Look closely and discover why more and more people are staying with Quest.

At first glance it's easy to think that Quest are the fastest growing serviced apartment accommodation group simply because of the money you save.

It's true that Quest allow you to forget about expensive tourist traps, hotel dinners and room service expenses you don't need – but the real truth is that Quest accommodation is something you feel at home in, instead of just staying at.

That's because the person who runs the Quest property is most likely to be the person who owns the business, and they're only happy when you say you'd love to stay again.

A place you'll feel at home in – instead of just staying at.

Freecall our central booking agency **1800 334 033**
Email: qrc@questapartments.com.au *Visit our website:* www.questapartments.com.au

QUEST

Australia's No. 1 accommodation group offers you

A strategic base for a busy executive. An imaginative setting for a romantic weekend. An accessible location for a memorable conference. The ideal destination for a family holiday. A good night's sleep at the end of a long day's drive. Flag Choice Hotels offer consistent quality and unrivalled value for money, irrespective of which brand you choose.

Check our website or phone for a directory. You'll enjoy the diversity of styles of our accommodation. As a guest you can earn rewards and points from a number of Flag Choice Hotels marketing partners. Because everyone at Flag Choice Hotels is dedicated to customer service we provide you with our 100% Satisfaction Guarantee*.

     * Full details available at all Flag Choice Hotels from 1 April 2001

Blue Dolphin

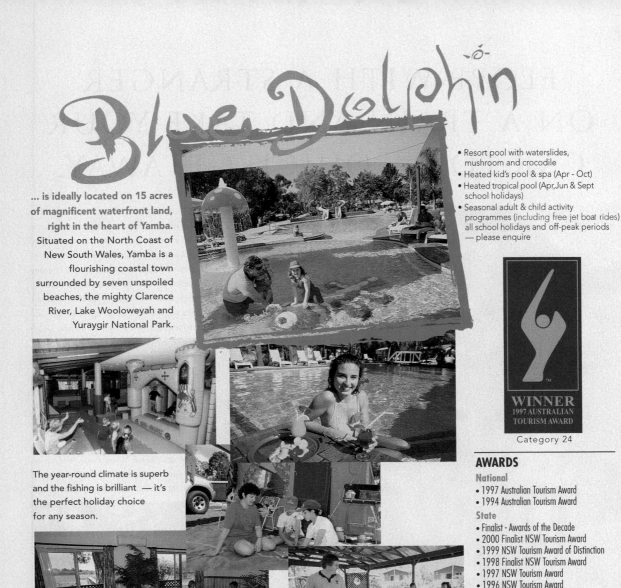

... is ideally located on 15 acres of magnificent waterfront land, right in the heart of Yamba. Situated on the North Coast of New South Wales, Yamba is a flourishing coastal town surrounded by seven unspoiled beaches, the mighty Clarence River, Lake Wooloweyah and Yuraygir National Park.

The year-round climate is superb and the fishing is brilliant — it's the perfect holiday choice for any season.

- Resort pool with waterslides, mushroom and crocodile
- Heated kid's pool & spa (Apr - Oct)
- Heated tropical pool (Apr, Jun & Sept school holidays)
- Seasonal adult & child activity programmes (including free jet boat rides) all school holidays and off-peak periods — please enquire

WINNER
1997 AUSTRALIAN TOURISM AWARD

Category 24

AWARDS

National
- 1997 Australian Tourism Award
- 1994 Australian Tourism Award

State
- Finalist - Awards of the Decade
- 2000 Finalist NSW Tourism Award
- 1999 NSW Tourism Award of Distinction
- 1998 Finalist NSW Tourism Award
- 1997 NSW Tourism Award
- 1996 NSW Tourism Award
- 1995 Finalist NSW Tourism Award
- 1994 NSW Tourism Award

Regional
- 2000 Hall of Fame
- 1999 North Coast Tourism Award
- 1998 North Coast Tourism Award
- 1997 North Coast Tourism Award
- 1996 North Coast Tourism Award
- 1995 North Coast Tourism Award
- 1994 North Coast Tourism Award

Industry
- 1999 CCIA Tourist Park Award
- 1998 CCIA Best North Coast Park
- 1997 CCIA Award of Distinction
- 1996 CCIA Special Award for Achievement
- 1995 CCIA Special Award for Achievement

FACILITIES

- Take-away food, cafe serving light meals and general store
- Recreation room — video games, snooker, table tennis
- Tennis court
- Indoor soft play room (Kidz Kave)
- Aquatic hire equipment — catamarans, motor boats, paddle boats & canoes
- Jetty & fishing pontoon
- Boat berthing & fish cleaning
- Villas, units & cabins with ensuite and full cooking
- Ensuite caravan & tent sites
- Powered caravan and tent sites
- Conference and meeting rooms
- Waterfront Deluxe Villas — 2 brms with spa, rev-cycle A/C, full cooking, d/washer, video & TV

PO Box 21, Yamba NSW 2464
Ph: (02) 6646 2194   Fax: (02) 6646 2274
email: enquiry@bluedolphin.com.au   http://www.bluedolphin.com.au

The Blue Dolphin
HOLIDAY RESORT
AAA Tourism ★★★★★

6089AG

ELOPE WITH A STRANGER ON A TRAIN AND TAKE YOUR CAR FOR A QUICK GETAWAY.

THE 🐫 GHAN   INDIAN PACIFIC

If the love of your life has begun to feel like a stranger lately, maybe its time to get away for a while together. Just the two of you. But extracting yourself from the demands of family, friends and finding your fortune sometimes calls for drastic measures. And a completely new kind of holiday. Trainways lets you take your car along for the ride and delivers you into a fabulous holiday which begins the moment you step aboard one of

the great train journeys of Australia. Trainways offers you tailored holidays with variety and flexibility. Travel one way by train, do your own thing, relax and enjoy and then drive home. If you prefer, you can do the same trip in reverse. And with our special $99* Motorail offer, taking your car on the

train is easily affordable. Choose a holiday which begins with a first class one way trip aboard the mighty Indian Pacific, the adventure that spans Australia. Or let your holiday begin with a journey into the heart of Australia aboard The Legendary Ghan. Savour the sights, the wines and dine in a beautiful

restaurant car. And afterwards, snuggle up beneath your doonas as the train races on starlit ribbons of steel through the crisp desert night. So whether it's a short, but oh-so-sweet affair or a longer holiday you're after, Trainways has a captivating collection of holiday packages to all the right places. Call 1300 13 21 47 for a free brochure and bookings, or see your licensed travel agent.

TRAINWAYS

Let's Make Tracks.

Reedcomm TR463 100139AG

Kosciuszko Alpine Way

Australia's great year-round scenic drive

Sydney - Snowy Mountains - Melbourne

The Kosciuszko Alpine Way through the Snowy Mountains offers a scenic alternative route from Sydney to Melbourne and vice versa. It is also one of Australia's greatest scenic drives, passing through the magnificent Kosciuszko National Park, a place of contrasts, of peaks covered with pure white snow, deep blue lakes full of trout, fields ablaze with wildflowers and beautiful autumn colours.

The Route

When travelling from **Sydney**, the route branches off the Hume Highway just south of Goulburn at the Federal Highway Canberra/Cooma turnoff. When travelling from **Melbourne**, the route branches off the Hume Highway at Albury and is signposted to the Hume Weir and Corryong.

The Northern Section

The route travels through the Monaro Plains and visits Jindabyne, Cooma and Canberra. Visit villages, historic huts and homesteads dating from the days when the first Europeans settled the Monaro Plains, or visit the many sites of Canberra, including Parliament House.

The Southern Section

From the Albury turnoff the route crosses the Hume Weir and heads towards the quaint town of Walwa on the banks of the Murray River. The route follows the Murray River and offers magnificent views of the western faces of the Snowy Mountains.

Just before Corryong the route turns off to Khancoban and Thredbo. The road is in good condition all the way.

Call us for a brochure. Take the alternative scenic route and enjoy the Snowy Mountains - Australia's High Country.

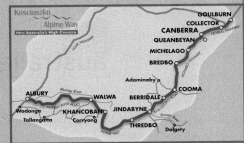

Visit the Snowies...

Thredbo Village

Spring, Summer and Autumn

Explore the many trails by horse, foot or bike. Fish the lakes and streams for rainbow and brown trout. The adventurous can try white water rafting, or mountain bike down some of the testing slopes.

Thredbo is an ideal spot to stop for a night or two. Nestled beneath Mt Kosciuszko, which at 2228 metres is Australia's highest mountain, Thredbo Village provides Mt Kosciuszko's most convenient access point.

The walk to the top of the summit is easy, particularly if you take the Kosciuszko Express chairlift from Thredbo. Relax afterwards at the Thredbo Alpine Training Centre. With a 50 metre pool, spa, fully equipped gymnasium, squash court and indoor sports hall, it's the perfect place to break the journey.

Thredbo boasts Australia's highest golf course and tennis courts and offers guided walks, mountain bike tuition and hire, fly fishing, abseiling, music and a place to inspire, invigorate and rejuvenate.

Ernie's holiday tip #25

All work and no play is very dull.

Too many hard-working Aussies have forgotten how to take a holiday. And all work and no play is no way to live. Taking a holiday in our beautiful country lets you unwind, reconnect with your family and helps you get in touch with your inner nice person again. An Aussie holiday is so easy too, because a host of delights are right there in your own backyard. So what are you waiting for? Put in that leave form, jump on our website and get out there.

see
australia
a national tourism initiative

See Australia proudly acknowledges Premium Sponsors Accor Asia Pacific and MasterCard International and Partners AAA Tourism (the national tourism body of the Australian motoring organisations), Ansett Australia, Avis, Captain Cook Cruises, Hazelton Airlines, Hertz, Qantas and travel.com.au Ltd.

Go on. Get out there.   **www.seeaustralia.com.au**

Pick up savings of 15% or more

Did you know that motoring organisation members are eligible for discounts on selected accommodation properties throughout Australia?

The National Accommodation Special Rates brochure contains information on over 300 accommodation properties throughout Australia, offering discounts of 15% or more to motoring organisation members. Pick up a brochure today at your local motoring organisation retail outlet.

Participating properties are indicated in this Accommodation Guide. Just look for the following symbol and quote your membership number when making a booking or show your membership card/tag on arrival.

DISCOVER...
MOVIES & TV

If you love the movies, you'll love the Fox Studios Backlot. Wander through this fantasy studio consisting of a series of exhibitions, attractions and live shows, each a discovery of the skills and craft behind some of your favourite movies and TV shows.

The Backlot is only part of the excitement at Fox Studios Australia. There's 20 restaurants, cafes and bars, 24 leading retailers, 4 live venues, 16 state of the art cinemas, plus markets, rock climbing, bungy trampoline, bowling plus Channel V and Fox Sports live broadcasts. It's all here!

PURCHASE YOUR DISCOUNTED TICKETS FROM YOUR NEAREST

AANT, NRMA, RAA, RACQ, RACT, RACV, RACWA.

Fox Studios Australia, Lang Road Moore Park, Sydney
www.foxstudios.com.au

Know your Destination
Experience More

**Where to go, what to see and how to get there
in six complete touring guides.**

Available from your local motoring organisation.

Accommodation Guide

2001 - 2002 Edition

This guide lists Hotel/Motels, Guest Houses, Bed & Breakfast, Apartments, Holiday Units/Flats, Chalets/Cottages, Lodges, Houseboats.

The companion Tourist Park Accommodation Guide lists Caravan Parks, Camping Areas and On-site Park Accommodation (which may include Lodges, Park Cabins, Holiday Flats, Chalets, On-Site Vans and Bunkhouses). Information collected up to February 13th, 2001.

AAA
TOURISM

Publisher

AAA Tourism Pty Ltd
ABN 79 087 199 504
Level 6/131,
Queen Street,
Melbourne, Victoria 3000
Phone (03) 8601 2200
Fax (03) 8601 2222
www.aaatourism.com.au

Advertising enquiries

AAA Tourism Pty Ltd
Level 6/131,
Queen Street,
Melbourne, Victoria 3000
Phone (03) 8601 2226
Fax (03) 8601 2222
advertising@aaatourism.com.au
www.aaatourism.com.au

Designed by

Design & Pre Press Consultants
Charlesworth Intermedia
- Melbourne Office
Level 5/131,
Queen St,
Melbourne, Victoria 3000

Printed by

PMP Print
2 Keys Road,
Moorabbin, Victoria 3189

Published for:

- National Roads and Motorists' Association Limited (NRMA Limited)
  388 George St, Sydney, NSW, 2000 - ABN 77 000 010 506
  Tel: 1300 13 11 22
  web: www.nrma.com.au/travel

- Royal Automobile Club of Victoria, (RACV)
  550 Princes Highway, Noble Park, Victoria 3174 - ABN 11 005 258 702
  Tel: (03) 9790 2211
  web: www.racv.com.au

- The Royal Automobile Club of Queensland Limited (RACQ)
  300 St Pauls Terrace, Fortitude Valley, Qld, 4006 - ABN 72 009 660 575
  Tel: 1800 629 501 (Country Queensland) or
  (07) 3361 2802 (Brisbane & Interstate) web: www.racq.com.au

- Royal Automobile Association of South Australia (RAA) -
  41 Hindmarsh Square, Adelaide, SA, 5000 - ABN 90 020 001 807
  Tel: (08) 8202 4540 or 1800 630 878 (outside Adelaide)
  web: www.raa.net

- Royal Automobile Club of Western Australia (RAC) -
  228 Adelaide Terrace, Perth, WA, 6000 - ABN 17 009 164 176
  Tel: 1800 807 011 (outside Perth) or (08) 9421 4400
  web: www.rac.com.au

- Royal Automobile Club of Tasmania (RACT)
  Cnr of Murray and Patrick Sts, Hobart, Tas, 7000 - ABN 62 009 475 861
  Tel: 13 27 22 (in Tasmania) or 03 6232 6300 (interstate calls)
  web: www.ract.com.au

- Automobile Association of the Northern Territory (AANT)
  AANT Building, 79–81 Smith St, Darwin, NT, 8000
  - ABN 13 431 478 529
  Tel: 08 8981 3837

- The Automobile Association
  Fannum House, Basingstoke, Hampshire, RG21 4EA, United Kingdom.
  Tel: 01256 491524
  web: www.theAA.com

- AA Guides Limited
  215 Wairau Rd, Glenfield, Auckland, New Zealand
  Tel: 09 441 2060
  web: www.aaguides.co.nz

Contents . . .

All about your Accommodation Guide

Town listings

This publication lists accommodation establishments under their appropriate town or suburb name. All Capital Cities (highlighted in red, detailed on facing page), Tourist Regions (highlighted in green, detailed below) and Towns are compiled, within each state in alphabetical order.

Tourist Regions

Abbreviations & symbols

Abbreviations

acc	accommodating
AE	American Express
a/c	air conditioning
BB	bed and breakfast
bbq	barbeque
BC	Bank Card
bedrm	bedroom
BLB	bed and light breakfast
blkts	blankets
BYO	bring your own liquor
cent heat	central heating
c/fan	ceiling fan
ch con	child concession
cnr	corner
conf fac	conference facilities
conv fac	convention facilities
cook fac	cooking facilities
cool	cooling (evaporative)
D	daily
DBB	dinner, bed and breakfast
DC	Diners Club
d/wash	dishwasher
E	east
EFT	electronic funds transfer
elec	electric
evap	evaporative
fac	facilities
fam con	family concession

fire pl	fire place
flr	floor
gr/fl	ground floor accommodation
heat	heating
iron brd	ironing board
JCB	Japanese credit card
ldry	laundry
ltd	limited
MC	Master Card
MCH	motorcharge
micro	microwave oven
min book	Minimum booking
MP	Motor Pass
N	north
pen con	Pensioner concession*
plygr	playground
pool	swimming pool
Pop	population
rec rm	recreation room
ref	reference
refrig	refrigerator
reqd	required
rm	room/s
RO	room only
S	south
sep	septic
serv	service
shwr	shower
stry	storeys

t/c mkg	tea and coffee making facilities
tel	telephone
tlt	toilet
TV	colour television
VI	Visa Card
W	west/weekly
w/end	weekend
w/mach	washing machine

(pensioner concession refers to aged pensioners. Other pension concessions are at proprietors' discretion.)

Symbols

☎	telephone number
✕	dining room/restaurant
⊠	fully licensed restaurant
♿	wheelchair access with assistance
♦	one person rate
♦♦	two persons rate
♦	extra person
✆	public phone
✉	postal address
✹	The CIA National Accreditation Program Member logo

Capital city & Suburb listings

18

User Guidelines

2001-2002
Accommodation Guide

Congratulations on purchasing your 2001/2002 Accommodation Guide. Over the next few pages you will find some useful information to help you plan your next holiday and ensure that you receive the most from this guide.

Your 2001/2002 Accommodation Guide includes accommodation establishments listed and rated by AAA Tourism. Listings in this publication are grouped into category types. The Accommodation Guide lists Motels/Hotels, Bed & Breakfast/Guest Houses, Self Contained Accommodation (Holiday Units, Holiday Flats, Apartments etc) and other types of accommodation such as Lodges, and Houseboats etc. The Tourist Park Accommodation Guide lists Caravan Parks, Camping Areas, and On-site Park Accommodation which may include Lodges, Park Cabins, Holiday Flats, Chalets, On-site Vans and Bunkhouses.

Establishments within each accommodation category are placed in descending order of rating (ie: highest rating establishment is listed first), and then in alphabetical order. The Accommodation & Tourist Park Guides are produced from a central database which is maintained by AAA Tourism. Information has been revised and updated prior to publication.

User Guidelines

To assist with quick reference each Australian state or territory is individually colour coded.

- Each state or territory commences with the listings of its capital city followed by the capital's suburbs in alphabetical order. The capital city and suburb town headings are presented in red to distinguish them from the majority of the book. After the suburbs most other towns in the state are listed in alphabetical order.
  An exception to this is where towns may be listed within a popular tourism region (eg Gold Coast). These towns (such as Surfers Paradise) are shown in green and will be alphabetical within the region.
- Pages have been alphabetically tabbed to assist locating towns.
- All town listings have map references, (see map pages at the start of each state and territory).
- Square brackets [ ], All data within the square bracket is available to each unit unless qualified by a number in brackets, eg. [shwr, tlt, cool(10), TV] means 10 units have cooling. Data outside of the square bracket refers to facilities shared by all guests.

Maps

Index maps showing towns listed in the Accommodation Guides are located at the start of each state and territory. Capital city and selected regional maps are located near the start of their relevant section.

- Indicates towns which are listed in the Accommodation Guide.
- Indicates towns which are listed in the Tourist Park Accommodation Guide.
- Indicates towns which are listed in both the Accommodation Guide and the Tourist Park Accommodation Guide.

Charges/Tariffs

Tariffs shown are a guide only and may change without notice. Check the tariff and other charges when making your reservation. Tariffs quoted are inclusive of GST (where applicable). Special discounted rates exist for motoring organisation members at selected accommodation properties throughout Australia. These properties are highlighted in the guide by the following symbol.

AAA TOURISM Special Rates

Operator comments & enhanced listings

Accommodation operators are invited to advertise in this directory in various forms. **Operator comments** may appear immediately after a main listing in red italic text.

Enhanced listings are highlighted in colour eg. in NSW a variation of blue, to make it stand out.

Operator comments and enhanced listings, do not in any way, represent property endorsement or the opinion of the Publisher.

Accommodation categories

For details of accommodation categories and star ratings see pages 22 and 23.

Every care but . . .

The publishers have produced this publication to provide assistance to motoring organisation members. The publication has been prepared from information available up to Feb 13th 2001.

The publishers endeavour to ensure that the information contained in this guide is true and correct at the time of publication. However, they cannot accept responsibility for mistakes in this guide, whether negligent or otherwise. In particular, they are not liable for any physical injury to persons or property arising from the publication of this guide, or for any other loss whatsoever.

The safety and first aid tips which appear in this directory are based on information from authoritative sources, and are intended as a guide only. The information is not a substitute for first aid courses or qualified professional assistance.

Advertisements in this guide are published and submitted by advertisers. The publishers have not verified the accuracy of the advertisements and accept no responsibility for their content. Some advertisements may offer discounts. The publishers are unable to verify the accuracy of the offers made or conditions, if any. Prior to making bookings, you should check the availability and conditions of any offers.

Acknowledgments

The publishers wish to acknowledge the invaluable input into the production of this directory which has come from all over Australia. Key sources of editorial, data and pictorial contribution include: Tourism NSW, Tourism Tasmania, Tourism Queensland, Tourism Victoria, South Australian Tourism Commmission, West Australian Tourism Commission, NRMA Limited, RAA Touring Services, RAC, RACQ, RACV, RACT, AANT, HMAA. **Our Cover -** Couple in hammock - Alma Bay, Magnetic Island, Queensland. Courtesy of Townsville Enterprise Limited.

How to use this directory

1. FINDING A TOWN

This directory has been broken into state sections which are colour coded. Within each state, capital city listings fall first, followed by the city suburbs and finally an alphabetical listing of towns for the rest of that state.

ACT NSW NT QLD SA TAS VIC WA

NEW SOUTH WALES
Home of modern Australia

SYDNEY NSW 2000

Pop 3,276,200. See Sydney map - page 56, ref A1. A vibrant and flourishing city, built around one of the most magnificent natural harbours in the world, Sydney is the capital of New South Wales and the oldest and largest city in Australia. Bowls, Fishing, Golf, Horse Racing, Horse Riding, Rowing, Sailing, Scenic Drives, Squash, Swimming, Tennis. See also Darlinghurst, Pyrmont & Woolloomooloo.

Hotels/Motels
★★★★★ **Bay Grand Hotel**, (LH), Previously ANA Hotel Sydney. 176 Cumberland St, The Rocks, 1km N of PO, ☎ 05 9250 6000, fax 05 9250 6250, (Multi-stry), 563 rms (40 suites) [shwr, bath, spa bath (5), tlt, hairdry, a/c, tel, cable tv, movie, t/c mkg, refrig, mini bar], lift, conv fac, ✕ (7), pool indoor heated, sauna, spa, rm serv, dinner to unit, ☏, gym-fee, cots, non smoking rms (166). D ♦ $430 - $675, ♦♦ $430 - $675, Suite D $705 - $4,800, ch con, AE BC DC JCB MC VI.

NEWCASTLE & SUBURBS - NSW

NEWCASTLE & SUBURBS - NEWCASTLE NSW 2300

Pop 270,300. (150km N Sydney), See map on page 55, ref D8. Newcastle is the capital of the Hunter region and has a fascinating past that contributes to its sense of identity today. Bowls, Fishing, Golf, Surfing, Swimming, Tennis.

Hotels/Motels

AAA
TOURISM
Special Value

★★★★☆ **Esplanade Holiday Inn**, (LH), Shortland Esp, 500m E of PO, ☎ 05 4929 5576, fax 05 4926 5467, (Multi-stry), 72 rms [shwr, tlt, hairdry, a/c, tel, cable tv, clock radio, t/c mkg, refrig, mini bar], lift, ldry, iron, iron brd, conv fac, ✕, pool, rm serv, dinner to unit, cots, non smoking units (24). RO ♦ $175 - $260, ♦♦ $165 - $260, ♦♦♦ $181 - $276, AE BC DC MC VI.

NERONG NSW 2423

Pop Nominal, (229km N Sydney), See map on page 54, ref B8. Small village on the shores of the Broadwater at the western edge of the Myall Lakes National Park. Boating, Bush Walking, Canoeing, Fishing, Scenic Drives, Swimming, Wind Surfing.

B&B's/Guest Houses
★★★★ **Chelsea Homestay**, (B&B), 61 Whimbrel Dve, 12km S of Bulahdelah, ☎ 05 4997 4180, fax 05 4997 4180, 1 rm [shwr, tlt, hairdry, fan, heat, clock radio, t/c mkg, refrig, cook fac, micro, toaster], lounge (TV), c/park (undercover), boat park, non smoking rms. BLB ♦♦ $60, RO ♦♦ $50.

Capital city and suburb town headings are in red.

Some towns are grouped into major tourist regions (eg Gold Coast). These areas are identified by green town headings.

Other town headings are listed in the relevant state colour (see above).

See pages 16-17 for further information.

If you know the geographical area you wish to visit, you can go directly to the maps at the start of each state section to find which towns have accommodation listed.

2. FINDING WHERE TO STAY

Accommodation listings in this publication are grouped into different categories; Hotels/Motels, Self Catering, B&B's/Guesthouses and Other Accommodation. Details of these styles of accommodation are explained on page 22.

3. CAN'T FIND WHAT YOU'RE LOOKING FOR

Should the town where you require accommodation be booked out or not have accommodation of the type you are looking for, there may be a town nearby that does. You may check nearby towns, by using relevant maps found at the start of each state. An Index Map may be found on the opposite page to help you quickly locate the map you are looking for. Every town listed in this guide is shown on one of the maps and has a map reference to make it easier to find.

Only towns listed in the Accommodation and Tourist Park Accommodation Guides are shown on these maps.

'Touring maps' are available in our state-based 'Experience' Guides or from your nearest motoring organisation office.

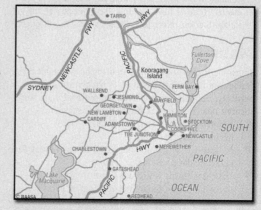

4. WHAT'S IN A LISTING?

Now that you have found the style of accommodation that you are after, we'd better explain how to obtain the most information out of each listing. Abbreviations & symbols utilised through this guide are detailed on page 16.

Star Rating

Most properties in this guide have a star rating.
See page 23 for rating definitions.

Accommodation Category

Describes what type of accommodation is listed.
See page 22 for category definitions.

Size of property

Detail how many rooms/suites etc.

CULCAIRN NSW 2660

Pop 1,200. (522km SW Sydney), See map on pages 52/53, ref E7. Handsome town at the heart of Morgan Country, an area that was terrorised by bushranger Dan 'Mad Dog' Morgan for years during the mid-1800s. Bowls, Fishing, Golf, Swimming, Tennis.

Hotels/Motels
★★★ **Country Motel**, (M), Cnr Olympic Way & Melrose St, 1km N of PO, ☎ 02 6029 8233, fax 05 6029 8413, 12 units [shwr, tlt, hairdry, a/c, heat, elec blkts, tel, TV, clock radio, t/c mkg, refrig, toaster], ldry, bar, pool (salt water), bbq, dinner to unit, cots-fee.
RO ♦ $50 - $60, ♦♦ $60 - $70, ♦ $10, AE BC DC MC VI, ⚹⚹.

CURRARONG NSW 2540

Pop 550. (188km S Sydney), See map on page 55, ref C5. South coast town at the foot of Crookhaven Bight that offers great opportunities for swimming, boating and fishing. Bowls, Fishing. See also Huskisson, Hyams Beach & Vincentia.

B&B's/Guest Houses
★★★★ **Comfort By The Beach**, (B&B), 68 Warrain Cres, 33km E of Nowra, ☎ 054448 3500, fax 05 4448 3500, (2 stry), 3 rms [ensuite, hairdry, elec blkts, tel, clock radio, refrig (communal)], ldry, iron, iron brd, TV rm, lounge (fire pl, spa, cook fac, t/c mkg shared, bbq, non smoking property. BB ♦♦ $121 - $187, ♦ $55, BC MC VI.

DARETON NSW 2717

Pop 560. (1036km W Sydney), See map on pages 52/53, ref B5. Small town on the Murray River between Wentworth and Mildura. Bowls, Fishing, Golf.

Hotels/Motels
Golden Club Motel, (M), Silver City Hwy, 1km W of PO, ☎ 05 5027 4737, fax 05 5027 4833, 26 units [shwr, spa bath (2), tlt, a/c-cool, heat, elec blkts, tel, TV, t/c mkg, refrig], ldry, pool, bbq, cots, non smoking rms (8). BLB ♦ $57, ♦♦ $62, ♦ $18, ch con, AE BC MC VI, ⚹⚹, (not yet classified).

Self Catering Accommodation
★★★☆ **Nanarewa Holiday Villas**, (HU), 28 Riverview Dve, 20km W of Mildura, or 05 5027 4868, fax 05 5027 4592, 5 units acc up to 6, [shwr, bath, tlt, evap cool, heat, elec blkts, TV, clock radio, cook fac, micro, toaster, ldry, blkts, linen, pillows], bbq, c/park (undercover), cots. D ♦ $70 - $80, ♦♦ $75 - $100, ♦♦♦ $91 - $110, ♦♦♦♦ $106 - $125
Operator Comment: 15 acres on river with boat ramp. 2 bedroom motels. 5 nights from $220 dble.
★★★☆ **Federation Motor Inn**, (M), 230 Warrain Ave, 1.5km N of PO, ☎ 02 6033 2022, fax 02 6033 2866, 22 units (3 suites) [shwr, spa bath (6), hairdry, a/c, elec blkts, tel, TV, video, clock radio, t/c mkg, refrig], ldry, ✕ (Tues to Sat), pool, sauna, bbq, dinner to unit, cots, non smoking units (7). RO ♦ $75 - $85, ♦♦ $85 - $90, ♦ $10 - $15, Suite RO ♦♦ $90 - $100, ch con, AE BC DC.

FLAG
FLAG CHOICE HOTELS

Facilities

Room facilities are detailed between square brackets **[ ]**. Property facilities are listed outside these brackets and are generally available for use by all guests. If a facility has limited availability a number in parenthesis **( )** indicates the number of facilities available.

Tariffs

Tariffs are generally listed as a range and include GST.

♦ indicates a single, ♦♦ double, ♦ extra person. Refer to page 19 for further information.

Wheelchair Access

This symbol identifies establishments with one or more units that provide wheelchair access with assistance. Refer to page 24 for further information.

Operator Comments

Operator comments refer to the listing immediately above. Operator comments are provided by properties as a promotional message and do not in any way reflect the opinions of the publisher.

---

5. INDEX MAP

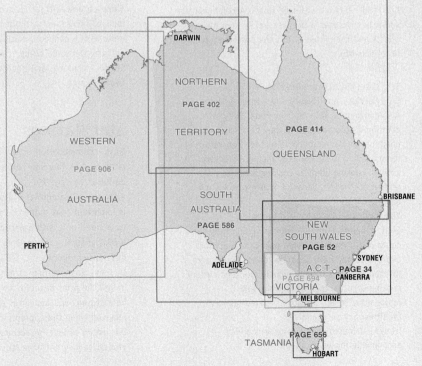

DARWIN

NORTHERN TERRITORY
PAGE 402

WESTERN AUSTRALIA
PAGE 906

PAGE 414

QUEENSLAND

SOUTH AUSTRALIA
PAGE 586

BRISBANE

NEW SOUTH WALES
PAGE 52

PERTH

ADELAIDE

A.C.T. **PAGE 34**
CANBERRA

SYDNEY

VICTORIA
PAGE 694

MELBOURNE

TASMANIA
PAGE 656

HOBART

Accommodation Categories

Accommodation listed under a town or suburb has been grouped into four major accommodation categories:

1. **Hotels / Motels**, which may include motels, motor inns, motor lodges, licensed hotels / motels & limited licensed hotels.
2. **Self Catering Accommodation,** which may include holiday units / flats, apartments, serviced apartments, houses, cottages, chalets, log cabins, villas.
3. **B&B's / Guest Houses,** which may include private hotels, B&B's and guest houses.
4. **Other Accommodation,** which may include lodges, bunkhouses, houseboats, cruisers & yachts. A definition of each accommodation type is detailed below:

Accommodation types

Hotels/Motels -
M - Motel, Motor Inn, Motor Lodge, mainly for motorists. All accommodation in units or suites. Adequate parking within or near the motel boundary.
All accommodation with individual bathing and toilet facilities. May be single or multi storey, and in some instances, converted buildings.
LH - Licensed Hotel. **LMH** - Licensed Motel Hotel. Fully licensed. Providing accommodation and meals, plus bar and lounge drinking facilities. The Motel Hotel has all or some accommodation with individual bathing and toilet facilities in a separate block, and adequate off street parking within the boundary.
Ltd LicH - Limited Licensed Hotel. Accommodation varies but includes a licensed bar or area for guests and their friends, not the customary public hotel amenity.

Self Catering Accommodation -
SA - Serviced Apartments, **HU** - Holiday Units
A - Apartments, **HF** - Holiday Flats. Fully self contained accommodation, may be a studio or a combination of bedrooms. May have separate lounge/living area. Normally includes crockery, cutlery, cooking utensils, cooking facilities and refrigerator/freezer. Serviced apartments include daily servicing.
Log Cabin/Cabin/Cotg - Cottages.
Chal - Chalets/Villas. A single dwelling fully self contained, may be a studio or a combination of bedrooms. May have separate lounge/living area. Kitchen facilities usually include crockery, cutlery, cooking utensils, cooking facilities and refrigerator/freezer. Private or shared laundry facilities may be available.
House - (House): Home used for holiday accommodation year round.

B&B's/Guest Houses -
B&B - Bed and Breakfast. Breakfast must be prepared and presented by the resident host(s) and included in the tariff. Other meals may be available. A separate bathroom for use by guests must be provided.
GH - Guest House. **PH** - Private Hotel. Usually non licensed holiday type accommodation often providing meals. Tea making facilities may be shared. Showers and toilets may be shared.

Other Accommodation -
Bunk - Bunkhouse. **Lodge** - Basic requirements including beds or bunks and is usually suitable for groups in dormitory style. May have cooking facilities, shower or toilet but these are normally shared.
Hbt - Houseboat. **Cruiser/Yacht** - Fully self contained with cooking and sleeping facilities.

Accommodation Variations

Farm - (Farm Type Property):
Accommodation which offers guests the opportunity to observe or become involved in farm life on a rural property. This type of accommodation offers a wide variety of standards and service. The category of accommodation is listed first, then the term "Farm" is added, eg (Cotg) (Farm) or (HF) (Farm).
Resort - (Resort):
A property situated in spacious ground which is self sufficient in service and facilities providing meals and a wide range of recreational facilities. It should have full time activities staff/guides, a tour activities desk and a variety of eating outlets on site. This type of accommodation will be listed as hotel, motel or caravan park as appropriate. The category of accommodation is listed first, then the term "Resort" is added, eg (M) (Resort) or (H) (Resort).

NOTE: In general context Unit indicates a room with shower/bath and toilet facilities.
Suite - a unit with at least one bedroom and a completely separate lounge/living room without beds. Interconnecting Unit - two separate units with a common lockable door between them to allow use of both units by the same guest/s.
Studio - cooking facilities/living room are incorporated in the bedroom area.

Star Ratings

Most accommodation listed in this publication has been inspected and rated by AAA Tourism. Further details regarding the rating definitions may be found on page 23.
Although all categories utilise STARS to describe the standard achieved, it is important that properties from different categories are not compared, eg a motel unit with a particular star rating should not be compared with a B&B of similar rating. This is why these properties are listed under different categories.
In some circumstances it may not be possible to assess new listings before the print deadline for a guide. In this instance, the words "Yet to be assessed" will appear as part of the listing text. This notation will be removed when the appropriate STARS are determined.
Our listing service for accommodation properties is voluntary. Unlisted properties may not have requested inclusion in the guide.

STARS Accommodation
classification schemes

AAA Tourism classification schemes

Currently AAA Tourism operates five different STARS Accommodation Classification Schemes – these are:

Hotel, Motel - Licensed Hotels, Hotels/Motels; Limited Licence Hotels.

Bed & Breakfast - Guest House & Private Hotel.

Self Catering - Holiday Units; Holiday Flats; Apartments; Cottages; Cabins; Log Cabins.

Caravan Park [see Tourist Park Accommodation guide]

Park Accommodation - Park cabins; On-site Vans; Cabins.[see Tourist Park Accommodation Guide].

The information and classification detailed in this guide is collected and maintained by AAA Tourism Pty Ltd.

The AAA Tourism STARS Accommodation Classification Schemes cover a wide range of accommodation and consist of ratings from one to five stars. One star offers clean basic accommodation, while five stars indicate outstanding accommodation offering international standards.

For properties to be eligible to participate in the AAA Tourism STARS Accommodation Classification Schemes they must meet minimum requirements. Some properties offer accommodation of more than one standard. The overall/prime rating is based on 50 per cent or the majority of the accommodation, while the remainder will appear in the relevant text listing with an indication of a higher or lower rating.

The star rating is allocated under **Primary** and **Secondary** categories.

Primary points determine the one to five star rating while **Secondary** points determine if the additional half star is warranted. Five star properties **must** achieve both primary and secondary points for the awarding of this rating, as it represents the benchmark for the industry and should satisfy the highest customer expectation.

Primary items include elements essential in the consumers choice of accommodation. These include, cleanliness, maintenance, condition, appearance and decor.

Secondary items are important in their own right. They represent additional items and facilities provided by properties which add comfort and value to a clients stay.

Allocation of items to primary and secondary categories are determined on a national basis, when each rating scheme is reviewed.

Properties offering special themes and concepts will be given due consideration for the theme when the assessment is made, providing the theme is consistent throughout the property and the comfort and convenience of guests is not compromised.

Some properties are identified as "Limited Facilities" listings, because they have only basic facilities.

The AAA Tourism STARS Accommodation Classification Schemes have been developed from information compiled throughout Australia. They are constantly under review. As the standards within the Tourism Accommodation Industry continually improve and have effect on the travelling public, standards will be adjusted to reflect these improvements.

HOTEL AND MOTEL RATINGS -

★ Establishments offering a basic standard of accommodation. Simply furnished. Resident manager.

★☆ Establishments offering similar standard to one star but offering more comfort and value by providing additional features and items.

★★ Well maintained establishments offering an average standard of accommodation with average furnishings, bedding, and floor coverings.

★★☆ Establishments offering similar standard to two star but offering more comfort and value by providing additional features and items.

★★★ Well appointed establishments offering a comfortable standard of accommodation, with above average furnishings and floor coverings.

★★★☆ Establishments offering similar standard to three star but offering more comfort and value by providing additional features and items.

★★★★ Exceptionally well appointed establishments with high quality furnishings and offering a high degree of comfort. High standard of presentation and guest services provided.

★★★★☆ Establishments offering similar standard to four star but offering more comfort and value by providing additional features and items. Reception, room service and housekeeping available 18 hours a day, with restaurant/bistro facilities available 7 nights a week.

★★★★★ International standard establishments offering superior appointments, furnishings and decor with an extensive range of first class guest services. A number and variety of room styles and/or suites available. Choice of dining facilities, 24 hour room service, housekeeping and valet parking. Porterage and concierge services available as well as a dedicated business centre and conference facilities.

HOLIDAY UNITS/APARTMENTS/COTTAGES RATINGS -

★ Clean basic accommodation with simple furnishings and facilities.

★★ Moderate accommodation with comfortable furnishings and facilities.

★★★ Well appointed establishments offering good comfortable accommodation and facilities.

★★★★ Excellent quality accommodation, furnishings and facilities.

★★★★★ International quality appointments, furnishings and decor with an extensive range of first class guest services and facilities. A benchmark under the applicable rating criteria.

☆ Establishments offering similar standard to the appropriate rating, but offering more comfort and value by providing additional features and items.

BED & BREAKFAST/GUEST HOUSE/PRIVATE HOTEL RATINGS -

★ Clean basic accommodation with simple furnishings and facilities.

★★ Moderate accommodation with comfortable furnishings and facilities.

★★★ Well appointed establishments offering good comfortable accommodation and facilities.

★★★★ Excellent quality of accommodation, furnishings and facilities. Must provide either individual or ensuite facilities for each bedroom.

★★★★★ International quality of appointments, furnishings and decor with an extensive range of first class guest services and facilities. Must provide ensuites to all bedrooms plus the communal areas and bedroom must be fully air-conditioned with individual controls in each bedroom.

☆ Establishments offering similar standard to the appropriate rating, but offering more comfort and value by providing additional features and items.

General Information

Child concessions

These generally apply to children sharing with two adults in the same room. Concessions may vary but generally apply to children under 12 years.

Office hours

Normal office hours are 8.00am to 6.00pm or 8.00pm - if you plan to arrive later than 6.00pm or leave earlier than 8.00am, we suggest you make prior arrangements.

Wheelchair access

The 'partial access' symbol identifies establishments with one or more units, with wheelchair access with assistance. People with mobility or other impairments have varying abilities and therefore AAA Tourism does not warrant that particular venues are, or are not accessible. AAA Tourism advises that before booking, you contact the venue to confirm that your needs can be catered for.

Power supply

The power supply is uniformly 220/240 volt 50 cycle alternating current with a few exceptions where special variations are available to meet the demands of international visitors (or some isolated purpose).

Pets

If you plan to take a pet with you, always make advance enquiries to check whether or not it will be admitted. Health regulations state that except for a guide dog with a person who is blind or a hearing dog for a person who is deaf, pets are prohibited in all accommodation. For health and humane reasons, do not lock or keep pets in cars in hot weather or for long periods.

Driving licences

Overseas driving licences held by bona fide tourists are accepted in Australia, usually for a maximum of one year, and valid for the same class of vehicle. International Driving Permits are also recognised. Drivers must carry licences/permits at all times while in charge of a motor vehicle.

Wandering stock

Stock and wildlife have all caused road accidents. Many Australian outback road are unfenced. Always look out for wandering animals on or near the road. Avoid driving at dusk, dawn or night time as this is when animals are at their most active.

Dust danger

Vehicles on unsealed roads can raise a dust cloud which will obscure your vision. Slow down and stop until the dust settles. Watch for approaching vehicles throwing up stones which may break your windscreen. Only overtake if is clear. Turn on your lights.

Australian Automobile Associations

Australian Automobile Associations provide road service, general motoring assistance, touring information and maps.
Members of organisations affiliated to the Alliance International de Tourism (AIT) or the Federation Internationale de L'Automobile (FIA) are entitled, during the validity of their home membership, to services provided by the Australian Automobile Associations.

Goods & Services Tax

The GST or Goods and Services Tax is a new tax levied by the Federal Government of Australia on almost all Goods and Services, including accommodation.

Information Services

Holiday Information :

NSW, NRMA –	1300 13 11 22
VIC, RACV –	HolidayLine – 13 13 29
QLD, RACQ –	1800 629 501 (Country Queensland) or (07) 3361 2802 (Brisbane & interstate calls)
SA, RAA –	Touring Services – (08) 8202 4540 (Adelaide Metro) or 1800 630 878 (outside Adelaide)
WA, RAC –	1800 807 011 (in Western Australia) or (08) 9421 4400
TAS, RACT –	13 27 22 (in Tasmania) or 03 62326 300 (interstate calls)
NT, AANT –	(08) 8981 3837

Special accommodation rates

Special discounted rates exist for motoring organisation members at selected accommodation properties throughout Australia. These properties are highlighted in the guide by AAA Tourism symbol. They offer a minimum 15% discount off the normal accommodation rate. Further information concerning the program including specific rates can be found within the National 'Special Rates' brochure. For a free copy of the brochure or for further program information contact your local automobile association office. The program is valid until 30 April, 2002.

AAA
TOURISM
Special Rates

Booking notes

Should you require special facilities make it clear that you will only book if they are definitely available, e.g. telephone, air conditioning, spa, etc. When booking accommodation, where linen, crockery, cutlery, cooking utensils, etc are optionally available, either take your own particular requirements or enquire what is available and how much it will cost. Long weekends (three days), Easter (five or more days) and Chrisas/New Year (week or fortnight) are sometimes treated as minimum booking periods. During these times single night accommodation may not be available. See page 27 for further booking advice.

Reader Feedback Page

Please help us!

AAA Tourism is dedicated to publishing quality touring information and your feedback is important to us. Please complete both sides of this Reader Feedback form in order to help AAA Tourism provide better products and services.

Had a good or bad experience?

We value your comments and feedback on the accommodation establishments you have experienced. If you have a specific complaint about an establishment, this should be directed to the proprietor. If you require AAA Tourism to investigate the complaint, please write to us with details, i.e. name, date of visit, room number, the issues. Please indicate if we have your permission to use your name in our investigation.

ABOUT OUR GUIDES:

1. Where did you pick up this guide?
❏ Auto Club Shop   ❏ Depot   ❏ Bookshop   ❏ Information Centre   ❏ Newsagent   ❏ Other _____
(please specify)

2. Where did you first find out about the Accommodation Guide?
❏ Family or Friend   ❏ Automobile Club   ❏ Advertising _____ *(please specify)*   ❏ Other _____
(please specify)

3. How often do you update your copy of this guide?
❏ First Time   ❏ Every Year   ❏ Every Two Years   ❏ Every Three or more years.

4. How often do you read this guide?
❏ First Time   ❏ Every Couple of weeks   ❏ Once a month   ❏ Four times per year
❏ Twice in a year   ❏ About once a year

5. When do you use this guide?
❏ prior to departure (for trip planning)   ❏ whilst travelling   ❏ both prior to departure & whilst travelling

6. Please rate the importance of the following content within this guide.

(0 is low 5 is very High Importance)	0	1	2	3	4	5
STAR Ratings	❏	❏	❏	❏	❏	❏
Colour Advertising	❏	❏	❏	❏	❏	❏
Maps	❏	❏	❏	❏	❏	❏
Town Information	❏	❏	❏	❏	❏	❏
Property Information	❏	❏	❏	❏	❏	❏
Number of listings	❏	❏	❏	❏	❏	❏
Other (please specify)	❏	❏	❏	❏	❏	❏

7. What other sources do you use when planning your travel? (please tick which ever are appropriate)
❏ Automobile Clubs   ❏ Travel magazines   ❏ Radio programmes
❏ Travel Agent   ❏ State/Territory tourism bodies   ❏ Friend/Family
❏ Tourism Information Centres   ❏ Free Tourism brochures   ❏ Television programmes
❏ Other Directories (eg. Yellow Pages, Citysearch)
❏ Other (please specify) . . . .
❏ Internet Site (please specify) . . . .
❏ Hotel/Motel/Tourist Park or other Accommodation Web-Sites (please specify) . . . .
❏ Travel/Tourism Web-Sites (please specify) . . . .

8. Is this guide easy to use?
❏ Yes Very Easy   ❏ Easy   ❏ Moderate   ❏ Not very easy   ❏ Very Difficult

ABOUT THE INTERNET:

9. Do you use the Automobile Club websites?
❏ No   ❏ Yes

10. If so, what information do you find valuable? (please comment)
. . . .

11. Do you have an Internet connected PC?
❏ No   ❏ Yes

12. If so, do you use it to plan you trips?
❏ No   ❏ Yes

13. What do you mainly research? (eg; maps, accommodation, attractions, weather etc)
. . . .(please comment)

14. Are property photographs helpful?
❑ No ❑ Yes

15. Have you ever booked your accommodation using email?
❑ No ❑ Yes

16. Have you ever booked accommodation over the Internet using a system that provides a secure credit-card payment facility?
❑ No ❑ Yes

17. Are you likely to do so in the future, and if not, why?
. . . .(please comment)

ABOUT YOUR TRAVELS:

18. Are you planning to travel within Australia in the next -
❑ - 3 months? ❑ - 6 months? ❑ - 9 months? ❑ - 12 months? ❑ - Yes but not within the next year
❑ - Not planning to travel... please go to q.26

19. Approximately what will be your month of departure?
❑ Jan- March ❑ April- June ❑ July-Sept ❑ Oct - Dec

20. What is your reason for travel?
❑ - visit family ❑ - visit friends ❑ - business ❑ - holiday ❑ - extended holiday
❑ - other . . . .(please specify)

21. What State/s are you going to visit?
❑ Victoria ❑ New South Wales ❑ Queensland ❑ South Australia ❑ Tasmania ❑ Northern Territory
❑ Western Australia ❑ ACT

22. How will you travel to your destination?
❑ Your car ❑ Hire car ❑ Aeroplane ❑ Bus ❑ Train ❑ Other . . . .(please specify)

23. What style of accommodation will you be booking, (choose as many as are applicable)
❑ Hotel ❑ Motel ❑ Guest House ❑ Bed and Breakfast ❑ friends/family
❑ Aparent ❑ Cabin ❑ Holiday Unit/ Flat ❑ Lodge ❑ Camping Area
❑ Chalet/Cottage ❑ Houseboat ❑ Caravan Park ❑ Park Cabin

24. Do you plan to book your accommodation before you travel?
❑ Yes, all accommodation ❑ Yes, some accommodation ❑ No

25. What is the duration of your travel? (from time of departure to arrival back at home)
❑ Less than a week ❑ One – two weeks ❑ Two – three weeks ❑ One month
❑ Two months ❑ Three months ❑ More than three months

ABOUT YOU:

26. What is your home State? ❑ ACT ❑ VIC ❑ NSW ❑ QLD ❑ TAS ❑ SA ❑ NT ❑ WA

27. Are you an automobile Club Member?
❑ Yes......... ❑ RACV ❑ NRMA ❑ RACQ ❑ RACT ❑ RAA ❑ AANT ❑ RACWA
❑ No

28. What Is Your Age?
❑ Under 25 ❑ 25-34 ❑ 35-44 ❑ 45-54 ❑ 55-64 ❑ 65-74 ❑ 75 plus

29. Sex- ❑ Male ❑ Female

30. Do you have children who generally travel with you? ❑ Yes ❑ No

31. What is your household income? (optional)
❑ Below 20000 ❑ 20000 – 29000 ❑ 30000 – 39000 ❑ 40000 – 49000 ❑ 50000- 59000
❑ 60000 – 69000 ❑ 70000 – 79000 ❑ 80000 – plus

32. Your employment Status
❑ Student ❑ Part Time/Casual Employed ❑ Full Time Employed ❑ Self Employed ❑ Unemployed ❑ Retired

Thank you for taking the time to complete this questionnaire.
Please return by fax to (03) 8601 2222 or mail to:
AAA Tourism Level 6/131 Queen Street, Melbourne, 3000

Some practical booking notes

HMAA AAA Tourism and the motoring organisations of Australia worked with the HMAA (Hotel Motel & Accommodation Association) to compile this consumer guide which highlights some industry practices.

Tariffs

Always check that tariffs are current, what is included, and in-room facilities, at the time of making your reservation. Check tariffs are GST inclusive. If you have additional guests staying check whether there is an extra person rate. It is important to also enquire about seasonal rates and surcharges

Deposits

Many properties request a deposit to confirm your booking. They may request credit card details as a guarantee, or to process a deposit for all or part of the anticipated tariff. Alternatively a cheque may be requested. During peak periods full payment may be requested for accommodation.

Cancellation fees

If the reservation is cancelled outside the timeframe stipulated by the accommodation establishment or booking service, or you fail to take up the reservation, for any reason, it is customary for a cancellation fee to be charged.

This cancellation fee is usually one night's room tariff. During peak periods an amount equal to the tariff for the full length of stay may be charged. It is important you request the cancellation policy at the time of making your reservation.

Time of arrival

In some instances you will be asked for an estimated time of arrival (ETA). If you are unable to arrive by your ETA, or expect to arrive ahead of your advised ETA, phone the property to let them know. This will ensure that your booking remains secured.

Payment on arrival

On arrival at the property a request may be made for full payment of accommodation or to take a "pre authorisation" of your credit card. In some instances the amount requested may exceed the accommodation costs to cover mini bar and food and beverage purchases during the stay.

Check in/ check out time

Usually accommodation is ready for occupation at 2pm on the day of arrival. Checkout at the end of your stay is normally between 10 am and 11 am. As these times vary from property to property, check the times that apply to your booking. Early arrival and late checkouts can sometimes be arranged, but additional charges may apply to the regular tariff.

Security

Safekeeping can be arranged for valuable items with the accommodation establishment. Refer to the Innkeepers Act in each state for further information. Before leaving your room or before retiring, check it is secure. If you have concerns, contact reception or your host.

Complaints

If some aspect of your accommodation is not to your satisfaction, bring the matter to the attention of the establishment immediately. This will give your host the opportunity to rectify the problem or meet your requirements.

Booking your accommodation

Consumers may book direct with properties and contact details are included in this guide. Some organisations offer booking services which may provide additional benefits.
Accommodation booking services are available through the RACQ, RAA, RAC, and RACT.

RACQ (Queensland) - (07) 3361 2802 Brisbane Metro) - 1800 629 501 (outside Brisbane).

RAA (South Australia) (08) 8202 4540 (Adelaide Metro) - 1800 630 878 (outside Adelaide).

RAC (Western Australia) - 08 9421 4400 (Perth Metro) - 1800 807 011 (outside Perth).

RACT (Tasmania) - 13 27 22 (in Tasmania) or (03) 6232 6300 (Interstate).

GOLDEN CHAIN ACCOMMODATION – FREE BOOKING SERVICE!

Each Golden Chain property has it's own Freecall service, so you can phone ahead and book direct.

This makes booking easier and more personal and allows you to find out 'first hand' about your destination.

This Golden Chain service applies to over 200 quality accommodation properties nationwide where you can stay year round in affordable comfort.

For a full colour accommodation directory of all Golden Chain locations and your free 'Gold Link' card, call the Golden Chain Head Office direct on **Freecall 1 800 023 966.**

CHOOSE YOUR NEXT DESTINATION AND FREECALL THE GOLDEN CHAIN NUMBER LISTED ON THESE TWO PAGES...IT'S THAT EASY.

A.C.T.

Canberra/Braddon. Canberra Rex Hotel	1 800 026 103
Canberra/O'Connor. Canberra Motor Village	1 800 026 199

NEW SOUTH WALES

Sydney:

Artarmon. Artarmon Inn	1 800 351 644
Chippendale. Noah Lodge	1 800 300 882
Chullora. Sleep-Inn Express Motel	1 800 111 245
Enfield. Burwood Motel	1 800 100 029
Glebe. Broadway University Motor Inn	1 800 263 909
Parramatta. Parramatta City Motel	1 800 227 410
Penrith. Penrith Motor Inn	1 800 001 358
Richmond. Colonial Motel Richmond	1 800 262 026
Sutherland. Sutherland Motel	1 800 817 246
Wahroonga. Ascot Motor Inn	1 800 111 243
Woolloomooloo. Mariners Court Hotel	1 800 359 295

Country:

Albury. Commodore Motel	1 800 674 555
Albury. Seaton Arms Motor Inn	1 800 152 552
Armidale. Armidale Motel	1 800 028 275
Ballina. Ballina Palms Motor Inn	1 800 221 812
Ballina. Richmond Motor Inn	1 800 639 993
Batemans Bay. Argyle Terrace Motor Inn	1 800 028 276
Bathurst. Ben Chifley Motor Inn	1 800 021 028
Berrima. Berrima Bakehouse Motel	1 800 670 370
Blue Mountains/Blackheath. Norwood Heritage Lodge	1 800 258 368
Broken Hill. Old Willyama Motor Inn	1 800 100 777
Casino. River Park Motor Inn	1 800 666 229
Coffs Harbour. Aquajet Motel	1 800 502 441
Coffs Harbour. Premier Motor Inn	1 800 622 096
Cootamundra. Southern Comfort Motor Inn	1 800 028 279
Cowra. Aalana Motor Inn	1 800 024 875
Cowra. Country Gardens Motor Inn	1 800 501 824
Deniliquin. Centrepoint Motel	1 800 677 490
Dubbo. Blue Gum Motor Inn	1 800 027 247
Dubbo. Endeavour Court Motor Inn	1 800 081 100
Forbes. Country Mile Motor Inn	1 800 803 748
Glen Innes. Clansman Motel	1 800 077 647

Gosford. Reece's Olympic Motel	1 800 243 217
Goulburn. Lilac City Motor Inn	1 800 654 124
Grafton. Jacaranda Motel	1 800 642 575
Gundagai. Garden Motor Inn	1 800 028 292
Gunnedah. Overlander Motor Lodge	1 800 422 677
Hay. Nicholas Royal Motel	1 800 333 563
Holbrook. Holbrook Town Centre Motor Inn	1 800 100 040
Junee. The Crossing Motel	1 800 248 227
Lismore. New Olympic Motel	1 800 000 298
Merimbula. Summerhill Motor Inn	1 800 024 946
Moama/Echuca. Sportslander Motor Inn	1 800 037 074
Molong. Molong Motor Inn	1 800 028 295
Moree. Billabong Motel	1 800 636 683
Mudgee. Horatio Motor Inn	1 800 001 404
Mulwala/Yarrawonga. Ashleigh Court Motor Inn	1 800 804 596
Murwillumbah. Poinciana Motel	1 800 353 987
Nambucca Heads. The Nambucca Resort	1 800 646 899
Narrabri. Aalbany Motel	1 800 024 211
Narrandera. Country Roads Motor Inn	1 800 028 591
Newcastle/Belmont. Lakeview Motor Inn	1 800 678 154
Newcastle/Raymond Terrace. Motto Farm Motel	1 800 131 735
Nowra. George Bass Motor Inn	1 800 649 270
Orange. Mid City Motor Lodge	1 800 047 906
Parkes. Hamilton's Henry Parkes Motor Inn	1 800 021 251
Port Macquarie. Beachpark Motel	1 800 224 438
Port Macquarie. Le George Motel	1 800 648 835
Queanbeyan. Hamilton's Town House Motel	1 800 020 629
Tamworth. Abraham Lincoln Motel	1 800 028 225
Tamworth. Town & Country Motor Inn	1 800 028 506
Taree/Cundletown. Cundle Motor Lodge	1 800 657 918
Tenterfield. The Peter Allen Motor Inn	1 800 803 559
Tocumwal. Bridge Motor Inn	1 800 266 268
Tumut. The Elms Motor Inn	1 800 819 497
Tuncurry/Forster. Tuncurry Motor Inn	1 800 637 166
Tweed Heads/Coolangatta. Las Vegas Motor Inn	1 800 807 351
Wagga Wagga. Golf View Motor Inn	1 800 352 900
Wagga Wagga. Heritage Motor Inn	1 800 028 508
Yass. Colonial Lodge Motor Inn	1 800 807 686

GOLDEN CHAIN

This bookmark highlights the best places to stay around Australia.

Use our listing of 1 800 nationwide freecall numbers on pages 28 & 29 of this directory to directly reach your next destination, free of charge.

Free lifetime membership in Gold Link Travel Club.
Book direct and present this card at any Golden Chain for your 10% discount.

GOLDEN CHAIN

This bookmark highlights the best places to stay around Australia.

Use our listing of 1 800 nationwide freecall numbers on pages 28 & 29 of this directory to directly reach your next destination, free of charge.

Free lifetime membership in Gold Link Travel Club.
Book direct and present this card at any Golden Chain for your 10% discount.

Every Golden Chain Wants You Back Again

GOLDEN CHAIN

Gold Link Club

10% DISCOUNT

NOT VALID UNLESS PRESENTED ON ARRIVAL

NORTHERN TERRITORY

Alice Springs. Alice Motor Inn	1 800 022 801
Alice Springs. The Outback Motor Lodge	1 800 896 133
Tennant Creek. Eldorado Motor Inn	1 800 888 010

QUEENSLAND
Brisbane:

Brisbane City. Metropolitan Motor Inn, Spring Hill	1 800 453 000
Ascot. Airport Ascot Motel	1 800 066 363
Carseldine. Carseldine Court Motel	1 800 634 822
Hamilton. Raceways Motel	1 800 077 474
Mt Gravatt. Viking Motel	1 800 625 811
South Brisbane. Park View Motel Southbank	1 800 642 511
Toowong. Club Crocodile Toowong Villas	1 800 777 092

Country:

Airlie Beach. Airlie Beach Motor Lodge	1 800 810 925
Ayr. Parkside Motel	1 800 831 244
Bundaberg. Bundaberg Coral Villa Motel	1 800 644 014
Cairns. All Round Motel – Inn The Pink	1 800 818 626
Cairns/Woree. Cannon Park Motel	1 800 110 555
Charters Towers. Charters Towers Heritage Lodge	1 800 880 444
Gympie. Fox Glenn Motor Inn	1 800 683 199
Hervey Bay/Pialba. Beachside Motor Inn	1 800 654 009
Hervey Bay/Torquay. Wanderer Villas	1 800 444 040
Longreach. Abajaz Motor Inn	1 800 081 288
Mackay. El-Toro Motel	1 800 687 186
Mackay. Sugar City Motel	1 800 645 525
Maroochydore. Beach Motor Inn	1 800 817 593
Maryborough. Kimba Lodge Motel	1 800 337 980
Miles. Miles Outback Motel	1 800 065 248
Mitchell. Berkeley Lodge Motor Inn	1 800 676 796
Rockhampton. Archer Park Motel	1 800 220 444
Rockhampton. Rocky Gardens Motor Inn	1 800 067 640
Roma. Mandalay Motel	1 800 069 698
St. George. Jacaranda Country Motel	1 800 332 585
Stanthorpe. Granite Court Motel	1 800 117 744
Toowoomba. Garden City Motor Inn	1 800 806 164
Toowoomba. Sunray Motor Inn	1 800 807 874
Townsville. Billabong Lodge Motel	1 800 627 757
Townsville. Ridgemont Executive Motel	1 800 804 168
Townsville. Summit Motel	1 800 645 138
Warwick. City View Motel	1 800 819 286

SOUTH AUSTRALIA
Adelaide:

North Adelaide. Regal Park Motor Inn	1 800 355 116
Pooraka. Pooraka Motor Inn	1 800 626 255

Country:

Bordertown. Dukes Motor Inn	1 800 088 109
Clare. Clare Central Motel	1 800 358 848
Goolwa. Goolwa Riverport Motel	1 800 155 033
Hahndorf. Hahndorf Inn Motor Lodge	1 800 882 682
Kadina. Kadina Gateway Motor Inn	1 800 665 005
McLaren Vale. McLaren Vale Motel	1 800 631 817
Mt. Gambier. Arkana Motor Inn	1 800 801 858
Mt. Gambier. Mid City Motel	1 800 807 277
Murray Bridge. Murray Bridge Oval Motel	1 800 641 689
Naracoorte. Country Roads Motor Inn	1 800 088 363
Penola. Coonawarra Motor Lodge	1 800 649 342
Renmark. Ventura Motel	1 800 626 721
Robe. Lake View Motel & Flats	1 800 819 997

TASMANIA
Hobart:

Montagu Bay. City View Motel	1 800 428 388

Country:

Burnie. Burnie Motor Lodge	1 800 252 025
Launceston. Parklane Motel	1 800 803 503
Queenstown. Queenstown Motor Lodge	1 800 684 997
Strahan. Sailors Rest	1 800 188 810
Swansea. Swansea Motor Inn	1 800 222 823

VICTORIA
Melbourne:

Abbotsford. Abbotsford Inn Motel	1 800 088 342
Beaconsfield. Melaleuca Lodge	1 800 812 603
Brunswick. Brunswick Tower Motel	1 800 802 470
Chadstone. Lamplighter Apartments	1 800 804 145
Essendon. Alexander Motor Inn	1 800 033 144
Fawkner. Hume Villa Motor Inn	1 800 063 990
Frankston. Frankston Colonial Motor Inn	1 800 155 044
Greensborough. Greensborough Motor Inn	1 800 807 782
Lilydale. Lilydale Motor Inn	1 800 181 222
Oakleigh. Lamplighter Motel	1 800 804 145
Richmond. Richmond Hill Hotel	1 800 801 618

Country:

Aireys Inlet. Lightkeepers Inn Motel	1 800 032 639
Apollo Bay. The Beachfront Motel & Cottages	1 800 815 973
Bairnsdale. Riverhill Motor Inn	1 800 651 027
Ballarat. Ambassador Motor Inn	1 800 811 782
Ballarat. Gold Sovereign Motor Inn	1 800 064 460
Beechworth. Golden Heritage Motor Inn	1 800 812 269
Benalla. Executive Hideaway Motel	1 800 033 128
Bendigo. Bendigo Haymarket Motor Inn	1 800 505 580
Bendigo/Eaglehawk. Bendigo Gateway Motel	1 800 032 263
Bendigo/Golden Square. Golden Square Motor Inn	1 800 033 129
Bendigo/Kangaroo Flat. Bendigo Motor Inn	1 800 032 941
Bright. Colonial Inn Motel	1 800 815 814
Camperdown. Manifold Motor Inn	1 800 816 915
Cann River. Cann River Hop Inn Motor Inn	1 800 675 874
Cobram. Regency Court Motel	1 800 035 321
Daylesford District. Hepburn Springs Motor Inn	1 800 249 939
Donald. Donald Motor Lodge	1 800 990 015
Echuca. Paddlewheel Motel	1 800 035 648
Echuca. Riverboat Lodge Motor Inn	1 800 033 134
Euroa. Jolly Swagman Motor Inn	1 800 221 664
Geelong/Grovedale. Grovedale Motel	1 800 033 136
Geelong/Waurn Ponds. Aristocrat-Waurnvale Motel	1 800 644 965
Gisborne. Gisborne Motel	1 800 893 127
Halls Gap. Mountain View Motor Inn	1 800 032 939
Hamilton. Bandicoot Motor Inn	1 800 679 926
Horsham. Country City Motor Inn	1 800 808 490
Horsham. Horsham Mid City Court Motel	1 800 033 141
Lakes Entrance. Cunningham Shore Motel	1 800 033 172
Lavers Hill. Otway Junction Motor Inn	1 800 138 139
Maldon. Maldon's Eaglehawk Motel	1 800 801 017
Maryborough. Golden Country Caratel	1 800 033 142
Marysville. Blackwood Cottages	1 800 014 545
Mildura. Mildura Plaza Motor Inn	1 800 033 146
Mildura. Murray View Motel	1 800 502 268
Morwell. Cedar Lodge Motor Inn	1 800 653 658
Ocean Grove. Ocean Grove Motor Inn	1 800 812 707
Orbost. Country Roads Motor Inn	1 800 636 873
Phillip Island/San Remo. The Quays Motel	1 800 033 149
Portland. Victoria Lodge Motor Inn	1 800 032 232
Queenscliff. Beacon Resort Motel	1 800 351 152
Rosebud. Admiral Motor Inn	1 800 627 262
Seymour. Wattle Motel	1 800 807 370
Shepparton. Bel-Air Motor Inn	1 800 063 815
Shepparton. Country Home Motor Inn	1 800 654 073
Swan Hill. Murray River Motel	1 800 008 300
Torquay. Torquay Tropicana Motel	1 800 032 131
Wangaratta. Wangaratta Motor Inn	1 800 811 049
Warrnambool. Anchor Belle Motel	1 800 033 151
Warrnambool. Gateway Motor Inn	1 800 808 051
Warrnambool. Hopkins House Motel	1 800 110 119
Wodonga. Border Gateway Motel	1 800 033 154
Wodonga. Motel Wellington	1 800 359 400
Yarragon. Yarragon Motel	1 800 332 655
Yarram. Ship Inn Motel	1 800 336 636

WESTERN AUSTRALIA
Perth:

West Perth. City Stay Apartment Hotel	1 800 819 191

Country:

Albany. Dog Rock Motel	1 800 017 024
Augusta. Georgiana Molloy Motel	1 800 180 288
Busselton. Gale Street Motel & Villas	1 800 685 412
Manjimup. Kingsley Motel	1 800 359 177
Margaret River. The Grange on Farrelly	1 800 650 100

Full details available on
www.goldenchain.com.au
For new locations (not listed)
call **1800 023 966**

GOLDEN

30

EVERY GOLDEN CHAIN WANTS YOU BACK AGAIN.

Non-smoking rooms now offered upon availability at Golden Chain properties.

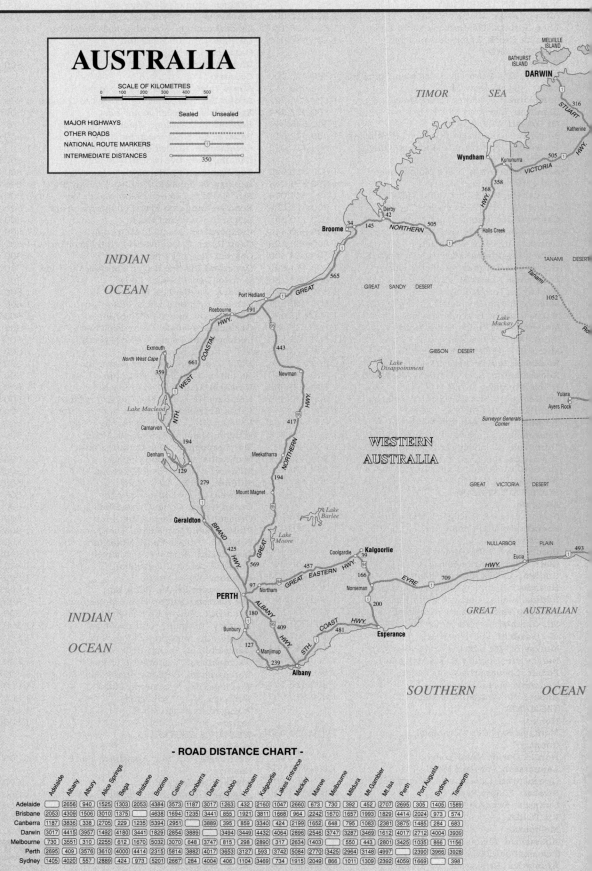

AUSTRALIA

SCALE OF KILOMETRES

0 100 200 300 400 500

MAJOR HIGHWAYS	Sealed	Unsealed
OTHER ROADS		
NATIONAL ROUTE MARKERS		
INTERMEDIATE DISTANCES	350	

TIMOR   SEA

MELVILLE ISLAND

BATHURST ISLAND

DARWIN

316

Katherine

Wyndham   Kununurra   505

368   358

Derby   42

Broome   34   145   *NORTHERN*   505   Halls Creek

VICTORIA HWY.

STUART HWY.

INDIAN

OCEAN

565

GREAT   SANDY   DESERT

TANAMI   DESERT

1052

Port Hedland

Roebourne   191   *GREAT*

443

Exmouth

North West Cape   661

359

WEST   COASTAL   HWY.

Newman

Lake Disappointment

GIBSON   DESERT

Yulara

Ayers Rock

Surveyor Generals Corner

Lake Macleod

Carnarvon   194

417   *NORTHERN   HWY.*

WESTERN

AUSTRALIA

Denham   129

279

Meekatharra

194

GREAT   VICTORIA   DESERT

Mount Magnet

Lake Barlee

Lake Moore

Geraldton   *BRAND   HWY.*

425

569   *GREAT*   457   Coolgardie   39   **Kalgoorlie**

97   Northam   *EASTERN   HWY.*   166   NULLARBOR   PLAIN   493

PERTH   *ALBANY*   Norseman   *EYRE*   709   Eucla   *HWY.*

180   200

Bunbury   409   *COAST   HWY.*   481   **Esperance**

127   Manjimup   *STH.   HWY.*

239

Albany

INDIAN

OCEAN

GREAT   AUSTRALIAN

SOUTHERN   OCEAN

- ROAD DISTANCE CHART -

	Adelaide	Albany	Albury	Alice Springs	Bega	Brisbane	Broome	Cairns	Canberra	Darwin	Dubbo	Horsham	Kalgoorlie	Lakes Entrance	Mackay	Maree	Melbourne	Mildura	Mt Gambier	Mt Isa	Perth	Port Augusta	Sydney	Tamworth
Adelaide		2656	940	1525	1303	2053	4384	3573	1187	3017	1263	432	2160	1047	2660	673	730	392	452	2707	2695	305	1405	1589
Brisbane	2053	4309	1506	3010	1375		4638	1694	1235	3441	855	1921	3811	1668	964	2242	1670	1657	1993	1829	4414	2024	973	574
Canberra	1187	3836	338	2705	229	1235	5394	2951		3889	395	859	3340	424	2199	1652	648	795	1083	2381	3875	1485	284	683
Darwin	3017	4415	3957	1492	4180	3441	1829	2854	3889		3494	3449	4432	4064	2896	2546	3747	3287	3469	1612	4017	2712	4004	3939
Melbourne	730	3551	310	2255	612	1670	5032	3070	648	3747	815	298	2890	317	2634	1403		550	443	2801	3425	1035	866	1156
Perth	2695	409	3576	3610	4000	4414	2315	5814	3882	4017	3653	3127	593	3742	5084	2770	3425	2964	3148	4997		2390	3966	3928
Sydney	1405	4020	557	2889	424	973	5201	2667	284	4004	406	1104	3469	734	1915	2049	866	1011	1309	2392	4059	1669		398

*All distances are in kilometres and are based on the most practical route.

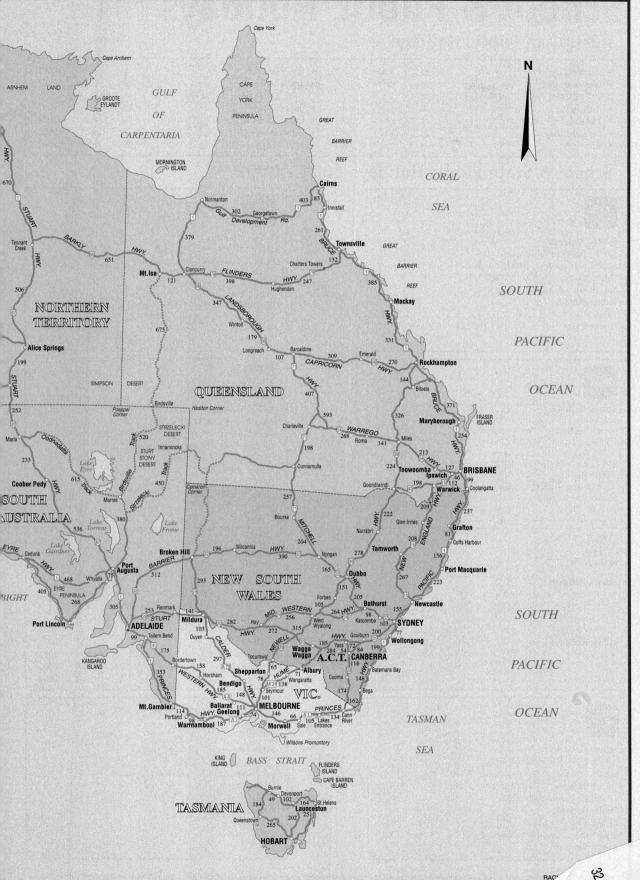

N

ARNHEM LAND
Cape Arnhem
GROOTE EYLANDT
GULF
OF
CARPENTARIA
MORNINGTON ISLAND

CAPE
YORK
PENINSULA
Cape York

GREAT
BARRIER
REEF

CORAL
SEA

670
STUART HWY.
Tennant Creek
BARKLY HWY.
651
506
HWY.
Normanton
302 Georgetown
Development Rd.
379
Gulf
261
Cairns
403 83
Innisfail

Townsville
GREAT
BARRIER
REEF

SOUTH
PACIFIC
OCEAN

Mt.Isa
121
Cloncurry
FLINDERS HWY.
398
Hughenden
347
Winton
179
Longreach
107
CAPRICORN HWY.
407
Charters Towers 132
247
385
Mackay
331
144
Rockhampton
Biloela
371
FRASER ISLAND

NORTHERN
TERRITORY
675
Alice Springs
199
STUART
SIMPSON DESERT
252
Birdsville
Poeppel Corner
Haddon Corner
593
Barcaldine
309
Emerald
270
LANDSBOROUGH
Barcaldine

QUEENSLAND

Marla
233
Oodnadatta
520
STRZELECKI DESERT
Innamincka
STURT STONY DESERT
450
Cameron Corner
257
Charleville
WARREGO
268 Roma 141
Miles
326
Maryborough
254
213
BRUCE HWY.
127
BRISBANE
99
Coolangatta

Coober Pedy
615
Lake Eyre
Birdsville Track
Strzelecki Track
198
Cunnamulla
224
Toowoomba
Ipswich
112
Warwick
Goondiwindi
198
209
237

SOUTH
AUSTRALIA
Marree
380
Lake Torrens
Lake Frome
536
Bourke
MITCHELL
204
Narrabri
222
Glen Innes
Grafton
81
Coffs Harbour
EYRE
Ceduna
Whyalla
75
468
Port Augusta
BARRIER
512
Broken Hill
196
Wilcannia
390
Nyngan
278
Tamworth
208
156
Port Macquarie
BIGHT
405
EYRE PENINSULA
268
Port Lincoln
305
293
NEW SOUTH
WALES
165
Dubbo
151
205
Forbes
105
Bathurst
264
155
Newcastle
267
223

Port Lincoln
253 Renmark
141
Mildura
282
Hay
256
West Wyalong
205
Katoomba
98
103
SYDNEY
Wollongong
77

ADELAIDE
99
Tailem Bend
175
Bordertown
158
297
Ouyen
103
Tocumwal
NEWELL HWY.
Wagga Wagga
A.C.T. CANBERRA
116
Batemans Bay
199
200

KANGAROO ISLAND
353
WESTERN HWY.
Horsham
78
Shepparton
65
Albury
71
138
Wangaratta
Cooma
148
Bega
Mt.Gambier
114
Ballarat
111
Bendigo
185
148
Seymour
101
VIC.
174
162
Portland
98
187
Geelong
146
74
MELBOURNE
66
105
Lakes Entrance
Cann River
TASMAN
Warrnambool
Morwell
Sale
Wilsons Promontory

SEA

KING ISLAND
BASS STRAIT
FLINDERS ISLAND
CAPE BARREN ISLAND

TASMANIA
Burnie
Devonport
49 102
St.Helens
184
164
Launceston
251
Queenstown
202
265
HOBART

OCEAN

School & Public Holidays

Australian Public Holidays

• Mothers Day	13	may	2001	• New Years Day	1	jan	2002
• Queens Birthday Holiday	11	june	2001	• Australia Day	28	jan	2002
(NT, QLD, SA, TAS, VIC, NSW, ACT)				(QLD, SA, TAS, NT, WA, ACT)			
• Fathers Day	2	sep	2001	• Good Friday	29	mar	2002
• Remembrance Day	11	nov	2001	• Easter Saturday	30	mar	2002
• Christmas Day	25	dec	2001	• Easter Monday	1	april	2002
• Boxing Day	26	dec	2001	• Anzac Day	25	april	2002

School & State Public Holidays 2001 - 2002

ACT

School Holidays
Sat 7 July - Sun 22 July 2001
Sat 29 September - Sun 14 October 2001
Sat 22 December - Thurs 31 Jan 2002
Sat 13 Apr - Sun 28 Apr 2002

Public Holidays

Labour Day	1	Oct	2001
Canberra Day	18	Mar	2002

SA

School Holidays
Sat 7 July - Sun 22 July 2001
Sat 29 September - Sun 14 October 2001
Sat 15 December - Sun 27 January 2002
Sat 13 Apr - Sun 28 Apr 2002

Public Holidays

Adelaide Cup Day	21	May	2001
Labour Day	1	Oct	2001
Proclamation Day	26	Dec	2001
Adelaide Cup Day	20	May	2002

NSW

School Holidays
Sat 7 July - Sun 22 July 2001
Sat 29 September - Sun 14 October 2001
Fri 21 December - Sun 27 January 2002 (Eastern Division)
Fri 21 December - Sun 3 January 2002 (Western Division)
Sat 13 Apr - Sun 28 Apr 2002

Public Holidays

Bank Holiday (Not state-wide)	6	Aug	2001
Labour Day	1	Oct	2001
Australia Day	26	Jan	2002

TAS

School Holidays
Sat 2 June - Sun 17 June 2001
Sat 8 September - Sun 23 September 2001
Fri 21 December - Wed 13 February 2002
Fri 29 Mar - Sun 7 Apr 2002

Public Holidays

Eight Hour Day	11	Mar	2002
(Possible change of date)			
Easter Tuesday	2	Apr	2002

NT

School Holidays
Sat 23 June - Sun 22 July 2001
Sat 29 September - Sun 7 October 2001
Sat 15 December - Sun 27 January 2002
Sat 6 Apr - Sun 14 Apr 2002

Public Holidays

May Day	7	May	2001
Picnic Day	6	Aug	2001
May Day	6	May	2002

VIC

School Holidays
Sat 30 June - Sun 15 July 2001
Sat 22 September - Sun 7 October 2001
Sat 22 December - Sun 27 Jan 2002
Fri 29 Mar - Sun 14 Apr 2002

Public Holidays

Melbourne Cup Day (Metro area only)	6	Nov	2001
Australia Day	26	Jan	2002
Labour day	11	Mar	2002

QLD

School Holidays
Sat 23 June - Mon 9 July 2001
Sat 22 September - Sun 7 October 2001
Sat 15 December - Sun 27 January 2002
Fri 29 Mar - Mon 8 Apr 2002

Public Holidays

Labour Day	7	May	2001
Royal National Show (Bris only)	15	Aug	2001
Labour Day	6	May	2002

WA

School Holidays
Sat 7 July - Sun 22 July 2001
Sat 29 September - Sun 14 October 2001
Fri 21 December - Sun 3 February 2002
Sat 20 Apr - Sun 5 May 2002

Public Holidays

Foundation Day	4	June	2001
Queens Birthday	1	Oct	2001
Labour Day	4	Mar	2002

DISCLAIMER: This information has been compiled from State and Federal Government sources throughout Australia and is subject to change without notice. No responsibility is accepted by the Publisher for the accuracy or omission of any information. Readers should rely on their own enquiries in making decisions touching their own or any other person's interest. **NOTE:** School holidays include weekends and public holidays.

If you need time out, or a short relaxing break with some champagne fresh air, there's no better place to head than the city in the bush - Canberra. It's a stress-free three hour drive from Sydney.

Canberra's a city like no other. Australia's only inland capital is set against the dramatic backdrop of the Brindabella mountains, dusted with snow in winter, misty blue in summer. It's a picture perfect capital where every season is celebrated, from crisp winter days with deep blue skies, to Canberra's Floriade festival – a vibrant explosion of spring colour and blossom.

In the national capital even the official buildings are fun. You can search for fossils at Parliament House – and there really are some embedded in its black limestone walls. You can wander through the War Memorial finding familiar names in the walls dotted with scarlet poppies. Take in a blockbuster exhibition at the Australian National Gallery, make your own coin at the Royal Australian Mint, and photograph stunning views over the city from Telstra Tower.

Kids will love Cockington Green's charming miniature world. They can immerse themselves in the world of movies and make-believe at ScreenSound Australia, or spend time absorbed in the fascinating hands-on and minds-on Questacon, the National Science and Technology Centre. Young – and old - astronomers can enjoy an expert introduction to star gazing at Stromlo Exploratory, or see space suits and moon rock at Tidbinbilla's Canberra Space Centre.

But Canberra offers more than official icons. It has a secret life. Over 40 per cent of the Australian Capital Territory is national parks and bushland.

Over 140 kilometres of bike and roller-blading paths meander through parks, woods and forests, there are quiet waters to canoe, and romantic secluded spots to picnic under the willows.

Take a picnic to the Cotter Reserve to relax beside the bubbling Murrumbidgee River; visit Tidbinbilla Nature Reserve to feed the wildlife; or venture further afield to Namadgi National Park for an unforgettable day of bushwalking. History buffs will love historic Lanyon homestead, and Bywong Gold Mining Village.

There's an abundance of birds in the national capital, from yellow tailed black cockatoos to endangered white winged choughs, to scarlet king parrots. If you are a serious bird watcher head for the Jerrabomberra Wetlands bird hides and watch the natural life as it unfolds in the lake shallows.

Canberra has another secret too. There are 21 boutique wineries in the area, with a big reputation for producing first-class cool climate whites, and some pretty fantastic reds too. Take a drive around the wineries; or contact a wine tour company to take the worry out of your driving.

As night falls over Canberra there's no better place to dine. Head for the trendy suburbs of Kingston and Manuka – if you haven't already had your café latté there during the morning, and perhaps spot a "polly" when Parliament is sitting. You will be assured of superb gastronomic treats, mouth-watering desserts, fresh produce, award winning Canberra wines – and capital service.

AUSTRALIAN CAPITAL TERRITORY

This is Canberra

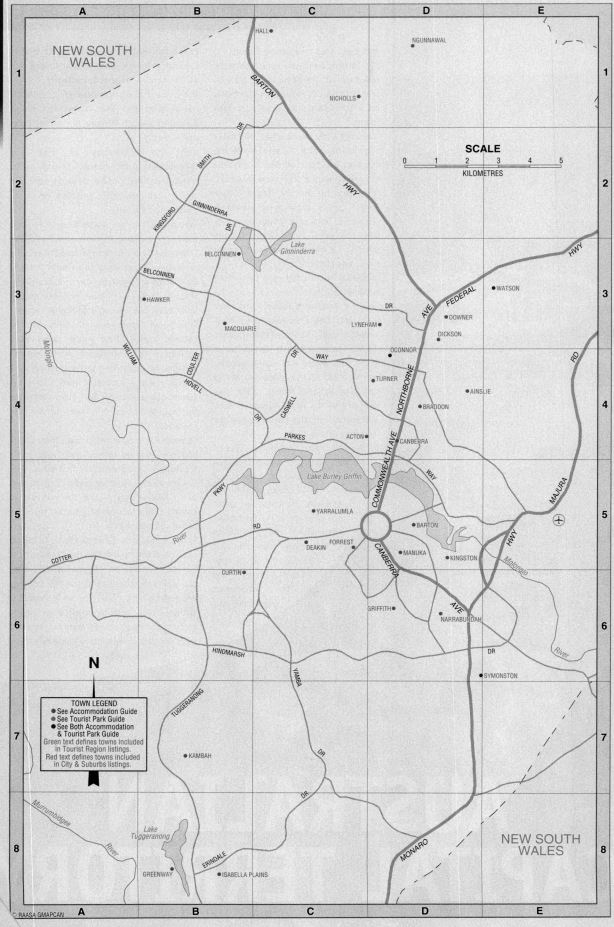

NEW SOUTH WALES

SCALE

0 1 2 3 4 5
KILOMETRES

HALL

NGUNNAWAL

NICHOLLS

BARTON DR

SMITH

KINGSFORD

GINNINDERRA

BELCONNEN

Lake Ginninderra

HWY

HWY

WATSON

BELCONNEN

HAWKER

WILLIAM

COULTER

HOVELL

DR

CASWELL

MACQUARIE

DR

WAY

LYNEHAM

DR

FEDERAL

AVE

DOWNER

DICKSON

OCONNOR

NORTHBORNE

TURNER

AINSLIE

BRADDON

Molonglo

River

PARKES

ACTON

CANBERRA

WAY

PKWY

Lake Burley Griffin

COMMONWEALTH AVE

RD

YARRALUMLA

BARTON

MAJURA

HWY

Molonglo

COTTER

DEAKIN

FORREST

MANUKA

KINGSTON

CURTIN

CANBERRA

GRIFFITH

AVE

NARRABUNDAH

RD

DR

River

HINDMARSH

YAMBA

SYMONSTON

N

DR

TUGGERANONG

TOWN LEGEND
● See Accommodation Guide
● See Tourist Park Guide
● See Both Accommodation
  & Tourist Park Guide
Green text defines towns included
in Tourist Region listings.
Red text defines towns included
in City & Suburbs listings.

KAMBAH

DR

Murrumbidgee

River

Lake Tuggeranong

ERINDALE

GREENWAY

ISABELLA PLAINS

MONARO

NEW SOUTH WALES

© RAASA GMAPCAN

CANBERRA ACT 2600

Pop 25,700. See map on page 34, ref D4, Canberra is the capital of Australia, a cosmopolitan and cultural place on the shores of Lake Burley Griffin.

Hotels/Motels

★★★★☆ **Parkroyal Canberra**, (LH), 1 Binara St, 300m SE of PO, ☎ 02 6247 8999, fax 02 6257 4903, (Multi-stry), 295 rms (6 suites) [shwr, bath, tlt, hairdry, a/c, tel, TV, video, movie, clock radio, t/c mkg, refrig], lift, iron, lounge, conv fac, ⊠, pool-heated, sauna, spa, rm serv, gym, cots, non smoking rms. **RO ♦ $158 - $290, ♦♦ $158 - $290, ♦ $33**, ch con, AE BC DC MC MP VI, ⅍.

★★★★☆ **Rydges Lakeside Canberra**, (LH), London Cir, ☎ 02 6247 6244, fax 02 6257 3071, (Multi-stry), 201 rms (13 suites) [shwr, bath (197), spa bath (5), tlt, hairdry, a/c, tel, TV, movie, clock radio, t/c mkg, refrig, mini bar], lift, ldry, lounge, conv fac, night club, ⊠ (2), pool indoor heated, 24hr reception, rm serv, cots, non smoking flr (8). **BB ♦ $150 - $178, ♦♦ $150 - $178, ♦♦♦ $180 - $208, ♦ $27, Suite BB $190 - $500**, ch con, AE BC DC MC VI, ⅍.

★★★★ **Capital Executive Apartment Hotel**, (M), 108 Northbourne Ave, Canberra City 2602, ☎ 02 6243 8333, fax 02 6248 8011, (Multi-stry), 83 units (24 suites) [shwr, bath, spa bath (24), tlt, a/c, heat, elec blkts, tel, cable TV, video, clock radio, t/c mkg, refrig, mini bar, cook fac], lift, ldry, ⊠, sauna, spa, rm serv, c/park (undercover), gym, cots, non smoking units. **RO ♦ $140.25 - $154, ♦♦ $140.25 - $154, ♦♦♦ $167.75 - $181.50, Suite RO $600 - $840**, ch con, AE BC DC EFT MC MP VI, ⅍.

★★★★ **Novotel Canberra**, (LH), 65 Northbourne Ave, 50m SW of GPO, ☎ 02 6245 5000, fax 02 6245 5100, (Multi-stry), 197 rms (37 suites) [shwr, tlt, a/c, tel, cable TV, clock radio, t/c mkg, refrig], lift, ldry, conf fac, ⊠, pool indoor heated, sauna, spa, dinner to unit, secure park (undercover), cots, non smoking rms (152). **RO ♦ $133 - $205, ♦♦ $133 - $205, ♦ $27, Suite RO $178 - $250**, ch con, AE BC DC EFT MC VI, ⅍.

For Accommodation Booking information - see p

Airport *Motor Inn*

57–73 Yass Road, Queanbeyan NSW 2620, PO Box 732, Tel: (02) 6297 7877, Fax: (02) 6299 2411

Reservations: 1800 647877

Canberra's convenient alternative

- 64 units of 4 and 3.5 star
- 8 family 2 and 3 bedroom apartments
- All rooms open onto unique garden atrium – absolutely no road noise
- In house movies
- Indoor heated pool
- Gym and sauna
- Games room
- Two full size tennis courts
- BBQ area

4 star facilities at 3 star prices

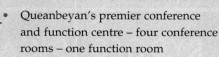

- Queanbeyan's premier conference and function centre – four conference rooms – one function room
- Licensed bar and restaurant
- Five minutes to Canberra airport
- Ten minutes to Canberra city
- Ample off street parking

FLAG
FLAG CHOICE HOTELS

Frequent *flyer*   *QANTAS*

Check out our web site on www.airportmotorinn.com.au for our monthly specials

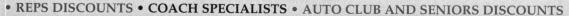

• **REPS DISCOUNTS** • **COACH SPECIALISTS** • AUTO CLUB AND SENIORS DISCOUNTS

Special capital country packages

- Two nights deluxe accommodation
- Buffet breakfast each morning
- A la carte dinner one night
- 2 for 1 entry into all of Canberra's attractions

$140pp
Conditions apply

es may change. Check before booking.

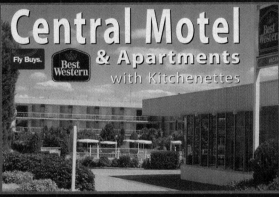

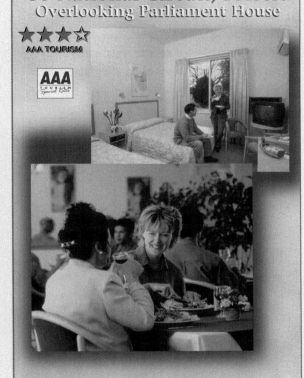

ACT

GRANDMANOR MOTORINN

**45 MACQUOID STREET,
QUEANBEYAN NSW 2620, TEL (02) 6299 2800**

Friendly personalised service, your home away from home, luxury rooms at an affordable price

- ★★★☆ star rating - AAA Tourism
- Quiet off highway location
- Licensed a la carte restaurant
- Free latest release in-house movies
- Family owned and operated
- Very large family rooms some with extra bedroom
- Romantic champagne package

Free Champagne and Breakfast, 2 nights Deluxe Accommodation Total Cost $105.00 per person inc GST

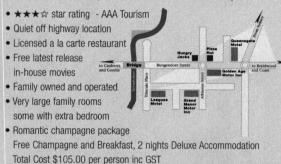

GOLDEN AGE MOTORINN

**Cnr of Bungendore Road & Atkinson Street
QUEANBEYAN NSW 2620, TEL (02) 6297 1122**

The motel for discerning travellers. A beautiful four star colonial style property, fully appointed rooms in business and deluxe standards, all modern facilities. Five minutes walk to shopping centre, clubs and bus interchange. Your gateway to the nations capital and the Snowy Mountains.

- 59 modern four star air-conditioned units, some interconnecting
- 10 minutes to Canberra's centre
- Five minutes to Canberra International Airport
- Spa bath units and salt water swimming pool
- Direct dial IDD/STD phones
- Cocktail bar and licensed restaurant
- Room service

- Free latest release in-house movies and colour TV's
- Disabled facilities
- Bubble Away Weekend Package - $165 per person.
- Relax in our Luxurious Deluxe rooms with bath for two nights. Free in house movies. Includes free fully cooked Breakfast for two. Dinner and Champagne for two to the value of $70 at the excellent Colonial restaurant.

4656AGa

 ★☆ **City Walk Hotel**, (M), 2 Mort St, 200m from PO, ☎ 02 6257 0124, fax 02 6257 0116, (Multi-stry), 39 units [shwr (12), bath (3), tlt (12), cent heat, fax, TV (5)], lift, ldry, lounge (TV), ✗, cook fac, t/c mkg shared, ✆, cots-fee. **RO** ⍊ **$45 - $65**, ⍊⍊ **$70**, ⍊ **$10**, BC MC VI.

Self Catering Accommodation

★★★★☆ **Canberra Quest Inn**, (SA), Melbourne Building, West Row, 150m E of GPO, ☎ 02 6243 2222, fax 02 6243 2288, 36 serv apts [shwr, bath (20), tlt, hairdry, a/c, tel, TV, video, clock radio, t/c mkg, refrig, cook fac, micro, d/wash, toaster, ldry, blkts, linen], lift, w/mach, dryer, iron, iron brd. **RO** ⍊ **$132 - $158**, ⍊⍊ **$178**, ⍊ **$17**, AE BC DC MC VI.

★★★★☆ **Capital Tower**, (SA), 2 Marcus Clarke St, ☎ 02 6276 3444, fax 02 6247 0759, (Multi-stry), 55 serv apts (55 suites) [shwr, bath, tlt, hairdry, a/c, tel, TV, video, clock radio, t/c mkg, refrig, cook fac, micro, d/wash, toaster], lift, pool (salt water), sauna, spa, bbq, secure park, gym, squash, tennis, cots. **RO** ⍊ **$155 - $220**, ⍊⍊ **$155 - $220**, AE BC DC EFT MC VI.

For Accommodation Booking information - see p

AAA TOURISM *Special Rates* ★★★★☆ **James Court Apartment Hotel**, (SA), 74 Northbourne Ave, 100m N of City Centre, ☎ 02 6240 1234, fax 02 6240 1235, 162 serv apts [shwr, spa bath, tlt, hairdry, a/c, elec blkts, tel, fax, TV, cable TV, movie, clock radio, t/c mkg, refrig, mini bar, cook fac, micro, d/wash, toaster, ldry, blkts, linen, pillows], lift, w/mach, dryer, iron, pool-heated, sauna, bbq, rm serv, dinner to unit, ☎, gym, cots, non smoking units. **RO $186 - $225**, AE BC DC MC VI.

★★★★☆ **Waldorf Apartment Hotel Canberra Pty Ltd**, (SA), 2 Akuna St, ☎ 02 6229 1234, fax 02 6229 1235, (Multi-stry), 133 serv apts acc up to 6, [shwr, bath, tlt, hairdry, cent heat, tel, TV, movie, clock radio, t/c mkg, refrig, mini bar, cook fac, micro, d/wash, toaster, ldry, blkts, linen], lift, w/mach, dryer, iron, iron brd, rec rm, TV rm, conf fac, pool (outdoor), pool indoor heated, sauna, spa, bbq, 24hr reception, ☎, gym, tennis (half court), cots, non smoking units. **RO ⋔ $132 - $209**, AE BC DC EFT JCB MC VI.

Other Accommodation

Canberra City Backpackers, 7 Akuna St, 500m SE of GPO, ☎ 02 6229 0888, fax 02 6229 0777, 65 rms [ensuite (8), a/c, cent heat, cable TV, movie, blkts, doonas, linen, pillows], lift, shared fac (61), ldry, lounge (TV), conf fac, ✗, bar, pool indoor heated, sauna, spa, cook fac, t/c mkg shared, refrig, bbq, ☎, bicycle, non smoking property. **D ⊹ $25 - $80**, AE BC DC EFT MC VI.

CANBERRA - ACTON ACT 2601

Pop Part of Canberra, (2km W Canberra), See map on page 34, ref C4, Inner suburb of Canberra, home to the main campus of the Australian National University.

Hotels/Motels

★★★☆ **University House at Aust National University**, (LH), Balmain Cres, 2km SW of Civic Centre, ☎ 02 6249 5211, fax 02 6249 5252, (Multi-stry gr fl), 143 rms (36 suites) [shwr, bath, tlt, hairdry, cent heat, tel, TV, clock radio, t/c mkg, refrig, cook fac (16), toaster], ldry, lounge (TV), conv fac, ✗, cafe, ☎. **RO ⊹ $68 - $106, ⋔ $118 - $128, ⋔⋔ $135 - $196, ⊚ $11, Suite D $124 - $196**, AE BC DC JCB MC VI.

Operator Comment: See our display advertisement at bottom of page.

CANBERRA - AINSLIE ACT 2602

Pop Part of Canberra, (3km NE Canberra), See map on page 34, ref D4, Inner northern suburb of Canberra.

Hotels/Motels

Best Western ★★★☆ **Tall Trees Motel**, (M), 21 Stephen St, ☎ 02 6247 9200, fax 02 6257 4479, 50 units [shwr, bath (32), tlt, hairdry (32), a/c, elec blkts, tel, TV, clock radio, t/c mkg, refrig, mini bar], ldry, iron, iron brd, cots, non smoking units (28). **RO ⊹ $82 - $120, ⋔ $92 - $130, ⋔⋔ $104 - $142, ⊚ $12**, 18 units at a lesser rating. AE BC DC EFT JCB MC MP VI.

CRESTVIEW TOURIST PARK

81 Donald Rd Queanbeyan/Canberra

TOP TOURIST PARKS

13km to Parliament House

PH: 1800 883 310

Ensuite Cabins	Non Smoking Cabins
Powered Sites	Non-Ensuite Cabins
Solar Heated Pool	Powered E/S Sites
Laundry	Playground
	EFTPOS available

*Sorry no pets
Resident owners assure satisfaction*

Trouble-free travel tips - Lights
Check the operation of all lights. If you are pulling a trailer of caravan make sure turning indicators and brake lights are working.

s may change. Check before booking.

CANBERRA - BARTON ACT 2600

Pop Part of Canberra, (3km E Canberra), See map on page 34, ref D5, Inner southern suburb of Canberra. Tennis.

Hotels/Motels

★★★★☆ **Hotel Kurrajong**, (LH), c1926. National Circuit, 5km E of Canberra Mail Centre, ☎ 02 6234 4444, fax 02 6234 4466, 26 rms [shwr, bath, tlt, hairdry, a/c, tel, TV, movie, clock radio, t/c mkg, refrig, mini bar], iron, iron brd, conv fac, rm serv, cots-fee, non smoking rms. RO ♦♦ $175 - $230, AE BC DC EFT MC VI, ♪&.

★★★★ **Brassey of Canberra**, (LH), Belmore Gdns, 1km E of Parliament House, ☎ 02 6273 3766, fax 02 6273 2791, (Multi-stry gr fl), 81 rms [shwr, tlt, cent heat, tel, clock radio, t/c mkg, refrig, mini bar], ldry, lounge, conv fac, ✕, 24hr reception, cots, non smoking rms (40). BB ♦ $110 - $138, ♦♦ $124 - $152, ◊ $15, ch con, 20 rooms yet to be assessed, AE BC DC MC VI.

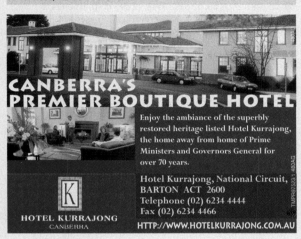

Enjoy the ambiance of the superbly restored heritage listed Hotel Kurrajong, the home away from home of Prime Ministers and Governors General for over 70 years.

Hotel Kurrajong, National Circuit, BARTON ACT 2600
Telephone (02) 6234 4444
Fax (02) 6234 4466

HOTEL KURRAJONG
CANBERRA

HTTP://WWW.HOTELKURRAJONG.COM.AU

★☆ **Macquarie Hotel**, (LH), 18 National Circuit, Cnr Sydney Ave, 700m from Parliament House, ☎ 02 6273 2325, fax 02 6273 4241, (Multi-stry gr fl), 530 rms [shwr (3), tlt (3), heat, TV (122), clock radio (3), cook fac (3)], shwr, tlt, ldry, rec rm, lounge (TV), ✕, bbq, ☎. BB ♦ $48.50 - $60.50, ♦♦ $84, D $199.50 - $420, 408 units not rated - blocks C,D,E,F, 3 units of a higher rating. BC EFT MC VI.

CANBERRA - BELCONNEN ACT 2617

Pop Part of Canberra, (10km NE Canberra), See map on page 34, ref B3, North-western suburb of Canberra.

Hotels/Motels

★★★★ **Belconnen Premier Inn**, (LMH), 110 Benjamin Way, ☎ 02 6253 3633, fax 02 6253 3688, (2 stry gr fl), 50 units (10 suites) [shwr, tlt, hairdry, a/c, tel, cable TV, clock radio, t/c mkg, refrig, mini bar], lift, ldry, iron, iron brd, lounge, conf fac, ✕, bar, rm serv, cots, non smoking units (25). RO ♦ $90 - $120, ♦♦ $90 - $120, ◊ $20, AE BC DC EFT JCB MC MP VI.

★★★★☆ **(Serviced Apartment Section)**, (2 stry gr fl), 10 serv apts acc up to 6, [shwr, tlt, hairdry, a/c-cool, tel, cable TV, clock radio, t/c mkg, refrig, mini bar, cook fac ltd, ldry], lift, iron, iron brd, lounge, conf fac, ✕, bar, rm serv, cots, non smoking units. D ♦ $120 - $215, ♦♦ $120 - $215, ◊ $20.

CANBERRA - BRADDON ACT 2612

Pop Part of Canberra, (1km NE Canberra), See map on page 34, ref D4, Inner northern suburb of Canberra.

Hotels/Motels

★★★★☆ **Saville Park Suites**, (LH), 84 Northbourne Ave, ☎ 02 6243 2500, fax 02 6243 2599, (Multi-stry), 176 rms (123 suites) [shwr, bath, tlt, hairdry, a/c, tel, TV, video (on request)-fee, movie, clock radio, t/c mkg, refrig, mini bar, cook fac (123), micro (56), toaster, ldry (123)], lift, iron, iron brd, business centre, conv fac, ✕, pool indoor heated, sauna, 24hr reception, rm serv, dinner to unit, secure park, ☎, gym, cots, non smoking flr (4), non smoking rms (88). RO ♦ $160, ♦♦ $160, ◊ $27.50, Suite RO ♦♦ $182 - $197, ◊ $27.50, ch con, AE BC DC EFT JCB MC VI.

For Accommodation Booking information - see page

B
ACT

★★★★☆ **The Chifley on Northbourne**, (LH), 102 Northbourne Ave, ☎ 02 6249 1411, fax 02 6249 6878, (2 stry gr fl), 78 rms (6 suites) [shwr, bath (38), spa bath (16), tlt, hairdry, a/c, tel, movie, clock radio, radio, t/c mkg, refrig, mini bar, toaster], lift, ldry, conv fac, ✕, pool, rm serv, dinner to unit, gym, cots, non smoking units (45). **RO** ♦ **$176**, ♦♦ **$176**, ⧉ **$25**, **Suite D $215 - $275**, ch con, AE BC DC EFT JCB MC VI.

★★★★ **Olims Canberra Hotel**, (LH), Cnr Ainslie & Limestone Ave, 1km NE of PO, ☎ 02 6248 5511, fax 02 6247 0864, (2 stry gr fl), 92 rms (33 suites) [shwr, tlt, a/c (88), cent heat, elec blkts, tel, cable TV, clock radio, t/c mkg, refrig, mini bar, cook fac (33)], ldry, lounge, conv fac, ✕, bar, 24hr reception, rm serv, cots, non smoking rms (49). **RO** ♦ **$110 - $180**, ♦♦ **$110 - $180**, ♦♦♦ **$198**, ⧉ **$18**, ch con, 37 rooms of a lower rating. AE BC DC EFT MC VI, ♿.

★★★☆ **Canberra Rex Hotel**, (LH), 150 Northbourne Ave, Canberra 2601, ☎ 02 6248 5311, fax 02 6248 8357, (Multi-stry), 154 rms (2 suites) [shwr, bath, tlt, a/c, heat, elec blkts, tel, TV, movie, clock radio, t/c mkg, refrig], lift, ldry, lounge, conv fac, ✕, bar, pool indoor heated, sauna, 24hr reception, rm serv, gym, cots. **BB** ♦ **$109**, ♦♦ **$124**, ⧉ **$32**, ch con, 74 units ★★☆. AE BC DC MC VI.

★★★☆ **Quality Inn Downtown**, (M), 82 Northbourne Ave, ☎ 02 6249 1388, fax 02 6247 2523, (Multi-stry gr fl), 65 units [shwr, tlt, hairdry, a/c, tel, TV, movie, clock radio, t/c mkg, cook fac (4)], ldry, ✕, c/park (limited undercover), gym, cots, non smoking units (50). **RO** ♦ **$110 - $145**, ♦♦ **$110 - $145**, ⧉ **$15**, ch con, AE BC DC MC VI.

★★★ **Kythera Motel**, (M), 98 Northbourne Ave, ☎ 02 6248 7611, fax 02 6248 0419, (Multi-stry gr fl), 72 units (2 suites) [shwr, tlt, a/c, heat, tel, TV, movie, radio, t/c mkg, refrig, cook fac (2)], lift, ldry, ✕, pool, c/park (undercover), cots. **RO** ♦ **$85**, ♦♦ **$85**, ♦♦♦ **$95**, AE BC DC MC VI.

★★☆ **Acacia Motor Lodge**, (M), 65 Ainslie Ave, 300m E of city centre, ☎ 02 6249 6955, fax 02 6247 7058, (2 stry gr fl), 53 units [shwr, tlt, heat, tel, TV, clock radio, t/c mkg, refrig], ldry, bbq, cots. **BLB** ♦ **$81**, ♦♦ **$87 - $92**, ♦♦♦ **$103**, ⧉ **$12**, AE BC DC MC VI.

Self Catering Accommodation

★★★ **Victoria Terrace Serviced Apartments**, (SA), 19 Fawkner St, 2km N of CBD, ☎ 02 6248 0833, fax 02 6230 4093, (Multi-stry gr fl), 15 serv apts acc up to 6, [shwr, bath, tlt, fan, heat, tel, TV, video, clock radio, t/c mkg, refrig, cook fac, micro, toaster, ldry, blkts, linen], w/mach, dryer, iron, iron brd, c/park (undercover), cots. **RO** ♦♦ **$100 - $150**, AE BC DC EFT MC VI.

CANBERRA - CURTIN ACT 2605

Pop Part of Canberra, (7km SW Canberra), See map on page 34, ref B6, Inner southern suburb of Canberra.

Hotels/Motels

★★★☆ **The Statesman**, (LMH), Cnr Strangway & Theodore Sts, ☎ 02 6281 1777, fax 02 6282 3938, (2 stry gr fl), 63 units (5 suites) [shwr, spa bath (13), tlt, hairdry, a/c, c/fan (29), elec blkts, tel, TV, clock radio, t/c mkg, refrig, doonas (8)], ldry, conv fac, ✕, rm serv, dinner to unit, cots, non smoking rms (25). **RO** ♦ **$88**, ♦♦ **$99**, ⧉ **$11**, **Suite D $126 - $140**, ch con, 29 units at a higher standard. AE BC DC EFT MC VI.

★★☆ **Curtin Budget Motel**, (M), 106 Cotter Rd, 8km S of Canberra City, ☎ 02 6281 5499, fax 02 6232 4034, (gr fl), 28 units [shwr, tlt, a/c-cool, elec blkts, TV, clock radio, t/c mkg, refrig, micro (communal), toaster], ldry, ✕, rm serv, ☎, cots. **RO** ♦ **$65**, ♦♦ **$65**, ⧉ **$10**, AE BC DC MC VI.

Operator Comment: See our display advertisement on opposite page.

B&B's/Guest Houses

★★★☆ **Birch Corner Bed & Breakfast**, (B&B), 31 Parker St, ☎ 02 6281 4421, fax 02 6260 4641, 4 rms [hairdry (2), a/c, cent heat, elec blkts, cable TV, clock radio, t/c mkg], ldry, lounge (TV), ✕, pool, bbq, courtesy transfer, cots, non smoking property. **BB** ♦ **$65**, ♦♦ **$95**, **DBB** ♦ **$90**, ♦♦ **$145**, ch con, BC MC VI.

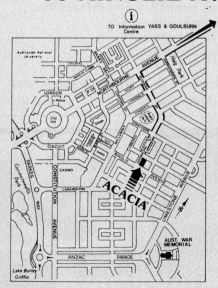

...tes may change. Check before booking.

CANBERRA - DEAKIN ACT 2600

Pop Part of Canberra, (5km SW Canberra), See map on page 34, ref C5, Inner southern suburb of Canberra.

Hotels/Motels

★★★☆ **Embassy Motel**, (M), Cnr Hopetoun Circuit & Adelaide Ave, ☎ 02 6281 1322, fax 02 6281 1843, (2 stry), 86 units (4 suites) [shwr, tlt, a/c-cool, cent heat, elec blkts, tel, TV, movie, clock radio, t/c mkg, refrig], ldry, conv fac, ⊠, pool, sauna, 24hr reception, rm serv, dinner to unit, cots, non smoking units (56). BLB ┆ **$125**, ┆┆ **$125**, ┆┆┆ **$140**, Suite D **$145 - $170**, 5 rooms of a higher standard. AE BC DC EFT JCB MC MP VI, ⅋.

Trouble-free travel tips - Jack
Check that the jack and wheel are on board and the jack works.

CANBERRA - DICKSON ACT 2602

Pop Part of Canberra, (3km N Canberra), See map on page 34, ref D3, Inner northern suburb of Canberra.

Hotels/Motels

★★★★ **Quality Inn Dickson**, (M), Previously Dickson Premier Inn Cnr Badham & Cape St, 2km N of CBD, ☎ 02 6247 4744, fax 02 6247 4455, (2 stry gr fl), 40 units [shwr, spa bath (12), tlt, hairdry, a/c, heat, tel, TV, movie, clock radio, t/c mkg, refrig, mini bar, micro (5), toaster], lift, ldry, iron, iron brd, ✆, gym-fee, squash-fee, cots-fee, non smoking units (21). BLB ┆ **$92 - $158**, ┆┆ **$107 - $160**, ┆ **$23**, AE BC DC EFT JCB MC VI.

★★★☆ **Pavilion on Northbourne**, (LH), 242 Northbourne Ave, ☎ 02 6247 6888, fax 02 6248 7866, (Multi-stry gr fl), 111 rms (41 suites) [shwr, bath, spa bath (10), tlt, hairdry, a/c, cent heat, tel, TV, movie, clock radio, t/c mkg, refrig, mini bar, cook fac (17), micro, toaster (17)], lift, ldry, conv fac, ⊠, pool, 24hr reception, rm serv, dinner to unit, ✆, cots, non smoking units (20). BB ┆ **$125 - $165**, ┆┆ **$125 - $165**, ┆ **$15 - $32**, RO ┆┆ **$145 - $198**, ┆ **$15**, Suite RO ┆┆ **$145 - $172**, ch con, 37 rooms of a higher standard, AE BC DC EFT JCB MC VI.

Self Catering Accommodation

★★★★☆ **The Parklands Apartment Hotel**, (SA), 1 Hawdon Pl, 3km N of GPO, ☎ 02 6262 7000, fax 02 6262 6000, (gr fl), 66 serv apts acc up to 6, [shwr, bath, spa bath, tlt, hairdry, a/c, heat, elec blkts, tel, TV, movie, clock radio, t/c mkg, refrig, mini bar, cook fac, micro, d/wash, toaster, ldry, blkts, linen], lift, w/mach, dryer, iron, iron brd, conf fac, pool-indoor, spa, bbq, courtesy transfer, gym, cots-fee, non smoking rms (6). RO **$99 - $270**, pen con, AE BC DC MC VI.

Budget International Hotel, (HU), 242 Northbourne Ave, 1.5km N of PO, ☎ 02 6247 6966, fax 02 6248 7823, (Multi-stry), 39 units acc up to 4, (Studio), [shwr, bath, tlt, a/c, TV, movie-fee, clock radio, t/c mkg, refrig, cook fac ltd, micro, toaster, blkts, linen, pillows], ldry, ⊠, pool, cots, non smoking units (20). D ┆ **$70 - $80**, ┆┆ **$70 - $80**, ┆ **$11**, ch con, AE BC DC EFT MC VI, (not yet classified).

CANBERRA - DOWNER ACT 2602

Pop Part of Canberra, (4km N Canberra), See map on page 34, ref D3, Inner northern suburb of Canberra.

B&B's/Guest Houses

★★★★ **Blue & White Lodge**, (B&B), 524 Northbourne Ave, 4km N of GPO, ☎ 02 6248 0498, fax 02 6248 8277, (2 stry gr fl), 10 rms [ensuite (10), spa bath (1), hairdry, a/c-cool, cent heat, fax, TV, clock radio, t/c mkg, refrig], ✕, bbq, ✎, cots, non smoking property. **BB ♦ $82.50, ♦♦ $93.50 - $104.50, ♦♦♦ $104.50, ◊ $16.50**, ch con, AE BC DC EFT MC VI.

★★★☆ **White Gum Place Bed & Breakfast**, (B&B), 23 Padbury Place, 4km N of GPO, ☎ 02 6248 9368, fax 02 6248 9368, (gr fl), 1 rm (1 suite) [shwr, tlt, hairdry, cent heat, elec blkts, tel, TV, video, clock radio, t/c mkg, refrig, cook fac ltd, micro, toaster], cots, non smoking rms. **BB ♦ $55 - $70, ♦♦ $70 - $85, ◊ $11 - $33, ♦♦ $400 - $450.**

Other Accommodation

★★★★ **Miranda Lodge**, (Lodge), 534 Northbourne Ave, 4km N of GPO, ☎ 02 6249 8038, fax 02 6247 6166, (2 stry gr fl), 22 rms [shwr, bath (3), spa bath (3), tlt, a/c-cool, c/fan (12), cent heat, tel, TV, video-fee, movie (12), clock radio, t/c mkg, refrig], iron, iron brd, cots, non smoking rms. **BB ♦ $80 - $90, ♦♦ $99 - $120, ♦♦♦ $120 - $140, ◊ $20**, AE BC DC EFT MC VI.

★★★☆ **Northbourne Lodge**, (Lodge), 522 Northbourne Ave, 4.5km N of city, ☎ 02 6257 2599, fax 02 6257 2599, (2 stry gr fl), 8 rms acc up to 4, [shwr, tlt, a/c-cool, cent heat, TV, t/c mkg, refrig], ✎, non smoking property, Pets allowed. **BB ♦ $85, ♦♦ $99 - $110, ◊ $25, W ♦ $350 - $450**, AE BC DC EFT MC VI.

CANBERRA - FORREST ACT 2603

Pop Part of Canberra, (4km S Canberra), See map on page 34, ref C5, Inner southern suburb of Canberra. Golf.

Hotels/Motels

★★★★☆ **Rydges Capital Hill**, (LH), Cnr Canberra Ave & National Cir, 1km SE of Manuka PO, ☎ 02 6295 3144, fax 02 6295 3325, (Multi-stry gr fl), 186 rms (36 suites) [shwr, bath (180), spa bath (37), tlt, a/c, tel, TV, video, clock radio, t/c mkg, refrig], lift, ldry, conv fac, ✕, pool, sauna, spa, rm serv, dinner to unit, gym, cots, non smoking rms (90). **RO ♦ $140 - $179, ♦♦ $140 - $179, ◊ $38.50, Suite RO ♦♦ $218.90**, ch con, 37 units at a higher standard. AE BC DC EFT JCB MC VI, ✍&.

 ★★★☆ **Forrest Inn & Apartments**, (M), 30 National Cir, ☎ 02 6295 3433, fax 02 6295 2119, (2 stry gr fl), 76 units (1 suite) [shwr, bath (2), tlt, a/c, elec blkts, tel, TV, clock radio, t/c mkg, refrig, mini bar], ldry, conv fac, ✕, bbq, cots, non smoking units (4). **RO ♦ $96.80, ♦♦ $96.80, ◊ $15, Suite D $145**, ch con, AE BC DC EFT MC VI.

★★★☆ **(Serviced Apartment Section)**, 26 serv apts acc up to 5, [shwr, tlt, a/c, heat, tel, TV, clock radio, t/c mkg, refrig, cook fac, toaster], ldry, bbq, plygr, cots. **D ♦ $110, ♦♦ $110, ◊ $15.**

 ★★☆ **Telopea Inn On The Park**, (M), 16 New South Wales Cres, ☎ 02 6295 3722, fax 02 6239 6373, (2 stry), 44 units (2 suites) [shwr, bath (12), tlt, a/c, tel, TV, radio, t/c mkg, refrig, cook fac ltd (12)], ldry, conv fac, ✕ (seasonal), pool indoor heated, spa, cots, non smoking units (30). **RO ♦ $103, ◊ $12, Suite D ♦ $134, ◊ $12**, ch con, 12 units at a higher standard. AE BC DC EFT MC VI.

Self Catering Accommodation

 ★★★★☆ **Bentley Suites**, (Apt), Cnr Canberra Ave & Dominion Circ, ☎ 02 6124 0000, fax 02 6124 0100, (gr fl), 107 apts acc up to 6, [shwr, spa bath (33), tlt, a/c, c/fan, tel, TV, video, clock radio, t/c mkg, refrig, cook fac, micro, d/wash, toaster, ldry, blkts, linen, pillows], w/mach, dryer, conf fac, pool-heated, sauna, bbq, dinner to unit, secure park (under cover), cots-fee, non smoking units (15). **D $157 - $221**, ch con, AE BC DC MC VI.

Rates may change. Check before booking.

CANBERRA - GREENWAY ACT 2900

Pop Part of Canberra, (14km SW Canberra), See map on page 34, ref B8, Outer south-western suburb of Canberra.

Hotels/Motels

  ★★★★ **Country Comfort Greenway**, (LMH), 46 Rowland Rees Cres, 200m W of Hyperdome, ☎ 02 6293 3666, fax 02 6293 3444, (2 stry gr fl), 100 units (4 suites) [shwr, spa bath (7), tlt, hairdry, a/c, elec blkts, tel, TV, clock radio, t/c mkg, refrig, mini bar, micro (1), ldry], lift, iron, iron brd, conf fac, lounge firepl, cafe, pool-heated, sauna, spa, bbq, rm serv, cots, non smoking units (60). **RO** ♦ $126, ♦♦ $126, ◊ $17.50, ch con, AE BC DC MC VI.
Operator Comment: See our display advertisement on previous page.

CANBERRA - GRIFFITH ACT 2603

Pop Part of Canberra, See map on page 34, ref D6, Inner southern suburb of Canberra.

Hotels/Motels

  ★★★★ **Quality Hotel Diplomat**, (M), Previously Diplomat Boutique Hotel Cnr Canberra Ave & Hely St, 2km S of Manuka, ☎ 02 6295 2277, fax 02 6239 6432, (Multi-stry gr fl), 67 units (10 suites) [shwr, bath (30), spa bath (8), tlt, hairdry, a/c, elec blkts, tel, TV, video-fee, movie, clock radio, t/c mkg, mini bar], lift, ldry, iron, iron brd, ⊠, pool (salt water), sauna, 24hr reception, rm serv, c/park (undercover), gym, cots. **RO** ♦ $160 - $220, ♦♦ $160 - $220, ◊ $20, ch con, AE BC DC MC MP VI.

CANBERRA - HALL ACT 2618

Pop Part of Canberra, (12km N Canberra), See map on page 34, ref C1, Historic village just south of the NSW border.

B&B's/Guest Houses

★★★★ **Last Stop Ambledown Brook**, (B&B), Brooklands Rd, 22km N of Canberra, ☎ 02 6230 2280, fax 02 6230 2280, (gr fl), 3 rms [shwr, tlt, fan, heat, elec blkts, tel, TV, radio, t/c mkg, refrig, cook fac ltd], pool, bbq, tennis. **BB** ♦ $66, ♦♦ $99, ◊ $10 - $60, **DBB** ♦ $91, ♦♦ $149, Train and Tram carriage accommodation.

CANBERRA - HAWKER ACT 2614

Pop Part of Canberra, (10km NW Canberra), See map on page 34, ref B3, North-western suburb of Canberra.

Hotels/Motels

★★★ **Belconnen Hotel Motel**, (LMH), Cnr Belconnen Way & Springvale Dve, ☎ 02 6254 2222, fax 02 6254 4505, (Multi-stry gr fl), 62 units (9 suites) [shwr, bath (4), spa bath (2), tlt, a/c, cent heat, tel, TV, clock radio, t/c mkg, refrig, cook fac (12)], lift, ldry, lounge, conv fac, ⊠, 24hr reception, rm serv, dinner to unit, cots-fee, non smoking rms (12). **RO** ♦ $90, ♦♦ $90, ◊ $20, **Suite D** $110 - $145, ch con, AE BC DC MC VI.

CANBERRA - ISABELLA PLAINS ACT 2905

Pop Part of Canberra, (18km S Canberra), See map on page 34, ref B8, Outer southern suburb of Canberra.

B&B's/Guest Houses

★★★☆ **Ironbark Cottage B&B**, (B&B), 4 Rabnor Pl, ☎ 02 6292 1563, fax 02 6292 1563, 2 rms [fan, heat, elec blkts, clock radio], ldry, iron, iron brd, lounge (TV), ✕, t/c mkg shared, bbq, cots, non smoking property. **BB** ♦ $75, ♦♦ $95, ◊ $50, **DBB** ♦ $100, ♦♦ $145, ◊ $75, fam con, BC MC VI.

CANBERRA - KAMBAH ACT 2902

Pop Part of Canberra, (16km S Canberra), See map on page 34, ref B7, Outer south-western suburb of Canberra.

Hotels/Motels

★★ **Kambah Inn**, (LMH), Marconi Cres, ☎ 02 6231 8444, fax 02 6231 2450, 11 units [shwr, tlt, hairdry, a/c, tel, TV, clock radio, t/c mkg, refrig, toaster], ⊠ (Mon to Sat), ✆, cots-fee. **BLB** ♦ $55, ♦♦ $66, ◊ $11, ch con, BC EFT MC VI.

CANBERRA - KINGSTON ACT 2604

Pop Part of Canberra, (4km S Canberra), See map on page 34, ref D5, Inner southern suburb of Canberra.

Hotels/Motels

 ★★★ **Motel Monaro**, (M), 27 Dawes St, 5km from City Centre, ☎ 02 6295 2111, fax 02 6295 2466, (2 stry gr fl), 29 units [shwr, tlt, hairdry, a/c, heat, elec blkts, tel, TV, video-fee, clock radio, t/c mkg, refrig, toaster], ldry, iron, iron brd, courtesy transfer (from train), cots-fee, non smoking units (25). **BLB** ♦ $99 - $105, ♦♦ $99 - $111, ♦♦♦ $110 - $125, ◊ $16, **RO** ♦ $89 - $99, ♦♦ $95 - $109, ♦♦♦ $105 - $120, ◊ $12, Min book all holiday times, AE BC DC EFT JCB MC MP VI.

Self Catering Accommodation

★★★★☆ **Kingston Court Serviced Apartments**, (SA), 4 Tench St, ☎ 02 6295 2244, fax 02 6295 5300, 36 serv apts acc up to 5, [shwr, bath, tlt, a/c, heat, elec blkts, tel, TV, video, clock radio, refrig, cook fac, d/wash, ldry (in unit), blkts, linen, pillows], w/mach, dryer, pool-heated-fee, bbq, c/park (undercover), tennis (half court). RO ♦ **$120**, ♦♦ **$135**, ♦♦♦ **$160**, ◊ **$15**, AE BC DC MC VI.

★★★★☆ **Kingston Terrace Serviced Apartments**, (SA), 16 Eyre St, ☎ 02 6239 9411, fax 02 6239 9499, (Multi-stry gr fl), 74 serv apts acc up to 6, [shwr, bath, spa bath (20), tlt, a/c, elec blkts, tel, TV, video (20), clock radio, t/c mkg, refrig, cook fac, micro, d/wash, toaster, ldry (in unit)], w/mach, dryer, pool-heated (solar), bbq, c/park (undercover), plygr, tennis (half court), cots. RO ♦ **$120**, ♦♦ **$135**, ♦♦♦ **$160**, ◊ **$15**, AE BC DC MC VI.

★★★★☆ **Medina Classic Canberra**, (SA), 11 Giles St, 2km SW of Parliament House, ☎ 02 6239 8100, fax 02 6239 7226, (Multi-stry gr fl), 50 serv apts (50 suites) acc up to 6, [shwr, bath (38), spa bath (3), tlt, hairdry, a/c, elec blkts, tel, TV, video-fee, clock radio, t/c mkg, refrig, cook fac, micro, d/wash, toaster, ldry, blkts, linen, pillows], lift, w/mach, dryer, iron, iron brd, conv fac, pool indoor heated, sauna, spa, bbq, c/park (garage), gym, cots. **Suite RO $134.20 - $242**, AE BC DC MC VI.

★★★★☆ **The Griffin Apartment Hotel**, (SA), 15 Tench St, 2km S of Parliament House, ☎ 02 6234 8000, or 02 6234 8111, fax 02 6239 5959, (2 stry gr fl), 83 serv apts acc up to 6, [shwr, spa bath (11), tlt, hairdry, a/c, tel, TV, movie, clock radio, t/c mkg, refrig, mini bar, cook fac, micro, d/wash, toaster, blkts, linen, pillows], ldry, iron, iron brd, conv fac, ⊠, rm serv, dinner to unit, gym, cots, non smoking rms (52). **D $192 - $292**, ch con, AE BC DC MC VI.

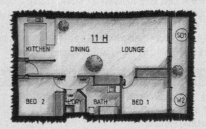
ACT
K

★★★★☆ **The York Canberra**, (SA), 31 Giles St, 2km E of Parliament House, ☎ 02 6295 2333, fax 02 6295 9559, (Multi-stry), 25 serv apts (2 suites) acc up to 6, [shwr, bath (18), tlt, hairdry, a/c (15), heat, elec blkts, tel, TV, video, clock radio, t/c mkg, refrig, cook fac (16), cook fac ltd (9), micro, toaster, ldry (in unit), blkts, linen, pillows], w/mach, dryer, iron, ⊠, bbq, secure park, cots, non smoking units. **Suite RO $170.50 - $242**, AE BC DC EFT MC VI.

★★★★ **Pinnacle Apartment Hotel**, (SA), 11 Ovens St, 500m N of PO, ☎ 02 6239 9799, fax 02 6239 6418, (gr fl), 97 serv apts acc up to 10, [shwr, bath, spa bath, tlt, a/c, heat, elec blkts, tel, TV, movie, clock radio, t/c mkg, refrig, cook fac, micro, d/wash, toaster, ldry, blkts, linen, pillows], w/mach, dryer, iron, conf fac, pool-heated, bbq, c/park (undercover), gym, cots. **RO $145, W $770**, AE BC DC EFT MC VI.

 ★★★☆ **Oxley Court**, (SA), Cnr Oxley & Dawes Sts, 1.5km E of Parliament House, ☎ 02 6295 6216, fax 02 6239 6085, 28 serv apts acc up to 6, (1 & 2 bedrm), [shwr, bath, tlt, a/c, heat, elec blkts, tel, TV, video, clock radio, refrig, cook fac, micro, d/wash, toaster, ldry], dryer, c/park (carport), plygr. **RO ♦ $130, ♦♦ $140, ◊ $12**, Min book long w/ends, AE BC DC EFT MC VI.

B&B's/Guest Houses

★★ **Victor Lodge**, (B&B), 29 Dawes St, ☎ 02 6295 7777, fax 02 6295 2466, 19 rms [fan, cent heat, tel, t/c mkg (communal), refrig (communal), cook fac, ldry, doonas], TV rm, ✕, bbq, cots (fee), non smoking property. **BB ♦ $44 - $50, ♦♦ $56 - $65**, BC EFT MC VI.

CANBERRA - LYNEHAM ACT 2602

Pop Part of Canberra, (3km N Canberra), See map on page 34, ref D3, Inner northern suburb of Canberra.

Hotels/Motels

★★★☆ **Canberra City Gateway Motel**, (M), Cnr Northbourne Ave & Mouat St, 3km N of Canberra City PO, ☎ 02 6247 2777, fax 02 6247 4871, (Multi-stry), 100 units [shwr, tlt, hairdry (25), a/c, cent heat, tel, TV, movie, clock radio, t/c mkg, refrig], lift, ldry, conv fac, ⊠, pool, rm serv, dinner to unit, cots-fee, non smoking units (17). **RO ♦ $130, ♦♦ $150, ◊ $11**, ch con, AE BC DC EFT MC VI, 🐾♿.

 ★★★☆ **Canberra Lyneham Motor Inn**, (M), 39 Mouat St, ☎ 02 6249 6855, fax 02 6247 6184, (2 stry gr fl), 32 units [shwr, bath (24), tlt, a/c, tel, TV, video, radio, t/c mkg, refrig], ldry, ⊠, rm serv, cots-fee. **RO ♦ $86, ♦♦ $97, ◊ $11**, ch con, 18 units not yet rated. AE BC DC MC VI.

★★★ **Yowani Country Club Motel**, (M), Northbourne Ave, 1km N of Dickson PO, ☎ 02 6241 3377, fax 02 6241 8561, 12 units [shwr, tlt, a/c, elec blkts, tel, TV, clock radio, t/c mkg, refrig, cook fac ltd], iron, iron brd, rec rm, ⊠ (Tue to Sat), bowls, golf. **RO ♦ $72, ♦♦ $77, ♦♦♦ $88**, ch con, AE BC DC EFT MC VI.

Australian Capital Motor Inn, (M), 193 Mouat St, 4km from City centre, ☎ 02 6257 8133, fax 02 6257 8144, (2 stry gr fl), 54 units [shwr, tlt, a/c, cent heat, tel (35), TV, video-fee, clock radio (35), t/c mkg, refrig, toaster], ldry, iron, iron brd, breakfast rm, pool, bbq, gym, cots, non smoking units (54). **RO ♦ $55 - $75, ♦♦ $65 - $85, ♦♦♦ $75 - $95, ◊ $5 - $10**, AE BC DC MC VI, (Rating under review).

CANBERRA - MACQUARIE ACT 2614

Pop Part of Canberra, (7km NW Canberra), See map on page 34, ref B3, Inner northern suburb of Canberra.

Hotels/Motels

★☆ **Jamison Inn**, (LH), 3 Bowman St, ☎ 02 6251 2111, fax 02 6251 4019, 25 rms [shwr, tlt, cent heat, elec blkts, tel, TV, clock radio, t/c mkg, refrig], ldry, conv fac, ⊠, rm serv, dinner to unit, cots. **RO ♦ $60 - $65, ♦♦ $70 - $75, ♦♦♦ $75 - $80, ◊ $10**, AE BC DC EFT MC VI.

CANBERRA - MANUKA ACT 2603

Pop Part of Canberra, (4km S Canberra), See map on page 34, ref D5, Inner southern suburb of Canberra. Bowls, Swimming, Tennis.

Self Catering Accommodation

★★★☆ **Manuka Park Serviced Apartments**, (SA), Cnr Manuka Circle & Oxley St, 1km S of Parliament House, ☎ 02 6239 0000, fax 02 6295 7750, (Multi-stry gr fl), 39 serv apts [shwr, tlt, hairdry, a/c, tel, TV, clock radio, t/c mkg, refrig, cook fac, micro, d/wash, toaster, ldry (in unit)], pool (salt water), secure park (undercover), cots. **RO ♦♦ $125 - $145, ◊ $10, W $805 - $910**, ch con, AE BC DC MC VI.

B&B's/Guest Houses

Manuka Cottage Bed & Breakfast, (B&B), 12 Stokes St, 300m W of PO, ☎ 02 6295 6984, fax 02 6295 6984, (gr fl), 1 rm (1 suite) [fan, heat (elec/wood), elec blkts, TV, radio, t/c mkg, refrig, doonas], bathrm, lounge firepl, ✕, pool, non smoking rms. **BB ♦ $98, ♦♦ $135, ◊ $60**, BC MC VI, (not yet classified).

Trouble-free travel tips - **Fluids**

Check all fluid levels and top up as necessary. Look at engine oil, automatic transmission fluid, radiator coolant (only check this when the engine is cold), power steering, battery and windscreen washers.

so much to see...
so much to do

canberra
HEART OF THE NATION

bentley suites
Style, Sophistication & Service

pinnacle apartments
Room to Move

heritage hotel
Something for Everyone

bentley suites

pinnacle apartments

hotel heritage

DOMA HOTELS CANBERRA

Central Reservations
Phone (02) 6295 2944 Fax: (02) 6239 6310
Freecall - 1800 026 346
email: reservations@hotelheritage.com.au
website: www.domahotelscanberra.com.au

CANBERRA - NARRABUNDAH ACT 2604

Pop Part of Canberra, (7km SE Canberra), See map on page 34, ref D6, Inner southern suburb of Canberra.

Hotels/Motels

  ★★★★ **Quality Inn Garden City**, (M), Previously Garden City Premier Inn Jerrabomberra Ave, opposite golf course, ☎ 02 6295 3322, fax 02 6239 6289, (2 stry gr fl), 72 units (3 suites) [shwr, tlt, a/c, tel, TV, movie, clock radio, t/c mkg, refrig], iron, iron brd, conv fac, ⊠, pool, rm serv, dinner to unit, cots-fee, non smoking rms (34). **RO ⋔ $120 - $150, ⋔ $15**, AE BC DC EFT MC MP VI, ⅍⅃.

★★★☆ **Crestwood Gardens Motor Inn**, (M), 39 Jerrabomberra Ave, adjacent German Club, ☎ 02 6295 2099, fax 02 6295 1240, (2 stry gr fl), 57 units [shwr, tlt, a/c (25), cent heat, elec blkts, tel, TV, clock radio, t/c mkg, refrig], ldry, ⊠, bbq, cots. **RO ⋔ $65, ⋔ $75, ⋔⋔ $85, ⋔⋔⋔ $95**, ch con, fam con, AE BC DC MC VI.

★★★☆ **Hotel Heritage**, (M), 203 Goyder St, adjacent golf course, ☎ 02 6295 2944, fax 02 6239 6310, 209 units [shwr, bath (73), spa bath (4), tlt, hairdry, a/c, heat, elec blkts, tel, TV, movie, clock radio, t/c mkg, refrig, cook fac (8)], ldry, conv fac, ⊠, bar, pool, sauna, spa, bbq, 24hr reception, rm serv, cots. **RO ⋔ $80 - $135, ⋔⋔ $80 - $135,** 67 rooms ★★★★, 40 dormitory rooms not rated. AE BC DC MC VI, ⅍⅃.

 ★★★☆ **Sundown Motel Resort**, (M), Previously Sundown Village Motel Jerrabomberra Ave, 5km S of GPO, ☎ 02 6239 0333, fax 02 6239 0288, 81 units (81 suites) [shwr, tlt, a/c, heat, elec blkts, tel, TV, clock radio, t/c mkg, refrig, cook fac, micro, toaster], ldry, conv fac, ⊠, pool, bbq, courtesy transfer, plygr, tennis. **Suite D ⋔ $99 - $115, ⋔⋔ $99 - $115, ⋔⋔⋔ $109 - $125, ⋔ $5 - $10**, ch con, AE BC BTC DC EFT JCB MC MP VI.

CANBERRA - NGUNNAWAL ACT 2913

Pop Part of Canberra, (14km N Canberra), See map on page 34, ref D1, Residential subur.

B&B's/Guest Houses

★★★ **Gungahlin Homestay Bed & Breakfast**, (B&B), Leita Court, 14km N of Canberra City, ☎ 02 6241 0776, fax 02 6241 0776, (gr fl), 1 rm [shwr, tlt, fan, cent heat, elec blkts, tel, TV, clock radio, t/c mkg], iron, iron brd, lounge (TV), c/park. **BB ⋔ $60, ⋔⋔ $80 - $90**, BC MC VI.

CANBERRA - NICHOLLS ACT 2913

Pop Nominal, (12km N Canberra), See map on page 34, ref C1, Residential suburb.

Hotels/Motels

Gold Creek Tourist Resort, (M), O'Hanlon Pl, 500m N of Cockington Green, ☎ 02 6241 3000, fax 02 6241 3300, (2 stry gr fl), 65 units [shwr, bath (5), spa bath (6), tlt, hairdry, a/c, tel, TV, clock radio, t/c mkg, refrig, mini bar (11), toaster], iron (6), iron brd (6), rec rm, conf fac, ✕, ⊠, pool (solar heated), cook fac, bbq, 24hr reception, rm serv, dinner to unit, cots, non smoking units. **BB ⋔ $90 - $130, ⋔⋔ $110 - $150, ⋔ $15 - $20**, pen con, AE BC DC EFT MC VI, (not yet classified).

CANBERRA - O'CONNOR ACT 2601

Pop Part of Canberra, (4km N Canberra), See map on page 34, ref D4, Inner northern suburb of Canberra.

Hotels/Motels

 ★★★ **Canberra Motor Village**, (M), Kunzea St, ☎ 02 6247 5466, fax 02 6249 6138, (2 stry gr fl), 38 units [shwr, tlt, a/c (28), heat (28), cent heat (10), tel, TV, clock radio, t/c mkg, refrig, cook fac (24)], ldry, ⊠, pool, bbq, tennis, cots. **BB ⋔ $73 - $98, ⋔⋔ $73 - $98, ⋔⋔⋔ $104 - $128.70, ⋔ $16.50**, AE BC DC MC VI.

B&B's/Guest Houses

★★★☆ **Pasmore Cottage Bed & Breakfast**, (B&B), 3 Lilley St, 3km from GPO, ☎ 02 6247 4528, fax 02 6247 4528, (gr fl), 3 rms [shwr, tlt, cent heat, elec blkts, tel, clock radio, t/c mkg], lounge (TV), c/park. **BB ⋔ $70 - $85, ⋔⋔ $85 - $105**, AE BC MC VI.

CANBERRA - SYMONSTON ACT 2609

Pop Part of Canberra, (7km SW Canberra), See map on page 34, ref D6, South-eastern suburb of Canberra.

Hotels/Motels

Canberra South Motor Park, (M), Canberra Ave, ☎ 02 6280 6176, fax 02 6239 2250, 21 units [shwr, tlt, heat, tel, t/c mkg, refrig, cook fac (1), cook fac ltd (4), toaster], ldry, rec rm, ✗, bbq, ✆, plygr, cots. **RO** ⨍ **$66 - $84**, ⨍⨍ **$66 - $84**, ⨍ **$10**, Min book long w/ends and Easter, BC EFT MC VI, (not yet classified).

Operator Comment: See our display advertisement opposite.

CANBERRA - TURNER ACT 2612

Pop Part of Canberra, (2km N Canberra), See map on page 34, ref D4, Inner northern suburb of Canberra.

Hotels/Motels

★★ **Canberra Central Apartments**, (M), Cnr Northbourne Ave & Barry Dr, 1 Block from PO, ☎ 02 6230 4781, fax 02 6230 6466, (Multi-stry gr fl), 158 units [shwr, bath (50), tlt, heat, TV, clock radio, t/c mkg, refrig, cook fac, micro (50), toaster], lift, ldry, ✆, cots, non smoking units (60). **D $110, W $290 - $550**, pen con, AE BC DC MC VI.

CANBERRA - WATSON ACT 2602

Pop Part of Canberra, (6km N Canberra), See map on page 34, ref E3, Inner northern suburb of Canberra.

Hotels/Motels

★★★ **National Capital Village Motel**, (M), Antill St, 6km N of PO, ☎ 02 6241 3188, fax 02 6241 2109, 20 units [shwr, bath, tlt, a/c, fan (on request), heat, elec blkts, tel, TV, video-fee, clock radio, t/c mkg, refrig, cook fac, toaster], ldry-fee, pool, bbq, plygr, cots. **RO** ⨍ **$55 - $63.80**, ⨍⨍ **$60.50 - $74.80**, ⨍ **$13.20**, AE BC BTC DC EFT MC VI, ♿.

★★★ **(Holiday Units Section)**, 40 units [shwr, bath, tlt, a/c-cool (29), heat, tel (19), TV, t/c mkg, refrig, cook fac, toaster, blkts, linen, pillows], ldry, lounge, bbq, cots. **RO $115 - $136.50**, ⨍ **$13.20**.

★★☆ **Canberra Carotel Motel**, (M), Federal Hwy, 7.2km N of GPO, ☎ 02 6241 1377, fax 02 6241 6674, (gr fl), 43 units (19 suites) [shwr, tlt, a/c, heat, TV, t/c mkg, refrig, cook fac (19), toaster], ldry, pool (salt water), bbq, shop (licensed), ✆, plygr, cots. **RO** ⨍⨍ **$64 - $110**, ⨍ **$6**, AE BC DC EFT MC VI.

Operator Comment: See our display advertisement on bottom of page.

★★☆ **Red Cedars Motel**, (M), Cnr Stirling Ave & Aspinall St, 4km E of Canberra City, ☎ 02 6241 1888, or 02 6241 8579, fax 02 6241 2944, 30 units [shwr, tlt, a/c (24), heat, elec blkts, tel, TV, clock radio, t/c mkg, refrig, cook fac ltd (8), toaster], cots-fee. **RO** ⨍ **$57 - $79**, ⨍⨍ **$68 - $90**, ⨍⨍⨍ **$79 - $99**, ⨍ **$15**, AE BC DC MC VI.

CANBERRA - YARRALUMLA ACT 2600

Pop Part of Canberra, (5km W Canberra), See map on page 34, ref C5, Inner southern suburb of Canberra beside Lake Burley Griffin in the heart of the 'consular belt'.

Hotels/Motels

★★★★★ **Hyatt Hotel Canberra**, (LH), Commonwealth Ave, 600m S of Commonwealth Ave bridge, ☎ 02 6270 1234, fax 02 6281 5998, (Multi-stry gr fl), 249 rms (18 suites) [shwr, bath, tlt, hairdry, a/c, elec blkts, tel, cable TV, movie, radio, t/c mkg, refrig, mini bar], lift, lounge, business centre, ✗, pool indoor heated, sauna, spa, 24hr reception, rm serv, bicycle, gym, tennis, cots, non smoking rms. **RO** ⨍ **$260 - $416**, ⨍⨍ **$260 - $416**, ⨍ **$43**, ch con, AE BC DC EFT JCB MC VI.

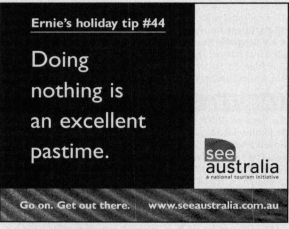

Sydney, capital of NSW, is Australia's biggest city in the state in which modern Australia has its roots. Roots which were first imbedded when the marvellous navigator, Captain James Cook, took possession for Britain in 1770.

The founding state has developed from the penal colony, of 1788 established by Governor Arthur Phillip at Sydney Cove, to a modern, sophisticated internationally famous destination.

NSW is a remarkable touring experience which ranges from bustling, beautiful sophisticated Sydney and its magnificent harbour, to the frontier lunar landscape of remote Mungo National Park in the west. It is a tribute to the tenacity of Australians that such change has been worked since 1813 when the explorers Blaxland, Lawson and Wentworth first made their way through the barrier of the Blue Mountains and settlers moved out from Sydney in their path.

The gold rush of the 1850's led to rapid development throughout the state and an increase in population which now makes NSW Australia's most populated state.

Superb beaches, the Hunter Valley wine region, the Hawkesbury, Central Coast and the Blue Mountains can be visited in an easy days drive from Sydney.

The North Coast of the state is sub-tropical. The west is striking in the "frontier" way with Lightning Ridge, Broken Hill and prehistoric Mungo part of an experience

which can lead to the junction of Australia's mightiest rivers, the Murray and the Darling near Wentworth and the border with Victoria and South Australia.

Kosciuszko National Park and the Snowy Mountains contain some of Australia's best ski resorts and a region which is a bushwalkers paradise in the warmer months.

The Southern coast is famous for its fishing and holiday towns and the Illawarra Coast and Southern Highlands attract beach and nature lovers like a magnet. The great outdoors is never far way in NSW and the countryside has a beauty all its own. Holidaying on a farm is a great way to both see and appreciate the "real" NSW.

Many farm families open their doors to city people to share their special life and depending on the property visitors can stay in their own cottage or in the homestead with the host family. Each property has its own specialties.

A caravan trip, camping, seaside holiday, theme park, museum or snow holiday are all within the scope of a weekend or short break. Follow the dolphins to the white beaches of Port Stephens. There are spectacular coastal walks and the chance of off-road adventure in the sand dunes.

The highway touring routes of NSW offer smooth travelling on links from Brisbane like the Newell, New England and Pacific Highways. Each has its own special attractions.

Outback the Kidman Way heads into Queensland via Cobar and Bourke. From Melbourne the Hume, Princes Olympic, Monaro and Snowy Mountains Highways provide access to touring options unique in the world.

From Adelaide the Barrier Highway sweeps from Broken Hill through Wilcannia, Cobar and Nyngan to Dubbo.

From Gawler in SA, the Sturt Highway strikes out to Hay and joins the Mid Western on the way to Bathurst and Lithgow and Sydney via the Great Western Highway.

NEW SOUTH WALES

Home of modern Australia

QUEENSLAND

AUSTRALIA

1

TIBOOBURRA

MILPARINKA

WANAARING

Narran Lake

Barwon

BOURKE

BREWARRINA

MITCHELL

2

WHITE CLIFFS

BYROCK

Bogan

R.

3

BARRIER

WILCANNIA

COBAR

HWY

NYNGAN

BROKEN HILL

SILVER

Menindee Lake

MENINDEE

Darling

Bogan

CITY

4

IVANHOE

CONDOBOLIN

Garnpung Lake

LAKE CARGELLIGO

R.

HWY

HILLSTON

Lake Cowal

5

Lake Victoria

WENTWORTH

DARETON

RANKINS SPRINGS

WESTERN

HWY

RIVER

BURONGA

GOL GOL

GOOLGOWI

WEETHALLE

CARAGABAL

STURT

TRENTHAM CLIFFS

WEST WYALONG

Lachlan

MID

GRIFFITH

ARDLETHAN

TEMORA

CALDER

EUSTON

ROBINVALE

HWY

BALRANALD

HAY

STURT

Murrumbidgee

DARLINGTON POINT

LEETON

MURRAY

GRONG GRONG

MALLEE

HWY

TOOLEYBUC

MOULAMEIN

COLEAMBALLY

NARRANDERA

COOLAMON

JUNEE

6

VICTORIA

Murray

Lake Urana

R.

HWY

WAGGA WAGGA

SOUTH

BARHAM

JERILDERIE

LOCKHART

THE ROCK

TARCUTTA

DENILIQUIN

URANA

YERONG CREEK

ADELONG

FINLEY

BERRIGAN

CULCAIRN

NEWELL

MATHOURA

TOCUMWAL

WALLA WALLA

HOLBROOK

VALLEY

MOAMA

BAROOGA

GEROGERY

WOOMARGAMA

HOWLONG

TUMBARUMBA

HWY

MULWALA

COROWA

BOWNA

Murray

ALBURY

WESTERN

HUME

Lake Hume

KHANCOBAN

FWY

7

HUME

VICTORIA

8

HWY

© RAASA

REFER TO PAGE 54
FOR MORE DETAIL

REFER TO PAGE 55
FOR MORE DETAIL

CANBERRA
For suburban listings,
refer to ACT-Canberra
& Suburbs sections.

REFER TO PAGE 34
IN ACT SECTION
FOR MORE DETAIL

ACT

SOUTH PACIFIC OCEAN

PACIFIC

TASMAN

SEA

N

TOWN LEGEND
● See Accommodation Guide
● See Tourist Park Guide
● See Both Accommodation
  & Tourist Park Guide
Green text defines towns included
in Tourist Region listings.
Red text defines towns included
in City & Suburbs listings.

SCALE
0   50   100   150   200
KILOMETRES

QUEENSLAND

BRUXNER

SEE MAP ON PAGE 53

BILAMBIL
TERRANORA
CHINDERAH
MURWILLUMBAH
TYALGUM
TWEED HEADS
FINGAL HEAD
BANORA POINT
KINGSCLIFF
CABARITA BEACH
HASTINGS POINT
POTTSVILLE BEACH
WOOYUNG BEACH
UKI
BILLINUDGEL
OCEAN SHORES
BRUNSWICK HEADS
MULLUMBIMBY
KYOGLE
NIMBIN
BANGALOW
BYRON BAY
SUFFOLK PARK
NEWRYBAR
GOOLMANGAR
CASINO
LISMORE
GOONELLABAH
ALSTONVILLE
MAROM CREEK
LENNOX HEAD
BALLINA
BALLINA EAST
BROADWATER

ASHFORD

TENTERFIELD

DRAKE

EVANS HEAD

TORRINGTON

EMMAVILLE
DEEPWATER

FINE FLOWER

JACKADGERY

PALMERS ISLAND
MACLEAN
BRUSHGROVE
TYNDALE
GRAFTON
ILUKA
YAMBA
ANGOURIE

INVERELL
GWYDIR
GLEN INNES

BROOMS HEAD

BEN LOMOND

MINNIE WATER

NYMBOIDA
WOOLI

HALFWAY CREEK
RED ROCK
ARRAWARRA
MULLAWAY
WOOLGOOLGA
EMERALD BEACH
MOONEE BEACH

GUYRA

NANA GLEN
LOWANNA
CORAMBA

ARMIDALE
THORA
EBOR
DORRIGO
KARANGI
TOORMINA
COFFS HARBOUR
SAWTELL
BONVILLE
REPTON
MYLESTOM
URUNGA
GLENIFFER
BELLINGEN

URALLA

BENDEMEER
NEW

VALLA BEACH
NAMBUCCA HEADS

OXLEY

MACKSVILLE
BELLBROOK

SCOTTS HEAD
GRASSY HEAD
STUARTS POINT
SOUTH WEST ROCKS

WALCHA

YARRAHAPINNI
COLLOMBATTI

KEMPSEY
HAT HEAD

CRESCENT HEAD

MOUNT SEAVIEW

DELICATE NOBBY

NOWENDOC

N

ELLENBOROUGH
BEECHWOOD
WAUCHOPE
PORT MACQUARIE

COMBOYNE
LAKE CATHIE
BONNY HILLS
NORTH HAVEN
DUNBOGAN

ELANDS

KENDALL
KEW
LAURIETON

HANNAM VALE

KNORRIT FLAT
MOORLAND
STEWARTS RIVER

WINGHAM
COOPERNOOK
CROWDY HEAD

GLOUCESTER
TAREE
OXLEY
ISLAND
HARRINGTON
MANNING POINT

TINONEE
OLD BAR

RAINBOW FLAT
DIAMOND BEACH
HALLIDAYS POINT

SALISBURY

NABIAC
FAILFORD

LOSTOCK DAM

WANG WAUK

DUNGOG
EAST
GRESFORD

TUNCURRY
FORSTER
COOMBA PARK

BULAHDELAH
PACIFIC PALMS
SMITHS LAKE

VACY

BOORAL
BUNGWAHL

PATERSON

NERONG
BOMBAH POINT

SEE MAP ON PAGE 53

NORFOLK ISLAND

OCEAN

PACIFIC

SOUTH

LORD HOWE ISLAND

TOWN LEGEND
● See Accommodation Guide
● See Tourist Park Guide
● See Both Accommodation
  & Tourist Park Guide
Green text defines towns included
in Tourist Region listings.
Red text defines towns included
in City & Suburbs listings.

SCALE
0 10 20 30 40 50   100
KILOMETRES

© RAASA

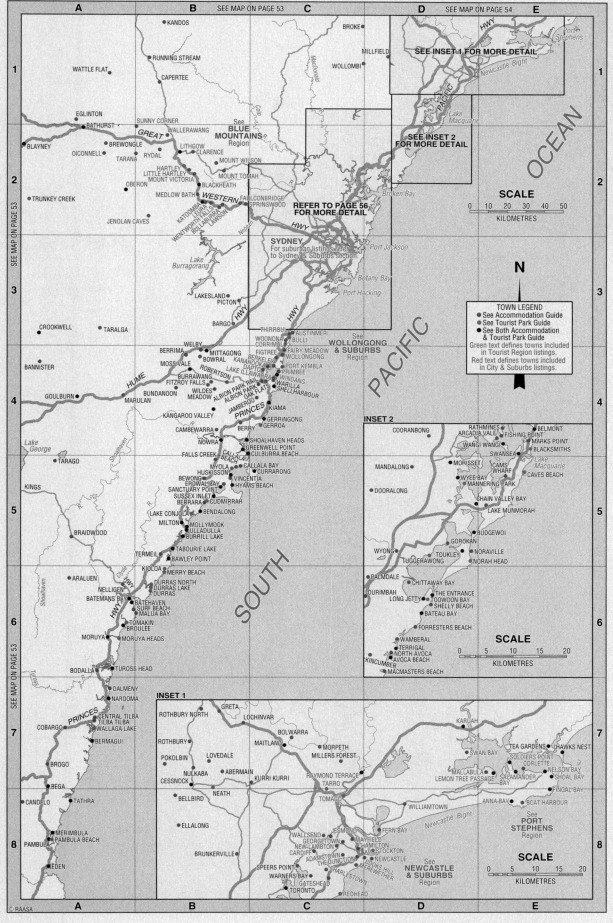

SEE MAP ON PAGE 53

SEE MAP ON PAGE 54

SCALE

0 10 20 30 40 50
KILOMETRES

N

TOWN LEGEND
● See Accommodation Guide
● See Tourist Park Guide
● See Both Accommodation
   & Tourist Park Guide
Green text defines towns included
in Tourist Region listings.
Red text defines towns included
in City & Suburbs listings.

INSET 2

SCALE

0 5 10 15 20
KILOMETRES

INSET 1

SCALE

0 5 10 15 20
KILOMETRES

© RAASA

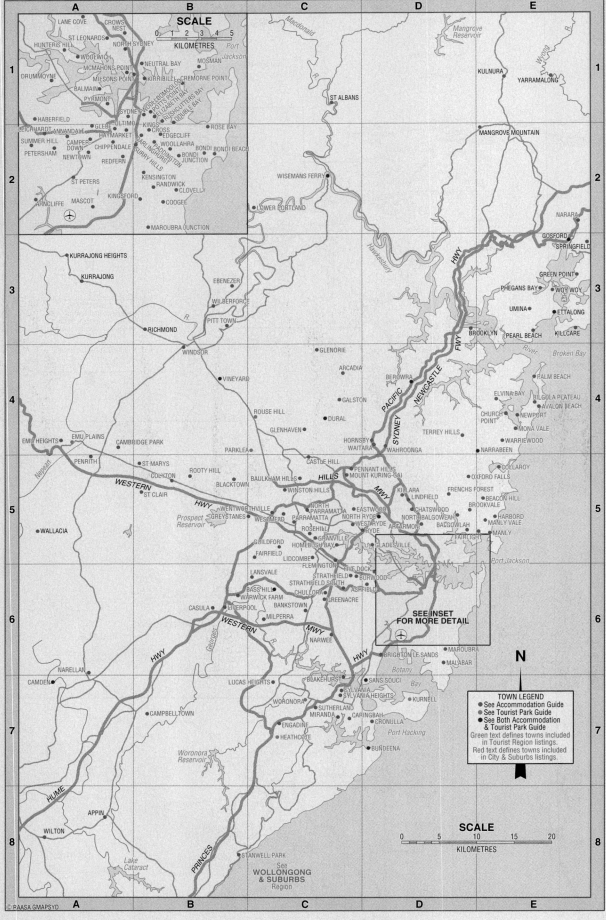

SCALE

A   B   C   D   E

0 1 2 3 4 5
KILOMETRES

Port Jackson

1

LANE COVE
CROWS NEST
ST LEONARDS
HUNTERS HILL
NORTH SYDNEY
WOOLWICH
MCMAHONS POINT
MILSONS POINT
NEUTRAL BAY
MOSMAN
DRUMMOYNE
BALMAIN
KIRRIBILLI
CREMORNE POINT
PYRMONT
WOOLLOOMOOLOO
POTTS POINT
ELIZABETH BAY
RUSHCUTTERS BAY
DOUBLE BAY
HABERFIELD
SYDNEY
ULTIMO
ROSE BAY
LEICHHARDT
ANNANDALE
GLEBE
HAYMARKET
KINGS CROSS
EDGECLIFF
WOOLLAHRA
SUMMER HILL
CAMPERDOWN
CHIPPENDALE
DARLINGHURST
BONDI
BONDI BEACH
PETERSHAM
NEWTOWN
REDFERN
SURRY HILLS
BONDI JUNCTION
ST PETERS
KENSINGTON
RANDWICK
CLOVELLY
ARNCLIFFE
MASCOT
KINGSFORD
COOGEE
MAROUBRA JUNCTION

Macdonald R

Mangrove Reservoir

Wyong R

ST ALBANS

KULNURA
YARRAMALONG

WISEMANS FERRY

NARARA
GOSFORD
SPRINGFIELD

MANGROVE MOUNTAIN

LOWER PORTLAND

GREEN POINT
PHEGANS BAY
WOY WOY
UMINA
ETTALONG

2

Hawkesbury R

KURRAJONG HEIGHTS

KURRAJONG

EBENEZER

WILBERFORCE

BROOKLYN
PEARL BEACH
KILLCARE

Broken Bay

3

RICHMOND

PITT TOWN

Hawkesbury River

PALM BEACH

WINDSOR

GLENORIE

ARCADIA

BEROWRA

ELVINA BAY
BILGOLA PLATEAU
AVALON BEACH

VINEYARD

GALSTON

CHURCH POINT
NEWPORT
MONA VALE

4

ROUSE HILL

DURAL

TERREY HILLS

WARRIEWOOD

EMU HEIGHTS
EMU PLAINS

CAMBRIDGE PARK

GLENHAVEN

HORNSBY
WAITARA

WAHROONGA

NARRABEEN

PENRITH

PARKLEA

CASTLE HILL

COLLAROY

ST MARYS
COLYTON

ROOTY HILL

PENNANT HILLS
MOUNT KURING-GAI

OXFORD FALLS

WESTERN
HWY
ST CLAIR

BLACKTOWN

BAULKHAM HILLS

HILLS

KILLARA
LINDFIELD

FRENCHS FOREST

BEACON HILL
BROOKVALE

5

WENTWORTHVILLE
GREYSTANES
WESTMEAD

WINSTON HILLS

NORTH
PARRAMATTA
PARRAMATTA

EASTWOOD
NORTH RYDE
WEST RYDE
RYDE

CHATSWOOD
NORTH BALGOWLAH
ARTARMON
BALGOWLAH

HARBORD
MANLY VALE
MANLY

Prospect Reservoir

ROSEHILL

GLADESVILLE

FAIRLIGHT

WALLACIA

GUILDFORD
FAIRFIELD

HOMEBUSH BAY

MWY

Port Jackson

LIDCOMBE

FLEMINGTON
FIVE DOCK
STRATHFIELD
BURWOOD

6

LANSVALE

BASS HILL
WARWICK FARM

STRATHFIELD SOUTH
CHULLORA
ASHFIELD

GREENACRE

SEE INSET
FOR MORE DETAIL

CASULA

LIVERPOOL

BANKSTOWN

MILPERRA

WESTERN

Georges R

NARWEE

MWY

HWY

MAROUBRA
MALABAR

BRIGHTON LE SANDS

N

NARELLAN

LUCAS HEIGHTS

BLAKEHURST

SANS SOUCI

Botany Bay

TOWN LEGEND
● See Accommodation Guide
● See Tourist Park Guide
● See Both Accommodation
   & Tourist Park Guide
Green text defines towns included
in Tourist Region listings.
Red text defines towns included
in City & Suburbs listings.

CAMDEN

WORONORA

SYLVANIA
SYLVANIA HEIGHTS

KURNELL

7

CAMPBELLTOWN

SUTHERLAND
MIRANDA

CARINGBAH

CRONULLA

ENGADINE

Port Hacking

HEATHCOTE

BUNDEENA

Woronora Reservoir

HUME

APPIN

WILTON

Lake Cataract

SCALE

0   5   10   15   20
KILOMETRES

8

PRINCES

STANWELL PARK

See
WOLLONGONG
& SUBURBS
Region

© RAASA GMAPSYD

A   B   C   D   E

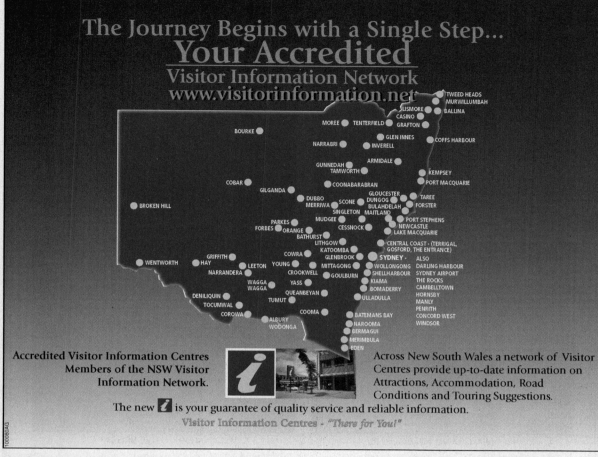

SYDNEY NSW 2000

Pop 3,276,200. See Sydney map - page 56, ref A1. A vibrant and flourishing city, built around one of the most magnificent natural harbours in the world, Sydney is the capital of New South Wales and the oldest and largest city in Australia. Bowls, Fishing, Golf, Horse Racing, Horse Riding, Rowing, Sailing, Scenic Drives, Squash, Swimming, Tennis. See also Darlinghurst, Pyrmont & Woolloomooloo.

Hotels/Motels

★★★★★ **ANA Harbour Grand Hotel**, (LH), Previously ANA Hotel Sydney. 176 Cumberland St, The Rocks, 1km N of PO, ☎ 02 9250 6000, fax 02 9250 6250, (Multi-stry), 563 rms (40 suites) [shwr, bath, spa bath (5), tlt, hairdry, a/c, tel, cable tv, movie, t/c mkg, refrig, mini bar], lift, conv fac, ✕ (7), pool indoor heated, sauna, spa, rm serv, dinner to unit, ☎, gym-fee, cots, non smoking rms (166). D ♦ $430 - $675, ♦♦ $430 - $675, Suite D $705 - $4,800, ch con, AE BC DC JCB MC VI.

★★★★★ **Hotel Inter-Continental Sydney**, (LH), 117 Macquarie St, 500m NE of GPO, ☎ 02 9253 9000, fax 02 9240 1240, (Multi-stry), 503 rms (29 suites) [shwr, bath, tlt, a/c, tel, TV, movie, clock radio, t/c mkg, refrig], lift, conv fac, ✕, pool-heated, rm serv, c/park (valet), gym. RO ♦♦ $457 - $555, ▯ $65, Suite W $887 - $4,352, Pedestrian entrance Cnr Phillip & Bridge Sts. AE BC DC JCB MC VI, ♿.

★★★★★ **Le Meridien**, (LH), 11 Jamieson St, 500m E of GPO, ☎ 02 9696 2500, fax 02 9696 2600, 415 rms (36 suites) [shwr, tlt, a/c, tel, TV, video-fee, clock radio, t/c mkg, refrig, doonas], lift, conf fac, ✕, pool indoor heated, sauna, rm serv (24hr), secure park (undercover), ☎, cots-fee, non smoking rms (200). RO ♦ $270, ♦♦ $270, Suite RO ♦ $270, ♦♦ $270, AE BC DC MC VI.

★★★★★ **Merchant Court Hotel, Sydney**, (LH), 68 Market St, Entrance opp State Theatre, ☎ 02 9238 8888, fax 02 9238 8899, (Multi-stry), 361 rms (19 suites) [shwr, bath, tlt, hairdry, a/c, heat, tel, TV, movie-fee, clock radio, t/c mkg, refrig, mini bar, cook fac ltd (11), micro (11), toaster (11)], lift, ldry, iron, iron brd, rec rm, lounge, business centre, conf fac, ✕, pool-heated, sauna, spa, steam rm, 24hr reception, rm serv, ☎, gym, cots, non smoking flr (8). RO ♦ $380, ♦♦ $380, ▯ $40, ch con, AE BC DC MC VI, ♿.

★★★★★ **Park Hyatt Sydney**, (LH), 7 Hickson Rd, The Rocks, 50m E of Harbour Bridge, ☎ 02 9241 1234, fax 02 9256 1555, (Multi-stry gr fl), 158 rms (5 suites) [shwr, bath, spa bath (2), tlt, hairdry, a/c, cent heat, elec blkts (on request), tel, TV, refrig, mini bar, doonas], lift, conv fac, ✕, pool-heated, sauna, spa, rm serv, dinner to unit, c/park (valet), gym, cots, non smoking rms (23). RO ♦ $600 - $5,000, ♦♦ $600 - $5,000, ▯ $50, Suite D ♦ $1,200 - $5,000, ♦♦ $1,200 - $5,000, ▯ $50, ch con, AE BC DC EFT JCB MC VI, ♿.

★★★★★ **Quay Grand Suites Sydney**, (LH), 61 Macquarie St, 200m S of Opera House, ☎ 02 9256 4000, fax 02 9256 4040, (Multi-stry), 65 rms (65 suites) [shwr, spa bath, tlt, hairdry, a/c, cent heat, tel, TV, video, movie, clock radio, t/c mkg, refrig, mini bar, cook fac, micro, toaster, ldry], lift, iron, iron brd, TV rm, lounge, conf fac, ✕, pool indoor heated, sauna, spa, 24hr reception, rm serv, ☎, gym, cots. D $515 - $765, ch con, AE BC DC MC VI.

★★★★★ **Quay West Sydney**, (LH), 98 Gloucester St, The Rocks, 1km N of GPO, ☎ 02 9240 6000, fax 02 9240 6060, (Multi-stry), 135 rms (132 suites) [shwr, bath, tlt, hairdry, a/c, tel, TV, video, clock radio, CD, t/c mkg, refrig, mini bar, cook fac, micro, d/wash, toaster, ldry (in unit)], lift, conv fac, ✕, bar, pool indoor heated, sauna, spa, rm serv, dinner to unit, c/park-fee, ☎, gym, cots. Suite D ♦ $380 - $1,650, ♦♦ $380 - $1,650, ♦♦♦ $410 - $1,680, ▯ $30, ch con, AE BC DC JCB MC VI.

★★★★★ **Sheraton On The Park**, (LH), 161 Elizabeth St, 100m E of Centrepoint Tower, ☎ 02 9286 6000, fax 02 9286 6686, (Multi-stry), 558 rms (48 suites) [shwr, bath, tlt, hairdry, a/c, elec blkts, tel, TV, movie, clock radio, t/c mkg, refrig, mini bar], conv fac, ✕, pool-heated (solar), sauna, spa, 24hr reception, rm serv, c/park (valet), ☎, gym, cots, non smoking rms (294). RO ♦ $370 - $450, ♦♦ $370 - $450, ▯ $45, Suite D ♦ $700 - $5,000, ♦♦ $700 - $5,000, ▯ $45, ch con, AE BC DC JCB MC VI, ♿.

★★★★★ **Sir Stamford at Circular Quay**, (LH), Previously The Ritz-Carlton Sydney 93 Macquarie St, 250m E of Circular Quay, ☎ 02 9252 4600, fax 02 9252 4286, (Multi-stry), 105 rms (13 suites) [shwr, bath, tlt, hairdry, a/c, cent heat, elec blkts, tel, TV, video, clock radio, t/c mkg, refrig, mini bar], lift, conv fac, ✕, pool-heated, sauna, rm serv, ☎, gym, cots. Suite RO $515 - $2,000, ch con, AE BC DC JCB MC VI.

Rates may change. Check before booking.

★★★★★ **The Observatory Hotel**, (LH), 89-113 Kent St, 500m N of The Rocks PO, ☎ 02 9256 2222, fax 02 9256 2233, (Multi-stry), 100 rms (21 suites) [shwr, bath, tlt, hairdry, a/c, cent heat, tel, TV, video-fee, clock radio, CD, t/c mkg, refrig, mini bar], rec rm, conv fac, ⊠, pool indoor heated, sauna, spa (heated), rm serv, dinner to unit, ☎, gym, tennis-fee, cots, non smoking rms (33). D ♦♦ **$415 - $665, Suite D $510**, ch con, AE BC DC JCB MC VI.

★★★★★ **The Regent Sydney**, (LH), 199 George St, 400m N of GPO, ☎ 02 9238 0000, fax 02 9251 2851, (Multi-stry), 531 rms (14 suites) [shwr, tlt, a/c, tel, TV, video, clock radio, t/c mkg, refrig, doonas], lift, conf fac, ⊠, pool indoor heated, sauna, spa, rm serv (24hr), dinner to unit, secure park (undercover), cots, non smoking rms (340). RO ♦ **$408 - $495, ♦♦ $408 - $528, ⸬ $55, Suite RO $539 - $4,356**, ch con, AE BC DC EFT JCB MC VI, &.

★★★★★ **The Westin Sydney**, (LH), 1 Martin Place, ☎ 02 8223 1111, fax 02 8223 1222, (Multi-stry), 416 rms (22 suites) [shwr, bath, tlt, hairdry, a/c, fire pl (48), cent heat, tel, TV, movie-fee, clock radio, t/c mkg, mini bar], lift, ldry, iron, iron brd, rec rm, lounge, business centre, conf fac, ⊠, pool-indoor, steam rm-fee, 24hr reception, rm serv, ☎, gym-fee, cots. RO ♦ **$236, ♦♦ $236, ⸬ $44**, ch con, AE BC DC EFT JCB MC VI, &.

★★★★☆ **Avillion Hotel Sydney**, (LH), 389 Pitt St, 200m SW of Hyde Park, ☎ 02 8268 1888, fax 02 9283 5899, (Multi-stry), 445 rms (12 suites) [shwr, bath (439), tlt, hairdry, a/c, heat, tel, TV, movie-fee, clock radio, t/c mkg, refrig, mini bar], lift, ldry, iron, iron brd, rec rm, lounge, business centre, conf fac, ⊠, 24hr reception, rm serv, dinner to unit, ☎, gym, cots. RO **$176 - $286, Suite RO $517 - $737**, AE BC DC JCB MC VI.

★★★★☆ **Four Points Hotel Sheraton Sydney**, (LH), Previously Hotel Nikko Darling Harbour 161 Sussex St, 500m W of Queen Victoria Building, ☎ 02 9299 1231, fax 02 9299 3340, (Multi-stry), 645 rms (47 suites) [shwr, bath, spa bath (4), tlt, hairdry, a/c-cool, cent heat, tel, TV, movie, clock radio, t/c mkg, refrig, mini bar, cook fac ltd (4), micro (4)], lift, ldry, business centre, conf fac, ⊠, rm serv, c/park (valet), ☎, gym, cots, non smoking rms (70). RO ♦ **$313 - $340, ♦♦ $313 - $340, Suite D $500 - $2,250**, AE BC DC JCB MC VI, &.

For Accommodation Booking information - see page 27

SYDNEY - continued...

★★★★☆ **Old Sydney Holiday Inn**, (LH), Previously Holiday Inn Old Sydney 55 George St, The Rocks, 500m N of Circular Quay, ☎ 02 9252 0524, fax 02 9251 2093, (Multi-stry), 174 rms [shwr, bath, tlt, a/c, tel, TV, movie, clock radio, t/c mkg, refrig, mini bar], lift, ldry, conv fac, ✕, coffee shop, pool, sauna, spa, rm serv, c/park (valet)-fee, cots, non smoking rms (96). **RO** ♦ **$247.50,** ♦♦ **$253,** ◊ **$33,** ch con, AE BC DC JCB MC MP VI, ⅋&.

★★★★☆ **Pacific International Suites - Sydney**, (LH), 433 Kent St, 50m from QVB, ☎ 02 9284 2300, fax 02 9264 6698, (Multi-stry), 112 rms (112 suites) [shwr, bath, spa bath (12), tlt, hairdry, a/c, cent heat, tel, TV, movie-fee, clock radio, t/c mkg, refrig, mini bar, cook fac, toaster], lift, ldry, iron, iron brd, lounge, ✕, 24hr reception, rm serv, c/park (limited)-fee, ✆, cots, non smoking rms (10). **RO** ♦ **$212 - $285,** ♦♦ **$212 - $285,** ◊ **$25,** AE BC DC EFT MC VI.

★★★★☆ **Pier One Parkroyal**, (LH), 11 Hickson Rd, Walsh Bay, ☎ 02 8298 9999, fax 02 8298 9777, (Multi-stry gr fl), 165 rms (10 suites) [shwr, bath, tlt, hairdry, a/c, tel, TV, movie-fee, clock radio, t/c mkg, refrig, mini bar], lift, iron, iron brd, lounge, business centre, conf fac, ✕, 24hr reception, rm serv, ✆, gym, cots, non smoking rms (avail). **RO** ♦ **$265 - $525,** ♦♦ **$265 - $525,** pen con, AE BC DC EFT JCB MC MP VI, ⅋&.

★★★★☆ **The Grace Hotel**, (LH), 77 York St, 100m fr PO, ☎ 02 9272 6888, fax 02 9299 8189, (Multi-stry), 382 rms (6 suites) [shwr, bath, tlt, a/c, tel, cable tv, clock radio, t/c mkg, refrig, mini bar, doonas], ldry, lounge, conf fac, ✕, pool indoor heated, sauna, spa, bbq, rm serv (24 hr), secure park (undercover), cots, non smoking flr (6). **RO** ♦ **$209 - $363,** ♦♦ **$209 - $363,** ◊ **$49.50,** Suite RO **$357 - $550,** ch con, AE BC DC EFT JCB MC VI.

★★★★☆ **The Wentworth**, (LH), 61 Phillip St, 500m E of PO, ☎ 02 9230 0700, fax 02 9228 9133, 431 rms (46 suites) [shwr, bath, tlt, hairdry, a/c, tel, TV, movie, clock radio, t/c mkg, refrig, mini bar, toaster], lift, ldry, iron, iron brd, conv fac, ✕, res liquor license, rm serv, c/park (valet), ✆, gym, cots, non smoking rms (126). **RO** ♦ **$299 - $709,** ♦♦ **$299 - $709,** ◊ **$30,** ch con, AE BC DC MC VI, ⅋&.

★★★★ **All Seasons Premier Menzies Hotel Sydney**, (LH), 14 Carrington St, 500m W of GPO, ☎ 02 9299 1000, fax 02 9290 3819, (Multi-stry), 446 rms (8 suites) [shwr, bath, tlt, a/c, elec blkts, tel, TV, clock radio, t/c mkg, refrig], lift, iron, iron brd, lounge, business centre, conv fac, ✕, bar, pool indoor heated, sauna, rm serv, c/park-fee, gym, cots, non smoking rms (263). **RO** ♦ **$200 - $350,** ♦♦ **$200 - $350,** ◊ **$35,** ch con, AE BC DC JCB MC VI, ⅋&.

★★★★ **Novotel Sydney on Darling Harbour**, (LH), 100 Murray St, Pyrmont 2009, adjacent Darling Harbour, ☎ 02 9934 0000, fax 02 9934 0099, (Multi-stry), 525 rms (24 suites) [shwr, bath, spa bath (8), tlt, hairdry, a/c, elec blkts, tel, TV, video, t/c mkg, mini bar], lift, iron, iron brd, lounge (gaming), business centre, conv fac, ✕, bar, pool, sauna, rm serv, ✆, gym, tennis, cots (avail), non smoking flr (5), non smoking rms (258). **D $280 - $544,** ch con, AE BC DC JCB MC VI, ⅋&.

★★★★ **Parkroyal at Darling Harbour**, (LH), 150 Day St, Haymarket 2000, opposite Darling Harbour Convention Centre, ☎ 02 9261 1188, fax 02 9261 8766, (Multi-stry), 349 rms (15 suites) [shwr, bath, tlt, hairdry, a/c, tel, TV, movie-fee, clock radio, t/c mkg, refrig, mini bar], lift, iron, conv fac, ✕, 24hr reception, rm serv, c/park (valet), ✆, gym, cots, non smoking flr (4). **RO** ♦ **$215 - $365,** ♦♦ **$215 - $365,** ♦♦♦ **$242 - $390,** ◊ **$27.50,** Suite D ♦ **$330 - $825,** ♦♦ **$330 - $825,** ◊ **$27.50,** AE BC DC JCB MC VI, ⅋&.

★★★★ **Pentura Hotel On Pitt**, (LH), 300 Pitt St, 750m S of GPO, ☎ 02 9283 8088, (Multi-stry), 115 rms [shwr, spa bath (7), tlt, hairdry, a/c, heat, tel, TV, movie, clock radio, t/c mkg, refrig, mini bar], lift, ldry, iron, iron brd, lounge, business centre, ✉, 24hr reception, rm serv, ☎, cots-fee, non smoking flr (4), non smoking rms (68). **RO** ♦♦ **$121 - $165**, ◊ **$20**, ch con, fam con, Minium booking New Years Eve & Day. AE BC DC MC VI.

★★★★ **Sydney Vista Hotel**, (LH), 7 York St, 500m W of GPO, ☎ 02 9274 1222, fax 02 9274 1274, (Multi-stry), 268 rms [shwr, bath, tlt, a/c, tel, fax (19), TV, movie-fee, radio, t/c mkg, refrig, cook fac (2)], lift, ldry, conv fac, ✗, bar, 24hr reception, rm serv, secure park, gym, cots, non smoking rms. **RO** ♦ **$154 - $265**, ♦♦ **$154 - $265**, ◊ **$27.50**, ch con, AE BC DC JCB MC VI, ♿.

★★★☆ **Harbour Rocks Hotel**, (LH), Heritage, 34 Harrington St, The Rocks, 500m W of The Rocks, ☎ 02 9251 8944, fax 02 9251 8900, (Multi-stry gr fl), 54 rms (1 suite) [shwr, tlt, hairdry, fan, tel, TV, movie, clock radio, t/c mkg, refrig, mini bar], iron, iron brd, ✉, cots. **RO** ♦ **$220**, ♦♦ **$220**, ◊ **$33**, ch con, AE BC DC JCB MC VI.

★★★☆ **Hotel Ibis World Square Sydney**, (LH), 384 Pitt St, 1km N of Central Station, ☎ 02 8267 3111, fax 02 8267 3100, (Multi-stry), 166 rms [shwr, tlt, hairdry, cent heat, tel, TV, movie-fee, clock radio, t/c mkg, refrig], lift, ldry, iron, iron brd, business centre, ✗, 24hr reception, ☎, cots, non smoking flr (8), non smoking rms (84). **RO** ♦ **$125**, ♦♦ **$125**, ◊ **$22**, ch con, fam con, pen con, AE BC DC JCB MC VI, ♿.

★★★☆ **Hyde Park Inn**, (M), 271 Elizabeth St, 1km S of GPO, ☎ 02 9264 6001, fax 02 9261 8691, (Multi-stry), 93 units (6 suites) [shwr, bath (5), tlt, hairdry, a/c, tel, TV, movie, clock radio, t/c mkg, refrig, cook fac (72), ldry], lift, ✉, c/park (limited), cots. **BLB** ♦ **$143**, ♦♦ **$159.50**, ♦♦♦ **$176**, ◊ **$16.50**, Suite D ♦♦ **$236.50**, ◊ **$16.50**, 24 units ★★☆. AE BC DC JCB MC VI.

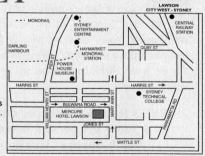

SYDNEY - continued...

AARONS HOTEL

Aarons Hotel is situated on Haymarket, one of Sydney's most vibrant and exciting areas. Newly renovated, our heritage listed boutique hotel is one of the friendliest and most professional 3.5 star hotels in the city. Our style of accommodation is fresh and appealing and, most importantly, our AAA packages unbeatable.

Close to Darling Harbour and Sydney Central Station, location is one of Aaron's greatest attributes.

You will find hundreds of shops, restaurants and entertainment venues close by, plus all five modes of transport within a five minute walking distance. As well as this, the airport shuttle bus picks up and drops off directly opposite the hotel.

RATES from $ 110.00 per double or $ 30.00 per person, based on Family Share of Five Rooms

Facilities include en-suite, 24 hr reception, restaurant + room service, air-conditioning/heating/fans/laundry and others.

AARONS HOTEL

37 Ultimo Rd, Haymarket, Sydney, 2000

PH: 02 9281 5555
FAX: 02 9281 2666
TOLL FREE: 1800 101 100

Email: aarons@acay.com.au
or Surf www.aaronshotel.citysearch.com.au

5021AG

Rates may change. Check before booking.

AAA TOURISM *Special Rates* ★★★☆ **Park Regis Hotel Sydney**, (M), 27 Park St, 500m S of GPO, ☎ 02 9267 6511, fax 02 9264 2252, (Multi-stry), 120 units (8 suites) [shwr, tlt, hairdry, a/c, tel, TV, clock radio, t/c mkg, refrig], lift, ldry, pool, 24hr reception, rm serv, c/park (limited), cots, non smoking flr (3). RO ♦ $165, ♦♦ $165, ◊ $22, Suite D ♦♦ $198, AE BC DC JCB MC VI.

★★★☆ **The Castlereagh Inn**, (LH), 169 Castlereagh St, ☎ 02 9284 1000, fax 02 9284 1999, (Multi-stry), 82 rms (2 suites) [shwr, tlt, hairdry, a/c, tel, TV, clock radio, t/c mkg, refrig], lift, ldry, conv fac, ✕, rm serv, dinner to unit, cots, non smoking rms (avail). BLB ♦ $126.50 - $159.50, ♦♦ $143 - $170.50, ◊ $27.50, Suite D $170.50 - $198, ch con, AE BC DC EFT MC VI.

★★★☆ **Travelodge Phillip St Sydney**, (LH), 165 Phillip St, Located within the NSW Leagues Club, ☎ 02 8224 9400, fax 02 8224 9500, (Multi-stry), 86 rms [shwr, tlt, hairdry, a/c, tel, TV, video-fee, movie, clock radio, t/c mkg, refrig, cook fac ltd, micro], lift, ldry, iron, iron brd, lounge, ✕, 24hr reception, ☏, gym-fee, cots. RO ♦ $119 - $149, ♦♦ $119 - $149, ♦♦♦ $135 - $165, ch con, AE BC DC EFT MC VI, ♿.

AAA TOURISM *Special Rates* ★★★☆ **Travelodge Wentworth Avenue Sydney**, (LH), Cnr Wentworth Ave & Goulburn St, 50m S of Hyde Park, ☎ 02 8267 1700, fax 02 8437 5345, (Multi-stry), 406 rms [shwr, tlt, hairdry, a/c, tel, TV, video-fee, movie-fee, clock radio, refrig, cook fac ltd, micro], lift, ldry, iron, iron brd, lounge, conf fac, ✕, 24hr reception, ☏, cots. RO ♦ $119 - $149, ♦♦ $119 - $149, ♦♦♦ $135 - $165, ch con, AE BC DC EFT MC VI, ♿.

★★★ **Hotel Ibis Darling Harbour**, (LH), 70 Murray St, Pyrmont 2009, 1km W of GPO, ☎ 02 9563 0888, fax 02 9563 0899, (Multi-stry), 256 rms [shwr, tlt, hairdry, a/c, tel, TV, movie-fee, clock radio, t/c mkg, refrig], lift, conv fac, ✕, 24hr reception, ☏, cots, non smoking rms (102). RO ♦ $135 - $155, ♦♦ $135 - $155, AE BC DC EFT JCB MC VI.

★★★ **The Lord Nelson Brewery**, (LH), Cnr Kent & Argyle Sts, The Rocks, 1km N of GPO, ☎ 02 9251 4044, fax 02 9251 1532, (2 stry), 9 rms [shwr (8), bath (8), tlt (8), a/c, tel, fax, TV, t/c mkg, refrig], shared fac (1 rm), iron, iron brd, ✕, non smoking rms. BLB ♦♦ $120 - $180, AE BC DC MC VI.

Cheap and Chic

Stay @ YWCA's
Y on the Park Hotel

Stylish and comfortable accommodation for all travellers in the vibrant heart of the city. Walking distance to Sydney's best attractions, shopping, Cafe's and nightlife. Choose from Deluxe, budget and share rooms. Light breakfast included.
Recommended by travellers around the world.

Freecall 1800 994 994 or Ph **(02) 9264 2451**
Fax (02) 9285 6288 email: yonthepark@ywca-sydney.com.au
web: www.ywca-sydney.com.au

5-11 Wentworth Ave, Sydney 2010

Cambridge
Park Inn®
I N T E R N A T I O N A L
SYDNEY
★★★☆ AAAT

NESTLED IN THE BEATING HEART OF SYDNEY, WITHIN WALKING DISTANCE TO CITY CENTRE, DARLING HARBOUR, TOURIST ATTRACTIONS, NIGHTLIFE AND HYDE PARK. WITHIN EASY REACH OF MAJOR SHOPPING AND BUSINESS DISTRICTS, PADDINGTON MARKETS, FOX STUDIOS, PUBLIC TRANSPORT AND FAMOUS OXFORD STREET.

FACILITIES INCLUDE :

- Indoor heated pool, spa, sauna, mini-gym
- In-room; hair-dryer, movies on demand
- Complimentary undercover security car parking
- One bedroom family suites available
- Spectacular Sydney skyline views

TOLL FREE 1800 251 901

EXCLUSIVE BENEFITS & DISCOUNTS, FROM $137.50 FOR MEMBERS.
- **Complimentary sumptuous gourmet breakfast 1-2 persons.**
- **Complimentary welcome drink per person.**
- **Best available room or suite.**
- **Complimentary welcome gesture in room.**

212 Riley Street, Surry Hills, Sydney NSW 2010 • Ph: 9212 1111
reservations@cambridgeparkinn.com.au • www.parkplaza.com.au

Experience Sydney Luxury

for just $125 per room

Mention this ad & receive 2 FREE breakfasts

Also, why not forget the hassle of traffic & parking, leave your car in our undercover security carpark & enjoy the short 3 minute shuttle bus ride to Darling Harbour & Circular Quay. Experience the heated pool & spa, restaurant & cocktail bar. The Haven is also a great place for kids, so bring them along!

THE HAVEN INN
PH: (02) 9660 6655
196 GLEBE POINT ROAD GLEBE, SYDNEY
EMAIL: bookings@haveninnsydney.com.au
WEBSITE: haveninnsydney.com.au

★★★ **YWCA's Y on the Park**, (M), 5 Wentworth Ave, 1km E of PO, ☎ 02 9264 2451, fax 02 9285 6288, (Multi-stry), 17 units [shwr, tlt, hairdry, tel, TV, clock radio, t/c mkg, refrig, micro (communal)], lift, ldry, lounge (TV), conv fac, cots, non smoking rms. RO ⫯ $108, ⫯⫯ $132, ⫯ $10, ch con, AE BC EFT MC VI.

★★☆ **(Hotel Section)**, 95 rms [micro (communal)], lift, bathrm, ldry, lounge (TV), conv fac, ✕, cafe, t/c mkg shared, 24hr reception, ✆, cots, non smoking rms. D ⫯ $29 - $68, ⫯⫯ $93, ⫯ $10, ch con, ⫯⬥.

★ **Mercantile Hotel**, (LH), 25 George St, 1.5km N of GPO, ☎ 02 9247 3570, fax 02 9247 7047, (2 stry), 19 rms [shwr (4), spa bath (4), tlt (4), a/c (4), fan, heat, TV, clock radio, t/c mkg, refrig], cots, 4 rooms of a higher standard. AE BC DC EFT JCB MC VI.

Hotel Coronation, (LH), 5 Park St, Sydney 1044, ☎ 02 9267 8362, fax 02 9267 6992, 21 rms [a/c-cool, heat, cent heat, tel, TV, clock radio, t/c mkg, refrig], ✕, rm serv, meals to unit, cots (fee). RO ⫯ $104.50, ⫯⫯ $121, AE BC DC EFT VI, (not yet classified).

Stamford Plaza Sydney, (LH), 187 Kent St, 800m N of PO, ☎ 02 9023 9888, fax 02 9023 9800, (Multi-stry), 143 rms (90 suites) [ensuite, spa bath (8), a/c, tel, cable tv, video, clock radio, t/c mkg, refrig, cook fac, micro, d/wash, toaster, ldry (135), doonas], lift, w/mach (135), dryer (135), lounge, conf fac, ✕, pool indoor heated, spa, steam rm, 24hr reception, rm serv (24hr), dinner to unit, secure park (undercover), ✆, cots-fee, non smoking rms (105). RO ⫯ $335 - $425, ⫯⫯ $335 - $425, ⫯ $55, Suite RO ⫯⫯ $425 - $755, ⫯ $55, ch con, AE BC DC JCB MC VI, (not yet classified).

The Wynyard Hotel, (LH), Cnr Clarence & Erskine Sts, 100m W of Wynyard Station, ☎ 02 9299 1330, fax 02 9299 5326, (Multi-stry), 14 rms [c/fan, TV, clock radio], ldry, ✕ (Mon to Fri), cook fac, t/c mkg shared, ✆. BLB ⫯ $93, ⫯⫯ $104, ch con, AE BC DC EFT MC VI.

Self Catering Accommodation

★★★★★ **Medina Grand Harbourside**, (SA), 55 Shelley St, 50m N of Sydney Aquarium, ☎ 02 9249 7000, fax 02 9249 6900, (Multi-stry), 114 serv apts acc up to 4, [shwr, bath, tlt, hairdry, a/c, tel, TV, movie-fee, clock radio, t/c mkg, refrig, mini bar, cook fac, micro, d/wash, toaster, ldry, doonas, linen], lift, w/mach, dryer, iron, iron brd, conf fac, pool (indoor), sauna, 24hr reception, gym, cots, non smoking rms (57). D $220 - $550, AE BC DC EFT MC VI.

★★★★★ **Medina Grand Sydney**, (SA), 511 Kent St, 500m E of Darling Harbour, ☎ 02 9274 0000, fax 02 9267 5655, (Multi-stry), 144 serv apts acc up to 6, [shwr, bath (90), tlt, hairdry, a/c, tel, cable tv, movie-fee, clock radio, t/c mkg, refrig, mini bar, cook fac, micro, d/wash, toaster, ldry (126), blkts, doonas, linen, pillows], lift, w/mach (126), dryer (126), iron, iron brd, conf fac, ✕, pool indoor heated, sauna, 24hr reception, rm serv, c/park-fee, ✆, gym, cots, non smoking flr (16). D $165 - $675, ch con, AE BC DC MC VI.

★★★★★ **Saville 2 Bond Street**, (SA), Previously 2 Bond Street Apartment Hotel Cnr George & Bond Sts, 300m N of GPO, ☎ 02 9250 9555, fax 02 9250 9556, (Multi-stry), 180 serv apts [shwr, bath (31), spa bath (6), tlt, hairdry, evap cool, cent heat, tel, TV, video, movie, clock radio, CD, t/c mkg, refrig, mini bar, cook fac, micro, d/wash, toaster, ldry, blkts, linen, pillows], lift, w/mach, dryer, iron, iron brd, cafe, pool-heated, spa, bbq, 24hr reception, rm serv, ✆, gym, cots, non smoking flr (6). D ⫯⫯ $242 - $990, ⫯ $28, W ⫯⫯ $1,694 - $6,930, ⫯ $196, ch con, AE BC DC EFT JCB MC VI.

★★★★☆ **Grand Mercure Apartments**, (SA), 50 Murray St, Pyrmont 2009, 1km W of GPO, ☎ 02 9563 6666, fax 02 9563 6699, (Multi-stry), 121 serv apts acc up to 4, [shwr, bath, tlt, hairdry, a/c, tel, TV, video, clock radio, CD, t/c mkg, refrig, mini bar, cook fac ltd, micro, d/wash, toaster, ldry], lift, pool indoor heated, sauna, spa, 24hr reception, dinner to unit, gym, cots. D $361 - $690, AE BC DC EFT JCB MC VI.

★★★★☆ **Medina Classic Martin Place**, (SA), 1 Hosking Pl, 50m S of Martin Place Railway Station, ☎ 02 9224 6400, fax 02 9224 6499, 49 serv apts acc up to 4, [shwr, tlt, hairdry, a/c, tel, TV, clock radio, t/c mkg, refrig, mini bar, cook fac, micro, d/wash, toaster, ldry, blkts, linen, pillows], lift, w/mach, dryer, iron, iron brd, 24hr reception, ch con, 7 studio units of a lower rating. D $165 - $198, AE BC DC EFT MC VI,

Operator Comment: See Medina Serviced Apartments advertisement under Sydney City.

★★★★☆ **Oakford Darling Harbour All-Suite Hotel**, (SA), 252 Sussex St, city side of Darling Harbour, ☎ 02 8280 5000, fax 02 8280 5050, (Multi-stry), 119 serv apts [shwr, spa bath (20), tlt, a/c-cool, tel, cable tv, movie, clock radio, t/c mkg, refrig, cook fac, micro, d/wash], w/mach, dryer, ✕, ⊠, pool-indoor, sauna, spa, 24hr reception, meals to unit, secure park (undercover), non smoking rms (70). RO ♦ **$228.80**, ♦♦ **$228.80**, ◊ **$27.50**, Suite RO **$248.80 - $2,191**, AE BC DC JCB MC VI.

★★★★☆ **The York Apartment Hotel**, (SA), 5 York St, 500m NW of GPO, ☎ 02 9210 5000, fax 02 9290 1487, (Multi-stry), 132 serv apts (101 suites) acc up to 4, [shwr, bath, tlt, hairdry, a/c, elec blkts, tel, TV, video, clock radio, t/c mkg, refrig, cook fac, micro, toaster, ldry], lift, w/mach, dryer, iron, ⊠, pool-heated, sauna, spa, 24hr reception, rm serv, secure park, gym, cots. RO ♦ **$258.50 - $324.50**, ♦♦ **$258.50 - $396**, ♦♦♦ **$374 - $605**, ◊ **$22**, Suite D **$374 - $605**, AE BC DC JCB MC VI.

★★★★ **Napoleon On Kent**, (SA), 219 Kent St, 500m S of The Rocks, ☎ 02 9299 5588, fax 02 9299 5788, 46 serv apts [shwr, bath (21), tlt, hairdry, a/c, tel, cable tv, clock radio, CD, t/c mkg, refrig, micro, d/wash, toaster, blkts, linen], ldry, iron, c/park-fee, cots-fee. D ♦♦ **$118 - $175**, ◊ **$33 - $66**, AE BC DC JCB MC VI.

★★★★ **Pacific International Apartments**, (Apt), 653 George St, 500m SE of GPO, ☎ 02 9284 4500, fax 02 9284 1411, (Multi-stry), 160 apts acc up to 6, (Studio, 1 & 2 bedrm), [shwr, bath, tlt, a/c-cool, heat, tel, TV, movie-fee, clock radio, t/c mkg, refrig, cook fac, micro, toaster, blkts, linen, pillows], ldry, w/mach, dryer-fee, ✕, ✆, cots, non smoking flr (10). RO ♦♦ **$242 - $302.50**, ◊ **$20**, ch con, AE BC DC EFT JCB MC VI.

★★★★ **The Stafford**, (SA), 75 Harrington St, The Rocks, 1km N of GPO, ☎ 02 9251 6711, fax 02 9251 3458, (Multi-stry), 40 serv apts (21 suites) acc up to 3, [shwr, bath, tlt, a/c, tel, TV, clock radio, t/c mkg, refrig, cook fac, toaster], lift, ldry, pool, sauna, spa, gym, cots. RO ♦ **$235**, ♦♦ **$235**, Suite D ♦ **$280**, ♦♦ **$280**, ch con, AE BC DC JCB MC VI,

Operator Comment: Please visit our Web Site www.thestafford.citysearch.com.au.

★★★★ **The Waldorf Apartment Hotel**, (SA), 57 Liverpool St, 1km S of GPO, 200m E of Darling Harbour, ☎ 02 9261 5355, fax 02 9261 3753, (Multi-stry), 60 serv apts [shwr, bath, tlt, hairdry, a/c, tel, TV, movie, clock radio, refrig, cook fac, d/wash], lift, w/mach, dryer, iron, pool, sauna, spa, rm serv, secure park, cots. D ∮ $193 - $462, ⚤ $193 - $462, ∮ $27.50, AE BC DC JCB MC VI.

  ★★★☆ **Carrington Sydney City Centre Apartments**, (SA), 57 York St, 100m W of GPO, ☎ 02 9290 1577, fax 02 9299 2727, (Multi-stry), 20 serv apts acc up to 6, [shwr, bath, tlt, a/c, tel, TV, clock radio, t/c mkg, refrig, cook fac, d/wash, toaster, ldry], lift, dryer, iron, cots-fee. D ∮ $220 - $275, ⚤ $220 - $275, ∮ $20, AE BC DC MC VI.

  ★★★☆ **Metro Suites On Sussex**, (SA), 132 Sussex St, 500m SW of GPO, ☎ 02 9290 9200, fax 02 9262 3032, (Multi-stry), 32 serv apts [shwr, bath, tlt, a/c, elec blkts, tel, TV, movie, clock radio, refrig, cook fac, ldry (in unit)], lift, dryer, iron, cots-fee. RO ⚤ $134 - $185, ch con, AE BC DC MC VI.

★★★☆ **The Savoy Apartments**, (SA), Cnr King & Kent Sts, 5min from Town Hall Station, ☎ 02 9267 9211, fax 02 9262 2023, (Multi-stry), 71 serv apts [shwr, bath, tlt, a/c-cool, tel, TV, clock radio, t/c mkg, refrig, cook fac, micro, d/wash, toaster, ldry], lift, cots. D ∮ $165, ⚤ $165, ∮ $16.50, AE BC DC EFT JCB MC VI.

★★★ **Downtown Serviced Apartments**, (HU), 336 Sussex St, 1km SW of GPO, ☎ 02 9261 4333, fax 02 9261 4988, 30 units acc up to 5, [shwr, bath, tlt, a/c, tel, TV, refrig, cook fac, toaster, ldry (in unit), blkts, linen, pillows], pool, spa, c/park (garage)-fee, tennis. D ⚤ $190 - $210, ∮ $20, AE BC DC MC VI.

  ★★★ **Metro Suites On King**, (SA), 27-29 King St, 500m SW of GPO, ☎ 02 9299 1388, fax 02 9299 1554, (Multi-stry), 17 serv apts acc up to 4, [shwr, bath, tlt, a/c-cool, heat, elec blkts, tel, TV, clock radio, t/c mkg, refrig, cook fac, micro, d/wash, ldry (in unit)], lift, dryer, iron, pool, cots. RO ⚤ $160 - $180, ∮ $20, ch con, Booking restrictions new years eve, AE BC DC MC VI.

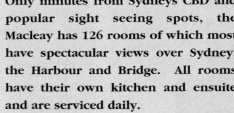

Alishan INTERNATIONAL GUEST HOUSE

100 Glebe Point Rd, Glebe, Sydney Australia 2037

- Reasonable accom. at an exceptional level
- Close to CBD & Darling Harbour
- Off street parking
- See listing under Glebe

Ph: (02) 9566 4048 Fax: (02) 9525 4686
Internet Address: www.alishan.com.au

Heritage Charm in bohemian Glebe

TRICKETTS

**Luxury
Bed & Breakfast**

270 Glebe Point Road, Glebe
Minutes to Sydney Centre on direct bus route.

Website: www.tricketts.com.au

RATES: $150 single, $176 - $198 double, incl GST & breakfast.
Self Contained Garden Apartment $198 double.

FEATURES: A beautifully restored Victorian Mansion with original ballroom, set in a large leafy garden. Antique furnishings, Persian carpets, charming large bedrooms, all with ensuites. This historic peaceful home offers all family comforts, in a warm friendly atmosphere.

AAAT ★★★★

Ph: (02) 9552 1141   Fax: (02) 9692 9462

 ★★★ **Stellar Suites On Wentworth**, (SA), 4 Wentworth Ave, Surry Hills 2010, 1km SE of GPO, ☎ 02 9264 9754, fax 02 9261 8006, (Multi-stry), 35 serv apts [shwr, tlt, a/c, heat, tel, TV, video (avail), clock radio, t/c mkg, refrig, cook fac], lift, ldry, cots. **D $127 - $140**, AE BC DC MC VI.

B&B's/Guest Houses

★★★★ **Bed & Breakfast Sydney Harbour**, (B&B), 140-142 Cumberland St, The Rocks, 500m SE of GPO, ☎ 02 9247 1130, fax 02 9247 1148, (Multi-stry), 7 rms [ensuite (5), fan, heat (elec), TV, clock radio], shared fac (2), ✕, t/c mkg shared, secure park, ☎, non smoking rms. **BB ♦ $110 - $185, ♦♦ $120 - $195**, BC EFT MC VI.

★★★★ **Central Park Hotel**, (PH), 185 Castlereagh St, 100m E of Sydney Town Hall, ☎ 02 9283 5000, fax 02 9283 2710, (Multi-stry), 36 rms (10 suites) [shwr, bath (16), spa bath (10), tlt, hairdry, a/c, tel, cable tv, video-fee, movie, clock radio, CD (7), t/c mkg, refrig, mini bar, micro (7), toaster], lift, ldry, rm serv, dinner to unit (5 Days), cots. **D $187 - $325**, AE BC DC JCB MC VI.

★★ **Sydney Central Private Hotel**, (PH), 75 Wentworth Ave, 300m N of Central station, ☎ 02 9212 0067, fax 02 9212 1005, (Multi-stry gr fl), 140 rms [shwr (20), tlt (20), a/c (15), c/fan (6), heat (4), TV (20), t/c mkg (20), refrig (80), micro (6)], lift, ldry, lounge (TV), lounge firepl (1), cook fac, t/c mkg shared, ☎, cots. **RO ♦ $45 - $100, ♦♦ $65 - $150, ♦ $20**, 20 rooms at 3 star rating, Min book Christmas Jan long w/ends and Easter, AE BC DC EFT JCB MC VI.

 **Captain Cook Cruises**, Ives Steps Dawes Point, ☎ 02 9206 1144, fax 02 9206 1178, 60 rms [shwr, tlt, a/c], conf fac, ✉, sauna, t/c mkg shared, bbq. **D all meals ♦ $292.50 - $338.50, ♦♦ $390 - $450**, Min book applies, AE BC DC MC VI.

Sydney Park Inn, (PH), 2-6 Francis St, ☎ 02 9360 5988, fax 02 9360 1085, (Multi-stry), 23 rms (1 suite) [shwr, spa bath (1), tlt, hairdry (23), a/c, tel, TV, movie, clock radio, t/c mkg, refrig, cook fac, micro, toaster], ldry, iron, iron brd, bbq, 24hr reception, rm serv, dinner to unit, plygr, tennis (half court), cots. **BLB ♦ $99, ♦♦ $105, D $115 - $125**, fam con, pen con, AE BC DC MC VI, (not yet classified).

Rates may change. Check before booking.

SYDNEY - ANNANDALE NSW 2038

Pop Part of Sydney, (5km W Sydney), See map on page 56, ref A2. Elegant, inner west suburb of Sydney.

Self Catering Accommodation

★★★ **Johnston Lodge**, (HF), 106 Johnston St, ☎ 02 9660 7075, fax 02 9660 6412, 9 flats acc up to 3, [shwr, tlt, fan, heat, tel, TV, refrig, cook fac (shared), micro, toaster, blkts, linen, pillows], ldry. **D $72 - $85**, Min book applies, BC EFT MC VI.

B&B's/Guest Houses

Inner City Lights B&B, (B&B), 133 Annandale St, ☎ 02 9692 0509, 2 rms (2 suites) [shwr, tlt, hairdry, a/c-cool, fan (1), elec blkts, tel, TV, clock radio, t/c mkg, refrig, cook fac ltd, micro, toaster], lounge firepl, bbq-fee, non smoking property. **BB ♦ $80 - $90, ♦♦ $100 - $120**, BC MC VI, (not yet classified).

SYDNEY - ARCADIA NSW 2159

Pop Part of Sydney, (40km N Sydney), See map on page 56, ref C4. Rural area in the north-western outskirts of Sydney. Scenic Drives.

B&B's/Guest Houses

★★★☆ **Willow Glen Cottage**, (B&B), 2 Marrakesh Place, ☎ 02 9653 2038, fax 02 9653 2874, 1 rm [shwr, tlt, hairdry, a/c-cool, c/fan, fire pl, heat, elec blkts, tel, TV, video, clock radio, t/c mkg, refrig, cook fac, micro, elec frypan, toaster], iron, iron brd, lounge (TV & firepl), c/park. **BB ♦ $110, ♦♦ $135**.

SYDNEY - ARNCLIFFE NSW 2205

Pop Part of Sydney, (11km S Sydney), See map on page 56, ref A2. Residential suburb in the St George area of Sydney. Fishing, Golf, Sailing.

Hotels/Motels

★★★★ **Hilton Sydney Airport**, (LH), Previously Sydney Airport Hilton 20 Levey St, opposite International Terminal, ☎ 02 9518 2000, fax 02 9518 2002, (Multi-stry), 266 rms [shwr, bath, tlt, a/c, elec blkts, tel, TV, movie-fee, clock radio, t/c mkg, refrig], lift, business centre, conv fac, ✉, pool-heated, rm serv, courtesy transfer, gym, squash, tennis, cots, non smoking flr (4). **RO ♦ $195 - $300, ♦♦ $240 - $345, ♦ $45**, ch con, 60 rooms of a lower rating. AE BC DC EFT JCB MC VI, ♦♦.

★★★☆ **Airport Sydney International Motor Inn**, (LMH), 35 Levey St, 500m S of Sydney Airport, ☎ 02 9556 1555, fax 02 9567 1309, (2 stry gr fl), 56 units [shwr, bath (45), spa bath (8), tlt, hairdry, a/c, tel, TV, clock radio, t/c mkg, refrig], ldry, iron, iron brd, lounge, business centre, conv fac, ✉, spa, rm serv, dinner to unit, courtesy transfer, ☎, cots-fee. **RO ♦ $109 - $199, ♦♦ $109 - $199, ♦ $20**, 4 family units of a lower rating. AE BC DC EFT JCB MC VI.

★★★ **Airport Motel Sydney**, (M), 33 Levey St, 500m S of Airport, ☎ 02 9599 9747, fax 02 9599 9777, (Multi-stry gr fl), 60 units [shwr, tlt, hairdry, a/c, tel, TV, clock radio, t/c mkg, refrig], lift, ldry, lounge, business centre, conf fac, ✉, rm serv, dinner to unit, courtesy transfer, ☎, cots-fee, non smoking rms. **RO ♦♦ $99, ♦ $20**, AE BC DC EFT MC VI.

SYDNEY - ARTARMON NSW 2064

Pop Part of Sydney, (10km N Sydney), See map on page 56, ref D5.

★★★★ **Artarmon Inn**, (M), 472 Pacific Hwy, 1km N of PO, ☎ 02 9412 1644, fax 02 9412 2112, (Multi-stry), 64 units [shwr, tlt, a/c, elec blkts, tel, TV, movie, clock radio, t/c mkg, refrig], lift, ldry, conv fac, ✉, pool, sauna, bbq, 24hr reception, rm serv, dinner to unit, cots, non smoking units (31). **RO $137 - $170**, ch con, AE BC BTC DC EFT JCB MC VI.

★★★★ **Twin Towers Inn**, (M), 260 Pacific Hwy, 1.5km N of St Leonards PO, ☎ 02 9439 1388, fax 02 9437 4171, (2 stry gr fl), 41 units [shwr, bath, spa bath (2), tlt, hairdry, a/c, elec blkts, tel, TV, video, clock radio, t/c mkg, refrig, mini bar], ldry, conv fac, ✉, pool, spa, rm serv, cots, non smoking units (27). **RO ♦ $131 - $199, ♦♦ $131 - $199, ♦♦♦ $151 - $219, ♦ $20**, AE BC DC MC VI.

★★★☆ **Linwood Lodge**, (M), 312 Pacific Hwy, 2km W of PO, ☎ 02 9439 6333, fax 02 9437 5936, (2 stry), 16 units [shwr, tlt, a/c, elec blkts, tel, TV, clock radio, t/c mkg, refrig, cook fac (some)], ldry, cots. **RO ♦ $55 - $105, ♦♦ $60 - $115**, AE BC DC EFT JCB MC VI.

SYDNEY - ASHFIELD NSW 2131

Pop Part of Sydney, (10km W Sydney), See map on page 56, ref D6. Inner-western suburb of Sydney. Bowls, Swimming.

★★★☆ **Ashfields Philip Lodge**, (M), 156 Parramatta Rd, 2km S of PO, ☎ 02 9797 9411, fax 02 9799 2918, (2 stry gr fl), 50 units [shwr, bath (2), spa bath (1), tlt, hairdry, a/c, fan, tel, TV, clock radio, t/c mkg, refrig], ldry, conv fac, ⊠, pool, rm serv, dinner to unit, cots-fee, non smoking units (6). **RO** ♠ **$118 - $129**, ♠♠ **$118 - $129**, ♠♠♠ **$129 - $139**, ◊ **$10**, AE BC DC EFT MC MP VI.

★★★ **Metro Motor Inn Ashfield**, (M), 63 Liverpool Rd, 1km W of PO, ☎ 02 9798 0333, fax 02 9716 6802, 38 units [shwr, tlt, a/c, tel, TV, movie, clock radio, t/c mkg, refrig], ldry, cots. **RO** ♠♠ **$90 - $150**, ch con, AE BC DC EFT MC VI.

★★☆ **Westside Motor Inn**, (M), 85 Hume Hwy (Liverpool Rd), 1Km E of Railway Station, ☎ 02 9797 7711, fax 02 9716 7282, (2 stry gr fl), 35 units [shwr, tlt, a/c, tel, TV, clock radio, t/c mkg, refrig, toaster], ldry, cots-fee. **RO** ♠ **$89 - $95**, ♠♠ **$89 - $95**, ◊ **$12**, ch con, AE BC DC MC VI.

SYDNEY - AVALON BEACH NSW 2107

Pop Part of Sydney, (35km N Sydney), See map on page 56, ref E4.
★★★★ **Avalon Beach Bed & Breakfast**, (B&B), 51 Riviera Ave, 2km NW of PO, ☎ 02 9918 7002, fax 02 9918 7002, (2 stry), 2 rms [hairdry, elec blkts, clock radio], lounge (TV), non smoking property. **BB** ♠ **$120 - $140**, ♠♠ **$140 - $160**.

SYDNEY - BALGOWLAH NSW 2093

Pop Part of Sydney, See map on page 56, ref D5.
★★★★ **Lillypilly Cottage**, (B&B), Previously Lillypilly B&B 72 Woodland St, 3km W of Manly Wharf, ☎ 02 9949 7090, fax 02 9949 4094, 1 rm [shwr, tlt, hairdry, fan, heat, TV, video, clock radio, t/c mkg, refrig, cook fac ltd, micro, toaster, ldry], iron, iron brd, courtesy transfer, non smoking rms. **BLB** ♠ **$100**, ♠♠ **$120**.

SYDNEY - BALMAIN NSW 2041

Pop Part of Sydney, (6km W Sydney), See map on page 56, ref A1. Historic inner western harbourside suburb.
★★★★ **Balmain Bed & Breakfast**, (B&B), 27 Lawson St, 3km W of Sydney City Centre, ☎ 0419 800 485, fax 02 9818 3228, 2 rms [shwr, tlt, cent heat, clock radio, t/c mkg, refrig]. **BB** ♠ **$120**, ♠♠ **$150**, BC MC VI.

★★★★ **Claremont**, (B&B), No children's facilities, 12 Claremont St, ☎ 02 9810 8358, fax 02 9810 8358, 2 rms [shwr, spa bath (1), tlt, hairdry, a/c, heat, elec blkts, TV, clock radio, t/c mkg, refrig], iron, iron brd. **BB** ♠ **$130**, ♠♠ **$165**, BC MC VI.

Balmain Village B&B Accommodation, (B&B), 54 Phillip St, 2.5km W of Sydney Centre, ☎ 02 9818 4587, fax 02 9818 4587, 1 rm [bath, a/c, c/fan, elec blkts, TV, video, clock radio, t/c mkg, refrig, micro, toaster, ldry, doonas], bathrm, ✕, cots (avail), non smoking rms. **BLB** ♠♠ **$139 - $165**, ◊ **$45**, ch con, Min book applies, BC MC VI, (not yet classified).
Balmain Lodge, (PH), 415 Darling St, ☎ 02 9810 3700, fax 02 9810 1500, (Multi-stry), 36 rms [shwr (2), tlt (2), TV, clock radio, t/c mkg, refrig, micro, toaster], ldry, iron brd, bbq, ✆, non smoking rms (avail). **RO** ♠ **$65**, ♠♠ **$75**, ♠ **$280**, ♠♠ **$330**, pen con, BC EFT MC VI.

SYDNEY - BANKSTOWN NSW 2200

Pop Part of Sydney, (21km SW Sydney), See map on page 56, ref C6. South-western suburb of Sydney. Swimming.

Hotels/Motels

★★★★☆ **Pacific International Hotel - Bankstown**, (LH), 477 Chapel Rd, 200m N of PO, ☎ 02 9790 4700, fax 02 9707 3359, (2 stry gr fl), 39 rms (21 suites) [shwr, bath (52), spa bath (8), tlt, hairdry, a/c, elec blkts, tel, cable tv, video, clock radio, t/c mkg, refrig, mini bar], lift, ldry, conv fac, ⊠, pool indoor heated, spa, 24hr reception, rm serv, c/park (valet), ✆, gym, cots, non smoking rms (2). **RO** ♠ **$252**, ♠♠ **$252**, ◊ **$10 - $25, Suite D** ♠ **$338**, ♠♠ **$338**, ◊ **$24.40**, ch con, fam con, pen con, AE BC DC EFT JCB MC MP VI, ♿.
★★★☆ **Travelodge Bankstown**, (LMH), Cnr Greenfield Pde & Mona St, ☎ 02 9793 0000, fax 02 9793 2439, 108 units [shwr, bath (4), tlt, hairdry, a/c, tel, TV, video-fee, movie-fee, clock radio, t/c mkg, refrig, cook fac ltd, micro], lift, ldry, iron, iron brd, lounge, conf fac, ✕, 24hr reception, ✆, cots. **RO** ♠ **$119 - $149**, ♠♠ **$119 - $149**, ♠♠♠ **$135 - $165**, ch con, AE BC DC EFT MC VI.

Self Catering Accommodation

★★★★ **Pacific International Apartments-Bankstown**, (SA), 513 Chapel Rd, ☎ 02 9798 8400, fax 02 9707 3359, (Multi-stry gr fl), 30 serv apts acc up to 6, [shwr, bath, tlt, hairdry, a/c, c/fan, elec blkts, tel, cable tv-fee, video, clock radio, t/c mkg, refrig, cook fac, micro, elec frypan, toaster, ldry, blkts, linen], w/mach-fee, dryer-fee, iron, iron brd, conf fac (100m from apts), pool indoor heated, spa, 24hr reception, ✆, gym, cots, non smoking units (10). **D** ♠ **$280**, ♠♠ **$280**, ◊ **$10**, AE BC DC EFT JCB MC MP VI.

Pacific International Apartments-Bankstown Sq, (SA), 59 Rickard Rd, 300m E from PO, ☎ 02 9790 4700, fax 02 9707 3359, (Multi-stry gr fl), 60 serv apts acc up to 5, (2 & 3 bedrm), [shwr, tlt, a/c, fan, cent heat, tel, TV, clock radio, t/c mkg, refrig, cook fac, micro, d/wash, blkts, linen], dryer, ✕, pool (outdoor), spa, secure park (undercover), non smoking units (30). **D ⃰ $211 - $280, ⃰⃰ $211 - $280, ⃰ $24.40**, ch con, weekly con, AE BC DC EFT MC VI, (not yet classified).

SYDNEY - BASS HILL NSW 2197

Pop Part of Sydney, (23km SW Sydney), See map on page 56, ref C6.

★★★★ **Gardenia Motor Inn**, (M), 850 Hume Hwy, 1.5km E of PO, ☎ 02 9644 9600, fax 02 9645 3146, (2 stry gr fl), 42 units [shwr, tlt, hairdry, a/c, elec blkts, tel, TV, video (avail), clock radio, t/c mkg, refrig], ldry, conv fac, ✕, rm serv, dinner to unit, cots-fee. **RO ⃰ $120, ⃰⃰ $120, ⃰ $10**, 16 units ★★★☆. AE BC DC MC VI, ⓗ.

★★★★ **Rydges Bankstown**, (LH), Cnr Hume Hwy & Strickland St, 1.5km E of PO, ☎ 02 9754 1099, fax 02 9754 1278, (Multi-stry), 119 rms [shwr, bath, spa bath (5), tlt, hairdry, tel, TV, video (avail), movie,

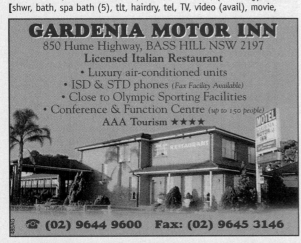

GARDENIA MOTOR INN
850 Hume Highway, BASS HILL NSW 2197
Licensed Italian Restaurant
• Luxury air-conditioned units
• ISD & STD phones *(Fax Facility Available)*
• Close to Olympic Sporting Facilities
• Conference & Function Centre *(up to 150 people)*
AAA Tourism ★★★★

☎ (02) 9644 9600   Fax: (02) 9645 3146

Rydges Bankstown ...continued
clock radio, t/c mkg, refrig, mini bar], lift, conv fac, ✕, pool (salt water), bbq, 24hr reception, rm serv, dinner to unit, cots, non smoking rms (71). **RO ⃰ $135 - $200, ⃰⃰ $135 - $200**, ch con, AE BC DC MC VI, ⓗ.

★★★ **Banksia Motel**, (M), 966 Hume Hwy, 1km W of PO, ☎ 02 9726 6666, fax 02 9724 4337, 38 units [shwr, tlt, a/c, tel, TV, clock radio, t/c mkg, refrig], ldry, cots-fee. **RO ⃰⃰ $99, ⃰ $10**, AE BC DC MC VI.

★★ **Bass Hill Tourist Park**, (M), 713 Hume Hwy, 6.5km E of Liverpool, ☎ 02 9724 9670, fax 02 9726 4777, 14 units [shwr, tlt, a/c, elec blkts, TV, t/c mkg, refrig, cook fac (2)], ldry, non smoking rms (4), **D $79.20**, BC EFT MC VI.

SYDNEY - BAULKHAM HILLS NSW 2153

Pop Part of Sydney, (20km W Sydney), See map on page 56, ref C5.

★★★★☆ **Norwest International Hotel**, (LH), 1 Columbia Crt, 500m fr PO, ☎ 02 9634 9634, 02 9634 9660, (Multi-stry), 132 rms [shwr, bath, tlt, a/c, elec blkts, tel, fax-fee, TV, video-fee, clock radio, t/c mkg, refrig, ldry, doonas], lift, ✕, 24hr reception, dinner to unit, secure park, ☏, cots, non smoking rms (33). **RO ⃰ $165 - $220, ⃰⃰ $165 - $220, ⃰ $30**, AE BC DC EFT MC VI, ⓗ.

SYDNEY - BEACON HILL NSW 2100

Pop Part of Sydney, (16km N Sydney), See map on page 56, ref E5.

★★★★☆ **Glan-Y-Mor**, (Villa), 20 Princess Mary St, 500m E of Governor Phillip Look-Out, ☎ 02 9983 0656, fax 02 9970 7570, 1 villa acc up to 4, (3 bedrm), [shwr, bath, tlt, fan, heat, elec blkts, tel, TV, t/c mkg, refrig, cook fac, micro, elec frypan, d/wash, toaster, ldry, blkts, linen, pillows], w/mach, dryer, iron, lounge, ✕, bbq, c/park (garage), non smoking property. **D $150 - $215, W $1,050 - $1,500**, Min book applies.

SYDNEY - BEROWRA NSW 2081

Pop Part of Sydney, (36km N Sydney), See map on page 56, ref D4.

★★☆ **Berowra Heights Hotel Motel**, (LMH), 1 Turner Rd, 2.6km W of Pacific Hwy, ☎ 02 9456 2193, fax 02 9456 3918, 6 units [shwr, tlt, c/fan, heat, TV, t/c mkg, refrig, toaster], ✕ (Wed to Sun), pool, bbq, rm serv, dinner to unit (5 days), ☏, plygr. **RO ⃰ $55, ⃰⃰ $66, ⃰ $10**, AE BC EFT MC VI.

SYDNEY - BILGOLA PLATEAU NSW 2107

Pop Part of Sydney, (35km N Sydney), See map on page 56, ref E4.
★★★★☆ **The Pittwater Bed & Breakfast**, (B&B), 15 Farview Rd,
☎ 02 9918 6932, fax 02 9918 6485, (2 stry), 2 rms (2 suites) [shwr,
spa bath (1), tlt, hairdry, a/c, elec blkts, tel, TV], ldry,
pool-heated (solar). **BB ⁑ $145, ⁑⁑ $165, DBB ⁑ $195, ⁑⁑ $265.**

SYDNEY - BLACKTOWN NSW 2148

Pop Part of Sydney, (36km NW Sydney), See map on page 56, ref B5.
Hotels/Motels
★★★☆ **Travelodge Blacktown**, (M), Cnr Reservoir & Holbeche Rd, 3km
S of Blacktown Railway Station, ☎ 02 8822 2000, fax 02 9672 4904,
(Multi-stry gr fl), 120 units [shwr, tlt, a/c, tel, TV, movie-fee, t/c mkg,
refrig, micro], ldry-fee, lounge, breakfast rm, ✕, coffee shop, 24hr
reception, plygr, tennis (5)-fee, cots, non smoking property. **RO ⁑ $119 -
$149, ⁑⁑ $119 - $149, ⁑⁑⁑ $135 - $165**, fam con, AE BC DC MC VI, ♿.
★★★ **Plumpton Motor Inn**, (LMH), Cnr Richmond Rd & Dublin St, 6km
W of PO, ☎ 02 9626 9766, fax 02 9626 5802, 21 units [shwr, tlt, a/c,
elec blkts, tel, TV, t/c mkg, refrig], ldry, ✕, cots-fee. **RO ⁑ $88, ⁑⁑ $88,
⁑⁑⁑ $104.50, ⁑ $16.50**, AE BC DC MC VI, ♿.

B&B's/Guest Houses
★★☆ **Allawah Street Guest House**, (B&B), 27 Allawah St, 500m W of
Blacktown Station, ☎ 02 9621 7953, fax 02 9621 2225, 2 rms [a/c,
tel (communal)], lounge (TV), t/c mkg shared, non smoking property.
BB ⁑ $80, ⁑⁑ $85, ⁑⁑⁑ $110, W ⁑ $525, ⁑⁑ $560, ch con.

SYDNEY - BLAKEHURST NSW 2221

Pop Part of Sydney, (18km S Sydney), See map on page 56, ref C7.

★★★☆ **Country Comfort - Blakehurst**, (M),
Cnr Woniora Rd & Princes Hwy, 1.5km W of PO,
☎ 02 9547 2177, fax 02 9546 5362, (2 stry
gr fl), 42 units [shwr, tlt, a/c, elec blkts, tel,
TV, video (avail), movie, clock radio, t/c mkg, refrig, mini bar (18), toaster],
ldry, ✕, pool, bbq, rm serv, dinner to unit, cots-fee. **RO $100 - $175**,
ch con, 16 units of a lower rating. AE BC DC MC VI.

★★☆ **Carss Park Motel**, (M), 384B Princes Hwy (Cnr Bunyala St),
2.5km S of Hurstville PO, ☎ 02 9546 3306, fax 02 9546 3306, 17 units
[shwr, tlt, a/c, elec blkts, TV, clock radio, refrig, cook fac], ldry, bbq,
cots (avail). **D ⁑ $88, ⁑⁑ $88, ⁑ $10, W ⁑⁑ $550, ⁑⁑⁑ $627, ⁑⁑⁑⁑ $693**,
AE BC EFT MC VI.

SYDNEY - BONDI NSW 2026

*Pop Part of Sydney, (7km E Sydney), See map on page 56, ref B2.
Famous eastern suburb of Sydney. Bowls, Golf, Scenic Drives,
Swimming. See also Bondi Beach.*
B&B's/Guest Houses
B.J. Guest House, (GH), 76 Old South Head Rd, 8km from CBD,
☎ 02 9389 9232, fax 02 9389 6091, (Multi-stry gr fl), 16 rms [TV-fee,
video-fee, t/c mkg-fee, refrig-fee, micro-fee], shared fac (16), ldry, ✕,
☏, non smoking rms. **RO ⁑ $30, ⁑⁑ $60**, AE BC DC EFT MC VI, (not yet
classified).

SYDNEY - BONDI BEACH NSW 2026

*Pop Part of Sydney, (8km E Sydney), See map on page 56, ref B2.
Famous beachside suburb of Sydney. Swimming.*
Hotels/Motels

★★★★☆ **Swiss-Grand Hotel Bondi
Beach**, (LH), Cnr Campbell Pde & Beach Rd,
☎ 02 9365 5666, fax 02 9365 5330,
(Multi-stry), 203 rms (203 suites) [shwr,
bath, spa bath, tlt, hairdry, a/c, cent heat,
tel, TV (2), movie, clock radio, t/c mkg,
refrig, mini bar], lift, iron, conv fac, ✕, pool-heated (2), sauna, 24hr
reception, ☏, gym, cots, non smoking suites (43). **Suite D ⁑ $229.90 - $715,
⁑⁑ $229.90 - $715, ⁑ $44**, ch con, AE BC DC JCB MC VI.
★★★ **City Beach Motor Inn**, (M), 99 Curlewis St, 350m N of PO,
☎ 02 9365 3100, fax 02 9365 0231, (2 stry gr fl), 26 units (2 suites)
[shwr, bath (4), spa bath (5), tlt, hairdry, a/c, tel, fax, TV, clock radio,
t/c mkg, refrig], ldry, pool, cots-fee. **RO ⁑ $140 - $195, ⁑⁑ $140 - $195,
⁑ $15, Suite D $195 - $210**, AE BC DC EFT MC MP VI, ♿.

Rates may change. Check before booking.

★★☆ **Alice Motel**, (M), 30 Fletcher St, 2km E of PO,
☎ 02 9130 5231, fax 02 9365 2099, (Multi-stry),
31 units [shwr, tlt, a/c, elec blkts, TV, clock radio,
t/c mkg, refrig], ldry, pool, cots. **RO ♦ $80 - $109,**
♦♦ $95 - $119, ♦♦♦ $120 - $130, $129 - $139, AE BC DC MC VI.

★★☆ **Bondi Hotel**, (LH), 178 Campbell Pde, 200m E of PO,
☎ 02 9130 3271, fax 02 9130 7974, (Multi-stry), 50 rms [shwr, bath (4),
tlt, a/c, tel, TV, t/c mkg, refrig], lift, ✉, c/park (limited), cots-fee.
RO ♦ $50, ♦♦ $95, ♦♦♦ $105, Suite D $125 - $190, AE BC DC MC VI.

★★ **Beach Road Hotel**, (LH), 71 Beach Rd, 1km NW of PO,
☎ 02 9130 7247, fax 02 9130 7084, 24 rms (1 suite) [shwr, bath (7),
tlt, a/c, TV, clock radio, t/c mkg, refrig, toaster], ✉ (Mon to Sun), ☎,
cots. **RO ♦ $70, ♦♦ $85, ◊ $15, $120,** BC MC VI.

★★ **Bondi Beachside Inn**, (M), 152 Campbell Pde, 100m N of PO,
☎ 02 9130 5311, fax 02 9365 2646, (Multi-stry), 67 units [shwr, tlt,
a/c, cent heat, tel, TV, clock radio, t/c mkg, refrig, cook fac (43),
toaster], lift, secure park. **RO ♦ $100 - $120, ♦♦ $100 - $120, ◊ $25,**
ch con, Vehicle entrance from Roscoe St. AE BC DC MC VI.

Self Catering Accommodation

Homaccom, (HU), 2/10 Ocean St, 150m N of Bondi Rd PO,
☎ 02 9389 9994, fax 02 9369 2232, 1 unit acc up to 4, [shwr, bath,
tlt, tel, TV, t/c mkg, refrig, cook fac, micro, toaster], lift, w/mach-fee,
dryer-fee, iron, iron brd, non smoking units. **RO ♦ $75, ♦♦ $55,** (not yet
classified).

B&B's/Guest Houses

★★ **Bondi Lodge**, (PH), 63 Fletcher St, 100m SE of PO,
☎ 02 9365 2088, fax 02 9365 2177, (Multi-stry), 68 rms (2 suites)
[shwr (2), tlt (2), c/fan, refrig], shared fac (66 rms), ldry, rec rm, ✕,
spa, t/c mkg shared, bbq, 24hr reception, ☎, cots, non smoking flr (3).
DBB ♦ $70, ♦♦ $100, ♦ $340, ♦♦ $470, RO ♦ $35, ♦ $185, BC EFT MC VI.

Before you travel

Before a trip have your vehicle serviced and checked over to
ensure reliable motoring. There are some checks you can make
yourself, generally the procedure can be found in the vehicle
owners manual.

*Pop Part of Sydney, (5km E Sydney), See map on page 56, ref B2.
Eastern suburb of Sydney.*

B&B's/Guest Houses

★★★ **Barron's Bed & Breakfast**, (B&B), 10 Stanley St, Queens Park,
500m S of PO, ☎ 02 9369 2717, fax 02 9387 1394, (2 stry gr fl),
3 rms [ensuite (1), fan, heat, TV, clock radio, t/c mkg, doonas],
shared fac (2), ldry, lounge firepl, ✕, non smoking rms. **BB ♦ $90 - $110,**
♦♦ $120 - $130, ch con.

★★★ **Sinclairs of Bondi**, (GH), 11
Bennett St, 500m E of Bondi Junction,
☎ 02 9744 6074, fax 02 9744 0664,
(2 stry gr fl), 22 rms [ensuite (8), fan,
heat, elec blkts-fee, TV, t/c mkg, refrig],
ldry, cook fac, ☎. **BLB ♦ $49.50 - $66,**
♦♦ $60.50 - $88, ◊ $27.50 - $33, BC MC VI.

*Pop Part of Sydney, (13km S Sydney), See map on page 56, ref D6.
Southern suburb on the western shores of Botany Bay. Bowls, Swimming.*

Hotels/Motels

★★★★☆ **Novotel Brighton Beach Sydney**, (LH), Cnr
The Grand Pde & Princess St, 12km S of GPO,
☎ 02 9597 7111, fax 02 9597 7877, (Multi-stry),
296 rms (196 suites) [shwr, bath, spa bath (avail), tlt,
hairdry, a/c, cent heat, tel, TV, movie-fee, t/c mkg, refrig, mini bar],
conv fac, ✉, cafe, pool-heated, sauna, spa, 24hr reception, rm serv, ☎,
gym, tennis, cots. **RO ♦ $211 - $236, ♦♦ $211 - $236, ◊ $33,** ch con,
AE BC DC EFT JCB MC VI.

*Pop Part of Sydney, (18km N Sydney), See map on page 56, ref D5.
Northern suburb of Sydney.*

Hotels/Motels

★★★☆ **Travelodge Manly Warringah**, (LH), 4 Victor Rd,
☎ 02 8978 1200, fax 02 8978 1300, (Multi-stry gr fl), 120 rms [shwr,
tlt, hairdry, a/c, tel, TV, movie-fee, clock radio, t/c mkg, refrig, micro],
lift, ldry, iron, iron brd, lounge, conf fac, ✉, pool-indoor (heated)-fee,
24hr reception, gym-fee, cots. **RO ♦ $119 - $149, ♦♦ $119 - $149,**
♦♦♦ $135 - $165, ch con, AE BC DC EFT MC VI.

*Pop 2,000. Part of Sydney, (41km S Sydney), See map on page 56,
ref D7. Southern suburb of Sydney situated across Port Hacking from
Cronulla, surrounded by the Royal National Park. Bowls, Bush
Walking, Fishing.*

Self Catering Accommodation

★★★★ **Jibbon View**, (HU), 6 Loftus St, 100m to Jibbon beach,
☎ 02 9523 1862, fax 02 9523 8381, 1 unit acc up to 4, [shwr, tlt,
hairdry, heat, elec blkts, TV, video, clock radio, t/c mkg, refrig,
cook fac, micro, toaster, ldry, doonas, linen reqd-fee], iron, iron brd,
bbq, non smoking property. **D ♦♦ $100 - $120, ◊ $20 - $25, W ♦♦ $560 -**
$900, ◊ $50, pen con, Min book long w/ends,
*Operator Comment: New brick veneer Beach House. Adjoins
Royal National Park - 80mts to Jibbon Beach. Superb ocean &
parkland views - at night the colored lights of Sydney CBD can
be seen! Modern kitchen. Northerly aspect - great sun deck.
www.ozemail.com.au/~jibbonview.*

B&B's/Guest Houses

★★★★☆ **Beachhaven Bed & Breakfast**, (B&B), 13 Bundeena Dve,
200m W of PO, ☎ 02 9544 1333, fax 02 9544 1333, (2 stry gr fl),
2 rms [shwr, spa bath, tlt, hairdry, heat, elec blkts, TV, video, clock
radio, CD, t/c mkg, refrig, mini bar, micro, toaster], ldry, iron, iron brd,
lounge, bbq, c/park (undercover). **BB ♦♦ $130 - $200,** Min book
applies, BC MC VI.

★★★☆ **Bundeena Bed & Breakfast**, (B&B), 2 Crammond Ave,
☎ 02 9527 2605, (2 stry gr fl), 1 rm [shwr, bath, tlt, hairdry, heat,
elec blkts, tel, TV, clock radio, cook fac, micro], bbq, c/park. **BB ♦♦ $90 -**
$150, ◊ $20 - $30.

SYDNEY - BURWOOD NSW 2134

Pop Part of Sydney, (13km W Sydney), See map on page 56, ref C6.

Hotels/Motels

★★★ **Burwood Motel**, (M), 117 Liverpool Rd, Enfield 2136, 1km S of PO, ☎ 02 9744 0521, fax 02 9744 0508, (2 stry gr fl), 27 units [shwr, tlt, hairdry, a/c, fan, heat, elec blkts, tel, TV, radio, t/c mkg, refrig, ldry]. RO ♦ $88, ♦♦ $88, AE BC DC MC VI.

B&B's/Guest Houses

★★★ **Sinclairs of Burwood Bed & Breakfast**, (B&B), 90 Shaftesbury Rd, 500m S of Burwood railway station, ☎ 02 9744 6074, fax 02 9744 0664, (2 stry gr fl), 21 rms [shwr (9), bath (3), tlt (9), fan, heat, TV, video-fee, clock radio, t/c mkg, refrig, cook fac ltd], ldry, dryer, iron, iron brd, lounge (TV), lounge firepl, ✕, courtesy transfer, ✆, cots, non smoking rms. BLB ♦ $55 - $66, ♦♦ $77 - $88, BC MC VI.

★★☆ **Burwood Boronia Lodge Private Hotel**, (PH), 7 Boronia Ave, 800m E of PO, ☎ 02 9744 9927, fax 02 9744 9927, (2 stry gr fl), 14 rms [shwr, tlt, hairdry, c/fan (8), fax, TV, clock radio, t/c mkg, refrig, micro, toaster], ldry, cook fac, c/park (limited), ✆, cots-fee. BLB ♦ $69.40 - $75.90, ♦♦ $73.80 - $80.30, W $390 - $430, BC MC VI.

SYDNEY - CAMBRIDGE PARK NSW 2747

Pop Part of Sydney, (52km W Sydney), See map on page 56, ref A4.

★★ **Overlander Licensed Motel Hotel**, (LMH), Cnr The Northern Rd & Boomerang Pl, 2km N of PO & Nepean District Hospital, ☎ 02 4730 2955, 20 units [shwr, bath (8), tlt, a/c-cool, fan, heat, TV, radio, t/c mkg, refrig, ldry], ✕, ✆. RO ♦ $55 - $65, ♦♦ $65 - $75, ◊ $10, BC EFT MC VI.

SYDNEY - CAMDEN NSW 2570

Pop 700. Part of Sydney, (61km SW Sydney), See map on page 56, ref A7.

Hotels/Motels

★★★ **Camden Country Club Motel**, (M), 277 Old Hume Hwy (Cnr Wire La), 4km SW of PO, ☎ 02 4655 8402, fax 02 4655 8456, 25 units (1 suite) [shwr, bath (1), spa bath (1), tlt, a/c, elec blkts, tel, TV, clock radio, t/c mkg, refrig], ldry, plygr, cots-fee. RO ♦ $60 - $77, ♦♦ $72 - $110, ♦♦♦ $88 - $105, ◊ $16.50, Suite D $165, AE BC DC EFT MC VI.

★★★ **Crown Hotel Motel**, (LMH), 187 Argyle St, 250m S of PO, ☎ 02 4655 2200, fax 02 4655 2279, (Multi-stry), 20 units [shwr, bath, spa bath (6), tlt, a/c, elec blkts, tel, TV, video (6), clock radio, t/c mkg, refrig, mini bar], ✕, cots. RO ♦ $76 - $99, ♦♦ $87 - $143, ◊ $17, AE BC DC EFT MC VI.

SYDNEY - CAMPBELLTOWN NSW 2560

Pop Part of Sydney, (55km SW Sydney), See map on page 56, ref B7.

Hotels/Motels

★★★★ **Macarthur Inn**, (M), Grange Rd, 2km NE of PO, ☎ 02 4628 1144, fax 02 4626 2409, (2 stry), 36 units [shwr, bath (9), spa bath (7), tlt, hairdry, a/c, heat, elec blkts, tel, TV, movie, clock radio, t/c mkg, refrig, cook fac (6), toaster], ldry, ✕ (Mon to Sat), bar (Mon to Sat), pool, sauna, steam rm, gym, cots-fee, non smoking rms (avail). RO ♦ $99, ♦♦ $99, ◊ $20, 2 family rooms of a lower rating, 12 units yet to be assessed. AE BC DC MC MP VI, ♿.

Macarthur Inn
Ph: (02) 4628 1144
Fax: (02) 4626 2409
FREE CALL 1800 025 435

Grange Road
(off Airds Rd) Leumeah
Free in house movies, Steam room, Gym, Queen size beds,
20M pool, Affordable luxury.
1169AG

1174AG
CENTRA
CAMPERDOWN
Missenden Rd and Marsden St,
Camperdown, NSW 2050
www.centra.com.au

Centra Camperdown is conveniently located within 5 minutes of Darling Harbour and Sydney's CBD.

Adjacent to Royal Prince Alfred Hospital and Sydney University.

Also within easy walking distance is the cafe and restaurant strip of Glebe, Newtown and Leichhardt.

Call the hotel direct on (02) 9516 1522.

Centra Hotels & Resorts. A division of Bass Hotels & Resorts

★★★☆ **Colonial Motor Inn**, (M), 20 Queen St, 1.5km E of PO, ☎ 02 4625 2345, fax 02 4627 1788, (2 stry gr fl), 31 units [shwr, bath (29), tlt, hairdry, a/c, elec blkts, tel, TV, clock radio, t/c mkg, refrig], ldry, conf fac, pool, cots, non smoking units (10). **RO 🚹 $82, 🚹🚹 $92, 🚹🚹🚹 $106, 🧒 $14**, ch con, AE BC DC EFT MC VI, ♿.

★★★ **Maclin Lodge**, (M), 38 Queen St, 800m N of PO, ☎ 02 4628 3788, fax 02 4628 3355, (2 stry gr fl), 87 units [shwr, spa bath (4), tlt, hairdry (40), a/c, elec blkts, tel, TV, clock radio, t/c mkg, refrig, cook fac (4)], ldry, iron, iron brd, conv fac, ✕, pool (salt water), rm serv, cots-fee. **RO 🚹 $82.50 - $209, 🚹🚹 $82.50 - $209, 🧒 $10**, ch con, AE BC DC EFT MC VI.

★★ **Motel Formule 1**, (M), 3 Rennie Rd, 3km N of PO, ☎ 02 4628 7340, fax 02 4628 7350, (Multi-stry gr fl), 72 units [shwr, tlt, a/c, TV], ✆, non smoking rms (avail). **RO 🚹 $59, 🚹🚹 $59**, AE BC DC EFT MC VI, ♿.

SYDNEY - CAMPERDOWN NSW 2050

Pop Part of Sydney, (5km S Sydney), See map on page 56, ref A2. Inner western Sydney suburb that's home to the University of Sydney and Royal Prince Alfred Hospital. Bowls.

Hotels/Motels

★★★☆ **Centra Camperdown**, (M), 9 Missenden Rd, 100m N of Royal Prince Alfred Hospital, ☎ 02 9516 1522, fax 02 9519 4020, (Multi-stry), 139 units [shwr, bath, tlt, a/c, tel, TV, clock radio, t/c mkg, refrig, mini bar], lift, ldry-fee, rec rm, conv fac, ☒, pool, wading pool, 24hr reception, rm serv, c/park (undercover), cots, non smoking units (84). **RO 🚹 $130 - $200, 🚹🚹 $130 - $200, 🧒 $33**, ch con, 32 units ★★★. AE BC DC JCB MC VI, ♿.

★★★ **Camperdown Towers**, (M), 144 Mallett St, 500m S of PO, ☎ 02 9519 5211, fax 02 9519 9179, (Multi-stry), 58 units [shwr, tlt, a/c, tel, cable tv, clock radio, t/c mkg, refrig, cook fac, micro], lift, ldry, pool, cots. **RO 🚹 $85, 🚹🚹 $90, 🚹🚹🚹 $110, $10**, ch con, 19 units ★★☆, 25 units of a lower rating, BC DC MC VI.

★ **(Serviced Apartment Section)**, 22 serv apts acc up to 5, [shwr, bath (12), tlt, hairdry, a/c, tel, cable tv, clock radio, t/c mkg, refrig, cook fac, micro, toaster, blkts, linen]. **D 🚹🚹 $155, RO 🧒 $10.**

Self Catering Accommodation

Oakford AUSTRALIA

★★★☆ **Oakford City West**, (SA), 23 Missenden Rd, ☎ 02 9557 6100, fax 02 9557 6099, (Multi-stry), 30 serv apts acc up to 5, [shwr, bath, tlt, hairdry, a/c, c/fan, cent heat, tel, cable tv, video (avail), clock radio, t/c mkg, refrig, cook fac, micro, d/wash, toaster, ldry, blkts, linen, pillows], lift, w/mach, dryer, iron, pool, bbq, c/park (garage), cots-fee. **D $130 - $215, W $875 - $1,400**, AE BC DC MC VI.

SYDNEY - CARINGBAH NSW 2229

Pop Part of Sydney, (24km S Sydney), See map on page 56, ref C7. Southern suburb of Sydney.

B&B's/Guest Houses

★★☆ **Bush Haven Bed & Breakfast**, (B&B), 31 Flide St, 250m W of station, ☎ 02 9525 4801, 3 rms [shwr, bath, tlt, hairdry, a/c, c/fan, tel, clock radio, t/c mkg], lounge (TV), lounge firepl, c/park. **BB 🚹 $60, 🚹🚹 $90.**

'House Munich' Bed & Breakfast, (B&B), 291 Burraneer Bay Rd, 1km S of PO, ☎ 02 9526 1564, fax 02 9524 6421, (2 stry), 2 rms [a/c, TV, clock radio], ldry, pool, spa, t/c mkg shared, refrig, bbq, non smoking property. **BB 🚹 $110 - $140, 🚹🚹 $120 - $150, 🧒 $50**, BC MC VI, (not yet classified).

SYDNEY - CASTLE HILL NSW 2154

Pop Part of Sydney, (35km NW Sydney), See map on page 56, ref C5. Fast growing residential suburb in the Hills district of Sydney. Tennis.

Hotels/Motels

★★★★ **The Hills Lodge Boutique Hotel**, (LH), Cnr Windsor & Salisbury Rds, 2km NW of Hills Private Hospital, ☎ 02 9680 3800, fax 02 9899 1182, (2 stry gr fl), 69 rms (7 suites) [shwr, bath (1), spa bath (1), tlt, hairdry, a/c, elec blkts, tel, TV, clock radio, t/c mkg, refrig, mini bar, cook fac ltd (3)], ldry, conv fac, ☒, pool, 24hr reception, rm serv, cots. **RO 🚹 $165 - $205, 🚹🚹 $165 - $205, 🧒 $15**, ch con, AE BC DC JCB MC MP VI, ♿.

69 LUXURIOUS ROOMS & SUITES • CLOSE TO PARRAMATTA • NOBLES RESTAURANT & BAR
FUNCTIONS & CONFERENCE FACILITIES • LOCATED IN THE HEART OF CASTLE HILL & NORWEST BUSINESS AREA

THE HILLS LODGE
BOUTIQUE HOTEL

THE HILLS LODGE – WINDSOR ROAD (CNR SALISBURY RD) CASTLE HILL NSW 2154 AUSTRALIA
PH: (02) 9680 3800 • FAX: (02) 9899 1182 • www.hillslodge.com.au
★★★★ AAA Tourism
1239AG

SYDNEY - CASULA NSW 2170

Pop Part of Sydney, (36km SW Sydney), See map on page 56, ref B6. Outer south-western suburb of Sydney.

Hotels/Motels

★★★☆ **Hunts Motel Function Centre**, (M), Camden Valley Way & Hume Hwy, 8km S of Liverpool PO, entry via York St, ☎ 02 9601 5088, fax 02 9602 6440, 120 units (11 suites) [shwr, bath (15), spa bath (9), tlt, a/c, tel, TV, clock radio, t/c mkg, refrig, cook fac (11), micro (11)], ldry, conv fac, ⊠, bar, pool-heated (solar), sauna, spa, bbq, 24hr reception, rm serv (ltd), tennis (2), cots (avail). RO ♦ $104.50 - $137.50, ♦♦ $104.50 - $137.50, ♦ $15, Suite D $187 - $198, AE BC DC JCB MC MP VI, ♦⟁.

★★ **Jolly Knight Motel**, (M), 568 Hume Hwy, 3km S of Liverpool, ☎ 02 9602 6815, 36 units [shwr, spa bath (1), tlt, a/c, tel, TV, t/c mkg, refrig, toaster], ldry, ⊠, ♦, cots-fee. RO ♦ $65 - $85, ♦♦ $65 - $85, ♦ $10, 12 units ★★★. AE BC DC EFT MC VI.

★☆ **Pop-In Motel**, (M), 6 York St (Hume Hwy), Crossroads, ☎ 02 9822 5131, fax 02 9602 0988, (2 stry gr fl), 24 units [shwr, spa bath (20), tlt, a/c, TV, video, movie, t/c mkg, refrig, micro (1)], 24hr reception, cots, AE BC DC EFT MC VI.

SYDNEY - CHATSWOOD NSW 2067

Pop Part of Sydney, (11km N Sydney), See map on page 56, ref D5. Part major business centre, part leafy northern suburb of Sydney. Bowls, Golf, Tennis.

Hotels/Motels

★★★★☆ **Saville Park Suites Chatswood**, (LH), Cnr Railway & Brown Sts, Opposite Chatswood train station, ☎ 02 9406 5500, fax 02 9406 5599, (Multi-stry), 165 rms [shwr, bath, tlt, hairdry, a/c, tel, TV, movie-fee, clock radio, t/c mkg, refrig, mini bar, cook fac (80), micro, d/wash (80), toaster, ldry (80)], lift, iron, iron brd, conf fac, ⊠, bar, pool-heated, spa, steam rm, 24hr reception, ♦, gym, cots, non smoking flr (5), non smoking units (90). D $176 - $363, W $1,232 - $2,541, ch con, AE BC DC EFT JCB MC VI.

Self Catering Accommodation

★★★★☆ **Chatsworth Plaza Suites**, (SA), 37 Victor St, Adjacent to Westfield Shopping Town, ☎ 02 9414 1600, fax 02 9411 6177, (Multi-stry), 54 serv apts acc up to 6, [shwr, bath, tlt, hairdry, a/c, cent heat, tel, TV, video, radio, t/c mkg, refrig, cook fac, micro, d/wash, toaster, ldry, blkts, linen, pillows], lift, w/mach, dryer, iron, conv fac, pool-heated, sauna, spa, bbq, gym, cots. D $240 - $355, W $1,680 - $2,485, ch con, AE BC DC MC VI.

SYDNEY - CHIPPENDALE NSW 2008

Pop Part of Sydney, (3km S Sydney), See map on page 56, ref A2. Inner city suburb of Sydney. Swimming.

Hotels/Motels

★★★☆ **Metro Motor Inn Chippendale**, (M), 1 Meagher St, ☎ 02 9319 4133, fax 02 9698 7665, (Multi-stry), 27 units [shwr, tlt, hairdry, a/c, tel, TV, movie, clock radio, t/c mkg, refrig, micro], ⊠, secure park (undercover), cots, non smoking units (avail). RO ♦♦ $102 - $120, ch con, AE BC DC EFT MC VI.

★★★☆ **Noah Lodge**, (LMH), 179 Cleveland St, 300m S of Central Station, ☎ 02 8303 1303, fax 02 8303 1300, (Multi-stry), 60 units [shwr, tlt, hairdry, a/c, tel, TV, clock radio, t/c mkg, refrig, mini bar], lift, ldry, rec rm, business centre, conf fac, ⊠, bbq-fee, rm serv, ♦, non smoking property. RO ♦♦ $89 - $94, BC EFT VI.

SYDNEY - CHULLORA NSW 2190

Pop part of Sydney, (18km W Sydney) See map on page 56, ref C6. Suburb of Sydney.

Hotels/Motels

★★★ **Sleep Inn Express Motel**, (M), 97 Hume Hwy, 1km E of PO, ☎ 02 9758 7999, fax 02 9758 8808, (2 stry), 88 units [shwr, tlt, a/c, elec blkts, TV, clock radio, t/c mkg, refrig], ✕, ♦, cots-fee, non smoking rms (20). RO ♦ $79 - $85, ♦♦ $79 - $85, ♦ $10, AE BC DC EFT MC VI.

SYDNEY - CHURCH POINT NSW 2105

Pop Part of Sydney, (35km N Sydney), See map on page 56, ref E4. Tranquil and picturesque spot on Pittwater in Sydney's north. Scenic Drives.

Hotels/Motels

★★☆ **Pasadena on Pittwater**, (M), 1858 Pittwater Rd, ☎ 02 9979 6633, fax 02 9979 6147, (2 stry), 14 units [shwr, tlt, cable tv, clock radio, t/c mkg, refrig], ⊠, jetty, cots. D $109 - $210, AE BC DC MC VI.

SYDNEY - CLOVELLY NSW 2031

Pop Part of Sydney, (8km E Sydney), See map on page 56, ref B2. Eastern beachside suburb of Sydney between Bronte and Coogee. Swimming.

Clovelly Bed and Breakfast, (B&B), 2 Pacific St, ☎ 02 9665 0009, (2 stry), 2 rms [shwr, tlt, fan, heat, elec blkts, TV, clock radio, doonas], t/c mkg shared. BB ♦ $105 - $120, ♦♦ $105 - $130, ♦ $50, BC MC VI, (not yet classified).

SYDNEY - COLLAROY NSW 2097

Pop Part of Sydney, (23km N Sydney), See map on page 56, ref E5. Northern beachside suburb of Sydney. Golf, Swimming.

★★★ **Scotters B & B**, (B&B), No children's facilities, 22 Collaroy St, ☎ 02 9982 6394, 2 rms [shwr, bath (1), tlt, hairdry, heat, elec blkts, clock radio], ldry, lounge (TV), t/c mkg shared, non smoking property. BB ♦♦ $95 - $105.

SYDNEY - COLYTON NSW 2760

Pop Part of Sydney, (45km W Sydney), See map on page 56, ref B5. Western suburb of Sydney near St Marys and St Clair.

★★☆ **Colyton Hotel**, (LMH), Cnr Great Western Hwy & Hewitt St, 4km E of PO, ☎ 02 9623 2266, fax 02 9623 7653, 30 units [shwr, tlt, a/c, TV, clock radio, t/c mkg, refrig], ldry, ⊠, plygr. BLB ♦ $77, ♦♦ $82, ♦♦♦ $88, ♦♦♦♦ $93, ♦ $5, AE BC DC MC VI.

SYDNEY - COOGEE NSW 2034

Pop Part of Sydney, (8km E Sydney), See map on page 56, ref B2. Eastern beachside suburb of Sydney with a laid back lifestyle and plenty of restaurants and cafes. Swimming.

Hotels/Motels

★★★★☆ **Crowne Plaza Coogee Beach**, (LH), 242 Arden St, 6km to airport, 7km to CBD, ☎ 02 9315 7600, fax 02 9315 9100, (Multi-stry), 207 rms (20 suites) [shwr, bath, tlt, hairdry, a/c, tel, TV, clock radio, t/c mkg, mini bar], lift, conv fac, ⊠, pool-heated, sauna, spa, dinner to unit, tennis, cots, non smoking rms (52). D ♦♦ $196 - $236, ♦ $38, Suite D $370 - $387, ch con, AE BC DC MC VI, ♦⟁.

★★★★ **Coogee Bay Boutique Hotel**, (LH), 9 Vicar St, ☎ 02 9665 0000, fax 02 9664 2103, (Multi-stry), 79 rms (19 suites) [shwr, bath (51), spa bath (10), tlt, hairdry (79), a/c, cent heat, tel, TV, video, movie, clock radio, t/c mkg, refrig, mini bar (79), cook fac (16), micro (16), toaster], lift, iron, iron brd, lounge, 24hr reception, ♦, cots-fee, non smoking rms (14). D ♦ $89 - $210, ♦♦ $89 - $210, ♦ $27.50, Suite D $149 - $300, 29 heritage rooms ★★★. AE BC DC EFT MC VI.

★★★★ **Coogee Sands Apartments**, (M), 161 Dolphin St,
☎ 02 9665 8588, fax 02 9664 1406, (Multi-stry), 80 units (1, 2 & 3 bedrm), [shwr, bath (26), tlt, hairdry, a/c, elec blkts (1), tel, TV, movie-fee, clock radio, t/c mkg, refrig, cook fac, micro], lift, iron, iron brd, conv fac, bbq, secure park (undercover), courtesy transfer, cots.
RO ♦ $155 - $215, ♦♦ $155 - $215, ◊ $20, ch con, AE BC DC MC VI.

Self Catering Accommodation

★★★★☆ **Medina Executive Coogee**, (SA), 183 Coogee Bay Rd, ☎ 02 9578 6000,
fax 02 9664 7122, (Multi-stry gr fl), 86 serv apts acc up to 5, [shwr, bath, tlt, hairdry, a/c, tel, cable tv-fee, video (avail), movie-fee, clock radio, t/c mkg, refrig, cook fac (53), cook fac ltd (33), micro, d/wash (53), toaster, ldry (53), blkts, doonas, linen, pillows], lift, ldry, w/mach (53), dryer (53), iron, iron brd, conf fac, pool indoor heated, sauna, gym, cots, non smoking flr (3).
D $155 - $260, ch con, Light breakfast available, AE BC DC MC VI.

SYDNEY - CREMORNE POINT NSW 2090

Pop Part of Sydney, (8km N Sydney), See map on page 56, ref B1. Exclusive area on a peninsula that juts into Sydney Harbour. See also Mosman & Neutral Bay.

Hotels/Motels

★★★ **Cremorne Point Manor**, (M), 6 Cremorne Rd, 1.5km S of PO,
☎ 02 9953 7899,
fax 02 9904 1265, (2 stry gr fl), 20 units [shwr, tlt, hairdry, fan, heat, elec blkts, TV, t/c mkg, refrig], ldry, cook fac, cots. BLB ♦ $49.50 - $88, ♦♦ $104.50 - $121, ♦♦♦ $121, Min book Christmas Jan and Easter, AE BC DC MC MCH VI.

SYDNEY - CRONULLA NSW 2230

Pop Part of Sydney, (26km S Sydney), See map on page 56, ref D7. Southern suburb renowned for its fine surfing beaches. Bowls, Swimming.

Hotels/Motels

★★★☆ **Cronulla Motor Inn**, (M), 85 Kingsway, 500m W of PO,
☎ 02 9523 6800, fax 02 9523 0314, (2 stry gr fl), 25 units [shwr, spa bath (1), tlt, hairdry, a/c, c/fan, heat, elec blkts, tel, TV, video-fee, clock radio, t/c mkg, refrig], ldry, iron, iron brd, pool, bbq, plygr, cots-fee. RO ♦ $154 - $184, ♦♦ $154 - $185, ch con, AE BC DC EFT JCB MC VI.

★★★☆ **Rydges Cronulla Beach**, (LH), 20-26 The Kingsway, 100m NE of PO,
☎ 02 9527 3100, fax 02 9523 9541, (Multi-stry), 84 rms (12 suites) [shwr, bath, spa bath (2), tlt, hairdry, a/c, tel, TV, movie, clock radio, t/c mkg, refrig, mini bar, cook fac ltd (44), micro (44), d/wash (2), toaster], lift, ldry, conv fac, ⊠, pool, sauna, spa, 24hr reception, rm serv, ☏, cots, non smoking rms (available). BB ♦♦ $180 - $209, RO ♦♦ $185, $164, Suite D ♦ $230 - $366, ◊ $27.50, ch con, AE BC MC VI.

★★★★★ *Trouble-free travel tips* - **Tyre wear**

Check tyre treads for uneven wear and inspect tyre walls and tread for damage.

SYDNEY - CROWS NEST NSW 2065

Pop Part of Sydney, (5km N Sydney), See map on page 56, ref A1. Lower north shore suburb with good eateries and restaurants.

Hotels/Motels

★★★★ **Sovereign Inn Motel**, (M), 220 Pacific Hwy, 400m S of PO,
☎ 02 9957 5744,
fax 02 9957 5394, (Multi-stry), 89 units (5 suites) [shwr, tlt, hairdry, a/c, tel, TV, clock radio, t/c mkg, refrig, mini bar], lift, iron, iron brd, conv fac, ⊠, pool, 24hr reception, rm serv, ☏, cots-fee, non smoking units (16). RO ♦ $170.50 - $203.50, ♦♦ $170.50 - $203.50, ◊ $16.50, Suite D $203.50, ch con, AE BC DC MC MP VI, ♿.

Self Catering Accommodation

★★★☆ **Medina Classic Crows Nest**, (SA), 167 Willoughby Rd, 400m S of PO, ☎ 02 9430 1400, fax 02 9436 2556, (Multi-stry), 36 serv apts acc up to 4, [shwr, tlt, hairdry, a/c, tel, TV, video-fee, clock radio, t/c mkg, refrig, cook fac, micro, toaster, blkts, doonas, linen, pillows], ldry, iron, iron brd, conf fac, pool (solar), spa, bbq, dinner to unit, c/park (undercover), cots. D $132 - $154, $137 - $160, AE BC DC MC VI.

SYDNEY - DARLINGHURST NSW 2010

Pop Part of Sydney, (2km E Sydney), See map on page 56, ref B2. See also Paddington & Potts Point.

Hotels/Motels

★★★★★ **Marriott Hotel**, (LMH), Previously Sydney Marriott 36 College St, ☎ 02 9361 8400, fax 02 9361 8599, 227 units (14 suites) [shwr, bath, spa bath (14), tlt, hairdry, a/c, tel, TV, movie, clock radio, t/c mkg, refrig, mini bar, cook fac ltd, micro, toaster], ldry, iron, iron brd, conv fac, ⊠, cafe, pool-heated, sauna, spa, steam rm, rm serv, c/park (undercover), ☏, gym, cots, non smoking rms (139). RO ♦ $246 - $281, ♦♦ $246 - $281, ♦♦♦ $271 - $314, ◊ $25, Suite D $306, ch con, AE BC DC JCB MC VI, ♿.

SYDNEY - DARLINGHURST continued...

★★★★ **Hyde Park Plaza Suites Sydney**, (LH), Previously Hyde Park Plaza Hotel 38 College St, opposite Hyde Park, ☎ 02 9331 6933, fax 02 9331 6022, (Multi-stry), 175 rms [shwr, bath, tlt, hairdry, a/c, tel, TV, movie, clock radio, t/c mkg, refrig, mini bar, cook fac], lift, ldry, conf fac, ⊠, pool-heated, sauna, spa, 24hr reception, gym, cots, non smoking rms (29). D ♦ $169, ♦♦ $169, ♦♦♦ $194, ◊ $25, ch con, Minium booking Dec 31- Jan 01 2001 & Feb 28 - Mar 04 2002, AE BC DC JCB MC VI.

★★★☆ **All Seasons On Crown**, (LH), 302-308 Crown St, 1km S of GPO, ☎ 02 9360 1133, fax 02 9380 8989, (Multi-stry), 94 rms [shwr, tlt, hairdry, a/c, tel, cable tv, clock radio, t/c mkg, mini bar, cook fac ltd (1), micro (1)], lift, ldry, iron, iron brd, ⊠, 24hr reception, rm serv (ltd), ☎, cots, non smoking rms (45). RO $147.40 - $184, AE BC DC EFT JCB MC VI, ⅁♿.

Self Catering Accommodation

AAA
T O U R I S M
Special Rates

★★★★ **Saville Park Suites**, (SA), 18 Oxford St, 100m SE of Hyde Park, ☎ 02 8268 2500, fax 02 8268 2599, (Multi-stry), 135 serv apts (135 suites) [shwr, bath, tlt, a/c, tel, TV, movie, clock radio, t/c mkg, refrig, mini bar, cook fac, d/wash, toaster, ldry], lift, ⊠, bar (cocktail), pool-heated, sauna, spa, rm serv, cots. Suite D ♦ $212 - $240, ♦♦ $212 - $240, ◊ $28, ch con, AE BC DC MC VI.

★★★ **Parkridge Corporate Apartments**, (Apt), 6-14 Oxford St, 1.5km SE of GPO, ☎ 02 9361 8600, fax 02 9361 8666, (Multi-stry), 40 apts [shwr, bath, tlt, hairdry, a/c, heat, tel, TV, video-fee, clock radio, t/c mkg, refrig, cook fac, micro, d/wash, toaster, ldry (in unit)], pool-heated, sauna, spa, cots. RO ♦♦ $120 - $160, ♦♦♦♦ $145 - $210, $945 - $1,155, BC EFT MC VI.

★★ **Kings Cross Holiday Apartments**, (HF), 169 William St, ☎ 02 9361 0637, 9 flats acc up to 5, [shwr, tlt, heat, TV, clock radio, refrig, cook fac, blkts, linen, pillows], ldry, AE BC DC JCB MC VI.

SYDNEY - DOUBLE BAY NSW 2028

Pop Part of Sydney, (4km E Sydney), See map on page 56, ref B1. Exclusive, leafy suburb in Sydney's east noted for its stylish shopping and eateries. Sailing.

Hotels/Motels

★★★★★ **The Ritz-Carlton Double Bay**, (LH), 33 Cross St, 6km E of GPO, ☎ 02 9362 4455, fax 02 9362 4744, (Multi-stry), 140 rms (15 suites) [shwr, bath, tlt, hairdry, a/c, elec blkts, tel, fax, TV, video (avail), movie, clock radio, refrig, mini bar], ldry, conv fac, ⊠, pool, 24hr reception, rm serv, dinner to unit, c/park (valet), ☎, gym, cots, non smoking rms (36). RO ♦ $185 - $3,000, ♦♦ $185 - $3,000, ◊ $35, ch con, AE BC DC EFT JCB MC VI, ⅁♿.

★★★☆ **Savoy Double Bay Hotel**, (M), 41 Knox St, 5km W of GPO, ☎ 02 9326 1411, fax 02 9327 8464, (Multi-stry), 38 units [shwr, bath (34), spa bath (2), tlt, hairdry, a/c, tel, video (available), clock radio, t/c mkg, refrig], lift, ldry, iron, iron brd, rm serv, dinner to unit, cots-fee. BB ♦♦ $119 - $189, ♦♦♦♦ $260, ◊ $17.50, ch con, 4 rooms of a higher rating, AE BC DC MC VI.

Self Catering Accommodation

Medina

★★★★ **Medina Executive Double Bay**, (SA), Cnr Ocean Ave & Guilfoyle St, 4km E of CBD, ☎ 02 9361 9000, fax 02 9332 3484, 10 serv apts acc up to 4, [shwr, spa bath, tlt, hairdry, a/c, tel, TV, video, clock radio, t/c mkg, refrig, cook fac, micro, elec frypan, d/wash, toaster, blkts, doonas, linen, pillows], ldry, iron, iron brd, cots. RO ♦ $165 - $346.50, ♦♦ $165 - $346.50, ch con, AE BC DC MC VI.

B&B's/Guest Houses

★★★★☆ **Sir Stamford Double Bay**, (PH), Previously Sir Stamford Hotel 22 Knox St, 6km E of CBD, ☎ 02 9363 0100, fax 02 9327 3110, (Multi-stry), 73 rms (9 suites) [shwr, bath, tlt, hairdry, a/c, cent heat, tel, TV, movie, t/c mkg, refrig, mini bar], lift, conv fac, ⊠, pool indoor heated, sauna, spa, rm serv, cots. RO ♦ $190 - $600, ♦♦ $190 - $600, ch con, AE BC DC JCB MC VI, ⅁♿.

★★★★ **Double Bay Bed & Breakfast**, (B&B), 63 Cross St, ☎ 02 9363 4776, fax 02 9363 1992, (2 stry), 3 rms [shwr, tlt, c/fan (2), elec blkts, tel, fax, clock radio, refrig (1)], ldry, iron, iron brd, lounge (TV & fireplace), t/c mkg shared, cots. BB ♦ $125 - $165, ♦♦ $145 - $185, ◊ $35, AE BC DC MC VI.

SYDNEY - DRUMMOYNE NSW 2047

Pop Part of Sydney, (6km W Sydney), See map on page 56, ref A1. Inner western suburb bounded by the waters of Iron Cove and the Parramatta River. Boating.

Self Catering Accommodation

★★☆ **Drummoyne Manor Hotel Apartments**, (SA), 35 Marlborough St, 150m N of Council Chambers, ☎ 02 9819 6166, fax 02 9819 7798, 25 serv apts acc up to 5, [shwr, bath (15), tlt, hairdry, a/c, c/fan, tel, cable tv, video (avail), clock radio, t/c mkg, refrig, cook fac, micro, toaster], ldry, iron, iron brd, pool, bbq, cots-fee. D ◊ $12, $125 - $180, AE BC DC MC VI, ⅁♿.

B&B's/Guest Houses

★★★★ **Wyncroft Bed & Breakfast**, (B&B), 57 Thompson St, 500m SE of PO, ☎ 02 9181 4274, fax 02 9181 4274, (2 stry), 3 rms [shwr, tlt, hairdry, fan (1), c/fan (2), heat, elec blkts, tel, t/c mkg], iron, iron brd, lounge (TV & firepl), ✕. BB ♦ $100, ♦♦ $132, BC MC VI.

SYDNEY - DURAL NSW 2158

Pop Part of Sydney, (36km N Sydney), See map on page 56, ref C4. Semi-rural suburb in Sydney's Hills district. Bowls, Scenic Drives.

Hotels/Motels

★★★★ **Dural Hotel Motel**, (LMH), 271 New Line Rd, 2km S of PO, ☎ 02 9651 1811, fax 02 9651 4345, 28 units [shwr, tlt, a/c, TV, clock radio, t/c mkg, refrig], ⊠, pool, spa (2), rm serv, dinner to unit, ☎. RO ♦ $75 - $135, ◊ $15, AE BC DC EFT MC VI.

B&B's/Guest Houses

★★★☆ **House at Round Corner**, (B&B), 679 Old Northern Rd, ☎ 02 9651 5777, fax 02 9651 5777, 4 rms [shwr (3), bath (1), tlt (4), a/c (1), c/fan (3), fire pl (1), heat, clock radio], ldry, rec rm, lounge (TV, video), ✕, pool, t/c mkg shared, bbq, non smoking property. **BB ♦ $65, ♦♦ $85, DBB ♦ $85, ♦♦ $125**, pen con.

SYDNEY - EASTWOOD NSW 2122

Pop Part of Sydney, (17km NW Sydney), See map on page 56, ref C5.

Hotels/Motels

★★★ **El-Rancho**, (LMH), Cnr Epping Hwy & Herring Rd, 2km W of North Ryde PO, ☎ 02 9887 2411, fax 02 9888 9145, 13 units [shwr, bath (2), tlt, a/c, tel, TV, clock radio, t/c mkg, refrig], conv fac, ✕, dinner to unit, cots. **BB ♦ $99, ♦♦ $110, ♀ $19**, ch con, AE BC DC MC VI.

SYDNEY - EBENEZER NSW 2756

Pop Part of Sydney, (69km N Sydney), See map on page 56, ref B3.

★★★★★ **Tizzana Winery Bed & Breakfast**, (B&B), 518 Tizzana Rd, 17km N of Windsor Po, ☎ 02 4579 1150, fax 02 4579 1216, 2 rms [bath, hairdry, a/c, c/fan, cent heat, TV, video, clock radio, t/c mkg], conf fac, lounge firepl, bbq, dinner to unit. **BB ♦♦ $180 - $220, DBB ♦♦ $310 - $350**, AE BC DC EFT JCB MC VI.

SYDNEY - EDGECLIFF NSW 2027

Pop Part of Sydney, (4km E Sydney), See map on page 56, ref B2.

★★★ **Metro Motor Inn Edgecliff**, (M), 230 New South Head Rd, opposite railway station, ☎ 02 9328 7977, fax 02 9360 1216, (Multi-stry), 34 units [shwr, bath, tlt, a/c, tel, TV, movie, clock radio, t/c mkg, refrig], lift, ldry, breakfast rm, c/park (limited), cots. **RO ♦♦ $108 - $118, ♀ $22**, ch con, AE BC DC MC VI.

SYDNEY - ELIZABETH BAY NSW 2011

Pop Part of Sydney, (3km E Sydney), See map on page 56, ref B1.

Hotels/Motels

★★★★☆ **Sebel of Sydney**, (M), 23 Elizabeth Bay Rd, 400m S of PO, ☎ 02 9358 3244, fax 02 9357 1926, (Multi-stry gr fl), 165 units (24 suites) [shwr, bath (146), tlt, hairdry, a/c, elec blkts, tel, TV, clock radio, t/c mkg, refrig], lift, ldry, iron, conv fac, ✕, bar, pool-heated, sauna, 24hr reception, rm serv, gym, cots. **RO ♦ $225 - $295, ♦♦ $280 - $340, ♀ $25, Suite D $595 - $825**, 24 rooms yet to be assessed, AE BC DC JCB MC VI.

★★★☆ **Gazebo Hotel**, (M), 2 Elizabeth Bay Rd, 200m SW of PO, ☎ 02 9358 1999, fax 02 9356 2951, (Multi-stry), 395 units (11 suites) [shwr, bath (200), tlt, hairdry, a/c, tel, TV, movie, clock radio, t/c mkg, refrig, mini bar], lift, conv fac, ✕, pool-heated, sauna, rm serv, cots, non smoking rms (66). **RO $124 - $252**, AE BC DC JCB MC VI, ♿.

★★★☆ **Madisons Central City Hotel**, (LH), 6 Ward Ave, 250m S of Potts Point PO, ☎ 02 9357 1155, fax 02 9357 1193, (Multi-stry gr fl), 39 rms (8 suites) [shwr, bath, tlt, hairdry, a/c, elec blkts, tel, cable tv, movie, clock radio, t/c mkg, refrig], lift, ldry, iron, iron brd, breakfast rm, 24hr reception, secure park, cots. **RO ♦♦ $108.90, ♀ $20, Suite D $126.50**, AE BC DC EFT JCB MC VI, ♿.

SYDNEY - ELIZABETH BAY continued...

★★☆ **Manhattan Park Inn International**, (LH), 8 Greenknowe Ave, 2km N of PO, ☎ 02 9358 1288, fax 02 9357 3696, (Multi-stry), 140 rms [shwr, tlt, hairdry, a/c, tel, TV, clock radio, t/c mkg, refrig], lift, ldry, ⊠, bar, 24hr reception, rm serv (ltd), c/park-fee, cots. **RO ♦ $88 - $110, ♦♦ $88 - $110, ◊ $16.50,** AE BC DC JCB MC VI.

★★☆ **Roslyn Gardens Motor Inn**, (M), 4 Roslyn Gardens, ☎ 02 9358 1944, fax 02 9357 7939, (Multi-stry gr fl), 29 units [shwr, tlt, hairdry, a/c, tel, cable tv, video-fee, clock radio, t/c mkg, refrig, mini bar, cook fac, micro], iron, secure park, cots. **RO ♦ $75 - $95, ♦♦ $75 - $110, ◊ $15,** ch con, AE BC DC EFT JCB MC VI.

Self Catering Accommodation

★★★☆ **Seventeen at Elizabeth Bay Boutique Apts**, (SA), Previously Seventeen Elizabeth Bay Quality Suites 17 Elizabeth Bay Rd, 250m S of PO, ☎ 02 9358 8999, 02 9356 2491, (Multi-stry gr fl), 30 serv apts acc up to 5, [shwr, bath, tlt, hairdry, a/c, tel, TV, clock radio, t/c mkg, refrig, cook fac, micro, toaster], lift, ldry, cots. **W ♦♦ $1,120, ♦♦♦♦ $1,400, RO ♦♦ $180, ♦♦♦♦ $230, ◊ $25,** Min book applies, AE BC DC JCB MC VI.

SYDNEY - ELVINA BAY NSW 2105

Pop Part of Sydney, (34km N Sydney), See map on page 56, ref E4.

★★★ **Elvina Bay Watch Cottage**, (Cotg), Accessible by boat only. 43 Sturdee Lane, 5 min by boat from Church Point, ☎ 02 9971 0283, fax 02 9981 2575, (2 stry gr fl), 1 cotg acc up to 8, [shwr, bath, tlt, fire pl, heat, tel, TV, video, clock radio, t/c mkg, refrig, cook fac, micro, toaster, ldry, linen reqd-fee], w/mach, iron, bbq, cots. **D $180 - $220, W $850 - $1,650,** Min book applies.

SYDNEY - EMU HEIGHTS NSW 2750

Pop Part of Sydney, See map on page 56, ref A4.

★★★☆ **Bell Bird Guest House**, (B&B), 38 Riverside Rd, ☎ 02 4735 7029, fax 02 4735 7902, (2 stry) 3 rms [shwr, tlt, a/c (1), fan (2), clock radio], ldry, rec rm, lounge (TV), lounge firepl, pool, bbq, non smoking property. **BB ♦♦ $75 - $135, ◊ $25,** ch con, AE.

SYDNEY - ENGADINE NSW 2233

Pop Part of Sydney, (32km S Sydney), See map on page 56, ref C7.

★★★☆ **Engadine Motor Inn**, (M), 1229 Princes Hwy, 1km S of PO, ☎ 02 9520 8166, fax 02 9520 8622, 25 units [shwr, spa bath (5), tlt, hairdry, a/c, tel, TV, video (avail) clock radio, t/c mkg, refrig, cook fac ltd (4)], ldry, pool indoor heated, plygr, cots, no smoking units (12). **W $600 - $850, RO ♦ $100, ♦♦ $110 - $165, ♦♦♦ $115 - $165, ◊ $10 - $30,** ch con, AE BC DC EFT MC VI, ♿.

SYDNEY - FAIRFIELD NSW 2165

Pop Part of Sydney, (30km SW Sydney), See map on page 56, ref C5.

★★☆ **Brown Jug Hotel Motel**, (LMH), 47 Stanbrook St, ☎ 02 9728 1435, fax 02 9724 3869, (2 stry), 14 units [shwr (6), tlt (6), a/c, tel, TV, clock radio, t/c mkg, refrig, toaster], shared fac (6 units), ldry, iron, iron brd, cook fac, ☎, cots-fee. **RO $68 - $79,** AE BC DC EFT MC VI.

SYDNEY - FAIRLIGHT NSW 2094

Pop Part of Sydney, (12km NE Sydney) See map on page 56, ref E5.

★★★★ **Manly View Apartments Fairlight**, (SA), 149 Sydney Rd, ☎ 02 9977 4188, fax 02 9977 0524, (Multi-stry gr fl), 21 serv apts acc up to 2, [shwr, tlt, hairdry, a/c, heat, tel, TV, clock radio, t/c mkg, refrig, cook fac, toaster, ldry, blkts, linen], w/mach, dryer, iron, iron brd, 24hr reception, cots, non smoking property. **D $150 - $165, W $976 - $1,070,** Min book applies, AE BC DC EFT JCB MC VI.

SYDNEY - FIVE DOCK NSW 2046

Pop Part of Sydney, (9km W Sydney), See map on page 56, ref D6.

B&B's/Guest Houses

★★★☆ **Majella Bed & Breakfast**, (B&B), 1 Wangal Pl, 7Km from city, ☎ 02 9712 5903, fax 02 9712 5903, (2 stry), 3 rms [shwr (1), bath (1), tlt (1), fan, tel, clock radio (1)], ldry, lounge (TV, video), ✕, t/c mkg shared, non smoking property. **BLB ♦ $65 - $95, ♦♦ $75 - $115.**

SYDNEY - FLEMINGTON NSW 2140

Pop Part of Sydney, (16km W Sydney), See map on page 56, ref C5.

★★★ **Flemington Markets Hotel Motel**, (LMH), 268 Parramatta Rd, 1km E of PO, ☎ 02 9764 3500, (2 stry), 16 units [shwr, tlt, hairdry, a/c, tel, TV, clock radio, t/c mkg, refrig], ☎. **RO ♦ $85, ♦♦ $99, ♦♦♦ $119, ◊ $20,** AE BC DC MC VI.

SYDNEY - FRENCHS FOREST NSW 2086

Pop Part of Sydney, (18km N Sydney), See map on page 56, ref D5.

★★☆ **Parkway Hotel**, (LMH), 5 Frenchs Forest Rd East, 1km E of PO, ☎ 02 9451 3699, fax 02 9975 1718, 10 units [shwr, tlt, heat, tel, TV, refrig], ⊠. **BLB ♦ $71, ♦♦ $82, ♦♦♦ $93, ◊ $10,** AE BC DC MC VI.

SYDNEY - GALSTON NSW 2159

Pop 1,200. Part of Sydney, (37km N Sydney), See map on page 56, ref C4.

★★★★☆ **Calderwood Bed & Breakfast**, (B&B), 16 Calderwood Rd, ☎ 02 9653 2498, fax 02 9653 2282, 1 rm (1 suite) [shwr, tlt, hairdry, a/c, c/fan, heat, elec blkts, tel, video, clock radio, refrig, micro, toaster], ldry, lounge (TV), spa, cook fac, dinner to unit, cots. **BB ♦ $90 - $100, ♦♦ $100 - $125, ◊ $30 - $60, Suite D ♦ $90 - $100, ♦♦ $100 - $125, ◊ $30 - $60,** ch con, BC MC VI.

SYDNEY - GLADESVILLE NSW 2111

Pop Part of Sydney, (9km NW Sydney), See map on page 56, ref D5.

 ★★★☆ **Sydney Huntley Inn Gladesville**, (M), 165 Victoria Rd, 250m E of PO, ☎ 02 9816 3333, fax 02 9816 2841, (Multi-stry), 66 units [shwr, bath (59), spa bath (3), tlt, hairdry, a/c (22), tel, TV, movie, clock radio, t/c mkg, refrig, mini bar], lift, conv fac, ⊠, pool, spa, bbq, 24hr reception, dinner to unit, c/park (undercover), courtesy transfer, cots, non smoking rms (avail). **BB ♦♦ $120,** AE BC DC EFT MC VI, ♿.

 ★★★ **Gladesville Motel**, (M), 157 Victoria Rd, 200m E of PO, ☎ 02 9816 4244, fax 02 9817 0158, (2 stry), 35 units [shwr, bath (5), tlt, hairdry, a/c, elec blkts, tel, TV, t/c mkg, refrig], ldry, cots, non smoking units (5). **RO ♦ $85, ♦♦ $85, ◊ $10,** AE BC DC EFT MC MCH VI.

SYDNEY - GLEBE NSW 2037

Pop Part of Sydney, (3km W Sydney), See map on page 56, ref A2. Inner western suburb of Sydney known for its alternative lifestyles and its many cafes and restaurants.

Hotels/Motels

  ★★★☆ **Broadway University Motor Inn**, (M), 25 Arundel St, Opposite University of Sydney, ☎ 02 9660 5777, fax 02 9660 2929, (2 stry gr fl), 45 units [shwr, tlt, hairdry, a/c, elec blkts, tel, TV, clock radio, t/c mkg, refrig, mini bar], ldry, iron, iron brd, ✕ (Mon - Fri), 24hr reception, dinner to unit (Mon-Fri), cots. **RO ♦ $139, ♦♦ $149, ◊ $16.50,** ch con, AE BC DC EFT JCB MC MP VI.

 ★★★ **Rooftop Motel**, (M), 146 Glebe Point Rd, 250m N of PO, ☎ 02 9660 7777, fax 02 9660 7155, (Multi-stry), 39 units [shwr, tlt, a/c, tel, TV, video (avail), t/c mkg, refrig], pool, bbq, 24hr reception, cots-fee. **RO ♦ $99 - $110, ♦♦ $99 - $110, ♦♦♦ $115 - $125,** ch con, AE BC DC JCB MC VI.

★★☆ **A-Line Hotel Sydney**, (LMH), 253 Broadway, ☎ 02 9566 2111, fax 02 9566 4493, (Multi-stry gr fl), 46 units [shwr, tlt, a/c, tel, TV, t/c mkg, refrig], 24hr reception, c/park (limited), ☎. **RO ♦ $100, ♦♦ $100, ◊ $20,** ch con, AE BC MC VI.

★★☆ **The Haven Inn Sydney**, (M), 196 Glebe Point Rd, 1km W of PO, ☎ 02 9660 6655, (Multi-stry), 51 units [shwr, spa bath (1), tlt, hairdry, a/c, heat, tel, TV, video, clock radio, t/c mkg, refrig, mini bar], pool-heated, spa, 24hr reception, rm serv, courtesy transfer, cots, non smoking units (10). **RO ♦ $110 - $120, ♦♦ $110 - $120, ◊ $15 - $18,** ch con, AE BC DC MC VI.

B&B's/Guest Houses

★★★★☆ **Glebe Bed & Breakfast**, (B&B), 192 St Johns Rd, 500m W of PO, ☎ 02 9552 6656, fax 02 9552 2556, 4 rms [ensuite, a/c-cool, fan, cent heat, tel, TV, clock radio, t/c mkg, refrig], ✕, non smoking rms (4). **BLB ♦ $100, ♦♦ $120,** weekly con, AE BC DC MC VI.

★★★★ **Tricketts Luxury Bed & Breakfast**, (B&B), 270 Glebe Point Rd, ☎ 02 9552 1141, fax 02 9692 9462, (2 stry gr fl), 7 rms [shwr, tlt, hairdry, a/c-cool, c/fan, cent heat, clock radio, t/c mkg], cook fac, non smoking property. **BB ♦ $150, ♦♦ $176, ◊ $35,** No facilities for children under 12.

★★★ **Alishan International**, (GH), 100 Glebe Point Rd, 1km NW of University, ☎ 02 9566 4048, fax 02 9525 4686, (2 stry gr fl), 14 rms [shwr, tlt, c/fan, TV, t/c mkg, refrig], ldry, rec rm, lounge (TV), cook fac, bbq, ☎, cots. **RO ♦ $88 - $99, ♦♦ $99 - $110, ◊ $16 - $20,** 5 rooms not included in rating. AE BC MC VI, ♿.

SYDNEY - GLENHAVEN NSW 2156

Pop Part of Sydney, (32km NW Sydney), See map on page 56, ref C4.

★★★☆ **Hathersage Bed & Breakfast**, (B&B), 10 Glenhaven Rd, 2km N of Castle Hill PO, ☎ 02 9634 4598, fax 02 9634 4438, (2 stry gr fl), 3 rms [shwr, spa bath (1), tlt, hairdry, a/c, heat, elec blkts, tel, TV, clock radio, t/c mkg, refrig, micro], iron, iron brd, lounge firepl, tennis, non smoking property. **BB** ♦ **$90**, ♦♦ **$105 - $120**, ◊ **$40**, BC MC VI.

SYDNEY - GLENORIE NSW 2157

Pop 800. Part of Sydney, (42km NW Sydney), See map on page 56, ref C4. Rural area on the road to Wisemans Ferry from Dural.

★★★★☆ **Camellia Haven**, (Cotg), 1395 Old Northern Rd, Dural 2158, ☎ 02 9652 1507, fax 02 9652 1507, 1 cotg acc up to 4, [shwr, tlt, hairdry, a/c, fire pl (combustion), tel, TV, clock radio, CD, t/c mkg, refrig, cook fac, micro, toaster], w/mach, iron, iron brd, c/park. **BLB** ♦ **$100**, ♦♦ **$125**, ◊ **$25**.

SYDNEY - GRANVILLE NSW 2142

Pop Part of Sydney, (23km W Sydney), See map on page 56, ref C5.

★★★★ **Parramatta View Serviced Apartments**, (SA), 10 Bridge St, 150m NW of Granville Railway Stn, ☎ 02 9499 4552, fax 02 9499 4553, (Multi-stry), 1 serv apt acc up to 4, [shwr, bath, tlt, hairdry, a/c, fan, heat, tel, TV, clock radio, t/c mkg, refrig, cook fac, micro, toaster, ldry, blkts, linen, pillows], lift, w/mach-fee, dryer-fee, iron, c/park (carport). **W $650 - $1,400**, Min book applies, AE BC DC MC VI.

SYDNEY - GREENACRE NSW 2190

Pop Part of Sydney, (18km SW Sydney), See map on page 56, ref C6.

★★★☆ **Bankstown Motel 10**, (M), Cnr Hume Hwy & Northcote Rd, ☎ 02 9523 9128, fax 02 9742 5879, (2 stry gr fl), 19 units [shwr, tlt, a/c, tel, TV, clock radio, t/c mkg, refrig], ldry, cots-fee, non smoking units (14). **RO** ♦ **$105 - $115**, ♦♦ **$115 - $125**, ◊ **$15**, AE BC DC EFT MC VI.

★★☆ **The Palms**, (LMH), 167 Hume Hwy, 4km N of Bankstown PO, ☎ 02 9642 7300, fax 02 9742 5021, 20 units [shwr, tlt, a/c, elec blkts, tel, TV, clock radio, t/c mkg, refrig], ldry, conv fac, ⊠, rm serv, cots. **RO** ♦ **$61 - $83**, ♦♦ **$72 - $93.50**, ♦♦♦♦ **$115**, AE BC DC MC VI.

SYDNEY - GREYSTANES NSW 2145

Pop Part of Sydney, (29km W Sydney), See map on page 56, ref C5.

★★☆ **Greystanes Inn**, (LMH), 701 Merrylands Rd, 100m W of PO, ☎ 02 9631 2266, fax 02 9636 5087, 6 units [shwr, tlt, fan, heat, TV, clock radio, t/c mkg]. **BLB** ♦ **$77**, ♦♦ **$90**, ♦♦♦ **$101**, AE BC DC MC VI.

SYDNEY - GUILDFORD NSW 2161

Pop Part of Sydney, (27km W Sydney), See map on page 56, ref C5.

Hotels/Motels

★★☆ **Sheridan Hotel**, (LMH), Cnr Fairfield & McCredie Rds, 2.5km NE of Fairfield PO, ☎ 02 9632 1888, fax 02 9632 8723, (2 stry gr fl), 15 units [shwr, tlt, a/c, tel, TV, radio, t/c mkg, refrig], lounge, conv fac, ⊠. **RO** ♦ **$66**, ♦♦ **$77**, ◊ **$11**, AE BC DC EFT MC VI.

★☆ **Guildford Golf View**, (LH), 150 Rawson Rd, ☎ 02 9632 9758, (2 stry), 9 rms [shwr, tlt, c/fan, heat, TV, t/c mkg, refrig, toaster], conv fac, ⊠, ✆, cots-fee. **BLB** ♦ **$66**, ♦♦ **$77**, **RO** ♦ **$55**, ♦♦ **$66**, BC MC.

SYDNEY - HABERFIELD NSW 2045

Pop Part of Sydney, (9km W Sydney), See map on page 56, ref A1.

Hotels/Motels

★★★☆ **Metro Motor Inn Haberfield**, (M), 171 Parramatta Rd, 1.5km N of PO, ☎ 02 9798 7666, fax 02 9716 7772, (Multi-stry gr fl), 44 units [shwr, tlt, a/c, tel, TV, movie, clock radio, t/c mkg, refrig], lift, ldry, conv fac, ⊠, pool, sauna, bbq, c/park (undercover), cots. **RO** ♦ **$90 - $120**, ch con, AE BC DC EFT MC VI.

★★★ **Palm Court Motor Inn**, (M), 17-23 Parramatta Rd, 2km E of PO, ☎ 02 9797 6111, fax 02 9798 6667, (2 stry gr fl), 32 units [shwr, spa bath (4), tlt, a/c, heat, tel (direct dial), TV, movie, clock radio, t/c mkg, refrig, mini bar], ldry, conv fac, ⊠, bbq, 24hr reception, rm serv, dinner to unit, cots. **BB** ♦ **$110**, ♦♦ **$120**, ◊ **$25**, **D $195**, ch con, 8 rooms at a lower rating. AE BC DC MC VI.

SYDNEY - HARBORD NSW 2096

Pop Part of Sydney, See map on page 56, ref E5.

Sandpiper Bed & Breakfast, (B&B), 58 Evans St, ☎ 02 9405 4837, fax 02 9905 4837, 1 rm [ensuite, a/c, TV, t/c mkg, refrig, doonas], cots, non smoking rms. **BLB** ♦ **$120 - $140**, ♦♦ **$120 - $140**, ◊ **$30**, BC MC VI, (not yet classified).

SYDNEY - HAYMARKET NSW 2000

Pop Part of Sydney, See map on page 56, ref A2. Inner city suburb of Sydney that encompasses Chinatown and part of Darling Harbour.

Hotels/Motels

★★★★☆ **Carlton Crest Hotel Sydney**, (LH), 169 Thomas St, Sydney 2000, 1.1km SW of PO, ☎ 02 9281 6888, fax 02 9281 6688, (Multi-stry), 247 rms (4 suites) [shwr, bath, tlt, a/c, elec blkts, tel, TV, video (5), clock radio, t/c mkg, refrig, mini bar], lift, iron, conv fac, ⊠, pool, spa, rm serv, c/park-fee, cots, non smoking rms (123). **RO** ♦ **$165 - $180**, ♦♦ **$165 - $180**, ♦♦♦ **$175 - $190**, ◊ **$28**, **Suite D $302**, ch con, AE BC DC JCB MC VI.

★★★★☆ **Southern Cross Sydney Hotel**, (LH), Cnr Goulburn & Elizabeth Sts, 1.5km SE of GPO, ☎ 02 9282 0987, fax 02 9211 8130, (Multi-stry), 192 rms (16 suites) [shwr, bath, spa bath (15), tlt, hairdry, a/c, elec blkts, tel, TV, movie-fee, clock radio, t/c mkg, refrig, mini bar, toaster], lift, ldry, iron, iron brd, lounge, ⊠, pool-heated, sauna, 24hr reception, rm serv, c/park (valet)-fee, ✆, gym, cots. **D** ♦ **$145**, ♦♦ **$145**, ◊ **$35**, ch con, AE BC DC MC VI, ⚹&.

★★★★ **All Seasons Darling Harbour**, (LH), 17 Little Pier St, Darling Harbour 2009, 200m S of Darling Harbour, ☎ 02 8217 4000, fax 02 8217 4400, (Multi-stry), 223 rms (5 suites) [shwr, bath, tlt, hairdry, a/c, tel, TV, movie-fee, clock radio, t/c mkg, refrig, mini bar], lift, iron, iron brd, business centre, conf fac, ⊠, pool-indoor (heated), 24hr reception, rm serv, gym, cots, non smoking rms (140). **D $240**, AE BC DC EFT JCB MC VI, ⚹&.

★★★★ **Furama Hotel Darling Harbour**, (LH), 68 Harbour St, opposite Sydney Entertainment Centre, ☎ 02 9281 0400, fax 02 9281 1212, (Multi-stry), 305 rms (14 suites) [shwr, bath, tlt, hairdry, a/c, cent heat, elec blkts, tel, TV, video, clock radio, t/c mkg, refrig, mini bar], ⊠, sauna, spa, rm serv, gym, cots, non smoking rms (58). **BB** ♦♦ **$184**, **RO** ♦♦ **$130**, ch con, AE BC DC JCB MC VI, ⚹&.

★★★☆ **Capitol Square Hotel Sydney**, (LH), Cnr Campbell & George Sts, 300m SE of Entertainment Centre, ☎ 02 9211 8633, fax 02 9211 8733, (Multi-stry), 94 rms [shwr, bath (91), tlt, hairdry, a/c, tel, TV, clock radio, t/c mkg, refrig, mini bar], lift, ⊠, 24hr reception, rm serv (ltd), dinner to unit, c/park-fee, ✆, cots, non smoking flr (3), non smoking rms (65). **BB** ♦ **$140 - $170**, ♦♦ **$140 - $170**, ◊ **$130**, AE BC DC MC VI, ⚹&.

★★★☆ **Country Comfort Sydney Central**, (LH), Cnr George & Quay Sts, 200m E of Railway Square, ☎ 02 9212 2544, fax 02 9281 3794, (Multi-stry), 114 rms [shwr, bath, spa bath (52), tlt, hairdry, a/c, fan, tel, fax, TV, movie, clock radio, t/c mkg, refrig, mini bar, micro (3)], lift, ldry, ⊠, cafe, pool, sauna, bbq, 24hr reception, rm serv, c/park (36), cots, non smoking flr (5). **RO** ♦ **$197**, ♦♦ **$197**, ◊ **$16.50**, ch con, AE BC DC EFT MC VI.

★★★☆ **Pacific International Inn - Sydney**, (LMH), 717 George St, 300m W of Central Railway Station, ☎ 02 9289 4400, fax 02 9281 5118, (Multi-stry), 163 units [shwr, bath (14), spa bath (5), tlt, hairdry, a/c, heat, tel, TV, movie-fee, clock radio, t/c mkg, refrig], lift, ldry, iron, iron brd, lounge, conf fac, ✗ (licensed), 24hr reception, ✆. **BLB** ♦ **$195**, ♦♦ **$195**, ◊ **$25**, 20 units ★★★★☆, AE BC DC EFT JCB MC MP VI, ⚹&.

Night driving

Clear vision is most important at night, when visibility is restricted. The newer and cleaner the windscreen, the easier it is to see. Clean your headlights and headlight covers, as dirt can severely reduce the brightness of your headlights. Have your headlights adjusted to suit the heaviest load you are likely to carry.

If the glare of oncoming headlights is troubling you, look slightly to the left of the road, to avoid the glare. Look at the edge of the road to make sure that you don't run off. Never drive with your high beams on if there is a vehicle travelling in either direction within 200 metres in front of you.

★★★ **Aarons Hotel**, (LH), 37 Ultimo Rd, 300m S of Darling Harbour, ☎ 02 9281 5555, fax 02 9281 2666, (Multi-stry), 94 rms [shwr, tlt, a/c-cool, tel, TV, clock radio, refrig], lift, ldry, 24hr reception, c/park (limited), cots. BB ♦ $130, ♦♦ $130, ♦♦♦ $140 - $155, ◊ $5 - $10, AE BC DC MC VI.

★★★ **Royal Garden International**, (LH), 431 Pitt St, 1.2km S of GPO, ☎ 02 9281 6999, fax 02 9281 6988, (Multi-stry), 215 rms (10 suites) [bath, tlt, hairdry, a/c, cent heat, tel, TV, clock radio, t/c mkg, refrig, mini bar], lift, conv fac, ⊠, cafe, pool, spa, 24hr reception, rm serv, ✆, cots. RO ♦ $121, ♦♦ $121, ◊ $22, Suite RO ♦ $165, ♦♦ $165, ◊ $22, AE BC DC MC VI.

Self Catering Accommodation

★★★★☆ **Medina Executive Sydney Central**, (SA), 2 Lee St, 100m W of Central Railway Station, ☎ 02 8396 9800, fax 02 9698 4855, (Multi-stry), 98 serv apts acc up to 4, [a/c-cool, tel, TV, movie (fee), clock radio, t/c mkg, refrig, cook fac (80), cook fac ltd, micro, d/wash, ldry, doonas, linen], lift, w/mach, conv fac, pool, sauna, spa, bbq, meals to unit, secure park (fee), gym, cots. D $165 - $275, AE BC DC MC VI.

★★★★☆ **Southern Cross Towers All Suite Hotel**, (SA), Cnr Goulburn & Wentworth Sts, 500m S of CBD, ☎ 02 9282 0987, fax 02 9277 3333, (Multi-stry), 120 serv apts acc up to 4, [shwr, bath, spa bath (15), tlt, hairdry, a/c, cent heat, elec blkts, tel, TV, movie-fee, clock radio, t/c mkg, refrig, mini bar, cook fac, micro, d/wash (14), toaster, blkts, linen], lift, ldry, w/mach, dryer, iron, iron brd, ⊠, sauna, 24hr reception, rm serv, ✆, gym, cots. D ♦ $145 - $230, ♦♦ $145 - $230, ◊ $35, ch con, AE BC DC MC VI.

SYDNEY - HOMEBUSH BAY NSW 2127

Pop part of Sydney (16km W Sydney) See Sydney map, ref C5. Suburb of Sydney, Site of the Sydney 2000 Olympic Games.

Hotels/Motels

★★★★☆ **Novotel Homebush Bay**, (LH), Olympic Blvde, ☎ 02 8762 1111, fax 02 8762 1211, (Multi-stry), 177 rms (28 suites) [shwr, bath (129), spa bath (28), tlt, hairdry, a/c, tel, TV, movie-fee, clock radio, t/c mkg, refrig, mini bar, cook fac ltd (28), micro (28)], lift, ldry, iron, iron brd, business centre, conf fac, ⊠, sauna-fee, spa, 24hr reception, rm serv, ✆, cots, non smoking units (152). RO ♦ $220, ♦♦ $220, ♦♦♦ $250, Suite RO ♦ $320, ♦♦ $320, ♦♦♦ $350, ch con, pen con, AE BC DC EFT JCB MC VI, ⅍⚌.

★★★☆ **Hotel Ibis Homebush Bay**, (LH), Olympic Blvde, ☎ 02 8762 1100, fax 02 8762 1211, (Multi-stry), 150 rms [shwr, tlt, hairdry, a/c, tel, TV, movie-fee, clock radio, t/c mkg, refrig], lift, ldry, lounge, business centre, conf fac, ⊠, sauna-fee, spa, ✆, cots, non smoking rms (125). RO ♦ $109, ♦♦ $109, ♦♦♦ $129, ch con, pen con, AE BC DC EFT JCB MC VI, ⅍⚌.

SYDNEY - HORNSBY NSW 2077

Pop Part of Sydney, (24km N Sydney), See map on page 56, ref D4. Major regional centre on Sydney's upper north shore. Bowls, Swimming.

Hotels/Motels

★☆ **The Hornsby Inn**, (LH), Cnr Hunter & Burdett Sts, 100m W of PO, ☎ 02 9477 5555, fax 02 9477 6738, (2 stry), 10 rms [shwr, tlt, a/c, fan, heat, TV, refrig]. BLB ♦ $82.50, ♦♦ $93.50, ◊ $11, AE BC DC MC VI.

mt.kuring-gai motel
RESTAURANT
(ONLY 5KM NORTH OF HORNSBY)
705 Pacific Highway, Mt. Kuring-gai, N.S.W. 2080
PHONE: (02) 9457 9393
LOWEST RATES IN HORNSBY AREA

SYDNEY - HUNTERS HILL NSW 2110

Pop Part of Sydney, (7km W Sydney), See map on page 56, ref A1.

★★★★ **Magnolia House Bed & Breakfast**, (B&B), 20 John St, ☎ 02 9879 7078, fax 02 9817 3705, 3 rms [ensuite (2), spa bath (1), hairdry (3), a/c, tel, clock radio (3)], shared fac (2), lounge, ✕, t/c mkg shared. BB ♦ $100 - $160, ♦♦ $120 - $210, DBB ♦ $120 - $180, ♦♦ $160 - $250, BC MC VI.

SYDNEY - KENSINGTON NSW 2033

Pop Part of Sydney, (5km SE Sydney), See map on page 56, ref B2.

Hotels/Motels

★★★ **Addisons on Anzac**, (M), 147 Anzac Pde, ☎ 02 9663 0600, fax 02 9313 6216, (Multi-stry), 42 units [shwr, tlt, hairdry, a/c, tel (direct in dial), TV, clock radio, t/c mkg, refrig, cook fac, micro, toaster], lift, ldry-fee, iron, rec rm, ⊠, c/park (undercover) (12), cots, non smoking units (14). RO ♦ $109, ♦♦ $120, ♦♦♦ $131, ◊ $11, AE BC DC EFT MC VI.

B&B's/Guest Houses

★★ **Parkview Private Hotel**, (PH), 7 Alison Rd, 500m NE of PO, opposite Centennial Park, ☎ 02 9662 1482, fax 02 9662 8661, 15 rms [shwr (9), tlt (9), fan, heat, TV, video-fee, t/c mkg, refrig], ldry, bbq, ✆, cots. BLB ♦ $43 - $50, ♦♦ $53 - $65, ♦♦♦ $66 - $78, ◊ $12, AE BC MC VI.

SYDNEY - KILLARA NSW 2071

Pop Part of Sydney, (15km N Sydney), See map on page 56, ref D5.

★★★☆ **Killara Inn Hotel & Conference Centre**, (M), 480 Pacific Hwy, 3km N of Chatswood, ☎ 02 9416 1344, fax 02 9416 6347, (2 stry), 39 units (1 suite) [ensuite, bath (3), a/c, tel, TV, video-fee, clock radio, t/c mkg, refrig], ldry, conf fac, ⊠, pool-heated, sauna, dinner to unit, cots-fee, non smoking property. RO ♦ $159.50 - $170.50, ♦♦ $159.50 - $170.50, ♦♦♦ $170 - $181.50, ◊ $11, Suite RO $220, AE BC DC MC VI.

SYDNEY - KINGS CROSS NSW 2011

Pop Part of Sydney, (2km E Sydney), See map on page 56, ref B2. There is actually no such suburb as 'Kings Cross' — the name refers to a locality that takes in parts of Darlinghurst, Potts Point and Rushcutters Bay.

Hotels/Motels

★★★★☆ **Holiday Inn Potts Point Sydney**, (LH), 203 Victoria St, Potts Point 2011, 2km E of GPO, ☎ 02 9368 4000, fax 02 8356 9111, (Multi-stry gr fl), 290 rms (6 suites) [shwr, bath, tlt, hairdry, a/c, heat, elec blkts, TV, clock radio, t/c mkg, refrig, mini bar], lift, conf fac, ⊠, 24hr reception, rm serv, gym, cots, non smoking flr (4). BB ♦ $158, ♦♦ $158, ♦♦♦ $201, ◊ $44, Suite D $267, AE BC DC JCB MC VI.

★★★★☆ **Millennium Hotel Sydney**, (LH), Top of William St, Potts Point 2011, top of William St, ☎ 02 9356 1234, fax 02 9356 4150, (Multi-stry), 390 rms [shwr, bath, tlt, a/c, tel, TV, movie, radio, t/c mkg, refrig, mini bar], lift, conf fac, ⊠ (2), coffee shop, pool, rm serv, gym, cots. BB ♦ $132, ♦♦ $132, ◊ $33, AE BC DC JCB MC VI.

★★★★☆ **The Crescent on Bayswater**, (LMH), 33 Bayswater Rd, Potts Point 2011, 1.5km E of GPO, ☎ 02 9357 7266, fax 02 9357 7418, (Multi-stry), 67 units (44 suites) [shwr, bath, tlt, hairdry, a/c, elec blkts, tel, TV, movie, clock radio, t/c mkg, refrig, mini bar, cook fac, micro, toaster], lift, ldry, night club, ⊠, bar, pool, 24hr reception, rm serv, secure park, cots. BB ♦ $200, ♦♦ $200, Suite BB ♦ $220, ♦♦ $220, ◊ $35, ch con, 23 rooms ★★★★. AE BC DC JCB MC VI.

THE CREST HOTEL
Spectacular Harbour, City & Rushcutters Bay views.
Surrounded by Restaurants, Bars and Nightclubs.
Close to major attractions & direct rail link to city.
Features the popular and unique Ginseng Bathhouse.

111 Darlinghurst Road, Kings Cross, NSW 2011
Ph: 02 9358 2755   Fax: 02 9358 2888
Email: reservations@thecresthotel.com.au

★★★☆ **The Crest Hotel**, (LH), Previously Hotel Capital 111 Darlinghurst Rd, Kings Cross 1340, opposite PO, ☎ 02 9358 2755, fax 02 9358 2888, (Multi-stry), 227 rms [shwr, bath, tlt, hairdry, a/c, tel, TV, clock radio, t/c mkg, refrig, mini bar], lift, ldry, conv fac, ⊠, bar, pool, sauna, spa, 24hr reception, rm serv, gym, cots, non smoking flr (18). **BB ⧎ $110 - $154, ⧎⧎ $137.50 - $154, ◊ $27.50**, 13 units of a lower rating, AE BC DC MC VI, ⌂⌂.

★★☆ **Kingsview Motel**, (M), 30 Darlinghurst Rd, Potts Point 2011, 300m E of PO, ☎ 02 9358 5599, fax 02 9357 3185, (Multi-stry), 67 units [shwr, tlt, hairdry, a/c, tel, TV, clock radio, t/c mkg, refrig], lift, iron, iron brd, cots-fee, non smoking units (11). **RO ⧎ $75 - $108, ⧎⧎ $75 - $108, ⧎⧎⧎ $85 - $115, ◊ $15**, AE BC DC MC VI.

FLAG
FLAG CHOICE HOTELS

Self Catering Accommodation

★★★☆ **New Hampshire Apartments**, (SA), Previously All Seasons New Hampshire Apartments 2 Springfield Ave, Potts Point 2011, 200m S of PO, ☎ 02 9356 3222, fax 02 9357 2296, 50 serv apts [shwr, bath, tlt, a/c, tel, TV, movie, clock radio, t/c mkg, refrig, cook fac, d/wash, ldry (in unit)], ✕, pool, 24hr reception, secure park, cots. **D ⧎ $135 - $175, ⧎⧎ $152.50 - $225**, ch con, AE BC DC JCB MC MCH MP VI.

B&B's/Guest Houses

★★★★☆ **Regents Court**, (PH), 18 Springfield Ave, Potts Point 2011, 200m S of PO, ☎ 02 9358 1533, fax 02 9358 1833, (Multi-stry), 31 rms [shwr, bath, tlt, hairdry, a/c, c/fan, tel, TV, video, clock radio, t/c mkg, refrig, cook fac, micro, toaster], lift, ldry, bbq, cots. **RO ⧎ $220 - $253, ⧎⧎ $220 - $253, ◊ $25**, ch con, AE BC DC JCB MC VI.

★★★☆ **Barclay**, (PH), 17 Bayswater Rd, Potts Point 2011, ☎ 02 9358 6133, fax 02 9358 4363, (Multi-stry), 41 rms [shwr (41), tlt (41), a/c, heat, tel, TV, t/c mkg, refrig], lift, spa, cots. **RO ⧎ $98, ⧎⧎ $120, ◊ $22**, ch con, AE BC DC MC VI.

★★★☆ **Hotel 59**, (PH), 59 Bayswater Rd, Potts Point 2011, 100m E of PO, ☎ 02 9360 5900, fax 02 9360 1828, (2 stry), 8 rms [shwr, bath (8), tlt, hairdry, tel, TV, refrig], lounge, cafe, cots. **BB ⧎ $115.50, ⧎⧎ $126.60 - $137.50**, BC EFT MC VI.

★★☆ **Astoria Private Hotel**, (PH), 9 Darlinghurst Rd, Potts Point 2011, 500m W of PO, ☎ 02 9356 3666, fax 02 9357 1734, 30 rms [shwr, tlt, a/c, heat, tel, TV, clock radio, t/c mkg, refrig], ldry, 24hr reception, cots, non smoking rms (4). **RO ⧎ $89, ⧎⧎ $94, ⧎⧎⧎ $105, ◊ $13**, ch con, fam con, No car parking, AE BC DC MC VI.

★★☆ **Cross Court Tourist Hotel**, (PH), 203 Brougham St, Potts Point 2011, 50m W of Kings Cross Railway Station, ☎ 02 9368 1822, fax 02 9358 2595, (Multi-stry gr fl), 20 rms (2 suites) [bath (2), c/fan, heat, fax, TV, clock radio, t/c mkg, refrig, mini bar, cook fac ltd (2)], shared fac (17), ldry, iron, iron brd, cots, non smoking property. **RO ⧎ $60 - $70, ⧎⧎ $70 - $80, ◊ $15**, AE BC MC VI.

SYDNEY - KINGSFORD NSW 2032

Pop Part of Sydney, (7km SE Sydney), See map on page 56, ref B2. South-eastern suburb of Sydney. Bowls.

Hotels/Motels

★★★☆ **Barker Lodge Motor Inn**, (M), 32 Barker St, 1km N of PO, opposite University of NSW, ☎ 02 9662 8444, fax 02 9662 2363, (2 stry gr fl), 60 units [shwr, bath (20), tlt, a/c, tel, TV, movie, clock radio, t/c mkg, refrig, mini bar], ldry, conv fac, ⊠, pool, sauna, spa, 24hr reception, rm serv, cots, non smoking units (30). **RO ⧎ $120 - $148, ⧎⧎ $125 - $154**, ch con, AE BC DC MC VI.

Operator Comment: See our advertisement at top of page.

SYDNEY - KIRRIBILLI NSW 2061

Pop Part of Sydney, (3km N Sydney), See map on page 56, ref B1. Pretty harbourside suburb on Sydney's lower north shore. Scenic Drives.

B&B's/Guest Houses

★ **Glenferrie Boutique Hotel**, (PH), 12a Carabella St, ☎ 02 9955 1685, fax 02 9929 9439, 70 rms [c/fan, TV-fee, refrig], TV rm, lounge, t/c mkg shared, 24hr reception, non smoking property. **DBB ⧎ $60, ⧎⧎ $80**, BC EFT MC VI.

Elite Private Hotel, (PH), 133 Carabella St, 200m NE of railway station, ☎ 02 9929 6365, fax 02 9925 0999, (Multi-stry gr fl), 20 rms [TV, t/c mkg, refrig], cook fac. **RO ⧎ $55, ⧎⧎ $66 - $88**, AE BC DC EFT MC VI.

Kirribilli Court, (PH), 45 Carabella St, 1.5km N of PO, ☎ 02 9955 4344, fax 02 9929 4774, 35 rms [refrig (10)], ldry, rec rm, lounge (TV), t/c mkg shared, bbq, ✆. **RO ⧎ $25, ⧎⧎ $30**, BC VI.

Tremayne Private Hotel, (PH), 89 Carabella St, 200m NE of Milsons Point railway station, ☎ 02 9955 4155, fax 02 9922 5228, (Multi-stry gr fl), 100 rms [shwr (16), tlt (16), TV (16), clock radio (16), t/c mkg (16), refrig], iron, iron brd, rec rm, lounge (TV), ✕, cook fac, t/c mkg shared. **BB ⧎ $33, ⧎⧎ $55, ⧎ $198, ⧎⧎ $340**.

SYDNEY - LANE COVE NSW 2066

Pop Part of Sydney, (9km N Sydney), See map on page 56, ref A1. Bushland northern suburb on the banks of the Lane Cove River. Bowls, Swimming.

Hotels/Motels

AAA TOURISM *Special Rates*   **COUNTRY COMFORT**

★★★☆ **Country Comfort Motel - Lane Cove**, (M), Gatacre Ave (off Pacific Hwy), 2km W of PO, ☎ 02 9427 0266, fax 02 9418 7016, (2 stry gr fl), 43 units [shwr, tlt, hairdry, a/c, elec blkts, tel, TV, movie, clock radio, t/c mkg, refrig, mini bar, toaster], ldry, ✕, cots, non smoking units (21). **RO ⧎ $125, ⧎⧎ $125, ◊ $15**, ch con, 15 units ★★★, AE BC DC MC VI.

SYDNEY - LANE COVE continued...

Self Catering Accommodation

★★★☆ **Linley Point Harbourview**, (Cotg), 16 Haughton St, 300m E of Fig Tree Bridge, ☎ 02 9427 0845, 1 cotg acc up to 3, [shwr, tlt, fan, heat, elec blkts, TV, clock radio, t/c mkg, refrig, cook fac, micro, ldry (in unit), blkts, linen, pillows], non smoking property. **RO** ♯♯ **$475**, Min book applies.

 ★★★☆ **Metro Suites Lane Cove**, (SA), 302 Burns Bay Rd, 2km E of PO, ☎ 02 9427 4000, fax 02 9427 2010, 23 serv apts acc up to 4, [shwr, bath, tlt, a/c, tel, TV, clock radio, t/c mkg, refrig, cook fac, ldry (in unit)], pool, sauna, bbq, c/park (undercover), squash, cots. **RO** ♯♯♯♯ **$212 - $232**, AE BC DC EFT MC VI.

B&B's/Guest Houses

★★★★☆ **Lane Cove's Jacaranda House**, (B&B), Previously Jacaranda House Lane Cove B&B 58 Richardson St West, 700m S of Lane Cove Plaza, ☎ 02 9427 4846, fax 02 9427 9019, (2 stry), 3 rms [shwr, tlt, hairdry, c/fan, heat, elec blkts, clock radio, t/c mkg], TV rm, bbq, non smoking property. **BB** ♯ **$110 - $135**, ♯♯ **$125 - $150**, AE BC MC VI.

SYDNEY - LANSVALE NSW 2166

Pop Part of Sydney, (27km SW Sydney), See map on page 56, ref C6. Suburb in south-western Sydney. Golf.

Hotels/Motels

★★★★ **Lansdowne Motor Inn**, (M), 161 Hume Hwy, 1km E of PO, ☎ 02 9727 5255, fax 02 9724 6304, 83 units (12 suites) [shwr, bath (38), spa bath (5), tlt, hairdry, a/c, elec blkts, tel, TV, movie, clock radio, t/c mkg, refrig], ldry, conv fac, ⊠, bar, pool, bbq, rm serv, cots. **RO** ♯ **$105 - $138**, ♯♯ **$105 - $138**, ◊ **$10**, Suite D **$138 - $165**, AE BC DC MC MP VI, ♿.

SYDNEY - LEICHHARDT NSW 2040

Pop Part of Sydney, (7km W Sydney), See map on page 56, ref A2. Cosmopolitan inner western suburb with a strong Italian influence. Bowls, Swimming.

B&B's/Guest Houses

★★ **Pensione Italia Bed & Breakfast**, (B&B), 73 Renwick St, ☎ 02 9560 2249, fax 02 9560 2249, (2 stry gr fl), 4 rms (2 suites) [shwr (2), tlt (2), hairdry, TV (2), clock radio, refrig, cook fac (2), toaster], shared fac (4 rooms), ldry, iron, iron brd, TV rm, lounge (TV), cook fac, t/c mkg shared. **BB** ♯ **$55**, ♯♯ **$85**, ♯♯♯ **$95**, Suite D ♯♯ **$95 - $105**, ♯♯♯ **$115**, ◊ **$10**.

SYDNEY - LIDCOMBE NSW 2141

Pop Part of Sydney, (20km W Sydney), See map on page 56, ref C5. Lidcombe adjoins the Olympic venue suburb of Homebush Bay.

Hotels/Motels

★★★ **Lidcombe Motor Inn**, (M), Cnr Mark & Taylor Sts, 100m E of PO, ☎ 02 9646 5799, fax 02 9749 1648, (Multi-stry gr fl), 25 units [shwr, tlt, hairdry, a/c, elec blkts, tel, TV, clock radio, t/c mkg, refrig, toaster], lift, ldry, secure park. **RO** ♯ **$108**, ♯♯ **$108**, ◊ **$12**, AE BC DC MC VI.

★★★ **(Serviced Apartment Section)**, 6 serv apts acc up to 4, [shwr, bath, tlt, hairdry, heat, elec blkts, tel, TV, clock radio, t/c mkg, refrig, cook fac, micro, toaster, ldry], cots-fee. **D** ♯♯♯♯ **$148**.

★★ **Liberty Plains Motor Inn**, (M), 5 Olympic Dve, 550m N of Lidcombe Railway Station, ☎ 02 9649 6554, fax 02 9646 1051, 34 units (1 suite) [shwr, tlt, a/c, heat, elec blkts-fee, tel, TV, video (3)-fee, clock radio, t/c mkg, refrig, cook fac (1), toaster], ldry, iron (6), iron brd (1), ⊠, pool, bbq, 24hr reception, rm serv, dinner to unit, plygr, cots, non smoking units (4). **RO** ♯♯ **$77 - $99**, ♯♯♯ **$99 - $120**, ◊ **$20**, AE BC DC EFT MC VI.

SYDNEY - LINDFIELD NSW 2070

Pop Part of Sydney, See map on page 56, ref D5. Leafy north shore suburb, one of the main access points to Lane Cove River National Park.

B&B's/Guest Houses

★★★★ **Coningsby**, (B&B), No children's facilities, 14 Beaconsfield Pde, 200m W of PO, ☎ 02 9416 4088, fax 02 9416 3557, (Multi-stry), 4 rms (3 suites) [shwr, bath (1), tlt, hairdry, a/c, elec blkts, tel, cable tv, video (1), clock radio, t/c mkg, refrig (1), ldry], ldry, lounge (TV) (3), lounge firepl (3), pool (salt water), courtesy transfer, gym, tennis, non smoking property. **BB** **$132 - $220**, AE BC DC MC VI.

SYDNEY - LIVERPOOL NSW 2170

Pop Part of Sydney, (32km SW Sydney), See map on page 56, ref B6. Thriving centre on the Georges River in Sydney's south-west. Golf, Swimming.

Hotels/Motels

 ★★★☆ **El Toro Motor Inn**, (LMH), Homepride Ave, 1km N of PO, ☎ 02 9602 7077, fax 02 9602 1392, (2 stry gr fl), 52 units (5 suites) [shwr, bath (33), spa bath (5), tlt, a/c, tel, TV, video (avail), movie, clock radio, t/c mkg, refrig, cook fac (2)], ldry, conv fac, ⊠ (Mon to Sat), pool, spa, rm serv, dinner to unit, cots, non smoking units (7). **W $672 - $1,092**, **RO** ♯ **$118 - $180**, ♯♯ **$118 - $180**, ♯♯♯ **$128 - $190**, ◊ **$10**, Min book applies, AE BC DC EFT MC VI.

★★★☆ **Fontainebleau Inn**, (M), 467 Hume Hwy, 3km S of PO, ☎ 02 9602 7455, fax 02 9821 2992, (2 stry gr fl), 30 units [shwr, bath (3), tlt, hairdry, a/c, elec blkts, tel, TV, clock radio, t/c mkg, refrig], ldry, iron, iron brd, conv fac, ⊠, pool (salt water), wading pool, spa, cots-fee. **RO** ♦ **$110 - $145**, ♦♦ **$115 - $145**, ◊ **$12**, ch con, AE BC DC JCB MC MP VI.

SYDNEY - LOWER PORTLAND NSW 2756

Pop Part of Sydney, (84km NW Sydney), See map on page 56, ref C2. Rural area on the Hawkesbury River between Wisemans Ferry and Sackville.

B&B's/Guest Houses

★★★★ **Jerimuda Guesthouse**, (B&B), 72 Laws Farm Rd, 19km N of Windsor PO, ☎ 02 4579 1028, fax 02 4579 1028, 1 rm (1 suite) [ensuite (1), spa bath (1), fan, heat (elec/wood), tel, TV, video, clock radio, t/c mkg, refrig, cook fac, ldry, doonas], shared fac (1), conf fac, pool (solar heated), spa, bbq, rm serv, dinner to unit, plygr, cots. **BB** ♦ **$60 - $85**, ♦♦ **$120 - $145**, ch con, weekly con.

★★★★ **Two Rivers Retreat**, (GH), 201 River Rd, ☎ 02 4575 5372, 2 rms [shwr, bath, spa bath (1), tlt, a/c, heat, elec blkts, TV, t/c mkg, cook fac], ldry, iron, iron brd, bbq, c/park. **BLB** ♦♦ **$120 - $375**, Min book applies.

Ferndale Private Hotel, (PH), River Rd, 2.5km N of Ferry, ☎ 02 4575 5223, 20 rms (20 suites) [shwr, tlt, a/c, heat, clock radio, t/c mkg, refrig], ldry, rec rm, lounge (TV), conv fac, pool, bicycle-fee, tennis, cots. **D** ♦ **$134.75 - $145**, AE BC DC MC VI.

SYDNEY - LUCAS HEIGHTS NSW 2234

Pop Part of Sydney, (42km SW Sydney), See map on page 56, ref C7. South-western suburb near the Woronora River and the Australian Military Reserve.

★★☆ **Lucas Heights Motel**, (M), New Illawarra Rd, 3.5km NW of Engadine PO, ☎ 02 9532 0335, fax 02 9532 0214, 18 units [shwr, tlt, a/c, heat, elec blkts, tel, TV, clock radio, t/c mkg, refrig, mini bar (6), cook fac (2), toaster], ldry, conv fac, ✗, pool, bbq, cots. **RO** ♦ **$71.50**, ♦♦ **$71.50**, BC MC VI.

SYDNEY - MALABAR NSW 2036

Pop Part of Sydney, (13km S Sydney), See map on page 56, ref D6. South-eastern beachside suburb of Sydney.

B&B's/Guest Houses

Bilga Bed & Breakfast, (B&B), 131 Bilga Crescent, ☎ 02 9661 5595, fax 02 9345 4070, 4 rms [shwr (2), tlt (2), fan (2), fire pl, heat, TV, video, t/c mkg, refrig], shared fac (2 rms), non smoking rms. **BB** ♦ **$82.50 - $93.50**, ♦♦ **$98 - $132**, ◊ **$30**, BC MC VI.

SYDNEY - MANLY VALE NSW 2093

Pop Part of Sydney, (16km N Sydney), See map on page 56, ref E5. Small northern suburb between Balgowlah and North Manly.

B&B's/Guest Houses

★★★☆ **The Possum Tree Guest House**, (GH), 83 King St, 500m E of Manly Dam, ☎ 02 9949 1984, fax 02 9949 1984, 3 rms [shwr (2), bath (1), tlt (2), hairdry (2), fan, heat, elec blkts, t/c mkg, refrig], shared fac (2 rms), lounge (TV), ✗, non smoking property. **BB** ♦ **$70**, ♦♦ **$120**, ch con.

SYDNEY - MANLY NSW 2095

Pop Part of Sydney, (15km NE Sydney), See map on page 56, ref E5. North-eastern beach and harbour suburb and one of Australia's most famous seaside resorts.

Hotels/Motels

★★★★ **Manly Pacific Parkroyal**, (LH), 55 North Steyne, 200m N of PO, ☎ 02 9977 7666, fax 02 9977 7822, (Multi-stry), 218 rms (11 suites) [shwr, bath (151), tlt, a/c, heat, tel, TV, movie, clock radio, t/c mkg, refrig], lift, ldry, conv fac, ⊠, pool-heated, sauna, spa, 24hr reception, rm serv, gym, cots, non smoking rms (112). **RO** ♦ **$190 - $220**, ♦♦ **$190 - $220**, ♦♦♦ **$215 - $245**, ◊ **$25**, **Suite D** ♦♦ **$370**, ch con, AE BC DC MC VI.

★★★★ **Radisson Kestrel Hotel on Manly Beach**, (LH), 8-13 South Steyne, 1km SE of PO, ☎ 02 9977 8866, fax 02 9977 8209, (Multi-stry), 83 rms (32 suites) [shwr, bath, spa bath (15), tlt, evap cool, tel, TV, movie, clock radio, mini bar, cook fac (24)], lift, ldry, conv fac, ✉, pool (2), sauna, spa, 24hr reception, rm serv, dinner to unit, cots. **RO** ♦ **$199 - $239,** ♦♦ **$199 - $239,** ♦♦♦ **$232 - $272,** ◊ **$33, Suite D** ♦ **$209 - $339,** ♦♦ **$209 - $339,** ch con, Min book Christmas and Jan, AE BC DC JCB MC VI.

★★★☆ **Manly Paradise Motel and Apartments**, (M), 54 North Steyne (Cnr Raglan St), 100m E of PO, ☎ 02 9977 5799, fax 02 9977 6848, (Multi-stry), 21 units [shwr, tlt, hairdry, a/c, elec blkts, tel, cable tv, clock radio, t/c mkg, refrig], lift, iron, iron brd, pool, c/park (undercover), cots. **RO** ♦ **$100 - $155,** ♦♦ **$100 - $155,** ♦♦♦ **$170,** AE BC DC JCB MC VI.

★★★★☆ **(Serviced Apartment Section)**, 20 serv apts acc up to 5, [shwr, bath, tlt, hairdry, a/c, fan, heat, elec blkts, tel, clock radio, refrig, cook fac, micro, d/wash, toaster, ldry, blkts, linen], cots. **D** ♦ **$285,** ♦♦ **$285,** ♦♦♦ **$310,** ◊ **$25.**

★★★ **Manly Beach Resort**, (M), 6 Carlton St, 500m N of PO, ☎ 02 9977 4188, fax 02 9977 0524, (2 stry), 40 units [shwr, tlt, a/c, heat, tel, TV, clock radio, t/c mkg, refrig, cook fac (1), micro (1)], ldry, pool-heated (solar), spa, cook fac, cots, non smoking units (10). **BLB** ♦ **$100 - $110,** ♦♦ **$125 - $140,** ♦♦♦ **$140 - $160,** ◊ **$10,** ch con, AE BC DC EFT JCB MC VI.

★★☆ **Manly Seaview Motel and Apartments**, (M), Cnr Pacific St & Malvern Ave, 500m fr North Steyne Surf Club, ☎ 02 9977 1774, fax 02 9977 5298, (2 stry gr fl), 20 units [shwr, spa bath (8), tlt, heat, tel, TV, clock radio, t/c mkg, refrig, cook fac (7)], c/park (undercover), cots. **D** **$95 - $300,** BC MC VI.

★☆ **Steyne Hotel**, (LH), 75 The Corso, Opposite Information Centre, ☎ 02 9977 4977, fax 02 9977 5645, (2 stry), 37 rms [shwr (4), spa bath (1), tlt (4), a/c (2), heat, tel, TV, t/c mkg (7), refrig (7)], ldry, lounge (TV), ✉, t/c mkg shared, cots. **BB** ♦ **$88 - $198,** ♦♦ **$110 - $242,** ♦♦♦♦ **$330,** ◊ **$33 - $44,** ch con, AE BC DC MC VI.

Self Catering Accommodation

★★★★☆ **Grande Esplanade Quest Establishment**, (SA), 54A West Esplanade, ☎ 02 9976 4600, fax 02 9976 4699, (2 stry), 54 serv apts acc up to 6, [shwr, bath, tlt, hairdry, a/c, cent heat, tel, TV, video, movie, clock radio, t/c mkg, refrig, cook fac (36), cook fac ltd (18), micro, d/wash, toaster, blkts, linen, pillows], lift, w/mach, dryer, iron, conv fac, sauna, gym, cots. **RO** ♦♦ **$199 - $260,** ch con, 18 units of a lower rating. AE BC DC JCB MC VI, ♿,

Operator Comment: Please visit our web site on www.grandeesplanade.citysearch.com.au

★★★★☆ **Manly Seaside Holiday Apartments**, (SA), Previously Manly Seaside Grande Esplanade Apts 68 West Esplanade, ☎ 02 9977 5213, fax 02 9977 7062, (Multi-stry), 15 serv apts acc up to 5, [shwr, spa bath, tlt, a/c, cent heat, tel, TV, video, clock radio, t/c mkg, refrig, cook fac, micro, d/wash, toaster, ldry (in unit), blkts, linen, pillows], lift, w/mach, dryer, iron, pool-heated, sauna, gym, cots-fee. **D** ♦ **$132 - $170.50,** ♦♦ **$132 - $170.50,** ◊ **$22,** Min book applies, AE BC MC VI.

★★★★ **Bella Vista**, (HU), 96 North Steyne, Cnr Pine St, ☎ 02 9977 2299, fax 02 9977 2569, 22 units [shwr, spa bath, tlt, heat, tel, TV, clock radio, t/c mkg, refrig, cook fac, micro, d/wash, toaster, ldry (in unit), blkts, linen, pillows], lift, secure park, cots. **D** **$285 - $465,** **W** **$1,540 - $2,695,** BC MC VI.

★★★☆ **Manly Ocean Royale**, (HU), 69 North Steyne, 500m N of Manly Corso, ☎ 02 9977 0099, fax 02 9977 0316, (Multi-stry gr fl), 15 units acc up to 6, [shwr, spa bath, tlt, hairdry, fan, heat, tel, cable tv, video, clock radio, refrig, cook fac, micro, elec frypan, d/wash, toaster, ldry (in unit), blkts, linen, pillows], lift, pool, pool-heated, sauna, spa, c/park (garage), tennis (half court), cots. **D** **$205 - $300,** **W** **$1,295 - $1,960,** AE BC DC MC VI.

★★★☆ **Mathew Bligh**, (HU), 33 East Esplanade, ☎ 02 9977 2299, fax 02 9977 2569, 2 units acc up to 6, [shwr, bath, tlt, heat, tel, TV, t/c mkg, refrig, cook fac, toaster, blkts, linen, pillows], lift, ldry, dryer, iron, cots. **D** **$242,** **W** **$1,155,** AE BC DC MC VI, ♿.

★★★☆ **Pacific Harbour Units**, (HU), 42 Victoria Pde, ☎ 02 9977 5213, fax 02 9977 7062, 6 units acc up to 5, [shwr, tlt, heat, tel, TV, radio, refrig, cook fac, micro, d/wash, toaster, ldry (in unit), blkts, linen, pillows], c/park (garage). **D** **$242 - $385,** Min book applies.

★★★ **Caprice**, (HU), 88 North Steyne, ☎ 02 9977 2299, fax 02 9977 2569, 4 units acc up to 5, [shwr, tlt, heat, tel, TV, t/c mkg, refrig, cook fac, toaster, ldry (in unit), blkts, linen, pillows], lift, dryer, iron, cots. **D** **$220 - $250,** **W** **$1,155,** BC MC VI, ♿.

★★★ **Santa-Fe**, (HU), 46 Victoria Pde, ☎ 02 9977 5213, fax 02 9977 7062, 6 units acc up to 7, [shwr, bath, tlt, heat, tel, TV, radio, refrig, cook fac, micro, toaster, blkts, linen, pillows], ldry, c/park. **D** **$115.50 - $280.50,** Min book applies.

★★★ **The Sands**, (HU), 114 North Steyne, ☎ 02 9977 5213, fax 02 9977 7062, 2 units acc up to 5, [shwr, bath, tlt, heat, tel, TV, radio, refrig, cook fac, micro, toaster, blkts, linen, pillows], ldry, c/park (garage). **D** **$176 - $330,** Min book applies.

★★★ **Waterside Apartments**, (HU), 48 Sydney Rd, ☎ 02 9977 5213, 12 units acc up to 2, [shwr, bath, tlt, a/c, tel, TV, radio, refrig, cook fac, micro, toaster, blkts, linen, pillows], ldry, spa, gym. **D** ♦♦ **$132 - $170.50,** ◊ **$22,** Min book applies.

★★☆ **Manly National**, (Apt), 22 Central Ave, ☎ 02 9977 6469, 160 apts acc up to 4, [shwr, bath, tlt, refrig, cook fac, linen reqd-fee], ldry, pool. **W** **$550 - $700,** Min book applies.

★★☆ **Strathaven Harbourfront**, (HU), 29 The Crescent, ☎ 02 9977 2299, fax 02 9977 2569, 4 units acc up to 5, [shwr, tlt, heat, tel, TV, t/c mkg, refrig, cook fac, toaster, ldry (in unit), blkts, linen, pillows], lift, dryer, iron, cots. **D** **$200,** **W** **$945,** ch con, BC MC VI.

★★☆ **Surfways**, (HU), 66 North Steyne, ☎ 02 9977 2299, fax 02 9977 2569, 2 units acc up to 3, [shwr, bath, tlt, heat, tel, TV, t/c mkg, refrig, cook fac, toaster, blkts, linen, pillows], lift, ldry, dryer, iron, cots, AE BC DC MC VI.

★★ **Merrivale**, (HU), 22 Ashburner St, ☎ 02 9977 5213, fax 02 9977 7062, 4 units acc up to 5, [shwr, bath, tlt, heat, tel, TV, radio, refrig, cook fac, toaster, blkts, linen, pillows], ldry, c/park (garage). **D** **$115.50 - $225.50.**

MANLY BEACH RESORT

6 CARLTON STREET MANLY
AFFORDABLE & FRIENDLY

- ➤ 40 modern air-conditioned rooms in double, twin or family format
- ➤ All rooms have modern ensuite bathroom, colour TV, clock radio, refrigerator, tea/coffee making facilities and direct-dial phones for local and international calls
- ➤ Inclusive continental breakfast
- ➤ Full breakfast available
- ➤ Fully equipped guests' kitchen and dining area
- ➤ Complete self-service laundry
- ➤ Solar-heated fresh water pool
- ➤ Sun terraces   ➤ On-site security parking

Experience MANLY
A world famous location

BOOKINGS & ENQUIRIES

CORRESPONDENCE:
PO BOX 221 MANLY NSW 2095

PHONE: (02) 9977 4188

FAX: (02) 9977 0524

EMAIL: manlybch@ozemail.com.au

WEBSITE: www.manlyview.com.au

100% AUSTRALIAN OWNED

149-153 SYDNEY ROAD
FAIRLIGHT

MANLY VIEW APARTMENTS FAIRLIGHT

LUXURIOUS ONE BEDROOM SERVICED APARTMENTS

- ➤ 22 Newly constructed one bedroom apartments on 3 levels
- ➤ Furnished to four star corporate standard
- ➤ Balconies with outdoor furniture setting
- ➤ Some units have harbour views
- ➤ Five minute walk to Manly Wharf
- ➤ Security underground parking
- ➤ Fully equipped kitchen with full sized refrigerator
- ➤ Laundry with washer, dryer, iron, ironing board
- ➤ Queen size bed with built in robe
- ➤ Sitting room equipped with leather lounge, TV, CD Player
- ➤ Dining area adjoining kitchen with dining setting
- ➤ Telephone with message bank

MANLY Seaside
HOLIDAY APARTMENTS

**Shop 2/39 East Esplanade
MANLY NSW 2095**

Phone: (02) 9977 5213
Fax: (02) 9977 7062
Email: reservations@manly-seaside.com
Web: www.manly-seaside.com

With over 130 fully self-contained apartments to choose from, Manly Seaside Holiday Apartments offers the largest variety of serviced apartments in Manly.

Apartment range includes studios, as well as one, two and three bedroom apartments, all in a variety of locations around Manly. Beach views, harbour views, central Manly. Budget through to Superior.

Apartment facilities include:
- Weekly servicing - Fully equipped kitchen - Laundry - Linen - Telephone and facsimile facilities - TV

★★ **Upper Grey Cliff**, (HU), 21 Upper Grey Cliff St, 1 km N of Manly, ☎ 02 9977 2299, fax 02 997 2569, 12 units acc up to 3, [heat, fan, TV, t/c mkg, refrig, cook fac, blkts, linen], ldry, dryer, cots-fee. D ⸷ $70, ⸷⸷ $70, ⸷ $70, weekly con, AE BC DC EFT MC VI.

Manly Waterside Holidays, (HU), 12 Arthur St, Fairlight 2094, ☎ 02 9977 4459, fax 02 8966 9975, (Multi-stry), 5 units acc up to 6, (Studio, 2 & 3 bedrm), [a/c-cool (2), a/c (2), c/fan (1), TV, video, clock radio, t/c mkg, refrig, cook fac, micro, d/wash (3), toaster, blkts, doonas, linen, pillows], ldry, w/mach, dryer, pool, bbq, secure park, cots. D $110 - $275, W $660 - $1,650, BC MC VI, (not yet classified).

Mystique Units, (HU), 82 North Steyne, ☎ 02 9977 2299, fax 02 9977 2569, 3 units acc up to 6, [shwr, spa bath (2), tlt, heat, tel, TV, clock radio, t/c mkg, refrig, cook fac, micro, d/wash, toaster, ldry (in unit), blkts, linen, pillows], lift, dryer, iron, secure park, cots. D $285 - $465, W $1,540 - $2,695, BC MC VI, (not yet classified).

B&B's/Guest Houses

★★★☆ **Francois Bed & Breakfast**, (B&B), 2/39 Quinton Rd, ☎ 02 9977 6196, (2 stry), 1 rm [shwr, tlt, hairdry, fan, heat, elec blkts, tel, clock radio, t/c mkg], iron, iron brd, lounge (TV), refrig, bbq, courtesy transfer. BB ⸷ $60 - $80, ⸷⸷ $90 - $110, Min book all holiday times.

★★★ **Manly Harbour Loft**, (B&B), 12 George St, ☎ 02 9949 8487, fax 02 9949 8487, (2 stry), 1 rm [shwr, tlt, hairdry, fan, heat, elec blkts, TV, t/c mkg, refrig], iron, iron brd, lounge, non smoking rms. BLB ⸷ $100 - $120, ⸷⸷ $120 - $140.

★★★ **Manly Lodge**, (GH), 22 Victoria Pde, 500m E of Manly Corso, ☎ 02 9977 8655, fax 02 9976 2090, (2 stry gr fl), 28 rms [shwr, bath, spa bath (14), tlt, a/c-cool, fan, heat, TV, video, t/c mkg, refrig, cook fac (19)], ldry, ⊠, sauna, spa, bbq, ☎, gym, cots. D ⸷ $20 - $35, $110 - $295, 15 rooms ★★. AE BC DC MC VI.

★★★ **Periwinkle - Manly Cove**, (GH), 18 East Esp, 500m S of PO, ☎ 02 9977 4668, fax 02 9977 6308, (2 stry), 18 rms [shwr (12), tlt (12), fan, heat, elec blkts, TV, refrig], shared fac (6 rooms), ldry, lounge (TV), cook fac, t/c mkg shared, bbq, ☎, cots. BB ⸷ $99 - $132, ⸷⸷ $126.50 - $165, BC MC VI.

SYDNEY - MAROUBRA JUNCTION NSW 2035

Pop Part of Sydney, (10km SE Sydney), See map on page 56, ref B2. Commercial centre north of Maroubra in Sydney's south-east.

Hotels/Motels

★★★★ **Trade Winds Hotel**, (M), 200 Maroubra Rd, 100m E of PO, ☎ 02 9344 5555, fax 02 9344 7372, (Multi-stry), 78 units [shwr, tlt, a/c, fan, tel, TV, video (avail), clock radio, t/c mkg, refrig, mini bar], lift, conv fac, cafe, pool, 24hr reception, dinner to unit, courtesy transfer, cots-fee, non smoking flr (4). RO ⸷ $145 - $195, ⸷⸷ $145 - 195, ⸷⸷⸷ $161.50 - $210, ⸷ $16.50, ch con, AE BC DC EFT MC MP VI, ⸷⸷.

Operator Comment: See our advertisement above.

SYDNEY - MAROUBRA NSW 2035

Pop Part of Sydney, (11km SE Sydney), See map on page 56, ref D6. Beachside suburb to the south of Coogee. Fishing, Swimming.

Hotels/Motels

★★☆ **Sands Hotel**, (LMH), 32 Curtin Cres, 2km S of PO, ☎ 02 9661 5953, fax 02 9661 9682, 15 units [shwr, bath, tlt, a/c-cool (6), heat, TV, clock radio, t/c mkg, refrig], ⊠, cots (avail). RO ⸷⸷⸷ $115 - $125, ⸷⸷⸷⸷ $125 - $135, AE BC DC EFT MC VI.

SYDNEY - MASCOT NSW 2020

Pop Part of Sydney, (7km S Sydney), See map on page 56, ref A2. Suburb north of Botany Bay, probably best known as the location of Sydney's International Airport, Kingsford Smith Airport. Bowls.

Hotels/Motels

★★★★☆ **Parkroyal Sydney Airport**, (LH), Cnr Bourke Rd & O'Riordan St, 1km N of Airport, ☎ 02 9330 0632, fax 02 9667 4517, (Multi-stry), 244 rms (4 suites) [shwr, bath, tlt, hairdry, a/c, tel, TV, movie-fee, clock radio, t/c mkg, refrig, mini bar], lift, conv fac, ⊠, 24hr reception, rm serv, dinner to unit, c/park (valet), courtesy transfer, gym, cots, non smoking flr (5). BB ⸷⸷ $187 - $209, ch con, 7 family rooms. Four star rating. AE BC DC JCB MC VI.

★★★★☆ **Stamford Sydney Airport**, (LH), Cnr O'Riordan & Robey Sts, 1km NE of Sydney Airport, ☎ 02 9317 2200, fax 02 9317 3855, (Multi-stry), 314 rms (12 suites) [shwr, bath, tlt, hairdry, a/c, tel, TV, movie, t/c mkg, refrig, mini bar], lift, conv fac, ⊠ (2), pool-heated, sauna, spa, rm serv, c/park (valet), courtesy transfer, ☎, gym, cots, non smoking flr (7). **BB** †† **$199, RO** †† **$130 - $204,** ⊙ **$30**, ch con, AE BC DC JCB MC VI.

★★★ **Hotel Ibis Sydney Airport**, (LH), 205 O'Riordan St, 1km N of domestic terminal, ☎ 02 8339 8500, fax 02 8339 8585, (Multi-stry gr fl), 200 rms [shwr, tlt, a/c, cent heat, tel, TV, movie, clock radio, t/c mkg], lift, ldry, ⊠, ☎, cots, non smoking rms (107). **RO** † **$109,** †† **$109,** ⊙ **$20**, AE BC DC EFT JCB MC VI, ⅙⅄.

SYDNEY - MCMAHONS POINT NSW 2060

Pop Part of Sydney, See map on page 56, ref A1. Lower north shore suburb on Lavender Bay, just west of the Harbour Bridge.

Self Catering Accommodation

★★★★ **Harbourside Apartments**, (SA), 2A Henry Lawson Ave, 1km S of North Sydney PO, ☎ 02 9963 4300, or 02 9963 4375, fax 02 9922 7998, (Multi-stry), 82 serv apts (62 suites) [shwr, bath (56), tlt, heat, elec blkts, tel, fax, TV, video (avail), clock radio, CD, t/c mkg, refrig, cook fac, micro], lift, ldry, pool, bbq, cots-fee. **D** † **$192.50 - $346.50,** †† **$192.50 - $346.50,** ⊙ **$10**, AE BC DC MC VI.

SYDNEY - MILPERRA NSW 2214

Pop Part of Sydney, (25km SW Sydney), See map on page 56, ref C6. South-western suburb on the Georges River near Bankstown. Golf.

Hotels/Motels

★★☆ **Milperra Palms Hotel Motel**, (LMH), 189 Beaconsfield St, 500m W of PO, ☎ 02 9771 2722, or 02 9771 2699, fax 02 9792 2962, 13 units [shwr, tlt, a/c, TV, clock radio, t/c mkg, refrig], conf fac, ⊠. **RO** † **$70,** †† **$85,** ⊙ **$15**, BC DC EFT MC VI.

SYDNEY - MILSONS POINT NSW 2061

Pop Part of Sydney, (2km N Sydney), See map on page 56, ref B1. Busy commercial and residential centre on the lower north shore beside the Harbour Bridge.

Hotels/Motels

★★★★☆ **Duxton Hotel**, (LH), 88 Alfred St, 1km S of PO, ☎ 02 9955 1111, or 02 9956 0748, fax 02 9955 3522, (Multi-stry), 129 rms (36 suites) [shwr, bath, tlt, hairdry, a/c, tel, TV, video-fee, clock radio, t/c mkg, refrig, mini bar, ldry], lift, business centre, conv fac, ⊠, bar, pool-heated, sauna, rm serv, secure park, ☎, cots, non smoking flr (4). **RO** † **$143 - $277,** †† **$143 - $277,** ⊙ **$25, Suite D $198 - $277**, 35 rooms ★★★. AE BC DC JCB MC VI.

Trouble-free travel tips - **Lights**

Check the operation of all lights. If you are pulling a trailer of caravan make sure turning indicators and brake lights are working.

SYDNEY - MIRANDA NSW 2228

Pop Part of Sydney, (24km S Sydney), See map on page 56, ref C7. Large urban centre in the Sutherland area.

Hotels/Motels

  ★★★ **Metro Motor Inn - Miranda**, (M), Cnr The Kingsway & Jackson Ave, 500m E of PO, ☎ 02 9525 7577, fax 02 9540 1593, (Multi-stry), 38 units [shwr, tlt, a/c, tel, TV, movie, clock radio, t/c mkg, refrig, micro (4)], lift, conv fac, cots. **RO** ♦♦ **$93 - $124**, ch con, AE BC DC EFT MC VI.

SYDNEY - MONA VALE NSW 2103

Pop Part of Sydney, (30km N Sydney), See map on page 56, ref E4. Major commercial centre for the Pittwater and upper northern beaches area.

Self Catering Accommodation

★★★ **Reef Resort**, (HU), 8-12 Terrol Cres, 1km NE of PO, ☎ 02 9979 5764, fax 02 9979 6856, (2 stry), 37 units acc up to 5, [shwr, bath, tlt, TV, clock radio, t/c mkg, refrig, cook fac, micro, toaster, blkts, linen, pillows], ldry, rec rm, pool, sauna, spa, bbq, c/park (garage), plygr, tennis (half court). **D** ♦♦♦♦ **$132 - $154**, **W** ♦♦♦♦ **$577.50 - $990**, Min book applies.

SYDNEY - MOSMAN NSW 2088

Pop Part of Sydney, (7km N Sydney), See map on page 56, ref B1. Stylish, lower north shore harbour suburb, home of Taronga Zoo.

Self Catering Accommodation

Ballantyne at Mosman, (Apt), 1 Ballantyne St, 1 km E of Mosman Ferry, mob 0425 200 700, fax 02 9968 1430, (Multi-stry), 8 apts acc up to 4, (Studio & 1 bedrm), [shwr, tlt, a/c, tel, cable tv, video, clock radio, t/c mkg, refrig, cook fac, micro, d/wash, toaster, blkts, linen, pillows], ldry, w/mach, dryer, c/park (undercover), cots, non smoking property. **D $99 - $150**, **W $695 - $1,050**, Min book applies, (not yet classified).

B&B's/Guest Houses

★★★☆ **Balmoral Bed & Breakfast**, (B&B), No children's facilities, 6 Kahibah Rd, ☎ 02 9969 6415, fax 02 9969 6415, 1 rm [shwr, tlt, c/fan, cent heat, elec blkts, tel, t/c mkg], lounge (TV, video), pool-heated (solar). **BB** ♦♦ **$100**, ◊ **$25**, Min book applies.

★★★☆ **Copperfield Place**, (B&B), No children's facilities, 9 Killarney St, 100m N of PO, ☎ 02 9969 5770, (2 stry), 3 rms [shwr, bath, tlt, elec blkts, clock radio], ldry, lounge (TV), t/c mkg shared, non smoking property. **BB** ♦ **$65 - $75**, ♦♦ **$90 - $95**.

SYDNEY - MOUNT KURING-GAI NSW 2080

Pop Part of Sydney, (32km N Sydney), See map on page 56, ref C5. Northern suburb flanked by the bushland of Ku-ring-gai Chase National Park.

Hotels/Motels

★★★☆ **Mt Kuring-Gai Motel**, (M), 705 Pacific Hwy, 5km N of Hornsby PO, ☎ 02 9457 9393, fax 02 9457 0483, 10 units [shwr, tlt, a/c, elec blkts, tel, TV, clock radio, t/c mkg, refrig], cots-fee. **RO** ♦ **$65**, ♦♦ **$75**, ◊ **$10**, ch con, AE BC DC MC VI.

SYDNEY - NARARA NSW 2250

Pop Part of Gosford, (79km SE Sydney), See map on page 56, ref E2. Central Coast suburb just north of Gosford.

B&B's/Guest Houses

★★★★ **Phoenix House**, (B&B), 68 Fountains Rd, 5km NW of PO, ☎ 02 4328 1631, fax 02 4328 1631, (2 stry gr fl), 4 rms (1 suite) [shwr (2), spa bath (1), tlt (4), a/c, tel, TV (2), video (2), clock radio, refrig], lounge (TV, video), pool (salt water), t/c mkg shared, bbq (2), cots-fee, non smoking rms. **BB** ♦ **$45 - $85**, ♦♦ **$90 - $140**, ◊ **$10 - $25**, ch con, fam con, pen con.

SYDNEY - NARELLAN NSW 2567

Pop Part of Sydney, (57km SW Sydney), See map on page 56, ref A6. Outer suburb of Sydney near the larger centre of Camden. Golf.

Hotels/Motels

★★★ **Angel Motel**, (M), 5 The Northern Rd off Camden Valley Way, 200m S of PO, ☎ 02 4646 1044, fax 02 4646 1429, (2 stry gr fl), 51 units (5 suites) [shwr, spa bath (1), tlt, hairdry, a/c, elec blkts, tel, TV, video-fee, clock radio, t/c mkg, refrig, cook fac (3), micro (5), toaster], ldry, iron, iron brd, ⊠, pool (salt water), cots-fee. **RO** ♦ **$75 - $99**, ♦♦ **$85 - $104.50**, ♦♦♦ **$100 - $132**, ◊ **$10**, **Suite D $130 - $198**, ch con, 13 rooms of 3.5 star rating. AE BC DC MC VI, ⚿.

SYDNEY - NARRABEEN NSW 2101

Pop Part of Sydney, (26km N Sydney), See map on page 56, ref E4. Northern beaches suburb blessed with fine waterways — long stretches of golden sand to the east, the shimmering Narrabeen Lakes to the west. Swimming.

Hotels/Motels

★★☆ **Narrabeen Sands Hotel**, (LMH), 1260 Pittwater Rd, ☎ 02 9913 1166, fax 02 9913 3215, (2 stry), 16 units (2 suites) [shwr, bath (2), spa bath (2), tlt, tel, TV, clock radio, t/c mkg, refrig, toaster], ⊠, ✆, cots (avail). **D** ♦ **$82.50**, ♦♦ **$99**, ♦♦♦ **$104.50**, **Suite D $132**, AE BC DC EFT MC VI.

SYDNEY - NARWEE NSW 2209

Pop Part of Sydney, (19km SW Sydney), See map on page 56, ref C6. Suburb of Sydney. Bowls.

Hotels/Motels

Narwee Hotel, (LH), 116 Penshurst Rd, ☎ 02 9533 3088, fax 02 9534 6879, (2 stry), 13 rms (1 suite) [shwr, tlt, a/c-cool, fan, cent heat, elec blkts, TV, clock radio, t/c mkg, refrig], ⊠, ✆, cots, non smoking rms (5). **BLB** ♦ **$55**, ♦♦ **$88**, ♦♦♦ **$110**, ♦♦♦♦ **$154**, **Suite BLB $176**, AE BC DC EFT MC VI, (not yet classified).

SYDNEY - NEUTRAL BAY NSW 2089

Pop Part of Sydney, (6km N Sydney), See map on page 56, ref B1. Fashionable harbourside suburb on Sydney's lower north shore.

B&B's/Guest Houses

 ★★ **Carnarvon Manor**, (PH), 51 Wycombe Rd, 300m N of ferry wharf, ☎ 02 9953 1311, fax 02 9953 8935, (2 stry gr fl), 20 rms [shwr (14), tlt (14), tel, TV, clock radio, t/c mkg, refrig], ldry, cook fac, bbq, cots. **RO** ♦ **$55 - $104.50**, ♦♦ **$99 - $148.50**, ◊ **$16.50**, AE BC DC MC MCH VI.

★ **Neutral Bay Motor Lodge**, (GH), 45 Kurraba Rd, 150m N of Neutral Bay Wharf, ☎ 02 9953 4199, fax 02 9953 4199, (2 stry gr fl), 20 rms [shwr (8), bath (2), tlt (8), fan, heat, tel, TV, clock radio, t/c mkg, refrig, toaster], ldry, iron, iron brd, cafe, cook fac, 24hr reception, ✆, cots-fee, non smoking property. **RO** ♦ **$65 - $70**, ◊ **$10**, AE BC DC MC VI.

SYDNEY - NEWPORT NSW 2106

Pop Part of Sydney, (34km N Sydney), See map on page 56, ref E4. Northern beaches suburb of Sydney situated on Pittwater. Swimming.

Hotels/Motels

 ★★★★ **Newport Mirage**, (M), Cnr Queens Pde & Kalinya St, ☎ 02 9997 7011, fax 02 9997 5217, (Multi-stry gr fl), 47 units (1 suite) [shwr, spa bath (9), tlt, hairdry, a/c, tel, TV, clock radio, t/c mkg, refrig], lift, ldry, conv fac, ✕, pool, sauna, spa, jetty, cots. **RO** ♦ **$160 - $250**, ♦♦ **$160 - $250**, ◊ **$15 - $20**, AE BC DC MC VI.

★★☆ **Newport Arms**, (LH), Kalinya St, opposite PO, ☎ 02 9997 4900, fax 02 9979 6919, (Multi-stry), 9 rms [shwr, tlt, a/c, fan, tel, TV, t/c mkg, refrig], ⊠, rm serv, cots. **BLB** ♦ **$88**, ◊ **$22**, AE BC DC MC VI.

B&B's/Guest Houses

★★★★★ **Blue Waters Penthouses B&B on Pittwater**, (B&B), 56 Prince Alfred Pde, 2km W of PO, ☎ 02 9999 1245, fax 02 9999 4530, (Multi-stry gr fl), 3 rms [shwr, bath (1), spa bath (2), tlt, a/c, fan, heat, elec blkts, tel, TV, clock radio, t/c mkg, refrig, cook fac (1), micro, toaster, ldry (1)], iron, iron brd, lounge (TV), lounge firepl, bbq, cots-fee, non smoking rms. **D** ♦♦ **$143 - $440**, ◊ **$55 - $65**, ch con, Min book applies, BC MC VI.

★★★☆ **April Cottage B&B**, (B&B), 94 Queens Pde East, ☎ 02 9999 4994, fax 02 9999 4994, 2 rms [hairdry (1), fan (1), c/fan, heat (1), tel, TV (1), video, clock radio (1), radio (1)], ldry, iron, iron brd, lounge (TV), cook fac, t/c mkg shared, c/park. **BLB** ♦ **$90**, ♦♦ **$120 - $180**.

★★★ **Nieafu Bed & Breakfast**, (B&B), 21 Myola Rd, ☎ 02 9997 3202, 1 rm [shwr, tlt, heat, TV, clock radio, t/c mkg, refrig, cook fac, toaster, ldry], lounge, non smoking property. **BB** ♦ **$100**, ♦♦ **$150**, ch con, fam con, pen con.

SYDNEY - NEWTOWN NSW 2042

Pop Part of Sydney, (5km SW Sydney), See map on page 56, ref A2. The essence of inner city Sydney, an eclectic blend of alternative lifestyles, university culture and inner city grunge.

B&B's/Guest Houses

Australian Sunrise Lodge, (PH), 485 King St, 600m S of PO, ☎ 02 9550 4999, (Multi-stry gr fl), 18 rms [shwr (14), tlt (14), hairdry (2), c/fan, heat, TV, video (3), t/c mkg, refrig, micro (6), toaster], cook fac, bbq, dinner to unit, ☏, cots. **RO** ♦ **$59 - $89**, ♦♦ **$69 - $99**, ♦♦♦ **$99 - $149**, ◊ **$29 - $49**, ch con, AE BC DC MC VI.

Billabong Gardens, (GH), 5-11 Egan St, ☎ 02 9550 3236, fax 02 9550 4352, (Multi-stry gr fl), 37 rms [shwr, tlt, c/fan, heat, tel, TV, clock radio, t/c mkg, refrig], ldry, rec rm, TV rm, lounge, ✕, pool-heated (solar), spa, cook fac, bbq, courtesy transfer (pick-up), ☏, plygr, gym (facilities), cots. **RO** ♦ **$49 - $88**, ♦♦ **$66 - $88**, ◊ **$17**, BC EFT MC VI.

SYDNEY - NORTH BALGOWLAH NSW 2093

Pop Part of Sydney, (12km N Sydney), See map on page 56, ref D5. North shore suburb on Middle Cove near Balgowlah and Garigal National Park.

B&B's/Guest Houses

★★☆ **Birdsong Bed & Breakfast**, (B&B), 46 Woolgoolga St, ☎ 02 9907 9028, fax 02 9949 4993, 3 rms [heat, elec blkts, tel, TV, clock radio, t/c mkg, refrig], ldry, iron, iron brd, rec rm, lounge (tv & firepl), pool-heated (solar), cook fac, bbq, non smoking rms.

SYDNEY - NORTH PARRAMATTA NSW 2151

Pop Part of Parramatta, (25km W Sydney), See map on page 56, ref C5. Western suburb adjacent to the historic city of Parramatta.

Self Catering Accommodation

★★★★ **Parramatta Furnished Apartments**, (HU), 18 Bellevue St, 3km N of PO, ☎ 0408 000 110, 8 units acc up to 5, [shwr, bath, tlt, a/c, tel, TV, movie, clock radio, t/c mkg, refrig, cook fac, micro, toaster, ldry, blkts, linen], w/mach, dryer, iron, iron brd, 24hr reception, plygr, cots, non smoking units (4). **W $650 - $850**, ch con, Min book applies, AE BC DC MC VI.

SYDNEY - NORTH RYDE NSW 2113

Pop Part of Sydney, (14km N Sydney), See map on page 56, ref D5. Leafy suburb on the Lane Cove River in Sydney's north. Golf.

Hotels/Motels

★★★☆ **Stamford North Ryde**, (LH), Cnr Epping & Herring Rds, 1km E of Macquarie University, ☎ 02 9888 1077, fax 02 9805 0655, (Multi-stry gr fl), 255 rms (227 suites) [shwr, bath (178), spa bath (77), tlt, a/c, tel, TV, movie, clock radio, t/c mkg, refrig, mini bar], lift, conv fac, ✕, pool-heated, spa, bbq, rm serv, dinner to unit, c/park (undercover), gym, tennis, cots. **RO** ♦ **$304**, ♦♦ **$304**, ◊ **$32**, **Suite D $458**, ch con, 26 rooms yet to be assessed, AE BC DC JCB MC VI.

★★★☆ **Travelodge Macquarie North Ryde**, (LMH), 81 Talavera Rd Macquarie University, 500m N of Macquarie shopping centre, ☎ 02 8874 5200, fax 02 8874 5300, (Multi-stry gr fl), 120 units [shwr, tlt, a/c, tel, TV, video-fee, movie-fee, clock radio, t/c mkg, refrig, cook fac ltd, micro], lift, ldry, iron, iron brd, lounge, conf fac, ✕, 24hr reception, ☏, cots. **RO** ♦ **$139**, ♦♦ **$139**, ◊ **$15**, ch con, AE BC DC EFT MC VI, ♿.

MGSM Executive Hotel and Conference Centre, (LH), 99 Talavera Rd, 500m W of Macquarie Centre, ☎ 02 9850 6094, fax 02 9850 6090, (2 stry gr fl), 40 rms (2 suites) [shwr, tlt, a/c, cent heat, tel, TV, clock radio, t/c mkg, refrig], ldry, conf fac, ✕, dinner to unit, secure park. **D** ♦♦ **$125 - $150**, AE BC DC EFT MC VI, (not yet classified).

Self Catering Accommodation

★★★★☆ **Medina Executive North Ryde**, (SA), 2-12 Busaco Rd, 1.2km W of PO, ☎ 02 9876 7000, fax 02 9876 7099, (2 stry), 58 serv apts acc up to 4, [shwr, bath, tlt, hairdry, a/c, heat, elec blkts, tel, TV, video, clock radio, t/c mkg, refrig, cook fac, micro, d/wash, toaster, ldry (in unit), blkts, linen, pillows], w/mach, dryer, iron, iron brd, conv fac, pool-heated (solar), sauna, spa, bbq, dinner to unit, c/park (undercover), plygr, gym, cots. **D $187 - $253**, ch con, Light breakfast available, AE BC DC MC VI.

SYDNEY - NORTH SYDNEY NSW 2060

Pop Part of Sydney, (4km N Sydney), See map on page 56, ref A1. Large business and shopping area located directly across the harbour from the city centre. Bowls.

Hotels/Motels

★★★★ **North Sydney Harbour View Hotel**, (M), Previously Harbour View Hotel North Sydney 17 Blue St, 500m S of PO, ☎ 02 9955 0499, fax 02 9955 4512, (Multi-stry), 211 units (2 suites) [shwr, bath, tlt, a/c, tel, TV, movie, clock radio, t/c mkg, refrig, mini bar], lift, ldry, iron, lounge, business centre, conv fac, ✕, rm serv, cots, non smoking flr (7). **D** ♦ **$231**, ♦♦ **$231**, ◊ **$30**, ch con, AE BC DC MC VI.

Operator Comment: See our display advertisement on page 92.

AAA
TOURISM
Special Rates

★★★★ **Rydges North Sydney**, (LH), 54 Mc Laren St, 500m N of PO, ☎ 02 9922 1311, fax 02 9922 4939, (Multi-stry), 166 rms (46 suites) [shwr, bath, tlt, hairdry, a/c, tel, TV, movie-fee, clock radio, t/c mkg, refrig, cook fac (suites only)], lift, ldry, ✕, bar, rm serv, cots. **RO** ♦ **$155 - $195**, ♦♦ **$155 - $195**, ♦♦♦ **$230 - $270**, ◊ **$27.50 - $38.50**, AE BC DC MC VI.

B&B's/Guest Houses

★★★☆ **The McLaren**, (GH), 25 McLaren St, 2km N of PO, ☎ 02 9954 4622, fax 02 9922 1868, (2 stry gr fl), 28 rms (2 suites) [shwr, bath (2), tlt, hairdry, a/c, tel, TV, clock radio, t/c mkg, refrig], c/park. **BLB** ♦ **$165,** ♦♦ **$165,** ◊ **$15,** AE BC DC MC VI, ⏃.

★★★ **Northshore Hotel**, (GH), 310 Miller St, 100m N of North Sydney Oval, ☎ 02 9955 1012, fax 02 9955 4212, (2 stry gr fl), 32 rms (1 suite) [shwr, tlt, a/c, tel, TV, clock radio, t/c mkg, refrig, cook fac (3)], ldry, cook fac, cots. **BB** ♦ **$92 - $150.**

SYDNEY - OXFORD FALLS NSW 2100

Pop Part of Sydney, (19km N Sydney), See map on page 56, ref D5. Bushland suburb north of Sydney between Frenchs Forest and Dee Why.

Hotels/Motels

★★★ **The Falls Resort & Convention Centre**, (M), 1110 Oxford Falls Rd, 500m E of Wakehurst Parkway, ☎ 02 9452 1300, fax 02 9975 1866, (2 stry), 12 units [shwr, tlt, a/c, TV, clock radio, t/c mkg, refrig], ldry, rec rm, conv fac, ✉ (for groups), pool-heated (solar), bbq, ⚲, plygr, tennis, cots. **BLB** ♦ **$88 - $99,** ♦♦ **$99 - $110,** ♦♦♦ **$110 - $121,** AE BC DC MC VI.

SYDNEY - PADDINGTON NSW 2021

Pop Part of Sydney, (3km E Sydney), See map on page 56, ref B2. Fashionable inner eastern suburb distinguished by its graceful rows of terrace houses. Bowls.

Hotels/Motels

★★★☆ **Sullivans Hotel**, (M), 21 Oxford St, 600m W of PO, ☎ 02 9361 0211, fax 02 9360 3735, (Multi-stry), 64 units [shwr, tlt, hairdry, a/c, tel, TV, movie, clock radio, t/c mkg, refrig], lift, ldry, ✗ (breakfast only), pool, 24hr reception, bicycle, cots. **RO** ♦ **$125 - $145,** ♦♦ **$125 - $145,** Min booking New Years Eve and Mardi Gras event. AE BC DC EFT MC VI.

Olympic Hotel, (LH), 308 Moore Park Rd, Opposite Sydney Football Stadium, ☎ 02 9361 6315, fax 02 9331 5396, (2 stry), 24 rms [shwr (14), tlt (14), fan (4), TV, clock radio, t/c mkg, refrig], shared fac (10 rms), ldry, iron, iron brd, ✗ (Tues to Sat), ✗ (Tues to Sat), cook fac, ⚲. **D** ♦♦ **$93.50, RO** ♦ **$71.50,** ◊ **$33,** AE BC DC EFT JCB MC VI.

Self Catering Accommodation

★★★★☆ **Medina Executive Paddington**, (SA), 400 Glenmore Rd, 2km E of PO, ☎ 02 9361 9000, fax 02 9332 3484, (Multi-stry gr fl), 48 serv apts acc up to 6, [shwr, bath, tlt, hairdry, a/c, tel, TV, video, clock radio, t/c mkg, refrig, cook fac, micro, d/wash, toaster, ldry (in unit), blkts, doonas, linen, pillows], w/mach, dryer, iron, iron brd, pool, bbq, dinner to unit, c/park (garage), tennis, cots. **D $286 - $350,** Light breakfast available, AE BC DC MC VI.

B&B's/Guest Houses

★★★★ **Marshalls of Paddington**, (B&B), 73 Goodhope St, 3km E of GPO, ☎ 02 9361 6217, fax 02 9361 6986, 2 rms (1 suite) [ensuite, fan, c/fan, heat, elec blkts, tel, TV, video, clock radio, t/c mkg, refrig, toaster, doonas], lounge (TV), lounge firepl, ✗, non smoking property. **BB** ♦♦ **$150,** ◊ **$40,** ch con, BC MC VI.

★★★ **Paddington Terrace Bed & Breakfast**, (B&B), 76 Elizabeth St, ☎ 02 9363 0903, fax 02 9327 1476, 2 rms [shwr, tlt, fan, heat, elec blkts, tel, TV, clock radio, t/c mkg], lounge (TV), ✗ (Breakfast only). **BB** ♦ **$115,** ♦♦ **$135,** Children by arrangement, AE BC JCB MC VI.

SYDNEY - PALM BEACH NSW 2108

Pop Part of Sydney, (43km N Sydney), See map on page 56, ref E4. Palm Beach, far up on the northern beaches, is a favourite coastal retreat for Sydney's well-to-do. Boating, Fishing, Golf, Scenic Drives, Swimming.

Self Catering Accommodation

★★☆ **The Ferry House**, (Cotg), 1120 Barrenjoey Rd, 100m N of Barrenjoey House, ☎ 02 9974 4342, 1 cotg acc up to 7, [shwr, tlt, hairdry, fan, heat, elec blkts, TV, t/c mkg, refrig, cook fac, micro, toaster, blkts, linen], iron, bbq, cots-fee, non smoking property. **D** ♦♦ **$140 - $175**, ◊ **$25, W $600 - $2,000**, ch con.

B&B's/Guest Houses

★★★★☆ **Palm Beach Bed & Breakfast**, (B&B), 122 Pacific Rd, ☎ 02 9974 1608, fax 02 9918 3201, (2 stry), 4 rms [shwr (3), bath, tlt (3), hairdry, c/fan, heat, tel, TV, clock radio], iron, iron brd, lounge (TV), ✕, t/c mkg shared, bbq, non smoking property. **BLB** ♦ **$90 - $110**, ♦♦ **$125 - $150.**

★★★★ **Palm Beach's 'Chateau Sur Mer' Exclusive B&B**, (B&B), No children's facilities, 124 Pacific Rd, 400m E of ferry wharf, ☎ 02 9974 4220, or 02 9974 1147, fax 02 9974 1147, 3 rms (3 suites) [shwr, bath (1), tlt, hairdry, a/c, elec blkts, tel, TV, video, clock radio, t/c mkg (3), refrig (3)], iron, iron brd, lounge (TV & firepl). **BLB** ♦ **$90**, ♦♦ **$140 - $250**, ◊ **$50**, BC MC VI.

Operator Comment: Paradise honeymoon location, ocean views, walks to beach.

★★★★ **Sails On Pittwater**, (B&B), 934 Barrenjoey Rd, ☎ 02 9974 1103, 1 rm [shwr, tlt, fan, heat, tel, TV, clock radio, t/c mkg, refrig, cook fac ltd, micro, toaster], iron, iron brd, bbq, c/park. **BLB** ♦ **$115**, ♦♦ **$145**, ◊ **$25, RO** ♦ **$100**, ♦♦ **$130**, ◊ **$20.**

★★★☆ **Jonah's Restaurant & Accommodation**, (GH), 69 Bynya Rd, ☎ 02 9974 5599, fax 02 9974 1212, 7 rms [shwr, tlt, a/c, tel (ISD), cable tv, t/c mkg, refrig], ✕, c/park. **BB** ♦♦ **$300 - $375, DBB** ♦♦ **$420 - $500, D** ◊ **$27.50**, AE BC DC MC VI.

★★ **Barrenjoey House**, (GH), 1108 Barrenjoey Rd, ☎ 02 9974 4001, fax 02 9974 5008, 5 rms [shwr (2), tlt (2), fan, heat], shared fac (4 rms), lounge (TV), ✕, cook fac, t/c mkg shared, plygr. **BLB** ♦♦ **$140 - $180**, AE BC DC MC VI.

SYDNEY - PARRAMATTA NSW 2150

Pop Part of Sydney, (24km W Sydney), See map on page 56, ref C5. Large business centre in Sydney's western suburbs, founded in 1788 and featuring some of Sydney's oldest buildings. Bowls, Swimming.

Hotels/Motels

★★★★☆ **Carlton Hotel Parramatta**, (LMH), (Previously Gazebo) 350 Church St, 500m N of PO, ☎ 02 9630 4999, fax 02 9630 0757, (Multi-stry), 202 units (7 suites) [shwr, bath, tlt, hairdry, a/c, elec blkts, tel, TV, movie, clock radio, t/c mkg, refrig, mini bar], lift, iron, conv fac, ✕, pool-heated, sauna, spa, rm serv, c/park (undercover), ☎, gym, cots, non smoking rms (avail). **RO** ♦ **$170 - $197.50**, ♦♦ **$170 - $197.50**, ◊ **$28**, ch con, AE BC DC MC MP VI.

★★★★☆ **Courtyard by Marriott**, (LH), 18 Anderson St, 250m SW of railway station, ☎ 02 9891 1277, fax 02 9687 1148, (Multi-stry gr fl) 181 rms (30 suites) [shwr, bath, spa bath (30), tlt, hairdry, a/c, tel, TV, movie, clock radio, t/c mkg, refrig, mini bar], lift, rec rm, ✕, pool-heated, spa (heat), rm serv, dinner to unit, secure park, ☎, cots, non smoking flr (3, 4, 5 &6). **RO** ♦ **$135 - $195**, ♦♦ **$135 - $195**, ◊ **$27.50, Suite RO** ♦ **$230**, ♦♦ **$230**, ◊ **$27.50**, AE BC DC JCB MC VI.

★★★★☆ **Parkroyal Parramatta**, (LH), 30 Phillip St, 200m N of PO, ☎ 02 9689 3333, fax 02 9689 3959, (Multi-stry), 196 rms (1 suite) [shwr, bath, tlt, hairdry, a/c, tel, TV, movie, clock radio, t/c mkg, refrig, mini bar], lift, iron, conv fac, ✕, pool, rm serv, dinner to unit, cots-fee, non smoking units (90). **RO** ♦ **$180 - $380**, ♦♦ **$180 - $380**, ◊ **$30**, ch con, AE BC DC EFT JCB MC VI, ♿.

★★★☆ **Parramatta City Motel**, (M), Cnr Great Western Hwy & Marsden St, ☎ 02 9635 7266, fax 02 9633 4216, (Multi-stry gr fl), 44 units [shwr, tlt, a/c, tel, TV, clock radio, t/c mkg, refrig], lift, ldry, conf fac, ✕, pool, rm serv, ☎, cots-fee. **RO** ♦ **$110 - $145**, ♦♦ **$120 - $145**, ◊ **$15 - $25**, ch con, AE BC DC EFT MC MCH VI.

★ **Argyle Street Hotel**, (LH), 111 Argyle St, 200m E of PO, ☎ 02 9635 8990, fax 02 9635 8207, 12 rms [shwr (5), spa bath (1), tlt (5), fan, heat], shared fac (7 rms), ✕, ☎. **RO** ♦ **$65 - $80**, ♦♦ **$65 - $110**, AE BC DC EFT MC VI.

Pacific International Suites, (LH), Cnr Parkes St & Valentine Ave, 1km SE of PO, ☎ 02 9685 1600, fax 02 9635 3388, (Multi-stry), 137 rms (6 suites) [shwr, spa bath (30), tlt, a/c-cool, cent heat, tel, TV, clock radio, t/c mkg, refrig], ldry, conf fac, ✕, ✕, pool (outdoor/heated), sauna, spa, rm serv, meals to unit, secure park (undercover), cots-fee, non smoking rms (70). **RO** ♦ **$190.30 - $224.40**, ♦♦ **$190.30 - $224.40**, ◊ **$27.50, Suite RO $239.80 - $282.70**, AE BC DC EFT JCB MC VI, (not yet classified).

(Serviced Apartment Section), 95 serv apts acc up to 5, (1 & 2 bedrm), [a/c-cool, cent heat, tel, TV, clock radio, t/c mkg, refrig, cook fac ltd, micro, blkts, pillows], w/mach, dryer, rm serv, meals to unit, cots-fee. **RO** ♦ **$222.20 - $304.70**, ♦♦ **$222.20 - $304.70**, ◊ **$27.50**, (not yet classified).

B&B's/Guest Houses

★★★☆ **Harborne Bed & Breakfast**, (GH), 21 Boundary St, ☎ 02 9687 8988, fax 02 9893 7018, 8 rms [shwr, bath (1), tlt, hairdry, a/c (4), tel, TV, clock radio], shared fac (4 rooms), ldry, iron, iron brd, t/c mkg shared, non smoking rms. **BB** ♦ **$95 - $130**, ♦♦ **$105 - $140**, 4 rooms ★★★★☆, AE BC DC MC VI.

★★ **Parramatta Central Motel**, (PH), 32 Station St East, 300m SE of railway station, ☎ 02 9633 4311, fax 02 9633 3563, (2 stry gr fl), 10 rms [shwr, c/fan, tel, TV, clock radio, t/c mkg, refrig], ldry, bbq, cots. **BLB** ♦ **$77**, ♦♦ **$77**, ◊ **$11**, AE BC DC MC VI.

★★☆ **(Serviced Apartment Section)**, 9 serv apts acc up to 6, [shwr, bath (8), tlt, fan, heat, tel, TV, clock radio, t/c mkg, refrig, cook fac, toaster], ldry, w/mach, dryer, iron, bbq. **BB $110 - $165**.

Trouble-free travel tips - **Hoses and belts**
Inspect the condition of radiator hoses, heater hose fan and air conditioner belts.

Your home away from home

AAAT ★★★☆ *4 Rooms* ★★★★☆

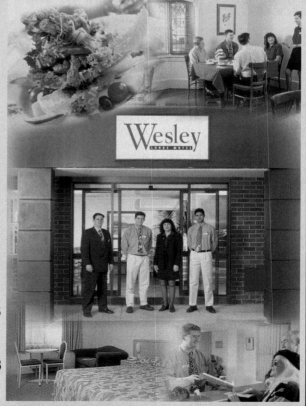

SYDNEY - PENNANT HILLS NSW 2120

Pop Part of Sydney, (24km W Sydney), See map on page 56, ref C5.

Hotels/Motels

★★★★☆ **The Chifley on City View**, (LH), Cnr Pennant Hills Rd & City View Rd, 150m W of PO, ☎ 02 9980 6999, fax 02 9980 6882, CHIFLEY (Multi-stry), 118 rms (35 suites) [shwr, spa bath (28), tlt, hairdry, a/c, tel, TV, movie, clock radio, t/c mkg, refrig, mini bar, micro (26), toaster], lift, ldry, iron, iron brd, conv fac, ⊠, cafe, pool, sauna, spa, bbq, 24hr reception, rm serv, dinner to unit, c/park (undercover), gym, cots-fee, non smoking rms (30). **RO $168 - $185**, ch con, AE BC DC EFT MC VI.

SYDNEY - PENRITH NSW 2750

Pop Part of Sydney, (56km W Sydney), See map on page 56, ref A5. Prosperous regional centre and Sydney's westernmost city at the foot of the Blue Mountains on the Nepean River.

Hotels/Motels

★★★★☆ **Penrith Motor Inn**, (LMH), Cnr Mulgoa Rd & Blaikie Rd, ☎ 02 4734 5555, fax 02 4734 5500, 28 units [shwr, tlt, hairdry, a/c, cable tv, t/c mkg, refrig, cook fac (1)], spa (4), 24hr reception. **RO ♦ $105 - $110, ♦♦ $130 - $140, ◊ $25**, BC EFT MC VI.

★★★★ **Panthers World of Entertainment**, (M), Resort, Cnr Mulgoa & Jamison Rds, 2km W of PO, ☎ 02 4720 5555, fax 02 4732 2928, (Multi-stry gr fl), 216 units (5 suites) [shwr, bath (80), tlt, hairdry, a/c, tel, TV, video (avail), t/c mkg, refrig, mini bar (124)], ldry, iron, iron brd, conv fac, night club, ⊠, coffee shop, pool, bbq, rm serv, golf (aqua), tennis, cots, non smoking rms (48). **RO ♦ $121 - $198, ♦♦ $121 - $198, Suite RO $181 - $330**, ch con, 102 rooms of 3.5 star rating, AE BC DC MC VI, ♿.

★★★☆ **Log Cabin**, (LMH), Memorial Ave, 1km from Penrith CBD, ☎ 02 4732 3122, fax 02 4721 4135, (2 stry), 39 units [shwr, bath (15), spa bath (1), tlt, hairdry, a/c, c/fan (24), tel, TV, clock radio, t/c mkg, refrig, mini bar (1)], ldry, iron, iron brd, conv fac, ⊠, bar (public), bbq, rm serv, cots-fee, non smoking units (3). **RO ♦ $115 - $130, ♦♦ $120 - $140, ♦♦♦ $135 - $145, ◊ $15**, AE BC DC EFT MC VI, ♿.

★★★☆ **Penrith Valley Inn**, (M), Cnr Great Western Hwy & Memorial Ave, 1km W of PO, ☎ 02 4731 1666, fax 02 4721 0321, (2 stry), 39 units [shwr, bath (2), spa bath (3), tlt, hairdry, a/c, elec blkts, tel, TV, clock radio, t/c mkg, refrig], ldry, conv fac, ⊠ (Wed - Sat), pool (salt water), spa, 24hr reception, rm serv, dinner to unit (6 nights), c/park (undercover), cots-fee, non smoking units (8). **BLB ♦ $105 - $170, ♦♦ $115 - $170, ◊ $15**, ch con, AE BC DC EFT MC VI, ♿.

★★ **Penrith Hotel**, (LH), 297 High St, opposite PO, ☎ 02 4721 2060, fax 02 4721 2735, (2 stry), 14 rms [shwr, tlt, a/c (4), fan (10), heat (10), TV, clock radio, t/c mkg, refrig], night club (Wed, Fri, Sat), ⊠. **RO ♦ $88 - $127, ♦♦ $99 - $127, ◊ $16.50**, 4 rooms ★★★, Min book applies, AE BC DC EFT MC VI.

★☆ **Jamison Hotel**, (LMH), Smith St, 2km S of PO, ☎ 02 4721 5764, fax 02 4732 3415, 7 units [shwr, tlt, a/c, fan, heat, tel, fax, TV, t/c mkg, refrig], ldry, ⊠. **BB ♦ $60, ♦♦ $60, ♦♦♦ $70, ◊ $5 - $10**, BC EFT MC VI.

Self Catering Accommodation

★★★☆ **Nepean Shores**, (SA), 6 Tench Ave, 3km SW of PO, ☎ 02 4721 4404, fax 02 4721 8368, 65 serv apts acc up to 5, [shwr, bath, tlt, a/c, elec blkts, tel, TV, movie, clock radio, t/c mkg, refrig, cook fac, toaster], conf fac, pool, bbq, tennis, cots. **RO ♦ $104.50 - $159.50, ♦♦ $104.50 - $159.50, ♦♦♦ $148.50 - $170.50, ◊ $11**, AE BC DC MC VI.

SYDNEY - PETERSHAM NSW 2049

Pop Part of Sydney, (9km W Sydney), See map on page 56, ref A2. Inner western suburb near Stanmore and Leichhardt. Bowls, Swimming.

B&B's/Guest Houses

★★★ **Brooklyn Bed & Breakfast**, (B&B), c1880. 25 Railway St, 300m N of railway station, ☎ 02 9564 2312, (2 stry gr fl), 5 rms [fan, heat, elec blkts, clock radio, pillows], bathrm (2), lounge (TV), t/c mkg shared, refrig, ☎. **BB ♦ $60 - $70, ♦♦ $80, ◊ $10**.

SYDNEY - PITT TOWN NSW 2756

Pop 650. (57km NW Sydney) See map on page 56, ref B3. Popular waterskiing area north-east of Windsor along the Hawkesbury River.

Self Catering Accommodation

★★★ **Hawkesbury Alpacas Bed & Breakfast**, (Farm), 64 Avondale Rd, ☎ 02 4573 6643, fax 02 4573 6643, 3 cabins acc up to 12, [shwr, bath (1), tlt, a/c, c/fan, fire pl, TV, clock radio, t/c mkg, refrig, micro, elec frypan, toaster, blkts, linen], iron, iron brd, rec rm, pool, bbq, shop, courtesy transfer, cots, Pets on application. **D $50 - $150, W $250 - $500**, BC MC VI.

SYDNEY - POTTS POINT NSW 2011

Pop Part of Sydney, (3km E Sydney), See map on page 56, ref B1. Cosmopolitan inner eastern suburb that takes in part of Kings Cross and is home to some of Sydney's best restaurants. Boating, Fishing, Sailing.

Hotels/Motels

★★★★☆ **The Landmark Parkroyal Hotel**, (LH), 81 Macleay St, 50m E of PO, ☎ 02 9368 3000, fax 02 9357 7600, (Multi-stry), 468 rms (10 suites) [shwr, bath, tlt, hairdry, a/c, elec blkts, tel, cable tv, clock radio, t/c mkg, refrig, mini bar], lift (4), business centre, conv fac, ⊠, pool, rm serv, courtesy transfer, gym, cots, non smoking rms. **RO ♦♦ $191, Suite D $315 - $950**, ch con, AE BC DC JCB MC VI, ♿.

★★★★☆ **The Rex Hotel Sydney**, (LH), 50-58 Macleay St, ☎ 02 9383 7788, fax 02 9383 7777, (Multi-stry), 254 rms (16 suites) [shwr, bath (252), tlt, hairdry, a/c, tel, TV, video-fee, movie-fee, clock radio, t/c mkg, mini bar], lift, iron, iron brd, conv fac, ⊠, pool-heated, spa, 24hr reception, rm serv, dinner to unit, ☎, gym, cots-fee, non smoking rms (65). **RO ♦ $280 - $490, ♦♦ $280 - $490**, AE BC DC EFT JCB MC VI.

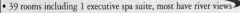

For Accommodation Booking information - see page 27

★★★☆ **De Vere Hotel**, (LH), 44 Macleay St, 40m N of PO, ☎ 02 9358 1211, fax 02 9358 4685, (Multi-stry), 100 rms [shwr, bath, tlt, a/c, tel, TV, clock radio, t/c mkg, refrig, cook fac ltd (10)], lift, 24hr reception, cots. P ♥♥ $97.90 - $206, RO ♦ $97.90 - $206, ch con, AE BC DC MC VI.

Self Catering Accommodation

★★★★ **Azure Executive Apartments**, (Apt), Previously Azure Macleay Executive Apartments 40 Macleay St, 100m W of PO, ☎ 02 9356 6900, or 02 9356 6903, fax 02 9356 6999, (Multi-stry), 40 apts (Studio & 1 bedrm), [shwr, tlt, a/c, tel, TV, clock radio, t/c mkg, refrig, cook fac, micro, ldry], lift, iron, secure park, cots. RO $137 - $192, ch con, 12 apartments of a lower rating, AE BC DC EFT MC VI.

Oakford AUSTRALIA

★★★★ **Oakford Potts Point**, (SA), 10 Wylde St, 5km E of PO, ☎ 02 9358 4544, fax 02 9357 1162, (Multi-stry), 35 serv apts acc up to 4, [shwr, bath (some), tlt, hairdry, a/c-cool, heat, tel, cable tv, video (avail), clock radio, t/c mkg, refrig, cook fac, micro, d/wash, toaster], lift, ldry, iron, pool, bbq, dinner to unit, secure park, cots-fee. RO ♥♥ $137 - $203.50, $885.50 - $347.50, AE BC DC MC VI.

★★★☆ **Macleay Serviced Apartments**, (SA), 28 Macleay St, 500m N of Kings Cross, ☎ 02 9357 7755, fax 02 9357 7233, (Multi-stry), 80 serv apts [shwr, bath (5), tlt, hairdry, a/c-cool, heat, tel, TV, video (9), movie, clock radio, t/c mkg, refrig, cook fac, micro, toaster], lift, ldry, iron, conf fac, pool, 24hr reception, cots, non smoking rms (28). W $732 - $798, RO ♦ $99 - $121, ♥♥ $110 - $143, AE BC DC EFT MC VI.

★★★☆ **The Grantham**, (SA), 1 Grantham St, opposite Navy Base, ☎ 02 9357 2377, fax 02 9358 1435, (Multi-stry gr fl), 38 serv apts acc up to 5, [shwr, tlt, hairdry, a/c, heat, tel, fax, cable tv, clock radio, t/c mkg, refrig, cook fac, toaster, ldry], lift, ldry, pool, rm serv (breakfast), dinner to unit, secure park, cots. RO ♦ $120 - $180, ♥♥ $120 - $180, ♦ $15, ch con, AE BC DC MC VI.

B&B's/Guest Houses

★★★★ **Victoria Court Sydney**, (PH), 122 Victoria St, 250m W of PO, ☎ 02 9357 3200, fax 02 9357 7606, (Multi-stry gr fl), 25 rms [shwr, tlt, a/c, c/fan, heat, tel, TV, clock radio, t/c mkg], lounge, secure park, cots-fee. BB ♦ $75 - $230, ♥♥ $99 - $230, ♥♥♥ $120 - $250, ♦ $20, AE BC DC MC VI.

★★ **Holiday Lodge**, (PH), 55 Macleay St, 3km E of PO, ☎ 02 9356 3955, fax 02 9356 3485, (Multi-stry gr fl), 15 rms [shwr (15), tlt (15), a/c, TV, t/c mkg, refrig], bbq, ✆, cots. D ♦ $86 - $97, ♥♥ $86 - $97, ♥♥♥ $98 - $110, ♦ $12 - $13, AE BC MC VI.

SYDNEY - PYRMONT NSW 2009

Pop Part of Sydney, (2km W Sydney), See map on page 56, ref A1.

Hotels/Motels

★★★★★ **Star City**, (LH), 80 Pyrmont St, 500m N of Darling Harbour, ☎ 02 9777 9000, fax 02 9657 8345, (Multi-stry), 352 rms [shwr, bath, tlt, hairdry, a/c, tel, TV, movie-fee, clock radio, t/c mkg, refrig, mini bar], lift, iron, iron brd, business centre, conv fac, ✉, pool-indoor (heated), sauna, spa, 24hr reception, rm serv, ✆, gym, cots, non smoking flr (3), non smoking rms (106). BB ♥♥ $290, ♦ $43, ch con, AE BC DC JCB MC VI, ♿.

Rates may change. Check before booking.

Star City ...continued
★★★★★ **(Serviced Apartment Section)**, 129 serv apts acc up to 6, [shwr, bath, tlt, hairdry, a/c, heat, tel, TV, movie-fee, clock radio, t/c mkg, refrig, mini bar, cook fac, micro, d/wash, toaster, ldry, blkts, linen], w/mach, dryer, iron, iron brd, non smoking flr (3), non smoking units (41). D ♦♦ $335 - $365, ◊ $43, ⑂&.

Self Catering Accommodation
★★★★☆ **Goldsbrough Apartments**, (SA), 243 Pyrmont St, Darling Harbour 2009, ☎ 02 9518 5166, fax 02 9518 5177, (Multi-stry), 60 serv apts acc up to 6, (Studio, 1, 2 & 3 bedrm), [shwr, tlt, a/c (47), heat (elec), tel, TV, clock radio, t/c mkg, refrig, cook fac, micro, d/wash, blkts, linen, pillows], lift, w/mach, dryer, pool indoor heated, sauna, spa, secure park-fee, cots-fee. D $131 - $250, weekly con, Min book applies, AE BC DC MC VI.

B&B's/Guest Houses
★★★☆ **Pyrmont Place**, (B&B), 109 Pyrmont St, ☎ 02 9660 7433, fax 02 9660 3618, 1 rm [shwr, tlt, hairdry, a/c, heat, tel, clock radio, t/c mkg, refrig], ldry, iron, iron brd, pool-heated (salt water), bbq, c/park. BB ♦ $120, ♦♦ $140, AE BC DC JCB MC VI.

★★ **Woolbrokers Arms**, (B&B), 22 Allen St (Cnr Pyrmont St), ☎ 02 9552 4773, fax 02 9552 4771, (2 stry gr fl), 26 rms [TV, t/c mkg, refrig], ldry, ✗, c/park-fee, ✆. BLB ♦ $66, ♦♦ $93, ♦♦♦ $107, ♦♦♦♦ $132, AE BC MC VI.

SYDNEY - RANDWICK NSW 2031
Pop Part of Sydney, (6km E Sydney), See map on page 56, ref B2. Situated in Sydney's eastern suburbs, Randwick is famous for its horse racing and the home of one of Australia's top courses. Art Gallery, Bowls, Golf, Squash.

Hotels/Motels
★★★☆ **Gemini Motel**, (LH), 65 Belmore Rd, 500m NE of Prince of Wales Hospital, ☎ 02 9399 9011, fax 02 9398 9708, (Multi-stry), 97 rms (1 suite) [shwr, tlt, a/c, heat, tel, TV, clock radio, t/c mkg, refrig], lift, ldry, conv fac, ✉, 24hr reception, rm serv, c/park (undercover), courtesy transfer, cots. RO ♦ $126.50, ♦♦ $126.50, ♦♦♦ $136.50, ◊ $16.50, AE BC DC MC VI.

★★★ **Esron Motel**, (M), Cnr Dudley & St Pauls Sts, 500m E of PO, ☎ 02 9398 7022, fax 02 9326 7011, (Multi-stry), 37 units [shwr, tlt, a/c, fan, heat, tel, TV, clock radio, t/c mkg, refrig, micro (12)], ldry, lounge, pool, cots. RO ♦ $85 - $94, ♦♦ $94 - $115, ♦♦♦ $95 - $132, ◊ $15, ch con, AE BC DC EFT MC VI.

Self Catering Accommodation

★★★☆ **Medina Classic Randwick**, (SA), 63 St Marks Rd, 1km E of racecourse, ☎ 02 9399 5144, fax 02 9399 4569, 60 serv apts acc up to 4, [shwr, bath, tlt, hairdry, a/c, elec blkts, tel, TV, video-fee, clock radio, t/c mkg, refrig, cook fac, micro, d/wash, toaster, ldry (in unit), blkts, linen, pillows], w/mach, dryer, iron, iron brd, conv fac, pool, sauna, spa, bbq, meals avail (breakfast & dinner), c/park (undercover), courtesy transfer, plygr, gym, cots. D $159 - $192, AE BC DC MC VI.

B&B's/Guest Houses
★★ **The Centre Bed & Breakfast**, (B&B), 14 Frances St, ☎ 02 9398 2211, fax 02 9326 6003, (2 stry gr fl), 34 rms [shwr (24), bath (2), tlt (24), c/fan, heat (22), elec blkts, tel, TV (27), t/c mkg (24), refrig (24), micro (1)], lift, ldry, iron, iron brd, TV rm, business centre, conf fac, ✗, pool (salt water), bbq-fee, ✆, non smoking flr (2). BLB ♦ $70, ♦♦ $90, ◊ $115, BC EFT MC VI.

SYDNEY - REDFERN NSW 2016
Pop Part of Sydney, (3km S Sydney), See map on page 56, ref A2. Inner suburb just to the south of the city centre. Art Gallery.

Hotels/Motels
★★★ **Central Railway Motel**, (M), 240 Chalmers St, 500m S of Central Station, ☎ 02 9319 7800, fax 02 9318 1004, (Multi-stry gr fl), 38 units [shwr, tlt, hairdry, fan, heat, tel, TV, clock radio, t/c mkg, refrig, cook fac ltd, micro, toaster], ldry, iron, iron brd, ✆, cots. D ♦ $95, ♦♦ $105, ♦♦♦ $150, ♦♦♦♦ $180, ch con, fam con, pen con, BC EFT MC VI.

B&B's/Guest Houses
★★ **Alfred Park Budget**, (PH), 207 Cleveland St, 600m S of Central Station, ☎ 02 9319 4031, fax 02 9318 4031, (Multi-stry gr fl), 38 rms [ensuite (20), TV, refrig], ldry, cook fac, bbq, cots. W $210 - $550, RO ♦ $45 - $65, ♦♦ $55 - $75, ♦♦♦ $70 - $90, ◊ $20.

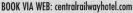

Trouble-free travel tips - **Windscreen wipers**

Check the operation of windscreen wipers and washers. Replace windscreen wiper rubbers if they are not cleaning the windscreen properly.

SYDNEY - ROOTY HILL NSW 2766
Pop Part of Sydney, (43km W Sydney), See map on page 56, ref B5. Rooty Hill is located in far western Sydney between Blacktown and Mount Druitt.

Hotels/Motels

★★★★☆ **Country Comfort Rooty Hill RSL Resort**, (LH), Resort, Cnr Railway & Sherbrooke Sts, 14km W of Parramatta, ☎ 02 9832 3888, fax 02 9832 1347, (Multi-stry), 165 rms (8 suites) [shwr, bath, spa bath (34), tlt, hairdry, a/c, cent heat, elec blkts, tel, movie, clock radio, t/c mkg, refrig, mini bar, micro (8), toaster], lift, ldry, rec rm, conv fac, ✉, pool indoor heated, sauna, spa, bbq, 24hr reception, rm serv, ✆, gym, tennis, cots. RO ♦ $142, ♦♦ $142, RO ◊ $16.50, ch con, AE BC DC JCB MC VI, ⑂&.

SYDNEY - ROSE BAY NSW 2029

Pop Part of Sydney, (8km E Sydney), See map on page 56, ref B2. An affluent suburb with many fine homes and gardens on the south-eastern shores of Sydney Harbour. Boat Ramp, Golf, Scenic Drives.

B&B's/Guest Houses

★★★ **Syls Sydney Homestay**, (B&B), 75 Beresford Rd, 2km W of PO, ☎ 02 9327 7079, fax 02 9362 9292, 3 rms (1 suite) [shwr (2), bath (1), tlt (2), heat (2), tel, t/c mkg, cook fac (1)], bbq, cots. **BB ♦ $85 - $95, ♦♦ $120 - $145, ♦♦♦ $150 - $200, ◊ $40, Suite D $160 - $320**, ch con, AE BC MC VI.

SYDNEY - ROSEHILL NSW 2142

Pop Part of Sydney, (23km W Sydney), See map on page 56, ref C5. Rosehill lies east of Parramatta on the Parramatta River and is home to one of Australia's premier horse racing venues.

Hotels/Motels

★★★★☆ **Mercure Hotel Parramatta**, (M), 106 Hassall St, Opposite Rosehill Racecourse, ☎ 02 9891 3877, fax 02 9891 3953, (Multi-stry), 165 units (2 suites) [shwr, bath, tlt, a/c, tel, TV, movie, clock radio, t/c mkg, refrig, mini bar], ldry, conv fac, ⊠, pool, spa, rm serv, c/park (undercover), ☎, tennis, cots, non smoking flr (4). **RO ♦ $175, ♦♦ $175, ♦♦♦ $195, ◊ $20, Suite D $245**, ch con, AE BC DC JCB MC VI, ♿.

★★★★☆ **Rydges Parramatta**, (LH), 116 James Ruse Dve, opposite racecourse, ☎ 02 9897 2222, fax 02 9897 2363, 151 rms (2 suites) [shwr, bath, tlt, hairdry, a/c, tel, TV, movie, clock radio, t/c mkg, refrig, mini bar], iron, iron brd, conv fac, ⊠, pool indoor heated, sauna, spa, rm serv, gym, cots, non smoking rms (78). **RO ♦ $120 - $240, ♦♦ $120 - $240, Suite D ♦ $195 - $290, ♦♦ $195 - $290**, AE BC DC JCB MC VI.

★★★★☆ **The Sebel Parramatta**, (LH), 110 James Ruse Dve, 2km SE of Parramatta PO, ☎ 02 8837 8000, fax 02 8837 8001, (Multi-stry), 174 rms (21 suites) [shwr, tlt, a/c, tel, cable tv, video, movie-fee, clock radio, t/c mkg, refrig], lift, conf fac, ⊠, pool-heated, spa, 24hr reception, rm serv (24hr), secure park (valet), cots, non smoking flr (4). **RO ♦ $140 - $305, ♦♦ $140 - $305, ◊ $25, Suite RO ♦♦ $240 - $600, ◊ $25**, AE BC DC MC VI, ♿.

Self Catering Accommodation

★★★★☆ **Quest Rose Hill**, (Apt), 8 Hope St, ☎ 02 9687 7711, fax 02 9687 7722, (Multi-stry gr fl), 53 apts acc up to 6, (1, 2 & 3 bedrm), [shwr, tlt, a/c, tel, TV, video, clock radio, t/c mkg, refrig, cook fac, micro, d/wash, toaster, ldry, blkts, linen, pillows], w/mach, dryer, conf fac, pool, bbq, c/park (undercover), cots, non smoking units (40). **D ♦♦ $166 - $245, ◊ $17**, AE BC DC EFT MC VI.

SYDNEY - RUSHCUTTERS BAY NSW 2011

Pop Part of Sydney, (3km E Sydney), See map on page 56, ref B1. Pretty harbour inlet to the east of Elizabeth Bay, comprising part of what's referred to as Kings Cross. Tennis.

Hotels/Motels

★★★★☆ **Rushcutters Harbourside Sydney**, (LMH), 100 Bayswater Rd, 200m E of Kings Cross PO, ☎ 02 8353 8988, fax 02 8353 8999, (Multi-stry), 260 units [shwr, bath, tlt, hairdry, a/c, elec blkts, tel, TV, movie-fee, clock radio, t/c mkg, refrig, mini bar], lift, ldry, iron, iron brd, conf fac, ⊠, pool-heated, spa, steam rm, 24hr reception, rm serv, courtesy transfer, ☎, plygr, gym, tennis-fee, cots-fee, non smoking rms (3). **RO ♦♦ $187 - $660**, ch con, AE BC DC JCB MC VI.

★★★ **The Bayside Hotel**, (LH), 85 New South Head Rd, 300m W of PO, ☎ 02 9327 8511, fax 02 9327 7808, (Multi-stry), 99 rms [shwr, bath (44), tlt, hairdry, a/c, tel, TV, clock radio, t/c mkg, refrig], lift, ldry, ⊠, cots. **D ♦♦ $139.50 - $157.50, ◊ $22, 24 rooms ★★★☆**, AE BC DC MC VI.

SYDNEY - RYDE NSW 2112

Pop Part of Sydney, (13km W Sydney), See map on page 56, ref D5.

Hotels/Motels

★★★★ **The Blaxland Accom & Conference Complex**, (LMH), 250 Blaxland Rd, mob 0417 295 289, fax 1300 363 067, (Multi-stry gr fl), 24 units [shwr, tlt, a/c, elec blkts, tel, TV, video, clock radio, t/c mkg, refrig, doonas], lift, ldry, conf fac, ⊠, bbq, rm serv, c/park (undercover), cots-fee, non smoking property. **RO ♦♦ $99 - $165, ◊ $15**, ch con, AE BC DC MC VI.

★★★☆ **Metro Motor Inn Ryde**, (M), Cnr Victoria Rd & Bowden St, 2km E of PO, ☎ 02 9807 4022, fax 02 9807 4020, (2 stry), 39 units [shwr, tlt, a/c, heat, elec blkts, tel, TV, movie, clock radio, t/c mkg, refrig], ldry, conv fac, ⊠, pool, bbq, rm serv, cots. **RO ♦♦ $99 - $125**, ch con, 19 units ★★★☆. AE BC DC EFT MC VI.

★★★ **Royal Hotel**, (LH), 68 Blaxland Rd, ☎ 02 9809 5956, fax 02 9809 2971, 12 rms (1 suite) [a/c, c/fan (5), TV (6), t/c mkg (6), refrig (6)], shared fac (11), bathrm (1), ldry, ✗, t/c mkg shared, dinner to unit, ☎, cots. **RO ♦ $60 - $80, ♦♦ $70 - $90, ◊ $15, Suite RO $90 - $110**, ch con, AE BC EFT MC VI.

Self Catering Accommodation

★★★ **The Maharlika Garden Serviced Apartments**, (SA), 17 William St, 400m N of PO, ☎ 02 9807 8695, fax 02 9807 1997, (Multi-stry gr fl), 52 serv apts acc up to 4, [shwr, tlt, hairdry, a/c, tel, TV, video-fee, clock radio, t/c mkg, refrig, cook fac, toaster, doonas, linen], ldry, iron, iron brd, bbq, ☎, cots. **D $80 - $140, W $490 - $840**, pen con, AE BC DC EFT MC VI.

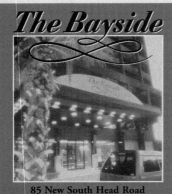

SYDNEY - SANS SOUCI NSW 2219

Pop Part of Sydney, (17km S Sydney), See map on page 56, ref D7. Suburb on a peninsula in southern Sydney between Kogarah and Botany Bays.

Hotels/Motels

★★★☆ **Sans Souci Motor Inn**, (M), 410 Rocky Point Rd, 320m S of PO, ☎ 02 9529 4600, fax 02 9529 4461, (2 stry gr fl), 28 units [shwr, spa bath (2), tlt, a/c, tel, TV, video, movie, clock radio, t/c mkg, refrig], ldry, pool, spa. RO ♦ $110, ♦♦ $120, ♦♦♦ $130, AE BC DC EFT MC VI.

SYDNEY - ST CLAIR NSW 2759

Pop Part of Sydney, (44km W Sydney), See map on page 56, ref B5. Western suburb of Sydney near St Marys and Penrith.

Hotels/Motels

★★★ **Blue Cattle Dog Hotel Motel**, (LMH), Cnr Mamre & Banks Dve, 3km S of PO, ☎ 02 9670 3050, fax 02 9670 3198, (2 stry), 18 units [shwr, spa bath (1), tlt, hairdry, a/c, tel, TV, clock radio, t/c mkg, refrig, mini bar, toaster], iron, conv fac, ✉, sauna, bbq, dinner to unit, c/park (undercover), ✆, gym, cots-fee, non smoking units (6). **BLB** ♦ $104.50, ♦♦ $121, ◊ $11 - $27.50, ch con, AE BC DC EFT MC VI.

SYDNEY - ST LEONARDS NSW 2065

Pop Part of Sydney, (6km N Sydney), See map on page 56, ref A1. A blend of commercial, business and residential areas situated on Sydney's lower north shore.

Hotels/Motels

AAA *TOURISM Special Rates* ★★★★ **Mercure Hotel St Leonards, Sydney**, (M), 194 Pacific Hwy, 300m W of Royal North Shore Hospital, ☎ 02 9439 6000, fax 02 9439 6442, (Multi-stry), 66 units (1 suite) [shwr, tlt, hairdry, a/c, tel, TV, clock radio, t/c mkg, refrig, mini bar], lift, ldry, conv fac, ✉, pool, bbq, 24hr reception, rm serv, dinner to unit, c/park (undercover), gym, cots, non smoking units (avail). RO ♦♦ $122 - $185, AE BC DC EFT MC VI.

★★★☆ **Greenwich Inn**, (M), 196 Pacific Hwy, 300m W of Royal North Shore Hospital, ☎ 02 9906 3277, fax 02 9436 2585, (Multi-stry gr fl), 29 units [shwr, spa bath (6), tlt, hairdry, a/c, heat, tel, TV, clock radio, t/c mkg, refrig], ldry, business centre, ✉, rm serv, dinner to unit, c/park (undercover), cots. RO ♦ $120 - $150, ♦♦ $125 - $160, ♦♦♦ $140 - $170, ◊ $10, ch con, 6 units ★★★★. AE BC DC MC VI.

Driver fatigue is a killer

While speed and alcohol are well known killers on the road, driver fatigue can be just as deadly, because of the subtle and insidious way it creeps up on a driver.

Nobody is immune to fatigue. To help in the fight against fatigue:

- Get a good night's sleep before the trip, and never drive when you would normally be asleep (not late at night or very early in the morning).
- Take rest breaks every two hours, or as soon as you feel drowsy.
- Do some light exercise and enjoy a light snack during your breaks.
- Don't pack too many driving hours into a day.
- Share the driving.

473-479 Liverpool Road
South Strathfield
NSW 2135

SYDNEY - ST MARYS NSW 2760

Pop 19,826. (47km W Sydney), See map on page 56, ref B5. Outer suburb of Sydney. Bowls, Golf, Swimming.
Hotels/Motels
★★★★ **St Marys Park View Hotel-Motel**, (LMH), 465 Great Western Hwy, ☎ 02 9623 1227, fax 02 9673 4667, (2 stry gr fl), 31 units [shwr, bath, spa bath (5), tlt, a/c, tel, TV, clock radio, t/c mkg, refrig], ldry, ✉, pool, bbq, ✆, cots, non smoking rms. **BLB** ♦ **$120 - $160**, ♦♦ **$120 - $160**, ♦ **$20**, ch con, AE BC DC EFT MC VI.

SYDNEY - ST PETERS NSW 2044

Pop Part of Sydney, (7km S Sydney), See map on page 56, ref A2. Inner Sydney suburb to the south of Newtown.
Hotels/Motels
★ **Motel Formule 1**, (M), 178 Princes Hwy, ☎ 02 9519 0685, fax 02 9519 0684, (Multi-stry gr fl), 80 units [shwr, tlt, a/c, TV], ✆, non smoking units (30). **RO** ♦ **$59**, ♦♦ **$59**, ♦♦♦ **$59**, AE BC DC EFT MC VI.

SYDNEY - STRATHFIELD SOUTH NSW 2136

Pop Part of Sydney, (14km W Sydney), See map on page 56, ref C6. Small suburb next to Strathfield in western Sydney. Bowls, Golf.
Hotels/Motels
★ **Motel Formule 1**, (M), 626 Hume Hwy, ☎ 02 9642 0666, fax 02 9642 0600, (Multi-stry gr fl), 80 units [shwr, tlt, a/c, TV], ✆, non smoking units (30). **RO** ♦ **$59**, ♦♦ **$59**, ♦♦♦ **$59**, AE BC DC EFT MC VI.

SYDNEY - STRATHFIELD NSW 2135

Pop Part of Sydney, (14km W Sydney), See map on page 56, ref C6.
Hotels/Motels

 ★★★★ **Spanish Inn Motor Lodge**, (M), 473 Liverpool Rd, opposite South Strathfield PO, ☎ 02 9642 8555, fax 02 9642 1885, (2 stry gr fl), 30 units [shwr, bath (4), tlt, a/c, elec blkts, tel, TV, clock radio, t/c mkg, refrig], ldry, conv fac, ✉ (Mon to Sat), spa (1), cots. **RO** ♦ **$118**, ♦♦ **$118**, ♦ **$20**, AE BC DC JCB MC MCH MP VI.
Operator Comment: See our advertisement at left.

 ★★★☆ **Town and Country Motel**, (M), 401 Liverpool Rd, 200m N of Enfield PO, ☎ 02 9642 0444, fax 02 9742 5486, (2 stry gr fl), 45 units (3 suites) [shwr, spa bath (1), tlt, a/c, tel, TV, video, clock radio, t/c mkg, refrig], ldry, lounge, conv fac, ✉, pool, spa, 24hr reception, rm serv, ✆, cots-fee, non smoking units (22). **BLB** ♦ **$126.50 - $198**, ♦♦ **$126.50 - $198**, ♦ **$22, Suite D $198**, ch con, AE BC BTC DC MC MP VI.

SYDNEY - SUMMER HILL NSW 2130

Pop art of Sydney, (10km W Sydney), See map on page 56, ref A2.
Hotels/Motels
★★☆ **Marco Polo Motor Inn**, (M), 42 Parramatta Rd, 500m N of railway station, ☎ 02 9798 4311, fax 02 9798 4466, (Multi-stry), 49 units [shwr, tlt, a/c, tel, TV, clock radio, t/c mkg, refrig], ✉ (Mon to Sat), c/park (undercover). **RO** ♦ **$95 - $105**, ♦♦ **$95 - $105**, ♦♦♦ **$110 - $115**, ♦ **$15**, ch con, AE BC DC MC VI.
Operator Comment: See our advertisement at top of page.

SYDNEY - SURRY HILLS NSW 2010

Pop Part of Sydney, (2km S Sydney), See map on page 56, ref B2.
Hotels/Motels

 ★★★★☆ **Furama Hotel Central**, (LMH), 28 Albion St, ☎ 02 9213 3820, fax 02 9281 0222, (Multi-stry), 270 units [shwr, bath, tlt, hairdry, a/c, tel, fax, TV, movie, clock radio, t/c mkg, refrig, mini bar], lift, conf fac, ✉, cafe, pool indoor heated, sauna, spa, 24hr reception, rm serv, dinner to unit, secure park, gym, non smoking rms (38). **RO** ♦ **$130**, ♦♦ **$130**, ch con, AE BC DC JCB MC VI, ⚷.

★★★☆ **Cambridge Park Inn International**, (LH), 212 Riley St, 2km SE of GPO, ☎ 02 9212 1111, fax 02 9281 1981, (Multi-stry), 170 rms (52 suites) [shwr, bath, tlt, a/c, tel, fax, TV, movie, clock radio, t/c mkg, refrig, mini bar], lift, ldry, conf fac, ✉, pool indoor heated, sauna, spa, 24hr reception, rm serv, secure park, gym, cots. **BB** ♦ **$137.50**, ♦♦ **$137.50**, ♦ **$11 - $27.50, Suite BB $159.50**, ch con, 8 units ★★★. AE BC DC JCB MC VI.

★★★ **Park Lodge Hotel**, (LMH), 747 South Dowling St, ☎ 02 9318 2393, fax 02 9318 2513, (Multi-stry gr fl), 20 units [shwr, tlt, hairdry, a/c, fan, heat, elec blkts, tel, TV, video, clock radio, refrig], ldry, iron brd, 24hr reception. RO ♀♀ **$82 - $154**, ⌷ **$22**, ch con, Light breakfast available. AE BC DC EFT MC VI, ⚅.

★★☆ **City Crown Lodge International**, (M), 289 Crown St, 1.5km SE of GPO, mob 0418 474 438, fax 02 9360 7760, (Multi-stry gr fl), 28 units [shwr, tlt, c/fan, heat, tel, TV, movie, clock radio, t/c mkg, refrig, cook fac (1)], ldry, c/park-fee. RO ♀ **$100**, ♀♀ **$100**, ♀♀♀ **$120**, ch con, AE BC DC JCB MC MCH VI.

★★☆ **Royal Exhibition**, (LH), 86 Chalmers St, 200m E of Central Railway Station, ☎ 02 9698 2607, fax 02 9690 1714, (2 stry), 16 rms [shwr, tlt, a/c, elec blkts, fax, TV, clock radio, t/c mkg, refrig], ✕, ☏, cots. RO ♀ **$80**, ♀♀ **$90 - $100**, ♀♀♀ **$125**, BC EFT MC VI.

Self Catering Accommodation

★★★★☆ **Medina on Crown**, (SA), 359 Crown St, 1.5km SW of CBD, ☎ 02 9360 6666, fax 02 9361 5965, 85 serv apts [shwr, bath, spa bath (16), tlt, hairdry, a/c, tel, TV, video, clock radio, t/c mkg, refrig, cook fac, micro, d/wash, toaster, ldry (in unit), blkts, doonas, linen, pillows], lift, w/mach, dryer, iron, iron brd, conv fac, ✕, pool, sauna, spa, bbq, 24hr reception, dinner to unit, c/park (garage), ☏, gym, tennis, cots, non smoking rms (16). D **$195 - $275**, AE BC DC MC VI, ⚅.

SYDNEY - SUTHERLAND NSW 2232

Pop Part of Sydney, (26km S Sydney), See map on page 56, ref C7.
Large urban centre between the Georges River and Port Hacking.

★★★☆ **Sutherland Motel**, (M), 2 Aldgate St, 1.5km SE of PO, ☎ 02 9545 1000, fax 02 9545 1065, (2 stry), 27 units [shwr, tlt, hairdry, a/c, heat, tel, TV, video (avail)-fee, clock radio, t/c mkg, refrig, toaster], ldry, ✕, pool, cots-fee. RO ♀ **$105 - $130**, ♀♀ **$105 - $130**, ⌷ **$10**, Some rooms of a lower rating, AE BC DC EFT MC VI, ⚅.

SYDNEY - SYLVANIA NSW 2224

Pop Part of Sydney, (21km S Sydney), See map on page 56, ref C7.
★★★ **ABA Motel**, (M), 131 Princes Highway, Opposite Southgate Shopping Centre, ☎ 02 9522 7388, fax 02 9522 5918, 20 units [shwr, tlt, hairdry, a/c, tel, TV, clock radio, t/c mkg, refrig, micro (1)], ldry, cots, non smoking units (7). RO ♀ **$96 - $118**, ♀♀ **$97 - $118**, ⌷ **$10**, ch con, AE BC EFT MC VI.

SYDNEY - SYLVANIA HEIGHTS NSW 2224

Pop Part of Sydney, (23km S Sydney), See map on page 56, ref C7.
Bushland suburb situated in the hills above Sylvania. Boating, Golf, Scenic Drives.

Hotels/Motels

★★★☆ **Abcot Inn**, (M), 410 Princes Hwy, opp Bates Dve, ☎ 02 9544 6444, or 02 9522 0444, fax 02 9522 4548, 46 units [shwr, bath (12), spa bath (13), tlt, hairdry, a/c, tel, TV, clock radio, t/c mkg, refrig, micro (3)], ldry, conv fac, ⊠ (6 nights), bar, pool, dinner to unit, cots-fee. RO ♀ **$80 - $180**, ♀♀ **$95 - $180**, ⌷ **$15**, ch con, 6 rooms of a lower rating. AE BC DC MC VI.

SYDNEY - TERREY HILLS NSW 2084

Pop Part of Sydney, (27km N Sydney), See map on page 56, ref D4.
Large suburb in the far north of Sydney that is surrounded by Ku-ring-gai Chase and Garigal National Parks. Bush Walking, Scenic Drives.

Hotels/Motels

★★★☆ **Checkers Resort & Conference Centre**, (M), 331 Mona Vale Rd, 200m E from Forest Way, ☎ 02 9450 2422, fax 02 9450 2778, (2 stry gr fl), 43 units [shwr, tlt, a/c, heat, tel, cable tv, clock radio, t/c mkg, refrig], ldry, conv fac, ⊠, pool, sauna, spa, bbq, rm serv, gym, tennis, cots. RO ♀♀ **$107.80**, ⌷ **$22**, ch con, AE BC DC EFT MC VI, ⚅.

SYDNEY - ULTIMO NSW 2007

Pop Part of Sydney, (2km SW Sydney), See map on page 56, ref A2.
Suburb of Sydney.

Hotels/Motels

★★★☆ **Hotel Unilodge Sydney**, (M), Cnr Broadway & Bay Sts, 2.5km S of City GPO, ☎ 02 9338 5000, fax 02 9338 5111, (Multi-stry), 115 units [shwr, tlt, a/c, fan, heat, tel, TV, clock radio, t/c mkg, refrig, micro, toaster], lift, ldry, rec rm, conv fac, pool indoor heated, sauna, spa, bbq, ☏, gym, cots. RO ♀ **$140 - $165**, ♀♀ **$140 - $165**, **$770 - $1,120**, ch con, AE BC DC MC VI.

★★★☆ **Mercure Hotel Lawson City West**, (LH), 383-389 Bulwara Rd, 2km SW of GPO, 200m W of Darling Harbour, ☎ 02 9211 1499, fax 02 9281 3764, (Multi-stry), 96 rms [shwr, bath, tlt, hairdry, a/c, tel, TV, clock radio, t/c mkg, refrig, mini bar], lift, iron, iron brd, lounge, conv fac, ⊠, 24hr reception, rm serv, c/park (undercover), cots, non smoking rms (70). BB ♀ **$155**, ♀♀ **$170**, ch con, AE BC DC JCB MC VI.

★☆ **The Lord Wolseley Hotel**, (LH), 265 Bulwara Rd, 500m from Darling Harbour, ☎ 02 9660 1736, fax 02 9692 0698, (Multi-stry), 9 rms [ensuite (1), c/fan, TV, clock radio, t/c mkg], ✕. BLB ♀ **$66 - $88**, ♀♀ **$93 - $115.50**, EFT.

B&B's/Guest Houses

★★★ **Vulcan Hotel Darling Harbour**, (B&B), 500 Wattle St, cnr Mary Ann St, ☎ 02 9211 3283, fax 02 9212 7439, (Multi-stry), 22 rms [heat, elec blkts], iron, lounge (TV), cook fac, t/c mkg shared, meals avail (for groups), ☏, non smoking property, 10 rooms ★, AE BC MC VI.

SYDNEY - VINEYARD NSW 2765

Pop 400. (52km NW Sydney), See map on page 56, ref B4.
Semi-rural area south-east of Windsor.

Hotels/Motels

★★★☆ **Gateway Motel Vineyard**, (M), Cnr Windsor & Boundary Rd, 6km SE of PO, ☎ 02 9627 6022, fax 02 9627 6035, (2 stry gr fl), 21 units [shwr, tlt, hairdry, a/c, tel, TV, clock radio, t/c mkg, refrig], iron, iron brd, ⊠, plygr, cots, non smoking units (4). RO ♀ **$85.90**, ♀♀ **$95 - $105**, ⌷ **$15**, AE BC EFT MC VI.

Operator Comment: See our display advertisement on page 103.

★★★ **Alexander The Great**, (M), 317 Windsor Rd, 2km E of Windsor PO, ☎ 02 4577 5555, fax 02 4577 3948, (2 stry gr fl), 25 units [shwr, tlt, a/c, tel, TV, video (avail), clock radio, t/c mkg, refrig, toaster], ldry, conv fac, ⊠, pool, dinner to unit, cots-fee. RO ♀ **$55 - $65**, ♀♀ **$60 - $70**, ⌷ **$10**, AE BC DC EFT MC MP VI.

SYDNEY - VINEYARD continued...

★★☆ **Tourmaline Hotel Motor Inn**, (LMH), Cnr Boundary & Windsor Rd, 6km SE of PO, ☎ 02 9627 1754, or 02 9627 2281, fax 02 9627 2790, (2 stry), 16 units [shwr, tlt, a/c, TV, clock radio, t/c mkg, refrig, toaster], lounge (TV), ⊠, ✆, plygr, cots. **RO** ♦ **$55 - $60**, ♦♦ **$65 - $70**, ⑂ **$15**, Units 1 to 7 not yet rated. AE BC DC EFT MC VI.

SYDNEY - WAHROONGA NSW 2076

Pop Part of Sydney, (23km N Sydney), See map on page 56, ref D4. Bushy, upper north shore suburb stretching from Ku-ring-gai Chase National Park down almost as far as Lane Cove River National Park. Bowls.

Hotels/Motels

GOLDEN CHAIN ★★★☆ **Ascot Motor Inn**, (M), 18 Ingram Rd, Pearces Cnr, ☎ 02 9487 3355, fax 02 9489 7559, 35 units (2 suites) [shwr, tlt, a/c, tel, TV, clock radio, t/c mkg, refrig], ldry, conv fac, ⊠, pool, rm serv, dinner to unit, courtesy transfer, cots-fee, non smoking units (12). **RO** ♦ **$99**, ♦♦ **$112 - $120**, ⑂ **$16**, **Suite D $169 - $189**, ch con, AE BC DC MC VI, ⅋⌂.

★★★ **Wahroonga Spanish**, (M), 33 Pacific Hwy, 13km S of Hornsby PO, ☎ 02 9487 3122, fax 02 9489 7786, (2 stry gr fl), 26 units [shwr, bath (1), tlt, hairdry, a/c, tel, TV, clock radio, t/c mkg, refrig, toaster], ldry, iron, ⊠, pool, bbq, dinner to unit, cots. **D** ♦ **$85**, ♦♦ **$95**, ♦♦♦ **$105**, 11 units ★★. AE BC DC EFT MC VI.

SYDNEY - WAITARA NSW 2077

Pop Part of Sydney, (23km N Sydney), See map on page 56, ref D4.

★☆ **Blue Gum**, (LH), 55 Pacific Hwy, 100m N of railway station, ☎ 02 9489 3220, or 02 9489 4205, fax 02 9489 3953, (2 stry), 11 rms [bath, hairdry, TV, t/c mkg], shared fac (7 rooms), conv fac, ⊠, ✆. **BLB** ♦ **$70**, ♦♦ **$80 - $95**, AE BC MC VI.

SYDNEY - WARRIEWOOD NSW 2102

Pop Nominal, (30km N Sydney), See map on page 56, ref E4.

B&B's/Guest Houses

★★★★☆ **By The Beach Bed & Breakfast**, (B&B), 126 Narrabeen Park Pde, Warriewood Beach 2102, 2km S of Mona Vale PO, ☎ 02 9979 1711, fax 02 9979 1722, 3 rms [ensuite, spa bath (1), a/c-cool, cent heat, elec blkts, tel, TV, video (1), clock radio, t/c mkg, refrig, ldry, doonas], ⊠, bbq, c/park. **BLB** ♦ **$85 - $110**, ♦♦ **$105 - $170**, weekly con, BC MC VI.

SYDNEY - WARWICK FARM NSW 2170

Pop Part of Sydney, (30km SW Sydney), See map on page 56, ref B6. South-western suburb and the venue of one of Sydney's major racecourses. Horse Racing.

Hotels/Motels

★★★★ **The Sunnybrook Hotel & Convention Centre**, (LH), 355 Hume Hwy, opposite racecourse, ☎ 02 9726 1222, fax 02 9728 4661, (Multi-stry gr fl), 138 rms (9 suites) [shwr, bath, spa bath (2), tlt, hairdry, a/c, heat, tel, TV, movie, clock radio, t/c mkg, refrig, mini bar], lift, ldry, iron, conv fac, ⊠, bar, pool, 24hr reception, rm serv, tennis-fee, cots. **RO** ♦ **$132**, ♦♦ **$132**, ⑂ **$22**, **Suite D $165**, ch con, AE BC DC JCB MC VI, ⅋⌂.

★ **Warwick Farm Grandstand Motel**, (M), 7 Hume Hwy, ☎ 02 9602 0100, fax 02 9602 0988, (2 stry gr fl), 37 units [shwr, spa bath (1), tlt, a/c, tel, TV, movie, t/c mkg, refrig], ldry, 24hr reception, cots. **RO** ♦ **$80**, ♦♦ **$90**, ⑂ **$20**, AE BC DC EFT MC VI.

SYDNEY - WENTWORTHVILLE NSW 2145

Pop Part of Sydney, (28km W Sydney), See map on page 56, ref C5. Busy residential area on the Cumberland Highway west of Parramatta.

Hotels/Motels

Motel Formule 1, (M), 377 Great Western Hwy, 3km W of Parramatta, ☎ 02 9769 1240, fax 02 9769 1250, (2 stry gr fl), 101 units [shwr, tlt, a/c, TV], ✗, ✆, non smoking units (50). **RO** ♦ **$59**, ♦♦ **$59**, ♦♦♦ **$59**, AE BC EFT MC VI, ⅋⌂.

SYDNEY - WEST RYDE NSW 2114

Pop Part of Sydney, (14km NW Sydney), See map on page 56, ref C5. Residential suburb near the Parramatta River west of Ryde. Golf.

Hotels/Motels

★★★★ **West Ryde Motor Inn**, (M), 1188 Victoria Rd, 1.5km W of PO, ☎ 02 9858 5333, fax 02 9874 0231, (2 stry gr fl), 41 units [shwr, tlt, a/c, tel, TV, movie, clock radio, t/c mkg, refrig], ldry, ⊠, pool, bbq, rm serv, dinner to unit, ✆, cots. **RO** ♦ **$115 - $135**, ♦♦ **$115 - $135**, ⑂ **$15**, 20 units ★★★☆, AE BC DC EFT MC MP VI.

SYDNEY - WESTMEAD NSW 2145

Pop Part of Sydney, (26km W Sydney), See map on page 56, ref C5. Western suburb between Blacktown and Parramatta, home of the Westmead Hospital and Westmead Children's Hospital. Golf, Squash.

Hotels/Motels

★★★☆ **Wesley Lodge**, (M), 175 Hawkesbury Rd, 100m E of PO, ☎ 02 9635 1233, fax 02 9893 7018, (2 stry gr fl), 57 units [shwr, bath (4), tlt, a/c, elec blkts, tel, TV, movie, clock radio, t/c mkg, refrig, cook fac (23), micro (20)], ldry, lounge, conv fac, ✗, dinner to unit, gym, cots, non smoking rms (43). **BB** ♦ **$100 - $120**, ♦♦ **$110 - $130**, ⑂ **$5 - $10**, ch con, AE BC DC MC VI, ⅋⌂.

SYDNEY - WILBERFORCE NSW 2756

Pop 1,950. (62km NW Sydney), See map on page 56, ref B3. Historic, rural area north of the Hawkesbury River beyond Windsor. Boating, Fishing, Horse Riding, Swimming, Water Skiing.

Hotels/Motels

★ **Tropicana Licensed Motel Hotel**, (LMH), Rose St, 1km NW of PO, ☎ 02 4575 1603, fax 02 4575 1379, 16 units [shwr, tlt, a/c, TV, clock radio, t/c mkg, refrig, toaster], ⊠, bbq, ✆. **RO** ♦ **$53**, ♦♦ **$53**, ♦♦♦ **$63**, ⑂ **$10**, ch con, BC DC MC VI.

SYDNEY - WINDSOR NSW 2756

Pop Part of Richmond-Win, (56km W Sydney), See map on page 56, ref B4. Pretty, historic town on the Hawkesbury River. Boating, Fishing, Horse Riding, Swimming, Water Skiing.

Hotels/Motels

★★★★ **Hawkesbury Lodge**, (LH), 61 Richmond Rd, 2km W of PO, ☎ 02 4577 4222, fax 02 4577 6939, (2 stry gr fl), 104 rms [shwr, bath (66), spa bath (44), tlt, hairdry, a/c, elec blkts, tel, cable tv, clock radio, t/c mkg, refrig, mini bar], ldry, iron, iron brd, lounge, conv fac, ⊠, pool indoor heated, sauna, spa, 24hr reception, rm serv, golf, tennis, cots, non smoking rms (30). **DBB** ♦♦ **$291 - $392**, **RO** ♦ **$164 - $215**, ♦♦ **$164 - $215**, ⑂ **$30**, ch con, 30 rooms ★★★★☆. AE BC DC MC VI, ⅋⌂.

★★★ **The Windsor Terrace**, (M), 47 George St, 400m NE of PO, ☎ 02 4577 5999, fax 02 4577 2708, (Multi-stry gr fl), 24 units [shwr, tlt, a/c, elec blkts, tel, TV, clock radio, t/c mkg, refrig, toaster], ldry, cots-fee. **RO** ♦ **$89**, ♦♦ **$99**, ⑂ **$12**, AE BC MC VI.

B&B's/Guest Houses
★★★★ **Rivers Edge B & B**, (GH), 39 George St, 1km N of PO, ☎ 02 4577 3149, fax 02 4577 2684, 1 rm [shwr, tlt, a/c-cool, heat, TV, clock radio, t/c mkg, refrig, micro, toaster], non smoking property. BLB ╫ $100, ╫╫ $100 - $150, AE BC DC EFT MC VI.
★★★☆ **The Doctors House B & B**, (B&B), 3 Thompson Square, ☎ 02 4577 8088, fax 02 4577 8004, (Multi-stry gr fl), 6 rms (1 suite) [shwr, tlt, hairdry, a/c, clock radio, t/c mkg, refrig (bar) (6)], iron, iron brd, TV rm, lounge, lounge firepl, cots-fee, non smoking property. BB ╫ $85, ╫╫ $110 - $195, Dinner by arrangement, AE BC DC MC VI.

SYDNEY - WINSTON HILLS NSW 2153

Pop Part of Sydney, (28km W Sydney), See map on page 56, ref C5.
★★☆ **Winston Hills Hotel**, (LH), Cnr Caroline Chisholm Dve & Junction Rd, adjacent to Winstons Hills Shopping Centre, ☎ 02 9624 4500, fax 02 9838 8418, 6 rms [shwr, tlt, a/c, tel, TV, radio, t/c mkg, refrig], ⊠. RO ╫ $100, AE BC EFT MC VI.

SYDNEY - WISEMANS FERRY NSW 2775

Pop Part of Sydney, (97km NW Sydney), See map on page 56, ref C2.
Hotels/Motels
★★★☆ **The Retreat at Wisemans**, (M), Previously Wisemans Ferry Country Retreat. Resort, Old Northern Rd, 50m N of PO, ☎ 02 4566 4422, fax 02 4566 4613, 54 units (2 suites) [shwr, spa bath (2), tlt, hairdry, a/c, tel, TV, clock radio, t/c mkg, refrig], iron, iron brd, conv fac, ⊠, pool (salt water), plygr, golf, tennis. D $110 - $150, Suite D $160 - $210, BC EFT MC VI, ⅋⚬.

Self Catering Accommodation
★★★★★ **Queen Victoria Inn**, (House), Previously Victoria Inn. Heritage. No facilities for children under 16. 177 Settlers Rd, 5km NW of PO, ☎ 02 4566 4554, fax 02 9879 5224, (2 stry gr fl), 1 house, acc up to 6 (3 bedrm). [shwr, bath, tlt, fan, heat, elec blkts, TV, video, CD, t/c mkg, refig, cook fac, micro, toaster, blkts, doonas, linen, pillows, towels], lounge firepl, bbq, breakfast ingredients, non smoking property. BB $450 - $1,195, W $3,445. Min book applies, AE BC MC VI.

Other Accommodation
Able Houseboats, (Hbt), Hawkesbury River, ☎ 02 4566 4308, or 02 4566 4299, fax 02 4566 4306, 25 houseboats acc up to 12, [shwr, tlt, TV, video, radio, refrig, cook fac, linen reqd-fee]. W $820 - $3,520.

SYDNEY - WOOLLAHRA NSW 2025

Pop Part of Sydney, (5km E Sydney), See map on page 56, ref B2. Wealthy, elegant suburb in Sydney's inner east.
B&B's/Guest Houses

FLAG
FLAG CHOICE HOTELS

★★★★ **The Historic Hughenden Boutique Hotel**, (GH), c1870. 14 Queen St, ☎ 02 9363 4863, fax 02 9362 0398, 36 rms (5 suites) [shwr, tlt, a/c, tel, TV, t/c mkg, refrig], ldry, conf fac, lounge firepl, ✕, ⊠, cots. BB ╫ $148, ╫╫ $174 - $284, ⅋ $30, ch con, AE MC VI.

Woollahra Terraces, (PH), 52 Edgecliff Rd, ☎ 02 9389 9777, fax 02 9389 6091, (Multi-stry gr fl), 31 rms [TV-fee, video-fee, t/c mkg-fee, refrig-fee, micro-fee], ldry, ✕, ✆, non smoking rms. D ⅋ $30, $110 - $200, AE BC DC EFT MC VI.

SYDNEY - WOOLLOOMOOLOO NSW 2011

Pop Part of Sydney, (1km E Sydney), See map on page 56, ref B1.
Hotels/Motels
★★★★☆ **The Sydney Boulevard**, (LH), 90 William St, 1km W of Australian Museum, ☎ 02 9383 7222, fax 02 9356 3786, (Multi-stry), 271 rms (6 suites) [shwr, bath, tlt, hairdry, a/c, tel, TV, movie, clock radio, t/c mkg, refrig, mini bar], lift, ldry-fee, iron, iron brd, business centre, conv fac, ⊠, bar, 24hr reception, rm serv, c/park-fee, cots, non smoking rms (avail). D $176 - $198, AE BC DC MC VI,
Operator Comment: See our colour advertisement under Sydney - Page 61.

★★★★☆ **W Hotel at Woolloomooloo**, (LH), 6 Cowper Wharf Rd, 2km N of Kings Cross PO, ☎ 02 9331 9000, fax 02 9331 9031, (Multi-stry gr fl), 104 rms (2 suites) [shwr, tlt, a/c-cool, cent heat, tel, TV, video-fee, clock radio, t/c mkg, refrig, doonas], lift, conf fac, ⊠, pool indoor heated, spa, rm serv (24hr), secure park (undercover), ✆, cots, non smoking rms (66). RO ╫ $324 - $513, ╫╫ $324 - $513, ⅋ $43, Suite RO $1,080, AE BC DC JCB MC VI.

★★★★☆ **Woolloomooloo Waters Apartment**, (LH), 88 Dowling St, off Cowper Wharf Rd, 250m W of Potts Point, ☎ 02 8356 1500, fax 02 9356 1500, (Multi-stry), 70 rms [shwr, bath, tlt, hairdry, a/c, tel, TV, clock radio, t/c mkg, refrig, mini bar, cook fac, micro], ldry, ⊠, bar, pool-indoor, sauna, spa, rm serv, secure park, cots. D ╫╫ $175 - $210, ⅋ $25, AE BC DC JCB MC VI.

GOLDEN CHAIN

★★★ **Mariners Court Hotel**, (M), 44-50 McElhone St, 200m N of Botanic Gardens, ☎ 02 9358 3888, fax 02 9357 4670, (Multi-stry), 40 units [shwr, tlt, fan, c/fan, heat, tel, TV, clock radio, t/c mkg, refrig], lift, ldry, rec rm, business centre, bbq, ✆, cots-fee, non smoking units (40). BLB ╫ $121, ╫╫ $121, ⅋ $10, ch con, fam con, pen con, AE BC DC EFT MC VI, ⅋⚬.

B&B's/Guest Houses
★★ **Harbour City Hotel**, (PH), 50 Sir John Young Cres, 400m E of Hyde Park, ☎ 02 9380 2922, fax 02 9380 2963, (Multi-stry gr fl), 13 rms [shwr (4), tlt (4), c/fan, heat, TV (9)], lift, ldry, rec rm, lounge (TV), ✕, cook fac, t/c mkg shared, 24hr reception, courtesy transfer, ✆, non smoking flr (4). D $73, BC EFT MC VI.

SYDNEY - WOOLWICH NSW 2110

Pop Part of Sydney, (6km W Sydney), See map on page 56, ref A1. Small suburb next to Hunters Hill, a genteel place on the peninsula that separates the Lane Cove and Parramatta Rivers.

B&B's/Guest Houses

★★★★ **Hunters Hill B&B**, (B&B), 4 Margaret St, Hunters Hill 2110, 150m N of Marina, ☎ 02 9816 1506, fax 02 9817 6891, (2 stry), 1 rm [shwr, tlt, hairdry, heat, elec blkts, TV, radio, t/c mkg, refrig], lounge (TV), bbq, non smoking rms. **BB ♦ $95, ♦♦ $140,** Min book applies.

End of Sydney & Suburbs

ABERDEEN NSW 2336

Pop 1,750. (308km N Sydney), See map on pages 52/53, ref H4. Small town on the Hunter River between Muswellbrook and Scone that dates from the 1830s. Bowls, Golf, Tennis, Water Skiing. See also Muswellbrook & Scone.

Hotels/Motels

★★★☆ **Aberdeen Motel**, (M), 205 New England Hwy, 600m S of Railway Station, ☎ 02 6543 7999, fax 02 6543 8120, 15 units [shwr, spa bath (2), tlt, hairdry, a/c, elec blkts, tel, TV, clock radio, t/c mkg, refrig, toaster], ldry, iron, iron brd, pool (salt water), bbq, dinner to unit, plygr, cots, non smoking units (5). **RO ♦ $62.70 - $73.70, ♦♦ $71.50 - $82.50, ♦ $13.20,** AE BC DC MC VI.

ABERMAIN NSW 2326

Pop Nominal, (153km N Sydney), See map on page 55, ref B7. Small coal mining village in the Hunter Valley between Cessnock and Kurri Kurri.

Hotels/Motels

Abermain Hotel, (LH), 27 Charles St, 500m S of PO, ☎ 02 4930 4201, fax 02 49308335
, (2 stry), 11 rms [fire pl, tel], shared fac (shwr, tlt & bath), lounge (TV), ✉, t/c mkg shared, bbq, ✆, non smoking rms. **BB ♦ $55, ♦ $55, DBB ♦ $85, ♦ $85,** ch con, fam con, (not yet classified).

ADAMINABY NSW 2630

Pop 350. (450km SW Sydney), See map on pages 52/53, ref F7. Snowy Mountains town close to the cross-country ski slopes of the Selwyn Snowfields. It also attracts people keen on horse riding, water sports and fishing the well-stocked waters of Lake Eucumbene. Boating, Bowls, Fishing, Sailing, Snow Skiing, Tennis, Water Skiing.

Hotels/Motels

★★★ **Adaminaby Country Inn**, (M), Snowy Mountains Hwy, 1km S of PO, ☎ 02 6454 2380, fax 02 6454 2462, 44 units (4 suites) [shwr, tlt, a/c-cool (22), cent heat, tel (22), TV, movie, clock radio, t/c mkg, refrig, cook fac (5)], ldry, rec rm, lounge (TV), conf fac, ✉, pool (Jan to mid Apr), spa (Jan to mid Apr), ✆, tennis, cots. **RO ♦ $55 - $99, ♦♦ $55 - $99, ♦♦♦ $66 - $116,** ch con, 22 rooms of a lower rating. AE BC EFT MC VI,

Operator Comment: Best 3-3 1/2 Star Motel Winner & Best Family Motel Finalist in the HMAA Awards for Excellence 2000.

Snow Goose, (LMH), Cnr Denison & Baker St, ☎ 02 6454 2202, fax 02 6454 2608, (2 stry gr fl), 10 units [shwr, tlt, heat, elec blkts, TV, t/c mkg, refrig], ✉, cots. **BB ♦ $25 - $55, ♦♦ $50 - $93.50, ♦♦♦♦ $75 - $137.50,** ch con, BC EFT MC VI.

Self Catering Accommodation

★★★ **Gooandra Alpine Cottages**, (Cotg), Snowy Mountains Hwy, 8km NW of Adaminaby, ☎ 02 6454 2327, or 02 6452 1811, fax 02 6454 2327, 4 cotgs acc up to 5, [shwr, tlt, fire pl (log), TV, t/c mkg, refrig, cook fac, micro, elec frypan, toaster, doonas, linen reqd-fee], w/mach, dryer, bbq. **D $110 - $165, W $660 - $1,155,** BC MC VI,

Operator Comment: When only the best will do. Secluded 100 acre bush setting, private trout lake. Adj Kosciusko N.P Lake, Eucumbene & Selwyn Snowfields.

★★ **Happy Valley Cottage**, (Cotg), (Farm), c1864, Yens Bay Rd, 3km S of PO, ☎ 02 6454 2439, fax 02 6454 2232, 3 cotgs acc up to 8, [shwr, bath (1), tlt, fan, fire pl (combustion), elec blkts, tel, TV, clock radio, t/c mkg, refrig, cook fac, micro, toaster, linen reqd-fee], iron, bbq, tennis, cots. **D ♦♦ $90, ♦ $10, W ♦♦ $450 - $630, ♦ $70,** Min book applies, BC MC VI.

(Bed & Breakfast Section), 3 rms [shwr, tlt, fan, heat, elec blkts, tel, clock radio], lounge (TV), ✕ (as reqd), cots. **BB ♦ $62, ♦♦ $124, DBB ♦ $84, ♦♦ $174.**

Koomulla Country Retreat, (Cotg), (Farm), Dry Plains, Cooma 2630, 23km SE of Adaminaby PO, ☎ 02 6453 7225, fax 02 6453 7254, 1 cotg acc up to 5, [shwr, tlt, heat, elec blkts, tel, TV, radio, t/c mkg, refrig, cook fac, micro, toaster, ldry, blkts, linen, pillows], w/mach, iron, bbq, cots-fee. **BB ♦ $70 - $85, ♦♦ $100 - $115, D ♦♦ $80 - $95, ♦ $20,** ch con, (not yet classified).

Snowy Mountains Alpine Cabins, Lot 7 Snowy Mountains Hwy, 8km NW of Adaminaby, ☎ 02 6454 1120, fax 02 6454 1123, 5 cabins acc up to 6, [shwr, bath, tlt, hairdry, heat, elec blkts, TV, video, clock radio, t/c mkg, refrig, cook fac, micro, elec frypan, toaster, ldry, doonas, linen], w/mach, dryer, iron, iron brd, bbq, 24hr reception. **D $65 - $190, W $420 - $1,300,** BC MC VI, (not yet classified).

Ashvale Cottage, (Cotg), Canberra Rd, 11km NE of Adaminaby, ☎ 02 6454 2063, 1 cotg acc up to 6, [shwr, tlt, fire pl (combustion), heat, elec blkts, TV, clock radio, t/c mkg, refrig, cook fac, micro, toaster, ldry, doonas, linen reqd-fee], iron, bbq, c/park. **D ♦ $82.50, ♦♦♦ $93.50, ♦ $11, W ♦♦ $412.50 - $577.50,** ch con, Min book applies.

Fontenoy Cottages, (Cotg), (Farm), Yaouk Rd, 9km N of PO, ☎ 02 6454 2227, 2 cotgs acc up to 9, [shwr, bath, tlt, heat, refrig, cook fac, toaster, linen reqd]. **D $90 - $120, W $400,** Min book applies.

Other Accommodation

★★☆ **Alpine Ash**, (Lodge), Cnr Lett & York Sts, 300m N of Giant Trout, ☎ 02 6454 2282, fax 02 6454 2329, (2 stry gr fl), 5 rms acc up to 16, [shwr (2), bath (1), tlt (2), heat, elec blkts, tel, TV, t/c mkg, refrig, cook fac, micro, d/wash, toaster, ldry, blkts, linen reqd-fee], w/mach, iron, dry rm, bbq (gas), cots. **D ♦♦ $95, ♦♦♦ $107, ♦ $15, W ♦♦ $475 - $665,** Min book applies.

Hide 'N' Rest Pyramids, (Lodge), Shannon's Flat Rd, 14km E of Adaminaby, ☎ 02 6454 2536, 2 rms acc up to 4, [shwr, tlt, heat, tel, TV, t/c mkg, refrig, cook fac, blkts, doonas, linen, pillows], ldry, w/mach, iron, rec rm, lounge, bbq, non smoking property. **D ♦♦ $85, ♦ $15, W ♦♦ $510,** (not yet classified).

Reynella Rides, (Lodge), (Farm), Bolaro Rd, 8km E of PO, ☎ 02 6454 2386, fax 02 6454 2530, 20 rms [fire pl, heat, elec blkts], ldry, rec rm, lounge (TV), ✕, tennis. **D $99,** AE BC MC VI.

Tanderra Lodge, (Lodge), Cnr Denison & Druitt Sts, 50m N of PO, ☎ 02 6454 2470, fax 02 6454 2042, 25 rms [shwr, tlt, heat, elec blkts, TV (6)], ldry, lounge (TV), ✉, t/c mkg shared, cots. **BB ♦ $45 - $71, ♦♦ $66 - $93, ♦ $25,** ch con, Min book applies, AE BC MC VI.

The Outpost Fly Fishing Lodge, (Lodge), (Farm), Yaouk Valley, 26km N of Adaminaby, ☎ 02 6454 2293, fax 02 6454 2612, 1 rm [ensuite, shwr (2), spa bath (1), heat, elec blkts], ldry, iron, iron brd, lounge (firepl), ✕ (1st Oct-30th April), pool, tennis, non smoking rms. **D all meals $250 - $280.**

ADAMSTOWN NSW

See Newcastle & Suburbs.

ADELONG NSW 2729

Pop 800. (425km SW Sydney), See map on pages 52/53, ref F6.

AAA TOURISM Special Rates ★★★☆ **Adelongs Beaufort House**, (GH), 77 Tumut St, 50m S of PO, ☎ 02 6946 2273, fax 02 6946 2553, (2 stry gr fl), 10 rms [shwr (1), tlt (1), fan, heat, elec blkts, tel, TV (1), t/c mkg], ldry, iron, iron brd, rec rm, lounge (TV, video), conf fac, lounge firepl, ✕, bbq, cots. **BLB 👤 $55 - $95, 👥 $75 - $110, +👤 $20 - $30, DBB 👤 $80 - $120, 👥 $125 - $155, +👤 $25 - $45**, ch con, BC MC VI.

★★☆ **(Motel Section)**, 4 units [shwr, tlt, hairdry, fan, heat, elec blkts, tel, fax, TV, video (avail), refrig, toaster], ldry, iron, iron brd, ✕. **BLB 👤 $55 - $75, 👥 $75 - $95, +👤 $20 - $30.**

ALBION PARK NSW 2527

Pop 6,500. (106km S Sydney), See map on page 55, ref C4.

B&B's/Guest Houses

★★★★★ **Calderwood Valley Retreat**, (B&B), 770 Calderwood Rd, Calderwood, ☎ 02 4257 4251, fax 02 425674250, 1 rm [shwr, tlt, hairdry, heat, elec blkts, tel, TV, clock radio, t/c mkg, refrig, cook fac, micro, toaster], lounge firepl, ✕, bbq, dinner to unit, courtesy transfer. **BB 👥 $145, +👤 $30**, BC MC VI.

★★★★ **Cooby Springs Country Retreat**, (B&B), 128 Cooby Rd (off Yellow Rock Rd), ☎ 02 4257 1960, fax 02 4257 3128, 2 rms [shwr, tlt, hairdry, fan (1), TV, clock radio, refrig (1)], iron, iron brd. **BB 👤 $80, 👥 $110, Suite BB 👥 $105 - $150.**

★★★☆ **Park Meadows B & B**, (B&B), 227 Tongarra Rd, 500m W of PO, ☎ 02 4256 5355, 3 rms [shwr, bath (1), tlt, hairdry (2), fan, heat, tel, TV, clock radio, t/c mkg], ldry, TV rm, ✕, pool (salt water), bbq, courtesy transfer, non smoking rms (2). **BB 👤 $55, 👥 $70, +👤 $15**, fam con, BC MC VI.

ALBION PARK RAIL NSW 2527

Pop 6,500. (106km S Sydney), See map on page 55, ref C4.

★★☆ **Oaks Motel Hotel**, (LMH), 249 Princes Hwy, 3km E of PO, ☎ 02 4257 1080, or 02 4257 1211, fax 02 4257 1088, (2 stry gr fl), 14 units [shwr, tlt, a/c, tel, TV, clock radio, t/c mkg, refrig, toaster], ldry, ☒, cots. **D $99, RO 👤 $55, 👥 $70**, ch con, AE BC MC VI, ♿.

ALBURY NSW 2640

Pop 41,500. (559km SW Sydney), See map on pages 52/53, ref E7. Flourishing city situated across the Murray River from Wodonga. Together, the two cities form the major centre for the Murray region. Bowls, Fishing, Golf, Scenic Drives, Swimming, Tennis. See also Wodonga.

Hotels/Motels

AAA TOURISM Special Rates, COUNTRY COMFORT ★★★★☆ **Country Comfort Albury**, (LH), Cnr Dean & Elizabeth Sts, 400m W of PO, ☎ 02 6021 5366, fax 02 6041 2848, (Multi-stry), 140 rms [shwr, bath, spa bath (5), tlt, hairdry, a/c, elec blkts, tel, cable tv, movie, clock radio, t/c mkg, refrig, mini bar], lift, ldry, iron, lounge, conv fac, ☒, pool-heated, sauna, spa, 24hr reception, rm serv, dinner to unit, cots, non smoking flr (5). **RO 👤 $130, 👥 $130, +👤 $16.50**, ch con, AE BC DC MC VI.

AAA TOURISM Special Rates, SUNDOWNER CHAIN MOTOR INNS ★★★★☆ **Sundowner Chain Motor Inns**, (M), Hovell Tree, Cnr Hume Hwy & Hovell St, ☎ 02 6041 2666, fax 02 6041 2883, (2 stry), 40 units (10 suites) [shwr, bath, spa bath (6), tlt, hairdry, a/c, tel, cable tv, clock radio, t/c mkg, refrig, mini bar, cook fac (8), micro (8), d/wash (8), toaster], lift, ldry, conv fac, ☒, pool (salt water), sauna, spa, bbq, rm serv, dinner to unit, c/park (undercover), 📞, gym, cots, non smoking units (20). **RO 👤 $115.50 - $202, 👥 $115.50 - $202, +👤 $11**, AE BC DC EFT MC MP VI, ♿.

FLAG, FLAG CHOICE HOTELS ★★★★☆ **The Motel Siesta Resort**, (M), 416 Wagga Rd (Hume Hwy), Lavington 2641, 1km N of Albury North PO, ☎ 02 6025 4555, fax 02 6040 1664, 88 units (5 suites) [shwr, spa bath (13), tlt, a/c, heat, elec blkts, tel, TV, video-fee, clock radio, t/c mkg, refrig, toaster], ldry, rec rm, read rm, conv fac, ☒, pool indoor heated, sauna, spa, bbq, rm serv, courtesy transfer, plygr, mini golf, gym, squash, tennis, cots-fee, non smoking units (34). **RO 👤 $100 - $129, 👥 $100 - $129, 👥👤 $111 - $140, +👤 $11, Suite D $129 - $159**, AE BC DC EFT MC VI, ♿.

For Accommodation Booking information - see page 27

 ★★★★ **Albury Manor House**, (M), 593 Young St, 1km NE of PO, ☎ 02 6041 1777, fax 02 6041 1617, (2 stry gr fl), 39 units (3 suites) [shwr, spa bath (9), tlt, a/c, tel, TV, movie, clock radio, t/c mkg, refrig, mini bar, toaster], lift, ldry, conv fac, ⊠, pool-heated, sauna, spa, rm serv, dinner to unit, cots. **RO** ⦿ $116 - $190, ⦿⦿ $116 - $190, ⦿ $10, **Suite D** $155 - $225, ch con, AE BC DC JCB MC MP VI.

★★★★ **Greentree Inn**, (M), 579 Olive St, 800m NE of PO, ☎ 02 6021 6100, fax 02 6041 1803, (Multi-stry), 60 units (4 suites) [shwr, bath (8), tlt, hairdry, a/c, elec blkts, tel, TV, movie, clock radio, t/c mkg, refrig, mini bar], lift, ldry, iron, iron brd, conv fac, ⊠, pool, bbq, 24hr reception, rm serv, plygr, non smoking rms (avail). **D** ⦿⦿ $110 - $135, ⦿ $15, 3rd floor rooms at a three star plus rating. AE BC DC MC VI.

   ★★★★ **Sundowner Chain Motor Inns**, (M), Paddlesteamer, 324 Wodonga Pl, ☎ 02 6041 1711, fax 02 6041 2161, (2 stry gr fl), 61 units [shwr, bath (8), spa bath (12), tlt, hairdry, a/c, tel, cable tv, video-fee, clock radio, t/c mkg, refrig, mini bar, toaster], ldry, iron, iron brd, conv fac, ⊠, bar, pool, sauna, spa, rm serv, cots, non smoking units (22). **RO** ⦿ $92 - $172, ⦿⦿ $92 - $172, ⦿ $11, ch con, AE BC DC EFT MC VI, ⅙.

 ★★★☆ **Albury Australia Park Motel**, (M), Cnr Wodonga Pl (Hume Hwy) & Ebden St, ☎ 02 6021 6000, or 02 6021 6189, fax 02 6041 2973, (2 stry gr fl), 37 units [shwr, bath (6), spa bath (2), tlt, a/c, elec blkts, tel, TV, video-fee, clock radio, t/c mkg, refrig], ldry, conf fac, ⊠ (Mon to Sat), pool-heated (solar), bbq, dinner to unit (Mon to Sat), cots, non smoking units (10). **RO** ⦿ $78 - $88, ⦿⦿ $86 - $96, ⦿ $10, ch con, AE BC DC MC VI.

★★★☆ **Albury Burvale Motor Inn**, (M), Previously Burvale Motor Inn 671 Young St (Hume Hwy), 1.5km N of PO, ☎ 02 6021 6911, fax 02 6021 6083, 28 units [shwr, tlt, hairdry, a/c, heat, elec blkts, tel, cable tv, movie, clock radio, t/c mkg, refrig, toaster], iron, pool, bbq, cots, non smoking units. **RO** ⦿ $60 - $70, ⦿⦿ $62 - $79, ⦿ $10, ch con, AE BC DC EFT MC VI.

★★★☆ **Albury Garden Court**, (M), 426 David St, 1km SE of PO, ☎ 02 6021 6244, fax 02 6021 6490, 17 units [shwr, tlt, hairdry, a/c, elec blkts, tel, TV, movie, clock radio, t/c mkg, refrig, toaster], pool, sauna, spa, bbq, cots-fee. **RO** ♦ **$60 - $72**, ♦♦ **$65 - $83**, ⱷ **$12**, AE BC DC EFT MC VI.

★★★☆ **Albury Georgian Motor Inn**, (M), 599 Young St, 1km NE of PO, ☎ 02 6021 8744, fax 02 6021 8320, (2 stry gr fl), 24 units (1 suite) [shwr, bath, spa bath (2), tlt, hairdry, a/c, elec blkts, tel, TV, video (avail), movie, clock radio, t/c mkg, refrig], ldry, ✕, pool-heated, spa, rm serv, cots. **RO** ♦ **$76 - $79**, ♦♦ **$82 - $85**, ⱷ **$12**, ch con, AE BC DC EFT MC MP VI, ♿.

★★★☆ **Albury Golf View Motor Inn** (M), Previously Albury Golf Club Motor Inn 530 North St, 1km N of PO, located on Golf Course, ☎ 02 6041 1211, fax 02 6041 2650, 17 units (2 suites) [shwr, bath (5), tlt,

Albury Golf View Motor Inn ...continued

hairdry, a/c, heat, elec blkts, tel, fax, TV, clock radio, t/c mkg, refrig, toaster], ldry, conv fac, ✕ (at Golf Club), pool-heated, bbq, plygr, cots-fee, non smoking units (10). **BLB** ♦ **$79 - $92**, ♦♦ **$89 - $100**, ⱷ **$10 - $16, Suite D $100 - $140**, Min book long w/ends, AE BC DC EFT MC VI, ♿.

★★★☆ **Albury Meramie Motor Inn**, (M), 595 Kiewa St, 500m N of PO, ☎ 02 6021 8100, fax 02 6041 2901, (2 stry gr fl), 27 units (2 suites) [shwr, tlt, a/c-cool, elec blkts, tel, TV, video-fee, clock radio, t/c mkg, refrig], ldry, pool (salt water), sauna, spa, dinner to unit, tennis (half court), cots-fee. **BLB** ♦ **$76**, ♦♦ **$86**, ⱷ **$10, Suite D** ♦♦♦♦ **$125 - $135**, AE BC DC MC VI.

★★★☆ **Albury Town House**, (M), 461 Wilson St, ☎ 02 6021 3000, fax 02 6021 6503, (2 stry gr fl), 21 units [shwr, bath (19), tlt, hairdry, a/c, elec blkts, tel, TV, video (avail), clock radio, t/c mkg, refrig], sauna, spa, bbq, dinner to unit, cots. **BLB** ♦ **$82**, ♦♦ **$98**, ⱷ **$15**, AE BC DC MC MP VI.

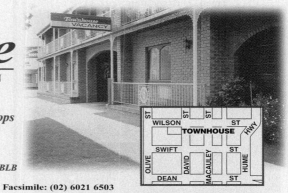

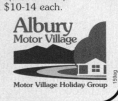

Crystal Fountain
ALBURY

410 Wagga Road (Hume Highway)
Lavington (Nth.Albury) 2641
Ph - (02) 6025 8033 Fax - (02) 6040 2243
Freecall 1800 021 909
Email - crystal@albury.net.au
Web Page - webeffects.com.au/awma/crystal

THE ESSENCE OF COMFORT
A boutique Motel that has spacious surrounds and
"Award winning" garden that will entice the
traveller to stay another night.
A FEW GOOD REASONS
• 24 Hour Check In
• Spacious Family Units With Cooking Facilities
• Indoor Spa, Sauna & Swimming Pool
• Licensed Room Service • Private Balcony Views
• Non Smoking Rooms • Trailer Parking

189AG

★★★☆ **Albury Winsor Park Motor Inn**, (M), 471 Young St, 800m E of PO, ☎ 02 6021 8800, fax 02 6041 2684, (2 stry gr fl), 18 units [shwr, bath, tlt, a/c, elec blkts, tel, TV, video-fee, clock radio, t/c mkg, refrig, toaster], pool, spa, cots-fee, non smoking rms (4). RO ∮ $66 - $75, ∮∮ $66 - $88, ∮ $10 - $15, 3 units of a three star rating. AE BC DC MC VI.

★★★☆ **Classic Motor Inn**, (M), 404 Wagga Rd (Hume Hwy), Lavington 2641, ☎ 02 6025 7177, fax 02 6040 1939, (2 stry gr fl), 24 units (0 suites) [shwr, bath (2), spa bath (1), hairdry, a/c, elec blkts, tel, TV, video, movie, clock radio, t/c mkg, refrig, toaster], ldry, iron, iron brd, pool (& children's), bbq, rm serv, cots, non smoking units (10). RO ∮ $64 - $70, ∮∮ $68 - $80, ∮∮∮ $78 - $90, ∮ $11, Suite D ∮∮ $88 - $99, AE BC DC EFT MC VI.

★★★☆ **Commodore Motel**, (M), 515 Kiewa St, opposite PO, ☎ 02 6021 3344, fax 02 6041 2947, (2 stry gr fl), 40 units [shwr, tlt, a/c, elec blkts, tel, TV, video-fee, clock radio, t/c mkg, refrig], ldry, ⊠, rm serv, cots-fee. RO ∮ $69 - $74, ∮∮ $80 - $85, ∮∮∮ $91 - $96, ∮ $11, ch con, AE BC DC EFT MC VI.

★★★☆ **Country Club Motor Inn**, (M), 1 Evesham Pl, Thurgoona 2640, 6km E of Lavington PO, ☎ 02 6043 1666, fax 02 6043 1850, (2 stry gr fl), 26 units [shwr, bath (8), spa bath (4), tlt, a/c, elec blkts, tel, TV, video-fee, clock radio, t/c mkg, refrig], ldry, conv fac, ⊠, bar, pool, sauna, spa, bbq, dinner to unit, golf, tennis, cots-fee. RO ∮ $101.20 - $123.20, ∮∮ $101.20 - $123.20, ∮∮∮ $125.40 - $134.20, ∮ $13.20, ch con, AE BC DC MC VI.

★★★☆ **Crystal Fountain Motel**, (M), 410 Wagga Rd (Hume Hwy), Lavington 2641, 500m N of Lavington PO, ☎ 02 6025 8033, fax 02 6040 2243, (2 stry gr fl), 21 units [shwr, tlt, hairdry, a/c, elec blkts, tel, cable tv, video-fee, clock radio, t/c mkg, refrig, cook fac (family rms), toaster], ldry, iron, iron brd, pool (salt water), sauna, spa, bbq, rm serv, cots, non smoking units (12). RO ∮ $71 - $83, ∮∮ $83 - $90, ∮∮∮ $91 - $105, ∮ $8, ch con, AE BC DC EFT MC MP VI.

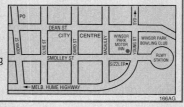

★★★☆ **Elm Court Motel**, (M), 435 Townsend St, 500m S of PO, ☎ 02 6021 8077, fax 02 6021 6974, 31 units [shwr, bath (1), tlt, hairdry, a/c, heat, elec blkts, tel, TV, movie, clock radio, t/c mkg, refrig, mini bar, toaster], ldry, ✕ (B'fast Only), pool indoor heated, spa, bbq, rm serv, dinner to unit, c/park (undercover), cots, non smoking units (4). RO ♦ $69 - $76, ♦♦ $79 - $86, ♦♦♦ $89 - $96, ♀ $10, ch con, 5 units of a lower rating. AE BC DC MC MP.

★★★☆ **Fountain Court Motor Inn**, (M), 568 David St, 1km NE of PO, ☎ 02 6021 8411, or 02 6021 8145, fax 02 6041 2265, 34 units [shwr, spa bath (2), tlt, hairdry, a/c, heat, elec blkts, tel, TV, video-fee, clock radio, t/c mkg, refrig], iron, iron brd, pool, sauna, spa, non smoking rms (avail). RO ♦ $77 - $89, ♦♦ $89 - $121, ♀ $14, AE BC DC MC MP VI.

★★★☆ **Hume Country Golf Club Motor Inn**, (M), 736 Logan Rd, 3km N of PO, on golf course, ☎ 02 6025 8233, fax 02 6040 4999, 21 units (4 suites) [shwr, spa bath (4), tlt, hairdry, a/c, elec blkts, tel, TV, video (2), clock radio, t/c mkg, refrig, toaster], ldry-fee, pool-heated, bbq, dinner to unit (incl liquor), plygr, cots, non smoking units (10). RO ♦ $62 - $75, ♦♦ $72 - $85, ♀ $11, Suite D $95 - $125, AE BC DC EFT MC VI.

★★★☆ **Matador Motor Inn**, (M), 617 Young St (Hume Hwy), 1km N of PO, ☎ 02 6021 1877, fax 02 6041 2625, (2 stry gr fl), 60 units [shwr, tlt, a/c-cool, heat, elec blkts, tel, TV, video, clock radio, t/c mkg, refrig], ldry, conv fac, ✕, bar, pool indoor heated, sauna, spa, bbq, gym, cots, non smoking units (25). RO ♦♦ $86.10 - $99, ♀ $11, AE BC DC MC MP VI, ৬.

★★★☆ **Mirrabooka Homestead Motor Inn**, (M), Burma Rd, Table Top 2640, opposite 'Ettamogah Pub', ☎ 02 6026 2271, or 02 6026 2415, fax 02 6026 2444, 25 units (2 suites) [shwr, spa bath (2), tlt, a/c, heat, elec blkts, tel, TV, clock radio, t/c mkg, refrig, toaster], ldry, conv fac, ✕, ✕, pool (salt water), spa, bbq, rm serv, dinner to unit, plygr, cots-fee, non smoking units (avail). W $350 - $500, RO ♦ $70 - $89, ♦♦ $79 - $120, ♦♦♦ $99, ♀ $15, Suite D ♦♦ $120, ch con, AE BC DC MC VI, ৬.

★★★ **Albury City Motel**, (M), 729 Young St, 2km N of PO, ☎ 02 6021 7699, fax 02 6041 2798, 18 units [shwr, tlt, a/c, cent heat, tel, cable tv, video-fee, clock radio, t/c mkg, refrig, toaster], ldry, pool, cook fac, bbq, dinner to unit, courtesy transfer, cots-fee. RO ♦ $59 - $65, ♦♦ $65 - $70, ♀ $10, ch con, AE BC DC EFT MC MP VI.

★★★ **Albury Coach House**, (M), 476 Wagga Rd (Hume Hwy), Lavington 2641, 2km N of Lavington PO, ☎ 02 6025 1233, or 02 6025 1465, fax 02 6040 1847, 17 units [shwr, tlt, a/c, heat, elec blkts, tel, TV, t/c mkg, refrig, cook fac (2), toaster], ldry, pool (solar), spa, bbq, dinner to unit, plygr, cots. RO ♦ $48 - $52, ♦♦ $57 - $62, ♦♦♦ $66 - $71, ♀ $9, ch con, AE BC DC MC MCH VI.

★★★ **Albury Hume Inn**, (M), 406 Wodonga Pl, 800m SW of PO, ☎ 02 6021 2733, fax 02 6041 2239, (2 stry gr fl), 44 units [shwr, bath (9), spa bath (1), tlt, hairdry, a/c, heat, elec blkts, tel, TV, movie, clock radio, t/c mkg, refrig], ldry, conv fac, ✕, pool, bbq, rm serv, cots, non smoking units (19). BLB ♦ $65 - $105, ♦♦ $65 - $105, ♀ $10, ch con, AE BC DC MC VI.

★★★ **Albury Viscount Motor Inn**, (M), 437 Young St (Hume Hwy), 1km SE of PO, 200m to railway station, ☎ 02 6021 2444, fax 02 6041 3830, (2 stry gr fl), 42 units [shwr, tlt, a/c, elec blkts, tel, TV, clock radio, t/c mkg, refrig, toaster], ldry, pool, bbq, cots. RO ♦ $50 - $64, ♦♦ $58 - $64, ♀ $9 - $10, ch con, 14 units ★★★, AE BC DC MC MCH VI.

★★★ **Allawa Motor Inn**, (M), Cnr Hume Hwy & Olive St, 500m S of PO, ☎ 02 6021 6133, fax 02 6021 6106, 16 units [shwr, tlt, a/c, elec blkts, tel, TV, video-fee, clock radio, t/c mkg, refrig, cook fac (1), toaster], ldry, pool-heated (solar), spa, bbq, dinner to unit, cots-fee, non smoking units (6), Dogs welcome on request. RO ♦ $60 - $73, ♦♦ $64 - $78, ♀ $12, BC DC EFT MC VI, ৬.

★★★ **Boomerang Motor Inn**, (LMH), Hume Hwy, Lavington 2641, ☎ 02 6025 1711, fax 02 6025 8886, (2 stry gr fl), 38 units [shwr, bath (21), tlt, a/c, elec blkts, tel, TV, video, clock radio, t/c mkg, refrig], ldry, rec rm, ✕, bar, pool indoor heated, sauna, spa, bbq, dinner to unit, cots-fee. RO ♦ $45 - $55, ♦♦ $55 - $66, ♦♦♦ $65 - $77, Min book applies, AE BC DC MC MP VI.

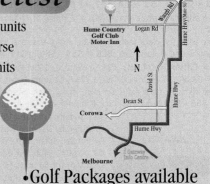

★★★ **Cottage Motor Inn**, (M), 527 Hume St (HumeHwy), 500m S of PO, ☎ 02 6021 3899, fax 02 6041 5277, (2 stry gr fl), 16 units [shwr, tlt, a/c, elec blkts, tel, TV, movie, clock radio, t/c mkg, refrig], sauna, spa, c/park (undercover) (6), cots. **RO** ♦ **$50 - $62**, ♦♦ **$62 - $67**, ♦♦♦ **$67 - $77**, ♦ **$10**, 3 units of a lower rating. AE BC DC MC MCH VI, ⚹&.

★★★ **Lake Hume Resort**, (M), Riverina Hwy, Lake Hume Village, 14km E of PO, ☎ 02 6026 4444, fax 02 6026 4572, 26 units [shwr, tlt, a/c, heat, elec blkts, tel, TV, clock radio, t/c mkg, refrig], ldry, conv fac, ⊠, pool, bbq, plygr, mini golf, tennis. **RO** ♦ **$75 - $91**, ♦♦ **$81 - $98**, AE BC DC MC VI, ⚹&.

★★★ **(Heritage Workers Cottages)**, 38 cabins acc up to 6, [shwr, tlt, a/c, tel, TV, refrig, cook fac, toaster, blkts, linen reqd, pillows], ldry-fee. **D $79 - $149**, 2 cottages at a higher rating.

★★★ **Seaton Arms Motor Inn**, (M), Cnr Olive & Wilson Sts, near S.S.A Club, ☎ 02 6021 5999, fax 02 6021 6520, (2 stry gr fl), 21 units [shwr, spa bath (1), tlt, a/c, tel, TV, clock radio, t/c mkg, refrig], iron, iron brd, conv fac, lounge firepl, ⊠ (Mon to Sat), dinner to unit (Mon to Sat), cots. **RO** ♦ **$84**, ♦♦ **$95**, ♦♦♦ **$106**, ♦ **$12**, AE BC DC MC VI.

★★★ **The Albury Regent**, (M), 666 Dean St, 250m W of PO, ☎ 02 6021 8355, or 02 6021 8032, fax 02 6021 8265, (2 stry), 24 units [shwr, bath (22), tlt, a/c, elec blkts, tel, TV, clock radio, t/c mkg, refrig, toaster], ldry, cots (avail), non smoking units (10). **RO** ♦ **$66**, ♦♦ **$71.50 - $82.50**, ♦ **$11**, AE BC DC MC VI.

★★☆ **Astor Motel**, (LMH), 629 Hume Hwy, 1km N of PO, ☎ 02 6021 1922, fax 02 6021 1669, (2 stry gr fl), 45 units [shwr, tlt, a/c, elec blkts, tel, cable tv, clock radio, t/c mkg, refrig], ldry, ⊠, pool-heated, bbq, rm serv, cots-fee. **RO** ♦ **$43**, ♦♦ **$54**, ♦♦♦♦ **$65**, ♦ **$6**, AE BC DC MC VI.

★★☆ **Barclay Gardens Motor Inn**, (M), 601 Hume Hwy, Lavington 2641, 2.5km N of Lavington PO, ☎ 02 6025 2466, fax 02 6040 1834, 24 units [shwr, tlt, hairdry, a/c, elec blkts, tel, TV, video, clock radio, t/c mkg, refrig, toaster], ldry, ⊠, pool, bbq, rm serv, dinner to unit, cots, non smoking units (9). **RO** ♦ **$48 - $58**, ♦♦ **$58 - $65**, ♦ **$8**, 8 units ★★★. AE BC DC EFT MC VI.

★★☆ **Southern Cross Motel - Lavington**, (M), 511 Hume Hwy, Lavington 2641, 2km N of Lavington PO, ☎ 02 6025 1622, fax 02 6040 4988, 18 units [shwr, tlt, a/c-cool, heat, fax, TV, clock radio, t/c mkg, refrig, toaster], pool, meals to unit, c/park (undercover) (14), cots-fee. **RO** ♦ **$44**, ♦♦ **$50 - $60**, ♦ **$7**, AE BC DC EFT MC VI.

★★ **Albury Central Motel**, (M), 473 Young St, 700m E of PO, ☎ 02 6021 3127, fax 02 6021 0564, 11 units [shwr, tlt, a/c, elec blkts, TV, clock radio, t/c mkg, refrig, toaster], ldry, pool-heated (solar), cots. **BLB** ♦♦ **$55 - $66**, ♦ **$11**, AE BC DC MC VI.

★★ **Clifton Motel**, (M), 424 Smollett St, 100m W of railway station, ☎ 02 6021 7126, fax 02 6021 7757, 11 units [shwr, tlt, a/c, heat, elec blkts, TV, clock radio, t/c mkg, refrig], ldry, cots-fee. **RO** ♦ **$50 - $55**, ♦♦ **$55 - $60**, ♦ **$11**, ch con, Min book applies, AE BC DC MC VI.

★☆ **Sodens Australia Hotel Motel**, (LMH), Classified by National Trust, Cnr David & Wilson Sts, 800m N of PO, ☎ 02 6021 2400, fax 02 6041 2838, (2 stry gr fl), 50 units [shwr (28), spa bath (1), tlt (28), a/c (29), elec blkts, TV (29), t/c mkg (29), refrig], ⊠, bbq. **BLB** ♦ **$22 - $35**, ♦♦ **$40 - $45**, ch con, 21 units not rated. AE BC DC EFT MC VI,

Operator Comment: We offer private gaming room & TAB facilities - www.sodens.com.au

Self Catering Accommodation

★★★ **Albury Central Serviced Apartments**, (HU), 252 Olive St, ☎ 02 6041 5755, fax 02 6021 7043, 6 units acc up to 6, [shwr, tlt, a/c, heat, elec blkts, tel, TV, refrig, cook fac, micro, linen], w/mach, dryer, iron, c/park (garage). **W $420 - $600**, **RO** ♦ **$65**, ♦♦ **$70**, ♦♦♦ **$80**, Min book applies, BC MC VI.

B&B's/Guest Houses

★★★★☆ **Elizabeth's Manor**, (B&B), 531 Lyne St, 1.5km S of PO, ☎ 02 6040 4412, fax 02 6040 5166, (2 stry), 3 rms [shwr, bath, tlt, hairdry, a/c, heat, elec blkts, tel, TV, clock radio, t/c mkg, refrig], ldry, iron, iron brd, rec rm, lounge firepl, ✕, bbq, meals avail, courtesy transfer, non smoking property. **BB** ♦ **$110**, ♦♦ **$140**, **DBB** ♦ **$155**, ♦♦ **$220**, AE BC DC MC VI.

★★★★☆ **Gundowring Bed & Breakfast**, (B&B), 621 Stanley St, 200m N of Botanical Gardens, ☎ 02 6041 4437, fax 02 6041 4229, 3 rms [shwr, bath, tlt, hairdry, c/fan, heat, elec blkts, tel, clock radio, t/c mkg], ldry, iron, iron brd, lounge (TV & firepl), non smoking property. **BB** ♦ **$110**, ♦♦ **$130**, BC MC VI.

★★★★ **Lorquon Bed & Breakfast**, (B&B), Tynan Rd, Table Top 2640, 20km N of Albury, ☎ 02 6026 2367, fax 02 6026 2267, 2 rms (1 suite) [shwr, bath (1), tlt, hairdry, evap cool, c/fan, fire pl, heat, elec blkts, tel, TV (1)], ldry, rec rm, lounge, ✕, pool (salt water), t/c mkg shared, bbq. **BB** ♦♦ **$140 - $185**.

ALSTONVILLE NSW 2477

Pop 4,750. (751km N Sydney), See map on page 54, ref E2. Picturesque township high on the Alstonville Plateau between Ballina and Lismore, renowned for its beautifully tended gardens and distinctive tibouchina trees. Bowls, Squash, Swimming, Tennis. See also Alstonville & Lennox Head.

Hotels/Motels

★★★★ **Garden Inn Wollongbar**, (M), Cnr Bruxner Hwy & Smith La, Wollongbar 2477, 2.8km W of Alstonville PO, ☎ 02 6628 5666, fax 02 6628 6966, 11 units [shwr, bath (2), spa bath (2), tlt, hairdry, a/c, c/fan, tel, cable tv, clock radio, t/c mkg, refrig, mini bar, toaster], ldry, iron, iron brd, conf fac (small), ⊠, rm serv (b'fast), dinner to unit, cots, non smoking property. **RO** ♦ **$73 - $120**, ♦♦ **$73 - $120**, ♦♦♦ **$93 - $130**, AE BC DC EFT MC VI.

★★★☆ **Alstonville Settlers**, (M), 188 Ballina Rd, 1km E of PO, ☎ 02 6628 5285, fax 02 6628 1669, 17 units [shwr, tlt, hairdry, a/c, tel, TV, clock radio, t/c mkg, refrig, toaster], ldry, iron, iron brd, pool, bbq, dinner to unit (Mon to Thu), cots, non smoking units (6). **RO** ♦ **$53 - $58**, ♦♦ **$60 - $70**, ♦ **$11**, ch con, 5 units of a lower rating, AE BC DC EFT MC VI.

B&B's/Guest Houses

★★★★☆ **Hume's Hovell**, (B&B), Dalwood Rd, 8km S of Alstonville, ☎ 02 6629 5371, fax 02 6629 5471, 2 rms [shwr, spa bath (1), tlt, hairdry, a/c-cool, heat, elec blkts, tel, TV, video, clock radio, CD, t/c mkg, refrig], pool (salt water), bbq, dinner to unit, tennis. **BB ♦ $130, ♦♦ $165 - $232, ◊ $33**, AE BC DC MC VI.

★★★★ **Serendip Plantation**, (B&B), 484 Gap Rd, ☎ 02 6628 3858, fax 02 6628 6205, 1 rm [shwr, tlt, hairdry, c/fan, heat, elec blkts, TV, clock radio, t/c mkg, refrig, toaster], iron, iron brd, pool (heated salt water), bbq, courtesy transfer, golf (putting green) (2), tennis (night lights), non smoking rms. **BLB ♦ $82.50, ♦♦ $104.50**, BC MC VI, *Operator Comment: Special Offer - 3rd night less 50%. Come & visit our beautiful secluded property on our website www.babs.com.au/serendip*

ANGLERS REACH NSW 2630

Pop Nominal, (483km SW Sydney), See map on pages 52/53, ref F7. Small village on the upper reaches of Lake Eucumbene.

★★ **Anglers Reach Lakeside Village**, (HU), Lot 3 Illawong Rd, 14km W of Adaminaby, ☎ 02 6454 2276, fax 02 6454 2270, 19 units [shwr, tlt, elec blkts, refrig, cook fac, micro, linen reqd-fee], ldry, w/mach (3), dryer (2), iron, iron brd, **D ♦♦ $59, ♦♦♦ $74, ◊ $15, W $347 - $840**, Min book all holiday times, BC EFT MC VI.

  (Bunkhouse Section), 1 bunkhouse acc up to 20, [shwr, tlt, elec blkts, refrig, cook fac, micro, linen reqd-fee], ldry, w/mach-fee, dryer-fee, iron, iron brd. **D ♦ $16**, Minimum booking - 15 people.

ANGOURIE NSW 2464

Pop 205. (280km N Sydney), See map on page 54, ref D3. Small settlement south of Yamba on the far north coast.

Self Catering Accommodation

★★★★ **Angourie Waves**, (HU), Cnr Bay & Barri St, ☎ 02 6646 2321, or 02 4959 5039, (2 stry gr fl), 3 units acc up to 8, [shwr, bath, tlt, c/fan, heat, TV, video, clock radio, t/c mkg, refrig, cook fac, micro, elec frypan, d/wash, toaster, ldry (in unit), blkts, linen, pillows], w/mach, dryer, iron, pool-heated (heated winter only), bbq, c/park (garage), cots. **D $120 - $150, W $520 - $1,600**, Min book applies.

★★★☆ **Nats at the Point**, (HU), The Crescent, ☎ 02 6646 1622, fax 02 6646 3827, 10 units acc up to 10, [shwr, bath, tlt, c/fan, TV, clock radio, t/c mkg, refrig, cook fac, micro, toaster, ldry (in unit), blkts, linen, pillows], w/mach, dryer, iron, ✕ (Sun to Sun), c/park. **D $95 - $150, W $570 - $900**, BC MC VI.

★★★☆ **The Beach House**, (Cotg), 5 Bay St, 100m SE of village store, ☎ 02 6684 3834, fax 02 6684 1834, (2 stry), 1 cotg acc up to 12, [shwr, bath, tlt, c/fan, heat, TV, video, clock radio, t/c mkg, refrig, cook fac, micro, d/wash, toaster, ldry, blkts], w/mach, iron, iron brd, bbq, cots, non smoking rms. **D $120 - $200, W $550 - $1,350.**

★★★ **Angourie Bay Villas**, (HU), 4 Bay St, 6km S of Yamba PO, ☎ 02 6646 2893, fax 02 6646 1542, 3 units acc up to 8, [shwr, bath, tlt, c/fan, TV, video, clock radio, t/c mkg, refrig, cook fac, micro, d/wash, toaster, blkts, linen, pillows], ldry, w/mach, dryer, iron, c/park (garage). **D $120 - $140, W $490 - $1,500.**

ANNA BAY NSW

See Port Stephens Region.

APPIN NSW 2560

Pop 1,350. (65km S Sydney), See map on page 56, ref A8. Rural area between Campbelltown and Wilton on the outskirts of Sydney. Bush Walking, Greyhound Racing, Horse Racing.

Hotels/Motels

★★☆ **Humes Explorer Motel**, (M), Appin Rd, opposite PO, ☎ 02 4631 1182, fax 02 4631 1167, 10 units [shwr, tlt, a/c, tel, TV, clock radio, t/c mkg, refrig], ldry, pool, bbq, cots-fee. **RO ♦ $40, ♦♦ $50**, ch con, AE BC DC MC VI.

ARALUEN NSW 2622

Pop Nominal, (298km S Sydney), See map on page 55, ref A6.

Self Catering Accommodation

Araluen Bush Retreat, (HU), (Farm), Kyminvale, 40km S of Braidwood, ☎ 02 4846 4025, or 02 4846 4096, fax 02 4846 4096, 3 units acc up to 4, [shwr, tlt, hairdry, heat, elec blkts, tlt, t/c mkg, refrig, doonas, linen], w/mach, iron, rec rm, plygr, non smoking units. **D all meals ♦ $77**, Min book applies, BC MC VI, (not yet classified).

ARCADIA VALE NSW 2283

Pop Part of Newcastle, (151km N Sydney), See map on page 55, ref E4. Settlement on the western side of Lake Macquarie on Eraring Bay.

B&B's/Guest Houses

★★★☆ **Lakeside Bed & Breakfast**, (B&B), 7 Alexander Pde, ☎ 02 4975 3298, fax 02 4975 3298, 2 rms [shwr, bath (1), tlt, hairdry, a/c, elec blkts, tel, clock radio], ldry, iron, iron brd, lounge (TV), pool (salt water), t/c mkg shared, bbq, non smoking rms. **BLB ♦ $55 - $65, ♦♦ $85 - $100**, BC MC VI.

ARDLETHAN NSW 2665

Pop 450. (563km W Sydney), See map on pages 52/53, ref E6. Small Riverina town that was once a large tin mining community and now acts as a service centre for the pastoralists and for travellers along the Newell Highway.

Hotels/Motels

★★ **London Hotel Motel**, (LMH), 12 Mirrool St, ☎ 02 6978 2300, fax 02 6978 2300, 7 units [shwr, tlt, a/c, elec blkts, TV, clock radio, t/c mkg, refrig, toaster], ✕, dinner to unit, ☎, cots. **RO ♦ $45, ♦♦ $55**, BC MC VI.

ARMIDALE NSW 2350

Pop 21,350. (569km N Sydney), See map on page 54, ref A5. Historic university city and heart of the New England region. Bowls, Fishing, Golf, Scenic Drives, Squash, Swimming, Tennis.

Hotels/Motels

★★★★ **Deer Park Motor Inn**, (M), 72-74 Glen Innes Rd, 2.5km N of PO, ☎ 02 6772 9999, fax 02 6772 8962, 24 units [shwr, bath (6), spa bath (2), tlt, hairdry, a/c, heat, elec blkts, tel, cable tv, video (avail), clock radio, t/c mkg, refrig, mini bar, toaster], ldry, iron, iron brd, conv fac, ✕ (Mon to Sat), bar, pool indoor heated, sauna, spa, bbq, rm serv, dinner to unit, cots, non smoking units (8), Dogs allowed by prior arrangement. **RO ♦ $89 - $120, ♦♦ $99 - $130, ◊ $7.50 - $15**, ch con, AE BC DC EFT MC MP VI, ⚹⚹.

Armidale Regency
HALLMARK INN
& Function Centre
AAA TOURISM ★★★☆

In a spacious, elevated parkland setting - the Regency is perfectly positioned to act as a base whilst exploring all the beautiful New England area offers. Close to cathedrals, museums, art galleries and numerous heritage buildings you will find that "a day is not enough". Armidale is surrounded by some of the best national parks and World Heritage areas in Australia. Our 2 day Escape Package below will allow you to get the most out of your stay.

❖ Quiet rooms with queen beds ❖ Some spa baths
❖ Family suites with kitchenettes ❖ 2 room executive suites
❖ Interconnecting rooms
❖ Internal access to reception & restaurant
❖ Austar satellite TV - **Free**
OUR RECREATIONAL FACILITIES
❖ 40ft swimming pool ❖ Indoor heated spa ❖ Sauna room
❖ 9 hole practice putting green
❖ Games room with billiards, table tennis & exercise bike

*applies most weekends

*Special Weekend Rates 20% OFF**

Lizabeth's Licensed A-la-carte Restaurant & Cocktail Bar
The Dumaresq Room   - catering for conferences
                     - weddings & parties

THE REGENCY ESCAPE
$ 150.00 incl. gst PER PERSON - TWIN SHARE
Two nights accommodation
- Two full hot breakfasts per person
One three course dinner per person
- Late Checkout

FREECALL
1800 650 798

FLAG
Phone: (02) 6772 9800 Fax: (02) 6771 2590
Email: regearmi@ozemail.com

AAA TOURISM *Special Rates*
208 Dangar Street,
(New England Hwy)
Armidale 2350, 1km South of city centre

★★★★ **Elite Motor Inn**, (M), 71 Marsh St, 600m N of PO, ☎ 02 6771 5377, fax 02 6771 5388, (2 stry gr fl), 14 units [shwr, tlt, hairdry, a/c, heat, elec blkts, tel, cable tv, video (avail), clock radio, t/c mkg, refrig, toaster], ldry, iron, iron brd, non smoking rms (3). **RO** ♦ **$65 - $75**, ♦♦ **$69 - $79**, ◊ **$10**, pen con, AE BC DC EFT JCB MC VI.

★★★★ **Moore Park Inn**, (M), Uralla Rd, 4km S of PO, ☎ 02 6772 2358, fax 02 6772 5252, 20 units [shwr, bath (10), spa bath (1), tlt, hairdry, a/c-cool, a/c, cent heat, elec blkts, tel, cable tv, video, clock radio, t/c mkg, refrig], iron, iron brd, conv fac, ⊠, pool, spa, rm serv, plygr, tennis, cots-fee. **RO** ♦ **$88 - $104**, ♦♦ **$98 - $114**, ◊ **$15**, AE BC DC JCB MC MP VI, ♿.

★★★★ **New England Motor Inn**, (M), 100 Dumaresq St, 400m NE of PO, ☎ 02 6771 1011, fax 02 6771 1011, (2 stry gr fl), 17 units (2 suites) [shwr, bath, spa bath (3), tlt, hairdry, a/c (19), cent heat, elec blkts, tel, cable tv (19), clock radio, t/c mkg, refrig, mini bar (19), cook fac (11), micro (19), toaster], ldry, iron, iron brd, rm serv, cots, non smoking units (11). **RO** ♦ **$72 - $85**, ♦♦ **$82 - $95**, ♦♦♦ **$89 - $105**, **Suite D $105 - $155**, AE BC DC EFT MC VI.

★★★★ **Sandstock Motor Inn**, (M), 101 Dumaresq St, 550m N of PO, opposite Bowling Club, ☎ 02 6772 9988, fax 02 6772 8490, 12 units [shwr, bath (11), tlt, hairdry, a/c, elec blkts, tel, TV, movie, clock radio, t/c mkg, refrig, toaster], iron, iron brd, dinner to unit, cots, non smoking units (10). **RO** ♦ **$66**, ♦♦ **$77 - $78**, ♦♦♦♦ **$93**, AE BC DC EFT MC VI, ♿.

★★★☆ **Abbotsleigh Motor Inn**, (M), 76 Barney St, 300m S of PO, ☎ 02 6772 9488, fax 02 6772 7066, (2 stry gr fl), 31 units [shwr, tlt, hairdry, fan, heat, elec blkts, tel, cable tv, video (3), movie, clock radio, t/c mkg, refrig, mini bar, micro (2), toaster], iron, iron brd, ⊠, rm serv, cots-fee, non smoking rms (7). **RO** ♦ **$50 - $100**, ♦♦ **$60 - $100**, 6 units of a lower rating. AE BC DC EFT MC MP VI.

★★★☆ **Acacia Motor Inn**, (M), 192 Miller St, 2km S of PO, ☎ 02 6772 7733, fax 02 6771 1901, 15 units [shwr, tlt, hairdry, a/c (6), fan, cent heat, elec blkts, tel, cable tv, video (avail), clock radio, t/c mkg, refrig, micro, toaster], ldry, rec rm, spa (indoor), bbq, dinner to unit, c/park (undercover), plygr, cots, non smoking rms (8). **RO** ♦ **$49.50 - $69.50**, ♦♦ **$60.50 - $71.50**, ♦♦♦ **$69.30 - $80.30**, ◊ **$8.80**, ♦♦ **$423.50**, AE BC DC EFT MC VI.

★★★☆ **Alluna Motel**, (M), 180 Dangar St (New England Hwy), 1km S of PO, ☎ 02 6772 6226, fax 02 6772 9022, 20 units [shwr, tlt, a/c-cool (11), fan (9), cent heat (18), elec blkts, tel, TV, video (avail), clock radio, t/c mkg, refrig], ldry, ⊠ (Mon to Sat), pool, cots-fee, non smoking units (avail). **RO** ♦ **$55 - $65**, ♦♦ **$65 - $75**, ◊ **$10**, ch con, AE BC DC EFT MC VI.

★★★☆ **Armidale Cattlemans Motor Inn**, (M), 31 Marsh St, 800m S of PO, ☎ 02 6772 7788, fax 02 6771 1447, (2 stry gr fl), 54 units (15 suites) [shwr, bath (26), spa bath (6), tlt, hairdry, a/c-cool, heat, elec blkts, tel, TV, clock radio, t/c mkg, refrig, mini bar, toaster], ldry, iron, conv fac, ⊠, pool-indoor (heated), sauna, spa, bbq, rm serv, cots, non smoking units (8). **RO** ♦ **$99 - $143**, ♦♦ **$99 - $143**, ◊ **$15**, 13 units ★★★★, Unit 17 not rated. AE BC DC MC MP VI, ♿.

Armidale
Heart of New England

- Free Heritage Trolley Tour
- Scenic Drives
- History and Heritage
- National Parks
- Gorges & Waterfalls

For all your information and accommodation needs call the Armidale Visitor Information Centre on
1800 627 736

Visit our Website at : www.new-england.org/armidale/
or email; armvisit@northnet.com.au
Armidale Visitor Information Centre,
82 Marsh Street, Armidale 2350.

5AG

★★★☆ **Armidale Motel**, (M), 66 Glen Innes Rd (New England Hwy), 2km N of PO, ☎ 02 6772 8122, fax 02 6772 1024, 21 units [shwr, tlt, hairdry (11), a/c (3), fan, cent heat, elec blkts, tel, TV, video (avail), clock radio, t/c mkg, refrig, cook fac (4), toaster], ldry, iron, rec rm, ⊠, pool-heated (solar), spa, bbq, c/park (undercover) (11), plygr, tennis (half court), cots-fee. D $82 - $122, RO ♦ $58 - $69, ♦♦ $65 - $79, ♦♦♦ $82 - $96, ◊ $11, ch con, AE BC DC MC VI.

★★★☆ **Armidale Regency Hallmark Inn**, (M), 208 Dangar St, 1km S of PO, ☎ 02 6772 9800, fax 02 6771 2590, 40 units (2 suites) [shwr, bath (9), spa bath (9), tlt, hairdry, a/c, elec blkts, tel, TV, video-fee, clock radio, t/c mkg, refrig, mini bar, cook fac (2)], ldry, rec rm, conv fac, ⊠, pool, sauna, spa, bbq, rm serv, cots-fee, non smoking units (14). RO ♦ $105 - $115, ♦♦ $110 - $120, ◊ $11, Suite D $165 - $175, AE BC DC MC MP VI, ⅋⅊.

★★★☆ **Cameron Lodge Motor Inn**, (M), Cnr Barney & Dangar Sts (New England Hwy), 600m S of PO, ☎ 02 6772 2351, fax 02 6772 5600, (2 stry gr fl), 40 units [shwr, tlt, hairdry, a/c-cool, cent heat, tel, TV, movie, clock radio, t/c mkg, refrig, mini bar (avail)], ldry, ⊠, rm serv, cots-fee, non smoking units (20). RO ♦ $70.40, ♦♦ $74.80, $82.50 - $115, AE BC DC EFT MC VI.

★★★☆ **Cedar Lodge**, (M), 119 Barney St, N.E.Hwy, 50m E of Armidale Central Park, ☎ 02 6772 9511, fax 02 6772 9516, (2 stry gr fl), 12 units [shwr, bath (4), tlt, hairdry, a/c-cool, heat, elec blkts, tel, cable tv, movie-fee, clock radio, t/c mkg, refrig, toaster], ldry, rm serv, cots, non smoking units (10). RO ♦ $65 - $75, ♦♦ $69 - $79, ♦♦♦ $79 - $89, ♦♦♦♦ $95 - $125, $12, ch con, AE BC DC EFT MC VI.

★★★☆ **Club Motel**, (M), 105 Dumeresq St, 500m N of PO, ☎ 02 6772 8777, fax 02 6772 8669, 18 units [shwr, bath (17), tlt, hairdry, a/c-cool, cent heat, elec blkts, tel, TV, movie, clock radio, t/c mkg, refrig, micro (2), toaster], ldry, iron, iron brd, rm serv, cots-fee, non smoking units (5). RO ♦ $66 - $76, ♦♦ $76 - $90, ♦♦♦ $80 - $100, ◊ $10, ch con, AE BC DC EFT MC MP VI, ⅋⅊.

★★★☆ **Cotswold Gardens Inn**, (M), 34 Marsh St, 800m N of PO, ☎ 02 6772 8222, fax 02 6772 5139, 24 units (1 suite) [shwr, spa bath (1), tlt, hairdry, fan, heat, elec blkts, tel, cable tv, video (avail), clock radio, t/c mkg, refrig, mini bar], iron, iron brd, lounge, ⊠, spa, bbq, rm serv, dinner to unit, plygr. RO ♦ $84 - $99, ♦♦ $94 - $143, ◊ $11, 4 units at a higher rating. AE BC DC MC MP VI.

★★★☆ **Country Comfort - Armidale**, (M), 86 Barney St (New England Hwy), 500m S of PO, ☎ 02 6772 8511, fax 02 6772 7535, (2 stry gr fl), 42 units [shwr, spa bath (5), tlt, hairdry, a/c, elec blkts, tel, fax, TV, movie, clock radio, t/c mkg, refrig, mini bar, micro (3)], ldry, conf fac, ⊠, rm serv, dinner to unit, cots, non smoking units (26). RO ♦ $99, ♦♦ $99 - $151, ◊ $15, ch con, 8 units of a higher rating. AE BC DC MC VI.

★★★☆ **Hideaway Motor Inn**, (M), 70 Glen Innes Rd, 2km N of PO, ☎ 02 6772 5177, fax 02 6771 2609, 22 units [shwr, tlt, hairdry, a/c-cool, cent heat (22), elec blkts, tel, TV, clock radio, t/c mkg, refrig, toaster], iron, iron brd, ⊠ (for groups only), pool, dinner to unit, plygr, cots-fee. RO ♦ $47 - $51, ♦♦ $51 - $55, ♦ $9, $73 - $107, AE BC EFT MC MCH VI.

★★★☆ **Westwood Motor Inn**, (M), 62 Barney St, 550m S of PO, ☎ 02 6772 8000, fax 02 6772 0953, 11 units [shwr, bath (1), tlt, hairdry, a/c (11), elec blkts, tel, cable tv, video-fee, clock radio, t/c mkg, refrig, toaster], ldry, bbq, cots-fee, non smoking units (avail). RO ♦ $60, ♦♦ $69 - $72, ♦ $7, ch con, AE BC DC EFT MC VI, ⚹⚹.

★★★☆ **(Serviced Apartments Section)**, 6 serv apts (6 suites) acc up to 7, [shwr, tlt, hairdry, fan, heat, elec blkts, tel, cable tv, video-fee, clock radio, t/c mkg, refrig, cook fac, micro, elec frypan, toaster], iron, iron brd. **Suite RO $72.**

AAA *TOURISM Special Rates*

★★★☆ **White Lanterns Motel**, (M), 22 Marsh St, 1km N of PO, ☎ 02 6772 5777, fax 02 6771 4294, 13 units [shwr, tlt, hairdry (7), a/c-cool, heat, elec blkts, tel, cable tv, video (avail), clock radio, t/c mkg, refrig, toaster], cots, non smoking units (9). RO ♦ $69 - $77, ♦♦ $75 - $82, ♦ $10, AE BC DC EFT MC VI, ⚹⚹.

★★★ **Armidale Rose Villa Motel**, (M), New England Hwy, 4km N of PO, ☎ 02 6772 3872, or 02 6772 1850, fax 02 6772 3872, 10 units [shwr, tlt, fan, cent heat, elec blkts, tel, TV, t/c mkg, refrig, toaster], bbq, meals to unit, c/park (undercover), boat park, trailer park, courtesy transfer, plygr, cots, Pets on application. D $70 - $95, RO ♦ $45 - $60, ♦♦ $50 - $75, ♦♦♦ $60 - $80, ♦ $10 - $15, AE BC DC EFT MC VI.

★★★ **The Estelle Kramer Motor Inn**, (M), 113 Barney St, 300m S of PO, ☎ 02 6772 5200, fax 02 6771 2507, 16 units (5 suites) [shwr, bath (1), spa bath (5), tlt, a/c-cool, heat, elec blkts, tel, TV, clock radio, t/c mkg, refrig, cook fac ltd (6), micro (5)], ldry, bbq, dinner to unit, cots-fee. RO ♦ $50 - $55, ♦♦ $60 - $66, ♦ $15, Suite D ♦ $60 - $65, ♦♦ $80 - $90, ♦ $15, 5 suites of a higher rating, AE BC DC MC VI.

★★☆ **Armidale Acres Motel**, (M), New England Hwy, 6km N of PO, ☎ 02 6771 1281, fax 02 6771 1281, (2 stry), 11 units (2 bedrm - 1xd.1xs.), [shwr, tlt, fan, heat, elec blkts, tel, TV, clock radio, t/c mkg, refrig, cook fac], ldry, pool, bbq, rm serv, plygr, tennis, cots. RO ♦ $53.90 - $60.50, ♦♦ $53.90 - $60.50, ♦ $9.90, AE BC DC MC VI.

Self Catering Accommodation

★★★☆ **Beambolong**, (Chalet), Harry McRae Dve, 6km NNE of PO, ☎ 02 6771 2019, fax 02 6771 2019, (2 stry gr fl) 1 chalet (1 suite) acc up to 10, [shwr, bath, spa bath, tlt, hairdry, fan, fire pl (combustion), elec blkts, tel, TV, video, clock radio, t/c mkg, refrig, cook fac, micro, toaster], bbq, rm serv, dinner to unit, plygr, cots. BB ♦ $50, ♦♦ $85, Suite D ♦♦ $160, ♦ $20, 2 rooms ★★. Min book applies.

★★★ **Creekside Cottages**, (Cotg), 5 Canambe St, 2km E of PO, ☎ 02 6772 2018, 2 cotgs acc up to 10, [shwr, bath (1), tlt, hairdry, heat, elec blkts, tel, TV, video, t/c mkg, refrig, cook fac, toaster, blkts, linen], ldry, w/mach-fee, dryer-fee, iron, iron brd, lounge firepl, bbq, courtesy transfer, plygr, tennis, cots, non smoking property. D ♦ $77, ♦♦ $95, ♦ $10 - $15, ch con.

B&B's/Guest Houses

★★★★★ **Lindsay House Hotel**, (GH), 128 Faulkner St, 1km S of PO, ☎ 02 6771 4554, fax 02 6772 4528, 8 rms [fan, cent heat, elec blkts, tel, TV, video, clock radio, t/c mkg, refrig (communal), ldry (communal)], w/mach, dryer, ✕ (guest), rm serv (24 hour), cots (fee), non smoking property. BB ♦ $143 - $220, ♦♦ $143 - $220, ♦ $44, ch con, weekly con, AE BC DC MC VI.

★★★★ **Comeytrowe**, (B&B), 184 Marsh St, 500m SE of PO, ☎ 02 6772 5869, fax 02 6772 5869, (2 stry gr fl), 2 rms [shwr, bath (1), tlt, heat, elec blkts, t/c mkg], ✕, tennis. BB ♦ $80, ♦♦ $100 - $110, ♦ $30 - $35, ch con, 1 room ★★★.

★★★★ **Glenhope Bed & Breakfast**, (B&B), Red Gum Lane, off Booralong Rd, 3.5km W of Armidale University, ☎ 02 6772 1940, fax 02 6772 0889, 1 rm (1 suite) [shwr, tlt, hairdry, cent heat, elec blkts, tel, TV, clock radio, t/c mkg, refrig, cook fac ltd, micro, elec frypan, toaster], ldry, bbq, c/park (garage). BB ♦ $65 - $75, ♦♦ $100 - $110, ♦ $35, D ♦ $60, ♦♦ $80, ♦ $20.

★★★☆ **Jindalee Bed & Breakfast and Farmstay**, (B&B), Biddulph Rd, 7km N of Armidale, ☎ 02 6771 1250, fax 02 6772 3467, 2 rms [shwr, bath, tlt, hairdry (1), fan, heat, elec blkts, tel, clock radio (1), t/c mkg, refrig, micro, toaster], ldry, lounge (TV), lounge firepl, cook fac, bbq, plygr, cots, non smoking property. BLB ♦♦ $85 - $100, ♦ $35 - $50, ch con, fam con.

★★★☆ **Poppys Cottage Farmstyle Bed & Breakfast**, (B&B), (Farm), Edwards Lne, off Dangarsleigh Rd, 10km S of PO, ☎ 02 6775 1277, fax 02 6775 1308, 2 rms [shwr, tlt, hairdry, fan, heat, elec blkts, tel, TV, clock radio, CD, t/c mkg, refrig, toaster], ldry, iron, iron brd, bbq, meals to unit, plygr, cots-fee. BB ♦ $75, ♦♦ $105, ♦♦♦ $140 - $150.

Monivea Bed & Breakfast, (B&B), 172 Brown St, 1km S of PO, ☎ 02 6772 8001, 2 rms [shwr, tlt, fan, heat, elec blkts, tel], lounge, t/c mkg shared, non smoking property. BB ♦ $55, ♦♦ $77, (not yet classified).

ARRAWARRA NSW 2456

Pop 1,500. (590km N Sydney), See map on page 54, ref D4.

B&B's/Guest Houses

★★★★☆ **Ocean View Guest House**, (GH), 17 Headland Rd, ☎ 02 6654 0338, fax 02 6654 0738, 4 rms [shwr, tlt, c/fan, heat, clock radio], lounge, ✕, pool, meals avail, courtesy transfer, non smoking rms (4). BB ♦♦ $126 - $143, BC MC VI.

ASHFORD NSW 2361

Pop 550. (728km N Sydney), See map on page 54, ref A2. Small New England town set in limestone country with plenty of local caves and rivers to explore.

Hotels/Motels

Commercial Hotel, (LH), 42 Albury St, ☎ 02 6725 4203, (2 stry), 14 rms [c/fan, elec blkts], ldry, lounge (TV), t/c mkg shared, c/park. BLB ♦ $25 - $30, ♦♦ $35 - $40.

AUSTINMER NSW

See Wollongong & Suburbs.

AVOCA BEACH NSW 2251

Pop Part of Sydney, (91km N Sydney), See map on page 55, ref D6.

Hotels/Motels

Bellbird Resort, (M), 360 Avoca Dve, 2km W of PO, 2km to beach, ☎ 02 4382 2322, fax 02 4382 3806, (2 stry) 36 units [shwr, tlt, a/c, fan, tel, TV, t/c mkg, refrig], conv fac, ✕, pool, rm serv, dinner to unit, plygr, tennis, cots-fee. **RO** ♦ **$75 - $95,** ♦♦ **$80 - $95,** ♦♦♦ **$92 - $107,** ⓘ **$7 - $12,** Rating under review. Min book applies, BC DC EFT MC VI.

(Serviced Apartment Section), 7 serv apts [shwr, tlt, a/c, elec blkts, tel, TV, clock radio, refrig, cook fac, toaster, ldry]. **D** ♦♦♦♦ **$145,** Rating under review.

Self Catering Accommodation

★★★☆ **Avoca Beach Heritage Villas**, (HU), 326 Avoca Dr, 2.0km W of PO, ☎ 02 4382 3618, fax 02 4382 3361, 20 units acc up to 4, [shwr, tlt, heat, TV, clock radio, refrig, cook fac, toaster, ldry, blkts, linen, pillows], ✕, pool, bbq, c/park (carport), ☎, tennis, cots, **W $550 - $1,255,** Min book applies, AE BC DC MC VI.

B&B's/Guest Houses

★★★★ **Avoca Treetops Bed & Breakfast**, (B&B), 18 Baronga Rd, ☎ 02 4382 3867, fax 02 4382 3867, (2 stry) 2 rms (1 suite) [shwr, tlt, elec blkts, tel, clock radio, t/c mkg (1), refrig (1), toaster (1)], lounge, non smoking property. **BB** ♦ **$130,** ♦♦ **$130,** BC EFT MC VI.

★★★ **Portofino By The Sea B&B**, (B&B), 125 Cape Three Points Rd, 800m NW of PO, ☎ 02 4382 1160, fax 02 4382 1163, 1 rm (1 suite) [shwr, tlt, hairdry, heat, TV, video, clock radio, t/c mkg, refrig, cook fac ltd, micro, toaster], iron, iron brd, bbq, cots. **BB** ♦ **$80,** ♦♦ **$110 - $130,** ⓘ **$25,** ch con, weekly con, BC MC VI.

★★☆ **Avoca- Lake- Side B&B**, (B&B), 9 Cape Three Points Rd, 11km from Gosford, ☎ 02 4382 1693, 5 rms [shwr (2), bath (2), tlt (3), c/fan, fire pl, heat, clock radio, t/c mkg, toaster], lounge (TV), ✕, c/park. **BB** ♦ **$55,** ♦♦♦ **$82.50.**

Pacific Sands Bed & Breakfast, (B&B), 50 Cape Three Point Rd, 1km S of Heazlett Park, ☎ 02 4382 6244, fax 02 4382 6299, (2 stry) 3 rms [ensuite (1), c/fan, heat (elec/gas), clock radio, micro, toaster, doonas], shared fac (2), lounge (TV), ✕, t/c mkg shared, refrig, non smoking rms. **BB** ♦ **$145 - $210,** ♦♦ **$145 - $210,** BC MC VI, (not yet classified).

BALLINA NSW 2478

Pop 16,050. (753km N Sydney), See map on page 54, ref E2.

Hotels/Motels

FLAG
FLAG CHOICE HOTELS

★★★★ **All Seasons Motor Inn**, (M), 301 Pacific Hwy, 1km W of PO, ☎ 02 6686 2922, fax 02 6686 4012, (2 stry gr fl), 38 units (2 suites) [shwr, tlt, hairdry, a/c, elec blkts, tel, TV, movie, clock radio, t/c mkg, refrig], ldry, conv fac, ✕, pool, spa, rm serv, dinner to unit, cots, non smoking units (16). **RO** ♦ **$96 - $145,** ♦♦ **$106 - $145,** ♦♦♦ **$117 - $156,** ⓘ **$11,** **$615 - $1,015,** Suite **D $130 - $174,** AE BC DC EFT MC MP VI.

★★★★ **Ballina Beach Resort**, (M), Compton Dve, Lighthouse Beach, 1km E of PO, ☎ 02 6686 8888, fax 02 6686 8897, (2 stry gr fl), 46 units [shwr, spa bath (10), tlt, hairdry, a/c, tel, TV, movie, clock radio, t/c mkg, refrig, cook fac ltd (16), toaster], ldry, iron, iron brd, conv fac, ✕, pool, sauna, spa, bbq, rm serv, dinner to unit, tennis, cots-fee. **D $159 - $215,** **RO** ♦ **$98 - $215,** ♦♦ **$109 - $215,** ⓘ **$11,** ch con, AE BC DC EFT MC VI, ♿.

★★★★ **Ballina Heritage Inn**, (M), 229 River St, opposite RSL, ☎ 02 6686 0505, or 02 6686 4123, fax 02 6686 0788, (2 stry gr fl), 26 units (2 suites) [shwr, spa bath (3), tlt, hairdry, a/c, tel, TV, video, clock radio, t/c mkg, refrig, toaster], ldry, iron, pool (salt water), c/park (undercover), cots. **RO** ♦ **$80 - $95,** ♦♦ **$90 - $140,** ♦♦♦ **$110 - $145,** ◊ **$15, Suite D $115 - $145,** ch con, Rooms of a higher standard available. AE BC DC EFT MC VI.

★★★★ **Ballina Island Motor Inn**, (M), Pacific Hwy, 2km S of Police Station, ☎ 02 6686 8866, fax 02 6686 8770, 40 units (3 suites) [shwr, bath, spa bath (4), tlt, hairdry, a/c, elec blkts, tel, cable tv, movie, clock radio, t/c mkg, refrig, mini bar, toaster], ldry, iron, iron brd, conv fac, ☒, pool, spa, dinner to unit, cots, non smoking units (26). **RO** ♦ **$105,** ♦♦ **$105 - $110,** ♦♦♦ **$120,** ◊ **$15, Suite D** ♦ **$150,** ◊ **$15,** AE BC DC EFT MC MCH MP VI.

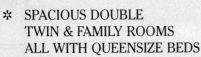

★★★☆ **Avlon Gardens Motel**, (M), 16 Bangalow Rd, 1km N of PO off Pacific Hwy, ☎ 02 6686 4044, fax 02 6686 4679, (2 stry gr fl), 10 units [shwr, spa bath (1), tlt, hairdry, a/c, fan, heat, elec blkts, tel, fax, cable tv, clock radio, t/c mkg, refrig, micro-fee, toaster], ldry, iron, iron brd, pool (salt water), bbq, rm serv, c/park (undercover), courtesy transfer, cots-fee, non smoking units (3). RO ♦ $61 - $95, ♦♦ $66 - $95, ◊ $12, 6 family rooms ★★★. AE BC DC EFT JCB MC VI.

GOLDEN CHAIN ★★★☆ **Ballina Palms Motor Inn**, (M), Cnr Bentinck & Owen Sts, 1.2km NE of PO, ☎ 02 6686 4477, fax 02 6686 4934, 13 units [shwr, tlt, hairdry, a/c, elec blkts, tel, fax (copier), TV, video (avail), clock radio, t/c mkg, refrig, micro, toaster], ldry, iron, iron brd, pool (salt water), bbq, dinner to unit, courtesy transfer, plygr, cots-fee, non smoking units (5). RO ♦ $73 - $110, ♦♦ $83 - $124, ◊ $12, ch con, AE BC DC EFT MC VI, ⚹&.

GOLDEN CHAIN ★★★☆ **Richmond Motor Inn**, (M), 227 River St, ☎ 02 6686 9100, fax 02 6686 9111, (2 stry gr fl), 13 units [shwr, spa bath (1), tlt, hairdry, a/c, tel, TV, video (avail), movie, clock radio, t/c mkg, refrig, toaster], iron, iron brd, pool (salt water), non smoking units (4). RO ♦ $85 - $105, ♦♦ $96 - $116, ◊ $11, AE BC DC EFT MC MP VI.

★★★ **Ballina Centre Point**, (M), 285 River St, 250m from RSL Club, ☎ 02 6686 6877, fax 02 6686 0542, (2 stry gr fl), 14 units [shwr, tlt, hairdry, a/c, tel, fax, TV, clock radio, t/c mkg, refrig], ldry, iron, pool. RO ♦ $45 - $75, ♦♦ $52 - $92, ◊ $10, ch con, AE BC DC EFT MC VI.

★★★ **Ballina Colonial Motel**, (M), Cnr Bangalow Rd & Skinner St, 1.5km N of Town Centre, ☎ 02 6686 7691, fax 02 6686 3163, 12 units [shwr, tlt, hairdry, a/c, fan, heat, tel, cable tv, clock radio, t/c mkg, refrig, toaster], ldry, pool, bbq, dinner to unit (Mon to Fri), cots, non smoking rms. RO ♦ $55 - $93.50, ♦♦ $60 - $99, ♦♦♦ $71.50 - $110, ♦♦♦♦ $77 - $115.50, $82.50 - $132, AE BC DC EFT MC MP VI.

★★★ **Ballina Travellers Lodge**, (M), 36 Tamar St, ☎ 02 6686 6737, or 02 6686 6342, fax 02 6686 6342, 12 units [shwr, tlt, a/c, fan (12), heat, elec blkts, tel, TV, clock radio, t/c mkg, refrig, toaster], ldry, rec rm, lounge (TV), pool (salt water), cook fac, bbq, cots-fee, non smoking units. RO ♦ $56 - $92, ♦♦ $62 - $105, ◊ $15, ch con, AE BC DC EFT MC VI.

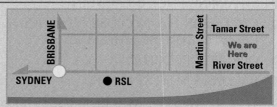

★★★ **Coast Inn Motel**, (M), 311 River St (Pacific Hwy), 1km W of PO, ☎ 02 6686 3300, fax 02 6681 4488, (2 stry gr fl), 10 units [shwr, tlt, a/c, fan, tel, TV, movie, clock radio, t/c mkg, refrig], c/park (undercover) (5), cots. RO ♦ $54, ♦♦ $55 - $65, ♦ $55 - $85, ♦♦♦ $66 - $95, ◊ $10, AE BC DC EFT MC VI.

★★★ **Fun'n'Sun Motel**, (M), Pacific Hwy, 500m N of The Big Prawn, ☎ 02 6686 3982, fax 02 6686 3982, 17 units (7 suites) [shwr, tlt, c/fan, heat, elec blkts, TV, clock radio, t/c mkg, refrig, cook fac (10), toaster], ldry, iron, iron brd, pool, bbq, c/park (undercover), cots-fee, non smoking units (avail). RO ♦ $49 - $77, ♦♦ $49 - $77, ◊ $10, Suite D ♦ $59 - $75, ♦♦ $59 - $75, 10 self contained units of a 2.5 star rating. AE BC EFT MC VI.

★★☆ **Almare Tourist Motel**, (M), 339 River St (Pacific Hwy), 1km W of PO, ☎ 02 6686 2873, or 02 6686 2833, fax 02 6686 6533, 13 units [shwr, tlt, a/c (9), fan (4), heat (4), tel, TV, clock radio, t/c mkg, refrig], pool, bbq, cots-fee. RO ♦ $42 - $48, ♦♦ $50 - $55, ◊ $10, AE BC EFT MC MCH VI.

★★☆ **Ballina Sundowner Motor Inn**, (M), 274 River St (Pacific Hwy), 150m from RSL Club, ☎ 02 6686 2388, fax 02 6686 0182, 27 units [shwr, tlt, a/c-cool (23), heat, tel, fax, TV, clock radio, t/c mkg, refrig, mini bar, toaster], ldry, ✉ (5 days), pool, bbq, rm serv (5 nights), cots-fee. RO ♦ $44, ♦♦ $55, ♦♦♦ $66, ◊ $12, AE BC DC EFT MC VI.

★★☆ **Chaparral Motel**, (M), Pacific Hwy, 2km S of PO, ☎ 02 6686 3399, fax 02 6686 3023, (2 stry gr fl), 18 units [shwr, tlt, hairdry, a/c, fan, elec blkts, tel, TV, movie, clock radio, t/c mkg, refrig], iron, iron brd, pool (salt water), bbq, c/park (undercover), plygr, cots. RO ♦ $48 - $80, ♦♦ $55 - $80, ♦♦♦ $68 - $92, ♦♦♦♦ $80 - $104, AE BC DC EFT MC VI.

★★☆ **Cubana Motel**, (M), 329 River St (Pacific Hwy), 500m W of PO, ☎ 02 6686 8366, fax 02 6686 8011, 25 units [shwr, tlt, a/c (11), c/fan, heat, tel, TV, video, movie, clock radio, t/c mkg, refrig, toaster], ldry, pool, bbq, c/park (undercover), cots, non smoking units (9). RO ♦♦ $53 - $60, ◊ $10, $318 - $360, 6 units of a higher rating, 4 units of a lower rating. AE BC DC EFT MC VI.

★★☆ **El Rancho Motor Inn**, (M), Cnr Cherry & Fox Sts, 1km N of PO, ☎ 02 6686 3333, fax 02 6686 0081, (2 stry gr fl), 25 units (3 suites) [shwr, spa bath (1), tlt, a/c-cool, fan, heat, elec blkts, tel, fax, TV, movie, clock radio, t/c mkg, refrig, cook fac (5), toaster], ldry, ✉ (6 nights), pool, bbq, rm serv, cots, non smoking units (2). W $360 - $560, RO ♦ $55 - $90, ♦♦ $60 - $100, ♦♦♦ $78 - $110, Suite D $90 - $120, ch con, AE BC DC EFT MC VI.

★★☆ **Hi Craft Motel**, (M), 297 River St (Pacific Hwy), 250m W of RSL Club, ☎ 02 6686 8868, fax 02 6686 3041, (2 stry gr fl), 26 units [shwr, tlt, hairdry, a/c (14), c/fan, heat, tel, fax, cable tv, clock radio, t/c mkg, refrig, cook fac (4)], ldry, iron, iron brd, ✕, pool, bbq, dinner to unit, cots-fee, non smoking units (8). RO ♦ $49 - $59, ♦♦ $49 - $89, ♦♦♦ $59 - $99, ◊ $10, 4 units of a lower rating. AE BC DC EFT MC MP VI.

★★☆ **Suntori**, (M), Pacific Hwy, 3km W of PO, ☎ 02 6686 2099, fax 02 6686 8594, 28 units [shwr, tlt, a/c, fan, heat, tel, TV, video (avail), clock radio, t/c mkg, refrig], ldry, rec rm, ✕, pool, bbq, rm serv, dinner to unit, plygr, cots-fee. RO ♦ $55 - $65, ♦♦ $55 - $65, ◊ $10, AE BC DC MC VI.

BALLINA NSW continued...

★☆ **Ballina Ferry Boat Motel**, (M), Previously Ballina Ferry Boat Budget Motel Pacific Pwy, 3km S of PO, ☎ 02 6686 2827, or 02 6681 3425, fax 02 6686 2827, 13 units [shwr, tlt, a/c-cool, fan, heat, tel, fax, cable tv (5), clock radio, t/c mkg, refrig, cook fac (5), toaster], pool, wading pool, bbq, plygr, cots, non smoking units (2). **RO** ♦ **$45 - $65**, ♦♦ **$46 - $70**, AE BC DC EFT JCB MC MCH VI.

★☆ **Ballina Motel**, (M), Pacific Hwy, 1km W of PO, ☎ 02 6686 2208, fax 02 6681 1774, 13 units [shwr, tlt, c/fan, heat, elec blkts, tel, fax, TV, movie, clock radio, t/c mkg, refrig, cook fac (1), toaster], iron, pool, bbq, plygr, cots-fee. **W $225 - $280**, **RO** ♦ **$42**, ♦♦ **$42**, ♦♦♦ **$45**, ♦ **$10**, AE BC DC EFT MC MP VI.

Self Catering Accommodation

★★★☆ **Club Resort Ballina**, (HU), 69 Jameson Ave, 5km NE of PO, ☎ 02 6686 7001, fax 02 6686 7473, 23 units acc up to 6, [shwr, bath (4), spa bath (4), tlt, a/c (8), c/fan, heat, tel, TV, movie, clock radio, t/c mkg, refrig, cook fac, micro, d/wash (5), toaster, blkts, linen, pillows], ldry, iron, rec rm, pool-heated (solar), sauna-fee, spa, bbq, golf, squash, tennis, cots-fee. **D** ♦♦ **$91 - $160**, ♦ **$11 - $16**, **W** **$485 - $1,265**, ♦ **$33 - $77**, Min book applies, AE BC DC MC VI.

★★★☆ **Leisure-Lee**, (Apt), 6 Easton Pl, Ballina East 2478, ☎ 02 6686 2426, fax 02 6686 2426, 6 apts acc up to 6, [shwr, tlt, heat, elec blkts, fax, TV, video, refrig, cook fac, linen reqd-fee], ldry, bbq, c/park (carport), courtesy transfer, ✆, cots. **D** ♦♦ **$99**, ♦ **$22**, **W $418 - $935**, BC MC VI.

★★★☆ **Shelly Pines**, (HU), 15 Pacific Terrace, ☎ 02 6686 2177, fax 02 6686 7460, 1 unit acc up to 6, [heat, fan, tel, TV, video, clock radio, refrig, cook fac, micro, d/wash, ldry, blkts], w/mach, dryer, pool, bbq, c/park. **W $420 - $1,000**, Min book applies.

★★★ **The Anchorage**, (HU), 60 Cedar Cres, Ballina East 2478, ☎ 02 6686 2177, (2 stry), 2 units acc up to 6, [shwr, bath, tlt, c/fan, heat, tel, TV, video, clock radio, t/c mkg, refrig, cook fac, micro, elec frypan, d/wash, toaster, ldry, linen reqd], pool (salt water), c/park (garage). **W $420 - $1,000**, Min book applies.

★★★ **The Shores**, (Cotg), 2 Fenwick Dve, Ballina East 2478, ☎ 02 6686 2177, 1 cotg acc up to 6, [bath, tlt, TV, refrig, cook fac, micro, toaster, ldry, linen reqd]. **W $320 - $700**, Min book applies.

★★☆ **De la Mer**, (HU), Cnr Mckinnon St & Cedar Cres, Ballina East 2478, ☎ 02 6686 2177, 5 units acc up to 6, [shwr, bath, tlt, TV, refrig, cook fac, ldry], pool, bbq, c/park (garage). **W $325 - $800**, Min book applies.

★★☆ **Hereford Court**, (HU), 72 Cedar Cres, Ballina East 2478, ☎ 02 6686 2177, 3 units acc up to 6, [shwr, bath, tlt, TV, video, refrig, cook fac, micro, ldry, linen reqd], w/mach, dryer, bbq, c/park (garage). **W $300 - $730**, Min book applies.

★★☆ **Pandanus Place**, (HU), 70 Cedar Cres, Ballina East 2478, ☎ 02 6686 2177, 1 unit acc up to 4, [shwr, bath, tlt, TV, refrig, cook fac, d/wash, toaster, ldry, linen reqd], pool, c/park (garage). **W $300 - $720**, Min book applies.

★★ **Cherry Court**, (HU), 60 Cherry St, 800m NE of PO, ☎ 02 6686 9545, fax 02 6686 9201, 3 units acc up to 4, [shwr, tlt, TV, refrig, cook fac, elec frypan, toaster, ldry, linen reqd], w/mach, dryer, iron, c/park (carport). **W $200 - $350**, Min book applies.

★★ **Haere Mai**, (HU), Cnr Pacific Terrace & Hindmarsh St, Ballina East 2478, ☎ 02 6686 2177, 2 units acc up to 4, [shwr, bath, tlt, heat, TV, clock radio, refrig, cook fac, toaster, linen reqd], w/mach. **W $235 - $600**, Min book applies.

★ **Pine Court**, (HU), 69 Crane St, 400m E of PO, ☎ 02 6686 9545, fax 02 6686 9201, 5 units acc up to 4, [shwr, tlt, heat, TV, refrig, cook fac, elec frypan, ldry, linen reqd], w/mach, dryer, iron, c/park. **W $180 - $300**, Min book applies.

Angels Beach Lodge B&B, (Cotg), 3 Sea Swallow Plc, Angels Beach, Ballina East 2478, 2km N of East Ballina PO, ☎ 02 6686 5253, fax 02 6686 5253, 1 cotg (1 suite) [shwr, tlt, fan (4), heat, clock radio, refrig, cook fac ltd, micro, ldry, doonas], lounge (TV/video), ✕, t/c mkg shared, bbq, non smoking suites. **BLB** ♦♦ **$95 - $145**, ♦ **$25**, ch con, weekly con, BC MC VI, (not yet classified).

B&B's/Guest Houses

★★★★★ **Ballina Manor**, (GH), 25 Norton St, ☎ 02 6681 5888, fax 02 6681 1900, (Multi-stry gr fl), 12 rms (4 suites) [shwr, bath (2), spa bath (3), tlt, hairdry, a/c, c/fan, heat, tel, TV, clock radio, t/c mkg, refrig], ldry, lounge, lounge firepl, ✕, rm serv, courtesy transfer, non smoking property. **BLB** ♦ **$115 - $175**, ♦♦ **$130 - $175**, **Suite BLB** ♦ **$175**, ♦♦ **$190**, ♦ **$20**, pen con, AE BC DC MC VI.

★★★☆ **The Yabsley**, (B&B), 5 Yabsley St, Ballina East 2478, 3km E of PO, ☎ 02 6681 1505, fax 02 6681 1505, 2 rms [shwr, bath (1), tlt, hairdry, c/fan, heat, elec blkts, tel, TV, clock radio], ldry, iron, iron brd, lounge (TV & fireplace), ✕, t/c mkg shared, bbq, non smoking property. **BB** ♦ **$100**, ♦♦ **$110**, **RO** ♦ **$90**, ♦♦ **$100**, BC MC VI.

★★★★ **Brundah**, (B&B), 37 Norton St, 400m E of Tourist Information, ☎ 02 6686 8166, 2 rms [shwr, tlt, hairdry, tel, TV, clock radio, t/c mkg, refrig], ldry, rec rm, lounge firepl, bbq, non smoking property. **BB** ♦ **$97.50 - $125**, ♦♦ **$110 - $145**, AE BC DC MC VI.

BALLINA EAST NSW 2478

Pop Part of Ballina, (755km N Sydney), See map on page 54, ref E2.
Self Catering Accommodation

★★★☆ **Harbourview**, (HU), Unit 2 / 11 Harbourview St, units (3 bedrm), [heat, fan, tel, TV, video, ldry], TV rm, pool, c/park. **W $430 - $1,100**.

BALRANALD NSW 2715

Pop 1,400. (852km SW Sydney), See map on pages 52/53, ref C6. Old river port on the Murrumbidgee River and one of the gateways to Mungo National Park. Fishing, Swimming.
Hotels/Motels

★★★☆ **Balranald Motor Inn**, (M), 154 Market St (Sturt Hwy), 1km W of PO, ☎ 03 5020 1104, fax 03 5020 1544, 23 units [shwr, tlt, hairdry, a/c, elec blkts, tel, cable tv, clock radio, t/c mkg, refrig], ldry, iron, iron brd, rec rm, ✉, pool, bbq, plygr, cots-fee. **RO** ♦♦ **$95**, ♦♦♦♦ **$142**, AE BC DC EFT MC VI.

★★★ **Balranald Colony Inn**, (M), 140 Market St, 300m N of PO, ☎ 03 5020 1302, fax 03 5020 1302, 6 units [shwr, tlt, a/c, elec blkts, TV, clock radio, t/c mkg, refrig, toaster], ldry, bbq, cots-fee, non smoking property. **RO** ♦ **$49.50**, ♦♦ **$55**, ♦♦♦ **$63.80**, AE BC EFT MC VI.

★★★ **Sturt Motel**, (M), 32 River St, ☎ 03 5020 1309, or 03 5020 0067, fax 03 6030 1802, 14 units [ensuite, a/c, heat (elec), elec blkts, tel, TV, clock radio, t/c mkg, refrig], ldry, pool, bbq, rm serv (breakfast), plygr, cots-fee, non smoking rms (2). **RO** ♦ **$46 - $50**, ♦♦ **$55 - $66**, ♦ **$8**, AE BC DC EFT JCB MC VI.

★★☆ **Balranald Shamrock Motel**, (LMH), Cnr Market & Mayall Sts, 400m E of PO, ☎ 03 5020 1107, or 03 5020 1304, fax 03 5020 1070, 18 units [shwr, bath (4), tlt, a/c-cool, heat, elec blkts, tel, TV, clock radio, t/c mkg, refrig], ✉ (6 nights), dinner to unit (6 nights), cots. **D $75 - $85**, **RO** ♦ **$46**, ♦♦ **$55**, BC DC MC VI.

★★ **Motel Capri**, (M), 207 Market St, 1km W of PO, ☎ 03 5020 1201, 12 units [shwr, tlt, a/c, elec blkts, TV, video (available), clock radio, t/c mkg, refrig, cook fac (1), toaster], ldry, pool, cots-fee, non smoking units (4). **RO** ♦ **$45**, ♦♦ **$55**, ♦ **$8**, ch con, 4 units ★★☆. AE BC DC MC VI.

BANGALOW NSW 2479

Pop 819. (778km N Sydney), See map on page 54, ref E2.
Self Catering Accommodation

★★★★ **Talofa Lodge**, (Cotg), 684 Bangalow Rd, 10km SW of Byron Bay, ☎ 02 6687 1494, fax 02 6687 1494, 5 cotgs acc up to 7, [shwr, tlt, fire pl (5), tel, TV, clock radio, t/c mkg, refrig, cook fac, micro, toaster, ldry, blkts, linen, pillows], w/mach, iron, bbq, non smoking property. **W $540 - $1,155**, ch con, Min book applies, BC MC VI.

B&B's/Guest Houses

★★★★☆ **Possum Creek Lodge**, (GH), Cedarvale Rd (off Possum Creek Rd), 2km W of PO, ☎ 02 6687 1188, fax 02 6687 1269, 3 rms [shwr, tlt, c/fan, fire pl (1), heat, elec blkts, TV], ldry, iron, iron brd, lounge (TV), ✕, pool (salt water), spa, non smoking property. **BB** ♦ **$130 - $170**, ♦♦ **$145 - $195**, **DBB** ♦ **$185 - $225**, ♦♦ **$265 - $310**, Min book applies, AE BC MC VI.

★★★★ **(Cottage Section)**, 1 cotg acc up to 6, [shwr, bath (1), tlt, a/c (1), heat, elec blkts, TV, video, t/c mkg, refrig, cook fac, micro, elec frypan, toaster, ldry, blkts, linen], w/mach, iron, iron brd, bbq. **D $110**, **W $495 - $1,100**, Meals by arrangement.

★★★★ **Green Mango Hideaway**, (B&B), Lofts Rd, off Coolamon Scenic Dve, 12km W of Byron Bay PO, ☎ 02 6684 7171, fax 02 6684 7181, (2 stry gr fl), 4 rms [shwr, tlt, c/fan, elec blkts], lounge (TV & firepl), ✕, pool (salt water), spa, t/c mkg shared, dinner to unit, non smoking property. **BB** ♦♦ **$140 - $210**, BC MC VI.

★★★★ **Riverview Guesthouse**, (GH), 99 Byron St, ☎ 02 6687 1317, fax 02 6687 2123, 3 rms [shwr, bath (1), tlt, hairdry, c/fan, heat, elec blkts], rec rm, lounge (TV), conv fac, ✕, spa. **BB** ♦ **$80 - $120**, ♦♦ **$90 - $160**, Min book all holiday times.

BANNISTER NSW 2580

Pop Nominal, (190km S Sydney), See map on page 55, ref A4.
Hillcrest B&B Farmstay Cottage, (Cotg), Hillcrest, 32km NW of Goulburn, ☎ 02 4844 3155, 1 cotg acc up to 5, [shwr, tlt, hairdry, heat, TV, clock radio, t/c mkg, refrig, cook fac, toaster], iron. **BB ♦ $45, ♦♦ $88, ⓥ $30**, ch con, fam con, pen con.

BANORA POINT NSW 2486

Pop Nominal, (854km N Sydney), See map on page 54, ref E1. See also Chinderah & Tweed Heads.

★★★★ Banora Point Motor Inn, (M), Cnr Pacific Hwy & Terranora Rd, ☎ 07 5524 2222, fax 07 5524 2143, (2 stry gr fl), 40 units [shwr, bath (3), spa bath (1), tlt, hairdry, a/c, tel, fax, cable tv, clock radio, t/c mkg, refrig, toaster], ldry, conv fac, ✕, pool, cots-fee, non smoking units (14). **RO ♦♦ $85 - $115, ⓥ $15**, ch con, AE BC DC EFT MC VI, ⓕ⌂.

BARADINE NSW 2396

Pop 600. Nominal, (493km NW Sydney), See map on pages 52/53, ref G3.
★★★☆ Warrigal Gardens, (B&B), Macquarie St, 1km NW of PO, ☎ 02 6843 1765, 2 rms [shwr, tlt, a/c-cool, c/fan, elec blkts, TV, clock radio, t/c mkg], non smoking rms (avail). **BB ♦ $55, ♦♦ $60, ⓥ $10**.

BARHAM NSW 2732

Pop 1,167. (848km SW Sydney), See map on pages 52/53, ref C6. Barham and its smaller twin town of Koondrook lie on the Murray River about halfway between Swan Hill and Echuca.

Hotels/Motels

★★★☆ Acacia Motor Inn, (M), 18 Thule St, 200m N of bridge, ☎ 03 5453 2955, fax 03 5453 2629, 16 units [shwr, tlt, a/c, c/fan (11), heat, elec blkts, tel, TV, clock radio, t/c mkg, refrig], conf fac, spa, bbq, cots-fee, non smoking units (5). **RO ♦ $50 - $60, ♦♦ $55 - $65, ♦♦♦ $71 - $76, ⓥ $12**, 5 units of a lower rating, AE BC DC EFT MC MCH VI.

BARHAM CLUB MOTOR INN

AAAT ★★★☆

- DIRECTLY OPPOSITE THE BARHAM SERVICES CLUB
- WELL APPOINTED ALL GROUND FLOOR UNITS • SALT WATER POOL AND BBQ FACILITIES • RC AIR CONDITIONING • SPA UNITS
- ALL REMOTE TV'S • QUEEN BEDS • NON SMOKING ROOMS
- A MINUTES WALK TO THE MURRAY

1 Niemur Street, Barham, NSW 2732
Ph: (03) 5453 2822 Fax: (03) 5453 3103
Email: clubinn@cybanet.net.au Web: www.goldenrivers.com

BARHAM GOLDEN RIVERS COUNTRY HOLIDAY APARTMENTS

AAA TOURISM ★★★★

...MORE THAN A MOTEL

21 NIEMUR ST. CHECK LISTING UNDER BARHAM
PH: 54532556 FAX: 54531134
RESERVATIONS: FREE CALL 1800 243355

★★★☆ Barham All Seasons Motor Lodge, (M), 45 Murray St (Cnr Niemur St), Opposite Services Club, ☎ 03 5453 2900, fax 03 5453 1055, (2 stry gr fl), 25 units [shwr, spa bath (4), tlt, a/c, heat, elec blkts, tel, TV, clock radio, t/c mkg, refrig, mini bar, toaster], ldry, pool-heated (solar), bbq, rm serv, cots, non smoking units (5). **W $360 - $600, RO ♦ $60 - $70, ♦♦ $70 - $90, ♦♦♦ $80 - $90, ⓥ $10**, ch con, AE BC DC MC VI.

★★★☆ Barham Club Motor Inn, (M), 1 Niemur St, Opposite Services Club, ☎ 03 5453 2822, fax 03 5453 3103, 25 units [shwr, spa bath (6), tlt, hairdry (25), a/c, heat, elec blkts, tel, TV, video (avail), clock radio, t/c mkg, refrig, toaster], pool, bbq, c/park (undercover), cots, non smoking units (avail). **RO ♦ $60 - $75, ♦♦ $66 - $86, ♦♦♦ $78 - $90, ⓥ $10**, 6 units of a lesser rating, AE BC DC EFT MC VI, ⓕ⌂.

★★★☆ Country Roads Motor Inn, (M), 45 Thule St, 500m N of PO, ☎ 03 5453 2811, fax 03 5453 2384, 20 units [shwr, tlt, hairdry (8), a/c-cool, heat, elec blkts, tel, TV, clock radio, t/c mkg, refrig, toaster], ldry, pool, bbq, dinner to unit, cots, non smoking units (3). **RO ♦ $56, ♦♦ $66, ⓥ $12**, AE BC DC EFT MC VI.

★★★ Barham Colonial Motel, (M), Cnr Murray & Chester Sts, 500m E of PO, ☎ 03 5453 3099, fax 03 5453 3114, 11 units [shwr, tlt, hairdry, a/c, elec blkts, tel, TV, video-fee, clock radio, t/c mkg, refrig, cook fac ltd (3), micro (3), toaster], ldry, pool, bbq, c/park. **RO ♦ $54 - $60, ♦♦ $60 - $75, ♦♦♦ $66 - $108**, ch con, Min book long w/ends and Easter, AE BC DC EFT MC VI.

★★☆ Barham Bridge Motor Inn, (M), 1 Murray St, 100m from bridge, ☎ 03 5453 2777, fax 03 5453 2212, (2 stry gr fl), 23 units [shwr, tlt, a/c-cool, elec blkts, tel, fax, TV, video, movie, clock radio, t/c mkg, refrig, cook fac (8)], pool-heated (solar), spa, bbq, cots-fee. **RO ♦ $44 - $62, ♦♦ $52 - $62, ♦♦♦ $52 - $77, ⓥ $15**, AE BC DC EFT MC VI.

Self Catering Accommodation

★★★★ Golden Rivers Country Holiday Apartments, (Apt), 21 Niemur St, 300m E of PO, ☎ 03 5453 2556, fax 03 5453 1134, (2 stry gr fl), 7 apts acc up to 7, [shwr, bath (3), spa bath (2), tlt, hairdry, a/c, c/fan, elec blkts, TV, video, clock radio, t/c mkg, refrig, cook fac, micro, d/wash, toaster], ldry, blkts, linen, pillows], w/mach, dryer, iron, pool-heated (solar/salt water), sauna, spa, bbq, c/park (carport), cots. **D ♦ $75 - $105, ♦♦ $75 - $105, ⓥ $16, W ♦♦ $450 - $750, ⓥ $108**, AE BC EFT MC VI.

Barham Golf Accommodation, (HU), Moulamein Rd, 2km NE of PO, ☎ 03 5453 2884, fax 03 5453 1077, 19 units acc up to 4, [shwr, tlt, a/c, elec blkts, TV, clock radio, refrig, cook fac, blkts, linen, pillows], ldry, w/mach (2), ✕, bbq, c/park (2), bowls, golf, tennis. **RO ♦ $46, ♦♦ $57 - $68, ⓥ $16**, ch con, AE BC DC EFT MC VI.

BAROOGA NSW 3644

Pop 1,000. (741km SW Sydney), See map on pages 52/53, ref D7. Barooga and its larger twin town of Cobram lie on the Murray River in a thriving fruit and dairy area. See also Cobram.

Hotels/Motels

★★★☆ Cobram Barooga Golf Club Motel, (M), Previously Cobram - Barooga Motel Golf Course Rd, ☎ 03 5873 4357, fax 03 5873 4772, 37 units [shwr, tlt, a/c, elec blkts, tel, TV, clock radio, t/c mkg, refrig, cook fac (3), micro (4), toaster], ldry, rec rm, pool, sauna, spa, bbq, golf, mini golf, tennis. **RO ♦ $60 - $94, ♦♦ $70 - $95, ♦♦♦ $90 - $110, ⓥ $20**, ch con, AE BC DC MC VI.

★★★☆ Cobram Barooga Golf Resort Motel, (M), Golf Course Rd, 1.2km W of PO, ☎ 03 5873 4523, fax 03 5873 4132, 16 units (1 suite) (1 bedrm), [shwr, tlt, a/c-cool, heat (elec), elec blkts, tel, TV, clock radio, t/c mkg, refrig, cook fac, micro, toaster], ldry, iron, iron brd, rec rm, pool, spa (communal), bbq, plygr, golf, tennis, cots. **RO ♦ $66 - $88, ♦♦ $77 - $90, ⓥ $17, Suite RO $143 - $165**, ch con, weekly con, BC EFT MC MCH VI,

Operator Comment: See our Main Advertisement listed under Cobram.

★★★☆ Sportsmans Motor Inn, (M), Cnr Golf Course Rd & Burkinshaw St, ☎ 03 5873 4444, fax 03 5873 4509, 20 units [shwr, tlt, a/c, fan, elec blkts, tel, TV, video, clock radio, t/c mkg, refrig, toaster], ldry, pool, spa, bbq, plygr, tennis, cots. **W $525 - $650, RO ♦ $65 - $93.50, ♦♦ $75 - $93.50, ♦♦♦ $97 - $115**, ch con, AE BC DC MC VI, ⓕ⌂.

★★★ **Barooga Golf View**, (M), Lot 11 Golf Course Rd, 1.7km NW of PO, ☎ 03 5873 4555, fax 03 5873 4556, 24 units [shwr, spa bath, tlt, a/c-cool, c/fan, heat, elec blkts, tel, TV, video (avail), clock radio, t/c mkg, refrig, toaster], ldry, pool, bbq. W $462 - $539, RO ♦ $66 - $80, ♦♦ $77 - $88, ♦♦♦ $99 - $110, ♦ $18 - $22, ch con, Min book applies, AE BC DC MC VI, ♠♿.

★★★ **Barooga River Gums Motor Inn**, (M), 15 Golf Course Rd, 300m S of PO, ☎ 03 5873 4575, fax 03 5873 4740, 16 units [shwr, tlt, a/c-cool (11), a/c (5), fan, heat (11), elec blkts, tel, TV, clock radio, t/c mkg, refrig, cook fac], ldry, pool-heated (solar), spa, bbq, c/park (undercover), cots. RO ♦ $63 - $77, ♦♦ $66 - $83, ♦ $13, ch con, 5 units ★★★☆, AE BC DC MC VI, ♠♿.

★★☆ **High Noon Motel**, (M), Berrigan Rd, 1km N of PO, ☎ 03 5873 4244, fax 03 5873 4749, 18 units (2 suites) [shwr, tlt, a/c, elec blkts, tel, TV, video (avail), clock radio, t/c mkg, refrig, cook fac (6), micro (10)], ldry-fee, pool, spa-fee, bbq, plygr, golf, cots-fee. RO ♦ $55 - $66, ♦♦ $55 - $70, ♦ $13, ch con, AE BC DC MCH VI.

Self Catering Accommodation

★★★☆ **Bullanginya Lodge**, (HU), 7 Banker St, 50m E of Barooga Sports Club, ☎ 03 5873 4636, fax 03 5873 4784, 6 units acc up to 5, [shwr, tlt, a/c, c/fan, elec blkts, tel, TV, video-fee, clock radio, t/c mkg, refrig, micro, elec frypan, toaster, blkts, linen, pillows], ldry, pool-heated (solar), bbq, ✆, cots-fee. D ♦♦ $60.50 - $80.30, ♦ $8.80 - $16.50, W ♦♦ $363 - $495, ♦ $55 - $77, ch con, BC MC VI.

★★★☆ **Wandeet Holiday Units**, (HU), 28 Barinya St, 200m N of PO, ☎ 03 5873 4881, fax 03 5873 4881, 3 units acc up to 3, [shwr, tlt, a/c, c/fan, elec blkts, TV, clock radio, refrig, cook fac, toaster, linen reqd-fee], ldry, pool, spa, bbq, c/park (carport). D ♦♦ $45 - $55, ♦ $5 - $8, W ♦♦ $265 - $295, ♦ $35 - $55.

★★☆ **Pepper-Corn Lodge**, (HU), Vermont St, 500m E of PO, ☎ 03 5873 4411, fax 03 5873 4411, 10 units acc up to 4, [shwr, tlt, a/c, elec blkts, TV, clock radio, refrig, cook fac, linen], ldry, pool, bbq, courtesy transfer, cots. D ♦ $45 - $50, ♦♦ $50 - $55, ♦♦♦ $60 - $70, ♦ $10 - $15, W $250 - $280, BC MC VI.

Townhouse Barooga, (HU), 44-46 Nangunia St, 1km N of PO, ☎ 03 5873 4024, fax 03 5873 4024, (2 stry gr fl), 9 units acc up to 8, [shwr, tlt, a/c, elec blkts, tel, TV, clock radio, t/c mkg, refrig, cook fac, micro, toaster, ldry, blkts, linen], w/mach, pool above ground, bbq, plygr, tennis, cots. D ♦♦ $55 - $70, ♦ $13 - $16, W ♦♦ $385 - $440, ♦ $44 - $65, ch con, pen con, BC MC VI, (not yet classified).

BARRABA NSW 2347

Pop 1,250. (548km NW Sydney), See map on pages 52/53, ref H2. Barraba nestles beside the Manilla River in the New England region and is a popular destination for fossickers and birdwatchers. Horton Falls. Mt.Kaputar National Park. Glen Riddle Reserve. Ironbark Fossicking Area. Rocky Creek Gorge & Glacial Forms. Bird Routes. Bird Watching, Bowls, Bush Walking, Fishing, Gem Fossicking, Golf, Scenic Drives, Tennis.

Hotels/Motels

★★ **Barraba Motel**, (M), 17 Edward St, 400m S of PO, ☎ 02 6782 1555, fax 02 6782 1802, 12 units [shwr, tlt, a/c-cool, fan, cent heat, elec blkts, tel, TV, clock radio, t/c mkg, refrig, toaster], ldry, ✗ (BYO), bbq, rm serv, cots. RO ♦ $54, ♦♦ $63, ♦ $11, AE BC MC VI.

BATEAU BAY NSW 2261

Pop Part of Wyong, (94km N Sydney), See map on page 55, ref D6. Central Coast town on the bay of the same name between Long Jetty and Forresters Beach. Golf, Surfing, Swimming. See also Shelly Beach.

Hotels/Motels

★★★☆ **Palm Court Motel**, (M), 61 Bateau Bay Rd, ☎ 02 4332 3755, fax 02 4332 8396, (2 stry gr fl), 10 units [shwr, tlt, fan, heat, elec blkts, tel, TV, clock radio, t/c mkg, refrig, toaster], ✗, pool, cots-fee. RO ♦ $70 - $115, ♦♦ $75 - $120, ♦ $11, AE BC DC MC VI.

Bateau Bay Hotel Motel, (LMH), The Entrance Rd, 1km S of PO, ☎ 02 4332 8022, fax 02 4334 3040, 6 units [shwr, tlt, c/fan, TV, clock radio, t/c mkg, refrig, toaster], ✉, bbq, plygr, cots. BLB ♦♦ $66 - $88, ♦ $10, AE BC MC VI.

BARRINGTON TOPS NSW

See Dungog, East Gresford, Gloucester, Paterson, Salisbury, Vacy.

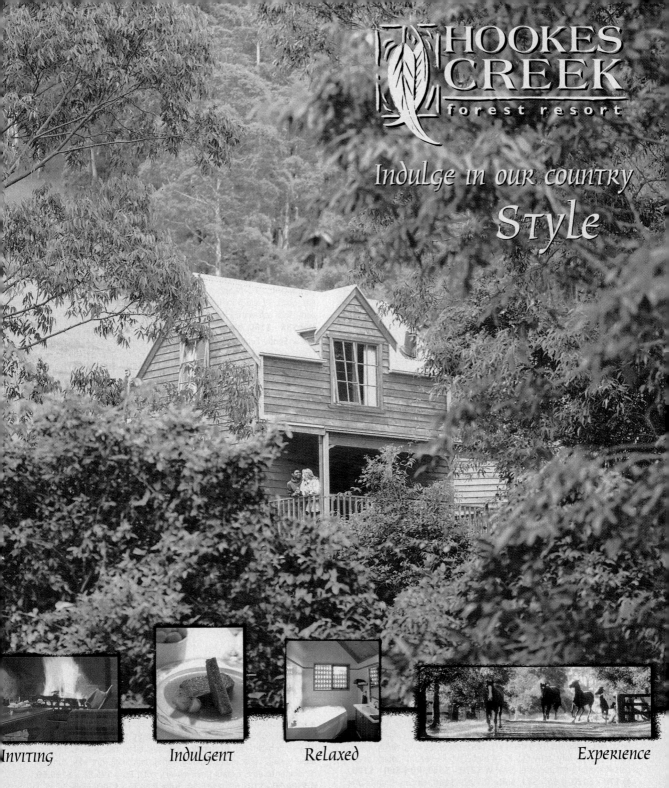

HOOKES CREEK
forest resort

Indulge in our country
Style

Inviting   **Indulgent**   **Relaxed**   **Experience**

Discover a tranquil valley in the foothills of the Barrington Tops where the views are breathtaking and just 25 guests share 2,000 acres (800 ha) of forest and wilderness teeming with wildlife.

Enjoy luxury private cottages with cosy fires and king size spa baths, casual to gourmet dining where every meal is a taste sensation and an inspirational setting for a range of outdoor activities including horseriding, tennis, bushwalking, fishing, birdwatching and swimming. A perfect retreat just 3½ hours drive north of Sydney in the Hunter region.

384 Jems Creek Road
Cobark via Gloucester NSW 2422 Australia
Tel: (02) 6558 5544 • Fax: (02) 6558 5552
Email: info@hookescreek.com.au
www.hookescreek.com.au

AAA Tourism ★★★★☆

BATEHAVEN NSW 2536

Pop Part of Batemans Bay, (302km S Sydney), See map on page 55, ref A6. Batehaven lies south-east of the township of Batemans Bay on the western shores of the bay itself. Boating, Fishing, Scenic Drives, Surfing, Swimming. See also Nelligen & Surf Beach.

Hotels/Motels

AAA
TOURISM
Special Rates

★★★☆ **Abel Tasman Motel**, (M), 222 Beach Rd, 3km E of PO, ☎ 02 4472 6511, fax 02 4472 4027, (2 stry gr fl), 14 units (1 suite) [shwr, tlt, hairdry, a/c, elec blkts, tel, TV, video-fee, clock radio, t/c mkg, refrig, micro (1), toaster (1)], cots-fee, non smoking units (6). W $301 - $805, RO ♦ $65 - $105, ♦♦ $75 - $115, ◊ $10, Suite D $102 - $149, ch con, Min book long w/ends, AE BC DC EFT JCB MC VI, ∱&.

★★★★ **(Serviced Apartment Section)**, (Multi-stry), 4 serv apts acc up to 6, [shwr, spa bath, tlt, hairdry, a/c, elec blkts, tel, TV, video-fee, clock radio, t/c mkg, refrig, cook fac, micro, d/wash, toaster, ldry, blkts, linen, pillows], w/mach, dryer, iron, secure park. D ♦♦ $159 - $194, ◊ $15, W ♦♦ $750 - $1,275, Min book long w/ends.

★★★☆ **Araluen Motor Lodge**, (M), 226 Beach Rd, ☎ 02 4472 6266, fax 02 4472 8791, 32 units (1 suite) [shwr, tlt, hairdry (14), a/c (32), heat, elec blkts, tel, TV, video (17), clock radio, t/c mkg, refrig, cook fac (7)], ldry, conv fac, ✗ (6 nights), pool-heated (solar), bbq, cots-fee, non smoking units (14). W $275 - $640, RO ♦ $60 - $100, ♦♦ $70 - $120, ◊ $6 - $11, Suite D $95 - $140, ch con, 9 units of a lesser rating, Min book applies, AE BC EFT MC VI, ∱&.

Self Catering Accommodation

★★★☆ **Aquarius**, (HU), 4 Matthew Pde, ☎ 02 4472 5793, fax 02 4472 8913, (Multi-stry), 18 units acc up to 7, [shwr, tlt, c/fan, heat, elec blkts, TV, video, clock radio, refrig, cook fac, micro, ldry, linen reqd-fee], pool (salt water), bbq, c/park (undercover), plygr, tennis (half court). W $240 - $950, BC MC VI.

★★★ **Edgewater Gardens Holiday Units**, (HU), 384-388 Beach Rd, Batemans Bay 2536, 3.5km E of Batemans Bay PO, ☎ 02 4472 4381, fax 02 4472 7966, (2 stry gr fl), 6 units acc up to 5, [shwr, tlt, heat, elec blkts, TV, clock radio, refrig, cook fac, micro, toaster, linen (fee) reqd-fee], ldry (fee), pool (salt water), bbq, ✆, cots-fee. D ♦♦ $55 - $120, ♦♦♦♦ $77 - $160, W ♦♦ $215 - $920, BC MC VI.

★★★ **Edgewater Gardens Serviced Apartments**, (SA), 384-388 Beach Rd, 3.5km E of Batemans Bay PO, ☎ 02 4472 4381, fax 02 4472 7966, (2 stry gr fl), 9 serv apts acc up to 5, [shwr, tlt, a/c (9), heat, elec blkts, TV, clock radio, refrig, cook fac, micro, toaster], ldry-fee, pool (solar salt water), bbq, ✆, cots-fee. D ♦ $60 - $120, ♦♦ $60 - $130, ♦♦♦♦ $88 - $160, W ♦♦ $230 - $720, BC MC VI.

★★★ **Sandy Feet Lodge**, (HF), 224 Beach Rd, ☎ 02 4472 4281, fax 02 4472 4281, 9 flats acc up to 6, [shwr, tlt, fan, elec blkts, TV, refrig, cook fac, micro, linen], ldry, bbq. D $50 - $90, W $175 - $520, BC MC VI.

★★ **Taliva Holiday Lodge**, (HU), 236 Beach Rd, 3km SE of Batemans Bay PO, ☎ 02 4472 4904, fax 02 4472 4904, 8 units acc up to 5, [shwr, tlt, c/fan, heat, elec blkts, tel, TV, t/c mkg, refrig, cook fac, micro, toaster, linen reqd-fee], ldry, ✉, pool-heated (solar), bbq, dinner to unit, cots. D ♦ $40 - $50, ♦♦ $50 - $90, ◊ $10 - $15, W ♦♦ $198 - $600, ◊ $15 - $20, ch con, BC MC VI.

BATEMANS BAY NSW 2536

Pop 9,550. (298km S Sydney), See map on page 55, ref A6. Popular south coast town that lies at the mouth of the Clyde River on a bay dotted by small islands. Boating, Bowls, Fishing, Golf, Tennis. See also Batehaven, Malua Bay, Nelligen & Surf Beach.

Hotels/Motels

GOLDEN
CHAIN

★★★★ **Argyle Terrace Motor Inn**, (M), 32 Beach Rd, 1km E of PO, ☎ 02 4472 5022, fax 02 4472 7722, (2 stry gr fl), 12 units (3 suites) [shwr, tlt, hairdry, a/c, elec blkts, tel, TV, video-fee, clock radio, t/c mkg, refrig], iron, iron brd, pool, cots-fee, non smoking units (8). RO ♦ $82 - $126, ♦♦ $92 - $136, ◊ $6.60 - $16.60, Suite D ♦ $114 - $158, ♦♦ $114 - $158, ch con, AE BC DC EFT MC MP VI.

★★★★ **Bridge Motel**, (M), 29 Clyde St, 500m NW of PO, ☎ 02 4472 6344, fax 02 4472 9329, (2 stry gr fl), 22 units [shwr, tlt, hairdry, a/c, elec blkts, tel, cable tv, video (avail), clock radio, t/c mkg, refrig], ldry, pool, bbq, dinner to unit, boat park, cots, non smoking units (8). RO ♦ $75 - $132, ♦♦ $85 - $170, ♦♦♦♦ $95 - $165, ◊ $5.50 - $13.20, AE BC DC EFT MC VI, ∱&.

★★★★ **Esplanade Motel**, (M), 23 Beach Rd, 200m SE of PO, ☎ 02 4472 0200, fax 02 4472 0277, (2 stry), 23 units (9 suites) [shwr, spa bath (15), tlt, hairdry, a/c, elec blkts, tel, cable tv, video (avail), clock radio, t/c mkg, refrig, mini bar], lift, ldry, conv fac, ✗, dinner to unit, c/park (undercover), cots. RO ♦ $96.80 - $115.50, ♦♦ $104.50 - $181.50, ◊ $16.50, Suite D $154 - $300, AE BC DC MC VI.

★★★★ **Lincoln Downs Country Resort**, (M), Princes Hwy, 800m N of
PO, ☎ 02 4472 6388, fax 02 4472 6821, (2 stry gr fl), 33 units [shwr,
bath (31), spa bath (6), tlt, hairdry, a/c, elec blkts, tel, TV, clock radio,
t/c mkg, refrig, mini bar], ldry, iron, iron brd, lounge, conv fac,
☒ (mon to sat), bar, pool, bbq, rm serv, tennis, cots-fee, non smoking
rms (15). **RO** ╫ **$95 - $160**, ╫╫ **$95 - $160**, ◊ **$15**, AE BC DC EFT MC VI.

★★★★ **Reef Motor Inn**, (M), 27 Clyde St, 450m NW of PO,
☎ 02 4472 6000, fax 02 4472 6059, (2 stry gr fl), 33 units
[shwr, spa bath (4), tlt, hairdry, a/c, elec blkts, tel,
cable tv, video-fee, clock radio, t/c mkg, refrig, mini bar,
toaster], ldry, iron, ☒, pool (salt water), spa, dinner to unit, cots-fee.
RO ╫ **$94 - $182**, ╫╫ **$105 - $193**, ╫╫╫ **$116 - $204**, ◊ **$11**, ch con,
AE BC DC MC MP VI, ♿.

Best Western

★★★★ **(Serviced Apartment Section)**, 7 serv apts (10 suites)
[shwr, spa bath, tlt, a/c, tel, TV, video-fee, t/c mkg, refrig, cook fac,
d/wash, toaster, ldry], secure park. **D $171.**

★★★☆ **Bay Breeze Motel**, (M), 21 Beach Rd, 300m SE of PO,
☎ 02 4472 7222, fax 02 4472 7313, (Multi-stry gr fl), 7 units [shwr, tlt,
hairdry, a/c, elec blkts, tel, TV, clock radio, t/c mkg, refrig], non smoking
units. **RO** ╫ **$88 - $132**, ╫╫ **$90 - $147**, ◊ **$12 - $17**, AE BC MC VI.

★★★☆ **Bayside Motel**, (M), 60 Beach Rd, 1km E of PO, ☎ 02 4472 6488, fax 02 4472 7195, 26 units [shwr, tlt, hairdry, fan, heat, elec blkts, tel, TV, video-fee, t/c mkg, refrig, cook fac (3), toaster], ldry, iron, iron brd, ⊠, pool, bbq, dinner to unit, cots, non smoking units (10). RO ⧫ $55 - $95, ⧫⧫ $60 - $120, ⧫⧫⧫ $75 - $130, ⧫ $10 - $14, ch con, 10 units of a lesser rating, AE BC DC EFT MC VI.

★★★☆ **Country Comfort - Batemans Bay**, (M), Cnr Princes Hwy & Canberra Rd, Surfside 2536, 1km N of PO, ☎ 02 4472 6333, fax 02 4472 6248, (2 stry) 56 units [shwr, spa bath (4), tlt, hairdry, a/c, elec blkts, tel, TV, movie, clock radio, t/c mkg, refrig, mini bar, toaster], ldry, iron, iron brd, rec rm, lounge, conv fac, ⊠, pool, spa, bbq, rm serv, dinner to unit, plygr, mini golf, tennis, cots, non smoking units (34). RO ⧫ $90, ⧫⧫ $90, ⧫ $15, ch con, 22 units ★★★. AE BC DC MC VI.

★★★ **Clyderiver Motor Inn**, (M), 3 Clyde St, 100m N of PO, ☎ 02 4472 6444, fax 02 4472 6854, (2 stry gr fl), 28 units [shwr, tlt, a/c, elec blkts, tel, TV, video (avail), movie, clock radio, t/c mkg, refrig, micro (2)], ⊠, pool, bbq, cots. RO ⧫ $6 - $85, ⧫⧫ $60 - $85, ⧫⧫⧫⧫ $85 - $110, Suite D $95 - $160, AE BC EFT MC VI.

★★★ **Pegasus Motor Inn**, (M), 31 Clyde St, 500m NW of PO, ☎ 02 4472 6077, fax 02 4472 8412, (2 stry gr fl), 20 units [shwr, tlt, a/c, elec blkts, tel, TV, video (avail), clock radio, t/c mkg, refrig], ldry, ⊠, rm serv, dinner to unit, boat park, jetty, cots, non smoking units (8). RO ⧫ $55 - $99, ⧫⧫ $59 - $120, ⧫⧫⧫ $69 - $139, AE BC DC EFT MC VI, 🛆.

★★★ **Zorba Motel**, (M), Orient St, 50m S of PO, ☎ 02 4472 4804, fax 02 4472 3866, (2 stry gr fl), 16 units (1 suite) [shwr, tlt, a/c, elec blkts, TV, t/c mkg, refrig, toaster], cots-fee. RO ⧫ $65 - $95, ⧫⧫ $75 - $110, ⧫ $10, ch con, 4 units of a lower rating, BC MC VI.

★★☆ **Cullendulla Park**, (M), Princes Highway, North Batemans Bay 2536, 6km N of Batemans Bay, ☎ 02 4478 6060, fax 02 4478 6744, 7 units [shwr, tlt, fan, heat, elec blkts, TV, video (available), clock radio, t/c mkg, refrig], ldry, rec rm, pool, bbq, plygr, cots, Pets alowed on leash. W $294 - $525, RO $49 - $75, D ⧫ $15 ch con, Units 2 and 3 not rated, Min book Christmas Jan and Easter, BC MC VI.

★★☆ **Mariners Lodge on the Waterfront Motel**, (LMH), Orient St, 100m S of PO, ☎ 02 4472 6222, fax 02 4472 7620, 31 units [shwr, bath (6), spa bath (5), tlt, hairdry, a/c, tel, TV, video (avail), clock radio, t/c mkg, refrig], iron, conv fac, ⊠, pool, dinner to unit. RO ⧫ $85 - $105, ⧫⧫ $105 - $140, ⧫ $10, 6 units ★★★, AE BC DC MC VI.

★★ **Hanging Rock Golf Club Family**, (M), Beach Rd, opposite golf club, ☎ 02 4472 4466, fax 02 4472 4066, 27 units [shwr, bath (1), tlt, hairdry, fan, heat, elec blkts, tel, TV, video (avail), t/c mkg, refrig, toaster], ldry, pool, bbq, car wash, plygr, cots. D ⧫ $50, ⧫⧫ $55, AE BC DC EFT MC VI.

Beach Drive Motel, (M), 24 Beach Rd, 500m S of PO, ☎ 02 4472 4805, fax 02 4472 4845, (2 stry gr fl), 18 units [shwr, tlt, fan (9), c/fan (9), elec blkts, tel, TV, clock radio, t/c mkg, refrig, micro (1), toaster], ldry, bbq-fee, rm serv, courtesy transfer, cots-fee, non smoking units (10). RO ⧫ $47 - $99, ⧫⧫ $56 - $110, ⧫ $12, pen con, AE BC DC EFT MC MP VI, (Rating under review).

Self Catering Accommodation

★★★☆ **Beach Road Holiday Units**, (HU), 45 Beach Rd, 2km E of PO, ☎ 02 6285 3880, fax 02 6285 3192, 1 unit acc up to 6, (3 bedrm), [shwr (2), bath, spa bath, tlt (3), a/c, fan, heat, TV, clock radio, refrig, cook fac, micro, d/wash, toaster, ldry, linen reqd], w/mach, dryer, iron, c/park (garage), cots. W $500 - $1,050, Min book applies, BC MC VI.

★★★☆ **The Beach House**, (Cotg), 22 Myamba Pde, ☎ 02 4472 4086, fax 02 4472 4086, 1 cotg acc up to 6, [shwr, spa bath, tlt, fire pl (combustion), elec blkts, TV, video, clock radio, refrig, cook fac, micro, elec frypan, d/wash, toaster, ldry, linen reqd], w/mach, dryer, iron, bbq, c/park (carport), cots. D $95 - $130, W $500 - $1,100, Min book applies.

★★★ **Avalon**, (HU), 3 Avalon St, 2km E of PO, ☎ 02 4472 4204, fax 02 4472 4204, 5 units acc up to 6, [shwr, tlt, fan, heat, elec blkts, TV, clock radio, refrig, cook fac, micro, linen reqd-fee], ldry-fee, pool-heated (solar), bbq, cots. D ⧫⧫ $50 - $110, ⧫ $11, W $220 - $770, BC MC VI.

WATERFRONT ZORBA MOTEL
BATEMANS BAY NSW 2536
PHONE (02) 4472 4804   FAX (02) 4472 3866

PICTURE TAKEN FROM MOTEL BALCONY

POSITION – POSITION – POSITION

Situated in a unique position facing the Clyde River. Spectacular views (throw a stone in the water from room distance).

Centre away from all traffic, 200 metres from R.S.L. Club. Walking distance to all facilities. Up graded rooms, tea & coffee fac, electric blankets, all units air conditioned, colour T.V., fridge, phone available, home cooked breakfast, personal service.

All Rooms Up Graded
A unique spot to stay, value for money
INSPECTION WELCOME

★★★ **Del Costa Holiday Villas**, (HU), 54 Beach Rd, ☎ 02 4472 6260, fax 02 4472 6260, 15 units acc up to 6, [shwr, tlt, heat, TV, video, refrig, cook fac, micro, ldry, linen reqd-fee], pool, spa, bbq, c/park (5), plygr, tennis (half court), cots. **D ♀♀ $65 - $130, ♀♀♀ $71 - $168, W $364 - $1,250**, BC EFT MC VI.

★★★ **The Riverside Townhouse**, (HU), Unit 1, 85 Timbara Cres, ☎ 02 4472 4086, fax 02 4472 4086, (2 stry), 1 unit acc up to 5, [shwr, tlt, fan, c/fan, heat (gas), elec blkts, TV, video, clock radio, refrig, cook fac, micro, elec frypan, toaster, ldry, blkts, linen reqd-fee], w/mach, dryer, iron, iron brd, bbq, cots. **D $79 - $110, W $375 - $795**, Min book applies.

★★☆ **Bay Surfside**, (HF), 662 Beach Rd, Surf Beach 2536, 7Km fr PO, ☎ 02 4471 1275, fax 02 4471 1275, 3 flats acc up to 4, [shwr, tlt, heat, elec blkts, TV, refrig, cook fac, micro, ldry (in unit), linen reqd], bbq, c/park (undercover). **D $60.50 - $110, W $242 - $770**, Min book all holiday times.

Merinda Cottage, (House), 63 Yowani Rd North Rosedale via, 2km S of Malua Bay, ☎ 02 4471 1235, fax 02 4471 3715, (2 stry gr fl), 1 house acc up to 6, (2 bedrm), [shwr, tlt, fire pl, heat, elec blkts, TV, video, t/c mkg, refrig, cook fac, micro, toaster, blkts, doonas, linen reqd-fee, pillows], w/mach, iron, iron brd. **D ♀♀ $100 - $170, W ♀♀ $300 - $1,050**, (not yet classified).

B&B's/Guest Houses

★★★★★ **Batemans Bay Manor**, (GH), No children's facilities, 22 Cor's Pde, 4km N of PO, ☎ 02 4472 9789, fax 02 4472 9395, (2 stry), 6 rms [bath (1), hairdry, a/c, c/fan, cent heat, elec blkts, TV, video, clock radio, refrig, doonas], ldry, iron, iron brd, lounge firepl, pool indoor heated, sauna, spa, bbq, c/park (undercover), gym, tennis (half size), non smoking property. **RO ♀ $130 - $180**, Meals by arrangement, AE BC EFT MC VI.

Other Accommodation

Bay River Houseboats, (Hbt), Wray St, ☎ 02 4472 5649, fax 02 4471 3333, 4 houseboats acc up to 10, [shwr, tlt, hairdry, heat, tel, TV, video, refrig, cook fac, micro, blkts reqd-fee, linen reqd-fee], iron, iron brd, bbq, cots. **W $800 - $1,730**, Min book applies, BC MC VI.

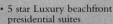

Clyde River Houseboats, (Hbt), Wray St, ☎ 02 4472 6369, or a/h 02 4472 8818, fax 02 4472 6369, 2 houseboats acc up to 10, [shwr, tlt, heat, TV, video, CD, refrig, cook fac, micro, doonas, linen reqd, pillows], bbq, c/park. **W $420 - $1,850**, Min book applies, BC EFT MC VI.

BATHURST NSW 2795

Pop 26,050. (205km W Sydney), See map on page 55, ref A2. The stately city of Bathurst was proclaimed in 1815 and is Australia's oldest inland settlement. Bowls, Golf, Scenic Drives, Swimming, Tennis.

Hotels/Motels

★★★★☆ **James Cook International Motor Inn**, (M), Cnr Mid Western & Great Western Hwys, 2km W of PO, ☎ 02 6332 1800, fax 02 6332 1890, 50 units [shwr, bath (13), spa bath (9), tlt, hairdry, a/c-cool, c/fan, heat, elec blkts, tel, cable tv, video, movie, clock radio, t/c mkg, refrig, mini bar], ldry, iron, iron brd, conv fac, ⊠, pool indoor heated (salt water), spa, bbq, 24hr reception, rm serv, dinner to unit, c/park (undercover), ☏, non smoking units (18). **RO $110 - $135**, Min book applies, AE BC DC MC MP VI, ⟨ﬔ.

★★★★ **Bathurst Motor Inn**, (M), 87 Durham St, ☎ 02 6331 2222, fax 02 6331 3568, 53 units (3 suites) [shwr, bath (4), spa bath (5), tlt, a/c (45), heat, elec blkts, tel, TV, video, clock radio, t/c mkg, refrig, mini bar (29), cook fac (3), toaster], ⊠, pool, spa, bbq, rm serv, dinner to unit, gym, cots. **RO ♦ $45 - $139, ♦♦ $55 - $149, ◊ $10, Suite D ♦♦ $136**, 11 units of two star plus rating, 13 units ★★★. AE BC DC MC VI.

AAA TOURISM *Special Rates* / FLAG FLAG CHOICE HOTELS / SUNDOWNER CHAIN MOTOR INNS

★★★★ **Sundowner Chain Motor Inns**, (M), 19 Charlotte St, 600m NE of PO, ☎ 02 6331 2211, fax 02 6331 4754, (2 stry gr fl), 37 units (2 suites) [shwr, bath (19), tlt, hairdry, a/c, elec blkts, tel, cable tv, video (avail), clock radio, t/c mkg, refrig, mini bar, toaster], ldry, iron, iron brd, ⊠ (6 nights), pool, c/park (off street), cots-fee, non smoking units (20). **RO ♦ $83 - $173, ♦♦ $83 - $173, ◊ $11**, ch con, 10 units ★★★☆. Min book applies during Bathurst car racing, AE BC DC EFT MC MP VI.

★★★☆ **Abercrombie Motor Inn**, (M), 362 Stewart St (Mid-Western Hwy), 2km W of PO, ☎ 02 6331 1077, fax 02 6331 8895, 16 units [shwr, tlt, hairdry, a/c, heat, elec blkts, tel, TV, video-fee, clock radio, t/c mkg, refrig, toaster], ldry-fee, iron, iron brd, bbq-fee, dinner to unit, cots-fee. **RO ♦ $54 - $68, ♦♦ $64 - $78, ◊ $10**, ch con, 4 units of a 2.5 star rating. AE BC DC EFT MC VI.

GOLDEN CHAIN ★★★☆ **Ben Chifley Motor Inn**, (M), 272 Stewart St (Great Western Hwy), 1km W of PO, ☎ 02 6331 5055, fax 02 6332 1429, (2 stry gr fl), 28 units [shwr, tlt, hairdry, a/c, heat, elec blkts, tel, cable tv, clock radio, t/c mkg, refrig, mini bar], iron, iron brd, ⊠, pool, dinner to unit, cots, non smoking units (10). **RO ♦ $82, ♦♦ $101, ◊ $12**, Min book applies, AE BC DC MC MP VI.

Best Western ★★★☆ **Coachmans Inn Motel**, (M), Cnr Gt Western Hwy & Oberon Rd, 3.5km E of PO, ☎ 02 6331 4855, fax 02 6331 7273, (2 stry gr fl), 26 units [shwr, tlt, a/c, elec blkts, tel, TV, video-fee, movie, clock radio, t/c mkg, refrig, toaster], iron, iron brd, ⊠ (Mon to Sat), dinner to unit (Mon to Sat), cots-fee, non smoking units (7). **RO ♦ $85, ♦♦ $95, ◊ $11**, ch con, 8 rooms of a 4 star rating. AE BC DC EFT MC VI.

★★★ **Country Lodge Motor Inn**, (M), 145 William St, 300m SW of PO, ☎ 02 6331 4888, fax 02 6331 4011, 30 units [shwr, tlt, a/c-cool, cent heat, tel, TV, video (avail), clock radio, t/c mkg, refrig], non smoking units (6). **RO ♦ $71 - $77, ♦♦ $77, ♦♦♦ $85 - $90, ◊ $10 - $15**, AE BC DC MC.

 Budget Motel Chain International ★★★ **Gold Panner Motor Inn**, (M), Sydney Rd (Great Western Hwy), Kelso 2795, 4km E of Bathurst PO, ☎ 02 6331 4444, fax 02 6331 4270, 32 units [shwr, tlt, hairdry (8), a/c, cent heat (22), elec blkts, tel, cable tv, video-fee, clock radio, t/c mkg, refrig, cook fac ltd (4), micro (2), toaster], ldry, iron (15), iron brd (15), pool, bbq, car wash, plygr, cots-fee, non smoking units (9). **RO ♦ $58 - $82, ♦♦ $68 - $92, ♦♦♦ $80 - $104, ◊ $12**, ch con, 8 units of a higher rating. AE BC DC EFT MC MCH VI, ⟨ﬔ.

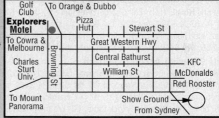

BATHURST NSW continued...

★★☆ **Panorama City Motor Lodge**, (LMH), 51 Durham St, 800m E of PO, ☎ 02 6331 2666, fax 02 6332 1439, (2 stry gr fl), 70 units [shwr, bath (15), tlt, a/c, elec blkts, tel, TV, clock radio, t/c mkg, refrig], ldry, conv fac, ⊠, pool, sauna, spa, bbq, rm serv (b'fast), ✆, cots-fee. **RO** ♦ **$66**, ♦♦ **$77**, ◊ **$11**, Min book applies, AE BC DC EFT MC VI.

★☆ **The Kelso**, (LMH), Sydney Rd (Great Western Hwy), Kelso, 4km E of PO, ☎ 02 6331 6675, fax 02 6331 6812, 12 units [shwr, tlt, a/c, TV, radio, t/c mkg, refrig, toaster]. **RO** ♦ **$50**, ♦♦ **$60**, ◊ **$5**.

★ **Park Hotel**, (LH), Cnr George & Keppel Sts, 200m NW of PO, ☎ 02 6331 3399, fax 02 6334 9099, (2 stry), 19 rms [shwr, tlt, fan, heat, elec blkts, TV, clock radio, t/c mkg], ldry, ⊠, ✆, cots-fee. **BB** ♦ **$43**, ♦♦ **$66**, ♦♦♦ **$90**, ch con, 1 room not rated. BC MC VI.

Self Catering Accommodation

★★★★☆ **Lochinvar - Mt Panorama**, (Cotg), 'Lochinvar' 448 Conrod Straight, Mt Panorama, 5km S of PO, ☎ 02 6331 2469, fax 02 6331 2469, 2 cotgs acc up to 4, [shwr (2), tlt (3), hairdry, c/fan, cent heat, elec blkts, tel, TV, video, clock radio, CD, t/c mkg, refrig, cook fac, micro, d/wash, toaster, ldry, blkts, linen, pillows], w/mach, iron, iron brd, bbq, c/park (garage) (1). **D** ♦♦ **$135 - $165**, ◊ **$30**, **W** ♦♦ **$550**, ◊ **$120**, *Operator Comment: Visit our website: members.optusnet.com.au/~lochinvar*

★★★★ **The Royal Apartments**, (HU), 108 William St, 300m E of PO, ☎ 02 6332 4920, fax 02 6323 3132, (Multi-stry), 6 units acc up to 5, [shwr, bath, tlt, fan, heat, elec blkts, tel, TV, clock radio, t/c mkg, refrig, cook fac, micro (1), toaster, ldry, blkts, linen, pillows], iron, non smoking units (2). **D** ♦ **$121 - $132**, ♦♦ **$132 - $143**, **W** **$720 - $990**, ch con, AE BC DC MC VI.

★★★ **Box Grove Cottages**, (Cotg), 119 Duramana Rd, ☎ 02 6337 1285, fax 02 6337 1285, 4 cotgs acc up to 6, [shwr, tlt, hairdry, TV, clock radio, t/c mkg, refrig, cook fac, micro, elec frypan, toaster, ldry, linen], w/mach, iron, cots (available). **D** ♦♦ **$75 - $90**, **W** ♦♦ **$380 - $495**.

★★ **David Jones Cottage**, (Cotg), 244 William St, 800m S of PO, ☎ 02 6332 4920, fax 02 6331 8566, 1 cotg acc up to 8, [shwr, bath, tlt, hairdry, fire pl, cent heat, elec blkts, tel, TV, clock radio, t/c mkg, refrig, cook fac, micro, d/wash, toaster, ldry, blkts, linen, pillows], w/mach, iron, c/park (carport), non smoking units. **D** ♦♦ **$143**, ◊ **$49**, **W** ♦♦ **$770**, ◊ **$110**, ch con, AE BC DC MC VI.

B&B's/Guest Houses

★★★★ **Blandford House**, (B&B), Heritage, No children's facilities, 214 Lambert St, ☎ 02 6331 9995, 3 rms [shwr, tlt, hairdry, c/fan, fire pl, heat, elec blkts, video, clock radio, refrig], iron, iron brd, lounge (TV), ✕, t/c mkg shared, bbq, non smoking property. **BB** ♦ **$90 - $100**, ♦♦ **$110 - $130**, BC MC VI.

★★★★ **Strathmore Victorian Manor**, (B&B), 202 Russell St, 600m SE of PO, ☎ 02 6332 3252, fax 02 6332 3819, 5 rms (5 suites) [shwr, bath (2), tlt, hairdry, heat, elec blkts, tel, TV, video (avail), clock radio], lounge (firepl), bbq, c/park. **BB** ♦ **$94**, ♦♦ **$110**, Suite D ♦ **$132**, AE BC DC MC VI.

★★★★ **The Old School B&B**, (B&B), 159 Seymour St, ☎ 02 6331 1206, 1 rm [shwr, tlt, hairdry, fan, heat, elec blkts, tel, TV, clock radio, t/c mkg, refrig, micro, toaster], iron, iron brd. **BB** ♦ **$70 - $100**, ♦♦ **$100 - $130**, ◊ **$20 - $30**, BC MC VI.

★★★☆ **A Winter-Rose Cottage Bed & Breakfast**, (B&B), 79 Morrissett St, 1km N of PO, ☎ 02 6332 2661, fax 02 6334 3322, 3 rms [ensuite (1), shwr (2), bath (1), tlt (2), hairdry, heat, elec blkts, clock radio, t/c mkg], lounge (TV & video), bbq, non smoking property. **BB** ♦ **$75**, ♦♦ **$85 - $100**, ◊ **$25**, Minimim booking race weekends, AE BC DC MC VI.

★★★☆ **(Cottage Section)**, 1 cotg acc up to 4, [shwr, tlt, heat, elec blkts, TV, clock radio, t/c mkg, refrig, cook fac ltd, micro, toaster, doonas, linen, pillows], w/mach, iron, iron brd. **BB** ♦♦ **$100**.

★★★☆ **Cherrywood by the River**, (B&B), 238 Eglinton Rd, 4km NW of PO, ☎ 02 6331 9427, 2 rms [hairdry, heat, elec blkts, tel, TV, clock radio, refrig], ldry, iron, lounge (TV & firepl), ✕, t/c mkg shared, bbq, c/park. **BB** ♦ **$50 - $60**, ♦♦ **$90 - $120**, Dinner by arrangement.

★★★☆ **Elm Tree Cottage**, (B&B), 270 Keppel St, 1.5km W of PO, ☎ 02 6332 4920, fax 02 6331 8566, 2 rms [shwr, tlt, heat, elec blkts, tel, TV, clock radio, t/c mkg, refrig, cook fac, micro, toaster], ldry, bbq. **BB** ♦ **$110**, ♦♦ **$132 - $150**, ♦♦♦ **$185**, ch con, weekly con, Dinner by arrangement. AE BC DC MC VI.

★★★☆ **Littlebourne**, (B&B), 4031 O'Connell Rd, 6km SE of PO, ☎ 02 6332 9094, fax 02 6332 9094, 3 rms [fan, heat (elec/wood), elec blkts, tel, TV, video, clock radio, ldry, doonas], rec rm, conf fac, ✕, t/c mkg shared, bbq, cots, non smoking property. BB ♦ $60 - $80, ♦♦ $110 - $120, ch con, weekly con, Dinner by arrangement, *Operator Comment: www.geocities.com/littlebourne*

★★★☆ **Pindari Emu Farm**, (B&B), 478 Timber Ridge Rd, Yetholme 2795, 25km E of Bathurst, ☎ 02 6337 5340, 3 rms [cent heat, elec blkts, clock radio], shared fac (shwr & tlt), ldry, iron, iron brd, rec rm, lounge (TV), ✕, cook fac, t/c mkg shared, bbq, plygr, cots, non smoking rms. BB ♦ $60, ♦♦ $105, ◊ $60, DBB ♦ $90, ♦♦ $160, ◊ $90.

★★★☆ **The Russells**, (B&B), 286 William St, 1.3km S of PO, ☎ 02 6332 4686, fax 02 6332 4686, 2 rms [shwr, tlt, hairdry, heat, elec blkts, clock radio, t/c mkg, cook fac (1), toaster], ldry, iron, iron brd, lounge (TV, video & firepl), ✕, non smoking rms. BB ♦ $65 - $70, ♦♦ $95 - $100, ♦♦♦ $135.

★★★ **Dinta Glen**, (B&B), 3 Strathmore Dve Forest Grove, 7km E of PO, ☎ 02 6332 6662, fax 02 6332 6662, 3 rms [hairdry, heat, elec blkts, tel, TV, clock radio], shared fac (shwr, tlt & bath), conf fac, ✕ (dinner available), pool (salt water), bbq, tennis, cots, non smoking property, Pets allowed. BB ♦ $50, ♦♦ $90, ch con, Dogs and horses welcome. Min book applies, AE BC MC VI,

Operator Comment: www.ix.net.au/~dinta

Paeton Place, (B&B), 1554 Mid Western Hwy, ☎ 02 6368 5846, fax 02 6368 5873, 3 rms [ensuite (1), a/c-cool, clock radio, doonas], ldry, w/mach, lounge (TV, video), t/c mkg shared, c/park (undercover), cots, non smoking property. BB ♦ $69, ♦♦ $95, ◊ $47.50, ch con, BC EFT MC VI, (not yet classified).

Rossmore Park Farm Holidays, (GH), (Farm), Limekilns Rd, 8km from PO, ☎ 02 6337 3634, 8 rms [shwr, tlt, c/fan, heat, elec blkts, t/c mkg, refrig], ldry, ✕, bbq, plygr. BB ♦ $42 - $58.80, ♦♦ $84, ♦♦♦ $126, ◊ $37.50, ch con. EFT.

Other Accommodation

★★★☆ **Secret Valley**, (Lodge), (Farm), 1459 Freemantle Rd, Eglinton 2795, 20km NW of Bathurst, ☎ 02 9683 2626, (2 stry gr fl), 1 rm acc up to 8, (3 bedrm), [shwr, bath, tlt, hairdry, heat, elec blkts, TV, video, clock radio (1), CD, t/c mkg, refrig, cook fac, micro, toaster, ldry], w/mach, iron, iron brd, bbq, non smoking property. D ♦♦ $86 - $220, W ♦♦ $350, ch con, fam con, Min book applies.

BATLOW NSW 2730

Pop 1,050. (478km SW Sydney), See map on pages 52/53, ref F7. Small town in the eastern Riverina, known as the 'apple capital' of New South Wales. Bowls, Fishing, Gem Fossicking, Gold Prospecting, Golf, Scenic Drives, Shooting, Swimming, Tennis.

B&B's/Guest Houses

Yellowin House, (B&B), 127 Yellowin Rd, 2.5km NE of PO, ☎ 02 6949 1043, fax 02 6949 1043, 3 rms [fan, fire pl (2), heat, elec blkts, clock radio, doonas], lounge (TV), lounge firepl, ✕, t/c mkg shared, refrig, bbq, tennis, non smoking property. BLB ♦ $75 - $100, ♦♦ $85 - $120, BC MC VI, (not yet classified).

BAWLEY POINT NSW 2539

Pop 450. (258km S Sydney), See map on page 55, ref B5. Old timber town on the south coast known for its arts and crafts and its good local beaches. Bush Walking, Fishing, Swimming. See also Termeil & Glennifer.

Self Catering Accommodation

★★☆ **Mimosa Hill Wildflowers**, (Cotg), 96 Bawley Point Rd, ☎ 02 4457 1421, fax 02 4457 1421, 3 cotgs acc up to 6, [shwr, tlt, fire pl (3), heat, elec blkts, clock radio, t/c mkg, refrig, cook fac, micro, linen reqd-fee], bbq, cots, non smoking property, Dogs allowed. D ♦♦ $82.50 - $121, ◊ $20, ch con, BC MC VI.

BEECHWOOD NSW 2446

Pop 450. Nominal, See map on page 54, ref C7. Village situated on the Hastings River west of Port Macquarie, close to the town of Wauchope.

B&B's/Guest Houses

★★★☆ **Telopea Bed & Breakfast**, (B&B), 657 Beechwood Rd, 6.5km W of Wauchope, ☎ 02 6585 6572, 2 rms [shwr, tlt, c/fan, heat, elec blkts, tel, TV, movie, clock radio, t/c mkg], ldry, iron, iron brd, TV rm, lounge, bbq, plygr, non smoking property. BB ♦ $50, ♦♦ $65, ◊ $10, RO ♦ $40, ♦♦ $50, ◊ $5, ch con.

BEGA NSW 2550

Pop 4,200. (446km S Sydney), See map on page 55, ref A7. Renowned as the 'cheese capital' of New South Wales, Bega is a busy commercial centre in the heart of the south coast's lush dairy country. Art Gallery, Bowls, Golf, Surfing, Swimming, Tennis.

Hotels/Motels

★★★★ **Bega Village Motor Inn**, (M), Princes Hwy, 150m S of PO, ☎ 02 6492 2466, fax 02 6492 1851, 27 units [shwr, spa bath (6), tlt, hairdry, a/c, elec blkts, tel, TV, video-fee, clock radio, t/c mkg, refrig], ldry, pool indoor heated, spa, cots-fee. RO ♦ $75 - $99, ♦♦ $85 - $99, ♦♦♦ $97 - $108, ◊ $11, 13 units ★★★☆. AE BC DC MC MP VI.

★★★☆ **Bega Downs Motel**, (M), Cnr High & Gipps Sts Princes Hwy, 500m S of PO, ☎ 02 6492 2944, fax 02 6492 2834, (2 stry gr fl), 27 units [shwr, spa bath (2), tlt, hairdry, a/c, heat, elec blkts, tel, cable tv, video, clock radio, t/c mkg, refrig, toaster], ldry, iron, iron brd, ✕, pool (salt water), bbq, rm serv, dinner to unit. RO ♦ $78 - $98, ♦♦ $88 - $118, ◊ $10, AE BC DC EFT MC MP VI.

★★★☆ **Bega Southtown Motor Inn**, (M), Princes Hwy, 1.7km S of PO, ☎ 02 6492 2177, fax 02 6492 2177, (2 stry gr fl), 13 units [shwr, tlt, hairdry (13), a/c, elec blkts, tel, TV, video-fee, clock radio, t/c mkg, refrig], iron, iron brd, pool (salt water), spa, bbq, dinner to unit (Mon to Sat), boat park, plygr, cots-fee, non smoking units (5). RO ♦ $52 - $87, ♦♦ $57 - $99, ♦♦♦ $68 - $110, ◊ $11, AE BC DC EFT MC VI.

★★★ **Princes Motel**, (M), Princes Hwy, cnr Auckland St, 1km S of PO, ☎ 02 6492 1944, fax 02 6492 1209, (2 stry gr fl), 34 units [shwr, tlt, hairdry, a/c, elec blkts, tel, TV, video (avail), clock radio, t/c mkg, refrig], ldry, iron, iron brd, ✕, cots. RO ♦ $51 - $70, ♦♦ $62 - $85, ♦♦♦ $65 - $85, ◊ $12, 10 units ★★☆, AE BC DC MC VI.

★★☆ **Northside Motel**, (M), Old Princes Hwy, 2km N of PO, ☎ 02 6492 1911, fax 02 6492 3334, 21 units [shwr, tlt, heat, elec blkts, tel, TV, video (15)-fee, clock radio, t/c mkg, refrig], ✕, bbq, dinner to unit, cots-fee. BLB ♦ $52 - $88, ♦♦ $58 - $88, ◊ $11, AE BC DC EFT MC MCH VI.

Self Catering Accommodation

★★★★ **Rock Lily Cottages**, (Cotg), 864 Warrigal Range Rd, Brogo, 25km N of Bega, ☎ 02 6492 7364, fax 02 6492 7364, 3 cotgs acc up to 11, [shwr, tlt, c/fan, heat, TV, clock radio, t/c mkg, refrig, cook fac, micro, toaster, ldry, blkts, linen], w/mach (1), iron, iron brd, lounge firepl, bbq, non smoking property. D ♦♦ $100 - $130, weekly con, BC MC VI.

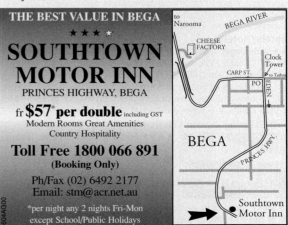

BEGA NSW continued...

B&B's/Guest Houses

★★★★ **The Pickled Pear**, (B&B), 62 Carp St, 300m E of PO, ☎ 02 6492 1393, fax 02 6492 0030, (2 stry gr fl), 3 rms (1 suite) [shwr, bath (1), spa bath (1), tlt, hairdry, a/c (2), heat (3), elec blkts, tel, TV, video (1), clock radio, t/c mkg, refrig (1)], iron, iron brd, lounge (TV & firepl), ✕, spa, non smoking property. **BB** ♦ **$80 - $115, ♦♦ $95 - $140, Suite D** ♦ **$115, ♦♦ $140**, Meals by arrangement, AE BC DC MC VI.

★★★☆ **Girraween Bed & Breakfast**, (B&B), 2 Girraween Crescent, 300m S of Bega R.S.L, ☎ 02 6492 1761, fax 02 6492 2877, 2 rms (1 suite) [shwr, tlt, a/c-cool, fan (2), heat (2), elec blkts, TV, video (1), clock radio, t/c mkg, refrig, cook fac, micro, toaster], ldry, iron, iron brd, lounge (TV), ✕, bbq, dinner to unit, c/park (garage), cots, non smoking units (2). **BB** ♦ **$42, ♦♦ $59,** ♦ **$15, RO** ♦ **$35, ♦♦ $45,** ♦ **$10**, fam con.

★★ **The Bega Central Motel**, (GH), 90 Gipps St, ☎ 02 6492 1263, fax 02 6492 1263, (2 stry gr fl), 9 rms [fire pl (3), heat, elec blkts], shwr, tlt, lounge (TV), conv fac, cafe (Mon to Sat), t/c mkg shared, cots. **BB** ♦ **$38, ♦♦ $48,** ♦ **$15**, ch con, BC MC VI.

　★☆ **(Motel Section)**, 6 units [shwr, tlt, heat, elec blkts, TV, t/c mkg, refrig, toaster]. **BB** ♦ **$45, ♦♦ $55,** ♦ **$15**.

BELLBIRD NSW 2325

Pop Part of Cessnock, (154km N Sydney), See map on page 55, ref B8. Bellbird lies south-west of Cessnock near the Hunter Valley vineyards.

Self Catering Accommodation

★★★★ **Hunter Valley Country Cabins**, Lot 2 Mount View Rd, 17km SW of Cessnock, ☎ 02 4990 8989, fax 02 4990 8936, 4 cabins acc up to 4, (2 bedrm), [shwr, tlt, a/c-cool, heat (wood), TV, refrig, cook fac, micro, blkts, doonas, linen, pillows], bbq, cots. **D** ♦ **$80 - $98.75, ♦♦ $80 - $98.75,** ♦ **$20 - $35**, ch con, BC EFT MC VI.

B&B's/Guest Houses

★★★☆ **Bellbird Heights Bed & Breakfast**, (B&B), 275 Wollombi Rd, 3km W of Cessnock PO, ☎ 02 4990 7219, 3 rms [shwr (1), tlt (2), fan, c/fan, heat, tel, TV, t/c mkg (1), refrig], iron, iron brd, rec rm, lounge firepl, pool (salt water), t/c mkg shared, non smoking property. **BLB ♦♦ $88 - $110**, ch con, BC MC VI.

　(Unit Section), 1 unit [shwr, tlt, c/fan, heat, TV, refrig, cook fac ltd, toaster, linen], iron, iron brd. **BLB ♦♦ $88 - $110**, (not yet classified).

BELLBROOK NSW 2440

Pop Nominal, (478km N Sydney), See map on page 54, ref C5. National Trust-classified village on the upper reaches of the Macleay River. Boating, Bush Walking, Fishing, Gem Fossicking, Scenic Drives, Swimming.

Self Catering Accommodation

★★ **Uralgurra Farmstay**, (Cotg), (Farm), 3871 Armidale Rd, 45kms W of Kempsey PO, ☎ 02 6563 1998, fax 02 6562 2944, 1 cotg acc up to 5, [shwr, bath, tlt, fan, heat, elec blkts, TV, clock radio, t/c mkg, refrig, cook fac, micro, elec frypan, toaster, ldry, linen reqd], w/mach, iron, pool, bbq, plygr, cots. **D ♦♦♦♦ $55,** ♦ **$10, W ♦♦♦♦ $275**.

BELLINGEN NSW 2454

Pop 2,690. (547km N Sydney), See map on page 54, ref C5. Small north coast town at the heart of the Bellinger Valley, which supports a blend of traditional farming and alternative communities. Bowls, Canoeing, Fishing, Golf, Scenic Drives, Swimming, Tennis, Vineyards, Wineries. See also Glennifer.

Hotels/Motels

★★☆ **Bellinger Valley Motor Inn**, (M), 1381 Waterfall Way, 1km W of PO, ☎ 02 6655 1599, fax 02 6655 1824, 27 units [shwr, tlt, hairdry, a/c, c/fan, elec blkts, tel, fax, TV, clock radio, t/c mkg, refrig, toaster], ldry, conv fac, ✉ (6 nights), pool, spa, bbq, rm serv, plygr, bowls (bocce), golf (3 rms), cots-fee, non smoking units (avail). **RO ♦♦ $60 - $95,** ♦ **$15**, 7 units of a higher standard. AE BC DC EFT MC VI.

Self Catering Accommodation

★★★★ **Fernridge Farm Cottage**, (Cotg), 1673 Waterfall Way, 4.5km W of PO, ☎ 02 6655 2142, fax 02 6655 2142, 1 cotg acc up to 6, [shwr, bath, tlt, c/fan, fire pl, TV, video, CD, t/c mkg, refrig, cook fac, micro, toaster, blkts, linen, pillows], bbq, cots, non smoking units. **D** ♦ **$110,** ♦ **$15, W ♦♦ $660,** ♦ **$90**, ch con.

★★★★ **Koompartoo Retreat**, (Chalet), Cnr Rawson & Dudley Sts, 1km S of PO, ☎ 02 6655 2326, fax 02 6655 2326, 4 chalets acc up to 3, [shwr, tlt, c/fan, heat, elec blkts, fax, TV, clock radio, t/c mkg, refrig, cook fac, elec frypan, toaster], iron, iron brd, lounge (TV), spa, bbq, c/park. **RO** ♦ **$115 - $125, ♦♦ $125 - $135,** ♦ **$25, ♦♦ $750 - $810**, BC MC VI.

★★★★ **Spicketts Creek Farm Holiday Cottages**, (Cotg), (Farm), Lot 177, Bowraville Rd Brierfield via, 16km from PO, ☎ 02 6655 1842, fax 02 6655 1842, 3 cotgs acc up to 6, [shwr, bath (1), tlt, c/fan, heat, elec blkts, TV, clock radio, t/c mkg, refrig, cook fac, micro, toaster, doonas, linen], bbq, non smoking property. **D ♦♦ $90 - $100,** ♦ **$20 - $25, W ♦♦ $550,** ♦ **$85 - $110**, fam con.

★★★☆ **Bellingen River Family Cabins**, (Cotg), 'Jemaree' Waterfall Way, 2km E of Bellingen, ☎ 02 6655 0499, fax 02 6655 0499, 2 cotgs acc up to 8, [shwr, tlt, c/fan, heat, fax, TV, clock radio, t/c mkg, refrig, cook fac ltd, micro, elec frypan, toaster, linen reqd-fee], ldry, bbq, plygr, canoeing, non smoking property. **D ♦ $77,** ♦ **$7 - $14, W ♦♦ $465**, ch con, Min book all holiday times, BC MC VI.

★★★☆ **Jelga River Retreat**, (Cotg), 1 Wheatley St, 1km NW of PO, ☎ 02 6655 2202, fax 02 6655 1486, 2 cotgs acc up to 6, [shwr, tlt, c/fan, heat (combustion), elec blkts, tel, TV, video, clock radio, refrig, cook fac, micro, toaster, ldry], bbq, plygr. **BB ♦ $90 - $100, ♦♦ $125 - $135,** ♦ **$30, W ♦♦ $725 - $785, RO ♦ $85 - $95, ♦♦ $115 - $125,** ♦ **$24, W ♦♦ $690 - $750**, ch con, 1 cottage yet to be assessed, Min book Christmas Jan and Easter, BC MC VI, ⅙.

★★★☆ **Maddefords Cottages**, (Cotg), North Bank Rd, ☎ 02 6655 9866, fax 02 6655 9866, 2 cotgs acc up to 6, [shwr, tlt, a/c, c/fan, tel, TV, video, CD, t/c mkg, refrig, cook fac, micro, toaster, blkts, linen, pillows], iron, bbq, cots-fee, non smoking units (2). **D ♦♦ $110,** ♦ **$22, W ♦♦ $660,** ♦ **$154**, BC MC VI.

★★★ **Crystal Creek Farm Stay**, (Cotg), 691 Promised Land Rd, 16km from Bellingen, ☎ 02 6655 1090, fax 02 6655 1090, 1 cotg acc up to 6, [shwr, bath, tlt, fan, heat, TV, video, radio, refrig, cook fac, micro, toaster, ldry, blkts, linen, pillows], bbq, c/park (carport). **D $100, W $550, High Season W $650**, Access road unsealed, enquire in wet weather. Min book applies.

★★★ **Mountside**, (Apt), 309 Roses Rd, 6km W of PO, ☎ 02 6655 2206, fax 02 6655 2276, 1 apt acc up to 4, [shwr, tlt, fan, heat, elec blkts, TV, video (avail), clock radio, t/c mkg, refrig, cook fac, micro, elec frypan, toaster], ldry, iron, iron brd, pool (salt water), bbq, tennis. **BLB ♦ $65, ♦♦ $85,** ♦ **$20, W $500**.

★★☆ **Bellingen Farmstay**, (Cotg), Previously Be Together Farmstay 417 Martells Rd, 15km SE of PO, ☎ 02 6655 2786, fax 02 6655 2830, 3 cotgs acc up to 6, [shwr, tlt, hairdry, fan, heat, tel, TV, clock radio, t/c mkg, refrig, cook fac, micro, elec frypan, toaster, blkts, linen], iron, bbq, c/park (carport). **D $100, W $450 - $700**, Min book applies, BC MC VI.

B&B's/Guest Houses

★★★★☆ **Bliss Lodge**, (GH), 355 Martells Rd, 13km SE of Bellingen, ☎ 02 6655 9111, fax 02 6655 0653, 4 rms [shwr, tlt, hairdry, fan, c/fan (1), heat, elec blkts, TV, clock radio, t/c mkg], ldry, iron, iron brd, lounge firepl, ✕, spa, bbq, canoeing, non smoking property. **BB ♦ $80 - $90, ♦♦ $130 - $140,** ♦ **$20 - $30**, Min book applies, AE BC DC MC VI.

★★★★☆ **Casa Belle Country Guest House**, (B&B), 90 Gleniffer Rd, 1.5km N of PO, ☎ 02 6655 9311, fax 02 6655 0155, 3 rms [shwr, bath (1), spa bath (2), tlt, hairdry, c/fan, fire pl (2), heat, tel, TV, video, clock radio, CD, t/c mkg], ldry, lounge, ✕, courtesy transfer, non smoking property. **BB ⋔ $95, ⋔⋔ $165**, AE BC DC MC VI.

★★★★ **Monticello Countryhouse Bed & Breakfast**, (B&B), 11 Sunset Ridge Dve, 1.5km NW of PO, ☎ 02 6655 1559, fax 02 6655 1559, 3 rms [shwr, bath (1), tlt, hairdry, c/fan, tel, TV, video (avail), clock radio, refrig], iron (1), iron brd (1), lounge firepl, t/c mkg shared. **BB ⋔ $100 - $120, ⋔⋔ $160 - $175**, Min book applies.

★★★★ **Rivendell Guest House**, (B&B), No children's facilities, 10-12 Hyde St, 50m E of PO, ☎ 02 6655 0060, fax 02 6655 0060, 4 rms [shwr, tlt, fan, fire pl, elec blkts, clock radio], lounge (TV & cd player), pool (salt water), t/c mkg shared. ☎ **BB ⋔ $99 - $150**, BC MC VI.

★★★☆ **Garden Guesthouse**, (GH), 39 John Glyde Rd, 5km NE of PO, ☎ 02 6655 2124, fax 02 6655 0626, 4 rms [fan, heat (1), tel, TV (3), clock radio (2), refrig, micro, toaster], iron, iron brd, lounge, cook fac, t/c mkg shared, bbq, cots-fee, non smoking property. **BLB ⋔⋔ $60 - $70, ◊ $20**, BC MC VI.

BELMONT NSW 2280

Pop Part of Lake Macquarie, (168km N Sydney), See map on page 55, ref E4. Town on the eastern shores of Lake Macquarie. Boating, Bowls, Fishing, Golf, Sailing, Scenic Drives, Surfing, Swimming, Tennis. See also Blacksmiths & Redhead.

Hotels/Motels

★★★☆ **Lake Macquarie Flag Motor Inn**, (M), 798 Pacific Hwy, 3km S of PO, ☎ 02 4945 8622, fax 02 4947 7149, 20 units [shwr, tlt, hairdry, a/c, elec blkts, tel, TV, video, clock radio, t/c mkg, refrig], ✕, pool (salt water), bbq, rm serv, dinner to unit, plygr, cots-fee. **RO ⋔⋔ $89 - $93, ◊ $11**, ch con, AE BC DC EFT MC VI, ⅙&.

★★★☆ **Lakeview Motor Inn**, (M), 749 Pacific Hwy, 1km S of PO, ☎ 02 4945 2847, fax 02 4945 2039, 16 units [shwr, spa bath, tlt, hairdry, a/c, elec blkts, tel, TV, movie, clock radio, t/c mkg, refrig, toaster], iron, iron brd, pool, bbq, cots-fee, non smoking units (5). **RO ⋔ $70 - $100, ⋔⋔ $80 - $110, ⋔⋔⋔ $90 - $130, ◊ $10**, AE BC DC MC VI, ⅙&.

★★★☆ **Squids Ink**, (M), 690 Pacific Hwy, 1km S of PO, ☎ 02 4947 7223, fax 02 4947 7276, (2 stry gr fl), 24 units (2 suites) [shwr, spa bath (2), tlt, hairdry, a/c (2), fan, heat, elec blkts, tel, TV, clock radio, refrig, cook fac (1), toaster], ldry, lounge (TV), conv fac, ✕, pool (salt water), spa, t/c mkg shared, bbq, rm serv, dinner to unit, plygr, canoeing, cots. **RO ⋔ $95 - $200, ⋔⋔ $105 - $220**, 4 units of a higher rating. Min book applies, AE BC DC MC VI.

★★★ **Belmont Aquarius Motor Inn**, (M), 813 Pacific Hwy, 2km S of PO, ☎ 02 4945 9899, fax 02 4945 1116, 13 units (1 suite) [shwr, tlt, hairdry, a/c, c/fan (12), elec blkts, tel, TV, video (avail), clock radio, t/c mkg, refrig, toaster], ldry, iron, pool, bbq, cots, non smoking units (8). **RO ⋔ $50 - $70, ⋔⋔ $55 - $80, ⋔⋔⋔ $66 - $95, ◊ $12**, AE BC DC EFT MC MCH VI.

★★★ **Winston Court Motel**, (M), 378 Pacific Hwy, 2km N of PO, ☎ 02 4945 2821, fax 02 4947 7646, 13 units [shwr, tlt, a/c, c/fan, heat, elec blkts, tel, TV, movie, clock radio, t/c mkg, refrig, toaster], ldry, pool, bbq, plygr, cots. **W $312 - $570, RO ⋔ $52 - $70, ⋔⋔ $63 - $82, ⋔⋔⋔ $82 - $92, ◊ $11**, ch con, AE BC DC MC MCH VI.

Operator Comment: See advertisement on next page

★★☆ **Pelican Palms Motor Inn**, (M), 784 Pacific Hwy, 3km S of PO, ☎ 02 4945 4545, fax 02 4945 8971, 13 units [shwr, tlt, hairdry, a/c, elec blkts, tel, TV, video-fee, clock radio, t/c mkg, refrig, toaster], ldry, pool, spa, bbq, courtesy transfer, cots, non smoking units (5). **RO ⋔ $46 - $60, ⋔⋔ $48 - $65, ⋔⋔⋔ $58 - $75**, ch con, AE BC DC EFT MC VI.

★★ **Gunyah Hotel Motel**, (LMH), 644 Pacific Hwy, ☎ 02 4945 4603, fax 02 4945 9878, (2 stry), 8 units [shwr, tlt, a/c, fan, TV, radio, t/c mkg, toaster], ✉, ☎. **BB ⋔ $50 - $60, ⋔⋔ $66 - $77, ◊ $15, RO ⋔ $44 - $55, ⋔⋔ $55 - $65, ◊ $15**, ch con.

WINSTON COURT
• M O T E L •

- Nearest Motel to 16's Club
- Free Movies
- Pool, BBQ, A/C
- Mins to Hosp, Beach, Lake
- 20km to Newcastle

PHONE: (02) 49 452 821

Budget Motel Chain International

378 Pacific Hway, Belmont 2280

656NW

'View before you choose'
www.spinnakers.com.au

AAAT ★★★★ Deluxe cabins

SPINNAKERS

687 Pacific Hwy Belmont 2280 Lake Macquarie
Reservations: 1800 352 303

654AG

Self Catering Accommodation
★★★☆ **Azure Waterfront Cottage**, (Cotg), 3 New St, mob 0410 485 217, fax 02 9817 4543, 1 cotg acc up to 4, (2 bedrm), [shwr, tlt, heat, fan (2), heat, tel, TV, video (on request) reqd-fee, refrig, cook fac, ldry, blkts, linen]. Pets allowed. **D** ♦ $70 - $90, ♦♦ $100 - $130, ♦ $20 - $30, ch con, pen con, weekly con.

★★★☆ **Lakeshores Self Catering Accommodation**, (Villa), Previously Lakeshores Self Contained Apartments 63 Tudor St, ☎ 02 4945 4224, fax 02 4945 4224, 3 villas acc up to 8, [shwr, bath, tlt, fan, heat, TV, clock radio, t/c mkg, refrig, cook fac, micro, elec frypan, d/wash, toaster, ldry, blkts, linen], w/mach, dryer, iron, iron brd, non smoking property. **D** $85 - $250, Min book applies, BC MC VI.

B&B's/Guest Houses
★★★★☆ **Lakeview Bed & Breakfast**, (B&B), 674 Pacific Hwy, ☎ 02 4945 8128, (2 stry gr fl), 2 rms [shwr, tlt, hairdry, fan, heat, TV, video, clock radio, t/c mkg, refrig]. **BB** ♦ $80 - $90, ♦♦ $110 - $130, ♦ $50 - $70.

BEMBOKA NSW 2550

Pop 250. Nominal, (466km S Sydney), See map on pages 52/53, ref G8. Historic village situated on the Bega Rive.

Self Catering Accommodation
Giba Gunyah Country Cottages, (Cotg), Pollocks Flat Rd Morans Crossing via, 10km E of PO, ☎ 02 6492 8404, fax 02 6492 8404, 2 cotgs acc up to 6, [shwr, tlt, fire pl, heat, elec blkts, TV, t/c mkg, refrig, cook fac, micro, elec frypan, toaster, blkts, linen], bbq, cots, Pets welcome. **D** ♦♦ $85 - $135, ♦ $20, **W** ♦♦ $575 - $995, ♦ $140 - $190, ♿, (not yet classified).

BEN LOMOND NSW 2365

Pop Nominal, (631km N Sydney), See map on page 54, ref B4. Small New England town midway between Guyra and Glen Innes with what's said to be the highest railway station in Australia — it sits at an altitude of 1363.4m. Gem Fossicking, Horse Riding, Scenic Drives.

Self Catering Accommodation
★★★ **Uncle Billys Retreat**, (Cotg), Yoolimba, ☎ 02 6779 4216, fax 02 6779 4266, 3 cotgs acc up to 4, [t/c mkg, refrig, cook fac ltd, blkts, doonas, linen reqd-fee, pillows], lounge firepl, bbq. **D** ♦ $30, ♦♦ $60, ♦ $30, ch con.

B&B's/Guest Houses
★★★☆ **Silent Grove Farm Stay B&B**, (B&B), Silent Grove, ☎ 02 6733 2117, fax 02 6733 2117, 3 rms [heat, elec blkts, tel, clock radio, micro (communal), toaster (communal)], ldry, iron, iron brd, lounge (TV & firepl), t/c mkg shared, refrig, tennis. **BB** ♦ $39, ♦♦ $72, ♦ $39, **DBB** ♦ $57, ♦♦ $108, ♦ $57, ch con, BC MC VI.

★★★☆ **(Cottage Section)**, 1 cotg acc up to 8, [shwr, bath, tlt, fire pl (combustion), TV, t/c mkg, refrig, cook fac, micro, elec frypan, toaster, ldry, linen reqd-fee], w/mach, iron, iron brd. **D** ♦♦ $72, ♦ $13, **W** ♦♦ $432, ♦ $78 - $90.

BENDALONG NSW 2539

Pop 500. (226km SW Sydney), See map on page 55, ref B5. Small seaside community near Lake Conjola, popular as a holiday base with families, scuba divers and anglers. Surfing, Swimming.

Self Catering Accommodation
★★ **Berringer Lake Holiday Cottages**, Berringer Rd, 3km SW of General Store, ☎ 02 4456 1640, fax 02 4456 1640, 4 cabins acc up to 5, [shwr, bath, tlt, heat, clock radio, refrig, cook fac, micro, elec frypan, toaster, linen reqd-fee], ldry, c/park. **D** ♦♦ $60 - $80, ♦ $10, **W** $370 - $520, Min book applies, BC MC VI.

Redhead House, (House), 4 Cherry St, ☎ 02 9517 1130, fax 02 9212 6386, (2 stry), 3 houses acc up to 8, [shwr, bath, tlt, heat, TV, video, clock radio, t/c mkg, refrig, cook fac, micro, toaster, ldry], w/mach, dryer, iron, iron brd, lounge firepl, non smoking property, **D** $200, **W** $650 - $1,200, Min book applies, (not yet classified).

BENDEMEER NSW 2353

Pop 250. (499km N Sydney), See map on page 54, ref A5. Historic town on the New England Highway between Tamworth and Uralla. Fishing, Golf, Shooting, Swimming.

Hotels/Motels
★☆ **Bendemeer**, (LH), Caroline St, 300m N of PO, ☎ 02 6769 6550, fax 02 6769 6692, (2 stry), 12 rms [shwr (7), bath (2), tlt (7), elec blkts, TV, t/c mkg], ldry, ✉, bbq, plygr, bowls. **RO** ♦ $20 - $35, ♦♦ $40 - $55, ♦ $10 - $20, ch con, 5 rooms ★.

BERKELEY NSW

See Wollongong & Suburbs.

BERMAGUI NSW 2546

Pop 1,196. (375km S Sydney), See map on page 55, ref A7. South coast fishing village renowned for its big game fishing, particularly for yellowfin tuna and marlin. Boating, Bowls, Bush Walking, Fishing, Golf, Surfing, Swimming, Tennis, Water Skiing. See also Wallace Lake.

Hotels/Motels

★★★★ **Beachview Motel**, (M), 12 Lamont St, 100m E of PO, ☎ 02 6493 4155, fax 02 6493 4879, (2 stry gr fl), 8 units [shwr, tlt, hairdry (8), a/c, fan, elec blkts, tel, fax, TV, video, clock radio, t/c mkg, refrig, toaster], ldry, iron, iron brd, bbq, boat park, cots, non smoking units (3). **RO** ♦ $66 - $132, ♦♦ $77 - $132, ♦♦♦ $83 - $132, ♦ $6, **W** $539 - $924, ch con, 1 unit of a lesser rating. AE BC DC EFT JCB MC VI.

★★★★ **Harbourview Motel**, (M), 56 Lamont St, 500m N of PO, ☎ 02 6493 5213, fax 02 6493 5209, 8 units [shwr, tlt, hairdry, fan, heat, elec blkts, tel, fax, TV, video (avail), clock radio, t/c mkg, refrig, toaster], ldry, iron, iron brd, bbq, boat park, cots (avail), non smoking rms (6). **D** ♦ $85 - $121, ♦♦ $99 - $145, ♦ $33, BC MC VI.

EASTVIEW MOTOR INN

AAAT ★★★☆

• *Absolute Ocean Views* • *1 & 2 bedroom Apartments*
• *Serviced apartments daily or midweek*
• *Discounts for Emergency Service Personnel*
• *Salt pool* • *Barbecue* • *Kitchen and Laundry*
• *Opposite Wetland Bird Sanctuary* • *200m from quiet beach*

46 Wallaga Lake Road, Bermagui NSW 2546

Fax: 02 6493 5176 **BERMAGUI** Ph: 02 6493 4777

Haven

★★★☆ **Eastview Motor Inn**, (M), 46 Wallaga Lake Rd, 600m N of Bridge, ☎ 02 6493 4777, fax 02 6493 5176, (2 stry gr fl), 9 units (1 bedrm2 bedrm), [shwr, bath (1), tlt, hairdry, fan, heat, elec blkts, tel, TV, video-fee, clock radio, t/c mkg, refrig, cook fac, micro (7), ldry], pool (salt water), bbq, boat park, courtesy transfer, non smoking units (5). **RO** ♦ **$70 - $110**, ♦♦ **$78 - $130**, ◊ **$15**, **W $350 - $800**, ch con, AE BC DC EFT MC VI.
★★☆ **Bermagui Motor Inn**, (M), 38 Lamont St, 100m W of PO, ☎ 02 6493 4311, fax 02 6493 3600, 17 units [shwr, tlt, heat, elec blkts, TV, video-fee, clock radio, t/c mkg, refrig, cook fac ltd (2), micro (2), toaster], bbq, cots-fee, non smoking rms (1). **RO** ♦ **$50 - $70**, ♦♦ **$50 - $95**, ◊ **$10**, ch con, fam con, BC MC VI.
Horseshoe Bay, (LMH), Lamont St, 400m E of PO, ☎ 02 6493 4206, fax 02 6493 4859, 3 units [shwr, tlt, heat, TV, t/c mkg, refrig], cots. **RO** ♦ **$50**, ♦♦ **$60**, ◊ **$10**, AE BC DC EFT MC VI.
(**Bunkhouse Section**), 1 bunkhouse **D** ♦ **$15**, (not yet classified).
(**Hotel Section**), (2 stry), 26 rms rec rm, lounge (TV), ⊠, bbq, dinner to unit, ✆, cots. **RO** ♦ **$25**, ♦♦♦ **$35**, ch con.

Self Catering Accommodation
★★★ **Anchorage Holiday Units Bermagui**, (HU), 2 West St, ☎ 02 6493 3308, fax 02 6493 3305, (2 stry gr fl), 17 units acc up to 5, [shwr, tlt, heat, elec blkts, TV, movie, clock radio, t/c mkg, refrig, cook fac, micro, elec frypan, toaster, blkts, doonas (4), linen] ldry, w/mach, dryer, iron, iron brd, pool-heated (solar, salt water), bbq, boat park, plygr, cots, non smoking units (8). **D $69.30 - $110**, **W $385 - $737**, BC EFT MC VI.
★★★ **Blue Pacific**, (HF), 73 Murrah St, East of Bermagui Bridge, ☎ 02 6493 4921, fax 02 6493 4921, 5 flats acc up to 6, [shwr, tlt, c/fan, heat, elec blkts, TV, video, clock radio, refrig, cook fac, micro, elec frypan, toaster, blkts, linen], ldry, bbq, cots. **D** ♦♦ **$50 - $83**, **W** ♦♦ **$300 - $540**, ch con, BC MC VI.
★★★ **Flats Elite**, (HF), 84 Murrah St, ☎ 02 6493 4274, fax 02 6493 5044, 12 flats acc up to 6, [shwr, tlt, fan, heat, elec blkts, TV, video-fee, clock radio, refrig, cook fac, elec frypan, toaster, blkts, doonas, linen, pillows], ldry, bbq, ✆. **D $44 - $140**, **W $264 - $880**, Min book Christmas Jan and Easter, BC MC VI, ♿.
★★★ **The Captains Quarters**, (HU), 4 George St, ☎ 02 6493 4946, fax 02 4993 5141, 3 units acc up to 6, [shwr, tlt, heat, TV, video, t/c mkg, refrig, cook fac, micro, d/wash, toaster, ldry, blkts, linen, pillows], w/mach, iron, pool (salt water), bbq, c/park. **D $65 - $120**, **W $400 - $750**, AE BC MC VI.

B&B's/Guest Houses
Sails, (B&B), 74 Fairhaven Point Way, 8km N of PO, ☎ 02 6493 4116, 2 rms (1 suite) [shwr, tlt, hairdry, heat, tel, TV], ldry, iron, iron brd, lounge, bbq, cots, non smoking rms. **BB** ♦♦ **$95 - $105**, (not yet classified).

BERRARA NSW 2540

Pop 550. Nominal, (207km S Sydney), See map on page 55, ref B5. Small village on the south coast near Sussex Inlet, known for its beach and rock fishing. Boating, Bush Walking, Canoeing, Fishing, Scenic Drives, Swimming.

Self Catering Accommodation
★★★★ **Berrara Beach Holiday Chalets**, (Chalet), Berrara Rd, 50km S of Nowra, ☎ 02 4441 2176, fax 02 4441 0001, 20 chalets acc up to 5, [shwr, tlt, a/c, heat (gas/slow comb.), TV, video, clock radio, t/c mkg, refrig, cook fac, micro, d/wash, toaster, linen reqd-fee], w/mach, dryer, iron, bbq, ✆. **D $120 - $250**, **W $715 - $1,375**, Min book applies.

BERRIDALE NSW 2628

Pop 1,300. (427km S Sydney), See map on pages 52/53, ref F7. Snowy Mountains town that acts as the administrative centre for the Snowy River Shire. It's a good base from which to go skiing or touring the mountains. Bowls, Fishing, Golf, Horse Riding, Scenic Drives, Swimming, Tennis.

Hotels/Motels
★★★☆ **Southern Cross Motor Inn & Tourist Park**, (M), Middlingbank Rd, 2km NW of PO, ☎ 02 6456 3289, fax 02 6456 3437, (2 stry gr fl), 22 units (4 suites) [shwr, bath (9), tlt, cent heat, elec blkts, tel (11), TV, clock radio, t/c mkg, refrig, cook fac (14)], ldry, dry rm, rec rm, lounge (bar), conv fac, ✕, ⊠ (chargrill), bbq, plygr, ski hire, cots. **RO** ♦ **$66 - $160**, ♦♦ **$77 - $160**, ◊ **$11 - $40**, **Suite D $110 - $335**, AE BC EFT MC VI.
Snowy Mountains Coach & Motor Inn, (M), Jindabyne Rd, 1km N of PO, ☎ 02 6456 3283, or 02 9985 1190, fax 02 6456 3049, (Multi-stry gr fl), 41 units [shwr, tlt, hairdry (12), cent heat, tel (12), TV, movie, clock radio, t/c mkg, refrig], ldry, rec rm, ⊠, pool indoor heated, sauna, bbq, rm serv, ✆, ski hire, cots. **RO** ♦ **$35 - $120**, ♦♦ **$55 - $130**, ♦♦♦ **$65 - $170**, ◊ **$20 - $40**, ch con, AE BC DC MC VI.

Self Catering Accommodation
★★☆ **Glenelm Cottage**, (Cotg), (Farm), Dalgety Rd, 4km SE of Berridale, ☎ 02 6456 3152, fax 02 6456 2628, 1 cotg acc up to 8, [shwr, bath, tlt, hairdry, fire pl (wood), elec blkts, TV, video, clock radio, t/c mkg, refrig, cook fac, elec frypan, toaster], w/mach, dryer, iron, bbq. **High Season D** ♦♦ **$90**, ◊ **$20**, **Low Season D** ♦♦ **$70**, ◊ **$20**, ch con, BC MC VI.
★★ **Coliro Flats**, (HF), 7 Cecil St, ☎ 02 4471 3176, 2 flats acc up to 9, [shwr, tlt, cent heat, TV, clock radio, t/c mkg, refrig, cook fac, micro, elec frypan, toaster, ldry, linen-fee], w/mach, dryer, iron. **D $130 - $160**, **W $600 - $850**, Min book applies.
★★ **Snowdale Flats**, (HU), 6 Thorwa Cl, 300m SE of PO, ☎ 02 4471 3176, 4 units acc up to 6, [shwr, bath, tlt, fire pl, cent heat, TV, clock radio, refrig, cook fac, micro, elec frypan, toaster, ldry, linen-fee], c/park (undercover). **D $110**, **W $500 - $700**, Min book applies.

B&B's/Guest Houses
★★★☆ **Ballantrae House**, (B&B), No children's facilities, 16 Myack St, 50m N of PO, ☎ 02 6456 3388, fax 02 6456 3388, 3 rms [shwr (2), bath (1), tlt (2), hairdry, heat, elec blkts, TV, t/c mkg, refrig, pillows], lounge, non smoking rms. **BB** ♦ **$60**, ♦♦ **$110**, Dinner by arrangement. BC MC VI.
★★★☆ **Cottonwood Bed & Breakfast**, (B&B), 3 William St, 100m S of PO, ☎ 02 6456 3374, fax 02 6456 3999, (2 stry gr fl), 14 rms (1 suite) [shwr, tlt, cent heat, elec blkts, TV, clock radio, t/c mkg, refrig], ldry, rec rm, lounge (TV), ⊠, ✆, cots. **BB** ♦ **$49 - $75**, ♦♦ **$58 - $110**, ♦♦♦ **$73 - $160**, ◊ **$15 - $45**, ch con, BC MC VI.

Other Accommodation
Cooba Lodge, (Lodge), Cootralantra Rd off Jindabyne Rd, 5km N of PO, ☎ 02 6456 3150, fax 02 6456 3691, (2 stry gr fl), 27 rms acc up to 7, [shwr, tlt, heat, elec blkts, TV, t/c mkg, refrig], ldry, rec rm, lounge, conv fac, ⊠, pool-heated, sauna, spa, bbq, ✆, plygr, gym, tennis, cots. **RO** ♦ **$40 - $65**, ♦♦ **$55 - $85**, ♦♦♦ **$65 - $95**, ◊ **$10**, BC MC VI.

BERRIGAN NSW 2712

Pop 1,000. (700km SW Sydney), See map on pages 52/53, ref D7. Attractive place between Finley and Corowa, well known for its country race meetings and typical of the smaller towns of this part of the Murray region. Bowls, Fishing, Golf, Horse Racing, Squash, Tennis.

Hotels/Motels
★★☆ **Berrigan Country Club Motor Inn**, (M), 18 Stewart St, 1km fr PO, ☎ 03 5885 2409, fax 03 5885 2600, 21 units [shwr, tlt, a/c, fan, elec blkts, tel, fax, TV, clock radio, t/c mkg, refrig, toaster], pool-heated (solar), bbq, bowls, golf, cots. **RO** ♦ **$50**, ♦♦ **$66**, ◊ **$11**, AE BC EFT MC VI, ♿.

BERRIMA NSW 2577

Pop 800. (122km S Sydney), See map on page 55, ref B4. Historic Southern Highlands village beside the Wingecarribee River. Scenic Drives.

Hotels/Motels

GOLDEN CHAIN

★★★☆ **Berrima Bakehouse**, (M), Cnr Wingecarribee St & Old Hume Hwy, 100m N of PO, ☎ 02 4877 1381, fax 02 4877 1047, (2 stry gr fl), 19 units [shwr, bath (1), tlt, a/c (2), fan, cent heat, elec blkts, tel, TV, clock radio, t/c mkg, refrig], ldry, pool, bbq, cots-fee, non smoking units (11). **RO** ♦ **$68 - $176**, ♦♦ **$82.50 - $176**, ◊ **$16.50**, pen con, Min book applies, AE BC DC EFT MC VI.

B&B's/Guest Houses

★★★★★ **Wanganderry Country House**, (B&B), No children's facilities, 61 Inverary Rd, Paddys River via, 25km S of Berrima, ☎ 02 4884 1502, fax 02 4884 1208, 2 rms [shwr, bath (1), spa bath (1), tlt, hairdry, a/c, elec blkts, tel, clock radio], iron, iron brd, rec rm, lounge (tv & firepl), t/c mkg shared, bbq, non smoking property. **BB** ♦♦ **$185 - $230**, **DBB** ♦♦ **$295 - $340**, Min book applies, AE BC MC VI.

★★★★☆ **Berrima Lodge**, (B&B), 22 Wilkinson St, 300m N of PO, ☎ 02 4877 1755, fax 02 4877 1756, 3 rms [shwr, tlt, heat, elec blkts], lounge firepl, t/c mkg shared, c/park. **BB** ♦ **$100 - $200**, ♦♦ **$135 - $340**, BC MC VI.

★★★★ **Walden Wood**, (B&B), Old Mandemar Rd, 1km N of PO, ☎ 02 4877 1164, fax 02 4877 1164, 2 rms [shwr, tlt, fire pl, heat, elec blkts, tel], lounge, t/c mkg shared, bbq, c/park. **BB** ♦ **$95 - $110**, ♦♦ **$110 - $165**, ♦♦♦ **$143 - $195**, **W $620**, Min book long w/ends.

★★★☆ **(Cottage Section)**, 1 cotg acc up to 6, [shwr, tlt, fire pl, heat, elec blkts, t/c mkg, refrig, cook fac, micro, elec frypan, toaster, blkts, linen, pillows], bbq, cots, non smoking units. **D** ♦♦ **$110 - $165**, ◊ **$55 - $90**, **W $770**, ch con.

★★★☆ **Valley View Bed & Breakfast**, (GH), Old Mandemar Rd, 2km NW of PO, ☎ 02 4877 1046, fax 02 4877 2076, 2 rms [shwr, tlt, radio, t/c mkg, refrig, cook fac, micro, elec frypan, toaster], lounge (TV & Stereo), breakfast ingredients. **BB** ♦♦ **$165 - $290**, ◊ **$90**, ch con.

Berrima Guest House, (GH), Cnr Oxley & Wilkinson Sts, 200m N of PO, ☎ 02 4877 2277, fax 02 4877 2345, 6 rms [shwr, tlt, c/fan, cent heat, elec blkts, TV, clock radio, doonas], conf fac, lounge firepl, ✕, t/c mkg shared, refrig, bbq, secure park, ☏, non smoking property. **BB** ♦ **$80 - $100**, ♦♦ **$150 - $198**, ◊ **$25**, BC MC VI, (not yet classified).

BERRY NSW 2535

Pop 1,600. (128km S Sydney), See map on page 55, ref B4. Historic south coast town that's a popular destination for antique hunters and people interested in local arts and crafts. Scenic Drives, Vineyards, Wineries.

Hotels/Motels

★★★★ **The Berry Village Boutique Motel**, (M), 72 Queen St, ☎ 02 4464 3570, fax 02 4464 3580, (2 stry gr fl), 24 units [shwr, spa bath (3), tlt, a/c, tel, cable tv, clock radio, t/c mkg, refrig], ldry, conf fac, lounge firepl, breakfast rm, pool-heated, c/park (undercover), cots-fee, non smoking property. **BLB** ♦ **$90 - $155**, ♦♦ **$98 - $177**, ◊ **$22**, AE BC DC EFT MC VI, 戌も.

★★★ **Bangalee Motel**, (M), Princes Hwy, 450m N of PO, ☎ 02 4464 1305, fax 02 4464 2139, 10 units [shwr, tlt, a/c (5), fan, heat, elec blkts, tel, TV, clock radio, t/c mkg, refrig], lounge, pool, bbq. **RO** ♦ **$55 - $100**, ♦♦ **$65 - $110**, ◊ **$15**, ch con, AE BC DC MC VI.

★★☆ **Berry Hotel**, (LH), 120 Princes Hwy, ☎ 02 4464 1011, fax 02 4464 2142, (2 stry), 14 rms ldry, rec rm, lounge (guest), conv fac, ✉, cafe, bbq, rm serv, dinner to unit, ☏, plygr, cots. **W $150**, **RO** ♦ **$40 - $50**, ♦♦ **$50 - $75**, ♦♦♦ **$60 - $80**, ◊ **$10 - $15**, ch con, AE BC EFT MC VI.

Self Catering Accommodation

★★★★ **Bundara Farm Cottages**, (Cotg), 18 Wire La, 3km E of PO, ☎ 02 4464 1565, fax 02 4464 2997, 2 cotgs acc up to 4, [shwr (2), bath (1), tlt (2), hairdry, fire pl, TV, video, t/c mkg, cook fac (2), blkts, linen], bbq, cots, Pets on application. **D** ♦♦ **$130 - $190**, ◊ **$30 - $55**, ch con, Min book applies, BC MC VI.

★★★☆ **Boronia Cottage Overnight Accommodation**, (Cotg), 285 Bryces Rd, 10km E of PO, ☎ 02 4464 2417, fax 02 4465 1150, 1 cotg acc up to 3, [shwr, tlt, hairdry, c/fan, heat, elec blkts, TV, clock radio, t/c mkg, refrig, cook fac, micro, elec frypan, toaster, doonas, linen], iron, iron brd, lounge firepl, bbq, non smoking property. **RO $100 - $130**, **W $610 - $710**, ch con.

★★★☆ **Figlea Cottages**, (Cotg), 165a Bong Bong Rd, ☎ 02 4464 1635, fax 02 4464 1635, 2 cotgs acc up to 4, [shwr, tlt, hairdry, fan, fire pl (1), heat, elec blkts, TV, video, radio, CD, t/c mkg, refrig, micro, elec frypan, toaster, blkts, linen, pillows], bbq, cots, non smoking property. **RO** ♦♦ **$100 - $140**, ◊ **$15**, ch con, Min book applies, BC MC VI.

★★★☆ **Jasper Cottage**, (Cotg), (Farm), 400 Strongs Rd Jaspers Rd, 8.6km S of Berry PO, ☎ 02 4448 6174, fax 02 4448 6174, 1 cotg acc up to 6, [shwr, bath, tlt, fire pl, elec blkts, tel, TV, video, radio, t/c mkg, refrig, cook fac, micro, toaster, ldry, blkts, linen, pillows], w/mach, dryer, iron. **RO $100 - $150**, **W $750 - $850**, Min book applies.

★★★☆ **Tullouch Loft**, (Chalet), 100 Tullouch Rd, Broughton Vale, 5km NW of Berry, ☎ 02 4464 1748, fax 02 4464 1748, 1 chalet acc up to 5, [shwr, tlt, hairdry, a/c, fan (1), heat, TV, video, CD, refrig, cook fac ltd, micro, elec frypan, toaster, ldry, blkts, linen, pillows], iron, iron brd, pool, bbq, c/park. **RO** ♦ **$85 - $120**, ♦♦ **$110 - $165**, ◊ **$15 - $40**.

Willowglen Farm, (House), (Farm), 218 Bundewallah Rd, 4km W of PO, ☎ 02 9130 4923, fax 02 9130 4923, 1 house acc up to 10, [shwr, bath, tlt, c/fan, fire pl, heat, tel, TV, video, t/c mkg, refrig, cook fac, micro, elec frypan, toaster, ldry], w/mach, dryer, iron, iron brd, bbq, cots, (not yet classified).

B&B's/Guest Houses

★★★★★ **Bimberdeen B&B**, (B&B), 580a Tourist Rd, ☎ 02 4464 2880, fax 02 4464 3283, 2 rms [shwr, bath, tlt, hairdry, a/c, c/fan, fire pl (1), heat, elec blkts, TV, video, clock radio, t/c mkg, refrig], bbq (undercover), courtesy transfer. **BB** ♦♦ **$170 - $200**, Min book applies, AE BC MC VI.

★★★★☆ **Abbeywood in the Fields**, (GH), Cnr Bryan Cl & Hillandale Rd, 4km N of PO, ☎ 02 4464 2148, fax 02 4464 2148, (2 stry gr fl), 2 rms [shwr, spa bath (1), tlt, hairdry, fan, tel, TV, t/c mkg], c/park. **BB** ♦ **$85**, ♦♦ **$110 - $140**.

★★★★☆ **Berry Mountain Bed & Breakfast**, (B&B), 150B Tourist Rd, Beaumont 2577, ☎ 02 4464 2485, fax 02 4464 2485, 4 rms (1 suite) [ensuite, shwr, bath (1), tlt, hairdry (1), c/fan, heat, elec blkts, TV (1), clock radio, t/c mkg, refrig (1), mini bar (1), micro (1)], TV rm, lounge firepl, non smoking property. **BB** ∮ **$140 - $180,** ∯ **$140 - $190,** BC MC VI.

★★★★☆ **Broughton Mill Farm**, (B&B), 78 Woodhill Mountain Rd, 1.5km N of PO, ☎ 02 4464 2446, fax 02 4464 1621, 5 rms [shwr, bath (3), spa bath (1), tlt, c/fan, cent heat, elec blkts, TV, radio, t/c mkg, doonas], conf fac, lounge firepl, ✕, pool, spa, refrig, bbq, ☏, non smoking property. **BB** ∯ **$180 - $250,** ◊ **$80,** Dinner by arrangement, Min book applies, BC MC VI.

★★★★☆ **Clunes of Berry**, (GH), No children's facilities, 24 Prince Alfred St, opposite old bank, ☎ 02 4464 2272, (2 stry gr fl), 5 rms [shwr, tlt, hairdry, c/fan, heat, elec blkts], lounge, t/c mkg shared, non smoking property. **BLB** ∮ **$110 - $190,** ∯ **$150 - $250,** Min book applies, AE BC DC MC VI.

★★★★☆ **Far Meadow Lodge**, (B&B), 199 Coolangatta Rd, 6km E of PO, ☎ 02 4448 5500, fax 02 4448 5500, 2 rms [shwr, spa bath, tlt, hairdry, heat, elec blkts, TV, video (1), radio, CD, t/c mkg, refrig, cook fac (1), micro (1), toaster (1)], lounge firepl, pool (salt water), bbq, non smoking property. **BB** ∮ **$100 - $115,** ∯ **$140 - $175,** ◊ **$25 - $30,** ch con, BC MC VI, ⓖ.

★★★★☆ **Mananga Homestead Bed & Breakfast**, (B&B), No children's facilities, A40 Princes Hwy, 1km N of Berry PO, ☎ 02 4464 1477, fax 02 4464 1477, 4 rms [ensuite, shwr, bath (2), tlt, fan, fire pl (3), heat, elec blkts, tel, clock radio, t/c mkg], lounge (TV), bbq, rm serv, c/park. **BB** ∮ **$100 - $198,** ∯ **$135 - $226,** ◊ **$50,** BC MC VI.

★★★★☆ **Woodbyne Luxury Accommodation**, (GH), 4 O'Keeffes La, Jaspers Brush 2535, 4km S of Berry, ☎ 02 4448 6200, fax 02 4448 6211, 7 rms [shwr, bath (5), tlt, hairdry, c/fan, heat, TV, video, t/c mkg, refrig], rec rm, lounge, lounge firepl, ✕, pool, bbq, c/park. **BB** ∯ **$253 - $275,** ◊ **$60,** AE BC DC MC VI.

★★★★ **Amelias Country House**, (B&B), No children's facilities, 67 Brogers Creek Rd, 7km N of PO, ☎ 02 4464 2534, fax 02 4464 2484, (2 stry gr fl), 3 rms [shwr, bath (1), tlt, hairdry, fan, heat, elec blkts], lounge (TV), ✕, t/c mkg shared, c/park. **BB** ∮ **$110 - $165,** ∯ **$155 - $175,** Min book applies, BC EFT MC VI.

★★★★ **Berry B&B in the Strawberry Fields**, (B&B), 35 Croziers Rd, 2km S of Berry, ☎ 02 4464 3430, fax 02 4464 3430, 2 rms (1 suite) [ensuite, spa bath, hairdry, fan (1), heat, cent heat, TV (1), clock radio, t/c mkg (1), refrig (1), cook fac ltd (1), micro (1), toaster (1), ldry], iron (1), iron brd (1), lounge, spa, cook fac, t/c mkg shared, bbq, cots, non smoking property. **BB** ∮ **$100 - $120,** ∯ **$120 - $150,** ◊ **$20 - $40,** BC MC VI.

★★★★ **Christopher's Our Place In Berry B & B**, (B&B), 146 Kangaroo Valley Rd, ☎ 02 4464 2771, fax 02 4464 3412, 3 rms [shwr, bath (1), tlt, hairdry, fan, heat, elec blkts], lounge (tv & firepl), ✕, pool-heated (salt water), t/c mkg shared, non smoking property. **BB** ∮ **$90 - $120,** ∯ **$140 - $170,** Dinner by arrangement, BC MC VI.

★★★★ **Elouera B & B**, (B&B), 5 Agars La, 1.5km N of PO, ☎ 02 4464 2668, fax 02 4464 2315, 3 rms [shwr, bath (2), spa bath (1), tlt, c/fan, heat], lounge, lounge firepl, ✕, t/c mkg shared, bbq, plygr, cots. **BB** ∮ **$90 - $110,** ∯ **$100 - $140,** ◊ **$15 - $30,** ch con, BC MC VI.

★★★★ **Swanlea Farm Bed & Breakfast**, (B&B), RMB 680 Bolong Rd, Bolong 2540, 6.8km E of Bomaderry, 10km NE of Nowra, ☎ 02 4421 7872, fax 02 4421 7872, 3 rms [ensuite, c/fan, heat, elec blkts, tel, clock radio, t/c mkg], lounge (TV), c/park. **BB** ∮ **$95,** ∯ **$140,** Min book long w/ends, AE BC MC VI.

★★★☆ **Bunyip Inn Guest House**, (GH), 122 Queen St, opposite old PO, ☎ 02 4464 2064, fax 02 4464 2324, (2 stry), 13 rms [shwr (10), bath (2), spa bath (2), tlt (10), c/fan, heat, elec blkts, TV, t/c mkg (5)], pool (salt water), t/c mkg shared, ☏. **BB** ∮ **$85 - $120,** ∯ **$100 - $198,** AE BC DC MC VI, ⓖ.

★★★☆ **Nightwinds of Berry**, (B&B), 44 Clarence St, 500m SE of Berry Public School, ☎ 02 4464 1845, fax 02 4464 2110, 1 rm (1 suite) [shwr, tlt, hairdry, c/fan, heat, elec blkts, clock radio, t/c mkg, refrig, micro, toaster, ldry], iron, iron brd, lounge (TV), pool (salt water), bbq, non smoking suites. **BB** ∮ **$80 - $90,** ∯ **$95 - $120.**

Ballindoch Park, (B&B), Lot 6, 140 Bryces Rd, 7km E of PO, ☎ 02 4464 3441, fax 02 4464 3442, 1 rm (1 suite) [ensuite (1), spa bath (1), a/c, elec blkts, clock radio, refrig, doonas], lounge (TV), pool-heated, bbq, non smoking suites. **Suite BB $154 - $176,** BC MC VI, (not yet classified).

Jaspers Brush B&B, (B&B), 465 Strongs Rd, Jaspers Brush, 10km S of PO, ☎ 02 4448 6194, fax 02 4448 6254, 3 rms [ensuite (2), c/fan, heat (elec), elec blkts, doonas], bathrm (1), ldry, conf fac, lounge firepl, ✕, refrig, bbq, non smoking rms. **BB** ∯ **$154 - $209,** BC MC VI, (not yet classified).

Sundance Park Bed & Breakfast, (B&B), 91 Wattamolla Rd, Woodhill Mountain, 8km NW of Apex Park, ☎ 02 4464 2008, fax 02 4464 2008, (Multi-stry gr fl), 3 rms (2 suites) [hairdry (2), tel, TV, t/c mkg (2), refrig (2), cook fac (1), cook fac ltd (2), micro (2), toaster (2)], ldry, iron, iron brd, rec rm, lounge firepl, pool (salt water), bbq, plygr, cots, non smoking property. **BB** ∮ **$105, Suite BB $210,** AE BC MC VI, (not yet classified).

BEWONG NSW 2540

Pop Nominal. (260km S Sydney) See map on page 55, ref B5. A quiet location near Wandandian, 5 km south of Tomerong. Boating, Canoeing.

B&B's/Guest Houses

★★★★ **Bottlebrush Cottage Bed & Breakfast**, (B&B), 18 Bottlebrush Ave, ☎ 02 4443 5999, fax 02 4443 5821, 1 rm [shwr, tlt, fan, heat, elec blkts, TV, clock radio, t/c mkg, refrig, cook fac ltd, toaster, doonas], non smoking property. **BLB** ♦♦ $66 - $80, ♦ $20, ch con, BC MC VI.

BILLINUDGEL NSW 2483

Pop Nominal, (803km N Sydney), See map on page 54, ref E2. Quaint far north coast town in a banana growing, cane harvesting and dairy farming area. Bush Walking, Scenic Drives. See also Ocean Shores.

Self Catering Accommodation

★★★★ **Pockets Cottage Resort**, (Cotg), Middle Pocket Rd, via Byron Bay, ☎ 02 6680 3300, fax 02 6680 3233, 4 cotgs acc up to 6, [shwr, spa bath, tlt, a/c, c/fan, cent heat, elec blkts, tel, TV, video, clock radio, t/c mkg, refrig, cook fac ltd, toaster], ldry, conv fac, ☒, pool (salt water), bbq, plygr, tennis, cots. **RO** ♦ $135 - $180, ♦♦ $135 - $180, ♦♦♦ $180 - $240, ch con, Min book applies, BC MC VI.

BINALONG NSW 2584

Pop 240. (316km SW Sydney), See map on pages 52/53, ref F6. Picturesque, historic town in the heart of Capital Country between Yass and Harden. Bush Walking.

Hotels/Motels

★★★ **Royal Tara**, (M), 27 - 37 Stephen St, 500m S of PO, ☎ 02 6227 4310, fax 02 6227 4323, 20 units [shwr, tlt, a/c, elec blkts, tel, TV, clock radio, t/c mkg, refrig], lounge (TV), conv fac, ☒, rm serv, cots. **RO** ♦ $75, ♦♦ $80, ♦ $15, AE BC DC MC VI.

BINGARA NSW 2404

Pop 1,250. (608km NW Sydney), See map on pages 52/53, ref H2. Pretty rural centre beside the Gwydir River on the Fossickers Way. Bowls, Fishing, Gem Fossicking, Golf, Scenic Drives, Swimming, Tennis.

Hotels/Motels

★★★ **Fossickers Way Motel**, (M), 2 Finch St, 300m N of PO, ☎ 02 6724 1373, fax 02 6724 1640, 12 units [shwr, tlt, a/c-cool, heat, elec blkts, tel, TV, clock radio, t/c mkg, refrig], ☒ (Mon to Sat), rm serv, dinner to unit, cots. **RO** ♦ $53 - $63, ♦♦ $60 - $70, ♦♦♦ $72 - $82, ♦ $11, Min book applies, AE BC DC MC VI.

B&B's/Guest Houses

The Hill Homestead, (B&B), Kiora Rd, 20km from PO, ☎ 02 6724 1686, fax 02 6724 1381, 2 rms [shwr, bath (1), tlt, hairdry, c/fan, elec blkts, tel, clock radio], ldry, iron, iron brd, rec rm, lounge (TV), lounge firepl, pool above ground, sauna, cook fac, t/c mkg shared, courtesy transfer, plygr, gym, cots, non smoking property. **BB** ♦ $55, ♦♦ $71.50, ♦ $30, **DBB** ♦ $77, ♦♦ $115.50, ♦ $55, ch con, pen con, AE BC DC EFT MC VI, (not yet classified).

BLACKHEATH NSW

See Blue Mountains Region.

BLAYNEY NSW 2799

Pop 2,650. (243km W Sydney), See map on page 55, ref A2. Historic town in picturesque sheep and cattle country south-west of Bathurst. Bowls, Fishing, Golf, Shooting, Tennis.

Hotels/Motels

★★★☆ **The Central Motel**, (M), 107 Adelaide St, 400m N of PO, ☎ 02 6368 3355, fax 02 6368 2844, 12 units (1 suite) [shwr, spa bath (1), tlt, hairdry (1), a/c, elec blkts, tel, TV, video-fee, clock radio, t/c mkg, refrig, toaster], dinner to unit, cots-fee. **RO** ♦ $55 - $68, ♦♦ $68 - $80, ♦♦♦ $75 - $95, ♦ $10, **Suite D** $100 - $130, Min book applies, AE BC DC MC VI.

★★★ **Blayney Goldfields Motor Inn**, (M), 48 Martha St, 800m S of PO, ☎ 02 6368 2000, fax 02 6368 3657, 21 units [shwr, tlt, hairdry, a/c, elec blkts, tel, TV, clock radio, t/c mkg, refrig, toaster], ldry, iron, ✕ (Mon to Sat), dinner to unit (Mon to Sat), cots-fee, non smoking units (avail). **RO** ♦ $58 - $78, ♦♦ $68 - $88, ♦ $10, ch con, pen con, Min book applies, AE BC DC EFT MC VI,

Operator Comment: Enjoy quality meals, comfortable units with quiet a/c exceptional heat/cooling in a relaxing tranquil setting adj to playground, tennis court & BBQ.

Self Catering Accommodation

★★★ **Blayney Leumeah Motel**, (HU), 29 Carcoar St, 600m W of PO, ☎ 02 6368 2755, fax 02 6368 2728, 23 units [ensuite (23), heat, elec blkts, tel, TV, clock radio, t/c mkg, cook fac, ldry], bbq (covered), dinner to unit, cots. **BLB** ♦ $52 - $62, ♦♦ $62 - $73, ♦ $18, Minium booking applies Bathurst long weekend, BC MC VI.

BLUE MOUNTAINS - NSW

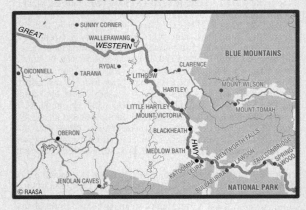

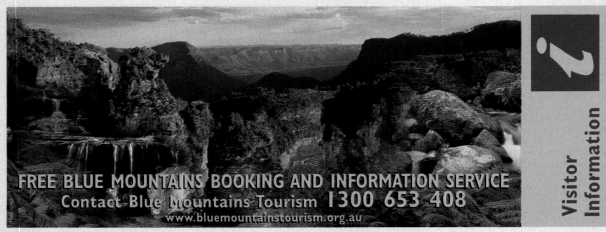

BLUE MOUNTAINS - BLACKHEATH NSW 2785

Pop 4,100. Part of Blue Mountains, (133km W Sydney), See map on page 55, ref B2. Historic village in the upper Blue Mountains, popularly known as the 'Rhododendron Town'. Bowls, Bush Walking, Golf, Horse Riding, Scenic Drives, Swimming, Tennis.

Hotels/Motels

FLAG
FLAG CHOICE HOTELS™

★★★☆ **Blackheath Motor Inn**, (M), 281 Great Western Hwy, 300m W of railway station, ☎ 02 4787 8788, fax 02 4787 8929, 18 units [shwr, tlt, hairdry, a/c-cool, cent heat (5), elec blkts, tel, cable tv, video-fee, clock radio, t/c mkg, refrig, toaster], ldry, spa, cots-fee, non smoking units (5). RO ⊦ $77 - $132, ⊦⊦ $88 - $132, ⊖ $16.50, AE BC DC EFT MC VI.

★★★☆ **High Mountains Motor Inn**, (M), 193 Great Western Hwy, 600m E of PO, ☎ 02 4787 8216, fax 02 4787 7802, 21 units [shwr, tlt, fan, heat, elec blkts, tel, TV, movie, clock radio, t/c mkg, refrig], ldry, ✕, BYO, rm serv (6 nights), cots-fee. RO ⊦ $65 - $115, ⊦⊦ $70 - $115, ⊦⊦⊦ $85 - $130, ⊖ $15, Min book applies, AE BC DC MC VI.

★★★★ **(Cottage Section)**, 3 cotgs acc up to 7, [shwr, spa bath, tlt, elec blkts, TV, movie, clock radio, t/c mkg, refrig, cook fac, blkts, linen, pillows], ldry, rm serv (6 nights), cots-fee. D ⊦ $170 - $200, ⊦⊦ $170 - $200, ⊖ $15, Min book applies.

★★★☆ **Redleaf Motor Lodge**, (M), Evans Lookout Rd, 2km E of PO, ☎ 02 4787 8108, fax 02 4787 8907, (2 stry gr fl), 46 units [shwr, bath (3), tlt, cent heat, elec blkts, tel, cable tv, clock radio, t/c mkg, refrig], ldry, rec rm, conv fac, ✕, pool indoor heated, sauna, spa, rm serv, tennis, cots-fee, non smoking units. RO ⊦ $78 - $110, ⊦⊦ $88 - $120, ⊖ $12, Min book applies, AE BC DC EFT MC VI.

Self Catering Accommodation

★★★★☆ **Some Days - Some Nights**, (Villa), 21 Days Cres, 200m N of PO, ☎ 02 4787 8585, fax 02 4787 8585, (Multi-stry gr fl), 1 villa acc up to 11, [shwr (4), bath (3), spa bath (1), tlt (5), cent heat, TV (3), video, clock radio, CD (2), t/c mkg, refrig, cook fac, micro, elec frypan, d/wash, toaster, ldry, blkts, linen], w/mach, dryer, iron, iron brd, lounge firepl, bar, bbq, gym, cots-fee, non smoking property. D $700, W $2,600, Min book applies, AE BC DC MC.

★★★★ **A Day's Delight**, (House), Previously Braeside, 38 Days Cres, ☎ 02 4787 7266, fax 02 4787 7058, (2 stry gr fl), 1 house acc up to 8, [shwr, bath, tlt, hairdry, fan, heat, TV, video, clock radio, t/c mkg, refrig, cook fac, micro, elec frypan, d/wash, toaster, ldry, linen reqd], w/mach, dryer, iron, iron brd, bbq, non smoking rms. D ⊦⊦ $180, ⊦⊦⊦ $220, W ⊦⊦ $500 - $800, ⊦⊦⊦ $600 - $1,000, Min book applies.

★★★★ **Secrets Hideaway**, (Cotg), Couples only. 173 Evans Lookout Rd, ☎ 02 4787 8453, fax 02 4787 8453, 3 cotgs acc up to 2, [shwr, spa bath, tlt, hairdry, fire pl, TV, video, clock radio, CD, t/c mkg, refrig, cook fac, micro, elec frypan, toaster, doonas, linen], bbq, breakfast ingredients. D $115 - $350,

Operator Comment: www.secretshideaway.com

★★★☆ **Werriberri Lodge**, (Cotg), Megalong Valley Rd, Megalong Valley, 10km S of PO, ☎ 02 4787 9127, fax 02 4787 7107, 6 cotgs acc up to 6, [shwr, bath, tlt, fire pl, cable tv, video (avail), movie, clock radio, refrig, cook fac, micro, linen reqd-fee], ldry, bbq, plygr, bicycle, tennis, D ⊦⊦ $72 - $92, ⊖ $10, Min book applies, BC MC VI.

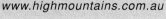

BLACKHEATH HOLIDAY CABINS

c/- New Ivanhoe Hotel
BLACKHEATH NSW 2780

Telephone:
(02) 4787 8158
Facsimile:
(02) 4782 2375

Ideal budget accommodation
for family or group holiday
(up to 50 people).
Quiet bush setting close to
Govetts Leap, National
Parks, bushwalks,
playground, swimming pool
and railway station.

• *Modern kitchen and combustion wood fire*

PER CABIN		2 BED	4 BED
Midweek	1 night Sun to Thurs	$105	$210
Weekend	2 nights Fri and Sat	$210	$420

• Supply own linen or hire

★★★ **Federation Gardens Lodge**, (HU), 185 Evans Lookout Rd, 4km E of PO, ☎ 02 4787 7767, fax 02 4787 7767, 13 units [shwr, heat, TV, video, clock radio, refrig, cook fac, micro, toaster, doonas, linen, pillows], ldry, rec rm, pool-indoor, bbq, tennis. **RO** ♦♦ **$110 - $171,** ♦♦♦ **$138 - $171,** ♦ **$28,** ch con, BC EFT MC VI.

★★★☆ **(Possums Hideaway Section),** 4 units [shwr, spa bath, tlt, TV, video, clock radio, cook fac, micro, toaster, linen]. **D** ♦♦ **$138 - $198.**

★★★ **Jemby-Rinjah Lodge**, 336 Evans Lookout Rd, 4km E of Great Western Hwy, ☎ 02 4787 7622, fax 02 4787 6230, 10 cabins acc up to 6, [shwr, tlt, heat, TV (1), video (1), refrig, cook fac, micro, toaster, linen], ldry-fee, bbq, cots-fee. **D $135 - $250,** ch con, 1 cabin yet to be assessed. AE BC DC EFT MC VI.

(Lodge Section), 3 rms acc up to 18, [shwr, tlt, c/fan, cent heat, refrig, blkts, linen, pillows], ldry-fee, w/mach-fee, dryer-fee, iron, rec rm, conv fac, ✕, ✆, cots, non smoking property, non smoking units (3). **BB** ♦ **$53 - $68, DBB** ♦ **$84 - $98.50,** Min book applies.

POSSUMS HIDEAWAY

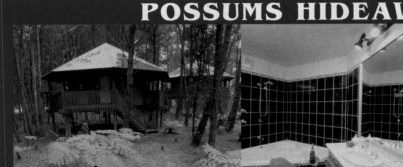

185 Evans Lookout Rd, Blackheath, NSW 2785
Tel/Fax 02 4787 7767
email: aaa@possumshideaway.com
web: www.possumshideaway.com

Self-contained studio suites for couples only. Close to spectacular bushwalks. Each suite contains TV/VCR, kitchen, wood heaters and two person spa.
• Tennis, table tennis, volley ball
• Billiard room
• Heated undercover pool
• Linen provided
• Gas BBQ's

FEDERATION GARDENS LODGE

185 Evans Lookout Rd Blackheath NSW 2785
Ph/Fax: (02) 4787 7767
Email: aaa@federationgardens.com
Web: www.federationgardens.com

Set in four acres of parkland, these two bedroom self-contained apartments are suitable for families or adult groups and sleep up to six. All apartments contain heaters, TV/VCR and kitchens.

• Linen provided

• Heated undercover swimming pool

• Tennis, table tennis, volley ball

• Five bedroom cottage available

• Gas BBQ's

• Communal Laundry

★★★ **Kanimbla View Environmental Retreat**, 113 Shipley Rd, 2.5km W of PO, ☎ 02 4787 8985, fax 02 4787 6665, 2 cabins acc up to 12, [radio, CD, cook fac, ldry, blkts, doonas, linen], conf fac, lounge firepl, spa (communal), bbq, plygr, tennis, non smoking property. RO ♦ $55 - $115, ♦ $55 - $115, ch con, weekly con, Min book applies, BC MC VI. *Operator Comment: Please visit our website: www.kanimbla.com*

★★☆ **Lakeview Holiday Park**, 63 Prince Edward St, ☎ 02 4787 8534, fax 02 4787 8534, 11 cabins acc up to 6, [shwr, tlt, elec blkts, refrig, cook fac, micro, linen reqd-fee], ldry, w/mach-fee, dryer-fee, rec rm, bbq. D ♦♦ $55 - $85, W ♦♦ $330 - $510, BC MC VI.

   ★★☆ **(Cottage Section)**, 1 cotg [shwr, tlt, fire pl, elec blkts, TV, refrig, cook fac, micro, linen reqd-fee], bbq. D ♦♦ $120 - $150, W ♦♦ $500 - $660.

B&B's/Guest Houses

★★★★☆ **Blue Mountains Bed and Breakfast**, (B&B), Previously Kalimna Bed & Breakfast, 200 Wentworth St, 1km W of PO, ☎ 02 4787 6660, fax 02 4787 6661, (2 stry), 3 rms [shwr, tlt, fan, heat, elec blkts, tel, TV, radio, t/c mkg, refrig (1), toaster (1)], iron, iron brd, c/park. BB ♦ $130, ♦♦ $130, BC MC VI.

★★★★☆ **Parklands Country Garden & Lodges**, (GH), 132 Govetts Leap Rd, 900m E of Great Western Hwy, ☎ 02 4787 7771, fax 02 4787 7211, (2 stry gr fl), 12 rms (6 suites) [shwr, bath, spa bath (5), tlt, hairdry, a/c-cool (6), fire pl, cent heat, tel, TV, radio, CD, t/c mkg, refrig, toaster], conv fac, cots. BLB ♦ $225 - $295, ♦♦ $225 - $295, Suite D ♦ $250 - $355, ♦♦ $250 - $355, AE BC DC MC VI.

★★★★ **Balquhain Country Guest House**, (GH), 161 Govetts Leap Rd, ☎ 02 4787 7026, fax 02 4787 7026, (2 stry gr fl), 4 rms [shwr, tlt, heat, elec blkts, clock radio, doonas], lounge (TV), lounge firepl, t/c mkg shared, refrig, tennis, non smoking property. BB ♦♦ $140 - $250, BC MC VI.

★★★★ **Glenella Guest House**, (GH), 56 Govetts Leap Rd, ☎ 02 4787 8352, fax 02 4787 6114, (2 stry gr fl), 9 rms (1 suite) [shwr, tlt, cent heat, tel, t/c mkg], lounge (TV), conf fac, lounge firepl, ✕, ✉, sauna, gym, cots, non smoking property. D ♦ $140, ♦♦ $180, Suite D ♦♦ $200, BC EFT MC VI.

★★★★ **Harrow Cottages**, (GH), 21 Brentwood Ave, 1km N of PO, ☎ 02 4787 8281, fax 02 4787 5772, 2 rms [shwr, spa bath, tlt, hairdry, fire pl, elec blkts, TV, video, clock radio, CD, t/c mkg, refrig, micro, toaster, pillows], ldry, iron, iron brd, bbq, non smoking units. BB ♦♦ $150, ♦♦ $1,000, Min book applies, BC MC VI.

★★★★ **Norwood Guest House**, (GH), No children's facilities, 209 Great Western Hwy, 300m E of PO, ☎ 02 4787 8568, fax 02 4787 8944, 7 rms [shwr, tlt, a/c, cent heat, elec blkts, TV, clock radio, t/c mkg, refrig], ✕. BB ♦ $90 - $120, ♦♦ $115 - $145, Min book applies, AE BC DC EFT MC VI.

★★★☆ **Kanangra Lodge Blue Mountains**, (B&B), 9 Belvidere Ave, ☎ 02 4787 8715, fax 02 4787 8748, 3 rms [shwr, bath (1), tlt, hairdry, fire pl, cent heat, elec blkts, TV (1), video (1), clock radio, cook fac ltd, micro (1), toaster (1)], lounge, t/c mkg shared, refrig. BB ♦ $125 - $165, ♦♦ $176 - $198, Min book applies, BC EFT MC VI.

★★★☆ **Kubba Roonga Blackheath**, (GH), 9 Brentwood Ave, ☎ 02 4787 8330, fax 02 4787 7540, 7 rms [shwr, spa bath (5), tlt, fire pl, heat, elec blkts, TV, t/c mkg], ✕. BB ♦ $125, ♦♦ $160, DBB ♦ $166, ♦♦ $236, BC EFT MC VI.

   ★★★★ **(Cottage Section)**, 3 cotgs acc up to 10, [shwr, spa bath, tlt, fire pl, elec blkts, TV, CD, t/c mkg, refrig, cook fac]. BB ♦♦ $165, ♦ $50.

   ★★★☆ **St Mounts Guest House**, (GH), 194 Great Western Hwy, 600m S of PO, ☎ 02 4787 6111, fax 02 4787 8165, 10 rms [shwr (8), bath (6), spa bath (1), tlt (8), fire pl (3), cent heat], shared fac (2), ldry, lounge (3), ✉, spa, bbq, ☏. D ♦ $110 - $190, Limited facilities for children. Min book applies, AE BC EFT MC VI.

   (Cottage Section), 3 cotgs acc up to 10, [shwr, bath (1), spa bath (1), tlt, fire pl, cent heat, TV, video (avail), clock radio, t/c mkg, refrig, cook fac, micro, toaster, blkts, linen, pillows], ldry, ✉, ☏, plygr, cots. RO $140 - $340, ch con.

BLUE MOUNTAINS - BULLABURRA NSW 2784

Pop Part of Blue Mountains, (109km W Sydney), See map on page 55, ref B2. Small Blue Mountains settlement between Lawson and Wentworth Falls.

B&B's/Guest Houses

★★★★ **Raleigh Country House**, (B&B), Previously Raleigh Lodge 88 Genevieve Rd, ☎ 02 4759 1300, fax 02 4759 2244, (2 stry gr fl), 3 rms (1 suite) [shwr, bath (1), spa bath (1), tlt, hairdry, elec blkts, TV, clock radio, t/c mkg], ldry, iron, iron brd, lounge (firepl), non smoking rms (3). BB $135, pen con, BC MC VI.

KUBBA ROONGA GUESTHOUSE&COTTAGES
FEATURING SPAS

GUESTHOUSE
• 7 Rooms, Spas
• Log fires
• Cooked breakfast
• Dinner available

COTTAGES
• Just for 2 or up to 10 people
• Spas
• Log fires
• Dinner available

FROM $70PP

FAX: (02) 4787 7540
TELEPHONE: (02) 4787 8330
EMAIL: mail@kubbaroonga.com.au
WEB: www.kubbaroonga.com.au

9 BRENTWOOD AVE, BLACKHEATH 2785, BLUEMOUNTAINS

BLUE MOUNTAINS - FAULCONBRIDGE NSW 2776

Pop Part of Blue Mountains, (92km W Sydney), See map on page 55, ref B2. Town situated in the central Blue Mountains. Bush Walking, Rock Climbing, Scenic Drives.

Hotels/Motels

★★★ **Pioneer Way Motel**, (M), 429 Great Western Hwy, 1.5km W of PO, ☎ 02 4751 2194, fax 02 4751 2194, (2 stry gr fl), 21 units [shwr, tlt, a/c (12), c/fan (9), heat, elec blkts, tel, TV, t/c mkg, refrig], ldry, ✉, cots-fee, non smoking rms (11). RO ♦ $66 - $100, ♦♦ $75 - $110, ♦♦♦ $90 - $125, ♦ $15, AE BC DC MC VI.

Self Catering Accommodation

★★★★☆ **The Studio Cottages Romantic Hideaway**, (Cotg), 169 Chapman Pde, 2.5km N of Great Western Hwy, ☎ 02 4751 4766, fax 02 4751 1240, 3 cotgs acc up to 6, [shwr, spa bath, tlt, hairdry, a/c, fire pl, tel, TV, video, clock radio, CD, t/c mkg, refrig, cook fac, micro, toaster], ldry, iron, iron brd, pool, bbq, meals avail, c/park (undercover). BB ♦ $150 - $200, ♦♦ $220 - $275, ♦ $55, BC EFT MC VI.

B&B's/Guest Houses

★★★★☆ **Theodora's Hideaway**, (B&B), 51 Summer Rd, ☎ 02 4751 9270, fax 02 4751 1186, (2 stry gr fl), 3 rms [shwr, spa bath, tlt, hairdry, a/c, elec blkts, tel, TV, t/c mkg, refrig, toaster], iron, iron brd, lounge firepl, pool (salt water), bbq, dinner to unit, non smoking rms. BB ♦♦ $195 - $275, Min book applies, AE BC MC VI.

   ★★★☆ **(Cottage Section)**, 1 cotg acc up to 4, [shwr, tlt, a/c, tel, TV, video, radio, t/c mkg, refrig, cook fac, micro, toaster, ldry, blkts, linen], iron, iron brd, spa. RO ♦♦♦♦ $165 - $195, ♦ $75.

★★★★ **Rose Lindsay Cottage**, (B&B), 113 Chapman Pde, 2km N of PO, ☎ 02 4751 4273, fax 02 4751 9497, 1 rm [heat, elec blkts, tel, clock radio, t/c mkg], bbq. BB ♦ $110 - $130, ♦♦ $154 - $286, ♦ $80, ♦♦ W $1,380 - $1,540, Min book applies.

★★★ **Kariwara Bed & Breakfast**, (B&B), 7 Tamara Rd, 2km N of PO, ☎ 02 4751 6855, 2 rms [fan, heat], lounge (TV), t/c mkg shared, refrig, non smoking property. BB ♦ $88, ♦♦ $110, BC MC VI.

BLUE MOUNTAINS - JENOLAN CAVES NSW 2790

Pop Nominal, (194km W Sydney), See map on page 55, ref B2. World-famous limestone caves situated a short distance south-west of the Blue Mountains. Bush Walking, Scenic Drives.

Self Catering Accommodation

★★★☆ **Jenolan Cabins**, (Cotg), Porcupine Hill, Edith Rd, 4km W of Jenolan Caves, ☎ 02 6335 6239, fax 02 6335 6239, 6 cotgs acc up to 6, [shwr, tlt, fire pl, TV, clock radio, refrig, cook fac, micro, toaster, linen reqd-fee], ldry, w/mach-fee, dryer-fee, bbq, ✆, cots. D ♦♦ **$98 - $105**, ⚲ **$6**, Min book applies, AE BC DC MC VI, ♿.

Operator Comment: See our Website www.bluemts.com.au/jenolancabins

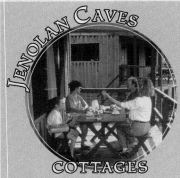

Set in bushland within the World Heritage listed Jenolan Caves Reserve, these comfortable cottages present a wonderful opportunity to be part of a special bushland environment close to Australia's premier cave system - Jenolan Caves.

Facilities detailed under listing for Jenolan Caves Cottages.

Bookings & Information:

Ph: 02 6359 3311   Fax: 02 6359 3307
Website: www.jenolancaves.org.au

2708AG

★★★ **Jenolan Caves Cottages**, Jenolan Caves Rd, 8km N of Jenolan Caves, ☎ 02 6359 3311, fax 02 6359 3307, 8 cabins acc up to 8, [shwr, tlt, fire pl, TV, clock radio, t/c mkg, refrig, cook fac, micro, toaster, linen-fee], ldry, bbq, plygr, cots-fee. D **$82.50 - $121**, AE BC DC EFT JCB MC VI.

★★★☆ **(Bellbird Cottage)**, cotgs.

B&B's/Guest Houses

★★★★ **Caves House**, (GH), adjacent to the caves, ☎ 02 6359 3322, fax 02 6359 3388, (Multi-stry gr fl) 50 rms [shwr (14), tlt (14), cent heat, t/c mkg], shared fac (16 shower, 16 toilet), ldry, rec rm, lounge (TV), conv fac, ✉, bbq, ✆, plygr, tennis, cots. D **$110 - $341**, 17 rooms of 4 star rating. AE BC DC EFT MC VI, ♿.

★★★★ **(Hotel - Motel Section)**, (2 stry gr fl), 28 units [shwr, bath, tlt, heat, TV, t/c mkg, refrig], cots. D **$60.50 - $209**, ♿.

★ **Forest Lodge**, (GH), Lot 11 Caves Rd, Oberon Plateau, 7km SW of Jenolan Caves, ☎ 02 6335 6313, fax 02 6335 6313, 8 rms [shwr, bath (1), tlt, heat, elec blkts, video (avail), t/c mkg, refrig (4), toaster], rec rm, lounge (TV), ✗, bbq, ✆, cots. D ♦ **$40**, ⚲ **$40**, ch con, 3 rooms of a basic standard.

Other Accommodation

★★ **Jenolan Caves Resort**, (Lodge), Previously The Gatehouse Jenolan Jenolan Caves, Situated behind Jenolan Caves House, ☎ 02 6359 3042, fax 02 6359 3037, 21 rms acc up to 6, [blkts, linen reqd-fee, pillows], rec rm, lounge (TV), cook fac, t/c mkg shared, bbq, ✆, plygr, tennis (half court). D **$60.50 - $341**, BC EFT MC VI.

★★★ **(Binoomea Cottage)**, 1 cotg acc up to 30, [heat, elec blkts (7), linen reqd-fee], lounge (TV), cook fac, t/c mkg shared, bbq, cots. D **$82.50 - $121**, ⚲ **$11**

BLUE MOUNTAINS - KATOOMBA NSW 2780

Part of BLUE MOUNTAINS region. Pop 17,700. Part of Blue Mountains, (122km W Sydney), See map on page 55, ref B2. The largest settlement and a popular holiday destination in the Blue Mountains. Bowls, Bush Walking, Golf, Horse Riding, Scenic Drives, Swimming, Tennis.

Hotels/Motels

★★★★★ **Lilianfels Blue Mountains**, (LH), Lilianfels Ave, ☎ 02 4780 1200, fax 02 4780 1300, (Multi-stry gr fl), 86 rms (5 suites) [shwr, bath, spa bath (7), tlt, hairdry, a/c, fire pl (2), cent heat, elec blkts, tel, TV, video, clock radio, t/c mkg, refrig, mini bar], conv fac, ✉, pool indoor heated, sauna, spa (1G-1L), 24hr reception, dinner to unit, c/park (undercover), ✆, gym, tennis, cots, non smoking rms (26). D **$346.50 - $418**, Suite D **$473 - $1,045**, Min book applies, AE BC DC EFT JCB MC VI, ♿.

AAA
TOURISM
Special Rates

★★★★☆ **Mountain Heritage Retreat**, (M), Previously Mountain Heritage Lovel & Apex Sts, ☎ 02 4782 2155, fax 02 4782 5323, (2 stry) 41 units (4 suites) [shwr, bath, spa bath (19), tlt, hairdry, a/c, fire pl (13), elec blkts, tel, TV, video, clock radio, t/c mkg, refrig, cook fac (4)], rec rm, conv fac, lounge firepl, ✉, bar, pool, bbq, plygr, cots-fee. D **$178 - $328**, Suite D **$308 - $418**, ch con, Min book applies, AE BC DC MC VI.

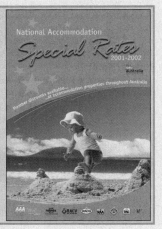

AAA Tourism ★★★★☆

Reward Yourself

- ✦ Enjoy breathtaking views of the spectacular cliff faces and tree-filled canyons of the World Heritage Listed Blue Mountains Wilderness.
- ✦ Absorb the romance and elegance of a bygone era without sacrificing the freshness, comforts and luxury of the 21st century, in this multi-award winning historic landmark.
- ✦ Situated in a secluded, yet convenient location, just a few minutes stroll from the hustle and bustle of Katoomba's shopping and tourist centre.
- ✦ All rooms and suites have a full size bath or luxurious spa.
- ✦ Many of the spa rooms and suites also have a romantic fireplace.
- ✦ Valley View suites are fully self-contained with separate lounge and fireplace, verandah, spa, kitchen and breathtaking views.
- ✦ Inquire about our selection of private cottages which offer a range of unique accommodation options.
- ✦ Superb dining in 'Jamison Views' a la carte restaurant.
- ✦ Piano lounge and cocktail bar.
- ✦ Cosy lounge rooms with fireplaces.
- ✦ Beautiful gardens, swimming pool, fitness centre and billiards lounge.
- ✦ Full Conference, Wedding and Function Facilities.

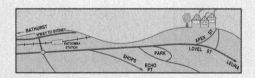

The MOUNTAIN HERITAGE

Ph: (02) 4782 2155   Fax: (02) 4782 5323
Apex and Lovel Sts, Katoomba NSW 2780
Website: www.mountainheritage.com.au
Email: contactus@mountainheritage.com.au

ALPINE MOTOR INN

Cnr Great Western Hwy
& Orient Street
(PO BOX 272)
KATOOMBA NEW SOUTH WALES 2780

Phone: 02 4782 2011 • Fax: 02 4782 2053
Email: alpineinn@bestwestern.com.au
Web site: www.bluemts.com.au/alpine
or www.bestwestern.com.au/alpine

Best Western Winner 1999

"Most modern Motel suites in town"

Category 4 star
★ ★ ★ ★ *AAU Tourism*
Special Rates Member

(Fully Refurbished Executive Suites)

- **Easy walk to** ... town
- **Three Sisters** ... 2 mins
- **Olympic site** ... 1 hour drive
- **All major credit cards** accepted
- **Discounted rates** for Seniors, Corporate travellers & Motoring Club Members

Right in the heart of the Blue Mountains

Indoor Heated Pool

Executive Suites

- Licenced Restaurant
- Elegant a la carte dining
- Restored Federation cottage (circa 1898)
- Open log fires

- 26 Luxurious units
- Executive suites with spas
- Interconnecting rooms
- Queen size beds
- Reverse cycle air conditioning/Central heating
- Electric blankets
- Colour TV
- Videos available
- Car washing facilities
- Childrens Playground
- Guest's Laundry
- Tea making facilities
- Indoor heated swimming pool & sauna (H/R)
- Bar fridges
- Incorporating our licenced "Rosewood Cottage Restaurant"
- Room service: meals

2810ag

Rosewood Cottage RESTAURANT

Blue Mountains

✱ *Special Packages*
•*Including midweek Rates*
•*Ask about our "Winter Yulefest"*

RESERVATIONS -   - 1800 622 017

★★★★ **Alpine Motor Inn**, (M), Cnr Great Western Hwy & Orient St, 1km E of PO, ☎ 02 4782 2011, fax 02 4782 2053, (2 story gr fl), 25 units (4 suites) [shwr, spa bath (1), tlt, hairdry, a/c, cent heat, elec blkts, tel, TV, video (12), clock radio, t/c mkg, refrig], ldry, ✕, pool indoor heated, sauna, dinner to unit, cots-fee, non smoking units (20). RO ♦ $99 - $204, ♦♦ $108 - $204, **Suite RO** ♦♦ $199 - $254, pen con, 10 rooms ★★★☆. Min book applies, AE BC DC MC MP VI.

★★★☆ **Katoomba Town Centre Motel**, (M), 218 Katoomba St, 500m S of PO, ☎ 02 4782 1266, fax 02 4782 4022, (2 story gr fl), 18 units [shwr, bath (2), spa bath (2), tlt, hairdry, a/c-cool, cent heat, elec blkts, tel, TV, video-fee, clock radio, t/c mkg, refrig, micro, toaster], ldry, rec rm, lounge, conv fac, breakfast rm, spa, bbq, plygr, cots-fee, non smoking units (4). **BB** ♦ $80 - $165, ♦♦ $105 - $195, ♦ $40 - $75, **RO** ♦ $70 - $155, ♦♦ $80 - $225, ♦♦♦ $101 - $195, ♦ $10 - $40, ch con, Min book Christmas Jan long w/ends and Easter, AE BC DC JCB MC VI,

Operator Comment: Website: www.katoombamotel.com Email: holiday@katoombamotel.com

Katoomba Town Centre Motel ...continued

★★★☆ **(St Elmo Heritage Guest House)**, (2 story gr fl), 13 rms [shwr, tlt, hairdry, fan, heat, elec blkts, tel, TV, video-fee, clock radio, t/c mkg, refrig, micro, toaster], ldry, rec rm, lounge, conv fac, breakfast rm, spa, bbq, plygr, cots-fee. **BB** ♦ $75 - $160, ♦♦ $99 - $185, ♦ $30 - $60, **RO** ♦ $65 - $150, ♦♦ $75 - $170, ♦ $10 - $35.

★★★☆ **The Clarendon Motor Inn**, (M), Cnr Lurline & Waratah Sts, 600m S of PO, ☎ 02 4782 1322, fax 02 4782 2564, (2 story gr fl), 14 units [shwr, tlt, hairdry, cent heat, elec blkts, tel, TV, clock radio, t/c mkg, refrig], shared fac (8), iron, iron brd, lounge (TV), ✕, pool-heated, sauna, dinner to unit, cots. **RO** ♦ $98, ♦♦ $130, ♦ $20, ch con, Min book applies, AE BC MC VI.

★★☆ **(Guest House Section)**, 21 rms [shwr (12), bath (4), spa bath (3), tlt (12), cent heat, tel, TV, clock radio, t/c mkg, refrig (12)], iron, iron brd, lounge (TV), pool-heated, sauna, dinner to unit, cots. **RO** ♦ $65, ♦♦ $90.

B

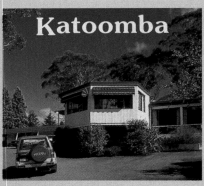

Self Catering Accommodation

★★★☆ **Echo Point Holiday Villas**, (Villa), 36 Echo Point Rd, 100m N of Three Sisters Lookout, ☎ 02 4782 3275, fax 02 4782 7030, 5 villas acc up to 6, [shwr, tlt, hairdry, fan, cent heat, elec blkts, cable tv, clock radio, CD, t/c mkg, refrig, cook fac, micro, elec frypan, toaster, ldry, blkts, linen], w/mach, dryer, iron, iron brd, bbq, c/park (undercover), ✆, non smoking units. **D ♦♦ $105 - $132, ♦♦♦♦ $132 - $154, W ♦♦ $788, ♦♦♦♦ $968**, Min book applies, AE BC MC VI.

★★★☆ **Milroy Holiday Apartments**, (SA), 15 Leichhardt St, 800m E of PO, ☎ 02 4782 1266, fax 02 4782 4022, 3 serv apts acc up to 6, [shwr, bath, tlt, hairdry, fan, heat, elec blkts, TV, video, clock radio, t/c mkg, refrig, cook fac, micro, toaster, blkts, linen, pillows], ldry, w/mach, dryer, iron, bbq, cots-fee. **BB ♦♦ $110 - $245, ◊ $45 - $75, W $595 - $945**, ch con, Min book long w/ends, AE BC DC JCB MC VI.

★★★ **Apple Tree Cottage - Katoomba**, (Cotg), 8 Warriga St, 500m W of PO, ☎ 02 4757 2226, fax 02 4757 2248, 1 cotg acc up to 6, [shwr, spa bath, tlt, cent heat, elec blkts, TV, video, clock radio, CD, t/c mkg, refrig, cook fac, micro, toaster, doonas, linen, pillows], lounge firepl, non smoking units. **D ♦♦ $100 - $160, ◊ $25 - $35, W ♦♦ $490 - $680, ◊ $50 - $70**, Min book applies, BC MC VI.

Cherry Cottage Echo Point, (Cotg), 193a Lurline St, ☎ 02 9567 4253, fax 02 9567 4253, 1 cotg acc up to 6, [shwr, bath, tlt, hairdry, fan, fire pl, heat, elec blkts, tel, clock radio, t/c mkg, refrig, cook fac, micro, elec frypan, toaster, ldry, blkts, doonas (4), linen, pillows], w/mach, dryer, iron, iron brd, TV rm (video), lounge firepl, bbq, ✆, non smoking property. **D $110 - $165, ◊ $25, W $650 - $950**, pen con, BC MC VI, (not yet classified).

B&B's/Guest Houses

★★★★★ **Palais Royale**, (GH), 228-230 Katoomba St, 400m S of Railway Station, ☎ 02 4784 6300, fax 02 4782 7444, (Multi-stry gr fl), 40 rms (1 suite) [shwr, bath (36), spa bath (1), tlt, hairdry, a/c, tel, TV, clock radio, t/c mkg, refrig], iron, iron brd, conf fac, lounge firepl, ⊠, sauna, spa, cots-fee, non smoking rms (20). **RO ♦ $132 - $277, ♦♦ $145 - $277, ◊ $45, Suite D ♦ $320 - $450, ♦♦ $320 - $450, ◊ $50**, ch con, Min book applies, AE BC EFT MC VI.

★★★★☆ **Edgelinks Bed & Breakfast**, (B&B), 138 Narrow Neck Rd, 1km fr PO, ☎ 02 4782 3001, fax 02 4782 9902, 3 rms [ensuite, spa bath, fan, cent heat, elec blkts, TV, video, clock radio, doonas], lounge firepl (2), t/c mkg shared, refrig, bbq, c/park (undercover) (2), cots, non smoking property. **BB ♦♦ $168 - $208**, BC MC VI.

★★★★☆ **Lurline Lavender Bed & Breakfast**, (B&B), 134 Lurline St, 1.5km S of PO, ☎ 02 4782 6230, fax 02 4782 1644, 2 rms [shwr, tlt, hairdry, fire pl, cent heat, elec blkts, TV, clock radio, t/c mkg], lounge, breakfast rm, non smoking rms. **BB** ¶ **$80 - $110,** ¶¶ **$100 - $150.**

★★★★☆ **The Loft Guesthouse**, (B&B), No children's facilities, 308 Katoomba St, 500m S of Town Centre, ☎ 02 4782 6165, fax 02 4782 6165, (2 stry gr fl), 4 rms [shwr, tlt, fan, heat, elec blkts, TV, clock radio, ldry], iron, iron brd, lounge (firepl), ✕ (breakfast), t/c mkg shared, non smoking rms. **BB** **$90 - $145, BLB $85 - $125,** BC MC VI.

★★★★☆ **Windradyne at Echo Point**, (B&B), No children's facilities, 6 Cliff Dve, ☎ 02 4782 9999, fax 02 4782 9999, 2 rms (2 suites) [shwr, bath, tlt, heat, elec blkts, tel, clock radio, refrig (1)], iron, iron brd, lounge (TV & firepl), breakfast rm, t/c mkg shared, c/park. **BB** ¶¶ **$150 - $210,** BC MC VI.

★★★★ **Blue Colony Luxury Bed & Breakfast**, (B&B), 286 Katoomba St, ☎ 02 4782 6910, 2 rms [shwr, tlt, hairdry, fan, heat, elec blkts, tel, TV], lounge firepl, spa, t/c mkg shared, non smoking property. **BB** ¶¶ **$120 - $170,** pen con, Min book applies.

★★★★ **Jamison House & The Rooster Restaurant**, (GH), 48 Merriwa St (Cnr Cliff Dve), 750m E of PO, ☎ 02 4782 1206, fax 02 4782 1206, 3 rms [shwr, bath (1), tlt, hairdry, fire pl, cent heat, elec blkts, tel, TV, clock radio, t/c mkg, refrig, toaster], ⊠, c/park. **BLB** ¶¶ **$132 - $308,** Min book applies, AE BC DC MC VI.

★★★★ **Leura Falls Bed & Breakfast**, (B&B), 56 Merriwa St, 1.2km E of PO, ☎ 02 4782 9660, fax 02 4782 9660, 2 rms [shwr, spa bath (1), tlt, fan, heat, elec blkts, TV, clock radio, micro (1), doonas], lounge firepl (1), t/c mkg shared, refrig, non smoking property. **BB** ¶ **$100 - $110,** ¶¶ **$120 - $140,** BC MC VI,

Operator Comment: Check out our secluded bush location at www.leurafalls.com

★★★★ **Lotus Lodge**, (GH), 83 Falls Rd, Wentworth Falls 2782, 1km S of PO, ☎ 02 4757 2590, fax 02 4757 4945, 3 rms [ensuite, spa bath, c/fan, cent heat, elec blkts, TV, video (avail), clock radio, micro, toaster], t/c mkg shared, refrig, non smoking property. **BLB** ¶¶ **$110 - $160,** BC MC VI.

★★★★ **McClintock The**, (GH), 15 Abbotsford Rd, 1km S of PO, ☎ 02 4782 4240, fax 02 4782 4858, 4 rms [shwr, tlt, hairdry, fire pl (2), cent heat, elec blkts, tel], iron, iron brd, lounge, breakfast rm, t/c mkg shared, non smoking property. **BB** ¶ **$115 - $125,** ¶¶ **$190 - $225,** BC MC VI.

★★★★ **Phoenix Lodge**, (B&B), 71 Seventh Ave, 1.5km N of PO, ☎ 02 4782 7848, fax 02 4782 9960, 4 rms (1 suite) [shwr, bath (1), spa bath (1), tlt, c/fan, fire pl (1), heat, elec blkts, doonas], ldry, lounge (cable TV, video), lounge firepl, spa, t/c mkg shared, refrig, bbq, cots, non smoking property. **BB** ¶ **$120 - $140,** ¶¶ **$120 - $140,** **Suite BB** ¶¶ **$200 - $240,** ch con, Minimum booking applies Mch 1 to Sep 30, BC MC VI.

Metropole Guesthouse

AAA Tourism ★★★☆

~ All rooms have Ensuites, T.V, Mini Bar, Tea/Coffee Bar,
  Electric Blankets, Heating, Fans (upgrade rooms available).
~ Fully Licensed Restaurant.
~ Games Room, Library with open Fire, Sun rooms, Lounge rooms
  with Log Fires, Guest Laundry.
~ Ask about our Special midweek & Weekend Packages.

Cnr Gang Gang & Lurline St Katoomba NSW
Ph: (02) 4782 5544   Fax: (02) 4782 6662
Email: metropol@pnc.com.au
Website: www.bluemts.com.au/metropole

RATES ~ Per person ~ Includes Dinner Accommodation & Full Breakfast

Midweek	1 night	Sun to Thurs	From	$92	per person
Weekend	2 nights	Fri & Sat	From	$199	per person

AAAT ★★

KATOOMBA MOUNTAIN LODGE

also *Yulefest 2001*
June - July - August

MID-WEEK PACKAGES (Twin/Dbl)
4 nights Mon to Fri OR Sun to Thurs
"Great budget Accommodation"

Bed, Light Breakfast	Bed, Full Breakfast	Dinner, Bed Light Breakfast	Dinner, Bed Full Breakfast
$132 p.p.	$136 p.p.	$212 p.p.	$220 p.p.

Share Facilities

• *Dining Room – BYO* • *Log Fires* • *Electric Blankets*
• *T.V. Lounge Room* • *Scenic Tours* • *Telephone*
• *Minutes from Railway, Town Centre & RSL Club*
• *Laundry* • *Games Room* • *Parking*

31 LURLINE STREET TEL (02) 4782 3933

★★★★ Sirens B&B, (B&B), 3 Duff St, 1km NW of PO, ☎ 02 4782 9386, fax 02 4782 9576, 3 rms [ensuite, heat (wood), cent heat, elec blkts, TV, video (1), radio], ✗, t/c mkg shared, bbq, non smoking rms. **BB ♦♦ $110 - $150**, BC MC VI.

★★★☆ Avonleigh Country House, (GH), 174 Lurline St, 2km S of PO, ☎ 02 4782 1534, (2 stry gr fl), 12 rms [shwr, tlt, cent heat], TV rm, conv fac, ✗ (BYO), t/c mkg shared, ✆, cots. **BB ♦ $90 - $145, ♦♦ $130 - $230**, ch con, Min book applies, AE BC DC MC VI.

★★★☆ Hermon Guest House, (GH), Previously Belgravia Mountain House 179 Lurline St, ☎ 02 4782 2998, fax 02 4782 4851, 6 rms [shwr, tlt, hairdry, fire pl, heat, elec blkts, TV, clock radio, t/c mkg], ldry, iron, iron brd, ✗, bbq. **BB ♦ $75 - $85, ♦♦ $96 - $132**, BC EFT MC VI.

★★★☆ Jasark Gum View Hideaway, (GH), 10 Miles Ave, 600m E of Railway Station, ☎ 02 4782 9804, 1 rm [shwr, tlt, hairdry, heat, elec blkts, cable tv, video, clock radio, t/c mkg, refrig, micro, toaster, doonas], w/mach-fee, dryer-fee, iron, iron brd, lounge, non smoking property. **D ♦♦ $100 - $120, ◊ $20**, BC MC VI,
Operator Comment: www.jasark.com.au

★★★☆ Kurrara Guesthouse, (GH), 17 Coomonderry St, ☎ 02 4782 6058, fax 02 4782 7300, (2 stry gr fl), 7 rms [shwr, tlt, cent heat, elec blkts, clock radio], ldry, lounge (TV), breakfast rm, spa, t/c mkg shared, non smoking rms. **BB ♦ $90 - $125**, BC EFT MC VI.

★★★☆ Megalong Lodge, (GH), Cnr Cliff Dve & Acacia Ave, ☎ 02 4782 2036, fax 02 4782 9841, (2 stry gr fl), 4 rms [shwr, bath, tlt, cent heat, elec blkts, TV], t/c mkg shared, bbq, ✆. **BB ♦ $70 - $95**, Min book applies, AE BC MC VI.

★★★☆ The Metropole Guesthouse, (GH), Cnr Gang Gang & Lurline Sts, 200m E of PO, ☎ 02 4782 5544, fax 02 4782 6662, (Multi-stry), 24 rms [shwr, tlt, heat, elec blkts, t/c mkg, refrig], ldry, rec rm, lounge, ⊠. **RO ♦ $60 - $80, ♦♦ $86 - $160, ◊ $35 - $55**, BC MC VI.

★★★ La Maison Guest House, (GH), 175 Lurline St, 1km SE of PO, ☎ 02 4782 4996, fax 02 4782 3595, (2 stry gr fl), 18 rms [shwr, bath (8), tlt, TV, clock radio, t/c mkg, refrig], conv fac, sauna, spa, c/park (undercover), cots. **BB ♦ $80 - $100, ♦♦ $110 - $150, ◊ $25**, BC EFT MC VI.

★★ Katoomba Mountain Lodge, (GH), 31 Lurline St, 100m S of PO, ☎ 02 4782 3933, fax 02 4782 3933, (Multi-stry gr fl), 12 rms [fire pl (open - communal), heat, elec blkts, TV (communal)], ldry, rec rm, lounge, ✗ (BYO), t/c mkg shared, ✆. **BB ♦ $53 - $62, ♦♦ $78 - $95, RO ♦ $45 - $54, ♦♦ $62 - $78**, BC MC VI.

★★ The Cecil Traditional Blue Mts G - House, (GH), 108 Katoomba St, opposite Town Centre Arcade, ☎ 02 4782 1411, fax 02 4782 5364, (2 stry gr fl), 23 rms [ensuite (5), heat, elec blkts], shared fac (18), ldry, rec rm, lounge (TV), ✗, t/c mkg shared, refrig, bbq, ✆, bush walking, tennis. **BB ♦ $45 - $65, DBB ♦ $70 - $90**, ch con, Min book applies, AE BC EFT MC VI.

Merrivale House, (B&B), 80 Waratah St, 400m E of PO, ☎ 02 4782 2437, fax 02 4782 2437, 3 rms [ensuite (2), bath (1), hairdry, c/fan (3), cent heat, elec blkts, TV (1), clock radio, t/c mkg], lounge (TV), refrig, non smoking property. **BB ♦ $70 - $100, ♦♦ $90 - $130**, (not yet classified).

Gales Waye Bed & Breakfast, (B&B), 156 Lurline St, ☎ 02 4782 2871, 3 rms [shwr, spa bath, tlt, hairdry, heat, TV, clock radio, t/c mkg], iron, iron brd, bbq, non smoking property. **BLB ♦♦ $70 - $120**, pen con.

BLUE MOUNTAINS - LAWSON NSW 2783

Pop 9,600. Part of Blue Mountains, (108km W Sydney), See map on page 55, ref B2. Town situated in the central Blue Mountains. Bush Walking, Scenic Drives.

B&B's/Guest Houses

★★★★★ Araluen B & B Lawson, (B&B), 59 Wilson St, 500m S of Police Station, ☎ 02 4759 1610, fax 02 4759 2554, (2 stry gr fl), 3 rms [shwr, tlt, hairdry, a/c, cent heat, elec blkts, clock radio], rec rm, TV rm, lounge firepl, t/c mkg shared, bbq, courtesy transfer, cots-fee. **BB ♦ $95 - $135, ♦♦ $135 - $210**, ch con, AE BC MC VI.

★★★☆ Pegums Guest House, (GH), 25 Honour Ave, 300m S of railway station, ☎ 02 4759 1844, fax 02 4759 1844, 9 rms [ensuite (1), cent heat, elec blkts], shared fac (8), rec rm, conv fac, ✗ (byo), t/c mkg shared, c/park. **BB ♦ $85 - $140, ♦♦ $110 - $140**, AE BC DC MC VI.

Night driving

Clear vision is most important at night, when visibility is restricted. The newer and cleaner the windscreen, the easier it is to see. Clean your headlights and headlight covers, as dirt can severely reduce the brightness of your headlights. Have your headlights adjusted to suit the heaviest load you are likely to carry.
If the glare of oncoming headlights is troubling you, look slightly to the left of the road, to avoid the glare. Look at the edge of the road to make sure that you don't run off. Never drive with your high beams on if there is a vehicle travelling in either direction within 200 metres in front of you.

BLUE MOUNTAINS - LEURA NSW 2780

Pop Part of Blue Mountains, (118km W Sydney), See map on page 55, ref B2. Historic Blue Mountains town with teahouses and craft shops, known as 'the Garden Village'. Bowls, Bush Walking, Golf, Scenic Drives, Swimming, Tennis.

Hotels/Motels

★★★★☆ **Peppers Fairmont Resort**, (LH), 1 Sublime Point Rd, 2km SE of PO, ☎ 02 4782 5222, fax 02 4784 1685, (Multi-stry gr fl), 210 rms (20 suites) [shwr, bath, spa bath (9), tlt, hairdry, a/c, tel, TV, movie, clock radio, t/c mkg, refrig], lift, iron, iron brd, conv fac, ✕, pool indoor heated, sauna, spa, rm serv, plygr, gym, squash, tennis, cots, non smoking rms (76). **RO** ♂♀ $240 - $338, ♀ $44, **Suite RO** ♂♀ $320 - $449, ♀ $44, 58 rooms of a lower rating, AE BC DC MC VI, ⚑&.

★★★☆ **Mercure Resort Blue Mountains**, (M), Fitzroy St, 2km SE of PO, ☎ 02 4784 1331, fax 02 4784 1813, (2 stry gr fl), 80 units (9 suites) [shwr, bath (16), tlt, hairdry, a/c, elec blkts, tel, TV, clock radio, t/c mkg, refrig, mini bar], lounge, conv fac, ✕, pool-heated, sauna, spa (2), 24hr reception, rm serv, dinner to unit, plygr, bicycle, gym, squash, tennis, cots. **RO** ♂ $130 - $168, ♂♀ $130 - $168, ♀ $22, **Suite D** $177 - $208, ch con, Min book applies, AE BC DC MC VI.

★★★ **Where Waters Meet**, (M), Portion 15 Mount Hay Rd, 2.5km off Great Western Hwy, ☎ 02 4784 3022, fax 02 4784 3343, 49 units (4 suites) [shwr, bath, tlt, c/fan, heat, elec blkts, tel, TV, t/c mkg, refrig, micro (4)], conv fac, ✕ (Fri & Sat), bicycle, tennis. **BB** ♂ $181.50, ♂♀ $181.50, ♀ $35, **Suite D** $209, ch con, Some rooms of a higher standard. Min book long w/ends and Easter, AE BC DC MC VI.

Self Catering Accommodation

★★★★ **Hills Havens Little Pomander**, (Cotg), Leura Mall, 600m S of PO, ☎ 02 4782 7777, fax 02 4782 9327, 1 cotg [shwr (2), spa bath, tlt (2), hairdry, fan, cent heat, elec blkts, TV, video, clock radio, t/c mkg, refrig, cook fac, micro, elec frypan, d/wash, toaster, ldry, blkts, linen], w/mach, dryer, iron, iron brd, lounge firepl, bbq, cots-fee, non smoking property. **D** ♂♀ $145 - $200, ♀ $35 - $50, **W** ♂♀ $770 - $900, ♀ $100, ch con, fam con, Min book applies.

★★★★ **Maples on the Mall**, (Cotg), 255 The Mall, 500m S of PO, ☎ 02 4784 2717, fax 02 4784 3388, 4 cotgs acc up to 8, (4 bedrm), [shwr, spa bath, tlt, c/fan, heat, elec blkts, tel, TV, video, clock radio, refrig, cook fac ltd, micro, toaster, blkts, doonas, linen, pillows], ldry, w/mach, secure park, plygr, breakfast ingredients, non smoking property. **D** ♂♀ $110 - $170, **W** ♂♀ $450 - $750, ♀ $100, ch con, AE BC DC MC VI.

★★★★ **The Manors Cottage at Leura**, (Cotg), 155 Megalong St, 500m SE of PO, ☎ 02 4784 2769, fax 02 4784 1624, 1 cotg acc up to 6, [shwr, tlt, hairdry, fire pl, cent heat, tel, TV, video, clock radio, CD, cook fac, linen], spa (hydro), c/park. **D** $150 - $200, BC MC VI.

★★★☆ **Bygone Beautys Cottages**, (Cotg), 20-22 Grose St, ☎ 02 4784 3117, fax 02 4784 3078, 17 cotgs acc up to 12, [shwr, spa bath (5), tlt, hairdry, fan (7), c/fan (2), cent heat (8), elec blkts, tel, TV, video, clock radio (6), radio (2), t/c mkg, refrig, cook fac, micro, elec frypan, d/wash (4), toaster, ldry, blkts, linen, pillows], w/mach (10), iron, cots-fee. **D** ♂ $67.50 - $150, ♀ $67.50 - $150, ch con, 2 cottages of a 4.5 star rating. Min book applies, AE BC EFT MC VI.

★★★☆ **Leuringa Holiday Cottage**, (Cotg), Beattie St, ☎ 02 9949 2823, fax 02 9949 1758, 1 cotg acc up to 7, [shwr, tlt, fan, fire pl (slow combustion wood), heat, elec blkts, tel, clock radio, t/c mkg, refrig, cook fac, micro, toaster, ldry], w/mach, dryer, iron, lounge (TV), c/park (carport). **D** ♂♀ $125 - $170.

★★★☆ **Talinga Holiday Cottage**, (Cotg), Tennyson Ave, 1km S of PO, ☎ 02 9949 2823, fax 02 9949 1758, 1 cotg acc up to 5, [shwr, bath, tlt, c/fan, fire pl (slow combustion wood), elec blkts, tel, TV, clock radio, t/c mkg, refrig, cook fac, micro, toaster, ldry], w/mach, dryer, iron. **D** ♂♀ $130 - $180.

Operator Comment: Two character filled cottages. Visit www.bluemts.com.au/leuringa

★★★ **Leura Lodge**, (HU), 7 Spencer St, 750m SE of PO, ☎ 02 4784 1462, fax 02 4784 1462, (2 stry gr fl), 1 unit acc up to 11, [shwr (2), bath (1), tlt (2), a/c-cool, heat (combustion), elec blkts, clock radio, t/c mkg, refrig, cook fac, micro, elec frypan, toaster, blkts, linen, pillows], ldry, lounge (TV), bbq. **D** ♂ $55 - $77, ch con, Group & family bookings only.

★★★ **Leura Traditional Cottages - Peartree Cottage**, (Cotg), 2 Hester Rd, ☎ 02 4784 1899, fax 02 4784 1899, 1 cotg acc up to 12, [shwr, bath, tlt, hairdry, fan, fire pl, heat, elec blkts, TV, video, clock radio, t/c mkg, refrig, cook fac, micro, toaster, blkts, linen], iron, iron brd, non smoking property. **D** ♂♀ $45 - $90, ♀ $25 - $55, **W** ♂♀ $800, ♀ $45 - $75, ch con, pen con, Min book applies.

★★★ **Sanjon Lodge**, (Cotg), 3 Russell Rd, 1km E of PO, ☎ 02 4782 2940, fax 02 4782 9327, 1 cotg acc up to 6, [shwr, spa bath, tlt, fire pl, heat, elec blkts, TV, video, clock radio, CD, t/c mkg, refrig, cook fac, micro, d/wash, toaster, ldry, linen], w/mach, dryer, iron, bbq, c/park (garage), cots-fee. **D** ♂♀ $125 - $170, ch con.

★★★ **Scribbly Gum Cottage**, (Cotg), 19 Blackheath St, ☎ 02 9418 7074, fax 02 9418 7074, 1 cotg acc up to 6, [shwr, bath, tlt (2), c/fan, fire pl (2), heat, elec blkts, tel, TV, clock radio, t/c mkg, refrig, cook fac, toaster, ldry, doonas, linen], iron, iron brd, lounge firepl, cots, non smoking property. **D 👥 $120 - $180, 🧒 $60**, ch con, Min book applies.

★★★ **The Cottage**, (Cotg), 11 Malvern Rd, 900m S of Railway Station, ☎ 02 4784 1668, 1 cotg acc up to 4, [shwr, bath, tlt, hairdry, fire pl, heat, elec blkts, TV, video, clock radio, t/c mkg, refrig, cook fac, micro, toaster, ldry, doonas, linen], iron, iron brd. **D $70 - $140, W $390 - $595**, Min book applies.

Leura Cottages, (Cotg), 76 Megalong St, 1km W of PO, ☎ 02 6359 3250, fax 02 6359 3251, 2 cotgs acc up to 11, [shwr, bath, tlt, fire pl, heat, elec blkts, TV, clock radio, t/c mkg, refrig, cook fac, micro, d/wash, toaster, blkts, linen], iron, iron brd, bbq, plygr, cots, non smoking property. **D 👤 $50 - $70**, ch con, fam con, pen con, BC MC VI, (not yet classified).

B&B's/Guest Houses

★★★★☆ **Argyll Guest House**, (B&B), No children's facilities, 11a Craigend St, 300m S of PO, ☎ 02 4784 1555, fax 02 4784 1566, 3 rms (3 suites) [shwr, spa bath (1), tlt, hairdry, cent heat, elec blkts, tel, TV, clock radio, t/c mkg], lounge (TV & firepl), bbq, c/park. **Suite D 👤 $100 - $140, 👥 $140 - $220**, MC VI.

★★★★☆ **Eastwicke Luxury Bed & Breakfast**, (B&B), 9 Balmoral Rd, 500m S of PO, ☎ 02 4784 1659, 1 rm (1 suite) [shwr, bath, tlt, heat, cent heat, elec blkts, tel, TV, clock radio, t/c mkg, refrig, micro, toaster], iron, iron brd, bbq, non smoking rms. **BLB 👥 $130 - $150**, Min book applies.

★★★★☆ **Fairway Lodge**, (B&B), 3 Sublime Point Rd, 2km SE of PO, ☎ 02 4784 3351, 3 rms [shwr, spa bath (1), tlt, hairdry, fan, fire pl, heat, elec blkts, TV, movie, clock radio, t/c mkg, refrig], lounge, ✕, bbq, cots, non smoking property. **BB 👤 $85 - $110, 👥 $110 - $170, 🧒 $20**, fam con, BC EFT MC VI.

★★★★☆ **Llandrindod Bed & Breakfast**, (B&B), 272 The Mall, 600m S of PO, ☎ 02 4784 3234, fax 02 4784 3234, (2 stry gr fl), 3 rms [shwr, tlt, hairdry, cent heat, elec blkts, TV, clock radio], iron, iron brd, lounge (tv vcr & firepl), c/park. **BB 👤 $110 - $165, 👥 $143 - $198**, Min book applies, BC MC VI.

★★★★☆ **Megalong Manor**, (B&B), 151 Megalong St, 500m SE of PO, ☎ 02 4784 1461, fax 02 4784 2716, 3 rms (3 suites) [shwr, bath, tlt, hairdry, heat, elec blkts, TV, clock radio, CD, t/c mkg, refrig, micro, toaster], c/park. **BLB 👤 $100 - $140, 👥 $140 - $190**, BC MC VI.

★★★★☆ **The Gatehouse**, (GH), 110 Craigend St, 2km SE of PO, ☎ 02 4782 2155, fax 02 4782 5323, 1 rm [shwr, spa bath, tlt, a/c, heat (open log fire), elec blkts, TV, video, clock radio, t/c mkg, refrig, cook fac, toaster], lounge, c/park (garage). **BLB $198 - $278**, Min book applies, AE BC DC MC VI.

★★★★☆ **The Greens**, (B&B), 26 Grose St, ☎ 02 4784 3241, fax 02 4784 3241, 5 rms [shwr (4), spa bath (1), tlt, hairdry, heat, elec blkts, clock radio], shared fac (2 rms), iron, iron brd, rec rm, lounge (TV), lounge firepl, t/c mkg shared, non smoking rms. **BB 👤 $85 - $165, 👥 $110 - $165**, BC MC VI.

★★★★☆ **Woodford of Leura**, (B&B), 48 Woodford St, ☎ 02 4784 2240, fax 02 4784 2240, (2 stry gr fl), 4 rms (2 suites) [shwr, bath (1), tlt, hairdry, cent heat, elec blkts, tel, TV, clock radio, t/c mkg], ldry, iron, iron brd, conv fac, lounge firepl, spa, non smoking rms (4). **BB 👥 $120 - $180, 🧒 $40**, BC MC VI.

★★★★ **Broomelea B&B**, (B&B), 273 Leura Mall, 500m S of PO, ☎ 02 4784 2940, fax 02 4784 2611, 3 rms [shwr, bath, spa bath, tlt, hairdry, fire pl, cent heat, elec blkts, tel, TV, video, t/c mkg], iron, iron brd, lounge firepl, spa, bbq, non smoking property. **BB 👤 $135 - $180, 👥 $154 - $200, 🧒 $35**, Min book applies, AE BC DC EFT MC VI.

★★★★ **Leura House**, (GH), 7 Britain St, 400m N of PO, ☎ 02 4784 2035, fax 02 4784 3329, (Multi-stry gr fl), 12 rms [shwr (11), bath (5), tlt (11), fire pl, cent heat, elec blkts, tel, TV, video, clock radio], ldry, lounge (TV), conv fac, ☒, t/c mkg shared, bbq, cots-fee. **BB 👤 $121 - $137.50, 👥 $152 - $174, 👥👤 $250**, ch con, AE BC DC MC VI.

★★★☆ **(Cottage Section)**, 3 cotgs acc up to 10, [shwr, bath, spa bath (1), tlt, heat, TV, video, radio, refrig, cook fac (2), d/wash (2), blkts, linen, pillows]. **BB 👤 $76 - $83**, ch con.

★★★☆ **Bed & Breakfast on Tennyson**, (GH), 1 Tennyson Ave, ☎ 02 4784 1661, 1 rm [shwr, tlt, hairdry, fan, heat, elec blkts, clock radio, t/c mkg, refrig, micro, toaster], iron, lounge (TV), non smoking property. **BB ♦ $90 - $110, ♦♦ $100 - $140**, Min book long w/ends.

★★★☆ **Bethany Manor Bed & Breakfast**, (B&B), 8 East View Ave, 800m NW of PO, ☎ 02 4782 9215, fax 02 4782 1962, 3 rms [ensuite, bath, spa bath (2), hairdry, fan, fire pl (1), cent heat, elec blkts, clock radio], iron, iron brd, lounge (TV), lounge firepl, breakfast rm, t/c mkg shared, tennis, non smoking property. **BB ♦ $85 - $130, ♦♦ $130 - $185**, Min book long w/ends, BC MC VI.

★★★☆ **Bunny's B&B**, (GH), 220 Leura Mall, 150m S of PO, ☎ 02 4782 7435, fax 02 4782 7435, 3 rms (1 suite) [hairdry (1), fire pl, cent heat, elec blkts, tel, TV, clock radio, refrig (1), micro (1), toaster (1)], iron (1), iron brd (1), rec rm, TV rm, lounge firepl, t/c mkg shared, courtesy transfer, cots, non smoking property. **BB ♦♦ $110 - $140**, AE BC MC VI.

★★★☆ **Gillians Bed & Breakfast Leura**, (B&B), 7 Coniston Rd, 1km E of PO, ☎ 02 4784 1133, fax 02 4782 5425, (2 stry), 2 rms [shwr, tlt, elec blkts, t/c mkg], rec rm, lounge (TV & firepl), non smoking rms. **BLB ♦♦ $145 - $155, ◊ $85.**

Gladstone Lodge Bed & Breakfast, (B&B), 75 Gladstone Rd, ☎ 02 4784 2518, fax 02 4784 1152, 3 rms [hairdry, fan, heat, elec blkts, clock radio, t/c mkg], lounge firepl, c/park (undercover), ✆, non smoking property. **BB $105**, AE BC MC VI, (not yet classified).

White Gables, (B&B), 63 Railway Pd, 300m W from PO, ☎ 02 4784 1008, 2 rms (1 suite) [fire pl (in guest lounge), cent heat, elec blkts, TV, video, clock radio, doonas], ldry, lounge, ✕, spa (communal), t/c mkg shared, refrig, non smoking property. **BB ♦ $85 - $135, ♦♦ $100 - $150, Suite BB ♦♦ $100 - $150, ◊ $35**, weekly con, Min book applies, BC MC VI, (not yet classified).

BLUE MOUNTAINS - LITHGOW NSW 2790

Pop 11,450. (161km W Sydney), See map on page 55, ref B2.
Historic mining town on the western slopes of the Blue Mountains.
Boating, Bowls, Fishing, Golf, Greyhound Racing, Scenic Drives,
Swimming, Tennis, Trotting, Water Skiing.

Hotels/Motels

★★★★ **Best Western Bowen Inn**, (M), Great Western Hwy, Bowenfels 2790, 4km E of Lithgow, ☎ 02 6352 5111, fax 02 6352 5100, 25 units [shwr, spa bath (5), tlt, hairdry, a/c, tel, cable tv, clock radio, t/c mkg, refrig, mini bar], iron, iron brd, conf fac, ✕, rm serv, dinner to unit, courtesy transfer, cots, non smoking rms (16). **RO ♦ $90 - $105, ♦♦ $90 - $105, ◊ $10 - $15**, pen con, AE BC DC EFT MC MP VI.

★★★☆ **Colonial Motor Inn**, (M), 526 Great Western Hwy, Marrangaroo, 6km W of PO, ☎ 02 6352 1655, fax 02 6352 2471, 34 units [shwr, tlt, a/c, tel, cable tv, video, clock radio, t/c mkg, refrig], ldry, ✕ (Mon to Sat), pool-heated (solar), meals to unit, cots-fee, non smoking units (22). **RO ♦♦ $85.80 - $96.80, ◊ $9.90 - $13.20**, AE BC DC MC VI.

★★★☆ **Zig Zag Motel**, (M), Cnr Chifley Rd & Clwydd St, 1.2km E of PO, ☎ 02 6352 2477, fax 02 6352 3654, 36 units [shwr, spa bath (1), tlt, a/c-cool, heat, tel, cable tv, video, clock radio, t/c mkg, refrig], ldry, conv fac, ✕, pool, plygr, cots-fee, non smoking units (12). **RO ♦ $75 - $95, ♦♦ $85 - $100, ◊ $90 - $110, ◊ $7 - $12, W $440 - $535**, ch con, 17 units of a higher standard, 9 units of a lower rating. AE BC DC EFT MC VI, ♿.

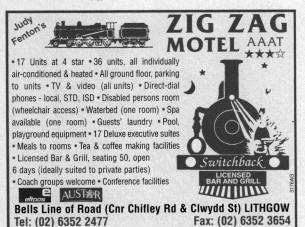
★★★ **Parkside Lodge**, (M), Great Western Hwy, 3km S of PO, ☎ 02 6351 2871, fax 02 6352 1232, 16 units [shwr, tlt, a/c-cool, heat, elec blkts, tel, TV, video-fee, clock radio, t/c mkg, refrig], ldry, cots, non smoking units (6). **RO ♦ $55 - $65, ♦♦ $66 - $77, ◊ $10**, AE BC DC EFT MC VI.

★★★☆ **Lithgow Valley Motel**, (M), 45 Cooerwull Rd, 4km W of PO, ☎ 02 6351 2334, fax 02 6352 3869, 16 units [shwr, tlt, heat, elec blkts, tel, cable tv (Sky), clock radio, t/c mkg, refrig], ☒ (Mon to Sat), cots-fee. **RO ♦ $55 - $65, ♦♦ $66, ◊ $11**, 3 units of a lower rating, Minimum booking long weekends and Bathurst race weekend. AE BC DC MC MCH VI.

Self Catering Accommodation

★★★ **No.1 Ferro**, (SA), 1 Ferro St, ☎ 02 6351 4524, fax 02 6351 4524, (2 stry), 5 serv apts acc up to 5, [shwr, tlt, heat, TV, clock radio, t/c mkg, refrig, cook fac, micro, toaster, blkts, linen, pillows], ldry, w/mach-fee, iron, c/park (carport), **D ♦♦ $60, ◊ $10, W ♦♦ $330, ◊ $60**, ch con.

★★★ **(Motel Section)**, 2 units [shwr, tlt, heat, TV, clock radio, t/c mkg, refrig, cook fac ltd, micro, toaster], ldry, c/park (garage). **RO ◊ $50, ◊ $10**, ch con.

BLUE MOUNTAINS - LITTLE HARTLEY NSW 2790

Pop Nominal, (143km W Sydney), See map on page 55, ref B2.
Small Blue Mountains village south-east of historic Hartley.
Boating, Bush Walking, Fishing, Horse Riding.

Self Catering Accommodation

★★★ **Mill Creek Cottage**, (House), 6 Mill Creek Rd, ☎ 02 4787 1400, fax 02 4787 1491, (2 stry), 1 house acc up to 6, (3 bedrm), [a/c, fan, TV, video, clock radio, t/c mkg, refrig, cook fac, micro, toaster, ldry-fee, blkts, doonas, linen], lounge firepl, bbq, ✆, non smoking property. **D ♦ $41.80 - $66, ♦♦ $94.60 - $132, ◊ $41.80 - $66**, MC VI.

Timberdell Cottage, (Cotg), Coxs River Rd, 4kms off Great Western Hwy, ☎ 02 6355 2437, 1 cotg acc up to 10, [shwr, tlt (2), fan (1), fire pl, elec blkts, tel, t/c mkg, refrig, cook fac, toaster, blkts reqd, linen reqd]. **D $100, W $400 - $480**, Min book applies, (not yet classified).

BLUE MOUNTAINS - MEDLOW BATH NSW 2780

Part of BLUE MOUNTAINS region. Pop 450. Part of Blue Mountains, (128km W Sydney), See map on page 55, ref B2. Upper Blue Mountains village probably best known for the Hydro Majestic Hotel, 'an Edwardian folly with a touch of Art Deco'. Bush Walking, Scenic Drives.

Hotels/Motels

★★★ **Hydro Majestic Hotel**, (LH), Great Western Hwy, ☎ 02 4788 1002, fax 02 4788 1063, (2 stry gr fl), 55 rms (0 suites) [shwr, bath (6), spa bath (1), tlt, hairdry (l), cent heat, tel, TV, clock radio, t/c mkg], ✕, pool, 24hr reception, ✆, tennis, cots-fee. **D ♦♦ $220 - $405, Suite D ♦♦ $800 - $1,350**, ch con, fam con, pen con, AE BC DC EFT MC VI.

Self Catering Accommodation

★★★☆ **Medlow Cottage**, (Cotg), 44 Portland Rd (Cnr Richmond Rd), 7km W of Katoomba, ☎ 02 9546 4719, 1 cotg acc up to 6, (3 bedrm), [shwr, bath, tlt, hairdry, fan, fire pl, heat, elec blkts, TV, video, clock radio, CD, t/c mkg, refrig, cook fac, micro, elec frypan, toaster, ldry (in unit), doonas, linen, pillows], iron, bbq, c/park (undercover), non smoking property, **BB** ♦♦ **$110**, ♦♦ **$500**, BC MC VI.

B&B's/Guest Houses

★★★ **Chalet Blue Mountains**, (GH), 46 Portland Rd, 500m E of railway station, ☎ 02 4788 1122, fax 02 4788 1064, 8 rms [shwr (4), bath (4), tlt (7), fire pl (open) (2), heat, cent heat, elec blkts], ✕, plygr, tennis. **BB** ♦ **$80 - $120**, ♦♦ **$130 - $150**, **DBB** ♦ **$125 - $145**, ch con, AE BC EFT MC VI.

BLUE MOUNTAINS - MOUNT TOMAH NSW 2758

Part of BLUE MOUNTAINS region. See map on page 55, ref B2. Located on the Bells Line of Road close to Mount Wilson. Botanic gardens and picnic areas. Bush Walking, Canoeing.

B&B's/Guest Houses

★★★★☆ **Tomah Mountain Lodge**, (B&B), Skyline Rd, 1km W of Botanic Garden, ☎ 02 4567 2111, fax 02 4567 2111, 3 rms [shwr, tlt, c/fan, heat, elec blkts, tel, TV, clock radio, t/c mkg], TV rm, lounge firepl, non smoking property. **BB** ♦ **$160**, ♦♦ **$175**, **DBB** ♦ **$197.50**, ♦♦ **$250**, AE BC DC EFT MC VI,

Operator Comment: Visit our website - www.tomahmountainlodge.com.au

BLUE MOUNTAINS - MOUNT VICTORIA NSW 2786

Part of BLUE MOUNTAINS region. Pop 750. (140km W Sydney), See map on page 55, ref B2. Small, historic town in the upper Blue Mountains. Scenic Drives.

Hotels/Motels

★★★☆ **Mount Victoria Motor Inn**, (M), Station St, 50m N of Great Western Hwy, ☎ 02 4787 1320, fax 02 4787 1543, 12 units [shwr, tlt, hairdry, a/c, heat, elec blkts, tel, fax, TV, video-fee, clock radio, t/c mkg, refrig], iron, iron brd, cots-fee, non smoking units (4). **RO** ♦ **$84 - $160**, ♦♦ **$94 - $160**, ♦♦♦ **$110 - $175**, ◊ **$16.50**, ch con, Min book applies, AE BC DC MC VI.

Self Catering Accommodation

★★☆ **Cedar Lodge Cabins**, 42 Great Western Hwy, ☎ 02 4787 1256, fax 02 4787 1956, 9 cabins acc up to 6, [shwr, spa bath (2), tlt, heat, elec blkts, TV, clock radio, t/c mkg, refrig, cook fac ltd, micro, linen], bbq. **D** ♦♦ **$71.50 - $330**, ◊ **$11**, **W** ♦♦ **$495 - $750**, ch con, BC MC VI.

(**Lodge Section**), 1 rm acc up to 20, [linen], TV rm, lounge, cook fac. **D** ♦ **$25 - $35**, (not yet classified).

B&B's/Guest Houses

★★★★ **Historic Closeburn House**, (GH), Cnr Mt York Rd & Closeburn Dr, ☎ 02 4787 1555, fax 02 4787 1318, (2 stry gr fl), 10 rms [shwr, bath, tlt, hairdry, cent heat, elec blkts, tel, clock radio], lounge (TV), conv fac, ✕, golf. **BB** ♦♦ **$159.50 - $231**, **DBB** ♦♦ **$255 - $332**, ◊ **$51 - $66**, Min book long w/ends, AE BC DC MC VI.

★★★☆ **The Hotel Imperial**, (GH), Cnr Great Western Hwy & Station St, Opposite PO, ☎ 02 4787 1233, fax 02 4787 1878, (2 stry gr fl), 24 rms [shwr (12), spa bath (1), tlt (12), heat (12), elec blkts], rec rm, lounge (TV), conv fac, ✕, t/c mkg shared, cots. **RO** ♦ **$51 - $161**, ♦♦ **$72 - $272**, ◊ **$29 - $44**, Rating excludes rooms A - E, AE BC EFT MC VI.

★★★☆ **The Manor House**, (GH), Montgomery St, 50m W of PO, ☎ 02 4787 1369, fax 02 4787 1585, (2 stry gr fl), 13 rms [shwr, bath (6), spa bath (1), tlt, cent heat, elec blkts], ldry, TV rm, conv fac, ✕, spa, t/c mkg shared, bbq, plygr, cots, non smoking rms. **BB** ♦♦ **$118 - $220**, **DBB** ♦♦ **$178 - $290**, ch con, 4 rooms ★★★. AE BC EFT MC VI.

(**Self Contained Section**), 1 unit acc up to 8, [shwr, bath, tlt, cent heat, elec blkts, TV, video, clock radio, refrig, cook fac, micro, d/wash, toaster, blkts, linen, pillows], w/mach, dryer, lounge firepl, breakfast ingredients. **D** ♦♦ **$175**, ◊ **$70**, (not yet classified).

★★★ **The Victoria & Albert**, (GH), Cnr Station St & Harley Ave, 100m W of PO, ☎ 02 4787 1241, or 02 4787 1396, fax 02 4787 1588, 30 rms (1 suite) [shwr (12), tlt (12), heat, elec blkts], shared fac (17), lounge, conv fac, ✕, pool, sauna, spa, t/c mkg shared, bbq, plygr, cots-fee, ch con. **BB** ♦ **$65 - $100**, ♦♦ **$90 - $170**, ◊ **$35 - $50** AE BC MC VI.

BLUE MOUNTAINS - MOUNT WILSON NSW 2786

Part of BLUE MOUNTAINS region. Pop Part of Blue Mtns, (167km W Sydney), See map on page 55, ref B2. Historic Blue Mountains village renowned for its cool climate gardens.

Self Catering Accommodation

★★★★ **Blueberry Lodge & The Loft**, (Chalet), Waterfall Rd, ☎ 02 4756 2022, fax 02 4756 2022, (2 stry gr fl), 2 chalets acc up to 6, [shwr, tlt, hairdry, fire pl, heat, elec blkts, tel, TV, radio, t/c mkg, refrig, cook fac, micro, elec frypan, toaster, blkts, linen, pillows] ldry, w/mach, dryer, iron, bbq, cots. **BB** ♦♦ **$165 - $185,** ♦ **$38.50 - $55,** ch con, BC MC VI.

BLUE MOUNTAINS - O'CONNELL NSW 2795

Part of BLUE MOUNTAINS region. Pop Nominal, (199km W Sydney), See map on page 55, ref A2. Small, National Trust-classified village between Bathurst and Oberon. Gem Fossicking.

B&B's/Guest Houses

★★★ **Yarrabin**, (GH), (Farm), 3253 Beaconsfield Rd, via BATHURST, ☎ 02 6337 5712, fax 02 6337 5628, 8 rms [ensuite, heat], rec rm, lounge (TV), pool, spa, tennis. **D** all meals ♦ **$95,** ♦♦ **$190,** ch con, Min book applies, AE BC MC VI.

The Church & School House B&B, (B&B), c1867, O'Connell Rd, ☎ 02 6337 5773, fax 02 6337 5778, 2 rms [shwr, tlt, heat, elec blkts, tel, clock radio, t/c mkg], ldry, iron, iron brd, meeting rm, cots, non smoking property. **BB** ♦ **$135 - $155,** ♦♦ **$155 - $175,** ♦ **$25 - $45,** **DBB** ♦ **$155 - $205,** ♦♦ **$205 - $275,** ♦ **$45 - $85,** BC MC VI, (not yet classified).

(School House Section), c1840, 1 cotg acc up to 4, [shwr, tlt, a/c-cool, fire pl, heat, elec blkts, tel, clock radio], ldry, iron, iron brd, bbq, cots, non smoking property. **D $275,** (not yet classified).

BLUE MOUNTAINS - OBERON NSW 2787

Part of BLUE MOUNTAINS region. Pop 2,550. (200km W Sydney), See map on page 55, ref A2. Small town on the scenic Oberon Plateau, surrounded by tracts of radiata pine forests and picturesque grazing country. Bowls, Bush Walking, Fishing, Gem Fossicking, Golf, Swimming, Tennis.

Hotels/Motels

★★★★ **Big Trout Motor Inn**, (M), Oberon St, 1km E of PO, ☎ 02 6336 2100, fax 02 6336 2114, 33 units [shwr, spa bath (avail), tlt, fan, heat, elec blkts, tel, TV, clock radio, t/c mkg, refrig, toaster], ldry, conv fac, ✉, rm serv, cots. **RO** ♦ **$78,** ♦♦ **$88,** ♦ **$12,** ch con, AE BC DC MC VI.

★★★☆ **Highlands Motor Inn**, (M), Cnr Dart & Fleming Sts, 300m N of PO, ☎ 02 6336 1866, fax 02 6336 1089, 15 units [shwr, bath (9), tlt, hairdry, fan, heat, elec blkts, tel, TV, clock radio, t/c mkg, refrig, toaster], ldry, iron, iron brd, bbq, dinner to unit, cots-fee, non smoking rms (8). **RO** ♦ **$77 - $80,** ♦♦ **$88 - $90,** ♦ **$10,** 7 units ★★★★. Min book long w/ends, AE BC DC MC VI, ♿.

★★☆ **Titania Motel**, (M), Tarana Crescent, 2km E of PO, ☎ 02 6336 1377, fax 02 6336 2174, 17 units [shwr, tlt, heat, elec blkts, tel, TV, clock radio, t/c mkg, refrig, toaster], breakfast rm, ✉, bbq, meals to unit, non smoking rms (2). **RO** ♦ **$55 - $72,** ♦♦ **$55.50 - $89,** ♦ **$11,** AE BC MC VI.

Self Catering Accommodation

★★★★★ **Allons Tarpeena Retreat**, (Cotg), 45 Titania Rd, 5km E of PO, ☎ 02 6336 2291, fax 02 6336 5330, 1 cotg [shwr, spa bath, tlt, hairdry, fire pl, heat, elec blkts, TV, video, clock radio, CD, t/c mkg, refrig, cook fac, micro, toaster, blkts, linen, pillows], ldry, non smoking property. **D $155 - $195, W $980,** Min book applies, BC MC VI.

★★★★☆ **Fernlee Cottage**, (Cotg), (Farm), 454 Dog Rocks Rd, Black Springs, 22kms from Oberon on the Abercrombie Rd, ☎ 02 6335 8192, fax 02 6335 8192, 1 cotg acc up to 6, [shwr (2), bath, tlt (2), hairdry, cent heat, elec blkts, tel, fax, TV, clock radio, refrig, cook fac, micro, toaster, ldry (in cotg), blkts, linen, pillows], w/mach, dryer, iron, bbq, c/park (garage), cots. **D** ♦ **$105,** ♦♦ **$105,** ♦♦♦ **$135,** ♦ **$15, W $525 - $825,** BC MC VI,

Operator Comment: Visit our website, www.fernlee.com.au

★★★★☆ **Melaleuca Mountain Chalets**, (Chalet), 935 Duckmaloi Rd, 9.3km E of PO, ☎ 02 6336 1158, fax 02 6336 2282, 6 chalets acc up to 6, [shwr, spa bath (4), tlt, fire pl, heat, elec blkts, TV, video, clock radio, t/c mkg, refrig, cook fac, micro, toaster, doonas, linen], iron, iron brd, bbq, cots-fee, non smoking property. **D** ♦♦ **$115 - $185,** ♦ **$15, W** ♦♦ **$710 - $950,** ♦ **$90,** BC MC VI.

★★★★ **Fitzpatricks At Oberon**, (Villa), 55 North St, 200m W of PO, ☎ 02 6336 5222, or 02 6336 1047, fax 02 6336 5222, 1 villa acc up to 4, [shwr, bath, tlt, cent heat, elec blkts, TV, clock radio, t/c mkg, refrig, cook fac, micro, elec frypan, d/wash, toaster, ldry, doonas, linen], w/mach, dryer, iron, iron brd, bbq, c/park. **D** ♦♦ **$120 - $140,** Min book applies, BC MC VI.

★★★★ **Stone Hedge**, (Cotg), 1028 Duckmaloi Rd, 12km E of PO, ☎ 0419 010 250, fax 02 9594 4345, 1 cotg acc up to 15, [c/fan, fire pl, cent heat, tel, t/c mkg, refrig, cook fac, micro, elec frypan, d/wash, toaster, ldry, blkts, linen, pillows], w/mach, iron, iron brd, rec rm, lounge firepl (tv/video), bbq, plygr, non smoking rms. **D $330 - $605, W $2,310 - $2,640,** Min book applies.

★★★☆ **Midlands Eco-Tourism Farmstay**, (HU), (Farm), O'Connell Rd, Midlands, ☎ 02 6336 3101, fax 02 6336 3101, 2 units acc up to 6, [shwr (2), bath (1), tlt (2), fire pl, heat, elec blkts, tel, TV, video (avail), t/c mkg, refrig, cook fac (2), toaster], ldry, lounge (TV), meeting rm, ✉, sauna, bbq, cots. **D $140, RO** ♦ **$55,** ♦♦ **$100,** AE BC MC VI.

B&B's/Guest Houses

★★★★★ **Lake View Ridge**, (B&B), 163 Harveys Lane, 7km S of PO, ☎ 02 6336 5277, fax 02 6336 0408, 3 rms (3 suites) [shwr, tlt, hairdry, a/c, cent heat, elec blkts, tel, TV, clock radio], ldry, rec rm, lounge, lounge firepl, ✕, non smoking property. **BB** ♦ **$110 - $130,** ♦♦ **$140 - $160, DBB** ♦ **$160 - $180,** ♦♦ **$240 - $260,** Min book Christmas Jan long w/ends and Easter, BC DC MC VI,

Operator Comment: www.bluemts.com.au/lakeviewridge

★★★★☆ **Tapio Guest House in a Garden**, (B&B), 36 Sydney Rd, 2km E of PO, ☎ 02 6336 2063, fax 02 6336 2063, 2 rms [shwr (2), bath (1), tlt (2), hairdry, a/c, fan, fire pl, heat, elec blkts, tel, TV, video, clock radio], lounge, ✕, secure park. **BB** ♦ **$85 - $93.50,** ♦♦ **$115 - $127.50,** Dinner by arrangement.

Duckmaloi Farm, (B&B), 54 Karawina Dve, Duckmaloi 2787 ☎ 02 6336 1375, fax 02 6336 1560, 2 rms [shwr, spa bath, tlt, heat, elec blkts, clock radio, cook fac ltd, doonas], lounge (TV, video), bbq, non smoking property. **BB** ♦♦ **$105 - $130,** ♦ **$35,** ch con, AE BC MC VI, (not yet classified).

(Cottage Section), 2 cotgs acc up to 6, (2 bedrm), [shwr, tlt, fan, heat, TV, video, clock radio, refrig, cook fac, toaster, blkts, doonas, linen, pillows], non smoking property. **BB** ♦♦ **$105 - $130,** ♦ **$20,** ch con, Min book applies, (not yet classified).

EagleView Escape

Exclusively for Couples

offering Luxury and Seclusion

Stunning 200 acre property 30 minutes west of the Blue Mountains, offering luxury and seclusion.
EagleView Escape offers 12 luxury self-contained suites in a unique earth-covered building carved into the hillside. Enter your private suite via our magical underground passageway and enjoy: 180 degree panoramic lake views, luxury 2 person spa, kitchenette, gas log fire, TV/VCR/CD player, queen-size bed, cedar shutters for privacy. Facilities include: billiard/lounge room, meals available, canoe hire, jet boating, wildlife and fishing. Local attractions: Jenolan Caves, Zig Zag Railway.

EAGLE VIEW
ESCAPE

Sandalls Drive, Rydal
via Lake Lyell NSW 2790
Phone: (02) 6355 6311
Fax: (02) 6355 6246
Web: www.eagleview.com.au

Rates may change. Check before booking.

BLUE MOUNTAINS - RYDAL NSW 2790

Part of BLUE MOUNTAINS region. Pop Nominal, (178km W Sydney), See map on page 55, ref B2. Small village west of Lithgow in the scenic Coxs River valley.

Self Catering Accommodation

★★★★ **Eagle View Escape**, (HU), No children's facilities, Lots 12 & 13 Sandalls Dve, 20km NW of Hartley Village, ☎ 02 6355 6311, fax 02 6355 6311, 12 units acc up to 2, [shwr, spa bath, tlt, hairdry, heat, TV, video, clock radio, t/c mkg, refrig, cook fac ltd, micro, elec frypan, toaster, blkts, linen, pillows], rec rm, lounge (TV), bbq, ✆. D $190 - $210, W $1,155, BC EFT MC VI.

Spirit of the Lake Retreat, (HU), Martins Rd, ☎ 02 6355 6300, fax 02 6355 6292, 6 units acc up to 2, (Studio), [shwr, spa bath, tlt, heat, elec blkts, TV, video, clock radio, t/c mkg, refrig, cook fac, micro, toaster, blkts, doonas, linen, pillows], lounge firepl, bbq, breakfast ingredients. BLB ♦♦ $150 - $185, ♦ $1,000, (not yet classified).

BLUE MOUNTAINS - SPRINGWOOD NSW 2777

Part of BLUE MOUNTAINS region. Pop Part of Blue Mtns, (92km W Sydney), See map on page 55, ref B2. Central Blue Mountains town that was named by Governor Macquarie in 1815. Bush Walking, Scenic Drives.

Hotels/Motels

★★★ **Royal Hotel**, (LH), 220 Macquarie Rd, ☎ 02 4751 1021, fax 02 4751 8697, (2 stry), 9 rms [shwr, tlt, a/c-cool, c/fan, heat, TV, toaster], rec rm, ✉, bar, cook fac, t/c mkg shared, ✆. RO ♦ $75, ♦♦ $95, 3 rooms of a lower rating. AE BC DC EFT MC VI.

B&B's/Guest Houses

★★★★★ **Storey Grange**, (B&B), 105 Lalor Dr, ☎ 02 4751 2672, fax 02 4751 2672, (2 stry gr fl), 2 rms [shwr, spa bath, tlt, hairdry, a/c (1), fan (1), c/fan (1), fire pl (3), heat (1), elec blkts, TV, video, clock radio, t/c mkg, refrig], iron, iron brd, TV rm, lounge firepl, non smoking property. BB ♦♦ $190 - $245, Minium booking applies weekends from May to Sept, AE BC EFT MC VI.

BLUE MOUNTAINS - SUNNY CORNER NSW 2795

Part of BLUE MOUNTAINS region. Pop Nominal, (191km W Sydney), See map on page 55, ref B2. Village nestled amongst vast pine forests between Lithgow and Bathurst, home to a fairly artistic community. Bush Walking.

B&B's/Guest Houses

★★★☆ **Sunny Corner Aussie Dreamer B&B**, (B&B), Vonlei Pines, 891 Sunny Corner Rd, 37km W of Lithgow, ☎ 02 6359 5313, 3 rms [elec blkts, clock radio], shared fac (shwr, tlt, spa), lounge (TV), ✕, spa, bbq, c/park. BB ♦ $50, ch con, Dinner by arrangement.

BLUE MOUNTAINS - TARANA NSW 2787

Part of BLUE MOUNTAINS region. Pop Nominal, (180km W Sydney), See map on page 55, ref B2. Small village between Bathurst and Lithgow. Bush Walking, Fishing, Horse Riding, Rock Climbing, Scenic Drives.

Self Catering Accommodation

★★★ **Tarana Hotel Cabins**, Main St, ☎ 02 6337 5841, fax 02 6337 5841, 3 cabins acc up to 5, [shwr, tlt, a/c, TV, t/c mkg, refrig, cook fac, micro, toaster], c/park. BLB ♦ $62, ♦♦ $88, ♦ $16.50.

BLUE MOUNTAINS - WALLERAWANG NSW 2845

Part of BLUE MOUNTAINS region. Pop 2,050. (174km W Sydney), See map on page 55, ref B2. Small town (pronounced 'wall-AIR-rewang') near Lithgow on the shores of Lake Wallace, which provides cooling water for Wallerawang Power Station and is a popular place for water sports.

Self Catering Accommodation

★★ **Black Gold Country Cabins**, Main St, 1km N of PO, ☎ 02 6355 7305, fax 02 6355 1550, 5 cabins acc up to 12, [shwr (2), bath (1), tlt (2), c/fan (4), heat, tel, TV, radio, t/c mkg, refrig, cook fac (4), micro (3), elec frypan (2), toaster, ldry (in unit) (2), blkts reqd, linen reqd-fee], ldry, w/mach (2), iron, rec rm, lounge (TV), conv fac, bbq, plygr, cots, non smoking units. D ♦♦ $50 - $60, ♦ $20, W ♦♦ $315 - $400, ♦ $20, ch con.

BLUE MOUNTAINS - WENTWORTH FALLS NSW 2782

Part of BLUE MOUNTAINS region. Pop Part of Blue Mountains, (114km W Sydney), See map on page 55, ref B2. Historic town in the central Blue Mountains. Bush Walking, Scenic Drives.

Hotels/Motels

Resteasy Motel, (M), Cnr Old Bathurst Rd & Great Western Hwy, 1km E of PO, ☎ 02 4757 1300, (2 stry gr fl), 35 units [shwr, bath, tlt, a/c, elec blkts, tel, TV, t/c mkg, refrig], rec rm, lounge (comm), ✉, pool, plygr, cots-fee. RO ♦ $66 - $100, ♦♦ $110 - $140, AE BC MC VI, (Rating under review). Jan 01.

Self Catering Accommodation

★★★★☆ **Brook Cottage**, (Cotg), No children's facilities, 2 Parkes St, ☎ 02 4784 3580, 1 cotg acc up to 4, [shwr (2), bath (2), fire pl, heat, elec blkts, tel, TV, video, clock radio (2), CD, t/c mkg, refrig, cook fac, micro, d/wash, toaster, ldry, blkts, linen], w/mach, dryer, iron, bbq, non smoking property. RO ♦♦ $180 - $220, Min book applies.

★★★★☆ **Weeroona House**, (House), 2 Fitzstubbs Ave, 500m S of shopping centre, ☎ 02 4757 2577, fax 02 4757 2577, 1 house acc up to 8, [shwr (2), bath (2), spa bath (1), tlt (2), hairdry, fire pl (2), heat, elec blkts, TV (2), video, clock radio, t/c mkg, refrig, cook fac, micro, elec frypan, d/wash, toaster, ldry, doonas, linen], w/mach, dryer, iron, iron brd, lounge firepl, bbq, cots, non smoking property. RO ♦♦ $250 - $500, ♦♦ $2,000, fam con.

★★★ **Gabbinbar Retreat**, (HU), 36-38 Pritchard St, 1km S of PO, ☎ 02 4757 4048, fax 02 4757 3963, 4 units (2 suites) acc up to 6, [shwr, spa bath (2), tlt, c/fan, fire pl, heat, elec blkts, TV, video, clock radio, t/c mkg, refrig, cook fac ltd, micro, elec frypan, toaster, blkts, linen, pillows], iron, iron brd, bbq, non smoking rms. D ♦♦ $80 - $175, ♦ $20 - $50, W ♦♦ $560 - $800, ch con, Min book applies, AE BC MC VI.

★★★ **Weeroona Cottage**, (Cotg), 31 Nelson Ave, ☎ 02 4757 2577, fax 02 4757 2577, 1 cotg acc up to 4, [shwr, bath, tlt, fire pl, TV, video, CD, cook fac, micro, linen]. D $120 - $160, W $700, fam con.

Cottage Fairways, (Cotg), 35 Beatty Rd, ☎ 02 4757 2182, fax 02 4757 4840, (2 stry), 1 cotg acc up to 7, (3 bedrm), [shwr, tlt, cent heat, elec blkts, TV, video, clock radio, refrig, cook fac, micro, toaster, ldry, blkts, linen, pillows], w/mach, lounge firepl, bar, bbq, c/park (undercover), cots, non smoking property. D ♦♦ $100 - $200, ♦ $25, W ♦♦ $650 - $700, ♦ $25, ch con, (not yet classified).

B&B's/Guest Houses

★★★★☆ **Blue Mountains Lakeside Lodge Bed & Breakfast**, (B&B), 30 Bellevue Rd, 1.3km N Station, ☎ 02 4757 3777, fax 02 4757 3444, 2 rms [shwr, spa bath, tlt, cent heat, elec blkts, TV, clock radio, t/c mkg], lounge firepl, breakfast rm, spa, non smoking property. BB ♦♦ $155 - $210, ♦ $50, BC MC VI.

★★★★☆ **Valley of the Waters Bed & Breakfast**, (B&B), 88 Fletcher St, 2km S of PO, 100m E of Conservation Hut, ☎ 02 4757 4860, fax 02 4757 4860, 3 rms [shwr, spa bath, tlt, hairdry, cent heat, elec blkts, cable tv, clock radio, t/c mkg, refrig], ldry, lounge firepl, ✕, bbq, rm serv, non smoking property. BB ♦♦ $160 - $220, BC MC VI.

★★★★ **Arabanoo Bed & Breakfast**, (B&B), 23 Taylor Avenue, 1km E of PO, ☎ 02 4757 2325, 2 rms [shwr, tlt, heat, elec blkts], TV rm, lounge firepl, t/c mkg shared, bbq, courtesy transfer, non smoking property. BB ♦ $95 - $130, ♦♦ $120 - $150, BC MC VI.

★★★★ **Falls Retreat**, (B&B), 63 Falls Rd, ☎ 02 4757 4749, fax 02 4757 4607, 3 rms [shwr, bath (1), tlt, fire pl (6), cent heat, elec blkts, t/c mkg, toaster], lounge, lounge firepl, non smoking rms. BB ♦♦ $145 - $185, BC EFT MC VI.

★★★★ **Whispering Pines by the Falls**, (B&B), c1898. 178 Falls Rd, 2km S of PO, ☎ 02 4757 1449, fax 02 4757 1219, (2 stry), 4 rms (4 suites) [shwr, tlt, cent heat, elec blkts, tel], rec rm, t/c mkg shared, bbq, c/park. BB ♦♦ $165 - $242, Min book applies, AE BC DC MC VI.

(Cottage Section), 1 cotg acc up to 8, [shwr, spa bath (2 pers), tlt, fire pl, heat, elec blkts, video, CD, t/c mkg, refrig, cook fac, elec frypan, d/wash, toaster, ldry, blkts, linen, pillows], w/mach, iron, rec rm, lounge (TV), bbq, c/park (garage). D $165 - $440, W $1,485, (not yet classified).

★★★☆ **Blue Glen Bed & Breakfast**, (B&B), 96 Waratah Rd,
☎ 02 4757 3817, 2 rms [shwr, tlt, hairdry, fan, heat, elec blkts, video (avail), clock radio, t/c mkg, refrig], iron, iron brd, TV rm, bbq, non smoking rms. **BB** ♦ **$65 - $90**, ♦♦ **$100 - $130**, ♦ **$30**, fam con, pen con, BC MC VI.

★★★☆ **Harford Bed & Breakfast**, (B&B), 32 Mulheran Lane,
☎ 02 4757 4264, 1 rm [shwr, tlt, elec blkts, clock radio, t/c mkg, refrig, toaster], iron, iron brd, lounge (TV & firepl), bbq, non smoking property. **BB** ♦♦ **$120 - $150**, Min book applies, BC MC VI.

★★★ **Monique's B & B**, (GH), 31 Falls Rd, 400m S of Railway Station,
☎ 02 4757 1646, fax 02 4757 2498, 3 rms [shwr (2), bath (1), tlt, heat, elec blkts, tel], ldry, lounge (TV, video), lounge firepl, cook fac, t/c mkg shared, refrig, bbq, non smoking rms. **BB** ♦ **$65 - $120**, ♦♦ **$80 - $140**, Min book applies, BC MC VI.

Moments, (B&B), 86 Fletcher St, ☎ 02 4757 4455, fax 02 4757 4555, 4 rms [shwr, spa bath, tlt, fire pl, cent heat, cable tv, video, clock radio, CD, t/c mkg, refrig], iron, iron brd, lounge firepl, non smoking rms. **BB** ♦♦ **$155 - $250**, BC EFT MC VI, (not yet classified).

End of Blue Mountains Region

BOAT HARBOUR NSW

See Port Stephens Region.

BODALLA NSW 2545

Pop 300. (330km S Sydney), See map on page 55, ref A6. Historic little south coast town set in a timber and dairying region.
Hotels/Motels
★★★ **Motel Bodalla**, (M), 52 Princes Hwy, 200m N of PO,
☎ 02 4473 5201, fax 02 4473 5201, 9 units [shwr, tlt, a/c, elec blkts, TV, radio, t/c mkg, refrig, toaster], bbq, cots. **RO** ♦ **$55**, ♦♦ **$55 - $70**, ♦♦♦ **$90**, ♦ **$15**, ch con, AE BC MC VI.

BOGGABILLA NSW 2409

Pop 650. (769km NW Sydney) (9km Goondiwindi), See map on pages 52/53, ref H1. Boggabilla lies at the junction of the Newell and Bruxner Highways on the banks of the Macintyre River. Fishing, Swimming, Water Skiing.
Hotels/Motels

★★☆ **Boggabilla Family Motel**, (M), Cnr Yeoman St & Newell Hwy, 900m SE of PO, ☎ 07 4676 2107, fax 07 4676 2333, 12 units [shwr, tlt, a/c, elec blkts, tel, TV, t/c mkg, refrig, cook fac (2)], pool, spa, bbq, c/park (carport), cots. **RO** ♦ **$49**, AE BC DC MC MCH VI.

BOGGABRI NSW 2382

Pop 900. (512km NW Sydney), See map on pages 52/53, ref H3. Cotton, coal and farming centre on the Namoi River in the foothills of the Nandewar Ranges. Fishing, Horse Riding, Swimming, Tennis.
Hotels/Motels
Boggabri Nestle Inn, (M), Cnr Merton & Grantham Sts, 500m S of PO,
☎ 02 6743 4308, fax 02 6743 4211, 9 units [shwr, tlt, hairdry, evap cool, c/fan, elec blkts, tel, TV, clock radio, t/c mkg, refrig, toaster], ldry, pool-heated (salt water), bbq, meals to unit, courtesy transfer, cots, non smoking rms. **RO** ♦ **$53.90**, ♦♦ **$63.80**, ♦♦♦ **$73.70**, ♦♦♦♦ **$83.60**, AE BC DC EFT MC VI, (Rating under review).

BOLWARRA NSW 2320

Pop Nominal, (167km N Sydney), See map on page 55, ref C7. Historic town situated across the Hunter River from Maitland.
B&B's/Guest Houses
★★★☆ **Maddies of Bolwarra**, (B&B), 35 Paterson Rd, 2km N of Maitland, ☎ 02 4930 1801, fax 02 4930 0734, 3 rms [shwr, bath (2), tlt, fan, heat, tel, clock radio, t/c mkg], iron, iron brd, lounge firepl, ✗, c/park. **BB** ♦ **$80 - $90**, ♦♦ **$100 - $120**, ♦ **$35**, **DBB** ♦ **$110 - $120**, ♦♦ **$150 - $180**, ♦ **$65**, Dinner by arrangement, BC MC VI.

BOMBALA NSW 2632

Pop 1,380. (485km SW Sydney), See map on pages 52/53, ref G8. Largest town in the eastern Monaro, situated midway between the Snowy Mountains and the coast. Bush Walking, Fishing, Golf, Swimming, Tennis.
Hotels/Motels

★★★ **Maneroo Motel**, (M), 129 Maybe St (Monaro Hwy), 200m S of PO,
☎ 02 6458 3500, fax 02 6458 3500, 21 units [shwr, tlt, hairdry, a/c, heat, elec blkts, tel, fax, TV, clock radio, t/c mkg, refrig, toaster], ✗, bbq, dinner to unit, cots-fee, non smoking rms (avail), Pets on application. **RO** ♦ **$47 - $52**, ♦♦ **$62 - $66**, ♦ **$15**, ch con, 5 units of a lower rating. AE BC EFT MC VI.
B&B's/Guest Houses
★★★☆ **Mailcoach Guest House**, (GH), 200 Maybe St, 500m S of PO,
☎ 02 6458 3721, fax 02 6458 3500, 3 rms [shwr, tlt, elec blkts, clock radio], ldry, lounge (TV), conv fac, ✉ (BYO), t/c mkg shared, ✆. **BLB** ♦♦ **$62.50**, BC EFT MC VI.

BONNY HILLS NSW 2445

Pop 1,450. (387km N Sydney), See map on page 54, ref C7. Coastal town just north of Laurieton and a popular holiday spot for fishing, swimming and surfing. Boating, Bowls, Bush Walking, Fishing, Scenic Drives, Surfing, Swimming, Tennis.
Self Catering Accommodation
★★★☆ **The Beach House**, (HU), 949 Ocean Dve, 100m S of surf club,
☎ 02 9387 2112, fax 02 9387 2112, 1 unit acc up to 8, [shwr (2), bath, tlt (2), hairdry, fan, heat, elec blkts, tel, TV, video, clock radio, CD, refrig, cook fac, micro, elec frypan, d/wash, toaster, ldry, linen reqd-fee], w/mach, iron, bbq, c/park (garage), cots. **W** **$595 - $1,090**, Min book applies.
B&B's/Guest Houses
★★★ **Beach Breakers (Upstairs)**, (B&B), 15 Beach St (upstairs),
☎ 02 6585 5552, fax 02 6584 8817, 1 rm (2 bedrm), [shwr, tlt, heat, fan, tel, TV, video, clock radio, t/c mkg, refrig, cook fac ltd, micro, ldry, doonas], ✗, bbq, cots, non smoking property, Pets on application. **BLB** ♦ **$60 - $80**, ♦♦ **$90 - $150**, ♦ **$10 - $15**, Min book Christmas Jan and Easter.

BONVILLE NSW 2441

Pop Nominal, (543km N Sydney), See map on page 54, ref D5. Service centre on the Pacific Highway, not far from Coffs Harbour and Sawtell, which is probably best known for its golf course. Fishing, Swimming.
Hotels/Motels
★★★☆ **Bonville International Golf Resort**, (LMH), North Bonville Rd, 11km S of Coffs Harbour, ☎ 02 6653 4002, fax 02 6653 4005, 30 units (13 suites) [shwr, bath (11), spa bath (8), tlt, hairdry, a/c, cent heat, tel, TV, clock radio, t/c mkg, refrig, mini bar], ldry, iron, iron brd, conf fac, ✉, pool, spa, bbq, courtesy transfer, ✆, plygr, tennis (3), cots. **RO** ♦ **$110 - $132**, ♦♦ **$132 - $176**, ♦ **$22**, Suite D ♦ **$132 - $154**, ♦♦ **$154 - $176**, ♦ **$22**, AE BC DC MC VI.
B&B's/Guest Houses
★★★★ **The Range**, (GH), 240 Crossmaglen Rd, ☎ 02 6653 4900, fax 02 6653 4900, 5 rms [shwr, bath (2), tlt, hairdry, c/fan, elec blkts, clock radio, refrig], ldry, rec rm, lounge (TV), lounge firepl, ✗, t/c mkg shared, non smoking property. **BB** ♦ **$90**, ♦♦ **$80 - $130**, **W** **$500 - $750**.

★★★☆ **Sunny Hill**, (B&B), 284 North Bonville Rd, 3km NW of PO,
☎ 02 6653 4422, fax 02 6653 4417, 3 rms [heat, fan, heat, elec blkts, video, clock radio, t/c mkg, cook fac ltd, ldry, doonas], w/mach, dryer, TV rm, pool-heated, bbq, non smoking property. **BB** ♦ **$90**, ♦♦ **$140 - $160**, AE BC MC VI.

BOORAL NSW 2425

Pop Nominal, See map on page 54, ref A8. Historic village on the Karuah River south of Stroud on the Bucketts Way.
B&B's/Guest Houses
Gundaine Forge, (GH), (Farm), River Rd, The Branch, 15km SE of Booral, ☎ 02 4997 6623, fax 02 4997 6623, 2 rms [shwr, tlt, c/fan, heat, tel, clock radio, t/c mkg, refrig], lounge (TV), ✗, courtesy transfer, non smoking rms (2). **BB** ♦ **$40 - $50**, ♦♦ **$75 - $100**, ♦ **$25 - $40**, **D** all meals ♦ **$70 - $90**, ♦♦ **$130 - $175**, fam con, pen con, (not yet classified).

BOOROWA NSW 2586

Pop 1,100. (348km SW Sydney), See map on pages 52/53, ref G6. Pretty town on the Boorowa River that services the surrounding pastoral, mainly wool growing region. Fishing, Golf, Swimming, Tennis.

Hotels/Motels

★★☆ **Boorowa Blue Metal Motel**, (M), 65 Queen St, 100m E of PO, ☎ 02 6385 3186, fax 02 6385 3921, 10 units [shwr, tlt, a/c (10), elec blkts, clock radio, t/c mkg, refrig, toaster], ldry, dryer, iron, bbq, rm serv, cots. **RO** ‡ $45 - $50, ‡‡ $57 - $66, ‡‡‡ $69 - $78, ◊ $10, AE BC EFT MC VI.

B&B's/Guest Houses

★★★☆ **Old School Bed & Breakfast**, (B&B), Yass St, Rye Park, 20km SE of Boorowa, ☎ 02 4845 1230, or 02 6227 2243, fax 02 4845 1260, 2 rms (2 suites) [shwr (3), bath (1), tlt (3), a/c (2), heat, elec blkts, tel], ldry, dryer, iron, lounge (4), ✕, t/c mkg shared, bbq, c/park. **BB** ‡ $90, ‡‡ $130, ◊ $40, **DBB** ‡ $135, ‡‡ $220, ch con, BC MC VI.

BOURKE NSW 2840

Pop 2,800. (780km W Sydney), See map on pages 52/53, ref E2. Historic outback port on the Darling River. Bowls, Fishing, Golf, Shooting, Swimming, Tennis.

Hotels/Motels

★★★☆ **Darling River Motel**, (M), 74 Mitchell St, 1km E of PO, ☎ 02 6872 2288, fax 02 6872 3288, 29 units [shwr, tlt, hairdry, a/c, heat, elec blkts, tel, TV, video, clock radio, t/c mkg, refrig, cook fac (3)], ldry, pool (salt water), spa, bbq, cots. **RO** ‡ $49 - $70, ‡‡ $62 - $83, ‡‡‡ $96, ◊ $13, 10 units ★★★★, 9 units ★★☆. AE BC DC EFT MC VI, 👶.

★★★ **Bourke Riverside Motel**, (M), 3 Mitchell St, 300m W of PO, ☎ 02 6872 2539, fax 02 6872 1471, 14 units (3 suites) [shwr, bath (3), tlt, a/c-cool (14), heat, elec blkts, TV, clock radio, t/c mkg, refrig, cook fac (3)], ldry, conf fac, breakfast rm, pool, bbq, courtesy transfer, tennis, cots-fee, non smoking units (5). **RO** ‡ $49.50 - $82.50, ‡‡ $55 - $82.50, ◊ $16.50, ch con, Dinner by arrangement, AE BC DC MC VI,

Operator Comment: With over 1 Ha spacious shady gardens this recently refurbished historic icon now offers new standards in country comfort. With deluxe heritage suites and the very comfortable budget accommodation. Why would you stay anywhere else!

★★☆ **The Outback Motel**, (M), 33 Mertin St, 100m S of PO, ☎ 02 6872 2716, fax 02 6872 2716, 13 units [shwr, tlt, a/c-cool, heat, TV, clock radio, t/c mkg, refrig], ldry, bbq. **RO** ‡ $50 - $60, ◊ $11, ch con, AE BC DC MC VI.

★☆ **The Port of Bourke Hotel**, (LH), 32 Mitchell St, 50m fr PO, ☎ 02 6872 2544, (2 stry), 17 rms [bath (7), a/c, heat], ldry, lounge (TV), cots. **RO** ‡ $34.10, ‡‡ $50.60 - $57.20, ‡‡‡ $61.60, ◊ $5.00. BC EFT MC VI.

Major Mitchell Motel, (M), 44 Mertin St (Mitchell Hwy), 200m fr PO, ☎ 02 6872 2311, fax 02 6872 2205, 16 units [shwr, spa bath (1), tlt, hairdry, a/c, elec blkts, tel, TV, video-fee, clock radio, t/c mkg, refrig, mini bar], ldry, pool (salt water), bbq, cots, non smoking rms (9). **RO** ‡ $72.60 - $123, ‡‡ $84.70 - $123, ◊ $16.50, ch con, 4 units of a higher standard. AE BC DC EFT MC VI, (Rating under review).

Self Catering Accommodation

★★★ **Bourke Cottage Accommodation**, (Cotg), 49 Hope St, 500m S of PO, ☎ 02 6872 2837, fax 02 6872 2837, 1 cotg acc up to 7, [shwr, bath, tlt, a/c-cool, a/c, c/fan, heat, elec blkts, TV, video, clock radio, CD, t/c mkg, refrig, cook fac, micro, toaster, blkts, linen, pillows], w/mach, iron, bbq, c/park (carport). **D** ‡‡ $70, ◊ $10, **W** ‡‡ $365, ◊ $70, Keys at 51 Hope St.

★ **Nulty Holiday**, (Cotg), Nulty Station, 45km W of PO, ☎ 02 6872 3163, 1 cotg acc up to 9, (3 bedrm), [shwr, bath, tlt, heat, TV, refrig, cook fac, ldry, linen reqd], bbq. **D** $80, **W** $450.

BOWRAL NSW 2576

Pop 8,700. (115km SW Sydney), See map on page 55, ref B4. Commercial centre of the Southern Highlands, famous for the Tulip Time Festival held in September. Bush Walking, Golf, Horse Riding, Swimming, Tennis. See also Welby.

Hotels/Motels

★★★★ **Briars Country Lodge**, (M), Moss Vale Rd, 5km S of PO, ☎ 02 4868 3566, fax 02 4868 3223, 30 units [shwr, bath, tlt, hairdry, a/c-cool, cent heat, tel, cable tv, clock radio, t/c mkg, refrig], ldry, iron, iron brd, lounge, conv fac, ✕, pool-heated, plygr, tennis, cots. **RO** ‡ $165 - $220, ‡‡ $165 - $220, ◊ $17.50, AE BC DC MC VI.

★★★★ **Grand Mercure Hotel Bowral Heritage Park**, (LH), 9 Kangaloon Rd, 1km S of PO, ☎ 02 4861 4833, fax 02 4861 4966, (2 stry gr fl), 82 rms (56 suites) [shwr, spa bath, tlt, c/fan, fire pl (56), heat, tel, cable tv, video (56), clock radio, CD, t/c mkg, refrig, mini bar], ldry, iron, iron brd, conv fac, ✕, pool indoor heated, sauna, spa, steam rm, 24hr reception, rm serv, plygr, bicycle, gym, squash, tennis (2), cots, non smoking rms. **RO** ‡‡ $190 - $290, **Suite D** $230 - $630, ch con, Min book applies, AE BC DC EFT JCB MC VI.

★★★★ **Manning Hotel**, (M), Kangaloon Rd, 1km S of PO, opposite golf club, ☎ 02 4861 2300, fax 02 4861 2328, 16 units [ensuite, shwr, tlt, hairdry, a/c, c/fan, heat, elec blkts, tel, TV, t/c mkg, refrig], bar (Brasserie - 7 days). **RO** ‡ $100 - $115, ‡‡ $115 - $150, ◊ $20, AE BC DC EFT MC VI.

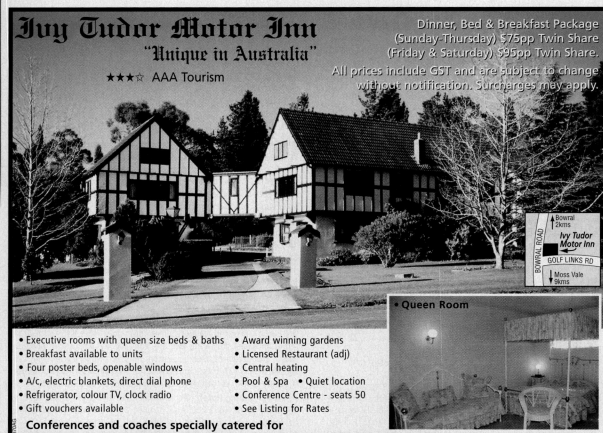

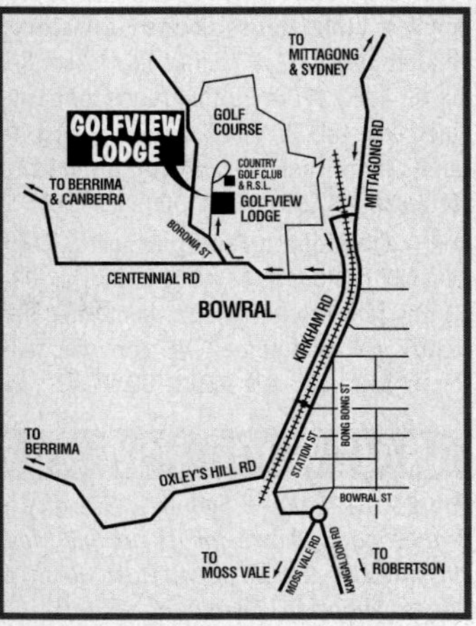

★★★☆ **Golf View Lodge**, (M), Boronia St, 1.5km NW of PO, ☎ 02 4861 2777, fax 02 4861 4863, (2 stry gr fl), 28 units (4 suites) [shwr, bath (1), spa bath (5), tlt, a/c, elec blkts, tel, TV, clock radio, t/c mkg, refrig, micro, toaster], ldry, conv fac, pool, bbq, tennis. **RO 👤👤 $88 - $135, Suite RO 👤👤 $145 - $155**, Min book long w/ends, BC MC VI.

AAA TOURISM Special Rates ★★★☆ **Ivy Tudor Motor Inn**, (M), Cnr Moss Vale & Links Rds, 1.5km S of PO, ☎ 02 4861 2911, fax 02 4861 4066, (2 stry gr fl), 32 units [shwr, bath (5), tlt, a/c-cool, cent heat, elec blkts, tel, TV, clock radio, t/c mkg, refrig, toaster], conf fac, ✕, pool, spa, bbq, cots-fee, non smoking units (15). **RO 👤 $69.50 - $82.50, 👤 $15**, ch con, Min book applies, AE BC DC EFT MC VI.

★★★☆ **Oxley View Motel**, (M), 535 Moss Vale Rd, 2km S of PO, ☎ 02 4861 4211, fax 02 4861 4211, 28 units [shwr, spa bath (11), tlt, hairdry (11), a/c, elec blkts, tel, TV, video (11), clock radio, t/c mkg, refrig], pool-heated (solar/ open summer), cots-fee. **RO 👤 $75 - $175, 👤👤 $75 - $180, 👤👤👤 $90 - $190**, AE BC DC EFT MC VI.

★★★ **Port O Call Motor Inn**, (M), Cnr Bong Bong & Bundaroo Sts, 100m N of PO, ☎ 02 4861 1779, fax 02 4861 1063, 20 units [shwr, tlt, fan, heat, elec blkts, tel, TV, clock radio, t/c mkg, refrig, toaster], ☒, cots-fee. **RO 👤 $55 - $93.50, 👤👤 $55 - $104.50, 👤 $11**, AE BC EFT MC VI.

Self Catering Accommodation

★★★☆ **Boronia Lodge Apartment Motel**, (SA), Boronia St, 1km NW of PO, ☎ 02 4861 1860, fax 02 4861 3667, 8 serv apts acc up to 5, [shwr, bath (2), tlt, hairdry, c/fan, heat, elec blkts, tel, TV, clock radio, t/c mkg, refrig, cook fac, micro, d/wash (5), ldry], bbq, c/park (undercover), cots, non smoking units (avail). **D 👤 $77 - $132, 👤👤 $82.50 - $132, 👤 $25, W 👤 $495 - $715, 👤👤 $495 - $715, 👤 $55**, ch con, Min book applies, BC MC VI.

Yellow House of Alderley Edge, (Cotg), (Farm), No children's facilities, Orchard Rd, 1km W of railway station, ☎ 02 4861 5750, fax 02 4861 5750, 1 cotg acc up to 2, [shwr, bath, tlt, hairdry, a/c, fire pl, cent heat, elec blkts, TV, video, clock radio, t/c mkg, refrig, cook fac, micro, toaster, doonas, linen], iron, iron brd, non smoking property. **D 👤👤 $420, W 👤👤 $900**, Min book applies, (not yet classified).

B&B's/Guest Houses

★★★★☆ **Byways Country House**, (B&B), Hamilton Ave, 1km NE of PO, ☎ 02 4861 3573, fax 02 4861 3573, 2 rms (1 suite) [shwr, bath (1), tlt, hairdry, cent heat, elec blkts, tel, TV (1), video (1), radio (1)], lounge firepl, t/c mkg shared, non smoking rms. **BB 👤👤 $100 - $150, Suite BB 👤👤 $130 - $170**, BC MC VI.

★★★★ **Berida Manor Country Resort**, (GH), 6 David St, 1km S of PO, ☎ 02 4861 1177, fax 02 4861 1219, (2 stry gr fl), 39 rms (16 suites) [shwr, tlt, a/c (10), heat, tel, TV, clock radio, t/c mkg, refrig], lounge (TV), conv fac, ☒, bar, pool indoor heated, sauna, spa, bicycle. **BB 👤 $116 - $138, 👤👤 $138 - $198, 👤👤👤 $171 - $231, 👤 $33 - $55, DBB 👤👤 $198 - $275, Suite BB 👤👤 $204 - $248, Suite DBB 👤👤 $259 - $325**, AE BC DC MC VI.

★★★★ **Glendale B&B**, (B&B), (Farm), Cnr Kangaloon & Sheepwash Rds, 9km SE of PO, ☎02 4887 1350, fax 02 4887 1350, 2 rms [shwr, bath, tlt, hairdry, fan, fire pl, cent heat, tel, TV, video, CD, t/c mkg, refrig, cook fac ltd, micro, toaster, pillows], dryer, iron, bbq, cots. **D $165 - $396**, Min book applies, BC MC VI.

BOWRAL NSW continued...

★★★★ **Links House Country Guesthouse**, (GH), No facilities for children under 12, 17 Links Rd, 1.5km S of PO, ☎ 02 4861 1977, fax 02 4862 1706, 15 rms [ensuite, bath (1), hairdry, cent heat, elec blkts, tel, TV, clock radio, t/c mkg, refrig], conv fac, lounge firepl, tennis, non smoking property. **BB ♦ $110 - $330, ♦♦ $132 - $330, ♦♦♦ $176 - $450**, AE BC DC EFT MC VI.

★★☆ **Craigieburn Family Resort & Conf Centre**, (GH), Centennial Rd, 2km NW of PO, ☎ 02 4861 1277, fax 02 4862 1690, (Multi-stry gr fl), 63 rms [shwr, bath (8), tlt, heat, elec blkts, clock radio, t/c mkg, refrig], rec rm, lounge (TV), conv fac, ☒, bbq, ✆, golf (9 hole), tennis (2), cots. **D ♦ $192**, BC MC VI.

BRAIDWOOD NSW 2622

Pop 950. (291km S Sydney), See map on page 55, ref A5. Braidwood is known for its art galleries, antiques and crafts and is classified by the National Trust. Bush Walking, Fishing, Golf, Scenic Drives, Shooting, Swimming, Tennis.

Hotels/Motels

★★☆ **Braidwood Cedar Lodge**, (M), Duncan St, 200m S of PO, ☎ 02 4842 2244, 10 units [shwr, tlt, fan, heat, elec blkts, TV, clock radio, t/c mkg, refrig, toaster], bbq, cots. **RO ♦ $53 - $58, ♦♦ $65 - $70, ♦ $13.20**, ch con, BC MC VI.

★★☆ **Braidwood Colonial Motel**, (M), 199 Wallace St, 500m N of PO, ☎ 02 4842 2027, fax 02 4842 2940, 10 units [shwr, tlt, hairdry, fan, heat, elec blkts, TV, video (avail), t/c mkg, refrig, toaster], ldry, iron, iron brd, bbq, cots-fee. **RO ♦ $60 - $77, ♦♦ $77, ♦ $11**, ch con, AE BC MC VI, ⚹⚹.

Torpy's Guest House & Motel, (M), Previously Torpys Motel 18 McKellar St, 500m N of PO, ☎ 02 4842 2551, fax 02 4842 2562, 6 units [shwr, tlt, fan, heat, elec blkts, TV, clock radio, t/c mkg, refrig, toaster], ldry, conv fac, ☒ (Thu to Mon), dinner to unit, cots-fee. **BLB ♦ $60, ♦♦ $75 - $85, ♦♦♦ $85 - $95, ♦ $15**, ch con, AE BC DC MC VI.

★★★☆ **(Bed & Breakfast Section)**, c1850, 4 rms (2 suites) [shwr, bath (1), tlt, cent heat, elec blkts, tel, t/c mkg], lounge (TV). **BB ♦ $80, ♦♦ $110 - $130.**

B&B's/Guest Houses

★★★★ **Settlers Flat Lodge Guest House**, (GH), No children's facilities, 112 Charleys Forest Rd Mongarlowe via, 13km E of PO, ☎ 02 4842 8085, fax 02 4842 8003, 7 rms [shwr, tlt, c/fan, cent heat, elec blkts, fax], lounge (TV), ✕, spa, t/c mkg shared, tennis. **BB ♦ $90 - $110, ♦♦ $160 - $200, DBB ♦ $110 - $130, ♦♦ $200 - $240**, BC MC VI.

★★★☆ **Doncaster Inn Guest House**, (GH), 1 Wilson St, ☎ 02 4842 2356, fax 02 4842 2521, (2 stry), 12 rms [fire pl, cent heat, tel], shared fac (7 rms), rec rm, lounge (TV), conv fac, ✕, t/c mkg shared. **BB ♦ $80 - $120, ♦♦ $130 - $160**, Min book long w/ends and Easter, AE BC MC VI.

★★★☆ **Rosewarne Cottage**, (B&B), Little River Rd, 12km E of PO, ☎ 02 4842 8145, fax 02 4842 8145, 2 rms [shwr, tlt, elec blkts], lounge firepl, t/c mkg shared, refrig, non smoking property. **BB ♦ $90, ♦♦ $120.**

Curraweena Lavender Farm, (B&B), Kings Hwy, 6km N of PO, ☎ 02 4842 2800, fax 02 4842 2800, 2 rms (2 suites) [shwr, bath, tlt, hairdry, fan, heat, elec blkts, tel, TV, clock radio, t/c mkg], ldry, iron, iron brd, bbq, non smoking rms. **BB ♦ $75, ♦♦ $110**, (not yet classified).

Sharing the roads - Trucks and cars

Trucks are different from cars. They take up more road space than cars, especially when turning, and are slower to accelerate, turn and reverse. Here are some hints in sharing our roads safely with trucks:

- Don't cut in on trucks. Because trucks need a greater braking distance than cars, truck drivers leave more space in front of them when approaching a red light or stop sign than a car.
- Allow extra time and space to overtake trucks. You will need about 1.5 kilometres of clear road space to pass a truck.
- Don't pass a left-turning truck on the inside. Trucks sometimes need more than one lane to turn tight corners, so watch for a truck swinging out near intersections.
- Be patient - follow at a safe distance. Truck drivers may not see you because of blind spots, particularly if you travel right behind them.

BRANXTON HOUSE MOTEL
AAA TOURISM ★★★☆ Rated

☎**(02) 4938 3099**

New England Highway, BRANXTON 2335

Situated in the centre of Branxton in the heart of The Hunter Valley. Central to Wyndham Estate Winery and Polkolbin- 5 mins. to Balloon Aloft . Vineyard tours arranged. Mid week special rates available.
Quite rooms, double brick with double glazed windows

Facilities include:
- Spacious Air Cond. Units
- Next to Tennis Court
- Queen Size Beds
- FREE In-House Movies

☆ **NEW MOTEL**
☆ **RURAL VIEWS**

BRANXTON NSW 2335

Pop 3,750. (174km N Sydney), See map on pages 52/53, ref J4. Historic town near the Hunter Valley wineries. Vineyards, Wineries.

Hotels/Motels

★★★☆ **Branxton House Motel**, (M), 69 Maitland Rd, ☎ 02 4938 3099, fax 02 4938 3104, 13 units [shwr, tlt, hairdry, a/c, c/fan, elec blkts, tel, TV, movie, clock radio, t/c mkg, refrig, toaster], ldry, iron, iron brd, cots-fee, non smoking units (5). **RO ♦ $55 - $95, ♦♦ $65 - $95, ♦ $10 - $15**, AE BC DC MC VI,
Operator Comment: Hunter Valley, Affordable Luxury.

B&B's/Guest Houses

★★★★☆ **Leconfield House**, (B&B), No children's facilities, 394 Dalwood Rd, 4km E of PO, ☎ 02 4938 1524, fax 02 4938 1524, 4 rms [ensuite, c/fan, elec blkts, t/c mkg, refrig], lounge (TV), non smoking units (avail). **BB ♦ $90 - $170, ♦♦ $110 - $195, ♦ $20 - $30**, BC MC VI.

BREWARRINA NSW 2839

Pop 1,100. (807km W Sydney), See map on pages 52/53, ref F2. The old river port of Brewarrina lies on the Barwon River, in an area rich in Aboriginal heritage and significance. Bowls, Fishing, Golf, Shooting, Swimming, Tennis.

Hotels/Motels

★★☆ **The Aboriginal Fisheries Motel**, (M), Previously Swancrest Motel Cnr Doyle & Sandon Sts, ☎ 02 6839 2397, 12 units [shwr, tlt, a/c, tel, TV, clock radio, t/c mkg, refrig]. **RO ♦ $55, ♦♦ $65, $70**, BC MC VI.

BREWONGLE NSW 2795

Pop Nominal, (188km W Sydney), See map on page 55, ref A2. Small village nestled in the picturesque Fish River valley between Bathurst and Lithgow.

Self Catering Accommodation

Adelong Park, (House), (Farm), Brewongle La, ☎ 02 6337 5562, fax 02 6337 5562, 1 house acc up to 10, [shwr (3), bath (1), spa bath (1), tlt (3), fan, elec blkts, tel, TV, video, clock radio, t/c mkg, refrig, cook fac, micro, elec frypan, d/wash, toaster, ldry, blkts, linen], w/mach, dryer, iron, iron brd, lounge firepl, bbq, canoeing, tennis, non smoking property. **D ♦♦ $120**, ch con, fam con, (not yet classified).

BROGO NSW 2550

Pop Nominal, (414km S Sydney), See map on page 55, ref A7. The gateway to Wadbilliga National Park, 25km N Bega. Bush Walking.

B&B's/Guest Houses

Bega Country B&B, (B&B), 624 Warrigal Range Rd, ☎ 02 6492 7205, fax 02 6492 7131, (2 stry), 2 rms [fan, heat, elec blkts, tel, clock radio, t/c mkg], ldry, lounge firepl, ✗, Pets on application. **BB ♦ $75 - $90, ♦♦ $95 - $120, ♦ $30 - $40, DBB ♦ $95 - $110, ♦♦ $135 - $160, ♦ $50 - $60,** ch con, fam con, pen con, BC MC VI, (not yet classified).

BROKE NSW 2330

Pop 300. (194km N Sydney), See map on page 55, ref C1. Pretty village on Wollombi Brook, off the beaten tourist trail yet still handy for exploring the Hunter Valley wineries.

Self Catering Accommodation

★★★ **Fordwich Olive Farm**, (Cotg), (Farm), 203 Fordwich Rd, 7km N of PO, ☎ 02 6579 1179, fax 02 6579 1256, 2 cotgs acc up to 8, [shwr, tlt, a/c, c/fan, radio, t/c mkg, refrig, cook fac, micro, toaster, blkts, linen, pillows], bbq, c/park. **BB ♦♦ $132, ♦ $33,** Min book applies, BC MC VI.

Elysium Vineyard Cottage, (Cotg), 393 Milbrodale Rd, 9km W of PO, ☎ 02 9664 2368, fax 02 9664 2368, 1 cotg acc up to 14, [shwr, bath, tlt, c/fan, elec blkts, TV, video, t/c mkg, refrig, cook fac, micro, elec frypan, toaster, linen reqd], iron, iron brd, TV rm, lounge firepl, pool, spa, bbq, c/park. **D ♦♦ $100 - $250, ♦ $50,** ch con, (not yet classified).

Monkey Place Country House, (House), 69 Wollombi St, 1.5km N of Village, ☎ 02 9713 2219, fax 02 9713 2136, 1 house acc up to 12, [shwr (2), bath, tlt (2), c/fan, fire pl, heat, tel, TV, video, t/c mkg, refrig, cook fac, micro, toaster, blkts, linen], w/mach, iron, iron brd, bbq, cots, non smoking property. **D ♦♦♦♦ $180 - $280, ♦ $45 - $70,** ch con, Min book applies, BC MC VI, (not yet classified).

B&B's/Guest Houses

★★★★★ **Green Gables Lodge**, (B&B), 558 Milbrodale Rd, 7.5km W of PO, ☎ 02 6579 1258, fax 02 6579 1258, (2 stry), 3 rms [shwr, tlt, hairdry, cent heat, TV, clock radio, t/c mkg, refrig], ldry, lounge firepl, spa, bbq. **BB ♦ $100, ♦♦ $185,** Helipad available. MC VI,

Operator Comment: Website: www.greengableslodge.com.au

BROKEN HILL NSW 2880

Pop 21,000. 23,500 approx, (1160km W Sydney), See map on pages 52/53, ref A3. Broken Hill is the mighty 'Silver City', queen of the New South Wales mining towns. Art Gallery, Bowls, Golf, Horse Racing, Scenic Drives, Squash, Swimming, Tennis.

Hotels/Motels

★★★★ **The Gateway Motor Inn**, (M), 201 Galena St, ☎ 08 8088 7013, fax 08 8087 0111, 12 units [shwr, spa bath (2), tlt, hairdry, a/c, tel, TV, clock radio, t/c mkg, refrig, toaster], ldry, pool-heated (solar, salt water), courtesy transfer, cots, non smoking units (6). **RO ♦ $80, ♦♦ $88, ♦ $10,** pen con, AE BC DC EFT MC VI.

 ★★★☆ **A Broken Hill Overlander Motor Inn**, (M), 142 Iodide St, ☎ 08 8088 2566, fax 08 8088 4377, 15 units [shwr, tlt, a/c, elec blkts, tel, TV, video, clock radio, t/c mkg, refrig, toaster], ldry, pool, sauna, spa, bbq, dinner to unit, cots. **RO ♦ $96, ♦♦ $82 - $105, ♦ $10,** ch con, 5 units of a higher standard, AE BC DC JCB MC MP VI, ⚲.

★★★☆ **Charles Rasp Motor Inn**, (M), 158 Oxide St, ☎ 08 8088 1988, fax 08 8088 4633, 20 units (3 suites) [shwr, spa bath (3), tlt, a/c, elec blkts, tel, TV, video-fee, clock radio, t/c mkg, refrig, toaster], ldry-fee, pool (salt water), spa, bbq, rm serv, cots-fee, non smoking units (2). **RO ♦ $82 - $96, ♦♦ $93 - $107, ♦ $12 - $15,** 8 units ★★★★. AE BC DC EFT MC VI.

 ★★★☆ **Crystal Motel**, (M), 326 Crystal St, ☎ 08 8088 2344, fax 08 8088 1887, 36 units [shwr, tlt, a/c, tel, TV, clock radio, t/c mkg, refrig, mini bar], ldry, conv fac, ✗, rm serv. **RO ♦ $70 - $145, ♦♦ $79 - $145, ♦ $15,** 5 units ★★★★. AE BC DC EFT MC VI.

 ★★★☆ **Hilltop Motor Inn**, (M), 271 Kaolin St, ☎ 08 8088 2999, fax 08 8088 4604, 29 units [shwr, tlt, hairdry, a/c, elec blkts, tel, TV, video, clock radio, t/c mkg, refrig, mini bar], ldry, w/mach, dryer, iron, iron brd, ✗, pool-heated, bbq, rm serv, cots, non smoking rms. **RO ♦ $90, ♦♦ $90, ♦ $12,** ch con, pen con, AE BC DC EFT MC MP VI.

★★★☆ **Mine Host Motel**, (M), 120 Argent St, ☎ 08 8088 4044, fax 08 8088 1313, (2 stry), 42 units [shwr, tlt, a/c, elec blkts, tel, TV, video-fee, clock radio, t/c mkg, refrig], ldry, pool, bbq, cots. **RO** ♦♦ **$88**, ◊ **$10**, ch con, 10 units ★★★. AE BC DC EFT MC VI.

★★★☆ **Old Willyama Motel**, (M), 30 Iodide St, ☎ 08 8088 3355, fax 08 8088 3956, (2 stry gr fl), 29 units (1 suite) [shwr, tlt, a/c, elec blkts, tel, TV, video-fee, clock radio, t/c mkg, refrig, mini bar], ⊠, pool, spa, bbq, rm serv, cots. **Suite RO** ♦ **$83 - $89**, ch con, 14 units ★★★☆. AE BC DC EFT MC VI, ৬.

★★★☆ **Silver Haven Motor Inn**, (M), 577 Argent St, ☎ 08 8087 2218, fax 08 8088 4494, 31 units [shwr, tlt, a/c, elec blkts, tel, TV, video, movie, clock radio, t/c mkg, refrig, toaster (6)], ldry, ⊠, pool-heated (solar), rm serv, cots. **RO** ♦ **$75 - $79**, ♦♦ **$79 - $84**, ♦♦♦ **$94 - $99**, ◊ **$15**, ch con, 10 units ★★☆. AE BC DC EFT MC VI.

★★★ **Annexe Motel**, (M), 76 Argent St, 500m W of PO, ☎ 08 8087 8495, fax 08 8088 5873, (2 stry), 8 units [shwr, tlt, a/c, elec blkts, TV, clock radio, t/c mkg, refrig], ✎, cots, non smoking rms (2). **RO** ♦ **$50 - $60**, ♦♦ **$55 - $65**, ♦♦♦ **$70 - $80**, AE BC DC MC MCH MP VI, ৬.

★★★ **Daydream Motel**, (M), 77 Argent St, ☎ 08 8088 3033, fax 08 8088 5873, 12 units [shwr, tlt, a/c, elec blkts, tel, TV, clock radio, t/c mkg, refrig], lounge, pool, bbq, rm serv (breakfast), non smoking units (6). **D** **$67 - $72**, **RO** ♦ **$57**, ♦♦ **$62**, ch con, AE BC DC EFT MC MCH MP VI.

★★★ **Silver Spade Hotel Motel**, (LMH), 151 Argent St, ☎ 08 8087 7021, fax 08 8088 1720, 14 units (1 suite) [shwr, tlt, a/c, elec blkts, tel, TV, video-fee, clock radio, t/c mkg, refrig, mini bar, micro (4), toaster], ldry, rec rm, lounge (TV), ⊠, pool, bbq, rm serv, plygr, cots-fee, non smoking units (2). **RO** ♦ **$52 - $55**, ♦♦ **$58 - $64**, ♦♦♦ **$64 - $72**, ◊ **$6 - $10**, **Suite D $64**, ch con, pen con, 3 units ★★★☆. AE BC DC EFT MC VI.

★★★ **Sturt Motel**, (M), 153 Rakow St, 4km W of PO, ☎ 08 8087 3558, fax 08 8087 3872, 19 units [shwr, tlt, a/c, elec blkts, TV, clock radio, t/c mkg, refrig, toaster], ldry, pool, bbq, cots-fee, non smoking units (7). **RO** ♦ **$48 - $54**, ♦♦ **$54 - $61**, ◊ **$9**, fam con, AE BC EFT MC MCH VI.

★★★ **(Cabin Section)**, 2 cabins acc up to 3, [a/c, elec blkts, TV, clock radio, refrig, cook fac, micro, toaster, blkts, linen, pillows], non smoking units. **D $53**, ♦♦ **$61**, ◊ **$9**.

★★★ **The Lodge Outback Motel**, (M), 252 Mica St, 500m N of PO, ☎ 08 8088 2722, fax 08 8088 2636, 22 units [shwr, bath (1), tlt, a/c, c/fan, elec blkts, tel, TV, video, clock radio, t/c mkg, refrig, toaster], ldry, pool (salt water), bbq, rm serv, cots, non smoking units (5). **RO** ♦ **$61 - $66**, ♦♦ **$61 - $72**, ◊ **$11**, **W $400 - $510**, ch con, fam con, AE BC DC EFT MC MP VI.

★★☆ **(Cottage Section)**, 1 cotg acc up to 6, [shwr, bath, spa bath, tlt, hairdry, evap cool, c/fan, heat, elec blkts, tel, TV, clock radio, t/c mkg, refrig, cook fac, micro, elec frypan, toaster, blkts, linen], w/mach, dryer, iron, iron brd, spa, cots. **D $88 - $143**, **W $550 - $990**.

★★☆ **Miners Lamp Motor Inn**, (M), Cnr Oxide & Cobalt Sts, ☎ 08 8088 4122, fax 08 8088 4419, (2 stry gr fl), 32 units [shwr, tlt, a/c-cool (10), a/c (22), heat (10), tel, cable tv, video-fee, clock radio, t/c mkg, refrig, mini bar, cook fac (1)], ldry, ⊠, pool, bbq, rm serv, cots. **RO** ♦ **$81**, ♦♦ **$91 - $98**, ◊ **$12**, ch con, pen con, AE BC DC EFT MC VI.

★ **Royal Exchange Hotel**, (LH), 320 Argent St, 100m N of Railway Station, ☎ 08 8087 2308, fax 08 8087 2191, (2 stry), 24 rms [shwr (9), tlt (9), a/c, elec blkts, TV (9), clock radio, t/c mkg, refrig (9)], lounge (TV), ⊠ (Mon to Sat). **BLB** ♦ **$25 - $35**, ♦♦ **$45 - $55**, ◊ **$8**, 9 rooms ★☆. AE BC DC MC VI.

Theatre Royal Hotel, (LH), c1890. 347 Argent St, ☎ 08 8087 3318, fax 08 8087 3511, (2 stry), 12 rms [a/c-cool, heat (1), elec blkts, TV (2), t/c mkg, refrig (2)], lounge (TV), ✕. **RO** ♦ **$26**, ♦♦ **$38**, ◊ **$10**, weekly con.

West Darling Hotel, (LMH), 400 Argent St, ☎ 08 8087 2691, fax 08 8087 1963, 27 units [shwr (9), bath (3), tlt (8), a/c-cool, heat, t/c mkg, refrig (9)], shared fac (23), TV rm, lounge (TV), cots. **BLB** ♦ **$30**, ♦♦ **$48 - $55**, ♦♦♦ **$60 - $64**, **W $150 - $300**, 1 rm ★. AE BC DC EFT MC VI.

Self Catering Accommodation

★★★★ **Broken Hill Historic Cottages**, (Cotg), The Olde Shoppe, 174A Cobalt St, ☎ 08 8087 9966, 1 cotg acc up to 2, (1 bedrm), [shwr, tlt, evap cool, heat, elec blkts, TV, clock radio, t/c mkg, refrig, cook fac, micro, toaster, ldry, doonas, linen, pillows], w/mach, dryer, iron, iron brd, non smoking property. **D** ♦♦ **$88**, AE BC MC VI.

★★★★ **(174 Cobalt St Section)**, Larissa, 1 cotg acc up to 6, (2 bedrm), [shwr, tlt, evap cool, heat, elec blkts, tel, TV, clock radio, t/c mkg, refrig, cook fac, micro, toaster, doonas, linen, pillows], w/mach, iron, iron brd, non smoking property. **D** ♦♦ **$88**, ◊ **$12**.

★★★★ **(402 Chappel St Section)**, Rose, 1 cotg acc up to 4, (1 bedrm), [shwr, tlt, evap cool, heat, elec blkts, tel, TV, clock radio, t/c mkg, refrig, cook fac, micro, toaster, ldry, doonas, linen, pillows], w/mach, dryer, iron, iron brd, c/park (garage), non smoking property. **D** ♦♦ **$88**, ◊ **$12**.

Broken Hill Historic Cottages ...continued

★★★★ **(92 Cobalt St Section)**, Lavender, 1 cotg acc up to 4, (1 bedrm), [shwr, tlt, evap cool, heat, elec blkts, tel, TV, clock radio, t/c mkg, refrig, cook fac, micro, toaster, ldry, doonas, linen, pillows], w/mach, iron, iron brd, c/park (garage), non smoking property. **D 👥 $88, 🧒 $12.**

★★★☆ **(430 Lane St Section)**, Casuarina, 1 cotg acc up to 6, (2 bedrm), [shwr, tlt, evap cool, heat, elec blkts, tel, TV, clock radio, t/c mkg, refrig, cook fac, micro, toaster, ldry, doonas, linen, pillows], w/mach, iron, iron brd, c/park (garage), non smoking property. **D 👥 $88, 🧒 $12.**

(161 Wolfram St Section), Pine, 1 cotg acc up to 6, (2 bedrm), [shwr, tlt, evap cool, heat, elec blkts, tel, TV, clock radio, t/c mkg, refrig, cook fac, micro, toaster, doonas, linen, pillows], w/mach, iron, iron brd, c/park (garage), non smoking property. **D 👥 $88, 🧒 $12**, (not yet classified).

(331 William St Section), Bottlebrush, 1 cotg acc up to 3, (1 bedrm), [shwr, tlt, c/fan, heat, elec blkts, TV, clock radio, t/c mkg, refrig, cook fac, micro, toaster, ldry, doonas, linen, pillows], w/mach, iron, iron brd, c/park (garage), non smoking property. **D 👥 $88, 🧒 $12**, (not yet classified).

★★★★ **Mulberry Vale Cabins**, Menindee Rd, 5km E of PO, ☎ 08 8088 1597, fax 08 8087 2710, 10 cabins acc up to 6, [shwr, tlt, a/c, elec blkts, TV (4), clock radio, t/c mkg (4), refrig (4), cook fac, micro (4), toaster, blkts, linen, pillows], ldry, w/mach (4), dryer (4), iron (4), pool, bbq (4), c/park (carport) (4), cots. **D $66 - $77**, 4 cabins ★★★☆. BC MC VI.

★★★★ **Outback Villas**, (HU), 2-4 Tramway Tce, 2.3km W of PO, ☎ 08 8088 7528, fax 08 8088 7529, 4 units acc up to 4, (2 bedrm), [shwr, tlt, hairdry, a/c, fan, heat, elec blkts, TV (satellite), clock radio, t/c mkg, refrig, cook fac, micro, toaster, blkts, doonas, linen, pillows], ldry, iron, iron brd, bbq, cots-fee. **D 👥 $77, 🧒 $9, W 👥 $485, 🧒 $56**, ch con, pen con, AE BC DC EFT MC VI.

★★★★ **The Desert Siesta Villa**, (Cotg), 12 Nicholls St, 2.5km SW of PO, ☎ 08 8088 4422, fax 08 8087 8673, 1 cotg acc up to 6, [shwr, bath, tlt, hairdry, a/c, heat, TV, clock radio, t/c mkg, refrig, cook fac, micro, toaster, ldry, blkts, linen, pillows], w/mach, dryer, iron, iron brd, bbq, c/park. **D 👥 $80, 🧒 $10, W 👥 $500**, ch con, BC EFT MC VI.

★★★☆ **Broken Hill Miners Rest Cottage**, (Cotg), 104 Piper St, ☎ 08 8087 7082, fax 08 8087 4522, 1 cotg acc up to 5, [shwr, tlt, hairdry, a/c-cool, fan, heat, elec blkts, TV, clock radio (cassette), t/c mkg, refrig, cook fac, micro, elec frypan, toaster, ldry, blkts, linen, pillows], w/mach, iron, iron brd, spa, bbq, c/park. **D $80 - $100, W $450**, ch con.

★★★☆ **Tarrawingee Holiday Units**, (HU), 253 Wills St, 1.5km SW of PO, ☎ 08 8088 4152, fax 08 8087 9350, 12 units acc up to 6, [shwr, bath, spa bath (1), tlt, a/c-cool, heat, TV, clock radio, t/c mkg, refrig, cook fac, toaster, ldry, blkts, linen, pillows], w/mach, iron, iron brd, pool-heated (solar), bbq, c/park (undercover), 📞, cots. **D 👥 $88, 🧒 $15**, ch con, AE BC DC EFT MC VI.

★★★ **Hydrangea Cottage of Broken Hill**, (Cotg), 482 Argent St, 1km E of PO, ☎ 08 8088 4422, fax 08 8087 8673, 1 cotg acc up to 9, [shwr, tlt, a/c, heat, TV, clock radio, t/c mkg, micro, elec frypan, toaster, ldry, blkts, linen, pillows], w/mach, dryer, iron, iron brd, bbq, c/park. **D 👥 $80, 🧒 $10, W 👥 $500**, BC EFT MC VI.

★★★ **Old Miners Home**, 25 Blende St, 2km SW of GPO, ☎ 08 8087 8205, fax 08 8087 8205, 1 cabin acc up to 6, (3 bedrm), [shwr, tlt, a/c-cool, heat, TV, clock radio, t/c mkg, refrig, cook fac, micro, blkts, doonas, linen, pillows], cots, non smoking rms. **D 👥 $80, 🧒 $10**, ch con, weekly con.

★★☆ **Country Rest Holiday Unit**, (HU), 2/37 Bonanza St, 3km S of PO, ☎ 08 8088 5374, 1 unit acc up to 4, [shwr, bath, tlt, a/c, c/fan, TV, clock radio, refrig, cook fac, micro, toaster, ldry, blkts, linen], iron, iron brd, non smoking units. **D $72.50, W $380.**

Bonanza Holiday Cottage, (Cotg), 124 Piper St, 1km NW of South Broken Hill PO, ☎ 0407 275 513, 1 cotg acc up to 5, [shwr, bath, tlt, a/c-cool, heat, tel, TV, clock radio, t/c mkg, refrig, cook fac, micro, elec frypan, toaster, ldry, blkts, linen, pillows], w/mach, iron, iron brd, cots, breakfast ingredients (on request). **D 👤 $33, 👥 $55, 🧒 $11**, ch con, pen con, Min book applies, (not yet classified).

Ruby's Cottage, (Cotg), 517 Argent St, ☎ 08 8088 4422, fax 08 8087 8673, 1 cotg acc up to 6, [shwr, tlt, hairdry, evap cool, heat, TV, clock radio, t/c mkg, refrig, cook fac, micro, elec frypan, toaster, ldry, doonas, linen], w/mach, dryer, iron, iron brd. **D 👥 $90, 🧒 $10**, ch con, BC EFT MC VI, (not yet classified).

B&B's/Guest Houses

★★★★☆ **The Imperial Fine Accommodation**, (GH), No children's facilities, 88 Oxide St, 500m NE of PO, ☎ 08 8087 7444, fax 08 8087 7234, (2 stry gr fl), 5 rms [shwr, tlt, hairdry, a/c, elec blkts, tel, TV, clock radio, refrig], iron, iron brd, rec rm, lounge firepl, pool-heated (salt water), t/c mkg shared, non smoking property. **BB 👤 $149 - $165, 👥 $149 - $165, RO 👤 $132, 👥 $132**, AE BC DC MC VI.

★★★☆ **Grand Guesthouse**, (GH), 313 Argent St, ☎ 08 8087 5305, fax 08 8087 5305, (2 stry), 18 rms [ensuite (6), a/c, heat, elec blkts, TV, t/c mkg, ldry, doonas], lounge (TV), lounge firepl, bbq, c/park (limited), non smoking property. **D 👤 $54.50 - $64.50, 👥 $64.50 - $74.50, 🧒 $15**, 6 rooms ★★★★. BC MC VI.

★★★ **Old Vic Bed & Breakfast**, (B&B), c1891. No children's facilities, 230 Oxide St (Cnr Oxide & Chapple Sts), 1.25km N of PO, ☎ 08 8087 1169, 8 rms [fan, heat, doonas, pillows], lounge (TV), t/c mkg shared, refrig, bbq, c/park. **BLB 👤 $40, 👥 $50.**

★★☆ **The Old Friary**, (GH), 118 Murton St, 2.5km N of GPO, ☎ 08 8087 1700, or 08 8087 9546, fax 08 8087 1700, 10 rms [a/c], ldry-fee, rec rm, lounge (TV), cook fac, t/c mkg shared, refrig, bbq, courtesy transfer, 📞, cots-fee. **BLB 👤 $27.50, 👥 $44, 🧒 $11**, ch con, AE.

Other Accommodation

The Tourist Lodge Guest House, 100 Argent St, ☎ 08 8088 2086, fax 08 8087 9511, 28 rms [a/c (16), fan, heat (11)], ldry, rec rm, lounge (TV), pool-heated (solar), cook fac, t/c mkg shared, refrig, bbq, c/park (limited), cots. **RO 👤 $28, 👥 $42, 👤 $135 - $180, 👥 $200 - $235**, ch con, AE BC MC VI.

BROOKLYN NSW 2083

Pop 700. (52km N Sydney), See map on page 56, ref D3. Small settlement on the southern banks of the Hawkesbury River. Boating, Bush Walking, Fishing, Rock Climbing, Sailing, Scenic Drives, Swimming, Water Skiing.

Self Catering Accommodation

★★★☆ **Brooklyn on Hawkesbury Apartments**, (SA), 3/55a Brooklyn Rd, 2km W of Railway Station, ☎ 02 9985 7892, fax 02 9985 7892, (2 stry gr fl), 8 serv apts acc up to 6, [shwr, bath (6), tlt, hairdry, c/fan, heat, elec blkts, tel, TV, video, clock radio, t/c mkg, refrig, cook fac, micro, elec frypan, toaster, ldry, doonas, linen], w/mach, dryer, iron, iron brd, conf fac, pool (salt water), bbq, courtesy transfer, gym, tennis (half court), cots. **D 👥 $85 - $130, 🧒 $20, W 👥 $510 - $910**, AE MC VI.

★★☆ **Hawkesbury River Marina**, (HU), Dangar Rd, McKell Park, ☎ 02 9985 7858, fax 02 9985 7851, 5 units acc up to 6, [shwr, tlt, a/c, TV, clock radio, refrig, cook fac, micro, toaster, blkts, linen, pillows], iron, conv fac, ⊠, 📞. **BLB $130 - $240, W $770 - $1,260**, AE BC DC MC VI.

Take extra care on long weekends

Road crashes are an unfortunate part of long weekends but motorists can improve their chances of survival with just a few sensible precautions.

- Don't take a long trip if you can take a short one; spend time relaxing closer to home instead of driving.
- Have the car serviced in advance. Do-it-yourself checks can include tyres (including the spare), brakes, lights, indicators, wipers, horn and exhaust system.
- Load heavy luggage as low and near the centre of the car as practical, while ensuring that hard or sharp items cannot fly around in a crash, and avoid blocking the view through mirrors or windows.
- Plan your route to reduce both travel time and safety hazards - freeways are by far the safest roads, while minor roads carrying heavy holiday traffic are dangerous.
- To ensure a safe drive home, don't jump into your car straight after a day at the beach or after an afternoon of full activity. Allow yourself time to relax and unwind before preparing for the journey home.

BROULEE NSW 2537

Pop 1,389. Part of Batemans Bay, (306km S Sydney), See map on page 55, ref A6. Peaceful place on the shores of Broulee Bay which features beaches for surfers, windsurfers and swimmers of all abilities. Fishing, Scenic Drives, Surfing.

Self Catering Accommodation

★★★ **Broulee Holiday Inn**, (SA), 18 Imlay St, 250m S of PO,
☎ 02 4471 6266, fax 02 4471 6266, (2 stry gr fl), 11 serv apts [shwr, bath, spa bath (1), tlt, heat, elec blkts, TV, video-fee, clock radio, t/c mkg, refrig, cook fac, micro, elec frypan, toaster], ldry, rec rm, pool-heated (solar), bbq, rm serv, ✆, plygr, cots. **RO ♦ $60 - $90, ♦♦ $70 - $95, ♦♦♦ $75 - $100, ♦ $10 - $15, W ♦♦ $400 - $700,** Min book Christmas Jan and Easter, BC MC VI.

★★ **Caraluki Flats**, (HF), 8 Clarke St, ☎ 02 4471 6441, 4 flats acc up to 6, [shwr, tlt, heat, elec blkts, TV, clock radio, refrig, cook fac, micro, linen (Fee) reqd], ldry, bbq, cots. **D $44 - $75, W $220 - $485,** BC MC VI.

BRUNKERVILLE NSW 2323

Pop Nominal, (151km N Sydney), See map on page 55, ref B8. Small settlement near the Watagan Mountains between Freemans Waterhole and Kurri Kurri. Scenic Drives.

Hotels/Motels

★★☆ **Watagan Forest**, (M), Main Rd, 2km N of Freemans Waterhole, ☎ 02 4938 0149, fax 02 4938 0504, 6 units [shwr, tlt, a/c, elec blkts, tel, TV, t/c mkg, refrig], ldry, ✕, rm serv, cots-fee. **RO ♦ $42 - $50, ♦♦ $55 - $65, ♦ $7 - $10,** ch con, AE BC DC MC VI.

BRUNSWICK HEADS NSW 2483

Pop 1,850. (797km N Sydney), See map on page 54, ref E2. North coast fishing town at the mouth of the Brunswick River. Boating, Bowls, Fishing, Golf, Scenic Drives, Surfing, Swimming, Tennis.

Hotels/Motels

★★★☆ **Chalet Motel**, (M), No children's facilities, Pacific Hwy, 500m S of PO, ☎ 02 6685 1257, fax 02 6685 1257, 12 units [shwr, tlt, a/c (4), fan, heat, elec blkts, tel, fax, TV, clock radio, t/c mkg, refrig, cook fac (3)], pool (salt water), cots, non smoking units (4). **RO ♦ $50 - $90, ♦♦ $55 - $120, ♦♦♦ $65 - $120,** 4 units ★★☆. AE BC EFT MC VI.

★★★ **Harbour Lodge Motel**, (M), 6 Old Pacific Hwy, 500m N of PO, ☎ 02 6685 1851, fax 02 6685 1089, (2 stry), 20 units [shwr, tlt, fan, tel, TV, movie, clock radio, t/c mkg, refrig], ldry, lounge, pool, cook fac, bbq, plygr, cots-fee. **RO ♦ $54 - $85, ♦♦ $54 - $110, ♦♦♦ $65 - $110, ♦ $11,** ch con, pen con, AE BC DC EFT MC MCH VI.

★★☆ **Heidelberg Holiday Inn**, (M), The Terrace, 300m NE of PO, ☎ 02 6685 1808, fax 02 6685 1673, (2 stry), 12 units [shwr, tlt, c/fan, heat, tel, TV, radio, t/c mkg, refrig], ✉, pool, dinner to unit, cots-fee. **RO ♦ $58 - $120, ♦♦ $62 - $120, ♦ $10,** AE BC DC EFT MC VI.

Self Catering Accommodation

★★ **Beach View**, (HU), 14 South Beach Rd, ☎ 02 6685 1206, 2 units acc up to 5, [shwr, tlt, TV, refrig, cook fac, ldry, linen reqd], c/park (garage). **W $352 - $693.**

★★ **Breakwater Villa**, (HU), 4 South Beach Rd, 750m E of PO, ☎ 02 6685 1206, 2 units acc up to 5, [shwr, tlt, TV, refrig, cook fac, linen reqd], ldry, bbq, c/park (carport). **W $341 - $605,** Min book applies.

★★ **Pacific View**, (HF), Mona St, ☎ 02 6685 1322, fax 02 6685 1016, 3 flats acc up to 5, [shwr, tlt, TV, refrig, cook fac, linen reqd], ldry, c/park (garage) (2). **W $200 - $510,** Min book applies.

BRUSHGROVE NSW 2460

Pop Nominal, (648km N Sydney), See map on page 54, ref D3. Small town on the Clarence River between Grafton and Maclean.

Other Accommodation

Clarence Riverboats, (Hbt), 60 Clarence St, ☎ 02 6647 6232, 3 houseboats acc up to 8, [shwr, tlt, TV, t/c mkg, refrig, cook fac, blkts, linen], courtesy transfer. **D $1,120 - $1,440,** Min book applies, BC MC VI, (not yet classified).

BUDGEWOI NSW 2262

Pop Part of Wyong, (114km N Sydney), See map on page 55, ref D5. Central Coast town on the spit of land that separates Lake Munmorah from Lake Budgewoi. Fishing, Surfing, Swimming.

Hotels/Motels

★★★☆ **Hibiscus Lakeside Motel**, (M), 2 Diamond Head Dve, 700m E of PO, ☎ 02 4390 9100, fax 02 4399 1452, 13 units [shwr, tlt, hairdry, a/c, elec blkts, tel, TV, movie, clock radio, t/c mkg, refrig], ldry, bbq, cots. **RO ♦ $72 - $127, ♦♦ $72 - $127, ♦♦♦ $83 - $138, ♦ $11,** Min book applies, AE BC DC MC VI.

B&B's/Guest Houses

Valen Cottage, (B&B), 159 Budgewoi Rd, 1km E of PO, ☎ 02 4390 0141, 1 rm [heat, elec blkts, tel, clock radio, t/c mkg, ldry, doonas], bathrm, lounge (TV/video), spa (communal), refrig, bbq, non smoking rms. **BB ♦ $55 - $75, ♦♦ $65 - $85,** weekly con, (not yet classified).

BULAHDELAH NSW 2423

Pop 1,113. (242km N Sydney), See map on page 54, ref B8. Highway service centre at the junction of the Myall and Crawford Rivers, the jump-off point for touring the Myall Lakes and surrounding forests. Bowls, Bush Walking, Fishing, Golf, Tennis.

Hotels/Motels

★★★ **Bulahdelah Motor Lodge**, (M), Pacific Hwy, 500m N of PO, ☎ 02 4997 4520, fax 02 4997 4258, 23 units (2 suites) [shwr, tlt, a/c, tel, TV, clock radio, t/c mkg, refrig], ldry, ⊠ (Mon to Sat), pool, sauna, dinner to unit. **RO** ♦ $55, ♦♦ $66, ⋔ $10, AE BC DC MC VI.

 ★★★ **Bulahdelah-Myall Motel**, (M), Pacific Hwy, 1km N of Bridge, ☎ 02 4997 4533, 12 units [shwr, tlt, a/c-cool (12), c/fan, heat, tel, TV, clock radio, t/c mkg, refrig], iron, iron brd, pool (salt water), bbq, dinner to unit, cots-fee. **RO** ♦ $50 - $59, ♦♦ $59 - $75, ♦♦♦♦ $72 - $85, ⋔ $10, ch con, Min book school holidays and Easter, Min book long w/ends, AE BC EFT MC VI.

★★☆ **Bulahdelah The Pines Motel**, (M), Pacific Hwy, 1km N of bridge, ☎ 02 4997 4274, fax 02 4997 4992, 18 units [shwr, tlt, a/c-cool, c/fan, fax, TV, movie, clock radio, t/c mkg, refrig], ⊠, pool, bbq, rm serv, dinner to unit, courtesy transfer, plygr, cots, non smoking units (6). **BLB** ♦ $40 - $80, ♦♦ $50 - $80, ♦♦♦♦ $70 - $100, ch con, pen con, BC EFT MC VI.

★★ **Mount View Motel**, (M), Pacific Hwy, 500m NE of bridge, ☎ 02 4997 4292, fax 02 4997 4292, 11 units [shwr, tlt, a/c, heat, elec blkts, TV, clock radio, t/c mkg, refrig], cots, non smoking units (1). **RO** ♦ $26 - $35, ♦♦ $36 - $45, ⋔ $7, pen con, AE BC EFT MC VI.

Self Catering Accommodation

★★★★ **FeKala Leisure Resort**, (Cotg), 22 Violet Hill Rd, 10km NE of PO, ☎ 02 4997 4454, fax 02 4997 4856, 4 cotgs acc up to 4, [shwr, tlt, fire pl, clock radio, refrig, blkts, linen, pillows], rec rm, pool, sauna, bbq, meals avail (on request), bicycle, canoeing, gym, tennis. **D** $895, Vegetarian meals & daily activities included in tariff. Min book applies, BC DC MC VI.

★★ **(Motel Section)**, 5 units [shwr, tlt, clock radio, refrig, micro (1), pillows], ✕, cook fac, bbq, meals avail (on request).

B&B's/Guest Houses

★★★★ **Stoneholme Farmstay Bed & Breakfast**, (B&B), 386 Old Inn Rd, 8km SW of PO, ☎ 02 4997 4698, fax 02 4997 4698, 2 rms [elec blkts, toaster], lounge (TV), lounge firepl, t/c mkg shared, refrig, non smoking property. **BB** ♦ $80, ♦♦ $110 - $121.

Other Accommodation

Luxury Houseboat Hire (Myall Lakes), (Hbt), Crawford St, ☎ 02 4997 4380, fax 02 4997 4664, 7 houseboats acc up to 10, [shwr, tlt, refrig, cook fac, blkts, linen, pillows], boat park. **W** $490 - $3,575, Min book applies, BC MC VI.

Myall Lakes Houseboats, (Hbt), Bulahdelah Marina, 90 Crawford St, ☎ 02 4997 4221, fax 02 4997 4221, 11 houseboats acc up to 12, [shwr, tlt, refrig, cook fac, linen reqd], bbq, c/park. **G** $250 - $1,900, **W** $370 - $3,230, Min book applies.

BULLABURRA NSW

See Blue Mountains Region.

BULLI NSW

See Wollongong & Suburbs.

BUNDANOON NSW 2578

Pop 1,750. (150km SW Sydney), See map on page 55, ref B4. Charming Southern Highlands town with a Scottish feel. Bowls, Bush Walking, Golf, Swimming.

Hotels/Motels

★★★☆ **Bundanoon Holiday Resort & Conference Centre**, (M), Previously Holiday Resort Bundanoon Anzac Pde, 100m SW of PO, ☎ 02 4883 6068, fax 02 4883 6729, 21 units [shwr, tlt, fan, cent heat, elec blkts, tel, TV, clock radio, t/c mkg, refrig], conf fac, pool, bbq, dinner to unit, tennis, cots-fee. **RO** ♦ $65 - $95, ♦♦ $75 - $100, ♦♦♦ $75 - $110, ⋔ $10, ch con, AE BC MC VI.

Self Catering Accommodation

★★★☆ **Inverard Cottage**, (Cotg), Cnr Gullies & Riverview Rd, 250m E of PO, ☎ 02 4883 7196, fax 02 4883 7196, 1 cotg acc up to 10, [shwr (2), bath (1), tlt (2), c/fan, fire pl (1), heat, elec blkts, radio, t/c mkg, refrig, cook fac, micro, toaster, ldry, blkts, linen, pillows], w/mach, iron, rec rm, lounge (TV), bbq, cots. **RO** $343 - $505, ch con, Min book applies.

B&B's/Guest Houses

★★★☆ **Mildenhall Guest House**, (GH), 10 Anzac Pde, 500m S of PO, ☎ 02 4883 6643, 5 rms [shwr (1), tlt (1), heat, elec blkts, tel], shared fac (4 rms), lounge (TV), t/c mkg shared, bbq, c/park. **BB** ♦ $70 - $80, ♦♦ $120 - $140, **DBB** ♦ $100 - $140, ♦♦ $200 - $240, BC MC VI.

★★★☆ **Tree Tops Guest House**, (GH), 101 Railway Ave, 1km NE of PO, ☎ 02 4883 6372, or 02 4883 6992, 20 rms [shwr, tlt, fan, heat, elec blkts, tel], lounge, conf fac, ✕, t/c mkg shared, refrig, plygr, cots. **BB** ♦ $110 - $150, ♦♦ $145 - $220, **DBB** ♦ $155 - $175, ♦♦ $235 - $315, ch con, BC MC VI.

Operator Comment: See our colour advertisement under Bowral. Home to Super Sleuth Murder Mysteries.

BUNGENDORE NSW 2621

Pop 1,350. (263km SW Sydney), See map on pages 52/53, ref G6. Bungendore is a small village dating back to the 1830s which has developed a thriving tourist trade in art, crafts and collectables. Horse Riding, Tennis.

Hotels/Motels

★★★☆ **The Carrington of Bungendore**, (M), 21 Malbon St, 1km SW of PO, ☎ 02 6238 1044, fax 02 6238 1036, 26 units (4 suites) [shwr, bath (17), spa bath (5), tlt, hairdry, c/fan, elec blkts, tel, TV, video, clock radio, t/c mkg, refrig, toaster], ldry, iron, iron brd, conv fac, ⊠, bbq, rm serv, cots. **BB** ♦♦ $165 - $235, **DBB** ♦♦ $305 - $355, AE BC DC EFT MC VI.

★★☆ **The Lake George**, (LMH), 20 Gibraltar St, Village Centre, ☎ 02 6238 1260, fax 02 6238 1960, 7 units [shwr, tlt, hairdry, fan, heat, elec blkts, TV, clock radio, t/c mkg, refrig, toaster], ldry, rec rm, ⊠, cots. **RO** ♦ $49, ♦♦ $60 - $66.

BUNGWAHL NSW 2423

Pop Nominal, (273km N Sydney), See map on page 54, ref B8. Tiny village on Myall Lake at the junction of the Lakes Way and the road to Seal Rocks. Boating, Fishing, Swimming.

Self Catering Accommodation

★★☆ **Bella Vista**, (Cotg), (Farm), Wattley Hill Rd, 6km from Lakes Way, ☎ 02 4997 7324, fax 02 4997 7369, 1 cotg acc up to 6, [shwr, bath, tlt, elec blkts, tel, TV, video, clock radio, refrig, cook fac, micro, elec frypan, toaster, linen], iron, cots, Dogs are welcome. **W** $275 - $385.

BURONGA NSW 2648

Pop 896. (1020km W Sydney), See map on pages 52/53, ref B5. Rural community on the Murray River across the border from the Victorian city of Mildura, at the heart of an extensive citrus and grape growing region. Bowls, Fishing, Shooting, Swimming, Tennis, Vineyards, Wineries.

Hotels/Motels

 ★★★ **Mildura's Sun River Motel**, (M), Junction of Mildura Bridge & Silver City Hwy, ☎ 03 5022 1784, fax 03 5022 1740, 26 units [shwr, tlt, a/c, elec blkts, tel, TV, movie, clock radio, t/c mkg, refrig, toaster], ⊠, pool, bbq, plygr, cots. **RO** ♦ $51 - $71, ♦♦ $55 - $75, ⋔ $11, ch con, AE BC BTC DC MC MCH VI.

Mungo Lodge, (M), Arumpo Rd, 104km NE of PO, close to Mungo National Park, ☎ 03 5029 7297, fax 03 5029 7296, 18 units [shwr, tlt, a/c-cool, heat, TV, t/c mkg, refrig, cook fac (2)], ⊠, ✆, cots. **D** ♦ $76 - $86, ♦♦ $86 - $96, ⋔ $11, ch con, BC MC VI.

B&B's/Guest Houses

★★★★ **Elizabeth Leighton B&B**, (B&B), 116 Sturt Hwy, ☎ 03 5021 2033, fax 03 5021 2033, (2 stry), 1 rm (1 suite) [shwr, tlt, hairdry (1), a/c-cool, heat, elec blkts, tel, clock radio (1), t/c mkg, refrig], ldry, iron, iron brd, rec rm, lounge (TV), bbq, non smoking rms. **BB** ♦ $65, ♦♦ $90, BC MC VI.

Other Accommodation

Acacia Family Houseboats, (Hbt), West Rd, Moored downstream fr Chaffey Bridge, ☎ 03 5022 1510, fax 03 5021 0909, 2 houseboats acc up to 6, (2 bedrm), [shwr, tlt, evap cool, heat, TV, video, radio, CD, refrig, cook fac, micro, blkts, doonas, linen, pillows], bbq. **W** $630 - $1,800, Security deposit - $200 & bond $300, BC MC VI.

BURRAWANG NSW 2577

Pop 204. (140km S Sydney), See map on page 55, ref B4. Small Southern Highlands village that dates from the 1860s. Scenic Drives.

B&B's/Guest Houses

★★★★ **The Keep Country House**, (B&B), Church Rd, 500m N of PO, ☎ 02 4886 4558, or 0412 228 601, fax 02 4886 4558, (2 stry), 4 rms [shwr, bath (1), tlt, hairdry, fire pl (6), cent heat, elec blkts, clock radio], iron, iron brd, lounge (firepl), ✕ (on request), t/c mkg shared, c/park. **BB** ♦ $185 - $250, ♦♦ $185 - $280, **DBB** ♦ $250 - $352, ♦♦ $360 - $610, AE BC EFT MC VI.

BURRILL LAKE NSW 2539

Pop 1,373. Part of Ulladulla, (251km S Sydney), See map on page 55, ref B5. Small south coast town on the shores of the lake of the same name. Boating, Fishing, Surfing, Swimming, Tennis.

Hotels/Motels

★★★☆ **Snuggle Inn**, (M), 155 Princess Hwy, 5km S Ulladulla PO, ☎ 02 4455 3577, fax 02 4454 4000, 11 units [shwr, tlt, hairdry, a/c, heat, elec blkts, tel, fax, TV, video-fee, clock radio, t/c mkg, refrig, cook fac (4), toaster], ldry, lounge firepl, pool-heated (salt water heated), bbq, cots. **W** $350 - $650, **RO** ♦ $60 - $100, ♦♦ $70 - $120, ◊ $12 - $15, BC DC MC VI.

★★☆ **Edgewater Motel**, (M), 1 Princess Ave, 200m N of PO, ☎ 02 4455 2604, fax 02 4454 4095, 10 units [shwr, tlt, fan, heat, elec blkts, TV, clock radio, t/c mkg, refrig], bbq, cots. **RO** ♦ $55 - $100, ♦♦ $60 - $130, ◊ $10, Min book Christmas Jan long w/ends and Easter, AE BC DC MC VI.

Self Catering Accommodation

★★★ **Lake Edge Holiday Units**, (HU), 27 Balmoral Rd, ☎ 02 4455 2478, fax 02 4454 3792, 7 units acc up to 7, [shwr, tlt, fan, heat, TV, clock radio, refrig, cook fac, micro, linen reqd-fee], ldry, pool (salt water), bbq, plygr, cots. **D** $50 - $120, **W** $320 - $700, Min book Christmas Jan and Easter.

BYROCK NSW 2831

Pop Nominal, (646km NW Sydney), See map on pages 52/53, ref E2. Small town on the Mitchell Highway between Nyngan and Bourke.

Hotels/Motels

★★ **Mulga Creek**, (LH), Mitchell Hwy, 300m S of PO, ☎ 02 6874 7311, 3 rms [shwr, tlt, a/c, fan, t/c mkg], rec rm, ✕, bbq, rm serv, dinner to unit, ☎, plygr. **BB** ♦ $48, ♦♦ $60 - $80, ◊ $26, AE BC MC VI.

BYRON BAY NSW 2481

Pop 6,100. (790km N Sydney), See map on page 54, ref E2. One of the most popular holiday destinations in Australia, situated in the far north coast on the most easterly point of the Australian mainland. Bowls, Fishing, Scenic Drives, Swimming, Tennis.

Hotels/Motels

★★★★☆ **Azabu Luxury Accommodation**, (LH), No children's facilities, 317 Skinners Shoot Rd, 3km SW of PO, ☎ 02 6680 9102, fax 02 6680 9103, 5 rms [shwr, spa bath (3), tlt, c/fan, heat, tel, TV, video, clock radio, t/c mkg, refrig, doonas], lounge firepl, ✕, pool-heated, spa, dinner to unit, non smoking property. **BB** ♦ $220 - $330, ♦♦ $220 - $330, AE BC EFT MC VI.

★★★★☆ **Beach Hotel**, (LMH), Bay St, 500m NE of PO, ☎ 02 6685 6402, fax 02 6685 8758, (2 stry gr fl), 25 units (5 suites) [shwr, bath (9), spa bath (5), tlt, hairdry, a/c, c/fan, tel, TV, video, radio, t/c mkg, refrig, mini bar, toaster], lift, ldry, rec rm, ✕, pool-heated, spa, rm serv, cots-fee. **RO** ♦ $190 - $380, ♦♦ $190 - $380, ◊ $20 - $40, **Suite D** ♦ $240 - $380, ♦♦ $240 - $380.

★★★★ **Byron Bay Holiday Inn Motel**, (M), 45 Lawson St, 500m E of PO, ☎ 02 6685 6373, fax 02 6685 5513, 16 units [shwr, tlt, hairdry, fan, heat, tel, cable tv, video-fee, clock radio, t/c mkg, refrig, mini bar], iron, iron brd, cots-fee, non smoking property. **RO** ♦ $150 - $220, ♦♦ $150 - $220, ◊ $20, AE BC DC MC VI.

★★★★ **Byron Bay Waves Motel**, (M), 35 Lawson St, ☎ 02 6685 5966, fax 02 6685 5977, 19 units (3 suites) [shwr, bath (17), tlt, hairdry, a/c, c/fan, tel, TV, movie-fee, clock radio, CD (1), t/c mkg, refrig, cook fac (1)], lift, iron, iron brd, secure park. **RO** ♦ $140 - $150, ♦♦ $140 - $495, ◊ $20 - $30, **Suite D** ♦♦ $225 - $325, Min book applies, AE BC DC EFT MC VI, ♿.

★★★★ **Lord Byron Resort**, (M), Resort, 120 Jonson St, 350m S of PO, ☎ 02 6685 7444, fax 02 6685 7120, (Multi-stry), 29 units [shwr, tlt, a/c, fan, heat, tel, TV, clock radio, t/c mkg, refrig], ldry, iron, iron brd, rec rm, lounge, conv fac, ⊠, pool-heated, sauna, spa (heated) (2), bbq, secure park, golf (practice nets), tennis, cots-fee. RO ♦ $99 - $220, ♦♦ $104 - $220, ♦♦♦ $124 - $240, ◊ $20, AE BC DC EFT MC MP VI.

★★★★ **(Apartment Section)**, 10 apts acc up to 6, [shwr, bath (8), tlt, c/fan, tel, TV, clock radio, t/c mkg, refrig, cook fac, micro, d/wash, toaster, ldry], w/mach, dryer, iron, iron brd. D $112 - $264, W $693 - $1,848.

★★★★ **Wollongbar Motor Inn**, (M), 19 Shirley St, 500m NW of PO, ☎ 02 6685 8200, fax 02 6685 8200, (2 stry gr fl), 17 units [shwr, tlt, a/c, c/fan, heat, elec blkts, tel, fax, TV, video (avail), clock radio, t/c mkg, refrig, cook fac (4)], ldry, pool (salt water), bbq, rm serv, cots, non smoking property. RO ♦ $85 - $165, ♦♦ $90 - $165, ♦♦♦ $105 - $180, ◊ $15 - $25, ch con, AE BC MC VI.

★★★☆ **Byron Sunseeker Motel**, (M), 100 Bangalow Rd, 1.5km S of PO, ☎ 02 6685 7369, fax 02 6685 5181, (2 stry gr fl), 12 units (4 suites) [shwr, tlt, a/c, c/fan, tel, cable tv, movie, clock radio, t/c mkg, refrig, cook fac ltd, toaster], ldry, rec rm, pool (salt water), bbq (covered), plygr, bicycle-fee, cots-fee. RO ♦ $85 - $165, ♦♦ $89 - $190, ◊ $12 - $25, Suite D $92 - $205, AE BC DC EFT MC VI.

★★★☆ **(Cottage Section)**, 6 cotgs acc up to 4, [shwr, tlt, hairdry, a/c, fan, tel, cable tv, movie, clock radio, t/c mkg, refrig, cook fac, toaster, blkts, linen, pillows], ldry, pool (salt water), bbq (covered), rm serv (b'fast), bicycle-fee, cots-fee. RO ♦ $89 - $195, ♦♦ $92 - $205, ◊ $12 - $25.

★★★☆ **The Bay Beach**, (M), 32 Lawson St, 500m E of PO, ☎ 02 6685 6090, or 02 6685 7220, fax 02 6685 7708, 16 units [shwr, tlt, hairdry, a/c, elec blkts, tel, cable tv, video-fee, clock radio, t/c mkg, refrig], ldry, ⊠, pool, bbq, dinner to unit, cots. RO ♦ $75 - $295, ♦♦ $75 - $295, ♦♦♦ $95 - $295, ◊ $10 - $15, AE BC DC MC VI.

★★★ **Baymist Motel**, (M), 12 Bay St, 400m N of PO, ☎ 02 6685 6121, fax 02 6685 7903, (2 stry gr fl), 10 units [shwr, tlt, hairdry, a/c, heat, elec blkts, cable tv, clock radio, t/c mkg, refrig, micro], ldry, cots, non smoking units. RO ♦ $135 - $250, ♦♦ $135 - $250, ♦♦♦ $145 - $280, BC EFT MC VI.

★★★ **Byron Hibiscus Motel**, (M), 33 Lawson St, 500m E of PO, ☎ 02 6685 6195, fax 02 6685 6195, 7 units (2 suites) [shwr, tlt, a/c, TV, clock radio, t/c mkg, refrig, micro, toaster], ldry, bbq, non smoking units. RO ♦ $135 - $275, ♦♦ $135 - $275, ♦♦♦ $145 - $310, Suite RO $195 - $385, BC EFT MC VI.

★★★ **Byron Motor Lodge Motel**, (M), 11-21Butler St, 400m W of PO, ☎ 02 6685 6522, fax 02 6685 8696, 14 units [shwr, tlt, hairdry, a/c (10), c/fan (11), heat, elec blkts, tel, TV, clock radio, t/c mkg, refrig, cook fac (5)], ldry, pool, bbq, cots. RO ♦ $80 - $140, ♦♦ $89 - $160, ◊ $10, Min book applies, AE BC DC EFT MC VI.

★★★ **Dolphins Motor Inn**, (M), 32 Bangalow Rd, ☎ 02 6680 9577, fax 02 6680 9511, 12 units [shwr, tlt, hairdry, a/c, tel, TV, clock radio, t/c mkg, refrig, cook fac (5), micro, toaster], iron, iron brd, spa, bbq, courtesy transfer, cots, non smoking rms (4). RO ♦ $75 - $130, ♦♦ $75 - $150, ◊ $10, Min book Christmas and Jan, AE BC EFT VI.

★☆ **Belongil by the Sea**, (M), 4 Childe St, 1.5km NW of PO, ☎ 02 6685 8111, fax 02 6685 5041, 15 units [shwr, tlt, c/fan, heat, TV, t/c mkg (11), refrig, cook fac (11), toaster], ldry, pool-heated, bbq, plygr, cots. D $55 - $189, BC MC VI.

Peppers, (LH), 139 Newes Rd, ☎ 02 6684 7348, 12 rms (1 & 2 bedrm), [shwr, tlt, c/fan, heat, tel, cable tv, clock radio, t/c mkg, refrig, doonas], ldry, ⊠, pool, spa, bbq, AE BC DC EFT MC VI, (not yet classified).

Self Catering Accommodation

★★★★☆ **Bay Royal Apartments**, (HU), 24-28 Bay St, ☎ 02 6680 9187, fax 02 6680 9205, (Multi-stry gr fl), 15 units acc up to 6, [shwr, bath, tlt, hairdry, c/fan, tel, TV, video, clock radio, t/c mkg, refrig, cook fac, micro, elec frypan, d/wash, toaster, ldry, blkts, linen], lift, w/mach, dryer, iron, iron brd, pool-heated (salt water), bbq, secure park. D $260 - $955, W $1,700 - $6,700, Min book applies, BC EFT MC VI.

★★★★☆ **Byron Lakeside**, (HU), 5 Old Bangalow Rd, 2.4km S of PO, ☎ 02 6680 9244, fax 02 6680 9243, 27 units acc up to 6, (1, 2 & 3 bedrm), [shwr, tlt, fan, TV, video, clock radio, t/c mkg, refrig, cook fac, micro, d/wash, toaster, blkts, linen, pillows], w/mach, dryer, pool, bbq, cots-fee. D ♦ $120 - $285, ♦♦ $120 - $285, Min book Christmas Jan and Easter, BC EFT MC VI.

★★★★☆ **The Links, Byron Bay**, (Apt), 64-70 Broken Head Rd, 4km S of PO, ☎ 02 6680 8451, fax 02 6680 8452, (2 stry), 12 apts acc up to 6, (1, 2 & 3 bedrm), [shwr, tlt, a/c (1), c/fan, heat (elec), tel, cable tv, video, clock radio, t/c mkg, refrig, cook fac, micro, d/wash, toaster, blkts, doonas, linen, pillows], w/mach, dryer, pool, bbq, cots-fee, non smoking units (6). **D** $135 - $420, **W** $560 - $2,850, weekly con, Min book applies, AE BC DC EFT MC VI.

★★★★ **Beaumonts Beach Houses**, (House), 1 Border St, 800m NW of PO, ☎ 02 6655 6656, fax 02 6655 6656, 1 house acc up to 8, (3 bedrm), [shwr, tlt, fan, heat, tel, cable tv, video, radio, refrig, cook fac, micro, d/wash, toaster, ldry, blkts, doonas, linen, pillows], w/mach, dryer, spa, bbq, c/park (undercover), cots, breakfast ingredients. **BB** ♦♦ $165 - $253, BC MC VI.

★★★★ **Byron Quarter**, (HU), 8 Byron St, 150m from PO, ☎ 02 6680 9900, fax 02 6680 9913, 23 units acc up to 6, (1 bedrm2 bedrm Studio), [shwr, tlt, fan, TV, video, clock radio, t/c mkg, refrig, cook fac, micro, d/wash, blkts, linen, pillows], w/mach, dryer, pool (outdoor), cots-fee. **D** ♦♦ $82 - $238, ♦♦♦ $110 - $328, ♦ $15, Min book applies, BC EFT MC VI.

★★★★ **Gosamara**, (Apt), 53 Shirley St, 1km N of PO, ☎ 02 6680 8711, fax 02 6685 8067, (2 stry), 13 apts acc up to 4, (1 & 2 bedrm), [shwr, tlt, a/c, c/fan, TV, video, clock radio, t/c mkg, refrig, cook fac, micro, d/wash, toaster, blkts, linen, pillows], w/mach, dryer, pool, spa, bbq, cots. **D** $90 - $160, Min book applies, BC EFT MC VI.

★★★★ **Julian's Apartments**, (HU), 124 Lighthouse Rd, 1.5km E of PO, ☎ 02 6680 9697, fax 02 6680 9695, (2 stry gr fl), 11 units acc up to 6, (Studio & 2 bedrm), [a/c-cool (10), a/c (8), fan (3), tel (6), TV, video, clock radio, CD (3), t/c mkg, refrig, cook fac, micro, d/wash, ldry, blkts, doonas, linen], w/mach, dryer, secure park (undercover), cots-fee, non smoking units. **D** ♦♦ $85 - $250, **W** ♦ $40 - $60, BC EFT MC VI.

★★★★ **Outrigger Bay**, (HU), 9 Shirley St, 500m E of PO, ☎ 02 6685 8646, fax 02 6685 6416, (2 stry gr fl), 23 units acc up to 6, (1, 2 & 3 bedrm), [shwr, tlt, a/c (4), fan, heat (elec), TV, video-fee, clock radio, t/c mkg, refrig, cook fac, micro, blkts, linen, pillows], w/mach, dryer, pool, spa, bbq, secure park, ✆, cots-fee, non smoking units (2). **D** ♦ $150 - $250, ♦♦ $160 - $270, ♦ $22 - $200, Min book applies, BC EFT MC VI.

★★★☆ **Byron Bay Beachfront Apartments**, (HU), 39-41 Lawson St, 400m E of PO, ☎ 02 6685 6354, fax 02 6685 6354, 12 units acc up to 6, [shwr, tlt, c/fan, heat, TV, video, CD, refrig, cook fac, micro, blkts, linen, pillows], ldry, bbq, c/park (undercover), cots-fee. **W** $550 - $2,500, $550 - $2,700, Min book applies, BC MC VI.

★★★☆ **Byron Central Apartments**, (Apt), 5 Byron St, ☎ 02 6685 8800, fax 02 6685 8802, 26 apts acc up to 5, [shwr, tlt, c/fan, heat, tel, TV, movie, clock radio, t/c mkg, refrig, cook fac, toaster, blkts, linen, pillows], ldry, w/mach, dryer, iron, pool, bbq, c/park (undercover), cots. **RO** ♦♦ $65 - $145, ♦♦ $445 - $1,050, Min book applies, AE BC DC EFT MC VI.

★★★☆ **Mariner Bay Apartments**, (HU), 43 Shirley St, 350m W of PO, ☎ 02 6685 5272, fax 02 6685 5424, 15 units acc up to 6, (2 & 3 bedrm), [shwr, bath (hip), tlt, c/fan, TV, video, clock radio, refrig, cook fac, micro, d/wash, toaster, ldry, blkts, linen, pillows], w/mach, dryer, iron, pool (salt water), bbq, c/park (garage), cots-fee. **D** $115 - $355, **W** $575 - $2,250, Min book applies, BC EFT MC VI, ♿.

★★★☆ **Murojum Farm**, (Cotg), Coopers Shoot Rd, 6km SW of PO, ☎ 02 6685 3602, fax 02 6685 3602, 3 cotgs acc up to 5, [shwr, tlt, heat, TV, video, t/c mkg, refrig, micro, elec frypan, toaster, blkts, linen, pillows], ldry, pool-heated, bbq, c/park (carport), cots. **D $150 - $230, W $700 - $1,200**, BC MC VI.

★★★☆ **Oasis Resort**, (HU), Scott St, 2km S of PO, ☎ 02 6685 7390, fax 02 6685 8290, 24 units acc up to 6, [shwr, bath, spa bath (5), tlt, c/fan, heat, tel, fax (4), TV, video (avail), CD (7), refrig, cook fac, d/wash, ldry, blkts, linen, pillows], rec rm, pool-heated, sauna, spa, bbq, c/park (undercover), plygr, gym, tennis, cots, **W $859 - $1,964**, Treetop House section of a higher standard, Min book applies, AE BC DC MC VI.

★★★★☆ **(Treetop House Section)**, 4 cotgs acc up to 6, [shwr, bath, spa bath, tlt, hairdry, a/c, c/fan, heat, tel, fax, TV, video, clock radio, CD, t/c mkg, refrig, cook fac, micro, d/wash, toaster, ldry, blkts, linen, pillows], w/mach, dryer, iron, cots. **D $1,845 - $3,135**.

★★★ **Bayview Lodge**, (HU), 22 Bay St, 300m E of PO, ☎ 02 6685 7073, fax 02 6685 8599, (Multi-stry gr fl), 16 units acc up to 6, [shwr, tlt, fan, heat, TV, video (avail), clock radio, t/c mkg, refrig, cook fac, micro, d/wash (15), ldry, blkts, linen, pillows], bbq, c/park (undercover). **D $130 - $145, W $575 - $1,800**, BC MC VI.

★★★ **Byron Bay Farmstay**, (Farm), 'Eastock' Bangalow Rd, 7km W of Byron Bay, ☎ 02 6685 3179, fax 02 6685 3179, 4 cabins acc up to 5, [shwr, tlt, c/fan, heat, TV, clock radio, t/c mkg, refrig, cook fac, micro, toaster, linen reqd-fee], ldry, bbq, cots. **D $80 - $132, W $450 - $900**, ch con, Min book applies, BC MC VI.

★★★ **Byron Bayside Holiday Accom**, (SA), 14 Middleton St, ☎ 02 6685 6004, fax 02 6685 8552, (2 stry gr fl) 20 serv apts acc up to 6, [shwr, tlt, c/fan, tel, TV, clock radio, t/c mkg, refrig, cook fac, toaster, ldry, blkts, linen, pillows], w/mach, dryer, iron, iron brd, c/park (garage), cots. **D ♦ $70 - $150, ♦♦ $75 - $155, ♦ $15, W ♦♦ $455 - $990**, AE BC DC EFT MC MCH VI, ♿.

★★★ **The Capes Holiday Apartments**, (HU), 39/41 Childe St, 500m NE of PO, ☎ 02 6687 1197, fax 02 6687 1566, (2 stry gr fl), 5 units (2 & 3 bedrm), [shwr, tlt, c/fan, TV, video, clock radio, t/c mkg, refrig, cook fac, micro, toaster, blkts, linen (2 persons), pillows], w/mach, dryer (1), bbq, cots-fee. **D ♦ $80 - $100, ♦♦ $80 - $100, ♦ $12**, weekly con, Min book applies, AE BC DC EFT MC VI.

★★☆ **Byron Bay Beach Resort**, (HU), Previously Byron Bay Beach Club Bayshore Dve, 3km N of PO, ☎ 02 6685 8000, fax 02 6685 6916, 78 units [shwr, tlt, fan, heat, TV, clock radio, t/c mkg, refrig, cook fac, toaster], ldry, lounge, conf fac, ✉, bar, pool-heated, bbq, bicycle, canoeing, golf, tennis. **D ♦ $109 - $204, ♦♦ $131 - $204**, Min book applies, AE BC DC EFT MC VI.

★★☆ **Byron Bay Rainforest Resort**, (HU), 39 Broken Head Rd, ☎ 02 6685 6139, fax 02 6685 8754, 7 units acc up to 7, [shwr, tlt, fan, heat, TV, movie, clock radio, refrig, cook fac, micro, blkts, linen, pillows], pool, spa, bbq, bush walking. **D ♦♦ $110 - $250, ♦♦♦ $110 - $250, W $650 - $1,900**, ch con, AE BC EFT MC VI, ♿.

★★★ **(Bed & Breakfast Section)**, 4 rms [shwr (4), tlt (4), a/c-cool, c/fan, heat, t/c mkg], shared fac (3), ldry, lounge, bbq. **BB ♦ $75 - $150, ♦♦ $85 - $150**.

BYRON BAY NSW continued...

B&B's/Guest Houses

★★★★★ **Wategos Watermark**, (GH), 29 Marine Pde, 3km S of PO, ☎ 02 6685 8999, fax 02 6685 8989, (2 stry), 5 rms [shwr, bath, tlt, hairdry, a/c, tel, TV], iron, iron brd, lounge, ✕. **BB ┆ $370, ┆┆ $395**, AE BC DC EFT MC VI.

★★★★☆ **Corys on Cooper**, (GH), 21 Cooper St, 1.5km S of PO, ☎ 02 6685 7834, fax 02 6685 7838, (2 stry gr fl), 4 rms [shwr, bath, tlt, a/c (1), c/fan, heat, elec blkts, TV], ldry, lounge, pool (salt water), spa, bbq, c/park. **BB ┆┆ $210 - $275**, BC MC VI.

★★★★☆ **Ewingsdale Country Guest House**, (GH), Top of McGettigans La, 6km W of PO, ☎ 02 6684 7047, fax 02 6684 7687, 4 rms (2 suites) [shwr, spa bath (2), tlt, a/c-cool (4), c/fan, heat, elec blkts, tel, TV (4), video], lounge (TV), pool (salt water), t/c mkg shared, c/park. **BB $160 - $319**, AE BC DC JCB MC VI.

★★★★☆ **Piccadilly Hill 'A Country Home for Guests'**, (B&B), Piccadilly Hill Rd, 10km S of PO, ☎ 02 6687 2068, fax 02 6687 2069, 3 rms [ensuite, bath (1), elec blkts, TV, clock radio, doonas], lounge firepl. **BB ┆┆ $180**.

★★★★☆ **Ruskin House**, (B&B), No children's facilities, 131 Jonson St, 500m S of PO, ☎ 02 6685 6144, fax 02 6685 6603, 5 rms [shwr, spa bath (4), tlt, hairdry, a/c, elec blkts, tel, TV, clock radio, t/c mkg], iron, iron brd, ✕, non smoking property. **BB ┆ $105 - $195, ┆┆ $135 - $220, RO ┆ $95 - $180, ┆┆ $110 - $200**, AE BC DC EFT MC VI.

★★★★☆ **Taylors a Country House for Guests**, (GH), No children's facilities, 160 McGettigans La, ☎ 02 6684 7436, fax 02 6684 7526, 6 rms [shwr, bath (2), spa bath (1), tlt, fire pl, video (1), clock radio, CD, cook fac (1)], lounge (TV), pool, dinner to unit. **BB ┆ $135, ┆┆ $160 - $195, ┆┆ $185 - $270, ┆ $50**, Min book applies, BC MC VI.

★★★★ **Collies Cottage**, (B&B), Lot 4, Picadilly Hill Rd via Coopers Shoot, ☎ 02 6687 1248, fax 02 6687 1248, (2 stry gr fl), 2 rms [hairdry, fan, elec blkts, tel, radio, refrig, d/wash], ldry, iron, iron brd, lounge (TV & firepl), ✕, t/c mkg shared, bbq, non smoking rms (2). **BB ┆┆ $160**, Min book applies.

★★★★ **Nirvana Lodge on the Beach**, (B&B), No children's facilities, 4 Beach Rd, Broken Head, 5km S of PO, ☎ 02 6685 4549, fax 02 6685 4155, (2 stry gr fl), 3 rms [shwr (3), bath (1), spa bath (1), tlt (3), c/fan (3), tel, TV, video (3), refrig, micro, toaster], ldry, iron, iron brd, TV rm, lounge firepl, cook fac, t/c mkg shared, bbq, courtesy transfer, non smoking property. **BLB ┆ $80, ┆┆ $100 - $180**, BC MC VI.

★★★★ **Teasdales on the Bay**, (B&B), 44 Lawson St, 500m E of PO, ☎ 02 6685 5125, fax 02 6685 5198, (Multi-stry), 5 rms [shwr, tlt, hairdry, fan, heat, tel, TV, movie, clock radio, t/c mkg, refrig], iron, iron brd, rec rm, ✕, pool (salt water), c/park. **BB ┆ $220 - $260, ┆┆ $220 - $260**, Min book applies, BC MC VI.

★★★☆ **Frangipani Cottage Bed & Breakfast**, (B&B), 49 Massinger St, 700m E of PO, ☎ 02 6685 8191, fax 02 6685 8191, 3 rms [shwr, bath (3), tlt, hairdry, c/fan, elec blkts, tel], ldry, lounge (TV & video), t/c mkg shared, c/park. **BB $132 - $175**, AE BC DC MC VI.

★★★☆ **Sandals Bed & Breakfast**, (B&B), 11 Carlyle St, ☎ 02 6685 8025, fax 02 6685 8599, (2 stry gr fl), 6 rms [shwr (2), tlt (2), c/fan, heat], ldry, iron, iron brd, lounge (TV), cook fac, t/c mkg shared, cots, non smoking property. **BLB ┆ $75 - $100, ┆┆ $110 - $180**, ch con, fam con, pen con, AE BC DC MC VI.

★★★ **Bamboo Cottage Guest House**, (B&B), 76 Butler St, 200m W of Tourist Centre, ☎ 02 6685 5509, fax 02 6680 8070, 5 rms [ensuite (1), c/fan, heat, tel, micro (1), toaster (1)], ldry, lounge (TV), t/c mkg shared, refrig, bbq. **BLB ┆ $40 - $100, ┆┆ $78 - $150**, Min book Christmas Jan and Easter.

★★★ **The Royal Oaks Guest House**, (GH), Previously Royal Oaks, 53 Broken Head Rd, 3km S of PO, ☎ 02 6685 8679, fax 02 6685 8679, 4 rms [ensuite, bath (1), c/fan, TV, clock radio, t/c mkg, refrig, micro, toaster, doonas], pool, spa, non smoking property. **BLB ┆ $60 - $150, ┆┆ $70 - $150, ┆ $15**, BC MC VI.

Other Accommodation

Middle Reef Beachouse, 13 Marvel St, 800m E of PO, ☎ 02 6685 5118, fax 02 6680 7430, 10 rms lounge (TV), cook fac, c/park. **RO ┆ $20 - $60, ┆┆ $45 - $130**, Min book all holiday times, AE EFT MC VI.

CABARITA BEACH NSW 2488

Pop Nominal, (840km N Sydney), See map on page 54, ref E1. Cabarita Beach (also known as Bogangar) is a charming village beside one of the Tweed Coast's most popular surfing beaches. Bowls, Fishing, Scenic Drives, Surfing, Tennis.

Hotels/Motels

★★★☆ **Cabarita Gardens Lake Resort**, (M), Tamarind Ave, ☎ 02 6676 2000, fax 02 6676 1108, (Multi-stry gr fl), 32 units (18 suites) [shwr, spa bath (18), tlt, a/c (2), c/fan, heat, tel, TV, video, clock radio, t/c mkg, refrig, cook fac (18), micro, elec frypan, d/wash (18), toaster, ldry (18)], ldry, conv fac, ✉, pool, sauna, spa, bbq, rm serv, dinner to unit, cots-fee. **D $80 - $320**, AE BC DC JCB MC MP VI.

★★★ **Cabarita Beachfront Hideaway**, (M), 21 Cypress Cres, ☎ 02 6676 1444, fax 02 6676 1203, (2 stry gr fl), 14 units (1 suite) [shwr, tlt, fan, heat, elec blkts, TV, clock radio, t/c mkg, refrig, cook fac (5), cook fac ltd (9)], ldry, pool (salt water), bbq, cots. **RO ♦ $76 - $132, ♦♦ $76 - $132, ♦ $11, Suite D $99 - $154**, AE BC DC MC VI.

★★☆ **Cabarita Beach Hotel Motel**, (LH), Coast Rd, ☎ 02 6676 1555, fax 02 6676 1208, (Multi-stry), 34 rms [shwr, spa bath (3), tlt, fan, tel, TV, clock radio, t/c mkg, refrig, micro (1)], w/mach (1), dryer (1), conv fac, ✉, pool, spa, rm serv, cots, non smoking units (10). **W $420 - $594, RO ♦ $70 - $110, ♦♦ $70 - $110, ♦ $11**, ch con, 12 units of a higher standard, AE BC DC MC VI.

★★ **Cabarita Beachouse Motel**, (M), Previously Cabarita Village Motel 39 Coast Rd, 100m N of PO, ☎ 02 6676 1633, (2 stry gr fl), 10 units [shwr, bath (1), tlt, c/fan, TV, movie, clock radio, t/c mkg, refrig], ldry, bbq, c/park. **RO ♦ $50 - $75, ♦♦ $55 - $75, ♦ $10**, ch con, Min book applies, BC MC VI.

Self Catering Accommodation

★★★★ **Diamond Beach Resort**, (HU), 105 Coast Rd, 500m S of PO, ☎ 02 6676 3232, fax 02 6676 3232, (Multi-stry gr fl), 32 units acc up to 6, [shwr, bath, tlt, TV, video (24), clock radio, t/c mkg, refrig, cook fac, micro, elec frypan, toaster, ldry, blkts, linen, pillows], rec rm, TV rm, pool-heated (solar), spa (heated), bbq, secure park, ☎, gym, cots. **D $95 - $155, W $465 - $1,090**, ch con, Min book applies, BC MC VI.

CALLALA BAY NSW 2540

Pop 1,750. See map on page 55, ref B5. Small town on the northern shores of Jervis Bay.

B&B's/Guest Houses

★★★★ **Greystone House Bed & Breakfast**, (B&B), 62 Emmett St, 20km E of Nowra, ☎ 02 4446 6123, fax 02 4446 6123, (2 stry gr fl), 4 rms (Studio), [ensuite, spa bath (1), heat, elec blkts, clock radio (4), t/c mkg (1 rm), refrig (2), cook fac (1), micro (1), toaster (1)], iron (1), TV rm, lounge firepl, t/c mkg shared (3 rooms), bbq, non smoking rms. **D $100**, ch con, VI.

Callala Beach View Apartments

Across the road from beach, 2 units, accom 6-8 people, fully self contained. Callala Beach 15 minutes from Nowra in Jervis Bay area. Approx 8km of beautiful white sand beach - excellent opportunities for swimming, boating and fishing, a good chance of seeing dolphins in the morning and afternoon.

Ideal for family fun.

Ph: (02) 9620 1251   Mobile: 0412 675 540

CALLALA BEACH NSW 2540

Pop 800. (177km S Sydney), See map on page 55, ref B5. South coast settlement on the shores of Jervis Bay. Bowls, Golf, Tennis. See also Callala Bay, Currarong, Hyams Beach & Vincentia.

Self Catering Accommodation

★★★ **Callala Beach View Apartments**, (HU), 3 Parkes Cres, ☎ 02 9620 1251, fax 02 9620 1274, 2 units acc up to 10, [shwr, bath, tlt, a/c (1), fan, heat, TV, t/c mkg, refrig, cook fac, toaster, ldry, linen reqd], w/mach, dryer, iron, bbq, c/park. **D $165, W $600 - $900**, AE BC DC MC.

CAMBEWARRA NSW 2540

Pop 1,000. (147km S Sydney), See map on page 55, ref B4. Small town nestled at the foot of Cambewarra Mountain, off the road to Kangaroo Valley. Bush Walking, Fishing, Horse Riding, Scenic Drives, Swimming, Vineyards, Wineries.

B&B's/Guest Houses

★★★★☆ **Illaroo Lodge Bed & Breakfast**, (B&B), 521 Illaroo Rd, ☎ 02 4446 0443, fax 02 4446 0443, 2 rms [shwr, bath (1), tlt, hairdry, a/c, cent heat, elec blkts, tel, TV, clock radio, t/c mkg, refrig], lounge firepl, pool-heated (solar), c/park. **BB ♦ $90 - $100, ♦♦ $120 - $175, ♦ $50**, AE BC MC VI.

★★★★ **Barefoot Springs**, (B&B), Carrington Rd, off Moss Vale Rd, 9.5km SE of Kangaroo Valley PO, ☎ 02 4446 0509, fax 02 2446 0530, 4 rms [shwr, bath (1), spa bath (3), tlt, hairdry, a/c-cool (3), fan, heat, elec blkts, clock radio, t/c mkg], ldry, iron, iron brd, lounge (firepl), c/park. **BB ♦ $110, ♦♦ $130 - $195, ♦ $30 - $60**, ch con, Dinner by arrangement. AE BC DC MC VI.

★★★★ **Fuchsia Gardens**, (B&B), 120 Tannery Rd, 1km N of PO, ☎ 02 4446 0733, 3 rms [ensuite (3), shwr, bath (1), tlt, hairdry, fan, heat, elec blkts, tel, TV (3), video (avail), clock radio, t/c mkg (comm), refrig], lounge (firepl) (1), ✗, non smoking property. **BB ♦ $95 - $125, ♦♦ $125 - $190, ♦♦♦ $190 - $235**, BC MC VI.

CAMS WHARF NSW 2281

Pop Part of Lake Macquarie, (129km N Sydney), See map on page 55, ref E5. Cams Wharf lies on the south-eastern shores of Lake Macquarie. Boating, Fishing. See also Narellan & Wilton.

Self Catering Accommodation

AAA
TOURISM
Special Rates

★★★★☆ **Rafferty's Resort - Lake Macquarie**, (SA), 1 Wild Duck Dve via Rafferty's Rd, ☎ 02 4972 5555, fax 02 4972 5253, 86 serv apts acc up to 6, [shwr, bath, tlt, hairdry, a/c, cent heat, tel, TV, video, clock radio, refrig, cook fac, micro, elec frypan, d/wash, toaster], conf fac, lounge firepl, ✉, pool (heated), spa, bbq, plygr, tennis, cots, non smoking units. **D $215 - $286**, 19 units yet to be assessed, Min book applies, AE BC DC MC VI.

CANDELO NSW 2550

Pop 350. (447km S Sydney), See map on page 55, ref A8. Old south coast dairying and timber village that retains many of its 19th century buildings. Bowls, Golf, Horse Riding, Scenic Drives, Swimming, Tennis.

Self Catering Accommodation

★★★ **Bumblebrook Farm**, (SA), Kemps La, 4km NW of PO, ☎ 02 6493 2238, fax 02 6493 2299, 4 serv apts [shwr, tlt, fan, heat, elec blkts, tel, TV, clock radio, t/c mkg, refrig, cook fac, micro, toaster], ldry, ✕ (in Homestead), bbq, plygr, cots, Pets on application. **BB** ♦ **$66 - $88**, ♦♦ **$82.50 - $99**, ◊ **$10**, **W $385 - $623.70**, ch con, Dinner by arrangement. BC MC VI.

B&B's/Guest Houses

Koinonia Pastimes, (B&B), 443 Kameruka La, 5km SE of PO, ☎ 02 6493 2227, fax 02 6493 2225, 4 rms [shwr, tlt, elec blkts, clock radio, toaster], lounge (TV), lounge firepl, t/c mkg shared, non smoking property. **BB** ♦ **$55**, ♦♦ **$85**, (not yet classified).

CANOWINDRA NSW 2804

Pop 1,650. (307km W Sydney), See map on pages 52/53, ref G5. Canowindra lies beside the Belubula River and is a pretty place, renowned for such diverse attractions as hot air ballooning and fish fossils. Bowls, Golf, Swimming, Tennis.

Hotels/Motels

 ★★★ **Canowindra Riverview Motel**, (M), 3 Tilga St, 400m E of PO, ☎ 02 6344 1633, fax 02 6344 2484, (2 stry gr fl) 13 units [shwr, bath (4), spa bath (1), tlt, hairdry, a/c, elec blkts, tel, TV, clock radio, t/c mkg, refrig, cook fac (1), micro (1), toaster], ldry, iron, iron brd, bbq, dinner to unit, cots, non smoking rms (11). **RO** ♦ **$66 - $82**, ♦♦ **$77 - $93**, ◊ **$12 - $20**, pen con, AE BC EFT MC VI.

★★☆ **Blue Jacket Motel**, (M), Cnr Bridge St & Cowra Rd, 2km S of PO, ☎ 02 6344 1002, fax 02 6344 1303, 12 units [shwr, tlt, a/c-cool, heat, elec blkts, tel, TV, clock radio, t/c mkg, refrig], ✕, non smoking units (4). **RO** ♦ **$55**, ♦♦ **$66**, ◊ **$10**, ch con, BC MC VI.

B&B's/Guest Houses

The Falls Guest House, (GH), Heritage, Belubula Way, 4km E of Canowindra, ☎ 02 6344 1293, fax 02 6344 1290, 5 rms [ensuite (1), shwr (1), tlt (1), a/c, fire pl (4), heat, elec blkts, tel], ldry, rec rm, lounge (TV), conv fac, ✕, t/c mkg shared, c/park. **BB** ♦ **$55**, ♦♦ **$110**, **RO** ♦ **$49.50**, ♦♦ **$99**, ch con, AE BC DC MC VI.

CAPERTEE NSW 2846

Pop Nominal, (221km NW Sydney), See map on page 55, ref B1. Sleepy, historic village on the road between Lithgow and Mudge.

Self Catering Accommodation

Turon Gates, (Log Cabin), Turon River Rd, 40km from Lithgow, ☎ 02 6359 0142, fax 02 6359 0188, 7 log cabins acc up to 8, [shwr, heat reqd, refrig, cook fac, doonas, linen], bbq. **D** ♦ **$29 - $35**, **W** ♦ **$198**, AE BC MC VI, (not yet classified).

CARAGABAL NSW 2810

Pop Nominal (369km W Sydney) See map on pages 52/53, ref F5. A small farming town situated between Grenfell and West Wyalong.

Self Catering Accommodation

Ben Lomond Country Retreat, (House), 6km N of PO, ☎ 02 6347 5235, fax 02 6347 5235, 1 house acc up to 7, (3 bedrm), [shwr, tlt, a/c-cool, heat, TV, video, clock radio, refrig, cook fac, micro, toaster, ldry, blkts, doonas, linen, pillows], lounge firepl, bbq, c/park (undercover). **D $140, W $350**, (not yet classified).

CARCOAR NSW 2791

Pop 200. (260km W Sydney), See map on pages 52/53, ref G5. Historic, well preserved little town that features buildings classified by the National Trust, arts and crafts galleries, antique shops and tea rooms. Fishing, Gem Fossicking.

B&B's/Guest Houses

★★★☆ **Dalebrook Guest House & Cottages**, (GH), Naylor St, ☎ 02 6367 3149, fax 02 6369 3113, (2 stry), 4 rms [shwr, bath, tlt, hairdry, fan, fire pl, heat, elec blkts, tel, TV, clock radio, t/c mkg, refrig, cook fac (2), micro (2), elec frypan (2), toaster (2), ldry, pillows], w/mach, dryer, iron, pool (salt water), bbq, plygr, tennis, cots. **D** ♦♦ **$80 - $110**, ◊ **$20**, ch con, BC MC VI.

CARDIFF NSW

See Newcastle & Suburbs.

CASINO NSW 2470

Pop 10,000. (726km N Sydney), See map on page 54, ref D2. Town on the Richmond River promoted as being the 'Beef Capital of Australia'. Bowls, Fishing, Golf, Swimming, Tennis.

Hotels/Motels

★★★☆ **Casino Motor Inn**, (M), 91 Hare St (Tenterfield Rd), 900m S of PO, ☎ 02 6662 1777, fax 02 6662 6223, (2 stry gr fl) 30 units [shwr, spa bath (1), tlt, a/c, tel, TV, movie, clock radio, t/c mkg, refrig, toaster], ldry, iron, iron brd, ✕ (Mon to Sat), pool, rm serv, cots-fee, non smoking units (8). **RO** ♦ **$64**, ♦♦ **$74**, ♦♦♦ **$85**, ◊ **$10**, AE BC BTC DC MC VI.

 ★★★☆ **River Park Motor Inn**, (M), 123 Centre St, 500m W of PO, ☎ 02 6662 2999, fax 02 6662 2158, (2 stry gr fl), 29 units (2 suites) [shwr, tlt, hairdry, a/c, heat, tel (direct dial), cable tv (19), clock radio, t/c mkg, refrig, ldry (guest)], iron (19), iron brd (19), ✕ (6 nights), rm serv, non smoking rms. **RO** ♦ **$61 - $90**, ♦♦ **$68 - $90**, ◊ **$11**, **Suite RO $90**, AE BC DC EFT MC VI.

★★★ **Clydesdale Motel**, (M), Cnr Johnston & Kent Sts (Bruxner Hwy), 2.5km NE of PO, ☎ 02 6662 5982, fax 02 6662 5997, 10 units [shwr, tlt, a/c, elec blkts, tel, TV, video (avail), clock radio, t/c mkg, refrig], ✕ (6 days), dinner to unit, cots. **D $82.50 - $93.50**, **RO** ♦ **$62**, ♦♦ **$72.50**, ◊ **$11**, AE BC DC MC VI.

★★★ **Squatters Homestead**, (M), 161 Centre St, ☎ 02 6662 3888, fax 02 6662 7377, 10 units [shwr, tlt, a/c, heat, elec blkts, tel, TV, movie, clock radio, t/c mkg, refrig, toaster], cots-fee. **RO** ♦ **$58 - $68**, ♦♦ **$68 - $78**, ◊ **$10**, AE BC DC EFT MC VI.

Milgate Motel, (M), Cnr Centre & North St, 700m N of PO, ☎ 02 6662 1828, fax 02 6662 1022, 16 units [ensuite, a/c-cool, c/fan, heat, elec blkts, tel, TV, radio, t/c mkg, refrig], pool, bbq, cots, non smoking units (12). **RO** ♦ **$69**, ♦♦ **$79 - $84**, ◊ **$10**, BC MC VI, (not yet classified).

B&B's/Guest Houses

Mongogarie Lodge, (B&B), 1310 Mongogarie Rd Mongogarie via, 23km SE of PO, ☎ 02 6664 1254, fax 02 6664 1254, 3 rms [ensuite, c/fan, micro], ldry, lounge (TV), lounge firepl, t/c mkg shared, refrig, bbq, cots-fee, non smoking property. **BB** ♦♦ **$120**, ◊ **$40**, ch con, MC VI, (not yet classified).

CASSILIS NSW 2329

Pop Nominal, (403km NW Sydney), See map on pages 52/53, ref H4. Cassilis (pronounce it with an emphasis on the first syllable — CASS-ilis) is a charming, historic village in the foothills of the Liverpool and Great Dividing Ranges. Bowls, Scenic Drives, Tennis.

B&B's/Guest Houses
Runnymede Homestead, (B&B), Merriwa Rd, Golden Hwy, 12km E of PO, 30km W of Merriwa, ☎ 02 6376 1183, fax 02 6376 1187, 3 rms [shwr (2), tlt (2), fan (1), c/fan (1), fire pl, heat, elec blkts, tel, clock radio], shared fac (2 rms), ldry, lounge (TV), ✕, pool (salt water), t/c mkg shared, meals avail, tennis. **BB** ♦ **$60 - $90,** ♦♦ **$90 - $110,** **DBB** ♦ **$80 - $100,** ♦♦ **$130 - $150,** Min book long w/ends.

CENTRAL TILBA NSW 2546

Pop Nominal, (360km S Sydney), See map on page 55, ref A7. National Trust-classified village that looks much as it did a hundred years ago and has developed into one of the major art and craft centres of the south coast.

Self Catering Accommodation
★★★ **Bellburra Cottages**, (Cotg), 318 Ridge Rd, 6km N of village, ☎ 02 4473 7157, fax 02 4473 7157, 4 cotgs acc up to 6, [shwr, tlt, heat, elec blkts, TV, video (2), clock radio, t/c mkg, refrig, cook fac, micro, toaster, doonas, linen reqd-fee], ldry, w/mach, bbq, cots. **D $65 - $95, W $300 - $650,** BC MC VI.

B&B's/Guest Houses
★★★★☆ **Fablewood Folly Bed & Breakfast**, (B&B), 64, Lot 15 Sunnyside Rd, 15km S of Narooma, ☎ 02 4473 7434, fax 02 4473 7434, 2 rms [shwr, tlt, hairdry, c/fan, heat, elec blkts, tel, TV, clock radio, t/c mkg], iron, iron brd, TV rm, lounge firepl, pool-heated (solar/salt water), refrig, bbq, non smoking property. **BB** ♦♦ **$120,** ♦♦ **$700 - $840,** fam con.

★★★☆ **The Two Story Bed & Breakfast**, (B&B), Bate St, ☎ 02 4473 7290, fax 02 4473 7290, (2 stry), 3 rms [shwr, tlt, elec blkts, t/c mkg], shared fac (2 rms), lounge (TV), cots. **BB** ♦ **$75 - $85,** ♦♦ **$95 - $105,** ◊ **$15 - $25,** ch con, BC EFT MC VI.

★★★☆ **Wirrina**, (B&B), Blacksmiths Lne (off Bate St), 50m E of Cheese Factory, ☎ 02 4473 7279, fax 02 4473 7279, 3 rms [shwr (1), tlt (1), fan, heat, elec blkts], shared fac (2), lounge, t/c mkg shared. **BB** ♦ **$75,** ♦♦ **$95,** ◊ **$45,** AE BC MC VI.

CESSNOCK NSW 2325

Pop 17,550. (149km N Sydney), See map on page 55, ref B7. Regional centre that is the major town for the Hunter Valley wine area and a large coal mining area. See also Kurri Kurri.

Hotels/Motels
★★★★ **Aussie Rest Motel**, (M), 43 Shedden St, 1km W of PO, ☎ 02 4991 4197, fax 02 4991 7099, 15 units [shwr, tlt, hairdry, a/c, elec blkts, tel, TV, clock radio, t/c mkg, refrig], ldry, iron, iron brd, ✕, pool (salt water), dinner to unit, c/park. **BLB** ♦ **$60 - $80,** ♦♦ **$80 - $120,** ◊ **$22 - $33, RO** ♦ **$55 - $77,** ♦♦ **$80 - $110,** ◊ **$11 - $22,** AE BC MC VI.

★★★☆ **Cessnock Motel**, (M), 13 Allandale Rd, 300m N of PO, ☎ 02 4990 2699, fax 02 4990 5834, 20 units [shwr, tlt, hairdry, a/c, elec blkts, tel, TV, video-fee, clock radio, t/c mkg, refrig, toaster], iron, iron brd, pool-heated (solar), bbq-fee, dinner to unit, cots-fee, non smoking units (7). **RO** ♦ **$59 - $89,** ♦♦ **$69 - $99,** ♦♦♦ **$89 - $119,** ◊ **$20,** Min book long w/ends, AE BC DC MC VI.

★★★☆ **Cessnock Vintage Motor Inn**, (M), 300 Maitland Rd, 600m E of PO, ☎ 02 4990 4333, fax 02 4991 1240, (2 stry gr fl), 23 units [shwr, tlt, hairdry, a/c, elec blkts, tel, TV, movie, clock radio, t/c mkg, refrig], ldry, pool-heated (solar), cook fac, bbq, dinner to unit, cots-fee, non smoking units (10). **RO** ♦ **$64 - $90,** ♦♦ **$75 - $105,** ◊ **$15,** ch con, Minimum booking long weekend and special events, AE BC DC EFT MC MCH VI.

★★★☆ **Cumberland Motor Inn**, (M), 57 Cumberland St, 1km S of PO, ☎ 02 4990 6633, fax 02 4991 1619, (2 stry gr fl), 29 units [shwr, bath (4), tlt, hairdry, a/c, c/fan, elec blkts, tel, TV, video-fee, clock radio, t/c mkg, refrig, toaster], ldry, iron, iron brd, ✕ (Mon to Sat), pool (salt water), dinner to unit, non smoking units (10). **D $84 - $142,** Min book applies, AE BC DC MC VI.

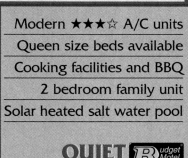

CESSNOCK NSW continued...

★★★ **Hunter Valley Motel**, (M), 30 Allandale Rd, 500m N of PO, ☎ 02 4990 1722, or 02 4990 1849, fax 02 4990 3025, (2 stry gr fl), 20 units [shwr, tlt, hairdry, a/c, fan, heat, elec blkts, tel, TV, video-fee, clock radio, t/c mkg, refrig, toaster], pool (salt water), bbq, dinner to unit, cots, non smoking rms (avail). **RO** ╫ $60 - $110, ╫ $82 - $125, ╫ $96 - $160, ╫ $18, ch con, Min book applies, AE BC DC EFT MC VI.

★★★ **Hunter Valley Travellers Rest**, (M), 35 Colliery St, 3km SE of PO, ☎ 02 4991 2355, fax 02 4991 2619, 17 units [shwr, tlt, a/c, c/fan, heat, elec blkts, tel, TV, clock radio, t/c mkg, refrig], ╳, bbq, cots, non smoking units. **BB** ╫ $75.80 - $95, ╫ $98.50 - $136.50, ╫ $32, ch con, AE BC DC EFT MC VI, ╠⚬.

Operator Comment: """Call about our fantastic getaway packages & indulge yourself not you wallet""".

★☆ **Bellbird Hotel**, (LH), 388 Wollombi Rd, Bellbird, 4km S of Cessnock, ☎ 02 4990 1094, fax 02 4991 5475, (2 stry), 18 rms [c/fan, heat, elec blkts, t/c mkg], lounge (TV), ╳, ╳, bbq, plygr, cots. **BB** ╫ $40 - $85, ╫ $59 - $95, ╫ $18, ch con, AE BC DC EFT MC VI.

★☆ **Chardonnay-Sky Motel**, (M), Lot 210 Allandale Rd, 5km N of PO, ☎ 02 4991 4812, fax 02 4991 2259, (2 stry gr fl), 20 units [shwr, tlt, a/c (7), c/fan, heat, elec blkts, TV, clock radio, t/c mkg, refrig], ldry, conv fac, pool, bbq, ╲, tennis, cots, non smoking units. **BLB** ╫ $65 - $99, ╫ $17, ch con, AE BC EFT MC VI.

★☆ **Royal Oak Hotel**, (LH), 221 Vincent St, 750m S of PO, ☎ 02 4990 2366, fax 02 4991 3366, (2 stry), 11 rms [elec blkts], shwr, tlt, iron, iron brd, lounge (TV), ╳, t/c mkg shared, ╲. **BLB** ╫ $30 - $35, ╫ $40 - $50, BC EFT MC VI.

Australia Hotel, (LH), All meals available on request. 136 Wollombi Rd, 1km W of PO, ☎ 02 4990 1256, fax 02 4990 6799, (2 stry), 15 rms [shwr (3), tlt (3)], ╳, ╳, bbq, ╲. **D** ╫ $30 - $35, ╫ $50 - $55, Rooms 1 and 4 not rated. BC EFT MC VI.

Neath Hotel, (LH), Classified by National Trust, Cessnock Rd, Neath 2326, 6km E of PO, ☎ 02 4930 4270, fax 02 4930 4195, (Multi-stry), 28 rms [elec blkts], ldry, lounge, ╳ (Fri to Sat), cots. **BB** ╫ $40 - $55, ╫ $60 - $90, ╫ $30, Min book applies.

Wentworth Hotel, (LH), 36 Vincent St, 100m S of PO, ☎ 02 4990 1364, fax 02 4990 7254, (2 stry), 21 rms [elec blkts], lounge (TV), ╳, t/c mkg shared, cots. **BB** ╫ $50 - $70, ╫ $80 - $95, ╫ $22 - $25, ch con, BC MC VI.

Self Catering Accommodation

★★★★ **Victoria Cottage**, (Cotg), 251 Maitland Rd, ☎ 02 4991 2120, fax 02 4990 6620, 1 cotg acc up to 6, [shwr, bath, tlt, a/c, elec blkts, TV, t/c mkg, refrig, cook fac, d/wash, toaster, ldry, doonas], w/mach, iron, iron brd, non smoking property. **D** $130 - $200.

B&B's/Guest Houses

★★★★ **Cessnock Heritage Inn**, (B&B), 167 Vincent St, 100m from Town Hall, ☎ 02 4991 2744, fax 02 4991 2720, (2 stry), 13 rms [shwr, tlt, hairdry, a/c, c/fan, elec blkts, tel, TV, clock radio, t/c mkg, refrig], iron, iron brd, lounge, ╳, c/park. **BB** ╫ $64 - $85, **DBB** ╫ $84 - $120, ╫ $130 - $160, Min book long w/ends, BC JCB MC MCH VI.

★★★★ **Danica House Bed & Breakfast**, (B&B), 27 Orient St, ☎ 02 4991 4893, 4 rms [shwr, tlt, c/fan, heat, TV, clock radio, t/c mkg, refrig, toaster], iron, iron brd, bbq, c/park. **BLB** ╫ $70 - $125, BC MC VI.

★★★★ **Greta Main Payoffice Guesthouse**, (B&B), No children's facilities, Lot 12 Wollombi Rd Greta Main via, 10km W of Cessnock, ☎ 02 4998 1703, fax 02 4998 1715, 3 rms [shwr, tlt, hairdry, a/c, c/fan, elec blkts, TV, clock radio, t/c mkg, refrig], lounge firepl, ╳, non smoking rms. **BB** ╫ $80 - $120, ╫ $85 - $130, **DBB** ╫ $110 - $150, ╫ $145 - $190, pen con, BC MC VI.

★★★☆ **Colliery House B&B**, (B&B), Lot 393 Colliery St, Neath 2326, 5km E of PO, ☎ 02 4930 8286, fax 02 4930 8286, 2 rms [shwr, spa bath (1), tlt, a/c (1), heat, TV (1), t/c mkg, refrig, toaster], iron, iron brd, lounge firepl, bbq, dinner to unit, non smoking property. **BB** ╫ $110 - $165, ╫ $55 - $77, **DBB** ╫ $187 - $242, ╫ $93.50 - $121, **Suite D** $165.

CHAIN VALLEY BAY NSW 2259

Pop 2,250. Part of Wyong, (124km N Sydney), See map on page 55, ref D5. Settlement that is actually on Lake Macquarie, but its situation on the northern boundary of Wyong Shire means that it is part of what's termed the Central Coast. Boating, Fishing, Swimming.

Self Catering Accommodation

★★★ **Teraglin Lakeshore Tourist Village**, Mulloway Rd, 3.5km W of Pacific Hwy, ☎ 02 4358 8267, fax 02 4358 8734, 13 cabins acc up to 6, [shwr, tlt, TV, refrig, cook fac, blkts reqd, linen reqd, pillows reqd], ldry, w/mach-fee, dryer-fee, iron-fee, pool, bbq, kiosk, LPG, ╲, tennis. **D** ╫ $55 - $80, ╫ $5 - $8, EFT.

CHARLESTOWN NSW

See Newcastle & Suburbs.

CHARLOTTE PASS NSW 2624

Pop Nominal, (521km S Sydney), See map on pages 52/53, ref F7. Snowy Mountains resort set deep within Kosciuszko National Park. At 1760m, it is the highest village in Australia (as opposed to Cabramurra, which is the highest town). Bush Walking, Snow Skiing.

Other Accommodation

Alitji Alpine Lodge, (Lodge), Charlotte Pass via, Perisher Valley 2624, ☎ 02 9971 0723, 8 rms acc up to 5, [shwr, tlt, heat, elec blkts, video (avail), blkts, linen, pillows], ldry, w/mach, dryer, iron, lounge (TV), ╳, bar, t/c mkg shared, refrig, ╲, cots. **D all meals** $450.

Kosciusko Chalet, (Lodge), Kosciuszko Rd, Snowy Mountains, ☎ 02 6457 5245, fax 02 6457 5362, (Multi-stry gr fl), 34 rms (3 suites) [shwr, bath, tlt, cent heat, t/c mkg], ldry, dry rm, lounge (TV), ✕, cots. DBB ∮ $95 - $113, ch con, Tariff includes oversnow transport, ski lift pass & ski tube tickets, Min book applies, AE BC DC MC VI.

CHINDERAH NSW 2487

Pop Nominal, (853km N Sydney), See map on page 54, ref E1. Small sugar growing township on the Tweed River between Tweed Heads and Murwillumbah. Bowls, Fishing, Golf, Surfing, Swimming, Tennis.

Hotels/Motels
★★★ **Chinderah Motel**, (M), 26 Chinderah Bay Dve, ☎ 02 6674 1660, fax 02 6674 4789, 11 units [shwr, tlt, a/c (8), fan, heat, tel, TV, clock radio, t/c mkg, refrig], ldry, pool, bbq, cots-fee, non smoking units (5). RO ∮ $45, ∮∮ $50, ∮∮∮ $60, ch con, Meals by arrangement.

CHITTAWAY BAY NSW 2261

Pop Part of Wyong, (81km N Sydney), See map on page 55, ref D6. Central Coast town on the bay of the same name in the south-western corner of Tuggerah Lake.

Hotels/Motels
★★★★ **Chittaway Motel**, (M), 98 Chittaway Rd, ☎ 02 4388 9110, fax 02 4388 9118, (2 stry gr fl), 20 units [shwr, bath (2), tlt, hairdry, a/c, tel, TV, movie, clock radio, t/c mkg, refrig, cook fac (2), micro (2), toaster], ldry, iron, iron brd, pool (salt water), bbq, cots, non smoking units (10). RO ∮ $95, ∮∮ $95, ∮ $15, pen con, AE BC DC EFT MC VI, ♿.

CHITTAWAY MOTEL

AAAT ★★★★

Situated in the heart of the Central Coast, just minutes from famous surf beaches, major shopping complexes, tourist attractions, licenced clubs and sporting facilities.

• Air Conditioning • In House Movies,
• Family Rooms with Cooking facilities • Pool & BBQ Area.

(02) 4388 9110

1303AG

B&B's/Guest Houses
★★★☆ **Chittaway Bay B & B Pelicans Rest**, (B&B), 68 Aloha Dve, ☎ 02 4388 6495, (2 stry gr fl), 2 rms [hairdry (1), fan (1), c/fan (1), heat, TV], ldry, iron (1), iron brd (1), lounge, t/c mkg shared, refrig, bbq, courtesy transfer, non smoking rms. BB ∮ $55 - $65, ∮∮ $75 - $85, fam con, pen con.

COBAR NSW 2835

Pop 4,500. (706km W Sydney), See map on pages 52/53, ref E3. Cobar is a bustling, thriving place offering many services to travellers and is a true frontier town — if you're heading north or west, from here on you're in the outback. Bowls, Golf, Shooting, Swimming.

Hotels/Motels

 ★★★☆ **Sundowner Chain Motor Inns**, (M), 67 Barrier Hwy (Marshall St), 1km W of PO, ☎ 02 6836 2304, fax 02 6836 2042, 43 units [shwr, spa bath, tlt, a/c, heat, elec blkts, tel, TV, clock radio, t/c mkg, refrig, mini bar], ldry, conv fac, ✕, pool (salt water), spa, bbq, cots, non smoking units (13). RO ∮ $87 - $189, ∮∮ $91 - $189, ∮ $11, ch con, 13 units of a lower rating. AE BC DC VI, ♿.
★★★☆ **Town & Country Motor Inn**, (M), 52 Marshall St, 500m NW of PO, ☎ 02 6836 1244, fax 02 6836 1383, (2 stry gr fl), 23 units [shwr, tlt, hairdry, a/c, elec blkts, tel, TV, movie-fee, clock radio, t/c mkg, refrig, toaster], ldry, iron, iron brd, conv fac, ✕ (Mon-Sat), pool (salt water), bbq, rm serv, dinner to unit (Mon-Sat), cots-fee, non smoking rms (6). RO ∮ $77, ∮∮ $88, pen con, AE BC DC EFT MC VI.

 ★★★ **Cobar Oasis**, (M), 76 Marshall St (Barrier Hwy), 500m W of PO, ☎ 02 6836 2452, fax 02 6836 1416, (2 stry gr fl), 20 units [shwr, tlt, hairdry (15), a/c, elec blkts, tel, TV, movie, clock radio, t/c mkg, refrig, toaster], iron (15), iron brd (15), pool, bbq, rm serv, meals to unit, cots-fee, non smoking units (5). RO ∮ $58, ∮∮ $70, ∮∮∮ $78, ∮ $8, AE BC DC EFT MC MCH VI, ♿.
★★★ **Copper City Motel**, (M), 40 Lewis St, Cnr Barrier Hwy & Kidman Way, ☎ 02 6836 2404, or 02 6836 2504, fax 02 6836 3680, 30 units [shwr, bath (2), tlt, a/c, elec blkts, tel, TV, video-fee, clock radio, t/c mkg, refrig, toaster], ldry, ✕, pool, bbq, rm serv, cots, non smoking units (8). RO ∮ $55, ∮∮ $66, ∮ $10, ch con, 5 units of a higher rating, AE BC DC EFT MC VI.

 ★★★ **Cross Roads**, (M), 21 Louth Rd, 650m N of State Bank, ☎ 02 6836 2711, fax 02 6836 1028, 17 units [shwr, tlt, a/c, elec blkts, tel, TV, clock radio, t/c mkg, refrig], pool, bbq, rm serv, cots, non smoking units (6). RO ∮ $60 - $66, ∮∮ $66 - $72, ∮∮∮∮ $84 - $92, ∮ $8, AE BC DC MC VI, ♿.
★★★ **Hi-Way Motel**, (M), Barrier Hwy, ☎ 02 6836 2000, fax 02 6836 1409, 12 units [shwr, tlt, hairdry, a/c, elec blkts, tel, TV, movie, clock radio, t/c mkg, refrig, mini bar, toaster], pool (salt water), bbq, rm serv, cots, non smoking units (6). RO ∮ $58, ∮∮ $62 - $74, AE BC DC EFT MC VI, ♿.

COBARGO NSW 2550

Pop 400. (380km S Sydney), See map on page 55, ref A7. Old south coast village in the heart of dairy country. It's a pretty place that's well known for its local arts and crafts. Scenic Drives.

Hotels/Motels
★★ **Cobargo Motel Hotel**, (LMH), Princes Hwy, ☎ 02 6493 6423, fax 02 6493 6730, 7 units [shwr, tlt, heat, elec blkts, tel, TV, video, t/c mkg, refrig], ldry, ✕, pool, spa. D ∮ $44, ∮∮ $55, ∮∮∮ $66, ∮ $10, BC EFT MC VI.

B&B's/Guest Houses

 ★★★★ **Eilancroft Country Retreat Bed & Breakfast**, (B&B), County Boundary Rd, 8km W of PO, ☎ 02 6493 7362, fax 02 6493 7362, 2 rms [shwr, tlt, fan, heat, elec blkts, tel, TV, clock radio], ldry, iron, iron brd, lounge (firepl), ✕, t/c mkg shared, dinner to unit, non smoking property. BB ∮ $80 - $90, ∮∮ $95 - $110, DBB ∮ $95 - $115, ∮∮ $160 - $170, BC MC VI.
The Old Cobargo Convent, (B&B), Wandella Rd, 500m W of PO, ☎ 02 6493 6419, fax 02 6493 6419, 1 rm [a/c, fire pl, elec blkts, clock radio, doonas], lounge (TV), lounge firepl, t/c mkg shared, non smoking property. BB ∮ $60, ∮∮ $100 - $110, ∮ $50, BC MC VI, (not yet classified).

COFFS HARBOUR NSW 2450

Pop 22,200. (558km N Sydney), See map on page 54, ref D5. Major north coast commercial and holiday centre. Bowls, Bush Walking, Canoeing, Croquet, Fishing, Golf, Horse Racing, Surfing, Swimming, Tennis.

Hotels/Motels
★★★★☆ **Aanuka Beach Resort**, (M), Resort, Firman Dve, Diggers Beach, 4km N of PO, ☎ 02 6652 7555, fax 02 6652 7053, 48 units (49 suites) [shwr, spa bath, tlt, hairdry, a/c, heat, tel, TV, video, t/c mkg, refrig, cook fac, toaster, ldry], conf fac, ✕ (2), pool indoor heated, sauna, spa, bbq, rm serv, plygr, gym, tennis, cots (avail). BB $204 - $390, AE BC DC MC VI.

★★★★☆ **(Beach Village - Holiday Unit Section)**, 47 units acc up to 6, [shwr, spa bath, tlt, tel, TV, video, refrig, cook fac, micro, d/wash, toaster, linen], pool-heated, spa, bbq, rm serv, plygr, tennis, cots. D $104 - $473.

Trouble-free travel tips - **Windscreen wipers**

Check the operation of windscreen wipers and washers. Replace windscreen wiper rubbers if they are not cleaning the windscreen properly.

C

NEW SOUTH WALES

ALL SEASONS PREMIER™
Pacific Bay Resort
C O F F S   H A R B O U R

AAA Tourism ★★★★☆

Set in 40 hectares of sub-tropical gardens on Charlesworth Bay, All Seasons Premier Pacific Bay Resort in Coffs Harbour offers guests the ultimate in a beachside getaway holiday.

RESORT ROOM
- King or twin bed option
- Private balcony
- Tea & Coffee making facilities
- Mini Bar
- Television

ONE BEDROOM SPA SUITE
- Luxury suite
- Large lounge area
- Separate bedroom with king bed
- Spacious bathroom with spa bath
- Private balcony

ONE BEDROOM FAMILY APARTMENT
- Fully self contained apartment
- Kitchen
- Laundry with dryer
- Separate bedroom with king bed
- Lounge area with sofa bed
- Private balcony

Pacific Bay Resort features extensive recreational facilities including tennis courts, 3 heated swimming pools, 9 hole golf course, Kids Club, gymnasium, indoor spa and sauna, massage & beauty retreat, hair salon and much more.

Cnr Pacific Highway & Bay Drive, Coffs Harbour, NSW 2450

Tel: (02) 6659 7000
Fax: (02) 6659 7100
email: pacific@allseasons.com.au

1333AG

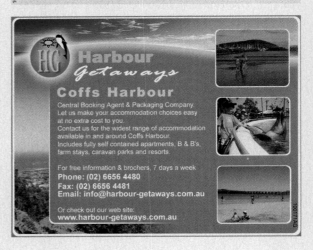

COFFS HARBOUR JETTY

Motel Caribbean
The place to stay in Coffs Harbour

Balcony rooms with ocean & harbour views, just a short walk to the historic jetty, marina, beaches & restaurants.

- Apartments
- Balcony rooms with spa
- Motel rooms
- All air-conditioned

353 High st, Coffs Harbour Jetty
Ph: (02) 6652 1500 Fax: (02) 6651 4158
caribean@tpgi.com.au

Allambie Holiday Apartments
The apartments with the superb harbour views
Experience the vibrant jetty area where you actually see the sea from your room.

- Self contained 1 & 2 bedroom apartments
- Pool • Spa
- Close to beaches, restaurants and marina

22 Camperdown St, Coffs Harbour Jetty
Ph: (02) 6652 6690 Fax: (02) 6652 9942

FLAG
FLAG CHOICE HOTELS

★★★☆ **Big Windmill Motor Lodge**, (M), 168 Pacific Hwy, 1km S of PO, ☎ 02 6652 2933, fax 02 6652 5872, 39 units (2 suites) [shwr, spa bath (2), tlt, hairdry, a/c-cool (39), fan (10), heat, elec blkts, tel, cable tv, clock radio, t/c mkg, refrig, mini bar, toaster], ldry, iron, iron brd, conf fac, ⊠, pool, sauna, spa, rm serv, cots-fee, non smoking units (15). **RO** ⸙ **$78 - $126,** ⸙⸙ **$80 - $130,** ⸙⸙⸙ **$85 - $135,** ⸙ **$10, Suite RO $110 - $135,** ch con, 8 units at a lower rating, AE BC DC EFT MC MP VI, ⟨☆⟩.

★★★☆ **Caribbean Motel**, (M), 353 High St, opposite Jetty PO, ☎ 02 6652 1500, fax 02 6651 4158, (Multi-stry gr fl), 22 units [shwr, spa bath (5), tlt, a/c, tel, fax, TV, clock radio, t/c mkg, refrig, cook fac (7)], iron, iron brd, pool, c/park (undercover) (10), cots. **RO** ⸙ **$60 - $75,** ⸙⸙ **$70 - $105,** ⸙⸙⸙ **$75 - $115,** ⸙ **$10,** AE BC DC JCB MC VI.

★★★☆ **Chelsea Motor Inn**, (M), 106 Grafton St (Pacific Hwy), 100m from RSL Club, ☎ 02 6652 2977, fax 02 6651 3467, (2 stry gr fl), 29 units [shwr, spa bath (1), tlt, a/c, tel, cable tv, movie, clock radio, t/c mkg, refrig], ldry, courtesy transfer, cots, non smoking units (10). **RO** ⸙ **$53 - $83,** ⸙⸙ **$64 - $94,** ⸙ **$11,** ch con, AE BC DC EFT MC VI, ⟨☆⟩.

★★★☆ **Coachmens Inn**, (M), 93 Park Beach Rd, 4km NE of PO, ☎ 02 6652 6044, fax 02 6651 2482, (2 stry gr fl), 41 units [shwr, tlt, a/c (20), fan, heat, tel, cable tv, clock radio, t/c mkg, refrig], ldry, rec rm, conf fac, pool, bbq, dinner to unit, c/park (undercover), car wash, cots-fee, non smoking units (20). **RO** ⸙ **$50 - $86,** ⸙⸙ **$54 - $96,** ⸙⸙⸙ **$64 - $105,** ⸙ **$11 - $17,** ch con, 9 units of a lower rating. AE BC DC EFT MC MP VI.

FLAG
FLAG CHOICE HOTELS

★★★☆ **Coffs Harbour Motor Inn**, (M), 22 Elizabeth St, 500m S of PO, ☎ 02 6652 6388, fax 02 6652 6493, (Multi-stry gr fl), 35 units [shwr, bath (5), spa bath (3), tlt, hairdry, a/c, elec blkts, tel, TV, movie, clock radio, t/c mkg, refrig, cook fac (3), toaster], ldry, iron, iron brd, ⊠, pool, spa, bbq, rm serv, cots-fee, non smoking rms (6). **RO** ⸙ **$88 - $138,** ⸙⸙ **$90 - $130,** ⸙ **$5 - $10,** AE BC DC EFT MC MP VI.

★★★☆ **Country Comfort - Coffs Harbour**, (M), 353 Pacific Hwy, 3.5km N of PO, ☎ 02 6652 8222, fax 02 6652 3832, 52 units [shwr, bath (12), spa bath (6), tlt, hairdry, a/c, tel, TV, movie, clock radio, t/c mkg, refrig, mini bar, cook fac (12)], ldry, conv fac, ⊠, pool, sauna, spa, bbq, rm serv, dinner to unit, plygr, tennis, cots, non smoking units (18). **RO** ⸙ **$90 - $123,** ⸙⸙ **$90 - $123,** ⸙ **$16.50,** ch con, AE BC DC MC VI, ⟨☆⟩.

AAA
T O U R I S M
Special Rates

COUNTRY COMFORT

1356AG

- ✦ Centre of Town
- ✦ Opposite Ex-Services Club
- ✦ 29 Air Conditioned Units
- ✦ 1 Disabled Unit
- ✦ Pay TV FREE to all units
- ✦ 1 Spa unit with double spa bath & Kingsize Bed
- ✦ Smoking or Non-Smoking Units available

Chelsea
Motor Inn

106 Grafton Street (Pacific Highway)
Coffs Harbour NSW 2450
PHONE **(02) 6652 2977**
FAX (02) 6651 3467
EMAIL: chelsea@key.net.au

COFFS HARBOUR MOTOR INN

1361AG

- ★ 300m to city centre, shops, cinemas and clubs opp. bus station
- ★ Pool, Heated Spa, BBQ area
- ★ Licensed restaurant and bar
- ★ Rooms with cooking facilities
- ★ Austar free to rooms, modem ports
- ★ All rooms renovated August 1998

RESERVATIONS:
1800 062 158

FLAG

22 Elizabeth Street Coffs Harbour 2450
Ph: (02) 6652 6388   Fax: (02) 6652 6493
Email: coffcoff@ozemail.com.au Internet: www.visitcoffsharbour.com/coffsinn

★★★☆ **Park Beach Resort**, (M), 111 Park Beach Rd, 500m E of Plaza PO, ☎ 02 6652 4511, fax 02 6652 4511, (2 stry gr fl), 16 units (2 suites) [shwr, spa bath (1), tlt, a/c (10), fan, heat, elec blkts, tel, cable tv, video-fee, clock radio, t/c mkg, refrig, cook fac (2), toaster], ldry, pool-heated (solar), spa, bbq, mini golf, gym, tennis (half court), cots-fee. RO ♦♦ $50 - $120, ♦♦♦ $65 - $139, ◊ $15, Suite D $89 - $239, AE BC DC EFT MC VI.

★★★☆ **Parkside Motor Inn**, (M), 14 Elizabeth St, 400m S of PO, ☎ 02 6652 4655, fax 02 6651 3616, (2 stry gr fl), 21 units [shwr, bath (9), tlt, hairdry, a/c, elec blkts (on request), tel, cable tv, clock radio, t/c mkg, refrig], ldry, ⊠, pool, spa, dinner to unit, cots-fee, non smoking units (10). RO ♦ $80 - $136, ♦♦ $93 - $136, ♦♦♦ $105 - $136, ◊ $12, AE BC DC MC MP VI.

AAA
T O U R I S M
Special Rates

★★★☆ **Pelican Beach Centra Resort**, (M), Resort, Pacific Hwy, 7km N of PO, ☎ 02 6653 7000, fax 02 6653 7066, (Multi-stry gr fl), 112 units [shwr, bath, tlt, hairdry, a/c, elec blkts, tel, TV, movie-fee, clock radio, t/c mkg, refrig, mini bar, cook fac (62)], lift, ldry, iron, iron brd, rec rm, lounge, conv fac, ⊠, pool (heated - winter), sauna, spa (2), bbq, 24hr reception, ✆, plygr, mini golf, gym, tennis (3), cots. RO ♦ $136 - $151, ♦♦ $136 - $151, ◊ $27, Min book applies, AE BC DC JCB MC VI, ♿.

GOLDEN CHAIN

★★★☆ **Premier Motor Inn**, (M), Pacific Hwy, 1km S of PO, ☎ 02 6652 2044, fax 02 6652 8516, 32 units [shwr, tlt, a/c, elec blkts, tel, TV, clock radio, t/c mkg, refrig, mini bar, micro, toaster], ldry, iron, iron brd, ⊠ (Mon to Sat), pool, bbq, rm serv, plygr, cots-fee, non smoking rms (avail). RO ♦ $56 - $110, ♦♦ $61 - $120, ♦♦♦♦ $90 - $130, 8 units ★★☆. AE BC DC MC VI.

★★★☆ **Royal Palms Motor Inn**, (M), 87 Park Beach Rd, 300m E of Park Beach Plaza, ☎ 02 6652 4422, fax 02 6651 2617, (2 stry gr fl), 30 units [shwr, tlt, hairdry, a/c, tel, TV, video, clock radio, t/c mkg, refrig, micro (3), toaster], ldry, pool, spa, bbq, dinner to unit, cots-fee, non smoking units (10). RO ♦ $49.50 - $99, ♦♦ $53 - $99, ◊ $11, AE BC DC MC VI, ♿.

Sanctuary Motor Inn & Resort

COFFS HARBOUR SOUTH
PHONE: (02) 6652 2111   FAX: (02) 6652 4725
visit our website at www.sanctuaryresort.com
email: info@sanctuaryresort.com

The Perfect choice for Business or Pleasure
★★★☆ AAA TOURISM

- ❀ Attractive bushland setting on 7 acres
- ❀ 37 luxurious rooms – Standard, Family, Kitchen, Deluxe
- ❀ Executive Suites with spa ❀ Pool/Waterslide, Spa and Sauna
- ❀ BBQ area ❀ Tennis and Squash Courts and Nine Hole Mini Putt Golf ❀ Wild Life Animal Sanctuary ❀ Licensed a-la carte Treehouse Restaurant overlooking gardens & mountains ❀ Courtesy vehicle available ❀ Ideally located 1.5km from city centre & 2km from airport

PACIFIC HIGHWAY COFFS HARBOUR SOUTH

Town Lodge Motor Inn
Centre of the City

[Map showing High St, Elbow St, Pacific Highway, Vernon St, Coffs St, To Sydney, City Centre PO, RSL, Bowling Club, To Brisbane]

Give your Hosts, TONY & ESME, a call on

Phone: (02) 6652 1288
Fax: (02) 6652 1306

110 PACIFIC HIGHWAY,
COFFS HARBOUR 2450

- **ADJACENT TO BOWLING AND EX-SERVICES CLUB**
- **FULLY AIR CONDITIONED**
- **ONLY 250 METRES FROM CITY CENTRE AND P.O.**
- **QUEEN SIZE BEDS**
- **FULLY FUNCTIONAL POOL**

Bananatown Motel
Budget Accommodation

- Undercover parking • 400m to CBD & clubs • Direct dial fax
- • Air conditioned • Swimming pool

AAA Tourism ★★★

PO Box 1638
15 Grafton Street, Coffs Harbour

Phone and Fax:
(02) 6652 4411

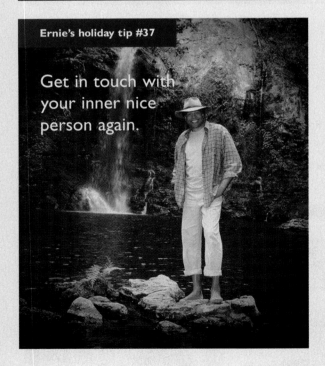

Ernie's holiday tip #37

Get in touch with your inner nice person again.

★★★☆ **Sanctuary Resort Motel**, (M), Pacific Hwy, 2km S of PO, ☎ 02 6652 2111, (2 stry gr fl), 37 units [shwr, spa bath (2), tlt, a/c (33), heat, tel, TV, movie, t/c mkg, refrig, mini bar, cook fac (4)], ldry, conf fac, ✕, pool (salt water), sauna, spa, bbq, rm serv, courtesy transfer, plygr, mini golf, squash, tennis, cots-fee. **RO** ♦ **$82.50 - $93.50,** ♦♦ **$88 - $104.50,** ♦♦♦ **$99 - $115.50,** ◊ **$13.50,** 15 units of a higher rating, AE BC DC EFT MC VI.

★★★☆ **Surf Beach Motor Inn**, (M), 25 Ocean Pde, Park Beach, 2km NE of PO, ☎ 02 6652 1872, fax 02 6652 1498, (2 stry gr fl), 11 units [shwr, tlt, fan, heat, tel, TV, clock radio, t/c mkg, refrig], ldry, pool, bbq, courtesy transfer, cots-fee, non smoking units. **D $88 - $140, RO** ♦♦ **$59 - $110,** ◊ **$11,** AE BC DC MC VI.

★★★☆ **Town Lodge Motor Inn**, (M), 110 Grafton St (Pacific Hwy), 350m N of PO, ☎ 02 6652 1288, fax 02 6652 1306, (2 stry gr fl), 20 units [shwr, tlt, a/c, tel (direct dial), cable tv, video (avail)-fee, clock radio, t/c mkg, refrig, toaster], pool, wading pool, non smoking units (7). **RO** ♦ **$58 - $104,** ♦♦ **$61 - $104,** ◊ **$11,** AE BC DC MC VI.

★★★ **Bananatown Motel**, (M), 15 Grafton St, 400m S of PO, ☎ 02 6652 4411, fax 02 6652 4411, 13 units [shwr, tlt, hairdry, a/c, fan, heat, tel, cable tv, clock radio, t/c mkg, refrig], pool, bbq, meals to unit, c/park (undercover), cots-fee. **RO** ♦ **$50 - $85,** ♦♦ **$50 - $89,** ♦♦♦ **$60 - $99,** ◊ **$5 - $14,** AE BC DC EFT MC VI.

★★★ **Bentleigh Motor Inn (Coffs Harbour)**, (M), Previously Plantation Inn, 94 Grafton St (Pacific Hwy), City Centre, ☎ 02 6652 2566, fax 02 6652 2566, (2 stry gr fl), 32 units [shwr, tlt, a/c, fan, heat, tel, TV, radio, t/c mkg, refrig], ldry, conv fac, ✕, cots. **RO** ♦ **$55 - $80,** ♦♦ **$58 - $90,** ♦♦♦ **$82 - $120,** AE BC DC MC VI.

 ★★★ **Bo suns Inn Motel**, (M), 37 Ocean Pde, 1.5km SE of Park Beach Plaza PO, ☎ 02 6651 2251, fax 02 6651 2251, (2 stry gr fl), 12 units (4 suites) [shwr, tlt, c/fan, heat, elec blkts, tel, TV, video-fee, clock radio, t/c mkg, refrig, cook fac (6), toaster], ldry, iron, iron brd, pool, spa, bbq, cots. **RO** ♦ **$61 - $99,** ♦♦ **$61 - $99,** ◊ **$11, Suite D $68 - $110,** Min book applies, AE BC DC EFT MC VI, ♿.

COFFS HARBOUR HOLIDAY VILLAGE

97 PARK BEACH RD • PHONE 02 6652 2055 • FAX 02 6652 2198 FLAG

Email: holicoff@fc-hotels.com.au

- Quiet off road location
- Standard & family rooms with cooking
- non-smoking & air conditioned rooms
- Licensed restaurant & bar - Room service
- Pool, hot spa, sauna, BBQ & trampoline
- Guest laundry
- 200m to beach, Bowls Club, specialty shops & take-aways
- Tour booking service
- Discounted rates for coaches & groups
- Bus & boat parking
- Family operated personalised service

Hosts: Larry, Lenie & Rinus, Sue

Toreador Motel

- Opposite Tourist Information & Coach Stop
- Stroll to City Centre, RSL, Clubs, Restaurants
- All Ground Floor Units with undercover parking
- Free Austar, remote TV, Air Conditioning
- Owner Operated

31 Grafton St (adj. Pacific Highway)

Phone: 02 6652 3887

Fax: 02 6652 5813

FLAG
FLAG CHOICE HOTELS

★★★ **Coffs Harbour Holiday Village**, (M), 97 Park Beach Rd, 2km NE of PO, ☎ 02 6652 2055, fax 02 6652 2198, (2 stry gr fl), 22 units [shwr, tlt, hairdry (6), a/c (6), fan, heat, elec blkts, tel, TV, video (avail), clock radio, t/c mkg, refrig, cook fac, toaster], ldry, w/mach-fee, dryer-fee, iron (10), iron brd (10), ✉, pool, sauna-fee, spa, bbq, rm serv, dinner to unit, plygr, gym, cots-fee, non smoking units (6). W $427 - $616, RO ♦ $61 - $88, ♦♦ $66 - $94, ◊ $10, ch con, 5 units ★★☆. AE BC DC MC MP VI.

★★★ **(Serviced Apartment Section)**, 9 serv apts acc up to 5, [shwr, tlt, hairdry (3), fan, c/fan (7), heat, elec blkts, tel, TV, video-fee, clock radio, t/c mkg, refrig, cook fac, micro (2), elec frypan, toaster, blkts, linen], iron, iron brd, cots-fee, non smoking units (2). D ♦♦ $79 - $142, ◊ $10, W $553 - $1,001.

★★★ **Golden Glow Motel**, (M), 19 Grafton St, 500m S of PO, ☎ 02 6652 2644, fax 02 6651 1436, 15 units [shwr, tlt, hairdry, a/c, fan, elec blkts, tel, cable tv, video, clock radio, t/c mkg, refrig, cook fac ltd (1), toaster, ldry], pool, bbq, dinner to unit, c/park (undercover), cots, non smoking rms (avail). RO ♦ $57 - $85, ♦♦ $57 - $85, ♦♦♦ $65 - $95, ◊ $7 - $10, 4 units at a higher standard. AE BC DC EFT MC VI,

Operator Comment: Bookings: Freecall 1800 659 869
Email: goldglow@key.net.au

Budget Motel Chain International

★★★ **Hawaiian Sands Motor Inn**, (M), Cnr Park Beach Rd & Ocean Pde, ☎ 02 6652 2666, fax 02 6652 2666, 17 units [shwr, tlt, a/c, elec blkts, tel, fax, TV, video-fee, clock radio, t/c mkg, refrig, cook fac (5), micro (5), toaster], iron, conv fac, ✉, pool, bbq, rm serv, courtesy transfer, cots-fee, non smoking units (8). RO ♦ $55 - $99, ♦♦ $64 - $99, ♦♦♦♦ $80 - $137, ◊ $13, Min book Christmas Jan long w/ends and Easter, AE BC DC MC MCH VI.

★★★ **Ocean Parade Motel**, (M), 41 Ocean Pde, 1km E of Plaza, ☎ 02 6652 6733, fax 02 6652 6733, (2 stry gr fl), 18 units [shwr, tlt, fan, heat, elec blkts, tel, TV, video, movie, clock radio, t/c mkg, refrig], ldry, pool (salt water), bbq, cots, non smoking units (2). RO ♦ $50 - $80, ♦ $50 - $80, ♦♦ $52 - $100, ♦♦♦ $55 - $130, ◊ $5 - $10, AE BC DC EFT MC VI.

COFFSHARBOUR

★★☆ AAA Tourism

- Motel Units are all Ground Level • 24hr Check In • Pool & BBQ Area • Playground
- Direct Dial Phone • Queen Beds • Games Room • Air Conditioning • Fax Facility
ALSO AVAILABLE • 2 BR FULLY SELF CONTAINED VILLAS • SLEEP UP TO 8 PRS

AROSA MOTEL 220 PACIFIC HWY
• PHONE: 0266523555 • FAX: 0266523276

★★★ **Paradise Palms Resort**, (M), 675 Pacific Hwy Korora via, 6km N of PO, ☎ 02 6653 6291, fax 02 6653 7351, 40 units [shwr, bath (9), spa bath (2), tlt, hairdry, fan, heat, TV, clock radio, t/c mkg, refrig, cook fac (30), toaster], ldry, rec rm, ✗, pool indoor heated, spa, bbq, ✆, plygr, tennis (half court), cots. RO ♦ $86 - $215, ♦♦ $86 - $215, ♦♦♦ $96 - $215, ◊ $15, Min book Christmas and Jan, AE BC DC MC VI, ♿.

★★★ **Toreador Motel**, (M), 31 Grafton St, opposite coach terminal & tourist info, ☎ 02 6652 3887, fax 02 6652 5813, 25 units [shwr, tlt, a/c, fan, heat, tel, cable tv, video (avail), clock radio, t/c mkg, refrig], pool, spa, cots-fee, non smoking rms. RO ♦ $54 - $85, ♦♦ $54 - $95, ♦♦♦ $64 - $98, ◊ $10, AE BC EFT MC VI.

★★☆ **Arosa Motel**, (M), 220 Pacific Hwy, ☎ 02 6652 3826, fax 02 6652 3276, 13 units [shwr, tlt, a/c-cool, fan, heat, tel, TV, video-fee, clock radio, t/c mkg, refrig], ldry, pool, bbq, dinner to unit, plygr, cots. RO ♦ $46 - $77, ♦♦ $50 - $77, ♦♦♦ $55 - $88, AE BC DC MC VI.

★★☆ **(Holiday Unit Section)**, 5 units acc up to 8, [shwr, tlt, a/c-cool, fan, heat, tel, TV, clock radio, refrig, cook fac, micro, blkts, linen, pillows], ldry, pool, bbq, c/park (carport). D ♦♦♦ $77 - $110, ◊ $11, W ♦♦ $385 - $840, Min book Christmas and Jan.

★★☆ **Australian Safari Motel**, (M), 29 Grafton St, 300m S of PO, ☎ 02 6652 1900, fax 02 6652 1689, 15 units [shwr, tlt, hairdry, a/c-cool, c/fan, heat, tel, TV, movie, clock radio, t/c mkg, refrig, toaster], pool, rm serv, dinner to unit, c/park (undercover), non smoking units (4). **RO** ♦ $55 - $79, ♦♦ $55 - $79, ♦♦♦ $60 - $99, ch con, AE BC DC EFT MC VI.

★★☆ **Matador Motor Inn**, (M), Cnr Grafton & Albany Sts (Pacific Hwy), 500m S of PO, ☎ 02 6652 3166, fax 02 6652 5072, (2 stry gr fl), 17 units [shwr, tlt, a/c, tel, cable tv, movie, clock radio, t/c mkg, refrig, micro (3)], ldry, ✕, pool, meals to unit, courtesy transfer, cots. **RO** ♦ $50 - $75, ♦♦ $55 - $85, ♦♦♦ $65 - $90, ◊ $10, AE BC DC EFT MC VI, *Operator Comment: Enquire about our "Seniors" Dinner Bed & Breakfast Packages. Also our Courtesy Pick up Train, Air, Bus.*

★★☆ **Ocean Palms Motel**, (M), Cnr Park Beach Rd & Ocean Pde, 2.5km N of PO, ☎ 02 6652 1264, fax 02 6651 5594, 12 units [shwr, tlt, c/fan, heat, elec blkts, TV, clock radio, t/c mkg, refrig, cook fac, micro, elec frypan, toaster], pool (salt water), bbq, ✆, cots. **W** $385 - $840, **RO** ♦ $50 - $110, ♦♦ $55 - $115, ♦♦♦ $70 - $120, ◊ $11 - $15, ch con, AE BC DC MC VI.

★★☆ **Sapphire Motel**, (M), Pacific Hwy, Korora North, 6km N of Coffs Harbour PO, ☎ 02 6653 6225, 10 units [shwr, tlt, fan, heat, tel, TV, clock radio, t/c mkg, refrig, micro (4), toaster], pool, bbq, plygr, cots-fee. **W** ♦♦ $250 - $500, **RO** ♦ $45 - $72, ♦♦ $45 - $72, ♦♦♦ $54 - $83, ◊ $9 - $11, AE BC MC VI.

★★ **Motel Formule 1**, (M), Previously Rest Inn Coffs Harbour. 1a McLean St, 100m N of Bus Terminal, ☎ 02 6650 9101, fax 02 6650 9102, (Multi-stry gr fl), 70 units [shwr, tlt, a/c, TV, clock radio], ldry, pool (salt water), ✆, non smoking rms (52). **D** ♦♦♦ $39 - $49, AE BC DC EFT MC VI.

★☆ **Midway Motor Inn**, (M), 209 Pacific Hwy, 1km N of PO, ☎ 02 6652 1444, fax 02 6652 1444, 33 units [shwr, tlt, a/c (18), fan, heat, TV, radio, t/c mkg, refrig], ldry, ✕, pool, bbq, cots-fee. **W** $200 - $400, **RO** ♦ $45 - $80, ♦♦ $45 - $80, ♦♦♦ $50 - $100, ◊ $5 - $10, ch con, AE BC DC MC VI.

★☆ **Star Motel**, (M), Pacific Hwy, 1.5km S of City Centre, ☎ 02 6652 1333, fax 02 6651 3048, (2 stry gr fl), 28 units [shwr, bath (1), tlt, a/c, fan, heat, TV, t/c mkg, refrig, cook fac (7)], ldry, rec rm, ✆, cots, AE BC DC MC VI.

Motel Formule 1, (M), 1A McLean St, 1km fr PO, ☎ 02 6650 9101, fax 02 6650 9102, (Multi-stry gr fl), 70 units [shwr, tlt, a/c, TV], ✆, non smoking units (30). **RO** ♦ $39 - $49, ♦♦ $39 - $49, ♦♦♦ $39 - $49, AE BC DC MC VI, (not yet classified).

Park Beach, (LMH), Ocean Pde, 2km NE of PO, ☎ 02 6652 3833, 24 units [shwr, tlt, fan, TV, t/c mkg, refrig], ldry, ✕, cots, BC MC VI.

Self Catering Accommodation

★★★★★ **Friday Creek Retreat**, (Cotg), 267 Friday Creek Rd, Upper Orara, 17km W of Coffs Harbour, ☎ 02 6653 8221, fax 02 6653 8535, 9 cotgs acc up to 5, [shwr, bath, spa bath (7), tlt, hairdry, a/c-cool (4), c/fan, fire pl, tel, TV, video, clock radio, CD, t/c mkg, refrig, cook fac, micro, elec frypan, toaster, blkts, linen, pillows], ldry, w/mach (1), dryer (1), iron, conv fac, pool, bbq, tennis, cots, non smoking units (9). **D** $180 - $340, **W** $1,260 - $2,380, AE BC MC VI.

★★★★ **Korora Bay Village**, (HU), James Small Dve Korora Bay via, 5km N of PO, ☎ 02 6653 6444, fax 02 6653 6486, (2 stry gr fl), 23 units acc up to 6, [shwr, bath, tlt, a/c (15), fan (7), heat (23), elec blkts, tel, TV, clock radio, t/c mkg, refrig, cook fac (2), blkts, linen, pillows], ldry, rec rm, pool, spa, bbq, c/park (undercover) (16), plygr, tennis, cots. **D** $85 - $170, **W** $464 - $1,146, BC MC VI, ⚟.

★★★★ **Pacific Towers Holiday Apartments**, (HU), 121 Ocean Pde, 1km E of Park Beach Plaza, ☎ 02 6652 3460, 26 units acc up to 7, [shwr, bath, tlt, heat, tel, TV, video, refrig, cook fac, micro, d/wash, ldry, blkts, linen, pillows], pool-heated, sauna, spa, bbq, secure park, tennis. D ♦♦ $108 - $210, ♦ $15, W ♦♦ $643 - $1,365, ♦ $65, Min book applies, BC MC VI.

★★★☆ **Allambie Apartments**, (SA), 22 Camperdown St, 300m S of Jetty PO, ☎ 02 6652 6690, fax 02 6652 9942, (Multi-stry gr fl), 6 serv apts acc up to 7, [shwr, tlt, c/fan, heat, tel, TV, video, clock radio, t/c mkg, refrig, cook fac, micro, d/wash, ldry], pool (salt water), spa, bbq, cots. RO ♦ $85 - $120, ♦♦ $105 - $145, ♦♦♦ $130 - $160, ♦ $15, W $695 - $1,290, ch con, AE BC DC JCB MC VI.

★★★☆ **Anchors**, (HU), 22 Boultwood St, ☎ 02 6652 4573, or 02 9712 1073, fax 02 6651 6665, 3 units acc up to 5, [shwr, tlt, fan, heat, TV, video, refrig, cook fac, micro, ldry, blkts, linen, pillows], pool-heated (solar), spa, c/park (carport), cots. D ♦♦ $70 - $100, W ♦♦ $330 - $660, ♦ $55 - $65, Min book applies.

★★★☆ **Aqua Villa Resort**, (HU), 56 Park Beach Rd, 2km N of PO, ☎ 02 6652 3539, fax 02 6652 2460, 22 units acc up to 6, [shwr, tlt, c/fan, TV, movie, clock radio, refrig, cook fac, micro, elec frypan, toaster, ldry, blkts, linen, pillows], iron, iron brd, rec rm, pool (solar heated), bbq, ✆, cots, non smoking property. D $50 - $190, W $195 - $1,065, 11 units of a lower rating. BC MC VI, ♿.

★★★☆ **Bangalow Waters**, (HU), 95 James Small Dve, Korora 2450, 5km N of PO, ☎ 02 6653 7999, fax 02 6653 6486, 7 units acc up to 6, (2 bedrm), [shwr, tlt, a/c, TV, refrig, cook fac, micro, toaster, ldry, blkts, doonas, linen, pillows], w/mach, bbq, c/park (undercover), plygr, cots, non smoking units (2). D ♦♦ $85 - $175, ♦ $10, W ♦♦ $420 - $1,100, ♦ $50, BC MC VI.

★★★☆ **Banyule Apartments**, (Apt), 5 Vincent St, ☎ 02 6652 1874, fax 02 6652 2264, 6 apts acc up to 6, [shwr, tlt, fan, heat, tel, TV, video, refrig, cook fac, micro, ldry, linen], pool, bbq, non smoking units (2). D ♦ $40 - $81, ♦♦ $44 - $90, ♦ $10, W $270 - $600, BC MC VI.

★★★☆ **Calypso Holiday Apartments**, (HU), 34-36 Prince St, 3km NE of PO, ☎ 02 6652 6468, fax 02 6652 6468, (2 stry), 10 units acc up to 4, [shwr, tlt, fan, c/fan, heat, elec blkts, TV, video, clock radio, refrig, cook fac, micro, ldry, blkts, linen, pillows], pool-heated (salt water), bbq, c/park (undercover), ✆, non smoking property. D ♦♦ $82, ♦♦♦♦ $187, W ♦♦ $446, ♦♦♦♦ $1,112, Min book applies.

★★★☆ **Harbour Terrace**, (HU), 38 Camperdown St, 200m S of Jetty PO, ☎ 02 6650 9499, fax 02 6651 5886, 4 units acc up to 6, [shwr, bath, tlt, c/fan, heat, TV, clock radio, t/c mkg, refrig, cook fac, micro, elec frypan, toaster, blkts, linen], ldry, w/mach-fee, dryer, iron, iron brd, pool, spa, bbq, courtesy transfer, cots, non smoking units (2). D $85 - $160, W $440 - $1,100, BC MC VI.

★★★☆ **Korora Court Holiday Apartments**, (HU), 39 Sandy Beach Rd Korora Bay, ☎ 02 6653 6438, 5 units acc up to 8, [shwr, tlt, fan, heat, tel, TV, video, refrig, cook fac, micro, ldry, blkts, linen, pillows], pool-heated (salt water), cots. W ♦♦ $400 - $1,400, ♦ $65, BC MC VI.

★★★☆ **Ocean Park**, (HU), 73 Ocean Pde, Park Beach, 1km N of Park Beach PO, ☎ 02 6652 3718, fax 02 6652 3718, 12 units [shwr, tlt, c/fan, heat, elec blkts, TV, video (avail), refrig, cook fac, micro], ldry, pool, bbq, plygr, cots (avail), non smoking units. D ♦ $55 - $120, ♦♦ $59 - $120, ♦♦♦ $71 - $132, ♦ $11, W $352 - $840, Min book applies, BC DC EFT MC VI.

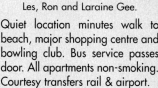

★★★☆ **Oceana Holiday Units**, (HU), 9 Prince St, ☎ 02 6651 1711, fax 02 6651 1711, 5 units acc up to 5, [shwr, spa bath (1), tlt, c/fan, heat, TV, video, clock radio, t/c mkg, refrig, cook fac, micro, elec frypan, toaster, ldry, blkts, linen], w/mach, dryer, iron, iron brd, pool, spa, bbq, courtesy transfer, cots, non smoking units (4). D ♦♦ $49 - $120, ♦ $11, W ♦♦ $295 - $720, ♦♦♦♦ $440 - $810, ♦ $55, pen con, BC MC VI.

★★★☆ **Sandcastles Holiday Apartments**, (HU), 63 Ocean Pde, 1km N of Jetty PO, ☎ 02 6652 6599, fax 02 6652 8918, (Multi-stry), 35 units acc up to 6, [shwr, tlt, c/fan, heat, tel, cable tv, video, clock radio, t/c mkg, refrig, cook fac, micro, elec frypan, d/wash, toaster, ldry, linen], dryer, iron, pool-heated, sauna, spa, bbq, secure park, courtesy transfer, cots-fee. D ♦ $96 - $160, ♦♦ $95 - $160, ♦ $15, W ♦♦ $540 - $1,120, BC MC VI.

★★★☆ **Sea Drift**, (HU), 5 Boultwood St, 1km N of Coffs Harbour Jetty, ☎ 02 6652 1957, fax 02 6652 1957, 10 units acc up to 6, [shwr, tlt, fan, heat, elec blkts, TV, video, clock radio, refrig, cook fac, micro, blkts, linen, pillows], ldry, rec rm, pool-heated (solar), spa, bbq, boat park, ✆, plygr, cots. RO ♦♦ $65 - $165, ♦ $8 - $11, W $385, ♦ $55, BC EFT MC VI.

★★★☆ **Smugglers**, (HU), Sandy Beach Rd, Korora Bay, 6km N from City Centre, ☎ 02 6653 6166, fax 02 6653 7636, (2 stry gr fl), 13 units (13 suites) acc up to 6, [shwr, bath (1), tlt, hairdry, fan, heat, elec blkts, tel, TV, video, clock radio, t/c mkg, refrig, cook fac, micro, toaster], ldry, pool-heated (solar), bbq, tennis (half court), cots. **Suite** D ♦ $100 - $120, ♦♦ $100 - $130, ♦♦♦ $110 - $140, ♦ $10, BC MC VI.

★★★☆ **Tahitian**, (HU), 27 Ocean Pde, 3km N of PO, ☎ 02 6652 2379, fax 02 6651 5817, (Multi-stry gr fl), 20 units acc up to 5, [shwr, tlt, hairdry, c/fan, heat, elec blkts, tel, TV, movie, clock radio, t/c mkg, refrig, cook fac, micro, toaster, blkts, linen, pillows], ldry, pool-heated (solar), sauna, spa, bbq-fee, c/park (undercover), cots. D ♦ $68 - $115, ♦♦ $73 - $115, ♦♦♦ $78 - $145, ♦♦♦♦ $85 - $145, ♦ $10, ch con, Min book applies, AE BC DC EFT MC VI.

★★★☆ **The Dunes at Park Beach**, (SA), 28 Fitzgerald St, 200m W of Park Beach, ☎ 02 6652 4522, fax 02 6652 3308, (Multi-stry gr fl), 19 serv apts acc up to 7, [shwr, tlt, c/fan, heat, elec blkts, tel, TV, movie, clock radio, refrig, cook fac, toaster, ldry], pool-heated, sauna, spa, bbq, plygr, tennis. **W $427 - $1,582, RO 🯅 $76 - $141, 🯅🯅 $76 - $141, 🯅🯅🯅 $93 - $215,** ⚲ **$10 - $20**, Min book all holiday times, AE BC DC MC VI.

★★★☆ **Torkee Holiday Apartments**, (Apt), 8 Prince St Park Beach via, 1km N of Jetty PO, ☎ 02 6652 6304, fax 02 6651 9670, 9 apts acc up to 4, [shwr, tlt, c/fan, heat, elec blkts, TV, video, clock radio, refrig, cook fac, micro, ldry, blkts, linen, pillows], rec rm, pool-heated (solar), sauna, spa, bbq, c/park (undercover), ☏, plygr, cots. **D 🯅🯅 $87 - $160,** ⚲ **$13, W 🯅🯅 $425 - $1,125,** ⚲ **$55**, Min book all holiday times, BC MC VI.

★★★☆ **Torrington Holiday Apartments Coffs Harbour**, (HU), Previously Torrington Hoiliday Units 27 Boultwood St, 1km N of Jetty PO, ☎ 02 6652 7546, fax 02 6652 8505, 9 units acc up to 5, [shwr, tlt, fan, heat, TV, video, clock radio, refrig, cook fac, micro, ldry, blkts, linen, pillows], pool, sauna, spa, bbq, c/park (undercover), ☏, plygr. **D 🯅 $55 - $115, 🯅🯅 $67 - $115, 🯅🯅🯅 $87 - $155,** ⚲ **$10**, Min book all holiday times, BC EFT MC VI.

★★★☆ **Tropic Oasis Holiday Villas**, (Villa), Previously Tropic Lodge Holiday Villas 10 Tropic Lodge Pl, Korora, 5km N of PO, ☎ 02 6653 6129, fax 02 6653 6129, 12 villas acc up to 14, [shwr, spa bath (8), tlt, fan, heat, TV, video, clock radio, refrig, cook fac, micro, elec frypan, d/wash (5), ldry, blkts, linen, pillows], rec rm, pool (heated salt water), spa, bbq, c/park (undercover), plygr (2), canoeing, gym, cots. D ♦♦ $80 - $150, ◊ $15 - $20, W $480 - $2,000, BC MC VI.

★★★ **Beachlander**, (HU), 47 Ocean Pde, 3km NE of PO, ☎ 02 6652 1439, 8 units acc up to 5, [shwr, tlt, fan, heat, TV, video, clock radio, refrig, cook fac, blkts, linen, pillows], ldry, pool, bbq, c/park (carport), ✆, plygr, cots. D ♦♦ $46, ◊ $7, W $266 - $711, BC MC VI.

★★★ **Dolphin Sands Holiday Cabins**, 16 Prince St, ☎ 02 6652 9550, 6 cabins [shwr, tlt, c/fan, tel, TV, clock radio, refrig, cook fac, micro, toaster, blkts, linen], ldry, iron, iron brd, pool (salt water), spa, bbq, courtesy transfer, cots. D ♦♦ $68 - $105, ◊ $10 - $17, W ♦♦♦♦ $380 - $835, ◊ $42 - $56, pen con, BC MC.

★★★ **Park Beach Cabins**, (HU), 14 Fitzgerald St, ☎ 02 6652 1095, fax 02 6652 0095, 10 units acc up to 6, [shwr, tlt, c/fan, heat, TV, clock radio, t/c mkg, refrig, cook fac, micro, elec frypan, toaster, linen reqd-fee], ldry, w/mach, dryer-fee, iron, pool, bbq, c/park (carport), cots. W ♦♦ $330 - $735, ◊ $30 - $95, BC EFT MC VI.

★★★ **Poperaperan Ridge**, 111 Convincing Ground Rd Karangi via, 15km NW of Coffs Harbour, ☎ 02 6653 8232, fax 02 6653 8732, 1 cabin [shwr, tlt, c/fan, fire pl, TV, clock radio, t/c mkg, refrig, cook fac, toaster, blkts, linen, pillows], non smoking property. D ♦♦ $66 - $88, ◊ $11, W ♦♦ $330 - $528, ◊ $66,

Operator Comment: Experience the bush, and abundant birdlife, in privacy and comfort just 15 mins from Coffs Harbour CBD. www.holidaycoast.com.au/poperaperan

★★★ **Sandboy Beachfront Holiday Apartments**, (HU), 69 Ocean Pde, 1km N of Jetty PO, ☎ 02 6652 5884, fax 02 6652 5884, 8 units acc up to 5, [shwr, tlt, fan, heat, TV, video, clock radio, refrig, cook fac, micro, ldry, blkts, linen, pillows], pool (salt water), sauna, spa, bbq, c/park (undercover), cots. D ♦♦ $68 - $145, ◊ $12, W ♦♦ $380 - $1,015, ◊ $55, BC EFT MC VI.

★★★ **Sunseeker**, (HU), 7 Prince St, ☎ 02 6652 2087, fax 02 6652 2087, 7 units acc up to 5, [shwr, tlt, fan, heat, TV, video, clock radio, refrig, cook fac, micro, ldry, blkts, linen, pillows], pool, bbq, c/park (carport), cots. **D ¶ $55 - $100, ♦♦ $55 - $100, ♦♦♦ $66 - $110,** ◊ **$11, W $308 - $797,** BC MC VI.

★★★ **Tradewinds Holiday Units**, (HU), 77 Ocean Pde, 1km N of Coffs Harbour Jetty PO, ☎ 02 6651 2212, fax 02 6651 2212, (Multi-stry), 10 units acc up to 8, [shwr, bath, tlt, heat, TV, video, clock radio, refrig, cook fac, micro, d/wash (3), toaster, ldry, blkts, linen, pillows], lift, pool, spa, bbq, secure park. **W ♦♦ $500 - $1,110,** ◊ **$50,** Min book applies, AE BC MC VI.

★★☆ **Airlie Court Holiday Apartments**, (HU), Cnr York & Boultwood Sts, 1km N of Jetty PO, ☎ 02 6652 4101, fax 02 6652 4101, 8 units acc up to 5, [shwr, tlt, c/fan, heat, elec blkts, TV, video (avail), clock radio, t/c mkg, refrig, cook fac, micro, ldry (4), blkts, linen, pillows], ldry, pool-heated (solar), spa, bbq, c/park (garage) (5), ✆, cots. **D ¶ $48 - $90, ♦♦ $50 - $95,** ◊ **$10,** BC MC VI.

★★☆ **Aruma Holiday Flats**, (HF), 3 Boultwood St, ☎ 02 6651 4666, fax 02 6651 4666, 4 flats acc up to 5, [shwr, tlt, fan, heat, TV, video, refrig, cook fac, micro, ldry, blkts, linen, pillows], bbq. **D ♦♦ $40 - $80,** ◊ **$10, W ♦♦ $220, ♦♦♦♦ $500,** BC MC VI.

★★☆ **Ceduna Court Apartments**, (HF), 23 Vincent St, Park Beach, ☎ 02 6652 2914, fax 02 6652 2914, 5 flats acc up to 5, [shwr, tlt, c/fan, heat, TV, video, clock radio, refrig, cook fac, micro, ldry, blkts, linen, pillows]. **D ♦♦ $45 - $73,** ◊ **$8 - $50, W $240 - $610.**

★★☆ **Island View Holiday Cabins**, (HU), 31 Split Solitary Rd, Nth Sapphire, 9km N of Coffs Harbour, ☎ 02 6653 6753, 12 units acc up to 8, [shwr, tlt, heat, TV, refrig, cook fac, ldry, blkts, linen, pillows], pool, spa, bbq, c/park (carport), plygr, tennis (half court), cots, **D ¶ $42 - $78, ♦♦ $42 - $78, ♦♦♦ $57 - $108,** ◊ **$7 - $28, W $259 - $798,** Min book applies.

★★☆ **Mt Brown Farm Country Cottages**, (Cotg), 90 Mt Brown Rd, Karangi, 8km W of City Centre, ☎ 02 6653 8408, fax 02 6653 8513, 4 cotgs acc up to 8, [shwr, tlt, heat, TV, refrig, cook fac, ldry, linen reqd-fee], pool, bbq, tennis. **D ♦♦ $65,** ◊ **$10, W $390 - $979,** BC VI.

★★ **Seabreeze Holiday Units**, (HU), 61 Ocean Pde, ☎ 02 6652 3651, 4 units acc up to 5, [shwr, tlt, fan, heat, elec blkts, tel, TV, video, clock radio, t/c mkg, refrig, cook fac, micro, elec frypan, toaster, blkts, linen, pillows], w/mach, iron, bbq, c/park. **D ♦♦ $45 - $80,** ◊ **$5 - $10, W ♦♦ $210 - $500,** ◊ **$30 - $60.**

Coral Court Holiday Units, (HU), 11 Vincent St, ☎ 02 6652 1461, 6 units acc up to 6, [shwr, tlt, c/fan, heat, TV, clock radio, refrig, cook fac, micro, elec frypan, toaster, ldry, blkts, linen], w/mach, iron, iron brd, 24hr reception, cots, non smoking units. **D ♦♦ $40 - $75,** ◊ **$10, W $210 - $450,** ◊ **$20,** EFT, (not yet classified).

Le Meadows, (HU), Previously The Meadows 14 Korora Bay Dve Korora via, 5km N of Plaza PO, ☎ 02 6653 6426, fax 02 6653 6329, 1 unit acc up to 6, (2 bedrm), [shwr, bath, tlt, fan, heat, cable tv, video, clock radio, t/c mkg, refrig, cook fac, micro, d/wash, toaster, ldry, blkts, doonas, linen, pillows], w/mach, dryer, pool, sauna, spa, bbq, c/park (undercover), ✆, plygr, cots, non smoking property. **D $115, W $675 - $1,400,** (not yet classified).

B&B's/Guest Houses

★★★★★ **The Waterside**, (GH), 80 Tiki Rd Off Pacific Hwy, 14km N of PO, ☎ 02 6653 7388, fax 02 6653 7300, (2 stry gr fl), 4 rms [shwr, bath (2), spa bath (1), tlt, hairdry, a/c, c/fan, heat, tel, TV, video, clock radio, t/c mkg, refrig], lounge (firepl), ✗, pool (salt water), bbq, tennis (half court), non smoking rms. **BB ¶ $125 - $240, ♦♦ $205 - $310,** AE BC DC MC VI.

★★★★☆ **Santa Fe Luxury Bed & Breakfast**, (B&B), 235 The Mountain Way off Gaudrons Rd, 9km N of Coffs Harbour PO, ☎ 02 6653 7700, fax 02 6653 7050, 3 rms [shwr, spa bath (suite) (1), tlt, hairdry, c/fan, heat, elec blkts, tel, video, clock radio, t/c mkg], ldry, rec rm, lounge (TV), pool (salt water), bbq, c/park. **BB $160 - $185,** AE BC DC MC VI.

★★★★ **Clissold Cottage**, (B&B), 4 Azalea Ave, 1km W of PO, ☎ 02 6651 2715, fax 02 6651 2715, 1 rm [shwr, bath, tlt, hairdry, a/c, c/fan, tel, TV, clock radio, t/c mkg, refrig], iron, iron brd, rm serv, non smoking rms. **BB ¶ $65 - $70, ♦♦ $80 - $90.**

★★★★ **Ferndahl Mountain Inn**, (B&B), Mt Browne Rd, 11.2km W of Coffs Harbour Mall, ☎ 02 6653 8449, fax 02 6653 8499, 4 rms (4 suites) [shwr, tlt, fan, fire pl, elec blkts, tel, clock radio], lounge (TV), conv fac, ✉ (Mon to Sun), pool (salt water), refrig, rm serv, c/park. **Suite BB ¶ $95, ♦♦ $120 - $140,** AE BC MC VI.

Beach Break B & B, (B&B), No children's facilities, 25A Charlesworth Bay Rd, 4km N of PO, ☎ 02 6651 6468, fax 02 6651 2565, (2 stry gr fl), 1 rm [ensuite, c/fan, heat, elec blkts, clock radio, t/c mkg, refrig, doonas], lounge (TV), pool-heated, non smoking property. **BB $150 - $180,** (not yet classified).

Medication and driving

Medication can effect your driving. Certain drugs can effect your mental alertness and/or co-ordination and therefore effect driving skills. Always check with your doctor the effect which any medication (over the counter or prescription) you are taking may have on your driving. There may be an alternative drug which will not affect your driving. It is best to avoid drinking alcohol while taking medication.

COLEAMBALLY NSW 2707

Pop 650. (623km SW Sydney), See map on pages 52/53, ref D6. Coleambally (pronounced 'Colly-AM-b'ly') is a modern little town on the Kidman Way at the heart of the Coleambally Irrigation Area. Bowls, Fishing, Golf, Horse Riding, Shooting, Swimming, Tennis.

Hotels/Motels
★ **Brolga Motel Hotel**, (LMH), Cnr Brolga Pl & Kingfisher Ave, opposite PO, ☎ 02 6954 4009, fax 02 6954 4406, 7 units [shwr, tlt, a/c, elec blkts, TV, t/c mkg, refrig], ldry.

COLLARENEBRI NSW 2833

Pop 550. (780km NW Sydney), See map on pages 52/53, ref G1. Collarenebri lies beside the Barwon River and is a favoured spot for fishing and water sports. Fishing, Shooting, Swimming.

Hotels/Motels
★★ **Tattersalls**, (LMH), Cnr Wilson & Walgett Sts, ☎ 02 6756 2205, fax 02 6756 2533, 12 units [shwr, tlt, a/c, heat, TV, t/c mkg, refrig], ldry, ✕, bbq. RO ⚹ $59, ⚹⚹ $69, ⚹ $10, AE BC MC VI.

COLLOMBATTI NSW 2440

Pop Nominal, (450km NW Sydney), See map on page 54, ref C6. Rural mid-north coast locality nestled in the shadow of the Collombatti, Ingalba and Tamban State Forests. Scenic Drives.

B&B's/Guest Houses
★★★☆ **Benbullen Farm Stay**, (B&B), 171 Swan La, ☎ 02 6566 8448, 3 rms [shwr, tlt, hairdry, fire pl, tel, clock radio], rec rm, lounge (TV), bbq, cots, Pets allowed. BB ⚹ $85, ⚹⚹ $170, ⚹⚹⚹ $225, ⚹ $85, DBB ⚹ $125, ⚹⚹ $250, ch con.

COMBOYNE NSW 2429

Pop Nominal, (437km NW Sydney), See map on page 54, ref B7. Pretty rural township set in the rich dairying country of the Comboyne Plateau. Bush Walking, Scenic Drives.

Other Accommodation
★★★★☆ **Comboyne Hideaway**, (Lodge), Cnr Koppinyarrat & Kendall Rd, 45km S of Port Macquarie, ☎ 02 6550 4230, 3 rms acc up to 6, [shwr, spa bath (on verandah) (3), tlt, hairdry, fire pl, elec frypan, tel, TV, video, t/c mkg, refrig, cook fac, micro, elec frypan, d/wash, toaster, blkts, linen, pillows], ldry, w/mach, dryer-fee, iron, ✕, pool-heated, bbq, dinner to unit, c/park (garage), cots. D $192 - $438, BC MC VI.

CONDOBOLIN NSW 2877

Pop 3,100. (477km W Sydney), See map on pages 52/53, ref F4. Regional centre on the Lachlan River and a major venue for sporting activities in western New South Wales. Bowls, Fishing, Golf, Swimming, Tennis.

Hotels/Motels
★★★ **Allambie Motel**, (M), William St, 500m W of PO, ☎ 02 6895 2722, fax 02 6895 4195, 25 units [shwr, tlt, a/c, elec blkts, tel, TV, video-fee, clock radio, t/c mkg, refrig], ldry, bbq, dinner to unit, cots-fee. RO ⚹ $59, ⚹⚹ $66 - $69, ⚹ $11, AE BC DC EFT MC VI.

★★☆ **Condobolin Motor Inn**, (M), 20 William St, 500m W of PO, ☎ 02 6895 2233, fax 02 6895 2965, 14 units [shwr, tlt, a/c, elec blkts, tel, TV, clock radio, t/c mkg, refrig], ldry, ✕ (Mon to Sat), pool, dinner to unit, cots-fee. RO ⚹ $61, ⚹⚹ $68, ⚹⚹⚹ $79, ⚹ $10, AE BC DC MC VI.

★☆ **Condobolin Hotel Motel**, (LMH), Cnr Bathurst & William Sts, 500m N of PO, ☎ 02 6895 2040, fax 02 6895 4154, 8 units [shwr, tlt, a/c, fan, TV, t/c mkg, refrig, toaster], ✕. RO ⚹ $45, ⚹⚹ $50, EFT.

COOKS HILL NSW

See Newcastle & Suburbs.

COOLAH NSW 2843

Pop 850. (388km NW Sydney), See map on pages 52/53, ref H4. This pretty town in the foothills of the Great Dividing and Warrumbungle Ranges lays claim to being the site of the original black stump of 'beyond the black stump' fame. Bowls, Fishing, Golf, Swimming.

Hotels/Motels
★ **The Coolah Black Stump**, (M), 10 Campbell St, 300m E of PO, ☎ 02 6377 1208, fax 02 6377 1208, 13 units [shwr, tlt, fan, heat, elec blkts, TV, clock radio, t/c mkg, refrig, doonas], pool, bbq (avail on request), cots-fee. RO ⚹ $49.50, ⚹⚹ $60.50, ⚹ $8, ch con, BC MC VI.

B&B's/Guest Houses
★★★ **Baladonga Bed & Breakfast**, (B&B), Gunnedah Rd, Blackstump Way, 10km N of Coolah, ☎ 02 6377 1390, fax 02 6377 1608, 3 rms [ensuite (36 holes), shwr, tlt, fan, heat, elec blkts, tel, cook fac (1)], ldry, rec rm, lounge (TV), pool (salt water), cook fac, plygr, tennis. BB ⚹⚹ $80, ⚹ $50, RO ⚹⚹ $80, ⚹ $50.

Gundare Bed & Breakfast, (B&B), via Coolah Creek & Cooks Rds, 10km NE of Coolah, ☎ 02 6377 1275, fax 02 6377 1777, 2 rms (2 suites) [shwr, tlt, elec blkts, tel, TV, t/c mkg, refrig], ldry, dinner to unit, tennis. BB ⚹ $30 - $35, ⚹⚹ $45 - $55, RO ⚹ $25 - $30, ⚹⚹ $40 - $45, ch con.

COOLAMON NSW 2701

Pop 1,250. (548km SW Sydney), See map on pages 52/53, ref E6. Charming town at the heart of the Riverina. Bowls, Swimming, Tennis.

B&B's/Guest Houses
★★☆ **Avondale Station**, (B&B), (Farm), Temora Rd, 4km N of PO, ☎ 02 6927 3055, fax 02 6927 3055, 3 rms [shwr, tlt, a/c, heat, elec blkts, TV, refrig, micro, elec frypan, toaster, pillows], iron, rec rm, bbq, tennis. BB ⚹ $60, ⚹⚹ $100, ch con, Dinner by arrangement. BC MC VI.

(Cottage Section), 1 cotg acc up to 4, [shwr, tlt, a/c, heat, elec blkts, t/c mkg, refrig, cook fac, toaster, blkts, linen, pillows], w/mach. BB ⚹ $60, ⚹⚹ $100, ch con.

COOMA NSW 2630

Pop 7,150. (394km SW Sydney), See map on pages 52/53, ref G7. Historic rural and service centre considered to be the 'capital' of the Snowy Mountains. Bowls, Bush Walking, Fishing, Golf, Horse Riding, Scenic Drives, Snow Skiing, Squash, Tennis. See also Nimmitabel.

Hotels/Motels

★★★★ **Cooma Motor Lodge**, (M), 6 Sharp St, 1km NE of PO, ☎ 02 6452 1888, fax 02 6452 3106, (2 stry gr fl), 44 units [shwr, tlt, hairdry (21), a/c, cent heat, tel, TV, clock radio, t/c mkg, refrig, doonas], iron, iron brd, ✕, sauna, rm serv. BLB ⚹ $60 - $150, ⚹⚹ $60 - $150, ⚹ $15, 11 units ★★★☆,13 units yet to be assessed. AE BC DC JCB MC MP VI.

★★★★ **Kinross Inn — Cooma**, (M), 15 Sharp St, 500m NE of PO, ☎ 02 6452 3577, fax 02 6452 4410, 17 units [shwr, spa bath (5), tlt, hairdry, a/c-cool, heat, elec blkts, tel, TV, video-fee, clock radio, t/c mkg, refrig, toaster, doonas], ldry-fee, iron, iron brd, pool indoor heated, bbq, dinner to unit, c/park (undercover), car wash, cots, non smoking units (10). RO ⚹⚹ $70 - $110, ⚹ $12, ch con, 8 units ★★★☆. AE BC DC MC VI.

★★★☆ **Alkira Motel**, (M), 213 Sharp St, 400m SW of PO, ☎ 02 6452 3633, fax 02 6452 7022, 13 units [shwr, tlt, hairdry, a/c-cool, cent heat, elec blkts, tel, TV, video-fee, movie, clock radio, t/c mkg, refrig, toaster], iron, iron brd, bbq, c/park (undercover), cots, non smoking units (4). RO ⚹ $60 - $110, ⚹⚹ $66 - $110, ⚹ $12 - $20, ch con, AE BC DC EFT JCB MC VI, &.

★★★☆ **Marlborough Motor Inn**, (M), Monaro Hwy, 1.5km N of PO, ☎ 02 6452 1133, fax 02 6452 4675, (2 stry gr fl), 60 units [shwr, spa bath (4), tlt, cent heat, tel, cable tv, video-fee, clock radio, t/c mkg, refrig, mini bar], ldry, lounge, conv fac, ✕, pool, sauna, spa, bbq, rm serv, dinner to unit, cots-fee, non smoking rms (21). RO ⚹ $77, ⚹⚹ $80, ⚹ $15, 30 units ★★★☆. AE BC DC EFT MC VI.

For Accommodation Booking information - see page 27

COOMA NSW continued...

★★★☆ **Nebula Motel**, (M), 42 Bombala St (Monaro Hwy), 500m SE of PO, ☎ 02 6452 4133, fax 02 6452 3397, 22 units [shwr, tlt, a/c-cool, heat, elec blkts, tel, cable tv, video (avail)-fee, clock radio, t/c mkg, refrig], dinner to unit, c/park (undercover), cots-fee, non smoking units (11). RO ♦ $62 - $82, ♦♦ $67 - $87, ◊ $11, High Season RO ♦ $113, ♦♦ $120, ♦♦♦ $131, ◊ $11, AE BC DC MC VI.

SOVEREIGN Motor Inns Chain

★★★☆ **Sovereign Motor Inn**, (M), 35 Sharp St, 500m NE of PO, ☎ 02 6452 1366, fax 02 6452 4965, 25 units [shwr, tlt, hairdry, c/fan, heat (electric), elec blkts, tel, TV, clock radio, t/c mkg, refrig], ldry, iron, iron brd, ⊠, rm serv, cots-fee. RO ♦ $72 - $94, ♦♦ $72 - $94, ◊ $11, Units 8 to 38 not rated. AE BC DC EFT MC VI.

★★★☆ **White Manor**, (M), 252 Sharp St, 1km W of PO, ☎ 02 6452 1152, fax 02 6452 1627, (2 stry gr fl), 12 units [shwr, tlt, hairdry, a/c, elec blkts, tel, cable tv, video, clock radio, t/c mkg, refrig, toaster], bbq, c/park (undercover), gym, non smoking rms. RO ♦ $55 - $85, ♦♦ $66 - $99, ◊ $11 - $16, AE BC DC EFT MC MCH VI.

★★★ **Cooma Country Club Motor Inn**, (M), 237 Sharp St, ☎ 02 6452 1884, fax 02 6452 2177, 32 units [shwr, tlt, a/c-cool, heat, elec blkts, tel, TV, clock radio, t/c mkg, refrig, toaster], ⊠, plygr. High Season D ♦ $80, ♦♦ $88 - $98, ◊ $15, Low Season D ♦ $55, ♦♦ $55 - $75, ◊ $10, Units 1 to 10, 12 & 15 not rated. AE BC DC MC VI.

★★☆ **High Country Motel**, (M), 12 Chapman St, 1.5km SW of PO, ☎ 02 6452 1277, fax 02 6452 3305, 40 units [shwr, tlt, cent heat, elec blkts, tel, TV, video (avail), clock radio, t/c mkg, refrig], rec rm, lounge, conv fac, ⊠, pool, bbq, courtesy transfer, plygr, cots-fee, non smoking units (12). RO ♦ $55 - $60, ♦♦ $60 - $77, ◊ $13 - $19, ch con, AE BC DC MC MCH VI.

★★☆ **The Alpine Angler Motel**, (M), Snowy Mountains Hwy, 5km W of PO, ☎ 02 6452 4537, fax 02 6452 7211, 9 units [shwr, tlt, heat, elec blkts, tel, TV, clock radio, t/c mkg, refrig, toaster], TV rm, lounge (TV), cots. **RO ♦ $50 - $60, ♦♦ $55 - $70, ◊ $10 - $15**, ch con, AE BC EFT MC VI.

★★ **Hawaii Motel**, (M), 192 Sharp St, 300m S of PO, ☎ 02 6452 1211, fax 02 6452 1211, 23 units [shwr, tlt, fan, heat, elec blkts, TV, radio, t/c mkg, refrig (16)], ✕. **RO ♦ $40 - $50, ♦♦ $50 - $60, ◊ $10**, ch con, AE BC DC MC VI.

★☆ **Coffey's Hotel Cooma**, (LH), 6 Short St, 1km E of PO, ☎ 02 6452 2064, fax 02 6452 6340, 6 rms [heat, elec blkts, doonas], TV rm, lounge, lounge firepl, t/c mkg shared, bbq, ✎, plygr, non smoking rms. **BLB ♦ $30, ♦♦ $50**, ch con, fam con, BC EFT MC VI.

★ **Bunkhouse Motel**, (M), 28 Soho St, 200m E of PO, ☎ 02 6452 2983, fax 02 6452 2983, 18 units [shwr, tlt, cent heat, elec blkts, tel, TV, video (avail), t/c mkg, refrig, toaster], ldry, ✎, cots-fee, BC MC VI.
    (Holiday Unit Section), 11 units acc up to 6, [shwr, tlt, TV, refrig, cook fac], (not yet classified).

B&B's/Guest Houses

★★★☆ **Springwell Bed & Breakfast**, (B&B), Bobundra Rd, ☎ 02 6453 5545, fax 02 6453 5539, 3 rms [shwr, tlt, heat, elec blkts, tel, cable tv], ldry, iron, iron brd, lounge (TV), lounge firepl, ✕, t/c mkg shared, bbq, tennis, cots, non smoking rms. **BB ♦ $50, ♦♦ $95, DBB ♦ $75, ♦♦ $145**, ch con.

★★ **Alpine Country Guest House**, (GH), 32 Massie St, 500m E of PO, ☎ 02 6452 1414, (2 stry gr fl), 13 rms [shwr, tlt, cent heat, TV], ✕, t/c mkg shared, cots, non smoking property. **RO ♦ $30 - $40, ♦♦ $30 - $60, ♦♦♦ $50, ◊ $15**, BC MC VI.

★★ **Lama World Bed & Breakfast**, (B&B), (Farm), Snowy Mountains Hwy, 19km SW of PO, ☎ 02 6452 4593, fax 02 6452 4692, 1 rm [shwr, tlt, heat, TV, t/c mkg], meals avail, Pets on application. **BB ♦ $55, ♦♦ $110, DBB ♦ $80, ♦♦ $160**, ch con, AE BC DC MC VI.

★★ **Litchfield**, (GH), (Farm), Carlaminda Rd, 21km E of PO, ☎ 02 6453 3231, 2 rms [shwr, bath, heat, elec blkts], ldry, rec rm, lounge (TV & Radio), bbq, plygr, tennis. **D all meals ♦ $90, ♦♦ $170**, ch con.
    (Bunk Section), 1 bunkhouse acc up to 6, [tlt, heat, elec blkts, blkts, linen, pillows], shared fac. **D all meals ♦ $75 - $80, ♦♦ $150 - $160**.

COOMBA PARK NSW 2428

Pop 250. Nominal, (301km N Sydney), See map on page 54, ref B8. Secluded mid-north coast community on the upper western shores of Wallis Lake. Boating, Bush Walking, Fishing, Scenic Drives.
★★★★☆ **Galway Downs Lakeside Country House**, (B&B), No children's facilities, 1788 Coomba Rd, 40km S of Forster, ☎ 02 6554 2019, fax 02 6554 2019, 5 rms (2 suites) [shwr (5), bath (3), tlt (6), fire pl, heat, elec blkts, tel], ✕ (dinner on request), pool, jetty. **BB ♦ $165 - $182, ♦♦ $198, Suite D $218**, AE BC MC VI.

COONABARABRAN NSW 2357

Pop 3,000. (451km NW Sydney), See map on pages 52/53, ref G3. Coonabarabran is a prosperous rural centre known both as the eastern gateway to Warrumbungle National Park and as 'the Astronomy Capital of Australia'. Bowls, Bush Walking, Golf, Swimming. See also Baradine.

Hotels/Motels

★★★★ **Acacia Motor Lodge**, (M), Newell Hwy, 150m S of PO, ☎ 02 6842 1922, fax 02 6842 2626, (2 stry gr fl), 22 units (2 suites) [shwr, bath, spa bath (4), tlt, a/c, heat, elec blkts, tel, TV, clock radio, t/c mkg, refrig, toaster], ldry, iron, iron brd, lounge, conv fac, ✕, pool, sauna-fee, spa, rm serv, gym, cots. **RO ♦ $87.45 - $135, ♦♦ $87.45 - $135, ◊ $10, Suite RO $145 - $150**, AE BC DC EFT MC VI.

★★★☆ **All Travellers Motor Inn**, (M), John St (Newell Hwy), 100m S of PO, ☎ 02 6842 1133, fax 02 6842 2505, 30 units (4 suites) [shwr, tlt, hairdry, a/c, c/fan, elec blkts, tel, TV, movie, clock radio, t/c mkg, refrig, toaster], iron, iron brd, pool, dinner to unit (Mon to Thu), car wash, cots-fee, non smoking units (10). **RO ♦ $60 - $86, ♦♦ $60 - $90, ♦♦♦ $70 - $100, ◊ $10, Suite D $99 - $130**, AE BC DC EFT MC VI.

Operator Comment: See advertisement on the following page.

★★★☆ **Amber Court Motor Inn**, (M), Oxley Hwy, 3km N of PO, ☎ 02 6842 1188, fax 02 6842 4239, 21 units [shwr, tlt, hairdry, heat, elec blkts, tel, TV, clock radio, t/c mkg, refrig, toaster], iron, ✕ (Mon to Sat), pool, dinner to unit, plygr, non smoking units (12). **D ♦ $55 - $68.20, ♦♦ $55 - $71.50, ◊ $10**, ch con, 6 units ★★☆. AE BC DC EFT MC MP VI.

★★★☆ **Clock Tower Motor Inn**, (M), 47 Dalgarno St, 75m N of PO, ☎ 02 6842 2444, fax 02 6842 2069, 17 units [shwr, tlt, a/c, elec blks, tel, TV, video (avail), clock radio, t/c mkg, refrig, toaster], pool-heated (solar), bbq, cots-fee. RO ♦ $57 - $77, ♦♦ $66 - $81, ♦♦♦ $77 - $92, ◊ $11, 4 units of a lower rating, AE BC DC MC VI.

 ★★★☆ **Coachmans Rest Motor Lodge**, (M), Newell Hwy, 1.5km S of PO, ☎ 02 6842 2111, fax 02 6842 2152, (2 stry gr fl), 20 units [shwr, bath (8), tlt, a/c, elec blks, tel, cable tv, clock radio, t/c mkg, refrig, mini bar, toaster], ✕, rm serv, dinner to unit, cots-fee, non smoking units (10). RO ♦ $84 - $94, ♦♦ $91 - $101, ♦♦♦♦ $130 - $140, ◊ $10, Min book all holiday times, AE BC DC EFT MC MP VI.

★★★☆ **El Paso Motel**, (M), Oxley Hwy, 1.5km S of PO, ☎ 02 6842 1722, fax 02 6842 2673, 21 units [shwr, tlt, a/c-cool (18), c/fan (3), heat, elec blks, tel, TV, video (available), clock radio, t/c mkg, refrig, toaster], conv fac, ✕ (6 nights), pool, rm serv, dinner to unit, plygr, cots-fee, non smoking units (available). RO ♦ $53 - $66, ♦♦ $55 - $77, ♦♦♦ $72 - $94, ◊ $9 - $13, AE BC DC EFT MC VI.

★★★☆ **Matthew Flinders Motor Inn**, (M), Oxley/Newell Hwy, 1.2km S of PO, ☎ 02 6842 1766, fax 02 6842 1613, 41 units (1 suite) [shwr, tlt, hairdry (28), a/c, elec blkts, tel (32), TV, clock radio, t/c mkg, refrig, toaster], ldry, iron, iron brd (28), ⊠, pool, rm serv, dinner to unit, plygr, cots-fee, non smoking units (11). RO ♦ $58 - $62, ♦♦ $58 - $68, ♦♦♦ $76 - $88, 11 units ★★★☆, 12 family units ★★☆, AE BC EFT MC VI.

★★★ **Country Gardens Motel Coonabarabran**, (M), Cnr John & Edwards St, 200m S of PO opp Information Centre, ☎ 02 6842 1711, fax 02 6842 2664, (2 stry gr fl) 37 units (2 suites) [shwr, tlt, hairdry, a/c-cool, cent heat, elec blkts, tel, TV, movie, clock radio, t/c mkg, refrig, toaster], ldry, ⊠ (6 nights), pool, rm serv, dinner to unit, cots, non smoking units (15). RO ♦ $55 - $72, ♦♦ $59 - $83, ⍭ $8, Suite D $110 - $145, ch con, 12 units ★★★☆, AE BC DC EFT JCB MC VI.

★★☆ **Poplars Motel**, (M), Oxley-Newell Hwy, 600m N of PO, ☎ 02 6842 1522, fax 02 6842 1578, 32 units (3 suites) [shwr, tlt, hairdry (30), a/c-cool, heat, elec blkts, tel, TV, movie, radio, t/c mkg, refrig, toaster], ldry, conv fac, ⊠, pool (salt water), bbq, cots, non smoking rms (26). D ♦ $55 - $66, RO ♦♦ $55 - $66, ⍭ $11, Suite D ♦♦ $66 - $77, AE BC DC MC MP VI.

★★☆ **Wagon Wheel Motel**, (M), Oxley Hwy, 2km S of PO, ☎ 02 6842 1860, fax 02 6842 1412, 14 units [shwr, tlt, a/c-cool, heat, elec blkts, tel, TV, video (available)-fee, clock radio, t/c mkg, refrig, toaster], pool, bbq, ✆, plygr, cots-fee, non smoking units (13). RO ♦ $60 - $70, ♦♦ $65 - $75, ⍭ $12, AE BC DC MC VI.

(Holiday Flat Section), 10 flats acc up to 8, [shwr, tlt, a/c-cool (2), fan, heat, elec blkts, TV, video-fee, refrig, cook fac, micro, blkts reqd, linen reqd-fee, pillows reqd-fee], bbq, ✆. D ♦♦ $45 - $70, ⍭ $10, (not yet classified).

★★☆ **Warrumbungles Mountain Motel**, (M), National Park Rd, 9km W of PO, ☎ 02 6842 1832, fax 02 6842 2944, 15 units [shwr, tlt, fan, heat, elec blkts, TV, clock radio, t/c mkg, refrig, mini bar, cook fac], ldry, conv fac (2), pool (salt water), bbq, ✆, plygr, golf (3 rms), tennis (half court). RO ♦ $47 - $60, ♦♦ $54 - $93, ♦♦♦ $65 - $71.50, ⍭ $8 - $11, 3 rooms of a higher standard, AE BC DC MC VI.

★★ **Castlereagh Village**, (M), Oxley Hwy, 2km N of PO, ☎ 02 6842 1706, fax 02 6842 2305, 10 units [shwr, tlt, fan, heat, elec blkts, TV, t/c mkg, refrig, cook fac], ldry, pool, bbq, plygr. D ♦♦ $47 - $55, ⍭ $9 - $11, ch con, BC EFT MC VI.

Self Catering Accommodation

★★★☆ **Timor Country Cottages**, (Cotg), National Park Rd, 12km W of PO, ☎ 02 6842 1055, 2 cotgs [shwr, bath, tlt, a/c-cool, fire pl, heat, elec blkts, TV, clock radio, t/c mkg, refrig, cook fac, micro, elec frypan, toaster, ldry, blkts, linen, pillows], bbq, c/park (undercover). D ♦♦ $80 - $100, ⍭ $10 - $20, W $450 - $540, ⍭ $60 - $120, ch con, 1 cottage yet to be assessed, Meals at homestead by arrangement. Min book applies,

Operator Comment: The only rated accommodation adjoining the Warrumbungle National Park. Ideal place to bring overseas visitors.

★★☆ **Brooklyn Cottage**, (Cotg), (Farm), Napier Lane, 39km E of Coonabarabran, ☎ 02 6842 8281, 1 cotg acc up to 8, [shwr, tlt, fan, fire pl, elec blkts, TV, t/c mkg, refrig, cook fac, micro, toaster, ldry, blkts, linen, pillows], w/mach, iron, bbq, c/park (garage), cots. D $90 - $100, W $450.

★☆ **Dalyup Cottage**, (Cotg), (Farm), River Rd, 8km E of Coonabarabran town, ☎ 02 6842 1929, or 02 6842 2875, 1 cotg acc up to 8, [shwr, bath, tlt, c/fan, fire pl, heat, elec blkts, tel, t/c mkg, refrig, cook fac, micro, elec frypan, toaster, ldry], w/mach, iron, bbq. D $65 - $85.

COONAMBLE NSW 2829

Pop 2,750. (590km NW Sydney), See map on pages 52/53, ref G3. Coonamble lies beside the Castlereagh River in one of the State's richest pastoral areas. Bowls, Fishing, Golf, Scenic Drives, Swimming, Tennis, Water Skiing.

Hotels/Motels

★★☆ **Castlereagh Lodge**, (M), 79-81 Aberford St (Castlereagh Hwy), 600m W of PO, ☎ 02 6822 1999, fax 02 6822 2297, 11 units [shwr, tlt, a/c, elec blkts, tel, TV, clock radio, t/c mkg, refrig], ldry, ⊠, dinner to unit, c/park (undercover), cots. RO ♦ $52, ♦♦ $62.70, ♦♦♦ $71.50, ♦♦♦♦ $79.20, ⍭ $8, 4 units of a higher standard. AE BC DC MC VI.

★★☆ **Cypress Motel**, (M), Castlereagh St, 1km S of PO, ☎ 02 6822 1788, fax 02 6822 2478, 21 units [shwr, tlt, a/c, elec blkts, tel, TV, clock radio, t/c mkg, refrig, toaster], conv fac, ⊠, pool, rm serv, dinner to unit, cots-fee, non smoking rms (1). RO ♦ $44 - $55, ♦♦ $55 - $66, ⍭ $11, 7 units of a lower rating. AE BC DC MC VI.

★★ **Coonamble Motel**, (M), Castlereagh St, 100m S of PO, ☎ 02 6822 1400, fax 02 6822 1400, 21 units [shwr, tlt, a/c, tel, TV, clock radio, t/c mkg, refrig], dinner to unit (Mon to Fri), cots-fee. RO ♦ $44.55, ♦♦ $55.66, ♦♦♦ $72.60 - $77, ⍭ $11, ch con, 4 units of a higher standard, 3 units of a lower rating. AE BC DC EFT MC VI.

Self Catering Accommodation
Thurn Holiday, (Cotg), 24km NE of Quambone, 45km W of Coonamble, ☎ 02 6824 2091, fax 02 6824 4048, 1 cotg acc up to 8, [shwr, bath, tlt, a/c, heat, tel, TV, refrig, cook fac, micro, ldry, linen reqd], bbq, tennis. D ♦ $60, ♦♦ $60, ♦♦♦ $60, ⍭ $10, W $300, ⍭ $10.

(Homestead Section), 2 apts acc up to 4, [shwr, bath, tlt, blkts, linen, pillows], lounge (TV), refrig. DBB ♦ $50, ♦♦ $90.

COOPERNOOK NSW 2426

Pop 350. (339km N Sydney), See map on page 54, ref C7. Old mid-north coast timber town beside the Pacific Highway, just north of the Lansdowne River. Boating, Fishing, Scenic Drives, Swimming.

Hotels/Motels
★★★ **Coopernook International Motor Inn**, (M), Pacific Hwy, ☎ 02 6556 3305, fax 02 6556 3413, 16 units [shwr, tlt, a/c, TV, clock radio, t/c mkg, refrig], ✕, bbq, dinner to unit, cots-fee. RO ♦ $68, ♦♦ $78 - $88, ♦♦♦ $78 - $98, ⍭ $12, AE BC DC MC VI.

COORANBONG NSW 2265

Pop 1,450. (137km N Sydney), See map on page 55, ref D4. Rural settlement to the west of Lake Macquarie, flanked by the forests of the Watagan Mountains. See also Mandalong.

Hotels/Motels
★★★★ **Watagan Lodge**, (M), 47 Kings Rd, Martinsville, 1km W of Cooranbong, ☎ 02 4977 3400, fax 02 4977 3774, 14 units [shwr, spa bath, tlt, a/c, tel, TV, clock radio, t/c mkg, refrig, micro (3), toaster], ldry, iron, iron brd, conv fac, conf fac, lounge firepl, pool, spa, bbq, plygr, cots, non smoking units (10). BB ♦♦ $93 - $110, ch con, fam con, pen con, AE BC DC EFT MC VI.

COOTAMUNDRA NSW 2590

Pop 5,900. (454km SW Sydney), See map on pages 52/53, ref F6. One of the Riverina's main stock handling and wheat growing centres, famous for wattle which grows profusely in the area. Bowls, Bush Walking, Golf, Swimming, Tennis. See also Wallendbeen.

Hotels/Motels

★★★☆ **Bradman Motor Inn**, (M), 196 Olympic Way, 1.5km S of PO, ☎ 02 6942 2288, fax 02 6942 1085, (2 stry gr fl), 20 units [shwr, tlt, hairdry, a/c, heat, elec blkts, tel, TV, video-fee, clock radio, t/c mkg, refrig, toaster], ldry, pool, bbq, dinner to unit, cots-fee, non smoking units (9). RO ♦ $52 - $58, ♦♦ $63 - $69, ⍭ $11, pen con, AE BC DC EFT MC MCH VI.

★★★☆ **Cootamundra Gardens Motor Inn**, (M), 96-102 Sutton St (Olympic Way), 600m S of PO, ☎ 02 6942 1833, fax 02 6942 1816, 23 units [shwr, tlt, a/c, elec blkts, tel, TV, video (avail), clock radio, t/c mkg, refrig, mini bar], ldry, ⊠ (Mon to Sat), pool, bbq, dinner to unit, cots, non smoking units (18). RO ♦ $77 - $88, ♦♦ $88 - $99, ⍭ $12, ch con, AE BC DC EFT JCB MC MP VI.

★★★☆ **Southern Comfort Motor Inn**, (M), 26 Parker St (Olympic Way), 700m N of PO, ☎ 02 6942 3366, fax 02 6942 3366, 15 units [shwr, bath (1), tlt, a/c, elec blkts, tel, TV, video, clock radio, t/c mkg, refrig], iron, iron brd, pool, bbq, dinner to unit (Mon to Thu), plygr, cots-fee, non smoking units (6). RO ♦ $73 - $85, ♦♦ $83 - $94, ♦♦♦ $93 - $104, ♦♦♦♦ $110, ⍭ $10, AE BC DC EFT MC VI, ⅏.

★★★ **Wattle Tree Motel**, (M), 66 Wallendoon St, 200m E of PO, ☎ 02 6942 2688, fax 02 6942 4273, (2 stry gr fl), 22 units [shwr, tlt, a/c-cool, a/c (8), cent heat, elec blkts, tel, TV, clock radio, t/c mkg, refrig, toaster], ldry, cots-fee, non smoking units (6). RO ♦ $50 - $60, ♦♦ $60 - $70, ⍭ $11, ch con, 8 units at a lower rating. AE BC EFT MC VI.

Self Catering Accommodation

★★★ **Woodies**, (Cotg), 56 Mackay St, 500m S of PO, ☎ 02 6942 4090, 1 cotg acc up to 8, [shwr, bath, tlt (2), heat, TV, refrig, cook fac, micro, toaster, ldry, blkts, linen, pillows], iron. RO ♦ $40, ♦♦ $45, ♦ $17, ch con.

B&B's/Guest Houses

White Ibis B & B, (B&B), 21 Wallendoon St, 350m of PO, ☎ 02 6942 1850, or 02 6942 3348, fax 02 6942 3850, (2 stry) 12 rms [ensuite (3), spa bath (1), a/c (3), fan (9), heat (9), elec blkts, tel (3), TV, clock radio, t/c mkg (3), refrig (3)], ldry, lounge (TV, video), conf fac, ✕, t/c mkg shared, refrig, bbq, ☎, non smoking rms. BB ♦ $45 - $50, ♦♦ $80 - $135, ♦ $20, ch con, BC EFT MC VI, (not yet classified).

CORLETTE NSW

See Port Stephens Region.

COROWA NSW 2646

Pop 5,150. (616km SW Sydney), See map on pages 52/53, ref E7. Historic town situated across the Murray River from the smaller Wahgunyah and just up the road from the winery town of Rutherglen. Bowls, Canoeing, Croquet, Fishing, Golf, Swimming, Tennis, Vineyards, Wineries. See also Wahgunyah & Rutherglen.

Hotels/Motels

★★★★ **Arcadia Motor Inn**, (M), 127 Federation Ave, 1km W of PO, ☎ 02 6033 2088, or 02 6033 2779, fax 02 6033 2088, 11 units [shwr, tlt, a/c, heat, elec blkts, tel, TV, video (avail), t/c mkg, refrig, cook fac ltd, micro (8), toaster], ldry, pool, bbq, plygr, cots-fee. RO ♦ $50 - $100, ♦♦ $55 - $100, ♦♦♦ $65 - $110, ♦ $12, W ♦♦ $230 - $450, ch con, Min book applies, AE BC DC MC VI, ৬.

★★★★ **Heritage Motor Inn**, (M), 25 Edward St, 1km SW of PO, ☎ 02 6033 1800, fax 02 6033 3491, 20 units (2 suites) [shwr, bath (7), spa bath (2), tlt, hairdry, a/c, elec blkts, tel, cable tv, video-fee, clock radio, t/c mkg, refrig, cook fac (12), toaster], ldry, iron, iron brd, conf fac, pool-heated (solar), bbq, plygr, cots-fee. RO ♦ $75 - $115, ♦♦ $85 - $125, ♦ $12, Suite D $115 - $135, Min book applies, AE BC DC MC VI, ৬.

The perfect place for a relaxing stay with all amenities. Walking distance (300m) to town centre and restaurants. Only minutes away from Rutherglen's wineries and Corowa's magnificent 27 hole golf course.

AAA TOURISM ★★★★

1577AG

Heritage Motor Inn
25 Edward Street Corowa NSW 2646
Phone: (02) 6033 1800 Fax: (02) 6033 3491

Tranquillity & Seclusion overlooking the Murray River

- Superior ground floor garden units with private courtyards
- King or queen beds
- Undercover parking
- Saltwater spa, pool, BBQ & gazebo
- Mins to golf, bowls & vineyards

MURRAY VIEW MOTEL
193 River St, Sth Corowa NSW
Ph: (02) 6033 2144
Fax: (02) 6033 1625

1582AG

★★★☆ **Bindaree Motel**, (M), 454 Honour Ave, 2km E of PO, ☎ 02 6033 2500, fax 02 6033 3826, 11 units [shwr, tlt, a/c, elec blkts, tel, TV, video-fee, clock radio, refrig, cook fac, micro], ldry, rec rm, pool, spa, bbq, plygr, tennis, cots. ♦♦ $55 - $108, ♦ $17, ch con, AE BC DC MC VI,

Operator Comment: 15 acres on river with boat ramp. 2 bedroom motels. 5 nights from $220 dble.

★★★☆ **Federation Motor Inn**, (M), 330 Honour Ave, 1.5km N of PO, ☎ 02 6033 2022, fax 02 6033 2866, 22 units (3 suites) [shwr, spa bath (6), hairdry, a/c, elec blkts, tel, TV, video, clock radio, t/c mkg, refrig], ldry, ✕ (Tues to Sat), pool, sauna, bbq, dinner to unit, cots, non smoking units (7). RO ♦ $75 - $85, ♦♦ $85 - $90, ♦ $10 - $15, Suite RO ♦♦ $90 - $100, ch con, AE BC DC EFT MC VI.

FLAG
FLAG CHOICE HOTELS

AAA TOURISM *Special Rates*

★★★☆ **Golfers Lodge Motel**, (M), Hume St, 3km SW of PO, ☎ 02 6033 1366, fax 02 6033 1391, 10 units [shwr, tlt, a/c, elec blkts, tel, TV, video (avail), clock radio, t/c mkg, refrig, mini bar (licensed)], ldry, pool, bbq. RO ♦ $55 - $66, ♦♦ $60 - $70, ♦ $11, AE BC DC MC VI.

★★★☆ **Murray View Motel Corowa**, (M), 193 River St, 3km S of PO, ☎ 02 6033 2144, fax 02 6033 1625, 10 units [shwr, tlt, a/c, elec blkts, tel, TV, clock radio, t/c mkg, refrig, cook fac (2), toaster], ldry, pool (salt water), spa, bbq, ☎, non smoking units (4). RO ♦ $55 - $77, ♦♦ $60.50 - $82.50, ♦ $11 - $16.50, BC EFT MC VI.

Budget Motel Chain *International*

★★★☆ **Ski Lodge Motel**, (M), 17 Lone Pine Ave, 1km E of PO, ☎ 02 6033 2966, fax 02 6033 2506, 10 units [shwr, tlt, hairdry, a/c-cool, heat, elec blkts, tel, fax, TV, clock radio, t/c mkg, refrig, cook fac, toaster], ldry, iron, pool, bbq, cots, non smoking units (3). RO ♦ $49 - $77, ♦♦ $55 - $77, ♦♦♦ $82 - $102, ♦ $14, Min book long w/ends, AE BC DC EFT MC MCH VI, ৬.

★★★☆ **Wingrove Motel**, (M), 147 Federation Ave, 1km S of PO, ☎ 02 6033 2055, fax 02 6033 2055, 10 units [shwr, tlt, hairdry, a/c-cool, heat, elec blkts, tel, TV, clock radio, t/c mkg, refrig, toaster], ldry, pool (salt water), bbq, cots. RO ♦ $55.78 - $74, ♦♦ $60.88 - $78, ♦♦♦ $72 - $100, ♦ $15, AE BC DC MC VI.

★★★ **Corowa Golf Club Motel**, (M), Hume St, 5km S of Clock Tower, ☎ 02 6033 4188, fax 02 6033 0634, (2 stry gr fl) 35 units [shwr, tlt, a/c, elec blkts, tel, TV, clock radio, t/c mkg, refrig, cook fac, toaster], ldry, rec rm, conf fac, ✕, pool-heated-fee, sauna-fee, spa-fee, bbq, rm serv (b'fast), ☎, gym-fee, squash-fee, tennis-fee, cots. RO ♦ $65 - $80, ♦♦ $72 - $88, ♦ $10 - $20, ch con, Min book applies, AE BC EFT MC VI, ৬.

★★★ **Green Acres Motel**, (M), 91 Federation Ave, 2km SW of PO, ☎ 02 6033 2288, fax 02 6033 2886, 20 units [shwr, tlt, a/c, heat, elec blkts, tel, TV, clock radio, t/c mkg, refrig, toaster], ldry, pool, spa (heated), bbq, rm serv, plygr, golf (practice area), tennis, cots-fee, non smoking units (6). RO ♦ $60 - $80, ♦♦ $66 - $88, ♦♦♦ $75 - $105, ♦ $14 - $20, ch con, AE BC DC MC VI, ৬.

Rates may change. Check before booking.

★★★ **Statesman Motor Inn**, (M), Cnr Edward St & Federation Ave, 1km S of PO, ☎ 02 6033 2411, fax 02 6033 2840, 25 units [shwr, bath (4), tlt, a/c, elec blkts, tel, TV, clock radio, t/c mkg, refrig, micro (4)], ldry, pool, sauna, spa, bbq, cots-fee, non smoking units (9). **RO** ⋕ $65 - $75, ⋕⋕ $70 - $85, ⋕⋕⋕ $75 - $95, ⋔ $12, AE BC DC EFT MC VI.

★★☆ **Corowa Motor Inn**, (M), 69 Riesling St, 100m N of GPO, ☎ 02 6033 1255, fax 02 6033 1605, 21 units (1 suite) [shwr, tlt, a/c, fan, heat (elec), elec blkts, TV, clock radio, t/c mkg, refrig], ldry, pool (outdoor/heated), sauna, spa, bbq, c/park. **RO** ⋕ $48 - $58, ⋕⋕ $55 - $70, ⋔ $10, **Suite RO** $70 - $100, ch con, weekly con, Min book applies, BC EFT MC VI.

★★☆ **Golfers Retreat Motel**, (M), 57 Hay St, 3km SW of PO, ☎ 02 6033 2059, fax 02 6033 2474, 7 units [shwr, tlt, a/c, fan, elec blkts, tel, TV, video (avail), clock radio, t/c mkg, refrig, cook fac, toaster], ldry, iron, iron brd, pool, bbq, cots. **RO** ⋕ $45 - $65, ⋕⋕ $50 - $70, ⋔ $11, fam con, AE BC DC MC VI.

★★☆ **Lovells Motel**, (M), 203 Sangar St, 300m N of PO, ☎ 02 6033 1566, fax 02 6033 2137, 14 units [shwr, tlt, a/c, elec blkts, tel, TV, clock radio, t/c mkg, refrig, cook fac (8)], ⊠, pool, bbq, cots-fee. **RO** ⋕ $57 - $67, ⋕⋕ $60 - $70, Min book applies, AE BC DC MC MP VI.

★★ **Westona Motel**, (M), 18 Edward St, 1km S of PO, ☎ 02 6033 2311, 5 units [shwr, tlt, a/c, heat, elec blkts, TV, clock radio, t/c mkg, refrig, toaster], ldry, bbq, c/park. **RO** ⋕ $42 - $60, ⋕⋕ $50 - $60, ⋔ $12, ch con, AE BC DC MC VI.

Motel Menere's, (M), Previously Macambo Motel 146 Federation Ave, 1km SW of PO, ☎ 02 6033 1066, 18 units (2 suites) [shwr, tlt, a/c, elec blkts, tel, TV, t/c mkg, refrig], rec rm, pool, sauna, bbq, plygr, tennis, cots, ch con, BC MC VI, (Rating under review).

Self Catering Accommodation
★★★★ **Mooratunka Farm Cottage**, (Cotg), (Farm), Enfield St, 5km SW of Clock Tower, ☎ 02 6033 4553, fax 02 6033 0135, 1 cotg acc up to 7, [shwr (2), bath, tlt (2), a/c, c/fan, heat, TV, t/c mkg, refrig, cook fac, micro, d/wash, toaster, ldry, doonas, linen], w/mach, lounge firepl, cots. **D** ⋕ $105, ⋔ $10, Min book applies, BC MC VI.

★★★☆ **Murray Bank Holiday Units & Yabby Farm**, (HU), 76 Federation Ave, ☎ 02 6033 2922, 5 units acc up to 6, (1 & 2 bedrm), [shwr, spa bath (1), tlt, a/c, elec blkts, tel, TV, clock radio, t/c mkg, refrig, cook fac, toaster, ldry, linen reqd-fee], bbq (covered), c/park (undercover), plygr, picnic facilities, canoeing, cots. **D** ⋕⋕ $45 - $66, ⋕⋕⋕⋕ $80 - $99, ⋔ $15, ch con, Min book applies, BC MC VI.

★★★☆ **Murray Lodge**, (HU), 43 Tower St, 1.5km W of PO, ☎ 02 6033 1712, fax 02 6033 0224, 9 units acc up to 6, [shwr, tlt, a/c, heat, elec blkts, TV, clock radio, refrig, cook fac, micro, ldry, linen], w/mach, pool, bbq, non smoking rms (4). **W** $455 - $840, **RO** ⋕⋕ $65 - $105, ⋕⋕⋕⋕ $90 - $130, ⋔ $8 - $15, Minimum booking Melbourne Cup weekend, BC MC VI.

★★☆ **Corowa Holiday Apartments**, (HU), 19 Lone Pine Ave, 2km NE of PO, ☎ 02 6033 2007, 7 units acc up to 6, [shwr, tlt, a/c, elec blkts, TV, refrig, cook fac, blkts, linen, pillows], w/mach, pool, bbq, cots. **RO** ⋕⋕ $45 - $50, ⋕⋕⋕ $300 - $335, ch con, Min book long w/ends, BC MC VI.

COWRA NSW 2794

Pop 8,550. (312km W Sydney), See map on pages 52/53, ref G5. Historic town on the Lachlan River renowned for its food, wine and the role it played in World War II. Boating, Bowls, Bush Walking, Fishing, Golf, Sailing, Swimming, Tennis, Water Skiing. See also Wyangala.

Hotels/Motels

GOLDEN CHAIN

★★★☆ **Aalana Motor Inn**, (M), 161 Kendal St, 400m E of PO, ☎ 02 6341 1177, fax 02 6341 1771, 19 units [shwr, tlt, hairdry, a/c, elec blkts, tel, TV, video-fee, clock radio, t/c mkg, refrig], bbq, dinner to unit, cots-fee, non smoking units (9). **RO** ⋕ $80, ⋕⋕ $95, ⋕⋕⋕ $105, ⋔ $10 - $15, ch con, AE BC DC JCB MC MP VI, ⅋⅋.

AAA TOURISM *Special Rates*

★★★☆ **Alabaster Motel**, (M), 20 Lynch St (Mid Western Hwy), 1km E of PO, ☎ 02 6342 3133, fax 02 6342 4075, 13 units [shwr, tlt, hairdry, a/c, heat, elec blkts, tel, TV, video, clock radio, t/c mkg, refrig, toaster], pool, spa, bbq, dinner to unit, cots-fee. **RO** ⋕ $79 - $86.70, ⋕⋕ $81.50 - $97, ⋕⋕⋕ $94.70 - $110.20, ⋔ $13.20, ch con, AE BC DC EFT MC VI.

Trouble-free travel tips - Lights
Check the operation of all lights. If you are pulling a trailer of caravan make sure turning indicators and brake lights are working.

CIVIC MOTOR INN and Oasis Restaurant

Young Road (Olympic Way) Cowra NSW 2794

Ph (02) 6341 1753   Fax (02) 6342 3296

TOLL FREE 1800 355 208

Quiet location 1km from PO, adjacent to Cowra's beautiful golf course

- air conditioned - reverse cycle
- licenced a la carté restaurant & bar Open 7 Days
- swimming pool • BBQ area
- extensive landscaped gardens
- quiet and relaxing dining room
- reps & motel guest menu
- Offering special packages including accommodation, dinner, breakfast and 18 holes of golf

75 GRENFELL ROAD, (MIDWEST HWY) COWRA

Spa Suites, Free Sat TV (6Ch), King and Queen size beds, Quiet edge of town on acreage, Pool BBQ, 7 New Suites. AAAT ★★★☆

1800 501 824   Phone (02) 6341 1100

GOLDEN CHAIN

COUNTRY GARDENS MOTOR INN ★★★☆

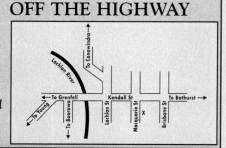

COWRA MOTOR INN

OFF THE HIGHWAY

ACCOMMODATION IN THE TOWN CENTRE CLOSE TO SHOPS & CLUBS
Privately owned and operated Check our Rates!

CLEAN & QUIET

3 Macquarie Street, COWRA, 2794 • Ph: 02 6342 2011 • Fax: 02 6342 2323

FLAG
FLAG CHOICE HOTELS

★★★☆ **Civic Motor Inn**, (M), Young Rd (Olympic Way), 2km SE of PO, ☎ 02 6341 1753, fax 02 6342 3296, 26 units [shwr, tlt, hairdry, a/c, elec blkts, tel, TV, video (avail), clock radio, t/c mkg, refrig], ldry, ⊠, pool, bbq, dinner to unit, plygr, cots-fee, non smoking units (9). **RO** ♦ $60 - $75, ♦♦ $66 - $82, ♦♦♦ $79 - $108, ⋔ $12 - $13, ch con, AE BC DC EFT JCB MC MP VI.

GOLDEN CHAIN

★★★☆ **Country Gardens Motor Inn**, (M), 75 Grenfell Rd, 3km W of PO, ☎ 02 6341 1100, fax 02 6341 1139, 18 units [shwr, bath (2), spa bath (3), tlt, hairdry, a/c, elec blkts, tel, cable tv, video-fee, clock radio, t/c mkg, refrig], ldry, iron, iron brd, pool, bbq, dinner to unit (Sun - Thur), cots, non smoking units (12). **RO** ♦ $82 - $130, ♦♦ $95 - $130, ♦♦♦ $107 - $142, ⋔ $12, Min book long w/ends, AE BC DC MC VI, ⅋.

Best Western

★★★☆ **Countryman Motor Inn**, (M), 164 Kendal St, ☎ 02 6342 3177, fax 02 6342 1748, 25 units [shwr, tlt, a/c-cool (7), a/c (18), cent heat (7), elec blkts, tel, cable tv, video-fee, clock radio, t/c mkg, refrig, mini bar], ⊠ (Mon to Sat), pool, dinner to unit, cots-fee. **RO** ♦ $73 - $100, ♦♦ $73 - $100, ♦♦♦ $103 - $113, 6 units ★★★☆. AE BC DC MC MP VI.

★★★☆ **Vineyard Motel**, (M), Chardonnay Rd, 4km SW of PO, ☎ 02 6342 3641, fax 02 6342 4916, 6 units [shwr, spa bath (1), tlt, heat, elec blkts, tel, TV, clock radio, t/c mkg, refrig, toaster], pool, bbq, rm serv, dinner to unit, bicycle, tennis, cots. **BB** ♦ $95 - $110, ♦♦ $105 - $130, ⋔ $10, AE BC DC EFT MC VI.

★★★ **Cowra Crest Motel**, (M), 133 Kendal St, 100m E of PO, ☎ 02 6342 2799, fax 02 6341 1653, 12 units [shwr, tlt, hairdry, a/c, elec blkts, tel, TV, video (6), clock radio, t/c mkg, refrig, micro-fee, toaster], pool, bbq, dinner to unit, cots-fee, non smoking units (6). **RO** ♦ $60 - $72, ♦♦ $66 - $78, ⋔ $7 - $11, AE BC DC EFT MC VI, ⅋.

Budget Motel Chain International

★★☆ **Cowra Motor Inn**, (M), 3 Macquarie St, 200m W of PO, ☎ 02 6342 2011, fax 02 6342 2323, (2 stry gr fl), 26 units [shwr, tlt, hairdry, a/c, elec blkts, tel, TV, clock radio, t/c mkg, refrig, toaster], ✗ (Closed Sun), pool, spa, dinner to unit, cots-fee, non smoking units (3). **RO** ♦ $46 - $48, ♦♦ $56 - $58, ⋔ $11, W $300 - $372, BC DC MC VI.

COWRA CREST MOTEL

133 Kendal Street, Cowra

AAA Tourism ★ ★ ★

- *Quiet central location*
- *Large well equipped rooms*
- *Non smoking rooms (6)*
- *Easy walking distance to clubs and restaurants*
- *Queensize beds (7)*

PHONE: (02) 6342 2799
FAX: (02) 6341 1653
EMAIL: thecrest@ix.net.au

Your hosts:
Bernie & Kathy Wallace

★★☆ **Town House**, (LMH), 15 Kendal St, 250m W of PO, ☎ 02 6342 1055, fax 02 6341 2930, 35 units [shwr, tlt, a/c-cool, cent heat, elec blkts, tel, TV, t/c mkg, refrig], ldry, conv fac, ✕, pool, bbq, rm serv, cots. RO ♦ $50, ♦♦ $60, ♦♦♦ $71, ⑂ $9 - $11, ch con, AE BC DC MC MCH VI, ⴕ⌷.

★☆ **Lachlan Valley**, (LMH), 162 Kendal St, ☎ 02 6342 2900, fax 02 6342 4050, 10 units [shwr, tlt, a/c-cool, cent heat, TV, t/c mkg, refrig], conv fac, ✕, rm serv. RO ♦ $55, ♦♦ $65, AE BC DC EFT MC VI.

Cowra Breakout Motor Inn, (M), 181 Kendal St, 500m E of PO, ☎ 02 6342 6111, fax 02 6342 6029, 17 units (4 suites) [ensuite, spa bath (1), a/c, heat, elec blkts, tel, cable tv-fee, video-fee, clock radio, t/c mkg, refrig, ldry], bbq, meals to unit, cots-fee, non smoking rms (13). RO ♦ $79, ♦♦ $95, ♦♦♦ $105, ⑂ $15, weekly con, BC EFT MC VI, (not yet classified).

Self Catering Accommodation

★★★ **Lachway Farm Villas**, (Villa), (Farm), 6406 Boorowa Rd (Lachlan Valley Way), 12.5km S of PO, ☎ 02 6345 3295, fax 02 6345 3296, 2 villas acc up to 4, [shwr, tlt, hairdry, a/c, elec blkts, TV, clock radio, t/c mkg, refrig, cook fac, micro, toaster, blkts, linen, pillows], bbq, courtesy transfer. D ♦ $95, ♦♦ $110, ⑂ $20, BC MC VI,

Operator Comment: Visit our website: www.cowra.org

B&B's/Guest Houses

★★★☆ **The Hart House**, (B&B), 90 Liverpool St, 2km E from Cowra, ☎ 02 6341 4588, fax 02 6341 4585, (2 stry), 3 rms [a/c-cool, heat (gas), elec blkts, t/c mkg, refrig, doonas], lounge (TV), conf fac, ✕, ✕, ✕, non smoking property, Pets on application. BB ♦ $140 - $155, ♦♦ $150 - $165, BC MC VI.

CRESCENT HEAD NSW 2440

Pop 1,200. (446km N Sydney), See map on page 54, ref C6. Mid-north coastal town situated on a headland at the southern end of Hat Head National Park. Bowls, Bush Walking, Fishing, Golf, Surfing, Swimming, Tennis.

Hotels/Motels

★★★☆ **Wombat Beach Resort**, (M), Pacific St, 400m W of PO, ☎ 02 6566 0121, fax 02 6566 0271, 25 units [shwr, bath (1), spa bath (1), tlt, hairdry, c/fan, heat, elec blkts, tel, TV, video, movie, clock radio, t/c mkg, refrig, cook fac (1)], ldry, rec rm, conv fac, ✕, pool-heated (solar), sauna, spa, bbq, plygr, gym, cots. RO ♦ $80 - $130, ♦♦ $90 - $140, ⑂ $10, AE BC DC EFT MC VI, ⴕ⌷.

★★★ **Mediterranean Motel**, (M), 35 Pacific St, ☎ 02 6566 0303, fax 02 6566 0858, (2 stry gr fl), 10 units [shwr, tlt, a/c (5), fan (5), heat (5), TV, t/c mkg, refrig], pool-heated, spa, bbq, meals to unit, plygr. D ♦♦ $55 - $88, ⑂ $9, AE BC DC MC VI.

★★☆ **Bush n Beach Retreat Motel**, (M), 353 Loftus Rd, 4km N of Crescent Head, ☎ 02 6566 0235, 6 units [shwr, tlt, hairdry-fee, tel, TV, clock radio, t/c mkg, refrig], ldry, conv fac, breakfast rm, pool (salt water), bbq, plygr, cots, non smoking units. D ♦ $75 - $85, ♦♦ $80 - $90, ⑂ $10.

(Lodge Section), 7 rms [tel], shared fac (shwr & tlt), ldry, breakfast rm, t/c mkg shared, bbq, non smoking rms. RO ♦ $25, ♦♦ $40, ⑂ $12.

Self Catering Accommodation

★★★☆ **Breakers 1**, (HU), 13 East St, 450m S of beach, ☎ 02 6566 0306, fax 02 6566 0546, (2 stry), 2 units acc up to 8, (2 bedrm), [shwr, tlt, fan, heat (elec), tel, TV, video, clock radio, t/c mkg, refrig, cook fac, micro, blkts, linen-fee], w/mach, bbq, c/park (garage), cots-fee. D $125 - $140, W $500 - $1,200, Min book applies, BC EFT MC VI.

★★★☆ **Crescent View**, (House), 12 May St, ☎ 02 4998 1576, fax 02 4998 0008, (2 stry), 1 house acc up to 10, (4 bedrm), [shwr (3), spa bath, tlt, c/fan, heat, tel, TV, video, clock radio, refrig, cook fac, micro, toaster, ldry], w/mach, iron, iron brd. W $320 - $1,400, AE BC MC VI.

★★★☆ **Endless Summer**, (House), 12 Main St, ☎ 02 6566 0306, fax 02 6566 0546, 1 house acc up to 6, (3 bedrm), [shwr, tlt, fan, heat (elec), tel, TV, radio, t/c mkg, refrig, cook fac, micro, ldry, blkts, linen-fee], w/mach, bbq, c/park (garage), cots-fee. D $100 - $110, W $320 - $950, BC EFT MC VI.

★★★☆ **Killuke Lodge Holiday Cottages**, (Cotg), Point Plomer Rd, 3km S of PO, ☎ 02 6566 0077, fax 02 6566 0318, 7 cotgs acc up to 5, [shwr, tlt, fan, fire pl, heat, tel (2), TV, video (3), clock radio, refrig, cook fac, micro, d/wash, toaster, linen reqd-fee], w/mach, dryer, iron, bbq, c/park (undercover) (6), ✆. W $295 - $995, Min book applies, AE BC DC MC VI.

★★★ **Driftwood House**, (Cotg), 32 Stewart St, 200m SE of PO, ☎ 02 6566 0306, fax 02 6566 0546, (2 stry gr fl), 1 cotg acc up to 7, [shwr, bath, tlt, fan, heat, TV, video, clock radio, t/c mkg, refrig, cook fac, micro, elec frypan, toaster, ldry, linen reqd-fee], w/mach, iron, iron brd, bbq, cots. D $100 - $110, W $320 - $950, Min book applies, BC EFT MC VI.

★★★ **Lakeview Units**, (HU), 25 Willow St, ☎ 02 6566 0306, fax 02 6566 0546, (2 stry gr fl), 6 units acc up to 6, [shwr, tlt, c/fan (2), heat, TV, video, clock radio, refrig, cook fac, micro, elec frypan, toaster, linen], w/mach, dryer, iron, bbq, cots-fee. D $85 - $120, W $250 - $1,000, Min book applies, BC EFT MC VI.

★★★ **Malibu 1**, (HF), 6 Dulconghi St, ☎ 02 6566 0306, fax 02 6566 0546, 1 flat acc up to 9, [shwr (2), tlt (2), TV, video, refrig, cook fac, micro, ldry, linen reqd-fee], w/mach, bbq, c/park (garage). D $100 - $130, W $400 - $1,100, Min book applies, BC EFT MC VI.

★★★ **Wallum Cottages**, (Cotg), Point Plomer Rd, Big Hill, 10km S of Crescent Head, ☎ 02 6566 0820, fax 02 6566 0820, (2 stry gr fl), 4 cotgs acc up to 6, [shwr, tlt, heat, tel, fax, TV, video, t/c mkg, refrig, cook fac, micro, d/wash, toaster, ldry, blkts, linen reqd-fee], w/mach, iron, iron brd, bbq, ✆, plygr, cots, non smoking property. **D** ♦♦ **$130 - $150**, ♦ **$28 - $55**, **W** ♦♦ **$430 - $750**, ♦ **$55 - $110**, BC MC VI.

★★★ **Willow Court**, (HU), 11 Willow St, ☎ 02 6566 0306, fax 02 6566 0546, 2 units acc up to 6, [shwr, tlt, TV, video, clock radio, t/c mkg, refrig, cook fac, micro, elec frypan, toaster, linen reqd], w/mach, iron, c/park (garage), cots-fee. **D $90 - $95, W $270 - $880**, Min book applies, BC EFT MC VI.

★★☆ **Bella Vista**, (House), 9 East Rd, ☎ 02 6566 0306, fax 02 6566 0546, houses [heat, tel, TV, video, clock radio, refrig, cook fac, micro, ldry, blkts, linen-fee], w/mach, bbq, cots-fee. **D $85 - $90, W $250 - $850**, weekly con, Min book applies, BC EFT MC VI.

★★☆ **Bellhaven**, (HU), 17 Willow St, ☎ 02 6566 0306, fax 02 6566 0546, 2 units acc up to 5, [shwr, tlt, TV, video, t/c mkg, refrig, cook fac, micro, elec frypan, toaster, linen reqd], w/mach, iron, bbq, c/park (carport), cots-fee. **D $85 - $90, W $250 - $850**, Min book applies, BC EFT MC VI.

★★☆ **Bournes Holiday Flats**, (HF), 1 Baker Dve, ☎ 02 6566 0293, 8 flats acc up to 5, [shwr, tlt, TV, refrig, cook fac, linen reqd-fee], ldry, bbq, c/park (undercover). **D $50 - $80, W $250 - $550**.

★★☆ **Caerula**, (House), 20 Stewart St, ☎ 02 6566 0306, fax 02 6566 0546, 1 house acc up to 7, [heat, tel, TV, video, radio, refrig, cook fac, micro, ldry, blkts, linen-fee], w/mach, bbq, secure park, cots-fee. **D $90 - $100, W $280 - $900**, weekly con, Min book applies, BC EFT MC VI.

★★☆ **Clareview**, (House), 8 Korogora St, ☎ 02 6566 0306, fax 02 6566 0546, 1 house acc up to 6, [heat, TV, radio, cook fac, micro, blkts, linen-fee], w/mach, bbq, cots-fee. **D $90 - $95, W $270 - $880**, BC EFT MC VI.

★★☆ **Harapan House**, (House), 23 Dulconghi St, ☎ 02 6566 0306, fax 02 6566 0546, 1 house acc up to 7, (2 bedrm), [heat, fan, TV, radio, micro, blkts, linen-fee], w/mach, cook fac, bbq, cots-fee. **D $90 - $100, W $280 - $900**, weekly con, Min book applies, BC EFT MC VI.

★★☆ **Pemberley**, (House), 30 Stewart St, ☎ 02 6566 0306, fax 02 6566 0546, 1 house acc up to 6, [heat, TV, video, radio, refrig, cook fac, micro, d/wash, blkts, linen-fee], w/mach, bbq, secure park, cots-fee. **D $90 - $100, W $280 - $900**, weekly con, Min book applies, BC EFT MC VI.

★★☆ **Sea Change**, (House), 27 Comara Tce, ☎ 02 6566 0306, fax 02 6566 0546, (2 stry), 1 house acc up to 8, (1 & 2 bedrm), [shwr, tlt, heat (elec), tel, TV, video, clock radio, t/c mkg, refrig, cook fac, micro, blkts, linen-fee], w/mach, bbq, c/park (garage), cots-fee. **D $100 - $110, W $320 - $950**, Min book applies, BC EFT MC VI.

★★☆ **Shiloh**, (House), 14 East St, ☎ 02 6566 0306, fax 02 6566 0546, 1 house acc up to 6, [shwr (2), tlt (2), heat, TV, video, radio, t/c mkg, refrig, cook fac, micro, elec frypan, toaster, ldry, linen reqd], ldry, w/mach, iron, bbq, c/park (garage), cots-fee. **D $90 - $100, W $280 - $900**, Min book applies.

★★☆ **Shorebreak**, (House), 13 Stewart St, ☎ 02 6566 0306, fax 02 6566 0546, 1 house acc up to 7, (4 bedrm), [shwr, tlt, heat (elec), TV, clock radio, t/c mkg, refrig, cook fac, micro, d/wash, blkts, linen-fee], w/mach, bbq, cots-fee. **D $90 - $100, W $360 - $900**, Min book applies, BC EFT MC VI.

★★ **Balarang**, (House), 11 Dulconghi St, ☎ 02 6566 0306, fax 02 6566 0546, 1 house acc up to 7, [heat, TV, video, clock radio, refrig, cook fac, micro, ldry, blkts, linen-fee], w/mach, bbq, cots-fee. **D $100 - $110, W $420 - $950**, weekly con, Min book applies, BC EFT MC VI.

★★ **Beach Point**, (HU), 22 Pacific St, ☎ 02 6566 0306, fax 02 6566 0546, 3 units acc up to 5, (1 & 2 bedrm), [shwr, tlt, heat (elec), TV, video, clock radio, t/c mkg, refrig, cook fac, micro, blkts, linen-fee], ldry, cots-fee. **D $45 - $65, W $160 - $550**, Min book applies, BC EFT MC VI.

★★ **By the Sea**, (HF), 13 Willow St, ☎ 02 6566 0306, fax 02 6566 0546, 2 flats acc up to 5, [shwr, tlt, TV, video, refrig, cook fac, micro, linen reqd-fee], ldry, cots-fee. **D $85 - $90, W $250 - $850**, BC EFT MC VI.

★★ **Fleur Cottage**, (House), 7 Willow St, ☎ 02 6566 0306, fax 02 6566 0546, 1 house acc up to 6, (3 bedrm), [shwr, tlt, heat (elec), TV, video, clock radio, t/c mkg, refrig, cook fac, micro, ldry, blkts, linen-fee], bbq, c/park (carport), cots-fee. **D $85 - $90, W $250 - $850**, Min book applies, BC EFT MC VI.

Holiday hazards

When holidaying away from home many drivers, cyclists and pedestrians are in unfamiliar territory. There are also many more children about than usual, so expect the unexpected.

Drivers should always be alert anywhere that children might run onto the road - and at holiday times this can be just about anywhere at all. Another holiday peril is the risk of out-of-town drivers making sudden turns and stops as they struggle to find their way, so it's wise to keep safe stopping distances.

Drivers who are "feeling their way" should pull over or stop in a side street rather than risk frustrating other drivers and perhaps causing an accident.

CROOKWELL NSW 2583

Pop 2,000. (267km SW Sydney), See map on page 55, ref A3. Picturesque town at the centre of prime merino and seed potato producing country. Bowls, Fishing, Golf.

Hotels/Motels

★★★ **Crookwell Upland Pastures Motor Inn**, (M), 2 Oram St, 200m N of PO, ☎ 02 4832 1999, fax 02 4832 1270, 12 units [shwr, tlt, hairdry, heat, elec blkts, tel, TV, clock radio, t/c mkg, refrig, toaster], bbq, cots. **RO** ♦ $64, ♦♦ $75, ◊ $11, AE BC DC EFT MC VI.

★★☆ **Crookwell**, (LMH), Cnr Spring & Goulburn Sts, 100m E of PO, ☎ 02 4832 1016, (2 stry), 8 units [shwr, tlt, a/c, elec blkts, TV, clock radio, t/c mkg, refrig], ⊠, c/park (undercover), ☎. **RO** ♦ $35, ♦♦ $45, ♦♦♦ $60.

Crookwell - UPLAND PASTURES MOTOR INN

2 Oram St, off Laggan Rd, Crookwell NSW 2583
Ph: (02) 4832 1999   Fax: (02) 4832 1270
AAAT ★★★
Quiet garden setting, short walk to town. 12 units - all ground floor, queen beds, electric blankets, room and bathroom heaters. See Australia's first wind farm, plus lavender farm, cool climate gardens and alpaca farms.

B&B's/Guest Houses

★★★☆ **Gundowringa Farm Stay**, (B&B), Gundowringa, 30km N of Goulburn PO, ☎ 02 4848 1212, fax 02 4848 1212, 6 rms (2 suites) [hairdry (1), cent heat, elec blkts, tel, TV (2), clock radio (1), refrig (1)], ldry, iron, iron brd, TV rm, lounge firepl, pool (salt water), cook fac, t/c mkg shared, bbq, dinner to unit, courtesy transfer, plygr, tennis, cots, non smoking property. **BB** ♦♦ $160, ◊ $15.

★★★☆ **Minnamurra Farmstay**, (B&B), (Farm), Minnamurra, 15km SE of PO, ☎ 02 4848 1226, fax 02 4848 1288, 4 rms [shwr (1), tlt (1), heat, elec blkts, tel], shared fac (3 rms), ldry, iron, iron brd, lounge (TV), ✕, t/c mkg shared, bbq, tennis, non smoking rms (4). **BB** ♦ $66, ♦♦ $132 - $141, **DBB** ♦ $115.50, ♦♦ $231 - $240, ch con.

CROWDY HEAD NSW 2427

Pop Nominal, (356km N Sydney), See map on page 54, ref C7. Small mid-north coastal settlement at the southern end of Crowdy Bay.

Hotels/Motels

★★★☆ **Crowdy Head Motel**, (M), 7 Geoffrey St, ☎ 02 6556 1206, fax 02 6556 1206, 6 units [shwr, tlt, fan, heat, elec blkts, TV, clock radio, t/c mkg, refrig], ✕, bbq, rm serv. **RO** ♦ $59 - $69, ♦♦ $64 - $84, 2 units at a higher standard, BC MC VI.

CUDAL NSW 2864

Pop 400. (316km W Sydney), See map on pages 52/53, ref G5. Cudal lies at the heart of Cabonne Country, one of the major food producing regions of New South Wales. Bowls, Swimming, Tennis.

Hotels/Motels

★★ **Cudal Motor Inn**, (M), 5 Main St, 100m W of PO, ☎ 02 6364 2175, 7 units [shwr, bath (1), tlt, a/c, fan, heat, elec blkts, TV, clock radio, t/c mkg, refrig], lounge, cafe, cots, Pets allowed. **RO** ♦ $50, ♦♦ $55 - $58, BC MC VI.

Trouble-free travel tips - Fluids

Check all fluid levels and top up as necessary. Look at engine oil, automatic transmission fluid, radiator coolant (only check this when the engine is cold), power steering, battery and windscreen washers.

CULBURRA BEACH NSW 2540

Pop 3,533. (172km Sydney), See map on page 55, ref B4. Popular south coast holiday town between the Crookhaven River and the sea. Fishing, Surfing, Swimming.

Hotels/Motels

★★☆ **Culburra Beach Motel**, (M), 56 Brighton Pde, 500 NE of PO, ☎ 02 4447 2053, fax 02 4447 2053, 10 units [shwr, tlt, c/fan, heat, elec blkts, TV, t/c mkg, refrig, cook fac ltd], ldry, rec rm, bbq, cots. **RO** ♦ $54.60 - $80.30, ♦♦ $55 - $88, ◊ $6 - $10, **W** ♦♦ $292 - $550, Min book applies, BC MC VI.

B&B's/Guest Houses

★★★★ **Ellesleigh Lodge Bed & Breakfast**, (B&B), 22 Fairlands St, 250m S of PO, ☎ 02 4447 2056, fax 02 4447 2056, (2 stry), 3 rms [shwr, tlt, hairdry, c/fan, heat, elec blkts, tel, t/c mkg], rec rm, lounge (TV), lounge firepl, ✕, pool, bbq, non smoking property. **BB** ♦ $80 - $100, ♦♦ $100 - $125, ◊ $65 - $85, pen con, BC MC VI.

CULCAIRN NSW 2660

Pop 1,200. (522km SW Sydney), See map on pages 52/53, ref E7. Handsome town at the heart of Morgan Country, an area that was terrorised by bushranger Dan 'Mad Dog' Morgan for years during the mid-1800s. Bowls, Fishing, Golf, Swimming, Tennis.

Hotels/Motels
★★★ **Morgan Country Motel**, (M), Cnr Olympic Way & Melrose St, 1km N of PO, ☎ 02 6029 8233, fax 02 6029 8413, 12 units [shwr, tlt, hairdry, a/c, heat, elec blkts, tel, TV, clock radio, t/c mkg, refrig, toaster], ldry, bar, pool (salt water), bbq, dinner to unit, cots-fee. **RO** ⭘ **$50 - $60**, ⭘⭘ **$60 - $70**, ⭘ **$10**, AE BC DC MC VI, ♿.

CURRARONG NSW 2540

Pop 550. (188km S Sydney), See map on page 55, ref C5. South coast town at the foot of Crookhaven Bight that offers great opportunities for swimming, boating and fishing. Bowls, Fishing. See also Huskisson, Hyams Beach & Vincentia.

B&B's/Guest Houses
★★★★ **Penny's By The Beach**, (B&B), 68 Warrain Cres, 33km E of Nowra, ☎ 02 4448 3500, fax 02 4448 3500, (2 stry), 3 rms [ensuite, hairdry, elec blkts, tel, clock radio, refrig (communal)], ldry, iron, iron brd, TV rm, lounge firepl, spa, cook fac, t/c mkg shared, bbq, non smoking property. **BB** ⭘⭘ **$121 - $187**, ⭘ **$55**, BC MC VI.

DALMENY NSW 2546

Pop 1,631. (351km S Sydney), See map on page 55, ref A7. South coast seaside town near Mummuga Lake. Bowls, Fishing, Surfing, Swimming, Tennis.

Self Catering Accommodation
★★★ **Cresswick Gardens**, (HU), 32 Cresswick Pde, 5km N of Narooma PO, ☎ 02 4476 7749, fax 02 4476 7749, (2 stry), 5 units acc up to 6, [shwr, tlt, fan, heat, elec blkts, TV, radio, refrig, cook fac, micro, linen reqd-fee], ldry, bbq. **D** ⭘ **$55 - $100**, ⭘⭘ **$60 - $105**, ⭘⭘⭘ **$65 - $110**, ⭘ **$10 - $20**, **W** ⭘⭘ **$275 - $850**, pen con.
★★★ **Dalmeny Shores**, (HU), 13 Cresswick Pde, ☎ 02 4476 8488, fax 02 4476 8489, (2 stry), 2 units acc up to 7, (2 bedrm3 bedrm), [shwr, bath, tlt, fan, heat, TV, clock radio, refrig, cook fac, micro, ldry, linen reqd-fee], w/mach, iron, iron brd, bbq, c/park. **W** ⭘⭘ **$330 - $750**, Min book applies.
★★★ **Noble Lodge**, (HU), 13 Mort Ave, 1km off Princes Hwy, ☎ 02 4476 7200, 7 units acc up to 4, [shwr, tlt, c/fan, heat, elec blkts, TV, clock radio, t/c mkg, refrig, cook fac, toaster, linen], ldry, bbq, c/park. **D** ⭘ **$40 - $60**, ⭘⭘ **$50 - $80**, ⭘⭘⭘ **$60 - $90**, ⭘ **$10 - $20**, **W** ⭘⭘ **$220 - $550**.

DARETON NSW 2717

Pop 560. (1036km W Sydney), See map on pages 52/53, ref B5. Small town on the Murray River between Wentworth and Mildura. Bowls, Fishing, Golf.

Hotels/Motels
Coomealla Club Motel, (M), Silver City Hwy, 1km W of PO, ☎ 03 5027 4737, fax 03 5027 4833, 26 units [shwr, spa bath (2), tlt, a/c-cool, heat, elec blkts, tel, TV, t/c mkg, refrig], ldry, pool, bbq, cots, non smoking rms (8). **BLB** ⭘ **$57**, ⭘⭘ **$62**, ⭘ **$18**, ch con, AE BC MC VI, ♿, (not yet classified).

Self Catering Accommodation
★★★☆ **Coomealla Holiday Villas**, (HU), 28 Riverview Dve, 20km W of Mildura, or 03 5027 4868, fax 03 5027 4592, 5 units acc up to 6, [shwr, bath, tlt, evap cool, heat, elec blkts, TV, clock radio, cook fac, micro, toaster, ldry, blkts, linen, pillows], bbq, c/park (undercover), cots. **D** ⭘ **$70 - $80**, ⭘⭘ **$75 - $100**, ⭘⭘⭘ **$91 - $110**, ⭘⭘⭘⭘ **$106 - $125**, ⭘ **$17.50 - $25**, **W** ⭘⭘ **$420**, ⭘⭘⭘⭘ **$575**, Min book applies, BC MC VI.

DAPTO NSW

See Wollongong & Suburbs.

DEEPWATER NSW 2371

Pop 250. (706km N Sydney), See map on page 54, ref B3. Small New England town and a popular spot for fly fishing. Fishing, Gem Fossicking, Scenic Drives. See also Torrington.

Hotels/Motels
★★ **Commercial Motel Hotel**, (LMH), Tenterfield St, 250m W of PO, ☎ 02 6734 5315, 6 units [shwr, tlt, heat, elec blkts, TV, t/c mkg, refrig, toaster], ✕ (Mon-Sat, L&D). **RO** ⭘ **$38.50**, ⭘⭘ **$49.50 - $55**, BC EFT MC VI.

DELUNGRA NSW 2403

Pop 300. (703km NW Sydney), See map on pages 52/53, ref J2. Small silo town on the Gwydir Highway between Inverell and Warialda.

B&B's/Guest Houses
★★★☆ **Myall Downs Farm Holidays**, (GH), (Farm), Reserve Creek Rd, 18km fr Delungra on Bingara Rd, ☎ 02 6723 6421, fax 02 6723 6425, 3 rms [shwr (2), bath (1), tlt (3), fan, heat, tel, TV, clock radio, micro], ldry, rec rm, bbq, c/park (garage), plygr, tennis, cots. **D all meals** ⭘ **$105 - $115**, ⭘⭘ **$210 - $230**, ⭘ **$105**, ch con, BC MC VI.
★★★ **(Cottage Section)**, 1 cotg acc up to 6, [shwr, bath, tlt (2), fan, heat, TV, clock radio, refrig, cook fac, toaster, linen reqd-fee], ldry, lounge firepl, bbq, c/park (garage), cots. **D** **$110**, **W** **$440**.

DENILIQUIN NSW 2710

Pop 7,800. (760km SW Sydney), See map on pages 52/53, ref D6. Thriving rural centre on the Edward River known for its rice and merino production. Bowls, Fishing, Golf, Swimming, Tennis, Water Skiing.

Hotels/Motels
★★★★ **Deniliquin Country Club Motor Inn**, (M), 68 Crispe St, ☎ 03 5881 5299, fax 03 5881 5274, 20 units [shwr, spa bath (1), tlt, hairdry, a/c, tel, TV, clock radio, t/c mkg, refrig, mini bar], ldry, conv fac, ✕, bbq, rm serv, dinner to unit, cots. **RO** ⭘ **$76 - $82**, ⭘⭘ **$88 - $94**, ⭘⭘⭘ **$107 - $113**, ⭘ **$19**, AE BC DC MC VI.

★★★☆ **Centrepoint Motel**, (M), 399 Cressy St, 500m N of PO, ☎ 03 5881 3544, fax 03 5881 4755, (2 stry gr fl), 17 units [shwr, spa bath (1), tlt, a/c, elec blkts, tel, cable tv, clock radio, t/c mkg, refrig, toaster], ldry, ✕, pool, spa, bbq, rm serv, dinner to unit, c/park (undercover), cots-fee, non smoking rms (avail). **RO** ⭘ **$56 - $66**, ⭘⭘ **$66 - $76**, ⭘ **$10**, AE BC MC MP VI, ♿.

★★★☆ **Settlement Motor Inn**, (M), 327 Victoria St, ☎ 03 5881 3999, fax 03 5881 1364, 13 units [shwr, bath (hip) (2), spa bath (1), tlt, a/c, elec blkts, tel, TV, video (avail), clock radio, t/c mkg, refrig, toaster], ldry, ✕, pool, spa, bbq, rm serv, dinner to unit (Mon to Thu), courtesy transfer, cots, non smoking units (4). **RO** ⭘ **$75 - $90**, ⭘⭘ **$75 - $90**, ⭘ **$16**, AE BC DC EFT MC MP VI.

★★★ **Coach House Hotel-Motel**, (LMH), 99 End St, 300m S of PO, ☎ 03 5881 1011, fax 03 5881 5492, 28 units [shwr, bath (4), tlt, a/c-cool, heat, elec blkts, tel, cable tv, clock radio, t/c mkg, refrig], ldry, ✕ (Mon to Sat), pool, rm serv, cots. **RO** ⭘ **$55**, ⭘⭘ **$60 - $66**, ⭘⭘⭘ **$76**, 4 units of a higher standard. BC MC VI.

★★★ **Deniliquin Motel**, (M), Cnr Wick & Crispe Sts, 600m S of PO, ☎ 02 5881 1820, fax 02 5881 5010, 16 units [shwr, tlt, a/c, elec blkts, tel, TV, video, clock radio, t/c mkg, refrig, micro, toaster], pool, spa, bbq, cots-fee. **RO ⸰ $57, ⸰⸰ $66, ⸰⸰⸰ $77, ⸰ $11**, ch con, AE BC DC EFT MC MCH VI.

★★★ **Peppin Motor Inn**, (M), Crispe St, 1km S of PO, ☎ 03 5881 2722, fax 03 5881 1661, 26 units [shwr, tlt, a/c, elec blkts, tel, TV, video-fee, clock radio, t/c mkg, refrig], ldry, ⊠, pool, bbq, rm serv, tennis, cots. **RO ⸰ $59, ⸰⸰ $65, ⸰⸰⸰ $74, ⸰ $9**, ch con, 2 Units of a higher standard 4 plus rating. AE BC DC JCB MC MP VI.

★★★ **Riviana Motel**, (M), Cnr Crispe & Hetherington Sts, 1km S of PO, ☎ 03 5881 2033, fax 03 5881 4920, 20 units [shwr, tlt, a/c-cool, heat, elec blkts, tel, fax, TV, clock radio, t/c mkg, refrig], pool, spa, bbq, dinner to unit, cots. **RO ⸰ $56, ⸰⸰ $66, ⸰ $10**, AE BC DC MC VI.

★★☆ **Deniliquin Golf Leisure Resort**, (M), Memorial Dve, 1km SE of PO, ☎ 03 5881 3835, or 03 5881 3660, fax 03 5881 4897, 14 units [shwr, tlt, a/c, heat, elec blkts, TV, clock radio, t/c mkg, refrig, cook fac (16), toaster], ldry, ⊠ (tue to sun), pool-heated, bbq, cots. **RO ⸰ $56, ⸰⸰ $62 - $73, ⸰ $17**, ch con, BC EFT MC VI.

★★☆ **Riverview Motel**, (M), Butler St, opposite Charlotte St, 1km N of PO, ☎ 03 5881 2311, fax 03 5881 3014, 24 units [shwr, tlt, a/c-cool, heat, elec blkts, tel, TV, video (avail), clock radio, t/c mkg, refrig, micro (1), toaster], ldry, ⊠, bbq, cots. **RO ⸰ $60, ⸰⸰ $72, ⸰ $11**, AE BC DC MC VI.

DENMAN NSW 2328

Pop 1,500. (250km N Sydney), See map on pages 52/53, ref H4. Small town handy to the vineyards of the Upper Hunter and the Goulburn River and Wollemi National Parks. Bowls, Golf, Scenic Drives, Swimming, Vineyards, Wineries.

Hotels/Motels

★★★☆ **Denman Motor Inn**, (M), 8 Crinoline St, 300m N of PO, ☎ 02 6547 2462, or 02 6547 2268, fax 02 6547 2976, 10 units [shwr, tlt, hairdry, a/c, elec blkts, tel, TV, video (avail), clock radio, t/c mkg, refrig], ldry, iron, iron brd, pool, bbq, plygr, cots-fee, non smoking rms (4). **RO ⸰ $60, ⸰⸰ $70, ⸰⸰⸰ $85, ⸰ $15**, AE BC DC EFT MC VI.

Self Catering Accommodation

Morna May Cottage, (Cotg), No children's facilities, 310 Rosemount Rd, 12km W of PO, ☎ 02 6547 2088, fax 02 6547 2066, 1 cotg acc up to 6, (2 bedrm), [shwr, tlt, a/c, c/fan, heat, TV, video, clock radio, refrig, cook fac, micro, toaster, ldry, blkts, doonas, linen, pillows], w/mach, bbq, cots, breakfast ingredients, non smoking property. **BLB ⸰ $80, ⸰⸰ $120, ⸰ $20**, BC MC VI, (not yet classified).

B&B's/Guest Houses

★★★★☆ **Kerrabee**, (B&B), Bylong Valley Way, Kerrabee, 35km W of Denman, ☎ 02 6547 5155, fax 02 9428 3514, 4 rms (4 suites) [bath (1), tlt, a/c (3), fire pl (4), elec blkts, tel, t/c mkg], ✕, bbq, cots, non smoking rms. **DBB ⸰ $110, ⸰⸰ $260**, BC DC MC VI.

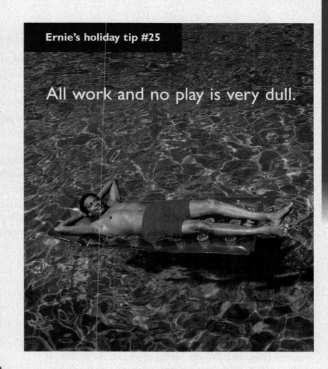

DIAMOND BEACH NSW 2430

Pop 450. (309km N Sydney), See map on page 54, ref B8. Small mid-north coastal township north of Hallidays Point, with a beach that's great for surfing and fishing. Bowls, Bush Walking, Fishing, Golf, Horse Riding, Surfing, Swimming, Tennis.

Self Catering Accommodation

★★★★ **Seashells**, (HU), Diamond Beach Rd, ☎ 02 6559 2779, fax 02 6559 2811, 38 units acc up to 8, [shwr, bath, tlt, c/fan, heat, TV, video, clock radio, refrig, cook fac, micro, toaster], ldry, rec rm, conf fac, ⊠, pool-heated, sauna, spa, bbq, plygr, golf, squash, tennis, cots. **D $90 - $180**, AE BC DC MC VI.

★★★☆ **Diamond Beach Resort**, (SA), Previously Albana Beach Resort, 394 Diamond Beach Rd, 5km N of Hallidays Point, ☎ 02 6559 2664, fax 02 6559 2675, 12 serv apts acc up to 5, [shwr, tlt, hairdry, a/c (1), fan, heat, tel, TV, video, clock radio, refrig, cook fac, micro, d/wash (1), toaster], ldry, rec rm, ✕, coffee shop, pool, bbq, dinner to unit, plygr, tennis, cots. **D ⸰ $80 - $165, ⸰⸰ $110 - $175, ⸰ $11, W $600 - $1,080**, 3 units of a higher standard, AE BC DC MC VI.

DOORALONG NSW 2259

Pop Part of Wyong, (104km N Sydney), See map on page 55, ref D5. Semi-rural area in the foothills of the Watagan Mountains. Horse Riding, Scenic Drives.

B&B's/Guest Houses

★★★★ **Dooralong Valley Resort**, (GH), Dooralong Rd, 20km W of Wyong, ☎ 02 4351 2611, fax 02 4355 1430, (2 stry gr fl), 66 rms (9 suites) [shwr, bath (38), tlt, hairdry, a/c, c/fan, fire pl (34), tel, TV (66), cable tv, clock radio, t/c mkg, refrig, mini bar], ldry, iron, iron brd, rec rm, lounge (TV), conv fac, ⊠, pool (2), ☏, bush walking, bicycle, canoeing, golf (Target), tennis, cots. **BB ♦♦ $169, ♦ $40**, ch con, Min book applies, AE BC DC JCB MC VI.

DORRIGO NSW 2453

Pop 1,000. (576km N Sydney), See map on page 54, ref C5.

Hotels/Motels

★★★☆ **The Lookout Motor Inn**, (M), Maynards Plain Rd, 3km E of PO, ☎ 02 6657 2511, fax 02 6657 2669, 25 units (1 suite) [shwr, tlt, a/c (11), fan (15), heat, elec blkts, tel, TV, clock radio, t/c mkg, refrig, mini bar], ldry, conv fac, ⊠, spa, bbq, plygr, tennis (half court), cots-fee, non smoking units (10), AE BC DC EFT MC VI, 🏃&.

★★☆ **Dorrigo Heritage Hotel Motel**, (LMH), Classified by National Trust, Cudgery St, opposite PO, ☎ 02 6657 2016, fax 02 6657 2059, 22 units (1 suite) [shwr (17), spa bath, tlt (17), a/c-cool (6), c/fan (11), heat, elec blkts, TV, clock radio (17), t/c mkg, refrig, toaster], shared fac (5), TV rm, lounge, conf fac, ✕, ⊠, ☏. **RO ♦ $39 - $54, ♦♦ $39 - $66, ♦♦♦ $60 - $66, ♦♦♦♦ $70 - $77**, 11 units of a lower rating. BC EFT MC.

★☆ **Commercial Hotel Motel**, (LMH), 15 Cudgery St, ☎ 02 6657 2003, 12 units [shwr, tlt, heat, elec blkts, TV, t/c mkg, refrig, toaster], ✕. **RO ♦ $32, ♦♦ $38, ♦♦♦ $55**, BC EFT MC.

Self Catering Accommodation

★★ **Laurina Farm Holidays**, (Cotg), (Farm), 5264 Waterfall Way, 11km W of PO, ☎ 02 6657 3251, 1 cotg acc up to 8, [shwr, tlt, TV, refrig, cook fac, ldry, blkts, linen, pillows], bbq, c/park (carport). **DBB ♦♦ $55, D ♦ $30, ♦ $30, W $440.**

B&B's/Guest Houses

★★★★ **Meriden Heights Retreat**, (B&B), 65 Everinghams Rd, ☎ 02 6657 2823, fax 02 6657 2823, 2 rms [shwr, tlt, hairdry, heat, elec blkts, tel, TV (2), clock radio, t/c mkg], ldry, lounge (TV), ✕, bbq, c/park. **BB ♦ $55 - $70, ♦♦ $95, ♦ $27.50, DBB ♦ $75 - $90, ♦♦ $135, ♦ $47.50**, BC MC VI.

★★★★ **Tallawalla Retreat**, (GH), 113 Old Coramba Rd South, 1.5km NE of PO, ☎ 02 6657 2315, 5 rms [shwr, tlt, heat, elec blkts, tel, TV, video, clock radio], ldry, lounge (TV), ✕, pool, sauna, t/c mkg shared, bbq, plygr, tennis, non smoking property. **BB ♦ $65, ♦♦ $125, ♦ $30.**

★★★☆ **Fernbrook Lodge**, (B&B), 4705 Waterfall Way (Armidale/Dorrigo Rd), 6km W of Dorrigo War Memorial, ☎ 02 6657 2573, fax 02 6657 2573, 4 rms [ensuite, bath (1), hairdry (1), fan, fire pl, heat, elec blkts, tel, TV, clock radio], ldry, lounge (TV), t/c mkg shared, bbq, non smoking rms. **BB ♦ $60, ♦♦ $90 - $100, ♦ $30, DBB ♦ $85, ♦♦ $140 - $150, ♦ $55**,
Operator Comment: See us at: www.midcoast.com.au/~fernbrooklodge

DRAKE NSW 2470

Pop Nominal, (808km N Sydney), See map on page 54, ref C2.
★★ **Drake Motel Hotel**, (LMH), Bruxner Hwy, ☎ 02 6737 6757, fax 02 6737 6757, 3 units [shwr, tlt, a/c, TV, clock radio, t/c mkg, refrig, toaster], ⊠ (Tues to Sun), bbq, ☏. **D ♦ $50, ♦♦ $60**, BC EFT MC VI.

DUBBO NSW 2830

Pop 30,100. (414km NW Sydney), See map on pages 52/53, ref G4. Dubbo is an important business and commercial regional centre and the home of the famous Western Plains Zoo.

Hotels/Motels

★★★★☆ **Cattlemans Country Motor Inn**, (M), 8 Whylandra St, 30m E of Dubbo West PO, ☎ 02 6884 5222, fax 02 6884 5299, (2 stry gr fl), 65 units [shwr, spa bath (15), tlt, a/c, elec blkts, tel, TV, video (avail), movie, clock radio, t/c mkg, refrig, mini bar, toaster], ldry, conv fac, ✕, pool indoor heated, bbq, dinner to unit, plygr, gym, cots-fee. **RO ♦ $65 - $83, ♦♦ $65 - $83, ♦♦♦ $76 - $95, ♦ $5 - $10**, ch con, AE BC DC EFT MC VI, 🏃&.

★★★★☆ **(Apartment Section)**, 10 apts acc up to 4, [shwr, tlt, a/c, elec blkts, tel, TV, movie, clock radio, t/c mkg, refrig, mini bar, cook fac, toaster]. **D $65 - $145.**

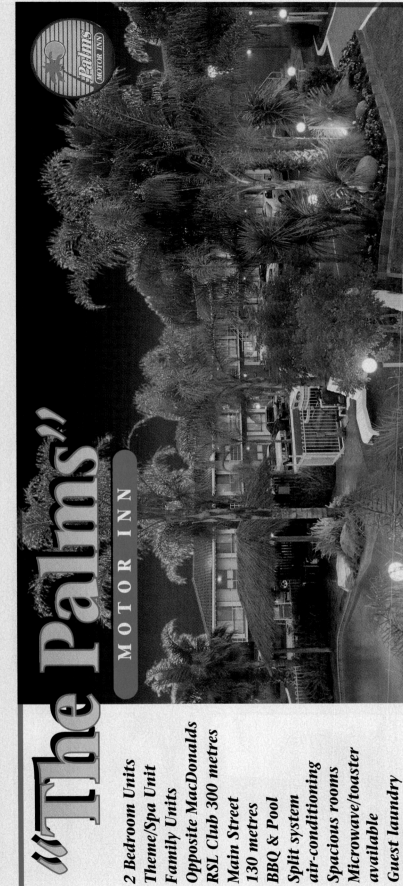

★★★★☆ ★★★★☆

DUBBO'S NEWEST AND LARGEST
"SET OVER 3 ACRES IN THE HEART OF THE CITY

Cattleman's Country

★★★★☆

MOTOR INN & SERVICED APARTMENTS

RESTAURANT & CONFERENCE CENTRE

4½ STAR RATING
AAA TOURISM

WHAT ROOM TYPE WOULD YOU LIKE?

- FAMILY SPA SUITES (1 OR 2 BEDROOM) • HONEYMOON SPA SUITES (HUGE IN ROOM OVAL SPAS)
- 2 BEDROOM FAMILY UNITS • SELF CONTAINED 2 & 3 BEDROOM UNITS • INTERCONNECTING
UNITS • EXECUTIVE SPA SUITES • EXTRA LARGE FAMILY ROOMS (WITH PRIVATE COURT YARDS)
- SERVICED APARTMENTS WITH FULL KITCHEN • QUIET UNITS • NON SMOKING

IF WE DON'T HAVE IT NOBODY DOES!
STAY IN A NEW MOTEL AND BE HAPPY.

Extensive children's playground for families.

Award winning a la carte restaurant (voted best restaurant west of the Blue Mountains) Full buffet breakfast room for your convenience.

Full gymnasium complete with rowing machine.

Luxury family, honeymoon or executive spa suites.

Saltwater pool and cabana area set in garden area.

Bicycle hire ride the famous zoo track.

★★★★☆ ★★★★☆

STAY IN DUBBO'S PREMIER MOTEL WITH IT'S FAMOUS FINE DINE RESTAURANT

The Reception and conference Centre

✱ SPECIAL ZOO PACKAGES

ASHWOOD Country Club

MOTEL RESTAURANT cocktail bar
FAMILY UNITS
TENNIS COURT SPA
AIR COND POOL
EXECUTIVE SUITES

**Corner Newell Hwy
& East Streets
Dubbo NSW 2830**

★ 39 Large reverse cycle air conditioned rooms ★ Room service also (A LA CARTE) ★ Executive rooms with spa bath ★ Honeymoon suites ★ Interconnecting Rooms ★ Disabled wheelchair access room plus assistant (1 unit) ★ Family Rooms ★ All queen beds ★ Direct dial phones – STD & ISD ★ Mini bar ★ Colour TV and in house movies ★ Guest laundry ★ Iron & Boards ★ Hairdryers ★ Tea and Coffee making facilities ★ Children's playground ★ Large saltwater pool ★ Heated outdoor spa and sauna ★ Full size tennis court ★ BBQ ★ Catering for Conferences, weddings and parties ★ Most credit cards accepted

★ *Special weekend rates*   *Everything You Want*
Proudly Australia owned and operated   AAA Tourism ★★★★

★ *Specials* for Company Representatives, Automobile & associated clubs.

Book direct on **Freecall 1800 805 875** or

(02) 6881 8700 or fax us on **(02) 6881 8930**

★ *We welcome you*

Email: ashwdubb@ozemail.com.au   **Website:** www.ashwood.com.au

★★★★ **Ashwood Country Club Motel**, (M), cnr Newell Hwy & East St, 1km W of PO, ☎ 02 6881 8700, fax 02 6881 8930, (2 stry gr fl), 39 units [shwr, bath (13), spa bath (2), tlt, hairdry, a/c, heat, elec blkts, tel, TV, video (avail), movie, clock radio, t/c mkg, refrig, mini bar], ldry, iron, iron brd, conv fac, ⊠, pool, sauna, spa, bbq, rm serv, dinner to unit, plygr, tennis, cots. **RO** ⸙ **$88 - $110,** ⸙⸙ **$88 - $130,** ⸙ **$15,** ch con, 2 units of a lower rating. AE BC DC MC MP VI, ⼋⼆.

★★★★ **Australian Heritage Motor Inn**, (M), Cnr Cobra & Brisbane Sts, 1km S of PO, ☎ 02 6884 1188, fax 02 6882 0184, (2 stry gr fl), 22 units [shwr, spa bath (5), tlt, a/c, tel, cable tv, video-fee, clock radio, t/c mkg, refrig, cook fac (1), toaster], ⊠ (Mon to Sat), pool, bbq, rm serv, dinner to unit, plygr, cots, non smoking units (10). **RO** ⸙ **$84 - $93.50,** ⸙⸙ **$105 - $143,** ⸙ **$6 - $10,** ch con, AE BC DC MC MP VI.

★★★★ **Blue Diamond Motor Inn**, (M), 113 Wingewarra St, 100m from RSL Club, ☎ 02 6882 0666, fax 02 6882 5851, 24 units [shwr, bath (3), tlt, hairdry, a/c, elec blkts, tel, fax, cable tv, clock radio, t/c mkg, refrig, mini bar, toaster], iron, iron brd, lounge, pool (salt water), bbq, rm serv, dinner to unit, car wash, cots, non smoking units (16). **RO** ⸙ **$74 - $94,** ⸙⸙ **$76 - $94,** ⸙ **$8 - $12,** 2 units ★★★☆. AE BC DC MC MP VI, ⼋⼆.

★★★★ **Dubbo R.S.L. Club Motel**, (M), Cnr Brisbane & Wingewarra Sts, 1km SE of PO, ☎ 02 6884 9099, fax 02 6884 2030, (Multi-stry gr fl), 34 units [shwr, bath (14), spa bath (4), tlt, hairdry, a/c, tel, TV, video, clock radio, t/c mkg, refrig, mini bar], ldry, ⊠ (R.S.L. Club), pool, rm serv, dinner to unit, cots, non smoking units (18). **RO** ⸙ **$89 - $136,** ⸙⸙ **$99 - $136,** ⸙⸙⸙⸙ **$137,** ⸙ **$10,** ch con, AE BC DC EFT MC VI, ⼋⼆.

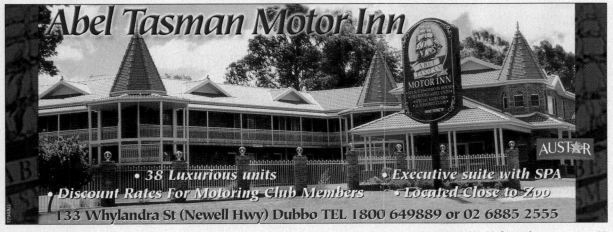

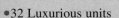

★★★★ **Endeavour Court Motor Inn**, (M), 94-98 Bourke St, 1 km NE of PO, ☎ 02 6881 1000, fax 02 6885 2266, (2 stry gr fl), 17 units [shwr, spa bath (1), tlt, hairdry, a/c, c/fan (1), elec blkts, tel, cable tv, clock radio, t/c mkg, refrig], ldry, iron, iron brd, pool, rm serv, dinner to unit, courtesy transfer, cots. **RO** ♦ **$85 - $95**, ♦♦ **$95 - $105**, ♦ **$10**, pen con, AE BC DC EFT MC VI.

★★★☆ **A A Golden West Motor Inn**, (M), 87 Cobra St, 1.5km SE of PO, ☎ 02 6882 2822, fax 02 6882 6800, (2 stry gr fl), 28 units [shwr, spa bath (2), tlt, hairdry, a/c, elec blkts, tel, TV, video, clock radio, t/c mkg, refrig], iron, iron brd, ✕, bar, pool, sauna, spa, bbq, rm serv, cots-fee, non smoking rms (5). **RO** ♦ **$67 - $79**, ♦♦ **$67 - $99**, ♦♦♦ **$97 - $107**, ♦ **$10**, 5 units of a lower rating. AE BC DC MC MP VI.

★★★☆ **Abel Tasman Motor Inn**, (M), 133 Whylandra St Newell Highway, 2km S of PO, ☎ 02 6885 2555, fax 02 6885 2544, 38 units [shwr, spa bath (8), tlt, hairdry, a/c, tel, cable tv, clock radio, t/c mkg, refrig], ldry, iron, iron brd, pool (salt water), dinner to unit, c/park. **RO** ♦ **$94 - $119**, ♦♦ **$99 - $133**, ♦ **$11 - $15**, AE BC DC EFT MC VI.

★★★☆ **Aberdeen Motor Inn**, (M), 25 Cobra St, ☎ 02 6884 1700, fax 02 6884 1636, (2 stry gr fl), 32 units [shwr, spa bath (6), tlt, hairdry, a/c, elec blkts, tel, TV, video (available), movie, clock radio, t/c mkg, refrig, mini bar], ldry, iron, iron brd, pool (salt water), bbq, rm serv, dinner to unit, cots-fee. **RO** ♦ **$90 - $97**, ♦♦ **$97 - $107**, ♦♦♦ **$107 - $117**, ♦ **$12**, ch con, AE BC DC JCB MC MP VI, ♿.

★★★☆ **All Seasons Motor Lodge**, (M), 78 Whylandra St (Newell Hwy), 1km SW of PO, ☎ 02 6882 6377, fax 02 6882 9198, 19 units [shwr, tlt, hairdry, a/c, elec blkts, tel, TV, video-fee, clock radio, t/c mkg, refrig, toaster], iron, iron brd, ✕ (6 nights), pool-heated (solar), sauna, spa, dinner to unit (6 nights), cots-fee, non smoking units (8). **RO** ♦ **$59.50 - $69.50**, ♦♦ **$69.50 - $74.50**, ♦ **$7**, 6 units ★★★★. AE BC DC EFT MC MP VI.

★★★☆ **Atlas Motel**, (M), 140 Bourke St, 300m from CBD, ☎ 02 6882 7244, fax 02 6882 7751, (2 stry gr fl), 31 units [shwr, tlt, hairdry, a/c, heat, elec blkts, tel, cable tv, video, clock radio, t/c mkg, refrig, toaster], ldry, iron, iron brd, pool (salt water), bbq, dinner to unit, cots-fee, non smoking units (15). **RO** ♦ **$74 - $86**, ♦♦ **$83 - $95**, ♦ **$10 - $12**, AE BC DC EFT MC VI, ♿.

Operator Comment: Avoid Driver Fatigue-get a good sleep away from the noisy transport highways.Zoo packs & Seniors rates available. Bookings 1800 024 972.

★★★☆ **Blue Gum Motor Inn**, (M), 109 Cobra St, 1km S of PO, ☎ 02 6882 0900, or 02 6882 0900, fax 02 6884 1133, (2 stry gr fl), 24 units [shwr, tlt, hairdry, a/c, elec blkts, tel, TV, video (avail)-fee, clock radio, t/c mkg, refrig, mini bar, toaster], ldry, iron, iron brd, pool, bbq, dinner to unit, cots-fee. **RO** ♦ **$69 - $75**, ♦♦ **$75 - $86**, ♦♦♦ **$86 - $97**, ♦ **$11**, Family rooms of a lower rating. AE BC DC EFT MC MP VI, ♿.

★★★☆ **Blue Lagoon Motor Inn**, (M), 81 Cobra St (Mitchell Hwy), 1km S of PO, ☎ 02 6882 4444, fax 02 6882 4084, (2 stry gr fl), 55 units [shwr, tlt, a/c, elec blkts, tel, cable tv, video, clock radio, t/c mkg, refrig, mini bar], ldry, iron, iron brd, ✕, pool, spa, bbq, rm serv, dinner to unit, plygr, cots, non smoking units (15). **RO** ♦ **$65 - $84**, ♦♦ **$65 - $94**, ♦ **$8**, ch con, Family rooms of a lower rating. Min book applies, AE BC DC EFT MC VI.

★★★☆ **Cascades Motor Inn**, (M), 147 Cobra St, 1.5km E of PO, ☎ 02 6882 3888, fax 02 6882 0906, (2 stry gr fl), 36 units [shwr, bath (13), spa bath (1), tlt, hairdry, a/c, tel, cable tv, video (avail), clock radio, t/c mkg, refrig, mini bar], ldry, iron, iron brd, conv fac, ✕ (6 nights), pool, rm serv, cots, non smoking units (20). **RO** ♦ **$73 - $83**, ♦♦ **$84 - $94**, ♦ **$11**, AE BC DC EFT MC VI.

★★★☆ **Country Comfort - Dubbo**, (M), Newell Hwy, 3km W of PO, ☎ 02 6882 4777, fax 02 6881 8370, (2 stry gr fl), 60 units [shwr, bath (20), spa bath (2), tlt, hairdry, a/c, tel, TV, video (on request), movie, clock radio, t/c mkg, refrig, mini bar, cook fac (1)], ldry, conv fac, ✕, pool, spa, bbq, rm serv, dinner to unit, tennis, non smoking units (20). **RO** ♦ **$87 - $147**, ♦♦ **$87 - $147**, ♦♦♦ **$93 - $147**, ♦♦♦♦ **$93 - $147**, ♦ **$16**, ch con, 10 units ★★★★, 8 units of a lower rating. AE BC DC EFT MC VI, ♿.

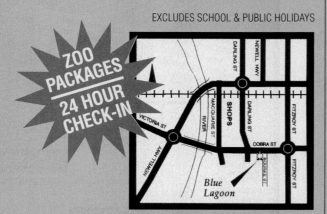

★★★☆ **Countryman Motor Inn**, (M), 47 Cobra St, ☎ 02 6882 7422, fax 02 6884 2432, (2 stry gr fl), 22 units [shwr, tlt, hairdry, a/c, elec blkts, tel, cable tv, video (available)-fee, clock radio, t/c mkg, refrig, mini bar], ldry, ⊠ (Mon to Sat), bar, pool, bbq, dinner to unit (6 nights), cots-fee, non smoking units (10). RO ♦ $81 - $112.50, ♦♦ $85 - $108, ♦♦♦ $92 - $112, ◊ $8 - $12, AE BC DC MC VI, ♿.

★★★☆ **Dubbo City Motor Inn**, (M), 57 Cobra St, 1km S of PO, ☎ 02 6882 7033, fax 02 6884 3608, (2 stry gr fl), 16 units [shwr, tlt, hairdry, a/c, elec blkts, tel, TV, video-fee, clock radio, t/c mkg, refrig], ✕ (6 nights), pool, dinner to unit (6 nights), cots. RO ♦ $63 - $86, ♦♦ $65 - $93, ♦♦♦ $77 - $107, ◊ $12, 5 units of a lower rating. AE BC DC MC MP VI.

★★★☆ **Forest Lodge Motor Inn**, (M), 248 Myall St, follow Base Hospital signs, ☎ 02 6882 6500, fax 02 6882 6075, 15 units [shwr, bath (4), tlt, a/c, elec blkts, tel, TV, video-fee, clock radio, t/c mkg, refrig, toaster], ldry, ⊠ (Mon to Sat), pool, cots, non smoking units (7). RO ♦ $65 - $82, ♦♦ $74 - $90, ♦♦♦ $83 - $99, ◊ $9, AE BC DC EFT MC MCH VI.

★★★☆ **Fountain View Motel**, (M), 113 Cobra St, 1.5km SE of PO, ☎ 02 6882 9777, fax 02 6884 3742, (2 stry gr fl), 27 units [shwr, tlt, a/c, elec blkts, tel, TV, video-fee, movie, clock radio, t/c mkg, refrig], ldry, pool, dinner to unit, cots, non smoking rms (8). RO ♦ $57 - $65, ♦♦ $66 - $74, ♦♦♦ $73 - $81, ◊ $8, AE BC DC MC MCH VI.

★★★☆ **Gallop Inn**, (M), 95 Cobra St, 1.5km S.E of PO, ☎ 02 6882 7888, fax 02 6884 1855, (2 stry gr fl), 33 units [shwr, spa bath (2), tlt, hairdry, a/c, elec blkts, tel, TV, clock radio, t/c mkg, refrig, toaster], ldry, iron, iron brd, ⊠ (6 nights), dinner to unit (6 days), cots, non smoking units (10). RO ♦ $55 - $77, ♦♦ $66 - $88, ◊ $11, 7 family rooms of a lower rating. AE BC DC EFT MC VI.

★★★☆ **Shearing Shed Motor Inn**, (M), 29-33 Cobra St, 250m S of Shopping Centre, ☎ 02 6884 2977, fax 02 6884 1249, (2 stry gr fl), 23 units [shwr, spa bath (6), tlt, hairdry, a/c, elec blkts, tel, cable tv, video-fee, clock radio, t/c mkg, refrig, toaster], ldry, iron, iron brd, pool (salt water), bbq, dinner to unit, cots-fee, non smoking units (7). RO ♦ $66 - $88, ♦♦ $72 - $99, ◊ $11, AE BC DC MC VI, ♿.

★★★☆ **The Homestead Motel**, (M), 101 Cobra St, 2km E of PO, ☎ 02 6882 4944, fax 02 6882 0188, 24 units [shwr, spa bath (1), tlt, hairdry, a/c-cool, cent heat, elec blkts, tel, TV, video-fee, clock radio, t/c mkg, refrig], ldry, iron, iron brd, ⊠ (6 nights), pool, dinner to unit (6 nights), cots, non smoking rms (8). RO ♦ $55 - $77, ♦♦ $66 - $88, ◊ $11, 6 family rooms of a lower rating. AE BC DC EFT MC VI.

★★★☆ **The Palms Motor Inn**, (M), 35 Cobra St, 1.5km S of PO, ☎ 02 6881 8155, fax 02 6881 8859, (2 stry gr fl), 24 units [shwr, spa bath (4), tlt, hairdry, a/c, elec blkts, tel, cable tv, video (avail), clock radio, t/c mkg, refrig, micro, toaster], ldry, iron, iron brd, pool, bbq, dinner to unit, cots. RO ♦ $76 - $126, ♦♦ $76 - $136, ◊ $12, AE BC DC EFT MC VI.

★★★ **Country Leisure Motor Inn**, (M), 86 Cobra St, 2km E of PO, ☎ 02 6882 3988, fax 02 6884 0887, 15 units [shwr, tlt, hairdry, a/c, elec blkts, tel, TV, video-fee, clock radio, t/c mkg, refrig, toaster], iron, iron brd, pool, dinner to unit, cots-fee, non smoking units (5). RO ♦ $54 - $66, ♦♦ $57 - $69, ◊ $9, 6 units of a lower rating. AE BC DC EFT MC VI.

HOMESTEAD MOTEL

101 Cobra St, Dubbo

AAAT ★★★☆

Phone: (02) 6882 4944 **Fax: (02) 6884 1855**

- 24 SPACIOUS UNITS
- LIC. RESTAURANT
- IRON & BOARDS
- CLOSE TO ZOO & RSL CLUB
- 2BR UNITS
- QUEEN SIZE BEDS
- HAIRDRYER
- COACH & GROUP SPECIALIST

		NORMALLY
Single from $55	NORMALLY	$66
Double from $61	NORMALLY	$85
Family from $77	NORMALLY	$99

Excludes school & public holidays

SHEARING SHED Motor Inn DUBBO

★★★☆ AAAT RATING

- Colour TV
- Dinner to Units
- Guest Laundry
- Direct Dial Phones
- Handicapped Suite
- Central Location

- Tea & Coffee Facilities
- Air Conditioned R/C Summer & Winter
- Hairdryers, Iron & Boards
- Saltwater Pool & Bush House BBQ Area
- Bedside Clock Radio
- Family Spa Units
- Executive & Honeymoon Spa Units

- Iron & Boards
- Queen Size Beds
- RSL Club 300 Metres
- Video Library & Players
- Opposite McDonalds
- Owner Operated

31 Cobra Street Dubbo NSW 2830 **Phone: (02) 6884 2977 Fax: (02) 6884 1249**

Gallop Inn Motel

95 Cobra Street, Dubbo (Mitchell Highway end)

Phone: (02) 6882 7888
Fax: (02) 6884 1855

FULLY LICENSED RESTAURANT
OWNER OPERATOR
WALK TO R.S.L. CLUB
10 MIN DRIVE TO ZOO

★★★☆
AAAT RATING
❖ 33 spacious

Interconnecting rooms ❖ Queens size beds

- ❖ Fridge
- ❖ Colour TV
- ❖ Spa Rooms
- ❖ Hairdryers, Iron & Boards
- ❖ Reversed cycle air-conditioning
- ❖ Tea & toast making facilities
- ❖ Direct dial phones
- ❖ Large salt water pool
- ❖ Guest Laundry
- ❖ Undercover parking

6 DAY + 5 NIGHTS TOUR EACH MONTH: FULLY INCLUSIVE
PHONE NOW FOR BOOKINGS ON **FREE CALL 1800 060 112**

★★★ **Dubbo Centrepoint**, (M), 146 Bourke St, 1km S of PO, ☎ 02 6882 7644, fax 02 6882 8002, (2 stry gr fl), 12 units [shwr, tlt, hairdry, a/c, elec blkts, tel, TV, video (avail), clock radio, t/c mkg, refrig], pool, bbq, cots-fee. **RO** ♦ $51 - $70, ♦♦ $55 - $75, ♦♦♦ $60 - $80, ◊ $9, ch con, AE BC DC MC VI.

★★★ **Green Gables Motel**, (M), 134 Bourke St, 1km SE of PO, ☎ 02 6882 5588, fax 02 6882 0785, 10 units [shwr, tlt, a/c-cool, c/fan, cent heat, tel, TV, clock radio, t/c mkg, refrig, toaster], ldry, dryer, pool, cots-fee. **RO** ♦ $53 - $62, ♦♦ $60 - $81, ♦♦♦ $68 - $84, ◊ $9, 2 units of a lower rating. AE BC DC MC VI.

★★★ **Tallarook Motor Inn**, (M), 17 Stonehaven Ave, 1km W of PO, ☎ 02 6882 7066, fax 02 6884 4778, (2 stry gr fl), 22 units (1 suite) [shwr, tlt, hairdry, a/c, tel, TV, video-fee, clock radio, refrig, cook fac], ldry, pool, c/park (undercover), cots-fee, non smoking units (10). **D** ♦ $57 - $66, ♦♦ $63 - $75, ♦♦♦ $69 - $83, ◊ $7, AE BC DC EFT MC VI.
Operator Comment: See our advertisement on next page.

 ★★☆ **Across Country Motor Inn**, (M), Cnr Newell Hwy & Baird St, 1km W of PO, ☎ 02 6882 0877, fax 02 6882 0480, 23 units [shwr, tlt, hairdry, a/c, c/fan, heat, elec blkts, tel, TV, clock radio, t/c mkg, refrig], ldry, pool, bbq, dinner to unit, cots, non smoking units (8). **RO** ♦ $49.50 - $60, ♦♦ $60.50 - $80, ◊ $10, 6 units ★★★☆, AE BC DC EFT MC MCH VI, ⌂&.

 ★★☆ **Matilda Motor Inn**, (M), 231 Darling St, 1km SE of PO, ☎ 02 6882 3944, fax 02 6884 3592, 38 units [shwr, bath (2), tlt, hairdry, a/c, c/fan (17), elec blkts, tel, TV, video-fee, clock radio, t/c mkg, refrig], ldry, conv fac, ⊠, pool, rm serv, cots-fee, non smoking units (14). **RO** ♦ $52 - $70, ♦♦ $57 - $77, ♦♦♦ $74 - $87, ◊ $6 - $10, ch con, 4 units of a higher standard. AE BC DC EFT MC MP VI.
Operator Comment: See our advertisement on next page.

★★ **Motel Formule 1**, (M), Previously Rest Inn Dubbo Cnr Mitchell & Newell Hwys, ☎ 02 6882 9211, fax 02 6882 9311, (Multi-stry gr fl), 65 units [shwr, tlt, a/c, TV, clock radio], ldry, iron, iron brd, breakfast rm, pool (salt water), refrig, 24hr reception, ☎ (2), cots, non smoking units (55). **RO** ♦ $39, ♦♦ $39, ♦♦♦ $39, 12 units ★★☆, AE BC DC MC VI, ⌂&.

★★ **Park Vue Motel**, (M), 131 Bourke St, 1km E of PO, ☎ 02 6882 4253, fax 02 6882 4253, 20 units [shwr, tlt, a/c, heat, elec blkts, TV, clock radio, t/c mkg, refrig, toaster], ldry, bbq, cots-fee. **RO** ♦ $43 - $49, ♦♦ $52 - $58, ◊ $9, ch con, AE BC MC VI.

★☆ **Merino Motel**, (M), 65 Church St, 100m S of Civic Centre 500m S of railway station, ☎ 02 6882 4133, fax 02 6884 3528, 21 units [shwr, tlt, a/c, elec blkts, tel, TV, radio, t/c mkg, refrig], ldry, cots-fee. **RO** ♦ $48, ♦♦ $58, ◊ $8 - $10, BC MC VI.

★☆ **Westside**, (LMH), Newell Hwy, 50m S of Dubbo West PO, ☎ 02 6882 3500, fax 02 6884 1980, 15 units [shwr, tlt, a/c, heat, elec blkts, TV, t/c mkg, refrig], ⊠, rm serv. **RO** ♦ $44, ♦♦ $55, ◊ $10, ch con, AE BC EFT MC VI.

★ **Castlereagh**, (LH), Cnr Brisbane & Talbragar Sts, 500m E of PO, ☎ 02 6882 4877, fax 02 6884 1520, (2 stry), 13 rms [shwr (13), tlt (13), fan, elec blkts], lounge (TV), ⊠ (Mon to Fri). **BB** ♦ $33 - $38.50, ♦♦ $55 - $66, **RO** ♦ $27.50, ♦♦ $55.

Self Catering Accommodation

★★★★☆ **Blizzardfield Country Retreat**, (Cotg), Richardson Rd, ☎ 02 6882 5909, fax 02 6882 1472, 1 cotg acc up to 8, [bath, fan, heat, tel, cable tv, video, clock radio, CD, refrig, cook fac, micro, d/wash, toaster, ldry], iron, iron brd, pool (salt water), spa, bbq, c/park. **D** $165, ◊ $20, ch con, Min book applies.

★★★★☆ **Grape Escape Dubbo**, (Cotg), Boora Warrie Rd, 14km SE of PO, ☎ 02 6884 2600, fax 02 6884 2600, 1 cotg acc up to 5, (2 bedrm), [shwr, spa bath, tlt, a/c-cool, c/fan, heat, elec blkts, tel, cable tv, video, clock radio, t/c mkg, refrig, cook fac, micro, toaster, blkts, doonas, linen, pillows], w/mach, dryer, lounge firepl, bbq, cots, breakfast ingredients, non smoking property. D ⚹ $99, ⚹⚹ $132, ⚹ $33, ch con, BC MC VI.

★★★★ **Country Apartments**, (SA), 230 Brisbane St, 1km S of PO, ☎ 02 6885 1141, fax 02 6885 3459, 9 serv apts acc up to 7, [shwr, spa bath (2), tlt, hairdry, a/c (8), c/fan, elec blkts, tel, TV, video, clock radio, t/c mkg, refrig, cook fac (5), cook fac ltd (3), micro (9), toaster, ldry, blkts, linen, pillows], w/mach (9), dryer (2), iron, pool, bbq, rm serv, dinner to unit (6 days), cots. RO ⚹ $95 - $180, ⚹⚹ $105 - $180, ⚹⚹⚹ $128 - $180, ⚹ $5 - $15, W $495 - $800, AE BC DC MC VI.

★★★☆ **Manera Heights Country Living**, (SA), Cnr Myall St & Cobbora Rd, 1.5km E of PO, ☎ 02 6884 3865, fax 02 6884 3436, (2 stry gr fl), 14 serv apts acc up to 6, [shwr, tlt, a/c, c/fan, heat, elec blkts, tel, TV, clock radio, t/c mkg, refrig, cook fac, micro, toaster], ldry, pool, bbq, cots-fee. RO ⚹ $55 - $60, ⚹⚹ $60 - $80, ⚹⚹⚹ $70 - $90, ⚹ $5 - $10, W $308 - $385, ch con, BC MC VI, ⚹♿.

B&B's/Guest Houses

★★★★★ **Pericoe Retreat Bed and Breakfast**, (B&B), 12R Cassandra Dr, 12km E of PO, ☎ 02 6887 2705, fax 02 6887 2705, 1 rm [a/c-cool, heat, fire pl, tel, video (avail), clock radio, t/c mkg, refrig, ldry], lounge (TV), ✕, pool, spa, bbq, meals to unit, tennis, cots, non smoking units (2). BB ⚹ $85, ⚹⚹ $135, ⚹ $30, weekly con, Min book long w/ends, BC MC VI.

★★★☆ **Gilbree Homestay Bed & Breakfast**, (B&B), 2R Winbar Rd, 8km E of PO, ☎ 02 6884 8003, fax 02 6884 8003, 2 rms [shwr, tlt, evap cool, heat, elec blkts, tel, TV, clock radio], iron, iron brd, rec rm, TV rm, lounge, cook fac, t/c mkg shared, bbq, cots, non smoking property. BB ⚹ $66, ⚹⚹ $100, ⚹ $30, ch con.

★★★☆ **Mayfair Cottage**, (B&B), 10 Baird St, 1km W of PO, ☎ 02 6882 5226, fax 02 6884 9462, 3 rms [shwr, bath, tlt, a/c-cool, heat, elec blkts, clock radio, t/c mkg], lounge (TV), pool (salt water), bbq. BB ⚹ $65, ⚹⚹ $95, ⚹ $30.

★★★☆ **Pinecrest Bed & Breakfast**, (B&B), 31L Camp Rd, 4km past Zoo turnoff, off Newell Hwy, ☎ 02 6884 0177, fax 02 6884 1117, 3 rms [shwr (3), tlt (2), hairdry, a/c-cool, c/fan, heat, elec blkts, tel, clock radio], shared fac (2 rms), iron, iron brd, lounge (tv & firepl), pool (salt water), t/c mkg shared, bbq, non smoking rms (3). BB ⚹ $85, ⚹⚹ $110 - $120, ⚹ $35, BC MC VI.

★★★★☆ **(Unit Section)**, 1 unit [shwr, tlt, a/c, TV, video, refrig, cook fac ltd, micro]. D ⚹⚹ $130.

Immarna Bed & Breakfast, (B&B), 12R Coolbaggie Rd, 23km W of PO, ☎ 02 6887 3131, 5 rms (1 suite) [shwr (2), bath (2), tlt (2), a/c (5), elec blkts (4), tel, clock radio, t/c mkg (2)], ldry, iron (available), iron brd (available), rec rm, lounge firepl (TV), ✕, t/c mkg shared, refrig, bbq, dinner to unit, ☏, plygr, non smoking rms (2). BB ⚹ $55, ⚹⚹ $99, ⚹ $10, BC MC VI, (not yet classified).

Other Accommodation

★★ **Dubbo YHA Backpackers**, (Lodge), Cnr Newell Hwy & Brisbane St, 250m S of PO, ☎ 02 6882 0922, fax 02 6882 0922, 6 rms [blkts, linen, pillows], bathrm, lounge, cook fac. RO ⚹ $17 - $20, ⚹⚹ $34, BC MC VI.

★ **The Hub of the West**, (Lodge), 79 Brisbane St, 500m NW of Railway Station, ☎ 02 6882 5004, fax 02 6882 5004, (2 stry gr fl), 52 rms [a/c-cool (24), elec blkts, blkts, linen, pillows], ldry, TV rm, cook fac, bbq, ☏. RO ⚹ $20, ⚹⚹ $40, ⚹ $5, W ⚹ $85, ⚹⚹ $130, ch con.

Aussie Cabins, (Lodge), Sheraton Rd, 5km E of City Centre, ☎ 02 6884 9504, fax 02 6884 4599, 20 rms [a/c, linen reqd-fee], rec rm, lounge (TV), conv fac, t/c mkg shared, bbq, ☏. D ⚹ $16.50, ⚹⚹ $49.50, ⚹ $3.30, ch con, BC MC VI.

DUNBOGAN NSW 2443

Pop Nominal, (381km N Sydney), See map on page 54, ref C7. Dunbogan is part of the Camden Haven region, an area of complex waterways and excellent fishing. Boating, Fishing, Swimming.

Self Catering Accommodation

★★☆ **Dunbogan Riverview Flats**, (HU), 55 The Boulevarde, 3km from PO, ☎ 02 6559 9137, fax 02 6559 7052, 7 units acc up to 6, [shwr, tlt, heat, TV, t/c mkg, refrig, cook fac, micro, elec frypan, toaster, linen reqd], ldry, w/mach, dryer, iron, bbq, c/park (carport).

★★ **Utopia Units**, (HU), 61 The Boulevarde, ☎ 02 6559 9212, 4 units acc up to 6, [shwr, tlt, TV, clock radio, t/c mkg, refrig, cook fac, micro, elec frypan, toaster, linen reqd], ldry, w/mach, iron, bbq, c/park (carport), cots. D $45, W $175 - $350.

B&B's/Guest Houses

★★★★ **Dunbogan Bed & Breakfast**, (B&B), 64 Camden Head Rd, 4km SE of Laurieton PO, ☎ 02 6559 6222, 3 rms [hairdry (1), fan, c/fan (2), heat, tel, t/c mkg, ldry], lounge (TV), lounge firepl, pool-heated (solar salt water), bbq, non smoking property. BB ⚹ $50 - $60, ⚹⚹ $80 - $100, fam con, AE BC MC VI.

DUNEDOO NSW 2844

Pop 800. (375km NW Sydney), See map on pages 52/53, ref G4. Dunedoo (pronounced 'Dunny-doo') is a charming town at the centre of beef, wool and wheat industries. Bowls, Gem Fossicking, Golf, Swimming.

Hotels/Motels

★★★ **Swan Motel Dunedoo**, (M), 58 Bolaro St, ☎ 02 6375 1112, fax 02 6375 1041, 8 units [shwr, tlt, a/c, c/fan, elec blkts, TV, clock radio, t/c mkg, refrig], bbq, ☏, cots. RO ⚹ $52.80, ⚹⚹ $66, ⚹⚹⚹ $71.50, AE BC EFT MC VI.

Self Catering Accommodation

★★★ **Digilah Station**, (HU), (Farm), Closed Jul 1 to Aug 31, Digilah Rd, 18km N of PO, ☎ 02 6375 1380, fax 02 6375 1380, 1 unit [shwr, tlt, heat, elec blkts, tel, TV, video, clock radio, t/c mkg, refrig, cook fac, toaster], ✕, pool, tennis. RO ⚹ $40 - $50, ⚹⚹ $80 - $90, ⚹⚹⚹ $115 - $125, ⚹ $28 - $40, Bookings essential.

DUNGOG NSW 2420

Pop 2,200. (202km N Sydney), See map on page 54, ref A8. Picturesque town in the Williams Valley, regarded as one of the main gateways to the Barrington Tops. Bowls, Bush Walking, Golf, Scenic Drives, Swimming, Tennis.

Hotels/Motels

★★★☆ **Tall Timbers Motel**, (M), 167 Dowling St, 100m N of PO, ☎ 02 4992 1547, fax 02 4992 3037, 12 units [shwr, tlt, hairdry, a/c, fan, tel, TV, video-fee, t/c mkg, refrig, cook fac (1)], iron, iron brd, ⊠ (char grill), cots, non smoking units (6). RO ⚹ $55 - $80, ⚹⚹ $77 - $115, ⚹⚹⚹ $93.50 - $120, ⚹ $20, AE BC EFT MC VI.

★☆ **The Royal Hotel**, (LH), 80 Dowling St, 200m S of PO, ☎ 02 4992 3070, fax 02 4992 3070, (2 stry), 21 rms lounge (TV), t/c mkg shared, bbq, cots. BLB ⚹ $22, ⚹⚹ $38, ch con.

Self Catering Accommodation

★★★☆ **Gumnut Glen Cabins**, 3620 Clarence Town Rd, Brookfield 2420, 15km S of Dungog, ☎ 02 4996 5515, fax 02 4996 5661, 4 cabins acc up to 4, [shwr, spa bath, tlt, hairdry, c/fan, fire pl (Gas log fire), elec blkts, TV, clock radio, refrig, cook fac, micro, toaster, blkts, linen], rec rm, pool (salt water), bbq, non smoking units. D ⚹ $90, ⚹⚹ $99 - $140, ⚹ $33, W ⚹ $425, ⚹⚹ $550, ch con, Min book applies, BC MC VI,

Operator Comment: Website: www.gumnutglen.bmr.com.au

★★★☆ **The Carriageway Resort**, Converted railway carriages. Clarencetown Rd, Crooks Park, 6km S of Dungog, ☎ 02 4992 1388, fax 02 4992 3888, 4 cabins acc up to 6, [shwr, spa bath (2), tlt, hairdry (2), a/c, c/fan (2), fire pl (2), tel, TV, clock radio (2), refrig, cook fac ltd, micro, toaster, blkts, linen, pillows], ldry, w/mach, dryer, iron, iron brd, pool (salt water), bbq, courtesy transfer, golf (6 hole), cots. D ⚹⚹ $110 - $253, W ⚹⚹ $275 - $616, ch con, 2 cabins of a higher rating. BC MC VI.

(Cottage Section), 1 cotg acc up to 8, [shwr, bath, tlt, a/c, c/fan, fire pl, heat, elec blkts, TV, clock radio, t/c mkg, refrig, cook fac, micro, toaster, ldry, doonas, linen], w/mach, iron, iron brd, non smoking property. D ⚹⚹ $130, W ⚹⚹ $600, (not yet classified).

★★★ **Dungog Country Apartments**, (HU), 262 Dowling St, 300m N of PO, ☎ 02 4992 2112, fax 02 4992 2112, (2 stry), 2 units acc up to 10, [shwr, tlt, c/fan, heat, elec blkts, TV, video, clock radio, t/c mkg, refrig, cook fac, micro, elec frypan, toaster, blkts, linen, pillows], iron, cots, non smoking rms (2). D ⚹ $50 - $60, ⚹⚹ $120, ⚹ $30, ch con.

★★★ **The Bower**, (House), 855 Main Creek Rd, 15km N of PO, ☎ 02 4992 1899, 1 house acc up to 8, (4 bedrm), [shwr, bath, tlt, a/c, fire pl, tel, TV, t/c mkg, refrig, cook fac, micro, elec frypan, toaster, ldry, blkts, linen], w/mach, iron, iron brd, pool (salt water), bbq, cots. D ♦♦ $85, ♦ $25, W ♦♦ $385, ♦ $110, ch con, fam con, Min book applies.

★★★ **Yeranda at Barrington Tops**, (Cotg), 117 Skimmings Gap Road Main Creek, 17km N of PO, ☎ 02 4992 1208, fax 02 4992 1208, 3 cotgs acc up to 6, [shwr, tlt, fire pl, tel, CD, refrig (2 gas, 1 electric), cook fac, linen reqd-fee], bbq, D ♦♦ $92 - $127, ♦ $28 - $63.50, W ♦♦ $420 - $566, 1 cottage yet to be rated, Solar power - 2, Min book applies, ♿.

★★☆ **Dingadee Cottage**, (Cotg), (Farm), Main Creek Rd, 5kms NE of Dungog, ☎ 02 4992 1731, 1 cotg acc up to 4, [shwr, tlt, a/c-cool, fan, heat, TV, clock radio, t/c mkg, refrig, cook fac, d/wash, toaster, ldry, blkts, linen, pillows], w/mach, lounge (TV), non smoking units. D ♦♦ $80 - $100, ♦ $10, W ♦♦ $450 - $500, ♦ $30.

★★ **Cangon Country Cottages**, (Cotg), (Farm), 'Cangon', ☎ 02 4992 1231, fax 02 4992 3061, 2 cotgs acc up to 9, [shwr, bath, tlt, c/fan, fire pl, elec blkts (2), TV, t/c mkg, refrig, cook fac, toaster, blkts, linen, pillows], bbq, c/park (garage). D ♦♦ $100, ♦ $15, W ♦♦ $500, ♦ $10, ch con.

★★ **Carawirry Cabins**, Cabbage Tree Rd, Main Creek, 19km N of Dungog, ☎ 02 4992 1859, fax 02 4992 3255, (2 stry), 2 cabins acc up to 8, [shwr, bath, tlt, fire pl, tel, refrig, cook fac, toaster, linen reqd-fee], bbq, non smoking units. D ♦♦ $99, ♦ $44, W ♦♦ $352, ♦ $176, ch con, Min book applies.

★★ **Yawata Accommodation**, Chichester Dam Rd, 16km NW of Dungog PO, ☎ 02 4995 9263, fax 02 4995 9263, 2 cabins [shwr, tlt, c/fan, heat, elec blkts, tel, clock radio, t/c mkg, refrig, micro, toaster, blkts, linen, pillows], lounge (TV), pool (salt water), bbq, plygr, cots. RO ♦ $40 - $60, ♦♦ $80 - $100, ♦ $10 - $20, BC MC VI.

★☆ **Melia Holiday Cottage**, (HU), Chichester Dam Rd, 22km N of Dungog, ☎ 02 4995 9265, fax 02 4995 9275, 1 unit acc up to 4, [shwr, tlt, c/fan, heat, refrig, cook fac ltd, micro, toaster], bbq, cots. D ♦♦ $60, ♦ $10, ch con, Min book applies.

Olivedale Farm, Cnr Sugarloaf Rd & Chichester Dam Rd, 2km N of PO, ☎ 02 4992 2090, fax 02 4992 2090, 1 cabin acc up to 2, (1 bedrm), [shwr, spa bath, tlt, a/c, heat (wood), cent heat, elec blkts, TV, clock radio, t/c mkg, refrig, cook fac, micro, blkts, doonas, linen, pillows], w/mach, dryer, pool, bbq, tennis, breakfast ingredients. D ♦♦ $100 - $140, weekly con, BC MC VI, (not yet classified).

Ironbark Hut, 99 Brewers Rd, Flat Tops via Dungog, 13km SE of PO, ☎ 02 4992 2092, 1 cabin acc up to 5, [shwr, tlt, fire pl, tel, t/c mkg, refrig (gas), cook fac, blkts, linen reqd-fee, pillows], bbq, Dogs and horses welcome. D ♦♦ $90, ♦ $15, Min book applies.

B&B's/Guest Houses

★★★★☆ **Jindabella Mountain Retreat**, (B&B), Flat Tops Rd, Flat Tops, 11km E of Dungog, ☎ 02 4992 2205, fax 02 4992 2206, 3 rms [spa bath, tlt, hairdry, a/c, c/fan, heat, tel], lounge (TV, video & firepl), ✕, t/c mkg shared, bbq. BB ♦♦ $150, BC MC VI.

★★★★☆ **Old Cambra School Bed & Breakfast**, (B&B), 583 Flat Tops Rd, Cambra, 16km SE of PO, ☎ 02 4992 3302, 3 rms [shwr, spa bath (1), tlt, hairdry, a/c, elec blkts, clock radio], TV rm, lounge firepl, pool (salt water), t/c mkg shared, courtesy transfer, non smoking rms. BB ♦♦ $140 - $150, BC MC VI,
Operator Comment: Luxury Romantic Retreat website www.barringtons.com.au\oldschool

★★★★☆ **Riverwood Downs Mountain Valley Lodge**, (GH), Monkerai Valley, 35km S of Gloucester PO, ☎ 02 4994 7112, fax 02 4994 7047, 20 rms [shwr, spa bath (8), tlt, hairdry, a/c, elec blkts, tel, TV, t/c mkg, refrig], ldry, iron, iron brd, rec rm, conv fac, ✕, bar, pool, bbq, ✆, canoeing, tennis (half court), cots. D all meals ♦ $144 - $245, ♦♦ $288 - $448, ♦♦♦ $432 - $576, ♦ $144 - $192, ch con, Min book applies, BC EFT MC VI.

★★★★ **Kirralee Bed & Breakfast**, (B&B), No children's facilities, 72 Dowling St, 200m S of PO, ☎ 02 4992 2210, fax 02 4992 2211, 4 rms [ensuite, bath (1), hairdry, c/fan, heat, elec blkts, tel], ldry, iron, iron brd, lounge firepl, t/c mkg shared, bbq, non smoking property. BB ♦ $110, ♦♦ $150, DBB ♦ $143, ♦ $216, BC MC VI.

★★★☆ **Barrington Guest House & Rainforest Cottages**, (GH), Salisbury, via Dungog, ☎ 02 4995 3212, fax 02 4995 3248, 40 rms [elec blkts], ldry, ✕, bush walking, tennis, cots. D all meals ♦♦ $158 - $304, ch con, Min book all holiday times, AE BC EFT MC VI.

★★★★ **(Rainforest Cottage Section)**, 20 cotgs [spa bath, fan, heat, elec blkts, TV, cook fac ltd, micro, elec frypan], ldry, cots. D ♦ $197.60, ♦♦ $304, ♦ $152.

Canningalla Bed & Breakfast, (B&B), Chichester Dam Rd, ☎ 02 4995 9230, fax 02 4995 9281, 4 rms [shwr (1), bath (1), tlt (1), fan (4), c/fan (1), heat, elec blkts, tel], shared fac (3 rooms), ldry, iron, iron brd, rec rm, lounge (tv & firepl), cook fac, t/c mkg shared, bbq, cots. BB ♦ $44 - $55, BC MC VI.

Tree Tops Healthy Lifestyle B&B, (B&B), 2928 Salisbury Rd, Salisbury 2420, 40km NW of PO, ☎ 02 4995 3295, fax 02 4995 3295, (Multi-stry), 3 rms [shwr, bath, tlt, tel], ldry, iron, iron brd, lounge (TV, video & firepl), ✕, t/c mkg shared, bbq, c/park. BB ♦ $50 - $65, Min book applies, BC MC VI.

Other Accommodation

★★★★☆ **The Barringtons Country Retreat**, (Lodge), Chichester Dam Rd, ☎ 02 4995 9269, fax 02 4995 9279, 24 rms acc up to 11, [shwr, bath, spa bath (24), tlt, a/c-cool, c/fan, fire pl (23), heat, tel, TV (20), video (20), clock radio, t/c mkg, refrig, cook fac (23), cook fac ltd (2), micro (23), elec frypan, toaster (23), blkts, linen, pillows], iron, ✕, pool (salt water), bbq, plygr, tennis, cots. DBB ♦♦ $286, RO ♦♦ $109, 6 cabins of a lesser rating, 4 cabins yet to be assessed. Min book applies, BC EFT MC VI.

DUNGOWAN NSW 2340

Pop Nominal, See map on pages 52/53, ref J3. Little town on the Fossickers Way south-east of Tamworth.

Hotels/Motels

Dungowan Tavern, (LH), Nundle Rd, 23km E of Tamworth, ☎ 02 6769 4206, fax 02 6769 4130, 5 rms [evap cool, fire pl (1), heat, elec blkts, clock radio], ldry, lounge (TV), ✕, t/c mkg shared, bbq, rm serv, ✆, plygr, non smoking property. BB ♦ $70, ♦♦ $90, RO ♦ $60, ♦♦ $80, AE BC EFT MC VI, (not yet classified).

DURI NSW 2344

Pop 530. Nominal, (448km NW Sydney), See map on pages 52/53, ref H3. Small village in the New England region between Tamworth and Werris Creek.

B&B's/Guest Houses

★★★☆ **Lalla Rookh Country House**, (B&B), No children's facilities, Werris Creek Rd, 20km S of Tamworth PO, ☎ 02 6768 0216, fax 02 6768 0330, 4 rms [shwr (3), tlt (3), evap cool, c/fan, fire pl (combustion), heat, elec blkts, TV, video, clock radio], ldry, lounge, t/c mkg shared, c/park (undercover). BB ♦ $74, ♦♦ $98, Dinner by arrangement, BC JCB MC VI.

EAST GRESFORD NSW 2311

Pop 308. See map on page 54, ref A8. Charming, historic town on the Allyn River between the Hunter Valley and Barrington Tops.

Self Catering Accommodation

★☆ **Leyburn Cottage East Gresford**, (Cotg), Bingleburra Rd, 10 km E of PO, ☎ 02 9337 2076, 1 cotg acc up to 6, [shwr, tlt, elec blkts, TV, video, CD, t/c mkg, refrig, cook fac, elec frypan, toaster, doonas, linen], read rm (library), lounge firepl, bbq. D $100, W $640.

B&B's/Guest Houses

★★★★ **Clevedon Bed & Breakfast**, (B&B), Gresford Rd, 1km SE of PO, ☎ 02 4938 9488, fax 02 4938 9488, 3 rms [shwr (2), tlt (2), a/c (2), elec blkts, TV (2), radio (2), t/c mkg (2)], ldry, iron, iron brd, lounge (TV), bbq, c/park. BB ♦♦ $55 - $85, ♦ $15, BC MC VI.

★★★★ **East Gresford Old Bank Building**, (B&B), Cnr Park St & Durham Rd, 100m S OF PO, ☎ 02 4938 9455, fax 02 4938 9389, 2 rms [shwr, tlt, hairdry, a/c, c/fan, elec blkts, TV, clock radio, t/c mkg, refrig, micro, toaster], iron, iron brd, cook fac, non smoking property. BB ♦♦ $90, ♦ $10.

EBOR NSW 2453

(647km N Sydney), See map on page 54, ref C5. Ebor lies on the Waterfall Way, the main route from Armidale to the coast that passes through scenes of breathtaking natural beauty. Fishing, Scenic Drives.

Hotels/Motels
★ **Ebor Falls**, (LMH), Grafton Rd, 300m W of PO, ☎ 02 6775 9155, fax 02 6775 9155, 4 units [shwr, tlt, heat, elec blkts, TV, t/c mkg, refrig, toaster], ✕, dinner to unit. RO ♦ $50, ♦♦ $55, ♦♦♦ $66, BC MC VI.

Self Catering Accommodation
★★★☆ **Marengo Chalet**, (Chalet), Marengo Rd, 32km N of PO, ☎ 02 6657 6175, fax 02 6657 6175, (2 stry gr fl), 1 chalet acc up to 8, [shwr (2), tlt (2), c/fan, fire pl, cent heat, elec blkts, tel, TV, video, clock radio (2), t/c mkg, refrig, cook fac, micro, elec frypan, toaster, ldry, blkts, linen, pillows], w/mach, dryer, iron, bbq, c/park (carport), plygr, tennis, cots. D ♦♦ $140, ◊ $20 - $30, W ♦♦ $784, ◊ $112 - $168, ch con, Min book applies.

EDEN NSW 2551

Pop 3,100. (500km S Sydney), See map on page 55, ref A8. Historic south coast fishing town on the shores of glorious Twofold Bay. Boating, Bush Walking, Fishing, Golf, Scenic Drives, Shooting, Swimming, Tennis.

Hotels/Motels
★★★★ **Twofold Bay Motor Inn**, (M), 166 Imlay St, 300m S of PO, ☎ 02 6496 3111, fax 02 6496 3058, (2 stry gr fl), 24 units (2 suites) [shwr, spa bath (2), tlt, hairdry, a/c, elec blkts, tel, cable tv (satellite), video-fee, movie, clock radio, t/c mkg, refrig, toaster], ldry, pool indoor heated, spa, rm serv, cots-fee, non smoking units (17). RO $77 - $165, Suite D $110 - $150, AE BC DC MC VI.

 ★★★☆ **Blue Marlin Resort & Motor Inn**, (M), Princes Hwy, 1km N of PO, ☎ 02 6496 1601, fax 02 6496 3498, 26 units (1 suite) [shwr, tlt, hairdry, a/c, fan, elec blkts, tel, TV, video (avail), clock radio, t/c mkg, refrig, cook fac], ldry, rec rm, conf fac, ✕, bar, pool indoor heated, spa, bbq, plygr, gym, cots, non smoking units (12). RO ♦ $50 - $95, ♦♦ $53 - $108, ♦♦♦♦ $75 - $122, ◊ $10, Suite D $148 - $198, AE BC DC EFT MC MCH VI.

 ★★★ **Bayview Motor Inn**, (M), Princes Hwy, 1km SW of PO, ☎ 02 6496 1242, fax 02 6496 1273, 30 units [shwr, tlt, heat, elec blkts, tel, TV, video-fee, clock radio, t/c mkg, refrig], ldry, conf fac, ✕, pool, spa, bbq, rm serv, plygr, cots, non smoking units (15). RO ♦ $60.50 - $126.50, ♦♦ $65 - $126.50, ♦♦♦ $71.50 - $120, ◊ $11, 12 units ★★☆, AE BC DC EFT MC VI,

Operator Comment: NSW Winner - Accommodation Industry Award for Excellence 2000.

★★★ **Golf View Motel**, (M), 34 Princes Hwy, 2.5km N of PO, ☎ 02 6496 1943, fax 02 6496 2712, 16 units [shwr, tlt, a/c, heat, elec blkts, tel, cable tv, clock radio, t/c mkg, refrig, cook fac (1)], ldry, pool, bbq, boat park, cots-fee, non smoking units (8). RO ♦ $45, ♦♦ $50, ♦♦♦ $59, ◊ $9, pen con, AE BC DC MC VI.

 ★★★ **Halfway Motel**, (M), 118 Imlay St, 200m W of PO, ☎ 02 6496 1178, fax 02 6496 3316, (2 stry gr fl), 30 units [shwr, spa bath (5), tlt, hairdry, a/c, elec blkts, tel, TV, video-fee, clock radio, t/c mkg, refrig, toaster], ✕, spa, bbq, rm serv, cots-fee, non smoking units (10). RO ♦ $53 - $95, ♦♦ $64 - $100, ♦♦♦ $75 - $180, ◊ $11, AE BC DC EFT JCB MC MP VI,

Operator Comment: Closest motel to the beach & centrally located. Friendly & informative. Whale watching Packages Oct. & Nov. 50m. to interstate coach stop.

★★★ **Whale Fisher Motel**, (M), 170 Imlay St, ☎ 02 6496 1266, fax 02 6496 1207, (2 stry gr fl), 16 units [shwr, tlt, hairdry, a/c, fan, elec blkts, tel, TV, video, clock radio, t/c mkg, refrig, toaster], ldry, iron, iron brd, bbq, rm serv, c/park. BB ♦ $55 - $80, ♦♦ $90 - $140, ◊ $35, RO ♦ $50 - $75, ♦♦ $60 - $90, ◊ $15, AE BC DC MC VI.

★★☆ **Centretown Motel**, (M), 167 Imlay St, ☎ 02 6496 1475, fax 02 6496 2088, 14 units [shwr, tlt, fan, heat, elec blkts, tel, TV, clock radio, t/c mkg, refrig], ldry, cots-fee. RO ♦ $45 - $80, ♦♦ $49 - $85, ♦♦♦ $59 - $95, ◊ $10, AE BC DC MC VI.

★★☆ **Coachmans Rest Motor Inn**, (M), Princes Hwy, 2km N of PO, ☎ 02 6496 1900, fax 02 6496 3398, 26 units (1 suite) [shwr, bath (6), spa bath (2), tlt, a/c, elec blkts, tel, TV, clock radio, t/c mkg, refrig, toaster], ldry, ✕, pool, spa, bbq, rm serv, cots-fee, non smoking units (16). RO ♦ $45 - $85, ♦♦ $65 - $120, ◊ $10 - $40, Suite D $85 - $125, AE BC DC EFT MC VI, ⚹&.

★★☆ **Sapphire Coast Motel**, (M), 48 Princes Hwy, 1.5km N of PO, ☎ 02 6496 1200, fax 02 6496 3464, 19 units [shwr, tlt, heat, elec blkts, tel, TV, video (avail), clock radio, t/c mkg, refrig], ✕, pool, spa, bbq, c/park (undercover) (10), boat park, plygr, cots. RO ♦ $44 - $77, ♦♦ $49 - $87, ♦♦♦ $57 - $93, ◊ $7 - $9, AE BC DC EFT MC VI.

Historic Sea Horse Inn, (LH), Classified by National Trust, Off Princess Hwy, Boydtown 2551, 8km S of PO, ☎ 02 6496 1361, fax 02 6496 1394, (2 stry), 14 rms [shwr (3), bath (1), tlt (3), heat, tel, TV, t/c mkg, refrig], shared fac (11 rms), lounge (TV), ✕, ✕, tennis, cots-fee. D ♦ $66 - $88, ♦♦♦♦ $132 - $176, Min book applies, AE BC DC EFT MC VI.

Self Catering Accommodation
★★☆ **Villa Eden**, (HU), 4 The Mews, 1km SW of PO, ☎ 02 6496 1790, 2 units acc up to 8, [shwr, bath, tlt, heat, TV, video, clock radio, refrig, cook fac, micro, d/wash, toaster, ldry, linen reqd-fee], bbq, c/park. D $80 - $210, W $375 - $1,000.

★★ **B Line**, (HF), 40 Bungo St, 600m N of PO, ☎ 02 6496 1790, 2 flats acc up to 5, [shwr, bath, tlt, heat, TV, refrig, cook fac, micro, ldry, linen reqd-fee], bbq, c/park (undercover). D $100 - $150, W $250 - $620.

B&B's/Guest Houses
★★★★ **Edens Bed & Breakfast**, (B&B), 13 Bellevue Pl, 1km S of PO, ☎ 02 6496 1575, or 02 6496 1445, fax 02 6496 1575, 2 rms [shwr, tlt, fan, heat, elec blkts, tel-fee, video, clock radio, t/c mkg], ldry, rec rm, lounge (TV), bbq, c/park. BB ♦ $65 - $85, ♦♦ $95 - $135, ♦♦♦ $130 - $175, ◊ $35 - $45, BC MC VI.

★★★★ **Gibson's By The Beach**, (B&B), 10 Bay St, Bay St, ☎ 02 6496 1414, (2 stry gr fl), 1 rm [spa bath, TV, video, refrig, cook fac ltd, micro]. BB ♦ $70 - $95, ♦♦ $105 - $130, ◊ $15 - $35.

★★★★ **The Crown & Anchor**, (B&B), Heritage, c1840, 239 Imlay St, ☎ 02 6496 1017, fax 02 9696 3878, 4 rms [shwr, bath (3), tlt, hairdry, fire pl (3), heat, elec blkts, tel], ldry, iron, iron brd, lounge (firepl), bbq, non smoking property. RO ♦ $90 - $150, ♦♦ $100 - $170, AE BC MC VI.

ELANDS NSW 2429

Pop Nominal, (367km N Sydney), See map on page 54, ref B7. Rural and artistic community on the Bulga Plateau, flanked by some of the most beautiful forests on the mid-north coast. Bush Walking, Fishing, Horse Riding, Scenic Drives.

Self Catering Accommodation
Tirrintippin Farm, (Cotg), Walcha Rd, Bulga Plateau via Elands, 41km W of Wingham, ☎ 02 6550 4533, fax 02 6550 4533, 1 cotg acc up to 10, [shwr, bath, spa bath, tlt, heat, elec blkts (1), tel, TV (1), clock radio, t/c mkg, refrig, micro, elec frypan, toaster], w/mach, iron, bbq, cots. **D all meals ♦ $65, ◊ $65, D ♦♦♦♦ $65, ◊ $5**, ch con.

ELLALONG NSW 2325

Pop 500. (139km N Sydney), See map on page 55, ref B8. Small rural and coal mining centre south of Cessnock near the Hunter Valley wineries.

Hotels/Motels
★ **Ellalong Hotel**, (LH), 80 Helena St, ☎ 02 4998 1217, (2 stry), 11 rms [elec blkts], ⊠, ✕, t/c mkg shared, ✆. **BB ♦ $38 - $50, ♦♦ $60 - $82, ♦♦♦ $100 - $121**, ch con, BC EFT MC VI.

ELLENBOROUGH NSW 2446

Pop Nominal, (440km NW Sydney), See map on page 54, ref B7. Small village on the Hastings River at the heart of rich timber and dairying country. Bush Walking, Canoeing, Horse Riding, Scenic Drives, Swimming.

Self Catering Accommodation
★★★★ **Forest Grange Mountain Retreat**, (Cotg), 223 Toms Creek Rd, 35km W of Wauchope, ☎ 02 6587 4313, fax 02 6587 4313, 3 cotgs acc up to 4, [shwr, tlt, fan, heat, elec blkts, tel, TV, radio, CD, t/c mkg, cook fac, blkts, linen, pillows], w/mach, dryer, iron, lounge (TV), bbq, meals avail, non smoking units. **D ♦♦ $100, W ♦♦ $700**, ch con, BC MC VI.
★★★☆ **Shute-Hill Country Retreat**, (Farm), 5690 Oxley Hwy, 36km W of Wauchope, ☎ 02 6587 4280, fax 02 6587 4280, 2 cabins acc up to 8, [shwr, tlt, fan, heat, elec blkts, tel, TV, clock radio, t/c mkg, refrig, cook fac, micro, elec frypan, toaster, ldry, linen reqd-fee], w/mach, bbq, cots. **D ♦♦♦♦ $75, ◊ $10 - $15, W ♦♦♦♦ $450, ◊ $60 - $90**, ch con.

EMMAVILLE NSW 2371

Pop 350. (706km N Sydney), See map on page 54, ref B3. Small New England town in an old tin mining area. It's a popular spot for fly fishing. Bush Walking, Fishing, Gem Fossicking.

Other Accommodation
Jimargie Hi-Country Holidays, (Lodge), Ashford/Emmaville Rd, 25.6km W of PO, ☎ 02 6733 7277, fax 02 6733 7277, 3 rms acc up to 10, [shwr, tlt, clock radio, refrig, cook fac, micro, elec frypan, toaster, linen reqd-fee], bbq, bush walking, cots. **D ♦ $33, W ♦ $198**.

(Bunkhouse Section), 2 bunkhouses acc up to 12, [shwr (outside), tlt (outside), refrig, cook fac, toaster], bbq, cots. **D ♦ $22, W ♦ $132**.

EROWAL BAY NSW 2540

Pop 500. (193km S Sydney), See map on page 55, ref B5. Secluded south coast village on St Georges Basin. Boating, Fishing, Swimming.

Self Catering Accommodation
Dungowan Holiday Flats, (HF), 99 Naval Pde, 500m W of PO, ☎ 02 4443 0333, (2 stry gr fl), 6 flats acc up to 5, [shwr, tlt, t/c mkg, refrig, cook fac, toaster, linen reqd], ldry, iron, bbq, cots. **D $70, W $490**, Min book applies.

(Cottage Section), 2 cotgs acc up to 9, [shwr, bath, t/c mkg, refrig, cook fac, toaster, linen reqd]. **D $75 - $110, W $525 - $770**.

ETTALONG NSW 2257

Pop Part of Gosford, (84km N Sydney), See map on page 56, ref E3. Central Coast town on a beach of the same name that connects Brisbane Water with Broken Bay. Boating, Bowls, Fishing, Swimming.

B&B's/Guest Houses
Ettalong Beach House Bed & Breakfast, (B&B), 129 The Esplanade, Ettalong Beach 2257, 1km S of PO, ☎ 02 4343 1895, fax 02 4343 1894, (2 stry gr fl), 4 rms [ensuite (4), c/fan, heat (elec/gas), elec blkts, TV, clock radio, t/c mkg, refrig, micro, toaster], ✕, spa, bbq, non smoking rms. **BB ♦♦ $120 - $135, ◊ $35**, BC MC VI, (not yet classified).

Motel Paradiso, (B&B), Cnr Schnapper Rd & Ocean View Rd, 1km E of PO, ☎ 02 4341 1999, fax 02 4342 7128, 1 rm (1 bedrm), [ensuite, spa bath, a/c, fan, cent heat, elec blkts, tel, TV, clock radio, t/c mkg, refrig, ldry], conf fac, ⊠, bbq, ✆, plygr, cots. **BB ♦♦ $75 - $135, ◊ $10**, Min book long w/ends and Easter, AE BC DC EFT MC VI, (not yet classified).

EUGOWRA NSW 2806

Pop 600. Nominal, (392km W Sydney), See map on pages 52/53, ref F5. Attractive and historic little town in central west New South South Wales.

B&B's/Guest Houses
★★☆ **Greylands B&B Farmstay**, (B&B), 'Greylands', Escort Way, 10km E of PO, ☎ 02 6859 5223, fax 02 6859 5223, 3 rms [hairdry (2), a/c, elec blkts, tel, clock radio, refrig, toaster], ldry, lounge (TV), ✕, t/c mkg shared, cots, non smoking property. **BB ♦ $50 - $60, ♦♦ $80 - $100**, pen con, Children by arrangement, AE BC MC.

EUSTON NSW 2737

Pop 450. (914km SW Sydney), See map on pages 52/53, ref B5. Community on the Murray River in a grape, citrus and sheep farming region. Fishing, Swimming.

Hotels/Motels
★★ **Euston Motel**, (M), Sturt Hwy, 500m from bowling club, ☎ 03 5026 3806, fax 03 5026 4202, 12 units [shwr, tlt, a/c-cool (6), a/c (6), heat, elec blkts, TV, t/c mkg, refrig, toaster], pool, bbq, dinner to unit, c/park (undercover), ✆ (available), cots. **RO ♦ $44, ♦♦ $55, ♦♦♦ $66**, BC MC VI.
Country Club Motor Inn, (M), 9 Murray Tce, ☎ 03 5026 4999, fax 03 5026 4998, 22 units [shwr, tlt, hairdry, a/c, tel, TV, clock radio, t/c mkg, refrig, mini bar], ldry, ⊠, bbq, meals to unit, tennis, cots. **RO ♦ $103 - $124, ♦♦ $103 - $124, ◊ $14**, ch con, pen con, AE BC DC EFT MC VI, (not yet classified).

EVANS HEAD NSW 2473

Pop 2,600. (727km N Sydney), See map on page 54, ref E3. Largest town in the Richmond River Shire, situated on the Evans River and favoured for its fishing, national parks and beaches. Boating, Bowls, Fishing, Golf, Surfing, Swimming, Tennis.

Hotels/Motels
★★★☆ **Evans Head Pacific Motel**, (M), Cnr Davis La & Woodburn St, 30m from PO, ☎ 02 6682 4318, fax 02 6682 5741, (2 stry gr fl), 16 units [shwr, tlt, a/c (12), fan, heat, elec blkts, tel, fax, TV, clock radio, t/c mkg, refrig, cook fac (8)], ldry, pool, bbq, cots. **RO ♦ $45 - $55, ♦♦ $49.50 - $85, ◊ $5.50 - $11**, ch con, AE BC DC MC VI.

Self Catering Accommodation
★★☆ **Avalon Court**, (HU), 46 Woodburn St, ☎ 02 6682 4611, 8 units acc up to 6, [shwr, tlt, fan, TV, refrig, cook fac, ldry, linen reqd], c/park (undercover). **W $190 - $550**.

★★☆ **Somerton**, (HU), 18 Mangrove St, ☎ 02 6682 4611, fax 02 6682 4405, 2 units acc up to 6, [shwr, bath, tlt, TV, t/c mkg, refrig, cook fac, elec frypan, d/wash, toaster, ldry, linen reqd], w/mach, dryer, iron, c/park (carport). **W $235 - $580**, Min book applies.

Rates may change. Check before booking.

★★ **Ocean Palms Holiday Units**, (HU), 1 Heath St, ☎ 02 6682 4611, 4 units acc up to 6, [shwr, tlt, TV, radio, refrig, cook fac, toaster, linen reqd], ldry, bbq, c/park. **W $235 - $580.**

★★ **The Anchorage**, (HU), 25 Beach St, ☎ 02 6682 4611, 7 units acc up to 4, [shwr, tlt, TV, refrig, cook fac, toaster, linen reqd], ldry. **W $180 - $550.**

Woodberry Units, (HU), 83 Woodburn St, 1km N of PO, ☎ 02 6682 4311, fax 02 6682 5164, 2 units acc up to 6, (3 bedrm), [shwr, tlt, fan, TV, clock radio, d/wash, ldry, blkts, linen], w/mach, secure park (garage). **W $270 - $700**, (not yet classified).

FAIRY MEADOW NSW

See Wollongong & Suburbs.

FALLS CREEK NSW 2540

Pop Nominal, See map on page 55, ref B5. Small village on the Princes Highway between Nowra and Jervis Bay.

Self Catering Accommodation

★★★ **Parma Farm Cottages**, (Cotg), 269 Parma Rd, 13km S of Nowra, ☎ 02 4447 8098, fax 02 4447 8201, 2 cotgs acc up to 8, [shwr, bath, tlt, c/fan, fire pl (open), heat, elec blkts, TV, video, radio, CD, t/c mkg, refrig, cook fac, micro, elec frypan, d/wash, toaster, ldry (in unit), linen reqd-fee], w/mach, iron, bbq, cots, non smoking rms. **D ♦♦ $110 - $165, ◊ $11 - $22, W ♦♦ $660 - $1,320, ◊ $55**, Min book applies, BC MC VI.

FAULCONBRIDGE NSW

See Blue Mountains Region.

FERN BAY NSW

See Newcastle & Suburbs.

FIGTREE NSW

See Wollongong & Suburbs.

FINE FLOWER NSW 2460

Pop Nominal, (699km N Sydney), See map on page 54, ref C3. Quiet rural locality on the back road from Grafton to Tabulam.

B&B's/Guest Houses

Wave Hill Station Farm Stays, (B&B), (Farm), Carnham Rd, 74km NW of Grafton, ☎ 02 6647 2145, fax 02 6647 2145, 2 rms [fan (1), c/fan (1), heat, tel, clock radio (1)], shared fac (shwr, tlt & bath), lounge (TV & firepl), ✗, t/c mkg shared, bbq, canoeing, tennis-fee, cots. **BB ♦ $50, D all meals ♦ $138, DBB ♦ $72**, ch con.

FINLEY NSW 2713

Pop 2,150. (598km SW Sydney), See map on pages 52/53, ref D7. Rural town in the Murray region at the heart of an extensive irrigation network and food producing area. Bowls, Golf, Shooting, Tennis.

Hotels/Motels

★★★☆ **Finley Palm Motor Inn**, (M), Cnr Newell Hwy & Berrigan Rd, 500m N of PO, ☎ 03 5883 2077, fax 03 5883 2037, 17 units [shwr, bath (2), tlt, a/c, heat, elec blkts, tel, fax, TV, video, movie, clock radio, t/c mkg, refrig], ldry, pool, bbq, cots-fee, non smoking units (avail). **D $130, RO ♦ $72, ♦♦ $83 - $88, ♦♦♦ $95, ◊ $15**, AE BC DC MC MP VI.

★★★ **Century Motor Inn**, (M), Newell Hwy, ☎ 03 5883 1466, fax 03 5883 2166, 18 units [shwr, tlt, a/c-cool, heat, elec blkts, tel, TV, clock radio, t/c mkg, refrig], ✗, pool, cots-fee. **RO ♦ $50, ♦♦ $55, ◊ $10**, ch con, AE BC EFT MC MCH MP VI.

★★☆ **Finley Motel**, (M), Newell Hwy, 500m N of PO, ☎ 03 5883 1088, fax 03 5883 1468, 21 units [shwr, tlt, a/c, elec blkts, tel, TV, clock radio, t/c mkg, refrig], ldry, ✗, bbq. **RO ♦ $48, ♦♦ $55**, AE BC DC EFT MC VI.

 ★★ **Country Club**, (LMH), 171 Murray St, 300m S of PO, ☎ 03 5883 1355, 11 units [shwr, tlt, a/c, elec blkts, TV, clock radio, t/c mkg, toaster], ldry, ✗ (Mod/Mediter Alacarte), ✗, cots, non smoking rms (4). **D $51, RO ♦ $39, ♦♦ $45**, AE BC DC MC MCH VI.

FINGAL BAY NSW

See Port Stephens Region.

FISHING POINT NSW 2283

Pop Part of Lake Macquarie, (157km N Sydney), See map on page 55, ref E4. Small community on the western shores of Lake Macquarie.

B&B's/Guest Houses

★★★★ **Beth's Bed & Breakfast**, (B&B), 205 Fishing Point Rd, 2km S of Rathmines, ☎ 02 4975 5144, fax 02 4975 5144, 1 rm [shwr, tlt, c/fan, heat (wood), TV, clock radio, t/c mkg, refrig], iron. **BB ♦ $65, ♦♦ $105**, ch con.

FITZROY FALLS NSW 2577

Pop Nominal, (150km SW Sydney), See map on page 55, ref B4. Fitzroy Falls is a pleasant spot at the northern end of Morton National Park.

Self Catering Accommodation

★★★☆ **Twin Falls Bush Cottages**, (Cotg), Throsby Rd, 1km NW from National Parks Information Centre, ☎ 02 4887 7333, fax 02 487 7148, 5 cotgs acc up to 8, [shwr, bath (3), tlt, fan, fire pl, elec blkts, TV, clock radio, t/c mkg, refrig, cook fac, micro, toaster, linen], w/mach, conv fac, bbq, plygr. **D $105**, BC MC VI.

B&B's/Guest Houses

★★★☆ **Cedarvale Health and Lifestyle Retreat Ltd**, (B&B), No children's facilities, 2999 Moss Vale Rd, 10km W of Kangaroo Valley, ☎ 02 4465 1362, fax 02 4465 1362, 5 rms [shwr, tlt, cent heat, video], ldry, lounge, ✗ (buffet), spa, t/c mkg shared, c/park. **BB ♦ $60, ♦♦ $110, ◊ $55, DBB ♦ $70, ♦♦ $130, ◊ $65**, BC MC VI.

FORBES NSW 2871

Pop 7,450. (384km W Sydney), See map on pages 52/53, ref F5. Forbes lies on the Lachlan River at the centre of a thriving pastoral region. It's a handsome town with many historic and ornate buildings, including some classic country pubs. Bowls, Fishing, Golf, Scenic Drives, Squash, Swimming, Tennis, Trotting, Water Skiing.

Hotels/Motels

 ★★★★ **Country Mile Motor Inn**, (M), 14 Cross St, 300m N of PO, ☎ 02 6852 4099, fax 02 6852 4099, 14 units [shwr, tlt, hairdry, a/c-cool, heat, elec blkts, tel, TV, video (avail), movie, clock radio, t/c mkg, refrig, toaster], ldry, iron, iron brd, pool (salt water), dinner to unit, cots-fee, non smoking units (5). **RO ♦ $71, ♦♦ $81, ♦♦♦ $91, ◊ $10**, ch con, 3 rooms ★★★☆, AE BC DC EFT JCB MC MP VI.

 ★★★☆ **Lake Forbes Motel**, (M), 8 Junction St, cnr Newell Hwy, 800m S of PO, ☎ 02 6852 2922, fax 02 6852 4483, (2 stry gr fl), 16 units [shwr, tlt, hairdry, a/c-cool, heat, elec blkts, tel, cable tv, clock radio, t/c mkg, refrig, toaster], iron, iron brd, cots-fee, non smoking units (5). **RO ♦ $56 - $62, ♦♦ $65 - $73, ♦♦♦ $75 - $83, ◊ $10**, AE BC DC EFT MC MCH VI.

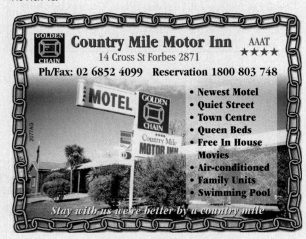

FORBES NSW continued...

★★★☆ **Town & Country Motor Inn**, (M), Newell Hwy, 1km N of PO, ☎ 02 6852 3444, fax 02 6852 4486, 19 units [shwr, spa bath (3), tlt, hairdry, a/c, elec blkts, tel, TV, video-fee, clock radio, t/c mkg, refrig], iron, iron brd, pool, bbq, rm serv, dinner to unit, golf, cots-fee, non smoking units (6). **RO ♦ $57, ♦♦ $68, ◊ $10**, AE BC DC MC VI.

Budget Motel Chain International

★★★ **Ben Hall Motor Inn**, (M), Cross St, 300m N of PO, ☎ 02 6851 2345, fax 02 6852 1654, 26 units [shwr, bath (1), tlt, a/c, c/fan, elec blkts, tel, TV, video-fee, clock radio, t/c mkg, refrig, toaster], bbq, meals to unit (breakfast & dinner), cots-fee, **RO ♦ $56 - $66, ♦♦ $63 - $73, ♦♦♦ $73 - $83, ◊ $10**, 6 units ★★★☆. AE BC DC EFT MC VI.

AAA Tourism Special Rates | FLAG Flag Choice Hotels | Sundowner Chain Motor Inns

★★★ **Sundowner Chain Motor Inns**, (M), 22 Sherriff St, Cnr Templar St, 100m E of PO, ☎ 02 6852 2466, fax 02 6852 3237, 40 units [shwr, spa bath (3), tlt, hairdry (11), elec blkts, tel, cable tv, video (14), clock radio, t/c mkg, refrig, mini bar (26)], ldry, ☒ (Mon to Sat), pool, c/park (off street), cots-fee, non smoking units (11). **RO ♦ $80 - $163, ♦♦ $85.50 - $163, ◊ $11**, ch con, AE BC DC EFT MC MP VI.

★★☆ **Adrian Motel**, (M), 3 Dowling St, Cnr Union St, ☎ 02 6852 2611, fax 02 6852 1767, 22 units [shwr, tlt, a/c, elec blkts, tel, TV, clock radio, t/c mkg, refrig, toaster], ldry, ☒, pool. **RO ♦ $48, ♦♦ $55, ♦♦♦ $60, ◊ $8**, AE BC DC EFT MC VI.

★☆ **Forbes Inn**, (LMH), Lawler St, 400m N of PO, ☎ 02 6852 1555, fax 02 6851 1701, 10 units [shwr, bath, tlt, a/c, elec blkts, TV, t/c mkg, refrig, toaster], ldry, conv fac, bbq, cots-fee. **RO ♦ $45, ♦♦ $49, ♦♦♦ $57, ◊ $12**, ch con, AE BC DC EFT MC VI.

FORRESTERS BEACH NSW 2260

Pop Part of Gosford, (89km N Sydney), See map on page 55, ref D6. Central Coast village near Terrigal backed by the Wamberal Lagoon Nature Reserve and Wyrrabalong National Park. Boating, Fishing, Scenic Drives, Swimming.

Hotels/Motels

★★★★ **Forresters Resort**, (M), 960 The Entrance Rd, 6km N of Terrigal, ☎ 02 4384 1222, fax 02 4385 3108, 34 units [shwr, bath (18), spa bath (4), tlt, hairdry, a/c, c/fan, elec blkts, tel, TV, video (avail), clock radio, t/c mkg, refrig, toaster], ldry, iron, iron brd, rec rm, conv fac, ☒, pool, spa, bbq, rm serv, dinner to unit, plygr, cots-fee. **RO ♦ $95 - $245, ♦♦ $100 - $245, ♦♦♦ $115 - $195, ◊ $15 - $20**, AE BC DC EFT MC VI.

Trouble-free travel tips - **Tyre pressures**

Check tyre pressures and set them to the manufacturer's recommendation, including the spare.

The specifications can generally be found on the tyre placard located in either the glove box or on the front door frame.

FORSTER NSW 2428

Pop 15,950. (312km N Sydney), See map on page 54, ref B8. Commercial centre of the Great Lakes region and an extremely popular holiday destination for swimming, surfing and fishing. Boating, Bowls, Fishing, Golf, Horse Riding, Squash, Surfing, Swimming, Tennis.

Hotels/Motels

★★★★ **Forster Palms Motel**, (M), 60 Macintosh St, 450m S of PO, ☎ 02 6555 6255, fax 02 6555 6255, 36 units [shwr, spa bath (4), tlt, hairdry, a/c, c/fan, elec blkts, tel, TV, video-fee, movie, clock radio, t/c mkg, refrig, mini bar (7)], ldry, iron, iron brd, pool (salt water), bbq, cots-fee. **RO ♦ $60 - $95, ♦♦ $65 - $140, ♦♦♦ $80 - $120, ◊ $11**, AE BC DC EFT MC VI, ♿.

★★★☆ **Bella Villa Motor Inn**, (M), 19 Lake St, 350m S of PO, ☎ 02 6554 6842, fax 02 6554 7102, (2 stry), 23 units [shwr, tlt, a/c, elec blkts-fee, tel, TV, video-fee, clock radio, t/c mkg, refrig, cook fac (21), toaster], ldry, pool, bbq, cots-fee. **RO ♦♦ $55 - $110, ◊ $10**, AE BC DC MC VI.

★★★☆ **Casita Motel**, (M), 91 Macintosh St, 1km S of PO, ☎ 02 6554 8033, fax 02 6555 8671, 19 units [shwr, tlt, c/fan, heat, elec blkts, tel, TV, movie, clock radio, t/c mkg, refrig, cook fac (5), micro (5), toaster], ldry, iron, pool, bbq, cots-fee. **RO ♦ $55 - $134, ♦♦ $55 - $134, ♦♦♦ $66 - $181, ◊ $11 - $16.50**, AE BC DC EFT MC VI.

AAA Tourism Special Rates

★★★☆ **Fiesta Motel**, (M), 23-25 Head St, 200m E of PO, ☎ 02 6554 6177, fax 02 6554 6982, (2 stry gr fl), 20 units [shwr, spa bath (2), tlt, hairdry (11), a/c (9), fan, heat, tel, TV, video-fee, clock radio, t/c mkg, refrig, cook fac ltd, micro (9), toaster], ldry, pool, spa, bbq, cots-fee, non smoking units (6). **RO ♦ $77 - $110, ♦♦ $80 - $123, ♦♦♦ $90 - $125, ◊ $12**, 9 units of a lower rating. AE BC DC MC VI.

★★★☆ **Forster Motor Inn**, (M), 11 Wallis St, 100m E of PO, ☎ 02 6554 6877, fax 02 6554 5061, (2 stry gr fl), 25 units (2 suites) [shwr, tlt, evap cool, cent heat, tel, TV, movie, clock radio, t/c mkg, refrig], ldry, ☒, pool-heated (solar), bbq, dinner to unit, c/park (undercover) (4), cots-fee, non smoking units (6). **RO ♦ $80 - $121, ♦♦ $80 - $121, ◊ $17 - $22, Suite D $96 - $154**, AE BC EFT MC VI, ♿.

Operator Comment: See advertisement on following page.

AAA Tourism Special Rates | Best Western

★★★☆ **Golden Sands Motor Inn**, (M), 6 Head St, 100m E of PO, ☎ 02 6554 6222, fax 02 6554 6797, (2 stry gr fl), 24 units [shwr, tlt, hairdry, a/c (13), c/fan, heat, elec blkts, tel, TV, video (avail), clock radio, t/c mkg, refrig, micro (7)], ldry, ☒, pool, bbq, dinner to unit, cots-fee. **RO ♦ $70 - $120, ♦♦ $75 - $132, ♦♦♦ $86 - $143, ◊ $12**, Min book applies, AE BC DC EFT MC VI, ♿.

★★★☆ **Jasmine Lodge Motel**, (M), 18 Wallis St, 90m E of PO, ☎ 02 6554 9838, fax 02 6554 9838, 11 units [shwr, tlt, hairdry, a/c (4), c/fan, heat, elec blkts, TV, movie, clock radio, t/c mkg, refrig, cook fac (5), toaster], ldry, pool, bbq, cots, non smoking units (4). **RO ♦ $55 - $90, ♦♦ $55 - $105, ♦♦♦ $71 - $125, ◊ $16, ♦♦ $330 - $700**, ch con, BC MC VI.

Operator Comment: See advertisement on following page.

FORSTER MOTOR INN

11 Wallis Street, Forster 2428
Ph: (02) 6554 6877 Fax: (02) 6554 5061
FORSTERS PREMIER MOTEL   AAA Tourism ★ ★ ★ ☆

Licenced Restaurant
★
27 Luxury Units
★
Competitive rates
★
Air conditioned
★
Pool
★
150 metres to
Beach, Lake & Town
★
Coaches Welcome

Jasmine Lodge Motel

QUALITY ACCOMMODATION AT AFFORDABLE PRICES
• 90m to beach, PO and shops • Spacious family units
• Some A/C • 5 self-contained units • Saltwater pool/BBQ area
• In-house movies • Close to all clubs.   AAAT ★ ★ ★ ☆ Rating

18 Wallis St, Forster, 2428. Ph/Fax: (02) 6554 9838

BARKLEY INN

FORSTERS NEWEST MOTEL

★ Affordable Luxury in the Heart
of Forster

★ 21 Luxury Airconditioned Suites

★ 10 Deluxe Spa Rooms with VCR

★ Free Satellite TV, In House Movies

★ 200m to main patrolled beach,
shops & restaurants

★ Walk to Aquatic Centre, Indoor
Heated Pool, Tennis & Squash
Courts, Clubs

★ ★ ★ ☆
AAA Tourism

38 HEAD STREET,
FORSTER
☎ (02) 65552552

AAA TOURISM **Special Rates** ★★★☆ **Lakesway Motor Inn**, (M), 26 The Lakes Way, 1.5km S of PO, ☎ 02 6554 8100, fax 02 6554 8480, (2 stry gr fl), 16 units [shwr, tlt, hairdry, fan, heat, tel, TV, video (avail), clock radio, t/c mkg, refrig, cook fac ltd], iron, iron brd, pool, bbq, dinner to unit, boat park, plygr, tennis (half court), cots, non smoking units (9). **RO ♦ $67 - $135, ♦♦ $67 - $135, ♦♦♦ $89 - $141**, AE BC MC VI.

★★★☆ **The Barkley Inn**, (M), 38 Head St, 200m from PO, ☎ 02 6555 2552, fax 02 6555 4801, (2 stry gr fl), 21 units [shwr, spa bath (7), tlt, hairdry, a/c, tel, fax, TV (satelite), video, movie, clock radio, t/c mkg, refrig, toaster], ldry, ✕, rm serv (b'fast), c/park. **RO ♦ $80, ♦♦ $88, ◊ $10**, AE BC DC MC.

★★★ **Great Lakes Motor Inn**, (M), Cnr West & Head Sts, 300m E of PO, ☎ 02 6554 6955, fax 02 6554 6955, (2 stry gr fl), 27 units [shwr, tlt, hairdry, fan, heat, elec blkts, tel, TV, video (avail), clock radio, t/c mkg, refrig, cook fac (4), toaster], ldry, iron, pool (salt water), bbq, cots-fee. **RO ♦ $45 - $80, ♦♦ $45 - $90, ♦♦♦ $63 - $95, ◊ $8**, AE BC DC EFT MC VI.

★★☆ **Island Palms Motor Inn**, (M), 115 The Lakes Way, 1.5km S of PO, ☎ 02 6554 5555, fax 02 6555 8835, 32 units [shwr, spa bath (8), tlt, fan, heat, tel, TV, movie, clock radio, t/c mkg, refrig, toaster], ldry, conv fac, ⊠, pool, dinner to unit, cots-fee, Min book Christmas Jan and Easter, AE BC DC MC VI.

★★☆ **Wallis Lake Motel**, (M), 5 Wallis St, 40m E of PO, ☎ 02 6555 5600, fax 02 6555 5600, 13 units [shwr, tlt, a/c-cool (7), fan, heat, tel, TV, clock radio, t/c mkg, refrig, cook fac (4), toaster], ldry, bbq, cots-fee. **RO ♦ $58 - $85, ♦♦ $60 - $95, ◊ $15**, BC MC VI.

Self Catering Accommodation

★★★★☆ **Beaches International**, (Apt), Cnr Head & Beach Sts, 200m N of PO, ☎ 02 6554 5160, fax 02 6555 9826, (Multi-stry), 10 apts acc up to 6, [shwr, spa bath, tlt, hairdry (1), c/fan, heat, cable tv (some), video, clock radio, t/c mkg, refrig, cook fac, micro, d/wash, toaster, ldry, doonas, linen], lift, w/mach, dryer, iron, iron brd, pool, spa, bbq, gym, non smoking units. **D $165 - $295, W $700 - $1,930**, BC MC VI.

Great Lakes Motor Inn

• 50m to Forster Main Beach and rock pool
• Walk to restaurants and shopping • Clubs nearby
• Salt water swimming pool • Family units available
• Guest BBQ in garden setting • All major credit cards accepted

24 HEAD ST, FORSTER, 2428
PH: (02) 6554 6955 FAX: (02) 6554 6955

LUXURY HOLIDAY ACCOMMODATION
1-5 Beach St, Forster NSW 2428

The 2 and 3 bedroom
fully self-contained apartments
all have large balconies offering glorious
ocean, harbour and lake views. These spacious
apartments are stylishly decorated and superbly
equipped. The visual security access leads you
into an elegant foyer with reception and
elevators to your room ℮

**BEACHES
INTERNATIONAL**

ph - 02 6554 5160 fax - 02 6555 9826
email - beachesinter@tpgi.com.au website - www.getnetted.com.au/beaches

AAA TOURISM ★ ★ ★ ★ ☆

★★★★☆ **Sails Apartments**, (HU), 7 Head St, 200m NE of PO, ☎ 02 6555 3700, fax 02 6555 9346, (Multi-stry), 18 units acc up to 6, (2 & 3 bedrm), [shwr, spa bath (4), tlt, tel, TV, video, clock radio, t/c mkg, refrig, cook fac, micro, blkts, doonas, linen, pillows], w/mach, dryer, pool, spa (communal), bbq, cots-fee, non smoking units. D ⚊ $165 - $175, ⚊⚊ $165 - $175, ⚊ $20, ch con, weekly con, BC EFT MC VI.

★★★★ **Coral Sands Holiday Apartments**, (HU), 96 Head St, 1km E of PO, ☎ 02 6554 8717, fax 02 6555 8664, 4 units acc up to 8, [shwr, bath, spa bath, tlt, heat, video, clock radio, refrig, cook fac, micro, elec frypan, d/wash, toaster, ldry, linen reqd-fee], w/mach, dryer, iron, bbq, c/park (garage), cots. D $80 - $150, W $290 - $1,670, Min book applies.

★★★★ **Horizons**, (HU), 8/84 Little St, 1km S of PO, ☎ 02 6554 8717, fax 02 6555 8664, (Multi-stry), 1 unit acc up to 6, [shwr, bath, tlt, fan, heat, TV, video, clock radio, refrig, cook fac, micro, elec frypan, d/wash, toaster, ldry, linen reqd-fee], lift, w/mach, dryer, iron, iron brd, bbq, c/park. D $80 - $130, W $470 - $1,250, Min book applies.

★★★☆ **Forster Gardens**, (HU), 1-5 Middle St, 400m SE of PO, ☎ 02 6554 6027, fax 02 6554 6027, 17 units acc up to 6, [shwr, tlt, c/fan, heat, TV, video, clock radio, t/c mkg, refrig, cook fac, micro, elec frypan, toaster, blkts, linen reqd-fee], ldry, iron, pool (s/water solar heated), bbq, ⚊ plygr, tennis (half court), cots, non smoking property. D $50, W $215 - $630, ch con, Min book applies, BC MC VI.

★★★☆ **Hi-Surf Holiday Apartments**, (HU), 92 Head St, 1km E of PO, ☎ 02 6554 8717, fax 02 6555 8664, 4 units acc up to 8, [shwr, bath, tlt, heat, TV, clock radio, refrig, cook fac, micro, elec frypan, d/wash, toaster, ldry, linen reqd-fee], w/mach, dryer, iron, bbq, c/park (garage), cots. D $70 - $130, W $290 - $1,300, Min book applies.

★★★☆ **Ocean Front Motor Lodge**, (SA), 22 North St, ☎ 02 6554 6587, fax 02 6555 2212, 8 serv apts acc up to 6, [shwr, tlt, hairdry, fan, heat, tel, TV, video, clock radio, t/c mkg, refrig, cook fac, micro, toaster, linen], ldry, iron, iron brd, bbq, plygr, cots. RO ⚊ $65 - $85, ⚊⚊ $85 - $150, ⚊ $10, ch con, AE BC MC VI.

★★★☆ **Sandbar Unit**, (HU), 1 Head St, 500m N of PO, ☎ 02 6554 8717, fax 02 6555 8664, 1 unit acc up to 6, [shwr, bath, tlt, heat, TV, clock radio, refrig, cook fac, micro, elec frypan, d/wash, toaster, ldry (in unit), linen reqd-fee], w/mach, dryer, iron, bbq, c/park (garage). W $280 - $800, Min book applies, AE.

★★★☆ **Twin Peaks Holiday Apartments**, (HU), 82 Head St, 1km E of PO, ☎ 02 6554 8717, fax 02 6555 8664, 3 units acc up to 8, [shwr, bath, tlt, heat, TV, clock radio, refrig, cook fac, micro, elec frypan, d/wash, toaster, ldry (in unit), linen reqd-fee], w/mach, dryer, iron, bbq, c/park (garage), cots. D $90 - $130, W $470 - $1,300, Min book applies.

★★★ **Blue Skies Holiday Units**, (HU), 17 West St, 150m N of PO, ☎ 02 6554 6899, (2 stry), 2 units acc up to 4, [shwr, tlt, fan, heat, TV, video, t/c mkg, refrig, cook fac, micro, elec frypan, toaster, ldry, doonas, linen], w/mach, dryer, iron, iron brd, c/park. D ⚊⚊ $45 - $55, ⚊ $10 - $12, W ⚊⚊ $140 - $380.

★★★ **Forster Holiday Villas**, (HU), 20 Bruce St, ☎ 02 6554 6837, fax 02 6554 6837, 13 units acc up to 6, [shwr, tlt, fan, heat, elec blkts, TV, video, clock radio, refrig, cook fac, micro, linen reqd-fee], ldry, pool (salt water), bbq, c/park (undercover), boat park, cots. D $55, W $190 - $900, Min book applies, AE BC MC VI.

★★★ **Gallipoli Court**, (HU), 6-12 Lake St, 1km W of PO, ☎ 02 6554 6264, fax 02 6555 8361, (2 stry gr fl), 18 units acc up to 6, [shwr, tlt, c/fan (6), heat, TV, clock radio, refrig, cook fac, micro, elec frypan, toaster, linen reqd], w/mach, dryer, iron, ⚊ W $220 - $813, Min book applies.

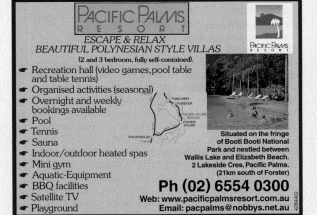

FORSTER NSW continued...

★★☆ **Ebbtide Units**, (HU), North St, 200m N of PO, ☎ 02 6554 6444, 5 units acc up to 6, [shwr, tlt, TV, video, refrig, cook fac, micro, ldry, linen reqd], w/mach, dryer, iron, pool, c/park. **W $225 - $880**, Min book applies, BC EFT MC VI.

★★☆ **Raffles**, (HU), 32 Bruce St, 1km S of PO, ☎ 02 6554 6444, fax 02 6555 6524, 2 units acc up to 6, [shwr, bath (1), tlt, heat, TV, video, clock radio, refrig, cook fac, micro, elec frypan, d/wash, toaster, ldry (in unit), linen reqd], dryer, iron, pool, bbq, c/park (garage). **W $220 - $735**, Min book applies, BC EFT MC VI.

★★ **Aaron Lodge**, (HF), Cnr Helen & MacIntosh Sts, 1.5km SE of PO, ☎ 02 6554 6444, 1 flat acc up to 5, [shwr, tlt, heat, TV, video, refrig, cook fac, micro, linen reqd], ldry, c/park (undercover). **W $145 - $485**, Min book applies, BC EFT MC VI.

★★ **Debra Court**, (HU), 20 North St, 250m from PO, ☎ 02 6554 6700, 3 units acc up to 5, [shwr, bath, tlt, TV, video, clock radio, t/c mkg, refrig, cook fac, micro, d/wash, toaster, blkts, linen reqd], w/mach, dryer, iron, iron brd, c/park. **D $230 - $700**.

★★ **Lakeshore Lodge**, (HU), 64 Little St, 700m S of PO, ☎ 02 6554 6444, 3 units acc up to 5, [shwr, tlt, heat, TV, video, refrig, cook fac, micro, ldry (in unit), linen reqd], w/mach, dryer, iron. **W $170 - $580**, Min book applies, BC EFT MC VI.

★★ **Riverside**, (HU), 4/40 Little St, 500m S of PO, ☎ 02 6554 6444, fax 02 6555 6524, 1 unit acc up to 5, [shwr, bath, tlt, heat, TV, video, refrig, cook fac, micro, elec frypan, toaster, ldry (in unit), linen reqd], dryer, iron, c/park (garage). **W $185 - $630**, Min book applies, BC EFT MC VI.

★★ **Riverview**, (HU), 42 Little St, 500m S of PO, ☎ 02 6554 6444, 1 unit acc up to 4, [shwr, bath, tlt, heat, TV, video, refrig, cook fac, micro, ldry (in unit), linen reqd], w/mach, dryer, iron, c/park (garage). **W $185 - $630**, Min book applies, BC EFT MC VI.

★★ **Wallis Court**, (HU), 44 Wallis St, 500m E of PO, ☎ 02 6554 6444, 1 unit acc up to 5, [shwr, bath, tlt, heat, TV, refrig, cook fac, ldry (in unit), linen reqd], w/mach, dryer, iron, c/park (garage). **W $190 - $660**, Min book applies, BC EFT MC VI.

★☆ **Carousel**, (HU), 6 Bruce St, ☎ 02 6554 6686, or 02 6552 9086, 6 units acc up to 5, [shwr, tlt, fan, heat, TV, refrig, cook fac, micro, toaster], ldry, w/mach, iron, bbq, cots-fee. **D $35 - $100, W $125 - $490**, Min book applies.

B&B's/Guest Houses

★★★☆ **The Tree Bed & Breakfast**, (B&B), 5 Sentry Cres, ☎ 02 6554 8365, 1 rm [shwr, tlt, hairdry, heat, elec blkts, tel, clock radio, t/c mkg, refrig, cook fac ltd, micro, toaster], ldry, iron, iron brd, lounge (tv & video), bbq, cots-fee. **BLB ╫ $40 - $60, ╫╫ $50 - $70, ◊ $10**.

★★★☆ **Tudor House Lodge**, (GH), 1 West St, 500m E of PO, ☎ 02 6554 8766, fax 02 6554 8453, (2 stry), 8 rms [shwr, bath, tlt, hairdry, c/fan, cent heat, tel, TV, clock radio, t/c mkg, refrig, mini bar], ✕, pool, sauna, spa, bbq, rm serv, dinner to unit, cots, Min book long w/ends and Easter, AE BC DC MC VI.

Lakeside Escape Bed and Breakfast, (B&B), 85 Green Point Drive, 10km S of PO, ☎ 02 6557 6400, fax 02 6557 6401, 3 rms [heat, fan, elec blkts, tel, video (lounge only), clock radio, t/c mkg (communal), refrig (communal)], lounge (TV), ✕, spa, rm serv (24 hr). **BB ╫ $100 - $125, ╫╫ $140 - $150, ◊ $100 - $125**, weekly con, BC MC VI, (not yet classified).

GATESHEAD NSW

See Newcastle & Suburbs.

GEORGETOWN NSW

See Newcastle & Suburbs.

GEROGERY NSW 2643

Pop Nominal, (548km SW Sydney), See map on pages 52/53, ref E7. Small town on the Olympic Highway between Albury and Culcairn. Scenic Drives.

B&B's/Guest Houses

★★★ **Table Top Mountain Retreat**, (B&B), 31km N of Albury, ☎ 02 6026 0529, fax 02 6026 0653, (2 stry gr fl), 3 rms [shwr (2), bath (1), tlt (2), fire pl, t/c mkg, refrig (2), cook fac (2)], lounge, ✕, pool (salt water), bbq, tennis, non smoking property. **BB ╫ $66 - $85**, ch con, BC MC VI.

GERRINGONG NSW 2534

Pop 2,900. (114km S Sydney), See map on page 55, ref C4. Pretty, popular tourist resort on the Illawarra coast south of Kiama. Boating, Bowls, Bush Walking, Scenic Drives, Squash, Surfing, Swimming, Tennis.

Hotels/Motels

★★★☆ **Seascape Manor**, (M), Fern St, 900m N of PO, ☎ 02 4234 1359, fax 02 4234 1495, 48 units (1 suite) [shwr, bath, spa bath (1), tlt, hairdry, a/c, elec blkts, tel, TV, video (avail), movie, clock radio, t/c mkg, refrig], iron, business centre, conv fac, ✉, pool (salt water), tennis, cots-fee. **RO ╫ $65, ╫╫ $80, ╫╫╫ $105, ◊ $25, Suite D ╫ $130, ╫╫ $150**, ch con, AE BC DC EFT MC VI, ﾤﾍ.

★★★ **Anchor Motel**, (M), 139 Belinda St, 50m S of PO, ☎ 02 4234 2222, fax 02 4234 0643, (Multi-stry gr fl), 29 units [shwr, bath (6), tlt, heat, elec blkts, tel, TV, video (avail), clock radio, t/c mkg, refrig, toaster], ldry, dinner to unit. **RO ╫ $55 - $90, ╫╫ $66 - $100, ╫╫╫ $77 - $110, ◊ $15**, AE BC DC MC VI, ﾤﾍ.

★★★ **Gerringong Motel Hotel**, (LMH), Cnr Belinda & Campbell Sts, 1km S of PO, ☎ 02 4234 1451, 16 units [shwr, tlt, a/c, TV, clock radio, t/c mkg, refrig]. **RO ╫ $66, ╫╫ $77, ◊ $10**, 6 units of a lower rating, AE BC EFT MC VI, ﾤﾍ.

GILGANDRA NSW 2827

Pop 2,800. (497km NW Sydney), See map on pages 52/53, ref G3. Gilgandra lies at the junction of the Newell, Castlereagh and Oxley Highways and is a handy base from which to explore the Warrumbungles. Bowls, Golf, Swimming, Tennis.

Hotels/Motels

★★★☆ **Cooee Motel**, (M), Cnr Newell Hwy & Hargraves La, 2km S of PO, ☎ 02 6847 2981, fax 02 6847 1511, 12 units [shwr, tlt, hairdry, a/c, elec blkts, tel, TV, clock radio, t/c mkg, refrig, toaster, ldry], iron, iron brd, bbq, dinner to unit, plygr, cots. **RO ╫ $49 - $54, ╫╫ $54 - $60, ◊ $10 - $12**, 3 units of a lower rating, AE BC DC EFT MC VI.

★★★☆ **Gilgandra Motel**, (M), 54 Warren Rd (Oxley Hwy), 50m E of PO, ☎ 02 6847 2500, fax 02 6847 2694, 24 units [shwr, tlt, a/c, elec blkts, tel, TV, clock radio, t/c mkg, refrig], ldry, ✉, pool, bbq, dinner to unit, plygr, cots. **RO ╫ $65, ╫╫ $73, ◊ $8**, ch con, AE BC DC EFT MC MP VI.

★★★☆ **Orana Windmill**, (M), 40 Warren Rd, 100m E of PO, ☎ 02 6847 2404, fax 02 6847 2844, 18 units [shwr, tlt, a/c, elec blkts, tel, TV, video-fee, clock radio, t/c mkg, refrig], ldry, ✕, pool (salt water), bbq, cots, non smoking units (6). **RO ╫ $56, ╫╫ $66, ╫╫╫ $78, ◊ $11**, ch con, 6 family units of a lower rating. AE BC DC EFT MC MCH VI.

★★★☆ **Three Ways Motel**, (M), Cnr Newell Hwy & Willie St, 200m SE of PO, ☎ 02 6847 2241, fax 02 6847 0122, 8 units [shwr, bath (2), tlt, hairdry, a/c, elec blkts, tel, fax, TV, video-fee, clock radio, t/c mkg, toaster], ldry, dinner to unit, cots. **RO ╫ $46.20 - $48.40, ╫╫ $52.80 - $55, ╫╫╫ $63.80 - $66, ◊ $11**, 2 family units of a lower rating. AE BC DC EFT MC MCH VI, ﾤﾍ.

★★★ **Alfa Motel**, (M), 7 Castlereagh St (Newell Hwy), 1km S of PO, ☎ 02 6847 1188, fax 02 6847 2154, 9 units [shwr, tlt, a/c, elec blkts, tel, TV, clock radio, t/c mkg, refrig, toaster], dinner to unit, c/park (undercover), cots-fee, non smoking units (3). **RO** ♦ $44 - $48, ♦♦ $50 - $55, ♦♦♦ $59 - $66, ◊ $9 - $10, ch con, BC MC VI.

★★★ **Castlereagh Motor Inn**, (M), Newell Hwy, 2.5km E of PO, ☎ 02 6847 2697, fax 02 6847 1537, 18 units [shwr, tlt, a/c-cool, heat, elec blkts, tel, TV, clock radio, t/c mkg, refrig, toaster], ldry, ⊠, rm serv, dinner to unit, car wash, cots-fee, non smoking rms (7). **RO** ♦ $48 - $53, ♦♦ $53 - $63, ♦♦♦ $68 - $73, ◊ $10, ch con, 3 rooms at a lower rating. AE BC DC EFT MC VI.

★★☆ **Akropolis Cafe & Accommodation**, (M), Coonamble Rd (Castlereagh Hwy), 2km N of PO, ☎ 02 6847 2636, fax 02 6847 2636, 6 units [shwr, tlt, a/c-cool, heat, elec blkts, TV, clock radio, t/c mkg, refrig, cook fac, toaster], ldry, bbq, ☎. **RO** ♦ $50, ♦♦ $55, ◊ $11, AE BC EFT MC VI, ⌂⚹.

★★☆ **Bungalow Motel**, (M), 19 Castlereagh St, ☎ 02 6847 1271, fax 02 6847 1879, 9 units [shwr, tlt, a/c, elec blkts, TV, clock radio, t/c mkg, refrig, toaster], bbq, cots-fee, non smoking units. **RO** ♦ $44 - $48, ♦♦ $46 - $56, ◊ $10, 3 rooms at a lower rating. AE BC EFT MC VI.

★★☆ **Gilgandra Lodge**, (M), 178 Warren Rd, 2km W of PO, ☎ 02 6847 2431, 8 units [shwr, tlt, a/c, elec blkts, TV, clock radio, t/c mkg, refrig, cook fac, toaster], ldry, pool, bbq, c/park (undercover). **RO** ♦ $42, ♦♦ $46, ◊ $8, BC MC VI.

★★☆ **Silver Oaks Motel**, (M), 1 Castlereagh St, 1km S of PO, ☎ 02 6847 0111, fax 02 6847 1375, 21 units [shwr, tlt, a/c, elec blkts, tel, TV, radio, t/c mkg, refrig, toaster, ldry], ⊠, pool, bbq, dinner to unit, cots-fee. **RO** ♦ $46 - $52, ♦♦ $49 - $58, ◊ $8 - $11, ch con, AE BC DC EFT MC VI.

★★☆ **The Village Motor Inn**, (M), Dubbo Rd, 2km S of PO, ☎ 02 6847 1433, fax 02 6847 2096, 31 units [shwr, tlt, a/c, elec blkts, TV, clock radio, t/c mkg, refrig, toaster, doonas], ⊠, pool, non smoking units (11). **RO** ♦ $40 - $45, ♦♦ $42 - $48, ♦♦♦ $51 - $60, ◊ $9 - $11, AE BC DC EFT MC VI.

B&B's/Guest Houses

★★☆ **Annas Place**, (B&B), 13 Morris St, ☎ 02 6847 2790, 2 rms [shwr, tlt, a/c-cool, c/fan, heat, elec blkts, TV, video, clock radio, t/c mkg, refrig, micro, toaster], pool-heated (solar), bbq, dinner to unit, cots, Pets allowed. **BB** ♦ $50, ♦♦ $90, ◊ $10 - $20, ch con.

★★☆ **Wyanna Farmstay Bed & Breakfast**, (B&B), 'Wyanna' Bearburg Rd, 32km NE of PO, ☎ 02 6848 8246, fax 02 6848 8246, 3 rms [shwr, tlt, evap cool, fan, heat, elec blkts, TV, clock radio, t/c mkg], lounge, ✕, bbq, cots. **BB** ♦ $55, ♦♦ $88, ♦♦♦♦ $110, Dinner by arrangement.

GLEN INNES NSW 2370

Pop 6,100. (667km N Sydney), See map on page 54, ref B3. Glen Innes is a New England town with strong Celtic associations, set in what's popularly known as 'Celtic Country'. Bowls, Gem Fossicking, Golf, Scenic Drives, Swimming.

Hotels/Motels

★★★☆ **Central Motel**, (M), Meade St, opposite PO, ☎ 02 6732 2200, or 02 6732 5607, fax 02 6732 1624, 16 units [shwr, tlt, hairdry, a/c, elec blkts, tel, cable tv, clock radio, t/c mkg, refrig], dinner to unit, cots-fee, non smoking units (5). **RO** ♦ $66, ♦♦ $72, ♦♦♦ $81, ◊ $9, AE BC DC EFT MC VI.

★★★☆ **Clansman Motel**, (M), New England Hwy, 2km S of PO, ☎ 02 6732 2044, fax 02 6732 5633, 12 units [shwr, tlt, fan, heat, elec blkts, tel, TV, clock radio, t/c mkg, refrig], ldry, ✕, dinner to unit, c/park (undercover), cots-fee, non smoking units (8). **RO** ♦ $68, ♦♦ $80, ♦♦♦ $92, ◊ $12, AE BC DC EFT MC VI.

★★★☆ **Glen Masterson Motel**, (M), 12 Church St (New England Hwy), 2km S of PO, ☎ 02 6732 1211, fax 02 6732 3110, 15 units [shwr, tlt, a/c, elec blkts, tel, TV, video, clock radio, t/c mkg, refrig, toaster], ldry, ✕, bbq, dinner to unit, cots-fee, non smoking rms (6). **RO** ♦ $50 - $55, ♦♦ $66 - $74, ◊ $8, AE BC DC EFT MC VI.

★★★☆ **New England Motor Lodge**, (M), Church St (New England Hwy), 100m N of PO, ☎ 02 6732 2922, fax 02 6732 2509, 38 units [shwr, spa bath (3), tlt, hairdry, evap cool (11), cent heat, elec blkts, tel, fax, TV, video (5), movie, clock radio, t/c mkg, refrig], ldry, ✕ (6 days), pool (salt water), spa, dinner to unit. **RO** ♦ $75 - $107, ♦♦ $80 - $120, ♦♦♦ $93 - $103, 5 units ★★★★, 9 units of 3 star rating. AE BC DC EFT MC MP VI.

★★★☆ **Rest Point Motel**, (M), Church St (New England Hwy), 1km S of PO, ☎ 02 6732 2255, fax 02 6732 1515, 25 units [shwr, spa bath (6), tlt, c/fan, heat, elec blkts, tel, cable tv, video (4), clock radio, t/c mkg, refrig], ldry, ✕, pool (salt water), spa, bbq, dinner to unit, plygr, cots. **RO** ♦ $79.20, ♦♦ $86.90, ◊ $11, AE BC DC MC MP VI.

Operator Comment: See advertisement on following page.

★★★ **Alpha Motel**, (M), New England Hwy, 1km S of PO, ☎ 02 6732 2688, fax 02 6732 4200, 15 units [shwr, tlt, heat, elec blkts, tel, TV, video (6), clock radio, t/c mkg, refrig], pool-heated (solar), bbq, dinner to unit, plygr, cots. **BLB** ♦ $55, ♦♦ $66, ♦♦♦ $77, ◊ $11, ch con, 6 units of a lower rating, AE BC DC EFT MC MP VI.

★★★ **Glen Haven Motor Inn**, (M), Cnr New England Hwy & Heron St, 2km S of PO, ☎ 02 6732 3266, fax 02 6732 3146, 14 units [shwr, spa bath (1), tlt, fan (14), cent heat, elec blkts, tel, TV, video (3), clock radio, t/c mkg, refrig], dinner to unit, cots-fee, non smoking units (3). **RO** ♦ $50 - $55, ♦♦ $58 - $63, ◊ $8, AE BC DC EFT MC MCH VI.

★★★ Jillaroo Motor Inn, (M), New England Hwy, 2km S of PO, ☎ 02 6732 3388, fax 02 6732 3378, 12 units [shwr, spa bath (1), tlt, a/c (2), c/fan (10), heat, elec blkts, tel, TV, clock radio, t/c mkg, refrig, toaster], bbq, dinner to unit, c/park (undercover), car wash, plygr, cots-fee, non smoking units (3). **RO** ♦ $50 - $52, ♦♦ $60 - $62, ♦♦♦ $68, ◊ $8, AE BC DC EFT MC MCH VI.

★★☆ Amber Motel, (M), 135 Meade St, 75m E of PO, ☎ 02 6732 2300, fax 02 6732 2423, 17 units [shwr, tlt, fan, heat, elec blkts, tel, TV, clock radio, t/c mkg, refrig], pool, bbq, cots. **RO** ♦ $50 - $56, ♦♦ $55 - $65, ◊ $8, 6 units ★★. AE BC DC EFT MC VI.

★☆ New Tattersalls, (LMH), Grey St, Off highway, ☎ 02 6732 3109, 33 units [shwr, tlt, a/c (2), fan, heat, elec blkts, tel (20), TV, clock radio, t/c mkg, refrig], ldry, conv fac, lounge firepl, ✕ (Mon to Sat). **RO** ♦ $41.80 - $49.50, ♦♦ $52.80 - $61.60, ◊ $5, 10 units ★★☆, A E BC DC MC VI.

B&B's/Guest Houses
★★★☆ Casa Del Banco, (B&B), 251B Grey St, ☎ 02 6732 5994, fax 02 6732 5996, (2 stry), 3 rms [shwr (1), spa bath (1), tlt (1), evap cool (1), fire pl, tel, TV (2), video (1)], ldry, lounge firepl, ✕, t/c mkg shared, non smoking property. **BB** ♦ $50 - $75, ♦♦ $100 - $120, ◊ $45, **DBB** ♦ $70 - $135, ♦♦ $140 - $160, ◊ $70.

GLENIFFER NSW 2454

Pop Nominal, (558km N Sydney), See map on page 54, ref C5. Rural locality on Never Never Creek, flanked by forests and the majestic Dorrigo escarpment. Bush Walking, Scenic Drives.

B&B's/Guest Houses
★★★☆ Blue Gum, (B&B), 770 Gleniffer, Rd Gleninffer via, Bellingen 2454, ☎ 02 6655 1592, 2 rms [shwr (1), tlt (1), hairdry, c/fan, heat, elec blkts, tel, TV, radio, t/c mkg, refrig, cook fac, micro, elec frypan, toaster], ldry, lounge (TV), bbq, c/park (carport), bicycle. **BB** ♦ $60 - $66, ♦♦ $85 - $94, ◊ $30, W ♦ $360 - $396, ♦♦ $510 - $560, ◊ $180 - $198, ch con.

GLOUCESTER NSW 2422

Pop 2,650. (468km N Sydney), See map on page 54, ref B7. Prosperous little town known as the eastern gateway to the Barrington Tops. Bowls, Bush Walking, Fishing, Golf, Shooting, Squash, Swimming, Tennis.

Hotels/Motels
★★★★ Gloucester Country Lodge, (M), Bucketts Way, 2km S of PO, ☎ 02 6558 1812, fax 02 6558 1411, 25 units [shwr, tlt, c/fan, heat, elec blkts, tel, TV, clock radio, t/c mkg, refrig, toaster], ldry, conv fac, pool (salt water), bbq, dinner to unit, non smoking units (13). **RO** ♦ $68 - $78, ♦♦ $80 - $90, ♦♦♦ $90 - $100, ◊ $11, Min book long w/ends, AE BC DC EFT MC VI.

★★★☆ Bucketts Way Motel, (M), 19 Church St, 200m W of PO, ☎ 02 6558 2588, fax 02 6558 1998, (2 stry gr fl), 28 units [shwr, tlt, cent heat, tel, TV, video (avail), clock radio, t/c mkg, refrig], ✕, pool, spa, bbq, rm serv (incl liquor), dinner to unit, cots. **RO** ♦ $65, ♦♦ $76, ◊ $11, AE BC DC MC VI.

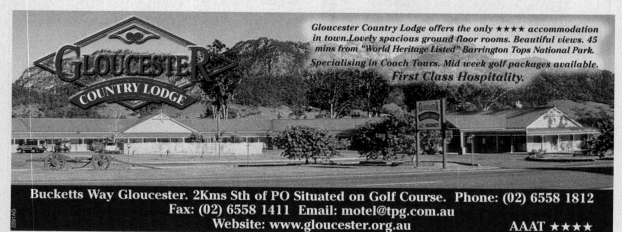

Bucketts Way MOTEL

The Bucketts Way MOTEL
Licensed RESTAURANT

OPEN • **WALK TO SHOPS, CLUBS, PARKS & SPORTS FACILITIES**

ONLY MOTEL IN THE CENTRE OF TOWN!

LICENSED THUNDERBOLT'S RESTAURANT & BAR - OPEN 7 DAYS
28 air conditioned rooms • central heating • direct dial phones
free pay TV • remote colour TVs • pool & spa • children's wading pool
room service seven days • dinner, bed & breakfast packages
specialising in group coach tours • Canoe & bike hire • Adventure tours
Email: bucketts@tpg.com.au

19 Church St
GLOUCESTER   **PH 02 6558 2588**   Facsimile:
02 6558 1998

Self Catering Accommodation

★★★★★ **The Great Escape Lofts**, (SA), 40-42 Hume St, 400m S of PO, ☎ 02 6558 9166, fax 02 6558 9177, 8 serv apts acc up to 4, [shwr, spa bath, tlt, hairdry, a/c, heat, elec blkts, tel, TV, video, clock radio, CD, t/c mkg, refrig, cook fac, micro, d/wash, toaster, doonas, linen], ldry, iron, iron brd, pool (salt water), spa, courtesy transfer, cots, non smoking property. **D $165, W ♥♥ $945**, ch con, AE BC DC EFT MC VI.

★★★☆ **Ashmar Country Cottage**, (Cotg), (Farm), 1581 Waukivory Rd, Waukivory, 15km SE of Gloucester, ☎ 02 6558 0949, 1 cotg acc up to 9, [shwr, tlt, hairdry, fan, fire pl, elec blkts, tel, TV, movie, clock radio, CD, t/c mkg, refrig, cook fac, micro, elec frypan, toaster, ldry (in unit), blkts, linen, pillows], w/mach, dryer, iron, ✕, bbq, meals avail, plygr, cots. **BB ♥♥ $120, DBB ♥♥ $164, D ♥ $99, ◊ $38 - $50.**

★★★☆ **Gloucester River Getaways**, (HU), 2 Church St, 200m N of PO, ☎ 02 6558 1528, 7 units acc up to 8, [shwr, bath, tlt, hairdry, a/c, c/fan (5), elec blkts, TV, video-fee, movie, clock radio, t/c mkg, refrig, cook fac, micro, elec frypan, d/wash (1), toaster, blkts, doonas, linen, pillows], w/mach, dryer, iron, iron brd, conf fac, bbq, courtesy transfer, cots-fee, non smoking property. **D ♥♥ $110, ◊ $20 - $25**, ch con, fam con, weekly con, BC EFT MC VI.

B&B's/Guest Houses

★★★★☆ **Hookes Creek Forest Resort**, (GH), 1800 Scone Rd, 36km W of PO, ☎ 02 6558 5544, fax 02 6558 5552, 10 rms (10 suites) [shwr, spa bath, tlt, hairdry, c/fan, fire pl (open), tel, TV, video, clock radio, CD, t/c mkg, refrig], ldry, ✕, pool, plygr, bush walking, bicycle, tennis, cots. **D all meals ♥♥ $340 - $420**, ch con, AE BC DC MC VI.

★★★★☆ **Peglynton Lodge Country Retreat**, (B&B), 127 Kia-Ora Rd, ☎ 02 6558 2582, fax 02 6558 2788, 3 rms [shwr, bath (1), tlt, hairdry, a/c (8), fire pl (2), heat, tel], ldry, iron, iron brd, rec rm, TV rm, lounge firepl, ✕, t/c mkg shared, bbq, courtesy transfer, plygr, cots, non smoking rms. **BB ♥ $70, ♥♥ $120 - $145, ◊ $30**, ch con, BC MC VI.

★★★★ **Barkeldine Farm Bed & Breakfast & The Cottage**, (B&B), 1177 Wallanbah Rd, 25km E of Gloucester, ☎ 02 6558 0222, fax 02 6558 0248, 3 rms [shwr (1), bath (1), tlt (2), hairdry (2), c/fan, heat, tel, clock radio (2)], lounge (TV), lounge firepl, ✕, pool (salt water), t/c mkg shared, refrig, bbq, tennis (half court), cots, non smoking property. **BB ♥ $80 - $120, ♥♥ $99.50 - $121**, ch con, pen con, BC MC VI.

★★★☆ **(Cottage Section)**, 1 cotg [shwr (2), tlt (2), fan, heat, tel, video, t/c mkg, refrig, cook fac, micro, elec frypan, d/wash, toaster, ldry, blkts, linen], w/mach, dryer, iron, iron brd, lounge firepl, cots, non smoking property. **D ♥ $104.50, ♥♥ $104.50, W ♥ $500, ♥♥ $500, Min book all holiday times.**

★★★★ **Valley View Bed & Breakfast**, (B&B), 1783 Bucketts Way, Wards River 2422, 20km from Gloucester, ☎ 02 4994 7066, fax 02 4994 7066, 3 rms (2 suites) [ensuite (1), hairdry (1), fan, c/fan (3), heat (1), tel, TV, clock radio, t/c mkg (2), refrig (2), cook fac (2), micro (2), toaster (2)], shared fac (4), ldry, iron, iron brd, rec rm, lounge, lounge firepl, ✕, pool (salt water), t/c mkg shared, refrig, bbq, cots. **BB ♥ $50, ♥♥ $90 - $100, ◊ $50**, ch con, 1 cottage ★★★★. MC VI.

★★★☆ **Gloucester Cottage Bed and Breakfast**, (B&B), 61 Denison St, 400m SE of PO, ☎ 02 6558 2658, fax 02 6558 2658, 3 rms [shwr (2), bath (1), tlt (2), hairdry (2), c/fan, heat, elec blkts, tel], lounge firepl (TV), c/park. **BB ♥ $50, ♥♥ $75**, ch con.

★★★ **Altamira Holiday Ranch**, (GH), (Farm), Bakers Creek Rd, 29km NE of PO, ☎ 02 6550 6558, fax 02 6550 6463, 20 rms [shwr, tlt, fan, elec blkts, t/c mkg, refrig], rec rm, lounge (TV), ✕, bar, pool, spa, bush walking, tennis, cots. **D all meals ♥ $137.50**, ch con, Min book applies, BC MC VI.

Other Accommodation

★★★ **Never-Never Lodge**, (Lodge), (Farm), 689 Manchester Rd via Barrington West Rd, 25km SW of Gloucester, ☎ 02 6558 1615, fax 02 6558 1615, 1 rm acc up to 10, [shwr, tlt, hairdry, c/fan, fire pl, t/c mkg, refrig, cook fac, micro, elec frypan, toaster, ldry, blkts, linen, pillows], w/mach, iron, lounge (TV & video), bbq, cots. **BB ♥♥ $80 - $100, ◊ $25, W ♥♥ $500, ◊ $140**, ch con, Min book applies.

GOL GOL NSW 2738

Pop 600. (1016km W Sydney), See map on pages 52/53, ref B5. Murray River township on the Sturt Highway near Mildura. Boating, Bowls, Fishing, Golf, Horse Riding, Scenic Drives, Swimming, Tennis, Water Skiing.

Hotels/Motels

Budget Motel Chain International

★★☆ **Mildura Riverside Motel**, (M), Cnr King & Adelaide Sts, 5km NE of Mildura, ☎ 03 5024 8778, fax 03 5024 8779, (2 stry gr fl), 19 units [shwr, tlt, a/c, elec blkts, tel, TV, movie, clock radio, t/c mkg, refrig, toaster], ldry, pool (salt water), bbq, dinner to unit, c/park. **RO ♥ $50 - $85, ♥♥ $60 - $85, ◊ $9**, AE BC DC EFT MC MCH VI, ⚹&.

GOODOOGA NSW 2831

Pop 400. (854km NW Sydney), See map on pages 52/53, ref F1. Small town on the Bokhara River, not far from the opal fields of Lightning Ridge.

Hotels/Motels

Telegraph Motel Hotel, (LMH), Adam St, 200m N of PO, ☎ 02 6829 6222, 4 units [shwr, tlt, a/c, elec blkts, tel, TV, clock radio, t/c mkg, refrig], ldry, ✕, bbq, rm serv, dinner to unit, c/park. **RO ♥ $44, ♥♥ $66, ♥♥♥ $88.**

GOOLGOWI NSW 2652

Pop 300. (617km W Sydney), See map on pages 52/53, ref D5. Small Riverina township at the junction of the Mid-Western Highway and the Kidman Way. Bowls, Bush Walking, Tennis.

Hotels/Motels

Highway Motel, (M), Lot 5 Zara St, 500m N of PO, ☎ 02 6965 1445, (2 stry gr fl), 12 units [shwr, tlt, a/c, TV, video, t/c mkg, refrig], ldry, ✕, cook fac, dinner to unit, c/park. **RO ♥ $55, ♥♥ $66, ◊ $10**, ch con, BC EFT MC VI.

GOOLMANGAR NSW 2480

Pop Nominal, (760km N Sydney), See map on page 54, ref D2. Small village on the far north coast between Lismore and Nimbin.

Hotels/Motels

★★★ **Klassic Lodge Country Retreat**, (M), 1597 Nimbin Rd, 16km N of Lismore, ☎ 02 6689 9350, fax 0 6689 9240, 11 units [shwr, tlt, hairdry, a/c, c/fan, heat, tel, TV, clock radio, t/c mkg, refrig], ldry, ✕, pool (salt water), spa, bbq, c/park (undercover), ✆, plygr, bush walking, cots-fee. **RO ♥ $65**, ch con, BC MC VI.

(Unit Section), 6 units acc up to 4, [shwr, tlt, a/c-cool, c/fan, tel, TV, clock radio, t/c mkg, refrig, cook fac, elec frypan, toaster, blkts, linen, pillows], ldry. **D $80.**

GOROKAN NSW 2263

Pop 8,850. Part of Wyong, (107km N Sydney), See map on page 55, ref D5. Central Coast town between Lake Budgewoi and Tuggerah Lake near the Wallarah Point Bridge. Boating, Bowls, Bush Walking, Fishing, Golf, Horse Riding, Sailing, Scenic Drives, Surfing, Swimming, Tennis, Water Skiing.

Hotels/Motels

★★★★ **Palms Reception Centre & Motel**, (LMH), 155-157 Wallarah Rd, ☎ 02 4393 2224, fax 02 4393 2397, 18 units [shwr, bath (17), spa bath (1), tlt, hairdry, a/c, c/fan (4), elec blkts, tel, cable tv, video (avail), clock radio, t/c mkg, refrig, cook fac (4), toaster], ldry-fee, iron, iron brd, ✕ (Tue & Sat), pool (salt water), bbq, cots. **RO ♥ $80 - $90, ♥♥ $80 - $100, ◊ $15**, fam con, AE BC DC MC VI, ⚹&.

GOROKAN NSW continued...

★★★☆ **Bridge View Motel**, (M), Cnr Wallarah Rd & The Corso, ☎ 02 4392 3355, fax 02 4392 3018, (2 stry gr fl), 18 units (1 suite) [shwr, tlt, hairdry, a/c, tel, TV, video-fee, clock radio, t/c mkg, refrig, toaster], ldry, pool, bbq, cots-fee, non smoking units (7). RO ♦ $66 - $85, ♦♦ $66 - $100, ♦ $10, Suite D $115 - $160, AE BC DC EFT MC VI.

★★★☆ **Tuggerah Lakes Motel**, (M), 54 Wallarah Rd, 100m from Masonic Club, ☎ 02 4392 3911, fax 02 4392 3011, 10 units [shwr, tlt, a/c, tel, TV, clock radio, t/c mkg, refrig], pool, bbq, cots-fee. RO ♦ $50 - $88, ♦♦ $60 - $99, ♦♦♦ $70 - $110, ♦♦♦♦ $80 - $132, AE BC DC MC VI.

Bridge View Motel

- Air Conditioned • Queen Size Available • Walk to Club
- 2 Bedroom Suite • Children's Playground & Park Opposite
- Non-Smoking Units • In House Movies & Video Available
- Pool & Barbecue • Remote TV • 18 Refurbished Rooms

AAA Tourism ★★★☆

Midweek Package Deals

Cnr Wallarah Road & The Corso, GOROKAN 2263
Phone: (02) 4392 3355   Fax: (02) 4392 3018
www.bridgeviewmotel.com.au
Email: reception@bridgeviewmotel.com.au
2304ag

Trouble-free travel tips - **Tyre pressures**
Check tyre pressures and set them to the manufacturer's recommendation, including the spare.
The specifications can generally be found on the tyre placard located in either the glove box or on the front door frame.

GOSFORD NSW 2250

Pop 128,956. (75km N Sydney). See map on page 56, ref E3. The major centre and bustling metropolis at the heart of the Central Coast. Boating, Bowls, Fishing, Golf, Sailing, Scenic Drives, Swimming, Tennis. See also Narara.

Hotels/Motels

★★★☆ **Bermuda Motor Inn**, (M), Cnr Henry Parry Dve & Pacific Hwy, ☎ 02 4324 4366, fax 02 4324 4055, 17 units [shwr, tlt, a/c, heat, tel, TV, clock radio, t/c mkg, refrig], ldry, pool, bbq, plygr, cots-fee. RO ♦ $66 - $85, ♦♦ $66 - $95, ♦♦♦ $95 - $107, ♦♦♦♦ $88 - $110, ♦ $13, fam con, 6 units ★★☆, AE BC DC MC MCH VI.

★★★☆ **Galaxy Motel**, (M), 26 Pacific Hwy, 2km W of PO, ☎ 02 4323 1711, fax 02 4322 0409, (2 stry gr fl), 49 units [shwr, bath (3), tlt, a/c, tel, TV, clock radio, t/c mkg, refrig], ldry, conf fac, ⊠, pool-heated (salt water), bbq, dinner to unit, plygr, cots-fee. RO ♦ $71 - $85, ♦♦ $83 - $94, ♦♦♦ $92 - $103, ♦♦♦♦ $101 - $112, ♦ $9, AE BC DC EFT MC VI, ♿.

Bermuda Motor Inn

Recently upgraded throughout plus
Foxtel (FREE)
★★★☆ AAA Tourism

Centrally located to:
Restaurants,
Hospitals,
Railway Station,
Tennis Courts,
Clubs, Shopping
Centres

Corner of Pacific Highway and Henry Parry Drive, Gosford North, 2250
PHONE: (02) 4324 4366; FAX: (02) 4324 4055
2309AG

GALAXY MOTEL

GALAXY MOTEL

Centrally located. Adjacent to and owned by Gosford RSL Club. 1 hour to Sydney and Newcastle by car or train.

Catering for all Corporate Business needs ... while also ideal for relaxed Family Group gatherings

26 PACIFIC HWY, GOSFORD WEST
PH: 02 4323 1711 FAX: 02 4322 0409
2313AG

AVOID THE SYDNEY TRAFFIC
Leave your car with us and enjoy the scenic air-conditioned hourly train ride to SYDNEY.

GOSFORD MOTOR INN

Best Western
Be our guest.

★★★☆
AAA Tourism

Phone: (02) 4323 1333
Fax: (02) 4323 3030
23 PACIFIC HIGHWAY
GOSFORD 2250
Sydney side of Gosford.
Easy walk to town
& Northpower Stadium

Discover Gosford's Water Wonderland.
3 Day Package Includes:

■ 3 nights luxury accommodation with panoramic waterviews together with 3 full hot breakfasts
■ Dinner 2 nights – different first class restaurants – each with magnificent water views
■ Fully narrated cruise on the Brisbane Waters

SPECIAL PRICE $209
per person twin share subject to availability

★★★☆ **Gosford Motor Inn**, (M), 23 Pacific Hwy, ☎ 02 4323 1333, fax 02 4323 3030, (2 stry gr fl), 36 units [shwr, bath (2), tlt, hairdry, a/c, heat, elec blkts, tel, TV, movie, clock radio, t/c mkg, refrig], ldry, lounge, pool-heated (solar), cook fac, bbq, dinner to unit, cots-fee, non smoking units (11). **RO** ♦ **$89.50 - $98.50**, ♦♦ **$94 - $103**, ◊ **$12**, ch con, AE BC DC EFT JCB MC MP VI.

★★★☆ **Gosford Palms Motor Inn**, (M), 7 Moore St, ☎ 02 4323 1211, fax 02 4323 4558, (2 stry gr fl), 18 units [shwr, tlt, hairdry, a/c, elec blkts, tel, cable tv, video-fee, clock radio, t/c mkg, refrig], ldry, iron, iron brd, pool (salt water), bbq, courtesy transfer, cots-fee, non smoking units (2). **RO** ♦ **$77 - $99**, ♦♦ **$80 - $99**, ♦♦♦ **$92 - $105**, ◊ **$12**, ch con, AE BC DC MC VI, ♿.

FLAG CHOICE HOTELS METRO INNS

★★★☆ **Metro Motor Inn Gosford**, (M), 512 Pacific Hwy, Gosford North 2250, ☎ 02 4328 4666, fax 02 4328 5787, (2 stry), 50 units (4 suites) [shwr, bath (22), spa bath (2), tlt, hairdry, a/c, elec blkts, tel, TV, video (7), movie, clock radio, t/c mkg, refrig, mini bar (25), cook fac (4), toaster], ldry, iron, conv fac, ✉, pool (salt water), spa, bbq, rm serv, dinner to unit, ☏, cots. **RO** ♦ **$96**, ♦♦ **$105**, ch con, 2 units of a lower rating. AE BC DC MC MP VI, ♿.

GOLDEN CHAIN

★★★☆ **Reeces Olympic**, (M), Masons Pde, 1km SE of PO, ☎ 02 4324 7377, fax 02 4323 4213, 29 units [shwr, bath (5), tlt, a/c, elec blkts, tel, TV, clock radio, t/c mkg, refrig], ldry, pool (salt water), spa, cook fac, bbq, cots-fee, non smoking units (14). **RO** ♦ **$77 - $95**, ♦♦ **$82 - $110**, ♦♦♦ **$94 - $120**, ◊ **$15**, AE BC DC MC VI.

★★★ **Rambler Motor Inn**, (M), 73 Pacific Hwy, 2km W of PO, ☎ 02 4324 6577, fax 02 4325 1780, 55 units [shwr, tlt, a/c, heat, elec blkts, tel, TV, clock radio, t/c mkg, refrig, toaster], pool, spa, bbq, plygr, non smoking units (27). **RO** ♦ **$60.50 - $82.50**, ♦♦ **$71.50 - $99**, ◊ **$11**, 13 units of a lower rating. AE BC DC EFT MC VI, ♿.

★★★ **Terranova Park Motel**, (M), 733 Pacific Hwy, Niagara Park, 5km N of PO, ☎ 02 4328 1222, fax 02 4329 1211, (2 stry gr fl), 28 units [shwr, tlt, a/c-cool, heat, elec blkts, tel, TV, clock radio, t/c mkg, refrig], conv fac, ✉, pool, rm serv, dinner to unit. **RO** ♦ **$55 - $80**, ♦♦ **$60 - $90**, ♦♦♦ **$70 - $95**, ◊ **$10 - $15**, 14 units of a lower rating. AE BC DC MC VI.

★★☆ **Bella Vista Motel**, (M), 5 Pacific Hwy, Kariong, ☎ 02 4340 1108, or 02 4340 1173, fax 02 4340 2250, (2 stry gr fl), 24 units [shwr, tlt, a/c, elec blkts, tel, TV, video-fee, clock radio, t/c mkg, refrig], ldry, ✉, pool, cots, non smoking units (6). **RO** ♦ **$65 - $85**, ♦♦ **$65 - $85**, ♦♦♦ **$75 - $105**, ◊ **$10**, ch con, AE BC DC MC VI.

★★☆ **Hotel Gosford**, (LH), 179 Mann St, 100m W of PO, ☎ 02 4324 1634, fax 02 4323 7150, (Multi-stry), 31 rms [shwr (4), tlt (per floor) (4), fan, elec blkts, TV, t/c mkg], lift. **RO** ♦ **$45**, ♦♦ **$64 - $72**, Min book applies, BC MC VI.

★★☆ **Villa Sorgenti Motel**, (M), Kowara Rd, off Debenham Rd, Somersby 2250, 2km W of West Gosford PO, ☎ 02 4340 1205, fax 02 4340 2758, 8 units [shwr, tlt, a/c, elec blkts, tel, TV, clock radio, t/c mkg, refrig], ✉, pool. **RO** ♦ **$60 - $71**, ♦♦ **$71 - $82**, ◊ **$11**, AE BC DC MC VI.

GOULBURN NSW 2580

Pop 21,300. (177km S Sydney), See map on page 55, ref A4. Known as the 'City of Roses', Goulburn has the distinction of being Australia's first inland city, declared as such by Queen Victoria on 14 March 1863. Bowls, Bush Walking, Fishing, Golf, Horse Racing, Scenic Drives, Swimming, Tennis.

Hotels/Motels

AAA TOURISM Special Rates Best Western

★★★★☆ **Best Western Centretown Goulburn**, (M), 77 Lagoon St, ☎ 02 4821 2422, fax 02 4821 9910, 37 units (12 suites) [shwr, bath (22), spa bath (12), tlt, hairdry, a/c, tel, video, movie, clock radio, t/c mkg, refrig, micro (25), toaster], ldry, iron, iron brd, business centre, conv fac, lounge firepl, ✉, pool indoor heated, spa, rm serv, cots-fee, non smoking units (21). **RO** ♦ **$75 - $131**, ♦♦ **$87 - $142**, ♦♦♦ **$115 - $153**, ◊ **$11**, **Suite RO** ♦ **$137 - $219**, ♦♦ **$148 - $230**, ◊ **$11**, 11 units ★★★☆, AE BC DC EFT JCB MC MP VI, ♿.

★★★☆ **(Cottage Section)**, 3 cotgs [shwr, tlt, a/c, heat, tel, TV, video, clock radio, t/c mkg, refrig, cook fac (2), micro, toaster], ldry, rm serv. **RO** ♦ **$137 - $169**, ♦♦ **$148 - $180**, ♦♦♦ **$159 - $191**, ◊ **$11**.
Operator Comment: See advertisement on following page.

Best Western

★★★★ **A Trappers Motor Inn**, (M), 2 Lockyer St, ☎ 02 4822 5445, fax 02 4822 5440, 39 units [shwr, bath (2), spa bath (4), tlt, hairdry, a/c, elec blkts, tel, cable tv, video-fee, clock radio, t/c mkg, refrig, mini bar, toaster], ldry, iron (10), iron brd (10), conf fac, lounge firepl, ✉, pool indoor heated, bbq, rm serv, dinner to unit, cots-fee, non smoking rms (21). **RO** ♦ **$82 - $125**, ♦♦ **$92 - $135**, ♦♦♦ **$125**, pen con, AE BC DC EFT MC VI.
Operator Comment: See advertisement on following page.

AAA TOURISM *Special Rates* **FLAG** FLAG CHOICE HOTELS

★★★★
Goulburn Heritage Motor Lodge, (M), Hume Hwy, 5km N of PO, ☎ 02 4821 9377, fax 02 4821 5991, (2 stry gr fl), 41 units [shwr, spa bath (5), tlt, hairdry, a/c, elec blkts, tel, TV, video (avail), clock radio, t/c mkg, refrig, mini bar], conv fac, ⌧, sauna, rm serv, dinner to unit, gym, cots-fee, non smoking units (6). **RO** ♦ **$88 - $100**, ♦♦ **$100 - $110**, ch con, AE BC DC EFT MC MP VI, 戊.

Quality FLAG CHOICE HOTELS
★★★★ **Posthouse Motor Lodge**, (M), 1 Lagoon St (Hume Hwy), 500m N of PO, ☎ 02 4821 5666, fax 02 4821 9975, (2 stry gr fl), 38 units (1 suite) [shwr, bath (3), spa bath (2), tlt, a/c-cool, cent heat, tel, cable tv, video, clock radio, t/c mkg, refrig], ldry, lounge, conv fac, ⌧, pool, rm serv, dinner to unit, cots-fee, non smoking units (8). **RO** ♦ **$82 - $92**, ♦♦ **$84 - $105**, ♦♦♦ **$101 - $118**, ◊ **$13**, **Suite RO $125**, ch con, AE BC DC EFT MC VI.

 Welcome MOTOR INNS
★★★☆ **Clinton Lodge Motel**, (M), 80 Clinton Street (Hume Hwy), 500m S of PO, ☎ 02 4821 4488, fax 02 4821 8442, (2 stry gr fl), 22 units [shwr, tlt, a/c, heat, elec blkts, tel, TV, video (avail), clock radio, t/c mkg, refrig], ldry, bbq, cots, non smoking units (18). **BLB** ♦ **$65 - $69**, ♦♦ **$76 - $80**, ◊ **$11**, AE BC DC EFT MC VI.

 GOLDEN CHAIN
★★★☆ **Lilac City Motor Inn**, (M), 126 Lagoon St (Hume Hwy), 1.5km N of PO, ☎ 02 4821 5000, fax 02 4821 8074, (2 stry gr fl), 28 units [shwr, tlt, hairdry (most), a/c, elec blkts, tel, TV, movie, clock radio, t/c mkg, refrig], ldry, conv fac, ⌧, dinner to unit, cots-fee, non smoking units (18). **RO** ♦ **$62 - $78**, ♦♦ **$73 - $90**, ◊ **$11**, AE BC DC EFT MC VI, 戊.

★★★ **Country Home Motel**, (M), 1 Cowper St (Old Hume Hwy), 2km S of PO, ☎ 02 4821 4877, fax 02 4821 4877, 11 units [shwr, tlt, a/c-cool, cent heat, tel, fax, cable tv, video-fee, clock radio, t/c mkg, refrig, toaster], cots-fee, non smoking units (7). **RO** ♦ **$45 - $58**, ♦♦ **$55 - $68**, ♦♦♦ **$65 - $78**, ◊ **$10**, AE BC DC EFT MC VI.

★★★ **Goulburn Central Motor Lodge**, (M), 120 Auburn St, 100m S of PO, ☎ 02 4821 1655, fax 02 4821 9242, (2 stry gr fl), 43 units [shwr, tlt, a/c-cool, cent heat, tel, TV, movie, clock radio, t/c mkg, refrig], ldry, ✕, rm serv, dinner to unit, cots-fee, non smoking units (22). **RO** ┆ $50 - $78, ┆┆ $78 - $89, ┆ $11, ch con, 6 units of a higher standard, 9 units of a lower rating, AE BC DC MC VI.

★★★ **Governors Hill Motel**, (M), 61 Sydney Rd, 3.5km N of PO, ☎ 02 4821 1766, fax 02 4821 4413, 18 units [shwr, tlt, a/c, elec blkts, tel, fax, TV, video-fee, clock radio, t/c mkg, refrig, toaster], ✕, bbq, rm serv, cots-fee, non smoking units (10). **RO** ┆ $49 - $59, ┆┆ $57 - $67, ┆┆┆ $67 - $77, ┆ $10, AE BC DC EFT MC MCH VI.

★★★ **Parkhaven Motel**, (M), 60 Lagoon St, 1km N of PO, ☎ 02 4821 4455, fax 02 4822 2807, 15 units [shwr, tlt, a/c-cool, fan, cent heat, elec blkts, tel, fax, TV, clock radio, t/c mkg, refrig, toaster], cots-fee, **RO** ┆┆ $65, ┆┆┆ $75, ch con, AE BC EFT MC VI.

★★★ **Southside Goulburn Budget Motel**, (M), Cnr Finlay & Hume Sts (Old Hume Hwy), 3km S of PO, ☎ 02 4821 1844, fax 02 4822 5616, 14 units [shwr, tlt, a/c, cent heat, elec blkts, tel, TV, t/c mkg, refrig, toaster], cots-fee, Pets allowed. **RO** ┆ $38 - $45, ┆┆ $42 - $50, ┆┆┆ $50 - $60, ┆ $6 - $10, AE BC DC MC VI.

★★☆ **Alpine Heritage Motel , Goulburn**, (M), Previously Alpine Lodge Motel 248 Sloane St, 200m SE of PO, ☎ 02 4821 2930, fax 02 4822 5455, (2 stry), 45 units [shwr, tlt, a/c, cent heat, elec blkts, tel, TV, movie, clock radio, t/c mkg, refrig, toaster, ldry], iron (8), iron brd, ✕, bbq, 24hr reception, cots-fee, non smoking rms (4). **RO** ┆ $35 - $55, ┆┆ $44 - $75, ┆┆┆ $55 - $99, ┆ $8, ch con, 20 units of a lower rating, AE BC DC EFT MC VI, *Operator Comment: Experience the Grandeur of a Heritage Listed Building, circa 1872.*

★★☆ **Hillview Motel**, (M), 2-4 Cowper St (Old Hume Hwy), 2km S of PO, ☎ 02 4821 3130, fax 02 4821 3693, 20 units [shwr, tlt, hairdry, a/c, heat, elec blkts, tel, fax, TV, video-fee, clock radio, t/c mkg, refrig, toaster], bbq, cots-fee, non smoking units (9). **RO** ┆ $39, ┆┆ $44 - $50, ┆┆┆ $44 - $59, ┆ $9, 5 units of a higher standard. AE BC DC EFT MC MCH VI.

★★☆ **Willows Motel**, (M), 21-23 Sydney Rd, 3km N of PO, ☎ 02 4821 4322, fax 02 4821 6295, 17 units [shwr, tlt, a/c, elec blkts, tel, TV, video, movie, clock radio, t/c mkg, refrig, toaster], ldry, pool-indoor (summer only), dinner to unit, cots-fee. **RO** ┆ $48 - $56, ┆┆ $55 - $60, ch con, AE BC DC EFT MC VI.

Self Catering Accommodation

Historic Lansdowne Park Farm & Vineyard, (Cotg), (Farm), Bungonia Rd cnr Memorial Dve, 2.7km SE of PO, ☎ 02 4821 8653, fax 02 4821 8092, 4 cotgs acc up to 4, [shwr, tlt, fan, fire pl, heat, elec blkts, TV, radio, refrig, cook fac, micro, toaster, ldry], rec rm, bbq, tennis, **D** $869.

B&B's/Guest Houses

★★★★☆ **Bentley Lodge Goulburn**, (B&B), 102 Clyde St, 4km W of PO, ☎ 02 4822 5135, fax 02 4822 5136, 6 rms [shwr, bath (2), tlt, hairdry, a/c, fan (6), c/fan (1), cent heat, elec blkts, TV, clock radio, refrig (1)], business centre, lounge firepl, ✕, pool (solar heated), sauna, spa (hottub), t/c mkg shared, courtesy transfer, tennis, non smoking rms. **BB** ┆ $75 - $85, ┆┆ $108, ┆ $33, **DBB** ┆ $108 - $118, ┆┆ $174 - $194, ┆ $66, BC MC VI.

★★★★☆ **Bishopthorpe Manor**, (GH), Bishopthorpe La, 6km SW of PO, ☎ 02 4822 1570, fax 02 4822 1571, (2 stry gr fl), 7 rms [shwr (2), bath (3), spa bath (2), tlt, hairdry, fan, fire pl (2), cent heat, elec blkts, clock radio, t/c mkg], shared fac (2 rms), iron, iron brd, conf fac, lounge firepl, ✕, bbq, courtesy transfer, non smoking rms. **BB** ┆┆ $150 - $235, 1 room ★★★★, BC MC VI.

★★★★ **(Cottage Section)**, 1 cotg [shwr, tlt, heat, refrig, cook fac ltd]. **RO** $200.

★★★ **(Lodge Section)**, 1 rm [fire pl, heat, clock radio], cook fac, t/c mkg shared, refrig, bbq. **BB** ┆┆ $75.

South Hill Homestead, (B&B), c1864, Garroorigang Rd, 3km S of PO, ☎ 02 4821 9591, fax 02 4821 9591, 5 rms [shwr (3), tlt (3), elec blkts, tel, TV, t/c mkg]. **BLB** ┆ $66, ┆┆ $110, ┆┆┆ $140, ┆ $39, ch con, BC MC VI.

Night driving

Clear vision is most important at night, when visibility is restricted. The newer and cleaner the windscreen, the easier it is to see. Clean your headlights and headlight covers, as dirt can severely reduce the brightness of your headlights. Have your headlights adjusted to suit the heaviest load you are likely to carry.

If the glare of oncoming headlights is troubling you, look slightly to the left of the road, to avoid the glare. Look at the edge of the road to make sure that you don't run off. Never drive with your high beams on if there is a vehicle travelling in either direction within 200 metres in front of you.

AAA TOURISM Special Rates
BENT STREET motor inn

62 Bent Street
SOUTH GRAFTON
Affordable 4 Star Luxury
★★★★
AAA TOURISM

- Superbly appointed spacious new units
- Fully Airconditioned, quiet and away from traffic noise
- AUSTAR free to all rooms
- Closest to clubs, restaurants, shops, tourist centre, rail, McDonalds and sporting fields
- Leisure area with pool, spa and guest BBQ
- Direct dial phones
- Conference and business facilities
- EFTPOS facilities with all major credit cards accepted
- Corporate rates and seniors discounts available

Whilst staying you can enjoy Grafton's premier licenced restaurant....

ZACKS
ON BENT STREET

for fine a la carte cuisine

Ph: 02 6643 4500
Fax: 02 6643 4555
email: bentst@key.net.au
www.bentstreetmotorinn.com.au
2384AG

GRAFTON NSW 2460

Pop 16,550. (625km N Sydney), See map on page 54, ref D3. Beautiful provincial city on the Clarence River, renowned for its graceful old buildings and jacaranda trees. Boating, Bowls, Fishing, Golf, Horse Racing, Scenic Drives, Swimming, Tennis. See also Halfway Creek, Jackadgery, Nymboida & Wooli.

Hotels/Motels

★★★★ **Abbey Motor Inn**, (M), 59 Fitzroy St, 250m E of PO, ☎ 02 6642 6122, fax 02 6643 1615, (2 stry gr fl), 24 units [shwr, tlt, hairdry, a/c, elec blkts, tel, fax, TV, movie, clock radio, t/c mkg, refrig, toaster], ldry, iron, rm serv (b'fast), cots, non smoking units (avail). **RO 👤 $56 - $59, 👥 $66 - $69**, AE BC DC MC VI.

AAA TOURISM Special Rates ★★★★ **Bent Street Motor Inn**, (M), 62 Bent St, South Grafton 2460, 300m S of Grafton Bridge, ☎ 02 6643 4500, fax 02 6643 4555, (2 stry gr fl), 20 units [shwr, tlt, hairdry, a/c, elec blkts, tel, TV, clock radio, t/c mkg, refrig, mini bar, toaster], ldry, iron, iron brd, ☒, pool, spa, bbq, cots, non smoking units (2). **BLB 👥 $90 - $107, RO 👥 $72 - $90**, ch con, pen con, AE BC DC EFT JCB MC MP VI.

FLAG Flag Choice Hotels ★★★★ **The Clarence Motor Inn**, (M), 51 Fitzroy St, ☎ 02 6643 3444, fax 02 6643 4622, (2 stry gr fl), 39 units (2 suites) [shwr, spa bath (4), tlt, hairdry, a/c, tel, cable tv, video (avail), movie, clock radio, t/c mkg, refrig, mini bar, micro (2), toaster], ldry, iron, iron brd, conv fac, ☒, pool, spa, bbq, rm serv (b'fast), dinner to unit, ☎, cots-fee, non smoking units (30). **RO 👤 $109 - $139, 👥 $104 - $134, 🧒 $15**, ch con, pen con, 4 rooms yet to be assessed. AE BC DC EFT JCB MC MP VI.

★★★★ **(Cottage Section)**, 3 cotgs acc up to 6, [shwr, bath, tlt, hairdry, a/c, fire pl (1), tel, cable tv, video-fee, movie, clock radio, t/c mkg, refrig, cook fac, micro, toaster]. **D 👤 $87 - $102, 👥 $92 - $122, 🧒 $10 - $15, W 👤 $490 - $595, 👥 $490 - $595, 🧒 $105 - $175.**

★★★☆ **Civic Motel**, (M), 153 Pound St, off Prince St, 600m W of PO, ☎ 02 6642 4922, fax 02 6642 4278, 10 units [shwr, tlt, a/c, c/fan, heat, elec blkts, tel, fax, cable tv, clock radio, t/c mkg, refrig, micro (2)], pool, c/park (carport), cots-fee. **RO 👤 $53 - $63, 👥 $64 - $74, 👥👤 $77 - $85, 🧒 $12**, ch con, AE BC DC MC VI.

Civic Motel ★★★☆ AAA Tourism

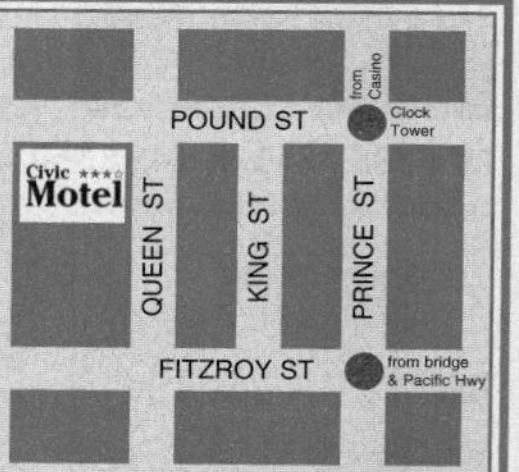

★ Close to RSL & Bowls Club
★ Away from highway noise
★ Close to CBD
★ Clean air conditioned units
★ Undercover parking
★ Cable TV, pool & BBQ
★ Reasonable rates

**153 Pound St.
GRAFTON**
Ph/Fax:
02 6642 4922
2371AG

FLAG
★★★☆ AAA Tourism
2376AG

FITZROY MOTEL
phone: (02) 6642 4477 fax: (02) 6643 1586
27 Fitzroy St. Grafton. (adj. to KFC).
Relax with us and enjoy our secluded pool and heated spa. Range of rooms available. We are centrally located close to quality restaurants and shops.

 ★★★☆ **Espana Motel**, (M), Pacific Hwy, South Grafton 2460, 2km S of PO, ☎ 02 6642 4566, fax 02 6642 1833, 28 units (1 suite) [shwr, tlt, a/c, c/fan, tel, cable tv, clock radio, t/c mkg, refrig], conv fac, ⊠, pool (salt water), spa, rm serv, cots. **RO ♦ $82 - $107, ♦♦ $87 - $112, ◊ $10, Suite D $107 - $132**, AE BC DC JCB MC MP VI.

 ★★★☆ **Fitzroy Motel**, (M), 27 Fitzroy St, 600m E of PO, ☎ 02 6642 4477, fax 02 6643 1586, (2 stry gr fl), 21 units [shwr, tlt, hairdry, a/c, elec blkts, tel, cable tv, video (avail), movie, clock radio, t/c mkg, refrig, toaster], ldry, iron, iron brd, pool, spa (heated), rm serv, dinner to unit, cots, non smoking units (16). **RO ♦ $66 - $95, ♦♦ $68 - $102, ◊ $10**, ch con, AE BC DC EFT MC MCH MP VI.

 ★★★☆ **Grafton Lodge Motel**, (M), Pacific Hwy, South Grafton 2460, 2km S of PO, ☎ 02 6642 7822, fax 02 6642 7954, 12 units (12 suites) [shwr, tlt, a/c, c/fan, elec blkts, tel, TV, clock radio, t/c mkg, refrig], ldry, pool, dinner to unit, cots-fee. **RO ♦ $66 - $71, ♦♦ $71 - $79, ◊ $12**, AE BC DC MC VI.

 ★★★☆ **Jacaranda Motel**, (M), Pacific Hwy, 3km N of Information Centre, ☎ 02 6642 2833, fax 02 6642 6351, 25 units [shwr, tlt, a/c, heat, tel, cable tv, t/c mkg, refrig], ldry, ⊠, pool, dinner to unit, plygr, cots-fee. **RO ♦ $65, ♦♦ $70 - $76, ♦♦♦ $79 - $88, ◊ $12**, AE BC DC EFT MC VI.

★★★☆ **Key Lodge Motel**, (M), 37 Fitzroy St, 600m E of PO, ☎ 02 6642 1944, fax 02 6642 1446, (2 stry gr fl), 30 units [shwr, bath (2), spa bath (2), tlt, a/c, tel, TV, video, clock radio, t/c mkg, refrig], ldry, ⊠, pool, sauna, spa, dinner to unit, cots, non smoking units (6). **RO ♦ $62 - $92, ♦♦ $72 - $79, ♦♦♦ $89 - $115**, AE BC DC EFT MC VI.

 ★★★ **Hi-Way Motel**, (M), Pacific Hwy, South Grafton 2460, ☎ 02 6642 1588, fax 02 6642 4417, (2 stry gr fl), 31 units [shwr, spa bath (1), tlt, a/c, heat, tel, TV, movie, clock radio, t/c mkg, refrig], ldry, pool, bbq, cots-fee, non smoking rms. **RO ♦ $50 - $70, ♦♦ $55 - $75, ♦♦♦ $70 - $85, ♦♦♦♦ $75 - $95**, BC EFT MC MCH VI.

★★★ **Hilldrop Motor Inn**, (M), 706 Gwydir Hwy, South Grafton 2460, ☎ 02 6644 9220, fax 02 6644 9992, 10 units [shwr, tlt, fan, heat, tel, TV, clock radio, t/c mkg, refrig], ✕, pool, cots-fee. **RO ♦ $35 - $45, ♦♦ $40 - $60, ◊ $10 - $15**, ch con, AE BC DC EFT MC VI,

Operator Comment: "Hilldrop is an affordable country style motel 10 mins drive from Grafton CBD".

★☆ **Crown Hotel Motel**, (LMH), 1 Prince St, ☎ 02 6642 4000, fax 02 6642 7996, (2 stry gr fl), 54 units [shwr (29), bath (2), tlt (29), a/c (18), fan (11), c/fan (22), tel (18), TV (18), clock radio (18), t/c mkg, refrig (18), toaster (18)], ldry, lounge (TV), ⊠ (2), bbq, rm serv, ✆, cots. **RO ♦ $20 - $85**, BC EFT MC MP VI.

★☆ **Roches Family Hotel**, (LH), 85 Victoria St, 300m W of PO, ☎ 02 6642 2866, fax 02 6643 1828, (2 stry), 14 rms [fan], lounge (TV), ⊠, t/c mkg shared, refrig, bbq. **RO ♦ $30, ♦♦ $38, ♦♦♦ $45**, AE BC DC MC VI.

Self Catering Accommodation

 ★★★☆ **Reilley's Hideaway Grafton Farmstay**, (Cotg), (Farm), 218 Reilley's La (Off Pacific Hwy), South Grafton 2460, ☎ 02 6642 6008, 1 cotg acc up to 6, [shwr, tlt, hairdry, a/c-cool, heat, elec blkts, tel, TV, video, clock radio, CD, t/c mkg, refrig, cook fac, elec frypan, toaster, blkts, linen], iron, iron brd, pool (salt water), spa, bbq, plygr, tennis (half court). **D ♦ $110, ♦♦ $110**, ch con, fam con.

B&B's/Guest Houses

★★★★☆ **Dovedale Bed & Breakfast**, (B&B), 3 Oliver St, 1.6km NE of PO, ☎ 02 6642 5706, (2 stry gr fl), 2 rms (1 suite) [shwr, tlt, a/c, c/fan, heat, TV, clock radio, t/c mkg, refrig], bbq, non smoking property. **BB ♦ $77 - $97, ♦♦ $97 - $107, ◊ $35 - $45**, AE BC MC VI.

★★★☆ **Seeview Farm**, (B&B), 440 Rogans Bridge Rd, Seelands, South Grafton 2460, ☎ 02 6644 9270, fax 02 6644 9270, 2 rms [shwr, tlt, hairdry, c/fan, elec blkts, tel], ldry, iron, iron brd, lounge (TV), t/c mkg shared, cots. **BB ♦ $40, ♦♦ $70 - $80**, ch con.

GRASSY HEAD NSW 2441

Pop Nominal, (474km N Sydney), See map on page 54, ref C5. Tiny mid-north coast seaside settlement. Bush Walking, Fishing, Scenic Drives, Swimming. See also Scotts Head & Yarrahapinni.

Self Catering Accommodation

★★★ **Grassy Head Hideaway**, (Cotg), 319 Grassy Head Rd, 15km E of Pacific Hwy, ☎ 02 6569 0811, 2 cotgs acc up to 4, [shwr, tlt, TV, clock radio, refrig, cook fac, micro, toaster, ldry (in unit), linen (bed)], pool (salt water), c/park (carport). **D ♦♦ $80 - $120, ◊ $10, W ♦♦ $300 - $730**, Min book applies.

GREEN POINT NSW 2251

Pop 128,956. See map on page 56, ref E3. Central Coast town on the north eastern shore of the Broadwater Fishing, Sailing, Scenic Drives, Swimming. See also Kincumber.

B&B's/Guest Houses

Binawee Bed & Breakfast, (B&B), 295 Avoca Dve, ☎ 02 4369 0981, fax 02 4369 0997, (2 stry gr fl), 3 rms [shwr, bath (1), tlt, hairdry (2), evap cool (1), fan (2), c/fan, cent heat, elec blkts, clock radio (2), t/c mkg], lounge (TV), lounge firepl, pool-heated (solar), spa, bbq, courtesy transfer, cots, non smoking property. **BB ♦ $60 - $75, ♦♦ $135 - $195, DBB ♦♦ $185 - $245**, AE BC MC VI, (not yet classified).

Tinkers Castle Bed & Breakfast, (B&B), 421 Avoca Dve, ☎ 02 4369 7769, (2 stry gr fl), 4 rms (1 suite) [shwr, bath (1), tlt, clock radio, t/c mkg], ldry, rec rm, lounge (TV), lounge firepl, ✕, bbq, cots, non smoking property. **BB ♦ $100 - $140, ♦♦ $125 - $160, ◊ $30 - $50**, BC MC VI, (not yet classified).

GREENWELL POINT NSW 2540

Pop 1,217. (173km S Sydney), See map on page 55, ref B4. Small south coast town renowned for its oysters. Boating, Bowls, Fishing, Swimming, Tennis.

Hotels/Motels

★★★ **Anchor Bay Motel**, (M), 113 Greenwell Point Rd, 100m E of PO, ☎ 02 4447 1722, 12 units [shwr, tlt, heat, elec blkts, TV, clock radio, t/c mkg, refrig, micro, toaster], ldry, bbq (covered), ✆, cots, non smoking units (4). **RO ♦ $60 - $85, ♦♦ $66 - $95, ◊ $10 - $15**, Min book applies, AE BC DC JCB MC VI, ♿.

Self Catering Accommodation

★★☆ **Glenn Allison**, (Cotg), 94 Greenwell Point Rd, 100m W of PO, ☎ 02 4447 1388, 3 cotgs acc up to 6, [shwr, tlt, heat, elec blkts, TV, clock radio, t/c mkg, refrig, cook fac, micro, elec frypan, toaster], ldry, bbq, c/park. **D ♦♦ $60, ♦♦♦ $70, W $300 - $500**, Min book applies.

GRENFELL NSW 2810

Pop 1,950. (391km W Sydney), See map on pages 52/53, ref F5. This charming central west town was the birthplace of author Henry Lawson back in 1867 and of another Australian author, Eric Rolls, in 1923. Bowls, Bush Walking, Fishing, Gold Prospecting, Golf, Scenic Drives, Swimming.

Hotels/Motels

★★ **Grenfell Motel**, (M), 84 Main St, 500m N of PO, ☎ 02 6343 1333, fax 02 6343 1889, 20 units [shwr, tlt, a/c-cool (4), a/c (16), c/fan, heat (4), elec blkts, tel, TV, video, clock radio, t/c mkg, refrig], dinner to unit (Mon to Thu), cots. **D ♦ $50, ♦♦ $61, ♦♦♦ $72, ◊ $11**, AE BC DC MC VI.

GRENFELL NSW continued...

B&B's/Guest Houses

★★★☆ **Grenfell House**, (B&B), No children's facilities, 7 Weddin St, ☎ 02 6343 2235, fax 02 6343 2235, (2 stry), 3 rms [shwr (3), bath (1), tlt (3), hairdry, c/fan (2), heat, elec blkts, clock radio], lounge (TV), lounge firepl, t/c mkg shared, non smoking property.
BB ⨁ **$90 - $100**, ⨁⨁ **$110 - $130**, Dinner by arrangement, Min book long w/ends and Easter.

GRETA NSW 2334

Pop 1,588. (224km N Sydney), See map on page 55, ref B7. Historic coal mining village between Branxton and Maitland, a good base from which to explore the Hunter wineries. Scenic Drives, Vineyards, Wineries.

B&B's/Guest Houses

★★★★☆ **The Table**, (GH), 3-5 Water St, ☎ 02 4938 7799, fax 02 4938 6011, (2 stry), 5 rms [shwr, tlt, hairdry, a/c, c/fan, heat, TV, clock radio, t/c mkg, refrig], ✕, non smoking rms (5).
DBB ⨁⨁ **$264 - $299**, AE BC MC VI.

GRIFFITH NSW 2680

Pop 14,200. (570km SW Sydney), See map on pages 52/53, ref E5. Thriving Riverina city at the centre of one of the most prosperous food and wine growing areas in Australia. Boating, Bowls, Golf, Sailing, Scenic Drives, Squash, Swimming, Vineyards, Wineries, Water Skiing.

Hotels/Motels

★★★★ **The Kidman Wayside Inn**, (M), 58-72 Jondaryan Ave, 1km S of PO, ☎ 02 6964 5666, fax 02 6962 4436, 60 units [shwr, bath (8), spa bath (8), tlt, hairdry, a/c, elec blkts (4), tel, TV, clock radio, t/c mkg, refrig, mini bar, toaster], ldry, iron, iron brd, lounge, conv fac, ✕, pool, rm serv, dinner to unit, cots, non smoking rms (40).
RO ⨁ **$77 - $132**, ◊ **$15**, ch con, AE BC DC EFT MC VI, ⅍⅄.

★★★★ **Yambil Inn**, (M), 155 Yambil St, 400m W of PO, ☎ 02 6964 1233, fax 02 6964 1355, 16 units [shwr, tlt, hairdry, a/c, elec blkts, tel, cable tv, video-fee, clock radio, t/c mkg, refrig], iron, iron brd, pool (solar, salt water), spa, bbq, cots-fee, non smoking units (10). **RO** ⨁ **$76**, ⨁⨁ **$81 - $87**, ◊ **$14**, ch con, AE BC DC EFT MC MP VI.

★★★☆ **Bagtown Inn Motel**, (M), 2 Blumer Ave, 1.5km SE of PO, ☎ 02 6962 7166, fax 02 6962 7981, 50 units (5 suites) [shwr, spa bath (15), tlt, a/c, heat, elec blkts, tel, TV, video, clock radio, t/c mkg, refrig], conv fac, ✕ (Closed Sundays), pool, sauna, spa, bbq, rm serv, car wash, plygr, tennis (half court), cots, Pet accommodation available. **RO** ⨁ **$90**, ⨁⨁ **$99**, ⨁⨁⨁ **$115**, ◊ **$10**, Suite D **$130 - $150**, AE BC DC MC MP VI.

FLAG
FLAG CHOICE HOTELS

★★★☆ **The Gemini Motel**, (LMH), 201 Banna Ave, ☎ 02 6962 3833, fax 02 6962 5619, (Multi-stry), 63 units [shwr, spa bath (4), tlt, a/c, tel, TV, movie, clock radio, t/c mkg, refrig, mini bar], lift, ldry, conv fac, ✕, rm serv, cots. **RO $175 - $120**, AE BC DC JCB MC MP VI.

★★★ **A-Line Motel**, (M), 187 Wakaden St, 800m E of PO, ☎ 02 6962 1922, fax 02 6964 1379, 23 units [shwr, tlt, a/c, tel, TV, video-fee, clock radio, t/c mkg, refrig], pool (salt water), bbq, cots-fee, non smoking rms (10). **RO** ⨁ **$62 - $78**, ⨁⨁ **$73 - $89**, ⨁⨁⨁ **$84 - $100**, ◊ **$11**, 9 rooms ★★★★. AE BC DC EFT MC VI, ⅍⅄.

★★★ **Acacia Motel**, (M), 923 Jondaryan Ave, 1km S of PO, ☎ 02 6962 4422, fax 02 6962 3284, 30 units [shwr, tlt, a/c, heat, elec blkts, tel, TV, video-fee, clock radio, t/c mkg, refrig], pool (salt water), cots. **RO** ⨁ **$70**, ⨁⨁ **$79**, ⨁⨁⨁ **$90**, ◊ **$11**, AE BC DC EFT MC VI.

Budget Motel Chain
International

★★★ **Citrus Motel**, (M), Jondaryan Ave, ☎ 02 6962 6233, fax 02 6964 1300, 28 units [shwr, tlt, a/c, elec blkts, tel, TV, video-fee, clock radio, t/c mkg, refrig, cook fac (2)], pool, sauna. **RO** ⨁ **$59 - $65**, ⨁⨁ **$69 - $75**, ⨁⨁⨁ **$75 - $80**, ◊ **$11**, AE BC DC EFT MC MP VI.

★★★ **Griffith Motor Inn**, (M), 96 Banna Ave, 500m E of PO, ☎ 02 6962 1800, fax 02 6962 7074, (2 stry gr fl), 40 units [shwr, spa bath (4), tlt, a/c, elec blkts, tel, TV, video-fee, clock radio, t/c mkg, refrig], ldry, ✕, pool, bbq, dinner to unit, cots-fee, non smoking units (4). **RO** ⨁ **$65 - $75**, ⨁⨁ **$72 - $85**, ⨁⨁⨁ **$85**, ◊ **$12**, AE BC DC MC VI.

Budget Motel Chain
International

★★★ **M I A**, (M), Leeton Rd, 2.5km SE of PO, ☎ 02 6962 1866, fax 02 6962 1715, 21 units [shwr, tlt, a/c, elec blkts, tel, TV, video-fee, clock radio, t/c mkg, refrig, toaster], ldry, pool, cook fac, bbq, dinner to unit, cots-fee. **RO** ⨁ **$61 - $68**, ⨁⨁ **$72 - $79**, ⨁⨁⨁ **$83 - $90**, ◊ **$11**, ch con, AE BC DC EFT MC MCH VI, ⅍⅄.

Self Catering Accommodation

★★★ **Griffith Northside Apartments**, (HU), 31 Edmondson Ave, 1km N of PO, ☎ 02 6964 5416, fax 02 6964 5417, (2 stry gr fl), 2 units acc up to 4, [shwr, tlt, hairdry, a/c, elec blkts, TV, video, clock radio, t/c mkg, refrig, cook fac, micro, toaster, blkts, linen], w/mach, iron, bbq, c/park (carport), non smoking property, BC MC VI.

GRONG GRONG NSW 2652

Pop Nominal, (534km SW Sydney), See map on pages 52/53, ref E6. Rural service centre on the Newell Highway between Narrandera and Ardlethan. Fishing.

Hotels/Motels

★★☆ **Grong Grong Motor Inn**, (M), Newell Hwy, 100m N of railway station, ☎ 02 6956 2109, 10 units [shwr, tlt, a/c, elec blkts, tel, TV, clock radio, t/c mkg, refrig], ✕, pool, bbq, dinner to unit, cots. **RO** ⨁ **$35.20**, ⨁⨁ **$49.50**, ⨁⨁⨁ **$55**, ◊ **$5.50**, Yet to be assessed. BC MC VI.

GULGONG NSW 2852

Pop 2,000. (310km NW Sydney), See map on pages 52/53, ref G4. Historic gold town that has been well preserved over the years and featured on the original $10 note. Bowls, Gold Prospecting, Golf, Scenic Drives, Squash, Swimming, Tennis, Vineyards, Wineries.

Hotels/Motels

★★★ **Ten Dollar Town Motel**, (M), Cnr Mayne & Medley Sts, 300m N of PO, ☎ 02 6374 1204, fax 02 6374 2188, 36 units [shwr, tlt, hairdry, a/c, elec blkts, tel, TV, clock radio, t/c mkg, refrig, toaster], iron, iron brd, ✕ (6 nights), dinner to unit (6 nights), cots-fee. **RO** ⨁ **$79 - $90**, ⨁⨁ **$79 - $90**, ⨁⨁⨁ **$89 - $110**, ◊ **$10**, AE BC DC EFT MC VI.

★ **Centennial Hotel**, (LMH), 141 Mayne St, 200m W of PO, ☎ 02 6374 1241, fax 02 6374 1241, 8 units [ensuite, bath (1), fan, heat, elec blkts, t/c mkg, toaster], lounge (TV), lounge firepl, ✕, bbq, ✆, cots. **RO** ⨁ **$45**, ⨁⨁ **$55**, ⨁⨁⨁⨁ **$75**, ◊ **$10**, BC EFT MC VI.

Goldfields Motor Inn, (M), Mayne St, 1km W of PO, ☎ 02 6374 1111, fax 02 6374 1086, 14 units [shwr, bath (2), tlt, a/c, elec blkts, tel, TV, video-fee, clock radio, t/c mkg, refrig, cook fac (7), micro (7)], ldry, pool, sauna, bbq, rm serv, dinner to unit, plygr, cots-fee. **RO** ⊧ **$52 - $59,** ⊧⊧ **$66 - $73,** ⊧⊧⊧ **$79 - $86,** ⊧ **$13,** ch con, AE BC DC EFT JCB MC VI, ⅋⅊.

Gulgong Motel, (M), 71 Medley St, 300m W of PO, ☎ 02 6374 1122, 20 units [shwr, bath (1), tlt, a/c (19), fan, heat, elec blkts, TV, video (avail), clock radio, t/c mkg, refrig], ldry, pool, bbq, dinner to unit, cots-fee. **BB** ⊧ **$50 - $57,** ⊧⊧ **$62 - $69,** ⊧⊧⊧ **$75 - $82,** ⊧ **$13,** ch con, AE BC DC MC VI.

B&B's/Guest Houses
★★★☆ **Lottie May Bed & Breakfast**, (B&B), Portion 220, Mayne St, 2km E of PO, ☎ 02 6374 1220, 3 rms [ensuite (1), fan, fire pl (combustion), heat (elec/wood), elec blkts, doonas], shared fac (2), lounge, t/c mkg shared, refrig, non smoking rms, Pets allowed. **BB** ⊧ **$50 - $60,** ⊧⊧ **$80 - $90,** weekly con, BC MC VI.

★★★☆ **Stables Guest House**, (B&B), 149 Mayne St, 200m W of PO, ☎ 02 6374 1668, fax 02 6374 1735, 5 rms [a/c (3), c/fan, fire pl, tel, TV (2), clock radio], lounge (TV), pool (salt water), t/c mkg shared, bbq, c/park. **BB** ⊧ **$78.60 - $93,** ⊧⊧ **$115.50 - $135, DBB** ⊧ **$140 - $210,** ⊧⊧ **$203.50 - $250,** ch con, AE BC EFT MC VI.

GUNDAGAI NSW 2722
Pop 2,050. (409km SW Sydney), See map on pages 52/53, ref F6. Historic town on the Murrumbidgee River, home to the famous 'dog on the tuckerbox'. Bowls, Fishing, Golf, Shooting, Swimming, Tennis.

Hotels/Motels

★★★☆ **Garden Motor Inn**, (M), West St, 1km N of Tourist Information Centre, ☎ 02 6944 1744, fax 02 6944 2085, 22 units [shwr, tlt, hairdry, a/c, elec blkts, tel, TV, clock radio, t/c mkg, refrig], ⊠, pool, bbq, cots-fee, non smoking units (avail). **RO** ⊧ **$70,** ⊧⊧ **$79,** ⊧⊧⊧ **$91,** ⊧ **$12,** 4 units of a lower rating, AE BC DC JCB MC MP VI.

★★★☆ **Poets Recall Motel**, (M), Cnr West & Punch Sts, 700m NW of PO, ☎ 02 6944 1777, fax 02 6944 2111, (2 stry gr fl), 23 units [shwr, tlt, a/c, elec blkts, tel, TV, video (8), clock radio, t/c mkg, refrig], ⊠ (Mon to Sat), pool, cots-fee, non smoking units (7). **RO** ⊧ **$59 - $69,** ⊧⊧ **$66 - $84,** ⊧⊧⊧ **$77 - $110,** ⊧ **$10 - $18,** ch con, AE BC DC MC VI.

★★★ **The Bushmans Retreat Motor Inn**, (M), Cnr Mount & Cross Sts, 3km S of PO, ☎ 02 6944 1433, fax 02 6944 1006, 18 units [shwr, tlt, a/c, elec blkts, tel, TV, video-fee, clock radio, t/c mkg, refrig], ⊠, pool, rm serv, plygr, cots-fee. **RO** ⊧ **$51 - $60,** ⊧⊧ **$55 - $71,** ⊧⊧⊧ **$68 - $84,** ⊧ **$12,** AE BC DC EFT MC MCH VI.

★★☆ **Gundagai Motel**, (M), Cnr West & Sheridan Sts, 500m W of PO, ☎ 02 6944 1066, fax 02 6944 2095, 27 units (2 bedrm), [shwr, tlt, a/c, heat, elec blkts, tel, TV, clock radio, t/c mkg, refrig], cots-fee. **RO** ⊧ **$46 - $53,** ⊧⊧ **$55 - $62,** ⊧ **$9,** 7 units of a higher rating, AE BC DC EFT MC VI.

★★ **Sheridan Motel**, (M), Cnr Sheridan & Otway Sts, 500m W of PO, ☎ 02 6944 1311, fax 02 6944 1881, 17 units [shwr, tlt, hairdry, a/c, heat, elec blkts, tel, TV, video, movie, clock radio, t/c mkg, refrig, toaster], dinner to unit, plygr, cots-fee, non smoking property. **RO** ⊧ **$48 - $58,** ⊧⊧ **$58 - $68,** ⊧⊧⊧ **$68 - $75,** ⊧ **$10,** ch con, 4 units of a higher standard. AE BC BTC MC VI.

★☆ **Criterion Hotel**, (LH), 172 Sheridan St, ☎ 02 6944 1048, or 02 6946 2342, (2 stry), 17 rms [c/fan, elec blkts], iron, iron brd, lounge (TV), ✕ (Mon to Sat), t/c mkg shared, ☎, cots. **BLB** ⊧ **$32, DBB** ⊧ **$49.**

Self Catering Accommodation
★☆ **Auto Cabins & Motel**, 108 West St, 1km N of Tourist Centre, ☎ 02 6944 1318, 5 cabins acc up to 7, [shwr, tlt, evap cool, heat, TV, clock radio, refrig, cook fac ltd, toaster, linen reqd-fee], Pets allowed under control. **D** ⊧⊧ **$38,** ⊧ **$5,** BC MC VI.

GUNNEDAH NSW 2380
Pop 8,300. (470km NW Sydney), See map on pages 52/53, ref H3. Picturesque town on the Namoi River that supports a prosperous agricultural industry. Each year, Gunnedah hosts one of the biggest rural expos in the country, the Ag-Quip Field Days; the town was also the home of poet Dorothea Mackellar. Bowls, Bush Walking, Fishing, Golf, Swimming, Tennis.

Hotels/Motels
★★★★ **Alyn Motel**, (M), 351 Conadilly St, 200m E of PO, ☎ 02 6742 5028, fax 02 6742 5029, 13 units [shwr, tlt, hairdry (7), a/c, c/fan, elec blkts, tel, TV, movie, clock radio, t/c mkg, refrig, toaster], pool (salt water), spa, bbq, dinner to unit, cots-fee, non smoking units (5). **RO** ⊧ **$65 - $75,** ⊧⊧ **$75 - $85,** ⊧⊧⊧ **$105,** ⊧ **$11,** AE BC DC EFT MC VI, ⅋⅊.

★★★★ **Maynestay Motel**, (M), 384 Connadilly St, 300m E of PO, ☎ 02 6742 7150, fax 02 6742 7152, (2 stry gr fl), 10 units (0 suites) [shwr, spa bath (2), tlt, hairdry, a/c, elec blkts, tel, TV, video (avail), clock radio, t/c mkg, refrig, micro (2), toaster], ldry, iron, iron brd, dinner to unit, cots. **RO** ⊧ **$75 - $85,** ⊧⊧ **$85 - $100,** ⊧⊧⊧ **$96 - $110, Suite RO $85 - $132,** AE BC DC EFT MC MP VI.

★★★☆ **The Overlander Motor Lodge**, (M), 40 Conadilly St, 2km W of PO, ☎ 02 6742 2677, fax 02 6742 4004, (2 stry gr fl), 16 units [shwr, tlt, a/c, elec blkts, tel, TV, clock radio, t/c mkg, refrig, toaster], ⊠ (Mon to Sat), pool, rm serv, dinner to unit, cots-fee. **RO** ⊧ **$63 - $68,** ⊧⊧ **$68 - $73,** ⊧⊧⊧ **$74 - $79,** ⊧ **$9,** ch con, AE BC DC EFT MC MP VI.

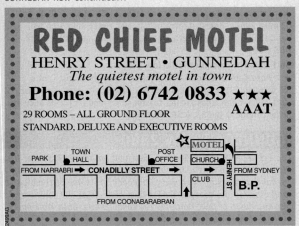

RED CHIEF MOTEL

HENRY STREET • GUNNEDAH

The quietest motel in town

Phone: (02) 6742 0833 ★★★
AAAT

29 ROOMS – ALL GROUND FLOOR
STANDARD, DELUXE AND EXECUTIVE ROOMS

★★★ Gunnedah Motor Inn, (M), 367 Conadilly St, 300m SE of PO, ☎ 02 6742 2377, fax 02 6742 6037, (2 stry gr fl), 20 units [shwr, bath (1), tlt, a/c, elec blkts, tel, TV, clock radio, t/c mkg, refrig, toaster], pool (salt water), dinner to unit, cots-fee. RO ♦ $50, ♦♦ $60, ♦♦♦ $70, ♦♦♦♦ $76, AE BC DC EFT MC MCH VI.

★★★ Harvest Lodge, (M), 404 Conadilly St, 1km E of PO, ☎ 02 6742 3400, fax 02 6742 3412, 15 units [shwr, spa bath (6), tlt, hairdry, a/c, elec blkts, tel, fax, cable tv, video (avail), movie, clock radio, t/c mkg, refrig, micro, toaster], ldry, conv fac, ⊠ (Mon to Sat), pool (salt water), dinner to unit, cots. RO ♦ $61 - $72, ♦♦ $61 - $72, ◊ $11, AE BC DC MC VI.

★★★ Plains Motor Inn, (M), 111 Conadilly St, Located in CBD, ☎ 02 6742 2511, fax 02 6742 4203, 15 units [shwr, tlt, a/c, heat, elec blkts, tel, TV, video (avail), clock radio, t/c mkg, refrig, toaster], ldry, pool, bbq, dinner to unit, cots. RO ♦ $55 - $65, ♦♦ $64 - $74, ♦♦♦ $75 - $85, ◊ $10, AE BC DC EFT MC MP VI, &.

AAA
TOURISM
Special Rates

★★★ Red Chief Motel, (M), Henry St, 200m SE of PO, ☎ 02 6742 0833, fax 02 6742 4872, 29 units [shwr, tlt, hairdry, a/c-cool, a/c (8), heat, elec blkts, tel, TV, clock radio, t/c mkg, refrig, cook fac (1), toaster], pool (salt water), bbq, cots, non smoking units (6). RO ♦ $55 - $61, ♦♦ $55 - $82, ◊ $11, ch con, 3 units of a lower rating, AE BC DC EFT MC VI, &.

★★☆ Billabong Motel, (M), 339 Conadilly St, 100m E of PO, ☎ 02 6742 2033, fax 02 6742 4360, (2 stry gr fl), 33 units [shwr, tlt, evap cool, heat, elec blkts, tel, TV, movie, clock radio, t/c mkg, refrig, toaster], pool, cots-fee. RO ♦ $50 - $54, ♦♦ $56 - $65, ♦♦♦ $70 - $75, ◊ $11, AE BC DC EFT MC VI.

Regal, (LH), 298 Conadilly St, ☎ 02 6742 2355, fax 02 6742 5185, (2 stry gr fl), 25 rms [shwr (8), bath (2), tlt (8), a/c-cool (21), elec blkts], ldry, iron, iron brd, lounge (TV & firepl), ✕, ⊠ (6 days), t/c mkg shared, ✆. RO ♦ $27, ♦♦ $35, ♦♦♦ $40, BC EFT MC VI.

GUNNING NSW 2581

Pop 500. (245km S Sydney), See map on pages 52/53, ref G6. Small town that dates from the 1830s. Its historic streetscape contains many old and interesting buildings and it's an enchanting place that sums up the essence of Capital Country. Bowls, Fishing, Golf, Swimming, Tennis.

Hotels/Motels

★★★☆ Gunning Motel, (M), Yass St, ☎ 02 4845 1191, fax 02 4845 1460, 24 units [shwr, tlt, hairdry, a/c, elec blkts, tel, fax, TV, movie, clock radio, t/c mkg, refrig], ldry, iron, iron brd, ⊠, pool (salt water), bbq, dinner to unit, cots-fee. RO ♦ $44 - $53, ♦♦ $55 - $65, ♦♦♦ $64 - $74, ◊ $9, AE BC DC MC VI.

B&B's/Guest Houses

★★★ Frankfield Guest House, (GH), 1-3 Warrataw St, 300m N of PO, ☎ 02 4845 1200, fax 02 4845 1490, 10 rms [ensuite (avail), fire pl (9), heat, elec blkts, refrig], iron, iron brd, conv fac, ✕, t/c mkg shared, bbq, plygr, cots. BB ♦ $60, ♦♦ $100, DBB ♦ $90, ♦♦ $160, pen con, AE BC MC VI.

Do Duck Inn Guesthouse, (GH), c1890, 22 Old Hume Hwy, 500m S of PO, ☎ 02 4845 1207, fax 02 4845 1207, 5 rms [shwr, bath (1), tlt, hairdry, fan, fire pl (2), heat, elec blkts, t/c mkg, refrig], iron, iron brd, lounge, ✕, bbq-fee, dinner to unit, courtesy transfer, non smoking property. BB ♦ $96.80 - $145.20, ♦♦ $121 - $154, DBB ♦ $126.50 - $181.50, ♦♦ $181.50 - $231.

GUYRA NSW 2365

Pop 1,800. (607km N Sydney), See map on page 54, ref B4. The New England town of Guyra is billed as 'the top of the range', due to its situation at the watershed of the Great Dividing Range at a height of 1320m. Bowls, Bush Walking, Fishing, Gem Fossicking, Golf, Scenic Drives, Swimming, Tennis.

Hotels/Motels

★★★☆ Shiralee Motel, (M), New England Hwy, 200m SE of PO, ☎ 02 6779 1380, fax 02 6779 1333, 11 units [shwr, spa bath (1), tlt, hairdry, heat, tel, cable tv, clock radio, t/c mkg, refrig, mini bar, toaster], iron, iron brd, meals to unit (incl liquor), c/park (undercover), cots, non smoking units (7). RO ♦ $62 - $100, ♦♦ $72 - $100, ◊ $10 - $12, AE BC DC EFT MC VI, &.

★★★ Guyra Park Motel, (M), New England Hwy, ☎ 02 6779 1022, fax 02 6779 1904, 20 units [shwr, tlt, heat, elec blkts, tel, TV, video, clock radio, t/c mkg, refrig, toaster], ldry, ⊠ (6 nights), bbq, dinner to unit, c/park (undercover), plygr, cots-fee. RO ♦ $47 - $50, ♦♦ $60 - $62, ◊ $10 - $20, pen con, AE BC DC MC VI.

Self Catering Accommodation

★★☆ Cabarfeidh Farmstay, (Cotg), (Farm), Inverell Rd, 20km W of PO, ☎ 02 6779 4235, fax 02 6779 4235, 2 cotgs [shwr, tlt, fan, fire pl, heat, elec blkts, TV, clock radio, t/c mkg, refrig, cook fac, micro, elec frypan, toaster, linen], w/mach, iron, bbq, c/park. D $95, W $475.

(Lodge Section), 6 rms [shwr (2), tlt (2), fan, fire pl, heat, elec blkts, TV, t/c mkg, refrig, cook fac, micro, elec frypan, toaster, linen reqd-fee], w/mach, iron, bbq, c/park. D $45 - $90, ch con.

HALFWAY CREEK NSW 2460

Pop Nominal, (595km N Sydney), See map on page 54, ref D4. Small northern rivers town on the Pacific Highway in the foothills of the Coast Range.

Self Catering Accommodation

★★★★☆ The Rainbows End Farm Resort, (Cotg), (Farm), 212 Grays Rd, ☎ 02 9153 8108, fax 02 9584 9137, 2 cotgs acc up to 7, [shwr, tlt, hairdry, c/fan, heat, elec blkts, tel, TV, video, clock radio, refrig, cook fac, micro, d/wash, toaster, blkts, linen, pillows], ldry, w/mach, dryer, iron, pool-heated, spa, bbq, tennis, cots, non smoking property. D $132 - $176, ◊ $33 - $66, W $660 - $935, Min book applies, BC MC VI.

★★★★☆ (Bed & Breakfast Section), 2 rms [shwr, spa bath (1), tlt, hairdry, c/fan, heat, elec blkts, tel, video, t/c mkg], lounge (TV). BB ♦♦ $121.

HALLIDAYS POINT NSW 2430

Pop 600. (308km N Sydney), See map on page 54, ref B8. Pretty coastal town between Forster and Taree at the northern end of Nine Mile Beach. Bowls, Fishing, Surfing, Swimming, Tennis.

Hotels/Motels

★★ Elga Blackhead Apartments & Motor Inn, (M), Blackhead Rd, 200m W of PO, ☎ 02 6559 2649, fax 02 6559 2649, (2 stry gr fl), 8 units [shwr, bath, tlt, a/c, heat, TV, clock radio, refrig, cook fac ltd, micro, toaster], ldry, iron, pool, bbq, plygr, cots. RO ♦ $70 - $95, ♦♦ $70 - $95, ◊ $11 - $15, ch con, AE BC DC MC VI.

B&B's/Guest Houses

★★★★ Blackhead Beach Bed & Breakfast, (B&B), 23 Woodlands Dve, 6km W of PO, ☎ 02 6559 2143, fax 02 6559 2104, 3 rms [ensuite (1), a/c (1), fan (2), fire pl, heat (elec) (2), elec blkts, TV (2), video, clock radio, doonas], shared fac (2), ldry, dryer, iron, iron brd, read rm, lounge (TV), ✕, pool (outdoore), spa (in pool), t/c mkg shared, refrig, bbq, rm serv, meals to unit, ✆, non smoking rms, Pets allowed. BB ♦ $105 - $140, ♦♦ $105 - $140, weekly con, AE BC MC VI.

★★★★ Waves On High St, (B&B), No children's facilities, 36 High St, Black Head Beach, ☎ 02 6559 3600, fax 02 6559 3263, (Multi-stry), 3 rms [shwr, bath (1), tlt, fan, heat, clock radio], TV rm, lounge, t/c mkg shared, non smoking rms. BB ♦♦ $125 - $135, BC MC VI.

HANNAM VALE NSW 2443

See map on page 54, ref C7.
B&B's/Guest Houses

AAA TOURISM *Special Rates* ★★★★☆ **Benbellen Country Retreat**, (B&B), Previously Benbellen Farmstay 60 Cherry Tree Lane, 30km S of Laurieton, ☎ 02 6556 7788, fax 02 6556 7778, (2 stry gr fl), 3 rms [ensuite, hairdry, c/fan, heat, tel, TV, t/c mkg, ldry], iron, iron brd, lounge, lounge firepl, ✕, 24hr reception, courtesy transfer, non smoking rms. BB ♦ $130 - $135, ♦♦ $165 - $175, AE BC DC JCB MC VI.

HAMILTON NSW

See Newcastle & Suburbs.

HARDEN NSW 2587

Pop 2,050. (361km SW Sydney), See map on pages 52/53, ref F6. Twin town of neighbouring Murrumburrah, an important rail and commercial centre for a flourishing mixed agricultural district. Bowls, Golf, Swimming, Tennis.
Hotels/Motels

★★☆ **Harden Motel**, (M), 42 Albury St, 400m E of PO, ☎ 02 6386 2377, fax 02 6386 2398, 15 units [shwr, tlt, a/c-cool (14), heat, elec blkts, tel, fax, TV, clock radio, t/c mkg, refrig], bbq, dinner to unit, cots-fee. RO ♦ $45 - $49, ♦♦ $55 - $66, ♦ $11, 5 units of a lower rating. AE BC DC MC VI.

HARRINGTON NSW 2427

Pop 1,400. (350km N Sydney), See map on page 54, ref C7. Mid-north coastal town on the northern shores of the Manning River mouth. Bowls, Fishing, Surfing, Swimming, Tennis.
Hotels/Motels

★★★☆ **Harrington Village Motel**, (M), 255 Beach St, 2km W of PO, ☎ 02 6556 1396, fax 02 6556 1386, (2 stry gr fl), 9 units [shwr, tlt, c/fan, heat, elec blkts, tel, fax, TV, clock radio, t/c mkg, refrig, cook fac (2), toaster], courtesy transfer, cots, non smoking units (3). RO ♦ $55 - $71, ♦♦ $61 - $71, ♦♦♦ $71.50 - $99, ♦ $11, ch con, Meals by arrangement, BC MC VI.

Self Catering Accommodation
Harrington Sea Breeze Apartments, (HU), 197 Beach St, ☎ 02 6556 1234, or 02 6556 3725, fax 02 6556 3725, 1 unit acc up to 5, [shwr, tlt, heat, TV, refrig, cook fac, blkts, linen, pillows], ldry, rec rm, pool, bbq, cots. W $220 - $550, Min book applies.

HAT HEAD NSW 2440

Pop 350. (459km N Sydney), See map on page 54, ref C6. Mid-north coastal village surrounded by the extensive heathland of Hat Head National Park. Bowls, Bush Walking, Fishing, Surfing, Tennis.
Self Catering Accommodation

Heatherlea Units, (HU), 46 Straight St, 500m E of PO, ☎ 02 6567 7665, 1 unit acc up to 5, (2 bedrm), [shwr, tlt, fan, heat (elec), TV, video, clock radio, t/c mkg, refrig, cook fac, micro, blkts, doonas, linen, pillows], w/mach, non smoking units, Pets on application. D ♦ $50, ♦♦ $50, weekly con, (not yet classified).

HAWKS NEST NSW 2324

Pop 1,200. (222km Sydney), See map on page 55, ref E7. Coastal resort on northern shores of Port Stephens, handy to the spectacular Myall Lakes National Park. Bowls, Bush Walking, Fishing, Golf, Scenic Drives, Surfing, Swimming.
Hotels/Motels

★★★☆ **Myall River Motor Inn**, (M), 3 Yamba St, 250m W of PO, ☎ 02 4997 1166, fax 02 4997 1957, (2 stry gr fl), 18 units (4 suites) [shwr, spa bath (4), tlt, hairdry, a/c, elec blkts, tel, TV, video (avail)-fee, clock radio, t/c mkg, refrig, cook fac, micro-fee, toaster], ldry, pool (salt water), bbq, cots-fee. W $329 - $790, RO ♦ $47 - $79, ♦♦ $59 - $119, ♦ $15, Suite D $79 - $119, Suite W $479 - $790, Min book all holiday times, AE BC EFT MC VI.

★★★ **Beachfront Motor Inn**, (M), Resort, 15 Beach Rd, ☎ 02 4997 0324, fax 02 4997 0324, (Multi-stry gr fl), 18 units [shwr, bath (1), tlt, a/c (4), c/fan, heat, elec blkts, tel, TV, clock radio, t/c mkg, refrig, cook fac, micro (3), toaster], ldry, pool, spa, bbq, cots. W $390 - $595, RO ♦ $50 - $88, ♦♦ $55 - $88, ♦♦♦ $84 - $111, ♦ $11, AE BC DC EFT MC VI.

HAWKS NEST NSW continued...

Self Catering Accommodation

★★★★ **Aquarius Holiday Units**, (HU), 9 Beach Rd, ☎ 02 4997 0262, fax 02 4997 1001, (Multi-stry gr fl), 6 units acc up to 4, [shwr, bath, tlt, fan, heat, TV, video, clock radio, CD, refrig, cook fac, micro, elec frypan, d/wash, toaster, ldry, linen reqd], w/mach, dryer, iron, iron brd, pool, bbq, non smoking property. **D $120 - $200, W $400 - $1,600.**

★★★☆ **Hawks Nest Lodge**, (HU), Cnr Booner & Bennett Sts, ☎ 02 4997 0941, fax 02 4997 1039, (Multi-stry gr fl), 43 units acc up to 6, [shwr, spa bath (1), tlt, hairdry, c/fan (39), heat, tel, TV, video-fee, clock radio, t/c mkg, refrig, cook fac (39), elec frypan (39), toaster, blkts, linen, pillows], ldry, w/mach (14), dryer (14), iron, rec rm, conv fac, ✉, pool, spa (unheated), bbq, ☎, gym, cots, non smoking units (18). **D $66 - $231, W $338 - $1,232**, AE BC DC EFT MC VI.

★★★ **Kururma Cottage**, (Cotg), 15 Kururma Cres, ☎ 02 4997 0262, fax 02 4997 1001, (2 stry) 1 cotg acc up to 4, [shwr, bath, tlt, heat, TV, video, refrig, cook fac, micro, d/wash, toaster, linen reqd], ldry, bbq, c/park (carport). **W $300 - $1,000.**

★★☆ **Blue Marlin Townhouse**, (HU), 26 Bennett St, ☎ 02 4997 0262, fax 02 4997 1001, (Multi-stry), 2 units acc up to 3, [shwr, bath, tlt, TV, video, refrig, cook fac, micro, d/wash, toaster, ldry, linen reqd], ldry, dryer, bbq, c/park (garage). **W $300 - $1,200.**

★★☆ **Carinya Units**, (HU), 4 Carinya Cl, 800m S of PO, ☎ 02 4997 0262, fax 02 4997 1001, 1 unit acc up to 3, [shwr, bath, tlt, heat, TV, refrig, cook fac, micro, d/wash, toaster, linen reqd], bbq, c/park (garage). **W $200 - $900.**

★★☆ **Jabiru Units**, (HU), 6-8 Bowral St, 700m S of PO, ☎ 02 4997 0262, fax 02 4997 1001, (2 stry) 8 units acc up to 2, [shwr, bath, tlt, heat, TV, clock radio, refrig, cook fac, toaster, ldry (in unit), linen reqd], bbq, c/park (garage). **W $200 - $800.**

★★☆ **The Anchorage Townhouse**, (HU), 1/84 The Anchorage, ☎ 02 4997 0262, fax 02 4997 1001, 1 unit acc up to 4, [shwr, spa bath, tlt, heat, TV, video, refrig, cook fac, micro, elec frypan, d/wash, toaster, linen reqd], bbq, c/park (garage). **W $300 - $1,200.**

★★☆ **The Boulevarde**, (Cotg), 81 The Boulevarde, ☎ 02 4997 0262, fax 02 4997 1001, 1 cotg acc up to 8, [shwr, tlt, heat, TV, refrig, cook fac, micro, elec frypan, toaster, linen reqd], ldry, cots. **W $400 - $1,200.**

★★ **Beachfront Units**, (HU), 17 Beach Rd, 900m E of PO, ☎ 02 4997 0262, fax 02 4997 1001, (Multi-stry), 2 units acc up to 4, [shwr, bath, tlt, TV, refrig, cook fac, micro, toaster, ldry (in unit), linen reqd], pool, bbq, non smoking property. **W $400 - $1,650**, Min book applies.

HAY NSW 2711

Pop 2,900. (730km SW Sydney), See map on pages 52/53, ref D6. Nestled on the banks of the Murrumbidgee River at the junction of three highways, Hay has been a welcome stop on the long overland haul since the days of Cobb & Co. Bowls, Bush Walking, Fishing, Golf, Swimming.

Hotels/Motels

★★★★ **Highway Inn Motel**, (M), Mid Western Hwy, 1km N of PO, ☎ 02 6993 2102, fax 02 6993 4299, 12 units [shwr, bath (1), spa bath (1), tlt, hairdry, a/c, elec blkts (available), tel, TV, video-fee, clock radio, t/c mkg, refrig, micro, toaster], pool (salt water), bbq, cots, non smoking rms (4). **RO ♦ $55 - $99, ♦♦ $66 - $110, ♦♦♦ $77 - $110, ⓘ $10.10**, AE BC DC EFT MC VI, ♿.

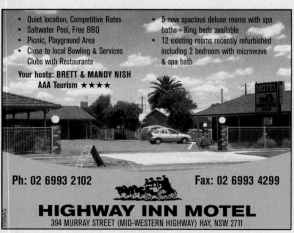

★★★☆ **Nicholas Royal**, (M), 152 Lachlan St, 50m N of PO, ☎ 02 6993 1603, or 02 6993 1603, fax 02 6993 1737, 16 units [shwr, tlt, hairdry, a/c, c/fan, elec blkts, tel, TV, movie, clock radio, t/c mkg, refrig, mini bar, toaster], ldry, iron, iron brd, pool, bbq, dinner to unit, trailer park, plygr, cots, non smoking units (8). **RO ♦ $68, ♦♦ $73 - $75, ⓘ $10**, AE BC DC EFT MC VI.

★★★☆ **Sundowner Chain Motor Inns**, (M), 35 Moama St (Sturt Hwy), 1.3km S of PO (South Hay), ☎ 02 6993 3003, fax 02 6993 1147, 35 units (6 suites) [shwr, bath (1), spa bath (2), tlt, hairdry, a/c, heat, elec blkts, tel, TV, video-fee, clock radio, t/c mkg, refrig], ldry, ✉, pool, spa, rm serv, plygr, tennis, cots-fee, non smoking units (9). **RO ♦ $84 - $138, ♦♦ $91 - $138, ⓘ $11**, ch con, Min book long w/ends, AE BC DC EFT JCB MC MP VI, ♿.

★★★ **Bidgee Motor Inn**, (M), 74 Lachlan St, 100m S of PO, ☎ 02 6993 2260, fax 02 6993 2261, 16 units [shwr, tlt, a/c, elec blkts, tel, TV, clock radio, t/c mkg, refrig, toaster], pool, plygr, cots-fee, non smoking units (6). **RO ♦ $56 - $59, ♦♦ $65 - $69, ⓘ $9**, AE BC DC EFT MC VI.

★★☆ **Cobb Inlander Motel**, (M), 83 Lachlan St, 100m S of PO, ☎ 02 6993 1901, fax 02 6993 3406, (2 stry gr fl), 42 units [shwr, tlt, a/c, elec blkts, tel, TV, clock radio, t/c mkg, refrig], ldry, conv fac, pool (salt water), rm serv, plygr, cots-fee, non smoking rms. **RO ♦ $52 - $64, ♦♦ $61 - $73, ♦♦♦♦ $76**, AE BC DC EFT MCH VI.

★★☆ **Hay Motel**, (M), Cnr Cobb & Sturt Hwy, 1km S of PO, ☎ 02 6993 1804, fax 02 6993 4696, 17 units [shwr, bath (2), tlt, a/c, elec blkts, tel, fax, TV, clock radio, t/c mkg, refrig], pool, dinner to unit, plygr, cots-fee. **RO ♦ $50 - $57, ♦♦ $55 - $63, ⓘ $8**, AE BC MC MCH VI.

★☆ **New Crown Hotel Motel**, (LH), 117 Lachlan St, opposite PO, ☎ 02 6993 1600, (2 stry), 8 rms [shwr, tlt, a/c, TV, clock radio, t/c mkg, refrig], ldry, ✕ (Mon to Sat), bbq, secure park, cots. **BLB ♦ $44, ♦♦ $55, ⓘ $11**, BC EFT MC VI.

Self Catering Accommodation

★★★☆ **A Twig in the Twilight Farm Holidays**, (Cotg), Previously Norwood Farm Holidays (Farm), 'Norwood', 80km NW of Hay, ☎ 02 6993 6742, fax 02 6993 6732, 1 cotg [shwr, tlt, a/c-cool, c/fan, fire pl, elec blkts, tel, clock radio, t/c mkg, refrig, cook fac, micro, elec frypan, toaster, blkts, linen, pillows], ldry, w/mach, rec rm, bbq, c/park (carport). **D ♦♦ $88 - $209, W ♦♦ $550**, Access road affected by weather.

HILLSTON NSW 2675

Pop 1,100. (693km W Sydney), See map on pages 52/53, ref D5. Pretty Riverina township on the banks of the Lachlan River. Boating, Bush Walking, Fishing, Gold Prospecting, Horse Racing, Swimming, Tennis.

Hotels/Motels

★★★ **Kidman Way Motor Inn**, (M), Cnr High & Keats St, 750m N of PO, ☎ 02 6967 2151, fax 02 6967 2351, 11 units [shwr, tlt, a/c, elec blkts, tel, TV, clock radio, t/c mkg, refrig, toaster], ldry, cots. **RO ♦ $55 - $60, ♦♦ $66 - $70, ⓘ $11 - $13**, AE BC DC MC VI.

Club House Hotel, (LH), 147 Hillston St, opposite PO, ☎ 02 6967 2514, fax 02 6967 2341, 18 rms ldry, lounge (TV), ✕, cook fac, t/c mkg shared, bbq, ☎. **RO ♦ $22, ♦♦ $35**, BC EFT MC VI.

HOLBROOK NSW 2644

Pop 1,350. (493km SW Sydney), See map on pages 52/53, ref E7.
Historic town on the Hume Highway roughly halfway between Sydney and Melbourne. Bowls, Golf, Horse Racing, Squash, Swimming, Tennis.

Hotels/Motels

★★★★ **Jolly Swagman Motor Inn**, (M), Cnr Bardwell & Albury Sts (Hume Hwy), 800m S of PO, ☎ 02 6036 3131, fax 02 6036 3068, 11 units (1 suite) [shwr, tlt, hairdry, a/c, elec blkts, tel, cable tv, clock radio, t/c mkg, refrig, toaster], iron, iron brd, ⊠, spa-fee, bbq, plygr, squash, cots-fee. RO ♦ $66 - $76, ♦♦ $79 - $89, ♀ $12, ch con, 2 units of a lower rating. AE BC DC MC VI.

★★★☆ **Holbrook Town Centre Motor Inn**, (M), 86 Albury St (Hume Hwy), 250m S of PO, ☎ 02 6036 2666, fax 02 6036 3549, (2 stry gr fl), 20 units [shwr, spa bath (2), tlt, a/c, elec blkts, tel, TV, video-fee, clock radio, t/c mkg, refrig], ldry, ⊠ (Mon to Sat), rm serv, cots-fee, non smoking units (9). RO ♦ $67 - $85, ♦♦ $79 - $97, ♦♦♦ $92 - $114, ♀ $13, ch con, AE BC DC EFT MC VI.

★★★ **Byer Motor Inn**, (M), Hume Hwy, 1.1km N of PO, ☎ 02 6036 2077, fax 02 6036 2581, 36 units [shwr, tlt, a/c, elec blkts, tel, TV, video (avail), clock radio, t/c mkg, refrig], ldry, ⊠, pool, rm serv, dinner to unit, cots-fee, non smoking units (available). RO ♦ $53 - $63, ♦♦ $60 - $70, ♀ $15, ch con, AE BC DC EFT MC VI.

★★★ **Glenndale Park Motel**, (M), 61 Albury St (Hume Hwy), 800m S of PO, ☎ 02 6036 2599, fax 02 6036 2231, 9 units [shwr, tlt, hairdry, a/c, fan, heat, elec blkts, tel, TV, clock radio, t/c mkg, refrig, toaster], pool, bbq, dinner to unit, kiosk, plygr, cots, non smoking units (3). RO ♦ $55 - $61, ♦♦ $64 - $71, ♀ $11, Min book all holiday times, EFT.

★★★ **Holbrook Skye Motel**, (M), 142 Albury St, ☎ 02 6036 2333, fax 02 6036 2333, 10 units [shwr, tlt, a/c, elec blkts, tel, TV, clock radio, t/c mkg, refrig, toaster], ldry, iron, iron brd, c/park (carport), ⬧, cots-fee, non smoking units (3). RO ♦ $60 - $70, ♦♦ $70 - $88, ♀ $12 - $20, AE BC DC MC VI.

Holbrook Settlers Motel, (M), Hume Hwy, 1.4km N of PO, ☎ 02 6036 2855, fax 02 6036 2857, 16 units [shwr, tlt, evap cool, heat, elec blkts, TV, clock radio, t/c mkg, refrig, toaster], pool, bbq, 24hr reception, dinner to unit, c/park (undercover), ⬧, plygr, cots-fee. RO ♦ $45 - $52, ♦♦ $52 - $60, ♀ $11, AE BC DC EFT MC VI, (not yet classified).

Other Accommodation

Glenfalloch, (Lodge), Four Mile La, 18km N on Hume Hwy, ☎ 02 6036 7203, or 02 6036 7215, fax 02 6036 7265, 11 rms acc up to 46, [fire pl, elec blkts, refrig (3), toaster (2), doonas reqd-fee, linen reqd-fee], shwr, tlt, ldry, w/mach, iron, lounge, pool, cook fac, t/c mkg shared, bbq, tennis. D ♦ $18, ch con, Tariff includes all farm activities. Camping & caravan sites available.

HOWLONG NSW 2643

Pop 1,697. (589km SW Sydney), See map on pages 52/53, ref E7.
Small town on the Murray River between Albury and Corowa. Bowls, Fishing, Golf, Squash, Swimming, Tennis.

Hotels/Motels

★★★☆ **Howlong Country Club**, (M), Golf Club Dve, ☎ 02 6026 5588, fax 02 6026 5941, 25 units [shwr, tlt, a/c, elec blkts, tel, TV, t/c mkg, refrig, toaster], ldry, ⊠, pool, sauna, spa, bbq, tennis, cots-fee. RO ♦♦ $75 - $86, ♀ $14, AE BC DC EFT MC VI, ♿.

★★☆ **Kismet Riverside Retreat**, (M), Riverina Hwy, 4km W of PO, ☎ 02 6026 5748, or 02 6026 5025, fax 02 6026 5025, 12 units [shwr, tlt, a/c, elec blkts, TV, t/c mkg, refrig, toaster], ldry, conf fac, ⊠, pool, bbq, plygr, tennis, cots-fee. RO ♦ $44, ♦♦ $55, ♀ $11, BC EFT MC VI.

Self Catering Accommodation

The Residence, (House), 37 Hawkins St, ☎ 02 6026 5192, fax 02 6026 5208, 3 houses acc up to 5, [shwr, bath, tlt, c/fan, heat, TV, clock radio, t/c mkg, refrig, cook fac, micro, toaster, ldry, doonas, linen-fee], iron, iron brd. D ♦♦ $44 - $66, ♀ $5 - $10, W ♦♦ $330 - $462, ♀ $35 - $70, (not yet classified).

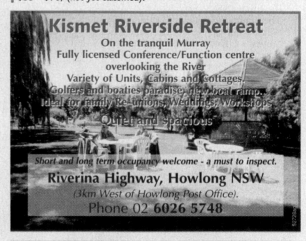
Medication and driving

Medication can effect your driving. Certain drugs can effect your mental alertness and/or co-ordination and therefore effect driving skills. Always check with your doctor the effect which any medication (over the counter or prescription) you are taking may have on your driving. There may be an alternative drug which will not affect your driving. It is best to avoid drinking alcohol while taking medication.

HUNTER VALLEY NSW

See: Aberdeen, Abermain, Bellbird, Branxton, Broke, Brunkerville, Cassilis, Cessnock, Denman, Ellalong, Kurri Kurri, Merriwa, Millfield, Moonan Flat, Mount View, Murrurundi, Muswellbrook, Nulkaba, Paterson, Pokolbin, Rothbury, Scone, Singleton, Vacy, Wollombi.

Seatbelts save lives

No one knows when a crash will occur and unless everyone in the car is properly restrained, there is a chance of unnecessary injury.

Even low-speed crashes can cause serious injury if people are not safely restrained, this highlights the need to wear those belts at all times, from the very start of every trip.

Get into the habit of not starting the car until all passengers are properly restrained.

Remember half of all crashes occur within five kilometres of home.

Hunter Wine Country is a world class vintage

As well as the famous Hunter Valley Wine Country and more than 80 vineyards, visitors find colonial townships, rich farming country, rugged National Parks, outstanding surf beaches and sparkling lakes and rivers in the Hunter Region of NSW.

The Hunter first gained prominence as a tourist region through its winemaking area centred on picturesque Polkolbin. Now Lake Macquarie, World Heritage listed Barrington Tops and the historic towns of Maitland and Morpeth in the geographic heart of the Hunter draw visitors. Cessnock is the gateway to Hunter Valley Wine Country. The winemaking tradition is over 150 years old.

Today, the hills around Cessnock and Pokolbin are a mecca for food and wine enthusiasts – visitors find many fine restaurants. In the Upper Hunter towns like Singleton, Muswellbrook and Scone reflect Australia's rural heritage with fine examples of early Australian architecture. The area also offers wineries, horse studs, forests and a wealth of outdoor activities.

A journey into the heart of the Hunter Valley Wine Country reveals wineries which offer some of the world's finest vintages. The seasons paint the Hunter with a vibrant brush. Wine Country has quaint villages, welcoming wineries, fine art galleries, craft stores and some of the best dining in Australia.

There is quality AAA Tourism STARS assessed accommodation available.

The many festival focus on the great local wines, food and music.

Most wineries specialise in Shiraz, Semillon, Chardonnay and increasingly Verdelho, Chambourcin and Merlot.

The Hunter Valley wine pedigree goes back to the early years of Australian history. The first grapes were planted in the 1830's near the Hunter River from vine cuttings shipped from Europe by pioneer viticulturist James Busby.

There are now more than 4,000 hectares under vine in the Hunter Region. Semillon grapes thrive in the warm, dry climate of the Hunter on sandy loam creek flats.

Two or three nights in the Hunter Valley Wine Country is a basic experience. The greater Hunter region is a destination for a week or more if its attractions are to be fully explored.

World class wine and AAA Tourism assessed accommodation are a welcoming combination in the Hunter.

HUSKISSON NSW 2540

Pop 3,350. (179km S Sydney), See map on page 55, ref B5. Old shipbuilding town on the sandy shores of Jervis Bay, commonly referred to as 'Husky'. Booderee National Park. Boating, Bowls, Bush Walking, Fishing, Golf, Scenic Drives, Swimming, Tennis. See also Callala Beach, Hyams Beach & Vincentia.

Hotels/Motels

★★★☆ **Huskisson Beach Motel**, (M), 9 Hawke St, 200m E of PO, ☎ 02 4441 6387, fax 02 4441 6129, (2 stry gr fl), 32 units [shwr, tlt, a/c (31), fan (1), heat, elec blkts, tel, TV, video-fee, clock radio, t/c mkg, refrig, toaster], ldry, conv fac, ✕, cots-fee, non smoking rms (12). **RO** ∮ **$70 - $175**, ∯ **$75 - $250**, ∮ **$15 - $25**, 6 units of a higher standard. Min book applies, AE BC DC MC VI.

★★★☆ **Jervis Bay Motel Huskisson**, (M), 41 Owen St, 100m W of PO, ☎ 02 4441 5781, fax 02 4441 7072, (2 stry gr fl), 15 units [shwr, tlt, a/c, elec blkts, tel, TV, clock radio, t/c mkg, refrig, toaster], ldry, pool, bbq, cots-fee. **RO** ∮ **$75 - $175**, ∯ **$75 - $175**, ∰ **$90 - $225**, ∮ **$25**, AE BC DC MC VI.

★★☆ **Bayside Motor Inn Huskisson**, (M), Cnr Hawke & Bowen Sts, 300m SE of PO, ☎ 02 4441 5500, fax 02 4441 7142, (2 stry gr fl), 30 units (1 suite) [shwr, tlt, a/c (10), fan, heat, elec blkts, TV, video-fee, clock radio, t/c mkg, refrig, cook fac (8)], ldry, ✕, pool-heated (solar), bbq, rm serv, cots. **RO** ∮ **$60 - $150**, ∯ **$65 - $190**, ∰ **$80 - $190**, ∮ **$12**, **W $450 - $1,200**, 11 units ★★★. Min book applies, AE BC BTC DC MC MCH VI.

Self Catering Accommodation

★★★★ **Woollamia Village Retreat**, (Apt), 21 Pritchard Ave, Woollamia 2540, 5.5km NW from Huskisson, ☎ 02 4441 6108, fax 02 4441 7055, 4 apts acc up to 6, (1 bedrm), [shwr, spa bath (2), tlt, a/c (1), fan, heat, TV, clock radio (2), radio (2), t/c mkg, refrig, cook fac (3), cook fac ltd (1), micro, ldry, blkts, doonas, linen, pillows], bbq, breakfast ingredients, non smoking property. **D** ∯ **$110 - $175**, ∮ **$25**, ch con, weekly con, BC MC VI.

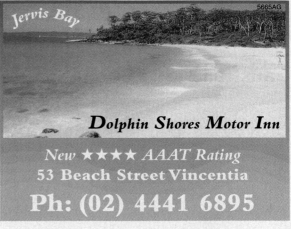

HUSKISSON NSW continued...

★★★☆ **Anglesea Lodges**, (SA), 2 Admiralty Cres, 500m N of PO, ☎ 02 4441 5057, or 02 4441 5251, fax 02 4441 5699, 6 serv apts acc up to 4, [shwr, tlt, hairdry, a/c, fan, heat, elec blkts, tel, TV, video, clock radio, t/c mkg, refrig, cook fac, micro, elec frypan, toaster], ldry, iron, pool (salt water), bbq, plygr, jetty, cots, non smoking units. **D $150 - $264, W $1,300 - $1,600**, Min book applies, AE BC MC VI.

Unit 10, The Promenade, (HU), Unit 10, The Promenade, ☎ 02 4421 7118, fax 02 4421 8947, 1 unit acc up to 5, [shwr, bath, tlt, TV, video, clock radio, CD, t/c mkg, refrig, cook fac, micro, toaster, ldry, doonas, linen reqd], w/mach, iron, iron brd, non smoking units. **D $115 - $165, W $650 - $990**, Min book applies, AE BC DC MC VI, (not yet classified).

B&B's/Guest Houses

★★★★☆ **Jervis Bay Guesthouse**, (GH), No children's facilities, 1 Beach St, ☎ 02 4441 7658, fax 02 4441 7659, (2 stry), 4 rms [shwr, spa bath (1), tlt, a/c, c/fan, heat], lounge firepl, t/c mkg shared, refrig, bbq, non smoking property. **BB ♦ $115 - $210, ♦♦ $130 - $225, ◊ $50**, AE BC DC EFT JCB MC VI,

Operator Comment: A charming B&B opposite an incredible white-sand beach on Jervis Bay. 1 spa room. Spectacular views. Great breakfast. Wonderful dolphins & wildlife.

★★★☆ **McArthurs At Jervis Bay**, (B&B), 17 McArthur Dve, Woollamia 2540, 2.5km from Falls Creek, ☎ 02 4447 8182, fax 02 4421 6197, (2 stry), 3 rms [spa bath (1), c/fan, heat, elec blkts, tel, refrig], rec rm, lounge (TV, video), lounge firepl, ✕, spa, t/c mkg shared, bbq, non smoking rms. **BB ♦ $80, ♦♦ $100 - $150.**

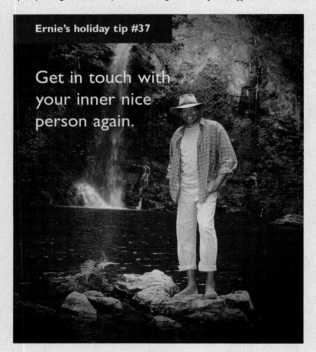

Trouble-free travel tips - Fluids

Check all fluid levels and top up as necessary. Look at engine oil, automatic transmission fluid, radiator coolant (only check this when the engine is cold), power steering, battery and windscreen washers.

HYAMS BEACH NSW 2540

Pop 170. (191km S Sydney), See map on page 55, ref B5. Village on the shores of Jervis Bay, with a beach said to have the whitest sand in Australia. Swimming. See also Vincentia.

Self Catering Accommodation

★★ **Kullindi**, (HU), Ellmoos Rd, 12km W of PO, ☎ 02 4441 2897, 5 units acc up to 6, [shwr, bath (1), tlt, c/fan (5), fire pl (open) (1), heat, elec blkts (dbl/beds only), fax, TV, refrig, cook fac, micro], ⊠, bbq, bush walking. **RO ♦♦ $95 - $280, W $550 - $1,050**, Min book applies, AE BC MC VI.

★★ **Walters**, (HF), 70 Cyrus St, ☎ 02 4443 0850, fax 02 4443 0850, 4 flats acc up to 5, [shwr, tlt, TV, video (avail), clock radio, refrig, cook fac, micro, linen reqd], ldry, cots. **D $70 - $115, W $470 - $700**, Min book applies.

ILUKA NSW 2466

Pop 1,850. (694km N Sydney), See map on page 54, ref D3. Quiet coastal town on the northern headland of the Clarence River mouth, flanked by Bundjalung National Park. Boating, Bowls, Bush Walking, Fishing, Golf, Surfing, Tennis.

Hotels/Motels

★★★☆ **Iluka Motel**, (M), 47 Charles St, 200m N of PO, ☎ 02 6646 6288, fax 02 6646 5777, 9 units [shwr, tlt, fan, heat, elec blkts, tel, TV, clock radio, t/c mkg, refrig, cook fac (4)], bbq, c/park (undercover). **RO ♦♦ $63 - $74, ◊ $6 - $11**, AE BC DC EFT MC VI.

Self Catering Accommodation

★★★☆ **Iluka Waterfront Holiday Units**, (HU), 14 Queen La, 200m W of PO, ☎ 02 6646 6330, 2 units acc up to 5, [shwr, tlt, fan, heat, TV, clock radio, t/c mkg, refrig, cook fac, d/wash, ldry (in unit), linen reqd-fee], c/park (undercover). **D $30 - $90, W $185 - $600**, Min book applies.

★★★ **Bream Court**, (HU), 38 Marandowie Dve, 1km N of PO, ☎ 02 6646 6210, fax 02 6646 6844, 2 units acc up to 5, [shwr, tlt, fan, heat, TV, video, clock radio, t/c mkg, refrig, cook fac, micro, elec frypan, toaster, ldry (in unit), linen], iron, bbq, c/park (garage). **D $80, W $375 - $690**, Min book applies, AE BC EFT MC VI.

★★★ **Camawood**, (HU), 2 Spenser St, ☎ 02 6646 6177, 7 units acc up to 6, [shwr, tlt, TV, refrig, cook fac, micro, toaster, ldry, linen reqd], pool, c/park (undercover), jetty. **W $395 - $695.**

★★☆ **Iluka Lodge Holiday Units**, (HU), 54 Charles St, 150m NE of PO, ☎ 02 6646 6177, 3 units acc up to 4, [shwr, tlt, fan, heat, TV, clock radio, refrig, cook fac, micro, toaster, ldry, linen reqd-fee], c/park. **W $250 - $460.**

★★☆ **Iluka Villas**, (HU), 4 Spenser St, ☎ 02 6646 6177, 8 units acc up to 6, [shwr, tlt, TV, refrig, cook fac, toaster], ldry, pool, bbq, c/park (carport), jetty. **D $290 - $660.**

★★☆ **The Dolphins**, (HU), 44 Spenser St, ☎ 02 6646 6013, 4 units acc up to 5, [shwr, bath, tlt, heat, TV, clock radio, refrig, cook fac, micro, blkts, linen reqd-fee], ldry, bbq, c/park (undercover), boat park. **D $40 - $60, W $200 - $375.**

INVERELL NSW 2360

Pop 9,400. (670km N Sydney). See map on page 54, ref A3. Attractive town on the Macintyre River. It's known as the 'Sapphire City', being at the heart of production of much of the world's supply of blue sapphire. Bowls, Fishing, Golf, Scenic Drives, Swimming, Tennis.

Hotels/Motels

★★★★ **Cousins Motor Inn**, (M), 9 Glen Innes Rd (Gwydir Hwy), adjacent to town centre, ☎ 02 6722 3566, fax 02 6722 5633, 18 units [shwr, spa bath (2), tlt, a/c, elec blkts, tel, cable tv, video, movie, clock radio, t/c mkg, refrig, toaster], pool, spa, dinner to unit, cots-fee, non smoking units (6). **RO ♦ $85, ♦♦ $95, ♦♦♦ $105, ◊ $10,** AE BC DC EFT JCB MC MP VI.

 ★★★☆ **Sapphire City Motel Inverell**, (M), 34 Glen Innes Rd (Gwydir Hwy), 1km E of PO, ☎ 02 6722 2500, fax 02 6722 2554, 17 units [shwr, tlt, a/c, elec blkts, tel, TV, clock radio, t/c mkg, refrig], dinner to unit, c/park (undercover) (13), cots-fee. **RO ♦ $63 - $68, ♦♦ $70 - $75, ♦♦♦ $81 - $86, ◊ $11,** Min book applies, AE BC DC EFT MC MCH MP VI.

 ★★★☆ **Top of the Town Motel**, (M), Gwydir Hwy, 2km W of PO, ☎ 02 6722 4044, fax 02 6722 5414, 21 units [shwr, tlt, a/c, elec blkts, tel, cable tv, video-fee, clock radio, t/c mkg, refrig], ✕ (Mon to Sat), pool, rm serv, dinner to unit, cots-fee, non smoking units (8). **RO ♦ $92, ♦♦ $92, ◊ $12,** ch con, AE BC DC MC MP VI.

★★★☆ **Twin Swans Motel**, (M), 189 Glen Innes Rd (Gwydir Hwy), 2km E of PO, ☎ 02 6722 2622, fax 02 6722 5479, (2 stry gr fl), 24 units (4 suites) [shwr, tlt, a/c, elec blkts, tel, cable tv, clock radio, t/c mkg, refrig], ✕ (Mon to Sat), pool (salt water), rm serv, dinner to unit (Mon to Sat), cots-fee. **RO ♦ $64, ♦♦ $72, ◊ $9, Suite RO ♦ $69, ♦♦ $78,** AE BC DC MC VI.

★★☆ **Inverell Motel**, (M), 49-57 Otho St, 100m NW of PO, centre of town, ☎ 02 6722 2077, fax 02 6751 0075, (2 stry gr fl), 24 units [shwr, tlt, a/c-cool, fan, elec blkts, tel, TV, clock radio, t/c mkg, refrig], ldry, meals to unit, cots-fee, non smoking units (3). **RO ♦ $49.50 - $60.50, ♦♦ $58.30 - $68.20,** AE BC DC MC VI.

IVANHOE NSW 2878

Pop 300. (840km W Sydney). See map on pages 52/53, ref C4. Isolated town on the Cobb Highway, at the junction of a number of unsealed roads that follow historic stock routes across the State. Bowls, Tennis.

Hotels/Motels

Ivanhoe Hotel, (LH), 10 Columbus St, 100 m of PO, ☎ 02 6995 1102, fax 02 6995 1447, 4 rms [shwr, tlt, a/c-cool, refrig, toaster], ✕ (as required), 24hr reception. **BLB ♦ $30 - $35, ♦♦ $50 - $60, DBB ♦ $45 - $55, ♦♦ $90 - $100,** EFT.

Other Accommodation

Gypsum Auto Port, (Lodge), Columbus St, ☎ 02 6995 1389, or 02 6995 1126, fax 02 6995 1389, 7 rms [shwr (3), tlt (3), a/c, cent heat, elec blkts, TV, clock radio, t/c mkg, refrig, cook fac (1), micro (1), toaster, blkts, linen, pillows], shared fac (4 units), ldry, iron, bbq (area), cots. **D ♦ $44, ♦♦ $71.50,** BC EFT MC VI.

JAMBEROO NSW 2533

Pop 724. (110km S Sydney). See map on page 55, ref C4. Small village on the Minnamurra River, first settled in the 1820s and still surrounded by pockets of rainforest. Bush Walking, Scenic Drives.

Hotels/Motels

★★☆ **Jamberoo Valley Lodge**, (M), Jamberoo Mountain Rd, 4km W of PO, ☎ 02 4236 0269, fax 02 4236 0446, 45 units [shwr, tlt, a/c, tel, TV, video (avail), clock radio, t/c mkg, refrig], ldry, rec rm, conv fac, ✕, pool, bbq, tennis, cots. **BB ♦♦ $125, ◊ $20, RO ♦♦ $100, ◊ $15,** ch con, Min book long w/ends and Easter, AE BC DC MC VI.

★☆ **Jamberoo Pub & Saleyard Motel**, (LH), 12 Allowrie St, ☎ 02 4236 0270, 9 rms shared fac (2), lounge (TV), conf fac, ✕, bbq, ✆, cots. **RO ♦ $35, ♦♦ $65, ♦♦♦ $75,** ch con, Light breakfast only available. AE BC EFT MC VI.

★★★☆ **(Motel Section)**, 9 units [shwr, tlt, a/c, tel, TV, clock radio, t/c mkg, refrig]. **RO ♦ $79 - $125, ♦♦ $110 - $125,** ♿.

JENOLAN CAVES NSW

See Blue Mountains Region.

JERILDERIE NSW 2716

Pop 900. (619km SW Sydney). See map on pages 52/53, ref D6. Historic town on the Newell Highway, famous for having been raided by Ned Kelly and his gang in 1879. Bowls, Fishing, Golf, Horse Racing, Shooting, Swimming.

Hotels/Motels

★★★ **Jerilderie Motor Inn**, (M), 4 Jerilderie St, ☎ 03 5886 1360, fax 03 5886 1235, 14 units [shwr, tlt, hairdry, a/c, elec blkts, tel, fax, TV, clock radio, t/c mkg, refrig, toaster], pool, bbq, plygr, cots-fee. **RO ♦ $55 - $65, ♦♦ $66 - $80, ◊ $10,** AE BC DC EFT MC VI.

 ★★ **Jerilderie Budget Motel**, (M), 1-5 Southey St (Newell Hwy), ☎ 03 5886 1301, 9 units [shwr, tlt, a/c-cool, heat, elec blkts, tel, TV, clock radio, t/c mkg, refrig, toaster], c/park (undercover), cots-fee. **RO ♦ $45, ♦♦ $54, ◊ $10,** AE BC DC MC VI.

★☆ **Colony Inn**, (LMH), Jerilderie St, ☎ 03 5886 1220, (2 stry gr fl), 12 units [shwr, tlt, a/c, elec blkts, tel, TV, clock radio, t/c mkg, refrig, toaster], ✕, cots-fee. **BLB ♦ $55, ♦♦ $60, ♦♦♦ $65, ◊ $10,** AE BC DC MC VI.

★ **Greenview Motel**, (M), Newell Hwy, 1km E of PO, ☎ 03 5886 1406, fax 03 5886 1537, 10 units [shwr, tlt, a/c-cool, heat, elec blkts, TV, clock radio, t/c mkg, refrig], ✕. **RO ♦ $32.50, ♦♦ $47.50,** AE BC MC VI.

Self Catering Accommodation

★★★ **Woodside Station**, (Cotg), (Farm), Woodside La, via Wilson Rd, off Bolton St, 38km N of PO, ☎ 03 5886 1560, fax 03 5886 1501, 1 cotg acc up to 8, [shwr (2), spa bath, tlt (2), a/c-cool, heat, TV, clock radio, t/c mkg, refrig, cook fac, micro, elec frypan, d/wash, toaster, ldry (in unit), blkts, linen, pillows], w/mach, dryer, iron, rec rm, bbq, plygr, canoeing, cots. **RO ♦ $80, ♦♦ $80, W $400.**

JESMOND NSW

See Newcastle & Suburbs.

JINDABYNE NSW 2627

Pop 4,320. See map on pages 52/53, ref F7. Year-round holiday resort situated in the Snowy Mountains. It's a good base from which to go skiing, exploring Kosciuszko National Park or casting a fishing line into Lake Jindabyne. Fishing, Golf, Scenic Drives, Snow Skiing, Squash, Swimming, Tennis, Water Skiing.

Hotels/Motels

★★★ **Alpine Resort Motel**, (M), 22 Nettin Cct, 1km W of PO, ☎ 02 6456 2522, fax 02 6456 2854, (Multi-stry gr fl), 29 units [shwr, bath (18), spa bath (18), tlt, hairdry (18), fan (18), cent heat, tel (18), TV, clock radio (18), t/c mkg, refrig, cook fac (2), micro (18), toaster (18)], ldry, iron (18), iron brd (18), rec rm, TV rm, conv fac, lounge firepl, ✕, spa, bbq, ✆, tennis, cots, non smoking rms (8). BB ♦ $80 - $200, ♦♦ $98 - $299, ◊ $15 - $30, RO ♦ $75 - $200, ♦♦ $75 - $280, ◊ $10 - $60, ch con, Min book applies, BC EFT MC VI.

★★★ **Banjo Paterson Inn**, (LMH), Previously Aspen Chalet Hotel Motel Kosciuszko Rd, ☎ 02 6456 2372, fax 02 6456 1138, (Multi-stry), 22 units [shwr, bath (27), spa bath (5), tlt, hairdry, cent heat, tel, cable tv, video-fee, t/c mkg, refrig], ldry, ✕, bar, courtesy transfer. D $65 - $750, Rating applies to lake view units, AE BC DC EFT MC VI.

★★☆ **Lake Jindabyne Motel Hotel**, (LMH), Kosciuszko Rd, ☎ 02 6456 2203, fax 02 6456 2807, (2 stry gr fl), 39 units [shwr, bath (5), tlt, a/c, cent heat, tel, TV, clock radio, t/c mkg, refrig], lounge, conv fac, ✕, pool indoor heated, sauna, spa, cots. BB ♦ $65 - $150, ♦♦ $75 - $200, ♦♦♦ $110 - $300, ♦♦♦♦ $110 - $300, ch con, 22 units not rated. AE BC DC EFT MC VI.

★★ **Lakeview Plaza Motel**, (M), 2 Snowy River Ave, opposite PO, ☎ 02 6456 2134, fax 02 6456 1372, (2 stry gr fl), 13 units [shwr, tlt, hairdry, cent heat, TV, movie, clock radio, t/c mkg, refrig, cook fac (2)], dry rm, ✕, bar, spa. RO ♦♦ $65 - $200, ch con, AE BC DC MC VI.

Alpine Gables Apartment Motel, (M), Cnr Kosciusko Rd & Kalkite St, 500m W of PO, ☎ 02 6456 2555, fax 02 6456 2815, (2 stry), 42 units [shwr, bath, tlt, fan, heat, tel, TV, movie, t/c mkg, refrig, cook fac, micro, elec frypan], ldry, ✕, sauna, spa, cots. D $93.50 - $267, W $676 - $1,716, ch con, AE BC DC MC VI.

Self Catering Accommodation

AAA
TOURISM
Special Rates

Quality
FLAG CHOICE HOTELS

★★★★ **Horizons Snowy Mountains Resort**, (SA), Kosciuszko Rd, 1.5km W of PO, ☎ 02 6456 2562, fax 02 6456 2488, 109 serv apts [shwr, bath, spa bath (36), tlt, heat, tel, cable tv, movie, clock radio, refrig, cook fac, micro, d/wash, toaster, ldry (in unit)], w/mach, dryer, lounge (firepl), conv fac, ✕, bar, pool indoor heated, c/park (undercover), non smoking units (95). **High Season D $176 - $406, Low Season D $103 - $180, High Season W $385 - $893**, AE BC DC EFT MC VI.

★★★☆ **Birken Apartments**, (HF), 21 Townsend St, 800m E of PO, ☎ 02 6456 2276, fax 02 6456 2276, 2 flats acc up to 5, [shwr, tlt, fan, heat, TV, refrig, cook fac, micro, blkts, linen, pillows], ldry, dry rm, sauna, bbq, plygr, cots, non smoking units (2). D $60 - $200, W $400 - $950, Min book applies, BC MC VI.

★★★☆ **Kalkite Villas**, (Cotg), 13 Magnolia Ave, Kalkite, 22km E of Jindabyne PO, ☎ 02 6456 7070, fax 02 6456 7073, (2 stry gr fl), 2 cotgs acc up to 7, [shwr, bath, tlt, heat, cent heat (1), TV, video, clock radio, t/c mkg, refrig, cook fac, micro, elec frypan, d/wash, toaster, ldry, blkts, linen, pillows], w/mach, dryer, iron, bbq, c/park (carport), non smoking units. D $100 - $180, W $500 - $1,100, BC MC VI.

★★★☆ **Pontis Lodge**, (HU), 27 Townsend St, 800m E of PO, ☎ 02 6456 2538, fax 02 6456 2538, 2 units acc up to 8, [shwr, bath, tlt, fan, heat, TV, video, refrig, cook fac, micro, ldry, linen reqd], bbq, c/park (garage), secure park, canoeing, cots. **RO $650 - $1,800**, Min book applies, BC MC VI.

★★★ **Arosa Apartmotel**, (SA), 3 Kosciuszko Rd, 350m N of PO, ☎ 02 6456 2189, fax 02 6456 2293, 4 serv apts acc up to 5, [shwr, bath, tlt, hairdry, cent heat, tel, TV, video, refrig, cook fac, micro], bbq, plygr. **High Season BB ♦♦♦♦ $240 - $280, ♦ $60 - $70, Low Season BB ♦♦ $80 - $100, ♦ $15**, Min book applies, BC MC VI.

★★☆ **Yowie Lodge**, (HU), Unit 3/26 Townsend St, 800m E of PO, ☎ 02 4328 4653, 1 unit acc up to 7, [shwr, bath, tlt, fan, heat, elec blkts, tel, TV, video, refrig, cook fac, micro, elec frypan, toaster, linen reqd], ldry, w/mach, dryer, iron, c/park. **W $429 - $935**, Min book applies, BC MC VI.

★★ **Chesa St Moritz**, (HU), Lot 10 Alpensee Weg, Tyrolean Village, 5km NE of PO, ☎ 02 6456 1856, fax 02 6457 1856, 1 unit acc up to 6, [shwr, tlt, heat, TV, refrig, cook fac, blkts, linen, pillows], ldry, dry rm, bbq. **High Season D $120 - $190, Low Season D $65 - $130, High Season W $700 - $1,050, Low Season W $310 - $520.**

★★ **Sonnblick Holiday Flats**, (HU), 47 Gippsland St, 1km SE of PO, ☎ 02 6456 1957, fax 02 6456 2057, 4 units acc up to 6, [shwr, tlt, heat, elec blkts, TV, video, refrig, cook fac, micro, toaster, linen], ldry, w/mach, dryer, iron, c/park. **D ♦♦ $60 - $140, W $300 - $1,050**, Min book applies, BC MC VI.

Aalberg Chalet, (Chalet), 8 Kirwan Cl, ☎ 02 6456 2647, fax 02 6457 2120, (2 stry gr fl), 1 chalet acc up to 7, [shwr, tlt, cent heat, tel, TV, clock radio, refrig, blkts, linen, pillows], lounge (TV), ✉, bar, spa, t/c mkg shared, bbq, ✆, cots. **Low Season BLB ♦ $55, ♦♦ $88, ♦ $17, High Season DBB ♦♦ $210 - $895, ♦♦ $350 - $1,540**, ch con, Min book applies, BC MC VI, (not yet classified).

Bogong Heights, (HU), 1 Bogong St, ☎ 02 6457 2208, fax 02 6457 2206, (2 stry gr fl), 3 units acc up to 9, [shwr, tlt, c/fan (2), heat, elec blkts, TV, video (3), refrig, cook fac, micro, elec frypan, toaster, linen reqd-fee], ldry, w/mach, dryer, iron, iron brd, courtesy transfer, cots, non smoking property. **D $100 - $500, W $380 - $1,470**, (not yet classified).

AAAT ★ ★ ★ ☆

Carinya Alpine Village, (HU), Dalgety Rd, Junction of Mowamba River & Dalgety Rd, ☎ 02 6456 2252, fax 02 6457 2252, 9 units acc up to 8, [shwr, bath (2), tlt, heat, TV, t/c mkg, refrig, cook fac, micro, elec frypan, toaster, ldry (5), blkts, linen reqd-fee], w/mach (5), rec rm, TV rm, conv fac, lounge firepl, bbq, ✆, plygr, tennis-fee, cots. **High Season D $92 - $282, Low Season D $50 - $100**, ch con, Min book applies, BC EFT MC VI, (not yet classified).

Highland Lodge, (HU), (Farm), Eucumbene Rd, Cnr Eucumbene & Kalkite Rds, ☎ 02 6456 7250, fax 02 6456 7220, 3 units acc up to 6, [shwr, tlt, cent heat, clock radio, t/c mkg, refrig, cook fac, micro, toaster, doonas, linen-fee], ldry, TV rm, lounge firepl, bbq, plygr, bicycle, cots, non smoking units. **D $80 - $150**, Min book applies, BC MC VI, (not yet classified).

The Swagmans Rest, (Cotg), Old School Rd via Hill Top Rd, 10km E of PO, ☎ 02 6456 7332, fax 02 6456 7332, 1 cotg acc up to 4, [shwr, tlt, c/fan, fire pl, heat, elec blkts (queen bed only), TV, t/c mkg, refrig, cook fac, micro, elec frypan, toaster, blkts, linen], w/mach, iron, iron brd, bbq, non smoking property. **D $100 - $180, W $450 - $900**, (not yet classified).

JINDABYNE NSW continued...

Cascades 8, (HU), 43 Flinders Pde, Redcliffe 4020, 500m W of PO, ☎ 02 6456 2368, 1 unit acc up to 4, [shwr, bath, tlt, heat, TV, video, clock radio, t/c mkg, refrig, cook fac, micro, toaster, linen], w/mach, dryer, iron, c/park (garage). **D $70 - $150.**

Highland Valley Apartments, (HU), 13 Ingebyra St, 300m S of PO, ☎ 02 6456 2265, fax 02 6456 1941, 3 units acc up to 8, [shwr, tlt, fan (1), cent heat, elec blkts, TV, video, clock radio, t/c mkg, refrig, cook fac, micro, elec frypan, toaster, doonas, linen reqd], ldry, iron, iron brd, dry rm, bbq, c/park (garage), cots. **D $70 - $330, W $360 - $1,210.**

B&B's/Guest Houses

★★★☆ **Sonnblick Lodge**, (GH), 49 Gippsland St, 1.5km SE of PO, ☎ 02 6456 2472, fax 02 6456 1688, (2 stry gr fl), 12 rms [shwr, tlt, hairdry, heat, elec blkts, clock radio], rec rm, lounge (tv, video & firepl), t/c mkg shared, refrig. **BB ╪ $40 - $95, ╫ $70 - $190, ⏦ $35 - $60,** ch con, AE BC DC MC VI.

★★★☆ **Upsan Downs Guest House**, (GH), Barry Way, 1.5km SW of PO, ☎ 02 6456 2421, fax 02 6456 1254, 7 rms [shwr, tlt, cent heat, elec blkts, TV, video], ldry, dry rm, rec rm, lounge (TV), pool indoor heated, sauna, steam rm, t/c mkg shared, refrig. **Low Season BB ╪ $60 - $65, High Season DBB ╪ $74 - $104, ╪ $483 - $696,** ch con, BC MC VI.

★★ **Enzian Lodge**, (GH), 42 Gippsland St, ☎ 02 6456 2038, fax 02 6456 1948, (2 stry gr fl), 8 rms [shwr, tlt, cent heat, TV], lounge (TV), t/c mkg shared, bbq, c/park (6), cots. **BB ╪ $75, ╫ $120, ╫╫ $150, ╫╫╫ $180,** ch con, BC MC VI.

Eagles Range Farmstay, (GH), Dalgety Rd, 13km S of PO, ☎ 02 6456 2728, fax 02 6456 2728, (2 stry gr fl), 4 rms [ensuite, bath (2), cent heat, tel, refrig, micro], ldry, iron, iron brd, lounge (TV & firepl), ✗, spa, t/c mkg shared, bbq, plygr, bicycle, cots, non smoking property. **BB ╫ $88, DBB ╫ $132, ⏦ $60,** ch con, fam con, Min book applies, BC MC VI, (not yet classified).

(**Chalet Section**), 3 chalets acc up to 8, [shwr, tlt, fire pl, tel, TV, video, clock radio, t/c mkg, refrig, cook fac, micro, elec frypan, toaster, linen reqd], bbq, cots, non smoking units. **D $88 - $150, W $528 - $660,** (not yet classified).

Kanga Lodge, (B&B), Resort, 33 Jerrara Dve, 8km NE of Jindabyne, ☎ 02 6456 7111, fax 02 6456 7307, (2 stry gr fl), 3 rms [shwr, bath (1), tlt, fan (2), heat], lounge (TV), lounge firepl, t/c mkg shared, refrig, courtesy transfer, non smoking property. **BB ╪ $50 - $85, ╫ $80 - $140,** ch con, Minimum booking winter weekends, BC MC VI, (not yet classified).

Troldhaugen Lodge, (B&B), 13 Cobbodah St, 500m SE of PO, ☎ 02 6456 2718, fax 02 6456 2718, (Multi-stry gr fl), 8 rms [shwr, bath (1), tlt, cent heat], rec rm, lounge (TV, video), lounge firepl, ✗, t/c mkg shared, refrig, bbq, courtesy transfer, ☎, cots, non smoking property. **BLB ╪ $25 - $70, ╫ $50 - $140, ⏦ $25 - $70,** ch con, fam con, (not yet classified).

Park Chalet Guest House, (GH), Barry Way, 15km S of Jindabyne, ☎ 02 6457 8177, fax 02 6457 8177, (2 stry gr fl), 8 rms [shwr, tlt, cent heat, elec blkts], rec rm, conv fac, lounge firepl (TV), ✗, pool-indoor, sauna, spa, t/c mkg shared, cots, AE BC MC VI.

Rimrock Bed & Breakfast, (B&B), 35 Jerrara Drive, ☎ 02 6456 2888, fax 02 6456 2888, (2 stry gr fl), 3 rms [shwr (1), bath (1), tlt (1), hairdry (2), heat, tel, clock radio, t/c mkg], shared fac (2 rms), ldry, iron, iron brd, lounge (TV & firepl), ✗, non smoking property. **BB ╪ $50 - $66, ╫ $100 - $132, ⏦ $33 - $50, DBB ╪ $77 - $94, ╫ $154 - $187, ⏦ $61 - $77,** ch con.

Other Accommodation

Hanna's Hutte Ski Lodge, (Lodge), 51 Gippsland St, 500m SE of PO, ☎ 02 9439 6333, fax 02 9437 5936, (2 stry gr fl), 1 rm acc up to 8, [shwr, tlt, heat (2), cent heat (10), elec blkts, refrig (5), mini bar (3), micro (5), doonas, linen], lounge (TV), lounge firepl, t/c mkg shared. **D ╫ $50 - $120, ⏦ $11 - $50, W ╫ $340 - $820, ⏦ $77 - $270,** ch con, AE BC DC MC VI, (not yet classified).

Nettin Chalet Lodge, (Lodge), 24 Nettin Cir, 1km W of PO, ☎ 02 6456 2692, fax 02 6456 1115, (2 stry gr fl), 36 rms [shwr, bath, tlt, cent heat, TV, movie, t/c mkg, refrig (20)], ldry, dry rm, rec rm, lounge, lounge firepl, ✗, bar, sauna, spa (winter), ☎, cots. **High Season BB ╪ $130, ╫ $130, Low Season BB ╪ $45, ╫ $70,** ch con, BC EFT MC VI.

Silvertop Lodge, (Lodge), Westons Rd via Alpine Way, ☎ 02 6456 1426, fax 02 6457 1537, (2 stry gr fl), 5 rms acc up to 11, [shwr, bath, tlt, heat, cent heat, TV, clock radio, t/c mkg, refrig, cook fac, micro, elec frypan, d/wash, toaster, ldry, doonas, linen], w/mach, dryer, iron, iron brd, dry rm, lounge firepl, bbq, cots, non smoking property. **BB ╫ $110,** BC MC VI, (not yet classified).

Ski Inn Lodge, (Lodge), 9 Nettin Cct, 1km W of PO, ☎ 02 6456 2918, fax 02 6456 1545, (2 stry), 1 rm [shwr, tlt, heat, TV, video, t/c mkg, linen], lounge, ✗, ☎, cots. **BB ╪ $37 - $90, ⏦ $37 - $90,** ch con, Min book applies, BC MC VI,

Operator Comment: Visit our web site at www.skiinn.com.au

The Jindy Inn, (Lodge), 18 Clyde St, 500m W of PO, ☎ 02 6456 1957, fax 02 6456 2057, (Multi-stry gr fl), 15 rms [shwr, tlt, hairdry, cent heat, elec blkts, video (avail), t/c mkg, refrig], ldry, ✉ (Winter only), cook fac. **RO ╪ $30 - $95, ╫ $50 - $190, ⏦ $25,** BC MC VI.

Thredbo Valley Lodge, (Lodge), Westons Rd, Jindabyne, 10km SE of PO, ☎ 02 6456 2511, fax 02 6456 2905, (2 stry gr fl), 1 rm [shwr, tlt, cent heat, doonas, linen], ldry, dry rm, rec rm, lounge (TV), conf fac, lounge firepl, pool-heated, sauna, bbq, courtesy transfer, ☎, tennis, cots. **BB ╫ $175 - $297, ⏦ $44 - $66, DBB ╫ $215 - $370, ⏦ $77 - $100,** ch con, BC EFT MC VI, (not yet classified).

JUGIONG NSW 2726

Pop Part of Gundagai, (340km SW Sydney), See map on pages 52/53, ref F6. Small Capital Country township that was for years a popular stop on the Hume Highway. Canoeing, Fishing.

Hotels/Motels

★★☆ **Jugiong Motor Inn**, (M), Cobb & Co Way, 1km N of PO, ☎ 02 6945 4269, fax 02 6945 4333, 18 units [shwr, tlt, a/c, elec blkts, TV, clock radio, t/c mkg, refrig], conv fac, ✗, pool, dinner to unit, ☎, plygr, cots-fee. **RO ╪ $50 - $56, ╫ $55 - $61, ╫╫ $61 - $67, ⏦ $6,** BC MC VI.

JUNEE NSW 2663

Pop 3,700. (505km SW Sydney), See map on pages 52/53, ref F6. Situated in the Murrumbidgee Murray district. Bowls, Golf, Shooting, Swimming, Tennis.

Hotels/Motels

 ★★★★ The Crossing Motel, (M), 39 Seignior St, 300m W of PO, ☎ 02 6924 3255, fax 02 6924 3210, (2 stry gr fl), 30 units (6 suites) [shwr, spa bath (4), tlt, hairdry, a/c, elec blkts, tel, TV, movie, clock radio, t/c mkg, refrig, toaster], ldry, ☒ (Mon - Sat), pool (salt water), dinner to unit, cots-fee, non smoking units (10). **RO** ♦ **$84 - $94**, ♦♦ **$94 - $104**, ◊ **$10**, Suite D **$122 - $167**, AE BC DC EFT MC MP VI.

★★★ Junee Motor Inn, (M), 61 Broadway, 800m NW of PO, ☎ 02 6924 1266, fax 02 6924 3045, 18 units [shwr, tlt, hairdry (10), a/c, heat, elec blkts, tel, TV (10), clock radio, t/c mkg, refrig, toaster], iron (10), iron brd (10), pool, non smoking units (6). **RO** ♦ **$72**, ♦♦ **$72**, ♦♦♦ **$84**, ◊ **$12**, 8 units ★★☆. AE BC DC EFT JCB MC VI.

KANAHOOKA - NSW

See Wollongong & Suburbs.

KANDOS NSW 2848

Pop 1,450. (247km W Sydney), See map on page 55, ref B1. Prosperous little mining town famous for producing cement. Bowls, Bush Walking, Fishing, Golf, Scenic Drives, Swimming, Tennis.

Hotels/Motels

★★ Fairway Motel, (M), Cnr Ilford Rd & Henbury Ave, 500m W of PO, ☎ 02 6379 4406, fax 02 6379 4996, 14 units [shwr, tlt, a/c, elec blkts, tel, TV, clock radio, t/c mkg, refrig], ldry, bbq, cots-fee. **RO** ♦ **$62**, ♦♦ **$73**, ♦♦♦ **$95**, ◊ **$16.50 - $22**, ch con, AE BC MC VI.

KANGAROO VALLEY NSW 2577

Pop 350. (177km S Sydney), See map on page 55, ref B4. Small village set amid mountains, valleys and waterfalls. Like nearby Berry, it has become a popular tourist destination and features a number of art and craft galleries. Bush Walking, Canoeing, Golf, Horse Riding, Swimming, Tennis.

Hotels/Motels

★★★★ Pioneer Motel Kangaroo Valley, (M), 152 Moss Vale Rd, 50m S of PO, ☎ 02 4465 1877, fax 02 4465 1413, (2 stry gr fl), 23 units [shwr, spa bath (11), tlt, hairdry, a/c, elec blkts, tel, TV, video, clock radio, t/c mkg, refrig, mini bar, cook fac ltd, micro, toaster, ldry], lift, ldry, iron, iron brd, conf fac, lounge firepl, ☒, pool-heated (salt water), rm serv, gym, cots-fee, non smoking rms (11). **RO** ♦♦ **$93.50 - $181.50**, ◊ **$5 - $10**, ch con, fam con, AE BC DC MC VI.

Self Catering Accommodation

★★★★☆ Minimbah Farm Cottages, (Cotg), Nugent's Creek Rd, 2km E of PO, ☎ 02 4465 1056, 2 cotgs [shwr, bath, tlt, fan, fire pl (1), heat, elec blkts, tel, TV, video, clock radio, t/c mkg, refrig, cook fac, micro, elec frypan, toaster, ldry, doonas, linen], w/mach, iron, iron brd, bbq, tennis (half court), cots, non smoking property. **RO $100 - $145**, BC MC VI.

★★★★ Loughmore Cottage, (Cotg), 164 Main Rd, ☎ 02 4465 1822, fax 02 4465 1812, 1 cotg acc up to 2, [shwr, tlt, hairdry, a/c, t/c mkg, refrig, cook fac ltd, toaster, doonas, linen], iron, iron brd, lounge firepl, non smoking property. **BLB** ♦♦ **$160**, Min book applies.

★★★☆ Jenoma Cottage, (Cotg), 27 Cullen Crescent, 1km N of PO, ☎ 02 9543 7030, fax 02 9543 9265, 1 cotg acc up to 6, [shwr, tlt, hairdry, fan, fire pl, heat, elec blkts, tel, TV, video, clock radio, t/c mkg, refrig, cook fac, micro, toaster, linen reqd], iron, bbq, plygr, non smoking units, **D $120 - $150**, **W $550 - $700**, Min book applies.

★★★☆ Jenoma Farm, (Cotg), (Farm), 65 Bendeela Rd, ☎ 02 9543 7030, fax 02 9543 9265, 1 cotg acc up to 10, (3 bedrm), [fan, heat (wood), elec blkts, tel, TV, video, clock radio, t/c mkg, refrig, cook fac, micro, ldry, blkts, doonas], bathrm, bbq, secure park, non smoking property. **D $170 - $200**, **W $980**, Min book applies.

★★★☆ The Big Bell Farm, 1666 Kangaroo Valley Rd, 3km SE of PO, ☎ 02 4465 1628, 2 cabins acc up to 4, [shwr, tlt, heat, TV, t/c mkg, refrig, cook fac, micro, toaster, blkts, linen-fee], bbq, cots non smoking property, Pets allowed. **D $70 - $90**, **W $350 - $375**, BC MC VI.

★★☆ Feriendorf Holiday Village, (Chalet), 55 Radiata Rd, 10km W of PO, ☎ 02 4465 1472, or 02 9713 9460, fax 02 4465 1801, 5 chalets acc up to 6, [shwr, tlt, heat, t/c mkg, refrig, cook fac, toaster], ldry, pool, bbq, plygr. **D $60 - $135**, **W $400 - $600**, Breakfast available. BC MC VI.

The Heavens Mountain Cottage, (Cotg), Paddington Lane, 5km N of PO, ☎ 02 4465 1400, fax 02 4465 1368, 1 cotg acc up to 4, (2 bedrm), [shwr, spa bath, tlt, a/c, heat, elec blkts, TV, video, clock radio, t/c mkg, refrig, cook fac ltd, micro, blkts, doonas, linen, pillows], w/mach, bbq, non smoking property. **D** ♦♦ **$132 - $198**, ♦♦♦♦ **$187 - $275**, BC EFT MC VI.

B&B's/Guest Houses

★★★★☆ Laurel Bank Bed & Breakfast, (B&B), 2501 Moss Vale Rd Barrengarry via, 4.2km N of Hampton Bridge, ☎ 02 4465 1616, fax 02 4465 1394, 4 rms [shwr, bath (1), tlt, c/fan, heat, elec blkts, tel, clock radio, t/c mkg, refrig (1), micro (1), toaster (1)], ldry, lounge (TV), lounge firepl, ✗, bbq, dinner to unit, non smoking property. **BB** ♦ **$90 - $150**, ♦♦ **$90 - $180**, Min book long w/ends, BC EFT MC VI.

★★★★☆ Rainbow on Morton Retreat Bed & Breakfast, (B&B), 438 Budgong Fire Trail, 19km SW of PO, ☎ 02 4465 1278, fax 02 4465 1761, 3 rms [shwr, tlt, hairdry, a/c-cool, fire pl (open log), heat, elec blkts, clock radio, t/c mkg, refrig], ldry, rec rm, TV rm, lounge, ✗, pool, spa, bbq, tennis, Small dogs welcome. **BB** ♦♦ **$145 - $160**, BC MC VI.

 **★★★★☆ Tall Trees**, (B&B), 8 Nugents Creek Rd, 1km E of PO, ☎ 02 4465 1208, fax 02 4465 1208, 3 rms (Studio), [shwr, spa bath (1), tlt, a/c (2), c/fan, elec blkts (4), tel, TV, clock radio, refrig, cook fac ltd (1), micro (1)], lounge firepl, breakfast rm, t/c mkg shared, bbq (1), c/park. **BB** ♦ **$75 - $135**, ♦♦ **$90 - $150**, ◊ **$45 - $65**, BC MC VI.

KARUAH NSW

See Port Stephens Region.

KATOOMBA NSW

See Blue Mountains Region.

KEMPSEY NSW 2440

Pop 8,600. (428km N Sydney), See map on page 54, ref C6. Commercial centre of the Macleay Valley and the home of the legendary Akubra hat. Boating, Bowls, Golf, Horse Riding, Scenic Drives, Squash, Swimming, Tennis, Water Skiing.

Hotels/Motels

  ★★★☆ All Nations Hallmark Inn, (M), 320 Pacific Hwy, 3km S of PO, ☎ 02 6562 1284, fax 02 6563 1907, 30 units [shwr, tlt, hairdry, a/c, tel, TV, video (8)-fee, clock radio, t/c mkg, refrig, toaster], ldry, iron (7), iron brd (7), rec rm, ☒ (6 nights), pool, spa, bbq, rm serv, plygr, cots-fee, non smoking units (10). **RO** ♦ **$80 - $100**, ♦♦ **$85 - $105**, ◊ **$10**, 8 units of a lower rating. AE BC DC JCB MC MP VI.

★★★☆ City Centre Motel, (M), 95 Smith St (Pacific Hwy), 500m N of PO, ☎ 02 6562 7733, fax 02 6562 8640, 43 units (2 bedrm), [shwr, bath (1), spa bath (4), tlt, hairdry, a/c, tel, TV, video (avail), clock radio, t/c mkg, refrig, cook fac (2), toaster], ldry, ☒ (2), pool, rm serv, dinner to unit, cots-fee, non smoking units (23). **RO** ♦ **$66**, ♦♦ **$77**, ◊ **$11**, AE BC DC EFT MC VI.

 ★★★☆ Colonial Court Motor Inn, (M), 155 Smith St (Pacific Hwy), 1km N of PO, ☎ 02 6562 6711, fax 02 6562 6636, 25 units [shwr, tlt, hairdry, a/c, tel, cable tv, video (10), clock radio, t/c mkg, refrig, toaster], iron, iron brd, pool, bbq, dinner to unit (6 nights), cots, non smoking units (16). **RO** ♦ **$70 - $105**, ♦♦ **$80 - $105**, ◊ **$10**, AE BC DC EFT JCB MC MP VI.

★★★☆ Kempsey Powerhouse Motel, (M), 465 Pacific Hwy, 5km S of PO, ☎ 02 6562 6988, fax 02 6562 6176, 21 units [shwr, spa bath (2), tlt, a/c, tel, TV, video, clock radio, t/c mkg, refrig], ☒, pool, bbq, rm serv, cots-fee. **RO** ♦ **$79**, ♦♦ **$75**, ♦♦♦ **$89**, ◊ **$12**, Undergoing refurbishment. AE BC BTC DC EFT JCB MC MP VI.

All Nations Hallmark Inn

AAA Tourism ★★★☆

A peaceful oasis in the heart of the lush Macleay Valley with 10 acres of lawns, gardens, pools & spa adjoining the golf course

★ Stardust

Licensed Restaurant featuring the freshest of local seafoods

AAA
TOURISM
Special Rates

All ground floor units with toasters and irons, set well back from the highway, ensuring quiet nights. Parking at your unit, games room with billiards, table tennis, electronic games. Trampoline, climbing frame. BBQ, boat and trailer parking.

Off Peak weekend rates 20% off!

320 Pacific Highway, South Kempsey 2440

FLAG

Freecall 1800 066 139   Email: allnkemp@ozemail.com
Ph: (02) 6562 1284   Fax: (02) 6563 1907

Fly Buys

Colonial Court Motor Inn

AAA Tourism ★★★☆

Quiet, elegant motel set in luxurious gardens on the banks of the beautiful Macleay River. Quality accommodation with personalised service is our speciality. Home cooked country breakfasts are also a feature. Accommodation includes executive suites, deluxe units and quality economy rooms. Close to restaurant and shops. For advice regarding your special needs or for further information contact June or Barry.

155 SMITH ST. (Pacific Hwy) KEMPSEY
Best Western and AAA (NRMA) Rates.

Best Western

AUSTAR

Ph: (02) 6562 6711   email: colcourt@bigpond.com   **Fax: (02) 6562 6636**

Moon River Motor Inn

Quiet Riverbank Motel & lic. Restaurant   157 Pacific Highw.

Riverview Rooms
Standard Rooms
Family Rooms
Self cont. Appartm.
Conference Room
Functions
Fax / Internet accessable

AAA TOURISM
★ ★ ★
KEMPSEY NSW

FREECALL 1800 627 415

Email: moonriver@tsn.cc   Web: moonriver.com.au

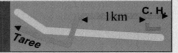

▸ 1km   **C. H.**
Taree

★★★ **Moon River Motor Inn**, (M), 157 Pacific Hwy, 1km N of PO, ☎ 02 6562 8077, fax 02 6562 7867, 31 units (1 suite) [shwr, tlt, hairdry (19), a/c, tel, TV, video (avail), clock radio, t/c mkg, refrig, mini bar, cook fac (1), micro (1), elec frypan (1), toaster (19)], ldry, ⊠, pool, rm serv (6 nights), cots-fee, non smoking units (25). **RO** ¶ **$55 - $77**, ¶¶ **$66 - $110**, ⍟ **$11**, AE BC DC EFT MC VI.

★★☆ **Fairway Lodge**, (M), 385 Pacific Hwy, 3km S of PO, ☎ 02 6562 7099, fax 02 6562 8645, 21 units [shwr, tlt, a/c, c/fan, tel, TV, t/c mkg, refrig, toaster], pool, bbq, dinner to unit, cots. **RO** ¶ **$38 - $40**, ¶¶ **$46 - $48**, ¶¶¶ **$52 - $55**, AE BC DC EFT MC MCH VI.

★★☆ **Park Drive Motel**, (M), 161 Pacific Hwy, 1km N of PO, ☎ 02 6562 1361, fax 02 6562 2394, (2 stry gr fl), 22 units [shwr, tlt, a/c, elec blkts, TV, clock radio, t/c mkg, refrig, toaster], ldry, pool, bbq, dinner to unit, ✆, cots (available). **RO** ¶ **$49.50 - $55**, ¶¶ **$55 - $60.50**, ⍟ **$5.50**, AE BC DC MC VI.

★★☆ **Skyline Motel**, (M), 40 Pacific Hwy, 1km S of PO, ☎ 02 6562 4888, 11 units [shwr, tlt, a/c, elec blkts, TV, clock radio, t/c mkg, refrig], dinner to unit, c/park (undercover) (5), cots-fee. **RO** ¶ **$44 - $50**, ¶¶ **$50 - $85**, ¶¶¶ **$85 - $105**, ⍟ **$10**, BC MC VI.

Self Catering Accommodation

Riverview Cabins, (Farm), Lower Creek, ☎ 02 6772 3328, fax 02 6772 3367, 2 cabins acc up to 6, [shwr, bath (1), tlt, fan, fire pl (combustion), tel, radio, refrig, cook fac, micro, elec frypan, toaster, blkts reqd-fee, linen reqd-fee, pillows reqd-fee], bbq, c/park. **D** ¶¶ **$44 - $66**, ⍟ **$11**, **W** ¶¶ **$264 - $396**, ⍟ **$11**, ch con.

B&B's/Guest Houses

★★★★ **Netherby**, (GH), 5 Little Rudder St, 250m E of PO, ☎ 02 6563 1777, fax 02 6563 1778, 4 rms [ensuite, bath (1), hairdry, a/c-cool, c/fan, heat, elec blkts, tel, TV, clock radio], ✕, cafe, t/c mkg shared, c/park. **BB** ¶ **$95.50**, ¶¶ **$143**, ch con, AE BC DC MC VI.

KENDALL NSW 2439

Pop 700. (371km N Sydney), See map on page 54, ref C7. Mid-north coast arts and crafts town situated on the Camden Haven River.

B&B's/Guest Houses

★★★★ **Mendip Lodge Gardens and B & B**, (B&B), 155 North Branch Rd, 6km from Kendall, ☎ 02 6559 0069, fax 02 6559 0039, 2 rms [fan, heat, elec blkts, tel, t/c mkg (communal), refrig (communal), ldry, doonas], TV rm, ✕, bbq, meals to unit, non smoking property, Pets on application. **BB** ¶¶ **$100**, ⍟ **$50**, ch con, weekly con, BC MC VI.

Dehra Doon Lodge, (B&B), 474 Batar Creek Rd, 4.74km SW of PO, ☎ 02 6559 4991, fax 02 6559 4956, 2 rms [ensuite (1), heat (elec/wood), TV, video, clock radio, t/c mkg (1), ldry, doonas], shared fac (1), ✕, refrig, bbq, meals avail, non smoking rms. **BB $80 - $110**, weekly con, Dinner by arrangement. (not yet classified).

KEW NSW 2439

Pop Part of Kendall, (371km N Sydney), See map on page 54, ref C7. Busy service centre on the Pacific Highway midway between Taree and Port Macquarie. Scenic Drives.

Hotels/Motels

★☆ **Kew Court**, (M), Pacific Hwy, ☎ 02 6559 4175, 13 units [shwr, tlt, c/fan, heat, TV, t/c mkg, refrig], ldry, pool (salt water), meals to unit, cots-fee. **RO** ¶ **$38.50**, ¶¶ **$44**, ⍟ **$11**, AE BC MC VI.

KHANCOBAN NSW 2642

Pop 400. (576km S Sydney), See map on pages 52/53, ref F7. Leafy town in the western foothills of the Snowy Mountains. Bush Walking, Canoeing, Fishing, Golf, Horse Riding, Scenic Drives, Snow Skiing, Swimming, Tennis. See also Corryong.

Hotels/Motels

★★★☆ **Khancoban Alpine Inn**, (LMH), Alpine Way, ☎ 02 6076 9471, fax 02 6076 9595, (2 stry gr fl), 36 units [shwr, spa bath (1), tlt, a/c-cool, heat, elec blkts, tel, TV, clock radio, t/c mkg, refrig, mini bar (16)], ldry, ⊠, pool, cots-fee. **RO** ¶ **$49.50**, ¶¶ **$66.50**, ⍟ **$9**, 10 units ★★☆. AE BC DC MC VI.

Self Catering Accommodation

★★★☆ **Khancoban Roadhouse**, Alpine Way, 600m S of PO, ☎ 02 6076 9400, fax 02 6076 9054, (2 stry gr fl), 1 cabin acc up to 4, [shwr, tlt, a/c, elec blkts, TV, clock radio, t/c mkg, refrig, micro, elec frypan, toaster, blkts, doonas, linen, pillows], cafe, bbq, ✆, plygr, cots. **D** ¶ **$50 - $55**, ¶¶ **$69 - $85**, ⍟ **$15**, **W $450 - $550**, BC EFT MC VI.

★★★ **Khancoban Rose Holiday Units**, (HU), Lot 2, Mitchell Ave, 60m E of Police Station, ☎ 02 6076 9530, fax 03 9444 0008, 4 units acc up to 5, [shwr, tlt, a/c, fan, elec blkts, TV, clock radio, t/c mkg, refrig, cook fac ltd, blkts, linen, pillows], iron, cots. **D** ¶ **$50 - $60**, ¶¶ **$60 - $70**, BC MC VI.

Bruno Nalepa Holiday Home, (House), 17 Mitchell Ave, 50m E of PO, ☎ 02 6076 9429, 2 houses acc up to 5, [fan (3), c/fan, heat (1), elec blkts (3), TV (1), clock radio (1), micro (1), toaster (1), doonas (3), linen], ldry, w/mach, iron, iron brd, cook fac, t/c mkg shared, refrig, bbq, ✆. **D** ¶ **$50**, ¶¶ **$50**, ¶¶¶ **$60**, ¶¶¶¶ **$60**, **W** ¶ **$300**, ¶¶ **$300**, ¶¶¶ **$360**, ¶¶¶¶ **$360**, (not yet classified).

Alpine Hideaway Village, (Cotg), Spillway Rd off Alpine Way, 2.5km W of PO, ☎ 02 6076 9498, fax 02 6076 9425, 2 cotgs acc up to 14, [shwr, tlt, heat, refrig, blkts, linen, pillows], ldry, lounge (TV), conv fac, ⊠, cook fac, bbq, plygr, tennis. **D** ¶ **$35**, Min book Christmas Jan and Easter, BC MC VI.

B&B's/Guest Houses

Cossettini's Bed & Breakfast, (B&B), Alpine Way, ☎ 02 6076 9332, 2 rms [shwr, spa bath, tlt, hairdry (1), c/fan, cent heat, refrig], TV rm, lounge, ✕, t/c mkg shared, bbq, non smoking rms. **BB** ¶ **$40**, ¶¶ **$60**, ch con, (not yet classified).

Other Accommodation

Lyrebird Lodge, (Lodge), Spillway Rd, 2.5km W of PO, ☎ 02 6076 9455, fax 02 6076 9455, 4 rms [shwr, tlt, fan, heat, elec blkts, refrig, toaster], ldry, lounge (TV), cook fac, bbq, cots. **BB** ¶ **$35.30 - $55**, ¶¶ **$77**, ch con, BC MC VI.

Queens Cottage Christian Retreat, (Lodge), Pendergast St, 500m from Fire Station, ☎ 02 6076 9033, fax 02 6076 9034, 6 rms acc up to 4, [shwr, bath, tlt, cent heat, elec blkts, t/c mkg], ldry, lounge (TV), conv fac, meals avail. ✆. **BB** ¶ **$52**, ¶¶ **$72.50**, ⍟ **$15**, **DBB** ¶ **$64**, ¶¶ **$96.50**, ⍟ **$27**, ch con, AE BC MC VI.

KIAMA NSW 2533

Pop 11,700. (106km S Sydney), See map on page 55, ref C4. Picturesque south coast seaside resort renowned for its blowhole. Bowls, Bush Walking, Fishing, Golf, Scenic Drives, Surfing.

Hotels/Motels

★★★★☆ **The Pines Flag Inn**, (M), 10 Bong Bong St, 200m S of PO, ☎ 02 4232 1000, fax 02 4233 1272, (2 stry gr fl), 29 units [shwr, bath (3), tlt, hairdry, a/c, elec blkts, tel, TV, clock radio, t/c mkg, refrig, mini bar], iron, iron brd, ⊠, bar, pool (salt water), rm serv, dinner to unit, cots-fee. **RO** ¶ **$99 - $179**, ¶¶ **$99 - $179**, ⍟ **$20**, Min book applies, AE BC DC EFT MC VI.

★★★★ **Kiama Terrace Motor Lodge**, (M), 45 Collins St, 1km NW of PO, ☎ 02 4233 1100, fax 02 4233 1235, (Multi-stry gr fl), 50 units [shwr, bath (23), spa bath (22), tlt, hairdry, a/c, tel, cable tv, video (available), clock radio, t/c mkg, refrig], ldry, iron, iron brd, conv fac, ⊠ (6 nights), pool, bbq, rm serv, dinner to unit (6 nights), cots-fee, non smoking rms (18). **RO** ¶ **$90 - $145**, ¶¶ **$99 - $155**, ¶¶¶ **$114 - $170**, ⍟ **$15**, Min book applies, AE BC DC EFT MC VI, ⅋.

★★★★ **Terralong Terrace**, (M), 129 Terralong St, 600m W of PO, ☎ 02 4232 3711, fax 02 4232 3811, (2 stry gr fl), 16 units [shwr, spa bath (14), tlt, hairdry, a/c, tel, TV, video-fee, movie, clock radio, t/c mkg, refrig, mini bar, cook fac, micro, d/wash, toaster, ldry], w/mach, dryer, iron, iron brd, pool (salt water), bbq, c/park (undercover), cots-fee, non smoking units (8). **D** ¶¶ **$115 - $260**, ⍟ **$15 - $20**, **W** ¶ **$665 - $1,680**, ⍟ **$84 - $112**, pen con, AE BC DC EFT JCB MC MP VI, ⅋.

★★★ **Kiama Ocean View Motor Inn**, (M), 9 Bong Bong St, 300m S of PO, ☎ 02 4232 1966, fax 02 4232 1010, (2 stry gr fl), 17 units [shwr, tlt, elec blkts, tel, TV, video (avail), clock radio, t/c mkg, refrig, toaster], ldry, bbq, cots. **RO** ¶ **$46 - $135**, ¶¶ **$46 - $135**, ⍟ **$11**, Min book applies, AE BC DC MC VI.

★★★ **Motel 617**, (M), 132 Manning St, 1km S of PO, ☎ 02 4232 1333, fax 02 4233 1214, (2 stry gr fl) 18 units [shwr, tlt, hairdry, a/c, elec blkts, tel, TV, video-fee, clock radio, t/c mkg, refrig, toaster], iron, iron brd, pool, bbq, plygr, cots-fee. **RO** ♦ $59 - $79, ♦♦ $65 - $89, ♦♦♦ $75 - $99, ⊘ $11, Min book Christmas Jan long w/ends and Easter, AE BC DC EFT JCB MC VI.

★★☆ **Kiama Beachfront Motel**, (M), 87 Manning St, 500m S of PO, ☎ 02 4232 1533, 22 units [shwr, tlt, a/c (7), fan, heat, elec blkts, tel, TV, clock radio, t/c mkg, refrig], ldry, bbq, cots. **RO** ♦ $55 - $85, ♦♦ $65 - $85, ⊘ $10, 5 rooms ★★. AE BC DC EFT MC VI.

B&B's/Guest Houses

★★★★★ **Spring Creek Retreat**, (B&B), 41 Jerrara Rd, 2.7km W of PO, ☎ 02 4232 2700, or 02 4232 2417, fax 02 4232 2600, 4 rms [shwr, bath, spa bath (3), tlt, fire pl, elec blkts, movie, clock radio, t/c mkg, refrig], iron, iron brd, lounge, lounge firepl, bbq-fee, courtesy transfer, non smoking rms. **BB** ♦♦ $165 - $225, ⊘ $45 - $95, BC EFT MC VI.

(Cottage Section), 3 cotgs [shwr, spa bath (2), tlt, hairdry, a/c, c/fan, heat, TV, clock radio, t/c mkg, refrig, cook fac, micro, elec frypan (1), toaster, doonas, linen], iron, iron brd, bbq, courtesy transfer, cots. **D** $125 - $220, **W** $850 - $1,200, pen con, Min book applies, (not yet classified).

KIAMA TERRACE MOTOR LODGE

LOCATED IN THE HEART OF KIAMA, WALKING DISTANCE TO KIAMA'S TOURIST ATTRACTIONS, SHOPPING & BUSINESS CENTRE.

The Kiama Terrace Motor Lodge offers friendly helpful service, along with the following facilities:

- Free Pay TV
- Salt Water Pool & BBQ
- Complimentary Laundry
- Full Conference Facilities
- Room Service Available on Breakfast & Dinner
- **Nearby Attractions:** Minnamurra Rainforest, Kangaroo Valley, Jamberoo & Berry

- Queen Size Beds
- 50 Rooms - 22 with Spas, some with Balconies
- Air Conditioned
- Video Players Available

AAA
TOURISM
Special Rates

AAA Tourism
★★★★

THE FULLY LICENSED TERRACE CAFÉ RESTAURANT IS OPEN FOR ALL MEALS (EXCEPT SUNDAY EVENING), HAS AN EXCELLENT COCKTAIL BAR & PROVIDES QUALITY FOOD IN A WARM FRIENDLY ATMOSPHERE.

Phone: 02 4233 1100   Fax: 02 4233 1235   Toll Free: 1800 64257

45-51 Collins Street, KIAMA 2533   Email: ktml@iearth.net

Discover...

Terralong Terrace KIAMA

the jewel in Kiama.

Luxury Serviced Apartments

★★★★ AAA Tourism

Walking distance to almost everything, a short drive to Minnamurra rainforest, golf courses & Jamberoo fun park. You can do as much as you want or nothing at all and just soak up the sunshine... *at very affordable prices.*

Recent Finalist in the Awards for Excellence in Tourism 2000

Reservations
Overnight & Long term
1800 683 711
129 Terralong Street
www.kiama.com.au/terralongterrace

Less than 2 hours from the centre of Sydney

★★★★☆ **Bed and Views Kiama**, (B&B), Previously Dux Guesthouse Bed & Breakfast 69 Riversdale Rd, 3km W of PO, ☎ 02 4232 3662, fax 02 4232 3662, 2 rms [shwr, tlt, hairdry, a/c-cool, heat, clock radio], ldry, lounge (TV), t/c mkg shared, bbq, courtesy transfer, non smoking rms. **BB** ♦ **$90 - $110**, ♦♦ **$110 - $140**, BC MC VI.

★★★★☆ **Elli's Bed & Breakfast**, (B&B), 126 Manning St (Corner Farmer St), 900m S of PO, ☎ 02 4232 2879, fax 02 4232 4338, 2 rms [shwr, bath, spa bath (1), tlt, hairdry, a/c-cool, a/c, c/fan, heat, elec blkts, tel, TV, clock radio, t/c mkg, refrig], ldry, iron, iron brd, lounge (tv & video), ✕, pool (salt water), bbq, c/park. **BB** ♦ **$80 - $120**, ♦♦ **$95 - $135**, ◊ **$30**, Limited facilities for children, BC MC VI.

★★★★☆ **Figtrees of Kiama**, (B&B), No children's facilities, 90 Barney St, ☎ 02 4232 4219, fax 02 4232 4848, (2 stry), 2 rms [shwr, bath (1), tlt, hairdry, fan, elec blkts, TV], iron brd, lounge, ✕, pool-heated (salt, solar), t/c mkg shared, refrig, secure park (undercover), non smoking property. **BB** ♦♦ **$140 - $165**, BC MC VI.

★★★★ **Cranford Lodge**, (B&B), Cnr Barney & Irvine Sts, 1km S of PO, ☎ 02 4232 1060, fax 02 4232 4188, 5 rms [shwr (5), bath (1), tlt, elec blkts, tel], lounge firepl (TV), t/c mkg shared, refrig, courtesy transfer, cots. **BB** ♦ **$95**, ♦♦ **$130**, ◊ **$30**, ch con, BC MC VI.

★★★★ **Kiama Bed & Breakfast & Cottage**, (B&B), 15 Riversdale Rd, 3km W of PO, ☎ 02 4232 2844, fax 02 4232 2868, (2 stry gr fl), 2 rms [shwr, bath (1), tlt, hairdry, a/c, fan, heat, elec blkts, TV, video, movie, clock radio, CD, t/c mkg, refrig, pillows], lounge, ✕, bbq-fee, dinner to unit, courtesy transfer, non smoking rms. **BB** ♦ **$100**, ♦♦ **$145 - $220**, ◊ **$35 - $40**, ch con, Min book all holiday times, BC MC VI.

★★★★★ **(Cottage Section)**, 2 cotgs [ensuite, shwr, bath (1), spa bath (1), tlt, hairdry, a/c, elec blkts, TV, video, CD, refrig, cook fac, micro, d/wash, toaster, linen], iron, iron brd, bbq. **BB** ♦ **$100**, ♦♦ **$145 - $220**, ◊ **$35 - $40**, Min book all holiday times.

★★★★ **Sage Cottage**, (B&B), No children's facilities, 62 Gipps St, 500m W of PO, ☎ 02 4233 1921, fax 02 4233 1921, 2 rms [ensuite, fan, heat, elec blkts, TV, video, clock radio, doonas], ✕, t/c mkg shared, refrig, bbq, non smoking rms. **BB** ♦♦ **$130**, ◊ **$40**.

KILLCARE NSW 2257

Pop Nominal, (91km N Sydney), See map on page 56, ref E3. Lovely spot on the Central Coast surrounded by Bouddi National Park.

Self Catering Accommodation

★★★★☆ **Granny's Cottage**, (HU), 16 Putty Beach Dve, 400m SE of PO, ☎ 02 4360 1950, fax 02 9654 9782, (2 stry gr fl), 3 units (2 suites) [shwr (2), spa bath (1), tlt, hairdry (2), a/c (1), fan, heat, elec blkts, TV, video (2), clock radio (2), t/c mkg, refrig, cook fac (1), cook fac ltd (1), micro (2), toaster], ldry, iron, iron brd, lounge firepl (1), bbq, non smoking property. **BB** ♦ **$90 - $110**, ♦♦ **$110 - $140**, ◊ **$28**.

KINCUMBER NSW 2251

Pop Gosford, (87km N Sydney), See map on page 55, ref D6. Central Coast town on the north-eastern shores of the Broadwater. Boating, Bowls, Fishing, Swimming, Vineyards, Wineries.

B&B's/Guest Houses

★★★★☆ **Cockle Bay House**, (B&B), 1 Calool St, 3km S of Old St Pauls Church, ☎ 02 4368 3394, fax 02 4368 4189, 4 rms (2 suites) [shwr, bath (1), tlt, hairdry, a/c, heat, elec blkts (available), tel, TV, t/c mkg, refrig], ldry, iron, iron brd, lounge (TV & firepl), pool-heated (salt water), bbq, tennis, non smoking property. **D $185 - $195**, Min book applies, BC EFT MC VI.

★★★ **Figtree Cottages Bed & Breakfast**, (B&B), 247 Avoca Dve, ☎ 02 4368 3056, 2 rms [ensuite, hairdry (1), c/fan, heat, tel, clock radio (1), refrig], ldry, lounge (TV), lounge firepl, ✕, pool (salt/solar heated), spa, t/c mkg shared, bbq, courtesy transfer, cots. **BB** ♦ **$80**, ♦♦ **$120 - $130**, BC MC VI.

KINGSCLIFF NSW 2487

Pop Nominal, (840km N Sydney), See map on page 54, ref E1. Beachside resort town located at the northern end of the Tweed Coast. Bowls, Fishing, Surfing, Swimming, Tennis.

Hotels/Motels

★★★★ **Pacific Sands Motel**, (M), Cnr Wommin Bay & Murphy Rds, 1km N of PO, ☎ 02 6674 2699, fax 02 6674 3662, (Multi-stry gr fl), 24 units [shwr, tlt, evap cool, tel, TV, clock radio, t/c mkg, refrig, toaster], ldry, ✉, pool, bbq, rm serv, dinner to unit, c/park (undercover), cots-fee. **D $77 - $132**, AE BC DC MC VI.

Pacific Sands Motel
KINGSCLIFF NSW

Absolute Beachfront Accommodation
- 10 mins south of Tweed Heads/Coolangatta • Air conditioned
- • Newly refurbished • Direct-dial telephones
- • Swimming pool and paved BBQ area • Undercover parking
Ph: (02) 6674 2699 Fax: (02) 6674 3662
1-3 Murphy's Rd Kingscliff NSW 2487

Budget Motel Chain International

★★★ **Blue Waters Motel**, (M), Cnr Wommin Bay Rd & Kingscliff St, 2km N of PO, ☎ 02 6674 2999, fax 02 6674 2999, 15 units [shwr, tlt, a/c, fan, elec blkts (2), tel, cable tv (2), video-fee, clock radio, t/c mkg, refrig, cook fac (6)], ldry, pool, bbq, dinner to unit, courtesy transfer, cots. **RO** ♦ **$44 - $77**, ♦♦ **$49 - $93**, ♦♦♦ **$60 - $105**, ◊ **$11**, ch con, AE BC BTC DC MC MCH VI, ♿.

★★★ **Kingscliff Motel**, (M), 80 Marine Pde, ☎ 02 6674 1780, fax 02 6674 4955, 12 units [shwr, tlt, a/c, c/fan, heat, tel, TV, clock radio, t/c mkg, refrig, toaster], pool, bbq, non smoking rms (7). **RO** ♦ **$50 - $90**, ♦♦ **$55 - $100**, ◊ **$10**, AE BC DC MC VI.

★★☆ **Pollys Motel**, (M), 148 Marine Pde, 8km fr Air Port, ☎ 02 6674 2888, fax 02 6674 2809, 10 units [shwr, tlt, fan, TV, video (3), clock radio, t/c mkg, refrig], iron, pool, cots. **RO** ♦ **$45 - $80**, ♦♦ **$55 - $100**, ♦♦♦ **$60.50 - $100**, ◊ **$10**, AE BC MC VI, ♿.

Self Catering Accommodation

★★★★ **Sunrise Cove Luxury Holiday Apts**, (HU), 13/28 Moss St, ☎ 02 6674 5046, fax 02 6674 5047, 17 units acc up to 8, [shwr (2), bath, tlt (2), c/fan, heat, tel, TV, video, clock radio, t/c mkg, refrig, cook fac, micro, elec frypan, d/wash, toaster, ldry, blkts, linen, pillows], w/mach, dryer, iron, pool (salt water), bbq, c/park (garage), cots-fee, non smoking units (1). **D $143 - $180**, **W $525 - $1,450**, Min book applies, BC MC VI.

★★☆ **Kingscliff Holiday**, 11 Pearl St, ☎ 02 6674 1526, 9 cabins acc up to 8, [shwr, tlt, c/fan, TV, refrig, cook fac, blkts, linen], ldry. **D** ♦♦ **$55**, **W $209 - $495**.

B&B's/Guest Houses

★★★★☆ **Wangaree Bed & Breakfast**, (B&B), Hattons Rd, Duranbah 2487, ☎ 02 6677 7496, fax 02 6677 7492, 3 rms [shwr, bath, tlt, hairdry, c/fan, heat, elec blkts, clock radio], lounge (TV), lounge firepl, t/c mkg shared, bbq, non smoking property. **BB** ♦ **$100 - $120**, ♦♦ **$120 - $150**.

KIOLOA NSW 2539

Pop Part of Bawley Point, (267km S Sydney), See map on page 55, ref B6. Kioloa lies on the south coast near some magnificent surf and swim beaches and Murramarang National Park. Bush Walking, Fishing, Surfing.

Self Catering Accommodation

★☆ **Kioloa Holiday**, Scerri Dve, 35km S of Ulladulla, ☎ 02 4457 1095, fax 02 4457 1095, 11 cabins [bath, tlt, refrig, cook fac, blkts reqd, linen reqd], shwr (4), ldry, w/mach, bbq, c/park (carport), plygr, No dogs or cats allowed. **D $45**, **W $220 - $400**, Min book all holiday times.

KOOTINGAL NSW 2352

Pop 1,400. (474km NW Sydney), See map on pages 52/53, ref J3. Kootingal is a satellite village of Tamworth surrounded by studs, orchards and small farms. Bowls, Horse Riding, Scenic Drives, Swimming, Tennis.

Hotels/Motels

★★★☆ **Kootingal Motor Inn**, (M), New England Hwy, 17km N of Tamworth, ☎ 02 6760 3382, fax 02 6760 5285, 12 units [shwr, tlt, a/c-cool, heat, elec blkts, tel, TV, clock radio, t/c mkg, refrig, toaster], ldry, bbq, dinner to unit, cots, non smoking units (9). **RO** ⊧ **$48 - $55,** ⊧⊧ **$55 - $66,** ⊧⊧⊧ **$60 - $75,** ⊧ **$8 - $10,** ch con, BC EFT MC VI.

★ **Kootingal Hotel**, (LH), 20 Gate St, adjacent to PO, ☎ 02 6760 3203, fax 02 6760 5240, 11 rms TV rm, lounge, meals avail (evening & lunch). **BLB** ⊧ **$33,** ⊧⊧ **$55,** ch con.

KULNURA NSW 2250

Pop Nominal, (82km N Sydney), See map on page 56, ref E1. Rural area in the foothills of the Watagan Mountains. Bowls, Bush Walking, Scenic Drives.

Self Catering Accommodation

★★★☆ **Kiah Retreat**, (Cotg), Finns Rd, 2km from PO, ☎ 02 4376 1348, fax 02 4376 1302, 1 cotg acc up to 4, [shwr, tlt, a/c, elec blkts, video, clock radio, t/c mkg, refrig, cook fac, micro, toaster, ldry], rec rm, lounge (TV), pool (saltwater), bbq, plygr, breakfast ingredients, Pets on application. **BB** ⊧ **$70 - $90,** ⊧⊧ **$125 - $150,** ⊧ **$15 - $25.**

KURRAJONG NSW 2758

Pop 1,200. (76km W Sydney), See map on page 56, ref A3. Rural area in the foothills of the Blue Mountains on the Bells Line of Road. Bowls, Scenic Drives.

B&B's/Guest Houses

★★★★☆ **Gumnut Cottage B&B**, (B&B), Grose Vale Rd, Northern Blue Mountains, ☎ 02 4573 2832, fax 02 4573 2932, 3 rms [ensuite, spa bath (1), hairdry (3), a/c (2), fan (1), elec blkts, TV, clock radio, CD, t/c mkg, refrig, doonas], ldry, iron, ✕, bbq, non smoking rms. **BB** ⊧ **$85 - $110,** ⊧ **$100 - $150,** ⊧ **$35 - $50, RO** ⊧ **$70 - $130,** ⊧⊧ **$70 - $130,** ⊧ **$30,** Min book long w/ends and Easter, BC MC VI.

KURRAJONG HEIGHTS NSW 2758

Pop 750. (77km W Sydney), See map on page 56, ref A3. Small town to the west of Kurrajong, further up the mountains.

Self Catering Accommodation

★★★★ **Madisons Mountain Retreat**, (Cotg), 1880 Bells Line Of Road, ☎ 02 4567 7398, fax 02 4567 7862, 8 cotgs acc up to 5, [shwr (8), spa bath (3), tlt (8), c/fan, fire pl, elec blkts, tel, TV, t/c mkg, refrig, cook fac ltd, micro, toaster, blkts, linen, pillows], ldry, w/mach, dryer, iron, pool-indoor, spa, bbq, ✆, gym, tennis, non smoking units (6). **D** ⊧⊧ **$132 - $187,** ⊧ **$27.50 - $44, W** ⊧⊧ **$800 - $850,** ch con, BC MC VI.

The Rustic Spirit, (Cotg), 23 Glenara Rd, ☎ 02 4567 7170, 3 cotgs acc up to 2, [shwr, spa bath, tlt, hairdry, fan, heat, elec blkts, TV, video, CD, t/c mkg, refrig, cook fac, micro, toaster, doonas, linen], ldry, iron, lounge firepl, bbq, courtesy transfer, breakfast ingredients. **BB** ⊧⊧ **$160 - $200,** pen con, (not yet classified).

B&B's/Guest Houses

★★★★ **Trellises Guest House**, (GH), 11 Warks Hill Rd, ☎ 02 4567 7313, fax 02 4567 7313, 6 rms [shwr, spa bath (3), tlt, a/c, fire pl (3), cent heat, tel, clock radio], ldry, iron, iron brd, rec rm, lounge (tv & firepl), conv fac, ✕, bbq, cots. **BB** ⊧ **$160,** ⊧⊧ **$190,** **DBB** ⊧ **$180,** ⊧⊧ **$250.**

KURRI KURRI NSW 2327

Pop 12,500. (150km N Sydney), See map on page 55, ref C7. Major regional centre between Cessnock and Maitland. Bowls, Golf, Swimming.

Hotels/Motels

★★★ **Kurri Motor Inn**, (M), Cnr Lang & Alexandra Sts, 600m W of PO, ☎ 02 4937 2222, fax 02 4936 2448, 14 units [shwr, tlt, a/c, c/fan, elec blkts, tel, TV, clock radio, t/c mkg, refrig, toaster], ldry-fee, ✕, pool, cots-fee, non smoking units (5). **RO** ⊧ **$68 - $95,** ⊧⊧ **$78 - $95,** ⊧⊧⊧ **$98 - $115,** ⊧ **$20,** BC MC VI.

Operator Comment: See advertisement at top of page.

KURRI MOTOR INN

Hunter Valley Wine Country   AAAT ★★★

Cnr. Lang & Alexandra Sts. Kurri Kurri NSW 2327

Ph (02) 4937 2222

www.kurrimotorinn.com.au

KYOGLE NSW 2474

Pop 2,850. (758km N Sydney), See map on page 54, ref D2. Centre of a dairy and mixed farming area on the upper reaches of the Richmond River. Bowls, Golf, Scenic Drives, Swimming, Tennis.

Hotels/Motels

★★☆ **Kyogle Motel**, (M), 295 Summerland Way, 2km S of PO, ☎ 02 6632 1070, fax 02 6632 1070, 9 units [shwr, tlt, a/c-cool (6), a/c (3), fan, heat, tel, TV, t/c mkg, refrig], ldry-fee, dinner to unit, cots-fee. **RO** ⊧ **$52.80 - $70.40,** ⊧⊧ **$61.60 - $79.20,** ⊧⊧⊧ **$66 - $86.90,** ⊧ **$11,** 3 units ★★★, AE BC MC VI.

LAKE CARGELLIGO NSW 2672

Pop 1,200. (576km W Sydney), See map on pages 52/53, ref E5. Small town on the shores of a large inland water storage system, popular for birdwatching and water sports. Boating, Fishing, Swimming.

Hotels/Motels

★★★ **Lachlan Way Motel**, (M), 2 Foster St, 150m E of PO, ☎ 02 6898 1201, fax 02 6898 1201, 12 units [shwr, tlt, a/c-cool, heat, elec blkts, tel, TV, video-fee, clock radio, t/c mkg, refrig], bbq. **RO** ⊧ **$55,** ⊧⊧ **$66,** ⊧ **$11,** 5 units ★★. AE BC DC MC VI.

★★☆ **Lake Cargelligo Motel**, (M), 28 Canada St, 300m S of PO, ☎ 02 6898 1303, fax 02 6898 1315, 10 units [shwr, tlt, a/c-cool, heat, elec blkts, tel, TV, movie, clock radio, t/c mkg, refrig], bbq, dinner to unit, boat park, cots-fee. **RO** ⊧ **$45,** ⊧⊧ **$50 - $55,** ⊧ **$11,** ch con, AE BC MC MCH VI.

LAKE CATHIE NSW 2445

Pop 1,800. (386km N Sydney), See map on page 54, ref C7. Lake Cathie (pronounced 'cat-eye') is a mid-north coastal settlement that is a popular holiday spot. Boating, Fishing, Swimming.

Hotels/Motels

★★★☆ **Country Surfside Motel Resort**, (M), Previously Country Surfside Resort 1379 Ocean Dve, 2km S of bridge, ☎ 02 6585 5430, fax 02 6585 4126, 15 units [shwr, tlt, fan, heat, elec blkts, tel, TV, clock radio, t/c mkg, refrig], ldry, rec rm, ✕, pool-heated (solar), spa, bbq, golf, tennis (half court), cots. **D** **$140 - $200, RO** ⊧ **$60 - $90,** ⊧⊧ **$70 - $100,** ⊧ **$15,** AE BC EFT MC VI, ♿.

CITY OF
Lake Macquarie

escape to long sun drenched beaches, a stunning lake and majestic mountain wilderness

experience swimming, boating, hiking, diving, fishing, jet skiing and surfing

explore delicious cafes and restaurant & quaint historic towns

Lake Macquarie

There are few places like it. A **vast blue waterway**, four times the size of Sydney Harbour, endless stretches of **pristine beaches** and an incredible **mountain wilderness** area. Just 90 minutes drive north of Sydney, you are invited to **escape, experience** and **explore** this beautiful area.

i Free Brochure: **1800 802 044**
Email: **tourism@lakemac.nsw.gov.au**
Website: **www.lakemac.com.au**

72 Pacific Highway, Blacksmiths NSW 2281,
ph: **02 4972 1172** (Open 7 days)   fax: **02 4972 1487**

escape experience explore

Phone: 1800 802 044

Self Catering Accommodation

★★★☆ **Teranga Holiday Apartments**, (HU), 1639 Ocean Dve, ☎ 02 6585 5285, 6 units acc up to 6, [shwr, tlt, a/c, c/fan, TV, refrig, cook fac, micro, linen reqd-fee], ldry, iron, pool, bbq, c/park (undercover), mini golf, tennis (3/4 court). **D** $55 - $130, **W** $220 - $770, Min book Christmas and Jan.

★★★ **Hamilton Rise**, (HU), 2 Elanora Dve, 300m S of PO, ☎ 02 6585 5777, (2 stry), 3 units acc up to 6, [shwr, bath, tlt, fan, heat, elec blkts, TV, refrig, cook fac, toaster, ldry (in unit), linen reqd-fee], c/park. **W** $175 - $485.

★★☆ **Campbells Beach Flats**, (HF), 28 Bundella Ave, ☎ 02 6585 5320, 2 flats acc up to 5, [shwr, tlt, TV, refrig, cook fac, linen reqd-fee], ldry. **W** $200 - $650.

★★☆ **Lakeview Lodge**, (HF), 1 Oxley St, ☎ 02 6585 5234, 5 flats acc up to 5, [shwr, bath, tlt, TV, refrig, cook fac, linen reqd-fee], ldry, c/park (carport), cots. **D ♦♦** $60, **W ♦♦** $165 - $500.

★★☆ **Pacific Waters**, (HU), 2 Aqua Cres, 200m S of PO, ☎ 02 6585 5777, fax 02 6585 5011, (2 stry), 1 unit acc up to 6, [shwr, bath, tlt, fan, heat, TV, refrig, cook fac, d/wash, toaster, ldry (in unit), linen reqd-fee], bbq, c/park. **W** $210 - $660.

★★☆ **Paradise Waters**, (HU), 18 Aqua Cres, ☎ 02 6585 5416, 5 units acc up to 5, (1 + 2 bedrm), [shwr, tlt, fan, heat, TV, refrig, cook fac, ldry, linen reqd-fee], bbq, c/park (carport). **D** $180 - $500, Min book applies.

★★ **Aqua Lodge Holiday Apartments**, (HU), Cnr Aqua Cres & Ocean Dve, ☎ 02 6585 5777, fax 02 6585 5011, 2 units acc up to 4, [shwr, bath, tlt, TV, refrig, cook fac, ldry, linen reqd-fee], c/park (carport). **W** $180 - $585.

★★ **Beachfront**, (HF), 12 Bundella Ave, ☎ 02 6585 5777, fax 02 6585 5011, 4 flats acc up to 5, [shwr, tlt, TV, refrig, cook fac, micro, ldry, linen reqd-fee], bbq, c/park (carport). **W** $210 - $630.

Cathie Court, (HU), 5 Boodgery St, 100m N of Bowling Club, ☎ 02 6585 5212, (2 stry gr fl), 4 units acc up to 6, [shwr, tlt, fan, heat, TV, clock radio, t/c mkg, refrig, cook fac, micro, elec frypan, toaster, blkts, linen reqd-fee], ldry, w/mach, dryer, iron, iron brd, bbq, cots. **D** $50 - $70, **W** $150 - $440, BC MC VI, (not yet classified).

LAKE ILLAWARRA NSW

See Wollongong & Suburbs.

LAKE MACQUARIE NSW

See: Arcadia Vale, (Belmont), Cams Wharf, Chain Valley Bay, Cooranbong, Fishing Point, Mandalong, Marks Point, Morisset, Rathmines, Speers Point, Swansea, Teralba, Toronto, Wangi Wangi, Warners Bay, Wyee Bay.

LAKE MUNMORAH NSW 2259

Pop 2,650. Wyong, (114km N Sydney), See map on page 55, ref E5. Central Coast town on the northern shores of a lake of the same name, flanked by the Munmorah State Recreation Area. Boating, Fishing, Swimming.

Hotels/Motels

★★☆ **Lake Munmorah Motel**, (M), Pacific Hwy, ☎ 02 4358 8108, 11 units [shwr, bath (1), tlt, fan, heat, elec blkts, tel, TV, t/c mkg, refrig], bbq, cots. **RO ♦** $71.50 - $88, **♦♦** $71.50 - $88, **♦♦♦♦** $150, ch con, AE BC MC VI.

LAKESLAND NSW 2572

Pop Nominal, (86km SW Sydney), See map on page 55, ref B3. Rural town situated near Picton.

Self Catering Accommodation

★★★☆ **Dilston Park**, (Cotg), 30 Lyons Rd, 11km W of Picton, ☎ 02 4680 9270, fax 02 4680 9371, 1 cotg acc up to 6, [shwr, tlt, hairdry, fan, heat, TV, t/c mkg, refrig, cook fac, micro, elec frypan, toaster, ldry, blkts, linen], w/mach, dryer, iron, iron brd, rec rm, TV rm, lounge firepl, pool (solar heated), spa, bbq, golf (Priv. 9 hole course), tennis, non smoking property. **D** $140 - $250, **W** $500 - $1,000, fam con.

LAURIETON NSW 2443

Pop Part of Camden Haven, (380km N Sydney), See map on page 54, ref C7. Coastal fishing village which, along with the neighbouring towns of Dunbogan and North Haven, makes up part of the Camden Haven area. Bowls, Fishing, Swimming, Tennis.

Hotels/Motels

★★★☆ **Mariner Motel**, (M), 12 Kew Rd, 400m N of PO, ☎ 02 6559 9398, fax 02 6559 9398, 12 units [shwr, tlt, a/c, tel, fax, TV, clock radio, t/c mkg, refrig], bbq, cots, non smoking rms (5). **RO ♦** $49.50 - $69.50, **♦♦** $58.50 - $95, ◊ $11, ch con, AE BC MC VI.

★☆ **Carawatha Country Resort**, (M), 146 Ocean Dve, 6km W of PO, 2km E of Kew, ☎ 02 6559 4209, 10 units [shwr, tlt, fan, heat, elec blkts, TV, clock radio (4), radio (6), t/c mkg, refrig, cook fac (4)], ldry, pool, bbq, plygr, tennis, cots. **D ♦** $55, **♦♦** $65, AE BC DC MC VI.

B&B's/Guest Houses

★★★★ **Stewarts River Bed & Breakfast**, (B&B), 14 Crosses La, Stewarts River 2443, 5km W of Pacific Hwy, ☎ 02 6556 5163, fax 02 6556 5163, 2 rms [shwr, tlt, hairdry, c/fan, heat, elec blkts], ldry, rec rm, TV rm, lounge, ✕, meals avail (dinner), non smoking rms. **BB ♦** $70, **♦♦** $90, pen con.

LAWSON NSW

See Blue Mountains Region.

Before you travel

Before a trip have your vehicle serviced and checked over to ensure reliable motoring. There are some checks you can make yourself, generally the procedure can be found in the vehicle owners manual.

LEETON NSW 2705

Pop 6,600. (565km SW Sydney), See map on pages 52/53, ref E6. The 'garden of the Riverina', nourished by the waters of the Murrumbidgee Irrigation Area (MIA) and part of the food bowl of New South Wales. Boating, Bowls, Fishing, Golf, Horse Racing, Scenic Drives, Swimming, Tennis, Vineyards, Wineries, Water Skiing.

Hotels/Motels

★★★★ **Bygalorie Motor Inn**, (M), 439 Yanco Ave, 1km SE of PO, ☎ 02 6953 4100, fax 02 6953 3445, 26 units [shwr, tlt, a/c, elec blkts, tel, fax, TV, clock radio, t/c mkg, refrig, toaster], ldry, conf fac, ⊠, pool, rm serv, non smoking units (12). RO ♦ $82 - $90, ♦♦ $92 - $100, ◊ $18, AE BC DC EFT MC VI, ⚹&.

★★★ **Motel Riverina**, (M), 1 Yanco Ave, 900m SE of PO, ☎ 02 6953 2955, fax 02 6953 2963, (2 stry gr fl) 38 units [shwr, tlt, a/c, heat, elec blkts, tel, TV (26), clock radio, t/c mkg, refrig], ldry, ⊠ (Mon to Sat), pool (salt water), bbq, c/park (undercover) (26), plygr, cots, non smoking units (5). BLB ♦ $68 - $78, ♦♦ $75 - $85, ♦♦♦ $85 - $95, ◊ $15, AE BC DC MC VI.

★★★ **Town Centre Motel**, (M), 22 Wade Ave, 50m S of PO, ☎ 02 6953 3044, fax 02 6953 7900, 23 units [shwr, tlt, a/c, heat, elec blkts, tel, TV, clock radio, t/c mkg, refrig, micro (5), toaster (5)], ✕ (Mon to Sat), pool (salt water), non smoking units (5). RO ♦ $65 - $70, ♦♦ $70 - $80, ♦♦♦ $85 - $95, ◊ $10, AE BC DC EFT MC VI.

B&B's/Guest Houses

★★★★ **The Madalock Country Bed 'N' Breakfast**, (B&B), 81 Kurrajong Ave, Opposite RSL Club, ☎ 02 6953 3784, fax 02 6953 3784, 3 rms [ensuite, spa bath (1), hairdry, evap cool, fire pl (2), cent heat, tel, TV, movie, clock radio, refrig, mini bar, toaster], ldry, iron, iron brd, lounge (TV), ✕, t/c mkg shared, bbq, dinner to unit, courtesy transfer, plygr, cots, non smoking rms. BB ♦ $79, ♦♦ $89, AE BC EFT MC VI.

★★★☆ **Historic Hydro Motor Inn**, (B&B), Classified by National Trust, Chelmsford Pl, ☎ 02 6953 1555, fax 02 6953 1500, (2 stry gr fl), 27 rms [shwr, tlt, a/c, elec blkts, tel, TV, clock radio, t/c mkg, refrig, cook fac (8)], lounge (TV), conv fac, ⊠, cots. BLB ♦ $68.50, ♦♦ $87, ◊ $19.50, RO ♦ $61, ♦♦ $72, ◊ $12, AE BC DC EFT JCB MC MCH MP VI, *Operator Comment: The Thomson family invites you to explore the wonders of the Hydro. Enjoy Eatons restaurant & bar. Meander through 2 acres of gardens. Relax on 700 sq m of verandahs. Enjoy 1 of 17 open fires.*

LEMON TREE PASSAGE NSW

See Port Stephens Region.

LENNOX HEAD NSW 2478

Pop 4,500. (765km N Sydney), See map on page 54, ref E2. Charming seaside village between Ballina and Byron Bay. Bowls, Fishing, Golf, Hangliding, Surfing, Swimming, Tennis.

Hotels/Motels

★★★ **Santa Fe Motel & Holiday Units**, (M), 8 Byron St, 250m NW of PO, ☎ 02 6687 7788, fax 02 6687 7788, (2 stry gr fl), 13 units (7 suites) [shwr, tlt, c/fan, heat, TV, clock radio, t/c mkg, refrig, cook fac (7), cook fac ltd (6), toaster], ldry, iron, iron brd, pool (salt water), bbq, cots, non smoking units. RO ♦ $65 - $140, ♦♦ $65 - $140, ♦♦♦ $76 - $151, ◊ $11, ch con, BC MC VI, ⚹&.

★★☆ **Lennox Head Motel**, (M), 49 Ballina St, 200m S of PO, ☎ 02 6687 7257, fax 02 6687 6344, 9 units [shwr, tlt, a/c, fax, TV, movie, clock radio, t/c mkg, refrig, cook fac (2), toaster], pool (salt water), courtesy transfer. RO ♦♦ $70 - $150, AE BC DC EFT JCB MC VI.

★★☆ **Lennox Head Motor Lodge & Holiday Units**, (M), 20 Byron St, ☎ 02 6687 7210, fax 02 6687 7210, 11 units (7 suites) [shwr, tlt, c/fan, heat, tel, TV, movie, clock radio, t/c mkg, refrig, cook fac (9), toaster], ldry, pool, bbq, cots. RO ♦ $48 - $110, ♦♦ $60 - $130, ♦♦♦ $70 - $140, ◊ $10 - $15, AE BC MC VI.

Self Catering Accommodation

★★★★☆ **Headland Beach Resort**, (HU), 7 Park Lane, 300m S of PO, ☎ 02 6618 0000, fax 02 6687 4143, 39 units acc up to 8, (1, 2 & 3 bedrm), [a/c-cool, heat, tel, TV, video-fee, clock radio, t/c mkg, refrig, cook fac, micro, d/wash, ldry, blkts, linen-fee], w/mach, dryer, conf fac, ⊠, pool-heated, sauna, spa, bbq, secure park, cots-fee. RO ♦♦ $120 - $140, ◊ $15, W ◊ $576 - $1,000, weekly con, AE BC DC EFT MC VI.

★★★★☆ **Newall's Apartments**, (HU), 10 Pinnacle Row, 1km S of PO, ☎ 02 6687 5144, fax 02 6687 6027, (2 stry), 4 units acc up to 6, [shwr, bath, tlt, hairdry, fan, heat, tel, TV, video, clock radio, CD, t/c mkg, refrig, cook fac, micro, elec frypan, d/wash, toaster, ldry, blkts, linen, pillows], w/mach, dryer, iron, pool (salt water), bbq, secure park, cots. D $120 - $350, W $720 - $2,124, Min book applies, AE BC DC MC VI.

★★★★ **Sandscape**, (House), 4 Killarney Cres, Skennars Head, 7km N of Ballina PO, ☎ 0418 163 153, 1 house acc up to 9, [shwr (3), bath (1), tlt (3), c/fan, elec blkts (3), tel, TV, video, clock radio, t/c mkg, refrig, cook fac, micro, d/wash, toaster, ldry, blkts, pillows], w/mach, dryer, iron, iron brd, bbq, courtesy transfer, cots-fee, non smoking property. W $450 - $2,040, Min book applies.

★★★ **Lennox Head Beachfront Apartments**, (HU), 77 Ballina St, ☎ 02 6687 7579, fax 02 6687 6035, 20 units acc up to 6, [shwr, tlt, TV, video-fee, refrig, cook fac, micro, ldry, linen reqd-fee], pool, bbq. W $300 - $880.

LEURA NSW

See Blue Mountains Region.

LIGHTNING RIDGE NSW 2834

Pop 1,800. (783km NW Sydney), See map on pages 52/53, ref F1. Famous opal town in the north-west of the State near the Queensland border. Bowls, Gem Fossicking, Swimming, Tennis.

Hotels/Motels

★★☆ **Black Opal Motel**, (M), Opal St, 50m W of PO, ☎ 02 6829 0518, fax 02 6829 0884, 11 units [shwr, tlt, a/c, tel, TV, t/c mkg, refrig, toaster]. RO ♦ $58.30, ♦♦ $69.30, ◊ $11, ch con, 3 rooms at a lower rating. AE BC MC VI.

★★☆ **Lightning Ridge Motel Hotel**, (LMH), Onyx St, 500m W of PO, ☎ 02 6829 0304, fax 02 6829 0306, 41 units [shwr, bath (28), tlt, a/c, fan, heat, tel, TV, clock radio, t/c mkg, refrig], ldry, iron, iron brd, ⊠ (Tue to Sat), pool (salt water), bbq, dinner to unit, ☎, cots. RO ♦ $57, ♦♦ $68, ♦♦♦ $80, 6 units of a three star rating, AE BC DC EFT MC VI, ⚹&.

★★☆ **Wallangulla Motel**, (M), Cnr Morella & Agate Sts, 200m W of PO, ☎ 02 6829 0542, fax 02 6829 0070, (2 stry gr fl), 42 units [shwr, spa bath (2), tlt, a/c, heat, tel, cable tv, clock radio, t/c mkg, refrig], ldry, bbq, cots-fee. RO ♦ $45 - $73, ♦♦ $56 - $84, ♦♦♦ $78 - $95, ♦♦♦♦ $89 - $122, ◊ $11, 11 units at three star rating. AE BC DC MC VI, ⚹&.

LISMORE NSW 2480

Pop 28,400. (757km N Sydney), See map on page 54, ref D2. Thriving northern rivers university city famed for its cultural life and physical beauty. Art Gallery, Bowls, Croquet, Golf, Greyhound Racing, Horse Racing, Horse Riding, Scenic Drives, Squash, Swimming, Tennis, Water Skiing.

Hotels/Motels

★★★★ **Lismore Wilson Motel**, (M), 119 Ballina St, 500m E PO, ☎ 02 6622 3383, fax 02 6622 3393, 25 units [shwr, bath (2), spa bath (4), tlt, hairdry, a/c, elec blkts, tel, TV, clock radio, t/c mkg, refrig, mini bar, cook fac (1), micro (4), toaster], ldry, iron, iron brd, bbq, dinner to unit, secure park, cots-fee, non smoking units (22). RO ♦ $74.50 - $132, ♦♦ $82.50 - $132, ◊ $11, AE BC DC EFT MC VI, ⚹&. *Operator Comment: "Lismore's newest and only 4 star motel - established 1997".*

★★★☆ **Centre Point Motel**, (M), 202 Molesworth St, ☎ 02 6621 8877, fax 02 6622 1409, (Multi-stry gr fl), 41 units (8 suites) [shwr, spa bath (3), tlt, hairdry, a/c, elec blkts, tel, TV, video (avail), clock radio, t/c mkg, refrig, mini bar, cook fac (3)], ldry, iron, iron brd, conv fac, ⊠, bbq, dinner to unit, cots-fee, non smoking units (15). **D** ♦ **$60 - $90, ♦♦ $60 - $90, ◊ $11, Suite D $95 - $130**, AE BC DC EFT MC MP VI, ⏚.

★★★☆ **Dawson Motor Inn**, (M), 25 Dawson St, 800m N of PO, ☎ 02 6621 8100, fax 02 6621 8929, 21 units (2 suites) [shwr, tlt, hairdry, a/c, elec blkts, tel, TV, t/c mkg, refrig, mini bar, toaster], ldry, iron, iron brd, pool (salt water), bbq, dinner to unit, cots, non smoking units (avail). **RO** ♦ **$60 - $80, ♦♦ $65 - $85, ◊ $10**, 5 rooms ★★★★. AE BC DC MC VI.

Operator Comment: Affordable luxury, in Lismore's most modern rooms.

★★★☆ **Lakeside Lodge Motel**, (M), Bruxner Hwy, 3.1km S of PO, ☎ 02 6621 7376, fax 02 6622 1799, 15 units [shwr, bath (4), tlt, hairdry, a/c, tel, cable tv, video-fee, clock radio, t/c mkg, refrig, toaster], ldry, iron, iron brd, dinner to unit, cots-fee. **RO** ♦ **$78, ♦♦ $89, ♦♦♦ $102, ◊ $8 - $13**, ch con, Min book applies, AE BC DC JCB MC MP VI.

★★★☆ **New Olympic Motel**, (M), 244 Molesworth St, 50m S of PO, ☎ 02 6621 9900, fax 02 6621 9968, (2 stry gr fl), 21 units [shwr, tlt, hairdry, a/c, tel, TV, video-fee, clock radio, t/c mkg, refrig], bbq, c/park (undercover), cots, non smoking units (7). **RO** ♦ **$58 - $78, ♦♦ $71 - $91, ◊ $13**, AE BC BTC DC EFT MC VI.

★★★☆ **Sisleys Inntown Motel**, (M), 111 Dawson St, 500m E of PO, ☎ 02 6621 9888, fax 02 6621 8812, (2 stry), 8 units [shwr, spa bath (1), tlt, hairdry, a/c, c/fan, elec blkts, tel, clock radio, t/c mkg, refrig, toaster], ldry, dinner to unit, cots. **RO** ♦ **$60 - $70, ♦♦ $70 - $100, ♦♦♦ $80 - $110, ◊ $11**, AE BC DC MC VI.

★★★ **A Z A Motel**, (M), 114 Keen St, 150m N of PO, ☎ 02 6621 9499, fax 02 6622 1554, (2 stry gr fl), 27 units [shwr, tlt, a/c, tel, TV, clock radio, t/c mkg, refrig], ldry, pool, cots-fee, non smoking rms (8). **RO** ♦ **$60 - $65, ♦♦ $70 - $75, ♦♦♦ $75 - $80, ◊ $10**, ch con, AE BC DC EFT MC MP VI.

L

NEW SOUTH WALES

★★★ **Arcadia Motel**, (M), Cnr James Rd & Ballina Rd, 6km E of PO, ☎ 02 6624 1999, fax 02 6624 1999, 10 units [shwr, tlt, a/c, fan, elec blkts, tel, TV, clock radio, t/c mkg, refrig], ldry, pool, dinner to unit (Mon to Thu), cots-fee, non smoking units (2). **RO** ♦ **$55**, ♦♦ **$63 - $66**, ◊ **$10**, AE BC DC EFT MC VI.

★★☆ **Karinga Motel**, (M), 258 Molesworth St, 100m S of PO, ☎ 02 6621 2787, fax 02 6622 1388, 31 units [shwr, tlt, a/c, elec blkts, tel, fax, TV, video-fee, clock radio, t/c mkg, refrig], ldry, ⊠ (Limited), dinner to unit (6 nights), cots, non smoking units (6). **RO** ♦ **$54 - $70**, ♦♦ **$64 - $80**, ♦♦♦ **$74 - $95**, ◊ **$12**, AE BC DC EFT MC VI.

Self Catering Accommodation

★★★☆ **Suzanne's Hideaway**, (Cotg), 20 Elliot Rd, Clunes 2480, 18km NE of Lismore, ☎ 02 6629 1228, fax 02 6629 1756, 1 cotg acc up to 2, (Studio), [shwr, tlt, hairdry, c/fan, heat, elec blkts, tel, TV, video, clock radio, CD, t/c mkg, refrig, cook fac, micro, toaster, blkts, linen, pillows], w/mach, dryer, iron, iron brd, pool (salt water), bbq, plygr, gym, tennis, cots (avail), non smoking property, **D** ♦♦ **$115 - $175**, **W** ♦♦ **$690 - $1,050**, ch con, BC MC VI.

★★★★☆ **(Villa Section)**, 2 villas acc up to 4, (2 bedrm), [shwr, spa bath, tlt, hairdry, c/fan, heat, elec blkts, tel, TV, video, clock radio, CD, refrig, cook fac, micro, d/wash, toaster, ldry, blkts, linen], w/mach, dryer, iron, iron brd, pool, bbq, c/park (undercover), gym, tennis, cots (available), non smoking rms. **D $150 - $270**, **W $900 - $1,620**.

B&B's/Guest Houses

★★★★ **Melville House**, (B&B), 267 Ballina St, 1.5km E of PO, ☎ 02 6621 5778, fax 02 6621 5778, (2 stry gr fl), 6 rms [ensuite (3), a/c (4), fan, heat (2), cent heat (4), TV, clock radio (4), doonas], ldry, ✕, pool, t/c mkg shared, refrig, bbq, ✆, plygr, cots, non smoking property, Pets on application. **BLB** ♦ **$45 - $110**, ♦♦ **$55 - $140**, ◊ **$15**, ch con, weekly con, 2 rooms ★★★☆. 2 rooms ★★★.

★★★★ **PJ's Bed & Breakfast**, (B&B), 152 Johnston Rd, Clunes 2480, 16km NE of Lismore PO, ☎ 02 6629 1788, fax 02 6629 1744, 3 rms [ensuite, fan, cent heat, elec blkts, TV, t/c mkg, refrig], ldry, pool, bbq, ✆, non smoking rms. **D** ♦ **$75 - $90**, ♦♦ **$90 - $120**, weekly con, AE BC EFT MC VI.

★★★☆ **Country Pumpkin Lodge**, (B&B), 8 Randle Rd, Marom Creek 2480, 25km SE of Lismore, ☎ 02 6629 8418, fax 02 6629 8418, 2 rms (1 suite) [shwr, tlt, hairdry, fan, heat, tel, TV, video, clock radio, t/c mkg, refrig, micro, toaster, ldry], iron, iron brd, bbq-fee, plygr, non smoking property. **BB** ♦ **$88**, ♦♦ **$110**, ◊ **$33**, ch con, BC MC VI.

★★★☆ **McDermotts Bed & Breakfast**, (B&B), 21 Sheridan Dve, Goonellabah 2480, 5km E of PO, ☎ 02 6624 1158, 2 rms [shwr, bath, tlt, fan, elec blkts, tel, t/c mkg], ldry. **BB** ♦ **$55 - $65**, ♦♦ **$65 - $75**, Dinner by arrangement.

★★★☆ **Top of the Town Apartments**, (GH), Cnr Pleasant & Fischer Sts, ☎ 02 6625 2693, fax 02 6625 1008, 7 rms [fan, heat (elec), tel, clock radio, doonas], shared fac (2), ldry, lounge (TV), ✕, pool (outdoor), spa (communal), t/c mkg shared, refrig, bbq, cots-fee, non smoking rms. **RO** ♦ **$21.50**, ♦♦ **$43**, weekly con.

(Apartments Section), 1 serv apt acc up to 6, (3 bedrm), [shwr, tlt, fan, heat (elec), tel, clock radio, t/c mkg, cook fac, micro, blkts, doonas, linen, pillows], w/mach, dryer, bbq, cots-fee, non smoking units. **D** ♦♦♦♦ **$88**, weekly con, (not yet classified).

LITHGOW NSW

See Blue Mountains Region.

LITTLE HARTLEY NSW

See Blue Mountains Region.

LOCHINVAR NSW 2321

Pop 500. (213km N Sydney), See map on page 55, ref B7. Small village in the Hunter region west of Maitland. Scenic Drives, Vineyards, Wineries.

Hotels/Motels

★☆ **Lochinvar Hotel Motel**, (LMH), New England Hwy, opposite PO, ☎ 02 4930 7216, 10 units [shwr, tlt, a/c, TV, refrig], ⊠. **BLB** ♦ **$38.50 - $49.50**, ♦♦ **$60 - $70**, ch con, BC EFT MC VI.

Self Catering Accommodation

★★★★☆ **Tranquil Vale**, (HU), 325 Pywells Rd, Luskintyre 2321. 6.5km N of PO, ☎ 02 4930 6100, fax 02 4930 6105, 3 units acc up to 5, (2 bedrm), [shwr, tlt, a/c, fan, cent heat, TV, video, t/c mkg, refrig, cook fac, micro, blkts, doonas, linen, pillows], ldry, pool, plygr, cots, breakfast ingredients, non smoking property. **BLB** ♦ **$60 - $70**, ♦♦ **$120 - $150**, AE BC MC VI.

LOCKHART NSW 2656

Pop 900. (520km SW Sydney), See map on pages 52/53, ref E6. Riverina township known as 'the Verandah Town' because of its National Trust-classified main street, a prime example of a turn-of-the-century rural business district. Bowls, Golf, Swimming, Tennis.

Hotels/Motels

★★ **Lockhart Motel**, (M), Cnr East & Green Sts, ☎ 02 6920 5357, fax 02 6920 5690, 9 units [shwr, tlt, a/c-cool, heat, elec blkts, TV, clock radio, t/c mkg, refrig, toaster], ldry, dinner to unit, cots-fee. **RO** ♦ **$59.40**, ♦♦ **$66**, ◊ **$6.60**, ch con, AE BC DC MC VI.

B&B's/Guest Houses

★★★☆ **The Bank & Stable Bed & Breakfast**, (B&B), Cnr Green & Matthews Sts, Opposite PO, ☎ 02 6920 5443, 3 rms [a/c-cool, a/c, c/fan, elec blkts, tel], TV rm, lounge (TV), lounge firepl, ✕, bar, bbq, non smoking property. **BB** ♦ **$66**, ♦♦ **$88**, BC MC VI.

LONG JETTY NSW 2261

Pop Part of Wyong, (96km N Sydney), See map on page 55, ref D6. Popular holiday spot just south of The Entrance on the south-east corner of Tuggerah Lake. Fishing, Golf, Sailing, Swimming.

Hotels/Motels

★★★☆ **Buccaneer Motel**, (M), 398 The Entrance Rd, 500m S of PO, ☎ 02 4334 3100, fax 02 4334 2806, 17 units (3 suites) [shwr, tlt, a/c-cool, fan, heat, elec blkts, tel, TV, clock radio, t/c mkg, refrig, micro (6), toaster, ldry (Guest laundry)], pool, non smoking units (8). **RO** ♦ **$77 - $98**, ♦♦ **$77 - $98**, ♦♦♦ **$92 - $113**, ◊ **$15**, Suite **D $98 - $120**, ch con, Min book applies, AE BC DC EFT MC VI.

★★★☆ **Jetty Motel**, (M), 353 The Entrance Rd, 1.5km S of The Entrance PO, ☎ 02 4332 1022, fax 02 4334 3515, 22 units [shwr, tlt, a/c, elec blkts, tel, cable tv, t/c mkg, refrig], pool (salt water), spa, cook fac, bbq, cots. **RO** ♦ **$55 - $100**, ♦♦ **$66 - $110**, ◊ **$11**, Min book applies, AE BC MC VI, ♿.

★★★☆ **Palm Gardens Resort**, (M), 44 Kitchener Rd, 2km S of The Entrance PO, ☎ 02 4333 1000, fax 02 4233 1161, (Multi-stry gr fl), 23 units (23 suites) [shwr, tlt, fan, heat, elec blkts, tel, TV, video (10)-fee, clock radio, t/c mkg, refrig, cook fac, micro, toaster], ldry-fee, rec rm, pool (salt water), sauna-fee, spa, steam rm-fee, bbq-fee, plygr, cots, non smoking suites (4). **RO** ♦ **$85**, ♦♦ **$90 - $200**, ♦♦♦ **$95**, ◊ **$8 - $18**, Suite **W $630 - $1,700**, ch con, Min book applies, AE BC EFT MC VI.

★★★☆ **The Coachman Motor Inn**, (M), 33 Gordon Rd, 2km S of The Entrance PO, ☎ 02 4332 3692, fax 02 4332 7650, (2 stry gr fl), 7 units (1 suite) [shwr, tlt, a/c, c/fan, heat, elec blkts, tel, TV, clock radio, t/c mkg, refrig, cook fac (4)], iron, iron brd, ✕, pool, bbq, c/park (undercover) (4), cots, non smoking rms. **RO** ♦♦ **$60.50 - $137.50**, ◊ **$11 - $16.50**, Min book applies, AE BC DC MC VI.

LORD HOWE ISLAND NSW 2898

Pop 350. (702km NE Sydney), See map on page 54, ref E7. Known as the 'Jewel of the Pacific', Lord Howe is a stunning place and one of the unsung wonders of New South Wales. Bird Watching, Bowls, Bush Walking, Golf, Scenic Drives, Swimming, Tennis.

Self Catering Accommodation

★★★☆ **Blue Lagoon Serviced Apartments**, (SA), ☎ 02 6563 2006, fax 02 6563 2150, 15 serv apts acc up to 3, [shwr, tlt, c/fan, tel, TV, clock radio, t/c mkg, refrig, cook fac, micro, elec frypan, toaster], ldry, rec rm, lounge (TV), bbq, rm serv, mini mart, ✆, tennis, cots-fee. **D** ♦ **$95**, Min book applies, BC MC.

★★★☆ **Lorhiti Apartments**, (HU), NE of PO, ☎ 07 3366 8000, or 02 6563 2081, 6 units acc up to 3, [shwr, tlt, hairdry, fan, heat, elec blkts, tel, TV, video, clock radio, t/c mkg, refrig, cook fac, micro, elec frypan, toaster, blkts, linen, pillows], ldry, w/mach, dryer, iron, lounge, ⊠, bbq, ✆. **D** ♦♦ **$130 - $252**, ◊ **$30**, **W** ♦♦ **$630 - $1,540**, ◊ **$315 - $770**, Min book applies, AE BC MC VI.

★★★☆ **Mary Challis Cottages**, (Cotg), ☎ 02 6563 2076, fax 02 6563 2159, 2 cotgs acc up to 2, [shwr, tlt, hairdry, c/fan, elec blkts, TV, radio, refrig, cook fac, micro, toaster, blkts, linen, pillows], ldry, iron. **D** ♦♦ **$83.50 - $143.**

★★★☆ **Somerset Apartments**, (HU), Neds Beach Rd, 200m E of PO, ☎ 02 6563 2061, fax 02 6563 2110, 25 units acc up to 3, [shwr, tlt, hairdry, fan, TV, clock radio, t/c mkg, refrig, micro, toaster, blkts, linen, pillows], ldry, bbq, ✆, cots. **D** ♦♦ **$142 - $310.**

★★★ **Leanda - Lei Apartments**, (HU), Middle Beach Rd, 500m S of PO, ☎ 02 6563 2195, fax 02 6563 2095, 15 units acc up to 6, [shwr, tlt, c/fan (7), TV, video, clock radio, t/c mkg, refrig, cook fac (9), cook fac ltd (6), micro, toaster, blkts, linen, pillows], ldry, w/mach, dryer, iron, rec rm, bbq, ✆, cots. **D** ♦ **$140 - $225,** ♦ **$40,** 4 units ★★★☆. AE BC MC VI.

★★★ **The Broken Banyan**, (HU), No children's facilities, Anderson Rd, ☎ 02 6563 2024, fax 02 6563 2201, 6 units acc up to 2, [shwr, tlt, elec blkts, TV, radio, t/c mkg, refrig, cook fac, micro, toaster, blkts, linen, pillows], ldry, bbq. **D** ♦♦ **$132 - $176,** Min book applies.

B&B's/Guest Houses
Capella Lodge, (B&B), Lagoon Rd, 1km S of Airport, ☎ 02 9544 2273, fax 02 9544 2387, 9 rms [shwr, bath, tlt, hairdry, c/fan, heat, tel, TV, radio, t/c mkg, refrig], ldry, ✉, ✆. **BB** ♦ **$260 - $345,** ♦♦ **$350 - $560,** AE BC MC VI, (not yet classified).

LOVEDALE NSW 2325
Pop Nominal, See map on page 55, ref B7. Village in the Hunter Valley between Cessnock and Branxton.
Self Catering Accommodation
★★★★ **Ironstone Cottage**, (Cotg), Londons Rd, ☎ 02 4990 3376, fax 02 4990 3376, 1 cotg acc up to 4, [shwr, bath, tlt, hairdry, a/c, c/fan, fire pl, TV, clock radio, t/c mkg, refrig, cook fac, micro, toaster, doonas, linen], iron, iron brd, bbq, non smoking property. **D** ♦♦ **$165,** **W** ♦♦ **$770,** BC MC VI.

LOWANNA NSW 2450
Pop Nominal, (560km N Sydney), See map on page 54, ref C4. A charming little village set in the mountains and rainforests 40km NW of Coffs Harbour.
Self Catering Accommodation
Wilkie's Wilderness, (House), 886 Camp Creek Rd, 10km N of PO, ☎ 02 6654 5216, 1 house acc up to 8, (2 bedrm), [shwr, tlt, heat (wood), clock radio, t/c mkg, refrig, ldry, blkts, doonas, linen], bbq, breakfast ingredients. **D** ♦♦ **$100 - $150,** ♦ **$10 - $15,** weekly con, (not yet classified).

LUE NSW 2850
Pop Nominal, (276km NW Sydney), See map on pages 52/53, ref H4. Lue (pronounced 'Loo-ey') lies roughly halfway between Mudgee and Rylstone and grew during the mid-1880s to service local pastoral concerns. Scenic Drives, Vineyards, Wineries.
B&B's/Guest Houses
★★★ **Lue Station**, (B&B), (Farm), Lue Station, ☎ 02 6373 6452, fax 02 6373 6465, 9 rms [shwr (7), bath (2), tlt (7), fan, fire pl, elec blkts, tel, TV, radio, t/c mkg, refrig, cook fac ltd, micro, toaster], rec rm, ✗, pool (salt water), bbq, plygr, tennis, cots. **BB** ♦ **$45 - $50,** ♦♦ **$90 - $100, DBB** ♦ **$65 - $75,** ♦♦ **$130 - $140,** ch con, BC MC VI.

LYNDHURST NSW 2797
Pop 250. (289km W Sydney), See map on pages 52/53, ref G5. Old gold town on the Mid-Western Highway between Blayney and Cowra.
Hotels/Motels
Royal Licensed Hotel, (LH), Main St, 60km W of Bathurst, ☎ 02 6367 5024, 4 rms [elec blkts, t/c mkg], ✗, meals avail, c/park. **RO** ♦ **$22,** ♦♦ **$45,** ♦ **$22,** ch con.

MACKSVILLE NSW 2447
Pop 2,700. (498km N Sydney), See map on page 54, ref C5. Old steamer port on the Nambucca River which now serves as the administrative and service centre for the area. Boating, Fishing, Swimming.
Hotels/Motels
★★★☆ **Mid Coast Motor Inn**, (M), Pacific Hwy, 800m S of PO, ☎ 02 6568 3544, fax 02 6568 1596, 25 units [shwr, tlt, a/c, elec blkts, tel, TV, clock radio, t/c mkg, refrig], ldry, pool (salt water), cots. **RO** ♦ **$45 - $55,** ♦♦ **$50 - $70,** ♦♦♦ **$55 - $80,** ♦ **$5 - $9,** AE BC DC MC VI.

★★★ **Golden Emblem Motel**, (M), Pacific Hwy, 800m S of PO, ☎ 02 6568 1977, fax 02 6568 2751, 19 units [shwr, tlt, a/c, c/fan, elec blkts, tel, TV, video (avail), movie, clock radio, t/c mkg, refrig, cook fac (1)], ✉ (open 6 days), pool, spa, bbq, rm serv, dinner to unit (6 days), cots-fee, non smoking units (12).
RO ♦ **$60 - $70,** ♦♦ **$68 - $78,** ♦ **$10,** AE BC DC EFT MC MP VI.

★★☆ **Belle Vue Riverside**, (M), Belle Vue Dve, N of PO over bridge, ☎ 02 6568 1363, fax 02 6568 3606, 9 units [shwr, tlt, fan, heat, elec blkts, TV, clock radio, t/c mkg, refrig], pool, bbq, plygr, cots-fee.
RO ♦ **$42 - $55,** ♦♦ **$46 - $60,** ♦ **$11,** AE BC MC VI.

Self Catering Accommodation
Cheviot Hills Farmstay, (House), 490 Congarinni South, 10km SE of PO, ☎ 02 6569 3190, fax 02 6569 3190, 1 house acc up to 8, (3 bedrm), [shwr, tlt, fan, heat, TV, clock radio, t/c mkg, refrig, cook fac, micro, toaster, ldry, blkts, doonas, linen, pillows], cots. **D** ♦ **$40,** ♦♦ **$70,** ♦ **$35,** ch con, Min book applies, (not yet classified).

B&B's/Guest Houses
★★★★ **Jacaranda Country Lodge**, (GH), Lot 6 Wilson Rd, 5km W of PO, ☎ 02 6568 2737, fax 02 6568 2769, 12 rms [shwr, tlt, c/fan (12), clock radio], TV rm, lounge, conf fac, pool, sauna, spa, courtesy transfer, ✆, jetty, tennis, non smoking property. **BLB** ♦ **$60 - $88,** ♦♦ **$100 - $132,** ♦ **$25,** BC MC VI.

MACLEAN NSW 2463
Pop 3,150. (667km N Sydney), See map on page 54, ref D3. Maclean has a proud Scottish heritage and is a self-proclaimed 'Scottish Town in Australia'. Bowls, Fishing, Golf, Surfing.
Hotels/Motels
★★★ **Maclean Motel**, (M), Old Pacific Hwy, 2km S of PO, ☎ 02 6645 2473, fax 02 6645 4299, 10 units [shwr, tlt, a/c, fan, heat, tel, TV, clock radio, t/c mkg, refrig, micro, toaster], ldry, pool, bbq, cots-fee. **W** **$265 - $400, RO** ♦ **$44 - $49.50,** ♦♦ **$49.50 - $55,** ♦ **$5.50,** AE BC DC MC VI.

★★☆ **Water View Motel**, (M), 121 River St, 700m N of PO, ☎ 02 6645 2494, fax 02 6645 2494, (2 stry gr fl), 14 units [shwr, tlt, a/c, elec blkts, TV, clock radio, t/c mkg, refrig], ldry, pool, bbq, ✆, cots. **RO** ♦ **$49,** ♦♦ **$56,** ♦♦♦ **$66,** ♦ **$11,** AE BC MC VI.

B&B's/Guest Houses
★★★☆ **Gables Bed & Breakfast**, (B&B), 2b Howard St, 1km N of PO, ☎ 02 6645 2452, fax 02 6645 2452, (2 stry), 4 rms [c/fan, fire pl, heat], lounge (TV), conv fac, t/c mkg shared, bbq, c/park. **BB** ♦♦ **$95,** BC MC VI.

MOTEL MACLEAN

Old Pacific Highway, P.O Box 101, Maclean 2463
Over the Clarence River, 350 metres off the Highway at the Southern Entrance

- River views from all rooms
- Economy Rates
- Meals to Rooms
- Walk to Restaurant
- Minutes to Town Centre
- Pool
- 20 – 30 minutes to Beaches
- BBQ
- Air Conditioning

Ph: (02) 6645 2473 Fax: (02) 6645 4299

MACMASTERS BEACH NSW 2251
Pop 750. Part of Gosford, (91km N Sydney), See map on page 55, ref D6. Central Coast seaside town on the shores of Allagai Bay. Boating, Fishing, Swimming. See also Kincumber.
B&B's/Guest Houses
★★★★☆ **The Bell's Guesthouse**, (B&B), Previously The Bells Bed & Breakfast, 7 Cripps Cl, 1km S of beach, ☎ 02 4382 4760, fax 02 4382 4761, 2 rms (1 suite) [ensuite, spa bath, hairdry, fan, fire pl (1), heat, elec blkts, tel, TV, video, clock radio, t/c mkg, refrig, cook fac (2), micro, toaster (2), ldry], iron, iron brd, lounge, lounge firepl, ✗, bbq, 24hr reception, rm serv, dinner to unit, courtesy transfer, non smoking property. **BB** ♦♦ **$220 - $265,** ♦ **$65,** pen con, Min book applies, AE BC EFT MC VI.

MAITLAND NSW 2320

Pop 50,100. (163km N Sydney), See map on page 55, ref C7. Historic city in the heart of the Hunter region on the banks of the Hunter River. Scenic Drives, Vineyards, Wineries. See also Kurri Kurri & Morpeth.

Hotels/Motels

 ★★★☆ Country Comfort Monte Pio, (M), Dwyer St (off New England Hwy), 2km NW of PO, ☎ 02 4932 5288, fax 02 4932 6788, (2 stry gr fl), 46 units [shwr, spa bath (4), tlt, hairdry, a/c, fire pl (1), tel, TV, movie, clock radio, t/c mkg, mini bar, toaster], iron, rec rm, lounge (TV), conf fac, ✖, pool, sauna, spa, 24hr reception, rm serv, dinner to unit, tennis, cots, non smoking rms (19). RO ♦ $105 - $148, ♦♦ $105 - $148, ◊ $15, ch con, 4 units of a higher standard, AE BC DC EFT JCB MC VI, ⟨⟩.

 ★★★☆ Endeavour Motel & Serviced Apartments, (M), New England Hwy, East Maitland 2323, 500m S of Maitland East PO, ☎ 02 4933 5488, fax 02 4934 2080, 28 units [shwr, spa bath (3), tlt, hairdry, a/c, tel, cable tv, clock radio, t/c mkg, refrig, cook fac (3), toaster], ldry, ✖, bar, pool (salt water), bbq, rm serv, dinner to unit, cots-fee, non smoking units (10). RO ♦ $80, ♦♦ $94, ◊ $7 - $14, AE BC DC EFT JCB MC MP VI.

 ★★★☆ Sundowner Chain Motor Inns, (M), 279 New England Hwy, 500m S of Rutherford PO, ☎ 02 4932 5255, fax 02 4932 8348, 40 units [shwr, tlt, hairdry, a/c, elec blkts, tel, cable tv, video, clock radio, t/c mkg, refrig, mini bar], ldry, iron, iron brd, ✖, pool (salt water), rm serv, dinner to unit, cots, non smoking units (20). RO ♦ $81.50 - $110.50, ♦♦ $93 - $110.50, ◊ $11, ch con, 13 units ★★★. AE BC DC EFT MC MP VI, ⟨⟩.

 ★★☆ Maitland City Motel, (M), 258 New England Hwy, Rutherford, 4km W of PO, ☎ 02 4932 8322, fax 02 4932 8343, (2 stry gr fl), 26 units [shwr, spa bath (1), tlt, hairdry, a/c, fan, heat, elec blkts, tel, cable tv, video-fee, clock radio, t/c mkg, refrig, toaster], ldry, cots-fee. D ♦ $63, ♦♦ $74 - $99, ♦♦♦♦ $99, ◊ $10, 3 units not included in listing, AE BC DC EFT MC MCH VI, ⟨⟩.

★★☆ Molly Morgan Motor Inn, (M), New England Hwy, East Maitland, 2km E of East Maitland PO, ☎ 02 4933 5422, fax 02 4933 2762, (2 stry gr fl), 38 units [shwr, bath (10), tlt, hairdry, a/c, tel, cable tv (22), clock radio, t/c mkg, refrig, mini bar (22)], ldry, conv fac, ✖, pool, bbq, rm serv, dinner to unit, plygr, cots. RO ♦ $65 - $140, ♦♦ $78 - $140, AE BC DC EFT MC VI, ⟨⟩.

★★ Shenanigans at The Imperial, (LH), 458 High St, 1km N of Station, ☎ 02 4933 6566, fax 02 4933 5855, (2 stry), 8 rms [a/c-cool, fan], ✖, t/c mkg shared, non smoking rms. BLB ♦ $50, ♦♦ $65, ◊ $15, AE BC DC EFT MC VI.

Self Catering Accommodation

 **★★★☆ 166 Apartments**, (Apt), 166 High St, East Maitland 2323, 500m N of PO, ☎ 02 4933 5488, fax 02 4934 2080, (2 stry gr fl), 5 apts (1 & 3 bedrm), [shwr, tlt, a/c, cable tv, clock radio, t/c mkg, refrig, cook fac, micro, toaster, blkts, linen, pillows], ldry, conf fac, ✖, pool, bbq, c/park (undercover), cots-fee, non smoking property. D $120 - $145, W $616 - $756, AE BC DC EFT MC VI.

 **★★★☆ Hunter River Retreat**, (Cotg), (Farm), 1090 Maitlandvale Rd, Rosebrook, 15km W of PO, ☎ 02 4930 1114, fax 02 4930 1690, 5 cotgs acc up to 6, [shwr, bath, spa bath (3), tlt, a/c, c/fan, fire pl, TV, clock radio, t/c mkg, refrig, cook fac, micro, elec frypan, toaster, blkts, linen, pillows], ldry, rec rm, pool (salt water), bbq, canoeing, tennis, cots. D $85 - $185, W $600 - $950, Min book applies, AE BC MC VI.

B&B's/Guest Houses

★★★★ The Old George & Dragon, (GH), 48 Melbourne St, East Maitland 2323, 3km E of Maitland PO, ☎ 02 4933 7272, fax 02 4934 1481, 4 rms [shwr, tlt, hairdry, a/c, fire pl (1)], lounge (guest), cook fac, t/c mkg shared, non smoking rms. DBB $253 - $324.50, AE BC DC MC VI.

★★★☆ Oxted Bed & Breakfast, (B&B), 4 Wakehurst Cres, Metford 2323, 1.5km E from East Maitland, ☎ 02 4933 1271, fax 02 4934 7966, 3 rms [fan (2), doonas], shared fac (3), ldry, lounge (TV/video), ✖, pool (outdoor), spa, t/c mkg shared, refrig, bbq, ☏, non smoking property. BB ♦ $85, ♦♦ $110, weekly con.

MALUA BAY NSW 2536

Pop 1,500. (297km S Sydney), See map on page 55, ref B6. South coast settlement at the southern extremity of Batemans Bay. See also Batehaven, Nilligen, Surf Beach.

Self Catering Accommodation

★★ Malua Bay Inn, (HU), 4 Kuppa Ave, ☎ 02 4471 1659, fax 02 4471 1659, 8 units acc up to 5, [shwr, tlt, a/c, TV, refrig, cook fac, toaster, blkts, linen, pillows], ldry. D $60 - $105, W $230 - $725, Min book long w/ends, BC MC VI.

★★ Sunrise Holiday Units, (HU), 31 Tallawang Ave, ☎ 02 4471 1638, fax 02 4471 1363, (2 stry gr fl), 2 units acc up to 4, (2 bedrm), [shwr, tlt, fan, heat, TV, radio, refrig, cook fac, micro, toaster, ldry, blkts, doonas, linen reqd, pillows], w/mach, bbq, c/park (undercover), cots. D ♦♦ $65 - $250, W ♦♦ $300 - $900, BC MC VI.

MANDALONG NSW 2264

Pop Part of Lake Macquarie, (153km S Sydney) See map on page 55, ref D5. Rural town in the Lake Macquarie hinterland between Morisset and Dooralong.

B&B's/Guest Houses

★★★☆ Kemeys Bed & Breakfast, (B&B), Sauls Rd, 10km W of PO, ☎ 02 4977 2525, fax 02 4977 2589, 3 rms (2 suites) [shwr, spa bath, tlt, hairdry, a/c, c/fan, clock radio, CD, t/c mkg, refrig, cook fac ltd], ldry, rec rm, lounge firepl (TV), ✖, bbq, dinner to unit, courtesy transfer, tennis, non smoking property. Suite BB ♦ $80 - $130, ♦♦ $90 - $160, Suite DBB ♦ $110 - $160, ♦♦ $150 - $220, AE BC MC VI,

Operator Comment: www.kemeys.com.au Luxurious, relaxing romantic hideaway, (7mins f/way). Unique country forest location, honeymoons, anniversaries, fabulous food, wildlife. Hosts, Robert & Jenny.

(Cottage Section), (2 stry), 1 cotg acc up to 5, [shwr, tlt, c/fan, TV, t/c mkg, refrig, cook fac ltd, micro, toaster, blkts, linen, pillows], lounge firepl, non smoking property. D ♦♦ $95 - $150, ◊ $25 - $35, W ♦♦ $480 - $580, ◊ $110, (not yet classified).

MANDURAMA NSW 2792

Pop 159. (285km W Sydney), See map on pages 52/53, ref G5. Small Central West town between Blayney and Cowra that originated during the gold boom of the 1850s. Scenic Drives.

B&B's/Guest Houses

★★★☆ **Millamolong Homestead**, (GH), (Farm), Millamolong Station, Millamolong Rd, 15km NW of PO, ☎ 02 6367 5241, fax 02 6367 5120, 8 rms (1 suite) [shwr (6), bath (3), tlt (6), fan, cent heat, elec blkts, t/c mkg], ldry, rec rm, lounge, ✕, pool (salt water), bicycle, canoeing, tennis. **D all meals** ♦ **$220**, ♦♦ **$352**, ♦ **$176**, ch con, AE BC MC VI.
(Millamolong Farmhouse), 9 rms [heat, elec blkts, TV, video], bicycle (hire). **D** ♦ **$55**, ♦♦ **$88**, ch con.

★★★☆ **Sunny Ridge Country Guest House**, (GH), Canowindra Rd, 1km W of PO, ☎ 02 6367 5092, fax 02 6367 5353, 6 rms (3 suites) [shwr, tlt, hairdry, cent heat, elec blkts, tel, TV, video-fee, clock radio, t/c mkg, refrig], rec rm, lounge, ✕, pool (salt water), bbq, golf, tennis. **BB** ♦ **$105**, ♦♦ **$140**, ♦ **$35**, BC MC VI.

MANGROVE MOUNTAIN NSW 2250

Pop Nominal, (115km N Sydney) See map on page 56, ref E2. Rural settlement situated in the Central Coast hinterland near Peats Ridge.

Self Catering Accommodation

Woodlands Country Stay, (Cotg), (Farm), 59 Baines Rd, ☎ 02 4374 1049, fax 02 4374 1649, 2 cotgs acc up to 4, [shwr, tlt, hairdry, c/fan, fire pl, heat, elec blkts, TV, video, movie, clock radio, t/c mkg, refrig, cook fac, micro, toaster, doonas, linen], rec rm, bar, spa, bbq, non smoking rms. **D $132 - $165**, ♦ **$40**, ch con, BC MC VI, (not yet classified).

MANILLA NSW 2346

Pop 2,100. (502km NW Sydney), See map on pages 52/53, ref H3. Pretty New England town at the junction of the Namoi and Manilla Rivers. Bowls, Fishing, Swimming, Tennis, Vineyards, Wineries.

Hotels/Motels

★★★ **Manilla Motel**, (M), Cnr Namoi & Court Sts, 300m SW of PO, ☎ 02 6785 1306, or 02 6785 1745, fax 02 6785 1306, 11 units [shwr, tlt, hairdry, a/c-cool, heat, elec blkts, tel, TV, video-fee, clock radio, t/c mkg, refrig, toaster], meals to unit. **RO** ♦ **$48 - $99**, ♦♦ **$58 - $99**, ♦ **$10**, AE BC DC EFT MC VI.

B&B's/Guest Houses

★★★★ **Oakhampton Homestead & Farmstay**, (B&B), (Farm), Oakhampton Rd, 21km N of Manilla, ☎ 02 6785 6517, fax 02 6785 6573, 3 rms [shwr, tlt, hairdry, a/c-cool, c/fan, heat, elec blkts, clock radio, t/c mkg, refrig], rec rm, lounge (TV), ✕, pool, bbq, plygr, tennis, cots. **BB** ♦ **$70**, ♦♦ **$120**, **D all meals** ♦ **$160 - $200**, BC MC VI.

★★★★☆ **(Unit Section)**, 1 unit acc up to 5, [a/c, elec blkts, tel, TV, clock radio, t/c mkg, refrig, cook fac, micro, toaster, blkts, linen], w/mach, dryer, dinner to unit. **DBB $180**, ch con.

★★★☆ **Ambleside B&B**, (B&B), Rushes Creek Rd, 1.5km S of PO, ☎ 02 6785 1517, fax 02 6785 1944, 3 rms [shwr, tlt, a/c, elec blkts, tel, TV, t/c mkg, refrig], ldry, rec rm, pool (solar), bbq-fee, cots, non smoking property. **BB** ♦ **$40 - $50**, ♦♦ **$50 - $60**, ♦♦♦ **$80**, ♦ **$25 - $30**, ch con, &.

★★★☆ **(Cottage Section)**, 1 cotg [shwr, tlt, a/c, elec blkts, tel, TV, t/c mkg, refrig, cook fac, micro], non smoking rms. **D $100**.

MANNERING PARK NSW 2259

Pop 2,350. See map on page 55, ref D5. Settlement on the southern shores of Lake Macquarie.
See advertisement at the bottom of page.

MARKS POINT NSW 2280

Pop Part of Belmont, (117km N Sydney), See map on page 55, ref E4. Eastern Lake Macquarie settlement on the peninsula between Swan and Village Bays. Boating, Fishing, Swimming.

B&B's/Guest Houses

★★★☆ **Top of The Point**, (B&B), 166 Marks Point Rd, ☎ 02 4947 7721, fax 02 4945 8579, 1 rm (1 suite) [shwr, tlt, fan, heat, elec blkts, TV, clock radio, t/c mkg, refrig, micro, toaster], lounge, ✕, pool, spa (indoor), c/park. **BLB** ♦♦ **$110 - $120**.

MARULAN NSW 2579

Pop 400. (165km SW Sydney), See map on page 55, ref A4. Small village and service centre on the Hume Highway, close to the Bungonia State Recreation Area.

Hotels/Motels

★ **Terminus Hotel**, (LH), 72 George St, 30km N of Goulburn, ☎ 02 4841 1504, fax 02 4841 1707, 5 rms [fire pl, cent heat, elec blkts, clock radio, t/c mkg, refrig, toaster], lounge (TV), ✉ (Fri & Sat night), ☎. **RO** ♦ **$27.50**, ♦♦ **$44**, ♦ **$10**, ch con, EFT.

MATHOURA NSW 2710

Pop 650. (795km SW Sydney), See map on pages 52/53, ref D7. Small town on the Cobb Highway between Deniliquin and Moama, and a starting point for forest drives that snake along the Murray and Edward Rivers. Boating, Fishing, Golf, Swimming.

Hotels/Motels

★★☆ **Red Gum Country Motor Inn**, (M), Cobb Hwy, 1km N of PO, 30km S of Deniliquin, ☎ 03 5884 3404, fax 03 5884 3404, 16 units [shwr, tlt, a/c, heat, elec blkts, tel, TV, clock radio, t/c mkg, refrig, toaster], ldry, pool, spa, bbq (covered), rm serv, plygr, cots-fee. **RO** ♦ **$55 - $66**, ♦♦ **$66 - $83**, ♦ **$11**, AE BC DC EFT MC VI.

Self Catering Accommodation

Tarragon Lodge, (Farm), Tarragon Lodge Rd, 11km E of PO, ☎ 03 5884 3387, fax 03 5884 3387, 15 cabins acc up to 6, [shwr, tlt, elec blkts, refrig, linen reqd-fee], ldry, rec rm, lounge, pool above ground, cook fac, bbq, plygr, bicycle, canoeing, tennis, cots. **D** ♦ **$20**, ch con, Min book applies.

Willow Bend Riverside Cabins, Picnic Point, 9km E of Mathoura, 40km N of Echuca, ☎ 03 5884 3388, fax 03 5884 3388, 10 cabins acc up to 8, (Powered Site), [shwr, tlt, a/c (6), fire pl (4), refrig, cook fac, toaster, blkts reqd-fee, linen reqd-fee, pillows reqd-fee], ldry, w/mach-fee, iron, bbq, plygr, tennis. **D** ♦♦ **$45 - $60**, ♦ **$16**, **W** ♦♦ **$315 - $410**, ♦ **$112**, ch con, Min book applies.

MAYFIELD NSW

See Newcastle & Suburbs.

MEDLOW BATH NSW

See Blue Mountains Region.

MENINDEE NSW 2879

Pop 400. (1271km W Sydney), See map on pages 52/53, ref B4. Historic river port on the Darling River, flanked by the massive water storage system of the Menindee Lakes. Boating, Fishing, Golf, Swimming.

Hotels/Motels

★★☆ **Burke & Wills Menindee**, (M), Yartla St, 200m S of PO, ☎ 08 8091 4313, fax 08 8091 4406, 15 units [shwr, tlt, a/c, elec blkts, TV, clock radio, t/c mkg, refrig, toaster], ldry, bbq, cots. RO ╢ $50, ╢╢ $61, ╢╢╢ $71, ╠ $10, ch con, BC MC VI, ╬╚.

MEREWETHER NSW

See Newcastle & Suburbs.

MERIMBULA NSW 2548

Pop 4,400. (457km S Sydney), See map on page 55, ref A8. One of the most popular holiday resorts on the south coast, renowned for its game fishing. Boating, Bowls, Fishing, Golf, Scenic Drives, Surfing, Tennis, Water Skiing.

Hotels/Motels

★★★★ **Fairway Motor Inn**, (M), 180 Arthur Kaine Dve, ☎ 02 6495 6000, fax 02 6495 1411, (2 stry gr fl) 20 units (5 suites) [shwr, spa bath (9), tlt, hairdry, a/c, c/fan (5), elec blkts, tel, TV, video (3), clock radio, t/c mkg, refrig, cook fac, micro, toaster], ldry, dryer, pool, spa, bbq, tennis, cots-fee. RO ╢ $60 - $100, ╢╢ $70 - $125, ╢╢╢ $80 - $130, ╠ $5, Suite D $85 - $140, ch con, AE BC DC EFT MC VI,

Operator Comment: Opposite Pambula/Merimbula Golf Club.

★★★★ **Merimbula Seaspray**, (M), 38 Merimbula Drive, 600m W of PO, ☎ 02 6495 3299, fax 02 6495 3176, (2 stry) 12 units (7 suites) [shwr, bath, spa bath (7), tlt, elec blkts, tel, TV, video-fee, clock radio, t/c mkg, refrig, cook fac (7), toaster], ldry, pool-heated, bbq, rm serv, cots-fee. RO ╢╢ $86 - $130, ╠ $15, Suite D ╢╢ $130 - $180, AE BC DC MC VI.

★★★☆ **Merimbula Motor Inn**, (M), Cnr Reid St & Merimbula Dve, 400m W of PO, ☎ 02 6495 3077, fax 02 6495 3517, (2 stry gr fl), 24 units (2 suites) [shwr, spa bath (1), tlt, hairdry, a/c, elec blkts, tel, cable tv, video (3)-fee, clock radio, t/c mkg, refrig, mini bar, toaster], ldry-fee, iron, iron brd, ⊠, pool, spa, bbq, rm serv, dinner to unit, cots-fee, non smoking units (16). D ╢ $99 - $178, ╢╢ $99 - $199, ╠ $10, Min book all holiday times, AE BC DC MC VI.

★★★☆ **Sapphire Waters Motor Inn**, (M), 32-36 Merimbula Drive, 250m W of PO, ☎ 02 6495 1999, fax 02 6495 3550, (2 stry gr fl), 29 units [shwr, spa bath (9), tlt, fan, heat, elec blkts, tel, TV, video-fee, clock radio, t/c mkg, refrig, cook fac (19)], ldry, pool, bbq, cots. RO ╢╢ $65 - $160, ch con, 7 budget units of a lower rating, AE BC DC MC VI.

★★★☆ **Summerhill Motor Inn**, (M), 24 Merimbula Dve, 100m W of PO, ☎ 02 6495 3111, fax 02 6495 3573, (Multi-stry gr fl), 18 units [shwr, spa bath (2), tlt, hairdry, a/c-cool, c/fan, heat, elec blkts, tel, TV, video (avail), clock radio, t/c mkg, refrig, cook fac, toaster], ldry, iron, iron brd, pool, bbq, cots-fee, non smoking units (6). RO ╢ $74 - $108, ╢╢ $89 - $120, ╢╢╢ $94.60 - $27.60, ╠ $10, AE BC DC MC VI.

★★★ **Black Dolphin Resort Motel**, (M), Arthur Kaine Drive, 2km S of PO, ☎ 02 6495 1500, fax 02 6495 1207, 44 units [shwr, tlt, hairdry (8), a/c (17), c/fan (30), elec blkts, tel, TV, clock radio, t/c mkg, refrig], ldry, conf fac, ⊠, pool (heated), spa, rm serv (b'fast), tennis (half court). RO ╢ $60 - $105, ╢╢ $65 - $145, ╠ $10, 5 units of a higher standard, AE BC DC MC VI.

★★★ **Kingfisher Motel**, (M), 105 Merimbula Dve, 1.4km N of PO, ☎ 02 6495 1595, fax 02 6495 1111, 14 units (0 suites) [shwr, tlt, a/c, elec blkts, tel, TV, movie, clock radio, t/c mkg, refrig, cook fac (2)], ldry, pool-heated, bbq, dinner to unit, cots. W $400 - $1,400, RO ╢ $55 - $80, ╢╢ $66 - $110, ╢╢╢ $77 - $120, Suite D $88 - $200, AE BC DC EFT MC VI,

Operator Comment: Every room has its own private balcony with outstanding ocean views.

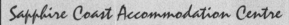

★★★ **Merimbula Motor Lodge**, (M), 131 Merimbula Dve (Princes Hwy), ☎ 02 6495 1748, fax 02 6495 2188, (2 stry gr fl), 18 units [shwr, tlt, fan, c/fan, heat, elec blkts, tel, TV, movie, clock radio, t/c mkg, refrig, cook fac, micro, toaster], ldry, pool, bbq, boat park, plygr, cots-fee. **RO** ♦ **$50 - $88,** ♦♦ **$55 - $110,** ♦♦♦ **$65 - $110,** ◊ **$11, W** **$308 - $693,** AE BC DC MC MCH MP VI.

★★★ **Ocean View Motor Inn**, (M), Cnr Merimbula Drive & View St, 800m N of PO, ☎ 02 6495 2300, fax 02 6495 3443, (2 stry gr fl), 20 units [shwr, tlt, heat, elec blkts, tel, TV, video (3)-fee, clock radio, t/c mkg, refrig, cook fac (14)], ldry, pool (salt water), bbq, cots-fee, non smoking units (4). **RO** ♦ **$55 - $100,** ♦♦ **$60 - $120,** ♦♦♦ **$77 - $136,** ◊ **$11,** Min book Christmas and Jan, BC EFT MC VI.

★★★ **Pelican Motor Inn**, (M), 18 Princes Hwy, 100m from PO, ☎ 02 6495 1933, fax 02 6495 3693, 25 units [shwr, tlt, fan, cent heat, elec blkts, tel, TV, video-fee, clock radio, t/c mkg, refrig], ldry, pool, spa-fee, bbq, plygr, cots. **W $385 - $693, RO** ♦ **$60.50 - $99,** ♦♦ **$66 - $99,** ♦♦♦ **$71.50 - $110,** ◊ **$8.80 - $11,** pen con, AE BC DC EFT MC VI.

★★★ **South Seas**, (M), Merimbula Dve, 100m N of PO, ☎ 02 6495 1911, fax 02 6495 1743, (2 stry gr fl), 30 units [shwr, tlt, fan, heat, elec blkts, tel, TV, video, clock radio, t/c mkg, refrig, cook fac], ldry, rec rm, pool-heated (solar), bbq, plygr, cots. **W** ♦♦ **$440 - $660, RO** ♦ **$60 - $90,** ♦♦ **$70 - $100,** ♦♦♦ **$80 - $110,** ◊ **$10 - $12,** 6 units of a higher standard, AE BC DC EFT MC VI.

★★★ **Town Centre Motor Inn**, (M), 8 Merimbula Dve (Old Princes Hwy), Opposite PO, ☎ 02 6495 1163, fax 02 6495 4422, (Multi-stry gr fl), 20 units [shwr, tlt, a/c-cool (5), c/fan (15), heat, elec blkts, tel, TV, video (avail), clock radio, t/c mkg, refrig, cook fac], ldry, rec rm, pool, bbq, courtesy transfer, cots. **RO** ♦ **$55 - $100,** ♦♦ **$66 - $110,** ♦♦♦ **$77 - $120,** ◊ **$11 - $15,** AE BC DC MC MP VI.

★★☆ **Hillcrest Motor Inn**, (M), 97 Merimbula Drive, 1.4km N of PO, ☎ 02 6495 1587, fax 02 6495 1869, (2 stry gr fl), 30 units [shwr, tlt, fan, heat, elec blkts, tel, cable tv, clock radio, t/c mkg, refrig, mini bar], ldry, ✗, pool, bbq, dinner to unit, plygr, tennis, cots-fee. **RO** ♦ **$55,** ♦♦ **$60,** ch con, AE BC DC MC MP VI, ♿.

★★☆ **Merimbula Gardens Motel**, (M), Merimbula Drive, 500m N of PO, ☎ 02 6495 1206, fax 02 6495 1206, 22 units [shwr, tlt, c/fan, heat, elec blkts, TV, t/c mkg, refrig, cook fac (1), toaster], ldry, ⊠, pool-heated, spa, bbq, ☏, cots, non smoking units (2). **RO** ♦ **$50 - $80,** ♦♦ **$60 - $90,** ◊ **$10,** ch con, BC EFT MC VI.

★★☆ **Norfolk Pine Motel**, (M), Princes Hwy, 1km N of PO, ☎ 02 6495 2181, fax 02 6495 2297, 19 units [shwr, tlt, hairdry, fan, heat, elec blkts, tel, TV, video (Video Hire), clock radio, t/c mkg, refrig, micro, toaster], ldry, iron, iron brd, pool, bbq, rm serv, dinner to unit, boat park, courtesy transfer, cots. **RO $45 - $80,** pen con, 6 units of a higher rating, BC DC MC VI.

Self Catering Accommodation

★★★★ **Albacore Luxury Holiday Apartments**, (HU), Previously Albacore Resort Market St, 500m S of PO, ☎ 02 6495 3187, fax 02 6495 3439, (Multi-stry), 20 units acc up to 4, [shwr, spa bath, tlt, a/c-cool (6), cent heat, tel, cable tv, video, clock radio, t/c mkg, refrig, cook fac, micro, elec frypan, d/wash, toaster, ldry (in unit)], lift, w/mach, dryer, iron, pool-heated (salt water), bbq, secure park. **W** ♦♦♦♦ **$500 - $1,540,** BC MC VI.

★★★★ **Azalea Court**, (HU), 27 Ocean Dve, 400m E of Merimbula Bridge, ☎ 02 6495 1611, fax 02 6495 3554, (2 stry gr fl), 8 units [shwr, spa bath (3), tlt, fan, heat, elec blkts, TV, video, clock radio, refrig, cook fac, micro, elec frypan, d/wash, toaster, ldry, blkts, linen, pillows], pool-heated (solar), bbq, c/park (garage), cots. **D** ♦♦ **$85 - $165,** ◊ **$15 - $20, W $350 - $1,165,** BC MC VI.

★★★★ **Tuscany Apartments**, (Apt), 10 Marine Pde, ☎ 02 6495 2030, fax 02 6495 3845, (2 stry gr fl), 17 apts acc up to 6, [shwr, bath, spa bath (6), tlt, hairdry, heat, elec blkts, tel, TV, video, refrig, cook fac, micro, d/wash, toaster, ldry (in unit), linen reqd-fee], w/mach, dryer, iron, pool-heated (solar), bbq, c/park (garage), plygr, cots-fee, non smoking units. **D $75 - $225, W $380 - $1,550,** Min book applies, BC MC VI.

★★★★ **Waterview Apartments**, (HU), 12 Arthur Kaine Dve, 1km S of PO, ☎ 02 6495 3408, fax 02 6495 4992, 11 units acc up to 6, [shwr, spa bath, tlt, heat, elec blkts, tel, cable tv (3), video, clock radio, refrig, cook fac, micro, elec frypan, d/wash, toaster, ldry (in unit), linen reqd-fee], w/mach, dryer, iron, pool-heated (salt water), bbq, c/park (undercover), plygr, cots-fee. **W $380 - $1,520,** BC MC VI.

★★★☆ **Apollo Apartments**, (HU), 61 Ocean Dve, 2km S of PO, ☎ 02 6495 3599, (2 stry), 11 units acc up to 5, [shwr, spa bath, tlt, fan, heat, elec blkts, TV, video, clock radio, refrig, cook fac, micro, elec frypan, d/wash, toaster, ldry (in unit), linen reqd-fee], w/mach, dryer, pool-heated (solar), bbq, c/park (undercover), ☏, plygr, tennis (half court), cots. **W $300 - $1,200.**

Trouble-free travel tips - **Tools**

It pays to carry some basic tools for emergency roadside repairs, such as an adjustable spanner, phillips head and flat blade screwdrivers, pliers and a roll of masking tape.

★★★☆ **Aquarius Apartments**, (HU), Cnr Dunns Rd & Princes Hwy, 2km SE of PO, ☎ 02 6495 3085, fax 02 6495 1822, (2 stry gr fl), 30 units [shwr, bath (3), spa bath (5), tlt, a/c (25), heat, elec blkts, tel, cable tv, video (6), t/c mkg, refrig, cook fac, toaster, ldry (in unit), linen], pool indoor heated, sauna, spa, bbq (covered), plygr, tennis, cots-fee. **D** $95 - $160, **W** $305 - $1,650, Min book applies, BC MC VI.

★★★☆ **Beach Haven**, (HU), 5 Calendo Ct, ☎ 02 6495 1273, 3 units acc up to 5, [shwr, bath (hip) (2), tlt, c/fan (2), heat, elec blkts, TV, video, clock radio, refrig, cook fac, micro, elec frypan, d/wash (1), toaster, ldry, linen reqd-fee], w/mach, dryer, iron, bbq, c/park (carport), cots. **W** $220 - $900, Min book all holiday times.

★★★☆ **Beachcomber Apartments**, (HU), 19 Ocean Dve, 2km S of PO, ☎ 02 6495 2143, (2 stry gr fl), 3 units acc up to 5, [shwr, spa bath, tlt, heat, elec blkts, TV, video, clock radio, t/c mkg, refrig, cook fac, micro, elec frypan, d/wash, toaster, ldry, linen reqd-fee], iron, bbq, c/park (carport), cots. **D** $50 - $145, **W** $275 - $1,050, Min book applies.

★★★☆ **Beachfront Units**, (HU), 53 Ocean Dve, 1km S of PO, ☎ 02 6495 3203, or 02 6495 3203, fax 02 6495 1419, 8 units acc up to 5, [shwr, bath, tlt, fan, heat, elec blkts, TV, video, clock radio, refrig, cook fac, micro, elec frypan, d/wash, toaster, ldry, linen reqd-fee], w/mach, dryer, iron, pool-heated (solar), bbq, plygr, cots. **W** $220 - $960, Min book applies.

★★★☆ **Calendo Apartments**, (HU), 7 Calendo Ct, 1.5km S of PO, ☎ 02 6495 2391, fax 02 6495 2391, 7 units acc up to 5, [shwr, tlt, fan, heat, elec blkts, TV, video, clock radio, refrig, cook fac, micro, toaster, ldry (in unit), linen reqd-fee], w/mach, dryer, iron, pool-heated (solar), bbq, plygr, cots. **W** $240 - $1,080.

★★★☆ **Gracelands**, (HU), Cameron St, ☎ 02 6495 2005, (2 stry gr fl), 7 units acc up to 4, [shwr, tlt, a/c, heat, elec blkts, TV, video, clock radio, refrig, cook fac, micro, d/wash (5), toaster, linen reqd-fee], dryer, iron, pool-heated (solar), spa, bbq, cots. **W** $225 - $860, Min book applies.

★★★☆ **Mandeni**, Sapphire Coast Dve, 8km N of PO, ☎ 1800 358 354, fax 02 6495 0192, 31 cabins acc up to 6, [shwr, tlt, heat, TV, clock radio, t/c mkg, refrig, cook fac, micro, toaster, ldry (in unit), blkts, linen, pillows], conv fac, pool (salt water), bbq, c/park (carport), ✆, plygr, golf (18 holes), mini golf, tennis, cots. **D** ♦♦ $70 - $180, ♦ $3 - $20, **W** ♦♦ $360 - $1,350, ♦ $20 - $40, BC EFT MC VI.

★★★☆ **Ocean Drive Apartments**, (Apt), 55 Ocean Dve, 1km S of PO, ☎ 02 6495 1006, (2 stry), 8 apts acc up to 5, [shwr, bath, tlt, heat, elec blkts, TV, video, clock radio, refrig, cook fac, micro, elec frypan, d/wash, toaster, ldry (in unit), linen], w/mach, dryer, iron, pool-heated (solar), bbq (covered), boat park. **W** $210 - $1,150, Min book applies.

★★★☆ **Pacific Heights Apartments**, (HU), 1 Ocean View Ave, 300m W of Market St, ☎ 02 6495 2366, fax 02 6495 2195, (2 stry), 24 units acc up to 6, [shwr, bath (2), spa bath (6), tlt, fan, heat, elec blkts, TV, video, clock radio, t/c mkg, refrig, cook fac, micro, d/wash, toaster, ldry (in unit), linen reqd-fee], w/mach, dryer, iron, pool-heated (salt water), bbq, c/park (carport), ✆, plygr, cots. **D** $50 - $100, **W** $265 - $1,055, 6 units yet to be rated. Min book applies.

★★★☆ **Panoramic Town Houses**, (HU), 13 Short St, 500m S of PO, ☎ 02 6495 3004, fax 02 6495 3004, (2 stry), 10 units acc up to 5, [shwr, bath, tlt, heat, elec blkts, TV, video-fee, clock radio, refrig, cook fac, micro, d/wash, toaster, ldry (in unit), linen reqd-fee], pool-heated (solar), wading pool, bbq, c/park. **DBB** $250 - $970, Min book applies.

★★★☆ **Pipers Lodge**, (SA), 107 Merimbula Dve, ☎ 02 6495 1440, fax 02 6495 3364, 9 serv apts acc up to 6, [shwr, tlt, heat, tel, TV, t/c mkg, refrig, cook fac, toaster], ldry, pool, bbq. **W** $315 - $950, **RO** ♦ $50 - $85, ♦♦ $50 - $85, ♦♦♦ $61 - $120, ♦ $10 - $20, BC MC VI.

★★★☆ **Surfside Merimbula**, (Apt), 37 Ocean Dve, 2km SE of PO, ☎ 02 6495 1317, fax 02 6495 1317, 8 apts acc up to 5, [shwr, bath (hip) (1), tlt, hairdry, fan, heat, TV, video, refrig, cook fac, micro, ldry, linen reqd-fee], pool-heated (solar), bbq, non smoking property. **W** $245 - $950, Min book applies, BC MC VI.

★★★☆ **Telopea Court Holiday Units**, (HU), 86 Main St, Opposite Bowling Club, ☎ 02 6495 1554, fax 02 6495 4544, (2 stry gr fl), 6 units acc up to 4, [shwr, tlt, hairdry, fan, heat, elec blkts, TV, video, clock radio, t/c mkg, refrig, cook fac, micro, elec frypan, toaster, blkts, linen reqd-fee], ldry, iron, iron brd, pool (solar/salt water), bbq, courtesy transfer, plygr, cots. **W** $247 - $935, BC MC VI.

★★★☆ **The Palms Apartments**, (HU), 63 Main St, ☎ 02 6495 1835, fax 02 6495 1835, (2 stry), 6 units acc up to 5, [ensuite, shwr, spa bath, tlt, elec blkts, TV, video, clock radio, t/c mkg, refrig, cook fac, micro, elec frypan, d/wash, toaster, ldry (in unit), linen reqd-fee], dryer, iron, pool-heated (solar), bbq, c/park (undercover), plygr, cots. **W $330 - $1,200**, BC MC VI.

★★★☆ **The Peninsular**, (HU), 57 Ocean Dve, 1km S of PO, ☎ 02 6495 3232, 12 units acc up to 5, [shwr, bath, tlt, hairdry, fan, heat, elec blkts, TV, video, clock radio, refrig, cook fac, micro, d/wash, toaster, ldry (in unit), linen reqd-fee], dryer, iron, pool-heated (solar), bbq, plygr, cots, non smoking units (4). **W $220 - $950**, Min book applies.

★★★ **All Seasons**, (HU), 39 Sapphire Coast Dve, ☎ 02 6495 1573, fax 02 6495 1573, 5 units acc up to 5, [shwr, tlt, heat, clock radio, refrig, cook fac, ldry (in unit), linen reqd-fee], pool, bbq, c/park (garage). **W $850**, AE BC EFT MC VI.

★★★ **Capri Apartments**, (HU), 38-40 Main St, 300m E of PO, ☎ 02 6495 2367, 11 units acc up to 6, [shwr, bath, tlt, a/c-cool, heat, elec blkts, TV, clock radio, refrig, cook fac, micro, elec frypan, d/wash (3), toaster, ldry (in unit), linen reqd-fee], w/mach, dryer, iron, pool (solar heated), spa, bbq, cots-fee. **D $65 - $80, W $260 - $900**, Min book applies.

★★★ **Fishpen**, (HU), 30 Fishpen Rd, 1km S of PO, ☎ 02 6495 1752, fax 02 6495 2820, 5 units acc up to 5, [shwr, tlt, heat, elec blkts, TV, clock radio, refrig, cook fac, micro, ldry, linen reqd-fee], bbq. **W $198 - $745**, Min book applies,Min book Christmas Jan and Easter.

★★★ **Harbour Lights**, (HU), 7 Cameron St, 500m E of PO, ☎ 02 6495 1028, fax 02 6495 4431, 3 units acc up to 5, [shwr, tlt, heat, elec blkts, TV, video (avail), clock radio, refrig, cook fac, micro, toaster, ldry, linen], w/mach, dryer, pool-heated (solar), bbq, c/park (garage). **D ♙ $55 - $110**, Min book applies, BC MC VI.

★★★ **Hillview Holiday Units**, (HU), 41 Sapphire Coast Dve, opposite Bowling Club, ☎ 02 6495 1764, fax 02 6495 1764, 7 units acc up to 5, [shwr, bath (6), tlt, fan, heat, elec blkts, tel, TV, clock radio, refrig, cook fac, micro, toaster, ldry, linen reqd-fee], w/mach, iron, iron brd, pool (solar heated), bbq, courtesy transfer, plygr, cots. **D $55 - $77, W $220 - $765**, pen con.

★★★ **Hydra**, (HU), 15 Short St, 500m S of PO, ☎ 02 6495 2310, fax 02 6495 3109, 8 units acc up to 5, [shwr, tlt, fan, heat, TV, video, refrig, cook fac, micro, linen reqd-fee], ldry, pool-heated (solar), bbq, cots. **W $200 - $795**, BC MC VI.

★★★ **Kanandah**, (HU), 21 Marine Parade, 500m E of Causeway, ☎ 02 6495 2038, fax 02 6495 2038, 1 unit acc up to 5, [shwr, tlt, heat, elec blkts, TV, clock radio, t/c mkg, refrig, cook fac, micro, elec frypan, toaster, linen reqd-fee], w/mach, dryer, iron, bbq, c/park (carport), cots. **D $45 - $105, W $185 - $800**.

★★★ **Lakeside Units**, (HU), 14 Fishpen Rd, 2km S of PO, ☎ 02 6495 1956, fax 02 6495 1956, 9 units acc up to 5, [shwr, tlt, heat, elec blkts, TV, video, clock radio, refrig, cook fac, micro, d/wash (5), toaster, linen reqd-fee], w/mach, dryer (Shared)-fee, iron, pool, bbq, c/park (undercover) (6), plygr, bicycle, canoeing, tennis (half court). **W $270 - $1,010**, Min book applies, BC MC VI.

★★★ **Margarita Manor**, (HU), Unit 3 19 Marine Pde, 1.5km SE of PO, ☎ 02 6495 2038, fax 02 6495 2038, 1 unit acc up to 7, [shwr (2), tlt (2), heat, elec blkts, TV (2), clock radio, t/c mkg, refrig, cook fac, micro, elec frypan, d/wash, toaster, ldry, linen reqd-fee], w/mach, dryer, iron, bbq, c/park (carport), cots. **W $290 - $1,100**, Min book applies.

★★★ **Marine Court**, (HU), 1 Marine Pde, 2km SE of PO, ☎ 02 6495 1904, fax 02 6495 1904, 8 units acc up to 5, [shwr, tlt, heat, elec blkts, TV, clock radio, refrig, cook fac, micro, ldry (in unit), linen reqd-fee], bbq. **W $240 - $990**, Min book applies.

★★★ **Merimbula Beach Cabins**, Short Point, 2km E of PO, ☎ 02 6495 1216, fax 02 6495 4206, 25 cabins acc up to 7, [shwr, tlt, fan, heat, elec blkts, TV, video-fee, clock radio, refrig, cook fac, micro-fee, linen (some) reqd-fee], ldry, bbq, ✆, plygr, tennis (half court), cots. **D $45 - $200, W $195 - $1,200**, Min book applies, BC EFT MC VI.

★★★ **Penguin Mews**, (HU), 27 Beach St, ☎ 02 6495 1660, fax 02 6495 1660, 11 units acc up to 6, [shwr, tlt, elec blkts, TV, video, refrig, cook fac, micro, d/wash (5), ldry (7), linen reqd-fee], pool-heated (solar), bbq. **W $250 - $1,150**, 5 units of a higher standard. Min book applies.

★★★ **Sandpiper Holiday Units**, (HU), 36 Sapphire Coast Dve, 300m W of PO, ☎ 02 6495 3415, fax 02 6495 3415, 4 units acc up to 5, [shwr, tlt, heat, elec blkts, TV, clock radio, refrig, cook fac, micro, elec frypan, toaster, linen reqd-fee], w/mach, dryer-fee, iron, bbq, cots-fee, non smoking units. **D $55 - $130, W $275 - $900**, Min book all holiday times.

★★★ **Southern Comfort**, (HU), 9 Marine Pde, 1.5km SE of PO, ☎ 02 6495 1778, fax 02 6495 1778, (2 stry gr fl), 4 units acc up to 5, [shwr, tlt, fan, heat, elec blkts, TV, clock radio, t/c mkg, refrig, cook fac, micro, toaster, ldry (in unit), linen reqd-fee], bbq, c/park (carport). **W $220 - $770**, Min book applies.

★★★ **The Fronds**, (HU), 4 Cameron St, 400m NE of PO, ☎ 02 6495 3792, 6 units acc up to 5, [shwr, tlt, heat, elec blkts, TV, video, clock radio, refrig, cook fac, micro, toaster, ldry, linen reqd-fee], w/mach, dryer, iron, bbq, cots. **D $49 - $110, W $220 - $750**, Min book applies.

★★★ **The Sands**, (HU), 4 Calendo Ct, 1.5km S of PO, ☎ 02 6495 2107, fax 02 6495 2107, (2 stry gr fl), 9 units acc up to 5, [shwr, bath (hip), tlt, fan, heat, elec blkts, fax-fee, TV, video-fee, clock radio, refrig, cook fac, micro, elec frypan, toaster, ldry (in unit) (2), linen reqd-fee], iron, pool-heated (salt water), spa, bbq, plygr, cots. **W $190 - $1,180**.

★★☆ **Admirals Lodge**, (HU), 2 Calendo Crt, 1.6km SE of PO, ☎ 02 6495 1121, fax 02 6495 3163, 6 units acc up to 5, [shwr, tlt, heat, elec blkts, TV, clock radio, t/c mkg, refrig, cook fac, micro, toaster, ldry, linen reqd-fee], w/mach, dryer-fee, iron, pool-heated (solar), bbq, plygr, cots. **D $40 - $65, W $275 - $1,010**, Min book applies, BC MC VI.

★★☆ **Anchor Bell Apartments**, (HU), 10 Cameron St, 500m NE of PO, ☎ 02 6495 1153, fax 02 6495 1153, 11 units acc up to 6, [shwr, bath, tlt, heat, TV, video, refrig, cook fac, micro, ldry (in unit), linen reqd-fee], pool-heated (solar), spa, bbq, tennis (half court). **W $250 - $1,100**, Min book applies, BC MC VI.

★★☆ **Banksia Court**, (HF), 22 Marine Pde, 1km S of PO, ☎ 02 6495 1663, 6 flats acc up to 5, [shwr, tlt, heat, elec blkts, TV, video (avail), clock radio, refrig, cook fac, micro, linen reqd-fee], ldry, bbq, cots. **W $160 - $685**.

★★☆ **Chapman Court**, (HU), 3 Chapman Ave, 1km S of PO, ☎ 02 6495 1780, 6 units [shwr, tlt, cent heat, elec blkts, TV, clock radio, refrig, cook fac, micro, linen reqd-fee], ldry, pool-heated, bbq, plygr. **W ♦♦♦♦ $220 - $880**.

★★☆ **Colonial Cove**, (HF), 17 Marine Pde, ☎ 02 6495 2038, fax 02 6495 2038, 5 flats acc up to 5, [shwr, tlt, heat, TV, clock radio, refrig, cook fac, micro, ldry, linen reqd-fee], bbq. **W $185 - $800**, 2 units of a higher standard.

★★☆ **Falcon Court**, (HF), 7 Chapman Ave, ☎ 02 6495 1231, 7 flats acc up to 9, [shwr, bath, tlt, heat, TV, clock radio (7), refrig, cook fac, micro, ldry (in unit) (2), linen], ldry, bbq. **W $180 - $900**, Min book applies.

★★☆ **Sunnyside Merimbula**, (HU), 12 Chapman Ave, 1.5km SE of PO, ☎ 02 6495 1124, fax 02 6495 1124, (2 stry gr fl), 4 units acc up to 7, [shwr, bath, tlt, a/c-cool, heat, elec blkts, TV, video, clock radio, refrig, cook fac, micro, elec frypan, toaster, ldry (in unit), linen reqd-fee], w/mach, iron, pool-heated (solar), bbq, cots. **D $40 - $156, W $210 - $1,055**, Min book applies.

★★☆ **Woodbine Park Holiday Cabins**, Sapphire Coast Drive, 8km N of PO, ☎ 02 6495 9333, fax 02 6495 9333, 20 cabins acc up to 6, [shwr, tlt, heat, TV, refrig, cook fac, micro, toaster, ldry, linen reqd-fee], pool (solar heated), bbq, ✆, plygr, golf, tennis, cots, **D ♦♦ $70 - $140, W ♦♦ $270 - $950**, AE BC EFT MC VI.

Bittangabee, (HU), 9 Cameron St, 500m E of PO, ☎ 02 6495 1028, fax 02 6495 4431, 5 units acc up to 5, [shwr, tlt, heat, elec blkts, TV, video-fee, clock radio, refrig, cook fac, micro, d/wash, toaster, ldry, linen], w/mach, dryer, pool-heated (solar), bbq, c/park (undercover). **D $65 - $130, W $230 - $1,000**, Min book applies, BC MC VI, (not yet classified).

Boardwalk Waterfront Holiday Units, (HU), 34 Oceanview Ave, 750m S of PO, ☎ 02 6495 4333, fax 02 6495 4333, 6 units acc up to 5, [shwr, tlt, fan, heat, TV, clock radio, t/c mkg, refrig, cook fac, micro, toaster, doonas, linen-fee], ldry, w/mach (2), dryer (2), iron, iron brd, bbq, plygr, cots, non smoking property. **D $50 - $100, W $200 - $850**, BC MC VI, (not yet classified).

Caribou Close, (HU), 1 Calendo Crt, 2km S of PO, ☎ 02 6495 2050, (2 stry), 4 units acc up to 6, (2 bedrm), [shwr, tlt, fan, heat, elec blkts, TV, video, clock radio, t/c mkg, refrig, cook fac, micro, blkts, linen (by arrangement), pillows], w/mach, dryer, bbq (communal), c/park (garage), cots. **W $240 - $880**, Min book applies, (not yet classified).

Crown Apartments, (Apt), 23 Beach St, ☎ 02 6495 2400, fax 02 6495 4800, (Multi-stry), 11 apts acc up to 4, [shwr, spa bath (10), tlt, hairdry, c/fan, heat, elec blkts, TV, video, clock radio, t/c mkg, refrig, cook fac, micro, d/wash (5), toaster, blkts, linen], lift, w/mach, dryer, iron, iron brd, pool above ground (salt water/solar), bbq, c/park. **D $120 - $185, W $400 - $1,300**, BC EFT MC VI, (not yet classified).

Lazydaze Units, (HU), 29 Ocean Dve, 2km S of PO, ☎ 02 6495 2143, 1 unit acc up to 5, [shwr, tlt, fan, cent heat, elec blkts, TV, video, clock radio, t/c mkg, refrig, cook fac, micro, elec frypan, toaster, ldry, linen reqd-fee], iron, bbq, cots. **W $250 - $800**, Min book applies, (not yet classified).

Seashells Merimbula, (HU), 5 Chapman Ave, ☎ 02 649454827, fax 02 6495 4837, (2 stry gr fl), 9 units acc up to 5, [shwr, tlt, fan, heat, TV, video, t/c mkg, refrig, cook fac, micro, toaster, blkts], ldry, iron, iron brd, pool, bbq, cots. **D $45 - $135, W $220 - $925,** BC MC VI, (not yet classified).

Coralyn Apartments, (HU), 1 Short St, 500m S of PO, ☎ 02 6495 4141, fax 02 6495 3439, (2 stry gr fl), 3 units acc up to 6, [shwr, spa bath, tlt, fan, cent heat, elec blkts, TV, video, clock radio, refrig, cook fac, micro, d/wash, ldry, linen reqd-fee], w/mach, dryer, iron, bbq-fee, c/park (garage), cots-fee. **W ** **$500 - $1,595**, Min book applies.

Kalindo Lodge, (HU), Cnr Marine Pde & Chapman Ave, 2km S of PO, ☎ 02 6495 1448, fax 02 6495 1448, 9 units acc up to 5, [shwr, tlt, elec blkts, TV, video, clock radio, refrig, cook fac, micro, linen reqd], ldry, pool-heated (solar), spa, bbq. **W $210 - $1,000**, Min book applies, BC MC VI.

B&B's/Guest Houses

Carltons of Casuarina, (B&B), 1 Casuarina Pl, Tura Beach 2548, 3km N of PO, ☎ 02 6495 0242, fax 02 6495 0271, 2 rms [ensuite, heat, elec blkts, clock radio, doonas], ldry, lounge (TV), t/c mkg shared, refrig, bbq, non smoking property. **BB ** **$110 - $130**, (not yet classified).

Bellbird Bed & Breakfast Merimbula, (B&B), 28 Tantawanglo St, ☎ 02 6495 3536, fax 02 6495 3536, 1 rm [shwr, tlt, hairdry, elec blkts, tel, TV, video, radio, t/c mkg, refrig, micro, toaster], iron, iron brd, lounge (tv & firepl), cots. **BB ** **$80 - $90, ** **$120 - $130,** **$55 - $60**, BC MC VI.

Seatbelts save lives

No one knows when a crash will occur and unless everyone in the car is properly restrained, there is a chance of unnecessary injury.

Even low-speed crashes can cause serious injury if people are not safely restrained, this highlights the need to wear those belts at all times, from the very start of every trip.

Get into the habit of not starting the car until all passengers are properly restrained.

Remember half of all crashes occur within five kilometres of home.

HOLIDAY HUB TOURIST PARK
PAMBULA BEACH NSW

BIG4 HOLIDAY PARKS

NSW AWARDS FOR EXCELLENCE IN TOURISM 2000 WINNER — Tourism Council Australia

Luxury & Family Villas
Caravan - Camping

1 800 677 808
holidayhub.com.au

Merimbula Holiday Park

- Heated Pool
- Slippery Dip
- Synthetic Grass Tennis Court
- Wading Pool
- Sparkling, clean amenities
- Caravan and Camping Sites

- Convenience Shop on site
- Metres to Beach
- Easy drive to five different Golf Courses
- Game Fishing
- Whale Watching

'LUXURY BY THE SEA'

- Fully Equipped Family Villas
- Honeymooner spa units
- Private BBQ's & Spa Baths
- Heated Pool • Queen Size Bed
- Colour TV - Microwave
- Plus a Million Dollar View over Beaches and the Ocean
- 2 Large undercover camp kitchens

Short Point, Merimbula. NSW. Ph: (02) 6495 1269 Fax: (02) 6495 3381

MERRIWA NSW 2329

Pop 956. (277km Sydney), See map on pages 52/53, ref H4. Pretty little town on the Golden Highway in the upper Hunter region, at the heart of rich wool, beef and wheat country. Bowls, Gem Fossicking, Golf, Tennis. See also Cassilis.

Hotels/Motels

★★☆ **El Dorando**, (M), 50 Bettington St, 500m E of PO, ☎ 02 6548 2273, fax 02 6548 2208, 12 units [shwr, tlt, a/c, heat, elec blkts, TV, clock radio, t/c mkg, refrig], pool, dinner to unit, cots. **RO** ♦ **$49.50**, ♦♦ **$58.30**, ♦♦♦ **$69.30**, ◊ **$11**, AE BC MC VI.

MICHELAGO NSW 2620

Pop Nominal, (342km SW Sydney), See map on pages 52/53, ref G7. Small village on the Monaro Highway between Canberra and Cooma.

Hotels/Motels

Michelago Village Inn, (M), Ryrie St, ☎ 02 6235 9088, fax 02 6235 9023, 6 units [shwr, tlt, fire pl (6), elec blkts, tel, clock radio, t/c mkg, refrig], lounge (TV, video), conf fac, ⊠. **RO** ♦ **$60**, ♦♦ **$60**, ◊ **$5**, AE BC MC VI.

MILLERS FOREST NSW 2324

Pop Part of Maitland, See map on page 55, ref C7. Dairying country on the Hunter River between Raymond Terrace and Maitland.

B&B's/Guest Houses

★★★★☆ **Martins Wharf Bed & Breakfast**, (B&B), 799 Duckenfield Rd, ☎ 02 4987 7241, fax 02 4987 6471, 2 rms (1 suite) [shwr, tlt, hairdry, a/c, elec blkts, tel, clock radio, refrig, cook fac ltd, micro, toaster], iron, iron brd, TV rm, lounge, t/c mkg shared, bbq, dinner to unit, courtesy transfer, cots, non smoking property. **BB $130**, BC MC.

MILLFIELD NSW 2325

Pop 500. (162km N Sydney), See map on page 55, ref D1. Small mining settlement between Cessnock and Wollombi, established in the 1830s.

Self Catering Accommodation

★★★★ **Bellbird Cottage**, (Cotg), (Farm), Lewis La off Mt View Rd, ☎ 02 4998 1705, fax 02 9361 6995, 1 cotg acc up to 6, [shwr, tlt, hairdry, a/c, fan, elec blkts, clock radio, CD, t/c mkg, refrig, cook fac, micro, elec frypan, toaster, blkts, linen, pillows], iron, lounge firepl, bbq, Dogs allowed. **BB** ♦♦ **$120 - $150**, ch con, Min book applies, AE BC MC VI.

   (Swallows Homestead Section), (Farm), 1 house acc up to 10, [shwr (2), tlt (2), hairdry, a/c, c/fan, elec blkts, TV, clock radio, CD, t/c mkg, refrig, cook fac, micro, elec frypan, toaster, blkts, linen, pillows], w/mach, dryer, iron, lounge firepl, bbq, c/park. **BB** ♦♦ **$100 - $130**.

MILLTHORPE NSW 2798

Pop 650. (263km W Sydney), See map on pages 52/53, ref G5. Pretty village with turn-of-the-century shopfronts, cottages and bluestone churches.

B&B's/Guest Houses

★★★☆ **Rosebank Guesthouse & Cottages**, (GH), 40 Victoria St, 40km W of Bathurst, 20km E of Orange, ☎ 02 6366 3191, fax 02 6366 3499, 9 rms [elec blkts], shared fac (shwr, tlt & bath), lounge, ✕, t/c mkg shared. **BB** ♦ **$82.50 - $93.50**, ♦♦ **$121 - $154**, DBB ♦ **$110 - $132**, ♦♦ **$187 - $231**, ch con, AE BC DC EFT MC VI.

MILPARINKA NSW 2880

Pop Nominal, (1456km NW Sydney), See map on pages 52/53, ref B1. Tiny township off the Silver City Highway about 40km south of Tibooburra. It's basically just a pub, some ruins and an old sandstone court house but is worth the diversion from the highway to see.

Hotels/Motels

Albert Hotel, (LH), Heritage, Loftus St, off Silver City Hwy adjacent airstrip, ☎ 08 8091 3863, fax 08 8091 3863, 7 rms [a/c-cool (3)], ⊠, bbq, ✆. **RO** ♦ **$20**, ♦♦ **$40**.

MILTON NSW 2538

Pop 1,050. (204km S Sydney), See map on page 55, ref B5. Historic village that's a popular stop on the south coast arts and crafts trail. Boating, Bowls, Bush Walking, Fishing, Golf, Horse Riding, Surfing, Swimming, Tennis.

Hotels/Motels

★★★☆ **Milton Village Motel**, (M), Princes Hwy, 500m N of PO, ☎ 02 4455 1944, fax 02 4455 3244, 9 units [shwr, tlt, hairdry, fan, heat, elec blkts, tel, TV, video-fee, clock radio, t/c mkg, refrig, toaster], pool, bbq, non smoking units (6). **RO** ♦ **$50 - $100**, ♦♦ **$60 - $105**, ◊ **$11 - $15**, AE BC DC EFT MC VI.

Self Catering Accommodation

★★★☆ **Narrawilly Farm Cottages**, (Cotg), (Farm), 'Narrawilly', 1.3km N of PO, ☎ 02 4456 4900, fax 02 4456 4072, 2 cotgs acc up to 10, [shwr, bath, tlt, c/fan, fire pl (combustion), heat, elec blkts, TV, radio, t/c mkg, refrig, micro, elec frypan, toaster, blkts, linen], iron, iron brd, bbq, cots, non smoking units. **D** ♦♦ **$120 - $175**, **W** ♦♦ **$700**, ch con, 1 cottage yet to be assessed. BC MC VI.

Milton Country Retreat, (Cotg), 142E Woodburn Rd, 14km W of PO, ☎ 02 4457 3497, fax 02 4457 3497, 2 cotgs acc up to 6, (3 bedrm), [shwr, tlt, elec blkts, TV, video, refrig, cook fac, micro, toaster, blkts, doonas, linen, pillows], ldry, w/mach, lounge firepl, pool, spa, cots, non smoking property. **D** ♦♦ **$110 - $150**, ◊ **$10 - $30**, **W** ♦♦ **$77 - $850**, ◊ **$70 - $210**, ch con, Min book applies, (not yet classified).

B&B's/Guest Houses

★★★★☆ **Milton Bed & Breakfast**, (B&B), No children's facilities, 124 Princes Hwy, ☎ 02 4455 4449, fax 02 4455 6325, 3 rms [shwr, tlt, hairdry, heat, elec blkts, tel, TV, video, clock radio, t/c mkg, refrig], lounge firepl, pool, bbq, non smoking property. **BB** ♦ **$112.20 - $132**, ♦♦ **$140 - $165**, Dinner by arrangement. BC MC VI.

★★★★ **Gabbi's Hollow**, (B&B), 63 Watson St, ☎ 02 4455 2099, fax 02 4455 2122, 4 rms [ensuite, a/c, c/fan, tel, TV, video, clock radio, t/c mkg, refrig, micro, toaster, doonas], ldry, lounge firepl, bbq, non smoking property. **BB** ♦ **$145**, ♦♦ **$165**, Min book applies, BC EFT MC VI.

MINNIE WATER NSW 2462

Pop 210. (678km N Sydney), See map on page 54, ref D4. Small north coast town surrounded by Yuraygir National Park. Boating, Fishing, Swimming.

Self Catering Accommodation

★★★ **Marima Holiday Units**, (HU), Wisteria Cres, 1km S of Store, ☎ 02 6642 1642, (2 stry), 3 units acc up to 6, [shwr, tlt, TV, t/c mkg, refrig, cook fac, micro, elec frypan, toaster, ldry], w/mach, iron, bbq, c/park (garage). **D $60**, **W $275 - $450**.

Medication and driving

Medication can effect your driving. Certain drugs can effect your mental alertness and/or co-ordination and therefore effect driving skills. Always check with your doctor the effect which any medication (over the counter or prescription) you are taking may have on your driving. There may be an alternative drug which will not affect your driving. It is best to avoid drinking alcohol while taking medication.

MITTAGONG NSW 2575

Pop 6,100. (109km SW Sydney), See map on page 55, ref B4. Mittagong, regarded by many as the gateway to the Southern Highlands, is full of antique outlets and arts and crafts galleries and houses the region's visitor information centre. Bowls, Bush Walking, Golf, Scenic Drives, Swimming, Tennis.

Hotels/Motels

★★★★ **Grand Country Lodge**, (M), Main St (Old Hume Hwy), 300m N of PO, ☎ 02 4871 3277, fax 02 4871 2923, (2 stry gr fl), 23 units [shwr, bath (20), spa bath (2), tlt, hairdry, cent heat, elec blkts, tel, TV (free Pay TV), clock radio, t/c mkg, refrig, mini bar], ldry, iron, iron brd, rm serv, dinner to unit, c/park (undercover), cots-fee. **RO** ♦ **$85 - $135,** ♦♦ **$85 - $135,** ◊ **$15,** AE BC DC EFT JCB MC MP VI,

Operator Comment: Guest comments: "Best Country Motel we have stayed at in years. We'll be back, Thankyou.".

★★★☆ **Mineral Springs Motel**, (M), Old Hume Hwy, 1km S of PO, adjacent to RSL club, ☎ 02 4871 1911, fax 02 4872 1085, (2 stry gr fl), 19 units [shwr, tlt, a/c, elec blkts, tel, TV, clock radio, t/c mkg, refrig], ⊠, bbq, rm serv (b'fast), cots, non smoking rms (5). **RO** ♦ **$55 - $66,** ♦♦ **$66 - $77,** ♦♦♦ **$77 - $88,** ◊ **$11,** AE BC DC EFT MC VI.

★★★☆ **Mittagong Motel**, (M), 7 Old Hume Hwy, 600m NE of PO, ☎ 02 4871 1277, fax 02 4871 1717, 28 units [shwr, tlt, a/c, elec blkts, tel, TV, clock radio, t/c mkg, refrig], ⚔, cots-fee, non smoking units (6). **RO** ♦ **$49.50 - $66,** ♦♦ **$53 - $88,** ♦♦♦ **$63 - $97,** ◊ **$10,** ch con, 11 units of a lower rating. AE BC BTC DC EFT MC VI.

★★★ **Poplars Motel**, (M), Old Hume Hwy, 4km NE of PO, ☎ 02 4889 4239, or 02 4889 5074, fax 02 4889 4239, 15 units [shwr, tlt, hairdry, a/c (13), fan (2), elec blkts, tel, TV, clock radio, t/c mkg, refrig], ldry-fee, bbq, rm serv, dinner to unit, plygr, cots-fee. **D $90 - $114, W $355 - $458, RO** ♦ **$66 - $90,** ♦♦ **$72 - $102,** ◊ **$9,** AE BC DC MC VI.

★★☆ **Melrose Motel**, (M), Old Hume Hwy, 150m NE of PO, ☎ 02 4871 1511, fax 02 4871 1511, 16 units [shwr, tlt, a/c, c/fan (12), elec blkts, tel, TV, clock radio, t/c mkg, refrig], ldry, bbq, plygr, cots-fee, non smoking units (8). **RO** ♦ **$65 - $75,** ♦♦ **$75 - $95,** ◊ **$15,** BC EFT MC VI.

B&B's/Guest Houses

★★★★☆ **Fitzroy Inn**, (B&B), 26 Ferguson Cres, ☎ 02 4872 3457, fax 02 4871 3451, (2 stry gr fl), 6 rms [ensuite, heat, elec blkts, video, doonas], ldry, lounge (TV), conf fac, ⊠, non smoking rms. **BB** ♦♦ **$170 - $220,** weekly con, AE BC DC MC VI.

Grey Cables Bed & Breakfast, (B&B), Lot 52, Spencer St, 700m SE of PO, ☎ 02 4871 3108, fax 02 4872 4006, 2 rms [ensuite (2), a/c, elec blkts, TV, clock radio, doonas], ⚔, spa, t/c mkg shared, refrig, bbq, non smoking rms. **BB** ♦♦ **$130 - $165,** weekly con, AE MC VI, (not yet classified).

Other Accommodation

★★☆ **Sturt Craft Centre - Ainsworth**, (Lodge), Range Rd, 1km S of PO, ☎ 02 4860 2083, fax 02 4860 2081, 2 rms acc up to 3, [shwr, tlt, heat, blkts, linen, pillows], cook fac, refrig. **RO** ♦♦ **$80,** ♦♦♦ **$90,** AE BC MC VI.

MOAMA NSW 2731

Pop 2,469. (840km SW Sydney), See map on pages 52/53, ref C7. Flourishing town on the Murray River which, along with its twin town of Echuca, offers excellent recreational opportunities. Boating, Bowls, Croquet, Fishing, Golf, Swimming, Tennis. See also Echuca.

Hotels/Motels

★★★★☆ **Madison Spa Motel Resort**, (LMH), 80 Meninya St, ☎ 03 5482 3011, fax 03 5482 3547, 40 units [shwr, spa bath (38), tlt, hairdry, a/c, fire pl (20), heat, tel, TV, video (4)-fee, movie-fee, clock radio, t/c mkg, refrig, mini bar, micro (4), toaster (4)], iron, iron brd, lounge, conf fac, lounge firepl, ⚔, ⊠, pool (outdoor/saltwater), pool-indoor (heated) (2), spa, steam rm, bbq-fee, gym, cots, non smoking rms. **RO** ♦ **$125 - $248,** ♦♦ **$138 - $275,** ◊ **$18,** AE BC DC EFT MC VI, ♿.

Operator Comment: The regions finest luxury motel resort, champagne, flickering log fire, poolside bar, imagine yourself. Madison Day Spa, what an experience this is. Roman bathhouse, steam room, solarium, massage, facials, body wraps and lots more. www.madisonspa.com.au

★★★☆ **Cadell on the Murray Motel**, (M), Perricoota Rd, 4km NW of PO, ☎ 03 5482 4500, fax 03 5482 6863, 26 units [shwr, bath (20), tlt, a/c, elec blkts, tel, TV, video-fee, clock radio, t/c mkg, refrig, micro], ldry, pool-heated (solar), bbq, plygr, tennis, cots-fee. **RO** ♦ **$77 - $104.50,** ♦♦ **$77 - $104.50,** ◊ **$11 - $22,** ch con, Min book long w/ends and Easter, AE BC MC VI, ♿.

Operator Comment: See our advertisement under Echuca VIC.

★★★☆ **Golden River Motor Inn**, (M), 34 Meninya St, Opposite the PO, ☎ 03 5480 9799, fax 03 5480 9917, 15 units [shwr, spa bath (2), tlt, a/c, c/fan, elec blkts, tel, TV, clock radio, t/c mkg, refrig, toaster], bbq, cots-fee. **BLB** ♦ **$69 - $97,** ♦♦ **$80 - $127,** ◊ **$14 - $16,** Min book long w/ends and Easter, AE BC DC EFT MC VI.

★★★☆ **Rich River Golf Club Resort**, (M), 24 Lane (off Perricoota Rd), 5.5km N of Moama bridge, ☎ 03 5480 9411, fax 03 5480 9713, 63 units [shwr, bath (6), spa bath (1), tlt, a/c, elec blkts, tel, TV, clock radio, t/c mkg, refrig], ldry, rec rm, lounge, conv fac, ⊠, pool, sauna, spa, bbq, c/park (undercover), plygr, bowls, golf, tennis, cots. **BLB** ♦ **$110 - $126.50,** ♦♦♦ **$132 - $148,** ◊ **$20,** ch con, 23 units ★★★★. AE BC DC EFT MC VI.

★★★☆ **River Country Inn**, (M), Meninya St, 500m N of PO, ☎ 03 5482 5511, fax 03 5482 2591, 27 units [shwr, spa bath (2), tlt, hairdry, a/c, elec blkts, tel, TV, video (avail), clock radio, t/c mkg, refrig, mini bar, toaster], ldry, iron, iron brd, conv fac, pool-heated (solar), bbq (covered), plygr, tennis, cots. **RO** ♦ **$75 - $105,** ch con, fam con, Min book long w/ends and Easter, AE BC DC MC VI, ♿.

★★★☆ **Sportslander Motor Inn**, (M), Cnr Cobb Hwy & Perricoota Rd, 900m N of PO, ☎ 03 5482 4366, fax 03 5480 6467, 30 units [shwr, bath (1), spa bath (6), tlt, hairdry, a/c, fan, elec blkts, tel, TV, video-fee, clock radio, t/c mkg, refrig, toaster], ldry, iron, iron brd, pool-heated (solar), bbq, plygr, cots, non smoking rms (4). **RO** ♦ **$64 - $106,** ♦♦ **$77 - $126,** ♦♦♦ **$88 - $137,** ◊ **$9 - $11,** Min book long w/ends and Easter, AE BC DC EFT MC VI, ♿.

M

★★★☆ **Sundowner Chain Motor Inns**, (M), 54 Meninya St (Cobb Hwy), 200m N of PO, ☎ 03 5482 3311, fax 03 5482 3758, 50 units (12 suites) [shwr, bath (4), spa bath (12), tlt, a/c, elec blkts, tel, TV, video (12)-fee, clock radio, t/c mkg, refrig, mini bar, toaster], ldry, iron, iron brd, conv fac, ☒ (Mon to Sat), pool (salt water) (2), sauna, spa, rm serv, plygr, tennis, cots-fee, non smoking units (25). **RO** ♦ **$102.50 - $153.50**, ♦♦ **$108 - $153.50**, ◊ **$11**, ch con, Min book long w/ends, AE BC DC EFT MC MP VI, ⚹⚹.

★★★ **Moama Central**, (M), 45 Meninya St, 100m N PO, ☎ 03 5482 5377, fax 03 5482 5093, 20 units [shwr, tlt, a/c, elec blkts, tel, TV, clock radio, t/c mkg, refrig, cook fac (1), toaster], bbq, cots, non smoking units (4). **BLB** ♦ **$58 - $85**, ♦♦ **$69 - $85**, ♦♦♦ **$84 - $100**, ◊ **$15**, ch con, Min book long w/ends and Easter, AE BC DC EFT MC MCH VI, ⚹⚹.

Self Catering Accommodation

★★★☆ **Riverview Cottages**, (Cotg), Perricoota Rd, 1km N of PO, ☎ 03 5480 0350, fax 03 5480 0360, 13 cotgs acc up to 6, [shwr, spa bath, tlt, a/c, heat, elec blkts, TV, video, clock radio, refrig, cook fac, micro, toaster, ldry, blkts, linen], w/mach, dryer, iron, iron brd, pool-heated (solar, salt water), bbq, 24hr reception, ✆, plygr, tennis, cots, non smoking property. **D** ♦♦ **$88 - $132**, ◊ **$11**, **W** ♦♦ **$616 - $924**, ◊ **$77**, Min book applies, AE BC DC EFT MC MP VI.

★★★★ **Birralee Holiday Villas**, (HU), 36 Shaw St, 250m E of PO, ☎ 03 5480 6257, fax 03 5482 6857, 16 units acc up to 6, [shwr, bath (9), spa bath, tlt, a/c, elec blkts, tel, TV, video, clock radio, refrig, cook fac, micro, toaster, ldry (in unit), blkts, linen, pillows], pool (salt water), spa, bbq, c/park (garage), plygr, tennis (half court), cots-fee. **D** ♦♦ **$66 - $125**, ◊ **$11 - $16.50**, **W** **$385 - $743**, ch con, BC EFT MC VI.

★★★★ **Carrington Holiday Units**, (HU), 40 Regent St, 1km NE of PO, ☎ 03 5480 6535, fax 03 5480 6535, 13 units acc up to 6, [shwr, tlt, hairdry, a/c, elec blkts, TV, video-fee, clock radio, refrig, cook fac, micro, toaster, ldry (in unit), blkts, linen, pillows], w/mach, dryer, iron, pool (salt water), bbq, c/park (carport), ✆, plygr, cots, non smoking property. **D** ♦♦ **$66 - $77**, ♦♦♦♦ **$88 - $110**, **W $407 - $693**, BC MC VI.

★★★★ **Perricoota Vines Retreat**, (HU), Lot 100 Perricoota Rd, 5km NW of PO, ☎ 03 5482 6655, fax 03 5482 4004, 12 units acc up to 8, (2 & 3 bedrm), [shwr, spa bath, tlt, a/c-cool, c/fan, heat, tel, TV, clock radio, t/c mkg, refrig, cook fac, micro, toaster, blkts, linen, pillows], ldry, w/mach, dryer, pool, bbq, c/park (undercover), cots, non smoking property. **D** ♦♦ **$95 - $165**, ◊ **$10 - $25**, **W $570 - $990**, ◊ **$70 - $175**, Min book Christmas Jan long w/ends and Easter, BC EFT MC VI.

★★★★ **Rich River Retreat**, (Apt), Lot 15, 24 Lane, 5km NW of PO, ☎ 03 5482 2431, fax 03 5482 2725, 10 apts acc up to 4, (2 bedrm), [shwr, tlt, a/c, elec blkts, TV, video, clock radio, t/c mkg, refrig, cook fac, micro, toaster, blkts, linen, pillows], w/mach, pool, bbq, cots, non smoking property. **D** ♦ **$85 - $120**, ♦♦ **$85 - $120**, ◊ **$10**, **W $550 - $840**, ♦♦ **$550 - $840**, ◊ **$70**, Min book applies, AE BC DC MC VI.

★★★★ **Winbi River Resort**, (SA), Perricoota Rd, 5km N of PO, ☎ 03 5480 9044, fax 03 5480 9726, 29 serv apts (29 suites) [shwr, bath, tlt, a/c, fan, heat, elec blkts, tel, TV, clock radio, t/c mkg, refrig, cook fac, micro, toaster], ldry, rec rm, pool, sauna, spa, bbq, plygr, tennis-fee, cots. **RO** ♦ **$65 - $75**, ♦♦ **$99 - $130**, ♦♦♦ **$139 - $154**, ◊ **$24**, ch con, Min book long w/ends and Easter, AE BC DC MC VI, ⚹⚹.

★★★☆ **Moama Holiday Villas**, (HU), 45 Chanter St, 1km E of PO, ☎ 03 5482 6229, fax 03 5480 6236, 6 units acc up to 6, [shwr, tlt, a/c, fan, heat, elec blkts, TV, video (avail), clock radio, refrig, cook fac, micro, toaster, ldry, blkts, linen, pillows], pool-heated (solar), bbq, c/park (carport), cots. **D** ♦ **$60 - $70**, ♦♦ **$60 - $70**, ♦♦♦ **$70 - $80**, ◊ **$10**, **W $360 - $700**, AE BC EFT MC VI.

★★★☆ **Murray River Resort**, (HU), Perricoota Rd, 4km NW of PO, ☎ 03 5480 9638, fax 03 5480 0183, 12 units acc up to 6, [shwr, spa bath, tlt, a/c, elec blkts, TV, video, clock radio, refrig, cook fac, toaster, ldry (in unit), blkts, linen, pillows], w/mach, dryer, iron, pool (salt water/solar), bbq, c/park (carport), plygr, tennis, cots (available). **D** ♦♦ **$85 - $110**, ◊ **$8 - $16**, **W $467 - $735**, ◊ **$48 - $77**, Min book long w/ends and Easter, AE BC MC VI.

★★★☆ **Old Charm Holiday Villas**, (HU), 1-7 Shaw St, 100m E of PO, ☎ 03 5480 9532, fax 03 5480 9060, (2 stry gr fl), 5 units acc up to 6, [shwr, bath (4), tlt, a/c, fan, elec blkts, tel (2), TV, video, clock radio, t/c mkg, refrig, cook fac, micro, d/wash, toaster, blkts, linen, pillows], w/mach, iron, bbq, c/park (undercover), cots. **RO** ♦ **$77 - $99**, ♦♦ **$77 - $99**, ♦♦♦ **$99 - $121**, ◊ **$11**, **W $485 - $1,155**, ch con, Min book applies, BC DC EFT MC VI.

★★★☆ **Tudorville**, (HU), Cnr Meninya & Echuca Sts, Opposite PO, ☎ 03 5480 9799, fax 03 5480 9917, (Multi-stry gr fl), 7 units acc up to 8, [shwr, bath (2), spa bath (5), tlt, a/c, elec blkts, TV, video, clock radio, refrig, cook fac, micro, toaster, ldry, blkts, doonas, linen, pillows], w/mach, dryer, iron, bbq, c/park (garage), cots. **D $75 - $160**, **W $455 - $980**, Min book applies, BC MC VI.

★★★ **Morning Glory River Resort**, (Cotg), Gilmours Rd, off Barmah Rd, 35km NE of Echuca, ☎ 03 5869 3357, fax 03 5869 3282, 7 cotgs acc up to 9, [shwr, bath (1), tlt, a/c-cool, fan, heat, elec blkts, TV, refrig, cook fac, micro, d/wash (1), toaster, linen reqd-fee], ldry, rec rm, pool-heated, bbq, kiosk, c/park (carport), plygr, jetty, golf, tennis, cots, Pets allowed. **D** ♦ **$50 - $90**, ♦♦ **$50 - $90**, ♦♦♦ **$64 - $104**, ◊ **$8 - $14**, 2 cottages not rated. BC EFT MC VI.

★★☆ **Always Welcome**, (HU), 16 Simms St, 150m SE of bridge, ☎ 03 5482 5835, (2 stry), 6 units acc up to 7, [shwr, tlt, a/c-cool, heat, elec blkts, TV, video (1), clock radio, refrig, cook fac, micro, toaster, ldry (in unit), blkts, doonas, linen, pillows], bbq, cots. **D** ♦ **$60.50 - $66**, ♦♦ **$60.50 - $88**, ♦♦♦ **$75.90 - $95.70**, ◊ **$11 - $16.50**, **W $363 - $500.50**, Min book Christmas Jan long w/ends and Easter, BC MC VI.

Misty Gum Cottages, (Cotg), 6 Berry St, 100m E of Moama Bowling Club, ☎ 03 5480 9292, fax 03 5480 9459, 4 cotgs acc up to 4, [shwr, spa bath (2), tlt, a/c, c/fan, elec blkts, tel, TV, video, clock radio, t/c mkg, refrig, cook fac, micro, toaster, ldry (in unit), blkts, linen, pillows], w/mach, iron, pool (salt water), bbq, c/park (carport), plygr, cots, non smoking rms. **D** ♦♦ **$85 - $105**, ◊ **$11**, **W** ♦♦ **$500 - $710**, ◊ **$60**, BC MC VI.

B&B's/Guest Houses

★★★☆ **Chiplands Bed & Breakfast**, (B&B), R.M.B. 2170 Perricoota Rd, 12km N of Moama, ☎ 03 5483 6284, fax 03 5483 6294, (2 stry), 3 rms [ensuite (2), a/c-cool, c/fan, heat, clock radio, toaster], shared fac (2), lounge firepl, pool, t/c mkg shared, refrig, bbq, cots, non smoking property, Pets allowed. **BLB** ♦ **$40 - $45**, ♦♦ **$85 - $90**, ◊ **$15**, ch con, weekly con, BC MC VI.

Other Accommodation

Bella Casa Houseboats, (Hbt), ☎ 03 5480 6211, fax 03 5480 6165, 3 houseboats acc up to 12, [shwr, spa bath, tlt, a/c-cool (ducted), fire pl, heat, tel (mobile), TV, video, refrig, cook fac, micro, d/wash, toaster, doonas, linen], w/mach, iron, iron brd, bbq. **D $1,446 - $3,850**, Min book applies, BC MC VI.

Dinky-Di, (Hbt), Lot 11 Maiden-Smith Dve, moored on NSW side of Murray, ☎ 03 5482 5223, or 03 5482 4686, fax 03 5482 4686, 15 houseboats acc up to 12, [shwr, tlt, a/c-cool, heat, TV, video, refrig, cook fac, micro, d/wash, doonas, linen reqd], ldry, w/mach. **W** ♦♦♦♦ **$870 - $3,000**, Security deposit - $300. BC MC VI.

MOLLYMOOK NSW 2539

Pop 3,000. (242km S Sydney), See map on page 55, ref B5. South coast seaside settlement between Milton and Ulladulla that dates back to the 1850s and was named after the mollymawk, a type of albatross. Boating, Bowls, Fishing, Golf, Scenic Drives, Squash, Surfing, Swimming, Tennis.

Hotels/Motels

★★★★ **Mollymook Shores by the Sea**, (M), Cnr Golf Ave & Shepherd St, 2km N of Ulladulla PO, ☎ 02 4455 5888, fax 02 4455 5636, (2 stry gr fl), 27 units (21 suites) [shwr, bath, spa bath (4), tlt, hairdry, a/c, tel, TV, video-fee, clock radio, t/c mkg, refrig, mini bar, cook fac (1)], iron, iron brd, conf fac, ☒, pool, sauna, bbq, dinner to unit, cots. **RO** ♦ **$93.50 - $170.50**, ♦♦ **$93.50 - $170.50**, ◊ **$16.50**, **Suite RO** ♦♦ **$88 - $176**, ◊ **$16.50**, AE BC DC EFT MC VI.

★★★☆ **Bannisters Point Lodge**, (M), 191 Mitchell Pde, 4.2km N of Ulladulla, ☎ 02 4455 3044, fax 02 4455 3451, (2 stry gr fl), 24 units [shwr, tlt, hairdry, fan, heat, elec blkts, tel, TV, video, clock radio, t/c mkg, refrig, toaster], ldry-fee, iron, iron brd, conv fac, ☒, cafe, pool (salt water), bbq, dinner to unit, cots-fee, non smoking units (18). **RO** ♦ **$85 - $140**, ♦♦ **$93.50 - $154**, ◊ **$10 - $15**, 6 rooms of a four star rating, AE BC MC VI.

Operator Comment: See advertisement under Ulladulla.

★★★☆ **Colonial Palms Motel**, (M), 15 Princes Hwy, 1km N of PO, ☎ 02 4455 1777, fax 02 4454 4033, 13 units [shwr, tlt, hairdry, a/c (3), fan, heat, elec blkts (available), tel, TV, video-fee, clock radio, t/c mkg, refrig, toaster], ldry, pool, bbq, dinner to unit, plygr. **RO** ♦ **$60 - $115**, ♦♦ **$65 - $120**, ◊ **$12**, ch con, AE BC DC EFT MC MCH VI.

★★★☆ **Mollymook Motel**, (M), Cnr Princes Hwy & Golf Ave, 1km N of Ulladulla PO, ☎ 02 4455 1877, fax 02 4454 2132, 11 units [shwr, tlt, hairdry, fan, heat, elec blkts, tel, cable tv, movie, clock radio, t/c mkg, refrig, cook fac ltd (3), toaster], bbq, cots. **RO ⚹ $60 - $135, ♦♦ $60 - $135, ⚹ $15 - $22**, AE BC DC MC VI,
*Operator Comment: * Balconies * Ocean & Golf Course Views * Latest In House Movies * AUSTAR Channels * Spacious Units *.*

★★★☆ **Mollymook Seascape Motel**, (M), 22 Princes Hwy, 2km N of Ulladulla PO, ☎ 02 4455 5777, fax 02 4455 3604, (2 stry gr fl), 14 units (4 suites) [shwr, spa bath (2), tlt, hairdry, fan, heat, elec blkts, tel, TV, video-fee, clock radio, t/c mkg, refrig, cook fac (4), toaster], ldry, pool-heated, bbq, dinner to unit, cots. **RO ⚹ $65 - $145, ♦♦ $65 - $200, Suite D $80 - $275, Suite W $315 - $1,650**, AE BC DC EFT MC VI.

★★★☆ **Mollymook Seaspray**, (M), 70 Ocean St, 2km N of Ulladulla PO, ☎ 02 4455 5311, fax 02 4455 1995, (2 stry gr fl), 9 units [shwr, spa bath (2), tlt, hairdry, c/fan, heat, elec blkts, tel, TV, video (avail), clock radio, t/c mkg, refrig, toaster], ldry, iron, iron brd, bbq, cots. **W $462 - $1,050, RO ⚹ $66 - $150, ♦♦ $77 - $150, ⚹ $10 - $20**, ch con, Min book applies, AE BC DC MC VI.

★★★ **Mollymook Surfbeach Motel and Apartments**, (M), 2 Shepherd St, ☎ 02 4455 3222, fax 02 4455 3342, (2 stry gr fl), 15 units (5 suites) [shwr, spa bath (2), tlt, hairdry, c/fan, heat, elec blkts, tel, TV, video, clock radio, t/c mkg, refrig, cook fac (5)], ldry, pool, spa, bbq, meals to unit, cots-fee, non smoking units (6). **RO ⚹ $77 - $137.50, ♦♦ $77 - $137.50, ⚹ $11**, AE BC DC EFT MC VI, ♿.

★★★ **Dolphins of Mollymook**, (M), 17 Shepherd St, 2km N of PO, ☎ 02 4455 3022, fax 02 4455 3022, 12 units (1 suite) [shwr, spa bath (1), tlt, c/fan, heat, elec blkts, tel, TV, clock radio, t/c mkg, refrig, micro], pool, bbq, non smoking units (6). **RO ⚹ $65 - $165, ♦♦ $65 - $165, ⚹ $15, Suite D $120 - $250**, AE BC DC MC VI.

★★☆ **Ocean View Motel**, (M), Princes Hwy, 2km N of PO, ☎ 02 4455 1283, fax 02 4455 5377, 12 units [shwr, tlt, fan, heat, elec blkts, tel, TV, movie, clock radio, t/c mkg, refrig, toaster], ldry, pool, bbq, dinner to unit, plygr, cots. **RO ⚹ $50 - $107, ♦♦ $55 - $112, ♦♦♦ $63 - $116, ⚹ $10**, ch con, AE BC DC MC VI.

Self Catering Accommodation

★★★★☆ **Breakers Apartments**, (SA), No children's facilities, 60 Ocean St, 2km N of Ulladulla PO, ☎ 02 4454 2154, fax 02 4454 2177, 7 serv apts acc up to 4, [shwr, bath, spa bath (4), tlt, hairdry, c/fan, heat, elec blkts, tel, TV, video-fee, clock radio, t/c mkg, refrig, cook fac, micro, toaster, blkts, linen, pillows], ldry, iron, cafe, bbq, c/park (carport), non smoking units. **D ♦♦ $160 - $225, ⚹ $50**, Min book applies, AE BC MC VI.

★★★★☆ **Mariners on Mollymook**, (HU), 1 Golf Ave, 3km N of Ulladulla PO, ☎ 02 4454 2011, fax 02 4454 2011, 5 units acc up to 5, [shwr, spa bath (2), tlt, hairdry, c/fan, heat, elec blkts, tel, TV, video, clock radio, t/c mkg, refrig, cook fac (2), cook fac ltd (3), micro, elec frypan (3), toaster, blkts, linen, pillows], ldry, iron, bbq, c/park. **D ♦♦ $115 - $195, ⚹ $15, W ♦♦ $550 - $1,550, ⚹ $55**, Min book applies, BC MC VI.

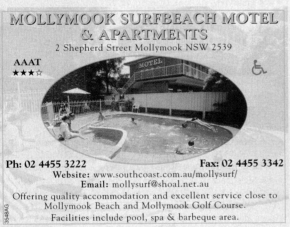

★★★★ **Mollymook Aquarius Motel Apartments**, (SA), 9 Shepherd St, 1.5km NE of Ulladulla PO, ☎ 02 4454 1400, fax 02 4454 2145, 8 serv apts acc up to 4, [shwr, tlt, hairdry, c/fan, heat, elec blkts, tel, TV, video-fee, clock radio, t/c mkg, refrig, cook fac, micro, toaster, blkts, linen, pillows], ldry, w/mach, dryer, iron, spa, bbq, c/park (undercover), cots-fee. **D** ♦♦ **$77 - $143**, ♦♦♦♦ **$110 - $187, W** ♦♦ **$495 - $1,001,** ♦♦♦♦ **$605 - $1,310**, Min book applies, AE BC MC VI, ⚐&.

★★★★ **Mollymook Beach Luxury Apartments**, (Apt), 46 Ocean St, 2km N of PO, ☎ 02 4454 2224, fax 02 4455 2221, (2 stry), 2 apts acc up to 6, (1, 2 & 3 bedrm), [c/fan, heat, elec blkts, TV, video, clock radio, t/c mkg, refrig, cook fac, micro, d/wash, toaster, blkts, linen, pillows], w/mach, dryer, spa, ☎, non smoking property. **D** ♦ **$130 - $185,** ♦♦ **$150 - $210,** ⚐ **$20**, weekly con, Min book applies, BC MC VI.

★★★★ **Mollymook Cove Holiday Apartments**, (HU), 17 Golf Ave, ☎ 02 4454 1892, fax 02 4455 4807, 8 units acc up to 6, [shwr, spa bath (1), tlt, hairdry, c/fan, cent heat, elec blkts, tel, TV, clock radio, t/c mkg, refrig, cook fac, micro, toaster, ldry, blkts, linen, pillows], w/mach, dryer, iron, spa, bbq, cots. **D** **$110 - $200, W** **$545 - $1,400**, AE BC MC VI.

★★★☆ **Forty Seven**, (HF), 47 Boag St, 2km N of Ulladulla PO, ☎ 02 4455 2814, 1 flat acc up to 6, [shwr, tlt, elec blkts, TV, video, clock radio, refrig, cook fac, micro, ldry, linen reqd-fee], bbq, plygr, cots. **D** **$40 - $70, W** **$245 - $470.**

★★★☆ **Mollymook Paradise Haven Apartment**, (HU), 39 Ocean St, 2km N of Ulladulla PO, ☎ 02 4455 5514, fax 02 4455 5091, (2 stry gr fl), 18 units [shwr, tlt, a/c, c/fan, elec blkts, tel, TV, video, clock radio, t/c mkg, refrig, cook fac, micro, toaster, ldry], bbq, cots-fee, non smoking units (8). **D** ♦♦ **$71.50 - $154,** ⚐ **$11 - $22, W** **$207.90 - $1,001**, Min book applies, AE BC DC MC VI, ⚐&.

★★★ **Biltaange Flats**, (HF), 79 Clyde St, ☎ 02 4455 2749, fax 02 4455 2749, 5 flats acc up to 6, [shwr, tlt, fan, heat, elec blkts, TV, video (avail), clock radio, refrig, cook fac, micro, elec frypan, linen], ldry, bbq, cots. **D** ♦ **$50 - $140,** ♦♦ **$60 - $140,** ♦♦♦ **$70 - $150, W** **$300 - $980**, 3 units not rated. Min book Christmas Jan long w/ends and Easter.

★★★ **Linksview**, (HU), 85 Clyde St, ☎ 02 4455 3922, fax 02 4455 1930, 5 units acc up to 6, [shwr, tlt, heat, TV, refrig, cook fac, linen reqd], ldry, bbq, c/park (garage). **W** **$200 - $900.**

★★★ **Mollymook Beach Units**, (HU), No 1 Ingold Ave, 2.5km N of PO, ☎ 02 4455 3925, (2 stry), 6 units acc up to 4, (2 bedrm), [shwr, tlt, heat, elec blkts, TV, t/c mkg, refrig, cook fac, micro, blkts, linen reqd-fee, pillows], w/mach, c/park. **D** ♦ **$66 - $150,** ♦♦ **$66 - $150**, weekly con, Min book Christmas Jan long w/ends and Easter, BC EFT MC VI.

★★★ **Palm Court Town Houses**, (HU), 14 Davies St, ☎ 02 4455 3922, fax 02 4455 1930, 5 units acc up to 6, [shwr, bath, tlt, heat, TV, refrig, cook fac, linen reqd], ldry, bbq, c/park (garage). **W** **$250 - $850.**

★★★ **Sues Place**, (Cotg), 125 Mitchell Pde, 3km N of Ulladulla PO, ☎ 02 4454 2011, fax 02 4454 2011, (2 stry), 1 cotg acc up to 6, [shwr (2), tlt (2), heat, refrig, cook fac, micro, elec frypan, d/wash, toaster, ldry, linen reqd-fee], bbq, c/park (carport). **D** ♦♦ **$115 - $150,** ⚐ **$15, W** **$495 - $1,400**, Min book applies.

★★☆ **Mollymook Beach Motor Inn**, (HU), 44 Ocean St, 2km N of Ulladulla PO, ☎ 02 4455 2221, fax 02 4455 2221, (2 stry gr fl), 8 units acc up to 5, [shwr, tlt, fan, heat, elec blkts, TV, video (avail), t/c mkg, refrig, cook fac], ldry, bbq, cots. **RO** ♦ **$55 - $100**, ♦♦ **$60 - $110**, ♦♦♦ **$75 - $125**, ◊ **$15**, **W $315 - $650**, ch con, BC MC VI.

★★ **Aldon**, (HU), 14 Wallace St, 200m W of golf club, ☎ 02 4455 2975, 2 units acc up to 4, [shwr, tlt, heat, elec blkts, TV, clock radio, refrig, cook fac, micro, toaster, ldry (in unit), linen reqd], cots. **W $250 - $650**, Min book applies.

Beach Retreat, (HU), 22 Beach Rd, ☎ 02 4455 2384, 3 units acc up to 6, [shwr, bath, tlt, c/fan, heat, TV, t/c mkg, refrig, cook fac, micro, elec frypan, d/wash (1), toaster, linen reqd], w/mach, dryer, iron, AE BC DC MC VI, (Rating under review).

B&B's/Guest Houses

★★★☆ **Beach House - Mollymook**, (GH), 3 Golf Ave, 2km N of Ulladulla PO, ☎ 02 4455 1966, fax 02 4455 3841, (2 stry gr fl), 17 rms (1 suite) [shwr, spa bath (1), tlt, hairdry, fan, heat, elec blkts, tel, TV, video, clock radio, t/c mkg, refrig, toaster], ldry, lounge, bar, pool (salt water), cook fac, bbq, cots-fee. **BLB** ♦ **$75 - $168**, ♦♦ **$85 - $168**, ♦♦♦ **$108 - $193**, ◊ **$25**, **Suite BLB** ♦♦ **$150 - $218**, ◊ **$25**, ch con, 1suite ★★★★, Min book applies, BC MC VI.

MOLONG NSW 2866

Pop 1,600. (314km W Sydney), See map on pages 52/53, ref G5. Historic, attractive town at the heart of Cabonne Shire whose name comes from an Aboriginal word meaning 'place of many rocks'. Bowls, Fishing, Golf, Swimming, Tennis.

Hotels/Motels

★★★ **Molong Motor Inn**, (M), 12 Gidley St, ☎ 02 6366 8099, fax 02 6366 8562, 16 units [shwr, bath (4), tlt, a/c, elec blkts, tel, TV, clock radio, t/c mkg, refrig, toaster], ldry, iron, iron brd, ⊠ (5 days), cots-fee, non smoking units (3). **RO** ♦ **$66**, ♦♦ **$77**, ♦♦♦ **$88**, ◊ **$11**, AE BC EFT MC VI.

Self Catering Accommodation

★★★ **Old Redbank Farm Holiday**, (Cotg), (Farm), "Old Redbank" Garra Rd, 10km W of Molong, ☎ 02 6366 8337, fax 02 6366 9071, 1 cotg acc up to 10, [shwr, bath, tlt, fan, fire pl, TV, video, clock radio, t/c mkg, refrig, cook fac, micro, elec frypan, toaster, ldry, blkts, linen], w/mach, iron, iron brd, bbq, tennis, cots. **D $115 - $160**, **W $550 - $850**, fam con.

B&B's/Guest Houses

★★★☆ **Lynro House Bed & Breakfast**, (B&B), 18 Phillip St, ☎ 02 6366 8746, fax 02 6366 8746, 4 rms (1 suite) [ensuite (1), fan, heat, elec blkts, ldry], ldry, iron, iron brd, lounge (TV, video), lounge firepl, ✕, non smoking property. **BB** ♦ **$55**, ♦♦ **$88 - $99**, **Suite D $95**.

★★★☆ **Nyrang Homestead**, (GH), Peabody Rd Borenore via, 30km W of Orange PO, ☎ 02 6364 2160, fax 02 6364 2063, (2 stry gr fl), 6 rms [spa bath, a/c, elec blkts, tel, clock radio], rec rm, lounge (TV), lounge firepl, tennis. **BB** ♦ **$90 - $121**, ♦♦ **$121 - $154**, ◊ **$55**, ch con, BC MC VI.

MOONAN FLAT NSW 2337

Pop Nominal, (280km N Sydney), See map on pages 52/53, ref J4. Historic village on the Hunter River on the western slopes of Barrington Tops. Canoeing, Horse Riding, Scenic Drives, Swimming.

Hotels/Motels

Victoria Hotel, (LH), 1 Mitchell St, 50m N of PO, ☎ 02 6546 3165, 3 rms [fan, heat (3), t/c mkg (3)], ldry, iron, iron brd, pool (salt water), bbq, c/park. **RO** ♦ **$30 - $35**, ♦♦ **$40 - $45**, ◊ **$5 - $10**, BC EFT MC VI.

Self Catering Accommodation

Garland Cottage, (Cotg), (Farm), "Karuah", 4km SW of PO, ☎ 02 6546 3132, fax 02 6546 3132, 1 cotg acc up to 12, [shwr (2), bath (1), tlt (2), fan, heat, elec blkts (3)-fee, TV, t/c mkg, refrig, cook fac, micro, toaster, ldry, blkts reqd-fee, linen reqd-fee], w/mach, iron, iron brd, lounge, freezer, bbq, cots. **D** ♦♦ **$50 - $100**, ◊ **$25**, ch con, BC MC VI, (not yet classified).

MOORLAND NSW 2443

Pop Nominal, (345km N Sydney), See map on page 54, ref C7. Farming community north of the Manning River between Taree and Camden Haven. Scenic Drives.

B&B's/Guest Houses

Wonga House, (B&B), Pacific Hwy, 28km N of Taree PO, ☎ 02 6556 5276, 2 rms [hairdry, fan, heat, tel, clock radio], ldry, TV rm, lounge firepl, ✕, pool (salt water), t/c mkg shared, bbq, non smoking property. **BB** ♦ **$85**, ♦♦ **$110**, (not yet classified).

MOREE NSW 2400

Pop 9,300. (665km NW Sydney), See map on pages 52/53, ref H2. This busy town at the junction of the Newell and Gwydir Highways is probably best known for its artesian spa baths. Bowls, Fishing, Golf, Shooting, Swimming, Tennis.

Hotels/Motels

★★★★ **Spa Village Travel Inn**, (M), 300 Warialda St, 1km S of PO, ☎ 02 6752 4033, fax 02 6752 4436, (2 stry gr fl), 52 units [shwr, spa bath (6), tlt, a/c, elec blkts, tel, TV, video, clock radio, t/c mkg, refrig, mini bar, cook fac (10), micro (21)], ldry, conv fac, ⊠, pool, spa, bbq, rm serv, dinner to unit, cots-fee, non smoking units (13). **RO** ♦ **$84 - $94**, ♦♦ **$94 - $105**, ◊ **$10**, AE BC DC MP VI.

★★★☆ **Alexander Motor Inn**, (M), Cnr Alice St & Newell Hwy, Adjacent to hospital, ☎ 02 6752 4222, fax 02 6752 4244, 22 units [shwr, tlt, hairdry, a/c, elec blkts, tel, cable tv (22), video, clock radio, t/c mkg, refrig], iron, iron brd, ✕ (Mon to Sat), pool-heated (solar), rm serv, cots-fee, non smoking rms (19). **RO** ♦ **$63 - $68**, ♦♦ **$70 - $79**, ♦♦♦ **$80 - $88**, ◊ **$12**, AE BC DC EFT MC VI.

★★★☆ **Burke and Wills Moree Motor Inn**, (M), Cnr Newell Hwy & Mungindi Rd, 1km N of PO, ☎ 02 6752 3377, fax 02 6752 5373, 74 units [shwr, spa bath (Executive) (2), tlt, a/c, heat, elec blkts, tel, cable tv, clock radio, t/c mkg], ldry, ⊠, pool, bbq, rm serv, cots, non smoking units (22). **RO** ♦ **$65 - $80**, ♦♦ **$70 - $90**, 26 units of a lower rating. AE BC DC EFT MC VI.

★★★☆ **Dragon and Phoenix Motor Inn**, (M), cnr Newell Hwy & Adelaide St, 1.5km S of PO, ☎ 02 6752 5555, fax 02 6752 5575, 38 units [shwr, spa bath (1), tlt, hairdry, a/c, elec blkts, tel, TV, movie, clock radio, t/c mkg, refrig, mini bar, cook fac (22), toaster], iron, iron brd, ⊠, pool, spa (thermal artesian), bbq, rm serv, dinner to unit, cots-fee. **RO** ♦ **$75 - $85**, ♦♦ **$88 - $98**, ◊ **$13**, 12 units ★★★★, AE BC DC EFT MC MP VI.

★★★☆ **Sundowner Chain Motor Inns**, (M), Newell Hwy, 500m N of PO, ☎ 02 6752 5321, fax 02 6752 5321, 32 units [shwr, tlt, a/c, tel, TV, video, clock radio, t/c mkg, refrig, toaster], ldry, ⊠, pool, bbq, rm serv, plygr, cots-fee, non smoking units (15). **RO** ♦ **$65.50 - $149.50**, ♦♦ **$65.50 - $149.50**, ◊ **$11**, ch con, 16 units of lower rating. Natural artesian thermal spa. AE BC DC EFT MC VI, 🕊.

★★★☆ **Winchester Motel**, (M), 54 Anne St (Newell Hwy), 1km S of PO, ☎ 02 6752 4666, fax 02 6752 3753, 15 units [shwr, tlt, hairdry, a/c, elec blkts, tel, TV, video-fee, movie, clock radio, t/c mkg, refrig, toaster], iron, iron brd, pool (salt water), rm serv, plygr, cots-fee, non smoking units (4). **RO** ♦ **$69**, ♦♦ **$79**, ♦♦♦ **$87**, ◊ **$8**, AE BC DC MC VI, 🕊.

★★★ **Billabong Motel**, (M), 353 Frome St (Newell Hwy), 1km S of PO, ☎ 02 6751 1000, fax 02 6751 1188, 26 units [shwr, tlt, a/c, c/fan (3), heat, elec blkts, tel, cable tv, video (avail), clock radio, t/c mkg, refrig, cook fac ltd, elec frypan, toaster], ldry, ✕, pool (salt water), bbq, rm serv, dinner to unit, cots-fee, non smoking units (9). **RO $60.50 - $97.90**, ch con, AE BC DC EFT JCB MC MP VI.

★★★ **Golden Harvest**, (M), 366 Frome St (Newell Hwy), ☎ 02 6752 2200, fax 02 6752 2200, 27 units [shwr, tlt, hairdry, a/c, fan (9), elec blkts, tel, cable tv, clock radio, t/c mkg, refrig, cook fac (9), toaster], ldry, iron, pool (salt water), bbq, meals to unit (Dinner & Breakfast), c/park (undercover), trailer park, cots-fee, non smoking units (8). **RO** ♦ **$58**, ♦♦ **$64**, ♦♦♦ **$73**, AE BC DC EFT MC VI.

MOREE NSW continued...

★★★ **Moree Lodge**, (M), 296 Warialda St, ☎ 02 6752 4504, fax 02 6752 4504, 15 units [shwr, tlt, a/c, TV, clock radio, t/c mkg, refrig, cook fac, toaster], ldry, bbq, c/park (undercover), ☎, cots-fee. **RO** ♦ $45 - $52, ♦♦ $58 - $68, ♦♦♦ $72 - $80, ◊ $15 - $20, BC MC VI.

★★☆ **Dover Motel**, (M), 20 Dover St, 40m E of artesian spa baths, ☎ 02 6752 2880, fax 02 6752 2880, 7 units [shwr, tlt, hairdry, a/c, heat, elec blkts, tel, TV, video (avail), t/c mkg, refrig, cook fac, micro, toaster], ldry, iron, iron brd, bbq, secure park, cots-fee, non smoking property. **RO** ♦ $55 - $60, ♦♦ $65 - $85, ♦♦♦ $105, ◊ $30, BC MC VI.

★★☆ **Jackaroo Motor Inn**, (M), 378 Newell Hwy, 1km S of PO, ☎ 02 6752 3233, fax 02 6752 3152, 13 units [shwr, tlt, a/c, elec blkts, tel, TV, clock radio, t/c mkg, refrig, toaster], pool, dinner to unit, c/park (undercover), cots-fee. **RO** ♦ $49, ♦♦ $55, ◊ $8, AE BC DC EFT MC VI.

★★☆ **Moree Spa Motor Inn**, (M), Cnr Alice & Gosport Sts, 1km E of PO, 500m from artesian spa baths, ☎ 02 6752 3455, fax 02 6752 3425, 30 units [shwr, tlt, a/c, elec blkts, tel, TV, clock radio, t/c mkg, refrig, cook fac (16)], ldry, bbq, c/park (undercover), cots-fee. **RO** ♦ $44 - $49, ♦♦ $55 - $60, ♦♦♦ $66 - $71, ◊ $11, ch con, AE BC DC MC VI.

★★ **The Baths Motel**, (M), 339 Warialda St, 100m from the spa baths, ☎ 02 6752 5155, 19 units [shwr, tlt, a/c-cool, heat, elec blkts, TV, clock radio, t/c mkg, refrig, cook fac, toaster], ldry, bbq, c/park (undercover), ☎. **RO** ♦ $44, ♦♦ $49.50, ♦♦♦ $60, BC MC VI.

MORISSET NSW 2264

Pop 1,050. (112km N Sydney), See map on page 55, ref D5. Regional centre on the south-western shores of Lake Macquarie. Boating, Fishing, Swimming.

Hotels/Motels

★★★☆ **The Bay Hotel/Motel**, (LMH), Fishery Point Rd, 6km NE of Morisset, ☎ 02 4973 3177, fax 02 4970 5553, 20 units [shwr, spa bath (2), tlt, a/c, elec blkts, tel, TV, clock radio, t/c mkg, refrig], lounge, ⊠, pool (salt water), bbq, plygr, tennis (2). **RO** ♦ $72 - $94, ♦♦ $77 - $99. AE BC DC EFT MC VI.

MORPETH NSW 2321

Pop Part of Maitland, (176km N Sydney), See map on page 55, ref C7. Historic riverboat town on the Hunter River. Scenic Drives.

B&B's/Guest Houses

★★★☆ **The Old Morpeth Convent Bed & Breakfast**, (B&B), 24 James St, 500m E of PO, ☎ 02 4934 5508, fax 02 4934 5508, (2 stry), 4 rms [hairdry (2), fan (1), c/fan, heat, elec blkts, clock radio, refrig (2)], ldry, rec rm, lounge (TV), lounge firepl, t/c mkg shared, non smoking property. **BB** ♦ $75, ♦♦ $110, BC MC VI.

MORUYA NSW 2537

Pop 2,602. (303km S Sydney), See map on page 55, ref A6. Pretty south coast town on the Moruya River, the headquarters of Eurobodalla Shire and a good base from which to explore Deua National Park. Boating, Fishing, Scenic Drives, Surfing, Swimming.

Hotels/Motels

★★★☆ **Moruya Motel**, (M), 2474 Princes Hwy, 1km N of bridge, ☎ 02 4474 2511, fax 02 4474 2511, 12 units [shwr, spa bath (1), tlt, a/c, heat, elec blkts, tel, TV, video-fee, clock radio, t/c mkg, refrig], ldry, bbq, dinner to unit, cots, non smoking units (6). **RO** ♦ $58 - $80, ♦♦ $69 - $100, ♦♦♦ $80 - $110, ◊ $11, AE BC DC EFT MC VI.

★★★ **Monarch**, (LH), 50 Vulcan St (Princes Hwy), 300m N of PO, ☎ 02 4474 2433, fax 02 4474 2419, 22 rms [shwr (15), spa bath (3), tlt (15), a/c (2), c/fan, heat, elec blkts, TV, t/c mkg, refrig], ldry, ⊠, cots. **RO** ♦ $24 - $42, ♦♦ $39 - $69, ◊ $10 - $15, ch con, 7 rooms ★★, 3 rooms ★★★☆. BC MC VI.

★★☆ **Luhana Motel**, (M), 82 Princes Hwy, 500m S of PO, ☎ 02 4474 2722, fax 02 4474 2664, 18 units [shwr, spa bath (2), tlt, hairdry, fan, heat, tel, TV, video-fee, clock radio, t/c mkg, refrig, cook fac (4)], ldry, conf fac, pool, bbq, plygr, tennis, cots, non smoking units (7). **RO** ♦ $59 - $74, ♦♦ $72 - $87, ◊ $11, 6 units ★★★☆. AE BC DC MC VI, ⟐.

★★☆ **Pearly Shells Motor Inn**, (LMH), Princes Hwy, 700m N of PO, ☎ 02 4474 4399, fax 02 4474 4509, 20 units [shwr, tlt, heat, elec blkts, TV, clock radio (8), t/c mkg, refrig, toaster], lounge firepl, ⊠ (Tue to Sun), meals to unit. **RO** ♦ $38.50, ♦♦ $44 - $66, ◊ $15, 4 units of a lower rating, 8 units yet to be rated. BC MC VI.

Self Catering Accommodation

★★★ **Mullimburra Beach House**, (House), 181 Mullimburra Point Rd, Bingie, 15km SE of Moruya, ☎ 02 4474 3347, fax 02 4474 4529, (2 stry gr fl), 1 house acc up to 6, [shwr, bath, tlt (2), fan, heat, TV, video, t/c mkg, refrig, cook fac, micro, toaster, ldry, blkts, linen reqd, pillows], w/mach, dryer, iron, iron brd, TV rm, bbq, cots, non smoking property. **D** $100 - $150, **W** $400 - $1,200, Min book applies.

★★☆ **Bakers Flat - The Cottages**, (Cotg), 3539 Araluen Rd, 35km NW of PO in Deua National Park, ☎ 02 4473 7279, fax 02 4473 7279, 2 cotgs acc up to 4, [shwr, tlt, fire pl, heat, refrig (1), cook fac, blkts, linen reqd-fee, pillows], non smoking property. **D** $70 - $110, **W** $310 - $620, AE BC MC VI.

Lucks Holiday Cottage, (Cotg), 14 Charles Moffit Dve, 10km S of Moruya Heads, ☎ 02 4474 4750, 2 cotgs acc up to 5, [shwr, bath, tlt, heat, TV, video, CD, refrig], w/mach, dryer, lounge firepl, bbq, cots, non smoking property. **D** ♦ $45 - $72, ♦♦ $75 - $110, **W** $225 - $715, ch con, (not yet classified).

B&B's/Guest Houses

★★★☆ **Post and Telegraph B&B**, (B&B), Cnr Page & Campbell Sts, ☎ 02 4474 5745, fax 02 4472 8866, (2 stry), 3 rms [shwr (1), tlt (1), hairdry, heat, elec blkts, clock radio], ldry, lounge (TV), lounge firepl, cook fac, t/c mkg shared, refrig, courtesy transfer, non smoking property. **BB** ♦ $88, ♦♦ $110 - $121, ◊ $22, AE BC MC VI.

Bri-Del Gardens B&B Homestay, (B&B), 9 Womban Rd, 3km W of PO, ☎ 02 4474 3736, fax 02 4474 3736, 1 rm [shwr, tlt, fan, heat, elec blkts, tel, clock radio, t/c mkg, refrig, cook fac, micro, toaster, ldry], lounge (TV), lounge firepl, ✕, bbq, non smoking property. **BB** ♦ $75, ♦♦ $100, **DBB** ♦ $100, ♦♦ $150 - $180, ◊ $25 - $65, ch con, fam con, pen con, BC MC VI, (not yet classified).

MOSS VALE NSW 2577

Pop 6,100. (129km SW Sydney), See map on page 55, ref B4. Major regional centre of the Southern Highlands. Bowls, Bush Walking, Golf, Scenic Drives, Swimming, Tennis.

Hotels/Motels

★★★★☆ **Peppers Manor House Southern Highlands**, (LH), Kater Rd, Sutton Forest 2577, 4km SW of PO, ☎ 02 4868 2355, fax 02 4868 3257, (2 stry gr fl), 43 rms (3 suites) [shwr, bath (30), spa bath (3), tlt, cent heat, tel, clock radio, t/c mkg], ldry, rec rm, lounge (TV), conv fac, ✕, pool, golf, tennis, cots. **RO** ♦ **$245 - $275**, ⚪ **$55**, **Suite RO $300 - $385**, ch con, AE BC DC MC VI, ♿.

★★★ **Bong Bong Motel**, (M), 238 Argyle St, ☎ 02 4868 1033, fax 02 4869 2393, 10 units [shwr, tlt, hairdry, fan, cent heat, elec blkts, tel, fax, TV, clock radio, t/c mkg, refrig], bbq, cots-fee. **RO** ♦ **$61 - $75**, ♦♦ **$72 - $89**, ⚪ **$10 - $15**, ch con, AE BC DC EFT MC VI.

★★☆ **Golf Ball Motel**, (M), Cnr Arthur & Spring Sts, ☎ 02 4868 1511, fax 02 4869 1215, (2 stry gr fl), 19 units [shwr, bath (6), tlt, heat, elec blkts, tel, TV, video-fee, clock radio, t/c mkg, refrig, mini bar], ldry, ✕, bbq, plygr, cots-fee. **RO** ♦ **$49.50 - $82.50**, ♦♦ **$60.50 - $82.50**, ♦♦♦ **$63.80 - $93.50**, ⚪ **$6.60 - $11**, ch con, AE BC DC MC VI.

B&B's/Guest Houses

★★★★ **Heronswood House**, (B&B), 165 Argyle St, 1km N of Railway Station, ☎ 02 4869 1477, fax 02 4869 4079, 5 rms [shwr, bath (1), tlt, cent heat, elec blkts, micro], lounge (TV), ✕, t/c mkg shared, bbq, non smoking property. **BB** ♦ **$71.50**, ♦♦ **$115.50 - $181.50**, ⚪ **$66 - $77**, BC MC VI.

★★★★ **Sutton Downs Bed & Breakfast**, (B&B), Golden Vale Rd, 1.5km NW of Sutton Forest - 4.3km E of Freeway, ☎ 02 4868 3126, fax 02 4868 3802, 3 rms [shwr, bath (1), tlt, hairdry, fan, heat, elec blkts], iron, iron brd, lounge (firepl), ✕, non smoking rms. **BB** ♦♦ **$140 - $180**, Min book applies, BC MC VI.

★★★☆ **Lynton Bed & Breakfast**, (B&B), 618 Argyle St, 750m S of Moss Vale Pk, ☎ 02 4868 2552, fax 02 4869 4519, 3 rms [shwr, bath (1), tlt, hairdry (2), fire pl (1), cent heat, elec blkts, tel, TV (2)], lounge (tv & firepl), meals avail, cots, non smoking rms (2). **BB** ♦♦ **$110 - $176**, AE BC MC VI.

HERONSWOOD HOUSE

HERONSWOOD HOUSE
Homestyle
ACCOMMODATION
(B&B)

Ph: (02) 4869 1477
www.acenet.com.au/~heron

- 5 large, welcoming double and twin rooms
- All rooms, with ensuites or own bathroom
- Richly decorated lounge and dining rooms
- Beautifully restored 1800's home
- Conference facilities available

165 Argyle Street, Moss Vale NSW 2577
Arrive as a visitor, leave as a friend

MOULAMEIN NSW 2733

Pop 450. (872km SW Sydney), See map on pages 52/53, ref C6. Historic port on the Edward River between Deniliquin and Balranald, close to the Murray River town of Swan Hill. Fishing, Swimming, Water Skiing.

Self Catering Accommodation

★★★ **Melness Host Farm**, (Cotg), (Farm), Moulemein Rd, 32km N of Swan Hill, ☎ 03 5034 0554, 1 cotg acc up to 6, [shwr, tlt, a/c, heat, TV, radio, t/c mkg, refrig, cook fac, micro, toaster, ldry], pool, bbq, plygr, cots. **D** ♦♦ **$70**, ♦♦♦ **$80**, Breakfast hamper available.

B&B's/Guest Houses

★★★★☆ **Riverview Bed & Breakfast**, (B&B), (Farm), Balpool Rd, 2.5km S of PO, ☎ 03 5887 5241, fax 03 5887 5454, 3 rms [shwr, tlt, hairdry, evap cool, c/fan, heat, elec blkts, tel, TV (1), clock radio], lounge firepl, ✕, spa, bbq, non smoking property. **BB** ♦ **$85**, ♦♦ **$99**, **DBB** ♦ **$112.50**, ♦♦ **$153**.

MOUNT SEAVIEW NSW 2446

Pop Nominal, (478km NW Sydney), See map on page 54, ref B6. Rural locality on the upper reaches of the Hastings River, close to Werrikimbe National Park. Bush Walking.

Hotels/Motels

★★★☆ **Mount Seaview Resort**, (M), Oxley Hwy, 55km W of Wauchope, ☎ 02 6587 7155, fax 02 6587 7195, 26 units [shwr, bath (15), spa bath (1), tlt, a/c, tel, clock radio, t/c mkg, refrig, cook fac (10)], ldry, lounge (TV), conv fac, ✕, bbq, tennis. **RO** ♦ **$54 - $76**, ♦♦ **$64 - $90**, ♦♦♦ **$74 - $105**, ⚪ **$10 - $15**, ch con, AE BC MC VI.

(Lodge Section), 24 rms acc up to 5, [shwr (3), tlt (3), linen reqd-fee], ldry, rec rm, cook fac. **D** ♦♦ **$32 - $47**, ⚪ **$4**.

MOUNT TOMAH NSW

See Blue Mountains Region.

MOUNT VICTORIA NSW

See Blue Mountains Region.

MOUNT VIEW NSW 2325

Pop Nominal, (187km N Sydney), Map GMAP03, Reference B8, Vineyards, Wineries.

Self Catering Accommodation

★★★★ **Hunter Valley Country Cabins**, Lot 2 Mount View Rd, 17km SW of Cessnock, ☎ 02 4990 8989, fax 02 4990 8936, 4 cabins acc up to 4, (2 bedrm), [shwr, tlt, a/c-cool, heat (wood), TV, refrig, cook fac, micro, blkts, doonas, linen, pillows], bbq, cots. **D** ♦ **$80 - $98.75**, ♦♦ **$80 - $98.75**, ⚪ **$20 - $35**, ch con, BC EFT MC VI.

MOUNT WILSON NSW

See Blue Mountains Region.

MUDGEE NSW 2850

Pop 8,200. (282km W Sydney), See map on pages 52/53, ref G4. Attractive wine, wool and honey town on the Cudgegong River, flanked by foothills of the Great Dividing Range. Bowls, Gem Fossicking, Golf, Horse Racing, Scenic Drives, Swimming, Tennis, Vineyards, Wineries. See also Windeyer.

Hotels/Motels

★★★★☆ **Country Comfort - Mudgee**, (M), Cassilis Rd, ☎ 02 6372 4500, fax 02 6372 4525, (2 stry gr fl), 66 units (4 suites) [shwr, tlt, hairdry, a/c, elec blkts, tel, TV, movie, clock radio, t/c mkg, refrig, mini bar], conv fac, ✕, pool indoor heated, sauna, spa, rm serv, tennis, cots, non smoking units (14). **RO** ♦ **$123 - $153**, ♦♦ **$123 - $153**, ⚪ **$15**, ch con, AE BC DC MC VI, ♿.

★★★★ **Horatio Motor Inn**, (M), 15 Horatio St, 2km S of PO, ☎ 02 6372 7727, fax 02 6372 7333, (2 stry gr fl), 22 units [shwr, tlt, hairdry, a/c, elec blkts, tel, TV, video (avail), movie, clock radio, t/c mkg, refrig, mini bar, micro, toaster], ldry, conf fac, pool-heated (solar), bbq, dinner to unit, cots, non smoking rms (avail). **RO** ♦ **$88 - $110**, ♦♦ **$88 - $110**, ⚪ **$12**, AE BC DC EFT MC VI, ♿.

★★★☆ **Cudgegong Valley Motel**, (M), 212 Market St, 2km W of PO, ☎ 02 6372 4322, fax 02 6372 3186, 16 units [shwr, tlt, hairdry, a/c, fan, heat, elec blkts, tel, TV, video, movie, clock radio, t/c mkg, refrig, micro (2), toaster, ldry], iron, iron brd, pool, bbq, dinner to unit (6 nights), plygr, cots, non smoking rms (12). **RO** ♦♦ **$59 - $88**, ⚪ **$10**, AE EFT MC VI, *Operator Comment: FREE BOOKING CALL 1800 813 769.*

Children and road safety

For the safety of children on the roads, the three main ingredients are supervision, teaching by example and talking with the children about how to use the road safely.

If your family is holidaying away from home, take a walk around the area when you arrive, show children the safest places to play and identify any potential dangers.

Because children pick up clues from adults around them, parents must be sure always to set a good example whether crossing a road, riding a bike or driving the car.

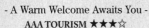

★★★☆ **Wanderlight Motor Inn**, (M), 107 Market St, ☎ 02 6372 1088, fax 02 6372 2859, (2 stry gr fl), 35 units (2 suites) [shwr, bath (12), tlt, a/c, elec blkts, tel, TV, video, clock radio, t/c mkg, refrig, toaster], ldry, ⊠ (Mon to Sat), pool, spa, bbq, dinner to unit, cots-fee. **RO** ⚹ **$77 - $90**, ⚹⚹ **$87 - $100**, ⚹ **$10, Suite D $112 - $172**, 10 units ★★★. AE BC DC JCB MC MP VI, ⅙⚹.

★★★☆ **Winning Post Motor Inn**, (M), 101 Church St, ☎ 02 6372 3333, fax 02 6372 1208, (2 stry gr fl), 43 units (3 suites) [shwr, bath (10), spa bath (3), tlt, hairdry, a/c, elec blkts, tel, TV, video (avail), movie, t/c mkg, refrig, cook fac (1)], ldry, iron, iron brd, conv fac, ⊠, bar, pool, spa (heated), rm serv, plygr, tennis (half court), cots-fee, non smoking units (13). **RO** ⚹ **$88 - $126.50**, ⚹⚹ **$99 - $137.50**, ⚹⚹⚹ **$113.30 - $148.50**, ⚹ **$11, Suite D $115 - $220**, AE BC DC EFT JCB MC VI.

★★★ **Hithergreen Motel**, (M), 252 Henry Lawson Dve, 4km N of PO, ☎ 02 6372 1022, fax 02 6372 6203, 16 units [shwr, tlt, a/c, elec blkts, tel, TV, movie, clock radio, t/c mkg, refrig], ✕ (Fri & Sat), pool (salt water), tennis, cots. **RO** ⚹ **$66**, ⚹⚹ **$77**, ⚹⚹⚹ **$88**, ch con, AE BC MC VI.

★★★ Motel Ningana, (M), Cnr Lewis & Mortimer Sts, ☎ 02 6372 1133, fax 02 6372 6326, 18 units [shwr, bath (2), tlt, a/c, elec blkts, tel, TV, video-fee, clock radio, t/c mkg, refrig, toaster], ldry, meals to unit, cots-fee. **RO** ⚹ $63 - $69, ⚹⚹ $69 - $71, ⚹⚹⚹ $77 - $83, ⚹ $6, AE BC EFT MC MCH VI.

 ★★★ Mudgee Motor Inn, (M), 1 Sydney Rd, 1.5km E from PO, ☎ 02 6372 1122, fax 02 6372 4404, 44 units [shwr, tlt, hairdry (14), a/c-cool, heat, elec blkts, tel, TV, video (fee), clock radio, t/c mkg, refrig, ldry, doonas], ✗, ✉, pool, bbq, rm serv, meals to unit, plygr, non smoking units (16), Pets on application. **RO** ⚹ $50 - $66, ⚹⚹ $66 - $88, ⚹ $11, ch con, weekly con, AE BC BTC DC EFT MC MCH VI.

★★★ Soldiers Motel, (M), 35 Perry St, 250m S of PO, ☎ 02 6372 4399, fax 02 6372 6596, (2 stry gr fl), 18 units [shwr, bath, spa bath (10), tlt, a/c, elec blkts, tel, TV, clock radio, t/c mkg, refrig, toaster]. **RO** ⚹ $62 - $68, ⚹⚹ $68 - $73, ⚹⚹⚹ $73 - $79, AE BC DC EFT MC VI, ♿.

★★ Central Motel, (M), 120 Church St, ☎ 02 6372 2268, fax 02 6372 2368, 8 units [shwr, tlt, elec blkts, TV, clock radio, t/c mkg, refrig, toaster], bbq. **RO** ⚹ $38 - $44, ⚹⚹ $49 - $55, AE BC DC EFT MC VI.

Federal Hotel, (LH), 34 Inglis St, 1.5km S of PO, ☎ 02 6372 2150, fax 02 6372 6393, (Multi-stry), 8 rms [c/fan, elec blkts, t/c mkg], ldry, lounge (TV), bbq, ☎, cots. **RO** ⚹ $22 - $27.50, ⚹⚹ $39.50 - $49.50, ⚹ $11, ch con, AE BC EFT MC VI.

Self Catering Accommodation

★★★★ Ilkley Cottages, (Cotg), 664 Black Springs Rd, 12km N of PO, ☎ 02 6373 3957, fax 02 6373 3958, 2 cotgs acc up to 10, [shwr, bath, tlt, hairdry, evap cool, fan (1), c/fan (1), fire pl, heat, elec blkts, TV, video (avail), clock radio, t/c mkg, refrig, cook fac, micro, elec frypan, toaster, blkts, linen], iron, bbq, plygr, cots, non smoking property. **D** ⚹⚹ $105 - $180, ch con, Min book applies, AE BC MC VI.

★★★ Kirima Cottages, (Cotg), Lot 2 Hill End Rd, ☎ 02 6372 0327, fax 02 6372 0347, 3 cotgs acc up to 6, [shwr, tlt, a/c-cool (2), fire pl, TV (1), video (2), clock radio, t/c mkg, refrig, cook fac, micro, toaster, linen], ldry, w/mach, bbq. **D** ⚹⚹ $100 - $140, ⚹ $25 - $40, **W** ⚹⚹ $440 - $550, fam con.

★★★ Primo Bed & Breakfast, (Cotg), 9 Court St, 500m W of PO, ☎ 02 6372 6990, fax 02 6372 6105, 3 cotgs [shwr, tlt, hairdry (1), fan, elec blkts, TV (1), clock radio, cook fac], shared fac (2 rms), ldry, iron, iron brd, lounge (TV & firepl), bbq, non smoking property. **BB** ⚹⚹ $110, BC MC VI.

Casita, (Cotg), 24 Henry Bayly Dve, 1.5km SW of PO, ☎ 02 6372 2237, 1 cotg acc up to 2, [shwr, tlt, hairdry, fan, heat, TV, clock radio, t/c mkg, refrig, micro, elec frypan, toaster, blkts, linen], iron, iron brd, non smoking property. **D** $90 - $150, **W** $500 - $1,050, (not yet classified).

Sherwood's Green, 435 Melrose Rd, 11km E of Mudgee, ☎ 02 6372 4574, fax 02 6372 4574, 1 cabin acc up to 4, (2 bedrm), [shwr, tlt, a/c, fan, heat (elec/wood), TV, clock radio, t/c mkg, refrig, cook fac, blkts, doonas, linen, pillows], bbq, cots, breakfast ingredients. **D** ⚹ $120, ⚹⚹ $140, ⚹ $20, weekly con, (not yet classified).

B&B's/Guest Houses

★★★★☆ Bed & Breakfast Pottier's Mudgee, (B&B), 9 Mulgoa Way, 1km E of Town Clock, ☎ 02 6372 1861, fax 02 6372 1841, 5 rms [ensuite, bath (1), hairdry (1), a/c, c/fan (1), fire pl (1), t/c mkg (1)], lounge (TV), lounge firepl, pool (saltwater), t/c mkg shared, non smoking rms. **BB** ⚹ $136 - $153, ⚹⚹ $153 - $170, AE BC DC EFT MC VI.

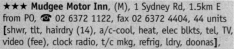
★★★★☆ The Mudgee Homestead Guest House, (GH), 3 Coorumbene Rd, 6km N of Mudgee, ☎ 02 6373 3786, fax 02 6373 3086, 6 rms [shwr, bath (2), tlt, hairdry, evap cool, c/fan, heat], rec rm, lounge (TV), lounge firepl, ✗, t/c mkg shared, bbq, courtesy transfer, non smoking property. **BB** ⚹ $155, ⚹⚹ $175, AE.

 **★★★★ Bellevue Park**, (B&B), Cassilis Rd, 2km N of Clock, ☎ 02 6372 7698, fax 02 6372 7738, 6 rms [shwr, spa bath (1), tlt (6), hairdry, c/fan (4), fire pl (2), heat, tel, clock radio, refrig (3)], iron brd, lounge firepl, ✗, pool, t/c mkg shared, tennis, non smoking property. **BB** ⚹ $120 - $180, ⚹⚹ $130 - $190, BC EFT MC VI.

★★★★ Karilla Guest Lodge, (B&B), (Farm), Mt Pleasant La, 6km N of Town Clock, ☎ 02 6372 6510, fax 02 6372 6595, 2 rms [shwr, tlt, hairdry, heat, elec blkts, tel, video, clock radio, t/c mkg, micro, toaster], ldry, iron, iron brd, lounge (tv & video), pool (salt water), cook fac, refrig, bbq, c/park (undercover). **BB** $140, Kennels and stables available.

★★★★ Kia-ora Bed & Breakfast, (B&B), No children's facilities, 92 Gladstone St, ☎ 02 6372 2529, 2 rms (1 suite) [shwr, tlt, hairdry, a/c, c/fan, elec blkts, tel, TV, t/c mkg]. **BB** ⚹ $80, ⚹⚹ $100.

★★★★ Old Wallinga Country House, (B&B), 65 Wallinga Lane, 7km S of Mudgee, ☎ 02 6372 3129, fax 02 6372 3129, 4 rms [shwr, tlt, hairdry, c/fan, fire pl (2), cent heat (2), elec blkts, tel, TV (2), t/c mkg, refrig], ldry, rec rm, TV rm, lounge firepl, pool (salt water), bbq, courtesy transfer, tennis, cots, non smoking rms, Dogs welcome. **BB** ⚹ $80 - $90, ⚹⚹ $144 - $165, ch con.

★★★☆ Galsworthy Park, (B&B), 8 Tuckermans Rd, 7km NW of Town Clock, ☎ 02 6372 7545, fax 02 6372 7106, 2 rms [hairdry, c/fan, heat, elec blkts, tel], iron, iron brd, lounge firepl, ✗, t/c mkg shared, refrig, bbq, plygr, cots, non smoking property. **BB** ⚹ $120, ⚹⚹ $150.

★★★☆ Lauralla Historic Guest House, (GH), Cnr Lewis & Mortimer Sts, 400m E of PO, ☎ 02 6372 4480, fax 02 6372 3320, 6 rms [shwr, spa bath (2), tlt, hairdry, fan, heat, elec blkts, tel, TV, clock radio, refrig], ldry, iron, iron brd, conv fac, lounge firepl, ✗, ✗, t/c mkg shared, bbq, cots. **BB** ⚹ $80 - $125, ⚹⚹ $125 - $210, ⚹ $45 - $55, ch con, AE BC DC EFT MC VI.

★★★☆ Lynch's Bed & Breakfast, (B&B), 146 Market St, ☎ 02 6372 4116, fax 02 6372 7925, 4 rms [shwr (3), tlt (3), hairdry, a/c-cool, c/fan (2), heat, elec blkts, tel, TV, clock radio, refrig (3)], shared fac (1 rm), lounge firepl, pool, bbq, non smoking property. **BB** ⚹ $90 - $120, ⚹⚹ $115 - $145.

★★★☆ Woodward Farm, (B&B), 829 Spring Flat Rd, 15km SE of Mudgee PO, ☎ 02 6373 1207, fax 02 6373 1207, (2 stry), 2 rms [shwr, tlt, a/c, fan, t/c mkg], bbq, Pets allowed. **BB** ⚹ $70, ⚹⚹ $100.

★★★ Tierney House, (B&B), Tierney La, off Henry Lawson Dve, ☎ 02 6373 3877, fax 02 6373 3027, 4 rms [shwr, tlt, a/c, c/fan], lounge (TV), lounge firepl, c/park. **BB** ⚹ $70, ⚹⚹ $90 - $120, BC MC VI.

⭐ *Trouble-free travel tips* - **Tyre pressures**
Check tyre pressures and set them to the manufacturer's recommendation, including the spare.
The specifications can generally be found on the tyre placard located in either the glove box or on the front door frame.

MULLAWAY NSW 2456

Pop Nominal, (591km N Sydney), See map on page 54, ref D4. Small village with a good surf beach, situated just north of Woolgoolga. Fishing, Surfing, Swimming.

Self Catering Accommodation

★★☆ **Mullaway Beach Cottages**, (Cotg), 33/35 The Boulevarde, ☎ 02 6654 2399, 2 cotgs acc up to 6, [shwr, bath, tlt, c/fan, TV, video (1), clock radio, t/c mkg, refrig, cook fac, micro, elec frypan, toaster, linen reqd], w/mach, iron, lounge (TV), pool (salt water), bbq, c/park (carport), plygr. **D ♦♦ $55**, ♦ **$10, W ♦♦ $350 - $650.**

★★ **Mullaway Beach Cabins**, 22 The Boulevarde, 4km N of PO, ☎ 02 6654 2644, 7 cabins acc up to 5, [tlt (2G-2L), heat, cook fac, blkts reqd, linen reqd], shwr (2G-2L), ldry, bbq, plygr, **D ♦♦ $31 - $59,** ♦ **$3 - $6, W ♦♦ $155 - $415,** ♦ **$15 - $42,** Min book Christmas and Jan.

MULLUMBIMBY NSW 2482

Pop 2,900. (798km N Sydney), See map on page 54, ref E2. North coast dairying and banana growing centre situated in spectacular sub-tropical country.

Hotels/Motels

★★★ **Mullumbimby Motel**, (M), 121 Dalley St, ☎ 02 6684 2387, fax 02 6684 4944, 10 units [shwr, tlt, a/c, fan, heat, cable tv, clock radio, t/c mkg, refrig], ldry, bbq, cots, non smoking units (5). **W $240, RO ♦ $50, ♦♦ $60, ♦♦♦ $70,** ♦ **$10,** AE BC MC VI.

★★☆ **Lyrebird Motel**, (M), 68 Dalley St, 50m N of PO, ☎ 02 6684 1725, fax 02 6684 1791, (2 stry gr fl), 16 units [shwr, tlt, hairdry, a/c-cool, heat, tel, TV, clock radio, t/c mkg, refrig, toaster], bbq. **RO ♦ $44 - $72, ♦♦ $55 - $88, ♦♦♦ $61 - $99,** ♦ **$11,** AE BC DC EFT MC VI, ♿.

Self Catering Accommodation

★★★☆ **Toolond Plantation**, (House), (Farm), Palmwoods via Main Arm Rd, ☎ 02 6684 5432, fax 02 6684 5432, 1 house acc up to 8, [shwr, bath, tlt, c/fan, TV, video, clock radio, refrig, cook fac, elec frypan, toaster, ldry, blkts, linen reqd-fee], w/mach, iron, iron brd, lounge firepl, bbq, cots, non smoking property. **D $100, W $610,** Min book applies.

★★★ **Mooyabil Farm Holidays**, (HU), (Farm), 448 Left Bank Rd, ☎ 02 6684 1128, fax 02 6684 1518, 5 units acc up to 7, [shwr, tlt, c/fan, fire pl, clock radio, refrig, cook fac, micro, toaster, blkts, linen, pillows], ldry, rec rm, lounge (tv & video), conv fac, pool (salt water), bbq, plygr, cots, non smoking units. **D $88 - $144, W $440 - $770,** BC MC VI, ♿.

B&B's/Guest Houses

★★★ **Fogartys Rural Retreat**, (B&B), Lavertys Gap, Wilsons Creek Rd, 7km W of Mullumbimby, ☎ 02 6684 0209, fax 02 6684 0209, 4 rms [shwr, bath, tlt, hairdry, fire pl, elec blkts, tel, radio], rec rm, lounge (TV), t/c mkg shared, tennis-fee. **BB ♦ $80, ♦♦ $100,** BC MC VI.

MULWALA NSW 2647

Pop 1,593. (736km SW Sydney), See map on pages 52/53, ref D7. Mulwala and its twin town of Yarrawonga lie on the shores of Lake Mulwala, an expansive body of water which was created on the Murray River in 1939 to form a major storage facility. Bowls, Croquet, Fishing, Golf, Rowing, Swimming, Tennis, Water Skiing. See also Yarrawonga.

Hotels/Motels

★★★★ **Capricorn Motor Inn**, (M), Melbourne Rd, 2.1km S of PO, ☎ 03 5744 3813, fax 03 5744 3816, 20 units [shwr, spa bath (4), tlt, hairdry, a/c, elec blkts, tel, TV, video-fee, clock radio, t/c mkg, refrig, toaster], ldry, pool-heated (solar), spa, bbq, cots-fee. **RO ♦ $60 - $100, ♦♦ $65 - $130,** ♦ **$10,** 9 units ★★★. Min book applies, AE BC DC EFT MC MP VI, ♿.

★★★★ **Services Club Motor Inn**, (M), Melbourne St, ☎ 03 5744 2333, fax 03 5743 1234, (2 stry gr fl), 60 units [shwr, bath (14), spa bath (24), tlt, hairdry (40), a/c, elec blkts, tel, TV, video-fee, clock radio, t/c mkg, refrig, mini bar, toaster], lift, ldry, lounge (TV), conv fac, ⊠, pool-heated (solar), bbq, ✆, plygr, cots. **W $630 - $1,015, RO ♦♦ $90 - $145,** ♦ **$45 - $72.50,** ch con, 20 units ★★★. Min book applies, AE BC DC MC VI, ♿.

GOLDEN CHAIN

★★★☆ **Ashleigh Court Motor Inn**, (M), 36 Corowa Rd, 1.4km E of PO, ☎ 03 5744 2261, fax 03 5744 2400, 12 units (3 suites) [shwr, spa bath (3), tlt, hairdry, a/c, elec blkts, tel, TV, video (avail), clock radio, t/c mkg, refrig], ldry, pool, sauna, bbq, cots, non smoking units (3). **RO ♦ $58 - $81, ♦♦ $65 - $81, ♦♦♦ $81 - $98,** ♦ **$10 - $17, Suite RO $80 - $120,** ch con, Min book applies, AE BC DC EFT MC VI.

★★★☆ **Mulwala Paradise Palms**, (M), Melbourne St, 600m S of PO, ☎ 03 5743 2555, fax 03 5744 2993, (2 stry gr fl), 12 units [shwr, tlt, a/c, heat, elec blkts, tel, TV, video, clock radio, t/c mkg, refrig, toaster], ldry, pool (salt water), spa, bbq, boat park, non smoking units (2). **RO ♦♦ $71.50 - $93.50,** ♦ **$11 - $16.50,** Min book Christmas Jan and Easter, AE BC DC MC VI.

★★★ **Murray River Motel**, (M), 211 Melbourne St, 1.5km S of PO, ☎ 03 5744 1245, fax 03 5743 3241, 14 units [shwr, tlt, hairdry, a/c, heat, elec blkts, tel, TV, clock radio, t/c mkg, refrig, toaster], pool-heated (solar), bbq, cots. **RO ♦ $55 - $75, ♦♦ $62 - $85,** ♦ **$10 - $15,** Breakfast available. AE BC DC MC VI.

★★☆ **Mulwala Motel Hotel**, (LMH), 88 Melbourne St, 100m S of PO, ☎ 03 5744 3204, 18 units [shwr, tlt, a/c, elec blkts, tel, TV, clock radio, t/c mkg, refrig, toaster], ldry, ✕ (5 nights), dinner to unit (5 nights), cots. **RO ♦♦ $55 - $72, ♦♦♦ $77 - $110,** ♦ **$10 - $15,** ch con, BC MC VI.

★★ **Aaroona Holiday Resort**, (M), Corowa Rd, 1.8km E of PO, ☎ 03 5744 1764, fax 03 5743 1599, 12 units [shwr, tlt, a/c, elec blkts, TV, clock radio, t/c mkg, refrig, elec frypan, toaster], ldry, pool, bbq. **RO ♦ $35 - $50, ♦♦ $60 - $71, ♦♦♦ $65 - $75,** ♦ **$11,** Light breakfast available. Min book long w/ends and Easter, BC MC VI.

Self Catering Accommodation

★★★★ **Lake Edge Resort**, (SA), Melbourne St, next to Mulwala Water Ski Club, ☎ 03 5743 8400, fax 03 5744 3742, 10 serv apts acc up to 6, [shwr, spa bath, tlt, a/c, elec blkts, tel, TV, clock radio, refrig, cook fac, micro, d/wash, toaster, blkts, linen, pillows], ldry, rec rm, pool, sauna, spa, bbq, cots. **D ♦♦ $88 - $132,** Min book long w/ends, BC MC VI.

★★★★ **Yarrawonga Lake Resort Villas**, (HU), Lake Resort Peninsula, Melbourne St, 200m N of Yarrawonga/Mulwala Bridge, ☎ 03 5743 1433, fax 03 5744 3576, (2 stry gr fl), 36 units acc up to 8, [shwr, spa bath (21), tlt, hairdry, a/c, elec blkts, tel, TV, video, clock radio, t/c mkg, refrig, cook fac (21), micro (21), d/wash (21), toaster, ldry (in unit) (21), blkts, linen, pillows], ldry, w/mach, rec rm, lounge (TV), ⊠, pool-heated (salt water heated), bbq, c/park (carport), cots. **D ♦♦ $150,** ♦ **$20, W ♦♦ $892.50,** ♦ **$140,** ch con, Min book applies, BC MC VI, ♿.

★★★ **Mulwala Colonial**, (HU), 9 Melbourne St, 500m N of PO, ☎ 03 5744 2526, 4 units acc up to 6, [shwr, tlt, a/c-cool, heat, elec blkts, TV, clock radio, t/c mkg, refrig, cook fac, toaster, linen reqd-fee], w/mach, iron, bbq-fee, c/park (carport). **D ♦♦ $40 - $75,** ♦ **$5 - $10, W ♦♦ $245 - $525,** Min book Christmas Jan long w/ends and Easter.

★★★ **Mulwala Lodge**, (HU), 126 Melbourne St, 1km S of PO, ☎ 03 5744 1178, 5 units acc up to 6, [shwr, tlt, a/c, heat, elec blkts, TV, refrig, cook fac, blkts, linen, pillows], ldry, bbq. **D ♦ $44 - $55, ♦♦ $59 - $66,** ch con, pen con, Min book Christmas Jan and Easter, BC MC VI.

★★★ **Parklake**, (HU), 37 Melbourne St, 300m N of PO, ☎ 03 5744 3965, fax 03 5744 3965, 3 units acc up to 4, [shwr, bath, tlt, evap cool, fan, heat, elec blkts, TV, refrig, cook fac, micro, ldry, linen reqd-fee], c/park (garage). **D ♦♦ $50 - $70, ♦♦♦ $60 - $80,** ♦ **$10, RO ♦♦ $350 - $500,** Min book applies.

★★★ **Regent Holiday Units**, (HU), 28 Lang St, 400m E of Mulwala Canal, ☎ 03 5744 3518, 4 units acc up to 6, [shwr, tlt, a/c-cool, c/fan, heat, elec blkts, tel, TV, clock radio, t/c mkg, refrig, cook fac, micro, elec frypan, toaster, ldry, linen reqd-fee], w/mach, iron, pool (salt water), bbq, c/park (carport), ✆, cots. **D $44 - $88,** ch con.

★★☆ **Lake Harbour**, (HU), Melbourne St, 1.6km S of PO, ☎ 03 5744 1171, 5 units acc up to 4, [shwr, tlt, a/c-cool, fan, heat, elec blkts, TV, clock radio, refrig, cook fac, blkts, linen, pillows], w/mach, bbq, c/park (carport). **D ♦ $46, ♦♦ $50,** ♦ **$10, W $340,** Min book Christmas Jan long w/ends and Easter, BC MC VI.

Akma Holiday Units, (HU), 12 Sturt St, ☎ 0412 819 326, 4 units acc up to 4, [shwr, tlt, evap cool, c/fan, heat, elec blkts, TV, clock radio, t/c mkg, refrig, cook fac, micro, elec frypan, toaster, ldry, blkts, linen-fee], w/mach, iron, iron brd, bbq, cots-fee. **D ♦♦ $45 - $65,** ♦ **$11, W ♦♦ $280 - $455,** ♦ **$11,** Min book Christmas Jan long w/ends and Easter, (not yet classified).

Other Accommodation

★★ **Yarrawonga & Border Golf Club**, (Lodge), Gulai Rd, 2.5km SW of PO, ☎ 03 5744 1911, fax 03 5744 2556, 68 rms (11 suites) acc up to 6, [shwr, spa bath (27), tlt, a/c, elec blkts, TV, refrig, cook fac, micro (27), elec frypan, toaster, ldry, blkts, linen, pillows], lounge, ✕, bbq (fee)-fee, bowls, golf, tennis. **D** ♦♦ **$63 - $105**, ◊ **$14 - $17**, **W** ♦♦ **$385 - $588**, ◊ **$85 - $108**, 24 rooms ★★★★. 14 rooms yet to be assessed.

MURRUMBATEMAN NSW 2582

Pop 1,100. (290km SW Sydney), See map on pages 52/53, ref G6. Small village midway between Yass and Canberra at the centre of a thriving cool climate wine industry. Vineyards, Wineries.

Hotels/Motels

★★☆ **Murrumbateman Country Inn**, (LMH), Cnr Hercules St & Barton Hwy, ☎ 02 6227 5802, fax 02 6227 5973, 14 units [shwr, bath (2), tlt, a/c, elec blkts, tel, TV, clock radio, t/c mkg, refrig, toaster], ⊠, ☎. **RO** ♦ **$50**, ♦♦ **$66**, ◊ **$11**, ch con, AE BC EFT MC VI.

MURRURUNDI NSW 2338

Pop 981. (309km NW Sydney), See map on pages 52/53, ref H4. National Trust-classified town on the slopes of the Liverpool Range in the upper Hunter. Bowls, Gem Fossicking, Golf, Horse Riding, Swimming, Tennis.

Hotels/Motels

★★★ **Valley View Motel**, (M), New England Hwy, 1.5km N of PO, ☎ 02 6546 6044, fax 02 6546 6684, 15 units [shwr, tlt, hairdry, a/c, heat, elec blkts, tel, TV, clock radio, t/c mkg, refrig, toaster], pool, bbq, dinner to unit, courtesy transfer, plygr, cots, non smoking units (6). **RO** ♦ **$46 - $51**, ♦♦ **$57 - $63**, ◊ **$9**, AE BC DC EFT MC MCH VI.

★★ **Murrurundi Motel**, (M), New England Hwy, 500m S of PO, ☎ 02 6546 6082, fax 02 6546 6600, 16 units [shwr, tlt, evap cool, heat, elec blkts, tel, TV, clock radio, t/c mkg, refrig], pool, bbq, courtesy transfer, plygr, cots. **RO** ♦ **$46.20**, ♦♦ **$57.20**, ◊ **$6.60 - $8.80**, BC EFT MC VI.

MURWILLUMBAH NSW 2484

Pop 7,650. (848km N Sydney), See map on page 54, ref E1. Northern rivers town situated on the banks of the Tweed River, against a backdrop of patchwork canefields and the spectacular Mount Warning. Bowls, Golf, Swimming, Tennis.

Hotels/Motels

AAA
TOURISM
Special Rates

★★★☆ **Murwillumbah Motor Inn**, (M), 17 Byangum Sts, 500m W of PO, ☎ 02 6672 2022, fax 02 6672 2143, (2 stry gr fl) 31 units [shwr, tlt, a/c, heat, elec blkts, tel, TV, movie, clock radio, t/c mkg, refrig, toaster], ldry, pool (salt water), bbq, cots-fee. **RO** ♦♦ **$64 - $104**, ◊ **$14 - $16**, ch con, AE BC DC MC VI, 🐾♿.

★★★☆ **Poinciana Motel**, (M), 453 Pacific Hwy, 1.5km S of Railway, ☎ 02 6672 3666, fax 02 6672 6101, (2 stry gr fl), 10 units [shwr, tlt, a/c, elec blkts, tel, TV, movie, clock radio, t/c mkg, refrig], ldry, pool (salt water), bbq, dinner to unit, cots-fee, non smoking units (6). **RO** ♦ **$55 - $66**, ♦♦ **$61 - $72**, ♦♦♦ **$73 - $77**, ♦♦♦♦ **$86**, AE BC DC EFT MC VI.

★★★ **Town Motel & Eatery**, (M), 3 Wharf St, 100m N of RSL Club, ☎ 02 6672 8600, fax 02 6672 8601, 10 units [shwr, tlt, a/c, c/fan, fax, TV, radio, t/c mkg, refrig, toaster], ldry, ✕ (BYO), rm serv, c/park (undercover). **RO** ♦ **$50 - $55**, ♦♦ **$55 - $65**, ◊ **$10**, AE BC DC EFT MC VI.

★★★ **Tweed River Motel**, (M), 55 Pacific Hwy, 3km N of PO, ☎ 02 6672 3933, fax 02 6672 5798, 15 units [shwr, tlt, a/c, tel, TV, video, clock radio, t/c mkg, refrig, mini bar, micro (2), toaster], ldry, lounge, pool, bbq, dinner to unit, plygr, cots, non smoking units (7). **D** **$74**, **RO** ♦ **$55**, ♦♦ **$59**, ♦♦♦ **$69**, AE BC DC EFT MC MCH VI.

Self Catering Accommodation

★★★★★ **Durobby Retreat**, (Cotg), Lot 3 Solomons Rd Mt Warning via, 10km S of PO, ☎ 02 6679 5570, fax 02 6679 5570, 2 cotgs acc up to 2, (1 bedrm), [shwr, tlt, a/c, c/fan, elec blkts, TV, video, radio, t/c mkg, refrig, cook fac, micro, toaster, blkts, doonas, linen, pillows], ldry, pool, bbq, c/park (undercover), breakfast ingredients, non smoking property. **BLB** ♦♦ **$220 - $242**, BC VI.

★★★★★ **Wollumbin Palms Retreat**, (Cotg), Lot 6, 112 Mount Warning Rd, ☎ 02 6679 5063, fax 02 6679 5278, 3 cotgs acc up to 2, [shwr, spa bath, tlt, a/c-cool, fire pl (3), heat, elec blkts (1), tel, TV, video, clock radio, CD, t/c mkg, refrig, cook fac, micro, toaster, blkts, linen, pillows], bbq, c/park (carport). **D** **$230 - $245**, Min book applies, BC MC VI.

★★★★☆ **Gibbyean Holiday Accommodation**, (Cotg), Kyogle Rd, Byangum, ☎ 02 6672 1087, 1 cotg acc up to 6, [shwr, bath (1), tlt, c/fan, fire pl (1), heat (1), TV, clock radio, t/c mkg, refrig, cook fac, micro, d/wash (1), toaster, ldry, blkts, linen, pillows], w/mach (2), dryer (1), iron, bbq, c/park (carport), non smoking property. **D** **$350**, Min book applies.

★★★★☆ **Torokina Cottage**, (House), off Pacific Hwy, 2km S of railway station, ☎ 02 6672 1218, fax 02 6672 6672, 1 house acc up to 6, (3 bedrm), [shwr (2), tlt (2), hairdry, c/fan, fire pl, elec blkts, tel, TV, video, clock radio, CD, t/c mkg, refrig, cook fac, micro, elec frypan, d/wash, toaster, ldry, doonas, linen], w/mach, dryer, iron, iron brd, bbq (2), c/park (carport), courtesy transfer (from airstrip), tennis, non smoking rms. **D** ♦ **$90**, ♦♦ **$120**, ◊ **$25**, **W** **$720**, Limited children's facilities. Breakfast available. BC MC VI.

Operator Comment: Visit our website on www.bigvolcano.com.au/custom/torokina

B&B's/Guest Houses

★★★★☆ **Hillcrest Bed & Breakfast**, (B&B), No children's facilities, Upper Crystal Creek Rd, Crystal Creek, 12km NW of PO, ☎ 02 6679 1023, 3 rms [ensuite, bath, hairdry, c/fan, heat, elec blkts, clock radio], iron, iron brd, lounge (TV, video, stereo), ✕, pool-heated, t/c mkg shared, refrig, bbq, c/park. **BB** ♦♦ **$100 - $130**, **DBB** ♦♦ **$170 - $200**, Min book Christmas and Jan, BC MC VI.

★★★★ **TreeTops Lodges**, (GH), Clothiers Creek Rd, 6km NE of Murwillumbah off Hwy, ☎ 02 6672 3068, fax 02 6672 5904, (2 stry), 15 rms (15 suites) [shwr, tlt, a/c, tel, TV, video, clock radio, t/c mkg, refrig, mini bar], conv fac, ⊠, non smoking rms. **BB** ♦ **$80 - $110**, BC DC EFT MC VI.

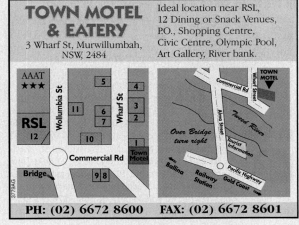

MURWILLUMBAH NSW continued...

★★★☆ Shiloh Coffee Bed & Breakfast, (B&B), Lot 3/22 Stokers Rd, 8km S of Murwillumbah PO, ☎ 02 6677 9554, (2 stry), 3 rms [hairdry, c/fan, tel, clock radio], ldry, lounge (TV), t/c mkg shared, refrig, bbq, non smoking property. **BB ♦ $60, ♦♦ $90**, Dinner by arrangement, BC MC VI.

Mount Warning Forest Hideaway, (GH), 460 Byrrill Creek Rd, 24km SW of PO, ☎ 02 6679 7277, fax 02 6679 7278, 7 rms [shwr, tlt, fan, heat, elec blkts, t/c mkg, refrig, cook fac, toaster], ldry, pool (salt water), bbq, c/park. **RO ♦♦ $66 - $155, ♦♦♦♦ $110 - $155, ♦♦♦♦ $550 - $1,085**, BC MC VI, (not yet classified).

Other Accommodation

Tweed River Houseboats, (Hbt), 161 Pacific Hwy, ☎ 02 6672 3525, fax 02 6672 8299, 2 houseboats [shwr, tlt, tel, TV, radio, refrig, cook fac, doonas, linen, pillows], bbq, c/park (garage). **W $685 - $1,395**, Min book applies, BC MC VI,

Operator Comment: Affordable comfort on the picturesque & peaceful Tweed River.

MUSWELLBROOK NSW 2333

Pop 10,550. (294km N Sydney), See map on pages 52/53, ref H4. Major centre of the upper Hunter, well placed as a base from which to tour the area's wineries. Art Gallery, Bowls, Golf, Horse Riding, Swimming, Tennis, Vineyards, Wineries.

Hotels/Motels

★★★☆ Baybrook Motor Inn, (M), New England Hwy, 2km S of PO, ☎ 02 6543 4888, fax 02 6541 1029, 12 units [shwr, tlt, hairdry, a/c, elec blkts, tel, cable tv, video (avail), clock radio, t/c mkg, refrig], ldry, iron, iron brd, pool, bbq, dinner to unit, courtesy transfer, cots, non smoking units (6). **RO ♦ $66 - $77, ♦♦ $77 - $88, ♦ $11**, AE BC DC MC VI.

　★★★★ (Serviced Apartment Section), 4 apts [shwr, tlt, hairdry, a/c, tel, cable tv, video (avail), clock radio, t/c mkg, refrig, cook fac ltd, micro, d/wash, toaster], w/mach, dryer, iron, iron brd, c/park (undercover), non smoking property. **D $100 - $180.**

★★★☆ Centabrook Motor Inn, (M), 111 Bridge St (New England Hwy), next to RSL Club, ☎ 02 6543 3444, fax 02 6541 1120, (2 stry gr fl), 16 units [shwr, tlt, hairdry, a/c, elec blkts, tel, cable tv, video (avail)-fee, clock radio, t/c mkg, refrig, toaster], ldry, iron, iron brd, pool, bbq, dinner to unit, cots, non smoking units. **RO ♦ $64 - $70, ♦♦ $75 - $80, ♦ $12**, ch con, AE BC DC EFT MC VI.

★★★☆ John Hunter Motel, (M), Maitland St (New England Hwy), 1.5km S of PO, ☎ 02 6543 4477, fax 02 6543 4962, (2 stry gr fl), 70 units [shwr, bath (4), tlt, hairdry, a/c, elec blkts, tel, cable tv, video (avail), clock radio, t/c mkg, refrig, mini bar], ldry, iron, iron brd, conv fac, ☒, pool, spa, bbq, rm serv, dinner to unit, cots-fee. **RO ♦ $85, ♦♦ $95, ♦♦♦ $105**, ch con, pen con, AE BC DC EFT JCB MC MP VI.

★★★☆ Muswellbrook Motor Inn, (M), New England Hwy, 600m S of PO, ☎ 02 6543 1531, fax 02 6543 3480, 10 units [shwr, tlt, hairdry, a/c, elec blkts, tel, TV, video (avail), movie, clock radio, t/c mkg, refrig, toaster], iron, iron brd, pool, bbq, meals to unit, courtesy transfer, cots-fee, non smoking units (7). **RO ♦ $54 - $59, ♦♦ $64 - $69, ♦ $6 - $11**, AE BC DC EFT MC VI.

★★★☆ Noah's In The Valley, (M), 91 Bridge St (New England Hwy), 200m N of PO, ☎ 02 6543 2833, fax 02 6543 2170, 36 units [shwr, bath (2), tlt, a/c, elec blkts, tel, TV, video-fee, clock radio, t/c mkg, refrig, mini bar, toaster], ☒ (Mon to Sat), pool, rm serv. **RO ♦ $64.90, ♦♦ $75.90, ♦♦♦ $86.90, ♦ $11**, ch con, AE BC DC MC VI, ♦&.

★★★☆ Sovereign Inn, (M), Cnr New England Hwy & Bell St, 1km S of PO, ☎ 02 6543 1188, fax 02 6543 1486, (2 stry gr fl), 37 units [shwr, tlt, hairdry, a/c, elec blkts, tel, cable tv, video-fee, clock radio, t/c mkg, refrig], ldry, iron, iron brd, ☒ (Mon to Sat), pool, bbq, dinner to unit, cots, non smoking units (13). **RO ♦ $76 - $86, ♦♦ $76 - $86, ♦ $11**, 6 family units of a lower rating, AE BC DC EFT MC VI.

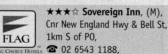

★★★☆ The Wayfarer Motel, (M), 124 Maitland St, 2km S of PO, ☎ 02 6541 1744, fax 02 6543 4655, 23 units [shwr, tlt, hairdry, a/c, elec blkts, tel, TV, video, clock radio, t/c mkg, refrig], ldry, iron, iron brd, pool, cook fac, bbq, dinner to unit, cots, non smoking units (9). **RO ♦ $60 - $67, ♦♦ $66 - $76, ♦ $11**, ch con, AE BC DC EFT MC MP VI.

★★★ Red Cedar Motel, (M), 12 Maitland St (New England Hwy), 500m S of PO, ☎ 02 6543 2852, fax 02 6543 2852, 10 units [shwr, tlt, hairdry, a/c, elec blkts, tel, fax, TV, video-fee, movie, clock radio, t/c mkg, refrig, toaster, ldry], iron, iron brd, cots-fee, non smoking units (5). **D $83 - $85, RO ♦ $53 - $55, ♦♦ $64 - $68, ♦♦♦ $72 - $75, ♦ $8**, AE BC EFT MC VI.

B&B's/Guest Houses

★★★★☆ Muswellbrook Rose Gardens Bed & Breakfast, (B&B), 14 Foley St, Upper Hunter Valley, ☎ 02 6543 2285, fax 02 6541 2111, (Multi-stry), 2 rms [shwr, tlt, hairdry, a/c, c/fan, cent heat, elec blkts, TV, clock radio, t/c mkg, refrig, ldry], pool (salt water), bbq, cots, non smoking rms. **BB ♦ $70, ♦♦ $90, ♦ $20**, ch con, 1 room yet to be rated, BC MC VI,

Operator Comment: www.rosegardens.com.au email: rosegardens@hunterlink.com.net.au. This quiet retreat is set in a beautiful garden with King Parrots and native birds.

★★★★ The Old Manse, (B&B), 106 Hill St, 500m N of PO, ☎ 02 6543 3965, fax 02 6541 1918, 1 rm (1 suite) [ensuite, bath, fan, heat (elec), elec blkts, TV, clock radio, t/c mkg, refrig, cook fac, micro, ldry], pool (outdoor), meals to unit, non smoking rms (1). **BB ♦ $70, ♦♦ $90**, BC MC VI.

NABIAC NSW 2312

Pop 550. (314km N Sydney), See map on page 54, ref B8. Pretty town just north of the junction of the Pacific Highway and the Bucketts Way. Bush Walking, Scenic Drives, Tennis.

Self Catering Accommodation

★★★★ Country Roads Farm Stay, 3736 Wallanbah Rd, 2.5km W of PO, ☎ 02 6554 1396, fax 02 6554 1001, 2 cabins acc up to 7, (2 bedrm), [shwr, tlt, a/c, fan, heat (wood), elec blkts, TV, video, clock radio, t/c mkg, refrig, cook fac, micro, blkts, doonas, linen, pillows], ldry, bbq, cots, breakfast ingredients, non smoking property. **D ♦♦ $125, ♦ $49**, ch con, weekly con, Min book applies.

B&B's/Guest Houses

★★★★★ Silver Gums Country Home, (B&B), 91 Cusack La, Dyers Crossing 2429 ☎ 02 6550 2318, fax 02 6550 2318, (2 stry), 4 rms [ensuite, a/c, heat, elec blkts, doonas], ldry, lounge (cable TV, video), lounge firepl, pool, t/c mkg shared, refrig, bbq, non smoking property. **BB ♦ $176, ♦♦ $198, ♦ $25**, Other meals by arrangement, BC MC VI.

★★★☆ Bundacreek Country Lodge, (GH), Minimbah Rd, ☎ 02 6554 1133, fax 02 6554 1133, 5 rms [shwr, tlt, c/fan, heat, tel, TV, clock radio, t/c mkg (3), refrig, cook fac (2), micro], ldry, rec rm, pool, bbq, rm serv, plygr, canoeing, golf. **RO ♦ $85 - $130, ♦♦ $95 - $140, ♦ $14**, ch con, Min book applies, BC MC VI.

NAMBUCCA HEADS NSW 2448

Pop 6,250. (512km N Sydney), See map on page 54, ref C5. Old north coast timber town that has been welcoming tourists since the 1920s. It's still a popular holiday destination with its beautiful waterways and plenty of things to see and do. Boating, Bowls, Fishing, Golf, Scenic Drives, Surfing, Tennis.

Hotels/Motels

★★★★ Destiny Motor Inn, (M), Cnr Pacific Hwy & Riverside Dve, 2km S of PO, ☎ 02 6568 8044, fax 02 6568 6083, 37 units [shwr, bath (6), tlt, hairdry, a/c, tel, TV, video, clock radio, t/c mkg, refrig, mini bar, toaster], ldry, iron brd, conv fac, ☒, pool (salt water), sauna, spa, bbq, rm serv, dinner to unit, cots. **RO ♦ $85 - $122, ♦♦ $97 - $122, ♦ $12**, AE BC DC MC MP VI.

★★★☆ Miramar Motel, (M), 1 Nelson St, 250m S of PO, ☎ 02 6568 7899, fax 02 6568 6591, 20 units (4 suites) [shwr, tlt, hairdry, fan, heat, tel, TV, clock radio, t/c mkg, refrig, cook fac (5), toaster], ldry, pool, spa, bbq, cots. **RO ♦ $52 - $74, ♦♦ $63 - $85, ♦♦♦ $74 - $107, ♦ $11, Suite D ♦♦ $74 - $107**, AE BC DC MC VI.

★★★☆ Nambucca Motor Inn, (M), 88 Pacific Hwy, 3km S of PO, ☎ 02 6568 6300, fax 02 6568 5546, 12 units [shwr, tlt, hairdry, a/c (4), c/fan, heat, elec blkts, tel, TV, video-fee, clock radio, t/c mkg, refrig, cook fac (1), micro (1)], ldry, rec rm, ☒, pool, bbq, dinner to unit, c/park (undercover) (8), boat park, trailer park, courtesy transfer, cots-fee. **RO ♦ $55 - $95, ♦♦ $55 - $95, ♦♦♦ $65 - $100, ♦ $12**, AE BC DC EFT MC MCH VI.

★★★☆ **The Nambucca Resort**, (M), Pacific Hwy, 4km S of PO, ☎ 02 6568 6899, fax 02 6568 8173, 27 units [shwr, tlt, hairdry, a/c, elec blkts, tel, TV, video, clock radio, t/c mkg, refrig, mini bar (8)], ldry, rec rm, conv fac, ✉, bar, pool, bbq, dinner to unit, plygr, canoeing-fee, golf (driving range), cots-fee, non smoking units (10). **RO** ┃ **$74 - $88**, ┇┇ **$88 - $99**, ┇┇┇ **$98 - $109**, ┃ **$10**, AE BC DC MC MP VI.

★★★ **Max Motel**, (M), 4 Fraser St (Old Pacific Hwy), 300m S of PO, ☎ 02 6568 6138, fax 02 6568 9478, (2 stry), 9 units [shwr, tlt, c/fan, heat, elec blkts, TV, clock radio, t/c mkg, refrig, toaster], cots-fee, non smoking units. **RO** ┃ **$45 - $102**, ┇┇ **$45 - $102**, ┃ **$11**, 2 units ★★★☆. 2 units ★★☆. Min book Christmas Jan and Easter, BC MC VI.

★★☆ **Coolawin Gardens Motel**, (M), Bellwood Dve, 1km SW of PO, ☎ 02 6568 6304, fax 02 6568 6304, 7 units [shwr, tlt, a/c-cool, fan, heat, elec blkts, TV, clock radio, t/c mkg, refrig, cook fac (1), micro, toaster], ldry, bbq, c/park (undercover), cots, non smoking units. **RO** ┃ **$44 - $60**, ┇┇ **$50 - $60**, ┃ **$10**, ch con, BC MC VI.

★★ **Blue Dolphin Motel**, (M), Fraser St, 75m N of RSL, ☎ 02 6568 6700, fax 02 6568 9235, (Multi-stry), 20 units (1 suite) [shwr, bath (1), tlt, a/c (6), c/fan, heat, tel, TV, video-fee, clock radio, t/c mkg, refrig, toaster], ldry, pool, bbq, rm serv, cots-fee. **D** ┃ **$50 - $60**, ┇┇ **$55 - $65**, ┃ **$11 - $16**, weekly con, AE BC DC EFT MC VI.

★★ **Jabiru Motel**, (M), Pacific Hwy, 3km S of PO, ☎ 02 6568 6204, fax 02 6568 6204, 8 units [shwr, tlt, hairdry (on request), c/fan, heat, elec blkts, TV, t/c mkg, refrig, cook fac (3), toaster], iron (on request), pool, bbq, meals to unit (breakfast), c/park (undercover), tennis (half court), non smoking units (7). **RO** ┃ **$39 - $50**, ┇┇ **$42 - $61**, ┇┇┇ **$53 - $66**, ┃ **$11**, AE BC MC VI.

B&B's/Guest Houses

★★★★ **Beilbys Beach House**, (GH), 1 Ocean St, ☎ 02 6568 6466, fax 02 6568 5822, (2 stry), 5 rms [ensuite (3), shwr (3), tlt (3), fan, heat, tel, TV], ldry, ✕, pool (salt water), cook fac, t/c mkg shared, refrig, bbq, plygr, bicycle, cots-fee, non smoking property. **BB** ┃ **$35 - $60**, ┇┇ **$44 - $82.50**, ┃ **$15 - $20**, weekly con, BC MC VI.

★★★☆ **Dunaber House B&B**, (B&B), 35 Piggott St, ☎ 02 6568 9434, fax 02 6569 4566, 2 rms [shwr, tlt, c/fan, heat, elec blkts, tel, TV, video, clock radio, t/c mkg, refrig], ldry, iron, iron brd, bbq, non smoking rms (2). **BB** ♦ **$50.50 - $70.50,** ♦♦ **$66 - $104.50,** ◊ **$16.50,** ch con.

★★★☆ **Scotts Bed & Breakfast**, (GH), 4 Wellington Dve, 500m S of PO, ☎ 02 6568 6386, fax 02 6569 4169, (2 stry), 8 rms [shwr, tlt, hairdry, fan, heat, elec blkts, TV, clock radio, t/c mkg, refrig], ✕ (Closed Sun), bbq, c/park (undercover). **BB** ♦ **$70 - $90,** ♦♦ **$70 - $110,** ◊ **$10 - $25,** AE BC DC MC VI.

Scotts Bed & Breakfast Guesthouse

AAAT ★★★☆

HISTORY • HOSPITALITY • QUALITY

Scotts Guesthouse offers eight deluxe ensuited guest rooms opening onto private balconies with spectacular ocean and river views. Each room features queen size beds, colour TV's, fans, fridges, hairdryers, clock radios, tea & coffee making facilities. Undercover parking provided. Walking distance to river, beaches, shops, clubs & next door to two seafood restaurants.

All major cards accepted

Cead Mile Failte

Hosts Robert & Joan Scott,
Wellington Drive, Nambucca Heads
Website: www.here.com.au/scotts

Phone: (02) 6568 6386 Fax: (02) 6569 4169

Trouble-free travel tips - Hoses and belts

Inspect the condition of radiator hoses, heater hose fan and air conditioner belts.

NANA GLEN NSW 2450

Pop Nominal, See map on page 54, ref D4. Small town in the Orara Valley between Glenreagh and Coramba, surrounded by lush north coast forests.

Self Catering Accommodation

★★★ **Kia-Ora Organic Certified Farm**, (Farm), Kia-Ora Farm, 28km NW of Coffs Harbour, ☎ 02 6654 3561, fax 02 6654 3561, 3 cabins acc up to 6, [shwr, tlt, heat, tel, TV, t/c mkg, refrig, cook fac, toaster, linen, pillows], iron, iron brd, pool above ground, bbq, courtesy transfer. **D** ♦♦ **$50,** ◊ **$9, W** ♦♦ **$300,** ch con, 1 cabin yet to be assessed, BC MC VI.

NAROOMA NSW 2546

Pop 3,400. (345km S Sydney), See map on page 55, ref A7. Narooma swirls around the hills and shores of Wagonga Inlet and is one of the gems of the south coast. Boating, Bowls, Bush Walking, Fishing, Golf, Squash, Surfing, Swimming, Tennis.

Hotels/Motels

★★★☆ **Amooran Court**, (M), 30 Montague St, 500m E of PO, ☎ 02 4476 2198, fax 02 4476 2374, 13 units [shwr, spa bath (4), tlt, a/c, elec blkts, tel, TV, video (9), clock radio, t/c mkg, refrig, cook fac, micro, elec frypan, toaster], ldry, pool-heated, bbq, plygr, cots, non smoking units (7). **W** **$385 - $1,300, RO** ♦ **$60 - $185,** ♦♦ **$65 - $200,** ◊ **$12,** 6 units ★★★. AE BC MC VI, ♿.

★★★☆ **(Holiday Unit Section)**, (Multi-stry gr fl), 14 units acc up to 6, [shwr, tlt, a/c, elec blkts, tel, TV, t/c mkg, refrig, cook fac, micro, toaster, blkts, linen, pillows], cots. **D** ♦ **$55 - $150,** ♦♦ **$65 - $135,** ◊ **$12, W** **$275 - $1,200.**

★★★☆ **Coastal Comfort Motel**, (M), Cnr Tilba St & Princes Hwy, 200m S of PO, ☎ 02 4476 2256, fax 02 4426 2256, (2 stry gr fl), 12 units (1 suite) [shwr, tlt, hairdry, fan, heat, elec blkts, tel, TV, video-fee, clock radio, t/c mkg, refrig, cook fac, micro], ldry, iron brd, pool, bbq, cots, non smoking rms (6). **RO** ♦ **$59 - $95,** ♦♦ **$68 - $99,** ◊ **$12,** AE BC DC EFT MC VI.

★★★☆ **Farnboro Motel**, (M), 206 Princes Hwy, 2km S of PO, ☎ 02 4476 4611, fax 02 4476 4294, 13 units (2 suites) [shwr, spa bath (1), tlt, fan, heat, elec blkts, tel, TV, video, clock radio, t/c mkg, refrig, cook fac (5), toaster], ldry, pool (solar heated), bbq, dinner to unit (breakfast), boat park (2), car wash, plygr, cots. **W $360, RO ♦ $60 - $95, ♦♦ $60 - $95, ♦♦♦ $72 - $110, ◊ $12, Suite D $75 - $145**, pen con, AE BC DC MC VI.

★★★☆ **Festival Motor Inn**, (M), 126 Princes Hwy, 100m S of PO, ☎ 02 4476 2099, fax 02 4476 2641, (2 stry gr fl), 28 units [shwr, tlt, hairdry, a/c, elec blkts, tel, TV, video (avail), clock radio, t/c mkg, refrig], ldry, ⊠, pool, rm serv, cots-fee. **D $77 - $110**, AE BC DC MC VI.

★★★☆ **Holiday Lodge Motel**, (M), Princes Hwy, 200m S of PO, ☎ 02 4476 2282, fax 02 4476 2425, (2 stry gr fl), 12 units [shwr, tlt, a/c, elec blkts, tel, TV, video-fee, clock radio, t/c mkg, refrig, cook fac (micro)], ldry, pool, bbq, cots. **W $310 - $600, RO ♦ $55 - $80, ♦♦ $65 - $95, ◊ $10 - $11**, AE BC DC EFT MC VI.

★★★☆ **Whale Motor Inn**, (M), Wagonga St (Princes Hwy), 50m N of PO, ☎ 02 4476 2411, (2 stry gr fl), 17 units [shwr, bath (1), spa bath (2), tlt, hairdry, a/c, heat, elec blkts, tel, movie, clock radio, t/c mkg, refrig], conv fac, ⊠ (Mon to Sat), pool, bbq, rm serv, cots. **RO ♦ $80, ♦♦ $90 - $145, ◊ $10**, AE BC DC EFT MC VI.

★★★ **Olympic Lodge**, (M), 76 Princes Hwy, 700m N of PO, ☎ 02 4476 2379, 4 units [shwr, tlt, fan, heat, elec blkts, TV, video, clock radio, t/c mkg, refrig, cook fac, toaster], ldry, bbq, rm serv. **RO ♦ $49.50 - $82.50, ♦♦ $55 - $88, ◊ $11 - $16.50**, ch con, BC MC VI.

★★★ **Tree Motel**, (M), 213 Princes Hwy, 1km S of PO, ☎ 02 4476 4233, fax 02 4476 3594, 13 units [shwr, tlt, a/c, fan, heat, elec blkts, tel, TV, video-fee, clock radio, t/c mkg, refrig, cook fac (4)], ldry, pool-heated, spa, bbq, cots. **RO ♦♦ $50 - $80, ◊ $8 - $10**, ch con, BC MC VI.

★★☆ **Forsters Bay Lodge**, (M), Forsters Bay Rd, 1.2km NW of PO, ☎ 02 4476 2319, fax 02 4476 1735, 6 units [shwr, tlt, heat, elec blkts, TV, t/c mkg, refrig, cook fac], ldry, bbq, cots. **RO ♦ $55 - $71.50, ♦♦ $55 - $71.50, ◊ $9.90 - $11.**

★★☆ **Narooma Motel**, (M), 243 Princes Hwy, 2km S of PO, ☎ 02 4476 4270, 14 units [shwr, tlt, fan, heat, elec blkts, TV, video-fee, t/c mkg, refrig, cook fac (4)], spa, bbq (area), cots-fee. **RO ♦ $49 - $69, ♦♦ $53 - $83**, 6 units of a lesser rating. AE BC DC EFT MC MCH VI.

Self Catering Accommodation

★★★★ **Mystery Bay Cottages**, (Cotg), 121 Mystery Bay Rd Mystery Bay, 10km S of Narooma, ☎ 02 4473 7431, 6 cotgs acc up to 5, [shwr, tlt, fire pl, TV, clock radio, t/c mkg, refrig, cook fac, micro, toaster, ldry (in unit), blkts, linen, pillows], w/mach, iron, rec rm, bbq, c/park (carport), tennis. **D ♦♦ $82.50, ◊ $11, W ♦♦ $462 - $825**, ch con, Min book applies.

★★★ **Apollo Units**, (HU), 16 McMillan Rd, 1km NW of PO, ☎ 02 4476 2461, (2 stry gr fl), 27 units acc up to 6, [shwr, tlt, heat, elec blkts, TV, clock radio, t/c mkg, refrig, cook fac, micro, elec frypan, toaster, ldry, linen reqd], iron, pool (salt water), bbq, ☎, tennis, cots-fee. **D ♦♦ $50 - $110, ◊ $5 - $11, W ♦♦ $205 - $650, ◊ $22 - $27,**

Operator Comment: Friendly family accommodation with 3 acres of room for the boat or the kids.

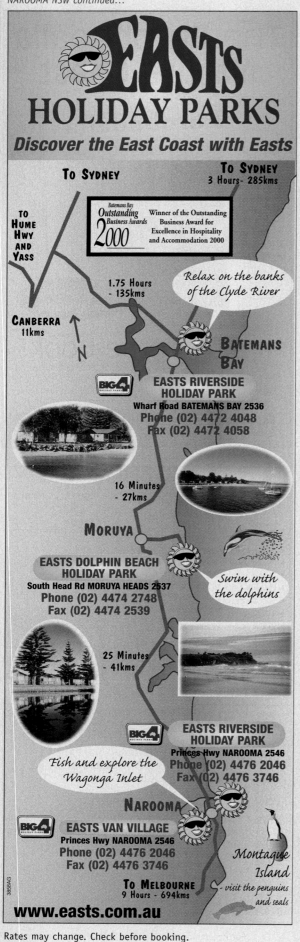

EASTS HOLIDAY PARKS

Discover the East Coast with Easts

Batemans Bay
Outstanding Business Awards
2000
Winner of the Outstanding Business Award for Excellence in Hospitality and Accommodation 2000

To Sydney

To Sydney
3 Hours- 285kms

To Hume Hwy and Yass

1.75 Hours - 135kms

Relax on the banks of the Clyde River

Canberra
11kms

N

BATEMANS BAY

BIG4

EASTS RIVERSIDE HOLIDAY PARK
Wharf Road BATEMANS BAY 2536
Phone (02) 4472 4048
Fax (02) 4472 4058

16 Minutes - 27kms

MORUYA

EASTS DOLPHIN BEACH HOLIDAY PARK
South Head Rd MORUYA HEADS 2537
Phone (02) 4474 2748
Fax (02) 4474 2539

Swim with the dolphins

25 Minutes - 41kms

BIG4

EASTS RIVERSIDE HOLIDAY PARK
Princes Hwy NAROOMA 2546
Phone (02) 4476 2046
Fax (02) 4476 3746

Fish and explore the Wagonga Inlet

NAROOMA

BIG4

EASTS VAN VILLAGE
Princes Hwy NAROOMA 2546
Phone (02) 4476 2046
Fax (02) 4476 3746

To Melbourne
9 Hours - 694kms

Montague Island - visit the penguins and seals

www.easts.com.au

★★★ **Clark Bay Farm**, (Farm), 467 Riverview Rd, 4.7km W of Narooma Bridge, ☎ 02 4476 1640, fax 02 4476 1640, 3 cabins acc up to 6, [shwr, spa bath (1), tlt, hairdry, a/c, TV, video, clock radio, t/c mkg, refrig, cook fac, micro, elec frypan, d/wash (1), toaster, ldry, blkts, linen], w/mach, dryer, iron, iron brd, rec rm, conf fac, pool-heated (salt water), spa, bbq, plygr, tennis, non smoking property. **D $99 - $154, W $900**, ch con, Min book applies, AE BC DC MC VI.

★★★ **Countess Court**, (HU), 10 Ballingalla St, 2km S of PO, ☎ 02 4476 2169, fax 02 4476 1677, (2 stry), 1 unit acc up to 5, [shwr, bath, tlt, TV, refrig, cook fac, micro, d/wash, toaster, ldry (in unit), linen reqd], pool, bbq, c/park (garage). **W $420 - $875**, Min book applies, BC EFT MC VI.

★★★ **Eastview**, (HU), 16 Tilba St, 350m S of PO, ☎ 02 4476 2169, fax 02 4476 1677, (2 stry), 1 unit acc up to 5, [shwr, bath, tlt, heat, TV, clock radio, t/c mkg, refrig, cook fac, micro, elec frypan, d/wash, toaster], w/mach, dryer, iron, c/park (garage). **W $385 - $875**, Min book applies, BC EFT MC VI.

★★★ **Grand Pacific**, (HU), 95-97 Wharf St, ☎ 02 4476 2169, fax 02 4476 1677, (2 stry), 1 unit acc up to 5, [shwr, bath, tlt, fan, heat, TV, refrig, cook fac, micro, d/wash, toaster, ldry, linen reqd], w/mach, dryer, iron, c/park (garage). **W $420 - $875**, Min book applies, BC EFT MC VI.

★★★ **Lavender Point Holiday Units**, (HU), 8 Lavender Point Rd, 1.5km N of po, ☎ 02 4476 2851, fax 02 4476 2159, 7 units acc up to 6, [shwr, tlt, fan, heat, elec blkts, TV, refrig, cook fac, micro, linen], ldry, bbq, c/park (undercover), boat park. **D ♦♦ $60 - $95, ♦ $12, W $260 - $630**, ch con.

★★★ **Nankeen Units**, (HU), 4 Burrawang St, ☎ 02 4476 2814, fax 02 4476 2814, 2 units acc up to 4, [shwr, tlt, fan, heat, TV, radio, refrig, cook fac, micro, toaster, ldry (in unit)], bbq. **W $250 - $500.**

★★★ **Narooma Golfers Lodge**, (HU), 8 Bluewater Dve, 500m E of PO, ☎ 02 4476 2428, 6 units acc up to 5, [shwr, tlt, tel, TV, refrig, cook fac, linen reqd-fee], ldry, bbq. **D ♦ $45 - $50, ♦♦ $50 - $55, ♦♦♦ $55 - $65, ♦ $5 - $10, W $230 - $510.**

★★★ **Narooma Palms**, (HU), 21a Tilba St, 500m E of PO, ☎ 02 4476 2928, fax 02 4476 2928, 9 units acc up to 5, [shwr, tlt, fan, heat, elec blkts, TV, refrig, cook fac, micro, elec frypan, toaster, linen reqd-fee], ldry, w/mach, dryer, iron, pool (salt water), spa, bbq, cots-fee. **D $55 - $120, W $225 - $700**, Min book Christmas Jan and Easter, BC MC VI.

★★★ **Roses Units**, (HU), 19 Tilba St, ☎ 02 4476 2079, fax 02 4476 1940, 7 units acc up to 5, [shwr, tlt, heat, TV, video, refrig, cook fac, micro, toaster, ldry], c/park (garage). **W $220 - $591.**

★★☆ **Cooinda Flats**, (HU), 170 Princes Hwy, 1km S of PO, ☎ 02 4476 2536, 6 units acc up to 6, [shwr, tlt, heat, elec blkts, TV, clock radio, t/c mkg, refrig, cook fac, elec frypan, toaster, linen reqd-fee], ldry, iron, bbq, cots. **D $50 - $80, W $200 - $500.**

★★☆ **Oakleigh Holiday Farm**, (Farm), Mystery Bay Rd, Mystery Bay, 11km S of Narooma, ☎ 02 4473 7219, fax 02 4473 7219, 6 cabins acc up to 15, [shwr, bath (2), tlt, c/fan (1), fire pl (3), heat (3), TV, radio, t/c mkg, refrig, cook fac, micro (5), elec frypan (2), toaster, ldry (in unit) (4), linen reqd-fee], ldry, w/mach (4), iron, rec rm, bbq, cots. **D $77 - $120, W $385 - $770**, ch con, Min book applies, BC MC VI.

★★☆ **Pacific Pines**, (HU), 4 Wharf St, ☎ 02 4476 2169, fax 02 4476 1677, (2 stry), 1 unit acc up to 5, [shwr, tlt, heat, TV, refrig, cook fac, micro, elec frypan, toaster, ldry (in unit), linen reqd], w/mach, dryer, iron, c/park (garage). **D $70 - $100, W $325 - $735**, Min book applies.

Inlet Views Holiday Lodge Motel, (HU), Previously Belvedere Lodge Motel. 15 Fosters Bay Rd, 1km W of PO, ☎ 02 4476 2483, fax 02 4476 5291, 6 units acc up to 2, [shwr, tlt, heat, TV, refrig, cook fac, blkts, linen, pillows]. **D ♦♦ $55, ♦ $10, W ♦♦ $250 - $500**, ch con, Min book Christmas Jan long w/ends and Easter, (Rating under review).

Kianga, (Cotg), 8 Pacific Ave, Kianga, ☎ 02 4476 2169, fax 02 4476 1677, 1 cotg acc up to 8, [shwr, bath, tlt, heat, elec blkts, tel, TV, clock radio, t/c mkg, refrig, cook fac, micro, elec frypan, d/wash, toaster, linen reqd], w/mach-fee, dryer-fee, iron, bbq, c/park (garage), cots. **D $100 - $150, W $490 - $1,015**, Min book applies, BC EFT MC VI, (not yet classified).

B&B's/Guest Houses

★★★★ **Bay Street Bed and Breakfast**, (B&B), 5 Bay St, 400m E of PO, ☎ 02 4476 3336, fax 02 4476 3336, (2 stry gr fl), 2 rms [ensuite, spa bath (1), heat, TV, video, clock radio, t/c mkg, refrig, micro (1), doonas], non smoking property. **BB ♦ $110 - $150, ♦♦ $120 - $160**, Min book long w/ends and Easter, BC MC VI.

**island view beach resort
Narooma**

holiday cabins
spa cabins
powered sites
camping sites
playground
bbq areas
beach front
25m heated pool
kids club
group bookings

Princes Hwy 2 km south of Narooma
Bookings
ph 1800 465 432
or visit
www.islandview.com.au
★ ★ ★ ★ AAAT

Award Winning Tourist Park

★★★★ **Bellbird Farm Cottage**, (B&B), (Farm), 30 Lilyvale Pl, 7km S of PO, ☎ 02 4476 3210, fax 02 4476 3210, 2 rms [shwr, tlt, c/fan, heat, elec blkts, TV, t/c mkg, refrig, cook fac ltd, micro, toaster, ldry], ✕, plygr, cots. BB ⋔ $70, ⋔⋔ $85 - $95, ◊ $20, ch con.

★★★ **(Cottage Section)**, (2 stry gr fl), 1 cotg acc up to 9, (3 bedrm), [shwr, bath, tlt, hairdry, c/fan, heat, elec blkts, tel, TV, clock radio, t/c mkg, refrig, cook fac, micro, elec frypan, toaster, linen, pillows], w/mach, dryer, iron, iron brd, bbq, plygr, cots. D ⋔⋔ $65 - $85, ◊ $15 - $20, W ⋔⋔ $375 - $600, ◊ $70 - $105.

★★★★ **Pub Hill Farm**, (B&B), (Farm), Scenic Dve, 8km W of PO, ☎ 02 4476 3177, fax 02 4476 3177, 4 rms [shwr, tlt, hairdry, fan, fire pl (1), heat, elec blkts, tel, TV, video (avail), clock radio, t/c mkg, refrig, micro], lounge (TV), bbq, Pets allowed. BB ⋔ $70, ⋔⋔ $80 - $105, Min book long w/ends and Easter.

NARRABRI NSW 2390

Pop 6,400. (568km NW Sydney), See map on pages 52/53, ref H2. Narrabri lies in the heart of the Namoi Valley and is one of the North West region's major administrative centres. Bowls, Fishing, Golf, Swimming, Tennis. See also Boggarbri & Wee Waa.

Hotels/Motels

★★★★ **Nandewar Motor Inn**, (M), Cnr Newell Hwy & Ann St, 1km W of PO, ☎ 02 6792 1155, fax 02 6792 2889, 44 units (2 suites) [shwr, spa bath (16), tlt, a/c, fan, heat, elec blkts, tel, TV, video, clock radio, t/c mkg, refrig], ldry, iron, iron brd, ✕ (Mon to Sat), pool, car wash, plygr, tennis (half court), cots-fee. RO ⋔ $77 - $99, ⋔⋔ $88 - $99, ⋔⋔⋔ $99 - $110, ◊ $11, Suite D $99 - $143, ch con, 20 units ★★★★, AE BC DC EFT MC MP VI.

★★★☆ **Aalbany Motel**, (M), 38 Cooma Rd (Newell Highway), 2.5km S of PO, ☎ 02 6792 4211, fax 02 6792 6142, 11 units [shwr, tlt, hairdry, a/c, elec blkts, tel, TV, movie, clock radio, t/c mkg, refrig, toaster], ldry, iron brd, pool (salt water), bbq, dinner to unit, cots. RO ⋔ $58, ⋔⋔ $68, ◊ $10, AE BC EFT MC VI.

★★★☆ **Aaron Inn Motel**, (M), 137 Barwan St (Newell Hwy), 700m N of PO, ☎ 02 6792 4000, fax 02 6792 1354, 11 units [shwr, tlt, hairdry, a/c, heat, elec blkts, tel, fax, cable tv, movie, clock radio, t/c mkg, refrig, toaster], ldry, iron, iron brd, pool (salt water), bbq, dinner to unit, plygr, cots, non smoking rms (6). RO ⋔ $63 - $68, ⋔⋔ $74, ⋔⋔⋔ $85, ◊ $10, AE BC DC EFT MC VI.

★★★☆ **Adelong Motel**, (M), 174 Maitland St, 200m N of PO, ☎ 02 6792 1488, fax 02 6792 1954, 27 units [shwr, spa bath (10), tlt, a/c, elec blkts, tel, TV, clock radio, t/c mkg, refrig], ldry, ✕ (Mon to Sat), pool, spa, c/park (undercover) (10), cots-fee. RO ⋔ $85 - $105, ⋔⋔ $85 - $105, ⋔⋔⋔ $105 - $125, ◊ $10, 5 units of a lower rating, AE BC DC EFT JCB MC MP VI.

★★★☆ **Bellview Motel**, (M), Newell Hwy (Cnr Barwan St), 200m N of PO, opposite Bowling Club, ☎ 02 6792 3844, fax 02 6792 3957, 16 units [shwr, tlt, hairdry, a/c, elec blkts, tel, cable tv, clock radio, t/c mkg, refrig, toaster], ldry, iron, iron brd, pool, bbq, boat park, cots, non smoking units (8). RO ⋔ $63 - $68, ⋔⋔ $68 - $76, ⋔⋔⋔ $79 - $86, ◊ $11, 8 units of a lower rating, AE BC DC EFT MC VI.

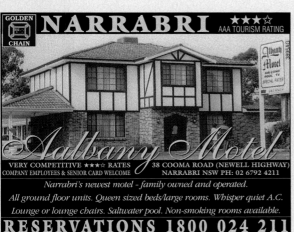

★★★☆ **Narrabri Mid Town Inn**, (M), 41 Maitland St, 600m S of PO, ☎ 02 6792 2233, fax 02 6792 3918, 19 units [shwr, tlt, a/c, elec blkts, tel, cable tv, video (avail), clock radio, t/c mkg, refrig], ldry, pool, dinner to unit (Mon - Thurs), cots-fee, non smoking units (7). **RO ♦ $74, ♦♦ $82, ♦♦♦ $92, ◊ $10**, AE BC DC EFT MC MP VI,

Operator Comment: Situated in town centre opposite police station. Quiet off highway location away from noise. Short walking distance to restaurants & RSL Club. Quality rooms to Flag standards at affordable rates. We pride ourselves on friendly country hospitality.

★★★ **Tommos Motor Lodge**, (M), 34 Cooma Rd (Newell Hwy), 2.5km S of PO, ☎ 02 6792 1922, fax 02 6792 4235, 12 units [shwr, tlt, a/c, elec blkts, tel, cable tv, video (avail), clock radio, t/c mkg, refrig, micro, toaster], ldry, pool (salt water), bbq, dinner to unit, meals to unit, boat park, trailer park, cots-fee, non smoking units (4).
RO ♦ $55 - $58, ♦♦ $66 - $70, ♦♦♦ $74 - $78, ◊ $9, AE BC DC EFT MC VI.

★★☆ **Kaputar Motel**, (M), 22 Cooma Rd (Newell Hwy), 3km S of PO, ☎ 02 6792 1550, fax 02 6792 4481, 13 units [shwr, tlt, a/c (4), heat (9), elec blkts, tel, cable tv, clock radio, t/c mkg, refrig, toaster], pool, bbq, dinner to unit (Mon to Sun), cots, non smoking units (6). **RO ♦ $50 - $55, ♦♦ $60 - $66, ◊ $10**, AE BC DC EFT MC VI.

★★ **Narrabri Motel**, (M), Newell Hwy, 2km SW of PO, ☎ 02 6792 2593, fax 02 6792 4559, (2 stry), 12 units [shwr, tlt, a/c-cool, heat, elec blkts, TV, t/c mkg, refrig, toaster], ldry, pool, bbq, cots. **RO ♦ $47 - $50, ♦♦ $54 - $58, ♦♦♦ $63 - $66, ◊ $9**, AE BC EFT MC VI.

B&B's/Guest Houses

★★★★ **Como Homestay**, (B&B), 26 Fraser St, 2km S of PO, ☎ 02 6792 3193, fax 02 6792 6066, 2 rms (1 suite) [shwr, bath (1), tlt, hairdry, evap cool (1), a/c (1), c/fan (1), heat, elec blkts, tel, TV, t/c mkg, refrig, micro], ldry, iron, iron brd, TV rm, lounge firepl, pool (salt water), bbq, dinner to unit, non smoking property. **BB ♦ $60 - $65, ♦♦ $80 - $85, ◊ $15**, ch con.

NARRANDERA NSW 2700

Pop 4,700. (556km SW Sydney), See map on pages 52/53, ref E6. Pretty rural centre on the Murrumbidgee River near the junction of the Sturt and Newell Highways. Boating, Bowls, Fishing, Golf, Swimming, Water Skiing. See also Grong Grong.

Hotels/Motels

★★★☆ **All Transit Motel**, (M), Sturt Hwy, at junction of Newell Hwy & Sturt Hwy, 2km S of PO, ☎ 02 6959 1155, fax 02 6959 1155, 14 units [shwr, tlt, a/c, heat, elec blkts, tel, TV, video-fee, clock radio, t/c mkg, refrig, toaster], pool, bbq, dinner to unit, cots, non smoking units (8). **RO ♦ $44 - $48, ♦♦ $53 - $58, ◊ $6.50**, AE BC DC EFT MC VI.

★★★☆ **Camellia Motel**, (M), 80 Whitton St, 700m N of PO, ☎ 02 6959 2633, fax 02 6959 2633, 15 units [shwr, tlt, hairdry (available), a/c, elec blkts, tel, TV, video-fee, clock radio, t/c mkg, refrig, toaster], pool, bbq, dinner to unit (sun to thurs), courtesy transfer, cots, non smoking units (5). **RO ♦ $46 - $51, ♦♦ $54 - $59**, AE BC DC EFT MC MCH VI.

★★★☆ **Country Roads Motor Inn**, (M), 92 Whitton St, 600m N of PO, ☎ 02 6959 3244, fax 02 6959 3245, 14 units [shwr, tlt, hairdry, a/c, heat, elec blkts, tel, TV, video, clock radio, t/c mkg, refrig, toaster], ldry, pool, bbq, dinner to unit, cots, non smoking units (5). **RO ♦ $63, ♦♦ $74, ♦♦♦ $85, ◊ $10**, AE BC DC EFT MC VI, &.

★★★☆ **Fig Tree Motel**, (M), Cnr King St & Newell Hwy, 700m NW of PO, ☎ 02 6959 1888, fax 02 6959 2261, (2 stry gr fl), 22 units (2 bedrm), [shwr, tlt, a/c, elec blkts, tel, cable tv, video (avail), clock radio, t/c mkg, refrig, toaster], ✉ (Mon to Sat), pool, dinner to unit, cots. **RO ♦ $55 - $65, ♦♦ $60 - $70, ◊ $8**, 6 units of a lower rating. AE BC DC MC MP VI.

★★★☆ **Gateway Motel**, (M), 152 East St, off Hwy, ☎ 02 6959 1877, fax 02 6959 1512, (2 stry gr fl), 38 units [shwr, tlt, hairdry, a/c, tel, TV, clock radio, t/c mkg, refrig, mini bar], ldry, conv fac, ✉ (6 days), bar, pool, rm serv, dinner to unit, c/park (undercover), cots. **RO ♦ $58 - $94.50, ♦♦ $65 - $94.50, ◊ $8**, AE BC DC EFT MC VI, *Operator Comment: Quiet off highway location.*

★★★☆ **Midtown Motor Inn**, (M), Cnr East & Larmer Sts, 200m S of PO, ☎ 02 6959 2122, fax 02 6959 3271, (Multi-stry gr fl), 20 units [shwr, tlt, hairdry, a/c, tel, cable tv, video-fee, clock radio, t/c mkg, refrig, toaster], iron, pool, bbq, dinner to unit, cots-fee, non smoking units (8). **RO ♦ $58 - $78, ♦♦ $68 - $78, ♦♦♦ $73 - $85, ◊ $10, $410 - $644**, AE BC EFT MC VI.

★★★☆ **Narrandera Club Motor Inn**, (M), Cnr Newell Hwy & Bolton St, 50m NW of PO, ☎ 02 6959 3123, fax 02 6959 3169, (2 stry gr fl), 30 units (4 suites) [shwr, spa bath (3), tlt, a/c, elec blkts, tel, TV, video, clock radio, t/c mkg, refrig, toaster], iron, iron brd, pool, cots. **RO ♦ $77 - $88, ♦♦ $82.50 - $126.50, ♦♦♦ $93.50 - $110, ◊ $7 - $10, Suite D $93.50 - $126.50**, AE BC DC MC MP VI.

★★★☆ **Newell Motor Inn**, (M), Newell Hwy, 2km SW of PO, ☎ 02 6959 2877, or 02 6959 2291, fax 02 6959 1381, 23 units [shwr, spa bath (3), tlt, a/c, elec blkts, tel, TV, video-fee, refrig, toaster], ✉ (6 nights), pool, bbq, rm serv, dinner to unit, cots-fee, non smoking units (8). **RO ♦ $51 - $83, ♦♦ $55 - $83, ♦♦♦ $64 - $88, ◊ $8**, 11 units ★★★. AE BC DC EFT MC VI, &.

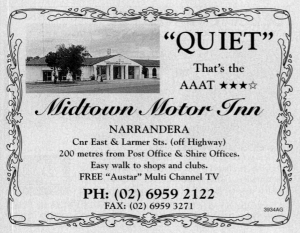

★★ Narrandera Motel, (M), Cnr Newell Hwy & Larmer St, 500m S of PO, opposite Police Station, ☎ 02 6959 1544, fax 02 6959 1445, (2 stry gr fl), 33 units [shwr, tlt, a/c, elec blkts, tel, TV, clock radio, t/c mkg, refrig], pool, cots, BC MC VI.

★ Charles Sturt Hotel, (LH), 77 East St, ☎ 02 6959 2042, fax 02 6959 4118, (2 stry), 10 rms [fan, elec blkts, t/c mkg], lounge (TV). **RO ♦ $20, ♦♦ $35**, ch con, BC.

New Criterion Hotel, (LH), Cnr Boulton & East Sts, 300m N of PO, 300m E of RSL, ☎ 02 6959 1122, fax 02 6959 4515, (2 stry), 17 rms [shwr (12), tlt (12), a/c (13), elec blkts, t/c mkg (11)], rec rm, lounge (TV), lounge firepl, ✕, bar, c/park (limited), cots-fee. **BLB ♦ $25 - $36, ♦♦ $36 - $46, ◊ $8**, pen con, BC EFT MC VI.

B&B's/Guest Houses

★★★★ Old Egerton Country Bed & Breakfast, (B&B), 48 Victoria Ave, 700m E of PO, ☎ 02 6959 3644, fax 02 6959 3288, 3 rms [shwr, bath (2), tlt, hairdry, evap cool, heat, elec blkts, tel, clock radio], ldry, TV rm, business centre, conf fac, lounge firepl, t/c mkg shared, bbq, courtesy transfer, tennis, non smoking property. **BB ♦ $92 - $108, ♦♦ $108 - $120**, AE BC DC MC VI.

★★★☆ Historic Star Lodge, (B&B), 64 Whitton St, ☎ 02 6959 1768, fax 02 6959 4164, 9 rms [shwr (1), tlt (1), a/c-cool (9), c/fan (1), heat, elec blkts, clock radio], lounge (TV), ✕, t/c mkg shared, c/park. **BLB ♦ $60, ♦♦ $90 - $110**, ch con, AE BC JCB MC VI.

NARROMINE NSW 2821

Pop 3,500. (472km W Sydney), See map on pages 52/53, ref F4. Narromine is a leafy town on the Macquarie River, renowned for its superb gliding conditions. Boating, Bowls, Golf, Squash, Swimming, Tennis.

Hotels/Motels

★★★ Peppercorn Motor Inn, (M), Mitchell Hwy, 800m W of PO, adjacent to golf club, ☎ 02 6889 1399, fax 02 6889 2582, 21 units [shwr, tlt, a/c-cool, fan, heat, elec blkts, tel, TV, clock radio, t/c mkg, refrig, toaster], ldry, pool, bbq. **RO ♦ $55, ♦♦ $66, ♦♦♦ $77, ◊ $8 - $11**, ch con, AE BC MC VI.

★★★ Stockman Motor Inn, (M), Mitchell Hwy, 1km E of PO, ☎ 02 6889 2033, fax 02 6889 2758, 16 units [shwr, tlt, hairdry, a/c, tel, TV, clock radio, t/c mkg, refrig, cook fac (1), toaster], ldry, ✕ (Mon to Sat), pool, bbq, rm serv, cots-fee. **RO ♦ $60, ♦♦ $70 - $100, ♦♦♦ $80 - $100, ◊ $10**, ch con, AE BC DC EFT MC VI, ⓘ&.

B&B's/Guest Houses

★★★★ The Abbey, (B&B), 24 Dandaloo St, 300m N of PO, ☎ 02 6889 2213, fax 02 6889 2122, (2 stry gr fl), 5 rms [shwr (3), bath (1), spa bath (2), tlt (4), hairdry, a/c, fire pl, cent heat, tel, clock radio, refrig, toaster], lounge (TV), lounge firepl, ✕, t/c mkg shared, bbq, non smoking property. **BLB ♦ $90, ♦♦ $110 - $130**, AE BC MC VI.

Camerons Farmstay, (B&B), Nundoone Park, Ceres Rd, 6km W of PO, ☎ 02 6889 2978, fax 02 6889 5229, 3 rms [hairdry (1), a/c, fan, heat, elec blkts, tel, clock radio, toaster (1)], lounge (TV, video), pool, t/c mkg shared, refrig, bbq, plygr, tennis, cots, non smoking property. **BB ♦ $60, ♦♦ $85 - $90, DBB ♦ $80, ♦♦ $120**, ch con, fam con, (not yet classified).

NELLIGEN NSW 2536

Pop Nominal, (289km S Sydney), See map on page 55, ref A6. Small, picturesque village on the Clyde River that was a thriving timber town and port in the latter half of the 19th century. Boating, Fishing, Swimming. See also Surf Beach.

Hotels/Motels

★☆ Steampacket Hotel/Motel, (LMH), 963 Kings Hwy, 9km NW from Batemans Bay, ☎ 02 4478 1066, fax 02 4478 1067, 4 units [shwr, tlt, a/c, fan, elec blkts, TV, clock radio, t/c mkg, refrig, toaster], iron, iron brd, lounge (TV & firepl), ✕, dinner to unit, ☎. **RO ♦ $50, ♦♦ $55, ♦♦♦ $60**, BC EFT MC VI.

Self Catering Accommodation

★★★☆ Sunlit Waters Leisure Retreat, (HU), 1 Bridgeview Rd, 8km NW of Batemans Bay, ☎ 02 4478 1007, fax 02 4478 1078, 11 units acc up to 4, [shwr, tlt, fan, heat, elec blkts, TV, clock radio, refrig, cook fac, micro, linen reqd-fee], ldry, pool, bbq, plygr, jetty, tennis, cots, non smoking units. **D ♦♦ $85 - $155, ◊ $15 - $40, W $345 - $850**, ch con, Min book applies.

B&B's/Guest Houses

★★★★☆ Nelligen Post Office Guest House, (GH), 7 Braidwood St, 9km NW of Batemans Bay, ☎ 02 4478 1079, fax 02 4478 1179, 3 rms [shwr, tlt, hairdry, a/c, c/fan, elec blkts, tel, TV, radio, t/c mkg, refrig], lounge (firepl), ✕, dinner to unit (on request), non smoking rms. **BB ♦ $80 - $100, ♦♦ $110 - $132, DBB ♦ $105 - $125, ♦♦ $160 - $182**, BC MC VI.

★★★★ The Nelligen Gallery Bed & Breakfast, (B&B), 13 Braidwood St, ☎ 02 4478 1163, 1 rm [shwr, bath, tlt, hairdry, a/c, fan, tel, TV, video, clock radio, CD, t/c mkg, refrig, cook fac ltd, micro, toaster], iron, iron brd, TV rm, lounge firepl, ✕, bbq, dinner to unit, courtesy transfer, non smoking property. **BB ♦ $100, ♦♦ $150**, BC MC VI.

NELSON BAY NSW

See Port Stephens Region.

NERONG NSW 2423

Pop Nominal, (229km N Sydney), See map on page 54, ref B8. Small village on the shores of the Broadwater at the western edge of the Myall Lakes National Park. Boating, Bush Walking, Canoeing, Fishing, Scenic Drives, Swimming, Wind Surfing.

B&B's/Guest Houses

★★★★ Harbourview Homestay, (B&B), 61 Whimbrel Dve, 12km S of Bulahdelah, ☎ 02 4997 4180, fax 02 4997 4180, 1 rm [shwr, tlt, hairdry, fan, heat, clock radio, t/c mkg, refrig, cook fac, micro, toaster], lounge (TV), c/park (undercover), boat park, non smoking rms. **BLB ♦♦ $60, RO ♦♦ $50**.

★★★☆ Annie's Waterfront Bed & Breakfast, (B&B), 13km S of Bulahdelah, ☎ 02 4997 4194, fax 02 4997 4194, 2 rms [shwr, tlt, c/fan, heat, tel, TV, t/c mkg, refrig, cook fac, micro, toaster], dinner to unit (by arrangement), plygr. **BB ♦ $61, ♦♦ $77, ◊ $19, RO ♦ $50, ♦♦ $61, ◊ $9**.

NEVILLE NSW 2799

Pop 100. Nominal, (276km W Sydney), See map on pages 52/53, ref G5. Historic central west village in the foothills of Stringybark Range.

Self Catering Accommodation

Neville Siding Accommodation, (HU), Crouch St, 500m E of PO, ☎ 02 6368 8455, fax 02 6368 8555, 4 units acc up to 4, [shwr, tlt, c/fan (1), heat, tel, TV, clock radio, refrig, cook fac, micro (1), elec frypan (1), blkts, linen, pillows], ldry, rm serv, c/park (carport), tennis, cots, breakfast ingredients, Pet allowed. **BLB ♦♦ $55**, Converted Rail Carriage & Station Accommodation.

NEW LAMBTON NSW

See Newcastle & Suburbs.

NEWCASTLE & SUBURBS - NEWCASTLE NSW 2300

Pop 270,300. (150km N Sydney), See map on page 55, ref D8. Newcastle is the capital of the Hunter region and has a fascinating past that contributes to its sense of identity today. Bowls, Fishing, Golf, Surfing, Swimming, Tennis.

Hotels/Motels

AAA TOURISM Special Rates ★★★★☆ **Holiday Inn Esplanade Newcastle**, (LH), Shortland Esp, 500m E of PO, ☎ 02 4929 5576, fax 02 4926 5467, (Multi-stry), 72 rms [shwr, tlt, hairdry, a/c, tel, cable tv, clock radio, t/c mkg, refrig, mini bar], lift, ldry, iron, iron brd, conv fac, ✉, pool, rm serv, dinner to unit, cots, non smoking units (24). **RO** ∮ $175 - $260, ♀♀ $165 - $260, ♀♀♀ $181 - $276, AE BC DC MC VI.

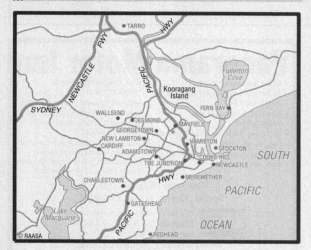

Located on a peninsular between Newcastle Harbour & the Pacific Ocean, Noah's sits in the heart of the historic East End. Enjoy Newcastle's spectacular beaches & unique heritage while also experiencing the rest of the Hunter.

Noah's features 91 air conditioned rooms with 24 hr reception, under cover parking, laundry facilities, licensed restaurant & cocktail bar. The Seaspray Restaurant is widely recognised as Newcastle's ultimate. A New Australian a la carte menu offers exquisite cuisine matched only by enchanting ocean views.

- Just 40 minutes to Port Stephens or Hunter vineyards
- 5 min. walk from Newcastle train/coach station & CBD
- **Opposite Newcastle Beach**

NOAH'S On the Beach NEWCASTLE

TOLL FREE: 1800 023 663
Ph: 02 4929 5181   Fax: 02 4926 5208
Email: reservations@noahsonthebeach.com.au
www.noahsonthebeach.com.au

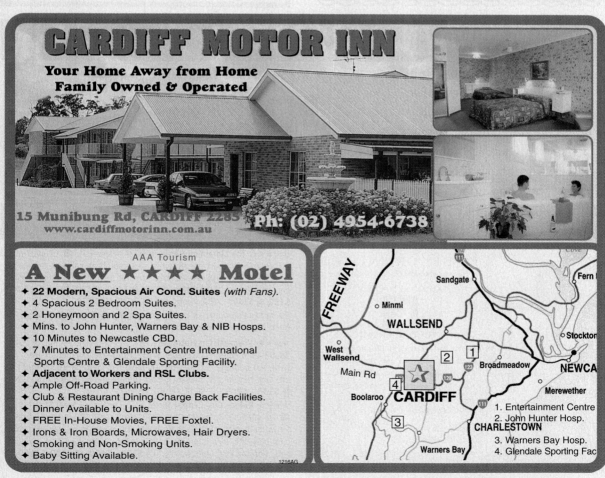

★★★★☆ **The Clarendon Hotel**, (LH), 347 Hunter St, ☎ 02 4927 0966, fax 02 4925 3900, 21 rms (8 suites) [a/c-cool, heat, cable tv, clock radio, t/c mkg, refrig, ldry], ✕, ⊠, meals to unit, secure park, cots (avail), non smoking rms. RO ╫ $129 - $139, ╫╫ $129 - $139, Suite RO ╫ $149 - $159, ╫╫ $149 - $159, weekly con, AE BC DC EFT MC VI,
Operator Comment: A new (opened March 2000) boutique hotel located in Newcastle's CBD.

★★★★ **Novocastrian Motor Inn**, (M), 21 Parnell Pl, 500m E of PO, ☎ 02 4926 3688, fax 02 4929 5795, (Multi-stry), 47 units [shwr, bath, spa bath (5), tlt, a/c, tel, TV, radio, t/c mkg, refrig, mini bar], lift, ldry, conf fac, ⊠, rm serv, c/park (limited), cots. RO ╫ $135 - $205, ╫╫ $135 - $205, AE BC DC MC VI.

★★★★ **Ridges City Central Hotel**, (M), Cnr King & Steel Sts, ☎ 02 4926 3777, fax 02 4926 4379, (Multi-stry), 122 units (6 suites) [shwr, bath, tlt, hairdry, a/c, heat, tel, TV, movie, radio, t/c mkg, refrig, mini bar], lift, ldry, iron, iron brd, conv fac, ⊠, pool, rm serv, gym, cots, non smoking units (avail). D ╫ $120 - $160, ╫╫ $120 - $160, ⋔ $27.50, AE BC DC MC MP VI, ⟨ᵬ⟩.

Rates may change. Check before booking.

★★★☆ **Junction Motel**, (M), 121 Union St, ☎ 02 4929 6677, fax 02 4929 4502, 30 units [shwr, bath, tlt, a/c, tel, TV, movie, clock radio, t/c mkg, refrig, mini bar], ldry, conv fac, ⊠, pool, ✆, cots, non smoking units (30). **RO** ♦ **$129**, ♦♦ **$129**, ◊ **$25**, ch con, AE BC DC JCB MC VI, ⅄&.

★★★☆ **Noahs on the Beach**, (M), Cnr Shortland Esp & Zaara St, 500m NE of PO, ☎ 02 4929 5181, fax 02 4926 5208, (Multi-stry), 90 units (1 suite) [shwr, bath, spa bath (6), tlt, a/c, tel, TV, radio, refrig, mini bar], lift, ldry, conv fac, ⊠, rm serv, c/park (undercover), cots. **RO** ♦ **$115.50**, ♦♦ **$137.50**, ◊ **$10**, Suite D **$219.50**, ch con, AE BC DC MC VI.

Self Catering Accommodation

★★★★☆ **Quest Newcastle**, (Apt), 575 Hunter St, Newcastle West 2302, ☎ 02 4927 8411, fax 02 4927 8441, (Multi-stry), 66 apts acc up to 6, (1, 2 & 3 bedrm), [shwr, tlt, a/c, cent heat, tel, TV, clock radio, t/c mkg, refrig, cook fac, micro, d/wash, toaster, ldry, blkts, linen, pillows], lift, w/mach, dryer, conf fac], ⊠, pool indoor heated, spa, dinner to unit, secure park (undercover), cots, non smoking property. **D** ♦♦ **$160 - $215**, ◊ **$17**, AE BC DC EFT MC VI.

★★★☆ **Beachside Luxury Accommodation**, (House), 2 Beach St, ☎ 02 4997 4524, fax 02 4997 4524, 1 house acc up to 7, [shwr, bath, tlt, hairdry, fan, heat, tel, TV, video, clock radio, t/c mkg, refrig, cook fac, micro, d/wash, toaster, ldry, doonas, linen], w/mach, dryer, iron, iron brd, cots. **D $160 - $180**, Min book applies.

B&B's/Guest Houses

★★★★☆ **Dunvegan House Bed & Breakfast**, (B&B), 4 Shepherds Place, 1km E of PO, ☎ 02 4929 4103, fax 02 4929 4141, (Multi-stry gr fl), 3 rms [shwr, tlt, c/fan, tel], ldry, iron, iron brd, TV rm, lounge, ✕, t/c mkg shared, bbq, courtesy transfer. **BLB** ♦ **$110 - $125**, ♦♦ **$143 - $165**, ◊ **$50**, AE BC EFT MC VI.

★★★★ **Anne's B&B At Ismebury**, (B&B), No children's facilities, 3 Stevenson Pl, ☎ 02 4929 5376, fax 02 4927 8404, (2 stry gr fl), 3 rms (1 suite) [shwr (2), spa bath (1), tlt (2), hairdry, fan, heat, elec blkts, tel, TV (2), clock radio, refrig, cook fac ltd (2), micro, toaster], ldry, iron (2), iron brd (2), lounge (TV & firepl), ✕ (combustion), t/c mkg shared, non smoking rms. **BB** ♦ **$88 - $132**, ♦♦ **$126.50 - $176**, ◊ **$44 - $55**, Suite D ♦♦ **$176 - $220**, ♦♦♦♦ **$275 - $330**, AE BC DC MC VI.

★★★★ **Newcomen Lodge**, (B&B), 70 Newcomen St, ☎ 02 4929 7313, fax 02 4929 7645, 1 rm [fan, heat (elec), elec blkts, TV, video, clock radio, t/c mkg, refrig, cook fac ltd, ldry, doonas], bathrm, ✕, pool (outdoor), bbq, non smoking rms (1). **BLB** ♦ **$90**, ♦♦ **$115**, ◊ **$20**, weekly con, VI.

NEWCASTLE & SUBURBS - ADAMSTOWN NSW 2289

Part of Pop Part of Newcastle, (167km N Sydney), See map on page 55, ref C8. Inner western suburb of Newcastle. Bowls, Greyhound Racing, Horse Racing, Swimming, Tennis.

Hotels/Motels

★★★☆ **Adamstown Elizabeth Motor Inn**, (M), 165 Brunker Rd, 100m N of PO, ☎ 02 4952 7111, fax 02 4952 9939, (2 stry gr fl), 23 units [shwr, tlt, a/c, tel, video, clock radio, t/c mkg, refrig], iron, iron brd, ⊠ (Mon to Thu), rm serv, cots-fee, non smoking rms (12). **RO** ♦ **$77 - $83**, ♦♦ **$88 - $93**, ◊ **$11**, 11 units ★★★☆. AE BC DC EFT MC VI.

★★ **Broadmeadow Motel**, (M), 144 Brunker Rd, 800m S of Broadmeadow Station, ☎ 02 4961 4666, fax 02 4962 1882, (2 stry gr fl), 27 units [shwr, tlt, a/c, heat, elec blkts, tel, TV, video-fee, clock radio, t/c mkg, refrig], ldry, pool (salt water), bbq, cots. **RO** ♦ **$69**, ♦♦ **$80**, ♦♦♦ **$91**, ♦♦♦♦ **$101**, AE BC DC MC VI.

★★ **Nags Head Hotel**, (LH), 272 Brunker St, 500m S of PO, ☎ 02 4952 5743, fax 02 4957 4584, (2 stry), 11 rms [c/fan, heat, t/c mkg, refrig, toaster], ldry, lounge (TV), ⊠ (Tue to Sat), ✆. **BLB** ♦ **$44**, ♦♦ **$55**, D ◊ **$11**, ch con, BC EFT MC VI.

B&B's/Guest Houses

★★★★☆ **B & B Glenrock**, (B&B), 10 Fernleigh Loop, Adamstown Heights 2289, 4km E of PO, ☎ 02 4942 2647, 1 rm [ensuite, bath, a/c, c/fan, elec blkts, tel, TV, clock radio, t/c mkg, refrig, toaster], pool, bbq, non smoking property. **BB** ♦ **$110**, ♦♦ **$140**, BC MC VI.

NEWCASTLE & SUBURBS - CARDIFF NSW 2285

Pop Part of Lake Macquar, (179km N Sydney), See map on page 55, ref C8. Bustling commercial and residential centre off the north-eastern tip of Lake Macquarie.

Hotels/Motels

★★★★ **Cardiff Motor Inn**, (M), 15 Munibung Rd, 300m SE of town centre, ☎ 02 4954 6738, fax 02 4956 6802, 22 units [shwr, spa bath (2), tlt, hairdry, a/c, fan, elec blkts, tel, cable tv, movie, clock radio, t/c mkg, refrig, micro], ldry, iron, iron brd, dinner to unit, cots-fee, non smoking rms (8). **RO** ♦ **$85 - $95**, ♦♦ **$95 - $105**, ◊ **$12**, AE BC DC MC VI.

NEWCASTLE & SUBURBS - CHARLESTOWN NSW 2290

Pop Part of Lake Macquarie, (163km N Sydney), See map on page 55, ref C8. One of the major centres of the Lake Macquarie region, situated about 5km north-east of the lake itself. Bowls, Golf, Swimming.

Hotels/Motels

★★★★☆ **Apollo International**, (M), 290 Pacific Hwy, 500m N of PO, ☎ 02 4943 6733, fax 02 4942 1149, (Multi-stry gr fl), 42 units (8 suites) [shwr, bath, spa bath (8), tlt, hairdry, a/c, tel, TV, clock radio, t/c mkg, refrig, mini bar], ldry, iron, iron brd, conv fac, ⊠, pool, bbq, 24hr reception, rm serv, tennis, cots, non smoking units (16). **D $138 - $234**, AE BC DC MC VI, ⅄&.

★★★★☆ **Madison Motor Inn**, (M), 109 Madison Dve, ☎ 02 4943 8899, fax 02 4942 1463, 50 units [shwr, bath, spa bath (2), tlt, hairdry, a/c, tel, cable tv, clock radio, t/c mkg, refrig, mini bar, toaster], ldry, iron, ⊠, pool, spa, 24hr reception, rm serv, cots, non smoking units (18). **RO** ♦♦ **$125 - $260**, ◊ **$11**, ch con, AE BC DC MC MP VI.

★★★ **Newcastle Heights**, (M), 270 Pacific Hwy, ☎ 02 4943 3077, fax 02 4943 3419, (2 stry gr fl), 18 units [shwr, tlt, a/c, heat, tel, TV, video (avail), clock radio, t/c mkg, refrig], ldry, ⊠ (Mon to Sat), pool (salt water), bbq, rm serv, cots, non smoking rms (4). **RO** ♦ **$67**, ♦♦ **$77**, ◊ **$11**, AE BC DC EFT MC VI.

★★ **Panorama Motor Inn**, (M), 256 Pacific Hwy, 400m N of PO, ☎ 02 4943 3144, fax 02 4943 5240, 33 units [shwr, tlt, hairdry, a/c, tel, TV, video (avail), clock radio, t/c mkg, refrig, cook fac (2)], ldry, iron, iron brd, ⊠, pool, bbq, rm serv, dinner to unit, cots. **RO** ♦ **$60 - $66**, ♦♦ **$66 - $77**, ◊ **$11**, ch con, AE BC DC MC VI.

Self Catering Accommodation

★★★ **Charlestown Serviced Apartments**, (SA), 39 Dickinson St, ☎ 02 4953 7323, fax 02 4961 5224, 4 serv apts acc up to 6, [shwr, bath, tlt, a/c, tel, TV, video, clock radio, t/c mkg, refrig, cook fac, micro, toaster, ldry, blkts, linen], w/mach, dryer, iron, iron brd, cots. **D $100**, W **$495**, BC VI.

NEWCASTLE & SUBURBS - COOKS HILL NSW 2300

Pop Part of Newcastle, (172km N Sydney), See map on page 55, ref D8. Inner suburb of Newcastle with a fashionable restaurant district.

Self Catering Accommodation

★★★★☆ **Darby Street Executive Apartments**, (SA), 55 Mitchell St, Merewether 2291, 150m S of PO, ☎ 02 4963 1118, or 02 4955 5888, fax 02 4955 5667, 4 serv apts acc up to 6, [shwr, bath, tlt, hairdry, a/c (2), fan, heat, tel, TV, video, clock radio, t/c mkg, refrig, cook fac, micro, d/wash, toaster, blkts, doonas, linen, pillows], lift, w/mach, dryer, iron, iron brd, bbq, courtesy transfer, cots, non smoking units. **D** ♦♦ **$99 - $125**, ◊ **$11**, W **$550 - $600**, weekly con, AE BC MC VI.

NEWCASTLE & SUBURBS - FERN BAY NSW 2295

Pop Nominal, (187km N Sydney), See map on page 55, ref D8. Village set on Fullerton Cove next to the Newcastle suburb of Stockton. Boating, Bowls, Fishing, Golf, Swimming.

Hotels/Motels

★★★ **Newcastle Links Motel**, (M), 51 Nelson Bay Rd, 6km N of Stockton, ☎ 02 4928 2366, fax 02 4920 1399, 26 units [shwr, bath (1), tlt, a/c, tel, TV, clock radio, t/c mkg, refrig], ldry, iron, pool (salt water), bbq, plygr, golf, cots-fee. **RO** ♦ **$49.50 - $81.40**, ♦♦ **$59.40 - $90.20**, ♦♦♦ **$70.40 - $101.20**, ◊ **$11**, ch con, 7 units ★★☆, 10 units not rated. AE BC DC MC VI.

NEWCASTLE & SUBURBS - GATESHEAD NSW 2290

Pop 8,500. (160km N Sydney), See map on page 55, ref C8. Gateshead lies directly to the south of Charlestown on Lake Macquarie.

Hotels/Motels

★★☆ **Gateshead Tavern**, (LMH), 9 Pacific Hwy, ☎ 02 4943 3944, fax 02 4943 3794, 23 units [shwr, tlt, a/c-cool (8), a/c (16), cable tv, clock radio, t/c mkg, refrig], ✆, cots. **RO ♦ $47, ♦♦ $63, ♀ $16.50,** AE BC EFT MC VI.

NEWCASTLE & SUBURBS - GEORGETOWN NSW 2298

Pop Part of Newcastle, See map on page 55, ref C8. North-western suburb of Newcastle.

Self Catering Accommodation

★★★ **Wentworth Cottage Serviced Accommodation**, (Cotg), 2 Wentworth St, ☎ 02 4958 8787, fax 02 4958 8784, 1 cotg acc up to 7, [shwr, bath, tlt, hairdry, heat, elec blkts, TV, t/c mkg, refrig, cook fac, micro, toaster, ldry, doonas, linen], w/mach, dryer, iron, iron brd, TV rm, lounge firepl, bbq, plygr. **D ♦♦♦♦ $110, ♀ $10, W ♦♦♦♦ $600**, BC MC VI.

NEWCASTLE & SUBURBS - HAMILTON NSW 2303

Pop Part of Newcastle, (164km N Sydney), See map on page 55, ref C8. Inner western suburb of Newcastle. Bowls, Greyhound Racing, Horse Racing, Tennis.

Hotels/Motels

★★★ **Tudor Inn Motel**, (M), Cnr Tudor & Steel Sts, 500m SW of PO, ☎ 02 4969 2533, fax 02 4961 4288, (Multi-stry), 31 units [shwr, tlt, a/c, tel, TV, radio, t/c mkg, refrig], ✕, cots-fee. **RO ♦ $77 - $86, ♦♦ $88 - $97, ♦♦♦ $99 - $108,** AE BC DC MC VI.

Self Catering Accommodation

★★★☆ **The Boulevard Apartments**, (SA), 22 Donald St, 300m N of PO, ☎ 02 4965 4716, (2 stry gr fl), 9 serv apts acc up to 6, [shwr, bath (1), tlt, hairdry, a/c, tel, TV, video, clock radio, CD, t/c mkg, refrig, cook fac, micro, toaster, ldry (in unit), blkts, linen, pillows], w/mach, dryer, iron, ✆, cots, non smoking units. **RO $143 - $198, $693 - $825,** ch con, AE BC DC MC VI.

The Boulevard
SERVICED APARTMENTS

22 Donald St, Hamilton, NEWCASTLE, NSW 2303.
Ph: (02) 4965 4716   Fax: (02) 4965 4709

Executive style luxurious serviced apartments located in the cosmopolitan suburb of Hamilton, Newcastle's premier restaurant district 5 minutes from beautiful beaches and a short walk to train and bus facilities.

2 b/r unit (RO)*	$143.00/night includes GST
2 b/r unit (RO)*	$693.00/week includes GST
3 b/r unit (RO)†	$198.00/night includes GST
3 b/r unit (RO)†	$825.00/week includes GST

* Accommodates up to 6 people. † Up to 8 people.

NEWCASTLE & SUBURBS - JESMOND NSW 2299

Pop Part of Newcastle, (170km N Sydney), See map on page 55, ref C8. Western suburb of Newcastle.

Self Catering Accommodation

Jesmond Executive Villas, (HU), 189 Newcastle Rd, 150m SE of Stockland Mall, ☎ 02 4955 5888, fax 02 4955 5667, 30 units acc up to 8, (1, 3 & 4 bedrm), [shwr, bath (15), spa bath (3), tlt, a/c, tel, TV, video-fee, clock radio, t/c mkg, refrig, cook fac ltd, micro, toaster], ldry, w/mach, dryer, iron, iron brd, bbq, cots, non smoking units (5). **D ♦ $66, ♦♦ $77, ♀ $11,** AE BC MC VI.

NEWCASTLE & SUBURBS - MAYFIELD NSW 2304

Pop Part of Newcastle, (181km N Sydney), See map on page 55, ref C8. Inner northern suburb of Newcastle. Bowls, Golf, Swimming, Tennis.

Hotels/Motels

★★★★ **Travellers Motor Village**, (M), 295 Maitland Rd, 1km W of PO, ☎ 02 4968 1394, fax 02 4968 8230, 20 units (2 suites) [shwr, spa bath (4), tlt, hairdry, a/c, tel, TV, video-fee, clock radio, t/c mkg, refrig, cook fac ltd, micro, toaster], ldry, iron, iron brd, pool, bbq, cots, non smoking units. **RO ♦ $89 - $106, ♦♦ $96 - $134, ♀ $8 - $10, Suite D ♦ $89 - $106, ♦♦ $96 - $134, ♀ $8 - $10,** ch con, fam con, AE BC EFT MC VI.

★★★★ **(Cabin Section)**, 10 cabins acc up to 4, [shwr, tlt, a/c, TV, refrig, cook fac, micro, toaster]. **D ♦♦ $76, ♀ $8.**

FLAG
FLAG CHOICE HOTELS

★★★☆ **Hospitality Motor Inn**, (M), 418 Maitland Rd (Pacific Hwy), 1km W of PO, ☎ 02 4967 1977, fax 02 4960 2085, (2 stry gr fl), 28 units [shwr, tlt, a/c, elec blkts, tel, TV, clock radio, t/c mkg, refrig, mini bar], ldry, iron, ✕, rm serv, dinner to unit, cots-fee. **RO ♦ $105 - $115, ♦♦ $118 - $126, ♀ $10,** AE BC DC JCB MC VI.

SOVEREIGN Motor Inns Chain

★★★☆ **Sovereign Motor Inn**, (M), 309 Maitland Rd (Pacific Hwy), 1km W of PO, ☎ 02 4968 4405, fax 02 4967 2975, 34 units [shwr, tlt, hairdry, a/c, tel, TV, video (avail), clock radio, t/c mkg, refrig], ldry, iron, iron brd, ✕, pool, cots-fee. **RO ♦ $86 - $97, ♦♦ $86 - $97, ♀ $11,** AE BC DC MC VI, ♿.

★★☆ **Mayfield Motel**, (M), 503 Maitland Rd (Pacific Hwy), 2km W of PO, ☎ 02 4968 2661, 22 units [shwr, tlt, a/c, tel, cable tv, clock radio, t/c mkg, refrig], iron, ✕ (Mon to Thu), pool (salt water), dinner to unit (Mon to Thu), cots-fee, non smoking rms (7). **RO ♦ $69 - $75, ♦♦ $75 - $83, ♀ $10,** ch con, AE BC DC MC VI.

B&B's/Guest Houses

★★★★ **Bella Vista Guest House**, (GH), 105 Crebert St, ☎ 02 4968 8512, fax 02 4968 8508, (2 stry), 6 rms (5 suites) [shwr (5), bath (5), tlt (5), hairdry, a/c (5), tel (5), TV (5), video (5), clock radio, refrig, toaster], iron, iron brd, lounge, conv fac, ✕ (by appointment), t/c mkg shared, non smoking property. **Suite BB ♦ $120, ♦♦ $130,** AE BC DC MC VI.

Other Accommodation

★★ **Hanbury Lodge**, (Lodge), 87 Hanbury St, ☎ 02 4960 8212, fax 02 4960 0598, (2 stry gr fl), 16 rms acc up to 4, [shwr, tlt, TV, clock radio (6), t/c mkg, refrig, blkts, linen], ldry, w/mach-fee, dryer-fee, iron, iron brd, rec rm, TV rm, meals avail, ✆, cots-fee, non smoking property. **D ♦ $75, ♦♦ $85, W ♦ $250, ♦♦ $300,** ch con, fam con, pen con, BC EFT MC VI.

NEWCASTLE & SUBURBS - MEREWETHER NSW 2291

Pop Part of Newcastle, (170km N Sydney), See map on page 55, ref C8. Beachside southern suburb of Newcastle. Boating, Bowls, Fishing, Hangliding, Swimming.

Hotels/Motels

★★★ **Aloha Motor Inn**, (M), 231 Glebe Rd, 1km NW of PO, ☎ 02 4963 1283, fax 02 4963 4483, (2 stry gr fl), 29 units [shwr, tlt, hairdry, a/c, tel, cable tv, clock radio, t/c mkg, refrig], ldry, iron, iron brd, cots-fee. **RO ♦ $83 - $95, ♦♦ $93 - $105, ♦♦♦ $102 - $115, ♀ $8 - $10,** 4 rooms of a higher standard. AE BC DC MC VI.

★☆ **Beach Hotel**, (LH), 99 Frederick St, 1km E of PO, ☎ 02 4963 1574, fax 02 4963 6602, (2 stry), 8 rms (1 suite) [c/fan, heat], rec rm, lounge (TV), conv fac, ✕, t/c mkg shared, refrig, c/park. **BLB ♦ $55, ♦♦ $65, Suite D ♦ $50, ♦♦ $65,** ◊ **$15,** AE BC EFT MC VI.

Self Catering Accommodation
★★★☆ **Merewether Serviced Apartments**, (Apt), 31-33 Merewether St, 400m S of PO, ☎ 02 4963 5065, fax 02 4963 5155, (2 stry), 5 apts acc up to 6, [shwr, bath, tlt, a/c, c/fan, tel, TV, video, clock radio, t/c mkg, refrig, cook fac, micro, elec frypan, d/wash, toaster, ldry (in unit), blkts, linen, pillows], w/mach, dryer, iron, c/park (garage). **D $132 - $154, W $660 - $770,** Min book applies, AE BC MC VI.

B&B's/Guest Houses
★★★★ **Merewether Beach B&B**, (B&B), 60 Hickson St, ☎ 02 4963 3526, fax 02 4963 7926, (2 stry gr fl), 1 rm [shwr, tlt, fan, heat, elec blkts, tel, TV, video, clock radio, t/c mkg, refrig, cook fac ltd, micro, toaster], ldry, iron, iron brd, c/park. **BB ♦ $100, ♦♦ $130,** ch con, BC MC VI.

NEWCASTLE & SUBURBS - NEW LAMBTON NSW 2305
Pop Part of Newcastle, (165km N Sydney), See map on page 55, ref C8. Leafy western suburb of Newcastle and the location of the popular Blackbutt Reserve. Bowls.

Hotels/Motels

AAA
T O U R I S M
Special Rates

★★★★☆ **The Executive Inn**, (LH), 10 Rugby Rd, 1km N of PO, ☎ 02 4935 1100, fax 02 4935 1481, 134 rms (32 suites) [shwr, bath (83), spa bath (32), tlt, hairdry, a/c, tel, cable tv, video-fee, clock radio, t/c mkg, refrig, mini bar], lift, ldry, conv fac, ✕, pool-heated (2), sauna, spa, rm serv, dinner to unit, c/park (undercover), gym, cots. **RO ♦ $120, ♦♦ $120,** ◊ **$20, Suite D ♦ $150 - $280,** ◊ **$20,** ch con, AE BC DC EFT JCB MC VI.

NEWCASTLE & SUBURBS - THE JUNCTION NSW 2291
Pop Part of Newcastle, (169km N Sydney), See map on page 55, ref C8. Suburb of Newcastle. Bowls, Horse Racing.

B&B's/Guest Houses
★★★★☆ **Fernwood Bed & Breakfast**, (B&B), 16 Ravenshaw St, 2.5 km W of Newcastle CBD, ☎ 02 4969 2912, fax 02 4969 2567, (2 stry), 3 rms [ensuite (2), spa bath (1), a/c-cool, heat, fan, heat (elec/wood), tel, TV, clock radio, ldry, doonas], bathrm (1), lounge (TV, video), t/c mkg shared, refrig, non smoking rms. **BB ♦ $90 - $99,** ch con, weekly con, BC EFT MC VI.

NEWCASTLE & SUBURBS - WALLSEND NSW 2287
Pop Part of Newcastle, (176km N Sydney). See map on page 55, ref C8. Suburb of Newcastle.

Hotels/Motels
★★ **Motel Formule' 1**, (M), Cnr Link & Lake Rds, 1km N of PO, ☎ 02 4950 0244, fax 02 4950 0524, (2 stry gr fl), 80 units [shwr, tlt, a/c-cool, TV], ✕, refrig, ✆, non smoking units (40). **BLB ♦ $59, ♦♦ $59, ♦♦♦ $59,** AE BC DC MC VI.

End of Newcastle & Suburbs

NEWRYBAR NSW 2479
Pop Nominal (773km N Sydney) See map on page 54, ref E2. A quaint village located between Byron Bay and Ballina.

Self Catering Accommodation
★★★ **Serenity Cottages**, (Cotg), 6 Brooklet Rd, ☎ 02 6687 2258, fax 02 6687 2259, 4 cotgs (4 bedrm), [shwr, tlt, c/fan, heat, TV, video, radio, t/c mkg, refrig, cook fac, micro, toaster, doonas, linen, pillows], w/mach, lounge firepl, spa, cots-fee. **D ♦♦♦♦ $130 - $190,** Min book applies, AE BC DC MC VI.

NIMMITABEL NSW 2631
Pop 250. (430km S Sydney), See map on pages 52/53, ref G8. Small, pretty township on the Monaro Highway that dates back to the 1830s. Fishing, Shooting, Tennis.

Hotels/Motels
★★ **Nimmitabel Motel**, (M), Snowy Mountains Hwy, ☎ 02 6454 6387, 10 units [shwr, tlt, heat, elec blkts, TV, t/c mkg, refrig, cook fac (2)], ✕, dinner to unit. **RO ♦ $46, ♦♦ $57,** ◊ **$11,** ch con, BC MC VI.

B&B's/Guest Houses
★★★☆ **Royal Arms Guest House**, (GH), c1850. Snowy Mountains Hwy, In the centre of town, ☎ 02 6454 6422, fax 02 6454 6433, (2 stry gr fl), 9 rms (1 suite) [shwr (4), bath (1), tlt (5), hairdry, fire pl, cent heat, elec blkts, tel, TV, clock radio, t/c mkg, refrig], ✕, rm serv, cots, non smoking rms. **BB ♦ $52, ♦♦ $93, Suite BB ♦♦ $130,** BC MC VI.

Other Accommodation
Riverglen Lodge, (Lodge), (Farm), Glen Allen Rd, 33km from Nimmitabel General Store, ☎ 02 6251 1267, fax 02 6253 5523, 1 rm acc up to 4, [heat, cook fac], lounge firepl, courtesy transfer, Pets allowed. **D $45,** ◊ **$20,** ch con, BC DC EFT MC VI. (not yet classified).

NORAVILLE NSW 2263
Pop 6,730. (111km N Sydney), See map on page 55, ref D5. Central Coast town next to Norah Head between Tuggerah Lake, Wyrrabalong National Park and the sea. Boating, Bowls, Fishing, Golf, Scenic Drives, Swimming.

Hotels/Motels
★★★ **Sea n Sun Motel**, (M), No children's facilities, 115 Budgewoi Rd, ☎ 02 4396 4474, fax 02 4396 4474, 12 units [shwr, tlt, hairdry, fan, heat, TV, clock radio, t/c mkg, refrig], ldry, bbq, ✆, mini golf. **RO ♦ $66 - $165, ♦♦ $71.50 - $165, ♦♦♦ $79 - $165,** ◊ **$10 - $15,** BC EFT MC VI.

NORFOLK ISLAND NSW 2899
Pop 2,000. (1676km NE Sydney), See map on page 54, ref E3. Beautiful sub-tropical Pacific island roughly halfway between Australia and New Zealand. Although it's a territory of Australia, a valid passport is required for entry to the island and re-entry into Australia. Bowls, Fishing, Golf, Scenic Drives, Swimming, Tennis.

Hotels/Motels
★★★☆ **Castaway Hotel**, (LH), Taylors Rd, ☎ 0011 672322625, fax 0011 672322785, 18 rms [shwr, bath (2), tlt, hairdry, fan (10), c/fan (13), elec blkts, tel, TV, video (avail), clock radio, t/c mkg, refrig, mini bar, ldry], ldry, rec rm, lounge (TV), conv fac, ✕, bbq, rm serv, dinner to unit, plygr, gym, cots-fee, 5 units of a lower rating, AE BC DC EFT MC VI.

★★★ **(Serviced Apartment Section)**, 5 serv apts acc up to 3, [shwr, bath (3), tlt, hairdry, c/fan, heat, elec blkts, tel, TV, video (avail), clock radio, t/c mkg, refrig, mini bar, cook fac, toaster, blkts, linen, pillows], ldry.

★★★☆ **Colonial of Norfolk**, (LH), Queen Elizabeth Ave, 700m SE of PO, ☎ 0011 672322177, fax 0011 672322831, 55 rms [shwr, tlt, hairdry, c/fan, elec blkts, tel, TV, clock radio, t/c mkg, refrig, cook fac (6)], ldry, iron, iron brd, TV rm, lounge (TV), conv fac, ✕, pool, bbq, ✆, cots. **RO ♦ $68 - $185, ♦♦ $136 - $185,** ◊ **$33 - $37,** 11 rooms of a 4 star rating. 9 rooms of a lower rating, AE BC DC EFT MC VI.

★★★☆ **South Pacific Resort Hotel**, (LH), Taylors Rd, 1km S of PO, ☎ 0011 6723 23154, fax 6723 22907, 37 rms [shwr, bath (12), tlt, hairdry, fan, elec blkts, tel, TV, video-fee, clock radio, t/c mkg, refrig, toaster], ldry, rec rm, conv fac, ✕, pool, bbq, dinner to unit, courtesy transfer, ✆, cots. **RO ♦ $110 - $130, ♦♦ $110 - $130, ♦♦♦ $130 - $150,** ◊ **$20,** 23 units of a higher standard, AE BC DC EFT MC VI.

★★★★ **(South Pacific Resort - Superior Rooms)**, 23 units **RO ♦ $130 - $150, ♦♦ $130 - $150, ♦♦♦ $150 - $170,** ◊ **$20.**

★★☆ **Hillcrest Gardens Hotel**, (LH), Taylors Rd, ☎ 0011 672322255, fax 0011 672322909, (Multi-stry gr fl), 28 rms (3 suites) [shwr, tlt, fan, elec blkts, tel, TV, video (3), clock radio, t/c mkg, refrig, cook fac (3), micro (3), toaster (3)], ldry, iron, iron brd, ✕, pool (salt water), bbq, courtesy transfer, tennis, cots. **RO ♦ $100 - $116, ♦♦ $100 - $116,** ◊ **$20,** ch con, AE BC DC EFT MC VI.

★★★☆ **(Serviced Apartments Section)**, 5 serv apts [shwr, tlt, elec blkts, tel, TV, video, clock radio, refrig, cook fac, micro, toaster, ldry], bbq, dinner to unit, cots. **D $155 - $238.**

★★☆ **Polynesian**, (LMH), New Cascade Rd, 80m from town centre, ☎ 0011 6723 2207, fax 0011 672323040, 17 units [shwr, tlt, fan, elec blkts, tel, TV, clock radio, t/c mkg, refrig, cook fac ltd, micro, elec frypan, toaster], ldry, ✕ (6 nights), pool, bbq, rm serv, dinner to unit, cots. **RO ♦♦ $88,** Tariff includes car hire. BC MC VI.

★★☆ **(Cottage Section)**, 1 cotg acc up to 6, [shwr, bath, tlt, fan, heat, elec blkts, tel, TV, video, clock radio, refrig, cook fac, micro, elec frypan, toaster, blkts, linen, pillows], ldry, pool, bbq, rm serv, dinner to unit, c/park (carport), cots. **D ♦♦♦♦ $185,** ch con.

Self Catering Accommodation
★★★★★ **Christians of Bucks Point**, (Cotg), Heritage, Martins Rd, Bucks Point, 1.5km NE of Kingston, ☎ 02 9525 7724, fax 02 501 1766, 1 cotg acc up to 6, [shwr, tlt, hairdry, fan, heat, elec blkts, tel, fax, cable tv, video, clock radio (5), t/c mkg, refrig, cook fac, micro, d/wash, toaster, ldry, blkts, linen, pillows], w/mach, dryer, iron, lounge, bbq, c/park. **D ♦♦ $275,** ◊ **$55,** Min book applies.

★★★★☆ **By the Bay**, (Cotg), Martins Rd Ball Bay, 6km E of PO,
☎ 0011 672323426, fax 0011 672322730, 1 cotg acc up to 4, (3 bedrm),
[shwr, spa bath, tlt, fan, heat, elec blkts, tel, TV, video, clock radio,
t/c mkg, refrig, cook fac, micro, d/wash, toaster, ldry, blkts, doonas,
linen, pillows], w/mach, dryer, lounge firepl, bbq, breakfast ingredients,
non smoking property. **BLB** ♦♦ **$250,** ◊ **$45.**

★★★★☆ **Dii Elduu**, (Cotg), Mission Rd, 3km W of PO,
☎ 0011 672323853, fax 0011 672323853, 2 cotgs acc up to 6, [shwr,
bath (1), tlt, hairdry, fan (1), c/fan (1), elec blkts, tel, TV, video, clock
radio, t/c mkg, refrig, cook fac, micro, elec frypan, d/wash (1), toaster,
ldry, blkts, linen], w/mach, iron, iron brd, bbq, cots, 1 cottage of a
4 star rating.

★★★★☆ **Endeavour Lodge**, (HU), Collines Head Rd, 3.5km E of PO,
☎ 0011 672322163, fax 0015 672322759, 4 units acc up to 3, (1 bedrm),
[shwr, tlt, fan, heat (gas), elec blkts, tel, TV, video, clock radio, t/c mkg,
refrig, cook fac, micro, toaster, blkts], w/mach, dryer, c/park. **D** ♦ **$150,**
♦♦ **$150,** ◊ **$30,** ch con, AE BC DC MC VI.

★★★★☆ **Fantasy Island Resort**, (HU), Taylors Rd, opposite Visitors
Centre, ☎ 0011 672323778, fax 0011 672323779, 10 units acc up to 4,
(Studio & 1 bedrm), [shwr, tlt, fan, heat (6), elec blkts, tel, TV, clock
radio, t/c mkg, refrig, cook fac, micro, toaster, blkts, linen, pillows],
ldry, w/mach, dryer, bbq, secure park (undercover), cots-fee, non
smoking property. **D** ♦ **$75 - $90,** ♦♦ **$95 - $145,** ◊ **$25 - $30,**
Min book applies.

★★★★☆ **Haydanblair House**, (House), Selwyn Pine Rd, 2km fr PO,
☎ 0011 672322625, fax 0011 672322785, 1 house acc up to 10, (4 bedrm),
[shwr, tlt, c/fan, elec blkts, tel, TV, video, clock radio, t/c mkg, refrig,
cook fac, micro, d/wash, toaster, ldry, blkts, linen, pillows], w/mach,
dryer, lounge firepl, bbq, c/park (undercover), plygr, cots. **D** ♦♦ **$238,**
◊ **$40,** AE BC DC EFT MC VI.

★★★★☆ **Lavendula of Norfolk Island**, (Cotg), off New Cascade Rd,
1km fr PO, ☎ 0011 672323654, or 0011 672322743,
fax 0011 672323587, 1 cotg acc up to 3, (2 bedrm), [shwr, tlt, fan,
heat, tel, TV, video, clock radio, t/c mkg, refrig, cook fac, micro,
toaster, ldry, blkts, doonas, linen, pillows], w/mach, spa, bbq, cots.
D ♦♦ **$192,** ◊ **$30,** Min book applies.

★★★★☆ **Oceanview Apartments**, (Apt), New Cascade Rd, 3km NE of PO,
☎ 0011 672322119, fax 0011 672322119, 2 apts acc up to 4, (1 bedrm),
[shwr, tlt, fan, tel, TV, video, clock radio, t/c mkg, refrig, micro, toaster,
blkts, linen, pillows], ldry, w/mach, lounge firepl, bbq, cots. **D $140 -
$260,** BC MC VI.

★★★★☆ **Shearwater Luxury Villas**, (HU), Point Ross, 5km SW of PO,
☎ 0011 672322539, fax 0011 672323359, 5 units acc up to 4, [shwr,
bath, tlt, hairdry, fan, heat, elec blkts, tel, TV, video (avail), clock radio,
refrig, cook fac, micro, d/wash, toaster, ldry (in unit), blkts, linen,
pillows], w/mach, bbq, cots. **D** ♦♦ **$220 - $240,** ♦♦♦ **$300,** ♦♦♦♦ **$320,**
W $1,640 - $2,240, 2 units yet to be assessed, Min book applies.

★★★★☆ **Shiralee Executive Cottages**, (SA), Taylors Rd, 500m S of PO,
☎ 0011 672322118, fax 0011 672323318, 6 serv apts acc up to 4,
[shwr, bath, tlt, hairdry, fan, heat, heat, elec blkts, tel, TV, video,
movie, clock radio, refrig, cook fac, micro, elec frypan, toaster, blkts,
linen, pillows], ldry, bbq, plygr, non smoking units. **RO** ♦♦ **$135 - $155,**
◊ **$35 - $40.**

★★★★☆ **Summerhouse**, (Cotg), Selwyn Pine Rd, 2km N of PO,
☎ 0011 672322573, fax 0011 672322889, 1 cotg acc up to 2, (1 bedrm),
[shwr, tlt, fan, heat, tel, TV, video, clock radio, cook fac, micro, toaster,
ldry, blkts, doonas, linen, pillows], w/mach, bbq, c/park (undercover).
D $210, Free use of hire car included, Min book applies, BC MC VI.

★★★★☆ **Tau Gardens**, (Cotg), Captain Quintal Dve, ☎ 0011 672322743,
fax 0011 672322743, 2 cotgs acc up to 5, [shwr, bath, tlt, hairdry, fan,
heat, elec blkts, tel, TV, video, clock radio, t/c mkg, refrig, cook fac,
micro, elec frypan, d/wash (2), toaster, ldry, blkts, linen, pillows],
w/mach, iron, bbq, cots. **D** ◊ **$25, $150 - $175, W $1,050 - $1,225,**
ch con, 1 unit of a lower rating, BC MC VI.

★★★★☆ **Tintoela of Norfolk**, (Cotg), Harpers Rd, Cascade,
☎ 0011 672322946, fax 0011 672322946, 2 cotgs acc up to 6, [shwr,
bath, tlt, hairdry, fan, fire pl, elec blkts, tel, TV, video, clock radio,
t/c mkg, refrig, cook fac, micro, elec frypan, d/wash, toaster, ldry,
blkts, linen], w/mach, dryer, iron, bbq, cots. **D** ♦♦ **$210 - $250,**
◊ **$35 - $40,** ch con, Tariff includes use of hire car.

★★★★☆ **Tradewinds**, (Cotg), Stockyard Rd, 4km E of PO,
☎ 0011 672322295, fax 0011 672322865, 5 cotgs acc up to 6, (2 & 3
bedrm), [shwr, tlt, c/fan, heat, tel, TV, video, clock radio, t/c mkg, refrig,
cook fac, micro, toaster, blkts, linen, pillows], ldry, w/mach, lounge firepl,
bbq, plygr, cots. **D** ♦♦ **$128,** ◊ **$20,** ch con, AE BC DC MC VI.

★★★★ **Bounty Lodge Apartments**, (Apt), Ferny La, 500m NW of PO,
☎ 0011 672322417, fax 0011 672323242, 5 apts acc up to 8, (1 & 2
bedrm), [shwr, tlt, c/fan, heat, elec blkts, tel, TV, video, clock radio,
t/c mkg, refrig, cook fac, micro, toaster, blkts, doonas, linen, pillows],
ldry, w/mach, ✉, cots, breakfast ingredients. **BLB** ♦ **$50 - $100,** ♦♦ **$100 -
$120,** ◊ **$20,** ch con, Free use of hire car included, BC MC VI.

★★★★ **Cobbys Gen Crystal Pool**, (Cotg), Rocky Point, 4km W of PO,
☎ 0011 672322693, fax 0011 672323124, 1 cotg acc up to 4, (2 bedrm),
[shwr, tlt, c/fan, heat, elec blkts, tel, TV, video, clock radio, refrig,
cook fac, micro, toaster, ldry, blkts, doonas, linen, pillows], w/mach,
bbq, cots, breakfast ingredients. **BLB** ♦♦ **$195,** ◊ **$25,** BC EFT MC VI.

★★★★ **Nine Pines**, (Cotg), Rocky Point Rd, 2.5km S of PO,
☎ 0011 672322417, fax 0011 672323242, 1 cotg acc up to 4, (2 bedrm),
[shwr, tlt, fan, heat, elec blkts, tel, TV, video, clock radio, refrig,
cook fac, micro, toaster, ldry, blkts, doonas, linen, pillows], w/mach,
bbq, cots. **BLB** ♦ **$100 - $162.50,** ♦♦ **$162.50,** ◊ **$20,** ch con.

★★★★ **Norfolk Holiday Apartments**, (Apt), Taylors Rd, 1km fr PO,
☎ 0011 672322009, fax 0011 672323851, (2 stry gr fl), 12 apts acc
up to 4, (1 & 2 bedrm), [shwr, tlt, c/fan, heat, elec blkts, tel, TV, clock
radio, t/c mkg, refrig, cook fac, micro, toaster, blkts, doonas, linen,
pillows], ldry, w/mach, cots. **D $118.50 - $149.50,** ◊ **$25.**

★★★★ **Riggers Retreat**, (Cotg), Cascade Rd, 2km fr PO,
☎ 0011 672324176, 1 cotg acc up to 3, (Studio), [shwr, tlt, c/fan,
heat, tel, TV, video, clock radio, t/c mkg, refrig, cook fac, micro, toaster,
ldry, blkts, doonas, linen, pillows], w/mach, bbq. **D $90 - $100,**
ch con, Min book applies, BC MC VI.

★★★★ **The Nobbs Apartments**, (HU), Grassy Rd, 500m W of PO,
☎ 0011 672322204, fax 0011 672323204, (2 stry gr fl), 8 units acc
up to 5, [shwr, tlt, fan, heat, elec blkts, tel, TV, video (avail), clock
radio, refrig, cook fac, micro, elec frypan, toaster, blkts, linen, pillows],
ldry-fee, pool, bbq, ☎, tennis-fee, non smoking units. **RO** ♦♦ **$110 - $135,**
◊ **$25.**

★★★☆ **Ainsley Lodge**, (HU), Grassy Rd, 500m NW of PO,
☎ 0011 672322269, fax 0011 672322376, 1 unit acc up to 5, [shwr,
tlt, hairdry, fan, elec blkts, tel, TV, radio, refrig, cook fac, micro, elec
frypan, toaster, blkts, linen, pillows], ldry, bbq, c/park. **RO** ♦♦ **$110,**
◊ **$15,** BC MC VI.

★★★☆ **Bligh Court Cottages**, (Cotg), Grassy Rd, 300m N of PO,
☎ 0011 672322114, fax 001167 232 3014, 7 cotgs acc up to 5, [shwr,
tlt, fan, heat, elec blkts, tel, TV, video (avail), clock radio, t/c mkg,
refrig, cook fac, micro, toaster, ldry, blkts, linen, pillows], w/mach, iron,
bbq, plygr, cots. **DBB** ♦♦ **$150,** ◊ **$30,** ch con, BC DC EFT MC VI, ♿.

★★★☆ **Callam Court**, (HU), New Cascade Rd, 2km E of shopping
centre, ☎ 0011 672322850, fax 0011 672322770, 4 units acc up to 6,
[shwr, tlt, fan, heat, elec blkts, tel, TV, video (avail), clock radio, refrig,
cook fac, micro, toaster, blkts, linen, pillows], ldry, iron, bbq, cots.
D ♦ **$88 - $106,** ♦♦ **$88 - $106,** ♦♦♦ **$133,** 1 unit of a higher standard.

★★★★☆ **(Cottage Section)**, 1 cotg acc up to 6, [shwr, tlt, hairdry, fan,
heat, elec blkts, tel, TV, video, clock radio, refrig, cook fac, micro, toaster,
blkts, linen, pillows], ldry. **D** ♦ **$155,** ♦♦ **$155,** ♦♦♦ **$198,** ♦♦♦♦ **$240.**

★★★☆ **Cascade Garden Apartments**, (HU), New Cascade Rd, 500m from shopping centre, ☎ 0011 672322625, fax 0011 672322785, 5 units acc up to 3, [shwr, tlt, fan, tel, TV, clock radio, CD, t/c mkg, refrig, cook fac, toaster, ldry, blkts, linen, pillows], ldry, bbq, cots. D ♦♦ $70 - $79, ◊ $25, W ♦♦ $490 - $553, ◊ $175, ch con, AE BC DC MC VI.

★★★☆ **Channers Corner Holiday Apartments**, (HU), Taylors Rd, ☎ 0011 672322532, fax 0011 672323329, (2 stry gr fl), 6 units acc up to 5, [shwr, tlt, fan, heat, elec blkts, tel, TV, video (avail), clock radio, refrig, cook fac, micro, elec frypan, toaster, blkts, linen, pillows], ldry, bbq, c/park (carport), cots. D ♦ $115, ◊ $25, ch con.

★★★☆ **Colony Lodge**, (HU), Queen Elizabeth Ave, 1.5 km E of PO, ☎ 0011 672322169, fax 0011 672323178, 4 units acc up to 4, [shwr, bath (1), tlt, fan, elec blkts, tel, TV, video, clock radio, refrig, cook fac, micro, elec frypan, toaster, blkts, linen, pillows], ldry, bbq, cots. RO ♦♦ $118, ♦♦♦♦ $140 - $152, 1 cottage of a higher standard, BC MC VI.

★★★☆ **Cumberland Close**, (HU), Taylors Rd, 500m E of PO, ☎ 0011 672322721, fax 0015 672323264, 7 units acc up to 5, [shwr, tlt, fan, heat, elec blkts, tel, TV, video, clock radio, refrig, cook fac, micro, elec frypan, toaster, blkts, linen, pillows], ldry, bbq, cots. RO ♦ $60 - $95, ♦♦ $95 - $150, ◊ $25, 1 unit of a 4 star rating. BC MC VI.

★★★★ **(Cottage Section)**, 1 cotg acc up to 7, [shwr, bath (1), tlt, hairdry (1), fan, heat, elec blkts, tel, TV, video, clock radio, refrig, cook fac, micro, elec frypan, toaster, ldry, blkts, linen, pillows], w/mach, iron, cots. D ♦♦ $150, ◊ $30.

★★★☆ **Cyathea Park Eco Tourist Lodge**, (Cotg), Red Rd, 2km from PO, ☎ 0011 672322636, fax 0011 672322636, 1 cotg acc up to 4, [shwr, tlt, heat, clock radio, t/c mkg, refrig, cook fac, ldry, blkts, linen], w/mach, iron, iron brd, bbq, courtesy transfer, ✆. D ♦♦ $110 - $130, ◊ $18 - $20.

★★★☆ **Daydreamer Holiday Apartments**, (HU), Grass Rd, 350m N of PO, ☎ 0011 672322114, fax 0011 672323014, 12 units acc up to 4, [shwr, tlt, fan, elec blkts, tel, TV, video, clock radio, t/c mkg, refrig, cook fac, micro, toaster, blkts, linen, pillows], ldry, w/mach, iron, bbq, cots. D ♦♦ $150, ◊ $30, ch con, BC DC EFT MC VI.

★★★☆ **Dolphin Inn**, (HU), New Cascade Rd, 2km N of shopping centre, ☎ 0011 672322269, fax 0011 672322376, 6 units acc up to 4, [shwr, tlt, fan, heat, elec blkts, tel, TV, video, refrig, cook fac, micro, toaster, blkts, linen, pillows], ldry, bbq, ✆, plygr. RO ♦♦ $80 - $90, ◊ $15, ch con, BC MC VI.

★★★☆ **Fletcher Christian Apartments**, (SA), Taylors Rd, 500m E of PO, ☎ 0011 672322169, fax 0011 672323178, 13 serv apts acc up to 4, [shwr, tlt, elec blkts, tel, TV, video, clock radio, refrig, cook fac, toaster], ldry, pool, bbq, non smoking property. D ♦♦ $134.50, ♦♦♦♦ $178.50, ◊ $25, Rates include car hire. BC MC VI.

★★★☆ **Hibiscus Aloha**, (HU), Taylors Rd, 100m from PO, ☎ 0011 672322908, fax 0011 672323298, 34 units acc up to 6, [shwr, tlt, heat, elec blkts, tel, TV, video-fee, radio, refrig, cook fac, toaster, blkts, linen, pillows], ldry, rec rm, conv fac, breakfast rm, pool, bbq, courtesy transfer, ✆, plygr, cots. D ♦♦ $100, ◊ $30, W ♦♦ $700, ◊ $210, ch con, MC VI.

★★★☆ **Hibiscus Tudor**, (HU), Taylors Rd, 1.5km S of PO, ☎ 0011 672322908, fax 0011 672322098, 5 units acc up to 8, [shwr, tlt, heat, elec blkts, tel, TV, video (avail), radio, refrig, cook fac, toaster, blkts, linen, pillows], ldry, conv fac, bbq, ✆, cots. RO ♦♦ $72 - $100, ◊ $30, ♦♦ $504 - $700, ◊ $210, ch con, BC MC VI.

★★★☆ **Highland Cottages**, (SA), Selwyn Pine Rd, 2km from shopping centre, ☎ 0011 672322625, fax 0011 672322785, 3 serv apts acc up to 6, [shwr, tlt, hairdry, fan, heat, elec blkts, tel, TV, clock radio, t/c mkg, refrig, cook fac, toaster, blkts, linen, pillows], ldry, w/mach, iron, rec rm, lounge (TV), ✉, pool, bbq, rm serv, dinner to unit, c/park (carport), tennis, cots-fee. D $128, W $896, ch con, AE BC DC MC VI.

★★★☆ **Islander Lodge Apartments**, (HU), Middlegate Rd, Kingston, 100m N of Historic Ruins, ☎ 0011 672322114, fax 0011 672323014, 5 units acc up to 3, [shwr, tlt, fan, elec blkts, tel, TV, video (avail), clock radio, t/c mkg, refrig, cook fac, micro, toaster, blkts, linen, pillows], ldry, iron, bbq, cots. D ♦♦ $150, ◊ $30, BC DC EFT MC VI.

★★★☆ **Kentia Holiday Apartments**, (HU), Collins Head Rd, 4km E of PO, ☎ 0011 672322280, fax 0011 672322977, 5 units acc up to 4, [shwr, tlt, hairdry, fan, heat, elec blkts, tel, TV, clock radio, refrig, cook fac, micro, elec frypan, toaster, ldry (in unit), blkts, linen, pillows], bbq, c/park (carport), cots. D ♦♦ $90, ◊ $20, ch con, AE BC DC MC VI.

★★★☆ **Kingston Apartments**, (Apt), Rooty Hill Rd, 4km SE of PO, ☎ 0011 672322529, fax 0011 672323284, 3 apts acc up to 4, (1 & 2 bedrm), [shwr, tlt, fan (2), c/fan (1), heat, tel, TV, video, clock radio, refrig, cook fac, micro, toaster, blkts, doonas, linen, pillows], ldry, bbq, cots. D ♦ $50 - $80, ♦♦ $100 - $160, ◊ $30, ch con, Min book applies.

★★★☆ **Mokutu Inn**, (HU), Stockyard Rd, 4.5km NE of shopping centre, ☎ 0011 672322262, fax 0011 6723223276, 12 units acc up to 6, [shwr, tlt, fan, heat, elec blkts, tel, video (avail), refrig, cook fac, micro, toaster, blkts, linen, pillows], ldry, t/c mkg shared, bbq, plygr. D ♦ $100, ♦♦ $100, ♦♦♦ $120, ♦♦♦♦ $135, ch con, BC EFT MC VI.

★★★☆ **Mulberry Valley Hideaway**, (Apt), Mill Rd, 3km NE of PO, ☎ 0011 672322433, fax 0011 672322433, 1 apt acc up to 2, (1 bedrm), [shwr, tlt, fan, heat, elec blkts, tel, TV, video, clock radio, refrig, cook fac, micro, toaster, ldry, blkts, doonas, linen, pillows], w/mach, bbq. D $95.

★★★☆ **Nuffka Apartments**, (HU), Ferny La, 500 m S of PO, ☎ 0011 672323513, fax 0011 672323734, 5 units acc up to 3, [shwr, bath, tlt, fan, heat, elec blkts, tel, TV, clock radio, refrig, cook fac, micro, toaster, blkts, linen, pillows], ldry, bbq, ✆. D ♦♦ $95, ◊ $30.

★★★☆ **Pacific Palms**, (HU), Duncombe Bay Rd, ☎ 0011 672323051, fax 0011 672322332, 2 units acc up to 4, [shwr, tlt, hairdry, fan, heat, elec blkts, tel, TV, video, radio, refrig, cook fac, elec frypan, toaster, blkts, linen, pillows], ldry, bbq, c/park (garage). D ♦♦ $68, ◊ $20.

★★★☆ **Peace Holiday Cottage**, (Cotg), Middlegate, 1km E of PO, ☎ 0011 672322822, fax 0011 672322822, 1 cotg acc up to 3, [shwr, tlt, fan, heat, elec blkts, tel, TV, video, clock radio, t/c mkg, refrig, cook fac, micro, toaster, ldry, blkts, linen, pillows], w/mach, dryer, iron, bbq, courtesy transfer, cots. RO ♦♦ $140, Tariffs includes car hire.

★★★☆ **Ponderosa Apartments**, (HU), Longridge, 7km N of PO, ☎ 0011 672322466, fax 0011 672323336, 8 units acc up to 4, [shwr, tlt, fan, elec blkts, tel, TV, clock radio, refrig, cook fac, micro, toaster, blkts, linen, pillows], ldry, pool (salt water), bbq, ✆. RO ♦♦ $85, ◊ $20.

★★★★☆ **(Cottage Section)**, 2 cotgs acc up to 4, [shwr, tlt, fan, elec blkts, tel, TV, video, refrig, cook fac, micro, toaster, blkts, linen, pillows]. D ♦♦ $165, ◊ $40.

★★★☆ **Seavista Holiday Apartments**, (HU), Taylors Rd, 1.5 km S of PO, ☎ 0011 672323539, fax 0011 672322105, 5 units acc up to 5, [shwr, tlt, fan, heat, elec blkts, tel, TV, video, clock radio, refrig, cook fac, micro, toaster, blkts, linen, pillows], ldry, bbq, c/park. RO ♦♦ $65 - $130, ♦♦♦ $65 - $150, ◊ $20, BC MC VI.

★★★☆ **The Crest Apartments**, (HU), Driver Christian Rd, 1.5km E of PO, ☎ 00 11672322280, fax 00 11672322977, 14 units [shwr, tlt, fan, heat, elec blkts, tel, TV, video (2)-fee, clock radio, t/c mkg, refrig, cook fac, micro, toaster, blkts, linen, pillows], ldry, bbq, cots. D ♦♦ $145 - $175, ◊ $25, 2 units of a higher standard, car hire included in tariff, BC MC VI.

★★★☆ **The Palms**, (Cotg), Cascade Rd Middlegate, 2km E of PO, ☎ 0011 672322529, fax 0011 672323284, 1 cotg acc up to 5, (2 bedrm), [shwr, tlt, tel, TV, video, refrig, cook fac, micro, d/wash, toaster, ldry, blkts, doonas, linen, pillows], w/mach, lounge firepl, bbq, cots. D ♦♦ $120 - $150, ◊ $30, ch con.

★★★☆ **Viewrest Inn**, (HU), Grassy Rd, 800m W of PO, ☎ 0011 672322269, fax 0011 672322376, 3 units acc up to 4, [shwr, bath (1), tlt, hairdry, fan, heat, elec blkts, tel, TV, video-fee, clock radio, refrig, cook fac, micro, toaster, blkts, linen, pillows], ldry, bbq, cots. RO ♦♦ $90, ◊ $15, ch con, BC MC VI.

★★★☆ **Whispering Pines**, (HU), Mt Pitt Rd, 2km W of PO, ☎ 0011 672322114, fax 0011 6723 2872, 7 units acc up to 4, [shwr, bath, tlt, hairdry, fan, elec blkts, tel, TV, radio, refrig, cook fac, micro, elec frypan, toaster, ldry (in unit), blkts, linen, pillows], bbq, cots. RO ♦ $210, ♦♦ $210, ◊ $40, BC DC EFT MC VI.

★★★ **Hibiscus Crown**, (HU), New Cascade Rd, 500 m from Town Centre, ☎ 0011 672322325, fax 0011 672322908, 9 units acc up to 6, [shwr, tlt, heat, elec blkts, TV, video-fee, clock radio, refrig, cook fac, toaster, blkts, linen, pillows], ldry, bbq, ✆, tennis, ch con, BC MC VI.

★★★ **Hibiscus Regal**, (HU), New Cascade Rd, 500m N of shopping centre, ☎ 0011 672322325, fax 0011 672322908, 8 units acc up to 3, [shwr, tlt, heat, elec blkts, tel, TV, video-fee, clock radio, refrig, cook fac, micro, toaster, blkts, linen, pillows], ldry, rec rm, pool, bbq, ✆, plygr, tennis, cots, ch con, BC MC VI.

NORFOLK ISLAND NSW continued...

★★★ **Panorama Garden Apartments**, (HU), Middlegate Rd, 400m from Coral Lagoon, ☎ 0011 672322625, fax 0011 672322785, (2 stry gr fl), 12 units acc up to 5, [shwr, tlt, c/fan, elec blkts, tel, TV, clock radio, t/c mkg, refrig, cook fac, toaster, blkts, linen, pillows], ldry, iron, bbq, cots. **D ♦♦ $70 - $128, ♦ $25, W ♦♦ $210 - $896, ♦ $175**, ch con, AE BC DC MC VI.

★★☆ **Anson Bay Lodge**, (HU), Bullocks Hut Rd, Anson Bay, 6.5km W of PO, ☎ 0011 672322897, fax 0011 672323198, 3 units acc up to 4, [shwr, tlt, tel, TV, clock radio, refrig, cook fac, elec frypan, toaster, blkts, linen, pillows], ldry, c/park (carport). **D ♦ $80, ♦ $25.**

★★☆ **Berganin's Cottage**, (Cotg), Burnt Pine, Next to Rawson Hall & PO, ☎ 0011 672322653, 1 cotg acc up to 3, [shwr, bath, tlt, TV, clock radio, t/c mkg, refrig, cook fac, elec frypan, toaster, ldry (in unit), blkts, linen, pillows], iron, cots. **RO ♦ $90, ♦♦ $90, ♦ $30.**

★★☆ **Central Garden Apartments**, (HU), The Village, 1km S of PO, ☎ 0011 672322625, fax 0011 672322785, 4 units acc up to 5, [shwr, tlt, fan, heat, elec blkts, tel (communal), TV, clock radio, t/c mkg, refrig, cook fac, micro, toaster, blkts, linen, pillows], ldry, bbq, cots. **D ♦♦ $97, ♦ $25**, ch con, AE BC DC MC VI.

★★☆ **Pine Valley Apartments**, (HU), New Cascade Rd, 150m N of shopping centre, ☎ 0011 672322202, fax 0011 672323207, 13 units acc up to 4, [shwr, tlt, fan, heat (gas), elec blkts, tel, TV, clock radio, refrig, cook fac, micro, elec frypan, toaster, blkts, linen, pillows], ldry, cots. **D ♦ $75, ♦♦ $89, ♦♦♦ $105, ♦ $18**, Car included with units $5 a day Insurance fee.

★★☆ **Saints Inn Apartments**, (SA), New Cascade Rd, 500m N of shopping centre, ☎ 0011 672323237, fax 0011 672323304, 4 serv apts acc up to 3, [shwr, tlt, fan, elec blkts, tel, TV, clock radio, t/c mkg, refrig, cook fac, toaster, blkts, linen, pillows], w/mach, dryer, iron, iron brd, pool, bbq, courtesy transfer, ☏, cots. **D ♦♦ $95 - $118**, fam con, BC MC VI.

B&B's/Guest Houses

★★★☆ **Aunt Ems Guest House**, (GH), Taylors Rd, opposite PO and Tourist Bureau, ☎ 0011 672322373, fax 0011 672322827, 7 rms [shwr, tlt, fan, elec blkts, tel, clock radio, t/c mkg], ldry, lounge (TV). **BB ♦ $70, ♦♦ $110.**

★★★☆ **Highlands Lodge**, (GH), Selwyn Pine Rd, 2km from Central PO, adjacent to National Park, ☎ 0011 672322741, fax 0011 672322045, (Multi-stry gr fl), 11 rms [shwr, bath (4), tlt, fan, heat, elec blkts, tel, TV, clock radio, t/c mkg, refrig], ldry, rec rm, lounge (TV), ✉, pool, bbq, dinner to unit, tennis, cots. **BB ♦ $117.50 - $169.50, ♦♦ $130 - $182, ♦ $37.50, RO ♦ $105 - $157, ♦♦ $105 - $157, ♦ $25**, ch con, 1 unit of a 4.5 star rating. AE BC DC MC VI.

NORTH AVOCA NSW 2260

Pop Part of Gosford, (90km N Sydney), See map on page 55, ref D6. Central Coast town between Avoca Beach and Terrigal with excellent surfing beaches. Fishing, Swimming.

B&B's/Guest Houses

★★★★☆ **Salty Rose Beach House Bed & Breakfast**, (B&B), 31 Surf Rider Ave, 1km S of Terrigal Shops, ☎ 02 4384 6098, fax 02 4385 1244, (2 stry), 2 rms [shwr, bath (1), tlt, hairdry, a/c, cent heat, elec blkts, tel, radio], iron, iron brd (available), lounge (tv & firepl), t/c mkg shared, bbq, non smoking property. **BB ♦♦ $185 - $249**, BC EFT MC VI.

NORTH HAVEN NSW 2443

Pop 1,650. (402km N Sydney), See map on page 54, ref C7. Part of an area referred to as Camden Haven, a place of complex waterways and excellent fisheries centred around the Camden Haven River. Bowls, Fishing, Swimming, Tennis.

Hotels/Motels

★★★☆ **Woongarra Motel**, (M), 5 The Parade, adjacent Bowls Club, ☎ 02 6559 9088, fax 02 6559 6426, 16 units [shwr, tlt, fan, heat, elec blkts, tel, TV, movie, clock radio, t/c mkg, refrig], ldry, pool, bbq, non smoking units (11). **RO ♦ $65 - $100, ♦♦ $65 - $100, ♦ $12, Suite D ♦♦ $80 - $125**, 6 units of a lower rating, AE BC DC EFT MC VI.

★★★ **Haven Waters**, (M), 9 The Parade, 50m N of PO, ☎ 02 6559 9303, fax 02 6559 9835, 14 units [shwr, tlt, a/c, fan, heat, elec blkts, tel, movie, clock radio, t/c mkg, refrig, toaster], ldry, pool, spa, bbq, cots-fee. **RO ♦♦ $69 - $190, ♦ $15**, ch con, AE BC DC MC VI.

Operator Comment: New Owner/Operators - (Formerly Lobster Pot Motel and Holiday Apartments).

★★★☆ **(Holiday Unit Section)**, 7 units [shwr, bath (6), tlt, hairdry, a/c, heat, tel, TV, movie, refrig, cook fac, micro, d/wash (1), toaster, ldry (in unit) (1)], pool, spa, bbq, plygr, cots-fee, non smoking units (2). **D $99 - $190, W $693 - $1,190, ⬛&.**

★★★ **North Haven Motel**, (M), 506 Ocean Dve, ☎ 02 6559 9604, fax 02 6559 9604, 6 units [shwr, tlt, fan, heat, elec blkts, tel, TV, clock radio, t/c mkg, refrig, toaster], bbq, rm serv, cots. **W ♦♦ $352 - $497, RO ♦ $46 - $64, ♦♦ $55 - $75, ♦♦♦ $64 - $86, ♦ $11**, ch con, AE BC EFT MC VI.

Operator Comment: Website: www.northhavenmotel.com.au

Self Catering Accommodation

★★★ **Japana Holiday Units**, (HU), 31 Alma St, opposite bowling club, ☎ 02 6559 9140, 5 units acc up to 6, [shwr, bath, tlt, fan, heat, TV, video (avail), clock radio, refrig, cook fac, micro, ldry, linen reqd-fee], bbq, c/park (garage), secure park, cots. **D $50 - $80, W $220 - $850**, Min book applies.

★★★ **Sundial Holiday Inn**, (HU), 591 Ocean Dve, 300m S of PO, ☎ 02 6559 9371, 4 units acc up to 5, [shwr, tlt, fan, heat, TV, refrig, cook fac, micro, linen reqd-fee], ldry, bbq, c/park (undercover). **D $50 - $80, W $230 - $550.**

★★☆ **Allinga**, (HU), 51 The Parade, ☎ 02 6559 9137, 5 units acc up to 6, [shwr, tlt, fan, heat, TV, video, radio, refrig, cook fac, micro, toaster, linen reqd], ldry, bbq, c/park (garage). **D $240 - $580.**

★★☆ **Laurieton Boat-o-Tel**, (HU), 3 Bridge St, ☎ 02 6559 9381, fax 02 6559 6547, 13 units acc up to 6, [shwr, tlt, TV, refrig, cook fac, toaster, linen reqd], ldry, bbq, c/park (undercover), jetty. **D $55 - $88, W $250 - $560**, BC MC VI.

★★☆ **Pioneer Holiday Units**, (HU), 3 Pioneer St, ☎ 02 6559 6586, 4 units acc up to 5, [shwr, bath, tlt, fan, heat, TV, refrig, cook fac, micro, elec frypan, toaster, ldry, linen reqd-fee], w/mach, iron, bbq, c/park (carport). **D $50 - $85, W $280 - $500.**

NORTH ROTHBURY NSW 2335

Pop 450. (169km N Sydney), See map on page 55, ref B7.

Hotels/Motels

★★★☆ **Hunter Country Lodge**, (M), 220 Branxton Rd, 12km N of Cessnock Airport, ☎ 02 4938 1744, fax 02 4938 1983, 16 units [shwr, tlt, hairdry, a/c, heat, tel, TV, video (avail), clock radio, t/c mkg, refrig, mini bar], ⊠, pool (salt water), bbq, cots. RO ♦♦ $120 - $180, ♦ $15, 4 units of a higher rating, AE BC DC MC VI.

NOWENDOC NSW 2354

Pop Nominal, (339km NW Sydney), See map on page 54, ref A7. Small village on the Thunderbolts Way, the main route from Walcha to Gloucester. Bush Walking, Scenic Drives.

Hotels/Motels

★★☆ **Nowendoc Country Motel**, (M), Wingham Rd, Midway Gloucester & Walcha, ☎ 02 6777 0952, fax 02 6777 0952, 4 units (4 suites) [shwr, tlt, heat, elec blkts, tel, TV, clock radio, t/c mkg, refrig, elec frypan, toaster], cots. BLB ♦ $30, ♦♦ $45.

★★☆ **(Cottage Section)**, 2 cotgs acc up to 8, [shwr (3), tlt (3), heat (wood), elec blkts, tel, TV, clock radio, t/c mkg, refrig, elec frypan, toaster, blkts, linen, pillows], ldry, iron, c/park. BLB ♦ $30, ♦♦ $55.

NOWRA NSW 2541

Pop 23,800. (144km S Sydney), See map on page 55, ref B4. Administrative and commercial centre of the Shoalhaven area, situated on the Shoalhaven River. Along with neighbouring Bomaderry, it forms the largest centre on the New South Wales coast south of Wollongong. Bowls, Canoeing, Fishing, Golf, Sailing, Scenic Drives, Squash, Swimming, Tennis, Water Skiing.

Hotels/Motels

★★★★ **George Bass Motor Inn**, (M), 65 Bridge Rd, 500m N of PO, ☎ 02 4421 6388, fax 02 4423 1909, 10 units [shwr, tlt, hairdry, a/c, elec blkts, tel, TV, video (avail), clock radio, t/c mkg, refrig, mini bar, toaster], ldry, iron, dinner to unit, cots, non smoking units (7). RO ♦ $72 - $98, ♦♦ $78 - $100, AE BC DC EFT MC VI, ♿.

★★★★ **Park Haven Motor Lodge**, (M), 150 Kinghorn St, 800m SE of PO, ☎ 02 4421 6444, fax 02 4421 5384, (2 stry gr fl) 30 units [shwr, spa bath (8), tlt, a/c, elec blkts, tel, fax, TV, video (avail), clock radio, t/c mkg, refrig, cook fac ltd (5)], ldry, conv fac, ⊠, pool (salt water), rm serv, cots-fee, non smoking units. RO ♦ $81 - $98, ♦♦ $92 - $159, ♦ $11, 15 units of a lower rating. AE BC DC MC VI.

★★★☆ **Archer Resort**, (LMH), Cnr Kalander St & Princes Hwy, 2km S of PO, ☎ 02 4421 5222, fax 02 4422 1788, 62 units (2 suites) [shwr, bath (7), spa bath (1), tlt, a/c, tel, TV, clock radio, t/c mkg, refrig], ldry, conv fac, night club (Thurs to Sat), ⊠, pool, sauna, spa, rm serv, dinner to unit, tennis, cots-fee. RO ♦ $49 - $99, ♦♦ $55 - $115, ♦♦♦ $62.20 - $128.20, ♦ $13.20, Suite D ♦♦ $85 - $115, ch con, 6 units subject to disco noise. AE BC DC MC VI, ♿.

★★★☆ **Avaleen Lodge Motor Inn**, (M), 317 Princes Hwy, Bomaderry, 3km N of PO, ☎ 02 4421 8244, fax 02 4421 8043, (2 stry gr fl) 6 units [shwr, tlt, hairdry, a/c, elec blkts, tel, TV, video, clock radio, t/c mkg, refrig, mini bar, cook fac (1), micro], baby bath, ldry, iron, iron brd, pool-heated (solar), bbq, dinner to unit, courtesy transfer, cots, non smoking units. RO ♦ $72 - $90, ♦♦ $76 - $90, ♦ $12, AE BC DC EFT MC VI.

Avaleen Lodge Motor Inn ...continued

★★★☆ **(Serviced Apartment Section)**, 4 serv apts [shwr, tlt, a/c, fan, heat, elec blkts, tel, TV, video-fee, clock radio, t/c mkg, refrig, mini bar, cook fac, micro, ldry (in unit)], baby bath, bbq, dinner to unit, courtesy transfer, cots. RO ♦ $108, ♦♦ $108 - $125, ♦ $12, ch con.

★★★☆ **Balan Village Motel**, (M), 175 Cambewarra Rd, 3km NE of PO, ☎ 02 4423 1111, fax 02 4423 1101, 25 units (11 suites) [shwr, spa bath (1), tlt, a/c, fan, elec blkts, tel, TV, movie, clock radio, t/c mkg, refrig, mini bar, cook fac (3), toaster], ldry, conv fac, ⊠, pool-heated (solar), bbq, rm serv, plygr, gym, non smoking units (3). RO ♦ $75 - $104, ♦♦ $87 - $150, ♦♦♦ $110 - $136, ♦ $6, Suite D $104 - $130, Min book long w/ends and Easter, AE BC DC EFT JCB MC MP VI, ♿.

★★★☆ **Bomaderry Motor Inn**, (M), 321 Princes Hwy, Bomaderry, 3km N of PO, ☎ 02 4421 0111, fax 02 4421 0126, 23 units [shwr, spa bath (1), tlt, hairdry, a/c, tel, TV, clock radio, t/c mkg, refrig, cook fac (6), toaster], ldry, iron, iron brd, pool (salt water), bbq, courtesy transfer, non smoking units (8). RO ♦ $60, ♦♦ $71, ♦ $6, AE BC DC MC VI, ♿.

★★★☆ **Bounty Motor Inn**, (M), 271 Princes Hwy, Bomaderry, 3km N of PO, ☎ 02 4421 2233, fax 02 4423 1844, 20 units [shwr, tlt, a/c, elec blkts, tel, cable tv, t/c mkg, refrig], iron, iron brd, ☒, pool, tennis, non smoking units (14). RO ♪ $60.50 - $82.50, ♪♪ $66 - $88, ♪♪♪ $77 - $99, ☼ $11, AE BC DC EFT MC VI.

Country Haven

★★★☆ **Nowra Motor Inn**, (M), 202 Kinghorn St, 800m S of PO, ☎ 02 4421 0555, fax 02 4423 1506, (2 stry gr fl), 30 units [shwr, bath (2), tlt, hairdry, a/c, fan (19), elec blkts, tel, TV, movie, clock radio, t/c mkg, refrig], ldry, ☒, pool (salt water), bbq, rm serv, trailer park, cots. RO ♪ $61 - $71, ♪♪ $69 - $79, ☼ $10, AE BC DC EFT MC MP VI.

Welcome MOTOR INNS

★★★☆ **Pleasant Way Motor Inn**, (M), Pleasant Way, 1km N of PO, ☎ 02 4421 5544, fax 02 4422 1743, (2 stry gr fl), 22 units [shwr, tlt, a/c, heat, elec blkts, tel, TV, video-fee, t/c mkg, refrig], ldry, rec rm, pool indoor heated, spa, bbq, plygr, cots-fee, non smoking units (9). RO ♪ $88 - $99, ♪♪ $93.50 - $109, ♪♪♪ $104.50 - $109, ☼ $11, ch con, Min book applies, AE BC DC JCB MC MP VI.

FLAG FLAG CHOICE HOTELS

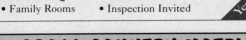

★★★ **Cross Country Motel**, (M), 242 Kinghorne St, 2km S of PO, ☎ 02 4421 7777, fax 02 4421 7306, 19 units [shwr, tlt, hairdry, a/c, elec blkts, tel, fax, TV, video-fee, clock radio, t/c mkg, refrig, toaster], ldry, pool, bbq, cots-fee, non smoking units (10). **RO** ♦ **$57 - $70**, ♦♦ **$68 - $80**, ♦♦♦ **$82 - $92**, ◊ **$14**, AE BC DC EFT JCB MC MCH MP VI.

★★★ **Marriott Park**, (M), Cnr Princes Hwy & Douglas Sts, 900m SE of PO, ☎ 02 4421 6999, fax 02 4423 2557, 16 units [shwr, tlt, a/c, elec blkts, tel, fax, TV, video-fee, clock radio, t/c mkg, refrig], ldry, bbq, cots-fee, non smoking units (5). **RO** ♦ **$64 - $75**, ♦♦ **$70 - $82**, ♦♦♦ **$84 - $100**, ◊ **$12**, ch con, Min book applies, AE BC DC MC VI.

★★★ **Riverhaven Motel**, (M), Scenic Dve, 1km N of PO, ☎ 02 4421 2044, fax 02 4421 2121, 22 units [shwr, bath (1), tlt, hairdry, a/c, elec blkts, tel, TV, video (1), clock radio, t/c mkg, refrig, cook fac (1), micro (1), toaster], ldry, rec rm, business centre, conv fac, ⊠, pool indoor heated, bbq, cots, non smoking units (3). **RO** ♦ **$60 - $75**, ♦♦ **$60 - $75**, ♦♦ **$60 - $75**, ♦♦♦ **$85 - $100**, ◊ **$10**, 9 units ★★☆. AE BC DC EFT MC VI.

Self Catering Accommodation

 ★★★★☆ **River Reflections**, (SA), 34 Illaroo Rd, ☎ 0410 488 067, 1 serv apt acc up to 6, [shwr, bath, tlt, hairdry, a/c, tel, TV, video, clock radio, t/c mkg, refrig, cook fac, micro, elec frypan, d/wash, toaster, ldry, blkts, linen], w/mach, dryer, iron, iron brd, bbq, non smoking property. **D** ♦♦ **$120 - $210**, ◊ **$25 - $35**, **W** ♦♦ **$480 - $1,500**, Min book applies.

★★★ **Mopoke Ridge Cottage**, (Cotg), 45b Mopoke Close, Longreach 2541 11km W of Nowra PO, ☎ 02 4422 0049, fax 02 4422 6064, 1 cotg acc up to 6, [shwr, bath, tlt, fan, heat, TV, video, t/c mkg, refrig, cook fac, micro, elec frypan, toaster, ldry, doonas, linen], w/mach, iron, iron brd, rec rm, pool (salt water), bbq, non smoking property. **D** ♦♦ **$126.50**, ◊ **$33**, **W** **$400 - $700**.

Tapitallee Retreat, (Cotg), Lilli Pilli Lne, 11km W of PO, ☎ 02 4446 0452, 2 cotgs acc up to 14, [tel, blkts, linen], rec rm, conv fac, t/c mkg shared, bbq, dinner to unit, c/park. **D** ♦ **$40 - $55**, ch con, weekly con.

B&B's/Guest Houses

★★★★ **Peachtree House Bed & Breakfast**, (B&B), 2 Peachtree Close, 5km SE of PO, ☎ 02 4423 3675, 1 rm [hairdry, fan, heat, TV, clock radio, t/c mkg, refrig], bathrm, iron, iron brd, bbq, non smoking property. **BB** ♦♦ **$90**, ◊ **$20**, BC MC VI.

★★★☆ **The White House**, (GH), 30 Junction St, 300m W of PO, ☎ 02 4421 2084, fax 02 4423 6876, (2 stry gr fl), 10 rms [hairdry, a/c-cool (5), fan, heat, elec blkts, TV, clock radio, t/c mkg, refrig], ldry, iron, iron brd, lounge (TV), lounge firepl, ⊠, bbq, cots-fee, non smoking property. **BB** ♦ **$55 - $77**, ♦♦ **$77 - $99**, ◊ **$11**, 2 rooms yet to be assessed, BC MC VI.

★★ **M&M'S Guest House**, (GH), 1a Scenic Dve, 200m W of Information Centre, ☎ 02 4422 8006, fax 02 4422 8007, 12 rms [a/c (9), c/fan, toaster (1)], ldry, rec rm, lounge (TV), lounge firepl, t/c mkg shared, refrig, bbq, cots, non smoking property. **BLB** ♦ **$25**, ♦♦ **$50**, ◊ **$10**, BC MC VI.

NULKABA NSW 2325

Pop Nominal, (180km N Sydney), See map on page 55, ref B7. Rural settlement in the Hunter Valley near Cessnock, established in the 1880s and once the centre of a large pottery making concern. Vineyards, Wineries.

Self Catering Accommodation

★★★★ **Wirral Grange Vineyard**, (Cotg), Lot 4, Lomas Lane, 7km S of Cessnock PO, ☎ 02 4990 5877, fax 02 4990 5877, 1 cotg acc up to 4, (2 bedrm), [shwr, tlt, fan, heat (elec), TV, video, t/c mkg, refrig, cook fac, micro, ldry, blkts, linen, pillows], pool, bbq, non smoking rms. **D** ♦ **$50 - $100**, ♦♦ **$100 - $200**.

★★★★ **Woodlane Cottages**, (Cotg), Lot 1971, Lomas La, 1km E of Rusa Park Zoo, ☎ 02 4991 3762, fax 02 4990 9586, 4 cotgs acc up to 8, [shwr, bath (2), tlt, a/c, c/fan, fire pl, TV, video, CD, t/c mkg, refrig, cook fac, micro, toaster, blkts, linen], bbq, non smoking property. **D** ♦♦ **$90 - $155**, ch con, BC MC VI.

B&B's/Guest Houses

★★★☆ **Nulkaba House**, (GH), 10 Austral St, ☎ 02 4991 4599, fax 02 4991 4599, (2 stry gr fl), 3 rms [ensuite (1), bath (1), tlt, hairdry, a/c, elec blkts, tel], iron, iron brd, lounge (TV & firepl), ⊠, bbq, non smoking rms (3). **BB** ♦ **$95 - $160**, ♦♦ **$95 - $160**, BC MC VI.

NUNDLE NSW 2340

Pop 250. (438km NW Sydney), See map on pages 52/53, ref J3. Historic gold village in the foothills of the Peel Ranges on the Fossickers Way. Bowls, Fishing, Gem Fossicking, Golf, Sailing, Scenic Drives, Tennis.

Hotels/Motels

★☆ **Hills of Gold**, (M), Jenkins St, Opposite post office, ☎ 02 6769 3222, fax 02 6769 3239, 6 units [shwr, tlt, fan, heat, elec blkts, TV, radio, t/c mkg, refrig, toaster], cots. **RO** ♦ **$45**, ♦♦ **$66 - $80**, ◊ **$10 - $25**, ch con, BC MC VI.

Peel Inn, (LH), Jenkins St, opposite PO, ☎ 02 6769 3377, fax 02 6769 3307, (2 stry), 9 rms [shwr (2), tlt (2), fan (4), c/fan (5), heat, elec blkts, TV, t/c mkg], ldry, ⊠. **BLB** ♦♦ **$65 - $70**, ch con, AE BC EFT MC VI.

B&B's/Guest Houses

★★★ **Jenkins Street Guesthouse**, (GH), 85 Jenkins St, 200m S of PO, ☎ 02 6769 3239, fax 02 6769 3239, 6 rms (3 suites) [shwr (4), bath (2), tlt (4), hairdry, heat, elec blkts], shared fac (2 rms), lounge firepl, ⊠, c/park. **BB** ♦♦ **$110 - $160**, BC DC MC VI.

★★ **Oak Cottage Hanging Rock**, (B&B), Barry Rd, Hanging Rock, 14km E of Nundle, ☎ 02 6769 3625, 1 rm [shwr, bath, tlt, fan, heat, elec blkts, t/c mkg, refrig, toaster], ldry, ⊠, bbq, dinner to unit, c/park (garage). **BB** ♦ **$55 - $65**, ♦♦ **$80 - $90**, **RO** ♦ **$35 - $45**, ♦♦ **$55 - $65**.

NYMBOIDA NSW 2460

Pop Nominal, (687km N Sydney), See map on page 54, ref C4. Small village on the Grafton-Armidale road, close to the wilderness area of Nymboida National Park. Bush Walking, Canoeing.

Hotels/Motels

★★★★ **Nymboida Coaching Station Inn & Restaurant**, (LMH), Armidale Rd, 40km SW of Grafton, ☎ 02 6649 4126, fax 02 6649 4187, 15 units [shwr, spa bath, tlt, a/c, tel, TV, clock radio, t/c mkg, refrig, toaster], ldry, conv fac, ⊠, rm serv, c/park. **BB** ♦ **$117.15**, ♦♦ **$125.40**, ◊ **$19.25**, **RO** ♦ **$108.90**, ♦♦ **$108.90**, ◊ **$11**, BC EFT MC VI.

NYNGAN NSW 2825

Pop 2,250. (599km W Sydney), See map on pages 52/53, ref F3. Nyngan lies on the banks of the Bogan River at the junction of the Mitchell and Barrier Highways. Bowls, Fishing, Golf, Swimming, Tennis, Water Skiing.

Hotels/Motels

★★★☆ **Country Manor Motor Inn**, (M), 145 Pangee St, opposite RSL Club, ☎ 02 6832 1447, fax 02 6832 2113, 20 units [shwr, tlt, hairdry, a/c, tel, cable tv, clock radio, t/c mkg, refrig], iron, iron brd, pool (salt water), cots-fee, non smoking units (1). **RO** ♦ **$54**, ♦♦ **$65**, ♦♦♦ **$76**, ◊ **$11**, AE BC DC EFT MC VI.

Operator Comment: See advertisement on next page.

 ★★★ **Alamo Motor Inn**, (M), Mitchell Hwy, 500m NW of PO, ☎ 02 6832 1660, fax 02 6832 1324, 24 units [shwr, tlt, hairdry, a/c, tel, TV, video-fee, clock radio, t/c mkg, refrig, toaster], ldry, pool, bbq, dinner to unit, cots. **RO** ♦ **$45 - $50**, ♦♦ **$55 - $60**, ch con, 4 units of a higher standard. AE BC DC EFT MC MCH VI.

N

NEW SOUTH WALES

★★★ **Sundowner Chain Motor Inns**, (M), Mitchell Hwy, 1.5km E of PO, ☎ 02 6832 1501, fax 02 6832 2004, (2 stry gr fl), 47 units [shwr, bath (2), tlt, a/c, tel, TV, video (avail)-fee, clock radio, t/c mkg, refrig, toaster], ldry, ⊠, pool, rm serv, dinner to unit, cots-fee, non smoking units (15). **RO** ♦ **$50 - $131**, ♦♦ **$56 - $131**, ♦ **$11**, ch con, 18 units of a lower rating. AE BC DC MC VI.

OAK FLATS NSW 2529

Pop 6,713. (106km S Sydney), See map on page 55, ref C4. Small town in the Shellharbour area. Fishing, Surfing, Swimming.

Hotels/Motels

★★★ **Lakeview Motel Hotel**, (LMH), Old Lake Entrance Rd, 1km E of PO, ☎ 02 4256 5292, fax 02 4257 3302, 25 units [shwr, tlt, a/c (13), fan, heat, TV, clock radio, t/c mkg, refrig, toaster], ldry, dryer, ⊠, bbq, plygr, cots. **RO** ♦ **$61**, ♦♦ **$72**, ♦♦♦ **$100**, ♦♦♦♦ **$135**, ch con, AE BC EFT MC VI, ♿.

OBERON NSW

See Blue Mountains Region.

O'CONNELL NSW

See Blue Mountains Region.

OCEAN SHORES NSW 2483

Pop 3,350. (800km N Sydney), See map on page 54, ref E2. Town renowned for its golf course on the far north coast near Brunswick Heads. Fishing, Golf, Scenic Drives, Surfing, Swimming.

Hotels/Motels

★★★ **Pacific Palms Motel**, (M), Cnr Orana Rd & Balemo Dve, 3km N of Brunswick Heads PO, ☎ 02 6680 2222, fax 02 6680 2018, 12 units [shwr, bath (1), tlt, a/c-cool (2), c/fan (10), heat, tel, TV, video-fee, clock radio, t/c mkg, refrig, micro (1), toaster], pool, bbq, c/park. **W $300 - $730, RO** ♦ **$55 - $90**, ♦♦ **$66 - $110**, ♦♦♦ **$77 - $122**, ♦ **$15**, AE BC DC MC VI.

OLD BAR NSW 2430

Pop 2,650. (321km N Sydney), See map on page 54, ref C8. Mid-north coastal town east of Taree. Surfing.

Self Catering Accommodation

★★★★☆ **Chiltern Lodge Country Retreat**, (Cotg), 139 Metz Rd, 10km SE of Taree PO, ☎ 02 6553 3190, fax 02 6553 3490, 4 cotgs acc up to 6, [shwr, tlt, c/fan, fire pl, elec blkts, TV, clock radio, refrig, cook fac, micro, elec frypan, toaster, ldry (in cabin), blkts, linen, pillows], iron, rec rm, lounge (TV), pool (salt water), spa, bbq, meals to unit, ☎.
D $148 - $198, W $790 - $1,590, ch con, Min book all holiday times, AE BC MC VI, ♿,
Operator Comment: See our Display advertisement under Taree.

SeaChange Holiday Cottage, (Cotg), 23 Bryan St, 200m fr PO, mob 0409 533 190, fax 02 6553 3490, 1 cotg acc up to 5, (3 bedrm), [shwr, tlt, fan, heat, elec blkts, tel, TV, video, clock radio, t/c mkg, refrig, cook fac, micro, toaster, ldry, blkts, doonas, linen, pillows], w/mach, dryer, bbq, c/park (undercover), plygr, non smoking property.
D ♦ **$85 - $145**, ♦ **$25, W** ♦♦ **$520 - $1,050**, ♦ **$100**, ch con, Minimum booking weekends & school holidays, BC MC VI, (not yet classified)
Operator Comment: Beautifully furnished, quiet seaside village atmosphere and top location! Walk to cafÈs, restaurants, bowling club, tennis, park pool & surf beach. Close to craft galleries, lagoon fishing, golf, river cruises & bushwalks. www.seachangecottage.com.au

B&B's/Guest Houses

★★★★ **Old Bar Beach Bed & Breakfast**, (B&B), 25 Old Bar Rd, 200m E of PO, ☎ 02 6553 7032, fax 02 6553 3717, (2 stry gr fl), 3 rms [shwr, bath (1), tlt, hairdry, c/fan, heat, elec blkts, TV, clock radio, t/c mkg, refrig], lounge firepl, bbq, dinner to unit, courtesy transfer, cots, non smoking property. **BB** ♦ **$100 - $140**, ♦♦ **$125 - $160**, ♦ **$25 - $40**, pen con, BC MC VI.

ORANGE NSW 2800

Pop 30,700. (276km W Sydney), See map on pages 52/53, ref G5. Major central west commercial centre for a rich and diversified district that is particularly suited to cold climate fruit growing. It lies at the foot of an extinct volcano, Mount Canobolas. Boating, Bowls, Fishing, Golf, Scenic Drives, Swimming, Tennis. See also Cudal.

Hotels/Motels

★★★★☆ **Central Caleula Motor Lodge**, (M), 60 Summer St, ☎ 02 6362 7699, fax 02 6362 7162, (2 stry gr fl), 59 units (2 suites) [shwr, bath (3), spa bath (10), tlt, a/c-cool (10), a/c, c/fan, heat, elec blkts, tel, TV, video-fee, clock radio, t/c mkg, refrig], ldry, conv fac, ⊠, pool (salt water), 24hr reception, rm serv, c/park (undercover), cots-fee, non smoking units (28).
RO ♦♦ **$110 - $170**, ♦♦♦ **$125 - $170**, ♦ **$15, Suite D $165 - $170**, AE BC DC JCB MC VI.

★★★★ **Apple City International Motor Inn**, (M), 146 Bathurst Rd, 2km E of PO, ☎ 02 6362 6033, fax 02 6362 6532, (2 stry gr fl), 50 units (3 suites) [shwr, bath (8), spa bath (3), tlt, hairdry, a/c, cent heat, elec blkts, tel, cable tv, movie, clock radio, t/c mkg, refrig, mini bar, toaster], ldry, iron, iron brd, conv fac, ⊠, rm serv, cots-fee, non smoking units (20). **RO** ♦ **$93.50 - $181.50**, ♦♦ **$104.50 - $181.50**, ♦ **$11**, ch con, Some units at a three star plus rating. Min book applies, AE BC DC EFT MC MP VI.

★★★★ **Town Square Motel**, (M), 246-248 Anson St, 250m N of PO, ☎ 02 6369 1444, fax 02 6361 3806, (2 stry gr fl), 29 units [shwr, bath (13), spa bath (1), tlt, hairdry, a/c, cent heat, elec blkts, tel, cable tv, video, clock radio, t/c mkg, refrig, mini bar, toaster], iron, iron brd, rec rm, lounge, conf fac, ✕, rm serv, courtesy transfer, cots, non smoking units (16). **RO** ♦ $92 - $105, ♦♦ $105 - $115, ◊ $10 - $15, ch con, fam con, pen con, AE BC DC EFT MC MP VI, ⟨⟩.

★★★☆ **Orange Motor Lodge**, (M), 110 Bathurst Rd, 2km E of PO, ☎ 02 6362 4600, fax 02 6362 0601, 27 units (1 suite) [shwr, tlt, a/c, heat (6), elec blkts, tel, TV, video (avail), clock radio, t/c mkg, refrig, cook fac (2)], ldry, bbq, rm serv (Mon to Thurs), cots-fee, non smoking units (6). **RO** ♦ $72 - $92, ♦♦ $81 - $102, ♦♦♦ $103 - $113, ◊ $11, ch con, Some units ★★★. Min book long w/ends and Easter, AE BC DC MC MP VI.

★★★☆ **Oriana Motor Inn**, (M), Woodward St, 1km of PO, ☎ 02 6362 3066, fax 02 6361 4977, (2 stry gr fl), 47 units [shwr, bath (2), tlt, a/c, heat, elec blkts, tel, TV, clock radio, t/c mkg, refrig], conv fac, ✕, pool, rm serv, non smoking units (13). **RO** ♦ $66 - $75, ♦♦ $72 - $83, ♦♦♦ $83 - $94, ◊ $11, 23 units of a 3 star rating. Minium booking Oct Field Days. AE BC DC EFT MC MCH VI.

Part of the Orange Ex-Services Club Leisure Centre

Awarded the NSW Tourism Award for Excellence

- Centrally located
- Executive suites with spas
- Disabled persons units
- Honorary membership to Orange Ex-services Club and full range of sporting facilities
- Full function facilities
- Full SKY Channel & Austar facilities

TEMPLERS MILL MOTEL
94 Byng St, Orange
Ph: (02) 6362 5611 Fax: (02) 6361 3714

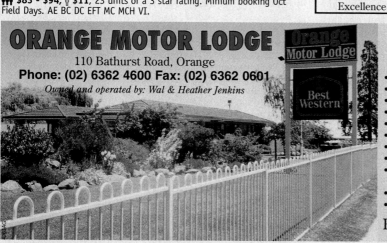

ORANGE MOTOR LODGE

110 Bathurst Road, Orange
Phone: (02) 6362 4600 Fax: (02) 6362 0601
Owned and operated by: Wal & Heather Jenkins

Economy to Deluxe and Self Contained Accommodation

AAAT ★★★☆

- All ground floor accommodation
- Friendly service
- Air conditioning
- Video hire
- Some queen size beds
- Electric Blankets
- Discount rates for extended stays
- Plenty of parking space
- Next door to McDonalds, Kentucky Fried and Restaurant
- Direct indial phones
- Room Service Monday-Thursday

Reservations Phone 1800 353 221

THE CENTRAL CALEULA MOTOR LODGE

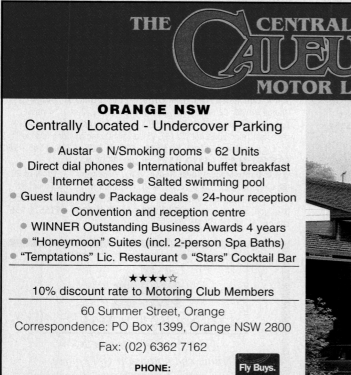

AAA Tourism ★★★★☆

ORANGE NSW
Centrally Located - Undercover Parking

- Austar ● N/Smoking rooms ● 62 Units
- Direct dial phones ● International buffet breakfast
- Internet access ● Salted swimming pool
- Guest laundry ● Package deals ● 24-hour reception
- Convention and reception centre
- WINNER Outstanding Business Awards 4 years
- "Honeymoon" Suites (incl. 2-person Spa Baths)
- "Temptations" Lic. Restaurant ● "Stars" Cocktail Bar

★★★★☆
10% discount rate to Motoring Club Members

60 Summer Street, Orange
Correspondence: PO Box 1399, Orange NSW 2800

Fax: (02) 6362 7162

PHONE:
(02) 6362 7699

Fly Buys.

FREE CALL
1800 024 845
Email:
caleula@bestwestern.com.au

Best Western
Be our guest.

★★★☆ **Sundowner Chain Motor Inns**, (M), Cnr Mitchell Hwy & Dalton St, 2km NW of PO, ☎ 02 6362 5755, fax 02 6362 9021, (2 stry), 41 units [shwr, tlt, hairdry, a/c-cool, heat, elec blkts, tel, cable tv, clock radio, t/c mkg, refrig, mini bar, toaster], iron, iron brd, ⊠ (Mon to Sat), pool indoor heated, sauna, spa, dinner to unit, plygr, cots-fee, non smoking units (11). RO ‡ $88 - $142, ‡‡ $95 - $142, ◊ $11, ch con, some units ★★★. Min book applies Bathurst w/end, AE BC DC EFT MC MP VI.

★★★☆ **Templers Mill Motel**, (M), 94 Byng St, 500m N of PO, adjoining Ex-Services Club, ☎ 02 6362 5611, fax 02 6361 3714, (2 stry gr fl), 31 units (6 suites) [shwr, spa bath (6), tlt, hairdry, a/c, elec blkts, tel, cable tv, video (17), clock radio, t/c mkg, refrig], ldry, conv fac, ⊠, pool indoor heated, rm serv, dinner to unit, cots-fee, non smoking units (6). RO ‡ $80, ‡‡ $92, ◊ $11, Suite D ‡ $105, ‡‡ $116, ◊ $11, ch con, AE BC DC EFT MC VI, ⚹&.

★★★ **Mid-City Motor Lodge**, (M), 243 Lords Pl, 300m NE of PO, ☎ 02 6362 1600, fax 02 6363 1714, (2 stry gr fl), 42 units [shwr, spa bath (2), tlt, a/c, cent heat, elec blkts, tel, TV, video (avail), clock radio, t/c mkg, refrig], ldry, ⊠, dinner to unit, cots-fee, non smoking units (6). RO ‡ $80 - $91, ‡‡ $91 - $101, ◊ $15, ch con, Some units ★★★☆. AE BC DC EFT MC MP VI.

★★☆ **Down Town Motel**, (M), 243 Summer St, opposite PO, ☎ 02 6362 2877, fax 02 6362 2877, 8 units [shwr, tlt, fan, heat, elec blkts, TV, clock radio, t/c mkg, refrig], dinner to unit, c/park (undercover) (5), cots-fee, non smoking units (3). RO ‡ $52 - $55, ‡‡ $64 - $67, ‡‡‡ $78 - $90, ◊ $12, ch con, AE BC DC MC VI.

★★ **Canobolas Licensed Hotel**, (LH), 248 Summer St, 200m E of PO, ☎ 02 6362 2444, fax 02 6362 9361, (Multi-stry), 92 rms (1 suite) [shwr (62), bath (10), tlt (62), cent heat, tel, TV, t/c mkg, refrig (80)], lift, ldry, conf fac, ⊠, cots. D ‡ $44 - $82.50, ‡‡ $82.50 - $132, Some units ★☆, 10 units ★★★. Min book long w/ends, AE BC DC EFT MC VI.

★★ **Ophir Tavern**, (LMH), Glenroi Ave, ☎ 02 6362 4995, fax 02 6362 8156, 4 units [shwr, tlt, a/c, heat, elec blkts, TV, clock radio, t/c mkg, refrig, toaster], conv fac, ⊠, ✆, BC EFT MC VI.

★ **Metropolitan Licensed Hotel**, (LH), 107 Byng St, 350m S of PO, ☎ 02 6362 1353, (2 stry), 16 rms [elec blkts, TV, cook fac (1)], shared fac (15 rms), ⊠, ✆, cots. BLB ‡ $40, ‡‡ $55, ◊ $15, AE BC DC EFT MC VI.

★ **Occidental Licensed Motel Hotel**, (LMH), Cnr Lords Pl & Kite St, 25m from PO, ☎ 02 6362 4833, fax 02 6361 3085, 20 units [shwr, tlt, elec blkts, TV, clock radio, t/c mkg, refrig, toaster], ⊠ (Mon to Thur), ✆. RO ‡ $55, ‡‡ $55, ◊ $10, BC MC VI.

Self Catering Accommodation
★★★ **Melview Greens**, (HU), Ploughmans La, 3.6km W of PO, ☎ 02 6362 0955, fax 02 6362 0855, 7 units acc up to 6, [shwr, tlt, heat, tel, TV, clock radio, t/c mkg, refrig, cook fac ltd, micro, elec frypan, toaster, blkts, linen], iron, iron brd, c/park. D ‡ $77 - $154, ‡‡ $88 - $154, ◊ $11, W ‡ $60.50 - $121, AE BC MC VI.

★★★ **Ridley Park Cottage**, (Cotg), 11 North St, 1km E of PO, ☎ 02 6365 3336, fax 02 6365 3000, 1 cotg acc up to 5, [shwr (1), tlt (1), fan, heat, elec blkts, TV, video, clock radio, t/c mkg, refrig, cook fac, micro, toaster, blkts, linen, pillows], w/mach, iron, c/park (garage), cots (avail), non smoking property. D ‡ $120, ‡‡ $120, ‡‡‡‡ $130, W $350, ch con, AE BC DC MC VI.

B&B's/Guest Houses
★★★★ **Clearview**, (B&B), Giles Rd Springside via, 10km fr PO, ☎ 02 6365 4224, fax 02 6365 4224, 3 rms (1 suite) [ensuite (1), spa bath (1), elec blkts, TV, clock radio, t/c mkg, refrig (1)], iron, iron brd, lounge, lounge firepl, t/c mkg shared, courtesy transfer, non smoking rms. BB ‡ $77, ‡‡ $110, Suite BB ‡‡ $132.

★★★★ **Greentrees Guesthouse**, (GH), 33 Pinnacle Rd, 4.5km SW of PO, ☎ 02 6361 4546, fax 02 6361 4566, 9 rms (1 suite) [shwr, spa bath (1), tlt, hairdry, a/c (7), fan (2), cent heat, elec blkts (2), TV (7), t/c mkg (7), refrig (7), cook fac ltd (4), micro (4), toaster (4)], ldry, iron (7), iron brd (7), lounge (TV), ✕, ✕, bbq, courtesy transfer, plygr, cots-fee, non smoking rms. BB ‡ $77 - $220, ‡‡ $99 - $220, RO ◊ $11 - $16.50, ch con, fam con, pen con, AE BC MC VI.

★★★★ **The Magistrates House Cotehele**, (B&B), 177 Anson St, 500m SW of PO, ☎ 02 6361 2520, fax 02 6361 2520, 5 rms [shwr (4), tlt (4), hairdry, a/c, fire pl, cent heat, tel, TV, t/c mkg, refrig], shared fac (2 rms), ldry, c/park. BB ‡ $110, ‡‡ $165, AE BC DC MC VI.

★★★☆ **Cleveland Bed & Breakfast**, (B&B), 9 Crinoline St, 1km N of PO, ☎ 02 6362 5729, fax 02 6361 2679, 3 rms [shwr, spa bath (1), tlt, hairdry, evap cool, heat (gas), elec blkts, tel, TV, video, clock radio], ldry, lounge (TV), ✕, t/c mkg shared, bbq, meals avail (by arrangement), cots (avail), non smoking property. BB ‡ $50 - $55, ‡‡ $80 - $90, ch con, AE BC MC VI.

★★★☆ **Huntley's Old Butter Factory**, (B&B), c1838. Cully Rd, Huntley, 12km E of Orange, ☎ 02 6365 5197, 2 rms [shwr, spa bath (double), tlt, fire pl (4), elec blkts, t/c mkg], ldry, lounge (TV), bbq, Pets allowed. BB ‡ $80, ‡‡ $120, ch con.

★★★☆ **Koolabah Farm B&B & Farmstay**, (B&B), (Farm), Cargo Rd, Lidster via Orange, 20km W of PO, ☎ 02 6365 6118, fax 02 6365 6120, 2 rms [c/fan, heat, elec blkts], ldry, iron, iron brd, lounge (tv & firepl), ✕, pool, t/c mkg shared, bbq, non smoking rms. BB ‡ $99 - $105, ‡‡ $135 - $155, ch con, AE BC DC MC VI.

★★★★ **(Cottage Section)**, 1 cotg acc up to 4, [shwr (1), bath (1), tlt (2), c/fan, fire pl, heat, elec blkts, TV, clock radio, t/c mkg, refrig, cook fac, micro, toaster, blkts, linen, pillows], iron. BB ‡‡ $135 - $155, ch con.

★★★☆ **Robin Hill Bed & Breakfast**, (B&B), 33 Neals La, Cargo Rd, 4.5km W of PO, ☎ 02 6365 3336, fax 02 6365 3000, 3 rms [shwr, bath (1), tlt, hairdry, fan, heat, elec blkts, clock radio], ldry, lounge (TV & firepl) (2), ✕, t/c mkg shared, cots, non smoking property, Pets allowed. BB ‡ $70, ‡‡ $95, ch con, Dinner by arrangement, AE BC DC MC VI.

★★★ **Campbell's Wyndhover Cottage**, (B&B), Cargo Rd, 5km W of Orange PO, ☎ 02 6365 3397, fax 02 6365 3397, (2 stry), 4 rms [ensuite (1), shwr (2), bath (1), tlt (3), fan (2), c/fan (1), fire pl (2), cent heat, elec blkts, tel, TV (2), video (avail), radio], ldry, lounge (TV), ✕, t/c mkg shared, c/park. BB ‡ $65 - $70, ‡‡ $95 - $125, ◊ $45 - $60, RO ‡ $55, ‡‡ $75 - $110, ◊ $35, ch con, BC DC MC VI.

★★★ **Duntryleague Guest House**, (GH), Woodward St, 2km W of PO, ☎ 02 6362 3822, fax 02 6361 7259, (Multi-stry), 14 rms [shwr, tlt, heat, elec blkts, tel, TV, t/c mkg, refrig], ldry, lounge (TV), conv fac, ⊠, bbq, golf, tennis, cots-fee. BB ‡ $80 - $115, ‡‡ $100 - $155, ◊ $35, ch con, AE BC DC EFT MC VI.

Turners Viveyard, (GH), Mitchell Hwy, 6km E of PO, ☎ 02 6369 1045, (2 stry gr fl), 30 rms (10 suites) [evap cool, cent heat, tel, cable tv, video, clock radio, t/c mkg, refrig, cook fac ltd, micro, toaster], ldry, conf fac, ✉, bbq, cots. **RO ♦ $145 - $210, ♦♦ $145 - $210, ♦ $15, Suite RO $195 - $265**, ch con, AE BC DC EFT MC VI, (not yet classified).

Strathroy Guest House Heritage Mansion, (GH), Heritage, No children's facilities, 26 Spring St, 2km E of PO, ☎ 02 6361 4493, (2 stry), 5 rms [shwr (4), bath (4), tlt (4), heat, elec blkts, tel, TV (5), clock radio, t/c mkg, refrig, micro], ldry, lounge firepl. **BB $95 - $130**, BC MC VI.

OURIMBAH NSW 2258

Pop 949. (84km N Sydney), See map on page 55, ref D6. Home of the Central Coast campus of the University of Newcastle. Bowls, Bush Walking, Tennis.

B&B's/Guest Houses

★★★ **Lilly Pilly Guesthouse**, (B&B), RMB 1240 Ourimbah Creek Rd, 3km N of Ourimbah PO & Railway Station, ☎ 02 4362 1910, 1 rm [shwr, tlt, c/fan (1), heat, tel], lounge (TV), cook fac, t/c mkg shared, c/park (limited). **BB ♦ $60, ♦♦ $85**.

OXLEY ISLAND NSW 2430

Pop Nominal, (334km N Sydney), See map on page 54, ref B7. Small village on an island near the mouth of the Manning River. Boating, Fishing, Scenic Drives, Swimming.

Self Catering Accommodation

Scotts Creek Homestead, (Cotg), (Farm), 150 Lauries La, ☎ 02 6553 2536, fax 02 6553 2434, 1 cotg acc up to 8, [shwr, tlt, fire pl, cable tv, radio, t/c mkg, refrig, cook fac, micro, elec frypan, toaster, ldry, blkts, linen, pillows], w/mach, iron, lounge, bbq, c/park. **D ♦♦ $125, ♦ $20 - $40, W ♦♦ $630 - $1,050**, ch con, BC MC VI, (not yet classified).

PACIFIC PALMS NSW 2428

Pop 550. (307km N Sydney), See map on page 54, ref B8. The area known as Pacific Palms features the gorgeous waterways of Wallis and Smiths Lakes and Blueys, Elizabeth and Boomerang Beaches. Boating, Bush Walking, Fishing, Surfing, Swimming, Water Skiing.

Hotels/Motels

★★★★ **Blueys By The Beach**, (M), 186 Boomerang Dve, 20km S of Forster, ☎ 02 6554 0665, fax 02 6554 0665, (2 stry gr fl), 9 units [shwr, tlt, hairdry, a/c (4), c/fan, heat, tel, TV, video, clock radio, t/c mkg, refrig, micro, toaster], pool, spa, bbq, c/park. **RO ♦ $65 - $130, ♦♦ $70 - $140, ♦ $12**, AE BC DC MC VI.

Self Catering Accommodation

★★★☆ **Pacific Palms Resort**, (SA), 2 Lakeside Cres, 3km NW of PO, ☎ 02 6554 0300, fax 02 6554 0272, 27 serv apts acc up to 6, [shwr, tlt, fan, heat, tel, TV (satelite), video, t/c mkg, refrig, cook fac, micro, toaster], ldry, rec rm, lounge (TV), pool, sauna, spa, bbq, plygr, gym, tennis, cots-fee, **D $120 - $242, W $720 - $1,452**, Min book applies, AE BC MC VI.

★★★☆ **St Clair by the Sea**, (Apt), 166 Boomerang Dve, ☎ 02 8850 1225, fax 02 8850 1225, 2 apts acc up to 8, [shwr, bath, tlt, fan, heat, tel, TV, video, clock radio, refrig, cook fac, micro, d/wash, toaster, ldry (in unit)], bbq, c/park (garage). **D $90 - $120, W $395 - $1,720**.

B&B's/Guest Houses

★★★★☆ **Karingal Bed & Breakfast**, (B&B), No children's facilities, 98 Coomba Rd, ☎ 02 6554 0122, fax 02 6554 0062, 2 rms [shwr, tlt, hairdry, c/fan, heat, elec blkts, clock radio], lounge (tv & firepl), t/c mkg shared, non smoking rms. **BB ♦ $85, ♦♦ $125**, AE BC JCB MC VI.

★★★★ **Pepper Tree Cottage**, (B&B), 106 Amaroo Dv, 2km S of PO, ☎ 02 6554 4522, 1 rm (1 suite) [shwr, tlt, hairdry, c/fan, heat, TV, video, clock radio, t/c mkg, refrig, cook fac ltd, micro, toaster, ldry], iron, iron brd, lounge, bbq. **BLB ♦ $65 - $75, ♦♦ $80 - $90, ♦ $10**.

PALMDALE NSW 2258

Pop Part of Wyong, (87km N Sydney), See map on page 55, ref D6. Rural community north of Ourimbah, flanked by the Ourimbah State Forest. Scenic Drives.

B&B's/Guest Houses

★★★☆ **Ambers Retreat**, (B&B), 4750 Fern Tree La, ☎ 02 4362 3403, fax 02 4362 9115, 4 rms [shwr, bath (1), tlt, hairdry, c/fan, elec blkts, tel, TV (1), clock radio], iron, iron brd, rec rm, lounge (TV, video), lounge firepl, pool (salt water), spa, t/c mkg shared, bbq, non smoking rms (4). **BB ♦ $88, ♦♦ $126.50 - $154, DBB ♦♦ $192.50 - $220**, BC MC VI.

PAMBULA NSW 2549

Pop 765. (463km S Sydney), See map on page 55, ref A8. Historic south coast dairying township that has altered little over the years and features many of its original, mainly weatherboard, buildings. Fishing, Surfing, Swimming.

Hotels/Motels

★★★☆ **Idlewilde Motor Inn**, (M), Princes Hwy, ☎ 02 6495 6844, fax 02 6495 7422, 16 units [shwr, tlt, c/fan, heat, elec blkts, tel, TV, video (5)-fee, clock radio, t/c mkg, refrig, cook fac (8), toaster], pool indoor heated, bbq, cots-fee, non smoking units (5). **RO ♦♦ $79 - $110, ♦♦♦ $84 - $120**, AE BC DC MC VI.

★★★ **The Colonial Motor Inn Pambula**, (M), Cnr Princes Hwy & Monaro St, 500m SW of PO, ☎ 02 6495 6700, fax 02 6495 6700, 14 units [shwr, tlt, c/fan, heat, elec blkts, tel, TV, video (available), clock radio, t/c mkg, refrig], pool (salt water), spa, bbq, cots. **RO ♦ $42.90, ♦♦ $49.50 - $77, ♦ $11**, ch con, AE BC DC MC VI.

Royal Willows Hotel Motel, (LMH), Princes Hwy, 50m S of PO, ☎ 02 6495 6005, fax 02 6495 7817, 14 units [shwr, tlt, heat, t/c mkg, refrig, toaster], rec rm, lounge (TV), ✉, bbq, ✆. **RO ♦ $30, ♦♦ $50, ♦ $10**, BC MC VI.

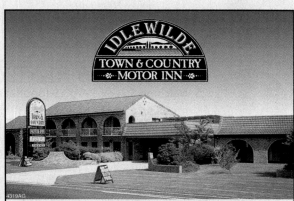

THE TOWN MOTEL WITH COUNTRY ATMOSPHERE
PAMBULA NSW 2549 Ph: (02) 6495 6844 Fx: (02) 6495 7422 (SEE LISTING UNDER PAMBULA)

PARKES NSW 2870

Pop 10,100. (364km W Sydney), See map on pages 52/53, ref F5. Major transport centre, bulkhead and wheat storage facility and a significant mining and commercial centre for the central west district. Bowls, Golf, Squash, Swimming, Tennis.

Hotels/Motels

FLAG
FLAG CHOICE HOTELS

★★★★ **Parkes International Motor Inn**, (M), Newell Hwy, 1.5km NE of PO, ☎ 02 6862 5222, fax 02 6862 2988, 26 units (1 suite) [shwr, bath (4), spa bath (3), tlt, hairdry, a/c, heat, elec blkts, tel, TV, video (3), clock radio, t/c mkg, refrig, mini bar], ldry, lounge, conv fac, ✉, pool, spa, rm serv, dinner to unit, cots, non smoking units (12). **RO ♦ $99, ♦♦ $105, ♦♦♦ $120, ♦ $15, Suite RO $100 - $150**, AE BC DC EFT MC VI, ♦♦.

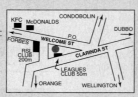

★★★☆ **All Settlers Motor Inn**, (M), 20 Welcome St, 100m S of PO, ☎ 02 6862 2022, fax 02 6862 4266, 17 units [shwr, spa bath (1), tlt, a/c, heat, elec blkts, tel, cable tv, video-fee, clock radio, t/c mkg, refrig, toaster], pool (salt water), bbq, dinner to unit, cots, non smoking rms (3). **RO** ♦ **$81**, ♦♦ **$88**, ◊ **$10**, AE BC DC EFT MC VI, ⟨&.

★★★☆ **Bushmans Motor Inn**, (M), Newell Hwy, 1km N of PO, ☎ 02 6862 2199, fax 02 6862 5261, 20 units [shwr, bath (3), tlt, hairdry, a/c, cent heat, elec blkts, tel, cable tv, video (avail), clock radio, t/c mkg, refrig, toaster], ldry, ⊠, pool (salt water), rm serv, cots-fee, non smoking units (9). **RO** ♦ **$85 - $89**, ♦♦ **$87 - $91**, ◊ **$8**, AE BC DC EFT MC MP VI, ⟨&.

★★★☆ **Court Street Motel**, (M), Cnr Court & Currajong Sts, 800m N of PO, ☎ 02 6862 3844, fax 02 6862 2483, 14 units [shwr, tlt, hairdry, a/c, elec blkts, tel, TV, clock radio, t/c mkg, refrig, toaster], iron, ✕, bar, rm serv, cots-fee, non smoking rms (3). **RO** ♦ **$64 - $70**, ♦ **$75 - $80**, ♦♦♦ **$90 - $98**, ◊ **$10**, AE BC DC EFT MC VI.

★★★☆ **Hamiltons Henry Parkes Motor Inn**, (M), 25 Welcome St, opposite PO, ☎ 02 6862 4644, fax 02 6862 4388, 20 units [shwr, spa bath (3), tlt, hairdry, a/c, elec blkts, tel, cable tv, video-fee, clock radio, t/c mkg, refrig, toaster], ldry, dinner to unit, car wash, cots, non smoking units (7). **RO** ♦ **$80**, ♦♦ **$90**, ♦♦♦ **$100**, AE BC DC EFT MC VI.

★★★☆ **Moonraker Motor Inn**, (M), 444 Clarinda St (Newell Hwy), 1.1km N of PO, ☎ 02 6862 2355, fax 02 6862 5230, 25 units (1 suite) [shwr, spa bath (2), tlt, a/c-cool, heat, tel, cable tv, clock radio, t/c mkg, refrig, ldry (valet)], ⊠, bar, pool, bbq, golf (driving range), tennis, cots-fee. **RO** ♦ **$89 - $93**, ♦♦ **$91 - $96**, ♦♦♦ **$98 - $103**, ◊ **$7**, Suite D **$120**, ch con, Min book applies, AE BC DC EFT MC MP VI.

★★★☆ **Parkview Motor Inn**, (M), 34 Forbes Rd (Newell Hwy), 1km S of PO, ☎ 02 6862 2888, fax 02 6862 5306, 39 units [shwr, tlt, a/c, elec blkts, tel, TV, clock radio, t/c mkg, refrig, toaster], ldry, ⊠ (Mon to Sat), pool, bbq, rm serv, plygr, cots. **RO** ♦ **$55 - $65**, ♦♦ **$65 - $77**, ◊ **$10**, 15 units ★★★☆, 8 family rooms of a 2.5 star rating. AE BC DC MC VI, ⟨&.

★★★☆ **Spanish Lantern Motor Inn**, (M), 62 Peak Hill Rd (Newell Hwy), 2km N of PO, ☎ 02 6862 3388, fax 02 6862 5121, 14 units [shwr, tlt, hairdry, a/c, elec blkts, tel, TV, clock radio, t/c mkg, refrig, toaster], ldry, iron, pool, bbq, dinner to unit (Mon to Thu), cots, non smoking units (10). **RO** ♦ **$56 - $62**, ♦♦ **$64 - $70**, ◊ **$10**, AE BC DC EFT MC MCH VI.

★★★ **Clarinda Motel**, (M), 72 Clarinda St, 1km E of PO, ☎ 02 6862 1655, fax 02 6862 3773, 23 units [shwr, bath (3), tlt, hairdry, a/c, heat, elec blkts, tel, TV, clock radio, t/c mkg, refrig, toaster], iron, iron brd, pool, cots-fee, non smoking units (18). **RO** ♦ **$55 - $63**, ♦♦ **$60 - $72**, ◊ **$10**, 3 units of a 3.5 standard. AE BC DC EFT MC VI.

★★★ **Coachman Hotel/Motel**, (LMH), Welcome St, 150m N of PO, ☎ 02 6862 2622, fax 02 6862 1839, (2 stry gr fl), 36 units [shwr, tlt, a/c, elec blkts, tel, TV, clock radio, t/c mkg, refrig], conf fac, ⊠ (Mon to Sat), pool, cots. **RO** ♦ **$55 - $71.50**, ♦♦ **$60.50 - $77**, ◊ **$10**, ch con, AE BC DC EFT MC VI, 14 units of a 2.5 star rating. (not yet classified).

★★★ **El Mexicali**, (M), 10 Station St, 1km S of PO, ☎ 02 6862 2555, fax 02 6862 1139, 12 units [shwr, tlt, hairdry, a/c, elec blkts, tel, TV, video (avail), clock radio, t/c mkg, refrig], ldry, pool (salt water), bbq, dinner to unit (Mon - Sat), cots. **RO** ♦ **$53**, ♦♦ **$60.50**, ♦♦♦ **$71.50**, ◊ **$11**, AE BC DC MC VI.

★★★ **North Parkes Motel**, (M), Newell Hwy, 1.5km N of PO, ☎ 02 6863 4333, fax 02 6863 5883, (2 stry gr fl), 35 units [shwr, tlt, hairdry, a/c, elec blkts, tel, TV, clock radio, t/c mkg, refrig, mini bar], iron, iron brd, ⊠ (6 nights), dinner to unit, non smoking units (11). **RO** ♦ **$77**, ♦♦ **$82.50**, ◊ **$8**, pen con, AE BC DC EFT MC MP VI.

B&B's/Guest Houses

★★★☆ **Kadina Bed & Breakfast**, (B&B), 22 Mengarvie Rd, ☎ 02 6862 3995, fax 02 6862 6451, 2 rms [hairdry, a/c, c/fan, elec blkts, movie, clock radio], ldry, lounge (TV), bbq, courtesy transfer, non smoking property. **BB** ♦ **$60**, ♦♦ **$90**, **DBB** ♦ **$78**, ♦♦ **$136**, ch con, BC MC VI.

PATERSON NSW 2421

Pop 350. (173km N Sydney), See map on page 54, ref A8. Historic little town between Maitland and Dungog which was established as a river port in the 1830s and retains many of its fine old buildings. Scenic Drives. See also Maitland.

Hotels/Motels

★★ **Court House Hotel**, (LMH), 23 King St, Next door to PO, ☎ 02 4938 5122, fax 02 4938 5309, 8 units [shwr, spa bath (1), tlt, a/c (5), fan (3), heat (3), TV (6), clock radio, t/c mkg, refrig], ⊠ (Closed Mon & Tue), bar, c/park. **RO** ♦ **$44**, ♦♦ **$66 - $99**, 3 rooms of a lesser rating. EFT.

PEAK HILL NSW 2869

Pop 1,050. (427km W Sydney), See map on pages 52/53, ref F4. Rural service centre on the Newell Highway between Parkes and Dubbo. Bowls, Golf, Swimming, Tennis, Trotting.

Hotels/Motels

★★★☆ **Country Roads Motor Inn**, (M), 34 Caswell St (Newell Hwy), 300m N of PO, ☎ 02 6869 1688, fax 02 6869 1504, 14 units [shwr, tlt, a/c-cool, heat, elec blkts, tel, TV, clock radio, t/c mkg, refrig], pool, bbq, dinner to unit (7 Days), cots, non smoking units (available). **RO** ♦ **$50**, ♦♦ **$60**, ◊ **$10**, BC MC VI, ⟨&.

★★★ **Oasis Motel and Cafe**, (M), 152 Caswell St (Newell Hwy), 1km S of PO, ☎ 1800 688 952, 11 units [shwr, tlt, hairdry, a/c-cool, heat, elec blkts, tel, TV, clock radio, t/c mkg, refrig, micro, toaster], bbq, dinner to unit, cots, non smoking rms. **RO** ♦ **$47.50**, ♦♦ **$48.50**, ♦♦♦ **$59.50**, ◊ **$9**, AE BC DC EFT MC VI.

★★★ **Peak Hill Golden Peak Budget Motel**, (M), 25 Caswell St (Newell Hwy), 400m N of PO, ☎ 02 6869 1429, fax 02 6869 1093, 14 units [shwr, tlt, hairdry, a/c-cool, heat, elec blkts, tel, TV, video (4), clock radio, t/c mkg, refrig, toaster], iron, iron brd, pool (salt water), bbq, dinner to unit, plygr, cots, non smoking units (5). **RO** ♦ **$48**, ♦♦♦ **$59**, ◊ **$10**, AE BC EFT MC MCH VI.

Self Catering Accommodation

★★★ **Westray Farmstay Bed & Breakfast**, (HU), (Farm), Westray Merino Stud Newell Highway, 5km N of PO, ☎ 02 6869 1540, fax 02 6869 1540, 1 unit acc up to 4, [shwr, spa bath, tlt, a/c-cool, heat, elec blkts, TV, t/c mkg, refrig, micro, toaster, blkts, linen, pillows], iron, bbq, c/park. **RO** ♦♦ **$65**, ◊ **$10**, Breakfast available, VI.

PEARL BEACH NSW 2256

Pop Part of Gosford, (84km N Sydney), See map on page 56, ref E3. One of the most exclusive areas on the Central Coast with a sunny aspect and beach frontage to Broken Bay.

B&B's/Guest Houses

P.B's B&B, (B&B), 108 Diamond Rd, ☎ 02 4342 9717, 1 rm (1 suite) [shwr, bath, tlt, fan, elec blkts, clock radio, t/c mkg, refrig, toaster], ldry, iron, iron brd, rec rm, lounge (TV, video), lounge firepl, tennis-fee, non smoking property. **BB** ♦♦ **$105**, ◊ **$55**, VI, (not yet classified).

PERISHER VALLEY NSW 2624

Pop 1,913. (489km SW Sydney), See map on pages 52/53, ref F7. Snowy Mountains ski village. Along with nearby Smiggin Holes, it's part of the Perisher Blue ski resort. Snow Skiing.

Self Catering Accommodation

★★★★ **The Stables**, (Chalet), Valhalla Rd, ☎ 02 6457 5755, fax 02 6457 5998, (2 stry gr fl), 18 chalets acc up to 6, [shwr, bath, spa bath, tlt, hairdry, fire pl, heat, tel, TV, video, t/c mkg, refrig, mini bar, cook fac, micro, d/wash, toaster, ldry, blkts, linen], w/mach, dryer, iron, c/park (summer), cots, non smoking property. **High Season D $220 - $1,155, Low Season D $120 - $375, High Season W $1,320 - $6,380**, Min book applies, AE BC DC EFT JCB MC VI.

Other Accommodation

Chalet Sonnenhof, (Lodge), Perisher Valley Village, off Kosciusko Rd, ☎ 02 6457 5256, fax 02 6457 5096, (Multi-stry), 17 rms acc up to 4, [shwr, bath (2), tlt, cent heat], w/mach-fee, dryer-fee, iron, ⊠ (Sun to Sun), sauna, spa, ✆, cots-fee. **BB ♦ $70, ♦♦ $110, DBB ♦ $95 - $205, ♦♦ $190 - $410, ♦♦♦ $285 - $570**, ch con, AE BC DC MC VI.

Sundeck Hotel, (Lodge), Front Valley, ☎ 02 6457 5222, fax 02 6457 5054, (2 stry gr fl), 36 rms acc up to 4, [shwr, tlt, cent heat, t/c mkg], lounge (TV), ⊠, ✆, cots. **High Season DBB ♦ $105 - $215**, Min book applies, BC MC VI.

Swagman Chalet, (Lodge), Perisher Valley Village, 400m SE of ski tube terminal, ☎ 02 6457 5275, (Multi-stry), 16 rms acc up to 4, [shwr, tlt, cent heat, elec blkts], ldry, dry rm, rec rm, lounge (TV), ⊠, spa, t/c mkg shared, courtesy transfer, ✆, cots-fee. **Low Season BB ♦ $45, High Season DBB $405 - $840**, BC MC VI.

PHEGANS BAY NSW 2256

Pop Part of Gosford, (79km N Sydney), See map on page 56, ref E3. Small Central Coast town on Woy Woy Bay in the south-western corner of Brisbane Water. Boating, Bush Walking, Fishing, Swimming.

B&B's/Guest Houses

★★★ **Minerva's Garden Cottage Bed & Breakfast**, (B&B), No children's facilities, 60 Phegans Bay Rd, off Woy Woy Bay Rd, 8km SE of Gosford Fwy turnoff, ☎ 02 4341 4295, 1 rm [shwr, tlt, fan, heat, TV, clock radio, t/c mkg, refrig, micro, toaster], ✆. **BB ♦ $55 - $65, ♦♦ $75 - $85, ◊ $25 - $30.**

PICTON NSW 2571

Pop 2,668. (79km SW Sydney), See map on page 55, ref B3. Rural centre on the south-western outskirts of Sydney. Swimming.

Hotels/Motels

★★☆ **Picton Village Motel**, (M), 1665 Old Hume Hwy, 2km N of PO, ☎ 02 4677 2121, fax 02 4677 1922, 25 units [shwr, spa bath (available), tlt, a/c, elec blkts, tel, TV, clock radio, t/c mkg, refrig, toaster], ldry, conv fac, ⊠, rm serv, dinner to unit. **RO ♦ $66 - $86, ♦♦ $76 - $96, ◊ $20**, ch con, AE BC DC MC VI.

B&B's/Guest Houses

★★★★ **Greenhills Picton B&B**, (B&B), 44 Argyle St, 500m N of PO, ☎ 02 4677 3298, fax 02 4677 3393, 1 rm [shwr, spa bath, tlt, hairdry, c/fan, elec blkts, tel, TV, video, clock radio, t/c mkg, refrig, mini bar, cook fac, micro, toaster, ldry], iron, iron brd, rec rm, lounge firepl, bbq, dinner to unit, courtesy transfer, plygr, cots. **BB ♦♦ $121 - $154**, AE BC MC VI.

★★★☆ **Mowbray Park Farm Holiday**, (GH), (Farm), Barkers Lodge Rd, 7km W of PO, ☎ 02 4680 9243, fax 02 4680 9224, 20 rms [shwr, bath, spa bath (2), tlt, a/c, fan, heat, clock radio, t/c mkg, refrig], rec rm, lounge (TV), pool, spa, bbq, plygr, canoeing, tennis, cots. **D all meals ♦ $105 - $135, W ♦ $735 - $819**, ch con, Min book applies, BC MC VI.

POKOLBIN NSW 2320

Pop Part of Cessnock, (195km N Sydney), See map on page 55, ref B7. Locality at the heart of the Hunter Valley wine region. Bowls, Golf, Greyhound Racing, Horse Racing, Swimming, Tennis, Trotting, Vineyards, Wineries. See also Cessnock & Rothbury.

Hotels/Motels

AAA TOURISM *Special Rates* ★★★★★ **Cypress Lakes Resort**, (LH), Cnr McDonalds & Thompson Rds, 1km S of McGuigan Bros Winery, ☎ 02 4993 1555, fax 02 4993 1599, (2 stry gr fl), 174 rms (80 suites) [shwr, bath, spa bath (20), tlt, hairdry, a/c, fire pl (40), tel, TV, movie, clock radio, t/c mkg, refrig, mini bar, micro], iron, iron brd, lounge (firepl), conv fac, ⊠, pool-heated (2), sauna, spa, 24hr reception, rm serv (24 hour), dinner to unit, c/park (valet), golf, gym, tennis, cots, non smoking units (16). **BB ♦♦ $216 - $324**, ch con, AE BC DC EFT JCB MC VI.

Operator Comment: See advertisement on page 312.

★★★★☆ **Harrigan's Irish Pub & Accommodation**, (LMH), Broke Rd, 15km NW of Cessnock, ☎ 02 4998 7600, or 02 4998 7854, fax 02 4998 7845, 48 units (6 suites) [shwr, spa bath (8), tlt, hairdry, a/c, tel, TV, movie, clock radio, t/c mkg, refrig, toaster], ldry, conv fac, ⊠, pool (salt water), ✆, plygr, cots-fee. **RO ♦ $120 - $165, ♦♦ $120 - $165, ◊ $20, Suite D $185 - $205**, ch con, Min book applies, AE BC DC MC VI.

★★★★☆ **Hunter Resort Country Estate**, (M), Hermitage Rd, 13km NW of Cessnock, ☎ 02 4998 7777, fax 02 4998 7787, 35 units (5 suites) [shwr (2), bath (2), spa bath (4), tlt (2), hairdry, a/c, elec blkts, tel, TV, video-fee, clock radio, CD (1), t/c mkg, refrig, micro (5), toaster], ldry, iron, iron brd, conv fac, ⊠, cafe, pool, spa, bbq, plygr, bush walking, bicycle, tennis, cots-fee. **BLB ♦ $175 - $300, ♦♦ $175 - $300, ◊ $22**, ch con, Min book applies, AE BC DC MC VI.

★★★★☆ **Hunter Valley Gardens Lodge**, (M), Broke Rd, 6km NW of Cessnock, ☎ 02 4998 7600, fax 02 4998 7710, (2 stry gr fl), 72 units (4 suites) [shwr, bath, tlt, hairdry, a/c, heat, tel, TV, movie, t/c mkg, refrig, mini bar], ldry, conv fac, ⊠, bar, pool-heated, sauna, spa, rm serv, tennis, cots, non smoking rms. **RO ♦ $195, ♦♦ $195, ◊ $25**, ch con, AE BC DC EFT JCB MC VI, ⅃க.

★★★★☆ **Pokolbin Village Resort & Conf Centre**, (M), Broke Rd, Opposite Rothbury Estate, ☎ 02 4998 7670, fax 02 4998 7377, 50 units (19 suites) [shwr, bath (1), spa bath (1), tlt, hairdry, a/c, fan, c/fan, elec blkts, tel, TV, video-fee, clock radio, t/c mkg, refrig, mini bar, cook fac (4), micro (17), toaster], conv fac, ⊠, cafe, pool-heated (solar), dinner to unit, ✆, plygr, tennis, cots-fee, non smoking units (25). **D ♦ $210 - $243, ♦♦ $210 - $243, ♦♦♦ $280 - $315, ♦♦♦♦ $342 - $380**, 26 units yet to be assessed, Min book applies, AE BC DC EFT MC VI.

★★★★ **Hermitage Lodge Motel**, (M), Cnr McDonalds & Gillards Rds, 12km NW of Cessnock, ☎ 02 4998 7639, fax 02 4998 7818, 10 units [shwr, spa bath (6), tlt, hairdry, a/c, elec blkts, tel, TV, clock radio, t/c mkg, refrig, toaster], ldry, iron, iron brd, ⊠, pool, bbq, dinner to unit, c/park. **BLB ♦ $80 - $170, ♦♦ $85 - $180, ♦♦♦ $95 - $190, ◊ $15**, Min book applies, AE BC MC VI.

★★★★ **Tuscany Estate Resort**, (M), Mistletoe La, Off Hermitage Rd, 9km W of Cessnock Airport, ☎ 02 4998 7288, fax 02 4998 7277, 26 units [shwr, bath, tlt, a/c, elec blkts, tel, TV, clock radio, t/c mkg, refrig, mini bar], conv fac, ⊠, pool, bbq, ☎, tennis, cots-fee, non smoking units. **BB** ♦ **$135 - $175,** ♦♦ **$135 - $175,** ◊ **$155 - $215, RO** ♦ **$120 - $160,** ♦♦ **$120 - $160,** ◊ **$20 - $40,** ch con, fam con, pen con, AE BC DC MC VI.

★★★☆ **Vineyard Hill Country Motel**, (M), Lovedale Rd, ☎ 02 4990 4166, fax 02 4991 4431, 8 units [shwr, tlt, a/c, c/fan, heat, elec blkts, tel, TV, video (avail), clock radio, t/c mkg, refrig, mini bar, cook fac, micro, toaster], pool (salt water), spa, bbq, meals avail, cots. **RO** ♦ **$97 - $141,** ♦♦ **$97 - $141,** ♦♦♦ **$114 - $218,** ◊ **$16.50,** AE BC MC VI.

★★★ **Elfin Hill Bed & Breakfast Motel**, (M), Marrowbone Rd, 6km W of Cessnock, ☎ 02 4998 7543, fax 02 4998 7817, 6 units [shwr, tlt, hairdry, a/c, tel, fax, TV, clock radio, t/c mkg, refrig], iron (available), iron brd (available), pool (salt water), bbq, cots. **BB** ♦ **$93 - $159,** ♦♦ **$93 - $159,** ◊ **$16.50 - $22,** ch con, BC MC VI.

★★☆ **Potters Inn Motel**, (M), Lot 181 De Beyers Rd, 5.5km NW of Nulkaba, ☎ 02 4998 7648, fax 02 4998 7648, 5 units [shwr, bath, tlt, a/c (1), c/fan, heat, elec blkts, TV, clock radio, t/c mkg, refrig], ⊠ (weekends only). **RO** **$85 - $115,** ch con, AE BC DC MC VI.

Self Catering Accommodation

★★★★★ **The Woods at Pokolbin**, (Cotg), Halls Rd, ☎ 02 4998 7368, fax 02 4998 7368, 2 cotgs acc up to 8, [shwr (4), spa bath (1), tlt (4), hairdry, a/c, cent heat, elec blkts, TV, video, t/c mkg, refrig, cook fac, micro, d/wash, toaster, ldry, blkts, linen], w/mach, dryer, iron, iron brd, conf fac, lounge firepl, bbq, c/park. **D** **$100 - $165,** Min book applies, BC MC VI.

★★★★☆ **Berenbell Vineyard Retreat**, (Cotg), 60 Mistletoe La, ☎ 02 4998 7468, fax 02 4998 7464, (2 stry gr fl), 5 cotgs acc up to 5, [shwr, bath (3), tlt, hairdry, a/c, c/fan, fire pl (5), heat, elec blkts, tel, TV, clock radio, t/c mkg, refrig, cook fac ltd, micro, toaster, blkts, linen], iron, iron brd, lounge, bbq, non smoking property. **BLB** ♦♦ **$132 - $198,** ♦♦♦♦ **$220 - $330,** ◊ **$30,** ch con, AE BC EFT MC VI.

★★★★☆ **(Guesthouse Section)**, 2 rms (1 suite) [a/c (2), c/fan, tel, TV (2), clock radio, toaster (2)], iron, iron brd, lounge firepl, t/c mkg shared, non smoking property. **BLB** ♦♦♦♦ **$198 - $275.**

_H_unter Resort Country Estate is a family owned and operated 41/2 star 35 room country inn. Taste beautiful food; sleep among the vines; sample great wines and beers; and actually experience the wine making process from grape to wine. The 2 hour **Hunter Valley Wine School** is a definite must! Also, the resort's horseback riding tour!

All rooms; Spa Suites and 2 Bedroom Cottage feature timber cathedral ceilings, bathtub and shower, air-conditioning and individual balconies. The restaurant is open each night, and for breakfast or lunch - Cafe San Martino and Wine Bar. There is tennis, a pool, heated spa, mountain bikes and walking tracks over the 70 secluded acres. Also on site is the Hunter's largest winery and The Hunter Valley Brewing Co.

HUNTER RESORT
C O U N T R Y   E S T A T E

Reservations: (02) 4998 7777
Hermitage Road, Pokolbin, NSW 2320
Website: www.HunterResort.com.au
4404AG

P

~ Hunter Valley Wine Country ~

Cypress Lakes Resort

"Just 90 minutes from Sydney and we were
in the heart of Hunter Valley Wine Country.

Our short break at Cypress Lakes Resort
was filled with promise; a private
luxury villa, stunning food and wine,
open fires...and five star service all the way.

Time to play – golf, laps in the heated pool,
boutique vineyards, famous wineries
and rustic restaurants to explore.
Time to relax – spa, aromatherapy,
and massage at The Golden Door Resort Spa.
Time to rediscover ourselves...Loved It!"

For reservations, call 1800 061 818 or visit our
website www.cypresslakes.com.au

CYPRESS LAKES

RESORT

Pokolbin - Hunter Valley Wine Country

5 star ~ 18 hole championship golf course
~ Unique villa style accommodation ~ Heated swimming pools
~Critters Club ~ The Golden Door Resort Spa
~ Pipette à la carte restaurant ~ Mulligans Brasserie ~ 3 bars
~ Short Break packages now available.
Corner McDonalds and Thompsons Roads Pokolbin,
Hunter Valley NSW 2320.

Peach 005899

4426AG

★★★★ **Cam-Way Serviced Apartments**, (SA), Campbells La, 14km N of PO, ☎ 02 4998 7655, 6 serv apts [shwr, tlt, a/c, clock radio, t/c mkg, refrig, cook fac], ldry, bbq, cots-fee, ch con, BC MC VI.

★★★★ **Kurrajong Vineyard Cottages**, (Cotg), 614 Hermitage Rd, 6km N of Broke Rd, ☎ 02 6574 7117, fax 02 6574 7006, 2 cotgs acc up to 6, [shwr, tlt, a/c, c/fan (1), fire pl, TV, video (1), clock radio, t/c mkg, refrig, cook fac ltd, micro, toaster, ldry, blkts, linen, pillows], iron, pool, bbq, ✆, non smoking property. **D** ♦♦ **$105 - $200**, ♦♦♦♦ **$150 - $265**, ch con, 1 cottage ★★★☆. AE BC JCB MC VI.

★★★★ **(Guest House Section)**, 1 rm [shwr, tlt, a/c, TV, video, clock radio, CD, t/c mkg, refrig, micro, toaster], pool, bbq, cots, non smoking suites. **BLB** ♦♦ **$93 - $110**, ch con.

★★★★ **Leonard Estate Guest House**, (Cotg), Leonard Estate, Lot 1, Palmers La, ☎ 02 4998 7381, fax 02 4997 0502, 4 cotgs acc up to 12, [a/c-cool, c/fan, heat, elec blkts], ldry, iron, iron brd, lounge (TV & firepl), pool (salt water), cook fac, bbq, non smoking property. **D** ♦ **$50 - $75**, fam con, BC MC VI.

★★★★ **Misty Glen Cottage**, (Cotg), Lot 6 Deasy Rd, ☎ 02 4998 7768, 1 cotg acc up to 6, [shwr, tlt, hairdry, a/c, c/fan, tel, TV, video, clock radio, t/c mkg, refrig, cook fac, micro, elec frypan, d/wash, toaster, blkts, linen], w/mach, iron, iron brd, bbq, non smoking property. **D $231 - $390**, Min book applies, BC MC VI.

★★★★ **Pokolbin Hill Chateau Resort**, (SA), Cnr Broke Rd & McDonalds Rd, ☎ 02 4998 7000, fax 02 4998 7011, 100 serv apts acc up to 4, [shwr, spa bath, tlt, hairdry, a/c, tel, TV, video, clock radio, t/c mkg, refrig, cook fac ltd, micro, toaster, blkts, linen], ldry, iron, iron brd, pool, tennis, cots. **D $115 - $210, W $728 - $1,323**, Min book applies, AE BC DC MC VI.

★★★★ **Pokolbin's Camway Cottages**, (Cotg), Previously Vineyard-n-Valley Campbell's La, 14km W of Cessnock PO, ☎ 02 4998 7655, fax 02 4998 7679, 3 cotgs acc up to 6, [shwr, tlt, a/c-cool, c/fan, elec blkts, TV, video, clock radio, t/c mkg, refrig, cook fac, micro (3), d/wash (3), toaster, ldry (3), blkts, linen, pillows], iron, cots. **D** ♦♦ **$110 - $135**, ◊ **$25 - $45**, ch con, 3 cabins of a lower rating. BC MC VI.

★★★★ **Twin Trees Country Cottages**, (Cotg), No children's facilities, Halls Rd, 10km NW of Cessnock PO, ☎ 02 4998 7311, fax 02 4998 7767, 10 cotgs acc up to 6, [shwr, tlt, a/c-cool (2), a/c (8), c/fan, fire pl, heat, elec blkts, tel, clock radio, CD, t/c mkg, refrig, cook fac, toaster, blkts, linen, pillows], ldry, pool, bbq, c/park. **D** ♦ **$110 - $165**, ♦♦ **$110 - $165**, ♦♦♦♦ **$220 - $300**, ◊ **$50 - $75**, Min book applies, BC MC VI.

★★★☆ **Belford Country Cabins**, 659 Hermitage Rd, 15km NW of Cessnock, ☎ 02 6574 7100, 5 cabins acc up to 12, [shwr, tlt, a/c, c/fan, fire pl (1), heat, elec blkts, TV, clock radio, CD, t/c mkg, refrig, cook fac, micro, toaster, blkts, linen, pillows], ldry, iron, iron brd, rec rm, conf fac, pool (salt water), bbq, dinner to unit, ✆, plygr, bicycle, cots, non smoking units. **D** ♦♦ **$90 - $220**, ◊ **$20 - $27.50**, ch con, Min book applies, BC MC VI.

★★★☆ **Duck Hollow Cottage**, (Cotg), 103 Deasys Rd, 1km E of Marsh Estate Wines, ☎ 02 9415 6656, fax 02 9415 6656, 1 cotg acc up to 10, [shwr, tlt, a/c-cool, fire pl (open), tel, refrig, cook fac, micro, elec frypan, d/wash, toaster, ldry, blkts, linen, pillows], w/mach, dryer, iron, lounge (TV & video), bbq. **D $780**, Min book applies.

★★★ **Araluen Mistletoe Cottages**, (Cotg), 108 Mistletoe La, ☎ 02 4998 7567, fax 02 4998 7567, 2 cotgs acc up to 6, [shwr, tlt, a/c, fire pl, TV, t/c mkg, refrig, cook fac, micro, toaster, blkts, linen], iron, iron brd, pool (salt water), bbq, cots, non smoking property. **D** ♦♦ **$95 - $330**, Min book applies, BC MC VI.

★★★ **Grapeview Villas**, (SA), Thompsons Rd, 13km N of Cessnock, ☎ 02 4998 7630, fax 02 4998 7644, 8 serv apts acc up to 5, [shwr, tlt, hairdry, fan, heat, elec blkts, fax, TV, clock radio, t/c mkg, refrig, cook fac, toaster], ldry, pool, bbq, cots-fee. **D** ♦♦ **$85**, ◊ **$25**, ch con, Min book applies, BC DC MC VI.

★★★ **Hunter Hideaway Cottages**, (Cotg), Tuckers La, 19km N of Cessnock, ☎ 02 4938 2091, fax 02 4938 2131, 3 cotgs acc up to 8, [shwr, tlt, a/c, c/fan, fire pl, tel, TV, clock radio, CD, t/c mkg, refrig, cook fac, micro, toaster], ldry, iron, bbq, cots. **D** ♦♦ **$85 - $110**, ♦♦♦ **$105 - $165**, ◊ **$25 - $55**, ch con, Min book applies, BC MC VI.

★★★ **The Hunter Habit**, (Cotg), Deasy's Rd, ☎ 02 4998 7290, fax 02 4998 7290, 4 cotgs acc up to 8, [shwr, tlt, hairdry, a/c, fire pl, TV, video, t/c mkg, refrig, cook fac, micro, toaster, ldry, blkts, linen, pillows], w/mach, dryer, iron, iron brd, conv fac, pool (mineral), spa, bbq, non smoking property. **D** ♦ **$66**, ◊ **$55**, Min book applies, AE BC DC EFT MC VI.

B&B's/Guest Houses

★★★★★ **Casuarina Country Inn**, (GH), No children's facilities, Hermitage Rd, 11km N of PO, ☎ 02 4998 7888, fax 02 4998 7692, 9 rms (8 suites) [shwr, bath, tlt, a/c, c/fan, elec blkts, tel, TV, clock radio, t/c mkg, refrig], lounge (TV), conv fac, ⊠, pool, sauna, tennis. RO ╪ $231 - $319, ╷ $33, AE BC DC MC VI.

　★★★★☆ **(Cottage Section)**, 3 cotgs acc up to 10, [shwr, spa bath (2), tlt, c/fan, elec blkts, TV, refrig, cook fac, micro, blkts, linen, pillows], ldry, bbq. **D $330 - $627.**

★★★★★ **Montagne View Estate**, (GH), Hermitage Rd, 9km N of PO, ☎ 02 4998 7822, fax 02 6574 7276, (2 stry gr fl), 8 rms (8 suites) [shwr, bath, spa bath (3), tlt, a/c, fire pl, tel, fax, TV, video, clock radio, t/c mkg, refrig, toaster], ⊠, pool (salt water), spa, tennis. **BB ╪ $175 - $195, ╫ $175 - $195, ╷ $33, DBB ╫ $305 - $325, ╷ $86,** Min book applies, AE BC MC VI.

★★★★★ **Patrick Plains Estate**, (GH), 647 Hermitage Rd, 3.5km from Pokolbin, ☎ 02 6574 7071, fax 02 6574 7074, 8 rms [shwr, bath, tlt, hairdry, a/c, elec blkts, tel, cable tv, clock radio, t/c mkg, refrig, toaster], ldry, iron, iron brd, lounge, lounge firepl, pool, bbq, cots, non smoking property. **BB $170 - $235,** AE BC DC EFT MC VI.

★★★★☆ **Catersfield House**, (GH), 96 Mistletoe Lane, ☎ 02 4998 7220, fax 02 4998 7558, 9 rms [shwr, bath (1), spa bath (1), tlt, hairdry, a/c, c/fan, TV, video, t/c mkg, refrig, micro (2)], ldry, iron, iron brd, rec rm, conv fac, lounge firepl, ✕, pool (salt water), bbq, cots, non smoking property. **BB ╫ $100 - $198, ╷ $25,** ch con, Meals by arrangement. AE BC DC JCB MC VI.

★★★★☆ **Peppers Convent Hunter Valley**, (B&B), Halls Rd, ☎ 02 4998 7764, fax 02 4998 7323, (2 stry gr fl), 17 rms [shwr, bath (16), tlt, hairdry, a/c, tel, TV, clock radio, t/c mkg, refrig, mini bar], conv fac, lounge firepl, pool, spa, bbq, tennis, cots. **RO $291 - $387, ╷ $55,** AE BC DC MC VI.

★★★★☆ **Peppers Guest House Hunter Valley**, (GH), Ekerts Rd, 10km NW of Cessnock, ☎ 02 4998 7596, fax 02 4998 7739, 47 rms [shwr, tlt, hairdry, a/c (25), c/fan (22), cent heat, tel, TV, clock radio, t/c mkg, refrig, mini bar], ldry, lounge, conv fac, ⊠, pool-heated, sauna, spa, bbq, ✆, tennis, cots. **RO $238 - $300, ╷ $55,** ch con, AE BC DC MC VI.

　★★★☆ **(Peppers Homestead)**, 1 cotg acc up to 8, [shwr (2), tlt (2), a/c, fire pl, tel, TV, refrig, cook fac, blkts, linen, pillows], lounge, ✕, pool, bbq.

★★★★☆ **Splinters Guest House**, (GH), 617 Hermitage Rd, 3km N of Hunter Estate Winery, ☎ 02 6574 7118, fax 02 6574 7280, 3 rms [shwr, tlt, a/c, c/fan, heat, tel, clock radio, t/c mkg, refrig, toaster], lounge (TV), pool, bbq, bicycle, golf. **BLB ╫ $95, ╫ $95 - $155,** BC MC VI.

　★★★★ **(Cottage Section)**, 2 cotgs acc up to 4, [shwr, tlt, a/c-cool, c/fan, heat, TV, clock radio, t/c mkg, refrig, cook fac, toaster, linen, pillows]. **BLB $130 - $620.**

★★★★☆ **The Carriages Guest House**, (GH), Halls La, 10km NW of Cessnock, ☎ 02 4998 7591, fax 02 4998 7839, 8 rms (8 suites) [shwr, bath, tlt, a/c, c/fan, fire pl, tel, TV, clock radio, t/c mkg, refrig, cook fac ltd, toaster], pool (salt water), bbq, tennis. **BB ╫ $170 - $270,** Min book applies, AE BC MC VI.

　★★★★☆ **(Cottage Section)**, 2 cotgs [shwr, spa bath, tlt, a/c, c/fan, tel, TV, video, clock radio, CD, t/c mkg, refrig, cook fac, toaster], iron, iron brd, lounge firepl (TV), bar, c/park. **BB ╫ $270.**

★★★★☆ **Thistle Hill Guest House**, (GH), 591 Hermitage Rd, ☎ 02 6574 7217, fax 02 6574 7217, 6 rms [shwr, tlt, a/c, c/fan, elec blkts, TV, t/c mkg, refrig, toaster], lounge, bbq. **BLB ╪ $260 - $850, ╫ $260 - $850,** AE BC MC VI.

　★★★★ **(Cottage Section)**, 1 cotg acc up to 4, [shwr (2), tlt (2), a/c, elec blkts, TV, video, clock radio, CD, refrig, cook fac, micro, elec frypan, toaster, ldry, linen], w/mach, dryer, iron, iron brd, bbq. **BLB ╫ $100 - $550, ╫╫ $200 - $550.**

★★★★☆ **Villa Provence Guest House**, (GH), No children's facilities, 15 Gillards Rd, 4km NW of Cessnock Airport, ☎ 02 4998 7404, fax 02 4998 7405, (2 stry gr fl), 9 rms (8 suites) [shwr, tlt, a/c-cool (9), c/fan (9), heat, elec blkts, tel, TV, video (9), clock radio, t/c mkg, refrig, cook fac ltd (8), micro (8), elec frypan, toaster], iron, iron brd, pool, bbq, cots, non smoking rms. **BLB ╫ $132 - $407,** ch con, fam con, Min book applies. AE BC MC VI.

P

POKOLBIN NSW continued...

★★★★ **Kirkton Park Country Hotel**, (GH), Oakey Creek Rd, 1km N of PO, ☎ 02 4998 7680, fax 02 4998 7775, 70 rms (3 suites) [shwr, bath (32), spa bath (2), tlt, hairdry, a/c (61), c/fan, heat, tel, TV, clock radio, t/c mkg, refrig, mini bar], rec rm, lounge (TV), conv fac, ⊠, pool-heated (indoor), sauna, spa, rm serv, gym, tennis. BB ♦ $225 - $335, ♦♦ $255 - $365, ♦♦♦ $315 - $425, ◊ $60, Suite BB ♦♦ $315 - $395, 23 rooms ★★★★☆. AE BC DC MC VI.

★★★★ **Sussex Ridge**, (GH), Off Deaseys Rd, ☎ 02 4998 7753, 14 rms [shwr, tlt, a/c-cool (4), c/fan, heat], lounge (TV), conv fac, pool, cook fac, t/c mkg shared, bbq, c/park. BB ♦♦ $132 - $215, ◊ $44 - $55, Min book applies. BC MC VI.

PORT KEMBLA NSW

See Wollongong & Suburbs.

PORT MACQUARIE NSW 2444

Pop 33,700. (398km N Sydney), See map on page 54, ref C7. Historic town on the Hastings River and one of the premier holiday destinations on the mid-north coast. Boating, Bowls, Fishing, Golf, Surfing, Swimming, Tennis.

Hotels/Motels

★★★★☆ **Sails Resort**, (M), Resort, 20 Park St, 1.5km N of PO, ☎ 02 6583 3999, fax 02 6584 0397, (2 stry gr fl), 83 units (6 suites) [shwr, bath, spa bath (6), tlt, hairdry, a/c, fan, elec blkts, tel, cable tv, video-fee, movie, clock radio, t/c mkg, refrig, mini bar, cook fac ltd (54), toaster], ldry, iron, iron brd, rec rm, lounge (TV), conv fac, ⊠, bar, pool (solar), spa, steam rm, bbq, 24hr reception, rm serv, dinner to unit, ☏, plygr, jetty, mini golf, tennis, cots-fee. RO ♦ $147 - $314, ♦♦ $147 - $314, ♦♦♦ $171 - $344, ◊ $30, Suite D $246 - $380, ch con, Min book long w/ends and Easter, AE BC DC JCB MC VI.

★★★★ **Best Western Macquarie Barracks Motor Inn**, (M), Previously Macquarie Barracks Motor Inn 103 Hastings River Dve, 3km W of PO, ☎ 02 6583 5333, fax 02 6583 5395, 34 units [shwr, spa bath (4), tlt, hairdry, a/c, fan, heat, tel, cable tv (satellite), clock radio, t/c mkg, refrig, cook fac (6), toaster], ldry, iron, iron brd, ⊠, pool, bbq, rm serv, cots-fee, non smoking units (16). RO ♦ $99 - $170, ♦♦ $99 - $170, ♦♦♦ $125 - $180, ◊ $15, 10 rooms of a 3.5 stardard. Min book long w/ends and Easter, AE BC DC MC MP VI, ₤&.

★★★★ **Country Comfort - Port Macquarie**, (M), Cnr Buller & Hollingworth Sts, 600m W of PO, ☎ 02 6583 2955, fax 02 6583 7398, (2 stry gr fl), 61 units [shwr, tlt, hairdry, a/c, tel, TV, clock radio, t/c mkg, refrig, mini bar, toaster], ldry, lounge, conv fac, ⊠, pool, spa, bbq, rm serv, dinner to unit, cots, non smoking units (12). RO ♦ $116 - $165, ♦♦ $116 - $165, ◊ $16.50, ch con, AE BC DC MC VI.

★★★★ **H W Motor Inn**, (M), Previously Historic Well Motel Cnr Stewart & Lord Sts, 800m E of PO, ☎ 02 6583 1200, fax 02 6584 1439, 44 units (2 suites) [shwr, tlt, elec blkts, tel, TV, clock radio, t/c mkg, refrig, toaster], ldry, lounge, pool, cots, non smoking units (15). RO $120 - $220, 21 units ★★★☆, AE BC MC VI.

★★★☆ **Aquatic Motel**, (M), 253 Hastings River Dve, 3km W of PO, ☎ 02 6583 7388, fax 02 6583 7913, (2 stry gr fl), 21 units [shwr, tlt, hairdry, fan, heat, elec blkts, tel, TV, clock radio, t/c mkg, refrig, cook fac (14), toaster], ldry, pool (salt water), bbq, dinner to unit, plygr, cots-fee. RO ♦ $70 - $140, ♦♦ $80 - $150, ◊ $12, 7 units ★★☆, AE BC DC EFT MC VI.

★★★☆ **Bayview Motor Inn**, (M), 22 Mort St, 1 km W of PO, ☎ 02 6583 3266, fax 02 6584 9003, (2 stry gr fl), 26 units [shwr, tlt, heat, elec blkts, tel, TV, video (avail), clock radio, t/c mkg, refrig, cook fac (25), micro], ldry, pool, bbq, plygr, cots, non smoking units (avail). RO ♦ $58 - $109, ♦♦ $58 - $109, ◊ $11, 11 units of a budget standard, AE BC DC MC VI.

affordable **luxury** priceless **view**

PORT MACQUARIE NSW continued...

★★★☆ Beach Park Motel, (M), 44 William St, 1km E of PO, ☎ 02 6583 2266, fax 02 6583 5226, (2 stry), 18 units [shwr, tlt, hairdry, a/c, elec blkts, tel, TV, video-fee, clock radio, t/c mkg, refrig, cook fac (8), toaster], ldry, iron, pool (salt water), bbq, dinner to unit, cots-fee. **RO** ♦ **$75 - $125**, ♦♦ **$85 - $125**, ♦♦♦ **$96 - $130**, ♦ **$11**, ch con, 4 units ★★★, Min book Christmas Jan long w/ends and Easter, AE BC DC MC VI.

★★★☆ Beachfront Regency Motor Inn, (M), 40 William St, 1km E of PO, ☎ 02 6583 2244, fax 02 6583 2868, (Multi-stry gr fl), 37 units [shwr, tlt, a/c, elec blkts, tel, TV, clock radio, t/c mkg, refrig], ldry, rec rm, ✉, pool, sauna, bbq, rm serv, cots-fee. **RO** ♦ **$60 - $70**, ♦♦ **$70 - $80**, ♦♦♦ **$77 - $87**, ♦ **$8**, ch con, AE BC DC MC VI.

★★☆ (Holiday Flat Section), 5 flats [shwr, tlt, heat, TV, clock radio, refrig, cook fac, blkts, linen, pillows], ldry, rec rm, pool, sauna, bbq. **D $35 - $85, W $245 - $595**.

★★★☆ Bermuda Breezes Resort, (M), cnr Bangalay Dve & Cathie Rd, 6km S of PO, ☎ 02 6582 0957, fax 02 6582 0691, 16 units [shwr, tlt, hairdry, a/c, heat, elec blkts, tel, TV, video (avail)-fee, clock radio, t/c mkg, refrig, cook fac ltd (10), micro (10), toaster], ldry, iron, iron brd, rec rm, pool, spa (heated), bbq, dinner to unit, plygr, gym, tennis, cots-fee. **RO** ♦ **$70 - $130**, ♦♦ **$75 - $190**, ♦♦♦ **$105 - $250**, **$410 - $1,650**, ch con, AE BC DC MC VI.

★★★☆ Burrawan Motel, (M), 24 Burrawan St, 2km E of PO, ☎ 02 6583 1799, fax 02 6583 9470, 10 units (2 bedrm), [shwr, tlt, fan, heat, elec blkts, tel, TV, clock radio, t/c mkg, refrig, cook fac (6), micro (6), toaster], ldry, rm serv, c/park (undercover). **RO** ♦ **$46 - $100**, ♦♦ **$48 - $175**, ♦♦♦ **$80 - $175**, ♦♦♦♦ **$90 - $175**, BC MC VI.

★★★☆ East Port Motor Inn, (M), Cnr Lord & Burrawan Sts, 1km E of PO, ☎ 02 6583 5850, fax 02 6583 5877, (Multi-stry gr fl), 22 units [shwr, tlt, a/c, tel, TV, clock radio, t/c mkg, refrig, toaster], ldry, conv fac, pool (salt water), bbq-fee, dinner to unit, cots, non smoking units (10). **RO $55 - $85**, ch con, AE BC EFT MC VI.

★★★☆ **El Paso Motor Inn**, (M), 29 Clarence St, 100m E of PO, ☎ 02 6583 1944, fax 02 6584 1021, (Multi-stry gr fl), 55 units (1 suite) [shwr, spa bath (2), tlt, hairdry, a/c, elec blkts, tel, TV, video (avail), movie, clock radio, t/c mkg, refrig, mini bar, cook fac (15), toaster], ldry, rec rm, conv fac, ⊠, pool-heated, sauna, spa, bbq, dinner to unit, cots-fee, non smoking units (6). RO ⧫ $90 - $115, ⧫⧫ $99 - $115, ⧫⧫⧫ $114 - $130, ⊘ $15, Suite D $185, AE BC DC JCB MC MP VI.

★★★☆ **Excelsior Motor Inn**, (M), Previously Pioneer Motor Inn 92 William St, 500m E of PO, ☎ 02 6584 5156, fax 02 6584 4144, (2 stry gr fl), 26 units (2 suites) [shwr, spa bath (2), tlt, a/c, tel, cable tv, t/c mkg, refrig, toaster], ldry, bbq, dinner to unit, cots-fee, non smoking units (20). RO ⧫ $55 - $60, ⧫⧫ $65 - $80, ⧫⧫⧫ $70 - $90, $100 - $120, Suite RO $90 - $120, fam con, AE BC EFT MC VI.

★★★☆ **Golden Beaches Motor Inn**, (M), Cnr Lord & Gordon Sts, 1km E of PO, ☎ 02 6583 8899, fax 02 6583 8408, (2 stry gr fl), 18 units [shwr, tlt, hairdry, a/c, elec blkts, tel, TV, video-fee, clock radio, t/c mkg, refrig, toaster], ldry, pool, spa, bbq, rm serv, cots, non smoking units (16). RO ⧫ $60 - $95, ⧫⧫ $65 - $105, ⧫⧫⧫ $65 - $105, ⊘ $10, ch con, AE BC DC EFT MC VI, ♿.

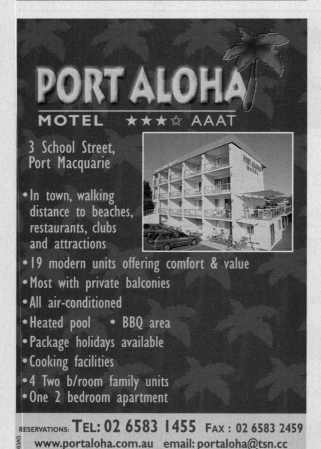
★★★☆ **Koala Tree Motel**, (M), 179 Gordon St (Oxley Hwy), 1km E of PO, ☎ 02 6583 2177, fax 02 6583 2177, 12 units [shwr, tlt, hairdry, c/fan, elec blkts, tel, cable tv, video-fee, movie, clock radio, t/c mkg, refrig, cook fac (1), toaster], ldry, pool, bbq, c/park (undercover), non smoking rms (7). **RO ⸙ $55 - $105, ⸙⸙ $55 - $105, ⸙⸙⸙ $70 - $120**, AE BC DC EFT MC MCH VI.

★★★☆ **Mercure Inn Sandcastle**, (M), 16-24 William St, 1km E of PO, ☎ 02 6583 3522, fax 02 6583 3465, (Multi-stry), 48 units (8 suites) [shwr, tlt, hairdry, a/c, tel, TV, video-fee, clock radio, t/c mkg, refrig, cook fac (8)], lift, ldry, rec rm, lounge, conv fac, ⊠, bar, pool, bbq, rm serv, cots-fee. **RO ⸙ $138 - $164, ⸙⸙ $138 - $164, ⸙⸙⸙ $149 - $175, Suite D $184 - $228**, ch con, 10 units ★★★. AE BC DC MC VI.

★★★☆ **Mid Pacific Motel**, (M), Cnr Clarence & Short Sts, 50m W of PO, ☎ 02 6583 2166, fax 02 6584 1191, (Multi-stry), 38 units (4 suites) [shwr, tlt, hairdry, a/c, elec blkts, tel, cable tv, video, clock radio, t/c mkg, refrig, cook fac], lift, ldry, iron, iron brd, pool (salt water), spa, bbq, dinner to unit, c/park (undercover) (12), cots-fee. **RO ⸙ $110 - $151, ⸙⸙ $110 - $151, ⸙⸙⸙⸙ $140 - $151, ⸙ $15**, ch con, AE BC DC MC VI.

★★★☆ **Palm Court Motor Inn**, (M), 138 William St, 1.5 km S of PO, ☎ 02 6583 5155, fax 02 6584 1128, 24 units (1 suite) [shwr, tlt, a/c, elec blkts, tel, TV, video (avail), movie, clock radio, t/c mkg, refrig, mini bar, toaster], ldry, ⊠, pool, sauna, spa, bbq, rm serv (6 nights), c/park (undercover), cots, non smoking units (avail). **RO ⸙ $105 - $140, ⸙⸙ $110 - $140, ⸙⸙⸙ $125 - $175, Suite RO $150 - $185**, AE BC DC JCB MC VI.

★★★☆ **Port Aloha Motel**, (M), 3 School St, 500m E of PO, ☎ 02 6583 1455, fax 02 6583 2459, (Multi-stry gr fl), 19 units [shwr, tlt, hairdry, a/c, elec blkts, tel, TV, video, movie, clock radio, t/c mkg, refrig, cook fac, toaster], ldry, conv fac, ✕, pool-heated (solar), bbq, rm serv, cots-fee, non smoking units (avail). **RO ⸙ $62 - $125, ⸙⸙ $62 - $125, ⸙⸙⸙ $88 - $160, ⸙ $10**, ch con, Min book applies, AE BC DC JCB MC MP VI.

★★★☆ **Port O Call Motel**, (M), 105 Hastings River Dve, 3km W of PO, ☎ 02 6583 5222, fax 02 6584 1277, 13 units [shwr, tlt, a/c (2), fan, heat, elec blkts, tel, TV, video (avail), clock radio, t/c mkg, refrig, cook fac (5), toaster], ldry, pool, bbq, dinner to unit, jetty, cots. **RO ⸙ $65 - $98, ⸙⸙ $70 - $115, ⸙ $12**, AE BC DC MC VI, .

★★★ **Arrowyn Motel**, (M), 170 Gordon St, 1km W of PO, ☎ 02 6583 1633, fax 02 6583 3040, 14 units [shwr, tlt, hairdry, a/c-cool (4), fan, heat, elec blkts, tel, fax, TV, video-fee, clock radio, t/c mkg, refrig, toaster], ldry, pool, cook fac, bbq, cots. **D $79 - $129, RO ⸙ $52 - $92, ⸙⸙ $55 - $95, ⸙ $12 - $17**, AE BC DC EFT MC VI.

★★★ **Horizon Motor Lodge**, (M), Cnr Buller & Hollingworth Sts, 300m SW of PO, ☎ 02 6583 2888, fax 02 6584 1965, (2 stry gr fl), 23 units [shwr, tlt, hairdry, a/c, tel, TV, clock radio, t/c mkg, refrig, toaster], pool, bbq, dinner to unit, plygr, cots. **RO ⸙ $70 - $90, ⸙⸙ $70 - $110, ⸙ $10**, AE DC EFT MC VI.

★★★ **John Oxley**, (M), 171 Gordon St, 1.5km W of PO, ☎ 02 6583 1677, fax 02 6583 1677, 11 units [shwr, tlt, a/c (6), fan, heat, TV, video (available), clock radio, t/c mkg, refrig, cook fac (2)], ldry, bbq, cots-fee. **W $266 - $630, RO ⸙ $48 - $88, ⸙⸙ $55 - $95, ⸙ $14**, AE BC EFT MC VI.

★★★ **Le George Motel**, (M), 4 Hollingworth St, 600m W of PO, ☎ 02 6583 3288, fax 02 6583 5236, (2 stry gr fl), 15 units [shwr, tlt, hairdry, a/c, elec blkts, tel, TV, movie, clock radio, t/c mkg, refrig], pool, bbq, dinner to unit, cots-fee, non smoking units (2). **RO ⸙ $75 - $109, ⸙⸙ $77 - $109, ⸙ $11**, ch con, AE BC MC VI.

★★★ **Shangri La Motel**, (M), 119 Gordon St, 700m W of PO, ☎ 02 6583 2500, fax 02 6583 1436, (2 stry gr fl), 12 units [shwr, tlt, a/c (11), c/fan, elec blkts, tel, fax, TV, clock radio, t/c mkg, refrig, toaster], ldry, pool (salt water), bbq. **RO** ♦ **$55 - $88,** ♦♦ **$55 - $88,** ⚹ **$11,** BC MC VI.

★★☆ **Central Views Motel**, (M), 2 Clarence St, 200m E of PO, ☎ 02 6583 1171, fax 02 6583 1171, 10 units [shwr, tlt, fan, heat, TV, clock radio, refrig, cook fac], ldry, pool, bbq. **D** ♦ **$49.50 - $110,** ♦♦ **$55 - $110,** ♦♦♦ **$66 - $120,** ⚹ **$7.70 - $11, W** **$330 - $990,** AE BC MC VI.

★★☆ **Hastings Valley Motel**, (M), 64 Burrawan St, 1km SE of PO, ☎ 02 6583 1303, fax 02 6583 1303, 9 units [shwr, tlt, a/c (7), c/fan (2), heat, elec blkts, tel, TV, clock radio, t/c mkg, refrig, cook fac], ldry, conf fac, bbq, courtesy transfer, cots. **W $275 - $840, RO** ♦ **$48 - $75,** ♦♦ **$52 - $90,** ♦♦♦ **$58 - $99,** ♦♦♦♦ **$62 - $105,** BC MC VI.

★★☆ **Major Innes Motel**, (M), 693 Oxley Hwy, 7km W of PO, ☎ 02 6581 0606, fax 02 6581 1931, 10 units [shwr, tlt, fan, heat, elec blkts, TV, clock radio, t/c mkg, refrig], ldry, pool, cook fac, bbq, c/park (undercover), tennis, cots. **RO** ♦ **$49 - $70,** ♦♦ **$49 - $70,** ⚹ **$11,** AE BC DC EFT MC VI.

★★☆ **Narimba Lodge Motel**, (M), 4 Narimba Cl, 4km SE of PO, ☎ 02 6583 3839, fax 02 6583 3839, 5 units [shwr, tlt, hairdry, fan, heat, elec blkts, fax, TV, video, clock radio, t/c mkg, refrig, micro, toaster], bbq, ✆, cots. **RO** ♦ **$51 - $77,** ♦♦ **$53 - $77,** ♦♦♦ **$66 - $88,** ⚹ **$11,** AE BC EFT MC MCH VI.

★★☆ **Rocky Beach Motel**, (M), 10 Pacific Dve, 2km S of PO, ☎ 02 6583 5881, fax 02 6583 5881, (2 stry gr fl), 10 units [shwr, tlt, hairdry, fan, heat, elec blkts, TV, clock radio, t/c mkg, refrig, cook fac, toaster], ldry, iron, iron brd, bbq, courtesy transfer, ✆, plygr, cots, non smoking units (3). **RO** ♦ **$58 - $80,** ♦♦ **$66 - $88,** ⚹ **$11 - $15,** BC EFT MC VI.

Macquarie Motel, (M), 21 Grant St, 1km SE of PO, ☎ 02 6583 1533, 30 units [shwr, tlt, fan, heat, tel, TV, video, clock radio, t/c mkg, refrig, cook fac], ldry, pool, bbq, plygr, cots-fee, **RO** ♦ **$38.50,** ♦♦ **$44 - $77,** ⚹ **$11,** BC MC VI.

Self Catering Accommodation

★★★★☆ **Port Pacific Resort**, (SA), 6 Clarence St, ☎ 02 6583 8099, fax 02 6584 9024, (Multi-stry), 79 serv apts acc up to 6, (1, 2 & 3 bedrm), [shwr, bath, tlt, fan, tel, TV, video, clock radio, t/c mkg, refrig, cook fac, micro, d/wash, toaster], lift, ldry, rec rm, lounge, conv fac, pool-heated, sauna, bbq, plygr, gym, tennis (half court), cots-fee, non smoking property, **D $132 - $214,** AE BC DC MC VI.

★★★★ **Beaches Holiday Resort**, (HU), 55 Pacific Dve, 3km E of PO, ☎ 02 6584 4433, fax 02 6584 4280, (Multi-stry gr fl), 19 units acc up to 6, [shwr, bath, spa bath (3), tlt, c/fan, cable tv, video-fee, t/c mkg, refrig, cook fac, micro, toaster, ldry, blkts, linen], w/mach, dryer, iron, iron brd, pool-heated (salt, solar), bbq, secure park, ✆, cots. **RO $110 - $185, W $380 - $1,370,** AE BC DC EFT MC VI.

Operator Comment: Visit our Website www.australiatravel.au.com/beachesresort

★★★★ **Harbour Watch**, (HU), 18-20 Burrawan St, ☎ 02 6584 1154, fax 02 6583 6202, (Multi-stry), 1 unit acc up to 6, [shwr, bath, tlt, c/fan, heat, TV, video, clock radio, refrig, cook fac, micro, elec frypan, d/wash, toaster, ldry (in unit), linen], lift, w/mach, dryer, iron, c/park (garage). **W $525 - $1,415,** Min book applies, AE BC MC VI.

★★★★ **River Haven Waterfront Cottage**, (Cotg), 82 Hibbard Dve, ☎ 02 6582 1267, fax 02 6582 3432, 1 cotg acc up to 6, [shwr, tlt, hairdry, fan, heat, TV, clock radio, CD, t/c mkg, refrig, cook fac, micro, d/wash, toaster, ldry, blkts, linen, pillows], w/mach, dryer, iron, lounge (TV), bbq, c/park (garage), jetty. **D** ♦♦ **$160 - $210,** ⚹ **$30, W** ♦♦ **$900 - $1,800,** Min book applies.

★★★★ **Vacation Village Apartments**, (Apt), 50 Settlement Point Rd, 5km NW of PO, ☎ 02 6583 5555, fax 02 6583 7373, 24 apts acc up to 6, [shwr, tlt, a/c-cool, heat, elec blkts, TV, video (avail), clock radio, refrig, cook fac, micro, d/wash, blkts, linen, pillows], ldry, rec rm, pool-heated, sauna, spa, bbq, c/park (carport), plygr, bicycle, bowls, mini golf, squash, tennis. **RO** ♦♦♦♦ **$130 - $250,** ⚹ **$11, W** ♦♦♦♦ **$780 - $1,500,** Min book applies, ♿.

AAA TOURISM Special Rates

★★★★ **Village Resort**, (Cotg), 288 Hastings River Dve, 7km W of PO, ☎ 02 6583 5544, fax 02 6584 0515, 32 cotgs acc up to 8, [shwr, bath, spa bath, tlt, hairdry, c/fan, heat, tel, TV, video, clock radio, t/c mkg, refrig, cook fac, micro, elec frypan, d/wash, toaster, ldry (in unit), blkts, linen, pillows], w/mach, dryer, iron, rec rm, lounge (TV), conv fac, pool indoor heated, sauna, spa, bbq, c/park (carport), plygr, gym, tennis, cots-fee. **D** ♦♦ **$110 - $265, ♦♦♦♦ $145 - $265,** ⬥ **$11, W** ♦♦ **$660 - $1,590, ♦♦♦♦ $870 - $1,590,** AE BC DC MC VI.

★★★☆ **Beach House Units**, (HU), 7 Lord St, 700m E of PO, ☎ 02 6584 1084, fax 02 6584 9924, 8 units acc up to 7, [shwr, bath, tlt, fan, heat, TV, clock radio, t/c mkg, refrig, cook fac, micro, toaster, ldry (in unit), blkts, linen, pillows], pool, bbq, ✆, cots. **W $330 - $1,390,** ch con, Min book applies, BC MC VI.

★★★☆ **Beach Lodge & Sea Spray Flats**, (HF), Cnr William & Owen Sts, opposite Bowling Club, ☎ 02 6583 6226, fax 02 6584 2721, 12 flats acc up to 6, [shwr, tlt, fan, heat, TV, clock radio, refrig, cook fac, micro, d/wash, toaster, blkts, linen, pillows], ldry, pool-heated, bbq, ✆, cots, **RO $71.50 - $165,** AE BC MC VI.

★★★☆ **Flynns Beach Townhouses**, (HU), Cnr Ocean & Chrisallen Sts, 3.2km S of PO, ☎ 02 6584 1166, fax 02 6584 1333, 10 units acc up to 6, [shwr, bath, tlt, c/fan, heat, TV, clock radio, t/c mkg, refrig, cook fac, micro, toaster, ldry (in unit), blkts, linen, pillows], w/mach, iron, pool (salt water), bbq, c/park (carport), non smoking units (4). **RO $50 - $160, W $450 - $1,120,** Min book all holiday times, BC MC VI.

★★★☆ **Oxley Cove Holiday Apartments**, (HU), 29 Owen St, ☎ 02 6583 1855, fax 02 6583 8695, 26 units acc up to 6, [shwr, tlt, hairdry, c/fan, heat, TV, video-fee, clock radio, t/c mkg, refrig, cook fac, micro, toaster, blkts, linen, pillows], ldry, pool-heated, bbq, c/park (undercover), ✆, cots-fee. **D $60 - $100, W $295 - $1,150,** Min book applies, AE BC MC VI.

★★★☆ **Port Macquarie Holiday Cabins**, 42/44 Flynn St, 2.5km S of PO, ☎ 02 6583 1747, fax 02 6584 3490, 7 cabins [shwr, tlt, c/fan, TV, refrig, cook fac, micro, toaster, linen-fee], w/mach-fee, dryer-fee, iron, iron brd, bbq. **D** ♦♦ **$49.50 - $99,** ⬥ **$5.50 - $7.50, W** ♦♦ **$346.50 - $850.50,** ⬥ **$5.50 - $7.50,** BC MC VI.

★★★☆ **Seychelles Holiday Units**, (HU), 135 Pacific Dve, 5km S of PO, ☎ 02 6582 3738, fax 02 6582 3864, 10 units acc up to 7, [shwr (2), bath, tlt (2), fan, heat, TV (2), video (avail), clock radio, refrig, cook fac, micro (10), d/wash (10), toaster, blkts, linen, pillows], ldry, w/mach, dryer, rec rm, pool-heated (solar), sauna, bbq, c/park (undercover), plygr, tennis (half court). **W $315 - $1,365,** Min book all holiday times, AE BC MC VI.

★★★☆ **Shelly Beach Resort**, (HU), 156 Pacific Dve, 5km SE of PO, ☎ 02 6582 3978, fax 02 6582 5680, 19 units acc up to 5, [shwr, tlt, hairdry, a/c-cool, TV, video (avail), clock radio, refrig, cook fac, micro, d/wash, ldry (in unit), linen], rec rm, pool-heated (solar), spa, bbq, ✆, plygr, tennis. **RO** ♦ **$75 - $95,** ♦ **$350 - $1,350,** Min book applies, AE BC MC VI.

★★★☆ **Strathmore Lodge**, (HU), 35 Watonga St, 7km S of PO, ☎ 02 6582 0848, fax 02 6582 1135, (2 stry gr fl), 3 units acc up to 6, (1, 2 & 3 bedrm), [shwr, bath (1), tlt, evap cool (1), a/c (2), fan, heat, TV, video, clock radio, t/c mkg, refrig, cook fac, micro, d/wash, toaster, ldry, blkts, doonas, linen, pillows], w/mach, dryer, lounge firepl, bbq, secure park (undercover). **D $115 - $260, W $600 - $1,400,** Min book applies.

★★★ **Airlie Palms**, (HU), 50 Pacific Dve, 2.5km S of PO, ☎ 1800 242 992, fax 02 6584 1253, (2 stry gr fl), 6 units acc up to 6, [shwr, tlt, hairdry, a/c (6), fax, TV, video, clock radio, refrig, cook fac, micro, toaster, blkts, linen], ldry, w/mach-fee, dryer-fee, bbq, c/park (undercover). **D $55 - $140, W $265 - $900,** Min book applies, ♿.

★★★ **Bay Park Gardens**, (HU), 1 Walters St, ☎ 02 6584 1154, fax 02 6583 6202, (2 stry), 1 unit acc up to 5, [shwr, bath, tlt, heat, TV, video, clock radio, refrig, cook fac, micro, elec frypan, toaster, ldry (in unit), linen reqd], w/mach, iron, pool, c/park (carport). **W $210 - $690,** Min book applies, AE BC MC VI.

★★★ **Blue Pacific**, (HF), 37 Pacific Dve, Flynns Beach, 2.5km SE of PO, ☎ 02 6583 1686, 4 flats acc up to 6, [shwr, tlt, c/fan, heat, TV, refrig, cook fac, micro, linen], ldry, c/park (carport), cots. **D** ♦ **$45 - $65,** ♦♦ **$45 - $80, ♦♦♦ $50 - $90,** ⬥ **$10,** ch con.

★★★ **La Mer**, (HU), Cnr Gordon & Owen Sts, 1km E of PO, ☎ 02 6584 1154, fax 02 6583 6202, (Multi-stry), 1 unit acc up to 4, [shwr, bath, tlt, fan, heat, TV, refrig, cook fac, micro, elec frypan, d/wash, toaster, ldry (in unit), blkts, linen, pillows], lift, w/mach, dryer, iron, c/park (undercover). **RO $350 - $920,** Min book applies, AE BC MC VI.

Shelly Beach Resort

Air-conditioned private and spacious fully self contained units. Colour TV, microwave, dishwasher, washing machine and dryer in each unit.

- Linen included
- Full-size floodlit tennis court
- Solar heated pool and spa
- BBQ area
- Children's playground
- Games room with table tennis and pool table
- Undercover parking
- Walk to beach and 5 minute drive to town

Shelly Beach Resort, 156 Pacific Drive, Port Macquarie 2444
PHONE: (02) 6582 3978 FREECALL: 1800 810 248

4584AG

★★★ **Sandringham Holiday Unit**, (HU), 9/66 Pacific Dve, ☎ 02 6584 1154, fax 02 6583 6202, (Multi-stry), 1 unit acc up to 4, [cook fac, ldry, linen], c/park. W $210 - $690, Min book applies.

★★★ **The Cottage**, (Cotg), 6 Elizabeth St, ☎ 02 6584 1154, fax 02 6583 6202, 1 cotg acc up to 8, [shwr, tlt, heat, TV, video, clock radio, t/c mkg, refrig, cook fac, micro, elec frypan, toaster, ldry (in unit), blkts, linen, pillows], w/mach, dryer, iron, bbq, c/park. W $265 - $850, Min book applies, AE BC MC VI.

★★★ **The Penthouse Holiday Unit**, (HU), 3/39 Matthew Flinders Dve, ☎ 02 6584 1154, fax 02 6583 6202, (2 stry), 1 unit acc up to 10, [shwr, bath, tlt, heat, TV, refrig, cook fac, micro, elec frypan, toaster, ldry (in unit), linen reqd], w/mach, dryer, iron, c/park (garage). W $315 - $1,350, Min book applies.

★★☆ **Breakers Holiday Units**, (HU), 2-4 Hill St, ☎ 02 6583 1625, fax 02 6584 6259, (2 stry gr fl), 6 units [shwr, tlt, c/fan, heat, TV, video, clock radio, t/c mkg, refrig, cook fac, micro, elec frypan, toaster, blkts, linen], ldry, iron, iron brd, bbq, 24hr reception, courtesy transfer, plygr, cots, non smoking units. D $44 - $130, W $220 - $800, pen con, AE BC MC VI.

★★☆ **Flynns Beach Holiday Units**, (HU), 51 Pacific Dve, 2.5 km S of PO, ☎ 02 6583 2528, fax 02 6583 2528, (2 stry gr fl), 6 units acc up to 4, [shwr, tlt, hairdry, c/fan, heat, TV, video, clock radio, refrig, cook fac, micro, elec frypan, toaster, blkts, linen, pillows], ldry, iron, bbq, cots, non smoking units (avail). RO $44 - $770, ⓟ $5, BC MC VI.

★★☆ **Golden Sands Apartments**, (HU), 9 Everard St, 2km S of PO, ☎ 02 6583 2067, fax 02 6583 2067, 5 units [shwr, tlt, heat, TV, clock radio, refrig, cook fac, micro, linen reqd-fee], ldry, bbq, c/park (undercover), cots. D ♀♀ $50, ⓟ $5, W $280 - $900, Min book applies.

★★☆ **Hastings River Holiday Units**, (HU), 6 Hastings River Drive, 1km W of PO, ☎ 02 6583 3084, fax 02 6583 9266, (2 stry gr fl), 10 units acc up to 6, [shwr, tlt, c/fan, heat, TV, video, clock radio, t/c mkg, refrig, cook fac, micro, elec frypan, toaster, blkts, linen reqd-fee], ldry, w/mach (3), dryer (1), iron, iron brd, pool (salt water), bbq, c/park (undercover), ☎, cots. D $55 - $140, W $250 - $880.

★★☆ **The Reef Holiday Unit**, (HU), 4/8 Burrawan St, ☎ 02 6584 1154, fax 02 6583 6202, (Multi-stry), 1 unit acc up to 4, [shwr, tlt, TV, refrig, cook fac, micro, elec frypan, toaster, ldry (in unit), linen reqd], w/mach, iron, c/park (garage). W $190 - $630, Min book applies, AE BC EFT MC VI.

★★ **Beach Park Apartments**, (HU), 58 Pacific Dve, ☎ 02 6584 1154, fax 02 6583 6202, (Multi-stry), 2 units acc up to 5, [shwr, bath, tlt, heat, TV, video (1), refrig, cook fac, micro, elec frypan, toaster, ldry (in unit), linen reqd], w/mach, dryer, iron, c/park (garage). W $170 - $730, Min book applies.

Beachcomber Resort, (SA), 54 William St, 500m E of PO, ☎ 02 6584 1881, fax 02 6584 1981, (Multi-stry gr fl), 22 serv apts acc up to 6, (1 & 2 bedrm), [shwr, spa bath (5), tlt, a/c, fan, elec blkts, TV, video, clock radio, t/c mkg, refrig, cook fac, micro, blkts, linen, pillows], w/mach, dryer, pool (outdoor/heated), bbq, plygr, cots, non smoking units. D ⓟ $90 - $125, ♀♀ $110 - $195, ⓟ $10 - $20, weekly con, AE BC DC EFT MC VI, (not yet classified).

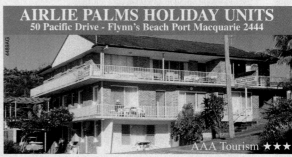

Beachside Holiday Apartments, (HU), 48 Pacific Dve, 3km S of PO, ☎ 02 6583 9544, fax 02 6582 2328, (Multi-stry gr fl), 29 units acc up to 6, (1, 2 & 3 bedrm), [shwr, spa bath (16), tlt, c/fan, cable tv, clock radio, t/c mkg, refrig, cook fac, micro, toaster, blkts, linen, pillows], ldry, w/mach, dryer, pool-heated, bbq, secure park (undercover), ✆, cots-fee, non smoking property. **W $320 - $1,470**, Min book all holiday times, BC MC VI, (not yet classified).

Koala Tree Apartments, (Apt), 2 New St, 500m W of PO, ☎ 02 6583 2177, fax 02 6583 2177, 3 apts acc up to 6, (2 bedrm), [shwr, bath, tlt, fan, heat, elec blkts, TV, clock radio, t/c mkg, refrig, cook fac, micro, toaster, blkts, linen, pillows], ldry, w/mach, bbq, secure park, plygr, non smoking property. **D ♦♦ $70 - $140, ◊ $15 - $20, W ♦♦ $420 - $840, ◊ $70 - $140**, AE BC DC EFT MC VI, (not yet classified).

Northpoint Luxury Waterfront Apartments, (Apt), 2 Murray St, 150m E of PO, ☎ 02 6583 8333, (Multi-stry gr fl), 40 apts acc up to 6, (2 & 3 bedrm), [shwr, tlt, fan, heat, elec blkts, cable tv, video, clock radio, refrig, cook fac, micro, d/wash, toaster, ldry, blkts, linen, pillows], lift, w/mach, dryer, ✉, pool-heated, spa, bbq, secure park (undercover), ✆, plygr, cots-fee, non smoking units (30). **D ♦♦ $138 - $310, ◊ $15 - $20, W ♦♦ $660 - $2,480, ◊ $120**, Min book applies, BC EFT MC VI, (not yet classified).

B&B's/Guest Houses

★★★★☆ **Belrina Bed & Breakfast**, (B&B), 22 Burrawong Dve, 7km S of PO, ☎ 02 6582 2967, fax 02 6582 2967, 2 rms [shwr, bath (1), spa bath (1), tlt, hairdry, c/fan, elec blkts, tel, fax, clock radio, t/c mkg], ldry, iron, iron brd, TV rm, lounge firepl, ✗, pool (salt water), refrig, bbq, non smoking property. **BB ♦ $88 - $100, ♦♦ $105 - $120, DBB ♦ $120 - $132, ♦♦ $170 - $185**, AE BTC DC MC VI.

★★★★☆ **Lighthouse Beach B & B Home Stay**, (B&B), No children's facilities, 91 Matthew Flinders Dve, 7km S of PO, ☎ 02 6582 5149, fax 02 6582 5882, 3 rms (1 suite) [shwr, spa bath (1), tlt, hairdry, a/c, heat, tel, TV, video (2), clock radio, t/c mkg, refrig], ldry, pool, spa, bbq, non smoking rms. **BB ♦ $75 - $110, ♦♦ $110 - $150**, BC MC VI.

★★★★☆ **Port Macquaries Newport Island B & B**, (B&B), 8 Francis St, 3.5km W of PO, ☎ 02 6584 0088, fax 02 6584 0577, (2 stry), 2 rms [ensuite, c/fan, heat, t/c mkg, refrig], lounge (cable TV), spa, non smoking property. **BB** ♦ **$99 - $110, BLB** ♦♦ **$110 - $148**, AE BC DC MC VI.

★★★★ **Azura Beach House Bed & Breakfast**, (B&B), 109 Pacific Dve, 3km S of PO, ☎ 02 6582 2700, fax 02 6582 2700, 2 rms [shwr, tlt, tel, TV, video, clock radio, refrig, micro], ldry, iron, iron brd, TV rm, lounge, lounge firepl, ✗, pool-heated, spa, t/c mkg shared, bbq, courtesy transfer. **BB** ♦ **$95 - $120**, ♦♦ **$110 - $135**, ◊ **$10 - $15**, BC MC VI.

★★★★ **Dolphin View Bed & Breakfast**, (B&B), No children's facilities, 53 Matthew Flinders Dve, 7km S of PO, ☎ 02 6582 3561, fax 02 6582 3561, (2 stry gr fl), 2 rms [shwr, bath (1), tlt, hairdry, c/fan, heat, elec blkts, TV (1), clock radio], ldry, iron, iron brd, lounge firepl (TV), ✗, pool (salt water), t/c mkg shared, non smoking property. **BB** ♦ **$88 - $110**, ♦♦ **$110 - $143**, BC MC VI.

★★★☆ **Joys Doo Drop Inn Bed & Breakfast**, (B&B), 29 Laguna Pl, Newport Island, 2km W of PO, ☎ 02 6583 3405, fax 02 6582 5910, 2 rms [ensuite (1), shwr, spa bath, tlt, hairdry, fan, heat, elec blkts, cable tv, clock radio, t/c mkg, refrig], lounge (TV & video), pool-heated (solar), bbq, c/park. **BB** ♦ **$65 - $75**, ♦♦ **$75 - $105**.

Port Macquarie Beachside B&B, (B&B), 60 Watonga St, ☎ 02 6582 3957, fax 02 6584 2550, (2 stry gr fl), 2 rms (1 suite) [heat (elec), elec blkts, TV, clock radio, t/c mkg, refrig, toaster, doonas], bathrm (2), lounge (TV), spa, non smoking rms (2). **BLB** ♦ **$60 - $85**, ♦♦ **$120 - $140**, ◊ **$40, Suite D $180**, BC MC VI, (not yet classified).

Telegraph Retreat, (B&B), 126 Federation Way, Telegraph Point 2441, 26km from Port Macquarie PO, ☎ 02 6585 0670, fax 02 6585 0671, 1 rm [shwr, bath, tlt, hairdry, c/fan, heat, elec blkts, tel, TV (2), video, clock radio, t/c mkg, refrig, mini bar, cook fac, micro, toaster, ldry], rec rm, lounge firepl, pool-heated, spa (pool), bbq, rm serv, dinner to unit, courtesy transfer, plygr, cots. **BLB** ♦ **$180**, ♦♦ **$160 - $200**, ◊ **$15 - $25, DBB** ♦ **$220**, ♦♦ **$240 - $280**, ◊ **$55 - $65**, ch con, BC MC VI, (not yet classified).

Other Accommodation

★★ **Limeburners Lodge**, (Lodge), 353 Shoreline Dve North Shore, 4km N of Port Macquarie Town Centre, ☎ 02 6583 3381, fax 02 6583 3683, (2 stry gr fl), 6 rms [hairdry, heat, TV, video, radio, toaster, linen reqd], shwr, tlt, ✗, pool, cook fac, t/c mkg shared, bbq, c/park. **RO** ♦ **$18.70**, ♦♦ **$37.40**, ◊ **$18.70**, ch con.

Beachside Backpackers YHA, 40 Church St, 500m from PO, ☎ 02 6583 5512, fax 02 6583 5512, 5 rms shwr, tlt, rec rm, cook fac. **RO $18 - $20**.

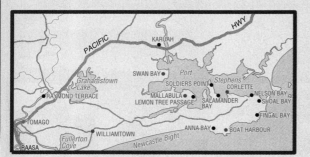

Sir Francis Drake Resort

Set on five acres of immaculate English gardens, Sir Francis Drake is the premier international ★★★☆ address in the Hunter Valley. Judged best function venue in the Hunter for 1998 and 99. Enjoy the fine food and service of two restaurants, cocktail lounge, spa, pool and tennis court. All this within 10 minutes of Newcastle Airport, with courtesy transport by arrangement. Central to Port Stephens, vineyards, golfing, botanic gardens, Morpeth and Newcastle.

Sir Francis Drake Resort
Conference and Training Centre

**204 Pacific Highway,
Motto Farm (South of
Raymond Terrace) 2324
Phone: (02) 4987 1444
Fax: (02) 4987 1393
Freecall: 1800 674 070**

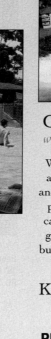
PORT STEPHENS - ANNA BAY NSW 2316

Pop 1,950. (211km N Sydney), See map on page 55, ref E8. Seaside town south of Port Stephens at the northern end of Stockton Beach. Boating, Fishing, Scenic Drives, Swimming.

Hotels/Motels
★★★★ **Bardots Resort**, (M), 288 Gan Gan Rd, 5km S of Nelson Bay, ☎ 02 4982 2000, fax 02 4982 2107, 12 units (3 suites) [shwr, tlt, hairdry, c/fan, heat, elec blkts, tel, TV, video (avail), clock radio, t/c mkg, refrig], rec rm, lounge (TV), ✕, pool-heated (salt water), spa, bbq, ✆, tennis, cots. **RO** ♦ $152, ♦♦ $152, ◊ $30, ch con, Clothing optional, Min book applies, AE BC MC VI.

Self Catering Accommodation
★★★ **The Retreat Port Stephens**, 266 Nelson Bay Rd, 8km SE of Nelson Bay, ☎ 02 4982 1244, fax 02 4982 2880, 7 cabins acc up to 6, [shwr, tlt, fan, heat, TV, video (4), clock radio, refrig, cook fac, micro, elec frypan, toaster, linen reqd-fee], ldry, w/mach, dryer, iron, pool, bbq, c/park (carport). **D** ♦♦ $53 - $118, ◊ $5.50 - $11, **W** ♦♦ $218 - $870, Min book applies, BC MC VI.

★★★★ **(Cottage Section)**, 3 cotgs acc up to 16, [shwr, bath, tlt, fan, fire pl (1), heat (2), TV, video, clock radio, refrig, cook fac, micro, elec frypan, toaster, ldry, linen reqd-fee], w/mach, dryer, iron, bbq, c/park (carport). **D** ♦♦ $99 - $150, ◊ $11 - $35, **W** ♦ $55 - $125.

★★☆ **Oceanfront Holiday Accommodation**, (HU), 15 Robinson St, ☎ 02 9428 4099, or 02 4982 1548, fax 02 9428 4099, (2 stry), 1 unit acc up to 6, [shwr, tlt, c/fan, heat, tel, TV, video, clock radio, t/c mkg, refrig, cook fac, micro, elec frypan, toaster, ldry, linen reqd-fee], w/mach, iron, iron brd. **D** $82 - $99, **W** $280 - $385.

B&B's/Guest Houses
★★★★☆ **Birubi Beach Luxury Accommodation**, (B&B), Previously Birubi Beach Bed & Breakfast 39 Ocean Ave, 1km S of PO, ☎ 02 4982 1520, fax 02 4982 1510, 1 rm [shwr, bath, tlt, a/c, c/fan, fire pl, tel, TV, video, radio, t/c mkg, refrig, toaster]. **BB** ♦ $120, ♦♦ $140 - $210, ◊ $40, BC MC VI.

★★★★ **Bays Holiday Park and B&B Taylors Beach**, (B&B), 23 Port Stephens Dve, 3km N of PO, ☎ 02 4982 1438, fax 02 4982 1438, 3 rms [shwr, tlt, a/c-cool, c/fan, heat, elec blkts, TV, clock radio, t/c mkg], bbq, non smoking property. **BB** $90 - $120, ch con, BC MC VI.

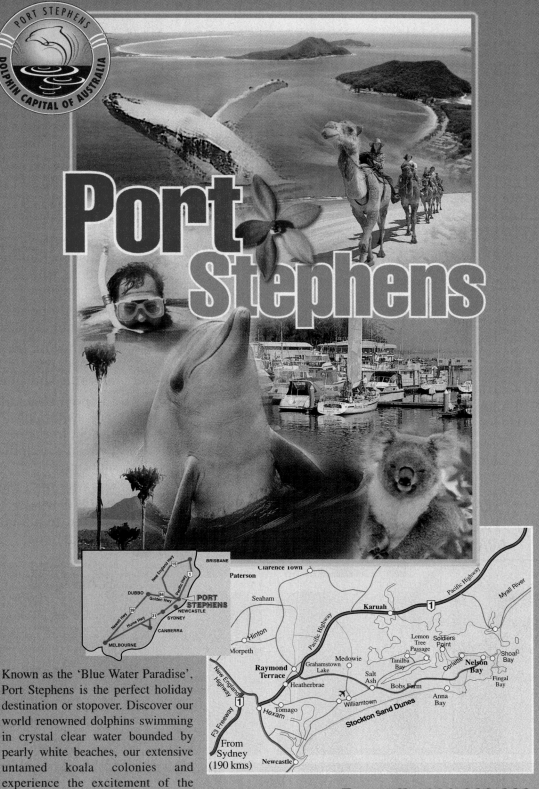

Port Stephens

Known as the 'Blue Water Paradise', Port Stephens is the perfect holiday destination or stopover. Discover our world renowned dolphins swimming in crystal clear water bounded by pearly white beaches, our extensive untamed koala colonies and experience the excitement of the many activities along our famous 32 kilometre Stockton sand dunes. It's the natural place to visit.

Freecall 1800 808 900
Email: tops@hunterlink.net.au
Port Stephens Tourism

Web Site: www.portstephens.org.au

Port Stephens Beachside Holiday Parks...
...it's no place like home!

Shoal Bay - central location opposite calm, aquamarine waters and white, sandy beaches.
- Short walk to beachside village with cafes, boutiques, restaurants & pub
- Quality camp & van sites, safari bungalows or luxury cabins some with disabled facilities
- Tennis, camp kitchen, in-house movies, cable TV, playground, rec room
- Conference, group & meeting facilities

shoal bay
holiday park

Fingal Bay - award winning park, directly opposite a stunning surf beach and surrounded by National Park.
- Huge tropical resort-style pool and kids wading pool
- Shady camp & van sites with cable TV, luxury beach houses, or budget cabins
- Camp kitchen, bbqs recreation room, and kids playground
- Great fishing, surfing, swimming, boating & bushwalking

fingal bay
holiday park

Halifax - absolute waterfront location in the heart of Nelson Bay.
- Surrounded by two unspoilt beaches
- Deep water boat ramp and jetty
- Quiet, friendly, atmosphere
- Great camp & van sites or luxury villas with spa
- Stroll to shops, clubs, marinas, restaurants, bowls and golf
- Top holiday & tourist attractions nearby

halifax
holiday park

Shoal Bay Rd, Shoal Bay NSW 2315
Email: shoalbay@beachsideholidays.com
Freecall: 1800 600 200
accommodation rating ★ ★ ★ ★

Marine Drive, Fingal Bay NSW 2315
Email: fingalbay@beachsideholidays.com
Freecall: 1800 600 203
accommodation rating ★ ★ ★ ★ ☆

Little Beach Rd, Little Beach, Nelson Bay 2315
Email: halifax@beachsideholidays.com
Freecall: 1800 600 201
accommodation rating ★ ★ ★ ★

Self-contained cabins from $49 double p.n. Up to 3 kids FREE! www.beachsideholidays.com.au*
*conditions apply

PS/1165

PORT STEPHENS - ANNA BAY NSW continued...

★★★★ **Clydesdale Bed & Breakfast**, (B&B), RMB 717A, Gan Gan Rd, 1.5km E of PO, ☎ 02 4982 1246, 1 rm [shwr, tlt, fan, heat, TV, radio, t/c mkg, refrig, toaster], lounge (TV), non smoking rms. **BB** ♦ **$100**, ♦♦ **$132**, ◊ **$30**, Min book applies, BC MC VI.

★★★☆ **Beachside Bed & Breakfast**, (B&B), 26 Fitzroy St, 1km S of PO, ☎ 02 4982 1399, fax 02 4982 1399, (2 stry), rms [shwr (1), spa bath (1), tlt (1), c/fan, tel], lounge (TV), lounge firepl, pool (salt water), t/c mkg shared, non smoking property. **BB** ♦♦ **$95 - $140.**

PORT STEPHENS - BOAT HARBOUR NSW 2316

Pop 500. (0km Sydney), See map on page 55, ref E8. Small settlement in the southern Port Stephens area.

B&B's/Guest Houses

★★★★ **Bagatelle Bed & Breakfast**, (B&B), 32 Andrew Close, ☎ 02 4981 9018, 3 rms (1 suite) [ensuite, hairdry, c/fan, heat (1), tel, clock radio], ldry, lounge (TV), pool indoor heated, t/c mkg shared, refrig, bbq, courtesy transfer. **BB** ♦ **$90 - $135**, ♦♦ **$100 - $155**, MC VI.

PORT STEPHENS - CORLETTE NSW 2315

Pop 2,200. (221km N Sydney), See map on page 55, ref E7. Town situated west of Nelson Bay on the southern shores of Port Stephens. Boating, Bowls, Fishing, Swimming, Tennis.

Hotels/Motels

★★★★☆ **Peppers Anchorage Port Stephens**, (LH), Corlette Point Rd, 4km W of Nelson Bay PO, ☎ 02 4984 2555, fax 02 4984 0300, (2 stry gr fl), 80 rms (25 suites) [shwr, bath, spa bath (27), tlt, hairdry, a/c, cent heat, tel, TV, video-fee, clock radio, t/c mkg, refrig, mini bar], ldry, rec rm, conv fac, ⊠, pool-heated, sauna, spa (heated), rm serv, plygr, gym, cots. **RO** ♦ **$248 - $323**, ◊ **$55**, Suite **RO** **$351 - $418**, ch con, AE BC DC JCB MC VI, ⚖.

★★☆ **Corlette Palms Motor Inn**, (M), 104 Sandy Point Rd, 4km W of Nelson Bay Police Station, ☎ 02 4981 1833, fax 02 4981 1845, 13 units [shwr, tlt, a/c-cool (1), c/fan, heat, elec blkts, TV, video-fee, clock radio, t/c mkg, refrig, micro (1), toaster], ldry, pool, cook fac, bbq, ☎, cots-fee. **RO** ♦ **$68 - $145**, ♦♦ **$68 - $145**, ◊ **$11 - $22**, ch con, fam con, pen con, Min book long w/ends, AE BC DC MC VI.

B&B's/Guest Houses

★★★★☆ **Anne's Waterfront Haven Bed & Breakfast**, (B&B), 44a Danalene Pde, ☎ 02 4984 1178, fax 02 4984 1178, (2 stry), 1 rm [shwr, bath, tlt, c/fan, heat, elec blkts, TV, video, clock radio, t/c mkg, refrig], ldry, TV rm, lounge, courtesy transfer, non smoking property. **BB** ♦♦ **$110 - $170**, BC MC VI.

★★★★☆ **Sandy Point Bed & Breakfast**, (B&B), 17 Mulubinda Pde, ☎ 02 4984 2964, fax 02 4984 4448, 2 rms (2 suites) [shwr, tlt, c/fan, heat, tel, TV, video, clock radio, t/c mkg, refrig, toaster], pool (solar heated), spa, bbq, c/park. **BLB** ♦♦ **$80 - $120**, ch con, BC MC VI.

★★★★ **Bonito Bed & Breakfast**, (B&B), 50 Bonito St, 5km N of Nelson Bay, ☎ 02 4981 5891, fax 02 4981 5891, (2 stry gr fl), 1 rm [ensuite, fan, TV, video, clock radio, t/c mkg, refrig], non smoking property. **BB** ♦♦ **$100 - $140**, BC MC VI.

★★★★ **Corlette Heights Bed & Breakfast**, (B&B), 44 The Peninsula, ☎ 02 4984 9539, fax 02 4984 9540, (2 stry gr fl), 2 rms (1 suite) [shwr, tlt, tel, TV, video, clock radio, t/c mkg, refrig, cook fac ltd], pool (salt water), bbq, non smoking property. **BB** ♦ **$80 - $90**, ♦♦ **$100 - $140**, ◊ **$30 - $35**, Suite BB ♦ **$80 - $90**, ♦♦ **$110 - $150**, ◊ **$30 - $40**, ch con, BC MC VI.

Operator Comment: Breakfast at Corlette Heights: on the balcony or by the pool, enjoying the views over beautiful Port Stephens-the perfect start to your day!.

PORT STEPHENS - FINGAL BAY NSW 2315

Pop 1,400. (242km N Sydney), See map on page 55, ref E8. Port Stephens fishing village set south of Nelson Bay on the sheltered sea waters of Fingal Bay. Boating, Fishing, Scenic Drives, Swimming.

Self Catering Accommodation

★★★ **The Dunes**, (HU), 38 Marine Dve, 300m N of PO, ☎ 02 4981 1999, 8 units acc up to 6, [shwr, bath, tlt, heat, TV, video, refrig, cook fac, toaster, linen reqd], ldry, pool, c/park (garage), tennis. **W** **$285 - $1,680**, Min book applies, BC MC VI.

★☆ **Taronga**, (HU), 18 Garuwa St, 1.5kms N of PO, ☎ 02 4981 1577, fax 02 4984 1204, 1 unit acc up to 7, [shwr, tlt, fan, heat, TV, refrig, cook fac, elec frypan, toaster, ldry, linen reqd-fee], iron, c/park (carport). **W** **$350 - $1,200**, Min book applies.

PORT STEPHENS - KARUAH NSW 2324

Pop 800. (194km N Sydney), See map on page 55, ref D7. Small village on the north-western reaches of Port Stephens. Boating, Bowls, Fishing, Golf, Tennis.

Hotels/Motels

★★★☆ **Country Life Motel**, (M), Pacific Hwy, 600m S of PO, ☎ 02 4997 5225, fax 02 4997 5225, 12 units [shwr, tlt, hairdry, a/c (12), fan, elec blkts, tel, TV, video (4), clock radio, t/c mkg, refrig], pool (salt water), bbq, cots-fee, non smoking units (8), **RO ♦ $52 - $60, ♦♦ $55 - $65, ◊ $11**, AE BC DC EFT MC MCH VI.

★★★ **Karuah Motor Inn**, (M), 19 Pacific Hwy, ☎ 02 4997 5336, fax 02 4997 5308, 14 units [shwr, tlt, hairdry (7), a/c, heat, elec blkts, tel, TV, clock radio, t/c mkg, refrig, mini bar, micro, toaster], iron, iron brd, cots-fee, non smoking units (7). **RO ♦ $56 - $76, ♦♦ $61 - $81, ♦♦♦ $79 - $90, ◊ $11**, AE BC EFT MC VI.

PORT STEPHENS - LEMON TREE PASSAGE NSW 2319

Pop 5,300. (194km N Sydney), See map on page 55, ref E7. Quiet town on the southern shores of Port Stephens where Tilligerry Creek flows into the bay. Boating, Bowls, Fishing, Golf, Sailing, Swimming, Tennis, Water Skiing.

Hotels/Motels

★★★★ **Lemon Tree Passage Motel**, (M), Previously Lemon Tree Motel. 47 Meredith Ave, 500m S of PO, ☎ 02 4982 3300, fax 02 4984 5999, 11 units [shwr, tlt, c/fan, heat, elec blkts, tel, TV, video-fee, clock radio, t/c mkg, refrig], ldry, pool, bbq, cots-fee, non smoking units (4). **RO ♦ $65 - $110, ♦♦ $66 - $110, ◊ $11 - $15**, BC MC VI, ⚹⚹.

Self Catering Accommodation

★★★★☆ **Bayside Lemon Tree Passage**, (HU), 99 Cook Pde, 700m W of Marina, ☎ 02 4984 5026, 1 unit acc up to 3, [shwr, tlt, hairdry, fan, heat, elec blkts, tel, TV, video, clock radio, t/c mkg, refrig, cook fac, micro, d/wash, toaster, ldry, blkts, linen], w/mach, dryer, iron, iron brd, cots, non smoking units. **D ♦♦ $45 - $75, ◊ $20, W ♦♦ $365, ◊ $140**.

B&B's/Guest Houses

★★★★ **Larkwood of Lemon Tree Bed & Breakfast**, (B&B), 1 Oyster Farm Rd, ☎ 02 4982 4656, fax 02 4982 4656, 3 rms [shwr, tlt, hairdry (1), c/fan, fire pl, heat, elec blkts, tel, TV, refrig], ✕, pool, bbq, non smoking property. **BB ♦ $70, ♦♦ $100, DBB ♦ $100, ♦♦ $150**, BC MC VI.

PORT STEPHENS - NELSON BAY NSW 2315

Pop 7,000. (209km N Sydney), See map on page 55, ref E7. Nelson Bay lies on the south-eastern shores of Port Stephens and is the major town for the area. It's a popular place with tourists, particularly in summer, and a superb snorkelling and scuba diving spot. Boating, Bowls, Fishing, Swimming, Tennis.

Hotels/Motels

★★★☆ **Admiral Nelson Motor Inn**, (M), Cnr Gowrie Ave & Achillies St, 200m E of RSL Club, ☎ 02 4984 9902, fax 02 4984 9904, (2 stry gr fl), 24 units [shwr, tlt, hairdry, a/c, tel, TV, clock radio, t/c mkg, refrig, micro (12), toaster], iron (available), iron brd (available), pool (salt water), cots-fee, non smoking units (18). **RO ♦ $80 - $200, ♦♦ $80 - $200, ◊ $15**, 12 units ★★★, AE BC DC EFT MC VI.

★★★☆ **Aloha Villa Motel**, (M), 30 Shoal Bay Rd, 1.5km E of PO, ☎ 02 4981 2523, fax 02 4984 1245, 16 units (5 suites) [shwr, tlt, a/c, heat, tel, TV, clock radio, t/c mkg, refrig, cook fac (11)], ldry, iron, pool (solar heated), spa (hot), bbq, plygr, cots. **RO $75 - $180, 👶 $20,** BC EFT MC VI.

★★★☆ **Central Motel**, (M), Cnr Government Rd & Church St, 300m W of PO, ☎ 02 4981 3393, fax 02 4981 5006, 10 units [shwr, tlt, hairdry, a/c, elec blkts, tel, TV, clock radio, t/c mkg, refrig, toaster], ldry, pool (salt water), non smoking units (5). **RO 👤 $72 - $132, 👥 $77 - $132, 👪 $88 - $143, 👶 $10 - $20**, ch con, Min book applies, AE BC MC VI.

AAA TOURISM *Special Rates* ★★★☆ **Nelson Lodge Motel**, (M), Resort, 1 Government Rd, 50m N of PO, ☎ 02 4981 1705, fax 02 4981 4785, (Multi-stry gr fl), 36 units [shwr, bath (8), spa bath (7), tlt, hairdry, a/c, tel, fax, TV, video, clock radio, t/c mkg, refrig, cook fac (4), micro (17), toaster], ldry, iron, iron brd, pool-heated, sauna, bbq, tennis, cots-fee. **RO 👤 $110 - $207, 👥 $110 - $207, 👪 $120 - $217, 👶 $10**, ch con, Min book long w/ends, AE BC DC MC VI, ♿.

AAA TOURISM *Special Rates* ★★★☆ **Nelson Towers Motel**, (M), 71A Victoria Pde, 50m N of PO, ☎ 02 4984 1000, fax 02 4984 1020, 16 units [shwr, spa bath (2), tlt, hairdry, a/c, tel, fax, TV, video, clock radio, t/c mkg, refrig, cook fac ltd (10), micro (10), toaster, ldry (in unit) (7)], lift, iron, iron brd, cafe, pool, cots-fee. **RO 👤 $123 - $266, 👥 $123 - $266, 👪 $133 - $276, 👶 $10**, ch con, AE BC DC MC VI.

★★★☆ **Peninsula Motor Inn**, (M), 52 Shoal Bay Rd, 1km E of PO, ☎ 02 4981 3666, fax 02 4981 1373, 27 units (1 suite) [shwr, spa bath (2), tlt, a/c, elec blkts, tel, TV, movie, clock radio, t/c mkg, refrig, cook fac (1)], ldry, ⊠, pool, cots. **W $390 - $1,100, RO 👤 $65 - $135, 👥 $70 - $150, 👪 $79 - $160, 👶 $15, Suite D $89 - $250**, Min book Christmas Jan long w/ends and Easter, AE BC DC EFT MC MP VI.

★★★★ **(Serviced Apartment Section)**, (2 stry), 4 serv apts acc up to 6, [shwr, bath, tlt, hairdry, a/c, elec blkts, tel, TV, video, clock radio, t/c mkg, refrig, cook fac, micro, toaster], cots. **W $590 - $1,600, RO 👤 $85 - $170, 👥 $95 - $190, 👪 $110 - $240, 👶 $20**, Min book applies.

★★★☆ **Westbury's Marina Resort**, (M), Previously Marina Resort 33 Magnus St, 200m E of PO, ☎ 02 4981 4400, fax 02 4981 1513, (Multi-stry gr fl), 44 units [shwr, bath (20), spa bath (22), tlt, a/c, tel, cable tv, video (avail), clock radio, t/c mkg, refrig, mini bar], lift, ldry, iron, iron brd, conv fac, ⊠, pool, sauna, spa, bbq, rm serv, cots. **RO 👤 $82 - $226, 👥 $82 - $226, 👶 $22**, ch con, Min book applies, AE BC DC JCB MC VI, ♿.

★★★ **Marlin Motel**, (M), 54 Shoal Bay Rd, 1km E of PO, ☎ 02 4981 1036, fax 02 4981 4722, 11 units [shwr, tlt, hairdry, a/c, elec blkts, tel, TV, video-fee, t/c mkg, refrig], ldry, iron, pool-heated (solar), spa, cook fac, bbq, cots-fee. **RO 👤 $68 - $128, 👥 $68 - $168, 👪 $68 - $168, 👶 $14 - $15**, ch con, weekly con, Min book applies, AE BC DC MC VI.

(Cottage Section), 1 cotg acc up to 6, [elec blkts, TV, video (avail), t/c mkg, cook fac, micro, linen], ldry, bbq, cots-fee. **W $300 - $1,400**, ch con.

AAA
TOURISM
Special Rates
★★★☆

Located in the centre of Nelson Bay
opposite the Marina. Take in the views
from a Waterview Suite or relax in the
private courtyard of a Standard
or Deluxe Motel Room

*Spa Rooms available by request
*TV, video and air conditioning
*Undercover parking *Elevator to rooms
*Room Service *Babysitting *Rooftop pool
Exclusively using Red Bellies at the Pub

*Holiday, weekend rates and minimum
2 night weekend bookings may apply*

71a Victoria Pde - PO Box 105
Nelson Bay NSW 2315

Ph (02) 4984 1000   Fax (02) 4984 1020
www.sandersgroup.citysearch.com.au

AAA
TOURISM
Special Rates
★★★☆

Standard and Family Accommodation

*Spa Rooms by request
*Heated swimming pool *Sauna
*Tennis Court *BBQ *Babysitting
*Air conditioned rooms *Room Service
*Coach and Group Accommodation
*Conference Facilities
Exclusively using Red Bellies at the Pub

*Holiday, weekend rates and minimum
2 night weekend bookings may apply*

1 Government Rd - PO Box 105
Nelson Bay NSW 2315

Ph (02) 4981 1705   Fax (02) 4981 4785
www.sandersgroup.citysearch.com.au

WESTBURY'S
MARINA
RESORT
Nelson Bay

Great Australian Hospitality

Located in the heart of Australia's Blue Water Paradise of Port Stephens, just $2^1/2$ hours north of Sydney - Westbury's Marina Resort is a boutique hotel offering great Australian Hospitality in a friendly and relaxed environment.

- Boutique hotel - 44 rooms all with views of the Bay and some with spas
- Private balconies and lift to all floors
- Free satellite TV
- Tour bookings - try 4WD safari, quad bikes, kayaking, camel rides, golf, dolphin and whale watch cruises, fishing charters and lots more
- Ketch's top floor restaurant with great food and great views
- Heated pool and kids wading pool, heated spa
- Exercise room and sauna
- Professional conference centre with on-site Coordinator

Packages

- **From $49.90**
  Bed & Breakfast
  - per person, twin share.

- **From $335.00**
  Dolphins in Paradise
  - per couple, all inclusive, 2 nights waterview accommodation, dinner one evening, from Ketch's special select menu breakfast each morning, wine tasting, cheese platter, 2 hour dolphin watch cruise plus a twin pack of Port Stephens Wines.

- **From $335.00**
  Romantic Rendezvous
  - per couple, all inclusive, 2 nights waterview accommodation, chilled champagne and chocolates on arrival, dinner one evening, breakfast each morning.

PACKAGE CONDITIONS - Subject to availability, conditions apply.
All rates include GST.

33 Magnus Street, Nelson Bay NSW 2315 Port Stephens
Phone (02) 4981 4400 Fax (02) 4981 1513
Toll Free 1800 659 949
Website: www.marinaresort.com.au

3986AG

★★★ **Port Stephens Motor Lodge**, (M), Cnr Magnus & Fingal Sts, ☎ 02 4981 3366, fax 02 4984 1655, (2 stry gr fl), 17 units [shwr, tlt, hairdry, a/c, elec blkts, tel, TV, movie, t/c mkg, refrig, cook fac (1), toaster], ldry, pool-heated (solar), bbq, c/park (undercover), cots. **RO** ∮ **$55 - $110,** ∯ **$66 - $125,** ⋔⋔⋔ **$77 - $135,** ◊ **$11,** ch con, Min book applies, AE BC DC MC VI.

★★☆ **Dolphins Motel**, (M), Dixon Dve, 1km E of PO, ☎ 02 4981 1176, fax 02 4981 1176, (2 stry gr fl), 25 units [shwr, tlt, heat, elec blkts, tel, TV, t/c mkg, refrig, cook fac (13), toaster], ldry, pool, bbq, cots-fee. **RO** ∮ **$59 - $88,** ∯ **$59 - $88,** ◊ **$11,** Min book applies, AE BC DC EFT MC VI.

★★☆ **Sandypoint Motor Lodge**, (M), 19 Sandypoint Rd, Corlette 2315, 2km W of Nelson Bay Marina, ☎ 02 4981 1315, fax 02 4981 1315, 6 units [shwr, tlt, a/c (1), c/fan (5), heat, elec blkts (6), TV, clock radio, t/c mkg, refrig, micro (4), elec frypan (4), toaster], ldry, bbq, cots. **RO** ∮ **$55,** ∯ **$66 - $100,** ◊ **$15,** weekly con, BC EFT MC VI.

Self Catering Accommodation

★★★★☆ **Beaches Serviced Apartments**, (SA), 12 Gowrie Ave, 200m first turn left after RSL Club, ☎ 02 4984 3255, fax 02 4984 3399, (2 stry), 10 serv apts (10 suites) [shwr, bath (9), tlt, hairdry, a/c, elec blkts, tel, TV, video, clock radio, t/c mkg, refrig, cook fac, micro, d/wash, toaster, ldry], pool, bbq, rm serv (b'fast), cots. **RO** ∯ **$100 - $175,** ◊ **$15, $650 - $1,700,** Min book applies, AE BC DC MC VI.

★★★★ **Casablanca at Little Beach**, (SA), Cnr Intrepid & Gowrie Ave, 2km W of PO, ☎ 02 4984 9100, fax 02 4984 4422, (2 stry), 14 serv apts acc up to 6, (1 & 2 bedrm), [shwr, spa bath, tlt, a/c-cool, fan, TV, video, t/c mkg, refrig, cook fac, micro, d/wash, blkts, doonas, linen], ldry, dryer, pool (heated), bbq, plygr, cots-fee. **RO** ∯ **$110 - $385,** ⋔⋔⋔⋔ **$154 - $473,** ◊ **$22,** ∯ **$693 - $1,232,** ⋔⋔⋔⋔ **$880 - $1,540,** AE BC DC EFT MC VI.

★★★☆ **Bay Parklands**, (HU), Gowrie Ave, 1km S of PO, ☎ 02 4981 1999, 41 units acc up to 6, [shwr, bath, tlt, heat, TV, video, refrig, cook fac, d/wash, toaster, linen-fee], ldry, pool, sauna, spa, c/park (garage), tennis. **W $340 - $1,520,** Min book applies, BC MC VI.

★★★☆ **Classic View**, (HU), 49 Victoria Pde via Nash La, ☎ 02 4981 1577, 2 units acc up to 7, [shwr, bath, tlt, a/c, TV, video, refrig, cook fac, micro, d/wash, ldry, linen reqd-fee], w/mach, dryer, iron, bbq, c/park. **W $630 - $1,800.**

★★★☆ **Florentine**, (HU), 11 Columbia Cl, 1km W of PO, ☎ 02 4981 1955, fax 02 4984 1256, (Multi-stry), 9 units acc up to 8, [shwr, bath, spa bath, tlt, heat, tel, TV, video, refrig, cook fac, micro, elec frypan, d/wash, toaster, ldry (in unit), linen reqd-fee], lift, w/mach, dryer, iron, pool, c/park (carport), cots-fee. **W $700 - $2,350**, Min book applies, BC MC VI.

★★★☆ **Le Vogue**, (HU), 16 Magnus St, 1km E of PO, ☎ 02 4981 1999, (Multi-stry), 6 units acc up to 6, [shwr, spa bath, tlt, TV, video, t/c mkg, refrig, cook fac, micro, elec frypan, d/wash, toaster, ldry, linen reqd-fee], lift, pool, sauna, c/park (garage), tennis, cots-fee. **W $700 - $2,350**, Min book applies.

★★★☆ **Leilani Serviced Apartments**, (SA), Gowrie Ave, Little Beach, 2km NE of PO, ☎ 02 4981 3304, fax 02 4984 1793, 8 serv apts acc up to 6, [shwr, spa bath (2), tlt, hairdry, a/c, elec blkts, tel, TV, video (avail), clock radio, t/c mkg, refrig, cook fac, micro, ldry], pool-heated (solar), bbq, cots. **RO ♦ $80 - $280, ♦♦ $80 - $280**, 1 cottages of a higher standard, Min book applies, AE BC DC MC VI, ♿.

CLASSIC VIEW

- Luxury 3 bed apt. Sleeps 6 with uninterrupted views over Nelson Bay Marina.
- Microwave, CD, Stereo, Air Cond, D/washer, TV and large balcony with sun lounge & BBQ.
- 3 min walk along waterfront to Marina and shops or cross road and relax on Nelson Bay Beach.

Classic View has everything you would expect. Children welcome.
Contact Dowling R/Estate

PH: (02) 4981 1577
FAX: (02) 4984 1204

Stay & Play in Paradise

Directly opposite Fly Point Marine Reserve, and the RSL club, and only a short walk to the beach, marina, restaurants and shops of one of Australia's leading tourist resorts.

Huge rooms

Luxury kitchen

- 1 & 2 bedroom loft apartments
- 2 bedroom suites
- All units have a two-person spa
- All units have a fully equipped kitchen, TV, VCR, large private balcony, direct dial telephone and air conditioning.

Heated Spa

NELSON BAY Breeze RESORT

Cnr Shoal Bay Rd and Trafalgar St
Nelson Bay NSW 2315
Phone   02 4984 3199
Fax   02 4984 9875

Nelson Bay is a 40 minute drive north of Newcastle.

Ph 1800 113 200   www.nelsonbaybreeze.homestead.com

Resort Luxury With The Relaxed, Laid Back Atmosphere of Serviced Apartments

Encore PR

SERVICED APARTMENTS

- 7 self contained air conditioned serviced apartments
- ideal for couples or small families
- Separate master bedroom
- Living area   • Fully equipped kitchen
- Laundry   • BBQ area
- Private sunny balcony or garden courtyard
- Solar heated pool
- Stroll to sandy beaches, Little Beach (100m) or Shoal Bay Beach (200m) within minutes
- Best location, perfect honeymoon/ anniversary destination
- Spa apartments
- 3, 5, & 7 day SPECIALS Winter and Summer
- 2 bedroom disabled apartments

GOWRIE AVE P.O Box 462 NELSON BAY 2315. 1st turn left after RSL

Leilani

PHONE (02) 4981 3304
FAX (02) 4984 1793

Website:
www.portstephens.org.au/leilani
Email: leilani@hunterlink.net.au

★★★☆ **Nelson Bay Breeze Resort**, (SA), 1 Trafalgar St, Near Nelson Bay RSL Club, ☎ 02 4984 3199, fax 02 4984 9875, 40 serv apts [shwr, spa bath, tlt, hairdry, a/c, tel, TV, video, clock radio, t/c mkg, refrig, cook fac ltd, micro, toaster, blkts, linen, pillows], ldry, ✗, pool (salt water), non smoking units (avail). D ♐ **$170 - $240**, ♐♐♐ **$180 - $260**, ♐ **$20**, W ♐♐ **$1,190 - $1,680**, ♐♐♐ **$1,260 - $1,820**, ch con, AE BC DC MC VI.

★★★☆ **The Anchorage**, (HU), 9 Laman St, 200m N of PO, ☎ 02 4981 1577, fax 02 4984 1204, (Multi-stry), 4 units acc up to 7, [shwr, bath, tlt, heat, elec blkts, tel, TV, video, clock radio, t/c mkg, refrig, cook fac, micro, d/wash, toaster, ldry, linen reqd-fee], lift, pool, cots-fee. W **$600 - $2,000**, Min book applies.

★★★ **Carindale**, (HU), Cnr Dowling & Fingal Sts, 500m E of PO, ☎ 02 4981 1955, fax 02 4984 1256, 9 units acc up to 6, [shwr, bath, tlt, heat, TV, video, refrig, cook fac, micro, elec frypan, toaster, linen reqd-fee], ldry, w/mach, dryer, iron, pool, bbq (gas), c/park (garage), tennis, cots-fee. W **$260 - $1,180**, Min book applies, BC MC VI.

★★★ **Commodore**, (HU), 11 Donald St, 500 E of PO, ☎ 02 4981 1577, fax 02 4984 1204, (Multi-stry gr fl), 11 units acc up to 5, [shwr, tlt, heat, TV, refrig, cook fac, elec frypan, toaster, ldry, linen reqd-fee], w/mach, dryer, iron, c/park. W **$260 - $850**, Units 5 and 9 not rated, Min book applies.

★★★ **Kiah Holiday Units**, (HU), 53 Victoria Pde, 700m E of PO, ☎ 02 4981 1577, fax 02 4984 1204, 2 units acc up to 4, [shwr, bath, tlt, c/fan, TV, video, clock radio, t/c mkg, refrig, cook fac, micro, elec frypan, d/wash, toaster, ldry, linen reqd-fee], w/mach, dryer, iron, iron brd, cots-fee. W **$385 - $1,300**, Min book applies, BC EFT MC VI.

★★★ **Luskin Lodge**, (HU), 29 Weatherley Cl, 2km NE of PO, ☎ 02 4981 1999, 8 units acc up to 5, [shwr, bath, tlt, heat, TV, refrig, cook fac, micro, elec frypan, d/wash, toaster, ldry (in unit), linen-fee], w/mach, bar, c/park (garage), boat park. W **$295 - $1,215**, Min book applies, BC MC VI.

★★★ **Mistral Court**, (HU), Mistral Cl, 1km S of PO, ☎ 02 4981 1955, 12 units acc up to 5, [shwr, bath, tlt, heat, TV, refrig, cook fac, toaster, ldry, linen-fee], c/park (garage), boat park. W **$255 - $1,005**, Min book applies, BC MC VI.

★★★ **Radburn**, (HU), 17 Ondine Cl, 300m W of Shoal Bay, ☎ 02 4981 1999, fax 02 4984 1256, 3 units acc up to 8, [shwr, bath (2), tlt, fan, heat, tel, TV, video, clock radio, t/c mkg, refrig, cook fac, micro, elec frypan, d/wash (1), toaster, ldry, blkts, linen reqd-fee], w/mach, dryer, iron, iron brd, cots-fee. W **$295 - $2,350**, Min book applies, BC EFT MC VI.

★★☆ **Bayview Towers**, (HU), 15 Victoria Pde, 750m E of PO, ☎ 02 4981 1577, fax 02 4984 1204, (Multi-stry), 1 unit acc up to 6, [shwr, tlt, fan, heat, tel, TV, video, t/c mkg, refrig, cook fac, micro, elec frypan, d/wash, toaster, ldry, linen reqd-fee], w/mach, dryer, iron, iron brd, c/park (carport), cots-fee. W **$350 - $1,200**, Min book applies, BC EFT MC VI.

★★☆ **Portside**, (HU), Donald St, 600m E of PO, ☎ 02 4981 1577, fax 02 4984 1204, (Multi-stry), 2 units acc up to 6, [shwr, bath, tlt, TV, video, refrig, cook fac, micro, toaster, ldry, linen reqd-fee], pool, bbq. W **$270 - $890**, Unit 11 not included in listing, Min book applies.

★★☆ **Shoalhaven Beachfront**, (HU), Voyager Close, 2km E of Nelson Bay PO, ☎ 02 4981 1999, 1 unit acc up to 4, [shwr, bath, tlt, fan, heat, TV, refrig, cook fac, micro, toaster, ldry (in unit), linen reqd], c/park (carport). W **$300 - $1,085**, Min book applies, BC MC VI.

★★☆ **Skyline**, (HU), 12 Thurlow Ave, 1km NW of PO, ☎ 02 4981 1577, fax 02 4984 1204, (Multi-stry), 4 units acc up to 6, [shwr, bath, tlt, TV, refrig, cook fac, micro, d/wash, toaster, ldry (in unit), linen reqd-fee], bbq, c/park. W **$350 - $1,100**, Min book applies.

★★☆ **The Poplars**, (HU), 36 Magnus St, 1km E of PO, ☎ 02 4981 1577, fax 02 4984 1204, (Multi-stry gr fl), 2 units acc up to 6, [shwr, bath, tlt, fan, TV, video, refrig, cook fac, micro, toaster, ldry, linen reqd-fee], pool. W **$250 - $1,100**, Min book applies.

★★☆ **Tradewinds**, (HU), 110 Victoria Pde, opposite marina, ☎ 02 4981 1955, 3 units acc up to 6, [shwr, bath, tlt, heat, TV, refrig, cook fac, d/wash, toaster, ldry (in unit), linen-fee], c/park (garage), cots-fee. W **$335 - $1,400**, Min book applies, BC MC VI.

★★☆ **Yachtsmans Rest**, (HU), 37 Victoria Pde, 500m E of PO, ☎ 02 4981 1999, fax 02 4984 1256, 4 units acc up to 6, [shwr, bath, tlt, a/c, heat, TV, video, refrig, cook fac, micro, elec frypan, d/wash, toaster, ldry, linen reqd-fee], w/mach, dryer, iron, c/park (carport), cots-fee. W **$480 - $1,690**, Min book applies, BC MC VI.

★★ **Promenade**, (HU), Intrepid Cl, 1km N of PO, ☎ 02 4981 1955, fax 02 4984 1256, (Multi-stry), 6 units acc up to 6, [shwr, bath, tlt, TV, refrig, cook fac, toaster, ldry (in unit), linen reqd-fee], c/park (garage), boat park, cots-fee. W **$230 - $1,490**, Min book applies, BC MC VI.

B&B's/Guest Houses

★★★★☆ **Nelson Bay Russell House**, (B&B), 114 Stockton St, 1.2km to PO, ☎ 02 4984 4246, fax 02 4981 3164, (2 stry), 4 rms (3 suites) [shwr, tlt, hairdry, a/c-cool, c/fan, TV, t/c mkg], TV rm, lounge, ✗, courtesy transfer. BB ♐ **$150 - $190**, BC MC VI.

★★★★☆ **Wisteria Cottage**, (GH), No children's facilities, 35 Thurlow Ave, 900m W of PO, ☎ 02 4984 9750, fax 02 4984 3338, 2 rms (2 suites) [shwr, tlt, a/c, fire pl (1), fax, TV (2), CD (2), t/c mkg, refrig, cook fac ltd, micro, toaster], ldry, bbq, ✆. Suite BLB ♐ **$170 - $250**, AE BC DC MC VI.

★★★★ **Croft Haven Bed & Breakfast**, (B&B), 202 Salamander Way, 4km SW of PO, ☎ 02 4984 1799, fax 02 4984 1799, 3 rms [ensuite (2), elec blkts, tel], bathrm (Private) (1), ldry, lounge (tv/fireplace), bbq, non smoking property. BB ♐ **$75 - $85**, ♐♐ **$85 - $145**.

★★★★ **Nelson Bay Bed & Breakfast**, (B&B), 81 Stockton St, ☎ 02 4984 3655, 3 rms [shwr, spa bath (1), tlt, hairdry, c/fan, fire pl, heat, elec blkts, tel, TV, clock radio, refrig, micro, toaster], ldry, iron, iron brd, ✗, t/c mkg shared, bbq, non smoking property. BB ♐ **$90 - $160**, ♐♐ **$100 - $180**, MC VI.

★★★☆ **Lorikeets B&B**, (B&B), 2 Wallawa Rd, 1km W of PO, ☎ 02 4984 3575, fax 02 4984 3575, 1 rm (1 bedrm), [ensuite, fan, heat (elec), TV, t/c mkg, refrig, ldry, doonas], bbq, cots, non smoking rms. BB ♐♐ **$95 - $125**, ch con.

PORT STEPHENS - RAYMOND TERRACE NSW 2324

Pop 12,350. (167km N Sydney), See map on page 55, ref C7.
Raymond Terrace is the administrative centre and gateway to Port Stephens located at the junction of the Hunter and Williams Rivers. Bowls, Golf, Swimming, Water Skiing.

Hotels/Motels

★★★☆ **Motto Farm Motel**, (M), 240 Pacific Hwy Motto Farm, 3km S of PO, ☎ 02 4987 1211, fax 02 4987 1214, 79 units (0 suites) [shwr, bath (10), spa bath (24), tlt, hairdry (4), a/c, tel, TV, video (50), clock radio, t/c mkg, refrig, micro (13), toaster], ldry, iron, iron brd, conv fac, ✉, pool (salt water), bbq, 24hr reception, rm serv, dinner to unit, plygr, tennis (half court), cots. RO **$74 - $95**, ♐ **$10**, Suite RO **$100 - $125**, Limited disabled facilities. AE BC DC EFT JCB MC VI.

★★★☆ **Sir Francis Drake Resort**, (M), 204 Pacific Hwy, 3km S of PO, ☎ 02 4987 1444, fax 02 4987 1393, 34 units (6 suites) [shwr, bath, spa bath (6), tlt, hairdry, a/c, heat, tel, TV, clock radio, t/c mkg, refrig, mini bar, toaster], ldry, conv fac, ✉, pool, spa, rm serv, dinner to unit, tennis, cots-fee, non smoking units (6). RO ♐ **$120**, ♐♐ **$125**, ♐ **$10**, Suite D **$165 - $175**, ch con, AE BC DC MC VI, ♿.

★★★☆ **Sleepy Hill Motor Inn**, (M), Previously Raymond Terrace Motor Inn. 92 Adelaide St (Old Pacific Hwy), 1km NE of PO, ☎ 02 4987 2321, fax 02 4983 1564, 30 units (6 suites) [shwr, tlt, a/c, heat, elec blkts, tel, TV, video (avail), clock radio, t/c mkg, refrig], ldry, ✉ (Mon to Sat), pool, rm serv, cots-fee. RO ♐ **$68 - $75**, ♐♐ **$74 - $90**, ♐ **$11**, Suite D **$105 - $135**, AE BC DC MC MCH VI.

★★★☆ Sundowner Chain Motor Inns, (M), 130 Adelaide St (Old Pacific Hwy), 100m E of PO, ☎ 02 4987 2244, fax 02 4983 1166, 30 units [shwr, tlt, hairdry, a/c, tel, cable tv, clock radio, t/c mkg, refrig, mini bar, cook fac (7), toaster], ldry, iron, iron brd, ⊠, bar, pool, 24hr reception, rm serv, plygr, cots-fee, non smoking units (avail). **RO ♦ $88 - $124, ♦♦ $93.50 - $124, ◊ $11**, ch con, AE BC DC MC MP VI.

★★ Kingston Motel, (M), 51 Kingston Pde, Motto Farm, 3km S of Raymond Terrace, ☎ 02 4983 1643, fax 02 4987 7754, 10 units [shwr, tlt, a/c, TV, clock radio, t/c mkg, refrig], secure park. **BLB ♦♦ $55 - $60, ♦♦♦ $70, ♦♦♦♦ $80**, 🕱♿.

Self Catering Accommodation

★★★☆ Musickas Bush Haven, (Cotg), 55 Italia Rd, Balickera 2324, 13km N of Raymond Terrace, ☎ 02 4988 6343, 1 cotg acc up to 5, [shwr, bath, tlt, c/fan, fire pl, TV, clock radio, t/c mkg, refrig, cook fac, micro, toaster, blkts, doonas, linen, pillows], w/mach, bbq, non smoking property. **D ♦♦ $80 - $120, ◊ $30**.

★★★ Hilltop Manor Accommodation, (SA), 14 Walker Cres, ☎ 02 4996 4446, 2 serv apts acc up to 8, [shwr, bath, tlt, hairdry, a/c, fan, heat, TV, video, clock radio, t/c mkg, refrig, cook fac, micro, elec frypan, toaster, ldry, doonas, linen, pillows], w/mach, dryer, iron, iron brd, bbq, non smoking property. **D ♦♦ $60 - $180**, fam con.

'Doribank' Farm Cottages, (Cotg), (Farm), Six Mile Rd, 9km N of PO, ☎ 02 4988 6205, fax 02 4988 6205, 1 cotg acc up to 5, [shwr, bath, tlt, a/c, c/fan, TV, clock radio, t/c mkg, refrig, cook fac, elec frypan, toaster, ldry, blkts, linen], iron, iron brd, bbq, **D ♦♦ $100, ◊ $15, W $600 - $700**, (not yet classified).

B&B's/Guest Houses

★★★☆ Bloomfields B & B, (B&B), 17 Ralston Rd, Nelsons Plains, 5km NW of PO, ☎ 02 4983 1839, 2 rms [shwr, bath, tlt, fan, heat, elec blkts, tel], lounge (TV), t/c mkg shared, cots. **BB ♦ $50, ♦♦ $80**, Dinner by arrangement.

THE TERRACE IS REMARKABLE

Raymond Terrace, two hours north of Sydney on the Pacific Highway has been a recognised spot to stop and kick back since Lieutenant Colonel Paterson called a halt on June 29, 1801 while surveying the Hunter.

Today Newcastle airport (Williamtown) is 15 minutes away, complete with the attraction of nine aircraft at Fighter World Museum for gung-ho war bird buffs. Raymond Terrace's off-beat name could be the result of an earlier impression from one of Lieutenant John Shortland's party, called Raymond, who remarked on the "terraced" nature of the tree tops while exploring the area in 1797.

As a base for a variety of 20 to 40 minute drive experiences, Raymond Terrace is impressive.

The town, which is now virtually a commuter belt township attached to Newcastle, 23 km to the south, is a historic experience in its own right. Nearby are attractions and destinations which include the Hunter Region Botanic Gardens, Nelson Bay and Tea Gardens, Dungog, Gloucester and the Barrington Tops, Newcastle City, Hunter Valley vineyards, Maitland, Morpeth, Paterson and other historic villages.

The Hunter Botanic Gardens are 4.5km south along the highway. Tomago House is an elegant sandstone mansion dating from 1843, just south of Raymond Terrace. Raymond Terrace is a logical link with the extensive waterways of beautiful Port Stephens, the Hunter Valley, and Barrington Tops World Heritage National Park.

MUST SEE AND DO IN THE AREA.

- Hunter Regional Botanic Gardens. *(pictured above)*
- Riverside Park and Picnic Grounds and Boomerang Historic Park are features of the town and of historic significance.
- Port Stephens.
- Hunter Valley vineyards.
- Newcastle's Nobbys and Stockton Beaches.
- Sketchley Cottage (circa 1850) and Pioneer Museum, in Adelaide St., Raymond Terrace (open Sunday 10am to 4pm).
- Fighter World Museum (RAAF Williamtown).

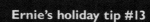

PORT STEPHENS - SALAMANDER BAY NSW 2317

Pop 2,840. (217km N Sydney), See map on page 55, ref E7. Resort town on the southern shores of Port Stephens.

Hotels/Motels

★★★☆ **Country Comfort - Port Stephens**, (M), Resort, 265 Sandy Point Rd, 5km W of Nelson Bay PO, ☎ 02 4984 1111, fax 02 4984 1222, 34 units (4 suites) [shwr, bath, spa bath (4), tlt, hairdry, a/c, tel, TV, movie, clock radio, t/c mkg, refrig, mini bar], ldry, iron, iron brd, rec rm, lounge (TV), conv fac, ⊠, pool (salt water), pool indoor heated, spa (heated), rm serv, dinner to unit, plygr, mini golf, gym, tennis (7), cots. **RO ♦ $142 - $164, Suite D $174 - $196**, ch con, Min book applies, AE BC DC MC VI.

★★★☆ **(Serviced Apartment Section)**, 23 serv apts [shwr, spa bath, tlt, hairdry, a/c, tel, TV, movie, clock radio, t/c mkg, refrig, cook fac], dinner to unit, cots-fee. **D $196 - $240**, Undergoing refurbishment. Rollaway beds avail @ $15 p/n.

Self Catering Accommodation

★★★★☆ **Horizons Golf Resort & Conference Centre**, (SA), 5 Horizons Dve, ☎ 02 4982 0502, fax 02 4982 0150, 58 serv apts acc up to 4, (1 & 2 bedrm), [shwr, tlt, hairdry, a/c, tel, TV, video, clock radio, t/c mkg, refrig, mini bar, cook fac ltd, micro, elec frypan, toaster], ldry, ⊠, cafe, pool (2), sauna, spa (2), bbq, ✆, plygr, tennis, cots. **BB ♦♦ $198 - $460**, ch con, AE BC DC EFT MC VI.

★★★☆ **Colonial Ridge Resort**, (SA), 4 Fleet St, ☎ 02 4982 0600, fax 02 4982 0611, 42 serv apts [shwr, tlt, a/c, tel, TV, clock radio, refrig, cook fac ltd, micro, elec frypan, toaster], pool (salt water), bbq, cots, non smoking units (10), Min book applies, AE BC DC EFT MC VI.

★★★☆ **Wanda Beach House Bed & Breakfast**, (HU), 171 Soldiers Point Rd, 4km N of Salamander Shopping Centre, ☎ 02 4982 7100, fax 02 4982 7123, 2 units acc up to 4, [shwr, tlt, hairdry, fire pl, heat, tel, TV, video, clock radio, t/c mkg, refrig, cook fac, micro, elec frypan, toaster, linen], ldry, iron, iron brd, bbq, c/park (undercover), canoeing, breakfast ingredients, non smoking property. **BLB ♦♦ $110 - $160**, BC MC VI.

B&B's/Guest Houses

★★★★☆ **Beachgarden Bed & Breakfast**, (B&B), 7 Randall Drive, 50m NE of Village Shops, ☎ 02 4982 0788, fax 02 4982 0789, 1 rm [shwr, tlt, hairdry, a/c, tel, TV, clock radio, t/c mkg, refrig, toaster], iron, iron brd, bbq, non smoking rms. **BB ♦ $110, ♦♦ $130 - $180**, BC MC VI.

★★★★☆ **Maggies on the Beach**, (B&B), 207 Soldiers Point Rd, ☎ 02 4984 7484, 2 rms (1 suite) [shwr, tlt, hairdry, fan, heat, TV, video, t/c mkg, refrig], ldry, iron, iron brd, lounge, bbq, courtesy transfer, non smoking rms. **BB ♦♦ $150 - $175**.

★★★★ **Kookaburra Lodge Bed & Breakfast**, (B&B), No children's facilities, 2 Fleet St, ☎ 02 4984 7418, fax 02 4984 7418, (2 stry gr fl), 3 rms [hairdry, fan, heat, elec blkts, clock radio], lounge (TV), lounge firepl, sauna, t/c mkg shared, refrig, bbq, boat park. **BB ♦ $65 - $75, ♦♦ $85 - $100**, BC MC VI.

★★★ **Salamander Way Bed & Breakfast**, (B&B), 108 Salamander Way, ☎ 02 4982 0376, fax 02 4982 0376, 1 rm [shwr, tlt, fan, heat, tel, TV, clock radio, t/c mkg, refrig, micro, toaster], pool (salt water), bbq, courtesy transfer, tennis, non smoking property. **BLB ♦ $60 - $100, ♦♦ $69 - $120**, pen con.

The Scented Garden Bed & Breakfast, (B&B), 84 Salamander Way, ☎ 02 4982 0433, (2 stry), 3 rms [ensuite (1), spa bath (1), heat, elec blkts, TV (1), clock radio, t/c mkg (1), refrig (1), doonas], lounge firepl, t/c mkg shared, refrig, secure park (1). **BB ♦ $90, ♦♦ $110 - $175**, BC MC VI, (not yet classified).

PORT STEPHENS - SHOAL BAY NSW 2315

Pop 2,026. (224km N Sydney), See map on page 55, ref E7. This little village occupies the southern headland of Port Stephens, is flanked by Tomaree National Park and has both ocean and harbour beaches. Boating, Bowls, Bush Walking, Fishing, Swimming, Tennis.

Hotels/Motels

★★★☆ **Shoal Bay Motel**, (M), 59-61 Shoal Bay Rd, 3km E of Nelson Bay PO, ☎ 02 4981 1744, fax 02 4984 1052, (2 stry gr fl), 18 units (4 suites) [shwr, tlt, a/c, c/fan (9), heat, elec blkts, tel, TV, clock radio, t/c mkg, refrig, cook fac (4 suites), micro, toaster], ldry, w/mach, dryer, iron, iron brd, rec rm, sauna-fee, cook fac, bbq, cots-fee. **RO ♦ $62 - $99, ♦ $73 - $200, ♦♦♦ $88 - $230, ◊ $15 - $25, Suite D $120 - $420**, ch con, pen con, AE BC DC MC VI.

★★☆ **Santa Catalina**, (M), 9 Shoal Bay Rd, ☎ 02 4981 1519, fax 02 4984 1602, (2 stry), 12 units [shwr, bath (12), spa bath (6), tlt, hairdry, a/c, c/fan, elec blkts, TV, clock radio, t/c mkg, refrig, cook fac, micro, toaster], ldry, pool (salt water), bbq. **RO ♦ $75 - $160, ♦♦ $75 - $160, ◊ $10 - $15**, AE BC DC EFT MC VI.

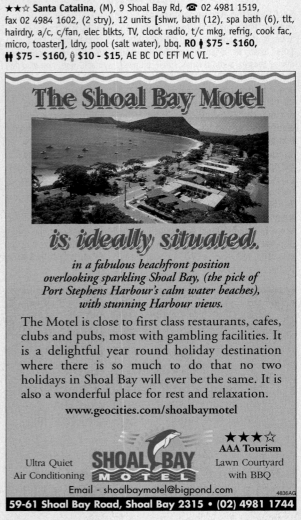

The Shoal Bay Motel

is ideally situated

in a fabulous beachfront position overlooking sparkling Shoal Bay, (the pick of Port Stephens Harbour's calm water beaches), with stunning Harbour views.

The Motel is close to first class restaurants, cafes, clubs and pubs, most with gambling facilities. It is a delightful year round holiday destination where there is so much to do that no two holidays in Shoal Bay will ever be the same. It is also a wonderful place for rest and relaxation.

www.geocities.com/shoalbaymotel

Ultra Quiet
Air Conditioning

SHOAL BAY MOTEL

★★★☆
AAA Tourism
Lawn Courtyard
with BBQ

Email - shoalbaymotel@bigpond.com

59-61 Shoal Bay Road, Shoal Bay 2315 • (02) 4981 1744

Experience the No.1 Resort Course in NSW

HORIZONS GOLF RESORT

Salamander Bay - Port Stephens

HORIZONS GOLF RESORT & CONFERENCE CENTRE

• Luxury self-contained condominiums • Fine dining Restaurant & Café
• Two swimming pools, spa's & sauna • Tennis court & volleyball court
• Kids Club & Children's playground • Conference facilities • Par 72 Championship Golf Course

5 Horizons Drive, Salamander Bay 2317. Tel: (02) 4982 0502 Fax: (02) 4982 0150 Toll Free: 1800 634 743 www.horizonsgolfresort.com.au

★★☆ **Shoal Bay Country Club Hotel**, (LH), Shoal Bay Rd,
☎ 02 4981 1555, fax 02 4984 1315, 64 rms [shwr, tlt, c/fan, heat, TV, clock radio, t/c mkg, refrig], ldry, lounge, conv fac, ⊠ (3), pool, cots. **BB ╂ $65, DBB ╂ $87**, ch con, Min book applies, AE BC DC MC VI.

Self Catering Accommodation
★★★ **Blue Waters**, (HU), 59 Ronald Ave, 3km E of PO, ☎ 02 4981 1999, fax 02 4984 1256, (Multi-stry), 4 units acc up to 5, [shwr, tlt, TV, refrig, cook fac, toaster, ldry (in unit), linen-fee], bar, cots-fee. **W $190 - $875**, Min book applies.

★★☆ **Del Rae**, (HU), 25 Shoal Bay Rd, 3km E of PO, ☎ 02 4981 1999, fax 02 4984 1256, 5 units acc up to 6, [shwr, bath, tlt, TV, refrig, cook fac, toaster, ldry (in unit), linen reqd-fee], c/park (undercover), cots-fee. **W $220 - $1,005**, Min book applies, BC MC VI.

★★☆ **Fleetwood 6**, (HU), 6/63 Shoal Bay Beachfront Rd, 3km E of Nelson Bay PO, ☎ 02 4981 1744, fax 02 4984 1052, (2 stry), 1 unit acc up to 6, [shwr, bath, tlt, fan, heat, elec blkts, TV, clock radio, t/c mkg, refrig, cook fac, micro, elec frypan, toaster, ldry (in unit), blkts, linen, pillows], w/mach, dryer, iron, iron brd, sauna-fee, secure park, cots. **D $150 - $295, W $575 - $1,450**, AE BC DC MC VI.

★★☆ **Sundeck Units**, (HU), 51 Ronald Ave, 400m E of PO, ☎ 02 4981 1999, 5 units acc up to 6, [shwr, tlt, heat, TV, video, refrig, cook fac, micro, toaster, ldry (in unit), linen reqd], pool, c/park (carport). **W $350 - $1,180**, Min book applies, BTC MC VI.

★★ **Bay Village**, (HU), 47 Shoal Bay Rd, 3km E of PO, ☎ 02 4981 1999, fax 02 4984 1256, 14 units acc up to 6, [shwr, bath, tlt, heat, TV, refrig, cook fac, toaster, linen-fee], ldry, secure park. **W $220 - $1,075**, Min book applies, BC MC VI.

★★ **Bella Vista**, (HU), 19 Shoal Bay Rd, ☎ 02 4981 1999, fax 02 4984 1256, (Multi-stry), 12 units acc up to 6, [shwr, bath, tlt, TV, t/c mkg, refrig, cook fac, elec frypan, toaster, linen reqd-fee], ldry, c/park (carport), cots-fee. **W $245 - $925**, Min book applies, BC MC VI.

★★ **Castaways Units**, (HU), 17 Shoal Bay Rd, 3km E of PO, ☎ 02 4981 1999, fax 02 4984 1256, 5 units acc up to 6, [shwr, tlt, heat, TV, refrig, cook fac, toaster, linen-fee], ldry. **W $265 - $1,380**, Min book applies, BC MC VI.

★★ **Mia Mia**, (HU), 2 Lillian St, 3km E of PO, ☎ 02 4981 1999, fax 02 4984 1256, (2 stry), 4 units acc up to 4, [shwr, tlt, heat, TV, refrig, cook fac, elec frypan, toaster, linen reqd-fee], ldry, c/park (carport), cots-fee. **W $175 - $755**, Min book applies, BC MC VI.

B&B's/Guest Houses
★★★★ **Shoal Bay B&B by the Beach**, (B&B), 85 Shoal Bay Rd, 4km E of Nelson Bay, ☎ 02 4984 9667, fax 02 4984 9668, 1 rm [fan, heat, elec blkts, TV, video, clock radio, t/c mkg, refrig, ldry], bbq, non smoking units. **BB ╂ $80 - $100, ╂╂ $120 - $145, ◊ $45**, ch con, weekly con, Min book all holiday times, BC MC VI.

★★★ **Beckys B&B**, (B&B), 51 Horace St, 2km E of Nelson Bay, ☎ 02 4984 1535, (2 stry gr fl), 1 rm [ensuite (1), fan, heat (elec), elec blkts, TV, video, radio, t/c mkg, refrig, cook fac ltd, ldry], bbq, meals to unit, plygr, cots, non smoking rms. **BB ╂ $50 - $80, ╂╂ $60 - $100, ◊ $40**, ch con, weekly con, Min book Christmas and Jan.

PORT STEPHENS - SOLDIERS POINT NSW 2317

Pop 1,055. (220km N Sydney), See map on page 55, ref E7. Popular holiday destination on the southern shores of Port Stephens. Boating, Bowls, Fishing, Swimming, Tennis.

Hotels/Motels
★★★☆ **Salamander Shores**, (LMH), 147 Soldiers Point Rd, ☎ 02 4982 7210, fax 02 4982 7890, (Multi-stry gr fl), 90 units (2 suites) [shwr, spa bath (34), tlt, hairdry, a/c, c/fan, tel, TV, movie, clock radio, t/c mkg, refrig], ldry, iron, iron brd, lounge, conf fac, ⊠ (2), bar, pool, rm serv, cots (avail on request). **RO ╂ $108 - $264, ╂╂ $108.90 - $264, ╂╂╂ $126 - $266.10, Suite D $230 - $265**, pen con, Spa Suites are of a 4 star rating. Min book applies, AE BC DC EFT MC VI, ⚹.

Operator Comment: The most spectacular water views! See our full-page ad under PORT STEPHENS.

Self Catering Accommodation
★★★☆ **Pelican Sands**, (HU), 83 Soldiers Point Rd, 8km W of PO, ☎ 02 4981 1577, fax 02 4984 1204, (2 stry), 1 unit acc up to 7, [shwr, bath, tlt, fan, heat, tel, TV, video, clock radio, t/c mkg, refrig, cook fac, micro, elec frypan, d/wash, toaster, ldry, linen reqd-fee], w/mach, dryer, iron, iron brd, pool (salt water), bbq, cots-fee. **W $540 - $1,700**, Min book applies, BC EFT MC VI.

★★☆ **Harbourside**, (HU), 7 Soldiers Point Rd, 50m E of PO, ☎ 02 4981 1955, 4 units acc up to 5, [shwr, bath, tlt, heat, TV, refrig, cook fac, toaster, linen reqd], ldry, c/park (garage). **W $260 - $1,060**, Min book applies, BC MC VI.

★★☆ **The Point**, (HU), 5 Mitchell St, 2km W of PO, ☎ 02 4981 1955, fax 02 4984 1256, 5 units acc up to 6, [shwr, bath, tlt, fan, TV, refrig, cook fac, elec frypan, toaster, linen reqd], ldry, w/mach, dryer, iron, cots-fee. **W $210 - $865**, BC EFT MC VI.

B&B's/Guest Houses

★★★★☆ **The Mitchells Waterfront B & B**, (B&B), 6 Mitchell St, ☎ 02 4982 0402, fax 02 4982 0402, 1 rm [shwr, bath, tlt, c/fan, heat, elec blkts, TV, clock radio, refrig], ldry, iron, iron brd, lounge (TV), bbq, non smoking rms. **BB ╂╂ $100 - $160**, BC MC VI.

★★★★ **Kent Kharma**, (B&B), 8 Kent Gardens, 5km W of Salamander, ☎ 02 4982 7554, (2 stry gr fl), 1 rm (1 suite) [ensuite (1), fan, heat, elec blkts, TV, radio, t/c mkg, refrig, doonas], ✗, pool, bbq, meals to unit, cots-fee, non smoking rms. **BB ╂ $80 - $120, ╂╂ $85 - $140, ◊ $50 - $85**, ch con, weekly con.

PORT STEPHENS - SWAN BAY NSW 2324

Pop Part of Port Stephen, (187km N Sydney), See map on page 55, ref D7. Sleepy fishing village on the western shores of Port Stephens. Boating, Fishing, Scenic Drives, Swimming, Water Skiing.

Self Catering Accommodation
★★★☆ **Fishermans Village**, Moffat Rd, 20km N of Raymond Terrace, ☎ 02 4997 5605, fax 02 4997 5433, 40 cabins acc up to 6, [shwr, bath (3), tlt, a/c (5), c/fan, heat, tel, TV, video-fee, clock radio, t/c mkg, refrig, cook fac ltd, micro, elec frypan, toaster, blkts, linen, pillows], ldry, iron, rec rm, lounge (TV), conv fac, ⊠, pool (salt water), bbq, c/park (carport), ✆, plygr, jetty, bush walking, golf, tennis (2), cots-fee. **RO ╂╂ $150, ◊ $45, W ╂╂ $550**, AE BC DC MC VI.

PORT STEPHENS - WILLIAMTOWN NSW 2301

Pop 1,375. (193km N Sydney), See map on page 55, ref D8. Gateway to the southern Port Stephens area and the site of a Royal Australian Air Force Base.

B&B's/Guest Houses

★★ **Altman Guest House**, (GH), 615 Cabbage Tree Rd, 3.4km from Williamtown Airport, ☎ 02 4965 1540, 2 rms (2 suites) [shwr, tlt, tel, TV, video, t/c mkg, refrig, micro], lounge (TV), ✕, pool (salt water), sauna, spa, bbq, plygr, gym. **BB 🧍 $45, 🧍🧍 $60, 🧍🧍🧍 $90, 👤 $20**, ch con.

End of Port Stephens

POTTSVILLE BEACH NSW 2489

Pop 2,000. (827km N Sydney), See map on page 54, ref E1. Far north coast settlement with one of the many excellent beaches to be found in this part of the world. Bowls, Fishing, Golf, Surfing, Swimming, Tennis.

Hotels/Motels

Budget Motel Chain International

★★★ **Pottsville Beach Motel**, (M), 30 Coast Rd, 300m NE of PO, ☎ 02 6676 1107, fax 02 6676 1251, (2 stry gr fl), 24 units [shwr, tlt, fan, heat, elec blkts, tel (10), TV, clock radio, t/c mkg, refrig, cook fac (3), micro (9), toaster, ldry], ldry, iron, iron brd, conv fac, ✕, ☒, pool, bbq, rm serv, dinner to unit, plygr, cots, non smoking units (11). **RO 🧍 $36 - $46, 🧍🧍 $40 - $50, 👤 $11**, ch con, weekly con, AE BC DC EFT JCB MC MCH VI.

Self Catering Accommodation

★★☆ **Beaches Pottsville Beach Holidays**, (HU), 11 Seabrae Crt, ☎ 02 6676 3204, (2 stry gr fl), 2 units acc up to 8, [shwr, bath, c/fan, TV, video (1), t/c mkg, refrig, cook fac, micro, elec frypan, d/wash (1), toaster, ldry, linen reqd-fee], w/mach, dryer (1), iron, iron brd, bbq, cots, non smoking property. **D 🧍🧍 $60 - $100, 👤 $10, W 🧍🧍 $260 - $700, 👤 $20**, pen con.

B&B's/Guest Houses

★★★★☆ **Nelly's Manor**, (B&B), No children's facilities, Lot 10 Spring Valley Rd, Cudgera, ☎ 02 6676 2094, 5 rms [ensuite (3), spa bath (2), fan, heat (gas), TV, video, clock radio, t/c mkg, refrig, ldry], conf fac, ✕, pool, non smoking property. **BLB 🧍🧍 $160 - $220**, ch con, BC MC VI.

QUEANBEYAN NSW 2620

Pop 25,689. (321km S Sydney), See map on pages 52/53, ref G7. Situated at the confluence of the Molonglo and Queanbeyan Rivers, the city of Queanbeyan lies just outside the Australian Capital Territory and is a thriving regional centre. Bowls, Fishing, Golf, Squash, Swimming, Tennis.

Hotels/Motels

AAA Tourism Special Rates — Best Western

★★★★ **Golden Age Motor Inn**, (M), 56 Macquoid St, 800m from PO, ☎ 02 6297 1122, fax 02 6299 1604, (2 stry gr fl), 59 units (2 suites) [shwr, bath (23), spa bath (2), tlt, a/c, elec blkts, tel, TV, video (avail), movie, clock radio, t/c mkg, refrig], iron, iron brd, conv fac, ☒, pool (salt water), rm serv, cots, non smoking units (30). **RO 🧍 $86.90 - $128.50, 🧍🧍 $94.60 - $135.50, 👤 $11**, 10 units of a lower rating, AE BC DC EFT JCB MC MP VI, ♿.

Quality — Flag Choice Hotels

★★★☆ **Airport Motor Inn**, (M), Previously Airport Premier Inn 57 Yass Rd, 3km E of PO, 5km E of Canberra Airport, ☎ 02 6297 7877, fax 02 6299 2411, (2 stry), 65 units (1 suite) [shwr, bath (54), spa bath (3), tlt, a/c, elec blkts, tel, TV, movie, clock radio, t/c mkg, refrig, mini bar], ldry, rec rm, conv fac, ☒, pool indoor heated, sauna, bbq, rm serv, plygr, gym, tennis (2), cots-fee, non smoking rms (17). **RO 🧍 $88 - $100, 🧍🧍 $88 - $100, 👤 $6 - $12, Suite D $105 - $120**, ch con, 21 units ★★★★, AE BC DC EFT MC VI, ♿.

★★★☆ **(Serviced Apartments Section)**, (2 stry gr fl), 8 serv apts [shwr, bath, spa bath, tlt, hairdry, a/c, t/c mkg, refrig, cook fac, micro, elec frypan, d/wash, toaster, ldry (in unit)], w/mach, dryer, iron, c/park (garage). **D $165 - $180, W $784.**

AAA Tourism Special Rates — Best Western

★★★☆ **Central Motel & Apartments**, (M), Previously Central Motel 11 Antill St, 400m N of PO, 6km E of Canberra Airport, ☎ 02 6297 2099, fax 02 6297 3619, (Multi-stry gr fl), 34 units [shwr, tlt, hairdry (34), a/c, cent heat, tel, TV, movie, clock radio, t/c mkg, refrig, cook fac (12), toaster], lift, ldry, conf fac, ☒, pool-heated (solar), bbq, dinner to unit, cots. **BLB 🧍 $69 - $78, 🧍🧍 $79 - $88, 🧍🧍🧍 $89 - $98, 👤 $10**, AE BC DC EFT JCB MC MP VI.

★★★☆ **(Serviced Apartment Section)**, 12 serv apts [shwr, tlt, a/c, cent heat, tel, TV, movie, clock radio, t/c mkg, refrig, cook fac, toaster], ldry, dinner to unit. **RO 🧍 $86 - $89, 🧍🧍 $96 - $99, 🧍🧍🧍 $106 - $109, 👤 $10.**

★★★☆ **Grand Manor Motor Inn**, (M), Cnr Macquoid & Atkinson Sts, 1km E of PO, ☎ 02 6299 2800, fax 02 6299 3780, (2 stry gr fl), 32 units [shwr, bath (16), tlt, hairdry, a/c, elec blkts, tel, TV, movie, clock radio, t/c mkg, refrig, doonas], ldry, iron, iron brd, ☒, pool (salt water), rm serv, dinner to unit, cots-fee, non smoking units (20). **RO 🧍 $76 - $87, 🧍🧍 $85 - $94, 👤 $11**, AE BC DC EFT MC MP VI.

Golden Chain

★★★☆ **Hamiltons Town House**, (M), Cnr Canberra Ave & Tharwa Rd, 800m SW of Tourist Info Centre, ☎ 02 6297 1877, fax 02 6297 1240, (2 stry gr fl), 18 units (2 suites) [shwr, spa bath (2), tlt, hairdry (available), a/c, elec blkts, tel, fax, TV, video (avail) (4), movie, clock radio, t/c mkg, refrig, micro (5), toaster], ldry, iron, iron brd, rm serv, dinner to unit (Mon to Fri), cots-fee, non smoking units (3). **RO 🧍 $63 - $81, 🧍🧍 $71 - $93, 👤 $13**, ch con, AE BC BTC DC EFT MC MCH MP VI, ♿,

Operator Comment: "See advertisement under Canberra".

★★★☆ **Leagues Motel**, (M), 1 Macquoid St, 600m E of PO, ☎ 02 6297 1355, fax 02 6299 2628, (2 stry gr fl), 44 units (13 suites) [shwr, bath (14), spa bath (6), tlt, hairdry, a/c, heat, elec blkts, tel, TV, clock radio, t/c mkg, refrig, micro, toaster], iron, iron brd, pool (salt water), spa, c/park (undercover) (12), cots-fee, non smoking units (20). **RO 🧍 $76 - $84, 🧍🧍 $86 - $94, 👤 $11, Suite RO 🧍🧍 $105 - $140**, ch con, 7 units ★★★, 12 units ★★★★. AE BC DC EFT MC MP VI.

★★★☆ **Mid City Motor Inn**, (M), 215 Crawford St, 400m N of PO, ☎ 02 6297 7366, fax 02 6299 3036, (2 stry gr fl), 20 units [shwr, tlt, hairdry, a/c-cool, cent heat, elec blkts, tel, TV, movie, clock radio, t/c mkg, refrig, toaster], ldry, iron, iron brd, cots. **BLB 🧍 $70, 🧍🧍 $77, 🧍🧍🧍 $87, 👤 $10**, AE BC DC EFT MC VI.

★★★☆ **Olympia Motel**, (M), 149 Crawford St, 100m N of PO, ☎ 02 6297 1777, fax 02 6299 2946, (2 stry gr fl), 25 units [shwr, tlt, hairdry, a/c, cent heat, elec blkts, tel, TV, video-fee, clock radio, t/c mkg, refrig, toaster], ldry, iron, bbq, cots-fee. **RO 🧍 $62 - $72, 🧍🧍 $66 - $77, 🧍🧍🧍 $77 - $88, 👤 $11**, AE BC DC EFT JCB MC MP VI.

★★★☆ **Queensgate Motel**, (M), 2 High St, 1.5km N of PO, ☎ 02 6297 7677, fax 02 6299 2543, (2 stry gr fl), 30 units [shwr, spa bath (2), tlt, a/c, elec blkts, tel, TV, video, clock radio, t/c mkg, refrig], ldry, ✉, pool, sauna, spa, rm serv, dinner to unit, cots-fee. RO ♦ $71 - $135, ♦♦ $71 - $135, ⚭ $11, 12 units ★★★, AE BC DC EFT JCB MC MP VI.

★★★☆ **Wallaby Motel**, (M), 88 Crawford St, 400m N of PO, ☎ 02 6297 1533, fax 02 6299 2985, 27 units [shwr, tlt, a/c, c/fan (13), cent heat (18), elec blkts, tel, TV, video-fee, movie, clock radio, t/c mkg, refrig, toaster], ldry, ✉, rm serv, car wash, cots-fee. BLB ♦ $55 - $65, ♦♦ $60 - $77, ⚭ $12 - $15, W ♦♦ $360 - $462, 8 units of a lower rating, BC EFT MC VI.

★★★ **Aussie Settler Motel**, (M), 5-9 High St, 500m E of PO, ☎ 02 6284 4637, fax 02 6284 4638, (2 stry gr fl), 10 units [shwr, tlt, a/c (8), heat (2), elec blkts, tel, TV, clock radio, t/c mkg, refrig, toaster, ldry], pool, bbq, cots. RO ♦ $53 - $77, ♦♦ $59 - $88, fam con, AE BC DC EFT MC VI.

QUEANBEYAN NSW continued...

★★★ **Burley Griffin Motel**, (M), 147 Uriarra Rd, cnr Young St, 2km W of PO, ☎ 02 6297 1211, fax 02 6297 3083, (2 stry gr fl), 22 units [shwr, bath (5), tlt, a/c-cool, fan, heat, elec blkts, tel, TV, clock radio, t/c mkg, refrig], ldry, pool, bbq, cots-fee, non smoking units (8). BLB ♦ $55 - $60, ♦♦ $60 - $66, ◊ $11, AE BC DC EFT MC MCH VI.

★★★ **Crest Motor Inn**, (M), 60 Crawford St, 500m N of PO, ☎ 02 6297 1677, fax 02 6299 3039, (2 stry gr fl), 25 units [shwr, tlt, c/fan, heat, elec blkts, tel, TV, video-fee, clock radio, t/c mkg, refrig, toaster], rec rm, cook fac, car wash, cots-fee. BLB ♦ $55, ♦♦ $61, ◊ $11, AE BC DC EFT MC VI.

★★★ **Margeurita Motel**, (M), Cnr Canberra Ave & Tharwa Rd, ☎ 02 6297 5531, fax 02 6297 6465, (2 stry gr fl), 10 units [shwr, tlt, a/c-cool, heat, elec blkts, tel, TV, clock radio, t/c mkg, refrig], cots-fee, non smoking units (4). RO ♦ $50 - $55, ♦♦ $55 - $60, ◊ $5, AE BC DC MC VI.

CREST MOTOR INN

AAAT ★★★   ♦ $55 ~ ♦♦ $61   Inspection Welcome

Tariff Includes: • Light breakfast • Tea & coffee facilities • Toaster • Refrigerator • Colour TV • Video players & video movies (fee) • Clock radio • Direct dial phones • Ceiling fans • Centrally heated • Electric blankets • Private facilities • Guest kitchen • Guest vacuum & car wash • Fax service

Tours organised
Bus to Canberra across street
2 minutes downtown
5 minutes walk to train station
2 minutes walk to Olympic Pool

Tel: (02) 6297 1677
Fax: (02) 6299 3039   60 Crawford Street, Queanbeyan NSW 2620

QUEANBEYAN PARKWAY HOMESTEAD

8 Lowe St. 2620   Ph (02) 6297 1411
Fax (02) 6297 6621.   Toll Free 1800 041 019
Please phone our TOLL FREE number to make your reservation

QUIET ACCOMMODATION AWAY FROM TRAFFIC NOISE

The Parkway is a quiet motel situated away from main streets yet only 3 mins from the centre of town, shops and clubs, and 10 mins drive from Canberra. Adjoining parkland the Parkway offers a sound nights sleep away from heavy traffic noise. Our rooms cater for the budget conscious traveller right up to our deluxe suites with two-person spas. Our restaurant provides excellent homestyle cuisine in a warm family atmosphere.

AUTO MOBILE MEMBERS DISCOUNT 10% (CONDITIONS APPLY.)

★★★ **Parkway Motel**, (M), 8 Lowe St, 500m N of PO, ☎ 02 6297 1411, fax 02 6297 6621, 30 units [shwr, bath (6), spa bath (2), tlt, hairdry, a/c-cool (21), a/c (9), heat (21), elec blkts, tel, TV, video-fee, clock radio, t/c mkg, refrig, toaster], ldry, ⊠, pool, rm serv, dinner to unit, plygr, cots-fee. D ♦ $52 - $80, ♦♦ $57 - $100, ◊ $10, ch con, 9 units of a higher standard. AE BC DC EFT MC MP VI, ♿.

★★★ **Rainbow Motel**, (M), 41 Bungendore Rd, 2km E of PO, ☎ 02 6297 2784, fax 02 6297 9836, 14 units (1 suite) [shwr, tlt, hairdry, a/c, elec blkts, tel, TV, video-fee, movie, clock radio, t/c mkg, refrig, toaster], bbq, cots-fee, non smoking units (8). RO ♦ $50 - $55, ♦♦ $55 - $66, ♦♦♦ $65 - $77, ◊ $10, Suite D $95, AE BC DC EFT MC MCH VI.

★☆ **Sunrise Motel**, (M), 9 Uriarra Rd, 1km N of PO, ☎ 02 6297 2822, fax 02 6297 2978, 22 units [shwr, tlt, a/c, cent heat, elec blkts, tel, TV, video, clock radio, t/c mkg, refrig], ldry, pool, bbq, plygr, cots-fee. RO ♦ $49.50, ♦♦ $55 - $60.50, ♦♦♦ $66, AE BC DC MC VI.

Self Catering Accommodation

The Village Cabins, (HU), 43 Canberra Ave, 300m S of Tourist Centre, ☎ 02 6297 1255, fax 02 6299 4145, 19 units [shwr, bath, tlt, c/fan, elec blkts, TV, refrig, cook fac, micro, blkts, linen, pillows], bbq. D ♦ $40 - $55, ♦♦ $49 - $59, ◊ $10, ch con, BC DC EFT MC VI, ♿.

B&B's/Guest Houses

★★★★☆ **Benbullen Bed & Breakfast**, (B&B), 75 The Ridgeway, 4.5 km E of PO, 11km E of Canberra Airport, ☎ 02 6297 6101, fax 02 6297 0262, 3 rms (3 suites) [shwr, bath, spa bath, tlt, a/c, fan, cent heat, elec blkts, tel, TV, video, clock radio, t/c mkg, refrig], pool, bbq, tennis, cots, non smoking property. BB ♦ $90, ♦♦ $120, ◊ $40, ch con, BC MC VI.

QUIRINDI NSW 2343

Pop 2,650. (393km NW Sydney), See map on pages 52/53, ref H3. Sunflower producing centre that is also regarded as the home of polo, which has been played in the district since the late 1800s. Bowls, Golf, Swimming, Tennis.

Hotels/Motels

★★★ **Heritage Motel**, (M), 88 George St, 100m S of PO, ☎ 02 6746 1742, fax 02 6746 1453, (2 stry gr fl), 12 units [shwr, tlt, a/c (10), c/fan, heat, tel, fax, TV, clock radio, t/c mkg, refrig, cook fac ltd (1), toaster], lounge (TV), conv fac, ⊠, bbq, dinner to unit, plygr, cots. BB ♦ $50 - $55, ♦♦ $66 - $80, ◊ $25, RO ♦ $44 - $55, ♦♦ $60 - $70, ♦♦♦ $77 - $82, ◊ $16, 3 units of a lower rating. AE BC DC MC VI.

★★ **Motel Quirindi**, (M), 147 Loder St, 2km S of PO, ☎ 02 6746 1777, fax 02 6746 3079, 17 units [shwr, tlt, a/c (10), fan, heat, elec blkts, tel, TV, clock radio, t/c mkg, refrig], bbq, rm serv, courtesy transfer, cots, non smoking units (1). RO ♦ $50 - $55, ♦♦ $60 - $66, ◊ $10, ch con, AE BC MC VI.

B&B's/Guest Houses

Karanilla Farm Bush Bungalows Complex, (GH), (Farm), Karanilla Farm, 12km NE of PO in wildlife sanctuary, ☎ 02 6746 5660, fax 02 6746 2548, 4 rms [shwr, tlt, a/c-cool (1), heat, elec blkts], ldry, conv fac, ✗, bbq, tennis, cots. D all meals ♦ $102.

(Cabin Section), 2 cabins acc up to 6, [shwr, tlt, a/c-cool (1), fan (available), heat, elec blkts, refrig, cook fac, elec frypan, toaster], conf fac, bbq, tennis, cots. D $88 - $108, W $616 - $750.

The Village Cabins

Please call TOLL FREE 1800 020 117

- 300m South of Tourist Office
- 19 Colonial style cabins
- Fully self contained
- Family size accommodates up to 5 people
- Cooking facilities
- Enjoy our BBQ area ● Laundromat for your convenience
- Workers and long stay welcome with special tariff
- All linen supplied
- Ensuite bathrooms
- Heaters, fans
- Colour TV
- Cabin for people with disabilities

Presentation & cleanliness our highest priority

43 CANBERRA AVE, QUEANBEYAN 2620
Phone: (02) 6297 1255 or Fax: (02) 6297 4145
Email: Jennym@netspeed.com.au

RAINBOW FLAT NSW 2430

Pop Part of Taree, (324km N Sydney), See map on page 54, ref B8. Located in the Lower North Coast region.

★★★★☆ **Rainbow Cottage B&B**, (B&B), 1535 The Lakes Way, 6Kms NW of Hallidays Point PO, ☎ 02 6553 6355, fax 02 6553 6356, 2 rms (1 suite) [ensuite, hairdry, fan, heat, TV, clock radio, t/c mkg, refrig, toaster], iron (on request), bbq, meals to unit, c/park. **BB ⫯ $85, ⫯⫯ $95 - $125,** ⫯ **$25,** ch con, fam con, pen con, BC MC VI.

RANKINS SPRINGS NSW 2669

Pop Nominal, (562km W Sydney), See map on pages 52/53, ref E5. Service centre on the Mid-Western Highway at the turnoff to Lake Cargelligo.

★☆ **Rankin Springs Boomerang Motel**, (M), Boomerang St, ☎ 02 6966 1240, fax 02 6966 1240, 11 units [shwr, tlt, a/c-cool, heat, elec blkts, TV, clock radio, t/c mkg, refrig], dinner to unit, plygr, cots-fee, No pets permitted. **W $176 - $203.50, RO ⫯ $38.50, ⫯⫯ $44 - $49.50, ⫯⫯⫯ $60.50,** ⫯ **$11,** AE BC MC VI.

RATHMINES NSW 2283

Pop Part of Newcastle, (155km N Sydney), See map on page 55, ref E4. Village on the western shores of Lake Macquarie just south of Toronto. Boating, Bowls, Fishing, Swimming.

B&B's/Guest Houses

★★★☆ **Overnight Reflections**, (B&B), 113 Fishing Point Rd, 1km S of Rathmines PO/Newsagent, ☎ 02 4975 1430, fax 02 4954 8484, 4 rms [shwr, bath, spa bath (1), tlt, hairdry, a/c, fire pl, elec blkts, tel, clock radio, t/c mkg], lounge (TV), bbq, c/park. **BB ⫯ $70, ⫯⫯ $100 - $180, DBB ⫯ $95, ⫯⫯ $160 - $190,** BC.

(Cottage Section), 1 cotg acc up to 2, [shwr, spa bath, tlt, hairdry, a/c, elec blkts, TV, clock radio, CD, t/c mkg, micro, elec frypan, toaster]. **BB ⫯⫯ $180,** (not yet classified).

(Lake House Section), 1 house acc up to 6, [shwr, tlt, TV, t/c mkg, refrig, cook fac, ldry, blkts, linen, pillows], c/park. **D $160,** (not yet classified).

RAYMOND TERRACE NSW

See Port Stephens Region.

RED ROCK NSW 2456

Pop 300. (600km N Sydney), See map on page 54, ref D4. Delightful coastal village between Coffs Harbour and Grafton. Bowls, Fishing, Swimming.

Redbank, (HF), 8 Schafer St, ☎ 02 6653 6418, 4 flats acc up to 8, [shwr, tlt, fan, heat, TV, video, refrig, cook fac, micro, doonas], ldry, bbq. **D $40 - $55, W $250 - $500,** (not yet classified).

RICHMOND NSW 2753

Pop 3,400. Part of Richmond-Win, (64km W Sydney), See map on page 56, ref B3. Pretty town at the foot of the Blue Mountains.

★★★☆ **The Colonial Motel**, (M), 161 March St, 100m fr railway station, ☎ 02 4578 1166, fax 02 4578 1811, (2 stry gr fl) 39 units [shwr, tlt, a/c, tel, TV, clock radio, t/c mkg, refrig], ldry, ⊠, pool (salt water), spa, bbq, rm serv, cots. **RO ⫯ $75 - $90, ⫯⫯ $88.50 - $100,** ⫯ **$15,** AE BC DC JCB MC VI.

ROBERTSON NSW 2577

Pop 248. (119km S Sydney), See map on page 55, ref B4. Quiet village in the Southern Highlands at the top of Macquarie Pass, situated in the largest potato growing area in New South Wales. Bowls, Bush Walking, Golf, Horse Riding, Swimming, Tennis.

Hotels/Motels

★★☆ **Robertson Country Motel**, (M), Illawarra Hwy, ☎ 02 4885 1444, fax 02 4885 1564, 6 units [shwr, tlt, fan, heat, elec blkts, tel, TV, clock radio, t/c mkg, refrig, toaster], ldry, coffee shop, cots. **RO ⫯ $60.50 - $82.50,** ⫯ **$11,** AE BC EFT MC VI.

B&B's/Guest Houses

★★★☆ **Rose Ella**, (B&B), McGuinness Dr, Mt Murray, 8km E of PO, ☎ 02 4885 1401, fax 02 4885 1717, 2 rms [ensuite, bath (1), hairdry, fan, heat, elec blkts, tel, clock radio, t/c mkg, ldry], iron, iron brd, TV rm, lounge (fireplace), ✗, bbq, courtesy transfer. **BB ⫯ $90 - $120, ⫯⫯ $120 - $150,** AE BC MC VI.

★★ **Ranelagh House**, (GH), Illawarra Hwy, 1km SE of Robertson, ☎ 02 4885 1111, fax 02 4885 1051, (Multi-stry), 42 rms (10 suites) [shwr, tlt, elec blkts, t/c mkg], shared fac (32), ldry, iron, iron brd, lounge (tv & firepl), conv fac, ✗, pool, ☎, cots. **DBB ⫯ $104.50 - $115.50,** ch con, 10 units of a higher standard. BC MC VI.

ROTHBURY NSW 2320

Pop 447. (200km N Sydney), See map on page 55, ref B7. Like neighbouring Pokolbin, Rothbury lies at the heart of the Hunter Valley wine region. Vineyards, Wineries. See also Cessnock & Pokolbin.

Self Catering Accommodation

★★★★☆ **Lothian Grange Luxury Cottage**, (Cotg), Cnr Branxton Rd & Littlewood Rd, North Rothbury 2335, 5km S of Branxton, ☎ 02 4938 1530, fax 02 4938 3649, 1 cotg acc up to 4, [shwr, tlt, hairdry, a/c, c/fan, fire pl, elec blkts, tel, TV, video, clock radio, t/c mkg, refrig, cook fac, micro, d/wash, toaster, ldry, blkts, linen], w/mach, dryer, iron, lounge, ✗, spa, bbq, c/park (undercover). **D ⫯⫯⫯⫯ $253 - $715,** Min book applies, AE BC MC VI.

★★★★ **Bluebush Estate**, (Cotg), Wilderness Rd Lovedale via, ☎ 02 4930 7177, fax 02 4930 7666, 3 cotgs acc up to 10, [shwr, bath (1), tlt, a/c, fan, heat, tel, TV, video, clock radio, t/c mkg, refrig, cook fac, micro, elec frypan, d/wash (2), toaster, ldry (1)], pool (salt water), bbq, tennis, cots. **D ⫯ $90 - $165, ⫯⫯ $110 - $175,** ch con, BC MC VI.

★★★★★ **(Bed & Breakfast Section)**, 4 rms [shwr, tlt, hairdry, a/c], ldry, lounge (TV, video), lounge firepl, non smoking property. **BB ⫯⫯ $110 - $175.**

★★★★ **Cambridge Retreat**, (Cotg), 25 Old North Rd, 9km NW of Cessnock Airport, ☎ 02 6574 7268, fax 02 6574 7046, (2 stry), 5 cotgs acc up to 8, [shwr, spa bath (2), tlt, hairdry, a/c, c/fan, fire pl, tel, TV, clock radio, CD, t/c mkg, refrig, cook fac, micro, elec frypan, toaster, ldry, blkts, linen, pillows], iron, iron brd, conf fac, pool (salt water), bbq, bicycle, cots. **BLB ⫯⫯ $143 - $179, ⫯⫯⫯⫯ $209 - $280,** ⫯ **$33 - $72,** BC MC VI.

★★★★ **Madigan Vineyard**, (Cotg), Lot 1, Wilderness Rd, 10km N of Cessnock, ☎ 02 4998 7111, fax 02 4998 7815, 3 cotgs acc up to 8, [shwr, bath (1), spa bath (1), tlt, hairdry, a/c, c/fan, heat (2), elec blkts, TV, video, clock radio, CD, refrig, cook fac, micro, elec frypan (1), toaster, blkts, linen, pillows], iron, c/park. **D ⫯⫯ $75 - $88,** ⫯ **$30,** ch con, MC VI.

★★★☆ **Wandin Valley Estate**, (Villa), Wilderness Rd, Lovedale 2325, 15km N of Cessnock, ☎ 02 4930 7317, fax 02 4930 7814, 4 villas acc up to 8, (2 & 4 bedrm), [shwr, bath, tlt, hairdry, c/fan, fire pl, tel, TV, t/c mkg, refrig, cook fac, toaster, blkts, linen, pillows], conf fac, cafe, pool, bbq, plygr, tennis. **D ⫯⫯ $150,** ⫯ **$75,** ch con, Min book applies, AE BC DC MC VI, &.

★★☆ **Claremont Country House**, (Cotg), Warraroong Estate, Wilderness Rd, 6km S of Greta PO, ☎ 02 4930 7594, fax 02 4930 7199, 1 cotg acc up to 10, [shwr (3), bath (1), tlt (3), t/c mkg, refrig, cook fac, micro, elec frypan, d/wash, toaster, ldry (in unit), blkts, linen, pillows], dryer, iron, pool (salt water), bbq, cots. **D ⫯ $44 - $71.50,** ch con, AE BC EFT MC VI.

ROTHBURY NSW continued...

B&B's/Guest Houses

★★★★☆ **Alleyn Court**, (GH), Lot 31 Talga Rd, ☎ 02 4930 7011, fax 02 4930 7022, 8 rms [shwr, tlt, hairdry, heat, elec blkts, tel, TV, video (1), clock radio, t/c mkg, refrig, micro (1), toaster], iron (1), iron brd (1), lounge (tv and fireplace), pool (salt water), cook fac, bbq, non smoking property. **BLB ♦ $110, ♦♦ $110 - $209**, BC MC VI.

★★★★ **Sovereign Hill Country Lodge & Vineyard**, (GH), Lot 34, Talga Rd, 15km N of Cessnock, ☎ 02 4930 7755, fax 02 4930 7715, 6 rms [shwr, tlt, hairdry, a/c, elec blkts, tel, TV, clock radio, t/c mkg, refrig, cook fac, toaster], iron, iron brd, lounge firepl, pool, bbq, 24hr reception, tennis, non smoking units. **BLB ♦ $88 - $176, ♦♦ $88 - $176, ◊ $12 - $22**, AE BC MC VI.

★★★☆ **Hill Top Country Guest House**, (GH), 81 Talga Rd, ☎ 02 4930 7111, fax 02 4930 7111, 6 rms (2 suites) [shwr, spa bath, tlt, hairdry (5), a/c, c/fan, clock radio, t/c mkg (2 rms)], iron, iron brd, lounge (tv & firepl), ✕, pool, t/c mkg shared, bbq, bicycle, canoeing.

BB ♦♦ $88 - $240, BC MC VI.

RUNNING STREAM NSW 2850

Pop Nominal, (304km NW Sydney), See map on page 55, ref B1. Small community situated roughly halfway between Lithgow and Mudgee. Scenic Drives.

Self Catering Accommodation

★★☆ **Wombat Hilltop**, (Cotg), Grunty Fen, 2.9km N of Cherry Tree Cafe, ☎ 02 6358 8211, fax 02 6358 8211, 2 cotgs acc up to 8, [shwr, tlt, c/fan, fire pl (combustion), elec blkts, radio, t/c mkg, refrig, cook fac, micro, toaster, blkts, doonas, linen reqd-fee, pillows], w/mach, iron, iron brd, lounge, bbq, cots. **D ♦ $25, ◊ $25**, ch con, Breakfast available, BC MC VI.

RYLSTONE NSW 2849

Pop 700. (254km W Sydney), See map on pages 52/53, ref H4. Pretty place on the Cudgegong River, with architecture that ranges from early slab construction to colonial sandstone. Bush Walking, Scenic Drives.

B&B's/Guest Houses

Mountain Valley Roo-Treat, (B&B), 25km S of Rylstone, ☎ 02 6379 4318, fax 02 6379 6180, 3 rms [ensuite, bath (1), hairdry (2), elec blkts (2), ldry], lounge, lounge firepl, ✕, pool, cots, non smoking rms. **BB ♦♦ $110, DBB ♦♦ $185**, ch con, (not yet classified).

RYDAL NSW

See Blue Mountains Region.

SALAMANDER BAY NSW

See Port Stephens Region.

SALISBURY NSW 2420

Pop Nominal, (225km N Sydney), See map on page 54, ref A8. Small settlement on the Williams River in the southern Barrington Tops area.

Self Catering Accommodation

Salisbury Lodges, (Chalet), 2930 Salisbury Rd, ☎ 02 4995 3285, fax 02 4995 3206, 3 chalets [shwr, spa bath, tlt, hairdry, fan (2), c/fan (1), fire pl, tel, TV (1), video (1), clock radio, t/c mkg, refrig, mini bar (2), cook fac, elec frypan, d/wash (1), toaster, ldry (1), doonas, linen, pillows], ldry, w/mach-fee, dryer-fee, iron, iron brd (1), rec rm, conf fac, lounge firepl, ✕, bbq, courtesy transfer, ✆, non smoking property. **BB ♦ $65 - $85**, ch con, Min book all holiday times, AE BC EFT MC VI, (not yet classified).

(Bed & Breakfast Section), 2 rms [shwr, spa bath, tlt, hairdry, c/fan, heat, tel, TV, clock radio, t/c mkg, refrig, toaster], ldry, iron, rec rm, lounge, conf fac, lounge firepl, ✕, bbq, dinner to unit, c/park. **BB ♦ $75**, Min book all holiday times, (not yet classified).

SANCTUARY POINT NSW 2540

Pop 5,988. (174km S Sydney), See map on page 55, ref B5. The largest of a series of towns dotted around the northern shores of St Georges Basin. Boating, Bowls, Fishing, Golf, Sailing, Squash, Swimming, Tennis.

Hotels/Motels

★★☆ **St Georges Basin Golf View**, (M), 49 Paradise Beach Rd, 25km S of Nowra PO, ☎ 02 4443 9502, fax 02 4443 8502, 10 units [shwr, tlt, c/fan, heat, TV, clock radio, t/c mkg, refrig], bbq. **RO ♦ $55 - $83, ♦♦ $61 - $94, ♦♦♦ $66 - $99, ◊ $11**, Min book Christmas Jan long w/ends and Easter, BC MC VI, ♿.

★★☆ **The Sanctuary Restaurant & Motel**, (M), 4 Paradise Beach Rd, Opposite St Georges Basin Country Club, ☎ 02 4443 0603, 7 units [shwr, tlt, a/c, TV, clock radio, t/c mkg, refrig], iron (1), iron brd (1), ✕, rm serv, dinner to unit, cots. **RO ♦ $65 - $95, ♦♦ $65 - $95, ◊ $15**, Min book all holiday times, BC MC VI.

Self Catering Accommodation

Jervis Bay Getaways, (Cotg), (Farm), Worrowing, Wool Rd, 2km S of Jervis Bay Roundabout, ☎ 02 4443 8912, fax 02 4443 7422, (2 stry gr fl), 2 cotgs acc up to 8, [shwr, spa bath, tlt, c/fan, elec blkts, TV, video, clock radio, CD, t/c mkg, refrig, cook fac, micro, elec frypan, d/wash, toaster, ldry, doonas, linen-fee], w/mach, iron, iron brd, lounge firepl, bbq, plygr, cots, non smoking property. **D ♦♦ $90 - $250, ◊ $30**, BC MC VI, (not yet classified).

SAWTELL NSW 2452

Pop 13,250. (546km N Sydney), See map on page 54, ref D5. North coast town which, although sizeable, retains a country town atmosphere. Bowls, Croquet, Fishing, Golf, Swimming, Tennis.

Hotels/Motels

★★★☆ **Beach Haven**, (M), 23 Twenty Second Ave, 1km N of PO, ☎ 02 6653 1659, fax 02 6653 1659, (2 stry gr fl), 17 units [shwr, tlt, a/c (7), fan, heat, elec blkts, tel, TV, video (avail), movie, clock radio, t/c mkg, refrig, cook fac ltd (7), toaster], ldry, pool-heated, spa, bbq, cots-fee. **W $450 - $1,050, RO ♦ $65 - $110, ♦♦ $69.30 - $120, ♦♦♦ $80.30 - $165, ◊ $11**, pen con, Min book applies, AE BC EFT MC VI.

★★☆ **The Coasters Motel**, (M), 77 First Ave, 100m N of the PO, ☎ 02 6653 1541, fax 02 6653 3233, (2 stry gr fl), 16 units [shwr, tlt, fan, heat, elec blkts, TV, clock radio, t/c mkg, refrig, cook fac (6)], ldry, rec rm, pool, bbq, ✆, gym, cots-fee. **RO ♦ $50, ♦♦ $55, ◊ $7.70**, pen con, AE BC MC VI, ♿.

★★☆ **(Holiday Unit Section)**, 10 units [shwr, tlt, fan, heat, elec blkts, TV, clock radio, refrig, cook fac, micro, ldry (in unit), blkts, linen, pillows], rec rm, pool, bbq, cots. **W $275 - $330**.

Self Catering Accommodation

★★☆ **Sundeck**, (HF), 66 First Ave, ☎ 02 6653 1064, 11 flats acc up to 5, [shwr, tlt, c/fan, TV, refrig, cook fac, linen reqd-fee], ldry, c/park (garage), cots. **D $66 - $77, W $198 - $550**, Min book applies, BC MC VI.

B&B's/Guest Houses

★★★★☆ **Alamanda Lodge**, (B&B), No children's facilities, 59 Boronia St, 100m SW of PO, ☎ 02 6658 9099, (2 stry), 4 rms [shwr, tlt, hairdry (1), c/fan, heat, elec blkts, TV, clock radio, t/c mkg, refrig, micro (1), toaster (1)], lounge, breakfast rm, bbq, courtesy transfer, ✆, non smoking property. **BLB ♦ $77 - $123, ♦♦ $93 - $143, ◊ $33**, BC DC MC VI.

Woodlands Beach House B & B, (B&B), 4 Boronia St, 300m S of PO, ☎ 02 6658 9177, fax 02 6658 9177, 2 rms [ensuite, c/fan, elec blkts, TV, clock radio, t/c mkg, refrig, doonas], non smoking property. **BB ♦ $55 - $66, ♦♦ $99 - $110**, BC MC VI, (not yet classified).

SCONE NSW 2337

Pop 3,450. (269km N Sydney), See map on pages 52/53, ref H4. Upper Hunter town that's widely acknowledged as the 'Horse Capital of Australia', a reference to the studs in the area that take advantage of fine pastures to produce champion breeds. Bowls, Golf, Horse Racing, Swimming, Tennis, Vineyards, Wineries, Water Skiing.

Hotels/Motels

★★★☆ **Airlie House Motor Inn**, (M), New England Hwy, 100m S of PO, ☎ 02 6545 1488, fax 02 6545 3061, 26 units (3 suites) [shwr, bath (9), tlt, hairdry, a/c, fan (10), fire pl, elec blkts, tel, TV, clock radio, t/c mkg, refrig], iron, iron brd, conv fac, ✕, bar, pool, rm serv, dinner to unit (6 nights), tennis (half court), cots-fee. **RO ♦ $75 - $85, ♦♦ $85 - $95, ◊ $10, Suite RO ♦ $105 - $115**, ch con, AE BC DC MC VI.

★★★☆ **Colonial Motor Lodge**, (M), Cnr Guernsey & Parker Sts, 800m N of PO, ☎ 02 6545 1700, fax 02 6545 3130, 24 units [shwr, bath (1), tlt, hairdry (14), a/c, fan (6), heat, elec blkts, tel, cable tv (24 rooms), video (10), clock radio, t/c mkg, refrig], ldry, iron, iron brd, ✕ (6 nights), dinner to unit (6 nights), cots-fee. **RO ♦ $75 - $80, ♦♦ $80 - $86, ◊ $10**, 10 units ★★★. AE BC DC JCB MC MP VI.

★★★☆ **Folly Foot Motel**, (M), New England Hwy, 500m N of PO, ☎ 02 6545 3079, fax 02 6545 3998, (2 stry gr fl), 18 units [shwr, bath (4), tlt, a/c, elec blkts, tel, fax, TV, movie, clock radio, t/c mkg, refrig], conv fac, ⊠, bar, dinner to unit, cots. **RO ∮ $62.70 - $77, ♔♔ $75.90 - $93.50, ◊ $11**, AE BC DC MC VI.

★★★ **Isis Motel**, (M), 250 New England Hwy, 600m S of PO, ☎ 02 6545 1100, fax 02 6545 1750, 18 units [shwr, tlt, a/c, elec blkts, tel, TV, video (avail), movie, clock radio, t/c mkg, refrig, toaster], ldry, pool, bbq, dinner to unit, cots. **RO ∮ $48 - $53, ♔♔ $54 - $64, ♔♔♔ $70, ◊ $10**, 6 family units of a lower rating, AE BC DC EFT MC MCH VI.

Self Catering Accommodation

★★☆ **Lake Glenbawn Holiday Village**, (Cotg), Glenbawn Rd, Lake Glenbawn, 14km E of Scone PO, ☎ 02 6543 7752, fax 02 6543 7829, 6 cotgs acc up to 6, [shwr, bath, tlt, a/c-cool (2), a/c (4), heat, t/c mkg, refrig, cook fac, micro, elec frypan, toaster, linen reqd-fee], w/mach, iron, bbq, kiosk, ☏, plygr, tennis. **D $66 - $110, W $363 - $495**, BC MC VI.

B&B's/Guest Houses

★★★☆ **Belltrees Country House**, (GH), Gundy Rd, 36km E of PO, ☎ 02 6546 1123, or 02 6546 1193, fax 02 6549 1193, 8 rms [shwr, bath (2), tlt, c/fan, heat, elec blkts, t/c mkg], ldry, lounge (TV, stereo, video), ✕, pool, tennis, cots. **DBB ∮ $255 - $285, ♔ $410 - $500, ◊ $150**, ch con, AE BC EFT MC VI.

(**Cottage Section**), 2 cotgs [shwr, spa bath (1), tlt, fire pl, refrig, cook fac, ldry (1)]. **D $70 - $110**, Min book applies.

SCOTTS HEAD NSW 2447

Pop 800. (494km N Sydney), See map on page 54, ref C5. Sleepy north coast seaside village with excellent beaches. Bowls, Fishing, Surfing, Tennis.

Self Catering Accommodation

★★★☆ **Grand View Holiday House**, (HU), 11 Vernon St, 200m W of PO, ☎ 02 6569 8008, fax 02 6569 8008, 1 unit acc up to 10, [fan, heat, TV, video, radio, CD, refrig, cook fac, micro, ldry, blkts, doonas, linen], w/mach, ✕, bbq, meals avail (on request only), non smoking property. **D ∮ $70 - $185, ♔ $100 - $260, W $700 - $1,400.**

★★★☆ **Ocean Blue Beach House**, (House), 3 Ocean St, ☎ 0407 230 217, fax 02 6568 2587, (2 stry gr fl), 1 house acc up to 12, [shwr (3), bath, tlt (3), c/fan, heat, TV, video, clock radio, refrig, cook fac, micro, d/wash, toaster, ldry, blkts, doonas, pillows], w/mach, dryer, iron, iron brd, bbq, c/park. **W $700 - $1,300**, Min book applies.

★★★☆ **Waratah Holidays Units**, (SA), Cnr Waratah & Vernon Sts, 150m S of PO, ☎ 02 6569 8228, 9 serv apts acc up to 5, [shwr, tlt, fan, heat, elec blkts, tel, TV, clock radio, t/c mkg, refrig, cook fac, toaster], ldry-fee, bbq, c/park (undercover). **D $60 - $105, W $250 - $630**, BC MC VI.

★★★ **Kooringal Cottage**, (Cotg), 18 Matthew St, 200m S of PO, ☎ 02 6568 1082, (2 stry gr fl), 1 cotg acc up to 12, [shwr, bath, tlt, c/fan, elec blkts, tel, TV, video, clock radio, refrig, cook fac, d/wash, toaster, ldry, blkts, linen, pillows], bbq, c/park (garage). **W $620 - $1,230**, Min book applies.

★★☆ **Scotts Head Holiday Units**, (HU), 4 Wallace St, 100m W of PO, ☎ 02 6569 8160, fax 02 4946 6160, (2 stry gr fl), 6 units acc up to 6, [shwr, tlt, TV, clock radio, refrig, cook fac, toaster, ldry (in unit), blkts reqd-fee, linen reqd-fee], pool (salt water), bbq, c/park (undercover), cots. **D $50 - $90, W $250 - $630**, Min book applies.

Benji's by the Sea, (House), 18 Vista Way, 1km W of PO, ☎ 02 6569 8326, 1 house acc up to 6, (3 bedrm), [shwr, tlt, c/fan, heat, TV, video, clock radio, t/c mkg, refrig, cook fac, toaster, ldry, doonas, linen reqd-fee, pillows], w/mach, lounge firepl, bbq, c/park (undercover), cots. **D $60 - $120, W $550 - $1,000**, (not yet classified).

B&B's/Guest Houses

★★★☆ **Scotts Head Bed & Breakfast**, (B&B), 16 Vista Way, ☎ 02 6569 8422, fax 02 6569 8499, 3 rms (1 suite) [shwr (1), spa bath (1), tlt (3), elec blkts, toaster], ldry, iron, iron brd, lounge (TV), lounge firepl, ✕, t/c mkg shared, bbq, non smoking rms. **BB ∮ $50, ♔♔ $70, ◊ $20**, AE BC MC VI.

SHELLHARBOUR NSW 2529

Pop 2,713. (103km S Sydney), See map on page 55, ref C4. Major residential centre on the Illawarra coast. Boating, Fishing, Swimming, Tennis.

Hotels/Motels

★★★☆ **Shellharbour Resort**, (M), Shellharbour Rd, 1km N of PO, ☎ 02 4295 1317, fax 02 4297 1040, 31 units [shwr, tlt, hairdry, a/c, elec blkts, tel, cable tv, clock radio, t/c mkg, refrig], ldry, conv fac, ⊠ (Open 7 days), pool, bbq, rm serv, dinner to unit, ☏, tennis, cots, non smoking units (8). **RO ∮ $95 - $110, ♔♔ $105 - $135, ♔♔♔ $120 - $140, ◊ $18 - $25**, ch con, AE BC DC EFT JCB MC VI.

★☆ **Ocean Beach Hotel**, (LH), 2 Addison St, ☎ 02 4296 1399, fax 02 4297 1486, (2 stry), 11 rms [shwr, tlt, TV, t/c mkg, refrig], ⊠, ☏, BC EFT MC VI.

B&B's/Guest Houses

★★★★ **Windradene Seaside Guest House**, (B&B), 29 Addison St, ☎ 02 4295 1074, fax 02 4297 7050, 4 rms [shwr, tlt (4), hairdry, c/fan, heat, TV, t/c mkg], ldry, iron, iron brd, lounge firepl, bbq, non smoking rms. **BB ∮ $90, ♔♔ $110 - $130, ◊ $35, RO ∮ $85, ♔♔ $100 - $110, ◊ $30**, ch con, BC MC VI.

SHELLY BEACH NSW 2261

Pop Part of Wyong, (95km N Sydney), See map on page 55, ref D6. Central Coast town between Toowoon Bay and Bateau Bay.

Self Catering Accommodation

★★★☆ **Shelly Beach Cabins**, Shelly Beach Rd, ☎ 02 4334 2900, fax 02 4334 7823, (2 stry gr fl), 28 cabins acc up to 6, [shwr, tlt, c/fan, heat, TV, video, t/c mkg, refrig, cook fac, micro, toaster, blkts, linen, pillows], bbq, ☏, cots. **D $93 - $173**, Min book applies, BC EFT MC VI.

Before you travel

Before a trip have your vehicle serviced and checked over to ensure reliable motoring. There are some checks you can make yourself, generally the procedure can be found in the vehicle owners manual.

SHOAL BAY NSW

See Port Stephens Region.

SHOALHAVEN HEADS NSW 2535

Pop 2,500. (129km S Sydney), See map on page 55, ref B4. South coast town situated where the Shoalhaven River meets the sea. It's a handy base from which to explore Seven Mile Beach National Park. Boating, Bowls, Bush Walking, Fishing, Surfing, Swimming, Tennis.

Hotels/Motels

★★★★ **Coolangatta Estate Resort**, (M), 1335 Bolong Rd, 12km NE of Nowra PO, ☎ 02 4448 7131, fax 02 4448 7997, 25 units (10 suites) [shwr, tlt, hairdry, a/c (14), fan, heat, elec blkts, tel, TV, clock radio, t/c mkg, refrig, mini bar], rec rm, conv fac, ✉, pool, bbq, plygr, bowls, golf, tennis, cots-fee. **RO** ♦ $90 - $150, ♦♦ $100 - $180, ◊ $20, ch con, Some units of a lower rating. Winery on site, Min book applies, AE BC DC EFT MC VI.

★★☆ **Shoalhaven Heads Motel Hotel**, (LMH), 51 River Rd, 500m S of PO, ☎ 02 4448 7125, 8 units [shwr, tlt, a/c, TV, t/c mkg, refrig, toaster], ✉, bbq, plygr, cots. **D** $75, **RO** ♦ $49.50 - $60.50, ♦♦ $55 - $66, ♦♦♦ $66 - $77, ◊ $11, Min book applies, BC MC VI.

SINGLETON NSW 2330

Pop 12,500. (248km N Sydney), See map on pages 52/53, ref J4. Main regional centre for the upper Hunter area. Scenic Drives, Vineyards, Wineries.

Hotels/Motels

★★★★☆ **Francis Phillip Motor Inn**, (M), 18 Maitland Rd, ☎ 02 6571 1991, fax 02 6571 2989, (2 stry gr fl) 35 units (4 suites) [bath (5), spa bath (6), a/c, tel, TV, t/c mkg, refrig, cook fac (5)], ldry, conv fac (2), ✉, bar, pool (salt water), rm serv, c/park (undercover), non smoking rms (21). **RO** ♦ $115.50 - $148.50, ♦♦ $126.50 - $160, **Suite D** $148.50 - $176, AE BC DC EFT MC VI.

★★★★ **Charbonnier Hallmark Inn**, (M), 44 Maitland Rd, 2.5km E of PO, ☎ 02 6572 2333, fax 02 6572 4975, (2 stry gr fl), 70 units (4 suites) [shwr, bath (68), tlt, hairdry, a/c, tel, TV, clock radio, t/c mkg, refrig, mini bar], lift, ldry, conv fac, ✉, pool, wading pool, sauna, spa, bbq, 24hr reception, rm serv, dinner to unit, tennis, cots-fee, non smoking rms (42). **RO** ♦ $110 - $125, ♦♦ $110 - $125, **Suite D** $170, ◊ $11, ch con, AE BC DC EFT JCB MC VI, ♿.

★★★★ **Mid City Motor Inn**, (M), 180 John St, 100m N of PO, ☎ 02 6572 2011, fax 02 6572 4414, (2 stry gr fl), 31 units (2 suites) [shwr, bath (8), tlt, hairdry, a/c, elec blkts, tel, cable tv, video, clock radio, t/c mkg, refrig, mini bar, cook fac (2)], ldry, iron, iron brd, ✉, pool (salt water), spa, rm serv, cots-fee. **RO** ♦ $129, ♦♦ $135, ♦♦♦ $147, ◊ $16, **Suite D** $156 - $197, ch con, AE BC DC JCB MC VI.

Operator Comment: See advertisement on page 346.

★★★☆ **Country Comfort Motel - Singleton**, (M), Cnr George & Hunter Sts, 500m E of PO, ☎ 02 6572 2388, fax 02 6572 2662, (2 stry gr fl) 49 units (1 suite) [shwr, tlt, a/c, heat, elec blkts, tel, TV, movie, clock radio, t/c mkg, refrig, mini bar], ldry, ✉, pool, rm serv, dinner to unit, cots-fee, non smoking units (10). **RO** ♦ $90 - $98, ♦♦ $90 - $98, ◊ $15, ch con, 23 units of a lower rating, AE BC DC MC VI.

★★★ **Benjamin Singleton Motel**, (M), 24 New England Hwy, 1km NE of PO, ☎ 02 6572 2922, fax 02 6571 2765, 10 units [shwr, tlt, a/c, elec blkts, tel, TV, movie, clock radio, t/c mkg, refrig, toaster], pool (salt water), cots-fee, Pets on application. **RO** ♦ $66 - $76, ♦♦ $75 - $86, ♦♦♦ $82 - $96, ◊ $10, AE BC DC EFT MC MCH VI.

★★☆ **Parkland Motel**, (M), New England Hwy, 4km N of bridge, ☎ 02 6572 3722, fax 02 6572 2151, 30 units [shwr, tlt, a/c, heat, tel, TV, video-fee, clock radio, t/c mkg, refrig, toaster], ldry, ✉ (Mon to Sat), pool (salt water), rm serv, cots-fee. **RO** ♦ $50, ♦♦ $60 - $65, ◊ $5, AE BC MC VI.

★ **Agricultural Motel Hotel**, (LMH), 4 Munro St, opposite railway station, ☎ 02 6572 1511, (2 stry) 12 units [shwr, tlt, fan, heat, elec blkts, TV, t/c mkg, refrig], ✉. **BLB** ♦ $35, ♦♦ $50, ◊ $12, BC EFT MC VI.

(Hotel Section), 13 rms [fan, heat, elec blkts], shared fac (shwr & tlt), lounge (TV). **BLB** ♦ $25, ♦♦ $40, ◊ $12.

★ **The Royal Hotel Motel**, (LMH), 84 George St, 500m S of PO, ☎ 02 6572 1194, fax 02 6572 3312, 7 units [shwr, tlt, c/fan, elec blkts, TV, t/c mkg, refrig, toaster], iron, iron brd, lounge (TV), ✉ (6 days), ✆. **RO** ♦ $35.20, ♦♦ $51.70, BC EFT.

(Hotel Section), 6 rms [c/fan, refrig (shared)], iron (available), iron brd (available), lounge (TV), ✉ (open 6 days), t/c mkg shared, ✆. **RO** ♦ $22, ♦♦ $35.20.

B&B's/Guest Houses

★★★★ **Fairoak Guest House**, (B&B), Raworth St, 1.5km E of PO, ☎ 02 6571 1586, 3 rms [shwr, bath (1), spa bath (1), tlt, a/c (3), c/fan, cent heat, tel, TV, clock radio], t/c mkg shared, bbq, cots. **BB** ♦ $77 - $82, ♦♦ $88 - $99, ch con, AE BC MC VI.

★★★★ **Singleton House Bed & Breakfast**, (B&B), 21 George St, 1km NE of PO, ☎ 02 6571 3152, fax 02 6571 5444, (2 stry), 3 rms [shwr, spa bath (1), tlt, hairdry, a/c, elec blkts, TV, video, clock radio, t/c mkg, refrig, ldry], ldry, iron, iron brd, lounge, pool (salt water), bbq, secure park, courtesy transfer, cots, non smoking rms. **BB** ♦ $85 - $95, ♦♦ $100 - $110, AE BC EFT MC VI.

Charbonnier HALLMARK INN

It's closer than you think!

★★★★ AAA Tourism Rating

★ 70 re-furbished rooms & suites
★ Baths in all units
★ Queen Size Beds
★ 24 Hr Reception/Room Service
★ Interconnecting Units
★ In House Video 24 Hours
★ Inside Access to all Units/Elevator
★ "Charades" Licensed Restaurant & Bar
★ Convention Facilities

Things to do...

Singleton, in the heart of the Hunter Valley, only 2.5 hours from Sydney & just 50 minutes from Newcastle - positioned between the vineyards of the Upper & Lower Hunter & only a 15 minute drive to the Wineries, is **"Closer than you think"**.

An ideal base for easy access to some of Australia's best vineyards, Historic Villages, Lake St. Clair, Barrington Tops, Upper Hunter Horse Studs, Mine Tours, Hot Air Balloon Flights

★★ Large Spacious Grounds
★★ Swimming Pool & Wading Pool
★★ BBQ - packs available
★★ Sail Covered Patio by Pool
★★ Full Size Floodlit Tennis Court
★★ Indoor Spa and Sauna
★★ **3pm Late Check-Out on Sunday**
★★ **1 to 3 night "Escape Holiday Packages"**

MID CITY MOTOR INN

AAAT ★★★★ SINGLETON

REGIONAL WINNER 98/99
Accommodation Industry Award for Excellence

WINNER 1998
Outstanding Business Award Best Restaurant

FINALIST 1998
NSW Tourism Award Superior Accom.

MINI BARS
Mini Bar

Non-smoking Rooms Available

Cocktail Bar

Licensed Restaurant

Business Facilities

Swimming Pool

In Room Movies

Limited Room Service

Laundry & Dry Cleaning

In Room Hairdryer

Heated Spa

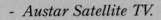

Visit the Hunter Region with its renowned vineyards and stay at Singleton's award winning Motor Inn, opposite shops overlooking the Hunter river and parkland. You can enjoy a delicious meal and fine wines of our region at Isabel's licensed restaurant.

- Austar Satellite TV.

RECEPTION

Sorry No Pets

Mention this advert for a 20% discount

Offer not to be used in conjunction with another discount or offer

MID CITY MOTOR INN
180 John St Singleton 2330
Ph: (02) 6572 2011 Fax (02) 6572 4414

4872AG

SMIGGIN HOLES NSW 2624

Pop Part of Perisher Val, (489km SW Sydney), See map on pages 52/53, ref F7. Snowy Mountains village which, along with Perisher Valley, is part of the Perisher Blue ski resort. Bush Walking, Scenic Drives, Snow Skiing.

Hotels/Motels

Smiggins, (LH), Kosciusko Rd, ☎ 02 6457 5375, (2 stry gr fl), 45 rms [shwr, tlt, cent heat, TV, video], ldry, dry rm, lounge (TV), conv fac, ⌧, sauna, t/c mkg shared, ski hire, cots-fee. **D $129 - $177, W $905 - $1,240**, ⚲ **$101 - $152**, AE BC DC MC VI.

★★★ **(Smiggins Hotel Chalet)**, (2 stry gr fl), 18 chalets [shwr, tlt, heat, TV, cook fac], ldry, dryer, lounge (TV), ☎, cots-fee, 4 rooms of a higher standard.

Other Accommodation

Astoria Alpine Chalet, (Lodge), Summit Rd, ☎ 02 6457 5365, fax 02 6457 5184, 20 rms acc up to 7, [shwr, tlt, cent heat, tel, t/c mkg], dry rm, lounge (TV), conv fac, ⌧, sauna, spa, cots. **High Season DBB** ⚲ **$95 - $180**, Min book applies, AE BC DC EFT VI.

Heidis Chalet, (Lodge), 6 Munyang Rd, 1km N of Perisher Valley PO, ☎ 02 9743 0911, (Multi-stry), 11 rms acc up to 6, [shwr, tlt, fire pl, cent heat], dry rm, lounge (TV & Video), ⌧, t/c mkg shared, cots. **DBB** ⚲⚲ **$180 - $330**, ⚲⚲⚲ **$180 - $320**, ch con, Minium booking June & October long weekends. BC MC VI.

Lodge 21 Ski Lodge, (Lodge), Munyang Rd, opposite Smiggins Hotel, ☎ 02 6457 5367, fax 02 6457 5142, (2 stry gr fl), 1 rm [shwr, tlt, heat, elec blkts, t/c mkg], lounge (TV), ✗, ✗, ☎, cots. **Low Season BB** ⚲ **$35, High Season DBB** ⚲ **$120**, MC VI.

Sponars Chalet, (Lodge), Kosciusko Rd, ☎ 02 6456 1111, fax 02 6456 1220, (Multi-stry), 32 rms acc up to 4, [shwr (26), tlt (26), heat, t/c mkg], lounge (TV), ⌧, pool, courtesy transfer, ☎, plygr, gym, ski hire. **DBB $65 - $145, $400 - $945**, ch con, Min book applies, AE BC MC VI.

The Lodge, (Lodge), 200m from Smiggins lifts, ☎ 02 6457 5341, fax 02 6457 5012, (2 stry gr fl), 1 rm acc up to 56, [ensuite, bath (6), cent heat], ldry, dry rm, lounge (TV), ⌧, sauna, spa (pool), t/c mkg shared, ☎, non smoking property. **DBB** ⚲ **$140 - $200**, ch con, AE BC DC MC VI.

SMITHS LAKE NSW 2428

Pop 850. See map on page 54, ref B8. Charming village on the shores of Smiths Lake in the beautiful Great Lakes area.

Self Catering Accommodation

★★★ **Sandpiper Lodges**, (HU), 113 Patsys Flat Rd, ☎ 02 6554 4050, 19 units acc up to 6, [shwr, bath (4), tlt, TV, video, refrig, cook fac, micro, d/wash (2)], ldry (2), bbq, canoeing-fee, tennis, **D $85 - $105, W $225 - $1,030**, Min book applies, BC EFT VI.

B&B's/Guest Houses

★★★ **Brookers B & B**, (B&B), 17 Macwood Rd, Pacific Palms 2428, 26km S of Forster/Tuncurry, ☎ 02 6554 4029, 1 rm (1 suite) [shwr, tlt, heat, TV, clock radio, t/c mkg, refrig, cook fac ltd, elec frypan, toaster], ldry, c/park. **BLB** ⚲ **$60 - $75,** ⚲⚲ **$75 - $85,** ⚲ **$12**.

SNOWY MOUNTAINS NSW

See Adaminaby, Anglers Reach, Berridale, Bombala, Buckenderra, Charlotte Pass, Cooma, Jindabyne, Nimmatabel, Perisher Valley, Smiggin Holes, Thredbo Village.

SOLDIERS POINT NSW

See Port Stephens Region.

SOUTH WEST ROCKS NSW 2431

Pop 3,500. (466km N Sydney), See map on page 54, ref C6. Mid-north coastal town magnificently positioned on the shores of Trial Bay, approached through the fertile dairy country that surrounds the Macleay River. Bowls, Bush Walking, Fishing, Golf, Sailing, Squash, Surfing, Swimming, Tennis, Wind Surfing.

Hotels/Motels

★★★☆ **Costa Rica Motel Resort**, (M), 134 Gregory St, 2km S of PO, ☎ 02 6566 6400, fax 02 6566 6802, 21 units [shwr, tlt, a/c, c/fan, heat, elec blkts, tel, TV, video (avail), clock radio, t/c mkg, refrig, cook fac (1), micro (6)], conv fac, ⌧, pool (salt water), sauna-fee, spa-fee, cook fac, bbq, squash-fee, tennis-fee. **D $115, RO** ⚲ **$61,** ⚲⚲ **$71,** ⚲ **$10**, AE BC DC MC VI.

SOUTH WEST ROCKS NSW continued...

★★☆ **Bay Motel**, (M), Prince of Wales Ave, ☎ 02 6566 6909, fax 02 6566 7088, 28 units [shwr, tlt, a/c, tel, cable tv, clock radio, t/c mkg, refrig], ⊠, cots-fee. **RO** ┆ **$50 - $70,** ┆┆ **$65 - $85,** ◊ **$11,** BC MC VI.

Motel South West Rocks, (M), 110 Gregory St, 1km S of PO, ☎ 02 6566 6330, fax 02 6566 5390, 22 units (0 suites) [a/c-cool, heat, fan, tel, TV, clock radio, t/c mkg, refrig, cook fac, ldry], conv fac, ⊠, pool, bbq, meals to unit, cots (fee), non smoking units (11). **D RO** ┆ **$41 - $62,** ◊ **$11,** ┆┆ **$52 - $73,** **Suite D $77 - $93.50,** ch con, weekly con, AE BC DC EFT MC MCH VI, (not yet classified).

Rockpool Motor Inn, (M), 45 McIntyre St, 1km E of PO, ☎ 02 6566 7755, fax 02 6566 7744, 28 units [ensuite, spa bath (5), a/c, cent heat, tel, TV, clock radio, t/c mkg, refrig, cook fac ltd], ldry, conv fac, ⊠, pool (outdoor), dinner to unit, c/park (undercover), cots, non smoking rms (27). **RO** ┆ **$65 - $130,** ┆┆ **$75 - $130,** ◊ **$15,** ch con, AE BC DC EFT MC VI, (not yet classified).

Self Catering Accommodation

★★★ **Pacific Court**, (HU), 33 Livingstone St, 200m E of PO, ☎ 1800 045 570, fax 02 6566 6356, 1 unit acc up to 5, [shwr, bath, tlt, hairdry, c/fan, heat, TV, video, clock radio, refrig, cook fac, micro, elec frypan, toaster, ldry, blkts, linen reqd, pillows], w/mach, iron, iron brd, c/park (garage). **W $270 - $740,** Min book applies, BC MC VI.

★★☆ **Birchgrove Terrace**, (HU), 8 Paragon Ave, 200m E of PO, ☎ 02 6566 6116, fax 02 6566 6165, (2 stry gr fl), 2 units acc up to 6, [shwr, bath, tlt, heat, TV, video, refrig, cook fac, micro, elec frypan, d/wash, toaster, linen reqd], w/mach, iron. **W $300 - $975,** Min book applies.

★★☆ **Main Beach**, (HU), 39 Livingstone St, 200m E of PO, ☎ 02 6566 6116, 6 units acc up to 5, [shwr, tlt, fan, heat, TV, refrig, cook fac, micro, toaster, linen reqd], ldry, bbq, c/park (carport). **W $225 - $925,** Min book applies.

★★☆ **Woody Wonder**, (HU), 49 Landsborough St, 300m SE of PO, ☎ 02 6566 6116, 2 units acc up to 5, [shwr, bath, tlt, fan, heat, TV, video (avail), refrig, cook fac, d/wash, toaster, linen reqd], ldry, c/park (garage). **W $245 - $730,** Min book all holiday times.

★★ **Trial Bay Lodges**, (HU), 24 Cardwell St, Arakoon, ☎ 02 6566 6594, 2 units acc up to 6, [shwr, tlt, fan, TV, clock radio, t/c mkg, refrig, cook fac, toaster, linen reqd], bbq, cots-fee, Min book applies.

★☆ **Ryder**, (HF), 22 McIntyre St, 400m E of PO, ☎ 02 6566 6116, 4 flats acc up to 9, [shwr, tlt, heat, TV, radio, refrig, cook fac, micro, toaster], ldry, bbq. **W $140 - $555,** Min book all holiday times.

Bayview Townhouses, (HU), 8 Bayview St, 500m SE of PO, ☎ 02 6566 6116, 1 unit acc up to 7, [shwr, bath, tlt, fan, heat, TV, video, clock radio, refrig, cook fac, toaster, linen reqd], ldry, bbq, c/park. **D $210 - $730,** Min book applies.

SOUTHERN HIGHLANDS NSW

See Berrima, Bowral, Bundanoon, Burrawong, Fitzroy Falls, Mittagong, Moss Vale, Robertson, Welby..

SPEERS POINT NSW 2284

Pop Part of Lake Macquarie, (170km N Sydney), See map on page 55, ref C8. Speers Point lies on the northern tip of Lake Macquarie on Warners and Cockle Bays.

Hotels/Motels

★★ **Pippi's at The Point**, (LH), The Esplanade & Main Rd, ☎ 02 4958 1022, fax 02 4958 3270, (2 stry), 15 rms [shwr, tlt, a/c-cool (3), heat, TV, t/c mkg, refrig], conv fac, ⊠, ☏, cots. **RO** ┆┆ **$66 - $77,** ◊ **$11,** ch con, AE BC DC EFT MC VI.

Night driving

Clear vision is most important at night, when visibility is restricted. The newer and cleaner the windscreen, the easier it is to see. Clean your headlights and headlight covers, as dirt can severely reduce the brightness of your headlights. Have your headlights adjusted to suit the heaviest load you are likely to carry.

If the glare of oncoming headlights is troubling you, look slightly to the left of the road, to avoid the glare. Look at the edge of the road to make sure that you don't run off. Never drive with your high beams on if there is a vehicle travelling in either direction within 200 metres in front of you.

Self Catering Accommodation

★★☆ **Secret Court**, (Apt), 2/40 Thompson Rd, 3km N of PO, ☎ 02 4950 8700, fax 02 4950 8699, (Multi-stry), 1 apt acc up to 4, [shwr, tlt, fan, heat, elec blkts, TV, clock radio, t/c mkg, refrig, cook fac, micro, toaster, ldry, blkts, doonas, linen, pillows], w/mach, lounge firepl, bbq, c/park (undercover). **D** ┆┆ **$110, W** ┆┆ **$650,** Min book applies, BC MC VI.

SPRINGFIELD NSW 2250

Pop Part of Gosford, (75km N Sydney), See map on page 56, ref E3. Suburb of Gosford.

B&B's/Guest Houses

Ibis House Bed & Breakfast, (B&B), 223 Wells St, 800m W of Barralong Rd Bridge, ☎ 02 4323 7747, fax 02 4323 7747, (2 stry gr fl), 2 rms (1 suite) [shwr, tlt, hairdry, c/fan, heat (1), TV, video, clock radio, t/c mkg, refrig, cook fac (1), micro], iron, iron brd, lounge firepl, bbq, dinner to unit, non smoking rms. **BLB** ┆┆ **$110, Suite BLB** ┆┆ **$125 - $150,** ◊ **$20,** pen con, BC MC VI, (not yet classified).

SPRINGWOOD NSW

See Blue Mountains Region.

ST ALBANS NSW 2775

Pop Nominal, (95km N Sydney), See map on page 56, ref C1. Small, historic village north of Wisemans Ferry on the Macdonald River. Bush Walking, Scenic Drives, Tennis.

Self Catering Accommodation

★★★☆ **Wellum's Lake Guest House**, (Cotg), Lot 1 Wellums Lake, Settlers Rd, 3km S of St Albans, ☎ 02 4568 2027, fax 02 4568 2027, 1 cotg acc up to 6, [shwr, tlt, a/c, radio, t/c mkg, refrig, micro, elec frypan, toaster, blkts, linen, pillows], iron, ✕, cafe, bbq, c/park. **D** ┆ **$95, W $230,** Min book applies, AE BC JCB MC VI.

★★★★ **(Homestead Section)**, 1 house acc up to 8, [shwr, spa bath, tlt, TV, refrig, cook fac, linen], lounge firepl, sauna. **D** ┆ **$125,** Min book applies.

B&B's/Guest Houses

★★★☆ **The Court House**, (GH), c1895. Upper Macdonald Rd, 100m W of St Albans Bridge, ☎ 02 4568 2042, fax 02 4568 2042, 4 rms [hairdry (2), fan, heat, cable tv, clock radio, refrig, cook fac], ldry, lounge (TV), conf fac, lounge firepl, spa, t/c mkg shared, bbq, tennis. **BB** ┆┆ **$145,** ┆┆┆┆ **$990,** Only group bookings on weekends, AE BC MC VI.

STANWELL PARK NSW

See Wollongong & Suburbs.

STEWARTS RIVER NSW 2443

Pop Nominal, See map on page 54, ref C7. Hinterland locality on the mid-north coast, on the banks of the Stewarts River.

Self Catering Accommodation

★★★★☆ **Penlan Cottage**, (Cotg), 661 Hannam Vale Rd, 30km S of Laurieton, ☎ 02 6556 7788, fax 02 6556 7778, 1 cotg [shwr, bath, tlt, hairdry, c/fan, heat, tel, TV, video, clock radio, t/c mkg, refrig, mini bar, cook fac, micro, elec frypan, toaster, blkts, doonas, linen, pillows], w/mach, dryer, iron, iron brd, TV rm, 24hr reception, courtesy transfer, non smoking property, Pets on application. **D** ┆┆ **$135, W** ┆┆ **$810,** ch con, fam con, AE BC DC JCB MC VI.

SUFFOLK PARK NSW 2481

Pop 2,550. (779km N Sydney), See map on page 54, ref E2. Far north coastal town just to the south of Byron Bay.

Hotels/Motels

★★★ **Tallow Beach Motel**, (M), Previously Sunaway Motel, 108 Alcorn St, 5km S of Byron Bay, ☎ 02 6685 3369, fax 02 6685 4568, 9 units [shwr, tlt, fan, heat, elec blkts, TV, clock radio, t/c mkg, refrig, cook fac (7)], pool-heated (solar), bbq, cots-fee. **RO** ┆ **$60 - $125,** ┆┆ **$60 - $125,** ◊ **$15,** Min book all holiday times, BC MC VI.

★★★ **The Park**, (LMH), 223 Broken Head Rd, 5km S of Byron Bay, ☎ 02 6685 3641, fax 02 6685 3553, 12 units [shwr, tlt, c/fan, heat, tel, TV, video-fee, clock radio, t/c mkg, refrig, cook fac (4), toaster], conv fac, ⊠, pool, plygr, cots-fee. **W $330 - $600, RO** ┆ **$55 - $88,** ┆┆ **$55 - $88,** ┆┆┆ **$66 - $99,** ◊ **$10,** ch con, Min book applies, AE BC MC VI, ♿.

SUNNY CORNER NSW

See Blue Mountains Region.

SURF BEACH NSW 2536

Pop Part of Batemans Bay, (284km S Sydney), See map on page 55, ref A6. Small community on Batemans Bay, situated between the larger centres of Batehaven and Malua Bay. Boating, Fishing, Golf, Scenic Drives, Surfing, Swimming.

Self Catering Accommodation

★★☆ **Sunrise Units**, (HU), 660 Beach Rd, ☎ 02 4471 1638, fax 02 4471 1363, 5 units acc up to 5, [shwr, bath, tlt, fan, heat, TV, clock radio, t/c mkg, refrig, cook fac, micro, toaster, ldry, blkts, doonas, linen reqd-fee, pillows], w/mach, bbq, c/park (undercover). **D $60 - $115, W $240 - $640**, BC MC VI.

B&B's/Guest Houses

★★★★☆ **Surf Beach Country Retreat**, (GH), 676 The Ridge Rd, 3km W of Surf Beach, ☎ 02 4471 3671, fax 02 4471 1671, (2 stry), 14 rms [shwr, spa bath (1), tlt, a/c (8), fan (9), c/fan (5), heat, elec blkts, TV, clock radio, t/c mkg, refrig (12), doonas], ldry, rec rm, lounge (TV), conf fac, ⊠, pool indoor heated, spa, ✆, bush walking, tennis. **BB ♦ $80 - $175, ♦♦ $110 - $220, ◊ $40**, ch con, AE BC DC EFT JCB MC VI,

Operator Comment: Please visit our Internet page - www.surfbeachretreat.com.au

★★★ **(Cabin Section)**, 3 cabins acc up to 5, (2 bedrm), [shwr, tlt, c/fan, TV, t/c mkg, refrig, cook fac ltd, micro, toaster, linen reqd-fee]. **D ♦♦ $90 - $150, ◊ $40 - $45.**

SUSSEX INLET NSW 2540

Pop 2,650. (188km S Sydney), See map on page 55, ref B5. Set on the western shores of the inlet that connects St Georges Basin with the sea, Sussex Inlet is a popular holiday destination for anglers and families keen on water sports. Boating, Bowls, Fishing, Golf, Swimming, Tennis.

Hotels/Motels

★★★☆ **Ranch Motel**, (M), 56 Iverson Rd, adjacent to Bowling Club, ☎ 02 4441 2007, 13 units [shwr, tlt, fan, heat, elec blkts, tel, TV, movie, clock radio, t/c mkg, refrig, cook fac (2), toaster], ldry, ⊠ (adjacent), pool, bbq, plygr, tennis, cots. **RO ♦ $62 - $82, ♦♦ $62 - $82, ◊ $12 - $10**, ch con, Min book Christmas Jan long w/ends and Easter, BC MC VI.

★★☆ **Bentley Waterfront Motel & Restaurant**, (M), 164 River Rd, 800m NW of PO, ☎ 02 4441 2052, 7 units [shwr, tlt, heat, elec blkts, TV, t/c mkg, refrig], pool indoor heated, bbq, jetty. **RO ♦♦ $57 - $76, ◊ $11**, weekly con, AE BC MC VI.

★★☆ **(Cottage Section)**, 7 cotgs acc up to 7, [shwr, tlt, a/c-cool, c/fan, heat, TV, clock radio, t/c mkg, refrig, cook fac ltd, micro, elec frypan, toaster, linen reqd-fee], ldry, w/mach, cots. **D ♦♦ $76 - $97, ◊ $11, W ♦♦ $349 - $660, ◊ $39.**

★★☆ **Sussex Inlet Motel**, (M), Jacobs Dve & River Rd, ☎ 02 4441 2711, (2 stry gr fl), 14 units [shwr, tlt, a/c, TV, t/c mkg, refrig], c/park. **RO ♦♦ $66, ◊ $11**, BC MC VI.

Self Catering Accommodation

★★★★ **Alonga Waterfront Cottages**, (Cotg), 166 River Rd, 750m N of PO, ☎ 02 4441 2046, fax 02 4441 3526, 8 cotgs acc up to 6, [shwr, tlt, a/c, TV (Video), clock radio, t/c mkg, refrig, cook fac, micro, toaster, linen reqd-fee], ldry, w/mach, dryer, iron, bbq (undercover), plygr, jetty, Small pets allowed in 1 cottage. **D ♦♦ $90 - $110, ◊ $10, W ♦♦ $330 - $770, ◊ $50**, BC MC VI.

★★★★ **(Alonga Waterfront Villas)**, 6 villas acc up to 4.

★★★☆ **Laguna Lodge Holiday Units**, (HU), 160 River Rd, 800m NW of PO, ☎ 02 4441 2315, fax 02 4441 3097, 6 units acc up to 4, [shwr, tlt, hairdry, fan, heat, elec blkts, TV, clock radio, refrig, cook fac, micro, elec frypan, toaster, linen reqd-fee], ldry, dryer-fee, iron, pool (salt water), bbq, jetty, non smoking property. **D ♦♦ $70 - $95, ◊ $10, W ♦♦ $295 - $690, ◊ $50**, ch con, Min book applies.

SUTTON NSW 2620

Pop Nominal, (286km SW Sydney), See map on pages 52/53, ref G6. Small village in the foothills of the Lake George Range, not far from the Australian Capital Territory border.

Hotels/Motels

AAA TOURISM Special Rates ★★★ **Rydges Resort Eagle Hawk Hill Canberra**, (M), Federal Hwy, ☎ 02 6241 6033, fax 02 6241 3691, 151 units (8 suites) [shwr, spa bath (8), tlt, a/c, heat, tel, TV, video, movie, clock radio, t/c mkg, refrig], ldry, rec rm, conv fac, ⊠ (2), pool, spa, bbq, 24hr reception, rm serv, plygr, gym, tennis, non smoking units. **RO ♦ $130, ♦♦ $130, ♦♦♦ $146.50, ◊ $16.50, Suite D $151**, AE BC DC MC VI.

Self Catering Accommodation

★★★★☆ **Goolabri Country Resort**, (SA), Previously Goolabri Park 100 Goolabri Dve, off Federal Hwy, 500m W of Sutton overpass, ☎ 02 6230 3294, fax 02 6230 3575, 12 serv apts acc up to 6, [shwr, tlt, heat, TV, video (6), clock radio, t/c mkg, refrig, cook fac, cook fac ltd (6), toaster], ldry, rec rm, conf fac, ✕ (Fri to Sat), pool-heated, bbq, ✆, plygr, golf, tennis, cots. **RO $154 - $204, ◊ $10**, Min book long w/ends, AE BC DC JCB MC VI.

SWAN BAY NSW

See Port Stephens Region.

SWANSEA NSW 2281

Pop 7,959. (113km N Sydney), See map on page 55, ref E4. Picturesque spot between the lake and the sea on the eastern shore of Lake Macquarie. Boating, Bowls, Fishing, Surfing, Swimming.

Hotels/Motels

★★★ **Black Swan Waterfront**, (M), 137 Bowman St, 300m S of PO, ☎ 02 4971 1392, fax 02 4972 1481, 12 units [shwr, tlt, hairdry, a/c, heat, tel, fax, TV, video, clock radio, t/c mkg, refrig], ldry, bbq, jetty (private), cots-fee. **RO** ⸙ **$55 - $75,** ⸙⸙ **$63 - $85,** ⸙⸙⸙ **$75 - $85,** ⸙ **$12**, AE BC DC EFT MC MCH VI.

★★★ **Blue Pacific Motor Inn**, (M), 82 Pacific Hwy, Blacksmiths 2281, 1km N of PO, ☎ 02 4971 1055, fax 02 4971 1296, (2 stry gr fl), 26 units (1 suite) [shwr, tlt, hairdry, a/c-cool (3), a/c (20), c/fan (16), heat (20), elec blkts, tel, TV, clock radio, t/c mkg, refrig, toaster (5)], ldry, conf fac, ⊠ (open 7 days), pool, rm serv, plygr, cots-fee, non smoking units (7). **RO** ⸙ **$60,** ⸙⸙ **$66 - $75,** ⸙ **$15, Suite RO $120 - $150**, ch con, AE BC DC MC MP VI.

★★☆ **Swansea Motel**, (M), 250 Old Pacific Hwy, 500m S of PO, ☎ 02 4971 1811, fax 02 4972 1417, 11 units [shwr, tlt, hairdry (6), a/c, fan, heat, elec blkts, tel, TV, video (available), clock radio, t/c mkg, refrig, cook fac (1), toaster], pool, bbq, meals to unit, cots, AE BC DC MC VI.

Self Catering Accommodation

★★★ **Selby Lakeside**, (Cotg), 66 Lakeside Dve, ☎ 02 4976 1414, 1 cotg acc up to 4, [shwr, bath, tlt, c/fan, fire pl, heat, elec blkts, TV, video, CD, t/c mkg, refrig, cook fac, micro, toaster, ldry, blkts, linen, pillows], iron, bbq, c/park (garage), cots. **D** ⸙⸙ **$85 - $135,** ⸙ **$20 - $40,** **W** ⸙⸙ **$550 - $625,** ⸙ **$140 - $160**.

TABOURIE LAKE NSW 2539

Pop 462. (244km S Sydney), See map on page 55, ref B5. South coast village nestled beside a lake of the same name. Boating, Canoeing, Fishing, Surfing, Swimming.

Hotels/Motels

★★★☆ **Tabourie Lake Motor Inn Resort**, (M), Princes Hwy, ☎ 02 4457 3133, fax 02 4457 3164, 20 units [shwr, tlt, hairdry, fan, heat, elec blkts, tel, TV, clock radio, t/c mkg, refrig, cook fac (16), toaster], ldry, rec rm, conv fac, ⊠, pool (solar heated), sauna, spa (heated), bbq, plygr, canoeing, gym, cots-fee. **W $365 - $840, RO** ⸙ **$58 - $95,** ⸙⸙ **$58 - $125,** ⸙ **$10**, AE BC DC MC VI, ⸙⸙.
Operator Comment: Please see our ad in Ulladulla Section.

Self Catering Accommodation

★★☆ **Sunseekers**, (HF), Cnr Beach & Dermal Sts, ☎ 02 4457 3017, fax 02 4457 3017, 5 flats acc up to 5, [shwr, tlt, fan, heat, TV, clock radio, refrig, cook fac, micro, linen reqd], ldry, bbq. **W $325 - $595**, Min book applies.

TALBINGO NSW 2720

Pop 300. (477km SW Sydney), See map on pages 52/53, ref F7. Small town in the western foothills of the Snowy Mountains.

★★★ **Country Club Motel**, (M), Bridle St, ☎ 02 6949 5260, fax 02 6949 5432, 6 units [shwr, tlt, hairdry, a/c-cool, c/fan, heat, elec blkts, tel, fax, TV, video, clock radio, t/c mkg, refrig, cook fac, toaster], ldry, conv fac, ⊠ (Tuesday to Sunday), ⸙, golf, tennis, cots. **RO** ⸙ **$70,** ⸙⸙ **$82,** ⸙ **$20**, ch con, BC EFT MC VI, ⸙⸙.

TAMWORTH NSW 2340

Pop 31,850. (420km NW Sydney), See map on pages 52/53, ref J3. Tamworth is billed as the Country Music Capital of Australia, famous for its Golden Guitar Awards and annual Australian Country Music Festival. Bowls, Golf, Scenic Drives, Swimming, Tennis. See also Duri.

Hotels/Motels

★★★★☆ **All Settlers Motor Inn**, (M), 191 Goonoo Goonoo Rd (Sydney Rd), 2km S of PO, ☎ 02 6762 1566, fax 02 6762 2316, 33 units [shwr, tlt, bath, spa bath (13), tlt, hairdry, a/c, heat, elec blkts, tel, TV, movie, clock radio, t/c mkg, refrig, mini bar, toaster], ldry, iron, iron brd, pool (salt water), bbq, rm serv, dinner to unit, car wash, cots-fee, non smoking units (22). **RO** ⸙ **$85 - $132,** ⸙⸙ **$95 - $155,** ⸙ **$15**, AE BC DC EFT JCB MC MP VI.

★★★★☆ **The Powerhouse Boutique Hotel**, (M), New England Hwy, 1.4km NE of PO, ☎ 02 6766 7000, fax 02 6766 7748, (2 stry gr fl), 81 units (8 suites) [shwr, bath, spa bath (24), tlt, hairdry, a/c, fan, tel, TV, video, clock radio, t/c mkg, refrig, mini bar, cook fac (2), toaster], ldry, conv fac, ⊠ (2), pool, sauna, spa, bbq, 24hr reception, rm serv, ⸙, plygr, gym, cots-fee. **RO** ⸙ **$116 - $121,** ⸙⸙ **$116 - $121,** ⸙⸙⸙ **$126.50 - $143,** ⸙ **$10 - $20, Suite D $176 - $198**, 25 units ★★★★. 8 rooms yet to be assessed. AE BC DC MC MP VI, ⸙⸙.

★★★★ **Golf Links Motel**, (M), Cnr Bridge St & Mahony Ave, N of golf club, ☎ 02 6762 0505, fax 02 6762 2247, (2 stry gr fl), 21 units (6 suites) [shwr, tlt, hairdry, a/c, elec blkts, tel, cable tv, clock radio, t/c mkg, refrig, toaster], ldry, ✕ (Mon to Sat), pool (salt water), dinner to unit (5 nights), cots. **RO** ⸙ **$75 - $95,** ⸙⸙ **$80 - $115,** ⸙ **$10 - $15, Suite D $95 - $150**, AE BC DC EFT MC VI.

GOLF LINKS MOTEL

AAAT ★★★★
260 Bridge Street, Tamworth
Phone: (02) 6762 0505
Fax: (02) 6762 2247

★ 21 Spacious Units
★ Family and Executive Suites with Spas
★ Split System Air Conditioning
★ Adjacent to Golf Course
★ Showground, Leagues Club
★ Salt Water Pool
★ Discounted Rates for Members

FREE AUSTAR IN ROOM SATELLITE TV

CADMAN MOTOR INN TAMWORTH

New England Highway (Sydney Side) Phone: (02) 6765 3333 Fax: (02) 6765 8287

Privately owned and operated by Steve & Lee Crelley
★★★☆ AAAT

• All ground floor units • Saltwater pool • 14 units • Close to sporting grounds • Walk to shops & clubs • Disabled unit/family unit • BBQ area • Courtesy pick up at station, airport & bus • Phone • r/c air/c • heat • tea/coffee & toaster. *FRIENDLY, PERSONAL SERVICE*

ABRAHAM LINCOLN MOTEL

New England Hwy (Armidale side) TAMWORTH
Email: abrahamlincoln@optusnet.com

GOLDEN CHAIN

• 15 quiet/clean ground floor units
• 12 non-smoking Units
• Queen Beds
• Salt water pool
• Adjacent Power House Function Centre
• Walking distance CBD
• R/C Air/Cond, Heating
• Free Pay TV

☎ **(02) 6766 1233**
Your Hosts: Christina and Klaas
1800 028 225
Fax: 02 6766 1613

AUSTAR
IN ROOM SATELLITE TV

Acacia Motel

235 New England Highway, Tamworth
Phone: (02) 6762 2277
Fax: (02) 6762 2284

• 1 & 2 Bedroom Units with cooking facilities available
• Heating and Cooling
• Pool, BBQ, and Play area.
• Close to Leagues Club.
Your Hosts Lorraine & Colin Adams

AUSTAR
Free Austar TV
in each unit

 GOLDEN CHAIN ★★★☆ **Abraham Lincoln**, (M), 343 Armidale Rd (New England Hwy), 1.5 km NE of PO, ☎ 02 6766 1233, fax 02 6766 1613, 15 units [shwr, tlt, hairdry, a/c, c/fan, heat, elec blkts, tel, TV, clock radio, t/c mkg, refrig, mini bar, toaster], ldry-fee, iron, iron brd, pool (salt water), cots-fee, non smoking units (12). RO ♦ $64, ♦♦ $75 - $78, ♀ $11, ch con, AE BC DC EFT MC VI, &.

★★★☆ **Acacia Motel**, (M), 235 New England Hwy, 2km S of PO, ☎ 02 6762 2277, fax 02 6762 2284, 20 units [shwr, tlt, hairdry (extra avail) (7), a/c, heat, elec blkts, tel, cable tv (Austar - free), clock radio, t/c mkg, refrig, cook fac (11), micro (12), toaster], ldry, pool (salt water), bbq, plygr, cots, non smoking rms (7). RO ♦ $50 - $60, ♦♦ $55 - $70, ♦♦♦ $68 - $75, ♀ $8 - $10, ch con, AE BC DC EFT MC VI.

  ★★★☆ **Alandale Flag Inn**, (M), Cnr New England Hwy & Burgmanns Ln, 6km S of PO, ☎ 02 6765 7922, fax 02 6765 2446, 25 units [shwr, tlt, a/c, elec blkts, tel, cable tv, video (avail), clock radio, t/c mkg, refrig], ldry, conv fac, ⊠, pool (salt water), spa, bbq, dinner to unit, plygr, tennis (half court), cots, non smoking units (18). RO ♦ $74.80 - $88, ♦♦ $83.60 - $100.10, ♦♦♦ $92.40 - $112.20, ch con, pen con, AE BC DC EFT MC MP VI, &.

 ★★★☆ **Ashby on Ebsworth Restaurant and Country Inn**, (M), New England Hwy, 1km S of PO, ☎ 02 6762 0033, fax 02 6762 0234, (2 stry gr fl), 21 units [shwr, spa bath (1), tlt, hairdry, a/c, heat, elec blkts, tel, TV, video, clock radio, t/c mkg, refrig, mini bar, toaster], ldry, ⊠, pool-heated (salt water), spa, rm serv, c/park (undercover), cots, non smoking units (2). RO ♦ $107, ♦♦ $107, ♦♦♦ $119, ♀ $12 - $20, ch con, AE BC DC EFT MC VI, &.

★★★☆ **Cadman Motor Inn**, (M), 103 Ebsworth St (New England Hwy), 1km S of PO, ☎ 02 6765 3333, fax 02 6765 8287, 14 units [shwr, tlt, hairdry, a/c, elec blkts, tel, TV, clock radio, t/c mkg, refrig, toaster], ldry, iron, iron brd, pool (salt water), bbq, dinner to unit (on request), courtesy transfer, cots-fee, non smoking units (7). RO ♦ $50 - $55, ♦♦ $60.50 - $66, ♦♦♦ $65 - $75, ♀ $5 - $8, AE BC EFT MC VI, &.

For Accommodation Booking information - see page 27

Stagecoach Inn Motel
TAMWORTH

- Queen Beds
- Free AUSTAR (Pay TV)
- EFTPOS Available
- Large Family Rooms
- Big Country Breakfast
- BBQs
- Salt Pool
- Safe Kiddies Playground
- Colour TV
- Video & Book Library
- DD Phones
- Guest Laundry
- Trailer Parking
- All Ground Floor & At Door Parking

AAA Tourism ★★★☆

02 6766 6311

Fax: 02 6766 6764
Email: stagecoach@bigpond.com

Your Hosts: Betty & Steve Stathis
401 Armidale Road (New England Hwy),
TAMWORTH NSW 2340

"Comfort at an affordable price"

5182AG

Tamworth Towers
on Ebsworth

- Tamworth's largest Motor Inn - 108 rooms
- 600m to city centre
- Close to sporting facilities, race course, showground & clubs
- Ground floor rooms
- Family units
- Spa suites
- Large swimming pool
- Oxley Function Centre (Weddings & Conferences)
- Venetians Cafe
- Newly refurbished property
- Guest laundry

Venetians cafe has a young team of talented & innovative chefs using the best fresh local produce to create a modern and exciting menu. All tastes are catered for and our little friends have their own special menu.

Cnr Oxley Highway and Ebsworth Street
Ph: (02) 6765 8361
Fax: (02) 6762 0894

5186AG

Town & Country
MOTOR INN
217 New England Highway (Sydney Side) Tamworth 2340

- Deluxe Units with Queen size beds
- Large Family units • Pool, spa, BBQ & Gazebo
- Close to Bowling Club, Golf Club, Leagues Club
- Close to New Entertainment Complex
- Courtesy Transport

AUSTAR

GOLDEN CHAIN

Ph: (02) 6765 3244   Fax: (02) 6762 0118
Reservations only 1800 028 506

Country Style Hospitality
Your Hosts Pam & Peter Varney

5194ag

★★★☆ **City Sider Motor Inn**, (M), 237 Marius St (New England Hwy), 500m N of PO, ☎ 02 6766 4777, fax 02 6766 4769, (2 stry gr fl), 38 units [shwr, spa bath (1), tlt, hairdry, a/c, elec blkts, tel, cable tv, clock radio, t/c mkg, refrig, toaster], ldry, ✉ (Mon to Sat), pool, spa (heated), rm serv, dinner to unit, cots-fee, non smoking rms (12). **RO ⋔ $69 - $85, ⋔ $80 - $95, ⋔ $11**, AE BC DC MC VI.

★★★☆ **Country Comfort - Tamworth**, (M), 293 Marius St (New England Hwy), 1km N of PO, ☎ 02 6766 2903, fax 02 6766 6317, 60 units (9 suites) [shwr, bath (15), spa bath (7), tlt, hairdry, a/c, elec blkts, tel, TV, video (avail), movie, clock radio, t/c mkg, refrig, mini bar, micro (10), toaster], ldry, iron, iron brd, conv fac, ✉, pool, spa, bbq, rm serv, dinner to unit, car wash, cots-fee, non smoking rms (20). **RO ⋔ $89, ⋔ $89, ⋔ $15**, ch con, 9 units of a higher standard. AE BC DC EFT MC VI, ⅋.

★★★☆ **Stagecoach Inn**, (M), 401 Armidale Rd (New England Hwy), 2km N of PO, ☎ 02 6766 6311, fax 02 6766 6764, 24 units [shwr, tlt, a/c-cool, heat, elec blkts, tel, fax, video (avail), movie, clock radio, t/c mkg, refrig, toaster], ldry, pool, bbq, plygr, cots, non smoking units (8), **RO ⋔ $57 - $70, ⋔ $63 - $75, ⋔ $10**, 6 family rooms of a lower rating. AE BC DC MC MCH VI.

★★★☆ **Tamwell Motel**, (M), 121 Johnston St, 2.5km N of PO, opposite Hospital, ☎ 02 6766 2800, fax 02 6766 5260, (2 stry gr fl), 16 units [shwr, tlt, hairdry, a/c, elec blkts, tel, TV, clock radio, t/c mkg, refrig, mini bar, toaster], ldry, iron, iron brd, ✗, rm serv, dinner to unit, secure park (under cover), ☎, cots-fee, non smoking property. **RO ⋔ $86.90, ⋔ $97.90, ⋔ $108.90, ⋔ $12**, ch con, AE BC DC MC VI, ⅋.

★★★☆ **Tamworth Flag Inn**, (M), 236 Goonoo Goonoo Rd (Sydney Rd), 2.5km S of PO, ☎ 02 6765 7022, fax 02 6765 8818, (2 stry gr fl), 60 units (2 suites) [shwr, bath (6), spa bath (2), tlt, hairdry, a/c, elec blkts, tel, cable tv, clock radio, t/c mkg, refrig, mini bar, micro (2), toaster], ldry, conv fac, ✉, pool, spa, rm serv, dinner to unit, plygr, cots-fee, non smoking units (25). **RO ⋔ $100 - $115, ⋔ $105 - $120, ⋔ $6 - $12, Suite D $155 - $170**, 8 units of a higher standard 17 units of a lower rating. AE BC DC EFT MC MP VI.

★★★☆ **Tamworth Motor Inn**, (M), 212 Goonoo Goonoo Rd, 2km S of PO, ☎ 02 6765 4633, fax 02 6765 4510, 29 units [shwr, tlt, a/c-cool, heat, elec blkts, tel, cable tv, clock radio, t/c mkg, refrig, toaster], ldry, conv fac, ✉, pool (salt water), spa, bbq, rm serv, dinner to unit, cots, non smoking units (10). **RO ⋔ $80, ⋔ $85, ⋔ $95 - $108, ⋔ $13**, 7 family units of a lower rating. AE BC DC EFT MC MP VI, ⅋.

★★★☆ **Tamworth Towers Motor Inn**, (M), Cnr Oxley Hwy & Ebsworth St, 1km S of PO, ☎ 02 6765 8361, fax 02 6762 0894, (2 stry gr fl), 108 units [shwr, spa bath (3), tlt, a/c, tel, TV, video-fee, clock radio, t/c mkg, refrig, mini bar], ldry, conv fac, cafe, pool, rm serv, cots, non smoking units (55). **RO ⋔ $84 - $94, ⋔ $89 - $99, ⋔ $99 - $109, ⋔ $10**, ch con, 26 units ★★★. AE BC DC MC VI.

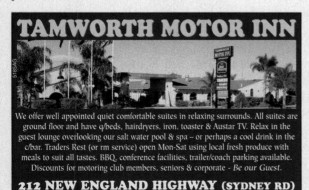

★★★☆ **Thunderbird Gardens Motel**, (M), Armidale Rd (New England Hwy), 6km N of PO, ☎ 02 6760 9200, fax 02 6760 9338, 22 units (3 suites) [shwr, bath (4), spa bath (1), tlt, hairdry, a/c, elec blkts, tel, TV, clock radio, t/c mkg, refrig, toaster], ldry, iron, iron brd, rec rm, conv fac, pool, bbq, dinner to unit, trailer park, car wash, cots, non smoking units (8). **RO** ♦ **$46**, ♦♦ **$56**, ◊ **$9**, **Suite D** ♦♦ **$90**, ch con, AE BC DC EFT MC MCH VI.

Operator Comment: "TAMWORTHS BEST KEPT SECRET".

★★★☆ **Town & Country Motor Inn**, (M), 217 Goonoo Goonoo Rd (New England Hwy), 2km S of PO, ☎ 02 6765 3244, fax 02 6762 0118, 18 units [shwr, tlt, a/c-cool, heat, elec blkts, tel, cable tv, video-fee, clock radio, t/c mkg, refrig, toaster], ldry, pool (salt water), spa, bbq, rm serv, dinner to unit (7 rms), courtesy transfer, cots-fee, non smoking units (6). **RO** ♦ **$60.50 - $72.50**, ♦♦ **$71.50 - $81.50**, ◊ **$6 - $11**, ch con, 5 units of a higher standard, 5 units of a lower rating. AE BC DC EFT MC MP VI.

★★★ **Colonial Motor Inn**, (M), 519 Armidale Rd (New England Hwy), 3km N of PO, ☎ 02 6766 1866, fax 02 6766 5145, 33 units [shwr, bath (2), tlt, hairdry, a/c, elec blkts, tel, cable tv, clock radio, t/c mkg, refrig], ldry, ⊠ (Mon to Sat), pool, bbq, rm serv, dinner to unit (Mon to Sat), cots, non smoking units (10). **RO** ♦ **$55**, ♦♦ **$61 - $66**, ◊ **$11**, ch con, AE BC DC EFT MC VI, ♿.

★★★ **Country Capital Motel**, (M), 193 Goonoo Goonoo Rd (Sydney Rd), 2km S of PO, ☎ 02 6765 5966, fax 02 6765 5812, (2 stry gr fl), 31 units (6 suites) [shwr, tlt, a/c-cool, heat, tel, TV, clock radio, t/c mkg, refrig, toaster], ldry, ⊠ (Mon to Thur), pool (salt water), plygr, cots-fee. **BLB** ♦ **$55 - $65**, ♦♦ **$55 - $65**, ♦♦♦ **$82.50 - $97.50**, ◊ **$7.50 - $27.50**, **Suite D** **$100 - $120**, AE BC DC MC VI.

★★★ **Golden Grain Motor Inn**, (M), New England Hwy, 2km S of PO, ☎ 02 6765 3599, fax 02 6762 0667, 13 units [shwr, bath (4), tlt, hairdry (4), a/c-cool, c/fan (9), heat, elec blkts, tel, TV, video-fee, movie, clock radio, t/c mkg, refrig, toaster], ldry, dryer-fee, iron, iron brd, pool (salt water), rm serv, dinner to unit, cots-fee, non smoking units (5). **RO** ♦ **$50 - $60**, ♦♦ **$54 - $66**, ♦♦♦ **$60 - $88**, ◊ **$10**, 4 units of a higher standard. AE BC DC EFT MC MP VI.

★★★ **Grande Motel**, (M), 117 Goonoo Goonoo Rd (New England Hwy), 1.5km S of PO, ☎ 02 6765 4444, fax 02 6762 0330, 10 units [shwr, tlt, a/c-cool, heat, elec blkts, tel, TV, video-fee, clock radio, t/c mkg, refrig, toaster], ldry-fee, iron, iron brd, pool (salt water), bbq, meals to unit (7 rms), courtesy transfer, cots-fee. **RO** ♦ **$50 - $60**, ♦♦ **$50 - $60**, ◊ **$10**, AE BC DC MC VI.

★★★ **Magnolia Motor Inn**, (M), Gunnedah Rd, 4km W of PO, ☎ 02 6760 7103, fax 02 6760 7276, 9 units [shwr, tlt, hairdry, a/c, elec blkts, tel, TV, clock radio, t/c mkg, refrig, toaster], iron, iron brd, meals avail, plygr, cots-fee. **RO** ♦ **$55 - $65**, ♦♦ **$64 - $75**, ◊ **$8**, ch con, BC MC VI.

★★★ **Motabelle**, (LMH), 303 Goonoo Goonoo Rd, (New England Hwy), 3km S of PO, ☎ 02 6765 7274, fax 02 6765 7274, 9 units [shwr, tlt, a/c-cool, heat, elec blkts, TV, clock radio, t/c mkg, refrig, cook fac, micro, toaster], bbq, cots-fee. **RO** ♦ **$52 - $60**, ♦♦ **$60 - $66**, ◊ **$7 - $11**, ch con, AE BC DC EFT MC MCH VI.

★★★ **Roydons Motel**, (M), Cnr New England Hwy & Church St, 1km S of PO, ☎ 02 6765 7355, fax 02 6765 7542, 12 units [shwr, tlt, a/c-cool, heat, elec blkts, tel, TV, video, clock radio, t/c mkg, refrig], cots. **RO** ♦ **$49.50**, ♦♦ **$55 - $60.50**, ♦♦♦ **$63.80 - $66**, ◊ **$10**, ch con, BC MC VI.

★★☆ **Almond Inn Motel**, (M), 389 Armidale Rd (New England Hwy), 2km N of PO, ☎ 02 6766 1088, fax 02 6766 9837, 27 units [shwr, spa bath (1), tlt, hairdry (14), a/c-cool, c/fan (14), heat (7), elec blkts, tel, TV, video (avail), clock radio, t/c mkg, refrig, micro (8)], ldry, iron, iron brd, ✗, pool, rm serv, cots, non smoking rms (13). **D** **$80 - $109**, **RO** ♦♦ **$53 - $95**, ◊ **$6**, 5 units of a higher standard, 7 units of a lower rating. AE BC DC EFT MC VI.

★★☆ **City Gate Motel**, (M), 300 New England Hwy, 2.2km S of PO, ☎ 02 6765 8368, fax 02 6765 8562, 11 units [shwr, tlt, a/c, heat, elec blkts, tel, TV, t/c mkg, refrig], pool, bbq, dinner to unit (5 nights), plygr, cots. **RO** ♦ **$50**, ♦♦ **$54 - $70**, ♦♦♦♦ **$80**, AE BC EFT MC VI.

★★☆ **Rileys Motel Australia**, (M), 354 New England Hwy, 3km S of PO, ☎ 02 6765 9258, fax 02 6765 4496, 31 units [shwr, tlt, a/c, tel, TV, clock radio, t/c mkg, refrig], ⊠ (5 nights), pool, dinner to unit (5 nights). BLB ♦ $49.50 - $120, ♦♦ $49.50 - $120, ◊ $14.30, AE BC DC MC VI.

★★ **Marion Motel**, (M), 159 Goonoo Goonoo Rd (New England Hwy), 2km S of PO, ☎ 02 6765 5585, fax 02 6762 5380, 14 units (2 suites) [shwr, tlt, a/c-cool, heat, elec blkts, TV, clock radio, t/c mkg, refrig, ldry], ldry-fee, bbq, ✆, cots. RO ♦ $44 - $48.40, ♦♦ $49.50 - $53.90, ♦♦♦ $60.50, ◊ $11, Suite D $71.50 - $82.50, ch con, 2 units of a higher rating, AE BC DC EFT MC MCH VI.

★☆ **Central Hotel**, (LH), Cnr Peel & Brisbane Sts, ☎ 02 6762 0686, fax 03 6761 2626, (Multi-stry), 36 rms [ensuite (6), shwr (6), tlt (8), fan, elec blkts, t/c mkg], lift, lounge (TV), ⊠ (Mon to Sat), c/park (limited), cots. RO ♦ $20 - $38.50, ♦♦ $44 - $49.50, 5 bunk rooms not rated. AE BC DC MC VI.

★☆ **Southgate Inn**, (LH), Cnr Kathleen & Kent Sts, 3km SW of PO, ☎ 02 6765 7999, 6 rms [shwr, tlt, a/c, heat, TV, clock radio, t/c mkg, refrig, toaster], ✗ (3 rms), ✆. RO ♦ $52.80, ♦♦ $58.30 - $63.80, ◊ $11, BC EFT MC VI.

Tamworth Hotel, (LH), 147 Marius St, 300m N of PO, ☎ 02 6766 2923, fax 02 6766 2847, (2 stry), 11 rms [elec blkts, t/c mkg], ⊠. RO ♦ $28, ♦♦ $38, BC MC VI.

Self Catering Accommodation

★★★★☆ **Quest Tamworth**, (Apt), 327 Armidale Rd, 1.4km N from PO, ☎ 02 6761 2366, fax 02 6761 2766, 40 apts (1, 2 & 3 bedrm), [a/c, tel, video-fee, clock radio, refrig, cook fac, micro, d/wash, blkts, linen], w/mach, dryer, lounge (TV), conf fac, ✗, ✗, pool (outdoor/solar), t/c mkg shared, bbq, cots-fee. D $130 - $192, ◊ $17, AE BC DC EFT MC VI.

★★★★☆ **The Roseville Apartments**, (SA), Cnr Ebsworth & Gipps St, 1km W of PO, ☎ 02 6765 3644, fax 02 6762 0420, (2 stry gr fl), 10 serv apts (8 suites) [shwr, bath, spa bath (1), tlt, hairdry, a/c-cool, heat, elec blkts, tel, TV, video, clock radio, t/c mkg, refrig, cook fac, micro, elec frypan, toaster, ldry (in unit)], w/mach, dryer, pool, bbq, secure park, cots-fee. Suite D ♦ $99 - $220, ♦♦ $99 - $220, ◊ $6 - $11, ch con, AE BC DC MC VI.

B&B's/Guest Houses

★★★★ **Beethovens Bed & Breakfast**, (B&B), 66 Napier St, 1km E of PO, ☎ 02 6766 2735, fax 02 6766 7523, 4 rms [shwr, bath (1), tlt, hairdry, a/c, cent heat, elec blkts, tel, TV, clock radio], business centre, conf fac, lounge firepl, t/c mkg shared, bbq, non smoking property. BB ♦ $100 - $160, ♦♦ $120 - $200, AE BC EFT MC VI.

★★★☆ **Helen's Bed & Breakfast Tamworth**, (B&B), Fresa Granja, RMB 516F, New England Hwy, 10km S of Tamworth, ☎ 02 6765 6766, fax 02 6766 7285, 4 rms (1 suite) [hairdry, evap cool, elec blkts-fee, TV (2), clock radio, t/c mkg], shared fac (bath, shwr, tlt), iron, iron brd, cook fac, bbq, dinner to unit, non smoking rms. BB ♦ $45, ♦♦ $85, ch con, fam con.

★★★☆ **Meldorn Pottery Bed & Breakfast**, (B&B), RMB 211C Meldorn La, 9km NW of Tamworth, ☎ 02 6761 8319, fax 02 6761 8319, 3 rms [hairdry, fan, elec blkts, tel, clock radio], ldry, iron, iron brd, lounge (TV), lounge firepl, ✗, t/c mkg shared, bbq, non smoking property. BB ♦ $65, ♦♦ $85, BC MC VI.

TARAGO NSW 2580

Pop Nominal, (216km S Sydney), See map on page 55, ref A5. Sleepy little village between Goulburn and Braidwood.

Hotels/Motels

Loaded Dog Hotel, (LH), Limited facilities, Wallace St, 25m N of PO, ☎ 02 4849 4499, fax 02 4849 4603, (2 stry), 10 rms [elec blkts, TV (7)], ⊠, t/c mkg shared, bbq, ✆, cots. BB ♦ $38.50, ♦♦ $71.50, EFT.

TARALGA NSW 2580

Pop 350. (222km SW Sydney), See map on page 55, ref A3. Picturesque village with poplar-lined streets that sprang up during the 1820s. The surrounding country produces fat lambs, fine wool, beef, berries and potatoes. Bush Walking, Fishing, Golf, Horse Riding, Tennis.

B&B's/Guest Houses

Taralga's Lilac Cottage B & B, (B&B), 28 Orchard St, opposite PO, ☎ 02 4840 2295, fax 02 4840 2410, 3 rms [ensuite, hairdry, fan, elec blkts, clock radio], lounge (TV), lounge firepl, t/c mkg shared, non smoking property. BB ♦ $75 - $105, ♦♦ $95 - $125, BC MC VI, (not yet classified).

Walton-Green Bed & Breakfast, (B&B), 35 Orchard St, ☎ 02 4840 2268, (2 stry), 3 rms [heat, clock radio], ldry, lounge firepl. BB ♦ $60, ♦♦ $90 - $100, ◊ $55, (not yet classified).

TARANA NSW

See Blue Mountains Region.

TARCUTTA NSW 2652

Pop 250. (424km SW Sydney), See map on pages 52/53, ref F6. Small town on the Hume Highway between Gundagai and Holbrook.

Hotels/Motels

★★☆ **Tarcutta Halfway Motor Inn**, (M), Sydney St, 1km E of PO, ☎ 02 6928 7294, fax 02 6928 7128, 25 units [shwr, tlt, a/c, tel, TV, clock radio, t/c mkg, refrig, toaster], ldry, ⊠, pool, bbq, plygr, cots-fee, non smoking units. RO ♦ $49.50, ♦♦ $55, ♦♦♦ $66, AE BC DC EFT MC VI.

TAREE NSW 2430

Pop 16,700. (312km N Sydney), See map on page 54, ref B7. Taree straddles the Manning River and is the commercial centre of the Manning Valley. Bowls, Fishing, Golf, Sailing, Scenic Drives, Surfing, Swimming, Tennis. See also Tinonee & Wingham.

Hotels/Motels

★★★☆ **Alabaster Motor Inn**, (M), 23-25 Oxley St, 2.4km N of PO, ☎ 02 6552 1455, fax 02 6551 2751, (2 stry gr fl), 20 units [shwr, tlt, hairdry, a/c, elec blkts, tel, TV, video, movie, clock radio, t/c mkg, refrig], ldry, iron brd, ⊠, pool, bbq, dinner to unit, plygr, cots-fee. RO ♦ $77 - $83, ♦♦ $85 - $93, ◊ $11, AE BC DC EFT JCB MC MP VI.

★★★☆ **Best Western Caravilla Motor Inn**, (M), 33 Victoria St (Pacific Hwy), 800m N of PO, ☎ 02 6552 1822, fax 02 6552 1904, 27 units [shwr, tlt, hairdry, a/c, tel, movie, clock radio, t/c mkg, refrig, toaster], iron, iron brd, ⊠ (Mon to Sat), pool (salt water), dinner to unit, plygr, cots, non smoking units (6). RO ♦ $73 - $85, ♦♦ $73 - $85, ◊ $12, AE BC DC MC VI.

★★★☆ **City Centre Motor Inn**, (M), 4 Crescent Ave, 1.5km N of PO, ☎ 02 6552 5244, fax 02 6551 3186, (2 stry gr fl), 20 units [shwr, tlt, hairdry, a/c, elec blkts, tel, TV, video, movie, clock radio, t/c mkg, refrig], iron, iron brd, pool (salt water), bbq, rm serv, dinner to unit, cots-fee, non smoking units (7). **D $110 - $121, RO ♦ $74 - $84, ♦♦ $80 - $90, ♦♦♦ $80 - $90,** AE BC DC EFT JCB MC MP VI.

★★★☆ **Cundle Motor Lodge**, (M), Old Pacific Hwy, 500m from the Taree bypass, ☎ 02 6553 9709, fax 02 6553 9706, 28 units (1 suite) [shwr, bath (3), spa bath (1), tlt, a/c, elec blkts, tel, TV, clock radio, t/c mkg, refrig], ldry, conv fac, ⊠, pool, spa, dinner to unit, cots-fee, non smoking units (10). **RO ♦ $60 - $70, ♦♦ $70 - $80, ♦♦♦ $80 - $90, Suite D $90 - $110,** AE BC DC EFT MC MP VI.

★★★☆ **In-Town Motor Inn**, (M), 77 Victoria St (Pacific Hwy), 300m W of PO, ☎ 02 6552 3966, fax 02 6551 0337, (2 stry gr fl), 20 units [shwr, bath, spa bath (2), tlt, a/c, heat, elec blkts, tel, TV, video-fee, clock radio, t/c mkg, refrig, cook fac (3), toaster], ldry, iron, iron brd, bbq, dinner to unit, cots, non smoking units (2). **RO ♦ $65 - $70, ♦♦ $70 - $80, ◊ $12,** AE BC DC MC VI.

★★★☆ **Marco Polo Motor Inn**, (M), Pacific Hwy, 1km N of PO, ☎ 02 6552 3866, fax 02 6551 3184, (2 stry gr fl), 19 units [shwr, tlt, hairdry, a/c, heat, elec blkts, tel, cable tv, clock radio, t/c mkg, refrig, mini bar], ldry, ⊠, res liquor license, pool (salt water), bbq, cots-fee, non smoking units (9). **D $123.20 - $176, RO ♦ $88 - $101, ♦♦ $99 - $110, ♦♦♦ $110 - $121, ◊ $11,** 5 units of a higher standard. AE BC DC JCB MC VI, ♨.

★★★☆ **Midlands Motel**, (M), Pacific Hwy, 800m N of Town Centre, ☎ 02 6552 2877, fax 02 6551 0127, 20 units (1 suite) [shwr, bath (4), tlt, a/c, heat, elec blkts, tel, fax, TV, movie, clock radio, t/c mkg, refrig, cook fac (4)], ldry, pool, bbq, cots-fee, non smoking units (8). **RO ♦ $66 - $99, ♦♦ $74 - $140, ♦♦♦ $86 - $151, ◊ $12, Suite RO $150 - $180,** ch con, Min book applies, AE BC DC MC MP VI.

★★★☆ **Pacific Motel**, (M), 51 Victoria St (Pacific Hwy), 600m N of PO, ☎ 02 6552 1977, fax 02 6552 5574, (2 stry gr fl), 24 units (9 suites) [shwr, tlt, hairdry, a/c, elec blkts, tel, fax, TV, video (avail), clock radio, t/c mkg, refrig, toaster], ldry, iron, iron brd, pool, bbq, dinner to unit, cots-fee, non smoking units (8). **RO ♦ $54 - $75, ♦♦ $62 - $84, Suite RO $84 - $170,** ch con, AE BC DC MC MP VI.

★★★☆ **Riverview Motor Inn**, (M), Old Pacific Hwy, 2km N of PO, ☎ 02 6552 2122, fax 02 6551 0098, (2 stry gr fl), 21 units (1 suite) [shwr, tlt, hairdry, a/c, elec blkts, tel, TV, video, clock radio, t/c mkg, refrig, mini bar], ldry, ⊠, pool, rm serv, dinner to unit, plygr, cots-fee. **RO** ♦ **$90**, ♦♦ **$100**, ◊ **$10**, **Suite RO** ♦♦ **$110**, AE BC DC JCB MC MP VI, ⚹&.

★★★ **Highway Motor Inn**, (M), 40 Pacific Hwy, 800m N of PO, ☎ 02 6552 5444, fax 02 6552 1903, 22 units (0 suites) [shwr, tlt, a/c, elec blkts, tel, TV, movie, clock radio, t/c mkg, refrig, toaster], bbq, boat park, car wash, cots-fee. **RO** ♦ **$45 - $50**, ♦♦ **$50 - $55**, ♦♦♦ **$60 - $65**, ◊ **$11**, **Suite RO $70 - $110**, AE BC DC MC MP VI.

★★★ **Rainbow Gardens Motel**, (M), 28 Crescent Ave (Pacific Hwy), 1.5km N of PO, ☎ 02 6551 7311, fax 02 6551 7312, 8 units [shwr, tlt, a/c, elec blkts, tel, TV, clock radio, t/c mkg, refrig], pool, bbq, cots-fee, non smoking units. **W $350, RO** ♦ **$47 - $53**, ♦♦ **$52 - $58**, ♦♦♦ **$69**, ◊ **$11**, ch con, AE BC EFT MC VI.

★★★ **Taree Country Motel**, (M), Old Pacific Hwy, Nearest to Freeway South Exit, ☎ 02 6552 2491, fax 02 6552 2337, 16 units [shwr, tlt, a/c (8), c/fan (8), heat (8), elec blkts, tel, TV (3 remote), movie, clock radio, t/c mkg, refrig, toaster], ldry, pool, bbq, dinner to unit, cots-fee. **W** ♦♦ **$320 - $400, RO** ♦ **$40 - $55**, ♦♦ **$48 - $60**, ♦♦♦ **$59 - $71**, ◊ **$11**, AE BC DC EFT MC VI.

★★☆ **Agincourt Motel**, (M), 9 Commerce St, 300m S of PO, ☎ 02 6552 1614, fax 02 6552 5257, (2 stry gr fl), 21 units [shwr, tlt, a/c, c/fan, elec blkts, TV, clock radio, t/c mkg, refrig], dinner to unit, ✆, cots-fee. **RO** ♦ **$30 - $40**, ♦♦ **$45 - $65**, ♦♦♦ **$60 - $75**, ch con, AE BC DC MC VI.

★★☆ **All Seasons Country Lodge**, (M), Pacific Hwy, 1.5km S of PO, ☎ 02 6552 1677, fax 02 6552 6760, 21 units [shwr, tlt, a/c, elec blkts, tel, TV, movie, clock radio, t/c mkg, refrig, cook fac (6), micro (6)], ldry, pool, sauna-fee, spa, bbq, courtesy transfer, plygr, cots-fee, non smoking units (4). **RO** ♦ **$48 - $65**, ♦♦ **$52 - $69**, ◊ **$10**, **Suite D $69 - $125**, AE BC DC EFT MC MP VI.

★★☆ **Arlite Motor Inn**, (M), Cnr Bligh St & Pacific Hwy, 3km N of PO, ☎ 02 6552 2433, fax 02 6552 2721, 20 units [shwr, tlt, a/c-cool, heat, elec blkts, tel, TV, clock radio, t/c mkg, refrig], pool, dinner to unit, cots-fee, 10 units of a lower rating. AE BC EFT MC VI.

TAREE NSW continued...

★★☆ **Jolly Swagman Motel**, (M), 1 Commerce St (Pacific Hwy), 300m S of PO, ☎ 02 6552 3511, fax 02 6553 4019, (2 stry gr fl), 21 units [shwr, tlt, a/c (17), fan, heat, elec blkts, tel, TV, clock radio, t/c mkg, refrig], ldry, ✗, pool, bbq, dinner to unit, plygr, cots. **W $200 - $320, RO ⬩ $45 - $80, ⬩ $10**, AE BC DC MC VI.

★★ **Chatham Motel**, (M), Pacific Hwy, 2km N of PO, ☎ 02 6552 1659, 10 units [shwr, tlt, fan, heat, TV, clock radio, t/c mkg, refrig], dinner to unit, cots-fee. **RO ⬩ $38.50 - $44, ⬩⬩ $38.50 - $44, ⬩⬩⬩ $55 - $66, ⬩ $11**, BC MC VI.

★ **Aquatic Motor Inn**, (M), Pacific Hwy, 2km N of PO, ☎ 02 6551 2822, (2 stry gr fl), 22 units [shwr, tlt, fan, TV, t/c mkg, refrig], pool, dinner to unit, cots-fee, AE BC DC MC VI.

Self Catering Accommodation

★★★★★ **Clarendon Forest Retreat**, (Cotg), Coates Rd via Possum Brush Rd, 21km S of PO, ☎ 02 6554 3162, fax 02 6554 3242, 6 cotgs acc up to 6, [shwr, bath, tlt, fan, heat, tel, TV, video, clock radio, refrig, cook fac, micro, d/wash, toaster, ldry, blkts, linen, pillows], w/mach, dryer, iron, pool, spa (6 pool spas), bbq, meals avail (On request), bush walking, tennis (half court), BC MC VI.

★★★★ **Kiwarrak Country Retreat**, (Cotg), 239 Half Chain Rd, 10km SE of PO, ☎ 02 6553 7391, fax 02 6553 7391, 2 cotgs [shwr, bath, tlt, hairdry, fan (1), c/fan (2), fire pl, TV, video, clock radio, CD, t/c mkg, refrig, cook fac, micro, elec frypan (1), toaster, blkts, linen], ldry, w/mach, iron, iron brd, spa (2), bbq, cots. **D ⬩⬩ $137.50 - $165, ⬩ $27.50, W ⬩⬩ $935 - $1,045**, BC MC VI.

★★★★ **Mansfield on the Manning**, (Cotg), Beauly Rd, Tinonee 2430, ☎ 02 6553 1800, fax 02 6553 1800, 2 cotgs acc up to 5, [shwr, tlt, heat, tel, TV, clock radio, t/c mkg, refrig, cook fac, micro, toaster, doonas, linen], w/mach, dryer, iron, iron brd, pool (salt water), bbq, courtesy transfer, cots, non smoking property. **D $110, W $600**, BC MC VI.

★★★☆ **Holiday Coast Taree Serviced Apartments**, (SA), 3 Little Wynter St, 600m S of PO, ☎ 02 6552 2016, fax 02 6551 0127, 2 serv apts acc up to 4, [shwr, bath, tlt, hairdry, heat, elec blkts, tel, TV, video, clock radio, t/c mkg, refrig, cook fac, micro, elec frypan, toaster, ldry, blkts, linen], w/mach, dryer, iron, dinner to unit, c/park (garage). **D ⬩⬩ $88 - $110, ⬩ $11, W ⬩⬩ $570 - $715, ⬩ $75**, Min book applies, AE BC DC EFT MC VI.

Other Accommodation

Manning River Holidays Afloat, (Hbt), 36 Crescent Ave (Pacific Hwy), 1km N of PO, ☎ 02 6552 6271, 8 houseboats acc up to 12, [shwr, tlt, radio, refrig, cook fac, blkts reqd-fee, linen reqd-fee, pillows reqd-fee], bbq. **D $50 - $800, W $355 - $1,870**.

TATHRA NSW 2550

Pop 1,700. (442km S Sydney), See map on page 55, ref A8. Picturesque south coast town at the southern tip of a bay that sweeps down from the mouth of the Bega River. Boating, Bowls, Fishing, Scenic Drives, Surfing, Swimming, Tennis.

Hotels/Motels

★★★ **Surfside Motel**, (M), Cnr Andy Poole & Francis Hollis Dve, ☎ 02 6494 1378, fax 02 6494 1378, 10 units [shwr, tlt, fan, heat, elec blkts, tel, TV, video-fee, clock radio, t/c mkg, refrig, cook fac, micro, toaster, doonas], w/mach, pool (solar), bbq, cots, non smoking units (4). **BLB ⬩ $52 - $160, ⬩⬩ $62 - $165, ⬩ $5**, ch con, AE BC EFT MC VI.

Self Catering Accommodation

★★★☆ **Esther Lodge**, (HU), 31 Esther St, ☎ 02 6494 1404, fax 02 6494 1406, 8 units acc up to 6, [shwr, tlt, heat, elec blkts, TV ((remote)), video, refrig, cook fac, micro, toaster, ldry (in unit), blkts, linen, pillows], dryer (shared), pool-heated (solar), bbq, boat park, plygr, cots-fee, non smoking units. **D ⬩⬩ $65 - $150, W ⬩⬩ $253 - $924, ⬩⬩⬩⬩ $303 - $999**, pen con, BC EFT MC VI.

★★★☆ **Kianinny Cabins Resort**, (Cotg), Tathra Rd, 2km W of PO, ☎ 02 6494 1990, fax 02 6494 1922, 25 cotgs acc up to 6, [shwr, tlt, elec blkts, TV, video-fee, clock radio, refrig, cook fac, micro, toaster, linen reqd-fee], ldry, lounge, conv fac, pool-heated (salt water), bbq, c/park (carport), ☎, plygr, canoeing, cots. **D ⬩⬩ $87 - $177, ⬩ $7, W ⬩⬩ $453 - $1,080, ⬩ $49**, ch con, Min book applies, BC EFT MC VI.

★★★☆ **Tathra Beach House Apartments**, (HU), 57 Andy Pool Dve, ☎ 02 6494 1944, (2 stry), 6 units acc up to 7, [shwr, tlt, fan, heat, elec blkts, tel, TV, video, clock radio, t/c mkg, refrig, cook fac, toaster, ldry, blkts, linen, pillows], pool-heated, spa, bbq, cots. **D ⬩⬩ $79 - $196, ⬩⬩⬩ $84 - $201, ⬩ $5, W $390 - $1,400**, BC MC VI.

SEABREEZE HOLIDAY PARK – TATHRA

Andy Poole Drive, Tathra Beach. 2550.

Phone: (02) 6494 1350 Fax: (02) 6494 4088

Email: info@seabreezetathra.com.au Web: www.seabreezetathra.com.au

Seabreeze Holiday Park is located directly opposite beautiful Tathra Beach.

- 2 BR Luxury Spa Villas
- 2 BR Deluxe Poly Cabin – 1 double and 2 single beds (linen, blankets, and towels supplied) microwave, remote Col TV/Video, ceiling fan/heater
- 2 BR Family Poly Cabins – 1 Double, 2 double bunks
- Ensuite Cabins – 1 double, 1 triple bunk
- Linen, electric blankets on all double beds
- On-site 4/6 Berth Caravans

- Large powered caravan and camping sites
- En-suite powered sites
- Tiled amenities block includes baths
- Separate babies/children's bathroom
- Laundry • TV/Games room • Camp kitchen
- Resort Pool & Toddler's pool (solar heated)
- Covered Gas BBQ area • Playground
- Park Boat & Bike Hire • Sorry, No pets
- Shop, Phone, LP Gas

AAA Tourism Rated ★★★★☆

BIG 4 HOLIDAY PARKS

★★★☆ **The Waves**, (HU), 8 Esther St, ☎ 02 6494 1465, 3 units acc up to 6, [shwr, bath, tlt, fan, heat, elec blkts, TV, video (avail), clock radio, t/c mkg, refrig, cook fac, micro, toaster, ldry (in unit), linen reqd-fee], w/mach, c/park (garage), cots. **D ♟ $50 - $140, W ♟♟ $250 - $1,000**, Min book applies.

★★★ **Sapphire Court**, (HU), Cnr Francis Hollis & Edna Dve, 3km N of PO, ☎ 02 6494 1980, fax 02 6494 5012, 10 units acc up to 6, [shwr, bath, tlt, heat, tel, TV, video, radio, refrig, cook fac, micro, toaster, ldry (in unit), linen reqd-fee], pool, sauna, spa, bbq, c/park (carport). **W $220 - $990**, Min book Christmas Jan and Easter, BC EFT MC VI.

Mogareeka Court Holiday Units, (HU), 9 Esther St, 2km N of PO, ☎ 02 6494 4847, fax 02 6494 4846, 5 units acc up to 6, (2 bedrm), [shwr, tlt, heat, TV, clock radio, t/c mkg, refrig, cook fac, micro, toaster, blkts, linen-fee, pillows], w/mach, bbq, cots, non smoking units. **D $66 - $110, W $330 - $770**, ch con, Min book Christmas Jan long w/ends and Easter, BC MC VI, (not yet classified).

TEA GARDENS NSW 2324

Pop 1,000. (219km N Sydney), See map on page 55, ref E7. Small resort town on the Myall River, on the northern shores of Port Stephens. Bowls, Bush Walking, Fishing, Golf, Scenic Drives, Squash, Surfing, Swimming, Tennis.

Hotels/Motels

★★★★☆ **Tea Gardens Club Inn Motel**, (M), 2 Yalinbah St, 500m SW of PO, ☎ 02 4997 0911, fax 02 4997 0910, 32 units [shwr, spa bath, tlt, hairdry, a/c, elec blkts, tel, TV, video-fee, clock radio, t/c mkg, refrig], ldry, ⊠, pool (salt water), bbq, cots-fee. **RO ♟ $127 - $145, ♟♟ $127 - $145, ⑨ $15**, AE BC DC EFT MC MP VI, ⚲⚲.

Self Catering Accommodation

★★★☆ **Riverside Gardens**, (HU), 154 Myall St, 50m W of PO, ☎ 02 4997 0262, fax 02 4997 1001, (2 stry), 1 unit acc up to 8, [shwr, spa bath, tlt, fan, c/fan, heat, elec blkts, TV, clock radio, t/c mkg, refrig, cook fac, micro, d/wash, toaster, blkts, doonas, pillows], w/mach, dryer, iron, iron brd, pool (inground), bbq, non smoking property. **W $400 - $1,000**.

B&B's/Guest Houses

★★★★☆ **The Bell Buoy Bed & Breakfast Studios**, (B&B), 117 Marine Drive, Opposite Marina on Waterfront, ☎ 02 4997 1688, fax 02 4997 1679, 2 rms (2 suites) [shwr, tlt, hairdry, fan, heat, tel, TV, video, clock radio, t/c mkg, refrig, toaster], ldry, iron, iron brd, bbq, cots. **BB ♟ $93.50 - $115.50, ♟♟ $104.50 - $154**, ch con, AE BC MC VI.

★★★★ **Lavender Grove Farm**, (B&B), 55 Viney Creek Rd, 3km N Hawks Nest turn off, ☎ 02 4997 1411, fax 02 4997 2001, 3 rms [shwr, spa bath, tlt, hairdry, c/fan, fire pl, elec blkts, tel, clock radio, t/c mkg, refrig], iron, iron brd, lounge (firepl, tv, video), pool (salt, solar heated), non smoking property (indoors). **BB ♟ $88 - $99, ♟♟ $121 - $143**, ch con, fam con, BC MC VI.

Other Accommodation

Tea Gardens, (Hbt), 22 Marine Dve, ☎ 02 4997 0555, 10 houseboats acc up to 10, [shwr, tlt, radio, refrig, cook fac, linen reqd-fee], bbq (10). **W $430 - $1,086**, Min book applies, AE BC MC VI.

Trouble-free travel tips - **Fluids**

Check all fluid levels and top up as necessary. Look at engine oil, automatic transmission fluid, radiator coolant (only check this when the engine is cold), power steering, battery and windscreen washers.

TEMORA NSW 2666

Pop 4,150. (469km SW Sydney), See map on pages 52/53, ref F6. Old Riverina gold town at the heart of good wheat and horse country, renowned for producing some of the finest harness racers in Australia. Boating, Bowls, Golf, Swimming, Tennis, Trotting, Water Skiing.

Hotels/Motels

★★★☆ **Goldtera Motor Inn**, (M), 80 Loftus St, 100m W of PO, ☎ 02 6977 2433, fax 02 6977 2319, 12 units [shwr, bath, tlt, hairdry, a/c, heat, elec blkts, tel, TV, video-fee, clock radio, t/c mkg, refrig, mini bar, toaster], ldry, iron, pool (salt water), cots-fee. RO ♦ $66 - $74, ♦♦ $77 - $85, ◊ $11, Min book applies, AE BC DC EFT MC VI, ♿.

★★★ **Aromet Motor-Inn**, (M), 132 Victoria St, 500m E of PO, ☎ 02 6977 1877, fax 02 6977 1181, 16 units [shwr, tlt, a/c, fan (9), heat, elec blkts, tel, TV, radio, t/c mkg, refrig], pool, bbq, cots. RO ♦ $55, ♦♦ $66, ◊ $12, ch con, AE BC DC MC VI.

 ★★☆ **Temora Motel**, (M), 21-23 Wagga Wagga Rd, 1km S of PO, next to Rural Museum, ☎ 02 6977 1866, fax 02 6978 1161, 8 units [shwr, tlt, a/c, elec blkts, tel, TV, clock radio, t/c mkg, refrig, toaster], bbq, cots-fee, non smoking rms (8). RO ♦ $54, ♦♦ $65, ♦♦♦ $76, ◊ $11, ch con, Not available Easter, AE BC DC EFT MC MCH VI.

TENTERFIELD NSW 2372

Pop 3,200. (758km N Sydney), See map on page 54, ref B2. Charming and historic New England town at the junction of the New England and Bruxner Highways. Bowls, Golf, Scenic Drives, Swimming, Tennis.

Hotels/Motels

 ★★★★ **Henry Parkes Motor Inn**, (M), Rouse St (New England Hwy), 100m S of PO, ☎ 02 6736 1066, fax 02 6736 2657, 31 units [shwr, bath (2), spa bath (7), tlt, hairdry, a/c-cool, fan (9), cent heat, elec blkts, tel, TV, video-fee, clock radio, t/c mkg, refrig, mini bar, micro (15), toaster, ldry (7)], iron, iron brd, rec rm, conv fac, ✕, pool-heated (solar), sauna, spa, bbq-fee, rm serv, dinner to unit, c/park (undercover) (10), plygr, gym, squash, cots-fee. RO ♦ $90.50 - $118.35, ♦♦ $105.50 - $127, ◊ $17, AE BC DC MC VI.

★★★★ **Settlers Motor Inn**, (M), Cnr Rouse & Douglas Sts, 400m S of PO, ☎ 02 6736 2333, fax 02 6736 2755, 18 units [shwr, spa bath (1), tlt, hairdry, a/c (18), cent heat, elec blkts, tel, TV, video (avail), clock radio, t/c mkg, refrig, toaster], ldry, iron, iron brd, pool-heated, spa, dinner to unit, c/park (undercover), cots-fee, non smoking units (avail). RO ♦ $40 - $85, ♦♦ $40 - $85, ♦♦♦ $50 - $90, ◊ $5 - $15, ch con, AE BC DC MC VI.

★★★☆ **Jumbuck Motor Inn**, (M), Cnr Rouse & Miles Sts (New England Hwy), 200m S of PO, ☎ 02 6736 2055, fax 02 6736 2863, 14 units [shwr, tlt, hairdry, a/c, heat, elec blkts, tel, cable tv, video, clock radio, t/c mkg, refrig, mini bar, toaster], ldry, c/park (undercover), cots-fee, non smoking units (avail). RO ♦ $55 - $70, ♦♦ $55 - $70, ♦♦♦ $66 - $80, AE BC DC MC MP VI.

★★★ **Golfers Inn**, (M), Cnr Pelham St & New England Hwy, 2.4km N of PO, ☎ 02 6736 3898, fax 02 6736 3898, 6 units [shwr, tlt, a/c, elec blkts, TV, t/c mkg, refrig, micro, toaster], ldry, ✕, bbq, cots, non smoking units (4). RO ♦ $40 - $45, ♦♦ $45 - $55, ◊ $10, 2 units of a lower rating, BC MC VI.

★★☆ **(Cabin Section)**, 5 cabins acc up to 4, [shwr, tlt, heat, elec blkts, TV, t/c mkg, refrig, micro, toaster], non smoking property. D $40, W $210 - $250.

 ★★★ **The Peter Allen Motor Inn**, (M), 177 Rouse St (New England Hwy), 100m S of PO, ☎ 02 6736 2499, fax 02 6736 2725, 20 units [shwr, tlt, hairdry, a/c (4), c/fan (16), cent heat, elec blkts, tel, TV, clock radio, t/c mkg, refrig, toaster], ldry, iron, iron brd, c/park (undercover), cots, non smoking units (5). RO ♦ $62.50, ♦♦ $71.50, ◊ $11, AE BC DC JCB MC VI, ♿.

 ★★☆ **Tally Ho Motor Inn**, (M), New England Hwy, 1.5km N of PO, ☎ 02 6736 1577, fax 02 6736 2864, 19 units [shwr, tlt, hairdry, fan, heat, elec blkts, tel, TV, clock radio, t/c mkg, refrig], ldry, ✕, bbq, c/park (undercover), plygr, cots-fee, non smoking rms (avail). RO ♦ $44 - $65, ♦♦ $49 - $70, ◊ $10, ch con, 7 units ★★★☆, AE BC DC EFT MC MCH VI.

★★☆ **Tenterfield Motor Inn**, (M), 114 Rouse St (New England Hwy), 500m S of PO, ☎ 02 6736 1177, fax 02 6736 1774, 19 units [shwr, tlt, a/c-cool (19), a/c (6), cent heat (16), elec blkts, tel, cable tv (Austar, Free), clock radio, t/c mkg, refrig, toaster], ldry, pool (salt water), sauna, dinner to unit, c/park (undercover), plygr, cots. RO ♦ $50, ♦♦ $55 - $66, ♦♦♦ $66 - $70, ◊ $7, AE BC DC EFT MC VI.

★★ **Royal Licensed Motel Hotel**, (LMH), High St, 500m N of PO, ☎ 02 6736 1833, fax 02 6736 2463, 12 units [shwr, tlt, heat, elec blkts, TV, radio, t/c mkg, refrig], ✕. BLB ♦ $31, ♦♦ $38.50, ♦♦♦ $49.50, ◊ $5.50 - $11, ch con, BC EFT MC.

★ **(Hotel Section)**, 18 units [elec blkts], lounge (TV). BLB ♦ $16.50.

★☆ **Telegraph**, (LMH), 139 Manners St, 90m E of PO, ☎ 02 6736 1015, fax 02 6736 3271, 5 units [shwr, tlt, cent heat, elec blkts, TV, t/c mkg, refrig], ✕ (Mon to Sat). RO ♦ $42, ♦♦ $51, ♦♦♦ $65, ◊ $15, BC EFT MC VI.

★☆ **(Hotel Section)**, 12 rms [elec blkts, refrig], lounge (TV), t/c mkg shared, ☎. RO ♦ $23, ♦♦ $34.

Bowling Club Motor Inn, (M), Cnr Scott & Molesworth Sts, 300m W of PO, ☎ 02 6736 1023, fax 02 6736 2925, 10 units [shwr, tlt, a/c, heat (elec), elec blkts, TV, clock radio, t/c mkg, refrig, micro, toaster, doonas], ✕, bbq, meals to unit, c/park (undercover), cots, non smoking rms (5). BLB ♦♦ $60.50, ◊ $11, weekly con, AE BC DC MC VI, (not yet classified).

B&B's/Guest Houses

★★★☆ **Henrys Bed & Breakfast**, (B&B), 144 Rouse St, ☎ 02 6736 1066, fax 02 6736 2657, 4 rms [shwr, bath (1), tlt, a/c-cool, c/fan, refrig, cook fac ltd, micro, doonas], lounge (TV, video), lounge firepl, ✕, pool-heated, spa, t/c mkg shared, non smoking property. BB ♦ $80 - $92, ♦♦ $95 - $100, ◊ $23.50, AE BC DC EFT MC VI.

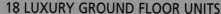

TERMEIL NSW 2539

Pop Nominal, (245km S Sydney), See map on page 55, ref B5.
Leafy south coast service centre located at the turnoff to the beachside town of Bawley Point. Boating, Fishing, Scenic Drives, Swimming.

B&B's/Guest Houses

★★★★☆ **Termeil Country Guest House**, (GH), Old Princes Hwy, 22km S of PO, ☎ 02 4457 1188, fax 02 4457 1498, 9 rms [shwr, tlt, heat, elec blkts], lounge, ✉, pool (salt water), spa, t/c mkg shared, ✆, bush walking, tennis, cots. **DBB** ♦♦ **$236 - $290**, ch con, AE BC DC MC VI, ⅁.

   ★★★★☆ **(Cottage Section)**, 2 cotgs [shwr, spa bath, tlt, TV, video, CD, cook fac ltd], lounge. **DBB** ♦♦ **$320 - $380**.

TERRANORA NSW 2486

Pop Nominal, (860km N Sydney), See map on page 54, ref E1.
Small town in the northern rivers area between Murwillumbah and Tweed Heads.

B&B's/Guest Houses

Tweed Manor, (B&B), Winchelsea Way, 10km S of Tweed Heads, ☎ 07 5590 5678, fax 07 5590 5679, (2 stry gr fl), 3 rms [ensuite, bath (2), spa bath (1), c/fan, heat, TV, clock radio, t/c mkg, refrig (1), doonas (2)], lounge firepl (2), pool-heated (solar), refrig, bbq, non smoking property. **BLB** ♦ **$145 - $245**, ♦♦ **$145 - $245**, Min book Christmas Jan long w/ends and Easter, BC MC VI, (not yet classified).

TERRIGAL NSW 2260

Pop Part of Gosford, (88km N Sydney), See map on page 55, ref D6. Classic seaside resort and one of the most popular holiday destinations on the Central Coast. Boating, Bush Walking, Fishing, Scenic Drives, Surfing. See also Wamberal.

Hotels/Motels

★★★★★ **Holiday Inn Resort Terrigal**, (LH), Pine Tree La, ☎ 02 4384 9111, fax 02 4384 5798, (Multi-stry), 196 rms (15 suites) [shwr, bath, spa bath (15), tlt, a/c, tel, movie, t/c mkg, refrig, mini bar], lift, conv fac, ✉, pool-heated, sauna, spa, rm serv, c/park (undercover), gym, tennis, cots. **RO** ♦ **$215 - $595**, ♦♦ **$215 - $595**, ♦♦♦ **$255 - $635**, ◊ **$40**, Suite D **$305 - $595**, ch con, AE BC DC EFT JCB MC VI.

★★★★ **Clan Lakeside Lodge**, (M), 1 Ocean View Dve, 1km N of PO, ☎ 02 4384 1566, fax 02 4385 2511, (2 stry gr fl), 32 units (6 suites) [shwr, tlt, a/c, heat, elec blkts, tel, TV, video (avail), clock radio, t/c mkg, refrig, cook fac (7)], ldry, conv fac, ✉ (Tue to Sat), bbq, cots. **RO** ♦ **$99 - $205**, ♦♦ **$99 - $220**, ◊ **$15**, ch con, Min book applies, AE BC DC EFT MC VI.

AAA TOURISM *Special Rates* **COUNTRY COMFORT** ★★★★ **Country Comfort Terrigal**, (M), 154 Terrigal Dve, 800m N of PO, ☎ 02 4384 1166, fax 02 4385 1480, (Multi-stry gr fl), 47 units (7 suites) [shwr, bath, tlt, a/c, tel, TV, movie, clock radio, t/c mkg, refrig, mini bar, toaster], ldry, conv fac, ✉, pool, sauna, spa, bbq, rm serv, dinner to unit, plygr, tennis, cots, non smoking units (23). **RO** ♦♦ **$173 - $217**, ◊ **$16.50**, ch con, Min book applies, AE BC DC MC VI, ⅁.

★★★★ **Terrigal Pacific Motel**, (M), 224 Terrigal Dve, 1km W of PO, ☎ 02 4385 1555, fax 02 4385 1476, (2 stry gr fl), 32 units [shwr, bath, tlt, hairdry, a/c, elec blkts, tel, TV, video (avail), clock radio, t/c mkg, refrig, micro (4), toaster (4)], conv fac, ✉, pool, sauna, spa, rm serv, dinner to unit, cots. **RO** ♦ **$130 - $240**, ♦♦ **$130 - $240**, Min book applies, AE BC DC EFT MC VI.

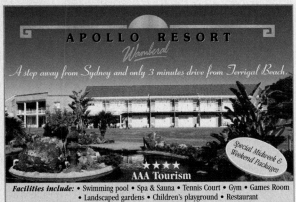

★★★★ **Terrigal Sails**, (M), 6 Maroomba Rd, 100m E of PO,
☎ 02 4384 7444, fax 02 4384 7222, (Multi-stry), 23 units (3 suites)
[shwr, spa bath (6), tlt, hairdry, a/c, tel, TV, clock radio, t/c mkg,
refrig, cook fac ltd, micro, toaster], lift, ldry, iron, iron brd, c/park.
RO ♚ $121 - $193, ♛ $30, Min book applies, AE BC EFT MC VI.
★★ **Terrigal Beach House**, (M), 1 Painter La, ☎ 02 4384 1423,
fax 02 4385 6325, 9 units [shwr, tlt, c/fan (7), heat, TV, clock radio,
t/c mkg, refrig], iron, rec rm, lounge, non smoking units (2).
RO ♙ $45 - $88, ♚ $45 - $88, ♛ $66 - $96, Min book all holiday times.

Self Catering Accommodation
★★★★ **Accom Terrigal Blue Haven Units**, (HU), 1/1 Maroomba Rd,
800m S of PO, ☎ 02 4385 9564, fax 02 4385 6325, (2 stry gr fl),
2 units acc up to 5, [shwr, bath, tlt, c/fan, heat, TV, video, clock radio,
t/c mkg, refrig, cook fac, micro, elec frypan, d/wash, toaster, ldry,
linen reqd], w/mach, dryer, iron, iron brd, bbq, c/park (undercover).
RO ♚ $110 - $185, ♛ $550 - $1,300, BC EFT MC VI.
★★☆ **Accom Terrigal Sunshine Units**, (HU), 1&5 Ocean View Dr, 2km
N of PO, ☎ 02 4385 9564, fax 02 4385 6325, (Multi-stry gr fl), 2 units
acc up to 6, [shwr, bath, tlt, TV, video, clock radio, t/c mkg, refrig,
cook fac, micro, elec frypan, d/wash (1), toaster, doonas, linen], iron,
iron brd, bbq, cots-fee, non smoking property. **RO** ♚ $82 - $160,
♛ $350 - $1,045, BC EFT MC VI.
★★☆ **Accom Terrigal Yarrara**, (HU), 4/17 Barnhill Rd,
☎ 02 4385 9564, fax 02 4385 6325, (Multi-stry), 1 unit acc up to 5,
[shwr, bath, tlt, heat, TV, video, clock radio, t/c mkg, refrig, cook fac,
micro, elec frypan, toaster, ldry, blkts, linen], w/mach, iron, iron brd,
c/park (undercover), non smoking rms. **D** ♚ $82 - $160, ♛ $5 - $10,
W ♚ $350 - $1,045, ch con, pen con, BC EFT MC VI.
★★☆ **Terrigal Beach Getaway**, (HU), 40 Havenview Rd, 1km NW of
PO, ☎ 02 4385 5995, fax 02 4324 3739, 4 units acc up to 5, [shwr,
tlt, a/c (2), c/fan (2), heat, TV, video, clock radio, t/c mkg, refrig,
cook fac, micro, toaster, ldry, blkts, linen], w/mach, iron, iron brd, bbq,
c/park. **W** $330 - $880.
★★☆ **Terrigal Beach Holiday Apartments**, (HU), 41 Barnhill Rd,
300m W of Surf Club, ☎ 02 4385 9564, fax 02 4385 6325, (2 stry gr fl),
3 units acc up to 6, [shwr, tlt, c/fan, heat, TV, video, clock radio,
t/c mkg, refrig, cook fac, micro, toaster, blkts, linen], ldry, w/mach,
iron, iron brd, bbq, c/park (undercover), cots. **D** ♚ $82 - $145,
W ♚ $350 - $950, pen con, BC MC VI.

B&B's/Guest Houses
★★★★☆ **An-Da-Cer House**, (B&B), 28 Serpentine Rd, 3km E of PO,
☎ 02 4367 8368, fax 02 4367 8368, 3 rms (2 suites) [shwr, bath (1),
tlt, a/c, tel, TV, video (2), t/c mkg, refrig], iron, iron brd,
lounge (firepl), ✗, pool-heated (salt water), c/park. **BB** ♚ $140 - $185,
BC EFT MC VI.
★★★★☆ **Terrigal Beach B&B**, (B&B), Cnr Tiarri Crc & Woolung Ave,
500m SE of PO, ☎ 02 4385 7853, fax 02 4385 7854, 7 rms [ensuite,
spa bath (2), a/c, cable tv, video, clock radio, t/c mkg, refrig, ldry (on
request), doonas], ✗, spa, bbq, non smoking rms (2). **BB** ♚ $220 - $260,
weekly con, Min book all holiday times,Min book long w/ends, AE BC
DC EFT MC VI.
★★★★ **Amber House Bed & Breakfast**, (B&B), 4 Country View Cl
Picketts Valley via, ☎ 02 4381 1709, fax 02 4381 1709, (2 stry), 1 rm
[shwr (1), tlt (1), a/c, fan, heat, TV (1)], ldry, lounge (TV), lounge firepl,
t/c mkg shared, non smoking property. **BB** ♙ $130, ♚ $150.
★★★★ **Terrigal Lagoon Bed & Breakfast**, (B&B), 58A Willoughby Rd,
600m N of Terrigal, ☎ 02 4384 7393, fax 02 4385 9763, (2 stry),
3 rms [ensuite, bath (1), a/c, fan, c/fan, heat, cent heat, TV, clock
radio, t/c mkg, refrig], rec rm, TV rm, pool (saltwater), t/c mkg shared,
non smoking rms. **BB** ♙ $100, ♚ $120 - $150, ♛ $20, BC MC VI.
★★★★ **Villa by the Sea**, (B&B), 27 Tabletop Rd, ☎ 02 4385 1170,
fax 02 4385 1170, 2 rms (2 suites) [shwr, tlt, hairdry, c/fan, tel, TV,
video, clock radio, t/c mkg, refrig, micro (1), toaster], iron, iron brd,
non smoking property. **BLB** ♚ $200 - $250, ♛ $65, BC MC VI.
★★★☆ **Terrigal Seaview Bed & Breakfast**, (B&B), 28 Table Top Rd,
1.2km S of PO, ☎ 02 4384 2329, fax 02 4384 2329, 1 rm [shwr, tlt,
hairdry, fan, heat, elec blkts, TV, video, clock radio, t/c mkg, refrig,
cook fac, micro, toaster, ldry], iron, iron brd, rec rm, pool (salt water),
bbq, non smoking property. **BB** ♙ $85 - $95, ♚ $115 - $125,
RO ♙ $80, ♚ $110.
Fairbanks Deer Park, (B&B), 250 Scenic Hwy, ☎ 02 4384 1752,
fax 02 4384 1573, (2 stry gr fl), 4 rms (1 suite) [ensuite, shwr, tlt, a/c,
tel, TV, t/c mkg], iron, iron brd, rec rm, TV rm, lounge firepl (5), pool,
spa, t/c mkg shared, non smoking property. **BB** ♙ $95, ♚ $165 - $195,
Min book applies, AE BC DC MC VI, (not yet classified).

THE ENTRANCE NSW 2261

*Pop 5,092. Part of Wyong, (98km N Sydney), See map on page 55,
ref D6. Popular Central Coast holiday spot between Tuggerah Lake
and the sea. Boating, Fishing, Golf, Scenic Drives, Surfing,
Swimming, Tennis.*

Hotels/Motels
★★★☆ **El Lago Waters Resort**, (M), 41 The Entrance Rd,
☎ 02 4332 3955, fax 02 4332 6188, (Multi-stry gr fl), 40 units [shwr,
bath (24), tlt, a/c, tel, TV, movie, clock radio, t/c mkg, refrig], ldry,
rec rm, conv fac, ✖, pool, spa, rm serv, tennis, cots-fee, non smoking
units (3). **RO** ♙ $77 - $154, ♚ $77 - $154, ♛ $11, pen con, Min book
applies, AE BC DC MC VI.
★★★☆ **Lake Front Motel**, (M), 16 Coogee Ave, 2km N of PO,
☎ 02 4332 4518, fax 02 4334 1212, 14 units [shwr, spa bath (2), tlt,
a/c, tel, TV, video-fee, clock radio, t/c mkg, refrig], ldry, pool, bbq,
cots-fee. **RO** ♙ $53 - $115, ♚ $68 - $115, ♙♙ $79 - $135, ch con,
Min book applies, AE BC EFT MC VI.

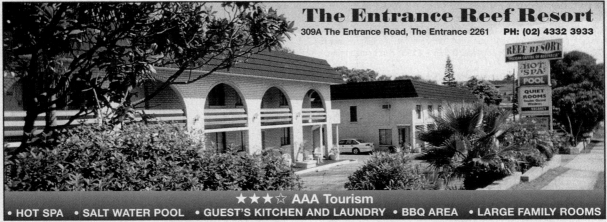
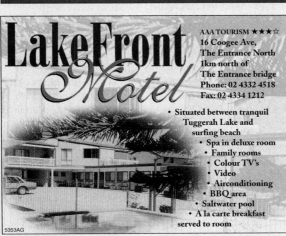

NEW SOUTH WALES

T

NEW SOUTH WALES · T

★★★☆ **Ocean Front Motel**, (M), 102 Ocean Pde, 1km E of PO, ☎ 02 4332 5911, fax 02 4334 2368, (Multi-stry gr fl), 31 units [shwr, spa bath (5), tlt, hairdry, a/c, elec blkts, tel, TV, video (4)-fee, clock radio, t/c mkg, refrig], ldry, iron, iron brd, conv fac, ⊠, bbq, dinner to unit, c/park (undercover), cots-fee. **D $95 - $195**, Min book applies, AE BC DC EFT MC VI, ⅋⌂.

★★★☆ **Sapphire Palms Motel**, (M), 180 The Entrance Rd, 1km S of PO, ☎ 02 4332 5799, fax 02 4332 5600, (2 stry gr fl), 20 units [shwr, tlt, hairdry, a/c, tel, TV, video-fee, clock radio, t/c mkg, refrig, toaster], ldry, pool-heated (solar), wading pool, spa (2), cook fac, bbq, cots. **RO ⍭ $53 - $58, ⍭⍭ $63 - $68, ⍭⍭⍭ $70 - $75, ⍭ $15**, Min book applies, AE BC MC VI, ⅋⌂.

★★★☆ **The Entrance Reef Resort**, (M), Previously Tienda Motel 309a The Entrance Rd, 1km S of PO, ☎ 02 4332 3933, fax 02 4334 2539, (2 stry gr fl), 30 units [shwr, tlt, a/c, tel, TV, clock radio, t/c mkg, refrig, toaster], ldry, pool (salt water), spa, bbq-fee, cots-fee, non smoking units (15). **RO ⍭ $55 - $110, ⍭⍭ $60.50 - $110, ⍭ $11 - $16.50**, ch con, Min book applies, AE BC DC EFT MC VI.

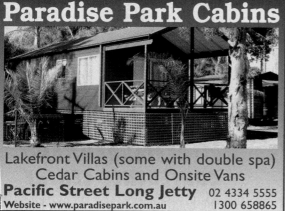

Paradise Park Cabins

Lakefront Villas (some with double spa)
Cedar Cabins and Onsite Vans
Pacific Street Long Jetty 02 4334 5555
Website - www.paradisepark.com.au 1300 658865

★☆ **The Entrance Hotel**, (LH), 87 The Entrance Rd, ☎ 02 4334 2411, or 02 4332 2001, fax 02 4334 2442, (Multi-stry), 10 rms [shwr (4), tlt (4), fan, c/fan, TV, radio (4), t/c mkg, refrig (6)]. **BB ⍭ $38.50, ⍭⍭ $77**, ch con, AE BC EFT MC VI.

Pacific International Waterfront Resort, (M), 89 The Entrance Rd, ☎ 02 4334 8000, fax 02 4334 6094, 145 units (85 suites) [spa bath (35), a/c, elec blkts (12), tel, TV, video, clock radio, t/c mkg, refrig, cook fac, ldry], conf fac, ⊠, ✕, pool, spa, bbq, rm serv (18 hr), meals to unit, secure park, cots, non smoking rms (75). **BB ⍭ $198 - $330, ⍭⍭ $198 - $330, Suite BB $220 - $330**, ch con, weekly con, AE BC DC EFT MC VI, (not yet classified).

Self Catering Accommodation

★★★★ **Pacific Breeze**, (HU), 10/71 Boondilla Rd, 1km SE of PO, ☎ 02 4332 8144, fax 02 4332 4776, (Multi-stry), 1 unit acc up to 5, [shwr, tlt, c/fan, TV, clock radio, refrig, cook fac, micro, elec frypan, toaster, ldry (in unit), linen reqd], w/mach, iron, c/park. **D $55 - $130, W $350 - $980**, Min book applies.

★★★☆ **Alvista Court**, (HF), 1 Fairport Ave, ☎ 02 4332 3404, 8 flats acc up to 4, [shwr, tlt, c/fan, heat, elec blkts, TV, refrig, cook fac, micro, blkts, linen, pillows], ldry, pool-heated (solar), bbq, cots. **D ⍭ $49 - $80, ⍭⍭ $58 - $90, ⍭⍭⍭ $70 - $100, ⍭ $9 - $12, W $210 - $870**, ch con, Min book all holiday times, BC MC VI.

★★★☆ **Ocean Palms Holiday Units**, (HU), 2/35 Ocean Pd, 200m NE of PO, ☎ 02 4332 8144, fax 02 4332 4776, (Multi-stry), 1 unit acc up to 6, [shwr, bath, tlt, heat, TV, video, clock radio, refrig, cook fac, micro, elec frypan, toaster, ldry (in unit), linen reqd], lift, w/mach, dryer, iron, c/park (garage). **D $55 - $130, W $390 - $920**, Min book applies.

★★★☆ **St Tropez**, (HU), 38 Dening St, ☎ 02 4332 8144, fax 02 4333 7388, 5 units acc up to 6, [shwr, bath, tlt, TV, refrig, cook fac, d/wash, toaster, linen reqd], ldry, pool, c/park (garage), tennis. **D $45 - $165, W $300 - $1,160**, Min book all holiday times.

★★★☆ **Surfside Palms Beach Resort**, (SA), 56-58 Ocean Pde, 1km S of PO, ☎ 02 4333 1902, fax 02 4334 5888, (Multi-stry gr fl), 16 serv apts acc up to 6, [shwr, spa bath (4), tlt, hairdry (4), c/fan, heat, tel, TV, video (9), clock radio (9), t/c mkg, refrig, cook fac, micro (9), elec frypan, toaster, doonas, linen], ldry, w/mach-fee, dryer-fee, iron, iron brd (6), rec rm, pool-heated (solar, salt water), spa, bbq, rm serv, c/park (carport) (5), ☎, plygr, cots-fee, non smoking rms (4). **D $90 - $285, W $680 - $1,055**, ch con, pen con, AE BC EFT JCB MC VI.

★★★ **Calypso Holiday Units**, (HU), 39 Marine Pde, opposite surf club, ☎ 02 4332 8144, fax 02 4333 7388, 4 units acc up to 8, [shwr, tlt, TV, refrig, cook fac, ldry (in unit), linen reqd], c/park (garage). **D $35 - $180, W $250 - $1,270**. Min book applies.

★★★ **Pinehurst**, (HU), 11 The Entrance Rd, 1km N of PO, ☎ 02 4332 2002, fax 02 4333 5550, 25 units acc up to 6, [shwr, bath, tlt, fan, heat, TV, refrig, cook fac, linen reqd-fee], ldry-fee, ⊠, bbq, kiosk, c/park (undercover), ☎, **D ♦ $80 - $135, ♦♦ $80 - $130, ♦♦♦ $85 - $130, ◊ $11, W ♦♦ $510 - $930**, AE BC MC VI.

★★★ **Sundowner**, (HU), 4/10 Marine Pde, 500m NE of PO, ☎ 02 4332 8144, fax 02 4332 4776, (Multi-stry), 1 unit acc up to 5, [shwr, bath, tlt, heat, TV, clock radio, refrig, cook fac, micro, elec frypan, d/wash, toaster, ldry], w/mach, dryer, iron, c/park (garage). **D $45 - $105, W $335 - $735**, Min book applies.

★★☆ **Foreshore Court**, (HU), 81 Hutton Rd, Nth Entrance, ☎ 02 4332 8144, 1 unit acc up to 7, [shwr, tlt, heat, TV, refrig, cook fac, ldry (in unit), linen reqd], pool, c/park (undercover). **D $50 - $115, W $330 - $810**, Min book applies.

★★☆ **Surf Side Six**, (HU), 1 Hutton Rd, ☎ 02 4332 5104, 5 units acc up to 6, [shwr, tlt, heat, TV, clock radio, refrig, cook fac, micro, toaster], pool, bbq, cots. **W $360 - $880**, 2 units ★★★. Min book applies.

B&B's/Guest Houses

★★★★☆ **Annabell's Bed & Breakfast - The Entrance**, (B&B), 5 Bent St, ☎ 02 4333 5669, fax 02 4333 7077, (2 stry gr fl), 4 rms (1 suite) [shwr, tlt, evap cool (1), c/fan (3), heat (2), cent heat (2), tel, TV, clock radio, t/c mkg, refrig, cook fac (1), micro (2), toaster (1)], ldry, lounge, ✕, bbq, non smoking property. **BB ♦♦ $80 - $150**, AE BC MC VI.

THE JUNCTION NSW

See Newcastle & Suburbs.

THE ROCK NSW 2655

Pop 900. (485km SW Sydney), See map on pages 52/53, ref E6. Riverina rural centre on the Olympic Highway dominated by the 554m peak that gives the town its name. Scenic Drives.

Hotels/Motels

★☆ **Kings Own**, (LMH), Olympic Way, 1km SE of PO, ☎ 02 6920 2011, fax 02 6920 2556, 12 units [shwr, tlt, a/c, elec blkts, tel, TV, clock radio, t/c mkg, refrig], ✕, ✕, pool, meals to unit, plygr, cots-fee. **D ♦ $35, ♦♦ $45**, BC MC VI.

B&B's/Guest Houses

Morningside Cottage Bed and Breakfast, (B&B), Mangoplah Rd, 1km E of PO, ☎ 02 6920 1102, fax 02 6920 1102, 1 rm (1 suite) [ensuite, evap cool, heat (elec), elec blkts, doonas], lounge (TV), lounge firepl, ✕, t/c mkg shared, refrig, non smoking suites. **BB $105 - $145**, (not yet classified).

THIRROUL NSW

See Wollongong & Suburbs.

THORA NSW 2454

Pop Nominal, See map on page 54, ref B5. Small village on the Bellinger River between Dorrigo and Bellingen.

B&B's/Guest Houses

Bellinger River Retreat, (B&B), 1498 Darkwood Rd, ☎ 02 6655 8632, fax 02 6655 8643, 6 rms (1 suite) [fan, heat, clock radio], ldry, lounge (TV), business centre, conf fac, ✕, cook fac, t/c mkg shared, bbq-fee, plygr, non smoking property. **BLB $75 - $105**, fam con, AE BC MC VI, (not yet classified).

THREDBO VILLAGE NSW 2625

Pop 2,100. (491km SW Sydney), See map on pages 52/53, ref F7. Thredbo, at the foot of the Crackenback Ridge in the Kosciuszko National Park, is the closest resort to Mount Kosciuszko. Bush Walking, Snow Skiing.

Hotels/Motels

★★★☆ **Thredbo Alpine**, (LH), Friday Dve, Village centre, ☎ 02 6459 4200, fax 02 6459 4201, (Multi-stry), 65 rms (3 suites) [shwr, bath, spa bath (2), tlt, hairdry, cent heat, tel, TV, movie, clock radio, t/c mkg, refrig, mini bar], ldry, conv fac, night club, lounge firepl, ⊠ (2), pool, sauna, spa, 24hr reception, cots. **High Season BB ♦♦ $152 - $498, Low Season BB ♦♦ $125 - $180**, ch con, 17 rooms ★★★. Min book applies, AE BC DC EFT MC VI.

★★★ **Snowgoose Lodge**, (M), Banjo Dve, ☎ 02 6457 6415, fax 02 6457 6349, 26 units [shwr, tlt, hairdry, TV, video, clock radio, t/c mkg, refrig], ldry, lounge, ⊠, sauna, ☎, cots, non smoking rms. **Low Season BB $99 - $155, High Season DBB ♦ $80 - $220**, Min book applies, AE BC DC MC VI.

★★★ **The River Inn**, (LH), Friday Dve, ☎ 02 6457 6505, fax 02 6457 6585, (2 stry gr fl), 53 rms [shwr, tlt, hairdry, heat, cent heat, TV, video, clock radio, t/c mkg, refrig], lift, iron, iron brd, dry rm, rec rm, TV rm, conv fac, lounge firepl, ⊠, pool indoor heated, sauna, steam rm, courtesy transfer, ☎, cots, non smoking property. **BB ♦♦ $135 - $240, ◊ $80 - $125**, ch con, fam con, Min book applies, AE BC DC EFT MC VI, 🅰.

Self Catering Accommodation

★★★★☆ **Ski In Ski Out Chalets**, (Chalet), Crackenback Dve, 500m W of PO, ☎ 02 6457 7030, fax 02 6457 7031, (2 stry gr fl), 19 chalets acc up to 10, (2, 3 & 4 bedrm), [ensuite, spa bath, heat (wood) (5), cent heat, tel, TV, video, clock radio, refrig, cook fac, micro, d/wash, ldry, blkts, doonas, linen], w/mach, dryer, sauna (steam room) (14), bbq, secure park, cots-fee, non smoking units. **D $275 - $1,337.50**, Min book applies, BC MC VI.

★★★★ **Lhotsky Apartments**, (HU), 10 Diggings Terrace, ☎ 02 6457 6600, fax 02 6457 6404, (Multi-stry gr fl), 5 units acc up to 6, [bath (2), spa bath (2), tlt, fan, tel, TV, video, clock radio, t/c mkg, refrig, cook fac, micro, d/wash, toaster, ldry, blkts, linen], w/mach, dryer, iron, iron brd, dry rm, cots. **High Season RO ♦ $40 - $195, Low Season RO ♦ $35 - $80**, Min book applies, BC MC VI.

★★★★ **Novotel Lake Crackenback Resort**, (SA), Alpine Way, 800m from Skitube, ☎ 02 6456 2960, fax 02 6456 1008, 45 serv apts [shwr, bath, tlt, hairdry, cent heat, tel, TV, movie-fee, clock radio, t/c mkg, refrig, cook fac, micro, d/wash, toaster, ldry, blkts, linen], w/mach, dryer, iron, iron brd, rec rm, conv fac, lounge firepl, ⊠, pool indoor heated, sauna, steam rm, bbq, ✆, plygr, canoeing, golf, gym, tennis, cots, non smoking property. **D ⅋ $199 - $340**, Min book applies, AE BC DC EFT MC VI.

★★★★ **Pender Lea Chalets**, (Cotg), Alpine Way, 20km N of Thredbo, ☎ 02 6456 2088, fax 02 6456 2088, 5 cotgs acc up to 10, [shwr, spa bath (5), tlt, hairdry, fire pl, cent heat, elec blkts, tel (Gold phone), TV, video, clock radio, t/c mkg, cook fac, micro, elec frypan, d/wash, toaster, ldry (in unit), linen reqd], sauna (4), c/park. **D $168 - $548, W $1,036 - $3,800**, pen con, Min book applies, BC MC VI.

★★★★ **(Cottage Section)**, 1 cotg acc up to 14, [shwr, bath (1), spa bath (1), tlt, hairdry, fire pl, cent heat, TV, video, clock radio, t/c mkg, refrig, cook fac, micro, elec frypan, d/wash, toaster, linen], ldry, ✆. **D $258 - $581, W $1,526 - $4,070.**

★★★ **(Park Cabin Section)**, 6 cabins acc up to 5, [shwr, tlt, hairdry, heat, TV, video, refrig, cook fac, micro, elec frypan, toaster, linen reqd-fee], ldry, c/park. **D $68 - $127, W $434 - $820.**

★★★★ **The Lantern Apartments**, (HU), 2 Banjo Dve, 200m SE of Thredbo Alpine Hotel, ☎ 02 6457 6600, fax 02 6457 6404, (Multi-stry gr fl), 35 units acc up to 4, [shwr, bath, spa bath (2), tlt, hairdry, heat, tel, cable tv, video, movie, CD, t/c mkg, refrig, cook fac, micro, d/wash, toaster, ldry], cots, non smoking units. **High Season D ⅋ $38 - $160, Low Season D ⅋ $25 - $70**, Min book applies, AE BC EFT MC VI.

★★★☆ **Thredbo Alpine Apartments**, (SA), Friday Dve, adjacent Thredbo Alpine Hotel, ☎ 02 6459 4194, fax 02 6459 4195, 36 serv apts acc up to 6, [shwr, bath, tlt, tel, TV, movie, clock radio, refrig, cook fac, micro, d/wash, toaster], ldry, cots. **D $127 - $770**, Limited service daily. Min book applies, AE BC DC MC VI.

★★★ **Silverwood Chalets**, (Chalet), 3 Diggings Tce, 400m S of PO, ☎ 02 9894 4044, fax 02 9899 3467, 4 chalets acc up to 6, [shwr, bath (2), tlt, fire pl, heat, tel, video (3), clock radio, refrig, cook fac, micro, d/wash, toaster, ldry, blkts, linen, pillows], w/mach, dryer, iron, cots-fee. **D $143 - $544, W $1,001 - $3,046**, Min book applies, BC EFT MC VI.

Aspect Chalets, (HU), Banjo Dve, 1km S of PO, ☎ 02 9894 4044, fax 02 9899 3467, 4 units acc up to 10, [shwr, bath, spa bath, tlt, fire pl, cent heat, tel (2), TV, video, clock radio, refrig, cook fac, micro, d/wash, toaster, ldry, blkts, linen, pillows], w/mach, dryer, iron, cots-fee. **D $220 - $1,292, W $1,540 - $7,235**, Min book applies, (not yet classified).

Rockpool Lodge, (Chalet), Mountain Dve, 1km NW of PO, ☎ 02 9894 4044, fax 02 9899 3467, 1 chalet acc up to 6, [shwr, bath, spa bath, tlt, fire pl, cent heat, tel, TV, video, clock radio, refrig, cook fac, micro, d/wash, toaster, ldry (in unit), blkts, linen, pillows], w/mach, dryer, iron, cots-fee. **D $253 - $935, W $1,771 - $5,236**, Min book applies, BC EFT MC VI, (not yet classified).

Sashas Apartments, (HU), 50m E of PO, ☎ 02 9894 4044, fax 02 9899 3467, 3 units acc up to 4, [shwr, bath (2), tlt, heat, tel (2), TV, video (1), refrig, cook fac, micro, d/wash (2), toaster, ldry (in unit) (1), blkts, linen, pillows], ldry, w/mach (1), iron, cots-fee. **D $99 - $660, W $693 - $3,696**, Min book applies, BC EFT MC VI, (not yet classified).

Sequoia Apartments, (HU), Banjo Dve, 300m SE of PO, ☎ 02 9894 4044, fax 02 9899 3467, 4 units acc up to 10, [shwr, bath, spa bath (2), tlt, fire pl, cent heat, tel, TV, video, clock radio, refrig, cook fac, micro, d/wash, toaster, ldry (in unit), blkts, linen, pillows], w/mach, dryer, iron, cots-fee. **D $143 - $1,292, W $1,001 - $7,235**, Min book applies, BC EFT MC VI, (not yet classified).

Steamboat Apartments, (HU), Banjo Dve, 200m S of PO, ☎ 02 9894 4044, fax 02 9899 3467, 2 units acc up to 5, [shwr, bath, tlt, cent heat, tel, TV, video (1), refrig, cook fac, micro, d/wash (1), toaster, blkts, linen, pillows], ldry, cots-fee. **D $154 - $566, W $1,078 - $3,170**, Min book applies, BC EFT MC VI, (not yet classified).

Woodridge Chalets, (Chalet), Mountain Dve, 1km NW of PO, ☎ 02 9894 4044, fax 02 9899 3467, 12 chalets acc up to 8, [shwr, bath, tlt, fire pl, cent heat, tel (8), TV, video (8), clock radio, refrig, cook fac, micro, d/wash, toaster, ldry, blkts, linen, pillows], w/mach, dryer, iron, cots-fee. **D $99 - $1,210, W $693 - $6,676**, Min book applies, BC EFT MC VI, (not yet classified).

Kasees Mountain Lodge & Apartments, (Apt), 4 Banjo Dve, ☎ 02 6457 6370, fax 02 6457 6432, 8 apts acc up to 4, [shwr, tlt, cent heat, TV, t/c mkg, refrig, cook fac, micro], ldry, dry rm, lounge firepl, sauna, bbq, cots. **D ⅋⅋ $88 - $176, ⅋⅋⅋ $120 - $188**, Min book applies, BC MC VI.

Mowamba Apartments, (HU), Mowamba Place, above the PO, ☎ 02 9894 4044, fax 02 9899 3467, 9 units acc up to 8, [shwr, bath (10), spa bath (2), tlt, fire pl (3), heat, tel (8), TV, video (4), refrig, cook fac, micro, d/wash (6), toaster, ldry, blkts, linen, pillows], w/mach, dryer, iron, cots-fee. **D $143 - $814, W $1,001 - $4,558**, Min book applies, BC EFT MC VI.

B&B's/Guest Houses

★★☆ **Berntis Mountain Inn**, (PH), Mowamba Pl, ☎ 02 6457 6332, fax 02 6457 6348, (Multi-stry), 29 rms [shwr, tlt, cent heat, tel, TV, clock radio, t/c mkg, refrig, cook fac (4)], dry rm, lounge, ⊠ (2), sauna, c/park (limited), cots. **High Season DBB ⅋ $195, Low Season DBB ⅋ $95**, ch con, AE BC DC EFT MC VI.

★☆ **Bursills Mountain Lodge**, (PH), Diggings Tce, ☎ 02 6457 6222, fax 02 6457 6461, (2 stry gr fl), 37 rms [shwr, tlt, cent heat, TV, t/c mkg, refrig], ldry, lounge, ⊠, bar, pool indoor heated, sauna, c/park (valet), cots. **Low Season BB $65 – $165, High Season DBB ♦ $95 – $200**, Min book applies, AE BC DC EFT MC VI.

Snowcloud B & B, (B&B), Riverview Tce, 500m fr PO, ☎ 02 6457 6428, fax 02 6457 6428, (Multi-stry), 3 rms [shwr, spa bath (1), tlt, cent heat, clock radio, refrig (1)], ldry, lounge (cable TV, video), lounge firepl, ✗, spa, steam rm, t/c mkg shared, ✆, non smoking property. **BB ♦♦ $140 – $510**, Minimum booking Jun 8 to Oct 1, BC EFT MC VI, (not yet classified).

Bimblegumbie Bed & Breakfast, (B&B), Alpine Way, Jindabyne 2627, 10km from Jindabyne, ☎ 02 6456 2185, fax 02 6456 2060, (2 stry gr fl), 8 rms [shwr, tlt, hairdry (4), c/fan, cent heat, clock radio, refrig (7), micro (3)], shared fac (6), ldry, iron, iron brd, rec rm, lounge (tv, video & firepl), ✗, cook fac, t/c mkg shared, meals avail, ✆, plygr, cots-fee, non smoking rms, Pets allowed. **BB $52 – $105**, ch con, fam con, weekly con, BC MC VI.

  (Cottage Section), 2 cotgs acc up to 10, [shwr, tlt, hairdry, fan, heat, TV, video, clock radio, refrig, cook fac, micro, blkts, doonas, linen, pillows], iron (available), iron brd (available), cots-fee, Dogs allowed on application. **D ♦♦ $88 – $180**, (not yet classified).

Crackenback Farm, (GH), Alpine Way, Thredbo Valley, Jindabyne 2627, 10km from Jindabyne, ☎ 02 6456 2198, fax 02 6456 2601, 6 rms [shwr, tlt, hairdry, elec blkts], dry rm, rec rm, lounge (TV), conv fac, ⊠, pool indoor heated, sauna, t/c mkg shared, ✆, plygr, tennis. **BLB ♦ $65 – $85, DBB ♦ $95 – $132**, AE BC DC EFT MC VI.

Other Accommodation

★★★☆ **Boali Lodge**, (Lodge), Mowamba Pl, 250m W of PO, ☎ 02 6457 6064, fax 02 6457 6054, (Multi-stry), 14 rms [shwr, tlt, cent heat], ldry, iron, iron brd, dry rm, rec rm, lounge (TV), lounge firepl, ✗, sauna, spa, t/c mkg shared, bbq, ✆, cots, non smoking property. **BB ♦ $55 – $60, D all meals ♦ $85 – $159**, BC MC VI.

Alpenhorn, (Lodge), Buckwong Pl, 150m S of Thredbo Alpine Hotel, ☎ 02 6457 6223, (Multi-stry gr fl), 20 rms [shwr, bath (3), tlt, cent heat, TV, movie, clock radio, t/c mkg, refrig, doonas, linen, pillows], dry rm, lounge, ⊠, bar, bbq, c/park (valet), cots, non smoking property. **BLB ♦♦ $90 – $330**, ch con, AE BC DC MC VI.

BlackBear Inn, (Lodge), 30 Diggings Tce, ☎ 02 6457 6216, fax 02 6457 6196, (Multi-stry), 15 rms [shwr, spa bath (4), tlt, cent heat, tel, TV, movie, t/c mkg], ldry, dry rm, lounge (TV), ⊠, refrig, cots-fee. **High Season D ♦ $200 – $1,100, Low Season D $70 – $160**, ch con, AE BC DC MC VI.

House of Ullr, (Lodge), Mowamba Pl, ☎ 02 6457 6210, fax 02 6457 6116, (Multi-stry), 20 rms acc up to 6, [shwr, tlt, cent heat, TV, t/c mkg, refrig], dry rm, ⊠, ✆, cots. **Low Season BB $75 – $175, High Season DBB ♦ $105 – $200**, ch con, Min book applies, AE BC DC EFT MC VI.

New Kirk Lodge, (Lodge), 8 Bobuck La, 500m NE of PO, ☎ 02 6457 6311, 1 rm acc up to 4, [shwr, tlt, heat, TV, t/c mkg, refrig, cook fac], dryer, lounge, c/park (limited), ✆, cots. **D $70 – $100, W $1,135 – $2,600**, Min book applies.

TIBOOBURRA NSW 2880

Pop 214. (1498km NW Sydney), See map on pages 52/53, ref B1. The remote town of Tibooburra lies at the heart of 'Corner Country', the north-western corner of New South Wales. Gem Fossicking.

Hotels/Motels

★★ **The Granites Motel**, (M), Cnr Brown & King Sts, adjacent PO, ☎ 08 8091 3305, fax 08 8091 3340, 10 units [shwr, tlt, a/c-cool, elec blkts, TV, t/c mkg, refrig], pool, cook fac, bbq, plygr, cots. **RO ♦ $48 – $52, ♦♦ $60 – $64**, ch con, BC MC VI.

Family Hotel, (LH), Briscoe St, ☎ 08 8091 3314, fax 08 8091 3430, 7 rms [a/c-cool], ldry, ⊠, bbq, ✆. **RO ♦ $22, ♦♦ $38.50 – $44**, ch con, BC EFT MC VI.

  (Motel Section), 10 units [shwr, tlt, a/c, elec blkts, tel, TV, video-fee, clock radio, t/c mkg, refrig], c/park. **RO ♦ $60.50, ♦♦ $66 – $77**, (not yet classified).

Tibooburra Licensed Hotel, (LH), Silver City Hwy, ☎ 08 8091 3310, fax 08 8091 3406, (2 stry gr fl), 8 rms [a/c, t/c mkg, refrig (some)], ldry, lounge, ⊠, cots-fee. **RO ♦ $28 – $35, ♦♦ $39 – $45, ◊ $11**, ch con, Rooms 9 to 14 not rated. BC EFT MC VI.

TILBA TILBA NSW 2546

Pop Nominal, (363km S Sydney), See map on page 55, ref A7. Historic south coast settlement nestled at the foot of the ancient volcano, Gulaga (Mount Dromedary). Bush Walking, Fishing, Golf, Horse Riding, Scenic Drives.

Self Catering Accommodation

★★★☆ **Couria Creek Farm Cottage**, (Cotg), (Farm), 9065 Princes Hwy, 6.5km S of Central Tilba PO, ☎ 02 4473 7211, fax 02 4473 7211, 2 cotgs acc up to 4, [shwr, tlt, fire pl, elec blkts, TV, clock radio, CD, t/c mkg, refrig, cook fac, micro, toaster, ldry, linen reqd], w/mach, iron, bbq, c/park (carport). **D ♦♦ $85 – $120, ◊ $20, W ♦♦ $520 – $750, ◊ $140**, Min book applies.

★★★ **Apple Tree Cottage**, (Cotg), (Farm), 'Fairview', 4km S of Tilba Tilba, ☎ 02 4473 7378, 1 cotg acc up to 2, [shwr, tlt, fan, fire pl (open), elec blkts, TV, radio, refrig, cook fac, toaster, blkts, linen, pillows], bbq. **D $65 – $75, W $415 – $485**.

Mountain View Tilba Farm Cottages, (Cotg), (Farm), Dromedary Trail, turn off Corkhill Dve at Pams Store, ☎ 02 4473 7207, fax 02 4473 7090, 2 cotgs acc up to 6, [shwr, bath, tlt, fire pl (1), TV, clock radio, t/c mkg, refrig, cook fac, toaster, ldry, blkts, linen, pillows], w/mach, iron, bbq, cots. **D $77 – $110, W $540 – $750**, ch con.

B&B's/Guest Houses

★★★★ **Green Gables**, (B&B), c1879. Corkhill Dve, ☎ 02 4473 7435, 3 rms [shwr, bath (1), tlt, hairdry, c/fan, cent heat, elec blkts, tel, TV, clock radio, t/c mkg, doonas], ldry, lounge, non smoking rms. **D ♦ $88, ♦♦ $121 – $132**, BC MC VI.

TINONEE NSW 2430

Pop 650. (341km N Sydney), See map on page 54, ref B7. Historic arts and crafts town on the Manning River near Taree.

B&B's/Guest Houses

★★★★ **Deans Creek Lodge**, (B&B), 2 Deans Creek Rd, 8km SW of Taree, ☎ 02 6553 1187, fax 02 6553 1187, 2 rms [hairdry (1), c/fan (2), heat (1), elec blkts, tel, TV (1), clock radio, t/c mkg (1), refrig (1)], ldry, iron, iron brd, lounge (TV), lounge firepl, ✗, pool (salt water), cots, non smoking property. **D ♦♦ $95, ◊ $40**, ch con, AE BC MC VI.

  ★★★☆ **(Bed & Breakfast Section)**, Kings Fisher Cottage, 1 rm **BB ♦♦ $110 – $130, ◊ $20**.

TOCUMWAL NSW 2714

Pop 1,450. (619km SW Sydney), See map on pages 52/53, ref D7. Small border town on the northern banks of the Murray River that was the site of the largest aerodrome in the South Pacific during World War II. It is now home to the largest soaring centre in Australia. Bowls, Fishing, Golf, Shooting, Swimming, Tennis, Water Skiing.

Hotels/Motels

★★★★ **Bridge Motor Inn**, (M), 26 Bridge St, 1km W of PO, ☎ 03 5874 2674, fax 03 5874 2223, (2 stry) 21 units [shwr, bath (4), tlt, a/c, c/fan, elec blkts, tel, TV, video-fee, clock radio, t/c mkg, refrig, micro, toaster], ldry-fee, pool-heated (solar), spa, bbq. **RO** ♦ $61 - $72, ♦♦ $72 - $83, AE BC DC EFT MC MP VI, ⅃⅁.

★★★☆ **Bakery Park Motor Inn**, (M), Deniliquin St, 200m E of PO, ☎ 03 5874 2490, fax 03 5874 2269, 15 units [shwr, spa bath (5), tlt, hairdry, a/c-cool, c/fan, heat, elec blkts, tel, fax, TV, video (avail), clock radio, t/c mkg, refrig, toaster], iron, iron brd, pool, spa, bbq, dinner to unit, boat park, trailer park, cots-fee, non smoking units (6). **RO** ♦ $45 - $65, ♦♦ $55 - $70, ♦♦♦ $60 - $75, ♦♦♦♦ $88 - $98, AE BC EFT MC VI.

★★★☆ **Kingswood Motel**, (M), Cnr Kelly St & Barooga Rd, 500m E of PO, ☎ 03 5874 2444, fax 03 5874 2840, 21 units (2 suites) [shwr, tlt, a/c, elec blkts, tel, TV, clock radio, t/c mkg, refrig, cook fac (7), toaster], ldry, conv fac, pool (salt water), bbq, car wash (bay), cots, non smoking rms (7). **RO** ♦ $62 - $92, ♦♦ $62 - $92, ♦♦♦ $72 - $102, ♦ $10, **Suite D** $96, AE BC DC EFT MC MCH VI, ⅃⅁.

★★★☆ **Tocumwal Motel**, (M), 11 Murray St, ☎ 03 5874 3022, fax 03 5874 3438, 10 units [shwr, tlt, hairdry, a/c, elec blkts, tel, TV, video, movie, clock radio, t/c mkg, refrig, toaster], ldry, iron, iron brd, pool, bbq, dinner to unit, cots. **BLB** ♦ $55 - $80, ♦♦ $60 - $80, ♦ $12, AE BC DC MC VI.

★★★ **Adams St Holiday Lodges**, (M), 67 Adams St, 2km E of PO, ☎ 03 5874 2423, fax 03 5874 3350, 16 units (2 bedrm), [shwr, tlt, a/c, c/fan, heat, elec blkts, TV, video (available), clock radio, t/c mkg, refrig, cook fac, micro, toaster], ldry, iron, iron brd, pool-heated (solar), spa, bbq, c/park (undercover), ☎, cots. **D** ♦ $44, ♦♦ $55 - $60.50, ♦ $11, **W** ♦♦ $340, BC EFT MC VI, ⅃⅁.

★★★ **Early Settlers Motel**, (M), Barooga Rd, 1.5km E of PO, ☎ 03 5874 2411, fax 03 5874 2667, 24 units [shwr, tlt, a/c, elec blkts, tel, TV, clock radio, t/c mkg, refrig, micro, toaster], ldry, pool, bbq, cots. **D** ♦ $55 - $88, ♦♦ $66 - $88, AE BC DC MC VI, ⅃⅁.

★★★ **Fairway Views Motor Inn**, (M), Barooga Rd, 1.8km E of PO, adjacent to golf course, ☎ 03 5874 2877, fax 03 5874 2605, 10 units [shwr, tlt, a/c, elec blkts, tel, TV, clock radio, micro, toaster], iron, pool (salt water), bbq, c/park. **D** ♦♦ $74 - $86, BC MC VI.

★★★ **Kanimbla Motor Inn**, (M), Newell Hwy, 500m W of PO, ☎ 03 5874 2755, fax 03 5874 2662, 20 units [shwr, spa bath (3), tlt, a/c, c/fan, elec blkts, tel, TV, clock radio, t/c mkg, refrig, cook fac (5), toaster], ldry, pool, bbq, cots-fee. **BLB** ♦ $55 - $75, ♦♦ $60 - $80, ♦ $12, AE BC DC MC MCH VI, ⅃⅁.

★★★ **Tocumwal Golf Motor Inn**, (M), Barooga Rd, 2km E of PO, ☎ 03 5874 2300, fax 03 5874 2665, 36 units [shwr, tlt, a/c, c/fan, elec blkts, tel, TV, clock radio, t/c mkg, refrig, micro, toaster], ldry, pool, bbq, cots. **RO** ♦ $60 - $70, ♦♦ $66 - $90, ♦♦♦ $82 - $100, ♦ $20, ch con, AE BC DC MC VI, ⅃⅁.

★★☆ **Thomas Lodge Motel**, (M), Cnr Barker & Deniliquin Sts, 400m E of PO, ☎ 03 5874 2344, fax 03 5874 3926, 14 units [shwr, tlt, a/c, elec blkts, tel, TV, clock radio, refrig, cook fac (1)], bbq, cots. **RO** ♦ $40, ♦♦ $49.50 - $55, ch con, AE BC DC MC VI.

★★ **Tocumwal Hotel Motel**, (LMH), 17-33 Deniliquin St, ☎ 03 5874 2025, fax 03 5874 3625, 7 units [shwr, tlt, a/c, fan, elec blkts, TV, clock radio, t/c mkg, refrig], ✗, bbq, cots-fee. **BLB** ♦ $44, ♦♦ $55, ♦♦♦ $66, AE BC DC EFT MC VI.

Self Catering Accommodation

★★★★☆ **Coachmans Cottages**, (HU), 16 Barooga Rd, 1.5km E of PO, ☎ 03 5874 2699, fax 03 5874 2722, 9 units acc up to 5, [shwr, bath, spa bath (2), tlt, hairdry, a/c, c/fan, heat, elec blkts, tel, TV, video, clock radio, refrig, cook fac, micro, toaster, ldry (in unit), blkts, linen, pillows], pool, bbq, plygr, tennis. **D** ♦♦ $88, ♦ $16, **W** $641, Light breakfast available. BC MC VI.

★★★ **Greenways**, (HU), Cnr Cobram & Kelly Sts, 1km SE of PO, ☎ 03 5874 2882, fax 03 5874 2882, 9 units acc up to 6, (1 & 2 bedrm), [shwr, spa bath (2), tlt, a/c, c/fan, elec blkts, TV, clock radio, refrig, cook fac, toaster, blkts, linen, pillows], ldry, pool, bbq, cots. **D** ♦ $60 - $80, ♦♦ $60 - $80, ♦ $11, **W** $420 - $476, ch con, BC MC VI.

B&B's/Guest Houses

River Park Bed & Breakfast, (B&B), No children's facilities, 1 Clement St, 1km N of PO, ☎ 03 5874 3425, fax 03 5874 3425, 1 rm (1 suite) [ensuite, spa bath, a/c-cool, fan, cent heat, elec blkts, TV, video, clock radio, t/c mkg, refrig, micro, ldry, doonas], lounge (TV), bbq, c/park. **BLB** ♦ $90, ♦♦ $110, ♦ $45, weekly con, Min book applies, BC MC VI, (not yet classified).

TOMAKIN NSW 2537

Pop 750. (302km S Sydney), See map on page 55, ref A6. Popular swimming, surfing and fishing spot situated on Broulee Bay between Batemans Bay and Moruya.

Self Catering Accommodation

★★★★ **The Moorings Resort**, (HU), George Bass Dve, ☎ 02 4471 7500, fax 02 4471 8125, (2 stry gr fl), 64 units acc up to 6, (Studio, 1, 2 & 3 bedrm), [shwr, spa bath (44), tlt, heat, elec blkts, TV, t/c mkg, refrig, cook fac, d/wash (44), ldry (in unit) (56)], ldry, rec rm, pool indoor heated, bbq, plygr, golf, tennis, cots. **D** $85 - $170, **W** $395 - $1,400, AE BC DC EFT MC VI.

TOMINGLEY NSW 2869

Pop Nominal, (484km NW Sydney), See map on pages 52/53, ref F4. Small village on the Newell Highway known as the gateway to the Macquarie Valley. Horse Racing, Scenic Drives.

Hotels/Motels

★★★ **Lucky Strike Motel**, (M), Newell Hwy, 500m N of PO, ☎ 02 6869 3211, fax 02 6869 3203, 26 units [shwr, tlt, a/c, heat, elec blkts, tel, TV, movie, clock radio, t/c mkg, refrig, toaster], pool, bbq, dinner to unit, plygr, cots-fee. **RO** ♦ $43 - $49, AE BC DC MC VI.

TOOLEYBUC NSW 2736

Pop 235. (907km W Sydney), See map on pages 52/53, ref C6. Delightful place nestled on the Murray among the river redgums. Boating, Bowls, Fishing, Golf, Shooting, Swimming.

Hotels/Motels

★★★★ **Club Motor Inn**, (M), Lockhart Rd, ☎ 03 5030 5502, fax 03 5030 5509, 20 units [shwr, bath (5), spa bath (2), tlt, hairdry (2), a/c, elec blkts, tel, TV, video (avail), clock radio, t/c mkg, refrig, mini bar, toaster], ldry, pool, bbq, plygr, golf, tennis, cots, non smoking units (7). **RO** ♦ $79, ♦♦ $92 - $108, AE BC DC EFT MC MP VI.

★★★☆ **Tooleybuc Golden Rivers Country Motel**, (M), 43 Murray St, 50m S of PO, ☎ 03 5030 5203, fax 03 5030 5370, 16 units [shwr, tlt, a/c, c/fan, elec blkts, tel, TV, video (avail), clock radio, t/c mkg, refrig, micro, toaster, ldry], pool, bbq, cots. **RO** ♦ $55 - $61, ♦♦ $66 - $72, ♦ $11, ch con, pen con, AE BC DC EFT MC MCH VI.

★★★ **Country Roads Motor Inn**, (M), Cnr Caddell St & Balranald Rd, 400m NW of PO, ☎ 03 5030 5401, fax 03 5030 5401, 14 units [shwr, tlt, a/c, elec blkts, tel, TV, video (available)-fee, clock radio, t/c mkg, refrig], ldry, meals to unit (breakfast), non smoking units. **RO** ♦ $50 - $55, ♦♦ $55 - $60, ♦♦♦ $70 - $75, pen con, AE BC DC MC VI.

TOOLEYBUC NSW continued...

Self Catering Accommodation

★★☆ **Tooleybuc River Retreat**, (HU), Lea St, 300m N of PO, ☎ 03 5030 5341, 4 units acc up to 4, [shwr, tlt, a/c, heat, elec blkts, TV, refrig, cook fac, micro, toaster, blkts, linen, pillows], bbq, cots. **D** ♦ $40, ♦♦ $50, ♦♦♦ $60, ◊ $11, **W** $300, ch con, Min book Christmas Jan long w/ends and Easter, BC MC VI.

Sharing the roads - Trucks and cars

Trucks are different from cars. They take up more road space than cars, especially when turning, and are slower to accelerate, turn and reverse. Here are some hints in sharing our roads safely with trucks:

- Don't cut in on trucks. Because trucks need a greater braking distance than cars, truck drivers leave more space in front of them when approaching a red light or stop sign than a car.
- Allow extra time and space to overtake trucks. You will need about 1.5 kilometres of clear road space to pass a truck.
- Don't pass a left-turning truck on the inside. Trucks sometimes need more than one lane to turn tight corners, so watch for a truck swinging out near intersections.
- Be patient - follow at a safe distance. Truck drivers may not see you because of blind spots, particularly if you travel right behind them.

TOORMINA NSW 2452

Pop Nominal, See map on page 54, ref D5. North coast town between Sawtell and Coffs Harbour.

Self Catering Accommodation

★★★☆ **Boambee Bay Resort**, (SA), Resort, 8 Barber Close, 1.5km NW of PO, ☎ 02 6653 2700, fax 02 6653 3389, (2 stry gr fl), 80 serv apts acc up to 6, [shwr, spa bath, tlt, hairdry, fan, heat, elec blkts, tel, TV, video, clock radio, refrig, cook fac, micro, d/wash, toaster, ldry (in unit)], rec rm, lounge, ✕ (3 rms), coffee shop, pool, sauna, spa (2), bbq, plygr, canoeing, mini golf, gym, tennis, cots. **RO** ♦ $135 - $220, ♦♦ $135 - $220, ♦♦♦ $150 - $245, ◊ $15, $945 - $2,240, ch con, Min book Christmas and Jan, AE BC DC EFT MC VI.

TOOWOON BAY NSW 2261

Pop Part of Wyong, (98km N Sydney), See map on page 55, ref D6. Central Coast community blessed with the upper reaches of Shelly Beach and the blue waters of Little and Toowoon Bays. Swimming.

★★★★☆ **Al Mare Beachfront Retreat**, (B&B), No children's facilities, 42 Werrina Pde, Blue Bay 2261, 2km SE of The Entrance town centre, ☎ 02 4333 7979, fax 02 4333 3778, 2 rms (2 suites) [ensuite, spa bath, c/fan, heat (gas), elec blkts, TV, video, clock radio, CD, t/c mkg, refrig, cook fac ltd, micro], iron, iron brd, bbq, meals to unit, secure park, non smoking suites. **BLB** ♦♦ $400, weekly con, Min book applies, AE BC EFT MC VI.

TORONTO NSW 2283

Pop 11,644. (160km N Sydney), See map on page 55, ref C8. Regional centre on the western shores of Lake Macquarie. Boating, Bowls, Fishing, Swimming, Tennis.

Hotels/Motels

Toronto, (LMH), 74 Victory Pde, 600m N of PO, ☎ 02 4959 1033, fax 02 4950 4804, 10 units [shwr, tlt, a/c, tel, TV, clock radio, t/c mkg, refrig, toaster], iron, cots-fee, Min book long w/ends, BC EFT MC VI.

Self Catering Accommodation

★★★☆ **Tranquil Shores Waterfront Cottage**, (Cotg), 6 Moore St, 2km N of PO, ☎ 02 4959 3673, fax 02 4959 3673, 1 cotg acc up to 4, (1 bedrm), [shwr, tlt, hairdry, a/c-cool, c/fan, heat, TV, video, clock radio, t/c mkg, refrig, cook fac, micro, toaster, ldry, blkts, doonas, linen, pillows], w/mach, dryer, bbq, c/park (undercover), cots, breakfast ingredients, non smoking property. **BB** ♦♦ $95 - $130, ◊ $10, ch con.

B&B's/Guest Houses

★★★★☆ **Anchorage Waterfront**, (GH), 104 Kilaben Rd, Kilaben Bay, ☎ 02 4950 5004, fax 02 4950 4229, 3 rms [a/c, fan, elec blkts, t/c mkg, micro, toaster], ldry, rec rm, lounge (TV), lounge firepl, ✕, pool (salt water), bbq, jetty, tennis. **BLB** ♦ $71.50, ♦♦ $88.

★★★★☆ **Bower Bird Bed & Breakfast**, (B&B), 74 Jarrett St, Kilaben Bay 2283, 2km S of Toronto PO, ☎ 02 4959 6060, fax 02 4959 6061, 3 rms (1 bedrm), [a/c, fan (2), heat (elec), elec blkts (3), clock radio, t/c mkg, ldry, doonas], shared fac (2), lounge (TV/video), pool (outdoor/solar heated), bbq, non smoking rms. **BB** ♦ $75, ♦♦ $95, ◊ $40, weekly con, BC MC VI.

★★★★ **Jacaranda Lodge Bed & Breakfast**, (B&B), 178 Coal Point Rd, Coal Point 2283, ☎ 02 4950 5494, fax 02 4950 5494, (2 stry gr fl), 2 rms (1 suite) [a/c (1), c/fan (1), heat, tel, TV, clock radio], ldry, lounge firepl, ✕, t/c mkg shared, non smoking property. **BB** ♦ **$50**, ♦♦ **$90**, ch con, pen con.

★★★☆ **Treetops Bed & Breakfast**, (B&B), 80 Coal Point Rd, ☎ 02 4959 2378, 2 rms [shwr, tlt, fan, heat, elec blkts, TV, clock radio, t/c mkg, refrig, toaster]. **BLB** ♦ **$49.50**, ♦♦ **$88**.

TOUKLEY NSW 2263

Pop 6,730. (110km N Sydney), See map on page 55, ref D5. Central Coast town between Budewoi and Tuggerah Lakes. Fishing, Scenic Drives, Swimming.

Hotels/Motels

★★★☆ **The Beachcomber**, (LMH), 200 Main Rd, ☎ 02 4397 1300, fax 02 4396 1128, (Multi-stry gr fl), 61 units [shwr, bath, spa bath (8), tlt, hairdry, a/c, tel, fax, TV, clock radio, t/c mkg, refrig], rec rm, conv fac, cafe, pool, sauna, spa, ✆, tennis, cots. **RO** ♦ **$80 - $190**, ♦♦ **$80 - $190**, ♦ **$16**, ch con, 18 units not rated, Min book long w/ends, AE BC DC MC VI.

★★★☆ **Toukley Motor Inn**, (M), 236 Main Rd, ☎ 02 4396 5666, fax 02 4396 5666, 13 units [shwr, tlt, hairdry, a/c, elec blkts, tel, TV, clock radio, t/c mkg, refrig], iron, pool. **RO** ♦ **$50 - $99**, ♦♦ **$55 - $105**, ♦ **$15**, ch con, AE BC DC EFT MC VI.

★★★ **Toukley Motel**, (M), 185 Main Rd, 500m W of PO, ☎ 02 4397 1999, (2 stry gr fl), 15 units [shwr, tlt, hairdry, a/c, elec blkts (available), tel (4), TV, clock radio, t/c mkg, refrig, toaster], cots. **RO** ♦ **$57 - $95**, ♦♦ **$62 - $95**, ♦♦♦ **$73 - $106**, ♦ **$6 - $17**, ch con, pen con, AE BC MC VI.

★★★ **Twin Lakes Motor Inn**, (M), 57 Main Rd, ☎ 02 4396 4622, fax 02 4396 4970, 11 units [shwr, bath (1), tlt, hairdry, a/c, elec blkts, tel, TV, video-fee, clock radio, t/c mkg, refrig, toaster], pool (salt water), bbq, cots-fee. **RO** ♦ **$50 - $78**, ♦♦ **$68 - $88**, ♦ **$8 - $12**, ch con, Min book applies, AE BC DC MC VI.

TOWAMBA NSW 2550

Pop Nominal, (502km S Sydney), See map on pages 52/53, ref G8. Small town located 50km inland from Eden.

Self Catering Accommodation
Fulligans, Fulligans Rd via Pericoe Rd, ☎ 02 6496 7156, fax 02 6496 7156, 4 cabins acc up to 6, [shwr, tlt, fire pl, refrig, cook fac, micro, linen reqd-fee], rec rm, conf fac, bbq, courtesy transfer, ✆, cots. **D** ♦ **$66**, ch con, Access road subject to weather conditions, BC MC VI, (not yet classified).

TRENTHAM CLIFFS NSW 2738

Pop Nominal, (1014km SW Sydney), See map on pages 52/53, ref B5. Citrus and grape growing area on the Murray River near Mildura. Boating, Fishing, Swimming, Water Skiing.

B&B's/Guest Houses
★★★☆ **Mildura's Linsley House**, (B&B), Sturt Hwy, 15km E of Mildura PO, ☎ 03 5024 8487, 3 rms [shwr (2), tlt (2), a/c-cool, c/fan, heat, clock radio, t/c mkg], lounge (TV), ✕, refrig. **BB** ♦ **$60**, ♦♦ **$88**, BC MC VI.

TUMBARUMBA NSW 2653

Pop 1,500. (511km SW Sydney), See map on pages 52/53, ref F7. Small town in the western foothills of the Snowy Mountains, surrounded by the forests and hills of the high country. Bush Walking, Fishing, Gem Fossicking, Golf, Scenic Drives, Shooting, Tennis.

Hotels/Motels
★★★☆ **Tumbarumba Motel**, (M), Cnr Mate St & Albury Cl, ☎ 02 6948 2494, fax 02 6948 2204, 31 units [shwr, spa bath (3), tlt, fan, c/fan, cent heat, elec blkts, tel, fax, TV, clock radio, t/c mkg, refrig], ldry-fee, conv fac, ✉, bbq, rm serv, cots-fee, non smoking units (9). **RO** ♦ **$58 - $68**, ♦♦ **$68 - $89**, ♦ **$15**, 6 units yet to be assessed. AE BC DC MC VI.

B&B's/Guest Houses
★★★ **Cayirylys Bed & Breakfast**, (B&B), The Parade, ☎ 02 6948 3228, 6 rms (1 suite) [shwr, tlt, a/c-cool, c/fan, cent heat, elec blkts, TV, t/c mkg], ✕, c/park. **BB** ♦ **$55**, ♦♦ **$76**.

TUMUT NSW 2720

Pop 5,900. (445km SW Sydney), See map on pages 52/53, ref F6. Attractive town in the western Snowy Mountains, situated on the Tumut River and dotted with deciduous trees. Bowls, Fishing, Golf, Horse Riding, Sailing, Scenic Drives, Shooting, Swimming, Tennis.

Hotels/Motels

★★★☆ **Ashton Townhouse Motel**, (M), 124 Wynyard St, 150m W of PO, ☎ 02 6947 1999, fax 02 6947 3777, (2 stry gr fl), 20 units [shwr, tlt, hairdry, a/c, heat, elec blkts, tel, fax, TV, video-fee, clock radio, t/c mkg, refrig], ldry, iron, iron brd, ⊠, bbq, rm serv, cots-fee, non smoking units (10). RO ♦ $90.20, ♦♦ $103, ◊ $16.50, 6 units of a lower rating. AE BC DC EFT JCB MC MP VI.

★★★☆ **Elms Motor Inn**, (M), Snowy Mountains Hwy, 200m E of PO, ☎ 02 6947 3366, fax 02 6947 3001, 10 units [shwr, tlt, hairdry, a/c, heat, cent heat, elec blkts, tel, TV (3), video-fee, clock radio, t/c mkg, refrig], ldry, iron, iron brd, bbq, rm serv, dinner to unit, cots-fee, non smoking units (8), BLB ♦ $68 - $74, ♦♦ $80 - $93, ♦♦♦ $93 - $102, ◊ $12, AE BC DC EFT MC VI.

★★★☆ **Tumut Motor Inn**, (M), Cnr Wynyard St & Snowy Mountains Hwy, 200m NE of PO, ☎ 02 6947 4523, fax 02 6947 4527, (2 stry gr fl), 19 units (1 suite) [shwr, tlt, hairdry, a/c (19), heat, elec blkts, tel, fax, cable tv, video-fee, clock radio, t/c mkg, refrig], ldry, iron, iron brd, conf fac, ✕, pool, rm serv, plygr, cots-fee, non smoking units (6). RO ♦ $70 - $90, ♦♦ $80 - $100, ◊ $10, Min book long w/ends, AE BC DC MC VI.

★★★☆ **Tumut Valley View Motor Inn**, (M), Snowy Mountains Hwy, 2km S of PO, ☎ 02 6947 2666, fax 02 6947 3960, 30 units (5 suites) [shwr, spa bath (5), tlt, a/c, elec blkts, tel, TV, clock radio, t/c mkg, refrig, cook fac (12)], ldry, conv fac, ✕, pool, bbq, plygr, cots, non smoking units (5). RO ♦ $58 - $80, ♦♦ $65 - $100, ♦♦♦ $78 - $110, ◊ $10 - $12, Suite D $90 - $110, 12 units of a lower rating. AE BC DC MC MP VI.

★★★ **Amaroo Motel**, (M), 55 Capper St, Cnr Merrivale St, 500m W of PO, ☎ 02 6947 7200, fax 02 6947 7254, 29 units [shwr, tlt, a/c-cool (12), a/c (17), heat, tel, fax, TV, video-fee, clock radio, t/c mkg, refrig], ⊠ (Mon to Sat), bbq, dinner to unit, squash-fee, cots-fee, non smoking units (14). RO ♦ $49 - $88, ♦♦ $55 - $100, ◊ $10 - $14, 14 units of a lower rating, Min book long w/ends and Easter, AE BC DC EFT MC VI.

★★★ **Farrington Motel**, (M), 71 Capper St, 500m W of PO, ☎ 02 6947 1088, fax 02 6947 3831, (2 stry gr fl), 23 units [shwr, tlt, a/c, elec blkts, tel, cable tv, clock radio, t/c mkg, refrig], ldry, pool, bbq, cots-fee, non smoking units (8). RO ♦ $70 - $85, ♦♦ $80 - $95, AE BC DC JCB MC MP VI.

Self Catering Accommodation

★★★ **Callemondah**, (HU), 49 Blowering Rd, 2km S of PO, ☎ 02 6947 1531, fax 02 6947 1534, 6 units acc up to 8, [shwr, tlt, a/c, elec blkts, tel, TV, clock radio, refrig, cook fac, micro, toaster, ldry (in unit), linen reqd], c/park (carport), No pets. D ♦♦ $60, ◊ $5, W $540, BC MC VI.

★★★ **Tumut Log Cabins**, (Log Cabin), 30 Fitzroy St, 300m N of PO, ☎ 02 6947 4042, fax 02 6947 9185, 5 log cabins acc up to 5, [shwr, tlt, a/c-cool (5), fan, heat, elec blkts, TV, clock radio, t/c mkg, refrig, cook fac, micro, elec frypan, toaster], ldry-fee, bbq, c/park. D $55 - $61, ◊ $5, W $345 - $385, BC MC VI.

B&B's/Guest Houses

★★★★ **Cramarric B&B**, (B&B), East St, 1.5km S of PO, ☎ 02 6947 2122, (2 stry), 3 rms [shwr, tlt, a/c-cool, fan, fire pl, heat, elec blkts, tel], ldry, lounge (TV), ✕, cook fac, t/c mkg shared, bbq, non smoking rms. BB ♦ $35 - $45, ♦♦ $60 - $80, ◊ $30 - $40.

★★★☆ **Willowbank B&B**, (B&B), 8 Sydney St, 1km SE of Tourist Information Centre, ☎ 02 6947 2678, fax 02 6947 2678, 3 rms [shwr (2), tlt, a/c (1), c/fan (2), heat, elec blkts, tel, TV (1), video (1), clock radio, refrig (1), cook fac (1), micro (1), toaster (1)], ldry, iron, iron brd, t/c mkg shared, cots, non smoking property. BB ♦ $45, ♦♦ $65, RO ♦ $45 - $65, ♦♦ $65.

★★ **Yurunga B&B Farmstay**, (B&B), Gocup Rd, 3km from Tumut, ☎ 02 6947 2306, fax 02 6947 2306, 3 rms [shwr, tlt, heat, elec blkts, tel, clock radio, t/c mkg, refrig, toaster], c/park. BLB ♦ $40, ♦♦ $75, ◊ $25.

TUNCURRY NSW 2428

Pop 5,018. (300km N Sydney), See map on page 54, ref B8. Along with its twin town, Forster, Tuncurry is the tourism and commercial centre of the Great Lakes region. Boating, Bowls, Fishing, Surfing, Swimming, Tennis.

Hotels/Motels

★★★☆ **South Pacific Palms Motor Inn**, (M), 36 Manning St, 300m S of PO, ☎ 02 6554 6511, fax 02 6554 5830, (2 stry gr fl), 26 units [shwr, tlt, hairdry, a/c, fan, heat, elec blkts, tel, TV, video-fee, clock radio, t/c mkg, refrig, micro (15), elec frypan (15), toaster], ldry, iron, ⊠, pool-heated (solar), bbq, rm serv, cots-fee. RO ♦ $82.50 - $143, ♦♦ $93.50 - $143, ♦♦♦ $104.50 - $159.50, ◊ $11, Min book applies, AE BC DC EFT JCB MC MP VI.

★★★ **Spanish Motel**, (M), Cnr Manning & Wallis Sts, 400m N of PO, ☎ 02 6554 7044, 22 units [shwr, spa bath (4), tlt, hairdry, a/c (9), c/fan, heat, elec blkts, tel, cable tv, video-fee, movie, clock radio, t/c mkg, refrig, cook fac (1), toaster, ldry-fee], ldry, pool, bbq, cots-fee. RO ♦ $52 - $75, ♦♦ $58 - $95, ◊ $10, ch con, AE BC DC MC VI.

★★★ **Tuncurry Motor Lodge**, (M), 132 Manning St, 500m N of PO, ☎ 02 6554 8885, fax 02 6555 5053, (2 stry), 18 units [shwr, tlt, a/c, tel, cable tv, clock radio, t/c mkg, refrig, cook fac (5), toaster], ldry, rec rm, pool (salt water), bbq, ☏, non smoking units (18). RO ♦ $55 - $88, ♦♦ $66 - $95, ♦♦♦ $77 - $100, ◊ $10, ch con, AE BC DC MC VI.

★☆ **Bali-Hi Motel**, (M), 65 Manning St, 500m N of PO, ☎ 02 6554 6537, 14 units [shwr, tlt, fan, heat, elec blkts, TV, movie, clock radio, t/c mkg, refrig], pool, bbq, dinner to unit, cots-fee. RO ♦ $45 - $95, ♦♦ $45 - $95, ♦♦♦ $65 - $95, ♦♦♦♦ $65 - $95, BC MC VI.

Self Catering Accommodation

★★★★ **Castillo Del Mar**, (HU), 11-15 Beach St, 500m E of PO, ☎ 02 6554 8717, fax 02 6555 8664, (Multi-stry), 2 units acc up to 6, [shwr, bath, tlt, fan, heat, TV, video, clock radio, refrig, cook fac, micro, elec frypan, d/wash, toaster, ldry, linen reqd-fee], w/mach, dryer, iron, iron brd, bbq, c/park. W $470 - $1,400, Min book applies.

★★☆ **Beachcourt Holiday Cottages**, (HF), 25 Beach St, ☎ 02 6554 7562, 3 flats acc up to 6, [shwr, bath (1), tlt, heat, TV, refrig, cook fac, micro, toaster, linen reqd-fee], ldry, bbq. D $160 - $480.

B&B's/Guest Houses

★★★★☆ **Rest Point Bed & Breakfast**, (B&B), 35 Rest Point Parade, 1km W of Forster/Tuncurry Bridge, ☎ 02 6554 9051, fax 02 6555 2266, 2 rms (1 suite) [hairdry (1), c/fan, heat, elec blkts, TV (1), clock radio, refrig (1)], ldry, rec rm, TV rm, lounge (TV), lounge firepl, cook fac, t/c mkg shared, bbq, non smoking rms (2). BB ♦ $120 - $130, ♦♦ $120 - $130, ◊ $50, AE BC DC MC VI.

★★★★☆ **Tokelau Guest House**, (B&B), 2 Manning St, opposite Forster/Tuncurry Bridge, ☎ 02 6557 5157, fax 02 6557 5158, (2 stry gr fl), 5 rms [shwr (4), bath (4), spa bath (1), tlt, a/c (2), c/fan (3), fire pl (2)], ldry, lounge firepl, ✕, t/c mkg shared, dinner to unit-fee, non smoking property. BB ♦♦ $121 - $176, Min book long w/ends, AE BC DC EFT MC VI.

TUROSS HEAD NSW 2537

Pop 1,800. (322km S Sydney), See map on page 55, ref A6. Spectacularly situated south coast town surrounded by the waters of the Tuross and Coila Lakes and the Pacific Ocean. Boating, Bowls, Fishing, Golf, Scenic Drives, Surfing, Swimming.

Hotels/Motels
★★ **Motel Tuross**, (M), Previously Tuross Head Motel 6 Trafalgar Rd, ☎ 02 4473 8112, fax 02 4473 9008, 9 units [shwr, tlt, heat, TV, t/c mkg, refrig], ldry, ✗, bbq, dinner to unit, cots. **RO** ♦ $55 - $71, ♦♦ $62.50 - $82, ♦ $7.50 - $11, ch con, BC MC VI.

Self Catering Accommodation
★★★ **Selwood Holiday Units**, (HU), 19 Craddock Rd, ☎ 02 4473 8294, 3 units acc up to 5, [shwr, tlt, heat, elec blkts, TV, refrig, cook fac, micro, linen reqd], pool, bbq. **D** ♦ $45 - $55, ♦♦ $50 - $95, ♦♦♦ $120, ♦ $15 - $25, **W** $155 - $600, Min book applies.

★★☆ **Cabarita**, (HF), 24 Hawkins Rd, ☎ 02 4473 8757, 1 flat acc up to 5, [shwr, tlt, heat, TV, refrig, cook fac, micro, ldry], bbq, c/park (carport). **W** $230 - $430, Min book applies.

★ **Ella May**, (HF), 15 Jellicoe Rd, ☎ 02 4473 8147, 2 flats acc up to 6, [shwr, tlt, TV, refrig, cook fac, micro, linen reqd], ldry. **W** $200, Min book applies.

The Hermitage, (Cotg), 3 Kitchener Rd, ☎ 02 9527 3627, (2 stry), 1 cotg acc up to 6, [shwr, bath, tlt, fan, heat, TV, radio, refrig, cook fac, elec frypan, toaster, ldry, linen reqd], w/mach, iron, cots. **D** $80, **W** $560.

TWEED HEADS NSW 2485

Pop 55,857. (862km N Sydney), See map on page 54, ref E1. Northernmost town in New South Wales, set on the Tweed River across the Queensland border from its twin town of Coolangatta. Boating, Bowls, Fishing, Golf, Scenic Drives, Surfing, Swimming, Tennis. See also Coolangatta.

Hotels/Motels

★★★★☆ **Bayswater Motor Inn**, (M), 129 Wharf St, ☎ 07 5599 4111, fax 07 5599 4044, (2 stry gr fl), 38 units [shwr, bath (32), spa bath (2), hairdry, a/c, tel, TV, movie, clock radio, t/c mkg, refrig, mini bar, toaster], conv fac, ✉, pool, spa, cots-fee, non smoking units (16). **RO** ♦ $82.50 - $130, ♦♦ $88 - $140, ♦ $16.50 - $22, Minium bookings apply New Years Eve & Wintersun Festival June 8th, 9th & 10th 2001, AE BC DC EFT MC VI.

★★★★ **Las Vegas Motor Inn**, (M), 123 Wharf St (Old Pacific Hwy), ☎ 07 5536 3144, fax 07 5536 9090, 21 units [shwr, spa bath (6), tlt, a/c, c/fan, elec blkts, tel, TV, video (6), movie, clock radio, t/c mkg, refrig], ldry, pool-heated, bbq, cots, non smoking units (6). **W** $399 - $499, **RO** ♦♦ $75 - $89, ♦ $10, 6 units of a higher standard. 2 family rooms of a lower rating. AE BC DC EFT MC VI.

★★★★ **Tweed Harbour Motor Inn**, (M), 135 Wharf St (cnr Brett St), Opposite Tweed Heads Bowls Club, ☎ 07 5536 6066, fax 07 5536 9811, (2 stry gr fl), 16 units [shwr, tlt, hairdry, a/c, tel, TV, clock radio, t/c mkg, refrig, toaster], ldry, iron, iron brd, pool (salt), meals avail (breakfast), non smoking units (7). **RO** ♦ $62 - $95, ♦♦ $65 - $95, ♦ $10 - $20, AE BC DC EFT MC VI.

★★★☆ **Blue Pelican Motel**, (M), 115 Wharf St (Old Pacific Hwy), ☎ 07 5536 1777, fax 07 5599 1987, (2 stry gr fl), 21 units [shwr, tlt, hairdry, a/c, elec blkts, tel, TV, video (available), clock radio, t/c mkg, refrig, micro (5), toaster], pool, spa, bbq, cots, non smoking units (8). **RO** ♦♦ **$55 - $99**, ◊ **$16.50**, ch con, 5 units of a lower rating. Min book applies, AE BC DC MC VI, ⅋.

★★★☆ **City Lights Motel**, (M), 35 Old Pacific Hwy, Tweed Heads South 2486, 500m N of PO, ☎ 07 5524 3004, fax 07 5524 1888, (2 stry gr fl), 17 units [shwr, spa bath (1), tlt, a/c, c/fan (9), tel, TV, movie, clock radio, t/c mkg, refrig], ldry, breakfast rm, pool, c/park (undercover), non smoking units (5). **RO** ♦ **$45 - $95**, ♦♦ **$45 - $95**, 7 units of a lower rating. AE BC DC EFT MC VI, ⅋.

★★★☆ **Cooks Endeavour Motor Inn**, (M), 26 Frances St, 200m S of PO, ☎ 07 5536 5399, fax 07 5536 5486, 21 units [shwr, tlt, hairdry (21), a/c, tel, TV, clock radio, t/c mkg, refrig, ldry], pool (salt water), spa, bbq, cots-fee, non smoking units (avail). **RO** ♦♦ **$72 - $105**, ♦♦♦ **$90 - $122**, ◊ **$13 - $18**, ch con, 7 units of a higher standard. Min book Christmas Jan long w/ends and Easter, BC MC VI.

★★★☆ **Jack Hi Motel**, (M), Cnr Brett & Powell Sts, 1km SE of PO, behind Bowling Club, ☎ 07 5536 1788, fax 07 5536 1596, 24 units [shwr, tlt, a/c, fan (1), tel, TV, clock radio, t/c mkg, refrig, toaster], ldry, pool, spa, cots-fee. **RO** ♦ **$58 - $78**, ♦♦ **$65 - $95**, ◊ **$12**, ch con, AE BC DC MC VI, ⅋.

★★★ **Calico Court Motel**, (M), 29/33 Old Pacific Hwy, Tweed Heads South 2486, 2km S of PO, ☎ 07 5524 3333, fax 07 5524 3604, (2 stry gr fl), 32 units [shwr, tlt, a/c, elec blkts, tel, TV, movie, clock radio, t/c mkg, refrig, toaster], ldry, iron (16), iron brd (16), pool (salt water), bbq, cots, non smoking units (16). **RO** ♦ **$45 - $75**, ♦♦ **$45 - $85**, ◊ **$10**, 16 units yet to be assessed, AE BC DC EFT MC VI.

★★★ **Kennedy Drive Motor Inn**, (M), 203 Kennedy Dve, Tweed Heads West 2485, 1km E of Seagulls League Club, ☎ 07 5536 1986, fax 07 5536 9272, (2 stry gr fl), 25 units [shwr, tlt, a/c, tel, TV, clock radio, t/c mkg, refrig, toaster], ldry, pool (salt water), bbq, cots-fee, non smoking units (10). **RO** ♦ **$52.50**, ♦♦ **$55**, ◊ **$10.50**, ch con, AE BC EFT MC VI.

★★★ **South Tweed Motor Inn**, (M), 9 Minjungbal Dr (Old Pacific Hwy), Tweed Heads South 2486, 1km N of PO, ☎ 07 5524 3111, fax 07 5524 2311, 20 units [shwr, tlt, a/c, tel, fax, TV, clock radio, t/c mkg, refrig, toaster], pool, bbq, cots, non smoking units (6). **RO** ♦ **$44 - $75**, ♦♦ **$46 - $80**, ♦♦♦ **$56 - $95**, ◊ **$7.50 - $15**, AE BC DC EFT MC VI.

★★★ **Twin Towns Motel**, (M), 21 Old Pacific Hwy, Tweed Heads South 2486, ☎ 07 5524 3108, fax 07 5524 3108, 16 units [shwr, spa bath (1), tlt, a/c (14), fan, TV, radio, t/c mkg, refrig, cook fac (1)], ldry, pool, bbq, ✆, cots. **RO** ♦ **$45 - $95**, ♦♦ **$48 - $95**, ch con, AE BC DC EFT MC VI.

★★☆ **Homestead Tweed**, (M), 58 Boyd St, 400m S of Bowls Club, ☎ 07 5536 1544, fax 07 5536 4123, (2 stry gr fl), 13 units [shwr, tlt, hairdry, a/c, tel, TV, clock radio, t/c mkg, refrig, toaster], ldry, pool, cots-fee, non smoking units (5). **D $90**, **RO** ♦ **$50**, ♦♦ **$55**, ♦♦♦ **$60**, ◊ **$10**, AE BC EFT MC VI.

★★☆ **Tweed Fairways Motel**, (M), Cnr Old Pacific Hwy & Soorley St, Tweed Heads South 2486, 600m S of Tweed Heads South PO, ☎ 07 5524 2111, fax 07 5524 9906, (2 stry gr fl), 44 units [shwr, tlt, a/c (26), fan (18), tel, TV, movie, clock radio, t/c mkg, refrig, micro (6), toaster], ldry, pool, cots. **RO** ♦♦ **$33**, ◊ **$11**, 6 units of a higher standard. AE BC DC EFT MC VI, ⅋.

Self Catering Accommodation

★★☆ **Carolina**, (HU), 42 Boundary St, Rainbow Bay, 300m E of PO, ☎ 07 5536 8855, fax 07 5599 2219, (2 stry), 5 units acc up to 6, [shwr, bath, tlt, fan, TV, radio, refrig, cook fac, micro, toaster, linen], ldry, c/park (carport). **W** ♦♦ **$260 - $600**, ◊ **$10 - $20**, Min book applies, AE BC DC EFT JCB MC VI.

★★ **Haven**, (HU), 40 Boundary St, Rainbow Bay, 300m E of Twin Towns RSL, ☎ 07 5536 5112, 6 units acc up to 6, [shwr, bath, tlt, fan, TV, radio, refrig, cook fac, toaster, linen reqd-fee], ldry, **D** ♦♦ **$260 - $660**.

★★ **Sea Drift**, (HU), 32 Boundary St, Rainbow Bay, ☎ 07 5536 4256, fax 07 5536 9109, (2 stry), 6 units acc up to 6, [tlt, fan, heat (avail), TV, movie, clock radio, refrig, cook fac, micro, linen reqd-fee], ldry, bbq. **W** ♦♦ **$240 - $600**, ◊ **$10 - $20**, Min book applies.

TYALGUM NSW 2484

Pop 250. (830km N Sydney), See map on page 54, ref D1. Picturesque village situated on the banks of the Oxley River.

★★★☆ **Tyalgum Tops Farm Resort**, (HU), (Farm), Tyalgum Creek Rd, 10km W of Mt Warning, 32km W of Murwillumbah, ☎ 02 6679 3370, fax 02 6679 3399, 5 units acc up to 6, [shwr, tlt, c/fan, heat, elec blkts, tel, t/c mkg, refrig, cook fac, toaster, blkts, linen, pillows], ldry, w/mach-fee, dryer-fee, iron-fee, rec rm, pool (salt water), bbq, ✆, plygr, tennis, cots. **D** ♦ **$77**, ◊ **$27.50**, **W** ♦♦ **$594**, ◊ **$165**, Min book applies, BC MC VI.

TYNDALE NSW 2460

Pop Nominal, (655km N Sydney), See map on page 54, ref D3. Small town between Grafton and Maclean.

★★☆ **Plantation**, (M), Pacific Hwy, 30km N of Grafton, ☎ 02 6647 6290, fax 02 6647 6290, (2 stry gr fl), 16 units [shwr, tlt, fan, heat, elec blkts, TV, clock radio, t/c mkg, refrig], ldry, lounge, conv fac, pool, bbq, cots. **RO** ♦ **$40 - $48**, ♦♦ **$45 - $55**, ♦♦♦ **$50 - $60**, ◊ **$6 - $12**, ch con, AE BC MC VI.

UKI NSW 2484

Pop 250. (820km N Sydney), See map on page 54, ref E1. Historic village on the Tweed River at the foot of Mount Warning.

Self Catering Accommodation

★★★ **Ecoasis**, 55 Tatyewan Ave Smiths Creek via, 5km E of PO, ☎ 02 6679 5959, fax 02 6679 5759, (2 stry gr fl), 2 cabins acc up to 12, (1 & 2 bedrm), [shwr, spa bath, tlt, c/fan, heat, TV, video, clock radio, t/c mkg, refrig, cook fac, d/wash, toaster, blkts, doonas, linen, pillows], bbq, cots, non smoking property. **D** ♦♦♦♦ **$231 - $357.50**, ◊ **$55**, **W** ♦♦♦♦ **$1,430 - $2,200**, ◊ **$330**, ch con, Min book all holiday times, BC MC VI.

B&B's/Guest Houses

Midginbil Hill Country Resort, (GH), Midginbil Rd, 30km SW of Murwillumbah, ☎ 02 6679 7158, fax 02 6679 7120, 8 rms [shwr, tlt, fan, heat], ldry, rec rm, conv fac, ✕, pool (salt water), t/c mkg shared, ✆, canoeing, tennis. **DBB** ♦♦ **$185**, ◊ **$47**, ch con, Min book all holiday times, BC MC VI.

ULLADULLA NSW 2539

Pop 8,400. (246km S Sydney), See map on page 55, ref B5. Ulladulla and neighbouring Mollymook form the largest settlement on the south coast between Nowra and Batemans Bay.

Hotels/Motels

FLAG
FLAG CHOICE HOTELS

★★★☆ **Albacore Motel - Holiday Apartments**, (M), Boree St, 200m S of PO, ☎ 02 4455 1322, fax 02 4455 2204, 19 units [shwr, bath, tlt, hairdry, a/c (8), c/fan (12), heat, elec blkts, tel, TV, video (avail), movie, clock radio, t/c mkg, refrig, cook fac (10), toaster], ldry, iron, iron brd, pool, bbq, cots-fee, non smoking units (6). **RO** ♦ **$82.50 - $150**, ♦♦ **$82.50 - $150**, ◊ **$16.50 - $22**, ch con, 8 units ★★★, Min book applies, AE BC DC JCB MC MP VI.

★★★☆ **Harbour Royal Motel**, (M), 29 Burrill St, ☎ 02 4455 5444, fax 02 4455 5993, (Multi-stry gr fl), 21 units (4 suites) [shwr, spa bath (4), tlt, hairdry, a/c, fan, heat, tel, TV, video (avail), clock radio, t/c mkg, refrig, mini bar, cook fac ltd (8), micro (10), toaster], ldry, pool indoor heated, bbq, rm serv, plygr, mini golf, cots. **RO** ♦ **$70 - $110**, ♦♦ **$75 - $144**, ◊ **$17**, Suite **RO** ♦♦ **$121 - $166**, ◊ **$17**, pen con, 8 rooms of a 4 star rating. AE BC DC EFT JCB MC MP VI, ⅋, *Operator Comment: 3 Day Package For 2 Persons From $228. B&B. Fully Air Conditioned.*

Best Western

★★★☆ **Pigeon House Motor Inn**, (M), 156 Princes Hwy, 600m S of PO, ☎ 02 4455 1811, fax 02 4455 5256, 16 units [shwr, tlt, hairdry, c/fan, heat, elec blkts, tel, TV, movie, clock radio, t/c mkg, refrig, toaster], iron, iron brd, pool (salt water), bbq, dinner to unit, cots-fee, non smoking units (5). **RO** ♦ **$63 - $120**, ♦♦ **$84 - $170**, ◊ **$15**, Min book applies, AE BC DC EFT JCB MC MP VI, *Operator Comment: Call about 3 day package from $198 per couple B & B.*

Winner
97, 98, 99 & 2000
Awards For
Excellence
in Tourism

Ulladulla Guest House Est. 1966

AAAT ★ ★ ★ ★ ★ www.guesthouse.com.au

• Heated pool, indoor and outdoor spas, sauna & gym
• Marble bathrooms with private spas available
• Lounge, library, conference room
• Air conditioned
• Elizans French Provincial Restaurant
• Surrounded by tropical gardens

39 Burrill St, Ulladulla NSW 2535

Ph: (02) 4455 1796

★★☆ **Windmill Harbour Foreshore Motel**, (M), Cnr Crescent St & Princes Hwy, ☎ 02 4455 5277, 9 units [shwr, tlt, a/c (3), fan, heat, elec blkts, tel, TV, clock radio, t/c mkg, refrig, ldry (service)], dinner to unit, c/park (garage) (3), bicycle, canoeing. **BLB ╬ $50 - $150, ╫ $50 - $150, ╫╫ $60 - $150, ◊ $10 - $20,** 3 units of a lower rating. AE BC DC MC VI.

Self Catering Accommodation

★★★★ **Ocean Point Resort**, (Cotg), Kings Point Dve, 2km S of PO, ☎ 02 4454 4261, fax 02 4454 2061, 28 cotgs acc up to 7, [shwr, tlt, heat, tel, TV, t/c mkg, refrig, cook fac, micro, toaster, linen-fee], ldry, rec rm, pool, sauna, spa, bbq, kiosk, plygr, squash, tennis, cots-fee. **D $72 - $145, W $504 - $1,015,** Min book applies, BC EFT MC VI.

B&B's/Guest Houses

★★★★★ **Ulladulla Guest House**, (GH), 39 Burrill St, 150m S of the harbour, ☎ 02 4455 1796, fax 02 4454 4660, (2 stry gr fl), 7 rms [shwr, bath (1), spa bath (2), tlt, hairdry, a/c-cool, c/fan, elec blkts, TV, video (avail), clock radio, t/c mkg, refrig, ldry (service)], iron, conv fac, ✗, pool-heated (salt water), sauna, spa (indoor /outdoor-heat), bbq, rm serv, dinner to unit, ✆, gym, non smoking property. **RO ╬ $100 - $160, ╫ $118 - $195, ◊ $40,** 2 units of a 4.5 star rating. Min book applies, AE BC DC EFT MC VI.

★★★☆ **(Holiday Unit Section)**, 2 units acc up to 4, [shwr, tlt, hairdry, a/c-cool, elec blkts, TV, video, clock radio, t/c mkg, refrig, cook fac ltd, micro, elec frypan, d/wash, toaster, blkts, linen, pillows], ldry. **D ╫ $105 - $204, ╫╫ $105 - $204, ◊ $40, W $590 - $710,** Min book applies.

UMINA NSW 2257

Pop Part of Gosford, (86km N Sydney), See map on page 56, ref E3. Central Coast town on the upper reaches of Broken Bay.
★★★★ **Ocean Beach Bed and Breakfast**, (B&B), 192 The Esplanade, ☎ 02 4342 8383, rms (0 suites) [a/c, video (in guest lounge), clock radio, t/c mkg (communal), refrig (communal), ldry, doonas], TV rm, ✗, spa, bbq, ✆, cots, Pets on application. **BB ╬ $60 - $80, ╫ $90 - $100, ◊ $50, Suite D $100 - $110,** ch con, Min book applies.

URALLA NSW 2358

Pop 2,450. (546km N Sydney), See map on page 54, ref A5. For years, Uralla was the stamping ground of bushranger Fred Ward (aka Thunderbolt) and there are plenty of reminders of him in this pretty New England town. Bowls, Fishing, Gem Fossicking, Golf, Scenic Drives, Shooting.

Hotels/Motels
★★★★ **Bushranger Motor Inn**, (M), 37-41 Bridge St (New England Hwy), Main St, ☎ 02 6778 3777, fax 02 6778 3888, 17 units [shwr, bath, spa bath (8), tlt, hairdry, a/c, elec blkts, tel, TV, clock radio, t/c mkg, refrig, mini bar, toaster], ldry, ✗, bar, rm serv, dinner to unit (6 nights), cots. **RO ╬ $67 - $75, ╫ $75 - $85, ◊ $13 - $16,** AE BC DC EFT MC VI, ♿.

★★★ **Altona Regency Motel**, (M), New England Hwy, 1km S of PO, ☎ 02 6778 4007, fax 02 6778 4599, 16 units [shwr, tlt, a/c-cool (5), fan (11), heat, cent heat, elec blkts, tel, TV, clock radio, t/c mkg, refrig, toaster], ldry, bbq, meals to unit, courtesy transfer, cots-fee. **RO ╬ $44.90 - $69, ╫ $49.90 - $79, ╫╫ $58.90 - $89, ◊ $11,** ch con, pen con, AE BC DC EFT MC VI.

★★☆ **Thunderbolt Inn Hotel**, (LH), 31 Bridge St, Main St, ☎ 02 6778 4048, fax 02 6778 3431, (2 stry), 9 rms [shwr (2), bath (1), tlt (2), elec blkts, clock radio], shared fac (7 rooms), ✉, t/c mkg shared, bbq, ✆. **RO ╬ $35, ╫ $35, ╫╫ $40,** BC EFT MC VI.

Self Catering Accommodation

★★★★ **Cruickshanks Cottage B & B and Farmstay**, (Cotg), Tourist Drive 19, ☎ 02 6778 2148, fax 02 6778 2148, 1 cotg acc up to 8, [shwr, bath, tlt, fire pl, elec blkts, tel, TV, clock radio, t/c mkg, refrig, cook fac, micro, elec frypan, toaster, ldry], iron, iron brd, bbq, meals avail. **BB ╬ $66, ╫ $110, ◊ $27.50 - $66,** ch con, AE BC MC VI.

★★★ **Lindon Cottage Bed & Breakfast**, (Cotg), (Farm), Lindon Rd via Kingstown Rd, 26km fr PO, 6 km dirt road. ☎ 02 6778 7120, fax 02 6778 7153, 1 cotg acc up to 6, [shwr (2), tlt (2), hairdry, fan, fire pl (1), heat, elec blkts, radio, t/c mkg, refrig, cook fac, micro, toaster], iron, iron brd, bbq, dinner to unit (by arrangement), tennis, non smoking rms. **BB ╬ $110, ╫ $110, ◊ $20,** ch con,
Operator Comment: "Please visit our website"
www.babs.com.au/lindon

B&B's/Guest Houses
Gwydir Getaway Farmstay Cottage, (B&B), Stony Batter North, 55km NW of Uralla, 65km S of Inverell, ☎ 02 6723 7234, fax 02 6723 7234, 3 rms [shwr, tlt, fire pl, heat, elec blkts, radio, t/c mkg, refrig, cook fac, micro, elec frypan, toaster], ldry, bbq, dinner to unit, canoeing, tennis, cots. **BB ╬ $80, ╫ $100, RO ╫ $80,** ch con, (not yet classified).

URUNGA NSW 2455

Pop 2,700. (530km N Sydney), See map on page 54, ref D5. Favourite north coast holiday spot at the mouth of the Bellinger and Kalang Rivers. Boating, Bowls, Fishing, Golf, Scenic Drives, Surfing, Swimming, Tennis.

Hotels/Motels
★★☆ **Kalang River**, (M), Pacific Hwy, 400m N of PO, ☎ 02 6655 6229, fax 02 6655 5184, 8 units [shwr, tlt, fan, heat, fax, TV, t/c mkg, refrig, toaster], ✗, ✗, bbq, rm serv, ✆. **RO ╬ $40 - $55, ╫ $45 - $65, ╫╫ $60 - $90, ◊ $10,** BC MC VI.

★★☆ **Sudden Comfort Motel**, (M), Pacific Hwy, 1.6km S of PO, ☎ 02 6655 6900, fax 02 6655 6900, 8 units [shwr, bath (1), tlt, c/fan, heat, TV, clock radio, t/c mkg, refrig, toaster], rm serv, meals avail, trailer park, non smoking property. **RO ╬ $40 - $66, ╫ $44 - $77, ╫╫╫ $55 - $88, ◊ $16.50 - $22,** AE BC EFT MC VI.

★★☆ **Westella Motel**, (M), 107 Pacific Hwy, 1.5km S of PO, ☎ 02 6655 6319, fax 02 6655 5242, 14 units [shwr, tlt, c/fan, heat, TV, clock radio, t/c mkg, refrig, cook fac (2)], ldry, pool, bbq, rm serv, c/park (undercover) (8), ✆, plygr, cots. **W $195 - $385, RO ╬ $35 - $45, ╫ $40 - $65, ╫╫ $45 - $65, ◊ $10 - $15,** ch con, BC EFT MC VI.

Brigalow Park, (M), Pacific Hwy, 3km S of PO, ☎ 02 6655 6334, fax 02 6655 3156, 8 units [shwr, tlt, fan, heat, elec blkts, TV, t/c mkg, refrig], ldry, pool, plygr, mini golf, tennis, cots, **RO ╫ $38 - $66, ◊ $5,** Min book Christmas and Jan, BC EFT MC VI (not yet classified).

Self Catering Accommodation
★★★☆ **Hungry Head Retreat**, (Cotg), 368 Hungry Head Rd, 1.6km E of Pacific Hwy, ☎ 02 6655 6736, fax 02 6655 6736, 1 cotg acc up to 6, [shwr, tlt, hairdry, c/fan, heat, tel, TV, CD, t/c mkg, refrig, cook fac, toaster], iron, spa, bbq, breakfast ingredients. **D $95 - $160, W $600 - $990,** BC MC VI.

★★★ **The Links**, (HU), 7 Bellingen St, ☎ 02 6655 6193, 3 units acc up to 6, [shwr, tlt, TV, refrig, cook fac, micro, toaster, ldry, linen reqd], bbq, c/park (carport). **W $180 - $420.**

★★☆ **Urunga Townhouse**, (HU), Bowra St, 120m NW of PO, ☎ 02 6655 6167, fax 02 6655 5998, 2 units acc up to 4, [shwr, bath, tlt, heat, TV, refrig, cook fac, micro, d/wash, toaster, ldry (in unit)], w/mach, c/park (garage). **W $260 - $490.**

URANGA NSW continued...

★★ **Paringa**, (HF), 5 Bellingen St, ☎ 02 6655 6305, 2 flats acc up to 6, [shwr, tlt, heat, TV, refrig, cook fac, micro, linen reqd], ldry, bbq, c/park (carport), plygr. **W $170 - $400**.

★☆ **Ernora Court**, (HU), 3 Bellingen St, 500m N of PO, ☎ 02 6655 6167, fax 02 6655 5998, 3 units acc up to 4, [shwr, tlt, TV, refrig, cook fac, ldry], c/park (carport). **W $220 - $390**, Min book applies.

★☆ **Greenview Court**, (HU), Bonville St, 20m S of PO, ☎ 02 6655 6167, 1 unit acc up to 4, [shwr, tlt, TV, refrig, cook fac, linen reqd], ldry, c/park (garage). **W $210 - $320**.

★ **Hungry Head Nature Reserve Cabins**, (HU), Hungry Head Rd, 4km S of PO, ☎ 02 6655 6208, fax 02 6655 6208, 10 units acc up to 6, [shwr, tlt, fan, heat, TV, refrig, cook fac, linen reqd], ldry, bbq. **D $59 - $69**, pen con, Min book applies.

B&B's/Guest Houses

★★★★ **Maino Gabuna**, (B&B), Wollumbin Dve, Hungry Head Urunga, ☎ 02 6655 6017, fax 02 6655 5955, (2 stry gr fl), 3 rms [shwr, tlt, fan (1), c/fan (2), heat, elec blkts, tel, clock radio], iron, iron brd, lounge (TV), lounge firepl, t/c mkg shared, bbq, plygr, cots, non smoking rms. **BB ♦ $95, ♦♦ $145**, AE BC MC VI, 🐾.

Newry Island Retreat, (B&B), 29 The Grove, Newry Island, 3 km W from Urunga PO, ☎ 02 6655 6050, fax 02 6655 6050, 2 rms [ensuite (2), heat, c/fan, elec blkts, TV, video, clock radio (1), radio, t/c mkg (1), refrig (1), cook fac ltd, doonas], t/c mkg shared, refrig, cots, non smoking rms. **BLB ♦ $55 - $70, ♦♦ $75 - $100, ◊ $25**, ch con, BC MC VI, (not yet classified).

VACY NSW 2421

Pop Nominal, (195km N Sydney), See map on page 54, ref A8. Small town on the Paterson River between Paterson and East Gresford. Bush Walking, Scenic Drives.

Hotels/Motels

★★★☆ **Vacy Village**, (M), Gresford Rd, opposite PO 25km N of Maitland, ☎ 02 4938 8089, 8 units [shwr, tlt, a/c, elec blkts, TV, clock radio, t/c mkg, refrig, cook fac (2), toaster], iron, iron brd, bbq, rm serv, dinner to unit, cots, non smoking units (5). **RO ♦ $49 - $55, ♦♦ $59 - $65, ◊ $12**, ch con, AE BC DC MC VI.

Self Catering Accommodation

★★★★★ **Banjo's Bushland Retreat**, (House), via Summerhill Rd, 10km fr PO, ☎ 02 9403 3388, fax 02 9449 5873, 2 houses acc up to 6, (2 & 4 bedrm), [shwr, bath (2), tlt, c/fan, heat, tel, clock radio, blkts, doonas, linen, pillows], ldry, w/mach, dryer, lounge (TV, video), lounge firepl, ⊠, pool, sauna, spa, cook fac, t/c mkg shared, refrig, bbq, c/park (undercover), plygr, cots, non smoking property. **RO ♦♦ $130 - $184, ◊ $75**, ch con, Min book applies.

★★★★★ **Eaglereach Wilderness Resort**, (Cotg), Summer Hill Rd, ☎ 02 4938 8233, fax 02 4938 8234, 38 cotgs acc up to 10, [shwr, spa bath (23), tlt, hairdry, a/c (9), c/fan, fire pl, elec blkts, TV, video, refrig, cook fac, micro, toaster, ldry (in unit), blkts, linen, pillows], iron, conv fac, ⊠, pool (salt water), bbq, shop, ☏, plygr, bush walking, bicycle, tennis, cots, non smoking units (avail). **BB ♦ $210 - $230, ♦♦ $210 - $230, ◊ $86 - $99**, ch con, 9 cottages of a higher standard. Min book applies, AE BC DC EFT JCB MC VI.

VINCENTIA NSW 2540

Pop Part of Huskisson, (182km S Sydney), See map on page 55, ref B5. Holiday town situated south of Huskisson on Jervis Bay. Boating, Bowls, Fishing, Golf, Scenic Drives, Swimming, Tennis.

Hotels/Motels

★★★★ **Jervis Bay Dolphin Shores Motor Inn**, (M), 53 Beach St, 400m NW of PO, ☎ 02 4441 6895, fax 02 4441 6895, 12 units [shwr, spa bath (4), tlt, hairdry, a/c, elec blkts, tel, TV, video (2)-fee, clock radio, t/c mkg, refrig, cook fac (4), cook fac ltd (4), micro (8), toaster], ldry, iron, iron brd, pool-heated (solar), spa, bbq, cots, non smoking units. **RO ♦ $85 - $170, ♦♦ $85 - $170, ♦♦♦ $93 - $190, ◊ $10 - $20**, ch con, Min book applies, AE BC EFT MC VI.

★★★★ **(Serviced Apartment Section)**, 4 serv apts [shwr, tlt, hairdry, a/c, elec blkts, tel, TV, video-fee, clock radio, t/c mkg, refrig, cook fac, micro, toaster], ldry, iron, bbq, cots, non smoking property. **RO ♦ $125 - $220, ♦♦ $125 - $220, ◊ $20, W $700 - $1,500**.

Self Catering Accommodation

★★★ **Collingwood on the Beach**, (House), 168 Elizabeth Dve, 500m N of shopping centre, ☎ 02 4421 7118, fax 02 4421 8947, 4 houses acc up to 10, [shwr, spa bath, tlt, c/fan, heat, TV, video, clock radio, CD, t/c mkg, refrig, cook fac, micro, d/wash, toaster, ldry, doonas, linen reqd-fee], w/mach, dryer, iron, iron brd, rec rm, bbq, non smoking property. **D $190 - $300, W $1,075 - $1,900**, Min book applies, AE BC DC MC VI.

Jervis Bay's Sea Change, (HU), 2/42 Elizabeth Dve, 1.5km S of Huskisson, ☎ 02 4441 6400, fax 02 4441 6636, (2 stry gr fl) 1 unit acc up to 6, (2 bedrm), [shwr, tlt, hairdry, fan, heat, TV, video, clock radio, CD, t/c mkg, refrig, cook fac, micro, d/wash, toaster, ldry, blkts, doonas, linen reqd-fee, pillows], w/mach, dryer, bbq, c/park (undercover), non smoking property. **D $125 - $170, W $720 - $1,200**, Min book all holiday times, (not yet classified).

B&B's/Guest Houses

★★★☆ **Bay View**, (B&B), 306 Elizabeth Dve, ☎ 02 4441 5805, 2 rms [shwr, tlt, fan, heat, elec blkts, tel, TV, clock radio, t/c mkg, refrig, micro, toaster], ldry, bbq, cots. **BLB ♦ $50, ♦♦ $95, ◊ $25**, ch con.

WAGGA WAGGA NSW 2650

Pop 42,850. (455km SW Sydney), See map on pages 52/53, ref E6. Flourishing city that is the major regional and cultural centre for the Riverina. It's also known as the 'Garden City of the South' because of its extensive parklands and floral displays. Bowls, Croquet, Fishing, Golf, Scenic Drives, Swimming, Tennis.

Hotels/Motels

★★★★☆ **Carriage House Motor Inn**, (M), Sturt Hwy, 4km E of PO, ☎ 02 6922 7374, fax 02 6922 7346, (2 stry gr fl), 37 units (4 suites) [shwr, spa bath (1), tlt, hairdry, a/c, elec blkts, tel, TV, movie, clock radio, t/c mkg, refrig, mini bar], ldry, iron, iron brd, conv fac, ⊠, bar, pool, sauna, spa, bbq, dinner to unit, plygr, tennis, cots. **RO ♦♦ $119 - $168, ◊ $12**, AE BC DC MC MP VI.

★★★★☆ **Townhouse International**, (M), 70 Morgan St, 50m from PO, ☎ 02 6921 4337, fax 02 6921 7509, (Multi-stry), 42 units (4 suites) [shwr, tlt, a/c, elec blkts, tel, TV, movie, clock radio, t/c mkg, refrig, mini bar], lift, ldry, lounge, conv fac, ⊠, pool, non smoking units (25). **RO $79 - $250, Suite RO $160**, AE BC DC JCB MC VI.

★★★★ **Ambassador Motor Inn**, (M), 313-315 Edward St, ☎ 02 6925 7722, fax 02 6925 6990, 22 units (0 suites) [shwr, spa bath (2), tlt, hairdry, a/c, elec blkts, tel, TV, video-fee, movie, clock radio, t/c mkg, refrig, mini bar, cook fac (3), micro (2), toaster], ldry, iron, iron brd, pool (salt water), bbq, dinner to unit (7am to 11pm), cots-fee, non smoking units (7), **RO ♦ $98, ♦♦ $110, ◊ $13, Suite D ♦♦ $120, ♦♦♦♦ $146**, AE BC DC EFT MC MP VI.

★★★★ **Boulevarde Motor Inn**, (M), 305 Edward St, ☎ 02 6925 5388, fax 02 6925 5603, 22 units [shwr, spa bath (2), tlt, hairdry, a/c, elec blkts, tel, TV, video (avail), movie, clock radio, t/c mkg, refrig, mini bar, micro (4), toaster], iron, iron brd, pool-heated (salt water), bbq, rm serv, dinner to unit, cots, non smoking units (14). **RO** ♦ $76 - $87, ♦♦ $87 - $100, ♦♦♦ $99 - $112, ◊ $13, AE BC DC MC VI.

★★★★ **Country Comfort Wagga Wagga**, (M), Cnr Morgan & Tarcutta Sts, 800m NE of PO, ☎ 02 6921 6444, fax 02 6921 2922, (2 stry gr fl), 90 units (3 suites) [shwr, bath (5), spa bath (7), tlt, a/c, elec blkts, tel, TV, video (44), clock radio, t/c mkg, refrig, mini bar], ldry, rec rm, conv fac, ⊠ (Mon-Sat), pool, sauna, spa, 24hr reception, rm serv, dinner to unit, courtesy transfer, cots-fee. **RO** ♦ $125, ♦♦ $125, ◊ $15, 37 units ★★★☆. AE BC DC MC VI.

★★★★☆ **(Serviced Apartment Section)**, 6 serv apts acc up to 6, [shwr, bath, tlt, hairdry, a/c, elec blkts, tel, TV, video, clock radio, t/c mkg, refrig, mini bar, cook fac, micro, toaster, blkts, linen, pillows], ldry, w/mach, dryer, iron, bbq, c/park (garage). **D $190 - $250.**

★★★★ Heritage Motor Inn, (M), 244 Edward St, 1km W of Wagga South, ☎ 02 6921 4099, fax 02 6921 6129, (2 stry gr fl), 22 units [shwr, spa bath (4), tlt, hairdry, a/c, elec blkts, tel, cable tv, video-fee, clock radio, t/c mkg, refrig], ldry, iron, iron brd, pool, sauna, spa, bbq, rm serv, dinner to unit, cots-fee, non smoking units (12). **RO ╪ $85 - $112, ╫ $95 - $120, ╬ $10**, AE BC DC MC MP VI.

★★★★ Lincoln Cottage Motor Inn, (M), 337 Edward St, 1km W of Wagga South, ☎ 02 6925 3833, fax 02 6925 3891, 22 units [shwr, spa bath (1), tlt, hairdry, a/c, heat, elec blkts, tel, TV, video-fee, clock radio, t/c mkg, refrig, cook fac (3), toaster], ldry, pool (salt water), bbq, meals to unit, courtesy transfer, plygr, cots-fee, non smoking units (11). **RO ╫ $105**, AE BC DC EFT MC MP VI.

★★★☆ (Serviced Apartment Section), 3 serv apts acc up to 4, [shwr, bath, tlt, a/c, c/fan, heat, elec blkts, tel, TV, video-fee, clock radio, refrig, cook fac, micro, elec frypan, toaster, ldry, blkts, linen, pillows], w/mach, iron, rm serv, cots-fee. **D ╫╫ $150**.

★★★★ Pavilion Motor Inn, (M), 22 Kincaid St, 2km N of PO, ☎ 02 6921 6411, fax 02 6921 6235, (Multi-stry gr fl), 45 units (16 suites) [shwr, bath (4), spa bath (5), tlt, hairdry, a/c, cent heat, elec blkts, tel, TV, movie, clock radio, t/c mkg, refrig, mini bar, cook fac (4)], lift, iron, conv fac, ⊠, pool-indoor, rm serv, dinner to unit, cots. **RO ╪ $130 - $190, ╫ $130 - $190, ╫╫ $140 - $190, ╬ $10, Suite D $130 - $175**, ch con, AE BC DC JCB MC MP VI.

★★★★ The Carlyle Motel, (M), 148 Tarcutta St, 500m N of PO, ☎ 02 6931 0968, fax 02 6931 0967, (2 stry gr fl), 21 units (4 suites) [ensuite, bath (14), spa bath (1), a/c, tel, TV, clock radio, t/c mkg, refrig, cook fac (2), cook fac ltd (2), micro (4), toaster (4)], ldry, cots-fee, non smoking rms (12). **RO ╪ $97 - $108, ╫ $97 - $108, ╬ $11, Suite RO ╫╫ $142 - $175**, ch con, AE BC DC EFT MC VI.

★★★☆ Allonville Motel, (M), Previously Allonville Gardens Motor Inn 3705 Sturt Hwy, Gumly Gumly, 7km E of Wagga, ☎ 02 6922 7269, fax 02 6922 7447, 29 units (4 suites) [shwr, tlt, hairdry, a/c, elec blkts, tel, TV, video-fee, clock radio, t/c mkg, refrig, mini bar], ldry, iron, iron brd, conv fac, ⊠, pool (salt water), bbq, dinner to unit, plygr, cots-fee, non smoking units (11), Pets welcome onto grounds, kennels & stables available. **RO ╪ $80, ╫ $92, ╬ $12, Suite D $150**, ch con, AE BC DC EFT MC VI.

★★★☆ Centralpoint Motel, (M), 164 Tarcutta St, ☎ 02 6921 7272, fax 02 6921 3446, (2 stry gr fl), 14 units [shwr, tlt, hairdry, a/c, heat, elec blkts, tel, fax, TV, clock radio, t/c mkg, refrig, cook fac, micro, toaster], ldry, iron, iron brd, ✆, cots-fee. **RO ╪ $83 - $100, ╫ $99 - $118, ╫╫ $120 - $138, ╬ $12**, AE BC DC MC VI.

★★★☆ (Serviced Apartment Section), (2 stry gr fl), 12 serv apts acc up to 6, [shwr, tlt, hairdry, a/c, heat, elec blkts, tel, TV, clock radio, t/c mkg, refrig, cook fac, micro, toaster, blkts, linen, pillows], ldry, dryer, iron, iron brd, ✆, cots. **D ╪ $83 - $100, ╫ $99 - $118, ╬ $12, W $434 - $588**.

★★★☆ Charles Sturt Motor Inn, (M), 82 Tarcutta St, ☎ 02 6921 8088, fax 02 6921 6279, 30 units (2 suites) [shwr, spa bath (2), tlt, a/c, elec blkts, tel, TV, clock radio, t/c mkg, refrig, toaster], ldry, conv fac, ⊠ (Mon-Sat), rm serv (Mon to Sat), cots-fee. **W ╪ $455, RO ╪ $89, ╫ $99, ╬ $12, Suite D $145**, AE BC DC MC MP VI.

★★★☆ Garden City Motor Inn, (M), 2 Day St, ☎ 02 6921 3646, fax 02 6921 3596, (2 stry), 30 units [shwr, tlt, a/c, elec blkts, tel, TV, video-fee, clock radio, t/c mkg, refrig], ⊠ (Mon to Sat), pool, rm serv, cots-fee, non smoking units (10). **RO ╪ $83, ╫ $90, ╬ $11**, AE BC DC MC VI,

Operator Comment: Quiet location off main roads, short stroll to CBD/Shopping, sports facilities, 2BR serviced apartment avail. Family operated.

★★★☆ Golfview Motor Inn, (M), Previously Ashmont Golf View Motel Cnr Sturt & McNickle Rd, 5km W of Wagga South, ☎ 02 6931 1633, fax 02 6931 4988, 16 units [shwr, tlt, hairdry, a/c, elec blkts, tel, cable tv, clock radio, t/c mkg, refrig, mini bar], pool, bbq, dinner to unit, plygr, tennis, cots-fee, non smoking units (7). **RO ╪ $68, ╫ $79, ╬ $11**, AE BC DC EFT MC MCH VI, ♿.

★★★☆ Junction Motor Inn, (M), 146 Ashmont Ave (Sturt Hwy), 4km W of PO, ☎ 02 6931 2900, fax 02 6931 5075, 19 units (1 suite) [shwr, tlt, a/c, elec blkts, tel, TV, video (avail), movie, clock radio, t/c mkg, refrig], ldry, ⊠ (3 rms), pool, bbq, rm serv, dinner to unit (Mon-Sat), cots-fee, non smoking units (9). **RO ╪ $66 - $71, ╫ $76 - $82, ╬ $11**, AE BC DC MC MCH VI.

★★★☆ Prince of Wales Motor Inn, (M), 143 Fitzmaurice St, 500m N of PO, ☎ 02 6921 1922, fax 02 6921 7016, (2 stry gr fl), 32 units [shwr, bath (25), spa bath (3), tlt, a/c, elec blkts, tel, fax, TV, video (avail), clock radio, t/c mkg, refrig, mini bar], iron, iron brd, ⊠ (6 rms), bar, pool, bbq, rm serv (pool), non smoking units (17). **RO ╪ $79 - $99, ╫ $79 - $99, ╫╫ $89, ╬ $10**, AE BC DC EFT MC MP VI.

★★★ Burringa Motel, (M), 39 Plumpton Rd, 5km S of Wagga South, ☎ 02 6922 3100, or 02 6922 3318, fax 02 6926 2603, 15 units [shwr, tlt, a/c, elec blkts, tel, TV, clock radio, t/c mkg, refrig, cook fac, doonas], ldry, pool, bbq, dinner to unit, cots-fee. **RO ╪ $66, ╫ $77, ╫╫ $88, ╬ $15**, ch con, 5 units of a lower rating. AE BC MC VI.

★★★ **City Park Motel**, (M), 1 Tarcutta St, ☎ 02 6921 4301, fax 02 6921 4739, 26 units [shwr, tlt, a/c, elec blkts, tel, fax, TV, video-fee, clock radio, t/c mkg, refrig], bbq, cots, non smoking rms (20). RO ∦ $59 - $69, ∦∦ $69 - $79, ⍭ $11, AE BC DC EFT MC MCH VI.

★★☆ **Astor Motor Inn**, (M), 104 Edward St, ☎ 02 6921 4328, fax 02 6921 7955, (Multi-stry gr fl), 43 units [shwr, bath (4), tlt, a/c, elec blkts, tel, TV, clock radio, t/c mkg, refrig], conv fac, ⊠, rm serv, cots-fee. RO ∦ $66 - $77, ∦∦ $77 - $88, ⍭ $11, AE BC DC MC VI.

★★☆ **Mercury Motor Inn**, (M), 3935 Sturt Hwy, Gumly Gumly, 5km E of Wagga South, ☎ 02 6922 7210, fax 02 6922 7101, 26 units [shwr, spa bath (1), tlt, a/c-cool (8), a/c (18), elec blkts, tel, TV, clock radio, t/c mkg, refrig], ldry, ✕ (5 nights), pool, bbq, dinner to unit (5 nights), plygr, cots-fee. BLB ∦ $55, ∦∦ $65, ∦∦∦ $70 - $80, ⍭ $12, ch con, BC MC VI.

★★☆ **Palm & Pawn Motor Inn**, (LMH), Hampden Av, 2km N of PO, ☎ 02 6921 6688, fax 02 6921 1839, 25 units [shwr, tlt, a/c, heat, tel, TV, clock radio, t/c mkg, refrig], ldry, ⊠, pool (salt water), bbq, dinner to unit, car wash, plygr, tennis (half court), cots-fee. RO ∦ $49, ∦∦ $59, ∦∦∦ $69, ⍭ $10, AE BC DC MC VI.

★☆ **William Farrer**, (LH), Cnr Peter & Edward Sts, Adjacent to Wagga South School, ☎ 02 6921 3631, (2 stry), 13 rms [shwr (7), tlt (7), a/c, fan, heat, elec blkts, t/c mkg], shared fac (6 rooms), lounge (TV), ⊠ (6 rms). BB ∦ $35 - $44, ∦∦ $44 - $55, ∦∦∦ $55 - $66.

★ **Romanos The Rugby Bar & Bistro**, (LH), Cnr Sturt & Fitzmaurice Sts, Opposite Police station & courthouse, ☎ 02 6921 2013, fax 02 6921 8357, (Multi-stry), 47 rms [ensuite (3), shwr (7), bath (1), tlt (3), a/c, fan (20), c/fan (5), heat (20), elec blkts, TV (3), clock radio, t/c mkg, refrig (3)], lift, lounge (TV), conv fac, ✕ (Mon-Sat), ☏ (2), cots-fee. RO ∦∦ $35 - $75, AE BC DC MC VI.

Self Catering Accommodation

★★★★ **Wagga Serviced Apartments**, (HU), Fitzmaurice St, ☎ 02 6922 9443, fax 02 6922 9403, 4 units acc up to 7, [shwr, bath, tlt, hairdry, a/c-cool, heat, elec blkts, tel, TV, video, clock radio, t/c mkg, refrig, cook fac, micro, d/wash, toaster, ldry (in unit), blkts, linen, pillows], w/mach, dryer, iron, bbq, c/park (garage). D $110 - $200, W $430 - $700, Min book applies, BC MC VI.

★★★★ **Wagga Wagga Country Cottages**, (Cotg), Hillary St, 5km NE of Tourist Centre, ☎ 02 6921 1539, fax 02 6921 1503, 3 cotgs acc up to 4, [shwr, spa bath, tlt, a/c-cool, heat, elec blkts, tel, TV, video, t/c mkg, refrig, cook fac ltd, micro, toaster, blkts, linen, pillows], w/mach, dryer, iron, pool (salt water), spa, bbq, c/park (carport), plygr. D ∦∦ $110, ⍭ $20, AE BC MC VI.

★★★☆ **Country House Motor Lodge**, (Apt), Sturt Hwy, Gumly Gumly, 5km E of Wagga South, ☎ 02 6922 7256, fax 02 6922 7205, 29 apts (1 suite) acc up to 5, [shwr, bath (10), spa bath (1), tlt, a/c, heat, elec blkts, tel, TV, movie, clock radio, t/c mkg, refrig, mini bar], ldry, ⊠ (Mon-Sat), pool, spa, plygr, cots-fee. BLB ∦ $59 - $135, ∦∦ $59 - $135, ⍭ $10, AE BC DC MC MP VI.

★★★ **Wagga Holiday Apartments**, (HU), Lindsay St, ☎ 02 6925 0026, fax 02 6925 0026, 4 units acc up to 6, [shwr, bath, tlt, a/c, cent heat, elec blkts, tel, clock radio, t/c mkg, refrig, cook fac, micro, toaster, ldry, blkts, linen, pillows], w/mach, dryer, iron, lounge (TV), bbq, c/park (garage), cots, non smoking units (1). D ∦∦ $75 - $100, ⍭ $16.50, W ∦∦ $380 - $800, Min book applies.

B&B's/Guest Houses

★★★☆ **Lagoonside Bed & Breakfast**, (B&B), 1 Beckwith St, 500m W of CBD, ☎ 02 6921 1308, fax 02 6921 1332, 3 rms [evap cool, cent heat, elec blkts], shared fac (shwr, bath & tlt), lounge (TV & firepl), ✕, c/park. BB ∦ $90, ∦∦ $110, AE BC MC VI.

★★★☆ **The Manor**, (GH), 38 Morrow St, ☎ 02 6921 5962, fax 02 6921 5962, (2 stry) 7 rms [a/c, heat, elec blkts, clock radio], ldry, lounge (TV), conv fac, ⊠, cook fac, bbq, dinner to unit, ☏. BLB ∦ $44 - $88, ∦∦ $88 - $160, ⍭ $25, AE BC DC MC VI.

Wagga Wagga Guest House, (GH), 149 Gurwood St, 1km W of Civic Centre, ☎ 02 6931 8702, fax 02 6931 8712, 7 rms [a/c (2), fan, heat (3), doonas], ldry, lounge (TV), ✕, cook fac, t/c mkg shared, refrig, bbq, c/park (5), non smoking property. RO ∦ $20, ∦∦ $38, ⍭ $15, Key Deposit $10, (not yet classified).

WALCHA NSW 2354

Pop 1,600. (435km N Sydney), See map on page 54, ref A6.
Walcha, the gateway to the spectacular Oxley Wild Rivers National Park.

Hotels/Motels

★★★ **Walcha Motel**, (M), 31 Fitzroy St, 100m W of PO, ☎ 02 6777 2599, fax 02 6777 1193, 20 units [shwr, tlt, hairdry (20), c/fan, cent heat, elec blkts, tel, fax, TV, clock radio, t/c mkg, refrig, mini bar], ⊠ (Mon to Sat), dinner to unit, cots-fee. RO ∦ $59.40 - $64.90, ∦∦ $70.40 - $81.40, ⍭ $13.20, 4 units ★★★☆. BC EFT MC VI, ⏃.

★★ **New England Motel**, (LMH), 51E Fitzroy St, 300m E of PO, ☎ 02 6777 2532, fax 02 6777 2532, 10 units [shwr, tlt, heat, elec blkts, TV, t/c mkg, refrig], ⊠ (Tue to Sun), cots-fee. RO ∦ $45, ∦∦ $55, ⍭ $15, ch con, BC MC VI.

Self Catering Accommodation

★★☆ **Cheyenne Wilderness Retreat**, (Cotg), (Farm), Winterbourne Rd, 40km NE of Walcha, ☎ 02 6777 9172, fax 02 6777 9117, 1 cotg acc up to 5, [shwr, tlt, fan, fire pl (combustion), elec blkts, tel, radio, t/c mkg, refrig, cook fac, elec frypan, toaster, linen reqd-fee], w/mach, bbq, cots. D ∦∦ $88, ⍭ $44, ch con.

Bloomfields Crossing, (Cotg), (Farm), 'Hole Creek', 33km NE of PO, ☎ 02 6777 9189, fax 02 6777 9188, 1 cotg acc up to 12, [shwr (2), bath (1), tlt (3), fire pl, elec blkts, tel, clock radio (2), t/c mkg, refrig, cook fac, micro, elec frypan, d/wash, toaster, blkts, linen, pillows], ldry, w/mach, dryer, iron, lounge (TV), bbq, meals avail, c/park (carport), tennis, cots. BB ∦ $75, RO ∦ $65, ∦∦ $130, ch con.

B&B's/Guest Houses

★★★☆ **Country Mood Bed & Breakfast**, (B&B), (Farm), Scrubby Gully Rd, 5km W of Walcha, ☎ 02 6777 2877, fax 02 6777 2877, 1 rm [shwr, tlt, hairdry, fan, heat, elec blkts, TV, radio, CD, t/c mkg, refrig], iron, iron brd, bbq, dinner to unit (on request), c/park (garage), tennis, cots. BB ∦ $65, ∦∦ $80, ⍭ $18.

★★☆ **Fenwicke House**, (B&B), 23E Fitzroy St, 100m E of Apsley River Bridge, ☎ 02 6777 2713, (2 stry), 3 rms [hairdry, elec blkts, tel, t/c mkg, cook fac, elec frypan, toaster], bathrm. BB ∦ $40, BLB ∦ $35, RO ∦ $25, BC MC VI.

WALGETT NSW 2832

Pop 2,000. (705km NW Sydney), See map on pages 52/53, ref G2.
Walgett, gateway to the opal fields of Lightning Ridge, Glengarry and Grawin, is situated at the junction of the Namoi and Barwon Rivers. Bowls, Fishing, Golf, Swimming, Tennis.

Hotels/Motels

★★☆ **Leisure World Motel**, (M), Brewarrina Rd, cnr Cumborah St, 7km W of PO, ☎ 02 6828 1154, fax 02 6828 2649, 18 units [shwr, tlt, a/c-cool, heat, tel, TV, clock radio, t/c mkg, refrig, toaster], conv fac, ⊠, pool, spa, bbq, rm serv, plygr, cots. RO ∦ $60, ∦∦ $75, ⍭ $15, ch con, AE BC DC MC VI.

★★ **Coolabah Motel**, (M), 95 Wee Waa St, 100m W of monument, ☎ 02 6828 1366, fax 02 6828 1982, 18 units [shwr, tlt, a/c, tel, TV, video (avail), clock radio, t/c mkg, refrig], ldry, bbq. **RO** $60.50 - $88, BC MC VI.

★★ **Walgett Motel**, (M), 14 Fox St, 300m N of PO, ☎ 02 6828 1355, fax 02 6828 1512, 25 units [shwr, bath (1), tlt, a/c, elec blkts, tel, cable tv, clock radio, t/c mkg, refrig], ldry, ✉, pool-indoor, cots-fee. **RO ♦** $50 - $60, **♦♦** $60 - $72, **♦♦♦** $70 - $82, ⚲ $10, 10 units of a higher standard. AE BC DC MC VI.

B&B's/Guest Houses
Bungle Gully Farmstay, (B&B), Walgett-Pilliga Rd, Come By Chance, 56km SE of Walgett, ☎ 02 6828 5288, fax 02 6828 5266, 5 rms [shwr (3), tlt (4), a/c-cool, c/fan, fire pl, heat, elec blkts, TV, t/c mkg], pool, bbq, tennis. **DBB ♦** $90.

WALLA WALLA NSW 2659

Pop 600. (565km SW Sydney), See map on pages 52/53, ref E7.
Walla Walla, (LMH), 81 Commercial St, ☎ 02 6029 2309, fax 02 6029 2309, 5 units [shwr, tlt, a/c, elec blkts, TV, t/c mkg, refrig, cook fac (1), toaster], ✗ (Thurs to Sat), meals avail, ☏. **BB ♦** $40, **♦♦** $50, ⚲ $10.

WALLACIA NSW 2745

Pop 1,000. (58km W Sydney), See map on page 56, ref A5. Rural village on the Nepean River south of Penrith.
★★★☆ **Hopewood Health Centre**, (GH), Health Retreat. 103 Greendale Rd, 2km S of PO, ☎ 02 4773 8401, fax 02 4773 8735, 48 rms [shwr (35), bath (10), tlt (35), fan, heat, tel, TV (22), video (22), clock radio (22)], shwr, tlt, shared fac (8), ldry, lounge (TV), ✗, pool-heated, gym, tennis. **D all meals ♦** $148 - $231, Vegetarian meals only, BC MC VI.

WALLENDBEEN NSW 2588

Pop Nominal, (434km W Sydney), See map on pages 52/53, ref F6.
★★★ **Old Nubba Schoolhouse**, (Cotg), (Farm), Old Nubba, 3km N of PO, ☎ 02 6943 2513, 3 cotgs acc up to 8, [shwr, bath, tlt, a/c (1), fan, fire pl, heat, elec blkts, clock radio, t/c mkg, refrig, cook fac, elec frypan, toaster, ldry], bbq, cots, Pets on application. **BB ♦** $75, **♦♦** $95, **♦♦♦** $125, **W** $495 - $650, ch con.

WALLSEND NSW

See Newcastle & Suburbs.

WALLERAWANG NSW

See Blue Mountains Region.

WAMBERAL NSW 2260

Pop Part of Gosford, (87km N Sydney), See map on page 55, ref D6. Beachside town between Terrigal and Forresters Beach.
Hotels/Motels
★★★★ **Apollo Resort Wamberal**, (M), 871 The Entrance Rd, 2km N of Terrigal PO, ☎ 02 4385 2099, fax 02 4385 2035, (2 stry gr fl), 44 units (3 suites) [shwr, bath (8), spa bath (3), tlt, hairdry, a/c, tel, TV, video, clock radio, t/c mkg, refrig, mini bar], ldry, rec rm, conv fac, ✉, bar, pool, sauna, spa, bbq, rm serv, dinner to unit, ☏, gym, tennis, cots. **D** $95 - $155, **Suite D** $155 - $200, AE BC DC EFT MC VI.

B&B's/Guest Houses
★★★★ **Coral Tree Cottage**, (B&B), 12 Carbeen Rd, 1km N of PO, ☎ 02 4384 7120, fax 02 4384 6191, 2 rms [a/c-cool, tel, TV, video, radio, t/c mkg, refrig, cook fac ltd], lounge firepl, ✗, spa, meals to unit, non smoking units (2). **BB ♦** $220, **♦♦** $240, AE BC MC VI.

WANAARING NSW 2840

Pop Nominal, (914km W Sydney), See map on pages 52/53, ref C1. Small town on the Paroo River between Bourke and Tibooburra.
Outback Inn, (LH), Vicary St, ☎ 02 6874 7758, fax 02 6874 7392, 4 rms [shwr, tlt].

WANG WAUK NSW 2429

Pop Nominal, (280km N Sydney), See map on page 54, ref B8.
★★★ **Unwinding Retreat Country Guest House**, (GH), 35 Bulby Close, 9km W of Wang Wauk River, ☎ 02 6550 2340, 5 rms [a/c-cool (1), elec blkts (2), clock radio (1), micro], shared fac (3 rms), lounge (TV & firepl), ✗, pool above ground, spa, t/c mkg shared, refrig, non smoking property. **BB ♦** $40, **♦♦** $70, **DBB ♦** $85, **♦♦** $150, BC MC VI.

WANGI WANGI NSW 2267

Pop 8,100. (154km N Sydney), See map on page 55, ref E4. Village on a narrow peninsula on the western shores of Lake Macquarie.
Self Catering Accommodation
★★★☆ **Rosella Lodge**, (Cotg), 56B Dobell Dve, 500m E of Workers Club, ☎ 02 4975 3454, fax 02 4975 2752, (2 stry gr fl), 1 cotg acc up to 8, [shwr (3), tlt (3), hairdry, a/c, fan (3), c/fan (2), heat (6), elec blkts, TV (2), video (1), clock radio (3), radio (1), t/c mkg, refrig, cook fac, micro, d/wash, toaster, ldry, blkts, linen, pillows], spa (heated), cots, non smoking rms. **RO ♦♦** $116 - $132, **♦♦** $616 - $854, ch con, fam con, Min book applies.

★★★ **Wangi Foreshore**, (HU), No children's facilities, Watkins Rd, 1.7km E of PO, ☎ 02 4975 3643, fax 024950 5526, 1 unit acc up to 5, [shwr, spa bath, tlt, fan, heat, elec blkts, TV, video, clock radio, t/c mkg, refrig, cook fac, micro, toaster, ldry (in unit), blkts, linen, pillows], w/mach, dryer, iron, non smoking units. **D ♦♦** $80 - $90, ⚲ $30 - $35, **W ♦♦** $460 - $520, ⚲ $150 - $175, Min book applies, BC MC VI.

B&B's/Guest Houses
★★★☆ **Kismet Lodge B&B**, (B&B), 103 Dobell Dve, 150m E of Police Station, ☎ 02 4975 1364, fax 02 4975 1031, (2 stry), 2 rms [shwr, bath, tlt, hairdry, fan, heat, elec blkts, tel, TV, t/c mkg], pool (salt water), bbq, non smoking property. **BB ♦** $55 - $95, **♦♦** $88 - $120, ⚲ $40, Min book applies.

WARIALDA NSW 2402

Pop 1,300. (648km NW Sydney), See map on pages 52/53, ref H2. New England town at the junction of the Gwydir Highway and the Fossickers Way. Bush Walking, Fishing, Gem Fossicking.
★★★ **The Sunflower Motel**, (M), Gwydir Hwy, West side of town, ☎ 02 6729 1344, 12 units [shwr, tlt, hairdry, a/c-cool, heat, elec blkts, tel, TV, video (avail), clock radio, t/c mkg, refrig], iron, iron brd, rm serv, dinner to unit, cots-fee, non smoking units (2). **RO ♦** $56 - $64, **♦♦** $67 - $75, **♦♦♦** $78 - $86, ⚲ $11, AE BC MC VI.

WARILLA NSW 2528

Pop 6,100. (104km S Sydney), See map on page 55, ref C4. Suburb of Shellharbour situated on the channel that connects Lake Illawarra with the sea.
Self Catering Accommodation
★★★☆ **Warilla Bowls & Recreational Club**, Lot 1, Jason Ave, 20km S of Wollongong, ☎ 02 4296 2000, or 02 4295 1811, fax 02 4297 1927, 19 cabins acc up to 6, [shwr, tlt, a/c, TV, clock radio, t/c mkg, refrig, micro, elec frypan, toaster, blkts, linen, pillows], ldry, conf fac, bbq, plygr, bowls, gym-fee, tennis-fee, cots. **DBB ♦♦♦♦** $77 - $88, ⚲ $11, weekly con, BC EFT MC VI.

B&B's/Guest Houses
★★★★ **Beachstay B&B**, (B&B), 16 Little Lake Cres, ☎ 02 4296 3636, 1 rm [shwr, tlt, fan, heat, tel, TV, clock radio, t/c mkg, refrig, micro, toaster, ldry], iron, iron brd, bbq, non smoking suites. **BLB ♦** $70 - $85, **♦♦** $90 - $110.

WARNERS BAY NSW 2282

Pop 6,230. (167km N Sydney), See map on page 55, ref C8. Town on the north-eastern shores of Lake Macquarie.

Hotels/Motels
★★☆ **Lakeside Motor Inn**, (M), 568 The Esplanade, 800m S of PO, ☎ 02 4948 9666, fax 02 4948 7633, 24 units [shwr, tlt, a/c, fan (8), elec blkts, tel, TV, video-fee, clock radio, t/c mkg, refrig], ldry, ✕ (Mon to Sat), pool, rm serv, cots-fee. **RO** ♦ **$62 - $70**, ♦♦ **$72 - $80**, ♦♦♦♦ **$92 - $100**, ◊ **$10**, ch con, AE BC DC EFT MC VI.

B&B's/Guest Houses
★★★★ **Warners Bay Bed & Breakfast**, (B&B), 364 The Esplanade, 1km W of PO, ☎ 02 4950 8598, fax 02 4950 8598, (2 stry), 2 rms [shwr, bath, tlt, hairdry, a/c, c/fan, heat, elec blkts, tel, TV, video, clock radio, t/c mkg, refrig], ldry, lounge, bbq, dinner to unit, courtesy transfer, non smoking property. **BB** ♦ **$60 - $70**, ♦♦ **$95 - $110**, ◊ **$25**, pen con.
★★★☆ **Bayside Bed and Breakfast**, (B&B), 57 Cherry Rd, 2km S of PO, ☎ 02 4948 9500, fax 02 4947 2057, 1 rm [shwr, tlt, hairdry, a/c, heat, elec blkts, TV, video, clock radio, t/c mkg, refrig, ldry], lounge, pool, bbq, bicycle, tennis, cots, non smoking rms. **BB** ♦ **$65**, ♦♦ **$90 - $110**, ch con, BC MC VI.

(Cottage Section), 1 cotg acc up to 4, [shwr, tlt, hairdry, a/c, elec blkts, TV, video, clock radio, CD, refrig, cook fac, micro, linen], iron, iron brd. **D $140**, (not yet classified).

WARREN NSW 2824

Pop 1,900. (559km W Sydney), See map on pages 52/53, ref F3. Prosperous town on the Macquarie River, heart of a cotton and wool producing area. Bowls, Fishing, Golf, Swimming, Tennis.

Hotels/Motels
★★★ **Macquarie Valley Motor Inn**, (M), Oxley Hwy, 400m N of PO, ☎ 02 6847 4396, fax 02 6847 4780, 15 units [shwr, tlt, hairdry (3), a/c, elec blkts, tel, TV, clock radio, t/c mkg, refrig], pool, rm serv, dinner to unit (Mon to Fri), cots, non smoking units (4). **RO** ♦ **$66**, ♦♦ **$77**, ◊ **$11**, AE BC DC MC VI.
★★★ **Warren Motor Inn**, (M), Cnr Chester & Stafford Sts, 400m W of PO, ☎ 02 6847 4404, or 02 6847 4508, fax 02 6847 3283, 18 units [shwr, tlt, a/c, heat, elec blkts, tel, TV, clock radio, t/c mkg, refrig, toaster], ldry, pool (salt water), plygr, cots-fee. **RO** ♦ **$55 - $66**, ♦♦ **$66 - $77**, ♦♦♦ **$77 - $88**, ◊ **$11**, AE BC DC MC VI.

Self Catering Accommodation
Webegong, (Farm), Coonamble Rd, 45km NE of PO, ☎ 02 6847 4896, fax 02 6847 4369, 1 cabin acc up to 45, [toaster, blkts, linen, pillows], shwr (5), tlt (4), cook fac, refrig, bbq. **D** ♦ **$15**, ◊ **$15**.

Other Accommodation
Haddon Rig - Jackaroo Lodge, (Lodge), Haddon Rig, ☎ 02 6847 4405, fax 02 6847 4656, 7 rms acc up to 12, [shwr (3), bath (1), tlt (3), hairdry, fan, fire pl (2), heat, tel, radio, blkts, linen, pillows], ldry, iron, rec rm, lounge (TV), conv fac, pool (salt water), t/c mkg shared, bbq, plygr, tennis, cots. **D all meals** ♦ **$150**, ch con, BC MC.
Willie Retreat, (Lodge), 'Willie Station', cnr Carinda Rd & Gibson Way, 110km N of PO, ☎ 02 6824 4361, fax 02 6824 4361, 5 rms acc up to 20, [c/fan, heat (combustion), elec blkts, video, radio, micro, doonas, linen, pillows], w/mach, iron, rec rm, lounge (TV), cook fac, t/c mkg shared, bbq, c/park. **D** ♦♦ **$55**, **W** ♦♦ **$330**, ch con.

(On-Site Van Section), 4 ⊡ acc up to 4, [fan, refrig, cook fac, toaster, doonas reqd-fee, linen reqd-fee]. **D** ◊ **$25**, ◊ **$6**, ch con, (not yet classified).

WARRUMBUNGLE NSW 2828

Pop Nominal, (550km NW Sydney), See map on pages 52/53, ref G3. Situated on western side of Warrumbungle National Park.

B&B's/Guest Houses

★★☆ **Gumin Gumin Homestead**, (GH), (Farm), 8km W of Warrumbungle. 9km W of Warrumbungle National Park.
☎ 02 6825 4368, 5 rms [fan, fire pl, elec blkts, radio, micro (1), doonas], lounge (TV), ✕, cook fac, t/c mkg shared, bbq, ✎, cots, Pets allowed. **RO** ♦ **$44**, ♦♦ **$71.50**, ◊ **$10 - $15**.

WATTLE FLAT NSW 2795

Pop Nominal, (170km NW Sydney), See map on page 55, ref A1.
★★★ **Ryder Homestead**, 130 Thompson St, 1.3km W of General Store, ☎ 02 6337 7171, fax 02 9770 4173, 1 cabin acc up to 6, [shwr, spa bath (1), tlt, c/fan, fire pl, heat, t/c mkg, refrig, cook fac, toaster, blkts, linen], ldry, rec rm, bbq, courtesy transfer, plygr, cots. **D $80 - $120**, BC MC VI.

(Bed & Breakfast Section), 1 rm [shwr, bath, tlt, fan, heat, elec blkts, refrig], ldry, rec rm, TV rm, lounge, lounge firepl, ✕, t/c mkg shared, bbq, dinner to unit, courtesy transfer, plygr, cots. **D $80 - $120**, (not yet classified).

WAUCHOPE NSW 2446

Pop 4,700. (394km N Sydney), See map on page 54, ref C7. Wauchope (pronounced 'war-hope') is a pretty, historic town at the centre of the mid-north coast's timber industry. Scenic Drives.

Hotels/Motels
★★★☆ **The Broad Axe Motel**, (M), Oxley Hwy, 2km W of PO, adjacent to Timbertown, ☎ 02 6585 1355, fax 02 6585 3776, 10 units [shwr, tlt, a/c (10), elec blkts, tel, TV, video, clock radio, t/c mkg, refrig], ldry, pool, bbq, tennis, cots-fee, non smoking units (6). **RO** ♦ **$50 - $70**, ♦♦ **$60 - $80**, ◊ **$11**, Dinner by arrangement, AE BC DC MC VI.
★★★ **Wauchope Motel**, (M), 84 High St, 200m W of PO, ☎ 02 6585 1933, fax 02 6586 1366, 12 units [shwr, tlt, a/c-cool, heat, tel, TV, clock radio, t/c mkg, refrig], bbq. **RO** ♦ **$44 - $70**, ◊ **$11**, AE BC DC MC VI.

Self Catering Accommodation
Cedar Grove, (HU), (Farm), 891 Upper Rolland Plains Rd, Rollands Plains 2441, 35km N of PO, 2km past Rolland Plains school, ☎ 02 6585 8257, fax 02 6585 8257, 2 units acc up to 10, [shwr, tlt, a/c, TV (2), clock radio, t/c mkg, refrig, cook fac, micro, elec frypan, toaster, ldry, blkts, linen, pillows], w/mach, iron, rec rm, bbq, plygr. **D $75 - $115**, **W $340 - $710**, Min book applies.

B&B's/Guest Houses
★★★☆ **Auntie Ann's Bed & Breakfast**, (B&B), 19 Bruxner Ave, 500m W of PO, ☎ 02 6586 4420, 3 rms [fan, heat, elec blkts (1), tel, clock radio], ldry, lounge (TV), pool (salt water), t/c mkg shared, bbq, courtesy transfer, non smoking property. **BB** ♦ **$50**, ♦♦ **$70**, BC MC VI.

WEE JASPER NSW 2582

Pop Nominal, (336km SW Sydney), See map on pages 52/53, ref F6. Small village.

Self Catering Accommodation
The Stables, Wee Jasper Rd, ☎ 02 6227 9619, fax 02 6227 9620, 3 cabins acc up to 5, [shwr, tlt, heat, elec blkts, t/c mkg, refrig, toaster, blkts, linen, pillows], ✕, Pets allowed. **D** ♦♦ **$65 - $75**, ◊ **$5**, AE BC EFT MC VI.

Other Accommodation
Wee Jasper Station, (Bunk), (Farm), Wee Jasper Station, 3.5km S of general store, ☎ 02 6227 9641, fax 02 6227 9603, 9 bunkhouses acc up to 39, [c/fan (1), fire pl, heat], lounge firepl, cook fac, t/c mkg shared, refrig. **D ∦ $10**, ch con, pen con, (not yet classified).

WEE WAA NSW 2388

Pop 1,900. (609km NW Sydney), See map on pages 52/53, ref H2. Wee Waa is the birthplace of the State's cotton industry and produces much of Australia annual crop today. Vineyards, Wineries.
★☆ **Wee Waa Motel**, (M), 148 Rose St, 100m E of PO, ☎ 02 6795 4522, fax 02 6795 3065, 19 units [shwr, bath (1), tlt, hairdry, a/c, tel, cable tv, t/c mkg, refrig], conv fac, ✖ (Mon to Sat), dinner to unit, cots, 8 units of a higher standard, AE BC DC EFT MC VI.

WEETHALLE NSW 2669

Pop 200. (545km W Sydney), See map on pages 52/53, ref E5. Small town on the Mid-Western Highway.
★★☆ **Travellers Rest**, (M), Mid Western Hwy, 750m W of PO, ☎ 02 6975 6193, fax 02 6975 6264, 4 units [shwr, tlt, a/c, heat, elec blkts, TV, radio, t/c mkg, refrig], pool, dinner to unit, ✆, cots, non smoking units (2). **RO ∦ $40.70, ∦∦ $50.60, ∦∦∦ $60.50, ◊ $9.90**, ch con, AE BC MC VI.

WELBY NSW 2575

Pop Nominal, (109km SW Sydney), See map on page 55, ref B4. A small town to the north-west of Mittagong.
★★★☆ **Welby Park Manor**, (B&B), Old Hume Hwy, 2km S of Mittagong PO, ☎ 02 4871 1732, (2 stry gr fl), 3 rms [shwr (1), bath (1), tlt (1), hairdry (1), a/c (2), fan (1), heat (1), elec blkts, clock radio, t/c mkg (1)], shared fac (2 rms), ldry, iron (1), iron brd (1), lounge (TV & firepl), ✖, courtesy transfer, non smoking property.
BB ∦∦ $130 - $240, ◊ $55, BLB ∦∦ $110, ◊ $50.

WELLINGTON NSW 2820

Pop 4,500. (382km W Sydney), See map on pages 52/53, ref G4. Charming rural centre that is best known for its fascinating caves.
Hotels/Motels
★★★☆ **Bridge Motel**, (M), 5 Lee St, 1km N of PO, on Macquarie River, ☎ 02 6845 2555, fax 02 6845 3560, 12 units [shwr, tlt, hairdry, a/c, heat, elec blkts, tel, TV, clock radio, t/c mkg, refrig], ✖, pool (salt water), meals to unit, tennis, cots, non smoking units (5). **RO ∦ $60 - $70, ∦∦ $70 - $80, ◊ $10**, AE BC DC MC VI.
★★★☆ **Garden Court Motor Inn**, (M), Mitchell Hwy, 1km N of PO, ☎ 02 6845 2288, fax 02 6845 2850, 22 units [shwr, tlt, a/c, elec blkts, tel, TV, video-fee, clock radio, t/c mkg, refrig], ldry, ✖, pool, dinner to unit, cots. **RO ∦ $55 - $70, ∦∦ $65 - $90, ◊ $10**, 10 units ★★☆. Min book long w/ends, AE BC DC EFT MC VI.
★★★☆ **Wellington Motor Inn**, (M), 37 Maxwell St, 300m S of PO, ☎ 02 6845 1177, fax 02 6845 1377, 11 units [shwr, tlt, a/c, heat, elec blkts, tel, TV, clock radio, t/c mkg, refrig, cook fac (1)], pool (salt water), cots-fee, non smoking units (6). **RO ∦ $55 - $77, ∦∦ $66 - $88, ∦∦∦ $77 - $99, ◊ $10**, Min book long w/ends, AE BC EFT MC VI.
★★☆ **Abel Macquarie Motel**, (M), 32 Mitchell Hwy, 1km N of PO, ☎ 02 6845 1011, fax 02 6845 2081, (2 stry gr fl), 22 units [shwr, tlt, a/c, fan, heat, elec blkts, tel, TV, clock radio, t/c mkg, refrig], cots. **RO ∦ $69, ∦∦ $79, ◊ $10**, AE BC DC MC VI.

B&B's/Guest Houses
★★★☆ **Carinya B&B**, (B&B), 111 Arthur St, 500m S of PO, ☎ 02 6845 4320, fax 02 6845 3089, 3 rms [hairdry, c/fan, heat, elec blkts, clock radio], shared fac (shwr & tlt), ldry, iron, iron brd, rec rm, lounge (tv & firepl), ✖, pool (salt water), t/c mkg shared, bbq, plygr, tennis, cots, non smoking property. **BB ∦ $59 - $75, ∦∦ $69 - $89, ◊ $20, DBB ∦ $84 - $100, ∦∦ $119 - $139, ◊ $45 - $50**, BC MC VI.
★★★☆ **Glen Mitchell**, (B&B), 18km N of Wellington, ☎ 02 6845 2287, fax 02 6845 2650, 3 rms (2 suites) [shwr (1), tlt (1), a/c, elec blkts, tel, video-fee, radio], shared fac (2 rms), ldry, lounge (TV), ✖, cook fac, t/c mkg shared, bbq, plygr, tennis. **BB ∦ $45, ∦∦ $90**, ch con, Dinner by arrangement.
★★★☆ **Narroogal Park Homestead**, (B&B), (Farm), c1880, Narroogal Rd, 24km S of Wellington, via Bakers Swamp, ☎ 02 6846 7223, fax 02 6846 7224, 3 rms ldry, rec rm, lounge (TV), pool, bbq, meals avail, tennis, Pets allowed. **BB ∦ $65 - $70, ∦∦ $110 - $125**, BC MC VI.
★★☆ **Argyle Bed & Breakfast**, (B&B), 'Argyle', 10km N of PO, ☎ 02 6845 1770, fax 02 6845 4092, 2 rms [shwr, tlt, fan, heat, elec blkts, clock radio, t/c mkg], lounge (TV), plygr, cots. **BB ∦ $45, ∦∦ $80, ◊ $15**, ch con, Dinner by arrangement. BC MC VI.

WENTWORTH NSW 2648

Pop 1,500. (1066km W Sydney), See map on pages 52/53, ref B5. Historic port at the junction of the Murray and Darling Rivers.
Hotels/Motels

★★★★☆ **Wentworth Grande Resort**, (M), 61-79 Darling St, ☎ 03 5027 2225, fax 03 5027 2235, (2 stry gr fl), 50 units (2 suites) [shwr, bath (30), spa bath (17), tlt, hairdry, a/c, tel, TV, movie, clock radio, t/c mkg, refrig, mini bar], lift, ldry, iron, iron brd, rec rm, lounge, conf fac, ✖, pool-heated (solar), spa, bbq, rm serv, dinner to unit, gym, cots, non smoking rms (31). **RO $95 - $135, Suite RO $95 - $135**, pen con, AE BC DC EFT JCB MC MP VI.
★★★☆ **Sportsmans Inn Motel**, (M), 120 Adams St, 500m NW of PO, ☎ 03 5027 3584, fax 03 5027 3166, 14 units (1 suite) [shwr, tlt, hairdry, a/c, elec blkts, tel, cable tv, movie, t/c mkg, refrig, cook fac (1)], ldry, pool-heated, spa, bbq, courtesy transfer, cots. **RO ∦ $50, ∦∦ $55 - $65, ∦∦∦ $66, ◊ $10, Suite D $80 - $90**, ch con, AE BC DC MC VI, ⚹⚐.
★★★☆ **Two Rivers Motel**, (M), Silver City Hwy, 1.6km N of PO, ☎ 03 5027 3268, fax 03 5027 2007, 25 units [shwr, tlt, a/c, elec blkts, tel, TV, movie, clock radio, t/c mkg, refrig], pool, spa, bbq, courtesy transfer, canoeing. **BLB ∦ $57, ∦∦ $68 - $78, ◊ $12**, ch con, AE BC EFT MC VI.
★★★☆ **Wentworth Central Motor Inn**, (M), Adam St, 100m W of PO, ☎ 03 5027 3777, fax 03 5027 3399, (2 stry gr fl), 25 units [shwr, tlt, a/c, c/fan, elec blkts, tel, TV, movie, clock radio, t/c mkg, refrig, toaster], ✖, pool, spa, cots. **BB ∦ $60, ∦∦ $75, ◊ $18, W $345 - $400, RO ∦ $50 - $60, ∦∦ $60 - $65, ∦∦∦ $70 - $80, ◊ $15 - $20**, ch con, AE BC MC VI.
★★★ **Wentworth Club Motel**, (M), Cnr Sandwych & Adams St, adjacent PO, ☎ 03 5027 3535, fax 03 5027 2018, 19 units [shwr, spa bath (4), tlt, a/c, heat, elec blkts, tel, TV, video-fee, clock radio, t/c mkg, refrig], ldry, cots. **BLB ∦∦ $58 - $60, RO ∦∦ $55 - $58**, AE BC EFT MC VI, ⚹⚐.
★★☆ **Darling Junction Motor Inn**, (M), Cnr Silver City Hwy & Armstrong Ave, 200m E of services club, ☎ 03 5027 3636, fax 03 5027 3166, (2 stry gr fl), 22 units [shwr, tlt, hairdry, a/c, elec blkts, tel, TV, movie, clock radio, t/c mkg, refrig, toaster], ldry, pool, bbq, courtesy transfer, cots. **BLB ∦ $50, ∦∦ $55, ∦∦∦ $70**, ch con, AE BC DC MC VI.
★☆ **Royal Motel Hotel**, (LMH), 41 Darling St, 100m S of PO, ☎ 03 5027 3005, fax 03 5027 2011, 7 units [shwr, tlt, a/c, elec blkts, tel (avail at office), TV, t/c mkg, refrig], lounge, ✖ (6 rms), cots. **RO ∦ $45, ∦∦ $50, ∦∦∦ $60**, BC EFT MC VI.

WENTWORTH NSW continued...

Self Catering Accommodation
★★★★ **Red Gum Lagoon Cottages**, (Cotg), 210 Adams St, 1.5km N of PO, ☎ 03 5027 2063, fax 03 5027 2224, 2 cotgs acc up to 6, [shwr, tlt, a/c-cool, fan, heat, elec blkts, TV, clock radio, t/c mkg, refrig, cook fac, micro, toaster, blkts, linen, pillows], w/mach, iron, bbq, c/park (carport), non smoking property. D ♥♥ $110 - $120, ♦ $30, W ♥♥ $700 - $820.

WENTWORTH FALLS NSW

See Blue Mountains Region.

WEST WYALONG NSW 2671

Pop 3,400. (497km W Sydney), See map on pages 52/53, ref E5. Administrative and service centre at the junction of the Newell and Mid-Western Highways. Bowls, Fishing, Golf, Swimming, Tennis, Trotting.

Hotels/Motels
★★★★ **Club Inn West Wyalong**, (M), Newell Hwy, 2.5 km S of PO, ☎ 02 6972 2000, fax 02 6972 2642, 42 units [shwr, spa bath, tlt, hairdry, a/c, elec blkts, tel, TV, video (library)-fee, clock radio, t/c mkg, refrig], ldry, conv fac, ⊠, pool, rm serv, golf, tennis, cots-fee, non smoking units (10). RO ♦ $79, ♥♥ $89, ♥♥♥♥ $125, ♦ $11, AE BC DC EFT MC VI, ⚹♿.

★★★☆ **Cameo Inn**, (M), 263 Neeld St, 1km E of PO, ☎ 02 6972 2517, or 02 6972 2255, fax 02 6972 3679, 18 units [shwr, spa bath (1), tlt, hairdry (5), a/c, elec blkts, tel, TV, video (avail), clock radio, t/c mkg, refrig, toaster], ldry, ⊠, pool indoor heated, spa, rm serv, cots-fee. RO ♦ $59 - $79, ♥♥ $69 - $89, ♦ $10, ch con, AE BC DC MC MP VI, ⚹♿.

★★★☆ **Colonial Motor Inn**, (M), Mid Western Hwy, 400m W of PO, ☎ 02 6972 2611, fax 02 6972 2950, 24 units [shwr, tlt, a/c, elec blkts, tel, cable tv, clock radio, t/c mkg, refrig], ldry, conv fac, pool, bbq, rm serv, cots. D $88 - $99, RO ♦ $60, ♥♥ $68 - $73, ♦ $10, ch con, pen con, 3 rooms of a lower rating. AE BC DC EFT MC VI.

★★★☆ **Country Roads Motor Inn**, (M), 268 Neeld St, 1km E of PO, ☎ 02 6972 2300, fax 02 6972 2865, 14 units [shwr, tlt, hairdry, a/c-cool, heat, elec blkts, tel, TV, video, clock radio, t/c mkg, refrig, toaster], pool, bbq, dinner to unit, boat park, cots-fee, non smoking units (7). RO ♦ $55 - $61, ♥♥ $64 - $70, ♦ $11, pen con, 3 units ★★★. AE BC DC EFT MC VI.

★★★☆ **The Palms Motel**, (M), Cnr Monash & Gladstone St, opposite Service & Citizen Club, ☎ 02 6972 2477, fax 02 6972 2363, (2 stry gr fl), 13 units (2 suites) [shwr, tlt, hairdry (10), a/c, c/fan, elec blkts, tel, cable tv, clock radio, t/c mkg, refrig, ldry], bbq, c/park (undercover) (10), cots, non smoking units (4). RO ♦ $72 - $82, ♥♥ $78 - $95, ♥♥♥ $103 - $118, ♦ $13, 3 units ★★★. AE BC DC MC VI.

★★★ **Acacia Golden Way**, (M), 45 Main St, 400m E of PO, ☎ 02 6972 2155, fax 02 6972 0157, (2 stry gr fl), 11 units [shwr, tlt, hairdry, a/c, elec blkts, tel, TV, clock radio, t/c mkg, refrig, toaster], ldry, pool, bbq, trailer park, cots. RO ♦ $50, ♥♥ $55 - $60, ♦ $10, AE BC DC EFT MC VI.

★★★ **Ambassadors True Blue Motor Inn**, (M), Main St, 1km E of PO, ☎ 02 6972 2588, fax 02 6972 3851, 32 units [shwr, tlt, a/c, fan, heat, elec blkts, tel, video (avail), clock radio, t/c mkg, refrig, mini bar], ⊠ (Mon to Fri), pool, rm serv, dinner to unit, cots, AE BC DC MC VI.

★★★ **Ardeanal Motel**, (M), Neeld St, 1km E of PO, ☎ 02 6972 2777, fax 02 6972 1080, 18 units [shwr, tlt, a/c-cool, heat, elec blkts, tel, TV, clock radio, t/c mkg, refrig], pool, bbq, dinner to unit, AE BC DC EFT MC VI.

★★★ **County Lodge Motor Inn**, (M), 25 Main St (Newell Hwy), 700m E of PO, ☎ 02 6972 2411, fax 02 6972 3289, 22 units [shwr, bath (1), tlt, a/c, fan, heat, elec blkts, tel, TV, video (avail), clock radio, t/c mkg, refrig, toaster (6)], pool, bbq, cots-fee, non smoking units (12). RO ♦ $50 - $60, ♥♥ $60 - $65, ♦ $10, 3 rooms ★★, AE BC DC EFT MC VI.

★★★ **Metropolitan Hotel**, (LH), 156 Main St, Next door to PO, ☎ 02 6972 0400, or 02 6972 3725, fax 02 6972 3547, 20 rms [bath, a/c-cool, c/fan (2), fire pl (2), heat, tel, TV, t/c mkg, refrig (12), toaster], iron, iron brd, ⊠, 24hr reception, cots, non smoking flr. BLB ♦ $25 - $35, ♥♥ $35 - $55, DBB ♦ $35 - $55, ♥♥ $55 - $75, ch con.

★★★ **Top Town Motel**, (M), Newell-Mid Western Hwy (Neeld St), 3km E of PO, ☎ 02 6972 2166, fax 02 6972 4476, 9 units [shwr, tlt, hairdry (7), a/c, heat, elec blkts, tel, TV, clock radio, t/c mkg, refrig], dinner to unit, cots-fee. RO ♦ $42 - $45, ♥♥ $48 - $53, ♦ $8, AE BC MC VI.

★★☆ **Charles Sturt Motor Inn**, (M), 295 Neeld St (Newell Hwy), 1.2km E of PO, ☎ 02 6972 2422, fax 02 6972 3782, 47 units [shwr, tlt, a/c, heat, elec blkts, tel, TV, clock radio, t/c mkg, refrig, toaster], ldry, ⊠, pool, sauna, bbq, rm serv, c/park (undercover), cots-fee, non smoking units (16). RO ♦ $50 - $60, ♥♥ $60 - $70, ♦ $12, ch con, AE BC DC EFT MC MCH VI, ⚹♿.

WHITE CLIFFS NSW 2836

Pop 207. (1061km W Sydney), See map on pages 52/53, ref C2. Historic opal mining town, full of hillocks housing mines and the famous 'dugout' or underground homes. Gem Fossicking.

Hotels/Motels

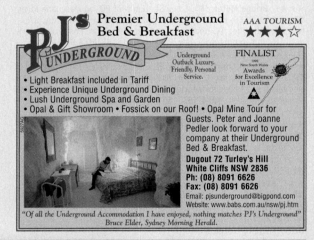

★★★ **White Cliffs Underground Dug-Out Motel**, (M), Accommodation underground, Smith's Hill, 1km S of PO, ☎ 08 8091 6647, fax 08 8091 6654, 32 units lounge (TV), conv fac, conf fac, ⊠, pool (salt water), t/c mkg shared, bbq, courtesy transfer, ☏, cots. D ♦ $54, ♥♥ $83, ♥♥♥ $105, ♦ $24, ch con, BC MC VI.

B&B's/Guest Houses

★★★☆ PJ's Underground Bed & Breakfast, (B&B), Accommodation underground. Dugout 72, Turleys Hill, 1.5km E of PO, ☎ 08 8091 6626, fax 08 8091 6626, 5 rms [tel, clock radio, t/c mkg, refrig], lounge (2), ✕, spa-fee, bbq-fee, c/park. **BB** ♦ **$81.50**, ♦♦ **$119**, ♦ **$33.50**, **BLB** ♦ **$71.50**, ♦♦ **$99**, ♦ **$24.50**, **DBB** ♦ **$108**, ♦♦ **$172**, ♦ **$61**, BC MC VI.

White Cliffs Family Inn at the Post Office, (B&B), Johnson St, ☎ 08 8091 6645, fax 08 8091 6645, 3 rms [fan (3), c/fan (1)], ✕, t/c mkg shared, ✆. **BLB** ♦ **$27.50**, ♦♦ **$44**, ♦ **$11 - $16.50**.

WILCANNIA NSW 2836

Pop 700. (965km W Sydney), See map on pages 52/53, ref C3. Historic river port on the Darling River.

Hotels/Motels

★★☆ Wilcannia Motel, (M), Barrier Hwy, ☎ 08 8091 5802, fax 08 8091 5001, 13 units [shwr, tlt, hairdry, a/c, elec blkts, tel, TV, video-fee, clock radio, t/c mkg, refrig], ldry, iron, iron brd, bbq, plygr, cots, non smoking units (8). **RO** ♦ **$64**, ♦♦ **$75**, ♦♦♦ **$86**, ♦ **$10**, AE BC DC EFT MC VI.

★★ Grahams Motel, (M), Cnr Woore St & Barrier Hwy, 500m W of PO, ☎ 08 8091 5040, fax 08 8091 5220, 10 units [shwr, tlt, a/c-cool, heat, tel, TV, video-fee, clock radio, t/c mkg, refrig], ldry, cots-fee. **BLB** ♦ **$60**, ♦♦ **$70**, ♦ **$10**, ch con, BC DC EFT MC MCH VI.

WILDES MEADOW NSW 2577

Pop Nominal, (134km S Sydney), See map on page 55, ref B4. Picturesque rural village on the Kangaroo Valley Escarpment.

Brookville, (Cotg), (Farm), Blencowes La, 3km S of Burrawang, ☎ 02 4886 4589, fax 02 4886 4589, 1 cotg acc up to 6, [shwr, bath, tlt, heat, elec blkts, tel, TV, radio, t/c mkg, refrig, cook fac, elec frypan, toaster, blkts, linen, pillows], pool (salt water), spa, bbq, cots. **D** ♦♦ **$125 - $220**, (not yet classified).

WILLIAMTOWN NSW

See Port Stephens Region.

WILTON NSW 2571

Pop 600. (82km SW Sydney), See map on page 56, ref A8. Rural village near Picton. Bowls, Golf, Greyhound Racing, Swimming, Vineyards.

Kedron Homestead B&B and Farmstay, (B&B), 305 Wilton Park Rd, 3min from Picton exit off freeway, ☎ 02 4677 3054, fax 02 4677 3054, 2 rms [shwr, hairdry, fan, heat, clock radio, t/c mkg, cook fac ltd, toaster], bbq, courtesy transfer, cots. **BLB** ♦ **$75 - $85**, ♦♦ **$90 - $120**, ♦ **$12 - $20**, ch con, fam con, (not yet classified).

WINDANG NSW

See Wollongong & Suburbs.

WINGHAM NSW 2429

Pop 4,450. (322km N Sydney), See map on page 54, ref B7. The oldest settlement on the Manning River, with many buildings classified by the National Trust. Scenic Drives.

★★★★ Wingham Country Lodge Motel, (M), Country Club Dve, Situated on Golf Course, ☎ 02 6553 0300, or 02 6553 0301, fax 02 6553 0075, 27 units [shwr, spa bath (1), tlt, hairdry, a/c, elec blkts, tel, TV, video (avail), clock radio, t/c mkg, refrig], ldry, iron, iron brd, conv fac, ✕, ⊠, pool (salt water), bbq, dinner to unit, non smoking units (10). **RO** ♦ **$64 - $96**, ♦♦ **$85 - $96**, ♦ **$15**, AE BC DC JCB MC VI.

★★★ Wingham Motel, (M), 13 Bent St, ☎ 02 6553 4295, fax 02 6553 4878, 16 units [shwr, tlt, a/c-cool, fan, heat, elec blkts, tel, TV, clock radio, t/c mkg, refrig, cook fac (3)], ldry, pool, bbq, plygr, cots-fee, non smoking units (5). **RO** ♦ **$51.70 - $57.20**, ♦♦ **$62.70 - $68.20**, ♦ **$11**, ch con, AE BC DC MC VI.

Australian Hotel, (LH), c1890. 24 Bent St, 100m W of PO, ☎ 02 6553 4511, fax 02 6553 4312, (2 stry), 12 rms lounge (TV), ⊠. **BLB** ♦ **$22**, ♦♦ **$38**, ch con, BC MC VI.

WOLLOMBI NSW 2325

Pop 50. (140km N Sydney), See map on page 55, ref C1. Charming little village that is one of the gateways to the Hunter Valley wine country.

Self Catering Accommodation

★★★☆ Cedar Creek Cottages, (Cotg), Wollombi Rd, Cedar Creek, 10km E of Wollombi, ☎ 02 4998 0008, 3 cotgs acc up to 12, [shwr, spa bath, tlt, a/c, c/fan, fire pl, elec blkts, tel, TV, clock radio, t/c mkg, refrig, cook fac (2), micro, elec frypan, toaster, blkts, linen, pillows], bbq, non smoking units. **D** ♦♦ **$99 - $143**, ♦ **$45**, ch con, BC MC VI.

B&B's/Guest Houses

★★★★★ Capers Country Guest House, (GH), Wollombi Rd, ☎ 02 4998 3211, fax 02 4998 3458, 5 rms [ensuite, spa bath (2), hairdry, a/c, fire pl (2), heat, elec blkts, tel, TV, video, movie, clock radio, t/c mkg], ldry, lounge firepl, ✕, refrig, courtesy transfer, non smoking property. **BB** ♦♦ **$195 - $250**, **DBB** ♦♦ **$295 - $360**, pen con, AE BC MC VI.

★★★★☆ (Cottage Section), 1 cotg acc up to 6, [shwr, spa bath (1), tlt (3), hairdry, a/c, heat, elec blkts, tel, fax, TV, video, clock radio, t/c mkg, refrig, cook fac, micro, d/wash, toaster, blkts, linen], w/mach, iron, lounge firepl, ✕, bbq, non smoking property. **BB** ♦♦ **$150**, ♦♦♦♦ **$220 - $275**.

★★★☆ Avoca House Bed & Breakfast, (B&B), Wollombi Rd, ☎ 02 4998 3233, fax 02 4998 3319, 3 rms [shwr (2), tlt (2), hairdry (2), a/c (1), c/fan, fire pl (1), heat, elec blkts, tel, video (1), CD (2), t/c mkg, refrig (2), micro (1), toaster (2)], bbq. **BB** ♦ **$50 - $80**, ♦♦ **$100 - $160**, ch con, Dinner by arrangement, BC MC VI.

★★★☆ Guest House Mulla Villa, (GH), Old North Rd, 2km SW of Wollombi PO, ☎ 02 4998 3254, fax 02 4998 3286, (2 stry gr fl), 4 rms [shwr, spa bath (2), tlt, a/c], lounge firepl, ✕, ✕, pool (salt water), cots-fee, non smoking rms. **BB** ♦ **$95 - $140**, ♦♦ **$180 - $280**, ♦ **$80 - $95**, **DBB** ♦ **$115 - $145**, ♦♦ **$230 - $285**, ♦ **$115 - $140**, Min book applies, AE BC DC EFT MC VI.

Other Accommodation

Yango Park House, (Lodge), 1 Upper Yango Creek Rd, 135km NW of Sydney, ☎ 02 4998 8322, fax 02 4998 8322, (Multi-stry gr fl), 1 rm acc up to 20, [fire pl, linen], sauna, tennis, Pets on application. **D** **$71.50**, ch con, Colonial style sandstone homestead ideal for groups 10-20. Min book applies, BC MC VI.

Trouble-free travel tips - **Tyre pressures**

Check tyre pressures and set them to the manufacturer's recommendation, including the spare.
The specifications can generally be found on the tyre placard located in either the glove box or on the front door frame.

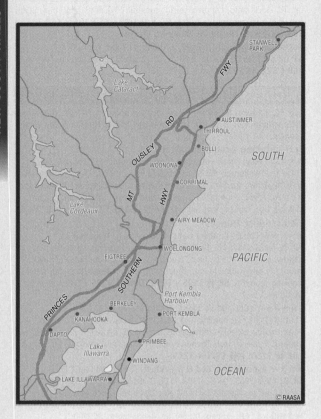

WOLLONGONG & SUBURBS - WOLLONGONG NSW 2500

Part of WOLLONGONG & SUBURBS region. Pop 219,750. (79km Sydney), See map on page 55, ref C4. This historic coal, iron and steel producing city on the coast south of Sydney is the third largest metropolis in New South Wales and the business centre of the Illawarra region. Boating, Fishing, Golf, Surfing, Tennis.

Hotels/Motels

★★★★ **Belmore All-Suite Hotel**, (LH), 39 Smith St, 500m N of city centre, ☎ 02 4224 6500, fax 02 4229 1860, (2 stry gr fl), 33 rms (30 suites) [shwr, bath, tlt, hairdry, a/c, tel, cable tv, video (avail), clock radio, t/c mkg, refrig, mini bar, cook fac, micro, d/wash], ldry-fee, sauna, spa, dinner to unit, cots. **D $133 - $161**, Min book applies, AE BC DC MC VI, ⓑ.

★★★★ **City Pacific Boutique Hotel**, (LH), 112 Burelli St, ☎ 02 4229 7444, fax 02 4228 0552, (Multi-stry), 61 rms [shwr, bath, spa bath (3), tlt, hairdry, a/c, heat, tel, TV, video (avail), radio, t/c mkg, refrig, mini bar], lift, iron, iron brd, conv fac, ⊠, bar, pool, 24hr reception, rm serv, secure park. **RO** ♦ **$75 - $250,** ♦♦ **$75 - $250,** ♦♦♦ **$93 - $270,** 15 rooms ★★★☆, AE BC DC MC VI, ⓑ.

★★★★ **Golden Pacific North Beach**, (M), 16 Pleasant Ave, 500m S of PO, ☎ 02 4226 3000, fax 02 4228 3853, (2 stry gr fl), 22 units (2 suites) [shwr, bath (4), spa bath (3), tlt, a/c, fan, heat, tel, TV, video-fee, radio, t/c mkg, refrig, cook fac ltd (9), micro (9)], ldry, cots-fee. **RO** ♦ **$83.50 - $104.50,** ♦♦ **$93.50 - $176,** ◊ **$15, Suite D $220**, ch con, Some rooms of a lower rating. AE BC DC MC VI, ⓑ.

★★★★ **Novotel Northbeach**, (LH), Cliff Rd, 1.5km N of PO, ☎ 02 4226 3555, fax 02 4229 1705, (Multi-stry), 204 rms (17 suites) [shwr, bath, spa bath (18), tlt, a/c, tel, TV, movie, t/c mkg, refrig, mini bar], lift, ldry-fee, conv fac, ⊠, pool, sauna, spa, rm serv, gym, tennis, cots, non smoking rms (108). **BB** ♦♦ **$227 - $360**, ch con, AE BC DC MC VI. *Operator Comment: See advertisement over page.*

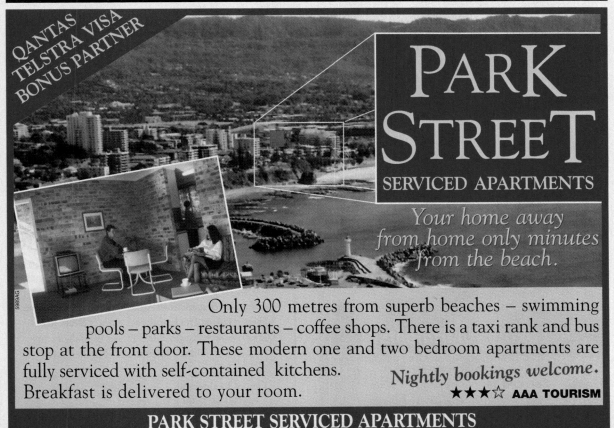

★★★☆ **Leisure Coast Park Inn**, (M), Carters La, Towradgi 2518, 3km N of Wollongong, ☎ 02 4283 5533, fax 02 4283 6750, 40 units (2 suites) [shwr, bath, spa bath (2), tlt, a/c, tel, TV, clock radio, t/c mkg, refrig, cook fac (2)], ldry, conv fac, ✕, pool, bbq, rm serv, cots. **RO ♦ $85 - $110, ♦♦ $95 - $140**, AE BC DC EFT JCB MC VI.

★★★☆ **Surfside 22 Motel**, (M), Cnr Crown & Harbour Sts, 1km E of PO, ☎ 02 4229 7288, fax 02 4228 9418, (2 stry), 16 units (1 suite) [shwr, bath, spa bath (1), tlt, a/c, elec blkts, tel, TV, video, clock radio, t/c mkg, refrig, cook fac (14)], dinner to unit, c/park (undercover), tennis, cots-fee. **RO ♦ $99 - $119, ♦♦ $109 - $129, ◊ $29, Suite RO $159 - $179**, ch con, Min book applies, AE BC DC MC VI.

★★★ **Beach Park Motor Inn**, (M), 10 Pleasant Ave, North Wollongong 2500, 2km N of PO, ☎ 02 4226 1577, fax 02 4226 1281, (Multi-stry gr fl), 18 units [shwr, spa bath (4), tlt, a/c (16), fan, tel, TV, video, clock radio, t/c mkg, refrig, cook fac (1)], iron, iron brd, cots. **RO ♦ $60 - $105, ♦♦ $60 - $170, ♦♦♦ $100 - $180, ◊ $15**, AE BC DC MC VI, ♿.

★★★ **Boat Harbour Motel**, (M), 7 Wilson St, 1km NE of PO, ☎ 02 4228 9166, fax 02 4226 4878, (Multi-stry), 42 units [shwr, tlt, a/c, tel, TV, clock radio, t/c mkg, refrig], lift, ldry, conv fac, ✉ (Mon to Sat), cots. **RO ♦ $101 - $120.50, ♦♦ $113 - $137**, AE BC DC JCB MC VI.

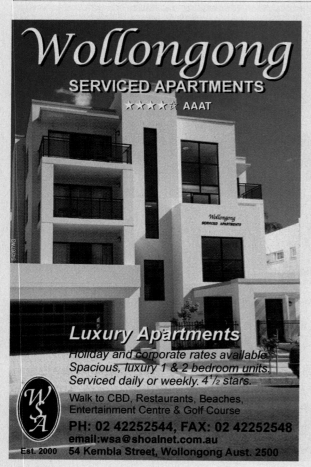
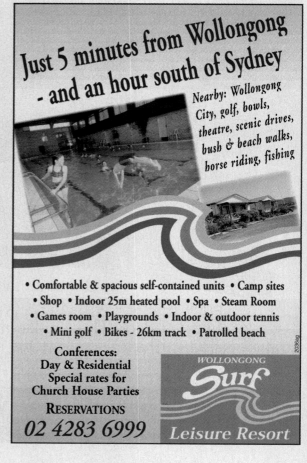

★★★ **Downtown Motel**, (M), 76 Crown St, 50m E of PO, ☎ 02 4229 8344, fax 02 4226 2675, (2 stry gr fl), 31 units [shwr, tlt, hairdry, a/c (19), fan, heat, tel, cable tv, radio, t/c mkg, refrig, toaster], conv fac, ✕ (Mon to Sat), rm serv, cots. RO ∮ $76 - $93, ∮∮ $76 - $98, ∮∮∮ $108, ⌂ $10, AE BC DC MC VI, *Operator Comment: A La Carte Restaurant with an extensive wine list. Located in the CBD.*

★★★ **Normandie Motel**, (M), 30 Bourke St, ☎ 02 4229 4833, or 02 4228 6030, fax 02 4229 4502, (2 stry gr fl), 17 units [shwr, tlt, c/fan, heat, elec blkts, tel, TV, t/c mkg, refrig], ldry, conf fac, ✕, dinner to unit. RO ∮ $75 - $99, ∮∮ $94 - $119, ∮∮∮ $139, AE BC DC JCB MC VI.

Self Catering Accommodation

★★★★☆ **Wollongong Serviced Apartments**, (SA), 54 Kembla St, 200m N of PO, ☎ 02 4225 2544, fax 02 4225 2548, 21 serv apts acc up to 6, (1 & 2 bedrm), [shwr, tlt, hairdry-fee, a/c, tel, TV, video-fee, clock radio, t/c mkg, refrig, cook fac, micro, blkts, doonas, linen, pillows], w/mach, dryer, bbq, rm serv, meals to unit, cots-fee, non smoking units (7). RO ∮ $115 - $121, ∮∮ $115 - $121, ∮∮∮∮ $133 - $146, ⌂ $11, ch con, weekly con, AE BC DC EFT MC VI.

★★★★ **Bel Mondo Luxury Accommodation**, (Apt), 10 Keira St, North Wollongong 2500, 200m S of Wollongong North PO, ☎ 02 4229 4199, fax 02 4227 4235, (2 stry gr fl), 9 apts acc up to 4, (1 & 2 bedrm), [shwr, spa bath (6), tlt, a/c, tel, TV, clock radio, refrig, micro, toaster], ldry, bbq, c/park (undercover), cots-fee. D ∮ $77 - $150, ∮∮ $94 - $185, ⌂ $25, Min book Christmas Jan long w/ends and Easter, AE BC DC MC VI.

★★★★ **North Point Luxury Apartments**, (SA), 6-8 Pleasant Ave, ☎ 02 4228 6666, fax 02 4225 2998, (Multi-stry gr fl), 15 serv apts (15 suites) [shwr, spa bath, tlt, c/fan, heat, tel, TV, video, movie, clock radio, CD, t/c mkg, refrig, cook fac, micro, d/wash, toaster, blkts, linen, pillows], lift, w/mach, dryer, iron, bbq, c/park (garage), cots. D $165 - $220, W $660 - $880, AE BC DC JCB MC VI.

★★★☆ **Park Street**, (SA), 1 Park St, North Wollongong, 300m W of North Beach, ☎ 02 4227 7999, fax 02 4227 7950, (Multi-stry) 17 serv apts [shwr, bath, tlt, heat, tel, TV, refrig, cook fac, toaster, ldry], bbq, c/park. D $100 - $150, AE BC DC MC VI.

★★★☆ **Smith St Apartments**, (SA), 38 Smith St, 300m W of Wollongong Harbour, ☎ 02 4227 2430, fax 02 4226 4708, (Multi-stry gr fl), 12 serv apts acc up to 7, [shwr, bath, tlt, heat, tel, TV, clock radio, t/c mkg, refrig, cook fac, micro, d/wash, toaster, ldry, blkts, linen, pillows], lift, w/mach, dryer, iron, non smoking units (2). D $130 - $180, W $650 - $980, AE BC MC VI.

★★★ **Sky Accommodation**, (SA), 5 Parkinson St, 200m S from West Wollongong PO, ☎ 02 4228 9320, fax 02 4225 3463, 14 serv apts acc up to 4, [fan, tel (public), TV, cook fac, micro, ldry, blkts, linen], w/mach, dryer, bbq, non smoking rms. D ∮ $60.50, ∮∮ $77, ∮∮∮ $88, ∮∮∮∮ $88, BC MC VI.

Trouble-free travel tips - Fluids

Check all fluid levels and top up as necessary. Look at engine oil, automatic transmission fluid, radiator coolant (only check this when the engine is cold), power steering, battery and windscreen washers.

B&B's/Guest Houses

★★★☆ **City Beach Bed & Breakfast**, (B&B), 2 Parkside Ave, ☎ 02 4228 3088, or 02 4228 8427, fax 02 4225 3658, (2 stry), 2 rms [hairdry (1), elec blkts, TV (1), video (1), clock radio, micro (1), toaster (1)], lounge, t/c mkg shared, refrig, bbq, non smoking property. BLB ∮∮ $90 - $110, AE BC DC EFT JCB MC VI.

★★★☆ **Peace Cottage**, (B&B), 30 Peace Cres, Balgownie 2519, 6.5 N of Wollongong PO, ☎ 02 4285 7113, fax 02 4285 7113, 1 rm [ensuite, heat (elec), clock radio, ldry, doonas], lounge (TV/video), ✕, t/c mkg shared, refrig, bbq, non smoking property. BB ∮ $44 - $55, ∮∮ $77 - $88, ch con, weekly con, Min book Christmas and Jan.

WOLLONGONG & SUBURBS - AUSTINMER NSW 2515

Pop Part of Wollongong, (69km S Sydney), See map on page 55, ref C3. Small seaside town north of Bulli on the south coast.

Self Catering Accommodation

Austinmer Holiday Accommodation, (HU), 44 Railway Ave, 300m N of Railway Station, ☎ 02 4268 0607, fax 02 4268 0607, 1 unit acc up to 4, [shwr, tlt, hairdry, heat, elec blkts, TV, video, clock radio, t/c mkg, refrig, cook fac, micro, elec frypan, toaster, ldry, blkts, linen reqd-fee], w/mach, iron, iron brd, bbq, non smoking rms. D $100 - $200, W $350 - $800, BC MC VI, (not yet classified).

B&B's/Guest Houses

★★★☆ **Ocean Break Bed & Breakfast**, (B&B), Resort, No children's facilities, 22 Lawrence Hargrave Dr, ☎ 0413 313 690, fax 02 4267 5051, (2 stry), 3 rms [shwr, spa bath, tlt, hairdry, fan, heat, elec blkts, tel, clock radio, t/c mkg, refrig, toaster], iron, iron brd, TV rm, lounge, bbq, cots, non smoking property. BB ∮ $75 - $85, ∮∮ $110 - $130, ⌂ $65 - $80, fam con.

WOLLONGONG & SUBURBS - BERKELEY NSW 2506

Part of WOLLONGONG & SUBURBS region. Pop Part of Wollongong, (93km S Sydney), See map on page 55, ref C4. Sizeable settlement on the northern shores of Lake Illawarra. Swimming.

Hotels/Motels

★★★ **Nan Tien Temple Pilgrim Lodge**, (M), Berkeley Rd, 9km S of Wollongong City, ☎ 02 4272 0500, fax 02 4272 0690, (Multi-stry gr fl), 100 units [shwr, bath (12), tlt, a/c (15), elec blkts, tel, TV, clock radio, t/c mkg, refrig (33), pillows], lift, ldry, conv fac, ✆, cots, non smoking rms. D $77 - $143, ch con, BC MC VI, ♿.

WOLLONGONG & SUBURBS - BULLI NSW 2516

Part of WOLLONGONG & SUBURBS region. Pop 5,521. (70km S Sydney), See map on page 55, ref C3. Historic coal mining town north of Wollongong. Fishing, Scenic Drives, Surfing, Swimming.

B&B's/Guest Houses

Beachside at Bulli, (B&B), 4 Jardine St, ☎ 02 4285 1815, fax 02 4283 5811, 1 rm [fan, heat, cable tv, video, clock radio, t/c mkg, refrig, cook fac ltd, micro, toaster, ldry, doonas], bbq, c/park (undercover), non smoking property. BLB ∮∮ $130, ⌂ $25, ch con, (not yet classified).

WOLLONGONG & SUBURBS - DAPTO NSW 2530

Part of WOLLONGONG & SUBURBS region. Pop 8,000. (97km S Sydney), See map on page 55, ref C4. Southern suburb of Wollongong that's renowned for its weekly greyhound races. Bowls, Fishing, Golf, Horse Riding, Sailing, Swimming, Tennis.

Hotels/Motels

★★★☆ **Elsinor Motor Lodge**, (M), Cnr Prince Edward Dr & Kanahooka Rd, off Princes Hwy, 2km N of PO, ☎ 02 4261 3366, fax 02 4261 6075, 25 units (4 suites) [shwr, spa bath (5), tlt, hairdry, a/c, elec blkts, tel, TV, video, clock radio, t/c mkg, refrig, mini bar (20), cook fac (5), toaster], conv fac, ✕ (Mon to Sun), pool indoor heated, sauna, spa, bbq, rm serv, cots. W $581 - $707, RO ∮ $98 - $109, ∮∮ $109 - $119, ⌂ $29, Suite D $168 - $199, ch con, 5 units of a higher standard, 6 units of a lower rating, Min book long w/ends and Easter, AE BC DC MC VI.

★☆ **Dandaloo Motel Hotel**, (LMH), Cnr Kanahooka Rd & Brownsville Ave, 2km NE of PO, ☎ 02 4261 1122, fax 02 4261 4680, (2 stry gr fl), 16 units [shwr, tlt, fan, heat, elec blkts, TV, t/c mkg, refrig, toaster], ✕, dinner to unit, BLB ∮ $44 - $77, ∮∮ $55 - $77, ∮∮∮ $77 - $88, ⌂ $11, BC EFT MC, ♿.

WOLLONGONG & SUBURBS - FAIRY MEADOW NSW 2519

Part of WOLLONGONG & SUBURBS region. Pop Part of Wollongong, (78km S Sydney), See map on page 55, ref C4. Beachside suburb of Wollongong. Boating, Fishing, Golf, Surfing, Tennis.

Hotels/Motels
Cabbage Tree Motel, (M), 1A Anama St, 500m S of PO, ☎ 02 4284 4000, fax 02 4284 4112, 35 units [shwr, tlt, heat, TV, t/c mkg, refrig, ldry], conf fac, pool, non smoking rms (10). RO ♦ $55 - $100, ♦♦ $65 - $100, ♀ $10, ch con, weekly con, AE BC DC EFT MC VI.

Self Catering Accommodation
★★★ **Wollongong Surf Leisure Resort**, (HU), Pioneer Rd, 1.5km E of PO, ☎ 02 4283 6999, fax 02 4285 1620, 102 units acc up to 7, [shwr, tlt, a/c-cool (66), fan (36), heat, tel, TV, video, clock radio, t/c mkg, refrig, cook fac, micro (66), blkts, linen, pillows], D $75 - $140, ch con, AE BC DC EFT MC VI.

★★★★ **(Caravan Section)**, (84 pwr), town water, shwr (10G-10L)-fee, tlt (12G-12L), baby bath (2), sullage (84), ldry, w/mach-fee, dryer-fee, iron, pool indoor heated, sauna, spa, bbq-fee, kiosk, LPG, ice, ✎, plygr, tennis-fee, No pets allowed. **pwr-site D ♦♦ $20 - $30, ♀ $5.50, un-pwr-site D ♦♦ $16.50 - $20, ♀ $5.50**, Min book applies.

WOLLONGONG & SUBURBS - FIGTREE NSW 2525

Part of WOLLONGONG & SUBURBS region. Pop Part of Wollongong, (80km S Sydney), See map on page 55, ref C4. Leafy inner suburb of Wollongong. Boating, Bowls, Fishing, Golf, Surfing, Tennis.

Hotels/Motels

★★★☆ **Sovereign Motor Inn**, (M), Lot 1, Princes Hwy, ☎ 02 4271 1122, fax 02 4271 4535, 42 units [shwr, bath (24), tlt, hairdry, a/c, tel, cable tv, video (avail), radio, t/c mkg, refrig], dry, conv fac, ☒ (Mon to Sat), bar, cots-fee, non smoking units (4). RO ♦ $92 - $103, ♦♦ $92 - $103, ♀ $11, AE BC DC VI.

B&B's/Guest Houses
★★★★☆ **Chapman's Wisteria Cottage**, (B&B), 75 Koloona Ave, 2km W of PO, ☎ 02 4229 8958, fax 02 4225 2110, 1 rm [shwr, tlt, hairdry, fan, heat, elec blkts, tel, TV, video, clock radio, t/c mkg], iron, iron brd, ✕, bbq, courtesy transfer. BB ♦ $75, ♦♦ $110, BC MC VI.

★★★★☆ **Greenhill at Figtree**, (B&B), 190 Princes Hwy, ☎ 02 4271 1120, fax 02 4272 8819, 17 rms (1 suite) [shwr, bath (2), tlt, hairdry, cent heat, tel, TV, clock radio, t/c mkg, refrig], ldry, iron, iron brd, rec rm, lounge (2), business centre, conf fac, cook fac, non smoking rms. BB ♦ $170, ♦♦ $190, AE BC MC VI.

WOLLONGONG & SUBURBS - KANAHOOKA NSW 2530

Pop Part of Wollongong, See map on page 55, ref C4. On the western shores of Lake Illawarra.

Self Catering Accommodation
★★★★ **Hillside View Apartment**, (Apt), 6 Field St, ☎ 02 4261 7498, fax 02 4261 7498, 1 apt acc up to 4, (1 bedrm), [shwr, tlt, TV, clock radio, t/c mkg, refrig, cook fac, micro, elec frypan, toaster, ldry, doonas, linen], w/mach, iron, iron brd, lounge, pool (salt water), bbq, courtesy transfer, non smoking property. D ♦♦ $95 - $110, ♀ $20, pen con, weekly con, MC VI.

WOLLONGONG & SUBURBS - LAKE ILLAWARRA NSW 2528

Pop part of Wollongong, (98km S Sydney), See map on page 55, ref C4.

B&B's/Guest Houses
★★★★ **Ebb-Tide By The Lake**, (B&B), 47 Reddall Pde, ☎ 02 4295 1297, fax 02 4295 3497, (2 stry), 2 rms [ensuite, shwr (2), tlt (2), hairdry (2), c/fan (3), elec blkts (4), tel, TV, clock radio, t/c mkg, refrig (2)], ldry, iron, iron brd, lounge (TV), bbq, courtesy transfer. BB ♦ $65, ♦♦ $85 - $95, ♀ $15, ch con, fam con, BC MC VI.

★★★★ **Lakeside Homestay B&B**, (B&B), 99 Madigan Blvd, 5Km NW of Shellharbour, ☎ 02 4296 5212, (2 stry), 2 rms [ensuite (1), shwr, bath (1), tlt, a/c, elec blkts (1), clock radio], ldry, lounge (TV, video), t/c mkg shared, refrig, bbq, courtesy transfer, non smoking property. BB ♦ $60 - $65, ♦♦ $80 - $90, ♀ $25 - $30, ch con.

WOLLONGONG & SUBURBS - PORT KEMBLA NSW 2509

Part of WOLLONGONG & SUBURBS region. Pop 5,062. (86km S Sydney), See map on page 55, ref C4. Famous harbour and steelworks that have been the economic pulse of the Illawarra region for many years.

B&B's/Guest Houses
★★★ **Wentworth Lodge**, (GH), Lots 1 & 2 Wentworth St, 200m N of PO, ☎ 02 4275 1915, fax 02 4275 1915, (Multi-stry gr fl), 36 rms [shwr (21), tlt (21), pillows], ldry, w/mach-fee, dryer-fee, iron, rec rm, lounge (TV), cook fac, t/c mkg shared, ✎, non smoking rms (10). D ♦ $30 - $40, W ♦ $99 - $110.

WOLLONGONG & SUBURBS - STANWELL PARK NSW 2508

Part of WOLLONGONG & SUBURBS region. Pop 1,300. (87km S Sydney), See map on page 56, ref B8. Beachside settlement at the foot of the Illawarra Escarpment below Stanwell Tops. Fishing, Surfing, Swimming.

Self Catering Accommodation
Cabbage Tree Cottage, (Cotg), 30 Beach Rd, ☎ 02 9953 0690, or 02 9955 4064, fax 02 9955 4085, 1 cotg acc up to 6, [shwr, bath, tlt, hairdry, c/fan, heat, elec blkts, TV, video, refrig, cook fac, micro, toaster, linen reqd], w/mach, dryer, iron, iron brd, lounge firepl, pool, bbq, non smoking property, Min book applies, AE BC MC VI, (not yet classified).

B&B's/Guest Houses
Kims Place, (B&B), 52a Lower Coast Rd, 500m E of PO, ☎ 02 4294 2929, fax 02 4294 2400, (2 stry), 1 rm [ensuite, fan, heat, TV, video, radio, CD, t/c mkg, refrig, cook fac ltd, micro, toaster, ldry, doonas], non smoking property. BB ♦♦ $140 - $180, Min book applies, (not yet classified).

Tudor Lodge Bed & Breakfast, (B&B), 3 Old Coast Rd, 500m S of Bald Hill lookout, ☎ 02 4294 4899, fax 02 4294 4899, (2 stry gr fl), 3 rms (1 suite) [shwr (2), tlt (2), fan, heat, elec blkts, cable tv, video (1), clock radio, t/c mkg, refrig (2), doonas], lounge firepl, ✕, bbq, c/park (undercover), non smoking property. BB ♦ $50, ♦♦ $90, ♀ $35, Suite BB $135, ch con, BC MC VI, (not yet classified).

WOLLONGONG & SUBURBS - THIRROUL NSW 2515

Part of WOLLONGONG & SUBURBS region. Pop 5,300. (65km S Sydney), See map on page 55, ref C3. Former coal mining town situated north of Bulli beside the sea. Bowls, Fishing, Scenic Drives, Surfing, Swimming.

Hotels/Motels
★★★ **Thirroul Beach**, (M), 222 Lawrence Hargrave Dr, ☎ 02 4267 2333, fax 02 4267 5904, (2 stry gr fl), 16 units [shwr, tlt, a/c, fan, elec blkts, tel, TV, clock radio, t/c mkg, refrig], ldry, bbq, plygr, cots. RO ♦ $45 - $55, ♦♦ $65 - $85, ♀ $10, ch con, BC EFT MC VI.

WOLLONGONG & SUBURBS - WINDANG NSW 2528

Part of WOLLONGONG & SUBURBS region. Pop 2,200. (98km S Sydney), See map on page 55, ref C4. Windang lies at the southern tip of the peninsula that separates Lake Illawarra from the sea. Boating, Bowls, Fishing, Golf, Surfing, Swimming, Tennis.

Hotels/Motels

★★★★☆ **Fairways Resort**, (M), 24 Golf Pl, Primbee 2502, 2km N of PO, adjacent to golf course, ☎ 02 4274 7274, fax 02 4274 6376, (2 stry gr fl), 26 units [shwr, bath (20), spa bath (4), tlt, a/c, tel, TV, clock radio, t/c mkg, refrig, mini bar, toaster], ldry, iron, iron brd, conv fac, ☒, pool, bbq, rm serv, tennis, cots. RO ♦ $123 - $160, ♦♦ $143 - $160, ♀ $20, AE BC DC MC VI, ᵬ.

Operator Comment: Special school holiday rates and packages available.

★★★☆ **Oasis Resort Best Western**, (M), 146 Windang Rd, 1km N of PO, opp golf course, ☎ 02 4295 1622, fax 02 4295 1459, 30 units [shwr, spa bath (3), tlt, hairdry, a/c, tel, cable tv, video (avail), clock radio, t/c mkg, refrig], ldry, iron, iron brd, conv fac, ⊠, pool, sauna, spa, bbq, rm serv, plygr, cots. RO ♦ $103 - $154, ♦♦ $116 - $165, ◊ $12, ch con, AE BC DC JCB MC MP VI.

WOLLONGONG & SUBURBS - WOONONA NSW 2517

Part of WOLLONGONG & SUBURBS region. Pop Part of Wollongong, (70km S Sydney), See map on page 55, ref C3. Beachside suburb of Wollongong situated south of Bulli. Boating, Fishing, Golf, Surfing, Swimming, Tennis.

Hotels/Motels
★★★☆ **Windmill Motor Inn**, (M), Cnr Princes Hwy & Gray St, 500m S of PO, ☎ 02 4284 8766, fax 02 4284 0494, 26 units (2 suites) [shwr, bath (10), spa bath (2), tlt, hairdry, a/c, elec blkts, tel, TV, movie, t/c mkg, refrig, cook fac (11), toaster, ldry (guest), doonas], iron, iron brd, conv fac, bbq, dinner to unit, cots-fee, non smoking rms (8). RO ♦ $93 - $119, ♦♦ $104 - $119, ◊ $29, Suite RO $145 - $169, ch con, Min book long w/ends, AE BC DC MC VI.

End of Wollongong & Suburbs

WONBOYN LAKE NSW 2551

Pop 200. Nominal, (534km S Sydney), See map on pages 52/53, ref G8. Small, quiet village on Wonboyn Lake, set deep in the forests of the far south coast. Boating, Fishing, Golf, Swimming.

Self Catering Accommodation
★★☆ **Wonboyn Lake Resort**, (Cotg), 1 Oyster Lane, 19km from Hwy, ☎ 02 6496 9162, fax 02 6496 9100, 14 cotgs [shwr, tlt, fan, heat, tel, TV, clock radio, refrig, cook fac, micro, blkts, linen, pillows], ldry, rec rm, conv fac, ⊠, pool, spa, bbq, ☎, plygr. D $70 - $150, W $400 - $980, BC MC VI.

Trouble-free travel tips - Jack
Check that the jack and wheel are on board and the jack works.

WOOLGOOLGA NSW 2456

Pop 3,750. (586km N Sydney), See map on page 54, ref D4. North coast seaside town that services local forestry, farming and tourism enterprises. Bowls, Fishing, Surfing, Swimming, Tennis.

Hotels/Motels
★★★☆ **Ocean Beach Motor Inn**, (M), 78 Beach St, 250m E of PO, ☎ 02 6654 1333, fax 02 6654 2966, 10 units [shwr, tlt, hairdry, a/c, c/fan, tel, TV, video-fee, clock radio, t/c mkg, refrig, micro, toaster], ldry, iron brd, pool-heated (solar), spa, bbq, dinner to unit, car wash, cots-fee, non smoking units (2). RO ♦ $55 - $110, ♦♦ $60.50 - $110, ♦♦♦ $73.70 - $125, ◊ $13 - $15.40, AE BC DC JCB MC VI.

★★★☆ **Rosebourne Gardens Motel**, (M), 48 Pacific Hwy, 1.2km NW of PO, ☎ 02 6654 1877, fax 02 6654 1970, 20 units [shwr, tlt, a/c, tel, TV, video-fee, clock radio, t/c mkg, refrig], ldry, ✕, pool, spa, dinner to unit, cots-fee, non smoking units (3). RO ♦ $50 - $70, ♦♦ $50 - $70, ♦♦♦ $61.50 - $85, ◊ $11 - $15, AE BC DC MC VI, ⅋.

★★★ **Balcony View Motor Inn**, (M), 62 Beach St, 100m E of PO, ☎ 02 6654 1289, fax 02 6654 1289, (2 stry gr fl), 10 units [shwr, tlt, fan, heat, tel, fax, TV, clock radio, t/c mkg, refrig, toaster], pool, bbq. W $380 - $610, RO ♦ $45 - $95, ♦♦ $55 - $100, ♦♦♦ $65 - $105, ◊ $10 - $15, AE BC DC MC VI.

★★★ **Woolgoolga Motor Inn**, (M), Pacific Hwy, 1.3km NW of PO, ☎ 02 6654 1534, 10 units [shwr, tlt, hairdry, fan, heat, tel, cable tv, video (hire), clock radio, t/c mkg, refrig], pool, bbq, plygr, cots-fee. RO ♦ $45 - $50, ♦♦ $50 - $55, ◊ $10, $65 - $70, AE BC DC MC MCH VI.

★★☆ **Pine Lodge Motel**, (M), Cnr Pacific Hwy & Clarence St, 850m W of PO, ☎ 02 6654 1532, fax 02 6654 1630, 10 units [shwr, tlt, a/c (4), fan, heat, elec blkts, tel, TV, video (avail), clock radio, t/c mkg, refrig], ldry, pool, bbq, dinner to unit, car wash, plygr, cots-fee. RO ♦ $44 - $72, ♦♦ $48 - $78, ♦♦♦ $55 - $93, ◊ $11 - $13, AE BC DC MC VI.

★★ **Go Bananas Motel**, (M), 53 Pacific Hwy, 1.2km NW of PO, ☎ 02 6654 1424, fax 02 6654 1424, 10 units (1 suite) [shwr, bath, tlt, a/c, fan, c/fan, heat, tel, TV, radio, t/c mkg, refrig], spa, bbq, c/park (undercover), car wash, plygr, cots-fee. W $250 - $480, RO ♦ $40 - $60, ♦♦ $40 - $60, ♦♦♦ $55, ◊ $8 - $10, Suite D $60 - $100, ch con, fam con, pen con, AE BC MC VI.

Self Catering Accommodation
★★★ **Safety Beach Ocean Bungalows**, (Cotg), 41a Safety Beach Dve, Safety Beach, 2km N of Woolgoolga, ☎ 02 6654 7445, 2 cotgs acc up to 5, [shwr, tlt, fan, heat, tel, TV, video, clock radio, t/c mkg, refrig, cook fac, micro, elec frypan, toaster, blkts, linen], ldry, iron, bbq, courtesy transfer, plygr, cots, non smoking rms (indoors). D ♦♦ $65 - $120, ◊ $12, W ♦♦♦♦ $440 - $740, ◊ $80, pen con.

WOOLI NSW 2462

Pop 550. (685km N Sydney), See map on page 54, ref D4. Coastal town between Coffs Harbour and Yamba surrounded by Yuraygir National Park. Boating, Fishing, Swimming, Tennis.

Hotels/Motels
★★☆ **Wooli Motel**, (LMH), Wooli Rd, 2km E of PO, ☎ 02 6649 7532, fax 02 6649 7711, 6 units [shwr, tlt, c/fan, heat, elec blkts, fax, TV, clock radio, t/c mkg, refrig, toaster], ldry, conv fac, ⊠, bbq, ☎, plygr, cots. RO ♦ $38.50 - $55, ♦♦ $55 - $66, ♦♦♦ $66 - $77, ◊ $11, Min book long w/ends, BC EFT MC VI.

Rates may change. Check before booking.

Self Catering Accommodation
★★☆ **Wooli River Lodges**, Lot 2 North Rd, ☎ 02 6649 7750, 8 cabins acc up to 6, [shwr, tlt, c/fan, TV, refrig, cook fac, micro, toaster], ldry, pool (salt water), bbq, canoeing. D ♦♦ $55 - $80, W $315 - $505, pen con, BC MC VI, ⅃⚹.

B&B's/Guest Houses
★★★☆ **Wooli Beachouse**, (B&B), 6 South Tce, 500m S of PO, ☎ 02 6649 7660, or 02 6642 7822, (2 stry) 3 rms [hairdry, fan, heat, elec blkts, tel, TV, video, clock radio, t/c mkg, refrig, micro, toaster], shared fac (shwr, tlt & spa), ldry, rec rm, lounge (TV), bbq, c/park. **BLB** ♦ $85 - $95.

WOOMARGAMA NSW 2644
Pop Nominal, (478km SW Sydney), See map on pages 52/53, ref E7. Convenient stopping place on the Hume Highway between Holbrook and Albury. Golf, Tennis.

Hotels/Motels
★★ **Woomargama Village**, (LMH), Hume Hwy, ☎ 02 6020 5232, fax 02 6020 5232, 10 units [shwr, tlt, a/c, heat, elec blkts, TV, clock radio, t/c mkg, refrig], ✕, pool (salt water), bbq, dinner to unit, plygr, cots. **RO** $45 - $77, ♦ $10, ch con, AE BC MC VI.

WOONOONA NSW
See Wollongong & Suburbs.

WOY WOY NSW 2256
Pop Part of Gosford, (82km N Sydney), See map on page 56, ref E3. One of the Central Coast's major centres, situated on Woy Woy Inlet and Brisbane Water. Boating, Bowls, Fishing, Golf, Swimming. See also Pearl Beach & Umina.

Hotels/Motels
★★★☆ **Glades Country Club Motor Inn**, (M), 15 Dunban Rd, 2km SW of PO, adjacent Country Club, ☎ 02 4341 7374, fax 02 4343 1170, 23 units [shwr, tlt, hairdry, a/c, elec blkts, tel, TV, movie, clock radio, t/c mkg, refrig, toaster], ldry, pool, bbq, cots, non smoking units (5). **RO** ♦ $70 - $110, ♦♦ $80 - $120, ch con, Min book applies, AE BC DC EFT MC VI, ⅃⚹.

★★★ **Watersedge Woy Woy**, (M), 18 The Boulevarde, 75m from Fishermen's Wharf, ☎ 02 4341 2888, fax 02 4341 8555, (2 stry), 17 units [shwr, tlt, a/c, tel, TV, clock radio, t/c mkg, refrig], ldry, ✕, dinner to unit, cots-fee, non smoking units (10). **D** ♦♦ $73 - $150, ♦ $7.70 - $11, ch con, fam con, pen con, BC EFT MC VI.

Self Catering Accommodation
Woy Woy Bed & Breakfast, (Apt), 132 Nth Burge Rd, 2km S of Railway Station, ☎ 02 4341 1744, fax 02 4341 1744, (2 stry gr fl) 1 apt acc up to 4, (3 bedrm) [shwr, tlt, heat, elec blkts (1), TV, radio, t/c mkg, refrig, cook fac ltd, micro, toaster, blkts, doonas, linen, pillows], w/mach, bbq, non smoking rms. **RO** ♦ $50, ♦ $50, ch con, Min book applies, (not yet classified).

B&B's/Guest Houses
★★★☆ **Blossoms Bed & Breakfast**, (B&B), 11 Koonora Ave, Orange Grove, 3km E of Woy Woy PO, ☎ 02 4341 8732, or 02 5452 2779, fax 02 4342 2778, 2 rms (2 suites) [shwr, bath, tlt, hairdry, fan, heat, elec blkts, tel, TV, video, clock radio, t/c mkg, refrig, cook fac, micro, elec frypan, toaster], ldry, iron, iron brd, pool (heated), bbq, non smoking rms. **BB** ♦ $85 - $105, ♦♦ $130 - $160, ♦ $50 - $60, BC MC VI.

★★★ **Elizabeths Waterfront Retreat**, (B&B), 1a Farnell Rd, 1km N of PO, ☎ 02 4341 1719, or 02 4343 1157, fax 02 4341 1719, 3 rms [shwr, tlt, a/c (1), fan, TV, clock radio, t/c mkg, refrig, cook fac (1), micro (2), toaster], bbq, courtesy transfer, non smoking rms. **BB** ♦ $50 - $65, ♦♦ $90 - $110, ♦ $15, BC MC VI.

★★★ **Pelicans' Nest**, (B&B), Previously Pelicans' Nest Waterfront Bed & Breakfast 322 Burge Rd, 1km S of PO, ☎ 02 4344 4660, 1 rm [shwr, tlt, a/c, fan, heat, elec blkts, TV, video, clock radio, CD, t/c mkg, refrig, micro, toaster], non smoking rms. **BLB** ♦ $88, ♦♦ $110, BC MC VI.

WYEE BAY NSW 2259
Pop 2,020. (124km N Sydney), See map on page 55, ref D5. Urban centre situated on the south-western shores of Lake Macquarie. Boating, Bowls, Fishing, Golf, Swimming.

Self Catering Accommodation
★★★★ **Waterfront Townhouses**, (HU), 77 Ruttleys Rd, 5km N of Doyalson RSL, ☎ 02 4359 1800, fax 02 4359 1800, (Multi-stry), 6 units acc up to 8, [shwr (2), bath (2), tlt (2), heat, TV (2), video, clock radio, t/c mkg, refrig, cook fac, micro, toaster, ldry (in unit), linen reqd-fee], w/mach, iron, pool, bbq, c/park (garage), boat park, tennis, non smoking units. **D** $154 - $220, Min book applies.

B&B's/Guest Houses
Hylands by the Lake, (B&B), 41 Kullaroo Rd, Summerland Point 2259 250m W of PO, ☎ 02 4976 1558, (2 stry gr fl) 1 rm [shwr, tlt, heat, TV, clock radio, t/c mkg, refrig, toaster, doonas], c/park (undercover), non smoking property. **BB** ♦ $75 - $90, ♦♦ $80 - $100, (not yet classified).

WYNDHAM NSW 2550
Pop Nominal, (465km S Sydney), See map on pages 52/53, ref G8. Small town in the heart of the south coast's dairy country. Bush Walking, Scenic Drives.

Self Catering Accommodation
★★★ **Warrawee Cottages**, (Cotg), 97 Burragate Rd, 5km S of Wyndham, ☎ 02 6494 2360, fax 02 6494 2450, 2 cotgs acc up to 6, [shwr, tlt, fire pl (wood heater), TV, clock radio, t/c mkg, refrig, cook fac, toaster, ldry, blkts, linen, pillows], w/mach, iron, bbq, tennis, cots. **D** ♦ $15, $50, **W** ♦♦ $300.

WYONG NSW 2259
Pop 100,468. (94km N Sydney), See map on page 55, ref D5. One of the main centres of the Central Coast, situated in the northern part of the region on the Wyong River and handy to Tuggerah Lake. Fishing, Golf, Greyhound Racing, Horse Racing, Scenic Drives, Swimming. See also Chittaway Bay, Dooralong & Palmdale.

Hotels/Motels
★★★☆ **Central Coast Motel**, (M), Cnr Pacific Hwy & Cutler Dve, 1Km N of PO, ☎ 02 4353 2911, fax 02 4352 1975, 18 units [shwr, tlt, a/c, fan, tel, TV, clock radio, t/c mkg, refrig, toaster], ldry, pool, bbq, cots-fee. **RO** ♦ $75 - $85, ♦♦ $77 - $95, ♦♦♦ $88 - $105, ♦ $5.50 - $11, ch con, AE BC DC EFT MC VI.

B&B's/Guest Houses
★★★☆ **Strathavon Heritage Resort**, (GH), 31 Boyce Ave, 1km E of PO, ☎ 02 4352 1161, fax 02 4351 2135, 46 rms [shwr, tlt, hairdry, c/fan, heat, TV, t/c mkg, refrig], ldry, ✕, bar, pool, ✆, mini golf, tennis. **BB** ♦♦ $125, **DBB** ♦♦ $195, **RO** ♦♦ $100, ch con, AE BC EFT MC VI.

YAMBA NSW 2464

Pop 4,700. (682km N Sydney), See map on page 54, ref D3. Delightful coastal resort at the mouth of the Clarence River.

Hotels/Motels

AAA TOURISM *Special Rates* ★★★★ **Aston Villa Motor Inn**, (M), 3 Mulgi St, 600m W of PO, ☎ 02 6646 2785, fax 02 6646 2399, (2 stry), 24 units [shwr, bath (1), spa bath (2), tlt, a/c (13), c/fan (12), heat, tel, fax, TV, video (all rooms), clock radio, t/c mkg, refrig, cook fac ltd (9), micro (6), toaster], ldry, pool (salt water), spa, bbq, cots-fee, non smoking rms (8). W $420 - $630, RO ♦♦ $70 - $105, ⓘ $10, ch con, AE BC DC EFT MC VI.

★★★★ **Moby Dick Waterfront Resort Motel**, (M), 27 Yamba Rd, 2km W of PO, ☎ 02 6646 2196, fax 02 6646 1383, (2 stry gr fl), 26 units [shwr, spa bath (2), tlt, c/fan, heat, elec blkts, tel, fax, TV, video, clock radio, t/c mkg, refrig, cook fac], ldry, conf fac, pool (salt water), spa, boat park, jetty, tennis, cots. RO ♦ $98, ♦♦ $98 - $140, ♦♦♦♦ $104 - $175, AE DC MC VI, ♿.

★★★★ **Pegasus Motel**, (M), Cnr Yamba & Angourie Rd, 1.1km W of PO, ☎ 02 6646 2314, fax 02 6646 1433, 6 units [shwr, tlt, c/fan, heat, tel, fax, TV, video, clock radio, t/c mkg, refrig, cook fac (6)], ldry, ✗, pool, bbq, c/park (undercover) (6), tennis, non smoking units (3). **RO** ♦ $55 - $65, ♦♦ $61 - $75, ♦ $11, ch con, AE BC DC EFT MC VI.

★★★★ **Surf Motel**, (M), 2 Queen St, 600m E of PO, ☎ 02 6646 2200, fax 02 6646 1955, (2 stry gr fl), 8 units [shwr, tlt, hairdry, a/c, c/fan, fax, cable tv, clock radio, t/c mkg, refrig, cook fac, micro, toaster], iron, iron brd, bbq, c/park (undercover). **RO** ♦ $80 - $165, ♦♦ $80 - $165, ♦ $15, BC DC MC VI,

Operator Comment: Brand new luxury 4 star self-contained apartments, right on main beach. Spectacular ocean views. Split-system Air Conditioning. Overnight and Weekly rates. Very reasonable tariffs - "You'll love it!".

★★★☆ **Oyster Shores Motel**, (M), 81 Yamba Rd, 2.6km W of PO, ☎ 02 6646 1122, fax 02 6646 8008, 26 units [shwr, tlt, fan, heat, elec blkts, tel, fax, TV, clock radio, t/c mkg, refrig, toaster], ldry, pool-indoor, spa, bbq, plygr, tennis (half court), cots, non smoking units (7). **RO** ♦ $55 - $77, ♦♦ $66 - $88, ♦♦♦ $77 - $110, ♦ $11, AE BC DC MC VI, ⚹.

(Villa Section), 2 villas [shwr, bath, tlt (2), elec blkts, tel, fax, TV, clock radio, refrig, micro, d/wash, toaster, ldry, blkts, linen], bbq. **D** ♦♦ $132, ♦ $11, **W** $770, (not yet classified).

★★★☆ **Yamba Oceanview Beachfront Resort Motel**, (M), 30 Clarence St, 500m E of PO, ☎ 02 6646 9411, fax 02 6646 9406, (Multi-stry gr fl), 26 units [shwr, tlt, c/fan, heat, tel, fax, TV, video, clock radio, t/c mkg, refrig, cook fac ltd, toaster], ldry, pool, bbq, c/park (carport) (13), cots. **RO** ♦ $59 - $150, ♦♦ $59 - $150, ♦ $10, AE BC DC EFT MC VI.

★★★☆ **Yamba Twin Pines Motel**, (M), 49 Wooli St, 600m N of Bowling Club, ☎ 02 6645 8055, fax 02 6645 8050, 16 units [shwr, tlt, c/fan, tel, TV, clock radio, t/c mkg, refrig, toaster], pool, bbq, courtesy transfer, cots, non smoking units (14). **RO** ♦ $65, ♦♦ $70, ch con, pen con, AE BC MC VI, ⚹.

★★★ **Inca Sun Motel**, (M), Cnr Wooli & Claude Sts, 700m W of PO, opposite XPT bus stop, ☎ 02 6646 2144, fax 02 6646 2144, (2 stry gr fl), 12 units [shwr, tlt, fan, heat, tel, fax, TV, video (avail), clock radio, t/c mkg, refrig], ldry, pool, bbq, cots, non smoking rms (6). **RO** ♦ $50 - $60, ♦♦ $60 - $99, ♦♦♦ $70 - $99, ♦ $10, AE BC DC MC VI.

★★★ **Yamba Beach Motel**, (M), 7 Queen St, 500m E of PO, ☎ 02 6646 9411, or 02 6646 2150, fax 02 6646 9406, (2 stry gr fl), 12 units [shwr, tlt, fan, heat, TV, clock radio, t/c mkg, refrig, cook fac, micro (6), toaster, ldry (guest)], pool, bbq, c/park (carport) (9), cots. **RO** ♦ $59 - $120, ♦♦ $59 - $120, ♦ $10, ch con, AE BC DC EFT MC VI.

★★☆ **Sea Spray Motel**, (M), Cnr Beach & Clarence Sts, 300m E of PO, ☎ 02 6646 2306, fax 02 6646 2306, (2 stry), 12 units [shwr, tlt, heat, fax, TV, clock radio, t/c mkg, refrig, cook fac ltd], ldry, bbq, c/park (carport) (5), cots. **RO** ♦ $45 - $110, ♦♦ $55 - $110, ♦♦♦ $70 - $115, ♦ $10, AE BC MC VI, *Operator Comment: Position ideal with fantastic ocean views opposite main beach.*

Self Catering Accommodation
★★ **Pembroke**, (HU), 29 Wooli St, 400m W of PO, ☎ 02 6646 2321, fax 02 6646 1583, 2 units acc up to 4, [shwr, tlt, fan, heat, TV, refrig, cook fac, micro, ldry, linen reqd], **D** ♦♦♦♦ $200 - $450, Min book applies, EFT.

Other Accommodation
Captain-A-Cruiser, (Hbt), Yamba Boatharbour Marina, ☎ 02 6645 8067, fax 02 6645 8167, 1 houseboat acc up to 8, [shwr, tlt, tel, TV, radio, cook fac, blkts reqd-fee, linen reqd-fee]. **W** $900 - $1,080, Aluminium dinghy with outboard motor available - no charge. Min book applies.

YARRAHAPINNI NSW 2441

Pop Nominal, (480km N Sydney), See map on page 54, ref C6. Small settlement at the foot of Mount Yarrahapinni, handy to beaches at Grassy Head, Scotts Head and Stuarts Point.
★★★☆ **Kurrabi Rainforest Retreat**, (GH), 140 Browns Rd, 6km W of Stuarts Point PO, ☎ 02 6569 0809, (2 stry gr fl), 4 rms [shwr (2), tlt (4), c/fan (2), tel, TV, video], shared fac (2 rms), ldry, rec rm, lounge (TV), pool, c/park. **BB** ♦♦ $110, **DBB** ♦♦ $180, BC MC VI.

YARRAMALONG NSW 2259

Pop 695. Part of Wyong, (109km N Sydney), See map on page 56, ref E1. Old timber town in a picturesque valley in the Watagan Mountains. Bush Walking, Horse Riding.
Self Catering Accommodation
★★★☆ **Yarradane Lodge**, (HU), (Farm), Bunning Creek Rd, 22km W of Yarramalong Fwy turnoff, ☎ 02 4356 1155, fax 02 4356 1323, 4 units [shwr (3), tlt (2), elec blkts, tel, clock radio, t/c mkg, refrig, cook fac, micro, elec frypan, toaster, blkts, linen], ldry, rec rm, pool (salt water), bbq, bicycle, tennis. **RO** ♦ $62 - $72, ♦♦ $124 - $144, ♦ $62 - $72, ch con, Min book applies.

B&B's/Guest Houses
★★★☆ **Yarramalong Manor**, (GH), Linga Longa Rd, 18km W of Wyong PO, ☎ 02 4356 1066, fax 02 4356 1066, (2 stry), 6 rms [shwr, tlt, fan, heat, elec blkts, tel, TV, clock radio, t/c mkg, refrig], lounge (TV), ✗, c/park. **BB** ♦ $50 - $60, AE BC DC EFT MC VI.

YASS NSW 2582

Pop 4,850. (279km SW Sydney), See map on pages 52/53, ref G6. Historic town promoted as being at the heart of 'Wine, Wool and Waterways'.
Hotels/Motels
★★★★ **Thunderbird Motel**, (M), 264 Comur St, 600m N of PO, ☎ 02 6226 1158, fax 02 6226 3045, 31 units [shwr, bath (3), spa bath (2), tlt, hairdry, a/c, elec blkts, tel, TV (27 rms remote), video (21), clock radio, t/c mkg, refrig], ldry, iron, iron brd, ✗, pool, bbq, rm serv, cots-fee, non smoking rms (12). **RO** ♦ $68 - $98, ♦♦ $77 - $110, ♦♦ $88 - $121, ♦ $88 - $121, 10 units at a lower rating, 9 units ★★★☆. AE BC DC EFT MC VI.
Operator Comment: See advertisement on next page.

★★★☆ **Colonial Lodge Motor Inn**, (M), Cnr McDonald St & Yass Valley Way, 1.5km N of PO, ☎ 02 6226 2211, fax 02 6226 2203, (2 stry gr fl), 15 units [shwr, spa bath (1), tlt, hairdry, a/c, cent heat, elec blkts, tel, TV, clock radio, t/c mkg, refrig, mini bar, toaster], iron, dinner to unit, courtesy transfer, non smoking units (8). **RO** ♦ $70 - $80, ♦♦ $80 - $90, ♦ $11, AE BC DC EFT MC MP VI.

★★★☆ **Sundowner Chain Motor Inns**, (M), Cnr Laidlaw & Castor Sts, 2km S PO, ☎ 02 6226 3188, fax 02 6226 3266, 30 units (2 suites) [shwr, spa bath (4), tlt, hairdry, a/c, elec blkts, tel, TV, video-fee, clock radio, t/c mkg, refrig, mini bar (25), micro (3), toaster], ldry, iron, iron brd, conv fac, ✗, rm serv, cots-fee, non smoking units (15). **RO** ♦ $79.50 - $153.50, ♦♦ $85 - $153, ♦ $11, ch con, AE BC DC EFT MC MP VI, ⚹.

Thunderbird

MOTEL AAA Tourism ★★★★

264 COMUR STREET, YASS NSW 2582 TEL: (02) 6226 1158 FAX: (02) 6226 3045

Be pampered with luxury accommodation set in a resort style atmosphere

★ 12 recently built executive rooms of international standard
★ Superbly appointed standard, deluxe and 2 bedroom units
★ Colour TV ★ Remote control TV & video players in deluxe
and executive Rooms ★ 2 Executive Rooms with large corner spas
★ Silent split system air conditioning ★ Queen size beds
★ Heating and electric blankets ★ Hair dryers ★ Irons and ironing boards
★ Direct dial telephones ★ Guest laundry
★ Quiet off-road units set in peaceful surroundings

★ Large free-form swimming pool
featuring sunbathing decks and
cascading waterfall
★ Paved and grassed entertaining area
with all weather BBQ facilities

Ewe'n me

Licensed Restaurant and Cocktail Bar
A renowned Restaurant set amongst relaxing surrounds with views of the lanscaped pool and gardens
in the summer months, and nestled around the blazing rock fireplace during winter.

615AG

YASS MOTEL

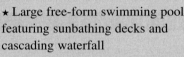

- Quiet off road units.
- Fully Licensed Restaurant with excellent choice of fine
  cuisine will ensure a hearty meal before retiring for the night.
- Friendly country environment and old fashion hospitality.
- Yass Motel is surrounded by tranquil grazing and pastures and
  cool mountain streams yet within walking distance to Clubs
  and Shopping Centre.
- Olympic Pool across the road. **Hume Hwy, Yass, NSW 2582.**
  Tel: 02 6226 1055

Bookings: 1800 685 383 **Fax: 02 6226 1425**

6158AG

HAMILTON YASS HUME
HOTEL INN

hosts:	Norma Templeman,
	Cheryl Cooke
no. rooms:	35
city centre:	1km
office hrs:	7am to 10.30pm
lic'd bistro:	Monday to Saturday
	(closed Sunday)

Activities & Attractions
Close to Olympic Pool, bowls, squash. Main centre 10 mins walk, Soldiers Club and
shops. Near Lake Burrinjuck, Cooma Cottage, Carey's Caves. Comfortable drive to
winter snowfield and wineries. Less than 30 minutes to our National Capital.

9 Laidlaw Street, Yass 2582
fax: 02 6226 3933 **BOOKINGS: 1800 020 559** ph: 02 6226 1722

Country *Haven*

★★★☆ **The Yass Motel**, (M), Hume Hwy, 800m S of PO,
☎ 02 6226 1055, or fax 02 6226 1425, 24 units [shwr, spa
bath (2), tlt, hairdry (12), a/c, heat, elec blkts, tel, fax, TV,
video (8), clock radio, t/c mkg, refrig], ⊠, rm serv, dinner to
unit, c/park (undercover), cots-fee, non smoking units (8).
RO ♦ $69 - $140, ♦♦ $69 - $140, ♦ $10, Suite D $108, AE BC DC EFT
MC MP VI.

★★☆ **Hamilton Hume Motor Inn**, (M), 9 Laidlaw St (Hume Hwy), 1km
S of PO, ☎ 02 6226 1722, fax 02 6226 3933, 36 units [shwr,
bath (19), spa bath (3), tlt, a/c, heat, elec blkts, tel, TV, video-fee,
clock radio, t/c mkg, refrig], ldry, ✕, ⊠, rm serv, plygr, cots, non
smoking rms. **RO ♦ $55 - $93.50, ♦♦ $66 - $137.50, ♦♦♦ $71.50 -
$148.50, ♦ $8,** ch con, 13 units ★★★. AE BC DC EFT MC VI, ⟨&⟩.

Budget Motel Chain International

★★☆ **Hi-Way Motor Inn**, (M), Cnr Grand Junction Rd &
Yass Valley Way, 2km N of PO, ☎ 02 6226 1300,
fax 02 6226 4184, 23 units [shwr, tlt, a/c-cool, heat,
elec blkts, tel, TV, clock radio, t/c mkg, refrig, toaster],
ldry, ✕, pool, dinner to unit, cots-fee, non smoking units (20).
RO ♦ $52 - $56, ♦♦ $60 - $82, ♦ $10, AE BC DC MC VI.

B&B's/Guest Houses
★★★☆ **Globe Bed & Breakfast**, (B&B), Classified by National Trust,
No children's facilities, 70 Rossi St, 500m N of PO, ☎ 02 6226 3680,
fax 02 6226 3680, (2 stry), 5 rms (4 suites) [shwr, bath (1), tlt,
c/fan (5), fire pl (2), cent heat, elec blkts], iron, iron brd, rec rm,
lounge (TV), lounge firepl, t/c mkg shared, cots, non smoking property.
BB ♦ $90, ♦♦ $120 - $130, AE BC DC MC VI.

YEOVAL NSW 2868

Pop 300. (359km NW Sydney), See map on pages 52/53, ref G4.
Carinya Farmstay, (Cotg), (Farm), 'Carinya', 27km W of PO, ☎ 02 6367 9244,
fax 02 6367 9244, 1 cotg acc up to 10, [shwr, bath, tlt, fan, fire pl,
elec blkts, TV, clock radio, t/c mkg, refrig, cook fac, micro, elec frypan,
toaster, ldry, linen reqd-fee], w/mach, iron, rec rm, lounge, pool above
ground, bbq, c/park (garage), cots. **D $99 - $165, W $495 - $880.**

YERONG CREEK NSW 2642

Pop 150. (500km SW Sydney), See map on pages 52/53, ref E6. Riverina village on the Olympic Highway between Henty and The Rock.
★★★☆ **Hanericka Farmstay**, (GH), (Farm), Fairfield, 5km NE of PO off Olympic Hwy, ☎ 02 6920 3709, fax 02 6920 3770, 8 rms [shwr, tlt, a/c-cool, elec blkts, clock radio], ldry, lounge (TV), pool (salt water), t/c mkg shared, bbq, tennis, cots. **BB** ⚭ **$65**, ⚭⚭ **$100, DBB** ⚭ **$80,** ⚭⚭ **$130**, ch con, BC MC VI.

YOUNG NSW 2594

Pop 6,800. (372km W Sydney), See map on pages 52/53, ref F6. Old goldrush town that has since become known as the 'Cherry Capital'.

Hotels/Motels
★★★★☆ **Young Federation Motor Inn**, (M), Main St, 300m from PO, ☎ 02 6382 5644, fax 02 6382 5672, 30 units (1 suite) [shwr, bath, spa bath (8), tlt, hairdry, a/c, elec blkts, tel, TV, video (6), clock radio, refrig, mini bar], conv fac, pool (salt water), rm serv, cots, non smoking units (11). **RO** ⚭ **$103 - $160,** ⚭⚭ **$103 - $160,** ⚭⚭⚭ **$117 - $174,** ⚭ **$14, Suite D** ⚭⚭ **$125 - $160**, ch con, AE BC DC EFT JCB MC MP VI, ♿.

★★★☆ **Best Western Tadlock Motor Inn**, (M), Olympic Hwy, 2km S of PO, ☎ 02 6382 3300, fax 02 6382 4699, 14 units [shwr, bath (1), spa bath (1), tlt, hairdry, a/c, elec blkts, tel, TV, movie, clock radio, t/c mkg, refrig], ldry, iron, iron brd, ✉ (Mon to Sat), rm serv, plygr, cots-fee, non smoking units (5). **RO** ⚭ **$74 - $102,** ⚭⚭ **$85 - $114,** ⚭ **$11 - $12**, AE BC DC EFT JCB MC MP VI, ♿.

AAA
TOURISM
Special Rates
★★★☆ **Cherry Blossom Motel**, (M), Olympic Way, 500m N of PO, ☎ 02 6382 1699, fax 02 6382 2841, 30 units [shwr, tlt, a/c-cool, heat, elec blkts, tel, TV, movie, clock radio, t/c mkg, refrig], ✗, pool (salt water), bbq, dinner to unit, cots-fee. **RO** ⚭ **$73,** ⚭⚭ **$83,** ⚭ **$11**, AE BC DC EFT MC MP VI.

★★★☆ **Colonial Motel**, (M), Olympic Way, 500m N of PO, ☎ 02 6382 2822, fax 02 6382 3698, 11 units [shwr, bath (4), tlt, hairdry, a/c, c/fan, elec blkts, tel, TV, movie, clock radio, t/c mkg, refrig, mini bar, toaster, ldry-fee], dinner to unit, cots-fee. **RO** ⚭ **$61 - $71.50,** ⚭⚭ **$69.30 - $82.50**, ch con, 4 units at four star rating, AE BC DC MC VI.

★★★★ **(Apartment Section)**, 4 apts acc up to 6, (Studio), [shwr, spa bath, tlt, hairdry, a/c-cool, heat, elec blkts, tel, TV, video-fee, movie, clock radio, t/c mkg, refrig, cook fac, micro, toaster], ldry, w/mach, iron, iron brd, dinner to unit. **RO** ⚭ **$82 - $93.50,** ⚭⚭ **$92 - $104.50,** ⚭ **$12**, ch con.

★★★ **Goldrush Motel**, (M), Olympic Way, 500m S of PO, ☎ 02 6382 3444, fax 02 6382 4458, 12 units [shwr, tlt, a/c, heat, elec blkts, tel, TV, video, movie, clock radio, t/c mkg, refrig, toaster], cots. **RO** ⚭ **$70,** ⚭⚭ **$80,** ⚭ **$10**, ch con, AE BC DC EFT MC VI.

★★★ **Town House Motor Inn**, (M), 23 Zouch St, 200m N of PO, ☎ 02 6382 1366, fax 02 6382 4366, 29 units [shwr, tlt, a/c, elec blkts, tel, TV, video (6), clock radio, t/c mkg, refrig, mini bar (3), toaster], ✉ (Mon to Sat), pool (salt water), bbq, rm serv (Mon to Sat), cots-fee, non smoking units (10). **RO** ⚭ **$62 - $72,** ⚭⚭ **$72 - $82,** ⚭ **$12**, 7 budget units of a 2.5 star rating. Minium booking Oct Long Weekend & Cherry Festival Weekend, AE BC DC MC MP VI.

Self Catering Accommodation
★★★ **Tilsawood Cottage**, (Cotg), 100 Pitstone Rd, Chinamans Dam, 3.5km S of PO, ☎ 02 6382 6275, fax 02 6382 6275, 1 cotg acc up to 4, [a/c, elec blkts, clock radio, t/c mkg, cook fac, micro], lounge (TV), bbq, cots (avail). **BLB** ⚭⚭ **$95,** ⚭ **$5 - $10**, ch con, BC MC VI.

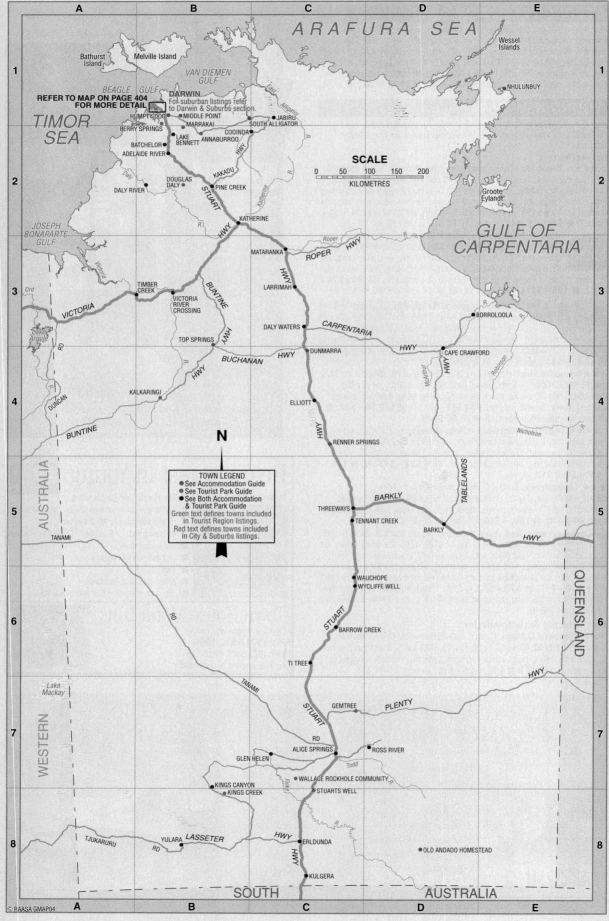

ARAFURA SEA

Wessel
Islands

Bathurst
Island

Melville Island

VAN DIEMEN
GULF

NHULUNBUY

BEAGLE GULF

TIMOR
SEA

DARWIN

REFER TO MAP ON PAGE 404
FOR MORE DETAIL

For suburban listings refer
to Darwin & Suburbs section.

HUMPTY DOO · MIDDLE POINT
BERRY SPRINGS · MARRAKAI
JABIRU
BATCHELOR · LAKE BENNETT · COOINDA · SOUTH ALLIGATOR
ADELAIDE RIVER · ANNABURROO

Groote
Eylandt

KAKADU

GULF OF
CARPENTARIA

DOUGLAS
DALY

DALY RIVER

PINE CREEK

STUART

JOSEPH
BONAPARTE
GULF

KATHERINE

MATARANKA

ROPER   HWY

SCALE

0   50   100   150   200
KILOMETRES

TIMBER
CREEK

VICTORIA

VICTORIA
RIVER
CROSSING

BUNTINE

LARRIMAH

HWY

BORROLOOLA

Lake
Argyle

TOP SPRINGS

DALY WATERS

CARPENTARIA   HWY

BUCHANAN   HWY

DUNMARRA

HWY

CAPE CRAWFORD

KALKARINGI

ELLIOTT

BUNTINE

HWY

RENNER SPRINGS

TABLELANDS

AUSTRALIA

N

TANAMI

TOWN LEGEND
● See Accommodation Guide
● See Tourist Park Guide
● See Both Accommodation
  & Tourist Park Guide
Green text defines towns included
in Tourist Region listings.
Red text defines towns included
in City & Suburbs listings.

BARKLY

THREEWAYS

TENNANT CREEK

BARKLY

HWY

QUEENSLAND

Lake
Mackay

WAUCHOPE
WYCLIFFE WELL

STUART

BARROW CREEK

WESTERN

TANAMI

TI TREE

STUART   RD

GEMTREE   PLENTY

HWY

GLEN HELEN

ALICE SPRINGS · ROSS RIVER

WALLACE ROCKHOLE COMMUNITY

KINGS CANYON
KINGS CREEK

STUARTS WELL

TJUKARURU
RD

YULARA   LASSETER

HWY

ERLDUNDA

OLD ANDADO HOMESTEAD

KULGERA

SOUTH   AUSTRALIA

© RAASA GMAP04

Covering one sixth of the Australian continent, the Northern Territory is a place of extremes, from its desert regions in the south to the tropics of the north.

In places the average rainfall is 15 cm a year while in others it can be more than 200 cm. The Territory has two major centres, the capital Darwin and Alice Springs. Other main centres are Katherine, Nhulunbuy and Tennant Creek. The main industries are mining and tourism. The Devils Marbles, Ayers Rock (Uluru), The Olgas (Kata Tjuta), Kings Canyon, the MacDonnell Ranges, Standley Chasm, the Simpson Desert, Katherine Gorge National Park (Nitmiluk), The Gulf, Mataranka with its thermal pool, the biggest bathtub in the Territory, are part of an ancient landscape which has been part of the Aboriginal culture for 30,000 years.

The Northern Territory's Kakadu National Park includes about 20,000 square kilometres of the Alligator River region in Australia's tropical north.

It is unique as almost all the catchment of the South Alligator River lies within its boundaries. Most of the habitat types of the Top End are found in this catchment producing a remarkable abundance and variety of plants and animals, many rare or found nowhere else.

New species continue to be discovered in the region. Kakadu qualifies for World Heritage listing on the basis of both natural and cultural value.

A large part of Kakadu is owned by Aboriginal people who maintain strong personal and spiritual links with their traditional land.

Most visitors prefer the "Dry" season from May to September when the humidity and temperatures are lowest (average daily max 30 deg. C. during the day). For those who can cope with the heat the "Wet" or "Green" season (November to March is a particularly beautiful time to see the park). If you travel in your own car plan to stay a few days. Visitors who enjoy Kakadu the most are those who stay the longest.

SAFETY NOTE:
There are hazards in Kakadu National Park, but if all park warnings are observed and caution and common sense exercised these will not spoil your visit.

NORTHERN TERRITORY

The Territory goes to extremes

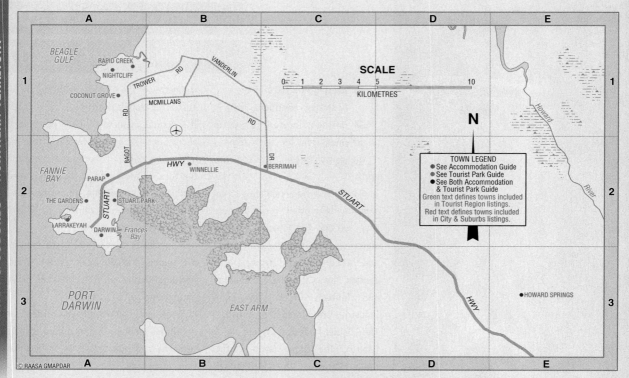

Map references:
A B C D E (top)
1 2 3 (sides)

BEAGLE GULF
RAPID CREEK
NIGHTCLIFF
COCONUT GROVE
TROWER RD
VANDERLIN
RD
MCMILLANS RD
BAGOT
HWY
WINNELLIE
FANNIE BAY
PARAP
THE GARDENS
STUART
STUART PARK
LARRAKEYAH
DARWIN
Frances Bay
DR BERRIMAH
STUART
HWY
PORT DARWIN
EAST ARM
HOWARD SPRINGS
Howard River

SCALE
0 1 2 3 4 5 10
KILOMETRES

N

TOWN LEGEND
● See Accommodation Guide
● See Tourist Park Guide
● See Both Accommodation & Tourist Park Guide
Green text defines towns included in Tourist Region listings.
Red text defines towns included in City & Suburbs listings.

© RAASA GMAPDAR

A B C D E (bottom)

DARWIN NT 0800

Pop 78,085. See map on page 404, ref A2. The capital city of the Northern Territory, and the Northern gateway of Australia. A rapidly expanding city first established in 1869 under the name of Palmerston. Art Gallery, Boating, Bowls, Fishing, Golf, Horse Racing, Scenic Drives, Squash, Swimming, Tennis.

Hotels/Motels

★★★★☆ **All Seasons Premier Darwin Central Hotel**, (LH), Cnr Smith & Knuckey Sts, ☎ 08 8944 9000, fax 08 8944 9100, (Multi-stry), 132 rms [ensuite, bath, hairdry, a/c, tel, TV, video, movie, clock radio, t/c mkg, refrig, mini bar, micro (30), elec frypan (30), toaster (30)], lift, ldry, w/mach-fee, dryer-fee, iron, iron brd, ✕, pool, rm serv, secure park, ✆, cots, non smoking units (110). RO ♦ **$138 - $174,** ♦♦ **$175 - $192,** ◊ **$40,** Function Centre. AE BC DC EFT JCB MC VI.

★★★★☆ **Novotel Atrium Darwin**, (LH), Cnr Peel St & The Esplanade, ☎ 08 8941 0755, fax 08 8981 9025, (Multi-stry), 138 rms [ensuite, bath (75), a/c-cool, c/fan, tel, TV, movie, clock radio, t/c mkg, refrig, toaster], lift, ldry, w/mach-fee, dryer-fee, lounge, conf fac, ✕, pool, spa, bbq, rm serv, cots. RO ♦ **$154,** ♦♦ **$154,** ◊ **$33, Suite D $254,** AE BC DC EFT MC VI.

★★★★☆ **Rydges Plaza Hotel Darwin**, (LH), 32 Mitchell St, 400m S of PO, ☎ 08 8982 0000, fax 08 8981 1765, (Multi-stry), 233 rms (12 suites) [ensuite, bath, spa bath (1), hairdry, a/c, tel, TV, movie, clock radio, t/c mkg, refrig, mini bar, ldry-fee], lift, lounge, conf fac, ✕, pool, spa (1), 24hr reception, rm serv, c/park (undercover), ✆, gym, cots, non smoking flr. RO ♦ **$162 - $260,** ♦♦ **$162 - $260,** ◊ **$27.50, Suite D $315 - $1,210,** ch con, AE BC DC EFT MC VI, ♿.

★★★★☆ **Saville Park Suites Darwin**, (LH), 88 The Esplanade, 1km SW of PO, ☎ 08 8943 4333, fax 08 8943 4388, (Multi-stry gr fl), 140 rms (140 suites) [ensuite, bath, hairdry, a/c-cool, tel, TV, clock radio, t/c mkg, refrig, mini bar, cook fac, micro (10), d/wash, toaster, ldry (in unit), pillows], lift, w/mach, dryer, iron, iron brd, conf fac, ✕, pool, spa, rm serv, ✆, cots. D **$177 - $355,** ch con, fam con, AE BC DC JCB MC VI.

★★★★☆ **The Carlton Hotel Darwin**, (LH), The Esplanade, 1.1km SW of PO, ☎ 08 8980 0800, fax 08 8980 0888, (Multi-stry), 197 rms (33 suites) [ensuite, bath, hairdry, a/c-cool, tel, cable tv, video, movie, clock radio, t/c mkg, refrig, mini bar, toaster], lift, ldry, lounge, conv fac, ✕, pool, sauna, spa, 24hr reception, rm serv, c/park (undercover), ✆, gym, cots, ch con, Function Centre. RO **$147, Suite $219,** AE BC DC EFT JCB MC VI.

Trouble-free travel tips - Fluids

Check all fluid levels and top up as necessary. Look at engine oil, automatic transmission fluid, radiator coolant (only check this when the engine is cold), power steering, battery and windscreen washers.

Rates may change. Check before booking.

★★★★ **Centra Darwin**, (LH), 122 Esplanade, 1km SW of GPO, ☎ 08 8981 5388, fax 08 8981 5701, (Multi-stry), 183 rms (2 suites) [ensuite, bath, hairdry, a/c-cool, tel, TV, movie, clock radio, t/c mkg, refrig, mini bar], lift, ldry, w/mach-fee, dryer-fee, iron, conf fac, ☒, pool, bbq, 24hr reception, rm serv, cots. RO ⚹ **$125 - $198**, ⚹⚹ **$125 - $198**, ⚹ **$25, Suite D $250**, ch con, AE BC DC EFT JCB MC MCH MP VI.

 ★★★★ **Mirambeena Resort Darwin**, (M), 64 Cavenagh St, 100m S of PO, ☎ 08 8946 0111, fax 08 8981 5116, 225 units [ensuite, a/c-cool, tel, TV, movie, clock radio, t/c mkg, refrig, cook fac (33)], ldry, rec rm, conv fac, ☒, pool (2), spa, pool bar, mini golf, cots. RO ⚹⚹ **$143 - $218.90**, ⚹⚹⚹ **$167.20 - $218.90**, ⚹ **$24.20**, 89 units ★★★. AE BC DC JCB MC VI, ⚹⚹.

 ★★★ **Asti Motel**, (M), Cnr Smith St & Packard Pl, 1.1km NW of GPO, ☎ 08 8981 8200, fax 08 8981 8038, (Multi-stry gr fl), 86 units [ensuite, bath (34), a/c-cool, fan (65), tel, TV, clock radio, t/c mkg, refrig, micro (34), toaster (34)], ☒, pool, spa, cots-fee. RO ⚹⚹ **$102 - $120**, ⚹⚹⚹⚹ **$114 - $143**, ⚹ **$10**, ch con, fam con, BC EFT MC VI.

  ★★★ **Metro Inn Darwin**, (M), 38 Gardens Rd, 1.3km N of GPO, ☎ 08 8981 1544, fax 08 8941 2541, (Multi-stry gr fl), 60 units [ensuite, a/c-cool, tel, TV, movie, clock radio, t/c mkg, refrig, cook fac (21), micro (21)], ldry, w/mach-fee, dryer-fee, ☒, pool, D **$87 - $170**, AE BC DC EFT JCB MC VI.

★★★ **Poinciana Inn**, (M), Cnr Mitchell & McLachlan Sts, 400m NW of GPO, ☎ 08 8981 8111, fax 08 8941 2440, (Multi-stry gr fl), 51 units [ensuite, bath (hip) (11), hairdry, a/c-cool, tel, TV, radio, t/c mkg, refrig], lift, ldry, iron, iron brd, ☒, pool, cots. BLB ⚹ **$92 - $119**, ⚹⚹ **$97 - $130**, ⚹ **$15 - $19**, ch con, AE BC DC EFT JCB MC VI.

 ★★★ **Top End Hotel**, (M), Cnr Mitchell & Daly Sts, 2km NW of GPO, ☎ 08 8981 6511, fax 08 8941 1253, (2 stry gr fl), 40 units [ensuite, a/c-cool, c/fan, tel, TV, movie, radio, t/c mkg, refrig, cook fac ltd], ldry, ☒ (5 Bars), pool (salt water), bbq, cots. RO ⚹⚹ **$85 - $152**, ⚹⚹⚹ **$95 - $163**, AE BC DC JCB MC VI.

★★☆ **All Seasons Frontier Darwin**, (LH), 3 Buffalo Ct, 1km N of GPO, ☎ 08 8981 5333, fax 08 8941 0909, (Multi-stry), 84 rms [ensuite, bath, a/c-cool, tel, TV, movie, clock radio, t/c mkg, refrig, mini bar], lift, ldry, iron, iron brd, lounge, conv fac, ☒, bar, pool, bbq, ✆, cots, non smoking rms (39). RO ⚹⚹ **$104.50 - $163**, ⚹ **$30**, ch con, AE BC DC JCB MC VI.

★★☆ **Palms Motel**, (M), 100 McMinn St, 1.4km N of GPO, ☎ 08 8981 4188, fax 08 8981 4415, (2 stry gr fl), 21 units [ensuite, a/c-cool, fan, tel, TV, clock radio, t/c mkg, refrig, cook fac (4)], ldry, pool, bbq, cots. RO ⚹ **$74.80 - $82.50**, ⚹⚹ **$74.80 - $132**, ⚹ **$11**, **Suite D $132**, ch con, fam con, pen con, AE BC DC EFT JCB MC VI.

 ★★ **Value Inn Motel**, (M), 50 Mitchell St, City Centre, ☎ 08 8981 4733, fax 08 8981 4730, (2 stry gr fl), 93 units [ensuite, a/c-cool, TV, refrig], lift, pool, ✆, non smoking units (62). RO ⚹ **$71 - $74**, ⚹⚹ **$71 - $74**, AE BC EFT MC VI,

Operator Comment: City Centre/Budget.Re:
www.valueinn.com.au

DARWIN NT continued...

★☆ **Don Hotel Motel**, (LMH), 12 Cavenagh St, 400m E of GPO, ☎ 08 8981 5311, fax 08 8981 5032, (2 stry gr fl), 38 units [ensuite, a/c-cool, c/fan, tel, TV, t/c mkg, refrig], night club (Mon to Sat), ✉ (Thurs to Sat), pool, bbq, cots. **BLB ♦ $60 - $70, ♦♦ $70 - $80, ◊ $10**, Restaurant has adult only entertainment. AE BC DC EFT MC VI.

Self Catering Accommodation

★★★★ **Cullen Bay Serviced Apartments**, (SA), 26 Marina Blvd, Cullen Bay, 2.5km W of GPO, ☎ 08 8981 7999, fax 08 8981 0171, (Multi-stry gr fl), 95 serv apts acc up to 6, [shwr, tlt, a/c-cool, c/fan, tel, TV, movie, clock radio, t/c mkg, refrig, cook fac, micro, toaster, ldry, blkts, linen, pillows], lift, w/mach, dryer, iron, iron brd, pool (saltwater), spa, bbq, 24hr reception, ✆, cots, **D ♦♦ $119.90 - $218.90**, AE BC DC EFT MC VI.

★★★★ **Marrakai Luxury All Suites**, (SA), 93 Smith St, 600m NW of GPO, ☎ 08 8982 3711, fax 08 8981 9283, (Multi-stry), 30 serv apts (30 suites) acc up to 4, [shwr, bath, tlt, a/c-cool, fan, tel, TV, clock radio, t/c mkg, refrig, cook fac, d/wash, ldry], lift, pool, spa, bbq, secure park, cots. **D ♦♦ $190, ♦♦♦ $205, ◊ $15**, AE BC DC MC VI.

★★★★ **Mediterranean All Suites Hotel**, (SA), Previously Emerald Hotel, 81 Cavenagh St, 500m SW of PO, ☎ 08 8981 7771, fax 08 8981 7760, (Multi-stry), 77 serv apts [ensuite, spa bath (50), hairdry, a/c, c/fan, tel, TV, movie, clock radio, t/c mkg, refrig, cook fac, toaster], ldry (3), w/mach, dryer-fee, iron, iron brd, ✉, bar, pool, ✆ (covered), non smoking units (28). **RO ♦ $132 - $175, ♦♦ $132 - $175, ◊ $22**, AE BC DC EFT MC MP VI.

★★★☆ **Alatai Holiday Apartments**, (Apt), Cnr McMinn St & Finniss St, ☎ 08 8981 5188, fax 08 8981 8887, (Multi-stry gr fl), 63 apts acc up to 4, (2 bedrm Studio), [shwr, tlt, a/c-cool, c/fan, tel, TV, movie, clock radio, t/c mkg, refrig, cook fac, micro (24), elec frypan (24), toaster], ldry, w/mach (51), dryer (51), rec rm, lounge (TV), ✉, pool, spa, bbq, c/park (undercover), cots-fee. **D $99 - $330**, AE BC DC EFT JCB MC VI.

★★★ **City Gardens Apartments**, (HU), Previously City Gardens Holiday Units, 93 Woods St, 900m N of PO, ☎ 08 8941 2888, fax 08 8981 2934, (2 stry gr fl), 16 units acc up to 6, (2 bedrm), [shwr, tlt, a/c-cool, fan, tel, TV, video (2), clock radio, refrig, cook fac, micro, toaster, ldry, blkts, linen, pillows], pool, bbq, cots. **D ♦♦♦♦ $136 - $150, ◊ $10**, fam con, AE BC DC MC VI.

★★★ **Peninsular Apartments**, (SA), 115 Smith St, 1km NW of GPO, ☎ 08 8981 1922, fax 08 8941 2547, (Multi-stry gr fl), 36 serv apts (Studio), [ensuite, a/c-cool, c/fan, tel, TV, movie, clock radio, t/c mkg, refrig, cook fac ltd, micro, toaster], lift, ldry, w/mach-fee, dryer-fee, iron, iron brd, bar (licensed), pool, cots. **D $80 - $140**, Breakfast available. AE BC DC MC VI.

★★☆ **Ti Tree Holiday Apartments**, (HU), 92 Woods St, 500m from PO, ☎ 08 8941 0568, fax 08 8981 5677, 8 units acc up to 4, [shwr, tlt, a/c-cool, c/fan, tel, TV, video-fee, clock radio, t/c mkg, refrig, cook fac, micro (4), toaster, blkts, linen, pillows], ldry, spa, **D ♦ $85 - $105, ♦♦ $101.50 - $121.50**, AE BC DC MC VI.

Other Accommodation

Air Raid City Lodge, (Lodge), 35 Cavenagh St, ☎ 08 8981 9214, fax 08 8981 6024, 24 rms [shwr, tlt, a/c-cool, TV, clock radio, t/c mkg, refrig], ldry, ✗, cook fac, 24hr reception, shop, ✆, cots. **RO ♦ $60, ♦♦ $70, ◊ $11**, AE BC DC EFT JCB MC VI.

Frogshollow Backpacker Resort, (Lodge), 27 Lindsay St, ☎ 08 8941 2600, fax 08 8941 0758, (2 stry gr fl), 26 rms acc up to 5, [ensuite (2), a/c-cool (17), fan, linen], ldry, iron, iron brd, lounge (tv, video), pool, spa, cook fac, t/c mkg shared, bbq, ✆. **D ♦ $18 - $20, ♦♦ $46 - $55**, ch con, AE BC DC EFT MC VI, ♿.

DARWIN - COCONUT GROVE NT 0810

Pop Part of Darwin, (9km N Darwin), See map on page 404, ref A1. A suburb of Darwin.

Self Catering Accommodation

★★☆ **Coconut Grove Holiday Apartments**, (Apt), 146 Dick Ward Dve, ☎ 08 8985 0500, fax 08 8985 0591, (Multi-stry gr fl), 35 apts acc up to 6, (1, 2 & 3 bedrm), [shwr, tlt, c/fan, tel, cable tv, refrig, cook fac], ldry, w/mach-fee, dryer-fee, iron brd, pool, cots. **D ♦ $100 - $158, ♦♦ $100 - $158, ◊ $12**, ch con, AE BC EFT MC VI.

DARWIN - HOWARD SPRINGS NT 0835

Pop Part of Darwin, (25km SE Darwin), See map on page 404, ref E3. An outer suburb of Darwin.

Hotels/Motels

★★ **Darwin Boomerang Motel**, (M), Lot 2, Virginia Rd, via Virginia, ☎ 08 8983 1202, fax 08 8983 3640, 9 units [ensuite, bath (hip) (1), a/c-cool, c/fan, TV, clock radio, t/c mkg, refrig, cook fac, toaster], ldry, w/mach-fee, dryer-fee, iron, iron brd, pool, bbq, ✆, cots, non smoking units. **RO ♦ $55 - $75, ♦♦ $60 - $75, ◊ $11**, ch con, BC MC VI.

B&B's/Guest Houses

★★★★☆ **Melaleuca Homestead Bed & Breakfast**, (B&B), 163 Melaleuca Rd, ☎ 08 8983 2736, fax 08 8983 3314, 2 rms [ensuite, a/c-cool, c/fan, t/c mkg], ldry, pool, spa, bbq, meals avail. **BB ♦ $132, ♦♦ $145**, BC MC VI.

★★★★ **(Cottage Section)**, No children's facilities, 2 cotgs acc up to 3, [shwr, tlt, hairdry, a/c, clock radio, t/c mkg, refrig, micro, elec frypan, toaster, blkts, linen, pillows], ldry, pool, spa, bbq, meals avail, c/park. **BB ♦♦ $155, ♦♦♦ $175**.

DARWIN - LARRAKEYAH NT 0820

Pop Part of Darwin, (2km W Darwin), See map on page 404, ref A2. A suburb of Darwin.

Other Accommodation

Banyan View Lodge, (Lodge), 119 Mitchell St, 1.2km NW of GPO, ☎ 08 8981 8644, fax 08 8981 6104, (Multi-stry gr fl), 44 rms acc up to 2, [ensuite (4), a/c-cool (16), fan, t/c mkg, refrig], ldry, lounge (TV), conf fac, spa, cook fac, bbq, ✆. **D ♦ $38 - $45, ♦♦ $45 - $61**, BC EFT MC VI.

(Bunkhouse Section), 3 bunkhouses acc up to 4, [linen]. **D ♦ $18, ◊ $18**.

DARWIN - NIGHTCLIFF NT 0810

Pop 3,431. (10km N Darwin) See map on page 404, ref A1. Suburb of Darwin.

Hotels/Motels

★★☆ **Darwin Phoenix Motel**, (M), 63 Progress Dve, ☎ 08 8985 4144, fax 08 8948 0425, 57 units [ensuite, bath, a/c-cool, tel, TV, movie, t/c mkg, refrig], ldry, conv fac, ✗, pool, 24hr reception, rm serv, cots. **RO ♦ $66 - $77, ♦♦ $77 - $88, ◊ $11**, ch con, AE BC DC EFT MC VI.

DARWIN - PARAP NT 0820

Pop Part of Darwin, (5km N Darwin), See map on page 404, ref A2. A suburb of Darwin.

Hotels/Motels

★★★ **Paravista Comfort Inn**, (M), 5 MacKillop St, ☎ 08 8981 9200, fax 08 8981 1049, (Multi-stry gr fl), 18 units [ensuite, bath (3), a/c, fan (9), tel, TV, clock radio, t/c mkg, refrig, mini bar], ldry, pool, rm serv. **RO ♦ $100 - $110, ♦♦ $110 - $121**, AE BC DC JCB MC VI.

★☆ **Motel Casablanca**, (M), 52 Gregory St, ☎ 08 8981 2163, fax 08 8981 8062, (2 stry), 45 units (2 suites) [ensuite, a/c-cool, c/fan, tel, TV, t/c mkg, refrig, cook fac, micro (9), toaster (9)], ldry, w/mach-fee, dryer-fee, rec rm, ✉ (Mon to Sat), pool, bbq, cots. **RO ♦ $71.50 - $93.50, ◊ $15, Suite D ♦♦ $85 - $148.50, ◊ $20**, ch con, pen con, AE BC DC MC VI.

Self Catering Accommodation

AAA TOURISM *Special Rates* ★★★☆ **Parap Village Apartments**, (SA), 39-45 Parap Rd, ☎ 08 8943 0500, fax 08 8941 3465, (Multi-stry gr fl), 44 serv apts acc up to 6, (2 & 3 bedrm), [shwr, tlt, a/c-cool, fan, tel, TV, video-fee, clock radio, t/c mkg, refrig, cook fac, micro, d/wash (20), toaster, ldry], iron, iron brd, pool, spa (2), bbq (3), car wash, plygr, cots. **D $154 - $220**, AE BC DC EFT MC VI.

DARWIN - RAPID CREEK NT 0810

Pop Part of Darwin, (9km N Darwin), See map on page 404, ref A1. A suburb of Darwin.

B&B's/Guest Houses

★★☆ **Frangipanni Bed & Breakfast**, (B&B), 6 Waters St, ☎ 08 8985 2797, fax 08 8985 2797, 1 rm [ensuite, a/c-cool, c/fan, TV, clock radio, t/c mkg, toaster], w/mach, iron, spa (outdoor), refrig, bbq, non smoking rms. **BLB ♦ $60 - $70, ♦♦ $70 - $80, ◊ $10**, ch con, BC MC VI.

DARWIN - STUART PARK NT 0820

Pop Part of Darwin, (4km N Darwin), See map on page 404, ref A2. A suburb of Darwin.

Self Catering Accommodation

★★★ **Stuart Park Holiday Apartments**, (Apt), 66 Stuart Hwy, ☎ 08 8981 6408, fax 08 8981 6418, (2 stry gr fl), 8 apts acc up to 4, (2 bedrm), [shwr, bath (hip) (4), tlt, a/c-cool, c/fan, TV, clock radio, t/c mkg, refrig, cook fac, toaster, blkts, linen, pillows], ldry, w/mach-fee, dryer-fee, iron, iron brd, spa, bbq, ✆. **D ♦♦♦♦ $82.50 - $99**, AE BC EFT MC VI.

The Summer House B&B, (HU), 3 Quarry Cres, ☎ 08 8981 9992, fax 08 8981 0009, 5 units acc up to 6, (1, 2 & 3 bedrm), [shwr, tlt, a/c-cool, c/fan, TV, video, clock radio, t/c mkg, refrig, cook fac, toaster, blkts, doonas, linen, pillows], w/mach-fee, dryer-fee, spa (communal) (1), meals to unit, ✆, cots, breakfast ingredients, non smoking property, ch con, **D ♦ $107 - $117, ♦♦ $117 - $137, ◊ $20 - $50**, AE BC MC VI, (not yet classified).

DARWIN - THE GARDENS NT 0820

Pop Part of Darwin, (2km N Darwin), See map on page 404, ref A2. A suburb of Darwin.

Hotels/Motels

AAA TOURISM *Special Rates* ★★★★★ **MGM Grand Darwin**, (LH), Gilruth Ave, Mindil Beach, ☎ 08 8943 8888, fax 08 8943 8999, (Multi-stry), 80 rms (16 suites) [ensuite, bath, spa bath (16), hairdry, a/c-cool, tel, cable TV, video, clock radio, t/c mkg, refrig, mini bar, toaster], lift, ldry, iron, iron brd, lounge, business centre, conv fac, ☒, pool, sauna, spa, 24hr reception, rm serv, ✆, gym, tennis, cots, non smoking flr (1), **RO ♦ $125 - $196, ♦♦ $125 - $196, ◊ $40, Suite D $187.50 - $299**, 16 suites ★★★★★. AE BC DC JCB MC VI, ⚹₺.

Self Catering Accommodation

★★★☆ **Botanic Gardens Apartments**, (Apt), 17 Geranium St, 2km N of GPO, ☎ 08 8946 0300, fax 08 8981 0410, (Multi-stry gr fl), 45 apts acc up to 5, (1, 2 & 3 bedrm), [shwr, tlt, a/c-cool, c/fan, tel, TV, clock radio, t/c mkg, refrig, cook fac, micro, toaster, ldry (in unit), blkts, linen, pillows], w/mach, dryer, iron, iron brd, pool (salt water) (2), spa, bbq, c/park (undercover), cots. **D $135 - $285**, 6 units yet to be rated. AE BC DC MC VI.

(Motel Section), 6 units [ensuite, a/c-cool, c/fan, TV, clock radio, t/c mkg]. **D $104 - $135**, (not yet classified).

End of Darwin & Suburbs

ADELAIDE RIVER NT 0846

Pop 365. (113km S Darwin), See map on page 402, ref B2. Situated on the river of the same name. Fishing.

B&B's/Guest Houses

★★★☆ **Mt Bundy Station Homestead Complex**, (B&B), Haynes Rd, 3km E of Stuart Hwy, ☎ 08 8976 7009, fax 08 8976 7113, 2 rms [hairdry, a/c-cool (1), c/fan, clock radio, t/c mkg, refrig], bathrm, ldry, w/mach, iron, iron brd, lounge (TV, Video & Stereo), bbq, meals avail (by arrangement), non smoking rms. **BB ♦ $100, ♦♦ $120 - $150, ◊ $50 - $80**, AE BC DC MC VI.

(Cottage Section), 1 cotg acc up to 6, (2 bedrm), [shwr, tlt, a/c-cool, c/fan, clock radio, t/c mkg, refrig, cook fac, elec frypan, toaster, ldry, blkts, linen, pillows], w/mach, iron, iron brd, ✆. **D $110, W $450**, (not yet classified).

ALICE SPRINGS NT 0870

Pop 27,488. (1490km S Darwin) See map on page 402, ref C7. Located in the heart of the MacDonnell Ranges. A tourist centre of international fame. Bowls, Golf, Hangliding, Horse Riding, Scenic Drives, Shooting, Squash, Swimming, Tennis.

Hotels/Motels

★★★★☆ **Alice Springs Resort**, (LH), 34 Stott Tce, 500m SE of PO, ☎ 08 8951 4545, fax 08 8953 0995, 144 rms [ensuite, bath (36), hairdry, a/c, tel, TV, video-fee, movie-fee, clock radio, t/c mkg, refrig, mini bar], ldry-fee, iron, iron brd, conf fac, ☒, pool, bbq, rm serv, cots, non smoking units (68). **RO ♦♦ $133 - $167, ◊ $25**, ch con, AE BC DC EFT JCB MC VI, ₺.

★★★★☆ **Lasseters Hotel Casino**, (LH), 93 Barrett Dve, 1.5km SE of PO, ☎ 08 8950 7777, fax 08 8953 1680, (2 stry gr fl), 74 rms [ensuite, bath, a/c, heat, elec blkts, tel, TV, movie, radio, t/c mkg, refrig, mini bar], lift, ldry, ☒, pool, bbq, rm serv, tennis, cots. **D ♦♦ $130 - $260, ◊ $30**, AE BC DC MC VI.

★★★★☆ **Mercure Inn Diplomat Alice Springs**, (M), Previously Fortland Diplomat Hotel Alice Springs Cnr Hartley St & Gregory Tce, 200m S of PO, ☎ 08 8952 8977, fax 08 8953 0225, (2 stry gr fl), 81 units [ensuite, spa bath (25), hairdry, a/c, tel, TV, video, movie, clock radio, t/c mkg, refrig, mini bar], ldry-fee, iron, iron brd, ☒ (bar), ✗, pool, rm serv, ✆, cots. **RO ♦♦ $100 - $189, ◊ $21**, ch con, AE BC DC JCB MC VI.

★★★★☆ **Rydges Plaza Resort**, (LH), Barrett Dve, 1.9km SE of PO, ☎ 08 8950 8000, fax 08 8952 3822, (Multi-stry gr fl), 235 rms (7 suites) [bath, hairdry, a/c, tel, video, movie, clock radio, t/c mkg, refrig, mini bar], lift, ldry, lounge, conv fac, ☒, pool-heated, sauna, spa, 24hr reception, rm serv, ✆, gym, tennis, non smoking units (109). **RO ♦ $209, ♦♦ $209, ◊ $27.50, Suite RO ♦♦ $396 - $506**, AE BC DC JCB MC VI, ₺.

 GOLDEN CHAIN ★★★☆ **Alice Motor Inn**, (M), 27 Undoolya Rd, 1km E of PO, ☎ 08 8952 2322, fax 08 8953 2309, (2 stry gr fl), 20 units [shwr, bath (15), tlt, a/c (16), tel, TV, video (21), clock radio, t/c mkg, refrig, mini bar, cook fac (7)], ldry-fee, pool, cots. **RO ♦ $85 - $105, ♦♦ $85 - $105, ◊ $15**, ch con, AE BC DC MC VI, ₺.

  ★★★☆ **Alice Springs Vista Hotel**, (M), Stephens Rd, ☎ 08 8952 6100, fax 08 8952 1988, (2 stry gr fl), 140 units [shwr, bath, tlt, a/c, tel, TV, movie, clock radio, t/c mkg, refrig, mini bar, ldry-fee], meeting rm, ☒, pool, spa, bbq, 24hr reception, rm serv, courtesy transfer (town), ✆, tennis, cots, non smoking rms (3). **RO ♦ $144.10, ♦♦ $144.10, ◊ $27.50**, ch con, AE BC DC EFT JCB MC VI, ₺.

★★★☆ **Desert Rose Inn**, (M), 15 Railway Tce, 450m W of PO, ☎ 08 8952 1411, fax 08 8952 3232, (Multi-stry gr fl), 45 units [ensuite, bath (37), a/c, tel, TV, clock radio, t/c mkg, refrig, micro (37), elec frypan], lift, ldry, ☒, pool, spa, bbq, ✆, cots. **RO ♦ $80 - $115, ♦♦ $96.40 - $125, ◊ $10**, ch con, 9 rooms ★★. BC EFT MC VI, ₺.

(Private Hotel Section), 28 rms [basin, shwr, tlt (1), a/c, tel, TV, radio, t/c mkg, refrig], shared fac. **RO ♦ $45 - $54, ♦♦ $45 - $54**, ch con.

★★★☆ **Elkira Court Motel**, (M), 65 Bath St, 200m S of PO, ☎ 08 8952 1222, fax 08 8953 1370, (2 stry gr fl), 58 units [ensuite, bath (15), a/c-cool (8), a/c (50), heat (8), tel, TV, clock radio, t/c mkg, refrig], ldry, conf fac, ☒ (Tue to Fri), pool, bbq, cots-fee, non smoking units (21). **RO ♦♦ $70 - $120**, 16 units of a lower rating. AE BC DC EFT MC VI, ♿.

★★★☆ **Gapview Resort Hotel Motel**, (LMH), Previously Queen of the Desert Resort. 115 Gap Rd, 2km S of PO, ☎ 08 8952 6611, fax 08 8952 8312, (2 stry gr fl), 52 units [ensuite, bath, a/c, tel, TV, video, clock radio, t/c mkg, refrig], ldry-fee, ☒, pool, bbq, rm serv, cots. **RO ♦♦ $85, ♦ $15**, ch con, AE BC DC EFT MC VI, ♿.

★★★☆ **Heavitree Gap Outback Resort**, (M), Palm Circ, 4.4km SW of PO, adjacent to Todd River, ☎ 08 8950 4444, fax 08 8952 9394, (2 stry gr fl), 80 units [shwr, tlt, a/c, tel, TV, movie, clock radio, t/c mkg, refrig, cook fac, toaster, doonas], ☒, pool, bbq, courtesy transfer (downtown), cots. **RO ♦ $110, ♦♦ $110, ♦ $10**, ch con, AE BC DC MC VI, ♿.

★★★☆ **Mercure Inn Oasis Alice Springs**, (M), Previously All Seasons Frontier Oasis, Alice Springs, 10 Gap Rd, 1km S of PO, ☎ 08 8952 1444, fax 08 8952 3776, (2 stry gr fl), 102 units [shwr, tlt, a/c, tel, TV, movie, clock radio, t/c mkg, refrig], ldry, ☒, pool, sauna, spa, bbq, rm serv, ☎, cots. **RO ♦ $88 - $135, ♦♦ $88 - $135, ♦ $30**, ch con, Function Centre. AE BC DC JCB MC VI.

★★★☆ **Red Centre Resort**, (M), North Stuart Hwy, 4km N of PO, ☎ 08 8950 5555, fax 08 8952 8300, 98 units [a/c, fan (50), tel, TV, clock radio, t/c mkg, refrig, cook fac (24), micro (24)], ldry-fee, rec rm, conf fac, ☒, pool, bbq (covered), courtesy transfer, ☎, tennis, non smoking units (30). **RO ♦ $113, ♦♦ $113, ♦ $15**, ch con, 19 units ★★☆. AE BC DC EFT MC VI, ♿.

★★★☆ **The Territory Inn**, (M), Leichhardt Tce, 300m E of PO, ☎ 08 8950 6666, fax 08 8952 7829, (Multi-stry gr fl), 108 units [ensuite, bath (hip) (35), a/c, heat, tel, cable tv, video-fee, clock radio, t/c mkg, refrig], ldry-fee, conv fac (first floor), ☒, pool-heated, spa, bbq, rm serv, dinner to unit, c/park (undercover) (35), cots, non smoking rms (7). **RO ♦♦ $140, ♦ $20**, ch con, AE BC DC EFT MC VI, ♿.

★★★ **Alice Tourist Apartments**, (M), Cnr Gap Rd & Gnoilya St, ☎ 08 8952 2788, fax 08 8953 2950, (2 stry gr fl), 24 units (1 & 2 bedrm), [shwr, bath (11), tlt, a/c, heat, tel, TV, clock radio, t/c mkg, refrig, cook fac, micro-fee], ldry-fee, pool, bbq, cots. **D $78 - $122**, Light breakfast available. BC EFT MC VI, ♿.

★★★ **Desert Palms Resort**, (M), 74 Barrett Dve, 1km S of PO, ☎ 08 8952 5977, fax 08 8953 4176, 80 units [shwr, tlt, a/c, tel, TV, clock radio, t/c mkg, refrig, cook fac ltd, micro, elec frypan], ldry-fee, pool, bbq, tennis (half court), cots-fee, non smoking rms. **RO ♦ $92, ♦♦ $92, ♦ $10**, AE BC DC EFT MC VI, ♿.

★★★ **Larapinta Lodge Motel**, (M), 3 Larapinta Dve, 1km W of PO, ☎ 08 8952 7255, fax 08 8952 7101, (2 stry gr fl), 31 units [shwr, tlt, a/c, tel, TV, clock radio, t/c mkg, refrig, micro, toaster, doonas], ldry, pool, cook fac, refrig, bbq, cots. **RO ♦ $67 - $77, ♦♦ $77 - $88, ♦ $5**, fam con, Light breakfast only available. AE BC DC MC VI.

★★★ **Melanka Lodge Motel**, (M), 94 Todd St, 500m S of PO, ☎ 08 8952 2233, fax 08 8952 2890, (Multi-stry gr fl), 55 units [ensuite (50), a/c, tel, TV, movie-fee, clock radio (22), t/c mkg, refrig, mini bar], ldry, rec rm, ☒, pool, bbq, c/park (limited), ☎, cots-fee. **RO ♦ $71 - $82.50, ♦♦ $79 - $88, ♦ $10**, ch con, AE BC DC EFT JCB MC VI.

(Backpackers Section), 110 rms acc up to 6, (Bunk Rooms), [basin, a/c-cool, heat, refrig, linen reqd-fee], cook fac. **D ♦ $15, ♦ $15**, ch con.

(Guest House Section), 34 rms [basin, shwr, tlt, a/c-cool, refrig], ldry. **D ♦♦ $38 - $60, ♦ $15.**

★★★ **Outback Motor Lodge**, (M), South Tce, 1.2km S of PO, ☎ 08 8952 3888, fax 08 8953 2166, 42 units [shwr, tlt, a/c, heat, tel, TV, video (4), movie, clock radio, refrig, cook fac, micro (23), elec frypan (12)], ldry, pool, bbq, cots. **RO ♦ $70 - $78, ♦♦ $82 - $92, ♦ $12**, ch con, AE BC DC EFT MC VI, ♿.

★★★ **The Swagmans Rest**, (M), 67 Gap Rd, ☎ 08 8953 1333, fax 08 8953 0404, 29 units [ensuite, bath, a/c, heat, tel, TV, t/c mkg, refrig, cook fac, toaster], ldry-fee, iron, iron brd, pool, bbq, cots-fee. **RO ♦ $71, ♦♦ $82, ♦ $11**, AE BC DC EFT MC MCH VI, ♿.

★★★ **White Gum Holiday Inn Motel**, (M), 17 Gap Rd, 1.5km S of PO, ☎ 08 8952 5144, fax 08 8953 2092, 24 units [shwr, tlt, a/c, tel, TV, clock radio, refrig, cook fac], ldry-fee, pool, bbq, cots-fee. **RO ♦ $60 - $70, ♦♦ $60 - $70, ♦ $10**, ch con, fam con, AE BC DC EFT MC VI.

★★☆ **Mount Nancy Motel**, (M), Stuart Hwy, 3km N of PO, ☎ 08 8952 9488, fax 08 8953 1279, 50 units [shwr, tlt, a/c-cool, heat, TV, t/c mkg, refrig, doonas], ldry-fee, pool, bbq, ☎, cots. **RO ♦ $64, ♦♦ $72, ♦ $11**, ch con, AE BC DC MC MCH VI.

Elkes Out Backpacker Resort, (M), 39 Gap Rd, 1.8km S of PO, ☎ 08 8952 8134, fax 08 8952 8143, (2 stry gr fl), 33 units [tlt, a/c, TV, clock radio, refrig, micro (6), toaster], shwr, ldry, pool, cook fac, t/c mkg shared, bbq, cots. **RO ♦ $18 - $82.50, ♦♦ $82.50**, ch con, AE BC DC MC VI.

Self Catering Accommodation

★★★★ **Jessica Court Townhouses**, (SA), 32 Gap Rd, 1.5km S of CBD, ☎ 08 8953 0164, fax 08 8952 0828, 5 serv apts acc up to 4, (2 bedrm), [shwr, bath, tlt (2), hairdry, a/c, c/fan, tel, TV, video, clock radio, t/c mkg, refrig, cook fac, micro, toaster, blkts, doonas, linen, pillows], w/mach, iron, iron brd, cots. **D ♦♦ $160 - $180, ♦ $10, W ♦♦ $840 - $980**, BC EFT MC VI.

B&B's/Guest Houses

★★★★☆ **Bond Springs Outback Retreat**, (B&B), Bond Springs Station, turnoff 14km N of PO, 7km E off Stuart Hwy, ☎ 08 8952 9888, fax 08 8953 0963, 2 rms (1 & 2 bedrm), [shwr, tlt, a/c, elec blkts, tel, radio], rec rm, lounge (TV), ✕, pool, t/c mkg shared, bbq, tennis, cots. **BB ♦♦ $200**, ch con, BC MC VI.

★★★★☆ **Hilltop Bed & Breakfast**, (B&B), 9 Zeil St, 5km W of PO, ☎ 08 8955 0208, fax 08 8955 0716, 1 rm [ensuite, a/c, c/fan, elec blkts, clock radio], w/mach, iron, iron brd, lounge (TV), bbq, non smoking rms. **BB ♦ $100, ♦♦ $130**, BC MC VI.

★★★★☆ **Orangewood Alice Springs Bed & Breakfast**, (B&B), 9 McMinn St, 1.5km E of PO, ☎ 08 8952 4114, fax 08 8952 4664, 4 rms [ensuite, bath (1), spa bath (1), hairdry, a/c-cool, c/fan, elec blkts], ldry, w/mach, iron, iron brd, lounge (TV), pool, t/c mkg shared, refrig, non smoking property. **BB ♦ $154 - $176, ♦♦ $154 - $176**, BC MC VI.

★★★☆ **Kathys Place B&B**, (B&B), 4 Cassia Crt, ☎ 08 8952 9791, fax 08 8952 0052, 1 rm [ensuite (1), a/c, TV], rec rm (pool table), pool, **BB ♦ $110 - $120, ♦♦ $110 - $120, ♦ $65**, BC MC VI.

★★ **Stuart Lodge Guesthouse YWCA**, (GH), Stuart Tce, 600m S of PO, ☎ 08 8952 1894, fax 08 8952 2449, (2 stry gr fl), 17 rms [a/c-cool, t/c mkg, refrig], ldry-fee, lounge (TV), pool, cook fac, bbq, secure park, ☎, cots, non smoking rms. **RO ♦ $38.50, ♦♦ $49.50, ♦ $11**, ch con, BC EFT MC VI.

Other Accommodation

Alice Lodge, (Lodge), 4 Mueller St, ☎ 08 8953 1975, fax 08 8953 0804, 13 rms acc up to 10, [a/c-cool, toaster (communal), blkts, linen, pillows], ldry, pool, cook fac, t/c mkg shared, bbq. **D ♦ $16, ♦ $16**, BC EFT MC VI.

Alice Springs Pioneer YHA Hostel, (Lodge), Cnr Parsons St & Leichhardt Tce, 100m E of PO, ☎ 08 8952 8855, fax 08 8952 4144, (2 stry gr fl), 15 rms acc up to 6, [a/c-cool, heat (oil), blkts, linen, pillows], ldry, rec rm, lounge (TV), pool, cook fac, t/c mkg shared, refrig, bbq, bicycle-fee. RO ⍾ $18 - $21.50, ⍾ $18 - $21.50, BC EFT MC VI.

Sandrifter Safari Lodge, (Lodge), 6 Kharlic St, 500m E of PO, ☎ 08 8952 8686, fax 08 8952 8686, 5 rms acc up to 2, [a/c-cool, heat, elec blkts, blkts reqd-fee, linen reqd-fee, pillows], ldry, spa, cook fac, t/c mkg shared, refrig, bbq, c/park. D ⍾ $20, ⍾ $15, BC MC VI, ⅙.

Toddys Resort, (Lodge), 41 Gap Rd, 1.5km S of PO, ☎ 08 8952 1322, fax 08 8952 1767, 15 rms acc up to 6, [shwr, a/c-cool, TV, refrig, blkts, linen, pillows], ldry-fee, rec rm, bar, pool, cook fac, t/c mkg shared, bbq, courtesy transfer, cots. RO ⍾ $52 - $73, ⍾⍾ $52 - $73, ⍾ $6, ch con, AE BC DC EFT MC VI.

 (Bunkhouse Section), 1 bunkhouse acc up to 8, [blkts, linen, pillows], cook fac. D ⍾ $10, ⍾ $10, ch con.

 (Cabin Section), 6 cabins acc up to 2, [basin, a/c-cool, refrig, blkts, linen, pillows], shwr, tlt, rec rm. RO ⍾ $40, ⍾⍾ $40.

 (Dormitory Section), 7 rms acc up to 8, [shwr (2), tlt (2), a/c-cool, blkts reqd-fee, linen, pillows], cook fac, refrig. D ⍾ $15 - $17, ⍾ $15 - $17, ch con.

BARKLY NT 0860

Pop Nominal, (1199km S Darwin) See map on page 402, ref D5. A small settlement at the junction of the Barkly & Tableland Hwys.
Hotels/Motels
★★☆ **Barkly Homestead Motel**, (M), Jnc Barkly & Tableland Hwys, 210km E of Tennant Creek, ☎ 08 8964 4549, fax 08 8964 4543, 10 units [shwr, tlt, a/c, fan, t/c mkg, refrig], ldry-fee, ⋈, bar, petrol, ⍾, cots-fee. RO ⍾ $75, ⍾⍾ $85, ⍾ $10, BC EFT MC VI.

BATCHELOR NT 0845

Pop 673. (99km S Darwin), See map on page 402, ref B2. Originally was a closed town servicing only employees of Rum Jungle Mine now a thriving pastoral area. Gateway to Litchfield Park. Bowls, Bush Walking, Canoeing, Fishing (Lake), Scenic Drives, Swimming (Pool), Tennis.
Hotels/Motels
★★☆ **Rum Jungle Motor Inn**, (LMH), Rum Jungle Rd, ☎ 08 8976 0123, fax 08 8976 0230, 22 units [ensuite, a/c-cool, c/fan, tel, TV, t/c mkg, refrig], ldry, w/mach-fee, dryer-fee, conf fac, ⋈, pool, kiosk, ⍾, cots. RO ⍾ $98, ⍾⍾ $110, ⍾ $11, BC EFT MC VI, ⅙.

BORROLOOLA NT 0854

Pop 1,500. (982km SE Darwin), See map on page 402, ref D3. Borroloola is a small settlement on the McArthur River. Boating, Fishing, Scenic Drives, Tennis.
Hotels/Motels
Gulf Wilderness Lodge, (LMH), Wollogorang Rd, 260km SE of PO, 250km W of Burketown, ☎ 08 8975 9944, fax 08 8975 9854, 6 units (Powered Site), [a/c-cool, c/fan, TV, t/c mkg, refrig, toaster], ldry, ✕, bbq, dinner to unit, shop, ⍾, plygr, cots. BB ⍾ $55, ⍾⍾ $77, BC EFT MC VI, (not yet classified).
Self Catering Accommodation
★☆ **Borroloola Holiday Village**, Robinson Rd, Centre of Town, opposite school, ☎ 08 8975 8742, fax 08 8975 8741, 8 cabins acc up to 5, [shwr, tlt, a/c-cool, TV, clock radio, t/c mkg, refrig, cook fac, toaster, blkts, linen, pillows], ldry, ice. D ⍾ $50 - $79, ⍾⍾ $92, ⍾⍾⍾ $96, AE BC DC EFT MC VI.

 ★ (Bunkhouse Section), 4 bunkhouses acc up to 4, [a/c, blkts, linen, pillows], lounge (TV), cook fac, refrig. D ⍾ $30, ⍾ $10, W ⍾ $180.
B&B's/Guest Houses
H & R Borroloola Guesthouse, (B&B), Lot 812, Robinson Rd, 300m E of Airport, ☎ 08 8975 8883, fax 08 8975 8877, 13 rms [ensuite (2), a/c-cool, c/fan (4), TV (3), t/c mkg (9), refrig (3), cook fac (3), cook fac ltd (1), micro (1), toaster (4), doonas], shared fac, ldry, ✕, t/c mkg shared, refrig, bbq, ⍾, BLB ⍾ $35, ⍾⍾ $50, (not yet classified).

CAPE CRAWFORD NT 0854

Pop Nominal, (872km SE Darwin), See map on page 402, ref D4. Situated at the junction of Carpentaria & Tableland Hwys.
Hotels/Motels
Heartbreak Hotel, (LH), Cnr Carpentaria & Tableland Hwys, ☎ 08 8975 9928, fax 08 8975 9993, 23 rms [a/c-cool, refrig (8)], iron, iron brd, ⋈, pool, t/c mkg shared, bbq, c/park. RO ⍾ $35 - $75, ⍾ $16.50, BC EFT MC VI.

COOINDA NT 0886

Pop Nominal, (207km SE Darwin), See map on page 402, ref C2. Located in Kakadu National Park. Bush Walking, Scenic Drives.
Hotels/Motels
★★☆ **Gagudju Lodge Cooinda**, (LMH), Off Kakadu Hwy, in Kakadu National Park, ☎ 08 8979 0145, fax 08 8979 0148, 48 units [ensuite, a/c-cool, fan, tel, cable tv, t/c mkg, refrig], ldry, w/mach-fee, dryer-fee, iron, iron brd, ⋈, pool, bbq, cots. RO ⍾ $198, ⍾⍾ $198, ⍾ $27.50, ch con, AE BC DC JCB MC VI.

DALY RIVER NT 0822

Pop 160. (240km S Darwin), See map on page 402, ref B2. A small settlement on the river of the same name. Boating, Bush Walking, Fishing.
Hotels/Motels
Daly River Pub, (LMH), Daly River Rd, ☎ 08 8978 2418, fax 08 8978 2418, 4 units [ensuite, a/c-cool, c/fan, TV, t/c mkg, refrig], ldry, ⋈, bbq. RO ⍾ $60, ⍾⍾ $77, ⍾ $5 - $10, BC EFT MC VI, (not yet classified).
Self Catering Accommodation
Woolianna Mango Plantation Fisherman's Lodge, (HU), Wooliana Rd, ☎ 08 8978 2478, fax 08 8978 2634, 1 unit acc up to 4, (2 bedrm), [shwr, tlt, c/fan, TV, cook fac, ldry, blkts, linen, pillows], pool, non smoking units, D ⍾ $100 - $170, ⍾⍾ $100 - $170, ⍾ $50 - $85, Closed for duration of Top End wet season. BC EFT MC VI, (not yet classified).

DALY WATERS NT 0852

Pop Nominal, (588km S Darwin), See map on page 402, ref C3. Situated 3km off the Stuart Hwy. Tennis.
Hotels/Motels
Daly Waters Pub, (LH), Historic Hotel. Stuart St, 3km W of Stuart Hwy, ☎ 08 8975 9927, fax 08 8975 9982, 10 rms [a/c-cool, fan], ldry, ⋈, pool, t/c mkg shared, bbq, cots, ch con, BC EFT MC VI. D ⍾ $33, ⍾⍾ $44, ⍾⍾⍾ $51, ⍾⍾⍾⍾ $57.

 (Motel Section), 4 units [ensuite, tel, TV, t/c mkg, refrig], RO ⍾ $95, ⍾⍾ $100, ⍾⍾⍾ $108, ⍾⍾⍾⍾ $115, (not yet classified).
Hi-Way Inn Motel, (M), Cnr Stuart & Carpentaria Hwys, ☎ 08 8975 9925, fax 08 8975 9984, 10 units [ensuite, bath (hip), a/c-cool, t/c mkg, refrig], ldry, ⋈, pool, bbq, ⍾. RO ⍾ $49.50, ⍾⍾ $60.50, ⍾⍾⍾ $71.50, AE BC DC EFT MC VI.

DUNMARRA NT 0852

Pop Nominal, (631km SE Darwin), See map on page 402, ref C4. Located on the Stuart Hwy on Barkly Tableland. Dunmarra Station built in 1926 and used as RAAF Base during World War 2.
Hotels/Motels
★★ **Dunmarra Wayside Inn Motel**, (M), Stuart Hwy, ☎ 08 8979 5522, 8 units [shwr, tlt, a/c, TV, t/c mkg, refrig], ⋈, pool, bbq, ⍾, cots-fee, RO ⍾ $55, ⍾⍾ $65, AE BC EFT MC VI.

ELLIOTT NT 0862

Pop 423. (772km S Darwin), See map on page 402, ref C4. Located on Stuart Hwy approximately halfway between Alice Springs & Darwin.
Hotels/Motels
Elliott Hotel, (LH), Stuart Hwy, ☎ 08 8969 2069, fax 08 8969 2083, 17 rms [shwr (7), tlt (7), a/c-cool, fan (7), t/c mkg (7), refrig (7)], ldry, ⋈, pool, bbq, ⍾, cots. RO ⍾ $38.50, ⍾⍾ $55, ⍾ $5.50, ch con, BC MC VI.

ERLDUNDA NT 0870

Pop Nominal, (1691km S Alice Springs), See map on page 402, ref C8. Situated on corner of Stuart & Lasseter Hwys 95km N of SA/NT border & 260km E of Ayers Rock at foot of Erldunda Range.

Hotels/Motels

★★☆ **Desert Oaks Motel**, (M), Cnr Stuart & Lasseter Hwys, ☎ 08 8956 0984, fax 08 8956 0942, 54 units [ensuite, a/c-cool (34), a/c, heat, elec blkts, TV (28), clock radio, t/c mkg, refrig], ldry, ⊠, pool, bbq, ✆, tennis, cots. RO ♦ $72, ♦♦ $86, ◊ $11, ch con, AE BC DC MC VI.

GLEN HELEN NT 0871

Pop Nominal, (112km W Alice Springs), See map on page 402, ref C7. A small settlement on the Finke River at Glen Helen Gorge, a scenically attractive part of the Western MacDonnell Ranges. Bush Walking, Scenic Drives, Swimming (Waterholes).

B&B's/Guest Houses

★★☆ **Glen Helen Resort**, (M), Namatjira Dve, ☎ 08 8956 7489, fax 08 8956 7495, 25 rms [ensuite, shwr, tlt, a/c-cool, doonas], lounge, ⊠, bbq, courtesy transfer, RO $121 - $143, AE BC DC MC VI.
(Bunkhouse Section), 10 bunkhouses acc up to 4, [a/c-cool, blkts reqd-fee, linen reqd-fee, pillows reqd-fee], shwr, tlt. D ♦ $16 - $19, ♦♦ $32 - $38, ◊ $16 - $19.

HUMPTY DOO NT 0836

Pop Nominal, (35km SE Darwin), See map on page 402, ref B1. A small coastal town.

Self Catering Accommodation

★★★ **Humpty Doo Homestay**, (Cotg), 45 Acacia Rd, 2.5km from PO, ☎ 08 8988 1147, fax 08 8988 1147, 1 cotg acc up to 4, (2 bedrm), [shwr, tlt, a/c, fan (4), TV, video, radio, CD, t/c mkg, refrig, cook fac, micro, blkts, doonas, linen, pillows], w/mach, pool, bbq, ✆, plygr, non smoking property. D $90 - $99, weekly con, BC MC VI.

JABIRU NT 0886

Pop 1,731. (252km E Darwin), See map on page 402, ref C1. Situated in the Kakadu National Park, this township was established in 1982 to house workers at the Ranger Uranium Mine. Tours of uranian mine are conducted from airport at Jabiru East. Boating, Bowls, Golf, Scenic Drives, Tennis.

Hotels/Motels

★★★☆ **Gagudju Crocodile Hotel**, (LH), Flinders St, Kakadu National Park, ☎ 08 8979 2800, fax 08 8979 2707, (2 stry gr fl), 110 rms [shwr, tlt, hairdry, a/c-cool, fan, tel, TV, movie, clock radio, t/c mkg, refrig, mini bar], ldry, conv fac, ⊠, pool, bbq, 24hr reception, rm serv, ✆, cots. RO ♦ $240, ♦♦ $240, ◊ $33, ch con, pen con, AE BC DC EFT JCB MC VI, ⚹.

KATHERINE NT 0850

Pop 10,500. (314km S Darwin), See map on page 402, ref B2. Situated on the Stuart Hwy a large modern town, the main industry being tourism. Katherine Gorge National Park, river cruises Cutta Cutta limestone caves - 27km S. Boating, Bowls, Bush Walking, Fishing, Golf, Horse Riding, Scenic Drives, Shooting, Swimming, Tennis.

Hotels/Motels

★★★☆ **Knotts Crossing Resort Motel**, (M), Cnr Giles & Cameron Sts, 2.5km NE of PO, ☎ 08 8972 2511, fax 08 8972 2628, 87 units [ensuite, bath (18), a/c-cool, c/fan, tel, fax (6), cable tv, clock radio, t/c mkg, refrig, cook fac (18)], ldry, w/mach-fee, dryer-fee, ⊠, pool, c/park (carport) (43), ✆, RO ♦ $110, ♦♦ $120, ◊ $10, AE BC DC EFT MC VI, ⚹.

★★★☆ **Pine Tree Motel**, (M), 3 Third St, 350m NE of PO, ☎ 08 8972 2533, fax 08 8972 2920, (2 stry gr fl), 50 units [shwr, tlt, hairdry, a/c-cool, fan, tel, TV, clock radio, t/c mkg, refrig], ldry, w/mach-fee, dryer-fee, iron, iron brd, ⊠, pool, bbq, rm serv, cots-fee. RO ♦ $69.40 - $87, ♦♦ $82.40 - $103, ◊ $9.60 - $12, AE BC DC EFT MC VI, ⚹.

★★★ **Katherine Hotel Motel**, (LMH), Cnr Katherine Tce (Stuart Hwy) & Giles St, opposite PO, ☎ 08 8972 1622, fax 08 8972 3213, 40 units [shwr, bath (28), tlt, a/c-cool, tel, TV, radio, t/c mkg, refrig], ⊠, bar, pool, bbq, cots. RO ♦ $85, ♦♦ $95, ♦♦♦ $105, fam con. AE BC DC EFT MC VI.

★★★ **Paraway Motel**, (M), Cnr O'Shea Tce & First St, 500m N of PO, ☎ 08 8972 2644, fax 08 8972 2720, (Multi-stry gr fl), 56 units [shwr, spa bath (1), tlt, a/c-cool, tel, TV, movie, clock radio, t/c mkg, refrig], ldry, w/mach-fee, dryer, iron, iron brd, ⊠, pool, spa, bbq, cots. RO ♦ $71 - $86, ♦♦ $81 - $97, ◊ $10, ch con, AE BC DC EFT JCB MC VI, ⚹.

★★☆ **Beagle Motor Inn**, (M), Cnr Fourth & Lindsay Sts, ☎ 08 8972 3998, fax 08 8972 3725, 29 units [ensuite, a/c-cool, TV, t/c mkg, refrig], ldry, w/mach-fee, dryer-fee, ⊠ (licensed), pool, spa, bbq, ✆, cots. RO ♦ $55 - $68, ♦♦ $65 - $78, ◊ $10, BC DC EFT MC VI, ⚹.
   ★☆ **(Budget Section)**, 10 units [a/c-cool, TV, t/c mkg, refrig], shared fac. RO ♦ $45 - $55, ♦♦ $55 - $65, ◊ $10.

★★★ **Crossways Hotel Motel**, (LMH), Katherine Tce (Stuart Hwy), 150m N of PO, ☎ 08 8972 1022, fax 08 8972 1591, (2 stry gr fl), 19 units [shwr, tlt, a/c-cool, cable tv, clock radio, t/c mkg, refrig, toaster], ldry, w/mach-fee, dryer-fee, iron, iron brd, night club (Fri & Sat), ⊠ (Mon to Sat), pool, bbq. RO ♦ $65 - $75, ♦♦ $75 - $90, ◊ $10.50, ch con, AE BC DC EFT MC VI.

★★☆ **Mercure Inn Katherine**, (M), Previously All Seasons Frontier Katherine Stuart Hwy, 3km S of PO, ☎ 08 8972 1744, fax 08 8972 2790, 100 units [shwr, tlt, a/c, fan (50), tel, TV, movie, clock radio, t/c mkg, refrig, cook fac (limited) (10)], ldry, w/mach-fee, dryer-fee, iron, iron brd, conf fac, ⊠, pool, bbq, ✆, bicycle-fee, tennis, cots. RO ♦ $109 - $124, ♦♦ $109 - $124, ◊ $30, ch con, pen con, 40 units ★★★☆. AE BC DC JCB MC VI, ⚹.

★★☆ **Riverview Motel**, (M), 440 Victoria Hwy, 2.4km SW of PO, ☎ 08 8972 1011, fax 08 8971 0397, 9 units [ensuite, a/c-cool, c/fan, tel, TV, t/c mkg, refrig, toaster], ldry, w/mach-fee, dryer-fee, iron, iron brd, pool, spa, bbq, ✆, cots. RO ♦ $61, ♦♦ $72, ♦♦♦ $83, ch con, BC EFT MC VI.

Springvale Homestead Motel, (M), Shadforth Rd, 9km NW of PO, off Victoria Hwy, ☎ 08 8972 1355, fax 08 8972 3201, 60 units [shwr, tlt, a/c-cool, fan, t/c mkg, refrig], ldry, ⊠, pool, bbq, ✆, cots. RO ♦ $39, ♦♦ $46, ◊ $7, BC EFT MC VI. (not yet classified).

Self Catering Accommodation

★★★★ **St Andrews Serviced Apartments**, (Apt), 27 First St, ☎ 08 8971 2288, fax 08 8971 2277, (2 stry gr fl), 14 apts acc up to 8, (2 bedrm), [shwr, tlt, hairdry, a/c-cool, c/fan, tel, TV, video, clock radio, t/c mkg, refrig, cook fac, micro, toaster, ldry, blkts, doonas, linen, pillows], w/mach, dryer, iron, iron brd, pool, bbq, c/park (undercover). D ♦♦♦♦ $111 - $212, AE BC DC EFT JCB MC VI.

★★ **Victoria Lodge**, (HU), 21 Victoria Hwy, 400m NW of PO, ☎ 08 8972 3464, fax 08 8971 1738, (2 stry gr fl), 6 units acc up to 4, [shwr, tlt, fan, TV, t/c mkg, refrig, cook fac, toaster], ldry, pool, bbq, D ♦ $35 - $50, ♦♦ $45 - $50, ◊ $10, BC MC VI.

B&B's/Guest Houses

★★★★ **Maud Creek Country Lodge**, (GH), Gorge Rd, 22km NE of PO, ☎ 08 8971 1814, fax 08 8972 2763, 3 rms [ensuite, a/c-cool, c/fan, t/c mkg, refrig, mini bar], lounge (TV), ✕, pool, bbq, non smoking property. BLB ♦ $84, ♦♦ $99, BC DC MC VI.

★★★☆ **Franz Weber's Bonrook Resort**, (GH), Previously Bonrook Lodge Guest House Stuart Highway, Pine Creek 0847, 7km S of PO, ☎ 08 8976 1232, fax 08 8976 1469, (2 stry gr fl), 17 rms (2 bedrm), [ensuite, a/c-cool, c/fan, t/c mkg], iron, iron brd, conf fac, ⊠, bar, pool (2), spa (2), ✆, bicycle-fee. D $179 - $180, RO ♦ $87, ♦♦ $105 - $155, ◊ $45, fam con, AE BC DC MC VI.

Kookaburra Lodge, (GH), Cnr Lindsay & Third Sts, ☎ 08 8971 0257, fax 08 8972 1567, 6 rms [shwr, tlt, a/c-cool, TV (6), t/c mkg, refrig (6), cook fac, micro, toaster], ldry, pool, RO ♦♦ $45, BC MC VI.

Other Accommodation

Palm Court Backpackers, (Lodge), Cnr Third & Giles Sts, 300m E of PO, ☎ 08 8972 2722, fax 08 8971 1443, 20 rms [shwr, tlt, a/c-cool, c/fan (19), refrig (communal)], ldry, w/mach-fee, dryer-fee, iron, iron brd, pool, cook fac, t/c mkg shared, bbq, courtesy transfer. RO ♦ $15, ♦♦ $45, BC DC EFT MC VI.

KINGS CANYON NT 0871

Pop Nominal, (320km W Alice Springs), See map on page 402, ref B7. Small township in the George Gill Ranges.

Hotels/Motels

★★★☆ **Kings Canyon Resort**, (M), Luritja Rd, Watarrka National Park, ☎ 08 8956 7442, fax 08 8956 7410, 128 units [ensuite, bath, spa bath (32), hairdry (32), a/c, tel, TV, movie, clock radio, t/c mkg, mini bar], ldry, iron (32), iron brd (32), conf fac, ⊠, ✕, bar (2), pool, bbq, ✆, cots-fee, ch con, **RO $269 - $378,** AE BC DC JCB MC VI.

KULGERA NT 0872

Pop Nominal, (262km S Alice Springs), See map on page 402, ref C8. There are rocky outcrops which surround the town, some rising up to 600 metres.

Hotels/Motels

★☆ **Kulgera Roadhouse Hotel Motel**, (LMH), Stuart Hwy, ☎ 08 8956 0973, fax 08 8956 0807, 10 units [shwr, bath (hip), tlt, a/c-cool, heat, TV, clock radio (1), t/c mkg, refrig], ⊠, bbq, ✆, Pets on application. **RO ♟♟ $66 - $77, ♙ $10**, ch con, AE BC DC EFT MC VI.

LAKE BENNETT NT 0822

Pop Nominal, (86km S Darwin), See map on page 402, ref B2. A man-made lake originally for irrigation now an area used for camping and outdoor nature studies. Boating, Bush Walking, Fishing, Swimming (Lake).

Self Catering Accommodation

★★★☆ **Lake Bennett Wilderness Resort**, (HU), 152 Chinner Rd, 25km NE of Batchelor PO, 7km off Stuart Hwy, ☎ 08 8976 0960, fax 08 8976 0256, 17 units acc up to 6, (1 bedrm 2 bedrm. Studio), [shwr, tlt, a/c-cool, c/fan, TV (5), video (5), t/c mkg, refrig, cook fac, micro], ldry, w/mach-fee, dryer-fee, ⊠, non smoking units. **D $121.50 - $248**, 5 units yet to be rated, BC EFT MC VI.

(Motel Section), 23 units [ensuite, spa bath (8), a/c-cool, c/fan, TV, t/c mkg, refrig], bbq, c/park (undercover) (8), non smoking property. **D ♟♟ $121.50 - $161.50, ♙ $22**, (not yet classified).

(Lodge Section), 1 rm acc up to 48, (Bunk Room), [ensuite (1), a/c-cool, c/fan, t/c mkg (1)], non smoking rms. **D $90 - $142.**

LARRIMAH NT 0852

Pop Nominal, (494km S Darwin), See map on page 402, ref C3. Small settlement and former main terminus for the rail service from Darwin, (service no longer in operation).

Hotels/Motels

Larrimah Wayside Inn Hotel, (LH), Stuart Hwy, ☎ 08 8975 9931, 7 rms [a/c-cool (6), fan], ldry, ✕, t/c mkg shared, bbq. **RO $25 - $50**, fam con, Family room $45.

MATARANKA NT 0852

Pop 250. (457km S Darwin), See map on page 402, ref C3. Located on the Stuart Hwy 106km S of Katherine. Scenic Drives.

Hotels/Motels

★★☆ **Territory Manor Motel**, (M), Martin Rd, 300m E of water tower, ☎ 08 8975 4516, fax 08 8975 4612, 26 units [ensuite, a/c-cool, tel, TV, t/c mkg, refrig], ldry, w/mach-fee, dryer-fee, conf fac, ⊠, pool, spa, cots-fee. **RO ♟ $74, ♟♟ $86, ♙ $11.50**, ch con, AE BC DC EFT MC VI.

★☆ **Mataranka Homestead Motel**, (M), Homestead Rd, 9km SE of PO, ☎ 08 8975 4544, fax 08 8975 4580, 24 units [ensuite, a/c-cool, fan, clock radio, t/c mkg, refrig], ldry, ⊠, bbq, ✆, cots, **RO ♟ $69.40 - $87, ♟♟ $82.40 - $103, ♙ $9.60 - $12**, Thermal bathing pool. AE BC DC EFT MC VI.

Self Catering Accommodation

★★☆ **Mataranka Cabins**, Lot 4705 Martin Rd, 2km E of Stuart Hwy, Bitter Springs, ☎ 08 8975 4838, fax 08 8975 4814, 2 cabins acc up to 5, [ensuite, a/c-cool, fan, TV, clock radio, refrig, cook fac, micro, toaster, blkts, linen, pillows], bbq, Pets on application. **D ♟♟ $70 - $82, ♙ $10**, BC MC VI.

MIDDLE POINT NT 0836

Pop Nominal, (68km E Darwin) See map on page 402, ref B1. A small township situated near the Djukbinj National Park.

B&B's/Guest Houses

★★★★ **Eden At Fogg Dam**, (B&B), 530 Middle Point Rd, Between Darwin & Kakadu National Park, ☎ 08 8988 5599, fax 08 8988 5582, 2 rms (1 suite) [ensuite (1), bath (1), a/c-cool, c/fan, TV, clock radio (2), t/c mkg (1), refrig (1), cook fac (1), micro (1), toaster (1), doonas], bathrm (1), ldry, lounge (TV), pool, spa, t/c mkg shared, refrig, bbq, non smoking property, **BB ♟ $110, ♟♟ $130, ♙ $60, Suite BB ♟♟ $130**, BC MC VI.

NHULUNBUY NT 0880

Pop 4,000. (996km E Darwin), See map on page 402, ref E1. Situated on the Gove Peninsula. The town was established as a service centre for Nabalco's bauxite mining and treatment plant.

Hotels/Motels

Gove Peninsula Motel, (M), 1 Matthew Flinders Way, 1.2km SW of PO, ☎ 08 8987 0700, fax 08 8987 0770, 19 units [shwr, tlt, a/c-cool, tel, TV, clock radio, t/c mkg, refrig, micro, toaster], ldry, w/mach-fee, dryer-fee, iron, iron brd, pool (salt water), bbq, cots-fee. **BLB ♟ $125.50, ♟♟ $152, RO ♟ $115.50, ♟♟ $132**, AE BC DC EFT MC VI, (not yet classified).

PINE CREEK NT 0847

Pop 600. (251km S Darwin), See map on page 402, ref B2. Gateway to Arnhem Land. The historic town was, during 1920's, a goldfield, yeilding more than $2,000,000. Modern day mining is still in progress. Boating, Fishing, Gold Prospecting, Swimming, Tennis.

Hotels/Motels

★★☆ **Pine Creek Hotel Motel**, (LMH), 40 Moule St, ☎ 08 8976 1288, 14 units [shwr, tlt, a/c-cool, fan, tel, TV, t/c mkg, refrig], ⊠, bbq, ✆, cots. **RO ♟ $65, ♟♟ $75, ♟♟♟ $85, ♙ $10**, AE BC DC MC VI, ♿.

Self Catering Accommodation

★★★ **Pine Creek Diggers Rest Motel**, 32 Main Tce, 220m N of PO, ☎ 08 8976 1442, fax 08 8976 1458, 8 cabins acc up to 5, [ensuite, bath (hip), a/c-cool, c/fan, tel, TV, movie, t/c mkg, refrig, toaster], ldry, w/mach-fee, dryer-fee, iron, iron brd, bbq, ✆. **D $75 - $90, W $450 - $540**, AE BC MC VI.

RENNER SPRINGS NT 0860

Pop Nominal, (866km S Darwin), See map on page 402, ref C4. Located in beef country on the Stuart Hwy. Many freshwater springs can be found in nearby rocky outcrops.

Hotels/Motels

★☆ **Renner Springs Desert Hotel Motel**, (LMH), Stuart Hwy, 160km N of Tennant Creek, ☎ 08 8964 4505, fax 08 8964 4525, 27 units [ensuite, a/c-cool, t/c mkg, refrig], ⊠, ✆. **RO ♟ $55 - $66, ♟♟ $66 - $77, ♙ $11**, AE BC EFT MC VI.

ROSS RIVER NT 0871

Pop Nominal, (80km E Alice Springs), See map on page 402, ref D7. A tourist area east of Alice Springs, in the East MacDonnell Ranges area. Bush Walking, Horse Riding, Swimming (Pool).

B&B's/Guest Houses

★☆ **Ross River Homestead**, (PH), Ross Hwy, ☎ 08 8956 9711, fax 08 8956 9823, 30 rms [ensuite, a/c-cool, heat, elec blkts], ⊠, pool, spa, ✆. **RO ♟♟ $80, ♙ $17**, ch con, AE BC EFT MC VI.

SOUTH ALLIGATOR NT 0886

Pop 1,602. (206km E Darwin), See map on page 402, ref B1. A small settlement located on the edge of Kakadu National Park. River cruises and wildlife safaris. Boating, Bush Walking, Fishing, Swimming (Pool).

Hotels/Motels

AURORA Resorts & Hotels — FLAG Flag Choice Hotels

★★★☆ **Kakadu Resort**, (M), Arnhem Hwy, ☎ 08 8979 0166, fax 08 8979 0147, 138 units [ensuite, bath (30), a/c-cool, tel, TV, clock radio, t/c mkg, refrig], ldry, iron, iron brd, conf fac, ⊠, pool, spa, bbq, tennis, cots-fee. **RO ♟ $138 - $185, ♟♟ $138 - $185, ♟♟♟ $33**, AE BC DC EFT MC VI, ♿.

TENNANT CREEK NT 0860

Pop 3,480. (964km S Darwin) See map on page 402, ref C5. A modern outback mining town, whose minerals include copper, gold and tin. Mary Ann Dam - 5km N of town offers excellent facilities for picnicing, swimming, canoeing & yachting. Bowls, Gold Prospecting, Golf, Horse Riding, Squash, Swimming, Tennis.

Hotels/Motels

★★★☆ **Bluestone Motor Inn**, (M), Paterson St, 500m S of PO, ☎ 08 8962 2617, fax 08 8962 2883, 65 units [shwr, tlt, a/c-cool, fan, tel (52), TV, t/c mkg, refrig], ldry, w/mach-fee, dryer-fee, ✕, pool, bbq, cots. **RO** ⍾ **$80 - $105,** ⍾⍾ **$85 - $115,** ⍾ **$10,** AE BC DC EFT MC VI, ⅃⅂.

★★★ **Eldorado Motor Lodge**, (M), Paterson St (Stuart Hwy), 1km N of PO, ☎ 08 8962 2402, fax 08 8962 3034, (2 stry gr fl), 80 units [shwr, tlt, a/c, tel, TV, t/c mkg, refrig], ✕, pool, bbq, courtesy transfer, cots-fee. **RO** ⍾ **$71 - $89,** ⍾⍾ **$76 - $94,** ⍾ **$5,** ch con, 8 rooms of a higher rating. 11 rooms ★★★☆. AE BC DC EFT MC VI, ⅃⅂.

★★☆ **Goldfields Hotel Motel**, (LMH), Paterson St (Stuart Hwy), 400m N of PO, ☎ 08 8962 2030, fax 08 8962 3288, (2 stry gr fl), 30 units [ensuite, a/c, tel, TV, clock radio, t/c mkg, refrig, toaster, doonas], ldry-fee, ✕ (chinese), cots. **RO** ⍾ **$55,** ⍾⍾ **$66,** ⍾ **$16.50,** BC EFT MC VI.

★★☆ **Safari Lodge Motel**, (M), Davidson St, 400m N of PO, ☎ 08 8962 2207, fax 08 8962 3188, 19 units [ensuite, a/c-cool, a/c, fan, heat (bar radiator), tel, TV, clock radio, t/c mkg, refrig, cook fac (1), cook fac ltd (5), toaster], ldry, iron, iron brd, spa, bbq, cots-fee. **RO** ⍾ **$75,** ⍾⍾ **$85,** ⍾ **$10,** AE BC DC MC VI.

(Safari Backpackers YHA Section), 1 rm acc up to 27, [a/c-cool, TV, linen-fee, pillows-fee], lounge, cook fac, ☏. **D $38**.

Self Catering Accommodation

★★☆ **Desert Sands Serviced Apartments**, (SA), 780 Paterson St, ☎ 08 8962 1346, fax 08 8962 1014, (2 stry gr fl), 13 serv apts acc up to 7, [shwr, tlt, a/c, TV, clock radio, t/c mkg, refrig, cook fac, micro (7), toaster, blkts, linen, pillows], w/mach, iron, iron brd, pool (salt water), spa, bbq, cots. **D** ⍾ **$60 - $65,** ⍾⍾ **$65 - $70,** ⍾ **$5,** BC EFT MC VI.

THREEWAYS NT 0860

Pop Part of Tennant Creek, (959km S Darwin) See map on page 402, ref C5. Situated at the junction of the Barkly & Stuart Hwys. John Flynn Memorial.

Hotels/Motels

Threeways Roadhouse Motel, (M), Cnr Stuart & Barkly Hwys, ☎ 08 8962 2744, fax 08 8962 2426, 8 units [shwr, tlt, a/c-cool, TV, t/c mkg, refrig], ldry, ✕, pool, bbq. **RO** ⍾ **$55 - $60.50,** ⍾⍾ **$55 - $60.50,** AE BC DC EFT MC VI.

TI TREE NT 0872

Pop Nominal, See map on page 402, ref C6. Situated on the Stuart Hwy. Swimming (Pool).

Hotels/Motels

★☆ **Ti Tree Roadhouse Hotel**, (Ltd Lic H), Stuart Hwy, ☎ 08 8956 9741, fax 08 8956 9780, 8 rms [ensuite, a/c-cool (4), a/c (6), heat (4), TV, t/c mkg, refrig], bar, pool, bbq, petrol, ☏. **RO** ⍾⍾ **$72,** fam con, AE BC DC EFT JCB MC MP VI.

TIMBER CREEK NT 0852

Pop Nominal, (602km S Darwin), See map on page 402, ref B3. Located on the Great Northern Hwy, once a remote station for the NT Mounted Police, surrounded by high bluffs.

Hotels/Motels

Timber Creek Hotel, (LH), Lot 94, Victoria Hwy, ☎ 08 8975 0722, fax 08 8975 0772, (2 stry gr fl), 5 rms [ensuite, a/c-cool, c/fan, TV, t/c mkg, refrig, toaster], ldry, w/mach, dryer, ✕, pool, spa, bbq, plygr, cots-fee, **RO $36.60 - $83.60,** AE BC DC EFT MC VI, (not yet classified).

Timber Creek Wayside Inn Hotel Motel, (LMH), Victoria Hwy, ☎ 08 8975 0722, fax 08 8975 0873, 16 units [shwr (6), bath (6), tlt (6), a/c-cool, c/fan, TV (6), t/c mkg, refrig (8)], ldry, w/mach-fee, dryer, ✕, pool, bbq, ☏, **RO $36.60 - $83.60,** BC EFT MC VI, (not yet classified).

VICTORIA RIVER CROSSING NT 0852

Pop Nominal, (507km S Darwin), See map on page 402, ref B3. Located on the Victoria Hwy.

Hotels/Motels

Victoria River Roadhouse Hotel Motel, (LMH), Victoria Hwy, ☎ 08 8975 0744, fax 08 8975 0819, 13 units [ensuite (8), a/c, fan, TV (6), t/c mkg (8), refrig], ldry. **D $35 - $71,** (not yet classified).

WAUCHOPE NT 0860

Pop Nominal, (1073km S Darwin) See map on page 402, ref C6. Located on the Stuart Hwy and noted for its mining and cattle. The town lies on the fringe of the Murchison & Davenport Ranges. Horse Riding.

Hotels/Motels

★☆ **Wauchope Hotel**, (LH), Stuart Hwy, ☎ 08 8964 1963, fax 08 8964 1567, 11 rms [ensuite (6), a/c-cool (5), a/c (6), heat (5), t/c mkg, refrig (10)], lounge, ✕, pool, bbq, tennis. **RO** ⍾ **$30 - $65,** ⍾⍾ **$70,** ⍾ **$7,** ch con, 5 rooms at list only. BC EFT MC VI.

WYCLIFFE WELL NT 0860

Pop Nominal, (135km S Tennant Creek) See map on page 402, ref C6. Located on the Stuart Hwy.

Hotels/Motels

★★ **Wycliffe Well Motel**, (M), Stuart Hwy, 135km S of Tennant Creek, ☎ 08 8964 1966, fax 08 8964 1961, 5 units [shwr, tlt, a/c, TV, t/c mkg, refrig], ldry, ✕, pool-indoor, bbq, LPG, petrol, plygr, cots. **RO** ⍾ **$67,** ⍾⍾ **$86,** ⍾ **$6,** AE BC EFT MC MCH VI.

YULARA NT 0872

Pop 2,367. (1983km S Darwin), See map on page 402, ref B8. A town established to cater for visitors to Ayers Rock (Uluru) & The Olgas. Situated in Uluru National Park. Ayers Rock is 18km S, The Olgas are 50km W. Scenic Drives.

Hotels/Motels

★★★★★ **Sails In The Desert Hotel**, (LH), Yulara Dve, ☎ 02 9339 1040, fax 02 9332 4555, (Multi-stry gr fl), 228 rms (2 suites) [ensuite, bath, spa bath (2), hairdry, a/c, tel, TV, movie, clock radio, t/c mkg, refrig, mini bar], lift, lounge, conv fac, ✕, pool, spa, 24hr reception, rm serv, ☏, tennis. **RO** ⍾ **$384 - $418,** ⍾⍾ **$384 - $418,** ch con, AE BC DC JCB MC VI, ⅃⅂.

★★★★☆ **Desert Gardens Hotel**, (M), Yulara Dve, ☎ 02 9339 1040, fax 02 9332 4555, (2 stry), 160 units [ensuite, a/c, tel, TV, clock radio, t/c mkg, refrig, mini bar], conv fac, ✕, pool, 24hr reception, rm serv, ☏, cots. **RO** ⍾⍾ **$320 - $345,** ⍾ **$22,** ch con, 60 units ★★★★☆. AE BC DC JCB MC MP VI, ⅃⅂.

★★★☆ **Outback Pioneer Hotel**, (LH), Yulara Dve, ☎ 02 9339 1040, fax 02 9332 4555, 125 rms [ensuite, bath, hairdry, a/c, tel, TV, movie, clock radio, t/c mkg, refrig, mini bar, cook fac ltd (25), micro], ldry-fee, iron, iron brd, ✕, pool, kiosk, ☏, cots (on request). **RO** ⍾ **$286 - $313,** ⍾⍾ **$286 - $313,** ⍾ **$20,** ch con, AE BC DC EFT JCB MC VI, ⅃⅂.

(Bunkhouse Section), 36 bunkhouses acc up to 4, [a/c, blkts, linen, pillows], cook fac, refrig. **D** ⍾ **$32 - $40,** ⍾ **$32 - $40.**

(Cabin Section), 12 cabins acc up to 4, [a/c, TV, t/c mkg, refrig, blkts, linen, pillows], shared fac. **D $138 - $146.**

Self Catering Accommodation

★★★☆ **Emu Walk Serviced Apartments**, (SA), Yulara Dve, ☎ 02 9339 1040, fax 02 9332 4555, 58 serv apts acc up to 8, (1 & 2 bedrm), [shwr, tlt, a/c, TV, clock radio, t/c mkg, cook fac, blkts, linen, pillows], w/mach, dryer, iron, iron brd, ☏. **D** ⍾⍾ **$297 - $323,** **D** ⍾⍾⍾⍾ **$369 - $401.**

Other Accommodation

Spinifex Lodge, (Lodge), Yulara Dve, ☎ 02 9339 1040, fax 02 9332 4555, (2 stry gr fl), 68 rms acc up to 4, [a/c, TV, video, movie, clock radio, t/c mkg, refrig, cook fac ltd, micro, toaster], shwr, tlt, ldry, bbq, cots. **D** ⍾⍾ **$297 - $323,** ⍾⍾⍾⍾ **$369 - $401,** AE BC DC JCB MC VI, ⅃⅂.

Rates may change. Check before booking.

Queensland is Australia's second biggest state after Western Australia and represents more than a quarter of Australia's total land mass. The "Sunshine State" holds five of Australia's 11 World Heritage areas. *They are:* **The Great Barrier Reef**, which stretches for about three-quarters of the length of the state's east coast. **Scenic Rim National Parks,** south of the capital Brisbane and the biggest area of sub-tropical rainforest in South-East Queensland. **Fraser Island,** the world's biggest sand island runs from south of Maryborough to north of Bundaberg and is noted for its sand dunes and pristine natural attractions. **Riversleigh Fossil Fields** in Lawn National Park in the north-west, recognised as one of the four most significant fossil sites in the world and; **The Wet Tropics**, which stretch from Townsville to Cooktown and nurture some of the world's oldest rainforests.

Tropical North Queensland is one of the few places on earth where rainforests actually grow down to meet coral reef. It is a special place where two World Heritage sites meet - The Great Barrier Reef and the ancient Daintree Rainforest.

Day trips head out from centres like Bundaberg, Mackay, Townsville, Cairns and Port Douglas to coral cays and pontoons anchored adjacent to reef outcrops.

The capital Brisbane is Australia's third biggest city after Sydney and Melbourne. To the south, the 70 km of Gold Coast beach front and adjacent Hinterland is nationally famed for its attractions both developed and natural.

North of Brisbane the Sunshine Coast is noted for surf, sand and scenery with the 13 peaks of the Glasshouse Mountains dominating the skyline. In the south-east, Toowoomba is Queenslands Garden City set in an area of mountains, rolling plains and national parks.

The vast Outback is the wide open road. The Matilda Highway stretches more than 2000 km's through small towns, cattle stations and striking countryside. Gladstone, 500 km's north of Brisbane, is a busy port which provides access to Heron and Lady Musgrave Islands.

It is part of the Capricorn region of which Rockhampton is the capital. The diverse attractions include towns like Emerald, Rubyvale and Sapphire, which reflect the attraction of the Gemfields.

Great Keppel Island is only 15 km off the coast. Mackay is the gateway to the Whitsunday Islands and behind the sugar port city is the rainforest wonderland of Eungella National Park.

The Whitsunday Islands – Daydream, South Molle, North Molle, Long, Dent, Hamilton, Whitsunday, Hook, Hayman and Lindeman are serviced from Airlie Beach.

Townsville is Australia's biggest tropical city with beautiful Mission Beach to the north, gold mining Charters Towers to the west, Bowen to the south and five resort islands in the east. Magnetic Islands is about 20 minutes from Townsville by fast ferry. Then Orpheus, Bedarra, Dunk and Hinchinbrook complete a range of island contrasts.

Cairns and Port Douglas enjoy magnificent beaches, Queensland's highest mountains, coral reef, 20 offshore islands and pristine World Heritage rainforest.

The Gulf Savannah extends from the Great Dividing Range to the Northern Territory border. It includes amazing natural attractions, including the world's biggest and longest lava tubes, 164 km in total, which formed in a volcanic eruption at Undara 190,000 years ago.

QUEENSLAND

Queensland Holds World Wonders

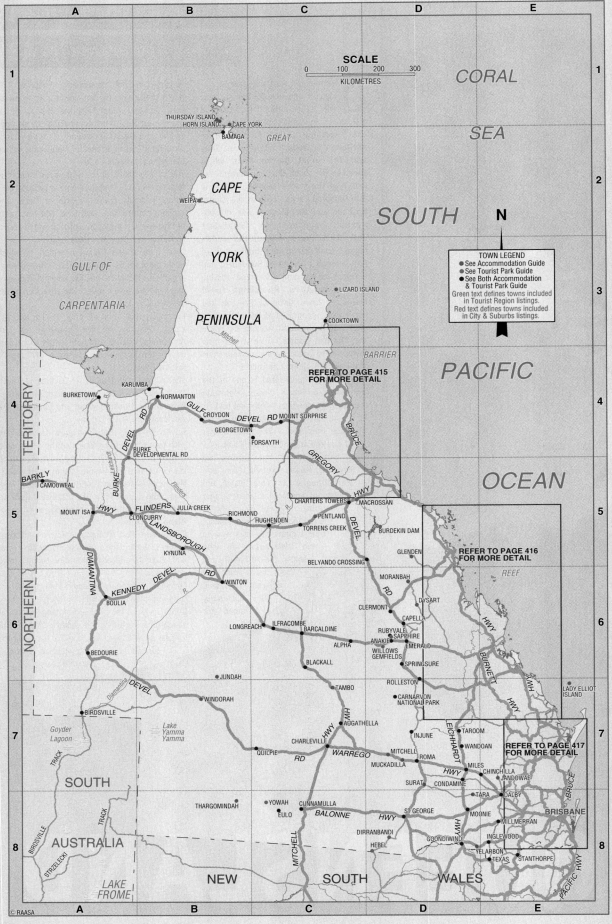

CORAL

SEA

SCALE
0   100   200   300
KILOMETRES

THURSDAY ISLAND
HORN ISLAND   CAPE YORK
BAMAGA

GREAT

CAPE

WEIPA

SOUTH

N

YORK

TOWN LEGEND
● See Accommodation Guide
● See Tourist Park Guide
● See Both Accommodation
   & Tourist Park Guide
Green text defines towns included
in Tourist Region listings.
Red text defines towns included
in City & Suburbs listings.

LIZARD ISLAND

PENINSULA

PACIFIC

Mitchell

COOKTOWN

BARRIER

REFER TO PAGE 415
FOR MORE DETAIL

GULF OF

CARPENTARIA

TERRITORRY

KARUMBA

BURKETOWN   NORMANTON

GULF   RD

CROYDON   DEVEL   RD   MOUNT SURPRISE

GEORGETOWN

FORSAYTH

BRUCE

GREGORY

OCEAN

BURKE
DEVELOPMENTAL RD

BARKLY

CAMOOWEAL

MOUNT ISA   HWY   FLINDERS

CLONCURRY

LANDSBOROUGH

JULIA CREEK

RICHMOND

HUGHENDEN

CHARTERS TOWERS   MACROSSAN

PENTLAND

TORRENS CREEK

DEVEL

BURDEKIN DAM

REFER TO PAGE 416
FOR MORE DETAIL

REEF

NORTHERN

DIAMANTINA

KENNEDY

DEVEL

RD

KYNUNA

WINTON

BOULIA

BELYANDO CROSSING

GLENDEN

MORANBAH

RD

CLERMONT

DYSART

BEDOURIE

LONGREACH   ILFRACOMBE   BARCALDINE

CAPELLA

HWY

JUNDAH

ALPHA   RUBYVALE   SAPPHIRE
ANAKIE
WILLOWS
GEMFIELDS   EMERALD

BLACKALL

SPRINGSURE

Diamantina   DEVEL

WINDORAH

TAMBO

ROLLESTON

CARNARVON
NATIONAL PARK

LADY ELLIOT
ISLAND

BURNETT

BIRDSVILLE

Goyder
Lagoon

Lake
Yamma
Yamma

QUILPIE   CHARLEVILLE   HWY   AUGATHELLA

RD   WARREGO

INJUNE

MITCHELL

TAROOM

WANDOAN

LEICHHARDT

HWY

MUCKADILLA

ROMA

MILES

CHINCHILLA

REFER TO PAGE 417
FOR MORE DETAIL

TRACK

SOUTH

THARGOMINDAH

YOWAH

EULO

CUNNAMULLA

BALONNE

HWY

SURAT

ST GEORGE

CONDAMINE

MOONIE

JANDOWAE

TARA   DALBY

HWY

BRUCE

MILLMERRAN

BRISBANE

BIRDSVILLE

STRZELECKI

AUSTRALIA

DIRRANBANDI

HEBEL

GOONDIWINDI

INGLEWOOD

YELARBON
TEXAS   STANTHORPE

PACIFIC HWY

LAKE
FROME

NEW

SOUTH

WALES

© RAASA

Rates may change. Check before booking.

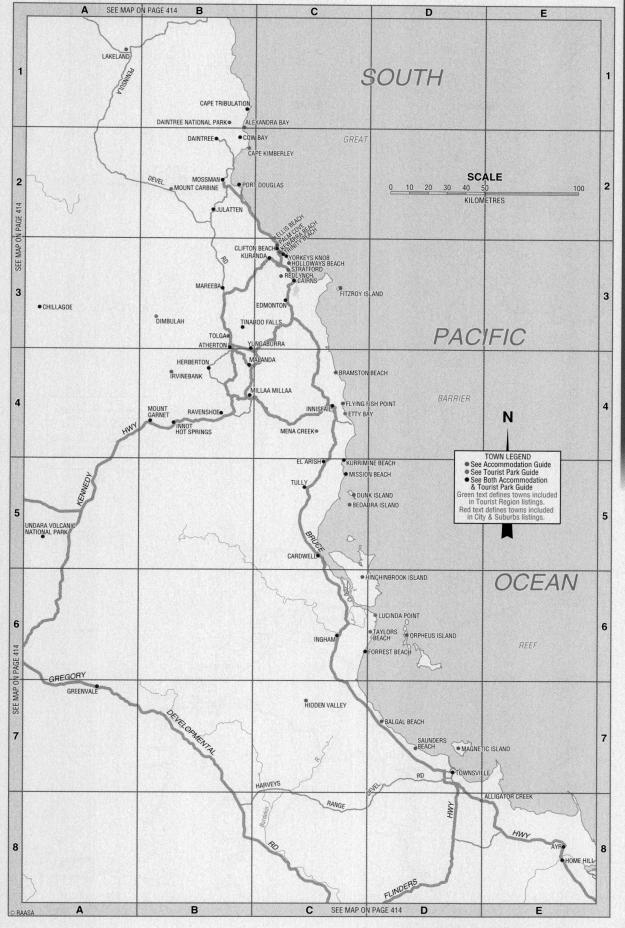

SOUTH

PACIFIC

OCEAN

GREAT

BARRIER

REEF

SCALE

0 10 20 30 40 50   100
KILOMETRES

N

TOWN LEGEND
● See Accommodation Guide
● See Tourist Park Guide
● See Both Accommodation
   & Tourist Park Guide
Green text defines towns included
in Tourist Region listings.
Red text defines towns included
in City & Suburbs listings.

LAKELAND

CAPE TRIBULATION
DAINTREE NATIONAL PARK   ALEXANDRA BAY
DAINTREE   COW BAY
           CAPE KIMBERLEY
DEVEL   MOSSMAN
           MOUNT CARBINE   PORT DOUGLAS
           JULATTEN
                            ELLIS BEACH
                            PALM COVE
                            KEWARRA BEACH
                            TRINITY BEACH
           CLIFTON BEACH
           KURANDA   YORKEYS KNOB
                      HOLLOWAYS BEACH
                      STRATFORD
                      REDLYNCH
           MAREEBA   CAIRNS
                                 FITZROY ISLAND
CHILLAGOE
           DIMBULAH   EDMONTON
                       TINAROO FALLS
           TOLGA
           ATHERTON   YUNGABURRA
           HERBERTON   MALANDA
           IRVINEBANK
                       BRAMSTON BEACH
                       MILLAA MILLAA
           MOUNT   FLYING FISH POINT
           GARNET   RAVENSHOE   INNISFAIL   ETTY BAY
                    INNOT
                    HOT SPRINGS
                    MENA CREEK
                           EL ARISH   KURRIMINE BEACH
                                      MISSION BEACH
                           TULLY
                                      DUNK ISLAND
                                      BEDARRA ISLAND
UNDARA VOLCANIC
NATIONAL PARK
                           CARDWELL
                                 HINCHINBROOK ISLAND
                                 LUCINDA POINT
GREGORY   TAYLORS
GREENVALE   BEACH   ORPHEUS ISLAND
                           INGHAM
                                 FORREST BEACH

HIDDEN VALLEY
                           BALGAL BEACH
DEVELOPMENTAL
                           SAUNDERS
                           BEACH
                                 MAGNETIC ISLAND
HARVEYS
                                 TOWNSVILLE
                      RANGE   ALLIGATOR CREEK
Burdekin

FLINDERS   AYR
                                 HOME HILL

KENNEDY
HWY
BRUCE
PENINSULA
RD

© RAASA

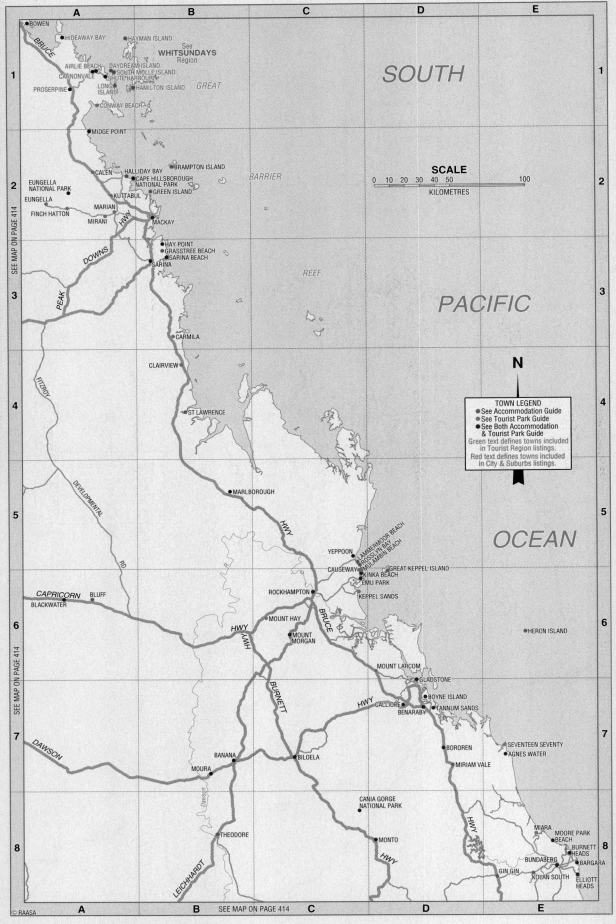

A B C D E

1

BOWEN
BRUCE
HIDEAWAY BAY
HAYMAN ISLAND
See
WHITSUNDAYS
Region
AIRLIE BEACH DAYDREAM ISLAND
CANNONVALE SOUTH MOLLE ISLAND
SHUTE HARBOUR
LONG
PROSERPINE ISLAND HAMILTON ISLAND
GREAT
CONWAY BEACH

MIDGE POINT

2

BRAMPTON ISLAND
EUNGELLA CALEN HALLIDAY BAY
NATIONAL PARK CAPE HILLSBOROUGH
EUNGELLA NATIONAL PARK
KUTTABUL GREEN ISLAND
MARIAN
FINCH HATTON
MIRANI MACKAY
HWY
BARRIER

SCALE
0 10 20 30 40 50 100
KILOMETRES

SOUTH

HAY POINT
GRASSTREE BEACH
SARINA BEACH
SARINA
DOWNS

3

PEAK
CARMILA
REEF
PACIFIC

CLAIRVIEW

4

FITZROY
ST LAWRENCE

N
TOWN LEGEND
● See Accommodation Guide
● See Tourist Park Guide
● See Both Accommodation
& Tourist Park Guide
Green text defines towns included
in Tourist Region listings.
Red text defines towns included
in City & Suburbs listings.

5

DEVELOPMENTAL
RD
MARLBOROUGH
HWY

OCEAN

LAMMERMOOR BEACH
YEPPOON ROSSLYN BAY
MULAMBIN BEACH
CAUSEWAY GREAT KEPPEL ISLAND
KINKA BEACH
ROCKHAMPTON EMU PARK
KEPPEL SANDS

6

CAPRICORN BLUFF
BLACKWATER
HWY MOUNT HAY
HWY MOUNT
MORGAN
BRUCE
HERON ISLAND

MOUNT LARCOM

GLADSTONE
BURNETT BOYNE ISLAND
HWY TANNUM SANDS
CALLIOPE
BENARABY

7

DAWSON
BOROREN SEVENTEEN SEVENTY
AGNES WATER
BANANA
MOURA BILOELA MIRIAM VALE

CANIA GORGE
NATIONAL PARK
HWY

8

Dawson R
THEODORE
MONTO
HWY
MIARA MOORE PARK
BEACH
BURNETT
HEADS
BUNDABERG BARGARA
GIN GIN
LEICHHARDT KOLAN SOUTH ELLIOTT
HEADS

A B C D E

© RAASA SEE MAP ON PAGE 414

SEE MAP ON PAGE 414

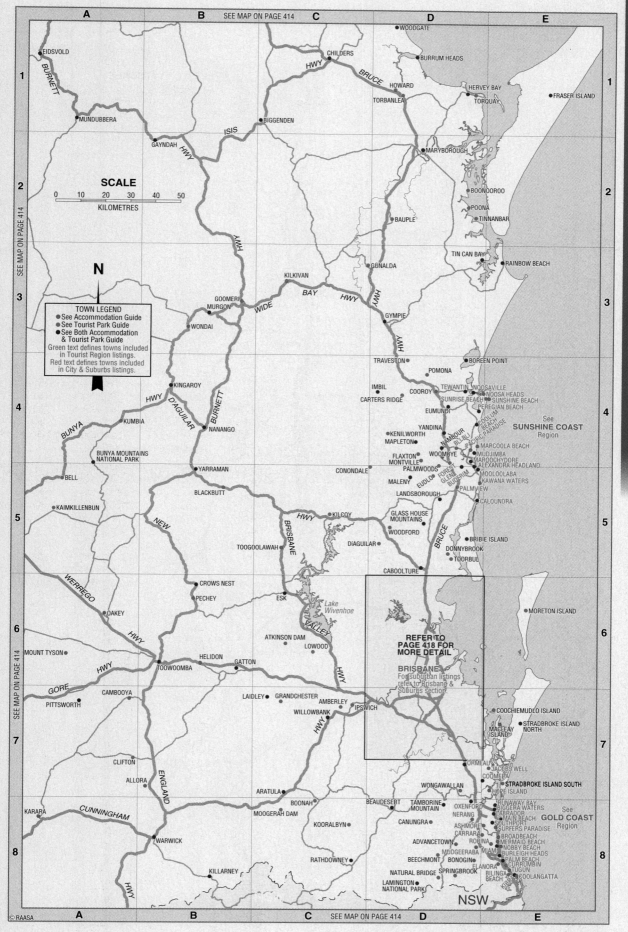

A   B   C   D   E

1

EIDSVOLD

BURNETT

WOODGATE

BURRUM HEADS

MUNDUBBERA

CHILDERS

HWY   HOWARD   HERVEY BAY

BRUCE   TORBANLEA   TORQUAY

FRASER ISLAND

ISIS   BIGGENDEN

MARYBOROUGH

2

GAYNDAH   HWY

SCALE

0   10   20   30   40   50
KILOMETRES

BOONOOROO

BAUPLE   POONA

TINNANBAR

N

KILKIVAN   GUNALDA   TIN CAN BAY

BAY   HWY   RAINBOW BEACH

3

WIDE   GYMPIE

GOOMERI
MURGON

WONDAI

HWY

TRAVESTON   BOREEN POINT

POMONA

TOWN LEGEND
● See Accommodation Guide
● See Tourist Park Guide
● See Both Accommodation
   & Tourist Park Guide
Green text defines towns included
in Tourist Region listings.
Red text defines towns included
in City & Suburbs listings.

IMBIL   COOROY   TEWANTIN NOOSAVILLE
CARTERS RIDGE   NOOSA HEADS
SUNRISE BEACH   SUNSHINE BEACH
EUMUNDI   PEREGIAN BEACH

4

KINGAROY

HWY   D'AGUILAR

KUMBIA

NANANGO

BUNYA   YANDINA
KENILWORTH   NAMBOUR
MAPLETON   WOOMBYE   PACIFIC PARADISE

See
SUNSHINE COAST
Region

COOLUM
BEACH

MARCOOLA BEACH
MUDJIMBA
MAROOCHYDORE
ALEXANDRA HEADLAND

BUNYA MOUNTAINS
NATIONAL PARK

YARRAMAN

FLAXTON
MONTVILLE
PALMWOODS

FOREST
GLEN   BUDERIM

MOOLOOLABA
KAWANA WATERS

BELL

BLACKBUTT

CONONDALE

MALENY   EUDLO

PALMVIEW

MOOLOOLABA

KAIMKILLENBUN

NEW

LANDSBOROUGH

CALOUNDRA

5

KILCOY

HWY

GLASS HOUSE
MOUNTAINS

BRISBANE

TOOGOOLAWAH

WOODFORD

BRUCE

BRIBIE ISLAND

DIAGUILAR   DONNYBROOK

TOORBUL

CABOOLTURE

6

WERREGO

CROWS NEST

PECHEY

ESK   Lake
Wivenhoe

VALLEY

MORETON ISLAND

OAKEY

HWY

REFER TO
PAGE 418 FOR
MORE DETAIL

MOUNT TYSON

GORE

HELIDON

ATKINSON DAM
LOWOOD

HWY

BRISBANE
For suburban listings
refer to Brisbane &
Suburbs section.

7

HWY   TOOWOOMBA   GATTON

COOCHIEMUDLO ISLAND

CAMBOOYA

PITTSWORTH

LAIDLEY   GRANDCHESTER

AMBERLEY

WILLOWBANK   IPSWICH

MACLEAY
ISLAND

STRADBROKE ISLAND
NORTH

CLIFTON

ENGLAND

HWY

ORMEAU

JACOBS WELL

COOMERA

ALLORA

ARATULA

STRADBROKE ISLAND SOUTH
HOPE ISLAND

8

KARARA

CUNNINGHAM

BOONAH

BEAUDESERT   TAMBORINE
MOUNTAIN

WONGAWALLAN

RUNAWAY BAY
BIGGERA WATERS
LABRADOR
MAIN BEACH
SOUTHPORT
SURFERS PARADISE

OXENFORD
NERANG

See
GOLD COAST
Region

MOOGERAH DAM

KOORALBYN

CANUNGRA

ASHMORE
CARRARA

BROADBEACH
MERMAID BEACH
NOBBY BEACH

WARWICK

ADVANCETOWN

ROBINA   MIAMI

BURLEIGH HEADS
PALM BEACH

KILLARNEY

RATHDOWNEY

BEECHMONT   BONOGIN
MUDGEERABA

ELANORA   CURRUMBIN
TUGUN

HWY

NATURAL BRIDGE   SPRINGBROOK

BILINGA
BEACH   COOLANGATTA

LAMINGTON
NATIONAL PARK

NSW

A   B   C   D   E

© RAASA

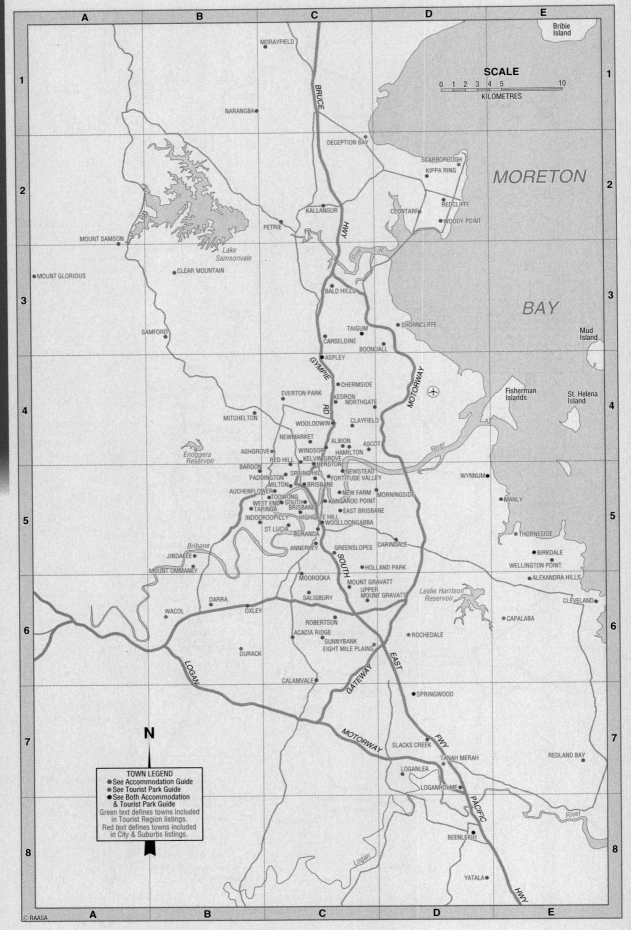

QUEENSLAND

SCALE
0 1 2 3 4 5   10
KILOMETRES

Bribie
Island

MORAYFIELD

BRUCE

NARANGBA

DECEPTION BAY

SCARBOROUGH
KIPPA RING

MORETON

KALLANGUR

CLONTARF
REDCLIFFE
WOODY POINT

PETRIE

HWY

MOUNT SAMSON

Lake
Samsonvale

Pine R.

BAY

MOUNT GLORIOUS

CLEAR MOUNTAIN

BALD HILLS

SHORNCLIFFE

Mud
Island

SAMFORD

TAIGUM
CARSELDINE
BOONDALL

GYMPIE

ASPLEY

EVERTON PARK
CHERMSIDE
KEDRON
NORTHGATE

RD

Fisherman
Islands

St. Helena
Island

MITCHELTON

WOOLOOWIN

CLAYFIELD

MOTORWAY

NEWMARKET

ALBION
ASCOT

ASHGROVE
WINDSOR
HAMILTON

River

Enoggera
Reservoir

BARDON
RED HILL
KELVIN GROVE
HERSTON

PADDINGTON
SPRING HILL
NEWSTEAD

WYNNUM

MILTON
FORTITUDE VALLEY

AUCHENFLOWER
BRISBANE

TOOWONG
NEW FARM
MORNINGSIDE

WEST END SOUTH
KANGAROO POINT

MANLY

TARINGA
BRISBANE
EAST BRISBANE

INDOOROOPILLY
HIGHGATE HILL
WOOLLOONGABBA

ST LUCIA
BURANDA

THORNESIDE

Bribane

ANNERLEY
GREENSLOPES
CARINDALE

JINDALEE

BIRKDALE
WELLINGTON POINT

MOUNT OMMANEY

HOLLAND PARK

ALEXANDRA HILLS

MOOROOKA
MOUNT GRAVATT
UPPER
MOUNT GRAVATT

Leslie Harrison
Reservoir

CLEVELAND

DARRA
SALISBURY

CAPALABA

WACOL
OXLEY

ROBERTSON
ROCHEDALE

LOGAN

ACACIA RIDGE
SUNNYBANK
EIGHT MILE PLAINS

DURACK

CALAMVALE

GATEWAY

EAST

SPRINGWOOD

MOTORWAY

FWY

SLACKS CREEK

N

TANAH MERAH

REDLAND BAY

TOWN LEGEND
● See Accommodation Guide
● See Tourist Park Guide
● See Both Accommodation
  & Tourist Park Guide
Green text defines towns included
in Tourist Region listings.
Red text defines towns included
in City & Suburbs listings.

LOGANLEA

LOGANHOLME

PACIFIC

River

Logan

BEENLEIGH

YATALA

HWY

© RAASA

Rates may change. Check before booking.

BRISBANE QLD 4000

Pop 1,300,000. See map on page 418, ref C5. The capital city of Queensland (the Sunshine State) is the state's centre for arts, culture, shopping, education and entertainment. The city hosted the 1988 World Expo. Boating, Bowls, Fishing, Golf, Horse Racing, Swimming, Tennis, Water Skiing.

Hotels/Motels

★★★★★ **Brisbane Hilton**, (LH), 190 Elizabeth St, ☎ 07 3234 2000, fax 07 3231 3199, (Multi-stry), 321 rms (6 suites) [shwr, bath, spa bath (1), tlt, hairdry, a/c, tel, TV, movie, clock radio, t/c mkg, refrig, mini bar], lift, iron, iron brd, business centre, conv fac, ✕, pool-heated, sauna, spa, 24hr reception, rm serv, secure park, gym, tennis, cots, non smoking flr (9), non smoking rms (172), ch con, AE BC CC DC JCB MC VI, ♿.

★★★★★ **Brisbane Marriott**, (M), 515 Queen St, CBD 800m city mall, ☎ 07 3303 8000, fax 07 3303 8088, (Multi-stry), 267 units (3 suites) [shwr, bath, tlt, H & C, hairdry, a/c, cent heat, tel (ISD), TV, video (suite only), movie, radio, CD, t/c mkg, refrig, mini bar, cook fac ltd, micro (3)], iron, iron brd, conf fac (suite only), ✕ (licensed), pool, pool indoor heated, sauna, spa, rm serv, dinner to unit, secure park, ☎, gym, cots. BB ♦ $169 - $201.50, ♦♦ $169 - $224, RO ♦ $145 - $179, ♦♦ $145 - $179, Suite BB ♦ $380, ♦♦ $380, ◊ $18.50, AE BC DC EFT JCB MC VI, ♿.

★★★★★ **Carlton Crest**, (LH), Cnr Ann & Roma Sts, ☎ 07 3229 9111, fax 07 3229 9618, (Multi-stry), 438 rms (7 suites) [shwr, bath (232), spa bath (7), tlt, hairdry, a/c, tel, TV, movie, clock radio, t/c mkg, refrig, mini bar], lift, ldry, iron, iron brd, business centre, conv fac, ✕, pool, 24hr reception, rm serv, c/park (undercover), gym, non smoking flr (4). RO ♦♦ $130 - $255, Suite RO $280 - $700, AE BC DC JCB MC VI, ♿.

★★★★★ **Conrad International Hotel & Treasury Casino**, (LH), William & George Sts, 800m W of PO, ☎ 07 3306 8888, fax 07 3306 8880, (Multi-stry), 134 rms (16 suites) [shwr, bath, tlt, hairdry, a/c, c/fan (24), tel, TV, movie, radio, t/c mkg, refrig, mini bar], lift, iron, iron brd, conf fac, ✕, sauna, 24hr reception, rm serv, secure park, ☎, gym, cots, non smoking rms (25). RO $195 - $305, AE BC DC JCB MC VI, ♿.

★★★★★ **Quay West Brisbane**, (LH), 132 Alice St, 100m W of City Botanic Gardens, ☎ 07 3853 6000, fax 07 3853 6060, (Multi-stry), 96 rms (1 & 2 bedrm), [shwr, bath, tlt, hairdry, a/c, tel, TV, movie, CD, t/c mkg, refrig, mini bar, cook fac, micro, toaster, ldry (in unit)], lift, dryer, iron, iron brd, conv fac, ✕, pool-heated, sauna, spa, rm serv, secure park, ☎, gym, cots, non smoking flr (8), non smoking rms (43). RO $209 - $292, ch con, AE BC DC JCB MC VI.

★★★★★ **Sheraton Brisbane Hotel & Towers**, (LH), 249 Turbot St, above Central Railway, ☎ 07 3835 3535, fax 07 3835 4960, (Multi-stry), 410 rms (25 suites) [shwr, bath, tlt, hairdry, a/c, tel, cable tv, movie, t/c mkg, refrig, mini bar], lift, business centre, conv fac, ✕, pool-heated, sauna, spa, 24hr reception, rm serv, c/park (undercover) (200), secure park (200), ☎, gym, cots, non smoking flr (3). RO ♦ $145 - $314, ♦♦ $145 - $314, Suite D $180 - $1,730, ch con, AE BC DC JCB MC VI, ♿.

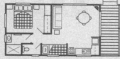

Pick up savings of 15% or more

Did you know that motoring organisation members are eligible for discounts on selected accommodation properties throughout Australia?

The National Accommodation Special Rates brochure contains information on over 300 accommodation properties throughout Australia, offering discounts of 15% or more to motoring organisation members. Pick up a brochure today at your local motoring organisation retail outlet.

Participating properties are indicated in this Accommodation Guide. Just look for the following symbol and quote your membership number when making a booking or show your membership card/tag on arrival.

★★★★★ **Stamford Plaza Brisbane**, (LH), Cnr Margaret & Edward Sts, 1km E of GPO, ☎ 07 3221 1999, fax 07 3221 6895, (Multi-stry), 252 rms (20 suites) [shwr, bath, spa bath (1), tlt, hairdry, a/c, tel, fax, TV, video (20), movie, radio, CD (20), t/c mkg, refrig, mini bar, cook fac (1), micro (1)], lift, ldry, iron, iron brd, business centre, conv fac, ⊠, pool-heated, sauna, spa, 24hr reception, rm serv, secure park, ✆, gym, cots, non smoking rms (39). **RO** ∮ **$273 - $416,** ⋕ **$273 - $416,** ⓭ **$39, Suite D $360 - $630,** AE BC DC JCB MC VI, ⅍.

★★★★☆ **Centra Brisbane**, (LH), Roma St, Brisbane Transit Centre, ☎ 07 3238 2222, fax 07 3238 2288, (Multi-stry), 191 rms (27 suites) [shwr, bath, tlt, hairdry, a/c, tel, cable tv, movie, clock radio, t/c mkg, refrig, mini bar], lift, ldry, dryer, iron, iron brd, conv fac, ⊠, sauna, spa, 24hr reception, rm serv, c/park (undercover), ✆, gym, cots, non smoking flr (4), non smoking rms (64). **RO** ∮ **$105 - $150,** ⋕ **$105 - $150,** ⓭ **$25,** ch con, AE BC DC JCB MC VI, ⅍.

★★★★☆ **Country Comfort Lennons Hotel**, (LH), 66 Queen St, City centre, ☎ 07 3222 3222, fax 07 3221 9389, (Multi-stry), 152 rms (35 suites) [shwr, bath (49), spa bath (8), tlt, hairdry, a/c, tel, TV, movie, clock radio, t/c mkg, refrig, mini bar, ldry (level 7)], lift, iron, iron brd, conv fac, ⊠, pool-heated, sauna, spa, 24hr reception, rm serv, secure park (36), ✆, cots, non smoking flr (11). **RO** ∮ **$122 - $180,** ⋕ **$122 - $180,** ⓭ **$16.50,** ch con, AE BC DC MC VI.

★★★★☆ **Hotel Grand Chancellor**, (LH), Cnr Leichhardt St & Wickham Tce, Spring Hill, 1km W of GPO, ☎ 07 3831 4055, fax 07 3831 5031, (Multi-stry), 180 rms (18 suites) [shwr, bath, tlt, hairdry, a/c, tel, TV, movie, clock radio, t/c mkg, refrig, mini bar], lift, ldry, iron, iron brd, conv fac, ⊠, pool, sauna, spa, 24hr reception, rm serv, secure park, ✆, gym, cots, non smoking flr (5). **RO** ⋕ **$121 - $160,** AE BC DC EFT JCB MC VI, ⅍.

Brisbane
City of Sun Days

To spend some time in the City of Sun Days or for further
Information 'SUNDIAL' Central Reservations ☎ 1800 077 777

QUEENSLAND

BRISBANE CITY QLD continued...

★★★★☆ **Royal Albert Boutique Hotel**, (Ltd Lic H), Cnr Elizabeth & Albert Sts, 20m from City Mall, ☎ 07 3291 8888, fax 07 3229 7705, (Multi-stry), 28 rms (31 suites) [shwr, tlt, hairdry, a/c, tel, TV, clock radio, t/c mkg, refrig, mini bar, cook fac, micro], lift, w/mach, dryer, iron, iron brd, 24hr reception, rm serv, dinner to unit, c/park (valet)-fee, cots. **RO** ♦ **$160 - $320**, ♦♦ **$160 - $320**, **Suite RO** ♦♦ **$220 - $300**, ◊ **$25**, AE BC DC MC VI.

★★★★☆ **Saville Abbey Hotel**, (Ltd Lic H), 160 Roma St, ☎ 07 3236 1444, fax 07 3236 1134, (Multi-stry), 70 rms [shwr, bath, tlt, hairdry, a/c, tel, TV, movie, clock radio, t/c mkg, refrig, mini bar, cook fac, micro, elec frypan, toaster], lift, ldry, iron, iron brd, conv fac, ⊠ (Mon - Sun), pool-heated, sauna, spa, 24hr reception, rm serv, secure park (35), ☎, cots, non smoking flr (8). **Suite D** ◊ **$115.50**, ◊ **$16.50**, Some units of a lower rating, AE BC DC JCB MC VI, ⚐⚑.

★★★★☆ **The Chifley on George**, (LH), 103 George St, opposite casino, ☎ 07 3221 6044, fax 07 3221 7474, (Multi-stry), 99 rms (6 suites) [shwr, spa bath (6), tlt, a/c, tel, TV, movie (3), clock radio, t/c mkg, refrig, mini bar], lift, ldry, conv fac, ⊠, cafe, pool, spa, 24hr reception, rm serv, c/park (undercover), ☎, cots, non smoking flr (5). **RO** ♦ **$120 - $136**, ♦♦ **$120 - $136**, ch con, AE BC CC DC MC VI.

★★★★☆ **The Sebel Suites Brisbane**, (LH), 95 Charlotte St Cnr Albert St, 300m W of GPO, ☎ 07 3224 3500, fax 07 3211 0299, 173 rms [a/c, cent heat, tel, TV, movie, clock radio, t/c mkg, refrig, mini bar, cook fac, micro, toaster, ldry, pillows], w/mach, dryer, conf fac, ✕, ⊠, pool, pool indoor heated, sauna, rm serv, dinner to unit, secure park, cots. **BB $151, RO $120 - $157, Suite BB $173, Suite RO $158 - $195**, ch con, AE BC DC EFT MC VI, ⚐⚑.

★★★★ **Novotel Brisbane**, (LH), 200 Creek St, 1km N of GPO, ☎ 07 3309 3309, fax 07 3309 3308, (Multi-stry), 293 rms (2 suites) [shwr, bath, spa bath (2), tlt, hairdry, a/c, tel, cable tv, movie, clock radio, t/c mkg, refrig, mini bar], lift, iron, iron brd, business centre, conv fac, ⊠, pool-heated, sauna, rm serv, c/park (undercover), ☎, gym, cots, non smoking rms (125). **RO** ♦ **$209 - $231**, ♦♦ **$209 - $231**, ◊ **$25, Suite D $290**, ch con, AE BC CC DC EFT MC VI, ⚐⚑.

★★★★ **Rendezvous Apartment Hotel**, (LH), 255 Ann St, 500m N of GPO, ☎ 07 3001 9888, fax 07 3001 9700, (Multi-stry gr fl), 139 rms (81 suites) [shwr, bath, tlt, hairdry, a/c, tel, TV, video, movie, clock radio, CD, t/c mkg, refrig, mini bar, cook fac ltd, micro, toaster], lift, iron, iron brd, conf fac, ⊠, rm serv, c/park (undercover)-fee, cots-fee, non smoking flr (1), non smoking units (38). **RO** ♦ **$128 - $238**, ♦♦ **$128 - $238**, ◊ **$33, Suite RO $153 - $238**, AE BC DC EFT JCB MC VI.

★★★☆ **Albert Park Hotel**, (LH), 551 Wickham Tce, Cnr Gregory Tce, ☎ 07 3831 3111, fax 07 3832 1290, (Multi-stry), 94 rms [shwr, bath (64), spa bath (5), tlt, hairdry (60), a/c, tel, TV, movie (60), clock radio, t/c mkg, refrig], lift, ldry, iron, iron brd, conv fac, ⊠, pool, 24hr reception, rm serv, c/park (undercover), cots, non smoking flr (3), non smoking units (51). **D** ♦♦♦ **$104 - $148**, **RO** ♦ **$104 - $148**, 30 units of a lower rating. AE BC DC MC VI.

★★★☆ **Goodearth Hotel**, (M), Previously Gazebo Hotel 345 Wickham Tce, ☎ 07 3831 6177, fax 07 3832 5919, (Multi-stry gr fl), 180 units (13 suites) [shwr, bath (90), tlt, hairdry, a/c, tel, TV, movie, clock radio, t/c mkg, refrig, mini bar, cook fac (13), micro (13)], lift, ldry-fee, dryer-fee, iron, iron brd, conv fac, cafe (licensed), pool, 24hr reception, rm serv (limited), dinner to unit, c/park (undercover), cots, non smoking flr (4), non smoking suites (6). **RO** ♦ **$87 - $155**, ◊ **$87 - $155, Suite RO $138 - $220**, ch con, AE DC JCB MC VI.

★★★☆ **Gregory Terrace Motor Inn**, (M), 397 Gregory Tce, Spring Hill 4000, ☎ 07 3832 1769, fax 07 3832 2640, (Multi-stry gr fl), 37 units [shwr, bath (21), tlt, hairdry, a/c-cool, heat, tel, TV, clock radio, t/c mkg, refrig, mini bar], lift, ldry-fee, dryer-fee, conv fac, ⊠, pool, 24hr reception, rm serv, dinner to unit, c/park (undercover), cots. **RO** ♦♦ **$108**, ◊ **$15**, ch con, AE BC DC MC VI, ⚐⚑.

★★★☆ **Hotel George Williams**, (LMH), 325 George St, ☎ 07 3308 0700, fax 07 3308 0733, 42 units [shwr, tlt, a/c-cool, tel, TV, clock radio, t/c mkg, refrig], lift, ldry-fee, conf fac, ✕ (non-smoking), bbq, secure park (undercover), gym, cots, non smoking rms (28). **RO** ♦ **$77 - $81**, ♦♦ **$77 - $81**, ◊ **$17**, ch con, AE BC DC EFT MC VI, ⚐⚑.

★★★☆ **Mercure Hotel Brisbane**, (Ltd Lic H), 85 North Quay, ☎ 07 3236 3300, fax 07 3236 1035, (Multi-stry), 175 rms (15 suites) [shwr, bath, tlt, hairdry, a/c, tel, TV, movie, clock radio, t/c mkg, refrig, mini bar], lift, iron, iron brd, conf fac, ⊠, pool, sauna, spa, 24hr reception, rm serv, c/park (limited undercover), ✆, cots, non smoking flr (5). **RO †** $128 - $176, **††** $128 - $176, **◊** $22, **Suite D** $220 - $275, ch con, AE BC DC MC VI.

★★★☆ **Metro Inn Tower Mill**, (Ltd Lic H), 239 Wickham Tce, ☎ 07 3832 1421, fax 07 3835 1013, (Multi-stry), 76 rms [shwr, bath (7), tlt, a/c, tel, TV, movie, clock radio, t/c mkg, refrig, mini bar (50)], lift, ldry-fee, dryer-fee, iron, iron brd, conf fac, ⊠, rm serv, c/park (undercover) (40), cots, non smoking rms (60). **RO** $97 - $119, AE BC DC MC VI.

★★★☆ **Metropolitan Motor Inn**, (M), 106 Leichhardt St, Cnr Little Edward St, ☎ 07 3831 6000, fax 07 3832 6198, (Multi-stry), 54 units [shwr, bath (6), tlt, a/c, tel, TV, movie, clock radio, t/c mkg, refrig], lift, ldry-fee, dryer-fee, iron, conv fac, ⊠ (Mon - Sun), bar, 24hr reception, rm serv, c/park (undercover) (35), ✆, cots. **RO †** $88, **††** $88, **◊** $11, ch con, AE BC DC MC VI.

★★★☆ **Royal on the Park**, (Ltd Lic H), Previously The Parkroyal Brisbane Cnr Alice & Albert Sts, ☎ 07 3221 3411, fax 07 3229 9817, (Multi-stry), 153 rms (8 suites) [shwr, bath, tlt, hairdry, a/c, tel, TV, movie, clock radio, t/c mkg, refrig, mini bar], lift, ldry, iron, iron brd, conf fac, ⊠, bar (cocktail), pool, spa, 24hr reception, rm serv, c/park (undercover) (75), gym, cots, non smoking rms. **RO †** $140 - $250, **††** $140 - $250, **◊** $30, **Suite D** $390 - $520, ch con, AE BC CC DC JCB MC VI.

★★★☆ **Wickham Terrace**, (M), 491 Wickham Tce, Spring Hill 4000, ☎ 07 3839 9611, fax 07 3832 5348, (Multi-stry gr fl), 47 units [shwr, bath (23), tlt, a/c, fan, tel, TV, movie, clock radio, t/c mkg, refrig], lift, ldry, dryer-fee, iron, iron brd, conv fac, ⊠, pool, spa, rm serv, c/park (undercover), cots-fee. **RO †** $97 - $103, **††** $106 - $109, **◊** $11, ch con, AE BC DC JCB MC VI.

★★★ **Astor**, (M), 193 Wickham Tce, Cnr Berry Street, ☎ 07 3831 9522, fax 07 3831 7360, (Multi-stry), 78 units (17 suites) [shwr, tlt, a/c, c/fan, tel, TV, movie, clock radio, t/c mkg, refrig, cook fac (23)], lift, ldry-fee, dryer-fee, iron, iron brd, ⊠ (Mon-Sat), 24hr reception, rm serv, c/park (limited) (40), ✆, cots. **RO †** $65 - $89, **◊** $12, **Suite D ††** $95, ch con, Units 11 to 23 ★★★. AE BC DC MC VI.

★★★ **Camelot Inn**, (M), 40 Astor Tce, ☎ 07 3832 5115, fax 07 3832 3775, (Multi-stry), 70 units [shwr, tlt, a/c, tel, TV, clock radio, t/c mkg, refrig, cook fac, micro (on request)], lift, ldry-fee, dryer-fee, iron, iron brd, ✕ (breakfast & dinner), pool, spa, bbq, rm serv (restaurant hours), secure park (30), plygr, cots. **RO †** $85, **††** $85, **◊** $11, ch con, AE BC DC MC VI.

★★★ **Explorers Inns**, (Ltd Lic H), 63 Turbot St (Cnr George St), 800m W of GPO, ☎ 07 3211 3488, fax 07 3211 3499, (Multi-stry gr fl), 58 rms [shwr, tlt, a/c, heat, tel, TV, clock radio, t/c mkg, refrig], lift, ldry-fee, dryer-fee, ⊠, cots, non smoking units (42). **RO †** $75, **††** $75, No off-street parking.

Operator Comment: "Explorers Inn is an award winning hotel with unique services and facilities specialising for the budget conscious traveller. We offer unbeatable rates and value for money in the heart of the CBD.
Email Address: explorer@powerup.com.au

★★★ **Hotel Ibis Brisbane**, (LH), 27 Turbot St, Central CBD, ☎ 07 3237 2333, fax 07 3237 2444, 218 rms [shwr, bath, tlt, hairdry, a/c-cool, tel, TV, movie, clock radio, t/c mkg, refrig, ldry], lift, ⊠, rm serv, cots. **RO †** $109 - $165, **††** $109 - $165, **◊** $22, ch con, AE BC DC MC VI, ♿.

For Accommodation Booking information - see page 27 **423**

★★★ **Soho**, (M), 333 Wickham Tce, ☎ 07 3831 7722, fax 07 3831 8050, (Multi-stry), 52 units [shwr, tlt, a/c-cool, heat, tel, TV, movie, clock radio, t/c mkg, refrig], ldry, ⊠ (7days), bar, mini mart, c/park (undercover) (7), cots-fee. RO ♦ $64, ♦♦ $76, AE BC DC JCB MC VI.

★★★ **Spring Hill Terraces**, (M), 260 Water S, Spring Hill 4000, ☎ 07 3854 1048, fax 07 3852 2121, (2 stry gr fl) 25 units [shwr, tlt, a/c-cool, heat, tel, TV, clock radio, refrig, cook fac (12)], ldry, pool, bbq, c/park (undercover), cots. RO ♦ $66 - $88, ♦♦ $66 - $88, ♦ $11, AE BC DC MC VI.

★★★ **(Budget Units Section)**, 4 apts [basin, c/fan, tel, TV, t/c mkg, refrig], shwr, tlt, shared fac. RO ♦ $50, ♦♦ $58.

Self Catering Accommodation

★★★★★ **City Park Apartments**, (SA), 251 Gregory Tce, Spring Hill, 2km N of CBD, ☎ 07 3839 8683, fax 07 3839 8616, (Multi-stry gr fl), 18 serv apts acc up to 4, (Studio, 1 & 2 bedrm), [ensuite, shwr, tlt, hairdry, a/c, fan (2), tel, fax, TV, video, CD (9), refrig, micro, d/wash, toaster, ldry, blkts, linen, pillows], dryer, iron, iron brd, pool (saltwater), bbq, secure park, cots. D $93 - $145.50, W $595 - $795, AE BC EFT MC VI.

★★★★☆ **Centrepoint Central Apartments**, (SA), 69 Leichhardt St, ☎ 07 3832 3000, fax 07 3832 1842, 38 serv apts acc up to 6, (1, 2 & 3 bedrm), [shwr, bath, tlt, a/c, tel, TV, video, clock radio, refrig, cook fac, micro, d/wash, ldry (in unit)], pool-heated, sauna, spa, bbq, secure park, cots-fee. D $135 - $210, W $672 - $1,036, Min book applies, AE BC DC MC VI.

★★★★☆ **Rothbury on Ann**, (SA), 301 Ann Street, 500m N of GPO, ☎ 07 3239 8888, fax 07 3239 8899, (Multi-stry), 55 serv apts acc up to 4, (1 & 2 bedrm), [ensuite, shwr, tlt, hairdry, a/c-cool, tel, TV, video, clock radio, CD, t/c mkg, refrig, cook fac, micro, d/wash, toaster, ldry, blkts, linen, pillows], lift, w/mach, dryer, iron, iron brd, sauna, spa, bbq, rm serv, gym, cots-fee. RO ♦♦ $770 - $1,036, ♦ $135 - $188, ch con, AE BC DC MC VI.

★★★★☆ **Spring Hill Mews**, (HU), 27 Birley St, Spring Hill 4000, 1.2km NW of Queen St Mall, ☎ 07 3232 0000, fax 07 3232 0099, (Multi-stry gr fl), 31 units acc up to 6, (1 & 2 bedrm), [ensuite, shwr, bath, tlt, hairdry, a/c, tel, TV, video, clock radio, refrig, micro, elec frypan, d/wash, toaster, ldry, blkts, linen, pillows], dryer, iron, iron brd, pool (salt water), bbq, c/park (undercover), cots. D ♦♦ $66 - $99, ♦ $5, ch con, AE BC DC MC VI.

★★★★☆ **The Astor Apartments**, (HU), 35 Astor Tce, ☎ 07 3839 9022, fax 07 3229 5553, (Multi-stry), 40 units acc up to 6, (1 & 2 bedrm), [ensuite, shwr, bath, tlt, a/c, tel, TV, refrig, cook fac, micro, d/wash, ldry (in unit), blkts, linen, pillows], lift, pool, sauna, spa, bbq, secure park, cots-fee. D ♦♦ $120, W ♦♦ $665, AE BC DC MC VI.

★★★★ **Summit Central Apartment Hotel**, (SA), 32 Leichhardt St, Spring Hill 4000, Cnr Allenby St, ☎ 07 3839 7000, fax 07 3832 2821, (Multi-stry), 72 serv apts acc up to 6, [shwr, bath (54), tlt, a/c, tel, TV, video-fee, clock radio, t/c mkg, refrig, cook fac, micro (54), ldry (in unit) (54)], lift, ldry, dryer, pool, sauna (2), spa, bbq, dinner to unit, meals avail, secure park, plygr, tennis (half court), cots. D $125 - $215, AE BC DC MC VI.

★★★★ The Manor Apartment Hotel, (HU), Previously The Manor Serviced Apartments. 289 Queen St, Next to GPO, ☎ 07 3229 2700, fax 07 3270 4747, (Multi-stry), 31 units acc up to 4, (1 + 2 bedrm), [ensuite, shwr, tlt, a/c, tel, TV, video, clock radio, refrig, cook fac, micro, ldry (in unit), blkts, linen, pillows], lift, dryer, c/park-fee. **RO $160 - $240, W $840 - $1,092**, AE BC DC MC VI, ♿,

Operator Comment: Continental Breakfast Included-Only a 60 meter stroll to Queen Street Mall!.

★★★☆ Alatai Apartments Spring Hill, (SA), 391 Wickham Tce, Spring Hill 500m N of CBD, ☎ 07 3831 5388, fax 07 3839 0060, (Multi-stry), 70 serv apts acc up to 7, (Studio, 2 & 3 bedrm), [ensuite, shwr, tlt, hairdry, a/c, tel, TV, movie, clock radio, refrig, cook fac, micro, toaster, ldry (in unit)], lift, dryer, iron, iron brd, rec rm, conv fac, c/park (undercover), cots-fee. **D $83 - $161**, ch con, AE BC DC MC VI,

Operator Comment: Family of 5 includes (1 Free)$161.00 (2 Bedroom Apartment.).

★★★☆ Bonapartes Serviced Apartments, (SA), Cnr Gipps St & St Pauls Tce, ☎ 07 3251 5000, fax 07 3257 1485, (Multi-stry gr fl), 42 serv apts acc up to 6, [shwr, tlt, hairdry, a/c (39), tel, TV, clock radio, refrig, cook fac, micro (27), ldry (in unit), blkts, linen, pillows], dryer, iron, iron brd, conv fac, pool (salt water), secure park, ☎, gym, cots-fee. **D $99 - $149, W $125 - $700**, ch con, AE BC DC MC VI.

★★★☆ Dahrl Court, (SA), 45 Phillips St, Spring Hill, ☎ 07 3832 1331, fax 07 3839 2591, (2 stry gr fl), 25 serv apts acc up to 6, (1 & 2 bedrm), [shwr, bath, tlt, a/c, fan, heat, tel, TV, clock radio, refrig, cook fac, micro], ldry, dryer, iron, pool, bbq, 24hr reception, c/park (undercover), gym, cots. **D ⚹ $75, ⚹⚹ $85, ⚹⚹⚹ $95 - $110**, ch con, AE BC DC MC VI.

★★★☆ Quest on North Quay, (Apt), 293 North Quay, ☎ 07 3236 1440, fax 07 3236 1582, (Multi-stry), 123 apts acc up to 3, (Studio, 1 & 2 bedrm), [shwr, bath, spa bath (106), tlt, hairdry, a/c, tel, TV, video (106), movie-fee, clock radio, CD (106), t/c mkg, refrig, mini bar, cook fac (106), micro (106)], lift, ldry-fee, dryer-fee, iron, iron brd, lounge, conv fac, ✉, pool, spa, 24hr reception, rm serv, secure park (47), gym, cots, non smoking flr. **D $259, RO ⚹⚹ $99 - $115**, 16 studio units of lower rating. AE BC DC JCB MC VI.

★★★☆ Sedgebrook on Leichhardt, (SA), 83 Leichhardt St, 50m W of main intersection, ☎ 07 3831 6338, fax 07 3832 8089, (Multi-stry), 43 serv apts acc up to 4, (1 & 2 bedrm), [shwr, spa bath, tlt, hairdry, a/c, tel, TV, clock radio, refrig, cook fac, micro, elec frypan, d/wash, toaster, ldry (in unit), blkts, linen, pillows], lift, dryer, iron, iron brd, ✉ (Tues - Sun), sauna, spa, secure park. **D $120 - $140, W $495 - $695**, ch con, AE BC CC DC MC VI.

★★☆ Dorchester, (HU), 484 Upper Edward St, 5 min walk city centre, ☎ 07 3831 2967, fax 07 3832 2932, (2 stry gr fl), 12 units acc up to 5, [shwr, bath, tlt, a/c-cool, fan, heat, tel, TV, t/c mkg, refrig, cook fac, micro, elec frypan, blkts, linen, pillows], ldry, cots. **D ⚹ $66, ⚹⚹ $77, $11**, ch con, AE BC DC EFT MC VI.

★★☆ SDK Central Apartments, (SA), 28 Fortescue St, Spring Hill ☎ 07 3832 3000, fax 07 3832 1842, (Multi-stry), 12 serv apts acc up to 3, (Studio & 1 bedrm), [shwr, tlt, a/c, tel, TV, refrig, cook fac, ldry (in unit)], lift, secure park. **D $89 - $109**, Min book applies, AE BC DC MC VI.

B&B's/Guest Houses

★★★★☆ Hawkesbury House Health, (B&B), 60 Hawkesbury Rd, Moggill, 35km SW of PO, ☎ 07 3202 9415, (2 stry gr fl), 3 rms [ensuite, a/c, cent heat, elec blkts, TV (2), video (2), clock radio, t/c mkg, doonas], ldry, lounge (cable TV), conf fac, lounge firepl, pool, sauna, refrig, bbq, golf, gym, tennis, non smoking property. **BB ⚹⚹ $190 - $240**, AE BC DC MC VI.

★★★★ Thornbury House, (B&B), 1 Thornbury St, Spring Hill, 1km N GPO, ☎ 07 3832 5985, fax 07 3832 7255, (Multi-stry gr fl), 6 rms [ensuite (3), a/c-cool, c/fan (5), heat, elec blkts (3), TV, clock radio (2), micro], bathrm (3), ldry, t/c mkg shared, refrig, ☎, non smoking rms (1). **BB ⚹ $77, ⚹⚹ $99, $20**, ch con, AE BC MC VI.

★★★ Annies Shandon Inn, (B&B), 405 Upper Edward St, ☎ 07 3831 8684, fax 07 3831 3073, (Multi-stry gr fl), 19 rms [ensuite (4), shwr (4), tlt (4), c/fan, heat], shwr, tlt, ldry, lounge (TV, airc), t/c mkg shared, c/park (limited) (4), ☎. **BB ⚹ $44 - $55, ⚹⚹ $55 - $66**, AE BC MC VI.

★★★ Gabba Guesthouse, (B&B), 18 Withington St, East Brisbane, ☎ 07 3392 3126, 1 rm [ensuite, hairdry, fan, TV, clock radio, t/c mkg, refrig, toaster], iron, iron brd, rec rm, lounge, pool (saltwater), spa, ☎, non smoking rms. **D ⚹ $40 - $50, ⚹⚹ $50 - $65**, Min book applies.

★★★ Ruth Fairfax House - QCWA Club, (B&B), 89 Gregory Tce, 1km from GPO, ☎ 07 3831 8188, (Multi-stry), 37 rms [basin, fan], lift, shwr, tlt, ldry, dryer, lounge (2 with TV), t/c mkg shared, refrig, ☎, cots-fee. **BB ⚹ $47, ⚹⚹ $65, ⚹ W $308, ⚹⚹ $427**, ch con, No off-street parking.

★★ Acacia Inner City Inn, (B&B), 413 Upper Edward St, ☎ 07 3832 1663, fax 07 3832 2591, (Multi-stry gr fl), 55 rms [shwr (3), tlt (3), a/c-cool (3), fan, TV-fee, t/c mkg (10)], shwr, tlt, ldry, lounge (TV), c/park (limited) (5), ☎. **BB ⚹ $40 - $70, ⚹⚹ $50 - $70, $15**, AE BC DC JCB MC VI.

Other Accommodation
New Brisbane City YHA, (Lodge), 392 Upper Roma St, 2km W of GPO, ☎ 07 3236 1004, fax 07 3236 1947, (2 stry), 52 rms acc up to 6, [ensuite (4), a/c (41), fan (13), linen], shwr, tlt, ldry, lounge (TV), ✗, cafe, cook fac, t/c mkg shared, refrig, c/park (limited), ☎. **D ⚹ $40 - $56, ⚹⚹ $40 - $56**, BC EFT JCB MC VI, ♿.

BRISBANE - ACACIA RIDGE QLD 4110

Pop 7,115. (15km S Brisbane), See map on page 418, ref C6. Residential suburb of Brisbane.

Hotels/Motels
★★★☆ Coopers Colonial Motor Inn, (M), 1260 Beaudesert Rd, 12km S of GPO, ☎ 07 3875 1874, fax 07 3275 1772, (2 stry gr fl), 42 units (3 suites) [shwr, spa bath (9), tlt, hairdry, a/c, tel, TV, video-fee, clock radio, t/c mkg, refrig, cook fac ltd (35), micro (35), toaster], ldry, conv fac, ✗ (Mon to Sat), pool, spa, dinner to unit, cots, non smoking units (avail). **RO ⚹ $82 - $100, ⚹⚹ $87 - $110, ⚹ $5**, ch con, AE BC DC MC VI, ♿.

★★☆ Acacia Ridge Functions & Convention Centre, (LMH), 1386 Beaudesert Rd, ☎ 07 3275 1444, fax 07 3277 8987, (2 stry gr fl), 27 units [shwr, tlt, a/c, tel, fax, TV, clock radio, t/c mkg, refrig], rec rm, conv fac, ✗ (Mon-Sat), ☎, cots-fee. **RO ⚹ $60, ⚹⚹ $71, ⚹⚹⚹ $82**, AE BC DC EFT MC VI, ♿.

B&B's/Guest Houses
★★★★☆ Grovely House, (GH), 1A Torrisi Tce, Stanthorpe 4380, 1.5km SW of PO, ☎ 07 4681 0484, fax 07 4681 0485, (2 stry gr fl), 4 rms [ensuite, heat, elec blkts, clock radio, doonas], lounge (cable TV, video), lounge firepl, t/c mkg shared, refrig, c/park (undercover), non smoking property. **BB ⚹ $115 - $145, ⚹⚹ $130 - $165**, BC EFT MC VI.

BRISBANE - ALBION QLD 4010

Pop 2,300. (8km N Brisbane), See map on page 418, ref C4. Suburb of Brisbane.

★★★★ **AAA Airport Albion Manor Apartments & Motel**, (M), Cnr Sandgate Rd & Camden St, 4km N of GPO, ☎ 07 3256 0444, fax 07 3256 0810, (2 stry), 17 units (2 suites) [shwr, tlt, hairdry, a/c, tel, TV, clock radio, t/c mkg, refrig, cook fac, micro, toaster, ldry-fee], dryer-fee, iron, iron brd, pool (saltwater), bbq, cots-fee. RO ♦ **$82.50**, ♦♦ **$86.90**, Suite RO ⊘ **$126.50**, ch con, AE BC DC MC VI, ⅙.

BRISBANE - ALEXANDRA HILLS QLD 4161

Pop 16,859. (25km E Brisbane), See map on page 418, ref E6. Outer Brisbane suburb overlooking bayside area.

★★★ **McGuires Alexandra Hills Hotel & Motel**, (LMH), Cnr Finucane & McDonald Rds, ☎ 07 3824 4444, fax 07 3824 4979, 12 units [shwr, tlt, a/c, tel, TV, clock radio, t/c mkg, refrig], conv fac, night club (Fri), ⊠, rm serv, c/park (undercover), cots. RO ♦ **$75**, ♦♦ **$75**, ⊘ **$15**, ch con, AE BC DC EFT JCB MC VI.

BRISBANE - ANNERLEY QLD 4103

Pop 8,871. (6km S Brisbane), See map on page 418, ref C5. Suburb of Brisbane.

AAA
TOURISM
Special Rates

★★★☆ **Annerley Motor Inn**, (M), 591 Ipswich Rd, ☎ 07 3892 1500, fax 07 3892 1703, (2 stry gr fl), 24 units (1 suite) [shwr, spa bath (1), tlt, hairdry (19), a/c, tel, fax (2), TV, clock radio, t/c mkg, refrig, mini bar, cook fac ltd (7)], ldry, conv fac, res liquor license, pool, bbq, rm serv, dinner to unit (Tue to Sat), c/park (undercover) (6), plygr, cots-fee, non smoking units (10). RO ♦ **$66 - $70**, ♦♦ **$68 - $75.50**, ⊘ **$10**, Suite RO **$95**, ch con, AE BC DC EFT MC VI.

★★★☆ **Lancaster Court**, (M), 521 Ipswich Rd, ☎ 07 3892 5700, fax 07 3848 6907, (2 stry gr fl), 15 units [shwr, tlt, hairdry (4 avail), a/c, tel, TV, clock radio, t/c mkg, refrig], pool (salt water), dinner to unit, c/park (undercover), cots-fee. RO ♦ **$71.50**, ♦♦ **$77**, ⊘ **$11**, AE BC DC EFT MC VI.

Self Catering Accommodation

★★★☆ **Cornwall Crest Apartments**, (HU), 63 Cornwall St, between Annerley & Ipswich Rds Opp P A Hospital, ☎ 07 3891 2411, fax 07 3891 2262, 5 units acc up to 6, (1 bedrm), [shwr, tlt, a/c (3), c/fan, tel, TV, clock radio, refrig, cook fac, micro, ldry (in unit)], dryer (3), iron, c/park (undercover), cots. D ♦♦♦ **$82.50 - $99**, ⊘ **$8**, W ♦♦♦ **$462 - $580**, ch con, BC MC VI.

B&B's/Guest Houses

★★★★ **Ridge Haven Bed & Breakfast**, (B&B), 374 Annerley Rd, 4km SE of GPO, ☎ 07 3391 7702, fax 07 3392 1786, 2 rms [shwr, tlt, hairdry, c/fan (1), t/c mkg, cook fac, ldry-fee], iron, iron brd, TV rm, lounge (Guest), bbq, c/park. BB ♦ **$85**, ♦♦ **$99**.

Don't Tailgate

Look Ahead! The closer you are to the car in front, the less you are able to see the road ahead, particularly when following large vehicles. Improve your view of the road ahead by increasing the distance between your vehicle and the one in front.

BRISBANE - ASCOT QLD 4007

Pop 4,821. (6km N Brisbane), See map on page 418, ref C4.

Hotels/Motels

★★★☆ **Airport 85**, (M), 40 Lamington Ave, 5km W of Airport, ☎ 07 3268 4966, fax 07 3268 3396, (2 stry gr fl), 25 units (1 & 2 bedrm), [shwr, bath (11), tlt, a/c, heat, tel, TV, clock radio, t/c mkg, refrig], ldry, iron, iron brd, ✕, pool, spa, rm serv, courtesy transfer-fee, cots. BLB ♦ **$88**, ♦♦ **$93.50**, ⊘ **$11**, ch con, AE BC DC EFT JCB MC VI, ⅙.

GOLDEN CHAIN

★★★☆ **Airport Ascot Motel**, (M), 99 Racecourse Rd, 4km W of airport, ☎ 07 3268 5266, fax 07 3268 5356, (2 stry gr fl), 20 units (1 suite) [shwr, spa bath (1), tlt, a/c, tel, TV, video (1), clock radio, t/c mkg, refrig], ldry, pool, rm serv, cots. RO ♦ **$79 - $87**, ♦♦ **$84 - $93**, Suite RO ♦ **$100 - $110**, ♦♦ **$100 - $110**, fam con, AE BC BTC DC EFT MC VI.

★★★ **Airway Motel**, (M), 6 Lamington Ave, 6km W of Airport, ☎ 07 3268 2457, fax 07 3868 1383, (2 stry gr fl), 21 units [shwr, bath (1), tlt, a/c-cool, heat, tel, TV, radio, t/c mkg, refrig, ldry], pool, dinner to unit (breakfast), c/park (undercover) (9), courtesy transfer (1 per only), cots-fee. RO ♦ **$75**, ♦♦ **$75**, ⊘ **$11**, ch con, AE BC BTC DC MC VI.

Self Catering Accommodation

★★★★ **Quest Ascot**, (SA), Cnr Duke St & Lancaster Rd, ☎ 07 3630 0400, fax 07 3630 3401, (2 stry gr fl), 24 serv apts acc up to 6, (Studio, 1 & 2 bedrm), [ensuite (14), shwr, bath (13), tlt, a/c, c/fan, tel (direct dial), TV, refrig, cook fac ltd (14), micro, toaster, ldry (13), blkts, linen, pillows], ldry, dryer (13), iron, iron brd, pool (saltwater), sauna, spa, bbq, c/park (undercover), cots-fee. RO ♦ **$86 - $162**, ♦♦ **$111 - $131**, AE BC DC MC VI.

★★☆ **Ascot Holiday Apartments**, (HU), 72 Racecourse Rd, 6 km W of Airport, ☎ 07 3268 6366, fax 07 3216 4140, (2 stry gr fl), 12 units (2 & 3 bedrm), [shwr, bath, tlt, fan, tel, TV, refrig, cook fac, blkts, linen, pillows], ldry, cots. RO ♦ **$60.50**, ♦♦ **$66**, W **$363 - $396**, AE BC DC EFT MC VI.

B&B's/Guest Houses

★★★☆ **Cheshunt House B & B**, (B&B), 259 Lancaster Rd, 100m E of Eagle Farm race course, ☎ 07 3268 4603, (2 stry), 2 rms [shwr, tlt, c/fan, tel, cable tv, video, clock radio], ldry, TV rm, lounge (cable TV, video), lounge firepl, t/c mkg shared, refrig, bbq, non smoking rms. BB ♦ **$55**, ♦♦ **$90**, ⊘ **$30**, ch con, BC MC VI, ⅙.

★★ **Ascot Budget Inn**, (B&B), 143 Nudgee Rd, 7km W of Airport, ☎ 07 3268 2823, fax 07 3268 4384, (2 stry gr fl), 10 rms [basin, a/c-cool, TV, t/c mkg, refrig], shwr, tlt, ldry, lounge (TV), ✕, cook fac, refrig, ☎, cots-fee. BB ♦ **$59**, ♦♦ **$64**, ♦ **$147 - $325**, ♦♦ **$292 - $358**, AE BC BTC DC EFT MC VI.

BRISBANE - ASPLEY QLD 4034

Pop 11,030. (6km N Brisbane), See map on page 418, ref C4.

Hotels/Motels

★★★☆ **Aspley Motor Inn**, (M), 1159 Gympie Rd, ☎ 07 3263 5400, fax 07 3263 5127, 17 units [shwr, tlt, a/c, heat, tel, TV, clock radio, t/c mkg, refrig, cook fac ltd (5), micro (6), toaster], ✕ (Mon-Frid), pool, bbq, dinner to unit, cots-fee, non smoking rms (8). RO ♦ **$65 - $75**, ♦♦ **$75 - $90**, ⊘ **$11**, ch con, AE BC DC JCB MC MP VI, ⅙.

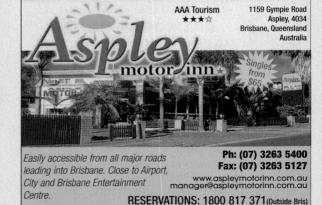

★★★ **Aspley Pioneer Motel**, (M), 794 Zillmere Rd,
☎ 07 3263 6122, fax 07 3263 6714, 15 units [shwr,
bath (1), tlt, a/c, tel, TV, movie, clock radio, t/c mkg,
refrig, toaster], pool, spa, bbq, cots. **RO** ♦ **$65**, ♦♦ **$70**,
♦ **$10**, AE BC DC EFT MC VI.

★★☆ **Alpha Motel**, (M), 1434 Gympie Rd, ☎ 07 3263 4011,
fax 07 3263 5150, 17 units [shwr, tlt, a/c-cool, c/fan, heat, tel, TV,
clock radio, t/c mkg, refrig, micro (8), toaster], ldry-fee, dryer-fee, ⊠,
rm serv, dinner to unit, courtesy transfer (hospital visitors), ☏, cots.
RO ♦ **$57**, ♦♦ **$60**, ♦ **$7**, ch con, AE BC DC MC VI.

★★☆ **Aspley Laurel**, (M), Cnr Darwin St & Gympie Rd,
☎ 07 3263 4322, fax 07 3862 9106, 12 units [shwr, tlt, a/c, c/fan,
heat, tel, TV, clock radio, t/c mkg, refrig, micro-fee], ldry, pool (salt
water), bbq, cots-fee. **RO** ♦ **$60**, ♦♦ **$66 - $72**, ♦ **$12**, AE BC DC MC VI.

BRISBANE - AUCHENFLOWER QLD 4066

Pop Part of Brisbane, (3km S Brisbane), See map on page 418, ref C5.
Hotels/Motels
★★★★ **Inn on the Park**, (M), 507 Coronation Dve Cnr Patrick Ln,
Toowong , ☎ 07 3870 9222, fax 07 3870 2246, (2 stry gr fl),
32 units (8 suites) [shwr, bath, tlt, a/c, tel, TV, clock radio, t/c mkg,
refrig, cook fac (8)], ldry, conv fac, ⊠, pool, c/park (undercover), cots.
RO ♦ **$130**, ♦♦ **$130**, **Suite RO $160**, AE BC DC MC VI.

Self Catering Accommodation
★★★★☆ **Fairthorpe Apartments**, (HU), 56 Dunmore Tce, 3km W of GPO,
250m fr Wesley Hospital, ☎ 07 3870 2777, fax 07 3870 5128,
(Multi-stry gr fl), 13 units acc up to 6, (2 bedrm), [shwr, bath, tlt, a/c,
tel, TV, clock radio, refrig, cook fac, micro, d/wash, toaster, ldry (in unit),
blkts, linen, pillows], lift, dryer, iron, pool (salt water), bbq,
c/park (undercover), secure park, tennis, cots-fee. **D** ♦♦ **$120**, ♦♦♦♦ **$140**,
W ♦♦ **$725**, ♦♦♦♦ **$800**, BC MC VI.

★★★★ **Metro Suites Milton Brisbane**,
(SA), 435 Coronation Dve, 2km SW of
Brisbane CBD opposite Wesley Hospital,
☎ 07 3217 8266, fax 07 3217 8299,
(Multi-stry), 35 serv apts acc up to 5, (1 & 2 bedrm), [shwr, bath, tlt,
a/c, tel, TV, movie, clock radio, refrig, cook fac, micro, ldry (in unit)],
lift, dryer, iron, sauna, spa, c/park (undercover), cots. **D $70 - $141**,
weekly con, AE BC DC EFT MC VI.

★★★☆ **Auchenflower Gardens**, (Apt), 39 Park Ave, 1km NW Wesley
Hospital, 2.5km fr CBD, ☎ 07 3870 8411, fax 07 3870 7664, (2 stry
gr fl), 22 apts acc up to 4, (Studio), [shwr, bath (21), tlt, hairdry, a/c,
tel, TV, clock radio, refrig, cook fac ltd (22), micro, elec frypan],
ldry-fee, dryer-fee, pool (salt water), bbq, secure park, non smoking
property. **BLB** ♦♦ **$75**, ♦ **$10**, ch con, AE BC DC EFT MC VI.

★★★ **Wesley Apartments**, (Apt), 420 Milton Rd, Cnr Ridley St, 1km E
of Wesley Hospital, ☎ 07 3870 7713, fax 07 3871 3984, 5 apts acc up
to 3, (Studio & 1 bedrm), [shwr, tlt, a/c-cool, c/fan, heat, tel, TV,
radio, CD, refrig, cook fac, blkts, linen, pillows], ldry, dryer,
c/park (undercover). **D $65 - $70**, BC MC VI.

BRISBANE - BALD HILLS QLD 4036

Pop 5,634. (18km N Brisbane), See map on page 418, ref C3.

★★☆ **Bald Hills**, (M), Cnr Gympie &
Telegraph Rds, ☎ 07 3261 1618,
fax 07 3261 2019, 6 units [shwr, tlt, a/c,
tel, TV, clock radio, t/c mkg, refrig], ldry,
pool, bbq, cots. **RO** ♦ **$55**, ♦♦ **$65**, ♦ **$10**,
ch con, AE BC DC EFT MC VI.

BRISBANE - BARDON QLD 4065

*Pop Part of Brisbane. (6km W Brisbane) See map on page 418, ref
B5. Situated at the base out Mount Cootha.*

Hotels/Motels
★★★★ **The Bardon Centre**, (M), 390 Simpsons Rd, 6km NW of GPO,
☎ 07 3217 5333, fax 07 3367 1350, (Multi-stry gr fl), 77 units [shwr,
tlt, a/c, heat, tel, TV, clock radio, t/c mkg, refrig, cook fac ltd], ldry,
dryer, rec rm, conv fac, ⊠, bar, pool (salt water), spa, bbq, rm serv,
dinner to unit, meals avail, gym, cots. **BB** ♦ **$81 - $124**, ♦♦ **$97 - $147**,
♦ **$16.50**, AE BC DC MC VI.

B&B's/Guest Houses
★★★★☆ **Tigh-na-Fios**, (B&B), 12 Leworthy St, 5km W of Brisbane PO,
☎ 07 3369 0111, fax 07 3369 4295, 2 rms [shwr (2), spa bath (1),
tlt (2), hairdry (1), a/c, fan, heat, tel, TV (1), video (1), clock radio,
t/c mkg, refrig (1), cook fac ltd, micro (1), toaster (1)], ldry, dryer,
iron (1), iron brd (1), lounge, c/park. **BB** ♦ **$70 - $80**, ♦♦ **$90 - $110**,
BC MC VI.

BRISBANE - BEENLEIGH QLD 4207

*Pop 8,108. (38km S Brisbane), See map on page 418, ref D8.
Satellite town on southern outskirts of Brisbane. Home of Australia's
oldest rum distillery, established in 1884. Beenleigh Rum Distillery.*

★★★ **Beenleigh Village Motel**, (M), 49 City Rd, 800m E of PO, Exit 34
Benleigh North City Road, ☎ 07 3807 3122, fax 07 3807 4903, 12 units
[shwr, tlt, a/c, tel, TV, clock radio, t/c mkg, refrig], pool, c/park (undercover),
cots-fee. **RO** ♦ **$65 - $75**, ♦♦ **$75 - $85**, ♦ **$11**, ch con, AE BC DC MC VI.

BRISBANE - BIRKDALE QLD 4159

*Pop 11,335. (26km SE Brisbane), See map on page 418, ref E5.
Outer suburb of Brisbane.*

★★★★ **Glentrace Bed & Breakfast**, (B&B), 3 Whitehall Ave, 17km E
Bne City 11km from Cleveland, ☎ 07 3207 4442, fax 07 3207 4442,
3 rms [ensuite (2), shwr, tlt, a/c, TV (1), t/c mkg (1), refrig (1)],
lounge (TV), ✗, t/c mkg shared, refrig, secure park, cots-fee,
non smoking rms. **BB** ♦ **$55 - $75**, ♦♦ **$70 - $80**, ♦ **$15**, ch con,
AE BC DC MC VI.

BRISBANE - BOONDALL QLD 4034

*Pop 6,883. (15km N Brisbane), See map on page 418, ref D3.
Suburb of Brisbane.*

Hotels/Motels
★★★ **Boondall**, (M), 2092 Sandgate Rd, ☎ 07 3265 1722, 6 units
[shwr, tlt, a/c, fan, tel, TV, clock radio, t/c mkg, refrig], ldry,
pool-heated, bbq, cots. **RO** ♦ **$55 - $66**, ♦♦ **$60.50 - $75**, ♦ **$11**, ch con,
AE BC DC MC VI.

Self Catering Accommodation
★★★★ **Virginia Palms Resort & Conference Centre**, (Villa),
Cnr Sandgate & Zillmere Rds, ☎ 07 3265 7066, fax 07 3865 1735,
85 villas (11 suites) acc up to 4, [shwr, bath (15), spa bath (15), tlt,
a/c, fan, tel, TV, movie, clock radio, t/c mkg, refrig, cook fac (28),
micro (11)], ldry, business centre, conf fac, ⊠ (Mon-Sun), bar, pool (2),
sauna, spa, rm serv, dinner to unit, cots-fee. **RO** ♦ **$115 - $165**,
♦♦ **$121 - $165**, ♦ **$15**, ch con, AE BC DC MC VI, ♿.

BRISBANE - BURANDA QLD 4102

*Pop Part of Brisbane, (5km S Brisbane), See map on page 418, ref
C5. Suburb of Brisbane.*

Hotels/Motels
★★☆ **Tottenham Court Motel**, (M), Cnr Tottenham & Wolseley Sts,
200m E of Princess Alexandra Hospital, ☎ 07 3391 0081,
fax 07 3391 0087, 23 units [shwr, tlt, c/fan, tel, TV, clock radio,
t/c mkg, refrig, micro, elec frypan, toaster], ldry-fee, dryer-fee, bbq.
RO ♦ **$44**, ♦♦ **$72**, ♦ **$10**, ch con, AE BC DC EFT MC VI.

Self Catering Accommodation
★★☆ **Alexandra Apartments**, (SA), 240 Ipswich Rd, opposite Princess
Alexandra Hospital, ☎ 07 3335 6600, fax 07 3391 7909, (Multi-stry),
33 serv apts acc up to 4, [shwr, tlt, fan, heat, tel, TV, clock radio,
refrig, cook fac, micro (6), ldry (in unit), blkts, linen, pillows], lift,
c/park (undercover), secure park. **D** ♦♦ **$59 - $79**, ♦ **$10**, ch con,
Units 21 to 36 ★★★☆. AE BC DC EFT MC MP VI, ♿.

★★★★ **(Serviced Apartment Section)**, 16 serv apts acc up to 6,
(1 & 2 bedrm), [shwr (4), bath (8), spa bath (4), tlt, hairdry, a/c,
c/fan, heat, tel, TV, clock radio, refrig, cook fac, micro, toaster, ldry,
blkts, linen, pillows], dryer, iron, iron brd, bbq, secure park.
RO $59 - $79, 3 types of accomoodation.

★★☆ **Wolseley Court**, (HU), 40 Wolseley St, ☎ 07 3891 5616,
fax 07 3366 3819, 6 units acc up to 6, (1 & 2 bedrm), [shwr, tlt, a/c,
fan, heat, tel, TV, t/c mkg, refrig, cook fac, micro (6), ldry (in unit),
blkts, linen, pillows], bbq, c/park (undercover). **D** ♦♦ **$60**, ♦ **$10**,
Min book applies, BC MC VI.

BRISBANE - CALAMVALE QLD 4116

Pop 5,396. (19km S Brisbane), See map on page 418, ref C6. Outer suburb of Brisbane.

★★☆ **McGuires Calamvale Hotel & Motel**, (LMH), Cnr Compton & Beaudesert Rds, ☎ 07 3273 4777, fax 07 3273 5661, 17 units [shwr, bath (1), tlt, a/c-cool, heat, tel, TV, clock radio, t/c mkg, refrig], night club, ⊠ (Fri & Sat/buffet), rm serv, ✆. **BB** ⊠ **$82.50**, ⊠ **$82.50**, ⊠ **$22.50**, **RO** ⊠ **$75**, ⊠ **$75**, ⊠ **$15**, AE BC DC EFT MC VI, ⅋⅁.

BRISBANE - CARINDALE QLD 4152

Pop 10,750. (9km E Brisbane), See map on page 418, ref D5. Suburb of Brisbane. Golf.

★★★☆ **Hotel Carindale**, (LH), Carindale St, Behind Carindale Shopping Centre, ☎ 07 3395 0122, fax 07 3398 6920, (Multi-stry), 59 rms (4 suites) [shwr, bath, tlt, a/c, tel, TV, clock radio, t/c mkg, refrig, mini bar], lift, ldry, dryer, ⊠, bar, 24hr reception, ✆, cots. **RO** ⊠ **$98**, ⊠ **$98**, ⊠ **$11**, **Suite D $120 - $136**, ch con, AE BC DC EFT JCB MC VI, ⅋⅁.

BRISBANE - CARSELDINE QLD 4034

Pop 5,572. (14km N Brisbane), See map on page 418, ref C3. Outer suburb of Brisbane.

Hotels/Motels

★★★★ **Carseldine Court**, (M), 1549 Gympie Rd, ☎ 07 3263 5988, fax 07 3862 9744, 21 units [shwr, tlt, a/c, c/fan, heat, tel, TV, clock radio, t/c mkg, refrig, cook fac ltd (4)], ldry, pool, spa (7), bbq, cots-fee. **RO** ⊠ **$65**, ⊠ **$74 - $80**, ⊠ **$9**, AE BC DC EFT MC VI.

★★★ **Carseldine Palms Motel**, (M), Cnr Gympie & Denver Rds, ☎ 07 3263 2255, fax 07 3263 2754, 56 units [shwr, bath (6), spa bath (7), tlt, a/c, tel, TV, clock radio, t/c mkg, refrig, cook fac ltd (11), micro (5)], ldry, conv fac, ⊠ (Mon to Sat), pool (salt water) (2), wading pool, dinner to unit, cots-fee, non smoking rms. **RO** ⊠ **$82 - $95**, ⊠ **$88 - $101**, ⊠ **$10**, ch con, AE BC DC MC VI, ⅋⅁.

BRISBANE - CHERMSIDE QLD 4032

Pop 6,271. (9km N Brisbane), See map on page 418, ref C4. Suburb of Brisbane.

Hotels/Motels

AAA TOURISM *Special Rates* ★★★★ **Chermside Motor Inn**, (M), 644 Gympie Rd, close Prince Charles Hospital & Kedron Wavell RSL, ☎ 07 3359 9255, fax 07 3359 8572, (2 stry gr fl), 22 units [shwr, tlt, a/c, tel, cable tv, video, t/c mkg, refrig, cook fac (3), ldry], pool, cook fac-fee, bbq, dinner to unit, plygr, cots-fee, non smoking units (14). **RO** ⊠ **$69 - $99**, ⊠ **$79 - $99**, ⊠ **$11**, ch con, AE BC DC EFT MC MP VI, ⅋⅁.

★★★ **Chermside Court**, (M), Cnr Farnell & Sparkes Sts, 500m NE PO & shopping centre, ☎ 07 3359 3988, fax 07 3359 4727, (2 stry gr fl), 16 units [shwr, tlt, a/c-cool (10), fan, heat, tel, TV, clock radio, t/c mkg, refrig, cook fac ltd, micro, elec frypan, toaster], ldry, lounge, bbq. **RO** ⊠ **$67**, ⊠ **$79**, ⊠ **$11**, **W** ⊠ **$460**, ⊠ **$518**, ⊠ **$46**, ch con, AE BC DC MC VI.

★★★ **Chermside Green**, (M), 949 Gympie Rd, ☎ 07 3359 1041, fax 07 3359 5952, (2 stry gr fl), 47 units [shwr, tlt, a/c, tel, TV, movie, clock radio, t/c mkg, refrig, mini bar, toaster], ldry, ⊠, pool, bbq, rm serv, dinner to unit, c/park (undercover) (22), cots-fee, non smoking units (20). **RO** ⊠ **$76 - $82**, ⊠ **$82 - $87**, ⊠ **$15**, ch con, Units 215 to 230 ★★★☆. AE BC DC EFT MC VI.

Self Catering Accommodation

★★★★ **Prince Charm Court**, (HU), 64 Hilltop Avenue, adjoins Prince Charles Hospital, ☎ 07 3350 2072, fax 07 3256 3922, (2 stry), 6 units acc up to 6, (2 bedrm), [shwr, bath, tlt, fan, TV, video, clock radio, refrig, micro, elec frypan, toaster, ldry, blkts, linen, pillows], dryer, iron, iron brd, secure park, cots-fee, non smoking units. **D** ⊠ **$70 - $85**, ⊠ **$10**, **W** ⊠ **$490**, ⊠ **$70**, Min book applies.

BRISBANE - CLAYFIELD QLD 4011

Pop 9,400. (7km N Brisbane), See map on page 418, ref C4. Metropolitan suburb of Brisbane.

Hotels/Motels

★★★☆ **Airport Clayfield Motel**, (M), 772 Sandgate Rd, 5km W of Airport, ☎ 07 3862 2966, fax 07 3862 2967, (Multi-stry), 22 units (1 suite) [shwr, bath (6), spa bath (1), tlt, hairdry, a/c, c/fan, tel, TV, video-fee, clock radio, t/c mkg, refrig], ldry, dryer, iron, pool (salt water), bbq, c/park (undercover), cots-fee, non smoking units (4). **RO** ⊠ **$67**, ⊠ **$75**, ⊠ **$10**, **Suite D $105**, AE BC DC MC VI.

★★★☆ **Bellevue Terrace**, (M), 592 Sandgate Rd, ☎ 07 3862 4065, fax 07 3862 4075, (2 stry gr fl), 27 units [shwr, tlt, a/c-cool, fan, heat, tel, TV, video-fee, clock radio, t/c mkg, refrig, cook fac ltd, micro, elec frypan, toaster], ldry, pool (salt water), bbq, c/park (undercover), cots-fee, non smoking units (5). **RO** ⊠ **$71.50**, ⊠ **$82.50**, ⊠ **$11**, AE BC DC EFT MC VI, ⅋⅁.

★★★☆ **(Serviced Apartment Section)**, 9 serv apts acc up to 4, (1 & 2 bedrm), [shwr, tlt, a/c-cool, tel, TV, clock radio, refrig, cook fac, micro, toaster, blkts, linen, pillows], dryer, iron, iron brd, pool (saltwater), bbq, c/park (undercover), gym. **D $99 - $132**, **W $462 - $589**.

★★★ **Turrawan Lodge**, (M), 657 Sandgate Rd, opposite Clayfield College, ☎ 07 3262 3811, fax 07 3262 8710, (Multi-stry gr fl), 11 units [shwr, tlt, a/c, tel, TV, radio, t/c mkg, refrig, micro], ldry, cook fac, c/park (undercover) (4), courtesy transfer (7am - 6pm), cots-fee, non smoking units. **BLB** ⊠ **$60**, ⊠ **$60**, ⊠ **$10**, AE BC DC EFT MC VI, ⅋⅁.

BRISBANE - CLEAR MOUNTAIN QLD 4500

Pop 407. (26km NW Brisbane), See map on page 418, ref B3. Outer suburb of Brisbane. Bush Walking.

★★★★ **Clear Mountain Health & Conference Centre**, (M), Resort, Clear Mountain Rd, ☎ 07 3298 5100, fax 07 3298 5435, 53 units [ensuite, shwr, tlt, fan, heat, tel, cable tv, video, clock radio, t/c mkg, refrig], ldry, rec rm, conv fac, ⊠, pool (salt water), sauna, bbq, bush walking, gym, tennis, non smoking property. **D all meals ▮ $170, ▮▮ $290,** Tariff includes massage and beauty treatments. AE BC DC EFT MC VI, ⟨&⟩.

BRISBANE - CLEVELAND QLD 4163

Pop 11,092. (26km E Brisbane), See map on page 418, ref E6. Outer bayside suburb of Brisbane.

Hotels/Motels

★★★★ **Pacific Resort Motel**, (M), 128 Middle St, 25 km E from GPO Brisbane, ☎ 07 3286 2088, fax 07 3286 7189, units (4 suites) [a/c, tel, TV, video, clock radio, t/c mkg, refrig, ldry], ✕, ⊠, pool-heated, sauna, cots-fee, non smoking rms (16). **RO ▮ $100, ▮▮ $100, ◗ $10, Suite RO $200,** ch con, AE BC DC EFT MC VI.

★★★☆ **Cleveland Motor Inn**, (M), Horation & Gordon Sts, Ormiston, 800m NW of Cleveland PO, ☎ 07 3286 3911, fax 07 3821 3033, 12 units [shwr, tlt, hairdry (7), a/c-cool (8), a/c (4), c/fan (5), heat, tel, TV, video-fee, clock radio, t/c mkg, refrig, cook fac (2), micro-fee, toaster], ldry, pool (salt water), bbq, rm serv, cots-fee, non smoking rms (4). **RO ▮ $60 - $71, ▮▮ $72 - $85, ◗ $11.50,** ch con, AE BC DC EFT MC VI.

★★★ **Cleveland Bay Air**, (M), 220 Middle St, ☎ 07 3286 2488, (Multi-stry gr fl), 17 units [shwr, tlt, a/c (5), c/fan (9), tel, TV, clock radio, t/c mkg, refrig], ldry, w/mach-fee, dryer-fee, ⊠, pool, dinner to unit, cots-fee. **RO ▮ $50, ▮▮ $55, ◗ $10,** ch con, AE BC DC MC VI.

Self Catering Accommodation

★★★★ **Cleveland Visitor Villas Motel**, (HU), 214 Bloomfield St, ☎ 07 3286 5756, fax 07 3821 4169, 8 units acc up to 6, (2 bedrm - Split level accommodation available.), [shwr, bath, tlt, fan, heat, tel, TV, cook fac, ldry (in unit), blkts, linen, pillows], dryer, res liquor license, pool, c/park (undercover), cots. **W $560 - $796, RO ▮ $77, ▮▮ $88, ◗ $11 - $33,** ch con, AE BC DC EFT MC VI.

B&B's/Guest Houses

★★★ **Bay View B & B**, (B&B), 96 Smith St, 1km S of PO, ☎ 07 3821 2475, fax 07 3821 2475, (2 stry gr fl), 2 rms [c/fan, heat, tel, clock radio, micro, toaster, ldry], lounge (TV, video), pool, cook fac, t/c mkg shared, refrig, bbq, non smoking property. **BB ▮ $35, ▮▮ $70, ◗ $10,** ch con.

BRISBANE - DARRA QLD 4076

Pop 4,107. (18km W Brisbane), See map on page 418, ref B6. Suburb of Brisbane.

Hotels/Motels

★★★ **Darra Motor Inn**, (M), 2855 Ipswich Rd, ☎ 07 3375 5468, fax 07 3375 5590, 17 units [shwr, tlt, a/c, c/fan, tel, cable tv, video, clock radio, t/c mkg, refrig], ldry-fee, dryer-fee, ⊠, pool (salt water), bbq-fee, dinner to unit, courtesy transfer, plygr, cots. **RO ▮ $60.50, ▮▮ $66, ◗ $10,** AE BC DC EFT MC VI.

★★☆ **Darra Universe**, (M), 2704 Ipswich Rd, ☎ 07 3375 5047, fax 07 3375 4253, 19 units [shwr, bath (1), tlt, a/c-cool (15), c/fan, heat (6), elec blkts, tel, TV, movie, clock radio, t/c mkg, refrig], ldry-fee, dryer-fee, ✕ (Mon to Sat), pool (salt water), spa, bbq, c/park (undercover) (12), plygr, cots-fee. **RO ▮ $45, ▮▮ $50, ◗ $8,** ch con, AE BC DC MC VI.

BRISBANE - EAST BRISBANE QLD 4169

Pop 4,809. (3km E Brisbane), See map on page 418, ref C5. Inner residential & light industrial suburb.

Hotels/Motels

★★★★☆ **The Wellington Boutique Hotel**, (M), 192 Wellington Rd, 1.8 km SE of CBD, ☎ 07 3891 1988, fax 07 3891 2200, (Multi-stry gr fl), 45 units [shwr, spa bath, tlt, hairdry, a/c, tel, cable tv, clock radio, t/c mkg, refrig, cook fac ltd, micro, toaster], lift, ldry, dryer, iron, iron brd, ⊠, pool above ground, rm serv, secure park, cots-fee, non smoking units (17). **RO ▮ $94 - $170, ▮▮ $94 - $170,** ch con, AE BC DC EFT MC VI, ⟨&⟩.

BRISBANE - EIGHT MILE PLAINS QLD 4113

Pop 7,961. (11km N Brisbane), See map on page 418, ref C4.
Operator Comment: See Dress Circle Mobile Village advertisement on previous page.

BRISBANE - EVERTON PARK QLD 4053

Pop 7,961. (11km N Brisbane), See map on page 418, ref C4.

Hotels/Motels

★★☆ **Everton Park**, (LMH), 101 Flockton St, ☎ 07 3353 2300, fax 07 3353 4247, 12 units [shwr, bath, tlt, a/c, tel, TV, clock radio, t/c mkg, refrig], ldry, conv fac, ☒ (Mon to Sun), c/park (undercover), ☏, plygr, cots-fee. **D 👤 $60, 👥 $75**, ch con, AE BC DC MC VI.

B&B's/Guest Houses

★★★☆ **Bridges Bed & Breakfast**, (B&B), 36 Henderson Rd, 12km NW of GPO, ☎ 07 3353 2604, fax 07 3353 4239, 3 rms [a/c, fire pl, heat, elec blkts, TV, clock radio], lounge (TV), t/c mkg shared, c/park (undercover), non smoking rms. **BB 👤 $50, 👥 $66, 🧒 $10.**

BRISBANE - FORTITUDE VALLEY QLD 4006

Pop 1,446. (2km N Brisbane), See map on page 418, ref C5

Hotels/Motels

★★★★ **Central Brunswick Apartment Hotel**, (LMH), 455 Brunswick St, ☎ 07 3852 1411, fax 07 3852 1015, (Multi-stry), 80 units (65 suites) [shwr, bath, tlt, hairdry, a/c, tel, TV, clock radio, t/c mkg, refrig, mini bar, cook fac, micro, toaster], ldry, dryer, iron, iron brd, conf fac, ☒, sauna, spa, bbq (covered), rm serv, dinner to unit, c/park (undercover), gym, cots, non smoking flr (3). **D $94 - $120**, ch con, AE BC DC EFT MC VI.

★★ **Tourist Guest House**, (M), 555 Gregory Tce, 500m fr Royal Brisbane Hospital, ☎ 07 3252 4171, fax 07 3252 2704, (2 stry gr fl), 40 units [basin (25), shwr (15), tlt (15), a/c-cool (15), fan (25), TV, t/c mkg, refrig], shwr (25), tlt (25), ldry, cook fac, meals to unit (breakfast)-fee, c/park (undercover) (6), ☏, cots. **D $40 - $65**, ch con, BC MC VI.

Self Catering Accommodation

★★★★☆ **Medina Executive Brisbane**, (SA), 45 Kemp Place, 5km NE of city, ☎ 07 3218 5800, fax 07 3218 5805, (Multi-stry), 162 serv apts acc up to 6, (Studio, 1, 2 & 3 bedrm), [ensuite (8), shwr, bath, spa bath (10), tlt, hairdry, a/c, tel, TV, video, clock radio, refrig, mini bar, cook fac, micro, d/wash (100), toaster, ldry (100), blkts, linen, pillows], lift, dryer (100), iron, iron brd, conf fac, pool, sauna, spa, 24hr reception, secure park (under cover), ☏, gym, tennis, cots, non smoking flr (4), non smoking rms (76). **D $105 - $385**, AE BC DC MC VI.

★★★☆ **Fortune Court in The Mall**, (SA), 8 Duncan St, Chinatown Mall, Cnr Ann St, ☎ 07 3332 8888, fax 07 3216 0802, (Multi-stry), 36 serv apts acc up to 4, [shwr, spa bath, tlt, a/c, tel, TV (satelite), movie, clock radio, refrig, micro, toaster, ldry (in unit), blkts, linen, pillows], lift, iron, iron brd, sauna, bbq (covered), gym. **RO $135 - $190**, AE BC DC MC VI.

B&B's/Guest Houses

Brisbane's B&B, (B&B), 1033 Ann St, 500m S of Fortitude Valley Mall, ☎ 07 3852 2001, fax 07 3852 2025, 5 rms [a/c-cool, c/fan, cable tv, clock radio, refrig, doonas], ldry, t/c mkg shared, bbq, secure park, ☏, cots, non smoking property. **BB 👤 $77, 👥 $88, 🧒 $10**, ch con, AE BC DC MC VI, (not yet classified).

Other Accommodation

★★ **Balmoral House**, (Lodge), 33 Amelia St, ☎ 07 3252 1397, fax 07 3252 5892, (2 stry gr fl), 18 rms acc up to 5, [shwr (6), tlt (6), fan, TV], shwr, tlt, ldry, lounge (TV), cook fac, t/c mkg shared, refrig, ☏, cots. **D $28 - $50**, ch con, fam con, AE BC MC VI.

BRISBANE - GREENSLOPES QLD 4120

Pop 7,043. (5km S Brisbane), See map on page 418, ref C5. Suburb of Brisbane. Bowls.

FLAG CHOICE HOTELS

★★★☆ **Greenslopes Motor Inn**, (M), 389 Cornwall St, Cnr Dansie St, ☎ 07 3394 3066, fax 07 3394 2936, (2 stry), 18 units [shwr, tlt, hairdry, a/c, tel, TV, movie, clock radio, t/c mkg, refrig], ldry-fee, dryer-fee, lounge, ☒, pool, bbq, dinner to unit, c/park (undercover), cots-fee. **RO 👤 $50 - $71, 👥 $50 - $82, 🧒 $11**, ch con, AE BC DC EFT MC VI.

BRISBANE - HAMILTON QLD 4007

Pop 4,158. (6km NE Brisbane), See map on page 418, ref C4. Suburb of Brisbane.

Hotels/Motels

★★★★★ **Powerhouse Boutique Hotel**, (Ltd Lic H), Cnr Hunt St & Kingsford Smith Dve, 8km to airport, 2km S of PO, ☎ 07 3862 1800, fax 07 3862 1219, (Multi-stry), 90 rms (14 suites) [shwr, bath (76), spa bath (14), tlt, hairdry, a/c, tel, fax (photocopier), TV, movie, t/c mkg, refrig], lift, ldry, dryer, conv fac, ☒ (2), coffee shop, pool, sauna, spa, bbq, rm serv, c/park (undercover), ☏, gym, cots. **RO 👥 $182 - $253, Suite RO $215 - $341**, ch con, AE BC DC EFT MC MP VI.

FLAG CHOICE HOTELS

★★★★☆ **Airport International Motel**, (M), 528 Kingsford Smith Dve, 5km to airport, Gateway Arterial Motorway nearby, ☎ 07 3268 6388, fax 07 3268 7395, (2 stry gr fl), 36 units (8 suites) [shwr, tlt, hairdry, a/c, heat, tel, cable tv, clock radio, t/c mkg, refrig, mini bar, micro (4), toaster (4)], lift, ldry, dryer, iron, conv fac, ☒, bar, pool (salt water), rm serv, dinner to unit, c/park (undercover) (10), courtesy transfer, cots. **D 👤 $110 - $115, 👥 $115 - $135, Suite RO $125 - $135**, ch con, pen con, AE BC DC MC VI, ♿.

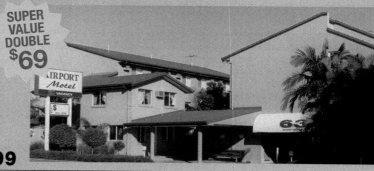

★★★★ **Airport**, (M), 638 Kingsford Smith Dve, 900m E of PO, 4km from airport, ☎ 07 3868 2399, fax 07 3868 2383, (2 stry gr fl), 33 units [shwr, bath (12), tlt, hairdry, a/c, tel, TV, clock radio, t/c mkg, refrig, cook fac (5)], ldry, dryer, dinner to unit, courtesy transfer (airport)-fee, non smoking rms (16). **RO** ♦ **$76 - $82**, ♦♦ **$76 - $82**, AE BC DC EFT MC VI.

★★★★ **Airport Admiralty**, (M), 95 Nudgee Rd, ☎ 07 3268 7899, fax 07 3268 4194, (2 stry gr fl), 38 units [shwr, spa bath (1), tlt, a/c, tel, TV, clock radio, t/c mkg, refrig, mini bar], ldry, dryer-fee, conv fac, ✗, bar, pool (salt water), bbq, rm serv, dinner to unit, c/park (undercover) (19), courtesy transfer (by arrangement)-fee, cots, non smoking rms. **RO** ♦ **$96.80**, ♦♦ **$103.40**, ch con, AE BC DC MC VI, 🐾.

★★★★ **Kingsford Smith**, (LH), 610 Kingsford Smith Dve, Cnr Nudgee Rd, ☎ 07 3868 4444, fax 07 3868 4555, (Multi-stry gr fl), 36 rms (36 suites) [shwr, spa bath (10), tlt, hairdry, a/c, tel, cable tv, movie, clock radio, t/c mkg, refrig, mini bar], lift, ldry-fee, dryer-fee, iron, iron brd, conv fac, bar, pool (salt water), bbq-fee, rm serv, dinner to unit, cots. **RO** ♦ **$110**, ♦♦ **$110**, ◊ **$16.50**, Suite D ♦♦ **$121**, ch con, fam con, AE BC DC EFT JCB MC VI, 🐾.

★★★★ **Pegasus Motor Inn**, (M), 71 Nudgee Rd, 5km from Airport, ☎ 07 3868 1900, fax 07 3868 1160, (2 stry gr fl), 27 units [basin, shwr, tlt, hairdry, a/c, tel, cable tv, clock radio, t/c mkg, refrig, mini bar], ldry-fee, dryer-fee, iron, iron brd, ✗ (Mon-Fri), pool-heated, spa, bbq (covered), rm serv, dinner to unit (Mon - Fri), secure park (undercover), cots-fee, non smoking units (8). **RO** ♦ **$99**, ♦♦ **$104**, ◊ **$10**, ch con, AE BC DC EFT MC VI, 🐾.

★★★★☆ **(Serviced Apartments)**, 20 serv apts acc up to 4, (1 bedrm), [ensuite, shwr, bath, tlt, hairdry, a/c, tel, cable tv, video, movie, clock radio, t/c mkg, refrig, micro, elec frypan, d/wash, blkts, linen, pillows], ldry, dryer, iron, iron brd, conv fac, ✗ (Mon-Fri), pool-heated (saltwater), sauna, spa, secure park (undercover), cots-fee. **RO** ♦ **$135**, ♦♦ **$135**, W **$750**.

★★★☆ **Airport Hamilton Hacienda**, (M), 560 Kingsford Smith Dve, 5km to airport, ☎ 07 3268 5011, fax 07 3268 5830, (Multi-stry gr fl), 42 units (1 suite) [shwr, bath (16), tlt, hairdry, a/c, tel, TV, clock radio, t/c mkg, refrig], ldry, dryer-fee, iron, iron brd, conv fac, ✗, pool, sauna, spa, dinner to unit, c/park (undercover) (23), gym, tennis, cots-fee. **RO** ♦ **$93**, ♦♦ **$98**, ch con, AE BC DC JCB MC MP VI, 🐾.

★★★☆ **Hamilton Motor Inn**, (M), 422 Kingsford Smith Dve, 5km to airport, ☎ 07 3268 5411, fax 07 3268 1979, (Multi-stry), 22 units (0 suites) [shwr, tlt, a/c, tel, TV, movie, clock radio, t/c mkg, refrig], lift, ldry, dryer-fee, conf fac, ✗, rm serv, c/park (undercover) (12), cots-fee. **RO** ♦ **$75**, ♦♦ **$82 - $94**, AE BC DC JCB MC VI.

★★★ **Airport Heritage**, (M), 620 Kingsford Smith Dve, 4km to airport, ☎ 07 3268 5899, fax 07 3268 1584, (2 stry), 32 units [shwr, bath, tlt, a/c, tel, TV, clock radio, t/c mkg, refrig, ldry], dryer, pool, dinner to unit, cots-fee. **RO** ♦ **$83.50**, ♦♦ **$89**, ch con, AE BC DC EFT MC VI.

★★★ **Raceways Motel**, (M), 66 Kent St, 6km from GPO, ☎ 07 3268 4355, fax 07 3868 1640, 12 units [shwr, tlt, a/c (9), tel, TV, clock radio, t/c mkg, refrig], ldry-fee, dryer-fee, pool, bbq, tennis (half court), cots. **RO** ♦ **$66**, ♦♦ **$70**, ◊ **$11**, AE BC DC MC MP VI.

★★★ **Riverview**, (M), 20 Riverview Tce, 5 km N from GPO, ☎ 07 3268 4666, fax 07 3268 6287, (2 stry gr fl), 14 units [shwr, tlt, a/c, tel, TV, clock radio, t/c mkg, refrig], ldry, dryer, spa, cots-fee. **D** **$80**, **RO** ♦ **$63**, ♦♦ **$69**, ch con, AE BC DC EFT MC MCH VI.

★★☆ **Airolodge Flight Deck Motel**, (M), 546 Kingsford Smith Dve, 5km from GPO, ☎ 07 3268 5355, fax 07 3268 2784, (2 stry), 20 units [shwr, tlt, a/c, tel, TV, clock radio, t/c mkg, refrig], lift, ldry, dryer, pool, rm serv, courtesy transfer (to/from airport), cots, Car storage. AE BC DC MC VI.

Self Catering Accommodation

★★★★ **Airport International Motel**, (SA), 528 Kingsford Smith Dve, 5km to airport, ☎ 07 3268 6388, fax 07 3268 7395, (2 stry gr fl), 6 serv apts acc up to 6, (1 & 2 bedrm), [shwr, bath, tlt, a/c, tel, TV, clock radio, refrig, mini bar, cook fac, d/wash], ldry, dryer, iron, iron brd, conv fac, ✗, pool (salt water), dinner to unit, courtesy transfer, cots. **RO** ♦ **$105 - $135**, ♦♦ **$110 - $135**, ch con, AE BC DC MC VI.

Other Accommodation

★★ **Kingsford Private Hotel**, (Lodge), 114 Kingsford Smith Dve, 1km from PO, 4km from GPO, ☎ 07 3862 1317, fax 07 3862 2658, (Multi-stry gr fl), 26 rms acc up to 4, [basin, a/c-cool (12), fan, TV, refrig], shwr, tlt, ldry-fee, dryer-fee, cook fac, t/c mkg shared, c/park (undercover), 📞, cots-fee. **BB** ♦ **$49**, ♦♦ **$55**, AE DC MC VI.

BRISBANE - HERSTON QLD 4006

Pop 3,075. (3km N Brisbane), See map on page 418, ref C5. Inner Brisbane suburb containing Royal Brisbane Hospital, Childrens Hospital, Womens Hospital and Medical School.

★★★ **Herston Place Motel**, (M), 27 Wyndham St, 2.5km fr PO, ☎ 07 3216 0111, fax 07 3216 0406, (2 stry gr fl), 22 units [shwr, tlt, a/c-cool (9), c/fan, tel, TV, clock radio, t/c mkg, refrig, micro, toaster, doonas], ldry, bbq, cots-fee, non smoking property. **RO** ♦ **$59 - $65**, ♦♦ **$69 - $75**, ◊ **$11**, ch con, AE BC DC EFT MC VI.

BRISBANE - HIGHGATE HILL QLD 4101

Pop 5,090. (3km S Brisbane), See map on page 418, ref C5. Suburb of Brisbane.

Hotels/Motels

★★★ **Ambassador Brisbane**, (M), 180 Gladstone Rd, ☎ 07 3844 5661, fax 07 3846 2031, (2 stry gr fl), 13 units [shwr, bath (1), tlt, a/c, tel, TV, clock radio, t/c mkg, refrig, cook fac (3)], ldry, pool (salt water), bbq, cots. **RO** $66, ch con, AE BC DC EFT MC VI.

Self Catering Accommodation

★★☆ **Riviera Apartments**, (HF), 5 Dudley St, ☎ 07 3844 4407, fax 07 3844 1638, (Multi-stry gr fl), 1 flat acc up to 6, [shwr, tlt, c/fan, tel (on request) (6), TV, refrig, cook fac, elec frypan, blkts, linen, pillows], ldry, dryer, pool, bbq, c/park (undercover) (3), ☏, plygr, cots. **RO** ♦ $53, ♦♦ $65, ♦♦ **W** $350 - $370, ch con, BC MC VI.

Other Accommodation

★★ **Somewhere to Stay(Backpackers)**, (Lodge), 45 Brighton Rd, ☎ 07 3846 2858, fax 07 3846 4584, (2 stry gr fl), 6 rms acc up to 3, [shwr, tlt, fan, TV, movie, t/c mkg, refrig], ldry, rec rm, lounge (TV), pool, bbq, c/park (limited), courtesy transfer, ☏. **D** $51, AE BC MC VI.

  (Budget Rooms Section), 66 apts acc up to 6, shwr, tlt, cook fac, t/c mkg shared, refrig. **RO** ♦ $14 - $18.

BRISBANE - HOLLAND PARK QLD 4121

Pop 12,950. (9km S Brisbane), See map on page 418, ref C5. Suburb of Brisbane. Mt Gravatt recreation reserve & lookout. Bowls, Tennis.

Hotels/Motels

★★★☆ **Holland Park Motel**, (M), 917 Logan Rd, Cnr Crown St, ☎ 07 3394 4422, fax 07 3394 4422, (2 stry), 12 units [shwr, tlt, a/c, tel, cable tv, clock radio, t/c mkg, refrig], ldry, dryer-fee, pool (salt water), bbq, cots, non smoking units (4). **RO** ♦ $66, ♦♦ $77, ♦ $10, AE BC DC JCB MC VI.

★★★☆ **Mt Gravatt Colonial Motor Inn**, (M), 1165 Logan Rd, ☎ 07 3849 4849, fax 07 3849 6434, (2 stry gr fl), 15 units [shwr, spa bath (1), tlt, hairdry (at reception), a/c, c/fan, tel, cable tv (11), video-fee, clock radio, t/c mkg, refrig, cook fac (5), micro (5)], ldry-fee, dryer-fee, iron (at reception), pool, spa, bbq, rm serv (dinner), meals to unit, cots-fee, non smoking units (8). **D** ♦♦♦ $75, Suite **D** ♦ $10, $85 - $160, ch con, AE BC DC EFT MC VI.

BRISBANE - INDOOROOPILLY QLD 4068

Pop 10,316. (7km SW Brisbane), See map on page 418, ref B5. Suburb of Brisbane.

Self Catering Accommodation

★★★★☆ **Brisbane's Best Indooroopilly**, (SA), 27 Russell Terrace, ☎ 07 3878 0222, fax 07 3878 0233, 25 serv apts (1, 2 & 3 bedrm), [ensuite, shwr, bath, tlt, hairdry, a/c, tel, TV, video, clock radio, t/c mkg, refrig, cook fac, micro, elec frypan, toaster, ldry, blkts, linen, pillows], iron, iron brd, pool, bbq, secure park, gym, cots-fee. **D** $100 - $125, **W** $485 - $525, Min book applies, AE BC DC MC VI.

★★★ **Forest Lodge**, (HU), 140 Central Ave, ☎ 07 3371 6600, fax 07 3371 6107, (2 stry gr fl), 31 units acc up to 5, [shwr, bath (8), tlt, a/c, c/fan, tel, TV, refrig, cook fac (full), blkts, linen, pillows], ldry-fee, iron, iron brd, pool, bbq, cots, non smoking units (7). **D** ♦ $65, ♦♦ $75, ♦ $10, **W** ♦ $375, ♦♦ $450, ch con, Light breakfast available, AE BC DC MC VI.

Other Accommodation

★★★ **Indooroopilly Lodge & Motel**, (Lodge), 21 Riverview Tce, 6.2km W GPO. 150m to railway station, ☎ 07 3378 4000, fax 07 3378 4577, 31 rms acc up to 6, [ensuite (9), a/c-cool (9), TV, t/c mkg (9), refrig], shwr, tlt, ldry, t/c mkg shared, c/park. **BB** ♦ $38, ♦♦ $80, ♦ $15, Some units ★★. AE BC EFT MC VI.

BRISBANE - JINDALEE QLD 4074

Pop 5,742. (13km W Brisbane), See map on page 418, ref B5.

★★☆ **Jindalee Hotel**, (LH), Cnr Sinnamon & Goggs Rds, ☎ 07 3376 2122, fax 07 3376 1933, (2 stry), 12 rms [shwr, tlt, a/c, tel, TV, t/c mkg, refrig], ldry, conv fac, ⊠, cots-fee. **D** ♦ $55, ♦♦ $65, ch con, AE BC DC EFT MC VI.

BRISBANE - KALLANGUR QLD 4503

Pop 14,740. (28km N Brisbane), See map on page 418, ref C2. Outer northern suburb of Brisbane.

★★ **Kallangur**, (LMH), 1517 Anzac Ave, ☎ 07 3886 2366, fax 07 3886 2355, 12 units [shwr, tlt, a/c, c/fan, TV, t/c mkg, refrig], ldry. **RO** ♦♦ **$50 - $55**, ♦ **$10**, BC MC VI.

BRISBANE - KANGAROO POINT QLD 4169

Pop 4,310. (3km E Brisbane), See map on page 418, ref C5. Inner suburb of Brisbane. Two minutes by ferry service to city.

Hotels/Motels

★★★★☆ **The Point on Shafston**, (LH), 21 Lambert St, 1.5km W of CBD, ☎ 07 3240 0888, fax 07 3392 1155, (Multi-stry), 106 rms (63 suites) [shwr, tlt, a/c-cool, cent heat, tel, TV, clock radio, t/c mkg, refrig, micro], lift, w/mach, dryer, conf fac, ⊠, pool-heated, bbq, rm serv, plygr, cots, non smoking rms (4). **D** $108 - $177, ch con, weekly con, AE BC DC EFT MC VI.

★★★★ **IL Mondo Boutique Hotel**, (M), 25-35 Rotherham St, ☎ 07 3392 0111, fax 07 3392 0544, (Multi-stry gr fl), 33 units (1 bedrm 2 bedrm), [ensuite, shwr, bath (some), tlt, hairdry, a/c-cool, tel, cable tv (11 channels), clock radio, t/c mkg, refrig], lift, iron, iron brd, lounge (TV), conf fac (for 30), ✕ (Mon to Sat), rm serv (restaurant hrs), c/park (undercover), secure park, cots, non smoking rms. **RO** ♦♦ **$75 - $210**, 12 rooms ★★★, AE BC DC EFT MC VI.

★★★☆ **Belvedere Motor Inn**, (M), Cnr Shafston Ave & Thorn St, ☎ 07 3891 5855, fax 07 3391 8794, (2 stry gr fl), 20 units (0 suites) [shwr, spa bath (3), tlt, a/c, tel, cable tv, clock radio, t/c mkg, refrig, ldry], pool. **RO** ♦ **$88**, ♦♦ **$109**, ♦ **$12**, Suite **RO** **$129**, AE BC DC EFT JCB MC VI.

★★★☆ **Ryans on the River**, (M), 269 Main St/Cnr Scott St, walkway to Southbank, 18km from airport, ☎ 07 3391 1011, fax 07 3391 1824, (Multi-stry gr fl), 23 units [shwr, tlt, hairdry, a/c, tel, TV, clock radio, t/c mkg, refrig], lift, ldry, iron, iron brd, pool (salt water), bbq, dinner to unit, secure park (undercover). **RO** ♦ **$139 - $199**, ♦♦ **$159 - $199**, AE BC BTC DC EFT MC VI.

★★★ **Paramount**, (M), 649 Main St, 500m N of Gabba Cricket Ground, ☎ 07 3393 1444, fax 07 3891 5592, 20 units [shwr, tlt, a/c, tel, TV, clock radio, t/c mkg, refrig, cook fac, toaster], ldry, iron, pool, cots. **RO** ♦ **$64.50 - $71**, ♦♦ **$69.50 - $83.50**, AE BC DC EFT MC VI.

★★★ **Southern Cross**, (M), 721 Main St, ☎ 07 3391 2881, fax 07 3391 2881, (Multi-stry gr fl), 25 units [shwr, tlt, a/c-cool, a/c, heat, tel, TV, movie, clock radio, t/c mkg, refrig], ldry, pool (salt water), bbq, cots. **RO** ♦ **$49.50**, ♦♦ **$55 - $60.50**, ♦ **$11**, ch con, AE BC DC EFT MC VI.

★★☆ **A 1 Motel**, (M), Cnr Main & Sinclair Sts, 500m N of Gabba Cricket Ground, ☎ 07 3391 6222, fax 07 3891 0720, (2 stry gr fl), 44 units (1 suite) [shwr, tlt, a/c, tel, TV, clock radio, t/c mkg, refrig, micro (2), toaster (6)], ldry, conf fac, pool, bbq, dinner to unit (Mon-Sat), meals to unit (7days), secure park (20), cots-fee, non smoking units (12). **RO** ♦ **$66**, ♦♦ **$71**, ♦ **$8 - $12**, Suite **RO** ♦ **$154**, ch con, fam con, AE BC DC EFT JCB MC MP VI.

Self Catering Accommodation

★★★★☆ **Bridgewater Quest Inn**, (Apt), 55 Baildon St, 1km E of CBD, ☎ 07 3391 5300, fax 07 3392 1513, (Multi-stry gr fl), 120 apts acc up to 6, (Studio, 1, 2 & 3 bedrm), [ensuite, shwr, bath, tlt, hairdry (at reception), a/c-cool, c/fan, tel, TV, clock radio, refrig, cook fac, micro, elec frypan, d/wash, toaster, ldry (in unit), blkts, linen, pillows], dryer, iron, iron brd, pool (salt water), sauna, spa, bbq (covered), 24hr reception, secure park, gym, cots-fee. **D** $132 - $240, AE BC DC MC VI.

★★★★ **Oakford All Suite Apartments**, (HU), 85 Deakin St, 600m E of GPO, ☎ 07 3249 8400, fax 07 3249 8499, (Multi-stry gr fl), 55 units acc up to 7, (1, 2 & 3 bedrm), [ensuite (24), shwr, bath, spa bath (2), tlt, hairdry, a/c, cent heat, tel, TV, video-fee, clock radio, refrig, cook fac, micro, d/wash, toaster, ldry (in unit) (18)], lift, ldry, dryer (18), iron, iron brd, rec rm, conv fac, pool, spa, bbq (covered), meals to unit (breakfast only)-fee, secure park, gym. **RO** $109 - $221, AE BC DC JCB MC VI, ♿.

★★★☆ **Kangaroo Point Holiday Apartments**, (HU), 819 Main St, 2km Sth of GPO, ☎ 07 3391 6855, fax 07 3391 3640, (2 stry), 28 units acc up to 9, (1, 2 & 4 bedrm), [shwr, bath (7), tlt, a/c (11), c/fan (17), heat, tel, TV, video-fee, clock radio, refrig, cook fac, micro, toaster, blkts, linen, pillows], ldry, dryer-fee, iron, iron brd, pool, bbq, c/park (undercover), cots-fee, non smoking units. **D** $71.50 - $143, **W** $352 - $880, 11 new units ★★★★, AE BC DC EFT MC VI.

Operator Comment: Please see our ad opposite

BRISBANE - KEDRON QLD 4031

Pop 11,328. (7km N Brisbane), See map on page 418, ref C4. Suburb of Brisbane.

Hotels/Motels

★★★★ **Kedron On The Brook**, (M), 700 Lutwyche Rd, 4km N of Royal Brisbane Hospital, ☎ 07 3857 8444, fax 07 3857 8977, 31 units (2 suites) [shwr, bath, tlt, hairdry, a/c-cool, a/c, heat, tel, TV, video (3), movie, clock radio, t/c mkg, refrig, cook fac ltd, micro, elec frypan, toaster], ldry, dryer-fee, iron, iron brd, rec rm, lounge (TV), conv fac, pool (salt water), bbq, c/park (undercover), gym, cots, non smoking units (5). **RO** ♦ **$71.50**, ♦♦ **$82.50**, Suite **RO** **$110**, AE BC DC EFT JCB MC VI.

Self Catering Accommodation

★★★ **Kedron Palms**, (SA), 642 Lutwyche Rd, 4 km N of Royal Brisbane Hospital, ☎ 07 3857 8033, fax 07 3857 8044, (2 stry gr fl), 28 serv apts acc up to 6, (Studio), [shwr, tlt, a/c (26), tel, TV, clock radio, t/c mkg, refrig, cook fac ltd, micro, elec frypan, toaster], ldry, dryer, iron, iron brd, ✕, bbq. **RO** ♦ **$64.90**, ♦♦ **$75.90**, AE BC DC EFT MC VI.

BRISBANE - KELVIN GROVE QLD 4059

Pop 3,704. See map on page 418, ref C4. Inner suburb of Brisbane.

★★★★ **Catherine House Bed & Breakfast**, (B&B), c1881. 151 Kelvin Grove Rd, 2.5km N Brisbane Transit Centre, ☎ 07 3839 6988, fax 07 3236 9093, (2 stry gr fl), 3 rms [shwr, tlt, a/c-cool, a/c, heat, TV, t/c mkg], ldry, lounge (TV), pool, bbq, non smoking property. **BB** ♦ **$77**, ♦♦ **$104.50**, ♦ **$25**, ch con, AE BC DC MC VI.

BRISBANE - KIPPA RING QLD 4021

Pop Part of Redcliffe, (30km N Brisbane), See map on page 418, ref D2. Suburb of Redcliffe.

Hotels/Motels

★★★☆ **Kippa Ring Village**, (M), 418 Elizabeth Ave, 500 km W of PO, ☎ 07 328 3393, fax 07 3283 2883, 10 units [shwr, tlt, a/c, heat, tel, TV, clock radio, t/c mkg, refrig, toaster], ldry, pool, bbq, c/park (undercover), cots-fee, non smoking units (6). **RO** ♦ **$66**, ♦♦ **$71.50**, ♦ **$11**, ch con, some units of a lower rating. AE BC MC VI.

Self Catering Accommodation

★★★ **Kippa Ring Village**, (HU), 418 Elizabeth Ave, 500km W of PO, ☎ 07 3283 3933, fax 07 3283 2883, 6 units acc up to 5, [shwr, tlt, a/c-cool, c/fan, tel, TV, clock radio, refrig, cook fac, micro, elec frypan, ldry (in unit), blkts, linen, pillows], pool, bbq, c/park (undercover), cots-fee. **RO** $71.50 - $93.50, ch con, Some units of a higher rating. AE BC MC VI.

BRISBANE - LOGAN CENTRAL QLD 4127

Pop Part of Brisbane, (22km S Brisbane). A major commercial suburb of Brisbane.

Hotels/Motels

★★★☆ **Logan City Motor Inn**, (M), 3725 Pacific Hwy, Logan City, ☎ 07 3209 7925, fax 07 3209 7607, (2 stry gr fl), 27 units [shwr, tlt, a/c, elec blkts, tel, TV, video, clock radio, t/c mkg, refrig, toaster], ldry, dryer, conv fac, ⊠, pool (salt water), spa, rm serv, dinner to unit, c/park (undercover) (13), cots-fee. **RO** ♦ **$95 - $130**, ♦♦ **$95 - $130**, ♦ **$15**, AE BC DC JCB MC VI, ♿.

BRISBANE - LOGANHOLME QLD 4129

Pop 11,273. (29km S Brisbane), See map on page 418, ref D7. Extreme southern district of Brisbane.

★★★★ **McNevins Logan Park**, (M), 4170 Pacific Hwy, ☎ 07 3209 8830, fax 07 3209 8835, 22 units [shwr, spa bath (12), tlt, hairdry, a/c, tel, TV, clock radio, t/c mkg, refrig, cook fac (5)], ldry, iron, iron brd, ⊠ (Mon to Sat), pool, dinner to unit, tennis, cots-fee, non smoking rms (5). **RO** ♦ **$60 - $75**, ♦♦ **$70 - $85**, ch con, 10 units ★★☆. AE BC DC MC VI, ♿.

BRISBANE - LOGANLEA QLD 4131

Pop part of Brisbane (26km S Brisbane) See map on page 418, ref D7. Outer suburb of Brisbane.

★★★ **Dooleys Hotel**, (LH), Cnr Loganlea Rd & Logandowns Drive, ☎ 07 3200 3777, fax 07 3200 3888, 20 rms [shwr, bath, spa bath (1), tlt, a/c, tel, TV, clock radio, t/c mkg, refrig], ⊠, rm serv, dinner to unit. **BLB** ♦ **$77**, ♦♦ **$88**, ◊ **$11**, ch con, BC DC EFT MC VI.

BRISBANE - MANLY QLD 4179

Pop 3,493. (19km NE Brisbane), See map on page 418, ref E5. Bayside Suburb of Brisbane. Boat harbour and yacht club.

Hotels/Motels

★★★★ **The Manly Hotel**, (LH), 54 Cambridge Pde, 100m fr boat harbour & council swimming pool, ☎ 07 3249 5999, fax 07 3893 1248, (2 stry), 18 rms [basin, shwr (7), spa bath (2), tlt (11), a/c-cool (2), a/c (9), fan (12), tel, TV], bathrm, ldry, dryer, iron (communal facilities), lounge, ⊠, ☎, cots. **RO** ♦♦ **$38.50 - $88**, 9 rooms of a lower rating. AE BC DC EFT MC VI.

Other Accommodation

Moreton Bay Lodge, 45 Cambridge Pde, Cnr Stanton Tce, ☎ 07 3396 3020, fax 07 3396 1355, (2 stry), 7 rms [shwr (3), tlt (3), c/fan, clock radio], shwr, tlt, ldry-fee, dryer-fee, lounge (TV), ⊠, cook fac, courtesy transfer. **RO** ♦ **$20 - $50**, AE BC MC VI.

BRISBANE - MILTON QLD 4064

Pop 1,599. (2km W Brisbane), See map on page 418, ref C5.

Hotels/Motels

★★★ **Coronation Boutique Hotel**, (M), 205 Coronation Dve, ☎ 07 3369 9955, fax 07 3369 5066, (Multi-stry gr fl), 54 units (5 suites) [shwr, bath (5), tlt, hairdry, a/c, tel, TV, clock radio, t/c mkg, refrig, mini bar], lift, ldry, conv fac, ⊠ (closed pub holidays), BYO, 24hr reception, rm serv, dinner to unit, c/park (undercover), cots. **RO** ♦ **$87 - $133**, ♦♦ **$87 - $133**, ◊ **$18 - $45**, Suite **RO $100 - $180**, ch con, AE BC DC MC VI.

Self Catering Accommodation

★★★★☆ **Cosmo on Park Road**, (SA), 60 Park Rd, 2km W of GPO, ☎ 07 3858 5999, fax 07 3858 5988, 74 serv apts acc up to 3, (Studio, 1 & 2 bedrm), [shwr, bath, tlt, hairdry, a/c, tel, TV, clock radio, t/c mkg, refrig, cook fac (59), micro (15), d/wash, toaster, ldry, blkts, linen, pillows], dryer, iron, iron brd, sauna, spa, bbq, dinner to unit, secure park, cots-fee. **D $120 - $165**, AE BC DC MC VI.

★★★★ **Milton Motel Apartments**, (SA), 19 Sheehan St, 100m W of Park Rd, ☎ 07 3876 2360, fax 07 3876 2359, 36 serv apts acc up to 6, (Studio, 1 & 2 bedrm), [shwr, tlt, a/c-cool, heat, tel, TV, clock radio, refrig, cook fac, toaster, ldry (in unit), blkts, linen, pillows], dryer, iron, iron brd, pool, c/park (undercover), cots-fee. **D $78 - $155**, Various units of a lower rating. AE BC EFT MC VI.

BRISBANE - MITCHELTON QLD 4053

Pop 6,070. (9km N Brisbane), See map on page 418, ref B4.

★★ **The Brook Hotel & Motel**, (LMH), Osborne Rd snr Samford Rd, ☎ 07 3355 5366, fax 07 3855 2562, 11 units [shwr, tlt, fan, TV, t/c mkg, refrig], ⊠ (Mon to Sat). **RO** ♦ **$50**, ♦♦ **$61**, ◊ **$11**, weekly con, AE BC DC EFT MC VI.

BRISBANE - MOOROOKA QLD 4105

Pop 8,573. (10km S Brisbane), See map on page 418, ref C6. Suburb of Brisbane.

Hotels/Motels

★★★☆ **Amaroo Motor Inn**, (M), 820 Ipswich Rd, ☎ 07 3892 1800, fax 07 3848 2600, (2 stry gr fl), 20 units [shwr, bath (1), tlt, a/c, tel, TV, clock radio, t/c mkg, refrig, cook fac (1), micro, toaster], ldry, iron, iron brd, conv fac, pool, bbq, dinner to unit, ☎, cots. **RO** ♦ **$68.50 - $71.50**, ♦♦ **$75 - $78**, ◊ **$11**, AE BC DC EFT JCB MC MP VI, ♿.

★★☆ **Moorooka Motel**, (M), 980 Ipswich Rd, ☎ 07 3848 9111, fax 07 3892 4831, 10 units [shwr, tlt, a/c, c/fan, elec blkts, tel, TV, clock radio, t/c mkg, refrig], ldry, pool, bbq, c/park (undercover), cots-fee. **RO** ♦ **$59**, ♦♦ **$64**, ◊ **$10**, ch con, AE BC DC MC MCH VI.

BRISBANE - MORAYFIELD QLD 4506

Pop part of Brisbane. (45km N Brisbane) See map on page 418, ref C1. Situated 2km from Caboolture, Morayfield has large shopping centres.

Morayfield Motel, (M), 146 Morayfield Rd, 100m W of Shopping Centre, ☎ 07 5495 2722, fax 07 5495 3680, (2 stry), 24 units [shwr, tlt, a/c, tel, TV, clock radio (8), t/c mkg, refrig, ldry], dryer, iron brd, ✗, pool, dinner to unit, ☎, cots. **RO** ♦ **$55**, AE BC DC EFT MC VI, (not yet classified).

BRISBANE - MORNINGSIDE QLD 4170

Pop 7,196. (8km E Brisbane), See map on page 418, ref C5.

★★☆ **McGuires Colmslie Hotel Motel**, (LMH),Cnr Wynnum & Junction Rds, ☎ 07 3399 8222, fax 07 3399 2947, 12 units [shwr, tlt, a/c, tel, TV, t/c mkg, refrig], night club (Fri & Sat), ⊠, rm serv, dinner to unit, cots. **RO** ♦ **$74.80**, ♦♦ **$85.80**, ◊ **$16.50**, ch con, AE BC DC MC VI.

BRISBANE - MOUNT GLORIOUS QLD 4520

Pop Part of Brisbane, (38km NW Brisbane), See map on page 418, ref A3. An outer suburb of Brisbane, Mt Glorious is a beautiful scenic area.

Self Catering Accommodation

★★★★ **Mt Glorious Getaways**, (Cotg), Browns Rd, 35km NW of Brisbane GPO, ☎ 07 3289 0172, fax 07 3289 0072, 4 cotgs acc up to 6, [shwr, tlt, heat (wood), elec blkts, TV, CD, refrig, cook fac, micro, toaster, blkts, linen, pillows], bbq, non smoking property. **D** ♦♦ **$120 - $145**, **W** ♦♦ **$610**, AE BC MC VI.

BRISBANE - MOUNT GRAVATT QLD 4122

Pop 3,115. (11km S Brisbane), See map on page 418, ref C6. Suburb of Brisbane.

★★★☆ **Viking Motel**, (M), 1207 Logan Rd (Pacific Hwy), ☎ 07 3349 7588, fax 07 3849 6838, (2 stry gr fl), 21 units [shwr, tlt, a/c-cool (10), a/c (11), c/fan, heat, tel, TV, clock radio, t/c mkg, refrig], ldry-fee, dryer-fee, pool, cots-fee. RO ♦ $81, ♦♦ $87, ♦♦♦♦ $120, ◊ $11, AE BC DC EFT MC VI.

★★☆ **Mount Gravatt Motel**, (M), 1750 Logan Rd, 800m N of Garden City Shopping Centre, ☎ 07 3349 6626, fax 07 3219 1898, 10 units [shwr, tlt, hairdry (5), a/c, c/fan, elec blkts, TV, clock radio, t/c mkg, refrig, cook fac ltd, micro (2)], non smoking units (4). RO ♦ $50, ♦♦ $63, ◊ $10, BC MC VI.

BRISBANE - MOUNT OMMANEY QLD 4074

Pop 1,910. (14km W Brisbane), See map on page 418, ref B5. Suburb of Brisbane.

★★★☆ **Mt Ommaney Plaza Hotel**, (M), Cnr Centenary Hwy & Dandenong Rd, ☎ 07 3279 1288, fax 07 3376 8729, (2 stry gr fl), 32 units (32 suites) [shwr, bath (32), tlt, hairdry, a/c, tel, TV, movie, clock radio, t/c mkg, refrig, mini bar, cook fac (32), micro (32), toaster (32)], iron, iron brd, conv fac, ⊠, pool, spa, 24hr reception, rm serv, c/park (undercover), ✆, tennis, cots. RO $115, Suite D ♦♦ $125, ◊ $20, Some units of a higher rating. AE BC DC MC VI, ⅟⅃.

BRISBANE - MOUNT SAMSON QLD 4520

Pop Nom, (32km Brisbane), See map on page 418, ref A2. Outer suburb of Brisbane. Bush Walking.

★★☆ **Trevena Glen**, (GH), (Farm), Winn Rd, 40 km NW of Brisbane PO, ☎ 07 3289 4257, fax 07 3289 4257, 3 rms (1 suite) [shwr, bath, tlt, c/fan (1), TV, clock radio, CD (1), t/c mkg, refrig, cook fac, cook fac ltd, micro, elec frypan, toaster], ldry, iron, iron brd, c/park (undercover), non smoking units. BLB ♦ $45, ♦♦ $80.

BRISBANE - NARANGBA QLD 4504

Pop part of Brisbane. (38km N Brisbane) See map on page 418, ref B1. A rural area, surrounded by golf courses.

★★★☆ **Richards B&B**, (B&B), 341 Boundary Road, 3km E of PO, ☎ 07 3888 3743, fax 07 3888 3938, 3 rms (1 suite) [c/fan, elec blkts, fax, TV, clock radio, refrig, ldry], shwr, tlt, dryer, rec rm, TV rm, business centre, t/c mkg shared, refrig, bbq, rm serv, tennis. BB ♦ $66, ♦♦ $88, Suite BB ♦♦ $165, deposit required. BC MC VI.

BRISBANE - NEW FARM QLD 4005

Pop 9,032. (3km N Brisbane), See map on page 418, ref C5. Inner suburb of Brisbane.

Hotels/Motels

★★★ **South Pacific Palms Motel & Hol Apts**, (M), Cnr Bowen Tce & Langshaw St, 2km Brisbane CBD, ☎ 07 3358 2366, fax 07 3358 3489, (2 stry gr fl), 19 units (2 bedrm), [shwr, bath (2), tlt, hairdry, a/c, tel, fax, TV, clock radio, t/c mkg, refrig, cook fac, micro (4), elec frypan (4)], ldry, pool, bbq, c/park (undercover), cots-fee. RO ♦ $68, ♦♦ $78, ◊ $11, ch con, AE BC DC MC VI.

Self Catering Accommodation

★★★★☆ **Kirribilli Apartments**, (HU), 150 Oxlade Dve, ☎ 07 3358 5622, fax 07 3254 1714, (Multi-stry gr fl), 26 units acc up to 7, [shwr, bath, tlt, a/c-cool, c/fan, heat, tel, cable tv, video-fee, clock radio, refrig, cook fac, micro, d/wash, ldry (in unit), blkts, linen, pillows], lift, pool, sauna, spa, bbq, secure park, tennis, cots-fee. D $140 - $208, W $805 - $1,029, AE BC DC EFT MC VI.

★★★☆ **Allender Apartments**, (HU), 3 Moreton St, 2km from Brisbane CBD, ☎ 07 3358 5832, fax 07 3254 0799, (2 stry gr fl), 10 units acc up to 5, [shwr, tlt, a/c (10), tel, TV, clock radio, refrig, cook fac, micro, blkts, linen, pillows], ldry, cots. D $77 - $121, ch con, AE BC DC EFT MC MCH VI.

BRISBANE - NEWMARKET QLD 4051

Pop part of Brisbane. (5km NW Brisbane), See map on page 418, ref C4.

★★ **Broadstairs**, (B&B), 65 Lansdowne St, 1km W of Wilston PO, ☎ 07 3356 6671, (2 stry), 1 rm [c/fan, heat (elec), tel, clock radio, micro, toaster, ldry, doonas], lounge (TV, video), ✗, pool-heated, t/c mkg shared, refrig, bbq, c/park. BLB ♦ $50, ♦♦ $80.

BRISBANE - NEWSTEAD QLD 4006

Pop 923. (3km N Brisbane), See map on page 418, ref C5. Inner riverside suburb of Brisbane.

★★★ **Newstead Gardens**, (M), 48 Jordan Tce, 3km N of GPO, ☎ 07 3252 7008, fax 07 3252 7828, (Multi-stry), 22 units [shwr, tlt, a/c, fan, tel, TV, movie, clock radio, t/c mkg, refrig, cook fac ltd, micro, toaster], ldry, bbq, c/park (undercover), non smoking units (12). BLB ♦ $75, ♦♦ $80, ch con, Light breakfast only available. AE BC DC MC VI.

BRISBANE - NORTHGATE QLD 4013

Pop 3,617. (11km N Brisbane), See map on page 418, ref C4. Suburb of Brisbane.

★★★★ **Northgate Airport Motel**, (M), 186 Toombul Rd, 2km SW Airport, ☎ 07 3256 7222, fax 07 3256 7277, (2 stry gr fl), 25 units (0 suites) [shwr, tlt, hairdry, a/c, tel, TV, movie, clock radio, t/c mkg, refrig, mini bar, cook fac ltd, micro (4)], ldry, dryer, conv fac, ⊠ (Mon-Sun), pool, bbq-fee, rm serv, dinner to unit, c/park (undercover) (3), cots. RO ♦ $90, ♦♦ $96, Suite RO ♦ $95.70, ♦♦ $103, ch con, AE BC DC EFT MC VI.

BRISBANE - OXLEY QLD 4075

Pop 6,033. (14km SW Brisbane), See map on page 418, ref B6. Suburb of Brisbane.

Hotels/Motels

★★★★ **Oxley Motor Inn**, (M), 2333 Ipswich Rd, ☎ 07 3375 3188, fax 07 3375 4052, 31 units [shwr, bath (8), tlt, hairdry, a/c, tel, TV, video (11), clock radio, t/c mkg, refrig], ldry, dryer, iron, iron brd, ⊠, pool, sauna, rm serv (7nights), dinner to unit, c/park (undercover), cots-fee. RO ♦ $60 - $71, ♦♦ $70 - $82, ◊ $8 - $10, AE BC DC MC VI.

★★☆ **Centenary Motor Inn**, (M), Access via Harcourt Rd ramp. 2479 Ipswich Rd, Cnr Portal St, ☎ 07 3375 3077, fax 07 3375 4914, (2 stry gr fl), 29 units [shwr, tlt, hairdry, a/c-cool, heat, tel, TV, video-fee, clock radio, t/c mkg, refrig], ldry, dryer-fee, conv fac, ⊠, bar, pool, bbq, rm serv, dinner to unit, c/park (undercover) (20), car wash, cots-fee. RO ♦ $60 - $65, ♦♦ $65 - $72, ◊ $10, AE BC DC MC VI, ⅟⅃.

BRISBANE - PADDINGTON QLD 4064

Pop 6,711. (2km NW Brisbane), See map on page 418, ref C5. Inner suburb of Brisbane.

B&B's/Guest Houses

★★★★ **Paddington B & B**, (B&B), 5 Latrobe Tce, 2.5 km NW of PO, ☎ 07 3369 8973, fax 07 3876 6655, (2 stry gr fl), 4 rms (2 suites) [shwr (4), bath (1), tlt (5), a/c (2), fan (2), TV (4), clock radio (4), radio (1), t/c mkg (3), refrig (2), cook fac (2), micro (2), toaster (2)], ldry, non smoking units. BB ♦ $77, ♦♦ $105, W $1,105, AE BC DC MC VI.

★★★☆ **Fern Cottage Bed & Breakfast**, (B&B), 89 Fernberg Rd, 3kms NW of Brisbane GPO, ☎ 07 3511 6685, or 07 3369 9030, fax 07 3511 6685, (2 stry gr fl), 4 rms [shwr (2), tlt (2), hairdry, a/c-cool, a/c, fan, c/fan, heat, TV, clock radio, t/c mkg, micro, ldry-fee, pillows], tlt, dryer-fee, iron, iron brd, lounge (TV), ✗, cook fac, non smoking property. BB ♦ $55, ♦♦ $70 - $80, ◊ $30, ch con, BC MC VI.

BRISBANE - PETRIE QLD 4502

Pop 7,350. (24km N Brisbane), See map on page 418, ref C2. Outer suburb of Brisbane.

★☆ **Pine Rivers**, (M), 1244 Anzac Ave, ☎ 07 3285 2253, 6 units [shwr, tlt, a/c, fan, heat, TV, clock radio, t/c mkg, refrig], pool, bbq, cots. **RO ♦ $40, ♦♦ $50, ◊ $7**, ch con, BC MC VI.

BRISBANE - RED HILL QLD 4059

Pop 4,653. (2.5km NW Brisbane), See map on page 418, ref C5. Inner suburb of Brisbane.

★★ **Avondale Private Hotel**, (PH), 179 Musgrave Rd, 300m W of PO, ☎ 07 3369 6565, (2 stry gr fl), 10 rms [c/fan, refrig], shwr, tlt, ldry, dryer, rec rm, lounge (TV), cook fac, t/c mkg shared, ✆. **RO ♦ $22, ♦♦ $36, ◊ $14.**

BRISBANE - REDCLIFFE QLD 4020

Pop 49,732. (34km N Brisbane), See map on page 418, ref D2. Seaside resort. Boat Ramp, Boating, Bowls, Fishing, Golf, Motor Racing, Sailing, Swimming, Tennis.

Hotels/Motels

★★☆ **Waltzing Matilda**, (M), 109 Margate Pde, ☎ 07 3284 5171, fax 07 3883 1006, (2 stry gr fl), 20 units [shwr, tlt, a/c-cool (6), a/c (14), tel, TV, clock radio, t/c mkg, refrig], ldry, ⊠ (Wed to Sun), pool, bbq, c/park (undercover) (10), cots-fee. **RO ♦ $50 - $60, ♦♦ $55 - $66, ◊ $5**, AE BC DC MC VI, ♿.

★★ **(Holiday Units Section)**, 8 units acc up to 5, [shwr, tlt, TV, clock radio, refrig, cook fac, micro, elec frypan, toaster, blkts, linen, pillows], w/mach, iron, iron brd, dinner to unit (Wed - Sun), cots. **D $94, W $385 - $495.**

★★ **Redcliffe Seabrae Hotel**, (LH), Cnr Anzac Ave & Marine Pde, 175m S of PO, ☎ 07 3284 2281, fax 07 3284 6263, (2 stry gr fl), 11 rms [shwr, tlt, a/c, tel, TV, t/c mkg, refrig], conv fac, ⊠. **RO ♦ $42, ♦♦ $55**, AE BC EFT MC VI.

B&B's/Guest Houses

★★★★☆ **The Palms Bed & Breakfast**, (B&B), 27 Macdonnell Rd, 1km from Redcliffe PO, ☎ 0732842741, fax 07 3885 6372, 5 rms [shwr, tlt, a/c, TV, clock radio, t/c mkg, refrig], iron, iron brd, ✗, secure park, cots. **BB ♦ $77 - $88, ♦♦ $77 - $88, ◊ $11**, ch con, BC EFT MC VI.

★★★ **Anna's Bed & Breakfast**, (B&B), 24 Sutton St, 500m S of PO, ☎ 07 3284 3290, (2 stry gr fl), 2 rms **BB ♦♦ $55 - $66**, ch con.

BRISBANE - REDLAND BAY QLD 4165

Pop 5,302. (42km SE Brisbane), See map on page 418, ref E7. Outer bayside suburb of Brisbane.

★★★ **Redland Bay Motor Inn**, (M), 152 Broadwater Tce, ☎ 07 3206 8188, fax 07 3829 0288, 16 units [shwr, bath (7), tlt, a/c-cool, heat, tel, TV, clock radio, t/c mkg, refrig, toaster], pool (salt water), bbq, cots. **RO ♦♦ $65 - $75**, ch con, AE BC DC EFT MC VI.

BRISBANE - ROBERTSON QLD 4109

Pop 3,998. (10km S Brisbane), See map on page 418, ref C6. Suburb of Brisbane, close to QEII Hospital & sporting complex.

Hotels/Motels

  ★★★☆ **Robertson Gardens Plaza Hotel**, (M), 281 Kessels Rd, 500m from QEII stadium & Hospital, ☎ 07 3875 1999, fax 07 3274 1428, (2 stry), 73 units (2 suites) [shwr, spa bath (2), tlt, a/c, tel, cable tv, clock radio, t/c mkg, refrig, toaster], ldry, iron, iron brd, ⊠, pool (salt water), rm serv, dinner to unit, cots. **RO ♦ $104, ♦♦ $104, ◊ $16.50**, AE BC DC MC MP VI, ♿.

★★★★ **(Villa Section)**, (2 stry gr fl), 60 serv apts acc up to 5, [shwr, tlt, a/c, c/fan, tel, cable tv, movie, clock radio, t/c mkg, cook fac], ldry, bbq, rm serv, cots. **D ♦♦ $104, W ♦♦ $497.**

BRISBANE - SALISBURY QLD 4107

Pop 5,109. (11km S Brisbane), See map on page 418, ref C6. Suburb of Brisbane.

Hotels/Motels

★★★ **Salisbury Hotel**, (LMH), 668 Toohey Rd, ☎ 07 3275 1922, fax 07 3275 1191, 16 units [shwr, tlt, a/c, TV, clock radio, t/c mkg, refrig, toaster], ldry-fee, ⊠, c/park (undercover), ✆, non smoking units (2). **RO ♦ $65, ♦♦ $75, ◊ $10**, ch con, AE BC DC EFT MC VI.

BRISBANE - SAMFORD QLD 4520

Pop 450. Nom, (21km NW Brisbane), See map on page 418, ref B3. Outer Suburb of Brisbane. Bush Walking, Horse Riding.

Self Catering Accommodation

★★★☆ **Haslemere Cottages**, (Cotg), Hulcombe Rd, Highvale, ☎ 07 3289 7190, fax 07 3289 7190, 2 cotgs [shwr, spa bath (1), tlt, hairdry, a/c-cool (2), c/fan, elec blkts, clock radio, refrig, cook fac, toaster, blkts, linen, pillows], iron, lounge firepl, dinner to unit. **W ♦♦ $561, RO ♦ $130 - $275, ♦♦ $130 - $275**, BC MC VI.

B&B's/Guest Houses

★★★★ **Beaumont House**, (B&B), 961 Eatons Crossing Rd, 2.5km N of PO, ☎ 07 3289 3000, fax 07 3289 3333, 6 rms [fan, fire pl (bedroom), heat, tel, cable tv, refrig, ldry, doonas], ✗, t/c mkg shared, dinner to unit, c/park. **BB ♦♦ $165 - $253**, AE BC DC EFT MC VI.

★★★★ **Haslemere Guest House**, (B&B), Hulcombe Rd, Highvale, 25 km NW of GPO, ☎ 07 3289 7190, fax 07 3289 7190, 3 rms [shwr, tlt, a/c-cool (1), fan, heat, elec blkts, radio, t/c mkg], ldry, lounge (TV & video), lounge firepl, c/park (undercover), non smoking rms (3). **BB ♦ $55 - $60, ♦♦ $95 - $105**, ch con, BC MC VI.

BRISBANE - SHORNCLIFFE QLD 4017

Pop 6,608. (27km N Brisbane) See map on page 418, ref D3. Northern suburb of Brisbane situated on Moreton Bay. Historical area of Brisbane.

B&B's/Guest Houses

★★★★ **Naracoopa Bed & Breakfast**, (B&B), 99 Yundah St, 21km NE of Brisbane GPO, ☎ 07 3269 2334, 2 rms [ensuite, shwr, tlt, a/c, c/fan, heat, TV (1), video, clock radio, t/c mkg, refrig], ldry-fee, w/mach, dryer, TV rm, spa. **BLB ♦ $75 - $85, ♦♦ $110 - $120, ◊ $25**, ch con, MC VI.

BRISBANE - SOUTH BRISBANE QLD 4101

Pop 2,497. (2km S Brisbane), See map on page 418, ref C5. Inner suburb of Brisbane. Site of World Expo '88. Qld Cultural Centre, Museum & Art Gallery. Qld Maritime Museum. South Bank.

Hotels/Motels

★★★★☆ **Rydges Southbank Brisbane**, (LH), Cnr Grey & Glenelg Sts, ☎ 07 3255 0822, fax 07 3255 0899, 305 rms (66 suites) [ensuite, a/c, cent heat, tel, TV, clock radio, t/c mkg, refrig, ldry], conf fac, ⊠, sauna, spa, rm serv (24hr), c/park (undercover), non smoking rms (194). **RO ♦ $169 - $398, ♦♦ $169 - $398, ◊ $27.50, Suite RO $253 - $398**, ch con, Min book Christmas and Jan, AE BC DC EFT MC VI, ♿.

★★★★ **Riverside Hotel Southbank**, (LH), Previously Metro Suites 20 Montague Rd, 1km S of GPO, ☎ 07 3846 0577, fax 07 3846 5433, 154 rms (95 suites) [shwr, bath, tlt, hairdry, a/c, tel, TV, movie, clock radio, t/c mkg, refrig, mini bar, cook fac ltd (92), micro (92), toaster, ldry], iron, iron brd, conf fac, ⊠, pool above ground (salt water), rm serv, secure park, cots, non smoking flr (6), non smoking rms (102). **D ♦ $104.50, ◊ $22, Suite D ♦ $88**, AE BC DC EFT JCB MC VI, ♿.

 ★★★★ **Sapphire Resort**, (M), 55 Boundary St, ☎ 07 3217 2588, fax 07 3217 2855, (Multi-stry gr fl), 56 units [shwr, bath, tlt, tel, TV, clock radio, t/c mkg, refrig, ldry-fee], dryer-fee, ✗ (Mon to Sun), cafe, pool, dinner to unit, c/park (undercover). **RO ♦ $60 - $75, ♦♦ $75 - $83, ◊ $10**, AE BC DC EFT MC VI, ♿.

 ★★★☆ **Parkview Motel Southbank**, (LMH), 41 Russell St, 500m from Southbank, ☎ 07 3846 2900, fax 07 3846 4933, 52 units [shwr, bath, tlt, a/c-cool, c/fan, tel, TV, t/c mkg, refrig, micro, toaster], ldry, pool (salt water), bbq, secure park. **RO ♦ $99, ♦♦ $99**, AE BC BTC DC EFT MC VI, ♿.

★★★☆ **Southbank Heritage All Suites Motel**, (M), 23 Edmonstone St, 1km S of City, ☎ 07 3846 5555, fax 07 3846 5422, (Multi-stry gr fl), 28 units [shwr, tlt, hairdry, a/c-cool, tel, TV, video (in house), clock radio, t/c mkg, refrig, cook fac, micro, toaster], ldry-fee, dryer-fee, iron, iron brd, pool (salt water), spa, bbq, c/park (undercover), cots-fee. **RO ♦ $98, ♦♦ $98, ◊ $11,** AE BC DC EFT MC VI.

★★★ **Edmondstone**, (M), 24 Edmonstone St, 2km S of Brisbane CBD, ☎ 07 3255 0777, fax 07 3255 0621, (2 stry gr fl), 21 units [shwr, tlt, a/c-cool, c/fan, heat, tel, cable tv, clock radio, t/c mkg, refrig, cook fac ltd, micro, toaster], ldry, dryer, pool (salt water), bbq, cots-fee, non smoking units (11). **RO ♦ $70, ♦♦ $70, ◊ $7,** AE BC DC MC MP VI.

★★★ **Mater Hill Place Motel**, (M), 1 Allen St, 2kms SE GPO, ☎ 07 3846 3188, fax 07 3846 3144, (2 stry) 20 units [shwr, bath, tlt, a/c (16), c/fan, tel, TV, clock radio, refrig, cook fac ltd, micro, elec frypan], ldry, lounge, bbq, c/park (undercover) (10), cots-fee. **RO ♦ $77, ♦♦ $88, ◊ $11,** AE BC DC EFT JCB MC VI.

★★★ **South Bank Mater Motel**, (M), Cnr Raymond Tce & Graham St, ☎ 07 3844 9133, fax 07 3844 7944, (2 stry gr fl), 33 units [shwr, bath (hip), tlt, a/c (18)-fee, c/fan (14), tel, TV, clock radio, t/c mkg, refrig, micro, elec frypan (7), toaster], ldry, w/mach-fee, dryer-fee, iron, bbq, c/park (undercover), cots (1), non smoking units. **D ♦♦ $83 - $94, W ♦♦ $581 - $658,** AE BC DC EFT MC VI, ♿.

Self Catering Accommodation

★★★★☆ **Hillcrest Central Apartment Hotel**, (SA), 311 Vulture St, Next to Southbank parklands, ☎ 07 3846 3000, fax 07 3846 3578, (Multi-stry), 80 serv apts acc up to 7, (Studio, 1, 2 & 3 bedrm), [shwr, bath (56), tlt, a/c, tel, TV, video-fee, clock radio, t/c mkg, refrig, cook fac (64), micro (24), ldry (in unit) (56)], lift, ldry, rec rm, conv fac, ✉, pool-heated, sauna, spa, bbq, secure park, ✆, tennis. **D $99 - $235,** AE BC DC MC VI.

B&B's/Guest Houses

★★★★ **La Torretta**, (B&B), 8 Brereton Street, 1.2 km S of Brisbane City Mall, ☎ 07 3846 0846, fax 07 3846 0846, 2 rms [shwr, tlt, fan, heat, clock radio], rec rm, cook fac, t/c mkg shared, bbq, cots-fee. **BLB ♦ $70 - $80, ♦♦ $85 - $95,** ch con, BC EFT MC VI.

★★★ **Adalong Lodge Guesthouse**, (GH), 81 Stephens Road, 2km S of City Centre, ☎ 07 3255 2888, fax 07 3255 3999, 22 rms [fan (11), clock radio], ldry, dryer-fee, rec rm, lounge (TV), t/c mkg shared, ✆, cots, non smoking property. **BB ♦ $30 - $40, ♦♦ $40 - $50,** BC MC VI.

BRISBANE - SPRING HILL QLD 4000

Pop part of Brisbane. (4km W Brisbane) See map on page 418, ref C5. Inner suburb of Brisbane.

Self Catering Accommodation

★★★☆ **Spring Hill Gardens Apartments**, (HU), 101 Bowen St, Brisbane, 1.5km fr GPO, ☎ 07 3839 0465, fax 07 3220 3444, (Multi-stry gr fl), 50 units acc up to 6, (1 & 2 bedrm), [ensuite, shwr, bath, tlt, a/c, c/fan, tel (STD), TV, clock radio, refrig, cook fac, micro, d/wash, toaster, ldry, blkts, linen, pillows], dryer, iron, iron brd, pool, c/park (undercover). **RO $110 - $150, $365 - $550,** BC EFT MC VI.

BRISBANE - SPRINGWOOD QLD 4127

Pop 6,742. (22km S Brisbane), See map on page 418, ref D7. Southern suburb of Brisbane.

Hotels/Motels

★★★★ **Springwood Motor Inn**, (M), 12 Hall Road, 20km S of GPO, ☎ 07 3299 5999, fax 07 3299 5988, 30 units (4 suites) [shwr, bath (9), spa bath (4), tlt, hairdry (30), a/c, tel, TV, movie, clock radio, t/c mkg, refrig, cook fac ltd (4), micro (4), toaster (4), ldry], dryer, iron, iron brd, conf fac, ✉, pool (saltwater), rm serv, dinner to unit, secure park, cots, non smoking rms (15). **RO ♦ $98, ♦♦ $98, Suite D ♦♦ $142,** AE BC DC EFT MC VI, ♿.

★★ **Springwood Motel & Hotel**, (LMH), Springwood Rd, ☎ 07 3208 4444, fax 07 3808 0022, 12 units [shwr, tlt, a/c, tel, cable tv, clock radio, t/c mkg, refrig], conv fac, ✕ (gaming, liquorbarn), c/park (undercover), ✆, cots. **D ♦♦ $75,** ch con, AE BC DC MC VI.

BRISBANE - ST LUCIA QLD 4067

Pop 9,924. (6km SW Brisbane), See map on page 418, ref C5. Suburb of Brisbane. Adjacent to University of Queensland.

Self Catering Accommodation

★★★★ **St Lucia Gardens**, (SA), 2 Gailey Rd, 4km SW of Brisbane GPO, ☎ 07 3870 7644, fax 07 3870 8332, (2 stry), 22 serv apts acc up to 5, (1 bedrm), [shwr, tlt, hairdry, a/c, tel, TV, refrig, cook fac, micro, toaster, ldry (in unit)], dryer, iron, pool, bbq, secure park, cots. **D ♦♦ $96.80, ◊ $12, W ♦♦ $654.50, ◊ $70,** AE BC DC MC VI.

BRISBANE - SUNNYBANK QLD 4109

Pop 7,733. (12km S Brisbane), See map on page 418, ref C6. Southern suburb of Brisbane. 15 Minutes to city & 35 minutes to Gold Coast Close access to Old Pacific Hwy & Gateway Arterial Rd.

Hotels/Motels

★★☆ **Sunnybank**, (LMH), Cnr Mains & McCullough Rds, ☎ 07 3345 1081, fax 07 3345 7336, 20 units [shwr, tlt, a/c, tel, TV, clock radio, t/c mkg, refrig], ldry, conv fac, ✉, pool, rm serv (dinner), ✆, cots-fee. **RO ♦ $66, ♦♦ $77, ◊ $8 - $18,** ch con, AE BC DC EFT MC VI.

★★☆ **Sunnybank Star Motel**, (M), 223 Padstow Rd, Eight Mile Plains 4113, Cnr Warrigal Rd, ☎ 07 3341 7488, fax 07 3341 7630, 60 units [shwr, bath (2), tlt, a/c, tel, TV, movie, clock radio, t/c mkg, refrig, cook fac (21), micro (7), elec frypan (7)], ldry, ✉, pool, bbq. **RO ♦ $71 - $108, ♦♦ $77 - $108, ◊ $11,** AE BC BTC DC EFT MC VI.

BRISBANE - TAIGUM QLD 4034

Pop 3,126. (14km N Brisbane), See map on page 418, ref C3. Suburb of Brisbane.

★★★★ **Colonial Village Motel**, (M), 351 Beams Rd, 13km N of GPO, ☎ 07 3865 0000, fax 07 3865 3587, (2 stry gr fl), 22 units [shwr, tlt, hairdry, a/c, tel, cable tv, clock radio, t/c mkg, refrig, mini bar], ldry, dryer, iron, iron brd, rec rm, ✉ (6 nights), pool, rm serv, tennis, cots. **RO ♦♦ $74 - $84,** AE BC DC EFT MC VI.

BRISBANE - TARINGA QLD 4068

Pop 6,232. (4km SW Brisbane), See map on page 418, ref B5. Inner suburb of Brisbane.

Self Catering Accommodation

★★★★☆ **Quest Taringa**, (SA), Cnr Waverly & Moggill Rds, 6km W of GPO, ☎ 07 3878 5500, fax 07 3878 5053, (Multi-stry), 33 serv apts acc up to 6, [shwr, tlt, a/c, c/fan, tel, TV, clock radio, refrig, cook fac, micro, elec frypan, d/wash, ldry (in unit)], dryer, iron, pool (salt water), bbq, c/park (undercover), secure park, cots-fee. **D $126 - $165,** AE BC DC MC VI.

BRISBANE - TOOWONG QLD 4066

Pop 12,928. (4km SW Brisbane), See map on page 418, ref C5. Inner suburb of Brisbane.

Hotels/Motels

★★★☆ **Benson Court Motel**, (M), 61 Benson St, ☎ 07 3870 4444, fax 07 3870 3244, (2 stry gr fl), 21 units [shwr, bath, tlt, hairdry (1), a/c (9), c/fan, tel, TV, clock radio, pillows], ldry, dryer, bbq, c/park (undercover) (7). **D ♦ $75 - $93, ♦♦ $75 - $93, ◊ $10, W ♦♦ $455 - $581,** ch con, AE BC DC EFT MC VI.

Self Catering Accommodation

★★★★☆ **Club Crocodile Toowong Villas**, (HU), 9 Ascog Tce, 4km to PO, ☎ 07 3371 4855, fax 07 3371 4661, (Multi-stry gr fl), 48 units acc up to 6, (Studio, 1, 2 & 3 bedrm), [shwr, bath, tlt, hairdry, a/c-cool, fan, tel, TV, clock radio, refrig, cook fac, micro, d/wash, ldry (in unit), blkts, linen, pillows], dryer, pool (2), bbq, c/park (undercover), plygr, cots-fee. **D $104 - $170,** AE BC DC MC VI.

★★★☆ **Quality Suites Toowong**, (SA), 24 Lissner St, 30m from Toowong Shopping Village, ☎ 07 3871 1633, fax 07 3871 1644, (2 stry gr fl), 36 serv apts acc up to 5, (1 & 2 bedrm), [shwr, bath, spa bath (2), tlt, a/c-cool, tel, TV, clock radio, t/c mkg, refrig, mini bar, ldry (in unit) (9)], lift, ldry, dryer, iron, iron brd, conv fac, pool (salt water), spa, c/park (undercover), secure park, cots. **D ◊ $15, $105 - $165,** ch con, AE BC DC EFT MC VI.

★★★ **Navarre Holiday Lodge**, (HU), 29 Elizabeth St, ☎ 07 3870 1011, fax 07 3371 1949, (2 stry gr fl), 9 units acc up to 6, (1, 2 & 3 bedrm), [a/c-cool, fan (8), heat, tel, TV, refrig, cook fac, micro, blkts, linen, pillows], ldry, dryer, pool, bbq, cots. **D ♦ $50, ♦♦ $60, ◊ $15, W ♦ $360 - $385,** BC MC VI.

Trouble-free travel tips - **Hoses and belts**

Inspect the condition of radiator hoses, heater hose fan and air conditioner belts.

BRISBANE - UPPER MOUNT GRAVATT QLD 4122

Pop 7,622. (14km SE Brisbane), See map on page 418, ref C6. Southern suburb of Brisbane.

Hotels/Motels

★★★★ **Travelodge Upper Mt Gravatt**, (LMH), 18 MacGregor St, 14km SE of GPO, ☎ 07 3347 7400, fax 07 3347 7500, (Multi-stry), 120 units [a/c-cool, cent heat, tel, TV, video, radio, t/c mkg, refrig, ldry], lounge (tv), ✕ (breakfast), meals to unit, 🐾, cots. **RO ♦ $79 - $109, ♦♦ $79 - $109, ♦♦♦ $95 - $125**, ch con, AE BC DC EFT JCB MC VI.

★★★☆ **Garden City Motor Inn**, (M), 2148 Logan Rd, opposite Garden City shopping centre, ☎ 07 3343 3655, fax 07 3343 7237, (2 stry), 20 units [shwr, tlt, a/c, c/fan (10), tel, TV, clock radio, t/c mkg, refrig, cook fac (4)], ldry, pool-heated (solar), c/park (undercover) (10), cots. **RO ♦ $76, ♦♦ $83, ♦ $12**, ch con, AE BC DC MC VI, ♿.

BRISBANE - WELLINGTON POINT QLD 4160

Pop 6,811. (25km SE Brisbane), See map on page 418, ref E5. Gateway to Moreton Bay. Fishing, Swimming.

Hotels/Motels

★★☆ **Wellington Point Hotel Motel**, (LMH), 391 Main Rd, ☎ 07 3207 2511, fax 07 3207 1719, (2 stry gr fl), 9 units [shwr, tlt, a/c (3), fan, c/fan (6), TV, radio, t/c mkg, refrig, toaster], ldry, ✉, 🐾, cots-fee. **RO ♦ $55, ♦♦ $66, ♦♦♦♦ $115.50**, AE BC DC EFT MC VI.

B&B's/Guest Houses

★★★★ **Wellington Point House**, (B&B), 25 The Esplanade, 1.5km S of PO, ☎ 07 3207 4355, fax 07 3207 4355, 3 rms [ensuite, spa bath (1), fan, heat, TV, video (1), t/c mkg, refrig, doonas], TV rm, refrig, non smoking rms. **BB ♦ $75 - $85, ♦♦ $85 - $100**, ch con, weekly con, BC MC VI,

Operator Comment: A big Queenslander with views across Moreton Bay to Stradbroke Island. Ph/ for brochure or visit www. wellingtonpointhouse.com.au.

BRISBANE - WEST END QLD 4101

Pop part of Brisbane. (5km SW Brisbane) See map on page 418, ref C5. A suburb of Brisbane.

Self Catering Accommodation

★★★★★ **Westend Central**, (SA), 220 Melbourne St, 1km S of GPO, ☎ 07 3011 8333, fax 07 3011 8399, 71 serv apts acc up to 6, (Studio, 1, 2 & 3 bedrm), [shwr, spa bath, a/c-cool, cent heat, tel, TV, clock radio, t/c mkg, refrig, micro, d/wash, blkts, linen, pillows], w/mach, dryer, pool, sauna, spa, bbq, cots-fee, non smoking units. **D ♦ $117 - $147, ♦♦ $117 - $220**, weekly con, AE BC DC MC VI.

B&B's/Guest Houses

★★★ **Eskdale Bed & Breakfast**, (B&B), 141 Vulture St, 2.5 km SW of GPO, ☎ 07 3255 2519, 4 rms [heat, fan, tel, TV, video, radio, refrig (communal), cook fac, micro, toaster, ldry], lounge (tv), ✕, t/c mkg shared, non smoking rms. **BB ♦ $55, ♦♦ $80**, ch con, BC MC VI.

BRISBANE - WINDSOR QLD 4030

Pop part of Brisbane. (2km N Brisbane) See map on page 418, ref C4. Inner suburb of Brisbane, easy access to all Brisbane has to offer.

Hotels/Motels

★★★★ **Windsor International Motel**, (M), Cnr Bryden St & Witwyche Rd, 700m N of Royal Brisbane Hospital, ☎ 07 3357 3456, fax 07 3357 3466, (Multi-stry gr fl), 60 units (1 suite) [shwr, bath (47), spa bath (10), tlt, hairdry, a/c, tel, TV, clock radio, t/c mkg, refrig, cook fac ltd (35), micro (35), pillows], lift, ldry-fee, dryer-fee, iron, iron brd, conf fac, ✉ (Mon to Sat), pool, sauna, rm serv, dinner to unit (Mon to Sat), c/park (undercover) (50), gym, cots, non smoking rms (43). **RO ♦ $109, ♦♦ $109, ♦ $11, Suite RO ♦ $85 - $115, ♦♦ $100 - $135**, AE BC DC EFT MC VI.

BRISBANE - WOODY POINT QLD 4019

Pop Part of Redcliffe, (28km N Brisbane), See map on page 418, ref D2. Bayside suburb of Redcliffe.

★☆ **Filmers Palace**, (LH), Gayundah Esp, ☎ 07 3284 6655, fax 07 3284 6878, (2 stry gr fl), 13 rms [basin, c/fan, TV (6)], shwr, tlt, ldry, lounge (TV & radio), ✉, 🐾, cots-fee. **RO ♦ $27.50, ♦♦ $50**, ch con, BC MC VI.

BRISBANE - WOOLLOONGABBA QLD 4102

Pop 4,143. (3km S Brisbane), See map on page 418, ref C5. Suburb of Brisbane.

★★★★ **Diana Plaza Hotel**, (Ltd Lic H), 12 Annerley Rd, opposite Mater Children's Hospital, ☎ 07 3391 2911, fax 07 3391 2944, (Multi-stry), 67 rms (9 suites) [shwr, bath, spa bath (9), tlt, hairdry, a/c, tel, TV, movie, clock radio, t/c mkg, refrig, mini bar, cook fac (9), cook fac ltd (3), micro (12), toaster], lift, ldry, conv fac, ✉, sauna, spa, rm serv, dinner to unit, 🐾, gym, cots-fee. **RO $115, Suite RO $155 - $220**, AE BC DC JCB MC VI.

BRISBANE - WOOLOOWIN QLD 4030

Pop Part of Brisbane, (5km N Brisbane), See map on page 418, ref C4. Suburb of Brisbane.

Self Catering Accommodation

★★★☆ **Matthew Flinders Apartments**, (HU), 45 Lisson Gr, 1km E of Lutwyche PO, ☎ 07 3262 6299, fax 07 3862 2772, (Multi-stry gr fl), 16 units acc up to 7, [shwr, tlt, a/c, tel, TV, clock radio, refrig, cook fac (1, 2 & 3 bedrm), cook fac ltd (studio), micro, blkts, linen, pillows], ldry, dryer-fee, iron, iron brd, pool (salt water), spa, bbq, cots. **RO ♦ $68 - $105, ♦♦ $68 - $105, W ♦ $410 - $630**, AE BC DC JCB MC VI.

★★☆ **Aabon Holiday Units**, (HF), 45 Lisson Gr, ☎ 07 3262 6462, fax 07 3862 2772, (2 stry), 12 flats [shwr, tlt, a/c-cool, fan, heat, tel, TV, clock radio, refrig, cook fac, blkts, linen], ldry, secure park (4), cots. **RO ♦ $80, ♦♦ $80**, ch con, BC MC VI.

BRISBANE - WYNNUM QLD 4178

Pop 10,845. (16km NE Brisbane), See map on page 418, ref D5. Bayside suburb of Brisbane.

Hotels/Motels

★★★ **Waterloo Bay Hotel Motel**, (LMH), 75 Berrima St, ☎ 07 3893 2344, fax 07 3393 4520, (2 stry gr fl), 18 units [shwr, tlt, a/c, tel, cable tv, clock radio, t/c mkg, refrig], ✉, c/park (undercover). **BB ♦ $55, ♦♦ $66, D ♦♦♦ $77**, AE BC DC MC VI.

★★☆ **Wynnum Anchor Motel**, (M), 14 Adam St, opposite RSL bowling club, ☎ 07 3396 3037, fax 07 3396 4808, 11 units [shwr, tlt, a/c, TV, t/c mkg, refrig, cook fac ltd (2)], ldry, pool, bbq, cots. **RO ♦ $50, ♦♦ $60, ♦ $6 - $11**, ch con, AE BC DC EFT MC VI.

Self Catering Accommodation

★★★ **Pelicans Nestle Inn**, (HU), 145 Esplanade, ☎ 07 3396 3214, fax 07 3396 3214, (2 stry gr fl), 8 units acc up to 5, (1 & 2 bedrm), [shwr, bath, tlt, a/c, TV, video, clock radio, t/c mkg, refrig, cook fac, micro, toaster, blkts, linen, pillows], ldry, dryer, iron, iron brd, bbq (2), c/park (undercover), cots. **D $75 - $100, W $420 - $650**, BC MC VI.

★★★☆ **(Townhouse Section)**, 5 units acc up to 5, (2 & 3 bedrm), [ensuite (4), shwr, bath, tlt, a/c, TV, video-fee, clock radio, t/c mkg, refrig, cook fac, micro, d/wash, toaster, ldry (in unit), blkts, linen, pillows], iron, iron brd, spa, bbq, secure park (garage). **D $145 - $185, W $750 - $1,120.**

BRISBANE - YATALA QLD 4207

Pop Nominal, (38km S Brisbane) See map on page 418, ref D8. Township at the base of Mount Tamborine.

★★★★ **Beenleigh Yatala Motor Inn**, (M), Cnr Stanmore Rd & Old Pacific Hwy, 3.6km S of PO, ☎ 07 3807 2555, fax 07 3287 5313, (2 stry gr fl), 34 units (3 suites) [shwr, bath (16), spa bath (3), tlt, a/c, tel, TV, video (3), clock radio, t/c mkg, refrig, cook fac (3), cook fac ltd (4), micro (7), toaster], ldry, dryer, conv fac, ⊠, pool, rm serv, dinner to unit, meals avail (dinner/breakfast), c/park (undercover) (25), cots. **RO ♦♦ $82,** ⋔ **$10, Suite D $120,** ch con, AE BC DC EFT MC VI, ⚘.
Operator Comment: 10KM North of Dreamworld & Movie World.

End of Brisbane & Suburbs

ADVANCETOWN QLD 4211

Pop Part of Beaudesert, (94km S Brisbane), See map on page 417, ref D8 Located in the Gold Coast Hinterland. The town was moved to its present site from the valley below before the valley was flooded by the Hinze Dam. Historic pioneer slab house. Gem Fossicking, Sailing.

Self Catering Accommodation
★★★★ **Cedar Lake Resort & Equestrian Centre**, (Apt), Resort, 555 Nerang-Murwillumbah Rd, 10km SW from Nerang, ☎ 07 5533 2255, fax 07 5533 2410, 60 apts (2 bedrm), [shwr, tlt, c/fan, TV, refrig, cook fac, blkts, linen, pillows], ldry, rec rm, conv fac, ⊠ (Tues-Sat), pool, sauna, spa, bbq, ✎, plygr, tennis, cots. **RO ♦♦♦♦ $137.50, ♦♦♦♦ W $654.50,** AE BC DC MC VI.

B&B's/Guest Houses
★★★☆ **Rumbalara**, (B&B), 72 Hoop Pine Crt, ☎ 07 5533 2211, fax 07 5533 2354, (2 stry gr fl), 4 rms [shwr, bath, tlt, c/fan, heat, tel, TV, video, t/c mkg], iron, iron brd, bbq, cots, non smoking rms. **BB ♦ $50, ♦♦ $85,** ch con.
Narrow Leaf Retreat & Healing Centre, (B&B), 118 Narrow Leaf Rd, 11k W Nerang, ☎ 07 5533 2573, fax 07 5533 2570, 12 rms [shwr, bath, tlt, hairdry, c/fan, t/c mkg, refrig], iron, iron brd, rec rm, conf fac, ✕, pool (salt water), spa, gym, non smoking property. **BB ♦♦ $110,** AE BC EFT MC VI, (not yet classified).

AGNES WATER QLD 4677

Pop 250. Nominal, (527km N Brisbane), See map on page 416, ref E7. The most northern surfing beach in Queensland - approximately halfway between Bundaberg and Gladstone - surfing, bush walks, fisihing, swimming, museum. Boating, Bush Walking, Fishing, Surfing, Swimming.

Hotels/Motels
★★★ **Mango Tree**, (M), 3 Agnes St, ☎ 07 4974 9132, 13 units [shwr, tlt, a/c-cool, c/fan, TV, clock radio, t/c mkg, refrig, cook fac, micro, toaster], ldry, bbq, dinner to unit, c/park (undercover) (6), ✎, cots-fee. **RO ♦ $60 - $75, ♦♦ $69 - $85,** ⋔ **$9,** BC EFT MC VI.

Self Catering Accommodation
★★★ **1770 Holiday Cabin Retreat**, (Cotg), 2276 Round Hill Rd, 7km from PO, ☎ 07 4974 9270, 8 cotgs acc up to 8, (1 & 2 bedrm), [shwr, tlt, heat, fan (3), c/fan (5), clock radio, refrig, cook fac, toaster, blkts, linen, pillows], ldry, iron, freezer (communal), bbq, plygr, cots. **D ♦♦ $65 - $80,** ⋔ **$11, W ♦♦ $390 - $480,** ⋔ **$66,** ch con, pen con, Library for guests. BC EFT MC VI.

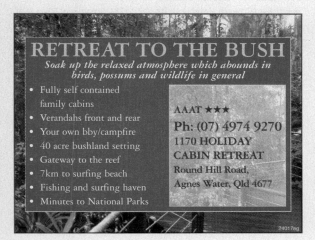

Agnes Palm Beachside Apartments, (HU), 12 Captain Cook Dr, 1.5km NE of PO, ☎ 07 4974 7200, fax 07 4974 7233, 9 units acc up to 6, (2 bedrm), [shwr, tlt, fan, TV, clock radio, t/c mkg, refrig, cook fac, micro, blkts, linen, pillows], w/mach, dryer, conf fac, cots, non smoking units. **D ♦♦ $77 - $88,** ⋔ **$5 - $10,** ch con, weekly con, (not yet classified).

B&B's/Guest Houses

★★★★ **Hobans Hideaway**, (B&B), No children's facilities, 2510 Round Hill Rd, 57km E of Miriam Vale ☎ 07 4974 9144, fax 07 4974 9144, 4 rms [shwr, tlt, c/fan, clock radio], ldry, lounge (TV & Cable), ✕, pool, t/c mkg shared (24 hr), bbq, ✎, bush walking. **BB ♦ $95, ♦♦ $110,** BC MC VI,
Operator Comment: Award winning retreat.Visit our website babs@com.au/qld/hoban.htm

Agnes by the Sea Bed & Breakfast, (B&B), 25 Captain Cook Dve, 200m N of PO, ☎ 07 4972 7273, (2 stry gr fl), 3 rms [c/fan, TV, video, clock radio, cook fac ltd, doonas], t/c mkg shared, refrig, bbq, non smoking property. **BB ♦ $88, ♦♦ $110,** BC MC VI, (not yet classified).

Pacific Crest Bed & Breakfast, (B&B), 15 Webster Crt, 1km S of PO, ☎ 07 4902 1770, fax 07 4902 1777, (2 stry gr fl), 4 rms [shwr, spa bath (3), tlt, c/fan (3), tel, cable tv, clock radio, t/c mkg, refrig, cook fac ltd, doonas], ldry, pool, spa, c/park (undercover), cots, non smoking property. **BB ♦ $190 - $250, ♦♦ $190-$250,** ⋔ **$20,** ch con, BC MC VI, (not yet classified).

AIRLIE BEACH QLD

See Whitsundays Region.

ALEXANDRA BAY QLD 4873

Pop Nominal, (1836km N Brisbane), See map on page 415, ref B1. Dense tropical rainforest area with abundant native flora & fauna, including brilliant orchids & butterflies. Birdwatching, Thorntons Peak nearby. Bush Walking.

★★★☆ **Daintree Wilderness Lodge**, (Chalet), 83 Cape Tribulation Rd, 13km N of Daintree ferry, tropical rainforest, ☎ 07 4098 9105, fax 07 4098 9021, 10 chalets acc up to 4, [shwr, tlt, c/fan, t/c mkg, refrig, mini bar], ⊠, bbq, rm serv, bush walking. **BLB ♦ $237, ♦♦ $237,** Chalets connected by boardwalks. Generated power only, AE BC DC MC VI.

ALEXANDRA HEADLAND QLD

See Sunshine Coast Region.

ALLORA QLD 4362

Pop 850. (152km SW Brisbane), See map on page 417, ref B7. Small agricultural township. Historic main street. Bush Walking, Golf, Scenic Drives, Tennis.

★★★★ **Talgai Homestead**, (GH), (Farm), Homestead c1868 on 300ha grazing property. Dalrymple Creek Rd, 6km W of Allora PO, ☎ 07 4666 3444, fax 07 4666 3780, 6 rms (6 suites) [shwr, bath (1), tlt, hairdry, fan, heat, elec blkts, TV, clock radio], lounge (fireplace), ⊠, t/c mkg shared, bush walking, tennis. **BB ♦♦ $120 - $285,** Meals by arrangement. Use of airstrip requires prior arrangement.

ALPHA QLD 4724

Pop 400. (1107km NW Brisbane), See map on page 414, ref C6. Located on Capricorn Hwy. Pastoral area known as 'The Gateway to the West'.

★★ **Alpha**, (LMH), Shakespeare St, ☎ 07 4985 1311, fax 07 4985 1173, 10 units [shwr, tlt, a/c, TV, t/c mkg, refrig], c/park (undercover), ✎, cots. **RO ♦ $49.50, ♦♦ $60.50,** ⋔ **$11,** ch con, AE BC MC VI.

Medication and driving

Medication can effect your driving. Certain drugs can effect your mental alertness and/or co-ordination and therefore effect driving skills. Always check with your doctor the effect which any medication (over the counter or prescription) you are taking may have on your driving. There may be an alternative drug which will not affect your driving. It is best to avoid drinking alcohol while taking medication.

ANAKIE QLD 4702

Pop 400. (947km NW Brisbane), See map on page 414, ref D6. Mining township renowned for its sapphires, rubies and the occasional diamond. Gem Fossicking.

Ramboda Homestead, (B&B), 'Ramboda', 0.5km N of Anakie, ☎ 07 4985 4154, fax 07 4985 4210, 4 rms [c/fan, elec blkts], shwr, tlt, lounge (TV), t/c mkg shared, tennis, cots, non smoking property. **DBB ♦ $50, ♦♦ $100, RO ♦ $33.50, ♦♦ $67**, ch con, Dinner by arrangement, BC MC VI, (not yet classified).

ARATULA QLD 4309

Pop Part of Boonah Shire, (89km SW Brisbane), See map on page 417, ref C7. Located on the Cunningham Hwy, close to Moogerah Dam, which provides irrigation water for the rich Warrill Valley. Parachute Club, water sports. Bush Walking, Gem Fossicking.

Hotels/Motels

★★☆ **Aratula**, (LMH), Cunningham Hwy, ☎ 07 5463 8100, 6 units [shwr, tlt, a/c, TV, clock radio, t/c mkg, refrig], ldry, conv fac, ⊠, c/park (undercover), ✆, cots. **RO ♦ $44, ♦♦ $55, ◊ $13**, ch con, BC MC VI.

★★ **Gap View Motel**, (M), Cunningham Hwy, ☎ 07 5463 8161, fax 07 5463 8161, 5 units [shwr, tlt, c/fan, heat, elec blkts, TV, t/c mkg, refrig], ldry, pool, c/park (undercover), plygr, cots-fee. **RO ♦ $46 - $52, ♦♦ $52 - $62, ◊ $7**, ch con, BC EFT MC VI.

ASHMORE QLD

See Gold Coast Region.

ATHERTON QLD 4883

Pop 5,700. (1749km N Brisbane), See map on page 415, ref B3. Heart of Atherton Tableland producing tobacco, peanuts, maize, and potatoes.

Hotels/Motels

★★★☆ **Atherton**, (M), Maunds Rd, 2km N of PO, ☎ 07 4091 1500, fax 07 4091 3234, 18 units [shwr, tlt, a/c-cool (3), fan, c/fan, heat, tel, TV, clock radio, t/c mkg, refrig], ldry, ⊠ (Tue-Sun), pool, c/park (undercover), cots. **RO ♦ $57.20, ♦♦ $68.20, ◊ $11**, ch con, AE BC DC MC VI.

★★★ **Hinterland**, (M), 44 Cook St, ☎ 07 4091 1885, fax 07 4091 4807, 16 units [shwr, tlt, a/c-cool (3), c/fan, heat, tel, TV, clock radio, t/c mkg, refrig], dinner to unit (Mon to Thur), c/park (undercover), cots. **RO ♦ $50, ♦♦ $58, ◊ $10**, ch con, AE BC DC MC VI.

★★★ **Wrights Motor Inn**, (M), Sims Rd, off Kennedy Hwy 2.5km N of PO, ☎ 07 4095 4141, fax 07 4095 4764, 38 units [shwr, tlt, a/c (17), c/fan, cent heat, tel, TV, movie, clock radio, t/c mkg, refrig, cook fac (5)], ldry, ⊠, pool (salt water), bbq, dinner to unit, c/park (undercover) (34), cots. **RO ♦ $48 - $53, ♦♦ $55 - $60, ♦♦♦♦ $80 - $85**, ch con, AE BC DC MC VI.

B&B's/Guest Houses

Atherton Blue Gum B & B, (B&B), 36 Twelfth Ave, 1.5km East of PO, ☎ 07 4091 5149, fax 07 4091 5149, 3 rms [shwr, tlt, c/fan (1), t/c mkg, refrig (1), toaster (1)], lounge (TV), cots. **BB ♦ $60.50 - $70.40, ♦♦ $70.40 - $80.30**, BC MC VI, (not yet classified).

AUGATHELLA QLD 4477

Pop 450. (745km NW Brisbane), See map on page 414, ref C7. Pastoral town on Warrego River. Cattle & Sheep industries rely on artesian bores. Bowls, Tennis.

★★★ **Augathella**, (M), Cavanagh St, ☎ 07 4654 5177, fax 07 4654 5353, 10 units [shwr, tlt, a/c, elec blkts, tel, TV, movie, clock radio, t/c mkg, refrig], bbq, dinner to unit, c/park (undercover), cots. **RO ♦ $49 - $53, ♦♦ $60 - $65, ◊ $10**, BC MC VI.

AYR QLD 4807

Pop 8,700. (1283km N Brisbane), See map on page 415, ref E8. Situated at the northern approach to the Burdekin Bridge (1097m long) in sugar Cane area. Ashworths Rock Shop, bowls, fishing, golf, swimming (pool), Bowls, Fishing, Golf, Swimming.

Hotels/Motels

★★★☆ **Country Ayr**, (M), 197 Queen St, ☎ 07 4783 1700, fax 07 4783 4934, 14 units [shwr, tlt, a/c-cool, tel, TV, movie, clock radio, t/c mkg, refrig], ldry, dryer, ⊠ (Mon-Sat), pool, cots-fee. **RO ♦ $84, ♦♦ $84 - $92, ◊ $12**, AE BC DC MC VI.

 ★★★☆ **Parkside**, (M), 76 Graham St, ☎ 07 4783 1244, fax 07 4783 4769, 18 units [shwr, tlt, a/c-cool, c/fan, tel, TV, clock radio, t/c mkg, refrig], ldry, dryer, ⊠ (Mon-Sat), bar, pool indoor heated, rm serv, dinner to unit, c/park (undercover), cots. **RO ♦ $61 - $69, ♦♦ $66 - $72, ◊ $9**, AE BC DC MC VI.

 ★★★ **Ayr Max Motel**, (M), 4 Edward St Bruce Hwy North, 2km N of PO opposite showgrounds, ☎ 07 4783 2033, fax 07 4783 3338, 12 units [shwr, tlt, a/c-cool, c/fan, tel, TV, movie, clock radio, t/c mkg, refrig, mini bar (no alcohol), toaster (4)], pool, spa, bbq, dinner to unit, c/park (undercover), cots-fee, non smoking units (5). **RO ♦ $49 - $54, ♦♦ $59 - $64, ◊ $9**, AE BC DC EFT MC MCH VI,

Operator Comment: Clean. Comfortable. Affordable. Your home away from home. We offer Auto club & Seniors discounts. To book your room Ph 07 4783-2033 NOW !

★★★ **Ayr Shamrock**, (M), 274 Queen St (Bruce Hwy), ☎ 07 4783 1044, fax 07 4783 4200, 10 units [shwr, tlt, a/c, c/fan, tel, TV, movie, clock radio, t/c mkg, refrig], ldry, pool (salt water), bbq, c/park (undercover). **RO ♦ $45, ♦♦ $50 - $55**, AE BC DC MC VI.

★★☆ **Ayrline**, (M), 129 Edward St, ☎ 07 4783 1100, fax 07 4783 4224, (2 stry gr fl), 12 units [shwr, tlt, a/c-cool, c/fan, tel, TV, clock radio, t/c mkg, refrig, cook fac (3), micro (3)], ldry, dryer, rec rm, pool (salt water), spa, bbq, dinner to unit, cots-fee. **RO ♦ $53 - $64, ♦♦ $59 - $64, ◊ $11**, AE BC DC EFT MC VI.

★★☆ **Tropical City Motor Inn**, (M), 121 Macmillan St, ☎ 07 4783 1344, fax 07 4783 1473, 16 units [shwr, tlt, a/c-cool, fan, tel, TV, clock radio, t/c mkg, refrig], ldry, conv fac, ⊠, pool, rm serv, dinner to unit, c/park (undercover) (6), cots. **RO ♦ $50 - $60, ♦♦ $56 - $68**, AE BC DC MC VI.

Self Catering Accommodation

★★★☆ **Country Ayr**, (SA), 135 Graham St, ☎ 07 4783 1700, fax 07 4783 4934, 4 serv apts acc up to 6, (2 bedrm), [shwr, tlt, a/c-cool, c/fan, TV, clock radio, t/c mkg, refrig, cook fac, ldry (in unit)], dryer, iron, c/park (undercover), cots-fee. **D ♦♦ $107, ◊ $20, W ♦♦ $589, ◊ $100**, AE BC DC MC VI.

BALGAL BEACH QLD 4816

Pop 550. (1,424km N Brisbane), See map on page 415, ref D7. Small tropical seaside resort between Townsville & Ingham. Crystal Creek-Mount Spec National Park. Fishing, Scenic Drives, Swimming.

Self Catering Accommodation

★★☆ **Balgal Beach Holiday Units**, (HU), 284 Ocean Pde, 50km N of Townsville, ☎ 07 4770 7296, 9 units acc up to 6, (1 bedrm), [shwr, tlt, a/c-cool, c/fan, TV, movie, clock radio, refrig, cook fac, toaster, blkts, linen, pillows], ldry, pool, spa, bbq, c/park (undercover), ✆. **D ♦♦ $55 - $66, ◊ $10, W ♦♦ $330 - $396, ◊ $60**, ch con, BC MC VI.

BAMAGA QLD 4876

Pop 750. (2720km N Brisbane), See map on page 414, ref B2. Township located 33km S of Cape York. Bamaga Aboriginal Community controls the Aboriginal Islander Community of Bamaga.

Other Accommodation

Seisia Seaview Lodge, (Lodge), Koroba Rd, Seisia, 8km NW of Bamaga Cape York, ☎ 07 4069 3243, fax 07 4069 3307, 6 rms [shwr, tlt, a/c, c/fan, t/c mkg, refrig, cook fac, elec frypan, toaster], ldry-fee, dryer-fee, iron, iron brd, ✕ (Mon to Sat), bbq (covered), ✆, cots. **RO ♦ $93, ♦♦ $105.50**, Breakfast available, BC EFT MC VI, (not yet classified).

BANANA QLD 4702

Pop 50. (618km N Brisbane), See map on page 416 , ref B7. Located at the junction of the Dawson and Leichardt Hwys. Scenic Drives.

B&B's/Guest Houses

★★★ **Cooper Downs Cattle Station**, (GH), (Farm), Working cattle property established 1860. 37km NE of Banana PO, ☎ 07 4996 5276, fax 07 4996 5259, 11 rms [shwr, bath, tlt, a/c (11), c/fan (6)], ldry, ☒, pool, bbq, kiosk, ✆, cots. AE BC MC VI.

Louise Cottage, (B&B), Leichhardt Highway, 12km S of Banana;40km N of Theodore, ☎ 07 4995 7237, fax 07 4995 7297, 3 rms [shwr, tlt, heat, fan, elec blkts, TV, clock radio, t/c mkg, refrig, cook fac, toaster], ✗, pool, bbq, dinner to unit. **BB ꭍ $65, ꭍꭍ $85, ꭍ $20**, ch con, (not yet classified).

BARCALDINE QLD 4725

Pop 1,600. (1152km NW Brisbane), See map on page 414 , ref C6. A wool growing and cattle raising district, known for its famous tree of knowledge (great shearers strike of 1891), the Australian Workers Heritage Centre (paying tribute to the working men and women of Australia), bowls, golf, tennis, cricket, swimming, Bowls, Golf, Tennis.

Hotels/Motels

★★★☆ **Landsborough Lodge**, (M), Landsborough Hwy, ☎ 07 4651 1100, fax 07 4651 1744, 23 units [shwr, bath (4), tlt, hairdry (14), a/c, c/fan, tel, cable tv, clock radio, t/c mkg, refrig, mini bar, cook fac (3), toaster], ldry, conf fac (40), ☒ (Mon-Sat), bar, pool (covered), dinner to unit, cots. **RO ꭍ $64, ꭍꭍ $75, ꭍ $11**, AE BC DC MC VI, 🖢.

★★★ **Barcaldine**, (M), Cnr Ash St (Landsborough Hwy), ☎ 07 4651 1244, fax 07 4651 1788, 11 units [shwr, tlt, a/c-cool (7), a/c (4), heat, tel, TV, movie, clock radio, t/c mkg, refrig, toaster], ldry, dinner to unit, kiosk, cots-fee. **RO ꭍ $50, ꭍꭍ $55, ꭍ $10**, ch con, AE BC DC EFT MC MCH VI.

★★★ **Ironbark Inn**, (M), Landsborough Hwy, 1km SE of PO, ☎ 07 4651 2311, fax 07 4651 2314, 18 units (2 suites) [shwr, tlt, a/c-cool (9), a/c (9), tel, TV, clock radio, t/c mkg, refrig], ldry-fee, dryer-fee, rec rm, conv fac, ☒, pool (salt water), c/park (undercover), cots-fee, non smoking units (6). **RO ꭍ $50, ꭍꭍ $65, ꭍ $10, Suite D $80 - $85, ꭍ $5**, AE BC DC EFT MC VI.

★★★ **Lee Garden**, (M), 1 Box St (Cnr Landsborough & Capricorn Hwys), ☎ 07 4651 1488, fax 07 4651 1847, 14 units [shwr, tlt, a/c, tel, TV, movie, clock radio, t/c mkg, refrig], ✗, BYO, c/park (undercover), courtesy transfer, cots-fee. **RO ꭍ $50, ꭍꭍ $55 - $65, ꭍ $10**, AE BC DC MC VI, 🖢.

★★ **Starlin**, (M), Pine St, opposite hospital, ☎ 07 4651 1353, fax 07 4651 1353, 6 units [shwr, tlt, a/c, c/fan, elec blkts (3), TV, clock radio (5), t/c mkg, refrig, cook fac ltd, micro, toaster], ldry, bbq. **RO ꭍ $35, ꭍꭍ $39**, ch con, BC MC VI.

Self Catering Accommodation

★★★☆ **The Blacksmiths Cottage**, (Cotg), c1900, 109 Elm Street, 1km from PO, ☎ 07 4651 1724, fax 07 4651 2243, 1 cotg acc up to 4, (2 bedrm), [shwr, tlt, fan, heat (oil), TV, t/c mkg, refrig, cook fac, micro, elec frypan, toaster, ldry (in unit), blkts, linen, pillows], iron, iron brd, c/park (carport). **BLB ꭍ $55, ꭍ $5, ꭍꭍ W $315.**

BARGARA QLD 4670

Pop 4,500. (384km N Brisbane), See map on page 416, ref E8. Popular seaside area close to Bundaberg. Boat Ramp, Boating, Bowls, Fishing, Golf, Scuba Diving, Surfing, Swimming.

Hotels/Motels

★★★ **Bargara Beach Motor Inn**, (M), 7a Bauer St, ☎ 07 4159 2395, fax 07 4159 2013, 8 units [shwr, spa bath (2), tlt, a/c (8), c/fan, tel, cable tv, clock radio, t/c mkg, refrig, cook fac (4), micro, toaster, ldry-fee], dryer-fee, iron, iron brd, bbq, c/park (undercover), plygr, cots-fee. **RO ꭍ $55 - $90, ꭍꭍ $55 - $95, ꭍ $10**, 2 self contained family units ★★★★, AE BC DC MC VI.

★★★ **Pacific Sun Motor Inn**, (M), 11 Bauer St, 13Km E of Bundaberg, ☎ 07 4159 2350, fax 07 4159 2350, 10 units [shwr, tlt, a/c-cool (10), c/fan, tel, cable tv (5), clock radio, t/c mkg, refrig, cook fac (8)], ldry, dryer, bbq, c/park (undercover), cots. **RO ꭍ $47 - $57, ꭍꭍ $51 - $66, ꭍ $12**, ch con, AE BC DC EFT MC MCH VI.

★★☆ **Pandanus Seafront**, (M), 105 The Esplanade, ☎ 07 4159 2313, 5 units [shwr, tlt, a/c-cool (4), a/c (1), c/fan, heat, cable tv, clock radio, t/c mkg, refrig], pool, bbq, c/park (undercover), cots. **RO ꭍ $45, ꭍꭍ $45 - $60, ꭍ $10**, BC MC VI.

Self Catering Accommodation

★★★★☆ **Don Pancho Beach Resort**, (SA), 62 Miller St, ☎ 07 4159 2146, fax 07 4159 2788, (Multi-stry gr fl), 42 serv apts acc up to 6, (Studio, 1 & 2 bedrm), [shwr, spa bath (15), tlt, a/c-cool (42), tel, cable tv, clock radio, t/c mkg, refrig, cook fac, micro, d/wash (18), ldry (in unit) (19)], ldry, ☒, bar, pool, spa, bbq, rm serv, c/park (undercover) (35), bicycle, gym, tennis (half court), cots-fee. **RO ꭍꭍ $88 - $160**, AE BC DC MC VI, 🖢.

★★★★ **Horizons**, (HU), 16 Miller St, beachfront, ☎ 07 4159 2736, fax 07 4159 1266, (Multi-stry gr fl), 3 units acc up to 6, (2 & 3 bedrm), [shwr, tlt, c/fan, heat, TV, video, clock radio, refrig, cook fac, micro, d/wash, ldry (in unit), blkts, linen, pillows], dryer, iron, bbq, c/park (undercover). **D $90 - $150, ꭍ $10, W ꭍꭍ $490 - $950, ꭍ $20**, BC EFT MC VI, 🖢.

★★★★ **Lakeview Park Holiday Townhouses**, (HU), Waimarie St, 1km S of PO opposite beach & golf course, ☎ 07 4159 1226, fax 07 4159 1050, 12 units acc up to 6, (2 & 3 bedrm), [shwr, bath (7), tlt, a/c-cool (6), fan, heat, tel, TV, video, clock radio, refrig, cook fac, micro, ldry (in unit), blkts, linen, pillows], dryer (8), bbq, c/park (garage), cots-fee. **D ꭍꭍꭍ $62 - $150, ꭍ $10, W ꭍꭍꭍ $435 - $735**, AE BC DC MC VI.

★★★☆ **Bargara Shoreline Serviced Apartments**, (SA), 104 Miller St, 30 m from golf course, ☎ 07 4159 1180, fax 07 4159 1588, (Multi-stry gr fl), 14 serv apts acc up to 6, (Studio & 2 bedrm), [ensuite, shwr, tlt, a/c, c/fan, heat, tel, cable tv, video, clock radio, refrig, cook fac, micro, ldry (in unit) (5)], ldry, iron, pool (salt water), bbq, c/park (undercover), cots-fee. **D ꭍꭍ $80 - $170, W ꭍꭍ $480 - $1,020**, AE BC DC EFT MC VI.

★★★☆ **Kellys Beach Resort**, (HU), 6 Trevors Rd, 3km S of PO, ☎ 07 4154 7200, fax 07 4154 7300, 26 units acc up to 7, [shwr, tlt, c/fan, TV, video, clock radio, refrig, cook fac, micro, toaster, pillows], ldry-fee, meeting rm, ✗ (BYO), bar, pool (2), sauna, spa, pool bar, bbq-fee, c/park (undercover), ✆, tennis (court fee), cots-fee, non smoking units (5). **RO ꭍ $70, ꭍꭍ $75 - $99, ꭍ $11**, ch con, Additional 15 hotel apartments-not rated. AE BC DC MC VI.

★★★☆ **Nieuport 54**, (HU), 54 Miller St, ☎ 07 4159 2164, fax 07 4159 2164, (2 stry), 6 units acc up to 6, (2 bedrm - Split level accommodation available.), [shwr, bath, tlt, a/c-cool (4), fan, TV, video, clock radio, refrig, cook fac, micro], ldry, sauna, spa, bbq, ✆, cots. **D ꭍꭍ $85 - $105, ꭍ $6, W ꭍꭍ $465 - $615, ꭍ $24**, BC MC VI.

★★★☆ **Ocean Court**, (HU), 6 Miller St, 900m S of PO, ☎ 07 4159 1513, fax 07 4159 1513, (Multi-stry gr fl), 4 units acc up to 6, (2 bedrm), [shwr, bath (hip), tlt, fan, TV, clock radio, refrig, cook fac, micro (5), d/wash (4), ldry (in unit), blkts, linen, pillows], dryer (5), bbq, secure park, cots. **D $80 - $100, W $300 - $600**, AE BC MC VI.

★★★☆ **Ocean Shores**, (HU), 33 Miller St, adjacent to golf course, ☎ 07 4159 1513, fax 07 4159 1593, 12 units, acc up to 4, (2 bedrm), [shwr, tlt, a/c-fee, c/fan, TV, refrig, cook fac, micro, ldry (in unit), blkts, linen, pillows], secure park, cots. **D $65 - $90, W $250 - $480**, AE BC MC VI.

BARGARA QLD continued...

★★★☆ **Sandcastles on the Beach**, (HU), 82 Miller St, opposite Golf Course, ☎ 07 4159 2175, (Multi-stry gr fl), 7 units acc up to 6, (2 bedrm), [shwr, tlt, c/fan, heat, tel, TV, video, clock radio, refrig, cook fac, micro, elec frypan, d/wash, ldry (in unit), blkts, linen, pillows], iron, bbq, c/park (undercover), cots-fee. **D ♦♦♦♦ $100 - $225, W ♦♦♦♦ $360 - $1,250**, BC EFT MC VI, ⚹占.

★★★☆ **Trelawney Beachfront Holiday Units**, (HU), 14 Miller Street, 13km E of Bundaberg, ☎ 07 4159 1266, fax 07 4159 1266, 3 units acc up to 4, [shwr, bath, tlt, fan, cable tv, clock radio, refrig, micro, toaster, blkts, linen, pillows], w/mach, dryer, iron, iron brd, bbq, c/park. **D ♦♦ $80 - $120, ◊ $10 - $20, W ♦♦ $375 - $790**, BC EFT MC VI, ⚹占.

★★★ **Bargara Gardens Motel**, (HU), 13 See St, ☎ 07 4159 2295, fax 07 4154 7555, 8 units acc up to 6, [shwr, tlt, a/c-cool (4), TV, refrig, cook fac (8), blkts, linen, pillows], pool (salt water), spa, bbq, cots. **RO ♦ $50 - $70, ♦♦ $55 - $85, ◊ $10**, BC MC VI.

★★★ **Causeway Flats**, (HU), 1 Miller St, ☎ 07 4159 1513, fax 07 4159 1513, 3 units acc up to 6, (1, 2 & 3 bedrm), [shwr, tlt, fan, TV, t/c mkg, refrig, cook fac, micro, toaster, blkts, doonas, linen, pillows], ldry, cots. **D ♦ $50 - $100, ♦♦ $70 - $100, W ♦ $250 - $590, ♦♦ $250 - $590**, ch con, AE BC EFT MC VI.

★★★ **Crystal Waters Beach Apartments**, (HU), 5 Miller St, adjoins 18 hole golf course, ☎ 07 4159 2667, fax 07 4154 7198, (2 stry gr fl), 12 units acc up to 6, [shwr, tlt, a/c-cool, c/fan, TV, movie, clock radio, refrig, cook fac, micro, elec frypan, blkts, linen, pillows], ldry, iron, pool, bbq, c/park (undercover), cots. **D $55 - $100, W $250 - $595**, BC MC VI.

★★★ **Sunrise Court**, (HU), 33 Miller St, adjacent to golf course ☎ 07 4159 1513, fax 07 4159 1513, 4 units acc up to 6, (2 bedrm), [shwr, bath (1), tlt, a/c-cool, fan, cable tv, clock radio, refrig, cook fac, micro, ldry (in unit) (1), blkts, linen, pillows], ldry, dryer, iron, spa, bbq, c/park (undercover), cots. **D ♦♦ $55 - $80, W $225 - $440**, AE BC MC VI.

B&B's/Guest Houses

★★★★ **Dunelm House Bed & Breakfast**, (B&B), 540 Bargara Rd, 9km E of Bundaberg PO, ☎ 07 4159 0909, fax 07 4159 0916, 3 rms [shwr, tlt, a/c, TV, clock radio], ldry, lounge (TV), pool-heated (salt water), spa, t/c mkg shared, bbq, c/park (undercover), non smoking property. **BB ♦ $55 - $60, ♦♦ $70 - $80**, BC MC VI.

BAUPLE QLD 4650

Pop Nominal, (222km N Brisbane), See map on page 417, ref D2. Small country town.

★★★☆ **The Quilt Country Lodge**, (B&B), Lot 2 Stottenville Rd, ☎ 07 4129 2611, fax 07 4129 2457, 3 rms [hairdry (1), c/fan, clock radio], iron, iron brd, rec rm, lounge (TV, video), t/c mkg shared, refrig, bbq (covered), c/park (undercover), non smoking rms (3). **BB ♦ $50, ♦♦ $100**, fam con.

BEAUDESERT QLD 4285

Pop 3,700. (64km S Brisbane), See map on page 417, ref D8. A commercial centre, west of Gold Coast Hinterland, surrounded by the mountains of the Scenic Rim. A rich agricultural, beef and dairying district. Bowls, Bush Walking, Golf, Horse Racing, Scenic Drives, Swimming, Tennis.

Hotels/Motels

★★★ **Beaudesert Motel**, (M), Cnr Brisbane & Tubber Sts, 200m N of PO, ☎ 07 5541 1244, fax 07 5541 1425, 8 units [shwr, tlt, a/c-cool, heat, elec blkts, tel, TV, clock radio, t/c mkg, refrig], bbq, dinner to unit, cots. **RO ♦ $46, ♦♦ $58, ◊ $12**, AE BC DC EFT MC VI.

★★☆ **Kerry Court**, (M), Cnr Brisbane Rd & Albert St, 500m S of PO, ☎ 07 5541 1593, fax 07 5541 1593, 8 units [shwr, tlt, a/c-cool, c/fan (2), heat, tel, TV, clock radio, t/c mkg, refrig, mini bar], bbq. **RO ♦ $44, ♦♦ $55, ◊ $11**, AE BC MC VI.

Self Catering Accommodation

★★☆ **Rim Fall Cottages**, (Cotg), (Farm), 1000 ha beef cattle property. Chingee Creek Rd, 50km S of Beaudesert, ☎ 07 5544 8235, fax 07 5544 8235, 2 cotgs acc up to 8, [shwr, tlt, refrig, cook fac, blkts, pillows], cots. **RO $60 - $120, ♦♦♦♦ $350 - $480**, ch con.

B&B's/Guest Houses

★★☆ **Cedar Glen**, (B&B), (Farm), Darlington via Beaudesert, 34km S of Beaudesert, ☎ 07 5544 8170, fax 07 5544 8240, 3 rms [heat, elec blkts], tlt, ldry, rec rm, lounge (TV/Video), cots. **D all meals ♦ $125**, ch con, BC MC VI.

★★★☆ **(Stinson Cottage)**, 1 cotg acc up to 5, [shwr, bath, tlt, hairdry, c/fan, elec blkts, TV, radio, refrig, cook fac, micro, elec frypan, d/wash, toaster, ldry (in unit), blkts, linen, pillows], dryer, iron, iron brd, cots. **D all meals ♦ $125**.

★★★☆ **(Tantallan Homestead)**, 1 rm [shwr, bath, tlt, c/fan, heat (wood fire), elec blkts, TV, radio, refrig, cook fac, micro, d/wash, toaster, ldry, pillows], lounge (TV), cots. **D $125 - $150, W $700 - $800**.

BEDOURIE QLD 4829

Pop 60. (1591km W Brisbane), See map on page 414, ref A6. A centre for the vast properties that surround the town and is the capital of the Diamantina Shire.

Simpson Desert Oasis, (M), Herbert St, 200km N of Birdsville, 200km S of Boulia, ☎ 07 4746 1291, fax 07 4746 1208, 4 units [shwr, tlt, a/c, tel, TV, radio, t/c mkg, toaster], iron, iron brd, ✕, res liquor license, rm serv, dinner to unit. **RO ♦ $65, ♦♦ $72 - $80, ◊ $18**, ch con, BC EFT MC VI, (not yet classified).

BEECHMONT QLD 4211

Pop Nominal, (108km S Brisbane), See map on page 417, ref D8. Located in Lamington National Park in the Gold Coast Hinterland. Bush Walking, Scenic Drives.

★★☆ **Wantalanya Chalets**, (HU), 2 Beechmont Rd, 11.8km from Advancetown turnoff, ☎ 07 5533 3520, 4 units acc up to 4, [shwr, tlt, heat, TV, refrig, cook fac, blkts, linen, pillows], ldry, bbq,c/park (undercover). **D ♦ $45, ♦♦ $75, W ♦♦ $450**.

BELYANDO CROSSING QLD 4820

Pop Nominal, (1187km NW Brisbane), See map on page 414, ref D5. Small outback area in central Queensland on banks of Belyando River.

Hotels/Motels

★★★ **Belyando Crossing Service Station Motel**, (M), Gregory Developmental Rd, 175km N of Clermont, 200km S of Charters Towers, ☎ 07 4983 5269, fax 07 4983 5269, 9 units [shwr, tlt, a/c-cool, TV, t/c mkg, refrig, pillows], meals to unit, cots-fee. **D ♦ $49.50, ♦♦ $60, ◊ $10**, AE BC EFT MC VI.

Self Catering Accommodation

★★★☆ **Plain Creek Host Farm**, (Cotg), (Farm), Plain Creek Station, via The Great Inland Wa, 26km NW of Belyando Crossing, ☎ 07 4983 5228, fax 07 4983 5314, 1 cotg acc up to 6, [shwr, tlt, a/c-cool, fan, c/fan, elec blkts, clock radio, t/c mkg, elec frypan, toaster], ldry, dryer, iron, iron brd, lounge (TV, video/homestead), ✕ (homestead), pool (salt water), spa, cook fac, refrig, bbq, cots. **D $66 - $195**, ch con. Tariff includes all activities and tours,

BENARABY QLD 4680

Pop 350. (514km N Brisbane), See map on page 416, ref D7. Located on the Bruce Hwy. Bowls, Fishing, Golf, Swimming, Tennis.

Hotels/Motels

★★★ **Benaraby Hilltop Motor Inn**, (M), Bruce Hwy, ☎ 07 4975 0211, fax 07 4975 0271, 11 units [shwr, tlt, a/c-cool, tel, TV, clock radio, t/c mkg, refrig], ✕, pool, spa, dinner to unit, c/park (undercover), gym, cots. **RO ♦ $44, ♦♦ $49.50, ◊ $5.50**, AE BC DC MC VI.

★★ **Greenacres Motel**, (M), Bruce Highway, 20km S of Gladstone PO, ☎ 07 4975 0136, fax 07 4975 0136, 7 units [shwr, tlt, a/c-cool (4), a/c (2), c/fan (2), tel (public), TV, clock radio, t/c mkg, refrig, toaster, ldry-fee], dryer-fee, iron, pool, bbq, dinner to unit, cots, non smoking units (4). **RO ♦ $44, ♦♦ $49.50, ◊ $5.50**, BC MC VI.

Trouble-free travel tips - Fluids

Check all fluid levels and top up as necessary. Look at engine oil, automatic transmission fluid, radiator coolant (only check this when the engine is cold), power steering, battery and windscreen washers.

Rates may change. Check before booking.

BIGGENDEN QLD 4621

*Pop 700. (284km N Brisbane), See map on page 417, ref C1.
Established in the Gold Rush of 1889, now a dairying, timber and
mining area. Mt Walsh and Coalstoun Lakes National Parks and the
Mt Woowoonga recreational reserve provide a scenic backdrop of
craggy peaks. Historic Chowey Bridge, Silver Bell Novelty Farm and
Museum. Bush Walking.*

Hotels/Motels

★★★ **Biggenden Motel Roadhouse**, (M), 44 Walsh St, ☎ 07 4127 1301,
fax 07 4127 1000, 7 units [shwr, tlt, a/c, tel, TV, clock radio,
t/c mkg, refrig], ✕, dinner to unit, shop, c/park (undercover).
RO ♦ $46, ♦♦ $56, ◊ $12, AE BC EFT MC VI.

B&B's/Guest Houses

★★★☆ **Rocky Creek Farm Stay**, (B&B), (Farm), 480ha cattle property,
Isis Hwy, 12km W of PO, ☎ 07 4127 1377, fax 07 4127 1377, 3 rms
shwr, tlt, rec rm, lounge (TV), pool, spa, bush walking, non smoking rms.
D all meals ♦ $110, ♦♦ $220, ch con.

BIGGERA WATERS QLD

See Gold Coast Region.

BILINGA BEACH QLD

See Gold Coast Region.

BILOELA QLD 4715

*Pop 5,200. (596km N Brisbane), See map on page 416, ref C7.
A constant growing rural town whose income is augmented by the
workforce of open cut coal mines, Teys Bros Meatworks and Cotton
Ginnery. Boating, Bowls, Fishing, Sailing, Swimming.*

Hotels/Motels

★★★★ **Biloela Motor Inn**, (LH), Cnr Dawson Highway & Clarke Drive,
1500m E of PO, ☎ 07 4992 4099, fax 07 4992 4011, 22 rms [shwr,
spa bath, tlt, a/c, tel, TV, clock radio, t/c mkg, refrig], ldry, dryer, iron,
iron brd, ✕, pool, bbq, rm serv, dinner to unit, cots, non smoking
rms (14). **RO ♦ $76, ♦♦ $86, ◊ $10**, ch con, AE BC DC EFT MC VI, ₰₲.

★★★☆ **Apollo**, (M), Cnr Gladstone Rd & Rainbow St,
☎ 07 4992 1122, fax 07 4992 1271, 28 units [shwr, tlt, a/c, c/fan,
heat (12), tel, TV, video-fee, radio, t/c mkg, refrig, cook fac (6)], ldry,
dryer, iron, ✕ (Mon to Sat), pool, bbq, rm serv, c/park (undercover) (20),
cots-fee. **RO ♦ $68, ♦♦ $75 - $79**, ch con, AE BC DC EFT MC VI, ₰₲.

★★★☆ **Biloela Centre**, (M), 52 Grevillea St, Town Centre,
☎ 07 4992 2622, fax 07 4992 3841, 15 units [shwr, tlt, a/c, tel, TV,
movie, clock radio, t/c mkg, refrig, toaster], ldry, dryer, iron, ✕ (Mon
to Sat), rm serv, dinner to unit, c/park (undercover), cots.
RO ♦ $68 - $75, ♦♦ $76 - $85, ◊ $11, AE BC DC MC VI.

★★★☆ **Settlers Inn Resort Style Motel**, (LMH), Dawson Hwy,
☎ 07 4992 2933, fax 07 4992 2627, 30 units [shwr, tlt, a/c, tel,
cable tv, clock radio, t/c mkg, refrig], ldry, iron, conv fac, ✕ (Mon to
Sat), pool, rm serv, dinner to unit, c/park (undercover), cots-fee.
RO ♦ $71 - $81, ♦♦ $80 - $90, ◊ $7, ch con, Units 17 to 30 ★★★☆.
AE BC DC MC VI, ₰₲.

★★★ **Biloela Countryman Motel**, (M), Burnett Hwy, ☎ 07 4992 1488,
fax 07 4992 2445, 28 units [shwr, tlt, a/c, heat, tel, cable tv, clock
radio, t/c mkg, refrig], ldry, w/mach-fee, dryer-fee, ✕ (Mon-Fri), pool,
dinner to unit, c/park (undercover), cots. **RO ♦ $52 - $55, ♦♦ $63 -
$68, ◊ $11**, AE BC BTC DC MC VI.

★★ **Sun Valley**, (M), 57 Dawson Hwy, ☎ 07 4992 1281,
fax 07 4992 3295, 8 units [shwr, tlt, a/c-cool, heat, TV, clock radio,
t/c mkg, refrig, toaster], ldry, dryer, pool, bbq, dinner to unit,
park (undercover), tennis, cots. **RO ♦ $45, ♦♦ $51, ◊ $10**, AE BC DC MC VI.

Silo Motor Inn, (M), 75 Dawson Hwy, 1km W of PO, ☎ 07 4992 5555,
fax 07 4992 3555, 25 units [ensuite, a/c, tel, TV, clock radio, t/c mkg,
refrig], ldry, conf fac, ✕, pool, meals to unit, cots, non smoking
units (22). **RO ♦ $85, ♦♦ $90 - $100, ◊ $15**, ch con, weekly con,
AE BC DC EFT MC VI, (not yet classified).

Self Catering Accommodation

★★★☆ **Biloela Countryman Motel**, (Cotg), Burnett Hwy,
☎ 07 4992 1488, fax 07 4992 2445, 14 cotgs acc up to 6, [shwr, tlt,
hairdry, a/c, tel, cable tv, clock radio, refrig, cook fac, micro, blkts, linen,
pillows], ldry, w/mach-fee, dryer-fee, iron, ✕ (Mon-Fri), pool, dinner to
unit, cots. **D ♦ $60.50, ♦♦ $71.50, ◊ $11**, AE BC BTC DC MC VI.

BIRDSVILLE QLD 4482

*Pop 100. (1586km W Brisbane), See map on page 414, ref A7.
Located between the Simpson & Sturt's Stony Deserts, at the
beginning of the Birdsville Track.*

★★☆ **Birdsville**, (LMH), 1 Adelaide St, ☎ 07 4656 3244,
fax 07 4656 3262, 18 units [shwr, tlt, a/c, heat, t/c mkg, refrig],
✕ (Mon-Sat), bbq. **RO ♦ $65, ♦♦ $92, ◊ $11**, BC MC VI, ₰₲.

BLACKALL QLD 4472

*Pop 1,400. (1045km NW Brisbane), See map on page 414, ref C6.
Small friendly town situated on the Landsborough Hwy. Original
Black Stump, Historic Woolscour, Jackie Howe Memorial. Bowls,
Golf, Swimming.*

Hotels/Motels

★★★★ **Blackalls Acacia Motor Inn**, (Ltd Lic H), Cnr Shamrock &
Short St, 800km W of Rockhampton, ☎ 07 4657 6022,
fax 07 4657 6077, 25 rms [shwr, tlt, a/c, tel, TV, movie, clock radio,
t/c mkg, refrig, toaster], ldry-fee, ✕, coffee shop, pool, spa (heated),
rm serv, dinner to unit, c/park (undercover), cots, non smoking units
(11). **RO ♦ $68 - $72, ♦♦ $79 - $83, ◊ $12**, AE BC DC EFT MC VI, ₰₲.

 ★★★ **Blackall Coolibah Motel**, (M), Matilda Hwy 36
Shamrock St, ☎ 07 4657 4380, fax 07 4657 4187,
15 units [shwr, tlt, a/c, c/fan, heat, tel, TV, t/c mkg,
refrig, toaster], ldry, pool (salt water), dinner to unit,
c/park (undercover), cots-fee. **RO ♦ $47 - $55, ♦♦ $58 - $65**, ch con,
AE BC DC EFT MC MCH VI.

★★ **Blackall Motel**, (M), Shamrock St, cnr Myrtle St, ☎ 07 4657 4491,
fax 07 4657 4611, 15 units [shwr, tlt, a/c-cool, heat, elec blkts, tel,
TV, movie, clock radio, t/c mkg, refrig], ldry, dryer-fee, dinner to
unit (Mon to Sat), kiosk, cots-fee. **RO ♦ $45, ♦♦ $56, ♦♦♦ $71**, ch con,
pen con, AE BC DC EFT MC VI.

B&B's/Guest Houses

★★★ **Avington Outback Holiday Station**, (GH), (Farm), Caravans.
Turn left off Landsborough Hwy, 75km NW of Blackall PO,
☎ 07 4657 5952, fax 07 4657 5025, 7 rms [shwr (2), tlt (2),
a/c-cool (4), elec blkts], shwr, tlt, ldry, lounge (Video), ✕ (BYO),
cook fac, t/c mkg shared, refrig, bbq, canoeing, golf, tennis, cots-fee.
D all meals ♦ $125, ch con, 6 Budget rooms in shearers' quarters
accommodation. BC MC VI.

BLACKBUTT QLD 4305

*Pop 500. (165km NW Brisbane), See map on page 417, ref B5.
District is popular with gemstone enthusiasts. Extensive State Forest
nearby. Bush Walking, Gem Fossicking, Scenic Drives.*

★☆ **The Blackbutt Motel**, (M), 69 Coulson St (D'Aguilar Hwy),
☎ 07 4163 0500, 6 units [shwr, tlt, fan, heat, TV, t/c mkg, refrig],
ldry, w/mach-fee, dryer-fee, bbq, dinner to unit (arrangement), shop, ✆.
RO ♦ $35, ♦♦ $45, ◊ $12.

BLACKWATER QLD 4717

*Pop 6,000. (861km NW Brisbane), See map on page 416, ref A6.
Known as the coal capital of Queensland. Open cut mining - Utah,
South Blackwater - inspections available. Swimming, Tennis.*

Hotels/Motels

★★☆ **Black Diamond**, (M), Capricorn Hwy, ☎ 07 4982 5944,
fax 07 4986 1525, 15 units [shwr, tlt, a/c-cool, elec blkts, tel, TV,
movie, clock radio, t/c mkg, refrig, mini bar], ✕, bbq (covered),
dinner to unit, c/park (undercover), cots-fee. **RO ♦ $77, ♦♦ $86, ◊ $11**,
ch con, 6 units ★★★☆. AE BC DC MC VI, ₰₲.

★★☆ **Bottletree Motel & Caravan Park**, (M), Cnr Capricorn Hwy &
Littlefield St, ☎ 07 4982 5611, fax 07 4982 5611, 11 units [shwr, tlt,
a/c, tel, TV, movie, clock radio, t/c mkg, refrig, cook fac ltd, elec frypan],
ldry, dryer, ✕ (BYO), bbq, dinner to unit, c/park (undercover), plygr,
cots. **RO ♦ $49, ♦♦ $60, ◊ $11**, ch con, AE BC DC MC VI.

★★☆ **Capricorn Hotel Motor Inn**, (LMH), Cnr Taurus & Arthur Sts,
☎ 07 4982 5466, fax 07 4986 1004, 36 units [shwr, tlt, a/c, tel, TV,
t/c mkg, refrig], conv fac, ✕, c/park (undercover), cots-fee. **RO ♦ $55,
♦♦ $65**, ch con, AE BC DC MC VI.

BLUFF QLD 4702

Pop 450. (829km NW Brisbane), See map on page 416, ref A6. Small railway town in mining area surrounded by brigalow country. A busy railway changeover centre. Activities include country races, football, rifle & pistol shooting. Blackdown Tableland National Park nearby. Bush Walking, Tennis.

Hotels/Motels
★★★ **Bluff Palms**, (M), North St, ☎ 07 4982 9133, fax 07 4982 9273, 15 units [shwr, tlt, a/c, tel, TV, clock radio, t/c mkg, refrig], ldry, ✉, pool (salt water), bbq. **RO** ♦ **$60.50**, ♦♦ **$66**, ◊ **$5.50**, AE BC MC VI.

BOONAH QLD 4310

Pop 2,250. (84km SW Brisbane), See map on page 417, ref C8. A rich agricultural area, located in the heart of Fassifern Valley.

Hotels/Motels
★★★ **Boonah**, (M), 1 Mt Carmel Rd, ☎ 07 5463 1944, fax 07 5463 4332, 16 units [shwr, tlt, hairdry, a/c-cool, c/fan, heat, elec blkts, TV, clock radio, t/c mkg, refrig, toaster], pool (salt water), bbq, meals to unit. **RO** ♦ **$60.50**, ♦♦ **$72.60**, **$12.10**, fam con, AE BC DC MC VI.

Self Catering Accommodation
★★★★ **Bilyana Cottages**, (Cotg) 1853 Boonah-Rathdowney Rd, Coochin, 18.5km E of Boonah, ☎ 07 5563 6249, fax 07 5463 6249, 3 cotgs acc up to 4, [shwr, tlt, c/fan, heat (wood fire), radio, CD, t/c mkg, refrig, cook fac, micro, toaster], non smoking rms (3). **D** ♦♦ **$85 - $135**, ◊ **$20**.

BOREEN POINT QLD 4565

Pop 300. Part of Tewantin, (185km N Brisbane), See map on page 417, ref D4. Located at Lake Cootharaba on the Sunshine Coast. Fishing, Sailing, Scenic Drives, Swimming, Water Skiing.

Apollonian Hotel, (LH) Lott 22 Laguna St, ☎ 07 5485 3100, fax 07 5485 3499, 10 rms [c/fan, t/c mkg], shwr, tlt, ✉, t/c mkg shared, ☎. **RO** ♦ **$14**, ♦♦ **$35**, BC MC VI.

BOROREN QLD 4678

Pop 350. (483km N Brisbane), See map on page 416, ref D7. A small suburb of Gladstone. Farming and timber area with scenic mountain backdrop. Hang gliding competitions off nearby mountain peaks. Dragonhall medieval fantasy tableaux.

Hotels/Motels
★★★★ **Bororen Hotel Motel**, (LMH) Bruce Hwy, ☎ 07 4974 4177, (2 stry) 12 units [shwr, tlt, a/c, tel, TV, clock radio, t/c mkg, refrig, toaster], ldry, ✉ (Fri- Sat), ✕, pool, c/park (undercover), ☎, cots. **RO** ♦ **$45 - $55**, ♦♦ **$55 - $65**, ◊ **$10**, BC EFT MC VI.

★★★★ **Koorawatha Homestead**, (M) Bruce Hwy, via Bororen, 2km S of PO, ☎ 07 4974 4188, fax 07 4974 4245, 22 units [shwr, tlt, hairdry, a/c-cool, heat (8), tel, TV, movie, clock radio, t/c mkg, refrig], iron, iron brd, conv fac, ✉ (6 nights), pool, bbq, rm serv, dinner to unit, c/park (undercover), cots-fee. **RO** ♦ **$68 - $78**, ♦♦ **$76 - $86**, ◊ **$11**, AE BC DC MC VI.

★★ **Bororen Motel**, (M) Bruce Hwy, ☎ 07 4974 4144, fax 07 4974 4144, 10 units [shwr, tlt, a/c-cool, c/fan (9), heat (8), TV, clock radio, t/c mkg, refrig], pool, plygr, cots. **RO** ♦ **$39**, ♦♦ **$45**, ◊ **$11**, ch con, BC MC VI.

BOULIA QLD 4829

Pop 250. (1903km NW Brisbane), See map on page 414, ref A6. Capital of the Channel Country, on the Burke River. Area mystery is the appearance of the 'Min Min'lights. The Stone Cottage, Min Min Hotel, Corroboree Tree, Cawnpore Hills, Last Hitching Post, Waddie Trees, the Red Stump, Dingo Fence.

Hotels/Motels
★★★ **Boulia Desert Sands**, (M) Herbert St, 100m from PO, ☎ 07 4746 3144, fax 07 4746 3144, 12 units [shwr, tlt, a/c, tel, TV, clock radio, t/c mkg, refrig, toaster]. **RO** ♦ **$60 - $70**, ♦♦ **$65 - $75**, ◊ **$10**, BC MC VI.

★ **Australian**, (LMH) Herbert St, ☎ 07 4746 3144, fax 07 4746 3191, (2 stry) 9 units [basin, a/c-cool, c/fan], shwr, tlt, ldry, lounge (TV), ✕ (Mon to Sat), ☎, cots. **RO** ♦ **$33**, ♦♦ **$38**, ch con.

★★ **(Motel Section)**, 4 apts [shwr, tlt, a/c, tel, TV, clock radio, t/c mkg, refrig, toaster], c/park (undercover). **RO** ♦ **$50**, ♦♦ **$60**.

BOWEN QLD 4805

Pop 9,000. (1165km N Brisbane), See map on page 416, ref A1. Known as the 'Climate Capital of Australia'. Boat Ramp, Bowls, Croquet, Fishing, Golf, Horse Racing, Sailing, Shooting, Squash, Swimming, Tennis.

Hotels/Motels
★★★☆ **Castle Motor Lodge**, (M) 6 Don St, 1.5km NW of CBD, ☎ 07 4786 1322, fax 07 4786 3097, 32 units [shwr, tlt, a/c-cool, tel, cable tv, video-fee, clock radio, t/c mkg, refrig], conv fac, ✉, pool, spa, rm serv, dinner to unit, c/park (undercover), cots-fee, non smoking units (7). **RO** ♦ **$68.20**, ♦♦ **$73.70**, ◊ **$11**, ch con, AE BC DC EFT MC VI.

★★★ **Ocean View**, (M) Bruce Hwy, Gordon Beach, 6km S of PO, ☎ 07 4786 1377, fax 07 4786 3818, 12 units [shwr, tlt, a/c-cool, c/fan, cable tv, clock radio, t/c mkg, refrig], ldry-fee, res liquor license, pool (salt water), bbq, dinner to unit (breakfast), c/park (undercover), ☎, cots. **RO** ♦ **$50**, ♦♦ **$58**, ◊ **$11**, AE BC EFT MC VI.

★★★ **Queens Beach Motor Hotel**, (LMH) 101 Golf Links Rd, Queens Beach, ☎ 07 4785 1555, fax 07 4785 1502, (2 stry gr fl), 50 units [shwr, tlt, a/c-cool, c/fan, tel, TV, movie, clock radio, t/c mkg, refrig, mini bar (10)], ldry, dryer, conv fac, ✉ (Mon-Sat), pool, rm serv, dinner to unit, ☎, cots-fee. **RO** ♦ **$41 - $54**, ♦♦ **$55 - $69**, ◊ **$15**, ch con, Units 1 to 22 ★★☆. AE BC DC EFT MC VI.

★★★ **Whitsunday Sands Resort**, (M) Horseshoe Bay, ☎ 07 4786 3333, fax 07 4786 3388, (2 stry gr fl), 20 units [shwr, bath, tlt, a/c-cool, c/fan, tel, cable tv, clock radio, t/c mkg, refrig, toaster], ldry, ✉ (Mon-Sat), pool (salt water), bbq, kiosk, boat park, plygr, cots-fee. **RO** ♦ **$55**, ♦♦ **$66**, ◊ **$11**, ch con, AE BC DC MC VI.

★★☆ **Pearly Shell**, (M) 2 Don St, ☎ 07 4786 1788, fax 07 4786 1788, 12 units [shwr, tlt, a/c-cool, c/fan, TV, radio, t/c mkg, refrig], pool (covered), c/park (undercover), ☎, cots-fee. **RO** ♦ **$44**, ♦♦ **$49.50 - $52.80**, ◊ **$8.80**, AE BC MC VI.

★☆ **North Australian**, (LMH) Cnr William & Herbert Sts, ☎ 07 4786 1244, fax 07 4786 2459, 16 units [shwr, tlt, a/c-cool, fan, tel, TV, movie, t/c mkg, refrig], meals avail (breakfast), ☎, cots-fee. **RO** ♦ **$40**, ♦♦ **$45**, ◊ **$8**, BC MC VI.

Self Catering Accommodation
★★★★ **Skyview Motel Family Units**, (HU) 49 Horseshoe Bay Rd, ☎ 07 4786 2232, fax 07 4786 3107, (2 stry gr fl), 14 units acc up to 6, (1 & 2 bedrm), [shwr, bath (hip), tlt, a/c-cool, c/fan, TV, clock radio, refrig, cook fac, micro, elec frypan, ldry (6 - no dryer), blkts, linen, pillows], ldry, dryer, pool (salt water), bbq (covered), c/park (undercover), ☎, plygr, cots. **D** ♦♦ **$64 - $80**, ◊ **$12 - $16**, **W** ♦♦ **$363 - $484**, ◊ **$56 - $70**, ch con, Min book Christmas Jan and Easter, AE BC DC EFT MC VI.

★★★☆ **Palm View**, (HU) Cnr Soldiers Rd & Howard St, ☎ 07 4785 1415, fax 07 4785 1421, 6 units acc up to 5, (1 bedrm), [shwr, tlt, a/c-cool, fan, heat, TV, video-fee, clock radio, refrig, cook fac, micro, blkts, linen, pillows], ldry, dryer, pool (salt water), bbq (covered), cots. **D** ♦♦ **$50 - $69**, ◊ **$11**, **W** ♦♦ **$286 - $396**, ◊ **$66**, BC MC VI.

★★★☆ **Whitsunday Sands Resort**, (HU) Horseshoe Bay Rd, ☎ 07 4786 3333, fax 07 4786 3388, 14 units acc up to 5, (1 & 2 bedrm), [shwr, bath (hip), tlt, a/c-cool, c/fan, tel, TV, refrig, cook fac, ldry (in unit) (10), blkts, linen, pillows], ✕ (Mon-Sat), pool (salt water), bbq, kiosk, boat park, plygr, cots-fee. **D** ♦♦ **$55 - $71.50**, ◊ **$11**, **W** ♦♦ **$330 - $451**, ch con, AE BC CC DC MC VI.

★★★ **Horseshoe Bay Resort**, (HU) Horseshoe Bay, ☎ 07 4786 2564, fax 07 4786 3460, 12 units acc up to 6, (Studio, 1 & 2 bedrm), [shwr, tlt, a/c-cool, c/fan, refrig, cook fac, blkts, linen, pillows], TV rm, ✉, pool, sauna, spa, mini golf, cots-fee, **D** ♦♦ **$59 - $77**, ◊ **$11**, AE BC EFT MC VI.

★★★ **Rod & Reel**, (HU) Horseshoe Bay Rd, Grays Bay, ☎ 07 4786 2421, 7 units acc up to 6, [shwr, tlt, fan, TV, refrig, cook fac, elec frypan, blkts, linen, pillows], ldry, pool, bbq, c/park (undercover), cots. **D** ♦♦ **$77**, ◊ **$11**, **W** ♦♦ **$385**, ch con, BC MC VI.

★★☆ **Rose Bay**, (HU) 51 Bluewater Pde, ☎ 07 4786 2434, (2 stry gr fl), 4 units acc up to 4, (1 bedrm), [shwr, tlt, c/fan, TV, refrig, cook fac, elec frypan, toaster, blkts, linen, pillows], ldry, w/mach, iron, bbq. **DBB** ◊ **$30**, **D** ♦♦ **$40 - $45**, ◊ **$5**, **W** ♦♦ **$240 - $270**.

BOYNE ISLAND QLD 4680

Pop 3,200. (515km N Brisbane). See map on page 416, ref D7.
A popular sporting and recreational area, situated at mouth of
Boyne River. Fishing, Water Skiing.

Hotels/Motels

★★★ **Boyne Island Motel and Villas**, (M), 3 Orana Ave, ☎ 07 4973 7444,
fax 07 4973 8983, 9 units [shwr, tlt, hairdry, a/c-cool, tel, TV, video,
clock radio, t/c mkg, refrig, toaster], ldry, dryer, pool, bbq, dinner to unit,
c/park (undercover), courtesy transfer, cots, ch con, AE BC DC MC VI.

Self Catering Accommodation

★★★★ **Boyne Island Motel And Villas**, (HU), Previously Boyne Island
Holiday Villas, 3 Orana Avenue, 1km S of PO, ☎ 07 4973 7444,
fax 07 4973 8983, (2 stry) 7 units acc up to 7, (1 & 2 bedrm), [shwr,
tlt, hairdry, a/c-cool, c/fan, tel, TV, video, clock radio, refrig, cook fac, micro,
ldry (in unit) (4), blkts, linen, pillows], ldry, iron, pool, bbq, c/park
(undercover), courtesy transfer, cots. D ♦♦ $58 - $80, AE BC DC MC VI.

★★★☆ **A Beach 'N Reef Motel**, (SA), 55-59 Wyndham Ave,
800m E of PO, ☎ 07 4973 8836, fax 07 4973 8165,
14 serv apts acc up to 4, (Studio), [shwr, tlt, a/c-cool,
tel, TV, video-fee, clock radio, t/c mkg, refrig, cook fac], ldry, dryer,
pool (salt water), spa, bbq, c/park (undercover), boat park, cots.
D ♦♦ $55 - $75, ♦ $15, ch con, AE BC MC VI.

BRAMPTON ISLAND QLD 4740

Pop Nominal, (975km N Brisbane). See map on page 416, ref B2.
Located on Great Barrier Reef (Cumberland Group). Mountainous island
(area of 8sq km) with forests, palm trees and white sandy beaches.
National Park & Wildlife Sanctuary. Surrounded by coral reefs.

Self Catering Accommodation

★★★☆ **Brampton Island**, (Apt), Resort, Brampton Island,
Via Mackay, ☎ 07 4951 4499, fax 07 4951 4097,
(Multi-stry), 108 apts acc up to 4, [shwr, tlt, a/c, c/fan,
tel, movie, clock radio, t/c mkg, refrig, blkts, linen, pillows],
ldry, rec rm, ⊠, cafe, pool (2), ☏, bush walking, golf, gym, tennis.
D all meals ♦ $294 - $360, ♦♦ $204 - $270, ♦ $140, ♦ W $1,230 -
$1,600, ♦♦ $780 - $1,150, ♦ $400, AE BC DC MC VI.

BRAMSTON BEACH QLD 4871

Pop 346. (1660km N Brisbane). See map on page 415, ref C4.
Seaside resort via Miriwinni. picnic areas. Boating, Canoeing,
Fishing, Golf, Swimming, Tennis.

Hotels/Motels

★★★ **Bramston Beach Holiday Motel**, (M), 1 Dawson
St, ☎ 07 4067 4139, fax 07 4067 4279, (2 stry gr fl),
12 units [shwr, tlt, a/c-cool-fee, fan, tel, TV, t/c mkg,
refrig, cook fac ltd, micro (5)], ldry, dryer, pool (salt water),
bbq (covered), c/park (undercover) (6), cots. RO ♦ $52, ♦♦ $62 - $66,
♦♦♦♦ $75, AE BC DC MC MCH VI.

BRIBIE ISLAND QLD 4507

Pop 10,743. (69km N Brisbane). See map on page 417, ref D5. An
island measuring 51km long by 7km wide, connected to the
mainland by a bridge across Pumiceston Passage which is a scenic
waterway running between the island and the mainland. Flora and
Fauna Sanctuary. Boat Ramp, Boating, Bowls, Bush Walking, Fishing,
Golf, Sailing, Squash, Surfing, Swimming, Tennis, Water Skiing.

Hotels/Motels

★★★ **Bribie Island Hotel**, (LMH), 29 Sylvan Beach Esp, opposite
Pumicestone Passage, ☎ 07 3408 7477, fax 07 3408 7501, 12 units
[shwr, tlt, a/c, c/fan, tel, TV, clock radio, t/c mkg, refrig, toaster],
ldry, conv fac, night club (Fri & Sat), ⊠, c/park (undercover), ☏, cots.
RO ♦ $60, ♦♦ $70, ♦ $10, AE BC DC EFT MC VI.

★★★ **Bribie Waterways Resort**, (M), 155 Welsby Pde, ☎ 07 3408 3000,
fax 07 3408 3076, (2 stry gr fl), 27 units [shwr, tlt, c/fan, tel, TV, clock
radio, t/c mkg, refrig, cook fac ltd (13), micro (13)], conv fac, ⊠,
pool (salt water), rm serv, cots-fee. RO ♦ $82.50 - $93.50, ♦♦ $82.50 -
$93.50, AE BC DC MC VI, ♿.

★★☆ **Koolamara Resort**, (M), Boyd St, 500m from golf course,
☎ 07 3408 1277, fax 07 3408 1204, (2 stry gr fl), 25 units [shwr, tlt,
a/c, c/fan, heat (10), tel, TV, clock radio, t/c mkg, refrig], ldry-fee,
dryer-fee, conv fac, ⊠ (Wed to Sun), pool, bbq (covered), rm serv,
dinner to unit, c/park (undercover), cots. RO ♦ $66 - $88,
♦♦ $77 - $88, ♦ $5 - $10, AE BC MC VI, ♿.

Self Catering Accommodation

★★★★ **Camelot Castle by the Sea on Bribie**, (HU), 12 Rickman Pde,
Woorim, Woorim 4507, 50km N of Brisbane, ☎ 07 3410 1414,
fax 07 3408 9980, (Multi-stry gr fl), 3 units acc up to 8, (2 bedrm).
D ♦ $70 - $90, ♦♦ $80 - $100, ch con, weekly con, BC MC VI, ♿.

★★★★ **Sylvan Beach Resort**, (HU), 19-23
Sylvan Beach Esplanade, 100m N of Bribie
Bridge, ☎ 07 3408 8300, fax 07 3408 8311,
(Multi-stry gr fl), 23 units acc up to 6, (2
& 3 bedrm), [ensuite (12), shwr, bath, tlt,
a/c-cool, tel, TV, video, clock radio, micro,
elec frypan, d/wash, toaster, ldry, blkts, linen, pillows], dryer, iron,
iron brd, pool (saltwater), bbq (covered), secure park, courtesy transfer,
bicycle, cots-fee. D $98 - $184, W $560 - $980, BC EFT MC VI.

★★★☆ **Placid Waters Holiday Apartments**, (HU), Cnr Toorbul &
Foster Sts, Bongareee 4507, adjacent to Pumicestone Passage
☎ 07 3408 2122, fax 07 3408 2244, (Multi-stry), 25 units acc up to 6,
(2 bedrm), [shwr, bath, tlt, c/fan, heat, tel, TV, video, clock radio,
refrig, cook fac, micro, d/wash, toaster, ldry (in unit), blkts, linen,
pillows], dryer, iron, iron brd, pool-heated (salt water), bbq, secure
park, cots. D ♦♦♦♦ $95 - $140, ♦ $10 - $40, W ♦♦♦♦ $380 - $800,
pen con, BC EFT MC VI.

★★☆ **Tanderra Lodge**, (HU), Nicholson Cl, ☎ 07 3408 3558,
fax 07 3408 1570, (Multi-stry), 7 units acc up to 6, (2 & 3 bedrm),
[ensuite, shwr, bath, tlt, TV, clock radio, refrig, cook fac, ldry (in unit),
linen reqd-fee], bbq, secure park, cots. D ♦♦ $70, ♦ $10, W ♦♦ $235 -
$485, Min book applies.

B&B's/Guest Houses

★★★☆ **Island Bed & Breakfast**, (B&B), 130 White Patch Esplanade,
69km N of Brisbane, ☎ 07 3408 9070, fax 07 3408 9071, 3 rms
[ensuite, fan, TV, clock radio], ldry, rec rm, spa, cook fac, t/c mkg
shared, bbq, dinner to unit, secure park, plygr. BB ♦ $55 - $60,
♦♦ $75 - $85, BC CC EFT MC VI.

BROADBEACH QLD

See Gold Coast Region.

BUDERIM QLD

See Sunshine Coast Region.

BUNDABERG QLD 4670

Pop 41,000. (368km N Brisbane), See map on page 416, ref E8. Large city established in 1867. Situated on the banks of the Burnett River, southern gateway to the Great Barrier Reef islands, whale watching and turtle tours in season. 'Whaling Wall' is a prominent feature of the City Centre. Sugar and small crops are important industries. Bundaberg Rum Distillery tours; Botanical Gardens; Hinkler House; Dreamtime Reptile Reserve. Boating, Bowls, Croquet, Fishing, Golf, Horse Racing, Shooting, Squash, Tennis, Water Skiing.

Hotels/Motels

★★★★☆ **Villa Mirasol Boutique Motel**, (M), 225 Bourbong St, 25m N of PO, ☎ 07 4154 4311, fax 07 4154 4011, 33 units [ensuite, spa bath (6), a/c, heat (elec), tel, TV, video, clock radio, t/c mkg, refrig], ldry, conf fac, ✗, pool, meals to unit, secure park (undercover), cots (fee), non smoking rms. RO ♦ $72 - $96, ♦♦ $82.50 - $104.50, ♦ $11, ch con, AE BC DC MC VI, ⅋⅄.

★★★★ **Alexandra Park Motor Inn**, (M), 66 Quay St & Cnr Bingera St, ☎ 07 4152 7255, fax 07 4152 9301, 19 units (9 suites) [shwr, bath (3), spa bath (2), tlt, hairdry, a/c-cool (6), a/c (13), tel, cable tv, clock radio, t/c mkg, refrig, mini bar, cook fac (1)], ldry, dryer, iron, iron brd, ⊠, pool, rm serv, dinner to unit, c/park (undercover), cots. RO $49.50 - $110, ch con, AE BC DC EFT MC VI.

★★★★ **Bert Hinkler Motor Inn**, (M), Cnr Takalvan & Warrell Sts, ☎ 07 4152 6400, fax 07 4151 3980, 32 units (3 suites) [shwr, bath (3), spa bath (1), tlt, hairdry, a/c-cool, tel, cable tv, clock radio, t/c mkg, refrig], ldry, iron, iron brd, conf fac, ⊠ (Mon - Thurs), pool, sauna, spa, rm serv, dinner to unit, c/park (undercover), tennis (half court), cots-fee. RO ♦ $77 - $115, ♦♦ $82 - $127, ♦ $5.50, AE BC DC MC MP VI.

★★★★ **Bundaberg International Motor Inn**, (M), 73 Takalvan St, ☎ 07 4151 2365, fax 07 4153 1866, (2 stry gr fl) 40 units (5 suites) [shwr, bath (6), spa bath (16), tlt, hairdry, a/c, tel, cable tv, video (2), clock radio, t/c mkg, refrig, mini bar, cook fac (4), micro (8)], ldry-fee, dryer-fee, iron, iron brd, conf fac, ⊠ (Mon to Sat), pool, spa, rm serv, c/park (undercover), non smoking units (19). RO ♦ $87 - $105, ♦♦ $90 - $110, ♦ $11, Suite D $150 - $185, AE BC DC MC VI, ⅋⅄.

★★★★ **Reef Gateway Motor Inn**, (M), 11 Takalvan St, ☎ 07 4153 2255, fax 07 4153 2294, 34 units (3 suites) [shwr, spa bath (3), tlt, hairdry, a/c-cool, a/c (11), heat, tel, TV, movie, clock radio, t/c mkg, refrig], ldry, ⊠ (Mon to Sat), pool (salt water), rm serv, c/park (undercover), cots-fee. RO ♦ $85 - $120, ♦♦ $92 - $120, ♦ $12, Suite RO ♦ $120 - $135, ♦♦ $120 - $135, AE BC DC EFT MC MP VI.

★★★★ **Sugar Country Motor Inn**, (M), 220 Bourbong St, ☎ 07 4153 1166, fax 07 4153 1726, (2 stry gr fl) 33 units [shwr, bath (4), spa bath (2), tlt, hairdry, a/c-cool, heat (6), tel, cable tv, clock radio, t/c mkg, refrig], ldry, conf fac, ⊠ (Mon to Sat), pool (salt water), rm serv, dinner to unit, c/park (undercover), cots-fee. RO ♦ $80, ♦♦ $88, ♦ $10, AE BC BTC DC EFT MC MP VI, ⅋⅄.

★★★☆ **Acacia Motor Inn**, (M), 248 Bourbong St, 500m W of PO, ☎ 07 4152 3411, fax 07 4152 2387, 26 units [shwr, tlt, a/c-cool, heat, tel, TV, movie, clock radio, t/c mkg, refrig], ldry-fee, dryer-fee, pool (salt water), bbq, dinner to unit (Mon to Sat), c/park (undercover), cots-fee. RO ♦♦ $79, ♦ $11, ch con, AE BC DC EFT MC MP VI.

★★★☆ **Bundaberg City Motor Inn**, (M), 246 Bourbong St, ☎ 07 4152 5011, fax 07 4152 5516, 17 units [shwr, tlt, hairdry, a/c-cool, a/c (8), tel, TV, movie, clock radio, t/c mkg, refrig], ldry-fee, dryer-fee, pool, bbq, dinner to unit, c/park (undercover), cots-fee. RO ♦ $76 - $84, ♦♦ $84 - $92, ♦ $11, AE BC DC EFT JCB MC MP VI.

★★★☆ **Bundaberg Coral Villa Motor Inn**, (M), 56 Takalvan St, ☎ 07 4152 4999, fax 07 4152 4541, 11 units (2 suites) [shwr, spa bath (1), tlt, hairdry (11), a/c (11), c/fan, heat, tel, TV, video (4), movie, clock radio, t/c mkg, refrig, cook fac ltd (5), toaster], iron, iron brd, pool, sauna (in unit) (1), bbq, c/park (undercover), cots-fee. RO ♦ $60 - $66, ♦♦ $69 - $82, ♦ $10, ch con, AE BC DC EFT MC VI.

★★★☆ **Bundaberg Spanish Motor Inn**, (M), Cnr Woongarra & Mulgrave Sts, ☎ 07 4152 5444, fax 07 4152 5970, 16 units [shwr, tlt, a/c-cool, heat (3), tel, TV, movie, clock radio, t/c mkg, refrig, cook fac], ldry, pool (salt water), bbq, dinner to unit, c/park (undercover), cots. RO ♦ $63, ♦♦ $75, ♦ $10, ch con, fam con, AE BC DC EFT MC VI.

★★★☆ **Butterfly Checkmate**, (M), 240 Bourbong St, ☎ 07 4152 2700, fax 07 4152 2424, 18 units (2 bedrm), [shwr, tlt, a/c, c/fan, heat, tel, TV, movie, clock radio, t/c mkg, refrig], ldry, dryer-fee, ✗ (Mon to Sat), pool (salt water), bbq, dinner to unit, c/park (undercover), cots. RO ♦ $58 - $64, ♦♦ $68 - $76, AE BC DC EFT MC VI.

★★★☆ **Sun City**, (M), 11a Hinkler Ave, ☎ 07 4152 1099, fax 07 4153 1510, 12 units [shwr, tlt, hairdry, a/c-cool, c/fan, heat, clock radio, t/c mkg, refrig, toaster], ldry, iron, iron brd, pool (salt water), bbq (covered), meals to unit, c/park (undercover), cots, non smoking units. D ♦ $50 - $55, ♦♦ $55 - $60, ch con, AE BC DC EFT MC MCH MP VI.

★★★ **Casper**, (M), 80 Takalvan St, ☎ 07 4153 1100, fax 07 4153 1100, 15 units [shwr, tlt, a/c-cool (14), c/fan, tel (14), TV, movie, clock radio, t/c mkg, refrig], pool, bbq, dinner to unit, c/park (undercover), cots-fee. RO ♦ $45 - $52, ♦♦ $52 - $58, ♦ $8 - $11, AE BC DC MC VI,

Operator Comment: Res.Owners-Personal Service-Clean Units-Relaxing Stay.

★★★ **Chalet Motor Inn**, (M), 242 Bourbong St, ☎ 07 4152 9922, fax 07 4153 5828, 14 units [shwr, spa bath (1), tlt, hairdry, a/c, tel, TV, movie, clock radio, t/c mkg, refrig, cook fac ltd (5), toaster], ldry-fee, dryer-fee, pool, spa, dinner to unit, c/park (undercover), cots. RO ♦ $60 - $70, ♦♦ $68 - $98, ♦ $8 - $12, ch con, AE BC DC EFT MC VI.

★★★ **Charm City**, (M), 23 Takalvan St, ☎ 07 4152 2284, fax 07 4153 1506, 11 units [shwr, tlt, a/c-cool, c/fan (8), heat, tel, TV, movie, clock radio, t/c mkg, refrig, cook fac (2), ldry (in unit) (1)-fee], dryer-fee, pool, bbq, dinner to unit, c/park (undercover), cots-fee. RO ♦ $50, ♦♦ $61, ♦ $11, ch con, AE BC DC MC VI.

★★★ **Kalua**, (M), 4a Hinkler Ave, ☎ 07 4151 3049, fax 07 4151 3303, 11 units [shwr, a/c-cool, fan, c/fan, tel, TV, movie, clock radio, t/c mkg, refrig, cook fac ltd (6)], ldry, pool, c/park (undercover), cots-fee. RO ♦ $44, ♦♦ $54, ♦ $10 - $12, ch con, BC MC VI.

★★★ **Matilda**, (M), 209 Bourbong St, ☎ 07 4151 4717,
fax 07 4153 1455, (2 stry gr fl), 14 units [shwr, tlt, a/c-cool, fan (3), heat, tel, TV, video (avail), clock radio, t/c mkg, refrig], pool. RO ⚊ $53 - $57.50, ⚊⚊ $64 - $66, ⚊ $11, ch con, Units 21 to 28 are ★★☆. AE BC DC EFT MC VI.

★★★ **Oscar**, (M), 252 Bourbong St, Cnr Branyan St, close to CBD,
☎ 07 4152 3666, fax 07 4152 6626, (2 stry gr fl), 21 units [shwr, tlt, a/c-cool, heat, tel, TV, movie, clock radio, t/c mkg, refrig], ldry, dryer-fee, pool, bbq, c/park (undercover), cots-fee, non smoking units (4). RO ⚊ $55 - $62, ⚊⚊ $62 - $74, ⚊ $12, 7 rooms of a 3.5 star rating. 4 rooms of a 4 star rating. AE BC DC EFT MC VI.

★★★ **Rum City**, (M), 52 Takalvan St, ☎ 07 4152 5722,
fax 07 4153 3964, 10 units [shwr, tlt, a/c-cool, c/fan, heat, tel, TV, movie, clock radio, t/c mkg, refrig, toaster], ldry, pool, bbq, dinner to unit, c/park (undercover), cots-fee. RO ⚊ $55 - $65, ⚊⚊ $60 - $70, ⚊ $10, ch con, AE BC DC EFT MC VI.

★★★ **Tropical Gardens Motor Inn**, (M), 123 Takalvan St, Opposite Brothers Sports Club, ☎ 07 4152 8822, fax 07 4153 5369, 23 units [shwr, tlt, a/c, c/fan, tel, TV, t/c mkg, refrig], ldry, conv fac, pool, spa, c/park (undercover), boat park, cots-fee. RO ⚊ $55, ⚊⚊ $60, ⚊ $12, AE BC DC MC VI.

★★☆ **Bourbong Street Motel**, (M), 265 Bourbong St,
☎ 07 4151 3089, fax 07 4151 3365, (2 stry gr fl), 17 units [shwr, tlt, a/c-cool, c/fan, heat (6), tel, TV, movie, radio, t/c mkg, refrig, cook fac (1)], ldry, dryer, cots-fee. RO ⚊ $49.50, ⚊⚊ $55, ⚊ $10, ch con, AE BC DC MC VI.

Park Lane, (M), 247 Bourbong St, ☎ 07 4151 2341, fax 07 4152 0066,
(2 stry gr fl), 27 units [shwr, tlt, hairdry, a/c-cool, fan (20), heat, tel, TV, clock radio, t/c mkg, refrig], ldry, dryer, ⊠ (Mon to Sat), pool, spa, bbq, rm serv, dinner to unit (Mon to Sat), c/park (undercover), cots-fee. RO ⚊ $54 - $59, ⚊⚊ $64 - $70, ⚊ $11, ch con, Units 1 to 4 ★★☆. AE BC DC EFT MC VI, (Rating under review).

Self Catering Accommodation

★★★★☆ **Waves on Sylvan**, (SA), 162 Sylvan Drive, Moore Park, 23km N of PO, ☎ 07 4159 8807, fax 07 4159 8611, 4 serv apts acc up to 8, (2 bedrm), [ensuite, fan, tel, TV, video, clock radio, t/c mkg, refrig, cook fac, micro, d/wash, ldry, blkts, linen], w/mach, lounge, pool, bbq, secure park (2 per unit), cots-fee. RO $108 - $137, $462 - $550, ch con, weekly con, BC MC VI.

★★★☆ **Wattle Cottage**, (Cotg), 46 Woods Rd, Alloway, 15km S of CBD, ☎ 07 4159 7355, fax 07 4159 7773, 1 cotg acc up to 4, (2 bedrm), [shwr, tlt, fan, heat, tel, TV, video, t/c mkg, refrig, cook fac, micro, toaster, ldry], iron, iron brd, bbq, cots. RO ⚊ $75, ⚊⚊⚊⚊ $75, ⚊ $10, ch con.

B&B's/Guest Houses

★★★☆ **Whiston House**, (B&B), 9 Elliott Heads Rd, 2km NW of PO, ☎ 07 4152 1447, fax 07 4152 1447, (2 stry), 3 rms [shwr (1), bath (1), tlt (1), hairdry, fan, elec blkts (1), TV (1), clock radio, t/c mkg, refrig], lift, ldry, dryer, iron, iron brd, lounge (tv, video, CD), ✗, pool (salt water), t/c mkg shared, bbq, c/park (undercover), non smoking rms (3). BB ⚊ $75 - $95, AE BC MC VI.

★★☆ **Bundaberg Farmstay Bed & Breakfast**, (B&B), 608 Bargara Rd, 12km E of PO, ☎ 07 4159 0900, (Multi-stry), 3 rms shwr, tlt, ldry, rec rm, lounge (TV), ✗, cook fac, t/c mkg shared, bbq (covered), cots, non smoking rms. BB ⚊ $40, ⚊⚊ $55, ⚊ $10, ch con.

★★ **Lyelta Lodge & Motel**, (GH), 8 Maryborough St, centre of city, ☎ 07 4151 3344, 15 rms [basin, a/c (2), c/fan, TV, t/c mkg, refrig], shwr, tlt, ldry, ✗, courtesy transfer, ✆. RO ⚊ $28, ⚊⚊ $36, ⚊ $10, BC MC VI.

 ★★ **(Motel Section)**, 5 units [shwr, tlt, c/fan, TV, t/c mkg, refrig], ldry, ✗, c/park (undercover), courtesy transfer. RO ⚊ $35, ⚊⚊ $45, ⚊ $10.

BUNYA MOUNTAINS NATIONAL PARK

Pop Part of Dalby, (248km NW Brisbane), See map on page 417, ref A4. Located on isolated spur of the Great Dividing Range, containing the largest stand of natural Bunya pine in Australia. Rainforest walks, waterfalls and wide variety of bird life. Bush Walking.

Self Catering Accommodation

★★★★ **No 1 Bunya Avenue**, (Chalet), Bunya Mountains, Dalby,
☎ 07 4668 3131, fax 07 4668 3171, (2 stry), 6 chalets acc up to 6, (2 & 3 bedrm), [ensuite, shwr (2), spa bath (1), tlt (3), c/fan, heat, elec blkts, TV, video, t/c mkg, refrig, cook fac, micro, elec frypan, toaster, ldry, blkts, linen, pillows], dryer, iron, iron brd, conf fac, ⊠, bbq, c/park (undercover). D ⚊⚊ $130 - $160, ⚊⚊⚊⚊ $130 - $160, ⚊ $15, Min book applies, AE BC EFT MC VI.

★★★ **Rices Holiday Cabins**, (Log Cabin), Bunya Mountains Rd,
☎ 07 4668 3133, 5 log cabins acc up to 5, [shwr, tlt, TV, clock radio, refrig, cook fac, micro, linen reqd-fee], business centre, casino, lounge firepl, bbq, c/park (undercover), plygr, cots. D ⚊⚊ $70, ⚊ $10, ch con.

★★☆ **Bunya Mtns Eco-Tourism Holidays**, (HU), Bunya Ave,
☎ 07 4668 3131, fax 07 4668 3171, 6 units acc up to 7, (Studio & 2 bedrm), [shwr, tlt, heat, elec blkts, TV, clock radio, refrig, cook fac (4), micro, elec frypan, toaster, linen (4) reqd-fee], ldry, ⊠ (Mon - Sun), cafe, c/park (undercover), cots-fee. D ⚊⚊ $65 - $85, ⚊ $10, AE BC BTC EFT MC VI.

B&B's/Guest Houses

★★★★ **Bunya Mountain Lodge**, (GH), No children's facilities,
3405 Bunya Mountains Park Rd, ☎ 07 4668 3134, fax 07 4668 3109, (2 stry), 4 rms (1 bedrm), [shwr, tlt, a/c-cool, fan, heat, elec blkts], ldry, lounge (TV), lounge firepl, t/c mkg shared, refrig, c/park (undercover). D all meals ⚊ $160, ⚊⚊ $215, DBB ⚊⚊ $310, AE BC MC VI.

BURKETOWN QLD 4830

Pop 200. (2174km NW Brisbane), See map on page 414, ref A4. Historical gulf savannah town. Fishing.

Escott Lodge, (Lodge), Working cattle station. 16km W of Burketown,
☎ 07 4748 5577, fax 07 4748 5551, 17 rms acc up to 8, [shwr, tlt, a/c-cool (13), fan, c/fan, fax, t/c mkg, refrig, cook fac (2), cook fac ltd (1), toaster (3)], ldry, ⊠ (Sun to Fri), bar, pool, ✆. D ⚊⚊ $77, ⚊ $33, ch con, AE BC EFT MC VI, (not yet classified).

BURNETT HEADS QLD 4670

Pop 2,100. (387km N Brisbane), See map on page 416, ref E8. Situated at the mouth of the Burnett River, marina and deepwater port. Port is departure point for reef cruises to Lady Musgrave Island; Poseidon's Seashells. Boating, Fishing, Surfing, Swimming.

★★★☆ **Anchorage House**, (B&B), 107 Sea Esplanade, 14km NE of Bundaberg PO. ☎ 07 4159 4781, fax 07 4159 4781, (2 stry), 3 rms [fan, heat, elec blkts, tel, TV, video, clock radio, cook fac ltd, doonas], ldry, ✗, t/c mkg shared, refrig, bbq, c/park (undercover) (1), non smoking property, Pets allowed. BB ⚊ $55 - $65, ⚊⚊ $70 - $80, ch con, weekly con, BC MC VI.

BURLEIGH HEADS QLD

See Gold Coast Region.

BURRUM HEADS QLD 4659

Pop 800. (298km N Brisbane), See map on page 417, ref D1. Seaside resort via Howard/Torbanlea located at the mouth of the Burrum River. National Park Fraser Island Day Tours. Boat Ramp, Bush Walking, Fishing, Swimming.

Self Catering Accommodation

★★★ **Burrum Sands**, (HU), Burrum St, beachfront, ☎ 07 4129 5275, fax 07 4129 5990, 8 units acc up to 5, (1 & 2 bedrm), [shwr, tlt, c/fan, TV, refrig, cook fac, micro, elec frypan, blkts, linen reqd-fee, pillows], ldry, pool-heated, bbq. D $58 - $78, W $250 - $480, BC MC VI.

San Marco Villas, (HU), 44 Esplanade, 37km N of Hervey Bay,
☎ 07 4129 5224, fax 07 4129 5999, 8 units (2 bedrm), [shwr, tlt, heat, c/fan, TV, video, clock radio, refrig, cook fac, micro, elec frypan, toaster, blkts, linen, pillows], ldry, w/mach-fee, dryer-fee, iron, iron brd, pool, spa, bbq (covered), c/park (undercover), ✆, plygr, cots-fee. RO ⚊⚊ $75, ⚊⚊ W $275 - $495, ch con, BC EFT MC VI, (not yet classified).

CABOOLTURE QLD 4510

Pop 17,600. (44km N Brisbane). See map on page 417, ref D5. Located just of the Bruce Hwy, on the Sunshine Coast. Caboolture Show (June). Bowls, Golf, Horse Riding, Scenic Drives, Swimming, Tennis.

Hotels/Motels

★★★ **Caboolture Motel**, (M), 4 Lower King St, 1.2km from PO, ☎ 07 5495 2888, fax 07 5495 2888, 35 units (7 suites) [shwr, tlt, a/c, c/fan, heat, tel, TV, clock radio, t/c mkg, refrig, cook fac ltd (5), micro, elec frypan, toaster], ldry, dryer, pool, bbq, rm serv, dinner to unit, c/park (undercover), cots-fee. RO ♦ $60 - $70, ♦ $15, Suite RO $110, ch con, Units 20 to 25 are ★★★☆. 10 Units yet to be assessed. AE BC DC MC VI, ⅋&.

★★★ **Caboolture Sundowner**, (LMH), Cnr Bribie Is & Aerodrome Rds, 4km E of PO, ☎ 07 5495 8666, fax 07 4695 7163, (2 stry gr fl), 10 units [shwr, spa bath (2), tlt, a/c, tel, TV, clock radio, t/c mkg, refrig], conv fac, ⊠, rm serv, dinner to unit, ☎, plygr, cots. RO ♦ $50 - $80, ♦♦ $60 - $85, ♦ $5, ch con, AE BC DC EFT MC VI.

★★☆ **Beachmere Palms**, (M), 30 Biggs Ave, Beachmere 4510, 12km from Caboolture, ☎ 07 5496 8577, fax 07 5496 2727, 6 units [shwr, tlt, a/c-cool, heat, tel, TV, clock radio, t/c mkg, refrig], ldry, dryer, pool, spa, bbq, dinner to unit, cots. RO ♦ $49.50 - $62, ♦♦ $55 - $66, ♦ $11, ch con, AE BC DC MC VI.

Self Catering Accommodation

★★★ **Caboolture Lodge**, (SA), 3 William St, 1.5km E of PO, ☎ 07 5495 3300, 6 serv apts acc up to 2, (1 bedrm), [shwr, tlt, a/c, TV, t/c mkg, refrig, blkts, linen, pillows], c/park. D ♦ $35 - $52, ♦♦ $40 - $60, ♦ $10, weekly con.

B&B's/Guest Houses

★★★☆ **Danby Hall Bed & Breakfast**, (B&B), 21 Riflebird Drive, 3km W of PO, ☎ 07 5495 7803, fax 0754281903, 4 rms [ensuite, hairdry (1), c/fan, elec blkts], ldry, dryer, iron (1), iron brd (1), TV rm, t/c mkg shared, bbq, secure park. BLB ♦ $30 - $40, ♦♦ $55 - $65.

CAIRNS QLD 4870

Pop 92,300. (1717km N Brisbane), See map on page 415, ref C3. Vibrant tropical city. Capital of Far North Queensland. Perfect base to enjoy the reef, rainforest and outback of the region. Australian Bird Park, Bulk Sugar Terminal, Cairns Show (Jul) Untouched World Heritage Listed Rainforests. Fishing, Golf, Horse Racing, Scenic Drives, Squash, Swimming, Trotting.

Hotels/Motels

★★★★★ **Cairns International Hotel**, (LH), 17 Abbott St, town centre 2 blocks E of PO, ☎ 07 4031 1300, fax 07 4031 1801, (Multi-stry), 321 rms (5 suites) [shwr, bath, spa bath (5), tlt, hairdry, a/c, tel, TV, video-fee, movie, clock radio, t/c mkg, mini bar], lift, ldry, conv fac, ⊠, pool (salt water), sauna (2), spa, 24hr reception, rm serv, c/park (undercover), gym, cots, non smoking rms (26). RO $315 - $430, Suite RO $640 - $1,690, ch con, AE BC DC JCB MC VI, ⅋&.

★★★★★ **Hilton Cairns**, (LH), Wharf St, ☎ 07 4050 2000, fax 07 4050 2001, (Multi-stry), 263 rms (5 suites) [shwr, bath, tlt, hairdry, a/c-cool, tel, TV, movie-fee, clock radio, t/c mkg, refrig, mini bar], lift, conv fac, ⊠, pool, sauna, spa, 24hr reception, rm serv, dinner to unit, c/park (garage), gym, cots, non smoking rms (68). RO ♦♦ $230 - $320, ch con, AE BC DC JCB MC VI, ⅋&.

★★★★★ **Radisson Plaza**, (LH), Pierpoint Rd, 300m fr PO, ☎ 07 4031 1411, fax 07 4031 3226, (2 stry), 219 rms (22 suites) [shwr, bath, tlt, hairdry, a/c-cool, c/fan, tel, TV, movie, clock radio, t/c mkg, refrig, mini bar], lift, ldry, conv fac, ⊠ (2), pool, sauna, spa, 24hr reception, rm serv, c/park (undercover), gym, cots, non smoking rms (avail). RO ♦ $368 - $407, ♦♦ $368 - $407, Suite RO $539 - $1,012, ch con, AE BC DC JCB MC VI, ⅋&.

★★★★★ **Sheridan Plaza**, (LH), 295 Sheridan St, 3km N of Cairns PO, ☎ 07 4031 6500, fax 07 4031 6226, (Multi-stry), 74 rms (10 suites) [shwr, bath, tlt, hairdry, a/c-cool, tel, cable tv, movie, clock radio, t/c mkg, refrig, mini bar], lift, ldry, dryer, iron, iron brd, conv fac, ⊠, pool, rm serv (24hr), dinner to unit, secure park, ☎, gym, cots, non smoking flr (1), non smoking rms (28). RO $125, ch con, AE BC DC JCB MC VI, ⅋&.

★★★★★ **The Reef Hotel Casino**, (LH), 35-41 Wharf St, 500m S of City Centre, ☎ 07 4030 8888, fax 07 4030 8777, (Multi-stry), 128 rms (3 suites) [shwr, spa bath, tlt, hairdry, a/c, c/fan, heat, tel, TV, video, movie, clock radio, t/c mkg, refrig, mini bar], lift, iron, iron brd, rec rm, conv fac, ⊠, pool, sauna, 24hr reception, rm serv, secure park, gym, cots. D ♦ $248 - $348, ♦ $33, ch con, AE BC DC JCB MC VI, ⅋&.

★★★★☆ **Country Comfort Sunlodge**, (M), Cnr Lake & Florence Sts, ☎ 07 4051 5733, fax 07 4031 2298, (Multi-stry gr fl), 75 units [shwr, tlt, hairdry, a/c, c/fan, tel, TV, movie, radio, t/c mkg, refrig, mini bar, micro (15), toaster], lift, ldry, iron, iron brd, ⊠, pool, 24hr reception, dinner to unit, cots-fee. RO ♦ $97 - $125, ♦♦ $97 - $125, ♦ $16.50, ch con, AE BC DC JCB MC VI.

★★★★☆ **Holiday Inn Cairns**, (LH), Cnr Esplanade & Florence St, ☎ 07 4050 6070, fax 07 4031 3770, (Multi-stry gr fl), 232 rms (6 suites) [shwr, bath, tlt, hairdry, a/c-cool, tel, cable tv, movie, clock radio, t/c mkg, refrig, mini bar], lift, ldry, conv fac, ⊠, bar, pool, spa, 24hr reception, rm serv, secure park, courtesy transfer, ☎, cots, non smoking rms (78). RO ♦ $260 - $287, ♦♦ $260 - $287, ♦ $27, Suite RO $390 - $435, AE BC DC JCB MC VI, ⅋&.

★★★★☆ **Matson Resort Cairns**, (LH), The Esplanade, ☎ 07 4031 2211, fax 07 4031 2704, (Multi-stry), 342 rms [shwr, bath, tlt, hairdry, a/c, fan, tel, TV, movie, clock radio, t/c mkg, refrig, mini bar, cook fac (78), cook fac ltd (22), ldry (in unit) (34)], lift, ldry, conf fac, ⊠ (2), pool (3), sauna, spa, bbq, 24hr reception, rm serv, c/park (undercover), courtesy transfer, gym, tennis, cots, non smoking flr (1). RO ♦ $175, ♦♦ $175, ♦ $25, ch con, AE BC DC JCB MC VI, ⅋&.

★★★★☆ **Mercure Hotel Harbourside**, (Ltd Lic H), 209 The Esplanade, ☎ 07 4051 8999, fax 07 4051 0317, (Multi-stry), 173 rms (25 suites) [shwr, bath, tlt, hairdry, a/c-cool, tel, TV, video-fee, movie, clock radio, t/c mkg, refrig, mini bar, cook fac (25), micro (25)], lift, ldry, dryer, iron, iron brd, conv fac, ⊠, bar, pool, spa, 24hr reception, rm serv, dinner to unit, c/park (undercover), courtesy transfer, ☎, cots. RO ♦♦ $170, ♦ $25, Suite D ♦♦ $191, ♦ $25, ch con, AE BC DC MC VI, ⅋&.

★★★★☆ **Pacific International**, (LH), Cnr Spence St & Esplanade, opposite Cairns Marlin Jetty, ☎ 07 4051 7888, fax 07 4051 0210, (Multi-stry), 173 rms (3 suites) [shwr, bath, tlt, hairdry, a/c, tel, TV, movie, clock radio, t/c mkg, refrig, mini bar], lift, ldry, conv fac, ⊠, bar, pool (salt water), spa, 24hr reception, rm serv, dinner to unit, cots. RO ♦ $220 - $320, ♦♦ $220 - $320, ♦ $35, ch con, AE BC DC JCB MC VI.

★★★★☆ **Palm Royale Cairns**, (LH), 7 Chester Ct, 6km W of Cairns City, ☎ 07 4032 2700, fax 07 4032 2800, (Multi-stry gr fl), 150 rms (16 suites) [shwr, bath (16), tlt, hairdry, a/c-cool, c/fan, tel, TV, movie, clock radio, t/c mkg, refrig], lift, ldry, dryer-fee, iron, iron brd, rec rm, lounge (tv), conv fac, ⊠, cafe, pool (salt water), spa, rm serv, secure park, courtesy transfer, ☎, cots-fee, non smoking rms (75). **RO $165 - $210**, ch con, AE BC DC JCB MC VI, ⓖ.

★★★★☆ **Rydges Plaza Cairns**, (LH), Cnr Spence & Grafton Sts, 500m N of PO, 450m to Casino,750m Convention Ctre, ☎ 07 4041 1022, fax 07 4041 1033, (Multi-stry), 101 rms (3 suites) [ensuite, a/c, tel, TV, movie, t/c mkg, mini bar, cook fac ltd (3)], lift, ldry, iron, iron brd, business centre, conv fac, ⊠, bar, bar (cocktail), pool, sauna, rm serv, c/park (undercover), non smoking rms (28). **RO ♀♀ $196 - $220, ♀♀♀♀ $196 - $220, ♀♀♀♀ $196 - $220**, AE BC DC JCB MC VI.

★★★★☆ **The Oasis Resort Cairns**, (Ltd Lic H), 122 Lake St, 800m N of PO, ☎ 07 4080 1888, fax 07 4080 1889, (Multi-stry gr fl), 314 rms (8 suites) [shwr, bath, spa bath (8), tlt, hairdry, a/c-cool, tel, TV, movie, clock radio, t/c mkg, refrig, mini bar], ldry-fee, dryer-fee, iron, iron brd, ⊠, pool, rm serv, secure park, gym, cots, non smoking units (150). **RO ♀♀ $195, ⓖ $33, Suite D ♀ $355, ⓖ $33**, ch con, AE BC DC EFT JCB MC VI, ⓖ.

  ★★★★ **Cannon Park Motel**, (M), 574 Bruce Hwy, Woree, 5km S Cairns City, ☎ 07 4033 5555, fax 07 4033 5444, (2 stry gr fl), 20 units [shwr, bath (hip), tlt, hairdry, a/c-cool, c/fan, tel, TV, movie, clock radio, t/c mkg, refrig, mini bar, cook fac ltd (4), micro (4), toaster (4)], ldry-fee, dryer-fee, iron, iron brd, ⊠, pool (salt water), dinner to unit, c/park (undercover), cots-fee, non smoking units (15). **RO ♀ $78 - $88, ♀♀ $86 - $95, ⓖ $10**, ch con, AE BC DC JCB MC MP VI, ⓖ.

 ★★★★ **Fig Tree Lodge**, (M), Cnr Sheridan & Thomas St, 2.5km N of PO, ☎ 07 4041 0000, fax 07 4041 0001, (2 stry gr fl), 46 units (3 suites) [shwr, bath, tlt, hairdry, a/c-cool, c/fan, tel, TV, clock radio, t/c mkg, refrig], ldry-fee, ⊠, pool, spa, rm serv, secure park (off-street), ☎, cots-fee. **RO ♀ $89, ♀♀ $89, ⓖ $15**, ch con, AE BC DC MC VI.

  ★★★★ **Rainbow Southside Inn**, (M), 450 Mulgrave Rd, 300m N of Earlville Shoppingtown, ☎ 07 4033 7722, fax 07 4033 5250, 61 units (8 suites) [shwr, bath, spa bath (2), tlt, hairdry, a/c-cool, c/fan, tel, TV, movie, clock radio, t/c mkg, refrig, mini bar, cook fac (10), micro (10)], ldry-fee, iron, iron brd, TV rm, conf fac, ⊠, pool (salt water), spa, rm serv, dinner to unit, secure park, cots-fee, non smoking units (30). **RO ♀♀♀ $87 - $116, ♀♀♀♀ $87 - $220, ⓖ $15**, AE BC DC EFT MC VI.

★★★★ **Reef Palms**, (M), 41 Digger St, ☎ 07 4051 2599, fax 07 4051 7676, (2 stry gr fl), 42 units (12 suites) [shwr, bath, spa bath (4), tlt, a/c-cool, c/fan, tel, TV, t/c mkg, refrig, cook fac ltd], ldry, pool (salt water), spa, bbq, cots. **RO ♀♀ $75 - $120, ⓖ $10**, ch con, AE BC DC JCB MC VI.

★★★★ **Royal Harbour Tradewinds**, (LH), 71 The Esplanade, Cairns central, ☎ 07 4080 8888, (Multi-stry), 46 rms [shwr, spa bath, tlt, hairdry, a/c-cool, tel, TV, video, clock radio, CD, refrig, mini bar, cook fac ltd, micro, toaster, ldry, pillows], w/mach, dryer, iron, conf fac, pool, bbq (2), cots. **RO ♀♀ $176 - $230, ⓖ $27.50**, AE BC DC JCB MC VI.

★★★★ **Tuna Towers**, (M), 145 Esplanade, ☎ 07 4051 4688, fax 07 4051 8129, (Multi-stry), 60 units (20 suites) [shwr, bath, tlt, hairdry, a/c-cool, tel, TV, movie, clock radio, t/c mkg, refrig, mini bar, cook fac ltd (30)], lift, ldry, iron, iron brd, ⊠, pool, spa, 24hr reception, rm serv, dinner to unit, c/park (undercover) (10), cots, non smoking rms (12). **RO $124 - $167**, ch con, AE BC DC JCB MC VI, ⅋.

★★★☆ **Acacia Court**, (Ltd Lic H), 223 The Esplanade, 2km N of PO, ☎ 07 4051 5011, fax 07 4051 7562, (Multi-stry gr fl), 150 rms [shwr, bath (134), tlt, a/c-cool, tel, TV, movie, clock radio, t/c mkg, refrig], lift, ldry, ⊠, pool, sauna, spa, 24hr reception, rm serv, c/park (undercover) (50), tennis, cots-fee. **RO ⚄ $91 - $108, ⚄⚄ $97 - $108, ⚄ $15**, 16 motel units ★★★. AE BC DC JCB MC VI.

★★★☆ **All Round Motel Inn The Pink**, (M), 263 Sheridan St, 2km N of Cairns City Place, ☎ 07 4051 4800, fax 07 4031 1526, (Multi-stry gr fl), 27 units [shwr, tlt, hairdry (13), a/c-cool, c/fan, tel, TV, movie, radio, t/c mkg, refrig, cook fac (14)], ldry, pool, bbq, dinner to unit, c/park (undercover) (8), cots-fee, non smoking units (15). **RO ⚄ $72 - $94, ⚄⚄ $77 - $94, ⚄ $6**, AE BC DC EFT MC VI.

★★★☆ **All Seasons Esplanade Hotel**, (M), Cnr The Esplanade & Aplin St, ☎ 07 4051 2311, fax 07 4031 1294, (Multi-stry gr fl), 80 units [shwr, bath (80), tlt, hairdry (80), a/c-cool, tel, TV, movie, t/c mkg, refrig, mini bar (80)], lift, ldry, dryer, pool (salt water), 24hr reception, cots, non smoking rms (30). **RO ⚄ $131 - $153, ⚄⚄⚄ $131 - $153, ⚄⚄⚄⚄ $131 - $153**, 47 rooms ★★★☆. AE BC DC JCB MC VI.

★★★☆ **All Seasons Sunshine Tower Hotel**, (M), 136 Sheridan St, ☎ 07 4051 5288, fax 07 4031 2483, (Multi-stry gr fl), 61 units [shwr, bath, tlt, a/c-cool, tel, TV, movie, clock radio, t/c mkg, refrig, mini bar, cook fac ltd (7)], lift, ldry, dryer, ⊠, pool (salt water), spa, bbq, 24hr reception, rm serv, secure park, ☏, cots. **RO ⚄ $107, ⚄⚄ $107, ⚄ $33**, ch con, AE BC DC JCB MC MP VI.

★★★☆ **Balaclava**, (LMH), 423 Mulgrave Rd, 7km E of Cairns city centre, ☎ 07 4054 3588, fax 07 4054 7537, 30 units [shwr, tlt, hairdry, a/c-cool, tel, TV, movie, clock radio, t/c mkg, refrig], ldry-fee, dryer-fee, iron, iron brd, conv fac, ⊠, pool (salt water), spa, bbq, rm serv, dinner to unit, c/park (undercover), ☏, plygr, cots. **RO ⚄ $60, ⚄⚄ $71, ⚄ $11**, ch con, AE BC DC EFT MC VI.

★★★☆ **Bay Village Tropical Retreat**, (LH), Lake St, Cnr Gatton St, lkm N of PO, 3km S of airport, ☎ 07 4051 4622, fax 07 4051 4057, (2 stry gr fl), 63 rms [shwr, tlt, a/c-cool, c/fan, tel, TV, clock radio, t/c mkg, refrig, mini bar, micro], ldry, ⊠, pool, bbq, 24hr reception, rm serv, dinner to unit, courtesy transfer, cots-fee. **RO ⚄⚄ $123.20 - $192.50**, ch con, AE BC DC MC VI.

★★★☆ **Cairns Tropical Gardens**, (M), 314 Mulgrave Rd, ☎ 07 4031 1777, fax 07 4031 2605, (2 stry gr fl), 55 units [shwr, tlt, a/c-cool, c/fan, tel, TV, movie, clock radio, t/c mkg, refrig, mini bar], ldry-fee, ⊠, pool (salt water), sauna, spa, rm serv, meals to unit, ☏, cots-fee. **RO ⚄⚄ $66 - $87, ⚄ $11**, AE BC DC MC VI.

★★★☆ **Cairns Village Resort**, (M), Resort, Cnr Bruce Hwy & Anderson Rd, opposite golf course, ☎ 07 4054 7700, fax 07 4054 7750, (2 stry gr fl), 195 units [shwr, tlt, hairdry, a/c-cool, c/fan, tel, TV, movie, clock radio, t/c mkg, refrig], ldry, ⊠, ✗, pool (salt water), spa, pool bar, bbq, c/park (undercover) (20), courtesy transfer, plygr, gym, tennis. **RO ⚄⚄ $81, ⚄ $30**, AE BC DC JCB MC VI, ⅋.

★★★☆ **Club Crocodile Hides Hotel**, (LH), Previously Hides Hotel 87 Lake St (Cnr Shields Sts), ☎ 07 4051 1266, fax 07 4031 2276, (2 stry), 102 rms [shwr, tlt, a/c-cool, c/fan, tel, TV, t/c mkg, refrig], lift, ldry, conv fac, ⊠, pool, 24hr reception, rm serv, c/park (undercover) (10), cots, non smoking rms (13). **BLB ⚄ $83 - $119**, ch con, 32 rooms yet to be assessd, AE BC DC JCB MC VI.

★★★☆ **Club Crocodile Lake Street**, (M), 183 Lake St, 600m from city centre, ☎ 07 4051 4988, fax 07 4051 6047, (2 stry gr fl), 54 units [shwr, bath (41), tlt, a/c-cool, c/fan, tel, TV, clock radio, t/c mkg, refrig, cook fac (5)], ldry, dryer, ⊠, pool, rm serv, cots, non smoking rms (16). **BLB ⚄ $100 - $120, ⚄⚄ $100 - $120, ⚄ $20**, ch con, AE BC DC JCB MC MP VI.

★★★☆ **Country Comfort Outrigger**, (M), Cnr Abbott & Florence Sts, ☎ 07 4051 6188, fax 07 4031 1806, (Multi-stry gr fl), 90 units [shwr, bath, tlt, hairdry, a/c-cool, c/fan, tel, TV, movie, clock radio, t/c mkg, refrig, mini bar], lift, ldry, dryer, iron, iron brd, conv fac, ⊠ (Mon - Sun), pool (salt water), spa, 24hr reception, rm serv, dinner to unit, c/park (undercover), cots, non smoking rms (16). **RO ⚄ $109 - $124, ⚄⚄ $109 - $124, ⚄ $16.50**, ch con, AE BC DC JCB MC VI.

★★★☆ **Flying Horseshoe**, (M), 281 Sheridan St, ☎ 07 4051 3022, fax 07 4031 2761, 50 units [shwr, tlt, hairdry, a/c-cool, c/fan, tel, TV, movie, clock radio, t/c mkg, refrig, mini bar], ldry, iron, ⊠, pool (salt water), spa, bbq, rm serv, dinner to unit, cots-fee. **RO $85 - $105**, ch con, 20 units ★★★. AE BC DC MC VI.

★★★☆ **Lake Central - A Greentree Inn**, (M), 137 Lake St, ☎ 07 4051 4933, fax 07 4051 9716, (Multi-stry gr fl), 57 units [shwr, tlt, a/c-cool, c/fan, tel, TV, clock radio, t/c mkg, refrig, micro, toaster], lift, ldry, dryer, breakfast rm, pool (salt water), bbq (1), cots, non smoking units (23). **RO $131 - $151**, ch con, AE BC DC JCB MC VI.

★★★☆ **Rainbow Palms**, (M), 157 Sheridan St, 500m N of City Mall, ☎ 07 4051 3555, fax 07 4051 3366, (2 stry), 32 units [shwr, tlt, a/c-cool, c/fan, tel, TV, movie, clock radio, t/c mkg, refrig, mini bar], ldry, ⊠, pool (salt water), bbq, rm serv, c/park (undercover), cots-fee, non smoking rms (32). **RO $80 - $110**, ch con, AE BC DC EFT MC VI.

★★★☆ **Tropical Queenslander**, (M), Previously Cairns Angler, 287 Lake St, ☎ 07 4031 1666, fax 07 4031 1491, (2 stry gr fl), 40 units [shwr, bath (26), tlt, a/c-cool, c/fan, tel, TV, clock radio, t/c mkg, refrig, cook fac ltd, micro, toaster], ldry, rec rm, bar, pool (2), spa, bbq, gym. **RO ⚄ $86, ⚄⚄ $86, ⚄ $14**, ch con, fam con, AE BC DC MC VI.

★★★ **A 1 Motel**, (M), 211 Sheridan St, 5 mins to airport, ☎ 07 4051 4499, fax 07 4031 1183, 31 units (1 suite) [shwr, tlt, a/c, c/fan, tel, TV, clock radio, t/c mkg, refrig], ldry, conf fac, ⌧, pool, rm serv, c/park (undercover) (10). **RO ♦ $66, ♦♦ $71, ◊ $8 - $12, Suite D ♦♦♦♦ $132**, ch con, fam con, AE BC DC EFT JCB MC MCH VI.

★★★ **Beltana**, (M), 380 Mulgrave Rd, ☎ 07 4054 3777, fax 07 4054 3101, (2 stry gr fl), 35 units [shwr, bath (11), tlt, a/c-cool, c/fan, tel, TV, clock radio, t/c mkg, refrig], ldry, ⌧ (Mon-Sat), pool, bbq, meals to unit (includes liquor), c/park (undercover) (12), cots-fee. **RO ♦ $50 - $55, ♦♦ $60 - $66, ◊ $6**, AE BC DC EFT MC VI.

★★★ **Cairns Holiday Lodge**, (M), 259 Sheridan St, Cnr Thomas St, ☎ 07 4051 4611, fax 07 4051 1926, (Multi-stry gr fl), 35 units [shwr, bath, tlt, a/c-cool, c/fan, tel, TV, video, clock radio, t/c mkg, refrig, cook fac (28), toaster], ldry, ⌧, pool (salt water), bbq, rm serv, dinner to unit, courtesy transfer, cots. **RO ♦ $85 - $95, ◊ $10**, ch con, AE BC DC JCB MC VI.

★★★ **Cairns Queens Court**, (M), 167 Sheridan St, ☎ 07 4051 7722, fax 07 4051 4811, (Multi-stry gr fl), 68 units [shwr, tlt, a/c-cool, c/fan, tel, TV, clock radio, t/c mkg, refrig, cook fac (24), cook fac ltd], ldry-fee, dryer-fee, ⌧, pool (salt water), bbq (covered), rm serv, c/park (undercover), cots, non smoking units (40). **RO $89**, ch con, AE BC DC EFT MC VI.

★★☆ **(Budget Rooms Section)**, 24 apts [a/c-cool, TV, clock radio, t/c mkg, refrig], shwr, tlt, cook fac. **RO $63**.

★★★ **Compass Bed & Breakfast Motel**, (M), 232 Mulgrave Rd, ☎ 07 4051 5466, fax 07 4051 5541, 26 units [shwr, tlt, a/c-cool, c/fan, tel, TV, movie, clock radio, t/c mkg, refrig, toaster], ldry, iron, iron brd, pool (salt water), bbq, cots. **RO ♦ $75 - $85, ♦♦ $85 - $95, ◊ $10**, AE BC DC MC MP VI.

★★★ **Coral Tree Inn**, (M), 166 Grafton St, 500m N of PO, ☎ 07 4031 3744, fax 07 4031 3064, (Multi-stry gr fl), 58 units (1 bedrm), [shwr, tlt, a/c-cool, c/fan, tel, TV, t/c mkg, refrig, cook fac ltd (8)], ldry, pool (salt water), cook fac, bbq, plygr, cots, non smoking rms (58). **RO $110 - $136**, AE BC DC MC VI, ⌸.

★★★ **G'Day Tropical Village Resort**, (M), 7-27 McLachlan St, Manunda, 4km fr city centre 7km fr airport, ☎ 07 4053 7555, fax 07 4032 1101, 68 units [shwr, tlt, a/c-cool, c/fan, tel, TV, clock radio, t/c mkg, refrig], ldry, ⌧, pool, ✆, cots-fee. **RO ♦ $88, ♦♦ $88, ◊ $11**, AE BC DC JCB MC VI, ⌸.

★★★ **Glenlee Motel**, (M), 560 Bruce Hwy, Woree 4868, 500m S of Earlville shopping centre, ☎ 07 4054 1009, fax 07 4054 7444, 8 units [shwr, tlt, a/c-cool, c/fan, tel, TV, movie, clock radio, t/c mkg, refrig], ldry, pool (salt water), spa, bbq, c/park (undercover), cots-fee. **D ♦ $55, ♦♦ $60.50**, AE BC DC MC VI.

★★★ **Great Northern Hotel**, (LH), 69 Abbott St, ☎ 07 4051 5151, fax 07 4051 3090, (2 stry), 33 rms [shwr, bath (3), tlt, a/c-cool, tel, TV, radio, t/c mkg, refrig, cook fac (1)], ldry, 24hr reception, cots. **RO ♦♦ $89 - $119, ◊ $11**, ch con, No off-street parking. AE BC DC MC VI.

★★★ **High Chaparral**, (M), 195 Sheridan St, ☎ 07 4051 7155, fax 07 4031 3527, (2 stry gr fl), 21 units [shwr, tlt, a/c-cool, c/fan, tel, TV, clock radio, t/c mkg, refrig, cook fac ltd (14)], ldry, pool, bbq, cots. **RO ♦ $65, ♦♦ $70, ◊ $10**, ch con, AE BC DC MC VI, ⌸.

★★☆ **(Unit Section)**, (Multi-stry gr fl), 22 units acc up to 6, (1 & 2 bedrm), [shwr, tlt, a/c-cool, c/fan, tel, TV, refrig, cook fac, blkts, linen, pillows], ldry, bbq, c/park (undercover) (12), cots-fee.

★★★ **Rainbow Inn**, (M), 179 Sheridan St, ☎ 07 4051 1022, fax 07 4051 1763, (2 stry gr fl), 126 units [shwr, bath (7), tlt, a/c-cool, fan, tel, TV, movie, clock radio (48), t/c mkg, refrig, mini bar], ldry, dryer, ⌧, bar, pool (salt water), spa, bbq, rm serv, cots. **RO $65 - $109, ◊ $15**, ch con, 43 rooms ★★☆. AE BC DC MC VI.

★★★ **The Leichhardt Motel Cairns**, (M), 468 Mulgrave Rd, 5.2km S of PO, ☎ 07 4054 5499, fax 07 4054 6573, 16 units [shwr, tlt, a/c-cool, c/fan, tel, TV, clock radio, t/c mkg, refrig], pool (salt water), bbq, cots-fee, non smoking units (5). **RO ♦ $55 - $60, ♦♦ $60 - $65, ◊ $10**, AE BC DC MC VI.

★★★ **Tree Tops Lodge Cairns**, (M), 7 Tanner Cres, Stratford 4872, ☎ 07 4039 9599, fax 07 4058 1129, 16 units [shwr, tlt, a/c-cool, fan, tel, TV, clock radio, t/c mkg, refrig, cook fac ltd (9), toaster], ldry, iron (9), iron brd (9), pool (salt water), cook fac, bbq, plygr, cots. **RO ♦ $55 - $66, ♦♦ $66 - $77**, ch con, fam con, Light breakfast only available. AE BC MC VI,

Operator Comment: Set in lush tropical gardens on the slopes of Mt Whitfield, Tree Tops enjoys panoramic vistas over the valley. Away from the constant drone of traffic, come and enjoy the peace and tranquility with us.

★★☆ **Adobe**, (M), 191 Sheridan St, 1.25km N of PO, ☎ 07 4051 5511, fax 07 4051 1451, (2 stry gr fl), 15 units [shwr, tlt, a/c-cool, cable tv, clock radio, t/c mkg, refrig], ldry, dryer-fee, ⌧, pool (salt water), rm serv, dinner to unit, ✆. **RO ♦ $50 - $65, ♦♦ $55 - $80, ◊ $10**, ch con, AE BC DC EFT MC VI.

★★☆ **Cairns Motor Inn**, (M), 187 Sheridan St, ☎ 07 4051 5166, fax 07 4051 3776, (2 stry gr fl), 21 units [shwr, tlt, a/c-cool, c/fan, tel, TV, radio, t/c mkg, refrig], ldry, pool, bbq, dinner to unit, c/park (undercover) (10), cots-fee. **RO ♦ $55 - $75, ♦♦ $55 - $75, ◊ $15**, ch con, AE BC DC MC VI.

★★☆ **Coolabah**, (M), 564 Mulgrave Rd, ☎ 07 4054 2711, fax 07 4033 5340, 9 units [shwr, tlt, a/c-cool, c/fan, tel, TV, clock radio, t/c mkg, refrig], ldry, pool, cots-fee. **RO ♦ $45 - $55, ◊ $11**, ch con, AE BC DC MC VI.

★★ **Bungalow**, (LMH), 200 Aumuller St, ☎ 07 4051 3277, fax 07 4051 3914, 8 units [shwr, tlt, a/c, fan, tel, TV, radio, t/c mkg, refrig], ⌧ (Mon to Sat), cots. **RO ♦♦ $55 - $65, ◊ $15**, AE BC EFT MC VI.

Heritage Motel Cairns, (M), 8 Minnie St, 500m S of City Centre, ☎ 07 4051 1211, fax 07 4031 4408, (Multi-stry gr fl), 44 units (4 suites) [ensuite, a/c, tel, TV, t/c mkg, refrig, toaster], ldry, cots-fee, non smoking flr (2). **BLB ♦ $90 - $120, ♦♦ $115 - $130, ♦ $40, Suite BLB $130**, ch con, AE BC DC EFT MC VI, (not yet classified).

Tradewinds Esplanade Hotel Cairns, (Ltd Lic H), 137 The Esplanade, ☎ 07 4053 0300, fax 07 4051 8649, (Multi-stry), 246 rms (13 suites) [shwr, bath, tlt, hairdry, a/c-cool, c/fan, tel, TV, movie, clock radio, t/c mkg, refrig, mini bar], lift, conv fac, ⊠ (2), pool (salt water), spa, 24hr reception, dinner to unit, c/park (garage), cots. **RO ♦♦ $260 - $300, ♦ $33, Suite RO ♦♦ $550 - $1,100**, 75 rooms ★★★☆, ⅋⅊.

Self Catering Accommodation

★★★★★ Waterfront Terraces, (HU), 233 The Esplanade, 1.5km N of CBD, ☎ 07 4031 8333, fax 07 4031 8444, (Multi-stry gr fl), 22 units acc up to 6, (1 & 2 bedrm), [shwr, bath, tlt, a/c-cool, c/fan, tel, video-fee, clock radio, refrig, cook fac, micro, d/wash, toaster, ldry (in unit), blkts, linen, pillows], dryer, iron, iron brd, pool (salt water), spa, bbq, c/park (undercover), secure park, cots-fee. **D $152 - $198, W $966 - $1,386**, ch con, Min book applies, AE BC DC JCB MC VI.

★★★★☆ Grosvenor in Cairns, (HU), 188 McLeod St, 1km N of PO, ☎ 07 4031 8588, fax 07 4031 8533, (Multi-stry), 38 units acc up to 4, (Studio, 1 & 2 bedrm), [ensuite (16), shwr, bath (22), tlt, hairdry, a/c-cool, fan, tel, cable tv, radio, refrig, micro (22), elec frypan (22), toaster, ldry (38), blkts, linen, pillows], ldry, dryer (22), iron (38), iron brd, pool (salt water), spa, bbq (covered), c/park (undercover), cots. **D $82 - $185**, AE BC DC MC VI.

★★★★☆ Il Centro Apartments, (SA), 30 Sheridan St, 50m from City Centre, ☎ 07 4031 6699, fax 07 4031 6777, (Multi-stry), 38 serv apts acc up to 4, [ensuite, shwr, bath, tlt, hairdry, a/c, tel, cable tv, clock radio, refrig, cook fac, micro, ldry (in unit)], lift, dryer, iron, iron brd, cafe, pool-heated (salt water), spa, bbq, rm serv, secure park (covered), cots-fee. **D ♦ $125, ♦♦ $125, ♦ $20**, ch con, AE BC DC MC VI.

★★★★☆ Il Palazzo Boutique Apartment Hotel, (SA), 62 Abbott St, ☎ 07 4041 2155, fax 07 4041 2166, (Multi-stry), 38 serv apts (38 suites) acc up to 2, [shwr, bath, tlt, hairdry, a/c, cent heat, tel, cable tv, video, clock radio, t/c mkg, refrig, mini bar, cook fac, micro, toaster], lift, iron, iron brd, ✕, pool-heated (salt water), bbq, rm serv (124), dinner to unit, c/park (undercover), secure park, cots. **RO $195**, AE BC DC JCB MC VI.

★★★★☆ Inn Cairns, (HU), 71 Lake St, 500m N/W of Casino Convention Centre, ☎ 07 4041 2350, fax 07 4041 2420, 38 units acc up to 4, [shwr, bath, tlt, a/c-cool, tel, TV, video, clock radio, refrig, cook fac, micro, toaster, ldry (in unit), blkts, linen, pillows], dryer, iron, iron brd, ✕, pool above ground (salt water), bbq, c/park (undercover), secure park, cots-fee. **D ♦♦ $120 - $158, ♦ $22, W ♦♦ $616 - $770, ♦ $44**, ch con, AE BC DC MC VI.

★★★★☆ Koala Court Holiday Apartments, (HU), 147/155 McLeod St, 500m N of PO, ☎ 07 4031 7887, fax 07 4041 1140, (Multi-stry gr fl), 19 units acc up to 5, (1, 2 & 3 bedrm), [shwr, bath (8), tlt, a/c-cool, c/fan, tel, cable tv, video-fee, movie, clock radio, refrig, cook fac, micro, ldry (in unit), blkts, linen, pillows], dryer, iron, pool (salt water), spa, bbq, secure park. **D ♦♦ $124 - $140, ♦ $20, W ♦♦ $948, ♦ $140**, AE BC DC MC VI.

★★★★☆ Mid City Luxury Suites, (HU), 6 McLeod St, opp Myer shopping centre, ☎ 07 4051 5050, fax 07 4051 5161, (2 stry), 19 units acc up to 4, [shwr, tlt, hairdry, a/c, c/fan, tel, cable tv, clock radio, refrig, mini bar, cook fac, micro, ldry (in unit), blkts, linen, pillows], dryer, iron, iron brd, pool, spa, bbq, meals to unit, secure park (undercover), cots. **D ♦♦ $99 - $125, ♦ $10**, ch con, AE BC BTC CC DC JCB MC VI, ⅋⅊.

★★★★☆ **Sunset Terrace**, (HU), 178 McLeod St, 1km N of Cairns central, ☎ 07 4031 9925, fax 07 4041 4851, (Multi-stry gr fl), 8 units acc up to 3, (1 & 2 bedrm), [ensuite, shwr, bath, spa bath (7), tlt, a/c-cool, c/fan, tel, TV, clock radio, refrig, cook fac, micro, d/wash, toaster, ldry, blkts, linen, pillows], dryer, iron, iron brd, pool (salt water), c/park (undercover), secure park (7). **D** ⓘ **$15 - $20, $130 - $150,** BC MC VI.

★★★★☆ **Tropic Towers All Suites Apartments**, (SA), 294 - 298 Sheridan St, 2km N of PO, ☎ 07 4031 3955, fax 07 4031 3738, (Multi-stry gr fl), 44 serv apts acc up to 6, (1 & 2 bedrm), [shwr, bath, tlt, a/c, tel, cable tv, clock radio, refrig, cook fac, micro, d/wash, ldry (in unit)], lift, dryer, iron, pool, spa, bbq, cots. **D** ⓘ **$105 - $135,** ⓘⓘ **$105 - $135,** ⓘ **$12,** ch con, AE BC DC MC VI, ⓘⓘ.

★★★★ **Cairns Aquarius**, (HU), 107 Esplanade, ☎ 07 4051 8444, fax 07 4031 1448, (Multi-stry), 38 units acc up to 4, [shwr, tlt, a/c-cool, c/fan, tel, TV, clock radio, refrig, cook fac, d/wash, ldry (in unit), blkts, linen, pillows], lift, pool, sauna, spa, bbq, secure park, tennis (half court), cots-fee. **RO** ⓘⓘⓘⓘ **$160 - $220,** Min book applies, AE BC DC MC VI.

★★★★ **Campus Apartment Motel**, (SA), 11 Faculty Close, Smithfield 4878, 15 km N of Cairns airport, ☎ 07 4057 7844, fax 07 4057 7370, (2 stry gr fl), 26 serv apts acc up to 4, (1 bedrm), [ensuite, shwr, tlt, hairdry, a/c, c/fan, tel, TV, video-fee, clock radio, refrig, cook fac, micro, d/wash, toaster, ldry (in unit), blkts, linen, pillows], dryer (in unit), iron, iron brd, pool (salt water), bbq, rm serv, c/park (undercover), cots. **D** **$80 - $90,** ⓘ **$15, W** ⓘⓘ **$480 - $520,** ⓘ **$90,** AE BC DC EFT MC VI.

★★★★ **City Terraces**, (HU), 63 McLeod St, 250m N of PO, ☎ 07 4051 8955, fax 07 4051 8744, (2 stry), 34 units acc up to 5, (1 & 2 bedrm), [shwr, tlt, hairdry, a/c-cool, c/fan, tel, cable tv, clock radio, t/c mkg, refrig, micro, d/wash (15), toaster, blkts, linen, pillows], w/mach-fee, dryer (15)-fee, iron, iron brd, pool, bbq, c/park (undercover). **D $110 - $190,** ⓘ **$20 W, $700 - $1,050,** ⓘ **$140,** AE BC DC MC VI.

★★★★ **Mango Paradise Apartments**, (HU), 30 Charles St, ☎ 07 4031 0185, fax 07 4031 9036, (2 stry gr fl), 5 units acc up to 6, (2 bedrm), [shwr, tlt, hairdry, a/c-cool, c/fan, tel, TV, clock radio, refrig, cook fac, micro, toaster, ldry, blkts, linen, pillows], iron, iron brd, pool, bbq, c/park (carport). **RO $79 - $99,** AE BC DC EFT MC VI.

★★★★ **Reef Gateway Apartments**, (HU), 239 Lake St, 1km N of PO, ☎ 07 4052 1411, fax 07 4051 6108, (Multi-stry gr fl), 17 units acc up to 5, (2 bedrm), [shwr, bath (20), tlt, a/c-cool, fan, tel, cable tv, video, clock radio, refrig, cook fac, micro, ldry (in unit), blkts, linen, pillows], pool (salt water), spa, bbq, c/park (undercover) (10), cots-fee. **D** ⓘⓘ **$110 - $128,** ⓘ **$22, W** ⓘⓘ **$600 - $896,** BC MC VI.

★★★★ **Regency Palms**, (HU), 225 McLeod St, 4km N of PO, ☎ 07 4031 4445, fax 07 4031 5415, (Multi-stry gr fl), 58 units acc up to 5, (2 bedrm), [shwr, tlt, a/c-cool, c/fan, tel, TV, movie, clock radio, refrig, cook fac, micro (52), d/wash, ldry (in unit), blkts, linen, pillows], lift, dryer, pool (salt water), c/park (undercover), cots. **D $120 - $160,** AE BC DC MC VI.

★★★★ **Rihga Colonial Club Resort**, (Apt), Resort, 18 Cannon St, 6km from city centre, ☎ 07 4053 5111, fax 07 4053 7072, 145 apts acc up to 4, [shwr, bath, tlt, a/c-cool, fan, tel, TV, movie, clock radio, t/c mkg, refrig, cook fac ltd, micro, elec frypan], ldry, conv fac, ⓧ (3), bar, pool (salt water) (3), 24hr reception, shop, courtesy transfer (airport/city shuttle), ⓘ, bicycle, gym, tennis, cots, non smoking rms (73). **D $221,** AE BC DC JCB MC VI.

★★★☆ **(Motel Section)**, 203 units [shwr, bath, tlt, hairdry, a/c-cool, fan, tel, TV, movie, clock radio, t/c mkg, refrig, pillows]. **RO** ⓘ **$147 - $173,** ⓘⓘ **$147 - $173.**

★★★★ **Royal Palm Villas**, (HU), 184 McLeod St, 1km Nth of CBD, ☎ 07 4052 1444, fax 07 4052 1255, (Multi-stry gr fl), 16 units acc up to 4, (1 bedrm), [shwr, tlt, a/c-cool, c/fan, tel, TV, clock radio, refrig, cook fac, micro, ldry (in unit), blkts, linen, pillows], dryer, iron, pool (salt water), bbq, cots-fee. **D** ⓘⓘ **$97 - $109,** ⓘ **$15, W** ⓘⓘ **$590 - $680,** ch con, pen con, AE BC DC MC VI.

★★★★ **The Citysider**, (HU), 17A Upward St, 1km NW of City Centre, ☎ 07 4051 2520, fax 07 4051 2503, (Multi-stry gr fl), 34 units acc up to 4, (2 bedrm), [shwr, bath (30), tlt, a/c-cool, c/fan, tel, TV, video-fee, clock radio, refrig, cook fac, micro, d/wash, ldry (in unit), blkts, linen, pillows], dryer, iron, pool, bbq, c/park (undercover), cots-fee. **D** ⓘ **$693 - $847,** ⓘⓘ **$770 - $847,** ch con, BC MC VI.

★★★★ **Villa Vaucluse**, (HU), 141-143 Grafton St, SE Civic Theatre, ☎ 07 4051 8566, fax 07 4051 8510, (Multi-stry), 18 units acc up to 4, (1 bedrm), [shwr, bath, tlt, a/c-cool, tel, TV, video, clock radio, refrig, cook fac, micro, ldry (in unit), blkts, linen, pillows], pool (salt water), bbq, secure park (undercover), cots. **D** ⓘⓘ **$120 - $154,** AE BC DC JCB MC VI.

★★★☆ **181 The Esplanade**, (SA), Previously Fortland 181 the Esplanade 181 The Esplanade, 1.5km N of Cairns PO, ☎ 07 4052 6888, fax 07 4031 6227, (Multi-stry), 37 serv apts acc up to 7, [shwr, bath, spa bath, tlt, hairdry, a/c-cool, tel, cable tv, video, clock radio, refrig, cook fac, micro, d/wash, ldry (in unit)], lift, pool, sauna, spa, bbq, secure park, cots. **D** ⓘⓘ **$120 - $240,** ⓘ **$22,** AE BC DC JCB MC VI.

★★★☆ **All Round Motel Inn The Pink**, (SA), 263-269 Sheridan St, 2km N of Cairns City Place, ☎ 07 4051 4800, fax 07 4031 1526, (Multi-stry gr fl), 15 serv apts acc up to 5, (2 bedrm), [shwr, tlt, a/c-cool, c/fan, tel, TV, movie, clock radio, refrig, cook fac, toaster], ldry, dryer-fee, iron, iron brd, pool (salt water), bbq (covered), dinner to unit (Mon to Sat), c/park (undercover) (8), cots-fee. **RO $101 - $123,** AE BC DC EFT MC VI.

★★★☆ **All Seasons Sunshine Tower Hotel Villa Apts**, (HU), 136 Sheridan St, ☎ 07 4051 5288, fax 07 4031 2483, (2 stry gr fl), 19 units acc up to 6, (1 & 2 bedrm), [shwr, tlt, a/c-cool, c/fan, tel, TV, movie, refrig, mini bar, cook fac, blkts, linen, pillows], ldry, ⓧ, pool (salt water), bbq, rm serv, ⓘ, cots. **D** ⓘⓘ **$127 - $162,** AE BC JCB MC MP VI.

FLAG
FLAG CHOICE HOTELS

★★★☆ **Cairns Queenslander**, (HU), Cnr Digger & Charles Sts, ☎ 07 4051 0122, fax 07 4031 1867, (Multi-stry gr fl), 51 units acc up to 4, (1 & 2 bedrm), [shwr, bath, tlt, a/c-cool, c/fan, tel, TV, clock radio, refrig, cook fac, blkts, linen, pillows], lift, ldry, ⓧ, pool, spa, bbq, c/park (undercover), cots-fee, non smoking units (35). **D** ⓘⓘ **$115 - $160,** ⓘ **$24,** AE BC DC EFT MC VI.

★★★☆ **Cairns Vacation Villas**, (HU), 8 Pease St, Manoora 4870, ☎ 07 4053 3149, (2 stry gr fl), 18 units acc up to 6, (1 bedrm), [shwr, tlt, a/c-cool, fan, TV, refrig, cook fac, ldry (in unit), blkts, linen, pillows], pool, bbq, c/park (undercover), car wash, ⓘ, cots. **D** ⓘⓘ **$70 - $85 W** ⓘⓘ **$420 - $525,** ch con, BC MC VI.

CAIRNS QLD continued...

★★★☆ **Cascade Gardens Apartments**, (HU), Cnr Lake & Minnie Sts, ☎ 07 4051 8000, fax 07 4052 1396, (Multi-stry gr fl), 47 units acc up to 4, (Studio & 1 bedrm), [shwr, tlt, a/c-cool, fan, tel, TV, clock radio, refrig, cook fac, ldry (in unit) (23), blkts, linen, pillows], ldry, dryer (in unit) (23), ✉, pool (salt water), spa, bbq, cots. **RO ⚭ $98 - $138, ⚲ $15** AE BC DC JCB MC VI, ⅋&.

★★★☆ **Coral Cay Villa**, (HU), 267 Lake St, ☎ 07 4046 5100, fax 07 4031 2703, (2 stry gr fl), 42 units acc up to 5, (Studio & 1 bedrm), [shwr, tlt, a/c-cool, c/fan, tel, TV, movie, clock radio, refrig, cook fac, micro, blkts, linen, pillows], ldry, dryer, pool, spa, bbq, cots. **D ⚭ $80 - $115, ⚲ $10**, AE BC DC JCB MC VI.

★★★☆ **Coral Reef Resort**, (HU), 192 Mann St, Westcourt 4870, 2.5km S of Cairns P O, ☎ 07 4051 9946, fax 07 4051 9946, (2 stry gr fl), 13 units acc up to 4, (1 & 2 bedrm), [shwr, tlt, a/c-cool (21), fan, tel, TV, clock radio, refrig, cook fac, ldry (in unit), blkts, linen, pillows], pool, spa, c/park (undercover), cots-fee. **D $46 - $95, W $320 - $600**, BC MC VI.

★★★☆ **Coral Towers**, (HU), 255 Esplanade, ☎ 074046 5465, fax 07 4031 2164, (Multi-stry gr fl),30 units acc up to 6, (1 & 2 bedrm), [shwr, bath, tlt, a/c-cool, c/fan, tel, TV, video, clock radio, refrig, cook fac, micro (10), d/wash, ldry (dryer), blkts, linen, pillows], lift, pool (salt water), spa, bbq, c/park (undercover), cots. **D $140 - $170, ⚲ $10**, AE BC DC EFT JCB MC VI.

★★★☆ **Flying Horseshoe**, (HU), 281 Sheridan St, ☎ 07 4051 3022, fax 07 4031 2761, (2 stry), 10 units acc up to 6, (Studio), [shwr, tlt, hairdry, a/c-cool, c/fan, tel, TV, movie, clock radio, t/c mkg, refrig, mini bar, cook fac ltd, micro, blkts, linen, pillows], ldry, iron, iron brd, ✉, pool (salt water), spa, bbq, cots-fee. **RO ⚲ $85 - $105, ⚭ $95 - $115**.

★★★☆ **Metro Inn Apartments Cairns**, (HU), 670 Bruce Hwy, 5.5km SW of Cairns PO, ☎ 07 4033 0522, fax 07 4033 0640, (Multi-stry gr fl), 28 units acc up to 6, (1 & 2 bedrm), [ensuite, shwr, bath, tlt, a/c, c/fan, tel, TV, movie, clock radio, refrig, micro, ldry (in unit), blkts, linen, pillows], dryer, lounge, pool (salt water), bbq, c/park (undercover), tennis, cots-fee. **D ⚭ $65 - $135**, ch con, AE BC DC MC VI.

★★★☆ **Rainforest Grove**, (HU), 40 Moody St, Manunda 4870, ☎ 07 4053 6366, fax 07 4032 1243, (2 stry gr fl), 32 units acc up to 6, (1 & 2 bedrm), [shwr, tlt, a/c, fan, tel, TV, clock radio, cook fac, micro, ldry (in unit), blkts, linen, pillows], pool (salt water), bbq, c/park (undercover), courtesy transfer, cots. **D ⚲ $90 - $105, ⚭ $100 - $115**, AE BC DC EFT MC VI.

★★★☆ **Trade Winds McLeod**, (HU), 191 McLeod St, ☎ 07 4031 2422, fax 07 4031 6727, (Multi-stry gr fl), 32 units acc up to 4, (2 bedrm), [shwr, tlt, a/c-cool, c/fan, tel, TV, clock radio, t/c mkg, refrig, cook fac, micro, d/wash, ldry (in unit), blkts, linen, pillows], pool, bbq, cots. **D $90 - $115, W $616 - $735**, AE BC DC MC VI.

★★★ **Arcadia**, (HU), 189 Sheridan St, 1km fr city, ☎ 07 4051 0908, (2 stry gr fl), 10 units acc up to 6, (1 & 2 bedrm), [shwr, tlt, a/c-cool, c/fan, TV, clock radio, refrig, cook fac, blkts, linen, pillows], ldry, pool (salt water), bbq, c/park (undercover), ☎, cots-fee. **D ⚭ $55 - $80, ⚲ $9, W ⚭ $385 - $540**, BC MC VI.

★★★ **City Walk**, (HU), 21 Upward St, 2km W of PO, ☎ 07 4051 2972, (2 stry), 12 units acc up to 7, (Studio, 2 & 3 bedrm), [shwr, bath (1), tlt, a/c-cool, c/fan, TV, clock radio, refrig, cook fac, blkts, linen, pillows], ldry, dryer, pool (salt water), bbq, c/park (undercover), cots. **D $50 - $100, W $320 - $630**, Min book applies, BC MC VI.

★★★ **El Dorado**, (HU), 243 Lake St, ☎ 07 4051 6122, fax 07 4031 6480, (2 stry gr fl), 17 units acc up to 6, (1 & 2 bedrm), [shwr, tlt, a/c-cool, fan, tel, TV, video-fee, refrig, cook fac, ldry (in unit) (11), blkts, linen, pillows], ldry, pool (salt water), bbq, c/park (undercover), courtesy transfer, cots. **D ⚭ $66, ⚭⚭ $88, W ⚭ $434, ⚭⚭ $565**, ch con, BC MC VI, *Operator Comment: El Dorado Apartments offers families and couples clean and comfortable accom at very comp prices.*

★★★ **Glenlee**, (SA), 560 Bruce Hwy, Woree 4868, 500m S of Earlville shopping centre, ☎ 07 4054 1009, fax 07 4054 7444, (2 stry gr fl), 4 serv apts acc up to 6, (2 bedrm), [shwr, tlt, a/c, c/fan, tel, TV, movie, clock radio, refrig, cook fac], ldry, dryer-fee, iron, iron brd, pool (salt water), spa, bbq, c/park (undercover), cots-fee. **D ⚲ $60, ⚭ $66**, AE BC DC MC VI.

★★★ **Oasis Inn**, (HU), 276 Sheridan St, ☎ 07 4051 8111, fax 07 4051 4073, (2 stry gr fl), 26 units acc up to 6, (1 & 2 bedrm), [shwr, bath, tlt, a/c-cool, c/fan, tel, TV, clock radio, t/c mkg, refrig, cook fac (20), blkts, linen, pillows], ldry, pool (salt water), bbq, c/park (undercover), cots-fee. **RO ⚭ $66 - $121, ⚲ $11.50, ⚭ W $450 - $810**, ch con, AE BC MC VI.

★★★ **Pacific Cay**, (HU), 193 Sheridan St, ☎ 07 4051 0151, fax 07 4051 0077, (2 stry gr fl), 17 units acc up to 6, (1 & 2 bedrm), [shwr, tlt, a/c-cool, c/fan, tel, TV, refrig, cook fac, blkts, linen, pillows], ldry, rec rm, pool, bbq, c/park (undercover), cots. **W $385 - $590**, AE BC MC VI.

★★★ **QCWA Holiday Units**, (HU), 258 Grafton St, 2km N of PO, ☎ 07 4031 2557, fax 07 4031 2557, 10 units acc up to 4, (2 bedrm), [shwr, bath, tlt, a/c, fan, TV, clock radio, t/c mkg, refrig, cook fac, toaster, blkts, linen, pillows], ldry, ☎, cots. **D ⚲ $35 - $50, ⚭ $45, ⚲ $10**, ⅋&.

★★★ **Tropic Sunrise**, (HU), 338 Sheridan St, 3km N of city centre, ☎ 07 4031 5664, fax 07 4051 2615, (2 stry gr fl), 21 units acc up to 5, (1 & 2 bedrm), [shwr, tlt, a/c-cool, c/fan, TV, clock radio, refrig, cook fac, micro, blkts, linen, pillows], ldry, dryer, iron, iron brd, pool, bbq, ☎, cots. **D ⚭ $75 - $90, ⚲ $10, W ⚭ $476 - $567, ⚲ $70**, pen con, BC DC MC VI.

★★★ **Villa Shangri La**, (HU), 288 Sheridan St, ☎ 07 4052 1333, fax 07 4051 2855, (Multi-stry gr fl), 34 units acc up to 5, [shwr, tlt, a/c-cool, c/fan, tel, TV, refrig, cook fac, blkts, linen, pillows], ldry, dryer, pool, bbq, cots-fee. **D ⚭ $72 - $82, W ⚭ $454 - $518**, BC MC VI.

★★☆ **Concord**, (HU), 183 Sheridan St, 1km fr city centre, ☎ 07 4031 4522, fax 07 4041 4970, (2 stry gr fl), 8 units acc up to 5, (1 bedrm), [shwr, tlt, a/c (8), c/fan, tel (8), TV, radio, t/c mkg, refrig, cook fac, blkts, linen, pillows], ldry, pool (salt water), bbq, c/park (undercover), cots-fee. **D $55 - $60**, ch con, AE BC DC MC VI.

★★☆ **Coolabah**, (HU), 564 Mulgrave Rd, ☎ 07 4054 2711, fax 07 4033 5340, 5 units (Studio & 1 bedrm), [shwr, tlt, a/c-cool, c/fan, tel, TV, refrig, cook fac ltd (5), blkts, linen, pillows], ldry, pool, c/park (undercover) (4), cots-fee. **D ⚭ $55 - $65, ⚲ $11**, AE BC DC MC VI.

★★☆ **High Chaparral**, (HU), 195 Sheridan St, ☎ 07 4051 7155, fax 07 4031 3527, (Multi-stry gr fl), 22 units acc up to 6, (1 & 2 bedrm), [shwr, tlt, a/c-cool, c/fan, tel, TV, refrig, cook fac, blkts, linen, pillows], ldry, pool, bbq, c/park (undercover) (12), cots-fee. **D ⚲ $65 - $90, ⚭ $70 - $90, ⚭⚭ $80 - $100, ⚭⚭⚭ $90 - $110**, AE BC DC MC VI.

B&B's/Guest Houses

★★★★★ **Nutmeg Grove Tropical Rainforest B&B**, (B&B), 7 Woodridge Cl, Crystal Cascades, via Redlync, 8km S of Redlynch PO, ☎ 07 4039 1226, fax 07 4039 1226, 2 rms [shwr, spa bath, tlt, hairdry, a/c, c/fan, tel, TV, video, clock radio, t/c mkg, refrig, pillows], ldry, dryer, lounge (TV), ✗, pool (salt water), ✆, non smoking property. **BB ♦♦ $120 - $150**, BC MC VI.

★★★★☆ **Peaceful Palms Bed & Breakfast**, (B&B), 128 Stanton Rd, Smithfield 4878, ☎ 07 4038 2146, fax 03 4035 4399, 2 rms [c/fan, elec blkts, t/c mkg, cook fac (limited), micro], lounge (TV, video), pool, spa, t/c mkg shared, refrig, bbq, cots (fee), non smoking property. **BB ♦ $55 - $65, ♦♦ $75 - $95**, ch con, VI.

★★★★ **Cairns Bed & Breakfast**, (B&B), 48 Russell St Edge Hill, 5km Cairns Centre & Airport, ☎ 07 4032 4121, fax 07 4053 6557, 3 rms [shwr, tlt, hairdry, a/c-cool, c/fan, clock radio, t/c mkg, refrig], ldry, dryer-fee, iron, iron brd, lounge (tv), ✗, pool, bbq, c/park (undercover), courtesy transfer (to airport), non smoking flr, non smoking rms (3). **RO ♦ $75, ♦♦ $95**.

★★★★ **Galvins Edge Hill B&B**, (B&B), 61 Walsh St, Edge Hill 4870, 250m N of PO, ☎ 07 4032 1308, 2 rms (2 suites) [a/c, fan, tel, TV, video, clock radio, t/c mkg, refrig, ldry, doonas], bathrm (2), pool, plygr, cots, non smoking suites. **RO $75 - $90**, ch con, Min book applies.

★★★☆ **Grange Cottage**, (B&B), 11 Elgata Cl, Woree 4868, ☎ 07 4054 6244, fax 07 4054 6244, 2 rms [shwr, bath, tlt, c/fan, TV, clock radio, t/c mkg, refrig, cook fac, micro, toaster, doonas, pillows], ldry, w/mach, dryer, bbq, cots, breakfast ingredients, non smoking property. **BLB ♦ $80, ♦♦ $90, ⓘ $25**, ch con, Min book applies.

★★★☆ **Jennys Home Stay Bed & Breakfast**, (B&B), 12 Leon Close, Brinsmead 4870, ☎ 07 4055 1639, 2 rms (1 & 2 bedrm), [ensuite (1), bath, hairdry (1), a/c-cool (1), c/fan, clock radio, refrig (1)], shwr, tlt, lounge (TV), pool (salt water), t/c mkg shared, bbq. **RO $50 - $80**.

Captain Cook Cruises, (GH), Trinity Wharf, 1 Wharf St, 750m NE of GPO, ☎ 07 4031 4433, fax 07 4031 6983, 75 rms [ensuite, hairdry, a/c-cool, tel, clock radio], lift, ldry, rec rm, TV rm, ✗, bar (3), pool (salt water), sauna, spa, t/c mkg shared, gym, cots-fee, non smoking units. **D all meals ♦♦ $2,300**, Cruise Vessel operating 3,4,& 7 night Great Barrier Cruises, AE BC DC JCB MC VI, (not yet classified).

Other Accommodation

Cairns McLeod St YHA, (Lodge), 20 McLeod St, 500m W of PO, ☎ 07 4051 0772, fax 07 4031 3158, (2 stry gr fl), 41 rms acc up to 8, [c/fan], shwr, tlt, ldry, lounge (TV), cafe, pool, cook fac, t/c mkg shared, refrig, kiosk, ✆. **D $18 - $44**, BC EFT MC VI.

Inn the Tropics, (Lodge), 141 Sheridan St, ☎ 07 4031 1088, fax 07 4051 7110, (2 stry gr fl), 51 rms [shwr (6), tlt (6), a/c-cool-fee, TV (6), t/c mkg, refrig], shwr, tlt, ldry, dryer, rec rm, lounge (TV), pool, cook fac, bbq, ✆. **RO ♦ $16.50 - $44, ♦♦ $44 - $55**, AE BC DC JCB MC VI.

Uptop Downunder Lodge (Backpackers), (Lodge), 164 Spence St, 1km S of City Centre, ☎ 07 4051 3636, fax 07 4052 1211, 47 rms acc up to 8, [c/fan, refrig], shwr, tlt, dryer-fee, rec rm, lounge (tv), pool, cook fac, t/c mkg shared, bbq, ✆, non smoking rms. **D $18 - $38**, AE BC MC VI.

CALLIOPE QLD 4680

Pop 1,200. (513km N Brisbane), See map on page 416, ref D7. Situated on the banks of the Calliope River in Queensland's tropical north. Boat Ramp, Boating, Bowls, Fishing, Gold Prospecting, Golf, Horse Racing, Horse Riding, Scenic Drives, Shooting, Swimming, Tennis.

★ **Calliope Cross Roads Motel**, (M), Cnr Bruce Hwy & Dawson Hwy, 19km from Gladstone, ☎ 07 4975 7207, fax 07 4975 7003, 6 units [shwr, tlt, a/c-cool, c/fan, TV, clock radio, t/c mkg, refrig], ldry, dryer-fee, bbq, rm serv, c/park (undercover), ✆, cots-fee, non smoking units. **RO ♦ $27.50 - $44, ♦♦ $38.50 - $52.80, ⓘ $11**, ch con, AE BC MC VI.

CALOUNDRA QLD

See Sunshine Coast Region.

CAMBOOYA QLD 4358

Pop 700. (149km W Brisbane), See map on page 417, ref A7. Small town in an agricultural district producing grain, cattle & dairying.

★★★☆ **Mendip Lodge**, (GH), (Farm), Working farm property. Todds Rd, 4km W of PO 8km off New England Hwy, ☎ 07 4696 1207, fax 07 4696 1696, 3 rms [elec blkts, clock radio], shwr, tlt, bathrm, ldry, lounge (TV), t/c mkg shared, bbq, c/park (undercover), cots. **BB ♦ $40, DBB ♦ $65**, ch con.

CAMOOWEAL QLD 4828

Pop 250. (2082km NW Brisbane), See map on page 414, ref A5. Last town encountered before crossing NT border.

Hotels/Motels

★★☆ **Camooweal Roadhouse**, (M), Barkly Hwy, ☎ 07 4748 2155, fax 07 4748 2132, 6 units [shwr, tlt, a/c, TV, movie, t/c mkg, refrig], ldry, ✗, non smoking units. **RO ♦ $60, ♦♦ $60, ⓘ $10**, ch con, AE BC MC VI.

Self Catering Accommodation

★★ **BP Camooweal Driveway**, Barkly Hwy, ☎ 07 4748 2137, fax 07 4748 2168, 4 cabins [shwr, tlt, a/c-cool, c/fan, TV, clock radio, t/c mkg, refrig, blkts, linen, pillows], ldry, dryer, ✗, bbq, dinner to unit, shop, petrol, ice, ✆. **D ♦ $50, ♦♦ $55, ⓘ $10**, ch con, AE BC DC EFT MC MP VI.

CANIA GORGE NATIONAL PARK

Pop Nominal, (549km NW Brisbane), See map on page 416, ref C8. Dramatic sandstone formations and rainforest pockets similar to Carnarvon Gorge. Sealed roads throughout. Many walking trails, abundant wildlife. The nearby Cania Dam has a picnic and recreation area.

Spring Creek Host Farm and Artist Retreat, 'Spring Creek', Monto 4630, 9km E of Cania Gorge National Park, ☎ 07 4167 8145, 2 cabins [shwr, tlt, heat, fan, elec blkts, t/c mkg], cook fac, bbq (covered). **BB ♦♦ $88, DBB ♦♦ $110, RO ♦♦ $80**, ch con, BC MC VI, (not yet classified).

CANNONVALE QLD

See Whitsundays Region.

CANUNGRA QLD 4275

Pop 400. (80km S Brisbane), See map on page 417, ref D8. This superb former timber town has a quaint village charm. Bird Watching, Bowls, Bush Walking, Golf, Hangliding, Scenic Drives.

Hotels/Motels

★★★ **Canungra Hotel**, (LH), 8 Kidston St, ☎ 07 5543 5233, fax 07 5543 5617, (2 stry), 11 rms [basin, ensuite (3), shwr (3), tlt (3), a/c], shwr, tlt, lounge (TV), ✗, cots. **RO ♦ $49.50 - $60.50, ♦♦ $55 - $66, ⓘ $11**, ch con, BC MC VI.

★★☆ **Canungra**, (M), Cnr Kidston & Pine Sts, 500 m E of PO, ☎ 07 5543 5155, fax 07 5543 5155, (2 stry gr fl), 10 units [shwr, tlt, fan, heat, TV, clock radio, t/c mkg, refrig], pool, cots. **RO ♦ $50, ♦♦ $60, ⓘ $10**, BC MC VI.

CANUNGRA QLD continued...

B&B's/Guest Houses

★★★★★ **Ferny Glen Cottage**, (B&B), (Farm), Ferny Glen Farm, Upper Coomera Rd, 10km SE of PO, ☎ 07 5543 7171, fax 07 5543 7118, 1 rm (2 bedrm), [ensuite (2), shwr, a/c, elec blkts, TV, video, CD, t/c mkg, refrig, cook fac, pillows], iron, iron brd, lounge, lounge firepl, pool (salt water), spa, bbq, c/park (undercover), tennis. **BB** ♦♦ **$180**, ⏧ **$35**, BC MC VI.

★★★★ **Baggs of Canungra**, (B&B), 12 King St, 300m SE of Police Station, ☎ 07 5543 5579, fax 07 5543 5579, 4 rms [ensuite (2), hairdry, fan (4), heat, cable tv, clock radio, t/c mkg, refrig (4)], bathrm (2), dryer, iron, iron brd, lounge firepl (& library), pool (salt water), sauna, spa, t/c mkg shared, bbq (covered), cots (avail), non smoking rms. **BB** ♦ **$75 - $95**, ♦♦ **$90 - $110**, ⏧ **$33**, ch con, BC MC VI.

★★★★ **Yandooya**, (GH), (Farm), 440ha cattle property, Table Top Rd, 18 km S of PO, ☎ 07 5543 5184, fax 07 5543 5140, 1 rm [ensuite, shwr, hairdry, c/fan, heat, clock radio, ldry], lounge (TV), t/c mkg shared, cots, non smoking rms. **D all meals** ♦ **$145**, ch con, BC MC VI.

   ★★★☆ **(Cottage Section)**, 2 cotgs (2 & 3 bedrm), [fan, TV, refrig, cook fac, elec frypan, toaster, ldry, blkts, linen, pillows], shwr, tlt, bbq, cots. **D all meals** ♦ **$145**, ch con.

★★ **Gumnuts Horseriding Resort**, (B&B), (Farm), Biddaddaba Creek Rd, 15km N of Canungra & 15km E of Beaudesert, ☎ 07 5543 0191, fax 07 055430191, 17 rms [fan, pillows], lounge (TV & video), conf fac, ✕ (with fireplace), pool, bbq, ☎, plygr, non smoking rms. **BB** ♦ **$50 - $70**, ♦♦ **$100 - $140**, ch con, Horseriding & activities included in tariff. AE BC MC VI.

CAPE HILLSBOROUGH NATIONAL PARK

Pop Nominal, (1,009km N Brisbane), See map on page 416, ref A2. Small town of Cape Hillsborough within the National Park received its name from Captain Cook. National Park includes Wedge Island.

★★★☆ **Cape Hillsborough Nature Resort**, (M), Previously Cape Hillsborough Holiday Resort, 47km N Mackay, ☎ 07 4959 0262, fax 07 4959 0500, (2 stry), 10 units [shwr, tlt, a/c-cool, TV, t/c mkg, refrig], ldry, w/mach-fee, ✕ (Mon-Sun), pool, bbq, rm serv, c/park (undercover), ☎. **RO** ♦ **$66**, ♦♦ **$77**, ⏧ **$11**, BC EFT MC VI.

CAPE TRIBULATION QLD 4873

Pop Nominal, (1867km N Brisbane), See map on page 415, ref B1. Located in World Heritage rainforest with beautiful coastal views. Boating, Fishing, Scenic Drives, Swimming.

Hotels/Motels

★★★★ **Coconut Beach Rainforest Resort**, (M), Resort, Cape Tribulation Rd, 150km N of Cairns PO, 32km N of Daintree Ferry, ☎ 07 4098 0033, fax 07 4098 0047, 40 units [shwr, tlt, hairdry, c/fan, clock radio, t/c mkg, refrig, mini bar, pillows], ldry, iron, iron brd, business centre, conv fac, ✕, bar, pool (3), shop, ☎. **BLB** ♦♦ **$345**, ⏧ **$49**, ch con, AE BC DC MC VI.

   ★★★☆ **(Unit Section)**, 27 units acc up to 5, [shwr, tlt, hairdry, c/fan, clock radio, t/c mkg, refrig, mini bar, blkts, linen, pillows], iron, iron brd. **BLB** ♦♦ **$230**, ⏧ **$49**, ch con.

★★★ **Ferntree Rainforest Resort**, (M), Resort, Camelot Cl, 38km N of Daintree Ferry close to beach, ☎ 07 4098 0000, fax 07 4098 0011, 42 units (8 suites) [shwr, tlt, a/c-cool, c/fan, tel, t/c mkg, refrig, pillows], rec rm, ✕, pool, c/park. **BLB** ♦ **$230**, ♦♦ **$230**, **Suite BLB** ♦ **$320**, ♦♦♦ **$320**, ch con, 8 suites ★★★★. AE BC DC MC VI.

Cape Trib Beach House, (LH), Cape Tribulation Rd, 138km N of Cairns, ☎ 07 4098 0030, fax 07 4098 0120, 21 rms [ensuite (9), a/c, fan, doonas], ldry, ✕, pool, t/c mkg shared, refrig, ☎, cots, non smoking property. **D** ♦ **$25 - $32**, ♦♦ **$99 - $109**, ch con, weekly con, AE BC DC EFT MC VI, (not yet classified).

B&B's/Guest Houses

Cape Tribulation Retreat, (B&B), Lot 19, Nicole Dr, 70km N of Mossman, ☎ 07 4098 0028, (Multi-stry), 2 rms [ensuite, fan, doonas], lounge (TV), t/c mkg shared, bbq. **BB** ♦ **$60**, ♦♦ **$90 - $100**, weekly con, BC MC VI, (not yet classified).

Other Accommodation

Daintree Cape Tribulation Heritage Lodge, (Lodge), Turpentine Rd, 18km N of Daintree Ferry, ☎ 07 4098 9138, fax 07 4098 9004, 16 rms acc up to 4, [shwr, tlt, hairdry, c/fan, t/c mkg, mini bar], ✕, bar, pool (salt water), spa, c/park (undercover), bush walking, bicycle, cots-fee. **BLB** ♦ **$176**, ♦♦ **$176**, ch con, BC JCB MC VI.

CAPE YORK QLD 4876

Pop Nominal, (2753km N Brisbane), See map on page 414, ref B1. The most northerly point of the Australian mainland. Fishing, Swimming.

Hotels/Motels

★★☆ **Pajinka Wilderness Lodge Cape York**, (M), Resort, Cape York, 400m S of Cape York, ☎ 07 4031 3988, fax 07 4031 3966, 24 units [shwr, tlt, c/fan], ldry, ✕, pool, t/c mkg shared, kiosk, shop. **D all meals** ♦ **$250 - $270**, ♦♦ **$460 - $500**, ch con, Dinghy, interpretation services. AE BC DC MC VI.

Other Accommodation

Lotus Bird Lodge, (Lodge), No children's facilities, Violet Vale Station Musgrave via, Coen 4871, 26km E of Musgrave, 133km S of Coen, ☎ 07 4059 0773, fax 07 4059 0703, 10 rms acc up to 4, [shwr, tlt, hairdry, c/fan, refrig], iron, iron brd, ✕, pool above ground, t/c mkg shared, bicycle, non smoking rms (4). **D all meals** ♦ **$247.50**, ♦♦ **$385**, AE MC VI, (not yet classified).

CAPELLA QLD 4702

Pop 750. (955km NW Brisbane), See map on page 414, ref D6. Centrally located in Queensland's Central Highlands, Gemfields and Coalfields regions. Bowls, Bush Walking, Golf, Horse Riding, Scenic Drives.

Hotels/Motels

★★★★ **Bottlebrush**, (M), 12 Abor St, ☎ 07 4984 9752, fax 07 4984 9754, 10 units [shwr, tlt, tel, TV, clock radio, t/c mkg, refrig, toaster], ✕ (Log Cabin Style), bbq, c/park (undercover). **RO** ♦ **$55**, ♦♦ **$65 - $70**, ch con, AE BC DC EFT JCB MC VI.

★★ **Hotel Capella**, (LMH), Peak Downs St, ☎ 07 4984 9433, fax 07 4984 9694, 8 units [shwr, tlt, a/c-cool, elec blkts (3), tel, TV, clock radio, t/c mkg, refrig], ✕ (Mon to Sat), dinner to unit. **RO** ♦ **$33 - $50**, ♦♦ **$44 - $61**, AE BC MC.

★ **Capella**, (M), Slider St, ☎ 07 4984 9177, fax 07 4984 9699, (2 stry gr fl), 17 units [shwr, tlt, a/c-cool, fan, heat, elec blkts, tel, TV, clock radio, t/c mkg, refrig, cook fac (6)], ldry-fee, cots. **RO** ♦ **$45**, ♦♦ **$55**, ch con, BC MC VI.

CARDWELL QLD 4849

Pop 1,400. (1533km N Brisbane), See map on page 415, ref C5. Gateway to Hinchinbrook Island region. Boating, Bowls, Bush Walking, Fishing, Golf, Scenic Drives, Swimming, Tennis.

Hotels/Motels

★★★ **Sunrise Village & Leisure Park**, (M), 43a Marine Pde, ☎ 07 4066 8550, fax 07 4066 8941, (2 stry gr fl), 28 units [shwr, tlt, a/c-cool, tel, TV, movie, clock radio, t/c mkg, refrig], ldry, iron, conv fac, ✕, cafe, pool, spa, bbq (covered), dinner to unit, c/park (undercover) (14), ☎, cots-fee. **RO** ♦ **$53 - $65**, ♦♦ **$68 - $80**, ⏧ **$11.50**, units 101 to 108 ★★☆. AE BC DC EFT MC VI.

   ★★☆ **(Cardwell Section)**, 12 units [shwr, tlt, a/c-cool, c/fan, tel, TV, clock radio, t/c mkg, refrig], pool (salt water), spa, c/park (undercover). **RO** ♦ **$45 - $56**, ♦♦ **$56 - $68**, ⏧ **$11.50**, ch con.

★★☆ **Lyndoch Motor Inn**, (M), 215 Victoria St, ☎ 07 4066 8500, fax 07 4066 8028, 19 units [shwr, tlt, a/c-cool, c/fan, tel (5), TV, t/c mkg, refrig, cook fac (5), ldry (in unit)], ldry, conv fac, ☒ (Mon to Sat), pool, bbq, courtesy transfer, ✆, cots-fee. **RO 👤 $25 - $50, 👥 $35 - $60, 🧍 $5**, Units 1 to 3, 6 to 12, 14, 16 to 18 & 26 to 29 ★. AE BC DC MC VI.

★☆ **Marine**, (LMH), Victoria St, ☎ 07 4066 8662, fax 07 4066 8697, 8 units [shwr, tlt, a/c, c/fan, TV, t/c mkg, refrig], ☒ (Mon to Sat), ✆. **RO 👤 $38.50, 👥 $44, 🧍 $10**, AE BC DC EFT MC VI.

Self Catering Accommodation

★★★ **Aquarius Motel & Holiday Units**, (HU), 25 Bruce Hwy, ☎ 07 4066 8755, fax 07 4066 2011, (2 stry gr fl), 5 units acc up to 6, [shwr, tlt, a/c-cool, c/fan, TV, clock radio, refrig, cook fac, blkts, linen, pillows], ldry, w/mach-fee, dryer-fee, pool, spa, c/park (undercover), cots-fee. **D 👥 $50 - $65, 🧍 $10**, ch con, BC MC VI.

CARNARVON NATIONAL PARK

Pop Nominal, (722km NW Brisbane), See map on page 414, ref D7. Controlled by the National Parks & Wildlife Service, this 217,000ha natural beauty is flanked by sheer white cliffs hiding cool crystal streams, waterfalls and mossy canyons. Famous for its ancient Aboriginal art Access is restricted during wet weather. Bush Walking, Scenic Drives.

★★★☆ **Oasis Lodge Carnarvon Gorge**, (GH), Carnarvon National Park, Rolleston 4702, ☎ 07 4984 4503, fax 07 4984 4500, 30 rms [shwr, tlt, a/c-cool, fan, heat, elec blkts, t/c mkg, refrig], ldry, lounge, ✕ (Licensed), bar, bbq, shop, petrol, ✆, cots. **D all meals 👤 $190 - $250, 👥 $292 - $370**, ch con.

CHARLEVILLE QLD 4470

Pop 3,300. (744km W Brisbane), See map on page 414, ref C7. Situated on the banks of the Warrego River. Experimental rain making site which failed. Vortex guns still on display outside Scout's Hall in Sturt St. Skywatch, School of Distance Education, Historic House Museum. Bowls, Golf, Horse Racing, Swimming, Tennis.

Hotels/Motels

★★★★ **Charleville**, (M), 148 King St, ☎ 07 4654 1566, fax 07 4654 2370, 28 units [shwr, tlt, a/c, elec blkts, tel, TV, movie, clock radio, t/c mkg, refrig, mini bar], ldry, conv fac, ☒ (Mon-Sat), bar, pool, spa, dinner to unit, c/park (undercover), car wash, cots-fee. **RO 👤 $65, 👥 $75, 👥👤 $95, 👥👥 $105**, ch con, Units 22 to 29 ★★★. AE BC MC VI.

★★★★ **Mulga Country Motor Inn**, (M), Cunnamulla Rd, ☎ 07 4654 3255, fax 07 4654 3381, 26 units [shwr, spa bath (1), tlt, hairdry, a/c, heat, tel, TV, movie, clock radio, t/c mkg, refrig], iron, iron brd, conv fac, ☒ (open Mon to Sat), pool (salt water), rm serv, dinner to unit (Mon to Sat), cots-fee, non smoking units (18). **RO 👤 $76, 👥 $87**, AE BC DC EFT MC VI, ♿.

★★★★ **Warrego**, (M), 75 Wills St, ☎ 07 4654 1299, fax 07 4654 2317, 12 units [shwr, tlt, a/c, fan, elec blkts, tel, TV, movie, clock radio, t/c mkg, refrig, mini bar], ldry, bbq, dinner to unit (6 nights), cots. **RO 👤 $64, 👥 $74, 🧍 $10**, AE BC DC MC VI.

★★ **Charleville Waltzing Matilda Motor Inn**, (M), 125 Alfred St, ☎ 07 4654 1720, fax 07 4654 3049, 29 units [shwr, tlt, a/c-cool, heat, elec blkts, tel (16), TV, movie, clock radio, t/c mkg, refrig], ldry, ✕, BYO, pool, spa, dinner to unit, cots. **RO 👤 $44, 👥 $55, 🧍 $10**, BC EFT MC VI.

★★ **Hotel Corones**, (LMH), 33 Wills St, 300m W of PO, ☎ 07 4654 1022, fax 07 4654 1756, 16 units [ensuite, tlt, a/c-cool (6), fan (6), refrig], ✕, ☒, cafe, coffee shop, c/park. **RO 👤 $45, 👥 $55, 🧍 $10**, ch con, AE BC MC VI.

CHARTERS TOWERS QLD 4820

Pop 8,900. (1386km N Brisbane), See map on page 414, ref C5. Known as the Heritage City of Queensland. Golf, Horse Racing, Shooting, Swimming.

Hotels/Motels

GOLDEN CHAIN

★★★★ **Charters Towers Heritage Lodge**, (M), 79-97 Flinders Hwy, 4-5km E of PO, ☎ 07 4787 4088, fax 07 4787 4358, 17 units [shwr, tlt, hairdry (2), a/c-cool, tel, cable tv, clock radio, t/c mkg, refrig, cook fac (4), micro (4), elec frypan (4)], ldry-fee, dryer-fee, iron (17), iron brd (17), pool (salt water), bbq, rm serv, c/park (undercover), plygr, cots, non smoking units(9). **RO 👤 $69, 👥 $80 - $96, 🧍 $10**, AE BC DC EFT VI, ♿.

★★★☆ **Cattlemans Rest Motor Inn**, (M), Cnr Bridge & Plant Sts, 500m from City Centre, ☎ 07 4787 3555, fax 07 4787 4039, 38 units [shwr, bath (14), tlt, a/c, tel, TV, movie, clock radio, t/c mkg, refrig], ldry, ☒ (Mon-Sat), pool, spa, bbq, rm serv, dinner to unit, c/park (undercover) (24), cots, non smoking units (5). **RO 👤 $73, 👥 $81, 🧍 $11**, AE BC DC MC VI.

★★★ **AAA Award Winning Park Motel**, (M), 1 Mosman St, ☎ 07 4787 1022, fax 07 4787 4268, 30 units [shwr, bath, tlt, a/c-cool, c/fan, tel, TV, radio, t/c mkg, refrig], ldry, iron, iron brd, conv fac, ☒ (Mon to Sat), pool (salt water), bbq, rm serv, dinner to unit, cots. **RO 👤 $69 - $72, 👥 $77 - $80, 🧍 $11**, AE BC DC EFT MC VI.

Budget Motel Chain International

★★★ **Country Road**, (M), Flinders Hwy, ☎ 07 4787 2422, fax 07 4787 7639, 18 units [shwr, tlt, a/c-cool, tel, cable tv, movie, clock radio, t/c mkg, refrig, cook fac (4)], ldry, pool, bbq, dinner to unit, c/park (undercover), cots. **RO 👤 $50 - $55, 👥 $56 - $65, 🧍 $11**, AE BC DC EFT MC MCH VI.

★★☆ **Hillview**, (M), Flinders Hwy, ☎ 07 4787 1973, fax 07 4787 4044, 11 units [shwr, tlt, a/c-cool, c/fan, tel, TV, clock radio, t/c mkg, refrig, cook fac (10), toaster], ldry, pool, bbq, dinner to unit, c/park (undercover) (9), plygr, cots-fee. **RO 👤 $56, 👥 $71, 🧍 $10**, ch con, AE BC DC MC VI.

B&B's/Guest Houses

★★★★ **Bluff Downs**, (GH), (Farm), c1862. A working stud cattle station with Quarter horses. 80km NW along Lynd H'way, 29km W on gravel rd, ☎ 07 4770 4084, fax 07 4770 4084, 4 rms (1 bedrm), [basin, hairdry, a/c-cool (4), heat, elec blkts, refrig], shwr, tlt, bathrm, dryer-fee, lounge (TV), ✕, t/c mkg shared, refrig, bbq, c/park (undercover), plygr, bush walking, cots, non smoking rms. **D all meals 👤 $121**, ch con.

★★★★ **York Street Bed & Breakfast**, (B&B), Queenslander c1900. No children's facilities, 58 York St, 1.2km SE of PO, ☎ 07 4787 1028, fax 07 4787 1085, 5 rms [ensuite, a/c-cool, TV, refrig, mini bar], ldry-fee, dryer-fee, pool (salt water), t/c mkg shared, ✆, non smoking rms. **BB 👤 $60, 👥 $72**, BC MC VI, ♿.

Historic Advent House B&B, (B&B), 29 Gordon St, 1.5 N of PO, ☎ 07 4787 3508, fax 07 4787 3163, 5 rms [ensuite (2), a/c, heat, cook fac ltd], ldry, lounge (TV), ✗, pool, spa, t/c mkg shared, refrig, bbq, non smoking property. **BB** ♦ **$56 - $67,** ♦♦ **$73 - $84,** ch con, weekly con, BC EFT MC VI, (not yet classified).

York Street Lodge, (GH), 58 York St, 1.2km SW of PO, ☎ 07 4787 1028, 17 rms [a/c-cool, c/fan, refrig], ldry, dryer, lounge (TV), ✗, pool (saltwater), t/c mkg shared, secure park, ✆, non smoking rms (5). **BB** ♦ **$33, RO** ♦ **$25,** (not yet classified).

CHILDERS QLD 4660

Pop 1,500. (315km N Brisbane), See map on page 417, ref C1. Rich canegrowing, fruit and vegetable area irrigated from the Monduran Dam. Pharmaceutical Museum, Isis Sugar Mill (tours Aug - Nov), Art Gallery, Hall of Memories. Bowls, Golf, Scenic Drives, Swimming, Tennis.

Hotels/Motels

★★★☆ **Gateway Motor Inn**, (M), Bruce Hwy, ☎ 07 4126 1288, fax 07 4126 1014, 19 units [shwr, tlt, a/c, tel, TV, clock radio, t/c mkg, refrig], pool, dinner to unit, cots. **RO** ♦ **$53 - $57,** ♦♦ **$62 - $68,** ◊ **$9,** ch con, AE BC DC EFT MC VI, ♿.

★★★ **Motel Childers**, (M), 136 Churchill St (Bruce Hwy), ☎ 07 4126 1177, fax 07 4126 2266, 14 units [shwr, tlt, hairdry, a/c, c/fan, tel, TV, clock radio, t/c mkg, refrig, toaster], ✗, c/park (undercover), cots-fee. **RO** ♦ **$56,** ♦♦ **$64,** ◊ **$10,** ch con, AE BC DC EFT MC VI.

★★ **Avocado Motor Inn**, (M), Bruce Hwy, 500m North of PO, ☎ 07 4126 1608, fax 07 4126 1190, 14 units [shwr, tlt, hairdry (4), a/c-cool, fan, heat, TV, clock radio, t/c mkg, refrig, toaster (4)], dinner to unit, c/park (undercover), cots, non smoking units (3). **RO** ♦ **$45 - $55,** ♦♦ **$52 - $60,** ◊ **$11,** AE BC DC EFT MC VI.

★★ **Panda**, (M), Bruce Hwy, ☎ 07 4126 1773, fax 07 4126 1773, 13 units [shwr, tlt, a/c-cool, c/fan, heat, TV, clock radio, t/c mkg, refrig], pool, dinner to unit, c/park (undercover), cots-fee. **RO** ♦ **$44,** ♦♦ **$52 - $56,** ◊ **$8,** AE BC DC EFT MC VI.

B&B's/Guest Houses

★★★★ **Mango Hill Bed & Breakfast**, (B&B), 1 Mango Hill Drive, 400m off Highway, mob 0408 875 305, fax 07 4126 1311, 2 rms [shwr, tlt, hairdry, c/fan, heat, TV, t/c mkg, refrig, toaster], ldry, dryer-fee, lounge (TV), ✗, pool (salt water), bbq, rm serv, dinner to unit, c/park (undercover), non smoking rms. **BB** ♦ **$77,** ♦♦ **$99,** ♦♦♦ **$121.**

CHILLAGOE QLD 4871

Pop 220. (1926km NW Brisbane), See map on page 415, ref A3. Former mining township located in northern Queensland on the Burke Developmental Road. National Park - limestone caves complex Historical Museum. Bush Walking.

Hotels/Motels

★★ **Chillagoe Caves Lodge**, (M), 7 King St, ☎ 07 4094 7106, fax 07 4094 7178, 6 units [shwr, tlt, a/c-cool, c/fan, t/c mkg, refrig], ✉, pool, cook fac, bbq. **RO** ♦ **$45 - $50,** ♦♦ **$55 - $60,** ◊ **$8 - $10,** BC MC VI.

★ **(Budget Rooms Section)**, 5 apts acc up to 3, [a/c-cool, c/fan], shwr, tlt, ✗ (Mon-Sun). **RO** ♦ **$25 - $30,** ♦♦ **$30 - $35,** ◊ **$5 - $8.**

Self Catering Accommodation

Chillagoe Cabins, (Cotg), Lot 22 Queen St, 200km W of Mareeba, ☎ 07 4094 7206, fax 07 4094 7226, 3 cotgs [shwr, tlt, hairdry, a/c-cool, TV, clock radio, t/c mkg, refrig, cook fac, micro, toaster], iron (1), iron brd (1), pool-indoor (salt water), bbq (covered), secure park, cots (1), non smoking property. **RO** ♦ **$82.50,** ♦♦ **$93.50,** BC MC VI, (not yet classified).

CHINCHILLA QLD 4413

Pop 3,250. (294km W Brisbane), See map on page 414, ref E7. Located on the Warrego Highway between Dalby and Miles. Gem Fossicking.

Hotels/Motels

★★★★ **Central Motor Inn**, (M), 131 Heeney St, 50m N of PO. Hotel adjacent, ☎ 07 4669 1100, fax 07 4668 9155, 14 units (1 suite) [shwr, tlt, hairdry, a/c, tel, TV, movie, clock radio, t/c mkg, refrig, cook fac, toaster], dryer, iron, iron brd, conv fac, ✉ (Mon to Sat), bbq-fee, rm serv, dinner to unit (Mon to Sat), c/park (undercover), trailer park (& Truck Parking), cots. **RO** ♦ **$71,** ♦♦ **$82,** ◊ **$11,** AE BC DC EFT MC VI.

★★★★ **Chinchilla Great Western Motor Inn**, (M), Warrego Hwy, ☎ 07 4662 8288, fax 07 4668 9050, 26 units [shwr, bath (4), tlt, hairdry, a/c, tel, TV, movie, clock radio, t/c mkg, refrig, toaster], ldry-fee, conv fac, ✉ (Mon to Sat), pool (salt water), bbq, rm serv, dinner to unit, cots-fee. **RO** ♦ **$70,** ♦♦ **$80 - $90,** ◊ **$20,** ch con, AE BC DC EFT MC VI, ♿.

★★★ **Barakula Motel Chinchilla**, (M), Warrego Hwy/West, 2km W of Town Centre, ☎ 07 4662 7323, fax 07 4668 9629, 10 units [shwr, tlt, hairdry, a/c, elec blkts, tel, TV, movie, radio, t/c mkg, refrig], dinner to unit, c/park (undercover), cots. **RO** ♦ **$48,** ♦♦ **$55 - $57,** ◊ **$12,** AE BC DC MC VI.

★★ **Commercial**, (LMH), Chinchilla St, ☎ 07 4662 7524, fax 07 4662 7755, 12 units [shwr, tlt, a/c, tel, TV, clock radio, t/c mkg, refrig], ✉, c/park (undercover), cots, AE BC MC VI.

★☆ **(Hotel Section)**, (2 stry), 11 units [basin], ✉, cots.

★★ **Vineyard**, (M), 96 Glasson St, 100m from Warrego Hwy, ☎ 07 4662 7379, fax 07 4662 7074, 13 units [shwr, tlt, a/c-cool, heat, TV, radio, t/c mkg, refrig, toaster], pool, bbq, c/park (undercover), ✆, plygr, cots-fee. **RO** ♦ **$42,** ♦♦ **$50,** ◊ **$15,** BC MC VI.

Chinchilla Mobile Park, (M), Wondai Rd, 400m off Warrego Hwy, ☎ 07 4662 7314, fax 07 4662 7248, 7 units [shwr, tlt, a/c, elec blkts, t/c mkg, refrig], c/park (undercover). **RO** ♦ **$45,** ♦♦ **$50,** BC MC VI, (not yet classified).

Self Catering Accommodation

★★★★ **Little Hollow**, (Cotg), Hereford cattle property. 'Bimbimbi' Greenswamp Rd, 20km from Chinchilla, ☎ 07 4665 8289, 1 cotg acc up to 10, [shwr, tlt, fan, heat, elec blkts, TV, t/c mkg, refrig, cook fac, linen]. **D** ♦♦♦♦ **$85,** ◊ **$10.**

CLERMONT QLD 4721

Pop 2,400. (1010km NW Brisbane), See map on page 414, ref D6. Situated amid beautiful pasture and agricultural land. It is an historical part of Central Queensland Highlands. Blair Athol Mine Tours. Bowls, Golf, Horse Racing, Shooting, Swimming.

Hotels/Motels

★★★★ **Peppercorn**, (M), 51 Capricorn St, ☎ 07 4983 1033, fax 07 4983 1679, 16 units [shwr, tlt, hairdry, a/c, heat, tel, TV, video-fee, clock radio, t/c mkg, refrig, mini bar], iron, iron brd, ✉ (Mon to Sat), pool, rm serv, dinner to unit, cots, non smoking rms (8). **RO** ♦ **$75 - $83,** ♦♦ **$83 - $89,** ◊ **$10,** ch con, Some units of a lower star rating. AE BC DC EFT MC VI.

★★★ **Clermont Motor Inn**, (M), Cnr Box & Capella Sts, 180m N of PO, ☎ 07 4983 3133, fax 07 4983 2699, 25 units [shwr, tlt, a/c, tel, TV, clock radio, t/c mkg, refrig], ✉ (Mon - Fri), pool, rm serv, dinner to unit, c/park (undercover), cots. **RO** ♦ **$60.50,** ♦♦ **$65,** ◊ **$5.50,** ch con, AE BC DC MC VI.

★★☆ **Grand**, (LMH), Capella St, ☎ 07 4983 1188, fax 07 4983 3105, (2 stry gr fl), 13 units [shwr, tlt, a/c, tel, cable tv, clock radio, t/c mkg, refrig], ldry, conv fac, ✉, cots. **RO** ♦ **$50,** ♦♦ **$60,** ◊ **$5,** ch con, AE BC DC EFT MC VI.

★ **Leo**, (LMH), Cnr Capella & Douglas Sts, ☎ 07 4983 1566, fax 07 4983 2663, 13 units [shwr, tlt, a/c-cool, heat, tel, TV, t/c mkg, refrig], ldry, ✉, dinner to unit, ✆. **RO** ♦ **$38,** ♦♦ **$45,** ◊ **$10,** ch con, AE BC DC EFT MC VI.

B&B's/Guest Houses

Wentworth Station Homestead, (GH), (Farm), Wuthung Rd, 45km W of Moranbah, ☎ 07 4983 5202, fax 07 4983 5358, 1 rm [shwr, bath (1), tlt, hairdry, a/c-cool, c/fan, heat, elec blkts, TV, video], ldry, iron, iron brd, rec rm, pool, bbq, plygr, cots. **D all meals** ♦ **$110,** ch con, (not yet classified).

CLIFTON BEACH QLD 4879

Pop 2,086. (1739km N Brisbane), See map on page 415, ref C3. A coastal resort located in Cairns. Paradise Palms International Golf Course located on Cook Hwy 2km S of Post Office.

Self Catering Accommodation

★★★★☆ **Argosy**, (HU), 119 Arlington Esp, ☎ 07 4055 3333, fax 07 4059 1279, (Multi-stry gr fl), 16 units acc up to 5, (2 bedrm), [shwr, bath, tlt, a/c-cool, fan, tel, TV, clock radio, refrig, cook fac, micro, d/wash, ldry (in unit), blkts, linen, pillows], lift, pool (salt water), sauna, spa, bbq, c/park (undercover), **D $85 - $150,** Min book applies, AE BC MC VI.

★★★★ **Agincourt Beachfront Apartments**, (HU), 69 Arlington Esp, 500metres from golf course, ☎ 07 4055 3500, fax 07 4055 3628, (Multi-stry gr fl), 45 units acc up to 3, (1 bedrm), [shwr, tlt, a/c-cool, fan, tel, TV, clock radio, refrig, cook fac, ldry (in unit), blkts, linen, pillows], lift, dryer, pool, bbq, c/park (undercover), courtesy transfer. **D $125 - $155,** Min book applies, AE BC DC JCB MC VI.

★★★☆ **Clifton Palms**, (HU), 35 Upolu Esp, ☎ 07 4055 3839, fax 07 4055 3888, (2 stry gr fl), 13 units acc up to 6, (1 & 2 bedrm), [shwr, tlt, a/c-cool, fan, TV, clock radio, refrig, cook fac, micro, blkts, linen, pillows], ldry, dryer, pool (salt water), bbq, c/park (undercover), ✆, cots. **RO** $49 - $130, AE BC MC VI.

★★★ **Clifton Sands**, (HU), Cnr Guide St & Clifton Rd, ☎ 07 4055 3355, fax 07 4059 1413, (Multi-stry gr fl), 18 units acc up to 4, [shwr, tlt, a/c-cool, fan, TV, refrig, cook fac, ldry (in unit), blkts, linen, pillows], pool (saltwater), bbq, c/park (undercover), ✆, cots. **D** ♦♦ $65 - $85, **W** ♦♦ $455, Min book applies, BC MC VI.

B&B's/Guest Houses

★★★★ **Kaikea**, (B&B), 16 Eddy St, 22km N of Cairns, ☎ 07 4059 0010, fax 07 4059 0975, 1 rm [shwr, bath, tlt, hairdry, a/c-cool, c/fan, TV, video, clock radio, CD, t/c mkg, refrig], ldry, lounge (tv), pool, spa, bbq, non smoking rms. **RO** ♦ $50, ♦♦ $75 - $85, ch con, BC MC VI.

CLONCURRY QLD 4824

Pop 2,500. (1776km NW Brisbane), See map on page 414, ref A5. Situated on the banks of the Cloncurry River. Bowls, Fishing, Swimming.

Hotels/Motels

★★★★ **Gidgee Inn**, (M), Matilda Highway, East of PO, ☎ 07 4742 1599, fax 07 4742 2431, 40 units [shwr, tlt, a/c-cool, c/fan, tel, TV, video, clock radio, t/c mkg, refrig, mini bar], ldry-fee, dryer-fee, iron, iron brd, conv fac, ✉ (Mon - Sat), rm serv, c/park (undercover), cots, non smoking units (36). **RO** ♦ $114 - $125, ♦♦ $114 - $125, ♦ $29, AE BC DC EFT JCB MC VI.

★★ **Oasis**, (LMH), Ramsay St, ☎ 07 4742 1366, fax 07 4742 1802, 12 units [shwr, tlt, a/c, tel, TV, video, movie, clock radio, t/c mkg, refrig], ✉, c/park (undercover), cots-fee. **RO** ♦ $50, ♦♦ $60, ♦ $10, ch con, BC EFT MC VI.

★★ **Wagon Wheel Motel**, (M), 54 Ramsay St, ☎ 07 4742 1866, fax 07 4742 1819, 27 units [ensuite, shwr, tlt, a/c-cool, c/fan, tel, TV, clock radio, t/c mkg, refrig], ldry-fee, ✉, pool, dinner to unit, ✆, cots. **RO** ♦ $43 - $69, ♦♦ $65 - $80, ♦ $11, ch con, Deluxe units 15 to 24 ★★★. AE BC DC EFT MC VI.

CONDAMINE QLD 4416

Pop Nominal, (334km W Brisbane), See map on page 414, ref D7. A large replica of the Condamine 'Bullfrog' bell in Condamine Park Condamine was known as Bonner Knob when established in 1856.

★★★☆ **Nelgai**, (GH), (Farm), A working cattle property. Redmarley Rd, 16km W Condamine, ☎ 07 4627 7124, fax 07 4622 7200, 2 rms [ensuite (1), shwr (1), bath (1), tlt (1), a/c-cool, heat, elec blkts], ldry, dryer, lounge (TV), bbq, cots. **DBB** ♦ $90, ♦ $180, ch con, DC.

COOCHIEMUDLO ISLAND QLD 4184

Pop Nominal, (31km SE Brisbane), See map on page 417, ref E7. A beautiful sub-tropical island boasting golden beaches, calm waters and a laidback atmosphere, within easy reach of Brisbane. Boating, Bush Walking, Fishing, Golf, Sailing, Swimming, Tennis.

Self Catering Accommodation

★★★☆ **Coochie Island Resort**, (HU), Dawn St, 100m fr beach, ☎ 07 3207 7521, fax 07 3207 0380, 11 units acc up to 6, (1 & 2 bedrm), [shwr, tlt, c/fan, TV, refrig, cook fac, micro (3), elec frypan, linen reqd-fee], ldry, ✉ (Wed to Sun), pool, bbq, c/park (undercover), courtesy transfer, cots, BC EFT MC VI.

Coochie Katandra Holiday Cabins, 76 Victoria Pde, ☎ 07 3207 7377, 4 cabins acc up to 5, [shwr, tlt, c/fan, TV, t/c mkg, refrig, cook fac, micro, toaster, ldry, blkts, linen reqd, pillows], bbq, c/park. **D** ♦ $40 - $50, ♦♦ $40 - $50, **W** ♦ $195 - $275, ♦♦ $195 - $275, (not yet classified).

COOKTOWN QLD 4871

Pop 1,400. (2051km N Brisbane), See map on page 414, ref C3. Situated on the Cape Yorke Peninsula on the banks of Endeavour River. It was the port for the Palmer River goldfields. Fishing, Swimming.

Hotels/Motels

★★★★ **The Sovereign Resort**, (LH), Cnr Charlotte & Green Sts, ☎ 07 4069 5400, fax 07 4069 5582, (2 stry gr fl), 29 rms (3 suites) [shwr, tlt, a/c-cool, fan, tel, cable tv, t/c mkg, refrig], ldry, dryer, ✉, pool, bbq, cots. **RO** ♦♦ $110 - $130, **Suite D** ♦♦ $130 - $165, AE BC DC EFT MC VI, ⚹⚹.

★★★ **Cooktowns River of Gold**, (M), Cnr Hope & Walker Sts, ☎ 07 4069 5222, fax 07 4069 5615, (2 stry gr fl), 23 units [shwr, tlt, a/c-cool, fan, tel, TV, video (in house), t/c mkg, refrig, cook fac (4)], ldry, ✉, pool, rm serv, dinner to unit, cots-fee. **RO** ♦♦ $84 - $102, ♦ $12, ch con, AE BC DC MC VI, ⚹⚹.

★★★ **Sea View**, (M), Webber Esp, ☎ 07 4069 5377, fax 07 4069 5807, 30 units [shwr, tlt, a/c-cool, tel, TV, movie, t/c mkg, refrig, toaster], ldry, w/mach, dryer, iron, pool, bbq, cots-fee. **RO** ♦ $45 - $87, ♦♦ $72 - $87, ♦ $11, ch con, 3 S/C Units ★★★★. BC EFT MC VI.

★★★★ **(Holiday Unit Section)**, 3 units acc up to 5, (2 bedrm), [shwr, bath, tlt, a/c-cool, c/fan, tel, TV, movie, clock radio, t/c mkg, refrig, cook fac, toaster, blkts, linen, pillows], iron, iron brd, bbq (covered), c/park (undercover). **D** $155 - $170, ch con.

★★☆ **Seagrens Inn**, (M), Heritage, 24 Charlotte St, ☎ 07 4069 5357, fax 07 4069 5085, (2 stry gr fl), 7 units [shwr, tlt, a/c-cool (4), fan, TV (6), t/c mkg, refrig, cook fac (1), micro (1)], ✉ (Wed-Mon), bar, pool, bbq, cots-fee. **RO** ♦♦ $45 - $65.

Self Catering Accommodation

★★★★ **Milkwood Lodge Rainforest Cabins**, Annan Rd, ☎ 07 4069 5007, fax 07 4069 5834, 6 cabins acc up to 4, (1 bedrm), [shwr, tlt, c/fan, clock radio, t/c mkg, refrig, cook fac, toaster, blkts, linen, pillows], iron, iron brd, bbq. **D** ♦♦ $99, ♦ $10, **W** ♦♦ $480, ♦ $60, BC MC VI.

★★★ **Cooktown Alamanda Inn**, (HU), Cnr Hope & Howard St, 1km S of PO, ☎ 07 4069 5203, fax 07 4069 5203, 5 units acc up to 5, [tlt, a/c-cool, c/fan, TV, clock radio, t/c mkg, refrig, cook fac ltd, micro, elec frypan, toaster, blkts, linen, pillows], ldry, w/mach-fee, dryer-fee, iron, ✗ (Fri-Sun B/fast only), pool, bbq, plygr. **D** ♦ $55, ♦♦ $75, ch con, BC MC VI.

(Lodge Section), 15 rms acc up to 5, [shwr (10), a/c-cool, c/fan, TV, t/c mkg, refrig, ldry], bathrm, ✗, pool, cook fac (5), bbq, boat park, plygr, cots. **RO** ♦ $28 - $40, ♦♦ $40 - $50, ch con.

B&B's/Guest Houses

★★★ **Hillcrest Bed & Breakfast**, (GH), Hope St, 600m N PO, ☎ 07 4069 5305, fax 07 4069 5893, 12 rms [c/fan], shwr, tlt, ldry, lounge (TV), ✗, pool, t/c mkg shared, bbq, cots, non smoking rms. **BLB** ♦ $40, ♦♦ $63, ♦ $10, ch con, AE BC MC VI.

★★☆ **(Motel Section)**, 6 units [shwr, tlt, a/c-cool, c/fan, TV, clock radio, t/c mkg, refrig, toaster], ldry, ✗, pool, bbq, rm serv, ✆, cots, non smoking units. **RO** ♦ $67, ♦♦ $85, ♦ $10, ch con.

Other Accommodation

Home Rule Rainforest, (Lodge), Rossville via Cooktown, 45km S of Cooktown Home Rule Falls nearby, ☎ 07 4060 3925, 10 rms acc up to 8, [fan, blkts, linen, pillows], shwr, tlt, ldry, ✉, cook fac, sink, refrig, bbq, shop, bush walking, cots. **D** ♦ $16.50, ♦ $16.50, ch con, Camping sites available, BC MC VI.

COOLANGATTA QLD

See Gold Coast Region.

COOLUM BEACH QLD

See Sunshine Coast Region.

COOMERA QLD

See Gold Coast Region.

COOROY QLD 4563

Pop 1,950. (131km N Brisbane), See map on page 417, ref D4. Small town in heart of Sunshine Coast Hinterland. Rail centre of Noosa Shire. Centre of fresh water fishing, sailing & canoes - Lake MacDonald and Lake Borumba Dams. Old Butter Factory - Arts & Crafts, Noosa Botanical Gardens. Bowls, Fishing, Golf, Squash.

Hotels/Motels
★★★ **Cooroy**, (M), 30 Elm St, opposite railway, ☎ 07 5442 6819, fax 07 5442 6821, 6 units [shwr, tlt, a/c, tel, TV, clock radio, t/c mkg, refrig], ldry, iron, bbq, c/park (undercover), cots, **RO** ♦♦ **$55 - $85**, BC MC VI.

Self Catering Accommodation
★★★★ **Cooroy Country Cottages**, (Cotg), 532 Black Mountain Rd, 9km W of PO, ☎ 07 5442 6819, fax 07 5442 6821, 2 cotgs acc up to 6, (2 & 3 bedrm), [shwr, tlt, a/c, c/fan, tel, TV, video, clock radio, t/c mkg, refrig, cook fac, micro, toaster, blkts, doonas, linen, pillows], ldry, w/mach, dryer, bbq, c/park (undercover), non smoking property. **D** ♦♦ **$110**, ♦ **$11**, **W** ♦♦ **$660**, ♦ **$66**, ch con, AE BC MC VI.

B&B's/Guest Houses
★★★★ **Boroloola**, (B&B), No children's facilities, 29 Pine Tree Dr, ☎ 07 5447 6608, fax 07 5447 6607, 2 rms [ensuite (2), shwr (2), tlt (2), a/c, c/fan, heat, elec blkts, TV, t/c mkg, doonas], ldry, lounge firepl, ✕, pool. **BB** ♦ **$100**, ♦♦ **$132**, AE BC MC VI.

★★★☆ **Cudgerie Homestead**, (GH), 42 Cudgerie Drive, Noosa Hinterland, ☎ 07 5442 6681, 4 rms [ensuite, shwr (3), tlt (4), c/fan, t/c mkg], ldry, lounge, ✕. **BB** ♦♦ **$100 - $130**.

COW BAY QLD 4873

Pop Nominal, (1832km N Brisbane), See map on page 415, ref B2. Tropical rainforest area.

Hotels/Motels
★★★ **Cow Bay Hotel**, (LMH), Cape Tribulation Rd, 11km N of Daintree River Ferry, ☎ 07 4098 9011, fax 07 4098 9022, 6 units [shwr, tlt, a/c-cool, c/fan, TV, t/c mkg, refrig], ldry, ✕, ✆, cots. **BLB** ♦ **$77**, ♦♦ **$77**, ♦ **$5**, ch con, Generated power, BC EFT MC VI.

★★☆ **The Rainforest Retreat**, (M), Cape Tribulation Rd, 10km N of Daintree Ferry, ☎ 07 4098 9101, fax 07 4098 9120, 10 units (1 bedrm), [shwr, tlt, a/c-cool-fee, c/fan, TV (4), t/c mkg, refrig, cook fac (8)], ldry, pool, bbq (covered), c/park (undercover), cots. **RO** ♦ **$15 - $50**, ♦♦ **$50 - $75**, ♦ **$10**, ch con, BC MC VI.

★☆ **(Bunkhouse Section)**, 1 bunkhouse acc up to 15, [blkts reqd, linen reqd, pillows reqd], shwr, tlt, ldry, pool, cook fac, t/c mkg shared, refrig, bbq (covered). **D** ♦ **$15**, ♦♦ **$30**.

B&B's/Guest Houses
Wait a While Bed & Breakfast, (B&B), 174 Buchanan Rd, 5km E of Cow Bay Turnoff, ☎ 07 4098 9195, fax 07 4098 9195, 2 rms [c/fan], lounge (TV), pool (salt water), bbq. **BB** ♦ **$60**, ♦♦ **$80**, (not yet classified).

Other Accommodation
Crocodylus Village Youth Hostel, (Lodge), Buchanan Creek Rd, 12km N of Daintree Ferry Rainforest Setting, ☎ 07 4098 9166, fax 07 4098 9131, 5 rms acc up to 8, [shwr, tlt, fan, c/fan], ldry, w/mach-fee, dryer-fee, ✕, pool, cook fac, t/c mkg shared, refrig, bbq (covered), ✆, bush walking, bicycle, cots. **D** ♦♦ **$65**, ♦ **$10**, ch con, BC EFT MC VI.

(Bunkhouse Section), 5 bunkhouses acc up to 18, [refrig (communal), blkts, linen], shwr, tlt, cook fac, t/c mkg shared. **D** ♦ **$20**.

Sharing the roads - Trucks and cars

Trucks are different from cars. They take up more road space than cars, especially when turning, and are slower to accelerate, turn and reverse. Here are some hints in sharing our roads safely with trucks:

- Don't cut in on trucks. Because trucks need a greater braking distance than cars, truck drivers leave more space in front of them when approaching a red light or stop sign than a car.
- Allow extra time and space to overtake trucks. You will need about 1.5 kilometres of clear road space to pass a truck.
- Don't pass a left-turning truck on the inside. Trucks sometimes need more than one lane to turn tight corners, so watch for a truck swinging out near intersections.
- Be patient - follow at a safe distance. Truck drivers may not see you because of blind spots, particularly if you travel right behind them.

CROWS NEST QLD 4355

Pop 1,200. (170km W Brisbane), See map on page 417, ref B6. Located 545m above sea level in grazing country. Scenic Drives.
★★★★ **Crows Nest**, (M), New England Hwy, 1km S of PO, ☎ 07 4698 1399, fax 07 4698 1959, 12 units [shwr, spa bath (1), tlt, a/c, elec blkts, tel, TV, clock radio, t/c mkg, refrig, cook fac (2), toaster (2)], ldry, dryer, bbq, dinner to unit, cots, Pets allowed. **RO** ♦ **$58**, ♦♦ **$70 - $76**, ♦ **$12**, AE BC DC EFT MC VI.

CROYDON QLD 4871

Pop 200. (2026km NW Brisbane), See map on page 414, ref B4. Former goldmining town in far north Queensland.
★★ **Croydon Club**, (LH), Cnr Brown & Sircom Sts, ☎ 07 4745 6184, fax 07 4745 6143, 16 rms [a/c, cable tv, t/c mkg, refrig], shwr, tlt, ldry, ✕, bbq, ✆. **RO** ♦ **$40**, ♦♦ **$55**, ch con, BC EFT MC VI.

★ **(Hotel Rooms Section)**, 10 apts [a/c-cool (6)], shwr, tlt, bar (cable-TV). **RO** ♦ **$35**, ♦♦ **$45**, ♦ **$12**, ch con.

CUNNAMULLA QLD 4490

Pop 1,450. (794km W Brisbane), See map on page 414, ref C8. Situated on the banks of the Warrego River.

Hotels/Motels
★★★☆ **Country Way Motor Inn**, (M), 17 Emma St, 5km E of P.O, ☎ 07 4655 0555, fax 07 4655 0455, 10 units [shwr, tlt, a/c-cool, c/fan, tel, TV, clock radio, t/c mkg, refrig], ldry-fee, iron, cots-fee. **RO** ♦ **$59**, ♦♦ **$69**, ♦ **$11**, AE BC MC VI.

★★ **Billabong Hotel Motel**, (LH), 5 Murray St, ☎ 07 4655 1225, fax 07 4655 1899, 12 rms [shwr, tlt, a/c-cool, heat, tel, TV, t/c mkg, refrig, ldry-fee], dryer-fee, iron, iron brd, conv fac, ✕, ✆, cots. **RO** ♦ **$50**, ♦♦ **$65**, ♦ **$11**, AE BC EFT MC VI.

★★ **Oxford Hotel Motel**, (LH), Railway St, ☎ 07 4655 1126, fax 07 4655 2166, 10 rms [basin, shwr, tlt, a/c-cool, heat, elec blkts, TV, t/c mkg, refrig], ✕, dinner to unit, ✆. **RO** ♦ **$33**, ♦♦ **$44**, ♦ **$11**, ch con, AE BC EFT MC VI.

★★ **Warrego**, (LMH), 9 Louise St, ☎ 07 4655 1737, fax 07 4655 2015, 10 units [shwr, tlt, a/c-cool (10), a/c (4), heat (6), tel, TV, clock radio, t/c mkg, refrig], ldry, conv fac, ✕, bbq, dinner to unit, ✆. **D** ♦ **$55 - $65**, ♦♦ **$65 - $70**, ♦ **$10**, Units 1 to 4 two star plus rating. BC MC VI.

★☆ **(Hotel Section)**, 11 apts [basin, shwr (1), tlt (1), a/c-cool, tel (2), TV (10), t/c mkg, refrig], lounge. **RO** ♦ **$28**, ♦♦ **$38**.

B&B's/Guest Houses
★★★☆ **Aldville Station**, (GH), Outback sheep & cattle property. M/S, Wyandra 4489, 120km NW of Cunnamulla PO, ☎ 07 4655 4814, fax 07 4655 4705, 4 rms [elec blkts], shwr, tlt, ldry, lounge (TV, video & radio), t/c mkg shared, refrig, bbq, petrol, bush walking, tennis. **D all meals** ♦ **$125**, ♦♦ **$205**, ch con, Tariffs include farm activities. BC MC VI.

CURRUMBIN QLD

See Gold Coast Region.

D'AGUILAR QLD 4514

Pop Nominal. (72km N Brisbane), See map on page 417, ref D5. Home of the Woodford Folk Festival, located in the D'Aguilar Range.
★★★ **D'Aguilar Motel**, (M), 2036 D'Aguilar Hwy, ☎ 07 5496 4060, fax 07 5496 4080, 8 units [shwr, tlt, hairdry, a/c, tel (ISD), TV, movie, clock radio, t/c mkg, refrig, ldry-fee], dryer-fee, iron, iron brd, conv fac, ✕, rm serv, dinner to unit, meals to unit, c/park (undercover), ✆, plygr, cots. **RO** ♦ **$55**, ♦♦ **$66**, ♦ **$11**, ch con, AE BC DC EFT MC VI, ♿.

DAINTREE QLD 4873

Pop Nominal, (1828km N Brisbane), See map on page 415, ref B2. Situated on the banks of the Daintree River. River cruises. Boating, Fishing.

Hotels/Motels
★★★★☆ Daintree Eco Lodge & Spa, (M), Daintree Rd, rainforest setting, ☎ 07 4098 6100, fax 07 4098 6200, 15 units [shwr, tlt, hairdry, a/c, c/fan, tel, TV, movie, clock radio, t/c mkg, mini bar], ⊠, pool-heated (solar), spa. **BB ♦ $412.50, ♦♦ $434.50, ◊ $66,** AE BC EFT MC VI, ⚹&.

Self Catering Accommodation
Daintree Valley Haven, (Cotg), No children's facilities, Stewart Creek Rd, 8km S of PO, ☎ 07 4098 6206, fax 07 4098 6106, 3 cotgs acc up to 3, (1 bedrm), [shwr, tlt, a/c-cool, c/fan, t/c mkg, refrig, cook fac ltd, micro, toaster, blkts, linen, pillows], bbq, breakfast ingredients, non smoking units. **D ♦ $110, ♦♦ $110, ◊ $33, W ♦ $660, ♦♦ $660, ◊ $198,** BC MC VI, (not yet classified).

Riverhome Cottages, (Cotg), Riverhome, 120km N of Cairns, ☎ 07 4098 6225, fax 07 4098 6225, 3 cotgs [shwr, bath, tlt, hairdry, a/c-cool, c/fan, clock radio, t/c mkg, refrig, cook fac ltd, toaster, ldry], dryer, bbq, c/park (undercover), non smoking property, Pets on application. **BB ♦♦ $120, ◊ $20,** ch con, BC MC VI, (not yet classified).

B&B's/Guest Houses
★★★★ Daintree Manor, (B&B), 27 Forest Creek Rd, North Daintree, ☎ 07 4090 7041, fax 07 4090 7041, (2 stry), 3 rms [shwr, tlt, c/fan], ldry, lounge (TV), t/c mkg shared, bbq, dinner to unit, c/park. **BB ♦ $85, ♦♦ $99,** ch con, MC VI.

★★★★ Kenadon Homestead Cabins, (GH), (Farm), Kenadon, via Daintree, ☎ 07 4098 6142, 7 rms [shwr, tlt, a/c-cool, c/fan, TV, t/c mkg, refrig, cook fac ltd, toaster, pillows], pool (salt water), bbq, cots. **BB ♦ $55, ♦♦ $80, ◊ $10,** BC MC VI.

★★★☆ Red Mill House, (B&B), No children's facilities, Stewart St, ☎ 07 4098 6233, fax 07 4098 6233, (2 stry gr fl), 7 rms [ensuite (4), bath (4), a/c-cool (4), c/fan], shwr, tlt, lounge (video), pool (salt water), t/c mkg shared. **BB ♦ $40, ♦♦ $66 - $88, ◊ $15,** BC MC VI.

Daintree Cloud 9, (B&B), Daintree Rd, 2km S of Daintree Village, ☎ 07 4098 6177, fax 07 4098 6177, 2 rms ldry, lounge (TV), ✕, spa, t/c mkg shared, bbq, c/park (undercover) (1), courtesy transfer, tennis (half court), non smoking property. **BB ♦♦ $250, ♦♦♦♦ $275,** Tariff includes massage, Min book applies, BC MC VI, (not yet classified).

Vistas Of The Daintree, (B&B), Previously Views Of The Daintree. 2 Stewart Creek Rd, 39km N of Mossman PO, ☎ 07 4098 6118, fax 07 4098 6118, 2 rms [ensuite, bath (1), a/c-cool, c/fan, fire pl, tel, cable tv, video, clock radio, t/c mkg, doonas], ldry, lounge (TV), ✕, spa, refrig, bbq, cots, non smoking property. **BB ♦ $90 - $100, ♦♦ $100 - $120, ◊ $15,** Min book applies, (not yet classified).

DAINTREE NATIONAL PARK

Pop Nominal, (1831km N Brisbane), See map on page 415, ref B1. Bush Walking.

Self Catering Accommodation
★★★☆ Bloomfield Wilderness Lodge, (SA), Resort, No facilities for children under 12, Weary Bay, Weary Bay 4871, 172km N of Cairns, ☎ 07 4035 9166, fax 07 4035 9180, 17 serv apts acc up to 3, (1 bedrm), [shwr, tlt, hairdry, c/fan, tel, t/c mkg, mini bar, ldry, linen, pillows], rec rm, lounge (TV), conv fac, ⊠, pool, bbq, courtesy transfer. **D all meals ♦ $209 - $365, ◊ $209 - $365,** Units 17 to 21 of a four star rating. Min book applies, BC DC MC VI.

DALBY QLD 4405

Pop 9,500. (211km W Brisbane), See map on page 414, ref E8. Centre of rich wheat growing district on the Warrego Hwy, featuring picturesque Thomas Jack Park, Pioneer Park Museum and nearby Jimbour House. Bowls, Golf, Horse Racing, Swimming.

Hotels/Motels

★★★★☆ Dalby Homestead, (M), 27 Drayton St, 20m N of Thomas Jack Park, ☎ 07 4662 5722, fax 07 4662 2988, 20 units (1 suite) [shwr, spa bath (1), tlt, hairdry, a/c, c/fan, elec blkts, tel, TV, video (1), clock radio, CD (1), t/c mkg, refrig, mini bar, cook fac (1), micro (1)], ldry, dryer, iron, iron brd, meeting rm, ✕, pool (salt water), bbq, c/park (undercover), non smoking units (8). **D ♦ $80, ♦♦ $91, ♦♦♦ $106,** ch con, AE BC DC EFT MC MP VI, ⚹&.

★★★☆ Country Pathfinder Motel, (M), Previously Pathfinder Motor Inn, 62 Condamine St, 100m W of PO, ☎ 07 4662 4433, fax 07 4662 5303, 16 units [shwr, tlt, hairdry, a/c, elec blkts, tel, TV, movie, clock radio, t/c mkg, refrig], ldry, iron, iron brd, dinner to unit, c/park (undercover), cots, non smoking units (8). **RO ♦ $69, ♦♦ $79, ◊ $13,** pen con, AE BC DC EFT JCB MC MP VI, ⚹&.

★★★☆ Dalby Manor Motor Inn, (M), Cnr Drayton & Pratten Sts, ☎ 07 4662 1011, fax 07 4662 1906, (2 stry) 28 units [shwr, tlt, hairdry, a/c, c/fan, elec blkts, tel, cable tv, clock radio, t/c mkg, refrig, mini bar, cook fac (2)], ldry, ⊠ (Mon to Sat), pool, spa, rm serv, dinner to unit, cots-fee. **RO ♦ $77, ♦♦ $88, ♦♦♦ $99, ♦♦♦♦ $110,** AE BC DC EFT MC MP VI, ⚹&.

★★★ Dalby Parkview Motel, (M), 31 Drayton St, ☎ 07 4662 3222, fax 07 4662 4997, 41 units [shwr, tlt, a/c, c/fan, elec blkts, tel, cable tv, clock radio, t/c mkg, refrig, toaster], ldry, pool, bbq, c/park (undercover), cots-fee. **RO ♦ $58, ♦♦ $66, ◊ $11,** ch con, AE BC DC EFT MC VI, ⚹&.

★★★ Myall, (M), Cnr Drayton & Myall Sts, ☎ 07 4662 3399, fax 07 4662 4004, 20 units [shwr, tlt, a/c, elec blkts, tel, TV, movie, clock radio, t/c mkg, refrig], spa, bbq, dinner to unit, c/park (undercover), courtesy transfer (Car), cots. **BLB ♦ $60, ♦♦ $66,** ch con, AE BC DC MC MCH VI.

DAYDREAM ISLAND QLD

See Whitsundays Region.

DIRRANBANDI QLD 4486

Pop 400. Nominal, (641km SW Brisbane), See map on page 414, ref D8. A wealthy cattle, sheep and cotton region beside the Balonne River.

Hotels/Motels
★★★ Dirranbandi, (M), Cnr Moore & Richardson Sts, ☎ 07 4625 8299, fax 07 4625 8299, 16 units [shwr, tlt, a/c, tel, TV, clock radio, t/c mkg, refrig], ⊠ (Mon to Sat), pool, rm serv, dinner to unit. **RO ♦ $60.50, ♦♦ $77 - $82.50, ◊ $13.50,** ch con, AE BC MC VI.

★☆ Dirran Pub, (LH), Railway St, 115km N/NE Lightning Ridge, ☎ 07 4625 8322, fax 07 4625 8270, (2 stry), 17 rms [a/c-cool, heat, ldry-fee], shwr, tlt, lounge (TV), ⊠, t/c mkg shared, bbq, ✆. **RO ♦ $28 - $60, ♦♦ $35 - $80, ◊ $10 - $15,** AE BC MC VI.

★★★ (Motel Section), 8 units **RO ♦ $60, ♦♦ $100, ◊ $17.**

DUNK ISLAND QLD 4810

Pop Nominal, (1602km N Brisbane), See map on page 415, ref C5. A popular Great Barrier Reef island with extensive walking tracks through 730ha of partly hilly National Park rainforest.

Hotels/Motels

★★★★ Dunk Island Resort, (M), Resort, Dunk Island, ☎ 07 4068 8199, fax 07 4068 8528, 24 units [shwr, bath, tlt, hairdry, a/c, c/fan, tel, TV, clock radio, t/c mkg, refrig, ldry, pillows], dryer, iron, iron brd, conv fac, ⊠, cafe, pool, spa, bush walking, golf (6 hole), squash, tennis (day/night) (4). **BB ♦ $295, ♦♦ $443,** ch con, AE BC DC MC VI.

★★★☆ (Banfields Units), 38 units [shwr, tlt, a/c, c/fan, tel, TV, clock radio, t/c mkg, refrig], ldry, dryer, iron, iron brd. **BB ♦ $220, ♦♦ $310, ◊ $130.**

★★★☆ (Beachfront Units), 50 units [shwr, bath, tlt, a/c, c/fan, tel, TV, clock radio, t/c mkg, refrig], ldry, dryer, iron, iron brd. **BB ♦ $300, ♦♦ $390.**

★★★☆ (Garden Cabanas), 36 units [shwr, tlt, a/c, c/fan, tel, TV, clock radio, t/c mkg, refrig], ldry, dryer, iron, iron brd. **BB ♦ $260, ♦♦ $350.**

DYSART QLD 4745

Pop 3,450. (973km N Brisbane), See map on page 414, ref D6. Service town for local mining area. Bowls, Golf, Horse Riding, Squash, Swimming, Tennis.

Hotels/Motels
★★★ Jolly Collier, (LMH), Queen Elizabeth Dve, ☎ 07 4958 1155, fax 07 4958 1001, 19 units (2 suites) [shwr, tlt, a/c, tel, TV, movie, radio, t/c mkg, refrig], ldry, conv fac, ⊠ (Mon to Sat), c/park (undercover), cots. **BB ♦ $85.50, ♦♦ $115.50, ♦♦♦♦ $150,** ch con, AE BC DC EFT MC VI.

EDMONTON QLD 4869

Pop 4,496. (1702km N Brisbane). See map on page 415, ref C3. Satellite town on Bruce Highway south of Cairns. Main industries are sugar growing and tourism. Speedway & BMX racing, Sugar World Tourist Attraction. Bowls, Fishing.

★★★ **Cairns Gateway Lodge**, (M), 35 Bruce Hwy, ☎ 07 4055 4394, (2 stry gr fl), 24 units [shwr, tlt, a/c-cool, tel, TV, movie, clock radio, t/c mkg, refrig, cook fac ltd, toaster], ldry, dryer, pool, bbq, c/park (undercover), ✆, cots. RO ⸋ $40, ⸋⸋ $45 - $50, ⸋ $7.50, ch con, AE BC DC MC VI.

EIDSVOLD QLD 4627

Pop 500. (437km NW Brisbane). See map on page 417, ref A1. Established as a gold mining town in 1888. Today, it produces top quality beef cattle. Historical Museum. Waruma Dam. Fishing, Golf, Scenic Drives, Swimming.

B&B's/Guest Houses

★★★☆ **Ormsary**, (GH), via Eidsvold, 8km W PO Eidsvold ☎ 07 4165 1127, fax 07 4165 1391, 3 rms [shwr, tlt, fan, heat], lounge (TV, video, stereo), pool, t/c mkg shared, bbq, bush walking, canoeing. BB ⸋ $45, DBB ⸋ $60, ch con, fam con.

Other Accommodation

Eidsvold Motel, (Lodge), Moreton St, ☎ 07 4165 1209, 6 rms acc up to 3, [fan, elec blkts, TV, video, radio, t/c mkg, refrig], shwr, tlt, ldry, lounge (TV), ✕, dinner to unit. RO ⸋ $22, ⸋⸋ $38.50, ⸋ $5.50, ch con, BC MC.

EL ARISH QLD 4855

Pop 300. (1594km N Brisbane). See map on page 415, ref C5. Located on the Bruce Hwy. Golf.

Hotels/Motels

★★☆ **Diggers Creek**, (M), Bruce Hwy, ☎ 07 4068 5281, fax 07 4068 5369, 6 units [shwr, tlt, a/c-cool, c/fan, tel, TV, clock radio, t/c mkg, refrig], ✕, pool, rm serv, dinner to unit, c/park (undercover), cots. RO ⸋ $35, ⸋⸋ $44, ⸋ $5.50, ch con, BC MC VI.

Self Catering Accommodation

Fish-O-Rama, 323 Cassowary Dr, 15km W of Mission Beach, ☎ 07 4068 5350, fax 07 4068 5021, 2 cabins acc up to 4, [shwr, tlt, a/c-cool, c/fan, TV, video, clock radio, t/c mkg, refrig, cook fac, toaster, blkts, linen, pillows], non smoking property. D ⸋ $50, ⸋⸋ $80, ⸋ $10, W ⸋⸋ $315, BC EFT MC VI, (not yet classified).

ELANORA QLD

See Gold Coast Region.

ELLIOTT HEADS QLD 4670

Pop 700. (389km N Brisbane). See map on page 416, ref E8. Popular with fisherman and surfers. Has the best of both worlds - river and open sea. Boating, Golf, Surfing, Swimming.

★☆ **Seaview**, (HF), 22 Lihs St, ☎ 07 4159 6388, (2 stry gr fl), 6 flats acc up to 4, (1 & 2 bedrm), [shwr, tlt, TV, refrig, cook fac, elec frypan, blkts reqd, linen reqd, pillows], ldry. D ⸋⸋ $40, W ⸋⸋ $140 - $220.

Safety first for younger cyclists

It's a sad fact of life that young cyclists are one of the high-risk groups on our roads, so it is vital that parents put safety first when their children start riding bicycles.

Only when parents are sure of a child's ability to handle traffic should they allow the child to take to the roads.

The best way to check that children are safe riding on the road is to go for a ride with them - a sort of road test, but without the child necessarily knowing it's a test.

If children are to ride to school, check out a safe route between home and school and familiarise the children with the route and any special problems. Helmets are now mandatory.

EMERALD QLD 4720

Pop 9,350. (918km NW Brisbane) (160km Alpha) (54km Capella). See map on page 414, ref D6. A fast growing town servicing the neigbouring properties, whose industry is predominantly cotton. Boating, Bowls, Gem Fossicking, Golf, Sailing, Shooting, Squash, Swimming, Water Skiing.

Hotels/Motels

★★★★ **Emerald Explorers Inn**, (M), Springsure Rd / Gregory Hwy, 2km N of Airport, ☎ 07 4982 2822, fax 07 4982 0389, 36 units [shwr, spa bath (1), tlt, hairdry, a/c, heat, tel, cable tv, movie, clock radio, t/c mkg, refrig, mini bar], ldry-fee, dryer-fee, iron, iron brd, conf fac, ⊠ (Mon - Sat), pool (salt water), bbq, rm serv, c/park (undercover), non smoking units. RO ⸋ $66 - $97, ⸋ $10, AE BC DC EFT JCB MC VI, ⓰⸋.

★★★★ **Emerald Maraboon Tavern & Motor Inn**, (LMH), Cnr Hospital & Esmond Sts, 2km NW of PO, ☎ 07 4982 0777, fax 07 4982 0700, (2 stry gr fl), 60 units [shwr, bath (4), tlt, a/c, tel, TV, movie, clock radio, t/c mkg, refrig, mini bar], ldry, dryer, conv fac, ⊠, pool (2), bbq, rm serv, dinner to unit, c/park (undercover) (7), ✆, cots-fee, non smoking units (17), ch con, AE BC DC EFT MC VI.

★★★☆ **Emerald Highlands**, (M), 5 Cypress Dve, opposite hospital and tavern, ☎ 07 4982 1922, fax 07 4982 0412, 12 units [shwr, tlt, a/c (12), c/fan (8), heat, tel, TV, video (3), movie, clock radio, t/c mkg, refrig, toaster (4)], ldry, dryer, dinner to unit (Mon to Fri), cots-fee. RO ⸋ $64 - $69, ⸋⸋ $72 - $76, ⸋ $8 - $12, ch con, AE BC DC EFT MC VI.

★★★☆ **The Emerald Meteor**, (M), Cnr Opal & Egerton Sts, ☎ 07 4982 1166, fax 07 4982 4422, (2 stry gr fl), 59 units (1 suite) [shwr, spa bath (1), tlt, a/c-cool, fan (10), heat, tel, TV, movie, clock radio, t/c mkg, refrig, mini bar], ldry, dryer, conv fac, ⊠ (2), pool, rm serv, ✆, cots-fee. RO ⸋ $90 - $99, ⸋⸋ $99 - $109, ⸋ $10, Suite D $115, AE BC DC MC VI.

★★★☆ **Western Gateway**, (M), Cnr Theresa St & Hospital Rd, ☎ 07 4982 3899, fax 07 4982 3107, (2 stry gr fl), 50 units (8 suites) [shwr, bath (4), tlt, a/c, tel, cable tv, clock radio, t/c mkg, refrig, mini bar], ldry, dryer, conv fac, ⊠ (2), coffee shop, bar (2), pool, bbq, rm serv, dinner to unit, cots-fee, non smoking units (26). RO ⸋ $103, ⸋⸋ $115, ⸋ $11.50, Suite D $140 - $158, Units 43 to 49 ★★★★. AE BC DC MC MP VI.

★★★ **A & A Lodge Motel Emerald**, (M), Clermont St, ☎ 07 4982 2355, fax 07 4982 3037, (2 stry gr fl), 14 units [shwr, tlt, a/c, tel, TV, movie, clock radio, t/c mkg, refrig], dinner to unit, cots-fee. RO ⸋ $61 - $65, ⸋⸋ $72 - $76, ⸋ $10, AE BC EFT MC VI.

★★★ **Emerald Tower Motor Inn**, (M), 71 Hospital Rd, Cnr Egan St (Clermont Hwy), ☎ 07 4982 2100, fax 07 4982 3272, 18 units [shwr, tlt, a/c, tel, cable tv, video, clock radio, t/c mkg, refrig, toaster (8), ldry], iron, iron brd, meals to unit, cots-fee. RO ⸋ $65 - $75, ⸋⸋ $75 - $85, ⸋ $10 - $12, AE BC DC MC VI.

★★★ **Motel 707**, (M), Ruby St cnr Clermont Highway, ☎ 07 4982 1707, fax 07 4982 4209, 43 units [shwr, tlt, a/c, tel, TV, movie, clock radio, t/c mkg, refrig], dinner to unit (Mon to Thur), cots-fee. RO ⸋ $49, ⸋⸋ $60, ⸋ $9, Units 33 to 43 of a lower rating. AE BC DC MC VI.

★★★ **Overflow Motor Inn**, (M), 77b Hospital Rd, 200m N of Water Tower, ☎ 07 4982 2156, fax 07 4982 2763, 16 units [shwr, spa bath (1), tlt, H & C, a/c, tel, TV, video (avail), clock radio, t/c mkg, refrig, cook fac ltd, micro, toaster, ldry], dryer, iron, iron brd, bbq, dinner to unit (Mon to Thur), cots, non smoking units (8). RO ⸋ $63, ⸋⸋ $77, ⸋ $10, ch con, AE BC DC EFT MC VI.

★★ **Emerald Star Hotel Motel**, (LMH), Cnr Clermont & Egerton Sts, ☎ 07 4982 1422, fax 07 4982 2060, (Multi-stry gr fl), 32 units [shwr, tlt, a/c, tel, TV, movie, t/c mkg, refrig], night club (Thur to Sat), ⊠ (Mon to Sun), ✆, cots. RO ⸋ $45, ⸋⸋ $55, ⸋ $10, ch con, AE BC DC MC VI.

B&B's/Guest Houses

★★★ **Central Inn**, (B&B), 90 Clermont St, 100m E of railway station, ☎ 07 4982 0800, fax 07 4982 0801, (2 stry), 20 rms [shwr, a/c, TV, clock radio, refrig], tlt, ldry-fee, dryer-fee, ✕, cook fac, non smoking rms. BLB ⸋ $39, ⸋⸋ $49, AE BC MC VI.

EMU PARK QLD 4702

Pop 2,800. (686km N Brisbane), See map on page 416, ref C6. Notable relic called Singing Ship in honour of Captain Cook, a soaring white sculpture that when the wind is caught in its sail-like formation a haunting yet melodious tune can be heard.

★★★☆ **Endeavour Inn Emu Park**, (M), 18 Hill St, ☎ 07 4939 6777, fax 07 4939 6733, (Multi-stry), 18 units [shwr, tlt, a/c, c/fan, tel, cable tv, clock radio, t/c mkg, refrig, cook fac ltd, toaster], ldry, dryer, ⊠, pool (salt water), bbq, rm serv, cots. **RO** ♦ **$53 - $64**, ♦♦ **$60 - $71**, ⋔ **$14**, ch con, AE BC DC EFT MC VI, ⟨⟩.

ESK QLD 4312

Pop 950. (100km NW Brisbane), See map on page 417, ref C6. Picturesque town surrounded by mountains. Somerset Dam, Wivenhoe Dam, Atkinson Dam, Splityard Creek Dam, Bellevue Homestead, Coominya, Caboonbah Homestead, south of Somerset. Boating, Scenic Drives, Swimming, Water Skiing.

Hotels/Motels
★★★ **Esk**, (M), 93 Ipswich St, ☎ 07 5424 1289, fax 07 5424 1289, 5 units [shwr, tlt, a/c-cool, heat, tel (Direct Dial), TV, clock radio, t/c mkg, refrig, toaster], pool, bbq, dinner to unit, cots. **RO** ♦ **$40 - $45**, ♦♦ **$50 - $55**, AE BC DC MC VI.

★★★ **Esk Wivenhoe Motor Inn**, (M), 2 Highland St, ☎ 07 5424 1677, fax 07 5424 2599, 10 units [shwr, tlt, a/c, tel, TV, clock radio, t/c mkg, refrig], ldry, dryer, dinner to unit, cots. **RO** ♦ **$45 - $49**, ♦♦ **$55 - $60**, ⋔ **$11**, AE BC DC MC VI.

★★★ **Glenn Rocks**, (M), 81 Brisbane Valley Hwy, ☎ 07 5424 1304, fax 07 5424 1489, 11 units [shwr, tlt, hairdry, a/c, elec blkts, tel, TV, video-fee, clock radio, t/c mkg, refrig], ⊠, pool, spa, dinner to unit, c/park (undercover), cots. **RO** ♦ **$44**, ♦♦ **$55 - $66**, BC MC VI, ⟨⟩.

EUDLO QLD 4554

Pop 1,253. (100km N Brisbane) See map on page 417, ref D5. Township part of Sunshine Coast Hinterland.

Hotels/Motels
★ **Chenrezig Institute**, (M), 33 Johnson Rd, 6km S of Eudlo PO, ☎ 07 5445 0077, fax 07 5445 0088, 10 units shared fac (shower/toilet), ldry, conf fac, ✕ (non smoking), t/c mkg shared, ☎, non smoking rms. **BLB** ♦ **$22 - $27**, **RO** ♦♦ **$19 - $22**, ch con, BC EFT MC VI.

B&B's/Guest Houses
★★★★ **Macaranga House**, (B&B), 23 Johnson Road, ☎ 07 5445 9347, fax 07 5445 9347, 4 rms [shwr, tlt, hairdry, heat, c/fan, TV, clock radio, t/c mkg, refrig, toaster, ldry], dryer, ✕, rm serv, dinner to unit, cots, non smoking flr. **BB** ♦ **$35 - $45**, ♦♦ **$65 - $85**, ⋔ **$10 - $25**, ch con, BC MC VI.

EULO QLD 4491

Pop Nominal, (862km W Brisbane), See map on page 414, ref C8. Small town on Paroo River. The Eulo mud springs (8km W) provide a safety valve for the pressures of the artesian basin. Fishing, Gem Fossicking.

★★☆ **Carpet Springs Tourist Retreat**, (GH), (Farm), Carpet Springs, Via Eulo, 19km W of Eulo, ☎ 07 4655 4064, fax 07 4655 4002, 1 rm [shwr, tlt, a/c-cool, heat, elec blkts, tel, t/c mkg, refrig, toaster], ✕. **D all meals** ♦ **$80**, ch con, AE BC MC VI.

EUMUNDI QLD 4562

Pop 450. (121km N Brisbane), See map on page 417, ref D4. Gateway to Noosa, situated on the Bruce Highway this rich coastal district produces pineapples, sugar, ginger, timber and dairy produce. Local craft market held at Old Butter Factory each Sunday. Home of Eumundi Brewery - brewery tours available Thunder Egg farm 1.5km from town Historical Museum.

Self Catering Accommodation
Parawanga Gardens Cottage, (Cotg), Lot 6 Ceylon Rd, 9km W of Eumundi, ☎ 07 5442 8956, 1 cotg acc up to 3, (2 bedrm), [shwr, bath, tlt, a/c-cool, tel, TV, video, clock radio, refrig, cook fac, blkts, linen, pillows], w/mach, dryer, iron, iron brd, lounge firepl. **D** ♦♦ **$89 - $109**, ⋔ **$15**, **W** ♦♦ **$489 - $689**.

B&B's/Guest Houses
★★★★☆ **Eumundi Rise Bed & Breakfast**, (B&B), 37-39 Crescent Rd, 200m W of PO, ☎ 07 5442 8855, fax 07 5442 8859, 4 rms [shwr, tlt, hairdry, c/fan, heat, elec blkts, clock radio, t/c mkg], lounge (TV), bbq, non smoking rms. **BB** ♦ **$70 - $90**, ♦♦ **$100 - $140**, AE BC DC MC VI.

★★★★ **Eumundi Country Cottage Bed & Breakfast**, (B&B), 47 Memorial Drive, ☎ 07 5442 7220, fax 07 5442 7320, 3 rms [ensuite, hairdry, c/fan, TV, radio, t/c mkg, refrig], iron (1), iron brd (1), bbq, non smoking property, non smoking rms. **BB** ♦ **$80 - $90**, ♦♦ **$110 - $130**, VI.

★★★★ **(Cottage Section)**, 1 cotg acc up to 5, (2 bedrm), [shwr, tlt, a/c, fan, heat, radio, t/c mkg, refrig, cook fac, micro, blkts, doonas, linen, pillows], w/mach, breakfast ingredients, non smoking property. **BLB** ♦♦ **$130**, ⋔ **$20**, ch con, weekly con, Min book applies.

★★★★ **Noosa Ridge Retreat**, (B&B), Previously King Protea Bed & Breakfast. 185 Sudholz Rd, Verrierdale, 10km E of Eumundi PO, ☎ 07 5449 1719, fax 07 5449 1577, (2 stry gr fl), 4 rms [ensuite, shwr (4), bath (1), tlt (4), c/fan, pillows], ldry, lounge (TV), ✕, pool, sauna, spa, cook fac, t/c mkg shared, bbq, non smoking flr (2). **BB** ♦ **$66 - $110**, ♦♦ **$88 - $165**, BC MC VI.

★★★★ **Toad Hall Bed & Breakfast**, (B&B), 358 Eumundi Range Rd, ☎ 07 5442 7426, 3 rms [ensuite, a/c-cool, TV, t/c mkg, refrig, doonas], ldry, ✕, pool, bbq, non smoking property. **BB** ♦♦ **$95 - $110**, ⋔ **$15 - $25**, weekly con, BC MC VI,

Operator Comment: Spectacular views. Visit us at: www.eumundi.com/toadhall.htm

EUNGELLA NATIONAL PARK

Pop Nominal, (1059km N Brisbane), See map on page 416, ref A2. Situated on Clark Range & Broken River, Platypus habitat. Picnic areas (Rainforest National Park & Eungella Dam) Bevans Lookout & Peases Lookout, Canoeing, Horseriding. Bush Walking, Scenic Drives, Swimming.

Hotels/Motels
★★★☆ **Broken River Mountain Retreat**, (M), Eungella National Park, 5km S of PO river frontage, ☎ 07 4958 4528, fax 07 4958 4564, 8 units [shwr, tlt, c/fan, fire pl (4), heat, TV, clock radio, t/c mkg, refrig, cook fac ltd], ldry, w/mach, dryer, iron, rec rm, ⊠, pool, bbq, ☎, plygr, bush walking, cots-fee. **RO** ♦♦ **$66 - $77**, ⋔ **$11**, 4 units ★★☆, AE BC MC VI.

★★★☆ **(Unit Section)**, 10 units acc up to 6, (1 & 2 bedrm), [shwr, bath (2), tlt, fan, fire pl, heat, TV, clock radio, refrig, cook fac, micro, toaster, blkts, linen, pillows], ldry, dryer, iron, rec rm, ⊠, pool, bbq, c/park (undercover) (4), ☎, plygr, cots-fee. **RO** ♦♦ **$88 - $110**, ⋔ **$11**.

★★★ **Historic Eungella Chalet Mountain Lodge**, (LH), Eungella National Park, Eungella 4757, ☎ 07 4958 4509, fax 07 4958 4503, (2 stry), 12 rms [basin (6), shwr (6), tlt (6), c/fan (6), heat (6), TV (6), t/c mkg (6), refrig (6)], ldry, rec rm, lounge (TV), ⊠, pool, ☎, plygr, cots. **RO** ♦ **$28 - $72**, ♦♦ **$50 - $88**, ch con, Rooms 1 to 6 ★☆ BC MC VI.

Self Catering Accommodation
★★★ **Historic Eungella Chalet Mountain Lodge**, Eungella National Park, ☎ 07 4958 4509, fax 07 4958 4503, 10 cabins acc up to 6, (1 & 2 bedrm), [shwr, tlt, heat, TV, refrig, cook fac (6), cook fac ltd (4), elec frypan (4), blkts, linen, pillows], ldry, lounge (TV), ⊠ (open all year), pool, bbq, ☎, plygr, bush walking, cots-fee. **D** ♦ **$88**, ♦♦ **$28 - $109**, ⋔ **$10**, ch con, BC MC VI.

FITZROY ISLAND QLD 4870

Pop Nominal, (1710km N Brisbane), See map on page 415, ref C3. Located on the Great Barrier Reef, this rainforest covered island is popular with bushwalkers, scuba divers, fishing and boating enthusiasts. Live-in dive courses available. National Park. Boating, Bush Walking, Fishing, Wind Surfing.

Self Catering Accommodation
★★★☆ **Fitzroy Island**, Resort, Via Cairns, ☎ 07 4051 9588, fax 07 4052 1335, 8 cabins acc up to 4, [shwr, tlt, hairdry, c/fan, TV, clock radio, t/c mkg, refrig, linen, pillows], iron, iron brd, ⊠, pool, kiosk, ☎, canoeing, cots. **DBB** ♦ **$220**, ch con, AE BC DC EFT MC VI.

(Beach Bunkhouses), 1 bunkhouse acc up to 4, [fan], shwr, tlt, cook fac, cots. **RO** ♦ **$31**, ⋔ **$31**, fam con.

FLAXTON QLD 4560

Pop Part of Nambour, (91km N Brisbane), See map on page 417, ref D4. Located on the Sunshine Coast Hinterland, offering antiques, local arts and crafts. Bush Walking, Scenic Drives.

Hotels/Motels

★★★ **Country Lodge**, (M), 332 Flaxton Dve, 3.5km S of Mapleton PO, ☎ 07 5445 7555, fax 07 5445 7250, 9 units [shwr, tlt, a/c, tel, TV, t/c mkg, refrig], ldry, ✕, pool, courtesy transfer, cots. RO ♦ $55 - $65, ♦♦ $60 - $80, ⓘ $15, ch con, BC EFT MC VI, ⌂&.

B&B's/Guest Houses

★★★★ **Avocado Grove Bed & Breakfast**, (B&B), 10 Carramar Court, off Ensbey Road, 4.5km N of Montville PO, ☎ 07 5445 7585, fax 07 5445 7585, 4 rms (4 suites) [shwr, tlt, c/fan, heat, TV (2), t/c mkg (2), refrig (2)], ldry, dryer, ✕, cook fac, bbq, non smoking property, non smoking flr (2). BB ♦ $90, ♦♦ $120 - $130,Suite BB ♦♦ $140 - $150, BC MC VI.

★★★★ **Tanderra On Flaxton**, (B&B), Flaxton Mill Rd, 3.5km N of P.O, ☎ 07 5445 7179, fax 07 5445 7120, 5 rms [shwr, bath (2), tlt, hairdry, c/fan (4), heat, elec blkts, clock radio (2), t/c mkg], TV rm, conf fac, bbq, non smoking rms. BB ♦ $85, ♦♦ $130 - $180, ⓘ $40, RO ♦ $70, ♦♦ $100 - $150, ⓘ $30, AE BC EFT MC VI.

FLYING FISH POINT QLD 4860

Pop 750. (1639km N Brisbane), See map on page 415, ref C4. Delightful little coastal town with a 3km long sandy beach.

★★★★ **Flying Fish Point Bed and Breakfast**, (B&B), 3 Alice Street, Flying Fish Point, Innisfail 4860, 7km E of Innisfail, ☎ 07 4061 8934, fax 07 4061 8394, 2 rms [shwr, tlt, a/c-cool, c/fan, TV, clock radio, ldry], dryer, TV rm, cook fac, t/c mkg shared, cots. BB ♦♦ $75, ⓘ $10.

FORREST BEACH QLD 4850

Pop 911. (1500km N Brisbane), See map on page 415, ref C6. Seaside town with wide expanse of beach.

Hotels/Motels

★★☆ **Forrest Beach**, (LMH), 1 Ash St, ☎ 07 4777 8700, 6 units [shwr, tlt, a/c-cool, c/fan, TV, t/c mkg, refrig, toaster], ldry, dryer, conv fac, ✕, pool (salt water), bbq, c/park (undercover), ✆, plygr, cots. RO ♦♦ $50, ♦♦♦♦ $65, ch con, BC EFT MC VI.

Self Catering Accommodation

★★ **Wilbry**, (HU), 8 Palm St Forest Beach, Ingham 4850, ☎ 07 4777 8755, 3 units acc up to 5, [shwr, tlt, a/c-cool, c/fan, TV, clock radio, refrig, cook fac, linen (weekly rates) reqd-fee], ldry, bbq, c/park (undercover), cots. D ♦♦ $50, ⓘ $5, W ♦♦ $230, ⓘ $10, BC MC VI.

FORSAYTH QLD 4871

Pop Nominal, (2020km NW Brisbane), See map on page 414, ref C4. Small historic town in far north Queensland. Former goldmining area & railway destination from Mt Surprise.

★★★☆ **Forsayth Homestay**, (B&B), Fourth St, ☎ 07 4062 5386, fax 07 4062 5464, 5 rms [a/c, c/fan, clock radio], shwr, tlt, ldry, iron, iron brd, TV rm, t/c mkg shared, bbq, secure park, cots, non smoking units (5). DBB ♦♦ $129.80, ⓘ $64.90, BC MC VI.

FRASER ISLAND QLD 4650

Pop Nominal, (250km N Brisbane), See map on page 417, ref E1. Coach services from Rainbow Beach $25 per person return. Security parking available at Rainbow Beach. World's largest sandmassed island. 44% of the island is State Forest and the remaining 56% is Regional Park. The island is World Heritage Listed.

Self Catering Accommodation

★★★★☆ **Fraser Island Beach Houses**, (House), Previously Villas on Fraser. Eliza St Eurong Second Valley, 60km SE Hervey Bay, ☎ 07 4127 9205, fax 07 4127 9207, (Multi-stry gr fl), 11 houses acc up to 8, (3 bedrm), [ensuite, shwr, bath, tlt, c/fan, cable tv, radio, refrig, cook fac, micro, d/wash, toaster, ldry, blkts, linen, pillows], dryer, iron, iron brd, pool, spa, bbq, c/park (carport), cots. RO ♦♦ $105 - $325, W ♦♦ $594 - $1,995, 6 units ★★★★. BC MC VI.

★★★★☆ **Kingfisher Bay Resort and Village**, (HU), Resort, Fraser Island, North White Cliffs, ☎ 07 3032 2805, fax 07 3221 3270, 39 units acc up to 4, (2 bedrm), [shwr, bath, spa bath, tlt, hairdry, heat, tel, TV, clock radio, t/c mkg, refrig, cook fac, micro, elec frypan, d/wash, toaster, ldry, blkts, linen, pillows], dryer-fee, iron, iron brd, rec rm, conv fac, ✉, pool (salt water), spa, 24hr reception, shop, ✆, bush walking, tennis. RO ♦♦ $275, AE BC DC EFT MC VI, ⌂&.

★★★☆ **(Hotel Section)**, (Multi-stry), 152 rms [shwr, bath, spa bath (38), tlt, hairdry, a/c, tel, TV, t/c mkg, refrig], iron, cots. RO ♦♦ $165 - $248.

★★★☆ **(Satinay Villa Section)**, 30 units acc up to 6, [shwr, spa bath, tlt, tel, TV, clock radio, cook fac, micro, elec frypan, d/wash, ldry (in unit)], dryer, iron, cots. D ♦♦ $275, Min book applies.

★★★ **(Villa Section)**, 10 units [shwr, bath, spa bath, tlt, fire pl (gas) (4), tel, TV, clock radio, ldry (in unit)], bathrm, dryer, cots. RO ♦ $33, Min book applies.

★★★★ **Eurong Beach Resort**, (HU), Eurong, ☎ 07 4127 9122, fax 07 4127 9178, (Multi-stry gr fl), 30 units acc up to 4, (Studio & 2 bedrm), [shwr, spa bath, tlt, c/fan, radio, t/c mkg, refrig, cook fac, blkts, linen, pillows], ldry, dryer, conv fac, ✉, pool, ✆, cots. D $88 - $222, W $440 - $1,100, 5 units ★★☆. Generated power.

★★★★ **Sailfish on Fraser**, (Apt), Happy Valley, ☎ 07 4127 9494, fax 07 4127 9499, (2 stry gr fl), 9 apts acc up to 6, (2 bedrm), [c/fan, tel, TV, clock radio, t/c mkg, refrig, micro, d/wash, toaster, ldry, blkts, doonas, linen, pillows], w/mach, dryer, pool, spa, bbq, c/park (undercover), cots. D $120 - $236, W $840 - $1,486, ch con, BC MC VI.

★★★ **Fraser Island Retreat**, (SA), Happy Valley, ☎ 07 4127 9144, fax 07 4127 9131, 9 serv apts acc up to 5, [shwr, tlt, c/fan, heat, TV, video, clock radio, t/c mkg, refrig, cook fac ltd, toaster, blkts, linen, pillows], ldry, dryer, ✉, pool, bbq, shop, petrol, ice, ✆, bush walking, cots. RO ♦ $125 - $154, ♦♦ $125 - $176, ♦♦♦ $125 - $192, Generated power, AE BC EFT MC VI.

★★ **Bow - Allum Place**, (HU), Lot 9 Anderson St Eurong, 300m s of Eurong Beach, ☎ 07 4127 9188, fax 07 4127 9184, 2 units acc up to 8, [t/c mkg, refrig, cook fac, ldry, blkts, linen reqd-fee, pillows], w/mach, bbq. RO ♦♦ $80 - $120, ♦♦ W $350 - $880.

Babbooyin Lodge, (Apt), Lot 11 Jarvis St Eurong, 300m S of Eurong Beach, ☎ 07 4127 9188, fax 07 4127 9184, 1 apt acc up to 8, (3 bedrm), [shwr, tlt, t/c mkg, refrig, cook fac, ldry, blkts, linen reqd-fee, pillows], w/mach, ✕, bbq. RO ♦♦ $80 - $120, ♦♦ W $350 - $880.

Waddy Lodge, (HF), 1.5km S of Orchid Beach, ☎ 07 4127 9206, 2 flats acc up to 8, [shwr, tlt, refrig (2 in each unit), cook fac (gas), blkts reqd, linen reqd], ldry, freezer, bbq. W $500 - $850, Min book applies.

GATTON QLD 4343

Pop 5,350. (90km W Brisbane), See map on page 417, ref B6. Situated on Lockyer Creek, known as Salad Bowl district. Also an important agricultural district. Queensland Agricultural College established in 1897, the college has fine buildings, crops, pastures and numerous stud animals, including Arab horses Brahman and Charolain cattle. Golf, Swimming.

Hotels/Motels

★★★ **Gatton**, (M), 74 Railway St, ☎ 07 5462 1333, fax 07 5462 3684, 20 units [shwr, tlt, hairdry (3), a/c, tel, TV, video (avail)-fee, clock radio, t/c mkg, refrig, toaster (3)], ldry-fee, bbq, cots-fee, non smoking units (10). RO ♦ $55 - $80, ♦♦ $60 - $90, ⓘ $11, AE BC DC EFT MC VI.

Driver fatigue is a killer

While speed and alcohol are well known killers on the road, driver fatigue can be just as deadly, because of the subtle and insidious way it creeps up on a driver.

Nobody is immune to fatigue. To help in the fight against fatigue:

- Get a good night's sleep before the trip, and never drive when you would normally be asleep (not late at night or very early in the morning).
- Take rest breaks every two hours, or as soon as you feel drowsy.
- Do some light exercise and enjoy a light snack during your breaks.
- Don't pack too many driving hours into a day.
- Share the driving.

GAYNDAH QLD 4625

Pop 1,750. (345km N Brisbane). See map on page 417, ref B2. Situated on the banks of the Burnett River and in the heart of an important citrus growing area, it is known as the 'Orange Capital'. Award winning Historical Museum. Claude Warton Weir Recreation Area. Ban Ban Springs. Bowls, Fishing, Golf, Horse Racing, Squash, Swimming.

Hotels/Motels

★★★☆ **Gayndah Colonial Motor Inn**, (M), 62 Capper St, ☎ 07 4161 1999, fax 07 4161 1052, 12 units [shwr, tlt, a/c, tel, fax, TV, movie, clock radio, t/c mkg, refrig, cook fac (1)], ldry, dryer-fee, ✕, pool (salt water), spa, bbq, dinner to unit, c/park (undercover), plygr, cots-fee. **RO ╽ $55, ╽╽ $66, ╽ $11**, ch con, Units 1,4,5,6 ★★★. AE BC DC MC VI, ♿.

★★★ **Gayndah Motel**, (M), 4 Mick Lutvey Street, 140km W Bundaberg, ☎ 07 4161 2500, fax 07 4161 2459, 9 units [shwr, tlt, a/c, tel, TV, clock radio, t/c mkg, refrig], ldry, dryer-fee, pool (salt water), bbq, c/park (undercover), cots. **RO ╽ $48 - $55, ╽╽ $55 - $62, ╽╽╽╽ $70 - $77**, BC.

GEORGETOWN QLD 4871

Pop 300. (1878km NW Brisbane). See map on page 414, ref C4. Former goldmining town in far north Queensland. Fishing, Gem Fossicking, Gold Prospecting, Golf, Scenic Drives, Swimming.

★★★ **Latara Resort**, (M), Gulf Developmental Rd, 1km W of PO, ☎ 07 4062 1190, fax 07 4062 1262, 25 units [shwr, tlt, a/c-cool, tel, TV, clock radio, t/c mkg, refrig], ldry, lounge, ✕, pool, bbq, rm serv, dinner to unit, cots. **RO ╽ $58, ╽╽ $76, ╽ $15**, ch con, AE BC DC MC VI.

GIN GIN QLD 4671

Pop 950. (371km N Brisbane). See map on page 416, ref E8. Agricultural and pastoral centre. Boating, Bowls, Fishing, Golf, Scenic Drives, Swimming, Tennis.

Hotels/Motels

 ★★★★ **Wild Scotsman Motor Inn**, (M), 5 Mulgrave St (Bruce Hwy), 1.5km N of PO, ☎ 07 4157 2522, fax 07 4157 2422, (2 stry gr fl), 16 units (1 suite) [shwr, bath (4), spa bath (1), tlt, hairdry, a/c-cool, tel, TV, movie, clock radio, t/c mkg, refrig, mini bar], ldry, dryer, iron, iron brd, ✕, pool (salt water), spa (bath), bbq, rm serv, dinner to unit, c/park (undercover), cots-fee, non smoking units (avail). **RO ╽ $82, ╽╽ $88, ╽ $11, Suite D ╽ $119, ╽╽ $119**, AE BC DC EFT MC MP VI, ♿.

 ★★★ **Gin Gin Central**, (M), 61 Mulgrave St, ☎ 07 4157 2444, fax 07 4157 2612, 14 units (1 & 2 bedrm), [shwr, tlt, a/c-cool, c/fan, heat, tel, TV, t/c mkg, refrig], ldry, ✕, bbq, rm serv, c/park (undercover), cots, non smoking units (7). **RO ╽ $50 - $55, ╽╽ $55 - $64**, AE BC DC EFT MC MCH VI.

★★★ **Gin Gin Village Motor Inn**, (M), 44 Mulgrave St, ☎ 07 4157 2599, fax 07 4157 3974, 10 units [shwr, tlt, a/c-cool, c/fan, heat, tel (8), TV (10), movie, clock radio, t/c mkg, refrig], ldry, spa (/pool), bbq, dinner to unit, c/park (undercover) (5), cots. **RO ╽ $48, ╽╽ $56, ╽ $10**, fam con, AE BC DC MC VI, ♿.

Sharing the roads - Trucks and cars

Trucks are different from cars. They take up more road space than cars, especially when turning, and are slower to accelerate, turn and reverse. Here are some hints in sharing our roads safely with trucks:

- Don't cut in on trucks. Because trucks need a greater braking distance than cars, truck drivers leave more space in front of them when approaching a red light or stop sign than a car.
- Allow extra time and space to overtake trucks. You will need about 1.5 kilometres of clear road space to pass a truck.
- Don't pass a left-turning truck on the inside. Trucks sometimes need more than one lane to turn tight corners, so watch for a truck swinging out near intersections.
- Be patient - follow at a safe distance. Truck drivers may not see you because of blind spots, particularly if you travel right behind them.

GLADSTONE QLD 4680

Pop 26,400. (534km N Brisbane). See map on page 416, ref D7. One of Queensland's busiest ports with a world class marina. Boating, Bowls, Fishing, Golf, Squash, Swimming, Tennis, Water Skiing. See also Boyne Island.

Hotels/Motels

 ★★★★☆ **Country Plaza International**, (M), 100 Goondoon St, City Centre, ☎ 07 4972 4499, fax 07 4972 4921, (Multi-stry), 80 units [shwr, bath, tlt, hairdry, a/c, tel, TV, movie, clock radio, t/c mkg, refrig, mini bar], lift, ldry, iron, iron brd, conv fac, ✕, bar, pool, 24hr reception, rm serv, dinner to unit, c/park (undercover), courtesy transfer, cots. **RO $109, ╽ $10**, ch con, AE BC DC MC VI.

(Business Suites), (2 stry gr fl), 6 units acc up to 6, (3 bedrm), [ensuite, bath, spa bath, hairdry, a/c, c/fan, cent heat, tel, TV, video, clock radio, refrig, mini bar, micro, d/wash, toaster, ldry, blkts, linen, pillows], w/mach, dryer, iron, iron brd, dinner to unit, cots. **D $129, W $623**, ch con, (not yet classified).

  ★★★★☆ **Metro Hotel & Suites Gladstone**, (M), 22-24 Roseberry St, ☎ 07 4972 4711, fax 07 4972 4940, (Multi-stry), 49 units (1 bedrm), [shwr, bath, tlt, a/c, tel, TV, movie, clock radio, t/c mkg, refrig, mini bar, cook fac, micro, ldry (in unit)], lift, ✕, pool (salt water), 24hr reception, dinner to unit, c/park (undercover), secure park, cots. **RO ╽╽ $99 - $137**, AE BC DC EFT MC VI.

★★★★ **Mid City Motor Inn**, (M), 26 Goondoon St, ☎ 07 4972 3000, fax 07 4972 3000, (2 stry gr fl), 25 units (1 suite) [shwr, tlt, a/c-cool, tel, TV, movie, clock radio, t/c mkg, refrig, toaster], iron, iron brd, pool (salt water), sauna, c/park (undercover), cots-fee, non smoking units (5). **RO ╽ $66, ╽╽ $77, Suite RO $121**, ch con, AE BC DC MC VI.

  ★★★★ **Sundowner Chain Motor Inns**, (M), Cnr Far St & Dawson Hwy, ☎ 07 4972 4322, fax 07 4972 4352, (2 stry gr fl), 36 units [shwr, tlt, hairdry, a/c-cool, tel, cable tv, clock radio, t/c mkg, refrig, mini bar], iron, iron brd, conf fac, ✕, pool, spa, rm serv, c/park (undercover), cots-fee, non smoking units. **RO ╽ $83.50 - $93.50, ╽╽ $83.50 - $93.50, ╽ $11**, ch con, AE BC DC MC MP VI, ♿.

 ★★★☆ **Camelot Motel**, (M), 19 Agnes St, Cnr Elizabeth St, ☎ 07 4979 1222, fax 07 4979 2700, (Multi-stry), 16 units (5 suites) [shwr, spa bath (3), tlt, a/c-cool, c/fan, tel, TV, movie, clock radio, t/c mkg, refrig], ldry, dryer, iron, iron brd, conv fac, ✕ (Mon to Sat), pool, rm serv, dinner to unit, cots. **D ╽ $68, ╽╽ $74, ╽ $10, Suite D ╽ $92, ╽╽ $92 - $120, ╽ $10**, ch con, AE BC DC MC MP VI.

★★★☆ **Mawarra**, (M), 6 Scenery St, ☎ 07 4972 1411, fax 07 4972 6889, (2 stry gr fl), 32 units [shwr, tlt, a/c-cool, heat, tel, TV, movie, clock radio, t/c mkg, refrig, cook fac (2)], ✕ (Mon to Sat), pool, bbq, rm serv, c/park (undercover), plygr, cots. **RO ╽ $52 - $54, ╽╽ $59 - $64, ╽ $10**, AE BC DC MC VI.

★★★☆ **Rusty Anchor Motor Inn**, (M), 167 Goondoon St, ☎ 07 4972 2099, fax 07 4972 2453, 22 units [shwr, tlt, a/c, tel, cable tv, clock radio, t/c mkg, refrig, mini bar (9)], ldry, ✕ (Mon to Sat), pool, bbq, rm serv, dinner to unit, cots-fee. **RO ╽ $52 - $60, ╽╽ $58 - $68**, AE BC DC MC VI.

★★★☆ **Siesta Villa Motor Inn**, (M), 104 Glenlyon St, 500m C.B.D, ☎ 07 4972 4922, fax 07 4972 4576, (2 stry gr fl), 10 units [shwr, tlt, hairdry, a/c, tel, TV, movie, clock radio, t/c mkg, refrig], ldry, iron, iron brd, pool (salt water), spa, bbq, meals to unit (dinner/breakfast), c/park (undercover), courtesy transfer, cots-fee. **RO ╽ $50 - $55, ╽╽ $58 - $70, ╽ $10**, AE BC DC EFT JCB MC VI.

★★★ **Amber Lodge**, (M), 129 Toolooa St, ☎ 07 4972 4144, fax 07 4972 7582, 15 units [shwr, tlt, a/c, tel, TV, movie, clock radio, t/c mkg, refrig, toaster], pool, c/park (undercover), cots-fee, non smoking rms. **RO ╽ $50 - $60**, ch con, AE BC DC MC VI.

★★★ **Gladstone Motel**, (M), 88 Toolooa St, ☎ 07 4972 2144, fax 07 4972 8081, 18 units [shwr, tlt, a/c-cool, tel, cable tv, clock radio, t/c mkg, refrig], pool, rm serv, dinner to unit, c/park (undercover), cots. **RO ╽ $49, ╽╽ $55 - $60, ╽ $8**, AE BC DC MC VI.

 ★★★ **Gladstone Reef**, (LMH), Cnr Goondoon & Yarroon Sts, ☎ 07 4972 1000, fax 07 4972 1729, (Multi-stry gr fl), 48 units [shwr, tlt, a/c, tel, TV, movie, clock radio, t/c mkg, refrig, mini bar (34)], lift, ldry, w/mach-fee, dryer, conv fac, night club (Wed, Fri & Sat), pool, rm serv, dinner to unit, cots. **RO ╽ $72 - $85, ╽╽ $80 - $94, ╽ $6.60**, ch con, AE BC DC MC VI.

GLADSTONE QLD continued...

★★★ **Gladstone Village Motor Inn**, (M), Cnr Dawson Hwy & Chapman Dve, ☎ 07 4978 2077, fax 07 4978 1869, 26 units [shwr, tlt, a/c, tel, TV, movie, clock radio, t/c mkg, refrig], ldry, conv fac, ✕, pool, bbq (covered), rm serv, c/park (undercover), courtesy transfer (airport/marina). **RO** ♦ **$55**, ♦♦ **$65**, ch con, fam con, AE BC BTC MC VI.

★★★ **Harbour Lodge Motel**, (M), 16 Roseberry St, ☎ 07 4972 6463, fax 07 4972 6463, (2 stry gr fl) 16 units [shwr, tlt, a/c-cool, c/fan, tel, TV, clock radio, t/c mkg, refrig, toaster], ldry, dryer, pool (salt water), cots-fee, non smoking rms (8). **RO** ♦ **$50 - $60**, ♦♦ **$62 - $70**, ♦ **$10**, AE BC DC MC VI.

★★★ **Park View Gladstone**, (M), 42 Roseberry St, ☎ 07 4972 3344, fax 07 4972 3344, (2 stry gr fl) 14 units [shwr, tlt, a/c, tel, TV, movie, clock radio, t/c mkg, refrig], pool, bbq, c/park (undercover), courtesy transfer, cots. **RO** ♦ **$53**, ♦♦ **$58 - $62**, ♦ **$8**, AE BC DC MC VI.

★★★ **Rocky Glen**, (LMH), Dawson Hwy, ☎ 07 4972 2977, fax 07 4972 2903, (2 stry gr fl), 21 units [shwr, tlt, a/c, c/fan, tel, TV, clock radio, t/c mkg, refrig, toaster], ldry, conv fac, ✕ (Mon to Sat), c/park (undercover), ☎, cots-fee. **RO** ♦ **$55**, ♦♦ **$65**, ♦ **$10**, ch con, AE BC DC MC VI.

 ★★★ **Why-Not Motor Inn**, (M), 23 Coon St, ☎ 07 4972 4222, fax 07 4972 5479, 11 units [shwr, tlt, a/c (11), c/fan, tel, TV, clock radio, t/c mkg, refrig, cook fac (7)], ldry, w/mach-fee, dryer-fee, pool, bbq, c/park (undercover) (9), cots-fee. **RO** ♦ **$50**, ♦♦ **$55**, ♦ **$6**, ch con, AE BC DC EFT MC MCH VI.

★★☆ **A 1 Motel**, (M), Toolooa St, ☎ 07 4972 1655, fax 07 4972 1655, 14 units [shwr, tlt, a/c, TV, clock radio, t/c mkg, refrig], ldry, pool, meals to unit (b/fast & dinner), c/park (undercover), ☎, cots-fee. **RO** ♦ **$49**, ♦♦ **$54**, ♦ **$8 - $10**, ch con, fam con, AE BC DC EFT JCB MC VI.

★★☆ **Sun Court Motor Inn**, (M), Far St, ☎ 07 4972 2377, fax 07 4972 2536, 12 units [shwr, tlt, a/c-cool, fan (7), c/fan (5), tel, TV, movie, radio, t/c mkg, refrig, cook fac ltd (4), toaster], ldry, dryer, pool, spa, bbq, dinner to unit, c/park (undercover), plygr, cots. **RO** ♦ **$60.50**, ♦♦ **$66**, ♦ **$8.80**, AE BC DC MC VI, ♿.

★★ **Queens**, (LMH), Cnr Goondoon & William Sts, ☎ 07 4972 6615, fax 07 4972 9550, (2 stry gr fl) 13 units [shwr, tlt, a/c-cool, TV, t/c mkg, refrig, toaster], ✕ (Mon to Sat), ☎. **RO** ♦ **$45**, ♦♦ **$50**, ♦ **$5**, Light breakfast only available. AE BC DC MC VI.

Harbour Sails Motor Inn, (M), 23 Goondoon St, ☎ 07 4972 3456, fax 07 4972 3567, 26 units (5 suites) [shwr, spa bath (2), tlt, hairdry, a/c, tel, TV, video (5), movie, clock radio, t/c mkg, refrig, mini bar, cook fac ltd (5), micro (5), toaster], ldry, iron, iron brd, ✕, pool (salt water), c/park (15), non smoking units (22). **RO** ♦ **$85**, ♦♦ **$85**, ♦ **$10**, AE BC DC EFT MC VI, (not yet classified).

Toolooa Gradens Motel, (M), 79 - 83 Toolooa St, 1km S of railway station, ☎ 07 4972 2811, fax 07 4972 1642, 17 units [shwr, tlt, a/c-cool, tel, TV, clock radio, t/c mkg, refrig, mini bar, cook fac ltd, toaster], ldry-fee, conf fac, ✕, pool, bbq, rm serv, dinner to unit, cots, non smoking units (4). **RO** ♦ **$42**, ♦♦ **$48**, ♦ **$7**, AE BC DC EFT MC VI, (not yet classified).

Self Catering Accommodation

★★★ **Why-Not Motor Inn**, (HU), Previously Why-Not 23 Coon St, ☎ 07 4972 4222, fax 07 4972 5479, 6 units acc up to 6, [shwr, tlt, a/c, c/fan, tel, TV, clock radio, refrig, cook fac, elec frypan, toaster, blkts, linen, pillows], ldry, w/mach-fee, dryer-fee, iron, pool, bbq, c/park (undercover), cots-fee. **D** ♦♦ **$66**, ♦ **$8**, ch con, AE BC DC EFT MCH VI.

B&B's/Guest Houses

Auckland Hill Bed & Breakfast, (B&B), 15 Yarroon St, opposite Police Station, ☎ 07 4972 4907, fax 07 4972 7300, (2 stry), 6 rms [shwr, spa bath (1), tlt, hairdry, c/fan, clock radio, t/c mkg, refrig (1)], dryer, lounge (TV), ✕ (1), pool, bbq, c/park (undercover), non smoking flr (1). **BB** ♦ **$90**, ♦♦ **$110 - $125**, AE BC DC MC VI, (not yet classified).

GLASS HOUSE MOUNTAINS QLD 4518

Pop 500. (65km N Brisbane), See map on page 417, ref D5. Unusual & spectacular volcanic range, said to be the oldest on the continent. National Park, State Forestry Lookouts. Bowls, Bush Walking, Gem Fossicking, Scenic Drives.

Hotels/Motels

★★★☆ **Glass House Mountains Motel**, (M), 1116 Glass House Mountains Rd, (Old Bruce Hwy, 2km S of Beerwah PO, ☎ 07 5496 9900, fax 07 5496 9900, 10 units [shwr, tlt, hairdry (5), a/c-cool, a/c (2), c/fan, heat, elec blkts, tel, fax, TV, video (videos avail) (2), clock radio, CD (3), t/c mkg, refrig, cook fac (1), micro (4), toaster], ldry (incl comm microwave), lounge, ✕ (Mon-Thurs), pool, bbq, rm serv, dinner to unit, c/park (undercover), plygr, bowls, mini golf, cots, non smoking property. **RO $55 - $66**, ch con, AE BC DC EFT MC VI.

B&B's/Guest Houses

★★★★☆ **The Mackisons of Glasshouse**, (B&B), 33 Heritage Dve, 3km SE of PO, ☎ 07 5493 0118, fax 07 5493 0218, 2 rms [shwr, bath, tlt, hairdry, a/c (1), c/fan, tel, TV (1)], lounge (TV), ✕, spa (Heated), non smoking rms. **BB** ♦ **$85.80**, ♦♦ **$125.85 - $137.30**, BC MC VI.

★★★☆ **Glass House Mountains Bed & Breakfast**, (B&B), 76 Kings Rd, 65km N of Brisbane, ☎ 07 5493 0031, fax 07 5493 0443, 2 rms [hairdry, c/fan, TV, clock radio, t/c mkg, refrig, cook fac, micro, toaster], shwr, tlt, ldry, iron, iron brd, TV rm, pool (saltwater), bbq, non smoking property, non smoking rms. **BB** ♦♦ **$95**, BC MC VI.

GLENDEN QLD 4743

Pop 1,350. (1116km N Brisbane), See map on page 414, ref D5. Developed as service town for nearby Steaming Coal Mine. Ludwig Leichhardt passed through this area in 1845. Shopping centre & medical centre amongst town facilities.

Hotels/Motels

★★★ **Glenden Country Motor Inn**, (M), Ewan Dve, ☎ 07 4958 9288, fax 07 4958 9942, 20 units [shwr, tlt, hairdry (7), a/c, tel, TV, video-fee, clock radio, t/c mkg, refrig, mini bar], ldry, iron (7), iron brd (7), ✕ (Mon-Thurs), rm serv, dinner to unit, c/park (undercover), cots. **RO** ♦ **$82.50 - $104.50**, ♦♦ **$104.50 - $132**, ♦ **$10**, ch con, AE BC DC MC VI.

GOLD COAST - QLD

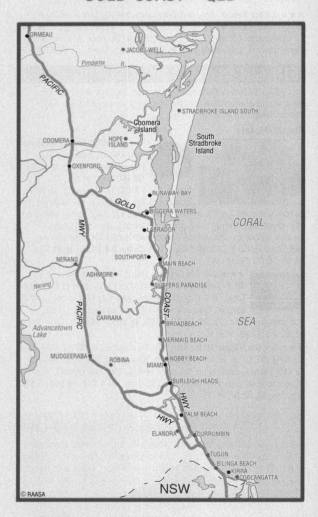

Before you travel

Before a trip have your vehicle serviced and checked over to ensure reliable motoring. There are some checks you can make yourself, generally the procedure can be found in the vehicle owners manual.

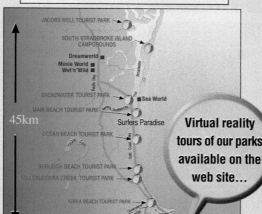

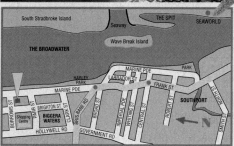

For Accommodation Booking information - see page 27

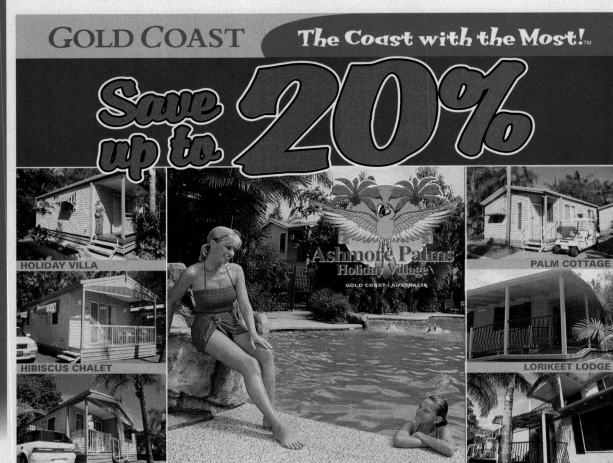

GOLD COAST

The Coast with the Most!™

Save up to 20%

HOLIDAY VILLA

HIBISCUS CHALET

FAMILY VILLA

Ashmore Palms Holiday Village
GOLD COAST · AUSTRALIA

PALM COTTAGE

LORIKEET LODGE

MACAW MANSION

Ashmore Palms offers your family more!

More Affordable

Holidaying at Ashmore Palms is now even more affordable! Simply mention your Automobile Association membership when making a reservation for accommodation and enjoy savings of up to 20%. During off peak times, you can take advantage of Ashmore Palms 7 Night Off Peak Specials (not subject to further discount). Each cabin is fully self-contained, featuring cooking facilities, air-conditioning (coin), ensuite, colour tv, private driveway and up to 3 bedrooms. Choose the cabin type that best suits your needs.

More Features

Ashmore Palms has an array of facilities. These include a large swimming lagoon, kids lagoon with mushroom fountains & shallow swim area (heated in winter), manmade rainforest walkway, full size tennis court, playground, barbecues, guest laundries, reception, tour desk, general store, South American Macaw parrots and more! During peak periods, take photographs with 2 tame Macaw parrots! Log on to Ashmore Palms' webcam for live photos of the lagoons.

You will soon discover why Ashmore Palms is a multi award winner, including the prestigious 1999 and 2000 Australian Tourism Awards for best "Budget Accommodation".

More Central

Only 8 minutes drive from Surfers Paradise and 8-12 minutes from most theme parks, Ashmore Palms is in a great, central location. Sea World, Movie World and Wet 'n Wild 12 mins, Dreamworld 18 mins. Close to restaurants, sporting venues, shops, entertainment, beaches and other tourist attractions. Walk to local shops, take-away food & public transport. Coach transfers to attractions available daily - ask for more information & prices.

WINNER
2000 AUSTRALIAN
TOURISM AWARDS
BUDGET
ACCOMMODATION

Ashmore Palms Holiday Village

71 Hinde St Ashmore 4214
Gold Coast · Queensland · Australia
For your "Coast with the Most" holiday, phone

Freecall 1800 065 222
(Australia only)

or (07) 5539 3222

Int'l Ph +61 7 5539 3222 • Int'l Fax +61 7 5597 1576
sales@ashmorepalms.com.au

www.ashmorepalms.com.au
Check out the new WebCam!

*Conditions apply: Automobile Club discount applies to nightly rates for first 2 persons. Surcharge of $20 per unit, per night applies during peak periods. Additional adults $9 each per night and children (3-13 yrs) $5 each per night. Discount does not apply to Off Peak Specials, linen hire or any other associated costs. Subject to change without notice.

24108AG

Rates may change. Check before booking.

GOLD COAST - ASHMORE QLD 4214

Pop 10,553. (74km S Brisbane), See map on page 417, ref E8. Suburb of Gold Coast. Golf, Shooting.

Self Catering Accommodation

★★★★★ **Royal Pines Resort**, (Apt), Resort, Ross St, 6km W of Surfers Parade, ☎ 07 5597 1111, fax 07 5597 2277, (Multi-stry), 330 apts (49 suites) acc up to 4, [shwr, bath, spa bath (47), tlt, hairdry, a/c, tel, TV, video, movie, clock radio, t/c mkg, refrig], lift, conv fac, ✉ (6), pool-heated, spa, 24hr reception, rm serv, c/park (undercover) (300), courtesy transfer, ☎, plygr, golf, gym, tennis (7), cots, non smoking flr (6). **RO ♦ $330 - $418, ♦♦ $330 - $418, Suite D $385**, ch con, Wildlife sanctuary, AE BC DC EFT JCB MC VI, ⚿.

★★★★★ **Royal Woods**, (HU), 16 Mulyan Place, 2km N Ashmore Plaza PO, ☎ 07 5597 0650, fax 07 5564 9833, 45 units acc up to 10, (1, 2 & 3 bedrm), [shwr, spa bath, tlt, a/c, cent heat, tel, TV, video-fee, movie, clock radio, t/c mkg, refrig, cook fac, micro, toaster, blkts, doonas, linen, pillows], w/mach, dryer, pool (outdoor), pool indoor heated, sauna, spa, bbq, secure park (undercover), gym, cots-fee. **RO ♦♦♦ $188 - $350**, weekly con, Min book applies, AE BC DC EFT MC VI.

★★★★☆ **Ashmore Palms Holiday Village**, (HU), 71 Hinde St, ☎ 07 5539 3222, fax 07 5597 1576, 51 units acc up to 6, (2 & 3 bedrm), [shwr, tlt, hairdry, a/c-cool-fee, c/fan, TV, clock radio, t/c mkg, refrig, cook fac, micro, toaster, blkts reqd-fee, linen reqd-fee, pillows], iron, iron brd. **D ♦♦ $100 - $120, ◊ $10**, ch con, Min book applies, AE BC DC EFT MC VI, ⚿.

★★★★☆ **(Apartment Section)**, (2 stry), 7 apts acc up to 6, (2 bedrm), [shwr, spa bath, tlt, hairdry, a/c-cool, c/fan, TV, video, clock radio, t/c mkg, refrig, cook fac, micro, toaster, blkts, linen, pillows], iron, iron brd. **D ♦♦ $190 - $210, ◊ $10**, ch con.

★★★☆ **(Villa Section)**, 21 villas acc up to 5, (2 bedrm), [shwr, tlt, a/c-cool, c/fan, TV, clock radio, refrig, cook fac ltd, micro, toaster, blkts reqd-fee, linen reqd-fee, pillows], iron, iron brd. **D ♦♦ $88 - $108, ◊ $10**, ch con, Min book applies.

GOLD COAST - BIGGERA WATERS QLD 4216

Pop 4,843. (73km S Brisbane), See map on page 417, ref E8. Suburb at northern end of Gold Coast, located near the Broadwater. Boat ramps for Broadwater. Boating, Fishing, Scenic Drives, Swimming, Water Skiing, Wind Surfing.

Hotels/Motels

★★★☆ **Sunburst Motel**, (M), 37 Brisbane Rd, 250m from Broadwater, ☎ 07 5537 9000, fax 07 5563 9249, 11 units [shwr, tlt, hairdry, a/c, c/fan, heat, TV, clock radio, t/c mkg, refrig, cook fac ltd, micro, toaster], pool (salt water), bbq, rm serv, meals avail (breakfast-on request), ☎, cots-fee, non smoking units (7). **RO ♦ $50 - $70, ♦♦ $65 - $85, ◊ $20**, ch con, AE BC EFT MC VI.

Self Catering Accommodation

★★★★☆ **Atrium Resort**, (HU), Cnr Marine Pde & Taylor St, ☎ 07 5537 9466, fax 07 5537 8197, (Multi-stry), 66 units acc up to 6, (1 & 2 bedrm), [shwr, spa bath, tlt, c/fan, tel, TV (2), cable tv, clock radio, refrig, cook fac, micro, d/wash, ldry (in unit), blkts, linen, pillows], lift, dryer, rec rm, ✗ (BYO), pool (salt water), pool-heated (salt water heated), sauna, spa (2), bbq, kiosk (Licensed), secure park, gym, tennis, cots-fee. **D $95 - $180, ◊ $17.50, W $545 - $1,225, ◊ $120**, Min book applies, AE BC DC MC VI.

★★★★☆ **Pelican Cove**, (HU), Cnr Back & Burrows Sts, 300m E of PO, ☎ 07 5537 7001, fax 07 5537 7438, (Multi-stry gr fl), 65 units acc up to 6, [shwr, bath, tlt, fan (pedestal), heat, tel, cable tv, clock radio, refrig, cook fac, micro, d/wash, ldry (in unit), blkts, linen, pillows], dryer, iron, pool (saltwater) (2), pool-heated (1), spa (1 heated) (2), bbq (2), dinner to unit, secure park, mooring (pontoon avail.), tennis (half court), cots-fee. **D ♦♦ $83 - $134, ◊ $12, W ♦♦ $462, ◊ $84**, Min book applies, BC MC VI.

★★★★☆ **Royal Pacific Resort**, (HU), 488 Marine Pde, 4km N of Southport, ☎ 07 5529 2288, fax 07 5563 8486, (Multi-stry gr fl), 54 units acc up to 6, (Studio, 1 & 2 bedrm), [ensuite (14), shwr, bath, spa bath (5), tlt, c/fan, tel, cable tv, clock radio, t/c mkg, refrig, cook fac, micro, elec frypan, d/wash, toaster, ldry, blkts, linen, pillows], lift, dryer, iron, iron brd, rec rm, pool-heated (salt water), sauna, spa, bbq, secure park, gym, cots-fee. **D $90 - $176, ◊ $15**, Min book applies, BC MC VI.

Operator Comment: See advertisement on page 470.

PELICAN COVE
Holiday Apartments

Heated pool & spa

Free pay TV in your apartment

Gold Coast
Absolute Waterfront

★★★★☆ RATING

10 mins to Surfers, Theme Parks & Sanctuary Cove
From $462/week for 2 people (except school holidays)

YOUR UNIT CONTAINS
- Fully self contained 2 & 3 bedroom apartments with ensuite set in tranquil tropical gardens with private balconies
- Microwave and dishwasher
- Colour TV, Telephone (STD, ISD)
- Linen provided and changed weekly
- Internal laundry, Free Pay T.V. in your apartment

OUR LOCATION
- 100 metres to fabulous Broadwater (popular fishing, windsurfing and swimming)
- 10 minutes to Surfers & Theme parks & Sanctuary Cove
- 300 metres to nearest shopping centre
- 5 minutes to Australia Fair and Harbour Town

Cnr Back & Burrows Streets
Biggera Waters Qld 4216
Ph: 07 5537 7001 Fax: 07 5537 7438
Website: www.pelicancove.com.au

OUR FACILITIES
- 2 pools (1 heated) & 2 spas (1 heated)
- Underground parking & intercom
- 2 BBQ's with undercover entertaining area
- Boat ramp & pontoon
- 1/2 court tennis
- Discount on your tours & tickets and we refund due to illness, wet weather etc.
- Dial-a-meal service
- Video hire available
- Regular local bus service

PELICAN
C·O·V·E
HOLIDAY APARTMENTS

For your "Beautiful One Day, Perfect the Next" stay call 1800 354 025

24269AG

GOLD COAST

The Coast with the Most!™

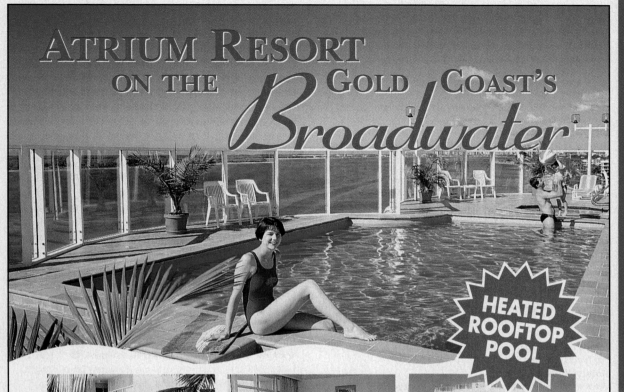
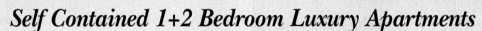

★★★★ **Bayview Beach on the Broadwater**, (HU), 418 Marine Pde, ☎ 07 5537 6770, fax 07 5537 8074, (Multi-stry), 22 units acc up to 6, [shwr, bath, tlt, fan, heat (16), tel, TV, refrig, cook fac, micro (20), d/wash (12), ldry (in unit), blkts, linen, pillows], lift, pool, spa, bbq, secure park, cots-fee. **D $164 - $185, W $638 - $924**, Min book applies, BC MC VI.

★★★★ **Runaway Cove**, (SA), 3/26 Back St. ☎ 07 5529 1000, fax 07 5571 4699, (Multi-stry gr fl), 6 serv apts acc up to 8, [ensuite, shwr, bath, tlt, fan, heat, tel, TV, clock radio, refrig, micro, d/wash, ldry (in unit)], dryer, pool, bbq, secure park, mooring, cots-fee. **D ♥♥ $90 - $125, ♥♥♥ $440 - $880**, ch con, Min book applies.

★★★★ **Windsurfer Resort**, (HU), 452 Marine Pde, 4km N of Southport, ☎ 07 5529 2300, fax 07 5529 2385, (Multi-stry gr fl), 39 units acc up to 4, (1 bedrm - One bedrm & split level townhouse units.), [shwr, tlt, a/c-cool, tel, TV, video-fee, clock radio, t/c mkg, refrig, cook fac, micro, toaster, ldry (in unit), blkts, linen, pillows], lift, dryer, iron, iron brd, rec rm, pool-heated, spa, bbq (covered), kiosk, secure park, cots-fee. **D $70 - $115.50, W $420 - $630**, Min book applies, BC MC VI.

★★★☆ **Broadwater Garden Village**, (HU), 490 Marine Pde, ☎ 07 5537 3969, fax 07 5537 3969, (Multi-stry), 15 units acc up to 4, (2 bedrm), [shwr, bath, tlt, fan (3), c/fan (12), TV, clock radio, refrig, cook fac, micro (15), d/wash (10), ldry (in unit), blkts, linen, pillows], dryer, pool, bbq, secure park, cots-fee. **D ♥♥♥ $225, W ♥♥♥♥ $385 - $750**, Min book applies.

GOLD COAST - BILINGA BEACH QLD 4225

Pop 1,125. (99km S Brisbane), See map on page 417, ref E8. Location of Coolangatta Airport. A southern suburb of Gold Coast. Joy flights, charters & sky diving.

Hotels/Motels

★★★★ **Bilinga Beach Resort**, (M), 281 Golden Four Dve, ☎ 07 5534 1241, fax 07 5534 1221, (2 stry gr fl), 16 units [shwr, tlt, a/c-cool, tel, TV, t/c mkg, refrig], pool, bbq, c/park(undercover), cots. **RO ♥ $60 - $150, ♥♥ $60 - $150, ◊ $15**, BC MC VI, ♿.

★★★★ **(Serviced Apartment Section)**, 6 serv apts [shwr, tlt, a/c, tel, TV, t/c mkg, refrig, cook fac], bbq, c/park (undercover), cots, ♿.

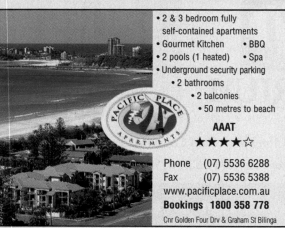

Self Catering Accommodation

★★★★☆ **Oceanside Resort**, (HU), 277 Golden Four Dve, 1.5 km S of Tugun PO☎ 07 5534 7000, fax 07 5598 3250, (Multi-stry gr fl), 13 units acc up to 8, [ensuite, shwr, bath, spa bath (6), tlt, a/c, tel, TV, video, clock radio, CD, refrig, cook fac, micro, elec frypan, d/wash, toaster, ldry (in unit), blkts, linen, pillows], lift, dryer, iron, pool, spa, bbq, secure park. **D ♥♥ $100 - $220, W ♥♥ $480 - $1,600**, BC MC VI.

★★★★☆ **Pacific Place**, (HU), 143 Golden Four Dve, ☎ 07 5536 6288, fax 07 5536 5388, (Multi-stry gr fl), 30 units acc up to 8, (2 & 3 bedrm), [ensuite, shwr, bath, tlt, hairdry, c/fan, heat, tel, TV, clock radio, refrig, cook fac, micro, d/wash, ldry (in unit), blkts, linen, pillows], dryer, iron, pool (salt water/1 heated) (2), spa, bbq, secure park, cots-fee. **D ♥♥ $130 - $230, ◊ $10, W ♥♥ $480 - $980**, BC EFT MC VI.

Other Accommodation

★★ **Coolangatta YHA**, (Lodge), 230 Coolangatta Rd, ☎ 07 5536 7644, fax 07 5599 5436, (2 stry gr fl), 15 rms acc up to 8, shwr, tlt, ldry, rec rm, lounge (TV), pool, cook fac, t/c mkg shared (free tea/coffee), refrig, bbq, courtesy transfer, ☎. **BLB ♥ $20, ♥♥ $105**, ch con.

GOLD COAST - BROADBEACH QLD 4218

Pop 3,375. (81km S Brisbane), See map on page 417, ref E8. Suburb of Gold Coast, with extensive variety of restaurants & shopping facilities.

Hotels/Motels

★★★★★ **Conrad Jupiters**, (LH), Broadbeach Island, ☎ 07 5592 1133, fax 07 5592 8219, (Multi-stry), 609 rms (31 suites) [shwr, bath, tlt, hairdry, a/c, tel, TV, clock radio, t/c mkg, refrig, mini bar], lift, conv fac, night club, ✉ (Mon - Sun) (6), bar (9), pool-heated, sauna, spa, 24hr reception, rm serv, c/park (undercover), gym, squash, tennis, cots, non smoking flr (3). **RO ♥ $175, ♥♥ $175, ◊ $38, Suite D $712 - $1,095**, AE BC DC JCB MC VI, ♿.

AAA TOURISM *Special Rates* ★★★★☆ **Grand Mercure Broadbeach**, (LH), 81 Surf Pde, direct access to beach - adjoins Oasis shop centre, ☎ 07 5592 2250, fax 07 5592 3747, (Multi-stry), 298 rms (5 suites) [shwr, bath, spa bath (23), tlt, hairdry, a/c, tel, TV, movie, clock radio, t/c mkg, refrig, mini bar], lift, conv fac, ✉ (2), bar, pool-heated, sauna, spa, 24hr reception, rm serv, c/park (undercover), gym, tennis (2), cots, non smoking rms (112). **RO $260, Suite D $365 - $710**, ch con, AE BC DC EFT JCB MC VI, ♿.

★★★☆ **Browns at Broadbeach**, (M), Previously Lukanda Motor Inn, 2591 Gold Coast Hwy, ☎ 07 5539 9292, fax 07 5537 5909, (2 stry gr fl), 17 units [shwr, spa bath (3), tlt, fan, TV, clock radio (6), t/c mkg, refrig, cook fac (11)], ldry, pool, spa, bbq, c/park (undercover), ☎, cots-fee. **RO ♥ $44 - $90, ♥♥ $59 - $99**, BC MC VI.

★★★☆ **Hi Ho Motel Apartments**, (M), 2 Queensland Ave, cnr Old Burleigh Rd, ☎ 07 5538 2777, fax 07 5538 9280, (Multi-stry), 20 units (1 & 2 bedrm), [shwr, bath, tlt, hairdry, fan, heat, tel, fax, TV, clock radio, t/c mkg, refrig, cook fac, micro], lift, ldry, w/mach, ✗ (Tues-Sat), pool-heated (solar), spa, secure park, cots. **RO ♥ $78 - $90, ♥♥ $78 - $90, ♥♥♥ $97 - $110, ◊ $10**, AE BC MC VI.

★★★☆ **Montego**, (M), 2671 Gold Coast Hwy, ☎ 07 5539 9956, fax 07 5538 1815, (2 stry gr fl), 25 units [shwr, tlt, a/c-cool (24), fan, heat, TV, clock radio, t/c mkg, refrig, micro (18)], pool (salt water), bbq, ☎, non smoking units (4). **RO ♥ $55 - $120, ♥♥ $55 - $130, ◊ $15 - $20**, AE BC DC EFT MC VI.

★★★ **Golden Rainbow**, (M), 2689 Gold Coast Hwy, ☎ 07 5570 3400, fax 07 5538 5603, (2 stry gr fl), 31 units (7 suites) [shwr, tlt, a/c, c/fan, tel, TV, clock radio, t/c mkg, refrig, ldry], pool, cots-fee. **D ♥ $50 - $90, ♥♥ $66 - $90, ♥♥♥ $85 - $140, ◊ $20**, ch con, BC MC VI.

★★ **Broadbeach Central Convention Motel**, (M), Previously Golden Nugget Motor Lodge 2733 Gold Coast Hwy, ☎ 07 5539 9495, (2 stry), 12 units [shwr, tlt, a/c-cool, heat, elec blkts, TV, t/c mkg, refrig], pool, c/park (undercover) (2), ☎, cots. **RO ♥ $44 - $95, ♥♥ $58 - $95, ◊ $15 - $25**, ch con, AE BC MC VI.

Self Catering Accommodation

★★★★★ **Belle Maison**, (HU), 129 Surf Parade, ☎ 07 5570 9200, fax 07 5570 9299, (Multi-stry), 40 units acc up to 7, (1, 2 & 3 bedrm), [ensuite, shwr, bath, spa bath (6), tlt, a/c-cool (10), fan (20), c/fan, tel, TV, radio, CD, refrig, cook fac, micro, elec frypan, d/wash, toaster, ldry (in unit), blkts, linen, pillows], lift, dryer, iron, iron brd, rec rm, pool-heated, sauna (2), spa (1 indoor & 1 outdoor) (2), bbq (covered) (2), c/park (undercover), secure park, gym, tennis (floodlit) (2), cots-fee. **W $750 - $2,380**, AE BC MC VI.

★★★★★ **Phoenician Resort Apartments**, (HU), 24 Queensland Ave, ☎ 07 5585 8888, fax 07 5585 8880, (Multi-stry gr fl), 195 units acc up to 6, (1 & 2 bedrm), [ensuite, shwr, bath, tlt, hairdry, tel, cable tv, video-fee, clock radio, CD, t/c mkg, refrig, micro, elec frypan, d/wash, toaster, ldry, blkts, linen, pillows], lift, dryer, iron, iron brd, rec rm, ✗ (breakfast only), pool-heated (indoor), sauna, spa, bbq, secure park, gym, cots-fee. **D ♥♥ $120 - $220, ♦ $25, W $847 - $2,198**, AE BC DC EFT MC VI.

★★★★☆ **Aruba Beach**, (HU), Cr Surf Pde & Queensland Ave, ☎ 07 5527 5933, fax 07 5527 5966, (Multi-stry), 64 units acc up to 12, (1 & 3 bedrm Studio), [shwr, tlt, hairdry (on application), c/fan, tel, TV, clock radio, refrig, cook fac, micro, d/wash, toaster, blkts, linen, pillows], pool, spa (communal), secure park, gym, cots-fee. **D $92 - $302**, AE BC DC MC VI.

★★★★☆ **Aruba Sands**, (HU), 11 - 17 Philip Ave, ☎ 07 5538 8155, fax 07 5538 8977, (Multi-stry), 46 units acc up to 6, (Studio, 1 & 2 bedrm), [ensuite (3), shwr, tlt, hairdry (on application), a/c, c/fan, tel, TV, clock radio, micro, d/wash, toaster, ldry, blkts, linen, pillows], dryer, iron, iron brd, pool, spa, bbq, secure park, gym, cots-fee. **D $92 - $206**, AE BC DC MC VI.

★★★★☆ **Aruba Surf**, (HU), 20 - 26 Anne Ave, ☎ 07 5539 0299, fax 07 5526 7066, (Multi-stry), 41 units acc up to 6, (Studio, 1 & 2 bedrm), [ensuite, shwr, tlt, hairdry (on application), a/c, c/fan, refrig, cook fac, cook fac ltd, micro, d/wash, ldry, blkts, linen, pillows], dryer, pool, spa (communal), bbq, secure park, gym, cots-fee. **D ♥♥ $78 - $180, ♦ $20**, AE BC DC MC VI.

BROADBEACH
EVERYTHING UNDER THE SUN

Broadbeach everything under the sun

FREE CALL 1800 785 364
www.broadbeachgoldcoast.com

The Fun Starts Here...

What's so special about Broadbeach? Basically, it has it all, and that makes it simply irresistible to locals and tourists alike. When thinking of Broadbeach, most people think of sun, sand, sparkling blue ocean, sumptuous cuisine, quality shopping and the chance of a flutter at the Casino. In recent years Broadbeach has acquired its own Gold Coast identity, one which allows visitors to enjoy all the very best of a cosmopolitan centre without losing the family holiday charm.

The Accommodation... From international hotels and luxury apartments through to budget units and motels, Broadbeach has the place for everybody. And one of the great bonuses of Broadbeach is that all the area's attractions are within easy walking distance.

The Beach... Broadbeach boasts one of the most beautiful beaches on the Gold Coast, if not Australia. The surf waves of Kurrawa Beach are spectacular, and best of all it is fully patrolled and safe for the family.

The Food... Broadbeach is the dining hub of the Gold Coast. An exciting range of alfresco restaurants, cafes and brasseries have turned Broadbeach into a truly cosmopolitan destination.

The Fun... There is well and truly enough to keep you occupied in Broadbeach itself - shop at Pacific Fair; visit Conrad Jupiters; browse the Sunday beachfront markets; enjoy a range of nightspots and heaps more. Discover the excitement and family atmosphere of Broadbeach - the dining and entertainment hub of the Gold Coast.

Beach Haven at Broadbeach

★★★★☆ Rating. Position, position. Beach and parklands. 300 shops. 62 restaurants. Jupiters Casino, Pacific Fair just a short walk. 32 levels of apartments with spectacular views from private balconies. Security parking, two pools, three spas, heated indoor pool, saunas, child wading pool, two full-sized tennis courts, games room and barbecues set in tropical grounds.

1 Albert Ave, Broadbeach Qld 4218
Phone (07) 5570 3888 Fax (07) 5570 3175
Email: bhaven@bhaven.com.au
Website: www.bhaven.com.au

Santa Anne by the Sea

★★★★☆ Rating. One bedroom and two storey holiday apartments for couples. Positioned 150m from beach, boardwalks, shops, cafes and Casino. Relax in the sauna, spa or pool set amongst tropical gardens. Lifts to all suites and security parking. All units have queen-size beds, sofa beds, television, kitchen and laundries. We also feature a comprehensive tour desk.

15 Anne Ave, Broadbeach Qld 4218
Phone (07) 5538 5455 Fax (07) 5538 5155
Email: santaanne@bigpond.com
Website: www.santaanne.com.au

La Grande

★★★★☆ Rating. The Mediterranean influence of La Grande Apartments offers a variety of spacious two and three bed-room fully equipped apartments adjacent to the patrolled golden sandy beach. With two bathrooms, laundry, cable television and balcony. Enjoy a barbecue by our heated pool, relax in the sauna or spa, work out in the gym or just stroll through the beautiful tropical gardens to the beach.

126 Old Burleigh Road, Broadbeach Qld 4218
Phone (07) 5592 5350 Fax (07) 5592 5130
Email: info@lagrande.com.au
Website: www.lagrande.com.au

South Pacific Plaza

★★★★☆ Rating. Opposite patrolled beach just on Oasis Shopping Resort plus monorail stop to Jupiters Casino. Sixty apartments on 16 levels. One and two bedrooms. All have ocean views, fully-equipped kitchens, microwave, ensuite, balcony, ceiling fans, hair dryer, phone, colour TV/Foxtel, separate laundry, security parking, sauna, full tennis, barbecue, heated spa.

157 Old Burleigh Road, Broadbeach Qld 4218
Phone (07) 5538 3911 Fax (07) 5592 0170
Email: sthpacplaza@bigpond.com

Markham Court

Set amongst lush tropical gardens and featuring two and three bedroom luxury units with air-conditioning or ceiling fans, fully-equipped kitchen and laundry facilities. Heated pool and spa and two barbecue areas. Central to the beach, Jupiters Casino, Pacific Fair, Oasis Shopping Centre and all restaurants.

36 Australia Ave, Broadbeach Qld 4218
Phone (07) 5592 3111 Fax (07) 5592 1424
Email: markhamcourt@hotmail.com
Website: www.broadbeachgoldcoast.com

Surf Parade Resort

★★★★ Rating. Fully self-contained Mediterranean style one bedroom apartments with in-room spa and wide curved balconies. Resort facilities include heated pool and spa, full size tennis court, gymnasium, sauna and barbecue. 200m to the beach and security parking. You'll want to stay forever!

210-218 Surf Pde, Broadbeach Qld 4218
Phone (07) 5538 8863 Fax (07) 5538 8862
Email: surfpde@onthenet.com.au
Website: www.surf-parade-resort.com.au

Ocean Royale

★★★★☆ Rating. Fifty metres to patrolled beaches and a short walk to shops, restaurants and casino. Fully self-contained one and two bedroom apartments all with private balconies and ocean views plus a three bedroom penthouse with own pool and sauna. Facilities include heated pool and spa, sauna, outdoor pool, barbecue area, half-size tennis court and security parking.

4 Britannia Ave, Broadbeach Qld 4218
Phone (07) 5570 1144 Fax (07) 5592 0703
Email: info@oceanroyale.com.au
Website: www.oceanroyale.com.au

The Pacific Resort Broadbeach

★★★★☆ Rating. Enjoy your holiday in uniformly and fashionably furnished apartments, all with ocean views, balconies, ceiling fans, fully equipped kitchens, washing machine and dryer. Your building faces the north east, the preferred aspect on the Gold Coast.

2 Albert Ave, Broadbeach Qld 4218
Phone 1800 074 511 Fax (07) 5570 2021
Email: pacificresort@bigpond.com
Website: www.pacificresort.com.au

Rates may change. Check before booking.

AAA TOURISM *Special Rates*

★★★★☆ **Beach Haven**, (HU), 1 Albert Ave, ☎ 07 5570 3888, fax 07 5570 3175, (Multi-stry), 147 units acc up to 6, (1 & 2 bedrm), [shwr, bath, tlt, c/fan, heat, tel, TV, clock radio, t/c mkg, refrig, cook fac, d/wash, ldry (in unit), blkts, linen, pillows], lift, rec rm, pool (3), pool indoor heated, wading pool, sauna, spa (3), bbq, secure park, tennis (2), cots-fee. **D ♦♦ $140 - $258, ♦ $25, W ♦♦ $980 - $1,806**, Min book applies, AE BC DC MC VI.

★★★★☆ **Boulevard North**, (HU), 1 Britannia Ave, ☎ 07 5538 7666, fax 07 5592 1060, (Multi-stry), 45 units acc up to 5, (1 & 2 bedrm), [shwr, bath (40), tlt, tel, TV, refrig, cook fac, micro, d/wash, ldry (in unit), blkts, linen, pillows], lift, pool-heated, sauna, spa, bbq, c/park (undercover), tennis. **D $145 - $275, W $700 - $1,400**, Min book applies, BC MC VI.

★★★★☆ **Capricornia Apartments**, (HU), 121 Surf Pde, 200m from beach, ☎ 07 5592 4252, fax 07 5592 4250, (Multi-stry), 24 units acc up to 6, (1, 2 & 3 bedrm), [shwr, bath, tlt, TV, video, refrig, cook fac, micro, d/wash, ldry (in unit), blkts, linen, pillows], lift, w/mach, dryer, iron, iron brd, rec rm, pool-heated, sauna, spa, bbq (covered) (2), secure park, tennis, cots-fee. **RO $640 - $1,628**.

★★★★☆ **Diamond Beach Resort**, (HU), 16 Alexandra Ave, ☎ 07 5570 0000, fax 07 5570 2222, (Multi-stry gr fl), 164 units acc up to 7, (1, 2 & 3 bedrm), [shwr, bath, spa bath (2), tlt, c/fan, heat, tel, TV, clock radio, refrig, cook fac, micro, d/wash, ldry (in unit)], dryer, iron, rec rm, pool (1 heated) (2), spa, bbq, kiosk, c/park (undercover), secure park, cots-fee. **RO $143 - $253, W $748 - $1,533**, BC MC VI.

★★★★☆ **Island Beach Resort**, (HU), 9 Margaret Avenue, ☎ 07 5592 4112, fax 07 5592 4550, (Multi-stry gr fl), 29 units acc up to 6, (1 & 2 bedrm), [ensuite, shwr, tlt, a/c-cool, TV, video-fee, clock radio, refrig, micro, d/wash, toaster, ldry, blkts, linen, pillows], dryer, iron, iron brd, pool-heated (saltwater), bbq, secure park, cots-fee. **RO ♦♦ $80 - $110, W ♦♦ $560 - $770**, ch con, AE BC DC EFT MC VI.

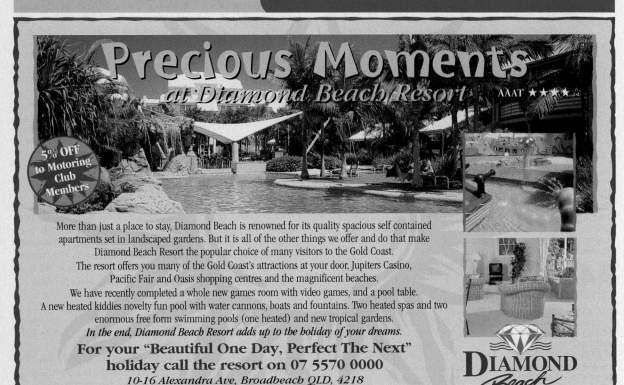

★★★★☆ **La Grande Luxury Apartments**, (HU), 126 Old Burleigh Rd, ☎ 07 5592 5350, fax 07 5592 5130, 30 units acc up to 6, (2 & 3 bedrm), [shwr, bath (hip), tlt, c/fan, tel, cable tv, video-fee, refrig, cook fac, micro, d/wash, ldry (in unit), blkts, linen, pillows], dryer, iron, pool-heated (salt water), sauna, spa, bbq, secure park, gym, cots-fee. **W $850 - $2,650**, BC MC VI.

★★★★☆ **Neptune Resort**, (Apt), 32 Surf Parade, opposite Casino 200m SW of Broadbeach surf beach, ☎ 07 5592 3555, fax 07 5592 3250, (Multi-stry gr fl), 116 apts acc up to 6, [shwr, bath, spa bath (50), tlt, hairdry, a/c-cool, elec blkts, tel, TV, video-fee, clock radio, refrig, mini bar, cook fac, elec frypan, d/wash, ldry (in unit), blkts, linen, pillows], lift, dryer, iron, iron brd, cafe, bar, pool-heated (salt water), sauna, spa, bbq (covered), secure park, gym, tennis (floodlit), cots. **BB $130 - $200, W $660 - $1,085**, ch con, AE BC DC MC VI.

★★★★☆ **Ocean Royale**, (HU), 4 Britannia Ave, Cnr Old Burleigh Rd, ☎ 07 5570 1144, fax 07 5592 0703, (Multi-stry), 46 units acc up to 7, (1 & 2 bedrm), [shwr, bath, tlt, hairdry, fan, c/fan, heat, tel, TV, clock radio, t/c mkg, refrig, cook fac, micro, d/wash, ldry (in unit), blkts, linen, pillows], lift, pool (salt water), pool-heated (indoor), sauna, spa (indoor), bbq, secure park, tennis (half court), cots-fee. **W $679 - $1,435**.

★★★★☆ **Pacific Resort Broadbeach**, (HU), 2 Albert Ave, ☎ 07 5570 1311, fax 07 5570 2021, (Multi-stry), 45 units acc up to 6, (1 & 2 bedrm), [shwr, bath, tlt, hairdry, fan, heat, tel, TV, clock radio, t/c mkg, refrig, cook fac, micro, ldry], lift, iron, pool, sauna, spa, bbq, secure park (undercover), tennis (half court), cots. **Suite D ♦ $121 - $225, ⑨ $20 - $75**, AE BC DC MC VI.

★★★★☆ **San Mateo on Broadbeach**, (Apt), Cnr Old Burleigh Rd & 2nd Av, ☎ 07 5561 0444, fax 07 5561 0445, (Multi-stry gr fl), 20 apts acc up to 8, [ensuite, shwr, tlt, a/c (5), c/fan, tel, TV, video (1)-fee, clock radio, refrig, micro, elec frypan, d/wash, toaster, ldry, blkts, linen, pillows], dryer, iron, iron brd, pool-heated (saltwater), spa, bbq, secure park, cots-fee. **W $492 - $1,400**, ch con, Min book applies, BC EFT MC VI.

★★★★☆ **Santa Anne By The Sea**, (HU), 15 Anne Ave, ☎ 07 5538 5455, fax 07 5538 5155, (Multi-stry gr fl), 18 units acc up to 5, (Studio & 1 bedrm), [shwr, spa bath (3), tlt, hairdry, a/c-cool (14), a/c (13), fan, tel, TV, video-fee, clock radio, refrig, cook fac ltd, micro, elec frypan, d/wash, toaster, ldry, blkts, linen, pillows], lift, dryer, iron, iron brd, pool, sauna, spa, bbq, secure park (covered), cots-fee. **D $65 - $153, W $455 - $1,071**, Min book applies, AE BC EFT MC VI.

★★★★☆ **South Pacific Plaza**, (HU), 157 Old Burleigh Rd, ☎ 07 5538 3911, fax 07 5592 0170, (Multi-stry), 60 units acc up to 6, (1 & 2 bedrm), [shwr, bath, tlt, hairdry, c/fan, tel, cable tv, refrig, cook fac, micro, d/wash (24), ldry (in unit), blkts, linen, pillows], lift, pool-heated, sauna, spa, secure park, tennis, cots-fee. **RO $155 - $228, W $784 - $1,489**, AE BC DC EFT JCB MC VI.

★★★★☆ **Talisman**, (HU), 67 Broadbeach Blvd, ☎ 07 5592 0100, (Multi-stry), 40 units (1 & 2 bedrm), [ensuite, shwr, bath, tlt, tel, cable tv, clock radio, refrig, cook fac, micro, elec frypan, d/wash, ldry (in unit), blkts, linen, pillows], lift, pool-heated, sauna (2), spa, bbq, secure park, tennis, cots-fee. **RO ♦♦ $145 - $210, W $1,475**, AE BC MC VI.

★★★★☆ **Victoria Square Apartments**, (HU), 15 Victoria Ave, ☎ 07 5592 1794, fax 07 5570 1184, (Multi-stry), 26 units acc up to 5, [ensuite, shwr, bath, tlt, a/c (5), c/fan, tel, cable tv, video-fee, clock radio, refrig, cook fac, micro, d/wash, ldry (in unit), blkts, linen, pillows], lift, dryer, iron, pool (salt water), sauna, spa, bbq, secure park, gym, cots-fee. **RO $120 - $440, W $840 - $3,080**, Min book applies, AE BC DC JCB MC VI.

★★★★ **Boulevard Towers**, (HU), 45 Broadbeach Blvd, ☎ 07 5538 8555, fax 07 5592 6427, (Multi-stry gr fl), 44 units acc up to 5, (1, 2 & 3 bedrm), [shwr, bath, tlt, c/fan, heat, tel, TV, video-fee, refrig, cook fac, micro, d/wash, ldry (in unit), blkts, linen, pillows], lift, pool, pool indoor heated, sauna, spa, bbq, secure park, tennis (half court), cots-fee. **D ♦♦ $85 - $127, ⑨ $20, W ♦♦ $595 - $896, ⑨ $140**, AE BC DC MC VI.

★★★★ **Jubilee Views**, (SA), 16 Jubilee Ave, 3km S Surfers Paradise, ☎ 07 5531 7335, fax 07 5538 7114, (Multi-stry), 12 serv apts acc up to 6, (2 & 3 bedrm), [shwr, bath, tlt, heat, TV, video-fee, clock radio, refrig, cook fac, micro, elec frypan, d/wash, toaster, ldry (in unit)], dryer, iron, pool (salt water), bbq, secure park, cots-fee. **W $490 - $1,320**, Min book applies, BC MC VI.

★★★★ **Portobello Beachside**, (HU), 2607 Gold Coast Hwy, ☎ 07 5538 7355, fax 07 5592 5219, (Multi-stry gr fl), 43 units acc up to 5, (1 & 2 bedrm), [ensuite (8), shwr, spa bath (8), tlt, c/fan, tel, TV, video-fee, clock radio, refrig, cook fac, micro, d/wash (8), toaster, ldry (in unit), blkts, linen, pillows], dryer, iron, iron brd, rec rm, pool-heated (salt water heated), spa, bbq (covered), dinner to unit, secure park, cots-fee. **D ♦ $65 - $129, ♦♦♦♦ $97 - $185, ⑨ $15**, BC MC VI.

★★★☆ **Barbados Holiday Apartments**, (HU), 12 Queensland Ave, ☎ 07 5570 1166, fax 07 5570 1894, (Multi-stry), 12 units (1 & 2 bedrm), [shwr, bath, tlt, c/fan (13), heat, tel, TV, clock radio, refrig, cook fac, d/wash, ldry (in unit), blkts, linen, pillows], lift, pool, sauna, spa, bbq, secure park, cots-fee. **RO ♦♦ $100 - $135, W ♦♦ $450 - $950**, Min book applies, BC MC VI.

★★★☆ **Broadbeach Central Holiday Units**, (HU), 18 Philip Ave, 6km S Surfers Paradise, ☎ 07 5592 6322, fax 07 5592 6323, (Multi-stry gr fl), 12 units acc up to 8, (1, 2 & 3 bedrm), [ensuite (2), shwr, bath (6), tlt, c/fan, tel, TV, video (1), clock radio, refrig, micro, ldry (in unit), blkts, linen, pillows], pool, bbq, secure park, cots-fee. **D $95 - $190, W $390 - $1,195**, BC MC VI.

★★★☆ **Broadbeach Motor Inn Apartments**, (SA), 2651 Gold Coast Hwy, ☎ 07 5570 1899, fax 07 5538 2602, (Multi-stry), 42 serv apts (12 suites) acc up to 4, [shwr, tlt, hairdry, c/fan, tel, cable tv, refrig, cook fac, micro], lift, ldry, pool, spa, bbq, secure park, plygr, mini golf. D ♦♦ $85 - $125, W ♦♦ $590 - $906, Suite D ♦♦♦♦ $704 - $1,198, AE BC MC VI.

★★★☆ **Grangewood Court Apartments**, (HU), Cnr Second Ave & Surf Pde, ☎ 07 5538 7782, fax 07 5538 7787, (Multi-stry gr fl), 14 units (2 & 3 bedrm), [shwr, bath (6), tlt, fan, heat, cable tv, refrig, cook fac, micro, d/wash, ldry (in unit), blkts, linen, pillows], rec rm, pool, spa, secure park. RO ♦♦ $385 - $1,350, Min book applies.

★★★☆ **Jadon Place**, (HU), 31 Hooker Blvd, Cnr Sunshine Blvd, ☎ 07 5572 3288, fax 07 5526 1230, (2 stry gr fl), 15 units acc up to 6, (1 & 2 bedrm), [shwr, tlt, fan, heat, tel, TV, clock radio, t/c mkg, refrig, cook fac, micro, ldry (in unit), blkts, linen, pillows], pool-heated (solar), spa, bbq, c/park (undercover), plygr, tennis (half court), cots-fee. RO ♦♦ $427 - $602, Min book applies.

★★★☆ **Le Lavandou Holiday Apartments**, (HU), 22 Jubilee Ave, ☎ 07 5539 0244, fax 07 5539 0244, (Multi-stry gr fl), 12 units acc up to 4, (2 bedrm), [shwr, bath, tlt, c/fan, tel, TV, video-fee, refrig, cook fac, micro, d/wash, ldry (in unit), blkts, linen, pillows], dryer, iron, pool (salt water), bbq, secure park, cots-fee. W $420 - $900, Min book applies.

★★★☆ **Mardi Gras Holiday Apartments**, (HU), 2755 Gold Coast Hwy, ☎ 07 5531 7522, fax 07 5592 0307, (Multi-stry gr fl), 24 units acc up to 6, (1 & 2 bedrm), [shwr, tlt, fan, heat, tel, fax, TV, clock radio, refrig, cook fac, micro, ldry (in unit), blkts, linen, pillows], dryer, iron, iron brd, pool, spa, bbq, secure park. D $90 - $135, W $385 - $970, BC MC VI.

★★★☆ **Markham Court**, (HU), 36 Australia Ave, ☎ 07 5592 3111, fax 07 5592 1424, 47 units (2 & 3 bedrm), [ensuite, shwr, bath, spa bath, tlt, a/c-cool (some), c/fan, tel, cable tv, clock radio, refrig, cook fac, micro, elec frypan, d/wash, toaster, ldry, blkts, linen, pillows], dryer, iron, iron brd, pool-heated, bbq, secure park, cots-fee. RO $525 - $1,375, BC MC VI.

★★★☆ **Old Burleigh Court Holiday Apartments**, (SA), 117 Old Burleigh Rd, ☎ 07 5570 2211, fax 07 5570 2516, (Multi-stry gr fl), 18 serv apts acc up to 6, (2 bedrm), [ensuite, shwr, bath, tlt, c/fan, heat, tel, TV, video-fee, clock radio, refrig, cook fac, micro, elec frypan, d/wash, ldry (in unit)], dryer, pool-heated, spa, secure park, cots-fee. W $510 - $1,000, BC MC VI.

★★★☆ **Queensleigh Holiday Apartments**, (HU), Cnr Queensland Ave & Old Burleigh Rd, ☎ 07 5538 4831, fax 07 5538 4007, (Multi-stry), 13 units acc up to 4, [shwr, tlt, tel, TV, clock radio, refrig, cook fac, micro, d/wash, ldry (in unit), blkts, linen, pillows], lift, pool, bbq, secure park, cots-fee. W $490 - $950.

★★★☆ **Sandpiper Holiday Apartments**, (HU), 155 Old Burleigh Rd, ☎ 07 5592 0144, fax 07 5592 1540, (Multi-stry gr fl), 46 units acc up to 6, (1, 2 & 3 bedrm), [shwr, bath (24), tlt, fan, tel, TV, movie, radio, refrig, cook fac, micro, d/wash (22), ldry (in unit), blkts, linen, pillows], lift, pool-heated, spa, bbq, secure park, cots-fee. D ♦♦ $110 - $220, ◊ $22 - $33, W ♦♦ $520 - $1,560, ◊ $88, Min book applies, BC EFT MC VI.

★★★☆ **Surfers Fairways Resort**, (HU), 1 Fairway Dve, Clear Island Waters, ☎ 07 5575 2533, fax 07 5578 5288, (Multi-stry), 9 units acc up to 4, (1 & 2 bedrm), [shwr, tlt, fan, heat, tel, TV, refrig, cook fac, d/wash, ldry (in unit), blkts, linen, pillows], lift, pool-heated, sauna, tennis, cots-fee. D ♦♦ $100 - $130, ◊ $10 - $20, W ♦♦ $450 - $550, ◊ $30 - $50, BC MC VI.

★★★ **Diana Motor Inn**, (HU), 56 Surf Pde, ☎ 07 5531 7508, fax 07 5531 7508, (Multi-stry gr fl), 10 units acc up to 4, (1 & 2 bedrm), [shwr, bath, tlt, fan, c/fan, heat, TV, refrig, cook fac, ldry (in unit), blkts, linen, pillows], pool, bbq, c/park (undercover). D ♦♦ $85 - $125, ◊ $20 - $25, W ♦♦ $385 - $850.

★★☆ **King Tide**, (HU), 65 Broadbeach Boulevard, ☎ 07 5531 7124, fax 07 5531 7124, (Multi-stry), 22 units acc up to 6, (2 & 3 bedrm), [shwr, bath, tlt, fan, TV, clock radio, refrig, cook fac, micro, ldry (in unit), blkts, linen, pillows], pool-heated, bbq, secure park, cots-fee. D $90 - $100, W $420 - $770.

Pop 6,430. (90km S Brisbane), See map on page 417, ref E8. A suburb of Gold Coast. Bowls, Croquet, Golf, Scenic Drives, Squash, Surfing, Swimming, Tennis, Water Skiing.

Hotels/Motels

★★★★ **Fifth Avenue**, (M), 1953 Gold Coast Hwy, Cnr 5th Ave, ☎ 07 5535 3588, fax 07 5535 0813, (2 stry gr fl), 38 units [shwr, spa bath (10), tlt, hairdry, a/c-cool, a/c (20), tel, cable tv, clock radio, t/c mkg, refrig, mini bar, cook fac (1)], ldry, conv fac, ⊠ (Mon to Sat), pool (salt water), 24hr reception, rm serv, c/park (undercover). RO $99 - $175, ch con, AE BC DC MC MP VI.

★★★★ **Outrigger Resort Gold Coast**, (M), 2007 Gold Coast Hwy, ☎ 07 5535 1111, fax 07 5576 3370, (Multi-stry gr fl), 68 units [shwr, bath, tlt, a/c-cool, heat, tel, TV, clock radio, t/c mkg, refrig], lift, ldry, conv fac, ⊠ (Mon-Sat), pool, spa, 24hr reception, rm serv, secure park, cots-fee. RO ♦ $75 - $126.50, ◊ $12.10, AE BC DC JCB MC VI, ♿.

★★★☆ **Burleigh International Motor Inn**, (M), 1896 Gold Coast Hwy, 500m S of Miami PO, ☎ 07 5535 0033, fax 07 5535 2044, (2 stry gr fl), 21 units [shwr, tlt, a/c-cool (5), c/fan, TV, clock radio, t/c mkg, refrig, cook fac ltd (3)], ldry, pool (salt water), bbq, cots-fee. RO ♦ $50 - $90, ♦♦ $60 - $105, ◊ $15, ch con, AE BC DC EFT MC VI, ♿.

★★☆ **Casino**, (M), 1761 Gold Coast Hwy, ☎ 07 5535 7133, fax 07 5576 8099, (2 stry gr fl), 12 units [shwr, bath (hip), tlt, c/fan, TV, movie, clock radio, t/c mkg, refrig, cook fac (3), micro (3), ldry], pool (salt water), meals to unit (breakfast), c/park (undercover), ☎. RO ♦ $38 - $95, ♦♦ $45 - $110, AE BC DC EFT MC VI.

★★ **Elite**, (M), 1935 Gold Coast Hwy, ☎ 07 5535 2920, (2 stry gr fl), 9 units [shwr, tlt, a/c-cool (7), TV, clock radio, t/c mkg, refrig, cook fac], bbq, ☎, cots-fee. RO ♦♦ $35 - $75, ◊ $10, BC MC VI.

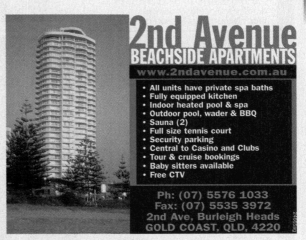

Self Catering Accommodation

★★★★☆ **2nd Avenue Beachside Apartments**, (HU), 2nd Ave, beachfront, ☎ 07 5576 1033, fax 07 5535 3972, (Multi-stry), 84 units acc up to 6, (1, 2 & 3 bedrm), [shwr, bath, spa bath, tlt, c/fan, heat, tel, TV, clock radio, refrig, cook fac, micro, d/wash, ldry (in unit), blkts, linen, pillows], lift, pool-heated (salt water heated), pool indoor heated, sauna (2), spa (2), bbq, secure park, tennis, cots-fee. W $585 - $1,890, Min book applies, BC MC VI.

★★★★☆ **Burleigh Beach Tower**, (HU), 52 Goodwin Tce, ☎ 07 5535 9222, fax 07 5576 1095, (Multi-stry gr fl), 86 units acc up to 5, (1 & 2 bedrm), [shwr, bath, tlt, fan, tel, TV, video (10), clock radio, refrig, cook fac, micro, d/wash, ldry (in unit), blkts, linen, pillows], lift, pool-heated, spa, kiosk, secure park, gym, tennis, cots-fee. D $132 - $220, AE BC DC JCB MC VI.

Welcome to Beautiful Burleigh

Burleigh Point Apartments

Modern 2 bedroom self contained apartments with everything to make your holiday complete. Swimming pool and heated spa, gazebo, BBQ and security parking. Faces beautiful Burleigh Beach and is opposite North Burleigh Surf Life Saving Club. Jupiters Casino and world class shopping are only minutes away.

300 The Esplanade, Burleigh Heads 4220.
Ph: (07) 5576 2233 Fax: (07) 5576 2650
email: bpoint@onthenet.com.au
Website: www.burleighpoint.com

Hillhaven Holiday Apartments

The perfect location for the perfect holiday with million dollar views from all balconies. Tranquil location nestled into the National Park with the blue Pacific at your front door. Fully self contained two and three bedroom holiday apartments.

2 Goodwin Terrace, Burleigh Heads 4220.
Ph: (07) 5535 1055 Fax: (07) 5535 1870
email: email@hillhaven.com.au
Web: www.hillhaven.com.au

Outrigger Resort

Superior hotel with all the facilities one would expect from a 4 star Flag Choice Hotel. The friendly staff are more than happy to direct you to places of interest and ensure you are not disturbed when its time to relax. Only 2 min. walk to beach. Gold Coast group specialists.

2007 Gold Coast Hwy, Burleigh Hds, 4220.
Free Call: 1800 641 153
Ph: (07) 5535 1111 Fax: (07) 5576 3370
email: info@outrigger.com.au
Web: www.outriggerresort.com.au

Paradise Grove

Set in six acres of landscaped gardens. Close to beach, shops, restaurants and clubs. Amenities include two pools, heated spa, tennis court, BBQ's, and licensed bar. Self contained units with fully equipped kitchens and laundries. Linen supplied and security parking.

7 West Burleigh Rd, Burleigh Heads, 4220
Phone: (07) 5576 3833 Fax: (07) 5576 3155
email: paradisegrove@onthenet.com.au
Web:www.goldcoastburleightourism.com.au

Southern Cross Apartments

Self contained luxury beachfront apartments with beautiful 2 bed-rooms and 2 bathrooms. Magnificent ocean views and situated in a beautiful garden setting. Heated outdoor pool, 2 spas, 2 half tennis courts, recreation room, gym equipment, undercover security parking, direct dial phones.

114–124 The Esplanade, Burleigh Hds 4220.
Phone: (07) 5535 3266 Fax: (07) 5535 1769
email: mail@sca.net.au
Web: www.sca.net.au

Sol na Mara Holiday Apartments

Large 2 and 3 bedroom apartments with ensuite, bathroom & private balcony all with ocean views. Fully equipped kitchen & laundry, wheel chair access, undercover security parking, security intercom, heated salt water swimming pool. Linen included in tariff. Children's playground opposite. Walk to shops & restaurants.

202 The Esplanade, Burleigh Heads, 4220
Phone: (07) 5535 1022 Fax: (07) 5535 1457
email: mail@solnamara.com.au
Web: www.solnamara.com.au

Burleigh Gardens North Hi Rise

Quality 1 & 2 bedroom fully self-contained units. Fully equipped kitchens, laundry, TV Cable (most units). Great location, easy walk to Burleigh shopping centre, patrolled beach (private access), clubs and restaurants. Heated pool, spa, 1/2 tennis court, games room, children's play area. BBQ. Security Parking. Tour Desk, Linen provided.

1855 Gold Coast Hwy, Burleigh Heads, 4220.
Ph: (07) 5535 4200 Fax: (07) 5576 1648
email: acc@burleighgardenshirise.com.au
Web: www.burleighgardenshirise.com.au

Burleigh Gardens Holiday Apartments

One and two bedroom, comfortable, fully self contained units, 2 with air/con., all with fans. Set in pleasant garden setting with solar heated pool. Children's play area, walkway to patrolled beach, undercover sec. parking and bus at front door. Handy to shops, bowling green and National Park. Free booking service for tours.

1849 Gold Coast Hwy, Burleigh Heads, 4220
Ph: (07) 5576 3955 Fax: (07) 5576 4372
email: bgha@bigpond.com.au
Web: www.burleighgardens.com.au

Burleigh Terraces

Modern, fully self contained 1, 2 or 3 bedroom apartments, ceiling fans, TV, laundry facilities, lift, undercover security parking, pool, spa, BBQ, in beautiful tropical setting. Right in the heart of beautiful Burleigh Heads. Easy walk to beach, shops, restaurants and bowling club. Central to all Gold Coast attractions.

1/1 Burleigh Street, Burleigh Heads, 4220.
Ph: (07) 5535 5311 Fax: (07) 5535 5344
email: burleigh_terraces@iprimus.com.au
Web: www.burleighterraces.cjb.net

Burleigh Beach Tower

Self contained apartments with full kitchen, separated bedrooms, bath/shower, ensuite, TV, w/machine, dryer, IDD/STD phone, swimming pool, spa, full size tennis court, security parking, gymnasium, kiosk. Opposite patrolled surf beach and close to Robina Shopping Town and golf courses.

52 Goodwin Terrace, Burleigh Heads 4220.
Ph: (07) 5535 9222 Fax: (07) 5576 1095
email: gwen@bbt.com.au
Website: www.bbt.com.au

Le Beach Apartments

On the beachfront with luxury 2 bedroom apartments with a sunny balcony overlooking a centrally located swimming pool and BBQ area set amongst beautifully landscaped gardens. Open and spacious units with stylish furnishings and modern amenities with magnificent views of the Pacific Ocean. Short walk to shops.

136 The Esplanade, Burleigh Heads, 4220.
Ph: (07) 5576 3777 Fax: (07) 5576 3777
email: enquiries@lebeach.com.au
Website: www.lebeach.com.au

Mariner Shores Resort & Beach Club

Affordable beachfront location. Conveniently located opposite the beach at North Burleigh Heads and offers a unique family holiday. There is a variety of recreational facilities and specialises in a complete holiday experience with organised activities including Kids Club and free use of surfboards & boogie boards .

260 The Esplanade, North Burleigh, 4220
Ph: (07) 5535 2177 Fax:(07) 5535 3691
email: mail@marinershores.com.au
Website: www.marinershores.com.au

GOLD COAST
The Coast with the Most!™

– Centre of the Gold Coast

Burleigh Heads gives you one of Australia's best surf breaks with protected beaches and headland national park. Stay in world class self-contained accommodation with spectacular ocean views. Visit wildlife parks, beachfront markets, restaurants and cafés – it's all waiting for you to discover at Burleigh Heads. Your holiday playground offers you easy driving access to exciting theme parks and all other Gold Coast attractions and shopping centres

BEAUTIFUL BURLEIGH
CENTRE OF THE GOLD COAST

Beautiful one Day...Perfect the Next

Burleigh On The Beach

All apartments air conditioned. Fully self contained 1 bedroom and 1 bedroom with family room apartments. 2 bedroom 2 level penthouses with rooftop terrace & spa. Fully equipped kitchen with m/wave and dishwasher, laundry with washing machine & dryer, linen supplied, weekly housekeeping & secure basement parking. Direct dial ISD/STD phones.

5, Fourth Ave cnr GC Hwy, Burleigh Heads, Q 4220.
Ph: (07) 5525 5999 Fax: (07) 5525 5900
email:holiday@burleighonthebeach.com.au
Web:www.burleighonthebeach.com.au

AAAT ★★★★

2nd Avenue Beachside Apartments

Beach front apartment building only 300m to Burleigh Shopping Centre. All units have private spa baths, fully equipped kitchens including microwave oven, ceiling fans, balconies. Indoor heated pool, spa & saunas, outdoor pool and wader, BBQs. Full size tennis court, security parking, ISD/STD phone, free Cable TV.

2nd Avenue, Burleigh Heads, Qld 4220.
Ph: (07) 5576 1033 Fax: (07) 5535 3972
email: 2ndavenue@better.net.au
Web: www.2ndavenue.com.au

AAAT ★★★★☆

Esplanade Apartments

Superior 25 level development providing one of the most spacious 2 & 3 bedroom apartments on the Gold Coast. Two apartments per floor, each 16sq, plus 6sq balcony. All have breathtaking views of beaches & spectacular hinterland mountains. Tennis, swimming pool, 2 spas, 2 saunas, BBQ amenities, secure car park.

146 The Esplanade, North Burleigh, 4220.
Ph: (07) 5535 0855 Fax: (07) 5576 3001
email: esplanade_apartments@bigpond.com.au
Web: www.travelaustralia.com.au/s/16736

AAAT ★★★★☆

Gemini Court Apartments

Large luxury self contained 1 & 2 bedroom apartments all with sunny balconies and magnificent ocean views. Full kitchen and laundry facilities, two bathrooms, ceiling fans. Large heated pool and spa, BBQ, sauna, tennis court, secure parking. Ideal family holiday location. Close to Burleigh Village, Nat. Park, patrolled beach, restaurants, cafés and shops.

45 Hayle Street, Burleigh Heads, Qld 4220
Free Call: 1800 636 036 Fax: (07) 5535 4755
email: info@geminicourt.com.au
Web: www.geminicourt.com.au

AAAT ★★★★☆

Cashelmara Beachfront Apartments

Seventeen stories with views of the Pacific Ocean. Spacious 2 and 3 bedroom apartments with ensuite, full kitchen facilities, s/pool (heated in winter), spa (heated), sauna, BBQ area, half court tennis, secure undercover parking, direct dial phone, security intercom, two lifts, linen included. Patrolled beach opposite.

170 The Esplanade, Burleigh Heads, 4220.
Ph: (07) 5535 0311 Fax: (07) 5535 0954
email:cashelmara@radd.com.au
www.travelaustralia.com.au/s/16735

AAAT ★★★★

Burleigh Surf Apartments

The perfect position for families. Directly opposite fully patrolled beach and surf club, with restaurants and shops nearby. All units have large balconies with ocean views, private spa baths, video player, hair dryer, heated indoor pool, large outdoor pool, gym, games room, full size tennis court, undercover security parking.

238 The Esplanade, Burleigh Heads, 4220.
Ph: (07) 5535 8866 Fax: ((07) 5535 8523
email: mail@burleighsurf.com.au
Web: www.burleighsurf.com.au

AAAT ★★★★☆

Key Largo Apartments

Key Largo is 100 metres from Burleigh Beach and a short stroll to Burleigh shops, restaurants and business houses. Key Largo has 4½ star luxury units set in a tropical garden setting with spacious lawns. A heated pool and spa, and BBQ area is central to the buildings grounds.

1911 Gold Coast Hwy, Burleigh Hds, 4220
Ph: (07) 5535 8022 Fax: (07) 5535 8080
email: info@keylargoapartments.com.au
Web: www.keylargoapartments.com.au

AAAT ★★★★☆

The Mediterranean

Comprises of 2 towers and a total of 110 elegantly appointed & fully equipped 1, 2 and 3 bedroom apartments. Features: outdoor pool, indoor heated pool and spa, children's paddling pool, sauna, gym, rooftop BBQ & gazebo, undercover security parking, security access building. Reception/tour desk hours 8am to 5.30pm.

220 The Esplanade, North Burleigh, 4220
Ph: (07) 5535 7188 Fax: (07) 5535 7166
email: mail@mediterraneanresort.com
Web: www.mediterraneanresort.com

AAAT ★★★★☆

GOLD COAST

The Coast with the Most!™

★★★★☆ **Burleigh Surf**, (HU), 238 The Esplanade, 1km N of PO, ☎ 07 5535 8866, fax 07 5535 8523, (Multi-stry), 60 units acc up to 6, (1 & 2 bedrm), [shwr, spa bath, tlt, hairdry, fan, tel, TV, video, clock radio, refrig, cook fac, micro, elec frypan, d/wash, ldry (in unit), blkts, linen, pillows], lift, rec rm, pool (salt water), pool indoor heated, sauna, spa, bbq, secure park, gym, tennis, cots-fee. W **$630 - $1,442**, ch con, Min book applies, BC MC VI.

★★★★☆ **Esplanade Apartments**, (HU), 146 The Esplanade, ☎ 07 5535 0855, fax 07 5576 3001, (Multi-stry), 29 units acc up to 6, (2 & 3 bedrm), [shwr, bath, tlt, heat, tel, TV, clock radio, refrig, cook fac, micro, d/wash, ldry (in unit), blkts, linen, pillows], lift, rec rm, pool indoor heated, sauna, spa, bbq, secure park, tennis, cots-fee. W **$600 - $1,465**, Min book applies.

★★★★☆ **Gemini Court**, (HU), Twin tower. 45 Hayle St, ☎ 07 5576 0300, fax 07 5535 4755, (Multi-stry), 65 units acc up to 6, (1 & 2 bedrm), [ensuite, shwr, bath, tlt, a/c-cool (3), fan, heat, tel, cable tv (36), video-fee, clock radio, refrig, cook fac, micro, d/wash, ldry (in unit), blkts, linen, pillows], lift, rec rm, pool-heated (salt water), sauna, spa, bbq, secure park, tennis, cots-fee. W **$630 - $1,330**, AE BC DC EFT MC VI.

Operator Comment: See our ad on opposite page.

★★★★☆ **Key Largo Apartments**, (HU), 1911 Gold Coast Hwy, Cnr 3rd Ave, ☎ 07 5535 8022, fax 07 5535 8080, (Multi-stry), 24 units acc up to 6, (2 bedrm), [shwr, bath, tlt, c/fan, tel, TV, video-fee, clock radio, refrig, cook fac, micro, d/wash, ldry (in unit)], pool-heated (salt water), spa, bbq, secure park, cots-fee. D ♦♦ **$410 - $880**.

★★★★☆ **Mediterranean on North Burleigh**, (HU), 220 The Esplanade, 200m S of N Burleigh Surfclub, ☎ 07 5535 7188, fax 07 5535 7166, (Multi-stry gr fl), 74 units acc up to 6, (1, 2 & 3 bedrm), [ensuite, shwr, bath, tlt, hairdry, a/c, fan (on request), tel, TV, video-fee, clock radio, refrig, cook fac, micro, elec frypan, d/wash, toaster, ldry (in unit), blkts, linen, pillows], lift, dryer, iron, iron brd, pool indoor heated (2), sauna, spa, bbq, c/park (undercover), secure park, gym, cots-fee. D **$150 - $335**, W **$750 - $2,345**, Min book applies, AE BC DC MC VI.

★★★★ **Burleigh Terraces**, (HU), 1 Burleigh St, ☎ 07 5535 5311, fax 07 5535 5344, (Multi-stry), 12 units acc up to 6, (1, 2 & 3 bedrm), [ensuite, shwr, bath, tlt, c/fan, tel, TV, video-fee, clock radio, refrig, cook fac, micro, elec frypan, d/wash, toaster, linen], lift, w/mach, dryer, iron, iron brd, pool, spa, bbq (covered), secure park, security gates, cots-fee. W **$420 - $1,120**, BC EFT MC VI.

★★★★ **Burleigh on the Beach**, (HU), Cnr Gold Coast Hwy & Fourth Ave, 1km N of PO, ☎ 07 5525 5999, fax 07 5525 5900, 34 units (1 & 2 bedrm), [ensuite (4), shwr, spa bath (4), tlt, a/c, c/fan, tel, TV, video-fee, clock radio, t/c mkg, refrig, micro, d/wash, toaster, ldry, blkts, linen, pillows], dryer, iron, iron brd, pool-heated (salt water), spa (heated), bbq, gym, cots-fee. D ♦♦ **$115 - $180**, ◊ **$10**, W ♦♦ **$450 - $1,190**, ◊ **$70**, BC EFT MC VI.

★★★★ **Cashelmara**, (HU), 170 The Esplanade, ☎ 07 5535 0311, fax 07 5535 0954, (Multi-stry gr fl), 25 units acc up to 7, (2 & 3 bedrm), [shwr, bath, tlt, fan, tel, TV, clock radio, t/c mkg, refrig, cook fac, micro, d/wash, ldry (in unit)], lift, pool-heated, sauna, spa, bbq, secure park, tennis (half court), cots-fee. D ♦♦ **$160**, ◊ **$20**, W ♦♦ **$520 - $1,150**, ◊ **$140**, Min book applies, BC MC VI.

★★★★ **Hillhaven Holiday Apartments**, (HU), 2 Goodwin Tce, ☎ 07 5535 1055, fax 07 5535 1870, (Multi-stry gr fl), 21 units acc up to 6, (2 & 3 bedrm), [shwr, bath (1), tlt, fan, heat, tel, TV, video-fee, clock radio, refrig, cook fac, micro, d/wash (10), ldry (in unit), blkts, linen, pillows], lift, secure park (14), cots-fee. D **$130 - $170**, W **$490 - $1,070**.

★★★★ **La Pacifique**, (HU), 60 Goodwin Tce, ☎ 07 5576 0799, fax 07 5576 3271, (Multi-stry), 23 units acc up to 6, [shwr, bath, tlt, fan (10), c/fan (19), heat, tel, TV, clock radio, refrig, cook fac, micro, d/wash, ldry (in unit), blkts, linen, pillows], lift, rec rm, pool (salt water), sauna, spa, bbq, secure park, tennis. W ♦♦ **$120 - $5,420**, Min book applies, BC MC VI.

★★★★ **Le Beach**, (HU), 136 The Esplanade, ☎ 07 5576 3777, fax 07 5576 3777, (Multi-stry), 29 units acc up to 5, (2 bedrm), [ensuite, shwr, bath, tlt, c/fan, heat, tel, TV, video-fee, clock radio, refrig, cook fac, micro, d/wash, ldry (in unit), blkts, linen, pillows], pool-heated, spa, bbq, secure park, cots-fee. W **$505 - $1,065**, AE BC DC EFT MC VI.

★★★★ **Oceanside Cove**, (HU), 1 First Ave, 300m N of PO, ☎ 07 5520 0040, fax 07 5576 7514, (Multi-stry gr fl), 12 units acc up to 6, [ensuite, shwr, bath, tlt, fan (3), c/fan (9), tel, TV, clock radio, refrig, micro, ldry (in unit), blkts, linen, pillows], dryer, iron, pool-heated (salt water), bbq, secure park, cots-fee. W ♦♦ **$395 - $630**, ◊ **$70**, Min book applies, BC MC VI.

★★★★ **Pacific Regis**, (HU), 30 The Esplanade, ☎ 07 5535 1692, fax 07 5535 6466, (Multi-stry), 40 units acc up to 6, [shwr, bath, tlt, tel, TV, video-fee, clock radio, refrig, cook fac, micro, elec frypan, d/wash, ldry (in unit), blkts, linen, pillows], lift, dryer, rec rm, pool, pool indoor heated, sauna (2), spa (2), bbq, secure park, gym, tennis (half court) (2), cots-fee. W **$460 - $1,050**.

★★★★ **Southern Cross Apartments**, (HU), 114-121 The Esplanade, ☎ 07 5535 3266, fax 07 5535 1769, (Multi-stry), 28 units acc up to 6, (2 bedrm), [shwr, bath, tlt, heat, tel, TV, video-fee, refrig, cook fac, micro, d/wash, ldry (in unit), blkts, linen, pillows], lift, rec rm, pool-heated, sauna, spa (2), secure park, gym, tennis (half court), cots-fee, W ♦♦ **$550 - $1,190**.

★★★☆ **Ambassador Apartments**, (HU), 100 The Esplanade, ☎ 07 5535 4089, (Multi-stry), 70 units acc up to 6, [shwr, bath, tlt, TV, video-fee, refrig, cook fac, micro, ldry (in unit), linen reqd-fee], lift, pool, secure park, cots-fee. W **$345 - $720**, Min book applies, EFT.

★★★☆ **Aussie Resort**, (HU), 1917 Gold Coast Hwy, ☎ 07 5576 2877, fax 07 5535 8034, (Multi-stry gr fl), 50 units acc up to 4, (1 bedrm), [shwr, tlt, c/fan, tel, TV, video-fee, clock radio, refrig, cook fac, micro, ldry (in unit), blkts, linen, pillows], rec rm, pool-heated (salt water heated), spa, bbq, c/park (undercover), cots-fee. D ♦♦ **$110**, ◊ **$15**, W **$465- $800**, BC MC VI.

★★★☆ **Burleigh Gardens Low Rise Holiday Aparts**, (HU), 1849 Gold Coast Hwy, ☎ 07 5576 3955, fax 07 5576 4372, (Multi-stry gr fl), 25 units acc up to 6, (1 & 2 bedrm), [shwr, tlt, a/c-cool (2), c/fan, heat, tel, TV, video-fee, clock radio, t/c mkg, refrig, cook fac, micro, d/wash (1), ldry (in unit), blkts, linen, pillows], pool-heated (solar), bbq, secure park, cots-fee. W ♦♦ **$400 - $680**, Min book applies, BC MC VI.

★★★☆ **Burleigh Gardens North**, (HU), 1855 Gold Coast Hwy, ☎ 07 5535 4200, fax 07 5576 1648, (Multi-stry), 31 units acc up to 5, (1 & 2 bedrm), [shwr, bath, tlt, c/fan, tel, TV, video-fee, clock radio, refrig, cook fac, micro, ldry (in unit), blkts, linen, pillows], lift, rec rm, pool, spa, bbq, secure park, plygr, tennis (half court), cots-fee. W **$434 - $896**, Min book applies, BC MC VI.

★★★☆ **Burleigh Point**, (HU), 300 The Esplanade, ☎ 07 5576 2233, fax 07 5576 2650, (Multi-stry gr fl), 18 units acc up to 5, (2 bedrm), [ensuite, shwr, bath, tlt, c/fan, heat, tel, TV, clock radio, refrig, cook fac, micro, d/wash, ldry (in unit), blkts, linen, pillows], pool (salt water), spa, bbq, secure park, cots-fee. D ♦♦ **$68 - $132**, ◊ **$14**, W ♦♦ **$460 - $920**, ◊ **$40**, BC MC VI.

★★★☆ **Horizons**, (HU), 1945 Gold Coast Hwy, ☎ 07 5535 6088, fax 07 5535 6557, (Multi-stry), 47 units acc up to 6, (1 & 2 bedrm), [shwr, tlt, fan, heat, tel, TV, clock radio, refrig, cook fac, micro, d/wash, ldry (in unit), blkts, linen, pillows], lift, pool (salt water, heated), sauna, spa, bbq, secure park, plygr, mini golf. W ♦♦ **$401 - $1,057**, Min book Christmas and Jan, BC EFT MC VI.

★★★☆ **Leyton Lodge**, (HU), 106 The Esplanade, ☎ 07 5535 7577, fax 07 5535 7422, (Multi-stry gr fl), 12 units acc up to 6, (2 & 3 bedrm), [shwr, bath (6), tlt, TV, clock radio, refrig, cook fac, micro, d/wash (11), ldry (in unit), blkts, linen, pillows], pool (salt water), spa, bbq, c/park (undercover) (6), secure park (6), cots-fee. D ♦♦ **$100**, W **$345 - $890**.

★★★☆ **Paradise Grove Apartments**, (HU), 301/7 West Burleigh Rd, 200m W of PO, ☎ 07 5576 3833, fax 07 5576 3155, 42 units acc up to 6, (2 & 3 bedrm), [ensuite (33), shwr, bath, tlt, c/fan, tel, TV, clock radio, t/c mkg, refrig, cook fac, micro, d/wash (15), toaster, ldry, blkts, linen, pillows], dryer, iron, iron brd, bar, pool above ground (salt water), spa, bbq (covered)-fee, secure park, tennis, cots-fee. D **$90**, W **$450 - $1,030**.

★★★☆ **Sol Na Mara**, (Apt), 202 The Esplanade, ☎ 07 5535 1022, fax 07 5535 1457, (Multi-stry), 25 apts acc up to 10, (1, 2 & 3 bedrm), [shwr, bath, tlt, hairdry, fan (6), c/fan (6), tel, TV, video-fee, clock radio, refrig, cook fac, micro, d/wash, ldry (in unit), blkts, linen, pillows], lift, dryer, pool-heated (salt water heated), secure park, cots-fee. **W** ♦♦ **$510 - $960,** ♦♦♦♦ **$560 - $960,** BC MC VI.

★★★☆ **St Marie**, (HU), 1901 Gold Coast Hwy, ☎ 07 5535 9006, fax 07 5576 7574, (Multi-stry gr fl), 17 units acc up to 5, (1 & 2 bedrm), [shwr, tlt, c/fan, tel, TV, video-fee, clock radio, refrig, cook fac, micro, ldry (in unit), blkts, linen, pillows], pool (salt water), spa, bbq, secure park, cots-fee. **W** ♦ **$350 - $630,** ♦♦ **$420 - $735,** Min book applies.

★★★☆ **Wyuna**, (HU), Cnr Esplanade & Second Ave, ☎ 07 5535 3302, fax 07 5535 3302, (Multi-stry), 17 units acc up to 6, (2 & 3 bedrm), [shwr, bath, tlt, heat, tel, TV, clock radio, refrig, cook fac, micro, ldry (in unit), linen reqd-fee], lift, secure park, cots-fee. **D** ♦♦♦♦ **$300 - $400.**

GOLD COAST - COOLANGATTA QLD 4225

Part of GOLD COAST region. Pop 3,511. (100km S Brisbane), See map on page 417, ref E8. Traditionally famous for its beach and surfing area. Rainbow Bay & Point Danger within walking distance from town. Excellent shopping and restaurant facilities. Bowls, Croquet, Golf, Horse Racing, Horse Riding, Scenic Drives, Squash, Surfing, Swimming, Tennis, Water Skiing.

Hotels/Motels

★★★★☆ **Calypso Plaza Coolangatta**, (LH), 87 Griffith Street, 800 metres E GPO, ☎ 07 5599 0000, fax 07 5599 0099, 156 rms (1 & 2 bedrm), [shwr, bath, spa bath (23), tlt, H & C, hairdry, a/c, c/fan, tel, TV, movie, clock radio, t/c mkg, refrig, cook fac, micro, toaster], dryer, iron, iron brd, conf fac, ⊠, pool-heated (salt water), spa, rm serv, secure park, gym, cots. **RO** ♦ **$110 - $220,** ♦♦ **$110 - $220,** AE BC CC DC EFT JCB MC VI.

Operator Comment: See our ad over page.

AAA
TOURISM
Special Rates

★★★☆ **Bombora on the Park**, (M), Carmichael Cl, Goodwin Park, ☎ 07 5536 1888, fax 07 5536 1828, (Multi-stry gr fl), 34 units [shwr, tlt, c/fan, tel, TV, clock radio, t/c mkg, refrig], ldry, rec rm, lounge (TV), ⊠, pool (salt water), bbq. **BB** ♦ **$75,** ♦♦ **$95,** ♦ **$25,** BC MC VI.

★★★☆ **Greenmount Beach Resort**, (Ltd Lic H), 3 Hill St, ☎ 07 5536 1222, fax 07 5536 1102, (Multi-stry), 151 rms [shwr, bath (48), tlt, a/c, c/fan, tel, TV, movie, t/c mkg, refrig], lift, ldry, rec rm, conf fac, ⊠, pool-heated (salt water), sauna, spa, 24hr reception, rm serv, c/park (limited), ✆, cots. **RO** ♦♦ **$110 - $137,** ♦ **$10,** ch con, AE BC DC MC VI.

★★ **Coolangatta Ocean View**, (M), Cnr Marine Pde & Clark St, ☎ 07 5536 3722, fax 07 5599 4057, (Multi-stry gr fl), 19 units [shwr, tlt, a/c, c/fan, tel, TV, t/c mkg, refrig, cook fac (6)], ldry, c/park (limited). **RO $55 - $126.50,** AE BC DC MC VI.

★★ **On the Beach**, (M), 118 Marine Pde, ☎ 07 5536 3624, fax 07 5536 3624, (2 stry gr fl), 16 units (1 & 2 bedrm), [shwr, bath (9), tlt, fan, tel, TV, clock radio, t/c mkg, refrig, cook fac (13), micro, toaster, pillows], ldry, cots. **RO** ♦ **$45 - $55,** ♦♦ **$50 - $60,** ♦ **$10,** ♦♦ **W $325 - $395,** BC EFT MC VI.

Self Catering Accommodation

★★★★☆ **Bayview Apartments**, (HU), 166 Marine Pde, Rainbow Bay 4225, ☎ 07 5536 9122, fax 07 5524 0244, (Multi-stry), 26 units acc up to 4, [ensuite, shwr, bath, tlt, heat, tel, cable tv, video-fee, refrig, cook fac, micro, d/wash, ldry (in unit), blkts, linen, pillows], lift, rec rm, pool (salt water), sauna, spa, bbq (covered) secure park, tennis, cots-fee. **W $615 - $1,230,** Min book applies.

★★★★☆ **Beach House Seaside Resort**, (HU), 58 Marine Pde, Cnr McLean St, ☎ 07 5588 8585, fax 07 5588 8525, (Multi-stry), 132 units acc up to 6, (2 bedrm), [ensuite, shwr, bath, spa bath (12), tlt, hairdry, c/fan, heat, tel, TV (2), video, movie, clock radio, refrig, cook fac, micro, d/wash, ldry (in unit), blkts, linen, pillows], lift, dryer, rec rm, ⊠, pool-heated, sauna, spa, bbq, secure park, gym, squash, tennis (half court). **D $135 - $215, W $876 - $1,435,** ch con, AE BC DC MC VI.

★★★★☆ **Beachcomber International Resort**, (HU), 122 Griffith St, 200m S of PO, ☎ 07 5588 8585, fax 07 5588 8525, (Multi-stry gr fl), 61 units acc up to 4, (1 & 2 bedrm), [shwr, bath, spa bath, tlt, hairdry, heat, tel, TV, video, clock radio, refrig, cook fac, micro, d/wash, ldry (in unit), blkts, linen, pillows], lift, rec rm, ⊠, pool (2), spa (2), bbq, secure park, gym, tennis (half court). **D $130 - $175, W $840 - $1,155,** ch con, AE BC DC JCB MC VI.

WHAT MORE COULD YOU ASK FOR?

As the southern Gold Coast's only four and a half star beachfront resort, Calypso Plaza offers guests the choice of studios and one or two bedroom suites. Enjoy an amazing array of recreational facilities, tropical lagoon with dual waterslides, al fresco dining at Reggae's Restaurant & Bar, plus 24 hour room service. What more could you ask for? For reservations call **1800 062 189**.

CALYPSO PLAZA
SUITES
COOLANGATTA

MIRVAC

87-105 Griffith Street, Coolangatta Qld 4225
Tel (07) 5599 0000 Fax (07) 5599 0099
Email reservationcalypsoplaza@mirvachotels.com.au
Website www.mirvachotels.com.au

CAL5575 90115ag

★★★★☆ **Bella Mare**, (HU), 5 Hill St, 30m S of Greenmount beach, ☎ 07 5599 2755, fax 07 5599 5719, 25 units acc up to 6, (2 & 3 bedrm), [ensuite, shwr, bath, tlt, a/c (4), c/fan, tel, TV, t/c mkg, refrig, micro, d/wash, toaster, ldry, blkts, linen, pillows], dryer, iron, iron brd, pool (salt water), sauna, spa, bbq, secure park, gym, cots-fee. **D $99 - $143, W $540 - $1,320**, BC EFT MC VI.

★★★★☆ **Ocean Plaza Resort**, (HU), Cnr Marine Pde & Warner St, 500m E of PO, ☎ 07 5536 9999, fax 07 5536 9111, (Multi-stry), 75 units acc up to 7, (1, 2 & 3 bedrm), [shwr, bath, tlt, fan, heat, tel, TV, clock radio, refrig, cook fac, micro, d/wash, ldry (in unit), blkts, linen, pillows], lift, dryer, rec rm, pool-heated, spa, secure park, golf (practice nets), gym, tennis (2), cots-fee. **D $135 - $173, W $665 - $1,925**, BC MC VI.

★★★★☆ **Outrigger Coolangatta Beach Resort**, (SA), 88 Marine Pde, 200m fr PO, ☎ 07 5506 8787, fax 07 5506 8888, (Multi-stry), 121 serv apts acc up to 7, (1, 2 & 3 bedrm), [ensuite, shwr, bath, tlt, hairdry, a/c, tel, TV, clock radio, refrig, cook fac, micro, d/wash, toaster, ldry, blkts, linen, pillows], lift, dryer, iron, iron brd, pool-heated, sauna, spa, bbq, secure park, gym, tennis, cots-fee. **RO** ♟ **$143 - $284,** ♟ **$30**, AE BC DC JCB MC VI.

★★★★☆ **Points North Apartments**, (HU), Cnr Marine Pde & Dutton St, ☎ 07 5536 0000, fax 07 5599 1010, (Multi-stry), 78 units acc up to 6, (1, 2 & 3 bedrm), [shwr, bath, tlt, c/fan, tel, TV, video-fee, clock radio, refrig, cook fac, micro, elec frypan, d/wash, ldry (in unit), blkts, linen, pillows], lift, dryer, rec rm, pool-heated (salt water heated), sauna, spa, secure park, tennis, cots-fee. **RO $581 - $1,743**, AE BC MC VI.

★★★★☆ **Rainbow Bay Resort**, (HU), 265 Boundary St, ☎ 07 5536 9933, fax 07 5536 9510, (Multi-stry gr fl), 21 units acc up to 8, (2, 3 & 4 bedrm), [shwr, spa bath (1), tlt, a/c (3), tel, TV, clock radio, t/c mkg, refrig, cook fac, micro, d/wash, blkts, linen, pillows], lift, w/mach, dryer, pool-heated, sauna, spa, bbq, secure park, cots-fee. **D $450 - $1,815**, BC MC VI.

★★★★ **The Bay Apartments**, (HU), 243 Boundary St, Rainbow Bay 4225, ☎ 07 5536 2988, fax 07 5536 7077, (Multi-stry gr fl), 30 units acc up to 6, (2 & 3 bedrm), [shwr, bath, spa bath (4), tlt, fan, c/fan, tel, TV, clock radio, refrig, cook fac, micro, d/wash, ldry (in unit), blkts, linen, pillows], dryer, iron, pool (salt water), spa, bbq, secure park, cots-fee. W $455 - $1,345, ⏏ $105, Min book applies, BC MC VI.

★★★☆ **Aries Apartments**, (HU), 82 Marine Pde, ☎ 07 5536 2711, fax 07 5536 2711, (Multi-stry), 14 units acc up to 5, [ensuite, shwr, bath, tlt, tel, TV, clock radio, refrig, cook fac, micro, d/wash, ldry (in unit), blkts, linen, pillows], lift, pool, sauna, spa, secure park, cots-fee. W $550 - $1,050, Min book applies.

★★★☆ **Carool Luxury Apartments**, (HU), Cnr Petrie St & Eden Ave, Rainbow Bay 4225, ☎ 07 5536 7154, fax 07 5536 7204, (Multi-stry), 22 units acc up to 8, [shwr, bath, tlt, fan, heat, tel, cable tv, video-fee, clock radio, refrig, cook fac, micro, elec frypan, d/wash, ldry (in unit), blkts, linen, pillows], lift, pool-heated, bbq, secure park, cots-fee. W $390 - $2,820, Min book applies, BC MC VI.

★★★☆ **Chateau Royale**, (HU), 1 Garrick St, ☎ 07 5536 8877, fax 07 5599 1509, (Multi-stry gr fl), 24 units acc up to 6, (1, 2 & 3 bedrm), [shwr, bath, tlt, fan, heat, tel, TV, video-fee, clock radio, refrig, cook fac, micro, d/wash, ldry (in unit), blkts, linen, pillows], lift, pool, sauna, spa, bbq, secure park, cots-fee. D $80 - $135, W $400 - $950, Min book applies, BC MC VI.

★★★☆ **Columbia Beachfront Apartments**, (HU), 184 Marine Pde, Rainbow Bay 4225, ☎ 07 5599 0666, fax 07 5599 0660, (Multi-stry), 36 units acc up to 4, (2 bedrm), [shwr, bath, tlt, tel, TV, refrig, cook fac, micro, elec frypan, d/wash, ldry (in unit), blkts, linen, pillows], lift, dryer, iron, pool, secure park, tennis (half court). W $550 - $1,330, Min book applies.

★★★☆ **Eden Tower**, (HU), 5 Ward St, 800m NE of PO, ☎ 07 5536 8213, (Multi-stry gr fl), 16 units acc up to 6, (1, 2 & 3 bedrm), [shwr, bath, tlt, tel, TV, video-fee, clock radio, refrig, cook fac, micro, elec frypan, d/wash, ldry (in unit)], lift, dryer, iron, pool, sauna, bbq, secure park. W ⏏⏏ $400 - $590, ⏏ $70, Min book applies.

★★★☆ **Rainbow Commodore Apartments**, (HU), 255 Boundary St, Rainbow Bay 4225, 100m fr beach, ☎ 07 5536 7758, fax 07 5536 9521, (Multi-stry), 38 units acc up to 5, [shwr, bath, tlt, tel, cable tv, video-fee, clock radio, refrig, cook fac, micro, d/wash, ldry (in unit), blkts, linen, pillows], lift, rec rm, pool, sauna, spa, secure park, tennis (half court), cots-fee. W $450 - $1,025, ch con, Min book applies.

★★★☆ **Rainbow Place Apartments**, (HU), 180 Marine Pde, Rainbow Bay 4225, 600m N of Tweed Heads PO, ☎ 07 5536 9144, fax 07 5599 0755, (Multi-stry gr fl), 36 units acc up to 5, (1 & 2 bedrm), [ensuite, shwr, bath, tlt, fan, tel, cable tv, video (2), clock radio, refrig, cook fac, micro, d/wash, ldry (in unit), blkts, linen, pillows], lift, pool-heated (solar), secure park, tennis (half court), cots-fee. W $425 - $1,245, Min book applies.

★★★ **Skyline**, (HU), 126 Musgrave St, entrance western end of Garrick St, ☎ 07 5536 8914, (Multi-stry), 12 units acc up to 6, (1 & 2 bedrm), [shwr, bath, tlt, fan, heat, TV, refrig, cook fac, elec frypan, ldry (in unit), blkts, linen, pillows], dryer, c/park (undercover), cots-fee. D $75 - $110, W $280 - $500, Min book applies.

★★★ **Sunset Strip**, (HF), 203 Boundary St, ☎ 07 5599 5517, fax 07 5536 7566, 9 flats acc up to 4, (1 & 2 bedrm), [shwr, tlt, c/fan, heat, TV, clock radio, refrig, cook fac, micro, elec frypan, toaster, blkts, linen, pillows], ldry, w/mach-fee, iron, pool, bbq, secure park, ☎. D ⏏⏏ $60 - $75, ⏏ $5 - $20, W ⏏⏏ $300 - $550, ⏏ $20 - $40, BC MC VI.

★☆ **Cashel Holiday Flats**, (HF), 209 Boundary St, 300m NE of Tweed Heads PO, ☎ 07 5599 2792, fax 07 5536 6886, (2 stry gr fl), 6 flats acc up to 6, (1 & 2 bedrm), [shwr, bath (1), tlt, c/fan, heat, TV, clock radio, refrig, cook fac (3), cook fac ltd (3), micro (6), elec frypan, toaster, blkts, linen reqd-fee, pillows], ldry, iron, iron brd, c/park (limited). W $220 - $600.

B&B's/Guest Houses

★★☆ **Sunset Strip Budget Resort**, (GH), 199 Boundary St, ☎ 07 5599 5517, fax 07 5536 7566, 43 rms [c/fan, TV, movie, radio, CD], shwr, tlt, ldry-fee, rec rm, lounge (TV), pool, cook fac, t/c mkg shared, bbq, secure park, ☎, plygr, non smoking rms. RO ⏏ $25 - $40, ⏏⏏ $40 - $60, ⏏ $25 - $30, ch con, BC MC VI.

GOLD COAST - COOMERA QLD 4209

Pop Part of the Gold Coast, (54km S Brisbane), See map on page 417, ref E7. Dreamworld - 80ha family theme park.

Hotels/Motels

★★★☆ **Coomera Motor Inn**, (M), Dreamworld Parkway, ☎ 07 5573 2311, fax 07 5573 2171, (2 stry gr fl), 31 units [shwr, tlt, hairdry, a/c, tel, TV, movie, clock radio, t/c mkg, refrig, toaster], ldry, dryer, ✉ (6 days), bar, pool-heated (solar), bbq, rm serv, courtesy transfer (to local theme parks), plygr, cots. RO ⏏ $75 - $85, ⏏⏏ $85 - $95, ⏏⏏⏏ $95 - $105, ch con, AE BC DC EFT MC VI, ♿.

GOLD COAST - CURRUMBIN QLD 4223

Pop 5,884. (94km S Brisbane), See map on page 417, ref E8. Picturesque suburb of Gold Coast. Animal & bird sanctuaries.

Self Catering Accommodation

AAA TOURISM Special Rates — ★★★★☆ **The Rocks Resort**, (HU), 828 Pacific Pde, ☎ 07 5534 4466, fax 07 5598 1460, (Multi-stry gr fl), 97 units acc up to 6, (1 & 2 bedrm), [shwr, bath, tlt, tel, cable tv, refrig, cook fac, micro, d/wash, ldry (in unit), blkts, linen, pillows], lift, rec rm, lounge, ✉, bar, pool-heated (2), sauna (2), spa (2), bbq, secure park, gym, tennis, cots-fee. D ⏏⏏ $158 - $225, W ⏏⏏ $672 - $1,575, ⏏⏏⏏⏏ $931 - $1,575, AE BC DC JCB MC VI.

★★★★ **Little Cove**, (HU), 26/36 Duringan St, ☎ 07 5534 4922, fax 07 5534 4977, (Multi-stry gr fl), 36 units acc up to 6, (2 & 3 bedrm), [ensuite, shwr, bath, tlt, tel, TV, clock radio, refrig, cook fac, micro, d/wash, toaster, ldry (in unit), blkts, linen, pillows], iron, iron brd, pool, sauna, spa, bbq, c/park (undercover), secure park, cots. **D ♦♦♦♦ $99 - $125, W ♦♦♦♦ $693 - $875**, BC MC VI.

★★★★ **Sanctuary Beach Resort**, (HU), 47 Teemangum St, ☎ 07 5598 2524, fax 07 5598 1611, (Multi-stry gr fl), 15 units (2 & 3 bedrm), [ensuite, shwr, bath, tlt, fan, tel, TV, video-fee, refrig, micro, d/wash, ldry (in unit)], dryer, iron, pool-heated (saltwater), spa, bbq, secure park, tennis, cots-fee. **D $90 - $110, W $510 - $1,500**, Min book applies, AE BC MC VI.

★★★★ **Sanctuary Lake Apartments**, (HU), 40 Teemangum St, ☎ 07 5534 3344, fax 07 5534 3377, (Multi-stry gr fl), 12 units acc up to 7, (2 & 3 bedrm), [ensuite, shwr, bath, tlt, c/fan, tel, TV, clock radio, refrig, cook fac, micro, d/wash, ldry (in unit), blkts, linen, pillows], dryer, iron, pool, spa, bbq, secure park, cots-fee. **D $105 - $175, W $575 - $1,050**, Min book applies, BC MC VI.

★★★★ **Sand Castles on Currumbin Beach**, (HU), 31 Teemangum St, ☎ 07 5598 2999, fax 07 5534 7699, (Multi-stry gr fl), 19 units acc up to 6, (2 & 3 bedrm), [shwr, bath, spa bath (4), tlt, c/fan, heat, tel, TV, video-fee, clock radio, refrig, cook fac, micro, d/wash, ldry (in unit), blkts, linen, pillows], pool, spa (heated), bbq, secure park, cots-fee. **RO $86.90 - $182.60, W $495 - $1,278**, BC EFT MC VI.

★★★☆ **Regent Court Currumbin**, (HU), 560 Gold Coast Hwy, ☎ 07 5534 2811, fax 07 5534 2567, (Multi-stry gr fl), 33 units acc up to 6, (2 & 3 bedrm), [ensuite, shwr, bath, tlt, c/fan, tel, TV, video-fee, clock radio, refrig, cook fac, micro, d/wash, toaster, ldry, blkts, linen, pillows], dryer, iron, iron brd, pool, bbq, secure park (under cover), cots-fee. **W $490 - $1,260**, ch con, AE BC DC EFT JCB MC VI.

★★★☆ **The Hill Apartments**, (HU), 38 Duringan St, ☎ 07 5598 1233, fax 07 5598 2079, (Multi-stry), 35 units acc up to 5, [shwr, bath, tlt, tel, TV, video-fee, clock radio, refrig, cook fac, d/wash, ldry (in unit), blkts, linen, pillows], pool, spa, bbq, secure park, cots-fee. **D $90 - $200, W $495 - $1,200**, Min book applies, BC EFT MC VI.

★★★ **Sunjarra Cottages on the Creek**, (Cotg), 1464 Currumbin Ck Rd, 14.6km SW of Currumbin, ☎ 07 5533 0449, fax 07 5533 0353, 2 cotgs acc up to 2, (1 bedrm), [ensuite, shwr, spa bath, tlt, fan, heat, TV, radio, CD, refrig, cook fac ltd, toaster, blkts, linen, pillows]. **RO ♦♦♦♦ $145 - $740**, Breakfast basket available, AE BC MC VI.

GOLD COAST - ELANORA QLD 4221

Pop part of Gold Coast (100km S Brisbane) See map on page 417, ref E8. Residential area west of Palm Beach.

Self Catering Accommodation

★★★☆ **Bay of Palms**, (HU), Coolgardie St, ☎ 07 5598 3055, fax 07 5598 3046, (2 stry gr fl), 60 units acc up to 8, (Studio, 1 & 2 bedrm), [shwr, tlt, c/fan, heat, tel, TV, clock radio, refrig, cook fac (32), blkts, linen, pillows], ldry, rec rm, bar, pool-heated (solar heated), spa, bbq, cots-fee. **D ♦♦ $55 - $120, ◊ $8 - $12, W ♦♦ $315 - $840**, Studio units not included in this rating. Min book applies, BC MC VI.

GOLD COAST - HOPE ISLAND QLD 4212

Pop 500. (65km S Brisbane), See map on page 417, ref E7. Located at northern end of Gold Coast. Rural area, developing into luxury housing estates, with Sanctuary Cove at its centre. Boating, Golf, Tennis.

Hotels/Motels

★★★★★ **Hyatt Regency Sanctuary Cove**, (LH), Manor Circle, Sanctuary Cove 4212, ☎ 07 5530 1234, fax 07 5577 8234, (Multi-stry gr fl), 247 rms (24 suites) [shwr, bath, tlt, hairdry, a/c, tel, TV, movie, clock radio, t/c mkg, refrig, mini bar], lift, conv fac, ⊠, pool, pool-heated, sauna, spa, 24hr reception, rm serv, plygr, bowls, golf (2), gym, tennis (10), cots. **RO ♦♦ $210 - $345, ◊ $40, Suite RO ♦♦ $310 - $1,800**, ch con, AE BC DC JCB MC VI, ♿.

★★★★☆ **Hope Harbour International**, (LH), Sickle Ave, ☎ 07 5530 1999, fax 07 5530 1205, 99 rms (0 suites) [shwr, bath, spa bath (4), tlt, hairdry, a/c-cool, tel, TV, movie, clock radio, t/c mkg, mini bar, pillows], lift, ldry, iron, iron brd, conf fac, ⊠, cafe, bar, pool-heated (salt water), sauna, spa, bbq, rm serv, dinner to unit, c/park (undercover), plygr, gym, tennis-fee, cots-fee. **D $122 - $169, Suite D $185 - $266**, ch con, AE BC DC EFT MC VI, ♿.

★★★☆ **Sanctuary Shores Resort**, (M), 1 Pinnaroo St, 2km W Sanctuary Cove, ☎ 07 5530 1111, fax 07 5530 1011, (2 stry), 12 units [shwr, tlt, hairdry, a/c-cool, c/fan, tel, TV, clock radio, refrig, cook fac, micro], ldry, ⊠, pool (salt water), spa. **RO ♦ $70, ♦♦ $80 - $85, ◊ $15**, BC EFT MC VI.

Self Catering Accommodation

★★★★★ **Hope Island Resort**, (HU), Oxenford Southport Rd, ☎ 07 5530 9000, fax 07 5530 9019, 26 units acc up to 6, (2 & 3 bedrm), [ensuite, spa bath, tlt, hairdry, tel, TV, clock radio, refrig, cook fac, micro, d/wash, toaster, ldry, blkts, linen, pillows], dryer, iron, iron brd, conv fac, ⊠, pool, bbq, tennis. **RO $195 - $355**, weekly con, Min book applies, AE BC DC JCB MC VI.

GOLD COAST - KIRRA QLD 4225

Pop Nominal, (97km S Brisbane), See map on page 417, ref E8. Suburb of Gold Coast. Fishing, Surfing, Swimming.

Hotels/Motels

★★★☆ **Gold Coast Airport Motel**, (M), 95 Golden Four Dve, ☎07 5536 6244, fax 07 5599 5545, (2 stry gr fl), 12 units [shwr, tlt, a/c-cool (4 units)-fee, c/fan, heat, TV, clock radio, t/c mkg, refrig], ldry, pool (salt water), spa, meals to unit (Breakfast only), c/park (undercover), courtesy transfer, ☎, cots. **RO ♦ $50 - $60, ♦♦ $55 - $65, ♦♦♦ $65 - $75**, ch con, AE BC DC EFT MC VI.

★★★☆ **Shipwreck Beach Motel**, (M), Gold Coast Hwy, ☎ 07 5536 3599, fax 07 5536 3742, (2 stry), 23 units [shwr, tlt, hairdry, a/c-cool, c/fan, heat, tel, TV, video, clock radio, t/c mkg, refrig, cook fac, micro], ldry, iron, iron brd, pool, spa (solar heated), non smoking units (17). **RO ♦ $54 - $75, ♦♦ $54 - $75, ♦♦♦♦ $80 - $105, ◊ $10**, ch con, AE BC DC MC VI.

★★★ **Kirra Beach**, (LH), Marine Pde, ☎ 07 5536 3311, (2 stry), 30 rms [shwr, tlt, a/c-cool, fan, TV, t/c mkg, refrig], ☎. **RO ♦ $30 - $40, ♦♦ $40 - $50, ◊ $10**, ch con, BC MC VI.

Self Catering Accommodation

★★★★☆ **Meridian Tower**, (HU), Cnr Coyne & Musgrave Sts, ☎ 07 5536 9400, fax 07 5599 5171, (Multi-stry), 32 units acc up to 5, (1 & 2 bedrm), [ensuite, shwr, bath, tlt, fan (20), heat (20), tel, TV, clock radio, refrig, cook fac, micro, d/wash, ldry (in unit), blkts, linen, pillows], lift, rec rm, pool-heated, sauna, spa, bbq, secure park, gym, tennis, cots-fee. **W ♦♦ $480 - $1,050, ◊ $70**, Min book applies, BC MC VI.

★★★★ **Kirra On The Beach**, (SA), 92 Musgrave St, ☎ 07 5599 2900, fax 07 5599 2444, (Multi-stry gr fl), 39 serv apts acc up to 6, (1 & 2 bedrm), [shwr, tlt, c/fan, tel, TV, clock radio, t/c mkg, refrig, mini bar, cook fac, micro, d/wash, toaster, ldry (in unit), blkts, linen, pillows], dryer, iron, iron brd, pool, bbq, secure park, cots-fee. **D ♦♦ $110 - $205, ◊ $15, W ♦♦ $440 - $1,155, ◊ $70**, BC MC VI.

★★★★ **Kirra Palms Holiday Apartments**, (HU), 112 Musgrave St, 500m N of Coolangatta PO, ☎ 07 5599 2888, fax 07 5599 2985, (Multi-stry gr fl), 20 units acc up to 7, (1, 2 & 3 bedrm), [ensuite, shwr, bath, spa bath (1), tlt, fan (20), c/fan (10), heat, tel, TV, video-fee, clock radio, refrig, cook fac, micro, elec frypan, d/wash, ldry (in unit), blkts, linen, pillows], dryer, iron, pool (salt water), spa, bbq, secure park. **D $130, W $455 - $1,200**, BC MC VI.

★★★☆ **San Chelsea**, (HU), 146 Pacific Pde, 2km N PO Coolangatta, ☎ 07 5536 3377, fax 07 5536 9151, (Multi-stry gr fl), 12 units acc up to 6, (2 & 3 bedrm), [ensuite (4), shwr, bath, spa bath (3), tlt, fan (11)-fee, c/fan (2), heat-fee, tel, TV, clock radio, refrig, cook fac, micro, d/wash (8), ldry (in unit), blkts, linen, pillows], dryer, pool-heated (solar), spa, bbq (covered), secure park, tennis (half court)-fee, cots-fee. W $450 - $1,200, BC MC VI.

GOLD COAST - LABRADOR QLD 4215

Pop 13,303. (71km S Brisbane), See map on page 417, ref E8. Located at the northern entrance of the Gold Coast. Boat Launching ramps. Boating, Golf, Scenic Drives, Squash, Swimming, Tennis, Water Skiing.

Hotels/Motels

★★★ **Limassol**, (M), 109 Frank St (Gold Coast Hwy), ☎ 07 5591 6766, fax 07 5591 2477, (2 stry gr fl), 14 units [shwr, tlt, a/c, c/fan, tel, TV, clock radio, t/c mkg, refrig], ldry, pool (salt water), cots-fee.
RO ⸙ $45 - $90, ⸙⸙ $50 - $110, ⸙ $11, AE BC DC MC VI.

★★ **Broadway**, (M), 128 Frank St (Gold Coast Hwy), ☎ 07 5531 3288, 16 units [shwr, bath (2), tlt, a/c-cool (9), c/fan (7), TV, movie, clock radio, t/c mkg, refrig, cook fac (7)], pool, bbq, ☎, cots-fee.
RO ⸙ $35 - $70, ⸙⸙ $45 - $105, ⸙ $10, BC MC VI.

Self Catering Accommodation

AAA TOURISM *Special Rates*

★★★★☆ **Crystal Bay Resort**, (HU), 182 Marine Pde, ☎ 07 5561 2200, fax 07 5525 5198, (Multi-stry gr fl), 137 units acc up to 6, [shwr, tlt, a/c-fee, c/fan, tel, TV, video-fee, clock radio, refrig, cook fac, micro, d/wash, ldry (in unit), blkts, linen, pillows], lift, dryer, iron, iron brd, pool-heated (salt water heated), sauna, spa, bbq, rm serv-fee, dinner to unit-fee, c/park (undercover), secure park, plygr, gym, cots-fee. D $82.50 - $106, ch con, BC MC VI.

★★★★☆ **Golden Shores Holiday Club**, (HU), 206 Marine Pde, ☎ 07 5574 2800, fax 07 5574 2810, (Multi-stry gr fl), 16 units acc up to 6, (2 bedrm), [shwr, spa bath, tlt, hairdry, c/fan, heat, tel, TV, video, clock radio, refrig, cook fac, micro, d/wash, ldry (in unit), blkts, linen, pillows], rec rm, pool (salt water), sauna, spa, bbq, secure park, gym, cots. D ⸙⸙ $115 - $155, ⸙ $10, W $665 - $1,015, AE BC DC MC VI.

★★★★ **Blue Waters Luxury Apartments**, (HU), 220 Marine Pde, ☎ 07 5591 1695, fax 07 5571 1159, 38 units acc up to 7, (2 & 3 bedrm), [ensuite, shwr, bath (21), tlt, fan, heat, tel, cable tv, video-fee, clock radio, refrig, cook fac, micro, d/wash, ldry (in unit), blkts, linen, pillows], dryer, iron, pool-heated (salt water heated), spa (pool), bbq, secure park, cots-fee. D ⸙⸙ $95, ⸙ $12, W ⸙⸙ $611 - $1,053, ⸙ $84, Min book applies, BC MC VI.

★★★★ **Mango Cove Resort**, (SA), 10 Bath St, ☎ 07 555638077, fax 07 5563 8107, (Multi-stry gr fl), 27 serv apts acc up to 2, (1 bedrm), [shwr, tlt, c/fan, tel, TV, video-fee, clock radio, refrig, cook fac, micro, d/wash, toaster, ldry, blkts, linen, pillows], dryer, iron, iron brd, pool-heated (salt water), spa, bbq, dinner to unit, secure park (undercover), cots-fee. W ⸙⸙ $315 - $699, Min book applies, BC EFT MC VI.

★★★☆ **Beaconlea**, (HU), 316 Marine Pde, ☎ 07 5532 9919, fax 07 5526 4211, (Multi-stry gr fl), 11 units acc up to 6, (2 bedrm), [ensuite, shwr, bath, tlt, fan, c/fan (1), heat, tel, cable tv, video-fee, radio, refrig, cook fac, micro, d/wash, ldry (in unit), blkts, linen, pillows], lift, dryer, rec rm, pool-heated (solar), bbq, c/park (undercover), tennis (half court), cots-fee. D $135 - $175, W ⸙ $574 - $1,225, BC MC VI.

Operator Comment: Visit our website: www.beaconleatower.com.au

★★★☆ **Broadwater Keys**, (HU), 125 Frank St, ☎ 07 5531 0839, fax 07 5591 3675, (Multi-stry gr fl), 30 units acc up to 6, (Studio, 1 & 2 bedrm), [shwr, tlt, c/fan, heat, tel, TV, refrig, cook fac, micro (24), elec frypan, ldry (in unit) (13), blkts, linen, pillows], ldry, dryer-fee, iron, iron brd, pool, bbq, c/park (undercover), cots-fee. D ⸙⸙ $70 - $110, ⸙ $15, W ⸙⸙ $350 - $700, ⸙ $105, ch con, BC MC VI.

★★★☆ **Champelli Palms Apartments**, (HU), 12 Whiting S Labrador, ☎ 07 5591 8155, fax 07 5527 0250, (Multi-stry gr fl), 10 units acc up to 5, (1 & 2 bedrm), [ensuite, shwr, bath, tlt, a/c (1), c/fan, heat, tel, TV, video-fee, clock radio, refrig, cook fac, micro, d/wash, ldry (in unit), blkts, linen, pillows], dryer, iron, pool (salt water), spa, secure park, cots-fee. W $375 - $975, Min book applies, BC MC VI.

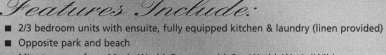

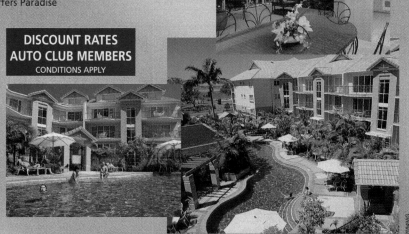

★★★☆ **Santa Fe Apartments By The Broadwater**, (SA), Cnr Frank & Robert Sts, 5km N Surfers Paradise, ☎ 07 5591 1433, fax 07 5591 1062, (Multi-stry gr fl), 15 serv apts acc up to 7, (2 & 3 bedrm), [ensuite, shwr, bath (hip), spa bath (1), tlt, fan, tel, TV, clock radio, refrig, cook fac, micro, d/wash, ldry (in unit)], dryer, pool-heated (salt water heated), spa, bbq, secure park. **D $85 - $210, W $385 - $1,390**, BC MC VI.

★★☆ **Villa Grande**, (HU), 372 Marine Pde, ☎ 07 5537 2624, fax 07 5577 4316, (2 stry gr fl), 7 units acc up to 6, [shwr, bath (4), tlt, c/fan (4), heat, TV, clock radio, refrig, cook fac, ldry (in unit) (4), blkts, linen, pillows], ldry, c/park (undercover) (7), cots-fee. **W ♦♦ $330 - $950**, Units 1 to 3 ★★☆. Min book applies.

GOLD COAST - MAIN BEACH QLD 4217

Pop 2,899. (77km S Brisbane), See map on page 417, ref E8. Located on the Spit at the northern end of the Gold Coast. Marina, hovercraft, bungee jumping & parasailing. Boating, Fishing, Scenic Drives, Squash, Swimming, Tennis, Water Skiing.

Hotels/Motels

★★★★★ **Palazzo Versace**, (LH), Seaworld Dr, ☎ 07 5509 8000, fax 07 5509 8888, 205 rms (59 suites) [shwr, bath, spa bath, tlt, a/c, tel, cable tv, radio, t/c mkg, refrig, cook fac (2)], conf fac, ⊠ (2), pool-heated (outdoor) (1), pool indoor heated (1), sauna (2), spa, rm serv, secure park, ✆, cots, non smoking rms (89). **RO ♦ $695 - $735, ♦♦ $695 - $735, Suite RO $795 - $4,000**, AE BC DC EFT JCB MC VI.

★★★★★ **Sea World Nara Resort**, (LH), Sea World Dve, ☎ 07 5591 0000, fax 07 5591 2375, (Multi-stry gr fl), 405 rms (13 suites) [shwr, bath, spa bath (6), tlt, hairdry, a/c, tel, TV, movie, clock radio, t/c mkg, refrig, mini bar, cook fac (145), micro (145), toaster (145)], ldry, iron, iron brd, business centre, conv fac, ⊠, bar (2), pool-heated (lagoon), sauna, spa, bbq, 24hr reception, rm serv (6am-midnight), dinner to unit, plygr, jetty, gym, tennis, cots, non smoking rms. **RO ♦♦♦♦ $190, ♦ $22, Suite RO $289**, ch con, Tariff includes entry to Sea World. AE BC DC JCB MC VI, ⅋⅊.

★★★★★ **Sheraton Mirage Gold Coast**, (LH), Sea World Dve, Broadwater Spit, ☎ 07 5591 1488, fax 07 5591 2299, (Multi-stry gr fl), 323 rms (30 suites) [shwr, bath, spa bath (84), tlt, hairdry, a/c, tel, TV, movie, clock radio, t/c mkg, refrig, mini bar], lift, conv fac, ⊠ (3), pool, spa, 24hr reception, rm serv, gym, tennis (4), cots, non smoking rms (24). **RO ♦♦ $470 - $690, Suite RO ♦♦ $870 - $3,176**, ch con, AE BC DC JCB MC VI, ⅋⅊.

★★★★ **Maldives on Main Beach**, (LH), Woodroffe Ave, Cnr Pacific St, ☎ 07 5557 7500, fax 07 5557 7599, (Multi-stry gr fl), 86 rms (86 suites) [shwr, tlt, hairdry, a/c, tel, TV, clock radio, t/c mkg, refrig, cook fac, micro, elec frypan, toaster, pillows], lift, ldry-fee, iron, iron brd, ⊠, pool (salt water), spa, bbq (covered), rm serv (breakfast / liquor), secure park (under cover), cots, non smoking flr (6), non smoking suites (36). **RO $110 - $250**, ch con, AE BC DC JCB MC VI.

Self Catering Accommodation

★★★★★ **Xanadu Resort**, (SA), 59 Pacific St, ☎ 07 5557 0400, fax 07 5571 1172, (Multi-stry), 72 serv apts acc up to 4, [ensuite, spa bath (3), hairdry, a/c, cent heat, tel, cable tv, video-fee, clock radio, t/c mkg, refrig, micro, d/wash, toaster, ldry, blkts, linen, pillows], lift, dryer, iron, iron brd, rec rm, conf fac, pool indoor heated (salt water), sauna, spa, steam rm, bbq-fee, rm serv, dinner to unit, c/park (undercover), gym, tennis, cots-fee. **D ♦♦ $150 - $280, W ♦♦ $805 - $2,030**, AE BC DC EFT MC VI.

★★★★☆ **Carrington Court**, (HU), 3576 Main Beach Pde, ☎ 07 5532 8822, fax 07 5532 8521, (Multi-stry), 17 units (2 bedrm), [ensuite, shwr, bath, tlt, fan, heat, tel, TV, clock radio, refrig, cook fac, micro, d/wash, ldry (in unit), blkts, linen, pillows], lift, pool (saltwater), sauna, bbq, secure park, tennis, cots-fee. **D $120 - $150, W $550 - $1,200**, Min book applies, BC MC VI.

★★★★☆ **Golden Sands on Main Beach**, (HU), 3575 Main Beach Pde, ☎ 07 5532 4811, fax 07 5532 4256, (Multi-stry gr fl), 32 units acc up to 6, (2 & 3 bedrm), [ensuite, shwr, bath, tlt, fan, tel, cable tv, video-fee, clock radio, refrig, cook fac, micro, d/wash, toaster, ldry (in unit), blkts, linen, pillows], lift, dryer, iron, iron brd, pool-heated (salt water heated), sauna, spa, bbq, c/park (undercover), secure park, tennis, cots-fee. **W $630 - $2,100**, AE BC DC EFT MC VI.

★★★★☆ **Meriton**, (HU), 29 Woodroffe Ave, ☎ 07 5591 3900, fax 07 5591 3628, (Multi-stry), 24 units acc up to 8, (1, 2 & 3 bedrm), [ensuite, shwr, bath, tlt, tel, TV, clock radio, cook fac, micro, d/wash, toaster, ldry, blkts, linen, pillows], lift, dryer, iron, iron brd, pool, pool-indoor, sauna, spa (communal), bbq (covered), gym, tennis, cots. **D $143 - $192.50, W $747 - $1,971**, Min book applies, BC MC VI.

★★★★☆ **Ocean Sands Resort**, (HU), 17 Hughes Ave, ☎ 07 5531 4188, fax 07 5531 4255, (Multi-stry gr fl), 25 units acc up to 2, [ensuite, shwr, bath, tlt, heat, tel, TV, clock radio, refrig, cook fac, micro, elec frypan, d/wash, toaster, ldry (in unit), blkts, linen, pillows], lift, dryer, iron, iron brd, rec rm, conv fac, pool-heated, pool-indoor, sauna, spa, bbq (covered), rm serv-fee, dinner to unit, c/park (undercover), secure park, gym, tennis, non smoking units (3). **D $165 - $326, W $870 - $1,625**, BC MC VI.

★★★★☆ **Oscar on Main Resort**, (HU), 1 Hughes Ave, 5km N of Surfers Paradise, ☎ 07 5527 0966, fax 07 5527 0933, (Multi-stry), 20 units acc up to 5, (1 & 2 bedrm), [ensuite (16), shwr, bath, spa bath, tlt, hairdry, TV, clock radio, refrig, cook fac, micro, elec frypan, d/wash, toaster, ldry (in unit), blkts, linen, pillows], dryer, iron, iron brd, conf fac, pool-indoor (heated salt water), spa (4), steam rm, bbq-fee, secure park, gym, tennis, cots. **D ♦♦ $245 - $315, ♦ $27.50, W ♦♦ $735 - $2,100**, ch con, Min book applies, BC MC VI.

★★★★☆ **Sunbird Beach Resort**, (HU), 3540 Main Beach Pde, Cnr Breaker St, ☎ 07 5532 9888, fax 07 5532 9266, (Multi-stry), 83 units acc up to 5, [shwr, bath, tlt, c/fan, tel, TV, video, clock radio, refrig, cook fac, micro, d/wash, ldry (in unit), blkts, linen, pillows], lift, dryer, pool, pool indoor heated, wading pool, sauna, spa, bbq, dinner to unit, secure park, ✆, squash, tennis, cots-fee. **W ♦♦ $665 - $1,449**.

★★★★ **Bougainvillea Luxury Apartments**, (HU), 3544 Main Beach Pde, ☎ 07 5571 0066, fax 07 5571 0066, (Multi-stry), 13 units acc up to 5, (2 bedrm), [ensuite, shwr, bath, tlt, tel, fax, cable tv, refrig, cook fac, d/wash, ldry (in unit), blkts, linen, pillows], lift, pool-heated, sauna, spa, bbq, secure park, tennis, cots-fee. **D ♦♦ $150, ♦ $15, W ♦♦ $655 - $1,450**, Min book applies, BC MC VI.

★★★★ **De Ville Apartments**, (HU), 3645 Main Beach Pde,
☎ 07 5591 6322, fax 07 5531 1983, (Multi-stry) 25 units acc up to 6, (1, 2 & 3 bedrm), [shwr, bath, tlt, fan, tel, cable tv (12), video-fee, clock radio, refrig, cook fac, micro, d/wash, ldry (in unit), linen, pillows], lift, dryer, iron, pool-heated, sauna, spa, bbq, c/park (undercover), tennis, cots-fee.
W $790 - $1,755, Min book applies, BC MC VI.

★★★ **Aloha Lane**, (HU), 11 Breaker St, ☎ 07 5591 5944, fax 07 5591 6062, (Multi-stry gr fl), 22 units acc up to 4, (2 bedrm), [shwr, bath, tlt, heat, c/fan, tel, TV, video-fee, t/c mkg, refrig, cook fac, micro, d/wash, ldry (in unit), blkts, linen, pillows], dryer, pool-heated (salt water), spa, bbq, secure park, cots-fee. **D $85 - $155, W $517 - $990**, Min book applies, BC MC VI, ♿.

★★★☆ **Beachside Tower**, (HU), 3545 Main Beach Pde,
☎ 07 5591 7033, fax 07 5532 2741, (Multi-stry gr fl), 18 units acc up to 6, (2 & 3 bedrm), [ensuite, shwr, bath, tlt, tel, TV, clock radio, refrig, cook fac, micro, d/wash, ldry (in unit), blkts, linen, pillows], lift, dryer, pool-heated, bbq, secure park, tennis (half court), cots-fee. **D $110 - $240, W $540 - $1,570**, Min book applies.

★★★☆ **Chidori Court**, (HU), 1 Cronin Ave, ☎ 07 5591 6544, fax 07 5591 6533, (Multi-stry gr fl), 36 units acc up to 6, [shwr, bath, tlt, tel, TV, refrig, cook fac, micro, elec frypan, d/wash, ldry (in unit), blkts, linen, pillows], dryer, pool-heated (salt water), spa, bbq, secure park, cots-fee. **D $140 - $199, W $455 - $1,225**, Min book applies, BC MC VI.

★★★☆ **Hibiscus on the Beach**, (HU), 3555 Main Beach Pde,
☎ 07 5591 4513, fax 07 5531 3995, (Multi-stry), 17 units acc up to 4, (2 bedrm), [shwr, bath, tlt, tel, TV, refrig, cook fac, micro, d/wash, ldry (in unit), blkts, linen, pillows], lift, pool, spa, bbq, secure park, cots-fee. **W $580 - $1,155**, Min book applies.

★★★☆ **Norfolk Luxury Beachfront Apartments**, (HU), 3534 Main Beach Pde, ☎ 07 5532 8466, fax 07 5591 4771, (Multi-stry), 18 units acc up to 6, (2 & 3 bedrm), [shwr, bath, tlt, fan, tel, fax, TV, video, clock radio, refrig, cook fac, micro, elec frypan, d/wash, toaster, ldry (in unit), blkts, linen, pillows], lift (2), dryer, iron, pool-heated (salt water heated), sauna, spa, bbq, secure park, tennis, cots-fee.
W ⧺ $695 - $1,750, 👤 $300, Min book applies.

GOLD COAST - MERMAID BEACH QLD 4218

Pop 4,554. (83km S Brisbane), See map on page 417, ref E8. Located on the Gold Coast. Bowls, Squash, Swimming, Tennis.
Hotels/Motels

AAA
TOURISM
Special Rates
★★★☆ **All Seasons Mermaid Waters Hotel**, (M), Cnr Markeri St & Sunshine Blvd, 1.5km W of PO,
☎ 07 5572 2500, fax 07 5572 9787, (Multi-stry gr fl), 102 units (14 suites) [shwr, bath, spa bath (14), tlt, hairdry, a/c, tel, TV, movie, clock radio, t/c mkg, refrig, cook fac (48)], lift, ldry, conv fac, ⊠ (Mon-Sat), pool (salt water), bbq, 24hr reception, rm serv, ✆, cots. **RO ⧺ $110 - $148.50, ⧺ $110 - $148.50, 👤 $33**, ch con, AE BC DC JCB MC VI, ♿.

★★★ **Camelot**, (M), 2289 Gold Coast Hwy, Cnr Surf St,
☎ 07 5572 7733, (2 stry gr fl), 11 units [shwr, tlt, a/c-cool, fan, TV, clock radio, t/c mkg, refrig], pool, bbq, cots-fee. **RO ⧺ $33 - $104.50, ⧺ $38.50 - $104.50, 👤 $5.50 - $11**, ch con, BC MC VI.

★★☆ **Camden Colonial Motor Inn**, (M), 2371 Gold Coast Hwy,
☎ 07 5575 1066, fax 07 5575 3841, (2 stry gr fl), 15 units [shwr, tlt, fan, tel, TV, video-fee, clock radio, t/c mkg, refrig, cook fac (on request), ldry-fee], pool-heated (salt water), spa (communal / heated), bbq, c/park (undercover) (10), cots-fee, non smoking rms (10). **RO ⧺ $50 - $90, ⧺ $59 - $110, 👤 $12**, AE BC DC MC VI.

★★☆ **Mermaid Beach Motel**, (M), 2395 Gold Coast Hwy,
☎ 07 5575 1577, fax 07 5575 5688, (2 stry gr fl), 22 units [shwr, spa bath (1), tlt, a/c-cool (5), a/c (1), fan, tel, TV, video, movie, clock radio, t/c mkg, refrig], ldry, pool (salt water), bbq, cots-fee. **RO ⧺ $28 - $65, ⧺ $38.50 - $75, 👤 $10**, ch con, AE BC DC MC VI.

★★☆ **Ocean Blue Motel**, (M), Previously Heron 2323 Gold Coast Hwy & Cnr Heron Ave, ☎ 07 5572 6655, fax 07 5575 3578, 14 units [shwr, tlt, a/c-cool (14), fan, tel, TV, clock radio, t/c mkg, refrig], ldry, pool (salt water), c/park (undercover) (6), cots-fee. **RO $45 - $120**, ch con, BC MC VI.

★★ **Classic Motel**, (M), 2429 Gold Coast Hwy, Cnr William St,
☎ 07 5575 2622, 8 units [shwr, tlt, a/c (4), c/fan, TV, clock radio, t/c mkg, refrig], ldry, pool, bbq, cots-fee. **RO ⧺ $45 - $55, ⧺ $65 - $75, 👤 $5**, ch con, AE BC MC VI.

★★ **Tropicana**, (M), 2595 Gold Coast Hwy, ☎ 07 5539 8151, (2 stry gr fl), 16 units [shwr, tlt, a/c-cool (7), fan (9), TV, clock radio, t/c mkg, refrig], pool, ✆, cots. **D ⧺ $45 - $120, ⧺ $50 - $130, 👤 $10 - $25**, ch con, BC MC VI.

★☆ **Captain Cook Colonial**, (M), 2283 Gold Coast Hwy, Cnr Surf St,
☎ 07 5572 7666, fax 07 5572 7655, 8 units [shwr, tlt, TV, clock radio, t/c mkg, refrig], pool, bbq, cots-fee, ch con, AE BC MC VI.

★☆ **Gold Coast Resort**, (M), 2333 Gold Coast Hwy, ☎ 07 5572 6466, fax 07 5572 0731, (2 stry gr fl), 31 units [shwr, tlt, a/c, tel, TV, clock radio, t/c mkg, refrig, cook fac (1)], ldry-fee, dryer-fee, ⊠, pool, spa, bbq (covered), secure park, cots. **RO $59 - $74**, ch con, AE BC MC VI.

★☆ **Red Emu**, (M), 2583 Gold Coast Hwy, 1km N of PO, ☎ 07 5575 2622, 7 units [shwr, tlt, c/fan, TV, t/c mkg, refrig, cook fac (2)], ldry. **RO ⧺ $45 - $55, ⧺ $65 - $75, 👤 $5**, BC MC VI.

★☆ **Van Diemen**, (M), 2267 Gold Coast Hwy, ☎ 07 5575 2622, 8 units [shwr, tlt, c/fan, TV, t/c mkg, refrig, cook fac (2)], ldry, pool, bbq, cots-fee. **RO ⧺ $45 - $55, ⧺ $65 - $75, 👤 $5**, ch con, AE BC DC MC VI.

Self Catering Accommodation

★★★★☆ **Diamond Cove Resort**, (HU), 16 Crescent Ave,
☎ 07 5572 2277, fax 07 5572 1492, (Multi-stry gr fl), 50 units acc up to 7, (1, 2 & 3 bedrm - Split level accommodation available.), [shwr, bath, tlt, a/c-cool (6), c/fan, tel, TV, clock radio, refrig, cook fac, micro, d/wash, toaster, ldry (in unit), blkts, linen, pillows], dryer, iron, pool-heated (salt water), spa, bbq, kiosk, secure park, cots-fee.
W ⧺ $645 - $1,400, Min book applies, BC MC VI.

★★★★☆ **Diamond Sands Resort**, (HU), 2342 Gold Coast Hwy,
☎ 07 5525 5199, fax 07 5525 5198, 63 units acc up to 6, (1, 2 & 3 bedrm), [ensuite, shwr, bath, tlt, c/fan, heat, tel, clock radio, refrig, cook fac, micro, elec frypan, d/wash, toaster, ldry (in unit), blkts, linen, pillows], dryer, iron, iron brd, rec rm, pool-heated (salt water heated), spa, bbq (covered), dinner to unit, secure park, cots-fee. **D $98 - $218, W $615 - $1,040**, ch con, Min book applies, BC MC VI.

★★★★☆ **Mermaid Beach Park View**, (Apt), 40 Ventura Rd,
☎ 07 5575 6100, fax 07 5575 6199, (2 stry gr fl), 20 apts acc up to 6, (1 & 2 bedrm), [ensuite, shwr, tlt, hairdry, a/c, fan, c/fan, tel, TV, video-fee, refrig, cook fac, micro, d/wash, ldry, blkts, linen, pillows], w/mach, dryer, iron, iron brd, pool (salt water), sauna, spa, bbq, secure park, cots-fee. **D $68 - $105, W $476 - $735**, ch con, BC MC VI.

MERMAID *Beach* PARK VIEW

www.mermaidparkview.com.au

Park View Resort is centrally located on the Gold Coast and offers a luxurious exclusivity that only a few are ever able to enjoy. The Coral Sea with pristine, patrolled surf beaches, aqua blue water with fine white sand, is just 70m away, while on the back door step is the park with shady trees and lush green grass. Close to cinemas, Casino, beach, restaurants & Pacific Fair shopping centre. 1&2 B/room apartments pool, spa, sauna, security parking & more. A relaxed holiday lifestyle option with the bonus of an enviable sub-tropical climate with 300 plus days of sunshine each year.

40-44 Ventura Road, Mermaid Beach, Gold Coast 4218
Ph: (07) 5575 6100 Fax: (07) 5575 6199
Email: parkview@onthenet.com.au

Park View Resort

G

QUEENSLAND

Visit Your Favourite Theme Park FREE!*
See our ad in the Gold Coast section
* Conditions Apply
3 PARK SUPER PASS

For Accommodation Booking information - see page 27   489

G

QUEENSLAND

★★★★☆ **Mermaid Cove Resort**, (HU), 45 Ventura Rd,
☎ 07 5526 1422, fax 07 5526 1433, (Multi-stry), 13 units acc up to 4, [shwr, tlt, c/fan, tel (ISD), TV, clock radio, refrig, micro, d/wash, toaster, ldry (in-unit), linen, pillows], dryer, iron, iron brd, pool-heated, spa, bbq, secure park. **D** †† **$120 - $132**, ◊ **$17**, **W** †† **$430 - $828**, AE BC EFT MC VI.

★★★★☆ **Montego Sands**, (Apt), 21 Peerless Av, 100m from beach,
☎ 07 5575 5822, fax 07 5575 5866, (Multi-stry gr fl), 24 apts acc up to 6, [shwr, bath (4), spa bath (4), tlt, hairdry, a/c, c/fan, tel, TV, video-fee, clock radio, refrig, cook fac, micro, toaster, ldry], iron, iron brd, pool (saltwater), spa, bbq, c/park (undercover), cots-fee. **W** †† **$364 - $775**, †††† **$504 - $1,064**, ch con, BC MC VI.

★★★★ **Montana Palms**, (HU), 32 Montana Rd, ☎ 07 5572 6833, fax 07 5572 8433, (Multi-stry gr fl), 19 units acc up to 5, (2 bedrm), [ensuite, shwr, bath, tlt, c/fan, heat, tel, TV, clock radio, refrig, cook fac, micro, d/wash, ldry (in unit), blkts, linen, pillows], dryer, iron, pool (salt water), sauna, spa (heated), bbq, secure park, cots-fee. **D** **$75 - $130**, **W** **$525 - $910**, Min book applies, BC DC MC VI.

★★★★ **Shaz Maisons**, (HU), 15 Surf St, ☎ 07 5572 6265, fax 07 5572 8190, (Multi-stry gr fl), 21 units acc up to 4, [ensuite, shwr, tlt, fan, tel, TV, refrig, cook fac, micro, toaster, ldry (in unit), blkts, linen, pillows], iron, iron brd, pool (salt water), bbq, secure park. **D** †† **$90 - $110**, **W** †† **$390 - $750**, BC MC VI.

★★★☆ **Foreshore Beachfront Apartments**, (HU), 67 Albatross Ave, ☎ 07 5572 7644, fax 07 5578 6458, (Multi-stry gr fl), 27 units acc up to 6, (1 & 2 bedrm), [shwr, bath, tlt, tel, TV, clock radio (5), radio (10), refrig, cook fac, micro, d/wash, ldry (in unit), blkts, linen, pillows], lift, dryer, iron, pool, spa, bbq, c/park (undercover), tennis (half court)-fee, cots-fee. **D** **$95 - $165**, **W** **$440 - $1,200**, Min book applies, BC MC VI.

★★★☆ **Sailfish Point Resort**, (HU), 300 Cottesloe Dve, Mermaid Waters 4218, ☎ 07 5572 0677, fax 07 5572 9501, (2 stry), 4 units acc up to 6, (2 & 3 bedrm), [shwr, bath, tlt, fan, tel, TV, refrig, cook fac, micro (7), ldry (in unit), blkts, linen, pillows], pool-heated, spa, bbq, secure park, tennis, cots-fee. **D** †††† **$75 - $115**, ◊ **$10**, **W** †††† **$490 - $700**, BC MC VI.

★★★☆ **Spindrift on the Beach Holiday Apartments**, (HU), Previously Spindrift Oceanfront Apartments, 37 Albatross Ave, ☎ 07 5572 5188, fax 07 5578 6320, (Multi-stry), 23 units acc up to 6, (1 & 2 bedrm), [shwr, bath, tlt, tel, TV, refrig, cook fac, micro, d/wash, ldry (in unit), blkts, linen, pillows], lift, pool-heated, spa, bbq, secure park, cots-fee. **W** **$375 - $1,100**, Min book applies,

Operator Comment: Visit our web site: www.spindriftonthebeach.com.au

★★★ **Nobbys Outlook**, (HU), 122-130 Marine Pde, ☎ 07 5572 8484, fax 07 5572 8038, (2 stry), 43 units acc up to 6, [shwr, bath, tlt, c/fan, heat, cable tv (5), clock radio (14), radio (13), refrig, cook fac, micro, elec frypan (1), d/wash (1), toaster, ldry (in unit), blkts, linen reqd-fee, pillows], dryer, iron, iron brd, pool (solar heated), bbq, c/park (undercover) (13), plygr. **D** **$60 - $120**, **W** **$300 - $1,670**.

Enjoy A Restful **Beachfront Holiday**
All units have ocean views
4 min. to Casino and 7 min. to Surfers Paradise
Right on patrolled beach • Security underground parking
Master bedroom with ensuite • Linen supplied
Two bedroom units with second bathroom
Fully equipped kitchen with dishwasher and garbage disposal
Separate laundry with washing machine and dryer
Swimming pool, spa and BBQ area
Half tennis court
24 hour direct dial telephone
67-71 Albatross Avenue, Mermaid Beach, Qld.
Phone: (07) **5572 7644**
Fax: (07) 5578 6458
Email: foreshor@onthenet.com.au

B&B's/Guest Houses

★★★★☆ **Mermaid Beachside Bed & Breakfast**, (B&B), 115 Seagull Av, 5km Sth of Surfers Paradise PO, ☎ 07 5572 9530, fax 07 5572 9530, (2 stry), 5 rms [shwr (4), bath (1), tlt (4), hairdry, a/c, tel, cable tv, radio, t/c mkg], ldry, dryer, iron, iron brd, TV rm, pool-heated (saltwater), cook fac (2), t/c mkg shared, bbq, c/park (undercover), non smoking flr (2), non smoking rms (5). **RO** ††† **$70 - $150**, ◊ **$40**, AE BC EFT MC VI.

GOLD COAST - MIAMI QLD 4220

Pop 5,426. (86km S Brisbane), See map on page 417, ref E8. Seaside location on the Gold Coast. Bowls, Golf, Squash, Swimming, Tennis.

Hotels/Motels

★★★☆ **Kristine Court**, (M), 2004 Gold Coast Hwy, ☎ 07 5572 7171, fax 07 5572 0977, (Multi-stry gr fl), 25 units [shwr, tlt, a/c-cool (25), c/fan, heat, tel, TV, clock radio, t/c mkg, refrig], ldry, pool (salt water), spa, secure park, cots, non smoking units (8). **RO** † **$40 - $120**, †† **$50 - $150**, ◊ **$10**, ch con, AE BC DC MC VI, ⚹.

★★★ **El Rancho**, (M), 2125 Gold Coast Hwy, Cnr Messines Cres, ☎ 07 5572 3655, fax 07 5575 4068, 8 units (1 suite) [shwr, spa bath (1), tlt, a/c-cool (8), fan, tel, TV, movie, clock radio, t/c mkg, refrig], ldry, pool, spa, bbq, plygr, cots. **RO** † **$35 - $40**, †† **$35 - $55**, BC MC VI.

★★★ **White Lanterns**, (M), 2121 Gold Coast Hwy, Cnr Messines Cres, ☎ 07 5572 8662, fax 07 5575 6900, (2 stry gr fl), 9 units [shwr, tlt, a/c-cool, c/fan, TV, clock radio, t/c mkg, refrig], ldry, pool, bbq. **RO** † **$40 - $120**, †† **$40 - $120**, ◊ **$10 - $20**, AE BC MC VI.

★★☆ **Miami Shore Motel and Apartments**, (M), 2016 Gold Coast Hwy, cnr Miami Shore Pde, ☎ 07 5572 4333, fax 07 5575 3988, (2 stry gr fl), 10 units [shwr, tlt, c/fan, heat, tel (9), TV, movie, clock radio, t/c mkg, refrig], ldry, pool (salt water), spa, bbq, cots-fee. **RO** † **$40 - $80**, †† **$40 - $100**, ◊ **$10 - $15**, ch con, Some units of a higher rating. AE BC EFT MC VI.

★★ **Miami**, (M), 2117 Gold Coast Hwy, ☎ 07 5572 3083, (2 stry), 5 units [shwr, tlt, fan, c/fan, TV, t/c mkg, refrig], ldry, cots-fee. **RO** † **$25 - $60**, †† **$30 - $75**, ◊ **$5**, ch con, BC MC VI.

Self Catering Accommodation

★★★★☆ **Grande Florida Beachside Resort**, (HU), 7 Redondo Ave, ☎ 07 5572 8111, fax 07 5572 8863, (Multi-stry gr fl), 150 units acc up to 6, (1, 2 & 3 bedrm), [shwr, bath, tlt, c/fan, heat, tel, TV, clock radio, refrig, cook fac, micro, d/wash, ldry (in unit), blkts, linen, pillows], dryer, iron, rec rm, pool-heated (lagoon style) (2), sauna, bbq, secure park, gym, cots. **W** **$395 - $1,490**, AE BC DC MC VI.

★★★★☆ **Mariner Shores Club**, (HU), 260 The Esplanade, ☎ 07 5535 2177, fax 07 5535 3691, (Multi-stry gr fl), 60 units acc up to 6, [ensuite (2 & 3 bedrms), shwr, spa bath (49), tlt, c/fan, tel, TV, video, clock radio, refrig, cook fac, micro, d/wash, ldry (in unit), blkts, linen, pillows], lift, dryer, iron, rec rm, ✉ (Mon-Fri), pool indoor heated, sauna, spa, bbq, c/park (undercover), ☏, plygr, gym, tennis, cots-fee. **D** **$131 - $175**, **W** **$821 - $1,095**, AE BC DC JCB MC VI.

★★★★ **Miami Beachside Apartments**, (HU), 15 Santa Monica Rd, ☎ 07 5575 5000, fax 07 5578 5999, 30 units acc up to 6, (2 bedrm), [ensuite, shwr, bath, tlt, fan (22), c/fan (20), tel, TV, refrig, cook fac, micro, elec frypan, d/wash, ldry (in unit), linen], dryer, iron, pool, spa, bbq, c/park (undercover), cots-fee. **W** **$490 - $1,050**, Min book applies, BC MC VI.

★★★☆ **Miami Pacific**, (HU), 3 Redondo Ave, ☎ 07 5578 6677, fax 07 5578 6367, 21 units acc up to 6, (Studio, 1 & 2 bedrm), [shwr, tlt, fan, tel, TV, video-fee, clock radio, refrig, cook fac (13), micro, elec frypan, blkts, linen, pillows], ldry, dryer, iron, pool-heated (salt water), bbq, c/park (undercover), cots-fee. **W** **$270 - $835**, Studio units ★★★. BC MC VI.

★★★☆ **Sanderling**, (HU), 40 Marine Pde, ☎ 07 5572 3576, fax 07 5572 3576, (Multi-stry gr fl), 14 units acc up to 6, (2 & 3 bedrm), [shwr, bath (hip), tlt, c/fan, TV, clock radio, refrig, cook fac, micro (14), elec frypan, d/wash, ldry (in unit), blkts, linen, pillows], lift, dryer, pool, bbq, secure park, ☏, tennis (half court), cots-fee. **D** †† **$49.50 - $66**, **W** **$390 - $975**, Min book applies, BC MC VI.

★★★ **El Rancho Holiday Apartments**, (HU), 2129 Gold Coast Hwy, ☎ 07 5572 3655, fax 07 5575 4068, (2 stry), 12 units acc up to 10, (1, 2 & 3 bedrm - Split level accommodation available.), [shwr, bath, tlt, tel, TV, clock radio, refrig, cook fac, micro, ldry (in unit), blkts, linen, pillows], bbq, c/park (undercover), plygr, cots. **D 👥 $45, 👤 $12.50, W 👥 $260**, BC MC VI.

★★★ **Miami Beach Apartments**, (HU), 12 Marine Pde, 1.5km S of Nobbys Beach PO, ☎ 07 5572 4444, fax 07 5572 3001, (Multi-stry gr fl), 18 units acc up to 6, (2 bedrm), [shwr, tlt, tel, TV, t/c mkg, refrig, cook fac, micro, toaster, blkts, linen, pillows], ldry, iron, c/park (undercover - 8) (22), cots-fee. **D 👥 $120 - $200, W $280 - $825**, BC MC VI.

★★★ **Miami Shore Motel and Apartments**, (HU), 2016 Gold Coast Hwy, ☎ 07 5572 4333, fax 07 5575 3988, (2 stry gr fl), 16 units acc up to 6, [shwr, tlt, c/fan, tel, TV, clock radio, refrig, cook fac (4), cook fac ltd (2), blkts, linen, pillows], ldry, pool (salt water), spa, bbq, c/park (undercover) (2). **D 👥 $50 - $120, 👤 $10 - $15, W 👥 $265 - $740**, AE BC EFT MC VI.

GOLD COAST - MUDGEERABA QLD 4213

Pop 7,741. (82km S Brisbane), See map on page 417, ref D8. Beginning of Gold Coast Hinterland. Closely settled commercial & shopping centre amid undulating dairying country. Gold Coast War Museum, Boomerang Farm nearby. Picnic areas. Bush Walking, Scenic Drives.

Hotels/Motels

★★★ **Wallaby Hotel**, (LMH), 45 Railway St, 300m N of PO, ☎ 07 5530 5600, fax 07 5530 3937, (2 stry), 10 units [shwr, tlt, a/c-cool, tel, TV, clock radio, t/c mkg, refrig, toaster], conv fac, ⊠, dinner to unit, c/park (undercover), cots, non smoking units (3). **BLB 👤 $60, 👥 $70**, AE BC DC EFT MC VI, ♿,

Operator Comment: Call today & ask us about staying 7 nights for the price of 6.

B&B's/Guest Houses

★★★★★ **Caprice Boutique Mountain Retreat**, (B&B), 40 Brackenfield Court, Bonogin 4213. 10km SW of PO, ☎ 07 5522 9187, fax 07 5522 9147, (2 stry), 3 rms [shwr, bath (2), tlt, hairdry, a/c, heat, elec blkts, TV, movie (DVD), clock radio], rec rm, ✕, pool (heated), spa, t/c mkg shared, non smoking flr (2). **BB 👤 $80 - $140, 👥 $90 - $150.**

★★★★☆ **Summer House Eco-Lodge**, (B&B), No children's facilities, Cnr Springbrook & Boomerang Rds, 6km S of Mudgeeraba PO, ☎ 07 5530 4151, fax 07 5530 7277, 1 rm [shwr, tlt, hairdry, c/fan, fire pl, TV, video, clock radio, CD, t/c mkg, refrig, micro, pillows], iron, pool, bbq, ☏. **RO 👥👥 $155 - $225, 👤 $10**, AE BC MC VI.

★★★★ **Meldrews of Mudgeeraba Bed & Breakfast**, (B&B), 18 Arkana St, ☎ 07 5530 3033, 3 rms [shwr, bath, tlt, fan, c/fan, heat, TV, video, clock radio, t/c mkg, refrig], iron, iron brd, TV rm, pool, non smoking property. **BB 👥 $80 - $110.**

★★★ **Hippocrates Health Centre of Australia**, (GH), Elaine Ave, 4km W of PO, ☎ 07 5530 2860, 14 rms [shwr, tlt, fan, heat, elec blkts], ldry, rec rm, ✕, pool-heated, sauna, spa, ☏, tennis. **D all meals 👥 $998 - $1,996**, Min book applies, BC MC VI.

GOLD COAST - NERANG QLD 4211

Pop 14,450. (72km S Brisbane), See map on page 417, ref D8. Gateway to the Gold Coast Hinterland on the Nerang River. Nerang State Forest, picnic areas. Fishing, Scenic Drives, Swimming.

Hotels/Motels

★★★ **Nerang Motor Inn**, (M), Cnr Pacific Hwy & Broadbeach Rd, ☎ 07 5578 2266, fax 07 5596 5446, 27 units [shwr, tlt, a/c, c/fan, tel, TV, clock radio, t/c mkg, refrig], ldry, pool, spa, bbq, plygr, cots. **RO 👤 $66 - $88, 👥 $66 - $88, 👤 $10**, AE BC DC MC VI.

★★☆ **Pelermans on the River**, (LMH), 53 Station St, ☎ 07 5557 1699, fax 07 5596 2339, (2 stry gr fl), 26 units [shwr, bath (16), tlt, a/c-cool, tel, TV, t/c mkg, refrig], ldry, conv fac, ⊠, pool, c/park (undercover) (16), cots. **BLB 👤 $60.50, 👥 $77 - $88, 👤 $16.50**, Units 17 to 25 ★★. AE BC DC EFT MC VI.

★★☆ **Town & Country**, (M), 2 Nerang Southport Rd, ☎ 07 5578 4488, fax 07 5596 5988, (2 stry gr fl), 30 units [shwr, tlt, a/c, tel, TV, clock radio, t/c mkg, refrig], ldry, conv fac, ⊠, pool, spa, dinner to unit, c/park (undercover) (19), cots-fee. **RO 👤 $77 - $100, 👥 $95 - $120**, ch con, AE BC DC EFT MC VI.

GOLD COAST - NOBBY BEACH QLD 4218

Pop Nominal, (83km S Brisbane), See map on page 417, ref E8. Seaside location on Gold Coast.

Self Catering Accommodation

★★★★☆ **Magic Mountain Resort**, (HU), Great Hall Dve, ☎ 07 5572 8088, fax 07 5572 8083, (Multi-stry gr fl), 100 units acc up to 6, (1, 2 & 3 bedrm), [ensuite, shwr, tlt, c/fan, tel, cable tv, clock radio, refrig, cook fac, micro, elec frypan, d/wash, toaster, ldry (in unit), blkts, linen, pillows], dryer, iron, iron brd, pool-heated, sauna, spa, bbq, kiosk, c/park (undercover), secure park, gym. **D** $120 - $133, **W** $553 - $1,757, BC MC VI.

★★★★ **Santorini by the Sea**, (HU), Chairlift Ave, ☎ 07 5527 7773, fax 07 5527 7774, 41 units acc up to 6, [ensuite, shwr, bath, tlt, hairdry, a/c (2), c/fan, heat (fan), tel, TV, video-fee, clock radio, CD-fee, refrig, cook fac, micro (30), elec frypan, d/wash (29), toaster, ldry (in unit), blkts, linen, pillows], dryer, iron, iron brd, ⊠, pool (salt water), spa, bbq (covered), secure park, cots-fee. **D** $80 - $200, **W** $546 - $1,400, AE BC MC VI.

★★★☆ **Sandrift Beachfront**, (HU), Previously Sandrift Apartments, 98 Marine Pde, Miami 4220, ☎ 07 5575 3677, fax 07 5572 1232, (Multi-stry gr fl), 22 units acc up to 6, (2 bedrm), [shwr, bath, tlt, fan (20), heat (19), tel, TV, clock radio (15), refrig, cook fac, micro, elec frypan, d/wash, ldry (in unit), blkts, linen, pillows], dryer, pool (salt water), spa (heated), bbq, secure park, cots-fee. **D ♦♦** $95 - $140, **W ♦♦** $380 - $980, BC EFT MC VI.

GOLD COAST - ORMEAU QLD 4208

Pop Nominal, (41km SE Brisbane), See map on page 417, ref D7. Small township within close proximity to Dreamworld, Movie World & Sea World.

Hotels/Motels

★★★ **Ormeau Motel and Cabin Park**, (M), Cnr Pacific Hwy & Goldmine Rd, ☎ 07 5546 6285, fax 07 5546 6031, 4 units [shwr, tlt, a/c, tel, TV, clock radio, t/c mkg, refrig, toaster], pool-heated (salt water). **RO ♦♦** $71 - $82, ♦ $5, AE BC EFT MC VI.

GOLD COAST - OXENFORD QLD 4210

Pop 2,500. (56km S Brisbane), See map on page 417, ref D8. Fishing, Swimming.

B&B's/Guest Houses

★★★★☆ **The Gold Coast Queenslander**, (B&B), 26 Clarence Drive, 'River Downs', ☎ 07 5573 2241, 2 rms [shwr, bath (hip) (1), tlt, hairdry, c/fan, clock radio], ldry, rec rm, lounge (TV, video), ✗, pool (salt water), t/c mkg shared, bbq, c/park (undercover), ☎, non smoking rms. **BB ♦** $75 - $80, **♦♦** $90 - $120, BC EFT MC VI.

★★★☆ **Kintail**, (B&B), 59 California Drive, ☎ 07 5573 7469, fax 07 5573 7919, 2 rms [shwr, bath, tlt, hairdry, c/fan, tel, TV, video, t/c mkg, refrig], iron, iron brd, pool, spa, secure park, gym. **BB ♦♦** $60 - $90, BC MC VI.

Wimbledon House, (B&B), 8 Wimbledon Way, ☎ 07 5573 5045, 2 rms [shwr, bath, tlt, hairdry, a/c, c/fan, heat, elec blkts, tel, cable tv, video, clock radio, CD, t/c mkg] iron, iron brd, bbq, c/park (undercover), cots. **BLB ♦** $60 - $80, **♦♦** $80 - $100, (not yet classified).

GOLD COAST - PALM BEACH QLD 4221

Pop 12,598. (93km S Brisbane), See map on page 417, ref E8. Located on southern area of the Gold Coast.

Hotels/Motels

★★★☆ **The Estuary Motor Inn**, (M), 1026 Gold Coast Hwy, ☎ 07 5534 5566, fax 07 5534 5476, (2 stry) 18 units [shwr, tlt, a/c (r/cyc), tel, TV, video, clock radio, t/c mkg, refrig, toaster], pool, cots-fee. **RO ♦** $55 - $88, **♦♦** $55 - $88, ♦ $11, AE BC DC MC VI.

★★★ **Palm Beach North**, (M), 1444 Gold Coast Hwy, ☎ 07 5576 1999, fax 07 5576 1955, (2 stry gr fl), 27 units [shwr, tlt, a/c-cool (21), c/fan, tel, TV, clock radio, t/c mkg, refrig, toaster], ldry, pool (salt water), spa, c/park (undercover). **RO ♦** $49.50 - $99, **♦♦** $49.50 - $104.50, ♦ $11 - $22, ch con, BC MC VI, ♿.

★★★ **Tropic Sands on the Beach**, (M), 1295 Gold Coast Hwy, ☎ 07 5535 1044, fax 07 5535 8313, (Multi-stry gr fl), 22 units [shwr, bath, spa bath (9), tlt, fan, heat, tel, TV, clock radio, t/c mkg, refrig], ldry, pool, spa, bbq, plygr, cots-fee. **RO ♦** $83 - $195, **♦♦** $83 - $195, ♦ $10, AE BC DC MC MP VI.

★★☆ **Surf N Sand**, (M), Cnr 1203 Gold Coast Hwy & 13th Ave, ☎ 07 5576 3804, fax 07 5576 3804, 9 units [shwr, tlt, c/fan, TV, clock radio, t/c mkg, refrig], bbq, c/park (undercover), ☎, cots. **RO ♦** $40 - $85, **♦♦** $40 - $100, ♦ $5 - $10, AE BC MC VI.

★★☆ **The Queenslander**, (M), Cnr 14th Ave & Gold Coast Hwy, ☎ 07 5535 3614, fax 07 5535 3614, (2 stry gr fl), 9 units [shwr, tlt, c/fan, TV, clock radio, t/c mkg, refrig, toaster], ldry, bbq, cots. **RO ♦** $33 - $90, **♦♦** $38.50 - $100, ♦ $5.50, BC MC VI.

★★ **Cheshire Cat**, (M), 1005 Gold Coast Hwy, ☎ 07 5534 2017, fax 07 5534 2017, (2 stry), 7 units [shwr, tlt, fan, heat, TV, t/c mkg, refrig, ldry], bbq, meals to unit (b/fast/dinner), c/park (undercover). **RO ♦** $45 - $105, **♦♦** $50 - $120, ♦ $10 - $20, ch con, AE BC MC VI.

Self Catering Accommodation

★★★★☆ **19th Avenue on the Beach**, (HU), 2, 19th Ave, ☎ 07 5576 3844, fax 07 5576 3929, (Multi-stry) 43 units acc up to 6, (3 bedrm), [shwr, spa bath, tlt, c/fan, tel, cable tv, video-fee, clock radio, refrig, cook fac, micro, d/wash, ldry (in unit), blkts, linen, pillows], lift, iron, rec rm, ⊠, pool indoor heated, sauna, spa, steam rm, bbq, secure park, gym, squash, tennis, cots-fee. **W ♦♦** $651 - $1,386, **♦♦♦♦** $770 - $1,386, ch con, Min book applies, BC MC VI.

★★★★☆ **Currumbin Sands Beachfront Apartments**, (HU), 955 Gold Coast Hwy, ☎ 07 5525 5000, fax 07 5525 5099, (Multi-stry), 36 units acc up to 7, (2 & 3 bedrm), [shwr, bath, tlt, c/fan, tel, TV, clock radio, refrig, cook fac, micro, d/wash, toaster, ldry (in unit), blkts, linen, pillows], dryer, iron, pool-heated (salt water heated), spa, bbq, secure park, cots-fee. **D** $90 - $225, Min book applies, BC MC VI.

★★★★☆ **Princess Palm on the Beach**, (HU), 969 Gold Coast Hwy, 5km N of Coolangatta Airport, ☎ 07 5534 5455, fax 07 5534 5702, (Multi-stry) 51 units acc up to 5, (2 bedrm), [ensuite, shwr, bath, spa bath (1), tlt, heat, c/fan (10), tel, cable tv, video, clock radio, refrig, cook fac, micro, d/wash, toaster, ldry, blkts, linen, pillows], lift, w/mach, dryer, iron, iron brd, rec rm, pool (salt water), sauna, spa, bbq, secure park, plygr, gym, tennis, cots-fee. **RO** $574 - $1,309, Min book applies, AE BC DC MC VI.

★★★★☆ **Regency on the Beach**, (SA), Previously Palm Beach Quest Resort. 1483-1489 Gold Coast Hwy, ☎ 07 5520 9888, fax 07 5520 9889, (Multi-stry), 62 serv apts acc up to 6, (Studio, 1, 2 & 3 bedrm), [ensuite, shwr, spa bath (5), tlt, hairdry, a/c, tel, cable tv, video, clock radio, refrig, micro, elec frypan, d/wash, toaster, blkts, linen, pillows], lift (2), w/mach, dryer, iron, iron brd, pool-heated (saltwater), sauna, spa (heated), steam rm, bbq (rooftop), dinner to unit, secure park (undercover), courtesy transfer, gym, cots-fee, non smoking rms (3). **RO** $95, AE BC DC EFT MC MP VI.

★★★★☆ **Royal Palm Resort**, (HU), 973 Gold Coast Hwy, ☎ 07 5534 5999, fax 07 5534 5849, (Multi-stry), 55 units (2 bedrm), [ensuite (master bedroom), shwr, bath, tlt, fan, heat-fee, tel, cable tv (45), video (43)-fee, clock radio, refrig, cook fac, micro (45), d/wash, toaster, ldry (in unit), blkts, linen, pillows], lift (3), dryer, iron, iron brd, rec rm, pool (salt water), sauna, spa (heated), bbq-fee, secure park, gym, tennis (2), cots-fee. **D** $150 - $230, **W** $595 - $1,295, ch con, Min book applies, AE BC DC MC VI.

★★★★☆ **Sea Mist Palms**, (HU), 1500 Gold Coast Highway, ☎ 07 5535 2955, fax 07 5520 3906, (Multi-stry gr fl), 17 units acc up to 4, (1 & 2 bedrm), [ensuite, shwr, tlt, c/fan, tel, TV, clock radio, refrig, micro, d/wash, toaster, ldry (in unit), blkts, linen] dryer, pool (saltwater), bbq, secure park, cots-fee. **D $100 - $150, W $420 - $910**, ch con, Min book applies, BC EFT MC VI.

★★★★☆ **The Estuary Motor Inn**, (HU), 1026 Gold Coast Hwy, ☎ 07 5534 5566, fax 07 5534 5476, (2 stry gr fl), 4 units acc up to 5, (2 bedrm), [shwr, bath (hip bath), tlt, a/c (r/cyc), c/fan, tel, TV, video, clock radio, refrig, cook fac, micro, elec frypan, toaster, ldry (in unit), blkts, linen, pillows], dryer, iron, iron brd, pool (salt water), cots. **D $120 - $165, W $600 - $1,100**, AE BC DC MC VI.

★★★★ **Casablanca Palms on the Beach**, (HU), Cnr 25th Ave & Gold Coast Highway, ☎ 07 5576 4299, fax 07 5576 4301, (Multi-stry gr fl), 12 units acc up to 8, (2 & 3 bedrm), [ensuite, shwr, bath, tlt, c/fan, TV, t/c mkg, refrig, cook fac, micro, d/wash, toaster, ldry (in unit), blkts, linen, pillows], lift, dryer, iron, iron brd, pool (salt water), spa, bbq, secure park, tennis, cots-fee. **D $110 - $260, W $500 - $1,300**.

FLAG
FLAG CHOICE HOTELS™

★★★★ **Isle of Palms Resort**, (HU), 2 Coolgardie St, Elanora, ☎ 07 5598 1733, fax 07 5598 1653, 55 units acc up to 6, (3 & 4 bedrm), [shwr, bath, spa bath (5), tlt, c/fan, tel, TV, refrig, cook fac, micro (50), d/wash (10), ldry (in unit), blkts, linen, pillows], rec rm, conv fac, ⊠, pool-heated, spa (2), bbq, secure park, ✆, tennis (2), cots-fee. **D ♯♯ $115 - $165, W $485 - $1,330**, Min book applies, AE BC DC MC VI.

★★★★ **Seascape Holiday Apartments**, (HU), 1189 Gold Coast Hwy, 500m N of PO, ☎ 07 5576 5575, fax 07 5535 4632, (Multi-stry), 20 units acc up to 6, (2 bedrm), [ensuite, shwr, tlt, tel, TV, video-fee, clock radio, refrig, cook fac, micro, d/wash, ldry (in unit), blkts, linen, pillows], lift, pool, sauna, spa, bbq, secure park, tennis (half court), cots-fee. **D $110 - $143, W $425 - $860**.

★★★★ **Surfers Horizons**, (HU), 2 17th Ave, 2km S of Burleigh Heads, ☎ 07 5535 5222, fax 07 5576 5035, (Multi-stry gr fl), 18 units acc up to 6, (2 & 3 bedrm), [ensuite, shwr, bath, tlt, c/fan, heat, tel, TV, clock radio, refrig, cook fac, micro, elec frypan, d/wash, toaster, ldry (in unit), blkts, linen, pillows], dryer, iron, pool (salt water/heated), spa, bbq, secure park, cots-fee. **W $590 - $990**, Min book applies, AE BC DC MC VI.

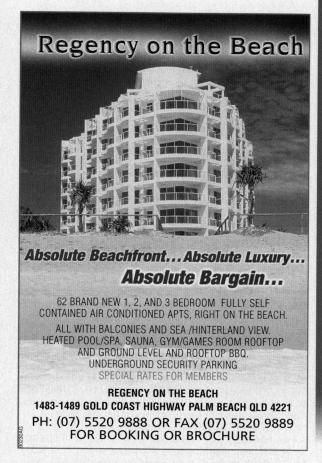
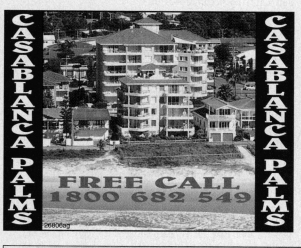

★★★☆ **Beach Palms**, (HU), 1111 Gold Coast Hwy, ☎ 07 5534 6888, fax 07 5534 6080, (Multi-stry gr fl), 20 units acc up to 6, [ensuite (19), shwr, tlt, c/fan, heat, tel, cable tv (19), clock radio, refrig, cook fac, micro, d/wash (10), ldry (in unit), blkts, linen, pillows], lift, rec rm, pool, sauna, spa, bbq, secure park, cots-fee. D $71 - $150, Min book applies, BC EFT MC VI. *Operator Comment: A three and half star resort at a family price. www.beachpalms.com.au or phone for brochure.*

★★★☆ **Palm Beach Resort**, (HU), 979 Gold Coast Hwy, ☎ 07 5598 2366, fax 07 5598 2246, (Multi-stry gr fl), 20 units acc up to 6, (1, 2 & 3 bedrm), [shwr, bath, tlt, fan (14), c/fan (6), heat, tel, TV, video-fee, refrig, cook fac, micro (17), d/wash, ldry (in unit), blkts, linen, pillows], pool (salt water), spa, bbq, secure park, tennis, cots-fee. W $415 - $1,200, Min book applies.

★★★☆ **Palm Gables**, (HU), Cnr Gold Coast Hwy & 16th Ave, ☎ 07 5576 5022, fax 07 5576 3851, (Multi-stry gr fl), 14 units acc up to 6, (2 bedrm), [shwr, bath (1), tlt, fan, heat, tel, TV, video (2)-fee, clock radio, refrig, cook fac, micro, ldry (in unit), blkts, linen, pillows], dryer, iron, pool-heated (salt water), bbq (2), secure park, cots-fee. D ♦♦♦♦ $299 - $845.

★★★☆ **Palm Winds**, (HU), 2 23rd Ave, ☎ 07 5576 5833, fax 07 5576 2896, (Multi-stry gr fl), 5 units acc up to 8, (2 & 3 bedrm), [shwr (2), bath, tlt (2), c/fan, tel, TV, clock radio, refrig, cook fac, micro, elec frypan, toaster, ldry (in unit), blkts, linen, pillows], dryer, iron, pool, bbq, c/park (undercover). D $93.50 - $209, W $572 - $1,320, BC MC.

★★☆ **Almo Apartments**, (HU), 3/24th Ave, North Palm Beach, 500m Tallabudgera Ck, ☎ 02 6281 4541, fax 02 6281 7641, (2 stry gr fl), 4 units acc up to 5, (2 bedrm), [shwr, tlt, a/c-cool (2), c/fan, TV, video-fee, clock radio, refrig, cook fac, micro, toaster], ldry, w/mach, iron, iron brd, bbq, c/park (carport). D $60 - $70, W $250 - $385, Min book applies.

GOLD COAST - ROBINA QLD 4226

Pop 3,506. (87km S Brisbane), See map on page 417, ref E8. Attractive residential suburb of Gold Coast featuring Robina Lake.
★★★★☆ **Radisson Resort Gold Coast**, (LH), Palm Meadows Drive, 8km W of Broadbeach, ☎ 07 5555 7700, fax 07 5555 7701, (Multi-stry), 308 rms (12 suites) [shwr, bath, tlt, hairdry, a/c, tel, TV, clock radio, t/c mkg, refrig], iron, iron brd, ⊠, pool-heated, sauna, spa, rm serv, dinner to unit, c/park (undercover), gym, tennis, cots, non smoking rms (102). RO $139 - $319, ch con, AE BC CC DC EFT JCB MC VI, ⟨&⟩.

GOLD COAST - RUNAWAY BAY QLD 4216

Pop 7,529. (71km S Brisbane), See map on page 417, ref E8. Canal-based suburb of Gold Coast close to Surfers Paradise.
Hotels/Motels

★★★★ **Runaway Bay Motor Inn**, (M), 429 Oxley Dve, ☎ 07 5537 5555, fax 07 5529 0244, (2 stry gr fl), 41 units (3 suites) [shwr, spa bath (6), tlt, hairdry, a/c, c/fan, tel, TV, movie, clock radio, t/c mkg, refrig, micro], ldry, conv fac, ⊠ (Tue - Sat), pool-heated (salt water), rm serv, dinner to unit, secure park, cots-fee. RO ♦ $105 - $165, ♦♦ $105 - $165, ♦ $16.50, Suite RO $182, AE BC DC MC VI, ⟨&⟩.

Self Catering Accommodation

★★★★☆ **Bayview Bay Apartments**, (HU), 37 Bayview St, ☎ 07 5537 7249, fax 07 5537 6882, (Multi-stry gr fl), 30 units acc up to 6, [shwr, bath, tlt, tel, TV, refrig, cook fac, d/wash, ldry (in unit), blkts, linen, pillows], dryer, pool (salt water), spa, bbq, secure park, cots-fee. D $125 - $150, ♦ $10, W $440 - $980, AE BC MC VI.

★★★★☆ **Bayview Waters**, (HU), 22 Jennifer Ave, ☎ 07 5537 6517, fax 07 5537 4929, (Multi-stry gr fl), 12 units acc up to 4, (2 bedrm), [ensuite, shwr, bath, tlt, heat (Fan), fan, c/fan (2), tel, TV, video-fee, clock radio, t/c mkg], refrig, cook fac, micro, elec frypan, d/wash, ldry, blkts, linen, pillows], dryer, iron, iron brd, pool-heated, spa (1), bbq (Covered), secure park (Undercover), cots-fee. W $425 - $890, BC MC VI.

★★★★☆ **Broadwater Shores**, (HU), 9 Bayview St, ☎ 07 5537 3555, fax 07 5537 3180, (Multi-stry), 13 units acc up to 7, (2 & 3 bedrm), [ensuite, shwr, bath, tel, TV, video-fee, cook fac, ldry], lift, rec rm, pool-heated (solar) (1), sauna, spa, bbq, secure park, tennis. W $580 - $1,355, 2 units of 3.5 star rating. Min book applies.

GOLD COAST - SOUTHPORT QLD 4215

Pop 20,252. (73km S Brisbane), See map on page 417, ref E8. Located on the Broadwater; the largest town and the commercial centre of the Gold Coast area.
Hotels/Motels

★★★☆ **Earls Court Motor Inn**, (M), 131 Nerang St, ☎ 07 5591 4144, fax 07 5591 1658, (2 stry), 34 units (3 suites) [shwr, bath (3), tlt, a/c-cool, c/fan, tel, TV, t/c mkg, refrig, cook fac (15), ldry (in unit) (3)], ldry, dryer, pool (salt water), bbq, c/park (undercover), cots-fee. RO ♦ $60.80 - $93.50, ♦♦ $65.45 - $93.50, ♦ $16.50, Suite D $76.65 - $117.70, ch con, Surcharge of $22.00 Big Day Out Concert, Homebake Concert, Indy Race, Gold Coast Marathon. AE BC DC MC VI.

★★☆ **Park Regis Hotel**, (Ltd Lic H), 2 Barney St, Cnr Brighton Pde 1km S of PO, ☎ 07 5532 7922, fax 07 5532 0195, (Multi-stry), 99 rms (1 bedrm), [shwr, bath (40), tlt, a/c-cool, tel, TV, clock radio, t/c mkg, refrig, micro (22)], lift, ldry, dryer, conv fac, ⊠, pool, cots. RO ♦ $210 - $280, ♦♦ $210 - $280, ◊ $15, ch con, Min book applies, AE BC DC MC VI, ⚹☐.

Self Catering Accommodation

★★★★☆ **Swan Lane Apartments**, (HU), Cnr Queens & Swan Lane, South Molle Island 4741, ☎ 07 5528 1900, fax 07 5528 1911, (Multi-stry gr fl), 19 units acc up to 4, [shwr, spa bath, tlt, a/c, fan (10), tel, TV, clock radio, micro, elec frypan, d/wash, toaster, ldry, blkts, linen, pillows], dryer, pool (solar heating), bbq, secure park, tennis-fee, cots-fee. D ♦ $115, ◊ $22, W ♦♦ $594 - $875, BC MC VI.

★★★★☆ **The Rays Resort on the Broadwater**, (HU), 106-108 Marine Parade, ☎ 07 5526 4999, fax 07 5526 4611, (Multi-stry gr fl), 88 units acc up to 4, [shwr, tlt, a/c, tel, TV, clock radio, refrig, cook fac, micro, elec frypan, toaster, ldry, blkts, linen, pillows], iron, iron brd, pool, spa (communal), bbq, secure park, gym, cots-fee. RO $110 - $132, W $581 - $924, AE BC DC MC VI.

★★★☆ **Palmerston Tower**, (HU), 114 Marine Pde (Gold Coast Hwy), ☎ 07 5532 0566, fax 07 5531 2202, (Multi-stry), 35 units acc up to 6, (1 & 2 bedrm), [shwr, bath, tlt, a/c-cool (3), c/fan, tel, TV, video-fee, clock radio, refrig, cook fac, micro, d/wash, ldry (in unit), blkts, linen, pillows], lift, dryer, pool-heated (saltwater), spa (heated), bbq, secure park, tennis (half court), cots-fee. D $120 - $165, W $551 - $1,103, BC DC MC VI.

GOLD COAST - STRADBROKE ISLAND SOUTH QLD 4183

Pop Nominal, (71km S Brisbane), See map on page 417, ref E7. Extends north from the Gold Coast for more than 20km.

Hotels/Motels

★★★ **South Stradbroke Island Resort**, (LMH), South Stradbroke Island, via Gold Coast, ☎ 07 5577 3311, fax 07 5577 3746, 40 units [shwr, tlt, a/c-cool (10), c/fan, TV, clock radio, t/c mkg, refrig], ldry, rec rm, conv fac, ⊠, pool, sauna, spa, kiosk, ☏, plygr, jetty, tennis, cots-fee. RO $95 - 140, ch con, Min book Christmas Jan and Easter, AE BC DC EFT MC VI.

Self Catering Accommodation

★★★★★ **Couran Cove Resort**, (Villa), Resort, ☎ 07 5597 9000, fax 07 5597 9090, 226 villas acc up to 8, (1, 2 & 4 bedrm Studio), [shwr, tlt, c/fan, tel, TV, movie, refrig, cook fac, micro, toaster, blkts, linen, pillows], iron, iron brd, rec rm, conf fac, ⊠, pool-heated (saltwater), bbq, secure park ((at Runaway Bay)), ☏, plygr, gym, tennis-fee, cots, non smoking units. D $205, W $1,292, AE BC CC DC JCB MC MP VI, ⚹☐.

★★★★☆ **(Nature Cabins)**, 93 cabins acc up to 8, (2 & 3 bedrm Studio), [shwr, tlt, c/fan, fire pl, tel, TV, movie, refrig, cook fac, micro, toaster, blkts, linen, pillows], iron, iron brd, non smoking units. W $989, Min book applies, ⚹☐.

GOLD COAST - SURFERS PARADISE QLD 4217

Part of GOLD COAST region. Pop 11,965. (78km S Brisbane), See map on page 417, ref E8. Vibrant heart of the Gold Coast. Bowls, Canoeing, Golf, Horse Racing, Sailing, Scenic Drives, Squash, Surfing, Swimming, Tennis, Water Skiing.

Hotels/Motels

★★★★★ **ANA Hotel Gold Coast**, (LH), 22 View Ave, ☎ 07 5579 1000, fax 07 5570 1260, (Multi-stry), 404 rms (18 suites) [shwr, bath, tlt, hairdry, a/c, tel, TV, movie, clock radio, t/c mkg, refrig, mini bar], lift, conv fac, ⊠, pool-heated, sauna, spa, rm serv, secure park, gym, tennis, cots, non smoking flr (2). RO ♦ $285 - $340, ♦♦ $285 - $340, ◊ $40, Suite D $412 - $1,865, ch con, AE BC DC JCB MC VI, ⚹☐.

★★★★★ **Gold Coast International**, (LH), Cnr Gold Coast Hwy & Staghorn Ave, ☎ 07 5584 1200, fax 07 5584 1280, (Multi-stry), 296 rms (21 suites) [shwr, bath, spa bath (21), tlt, hairdry, a/c, tel, TV, video-fee, movie-fee, clock radio, t/c mkg, refrig, mini bar], lift, ldry, conv fac, ⊠, pool, sauna, spa, rm serv, c/park (undercover), gym (2), tennis (2), cots, non smoking flr (2). RO ♦ $210 - $230, ♦♦ $210 - $230, ◊ $22, Suite D $360, ch con, AE BC DC JCB MC VI, ⚹☐.

★★★★★ **Parkroyal Surfers Paradise**, (LH), 2807 Gold Coast Hwy, 2km S of PO, ☎ 07 5592 9900, fax 07 5592 1519, (Multi-stry), 379 rms (25 suites) [shwr, bath, spa bath (152), tlt, hairdry, a/c, tel, cable tv, movie, clock radio, t/c mkg, refrig, mini bar], lift, ldry, iron, iron brd, conv fac, ⊠ (3), cafe, pool (2), pool-heated, sauna, spa, 24hr reception, rm serv, c/park (undercover), ☏, plygr, gym, tennis, cots. BB ♦ $153 - $224, ♦♦ $165 - $236, AE BC DC MC VI, ⚹☐.

★★★★★ **Surfers Paradise Marriott Resort**, (Ltd Lic H), 158 Ferny Ave, 1km N of PO, ☎ 07 5592 9800, fax 07 5592 9888, (Multi-stry), 300 rms (30 suites) [shwr, bath, spa bath (30), tlt, a/c, tel, TV, video, movie, radio, t/c mkg, refrig, mini bar], lift, rec rm, lounge, conv fac, ⊠, pool-heated, sauna, spa, bbq, 24hr reception, rm serv, c/park (undercover), ☏, plygr, gym, tennis, cots. RO $195 - $495, ch con, AE BC DC JCB MC VI, ⚹☐.

AAA Australis
TOURISM HOTELS·RESORTS·APARTMENTS
Special Rates

★★★★☆ **Australis Sovereign Hotel**, (LH), Cnr Birt & Ferny Ave, ☎ 07 5579 3888, fax 07 5579 3877, (Multi-stry gr fl), 204 rms (153 suites) [shwr, bath, spa bath (12), tlt, hairdry, a/c, c/fan, tel, TV, movie, clock radio, t/c mkg, refrig, mini bar, cook fac ltd, micro, elec frypan, toaster], lift, ldry-fee, dryer-fee, iron, iron brd, conv fac, ⊠, pool, sauna, spa, rm serv, secure park, gym, cots-fee. D ♦♦ $105 - $125, ◊ $30, ch con, AE BC DC MC VI. *Operator Comment: Please see ad on next page.*

★★★★☆ **Concorde Hotel Gold Coast**, (LH), Ferny Ave, ☎ 07 5539 0444, fax 07 5592 3757, (Multi-stry), 199 rms (4 suites) [shwr, bath, tlt, hairdry, a/c, tel, TV, movie, clock radio, t/c mkg, refrig], lift, ldry-fee, lounge (piano), ⊠ (Wed to Sun), bar, pool (salt water), spa, 24hr reception, rm serv, secure park, ☏, cots. RO ♦ $121 - $187, ♦♦ $121, ◊ $33, Suite RO $275 - $385, ch con, AE BC DC JCB MC VI, ⚹☐.

★★★★☆ **Courtyard Surfers Paradise Resort**, (Ltd Lic H), Cnr Gold Coast Hwy & Hanlan St, ☎ 07 5579 3499, fax 07 5592 0026, (Multi-stry), 405 rms (4 suites) [shwr, bath, spa bath (14), tlt, hairdry, a/c, tel, TV, movie-fee, clock radio, t/c mkg, refrig, mini bar], lift, ldry, iron (on each floor), iron brd (on each floor), conv fac, ⊠, pool-heated, spa, 24hr reception, rm serv, c/park (undercover), gym, tennis, non smoking flr. RO ♦ $110 - $310, ♦♦ $110 - $310, ◊ $33, Suite RO $350 - $3,000, AE BC DC JCB MC VI, ⚹☐.

★★★★☆ **Legends Hotel**, (LH), Cnr Gold Coast Hwy & Laycock St, ☎ 07 5588 7888, fax 07 5588 7885, (Multi-stry), 403 rms (16 suites) [shwr, bath, spa bath (16), tlt, hairdry, a/c, tel, TV, movie-fee, clock radio, t/c mkg, refrig, mini bar], lift, ldry, conv fac, ⊠, pool, sauna, rm serv, c/park (undercover), secure park, ☏, gym, cots, non smoking rms (40). RO ♦ $110 - $240, ♦♦ $110 - $240, ◊ $25, ch con, AE BC DC JCB MC VI, ⚹☐.

★★★★☆ **Outrigger Sun City Resort**, (LH), Cnr Ocean Ave & Gold Coast Hwy, ☎ 07 5584 6000, fax 07 5584 6666, (Multi-stry), 192 rms (28 suites) [shwr, bath, tlt, hairdry, fan, tel, TV, video-fee, movie, clock radio, CD-fee, t/c mkg, refrig, cook fac, micro, elec frypan], lift, iron, iron brd, conv fac, ✕, pool indoor heated, sauna, spa (communal), steam rm, bbq (covered), secure park (undercover), gym, tennis, cots-fee. RO ♦♦ $275 - $385, ♦ $30, AE BC DC EFT MC VI.

★★★★☆ **Watermark Gold Coast**, (LH), Cnr Hamilton Ave & Gold Coast Hwy, 500m SW of PO, ☎ 07 5588 8333, fax 07 5588 8300, (Multi-stry), 410 rms (4 suites) [shwr, bath, spa bath (2), tlt, hairdry, a/c, tel, TV, movie-fee, clock radio, t/c mkg, refrig, mini bar], lift, iron, iron brd, conv fac, ✕ (Mon-Sun) (2), bar (2), pool-heated, sauna, spa, rm serv, c/park (undercover), secure park, ✆, gym, cots, non smoking flr (2), non smoking rms (44), ch con, AE BC DC JCB MC VI, ♿.

★★★★ **Chateau Beachside**, (Ltd Lic H), Cnr The Esplanade & Elkhorn Ave, ☎ 07 5538 1022, fax 07 5538 5460, (Multi-stry), 78 rms (58 suites) [shwr, bath (77), tlt, a/c (58), fan, tel, TV, clock radio, t/c mkg, refrig, cook fac (76)], lift, ldry, rec rm, ✕, bar, pool, sauna, spa, steam rm, secure park, tennis, cots. RO ♦♦ $99 - $159, Suite RO ♦♦ $109 - $169, ♦ $28, AE BC DC MC VI.

★★★★ **Novotel Beachcomber Surfers Paradise**, (Ltd Lic H), 18 Hanlan St, ☎ 07 5570 1000, fax 07 5538 4968, (Multi-stry), 302 rms (144 suites) [shwr, bath (247), tlt, a/c, fan, tel, cable tv, video-fee, clock radio, t/c mkg, refrig, mini bar, cook fac (220), ldry (in unit) (220)], lift, ldry, rec rm, conf fac, ✕, bar, pool, pool indoor heated, sauna, spa, bbq, 24hr reception, rm serv, c/park (undercover), gym, tennis, cots. RO ♦ $202 - $224, ♦♦ $202 - $224, ♦ $21, Suite D $246, ch con, AE BC DC JCB MC VI.

★★★★ **Paradise Island Resort Apartments**, (LH), Previously Paradise Island Central Resort, 1 Paradise Island, ☎ 07 5531 5600, fax 07 5592 5552, (Multi-stry gr fl), 195 rms (130 suites) [shwr, bath, tlt, hairdry, a/c, c/fan, tel, cable tv, clock radio, t/c mkg, refrig, cook fac (132), micro, d/wash, toaster, ldry (in unit) (132)], lift, ldry, dryer, rec rm, conv fac, ✕, pool-heated, sauna, spa, bbq, 24hr reception, rm serv, dinner to unit, secure park, ✆, plygr, tennis, cots. D ♦♦ $89 - $179, ♦ $28, Suite D ♦♦ $99 - $239, ♦ $28, AE BC DC JCB MC VI.

★★★☆ **Iluka Beach Resort**, (LH), Cnr The Esplanade & Hanlan St, ☎ 07 5539 9155, fax 07 5592 2037, (Multi-stry), 100 rms (32 suites) [shwr, bath (30), tlt, hairdry, c/fan, tel, TV, clock radio, t/c mkg, refrig, cook fac (suites only), micro (suites only)], lift, ldry, dryer, iron, iron brd, conv fac, ✕, bar, pool-heated, sauna, spa, cots. RO ♦ $77 - $99, ♦♦ $77 - $99, Suite D $99 - $143, AE BC DC MC VI.

★★★☆ **International Beach Resort**, (LH), 84 The Esplanade, 500m N of PO, ☎ 07 5539 0099, fax 07 5538 9613, (Multi-stry), 120 rms [shwr, bath (hip), tlt, a/c, c/fan, tel, TV, refrig, cook fac], lift, ldry-fee, dryer-fee, conv fac, ✕, pool, sauna, spa, bbq, 24hr reception, rm serv, secure park, ✆, gym, tennis, cots-fee. D $80 - $220, AE BC DC MC VI.

★★★☆ **Islander Resort Hotel**, (LH), 6 Beach Rd, ☎ 07 5538 8000, fax 07 5592 2762, (Multi-stry), 101 rms (1 bedrm), [shwr, bath (50), tlt, hairdry (40), a/c, tel, TV, movie, clock radio, t/c mkg, refrig, cook fac (50)], lift, ldry, conv fac, ✕, bar, pool, sauna, spa, 24hr reception, c/park (undercover), ✆, squash, tennis, cots. RO ♦ $85, ♦♦ $85 - $105, ♦ $22, 49 rooms ★★★☆. AE BC DC MC VI.

★★★☆ **Mercure Resort Surfers Paradise**, (M), 122 Ferny Ave, ☎ 07 5579 4444, fax 07 5579 4492, (Multi-stry), 405 units [shwr, bath, tlt, a/c, tel, cable tv, movie, clock radio, t/c mkg, refrig, mini bar, micro (17), toaster (17)], lift, ldry, conv fac, ✕ (2), pool (4), wading pool, sauna, c/park (undercover), plygr, gym, tennis (2), cots. RO $170 - $260, fam con, AE BC DC EFT MC VI, ♿.

★★★☆ **Pink Poodle**, (M), 2903 Gold Coast Hwy, ☎ 07 5539 9211, fax 07 5539 9136, (2 stry gr fl), 21 units [shwr, spa bath (1), tlt, a/c-cool, c/fan, heat, tel, TV, clock radio, t/c mkg, refrig], ldry, dryer, ✕ (Wed to Mon), pool (salt water), spa, dinner to unit, cots. RO ♦ $68 - $129, ♦♦ $78 - $129, ♦ $10, ch con, AE BC DC JCB MC MP VI.

★★★☆ **Trickett Gardens Holiday Inn**, (M), 24 Trickett St, ☎ 07 5539 0988, fax 07 5592 0791, (Multi-stry gr fl), 31 units (1 & 2 bedrm), [shwr, tlt, a/c, tel, TV, clock radio, t/c mkg, refrig, cook fac, micro, ldry (in unit)], dryer, iron, pool-heated, spa, bbq, secure park, cots-fee. Suite D ♦♦ $100 - $132, ♦ $17, ch con, Minium booking Christmas/Jan & Indy race. BC EFT JCB MC VI.

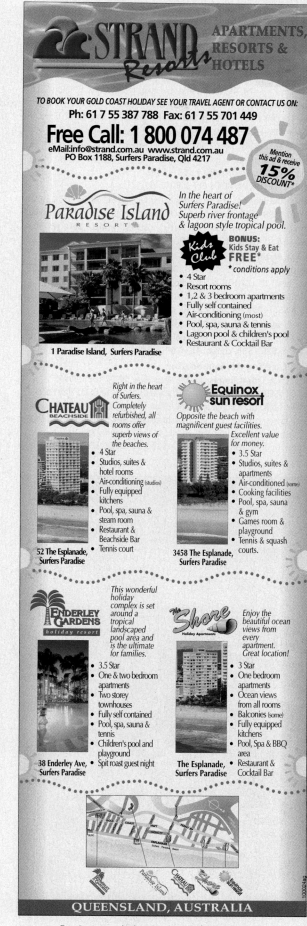

G

QUEENSLAND

★★★ **Cavill Inn**, (M), 25 Cavill Ave, ☎ 07 5531 5559, (2 stry), 12 units [shwr, tlt, a/c, fax, TV, t/c mkg, refrig, toaster], ldry-fee, dryer, bar, c/park (undercover), ⬩, **D** ♯♯ **$60, RO** ♦ **$50,** ⬩ **$15,** ch con, AE BC MC VI.

★★★ **D'Arcy Arms**, (M), 2923 Gold Coast Hwy, ☎ 07 5592 0892, fax 07 5592 2727, (2 stry gr fl), 17 units (1 suite) [shwr, tlt, a/c-cool, fan, c/fan, heat, tel, TV, clock radio, t/c mkg, refrig], ldry, ⊠ (Mon-Sat), pool-heated, spa, rm serv, dinner to unit, c/park (undercover), ⬩, cots-fee. **RO** ♦ **$55 - $90,** ♯♯ **$70 - $110,** ⬩ **$10,** ch con, AE BC DC MC VI.

★★★ **Silver Sands**, (M), 2985 Gold Coast Hwy, Cnr Markwell Ave ☎ 07 5538 6041, fax 07 5538 6041, (2 stry gr fl), 11 units [shwr, tlt, c/fan, TV, clock radio, t/c mkg, refrig, cook fac ltd], pool, spa, bbq (covered), ⬩, cots. **RO** ♦ **$53 - $99,** ♯♯ **$64 - $104,** AE BC DC EFT JCB MC VI.

★★☆ **Delilah**, (M), 72 Ferny Ave & Cnr Cypress St, ☎ 07 5538 1722, fax 07 5538 1722, (2 stry), 11 units [shwr, tlt, fan, TV, radio, t/c mkg, refrig, toaster], ldry, pool (salt water), cots. **RO** ♦ **$40 - $80,** ♯♯ **$50 - $95,** ⬩ **$10 - $15,** ch con, BC MC VI.

★★☆ **Paradise Inn**, (M), 2826 Gold Coast Hwy, ☎ 07 5592 0585, fax 07 5592 1182, (2 stry gr fl), 30 units [shwr, bath (1), tlt, a/c (20), fan, heat, tel (24), TV, clock radio, t/c mkg, refrig, cook fac (21), micro (9)], ldry, dryer, ⊠, pool, spa, c/park (undercover), cots. **RO** ♦ **$55 - $99,** ♯♯ **$66 - $110,** ch con, BC MC VI, ⬩⬩.

★★☆ **Surfers City**, (M), 3314 Gold Coast Hwy, tlt, c/fan, heat, TV, t/c mkg, refrig, toaster], lift, pool, cots-fee. **RO** ♦ **$75 - $95,** ♯♯ **$75 - $105,** ⬩ **$25 - $35,** ch con, AE BC DC JCB MC VI.

Self Catering Accommodation

★★★★★ **Crown Towers**, (SA), 5 Palm Ave, ☎ 07 5555 9999, fax 07 5555 9998, (Multi-stry), 233 serv apts acc up to 6, (1, 2 & 3 bedrm), [shwr, bath, tlt, hairdry, a/c-cool, c/fan, tel, TV, clock radio, CD, refrig, cook fac, micro, elec frypan, d/wash, toaster, ldry, blkts, linen, pillows], lift (6), dryer, iron, iron brd, rec rm, ⊠, pool, sauna, spa, steam rm, dinner to unit, gym. **RO** ♯♯ **$193 - $260,** AE BC DC EFT JCB MC VI.

★★★★★ **Moroccan Beach Resort**, (HU), 14 View Ave, ☎ 07 5526 9400, fax 07 5526 9700, (Multi-stry gr fl), 180 units acc up to 6, (Studio, 1 & 2 bedrm), [ensuite, shwr, bath, tlt, hairdry, a/c-cool, a/c, fan, c/fan, tel, cable tv, clock radio, refrig, cook fac, micro, elec frypan, d/wash, toaster, ldry (in unit), blkts, linen, pillows], lift, tlt, dryer, iron, iron brd, rec rm, ⊠, ✕, pool-heated (salt water heated), pool-indoor, sauna, spa, bbq (covered), rm serv, dinner to unit, c/park (undercover), secure park, ⬩, plygr, gym, cots-fee. **D $139 - $329,** Min book applies, AE BC DC JCB MC VI.

★★★★☆ **Acapulco on the Beach Resort**, (HU), 2 Thornton St, 1km S of PO, ☎ 07 5570 1555, fax 07 5592 2712, (Multi-stry), 70 units acc up to 5, [ensuite, shwr, bath, tlt, c/fan (12), tel, cable tv, video, refrig, cook fac, micro, d/wash, ldry (in unit), blkts, linen, pillows], lift, dryer, iron, rec rm, pool-heated, pool indoor heated, sauna, spa (2), bbq, rm serv, dinner to unit, secure park, tennis (full & half court), cots-fee. **D $135 - $242,** AE BC DC MC VI.

★★★★☆ **Aegean**, (HU), 30 Laycock St, ☎ 07 5570 2388, fax 07 5538 1419, (Multi-stry), 125 units acc up to 5, [shwr, bath, tlt, a/c-cool (40), fan, heat, tel, cable tv, video-fee, refrig, cook fac, micro, d/wash, ldry (in unit), blkts, linen, pillows], lift, dryer, ⊠, pool, pool indoor heated, sauna, spa, bbq, dinner to unit, secure park, gym, tennis, cots-fee. **D** ♯♯ **$143,** ⬩ **$22, W** ♯♯ **$1,001 - $1,190,** 60 units yet to be assessed. Min book Christmas and Jan, AE BC DC MC VI.

★★★★☆ **Dorchester On The Beach**, (HU), 3 Garfield Tce, 1km S of PO, ☎ 07 5539 8199, fax 07 5538 9369, (Multi-stry), 8 units acc up to 6, (3 bedrm), [shwr, tlt, c/fan, tel, TV, video-fee, radio, refrig, cook fac, micro, d/wash, ldry (in unit), blkts, linen, pillows], lift, pool-heated (salt water heated), sauna, bbq, secure park, tennis (half court), cots-fee. **W $1,015 - $1,750,** Min book applies, BTC MC VI.

★★★★☆ **Emerald Resort**, (HU), 7 Mallana St, 800m SW of PO, ☎ 07 5538 2678, fax 07 5538 2654, (Multi-stry), 26 units acc up to 4, (2 bedrm), [ensuite, shwr, spa bath, tlt, hairdry, tel, TV, clock radio, refrig, cook fac, d/wash, ldry (in unit), blkts, linen, pillows], lift, dryer, iron, rec rm, pool (salt water), pool-heated, sauna, spa, bbq, secure park. **D $130 - $155, W $833 - $1,001,** AE BC DC MC VI.

★★★★☆ **Focus**, (HU), 114 The Esplanade, ☎ 07 5538 5999, fax 07 5539 8457, (Multi-stry), 65 units acc up to 7, (2 & 3 bedrm), [shwr, bath, tlt, tel, TV, clock radio, refrig, cook fac, d/wash, ldry (in unit), blkts, linen, pillows], lift, pool-heated, sauna, spa, bbq, secure park, tennis, cots-fee. **D** ♯♯ **$123 - $211,** Min book applies, AE BC DC MC VI.

★★★★☆ **Hi Surf Luxury Apartments**, (HU), 150 The Esplanade, ☎ 07 5538 8011, fax 07 5538 3808, (Multi-stry), 50 units acc up to 6, (2 bedrm), [shwr, bath, tlt, tel, cable tv, clock radio, refrig, cook fac, micro, d/wash, ldry (in unit), blkts, linen, pillows], lift, dryer, pool-heated, pool indoor heated, wading pool, sauna, spa, bbq, secure park, plygr, mini golf, gym, tennis, cots-fee. **D** ♯♯ **$125,** ⬩ **$20, W** ♯♯♯♯ **$980,** Min book applies, AE BC DC JCB MC VI.

★★★★☆ **Imperial Surf**, (HU), 80 The Esplanade, ☎ 07 5570 2555, fax 07 5592 2044, (Multi-stry), 100 units acc up to 5, (1 & 2 bedrm), [shwr, bath, tlt, fan, tel, TV, clock radio, refrig, cook fac, micro, d/wash, ldry (in unit), blkts, linen, pillows], lift, dryer, pool-heated, sauna, spa, bbq, secure park, tennis, cots-fee. **D** ♯♯ **$135 - $175, W** ♯♯ **$825 - $1,085,** Min book applies, AE BC DC JCB MC VI.

★★★★☆ **Paradise Centre Apartments**, (HU), Previously Paradise Centre Outrigger Beachside Apartments. Hanlan St, ☎ 07 5579 3399, fax 07 5570 2077, (Multi-stry), 89 units acc up to 7, (1, 2 & 3 bedrm), [shwr, bath, tlt, hairdry, a/c, tel, TV, clock radio, refrig, cook fac, micro, d/wash, ldry (in unit), blkts, linen, pillows], lift, pool-heated, sauna, spa, bbq, secure park, gym, tennis, cots-fee. **D $134 - $232,** AE BC DC JCB MC VI.

★★★★☆ **Surfers Hawaiian**, (HU), 2890 Gold Coast Hwy, 1km from casino, ☎ 07 5592 2380, fax 07 5592 3967, (Multi-stry), 35 units acc up to 5, (2 bedrm), [ensuite, shwr, bath, tlt, fan, c/fan, tel, TV, video-fee, clock radio, refrig, cook fac, micro, d/wash, toaster, ldry (in unit), blkts, linen, pillows], lift, dryer, iron, iron brd, ⊠ (Wed-Sun), pool-heated (salt water), wading pool, sauna, spa (2), bbq, rm serv-fee, dinner to unit-fee, secure park, gym, cots-fee. **D $165 - $247.50, W $770 - $1,732.50,** BC JCB MC VI.

★★★★☆ **Surfers Mayfair**, (HU), 19 Riverview Pde, Cnr Cypress Ave, 1km N of PO, ☎ 07 5592 3520, fax 07 5539 8444, (Multi-stry), 23 units acc up to 5, [shwr, spa bath, tlt, tel, cable tv, refrig, cook fac, micro, d/wash, ldry (in unit), blkts, linen, pillows], lift, pool-heated, sauna, spa, bbq, secure park, tennis, cots-fee. **D $125 - $275,** Min book applies, BC MC VI.

★★★★☆ **Viscount Towers**, (HU), 1 First Ave, 2km S of PO, ☎ 07 5538 7222, fax 07 5538 7439, (Multi-stry), 22 units acc up to 6, (2 & 3 bedrm), [ensuite, shwr, bath, heat, tel, cable tv, video-fee, refrig, cook fac, micro, d/wash, ldry (in unit), blkts, linen, pillows], dryer, pool-heated, sauna (2), spa, bbq (covered), secure park, cots-fee. **W $725 - $830,** BC EFT MC VI.

★★★★ **Anacapri Holiday Resort Apartments**, (HU), 43 Enderley Ave, ☎ 07 5592 0966, fax 07 5592 2469, (Multi-stry gr fl), 58 units acc up to 7, (1, 2 & 3 bedrm), [shwr, bath, tlt, c/fan, tel, TV, refrig, cook fac, micro, d/wash, ldry (in unit), blkts, linen, pillows], lift, dryer, pool-heated, sauna, spa, bbq, secure park, gym, tennis, cots-fee. D, W ♦♦ **$490 - $1,743**, ⊘ **$22**, Min book applies, BC MC VI.

★★★★ **Aquarius on the Beach**, (HU), 4 Old Burleigh Rd, ☎ 07 5538 9466, fax 07 5538 5251, (Multi-stry), 114 units acc up to 5, (1 & 2 bedrm), [shwr, bath, tlt, c/fan (24), heat (24), tel, TV, video-fee, clock radio, cook fac, d/wash, ldry (in unit), blkts, linen, pillows], lift, dryer, pool-heated, pool indoor heated, sauna, spa, bbq, secure park, plygr, gym, squash, tennis, cots-fee. W ♦♦ **$770 - $1,301**, Min book applies, AE BC DC MC VI.

★★★★ **Baronnet Apartments**, (HU), 10 Enderley Ave, ☎ 07 5592 1099, fax 07 5592 2861, (Multi-stry), 30 units acc up to 4, (1 & 2 bedrm), [shwr, bath, tlt, fan (30), heat (30), tel, TV, clock radio, t/c mkg, refrig, cook fac, micro, d/wash, ldry (in unit), blkts, linen, pillows], lift, dryer, pool-heated, sauna, spa, bbq, secure park, tennis (half court), cots-fee. D ♦♦ **$70 - $200**, W ♦♦ **$588 - $945**, ch con, AE BC DC MC VI.

★★★★ **Berkley Square**, (HU), 23 Northcliffe Tce, Cnr Hamilton Ave, ☎ 07 5538 9099, fax 07 5531 7802, (Multi-stry), 22 units acc up to 5, (1 & 2 bedrm), [shwr, bath, tlt, fan, heat, tel, TV, video (6), clock radio, refrig, cook fac, micro, d/wash, ldry (in unit), blkts, linen, pillows], lift, pool-heated, sauna, spa, bbq, secure park, tennis (half court), cots-fee. D **$115 - $200**, W **$715 - $1,760**, Min book applies, BC MC VI.

★★★★ **Biarritz Luxury Apartments**, (HU), Cnr Old Burleigh Rd & First Ave, ☎ 07 5570 1377, fax 07 5570 2480, (Multi-stry), 55 units acc up to 6, (1, 2 & 3 bedrm), [shwr, bath, tlt, fan, tel, cable tv, clock radio, refrig, cook fac, micro, d/wash, ldry (in unit), blkts, linen, pillows], lift, dryer, rec rm, pool, pool indoor heated, sauna (2), spa, bbq, secure park, tennis. D ♦♦ **$90 - $170**, ⊘ **$20**, W ♦♦ **$630 - $1,590**, 43 Units not rated. BC DC MC VI.

★★★★ **Breakers North**, (HU), 50 Old Burleigh Rd, ☎ 07 5538 8888, fax 07 5538 9126, (Multi-stry), 50 units acc up to 4, (1 & 2 bedrm), [shwr, bath, tlt, fan (40), tel, cable tv, clock radio, t/c mkg, refrig, cook fac, micro, d/wash, ldry (in unit), blkts, linen, pillows], lift, dryer, rec rm, pool-heated, sauna, spa, bbq, secure park, tennis, cots-fee. D ♦♦ **$99 - $223**, ⊘ **$25**, W ♦♦ **$690 - $1,560**, ch con, Min book applies, AE BC DC MC VI.

★★★★ **Capricorn One**, (HU), 198 Ferny Ave, ☎ 07 5570 2344, fax 07 5531 5373, (Multi-stry), 30 units acc up to 5, (2 bedrm), [ensuite, shwr, bath, tlt, fan, tel, cable tv, clock radio, refrig, cook fac, micro, d/wash, ldry (in unit), blkts, linen, pillows], lift, pool, sauna, spa, bbq, secure park, tennis (half court), cots-fee. W **$628 - $3,000**, Min book applies, BC MC VI.

★★★★ **Chevron Palms**, (SA), 50 Stanhill Drive, Chevron Island, ☎ 07 5538 7933, fax 07 5538 7966, (Multi-stry gr fl), 40 serv apts acc up to 4, (1 bedrm), [ensuite, shwr, tlt, c/fan, heat, tel, cable tv, clock radio, refrig, cook fac, micro, toaster, ldry (in unit), blkts, linen, pillows], dryer, iron, iron brd, pool (saltwater, heated), bbq, secure park, cots-fee. D **$60 - $100**, W **$840**, BC EFT MC VI.

★★★★ **Emerald Sands**, (HU), Cnr Fern St & Garfield Tce, ☎ 07 5526 7588, fax 07 5538 6522, (Multi-stry gr fl), 19 units acc up to 4, (1 & 2 bedrm), [shwr, tlt, c/fan, heat, tel, TV, video-fee, clock radio, refrig, cook fac, micro, d/wash, toaster, ldry (in unit), blkts, linen, pillows], lift, dryer, iron, iron brd, cots-fee. D **$121 - $165**, W **$646 - $1,309**, BC EFT MC VI.

★★★★ **Florida Apartments**, (Apt), 2916 Gold Coast Hwy, ☎ 07 5592 0461, fax 07 5570 3476, (Multi-stry gr fl), 33 apts acc up to 5, (1 & 2 bedrm), [shwr, tlt, c/fan, tel, TV, clock radio, t/c mkg, refrig, cook fac, micro, d/wash, toaster, blkts, doonas, linen, pillows], lift, w/mach, dryer, pool, sauna, spa, bbq, secure park, tennis (half court), cots-fee. D ♦♦ **$92 - $128**, ⊘ **$23**, W ♦♦ **$552 - $768**, ⊘ **$138**, Min book applies, BC EFT MC VI.

★★★★ **Genesis Luxury Apartments**, (HU), Cnr Markwell Ave & Gold Coast Hwy, ☎ 07 5538 2099, fax 07 5592 3494, 34 units acc up to 7, (2 & 3 bedrm), [shwr, bath, tlt, c/fan, heat, tel, TV, video-fee, clock radio, refrig, cook fac, micro, ldry (in unit), blkts, linen, pillows], dryer, rec rm, pool, pool-heated, sauna (2), spa, bbq, secure park (2), gym, tennis (half court) (2), cots-fee. D **$104 - $332**, W **$700 - $2,324**, Min book applies, BC MC VI,

Operator Comment: Visit our website at: www.genesisapartments.com.au

★★★★ **K Resort**, (HU), 55 Whelan St, ☎ 07 5531 6655, fax 07 5538 3161, (Multi-stry gr fl), 57 units acc up to 7, (1, 2 & 3 bedrm), [shwr, spa bath (33), tlt, c/fan, tel, TV, video, clock radio, refrig, cook fac, micro, d/wash, ldry (in unit), blkts, linen, pillows], dryer, iron, pool-heated (salt water heated), spa, bbq, secure park, cots-fee. D **$69 - $293**, Min book applies, AE BC MC VI.

★★★★ **Karana Palms**, (HU), 40 Tarcoola Cres, ☎ 07 5592 4554, fax 07 5592 4552, (Multi-stry gr fl), 17 units acc up to 2, (1 bedrm), [shwr, tlt, c/fan, tel, TV, video, clock radio, refrig, cook fac, micro, ldry, blkts, linen, pillows], dryer, iron, iron brd, pool (salt water), bbq, secure park, cots. RO ♦♦ **$80 - $125**, ♦♦ **$385 - $850**, AE BC DC EFT MC VI.

★★★★ **Kupari Boutique Apartments**, (Apt), 3303 Gold Coast Hwy, 500m N of PO, ☎ 07 5526 2911, fax 07 5504 6994, 17 apts acc up to 6, (1 & 2 bedrm), [shwr, tlt, fan, tel, TV, clock radio, t/c mkg, refrig, cook fac, micro, d/wash, toaster, blkts, linen, pillows], ldry, w/mach, dryer, pool, spa, bbq, secure park (undercover), cots-fee. D ♦♦ **$70 - $115**, ⊘ **$10 - $15**, W ♦♦ **$490 - $790**, ⊘ **$70**, AE BC DC EFT MC VI.

★★★★ **Mari Court**, (HU), 23 Wharf Rd, 1.5km S of PO, ☎ 07 5592 2122, fax 07 5592 1916, (Multi-stry gr fl), 59 units acc up to 8, (1, 2 & 3 bedrm), [shwr, bath, tlt, c/fan, tel, TV, video-fee, refrig, cook fac, micro, d/wash, ldry (in unit), blkts, linen, pillows], dryer, rec rm, pool-heated (salt water heated), spa, bbq, secure park, cots-fee. D **$100 - $240**, W **$700 - $1,680**, ch con, Min book applies, BC EFT MC VI.

★★★★ **Marriner Views**, (HU), Cnr Garfield Tce & Fern St, ☎ 07 5538 4333, fax 07 5538 7388, (Multi-stry), 21 units acc up to 6, [shwr, bath, tlt, tel, TV, video, refrig, cook fac, micro, d/wash, ldry (in unit), blkts, linen, pillows], lift, rec rm, pool-heated, pool-indoor (plunge pool), sauna, spa, bbq, secure park (covered), tennis. W **$809 - $1,502**, Min book applies, BC EFT MC VI.

★★★★ **Narrowneck Court**, (HU), 204 Ferny Ave, ☎ 07 5592 2455, fax 07 5538 4153, (Multi-stry gr fl), 27 units acc up to 6, (2 & 3 bedrm), [shwr, bath, tlt, fan, heat, tel, cable tv, clock radio, refrig, cook fac, micro (12), d/wash, ldry (in unit), blkts, linen, pillows], lift, dryer, pool-heated, bbq, secure park, cots. D **$495 - $1,400**, Min book applies.

★★★★ **Paradise Isles**, (SA), 40 Burra St, Chevron Island 4217, ☎ 07 5539 9907, fax 07 5539 9912, 39 serv apts acc up to 4, [shwr, tlt, c/fan, tel, TV, clock radio, refrig, cook fac, micro, d/wash, toaster, ldry, blkts, linen, pillows], dryer, iron, iron brd, pool, spa, bbq, secure park, cots-fee. D ♦♦ **$66 - $120**, ⊘ **$16.50**, W ♦♦ **$349 - $840**, ⊘ **$115**, BC JCB MC VI.

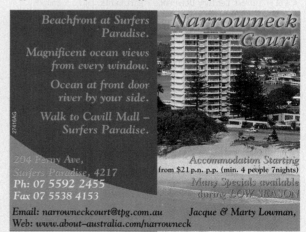

★★★★ **Paros on the Beach**, (HU), 26 Old Burleigh Rd, ☎ 07 5592 0780, fax 07 5592 1421, (Multi-stry gr fl), 35 units acc up to 8, (1, 2 & 3 bedrm), [ensuite, shwr, bath (6), spa bath (2), tlt (2), a/c (13), c/fan, tel, TV, video-fee, clock radio, refrig, cook fac, micro, d/wash, ldry (in unit), blkts, linen, pillows], lift, dryer, pool-heated, spa, bbq (2), secure park, tennis, cots-fee. D ♦♦♦♦ $110 - $200, ♦ $18, W ♦♦♦♦ $735 - $1,500, Min book applies, AE BC DC MC VI.

★★★★ **Peninsula Apartments**, (HU), Previously Peninsula Outrigger Beachside Apartments. Cnr The Esplanade & Clifford St, ☎ 07 5570 2777, fax 07 5592 2539, (Multi-stry), 127 units acc up to 5, (1, 2 & 3 bedrm), [shwr, bath, tlt, hairdry, c/fan, heat (5), tel, TV, clock radio, refrig, cook fac, micro, d/wash, ldry (in unit), blkts, linen, pillows], lift, dryer, ⊠, pool-heated, sauna, spa, bbq, secure park, squash, tennis (half court), cots-fee. DBB $165 - $325, AE BC DC JCB MC VI.

★★★★ **President Apartments**, (HU), 29 Northcliffe Tce, 400m S of PO, ☎ 07 5538 1944, fax 07 5538 4880, (Multi-stry gr fl), 23 units acc up to 5, (1 & 2 bedrm), [shwr, bath (2), tlt, heat, tel, cable tv, clock radio, refrig, cook fac, micro, d/wash (6), ldry (in unit), blkts, linen, pillows], lift, pool-heated, bbq, c/park (undercover), cots-fee. D ♦♦ $104 - $218, ♦ $20, W ♦♦ $728 - $1,526, Min book applies, BC MC VI.

★★★★ **Silverton**, (HU), 2940 Gold Coast Hwy, ☎ 07 5538 2188, fax 07 5592 0714, (Multi-stry), 40 units acc up to 4, (1 & 2 bedrm), [shwr, bath, tlt, c/fan, tel, cable tv, clock radio, refrig, cook fac, d/wash, ldry (in unit), blkts, linen, pillows], lift, dryer, pool-heated, sauna, spa, bbq, kiosk, jetty, gym, tennis, cots-fee. W ♦♦ $630 - $1,484, Min book all holiday times, AE BC DC MC VI.

★★★★ **St Tropez**, (HU), 27 Orchid Ave, ☎ 07 5538 7855, fax 07 5538 6803, (Multi-stry gr fl), 53 units acc up to 6, [shwr, tlt, tel, TV, clock radio, refrig, cook fac, ldry (in unit), blkts, linen, pillows], dryer, pool-heated, sauna, spa, bbq, secure park, cots-fee. D $89 - $185, Min book applies, AE BC MC VI.

★★★★ **Surf Parade Resort**, (SA), 210 -216 Surf Parade, ☎ 07 5538 8863, fax 07 5538 8862, (Multi-stry gr fl), 98 serv apts acc up to 3, [ensuite, shwr, spa bath, tlt, a/c, heat, c/fan, tel, TV, video-fee, clock radio, refrig, micro, toaster, ldry, blkts, linen, pillows], dryer, iron, iron brd, rec rm, pool-heated, sauna, spa (heated), bbq, rm serv-fee, dinner to unit-fee, secure park, gym, tennis-fee, cots-fee. W $539 - $847, Min book applies, BC EFT MC VI.

★★★★ **Surfers Beach Holiday Apartments**, (HU), 33 Beach Pde, 1km S of PO, 250m to beach, ☎ 07 5538 3700, fax 07 5539 9605, (Multi-stry gr fl), 18 units acc up to 8, (1, 2 & 3 bedrm), [shwr, bath, tlt, tel, TV, video-fee, clock radio, refrig, cook fac, micro, d/wash, ldry (in unit), blkts, linen, pillows], dryer, pool-heated (salt water), spa, bbq, secure park, cots-fee. D $95 - $205, W $665 - $1,435, Min book applies, BC MC VI.

★★★★ **Surfers Century Oceanside Apartments**, (HU), 5 Enderley Ave, ☎ 07 5570 2122, fax 07 5570 2296, (Multi-stry), 50 units acc up to 5, (1 & 2 bedrm), [shwr, bath, tlt, tel, TV, radio, refrig, cook fac, micro, d/wash, ldry (in unit), blkts, linen, pillows], lift, dryer, iron, pool-heated (salt water heated), sauna, spa, bbq, secure park, plygr, gym, tennis (2), cots. D ♦♦ $117 - $194, ♦ $20, W ♦♦ $819 - $1,358, ♦ $140, Min book applies, BC MC VI.

★★★★ **Surfers Chalet**, (HU), Cnr Aubrey St & Garfield Tce, ☎ 07 5538 8488, fax 07 5538 8818, (Multi-stry), 17 units acc up to 8, (2 & 3 bedrm), [shwr, bath, tlt, fan, c/fan (6), heat, tel, TV, clock radio, refrig, cook fac, micro (12), d/wash, ldry (in unit), blkts, linen, pillows], lift, dryer, pool, sauna, spa, secure park, cots-fee. W $440 - $1,100, BC MC VI.

★★★★ **Surfers Plaza Resort**, (HU), 4 Ferny Ave, ☎ 07 5592 3888, fax 07 5538 4228, (Multi-stry), 60 units acc up to 5, [shwr, bath, spa bath (30), tlt, c/fan, tel, TV, clock radio, t/c mkg, refrig, cook fac, micro, d/wash, ldry (in unit), blkts, linen, pillows], lift, dryer, ⊠, pool-heated, sauna, bbq, kiosk, secure park, ☎, bowls, cots-fee. D $120 - $235, W $625 - $1,645, BC MC VI.

★★★★ **The Moorings on Cavill**, (HU), 63 Cavill Ave, ☎ 07 5538 6711, fax 07 5592 2103, (Multi-stry), 28 units acc up to 6, (1 & 2 bedrm), [shwr, bath, tlt, a/c-cool (on request), c/fan, heat, tel, TV (Foxtel on request), clock radio, refrig, cook fac, micro, d/wash (12), ldry (in unit)], lift, rec rm, pool-heated, wading pool, sauna, spa, bbq, secure park, cots-fee. D $112 - $220, Min book applies, AE BC MC VI.

★★★★ **The Penthouses**, (HU), 20 Old Burleigh Rd, ☎ 07 5538 9100, fax 07 5531 7525, (Multi-stry), 25 units acc up to 6, (2 & 3 bedrm), [shwr, bath, tlt, fan (13), heat, tel, TV, video-fee, refrig, cook fac, micro (20), d/wash, ldry (in unit), blkts, linen, pillows], lift, dryer, rec rm, pool-heated, sauna, spa, secure park, tennis, cots-fee. D $132 - $286, W $924 - $2,002.

★★★★ **The Regent**, (HU), 18 Aubrey St, ☎ 07 5570 2255, fax 07 5538 8408, (Multi-stry), 45 units acc up to 5, [shwr, bath, tlt, tel, cable tv, clock radio, refrig, cook fac, micro, d/wash, ldry (in unit), blkts, linen, pillows], lift, dryer, rec rm, pool (2), pool indoor heated, sauna, spa, bbq, secure park, plygr, tennis, cots-fee. D ♦♦♦♦ $147 - $268, ♦ $22, W ♦♦♦♦ $1,024 - $1,878, Min book applies, BC MC VI.

★★★★ **Warringa Surf**, (HU), 219 Surf Pde, ☎ 07 5570 2466, fax 07 5570 2466, (Multi-stry), 20 units acc up to 5, (1 & 2 bedrm), [shwr, bath, tlt, fan (14), tel, fax, TV, clock radio, refrig, cook fac, micro, ldry (in unit), blkts, linen, pillows], lift, pool (salt water), sauna, bbq, secure park, cots-fee. W ♦♦ $490 - $840, BC EFT MC VI.

★★★★ **Zenith**, (HU), 20 The Esplanade, ☎ 07 5527 6045, fax 07 5527 6956, (Multi-stry), 47 units acc up to 7, (1, 2 & 3 bedrm), [shwr, bath, tlt, tel, TV, refrig, cook fac, micro, d/wash, ldry (in unit)], lift, dryer, pool, pool indoor heated, sauna, spa, bbq (covered), secure park, tennis, cots-fee. D ♦♦ $135 - $244, ♦ $20, Min book applies, AE BC DC MC VI.

★★★☆ **Aarons Holiday Inn**, (HU), 3355 Gold Coast Hwy, ☎ 07 5538 8366, fax 07 5592 0242, (Multi-stry gr fl), 44 units acc up to 8, (1, 2, 3 & 4 bedrm), [shwr, tlt, c/fan, heat-fee, tel, TV, video-fee, clock radio, refrig, cook fac, ldry (in unit), blkts, linen, pillows], rec rm, pool-heated, spa, bbq, kiosk, secure park, tennis (half court), cots-fee. D ♦♦ $60 - $100, ♦ $15, W ♦♦ $410 - $580, ♦ $105, AE BC DC MC VI.

★★★☆ **Alexander Apartments**, (HU), 2943 Gold Coast Hwy, ☎ 07 5538 7777, fax 07 5539 0200, (Multi-stry), 52 units acc up to 6, (1 & 2 bedrm), [shwr, tlt, c/fan, tel, TV, video-fee, refrig, cook fac, micro (50), d/wash (27), ldry (in unit), blkts, linen, pillows], lift, pool-indoor, sauna, spa, bbq, secure park, tennis (half court), cots-fee. W $580 - $1,400, Min book applies, AE BC DC MC VI.

★★★☆ **Aloha**, (HU), 8 Trickett St, ☎ 07 5538 1922, fax 07 5538 1611, (Multi-stry), 55 units acc up to 5, (1 & 2 bedrm), [shwr, tlt, fan, tel, TV, clock radio, refrig, cook fac, ldry (in unit), blkts, linen, pillows], lift, dryer, ⊠, pool-heated, sauna, spa, bbq, secure park, plygr, tennis (half court). **RO $805 - $1,001**, Min book applies, BC MC VI.

★★★☆ **Anchor Down Apartments**, (HU), 27 Whelan St, 500m SW of PO, ☎ 07 5592 0914, fax 07 5539 9679, (Multi-stry gr fl), 29 units acc up to 5, (2 bedrm), [shwr, bath, tlt, c/fan, tel, cable tv, video-fee, clock radio, refrig, cook fac, micro, ldry (in unit), blkts, linen, pillows], dryer, pool-heated (salt water), spa, bbq (covered), secure park, cots-fee. **D $90 - $170, W $600 - $1,190**, ch con, Min book applies, BC MC VI.

★★★☆ **Aristocrat Apartments**, (HU), 19 Aubrey St, ☎ 07 5570 1100, fax 07 5592 2558, (Multi-stry), 46 units acc up to 5, (1 & 2 bedrm), [shwr, bath (34), tlt, c/fan, tel, TV, video-fee, clock radio, refrig, cook fac, micro, d/wash, ldry (in unit), blkts, linen, pillows], lift, dryer, pool-heated (salt water), pool indoor heated, sauna, spa, bbq, secure park, ☏, gym, tennis (half court), cots-fee. **D ♦♦ $110 - $195, ◊ $22, W ♦♦ $600 - $1,209**, AE BC DC MC VI.

★★★☆ **Bahia Beachfront Apartments**, (HU), 154 The Esplanade, 800m fr PO, ☎ 07 5538 3322, fax 07 5592 0318, (Multi-stry), 35 units acc up to 6, (1 & 2 bedrm), [shwr, bath, tlt, fan, c/fan (10), heat, tel, TV, video-fee, clock radio, refrig, cook fac, micro, d/wash (25), ldry (in unit), blkts, linen, pillows], lift, dryer, rec rm, pool-heated, sauna, spa, bbq, secure park, cots-fee. **D ♦♦ $85 - $127, ◊ $10**, Min book all holiday times, AE BC DC MC VI.

★★★☆ **Bay Lodge Apartments**, (HU), 35 Palm Ave, ☎ 07 5592 2811, fax 07 5592 2557, 51 units acc up to 5, (1 & 2 bedrm), [shwr, bath, tlt, c/fan, tel, TV, clock radio, refrig, cook fac, micro, ldry (in unit), blkts, linen, pillows], dryer, iron, pool-heated (salt water heated), spa, bbq, secure park, tennis (half court). **D $80 - $248, W $562 - $1,509**, AE BC MC VI.

★★★☆ **Beachpoint Apartments**, (HU), Cnr The Esplanade & Staghorn Ave, ☎ 07 5538 4355, fax 07 5592 2881, (Multi-stry), 142 units acc up to 5, (1 & 2 bedrm), [shwr, bath, tlt, a/c-cool (10), fan, heat, tel, TV, clock radio, refrig, cook fac, micro, d/wash (20), ldry (in unit), blkts, linen, pillows], lift (3), dryer, pool-heated, pool indoor heated, wading pool, sauna, spa, bbq, secure park, tennis, cots-fee. **D ♦♦ $132, ◊ $22, W ♦♦ $748 - $1,155**, AE BC DC MC VI.

★★★☆ **Brentwood**, (HU), 11 Paradise Is, ☎ 07 5592 2277, fax 07 5592 2240, (Multi-stry), 12 units acc up to 6, (1 & 2 bedrm), [shwr, bath, tlt, a/c-cool, TV, clock radio, refrig, cook fac, micro, elec frypan, ldry (in unit), blkts, linen, pillows], lift, dryer, pool, bbq, cots. **W ♦♦♦♦ $490 - $1,000.**

★★★☆ **Budds Beach Apartments**, (HU), 1/43 Cypress Ave, ☎ 07 5592 2779, fax 07 5592 2989, 10 units acc up to 3, (1 bedrm), [shwr, tlt, c/fan, tel, TV, clock radio, refrig, cook fac, micro, toaster, ldry (in unit), blkts, linen, pillows], dryer, iron, iron brd, pool (salt water), bbq (covered), secure park, cots-fee. **D ♦♦ $66 - $109, ◊ $22**, 20 units to be assessed. Min book applies, BC MC VI.

★★★☆ **Candlelight Holiday Apartments**, (HU), 22 Leonard Ave, ☎ 07 5538 1277, fax 07 5592 2376, (Multi-stry), 13 units acc up to 6, (1 & 2 bedrm), [shwr, bath (hip), tlt, fan, heat, tel, TV, clock radio, refrig, cook fac, ldry (in unit), blkts, linen, pillows], pool-heated (solar), bbq, c/park (undercover), cots-fee. **D ♦♦ $79 - $115, ◊ $11, W ♦♦ $476 - $805**, Min book applies, BC MC VI.

★★★☆ **Cannes Court**, (HU), 17 Genoa St, 1.5km S of PO, ☎ 07 5538 1288, fax 07 5538 0317, (Multi-stry gr fl), 44 units acc up to 6, (2 bedrm), [shwr, bath, tlt, fan, heat-fee, tel, TV, video-fee, clock radio, refrig, cook fac, micro (12), ldry (in unit), blkts, linen, pillows], dryer, pool (salt water/solar htd), spa, bbq, secure park, cots-fee. **D ♦♦ $100 - $165, ◊ $20, W ♦♦ $490 - $900**, BC MC VI.

★★★☆ **Carlton**, (HU), Cnr Clifford St & Northcliffe Tce, ☎ 07 5538 5877, fax 07 5570 2331, (Multi-stry gr fl), 19 units acc up to 5, (1 & 2 bedrm), [shwr, bath (16), tlt, fan, heat, tel, TV, refrig, cook fac, micro, ldry (in unit), blkts, linen, pillows], lift, dryer, pool, secure park, cots-fee. **W $462 - $1,194**, Min book applies, BC JCB MC VI.

★★★☆ **Casa del Sol**, (HU), 35 Old Burleigh Rd, ☎ 07 5538 8571, fax 07 5592 3095, (Multi-stry), 15 units acc up to 6, (2 bedrm), [shwr, bath, tlt, fan, heat, tel, TV, refrig, cook fac, micro, d/wash, ldry (in unit), blkts, linen, pillows], dryer, pool, bbq, secure park, cots-fee. **D $80 - $130, W $350 - $850**, Min book applies, BC MC VI.

★★★☆ **Cascade Gardens Apartments**, (HU), 26 Monaco St, ☎ 07 5592 0567, fax 07 5570 1520, (Multi-stry gr fl), 54 units acc up to 6, (2 bedrm), [ensuite, shwr, bath, tlt, a/c (11)-fee, fan, heat-fee, tel, TV, video-fee, clock radio, refrig, cook fac, micro, d/wash, ldry (in unit), blkts, linen, pillows], dryer, iron, pool (salt water), spa, bbq, c/park (undercover), cots-fee. **RO $94 - $160, W $630 - $1,085**, Min book applies, BC MC VI.

★★★☆ **Centrepoint Resort Surfers Paradise**, (HU), 67 Ferny Ave, ☎ 07 5538 9955, fax 07 5570 1018, (Multi-stry), 69 units acc up to 5, (1 & 2 bedrm), [shwr, bath (40), tlt, hairdry, a/c, tel, TV, clock radio, refrig, cook fac, micro, ldry (in unit), blkts, linen, pillows], lift, pool (2), pool indoor heated, sauna (2), spa, bbq, secure park, tennis (half court), cots-fee. **D $96 - $220, W $672 - $1,540**, Min book applies, AE BC DC MC VI.

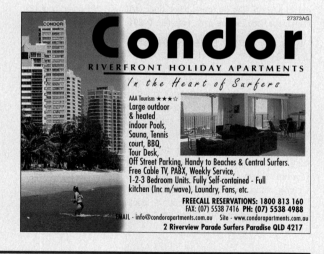

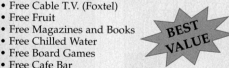

★★★☆ **Columbia Tower Apartments**, (HU), 19 Fern St, ☎ 07 5570 2088, fax 07 5592 1373, (Multi-stry), 13 units acc up to 5, (1 & 2 bedrm), [shwr, bath (8), tlt, tel, TV, clock radio, refrig, cook fac, micro (14), d/wash, ldry (in unit), blkts, linen, pillows], lift, w/mach, dryer, iron, pool (salt water), sauna, bbq, secure park, tennis (half court), cots-fee. W ♦♦♦♦ $420 - $900, ◊ $15, BC MC VI.

★★★☆ **Condor**, (HU), 2 Riverview Pde, 300m W of PO, ☎ 07 5538 4988, fax 07 5538 7416, (Multi-stry), 28 units acc up to 7, (1, 2 & 3 bedrm), [shwr, bath, tlt, fan, tel, cable tv (free colour cable TV), video-fee, clock radio, refrig, cook fac, micro, d/wash (20), ldry (in unit), blkts, linen, pillows], lift, dryer, iron, pool-heated (solar), pool indoor heated, sauna, bbq, tennis, cots-fee. D $85 - $230, min booking 2 nights. AE BC DC EFT MC VI.

★★★☆ **Coolamon Apartments**, (HU), 16 Genoa St, ☎ 07 5538 9600, fax 07 5538 9700, (Multi-stry gr fl), 30 units acc up to 4, [shwr, tlt, tel, TV, refrig, cook fac, micro, d/wash, ldry (in unit), blkts, linen, pillows], dryer, pool-heated (saltwater), bbq, c/park (undercover), cots-fee. D ♦♦ $60, ◊ $10, W ♦♦ $420, ◊ $70, Min book applies, BC MC VI.

★★★☆ **Copacabana**, (HU), 24 Hamilton Ave, ☎ 07 5592 1866, fax 07 5538 5059, (Multi-stry), 40 units acc up to 6, (1, 2 & 3 bedrm), [shwr, bath (17), tlt, tel, TV, video-fee, clock radio, refrig, cook fac, micro, d/wash (18), ldry (in unit), blkts, linen, pillows], dryer, rec rm, pool-heated, sauna, spa, bbq, secure park, cots-fee. D ♦♦ $110 - $170, W ♦♦ $699 - $1,043, Min book applies, AE BC MC VI.

★★★☆ **Cosmopolitan Holiday Apartments**, (HU), Previously Cosmopolitan Outrigger Holiday Apartments. Cnr Surfers Paradise Boulevard & Beach Rd, ☎ 07 5570 2311, fax 07 5570 2389, (Multi-stry), 49 units acc up to 5, [shwr, bath, tlt, hairdry, a/c-cool (to some units), fan, heat, tel, TV, movie, clock radio, refrig, cook fac, micro, d/wash, ldry (in unit), blkts, linen, pillows], lift, dryer, pool (2), sauna, spa, bbq, secure park, cots-fee. D $98 - $216, AE BC DC MC VI.

AAA TOURISM *Special Rates* ★★★☆ **Cypress Avenue Apartments**, (HU), 33 Cypress Ave, ☎ 07 5539 8855, fax 07 5539 8877, (Multi-stry gr fl), 19 units acc up to 4, (1 bedrm), [ensuite, shwr, tlt, hairdry, c/fan, heat, tel, cable tv, clock radio, refrig, cook fac, micro, elec frypan, toaster, ldry (in unit), blkts, linen, pillows], dryer, iron, iron brd, pool (salt water), bbq (covered), dinner to unit, c/park (undercover), secure park, cots-fee. D ♦♦ $89 - $137, ◊ $20, W ♦♦ $595 - $980, ch con, Min book applies, BC MC VI.

★★★☆ **Diamonds Resort**, (HU), 19 Orchid Ave, ☎ 07 5570 1011, fax 07 5570 1118, (Multi-stry), 21 units acc up to 6, (Studio & 1 bedrm), [ensuite (1), shwr, tlt, a/c-cool, c/fan, tel, TV, video (1), clock radio, t/c mkg, refrig, cook fac (11), micro (11), ldry (in unit) (11), blkts, linen, pillows], lift, ldry, night club, ✉, pool-heated (salt water), spa, secure park. D ♦♦ $82.50 - $137.50, ◊ $11, W ♦♦ $577.50 - $962.50, AE BC DC JCB MC VI.

★★★☆ **Enderley Gardens**, (HU), 38 Enderley Ave, ☎ 07 5570 1511, fax 07 5592 3878, (Multi-stry gr fl), 76 units acc up to 5, (1 & 2 bedrm), [shwr, tlt, c/fan, tel, TV, clock radio, refrig, cook fac, ldry (in unit), blkts, linen, pillows], dryer, pool-heated, wading pool, sauna, spa, bbq, secure park, plygr, tennis (half court), cots-fee. D ♦♦ $83 - $139, ◊ $28, W ♦♦ $581 - $973, Min book applies, AE BC DC MC VI.

★★★☆ **Equinox Sun Resort**, (HU), 3458 The Esplanade, ☎ 07 5538 3288, fax 07 5538 6862, (Multi-stry), 125 units acc up to 4, (Studio & 1 bedrm), [shwr, bath, tlt, c/fan, tel, TV, clock radio, refrig, cook fac (98), micro (27), blkts, linen, pillows], lift, ldry, rec rm, pool-heated (winter), sauna, spa, bbq, secure park, gym, squash, tennis (half court) (2), cots-fee. D ♦♦ $79 - $115, ◊ $25, W $553 - $805, Min book applies, AE BC DC MC VI.

★★★☆ **Grosvenor Beachfront Apartments**, (HU), 26 The Esplanade, ☎ 07 5570 3111, fax 07 5539 8799, (Multi-stry), 57 units acc up to 6, (1 & 2 bedrm), [shwr, bath (28), tlt, c/fan, heat, tel, cable tv, clock radio, refrig, cook fac, micro, d/wash, ldry (in unit), blkts, linen, pillows], lift, dryer, pool-heated, sauna, spa, bbq, secure park, tennis, cots-fee. D $123 - $240, Min book applies, BC MC VI.

★★★☆ **Holiday North**, (HU), 30 Aubrey St, ☎ 07 5538 0044, fax 07 5570 3013, (Multi-stry gr fl), 29 units acc up to 7, (1 & 2 bedrm), [shwr, tlt, a/c-cool-fee, c/fan (1), heat, tel, cable tv-fee, video-fee, clock radio, refrig, cook fac, micro, ldry (in unit), blkts, linen, pillows], pool-heated, spa, bbq, secure park, cots-fee. D $336 - $600, Min book applies, BC MC VI.

★★★☆ **Le Chelsea**, (HU), 11 Frederick St, ☎ 07 5538 3366, fax 07 5531 7365, (Multi-stry gr fl), 17 units acc up to 5, (2 bedrm), [shwr, bath (4), tlt, fan, heat, tel, TV, video-fee, clock radio, refrig, cook fac, micro, d/wash, ldry (in unit), blkts, linen, pillows], dryer, pool-heated, bbq, secure park. D $77 - $132, W $539 - $924, ch con, Min book applies, BC MC VI.

★★★☆ **Markwell Surf**, (HU), 14 Markwell Ave, ☎ 07 5538 8098, fax 07 5538 8098, (Multi-stry gr fl), 8 units acc up to 6, (1 & 2 bedrm), [shwr, bath (6), tlt, fan, heat, TV, refrig, cook fac, ldry (in unit), blkts, linen, pillows], w/mach, dryer, pool-heated, bbq, c/park (undercover), cots-fee. BB ◊ $55 - $60, ♦♦ $93 - $110, Min book applies.

★★★☆ **Monte Carlo Sun Resort**, (HU), 38 Orchid Ave, ☎ 07 5538 0777, fax 07 5538 1830, (Multi-stry), 27 units acc up to 6, [shwr, bath (9), tlt, tel, TV, video-fee, radio, refrig, cook fac, micro (20), d/wash (9), ldry (in unit), blkts, linen, pillows], lift, pool-heated, sauna, spa, bbq, secure park, tennis (half court), cots-fee. D ♦♦ $93, W ♦♦ $655 - $1,120, AE BC DC MC VI.

★★★☆ **Murray Court**, (HF), 59 Paradise Island, ☎ 07 5538 2107, 1 flat acc up to 6, [shwr, tlt, fan, heat, TV, clock radio, refrig, cook fac, blkts, linen, pillows], ldry, pool, bbq, c/park (undercover), cots. D ♦♦ $55 - $80, ◊ $10, W ♦♦ $365 - $500.

★★★☆ **Mykonos Apartments**, (HU), 28 Old Burleigh Rd, ☎ 07 5538 4566, fax 07 5538 4566, (Multi-stry gr fl), 10 units acc up to 8, (2 & 3 bedrm), [shwr, bath, tlt, fan (4), heat, tel, TV, clock radio, refrig, cook fac, d/wash, ldry (in unit), blkts, linen, pillows], dryer, rec rm, pool-heated, sauna, bbq, secure park, cots-fee. D $110, W $700 - $1,320, AE BC DC MC VI.

★★★☆ **North Surf**, (HU), 220 Surf Pde, ☎ 07 5538 9177, fax 07 5538 9177, (Multi-stry), 3 units acc up to 6, (2 bedrm), [shwr, bath, tlt, fan, heat, tel, TV, clock radio, refrig, cook fac, micro, d/wash, ldry (in unit), blkts, linen, pillows], lift, dryer, pool, bbq, secure park, cots-fee. D $90 - $130, W $460 - $900, Min book applies, BC MC VI.

★★★☆ **Oak Lodge**, (HU), Cnr Oak & Palm Aves, ☎ 07 5538 4420, fax 07 5538 1665, (Multi-stry), 13 units acc up to 7, (2 & 3 bedrm), [shwr, bath, tlt, fan, cable tv, refrig, cook fac, d/wash, ldry (in unit), blkts, linen, pillows], lift, pool, spa, bbq, c/park (undercover), ☎, cots-fee. W $400 - $900, Min book applies.

★★★☆ **Olympus**, (HU), Cnr View Ave & 62 Esplanade, ☎ 07 5538 7288, fax 07 5592 0769, (Multi-stry gr fl), 30 units acc up to 4, (1 & 2 bedrm), [shwr, bath (9), tlt, c/fan, heat, tel, TV, clock radio, refrig, cook fac, micro, ldry (in unit), blkts, linen, pillows], lift, dryer, pool-heated, sauna, bbq, dinner to unit, c/park (undercover), tennis (half court), cots-fee. RO ♦ $110, weekly con, Min book applies, AE BC DC MC VI.

★★★☆ **Oriana**, (HU), 44 Old Burleigh Rd, beachfront, ☎ 07 5538 0544, fax 07 5531 6360, (Multi-stry), 22 units acc up to 6, [ensuite, shwr, bath, tlt, tel, TV, video-fee, clock radio, refrig, cook fac, micro, d/wash, ldry (in unit), blkts, linen, pillows], lift, dryer (in unit), pool-heated, sauna, spa, bbq, secure park, cots-fee. D $92 - $160, Min book applies.

★★★☆ **Pacific Point**, (HU), 3468 Main Beach Pde, ☎ 07 5531 7120, fax 07 5531 7120, (Multi-stry), 14 units acc up to 4, [ensuite, shwr, bath, tlt, c/fan, tel, TV, clock radio, refrig, cook fac, micro, d/wash, ldry (in unit), blkts, linen, pillows], lift, pool-heated, sauna, spa, bbq, secure park. D $490 - $1,120, Min book applies, BC MC VI.

★★★☆ **Paradise Royal**, (HU), 31 Old Burleigh Rd, ☎ 07 5531 7639, fax 07 5531 6224, (Multi-stry gr fl), 20 units acc up to 6, (1, 2 & 3 bedrm), [shwr, bath, tlt, fan, heat, tel, TV, clock radio, refrig, cook fac, micro, ldry (in unit), blkts, linen, pillows], pool-heated, bbq, c/park (undercover), secure park, cots-fee. W $320 - $900, BC MC VI.

★★★☆ **Paradise Sands**, (HU), 42 Old Burleigh Rd, ☎ 07 5539 9793, fax 07 5531 6167, (Multi-stry gr fl), 17 units acc up to 6, [shwr, bath, tlt, fan (8), TV, radio, refrig, cook fac, micro (14), ldry (in unit), blkts, linen, pillows], dryer, pool, bbq, c/park (undercover), cots-fee. W $465 - $965, Min book applies.

★★★☆ **Paradise Towers AAA**, (HU), 3049 Gold Coast Hwy, 20m from PO, ☎ 07 5592 3336, fax 07 5592 3337, (Multi-stry), 18 units acc up to 4, [shwr, tlt, fan, TV, refrig, cook fac, micro (15), elec frypan, blkts, linen, pillows], lift, ldry-fee, dryer-fee, iron, pool-heated, secure park, ☎. D $70 - $110, W $385 - $750, ch con, Reception 13th floor, AE BC DC MC VI.

★★★☆ **Promenade Apartments**, (HU), 18 Orchid Ave, ☎ 07 5538 6799, fax 07 5538 6879, (Multi-stry), 31 units acc up to 6, (1 & 2 bedrm), [shwr, spa bath (penthouse), tlt, c/fan, heat, tel, TV, clock radio, t/c mkg, refrig, cook fac, d/wash, ldry (in unit)], lift, dryer, pool, sauna (penthouse), spa, bbq, secure park (undercover), plygr, tennis (half court), cots. D $115 - $184, W $616 - $1,288, AE BC DC EFT JCB MC VI.

★★★☆ **Quarterdeck Apartments**, (HU), 3263 Gold Coast Hwy, ☎ 07 5592 2200, fax 07 5538 0282, (Multi-stry), 54 units acc up to 4, (1 bedrm), [shwr, tlt, a/c (avail), c/fan, heat, tel, TV, clock radio, refrig, cook fac, micro, ldry (in unit), blkts, linen, pillows], lift, dryer, rec rm, pool (salt water), pool indoor heated, sauna (2), bbq, secure park, cots-fee. W ♦♦ $476 - $784, ♦ $126, BC MC VI.

★★★☆ **Raffles Royale**, (HU), 69 Ferny Ave, ☎ 07 5538 0099, fax 07 5538 0688, (Multi-stry gr fl), 53 units acc up to 6, (1 & 2 bedrm), [shwr, tlt, c/fan, tel, TV, video-fee, clock radio, refrig, cook fac, micro, ldry (in unit), blkts, linen, pillows], dryer, iron, pool, bbq, secure park, cots-fee. D ♦♦ $101 - $165, W ♦♦ $567 - $1,000, AE BC DC MC VI.

★★★☆ **River Park Towers**, (HU), 40 Watson Esp, ☎ 07 5539 9588, fax 07 5592 2096, (Multi-stry), 12 units acc up to 4, (1 & 2 bedrm), [shwr, bath (9), tlt, fan, heat, tel, TV, clock radio, refrig, cook fac, micro, ldry (in unit), blkts, linen, pillows], lift, dryer, pool-heated, bbq, secure park, cots-fee. W $500 - $1,100, ch con, BC MC VI.

★★★☆ **Seacrest Apartments**, (HU), Cnr Higman St & Main Beach Pde, ☎ 07 5538 7755, fax 07 5592 0823, (Multi-stry), 43 units acc up to 6, (1 & 2 bedrm), [ensuite, shwr, bath, tlt, hairdry, c/fan, heat, tel, TV, video-fee, clock radio, refrig, cook fac, micro, d/wash (30), ldry (in unit), blkts, linen, pillows], lift, dryer, rec rm, pool (salt water), pool indoor heated, sauna, secure park, tennis (half court), cots-fee, Min book Christmas and Jan, AE BC DC MC VI.

★★★☆ **Shangri La Gold Coast**, (HU), 28 Northcliffe Tce, ☎ 07 5570 2366, fax 07 5592 3929, (Multi-stry), 109 units acc up to 6, (1, 2 & 3 bedrm), [shwr, bath, tlt, a/c, tel, TV, movie, refrig, cook fac, d/wash, ldry (in unit), blkts, linen, pillows], lift, dryer, rec rm, ⊠, pool, pool indoor heated, sauna, spa, bbq, secure park, tennis, cots. D $123 - $259, W $112 - $238, AE BC DC MC VI.

★★★☆ **Shore Apartments**, (HU), Cnr Esplanade & Ocean Ave, 600m N of PO, ☎ 07 5539 0388, fax 07 5539 0004, (Multi-stry), 40 units acc up to 3, (1 bedrm), [shwr, tlt, fan (7), c/fan (22), tel, TV, video-fee, clock radio, refrig, cook fac ltd, micro (7), blkts, linen, pillows], lift, ldry-fee, dryer-fee, iron, ⊠ (Mon - Sat), pool-heated (salt water heated), spa, bbq, dinner to unit, secure park, cots-fee. D ♦♦ $92 - $139, W ♦♦ $553 - $973, AE BC DC MC VI.

★★★☆ **Surf Regency**, (HU), 9 Laycock St, ☎ 07 5538 0888, fax 07 5592 3568, (Multi-stry gr fl), 40 units acc up to 5, (1 & 2 bedrm), [shwr, tlt, fan, heat, tel, TV, clock radio, refrig, cook fac, micro, ldry (in unit), blkts, linen, pillows], dryer, pool-heated (winter), sauna, spa (2), bbq (elec) (3), secure park, cots-fee. D $122 - $220, ♦ $28, W $770 - $1,540, ♦ $196, Min book applies, AE BC DC EFT MC VI.

★★★☆ **Surfers Beachside**, (HU), Cnr Vista St & Garfield Tce, ☎ 07 5570 3000, fax 07 5570 3955, 23 units acc up to 5, (1 & 2 bedrm), [shwr, bath, tlt, tel, TV, refrig, cook fac, micro, d/wash, ldry (in unit), blkts, linen, pillows], dryer, pool-heated, sauna (2), spa, bbq, secure park, tennis (half court), cots-fee. D $110 - $140, W $840 - $1,085, Min book applies, BC JCB MC VI.

Operator Comment: See our ad on page following.

★★★☆ **Surfers Del Rey**, (SA), 37 Whelan St, ☎ 07 5592 0877, fax 07 5592 2112, (Multi-stry gr fl), 28 serv apts acc up to 5, (1 & 2 bedrm), [shwr, bath, tlt, fan, heat, tel, TV, video-fee, clock radio, t/c mkg, refrig, cook fac, micro, d/wash, ldry (in unit)], pool-heated (salt water heated), spa, bbq, secure park, jetty, cots-fee. D ♦♦ $70 - $175, ♦ $10, W ♦♦ $500 - $1,225, BC MC VI.

★★★☆ **Surfers International Resort**, (HU), 7 Trickett St, ☎ 07 5579 1299, fax 07 5579 1230, (Multi-stry), 65 units acc up to 5, (1 & 2 bedrm), [shwr, bath (25), tlt, tel, radio, refrig, cook fac, ldry, blkts, linen, pillows], lift, ldry, pool-heated, sauna, spa, secure park, gym, cots-fee. D ♦♦ $110 - $150, ♦ $20, W ♦♦ $770 - $1,400, AE BC DC MC VI.

★★★☆ **Surfers Royale**, (HU), 9 Northcliffe Tce, ☎ 07 5538 4744, fax 07 5538 4016, (Multi-stry), 43 units acc up to 6, [shwr, bath (28), tlt, tel, TV, video, clock radio, refrig, cook fac, micro, d/wash, ldry (in unit), blkts, linen, pillows], lift, dryer, rec rm, pool indoor heated, sauna, spa, bbq, secure park, tennis (half court). D $110 - $175, W $660 - $1,280, BC MC VI.

★★★☆ **Surfers Tradewinds**, (HU), Cnr Wharf Rd & Beach Pde, 200m fr beach, ☎ 07 5592 1149, fax 07 5538 9330, (Multi-stry gr fl), 42 units acc up to 8, (1, 2 & 3 bedrm), [shwr, bath, tlt, c/fan, heat, tel, TV, video-fee, refrig, cook fac, d/wash, ldry (in unit), blkts, linen, pillows], dryer, pool-heated (salt water heated), spa (heated), bbq, secure park, cots-fee. W **$672 - $1,610**, Min book applies.

AAA TOURISM *Special Rates*

★★★☆ **Surfers Tropique**, (HU), 27 Wharf Rd, 250m fr beach, ☎ 07 5592 1575, fax 07 5592 2669, (Multi-stry gr fl), 44 units acc up to 6, (2 bedrm), [shwr, bath, tlt, c/fan, heat, tel, TV, t/c mkg, refrig, cook fac, micro, d/wash, ldry (in unit), blkts, linen, pillows], pool-heated, spa, bbq, secure park. D **$88 - $200**, W **$616 - $1,400**, Min book applies. BC MC VI.

★★★☆ **Surfspray Court Holiday Apartments**, (HU), 21 Old Burleigh Rd, ☎ 07 5592 2744, fax 07 5531 5502, (Multi-stry gr fl), 16 units acc up to 6, [shwr, tlt, c/fan, heat, tel, TV, clock radio, refrig, cook fac, micro, ldry (in unit), blkts, linen, pillows], pool-heated, bbq, secure park, cots-fee. D ♥♥ **$65 - $85**, ♀ **$20**, W ♥♥ **$385 - $770**, ♀ **$50**, Min book applies. BC MC VI.

★★★☆ **The Breakers**, (HU), 60 Old Burleigh Rd, absolute beachfront, ☎ 07 5538 5311, fax 07 5592 1668, (Multi-stry), 36 units acc up to 5, (1 & 2 bedrm), [shwr, bath, tlt, fan, heat, tel, TV, clock radio, refrig, cook fac, micro, d/wash, ldry (in unit), blkts, linen, pillows], lift, pool-heated, bbq, secure park, cots-fee. D **$85 - $220**, Min book applies. BC MC VI.

★★★☆ **The Sands**, (HU), 40 The Esplanade, ☎ 07 5539 8433, fax 07 5531 6490, (Multi-stry), 35 units acc up to 6, (1 & 2 bedrm), [shwr, bath, tlt, c/fan, tel, refrig, cook fac, micro, ldry (30, dryer 30), blkts, linen, pillows], lift, ldry, pool-heated, secure park. D **$60**, W **$315**, 33 units ★★★. BC MC VI.

★★★☆ **Thornton Tower**, (HU), Cnr Thornton St & Gold Coast Hwy, ☎ 07 5592 0043, fax 07 5538 2947, (Multi-stry), 35 units acc up to 5, (1 & 2 bedrm), [shwr, bath, tlt, c/fan, tel, TV, refrig, cook fac, micro, ldry (in unit), blkts, linen, pillows], lift, pool (salt water), pool indoor heated, sauna, spa, bbq, secure park, tennis, cots-fee. D **$81 - $159**, W **$512 - $1,113**, AE BC DC MC VI.

★★★☆ **Top of the Mark**, (HU), 3-15 Orchid Ave, ☎ 07 5538 7944, fax 07 5538 7475, (Multi-stry), 65 units acc up to 5, [shwr, tlt, c/fan, tel, TV, clock radio, refrig, cook fac, d/wash (60), ldry (in unit), blkts, linen, pillows], lift, rec rm, pool-heated, sauna, spa, bbq, secure park, tennis (half court), cots-fee, Min book applies, AE BC DC MC VI.

★★★☆ **Villa Vera Resort**, (HU), 41 Watson Esp, ☎ 07 5592 1924, (2 stry), 10 units acc up to 8, [ensuite, a/c, c/fan, TV, t/c mkg, refrig, mini bar, cook fac, micro, blkts, linen, pillows], w/mach, dryer, pool, bbq, secure park, ☎, cots-fee, ch con, BC MC VI.

★★★☆ **Whelan Waters**, (HU), 41 Whelan St, 500m E of Town centre, ☎ 07 5527 5575, fax 07 5527 5099, (Multi-stry gr fl), 15 units acc up to 5, (1 & 2 bedrm), [ensuite, shwr, tlt, fan, tel, TV, clock radio, refrig, cook fac, micro, d/wash, toaster, ldry (in unit), blkts, linen, pillows], dryer, iron, iron brd, pool-heated (salt water), bbq, cots-fee. W ♥♥ **$350 - $950**, Min book applies, BC MC VI.

★★★ **Ashleigh Lodge**, (HU), 19 Vista St, ☎ 07 5539 8541, fax 07 5539 8541, (2 stry gr fl), 6 units acc up to 4, (1 & 2 bedrm), [shwr, tlt, fan, heat, TV, radio, refrig, cook fac, blkts, linen, pillows], ldry, pool, bbq, c/park (undercover), cots-fee. D ♥♥ **$45**, ♥♥♥♥ **$66**, ♀ **$10**, W ♥♥ **$490**, ♥♥♥♥ **$630**, BC MC VI.

★★★ **Durham Court**, (HU), 21 Clifford St, ☎ 07 5592 1855, fax 07 5539 0135, (Multi-stry), 16 units acc up to 6, (1 & 2 bedrm), [shwr, tlt, c/fan, heat, tel, TV, clock radio, refrig, cook fac, ldry (in unit), blkts, linen, pillows], lift, dryer, pool, wading pool, secure park, cots-fee. D **$50 - $150**.

★★★ **Sea Shell**, (HU), 12 Hamilton Ave, ☎ 07 5539 0695, fax 07 5539 0051, (2 stry gr fl), 8 units acc up to 6, (1 & 2 bedrm), [shwr, tlt, fan, heat, TV, t/c mkg, refrig, cook fac, blkts, linen, pillows], ldry, pool, bbq, c/park (undercover), cots-fee. W ♥♥ **$350 - $620**, ch con, Min book applies, BC MC VI.

★★★ **Spectrum**, (HU), 3 River Dve, ☎ 07 5570 2400, fax 07 5538 6228, (Multi-stry), 22 units acc up to 5, (1 & 2 bedrm), [shwr, bath, tlt, tel, TV, refrig, cook fac, micro, d/wash, ldry (in unit), blkts, linen, pillows], lift, pool, sauna, spa, bbq, secure park, tennis (half court), cots-fee. W **$504 - $1,050**.

★★★ **Sunset Court**, (HU), Cnr Watson Esp & Whelan St, 1 Block from Centre of Surfers, ☎ 07 5539 0266, fax 07 5561 0691, (Multi-stry), 17 units acc up to 6, [shwr, tlt, fan, heat, TV, radio, refrig, cook fac, micro, blkts, linen, pillows], ldry, pool, bbq, c/park (undercover), cots. W ♥♥ **$367 - $695**, ch con, BC JCB MC VI.

★★★ **Suntower**, (HU), 64 The Esplanade, ☎ 07 5531 7377, fax 07 5531 5890, (Multi-stry), 22 units acc up to 4, (2 bedrm), [shwr, tlt, TV, refrig, cook fac, micro, ldry (in unit), linen], lift, dryer, pool, c/park (undercover), cots-fee. **D** $90 - $120, **W** $510 - $890, Min book applies.

★★★ **Surfers Pacific Towers**, (HU), 3 Northcliffe Tce, absolute beachfront, ☎ 07 5539 9611, fax 07 5539 9125, (Multi-stry), 19 units acc up to 6, (1, 2 & 3 bedrm), [shwr, tlt, heat, tel, cable tv, refrig, cook fac, micro, ldry (in unit), blkts, linen, pillows], lift, pool-heated, bbq, secure park, cots-fee. **W** $460 - $1,500, Min book applies, BC MC VI.

★★★ **Surfers Paradise Beach Units**, (HU), 22 Trickett St, 300m S of PO 150m to beach, ☎ 07 5531 7661, fax 07 5592 1436, (Multi-stry), 15 units acc up to 6, (1 & 2 bedrm), [shwr, bath (hip), tlt, c/fan, heat, tel, TV, refrig, cook fac, micro, ldry (in unit), blkts, linen, pillows], lift, dryer, pool-heated (solar), secure park (undercover), cots-fee. **W** $475 - $910, AE BC MC VI.

★★★ **View Pacific Holiday Apartments**, (HU), 5 View Ave, ☎ 07 5570 3788, fax 07 5531 5995, (Multi-stry gr fl), 34 units acc up to 4, [shwr, tlt, c/fan, tel, TV, clock radio, refrig, cook fac, ldry (in unit), blkts, linen, pillows], lift, dryer, pool, bbq, secure park, cots-fee. **D** $60 - $110, **W** $390 - $770, Min book applies, BC MC VI.

★★☆ **Admiral Motor Inn**, (HF), 2965 Gold Coast Hwy, ☎ 07 5539 8759, fax 07 5539 8759, (2 stry gr fl), 14 flats acc up to 10, (1, 2 & 3 bedrm), [shwr, tlt, c/fan, heat, TV, t/c mkg, refrig, cook fac, blkts, linen, pillows], ldry, pool, dinner to unit, c/park (limited), cots-fee. **D ⋔** $55 - $120, ⋔ $15, ch con, AE BC DC MC VI.

★★☆ **Club Surfers**, (HU), 2877 Gold Coast Hwy, 3km S of PO, ☎ 07 5531 5244, fax 07 5531 5249, (Multi-stry gr fl), 60 units acc up to 4, (Studio & 2 bedrm), [shwr, tlt, c/fan, TV, radio, refrig, cook fac, ldry, blkts, linen, pillows], dryer, iron, pool-heated (salt water heated), sauna, spa, bbq, secure park (covered), ✆ plygr, squash-fee, tennis-fee, cots-fee. **D** $55 - $100, ch con, BC MC VI.

★★☆ **Delilah**, (HU), 72 Ferny Ave, Cnr Cypress St, ☎ 07 5538 1722, (Multi-stry), 14 units acc up to 6, [shwr, bath, tlt, fan, TV, clock radio, refrig, cook fac, blkts, linen, pillows], ldry, pool (salt water), secure park, ✆, cots. **D ⋔** $70 - $150, ⋔ $10, **W ⋔** $300 - $550, ⋔ $30, BC MC VI.

GOLD COAST - TUGUN QLD 4224

Part of GOLD COAST region. Pop 3,558. (103km S Brisbane), See map on page 417, ref E8. Seaside suburb on southern section of Gold Coast. Bowls, Golf, Scenic Drives, Squash, Surfing, Swimming, Tennis.

Self Catering Accommodation

★★★★☆ **Golden Riviera Beach Resort**, (HU), Golden Four Dve, 200m S of PO, ☎ 07 5525 9800, fax 07 5525 0566, 66 units acc up to 5, (1 & 2 bedrm), [shwr, tlt, a/c, fan, tel, TV, video-fee, clock radio, t/c mkg, refrig, cook fac, micro, d/wash, blkts, linen, pillows], w/mach, dryer, ⊠, pool, spa, secure park, cots-fee. **D** $125 - $165, **W** $455 - $1,235, BC EFT MC VI.

★★★★☆ **Pelican Sands Beach Resort**, (HU), 335 Golden Four Drive, 2km N Airport, ☎ 07 5534 7744, fax 07 5534 7431, (Multi-stry gr fl), 26 units acc up to 6, [shwr, bath, spa bath, tlt, tel, TV, video, refrig, cook fac, micro, d/wash, ldry (in unit), blkts, linen, pillows], rec rm, pool (salt water), sauna, spa, bbq, secure park, cots. **D** $155 - $285, **W** $1,010 - $1,725, BC MC VI.

★★★★ **Pacific Surf Absolute Beachfront Apartments**, (HU), 373 Golden Four Dr, 300m S of PO, ☎ 07 5534 6599, fax 07 5534 6865, (Multi-stry gr fl), 22 units acc up to 6, [shwr, tlt, c/fan, heat, tel, TV, video-fee, clock radio, t/c mkg, refrig, cook fac, micro, d/wash, toaster, blkts, linen, pillows], w/mach, dryer, pool, bbq, secure park, cots-fee. **W ⋔** $350 - $990, **⋔** $350 - $990, Min book applies, BC EFT MC VI.

★★★★ **San Simeon Beachfront Apts**, (HU), 387 Golden Four Dve, absolute beachfront, ☎ 07 5534 5077, fax 07 5534 7340, (Multi-stry gr fl), 40 units acc up to 6, (2 bedrm), [shwr, bath, tlt, c/fan, tel, TV, clock radio, refrig, cook fac, micro, d/wash, ldry (in unit), blkts, linen, pillows], lift, pool-heated, sauna, spa, bbq, secure park, tennis, cots-fee. **D ⋔** $165, ⋔ $11, **W** $495 - $1,120, Min book applies, BC MC VI.

★★★☆ **Crystal Beach Apartments**, (HU), 329 Golden Four Dve, beachfront, ☎ 07 5534 6633, fax 07 5534 7437, (Multi-stry gr fl), 30 units acc up to 7, [shwr, bath, tlt, tel, TV, video-fee, refrig, cook fac, micro, d/wash, ldry (in unit), blkts, linen, pillows], pool (salt water), spa, bbq, secure park, cots-fee. **W** $500 - $1,385, Min book applies.

End of Gold Coast

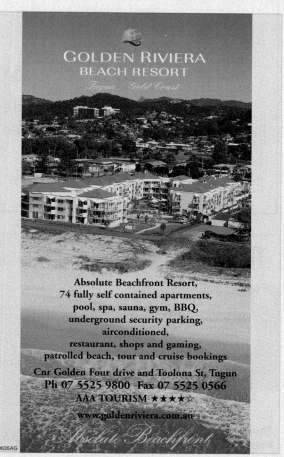

GOOMERI QLD 4601

Pop 450. (243km N Brisbane), See maps on page 417, ref B3. Agricultural, dairying, pastoral and timber township.

Hotels/Motels

★★☆ **Goomeri Motel**, (M), Cnr Boonara & McGregor Sts, ☎ 07 4168 4141, 10 units [shwr, tlt, a/c-cool, fan, heat, tel (4), TV, clock radio, t/c mkg, refrig, mini bar], ldry, meals to unit, c/park (undercover), non smoking units (3). **RO** ♦ $50, ♦♦ $60, ♦ $10, ch con, Units 7,8,9,10 ★★★. AE BC MC VI.

B&B's/Guest Houses

★★☆ **Springbrook Host Farm**, (B&B), Working cattle property & Murray Grey stud. Burnett Hwy, Booubyjan, 28km N of Goomeri, ☎ 07 4168 6106, fax 07 4168 6155, 3 rms [hairdry, fan, heat, elec blkts, tel, clock radio, t/c mkg], shwr, tlt, bathrm, ldry, dryer, lounge (TV & video), ✕, pool (salt water), cots-fee. **DBB** ♦ $100, ♦♦ $180, ch con.

GOONDIWINDI QLD 4390

Pop 4,400. (360km W Brisbane), See maps on page 414, ref D8. Located on the Queensland/New South Wales border, on the banks of the MacIntyre River. Is a major commercial centre for wool, beef, cotton and grain. One of Australia's largest cotton gins and grain storage facility. Bowls, Golf, Horse Racing, Shooting, Swimming, Tennis.

Hotels/Motels

★★★★☆ **At the Town House Motor Inn**, (M), 110 Marshall St, ☎ 07 4671 1855, fax 07 4671 2918, 21 units [shwr, tlt, hairdry, a/c, c/fan, elec blkts, tel, cable tv, clock radio, t/c mkg, refrig, mini bar, toaster], iron, iron brd, conv fac, ✕, pool, spa, bbq, rm serv, cots-fee, non smoking units (7). **RO** ♦ $85, ♦♦ $87, ♦ $8, AE BC DC MC MP VI, ♿.

★★★★☆ **Jolly Swagman Motor Inn**, (Ltd Lic H), Andersen St, 1.5km S of PO, ☎ 07 4671 4560, fax 07 4671 3708, 55 rms [shwr, tlt, hairdry, a/c, tel, TV, movie, clock radio, t/c mkg, refrig], conf fac, ✕, pool, spa, rm serv, c/park (undercover), cots, non smoking rms (6). **RO** ♦ $61.60 - $93.50, ♦♦ $81.40 - $126.50, AE BC MC VI, ♿.

★★★★ **Goondiwindi**, (M), Old Cunningham Hwy, ☎ 07 4671 1544, fax 07 4671 3296, 32 units [shwr, tlt, hairdry, a/c, elec blkts, tel, TV, clock radio, t/c mkg, refrig, mini bar], ldry, iron, iron brd, conf fac, ⊠, pool, dinner to unit, c/park (undercover), cots-fee, non smoking units (11). RO ⵚ $79, ⵜⵜ $89, ⵚ $10, AE BC DC MC VI.

★★★★ **MacIntyre Motor Inn**, (M), 15 McLean St, ☎ 07 4671 2477, fax 07 4671 3051, 18 units [shwr, tlt, hairdry, a/c, elec blkts, tel, cable tv, clock radio, t/c mkg, refrig, mini bar], pool (salt water), spa, meals to unit, c/park (undercover), cots-fee, non smoking units (12). RO ⵚ $73, ⵜⵜ $75 - $85, ⵚ $10, AE BC DC MC VI.

 ★★★★ **Pioneer Motor Inn**, (M), 145 Marshall St, ☎ 07 4671 2888, fax 07 4671 3050, 16 units [shwr, tlt, hairdry, a/c, elec blkts, tel, cable tv, clock radio, t/c mkg, refrig, mini bar], ldry, pool, rm serv, cots-fee. RO ⵜⵜ $79 - $93, ⵚ $8, AE BC DC MC VI, ⅄⅃.

★★★☆ **Gunsynd Motor Inn**, (M), 10 McLean St, ☎ 07 4671 1555, fax 07 4671 2841, 16 units [shwr, tlt, a/c, c/fan, elec blkts, tel, TV, movie, clock radio, t/c mkg, refrig, toaster], pool, dinner to unit, c/park (undercover), trailer park, cots-fee. RO ⵚ $60 - $68, ⵜⵜ $68 - $75, ⵚ $10, AE BC DC MC VI.

 ★★★ **Binalong**, (M), 30 McLean St, ☎ 07 4671 1777, fax 07 4671 1617, (2 stry gr fl), 18 units [shwr, tlt, a/c, tel, TV, clock radio, t/c mkg, refrig], pool, bbq, dinner to unit (Mon - Thurs), cots-fee, non smoking units (5). RO ⵚ $54, ⵜⵜ $64, ⵚ $10, AE BC DC EFT MC VI.

 ★★★ **Border Motel**, (M), 126 Marshall St, ☎ 07 4671 1688, fax 07 4671 3143, 18 units [shwr, tlt, a/c, heat, elec blkts, tel, TV, movie, clock radio, t/c mkg, refrig], ✕, pool, c/park (undercover), cots, non smoking units (6). RO ⵚ $59 - $64, ⵜⵜ $69 - $74, ⵚ $9, AE BC DC EFT MC VI.

★★☆ **Railway**, (LMH), 69 Herbert St, ☎ 07 4671 1035, fax 07 4671 3571, 9 units [shwr, tlt, a/c, tel, TV, clock radio, t/c mkg, refrig], conf fac, meals avail, ☏. RO ⵚ $50, ⵜⵜ $60, ⵚ $5.50, BC EFT MC VI.

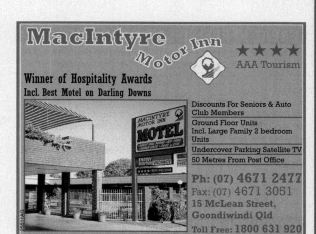

GRANDCHESTER QLD 4340

Pop Nominal, (66km W Brisbane), See maps on page 417, ref C7. Located near Laidley. Bush Walking, Horse Riding.

B&B's/Guest Houses

★★★★ **Peppers**, (GH), Previously Old Hidden Vale 3,645ha cattle property. Mt Mort Rd, Lockyer 4344, 6km S of PO, ☎ 07 5465 5900, fax 07 5465 5999, 25 rms [shwr, spa bath (4), tlt, a/c-cool (9), a/c (1), c/fan (20), fire pl (2), heat, tel, TV, clock radio, t/c mkg, refrig, mini bar], ldry, dryer, lounge, conf fac (1), lounge firepl (5), ⊠, pool (salt water), dinner to unit, tennis, cots, non smoking property. RO ⵚ $210 - $282, ⵜⵜ $210 - $282, ⵚ $44, AE DC MC VI.

GRASSTREE BEACH QLD 4740

Pop 400. Nominal, (954km N Brisbane), See maps on page 416, ref B3. Small seaside area located near Sarina. Fishing, Swimming.

Self Catering Accommodation

★★★★ **Zelma Court Holiday Units**, (Cotg), 58 Zelma St, 35km S Mackay, ☎ 07 4956 6180, fax 07 4956 6180, 5 cotgs acc up to 6, (2 bedrm), [shwr, bath (1), tlt, c/fan, heat, TV, clock radio, refrig, cook fac, micro, ldry (in unit), blkts, linen, pillows], iron, pool, bbq, c/park (undercover) (4), secure park (1), cots. D ⵜⵜ $50, ⵚ $5, W ⵜⵜ $300.

GREAT KEPPEL ISLAND QLD 4700

Pop Nominal, (681km N Brisbane), See maps on page 416, ref D6. Located on Great Barrier Reef, 12km off the Capricorn Coast with secluded white beaches. Underwater Observatory for coral viewing.

Hotels/Motels

★★★★ **Great Keppel Island Resort**, (M), Resort, Hillside Villas, ☎ 07 4939 5044, fax 07 4939 1775, (2 stry gr fl), 60 units [shwr, bath, tlt, a/c, c/fan, tel, TV, clock radio, t/c mkg, refrig, ldry, pillows], ldry, iron, iron brd, conv fac, night club, ✕, cafe, pool (1 heated), spa, bush walking, golf, squash, tennis, cots. D ♯♯ **$255 - $468**, AE BC DC EFT MC VI.

   ★★★☆ **(Beachfront Units Section)**, 57 units [shwr, tlt, c/fan, tel, TV, clock radio, t/c mkg, refrig], ldry, dryer. D ♯♯ **$218 - $410**.

   ★★★☆ **(Garden Units Section)**, 75 units [shwr, tlt, c/fan, tel, TV, clock radio, t/c mkg, refrig], ldry. D ♯♯ **$170 - $329**.

GREEN ISLAND QLD 4871

Pop Nominal, (1720km N Brisbane), See maps on page 416, ref B2. Located on Great Barrier Reef. Snorkelling, glass bottom boats, underwater observatory, Barrier Reef theatre, Marineland. Bush Walking, Swimming.

Self Catering Accommodation

★★★★★ **Green Island Resort**, (HU), 27km E of Cairns, ☎ 07 4031 3300, fax 07 4052 1511, 46 units acc up to 3, [shwr, bath, tlt, hairdry, a/c-cool, c/fan, tel, TV, t/c mkg, mini bar, blkts, linen, pillows], ldry, iron, ✕, pool (2), bbq-fee, rm serv, ✆. D ♯♯ **$440 - $550**, AE BC DC EFT JCB MC VI.

GREENVALE QLD 4816

Pop 100. (1586km N Brisbane), See maps on page 415, ref A7. Cattle Country, located on the Gregory Development Rd 203km N of Charters Towers.

Self Catering Accommodation

★★☆ **Three Rivers Hotel**, (Apt), Redbank Drive, 200km NW of Charters Towers, ☎ 07 4788 4222, fax 07 4788 4233, 7 apts (1 suite) acc up to 8, [shwr, bath (1), tlt, a/c, c/fan, TV, t/c mkg, refrig, cook fac (suite), toaster], ldry-fee, dryer-fee, iron, iron brd, conv fac, ✕, pool, bbq, c/park (undercover), ✆, tennis, non smoking units (4). RO ♦ **$48**, ♯♯ **$66**, ◊ **$10**, Suite D ♦ **$66**, ♯♯ **$78**, ◊ **$15**, BC EFT MC VI.

GUNALDA QLD 4570

Pop 400. (196km N Brisbane), See maps on page 417, ref C3. Rich farming area situated on Mary River - dairying, small crops, tropical fruit farms and cattle breeding. Mt Kanighan Lookout. Bush Walking, Canoeing, Fishing, Gold Prospecting, Horse Riding, Scenic Drives, Swimming.

B&B's/Guest Houses

★★★☆ **Mary River Homestead**, (GH), (Farm), 166ha cattle breeding property. Scotchy Pocket, 30km N of Gympie, ☎ 07 5484 6163, fax 07 5482 2800, 1 rm [shwr (2), tlt (2), a/c-cool, c/fan, heat, tel, TV], ldry, rec rm, lounge (TV), ✕, cook fac, bbq, meals to unit, bush walking, canoeing, cots. RO ♦ **$30**, ch con.

GYMPIE QLD 4570

Pop 10,800. (166km N Brisbane), See maps on page 417, ref D3. Centre of a rich agricultural & pastoral district situated on the Mary River. Bowls, Fishing, Golf, Horse Racing, Swimming, Tennis.

Hotels/Motels

★★★★ **Great Eastern Motor Inn**, (M), 27 Geordie Rd, ☎ 07 5482 7288, fax 07 5482 6445, (2 stry), 32 units (6 suites) [shwr, bath (3), spa bath (1), tlt, a/c, tel, cable tv, movie, clock radio, t/c mkg, refrig, mini bar, cook fac (5), micro (5)], ldry, w/mach-fee, dryer-fee, conv fac, ✕, pool (salt water), rm serv, c/park (undercover) (24), cots, non smoking rms (5). RO ♦ **$77 - $85**, ♯♯ **$85 - $96**, ◊ **$13**, Suite D ♦ **$102**, ♯♯ **$112**, ch con, AE BC DC MC MP VI, ✆.

★★★★ **Gympie Muster Inn**, (M), 21 Wickham St (Bruce Hwy), 500m W of PO, ☎ 07 5482 8666, fax 07 5482 8601, (2 stry gr fl), 22 units (1 suite) [shwr, bath (1), spa bath (4), tlt, a/c, c/fan, tel, cable tv, clock radio, t/c mkg, refrig, mini bar], ldry, conv fac, ✕ (Mon-Sat), pool (salt water), spa, rm serv, c/park (undercover), cots. RO ♦ **$80 - $90**, ♯♯ **$85 - $95**, ◊ **$12**, Suite D ♦ **$80**, ♯♯ **$90**, AE BC DC JCB MC VI, ✆.

★★★☆ **Hilltop**, (M), Bruce Hwy, 2km NW of PO, ☎ 07 5482 3577, fax 07 5482 4077, 15 units [shwr, tlt, a/c, tel, TV, movie, clock radio, t/c mkg, refrig, toaster], pool, bbq, dinner to unit, c/park (undercover), cots, non smoking rms. RO ♦ **$61**, ♯♯ **$68**, AE BC DC MC VI, ✆.

★★★☆ **Shady Rest**, (M), 17 Violet St (Bruce Hwy), 800m NW of PO, ☎ 07 5482 1999, fax 07 5482 8696, 14 units [shwr, tlt, hairdry, a/c-cool, c/fan, heat, tel, cable tv, video, movie, clock radio, t/c mkg, refrig, ldry (service)], iron, iron brd, pool, bbq, dinner to unit, c/park (undercover), trailer park, cots-fee. RO ♦ **$52 - $63**, ♯♯ **$57 - $72**, ◊ **$11 - $13**, AE BC CC DC EFT MC VI.

★★★ **Fox Glenn Motor Inn**, (M), Bruce Hwy, 1.6km S of PO, ☎ 07 5482 3199, fax 07 5482 8468, 20 units [shwr, tlt, a/c, elec blkts, tel, TV, movie, clock radio, t/c mkg, refrig, mini bar], ldry, lounge, conf fac, ✕, pool, bbq, rm serv, boat park, cots, non smoking units (6). RO ♦ **$63**, ♯♯ **$70**, ◊ **$11**, ch con, AE BC DC EFT MC MP VI.

★★★ **Golden Gate Motor Inn**, (M), Bruce Hwy, 2.5km S of PO, ☎ 07 5482 3611, fax 07 5483 8055, 10 units [shwr, tlt, a/c, c/fan, tel, TV, movie, clock radio, t/c mkg, refrig], pool, bbq, dinner to unit (6pm to 7pm), c/park (undercover), boat park, plygr, cots. RO ♦ **$55**, ♯♯ **$60 - $64**, ◊ **$10**, AE BC DC EFT MC VI.

★★☆ **Gympie Motel**, (M), 83 Bruce Hwy, 600m from town centre, ☎ 07 5482 2722, fax 07 5482 2175, 29 units [shwr, tlt, a/c-cool, a/c (6), c/fan, heat (2), tel, TV, clock radio, t/c mkg, refrig, cook fac ltd (2)], ldry, dryer, ✕, pool-heated (solar), rm serv, dinner to unit, c/park (undercover), cots. RO ♦ **$46**, ♯♯ **$54**, ◊ **$10**, ch con, AE BC DC MC VI.

★★☆ **Nation Wide**, (M), Bruce Hwy, 1.5km NW of PO, ☎ 07 5482 5777, fax 07 5483 6088, 20 units [shwr, a/c, fan, heat, elec blkts, TV, video, movie, clock radio, t/c mkg, refrig, cook fac ltd, toaster], ldry, breakfast rm, ✕, pool, bbq, 24hr reception, rm serv (24hr), meals to unit, c/park (undercover), boat park, plygr, cots, non smoking rms (8), Pets allowed. RO ♦ **$41.80**, ♯♯ **$49.50**, ◊ **$8.80**, ch con, AE BC DC MC VI.

★★ **Ampol Curra Country**, (M), Cnr Bruce Hwy & David Dve, Curra 4570, 17km N of Gympie, ☎ 07 5483 1388, 5 units [shwr, tlt, a/c, TV, clock radio, t/c mkg, refrig], ✕, petrol, c/park (undercover), ✆, cots. RO ♦ **$35**, ♯♯ **$40**, ◊ **$5**, ch con, BC MC VI.

★★ **Northumberland**, (LMH), 29 Channon St, 500m N of PO, ☎ 07 5482 2477, fax 07 5483 7328, 8 units [shwr, tlt, a/c, c/fan, TV, clock radio, t/c mkg, refrig], conv fac, ✕ (Mon to Sat), rm serv, ✆, cots. D ♦ **$50**, ◊ **$8**, RO ♦ **$42**, ch con, BC MC VI.

★☆ **The Empire**, (LH), 196 Mary St, ☎ 07 5482 8444, fax 07 5482 8983, (2 stry), 12 rms [basin, fan], shwr, tlt, rec rm, lounge (tv), ✕ (Mon-Sat), t/c mkg shared. RO ♦ **$20**, ♯♯ **$30**, ◊ **$10**, AE BC DC EFT MC VI.

B&B's/Guest Houses

★★★ **Curtis Park**, (B&B), (Farm), Working cattle & olive grove property. No children's facilities, 521 Beckmanns Rd, Glenwood, 45km N of Gympie bordering Tuan State Forest, ☎ 07 5485 7266, fax 07 5485 7200, 3 rms [c/fan, heat], shwr, tlt, lounge (TV & radio), pool (salt water), t/c mkg shared, refrig, bbq, meals avail (by arrangement), bush walking (& birdwatching), non smoking rms. BLB ♦ **$90**, BC MC VI.

HALLIDAY BAY QLD 4741

Pop Nominal, (1018km N Brisbane), See maps on page 416, ref A2. Excellent beach and fishing area. Turtle Rookery Overlooking Brampton Island Group.

Self Catering Accommodation

★★★☆ **Halliday Bay**, (HU), Resort, Headland Drive, 48km N of Mackay via Seaforth, ☎ 07 4959 0322, fax 07 4959 0422, 54 units acc up to 6, (1 bedrm), [shwr, tlt, c/fan, TV, refrig, cook fac, ldry, blkts, linen, pillows], dryer, rec rm, ✕, pool, bbq, kiosk, ✆, plygr, tennis, cots. D **$65**, AE BC DC MC VI.

   (Holiday Unit Section), (2 stry gr fl) 18 units acc up to 4, (Studio), [shwr, tlt, c/fan (12), TV, refrig, cook fac ltd, blkts, linen, pillows], cots. D **$55**.

Rates may change. Check before booking.

HAMILTON ISLAND QLD

See Whitsundays Region.

HAY POINT QLD 4740

Pop Part of Mackay Area, (961km N Brisbane), See maps on page 416, ref B3. Largest coal exporting port in Australia.

Hotels/Motels

★★☆ **Hay Point**, (LMH), The Esplanade, ☎ 07 4956 3266, 12 units [shwr, bath (2), tlt, a/c, tel, TV, clock radio, t/c mkg, refrig, cook fac (2)], ldry, conv fac, pool, bbq, dinner to unit, c/park (undercover), cots. **RO** ♦ **$45**, ♦♦ **$50**, ♦ **$5**, AE BC EFT MC VI.

HAYMAN ISLAND QLD

See Whitsundays Region.

HELIDON QLD 4344

Pop 600. (107km W Brisbane), See maps on page 417, ref B6. Located in the Lockyer Valley and noted for its mineral waters and sandstone.

Hotels/Motels

★★★☆ **Helidon Natural Springs Spa Resort**, (M), Warrego Hwy, 2km W of PO, ☎ 07 4697 6066, fax 07 4697 6723, 17 units [shwr, spa bath, tlt, a/c, heat, elec blkts, tel, TV, video (7), clock radio, t/c mkg, refrig, toaster], ✉ (Mon to Sat), pool (salt water), pool-heated (hot hydrotherapy), sauna, bbq, dinner to unit, gym, cots-fee. **RO** ♦ **$43 - $87**, ♦♦ **$54 - $87**, ♦ **$11**, AE BC DC EFT MC VI.

B&B's/Guest Houses

★★★★ **Silver Ridge B&B**, (B&B), 103 Silver Pinch Rd, 3km SE from Toowoomba, ☎ 07 4635 7725, fax 07 4635 7725, 2 rms [ensuite, heat, TV, video, cook fac ltd, doonas], ldry, t/c mkg shared, refrig, bbq. **BLB** ♦ **$45 - $60**, ♦♦ **$90 - $120**, ch con, weekly con, BC MC VI, ♿.

HERBERTON QLD 4872

Pop 1,000. (1730km N Brisbane), See maps on page 415, ref B4. Historic tin mining town on the Atherton Tableland.

Self Catering Accommodation

★★★☆ **Greensprings Holiday Farm**, (Apt), Off Wieland Rd Wondecla via Herberton F.N.Q. 24km S of Atherton, ☎ 07 4096 2292, fax 07 4096 2292, (2 stry), 4 apts acc up to 8, [shwr (1), bath (hip) (1), tlt (2), fan (2), c/fan (2), fire pl, heat (oil, fireplace), tel, video, movie, clock radio, CD, refrig (4), cook fac ltd, micro (2), elec frypan, toaster], shwr, tlt, ldry-fee, dryer-fee, iron, iron brd, rec rm, lounge (TV), t/c mkg shared, bbq (covered), non smoking flr, non smoking rms. **BB** ♦ **$66**, ♦♦ **$88**, BC EFT MC VI.

HERON ISLAND QLD 4680

Pop Nominal, (534km N Brisbane), See maps on page 416, ref E6. Near southern end of Great Barrier Reef, a true coral cay 1km in width, with partly exposed reef at low tide. Island & reef - National Prk/Wildlife Sancturay-prolific birdlife. Marine Geology Station.

Hotels/Motels

★★★ **Heron Island**, (M), Resort, via Gladstone, Coral cay located on Great Barrier Reef, ☎ 07 4972 9055, fax 07 4972 0244, 4 units [shwr, tlt, fan, clock radio, t/c mkg, refrig, mini bar (on request), pillows], ldry, conv fac, ✉, cafe, pool (2), shop, ✆, tennis, cots. **D all meals** ♦ **$170 - $360**, ch con, AE BC DC JCB MC VI.

★★★ **(Heron Units)**, 44 units [shwr, tlt, hairdry, c/fan, clock radio, t/c mkg, refrig], cots. **D all meals** ♦ **$300**, ch con.

★★★ **(Point Units)**, 4 units [shwr, tlt, fan, clock radio, t/c mkg, refrig, mini bar (on request)], cots. **D all meals** ♦ **$400**, ch con.

★★☆ **(Reef Units)**, 32 units [shwr, tlt, hairdry, clock radio, refrig], cots. **D all meals** ♦ **$260**, ch con.

★★ **(Turtle Cabins)**, 35 cabins acc up to 4, [basin, fan, t/c mkg], shwr, tlt, shared fac. **D all meals** ♦ **$180**, ch con.

HERVEY BAY QLD 4655

Pop 32,050. (289km N Brisbane), See maps on page 417, ref D1. The large area of water, and pleasant strip of seaside resorts, between Maryborough and Bundaberg that is protected by Fraser Island. Boat Ramp, Boating, Bowls, Fishing, Golf, Sailing, Swimming, Tennis.

Hotels/Motels

★★★★ **Ambassador Motor Lodge**, (M), 296 Esplanade, Pialba 4655, ☎ 07 4124 0044, fax 07 4124 8199, (2 stry gr fl), 21 units [shwr, bath, spa bath (2), hairdry, a/c (r/cyc), c/fan, tel, cable tv, movie, clock radio, t/c mkg, refrig, mini bar], ldry, dryer, iron, iron brd, ✉ (Mon to Fri non-smoki), spa, bbq, rm serv, dinner to unit, c/park (undercover), non smoking units (15). **RO** ♦ **$73 - $78**, ♦♦ **$83 - $95**, ♦ **$10**, AE BC DC JCB MC MP VI, ♿.

★★★★ **Beachside Motor Inn**, (M), 298 Esplanade, Pialba, 200m from CBD, ☎ 07 4124 1999, fax 07 4124 1055, (2 stry gr fl), 16 units (2 suites) [shwr, tlt, hairdry, a/c (14), c/fan, tel, cable tv, clock radio, t/c mkg, refrig, cook fac (2), cook fac ltd (3), micro (2), toaster], ldry, w/mach, dryer-fee, iron, iron brd, pool (salt water), spa, bbq, rm serv, cots-fee, non smoking units (8). **RO** ♦ **$75 - $82**, ♦♦ **$85 - $104.50**, ♦ **$11 - $16.50**, **Suite RO $104.50 - $143**, AE BC DC EFT MC VI.

★★★★ **Fraser Gateway Motor Inn**, (M), 68 Main St, Pialba 4655, ☎ 07 4128 3666, fax 07 4128 3802, 28 units [shwr, tlt, a/c, tel, TV, movie, clock radio, t/c mkg, refrig, mini bar], ldry, ✉ (Mon-Thurs), pool, bbq, rm serv, cots. **RO** ♦ **$75 - $85**, ♦♦ **$85 - $115**, ♦ **$11**, ch con, AE BC DC EFT MC VI.

★★★★ **Kondari Resort**, (LMH), 49 Elizabeth St, Urangan 4655, ☎ 07 4128 9702, fax 07 4125 3031, 97 units (1 bedrm), [shwr, tlt, a/c (97), c/fan (60), heat (97), tel, TV, movie, clock radio, t/c mkg, refrig, mini bar, cook fac], ldry, conv fac, ✉, pool, bbq, c/park (undercover) (14), ✆, tennis (half court) (2), cots. **D $99 - $129**, ♦ **$20**, ch con, 24 units ★★★★, Light breakfast available. AE BC DC MC VI.

★★★★ **Sunseeker**, (M), 354 Esplanade, Scarness 4655, ☎ 07 4128 1888, or 07 4128 1388, fax 07 4128 1744, (2 stry gr fl), 10 units [shwr, tlt, hairdry, a/c, c/fan, tel, cable tv, clock radio, t/c mkg, refrig, cook fac (4)], ldry, dryer-fee, pool, bbq, meals to unit, boat park (& trailer), car wash, cots, non smoking units (4). **RO** ♦ **$78 - $108**, ♦♦ **$88 - $120**, ♦ **$15**, AE BC DC EFT MC VI.

★★★☆ **Hervey Bay**, (M), 518 Esplanade, Urangan 4655, ☎ 07 4128 9277, fax 07 4125 3675, (2 stry gr fl), 18 units [shwr, tlt, a/c, c/fan, tel, cable tv, video (avail), clock radio, t/c mkg, refrig, cook fac (10), toaster (18)], dryer (fee), pool, bbq, cots. **RO** ♦ **$55 - $72**, ♦♦ **$66 - $88**, ♦ **$8**, AE BC DC EFT MC VI.

★★★☆ **Hervey Bay Resort**, (M), 249 Esplanade, Pialba 4655, ☎ 07 4128 1555, fax 07 4128 4688, (Multi-stry gr fl), 24 units (1 suite) [ensuite (1), shwr, bath, spa bath (3), tlt, a/c, c/fan, tel, TV, clock radio, t/c mkg, refrig], lift, ldry, conv fac, ✉, pool (salt water), spa, rm serv, dinner to unit, c/park (undercover), cots. **RO** ♦ **$75 - $92**, ♦♦ **$87 - $102**, ♦ **$13**, **Suite D $210 - $250**, AE BC DC MC VI, ♿.

H

QUEENSLAND

★★★☆ **Playa Concha Resort**, (M), 475 Esplanade, Cnr Ann St, Torquay 4655, ☎ 07 4125 1544, fax 07 4124 9232, (2 stry gr fl), 40 units (16 suites) [shwr, spa bath (16), tlt, hairdry, a/c, c/fan, tel, TV, clock radio, t/c mkg, refrig, cook fac (16)], ldry-fee, ⊠, pool-heated (salt water heated), spa, bbq, rm serv, dinner to unit, cots-fee. **RO** ♦ **$88,** ♦♦ **$88, Suite D $105,** fam con, Units 54 to 69 are ★★★★. AE BC DC MC VI.

★★★☆ **Shelly Beach**, (M), 510 Esplanade, Urangan 4655, ☎ 07 4128 9888, fax 07 4128 9883, (2 stry gr fl), 12 units [shwr, tlt, hairdry, a/c (12), c/fan (13), heat, tel, cable tv, clock radio, t/c mkg, refrig, cook fac, micro, elec frypan, toaster], ldry, iron, iron brd, bbq, c/park (undercover) (9), boat park, non smoking units (8). **RO** ♦ **$66 - $99,** ♦♦ **$68 - $99,** ♦ **$11,** AE BC DC MC VI.

★★★☆ **Tower Court**, (M), 460 The Esplanade, Torquay 4655, ☎ 07 4125 1322, fax 07 4125 5124, (2 stry gr fl), 15 units [shwr, tlt, a/c (15), fan (4), tel, cable tv, clock radio, t/c mkg, refrig, cook fac (8), elec frypan (8), toaster], ldry, dryer-fee, pool (salt water), bbq, meals to unit (breakfast), c/park (undercover) (12), cots. **RO** ♦ **$62 - $80,** ♦♦ **$68 - $85,** ♦ **$10,** AE BC DC MC VI.

★★★ **Emeraldene Motel**, (M), 166 Urraween Rd, Pialba 4655, 300m W of Hospital, ☎ 07 4124 7952, fax 07 4124 0218, 14 units [shwr, bath (2), tlt, a/c-cool, heat, fan, tel, TV, video, t/c mkg, refrig, micro, ldry], dryer, iron, iron brd. **D** ♦ **$53,** ♦♦ **$68,** BC MC VI, ⌂&.

★★★ **Fairway**, (M), 29 Boat Harbour Dve, Pialba 4655, ☎ 07 4128 1911, or 07 4128 1008, fax 07 4124 5624, 10 units [shwr, tlt, a/c-cool, c/fan, heat, tel, fax, TV, clock radio, t/c mkg, refrig], ldry, iron, iron brd, pool, bbq, boat park, trailer park. **RO** ♦ **$64 - $84,** ♦♦ **$68 - $88,** ♦ **$11,** BC EFT MC VI.

★★☆ **Reef**, (M), 410 The Esplanade, Torquay 4655, ☎ 07 4125 2744, fax 07 4125 2744, 25 units [ensuite (all rooms), a/c-cool, fan, c/fan (3), heat, tel, TV, clock radio, t/c mkg, refrig, cook fac (5), toaster], ldry, w/mach-fee, pool (salt water), bbq-fee, rm serv, meals avail (Continental Brfst), cots-fee. **RO** ♦ **$50 - $65,** ♦♦ **$55 - $85,** ch con, AE BC DC MC MP VI.

★★☆ **Urangan Motor Inn**, (M), 573 Esplanade, Urangan 4655, ☎ 07 4128 9699, fax 07 4128 9278, (2 stry gr fl), 42 units [shwr, tlt, a/c-cool, c/fan, heat, tel, TV, radio, t/c mkg, refrig, cook fac ltd (5), micro (5), toaster (5)], ldry, ⊠, bar, pool (salt water), spa, rm serv, dinner to unit, c/park (undercover) (26), cots, non smoking units (4). **RO** ♦ **$25 - $66,** ♦♦ **$63 - $72,** ♦ **$11,** Some units of a 3 star rating. AE BC EFT JCB MC VI.

★★ **Point Vernon**, (M), 189 Esplanade, ☎ 07 4128 1418, 7 units [shwr, tlt, a/c-cool, fan, TV, t/c mkg, refrig, cook fac ltd (4), toaster (4)], ldry, pool, cots-fee. **BLB** ♦ **$43 - $48,** ♦♦ **$53 - $60,** ♦ **$12,** ch con.

Self Catering Accommodation

★★★★☆ **Alexander Luxury Apartments**, (HU), 496 Esplanade, Torquay, 1000m W of Urangan Pier, ☎ 07 4125 6555, fax 07 4124 9100, (Multi-stry gr fl), 11 units acc up to 6, (2 bedrm), [shwr, bath, tlt, hairdry, a/c, c/fan, tel, cable tv, video, clock radio, t/c mkg, refrig, cook fac, micro, elec frypan, d/wash, toaster, ldry (in unit), blkts, linen, pillows], lift, dryer, iron, iron brd, pool (salt water), spa (2), boat park, secure park (undercover), courtesy transfer, cots-fee. **RO** ♦♦ **$132 - $205,** **W** ♦♦ **$595 - $1,150,** AE BC DC EFT MC VI.

★★★★☆ **Charlton Luxury Apartments**, (HU), 451 Esplanade, Torquay 4655, ☎ 07 4125 3661, fax 07 4125 1221, (Multi-stry), 19 units acc up to 6, (2 & 3 bedrm), [ensuite, shwr, bath, spa bath (4), tlt, hairdry, a/c, c/fan, tel, cable tv, video, clock radio, CD (5), refrig, cook fac, micro, elec frypan, d/wash, toaster, ldry (in unit), blkts, linen, pillows], lift, dryer, iron, iron brd, pool (saltwater), bbq, c/park (undercover), boat park, secure park. **RO** ♦♦ **$125 - $280,** **W** ♦♦ **$605 - $1,600,** AE BC DC EFT MC VI.

★★★★☆ **Great Sandy Straits Marina Resort**, (HU), Buccaneer Dve, Urangan 4655, ☎ 07 4128 9999, fax 07 4125 1688, (Multi-stry gr fl), 110 units acc up to 2, [shwr, bath, tlt, c/fan, TV, video, refrig, cook fac, micro, d/wash, ldry (in unit), blkts, linen, pillows], iron, rec rm, pool (2), sauna, spa, bbq, c/park (undercover), plygr, tennis, cots-fee. **RO** **$100 - $220,** **W** **$490 - $1,190,** AE BC DC MC VI.

★★★★☆ **Riviera Resort Hervey Bay**, (HU), 385 Esplanade, Torquay 4655, 500m N of PO, ☎ 07 4124 3344, fax 07 4125 0500, (Multi-stry gr fl), 54 units acc up to 6, [ensuite (20), shwr, bath, tlt, hairdry, a/c (31), c/fan, tel, TV, video, clock radio, refrig, cook fac, micro, d/wash, ldry (in unit), blkts, linen, pillows], lift, dryer, iron, iron brd, conv fac, ⊠ (open 7 days), pool (salt water), sauna, spa, bbq, secure park, plygr, tennis, cots-fee. **RO $115 - $200,** **W $530 - $1,175,** AE BC DC EFT JCB MC VI.

★★★★☆ **Santalina**, (HU), 566 Esplanade, Urangan 4655, 75m W Urangan Pier, ☎ 07 4125 4500, fax 07 4125 4708, (2 stry gr fl), 13 units acc up to 6, (2 bedrm), [shwr, bath, tlt, c/fan, tel, TV, video, clock radio, refrig, cook fac, micro, elec frypan, d/wash (12), ldry (in unit), blkts, linen, pillows], pool (salt water), spa, bbq, ✆, cots. **D $100 - $155,** **W $400 - $895,** BC EFT MC VI.

★★★★☆ **White Crest**, (HU), 397 Esplanade, Torquay 4655, ☎ 07 4124 3938, fax 07 4124 1378, (Multi-stry gr fl), 28 units acc up to 8, (1, 2 & 3 bedrm), [shwr, bath, spa bath (1), tlt, a/c (27), c/fan, tel, cable tv, video (avail), clock radio, refrig, cook fac, micro, d/wash, ldry (in unit), blkts, linen, pillows], lift, dryer, iron, rec rm, pool, spa, bbq, secure park, tennis (day & night), cots (highchairs). **D $100 - $220,** **W $425 - $1,045,** BC EFT MC VI.

★★★★ **Hervey Bay Colonial Lodge**, (HU), 94 Cypress St, Torquay 4655, 50m fr beach, ☎ 07 4125 1073, fax 07 4125 5387, 8 units acc up to 6, (1 & 2 bedrm), [shwr, tlt, a/c, c/fan (8), cable tv, clock radio, refrig, cook fac, micro, blkts, linen, pillows], ldry, pool, bbq, c/park (undercover), courtesy transfer, ✆, cots, non smoking rms. **D** ♦♦ **$65 - $140,** ♦ **$10 - $15,** **W $285 - $750,** ch con, AE BC EFT MC VI.

★★★★ **Kalyan**, (HU), 99 Cypress St, Torquay 4655, ☎ 07 4124 9666, fax 07 4124 9666, (2 stry), 8 units acc up to 5, (2 bedrm), [shwr, bath, tlt, c/fan, TV, clock radio, refrig, cook fac, micro, ldry (in unit), linen], pool, bbq, c/park (undercover). **RO** ♦♦ **$85 - $120,** ♦♦♦♦ **$400 - $750.**

★★★★ **Ocean View Holiday Apartments**, (HU), 548 Esplanade, Urangan 4655, 1km W of jetty, ☎ 07 4124 4239, (Multi-stry gr fl), 4 units acc up to 6, (1 & 2 bedrm), [shwr, tlt, c/fan, heat, cable tv, clock radio, refrig, cook fac, micro, elec frypan, d/wash (3), toaster, ldry (in unit), blkts, linen, pillows], iron, iron brd, bbq, c/park (carport), cots. **D** ♦♦ **$60 - $100,** ♦ **$10,** **W** ♦♦ **$330 - $670.**

★★★★ **Ocean Waves Beachfront Holiday Units**, (HU), 235 Esplanade, Pialba 4655, 2 km NW of Coles Shop Cntre, ☎ 07 4124 5760, fax 07 4124 5760, (2 stry gr fl), 5 units acc up to 6, [ensuite, shwr, bath, tlt, a/c-cool, c/fan, TV, video, clock radio, refrig, cook fac, micro, d/wash, ldry (in unit), blkts, linen, pillows], dryer, iron, iron brd, pool, bbq, c/park (undercover), secure park, ✆, cots. **D** ♦♦ **$77 - $99,** ♦ **$10,** **W** ♦♦ **$440 - $693,** BC EFT MC VI.

★★★★ **Playa Concha Apartments**, (HU), 477 Esplanade, Torquay 4655, ☎ 07 4125 1544, fax 07 4125 3413, (2 stry gr fl), 12 units acc up to 6, (2 bedrm), [shwr, tlt, hairdry, a/c, c/fan, tel, TV, movie, clock radio, refrig, cook fac ltd, micro, elec frypan, toaster, blkts, linen, pillows], ldry, w/mach-fee, dryer-fee, iron, iron brd, ⊠, pool (salt water), bbq-fee, c/park (carport), cots-fee. **D $88 - $105,** AE BC DC EFT MC VI.

★★★★ **Shelly Bay Resort**, (HU), 466 The Esplanade, Torquay 4655, 3km E PO, ☎ 07 4125 4533, fax 07 4125 4878, (Multi-stry gr fl), 28 units acc up to 6, (1 & 2 bedrm), [shwr, tlt, a/c-cool, c/fan, tel, cable tv (18), clock radio, refrig, cook fac, micro, elec frypan, ldry (in unit), blkts, linen, pillows], lift, dryer, ⊠, pool (salt water), bbq, secure park, tennis (half court). **D $85 - $155,** ♦ **$10,** **W $395 - $900,** ♦ **$50,** ch con, AE BC DC EFT MC VI.

★★★★ **St Tropez on the Esplanade**, (HU), 367 Esplanade, Scarness 4655, 1km E of PO, ☎ 07 4124 4911, fax 07 4128 3909, (Multi-stry gr fl), 4 units acc up to 4, (2 bedrm), [ensuite, shwr, bath, tlt, c/fan, heat, elec blkts, TV, video, clock radio, refrig, cook fac, micro, elec frypan, d/wash, ldry (in unit), blkts, linen, pillows], dryer, iron, pool (salt water), bbq, c/park (undercover), secure park, cots. **RO** ♦♦ **$75 - $110**, ⚲ **$10**, **W** ♦♦ **$420 - $650**, BC MC VI.

★★★☆ **Atlantis On the Bay**, (HU), 458 Esplanade, Torquay 4655, 500m SE of PO, ☎ 07 4125 1322, fax 07 4125 5124, (Multi-stry gr fl), 4 units (2 bedrm), [shwr, bath, tlt, c/fan, cable tv, clock radio, refrig, cook fac, micro, d/wash, ldry (in unit), blkts, linen reqd-fee, pillows], dryer, iron, pool (salt water), secure park, courtesy transfer. **RO $95 - $140**, **W $385 - $650**, AE BC DC MC VI.

★★★☆ **Bay Hideaway Resort**, (HU), 1 Ibis Blvd, Pialba 4655, 50m E Shopping Centre, ☎ 07 4124 2621, fax 07 4124 5804, (2 stry gr fl), 18 units acc up to 4, [ensuite (3), shwr, bath, spa bath (9), tlt, hairdry (9), a/c (9), c/fan, tel (9), TV, video, movie, clock radio, CD, refrig, cook fac, micro, elec frypan, d/wash, ldry (in unit), blkts, linen, pillows], dryer, iron, iron brd, pool (salt water), bbq, c/park (undercover), cots. **D $99 - $330**, **W $490 - $1,100**, ch con, AE BC DC MC VI.

★★★☆ **Delfinos Bay Resort**, (HU), 383 Esplanade, Torquay 4655, 1km from PO, ☎ 07 4124 1666, fax 07 4128 3019, (Multi-stry gr fl), 21 units acc up to 7, [shwr, bath, tlt, a/c-cool, c/fan, tel, TV, movie, clock radio, refrig, cook fac, micro, ldry (in unit), blkts, linen, pillows], lift, dryer, iron, iron brd, rec rm, ✕, pool (salt water), sauna, bbq, rm serv, meals to unit (breakfast/dinner), c/park (undercover), cots. **D $60 - $130**, **W $385 - $750**, AE BC DC EFT MC VI.

★★★☆ **Monango**, (HU), 13 Ann St, Torquay 4655, ☎ 07 4125 1288, (2 stry gr fl), 16 units acc up to 5, (1 & 2 bedrm), [shwr, tlt, c/fan, TV, clock radio, refrig, cook fac, micro-fee, elec frypan, blkts, linen reqd-fee, pillows], ldry, rec rm, pool, spa, bbq, c/park (undercover), boat park, ⚓, plygr, cots. **D** ♦♦ **$55 - $121**, **W $198 - $583**, BC MC VI.

★★★☆ **Palm Court - Hervey Bay**, (HU), 368 Esplanade, Scarness 4655, 1km E of PO, ☎ 07 4128 3909, fax 07 4128 3909, (2 stry gr fl), 6 units acc up to 6, [shwr, tlt, a/c-cool, c/fan, heat, cable tv, clock radio, refrig, cook fac, micro, toaster, ldry (in unit), linen], w/mach, iron, pool, bbq, c/park (undercover), cots. **D** ♦♦ **$60 - $100**, ⚲ **$10**, **W** ♦♦♦♦ **$340 - $620**, ⚲ **$10**, ch con, BC MC VI.

★★★ **(Beach House Section)**, 1 house acc up to 6, (3 bedrm), [shwr, tlt, a/c, fan, c/fan, cable tv, clock radio, t/c mkg, refrig, cook fac, micro, toaster, blkts, doonas, linen, pillows], w/mach, bbq, cots. **D** ♦♦ **$60 - $100**, **W** ♦♦ **$360 - $620**, ch con.

(Beach Hut Section), 1 cotg acc up to 2, (Studio), [shwr, tlt, c/fan, heat, TV, clock radio, t/c mkg, refrig, cook fac ltd, micro, toaster, blkts, doonas, linen, pillows]. **D** ♦ **$50 - $80**, ♦♦ **$55 - $85**, (not yet classified).

★★★☆ **Pine Lodge Holiday Apartments**, (HU), 359 Esplanade, Scarness 4655, 300m E Shopping Centre, ☎ 07 4124 4239, (2 stry gr fl), 4 units acc up to 5, (2 bedrm), [shwr, tlt, c/fan, cable tv, clock radio, refrig, cook fac, micro, elec frypan, blkts, linen reqd, pillows], ldry, iron, iron brd, bbq, c/park (undercover), cots. **RO** ♦♦ **$55 - $100**, **W** ♦♦ **$340 - $650**, ch con.

★★★ **(Cottage Section)**, 1 cotg acc up to 7, [shwr, bath, tlt, c/fan, TV, clock radio, refrig, cook fac, micro, elec frypan, toaster, ldry (in unit), blkts, linen reqd, pillows], iron, iron brd, bbq (covered), c/park (undercover), cots. **RO** ♦♦ **$55 - $100**, ⚲ **$10**, **W** ♦♦ **$340 - $650**.

★★★☆ **St Tropez Apartments Hervey Bay**, (HU), 367 Esplanade, Scarness 4655, 1km E of PO, ☎ 07 4124 4911, fax 07 4128 3909, (2 stry gr fl), 4 units acc up to 4, (2 bedrm), [ensuite, shwr, bath, tlt, c/fan, TV, video, clock radio, refrig, cook fac, micro, elec frypan, d/wash, toaster, ldry, blkts, linen, pillows], dryer, iron, iron brd, pool, bbq, c/park (undercover). **RO** ♦♦ **$65 - $120**, ⚲ **$10**, **W** ♦♦ **$420 - $650**, ♦♦♦♦ **$520 - $750**, BC MC VI.

★★★☆ **Sunnynook Apartments**, (HU), 479 Esplanade, Torquay 4655, 50m E Ann St, ☎ 07 4125 6159, (Multi-stry), 8 units acc up to 7, (2 bedrm), [shwr, bath, tlt, c/fan, TV, clock radio, refrig, cook fac, micro, elec frypan, ldry (in unit), blkts, linen, pillows], pool (salt water), spa, bbq, secure park, cots. **D** ♦♦ **$65 - $85**, ⚲ **$15**, **W** ♦♦ **$300 - $475**, BC MC VI.

★★★ **Ace Holiday Homes**, (House), 17 Hibiscus St, Urangan 4655, 50m fr beach, ☎ 07 4125 6919, fax 07 4125 3658, 2 houses acc up to 8, (2 & 4 bedrm), [shwr, tlt, c/fan, heat, TV, video, clock radio, t/c mkg, refrig, cook fac, micro, toaster, ldry, blkts, doonas, linen, pillows], w/mach, bbq, c/park (undercover). **W $350 - $600**, 1 house ★★★★, Min book applies.

★★★ **Bay View Court Holiday Apartments**, (HF), 494 Esplanade, Torquay 4655, ☎ 07 4125 2418, (2 stry gr fl), 8 flats acc up to 5, (2 bedrm), [shwr, tlt, c/fan, TV, movie, clock radio, refrig, cook fac, micro], ldry, w/mach-fee, pool (salt water), bbq, c/park (undercover) (6), boat park, plygr, cots. **D** ♦♦ **$60 - $85**, ⚲ **$20**, **W $300 - $600**, ch con, BC EFT MC VI.

★★★ **Calypso Units**, (HU), 480 Esplanade, Torquay 4655, ☎ 07 4125 2688, (2 stry gr fl), 6 units acc up to 6, (2 bedrm), [shwr, tlt, fan (3), c/fan (3), heat (6), TV, clock radio, t/c mkg, refrig, cook fac, micro, blkts, linen, pillows], ldry, pool (salt water), bbq, c/park (undercover), courtesy transfer, cots. **RO** ♦♦ **$75 - $175**, **W $300 - $850**, AE BC DC EFT MC VI.

★★★ **Colonial Log Cabin Resort**, (HU), Cnr Pulgul St & Boat Harbour Dve, Urangan 4655, ☎ 07 4125 1844, fax 07 4125 3161, 11 units acc up to 6, (1 & 2 bedrm), [shwr, tlt, a/c-cool (2), c/fan, TV, refrig, cook fac, blkts, linen, pillows], ldry, rec rm, ✕, bar, pool (salt water), bbq, tennis. **D** ♦♦ **$63 - $93**, ⚲ **$10**, BC MC VI.

(Backpackers Bunkhouse Section), 1 bunkhouse acc up to 3, [linen], shwr, tlt, lounge (TV), cook fac, refrig. **D** ♦ **$15**.

★★★ **Golden Sands Motor Inn**, (HU), 44 Main St, Pialba 4655, ☎ 07 4128 3977, fax 07 4128 4292, 10 units acc up to 6, [shwr, tlt, tel, TV, clock radio, t/c mkg, refrig, cook fac ltd], ldry, dryer, pool, bbq, meals to unit (breakfast), cots. **RO** ♦ **$60**, ♦♦ **$70 - $80**, ⚲ **$10**, AE BC DC EFT MC VI.

★★★ **Lisianna**, (HU), 338 Esplanade, Scarness 4655, ☎ 07 4124 2950, fax 07 4124 2950, (2 stry gr fl), 6 units acc up to 4, (2 bedrm), [shwr, tlt, a/c-cool (5), c/fan, TV, clock radio, refrig, cook fac, micro, elec frypan], ldry, iron, bbq, c/park (undercover), cots. **D $55 - $90**, **W $275 - $525**, BC EFT MC VI.

HERVEY BAY QLD continued...

★★☆ **Kingfisher Court**, (HU), 374 Esplanade, Scarness 4655,
☎ 07 4124 1876, (2 stry gr fl), 7 units acc up to 4, [shwr, tlt, c/fan, TV, clock radio, refrig, cook fac, linen], ldry, pool, bbq, c/park (undercover), cots. **D ♀♀ $55 - $85, W $230 - $595**, BC MC VI.

★★☆ **Sun Bay Palms**, (HU), 3 McKean Rd, Scarness 4655, 500m S of PO, ☎ 07 4128 4088, fax 07 4124 8484, (2 stry), 5 units acc up to 6, (2 bedrm - Split level accommodation available.), [shwr, tlt, fan, heat, TV, clock radio, refrig, cook fac, micro, elec frypan, ldry (in unit), linen-fee], bbq, boat park, secure park, cots. **D ♀♀ $55 - $90, W $250 - $530, ⓦ $12.**

★☆ **Jetty View Flats**, (HU), 583 Esplanade, Urangan 4655, 200m E of Urangan Pier, ☎ 07 4128 9255, fax 07 4128 9255, (2 stry gr fl), 4 units acc up to 5, (2 bedrm), [shwr, bath, tlt, fan, TV, refrig, cook fac, elec frypan, toaster, blkts, linen reqd-fee, pillows], ldry, iron, bbq, c/park (undercover). **D $40 - $55, W $220 - $350**, BC MC VI.

B&B's/Guest Houses

★★★★ **Oceanic Palms B & B**, (B&B), 50 King St, Urangan 4655, ☎ 07 4128 9562, fax 07 4128 9562, 2 rms [shwr, tlt, H & C, heat, c/fan, elec blkts, t/c mkg, refrig, toaster], bathrm, rec rm, TV rm, pool-heated, spa (communal), bbq, secure park. **BLB ♀ $40 - $55, ♀♀ $75 - $95**, ch con, BC EFT MC VI.

★★★☆ **Mirambeena Bed and Breakfast**, (B&B), 76 Boundary Rd, Urangan 4655, ☎ 07 4124 9865, 3 rms [hairdry, a/c, c/fan, clock radio, ldry-fee], tlt, bathrm, dryer-fee, TV rm, lounge, pool (saltwater), t/c mkg shared, bbq (covered), courtesy transfer, non smoking rms. **BB ♀ $50, ♀♀ $70.**

★★★☆ **The Bay Bed & Breakfast**, (B&B), 180 Cypress St Urangan via, ☎ 07 4125 6919, fax 07 4125 3658, (2 stry), 5 rms [ensuite (1), shwr (2), tlt (2), a/c, c/fan, TV (2), clock radio, t/c mkg, refrig (1), micro (communal) (1)], shwr, tlt, lounge (TV & video), pool-heated (salt water), bbq (covered), non smoking rms. **BB ♀ $50, ♀♀ $70 - $100.**

Lakeside Bed and Breakfast, (B&B), 27 Lido Pde Urangan, ☎ 07 4128 9448, fax 07 4128 9448, 2 rms [shwr, tlt, c/fan, cable tv, video, clock radio, cook fac ltd, doonas], ldry, lounge firepl, spa, t/c mkg shared, refrig, bbq, c/park (undercover), cots-fee, non smoking property. **BB ♀ $50 - $60, ♀♀ $75 - $95**, ch con, AE BC DC EFT MC VI, (not yet classified).

HIDDEN VALLEY QLD 4861

Pop Nominal, (1491km NW Brisbane), See maps on page 415, ref C7. Cattle Farming District Falls on Running River.

Hotels/Motels

Hidden Valley Cabins, (LMH), Pine Creek Rd. 120km NW Townsville, ☎ 07 4770 8088, fax 07 4770 8088, 6 units [shwr, tlt, t/c mkg], rec rm, lounge (TV), conv fac, ⊠, pool (salt water), spa, ✆, plygr, cots, non smoking rms (4). **D $38.50 - $66**, ch con, BC EFT MC VI.

HIDEAWAY BAY QLD

See Whitsundays Region.

HINCHINBROOK ISLAND QLD 4816

Pop Nominal, (1533km N Brisbane), See maps on page 415, ref C6. One of the largest National Park islands in the world.

Hotels/Motels

★★★ **Hinchinbrook Island**, (M), Resort, ☎ 07 4066 8270, fax 07 4066 8271, 15 units [shwr, tlt, c/fan, t/c mkg, refrig, pillows], ldry, ⊠, pool, shop, bush walking, canoeing. **D all meals ♀ $341.50**, ch con, Transfers by resort launch - prior arrangement necessary. AE BC DC MC VI.

★★★ **(Treehouse Units)**, 15 units [shwr, tlt, c/fan, t/c mkg, refrig]. **D all meals ♀ $369.50.**

★★☆ **(Cabin Section)**, 3 units [shwr, tlt, c/fan, t/c mkg, refrig]. **D all meals ♀ $247.50.**

Trouble-free travel tips - Tyre pressures

Check tyre pressures and set them to the manufacturer's recommendation, including the spare.

The specifications can generally be found on the tyre placard located in either the glove box or on the front door frame.

HOLLOWAYS BEACH QLD 4878

Pop 3,174. (1730km N Brisbane), See maps on page 415, ref C3. Part of Marlin Coast and popular holiday destination.

Self Catering Accommodation

★★★★ **Cairns Beach Resort**, (HU), 129 Oleander St, 9km Nth of Cairns Inter. & Dom. Airports, ☎ 07 4037 0400, fax 07 4037 0600, (Multi-stry), 73 units acc up to 4, (1 bedrm), [shwr, bath, tlt, hairdry, a/c, tel, TV, clock radio, refrig, cook fac, micro, d/wash (73)], toaster, ldry, blkts, linen, pillows], iron, iron brd, pool, bbq, cots. **D $75 - $130**, AE BC DC MC VI.

★★★☆ **Pacific Sands Holiday Apartments**, (HU), 1 Poinciana St, 50m from beachfront, ☎ 07 4055 0277, fax 07 4055 0899, (2 stry gr fl), 37 units acc up to 4, (2 bedrm), [shwr, tlt, c/fan, tel, TV, clock radio, refrig, cook fac, micro, d/wash, ldry (in unit), blkts, linen, pillows], dryer, iron, pool (salt water), bbq, c/park (undercover). **D $95, W $608**, AE BC DC MC VI.

★★★ **Welzheimer Holiday Units**, (HF), 9 Mimosa St, ☎ 07 4055 9586, fax 07 4055 9789, 6 flats acc up to 4, (1 & 2 bedrm), [shwr, tlt, a/c-cool, c/fan, TV, radio, refrig, cook fac], ldry-fee, dryer-fee, iron, pool (salt water), bbq, c/park (undercover), cots. **D $45 - $60**, Min book applies.

HOME HILL QLD 4806

Pop 3,050. (1271km N Brisbane), See maps on page 415, ref E8. Located on the Burdekin River, it is the centre of a rich sugar cane district. Boating, Bowls, Fishing.

Hotels/Motels

★★☆ **Burdekin Motor Inn**, (M), 14 Eighth Ave, South of PO, ☎ 07 4782 1511, fax 07 4782 1606, 14 units [shwr, tlt, a/c-cool, c/fan, tel, TV, clock radio, t/c mkg, refrig, toaster], ldry, dryer, ⊠ (Fri to Sat), bar, pool, bbq, rm serv, dinner to unit (Mon to Thurs), c/park (undercover), cots-fee. **RO ♀ $46.20, ♀♀ $55, ⓦ $8.80**, AE BC DC MC VI.

HOPE ISLAND QLD

See Gold Coast Region.

HORN ISLAND QLD 4875

Pop Nominal, (2938km N Brisbane), See maps on page 414, ref B1. A unique tropical island surrounded by over 100 other Torres Strait Islands. Fishing, Gold Prospecting.

Hotels/Motels

★★ **Gateway Torres Strait Resort**, (M), 24 Outie St, 7km W of Airport 500m from Wharf, ☎ 07 4069 2222, fax 07 4069 2211, 22 units [basin, shwr, tlt, a/c-cool, c/fan, tel (4), TV, movie, t/c mkg, refrig, cook fac ltd, micro, toaster], ldry-fee, lounge (TV), conv fac, ⊠, courtesy transfer, ✆, cots. **RO ♀ $99, ♀♀ $125, ⓦ $25**, ch con, AE BC MC VI.

HOWARD QLD 4659

Pop 950. Part of Hervey Bay, (281km N Brisbane), See maps on page 417, ref D1. Pleasantly quiet country town, featuring Brooklyn the superb colonial house once the home of Senator Dame Annabel Rankin.

B&B's/Guest Houses

Melvos B & B Country House, (B&B), Lot 84 Pacific Haven Circuit, 6.5km N of PO, ☎ 07 4129 0201, fax 07 4129 0201, 3 rms [shwr (2), bath (1), spa bath (1), tlt (2), hairdry, c/fan (5), elec blkts, TV, clock radio, t/c mkg, refrig (1)], ldry, dryer, iron, iron brd, lounge (TV), pool-heated, spa, bbq. **BB ♀ $55, ♀♀ $88**, (not yet classified).

HUGHENDEN QLD 4821

Pop 1,450. (1645km NW Brisbane), See maps on page 414, ref C5. Major centre for wool, cattle and grain. Also a popular fossil finding area. Porcupine Gorge, Dinosaur Display Centre. Bowls, Swimming.

Hotels/Motels

★★★ **Hughenden Rest Easi**, (M), Flinders Hwy (West), ☎ 07 4741 1633, 11 units [shwr, tlt, a/c-cool, elec blkts (4), tel, TV, clock radio, t/c mkg, refrig, ldry], pool, bbq, dinner to unit, ✆, cots-fee, non smoking rms (6). **RO ♀ $55 - $61, ♀♀ $66 - $73, ⓦ $13**, BC MC VI.

★★★ **Royal**, (LMH), Moran St, ☎ 07 4741 1183, fax 07 4741 1731, 34 units (1 & 2 bedrm), [shwr, tlt, a/c, c/fan, tel, TV, clock radio, t/c mkg, refrig], ldry, ✉, dinner to unit, cots. **RO** ♦ **$55 - $60.50**, ♦♦ **$66 - $71.50**, ⬩ **$13 - $18**, ch con, AE BC MC VI.

★ **Wrights Motel & Rest**, (M), 20 Gray St, ☎ 07 4741 1677, fax 07 4741 1677, 16 units [shwr, tlt, a/c-cool, c/fan, tel, TV, clock radio, t/c mkg, refrig], ✉, dinner to unit (Mon to Sat), cots-fee. **RO** ♦ **$41.80**, ♦♦ **$49.50**, ⬩ **$11**, ch con, AE BC DC MC VI.

ILFRACOMBE QLD 4727

*Pop 322. (1143km NW Brisbane), See maps on page 414, ref C6.
Small outback township on the Landsborough (Matilda) Hwy situated on former site of Wellshot Station, once the largest stocked sheep station in the world. Extensive Folk Museum open daily - entrance by donation. Township facilities include Railway Station, Post Office, General Stores and Police Station; also 100 year old Wellshot Hotel.*

Hotels/Motels
Historic Wellshot Hotel, (LH), Matilda Hwy, 25km E of Longreach Hall of Fame, ☎ 07 4658 2106, fax 07 4658 3926, 7 rms [fan, t/c mkg], shwr, tlt, ldry, ✉, ☎, non smoking flr. **RO** ♦ **$25**, ♦♦ **$43**, BC EFT MC VI.

IMBIL QLD 4570

*Pop 450. (148km N Brisbane), See maps on page 417, ref D4.
Small town in rich dairying & fruit growing area. Lake Borumba & Borumba Dam 13km SW. Bowls, Bush Walking, Scenic Drives.*

Hotels/Motels
★★ **Imbil**, (M), The Island Rd, ☎ 07 5484 5191, 5 units [shwr, tlt, a/c, elec blkts, TV, clock radio, t/c mkg, refrig]. **RO** ♦ **$33**, ♦♦ **$44**, ⬩ **$9.90**.

INGHAM QLD 4850

*Pop 5,000. (1481km N Brisbane), See maps on page 415, ref C6.
Sugar township located within the southern Wet Tropics World Heritage Region. Bush Walking, Fishing, Golf, Horse Racing, Scenic Drives, Swimming.*

Hotels/Motels
★★★ **Herbert Valley**, (M), Bruce Hwy, ☎ 07 4776 1777, fax 07 4776 3646, 30 units [shwr, tlt, a/c-cool, c/fan, tel, TV, clock radio, t/c mkg, refrig], ldry, ✉ (Mon to Sat), pool-heated (solar), dinner to unit (Mon to Sat), cots ($4.50)-fee. **RO** ♦ **$49.50 - $52.80**, ♦♦ **$55 - $60.50**, ⬩ **$7.70**, ch con, AE BC DC MC VI.

★★☆ **Ingham**, (M), 62 Townsville Rd, ☎ 07 4776 2355, fax 07 4776 3015, 19 units [shwr, spa bath (4), tlt, a/c-cool, c/fan, tel, TV, movie (15), radio, t/c mkg, refrig], pool, dinner to unit (prior arrangement), cots-fee. **D** ♦ **$49.50 - $82.50**, ♦♦ **$55 - $82.50**, ♦♦♦ **$61.60 - $89.10**, ♦♦♦♦ **$68.20 - $89.10**, AE BC MC VI.

★☆ **Lees**, (LH), 58 Lannercost St, ☎ 07 4776 1577, fax 07 4776 1503, (2 stry) 22 rms [shwr, bath (2), tlt, a/c-cool, c/fan, TV, t/c mkg, refrig (3)], ✉ (Mon to Sat), refrig. **D** ♦ **$45**, ♦♦ **$55**, ch con, No off-street parking. AE BC DC EFT MC VI.

B&B's/Guest Houses
★★★ **Como Estate Homestay**, (B&B), (Farm), 80ha sugar cane farm, Como Rd, 7km S of PO, ☎ 07 4777 2165, fax 07 4777 2335, 4 rms [hairdry, c/fan, radio], shwr, tlt, ldry, dryer, lounge (TV), pool, t/c mkg shared, c/park (undercover), non smoking rms (4). **BB** ♦ **$30**, ♦♦ **$60**.

INGLEWOOD QLD 4387

*Pop 950. (270km SW Brisbane), See maps on page 414, ref E8.
District produces a diversity of primary products - wheat, lucerne, timber, fat cattle, sheep and dairy produce. Coolmunda Dam. Boating, Bowls, Fishing, Golf, Swimming, Tennis, Water Skiing.*

Hotels/Motels
★★★☆ **Motel Olympic**, (M), 83 Albert St, ☎ 07 4652 1333, fax 07 4652 1646, 12 units [shwr, tlt, hairdry, a/c, elec blkts, tel, TV, movie, clock radio, t/c mkg, refrig, toaster, ldry (service)], ✉, pool, bbq, plygr, cots-fee, non smoking rms (6). **BLB** ♦ **$40**, ♦♦ **$51 - $53**, ⬩ **$8**, ch con, AE BC DC EFT MC VI.

★★★ **Inglewood Motel**, (M), Albert St, ☎ 07 4652 1377, fax 07 4652 1477, 11 units [shwr, tlt, hairdry, a/c, elec blkts, tel, fax, cable tv, clock radio, t/c mkg, refrig, micro, toaster], ldry, iron, iron brd, pool, bbq, dinner to unit, c/park (undercover), cots-fee. **RO** ♦ **$44**, ♦♦ **$53**, ⬩ **$8**, AE BC DC EFT MC MCH VI.

INJUNE QLD 4454

*Pop 400. (568km NW Brisbane), See maps on page 414, ref D7.
Hub of a vast cattle and sheep district. Referred to as the 'southern gateway' to Carnarvon and Mount Moffat National Parks. Nearby is Mt Moffatt National Park. Bush Walking.*

Hotels/Motels

★★★ **Injune**, (M), 60 Hutton St, ☎ 07 4626 1328, fax 07 4626 1168, 16 units [shwr, tlt, a/c-cool (8), a/c (8), heat (8), elec blkts, tel, cable tv, clock radio, t/c mkg, refrig, cook fac (2), micro, toaster]. **RO** ♦ **$55 - $66**, ♦♦ **$69 - $75**, ⬩ **$11**, ch con, AE BC DC EFT MC VI.

INNISFAIL QLD 4860

*Pop 9,000. (1629km N Brisbane), See maps on page 415, ref C4.
Johnstone River Crocodile Farm (halfway to Flying Fish Point) - open daily. Paronella Park Sugar Museum, Johnstone River Crocodile Farm - open daily. Boating, Bowls, Fishing, Golf, Horse Racing, Scenic Drives.*

Hotels/Motels

★★★☆ **Barrier Reef**, (M), 2 River Ave (Bruce Hwy), 1km S of PO, ☎ 07 4061 4988, fax 07 4061 2896, (2 stry gr fl), 41 units [shwr, tlt, a/c-cool, fan, tel, cable tv, clock radio, t/c mkg, refrig, cook fac (2), micro (2)], ldry, ✉, pool, c/park (undercover), cots-fee, non smoking rms (17). **RO** ♦ **$63 - $70**, ♦♦ **$70 - $85**, ⬩ **$11**, ch con, AE BC DC EFT MC VI.

INNISFAIL QLD continued...

★★★ **Moondarra**, (M), 21 Ernest St, Bruce Hwy, ☎ 07 4061 7077, fax 07 4061 3231, 14 units [shwr, tlt, a/c, fan, tel, TV, clock radio, t/c mkg, refrig, cook fac (3)], ldry, meals to unit, cots, non smoking rms (3). **RO** ⧍ **$50**, ⧍⧍ **$55**, ⧍ **$10**, AE BC DC MC VI.

★★☆ **The Robert Johnstone**, (M), Cnr Fitzgerald Esp & Grace St, ☎ 07 4061 2444, fax 07 4061 3639, (2 stry gr fl), 25 units [shwr, tlt, a/c-cool, fan, tel, TV, movie, clock radio, t/c mkg, refrig, cook fac], ldry, dryer, c/park (undercover) (12), cots-fee. **RO** ⧍ **$55**, ⧍⧍ **$66 - $75**, ⧍ **$15**, ch con, Units 6 to 10 and 11 to 16 ★★★. AE BC DC EFT MC VI, ⌂&.

★★☆ **Walkabout**, (M), 20 McGowan Dve, ☎ 07 4061 2311, fax 07 4061 4919, 18 units [shwr, tlt, a/c-cool, fan, tel, TV, movie, t/c mkg, refrig], ldry, w/mach-fee, dryer-fee, c/park (undercover), ch con, AE BC DC MC VI.

 ★★ **Black Marlin**, (M), 26 Glady St, ☎ 07 4061 2533, fax 07 4061 6899, 10 units [shwr, tlt, a/c-cool, fan, tel, TV, clock radio, t/c mkg, refrig], pool. **D** ⧍ **$48**, ⧍⧍ **$53**, ⧍ **$12**, ch con, BC MC VI.

★☆ **Carefree**, (M), 14 Owen St, ☎ 07 4061 2266, fax 07 4061 4164, (2 stry gr fl), 15 units [shwr, tlt, a/c-cool, fan, tel, cable tv, movie, clock radio (some), t/c mkg, refrig], cots, AE BC DC EFT MC VI.

INNOT HOT SPRINGS QLD 4872

Pop Nominal, (1766km NW Brisbane), See maps on page 415, ref B4. Small agricultural township noted for its hot mineral springs.

Hotels/Motels
★★ **Hot Springs Hotel-Motel**, (LMH), Kennedy Hwy, ☎ 07 4097 0203, 5 units [ensuite, shwr, tlt, fan, TV, t/c mkg, refrig], ldry, conv fac, ⌧, dinner to unit, c/park (undercover), plygr. **RO** ⧍⧍ **$55**, ch con.

IPSWICH QLD 4305

Pop 131,514. (44km W Brisbane), See maps on page 417, ref C7. Ipswich - the oldest provincial city in Queensland. Queens Park and Limestone Park. Bowls, Croquet, Golf, Horse Riding, Swimming, Tennis, Water Skiing.

Hotels/Motels
 ★★★☆ **Ipswich Flag Inn**, (M), 86 Warwick Rd, ☎ 07 3281 2633, fax 07 3202 4418, 19 units [shwr, spa bath (1), tlt, a/c, tel, TV, video, clock radio, t/c mkg (14), refrig, cook fac (5)], ldry, w/mach, dryer, pool, bbq, meals to unit, plygr, cots, non smoking rms (6). **RO** ⧍ **$77 - $100**, ⧍⧍ **$88 - $110**, ⧍ **$10**, AE BC DC MC VI.

★★★☆ **Ipswich Heritage Motor Inn**, (M), 51 - 55 Warwick Rd, ☎ 07 3202 3111, fax 07 3202 3692, (2 stry gr fl), 24 units (8 suites) [shwr, tlt, a/c, tel, TV, clock radio, t/c mkg, refrig, ldry (Guest)], ⌧, pool, bbq, plygr, cots. **RO** ⧍ **$75**, ⧍⧍ **$85**, ⧍ **$10**, Suite D **$95 - $135**, AE BC DC MC VI, ⌂&.

 ★★★☆ **Sundowner Chain Motor Inns**, (M), 250 South Station Rd, ☎ 07 3202 4622, fax 07 3812 1447, (2 stry gr fl), 34 units (2 suites) [shwr, bath (7), spa bath (3), tlt, a/c, c/fan (4), elec blkts, tel, TV, clock radio, t/c mkg, refrig, mini bar, toaster], ldry, w/mach-fee, dryer, conf fac, ⌧, pool, spa, bbq, rm serv, dinner to unit, c/park (undercover), plygr, cots-fee. **RO** ⧍ **$85.50 - $195**, ⧍⧍ **$95.50 - $195.50**, ⧍ **$11**, Suite D **$180.50**, ch con, Min book applies, AE BC DC MC VI, ⌂&.

★★★ **Mary Ellen Motel**, (M), Cnr Limestone & Thorn Sts, adjacent Queens Park, ☎ 07 3281 2100, fax 07 3281 0772, (2 stry gr fl), 14 units [shwr, tlt, hairdry, a/c, heat, tel, TV, movie, clock radio, t/c mkg, refrig], w/mach-fee, dryer-fee, iron, iron brd, bbq, c/park (undercover), non smoking rms. **RO** ⧍ **$71.50**, ⧍⧍ **$82.50 - $88**, ⧍ **$11**, pen con, AE BC DC EFT MC VI.

 ★★☆ **Motel Monaco**, (M), 28 Downs St, North Ipswich 4305, ☎ 07 32814200, fax 07 3281 1641, 20 units [shwr, tlt, a/c, tel, TV, clock radio, t/c mkg, refrig, cook fac ltd (3), toaster], ldry, dryer, pool, bbq, plygr, cots-fee. **RO** ⧍ **$58 - $62**, ⧍⧍ **$65 - $69**, ⧍ **$10**, ch con, AE BC BTC DC EFT MC MP VI.

B&B's/Guest Houses
★★★☆ **Villiers Bed & Breakfast**, (B&B), 14 Cardew St, 3km E of PO, ☎ 07 3281 7364, 2 rms [shwr, bath, tlt, hairdry, a/c-cool, fan, heat, elec blkts, clock radio, t/c mkg], ldry, dryer, iron, iron brd, lounge (TV), bbq, c/park (undercover), cots-fee, non smoking rms. **BB** ⧍ **$42**, ⧍⧍ **$72**, ⧍ **$17**, ch con.

IRVINEBANK QLD 4872

Pop Nominal (1,758km N Brisbane) See maps on page 415, ref B4. Historic tin mining town set in the hills west of Herberton.

Hotels/Motels
Irvinebank Tavern & Motel, (LMH), McDonald Street, 27 Kms W of Herberton, ☎ 07 4096 4176, fax 07 4096 4050, 2 units [shwr, tlt, heat, c/fan, TV, t/c mkg, refrig, toaster, ldry], dryer, iron, iron brd, ⌧, bbq (covered), ☏, plygr. **RO** ⧍ **$25**, ⧍⧍ **$45**, ⧍ **$10**, EFT, (not yet classified).

JANDOWAE QLD 4410

Pop 700. (270km W Brisbane), See maps on page 414, ref E7. Located in a large grain growing belt. Bowls, Golf, Squash, Swimming, Tennis.

B&B's/Guest Houses
★★★☆ **Diamondy**, (GH), (Farm), Jandowae via Dalby, 300km W Brisbane, ☎ 07 4668 6124, fax 07 4668 6124, 3 rms [shwr, bath, tlt, c/fan, elec blkts], pool, tennis. **D all meals** ⧍⧍ **$200**.

JULATTEN QLD 4871

Pop Nominal, (1821km N Brisbane), See maps on page 415, ref B2. Timber, mining (wolfram) township. Rural farming community. High level rainforest with emphasis on birdwatching. Native fauna & flora.

Self Catering Accommodation
★★★ **Kingfisher Park Birdwatchers Lodge**, (HU), No children's facilities, Lot 1 Mt Kooyong Rd, 22kms W of Mossman, ☎ 07 4094 1263, fax 07 4094 1466, 6 units acc up to 3, [shwr, tlt, clock radio, refrig, cook fac, micro, blkts, linen, pillows], ldry, dryer, bbq (covered). **D** ⧍⧍ **$104 - $110**, ⧍ **$30**, **W** ⧍⧍ **$538 - $624**, BC MC VI. **(Bunkhouses)**, 3 bunkhouses acc up to 2, [blkts, linen, pillows]. **RO** ⧍⧍ **$48 - $58**.

JULIA CREEK QLD 4823

Pop 500. (1713km NW Brisbane), See maps on page 414, ref B5. Centre of a rich pastoral area.

Hotels/Motels
★★ **Julia Creek**, (M), Flinders Hwy, ☎ 07 4746 7305, 11 units [shwr, tlt, a/c-cool, heat, tel, TV, movie, clock radio, t/c mkg, refrig], pool, bbq, c/park (undercover), plygr, cots-fee. **RO** ⧍ **$60.50**, ⧍⧍ **$66**, ⧍ **$11**, AE BC DC MC VI.

★☆ **Gannons**, (M), 36 Burke St, opposite PO, ☎ 07 4746 7103, fax 07 4746 7603, 13 units [shwr, tlt, a/c-cool, tel, TV, clock radio, t/c mkg, refrig], ldry, dryer, ⌧, t/c mkg shared, rm serv, dinner to unit (Mon to Sat), c/park. **RO** ⧍ **$55**, ⧍⧍ **$65**, ⧍ **$10**, AE BC DC EFT MC VI.

JUNDAH QLD 4736

Pop Nominal, (1,251km NE Brisbane), See maps on page 414, ref B6. Small rural town on banks of Thomson River. Council administration centre.

Hotels/Motels
Jundah Hotel Motel, (LMH), Dickson St, 217 SW of Longreach, ☎ 07 4658 6166, fax 07 4658 6166, 7 units [a/c-cool], ldry, lounge (TV), ⌧, t/c mkg shared, bbq, secure park, ☏, plygr. **RO** ⧍ **$30**, ⧍⧍ **$50**, ⧍ **$70**, ch con, BC EFT MC VI, (not yet classified).

KARARA QLD 4352

Pop Nominal, (210km SW Brisbane), See maps on page 417, ref A8. Situated in sheep, cattle and gold mining area.

B&B's/Guest Houses
Warahgai, (B&B), Karara, 57km W of Warwick, ☎ 07 4667 4166, fax 07 4667 4122, 3 rms [shwr, bath, tlt, hairdry, c/fan, elec blkts, TV, clock radio], ldry, dryer, iron, lounge (TV), lounge firepl, ✗, t/c mkg shared, bbq, tennis, non smoking rms (2). **BB** ⧍ **$55**, **DBB** ⧍ **$82.50**, (not yet classified).

Rates may change. Check before booking.

KARUMBA QLD 4891

Pop 1,050. (2222km NW Brisbane), See maps on page 414, ref B4. Situated at the mouth of the Norman River, it is the base for the southern gulf's prawn trawlers. Fishing.

Hotels/Motels

★★ **Karumba Lodge**, (LMH), Yappar St, 50m N of PO,
☎ 07 4745 9121, fax 07 4745 9379, (2 stry gr fl) 24 units [shwr, tlt, a/c-cool, a/c, tel (18), TV, t/c mkg, refrig, ldry], conv fac, ⊠ (Tues to Sat), bar, bbq, c/park (undercover), cots. **RO** ⬥ **$71.50**, ⬥⬥ **$82.50**, ch con, AE BC MC VI.

Self Catering Accommodation

★★★ **Ashs Holiday Units**, (HU), Palmer St, 8km W of PO,
☎ 07 4745 9132, fax 07 4745 9134, 12 units acc up to 6, [shwr, tlt, a/c-cool, c/fan, TV, clock radio, refrig, cook fac ltd, micro, blkts, linen, pillows], ldry, dryer-fee, pool (salt water), spa, bbq, c/park (undercover), ⬥, cots. **RO** ⬥ **$60**, ⬥⬥ **$66**, ⬥⬥⬥ **$71.50**, ⬥⬥⬥⬥ **$77**, **W** ⬥ **$346.50**, ⬥⬥ **$385**, ⬥⬥⬥ **$423**, ⬥⬥⬥⬥ **$462**, BC MC VI.

★★☆ **Matildas End**, (HU), 62 Yappar St, opposite supermarket, ☎ 07 4745 9368, fax 07 4745 9319, 10 units acc up to 6, (1, 2 & 3 bedrm), [shwr, tlt, TV, cook fac, blkts, linen, pillows], ldry, pool, spa, bbq. **D** ⬥ **$50**, ⬥⬥ **$60**, ⬥ **$10**, **W** ⬥⬥ **$310**, AE BC EFT MC VI.

KAWANA WATERS QLD

See Sunshine Coast Region.

KENILWORTH QLD 4574

Pop 300. (154km N Brisbane), See maps on page 417, ref D4. A centre for the dairying industry located in the Mary River region. Bellbird Sanctuary The Breadknife Waterfalls Kenilworth Country Foods (Cheese Factory). Bush Walking, Fishing, Gem Fossicking.

B&B's/Guest Houses

★★★☆ **House Landwehr**, (B&B), 108 Jubilee Rd, Carters Ridge 4563. 24km N of PO, 21km W of Cooroy, ☎ 07 5447 9253, fax 07 5447 9253, 2 rms [elec blkts, tel, radio, ldry, doonas], lounge (TV), ✕, spa, t/c mkg shared, refrig, bbq, non smoking property, Pets on application. **BB** ⬥ **$45**, ⬥⬥ **$75**, weekly con.

★★★ **Kenilworth House**, (B&B), 23 Elizabeth St, 50m N of PO,
☎ 07 5446 0500, fax 07 5446 0444, 4 rms [shwr (2), tlt (2), fan, elec blkts], shwr, lounge (TV), lounge firepl, ✕, t/c mkg shared, c/park (undercover) (2), non smoking property. **BB** ⬥ **$40**, ⬥⬥ **$77 - $95**, BC MC VI.

KEWARRA BEACH QLD 4879

Pop 1,331. (1738km N Brisbane), See maps on page 415, ref C3. Part of Marlin Coast, where the rainforest meets the Coral Sea. Water activities (Jun-Sept).

Hotels/Motels

★★★★☆ **Kewarra Beach Resort**, (LH), Resort, Kewarra Beach, 20km N Cairns off Captain Cook Hwy, ☎ 07 4057 6666, fax 07 4057 7525, 76 rms (1 suite) [shwr, bath, tlt, hairdry, a/c-cool, c/fan, tel, TV, clock radio, t/c mkg, refrig, mini bar], ldry-fee, dryer-fee, ⊠, pool (salt water), 24hr reception, rm serv (6am-11pm), ⬥, tennis, cots, non smoking units (25). **RO** ⬥ **$176 - $292**, ⬥⬥ **$224 - $368**, ⬥ **$50**, **Suite D** ⬥ **$384**, ⬥⬥ **$452**, ⬥ **$100**, ch con, AE BC DC MC VI.

KILCOY QLD 4515

Pop 1,500. (94km NW Brisbane), See maps on page 417, ref C5. Located on the Sunshine Coast, close to Lake Somerset - a major water storage area for Brisbane. Boating, Fishing, Scenic Drives, Swimming.

Hotels/Motels

★★★☆ **Kilcoy Gardens Motor Inn**, (M), Cnr Hope & Ethel Sts,
☎ 07 5497 1100, fax 07 5497 1177, 8 units [shwr, tlt, a/c, tel, TV, clock radio, t/c mkg, refrig, mini bar], ⊠ (Mon to Sat), rm serv, dinner to unit, c/park (undercover), cots-fee, non smoking units (6). **RO** ⬥ **$54**, ⬥⬥ **$65**, ⬥ **$12**, ch con, AE BC DC EFT MC VI, ♿.

★★ **Kilcoy**, (M), 6 William St, ☎ 07 5497 1433, 8 units [shwr, tlt, a/c, fan, elec blkts, TV, clock radio, t/c mkg, refrig, toaster], ldry, pool, c/park (undercover), cots-fee. **RO** ⬥ **$38**, ⬥⬥ **$45**, ⬥ **$8**, BC MC VI.

KILLARNEY QLD 4373

Pop 850. (198km SW Brisbane), See maps on page 417, ref B8. Scenic district located at the foot of the Great Dividing Range. Queen Mary Falls National Park. Dagg's and Brown's Falls. Bush Walking, Fishing, Scenic Drives, Swimming.

Hotels/Motels

★★★ **Sundown**, (M), Pine St, ☎ 07 4664 1318, fax 07 4664 1544, 6 units [shwr, tlt, fan, heat, elec blkts, TV, radio, t/c mkg, refrig, cook fac], ldry. **RO** ⬥ **$44**, ⬥⬥ **$55**, ⬥ **$11**, Light breakfast only available. AE BC MC VI.

B&B's/Guest Houses

★★★☆ **Oaklea**, (B&B), (Farm), Working beef & cattle property, The Head, via Killarney, 27km E of PO, ☎ 07 4664 7161, fax 07 4664 7161, 2 rms [shwr, tlt, elec blkts], ldry, lounge (TV), ✕, bush walking, non smoking rms. **BB** ⬥ **$45**, ⬥⬥ **$75**, ch con, Other meals by arrangement.

★★★☆ **(The School Cottage Section)**, 1 cabin acc up to 4, [ensuite, bath, fan, heat, elec blkts, TV, clock radio, CD, t/c mkg, refrig, cook fac]. **BB** ⬥ **$45**, ⬥⬥ **$70**.

KINGAROY QLD 4610

Pop 7,000. (210km NW Brisbane), See maps on page 417, ref B4. Capital of the Australian peanut industry. Commercial centre of Queensland's rich South Burnett District. Bunya Mountains National Park. Bicentennial Heritage Museum. Scenic Drives.

Hotels/Motels

★★★☆ **Burke & Wills Motor Inn**, (M), 95 Kingaroy St,
☎ 07 4162 2933, fax 07 4162 5131, 50 units [shwr, bath (12), tlt, hairdry, a/c, elec blkts, tel, cable tv, movie, clock radio, t/c mkg, refrig], ldry, ⊠ (Mon to Sat), pool, rm serv (mon-sat), dinner to unit, cots-fee. **RO** ⬥ **$69**, ⬥⬥ **$80**, ⬥ **$11**, AE BC DC JCB MC VI.

★★★ **Oasis**, (M), 50 Walter Rd (Brisbane Hwy),
☎ 07 4162 2399, fax 07 4162 3577, 24 units [shwr, tlt, a/c (24), elec blkts (6), tel, TV, clock radio, t/c mkg, refrig], ldry, conv fac, ⊠, pool, bbq, rm serv, dinner to unit, c/park (undercover), plygr, cots. **RO** ⬥ **$49**, ⬥⬥ **$57 - $61**, AE BC DC MC VI.

★★★ **Pioneer Lodge**, (M), 100 Kingaroy St, ☎ 07 4162 3999, fax 07 4162 4813, 20 units [shwr, tlt, hairdry, a/c, tel, TV, movie, clock radio, t/c mkg, refrig, mini bar], ldry, dryer, conv fac, ⊠, rm serv, c/park (undercover) (7), cots-fee. **RO** ⬥ **$68 - $73**, ⬥⬥ **$73 - $80**, ⬥ **$11**, AE BC DC MC MP VI.

★★☆ **Holliday**, (M), 175 Youngman St, ☎ 07 4162 1822, fax 07 4162 4002, 13 units [shwr, tlt, hairdry, a/c-cool, c/fan, heat, elec blkts, tel, TV, clock radio, t/c mkg, refrig, cook fac (3)], pool (salt water), bbq, rm serv, dinner to unit (Mon-Thur), c/park (undercover), cots. **RO** ⬥ **$45 - $55**, ⬥⬥ **$55 - $65**, ⬥ **$8**, AE BC DC EFT MC VI.

★★☆ **Motel Kingaroy**, (M), 38 Knight St, ☎ 07 4162 1966, fax 07 4162 1966, 19 units [shwr, tlt, a/c-cool (18), a/c (1), fan, heat, elec blkts, tel, TV, clock radio, t/c mkg, refrig], ldry, conf fac, ⊠, bar (cocktail), pool, bbq, rm serv, c/park (undercover), cots. **RO** ⬥ **$48 - $52**, ⬥⬥ **$58 - $62**, ⬥ **$11**, fam con, AE BC DC MC VI.

Self Catering Accommodation

★★★ **Passchendaele Farm Holidays**, (Cotg), 2900ha working cattle property, Ironpot Rd, 66km W of PO, ☎ 07 4164 8147, fax 07 4164 8218, 1 cotg acc up to 9, [shwr, bath, tlt, fan, heat, elec blkts, TV, clock radio, t/c mkg, refrig, cook fac, micro, elec frypan, toaster], ldry, iron, iron brd, ✕, bbq, cots, non smoking property. **RO** ⬥⬥ **$99**, ⬥ **$16.50**, ch con, Min book applies.

★★★☆ **(Bed and Breakfast Section)**, 2 rms [shwr, bath, tlt, fan, heat, elec blkts, TV, clock radio, t/c mkg, refrig, cook fac, micro, elec frypan, toaster], ldry (1), iron, iron brd. **BB** ⬥ **$55**, **D all meals** ⬥ **$148**.

B&B's/Guest Houses

★★★ **Minmore**, (GH), (Farm), Minmore Homestead, 20km W of Kingaroy 250km W of Brisbane, ☎ 07 4164 3196, fax 07 4164 3196, 3 rms [fan, heat, radio (1), CD], shwr, tlt, bathrm, lounge (TV), t/c mkg shared. **D all meals** ⬥ **$148.50**, ch con.

(Cottage Section), 1 cotg acc up to 3, [shwr, bath, tlt, fan, heat, refrig, cook fac, micro, blkts, linen, pillows], ldry, cots. **D** ⬥⬥⬥⬥ **$80**, ⬥ **$5 - $10**, ch con, Dinner by arrangement.

KINKA BEACH QLD 4703

Pop Nominal, (693km N Brisbane), See maps on page 416, ref C6. Coastal seaside area and part of Capricorn Coast. Coral Life Marine Land provides all-weather viewing of marine life.

Self Catering Accommodation

★★★☆ **Sunlover Lodge**, (HU), 3 Camellia St, 5km N of Emu Park, ☎ 07 4939 6727, fax 07 4939 6358, 4 units acc up to 6, (1 & 2 bedrm), [shwr, tlt, hairdry, a/c-cool, fan, TV, video, clock radio, refrig, cook fac, micro, blkts, linen, pillows], ldry, pool, bbq, c/park (undercover), plygr, cots. D ♦♦ $55 - $75, ♦ $10, W ♦♦ $330 - $525, ch con, AE BC MC VI. *Operator Comment: New! Ensite Cabins available from 2001. Ring 1800 666 445 for details.*

★★★ **Elgan**, (HU), 934 Scenic Hwy, ☎ 07 4939 6437, fax 07 4939 6437, 13 units acc up to 6, [shwr, tlt, a/c-cool, c/fan, TV, refrig, cook fac, micro, blkts, linen, pillows], ldry, pool, spa, bbq. D ♦♦ $58 - $85, ♦ $11, AE BC MC MCH VI.

KIRRA QLD

See Gold Coast Region.

KOLAN SOUTH QLD 4670

Pop 3,677. (396km N Brisbane), See maps on page 416, ref E8. A small country town in sugar cane area on outskirts of Bundaberg.

Hotels/Motels

★★☆ **South Kolan**, (LMH), Gin Gin Hwy, 25km W of Bundaberg. Midway btwn Bund. & Gin Gin, ☎ 07 4157 7235, 6 units [shwr, tlt, a/c, TV, clock radio, t/c mkg, refrig, toaster], ldry, ⊠ (Fri & Sat), dinner to unit, ✆, cots. RO ♦ $40, ♦♦ $50, ♦ $10, ch con, BC EFT MC VI.

KOORALBYN QLD 4285

Pop 800. (95km S Brisbane), See maps on page 417, ref C8. Leisure orientated resort of a unique semi-rural lifestyle. Bowls, Bush Walking, Golf, Horse Riding, Scenic Drives, Swimming, Tennis.

Hotels/Motels

★★★★ **The Kooralbyn Hotel**, (M), Routley Dve, ☎ 07 5544 6222, fax 07 5544 6260, 100 units [shwr, bath, spa bath (45), tlt, hairdry, tel, TV, video, movie, radio, t/c mkg, refrig, mini bar, ldry, pillows], conf fac, ⊠ (4), pool, sauna, spa, bbq, 24hr reception, rm serv, ✆, bowls, golf, mini golf, gym, tennis. D $132 - $198, ch con, AE BC DC EFT JCB MC VI, ♿.

★★★☆ **(Countryside Villa Section)**, 10 units acc up to 20, [shwr, tlt, fan, tel, TV, clock radio, refrig, cook fac, ldry (in unit), blkts, linen, pillows]. D $110.

★★★☆ **(Hillside Villa Section)**, 38 units [shwr, bath, tlt, a/c, tel, TV, clock radio, refrig, cook fac, ldry (in unit), blkts, linen, pillows]. RO ♦ $132 - $176, ♦♦ $132 - $176.

★★☆ **(Lodge Section)**, 24 rms [shwr, bath, tlt, hairdry, a/c, tel, TV, clock radio, t/c mkg, refrig], cots-fee. RO ♦ $66, ♦♦ $66.

Self Catering Accommodation

★★★☆ **Kooralbyn Holiday Rentals**, (HU), 11 Haygarth Dve, ☎ 07 5544 6377, fax 07 5544 6132, 10 units (2 bedrm), [shwr, bath, tlt, c/fan, heat, TV, clock radio, refrig, cook fac, micro (1), ldry (in unit), blkts, linen, pillows], dryer, iron, cots-fee.

★★★☆ **(Hillside Villas)**, 10 units (1 bedrm), [shwr, bath, tlt, a/c, TV, clock radio, refrig, cook fac, micro (3), ldry (in unit), blkts, linen, pillows], dryer, iron, cots-fee.

KUMBIA QLD 4610

Pop 225. (238km NW Brisbane), See maps on page 417, ref A4. Situated on Bunya Hwy midway between Kingaroy and the Bunya Mountains (National Park). A tidy towns award winner. Taabinga Homestead (listed by National Trust) is nearby Popular Boondooma Dam (1 hour drive) has fishing for yellow belly & silver perch also boating, waterskiing and picnic areas. Horse Racing.

Self Catering Accommodation

Old Boyneside, (Cotg), (Farm), Bunya Hwy, 12km S of PO at foothills of Bunya Mountains, ☎ 07 4164 4262, fax 07 4164 4121, 1 cotg acc up to 8, [shwr, bath, tlt, heat (combustion stove), elec blkts, TV, radio, refrig, cook fac, ldry (in unit), blkts, linen, pillows], bbq, cots. D $90 - $140, W $580 - $930, fam con, BC MC VI.

★★★☆ **(Homestead Section)**, (Farm), Historic Homestead, 2 rms [shwr, tlt, fan, elec blkts, video, radio, t/c mkg], lounge (TV), lounge firepl. D all meals ♦ $145, ch con.

KURRIMINE BEACH QLD 4871

Pop 850. (1594km N Brisbane), See maps on page 415, ref C5. Located east of Silkwood with a wide sandy beach protected by King Reef. Barnard Islands nearby. Short drive to Palmerstone National Park and Atherton Tableland. Bowls, Fishing, Golf, Sailing, Snorkelling, Swimming, Tennis.

Hotels/Motels

★★★ **King Reef Resort Hotel**, (M), Jacobs Rd, ☎ 07 4065 6144, fax 07 4065 6172, (2 stry) 4 units [shwr, tlt, a/c-cool, c/fan, TV, t/c mkg, refrig], ldry-fee, dryer-fee, ⊠, pool, bbq, c/park (undercover), ✆, cots-fee, non smoking units. RO ♦ $50, ♦♦ $55, ch con, BC EFT MC VI.

★★★ **(Holiday Unit Section)**, (2 stry gr fl), 11 units acc up to 6, [shwr, tlt, a/c-cool, fan, TV, clock radio, refrig, cook fac ltd, micro, toaster, blkts, linen, pillows], ldry, dryer, ⊠, pool, bbq, c/park (undercover), ✆, cots. D ♦♦ $55 - $70, ♦ $10, W ♦♦ $380 - $390, ch con.

★★★ **Villa Monaco Motor Lodge**, (M), 4 Hawthorne Dve, ☎ 07 4065 6311, fax 07 4065 6344, (2 stry), 28 units [shwr, spa bath (1), tlt, a/c-cool, tel, TV, video, t/c mkg, refrig, cook fac (11)], ldry, conf fac, ⊠, pool, bbq, cots. RO ♦ $55, ♦♦ $55, ♦ $5, ch con, Units 2 to 5 ★★☆. AE BC DC EFT MC VI.

Self Catering Accommodation

★★★ **QCWA**, (HU), Robert Johnstone Pde, ☎ 07 4065 6110, or 07 4061 4600, fax 07 4065 6404, 6 units acc up to 6, (2 bedrm), [shwr, tlt, a/c-cool, c/fan, TV, t/c mkg, refrig, toaster, ldry, blkts, linen, pillows], iron, iron brd, cots, ♿.

KYNUNA QLD 4736

Pop Nominal, (1597km NW Brisbane), See maps on page 414, ref B5. A small, remote town.

Hotels/Motels

★☆ **Blue Heeler**, (LMH), Matilda Hwy, ☎ 07 4746 8650, fax 07 4746 8643, 21 units [a/c], shwr, tlt, lounge (TV), ✕, bbq, dinner to unit, ✆. RO ♦♦ $33, ♦ $5.50, AE BC DC EFT MC VI.

(Motel Section), 4 apts [shwr, a/c-cool, TV, t/c mkg, refrig]. RO ♦♦ $55, ♦ $5.50.

LABRADOR QLD

See Gold Coast Region.

LADY ELLIOT ISLAND QLD 4670

Pop Nominal, (371km N Brisbane), See maps on page 414, ref E7. Island Resort located at the southern end of Great Barrier Reef. 42ha marine park is a true coral cay. Snorkelling, scuba diving, glass bottom boats. The island is also a popular birdlife sanctuary. Turtle or bird watching season October to April. Whale watching season June to November.

Self Catering Accommodation

★★☆ **Lady Elliot Island Reef Resort**, Resort, ☎ 1800 072 200, fax 07 4125 5778, 5 cabins acc up to 4, (1 & 2 bedrm), [shwr, tlt, fan, t/c mkg, refrig, blkts, linen, pillows], ⊠, pool, shop, ✆, plygr, cots. D ♦ $242, ♦♦ $396, ch con, Reef Education Centre. Tariff includes breakfast and dinner, AE BC DC JCB MC VI.

★★ **(Reef Units)**, 24 cabins acc up to 4, (1 bedrm), [shwr, tlt, fan, t/c mkg, blkts, linen, pillows]. D ♦ $214, ♦♦ $352.

(Tent Cabins), 14 cabins acc up to 4, [fan, blkts, linen, pillows], shwr, tlt, shared fac. D ♦ $203, ♦♦ $274.

LAIDLEY QLD 4341

Pop 2,350. (87km W Brisbane), See maps on page 417, ref C7. Located 10km off the Warrego Hwy between Ipswich & Toowoomba. Pioneer Village.

Hotels/Motels

★★★ **Hatton Vale**, (M), Cnr Shaw Rd & Warrego Hwy, Hatton Vale, ☎ 07 5465 6611, fax 07 5465 6043, 10 units [shwr, tlt, a/c, tel, TV, video, clock radio, t/c mkg, refrig], conv fac, ⊠ (Tues to Sun), pool, bbq (covered), dinner to unit, c/park (undercover), plygr, cots-fee. D ♦ $50 - $58, ♦♦ $60 - $70, ♦ $10, AE BC DC MC VI.

B&B's/Guest Houses

★★★★ **Denbigh Farm**, (GH), Historic country home on 7ha working farm property. 220 Mulgowie Rd Thornton via, 22km S of PO, ☎ 07 5466 7190, fax 07 5466 7190, 1 rm [shwr, bath, tlt, elec blkts, radio], ldry, lounge (TV & radio), ✕, c/park (undercover). **BB ♦ $50, D all meals ♦ $120.**

★★★☆ **(Cottage Section)**, 1 cotg acc up to 5, [shwr, bath, tlt, fan, heat, elec blkts, clock radio, t/c mkg, refrig, cook fac ltd, micro, elec frypan, toaster, blkts, linen, pillows], ldry, dryer, iron, iron brd, ✕, bbq, c/park (undercover), cots. **BB ♦ $50, $75 - $100.**

★★★★ **Twelve Oaks**, (B&B), 39 Donaldson Rd, Plainland, 1.5km from Plainland 8km from Laidley, ☎ 07 5465 6332, 2 rms [ensuite (2), shwr, spa bath (1), tlt, a/c-cool (1), fan, heat, TV (1)], lounge (TV), ✕, c/park (undercover), non smoking property. **BB ♦ $50, ♦♦ $135.**

LAKELAND QLD 4880

Pop Nominal, (1967km N Brisbane), See maps on page 415, ref A1. Small township located in pastoral area. Scenic Drives.

Hotels/Motels

★ **Lakeland Downs**, (LMH), Jnct Peninsula & Cooktown Developmental Rds, 146km N of Mt Molloy, ☎ 07 4060 2142, 18 units [shwr, tlt, fan, t/c mkg], ldry, dryer, iron, ✕, pool, bbq, ✆, BC MC VI.

LAMINGTON NATIONAL PARK

Pop Part of Nerang, (108km S Brisbane), See maps on page 417, ref D8. Subtropical rainforest area (including Binna Burra & Green Mountains), located in Gold Coast Hinterland. Caves, falls, abseiling, birdwatching. Bush Walking, Scenic Drives, Swimming.

B&B's/Guest Houses

★★★★☆ **O'Reillys Rainforest Guesthouse**, (GH), Lamington National Park Rd, O'Reilly's Plateau, ☎ 07 5544 0644, fax 07 5544 0638, 70 rms [shwr, tlt, fire pl (3), elec blkts, t/c mkg, refrig], ldry, rec rm, lounge firepl, ✕, pool (heated plunge), sauna, spa, cots. **D all meals ♦ $127 - $210, ♦ $127 - $210,** ch con, Tariff includes entertainment, tree top walk, morning & afternoon teas, Minium booking Bird Week - Nov, AE BC DC EFT MC VI, ♿.

★★ **(Budget Rooms)**, 6 rms [elec blkts, t/c mkg], shwr, tlt, cots. **RO ♦ $119,** ch con.

★★★★ **Binna Burra Mountain Lodge**, (GH), Beechmont 4211, ☎ 07 5533 3758, fax 07 5533 3658, 26 rms [ensuite (25), shwr (25), tlt (25), fire pl, heat, elec blkts, t/c mkg, refrig, mini bar, ldry, doonas], rec rm, lounge, conf fac, ✕ (licensed), cots. **D all meals ♦ $170 - $211, ♦♦ $318 - $378,** ch con, 15 rooms ★★★, AE BC DC MC VI.

★★★ **(Casuarina Cabins)**, 14 rms [shwr, tlt, fire pl, heat, elec blkts, t/c mkg, refrig, mini bar, doonas], bathrm, ldry, rec rm, lounge, ✕. **D all meals ♦ $136 - $181, ♦♦ $250 - $318.**

AAA TOURISM *Special Rates*

LAMMERMOOR BEACH QLD 4703

Pop Nominal, (686km N Brisbane), See maps on page 416, ref C5. Seaside resort on the Capricorn Coast.

Self Catering Accommodation

★★★★ **Lammermoor Lodge**, (HU), 130 Scenic Hwy, beachfront 4km S of Yeppoon PO, ☎ 07 4933 6190, (2 stry gr fl), 6 units acc up to 8, (2 & 3 bedrm), [shwr, tlt, a/c-cool, fan, TV, video, refrig, cook fac, micro, d/wash, ldry (in unit), blkts, linen, pillows], dryer-fee, pool, bbq, c/park (undercover), cots. **D ♦♦ $65 - $80, ♦ $10, W ♦♦ $350 - $600,** ch con, BC EFT MC VI.

★★★☆ **L'Amor Holiday Apartments**, (HU), 100 Scenic Hwy, ☎ 07 4933 6255, fax 07 4933 6661, (Multi-stry gr fl), 16 units acc up to 6, (1, 2 & 3 bedrm), [shwr, tlt, a/c-cool, c/fan, tel, TV, video, clock radio, refrig, cook fac, blkts, linen, pillows], ldry, dryer, rec rm, pool (salt water), sauna, spa-fee, bbq, c/park (undercover), plygr, gym, tennis (half court), cots-fee. **D ♦♦ $71, ♦ $16,** ch con, AE BC MC VI.

★★★ **Allamanda Court**, (HU), Scenic Hwy, 30m to beach, ☎ 07 4933 6454, fax 07 4933 6454, (2 stry gr fl), 4 units acc up to 4, [shwr, tlt, a/c-cool-fee, c/fan, heat-fee, TV, clock radio, refrig, cook fac, micro, blkts, linen, pillows], ldry, pool-heated (salt water heated), bbq, c/park (undercover), cots. **D ♦♦ $66 - $88, ♦ $11, W ♦♦ $396 - $616, ♦ $66,** Min book applies, AE BC BTC MC VI.

★★★ **Allamanda Lodge**, (HU), Scenic Hwy, 30m to beach, ☎ 07 4933 6454, fax 07 4933 6454, (2 stry), 3 units acc up to 4, [shwr, tlt, a/c-fee, c/fan, TV, clock radio, refrig, cook fac, micro, blkts, linen, pillows], ldry, pool-heated (salt water heated), bbq, c/park (undercover), cots. **D ♦♦ $55 - $77, ♦ $11, W ♦♦ $330 - $539, ♦ $66,** Min book applies, AE BC BTC MC VI.

★★★ **Golden Sands**, (HU), Scenic Hwy, 4km S of Yeppoon, ☎ 07 4933 6193, (2 stry gr fl), 4 units acc up to 5, [shwr, bath (hip), tlt, fan, TV, clock radio, refrig, cook fac, micro, blkts, linen, pillows], ldry, pool-heated, bbq, c/park (undercover), cots. **D ♦♦ $55 - $60, ♦ $10, W ♦♦ $330 - $420, ♦ $60 - $70,** 1 unit ★★★☆, BC MC VI.

LANDSBOROUGH QLD 4550

Pop 1,350. (76km N Brisbane), See maps on page 417, ref D5. Located on Glass House Mountains Rd 21km SW of Caloundra. Historical museum, aboriginal axe grinding grooves, pottery. Fishing, Golf, Scenic Drives.

Hotels/Motels

★★★ **Beerwah Motor Lodge**, (M), Glass House Mountains Rd (Old Bruce Hwy), 3km N of PO, ☎ 07 5494 1911, fax 07 5494 8072, 9 units [shwr, tlt, hairdry, a/c-cool, c/fan, heat, elec blkts, tel, TV, movie, clock radio, t/c mkg, refrig], ldry, pool, cook fac, bbq, dinner to unit, plygr, cots. **RO ♦ $50 - $55, ♦♦ $55 - $66, ♦ $11,** AE BC DC MC VI, ♿.

LIZARD ISLAND QLD 4870

Pop Nominal, (1717km N Brisbane), See maps on page 414, ref C3. Discovered & named by Captain James Cook August 1770. Situated in the Coral Sea surrounded by coral reefs. Temperature ranges between 23 & 32 degrees Centigrade. Twenty-four island beaches with safe boat anchorages. World famous 'Giant Cod Hole'. Island also famous as a base for game fishing (black marlin). Listed as a National Park with large variety of fish & bird life. Fishing, Sailing, Tennis.

Self Catering Accommodation

★★★★★ **Lizard Island Lodge**, (Villa), Resort, No facilities for children under 6, Lizard Island, via Cairns, Overlooking Anchor Bay, ☎ 07 4060 3999, fax 07 4060 3991, 40 villas acc up to 2, [shwr, bath, tlt, hairdry, a/c-cool, c/fan, tel, t/c mkg, refrig, mini bar, ldry, linen, pillows], dryer, iron, ✉, bar, pool, bush walking, tennis. **D all meals** ♦ **$800 - $1,150**, ♦♦ **$600 - $950**, ◊ **$350**, Medical clinic and Royal Flying Doctor Service available. AE BC DC JCB MC VI.

★★★★★ **(Unit Section)**, 40 units [shwr, tlt, hairdry, a/c-cool, c/fan, tel, t/c mkg, refrig, mini bar], ldry, dryer, iron. **D all meals** ♦ **$800 - $1,150**, ♦♦ **$600 - $950**, ◊ **$350**.

LONG ISLAND QLD

See Whitsundays Region.

LONGREACH QLD 4730

Pop 3,750. (1260km NW Brisbane), See maps on page 414, ref C6. Famous for the Australian Stockman's Hall of Fame. Bowls, Fishing, Golf, Horse Racing, Swimming, Tennis.

Hotels/Motels

★★★★ **Albert Park**, (M), Sir Hudson Fysh Dve, 500m W of Hall of Fame/walk dist opposite airport, ☎ 07 4658 2411, fax 07 4658 3181, 56 units [shwr, tlt, a/c, tel, TV, movie, clock radio, t/c mkg, refrig], ldry, conv fac, ✉, pool (salt water), spa, rm serv, c/park (undercover), cots-fee. **RO** ♦ **$68.20**, ♦♦ **$79.20**, ◊ **$11**, AE BC DC MC VI, ⓕ&.

★★★☆ **Abajaz Motor Inn**, (M), Previously Starlight Motel 11 Wonga St, ☎ 07 4658 1288, fax 07 4658 3277, 19 units [shwr, tlt, a/c, tel, TV, movie, t/c mkg, refrig], iron, pool, bbq, c/park (undercover), cots-fee. **RO** ♦ **$66**, ♦♦ **$77**, ◊ **$8**, AE BC DC EFT MC MP VI.

★★★☆ **Longreach Motor Inn**, (M), 84 Galah St, opposite railway station 300m E of PO, ☎ 07 4658 2322, fax 07 4658 1828, (2 stry gr fl), 57 units [shwr, tlt, a/c, tel, TV, movie, clock radio, t/c mkg, refrig], ldry, w/mach-fee, dryer-fee, ✉, pool, bbq, rm serv, c/park (undercover), cots-fee. **RO** ♦ **$82**, ♦♦ **$93**, ◊ **$10**, AE BC DC EFT MC VI, ⓕ&.

★★★ **Jumbuck**, (M), Sir Hudson Fysh Dve (Ilfracombe Rd), 400m from Hall Of Fame, ☎ 07 4658 1799, fax 07 4658 1832, 36 units [shwr, bath (2), tlt, a/c-cool, heat (18), elec blkts (18), tel, TV, movie, clock radio (18), t/c mkg, refrig, mini bar], ldry, conv fac, ✉, pool, rm serv, courtesy transfer, ✆, plygr, cots, non smoking rms (7). **RO** ♦ **$66 - $72.50**, ♦♦ **$77 - $84.50**, BC MC VI.

★★★ **Longreach**, (M), 127 Eagle St, centre of town, ☎ 07 4658 1996, fax 07 4658 3035, 14 units [shwr, tlt, a/c, tel, TV, clock radio, t/c mkg, refrig], ldry, w/mach-fee, meals to unit, c/park (undercover), courtesy transfer, cots. **RO** ♦ **$62 - $68**, ♦♦ **$73 - $79**, ♦♦♦ **$80 - $90**, ◊ **$6 - $9**, AE BC MC VI.

Self Catering Accommodation

★★★ **Aussie Betta Cabins**, Ilfracombe Rd, 2km E of PO, ☎ 07 4658 3811, fax 07 4658 3812, 16 cabins acc up to 5, [shwr, tlt, a/c, TV, refrig, cook fac, toaster, blkts, linen, pillows], w/mach-fee, dryer-fee, iron, pool (salt water), bbq-fee, ✆, cots-fee. **D** ♦ **$58.30**, ♦♦ **$67.10**, ♦♦♦ **$75.90**, ◊ **$8.80**, **W** ♦♦ **$469.70**, ◊ **$61.60**, BC MC VI, ⓕ&.

MACKAY QLD 4740

Pop 44,900. (975km N Brisbane), See maps on page 416, ref B2. Centre of the largest sugar producing region in Australia, with the largest bulk sugar facilities in the world. Bowls, Croquet, Fishing, Golf, Motor Racing, Sailing, Scuba Diving, Shooting, Squash, Swimming, Tennis, Trotting.

Hotels/Motels

★★★★☆ **Ocean International Hotel**, (Ltd Lic H), 1 Bridge Rd, ☎ 07 4957 2044, fax 07 4957 2636, (Multi-stry gr fl), 46 rms [shwr, bath, spa bath (13), tlt, hairdry, a/c-cool, tel, cable tv, movie, clock radio, t/c mkg, refrig, mini bar, cook fac (7), micro (7)], lift, ldry, dryer, conv fac, ✉, pool, sauna, spa, bbq, 24hr reception, rm serv, dinner to unit, cots. **RO** ♦ **$164 - $264**, ♦♦ **$164 - $264**, ◊ **$22**, ch con, AE BC DC MC VI.

★★★★☆ **Shakespeare International**, (M), 309 Shakespeare St, 1km SW of PO, ☎ 07 4969 0200, or 07 4953 1111, fax 07 4957 3826, (2 stry gr fl), 37 units (17 suites) [shwr, bath (18), spa bath (2), tlt, hairdry, a/c-cool, tel, cable tv, movie, clock radio, t/c mkg, refrig, mini bar, cook fac (19)], ldry, dryer, iron, iron brd, conv fac, ✉, pool (salt water), spa, 24hr reception, rm serv, dinner to unit, c/park (undercover), cots-fee. **RO** ♦ **$93.50**, ♦♦ **$99**, **Suite D** ♦ **$104.50**, ♦♦ **$110**, ch con, AE BC DC MC MP VI.

★★★★☆ **White Lace Motor Inn**, (M), 73 Nebo Rd, ☎ 07 4951 4466, fax 07 4951 4942, (2 stry gr fl), 35 units (1 suite) [shwr, bath (3), tlt, a/c, tel, TV, movie (24 hrs), clock radio, t/c mkg, refrig, mini bar, cook fac (1)], ldry, dryer, iron, ✉, pool, spa (7), 24hr reception, rm serv, dinner to unit, c/park (undercover), cots-fee. **RO** ♦ **$89 - $120**, ♦♦ **$89 - $120**, ◊ **$10 - $12**, **Suite D** **$109**, ch con, AE BC DC MC MP VI, ⓕ&.

★★★★☆ **Windmill Motel and Reception Centre**, (M), 5 Highway Plaza, Bruce Highway, 3.5km N of City Centre, ☎ 07 4944 3344, fax 07 4944 3355, (2 stry gr fl), 42 units (8 suites) [shwr (17), bath (21), spa bath (4), tlt, hairdry, a/c-cool, c/fan (8), tel, TV, video, movie, clock radio (8), t/c mkg, refrig, mini bar, cook fac (8), cook fac ltd (8), micro (8), elec frypan (8), toaster (8), ldry (guest)], dryer-fee, iron, iron brd, rec rm, conf fac (seat 400), ✉, cafe, coffee shop, pool, bbq (covered)-fee, rm serv (6.30am-12pm), dinner to unit, c/park (undercover), tennis, cots, non smoking units (29). **RO** ♦♦ **$94**, ♦♦♦ **$104**, ♦♦♦♦ **$120**, **Suite DBB** ♦♦ **$110 - $120**, ch con, AE BC DC EFT MC VI.

★★★★ **Alara Motor Inn**, (M), 52 Nebo Rd, ☎ 07 4951 2699, fax 07 4951 4785, 34 units [shwr, spa bath (3), tlt, hairdry, a/c-cool, c/fan, tel, cable tv, video, clock radio, t/c mkg, refrig, mini bar], ldry, iron, iron brd, conv fac, ✉ (Mon - Sun), pool, sauna, spa, rm serv, dinner to unit, c/park (undercover), cots, non smoking rms (17). **RO** ♦ **$79 - $87**, ♦♦ **$84 - $98**, ◊ **$10**, fam con, AE BC DC EFT MC VI.

★★★★ **Blue Ribbon Motor Inn**, (M), 34 Nebo Rd, ☎ 07 4957 7995, fax 07 4957 8885, 32 units (5 suites) [shwr, tlt, a/c, c/fan (8), tel, cable tv, clock radio, t/c mkg, refrig, cook fac (10)], ldry, ✉ (Mon - Fri), pool, spa, rm serv, dinner to unit, c/park (undercover), cots, non smoking units (13). **RO** ♦ **$58**, ♦♦ **$65**, ◊ **$11**, **Suite D** ♦ **$66**, ♦♦ **$70**, ch con, Units 2 to 17 of a lower rating. AE BC DC MC VI.

★★★★ **Country Plaza Motor Inn**, (M), 40 Nebo Rd, ☎ 07 4957 6526, fax 07 4957 3628, 38 units [shwr, tlt, hairdry, a/c, c/fan (16), tel, cable tv, movie, clock radio, t/c mkg, refrig, toaster], ldry, dryer, iron, iron brd, ✉ (Mon-Sat 6pm), pool, spa, bbq, dinner to unit, c/park (undercover), cots-fee. **RO** ♦ **$66 - $73**, ♦♦ **$73 - $78**, ch con, AE BC DC MC VI.

★★★★ **El Toro**, (M), 14 Nebo Rd, 500m S of showgrounds, ☎ 07 4951 2722, fax 07 4957 3944, (2 stry gr fl), 19 units [shwr, bath (2), tlt, hairdry (9), a/c-cool (10), a/c (9), tel, TV, video (2), movie, clock radio, t/c mkg, refrig], ldry-fee, dryer-fee, pool, cook fac-fee, bbq, dinner to unit (licensed), c/park (undercover), plygr, cots-fee. **RO** ♦ **$60 - $70**, ♦♦ **$70 - $80**, ◊ **$5 - $10**, fam con, Units 1 to 7 of a 3 star plus. AE BC DC EFT MC VI.

★★★★ **Marco Polo**, (M), 46 Nebo Rd, 2km S of PO, ☎ 07 4951 2700, fax 07 4951 3440, (2 stry gr fl), 30 units (4 suites) [shwr, bath (2), spa bath (2), tlt, hairdry, a/c, tel, cable tv, video-fee, clock radio, t/c mkg, refrig, mini bar], ldry, iron, iron brd, conf fac, ✉, pool (salt water), sauna, spa, rm serv, c/park (undercover), gym, non smoking units (15). **RO** ♦ **$99**, ♦♦ **$99**, ◊ **$11**, AE BC DC JCB MC VI.

Rates may change. Check before booking.

★★★★ **Mercure Inn Mackay**, (M), Previously Fortland Four Dice 166 Nebo Rd, ☎ 07 4951 1555, fax 07 4951 3655, (2 stry gr fl), 34 units (2 suites) [shwr, spa bath (2), tlt, a/c, tel, TV, movie, clock radio, t/c mkg, refrig, mini bar, toaster], ldry, iron, iron brd, conv fac, ⊠, pool, rm serv, c/park (undercover), cots-fee. **RO** ♦ **$126,** ♦ **$18, Suite D $237,** AE BC DC MC VI, ﾟ&.

★★★★ **The Lantern Motor Inn**, (M), 149 Nebo Rd, ☎ 07 4951 2188, fax 07 4957 2794, (2 stry gr fl), 16 units [shwr, tlt, a/c-cool, c/fan, tel, cable tv, clock radio, t/c mkg, refrig, mini bar], ldry, ⊠ (Mon to Sat), pool (salt water), spa, bbq, rm serv, dinner to unit, c/park (undercover), cots. **D** ♦ **$78,** ♦♦ **$83,** ch con, AE BC DC EFT MC VI.

★★★★ **The Rose Motel**, (M), 164 Nebo Rd, ☎ 07 4957 6572, fax 07 4957 2070, (2 stry gr fl), 28 units [shwr, tlt, a/c, c/fan, tel, cable tv, movie, clock radio, t/c mkg, refrig, toaster], ldry, conv fac, conf fac, ⊠ (Mon-Sat), pool (salt water), bbq, rm serv, c/park (undercover), cots-fee. **RO** ♦ **$60 - $100,** ♦♦ **$70 - $100,** ♦ **$6,** ch con, AE BC DC MC VI.

★★★★ **Whitsunday Waters Resort**, (M), Beach Rd, Dolphin Heads, beach frontage, ☎ 07 4954 9666, fax 07 4954 9341, 84 units [shwr, tlt, hairdry, a/c-cool, c/fan, tel, cable tv, clock radio, t/c mkg, refrig, micro, elec frypan, toaster], ldry, iron, iron brd, cots. **RO** ♦ **$82 - $103,** AE BC DC MC VI.

★★★☆ **Coral Sands**, (M), 44 Macalister St, ☎ 07 4951 1244, fax 07 4957 2095, (2 stry gr fl), 46 units (2 suites) [shwr, spa bath (2), tlt, a/c-cool, tel, TV, video (15), clock radio, t/c mkg, refrig, mini bar (29)], ldry, dryer, conv fac, ⊠ (Mon to Sat), pool (salt water), sauna, bbq, rm serv, dinner to unit, c/park (undercover), cots-fee. **RO** ♦ **$60 - $68,** ♦♦ **$68 - $75,** ♦ **$10, Suite D $90 - $200,** ch con, 16 units ★★☆. AE BC DC MC VI.

★★★☆ **Gorries**, (M), 186 Nebo Rd, ☎ 07 4952 2033, fax 07 4952 4706, 20 units [shwr, tlt, a/c-cool, tel, TV, movie, clock radio, t/c mkg, refrig, cook fac ltd (7), micro (7), elec frypan (7), toaster (7)], ldry, pool (salt water), bbq, rm serv, dinner to unit, c/park (undercover), cots. **RO** ♦ **$47 - $52,** ♦♦ **$50 - $59,** ♦ **$11,** AE BC DC MC VI.

★★★☆ **Mackay Motor Inn**, (M), 208 Nebo Rd, ☎ 07 4952 2822, fax 07 4952 2880, 22 units [shwr, tlt, a/c, tel, TV, movie, clock radio, t/c mkg, refrig, cook fac ltd (8), micro (8)], ldry, w/mach-fee, dryer-fee, pool, bbq, 24hr reception, rm serv, dinner to unit, c/park (undercover), cots, non smoking rms (13). **RO** ♦ **$64 - $74,** ♦♦ **$64 - $74,** ch con, AE BC DC EFT MC VI.

★★★☆ **Miners Lodge Motor Inn**, (M), 60 Nebo Rd, ☎ 07 4951 1944, fax 07 4957 2737, (2 stry gr fl), 28 units [shwr, bath, tlt, a/c-cool, c/fan (8), tel, TV, movie, clock radio, t/c mkg, refrig, cook fac-fee, elec frypan (3), toaster], ldry, dryer, ⊠, pool, bbq, dinner to unit, c/park (undercover), cots-fee. **RO** ♦ **$72 - $83,** ♦♦ **$83 - $94,** ♦ **$11,** ch con, AE BC DC MC MP VI, ﾟ&.

★★★☆ **Northview**, (M), Cnr Bruce Hwy & Phillip St, ☎ 07 4942 1077, fax 07 4942 2532, 14 units [shwr, tlt, hairdry, a/c-cool, tel, TV, movie, clock radio, t/c mkg, refrig, mini bar], ldry, pool, bbq, meals to unit, c/park (undercover), non smoking rms. **RO** ♦ **$49.50,** ♦♦ **$60.50,** ♦ **$11,** ch con, AE BC DC EFT MC VI.

★★★☆ **Sugar City**, (M), 66 Nebo Rd, ☎ 07 4968 4150, fax 07 4968 4189, 21 units [shwr, tlt, hairdry, a/c-cool, tel, cable tv, clock radio, t/c mkg, refrig], ldry, iron, iron brd, ⊠ (Mon-Sat), pool (salt water), bbq, rm serv, c/park (undercover), plygr, cots, non smoking units (3). **RO** ♦ **$66 - $78,** ♦♦ **$76 - $88,** ♦ **$10,** ch con, 5 units ★★★★. AE BC DC EFT MC MP VI.

★★★☆ **Sun Plaza**, (M), 35 Nebo Rd, 1km from CBD, ☎ 07 4951 2688, fax 07 4951 2651, (2 stry gr fl), 32 units [shwr, tlt, a/c, c/fan, tel, TV, movie, clock radio, t/c mkg, refrig], ldry, ⊠ (Mon to Sat), pool, sauna, bbq, rm serv, dinner to unit, c/park (undercover), cots-fee. **RO** ♦ **$52.80 - $58,** ♦♦ **$55 - $66,** ♦ **$12,** ch con, AE BC DC MC VI.

★★★☆ **Sundowner Chain Motor Inns**, (M), 2 Macalister St, ☎ 07 4951 1666, fax 07 4951 1968, (2 stry gr fl), 33 units (6 suites) [shwr, spa bath (8), tlt, a/c, c/fan, tel, TV, video, clock radio, t/c mkg, refrig, micro (6), toaster], ldry, iron, iron brd, ⊠ (Mon-Fri), pool, bbq, rm serv, dinner to unit, plygr, cots-fee. **RO** ♦ **$77 - $98.50,** ♦♦ **$81.50 - $98.50,** ♦ **$11, Suite D $98.50,** AE BC DC MC MP VI.

★★★ **Bel Air**, (M), 10 Nebo Rd, ☎ 07 4957 3658, fax 07 4953 1927, 18 units [shwr, tlt, a/c-cool, c/fan, tel, TV, movie, clock radio, t/c mkg, refrig, toaster], ldry, pool, bbq, dinner to unit, c/park (undercover), plygr, cots-fee. **RO** ♦ **$49,** ♦♦ **$48,** ♦ **$10,** ch con, AE BC DC EFT MC VI.

★★★ **City Gates**, (M), 9 Broadsound Rd (Bruce Hwy), 200m S of Tourist Info Centre, ☎ 07 4952 5233, fax 07 4952 3666, 6 units [shwr, tlt, a/c-cool, TV, t/c mkg, refrig], ldry, dryer, bbq, c/park (undercover), non smoking units (3). **RO** ♦ **$41.80,** ♦♦ **$47.30,** ♦ **$13.20,** ch con, BC MC VI.

★★★ **Culbara**, (M), Bruce Hwy South, 1/2 way between Mackay & Sarina, ☎ 07 4959 5251, fax 07 4959 5568, 9 units [shwr, tlt, a/c-cool, c/fan, tel, TV, movie, clock radio, t/c mkg, refrig, cook fac, micro, elec frypan, toaster], ldry, dryer, pool, bbq, rm serv, dinner to unit, boat park, plygr, cots-fee. **RO** ♦ **$40,** ♦♦ **$40 - $55,** ♦ **$8 - $10, W $210 - $245,** ♦ **$35,** ch con, AE BC EFT MC VI,

Operator Comment: Good overnight stop-Book direct 1800 645 395-Qld call only.

★★★ **Farview Motel**, (M), 22 Chidlow Street, Farleigh, ☎ 07 4959 8803, fax 07 4959 8166, 10 units [shwr, tlt, c/fan, TV, clock radio, t/c mkg, refrig, cook fac, micro, elec frypan, toaster], ldry, iron, iron brd, conf fac, ⊠, rm serv, dinner to unit, cots, non smoking units (4). **RO** ♦ **$48 - $52,** ♦♦ **$56 - $60,** ♦ **$10.**

★★★ **Metropolitan**, (LH), Cnr Gordon & Carlyle Sts, ☎ 07 4957 2802, fax 07 4957 3477, (2 stry), 7 rms [shwr, tlt, a/c-cool, TV, t/c mkg, refrig], ⊠, ✆, plygr, cots. **RO** ♦ **$40,** ♦♦ **$45,** Light breakfast only available. AE BC EFT MC VI.

★★★ **Milton**, (M), Cnr Milton & George Sts, ☎ 07 4951 1377, fax 07 4953 3020, 16 units [shwr, tlt, a/c-cool, c/fan, tel, TV, movie, clock radio, t/c mkg, refrig, cook fac ltd (5), toaster], ldry, pool, bbq, dinner to unit (prior arrangement), c/park (undercover), cots-fee. **RO** ♦ **$55,** ♦♦ **$55 - $65,** ♦ **$10,** ch con, AE BC DC MC VI.

(Holiday House Section), 1 cotg acc up to 8, [shwr, tlt, c/fan, tel, TV, video-fee, clock radio, refrig, cook fac, micro, elec frypan, toaster, ldry (in unit), blkts, linen, pillows], dryer, iron, iron brd. **D $120.**

(Townhouse Section), 1 unit acc up to 6, [shwr, tlt, a/c-cool, c/fan, tel, TV, video-fee, clock radio, refrig, cook fac, micro, elec frypan, toaster, ldry (in unit), blkts, linen, pillows], dryer, iron, iron brd. **D $150.**

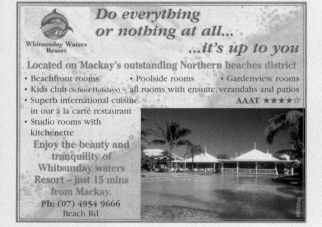

★★★ **Paradise Lodge**, (M), 19 Peel St, opposite bus terminal, ☎ 07 4951 3644, fax 07 4953 1341, (2 stry gr fl), 12 units [shwr, tlt, a/c-cool, fan, tel, TV, clock radio, t/c mkg, refrig], ldry, c/park (undercover), non smoking rms (4). RO ♦ $55, ♦♦ $60 - $64, ch con, AE BC DC EFT MC MCH VI.

★★★ **Pioneer Villa**, (M), 30 Nebo Rd, ☎ 07 4951 1288, fax 07 4957 3647, 18 units [shwr, tlt, a/c-cool, heat, tel, TV, movie, clock radio, t/c mkg, refrig, cook fac (6), micro (4)], ldry, dryer, ✉, pool, bbq, rm serv, dinner to unit, c/park (undercover), cots. RO ♦ $60.50, ♦♦ $66, ♦ $10, AE BC DC MC VI.

★★☆ **Bona Vista**, (M), Cnr Malcomson St & Norris Rd (Old Bruce Hwy), ☎ 07 4942 2211, fax 07 4942 5227, (2 stry gr fl), 18 units [shwr, tlt, a/c-cool, tel, TV, t/c mkg, refrig, micro (4)], ldry, ✉, pool, bbq, cots-fee. BLB ♦ $38 - $42, ♦♦ $45 - $55, ♦ $5 - $10, ch con, AE BC DC MC VI.

★★☆ **Boomerang**, (LMH), South Nebo Rd, ☎ 07 4952 1755, fax 07 4952 1104, 23 units [shwr, tlt, a/c-cool, tel (20), TV, clock radio, t/c mkg, refrig], ldry, dryer, ✉, pool, plygr. RO ♦ $38, ♦♦ $40 - $45, ♦ $12, BC MC VI.

★★☆ **Cool Palms**, (M), 4 Nebo Rd, ☎ 07 4957 5477, fax 07 4951 4660, 14 units [shwr, tlt, a/c-cool (14), a/c (2), c/fan, tel, TV, clock radio, t/c mkg, refrig, cook fac (5), toaster], pool, spa, c/park (undercover), cots-fee. RO ♦ $44 - $50, ♦♦ $44 - $50, ♦ $12, ch con, BC DC EFT MC VI.

★★☆ **Hi Way Units**, (M), Nebo Rd, Cnr Webberley St, ☎ 07 4952 1800, fax 07 4952 1172, 7 units [shwr, tlt, a/c, c/fan, tel, TV, movie, t/c mkg, refrig, cook fac, micro, elec frypan, toaster], ldry, dryer, pool (salt water), c/park (undercover), cots. RO ♦ $42, ♦♦ $47, ♦ $10, ch con, BC MC VI.

★★☆ **Mackay Townhouse Motel**, (M), 73 Victoria St, Imperial Arcade, 1st Floor, ☎ 07 4957 6985, fax 07 4957 6249, 17 units [shwr, bath (2), tlt, a/c, TV, clock radio, t/c mkg, refrig], cots. RO ♦ $44, ♦♦ $55, ch con, fam con, BC DC EFT MC VI.

★★☆ **Mia Mia**, (M), 191 Nebo Rd, Cnr McGinn St, ☎ 07 4952 1466, fax 07 4952 5557, 16 units [shwr, tlt, a/c, tel, TV, movie, clock radio, t/c mkg, refrig], ldry, dryer, pool, bbq, rm serv, c/park (undercover), cots. RO ♦♦ $48, ♦ $14, ch con, BC EFT MC VI.

★★☆ **Star**, (M), 175 Nebo Rd, Cnr Donaldson St, ☎ 07 4952 2444, fax 07 4952 5005, 8 units [shwr, tlt, a/c-cool, fan, tel, TV, clock radio, t/c mkg, refrig], ldry, dryer, pool, c/park (undercover). RO ♦ $49, ♦♦ $53 - $60, ♦ $10, ch con, AE BC DC MC VI.

★★☆ **Tropic Coast Motel**, (M), 158 Nebo Rd, ☎ 07 4951 1888, fax 07 4957 2694, 36 units [shwr, tlt, a/c-cool, c/fan, tel, TV, movie, clock radio, t/c mkg, refrig], ldry, dryer, pool, rm serv, dinner to unit, c/park (undercover), cots-fee. RO ♦ $55, ♦ $10, fam con, Units 1 to 16 of a lower rating (1.5). AE BC DC MC VI.

★★ **Hotel Whitsunday International**, (LH), Cnr Macalister & Victoria Sts, ☎ 07 4957 2811, fax 07 4951 1785, (Multi-stry), 12 rms [shwr, tlt, a/c-cool, tel, TV, radio, t/c mkg, refrig], lift, ldry, ✆, cots, AE BC DC MC VI.

★★ **International Lodge**, (M), 40 Macalister St, city centre, ☎ 07 4951 1022, fax 07 4951 1022, (2 stry gr fl), 16 units [shwr, tlt, a/c-cool, c/fan, tel, TV, movie, radio, t/c mkg, refrig], ldry, cots. RO ♦ $45, ♦♦ $50 - $55, ♦ $10, BC MC VI.

Self Catering Accommodation

Best Western

★★★★☆ **Blue Pacific Resort**, (HU), Previously Blue Pacific Village 26 Bourke St, Blacks Beach 4740, ☎ 07 4954 9090, fax 07 4954 8385, 38 units acc up to 8, (Studio, 1, 2 & 3 bedrm), [shwr, bath (13), tlt, a/c-cool, c/fan, tel, TV, clock radio, refrig, cook fac, micro (32), ldry (in unit), blkts, linen, pillows], rec rm, conv fac, ✉, pool-heated (salt water heated), spa, bbq, rm serv, c/park (undercover), plygr, tennis (half court), cots. D ♦♦ $88 - $138, ♦ $18, ch con, Units 1 to 5 & 8 to 9 ★★★, Units 10 to 15 ★★★☆. AE BC DC JCB MC VI, ♿.

★★★★☆ **Illawong Beach Resort**, (HU), Previously Illawong Lakes Resort Resort, Illawong Dr, 3.5km E of Airport, ☎ 07 4957 8427, fax 07 4957 8460, 37 units acc up to 5, (2 bedrm), [shwr, tlt, hairdry, a/c-cool, c/fan, tel, TV, clock radio, t/c mkg, refrig, mini bar, cook fac, micro, toaster], ldry-fee, dryer-fee, iron, iron brd, rec rm, conv fac, ✉, pool, spa, bbq, rm serv, dinner to unit, secure park, plygr, tennis, cots, non smoking units (20). D $130 - $160, W $780 - $960, ch con, AE BC DC EFT MC VI.

★★★★☆ **Sea Eagles Beach Resort**, (SA), Beachfront Peninsula Drive, Salonika Beach, 25km S Mackay, ☎ 07 4956 3388, fax 07 4956 3245, 19 serv apts acc up to 6, [shwr, bath, tlt, a/c-cool, c/fan, tel, TV, video, clock radio, refrig, cook fac, micro, d/wash, ldry (in unit), blkts, linen, pillows], dryer, ✉, pool (salt water), spa, freezer, bbq, c/park (undercover), plygr, tennis (half court), cots. D ♦ $110, ♦♦ $119, ♦♦♦♦ $129, ♦ $10, AE BC DC EFT MC VI.

★★★★ **La Solana**, (HU), 15 Pacific Dve & Cnr Pitt St, Blacks Beach 4740, 50m from beach, ☎ 07 4944 4600, fax 07 4954 9578, (2 stry gr fl), 12 units acc up to 6, (Studio, 1 & 2 bedrm), [shwr, tlt, a/c-cool, c/fan, tel, TV, clock radio, refrig, cook fac, micro, ldry (in unit), blkts, linen, pillows], dryer (6), pool (salt water), bbq (covered), c/park (undercover), plygr, tennis (half court), cots. D ♦♦ $60.50 - $93.50, ♦ $10, W ♦♦ $363 - $654.50, ch con, Units 1 to 5 ★★★. AE BC MC VI.

★★★★ **Ocean Resort Village**, (HU), 5 Bridge Rd, 3.5kms from city centre 1.5kms from airport, ☎ 07 4951 3200, fax 07 4951 3246, 34 units acc up to 6, (Studio, 1 & 2 bedrm), [shwr, tlt, hairdry, a/c-cool, c/fan, tel, cable tv, clock radio, t/c mkg, refrig, cook fac, micro, toaster], pool, bbq (2), kiosk, c/park (undercover), tennis (half court), cots-fee. D ♦♦ $79, ♦ $8, AE BC DC MC VI.

15 Pacific Drive,
Blacks Beach
Mackay QLD 4740
Ph: 07 4944 4600
Fax: 07 4954 9578

Refer to listing under Mackay

The fully self-contained units have:-
• One or two bedrooms • All Air conditioned • Linen supplied • Large lounge-dining area • Fully equipped kitchen with large stove and fridge • Colour TV • Clock radio • Own laundry • Fully screened • Ceiling fans • Pool • Covered barbeque and children's play area • ½ Court tennis • Undercover parking • Tour desk • 50m to beach • Long and short term stays

Email: lasona@telstra.easymail.com.au

★★★★ **The Shores**, (HU), 9 Pacific Dve, Blacks Beach, absolute beach frontage, ☎ 07 4954 9444, fax 07 4954 8580, (2 stry gr fl), 36 units acc up to 7, [shwr, bath, spa bath (2), tlt, a/c-cool, tel, cable tv, video (14), clock radio, t/c mkg, refrig, cook fac, micro, d/wash (2), ldry (in unit), blkts, linen, pillows], dryer, pool (salt water) (2), wading pool, spa, bbq, c/park (undercover), tennis (floodlit), cots. D †† $100 - $165, ◊ $17, ch con, AE BC DC MC VI.

★★★☆ **Elanora Units**, (HU), 182 Shoal Pt Rd, 16km N, ☎ 07 4954 6247, fax 07 4954 6247, 4 units acc up to 5, (2 bedrm), [shwr, tlt, a/c-cool-fee, c/fan (4), TV, clock radio, t/c mkg, refrig, cook fac, micro, elec frypan, toaster, blkts, linen, pillows], ldry, iron, pool, bbq, c/park (undercover) (2). D †† $49.50 - $66, ◊ $5.50, W †† $308 - $423.50, BC MC VI.

★★★☆ **Pacific Palms**, (HU), Symons Ave (off Waverley St), Bucasia Beach 15km N of Mackay PO, ☎ 07 4954 6277, fax 07 4954 6508, 6 units acc up to 5, [shwr, tlt, a/c-cool, tel, TV, clock radio, refrig, cook fac, micro, elec frypan, ldry (in unit), blkts, linen, pillows], dryer-fee, pool (salt water), bbq, c/park (undercover), cots. D $68.20 - $75.90, W $409.20 - $477.40, ch con, BC MC VI.

★★★☆ **Riverside**, (SA), 480 Bridge Rd, opposite Base Hospital, ☎ 07 4957 2501, fax 07 4957 2025, 15 serv apts acc up to 4, (Studio), [shwr, tlt, a/c-cool, tel, cable tv, clock radio, refrig, cook fac, micro, elec frypan, toaster], ldry, pool, spa, bbq, meals avail (breakfast), c/park (undercover), cots-fee, non smoking rms (4). D † $55, †† $60 - $62, ◊ $13, W †† $360 - $372, ◊ $78, ch con, BC MC MCH VI.

Stoney Creek Cottages & Trail Rides, (Cotg), Stoney Creek Rd, Eton, 30km SW of Mackay, ☎ 07 4954 1177, 1 cotg acc up to 2, (1 bedrm), [shwr, tlt, radio, refrig, cook fac], TV rm, bbq. D † $80 - $96, †† $96, ◊ $15, BC MC VI.

(Budget Accommodation Section), 1 rm (2 bedrm), [shwr, tlt, radio], cook fac, t/c mkg shared, bbq. RO † $15, fam con.

B&B's/Guest Houses
★★★★ **Eagle Nest Farm**, (B&B), Gormleys Rd, Seaforth 4741, ☎ 07 4959 0552, fax 07 4959 0552, 5 rms [shwr, tlt, c/fan], ldry, lounge (TV), ✗, pool (salt water), cook fac, t/c mkg shared, bbq, secure park, ✆, non smoking rms. BB † $45, †† $65.

MACLEAY ISLAND QLD 4184

Pop Nominal (40km S Brisbane) See maps on page 417, ref E7. In Moreton Bay. Macleay Island is the second largest island in the South Moreton Bay Islands group. Accessible only by water.

Self Catering Accommodation
Stolpje on Macleay, (Cotg), 4 Natone Terrace, 3 km north of jetty, ☎ 07 3409 5881, or 07 3409 5950, 1 cotg acc up to 6, [shwr, bath, tlt, c/fan, heat, tel, TV, CD, refrig, micro, elec frypan, toaster, ldry, blkts, linen, pillows], iron, iron brd. D $71.50, W $330, (not yet classified).

Trouble-free travel tips - **Tyre pressures**
Check tyre pressures and set them to the manufacturer's recommendation, including the spare.
The specifications can generally be found on the tyre placard located in either the glove box or on the front door frame.

MAGNETIC ISLAND QLD 4819

Pop 2,250. (1371km N Brisbane). See maps on page 415, ref D7. A World Heritage National Park 8km from Townsville, bowls, bush walks, fishing, golf, horse riding, sailing, swimming, tennis, water skiing, jet skiing, galleries and wildlife. Bowls, Bush Walking, Fishing, Golf, Horse Riding, Sailing, Swimming, Tennis, Water Skiing.

Hotels/Motels

FLAG
FLAG CHOICE HOTELS™

★★★★ **Magnetic Island International Hotel**, (LMH), Resort, Mandalay Ave, Nelly Bay, 20 minutes by Ferry from Townsville, ☎ 07 4778 5200, fax 07 4778 5806, 80 units (0 suites) [shwr, tlt, hairdry, a/c, c/fan, tel, TV, video, clock radio, t/c mkg, refrig, mini bar, micro, toaster, pillows], ldry-fee, dryer-fee, iron, iron brd, conv fac, ✉, pool, bbq, ✆, gym, tennis, cots-fee. RO † $120, ◊ $20, Suite RO † $160, †† $160, ◊ $20, ch con, AE BC DC MC VI, ﾃ&.

★★☆ **Arcadia Hotel Resort**, (LH), 7 Marine Pde, Arcadia, ☎ 07 4778 5177, fax 07 4778 5939, (2 stry gr fl), 27 rms [shwr, tlt, a/c-cool, c/fan, tel, TV, radio, t/c mkg, refrig], ldry, ✗, ✉, pool, spa, courtesy transfer, ✆. D † $77 - $99, †† $77 - $99, BC EFT MC VI.

Magnetic Island Tropical Resort, (M), Yates St, Nelly Bay, ☎ 07 4778 5955, fax 07 4778 5601, 30 units [shwr, bath (hip), tlt, a/c-cool (7), c/fan, TV (19), clock radio (19), t/c mkg (19), refrig (19)], ldry, dryer, lounge (TV), conv fac, ✉, pool, spa, bbq, ✆, non smoking units. RO † $55 - $104.50, †† $55 - $104.50, ◊ $11, BC EFT MC VI.

Self Catering Accommodation
★★★★☆ **Sails on Horseshoe**, (HU), 13 Pacific Drive, Horseshoe Bay, 13km E of Townsville PO, ☎ 07 4778 5117, fax 07 4779 1158, (2 stry), 11 units acc up to 6, [ensuite (1), shwr, spa bath (9), tlt, a/c-cool, c/fan, tel, cable tv, video, clock radio, refrig, cook fac, micro, elec frypan, d/wash, toaster, ldry (in unit), blkts, linen, pillows], dryer, iron, iron brd, pool (salt water), bbq (covered), c/park (undercover), cots. D $204.50, W $1,323, Min book applies, BC MC VI.

★★★★ **Champagne Apartments**, (HU), 38 Marine Pde, Arcadia, ☎ 07 4778 5077, fax 07 4778 5244, (2 stry gr fl), 4 units acc up to 7, (2 & 3 bedrm), [ensuite, shwr, spa bath, tlt, a/c-cool, c/fan, TV, video, clock radio, refrig, cook fac, micro, elec frypan, d/wash, ldry (in unit), blkts, linen, pillows], dryer, pool (salt water), bbq, c/park (undercover). D $140 - $160, Min book applies.

★★★★ **Island Leisure Resort**, (HU), 4 Kelly St, Nelly Bay, 3 km from PO, ☎ 07 4778 5000, fax 07 4778 5042, 17 units acc up to 3, (Studio), [shwr, tlt, a/c, c/fan, tel, TV, video, movie, clock radio, t/c mkg, refrig, cook fac, micro, blkts, linen, pillows], ldry, rec rm, pool (salt water), spa, bbq, kiosk, shop, courtesy transfer, tennis, cots. D † $110, †† $120, W † $693, ◊ $63, ch con, pen con, Min book applies, AE BC DC MC VI, ﾃ&.

★★★☆ **Dunoon Beachfront Apartments**, (HU), The Esplanade, Picnic Bay, 250m N of Picnic Bay Jetty, ☎ 07 4778 5161, fax 07 4778 5532, 22 units acc up to 5, [shwr, tlt, a/c-cool-fee, c/fan, TV, clock radio, refrig, cook fac, micro, blkts, linen, pillows], ldry, dryer, iron, pool (salt water), spa, bbq, ✆, plygr, cots. D † $89 - $108, †† $89 - $108, ch con.

★★★☆ **Island Palms Resort**, (HU), 13 The Esplanade, Nelly Bay, ☎ 07 4778 5571, fax 07 4778 5599, (Multi-stry), 12 units acc up to 6, [shwr, bath (6), tlt, a/c-cool, fan, TV, clock radio, refrig, cook fac, micro, elec frypan, ldry (in unit), doonas, linen, pillows], dryer, pool (salt water), spa, bbq, c/park (undercover), ✆, tennis (half court), cots. D $85 - $110, AE BC MC VI.

★★★☆ **Tropical Palms Inn**, (SA), 34 Picnic St, Picnic Bay, 150m from beach, ☎ 07 4778 5076, fax 07 4778 5897, (2 stry gr fl), 12 serv apts acc up to 4, (Studio), [shwr, tlt, a/c, c/fan, TV, video (12), clock radio (12), t/c mkg, refrig, cook fac ltd], ldry, pool, bbq, shop, c/park (5), ✆, cots. D †† $75 - $83, W †† $462 - $580, ch con, AE BC BTC DC EFT MC VI.

★★★ **Dandaloo Gardens**, (HU), 40 Hayles Ave, Arcadia, 8km fr Townsville, ☎ 07 4778 5174, fax 07 4778 5185, 8 units acc up to 5, (1 bedrm), [shwr, tlt, a/c-cool, c/fan, TV, video (4), clock radio, refrig, cook fac, micro, blkts, linen, pillows], ldry, dryer, pool (salt water), bbq, plygr, cots. D $71.50 - $82.50, W $462 - $539, Units 5 to 8 ★★☆. AE BC DC MC VI.

★★★ **Island Magic Apartments**, (HU), Armand Way, Arcadia, 100m from Hotel Arcadia, ☎ 07 4778 5077, fax 07 4778 5244, (2 stry), 6 units acc up to 5, (2 bedrm - Split level accommodation available.), [shwr, tlt, a/c-cool, c/fan, TV, clock radio, refrig, cook fac, micro, ldry (in unit), blkts, linen, pillows], dryer, bbq, c/park (undercover), cots. D $100 - $110, W $665 - $700, Min book applies.

★★★ **Magnetic Island Holiday Units**, (HU), 16 Yule St, Picnic Bay, ☎ 07 4778 5246, fax 07 4758 1503, 6 units acc up to 6, (1 & 2 bedrm), [shwr, tlt, a/c-cool (4), c/fan, TV, clock radio, refrig, cook fac, blkts, linen, pillows], ldry, pool-heated (Solar), bbq, c/park (undercover), courtesy transfer, cots. D ♦♦ $77, ◊ $19, W ♦♦ $462, BC MC VI.

★★★ **Magnetic Retreat**, (HU), 11 Rheuben Tce, Arcadia, 150m fr Alma Bay beach, ☎ 07 4778 5357, fax 07 4778 5357, 7 units acc up to 6, (1 & 2 bedrm), [shwr, tlt, a/c-cool, c/fan, TV, clock radio, refrig, cook fac, ldry (in unit) (3), blkts, linen, pillows], ldry, dryer, pool (salt water), spa, bbq, c/park (undercover), courtesy transfer, cots. D $95 - $120, Min book applies.

★★★ **Palm View Chalets**, (HU), 114 Sooning St, Nelly Bay, ☎ 07 4778 5596, fax 07 4778 5256, 10 units acc up to 10, (1, 2 & 3 bedrm), [shwr, bath (1), spa bath (1), tlt, a/c-cool, c/fan, TV, clock radio, refrig, cook fac, micro, elec frypan, blkts, linen, pillows], ldry, dryer, iron, iron brd, rec rm, pool (salt water), bbq, c/park (undercover), ✎, cots. D ♦♦ $50 - $75, W ♦♦ $300 - $489, BC MC VI.

★★☆ **Magnetic North Holiday Apartments**, (HU), 2 Endeavour Rd, Arcadia, 300m W of Alma Bay beach, ☎ 07 4778 5647, or 03 6224 1478, fax 07 4778 5647, (2 stry gr fl), 6 units acc up to 6, (2 bedrm), [shwr, tlt, a/c-cool, c/fan, TV, refrig, cook fac, micro, ldry, blkts, linen, pillows], iron, pool, bbq, c/park (undercover), plygr. W $595, BC MC VI.

B&B's/Guest Houses

★★★ **Marshalls Bed & Breakfast**, (B&B), 3 Endeavour Rd, Arcadia Bay, 8km NE of Townsville, ☎ 07 4778 5112, 4 rms [c/fan, clock radio], shwr, tlt, ldry, lounge (TV), t/c mkg shared, c/park. BLB ♦ $40, ♦♦ $60, ◊ $20, ◊ $20, BC MC VI.

MAIN BEACH QLD

See Gold Coast Region.

MALANDA QLD 4885

Pop 850. (1702km N Brisbane), See maps on page 415, ref B4.
Large dairy industry and milk production centre.

Hotels/Motels

★★★☆ **Malanda Lodge**, (M), Millaa Millaa Rd, 1.5km SW of PO, ☎ 07 4096 5555, fax 07 4096 5516, 17 units [shwr, bath (12), tlt, a/c, tel, TV, movie, clock radio, t/c mkg, refrig, ldry], conv fac, ✖ (Mon-Sat), pool, spa, dinner to unit, golf (par 3). RO ♦ $65, ♦♦ $75, ◊ $10, AE BC DC MC VI.

Self Catering Accommodation

★★★★☆ **Fur n Feathers Rainforest Tree Houses**, (Cotg), Hogan Rd, Tarzali via Malanda, 10km S of Malanda PO, ☎ 07 4096 5364, (Multi-stry gr fl), 6 cotgs acc up to 8, [shwr, spa bath (4), tlt, hairdry, c/fan (3), fire pl (wood fire), cent heat, tel, TV, clock radio, refrig, cook fac, micro, elec frypan, d/wash (3), toaster, ldry (in unit), blkts, linen, pillows], dryer, iron, iron brd, bbq, c/park (undercover), cots, RO ♦♦ $130 - $220, ◊ $15 - $30, ♦♦ $780 - $1,320, 1 cottage ★★★★. BC MC VI, ⚹.

Operator Comment:
refer our website: www.rainforesttreehouses.com.au

Rose Gums Wilderness Retreat, (Cotg), Land Rd Butchers Creek via, 16km E of PO, ☎ 07 4096 8360, fax 07 4096 8230, (2 stry gr fl), 4 cotgs acc up to 6, (1 & 2 bedrm), [shwr, spa bath, tlt, c/fan, heat, elec blkts, TV, clock radio, t/c mkg, refrig, cook fac, micro, toaster, blkts, doonas, linen, pillows], w/mach, dryer, lounge firepl, plygr, cots-fee, breakfast ingredients, non smoking property. D ♦♦ $150, ◊ $25, W ♦♦ $945, ◊ $20, ch con, Min book Christmas and Jan, BC MC VI, (not yet classified).

B&B's/Guest Houses

★★★★☆ **Honeyflow Homestead**, (B&B), Heidke Rd, 8km E of PO, ☎ 07 4096 8173, 4 rms (4 suites) [ensuite (4), shwr (2), bath (3), tlt, fan, heat, elec blkts, clock radio, t/c mkg, refrig, ldry], spring water, rec rm, lounge firepl, ✖, bbq. BB ♦ $126.50 - $137.50, ◊ $49.50, ch con, AE BC DC MC VI.

★★★☆ **Fairdale Farmstay**, (B&B), (Farm), Dairy farming property. Hillcrest Rd, 3km SE of PO, ☎ 07 4096 6599, fax 07 4096 6597, 3 rms (3 bedrm), [shwr, bath, tlt, hairdry, heat (woodfire), tel, TV, clock radio, refrig, cook fac, cook fac ltd, micro, elec frypan, toaster], ldry, dryer, iron, iron brd, TV rm, ✖ (open by arrangement), pool (salt water), bbq (covered), dinner to unit, meals avail (on request), c/park (undercover), courtesy transfer, plygr, cots-fee. BB ♦ $49 - $70, ♦♦ $72 - $95, ◊ $22.

★★★★ **(Cottage Section)**, 3 cotgs acc up to 6, [shwr, bath, tlt, fan, heat, TV, clock radio, refrig, cook fac, micro, blkts, linen, pillows], ldry, dryer, meals avail. D ♦♦ $120, ♦♦♦♦ $165, ◊ $22.

★★★☆ **Travellers Rest**, (B&B), Millaa Millaa Rd, 5km s of Malanda, ☎ 07 4096 6077, fax 07 4096 6077, 6 rms [fan, t/c mkg (communal), ldry-fee], shwr, tlt, rec rm, TV rm, ✖, non smoking rms. BB ♦ $40, ♦♦ $70, ◊ $15, BC MC VI.

Hattons Hideaway, (B&B), 37 Whiteing Cl, ☎ 07 4096 5239, fax 07 4096 5239, 1 rm (1 suite) [shwr, tlt, fan, heat, elec blkts, TV, video, clock radio, t/c mkg, refrig, cook fac, doonas], bbq, non smoking property. BB ♦ $110, ♦♦ $150, weekly con, BC EFT MC VI, (not yet classified).

MALENY QLD 4552

Pop 900. (90km N Brisbane), See maps on page 417, ref D5. Dairying area, overlooking Glass House Mountains. Pottery, art & craft. Baroon Pocket Dam, Mary Cairncross Park, Gardiner's Falls. Bush Walking, Horse Riding, Scenic Drives.

Hotels/Motels

★★★☆ **Tranquil Park Resort**, (M), 152 Mountain View Rd. 3km W of Mary Cairncross Park, ☎ 07 5494 4544, fax 07 5494 3916, (2 stry gr fl), 31 units [shwr, bath (4), spa bath (3), tlt, heat (30), tel, TV, t/c mkg, refrig], rec rm, lounge, conv fac, ✖, pool-indoor (heated), c/park (undercover), tennis, non smoking units. D $145 - $165, RO ♦♦ $88 - $106, BC EFT MC VI, ⚹.

★★★ **Maleny Loggers Rest**, (M), Landsborough-Maleny Rd, 8km W Landsborough, ☎ 07 5494 2944, fax 07 5494 2279, 10 units [shwr, spa bath (2), tlt, c/fan, heat, elec blkts, tel, TV, clock radio, t/c mkg, refrig], ldry, pool, bbq, c/park (undercover), cots-fee. RO ♦ $60 - $72, ♦♦ $77 - $110, ◊ $11 - $16.50, ch con, AE BC EFT MC VI.

★★☆ **Maleny Hills**, (M), Montville Rd, 6km S of PO, ☎ 07 5494 2551, 5 units [shwr, tlt, fan, heat, elec blkts, TV, clock radio, t/c mkg, refrig, cook fac, toaster, ldry (in unit)], bbq, c/park (undercover). D ♦ $50, ♦♦ $60, ch con, BC MC VI.

Self Catering Accommodation

★★★☆ **Tranquil Park Resort**, (SA), 152 Mountain View Rd, 3km W of Mary Cairncross Park, ☎ 07 5494 2544, (2 stry gr fl), 30 serv apts (1, 2 & 3 bedrm), [shwr, bath, tlt, refrig], conv fac, ✖, pool-indoor (heated), c/park (undercover), ✎, tennis. D ♦♦ $77 - $154, BC MC VI.

★★★ **Maleny Country Cottages**, (Cotg), Cork's Pocket Rd, 10km W of Maleny PO, ☎ 07 5494 2744, fax 07 5429 6195, 4 cotgs acc up to 4, (1 & 2 bedrm), [shwr, spa bath (4), tlt, hairdry, fan, c/fan, fire pl, TV, clock radio, CD, t/c mkg, refrig, cook fac, micro, ldry, blkts, doonas, linen, pillows], iron, iron brd, bbq (covered), c/park (undercover), non smoking rms. D ♦♦ $93 - $175, ◊ $25 - $100, W $750 - $1,150, ch con, AE BC DC EFT MC VI.

★★★ **Solothurn Maleny Rural Resort**, (Cotg), (Farm), 160ha cattle property. Reesville Rd, 7km W of PO, ☎ 07 5494 2438, fax 07 5499 9279, (2 stry), 15 cotgs [shwr, spa bath (1), tlt, fire pl, tel, TV, video (1), t/c mkg, refrig, cook fac], ldry, rec rm, conv fac, ✖, pool, sauna, plygr, tennis, cots. D ♦♦ $100 - $165, ♦♦♦♦ $190 - $225, ch con, BC MC VI, ⚹.

★★ **Frasers Selection**, (Cotg), (Farm), 86ha working mountain property on the edge of Conondale Forest and Blackall Range. Corks Pocket Rd, 8km W of PO, ☎ 07 5494 2735, fax 07 5499 9044, 2 cotgs acc up to 6, [shwr, tlt, heat, radio, t/c mkg, refrig, cook fac, toaster], bbq, c/park (undercover). D $121, W $605 - $765, BC MC VI.

Jacaranda Cottages, (Cotg), 13 Tuetoberg Ave Witta via, 7km N of PO, ☎ 07 5435 8183, fax 07 3366 7487, 2 cotgs acc up to 6, (2 bedrm), [shwr, tlt, fan, heat, TV, clock radio, refrig, cook fac, micro, toaster, blkts, doonas, linen, pillows], ldry, w/mach, lounge firepl, bbq, c/park (undercover), cots, non smoking property. D $80 - $130, W $500 - $700, Min book applies, (not yet classified).

B&B's/Guest Houses

★★★★★ **Chateau Cedarton Australia**, (GH), 2 Cedarton Drive, Cedarton, 15 km SW of Maleny, ☎ 07 5496 1789, fax 07 5496 1789, (2 stry gr fl), 5 rms [ensuite (4), elec blkts, TV, clock radio, t/c mkg, refrig, mini bar, ldry], shwr (2), tlt (2), dryer, read rm (library), ✕, pool (salt water), sauna, spa, bbq (covered). **BB ♦ $154 - $176, ♦♦ $154 - $176**, BC MP VI.

★★★★★ **Eyrie Escape**, (B&B), Bradenburg Rd Bald Knob, 3km S of Mooloolah, ☎ 07 5494 8242, fax 07 5439 9666, 3 rms [shwr, bath (1), tlt, hairdry, a/c, c/fan, elec blkts, clock radio, t/c mkg, refrig], ldry, dryer, lounge (TV, dvd), pool-heated, spa, bbq (covered), rm serv (24 hrs), dinner to unit, ✆, tennis, non smoking property. **BB ♦ $150, ♦♦ $195**, AE BC DC MC VI, ⌖.

Operator Comment: Luxury Accomodation Award Excellence in Tourism.

★★★★☆ **Bendles Cottages & Country Villas**, (B&B), 41 Montville Rd, 3km SW of PO, ☎ 07 5494 2400, fax 07 5494 2048, 5 rms [shwr, spa bath, tlt, hairdry, c/fan, heat, tel, TV, video, clock radio, CD, t/c mkg, refrig, cook fac ltd, micro, elec frypan, toaster], iron, iron brd, lounge firepl, bbq, tennis. **BB ♦♦ $160 - $225**, AE BC DC EFT MC VI.

★★★★ **(Apartment Section)**, 4 apts acc up to 4, (1 & 2 bedrm), [shwr, spa bath, tlt, hairdry, c/fan, TV, video, CD, refrig, cook fac (2), cook fac ltd (2), micro, elec frypan, toaster, ldry (in unit) (2), blkts, linen, pillows], w/mach, dryer, iron, iron brd, lounge firepl, bbq, c/park (carport), tennis. **D $209 - $275, W $1,200 - $1,400**, Min book applies.

★★★★ **Lillypilly's Country Cottages**, (B&B), No children's facilities, 260 Maleny Montville Rd, 6km S of Montville, ☎ 07 5494 3002, fax 07 5494 3499, 5 rms [shwr, spa bath, tlt, c/fan, fire pl, tel, TV, video, clock radio, CD, t/c mkg, refrig, cook fac ltd, micro, toaster], iron, iron brd, pool, bbq, dinner to unit (5 days), non smoking rms (5). **BB ♦♦ $143 - $203.50**, AE BC DC EFT MC VI.

★★★★☆ **Nunkeri Avocado Orchard**, (B&B), 51 McCarthy's Road, 2km S of PO, ☎ 07 5494 3494, fax 07 5429 6121, 1 rm [shwr, tlt, hairdry, a/c, c/fan, elec blkts, TV, video, clock radio, t/c mkg, refrig, micro, toaster, ldry], dryer, iron, iron brd, rec rm, TV rm, pool-heated, cook fac, bbq, secure park (Undercover). **BB ♦ $85, ♦♦ $105**, BC MC VI.

★★★★☆ **Roseville House**, (B&B), 226 Maleny Montville Rd, ☎ 07 5494 3411, 4 rms [c/fan, heat, clock radio, t/c mkg, refrig], ldry, w/mach, lounge (cable TV, video), lounge firepl, refrig, plygr, non smoking property. **BB ♦ $100 - $110, ♦♦ $140 - $160**, BC MC VI.

★★★★ **Glencliff Guesthouse Bed & Breakfast**, (B&B), Lot 3 Corks Pocket Rd, ☎ 07 5499 9930, fax 07 5494 3989, 4 rms (Ensuite Site), [shwr (2), bath, tlt (2), hairdry, a/c, heat (oil) (3), TV (5), video (2), clock radio (4), t/c mkg (4), refrig, micro], shwr (2), tlt (2), ldry, dryer, iron, iron brd, rec rm, TV rm, spa, t/c mkg shared, bbq, dinner to unit, c/park (undercover) (1), golf (10 hole), gym, tennis (half). **D ♦ $70 - $95, ♦♦ $110 - $125, ◊ $40**, BC MC VI.

★★★★ **Maleny Lodge Guest House**, (B&B), No children's facilities, 58 Maple St, ☎ 07 5494 2370, fax 07 549443407, 7 rms [ensuite, fire pl, heat, elec blkts, video, doonas], lounge (TV,cdplayer), pool, t/c mkg shared. **BB ♦♦ $132 - $181**, AE BC MC VI.

★★★★ **Rowan House**, (GH), Heritage, 36 Rowan Lane, Rowan Lane, ☎ 07 5494 1042, fax 07 5494 1345, 4 rms (4 suites) [shwr, bath, tlt, hairdry, a/c-cool, heat, TV, clock radio, CD, t/c mkg, refrig, cook fac (1), ldry], dryer, lounge, conf fac, ✕, pool, bbq, c/park (undercover), ✆, tennis, non smoking suites. **Suite D ♦ $154, ♦♦ $187, ◊ $38.50**, BC EFT MC VI.

★★★☆ **Cairncross Lodge**, (B&B), 33 Mary Cairncross Ave, 6km S of PO, ☎ 07 5494 3633, fax 07 5494 3633, (2 stry gr fl), 5 rms [ensuite (2), shwr, tlt, a/c (1), heat, elec blkts, TV, t/c mkg], ldry, dryer, rec rm, lounge, ✕, non smoking rms. **BB ♦ $55, ♦♦ $90 - $110, ◊ $45**, AE BC MC VI.

Pop 550. Part of Nambour, (96km N Brisbane), See maps on page 417, ref D4. Located in the Blackall Range amid lush rainforest. Mapleton Falls National Park. Bowls, Scenic Drives.

Self Catering Accommodation

★★★☆ **Tanglewood Gardens**, Montville Rd (Flaxton Dve), 1.5km from PO, ☎ 07 5445 7100, fax 07 5445 7528, 12 cabins acc up to 4, (1 & 2 bedrm), [shwr, tlt, hairdry (4), c/fan, fire pl (7), heat, tel, TV, video (4), clock radio, refrig, cook fac, micro (9), ldry (in unit) (6), blkts, linen, pillows], iron, iron brd, pool, sauna, spa, bbq, c/park (undercover), bowls, tennis, cots-fee, non smoking rms (6). **D ♦♦ $110 - $165, ◊ $27.50, W ♦♦ $680 - $870**, BC EFT MC VI.

B&B's/Guest Houses

★★★★☆ **Obilo Lodge Bed & Breakfast**, (B&B), Obi Obi Rd, 2.2km W of PO, ☎ 07 5445 7705, fax 07 5445 7705, 3 rms [shwr, spa bath (1), tlt, c/fan, heat, elec blkts, clock radio], lounge (TV), ✕, pool, t/c mkg shared, non smoking rms. **BB ♦♦ $85 - $150, ♦♦ $150**, BC MC VI.

★★★★ **Mapleton Eden Lodge**, (B&B), 97 Flaxton Dve, 1.3km S of PO, ☎ 07 5445 7678, fax 07 5445 7653, 5 rms [ensuite (2), shwr, tlt, hairdry (2), fan, c/fan (2), heat, TV (2), t/c mkg (2), refrig (2)], bathrm (2), ldry, lounge (TV, with fireplace), t/c mkg shared, refrig, c/park. **BB ♦ $68, ♦♦ $88 - $110**, BC MC VI.

See Sunshine Coast Region.

Pop 6,900. (1781km N Brisbane), See maps on page 415, ref B3. Famous for meeting of the waters. Name is aboriginal for meeting of the waters. Davies Creek Falls Emerald Creek Falls Granite Gorge Ant-Hill Park Mareeba Trainland (open weekdays only). Boating, Bowls, Bush Walking, Fishing, Golf, Horse Racing, Scenic Drives, Swimming.

Hotels/Motels

★★★★ **Jackaroo**, (M), 340 Byrnes St, ☎ 07 4092 2677, fax 07 4092 3837, 25 units [shwr, tlt, a/c-cool, c/fan, tel, cable tv, clock radio, t/c mkg, refrig], ldry, pool, meals to unit, c/park (undercover) (20). **RO ♦ $50 - $67, ♦♦ $60 - $80, ◊ $12**, ch con, AE BC DC MC VI, ⌖.

★★★★ **Mareeba Motor Inn**, (M), Kennedy Highway, 2km S of GPO, ☎ 07 4092 2451, fax 07 4092 2338, 15 units [shwr, tlt, a/c-cool, c/fan, tel, TV, video, movie, clock radio, t/c mkg, refrig, mini bar], ldry-fee, dryer-fee, ✕, pool above ground (salt water), bbq-fee, rm serv, dinner to unit, cots-fee, non smoking units (7). **RO ♦ $60.50, ♦♦ $60.50, ◊ $11**, AE BC EFT VI.

★★★ **Mareeba Motel Golden Leaf**, (M), 261 Byrnes St, ☎ 07 4092 2266, fax 07 4092 2207, 14 units [shwr, tlt, a/c-cool, c/fan, tel, TV, clock radio, t/c mkg, refrig], ldry, pool, bbq, c/park (undercover), cots. **RO ♦ $65, ♦♦ $75, ◊ $10**, AE BC DC MC VI.

B&B's/Guest Houses

★★★★ **Arriga Park**, (GH), (Farm), Working sugar cane farm property. Dimbulah Rd, 10km W of Mareeba, ☎ 07 4093 2114, fax 07 4093 2114, 2 rms [shwr, bath, tlt], ldry, lounge (TV), spa (outdoor), c/park (undercover). **BB ♦ $60, ♦♦ $120, ◊ $60**, Other meals by arrangement. Min book applies, ⌖.

MARLBOROUGH QLD 4705

Pop Nominal, (743km N Brisbane), See maps on page 416, ref B5. Pastoral and cattle district located on Bruce Hwy. Chrysophase mine located on private property. Historical museum. Public swimming pool. Arts & crafts; fuel.

Hotels/Motels

★★★ **Marlborough Motel**, (M), Bruce Hwy, ☎ 07 4935 6112, fax 07 4935 6339, 7 units [shwr, tlt, a/c, tel, TV, clock radio, t/c mkg, refrig], ldry, rec rm, conf fac, ✗ (Licensed), bbq, dinner to unit, \. RO ♦ $53, ♦♦ $57 - $62, ◊ $6 - $9, ch con, AE BC EFT JCB MC VI.

MAROOCHYDORE QLD

See Sunshine Coast Region.

MARYBOROUGH QLD 4650

Pop 21,300. (255km N Brisbane), See maps on page 417, ref D2. One of Queensland's oldest cities, first settled in 1843. Boating, Bowls, Fishing, Golf, Motor Racing, Sailing, Squash, Tennis, Water Skiing.

Hotels/Motels

★★★★ **Blue Shades Motor Inn**, (M), Cnr Ferry & Queen Sts(Bruce Hwy), ☎ 07 4122 2777, fax 07 4122 3514, 36 units (3 suites) [shwr, bath (3), tlt, hairdry (34), a/c, tel, cable tv, video-fee, clock radio, t/c mkg, refrig], dryer-fee, iron, iron brd (18), conf fac, ✉, pool, rm serv, dinner to unit, c/park (undercover), cots-fee, non smoking units (30). RO ♦ $66 - $77, ♦♦ $71.50 - $82.50, Suite RO $93.50 - $121, ch con, Split rating. 4 star Units 18-36. 3and 1/2 star rating for units 1-17. AE BC DC MC MP VI, ♿.

★★★★ **Kimba Lodge**, (M), 177 John St, closest to CBD, ☎ 07 4123 3999, fax 07 4123 6458, (2 stry) 25 units (1 suite) [shwr, a/c-cool, c/fan, tel, TV, movie, clock radio, t/c mkg, refrig, cook fac (1)], pool (salt water), bbq (covered), c/park (undercover) (9), cots-fee, non smoking rms. RO ♦ $69, ♦♦ $78, ◊ $12, Suite D $143, AE BC DC EFT MC VI.

★★★★ **McNevins Parkway**, (M), 188 John St, ☎ 07 4122 2888, fax 07 4122 2546, 35 units [shwr, spa bath (4), tlt, hairdry, a/c, tel, TV, movie, clock radio, t/c mkg, refrig, mini bar, micro (2), toaster], ldry-fee, iron, iron brd, ✉, pool, sauna, spa, rm serv, dinner to unit, c/park (undercover), cots-fee. RO ♦ $68, ♦♦ $78, ◊ $10, ch con, 13 units of a 4 star rating (Units 2, 36 to 43 and 47 to 50). AE BC DC MC VI.

★★★☆ **(Motel Section)**, 15 units [shwr, tlt, hairdry, a/c, tel, TV, movie, clock radio, t/c mkg, refrig], ✉ (Wed-Sat), rm serv, dinner to unit, c/park (undercover), cots-fee. RO ♦ $58, ♦♦ $68, ch con.

★★★ **Cara**, (M), 196 Walker St, opposite Base Hospital, ☎ 07 4122 4288, fax 07 4123 3616, 14 units [shwr, bath (1), spa bath (1), tlt, hairdry, a/c (r/cyc), c/fan, tel, cable tv, clock radio, t/c mkg, refrig, cook fac (2), micro (5)], ldry, dryer, pool (salt water), dinner to unit (Mon to Fri), meals avail (Breakfast & Dinner), c/park (undercover), cots, non smoking units (7). RO ♦ $54 - $64, ♦♦ $60.50 - $75, ◊ $5.50 - $11, AE BC DC MC VI.

★★★ **Mineral Sands**, (M), Cnr 75 Ferry St & Albert St, ☎ 07 4121 2366, fax 07 4122 1726, (2 stry gr fl) 20 units [shwr, tlt, a/c, tel, TV, movie, clock radio, t/c mkg, refrig], ldry, dryer, ✉, pool, dinner to unit, plygr, cots-fee. RO ♦ $62 - $68, ♦♦ $68 - $74, ◊ $10, ch con, Units 11 to 21 ★★★. AE BC DC MC MP VI.

★★★ **Royal Centre Point**, (LMH), 326 Kent St, 100m S of PO, ☎ 07 4121 2241, fax 07 4123 2500, (2 stry) 18 units [shwr, tlt, hairdry, a/c-cool, fan, tel, TV, video, clock radio, t/c mkg, refrig, micro], ldry, dryer, iron, iron brd, ✉, ✗, cook fac, secure park, cots. RO ♦ $47.50 - $70, ♦♦ $52.50 - $80, ◊ $7 - $10, ch con, 8 rooms at a 2.5 star rating. AE BC DC MC VI.

★★★ **Spanish Motor Inn Maryborough**, (M), 499 Alice St, ☎ 07 4121 2858, or 07 4121 2073, fax 07 4121 2859, 22 units [shwr, tlt, a/c-cool, heat, tel, TV, movie, clock radio, t/c mkg, refrig, mini bar], ldry, ✉ (Mon to Sat), pool, rm serv, dinner to unit, c/park (undercover), courtesy transfer, plygr, cots-fee, non smoking units (9). RO ♦ $50.60 - $56, ♦♦ $60.50 - $66, ◊ $11, AE BC DC EFT MC VI.

★★★ **Susan River Homestead Ranch Resort**, (M), Resort, Fraser Coast Hwy, via Maryborough, Hervey Bay 4655, 20km S of Hervey Bay, ☎ 07 4121 6846, fax 07 4122 2675, 16 units [shwr, tlt, c/fan, TV, t/c mkg, refrig, pillows], ldry, rec rm, conv fac, lounge firepl, ✉, bar, pool, sauna, spa, bbq, courtesy transfer, bush walking, gym, tennis, cots. BB ♦ $82.50, ♦♦ $122, ch con, AE BC DC MC VI.

★★☆ **Arkana Inn**, (M), 46 Ferry St, ☎ 07 4121 2261, fax 07 4123 1807, 32 units [shwr, tlt, a/c-cool, fan (6), heat, tel, TV, movie, clock radio, t/c mkg, refrig], ldry-fee, dryer-fee, ✉, pool, rm serv, cots-fee. RO ♦ $49.50 - $58, ♦♦ $59.50 - $68, ◊ $10, AE BC DC EFT MC MP VI.

★★☆ **Maryborough City**, (M), 138 Ferry St, ☎ 07 4121 2568, fax 07 4121 2259, 17 units [shwr, tlt, a/c-cool, a/c (7), c/fan, heat, tel, TV, clock radio, t/c mkg, refrig], ldry, dryer, ✉ (Mon to Sun), pool, bbq, rm serv, c/park (undercover), cots-fee. RO ♦ $49, ♦♦ $58, ◊ $9, BC MC VI.

★★☆ **Wide Bay Lodge & Conference Centre**, (M), Cnr Walker & Croyden Streets, 500m W of Base Hospital, ☎ 07 4121 5255, fax 07 4123 1082, 22 units [shwr, tlt, c/fan (12), TV (6), cable tv, t/c mkg, refrig (6)], ldry, dryer-fee, rec rm, TV rm, conf fac, ✗, pool, bbq, dinner to unit, \. RO ♦ $38 - $38, ♦♦ $45 - $45, ◊ $10, ch con, BC MC VI.

B&B's/Guest Houses

★★★☆ **Jacaranda Retreat**, (B&B), 64 Woongool Rd, Tinana, 270km N of Brisbane GPO, ☎ 07 4121 3567, fax 07 4121 3567, 2 rms [hairdry, c/fan, TV, video, clock radio, t/c mkg], shwr, tlt, bathrm, bathrm (1). BB ♦ $75, ♦♦ $95.

MERMAID BEACH QLD

See Gold Coast Region.

MIAMI QLD

See Gold Coast Region.

MIDGE POINT QLD 4799

Pop Nominal, (1157km N Brisbane), See maps on page 416, ref A2. Small seaside tourist resort in Whitsunday Passage. Boating, Fishing, Scenic Drives, Swimming.

Self Catering Accommodation

★★★ **Whitsunday Cabins**, 12 Patterson St, Repulse Bay, adjacent to Laguna Quays, ☎ 07 4947 6161, fax 07 4947 6161, 10 cabins acc up to 4, [ensuite (4), shwr (6), tlt (5), c/fan, TV, refrig, cook fac, micro, toaster, blkts, linen, pillows], shwr, tlt, ldry, dryer, pool (salt water), bbq, boat park, car wash, tennis. D ♦♦ $38.50 - $49.50, ◊ $5.50, W ♦♦ $198 - $231, ◊ $16.50.

MILES QLD 4415

Pop 1,200. (339km W Brisbane), See maps on page 414, ref D7. Known as the 'Crossroads of the Golden West'. Local primary production includes dairying, fruit growing, wheat, sheep, cattle and timber. Best known for the Miles Historical Village, Possum Park and Wildflower Festival. Bowls, Golf, Tennis.

Hotels/Motels

★★★★ **Miles Outback Motel**, (M), 11 Murilla St, Warrego Hwy, western end of CBD, ☎ 07 4627 2100, fax 07 4627 2172, 18 units [shwr, tlt, a/c, tel, TV, clock radio, t/c mkg, refrig], ldry, dryer, iron, iron brd, bbq, dinner to unit, c/park (undercover), secure park (10). RO ♦ $68, ♦♦ $77 - $79, ◊ $11, ch con, AE BC DC EFT MC VI.

★★★ **Golden West Motor Inn**, (M), 50 Murilla St, ☎ 07 4627 1688, fax 07 4627 1407, 12 units [shwr, tlt, a/c, elec blkts, tel, cable tv, clock radio, t/c mkg, refrig], pool, dinner to unit (Mon to Sat), cots-fee. RO ♦ $61.60, ♦♦ $72.60, ch con, AE BC DC MC VI, ♿.

★★★ **Starline Motor Inn**, (M), 97-99 Murilla St, ☎ 07 4627 1322, fax 07 4627 1632, 22 units [shwr, tlt, hairdry, a/c-cool, heat, tel, TV, clock radio, t/c mkg, refrig], iron (5), iron brd (5), pool, bbq, dinner to unit, trailer park, cots-fee. RO ♦ $54, ♦♦ $64, ◊ $11, ch con, AE BC DC MC MCH VI.

Self Catering Accommodation

★★★☆ **Possum Park Underground**, (HU), Historical World War II RAAF ammunition bunkers. Leichhardt Hwy, 20km N of Miles on Hwy 39, ☎ 07 4627 1651, fax 07 4627 1651, 3 units [shwr, tlt, fan, heat, elec blkts, TV, clock radio, refrig, cook fac, micro, blkts, linen, pillows], ldry, dryer, rec rm, bbq, c/park (undercover), bush walking. RO ♦ $55, ♦♦ $60, ◊ $10, W ♦♦ $300, BC MC VI.

MILLAA MILLAA QLD 4886

Pop 300. (1693km N Brisbane), See maps on page 415, ref B4. At the heart of Waterfall Country.

B&B's/Guest Houses

★★★★☆ **Iskanda Park Farmstay**, (B&B), (Farm), Nash Rd, 7km N of PO, ☎ 07 4097 2401, or 07 4097 2387, fax 07 4097 2401, 1 rm [ensuite, hairdry, a/c-cool, fan, clock radio], ldry, dryer, lounge (TV), t/c mkg shared, bbq, meals avail. **BB ♦♦ $120**, BC MC VI.

　★★★ **(Cottage Section)**, 1 rm (1 bedrm), [shwr, tlt, hairdry, fan, TV, clock radio, refrig, cook fac, toaster, ldry, pillows], dryer, meals avail. **D ♦♦ $120, ◊ $20**.

MILLMERRAN QLD 4357

Pop 1,050. (210km SW Brisbane), See maps on page 414, ref E8. Located in agricultural district - sheep, cattle, poultry & pig farming, grain & cotton. Several host farm properties nearby. Bicentennial Water Park, sporting & services clubs. Historical Society Museum - open Sundays 12noon to 5pm. Bowls, Golf, Swimming, Tennis.

Hotels/Motels

★★☆ **Millmerran**, (M), 62 Campbell St, next to Shell Roadhouse, ☎ 07 4695 1155, fax 07 4695 1780, 10 units [shwr, tlt, a/c, c/fan (5), heat, elec blkts, tel, TV, clock radio, t/c mkg, refrig], ldry, dinner to unit, cots-fee. **RO ♦ $50, ♦♦ $58, ◊ $8**, ch con, AE BC DC EFT MC VI.

MIRIAM VALE QLD 4677

Pop 400. (470km N Brisbane), See maps on page 416, ref D7. Northern gateway to the tranquil resorts of Agnes Water, 1770 and Round Hill Head.

Hotels/Motels

★★☆ **Miriam Vale**, (M), Bruce Hwy, opposite Miriam Vale State School, ☎ 07 4974 5233, fax 07 4974 5134, 16 units [shwr, tlt, a/c (16), c/fan, heat (16), TV, t/c mkg, refrig], pool, bbq, dinner to unit, cots-fee. **RO ♦♦ $44 - $55**, Units 5 to 8 and 14 to 16 are ★★. AE BC DC MC VI.

★☆ **Colosseum**, (M), Bruce Hwy, Colosseum Creek, 16km S of PO, ☎ 07 4974 5244, 12 units [shwr, tlt, a/c-cool, c/fan, TV, clock radio, t/c mkg, refrig], ⊠, ✆, cots. **RO ♦ $35, ♦♦ $45, ◊ $10**, AE BC EFT MC VI.

MISSION BEACH QLD 4852

Pop 1,000. (1602km N Brisbane), See maps on page 415, ref C5. A palm fringed beach with a backdrop of World Heritage Rainforest. Reef Cruises, Access to Dunk Island. White water rafting. Tandem parachuting. Aboriginal Cultural Experiences. Boating, Fishing, Golf, Sailing, Swimming, Water Skiing, Wind Surfing.

Hotels/Motels

 ★★★★ **The Horizon at Mission Beach**, (Ltd Lic H), Resort, Explorer Dve, Mission Beach South 4852, overlooking Dunk Island & Coral Sea, ☎ 07 4068 8154, fax 07 4068 8596, 55 rms [shwr, bath, tlt, hairdry, a/c-cool, c/fan, tel, cable tv, movie, clock radio, t/c mkg, refrig, mini bar, pillows], iron, iron brd, conv fac, ⊠, pool (salt water), rm serv, shop, bush walking, tennis. **RO $220 - $350**, ch con, AE BC DC EFT MC VI.

★★★☆ **Castaways On The Beach Resort**, (M), Previously Castaways Beach Resort Cnr Pacific Pde & Seaview St, Beach frontage, ☎ 07 4068 7444, fax 07 4068 7429, (Multi-stry gr fl), 52 units (15 suites) [shwr, bath, tlt, a/c-cool, tel, TV, movie, clock radio, t/c mkg, refrig, cook fac ltd (15)], lift, ldry, dryer, ⊠, bar, pool, spa, bbq, rm serv, c/park (undercover) (20), ✆, cots. **RO ♦♦♦ $110 - $130, ◊ $16, Suite D $130 - $190**, ch con, AE BC DC EFT MC VI, ⚹&.

★★★☆ **Mackays Mission Beach**, (M), 7 Porter Prom, ☎ 07 4068 7212, fax 07 4068 7212, 22 units [shwr, bath (12), tlt, a/c-cool (12), c/fan, tel, TV, clock radio, t/c mkg, refrig, cook fac (4)], ldry-fee, dryer-fee, pool, dinner to unit, c/park (undercover) (6), cots-fee. **D $80 - $110**, ch con, Units 101 to 106 ★★★. BC MC VI.

★★★ **Mission Beach Resort**, (LMH), Cnr Cassowary Dve & Wongaling Beach Rd, ☎ 07 4068 8288, fax 07 4068 8429, 73 units [shwr, tlt, a/c-cool, c/fan, tel, TV, movie, t/c mkg, refrig], ldry, dryer, rec rm, conv fac, ⊠, bar, pool (salt water) (4), spa (3), bbq, shop, c/park (undercover), ✆, plygr, tennis, cots, non smoking rms (51). **RO ♦ $100, ♦♦ $110**, ch con, AE BC DC EFT MC VI.

Self Catering Accommodation

★★★★☆ **Eco Village Mission Beach**, (Cotg), Clump Point Rd, 1km N Information Centre, ☎ 07 4068 7534, fax 07 4068 7538, 11 cotgs acc up to 5, (Studio), [shwr, spa bath (2), tlt, hairdry, a/c-cool, c/fan, tel, TV, movie, clock radio, refrig, cook fac, micro, blkts, linen, pillows], ldry, w/mach-fee, dryer-fee, iron, ⊠, pool (salt water), spa, bbq, plygr, cots. **D $130 - $141, W $910 - $987**, ch con, AE BC DC MC VI.

★★★★☆ **The Wongalinga Apartments**, (HU), 64 Reid Rd, Wongaling Beach 4852, 10km S of Mission Beach PO Beachfront, ☎ 07 4068 8221, fax 07 4068 8180, (2 stry gr fl), 9 units acc up to 6, (1, 2 & 3 bedrm), [shwr, bath, tlt, a/c-cool, c/fan, tel, TV, clock radio, refrig, cook fac, micro, d/wash, ldry (in unit), blkts, linen, pillows], dryer, pool, wading pool, spa, bbq, secure park, cots. **D $143 - $220, W $858 - $1,320**, BC EFT MC VI.

★★★★ **Beaches**, (HU), 82 Reid Rd Wongaling Beach, Beachfront, ☎ 07 4068 7411, fax 07 4068 7308, (2 stry gr fl), 4 units acc up to 9, (2 & 3 bedrm), [ensuite, shwr, bath, tlt, a/c-cool (1), c/fan, TV, refrig, cook fac, micro, d/wash, ldry (in unit), blkts, linen, pillows], dryer, iron, iron brd, pool (salt water), bbq, c/park (undercover), cots-fee. **D $110 - $165, W $500 - $1,375**, Min book applies, BC MC VI.

★★★★ **Bedarra Lodge**, (HU), Previously Lugger Bay Eco Suites & Lodges 18 Explorers Dve, Mission Beach South 4852, Tropical rainforest overlooking beach, ☎ 07 4068 8400, fax 07 4068 8586, 17 units acc up to 8, (1 & 3 bedrm), [shwr, spa bath, tlt, a/c-cool, c/fan, tel, TV, CD, t/c mkg, refrig, blkts, linen, pillows], conv fac, pool (salt water), c/park (undercover). **W $686 - $4,548**, 6 units rated at two stars plus, AE BC DC MC VI.

★★★★ **Montage Beach Apartments**, (HU), 42 Mitchell St, 12km from PO, ☎ 07 4068 8204, or 07 4066 9251, fax 07 4066 9213, 4 units acc up to 6, (1, 2 & 3 bedrm), [ensuite (1), shwr, tlt, a/c-cool, c/fan, TV, clock radio, refrig, cook fac, micro, d/wash, ldry (in unit), blkts, linen, pillows], w/mach, dryer, iron, pool, spa, bbq, c/park (undercover), cots. **D ♦♦ $110 - $180, ◊ $25**, Min book applies, BC MC VI.

★★★☆ **Kirrama**, (HU), 157 Reid Rd, ☎ 07 4068 7411, fax 07 4068 7308, (2 stry gr fl), 4 units acc up to 5, (2 bedrm), [shwr, tlt, a/c-cool, c/fan, TV, video (1), refrig, cook fac, micro (2), ldry, blkts, linen, pillows], dryer, iron, iron brd, pool (salt water), bbq, c/park (undercover), cots-fee. **RO ♦♦♦♦ $55 - $100, ♦♦♦♦ $390 - $660**, BC EFT MC VI.

★★★☆ **Liana Place**, (HU), Cnr Boyett Rd & Porter Prom, ☎ 07 4068 7411, fax 07 4068 7308, (2 stry gr fl), 4 units acc up to 5, (1 & 2 bedrm), [shwr, bath (2), tlt, a/c-cool (1), c/fan, TV, video (2), refrig, cook fac, micro (2), d/wash (1), ldry, blkts, linen, pillows], dryer, iron, iron brd, pool (salt water), bbq, c/park (undercover), ✆, plygr, cots-fee. **RO ♦♦♦♦ $60 - $100, ♦♦♦♦ $390 - $700**, Min book applies, BC EFT MC VI.

★★★ **Banfield**, (HU), 16-20 Reid Rd, Wongaling Beach, ☎ 07 4068 7411, fax 07 4068 7308, 5 units acc up to 8, (3 bedrm), [shwr, bath (hip), c/fan, TV, video (1), CD (1), t/c mkg, refrig, cook fac, micro (4), d/wash, toaster, blkts, linen, pillows], iron, iron brd, pool (saltwater), cots-fee. **D $55 - $154, W $385 - $770**, Min book applies, BC EFT MC VI.

★★★ **Ceud Mile Failte**, (HU), Porter Prom, ☎ 07 4068 7144, 4 units acc up to 6, (2 bedrm), [shwr, tlt, c/fan, TV, refrig, cook fac, blkts reqd-fee, linen reqd-fee], ldry, pool, bbq, c/park (undercover), cots. **D ♦♦ $70, ◊ $12, W ♦♦ $400, ◊ $72**, ch con.

MISSION BEACH QLD continued...

★★★ **Del Rio Apartments**, (HU), 150 Kennedy Esp, Mission Beach South 4852, ☎ 07 4068 8270, fax 07 4068 8276, (2 stry gr fl), 8 units acc up to 6, (2 bedrm), [shwr, tlt, fan, TV, clock radio, refrig, cook fac, ldry (in unit), blkts, linen, pillows], pool, bbq, c/park (undercover), cots. D ♦♦ $55 - $88, ♦ $16.50, W ♦♦ $385 - $544.50, ♦ $77, ch con, Min book applies, BC MC VI.

★★★ **The Coral Trout on Mission Beach**, (HU), 40 Reid Rd, Beachfront, ☎ 07 4068 9222, fax 07 4068 9333, 6 units acc up to 8, (1 & 2 bedrm), [shwr, tlt, hairdry, c/fan, TV, video-fee, radio, refrig, micro], ldry, pool (2), spa, bbq, courtesy transfer, ☎. D $88, ch con, BC DC EFT MC VI.

★★☆ **Golden Sands**, (HU), 54 Seafarer St, Mission Beach South 4852, ☎ 07 4068 1013, fax 07 4068 2520, (2 stry gr fl), 6 units acc up to 6, (Studio & 2 bedrm), [shwr, tlt, a/c-cool, c/fan, TV, refrig, cook fac, blkts, linen, pillows], ldry, pool, bbq, c/park (undercover), cots-fee. D ♦♦ $55 - $88, ♦ $11, W ♦♦ $330 - $550, ch con, BC MC VI.

B&B's/Guest Houses

★★★★★ **Collingwood House**, (B&B), No children's facilities, 13 Spurwood Close, 5km S of Mission Beach PO, ☎ 07 4068 9037, fax 07 4068 9037, 3 rms [ensuite (3), a/c-cool, c/fan, clock radio], ldry, dryer, rec rm, lounge (TV), pool (salt water), t/c mkg shared, bbq (covered), ☎, non smoking property. BB ♦ $75 - $85, ♦♦ $89 - $99, BC MC VI.

★★★★ **Bed and Beachfront Holiday Accommodation**, (B&B), 92 Reid Road, ☎ 07 4068 9990, fax 07 4068 9990, 1 rm [shwr, tlt, a/c-cool, a/c, c/fan, TV, clock radio, t/c mkg, refrig, toaster], pool (saltwater), bbq (covered). BLB ♦♦ $71.50, BC MC VI.

★★★★ **Kennedy Cottage**, (B&B), 134 Kennedy Esp, 10km S of North Mission Beach, ☎ 07 4068 8654, fax 07 4068 8276, 1 rm [shwr, tlt, c/fan, TV, clock radio, t/c mkg, refrig, toaster], ldry, iron, iron brd, c/park (undercover). BB ♦ $55, ♦♦ $77.

Sejala On The Beach, (B&B), 1 Pacific St, 500m S of P.O, ☎ 07 4068 7241, fax 07 4068 7241, 3 rms [shwr, tlt, hairdry, a/c-cool, c/fan, TV, video, clock radio, t/c mkg, refrig, cook fac ltd, micro, toaster], ldry-fee, dryer-fee, iron, iron brd, pool, bbq, secure park, cots. BB ♦♦ $87 - $98, ♦ $55, D ♦♦ $65 - $76, ♦ $33, ch con, (not yet classified).

Other Accommodation

Bingil Bay Resort, The Esplanade, Bingil Bay, enter off Cutten St, ☎ 07 4068 7208, fax 07 4068 7226, (2 stry gr fl), 16 rms acc up to 4, [shwr, tlt, a/c-cool (11), c/fan, TV, clock radio, t/c mkg, refrig], ☒, pool, ☎. RO ♦ $25 - $75, ♦♦ $64 - $75, ♦♦♦ $75, Units 2 to 6 ★★. BC MC VI.

MITCHELL QLD 4465

Pop 950. (566km W Brisbane), See maps on page 414, ref D7. Situated on the banks of the Maranoa River, it is the centre of a sheep, cattle and wheat growing district.

Hotels/Motels

★★★☆ **Berkeley Lodge Motor Inn**, (M), 20 Cambridge St, ☎ 07 4623 1666, fax 07 4623 1304, 27 units [shwr, tlt, a/c, tel, TV, clock radio, t/c mkg, refrig], ldry, conv fac, ☒ (Mon to Sat), pool, spa, rm serv, dinner to unit, cots-fee. RO ♦ $69, ♦♦ $82, ♦ $13, ch con, AE BC DC EFT MC VI, ♿.

★★☆ **Mitchell**, (M), Cnr Oxford & Caroline Sts, ☎ 07 4623 1355, fax 07 4623 1355, 12 units [shwr, tlt, a/c, fan, cable tv, clock radio, t/c mkg, refrig], bbq (covered), c/park (undercover), cots-fee. RO ♦ $45 - $70, ♦♦ $55 - $70, ♦ $11 - $12, BC MC MCH VI.

MONTO QLD 4630

Pop 1,300. (503km NW Brisbane), See maps on page 416, ref D8. Young country town established in 1924.

Hotels/Motels

★★★ **Monto Colonial Motor Inn**, (M), Historicl building - c1880, 6 Thomson St, ☎ 07 4166 1377, fax 07 4166 1437, (2 stry) 22 units [shwr, tlt, tel, cable tv, clock radio, t/c mkg, refrig], ldry, dryer, ☒ (Mon - Sat), bar, cots. RO ♦ $53, ♦♦ $63, ♦ $8, ch con, AE BC DC EFT MC VI.

★★★ **Monto Three Moon Motel**, (M), 4 Flinders St, ☎ 07 4166 1777, fax 07 4166 1712, (2 stry gr fl), 21 units [shwr, tlt, a/c, elec blkts, tel, cable tv, clock radio, t/c mkg, refrig], ✕, dinner to unit, cots. RO ♦ $53, ♦♦ $63 - $64, ch con, AE BC MC VI.

MONTVILLE QLD 4560

Pop Part of Nambour, (88km N Brisbane), See maps on page 417, ref D4. Situated on the crest of the Blackall Range, overlooking the Sunshine Coast. Old English Village atmosphere.

Hotels/Motels

★★★★ **Clouds of Montville**, (M), 166 Balmoral Rd, 2.5km S of PO, ☎ 07 5442 9174, fax 07 5442 9485, (2 stry gr fl) 10 units [shwr, tlt, a/c, tel, TV, clock radio, t/c mkg, refrig, micro, elec frypan, toaster], ldry, pool (salt water), bbq, tennis, cots-fee, non smoking rms. RO ♦♦ $82.50 - $121, ch con, Min book applies, AE BC DC EFT MC VI.

★★★☆ **Montville Mountain Inn**, (M), Main St, 3km S of Kondalilla Nationa, ☎ 07 5442 9499, fax 07 5442 9303, (2 stry gr fl), 26 units [shwr, spa bath (1), tlt, a/c, elec blkts, tel, TV, clock radio, t/c mkg, refrig], ldry, conv fac, ☒, pool (salt water), rm serv, tennis, cots-fee. RO ♦ $55 - $93, ♦♦ $77 - $93, BC JCB MC VI.

Self Catering Accommodation

★★★★★ **The Falls Rainforest Cottages**, (Cotg), 20 Kondalilla Falls Rd, 1.5km N of PO, ☎ 07 5445 7000, fax 07 5445 7001, 6 cotgs acc up to 3, (1 bedrm), [shwr, spa bath, tlt, hairdry, a/c, c/fan, fire pl (wood), elec blkts, TV, video, clock radio, CD, refrig, micro, toaster, blkts, linen, pillows], w/mach-fee, iron, iron brd, bbq (covered), non smoking units. D $190 - $280, BC MC VI.

★★★★☆ **The Narrows Escape**, (Cotg), No children's facilities, Narrows Rd, 4km W of Montville, ☎ 07 5478 5000, fax 07 5442 9472, 6 cotgs acc up to 3, (1 bedrm), [shwr, spa bath, tlt, hairdry, c/fan, heat, elec blkts, TV, video, clock radio, CD, refrig, cook fac, micro, blkts, linen, pillows], ldry, dryer, pool (salt water), bbq, c/park (undercover). D ♦♦ $160 - $225, ♦ $50, BC MC VI.

★★★★☆ **Treetops Cabins on the Lake**, Narrows Rd, 5.5km W of Montville, ☎ 07 5478 5888, fax 07 5478 5166, 6 cabins acc up to 2, (1 & 2 bedrm), [shwr, spa bath, tlt, fan, c/fan, heat, elec blkts, TV, video, clock radio, CD, t/c mkg, refrig, cook fac ltd, micro, toaster, blkts, linen, pillows], ldry, dryer, iron, iron brd, rec rm, bbq, c/park (undercover). D $240 - $270, BC MC VI.

Rates may change. Check before booking.

★★★☆ **Montville Country Cabins**, 396 Western Ave, 4km W from main road turnoff, ☎ 07 5442 9484, (2 stry), 10 cabins acc up to 6, [shwr, bath, spa bath (8), tlt, c/fan, TV, video (5), CD, refrig, cook fac, blkts, linen, pillows], ldry, dryer, lounge firepl, bbq, cots-fee. **D** �H **$132 - $198, W** �H **$863 - $1,280**, AE BC DC MC VI.

★★★ **Montville Holiday Apartments**, (HU), 60-68 Western Avenue, 0.6km from village, ☎ 07 5442 9108, fax 07 5478 5265, 11 units acc up to 7, [shwr, tlt, fire pl (8), TV, radio, refrig, cook fac (5), micro (3), elec frypan (3), ldry, blkts, linen, pillows], iron (7), iron brd (7), pool, spa, bbq, c/park (undercover) (7), mini golf, cots (fee). **D** �H **$50 - $135,** ⓘ **$12, W** �H **$290 - $520,** ⓘ **$60**, AE BC DC EFT MC VI.

★★★ **Tree Houses of Montville**, (HU), Lot 5 Kondalilla Falls Rd, entrance to Kondalilla National Park, ☎ 07 5445 7650, fax 07 5445 7650, 20 units acc up to 5, (1 & 2 bedrm), [shwr, spa bath, tlt, c/fan, fire pl, TV, video, CD, refrig, cook fac, micro, blkts, linen, pillows], ldry, lounge firepl, ✕, pool (salt water). **BB $110 - $300**, BC EFT MC VI.

B&B's/Guest Houses

★★★★☆ **Montville Misty View Cabins Resort**, (B&B), 284 - 296 Western Ave, 3km (along Avenue) SW Montville Village, ☎ 07 5442 9522, fax 07 5442 9522, 3 rms [shwr, bath, spa bath, tlt, hairdry, fan, cent heat, TV, video, movie, clock radio, CD, t/c mkg, refrig, cook fac, micro, toaster], ldry, dryer, rec rm, ✕ (Tues to Sun), pool (salt water), bbq, rm serv, meals to unit, c/park (undercover), tennis. **BB** �H **$150 - $220**, AE BC DC EFT JCB MC VI.

★★★★☆ **Montville Provencal** (GH) 37 Western Ave, ☎ 07 5478 5054, fax 07 5478 5054, 5 rooms [ensuite, spa, elec blkts, hairdry, heat (wood fire),TV, clock radio, refrig, t/cmkg] lounge, pool, non smoking rooms. **D $125- 210**, BC,EFT, MC, VI.

★★★★☆ **The Falls Bed & Breakfast**, (B&B), 20 Kondalilla Falls Rd, 1.5km N of Montville, ☎ 07 5445 7000, fax 07 5445 7001, 4 rms [shwr, tlt, a/c-cool, c/fan, heat, elec blkts], ldry, dryer, lounge (TV), ✕, t/c mkg shared, bbq, non smoking rms. **BB** �H **$130 - $170**, BC MC VI.

★★★☆ **The Spotted Chook Ferme Auberge**, (GH), 176 Western Ave, 2km W 0of P.O. ☎ 07 5442 9242, fax 07 5478 5811, 4 rms [shwr, bath, tlt, hairdry, cent heat, TV, video, clock radio, CD, t/c mkg, refrig], iron, iron brd, ✗, non smoking property. **BB ♦ $110 - $180, ♦♦ $120 - $220, ◊ $40**, ch con, BC EFT MC VI.

★★★★ **Montville Grove Luxury Cabins**, (B&B), No children's facilities, 318 Western Ave, 4km W of PO, ☎ 07 5442 9186, fax 07 5442 9469, 2 rms [shwr, tlt, c/fan, heat (combustion fireplace), elec blkts, TV, video, clock radio, CD, refrig, cook fac, micro, ldry, pillows], bbq, non smoking property. **BB ♦♦ $110 - $185**, AE BC DC MC VI.

MOOLOOLABA QLD

See Sunshine Coast Region.

MOONIE QLD 4406

Pop Nominal, (321km SW Brisbane), See maps on page 414, ref D8.
Hotels/Motels
★☆ **Moonie Travelstop Hotel Motel**, (M), Moonie & Leichardt Hwys, 100km N of Goondiwindi, ☎ 07 4665 0200, fax 07 4665 0250, 16 units [shwr, tlt, a/c, TV, t/c mkg, refrig], ✉, ✗, ✆. **RO ♦ $27.50 - $40, ♦♦ $50, ◊ $11 - $16.50**, ch con, BC EFT MC VI.

MOORE PARK BEACH QLD 4670

Pop 650. (391km N Brisbane), See maps on page 416, ref E8. Small coastal town with long sandy beach. Bowls, Fishing, Surfing, Swimming.
Hotels/Motels
★★★ **Moore Park Beach Motel**, (M), Previously Moore Park Beach 29 Club Ave, 200m fr beach, ☎ 07 4159 8332, fax 07 4159 8520, 6 units [shwr, tlt, a/c, c/fan, heat, tel, cable tv, clock radio, t/c mkg, refrig, toaster], ldry, pool (salt water), spa, bbq, dinner to unit, c/park (undercover), cots. **RO ♦ $50, ♦♦ $58.30, ◊ $10**, BC EFT MC VI.

MORANBAH QLD 4744

Pop 6,508. (1120km N Brisbane), See maps on page 414, ref D6. Small town on Denham Range. Bowls, Bush Walking, Golf, Swimming.
Hotels/Motels
★★★ **Black Nugget**, (LMH), Griffin St, ☎ 07 4941 7185, fax 07 4941 5541, 28 units [shwr, tlt, a/c, tel, TV, movie, radio, t/c mkg, refrig], ldry, iron, iron brd, conv fac, night club (Fri), ✉ (Mon-Sat), cots-fee. **BB ♦ $93.50, ♦♦ $110**, ch con, AE BC DC EFT MC VI.

MORETON ISLAND QLD 4025

Pop 262. (37km NE Brisbane), See maps on page 417, ref E6. Holiday orientated sand island (89%) National Park, with superb surfing beaches & world's highest sandhills. Strictly 4WD. scubadiving, snorkelling, sand toboganning. Camping & vehicle permit essential for National Park. Parking at Brisbane Terminal (fee). Highspeed catamaran transfers to island. Fishing, Squash, Surfing, Swimming, Tennis.
Self Catering Accommodation
★★★☆ **Tangalooma Wild Dolphin Resort**, (Villa), Resort, ☎ 07 3268 2666, fax 07 3268 6299, 56 villas acc up to 8, (2 bedrm), [shwr, tlt, c/fan, tel, TV, clock radio, refrig, cook fac, micro, ldry, blkts, linen, pillows], lounge, conv fac, ✉, pool, bbq, ✆, plygr, squash, tennis, cots. **D ♦♦ $290 - $370, ◊ $20, W ♦♦ $1,750 - $2,310**, AE BC DC EFT MC VI.

★★★☆ **(Holiday Units Section)**, Resort, (2 stry gr fl), 134 units acc up to 5, (Studio & 1 bedrm), [shwr, tlt, c/fan, tel, TV, t/c mkg, refrig, cook fac ltd, micro, blkts, linen, pillows], bar, plygr. **D ♦ $160 - $200, ♦♦ $190 - $230.**

★★ **Bulwer**, (HF), 100 Morton St Bulwer, 150m from Barge landing point, ☎ 07 3408 2202, fax 07 3880 1725, (2 stry gr fl), 6 flats (2 bedrmBunk Rooms), [shwr, bath, tlt, c/fan, refrig, cook fac, micro, ldry (in unit) (4), linen reqd-fee], ldry, dryer, bbq, kiosk (licenced), ✆. **W $496 - $550**, Access by vehicular & passenger Combie Trader Barge from Scarborough, BC EFT MC VI.

Moreton Moorings, (HF), 55 The Esplanade, Kooringal, ☎ 07 3409 0148, (2 stry gr fl), 6 flats acc up to 8, (1, 2 & 3 bedrm), [shwr, bath, tlt, TV, refrig, linen reqd, pillows], ldry, ✆. **D $60 - $110, W $300 - $650**, 4WD vehicles only. (Rating under review).

MOSSMAN QLD 4873

Pop 1,900. (1792km N Brisbane), See maps on page 415, ref B2. Most picturesque and northerly sugar region. Mount Demi 1,158m, Mossman Gorge National Park, Mossman Central Sugar Mill High Falls Farm (exotic fruit) Kuku Yalangi Dreaming Trail. Boat Ramp, Boating, Bowls, Bush Walking, Fishing, Golf, Scenic Drives.
Hotels/Motels
★★★ **Demi View**, (M), 41 Front St, ☎ 07 4098 1277, fax 07 4098 2102, 24 units [shwr, tlt, a/c-cool, c/fan, tel, TV, clock radio (10), t/c mkg, refrig], ldry, ✉ (Tues-Sun), pool (salt water), bbq, dinner to unit, c/park (undercover). **RO ♦ $62, ♦♦ $72, ◊ $10**, ch con, AE BC MC VI.

★★ **O'Malleys @ Mossman**, (LH), 2 Front St, 500m N of P.O. ☎ 07 4098 1410, fax 0740981958, 22 rms [a/c-cool (14), c/fan, TV (4), t/c mkg, refrig (10)], ✗, pool (salt water), ✆. **RO ♦ $15, ◊ $15**, AE BC DC EFT MC VI.

Self Catering Accommodation

★★★★ **Silky Oaks Lodge**, (Chalet), Finlayvale Rd,Mossman River Gorge, 7km NW of PO, ☎ 07 4098 1666, fax 07 4098 1983, 60 chalets acc up to 3, [shwr, spa bath (14), tlt, hairdry, a/c-cool, c/fan, tel, clock radio, refrig, mini bar], ldry, dryer, iron, iron brd, conf fac, ✉, bar, pool (salt water), shop, bush walking, bicycle, canoeing, tennis. **BLB $426**, AE BC DC JCB MC VI.

★★★★ **Tropical Beachside**, (HU), 59 Wonga Beach Rd, Wonga Beach 4873, 30km N of Port Douglas, ☎ 07 4098 7500, fax 07 4098 7600, (Multi-stry gr fl), 8 units acc up to 6, (1, 2 & 3 bedrm), [ensuite (1), shwr, bath (5), tlt, hairdry, a/c-cool, c/fan, tel, TV, clock radio, cook fac, micro, d/wash (5), toaster, ldry (in-unit) (2), blkts, linen, pillows], ldry, dryer (in-unit) (2), iron (2), iron brd (2), pool, bbq, ✆, cots-fee. **RO ♦♦ $152, ♦♦ $890.75**, Min book applies, BC EFT MC VI.

★★★ **White Cockatoo**, 9 Alchera Dve, 1km S of PO, ☎ 07 4098 2222, fax 07 4098 2221, 23 cabins acc up to 6, [shwr, tlt, a/c-cool, tel, TV, refrig, cook fac, blkts, linen, pillows], ldry, dryer, pool (salt water), spa, bbq (covered), kiosk, c/park (undercover), cots. **RO ♦ $55 - $66, ♦♦ $66 - $77, ◊ $11**, ch con, weekly con, Breakfast available, AE BC DC MC VI.
B&B's/Guest Houses
★★★★ **Side The Sea Bed & Breakfast**, (B&B), 148 Marine Pde, 7k N Mossman PO, ☎ 07 4098 1213, fax 07 4098 3452, 1 rm [shwr, tlt, hairdry, c/fan, TV, clock radio, t/c mkg, refrig], ldry, TV rm, pool, bbq, cots, non smoking rms. **BB ♦ $60 - $65, ♦♦ $80 - $90, ◊ $20**, ch con.

★★★☆ **Wonga Beach Independent Homestay**, (B&B), 10 Yarun Close, Wonga Beach, 17km N of Mossman, ☎ 07 4098 7677, fax 07 4098 7677, 2 rms [hairdry, fan, clock radio], shwr, tlt, TV rm, pool, t/c mkg shared, bbq, cots. **BB ♦ $66, ♦♦ $88**, ch con, BC MC VI.

MOUNT GARNET QLD 4872

Pop 400. (1796km N Brisbane), See maps on page 415, ref B4. Tin production with extensive alluvial deposits. Topaz fields are a feature of the region. Gem Fossicking.
Hotels/Motels
★★ **Mt Garnet Motel & BP Roadhouse**, (M), Kennedy Hwy, 500m W of PO, ☎ 07 4097 9249, fax 07 4097 9018, 10 units [shwr, tlt, fan, TV, t/c mkg, refrig], ✗, ✆, cots. **RO ♦ $44, ♦♦ $50, ◊ $11**, ch con, BC EFT MC VI.

MOUNT ISA QLD 4825

Pop 21,750. (1867km NW Brisbane), See maps on page 414, ref A5. Set on Leichhardt River - NW Qld's major industrial, commercial & administrative centre. One of world's largest silver and lead mines, also a major copper and zinc mining area. Mount Isa Museum, Royal Flying Doctor Base, School of the Air Kalkadoon Tribal Centre, Lake Moondarra, Riversleigh Fossils Display, National Trust Tent House, Mount Isa Mines Display & Visitors Centre. Boating, Bowls, Gem Fossicking, Golf, Sailing, Shooting, Swimming, Tennis, Water Skiing.
Hotels/Motels
★★★★ **Mercure Hotel Verona**, (M), Cnr Camooweal & Marian Sts, ☎ 07 4743 3024, fax 07 4743 8715, (Multi-stry), 57 units [shwr, bath (32), tlt, hairdry, a/c, tel, movie, clock radio, t/c mkg, refrig, mini bar], lift, ldry, iron, iron brd, conv fac, ✉, pool, rm serv, dinner to unit, c/park (undercover), cots. **RO ♦ $141 - $150, ♦♦ $141 - $150**, AE BC DC MC VI.

Rates may change. Check before booking.

★★★★ **Mt Isa Outback Motor Inn**, (M), 45 West St, 200m N Town Centre, ☎ 07 4743 2311, fax 07 4743 5411, 26 units [shwr, bath (11), spa bath (1), tlt, hairdry, a/c, tel, cable tv, movie, clock radio, t/c mkg, refrig], ldry, w/mach-fee, dryer, ✉, pool (salt water), bbq, rm serv, dinner to unit, c/park (undercover) (5), non smoking units (10), AE BC DC EFT MC VI, ⚹🛇.

★★★☆ **Mercure Inn Burke & Wills, Mt Isa**, (M), Previously Burke & Wills Motor Inn Cnr Grace & Camooweal Sts, ☎ 07 4743 8000, fax 07 4743 8424, (2 stry gr fl), 56 units [shwr, bath (46), tlt, a/c, tel, TV, movie, clock radio, t/c mkg, refrig, mini bar], ldry, ✉, bar, pool, spa (1), rm serv. **RO** ⚹ **$182,** ⚹⚹ **$182,** ⚹ **$16,** AE BC DC MC VI.

★★★☆ **Townview**, (M), 116 Kookaburra St, ☎ 07 4743 3328, fax 07 4749 0409, 24 units (3 suites) (1, 2 & 3 bedrm), [shwr (20), bath (4), spa bath (3), tlt (20), a/c-cool, tel, cable tv, movie, clock radio, t/c mkg, refrig, cook fac (4), cook fac ltd (2), micro (2), toaster], ldry-fee, dryer-fee, pool (salt water), dinner to unit, c/park (undercover) (6). **RO** ⚹ **$55 - $93.50,** ⚹⚹ **$55 - $93.50,** ⚹ **$5, Suite D** ⚹ **$105 - $135,** AE BC DC EFT MC VI.

★★★ **4th Ave Motor Inn**, (M), 20 Fourth Ave, ☎ 07 4743 3477, fax 07 4743 8372, 25 units [shwr, tlt, a/c, c/fan (8), tel, TV, t/c mkg, refrig], ldry, pool. **RO** ⚹ **$61.50,** ⚹⚹ **$71.50,** ⚹ **$10,** AE BC DC MC VI.

★★★ **Copper City**, (M), 105 Butler St, 1.2km E of PO, ☎ 07 4743 2033, fax 07 4743 2290, 11 units [shwr, tlt, fan, tel, cable tv, clock radio, t/c mkg, refrig, toaster], ldry-fee, dryer-fee, iron, iron brd, pool-heated (salt water), bbq, dinner to unit (Mon to Fri), meals to unit (Breakfast), c/park (undercover), cots. **RO** ⚹ **$66,** ⚹⚹ **$76,** ⚹ **$10,** ch con, AE BC DC MC VI.

★★★ **Motel Central Point**, (M), 6 Marian St, 100m E of K Mart Plaza, ☎ 07 4743 0666, fax 07 4743 0611, (2 stry) 19 units [shwr, tlt, a/c-cool, fan, tel, cable tv, clock radio, t/c mkg, refrig, cook fac ltd, micro, toaster, ldry-fee], dryer-fee, pool (saltwater), spa, bbq, ⚹. **RO** ⚹ **$66,** ⚹⚹ **$77,** ⚹ **$11,** ch con, AE BC DC EFT MC VI.

★★★ **The Overlander**, (LMH), 119 Marian St, ☎ 07 4743 5011, fax 07 4743 7160, 20 units [shwr, tlt, a/c, tel (deposit), cable tv, movie, t/c mkg, refrig, mini bar], ldry, conv fac, ✉, c/park (undercover), plygr, cots. **RO** ⚹ **$66,** ⚹⚹ **$82,** ch con, AE BC DC EFT MC VI.

★★☆ **Mount Isa Hotel**, (LH), Cnr Miles & Marian Sts, ☎ 07 4743 2611, fax 07 4743 0136, 24 rms [shwr, tlt, a/c-cool, tel, TV, movie, t/c mkg, refrig], ldry, dinner to unit, secure park, cots. **RO** ⚹ **$69,** ⚹⚹ **$79,** ⚹ **$15,** AE BC DC MC VI.

★★ **Inland Oasis**, (M), 195 Barkly Hwy, airport side of Mt Isa, ☎ 07 4743 3433, fax 07 4743 5569, 23 units [shwr, tlt, a/c-cool, tel, TV, radio, t/c mkg, refrig], ldry, ✉ (Mon to Sat), pool (salt water), bbq, rm serv, cots-fee. **RO** ⚹ **$61,** ⚹⚹ **$70,** ⚹ **$5.50 - $8.80,** AE BC DC MC VI.

★★☆ **(Economy Units Section)**, 18 units [shwr, tlt, a/c-cool, tel, TV, movie, clock radio, t/c mkg, refrig]. **RO** ⚹ **$44,** ⚹⚹ **$52.80.**

Barkly Hotel, (LMH), 55-65 Barkly Highway, 1 km from GPO, ☎ 07 4743 2988, fax 07 4743 9103, (Multi-stry), 42 units (2 suites) [shwr, tlt, a/c-cool, tel, TV, t/c mkg, refrig, ldry], dryer, conf fac, pool, bbq, secure park, ⚹, cots. **RO** ⚹ **$55,** ⚹⚹ **$70, Suite RO** ⚹ **$90,** ⚹⚹ **$90,** ch con, AE BC DC EFT JCB MC VI, (not yet classified).

Self Catering Accommodation
★★★ **Copper City Motel Holiday Units**, (HU), 105 Butler St, 1.2km E of GPO, ☎ 07 4743 2033, fax 07 4743 2290, 4 units acc up to 6, (1 & 2 bedrm), [shwr, tlt, a/c-cool, c/fan, tel, cable tv, clock radio, refrig, cook fac, micro, elec frypan, toaster, blkts, linen, pillows], w/mach-fee, dryer-fee, iron, iron brd, pool-heated (salt water heated), bbq, c/park (undercover), cots. **RO** ⚹⚹ **$90 - $150,** AE BC DC MC VI.

MOUNT MORGAN QLD 4714

Pop 2,500. (724km N Brisbane), See maps on page 416, ref C6. A small historical town full of history, established in the gold rush days. Museum Mine and Caves Tour The Swinging Bridge Gold Mount Railway. Bush Walking, Scenic Drives.

Hotels/Motels

★★☆ **Mt Morgan Motel & Van Park**, (M), Cnr Burnett Hwy & Showgrounds Rd, 1.5km S of PO, ☎ 07 4938 1952, fax 07 4938 1952, 5 units [shwr, tlt, a/c (5), c/fan (2), TV, t/c mkg, refrig, cook fac ltd, toaster], ldry-fee, dryer-fee, pool (salt water), bbq, meals avail (Dinner/Breakfast), c/park (undercover), ⚹, plygr. **D** ⚹⚹ **$44 - $50,** ⚹ **$10,** AE BC EFT MC MCH VI.

MOUNT SURPRISE QLD 4871

Pop Nominal, (1860km NW Brisbane), See maps on page 414, ref C4. Small town on the banks of Elizabeth Creek. Obrien's Creek gemfields (Topaz). Undara Lava Tubes located approximately 55km east of Mt Surprise. All entry to Lava Tubes system by prior arrangement with Savannah Guide. The terminus for the Savannahlander Train - Mount Surprise to Forsayth. Bush Walking, Gem Fossicking.

Hotels/Motels
★☆ **Mount Surprise**, (LH), Garland St, 92km E of Georgetown 294km, ☎ 07 4062 3118, 7 rms [c/fan, elec blkts], shwr, tlt, ldry, dryer, lounge (TV), ✉, t/c mkg shared, refrig, bbq, rm serv, dinner to unit, secure park, ⚹, plygr. **RO** ⚹ **$25,** ⚹⚹ **$40,** ch con, BC EFT MC VI.

MOUNT TYSON QLD 4356

Pop Nominal, (168km W Brisbane), See maps on page 417, ref A6. Cattle, grain & cotton producing district. Located between towns of Oakey & Pittsworth A frequent 'Tidy Towns' winner.

B&B's/Guest Houses
★★★ **Adora Downs Farm Stay**, (GH), (Farm), Via Mount Tyson 4356, 4km W of Mount Tyson PO, ☎ 07 4693 7148, fax 07 4693 7267, 3 rms [shwr, bath, tlt, elec blkts], lounge (TV), pool, bicycle, tennis. **D** all meals ⚹ **$95.70,** ⚹⚹ **$120.**

★★ **(Lodge Section)**, 10 rms [elec blkts], shwr (2), tlt (3), bathrm (2). **D** all meals ⚹ **$95.70.**

MOURA QLD 4718

Pop 2,000. (637km NW Brisbane), See maps on page 416, ref B7. Located in the heart of the rich Dawson Valley, it produces beef, wheat, sorghum sunflower, cotton and most importantly coal. Blackdown Tablelands and Coal Mines. Bowls, Swimming, Tennis.

Hotels/Motels
★★★ **Moura Burradoo**, (M), Dawson Hwy, ☎ 07 4997 1588, fax 07 4997 1062, 16 units [shwr, tlt, a/c, c/fan, tel, TV, movie, clock radio, t/c mkg, refrig], ldry, ✉ (Mon to Thur), pool, dinner to unit (Mon-Thu). **RO** ⚹ **$71,** ⚹⚹ **$83,** ⚹ **$12,** AE BC DC EFT MC VI.

★★☆ **Coal & Cattle**, (LMH), Dawson Hwy, ☎ 07 4997 1511, fax 07 4997 1324, 22 units [shwr, tlt, a/c, tel, TV, clock radio, t/c mkg, refrig], conv fac, ✉ (Mon - Sat), cots. **BB** ⚹ **$71.50,** ⚹⚹ **$93.50, RO** ⚹ **$22,** ch con, AE BC DC EFT MC VI.

MUCKADILLA QLD 4461

Pop Nominal, (520km W Brisbane), See maps on page 414, ref D7. Situated on the Warrego Hwy. A small western town once famous for its artesian bore water baths. Town is centre for surrounding wheat, sheep & cattle farming.

Hotels/Motels
★☆ **Muckadilla**, (LMH), Warrego Hwy, ☎ 07 4626 8318, 9 units [shwr, bath, tlt, fan, heat, elec blkts, TV, t/c mkg], ✉, pool (salt water), bbq, ⚹, cots. **RO** ⚹ **$25,** ⚹⚹ **$35,** ⚹ **$10.**

MUDGEERABA QLD

See Gold Coast Region.

MUDJIMBA QLD

See Sunshine Coast Region.

MUNDUBBERA QLD 4626

Pop 1,250. (426km NW Brisbane), See maps on page 417, ref A1. Citrus growing and dairying area. Auburn River National Park. The Big Mandarin. Canoeing, Horse Riding, Water Skiing.

Hotels/Motels
★★★☆ **Billabong Motor Inn**, (M), Mundubbera-Durong Rd, ☎ 07 4165 4533, fax 07 4165 4130, 17 units [shwr, tlt, a/c, tel, TV, movie, clock radio, t/c mkg, refrig, mini bar], ldry, dryer, ✉, pool (salt water), bbq, meals to unit, c/park (undercover), cots-fee. **RO** ⚹ **$61.05,** ⚹⚹ **$69.75,** ⚹ **$11,** ch con, AE BC DC MC VI.

★★★ **Mundubbera**, (M), 42 Strathdee St, ☎ 07 4165 4399, fax 07 4165 3111, 20 units [shwr, tlt, a/c-cool, c/fan, heat, elec blkts, tel, cable tv, movie, clock radio, t/c mkg, refrig], ldry, pool, bbq, dinner to unit, c/park (undercover), cots-fee. **RO** ⚹ **$58 - $72,** ⚹⚹ **$65 - $80,** ⚹ **$11,** ch con, AE BC DC EFT MC VI.

MURGON QLD 4605

Pop 2,100. (258km NW Brisbane), See maps on page 417, ref B3. Agricultural area known as the beef centre of the Burnett. Freshwater recreation at Bjelke Petersen Dam & Queensland Dairy Museum. Bowls, Bush Walking, Fishing, Golf, Swimming.

Hotels/Motels

★★★ **Murgon Motor Inn**, (M), 193 Lamb St (Bunya Hwy), opposite golf course, ☎ 07 4168 1400, fax 07 4168 1400, 20 units [shwr, tlt, hairdry (8), a/c, c/fan (8), tel, TV, clock radio, t/c mkg, refrig, mini bar], dryer-fee, iron (4), iron brd (4), ⊠, pool (salt water), bbq, rm serv, dinner to unit, cots-fee. **RO** ⏚ **$53.90 - $64.90,** ⏚⏚ **$61.60 - $75.90,** ⏚ **$11,** ch con, Unit 13 to 20 ★★★★. AE BC DC MC VI.

★☆ **Australian**, (LMH), Cnr Gore & Lamb Sts, ☎ 07 4168 1077, (2 stry gr fl), 11 units [shwr, tlt, a/c, tel, TV, radio, t/c mkg, refrig], conv fac, ⊠ (Mon to Sat), rm serv, dinner to unit, cots. **RO** ⏚ **$42.50,** ⏚⏚ **$52.80,** ⏚ **$10,** ch con, AE BC DC EFT MC VI.

B&B's/Guest Houses

★★★★ **Bridgeman Downs**, (B&B), (Farm), 866 Barambah Rd via Moffatdale, 10km from PO, ☎ 07 4168 4784, fax 07 4168 4767, 2 rms [shwr (2), tlt (2), c/fan, heat, elec blkts], shwr, tlt, bathrm, ldry, lounge (TV & Video), bbq. **BB** ⏚ **$50,** ⏚⏚ **$95,** ch con.

  (Cottage Section), 1 cotg [shwr, tlt, heat (1), c/fan (1), elec blkts, tel (1), TV, video, clock radio, refrig, cook fac (1), cook fac ltd (1), elec frypan (1), toaster (1), blkts, linen, pillows], iron (1), iron brd (1), TV rm, bbq, rm serv, cots (1)-fee. **D** ⏚ **$10, $75,** (not yet classified).

NAMBOUR QLD 4560

Pop 12,200. (100km N Brisbane), See maps on page 417, ref D4. Commercial and administrative centre of Maroochy Shire, surrounded by sugar cane, pineapples and other plantations. Moreton Central Sugar Mill. Bowls, Croquet, Golf, Squash, Swimming.

Hotels/Motels

★★★☆ **Nambour Motor Inn**, (M), Cnr Coronation Ave & Rigby St, ☎ 07 5441 5500, fax 07 5441 4520, 14 units [shwr, tlt, a/c, tel, TV, movie, clock radio, t/c mkg, refrig, toaster], ldry, pool, spa (unheated), bbq-fee, dinner to unit, cots. **RO** ⏚ **$59 - $65,** ⏚⏚ **$69 - $75,** ⏚ **$10,** AE BC DC EFT MC VI.

★★★ **Centrepoint**, (M), 26 Coronation Ave, ☎ 07 5441 4811, fax 07 5441 4315, 12 units [shwr, tlt, a/c, c/fan, tel, TV, clock radio, t/c mkg, refrig], pool, bbq, meals to unit (dinner/breakfast), cots. **RO** ⏚ **$55 - $66,** ⏚⏚ **$66 - $77,** ⏚ **$11,** ch con, AE BC DC MC VI.

★★☆ **Ambor Court**, (M), 171 Currie St, ☎ 07 5441 2611, fax 07 5441 2123, (2 stry gr fl), 19 units [shwr, tlt, a/c-cool, c/fan, heat, tel, TV, clock radio, t/c mkg, refrig], ldry, pool, bbq, dinner to unit, c/park (undercover), cots-fee. **RO** ⏚ **$49.50,** ⏚⏚ **$60,** ⏚ **$11,** ch con, AE BC DC MC VI.

★★☆ **Koala Welcome Inn**, (M), McKenzie Rd, 2.5km S of town centre, ☎ 07 5442 1411, fax 07 5442 1077, 22 units [shwr, tlt, a/c (18), tel, TV, clock radio, t/c mkg, refrig], ldry, pool, bbq, c/park (undercover). **RO** ⏚ **$38.50 - $49.50,** ⏚⏚ **$44 - $60.50,** ⏚ **$11,** Budget units 21 to 24 ★★☆. AE BC DC MC VI.

★★☆ **Nambour Midway Motel**, (M), 89 Howard St, ☎ 07 5441 2322, fax 07 5441 2243, 17 units [shwr, spa bath (6), tlt, a/c-cool, c/fan, heat, tel, TV, clock radio, t/c mkg, refrig], ldry, conv fac, ⊠, pool, bbq, dinner to unit, c/park (undercover), cots-fee. **P** ⏚ **$55 - $88, RO** ⏚⏚ **$60.50 - $88,** ⏚ **$11,** AE BC DC MC VI.

★☆ **Commercial**, (LH), 35 Currie St, ☎ 07 5441 1144, fax 07 5441 4969, 13 rms [shwr, tlt, a/c, TV, t/c mkg, refrig], conv fac, ⊠, meals avail (Full B/fast), c/park (undercover) (5), ☏, cots. **RO** ⏚ **$33,** ⏚⏚ **$45 - $49.50,** ch con, BC EFT MC VI.

Self Catering Accommodation

★★★★ **Hospital Grove Apartments**, (HU), 31 Hospital Road, 50m S of Nambour Hospital, ☎ 07 5441 7200, fax 07 5441 3977, (2 stry gr fl), 8 units acc up to 4, [shwr, bath (1), tlt, a/c (4), tel, TV, clock radio, refrig, micro, elec frypan, toaster, ldry, blkts, linen, pillows], dryer, iron, iron brd, c/park (undercover). **RO** ⏚⏚ **$79,** ⏚ **$10,** **W** ⏚⏚ **$415 - $460,** AE BC DC EFT MC VI.

NANANGO QLD 4615

Pop 2,700. (186km NW Brisbane), See maps on page 417, ref B4. Located on the Burnett Hwy with many gem-fossicking areas nearby. Bush Walking, Gem Fossicking, Gold Prospecting, Scenic Drives.

Hotels/Motels

★★★★ **Copper Country Motor Inn**, (M), Vineyard, Kingaroy Rd, opposite golf course, ☎ 07 4163 1011, fax 07 4163 1122, 11 units [shwr, tlt, hairdry, a/c, tel, cable tv, clock radio, t/c mkg, refrig], conf fac, ⊠, rm serv, c/park (undercover), cots. **RO** ⏚ **$70,** ⏚⏚ **$79,** ⏚ **$10,** ch con, AE BC DC EFT MC VI.

★★★☆ **Nanango Fitzroy Motel**, (M), 55 Fitzroy St, Off Highway, ☎ 07 4163 1100, fax 07 4163 1302, (2 stry) 20 units [shwr, tlt, a/c, tel, TV, clock radio, t/c mkg, refrig, cook fac (10)], ldry, dryer, iron, ✕, pool, bbq, dinner to unit, c/park (undercover), cots-fee. **RO** ⏚ **$50 - $56,** ⏚⏚ **$55 - $66,** ⏚ **$11,** ch con, AE BC DC EFT MC VI.

★★ **Antler**, (M), 33 Henry St, ☎ 07 4163 1444, fax 07 4163 1444, 12 units [shwr, tlt, a/c, c/fan (2), TV, clock radio, t/c mkg, refrig], pool, bbq, c/park (undercover), cots. **RO** ⏚ **$42,** ⏚⏚ **$53,** ⏚ **$11,** ch con, AE BC DC MC VI.

★★ **Nanango Star**, (M), 43 Drayton St, ☎ 07 4163 1666, fax 07 4163 1309, 12 units [shwr, tlt, a/c, c/fan, tel, TV, clock radio, t/c mkg, refrig], bbq, meals to unit, c/park (undercover) (8), cots. **RO** ⏚ **$45,** ⏚⏚ **$55 - $57,** ⏚ **$11,** ch con, AE BC DC MC VI.

NATURAL BRIDGE QLD 4211

Pop Nominal, (103km S Brisbane), See maps on page 417, ref D8. Small mountain village on the Nerang River situated in the Gold Coast Hinterland. Bush Walking, Scenic Drives.

Self Catering Accommodation

★★★★ **Solitude**, (Chalet), 3376 Nerang-Murwillumisoh Rd M.S 208, ☎ 07 5533 6138, fax 07 5533 6138, 4 chalets acc up to 8, [shwr, tlt, fan, heat, refrig, cook fac, micro, blkts, linen, pillows], bbq, c/park (undercover), breakfast ingredients, non smoking units (4). **D** ⏚⏚ **$102 - $112, W** ⏚⏚ **$715,** Min book applies.

NERANG QLD

See Gold Coast Region.

NOBBY BEACH QLD

See Gold Coast Region.

NOOSA HEADS QLD

See Sunshine Coast Region.

NOOSAVILLE QLD

See Sunshine Coast Region.

NORMANTON QLD 4890

Pop 1,350. (2152km NW Brisbane), See maps on page 414, ref B4. Main centre of Carpentaria Shire, established in 1868. The home of the Gulflander Traveltrain -Historical scenic train service connecting Normanton to Croydon. Fishing, Golf, Scenic Drives, Swimming, Tennis.

Hotels/Motels

★★★ **Brolga Palms Motel**, (M), 92 Landsborough St, ☎ 07 4745 1009, fax 07 4745 1626, 17 units [shwr, tlt, a/c-cool, c/fan, tel, TV, clock radio, refrig], ldry, ⊠, pool (salt water), spa. **RO** ⏚ **$65 - $75,** ⏚⏚ **$75 - $85,** ⏚ **$10 - $15,** AE BC EFT MC VI.

★★☆ **The Gulfland Motel**, (M), Previously Gulfland Motel & Caravan Park 11 Landsborough St, 1.5km S of PO, ☎ 07 4745 1290, fax 07 4745 1138, 28 units [shwr, tlt, a/c-cool, fan, TV, t/c mkg, refrig], ⊠, pool. **RO** ⏚ **$66 - $77,** ⏚⏚ **$77 - $88,** AE BC MC VI.

★★ **Albion**, (LMH), Haig St, 200m E of PO, ☎ 07 4745 1218, fax 07 4745 1675, 7 units [shwr, tlt, a/c-cool, fan, TV, t/c mkg, refrig], ldry, iron, ⊠ (Mon to Sat - counter), bbq, courtesy transfer, ☏. **RO** ⏚ **$55,** ⏚⏚ **$60,** ⏚⏚⏚ **$70,** ch con.

OAKEY QLD 4401

Pop 3,400. (157km W Brisbane), See maps on page 417, ref A6. Located on the Warrego Hwy. Bernborough racehorse monument Army airfield - Museum of Australian Army Flying Close to Jondaryan Woolshed Heritage Museum. Bowls, Golf, Horse Riding, Swimming, Tennis.

Hotels/Motels

★★★☆ **Kellys**, (M), Campbell St, opposite Community Centre, ☎ 07 4691 1109, fax 07 4691 2389, 11 units [shwr, tlt, hairdry, a/c, fan, tel, TV, clock radio, t/c mkg, refrig, cook fac (2), toaster], ldry, iron (6), iron brd (6), ✕, bar, bbq, dinner to unit, c/park (undercover), cots, non smoking property. **RO 👤 $60, 👥 $66 - $70, ⓘ $11**, ch con, AE BC DC EFT MC VI, ♿.

Budget Motel Chain International

★★★☆ **Oakey**, (M), 1 Toowoomba Rd, ☎ 07 4691 1000, fax 07 4691 1034, 12 units [shwr, tlt, a/c, elec blkts, tel, TV, clock radio, t/c mkg, refrig], ldry, ✕, ⊠, bbq, dinner to unit, c/park (undercover), cots. **RO 👤 $52, 👥 $62, ⓘ $12**, AE BC DC MC VI.

★★★☆ **Park House Motor Inn**, (M), 27 Campbell St, 1km S of PO, ☎ 07 4691 1877, fax 07 4691 2504, 8 units [shwr, tlt, hairdry, a/c, heat, elec blkts, tel, TV, video, clock radio, t/c mkg, refrig, cook fac (2), micro (3), toaster (8)], ldry, c/park (undercover), cots. **RO 👤 $60, 👥 $66, ⓘ $11**, AE BC DC EFT MC VI.

ORMEAU QLD

See Gold Coast Region.

ORPHEUS ISLAND QLD 4850

Pop Nominal, (1371km N Brisbane), See maps on page 415, ref D6. A small island surrounded by coral reefs. A National Park with some 50 varieties of birds & nesting turtles. Seasonal whale migration. Viewing of coral and marine life by glass-bottomed boat Secluded tropical surroundings, 45 nautical miles from Townsville. Boating, Bush Walking, Sailing, Swimming, Tennis, Water Skiing.

Hotels/Motels

★★★★ **Orpheus Island**, (M), Resort, No children's facilities, ☎ 07 4777 7377, fax 07 4777 7533, 6 units [shwr, bath, spa bath, tlt, hairdry, c/fan, t/c mkg, refrig, mini bar, ldry, pillows], rec rm, conv fac, ⊠, pool (2), spa, bush walking, tennis. **D all meals 👥 $1,430**, AE BC DC MC VI.

★★★★ **(Beachfront Studio Section)**, 15 units [shwr, bath, spa bath, tlt, hairdry, a/c, c/fan, radio, t/c mkg, refrig, mini bar, pillows]. **D all meals 👤 $750, 👥 $1,220.**

★★★★ **(Bungalow Section)**, 2 units [shwr, bath, spa bath, tlt, hairdry, a/c-cool, c/fan, t/c mkg, refrig, mini bar, pillows]. **D all meals 👥 $1,370.**

★★★☆ **(Beachfront Terrace Suites)**, 8 units [shwr, tlt, hairdry, a/c, c/fan, radio, t/c mkg, refrig, mini bar, pillows]. **D all meals 👤 $635, 👥 $1,020, ⓘ $360.**

OXENFORD QLD

See Gold Coast Region.

PACIFIC PARADISE QLD

See Sunshine Coast Region.

PALM BEACH QLD

See Gold Coast Region.

PALM COVE QLD 4879

Pop 1,993. (1746km N Brisbane), See maps on page 415, ref C3. Popular palm-fringed sandy beach on the Marlin Coast. Tourist centre for the Great Barrier Reef, Rainforest, Daintree River and the Atherton Tablelands. Fishing, Golf, Horse Riding, Sailing, Scenic Drives, Swimming, Tennis.

Hotels/Motels

★★★★☆ **Azure Waters Beachfront Apartments**, (LH), 139 Williams Espl, 26km N of Cairns, ☎ 07 4059 1550, fax 07 4059 1551, 16 rms [shwr, tlt, a/c-cool, c/fan, tel, cable tv, clock radio, t/c mkg, refrig, toaster], ldry, ⊠, spa, dinner to unit, cots-fee, non smoking rms. **RO 👥 $140 - $200**, AE BC DC EFT MC VI.

Azure Waters Beachfront Apartments ...continued

★★★★☆ **(Apartment Section)**, 36 apts acc up to 6, (1, 2 & 3 bedrm), [shwr, tlt, a/c-cool, c/fan, tel, cable tv, clock radio, t/c mkg, refrig, cook fac ltd, micro, toaster], ldry, ⊠, pool (plunge pool), spa, bbq, dinner to unit, cots-fee, non smoking units. **D $195 - $385, W $1,260 - $2,555.**

★★★★☆ **Courtyard by Marriott Great Barrier Reef Rsrt**, (Ltd Lic H), Cnr Veivers Esp & Williams Rd, 25km N of Cairns, ☎ 07 4059 9507, fax 07 9055 3202, (Multi-stry), 189 rms (4 suites) [shwr, bath, tlt, hairdry, a/c-cool, tel, TV, movie-fee, clock radio, t/c mkg, refrig, mini bar (189)], lift, ldry, dryer, iron, iron brd, conv fac, ⊠, pool, spa, 24hr reception, rm serv, plygr, tennis, non smoking rms (85). **RO 👤 $237 - $269.50, 👥 $237 - $296.50, ⓘ $32.50, Suite D $312 - $388**, ch con, AE BC DC MC VI, ♿.

★★★★☆ **Novotel Palm Cove Resort**, (LH), Resort, Coral Coast Dve, 25km north of Cairns, ☎ 07 4059 1234, fax 07 4059 1297, (Multi-stry gr fl), 224 rms (72 suites) [shwr, bath, tlt, hairdry (224), a/c-cool, tel, cable tv, movie, clock radio, t/c mkg, refrig, cook fac (116)], lift, ldry, iron, iron brd, conv fac, ⊠, pool (10), sauna, spa, bbq, 24hr reception, 📞, plygr, golf, gym, squash (2), tennis (3), non smoking rms (156). **RO $220 - $460**, ch con, AE BC DC EFT JCB MC VI, ♿.

★★★★☆ **(Apartment Section)**, 106 apts acc up to 6, (1, 2 & 3 bedrm), [shwr, bath, spa bath (8), tlt, hairdry, a/c, c/fan, tel, TV, movie, clock radio, t/c mkg, refrig, mini bar, cook fac], dryer, iron, iron brd, rm serv, cots-fee. **RO $220 - $460**, ♿.

★★★★☆ **Palm Cove Beach Sarayi**, (M), 95 Williams Esp, beachfront 26km N of Cairns, ☎ 07 4055 3734, fax 07 4059 1022, 23 units [shwr, tlt, a/c-cool, c/fan, tel, cable tv, movie, clock radio, refrig, cook fac, pillows], ldry, iron, ✕, spa, bbq, c/park. **RO 👥 $79 - $215, ⓘ $17.50**, ch con, AE BC DC MC VI.

Self Catering Accommodation

★★★★☆ **Angsana Resort & Spa**, (SA), Previously The Allamanda Palm Cove 1 Veivers Rd, absolute beachfront, ☎ 07 4055 3000, fax 07 4059 0166, (Multi-stry gr fl), 69 serv apts (1, 2, 3 & 4 bedrm), [shwr, bath (50), tlt, a/c-cool, fan, tel, TV, movie, clock radio, refrig, mini bar, cook fac, micro, d/wash, ldry (in unit)], conf fac, ⊠, pool, spa (indoor/outdoor), bbq, 24hr reception, secure park, cots. **D 👥 $330 - $800**, AE BC DC MC VI.

★★★★☆ **Coral Horizons**, (HU), 137 William Esp, ☎ 07 4059 1565, fax 07 4059 1551, (Multi-stry gr fl), 7 units acc up to 4, (2 bedrm), [shwr, tlt, a/c-cool, c/fan, cent heat, TV, clock radio, t/c mkg, refrig, cook fac, micro, toaster, ldry, blkts, linen, pillows], lift, w/mach, dryer, pool, bbq, c/park (undercover), cots-fee, non smoking property. **D $265 - $295, W $1,750 - $1,960**, Min book applies, AE BC DC EFT MC VI.

★★★★☆ **Marlin Waters Beachfront Apartments**, (HU), 131 Williams Esp, ☎ 07 4055 3933, fax 07 4055 3935, (Multi-stry gr fl), 21 units acc up to 5, (1 & 2 bedrm), [shwr, bath, tlt, a/c-cool, fan, tel, TV, clock radio, refrig, cook fac, ldry (in unit), blkts, linen, pillows], lift, pool, spa, bbq, c/park (undercover). **D 👥 $114 - $220, ⓘ $28, W $800 - $1,080**, Min book applies, BC MC VI.

★★★★☆ **Oasis at Palm Cove**, (HU), McDonald Close, 20km N of Cairns, ☎ 07 4059 0522, fax 07 4059 0577, 36 units acc up to 6, (3 bedrm), [ensuite, shwr, bath, tlt, hairdry, a/c-cool, c/fan, tel, cable tv, video, clock radio, CD, refrig, cook fac, micro, d/wash, toaster, ldry, blkts, linen, pillows], dryer, iron, iron brd, pool (saltwater), spa, bbq, c/park (undercover), secure park, plygr, tennis, cots. **D 👥 $195 - $370, ⓘ $25**, AE BC DC MC VI.

★★★★☆ **Palm Beach Villas (Palm Cove)**, (HU), Previously Palm Beach Villas 24 Warren St, 1km W of PO, ☎ 07 4059 0900, fax 07 4059 0300, 23 units acc up to 6, (2 & 3 bedrm), [shwr, tlt, hairdry (on request), a/c-cool, c/fan, tel, TV, clock radio, refrig, cook fac, micro, d/wash, toaster, ldry, blkts, linen, pillows], dryer, iron, iron brd, pool (6), spa (communal), freezer, bbq (7), secure park, cots-fee. **RO $128 - $178**, ch con, AE BC DC MC VI.

★★★★☆ **Sebel Reef House**, (SA), 99 Williams Esp, 25km N of Cairns, ☎ 07 4055 3633, fax 07 4055 3305, (Multi-stry), 69 serv apts (4 suites) acc up to 5, [shwr, bath (56), spa bath (4), tlt, hairdry, a/c-cool, c/fan, tel, TV, video, clock radio, CD, t/c mkg, refrig, mini bar, micro (55)], lift, ldry-fee, iron, iron brd, conv fac, ⊠, pool (3), spa (2), c/park (undercover), cots. **RO $265 - $550**, AE BC DC JCB MC VI.

★★★★☆ **The Reef Retreat**, (HU), 10 - 14 Harpa St, 50m to beach, ☎ 07 4059 1744, fax 07 4059 1745, (Multi-stry gr fl), 36 units acc up to 6, (1 & 2 bedrm), [shwr, spa bath (13), tlt, a/c-cool, fan, tel, TV, clock radio, refrig, cook fac, blkts, linen, pillows], ldry, pool, spa, bbq, c/park (undercover). **D $130 - $250**, AE BC DC MC VI.

PALM COVE QLD continued...

★★★★☆ **Villa Paradiso**, (HU), 111 Williams Esp, 25km N of Cairns PO, ☎ 07 4055 3838, fax 07 4055 3991, (Multi-stry), 19 units acc up to 8, (2 & 3 bedrm), [shwr, tlt, a/c-cool, fan, tel, TV, refrig, cook fac, micro, d/wash, ldry (in unit), blkts, linen, pillows], iron, pool, spa, bbq, secure park, cots-fee. **RO $278 - $378**, BC MC VI.

★★★★ **Melaleuca Resort**, (HU), 85 Williams Esp, ☎ 07 4055 3222, fax 07 4055 3307, (2 stry), 22 units acc up to 4, (1 bedrm), [shwr, tlt, a/c-cool (Split System), fan, tel, TV, clock radio, refrig, cook fac, ldry (in unit), blkts, linen, pillows], pool (salt water), spa, bbq, c/park (undercover), courtesy transfer. **D** ♦♦ **$111 - $168**, ◊ **$25**, Min book applies, AE BC DC MC VI.

★★★★ **Palm Cove Tropic Apartments**, (SA), 6 Triton St, ☎ 07 4055 3555, fax 07 4055 3566, (2 stry gr fl), 19 serv apts acc up to 5, (1 & 2 bedrm), [shwr, tlt, a/c, fan, tel, TV, video, clock radio, t/c mkg, refrig, cook fac, micro, blkts, linen, pillows], w/mach, dryer, pool, bbq, cots-fee. **D** ♦ **$120 - $165**, ♦♦ **$120 - $165**, ◊ **$10 - $20**, BC EFT MC VI.

★★★☆ **Paradise Village Resort**, (HU), 119 Williams Esp, adjacent PO, ☎ 07 4055 3300, fax 07 4055 3991, (Multi-stry gr fl), 28 units [shwr, tlt, a/c, c/fan, tel, TV, movie, clock radio, refrig, cook fac (14), ldry (in unit) (1), blkts, linen, pillows], ldry-fee, dryer-fee, ⊠, pool, spa, rm serv, c/park (undercover), courtesy transfer, cots-fee. **RO** ♦♦ **$165**, ♦♦♦♦ **$195**, ◊ **$22**, 14 studio units not part of this rating. AE BC DC MC VI.

★★★☆ **Silvester Palms**, (HU), 32 Veivers Rd, 300m fr beach, ☎ 07 4055 3831, fax 07 4055 3598, (2 stry gr fl), 9 units (1, 2 & 3 bedrm), [shwr, tlt, a/c-cool (1), fan, TV, clock radio, cook fac, micro, blkts, linen, pillows], ldry, pool, bbq, ✆, cots. **RO $80 - $120**, BC MC VI.

PALMVIEW QLD

See Sunshine Coast Region.

PECHEY QLD 4355

Pop Nominal, (168km W Brisbane), See maps on page 417, ref B6. Located 545m above sea level in grazing area.

Self Catering Accommodation

★★ **Listening Ridge**, (Farm), Working cattle property. Lake Perserverance Rd, 40km N of Toowoomba, ☎ 07 4698 1424, fax 07 4698 1424, 2 cabins acc up to 4, [shwr, bath (1), tlt, c/fan, elec blkts, refrig, cook fac]. **D** ♦♦ **$90**, Meals by arrangement.

PERIGIAN BEACH QLD

See Sunshine Coast Region.

PITTSWORTH QLD 4356

Pop 3,250. (169km SW Brisbane), See maps on page 417, ref A7. Rich grain & dairying district. Location of the Pittsworth Folk Museum and Home of annual truck pulling championships. Bowls, Fishing, Golf, Scenic Drives, Squash, Swimming, Tennis.

Hotels/Motels

★★☆ **Pittsworth**, (LMH), Cnr Yandilla & Briggs Sts, ☎ 07 4693 1999, fax 07 4693 1347, 9 units [shwr, tlt, fan, heat, elec blkts, TV, t/c mkg, refrig], conv fac, ⊠ (Mon to Sat), dinner to unit, ✆, cots-fee. **RO** ♦ **$44**, ♦♦ **$52.80**, ♦♦♦ **$56**, ♦♦♦♦ **$60**, AE BC DC MC VI.

★★ **Golden Grain**, (M), Yandilla St, ☎ 07 4693 1206, fax 07 4693 2488, 9 units [shwr, tlt, a/c, fan, c/fan, heat, elec blkts, tel (1), TV, t/c mkg, refrig, cook fac (1)], pool-heated, bbq, cots-fee. **RO** ♦ **$44**, ♦♦ **$50**, ◊ **$10**, ch con, AE BC MC VI.

POMONA QLD 4568

Pop 950. (141km N Brisbane), See maps on page 417, ref D4. Small town nestled in picturesque valley at base of Mt Cooroora in the northern Sunshine Coast Hinterland. A rural district of small farms and country homes. The Majestic Theatre is over 80 years old & is the oldest continually running cinema in Australia. The Cooroora Historical Museum contains many records of local timber & dairying industries. Bowls, Bush Walking, Tennis.

Hotels/Motels

Pomona Hotel, (LH), Station St, 500m S of PO, ☎ 07 5485 1187, fax 07 5485 0087, (2 stry), 11 rms [basin, c/fan, t/c mkg, toaster], shwr, tlt, ldry, lounge (TV), ⊠ (Mon to Sat), bbq, dinner to unit, ✆. **RO** ♦ **$20**, ♦♦ **$30**, ◊ **$10**, ch con.

PORT DOUGLAS QLD 4871

Pop 3,650. (1792km N Brisbane), See maps on page 415, ref B2. Port for Mossman 20km. Sugar cane & grazing area. One of the oldest towns in North Queensland, being originally a landing point for miners. A big game fishing centre and base for prawn trawlers working the waters off Cape York Peninsula. The Court House Museum, Ben & Lynn Cropp Museum of shipwreck relics, Flagstaff Hill Lookout Four Mile Beach Marina Mirage.

Hotels/Motels

★★★★★ **Thala Beach Lodge**, (LH), Private Rd Oak Beach via, 16km S of PO, ☎ 07 4098 5700, fax 07 4098 5837, 85 rms (1 suite) [ensuite, a/c-cool, c/fan, tel, TV, clock radio, t/c mkg, refrig], ldry, conf fac, ⊠, pool, spa, rm serv (24hr), dinner to unit, secure park, non smoking rms (20). **RO** ♦ **$225 - $290**, ♦♦ **$293 - $377, Suite D $463**, AE BC DC MC VI.

★★★★☆ **Radisson Treetops Resort**, (LH), Resort, Port Douglas Rd, ☎ 07 4030 4333, fax 07 4030 4323, (Multi-stry gr fl), 306 rms (9 suites) [shwr, bath, tlt, hairdry, c/fan, tel, TV, movie, clock radio, t/c mkg, mini bar], lift, iron, iron brd, ⊠, pool (salt water), rm serv, dinner to unit, ✆, cots, non smoking rms (30). **RO** ♦ **$219 - $239**, ♦♦ **$219 - $239**, ◊ **$22, Suite D $349 - $469**, ch con, AE BC DC JCB MC VI, ♿.

★★★★ **Lazy Lizard Motor Inn**, (M), 121 Davidson St, ☎ 07 4099 5900, fax 07 4099 5105, 22 units (2 bedrm), [shwr, bath, tlt, hairdry, a/c-cool, c/fan, tel, TV, video, clock radio, t/c mkg, refrig, cook fac ltd, micro, toaster], ldry, dryer, pool (salt water), spa, bbq (covered), c/park (undercover), cots-fee. **RO** ♦ **$94 - $116**, ♦♦ **$94 - $116**, ◊ **$15**, AE BC DC MC VI, ♿.

★★★★ **Pelican Inn Port Douglas**, (M), 123 Davidson St, ☎ 07 4099 5266, fax 07 4099 5821, 17 units [shwr, bath, tlt, a/c-cool, c/fan, tel, cable tv, radio, t/c mkg, refrig, mini bar, micro, toaster], ldry, ⊠ (Mon - Sat), bar, pool (salt water), rm serv, dinner to unit, c/park (undercover), cots (avail). **RO** ♦ **$99 - $115**, ♦♦ **$99 - $115**, ◊ **$15**, ch con, AE BC DC MC VI.

★★★ **Port Douglas**, (M), 9 Davidson St, ☎ 07 4099 5248, fax 07 4099 5504, 19 units [shwr, bath (2), tlt, a/c-cool, c/fan, tel, TV, clock radio, t/c mkg, refrig], pool (salt water), bbq (covered), c/park (undercover), cots-fee. **RO** ♦ **$72 - $84**, ♦♦ **$72 - $84**, ◊ **$16**, ch con, Units 14 to 20 are ★★☆. AE BC DC MC VI, ♿.

★★★ **Port O'Call**, (M), Port St, ☎ 07 4099 5422, fax 07 4099 5495, 10 units [shwr, tlt, a/c-cool, c/fan, TV (6), clock radio (6), t/c mkg, refrig (6), pillows], ldry, rec rm, lounge, ✕, bar, bar, pool, kiosk, ✆, cots. **D** ♦ **$65 - $95**, ♦♦ **$65 - $85**, ◊ **$11**, 4 units of a lower rating. BC EFT MC VI.

(Unit Section), 18 bunkhouses acc up to 4, [shwr, tlt, a/c-cool-fee, c/fan, linen]. **D** ♦ **$19.50 - $21**, ◊ **$19.50 - $21**.

★★☆ **Coconut Grove Motel/Backpackers**, (M), 58 Macrossan St, ☎ 07 4099 5124, fax 07 4099 5144, (2 stry gr fl), 24 units [shwr, tlt, a/c-cool-fee, c/fan, TV, t/c mkg, refrig, cook fac (1)], ldry, dryer, ⊠, pool, c/park (undercover), ✆. **RO** ♦♦ **$85**, ◊ **$10**, Units 1 to 6 are ★★. AE BC DC MC VI.

Self Catering Accommodation

★★★★☆ **Balboa Apartments**, (HU), 1 Garrick St, Cnr Macrossan St, ☎ 07 4099 5222, fax 07 4099 5023, (Multi-stry gr fl), 10 units acc up to 6, (2 & 3 bedrm), [shwr, bath, tlt, hairdry, a/c-cool, c/fan, tel, TV, clock radio, CD, refrig, cook fac, micro, d/wash, ldry (in unit), blkts, linen, pillows], dryer, pool (salt water), spa, bbq, c/park (undercover), cots-fee. **D $230 - $385**, Min book applies, AE BC DC MC VI.

★★★★☆ **Beaches**, (HU), 19 The Esplanade, 500m E of PO, ☎ 07 4099 4150, fax 07 4099 5206, 27 units acc up to 8, (2 & 3 bedrm), [shwr, spa bath, tlt, hairdry, a/c-cool, c/fan, tel, TV, video, clock radio, refrig, cook fac, micro, d/wash, ldry (in unit), blkts, linen, pillows], dryer, iron, iron brd, coffee shop, pool (salt water), bbq, c/park (undercover), courtesy transfer (from Cairns). **D** ♦♦ **$240 - $299**, ◊ **$38, $1,680 - $2,093**, AE BC DC JCB MC VI.

★★★★☆ **Le Cher Du Monde**, (HU), 34 Macrossan St, 100m NW of PO, ☎ 07 4099 6400, fax 07 4099 6411, (Multi-stry gr fl), 27 units acc up to 3, (1 bedrm), [ensuite, shwr, bath, spa bath, tlt, hairdry, a/c-cool, c/fan, tel, cable tv, video, clock radio, refrig, cook fac, micro, toaster, blkts, linen, pillows], ldry, dryer, pool (salt water), bbq, c/park (undercover), secure park, cots-fee. **D** ♦♦ **$165, W** ♦♦ **$1,045**, AE BC DC EFT MC VI.

★★★★☆ **Mandalay Shalimar Apartments**, (Apt), Cnr Garrick & Beryl Sts, 700m SE of PO, ☎ 07 4099 6188, fax 07 4099 3461, (Multi-stry gr fl), 34 apts acc up to 6, (2 & 3 bedrm), [ensuite, a/c-cool, fan, tel, TV, video, clock radio, refrig, cook fac, micro, d/wash, ldry, blkts, linen], dryer, pool, spa, bbq, secure park (undercover), cots-fee, non smoking units (4), Pets on application. **RO $265 - $395**, Min book applies, ♿.

  ★★★★☆ **Metro Suites Port Douglas**, (HU), 9 Port Douglas Rd, 2km S of PO, ☎ 07 4099 6000, fax 07 4099 6300, (Multi-stry), 23 units acc up to 6, (Studio, 1, 2 & 3 bedrm), [ensuite, shwr, bath (5), spa bath (1), tlt, a/c-cool, c/fan, tel, TV, video (3), movie, clock radio, CD (1), mini bar, ldry, blkts, linen, pillows], dryer, iron, iron brd, pool, spa (communal), bbq, cots. **D $98 - $360.**

★★★★☆ **Port Douglas Apartments**, (Apt), 63 Macrossan Street, Port Douglas, ☎ 0740996199, fax 074099 6299, 17 apts acc up to 4, (1 bedrm), [shwr, bath, tlt, hairdry, a/c-cool, fan, tel, TV, video, clock radio, refrig, cook fac, micro, d/wash, toaster, blkts, linen, pillows], ldry, iron, iron brd, pool (saltwater), spa, bbq, c/park (undercover), cots-fee. **D ♦ $22, ♦♦ $44**, ch con, Min book applies, AE BC DC MC VI.

★★★★☆ **Port Douglas Coral Apartments**, (HU), 9 Blake St, 800m S of town centre, ☎ 07 4099 6166, fax 07 4099 6177, (Multi-stry gr fl), 23 units acc up to 4, [shwr, tlt, hairdry, a/c-cool, c/fan, tel, TV, clock radio, refrig, cook fac, micro, toaster, blkts, linen, pillows], pool (salt water), bbq (covered), c/park (undercover), cots. **RO ♦♦ $133 - $156, ◊ $17, W ◊ $665 - $1,092**, ch con, Min book applies, AE BC DC EFT MC VI.

★★★★☆ **Port Douglas Plantation Resort**, (HU), 1 Captain Cook Highway, 6km S of Port Douglas PO, ☎ 07 4099 3522, fax 07 4099 3544, 65 units acc up to 6, [ensuite, shwr, bath (hip) (10), tlt, hairdry, a/c-cool, c/fan, tel, cable tv, clock radio, t/c mkg, refrig, cook fac ltd, micro, toaster, ldry], iron, iron brd, ✉, coffee shop, pool (salt water), bbq (covered), mini mart, c/park (undercover), golf, gym, tennis, cots. **D ♦♦ $165 - $215, ◊ $20**, ch con, BC MC VI.

★★★★☆ **Port Douglas Quest Resort**, (SA), Cnr Mahogany & Port Douglas Rds, 2km S of PO, ☎ 07 4099 4500, fax 07 4099 4766, (Multi-stry), 52 serv apts acc up to 6, (1, 2 & 3 bedrm), [ensuite (3), shwr, tlt, hairdry, a/c, c/fan, tel, TV, clock radio, refrig, cook fac, d/wash, toaster, ldry (in unit)], lift, dryer, iron, iron brd, pool (salt water), spa, bbq (covered), c/park (undercover), secure park, cots-fee, non smoking rms (17). **D $176 - $264**, AE BC DC EFT MC VI.

★★★★☆ **Reflections of Port Douglas**, (SA), 70 Macrossan St, 150m E PO, ☎ 07 4099 4555, fax 07 4099 4050, (2 stry gr fl), 8 serv apts acc up to 7, (2 & 3 bedrm), [ensuite, shwr, bath, tlt, hairdry, a/c, c/fan, tel, TV, video, CD, refrig, cook fac, micro, d/wash, ldry (in unit)], dryer, pool (salt water), bbq, c/park (undercover), cots-fee. **D $198 - $396**, ch con, Min book all holiday times, AE BC DC MC VI.

 ★★★★☆ **Rydges Reef Resort Port Douglas**, (Apt), Previously Radisson Reef Resort Resort, 87-109 Port Douglas Rd, ☎ 07 4099 5577, fax 07 4099 5559, (2 stry), 180 apts acc up to 6, (1, 2 & 3 bedrm), [ensuite, shwr, bath, tlt, a/c-cool, c/fan, tel, TV, clock radio, refrig, cook fac, micro (on request), d/wash, toaster, ldry, linen, pillows], iron, iron brd, conv fac, ✉ (2), pool (lagoon style) (4), plygr, gym, tennis (2), cots. **D ♦♦ $180 - $380, ◊ $27**, ch con, AE BC DC JCB MC VI.

★★★★☆ **(Hotel Section)**, (Multi-stry gr fl) 299 rms (15 suites) [shwr, bath, tlt, hairdry, a/c-cool, c/fan, tel, TV, movie-fee, clock radio, t/c mkg, refrig, mini bar], ldry, lounge (TV), rm serv, ☏, cots. **RO $240 - $380**, ch con.

★★★★☆ **Sunseeker**, (HU), 7 Garrick St, 50m from beach, ☎ 07 4099 5055, fax 07 4099 5446, 9 units acc up to 5, (2 bedrm), [ensuite, shwr, spa bath, tlt, a/c, c/fan, tel, TV, clock radio, refrig, cook fac, micro, d/wash, ldry (in unit)], bathrm (2), dryer, pool (salt water), bbq, c/park (undercover), cots-fee. **D ♦♦♦♦ $165 - $228**, unit 2 is a three star plus rating. AE BC MC VI.

★★★★☆ **The Pavilions Port Douglas**, (HU), 35 Macrossan St, 600m W of 4 Mile Beach, ☎ 07 4099 4888, 20 units acc up to 2, (Studio, 1 & 2 bedrm), [shwr, spa bath, tlt, a/c-cool, a/c (2), c/fan, tel, cable tv, clock radio, t/c mkg, refrig, cook fac, micro, toaster, blkts, linen, pillows], ldry, ✉, pool, spa, bbq, c/park. **D ♦ $115 - $250, ♦♦ $115 - $250, ◊ $35**, AE BC DC EFT MC VI.

★★★★ **Beach Terraces**, (HU), 15 - 17 Garrick St, 600m S of PO, ☎ 07 4099 5998, fax 07 4099 4113, (Multi-stry gr fl), 20 units acc up to 6, [shwr, spa bath (2), tlt, a/c-cool, c/fan, tel, TV, video, clock radio, refrig, cook fac, micro, d/wash, ldry (in unit), blkts, linen, pillows], dryer, pool (salt water), spa, bbq (covered), c/park (undercover), cots-fee. **D $143 - $323**, Min book applies, AE BC DC MC VI.

★★★★ **Club Tropical Resort**, (Apt), Resort, Cnr Wharf & Macrossan Sts, ☎ 07 4099 5885, fax 07 4099 5868, 51 apts acc up to 6, [shwr, bath, tlt, hairdry, a/c-cool, c/fan, tel, TV, video, movie, CD, t/c mkg, refrig, mini bar, cook fac, micro], lift, iron, iron brd, meeting rm, ✉, pool (salt water), sauna, spa (hot) (2), 24hr reception, rm serv, c/park (undercover), cots. **D $220 - $430**, ch con, AE BC MC VI, ♿.

Operator Comment: Located in the centre of Port Douglas.

★★★★ **Coral Sea Villas**, (Villa), 68 Macrossan St, 200m from town centre, ☎ 07 4099 5511, fax 07 4099 5523, 9 villas acc up to 6, [shwr, bath (4), tlt, a/c-cool, c/fan, tel, TV, video (4), clock radio, refrig, cook fac, micro, ldry (in unit), blkts, linen, pillows], dryer, iron, iron brd, pool (salt water), bbq, c/park (undercover), cots-fee. **D ♦♦ $125 - $170, ◊ $20**, Min book applies, BC MC VI.

★★★★ **Driftwood Mantaray on Macrossan**, (HU), 65 Macrossan St, ☎ 07 4099 5119, fax 07 4099 5272, (2 stry gr fl), 17 units acc up to 6, (1, 2 & 3 bedrm), [shwr, bath, spa bath (14), tlt, hairdry, a/c-cool, c/fan, tel, TV, video, clock radio, refrig, cook fac, micro, ldry (in unit), blkts, linen, pillows], dryer, pool, spa, bbq, c/park (undercover), cots-fee. **D $125 - $305**, Min book applies, BC MC VI.

★★★★ **Garrick House**, (HU), 11 Garrick St, ☎ 07 4099 5322, fax 07 4099 5021, (Multi-stry gr fl), 19 units acc up to 4, (Studio, 1 & 2 bedrm), [shwr, bath, tlt, hairdry, a/c-cool, c/fan, tel, TV, video, clock radio, refrig, cook fac, micro, elec frypan, d/wash (15), toaster, ldry (in unit), blkts, linen, pillows], dryer, iron, iron brd, pool (salt water), t/c mkg shared, bbq, c/park (undercover), plygr, cots. **D $95 - $215**, AE BC DC MC VI.

★★★★ **Hibiscus Gardens**, (HU), Cnr Owen & Mowbray Sts, ☎ 07 4099 5315, fax 07 4099 4678, (Multi-stry gr fl), 68 units acc up to 7, (Studio, 1 & 2 bedrm), [ensuite (75), shwr, bath (66), tlt, hairdry, a/c-cool, c/fan, tel, TV, video, clock radio, refrig, cook fac, micro, toaster, blkts, linen, pillows], ldry, dryer, iron, pool (salt water), spa, bbq, c/park (undercover), cots. **D $90 - $335, W $630 - $2,345**, AE BC DC MC VI.

★★★★ **Macrossan House**, (HU), No children's facilities, 19 Macrossan St, 300m N of PO, ☎ 07 4099 4366, fax 07 4099 4377, 16 units acc up to 2, (1 bedrm), [shwr, tlt, hairdry, a/c-cool, c/fan, tel, TV, video, clock radio, refrig, cook fac, micro, toaster, ldry, blkts, linen, pillows], dryer, iron, iron brd, pool, spa, freezer, bbq, c/park. **D $130 - $157**, AE BC DC MC VI, ♿.

★★★★ **Marina Terraces**, (HU), 16 Davidson St, ☎ 07 4099 5188, fax 07 4099 5136, (Multi-stry gr fl), 17 units acc up to 5, (1 & 2 bedrm), [shwr, tlt, a/c-cool, c/fan, tel, TV, clock radio, refrig, cook fac, micro (17), d/wash (2), ldry (in unit), blkts, linen, pillows], dryer, pool (salt water), spa (1), bbq, c/park (undercover), cots-fee. **D ♦ $135 - $180, ♦♦ $135 - $180, ♦♦♦ $164 - $180, ♦♦♦♦ $164 - $180, ◊ $22**, Min book applies, AE BC DC MC VI.

★★★★ **Martinique on Macrossan**, (HU), 66 Macrossan St, 100m fr PO, ☎ 07 4099 6222, fax 07 4099 6233, (2 stry gr fl), 19 units acc up to 2, [shwr, tlt, a/c-cool, c/fan, tel, TV, video, t/c mkg, refrig, cook fac, micro, elec frypan, toaster], iron, iron brd, pool (salt water), bbq, c/park. **D $132 - $154, ◊ $20**, AE BC EFT VI.

Children in cars

Here are some hints to make things safer and more comfortable when travelling with children in your car.

- Ensure that child restraints are correctly fitted and adjusted, and suitable for the size of the children. Nothing will irritate a child more on a long trip than being uncomfortable in their child restraint and an irritated child means extra stress and distraction for the driver.
- Make sure to take a supply of games that children can play in the car without distracting the driver. Card games and board games with magnetic pieces are useful. Avoid sharp toys as these can be dangerous missiles in a crash.
- Remember that children require more frequent breaks for toilet stops and drinks.
- Don't leave children in the car while you attend to other business, especially in hot weather. Children dehydrate much more easily than adults. Even in the shade, the temperature inside a parked car can build up to dangerously high levels.

PORT DOUGLAS QLD continued...

★★★★ **Mowbray By The Sea**, (HU), 36 Mowbray St, 450m E of P.O, ☎ 07 4099 4599, fax 07 4099 4688, 16 units acc up to 4, (2 bedrm), [ensuite, shwr, bath, tlt, hairdry, a/c, c/fan, tel, TV, video, clock radio, t/c mkg, refrig, micro, d/wash, toaster, ldry, blkts, linen, pillows], dryer, iron, iron brd, pool-indoor (salt water), spa, bbq, secure park, cots-fee. D ♦♦ $185 - $240, ◊ $20, W ♦♦ $1,295 - $1,680, weekly con, Min book applies, AE BC DC EFT MC VI.

★★★★ **Nimrod Apartments**, (HU), 31 Nautilus St, Four Mile Beach, 4km S of PO, ☎ 07 4099 3399, fax 07 4099 3442, 29 units acc up to 6, (2 & 3 bedrm), [shwr, bath, tlt, a/c-cool (48), c/fan, tel, TV, refrig, cook fac, ldry (in unit), blkts, linen, pillows], dryer, iron, pool (salt water), wading pool, spa, bbq (covered), c/park (undercover), plygr, tennis, cots-fee. D $110 - $175, Min book applies, AE BC DC MC VI.

★★★★ **Port Douglas Palm Villas**, (HU), 40 Warner St, 500m W of PO, ☎ 07 4099 4822, fax 07 4099 5840, (2 stry gr fl), 21 units acc up to 2, (1 bedrm), [ensuite, shwr, tlt, a/c-cool, c/fan, tel, TV, video, clock radio, refrig, cook fac, micro, toaster, blkts, linen, pillows], ldry, iron, iron brd, pool. D $80 - $132, BC MC VI.

★★★★ **Port Douglas Reef Club**, (HU), 62 Davidson St, 800m S of PO, ☎ 07 4099 4900, fax 07 4099 4700, (2 stry gr fl), 59 units acc up to 4, (1 & 2 bedrm), [shwr, bath, tlt, hairdry, a/c, c/fan, tel, cable tv, video, clock radio, refrig, cook fac, micro, toaster, blkts, linen, pillows], ldry, dryer, iron, iron brd, pool (saltwater), spa, bbq, c/park (undercover), cots-fee. D ♦♦ $119 - $149, ♦♦♦♦ $159 - $199, ◊ $15, AE BC DC EFT MC VI, ⅃⅃.

★★★★ **Port Douglas Tropic Sands**, (HU), 21 Davidson St, 300m S of GPO, ☎ 07 4099 4533, fax 07 4099 4449, (2 stry gr fl), 14 units acc up to 4, (1 bedrm), [ensuite, shwr, tlt, hairdry, a/c-cool, c/fan, tel, TV, clock radio, refrig, cook fac, micro, toaster, blkts, linen, pillows], baby bath, ldry, iron, iron brd, pool (salt water), bbq (covered), c/park (undercover), cots-fee. D $105 - $148, W $735 - $1,036, ch con, AE BC MC VI.

★★★★ **The White House**, (HU), 19 Garrick St, 100m fr beachfront, ☎ 07 4099 5600, fax 07 4099 5006, (2 stry gr fl), 9 units acc up to 6, (1, 2 & 3 bedrm), [shwr, bath (6), tlt, hairdry, a/c-cool, c/fan, tel, TV, video, clock radio, refrig, cook fac, micro, d/wash, ldry (in unit), blkts, linen, pillows], dryer, pool (salt water), spa, bbq (covered), c/park (undercover), cots. D ♦♦ $120 - $235, ◊ $20, Min book applies, AE BC DC MC VI.

The most popular position for holiday makers. Just a short stroll to the Village of Port Douglas & only a few steps to Four Mile Beach !

Yes! We are the newest ★★★★ Holiday Accommodation in Port Douglas

• Fully self-contained, Ensuites to both rooms, main has Spa bath
• Large Balcony with fan • 26m Lap Pool and Huge Spa • Atrium between Units and pool area • Gazebo BBQ area • Under ground security Parking

Cnr Garrick & Mowbray Streets, Port Douglas, Queensland 4871
Ph: 07 4099 4599 Fax: 07 4099 4688
Email: sales@mowbraybythesea.com.au
Web Site: mowbraybythesea.com.au

mowbray
BY THE SEA

NIMROD
RESORT
APARTMENTS
AAAT ★★★★
31 Nautilus Street
Four Mile Beach
PORT DOUGLAS
Ph: 07 4099 3399
Fax: 07 4099 3442
nimrodresort@internetnorth.com.au
www.nimrod-apartments.com.au

Surrounded by a unique atmosphere and set in 1.2 hectares of lush tropical gardens located at tranquil Four Mile Beach, Nimrod Resort Apartments provide an ideal base to explore the village of Port Douglas and its surrounds, the Marlin Coast, the Great Barrier Reef and the Daintree Rainforest. 1, 2 & 3 bedrooms, fully self contained.

★★★★ **Ti Tree Resort**, (HU), 1 Barrier St, 4km S of PO 400m fr beach, ☎ 07 4099 3444, fax 07 4098 5025, (2 stry gr fl), 38 units acc up to 5, [shwr, bath (14), tlt, a/c-cool, c/fan, tel, TV, clock radio, refrig, cook fac, micro, ldry (in unit), blkts, linen, pillows], pool (salt water), spa, bbq (covered), c/park (undercover), tennis, cots-fee. D ♦♦ $121 - $165, W ♦♦ $770 - $1,155, Min book applies, BC MC VI.

★★★★ **Villa San Michele**, (HU), 39-41 Macrossan St, ☎ 07 4099 4088, fax 07 4099 4975, (Multi-stry gr fl), 40 units acc up to 4, [ensuite, shwr, bath, tlt, hairdry, a/c-cool, c/fan, tel, TV, video, clock radio, refrig, cook fac ltd, micro, toaster, blkts, linen, pillows], ldry, dryer, iron, iron brd, pool (salt water), spa, bbq, c/park (undercover), cots-fee. D $155 - $255, AE BC DC MC VI.

Operator Comment: The most central location in town, cool self contained apartments styled in a Mediterranean theme with the convenience of the restaurants at our doorstep yet only 400 meters to Four mile Beach or the Marina. Visit us today www.villasanmichele.com.au

★★★☆ **Archipelago Studio Apartments**, (HU), 72 Macrossan St, 300m to town centre, ☎ 07 4099 5387, fax 07 4099 4847, (Multi-stry gr fl), 21 units acc up to 4, (Studio), [shwr, tlt, a/c-cool, c/fan, tel, TV, clock radio, refrig, cook fac ltd, blkts, linen, pillows], ldry-fee, dryer-fee, iron, pool (salt water), bbq, c/park (undercover). D ♦♦ $89 - $159, ◊ $20, Min book applies, AE BC MC VI.

★★★☆ **Port Douglas Retreat**, (HU), 31-33 Mowbray St, 250mtrs S of PO, ☎ 07 4099 5053, fax 07 4099 5033, (2 stry gr fl), 36 units acc up to 2, [shwr, tlt, a/c, c/fan, tel, TV, movie, clock radio, refrig, cook fac, micro, toaster, ldry, blkts, linen, pillows], dryer, iron, iron brd, pool, bbq, c/park (undercover), cots. D $102 - $143, BC MC VI, ⅃⅃.

★★★☆ **Port Douglas Terrace**, (HU), 17 Esplanade, ☎ 07 4099 5397, fax 07 4099 5206, (2 stry gr fl), 17 units acc up to 5, (1 & 2 bedrm), [shwr, bath (6), tlt, a/c-cool, c/fan, tel, TV, video, clock radio, refrig, cook fac, micro, d/wash (6), ldry (in unit), linen, pillows], pool (salt water), bbq, c/park (undercover), courtesy transfer (from Cairns), tennis. D ♦♦ $120 - $240, ◊ $25, W $840 - $1,680, AE BC DC JCB MC VI.

★★★☆ **Port Douglas Vacation Village**, (HU), 71 Port Douglas Rd, 3km S of PO, ☎ 07 4099 5183, fax 07 4099 5563, 18 units acc up to 8, (2 & 4 bedrm), [shwr, tlt, hairdry, a/c-cool (17), c/fan, TV, refrig, cook fac, ldry (in unit), blkts, linen, pillows], dryer, pool (salt water), bbq (covered), c/park (undercover), ✆, tennis (half court), cots. D ♦♦ $85 - $105, W ♦♦ $510 - $630, AE BC DC MC VI.

Budget Motel Chain International

★★★☆ **Talofa**, (HU), 115 Davidson St, ☎ 07 4099 5416, fax 07 4099 5574, 12 units acc up to 4, [shwr, tlt, a/c-cool, c/fan, TV, video (5), clock radio, refrig, cook fac, blkts, linen, pillows], ldry, pool (salt water), bbq (covered), c/park (undercover), ✆, cots. D ♦♦♦ $86 - $160, ◊ $16.50, BC MC VI.

★★★☆ **The Lychee Tree**, (HU), 95 Davidson St, ☎ 07 4099 5811, fax 07 4099 5175, 20 units acc up to 5, [shwr, bath, tlt, a/c-cool, c/fan, tel, TV, video (10), clock radio, refrig, cook fac, micro, ldry (in unit), blkts, linen, pillows], dryer, pool (salt water), bbq (covered), c/park (undercover), cots-fee. D ♦♦ $115, ♦♦♦♦ $140, BC MC VI.

★★★☆ **The Mango Tree**, (HU), 91 Davidson St, 1.3km SE of PO, ☎ 07 4099 5677, fax 07 4099 5125, (2 stry gr fl), 19 units acc up to 6, (2 bedrm), [shwr, bath, tlt, a/c-cool, c/fan, tel, TV, clock radio, refrig, cook fac, micro, ldry (in unit), blkts, linen, pillows], pool (salt water), spa, bbq (covered), c/park (undercover), tennis, cots-fee. D ♦♦ $105 - $176, ◊ $11 - $22, Min book all holiday times, AE BC MC VI.

★★★☆ **The Port Douglas Outrigger**, (HU), 16 Mudlo St, 500m SE of PO, ☎ 07 4099 5662, fax 07 4099 5717, (Multi-stry gr fl), 17 units acc up to 5, (1 & 2 bedrm), [shwr, bath (2), tlt, a/c-cool, c/fan, tel, TV, movie, clock radio, refrig, cook fac, micro, d/wash, ldry (in unit), blkts, l inen, pillows], dryer, pool (salt water), bbq (covered), c/park (undercover), cots-fee. D $110 - $170, W $693 - $1,120, AE BC DC MC VI.

★★★☆ **The Port Douglas Queenslander**, (HU), 8-10 Mudlo St, 400m SW PO, ☎ 07 4099 5199, fax 07 4099 5353, (2 stry gr fl), 17 units acc up to 5, (Studio, 1 & 2 bedrm), [shwr, bath (2), spa bath (2), tlt, a/c-cool, c/fan, tel, TV, movie, clock radio, refrig, cook fac, micro, d/wash (15), ldry (in unit), blkts, linen, pillows], dryer, iron, pool-heated (solar), bbq, c/park (undercover), cots-fee. D ♦♦ $92 - $176, ◊ $16.67, W ♦♦ $644 - $1,232, BC MC VI.

★★★☆ **Tropical Nites**, (HU), 119 Davidson St, 1.5km S of PO, ☎ 07 4099 5666, fax 07 4099 5079, (2 stry), 12 units acc up to 8, (3 bedrm), [shwr, bath, tlt, a/c-cool, c/fan, tel, TV, refrig, cook fac, micro, d/wash (3), ldry (in unit), blkts, linen, pillows], dryer, pool (salt water), bbq (covered), c/park (undercover), cots-fee. D $107 - $165, W $749 - $1,155, Min book applies, AE BC MC VI. *Operator Comment: 1,2 or 3 bedroom Townhouses. Ask regarding Superior Townhouse tariffs.*

★★★☆ **Tropical Reef Apartments**, (HU), 10 Davidson St, ☎ 07 4099 5533, fax 07 4099 5642, 16 units acc up to 6, (3 bedrm), [shwr, bath, tlt, hairdry, a/c-cool, c/fan, tel, TV, video, clock radio, refrig, cook fac, micro, ldry (in unit), blkts, linen, pillows], dryer, pool (salt water) (2), bbq (covered), c/park (undercover), cots-fee. D ♦♦ $121 - $198, ♦ $18, Min book applies, BC MC VI.

★★★☆ **Whispering Palms**, (HU), 20 Langley Rd, 3km S of PO, ☎ 07 4098 5128, fax 07 4098 5762, (2 stry gr fl), 39 units acc up to 6, (Studio, 1 & 2 bedrm), [shwr, tlt, a/c-cool (22), c/fan, tel, TV, clock radio, refrig, cook fac, blkts, linen, pillows], ldry, dryer, ⊠ (Wed to Mon), bar, pool (salt water), spa, bbq, kiosk, c/park (undercover), cots-fee. D $128 - $154, ♦ $17.60, AE BC DC MC VI.

Cayman Villas Port Douglas, (Apt), 35 Mowbray St, 300m N of PO, ☎ 07 4087 2300, fax 07 4087 2350, (Multi-stry gr fl), 26 apts acc up to 7, (2 & 3 bedrm), [shwr, spa bath, tlt, a/c, c/fan, tel, cable tv, clock radio, t/c mkg, refrig, cook fac, micro, d/wash, toaster, ldry, blkts, linen, pillows], w/mach, dryer, pool, spa, bbq, secure park (undercover), cots-fee, non smoking property. D ♦♦ $198 - $326, ♦ $22, Min book applies, AE BC DC EFT MC VI, (not yet classified).

Freestyle Port Douglas, (Apt), 47 Davidson St, 400m S of PO, ☎ 07 4099 6055, fax 07 4099 5713, (2 stry gr fl), 31 apts acc up to 5, (1 & 2 bedrm), [shwr, tlt, a/c-cool, c/fan, tel, cable tv, clock radio, t/c mkg, refrig, cook fac, micro, d/wash, toaster, ldry, blkts, linen, pillows], pool, bbq, cots. D ♦ $110 - $195, ♦♦ $110 - $195, ♦ $20, ch con, AE BC DC EFT MC VI, (not yet classified).

Nautilus Holiday Apartments, (Apt), 69 Davidson St, 800m S of PO, ☎ 07 4099 4100, fax 07 4099 6099, (2 stry gr fl), 15 apts acc up to 6, (2 & 3 bedrm), [shwr, tlt, a/c-cool, c/fan, tel, TV, clock radio, t/c mkg, refrig, cook fac, micro, blkts, linen, pillows], w/mach, dryer, pool, bbq, secure park, cots-fee, non smoking units (2). D $160 - $225, Min book applies, AE BC DC EFT MC VI, (not yet classified).

Peppers, (Villa), Old Port Rd, ☎ 07 4099 1511, fax 07 4099 1499, (2 stry gr fl), 14 villas acc up to 8, (2, 3 & 4 bedrm), [shwr, spa bath, tlt, a/c, c/fan, tel, cable tv, video, clock radio, t/c mkg, refrig, cook fac, micro, d/wash, toaster, blkts, linen, pillows], ldry, w/mach, dryer, conf fac, ⊠, bbq, c/park (undercover), cots-fee. D ♦ $385 - $495, ♦♦ $385 - $495, ♦ $44, AE BC DC EFT JCB MC VI, (not yet classified).

The Regal on Macrossan, (HU), 51 Macrossan St, City centre, ☎ 07 4099 4421, fax 07 4099 4412, (Multi-stry gr fl), 30 units acc up to 4, (Studio, 1 & 2 bedrm), [ensuite, shwr, spa bath (30), tlt, hairdry, a/c, c/fan, tel, TV, video, clock radio, refrig, cook fac ltd, micro, toaster, blkts, linen, pillows], dryer, iron, iron brd, conf fac, pool, spa, bbq, secure park, cots-fee. D $125 - $285, AE BC DC MC VI, (not yet classified).

B&B's/Guest Houses

★★★★★ **Cassowary Ridge B&B**, (B&B), 12 Ocean View Rd, 6km N of Port Douglas, ☎ 07 4098 4115, fax 07 4098 4115, 2 rms [ensuite, a/c-cool, c/fan, TV, clock radio, t/c mkg, refrig], spa (plunge), secure park, non smoking rms (2). BB ♦♦ $100, MC VI.

★★★★★ **Marae Bed & Breakfast**, (B&B), Lot 1, Chooks Ridge, Shannonvale, 15km N of Port Douglas PO, ☎ 07 4098 4900, fax 07 4098 4099, (Multi-stry gr fl), 3 rms [shwr, bath (1), tlt, a/c, c/fan, TV], ldry-fee, dryer-fee, rec rm, lounge (TV), ✕, pool (salt water), t/c mkg shared, c/park (undercover) (2). BB ♦ $90, ♦♦ $130, BC MC VI.

★★★★★ **Paradise Villa**, (B&B), 63 Reef St, 25m to beach; 4km S of PO, ☎ 07 4099 3604, fax 07 4099 3604, 1 rm (1 suite) [shwr, bath, tlt, hairdry, a/c-cool, c/fan, TV, video, clock radio, t/c mkg, refrig, cook fac ltd, toaster, ldry], dryer, iron, iron brd, pool (salt water), c/park (undercover), non smoking rms. BLB ♦ $100 - $120, ♦♦ $110 - $120, BC MC VI.

Other Accommodation

Dougies Backpacker Resort, 111 Davidson St, ☎ 07 4099 6200, fax 07 4099 6047, 8 rms [a/c, c/fan, TV, refrig, ldry], shwr, tlt, dryer, iron, iron brd, rec rm, TV rm, lounge, bar, pool, cook fac, bbq, shop, ✆. D ♦♦ $55, $18, EFT MC VI.

PROSERPINE QLD

See Whitsundays Region.

QUILPIE QLD 4480

Pop 750. (954km W Brisbane), See maps on page 414, ref C7. Known as the 'Gateway to the Channel Country', Quilpie services a large sheep and cattle grazing area.

Hotels/Motels

★★★ **Quilpie Motor Inn**, (M), Brolga St, ☎ 07 4656 1277, fax 07 4656 1231, 14 units [shwr, tlt, a/c, tel, TV, movie, clock radio, t/c mkg, refrig, toaster], ldry, ⊠, bbq, dinner to unit, c/park (undercover), plygr. RO ♦ $60, ♦♦ $70, AE BC DC EFT MC VI.

★★☆ **Imperial**, (LMH), Cnr Brolga & Buln Buln Sts, ☎ 07 4656 1300, fax 07 4656 1325, 8 units [shwr, tlt, a/c, tel, TV, t/c mkg, refrig], ldry, dryer, ⊠, bbq, dinner to unit, c/park (undercover), plygr. RO ♦ $50, ♦♦ $55, ch con, AE BC DC EFT MC VI.

RAINBOW BEACH QLD 4581

Pop 850. (243km N Brisbane), See maps on page 417, ref E3. Coastal town taking its name from the towering coloured sandcliffs nearby. Bush Walking, Fishing, Scenic Drives, Surfing.

Hotels/Motels

★★★ **Rainbow Beach Motor Inn Motel**, (M), Spectrum Ave, 400m from beachfront, ☎ 07 5486 3255, fax 07 5486 3317, (Multi-stry gr fl), 19 units [shwr, bath (5), tlt, c/fan, tel, TV, clock radio, t/c mkg, refrig, micro], ⊠ (Tues-Sat), pool, dinner to unit, cots. RO ♦ $55 - $78, ♦♦ $65 - $88, ♦ $10, AE BC MC VI.

★★★ **Rainbow Sands**, (M), 42 Rainbow Beach Rd, 250m W of PO, ☎ 07 5486 3400, fax 07 5486 3492, (Multi-stry gr fl), 12 units [shwr, tlt, c/fan, tel, TV, clock radio, t/c mkg, refrig], dryer, conv fac, pool (salt water), sauna, spa, bbq, c/park (undercover), cots. D $85 - $176, W $325 - $765, RO $59 - $82.50, AE BC DC EFT MC VI.

★★☆ **Mikado Motor Inn**, (M), Cooloola Dve, ☎ 07 5486 3211, fax 07 5486 3283, (Multi-stry gr fl), 19 units [shwr, tlt, a/c-cool (10), c/fan, tel, TV, t/c mkg, refrig], ldry, w/mach-fee, ⊠ (Mon-Sat), pool, bbq, rm serv. RO ♦ $71, ♦♦ $71, ♦ $15, ch con, pen con, AE BC MC VI.

★☆ **Rainbow Beach**, (LMH), Wide Bay Esp, beachfront, ☎ 07 5486 3125, fax 07 5486 3168, 12 units [shwr, tlt, tel, TV, t/c mkg, refrig], ldry, w/mach-fee, dryer-fee, ⊠, courtesy transfer, cots. RO ♦ $45, ♦♦ $60, ♦ $15, BC EFT MC VI.

Self Catering Accommodation

★★★★ **Rainbow Getaway Holiday Apartments**, (HU), Cnr Rainbow Beach Rd & Double Island Dve, 500m E of Beach & Surf Club, ☎ 07 5486 3500, fax 07 5486 3050, (2 stry gr fl), 29 units acc up to 6, [ensuite (29), shwr, spa bath (19), tlt, fan, tel, TV, video, clock radio, refrig, cook fac, micro, elec frypan, d/wash, toaster, ldry (in unit), blkts, linen, pillows], dryer, iron, iron brd, pool-heated (salt water), bbq (covered), secure park (garage), plygr, gym. D $80 - $170, W $450 - $1,050.

★★★☆ **Rainbow Sands**, (HU), 42 Rainbow Beach Rd, 250m W of PO, ☎ 07 5486 3400, fax 07 5486 3492, (Multi-stry gr fl), 12 units acc up to 6, (Studio & 2 bedrm), [shwr, bath, tlt, c/fan, tel, TV, clock radio, refrig, cook fac, micro, d/wash, ldry (in unit), blkts, linen, pillows], dryer, iron, conv fac, pool (salt water), sauna, spa, bbq, c/park (undercover), cots. D ♦♦ $85 - $175, W ♦♦ $359 - $825, AE BC DC EFT MC VI.

★★★☆ **Rainbow Shores Baden**, (HU), Rainbow Shores Dve, 10k S Fraser Island, ☎ 07 5486 3999, fax 07 5486 3111, (Multi-stry gr fl), 40 units acc up to 8, [shwr, tlt, c/fan, heat, TV, refrig, cook fac, micro, d/wash, blkts, linen, pillows], ldry, w/mach, dryer, iron, pool (salt water), bbq, ✆, mini golf, cots-fee. D ♦♦ $100 - $120, RO ♦ $10, W ♦♦ $440 - $710, BC MC VI.

★★ **Rainbow Beach**, (HF), Wide Bay Esp, ☎ 07 5486 3125, fax 07 5486 3168, (2 stry gr fl), 8 flats acc up to 5, (2 bedrm), [shwr, tlt, TV, refrig, cook fac, blkts, linen, pillows], cots. D $80, BC EFT MC VI.

RATHDOWNEY QLD 4287

Pop 250. (102km S Brisbane), See maps on page 417, ref C8. Gateway to the wilderness areas of Mt Lindesay & Mt Barney.

Hotels/Motels

★★★ **Rathdowney**, (LMH), Mt Lindesay Hwy, opposite PO, ☎ 07 5544 1121, 6 units [shwr, tlt, a/c (1), c/fan, heat, elec blkts, TV, clock radio, t/c mkg, refrig, cook fac ltd, toaster], ldry, ⊠, pool, dinner to unit, cots. RO ♦ $45, ♦♦ $55, ♦ $5, BC MC VI.

RAVENSHOE QLD 4872

Pop 850. (1719km N Brisbane), See maps on page 415, ref B4. Industrial & tourist town on the western edge of Evelyn Tableland. Timber forests nearby - Maple, Silver Ash, Walnut. Timber mill 2km S. Little Millstream Falls, 2km down Tully Falls Road. Bowls, Golf, Scenic Drives.

Hotels/Motels

★★☆ **Club**, (LMH), Grigg St, ☎ 07 4097 6109, 8 units [shwr, tlt, fan, heat, elec blkts, tel, TV, clock radio, t/c mkg, refrig], ldry, ✗, rm serv, dinner to unit, c/park (undercover), cots. RO ∮ $35, ∮∮ $50, ∮ $10, ch con, AE BC DC MC VI.

★★☆ **Tall Timbers**, (M), Kennedy Hwy, ☎ 07 4097 6325, 4 units [shwr, tlt, fan, heat, TV, t/c mkg, refrig], ldry, ✗, c/park (undercover), ✆, cots. RO ∮ $40, ∮∮ $50, ∮ $9, BC EFT MC VI.

Self Catering Accommodation

★★★★ **Millstream Retreat**, (Cotg), Kennedy Hwy, 12km N of Ravenshoe, ☎ 07 4097 6785, fax 07 4097 6785, 2 cotgs acc up to 5, [shwr, tlt, c/fan, heat, clock radio, refrig, cook fac, micro, toaster, ldry (in unit), blkts, linen, pillows], dryer, iron, iron brd, c/park (carport), cots. D ∮∮ $105, ∮ $20, W ∮∮ $630, ∮ $80, BC MC VI.

★★★★ **The Pond Cottage**, (Cotg), Tully Falls Rd, 9km S of Kennedy Hwy junction, ☎ 07 4097 7189, fax 07 4097 7189, 1 cotg acc up to 6, [shwr, tlt, hairdry, fan, heat (pot belly stove), TV, clock radio, t/c mkg, refrig, cook fac, micro, elec frypan, toaster, blkts, linen, pillows], iron, iron brd, spa (private outdoor htd). BLB ∮∮ $115, ∮ $11, $450, BC MC VI.

Possum Valley Rainforest Cottages, (Cotg), Evelyn Central, via Ravenshoe, 30km S of Atherton, ☎ 07 4097 8177, fax 07 4097 8177, 2 cotgs acc up to 6, (3 bedrm), [shwr, bath (1), tlt, heat, t/c mkg, refrig, cook fac, blkts, linen, pillows], bbq, c/park (1). D ∮∮ $75, ∮ $5, W ∮∮ $350, ∮ $20, ch con, BC MC VI, (not yet classified).

B&B's/Guest Houses

Hoe's Point, (B&B), No children's facilities, Lot 904 Park Lane, 12km W of PO, ☎ 07 4097 7467, fax 07 4097 7467, 1 rm [bath, tlt, hairdry, c/fan, wood heat, t/c mkg, refrig, mini bar, toaster], sauna, bbq (covered), c/park (undercover), non smoking property. BB ∮ $110, ∮∮ $130, MC VI, (not yet classified).

Jacklin Park Host Farm, (B&B), (Farm), Greys Lane, ☎ 07 4097 6379, (2 stry gr fl), 2 rms [shwr, spa bath, tlt, hairdry, heat, elec blkts, clock radio, t/c mkg, refrig, cook fac ltd, micro, elec frypan, toaster], ldry, dryer, iron, iron brd, lounge (TV, cd), ✗, bbq (covered), c/park (undercover), tennis-fee, cots, non smoking property. BB ∮∮ $85, ∮ $10, ch con, (not yet classified).

REDLYNCH QLD 4870

Pop 1,002. (1732km N Brisbane), See maps on page 415, ref C3. Satellite suburb of Cairns.

B&B's/Guest Houses

★★★☆ **Zanzoo Retreat**, (B&B), Lot 4 Mary Parker Dve, ☎ 07 4039 2842, fax 07 4039 0450, (2 stry gr fl), 6 rms [ensuite (3), spa bath (1), a/c-cool (2), a/c (4), c/fan (3), clock radio, doonas], ldry, w/mach, dryer, lounge, ✗, spa, t/c mkg shared, refrig, bbq, c/park (undercover), non smoking property. BB ∮ $90 - $120, ∮∮ $110 - $140, ∮ $25, ch con, 3 rooms ★★★★★, Min book applies, BC EFT MC VI.

RICHMOND QLD 4822

Pop 750. (1660km NW Brisbane), See maps on page 414, ref B5. Important pastoral centre.

Hotels/Motels

★★ **Entrikens Pioneer**, (M), 82 Goldring St, Opposite Marine Fossil Display, ☎ 07 4741 3188, fax 07 4741 3358, 16 units [shwr, tlt, a/c-cool, heat, tel, TV, clock radio, t/c mkg, refrig], ldry, bbq, c/park (undercover), cots-fee. RO ∮ $61, ∮∮ $72, ∮ $11, ch con, Units 14 to 17 ★★★. AE BC MC VI.

★★ **Midway**, (M), Flinders Hwy, ☎ 07 4741 3192, fax 07 4741 3221, 7 units [shwr, tlt, a/c-cool, c/fan, TV (direct dial), radio, t/c mkg, refrig], ldry, w/mach-fee, dryer-fee, ✗, dinner to unit, petrol, c/park (undercover), ✆, plygr. RO ∮ $49.50, ∮∮ $60.50, ∮ $11, ch con, AE BC DC EFT MC VI.

ROBINA QLD

See Gold Coast Region.

Rates may change. Check before booking.

ROCKHAMPTON QLD 4700

Pop 57,800. (637km N Brisbane), See maps on page 416, ref C6. Known as the Beef Capital of Australia. A huge metal sundial 'The Capricorn Spire' marks the crossing of the Tropic of Capricorn. Boat cruises on the Fitzroy River, Aboriginal Dreamtime centre, Civic Theatre, two botanic gardens (one with a zoo), Cultural Centre, Museums. Historic buildings in Quay St, alongside the Fitzroy River, includes ANZ Bank (1864) and the nearby Customs House (1901). Olsens and Cammoo Caves - 22km north of Rockhampton off the Bruce Hwy. Mt Morgan Mine (40km SW) is the largest man-made hole in the southern hemisphere. Mt Hay Gemstone Tourist Park. Harley Davidson Tours. Art Gallery, Bowls, Fishing, Golf, Greyhound Racing, Horse Racing, Shooting, Squash, Swimming, Tennis, Water Skiing.

Hotels/Motels

★★★★☆ **Cattle City Motor Inn**, (M), 139 Gladstone Rd, ☎ 07 4927 7811, fax 07 4922 5448, (2 stry gr fl), 26 units (4 suites) [shwr, bath, spa bath (3), tlt, hairdry, a/c, c/fan (20), tel, TV, video, clock radio, t/c mkg, refrig, mini bar, micro (3)], ldry, w/mach-fee, dryer-fee, iron, conv fac, ✗, pool, bbq, rm serv, c/park (undercover) (20), gym, cots-fee. RO ∮ $84 - $95, ∮∮ $95 - $105, ∮ $11, Suite D $113 - $146, ch con, Some rooms of a 3.5 star rating. AE BC DC JCB MC VI, ♿.

★★★★☆ **Centre Point Motor Inn**, (M), 131 George St (Bruce Hwy), ☎ 07 4927 8844, fax 07 4927 8732, (2 stry gr fl), 60 units [shwr, spa bath (3), tlt, hairdry (30), a/c, tel, TV, movie, clock radio, t/c mkg, refrig, mini bar], ldry, dryer, ✗, pool, 24hr reception, rm serv, dinner to unit, c/park (undercover), cots-fee. RO ∮ $89, ∮∮ $99, ∮ $11, ch con, AE BC DC MC MP VI, ♿.

★★★★☆ **Country Comfort Rockhampton**, (M), 86 Victoria Pde, ☎ 07 4927 9933, fax 07 4927 1615, (Multi-stry), 72 units (6 suites) [shwr, bath, tlt, hairdry, a/c, tel, TV, movie, clock radio, t/c mkg, refrig, mini bar], lift, ldry, iron, iron brd, conv fac, ✗, pool, bbq, 24hr reception, rm serv, c/park (undercover) (15), ✆, cots, non smoking flr (3). RO ∮ $102, ∮∮ $102, ∮ $15, ch con, fam con, AE BC DC MC VI.

★★★★☆ **Sun Palms Hotel Motel**, (LMH), 160 Gladstone Rd, 300m N Tourist Information Centre, ☎ 07 4927 4900, fax 07 4927 9643, 45 units (1 & 2 bedrm), [shwr, spa bath, tlt, hairdry, a/c, c/fan, tel, fax (18), cable tv, video, clock radio, t/c mkg, refrig, micro, toaster], ldry-fee, dryer-fee, iron, iron brd, conv fac, ✗, pool (salt water), rm serv, dinner to unit, c/park (undercover), cots. RO ∮ $78, ∮∮ $88 - $90, ∮ $12 - $16, ch con, AE BC DC EFT MC VI, ♿.

★★★★☆ **Tropical Wanderer Resort**, (M), 394 Yaamba Rd (Bruce Hwy) North Rockhampton, ☎ 07 4926 3822, fax 07 4928 8510, 24 units [shwr, tlt, a/c-cool (29), c/fan, tel, TV, radio (29), t/c mkg, refrig, cook fac (10), toaster], ldry, rec rm, conv fac, ✗, pool, bbq, dinner to unit, c/park (undercover) (10), plygr, tennis (half court), cots-fee. RO ∮ $80 - $110, ∮∮ $91 - $110, ∮ $11, ch con, AE BC DC JCB MC MP VI, ♿.

★★★★ **Ambassador on the Park**, (M), 161 George St, ☎ 07 4927 5855, fax 07 4922 2172, (Multi-stry gr fl), 70 units (3 suites) [shwr, bath, tlt, hairdry, a/c-cool, heat, tel, cable tv, movie, clock radio, t/c mkg, refrig, mini bar (44)], lift, ldry, conv fac, ✗, pool, rm serv, dinner to unit, secure park, ✆, cots-fee. BLB ∮ $77 - $88, ∮∮ $99 - $121, ∮ $16.50, RO ∮ $66, ∮∮ $88 - $99, ∮ $16.50, ch con, 4 rooms ★★☆, 22 rooms ★★★☆, AE BC DC MC VI.

★★★★ **Central Park**, (M), 224 Murray St, ☎ 07 4927 2333, fax 07 4927 3237, (2 stry gr fl), 45 units [shwr, spa bath (2), tlt, hairdry (20), a/c-cool (20), a/c (25), heat (3), tel, cable tv (20), video, clock radio, t/c mkg, refrig], ldry, dryer, iron, ✗ (Mon-Sat), pool (salt water), pool, rm serv, dinner to unit, c/park (undercover), cots-fee. RO ∮ $57 - $74, ∮∮ $68 - $85, ∮ $12, ch con, 22 units of a 3 star plus rating. AE BC DC EFT MC MP VI, ♿.

★★★★ **Dreamtime Lodge**, (M), Bruce Hwy, 6km N of Rockhampton, ☎ 07 4936 4600, fax 07 4936 4611, 30 units (1 suite) [shwr, tlt, hairdry, a/c, tel, cable tv, clock radio, t/c mkg, refrig], ldry, dryer, iron, iron brd, conf fac, ✗, pool, dinner to unit (Mon to Sat), ✆, cots. RO ∮ $64 - $68, ∮∮ $64 - $72, Suite RO $110, BC MC VI, ♿.

★★★★ **Regency on Albert Street**, (M), Cnr Albert & Campbell Sts, ☎ 07 4922 6222, fax 07 4922 2573, (2 stry gr fl), 45 units (4 suites) [shwr, bath (6), spa bath (3), tlt, hairdry, a/c-cool, c/fan, heat, tel, TV, movie, clock radio, t/c mkg, refrig, mini bar, cook fac (4)], ldry, dryer-fee, conv fac, ⊠, pool, 24hr reception, c/park (undercover), cots-fee. **RO 👤 $77, 👥 $81 - $110, Suite D 👥 $91 - $110**, AE BC DC EFT MC VI.

★★★★ **Rockhampton Palms Motor Inn**, (M), 55 George St, 1.5k S.W of P.O, ☎ 07 4922 6577, fax 07 4922 6889, 21 units [shwr, tlt, hairdry, a/c-cool, tel, cable tv, movie, clock radio, t/c mkg, refrig, mini bar, micro, toaster], ldry, iron, iron brd, pool (salt water), bbq, rm serv, dinner to unit, c/park (undercover), cots-fee, non smoking units (8). **RO 👤 $69, 👥 $79**, ch con, AE BC DC EFT JCB MC VI, ♿.

★★★★ **True Blue Motor Inn**, (M), Bruce Hwy, Parkhurst, 3km N of Yeppoon turnoff, ☎ 07 4936 1777, fax 07 4936 1951, 25 units [shwr, bath (5), spa bath (2), tlt, a/c, tel, cable tv, movie, clock radio, t/c mkg, refrig], ldry, dryer, pool, spa, bbq, dinner to unit, c/park (undercover), boat park, plygr, cots. **RO 👤 $50, 👥 $60, ♙ $10**, ch con, AE BC DC EFT MC VI, ♿.

GOLDEN CHAIN

★★★☆ **Archer Park**, (M), 39 Albert St, ☎ 07 4927 9266, fax 07 4922 5750, (2 stry gr fl), 26 units [shwr, bath, spa bath (5), tlt, a/c, tel, TV, video, clock radio, t/c mkg, refrig, cook fac (2)], ldry, dryer, iron, iron brd, conv fac, ⊠ (Mon to Sat), pool, rm serv, dinner to unit, c/park (undercover) (18), cots. **RO 👤 $69, 👥 $79 - $85, 👥👥 $97 - $18, ♙ $10**, AE BC BTC DC EFT MC VI, ♿.

FLAG Flag Choice Hotels

★★★☆ **Club Crocodile Motor Inn**, (M), Cnr Albert & Alma Sts, ☎ 07 4927 7433, fax 07 4927 3815, (2 stry gr fl), 44 units [shwr, spa bath (2), tlt, a/c, tel, TV, video-fee, movie, clock radio, t/c mkg, refrig], ldry, dryer, conv fac, ⊠ (Mon - Sat), pool, rm serv, dinner to unit, c/park (undercover), cots-fee. **RO 👤 $89 - $115, 👥 $78 - $95, ♙ $12**, ch con, AE BC DC MC MP VI, ♿.

Best Western

★★★☆ **Fitzroy Motor Inn**, (M), 78 Fitzroy St, Cnr Campbell St 2 minutes to city centre, ☎ 07 4927 9255, fax 07 4922 1828, 22 units [shwr, bath (1), spa bath (5), tlt, a/c, tel, TV, movie, clock radio, t/c mkg, refrig], ldry, w/mach-fee, dryer-fee, conv fac, ⊠ (Mon-Sat), pool (salt water), rm serv, c/park (undercover), cots-fee. **RO 👤 $74 - $85, 👥 $85 - $96, ♙ $12**, ch con, AE BC DC EFT MC VI.

AAA Tourism Special Rates

★★★☆ **Glenmore Palms**, (M), 520 Bruce Hwy, Glenmore, ☎ 07 4926 1144, fax 07 4926 1789, 38 units [shwr, tlt, a/c, tel, cable tv, clock radio, t/c mkg, refrig, cook fac (2), cook fac ltd (4)], ldry, conv fac, ⊠, pool (salt water), spa, rm serv, dinner to unit, cots-fee. **RO 👤 $75.50 - $89, 👥 $80.50 - $100, ♙ $10 - $11**, ch con, AE BC DC MC VI, ♿.

AAA Tourism Special Rates

★★★☆ **Golden Fountain**, (M), 166 Gladstone Rd, ☎ 07 4927 1055, fax 07 4927 4398, 31 units [shwr, tlt, hairdry, a/c, c/fan (5), tel, TV, movie, clock radio, t/c mkg, refrig, cook fac (9), micro (11)], ldry, dryer, iron, iron brd, pool, bbq, rm serv, dinner to unit, c/park (undercover) (27), plygr, cots-fee. **RO 👤 $70 - $88, ♙ $11**, ch con, Units 15, 16 & 23 to 26 ★★☆. AE BC DC EFT MC VI.

★★★☆ **Gracemere Motor Inn**, (M), O'Shanesy St, Gracemere 4702, 8km S of Rockhampton PO, ☎ 07 4933 2233, 17 units [shwr, bath, spa bath (2), tlt, hairdry, a/c-cool, tel, TV, video, clock radio, t/c mkg, refrig, mini bar], ldry, dryer, conv fac, ⊠ (Tues-Sat), pool, rm serv, dinner to unit, c/park (undercover), cots-fee. **RO 👤 $58 - $64, 👥 $62 - $66, ♙ $11**, ch con, AE BC DC MC VI, ♿.

★★★☆ **Leichhardt Hotel - Rockhampton**, (LH), Cnr Bolsover & Denham Sts, ☎ 07 4927 6733, fax 07 4927 8075, (Multi-stry gr fl), 89 rms (8 suites) [shwr, bath (60), tlt, hairdry, a/c-cool (29), a/c (60), tel, cable tv, radio, t/c mkg, refrig, mini bar (60)], lift, ldry, dryer, iron, business centre, conv fac, ⊠, pool, 24hr reception, rm serv, dinner to unit, ☏, cots. **D $53 - $136**, 22 rooms ★★☆ & 16 units ★☆. AE BC DC EFT MC VI.

GOLDEN CHAIN

★★★☆ **Rocky Gardens Motor Inn**, (M), 292 Lower Dawson Rd, 500m S Capricorn Spire, ☎ 07 4922 9200, fax 07 4921 3717, (2 stry gr fl), 28 units [shwr, bath (3), tlt, a/c, tel, cable tv, video, clock radio, t/c mkg, refrig], ldry, dryer, iron, iron brd, ⊠, pool (salt water), bbq, rm serv, dinner to unit, cots. **RO 👤 $64, 👥 $70, ♙ $10**, ch con, AE BC DC MC VI, ♿.

AAA Tourism Special Rates — Sundowner Chain Motor Inns

★★★☆ **Sundowner Chain Motor Inns**, (M), 112 Gladstone Rd, ☎ 07 4927 8866, fax 07 4927 9711, (2 stry gr fl), 32 units [shwr, tlt, hairdry (17), a/c, tel, cable tv, movie, clock radio, t/c mkg, refrig, mini bar, cook fac (2)], ldry, dryer, ⊠, pool, rm serv, dinner to unit, c/park (undercover), ☏, cots-fee. **RO 👤 $57 - $110.50, 👥 $62 - $110.50, ♙ $11**, ch con, AE BC DC MC VI, ♿.

FLAG Flag Choice Hotels

★★★☆ **Travellers Motor Inn**, (M), 110 George St, ☎ 07 4927 7900, fax 07 4922 2100, (2 stry gr fl), 28 units [shwr, tlt, hairdry (20), a/c, tel, TV, video-fee, clock radio, t/c mkg, refrig, mini bar, toaster], ldry, iron (20), iron brd, conf fac, ⊠ (Except Public Hols), bar, pool, rm serv, c/park (undercover), cots. **RO 👤 $63 - $88, 👥 $69 - $94, ♙ $6**, AE BC DC EFT MC VI.

★★★☆ **Tropical Gateway Motor Inn**, (M), 122 Gladstone Rd, ☎ 07 4927 8822, fax 07 4922 1148, (2 stry gr fl), 28 units [shwr, tlt, a/c-cool, tel, TV, movie, clock radio, t/c mkg, refrig, ldry], ⊠ (Mon-Sat), pool, rm serv, dinner to unit, c/park (undercover) (10), cots-fee. **RO 👤 $55, 👥 $60 - $65, ♙ $10**, ch con, AE BC DC MC VI, ♿.

★★★☆ **Wintersun**, (M), Bruce Hwy, ☎ 07 4928 8722, fax 07 4926 1036, (2 stry gr fl), 27 units [shwr, tlt, hairdry, a/c, tel, TV, clock radio, t/c mkg, refrig, toaster], ldry, dryer, ⊠ (Mon to Sat), pool, spa, rm serv, dinner to unit, c/park (undercover), cots-fee. **RO 👤 $66, 👥 $71 - $77, 👤👥 $88, 👥👥 $99, ♙ $10**, ch con, AE BC DC EFT MC VI.

★★★ **Ambassador Motor Inn**, (M), Yaamba Rd, ☎ 07 4928 2222, fax 07 4926 1873, (2 stry gr fl), 32 units [shwr, tlt, a/c-cool, c/fan, tel, TV, clock radio, t/c mkg, refrig, cook fac (2)], ldry, dryer, conv fac, ⊠ (Mon to Fri), pool, rm serv, dinner to unit, c/park (undercover), cots, non smoking units (2). **D 👤 $53, 👥 $57, ♙ $12**, AE BC DC MC VI.

★★★ **Cambridge**, (LMH), Cnr Bolsover & Cambridge Sts, ☎ 07 4922 3006, fax 07 4922 4051, (2 stry gr fl), 15 units (3 suites) [shwr, bath, tlt, a/c, tel, cable tv, movie, clock radio, t/c mkg, refrig], ldry, dryer, conv fac, ⊠, rm serv, dinner to unit, c/park (undercover) (6), ☏, cots. **RO 👤 $65, 👥 $75, ♙ $5, Suite RO $95**, ch con, AE BC DC EFT MC VI.

★★★ **Castle Court Motor Inn**, (M), 75 Gladstone Rd, 450m fr Railway station, ☎ 07 4927 5377, fax 07 4921 2395, 23 units [shwr, tlt, a/c, c/fan (8), tel, TV, video-fee, t/c mkg, refrig], ✕ (except Sat & P/hols), pool, rm serv, c/park (undercover), cots-fee. **RO 👤 $52, 👥 $57, ♙ $11**, ch con, AE BC DC MC VI, ♿.

For Accommodation Booking information - see page 27

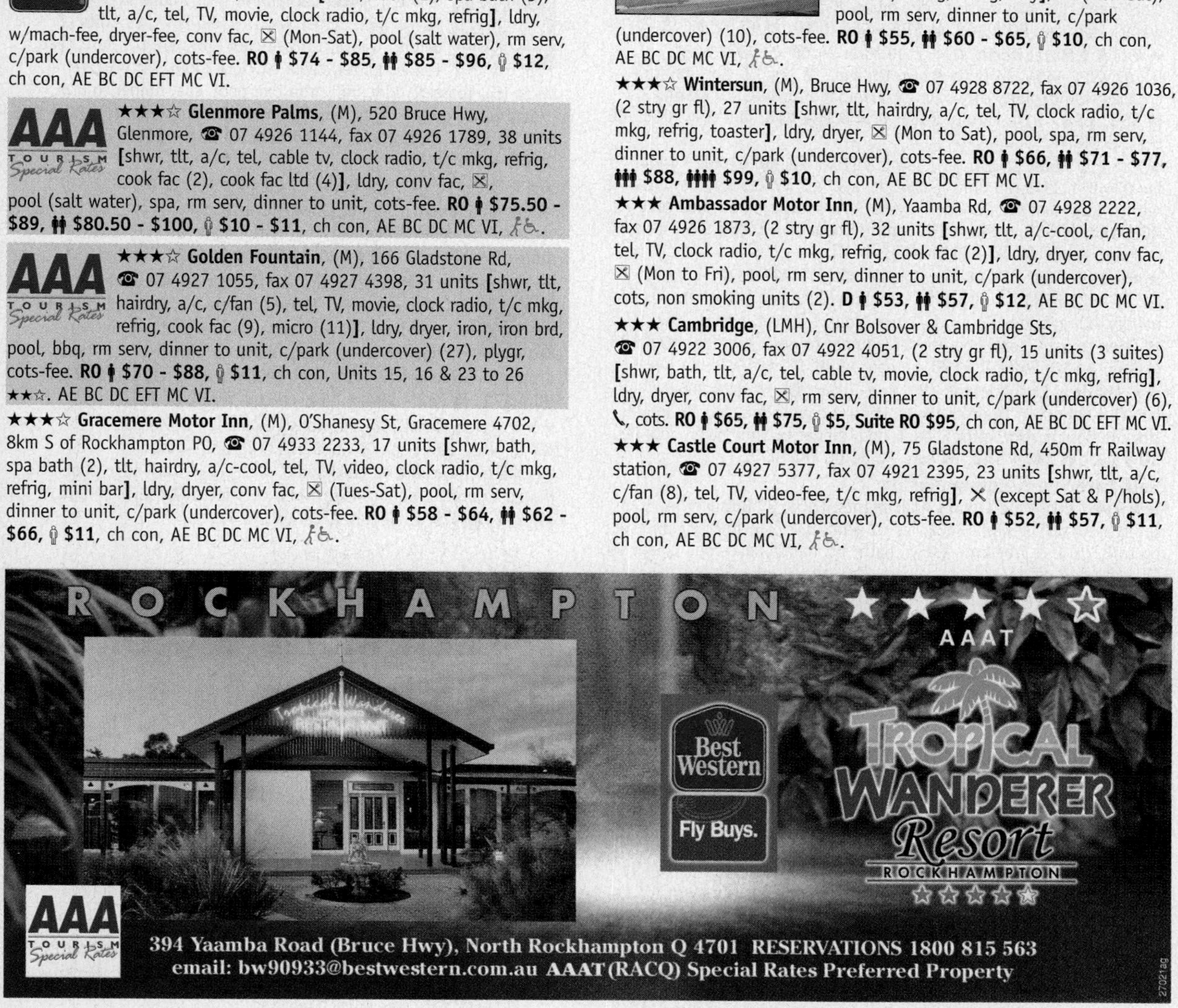

ROCKHAMPTON QLD continued...

★★★ **Citywalk Motor Inn Rockhampton**, (M), Cnr Campbell & William Sts, 800m W of PO, ☎ 07 4922 6009, fax 07 4922 6009, (2 stry gr fl), 16 units [shwr, tlt, a/c-cool, c/fan, tel, TV, clock radio, t/c mkg, toaster], ldry. **BLB ♦ $52, ♦♦ $57, ◊ $11**, AE BC DC EFT MC VI.

★★★ **Motel Lodge**, (M), 100 Gladstone Rd, ☎ 07 4922 5726, fax 07 4927 3130, (2 stry gr fl), 15 units [shwr, tlt, hairdry (6), a/c-cool, c/fan, heat (9), tel, cable tv, clock radio, t/c mkg, refrig, cook fac ltd, micro (9)], pool, cots-fee. **RO ♦ $52, ♦♦ $58**, ch con, BC MC VI.

★★★ **Parkhurst Motel**, (M), 1434 Bruce Hwy, Parkhurst, ☎ 07 4936 1126, fax 07 4936 1897, 12 units [shwr, tlt, a/c, c/fan, tel, TV, clock radio, t/c mkg, refrig], ldry, pool, dinner to unit, c/park (undercover), cots-fee. **RO ♦ $32 - $40, ♦♦ $39 - $49, ◊ $8**, ch con, Units 1 to 6 are ★★☆. BC EFT MC VI.

★★★ **Porkys**, (M), 141 George St, 800m SW from PO, city centre & Rail Station, ☎ 07 4927 8100, 10 units [shwr, tlt, a/c, tel, TV, clock radio, t/c mkg, refrig], ldry, iron, c/park (undercover), cots. **BB ♦♦ $48 - $53, BLB ♦ $43 - $48**, AE BC MC VI.

★★★ **Rockhampton Court Motor Inn**, (M), 78 George St, ☎ 07 4927 8277, fax 07 4927 8277, (2 stry gr fl), 20 units [shwr, spa bath (2), tlt, hairdry, a/c, tel, TV, video (2), clock radio, t/c mkg, refrig, cook fac ltd, toaster], ldry, w/mach-fee, dryer-fee, pool (salt water), spa, bbq, c/park (undercover), cots. **RO ♦ $58, ♦♦ $68, ◊ $11**, ch con, AE BC DC MC VI.

★★★ **Rocky City**, (M), 11 Albert St, ☎ 07 4922 6800, fax 07 4922 6805, 23 units (1 & 3 bedrm), [a/c-cool, tel, cable tv, clock radio, t/c mkg, refrig, cook fac (1), micro, pillows], ldry, w/mach, dryer, ⊠, pool, meals to unit, c/park (undercover), cots-fee, Pets allowed. **BB ♦ $68 - $75, ♦♦ $75 - $82, ◊ $23**, ch con, weekly con, AE BC DC EFT MC VI, ♿.

★★★ **Simpsons**, (M), 156 George St, ☎ 07 4927 7800, (2 stry gr fl), 17 units [shwr, tlt, a/c, tel, TV, clock radio, t/c mkg, refrig], ldry, w/mach-fee, dryer-fee, pool, cots-fee. **RO ♦♦ $58, ◊ $7**, AE BC DC MC VI.

★★★ **The David**, (M), 209 Musgrave St, ☎ 07 4927 4333, fax 07 4927 4333, (2 stry gr fl), 36 units [shwr, tlt, a/c, tel, TV, video, clock radio, t/c mkg, refrig], ldry, dryer, ⊠ (Mon to Sat), pool (salt water), cots-fee. **RO ♦ $49, ♦♦ $55 - $58, ◊ $9**, AE BC DC MC VI.

★★☆ **A 1 Motel North**, (LMH), 30 Main St, ☎ 07 4922 4251, fax 07 4922 4454, 14 units [shwr, tlt, a/c, tel (7), TV, clock radio, t/c mkg, refrig], ldry, conv fac, ⊠ (Mon-Sat), rm serv. **RO ♦ $44, ♦♦♦ $53, ◊ $8 - $10, Family Room of 4 D ♦♦♦♦ $68**, fam con, AE BC DC EFT JCB MC VI.

★★☆ **A 1 Motel South**, (M), 134 Gladstone Rd, ☎ 07 4927 4944, fax 07 4921 2343, 25 units [shwr, tlt, a/c, tel, TV, clock radio, t/c mkg, refrig], ldry, conf fac (function rooms), ✕, pool, c/park (undercover). **RO ♦ $53, ♦♦ $58, ◊ $8 - $10, Family Room of 4 D ♦♦♦♦ $74**, ch con, fam con, AE BC DC EFT JCB MC MCH MP VI.

★★☆ **Motel 98**, (M), 98 Victoria Pde, ☎ 07 4927 5322, fax 07 4927 5883, (2 stry gr fl), 26 units (2 suites) [shwr, tlt, hairdry (1), a/c, tel, TV, movie, clock radio, t/c mkg, refrig], ldry, ⊠ (Mon to Sat), pool, bbq, rm serv, dinner to unit, cots-fee. **RO ♦ $85, ♦♦♦ $95, ◊ $10, Suite D $120**, ch con, AE BC DC MC VI.

★★ **Charlton Lodge Motel**, (M), Bruce Hwy, ☎ 07 4928 2066, fax 07 4928 4000, 10 units [shwr, tlt, a/c-cool, c/fan, tel, TV, movie, clock radio, t/c mkg, refrig], pool, bbq, dinner to unit, plygr, cots-fee. **RO ♦ $43, ♦♦ $47 - $49**, ch con, AE BC DC EFT MC VI.

Self Catering Accommodation

★★★★☆ **City Ville Luxury Apartments**, (HU), 21 Bolsover St, 1 km N City Mall, ☎ 07 4922 8322, fax 07 4922 8316, (2 stry), 17 units acc up to 8, (1, 2 & 3 bedrm), [shwr, bath, tlt, hairdry, a/c-cool, c/fan, tel, TV, video-fee, refrig, cook fac, micro, d/wash (4), ldry (in unit) (4), blkts, linen, pillows], ldry, dryer, pool (salt water), spa, bbq, c/park (undercover), cots-fee. **D $75 - $190**, AE BC DC MC VI.

★★★★☆ **The Coffeehouse Apartment Hotel**, (Apt), Cnr Williams & Bolsover Sts, 150m E of PO, ☎ 07 4927 5722, fax 07 4927 5186, (2 stry), 11 apts (1 bedrm), [shwr, tlt, hairdry, a/c, tel, fax, TV, movie, clock radio, CD, t/c mkg, refrig, mini bar, cook fac, micro, toaster], ldry-fee, iron, iron brd, ⊠, pool (salt water), rm serv, dinner to unit, c/park (undercover), cots-fee, non smoking units. **D $132**, AE BC DC EFT MC VI.

★★★★ **(Motel Section)**, 11 units [shwr, tlt, hairdry, a/c, tel, TV, movie, clock radio, CD, t/c mkg, refrig, mini bar, toaster], iron, iron brd, non smoking units. **RO ♦♦ $104 - $115, ◊**.

★★★★ **Rockhampton Serviced Apartments**, (HU), 128 Denham St, 500m W of PO, ☎ 07 4922 9222, fax 07 4922 9333, (2 stry gr fl), 9 units acc up to 6, (1 & 2 bedrm), [shwr, tlt, a/c, c/fan, tel, TV, video, clock radio, refrig, cook fac, micro, toaster, ldry (in unit), blkts, linen, pillows], dryer, iron, iron brd, pool (salt water), c/park (undercover), cots. **D $88 - $115.50, W $550 - $748, RO $71.50**, AE BC DC MC VI.

Pop Nominal, (739km NW Brisbane), See maps on page 414, ref D6. Gateway to Carnarvon Gorge.

Hotels/Motels

★★ **Rolleston**, (LMH), Cnr Warrijo & Comet Sts, ☎ 07 4984 4544, fax 07 4984 3445, 6 units [shwr, tlt, a/c-cool, TV, t/c mkg, refrig, toaster], ⊠ (Mon - Sat), bbq, ☏. **RO ♦ $55, ♦♦ $65, ◊ $10**, BC EFT MC VI.

Pop 5,750. (479km W Brisbane), See maps on page 414, ref D7. Known as the Gateway to the Outback. Commercial centre of the Maranoa District producing wool, wheat and beef.

Hotels/Motels

★★★★ **Overlander Homestead**, (M), Warrego Hwy, 2 km E of McDonalds, ☎ 07 4622 3555, fax 07 4622 2805, 33 units [shwr, bath (10), tlt, hairdry, a/c, elec blkts, tel, cable tv, video, clock radio, t/c mkg, refrig, mini bar], ldry, conv fac, ⊠, pool, spa, bbq, rm serv, dinner to unit, cots-fee. **RO ♦ $77 - $80, ♦♦ $88 - $91, ◊ $11**, Stables for horses available. AE BC DC MC VI, ♿.

★★★★ **Starlight Motor Inn**, (M), 20B Bowen St, 5 km E of McDonalds, ☎ 07 4622 2666, fax 07 4622 2111, 18 units (2 bedrm), [shwr, spa bath (2), tlt, a/c, c/fan, tel, TV, clock radio, t/c mkg, refrig, cook fac ltd, micro, toaster], ldry-fee, dryer-fee, iron, iron brd, conv fac, ✕ (Mon to Fri), rm serv, dinner to unit, cots-fee, non smoking units (10). **RO ♦ $71.50, ♦♦ $82.50 - $85.80, ◊ $11**, AE BC CC DC EFT MC VI, ♿.

★★★☆ **Bottle Tree Gardens Motel**, (M), 22 Bowen St, ☎ 07 4622 6111, fax 07 4622 6499, 18 units [shwr, spa bath (6), tlt, a/c, c/fan, tel, cable tv, clock radio, t/c mkg, refrig, cook fac ltd, micro, toaster], bbq, dinner to unit, cots, non smoking rms (6). **RO ♦ $62.70 - $71.50, ♦♦ $68.20 - $77, ◊ $10**, AE BC DC EFT MC VI, ♿.

 ★★★☆ **Motel Carnarvon**, (M), Injune Rd, ☎ 07 4622 1599, fax 07 4622 4147, 20 units (2 bedrm), [shwr, tlt, a/c-cool (16), a/c (4), fan, heat, elec blkts, tel, cable tv, clock radio, t/c mkg, refrig, micro (5), toaster], ldry, iron, iron brd, pool, spa, dinner to unit, c/park (undercover), plygr, cots-fee, non smoking units (9). **RO ♦ $55 - $59, ♦♦ $62 - $68, ◊ $10, 2 Bedroom RO $98 - $110**, ch con, AE BC DC EFT MC MCH VI.

★★★ **Bryants**, (M), Cnr Bowen & Gregory Sts, ☎ 07 4622 3777, fax 07 4622 2683, 10 units [shwr, tlt, a/c-cool (6), a/c (4), elec blkts, tel, cable tv, clock radio, t/c mkg, refrig, cook fac (1), toaster], ldry, dinner to unit, cots. **RO ♦ $65, ♦♦ $75, ◊ $11**, AE BC DC MC VI.

 ★★★ **Mandalay**, (M), 39 Quintin St, ☎ 07 4622 2711, fax 07 4622 2692, 12 units [shwr, tlt, a/c, tel, cable tv, clock radio, t/c mkg, refrig, toaster], ldry, iron, iron brd, res liquor license, pool, dinner to unit (Mon to Thurs), c/park (undercover) (3), cots, non smoking units (11). **D $121, RO ♦ $71, ♦♦ $82 - $84, ◊ $11**, ch con, AE BC DC MC MP VI.

★★★ **Roma Motel**, (M), Previously Roma. 11 Bowen St, ☎ 07 4622 2288, fax 07 4622 4723, 25 units [shwr, tlt, a/c, elec blkts, tel, cable tv, clock radio, t/c mkg, refrig], ldry, pool, bbq, dinner to unit, c/park (undercover), cots-fee. **RO ♦ $57, ♦♦ $66, ♦♦♦ $72, ♦♦♦♦ $79**, ch con, AE BC DC MC VI.

ROMA'S NEWEST MOTEL

STARLIGHT MOTOR INN

* 18 Luxury Units
  - Inc.2 family rooms
* Dining/conference facilities & equipment
* Free Austar cable TV
* Non smoking rooms
* Centre of town

AAA Tourism ★★★★

20B BOWEN STREET, ROMA, QLD

PHONE: (07) 4622 2666
FAX: (07) 4622 2111
RESERVATION FREECALL 1800 066 022

Quietest Location Best Value

AAAT ★★★☆

Budget Motel Chain International

Motel Carnarvon

FREECALL 1800 621 155
FAX: 07 4622 4147
INJUNE RD, ROMA

★ 20 Three Star Plus Spacious Ground Floor Units
★ New Sealy Queen Size Beds
★ Austar ★ 14 TV Channels ★ Pool ★ Spa
★ Air-Conditioned ★ Non-Smoking Rooms Avail
★ Large Divided Family Units Sleep 6
★ Budget Family Rooms ★ Playground
★ Licensed ★ Evening Meals to Units
★ Undercover Parking in front of every unit
★ Oversize Parking ★ Opposite Bowls Club

★★☆ **A Wishing Well**, (M), 77 Quintin St, ☎ 07 4622 2566, fax 07 4622 3606, 26 units [shwr, tlt, a/c, tel, cable tv, movie, clock radio, t/c mkg, refrig, toaster], ⊠, pool, bbq, rm serv, meals to unit, trailer park, cots-fee. RO ♦ $47.30 - $58.30, ♦♦ $58.30 - $69.30, ♦ $12.10, ch con, 4 units of a 3.5 star rating. AE BC DC EFT MC VI.

★★☆ **Palms**, (M), 6 Bowen St, 1.5km E of PO, ☎ 07 4622 6464, fax 07 4622 6263, 6 units [shwr, tlt, a/c-cool, heat, elec blkts, tel, TV, clock radio, t/c mkg, refrig, toaster], ldry, bbq, rm serv, dinner to unit. RO ♦ $38.50, ♦♦ $48.40, ♦♦♦ $57.20, ♦♦♦♦ $66, ch con, BC MC VI.

B&B's/Guest Houses

★★★★ **Richmond Downs Bed & Breakfast**, (B&B), Richmond Downs, 10.5 km S of Roma on Carnarvon Hwy, ☎ 07 4622 2731, fax 07 4622 3512, 1 rm [shwr (1), tlt (1), a/c (1), c/fan (1), heat, elec blkts], ✕, cots. BB ♦ $100, ♦♦ $120, DBB ♦♦ $200, ch con.

ROSSLYN BAY QLD 4703

Pop Nominal, (677km N Brisbane), See maps on page 416, ref C5. Popular boat harbour just south of Yeppoon on Capricorn Coast, where cruise boats depart daily for Great Keppel Island.

Hotels/Motels

★★★☆ **Rosslyn Bay Inn Resort**, (M), Rosslyn Bay, 10km S of PO, ☎ 07 4933 6333, fax 07 4933 6297, (Multi-stry gr fl) 36 units [shwr, tlt, a/c-cool, c/fan, tel (33), TV, movie (29), clock radio, refrig, cook fac ltd (33)], ldry, w/mach-fee, dryer-fee, conv fac, ⊠, pool, bbq, c/park (undercover) (20), secure park, mini golf, tennis, cots-fee. RO ♦♦ $90 - $105, ♦ $20 - $25, ch con, AE BC DC MC VI.

Self Catering Accommodation

★★★★ **Rosslyn Bay Inn Resort**, (SA), Rosslyn Bay via Yeppoon, ☎ 07 4933 6333, fax 07 4933 6297, (Multi-stry gr fl), 6 serv apts acc up to 7, (2 bedrm), [shwr, tlt, a/c, tel, TV, movie, refrig, cook fac, ldry (in unit)], conv fac, ⊠, pool, bbq, c/park (undercover), secure park, tennis, cots-fee. D ♦♦♦ $130 - $160, ♦ $20 - $25, W ♦♦♦♦ $900 - $1,000, ch con, AE BC DC MC VI.

RUBYVALE QLD 4702

Pop 600. (965km NW Brisbane), See maps on page 414, ref D6. Small township in the Central Highlands. Gem Fossicking.

Self Catering Accommodation

★★★ **Bedford Gardens**, (HU), Vane Tempest Rd, 300m NW of PO, ☎ 07 4985 4175, fax 07 4985 4175, 5 units acc up to 8, (Studio, 1 & 2 bedrm), [shwr, tlt, a/c-cool, c/fan, heat, tel, TV, cook fac, blkts, linen, pillows], ldry, bbq. D ♦ $55, ♦♦ $60.50, ♦ $8.25, AE BC MC VI.

The Castle Casuarina Hill, (HU), Old Airport Road, ☎ 07 4985 4118, fax 07 4985 4130, 8 units acc up to 6, (Studio), [shwr, tlt, TV, radio, blkts, pillows], rec rm, cook fac, t/c mkg shared, bbq (covered), ✆. RO ♦♦ $55, ♦ $27.50, ♦♦ $330, ♦ $165, (not yet classified).

RUNAWAY BAY QLD

See Gold Coast Region.

Trouble-free travel tips - Lights

Check the operation of all lights. If you are pulling a trailer or caravan make sure turning indicators and brake lights are working.

SARINA QLD 4737

Pop 3,200. (939km N Brisbane), See maps on page 416, ref B3. Located on the foothills of the Connors range, this town possesses a host of natural attractions including a series of spectacular mountain ranges and lush rainforest areas. Golf, Shooting, Squash, Swimming, Tennis.

Hotels/Motels

★★★☆ **Sarina Motor Inn**, (M), Bruce Hwy, ☎ 07 4943 1431, fax 07 4943 1541, 16 units [shwr, tlt, a/c-cool, tel, cable tv, clock radio, t/c mkg, refrig, toaster], conv fac, ⊠, bar, pool, rm serv, c/park (undercover) (12), cots-fee. RO ♦ $55 - $60.50, ♦♦ $60.50 - $71.50, ♦ $5.50 - $11, ch con, AE BC DC EFT MC VI, ♿.

★★★☆ **Tramway**, (M), 110 Broad St (Bruce Hwy), ☎ 07 4956 2244, fax 07 4943 1262, 12 units [shwr, tlt, a/c-cool, c/fan, heat, tel, TV, movie, clock radio, t/c mkg, refrig, cook fac (2)], ldry, pool, bbq, dinner to unit, c/park (undercover), boat park, trailer park, cots, non smoking units (5), Pets allowed (grounds only). RO ♦ $50 - $65, ♦♦ $55 - $70, ♦ $11, ch con, AE BC DC EFT MC VI.

★★ **Tandara**, (LMH), Broad St (Bruce Hwy), ☎ 07 4956 1323, fax 07 4943 1027, 15 units [shwr, tlt, a/c-cool, c/fan, tel, fax, cable tv, t/c mkg, refrig], ldry, conv fac, ⊠, c/park (undercover), trailer park (& large vehicles), cots-fee. RO ♦ $45, ♦♦ $50 - $52, ♦ $8, BC MC VI.

SARINA BEACH QLD 4737

Pop 400. (952km N Brisbane), See maps on page 416, ref B3. Attractive seaside area located near Sarina. Fishing, Swimming, Water Skiing.

Hotels/Motels

★★★☆ **Sandpiper**, (M), Owen Jenkins Dve, ☎ 07 4956 6130, fax 07 4956 6601, (Multi-stry), 23 units [shwr, tlt, a/c-cool, c/fan, tel, TV, clock radio, t/c mkg, refrig, cook fac], ldry, pool, spa, bbq, c/park (undercover), cots. RO ♦♦ $50 - $75, ♦ $10 - $12, ch con, AE BC DC EFT MC VI.

★★★☆ **Sarina Beach**, (M), The Esplanade, ☎ 07 4956 6266, fax 07 4956 6197, (2 stry gr fl) 17 units (2 suites) [shwr, tlt, a/c-cool, c/fan, tel, TV, clock radio, t/c mkg, refrig, cook fac (12)], ldry, ⊠, bar, pool (salt water), bbq, rm serv, dinner to unit, plygr, tennis (half court), cots-fee. RO ♦ $55 - $82.50, ♦♦ $64 - $93, ♦ $11, Suite D ♦ $82.50 - $93.50, ch con, AE BC DC JCB MC VI.

B&B's/Guest Houses

★★★☆ **Sarina Beach Bed & Breakfast**, (B&B), 8 W.E. Owen Cres, ☎ 07 4956 6269, fax 07 4956 6965, 3 rms [a/c-cool, c/fan, heat, clock radio, t/c mkg, refrig (shared), toaster], iron, iron brd, rec rm, TV rm, non smoking rms (3). BLB ♦ $52.80, ♦♦ $71.50, ♦ $20, BC MC VI.

SAUNDERS BEACH QLD 4818

Pop Nominal, (1400km N Brisbane), See maps on page 415, ref D7. Seaside resort opposite Magnetic Island. Fishing, Swimming.

Self Catering Accommodation

★★★ **Saunders Beach Ocean View**, (HU), 23 Cay St, 22km N of Townsville Airport off Bruce Hwy, ☎ 07 4778 6486, fax 07 4778 6486, 8 units acc up to 4, [shwr, tlt, a/c-cool-fee, fan, TV, radio, refrig, cook fac, blkts, linen, pillows], ldry, pool (salt water), bbq, c/park (undercover), ✆, cots. D ♦♦ $55 - $66, ♦ $11, W ♦♦ $330 - $396, ♦ $66, ch con, BC MC VI.

SHUTE HARBOUR QLD

See Whitsundays Region.

SOUTH MOLLE ISLAND QLD

See Whitsundays Region.

SOUTHPORT QLD

See Gold Coast Region.

SPRINGBROOK QLD 4213

Pop Nominal, (108km S Brisbane), See maps on page 417, ref D8.
Located in the Gold Coast Hinterland amid many national parks.

★★★ **English Country Gardens**, (LMH), 2932 Springbrook Rd, 29.3 km SW of Medgeeraba round a bout, ☎ 07 5533 5244, fax 07 5533 5778, 1 unit [shwr, bath, tlt, fire pl, elec blkts, TV, movie, clock radio, t/c mkg, refrig, cook fac, micro, toaster, ldry], ⊠, pool (salt water), secure park, non smoking units. **RO ♦♦ $120 - $140, ◊ $10**, BC MC VI.

★★★★☆ **Purlingbrook Cottage**, (Cotg), 27 Forestry Rd, 100m W of falls, ☎ 07 5533 5527, fax 07 5533 5500, 1 cotg acc up to 4, (2 bedrm), [shwr, spa bath, tlt, elec blkts, radio, t/c mkg, refrig, cook fac ltd, micro, d/wash, toaster, ldry, blkts, doonas, linen, pillows], w/mach, dryer, lounge (TV, video), lounge firepl, bbq, c/park (undercover), non smoking property. **D ♦♦ $150 - $180, ◊ $20 - $25, W $800 - $945**, BC EFT MC VI.

★★★★ **Mouses House**, (Chalet), Springbrook Rd, ☎ 07 5533 5192, 10 chalets (1 & 2 bedrm), [shwr, spa bath (7), tlt, fire pl, heat, TV, video (on request)-fee, clock radio, refrig, cook fac, micro, blkts, linen, pillows], ldry, sauna, spa, bbq, bicycle, tennis (half court). **RO ♦♦ $142.50 - $165, ◊ $55, ♦♦ $815 - $925**, Min book applies. BC MC VI.

★★★★ **Springbrook Rainforest Cabins**, (Cotg), 317 Repeater Station Rd, ☎ 07 5533 5366, 3 cotgs acc up to 11, [shwr, tlt, fan, fire pl, heat, TV, clock radio, refrig, cook fac, micro, elec frypan, ldry (in unit), blkts, linen, pillows], iron, ✆. **D ♦ $88 - $132, ◊ $22, W ♦♦ $704, ◊ $154**, fam con, AE BC MC VI.

★★★ **(Mountain Lodge Section)**, 5 rms [shwr, bath (1), tlt, heat, TV, t/c mkg, refrig, cook fac (1), micro, elec frypan, pillows], ldry, iron, rec rm, lounge firepl, cook fac, bbq, ✆. **D ♦ $44, ♦♦ $56 - $88, ◊ $22, W ♦ $308, ♦♦ $456, ◊ $154**.

★★★☆ **Springbrook Mountain Chalets**, (Chalet), 2058 Springbrook Rd, 19km W of Mudgeeraba PO, ☎ 07 5533 5205, fax 07 5533 5156, 5 chalets acc up to 6, (1 & 2 bedrm), [shwr, spa bath (5), tlt, fire pl (pot belly) (3), heat (slow combustion) (1), elec blkts, TV, CD, t/c mkg, refrig, cook fac, micro, blkts, linen, pillows], bbq, bush walking, bicycle. **D ♦♦ $132 - $198, ◊ $44**, 2 chalets ★★★★☆, Breakfast basket available. Min book applies.

Forget Me Not Cottages, (Cotg), 20 Pine Creek Rd, 20km W of Mudgeeraba, ☎ 07 5533 5150, fax 07 5533 5155, 2 cotgs acc up to 2, (1 bedrm), [shwr, spa bath, tlt, hairdry, fan, c/fan, TV, video, clock radio, CD, refrig, micro, elec frypan, d/wash, toaster, ldry], iron, iron brd, bbq, tennis. **D $187 - $203.50, W $1,155**, BC MC VI, (not yet classified).

★★★★☆ **Hardy House**, (B&B), Old School Rd, 28km SW of Mudgeeraba, ☎ 07 5533 5402, fax 07 5533 5403, 2 rms (1 suite) [shwr, tlt, a/c-cool (1), fire pl (wood), heat, refrig, ldry], TV rm, t/c mkg shared. **BB ♦ $45, ♦♦ $90**, ch con, BC EFT MC VI.

★★★★ **Canyon Lookout Guest House**, (B&B), Canyon Pde, ☎ 07 5533 5120, (2 stry gr fl), 2 rms [shwr (2), tlt, heat, elec blkts, TV, t/c mkg, refrig], lounge (fireplace), ✗ (Wed to Sun). **BB ♦ $75, ♦♦ $85**.

★★★☆ **Tulip Gardens Guesthouse**, (GH), No children's facilities, 2874 Springbrook Rd, 28.7km from Mudgeeraba, ☎ 07 5533 5125, fax 07 5533 5125, 5 rms [heat (3), elec blkts, clock radio], shwr, tlt, lounge (TV), ✗, BYO, t/c mkg shared, refrig, bbq, non smoking rms. **BB ♦ $49.50, ♦♦ $99**.

SPRINGSURE QLD 4722

Pop 650. (809km N Brisbane), See maps on page 414, ref D6.

★★☆ **Springsure Zamia**, (M), 27 Charles St, ☎ 07 4984 1455, fax 07 419841587, 10 units [shwr, tlt, a/c-cool, tel, TV, t/c mkg, refrig, cook fac], ldry, cafe, bbq, dinner to unit, cots. **RO ♦ $53, ♦♦ $64, ◊ $11**, ch con, AE BC MC VI.

ST GEORGE QLD 4487

Pop 2,450. (503km SW Brisbane), See maps on page 414, ref D8.
Located south west of Toowoomba on the Balonne River.

★★★★ **Jacaranda Country Motel**, (M), 78-80 Grey Street, 600m S of RSL, ☎ 07 4625 1011, fax 07 4625 1015, 18 units [shwr, tlt, hairdry, a/c, tel, cable tv, clock radio, t/c mkg, refrig, mini bar, toaster], ldry-fee, iron, iron brd, pool (saltwater), bbq (covered), rm serv, dinner to unit, c/park (undercover), plygr, cots-fee, non smoking units (9). **RO ♦ $75, ♦♦ $85, ◊ $11**, ch con, AE BC DC EFT MC VI.

★★★★ **Riverland Motor Inn**, (M), 72 Victoria St, ☎ 07 4625 1229, fax 07 4625 1227, 26 units [shwr, tlt, hairdry, a/c, c/fan, tel (direct dial), TV, clock radio, t/c mkg, refrig, mini bar, cook fac ltd (1), micro (3), toaster], ldry-fee, iron, iron brd, ⊠ (Mon-Sat), pool (salt water), bbq, dinner to unit (Mon-Sat), car wash, cots-fee, non smoking units (17). **RO ♦ $76, ♦♦ $86, ◊ $10**, AE BC DC EFT MC VI.
Operator Comment: Opened February 2000. Newest Motel in St George.

★★★☆ **Balonne**, (M), 52 Victoria St, ☎ 07 4625 5155, fax 07 4625 4241, 16 units [shwr, tlt, hairdry, a/c, elec blkts, tel, cable tv, clock radio, t/c mkg, refrig, toaster], pool, bbq, dinner to unit, c/park (undercover), cots-fee, non smoking units (6). **RO ♦ $52 - $57, ♦♦ $62 - $68, ◊ $10**, ch con, AE BC DC EFT MC MCH VI.

★★★☆ **Merino Motor Inn**, (M), 78 Victoria St, 5 km E of Town Centre, ☎ 07 4625 3333, fax 07 4625 3574, 27 units [shwr, tlt, a/c, tel, cable tv (6 channels), clock radio, t/c mkg, refrig, cook fac (1)], ldry-fee, conv fac, ⊠ (Mon to Sat), pool, bbq, rm serv, dinner to unit (Mon to Sat), c/park (undercover), car wash, cots-fee. **RO ♦ $69 - $82, ♦♦ $77 - $92, ◊ $11**, AE BC DC EFT MC VI.

ST LAWRENCE QLD 4707

Pop Nominal, (832km N Brisbane), See maps on page 416, ref B4.
Ripplebrook Host Farm, (GH), (Farm), A working beef cattle property. via St Lawrence, 18km W St Lawrence 155km S Mackay, ☎ 07 4956 9202, fax 07 4956 9202, 2 rms [fan], ldry, rec rm, lounge (TV), ✗, t/c mkg shared, bush walking, cots, non smoking property. **BB ♦ $55, ♦♦ $88, DBB ♦♦ $110**, BC MC VI, (not yet classified).

STANTHORPE QLD 4380

Pop 4,150. (221km SW Brisbane), See maps on page 414, ref E8.
Hotels/Motels

★★★★ **Murray Gardens Motel & Cottages**, (M), Pancor Rd, 800m NW of PO, ☎ 07 4681 4121, fax 07 4681 4083, 14 units [shwr, spa bath (1), tlt, fan, heat, elec blkts, TV, clock radio, t/c mkg, refrig, cook fac, toaster], ldry, iron, iron brd, ⊠ (Mon to Sat), spa, bbq, c/park (undercover), ✆. **RO ♦ $49.50, ♦♦ $61.50**, ch con, AE BC DC MC VI, ﬛.

★★★★ **The Vines**, (M), 2 Wallangarra Rd, 300m S of PO, ☎ 07 4681 3844, fax 07 4681 3843, (2 stry gr fl), 26 units [shwr, tlt, a/c, elec blkts, tel, cable tv, clock radio, t/c mkg, refrig, cook fac ltd (2), micro (2), toaster (2)], ldry, dryer, conv fac, dinner to unit, c/park (undercover) (19), cots. **RO ♦ $70 - $85, ♦♦ $77 - $97**, ch con, AE BC DC MC MP VI, ﬛.

★★★☆ **Apple & Grape**, (M), 63 Maryland St, ☎ 07 4681 1288, fax 07 4681 3855, (2 stry gr fl), 19 units [shwr, tlt, hairdry, a/c, c/fan, elec blkts, tel, TV, clock radio, t/c mkg, refrig], ldry, rec rm, c/park (undercover) (8), plygr, cots-fee. **RO ♦♦ $66 - $93.50, ◊ $11**, ch con, AE BC DC MC VI.

★★★☆ **Granite Court**, (M), 34 Wallangarra Rd, ☎ 07 4681 1811, fax 07 4681 2916, 19 units [shwr, tlt, hairdry, a/c, elec blkts, tel, TV, clock radio, t/c mkg, refrig, cook fac (1), toaster], ldry, pool, bbq, rm serv (residential lic), dinner to unit, c/park (undercover), cots-fee. **RO ♦ $53 - $60, ♦♦ $59 - $72, ◊ $11**, AE BC DC EFT MC VI.

★★★☆ **High Street Motor Inn**, (M), 1 High St, ☎ 07 4681 1533, fax 07 4681 1614, 18 units [shwr, tlt, hairdry, a/c (3), fan, fire pl (in Restaurant), heat, elec blkts, tel, TV, clock radio, t/c mkg, refrig, toaster], ldry, ⊠ (Mon to Sat), bbq, rm serv, c/park (undercover), plygr, cots-fee. **RO ♦ $50 - $65, ♦♦ $65 - $90, ◊ $11**, ch con, AE BC DC EFT MC VI, ﬛.

★★★☆ **Stannum Lodge Motor Inn**, (M), 12 Wallangarra Rd, ☎ 07 4681 2000, fax 07 4681 1045, 12 units [shwr, tlt, a/c-cool, c/fan, heat, elec blkts, tel, TV, clock radio, t/c mkg, refrig, micro, toaster], ldry, ✗ (charge back), pool, bbq, dinner to unit, c/park (undercover), cots-fee. **BLB ♦ $55 - $66, ♦♦ $64 - $72, ◊ $11**, AE BC DC EFT MC VI.

★★★ **Boulevard**, (M), 76 Maryland St, ☎ 07 4681 1777, fax 07 4681 3218, 14 units [shwr, tlt, a/c (9), fan, heat, elec blkts, tel, TV, video (4), clock radio, t/c mkg, refrig, toaster], ldry, c/park (undercover), cots. **RO ♦ $41 - $49, ♦♦ $47 - $55, ◊ $8**, AE BC DC MC MCH VI.

★☆ **Country Club**, (LMH), 26 Maryland St, ☎ 07 4681 1033, fax 07 4681 3186, (2 stry gr fl), 8 units [shwr, tlt, heat, TV, clock radio, t/c mkg, refrig], conv fac, ⊠ (Mon to Sat), ✆, cots. **RO ♦ $35, ♦♦ $50**, ch con, BC MC VI.

(Hotel Section), 10 apts [basin], shwr, tlt, cots. **RO ♦ $20, ♦♦ $30**, ch con.

Self Catering Accommodation

★★★★☆ **Diamondvale B & B Cottages**, (Cotg), Diamondvale Rd, 4km E of PO, ☎ 07 4681 3367, fax 07 4681 3367, 3 cotgs acc up to 4, (1 & 2 bedrm), [ensuite (1), shwr, bath (1), tlt, hairdry, c/fan, fire pl (in living room), heat, elec blkts, TV, video, clock radio, t/c mkg, cook fac, micro (1), toaster], ldry, iron, iron brd. **BB ⋔ $88 - $99, ⋔⋔ $154 - $165, ⦿ $44 - $50**, ch con.

★★★★☆ **Happy Valley Vineyard Retreat**, (Cotg), Resort, Glenlyon Dve, 3km W of PO, ☎ 07 4681 3250, fax 07 4681 3082, 10 cotgs acc up to 12, [shwr, tlt, c/fan, elec blkts, t/c mkg, blkts, linen, pillows], iron, iron brd, lounge (TV), lounge firepl, ⊠, courtesy transfer, bush walking. **BB ⋔⋔ $99 - $139**, ch con, Meals by arrangement. AE BC MC VI.

 ★★★★ **(Wildflower Cottages Section)**, 10 rms [shwr, tlt, c/fan, heat, elec blkts, t/c mkg, pillows], iron, iron brd. **BB ⋔⋔ $99 - $139, ⦿ $49.50 - $69.50**.

 ★★★☆ **(Cabin Section)**, 2 rms [shwr, tlt, heat, elec blkts, refrig, cook fac ltd, pillows], iron, iron brd. **BB ⋔⋔ $99 - $139**.

★★★★ **Alpaca Cottage**, (Cotg), (Farm), Working Alpaca stud property. Ridge Rd The Summit via, 13km NE Stanthorpe, ☎ 07 3256 7333, fax 07 3256 7900, 1 cotg acc up to 3, [shwr, bath, tlt, hairdry, heat, elec blkts, TV, t/c mkg, refrig, cook fac], bush walking. **RO ⋔ $120**, AE BC MC VI.

★★★☆ **Radford Cottages**, (Cotg), 63 Wallangarra Rd, ☎ 07 4681 1310, 6 cotgs acc up to 6, (2 bedrm), [shwr, bath, tlt, fan, fire pl, heat, TV, refrig, cook fac, toaster, ldry (in unit), blkts, linen, pillows], iron, iron brd, c/park (undercover), cots. **BB ⋔⋔ $66 - $99, ⋔⋔⋔⋔ $132 - $198**, BC MC VI.

 (Johnson Cottage Section), 17 Johnson St, 1 cotg [shwr, bath, tlt, fan, fire pl, heat (fan), TV, t/c mkg, refrig, cook fac, elec frypan, toaster, ldry], iron, iron brd, c/park (undercover), cots. **BLB ⋔ $66 - $99, ⋔⋔ $66 - $99**, (not yet classified).

 (Pinewood Cottage Section), 1 cotg acc up to 8, [shwr, tlt, fan, fire pl, heat (fan), TV, t/c mkg, refrig, cook fac, elec frypan, toaster, ldry], iron, iron brd, c/park (undercover). **BLB ⋔ $66 - $99, ⋔⋔ $66 - $99, ⦿ $22**, (not yet classified).

★★ **Callemondah Host Farm**, (Cotg), (Farm), Working sheep and cattle property, 'Callemondah', Stanthorpe, 58km W of PO (Texas Rd.), ☎ 07 4685 6162, fax 07 4685 6156, 1 cotg acc up to 8, [shwr, bath, tlt (2), heat, elec blkts, TV, refrig, cook fac, elec frypan, toaster], ldry. **D ⋔ $33**, ch con.

★★★★
AAAT

The Vines

MOTEL & COTTAGES

2 Wallangarra Road Stanthorpe Qld. Phone 07 4681 3844
www.thevinesmotel.com.au *Email:* thevines@halenet.com.au

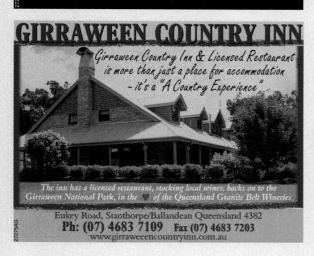

GIRRAWEEN COUNTRY INN

Girraween Country Inn & Licensed Restaurant is more than just a place for accommodation - it's a "A Country Experience"

The inn has a licenced restaurant, stocking local wines, backs on to the Girraween National Park, in the ♥ of the Queensland Granite Belt Wineries

Eukey Road, Stanthorpe/Ballandean Queensland 4382
Ph: (07) 4683 7109   Fax (07) 4683 7203
www.girraweencountryinn.com.au

B&B's/Guest Houses

★★★★★ **Smiths Vineyard**, (B&B), Zambelli Rd, Ballandean 4382, 19km S of Stanthorpe 800m W of Ballandean PO, ☎ 07 4684 1139, fax 07 4684 1261, 3 rms [shwr, tlt, hairdry, heat, elec blkts, TV, t/c mkg], ldry, dryer, lounge firepl, c/park (undercover), non smoking rms. **D ⋔ $90, ⋔⋔ $130**, BC MC VI.

★★★★★ **Vineyard Cottages**, (B&B), No children's facilities, New England Hwy, Ballandean 4382, 15km S of Stanthorpe, ☎ 07 4684 1270, fax 07 4684 1324, 7 rms (4 suites) [shwr, bath (hip), spa bath (6), tlt, hairdry, a/c-cool (4), c/fan (1), cent heat, elec blkts, TV, t/c mkg, refrig], conv fac, lounge firepl, ⊠ (Mon-Sun), dinner to unit, non smoking property. **BB ⋔⋔ $145 - $215**, AE BC MC VI.

★★★★☆ **Das Helwig Haus**, (B&B), 14ha farm & orchard, Mt Stirling Rd, Glen Aplin 4381, 9km S of Stanthorpe, ☎ 07 4683 4227, fax 07 4683 4227, 8 rms (4 suites) [ensuite (6), shwr, bath, tlt, hairdry, fan (4), c/fan (4), heat (4), elec blkts, TV (1), clock radio (4), t/c mkg (5), refrig (5), cook fac ltd (4), micro (4)], ldry, dryer, iron (2), iron brd (2), lounge (TV), lounge firepl, ✗, BYO, bbq, c/park (undercover), non smoking rms. **BB ⋔⋔ $110 - $130, Suite D ⋔ $130 - $160, ⋔⋔ $130 - $160, ⦿ $40**, BC MC VI.

★★★★☆ **Honeysuckle Cottages**, (B&B), Mayfair Lane, 3km N PO, ☎ 07 4681 1510, fax 07 4681 1454, 7 rms [shwr, spa bath (3), tlt, hairdry, heat (combustion log fire), elec blkts, TV, clock radio, refrig, cook fac, micro, ldry (in unit) (5), pillows], dryer (5), iron, iron brd, dinner to unit-fee, cots. **BLB ⋔⋔⋔⋔ $125 - $170, ⦿ $44**, ch con, AE BC DC MC VI.

★★★★ **Amberley Edge**, (B&B), Homestead on working vineyard property. Clark Lane, 8km W of Stanthorpe, ☎ 07 4683 6203, fax 07 4683 6203, 3 rms [ensuite (3), t/c mkg], lounge (TV), lounge firepl (log), c/park (undercover), bush walking, non smoking rms. **BB ⋔⋔ $125**.

★★★★ **Ballandean Lodge**, (B&B), Children by arrangement, Rees Rd, Ballandean 4382, ☎ 07 4684 1320, fax 07 4684 1340, 3 rms [ensuite (3), c/fan, heat, elec blkts], ✗, non smoking units. **BB ⋔ $70 - $85, ⋔⋔ $115 - $130**, BC MC VI.

★★★★ **Girraween Country Inn**, (GH), Eukey Rd, Ballandean 4382, 22km S Stanthorpe PO, ☎ 07 4683 7109, fax 07 4683 7203, (2 stry), 7 rms (1 suite) [shwr, bath (1), tlt, c/fan, heat, elec blkts, TV, t/c mkg], conv fac, lounge firepl, ⊠, non smoking property. **BB ⋔ $49 - $80, ⋔⋔ $88 - $165, DBB ⋔ $82 - $115, ⋔⋔ $138 - $230**, ch con, BC MC VI.

★★★★ **Tin Kettling**, (B&B), 94 Hale Haven Dve, 3km SE of PO, ☎ 07 4681 1584, fax 07 4681 4584, 2 rms [shwr, bath, tlt, heat, elec blkts, t/c mkg, refrig], ldry, lounge (TV), lounge firepl, bbq, c/park (undercover), non smoking rms. **BB ⋔ $75, ⋔⋔ $115**.

★★☆ **Riversdale Homestead**, (GH), (Farm), Cattle, sheep & crop producing property. 'Riversdale', Glenlyon Dam Rd via, 90km SW of Stanthorpe, ☎ 02 6737 5277, fax 02 6737 5260, 2 rms [fan, heat, elec blkts], shwr, tlt, ldry, lounge (TV), t/c mkg shared, bbq, tennis. **BB ⋔ $50, D all meals ⋔ $88, DBB ⋔ $65**, ch con.

Mt Stirling Olives, (B&B), Collins Rd, Glen Aplin 4381, 4k W Glen Aplin P.O, ☎ 07 4683 4270, fax 07 4683 4270, 2 rms [shwr, bath, tlt, hairdry, fan, fire pl, radio, CD, t/c mkg, refrig, cook fac, micro, toaster], iron, iron brd. **BB ⋔⋔ $130, ⦿ $5**, BC MC VI, (not yet classified).

St Ignatius Vineyard Retreat, (B&B), Lot 133 New England Highway, Severnlea 4352, 9km S of Stanthorpe PO, ☎ 07 4683 4382, fax 07 3397 5280, 4 rms (3 suites) [shwr (2), bath, spa bath (1), tlt (3), hairdry (3), heat, elec blkts, TV (2), video (2), movie (1), t/c mkg, refrig, elec frypan, toaster], ldry, dryer, iron (1), iron brd (1), conf fac, ⊠, cook fac, bbq, non smoking property. **D $150**, (not yet classified).

STRADBROKE ISLAND NORTH QLD 4183

Pop 2,289. (30km SE Brisbane), See maps on page 417, ref E7. Is the biggest island in Moreton Bay.

Self Catering Accommodation

★★★★☆ **Whale Watch Ocean Beach Resort**, (HU), 7 Samarinda Dve Point Lookout, Stradbroke Island North, direct ocean access, ☎ 07 3409 8555, fax 07 3409 8666, (Multi-stry), 38 units acc up to 6, (3 bedrm), [ensuite, shwr, bath, tlt, a/c (24), c/fan, tel, TV, video, clock radio, refrig, cook fac, micro, d/wash, toaster, ldry, blkts, linen, pillows], lift, dryer, iron, iron brd, rec rm, pool, spa, bbq-fee, secure park (undercover), gym, cots-fee. **D $195 - $315, W $650 - $1,850**, BC CC EFT MC VI.

Operator Comment: See our display advertisement on page 542.

★★★★ **Pandanus Palms Resort**, (HU), 21 Cumming Pde, Point Lookout 4183, ☎ 07 3409 8106, fax 07 3409 8339, 28 units acc up to 6, (2 & 3 bedrm), [ensuite (1), shwr, bath, tlt, fan (4), c/fan (6), heat (4), TV, video, clock radio, refrig, cook fac, micro, d/wash, ldry (in unit), blkts, linen, pillows], dryer, ⊠ (Tue - Sat. Dinner), pool (salt water), bbq, c/park (undercover), ☎, gym-fee, tennis, cots-fee. **D $122.50 - $195, W $495 - $1,350**, Min book applies, BC EFT MC VI.

★★★★ **Samarinda Jewel By The Sea**, (HU), 1 Samarinda Dve, Point Lookout 4183, 1km E PO, ☎ 07 3409 8785, fax 07 3409 8847, (Multi-stry gr fl), 15 units acc up to 6, (2 & 3 bedrm), [ensuite, shwr, bath, tlt, TV, video, clock radio, refrig, micro, elec frypan, d/wash, ldry (in unit), linen], dryer, iron, pool (salt water), bbq, c/park (undercover), cots-fee. **D ♦♦ $200, ♦ $25, W ♦♦ $695 - $1,450, ♦ $30**, ch con, Min book applies, BC EFT MC VI.

★★★☆ **Anchorage Village Beach Resort**, (HU), 25 East Coast Rd, Point Lookout 4183, North Stradbroke Island, ☎ 07 3409 8266, fax 07 3409 8304, (Multi-stry), 29 units acc up to 6, (Studio, 1 & 2 bedrm), [shwr, bath (3), tlt, c/fan, tel, TV, clock radio, t/c mkg, refrig, cook fac, micro (12), d/wash (7), ldry (in unit) (7), blkts, linen, pillows], ldry, dryer, conv fac, ⊠ (Wed-Sun), pool, sauna, bbq, rm serv-fee, dinner to unit-fee, c/park (undercover) (7), mini golf, cots. **D ♦♦ $175 - $280, W $470 - $840**, Min book applies, BC MC VI.

★★★☆ **The Islander**, (HU), East Coast Rd, Point Lookout 4183, 100m fr beach, ☎ 07 3409 8388, fax 07 3409 8730, (Multi-stry gr fl), 29 units acc up to 7, (Studio, 1 & 2 bedrm), [shwr, tlt, TV, video, refrig, cook fac, micro, d/wash (19), ldry (in unit), blkts, linen, pillows], dryer (23), pool, bbq, c/park (undercover) (21), plygr, tennis. **D ♦♦ $150 - $200, ♦♦♦♦ $230 - $300, W ♦♦♦♦ $550 - $1,050, $320 - $580**, Min book applies, AE BC EFT MC VI.

★★★ **Raine & Horne Stradbroke Island**, (HU), Kennedy Dve, Point Lookout 4183, 300m S of beach, ☎ 07 3409 8213, fax 07 3409 8733, (2 stry), 12 units acc up to 8, (2 & 3 bedrm), [shwr, tlt, c/fan, TV, video, clock radio, t/c mkg, cook fac, micro, toaster, blkts, linen, pillows], ldry, w/mach, dryer, pool, spa, c/park (undercover). **D $90 - $180, W $365 - $950**, ch con, Min book applies, BC EFT MC VI.

★ **Cosy**, (Cotg), Cnr Mirimar & Ballow Sts, Amity Point 4183, North Stradbroke Island, ☎ 07 3409 7119, fax 07 3288 2021, 5 cotgs acc up to 6, (2 & 3 bedrm), [shwr (3-ext), tlt (3-ext), refrig, cook fac, elec frypan, ldry (in unit) (2), blkts reqd, linen reqd], ldry, cots. **D $50 - $100, W $240 - $600**.

Amity Bungalows, 33 Ballow St, Amity Point 4183, 500m N of Amity Point PO, ☎ 07 3409 7126, fax 07 5573 2505, 3 cabins acc up to 6, (1 & 2 bedrm), [shwr, tlt, TV, video, clock radio, t/c mkg, cook fac, micro, blkts, doonas, linen reqd-fee, pillows], ldry, w/mach, dryer, bbq, c/park (undercover), plygr. **D $100, W $400 - $600**, Min book applies, BC EFT MC VI, ♿, (not yet classified).

B&B's/Guest Houses

★★★★ **Sunsets at Point Lookout**, (B&B), 6 Billa St, Point Lookout 4183, 150m S of beach, ☎ 07 3409 8823, fax 07 3409 8873, (2 stry gr fl), 3 rms [ensuite, c/fan, heat, TV, toaster, doonas], ldry, t/c mkg shared, refrig, bbq, non smoking property. **BB ♦♦ $90 - $120**, BTC MC VI.

Other Accommodation

Minjerribah Holiday Camp, (Lodge), Cnr Oxley Pde & Cunningham St, Dunwich 4163, ☎ 07 3409 9445, (2 stry gr fl), 80 rms acc up to 2, [basin], shwr, tlt, ldry, lounge (TV), cook fac, bbq, meals avail. **D ♦ $10 - $15**, ch con.

STRADBROKE ISLAND SOUTH QLD 4183

Pop Nominal, (71km S Brisbane), See map on page 417, ref E7. Extends north from the Gold Coast for more than 20km.

Hotels/Motels

AAA TOURISM Special Rates ★★★ **South Stradbroke Island Resort**, (LMH), South Stradbroke Island, via Gold Coast, ☎ 07 5577 3311, fax 07 5577 3746, 40 units [shwr, tlt, a/c-cool (10), c/fan, TV, clock radio, t/c mkg, refrig], ldry, rec rm, conv fac, ⊠, pool, sauna, spa, kiosk, ☎, plygr, jetty, tennis, cots-fee. **RO $95 - 140**, ch con, Min book Christmas Jan and Easter, AE BC DC EFT MC VI.

Self Catering Accommodation

★★★★★ **Couran Cove Resort**, (Villa), Resort, ☎ 07 5597 9000, fax 07 5597 9090, 226 villas acc up to 8, (1, 2 & 4 bedrm Studio), [shwr, tlt, c/fan, tel, TV, movie, refrig, cook fac, micro, toaster, blkts, linen, pillows], iron, iron brd, rec rm, conf fac, ⊠, pool-heated (saltwater), bbq, secure park ((at Runaway Bay)), ☎, plygr, gym, tennis-fee, cots, non smoking units. **D $205, W $1,292**, AE BC CC DC JCB MC MP VI, ♿.

★★★★☆ **(Nature Cabins)**, 93 cabins acc up to 8, (2 & 3 bedrm Studio), [shwr, tlt, c/fan, fire pl, tel, TV, movie, refrig, cook fac, micro, toaster, blkts, linen, pillows], iron, iron brd, non smoking units. **W $989**, Min book applies, ♿.

STRATFORD QLD 4872

Pop 1,142. (1731km N Brisbane), See maps on page 415, ref C3. Suburb of Cairns.

B&B's/Guest Houses

★★★★ **Lilybank**, (B&B), Historic Queenslander home. 75 Kamerunga Rd, 8km N of Cairns PO, ☎ 07 4055 1123, fax 07 4058 1990, (2 stry), 3 rms [ensuite, shwr, bath (2), tlt, hairdry (3), a/c-cool, c/fan, video (1), clock radio], ldry, lounge (TV), pool, t/c mkg shared, refrig, ☎. **BB ♦ $66, ♦♦ $88 - $99, ♦ $27.50**, AE MC VI.

SUNRISE BEACH QLD

See Sunshine Coast Region.

SUNSHINE BEACH QLD

See Sunshine Coast Region.

SUNSHINE COAST REGION - QLD

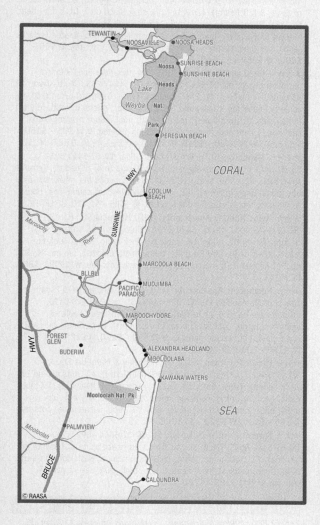

© RAASA

Self Catering Accommodation

★★★★☆ **Alex Seaside Resort**, (HU), 146 Alexandra Pde, 1km N of Mooloolaba, ☎ 07 5479 5055, fax 07 5475 5155, (Multi-stry gr fl), 31 units acc up to 6, (Studio, 1 & 2 bedrm), [ensuite, shwr, spa bath, tlt, hairdry, a/c, c/fan, tel, video, clock radio, refrig, mini bar, cook fac, micro, elec frypan, d/wash, toaster, blkts, linen, pillows], lift, ldry, dryer, iron, iron brd, pool-heated (saltwater), spa (heated), bbq, secure park, cots-fee. D ♦♦ $130 - $320, ♦ $25, W ♦♦ $535 - $1,600, ♦ $65, BC DC EFT MC VI.

★★★★☆ **Alexandra Beach Resort**, (HU), Resort, Cnr Alexandra Pde & Pacific Tce, 1km N of PO, ☎ 07 5475 0600, fax 07 5475 0611, 215 units acc up to 6, (Studio, 1, 2 & 3 bedrm), [ensuite, shwr, bath, tlt, hairdry, a/c-cool, heat, tel, movie-fee, clock radio, refrig, mini bar, cook fac (177), cook fac ltd (36), micro, elec frypan, d/wash, toaster, ldry, blkts, linen, pillows], lift, iron, iron brd, conf fac, pool (salt water/2 heated) (3), spa (2), pool bar, bbq, rm serv, dinner to unit, secure park, gym, cots. D ♦ $32, $125 - $280, AE BC DC JCB MC VI.

★★★★☆ **Alexandra on the Pacific**, (HU), 4 Buderim Ave, ☎ 07 5444 1600, (Multi-stry gr fl), 24 units acc up to 8, (1, 2 & 3 bedrm), [ensuite, shwr, spa bath (20), tlt, a/c, c/fan, tel, cable tv, video, clock radio, refrig, mini bar, cook fac, micro, d/wash, toaster, ldry (in unit), blkts, linen, pillows], lift, dryer, iron, iron brd, rec rm, conv fac, pool-heated (salt water), sauna, spa, bbq, rm serv, secure park, cots-fee. D $130 - $220, W $670 - $1,580, AE BC DC EFT MC VI.

★★★★☆ **Aquarius Resort**, (HU), 13/140 Alexander Pde, 100m N of SLSC, ☎ 07 5443 3330, fax 07 5443 1954, 19 units acc up to 6, [ensuite, shwr, spa bath, tlt, hairdry, a/c, c/fan, tel, TV, video, movie, clock radio, CD, t/c mkg, refrig, mini bar, micro, d/wash, toaster, ldry, blkts, linen, pillows], lift, iron, iron brd, rec rm, conv fac, ✕ (Tues - Sat), pool-heated (salt water), spa, bbq, rm serv, dinner to unit (Tues - Sat), secure park, gym, cots. D $125 - $340, W $630 - $2,730, AE BC DC MC VI.

★★★★☆ **Grand Palais Beachside**, (HU), Cnr Alexandra Pde & Mary St, 20m W of beach, ☎ 07 5444 8861, fax 07 5444 6758, (Multi-stry gr fl), 60 units acc up to 6, (1, 2 & 3 bedrm), [shwr, spa bath, tlt, a/c, heat, tel, TV, clock radio, t/c mkg, refrig, cook fac, micro, toaster, blkts, linen, pillows], ldry, ✕, pool, sauna, spa, bbq, c/park (undercover), cots-fee, non smoking units (4). D $130 - $180, Min book applies, AE BC DC MC VI.

SUNSHINE COAST - ALEXANDRA HEADLAND QLD 4572

Pop 2,783. (104km N Brisbane), See maps on page 417, ref D5.

Hotels/Motels

★★★ **Alexandra Sunshine Motor Inn**, (M), 122 Alexandra Pde, ☎ 07 5443 6899, (2 stry gr fl), 13 units [shwr, bath (6), tlt, c/fan, heat (10), tel, TV, clock radio, t/c mkg, refrig, toaster], ldry, dryer, pool (salt water), bbq, cots. RO ♦ $60 - $110, ♦♦ $75 - $130, ♦ $10, ch con, AE BC DC EFT MC VI, ♿.

S
QUEENSLAND

★★★★☆ **The Mirage Alexandra Headland**, (HU), 8 Mari St, 300m fr lifesaving club, ☎ 07 5443 9400, fax 07 5451 7979, (Multi-stry), 27 units acc up to 6, (1, 2 & 3 bedrm), [shwr, tlt, a/c-cool, c/fan, tel, cable tv, video, clock radio, refrig, cook fac, micro, d/wash, toaster, ldry, blkts, linen, pillows], lift, w/mach, dryer, pool-heated, wading pool, sauna, spa, bbq, secure park (undercover), plygr, gym, tennis, cots-fee. **D** $120 - $350, **W** $595 - $1,390, AE BC DC EFT MC VI.

★★★★ **Ocean Boulevarde**, (HU), 136 Alexandra Pde, 100m N of Surf Club, ☎ 07 5443 3229, fax 07 5443 4933, (Multi-stry gr fl), 33 units acc up to 3, (1 bedrm), [shwr, spa bath, tlt, hairdry, a/c, c/fan, tel, cable tv, video, clock radio, refrig, micro, toaster, ldry, blkts, linen, pillows], dryer, iron, iron brd, pool-heated (in winter), spa, bbq, rm serv (liquor), courtesy transfer, cots-fee. **D** ♦♦ $140 - $160, ♦ $20, AE BC DC EFT MC VI.

★★★☆ **Alexandria Apartments**, (HU), Cnr Alexandra Pde & Mayfield St, ☎ 07 5444 2700, fax 07 5444 6670, (Multi-stry), 27 units acc up to 6, [shwr, bath, tlt, a/c-cool, c/fan, tel, cable tv, clock radio, refrig, cook fac, micro, d/wash, ldry (in unit), blkts, linen, pillows], dryer, rec rm, pool-heated, sauna, bbq, secure park, cots-fee. **D** ♦♦ $125 - $195, **W** $500 - $1,260, BC EFT MC VI.

AAA Tourism
★★★★☆

6 Mari Street
Alexandra Headland Qld 4572
LOCAL CALL 1300 135 990
Email: accom@miragealex.com.au
www.miragealex.com.au

Alexandria Holiday Apartments

• 27 Spacious, fully self contained 1,2 & 3 bedroom Beachfront Units • Private Balconies all with Ocean Views facing north • Colour TV, PABX Phones • Gas Heated Pool, Putting Green, Sauna, Games Room, BBQ • Security Parking • Opposite patrolled Beach • Walking distance to Restaurants & Clubs • Cable TV

PO Box 280 Mooloolaba 4557   Web: www.alexapartments.com
Cnr Alexandra Parade & Mayfield Street, Alexandra Headland
PHONE 07 5444 2700 Fax 07 5444 6670

174 Alexandra Pde
Alexandra Headland
Sunshine Coast 4572
Ph: 07 5443 5011
Fax: 07 5443 6512
www.mandolin.com.au

★★★☆ **Headland Gardens**, (HU), 7 Juan St, 70m to beach, ☎ 07 5444 4655, fax 07 5444 4655, (Multi-stry gr fl), 23 units acc up to 6, (1, 2 & 3 bedrm), [ensuite (14), shwr, bath (20), tlt, c/fan, heat, tel (23), TV, video-fee, clock radio, refrig, cook fac, micro, d/wash, ldry (in unit), blkts, linen, pillows], dryer, rec rm, pool-heated (solar), sauna, spa, bbq, secure park, tennis (half court), cots-fee. **D** $90 - $200, **W** $350 - $1,060, BC MC VI.

★★★☆ **Headland Tropicana**, (HU), 274 Alexandra Pde, 500m to patrolled beach, ☎ 07 5444 2888, fax 07 5444 5233, (Multi-stry gr fl), 36 units acc up to 6, (1, 2 & 3 bedrm), [shwr, bath, tlt, c/fan (29), tel, cable tv, video-fee, clock radio, refrig, cook fac, micro, d/wash, ldry (in unit), blkts, linen, pillows], rec rm, pool, pool indoor heated, sauna, spa, bbq, secure park, tennis (half court), cots-fee. **D** ♦♦ $95 - $150, ♦ $16.50, **W** ♦♦ $530 - $810, Min book applies, AE BC DC EFT MC VI.

★★★☆ **Mandolin**, (HU), 174 Alexandra Pde, ☎ 07 5443 5011, fax 07 5443 6512, (Multi-stry), 47 units acc up to 4, (2 bedrm), [ensuite, shwr, bath, tlt, c/fan, heat, tel, cable tv, refrig, cook fac, micro, d/wash, ldry, blkts, linen, pillows], lift, rec rm, pool-heated, sauna, spa, bbq, secure park, tennis, cots-fee. **RO** ♦♦ $130, ♦♦ $465 - $1,210, BC EFT MC VI.

★★★ **Mylos Holiday Apartments**, (HU), Maroubra St, ☎ 07 5443 4077, fax 07 5479 2737, (Multi-stry), 36 units (2 & 3 bedrm), [shwr, tlt, c/fan, tel, cable tv, clock radio, refrig, cook fac, micro, d/wash (9), ldry (in unit), blkts, linen, pillows], rec rm, ✕, BYO, pool (1 heated) (2), sauna, bbq, secure park, cots-fee. **W** $399 - $800, BC MC VI.

★★★ **Northpoint Apartments**, (HU), Cnr Alexandra Pde & Pacific Tce, 1km N of Mooloolaba PO, ☎ 07 5444 4451, fax 07 5478 0430, 15 units acc up to 6, (2 bedrm), [shwr, tlt, fan, heat, cable tv, video-fee, refrig, cook fac, micro, ldry (in unit), blkts, linen, pillows], dryer, pool, bbq, secure park, ☎. **D** ♦♦ $90 - $220, ♦ $12 - $15, **W** $350 - $600, BC MC VI.

★★★ **Pacific Horizons**, (HU), Cnr Wirraway & Maroubra Sts, ☎ 07 5443 7166, fax 07 5443 9736, (Multi-stry), 42 units acc up to 7, (2 bedrm), [shwr, bath, tlt, fan (21), c/fan (6), heat (21), TV, clock radio, t/c mkg, refrig, cook fac, micro, elec frypan, d/wash, ldry (in unit), blkts, linen, pillows], dryer, pool (3), bbq, secure park, cots-fee. **D** $90 - $130, **W** $320 - $720, BC MC VI.

★★★ **Sorrento**, (HU), 29 Edward St, ☎ 07 5444 4099, fax 07 5444 4099, (Multi-stry gr fl), 11 units acc up to 4, [shwr, bath, tlt, heat, TV, clock radio, refrig, cook fac, micro, d/wash, ldry (in unit), blkts, linen, pillows], pool-heated, bbq, boat park, secure park, ☎, cots-fee.**W** ♦♦♦♦ $385 - $720.

SUNSHINE COAST - BUDERIM QLD 4556

Pop 12,500. (99km N Brisbane), See maps on page 417, ref D5. Centre of a fruitgrowing district.

Hotels/Motels

★★★ **Buderim Ginger Mountain Motel**, (M), 45 King St, ☎ 07 5445 1699, fax 07 5445 5101, (2 stry gr fl), 43 units [shwr, tlt, fan (43), c/fan (46), heat, tel, TV, clock radio, t/c mkg, refrig, cook fac (2), toaster], ldry, conv fac, ✕, pool, rm serv, c/park (undercover) (12). **RO** ♦ $52.80 - $78, ♦♦ $63.80 - $104.50, ♦ $11, AE BC EFT MC VI, ♦♦.

★★★ **Fiesta Motel**, (M), Tanawha Tourist Dve, via Buderim, 5 km W of Buderim, ☎ 07 5445 1874, fax 07 5445 8452, 6 units [shwr, tlt, a/c-cool (3), fan, TV, t/c mkg, refrig, micro, toaster], ldry, pool, bbq, ☎, cots-fee. **RO** ♦♦ $58 - $72, ♦ $10, AE BC DC MC VI.

Fiesta Motel
...nestled in the foothills of Buderim

★★★ AAA Tourism

Small, Secure, Private,
Clean & Friendly
Tranquil Gardens,
BBQ & Pool
Queen Beds, A/C &
Non-smoking Units
Moderate Tariff
Specials for Seniors

Central to everything
on the Sunshine Coast

(07) 5445 1874
Fax: (07) 5445 8452
Email: fiesta@ozemail.com

★★☆ **Buderim Pines**, (M), 92 Burnett St, ☎ 07 5445 1119, fax 07 5445 1119, (2 stry gr fl), 13 units [shwr, tlt, fan (4), c/fan, heat, TV, t/c mkg, refrig, cook fac (3), toaster], ldry, LPG, ☏, cots. **RO ♦ $55 - $65, ♦♦ $55 - $65**, ch con, BC MC VI.

B&B's/Guest Houses

★★★★★ **Buderim White House Bed & Breakfast**, (B&B), 54 Quorn Close, 93km N Brisbane, ☎ 07 5445 1961, fax 07 5445 1994, 4 rms [ensuite, spa bath (2), hairdry, a/c, heat, fire pl, TV, video, clock radio, t/c mkg, refrig], iron, iron brd, lounge (fireplace), c/park (undercover) (3), non smoking rms. **BB ♦♦ $150 - $190**, BC MC VI.

★★★★ **Buderim Suncoast Bed & Breakfast**, (B&B), 168 Mons School Rd, 3km E of Forest Glen turnoff, ☎ 07 5476 8423, fax 07 5476 8774, 2 rms [ensuite (2), shwr, bath (1), tlt, hairdry, a/c-cool, heat (fan), elec blkts, tel, TV, video (avail)], clock radio, ldry], iron, iron brd, TV rm, pool, bbq, non smoking rms. **BB ♦♦ $75 - $115**, AE BC BTC DC MC VI.

★★★☆ **Buderim Rainforest Cabins B & B**, (B&B), 27 Earlybird Drive, 6km W of Mooloolaba beach, ☎ 07 5445 4050, 2 rms [ensuite, shwr, tlt, c/fan, fire pl, CD, refrig], w/mach, dryer, iron, ✕, pool (saltwater), t/c mkg shared, bbq. **BB ♦ $100, ♦♦ $125 - $132**, AE BC DC MC VI.

★★★ **(Cabin Section)**, 3 cabins acc up to 2, (Studio), [shwr, tlt, c/fan, fire pl, elec blkts, TV, video, clock radio, CD, refrig, micro, toaster, blkts, linen, pillows], w/mach, dryer, iron, pool (saltwater), spa (double), bbq. **D ♦♦ $190, W ♦♦ $1,090**.

Aquila Guest House, (GH), 21 Box St, 1km E of PO, ☎ 07 5445 3681, fax 07 5445 3681, (2 stry gr fl), 7 rms [ensuite, spa bath (1), c/fan, heat, TV, clock radio, refrig, cook fac ltd, toaster, doonas], conf fac, ✕, t/c mkg shared, refrig, bbq, secure park, non smoking property. **BLB ♦ $100 - $155, ♦♦ $110 - $165**, Min book applies, AE BC DC MC VI, (not yet classified).

SUNSHINE COAST - CALOUNDRA QLD 4551

Pop 28,300. (91km N Brisbane), See maps on page 417, ref D5. A resort of estuaries and beaches located at the northern end of Pumiceston Channel.

Hotels/Motels

★★★☆ **Anchorage Motor Inn & Resort**, (M), 18 Bowman Rd, ☎ 07 5491 1499, fax 07 5491 7279, (2 stry gr fl), 26 units [shwr, spa bath (3), tlt, hairdry, a/c, c/fan, tel, TV, video (13), clock radio, t/c mkg, refrig, cook fac (6), micro (6), elec frypan (6), toaster (6)], ldry-fee, dryer-fee, conv fac (up to 50pp), ✕, pool, spa, bbq, rm serv, dinner to unit, c/park (undercover) (18), plygr, tennis, cots-fee. **RO ♦ $70 - $103, ♦♦ $75 - $125**, ch con, AE BC DC MC VI.

★★★☆ **Caloundra Suncourt**, (M), 135 Bulcock St, ☎ 07 5491 1011, fax 07 5491 9118, (2 stry gr fl), 12 units [shwr, tlt, a/c-cool, heat, tel, TV, video-fee, clock radio, t/c mkg, refrig, cook fac (4)], ldry, dryer, pool, c/park (undercover). **RO ♦ $65 - $99, ♦♦ $66 - $120, ♦ $12 - $18**, AE BC DC MC VI.

★★★☆ **Wandalua Motel**, (M), Cnr Roderick & Buccleugh Sts, 400 m W of Moffat Beach, ☎ 07 5491 2122, fax 07 5492 8015, (2 stry gr fl), 12 units [shwr, tlt, a/c-cool, heat, tel, TV, clock radio, t/c mkg, refrig], ldry-fee, dryer-fee, iron, iron brd, pool, bbq, c/park (undercover), cots-fee, non smoking units (6). **RO ♦ $66 - $99, ♦♦ $71 - $99**, Min book long w/ends, AE BC DC EFT MC VI.

★★★ **Caloundra Ocean Views Motor Inn**, (M), 115 Bulcock St, ☎ 07 5491 1788, fax 07 5492 5564, (2 stry gr fl), 15 units [shwr, tlt, a/c-cool, heat, tel, TV, video-fee, clock radio, t/c mkg, refrig, cook fac (5), elec frypan (5), toaster (5)], ldry, dryer-fee, pool, bbq, c/park (undercover), cots. **RO ♦ $55 - $86, ♦♦ $60 - $90**, ch con, AE BC CC DC EFT MC VI.

★★☆ **Altons Palm Breeze**, (M), 105 Bulcock St, ☎ 07 5491 5566, fax 07 5491 5115, (2 stry gr fl), 21 units [shwr, tlt, a/c-cool, c/fan, heat, tel, TV, clock radio, t/c mkg, refrig], ldry, dryer, rec rm, pool, c/park (undercover), cots-fee. **RO $55 - $75**, ch con, AE BC DC EFT MC MP VI.

★★☆ **Caloundra North Motor Inn**, (LMH), 32 Buderim St, Currimundi 4551, 500m E of Shopping Centre, ☎ 07 5491 5200, fax 07 5491 7381, 22 units [shwr, tlt, a/c, tel, cable tv, clock radio, t/c mkg, refrig], ldry, conf fac, ✕, pool-heated, bbq, c/park (undercover), plygr, cots-fee. **RO ♦ $55 - $65, ♦♦ $60 - $70, ♦ $8**, AE BC DC EFT MC VI.

★★☆ **City Centre Motel**, (M), Previously Caloundra Safari, Cnr Orsova Tce & Minchinton St, 200m NW of city centre, ☎ 07 5491 3301, (2 stry gr fl), 7 units [shwr, tlt, a/c (8), c/fan, heat, tel, TV, t/c mkg, refrig], ldry, dryer, bbq, c/park (undercover), cots. **RO ♦ $55 - $60.50, ♦♦ $66 - $77, ♦ $11 - $16.50**, ch con, fam con, BC MC VI.

★★ **Caloundra Motel**, (M), 30 Bowman Rd, 100m W of Sundland Shopping Centre, ☎ 07 5491 1411, fax 07 5492 7411, (2 stry gr fl), 14 units [shwr, tlt, a/c-cool, heat, TV, t/c mkg, refrig], pool, bbq, c/park (undercover), boat park. **RO ♦ $45 - $55, ♦♦ $55 - $65, ♦ $10**, AE BC DC EFT MC VI.

Self Catering Accommodation

★★★★☆ **La Promenade Apartments**, (SA), 4 Tay Ave, waterfront, 150m from town centre, ☎ 07 5499 7133, fax 07 5499 7144, (Multi-stry gr fl), 21 serv apts [shwr, spa bath, tlt, hairdry, a/c, tel, cable tv, video, movie, clock radio, CD, refrig, cook fac ltd, micro, elec frypan, toaster, ldry, blkts, linen, pillows], lift, w/mach, dryer, iron, iron brd, ✕ (Clsd.Good Fri & Xmas), pool-heated, spa, secure park (under cover), cots-fee. **D $122 - $242, W $654 - $1,228**, AE BC DC EFT MC VI, ♿.

★★★★☆ **Meridian Luxury Apartments**, (Apt), Cnr Burgess & Albert Sts, 250m from Kings Beach, ☎ 07 5491 0600, fax 07 5491 0666, (Multi-stry), 20 apts acc up to 6, (2 & 3 bedrm), [ensuite, shwr, bath, tlt, hairdry, heat, c/fan, tel, TV, video, clock radio, t/c mkg, refrig, micro, d/wash, ldry, blkts, linen, pillows], lift, dryer, iron, iron brd, pool (saltwater), bbq, secure park (undercover), cots-fee. **D $135, W $410 - $615**, BC EFT JCB MC VI.

★★★★☆ **Pandanus Shores**, (HU), 1 The Esplanade, Cnr Dingle Av, 1km N of PO, ☎ 07 5492 8922, fax 07 5492 6628, (Multi-stry gr fl), 9 units [ensuite, shwr, bath, tlt, c/fan (8), tel, TV, video, clock radio, CD (3), refrig, cook fac, micro, d/wash, toaster, ldry (in unit), blkts, linen, pillows], lift, dryer, iron, iron brd, pool (salt water), bbq, c/park (undercover), secure park, cots-fee. **RO ♦ $97 - $205, ♦♦ $97 - $205, W $455 - $1,400**, BC MC VI,

Operator Comment: View our Destination Queensland Web Site at http://www.queensland-holidays.com.au

★★★★☆ **Portobello By The Sea**, (HU), 6 Beerburrum St, ☎ 07 5491 9038, fax 07 5439 4199, (Multi-stry gr fl), 55 units acc up to 6, [ensuite (21), shwr, bath (21), spa bath (8), tlt, c/fan, tel, cable tv, video, clock radio, t/c mkg, refrig, micro, elec frypan, d/wash, toaster, ldry, blkts, linen, pillows], lift, dryer, iron, iron brd, ✕, pool-heated (salt water), bbq, secure park (covered), cots-fee. **D ♦♦ $100 - $300, ♦ $15, W ♦♦ $420 - $700, ♦ $45**, AE BC DC EFT MC VI, ♿.

★★★★☆ **Rendezvous Golden Beach Resort**, (SA), 75 The Esplanade, Golden Beach, 50m E of Golden Beach P O, ☎ 07 5437 4100, fax 07 5437 4237, (Multi-stry gr fl), 134 serv apts (1, 2 & 3 bedrm), [shwr, spa bath, tlt, hairdry, a/c, tel, TV, movie, clock radio, refrig, mini bar, cook fac, micro, elec frypan, toaster, blkts, linen, pillows], lift, ldry, dryer-fee, iron, iron brd, rec rm, conf fac, ✕, pool-heated, spa, steam rm, bbq-fee, rm serv, dinner to unit, secure park (undercover, overflow), plygr, gym, tennis, cots-fee. **RO $149 - $210**, AE BC DC EFT MC VI, ♿.

★★★★☆ **Riviere on Golden Beach**, (Apt), 72 Esplanade, Opposite PO, ☎ 07 5492 3200, fax 07 5492 4422, (Multi-stry), 26 apts acc up to 6, (2 & 3 bedrm), [ensuite, shwr, bath, spa bath, tlt, hairdry, c/fan, tel (ISD), cable tv, video, clock radio, refrig, micro, elec frypan, d/wash, toaster, ldry, blkts, linen, pillows], dryer, iron, iron brd, pool-heated, bbq, secure park (undercover), cots-fee. **D ♦♦♦♦ $150, RO ♦ $130 - $210, ♦♦ $130 - $210, W $595 - $1,150**, BC MC VI,

Operator Comment: Affordable luxury on the beachfront. Ring and enquire about our special offer.

SAILS RESORT ON GOLDEN BEACH

Panoramic views and absolute waterfront, 200m to local shopping centre

3 Landsborough Parade, Caloundra QLD 4551
Email: stay@sailsresort.com
Web: www.sailsresort.com
Ph: **07 5492 7888**
Fax: **07 5492 7900**
Reservations: **1800 358 288**

★★★★☆ **Sails Resort on Golden Beach**, (HU), 3 Landsborough Pde, 200m S Sunland Shopping Centre, ☎ 07 5492 7888, fax 07 5492 7900, (Multi-stry), 24 units (2 & 3 bedrm), [ensuite, shwr, bath, spa bath (1), tlt, tel, TV, video, clock radio, CD (8), refrig, cook fac, micro, d/wash, ldry (in unit), blkts, linen, pillows], lift, dryer, iron, iron brd, pool-heated (saltwater), spa, bbq, secure park, cots-fee. **D $135 - $230, W $460 - $650**, BC EFT MC VI.

★★★★☆ **The Entrance**, (HU), 13 Westaway Pde, Currimundi 4551, 5km N of Caloundra PO, ☎ 07 5493 6994, fax 07 5493 6954, (Multi-stry), 9 units acc up to 6, (3 bedrm), [shwr, spa bath (2), tlt, c/fan, tel, TV, video, clock radio, refrig, cook fac, micro, elec frypan, d/wash, toaster, ldry, blkts, linen, pillows], lift, dryer, iron, iron brd, pool (salt water), bbq, secure park (garage), cots-fee. **W $574 - $1,960**, BC EFT MC VI, ♿.

★★★★☆ **The Jetty Pelican Waters**, (HU), 1 Raleigh St, Golden Beach 4551, ☎ 07 5492 4077, fax 07 5492 4088, 9 units acc up to 6, (3 bedrm), [shwr, tlt, c/fan, tel, TV, clock radio, t/c mkg, refrig, cook fac, micro, d/wash, toaster, blkts, linen, pillows], ldry, w/mach, dryer, pool-heated, c/park (undercover), cots-fee, non smoking property. **D ♂♀ $128 - $150, ♿ $16, W ♂♀ $585, ♿ $70**, BC EFT MC VI.

★★★★☆ **Windward Passage**, (HU), 31 Landsborough Pde Golden Beach via, 400m S of Sunland Shopping Centre, ☎ 07 5492 3666, fax 07 5492 3422, (Multi-stry gr fl), 22 units acc up to 7, (1 & 2 bedrm), [ensuite, shwr, bath, spa bath (12), tlt, fan (10), c/fan, heat, tel, cable tv, video, clock radio, t/c mkg, refrig, cook fac, micro, elec frypan, d/wash, toaster, ldry, blkts, linen, pillows], dryer, iron, iron brd, pool-heated, bbq (covered), secure park, cots-fee. **D $135 - $170, W $445 - $1,250**, Min book applies, BC EFT MC VI, ♿.

Operator Comment:
Visit our website at: www.windwardpassage.com.au

★★★★ **Belaire Place Caloundra**, (HU), 34 Minchinton St, ☎ 07 5491 8688, fax 07 5491 7447, (Multi-stry), 20 units acc up to 4, (1 bedrm), [shwr, bath, spa bath (1), tlt, a/c (2), c/fan, tel, cable tv, video-fee, clock radio, t/c mkg, refrig, cook fac, micro, toaster, blkts, linen, pillows], ldry, w/mach-fee, dryer-fee, iron, iron brd, conf fac, ⊠, pool-heated (salt water), secure park, gym. **RO ♂ $95 - $150, ♂♀ $95 - $150, W $370 - $820**, AE BC DC EFT MC VI, ♿.

★★★★ **Belvedere Apartments**, (HU), 61 Esplanade, Golden Beach, Golden Beach 4551, 1km S of Shopping Centre, ☎ 07 5492 3963, fax 07 5492 3415, (Multi-stry) 18 units acc up to 6, (2 & 3 bedrm), [ensuite, shwr, bath, tlt, c/fan, heat, tel, cable tv (7 channels), video (7 units), clock radio, refrig, cook fac, micro, elec frypan, d/wash, ldry (in unit), blkts, linen, pillows], lift, dryer, pool (salt water), bbq (covered), c/park (undercover), secure park, cots-fee. **D $135, W $375 - $535**, BC EFT MC VI, ♿.

★★★★ **Centrepoint Apartments Caloundra**, (HU), cnr Minchinton St & Leeding Tce, 20m from town centre, ☎ 07 5492 0100, fax 07 5492 0101, (Multi-stry), 58 units acc up to 6, (1, 2 & 3 bedrm), [ensuite, shwr, bath (29), tlt, fan, heat, tel, cable tv, movie, clock radio, refrig, cook fac, micro, d/wash, ldry (in unit), blkts, linen, pillows], lift, dryer, ⊠, cafe, pool-heated, sauna, bbq, rm serv, secure park. **RO $130 - $180, W $665 - $1,400**, AE BC DC MC VI.

★★★★ **Fairseas Apartments**, (Apt), 68 The Esplanade Golden Beach via, 1.7km SW of PO, ☎ 07 5492 4237, fax 07 5492 4271, (Multi-stry), 9 apts acc up to 6, (2 & 3 bedrm), [shwr, bath, tlt, hairdry (1), heat, c/fan (9), TV, video, clock radio, refrig, micro, d/wash, toaster, ldry, blkts, linen, pillows], dryer, iron, iron brd, pool, spa, bbq, secure park, cots-fee. **RO ♂ $105 - $135, ♂♀ $105 - $135, W $365 - $845**, BC EFT MC VI.

★★★★ **Gemini Resort**, (HU), 49 Landsborough Pde, 500m S of Sunland Shopping Centre, ☎ 07 5492 2200, fax 07 5492 1000, (Multi-stry gr fl), 90 units [shwr, bath, tlt, fan, heat, tel, cable tv, movie, clock radio, refrig, cook fac, micro, d/wash, ldry (in unit), blkts, linen, pillows], dryer, rec rm, ⊠ (Tues to Sun), bar, pool-heated (salt water) (2), sauna, spa (2), bbq, secure park, tennis, cots-fee. **RO $125 - $160, W $540 - $1,490.**

★★★★ **Kings Bay Apartments**, (HU), 18 Mahia Tce Kings Beach via, Cnr Moreton Pde, 1 km E of PO, ☎ 07 5438 0600, fax 07 5438 0700, (Multi-stry), 11 units acc up to 6, (2 & 3 bedrm), [shwr, bath, tlt, fan, heat, TV, video, clock radio, t/c mkg, refrig, cook fac, micro, d/wash, toaster, blkts, linen, pillows], shwr (external), tlt (external), w/mach, dryer, iron, iron brd, pool-heated (saltwater), spa (heated), bbq (covered), secure park, cots. **D $150 - $231, W $418 - $979**, BC EFT MC VI.

★★★★ **Kings Row Holiday Apartments**, (Apt), 10 Warne Tce, Kings Beach 4551, ☎ 07 5438 0088, fax 07 5492 8999, (Multi-stry), 7 apts acc up to 6, (2 bedrm), [shwr, spa bath, tlt, a/c-cool (3), fan (1), heat (2), tel, TV, video, clock radio (5),t/c mkg, refrig, cook fac, micro, d/wash, toaster, ldry (in unit), blkts, linen, pillows, towels]. lift, w/mach, dryer, pool heated, spa, bbq, cots-fee. **D ♂♀ $140 to $190, ♿ $25 - $35**, Min book all holiday times, BC EFT MC VI.

★★★★ **Rydges Oasis Resort Caloundra**, (Apt), Resort, Cnr 2 North St & Landsborough Pde, 500m S of PO, ☎ 07 5491 0333, fax 07 5491 0300, (Multi-stry gr fl), 200 apts acc up to 7, (1, 2 & 3 bedrm), [shwr, bath, spa bath (128), tlt, hairdry (110), a/c (158), c/fan (50), tel, TV, video, movie, clock radio, t/c mkg, refrig, mini bar (on request), cook fac (50), cook fac ltd (48), micro (100), elec frypan (98), toaster (98), ldry (in unit)], lift, dryer-fee, iron, iron brd, conv fac, ⊠ (7am-10pm/non smoking) (2), pool, spa, 24hr reception, dinner to unit, secure park, ☎, plygr, tennis-fee, cots-fee, non smoking flr (1), non smoking units (37). **D $147 - $202**, ch con, 61 units of 3.5 star rating. Min book all holiday times, AE BC DC EFT MC VI, ♿.

★★★★ **Sandy Shores**, (HU), 7 The Esplanade Golden Beach via, 500m S of Sunland Shopping Complex, ☎ 07 5492 3400, fax 07 5492 3399, (Multi-stry gr fl), 5 units acc up to 6, (2 & 3 bedrm), [shwr, bath, tlt, hairdry, a/c, tel, TV, video, clock radio, t/c mkg, refrig, cook fac, micro, d/wash, toaster, blkts, linen, pillows], lift, w/mach, dryer, iron, iron brd, pool-heated (saltwater), bbq, secure park (undercover), cots-fee. **RO ♂ $125 - $145, ♂♀ $125 - $145, W $470 - $1,025**, BC EFT MC VI.

★★★★ **Sea Eagle Apartments**, (HU), 38 Victoria Tce Kings Beach, 1 km N of GPO, ☎ 07 5492 5552, fax 07 5491 9122, (Multi-stry gr fl), 9 units (2 & 3 bedrm), [ensuite, shwr, spa bath (8), tlt, c/fan, heat (fan), TV, video, refrig, cook fac, micro, elec frypan, d/wash, toaster, ldry (in unit), blkts, linen, pillows], lift, w/mach, dryer, iron, pool, bbq, c/park (undercover), secure park, ☎. **W $485 - $1,230, RO ♂ $140 - $195, ♂♀ $140 - $195**, BC EFT MC VI.

★★★☆ **Burgess Apartments**, (HU), Cnr Burgess & Albert Sts, Kings Beach, 150m N of Kings Beach, ☎ 07 5491 4594, fax 07 5491 8050, (Multi-stry gr fl), 20 units acc up to 3, [shwr, bath, spa bath (1), tlt, c/fan (12), heat, tel, cable tv, video, clock radio, cook fac, micro, d/wash, ldry (in unit), blkts, linen, pillows], lift, pool, sauna, spa, bbq, secure park, tennis (half court), cots-fee. **RO ♂ $120 - $160, ♂♀ $120 - $160, $420 - $1,090, Penthouse RO $390 - $1,620**, BC EFT MC VI.

★★★☆ **Campbells Cove**, (HU), 30 Esplanade Headland, Kings Beach, 1km E CBD, ☎ 07 5491 5288, fax 07 5491 5936, (Multi-stry), 10 units acc up to 6, (2 bedrm3 bedrm), [ensuite, shwr, bath, tlt, c/fan (5), heat, tel, TV, video (7), clock radio, refrig, cook fac, micro, d/wash, ldry (in unit), blkts, linen, pillows], lift, dryer, iron, iron brd, pool, bbq, secure park. **D $130, RO $435 - $1,375**, BC DC EFT MC VI.

★★★☆ **Capeview Apartments**, (HU), 26 Orvieto Tce, Cnr Ormonde Tce, 1km NE of PO, ☎ 07 5491 6436, fax 07 5491 9705, (Multi-stry gr fl), 14 units acc up to 7, (2 & 3 bedrm), [ensuite, shwr, bath, tlt, fan, c/fan, heat, tel, TV, video, clock radio, refrig, cook fac, micro, elec frypan, d/wash, ldry (in unit), blkts, linen, pillows], dryer, iron, pool, bbq, c/park (garage), secure park, plygr, cots-fee. **RO ♂♀ $140 - $160, ♂♀♂♀ $140 - $160, $480 - $1,150**, BC EFT MC VI.

★★★☆ **Casablanca Beachfront Holiday Apartments**, (HU), Cnr Edmund St & Ormonde Tce, 20m from Kings Beach, ☎ 07 5491 4323, fax 07 5491 4323, (Multi-stry gr fl), 22 units acc up to 8, [shwr, bath, tlt, fan, c/fan, heat, tel, TV, clock radio, refrig, cook fac, micro, d/wash, ldry (in unit), blkts, linen, pillows], dryer, pool-heated, bbq, boat park, secure park, tennis (half court), cots-fee. **D $110, W $440 - $900**, BC EFT MC VI.

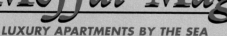

★★★☆ **Cheltenham Apartments**, (HU), 40 King St, 300m from Kings Beach, 1.5km NE of PO, ☎ 07 5491 6564, fax 07 5491 6564, (Multi-stry), 10 units acc up to 6, [shwr, bath, tlt, fan, heat, tel, cable tv, video (2), clock radio, refrig, cook fac, micro, d/wash, ldry (in unit), blkts, linen, pillows], dryer, iron, pool, spa (roof top), bbq, secure park, cots-fee. **D $110 - $143, W $385 - $803,** BC MC VI.

★★★☆ **Dulkara Units**, (HU), 6 Merrima Ave Kings Beach, 30m from patrolled beach, ☎ 07 5491 3201, fax 07 5491 3280, (Multi-stry), 15 units acc up to 7, (2 & 3 bedrm), [shwr, bath (2), tlt, tel, TV, clock radio, refrig, cook fac, micro, elec frypan, d/wash (2), ldry (in unit), blkts, linen, pillows], lift, dryer, pool, bbq, secure park, car wash, cots-fee. **RO ☗ $105, ☗☗ $105, W $350 - $850, BC MC VI.**

★★★☆ **Joanne Apartments**, (HU), Cnr Cooma Tce, Knox Ave & The Esplanade, 5 km N of PO, ☎ 07 5491 3245, fax 07 5491 7249, (Multi-stry gr fl), 27 units [shwr, bath, tlt, fan, c/fan, heat, tel, TV, video, clock radio, refrig, cook fac, micro, d/wash (23), ldry (in unit), blkts, linen, pillows], dryer, pool (2), c/park (undercover), secure park (23), cots-fee. **D $120, W $370 - $795,** BC EFT MC VI.

★★★☆ **Kings Cove Apartments**, (HU), 33 Burgess St Kings Beach, 1.5 km N of PO, ☎ 07 5492 7611, fax 07 5492 7611, (Multi-stry), 5 units acc up to 6, (2 bedrm), [shwr, bath, tlt, a/c-cool (1), fan (4), c/fan (4), heat, TV, video (4), clock radio, refrig, cook fac, micro, elec frypan, d/wash (4), toaster, ldry (in unit), blkts, linen, pillows], dryer, iron, iron brd, pool, bbq (covered), c/park (undercover), cots-fee. **D $95 - $120, W $360 - $760.**

★★★☆ **Kings Way Apartments**, (HU), 20 Warne Tce (entry Dingle Ave), 500m E of PO, ☎ 07 5491 7500, fax 07 5491 7504, (Multi-stry), 12 units acc up to 5, (2 bedrm), [shwr, bath, tlt, fan (7), c/fan (5), TV, video (6), clock radio, refrig, cook fac, micro, d/wash, ldry (in unit), blkts, linen, pillows], dryer, iron, pool (salt water), spa, bbq, secure park, cots-fee. **W $305 - $800, RO ☗ $95 - $120, ☗☗ $95 - $120,** BC MC VI.

Trouble-free travel tips - Hoses and belts

Inspect the condition of radiator hoses, heater hose fan and air conditioner belts.

★★★☆ **Lindomare Holiday Apartments**, (HU), 11-13 Orvieto Tce, Kings Beach, 100m W of patrolled Kings Bch, ☎ 07 5492 5922, fax 07 5492 5808, (Multi-stry gr fl), 16 units (2 & 3 bedrm - some units with ensuite), [shwr, bath, tlt, c/fan, heat, tel, TV, video, clock radio, refrig, cook fac, micro, d/wash, ldry (in unit), blkts, linen, pillows], dryer, iron, pool (heated), sauna, bbq, secure park, cots-fee. **D $123 - $230, W $413 - $889**, BC MC VI.

★★★☆ **Norfolks on Moffat Beach**, (HU), 32 Queen of Colonies Pde Moffat Beach, 50m S of Moffat Beach, ☎ 07 5492 6666, fax 07 5492 6262, (Multi-stry gr fl), 34 units acc up to 6, [ensuite (23), shwr, bath, tlt, fan (24), c/fan (11), heat, tel, cable tv, video (35), clock radio, refrig, cook fac, micro, d/wash, ldry (in unit), blkts, linen, pillows], lift, dryer, iron, pool-heated (gas), sauna, spa, bbq, cots-fee. **RO ♦ $145 - $195, ♦♦ $145 - $195, W $450 - $570**, Min book applies, BC EFT MC VI.

★★★☆ **Seapoint Ocean Apartments**, (HU), 32 Victoria Tce, adjacent to oceanfront, ☎ 07 5491 2433, fax 07 5491 7270, (Multi-stry gr fl), 14 units (2 & 3 bedrm), [ensuite, shwr, bath, tlt, c/fan, heat, TV, video-fee, clock radio, refrig, cook fac, micro, d/wash, ldry (in unit), blkts, linen, pillows], dryer, pool-heated (solar), bbq, secure park, ✆, cots-fee. **RO ♦ $120, ♦♦ $120, W $380 - $890**, BC EFT MC VI.

★★★☆ **The Retreat Lakeside Currimundi**, (HU), 9 Westaway Pde, 5km N of Caloundra PO, ☎ 07 5493 6833, fax 07 5493 7488, (Multi-stry), 10 units acc up to 7, (2 bedrm), [ensuite, shwr, bath, spa bath (3), tlt, c/fan, TV, video, clock radio, refrig, cook fac, micro, elec frypan, d/wash, ldry (in unit), blkts, linen, pillows], lift, dryer, iron, pool (salt water), spa, secure park, cots-fee. **RO ♦ $100, ♦♦ $100, W $400 - $1,470, BC MC VI.**

★★★☆ **Tranquil Shores**, (HU), 57 Minchinton St, 50m N of Bulcock Beach, ☎ 07 5491 8509, fax 07 5491 5363, (Multi-stry), 18 units acc up to 4, (2 bedrm), [ensuite (12), shwr, bath (6), tlt, fan, heat, tel, TV, clock radio, refrig, cook fac, micro, elec frypan, d/wash, ldry (in unit), blkts, linen, pillows], dryer, iron, iron brd, pool-heated (solar), spa, secure park, cots-fee. **W $405 - $765**, Min book applies, BC MC VI.

★★★☆ **Tripcony Quays**, (HU), 42 Maloja Ave, ☎ 07 5491 1166, fax 07 5491 9838, (Multi-stry), 13 units acc up to 7, (2 & 3 bedrm), [shwr, bath, tlt, fan, heat, tel, TV, clock radio, refrig, cook fac, micro, d/wash, ldry (in unit), blkts, linen, pillows], dryer, iron, pool (gas heated), bbq, boat park, secure park. **RO ♦ $115 - $160, ♦♦ $115 - $160, ♦ $390 - $1,050, ♦♦ $390 - $1,050**, AE BC MC VI.

★★★☆ **Whitecaps Apartments**, (HU), 44 Edmund St, 1km NE of PO, ☎ 07 5492 5254, fax 07 5491 5868, (Multi-stry gr fl), 12 units acc up to 6, (2 & 3 bedrm), [ensuite (2), shwr, bath, tlt, fan (9), c/fan (3), heat, tel, TV, video, clock radio, refrig, cook fac, micro, d/wash, toaster, ldry (in unit), blkts, linen, pillows], dryer, iron, iron brd, pool-heated (salt water), spa, bbq, secure park, cots-fee. **RO $170, $300 - $350**, BC EFT MC VI.

★★★☆ **Windbourne Holiday Apartments**, (HU), 101 Esplanade, Golden Beach, ☎ 07 5492 3365, fax 07 5492 3633, (Multi-stry), 15 units acc up to 6, [shwr, bath, tlt, fan, heat, TV, t/c mkg, refrig, cook fac, micro, d/wash, ldry (in unit), blkts, linen, pillows], dryer, pool, sauna, bbq, c/park (garage). **RO $345 - $715**, BC MC VI.

★★★ **Beachside Court**, (HU), 33A Burgess St, Kings Beach, 3km NE of Caloundra PO, ☎ 07 5491 7454, fax 07 5491 5434, 12 units acc up to 5, (2 bedrm), [shwr, bath, tlt, fan (2), c/fan, heat, TV, video (avail) (2)-fee, clock radio, refrig, cook fac, micro, toaster, ldry (in unit), linen, pillows], dryer, iron, iron brd, pool (solar heated), bbq (covered), secure park, ✆, cots-fee. **D ♦♦ $89 - $115, W $335 - $640**, BC EFT MC VI.

★★★ **Estoril on Moffat**, (HU), 38 McIlwraith St, Moffat Beach, 200m E of Moffat Beach PO, ☎ 07 5491 5988, fax 07 5491 5799, (Multi-stry gr fl), 20 units acc up to 4, [shwr, bath, tlt, tel, cable tv, video-fee, clock radio, refrig, cook fac, d/wash, ldry (in unit), blkts, linen, pillows], dryer, rec rm, pool-heated, sauna, spa, bbq, secure park, cots-fee. **RO ♦ $110, ♦♦ $110, W $560 - $980**, , AE BC DC EFT MC VI.

★★★ **Raintrees Resort**, (HU), 1 Bryce St, Moffat Beach, beachfront, ☎ 07 5491 5555, fax 07 5491 1284, (Multi-stry gr fl), 39 units [shwr, bath, tlt, c/fan, tel, cable tv, video-fee, clock radio, refrig, cook fac, micro, d/wash, ldry (in unit), blkts, linen, pillows], pool-heated (2), spa (heated), bbq (4), secure park, cots-fee. **RO ♦ $220 - $540, ♦♦ $220 - $540, W $540 - $1,210,** Min book applies, AE BC DC EFT MC VI.

★★★ **Seafarer Chase**, (HU), 41 Canberra Tce, 700m E of PO, 150m W of Kings Beach, ☎ 07 5491 7155, fax 07 5491 7155, (Multi-stry), 6 units acc up to 4, [ensuite, shwr, bath, tlt, fan, heat, TV, clock radio, refrig, cook fac, micro, elec frypan, d/wash, toaster, ldry (in unit), blkts, linen, pillows], dryer, iron, iron brd, pool (salt water), secure park. **RO ♦ $350 - $805, ♦♦ $350 - $805,**

Operator Comment: Email: seachase@caloundra.net

★★☆ **Mainsail Holiday Apartments**, (HU), 1 Saltair St, 1km NE of PO, ☎ 07 5491 5600, fax 07 5492 7420, (Multi-stry), 13 units acc up to 7, (2 bedrm), [shwr, bath, tlt, c/fan (3), tel, TV, video (5)-fee, refrig, cook fac, micro, d/wash (12), ldry (in unit), blkts, linen, pillows], dryer, rec rm, pool, sauna, spa, bbq, secure park (garage), cots-fee. **RO $220 - $360**, BC EFT MC VI.

Maritime Holiday Apartments, (Apt), 1/38a King St, 250m S of Kings Beach, ☎ 07 5492 8255, fax 07 5499 7823, (Multi-stry), 15 apts acc up to 4, (2 bedrm), [shwr, tlt, fan (10), c/fan (5), heat, tel, cable tv, video (4)-fee, t/c mkg, refrig, cook fac, micro, d/wash, toaster, ldry, blkts, linen, pillows], w/mach, dryer, pool, bbq, secure park (undercover), cots-fee. **D $110, W $430 - $720**, BC MC VI, (not yet classified).

SUNSHINE COAST - COOLUM BEACH QLD 4573

Pop 7,000. (132km N Brisbane), See maps on page 417, ref D4. Boating, Bowls, Fishing, Golf, Scenic Drives, Surfing, Swimming.

Self Catering Accommodation

★★★★☆ **Clubb Coolum Beach Resort**, (HU), 89-97 The Esplanade, 1Km S of PO, ☎ 07 5446 3888, fax 07 5446 3369, 54 units acc up to 6, (2 & 3 bedrm), [basin, ensuite, shwr, bath, tlt, c/fan, tel, TV, clock radio, refrig, cook fac, micro, elec frypan, d/wash, toaster, ldry (in unit)], dryer, iron, pool-heated, sauna, spa, bbq, secure park, gym, tennis, cots-fee. **D $140 - $190, W $700 - $1,400**, AE BC DC EFT MC VI.

★★★★☆ **Coolum Baywatch**, (HU), The Esplanade, 1766 David Low Way, 100m S of Surf Club, ☎ 07 5446 5500, fax 07 5446 4455, (Multi-stry), 11 units acc up to 4, (1 & 2 bedrm), [ensuite, shwr, spa bath, tlt, a/c, tel, TV, video, clock radio, t/c mkg, refrig, cook fac, micro, elec frypan, d/wash, toaster, blkts, linen, pillows], lift, w/mach, dryer, iron, iron brd, pool-heated (salt water), sauna, spa, bbq, secure park. **D $150 - $210, W $500 - $1,470**, AE BC DC MC VI.

★★★★☆ **Coolum Beach Mediterranean Resort**, (SA), 7-13 Beach Rd (Cnr Beach & Frank Sts), 2km from PO, ☎ 07 5471 7744, fax 07 5455 7177, (Multi-stry), 14 serv apts (1 & 2 bedrm), [shwr, tlt, hairdry, c/fan, tel, TV, video, clock radio, refrig, cook fac, elec frypan, d/wash, toaster, ldry, blkts, linen, pillows], iron, iron brd, rec rm, ✗, pool-heated (saltwater/solar), sauna, spa (comm), bbq, c/park (undercover), secure park, ☎ cots-fee. D ┇ $125 - $170, W ┇ $480 - $1,050, AE BC DC EFT MC VI.

★★★★☆ **Coolum Caprice**, (HU), 1770 David Low Way, opposite patrolled beach, ☎ 07 5446 2177, fax 07 5446 3559, (Multi-stry), 68 units acc up to 7, (1, 2 & 3 bedrm), [ensuite, shwr, bath, tlt, c/fan, heat, tel, cable tv, video, clock radio, refrig, cook fac, micro, d/wash, ldry (in unit), blkts, linen, pillows], lift, iron, iron brd, rec rm, pool-heated, sauna, spa, bbq, secure park, plygr, gym, cots-fee. D ♦♦ $115 - $200, W ♦♦ $476 - $815, BC EFT MC VI.

★★★★☆ **Endless Summer Resort**, (HU), 9 Frank St, 100m W of beach, ☎ 07 5471 9800, fax 07 5471 9888, (Multi-stry gr fl), 31 units acc up to 7, (1, 2 & 3 bedrm), [shwr, spa bath, tlt, a/c (5), c/fan, tel, cable tv, video-fee, clock radio, t/c mkg, refrig, cook fac, micro, d/wash, toaster, blkts, linen, pillows], lift, ldry, w/mach, dryer, rec rm, pool-heated, sauna, spa, bbq, secure park (undercover), plygr, cots-fee. D $95 - $220, W $495 - $1,475, ch con, AE BC DC EFT MC VI.

★★★★☆ **The Beach Retreat Coolum**, (HU), Resort, 1750 David Low Way, 1.2km S of PO, ☎ 07 5471 7700, fax 07 5471 7711, 87 units acc up to 5, (Studio, 1 & 2 bedrm), [ensuite (32), shwr, spa bath (55), tlt, a/c, tel, TV, movie, clock radio, refrig, mini bar, cook fac ltd, micro, toaster, blkts, linen, pillows], w/mach, dryer, iron, iron brd, ✗, pool-heated (salt water), sauna, spa, bbq, dinner to unit, secure park, cots-fee. D ♦♦ $87 - $132, ▯ $12, W ♦♦ $485 - $924, ♦♦♦♦ $725 - $1,190, AE BC DC MC VI, ♿.

★★★★☆ **The Point**, (Villa), 1 Bay Tce, 1km S of Coolum Beach, ☎ 07 5440 9888, fax 07 5440 9889, 60 villas acc up to 8, [ensuite, shwr, bath, spa bath, tlt, hairdry, c/fan, heat, tel, TV, video, clock radio, CD (14), t/c mkg, refrig, micro, elec frypan, d/wash, toaster, ldry, blkts, linen, pillows], dryer, iron, iron brd, pool (2), bbq-fee, c/park (undercover), cots-fee. RO $155 - $260, W $840 - $1,435, AE BC DC EFT MC VI.

★★★★ **Coolum Beach Getaway Resort**, (HU), 3 First Ave, ☎ 07 5471 6759, fax 07 5471 6222, 15 units acc up to 6, (1, 2 & 3 bedrm), [ensuite, shwr, tlt, fan, TV, video, clock radio, t/c mkg, cook fac, micro, elec frypan, d/wash, toaster, ldry, blkts, linen, pillows], dryer, iron, iron brd, pool-heated (salt water), spa, bbq (covered), secure park (garage), tennis (half court). RO $120 - $180, W $435 - $1,200, BC EFT MC VI.

★★★★ **Coolum Blueseas**, (HU), 59-63 Coolum Tce, 300m S of beachfront, shops & restaurants, ☎ 07 5446 4100, fax 07 5446 5090, (Multi-stry gr fl), 6 units acc up to 6, (2 & 3 bedrm), [ensuite, shwr, spa bath, tlt, c/fan, tel, TV, video, clock radio, refrig, cook fac, micro, elec frypan, d/wash, toaster, ldry (in unit), blkts, linen, pillows], iron, iron brd, pool (salt water), spa, bbq (covered), secure park, cots-fee. D $160 - $190, W $495 - $1,190, BC MC VI, ♿.

★★★☆ **Pandanus Coolum Beach**, (SA), 1 Coolum Esp, 500m S of PO, ☎ 07 5446 3905, fax 07 5446 4669, (Multi-stry gr fl), 20 serv apts acc up to 6, (2 & 3 bedrm), [shwr, bath (hip), tlt, c/fan, tel, TV, video, clock radio, refrig, cook fac, micro, elec frypan, d/wash, ldry (in unit)], dryer, pool-heated (salt water), spa, bbq, secure park, courtesy transfer-fee, cots-fee. W $500 - $1,020, BC EFT MC VI.

★★★☆ **Surf Dance**, (HU), 29 Coolum Tce, 500m S of PO, ☎ 07 5446 1039, fax 07 5446 1039, (Multi-stry), 14 units acc up to 6, (1 & 2 bedrm), [shwr, bath, tlt, c/fan, heat, TV, clock radio, refrig, cook fac, micro, d/wash, ldry (in unit), blkts, linen, pillows], pool-heated (salt water heated), bbq, c/park (garage), ☎, cots-fee. RO $80 - $140, W $300 - $840.

★★☆ **Villa Coolum**, (HU), 102 Coolum Tce, 250m from beach, ☎ 07 5446 1286, fax 07 5446 4049, 10 units acc up to 4, (1 bedrm), [shwr, tlt, c/fan, heat, TV, clock radio, refrig, cook fac, micro, elec frypan, blkts, linen, pillows], ldry, pool, bbq, c/park (undercover). D ♦♦ $59 - $100, ▯ $10, W ♦♦ $300 - $600, AE BC DC MC VI.

B&B's/Guest Houses

★★★★ **Coolum Dreams Bed & Breakfast**, (B&B), No children's facilities, 28 Warran Rd, 4km S of Coolum PO, ☎ 07 5446 3868, fax 07 5446 3868, (2 stry gr fl), 3 rms [ensuite, shwr, tlt, a/c-cool (1), c/fan, heat, TV (3), clock radio, refrig], ldry, dryer, lounge (TV), spa, t/c mkg shared, bbq, non smoking rms. BB ♦ $70 - $85, ♦♦ $90 - $130, AE BC MC VI.

★★★★ **Mt Coolum Retreat**, (B&B), 77 Mountain View Drive, ☎ 07 5471 6532, fax 07 5471 6532, 4 rms [shwr, bath (1), tlt, hairdry, c/fan, elec blkts, TV, video, t/c mkg, refrig, cook fac, micro], iron, iron brd, TV rm, spa, cook fac, bbq. BB ♦ $50 - $65, ♦♦ $80 - $100, BC EFT MC VI.

SUNSHINE COAST - KAWANA WATERS QLD 4575

See maps on page 417, ref D5. A northern suburb of Caloundra.

Hotels/Motels

★★★☆ **Kawana International Motor Inn**, (M), 18 Nicklin Way, ☎ 07 5444 6900, fax 07 5444 6424, (2 stry gr fl), 23 units [shwr, bath (5), tlt, a/c-cool (23), tel, TV, clock radio, t/c mkg, refrig], ldry, dryer, ☒, pool (salt water), c/park (undercover), cots, non smoking units. **RO 👤 $60 - $75, 👥 $66 - $90, 👤 $11**, AE BC DC MC VI, ♿.

★★☆ **Stewarts Kawana Waters**, (LMH), Nicklin Way, ☎ 07 5444 6699, fax 07 5444 7053, (2 stry gr fl), 15 units [shwr, tlt, a/c, tel, TV, clock radio, t/c mkg, refrig], conv fac, ☒, pool, c/park (undercover), plygr, cots-fee. **BB 👤 $49 - $60, 👥 $68 - $80, 👤 $19**, ch con, AE BC DC MC VI.

★★☆ **Sun Surf**, (M), 56 Nicklin Way, cnr Sunbird Chase, ☎ 07 5493 3377, fax 07 5493 3377, 15 units [shwr, tlt, a/c, heat, tel, TV, movie, clock radio, t/c mkg, refrig, cook fac (1)], ldry, dryer, pool, spa, c/park (undercover), cots-fee. **RO 👤 $53 - $90, 👥 $58 - $95, 👤 $11**, ch con, AE BC EFT MC VI, ♿.

Self Catering Accommodation

★★★★☆ **Beachside Resort**, (HU), Cnr Pacific Boulevarde & Weema St, 200m E of Shoppingtown, ☎ 07 5478 4000, fax 07 5477 9399, (Multi-stry gr fl), 36 units acc up to 6, (1, 2 & 3 bedrm), [ensuite (24), shwr, bath, tlt, a/c-cool (10), heat, tel, cable tv, video (5), clock radio, refrig, cook fac, micro, elec frypan, d/wash, toaster, ldry (in unit), blkts, linen, pillows], lift, dryer, iron, iron brd, rec rm, pool-heated, sauna, spa, bbq, secure park, gym, tennis (night), cots-fee, non smoking flr. **D $130 - $212, W $549 - $1,485**, AE BC EFT MC VI.

AAA TOURISM *Special Rates* ★★★★ **Surfside on the Beach**, (HU), 143 Lowanna Dve, Buddina 4575, 1.5km E Kawana PO, ☎ 07 5444 0044, fax 07 5444 0668, (Multi-stry gr fl), 63 units acc up to 6, [ensuite, shwr, bath, tlt, c/fan, heat, tel, TV, clock radio, refrig, cook fac, micro, elec frypan, d/wash, ldry (in unit), blkts, linen, pillows], lift, pool-heated, bbq, secure park, cots-fee. **D $132 - $180, W $595 - $1,475**, ch con, BC MC VI.

B&B's/Guest Houses

★★★☆ **Beachfront Palms B & B**, (B&B), 61 Oceanic Drive, 105 km N Brisbane, ☎ 07 5493 4131, fax 07 5493 3829, 2 rms [a/c-cool (1), fan, elec blkts, TV (1), clock radio], shwr, tlt, TV rm (video, cd & radio), ✕, cook fac (incl toaster, refrig), t/c mkg shared, bbq (covered), c/park (garage), non smoking flr, non smoking rms. **BB 👤 $70, 👥 $85 - $110, 👤 $10**, ch con, BC DC MC VI,

Operator Comment:
Visit our web site at: www.babs.com.au/beachfront

SUNSHINE COAST - MARCOOLA BEACH QLD 4564

Pop 1,150. (125km N Brisbane), See maps on page 417, ref D4.

Hotels/Motels

★★★☆ **Discovery Beach Hotel Resort**, (LH), David Low Way, between Twin Waters & Hyatt Coolum, ☎ 07 5448 8900, fax 07 5448 8966, (Multi-stry), 86 rms [shwr, tlt, a/c, tel, cable tv, video, t/c mkg, refrig], lift, conv fac, conf fac, night club, ☒ (3), pool, spa, bbq, secure park, gym, tennis (half court), cots. **RO 👥 $100, 👤 $20**, ch con, EFT MC VI.

★★★☆ **Pacific Palms Motor Inn**, (M), 1051 David Low Way, 80m fr beach, ☎ 07 5448 7655, fax 07 5448 7655, 10 units [shwr, tlt, a/c-cool, tel, TV, clock radio, t/c mkg, refrig, cook fac (4)-fee, toaster], ldry-fee, pool, bbq. **RO 👤 $55 - $100, 👥 $55 - $100, 👤 $10**, BC MC VI.

★★☆ **Marcoola**, (M), 900 David Low Way, ☎ 07 5448 7313, fax 07 5448 7211, 10 units [shwr, tlt, c/fan, heat, tel, TV, clock radio, t/c mkg, refrig, micro (4), elec frypan (6), toaster], pool, bbq, dinner to unit, cots. **RO 👤 $45 - $50, 👥 $55 - $70, 👤 $15**, BC MC VI.

Self Catering Accommodation

★★★★☆ **Atlantis Marcoola**, (HU), 903 David Low Way, ☎ 07 5450 9800, fax 07 5450 9888, (Multi-stry), 20 units acc up to 6, (1, 2 & 3 bedrm), [shwr, tlt, a/c-cool, c/fan, tel, cable tv, video, clock radio, refrig, cook fac, micro, d/wash, toaster, blkts, linen, pillows], lift, ldry, w/mach, dryer, rec rm, pool-heated, wading pool, spa, bbq, secure park (undercover), plygr, tennis, cots-fee. **D 👥 $90 - $160, 👤 $15, W 👥 $395 - $650, 👤 $105**, ch con, AE BC DC EFT MC VI.

★★★★☆ **Salerno on the Beach**, (HU), 939 David Low Way, 6km N of Maroochydore PO, ☎ 07 5448 9699, fax 07 5448 8594, (Multi-stry), 22 units acc up to 6, (2 & 3 bedrm), [ensuite, shwr, bath, spa bath (6), tlt, hairdry (3), a/c (9), c/fan (16), heat (9), tel, TV, video, clock radio, CD (3), t/c mkg, refrig, micro, elec frypan, d/wash, toaster, ldry, blkts, linen, pillows], lift, dryer, iron, iron brd, pool-heated (salt water), bbq (covered), c/park (undercover), plygr, tennis, cots-fee. **RO $125 - $250**, BC EFT MC VI.

★★★★☆ **San Marino by the Sea**, (HU), 917 David Low Way, 1km from airport, ☎ 07 5450 6144, fax 07 5450 6411, (Multi-stry), 25 units acc up to 6, (2 & 3 bedrm), [shwr, spa bath (12), tlt, a/c (4), fan, tel, cable tv (7), video (12), clock radio, t/c mkg, refrig, cook fac, micro, d/wash, blkts, linen, pillows], w/mach, dryer, bar, pool-heated, bbq, secure park, plygr, cots-fee, non smoking units (3). **D 👥 $110 - $290, 👤 $15, W 👥 $395 - $790**, ch con, weekly con, Min book Christmas and Jan, BC EFT MC VI, ♿.

★★★★ **Surf Club Apartments**, (HU), 63 Marcoola Esplanade, 30m to beach, ☎ 07 5448 9877, fax 07 5450 9199, (Multi-stry gr fl), 20 units acc up to 6, (2 & 3 bedrm), [ensuite, shwr, bath, spa bath, a/c (2), c/fan (14), tel, TV, video, clock radio, cook fac, micro, d/wash, ldry, blkts, linen, pillows], iron, iron brd, pool (1 Heated) (2), spa (communal), bbq, meals to unit, secure park, courtesy transfer, cots-fee. **D $120 - $200, W $400 - $1,480**, BC MC VI, ♿,

Operator Comment:
Visit our web site: www.surfclubapartments.com.au

SUNSHINE COAST - MAROOCHYDORE QLD 4558

Pop 36,400. (112km N Brisbane), See maps on page 417, ref D4.
Horton Park Golf Club Alinga Tennis Centre. Boating, Bowls, Golf,
Sailing, Squash, Surfing, Swimming, Water Skiing.

Hotels/Motels

★★★☆ **Coachmans Courte Motor Inn**, (M), Resort, 94 Sixth Ave, ☎ 07 5443 4099, fax 07 5443 5876, (2 stry gr fl), 14 units [shwr, tlt, hairdry, a/c-cool, heat, tel, TV, video, clock radio, t/c mkg, refrig], pool, spa (unheated), c/park (undercover), cots-fee, non smoking units (9). **RO ♦ $81, ♦♦ $91,** ♦ **$12**, Min book Christmas Jan and Easter, AE BC DC JCB MC MP VI.

★★★☆ **Heritage Motor Inn**, (M), 69 Sixth Ave, ☎ 07 5443 7355, fax 07 5443 3794, 18 units [shwr, tlt, hairdry (9), a/c, tel, TV, video-fee, clock radio, t/c mkg, refrig], pool, spa, bbq, cots-fee. **RO ♦♦ $85 - $110,** ♦ **$10**, AE BC DC MC MP VI.

★★★ **Beach Motor Inn**, (M), 61 Sixth Ave, cnr Kingsford Smith Pde 100m to beach, ☎ 07 5443 7044, fax 07 5443 8490, 18 units [shwr, tlt, hairdry, a/c-cool, heat, tel, TV, video-fee, clock radio, t/c mkg, refrig], iron, iron brd, conf fac, pool, bbq, dinner to unit, cots-fee. **RO ♦ $88 - $132,** ♦♦ **$88 - $132,** ♦ **$22**, AE BC DC MC VI.

★★★ **Blue Waters**, (M), 64 Sixth Ave, ☎ 07 5443 6700, fax 07 5443 6242, (2 stry gr fl), 20 units [shwr, bath, tlt, a/c, tel, TV, t/c mkg, refrig, cook fac ltd (avail-10)], ldry, pool (salt water), c/park (undercover), cots. **RO ♦ $55 - $85,** ♦♦ **$60 - $105,** ♦ **$20**, ch con, AE BC DC MC MP VI.

★★★ **Wun Palm Motel**, (M), Cnr Duporth Ave & Phillip St, 1km W of PO, ☎ 07 5443 4677, fax 07 5443 4158, (2 stry gr fl), 12 units [shwr, tlt, a/c-cool, heat, tel, TV, video-fee, clock radio, t/c mkg, refrig], pool, bbq, cots, non smoking rms (4). **RO ♦ $54 - $64,** ♦♦ **$60 - $94,** ♦ **$11**, ch con, AE BC DC MC VI.

★★☆ **Avenue Motor Inn**, (M), 106 Sixth Ave, ☎ 07 5443 3600, fax 07 5443 3460, (2 stry), 16 units [shwr, tlt, hairdry (6), a/c-cool, heat, tel, TV, movie, clock radio, t/c mkg, refrig], pool, bbq, c/park (undercover), cots-fee. **RO ♦ $73 - $112,** ♦♦ **$84 - $112,** ♦ **$12**, AE BC DC JCB MC MP VI.

★★ **Maroochy River**, (M), 361 Bradman Ave, ☎ 07 5443 3142, 8 units [shwr, tlt, a/c (6), c/fan (8), TV, clock radio, t/c mkg, refrig, cook fac (8), micro (3), toaster], pool, ✆, cots-fee, Pets allowed. **RO ♦ $50 - $55,** ♦♦ **$55 - $95,** ♦ **$10**, ch con, AE BC MC VI.

Self Catering Accommodation

★★★★☆ **Argyle on the Park**, (HU), 31 Cotton Tree Pde, Off Moroochy River, ☎ 07 5443 3022, fax 07 5443 4941, (Multi-stry), 23 units acc up to 6, (1, 2 & 3 bedrm), [ensuite (3), shwr, tlt, a/c, tel, cable tv, clock radio, refrig, micro (convection), elec frypan, d/wash, toaster, ldry (in unit), blkts, linen, pillows], lift, dryer, iron, iron brd, pool (salt water), bbq, c/park (undercover), secure park, cots-fee. **D ♦♦ $115 - $160,** ♦ **$15,** **W ♦♦ $430 - $780,** ♦ **$40**, AE BC DC MC VI.

Operator Comment:
Visit our website on http://www.argyleonthepark.com.au

★★★★ **Catalina Resort**, (HU), Sixth Ave, 40m from patrolled beach, ☎ 07 5443 8666, fax 07 5443 7942, (Multi-stry), 49 units acc up to 6, [shwr, spa bath, tlt, tel, cable tv, video-fee, clock radio, refrig, cook fac, micro, d/wash (43), ldry (in unit), blkts, linen, pillows], lift, dryer, rec rm, pool-heated, wading pool, sauna, spa, bbq, secure park, car wash, tennis, cots-fee. **W $420 - $798, RO $95 - $175,** Min book all holiday times, AE BC DC MC VI.

★★★★ **Chateau Royale Beach Resort**, (HU), Cnr Sixth & Memorial Aves, 50m fr beachfront, ☎ 07 5443 0300, fax 07 5443 0371, (Multi-stry), 45 units acc up to 6, (2 & 3 bedrm), [shwr, bath, tlt, c/fan, tel, TV, video-fee, clock radio, refrig, cook fac, micro, d/wash, ldry (in unit), blkts, linen, pillows], lift, dryer, pool-heated, sauna, spa, bbq, secure park, cots-fee, non smoking flr (3). **D $150 - $210,** **W $620 - $1,940,** Min book applies, BC MC VI.

★★★★ **Crystal Waters Picnic Point**, (HU), 12 Picnic Point Esplanade, 1.25km NW of Maroochydore PO, ☎ 07 5479 4226, fax 07 5479 4237, 8 units acc up to 6, (1, 2 & 3 bedrm), [ensuite, shwr, bath (8), tlt, a/c-cool (1), fan (1), c/fan, TV, video (5), clock radio (5), CD (4), t/c mkg, refrig, cook fac, micro, elec frypan, d/wash, toaster, ldry, blkts, linen, pillows], lift, dryer, iron, iron brd, pool, spa, bbq, secure park. **D $175 - $230, W $395 - $1,300,** Min book applies, BC EFT MC VI.

★★★★ **Key Largo Maroochydore**, (HU), Previously Key Largo 6 Aerodrome Rd, ☎ 07 5443 7774, fax 07 5443 4765, (Multi-stry), 30 units acc up to 6, (1, 2 & 3 bedrm), [ensuite, shwr, bath, tlt, c/fan, tel, TV, video, clock radio, refrig, cook fac, micro, d/wash, toaster, ldry (in unit), blkts, linen, pillows], lift, dryer, iron, iron brd, pool-heated (salt water heated), sauna, spa, bbq, secure park (covered), gym, cots-fee. **W $450 - $1,575,** BC MC VI.

★★★★ **Picture Point Luxury Apartments**, (Apt), 24 Picnic Point Esp, 1km N of PO, ☎ 07 5479 1512, fax 07 54793116, (Multi-stry gr fl), 5 apts acc up to 6, (2 & 3 bedrm), [ensuite, shwr, bath, spa bath (1), tlt, a/c-cool, a/c (1), tel, TV, video, clock radio, refrig, micro, d/wash, toaster, ldry, blkts, linen, pillows], lift, shwr, tlt, dryer, iron, iron brd, pool, spa, secure park, cots-fee. **D $150 - $160,** ♦ **$10 - $15,** **W $520 - $1,150,** ch con, BC EFT MC VI.

Operator Comment: Reservations at: jbussell@bigpond.com

★★★★ **Reflections**, (HU), 2-4 Picnic Point Esp, 1km N of PO, ☎ 07 5443 9707, fax 07 5443 9079, (Multi-stry gr fl), 14 units acc up to 6, (2 & 3 bedrm), [ensuite, shwr, bath, spa bath (4), tlt, c/fan, tel, TV, video (8), clock radio, refrig, cook fac, micro, elec frypan, d/wash (14), toaster, ldry (in unit), blkts, linen, pillows], dryer, iron, iron brd, pool, spa, bbq (covered), secure park, cots-fee. **D ♦ $120 - $200, W $390 - $1,100,** BC EFT MC VI.

★★★★ **River Sands Holiday Apartments**, (HU), 271 Bradman Avenue, ☎ 07 5443 1179, fax 07 5479 2011, (2 stry), 12 units acc up to 4, [ensuite, shwr, bath, tlt, c/fan, tel (ISD), TV, video, clock radio, refrig, cook fac ltd, micro, elec frypan, d/wash, toaster, blkts, linen, pillows], ldry, w/mach, dryer, iron, pool (saltwater), bbq, c/park (undercover). **RO $110 - $135,** ♦ **$10**, AE MC VI.

Trouble-free travel tips - Windscreen wipers
Check the operation of windscreen wipers and washers. Replace windscreen wiper rubbers if they are not cleaning the windscreen properly.

★★★★ **Seashapes**, (HU), 44 Fourth Ave, 1km S of Cotton Tree P.O, ☎ 07 5451 1311, fax 07 5451 1311, 5 units acc up to 6, (2 & 3 bedrm), [ensuite, shwr, bath, spa bath (1), tlt, hairdry (1), c/fan, tel (3), TV, video, clock radio, t/c mkg, refrig, cook fac, micro, d/wash, toaster, lndry, blkts, linen, pillows], iron, iron brd, pool (salt water), bbq, secure park, cots-fee. D $120 - $195, W $385 - $880, BC MC VI.

★★★★ **Sunshine Towers**, (HU), 33 Sixth Ave, 150m S of Cotton Tree PO, ☎ 07 5443 1722, fax 07 5451 1386, (Multi-stry), 4 units acc up to 6, (2 & 3 bedrm), [ensuite, shwr, spa bath (3), tlt, a/c-cool (2), c/fan, tel, cable tv (2), video, clock radio, refrig, cook fac, micro, elec frypan, d/wash, toaster, lndry, blkts, linen, pillows], lift, dryer, iron, iron brd, pool (salt water), bbq (covered), secure park, cots-fee. RO ♦♦ $140 - $220, ♦♦ $460 - $1,250, AE BC DC EFT MC VI.

★★★★ **The Esplanade Picnic Point**, (HU), 18-22 Picnic Point Esp, ☎ 07 5479 4166, fax 07 5479 4396, (Multi-stry gr fl), 14 units acc up to 6, [ensuite, shwr, bath, tlt, c/fan, tel, TV, video, clock radio, refrig, cook fac, micro, d/wash, toaster, lndry (in unit), blkts, linen, pillows], lift, dryer, iron, iron brd, pool, spa, bbq, c/park (undercover), secure park, courtesy transfer, cots-fee. D $145 - $185, W $485 - $1,245, BC DC MC VI.

★★★☆ **Banyandah Towers**, (HU), 150 Duporth Ave, ☎ 07 5443 6911, fax 07 5443 5841, (Multi-stry), 56 units acc up to 5, (2 bedrm), [shwr, bath, spa bath, tlt, c/fan, heat, tel, cable tv, video-fee, clock radio, cook fac, micro, d/wash, lndry (in unit), blkts, linen, pillows], lift, dryer, rec rm, pool-heated, sauna, spa, bbq, secure park, jetty, cots-fee. D $170, W $490 - $1,030, ch con, Min book applies, BC DC MC VI.

★★★☆ **Beach Houses**, (HU), Cnr Sixth Ave & Beach Pde, 200m S of Cotton Tree PO, ☎ 07 5443 3049, fax 07 5443 8046, (Multi-stry gr fl), 16 units acc up to 8, (2 & 3 bedrm), [ensuite, shwr, bath, tlt, fan (15), tel, TV, video, clock radio, refrig, cook fac, micro, elec frypan, d/wash, lndry (in unit), blkts, linen, pillows], dryer, iron, pool, bbq, secure park, cots. D $120 - $240, W $400 - $990, $440 - $1,070, AE BC DC MC VI.

★★★☆ **Beachfront Towers**, (HU), 4 Aerodrome Rd, ☎ 07 5443 3443, fax 07 5443 9194, (Multi-stry), 40 units acc up to 4, (2 bedrm), [shwr, bath, tlt, fan (35), heat (32), tel, cable tv, cook fac, micro, d/wash, lndry (in unit), blkts, linen, pillows], lift, rec rm, ⊠, pool-heated, sauna, bbq, secure park, cots-fee. D $120, W $420 - $840, BC MC VI.

★★★☆ **Burlington Holiday Apartments**, (HU), 75 Sixth Ave. ☎ 07 5443 7088, fax 07 5456 7444, (Multi-stry gr fl), 16 units acc up to 5, [ensuite (4), shwr, bath (11), tlt, c/fan, tel, cable tv, clock radio, refrig, cook fac, micro, d/wash, lndry (in unit), blkts, linen, pillows], dryer, pool (salt water, heated), bbq, secure park, cots-fee. D $120 - $175, W $365 - $1,015, BC MC VI,

Operator Comment: Discount for AAA members staying 2 or more nights.

★★★☆ **Camargue**, (HU), 52 Alexandra Pde, Cnr Kingsford Smith Pde, ☎ 07 5443 6656, fax 07 5479 2066, 18 units acc up to 6, (2 bedrm), [ensuite, shwr, bath, tlt, a/c, tel, cable tv, video, refrig, cook fac, micro, d/wash, lndry (in unit), linen], lift, pool-heated, sauna, spa, bbq, secure park. RO $130 - $140, W $520 - $1,145, Min book applies, BC EFT MC VI.

★★★☆ **Coral Sea Apartments**, (HU), 35 Sixth Ave, 300m S of Cotton Tree PO, ☎ 07 5479 2999, fax 07 5479 2999, (Multi-stry), 20 units acc up to 6, (2 & 3 bedrm), [ensuite, shwr, bath, tlt, fan, TV, clock radio, refrig, cook fac, micro, elec frypan, d/wash, toaster, lndry (in unit), blkts, linen, pillows], dryer, iron, pool (salt water), bbq, secure park, cots-fee. D $125 - $180, W $350 - $1,150, BC MC VI.

★★★☆ **Elouera Tower**, (HU), 81 Sixth Ave, ☎ 07 5443 5988, fax 07 5443 0777, (Multi-stry), 49 units acc up to 6, (1, 2 & 3 bedrm), [ensuite, shwr, bath, tlt, c/fan (41), tel, cable tv, video-fee, refrig, cook fac, micro, d/wash, lndry (in unit), blkts, linen, pillows], lift, pool-heated, sauna, spa, bbq, secure park, tennis, cots-fee. D $95, W $385 - $1,600, Min book applies, BC EFT MC VI.

★★★☆ **Langley Park Holiday Apartments**, (HU), 12 Parker St, ☎ 07 5443 6057, fax 07 5443 6057, (Multi-stry), 18 units acc up to 5, (1 & 2 bedrm), [ensuite, shwr, bath, tlt, tel, cable tv, refrig, cook fac, micro, d/wash, lndry (in unit), blkts, linen, pillows], lift, pool-heated, bbq, c/park (undercover). W $280 - $820, Min book applies, 🐾,

Operator Comment: http://www.travelaustralia.com.au

★★★☆ **Majorca Isle**, (HU), 27 Sixth Ave, ☎ 07 5443 9437, fax 07 5443 1514, (Multi-stry), 44 units acc up to 6, (2 & 3 bedrm), [shwr, tlt, c/fan, tel, TV, video-fee, refrig, cook fac, micro, d/wash, lndry (in unit), blkts, linen, pillows], lift, dryer, rec rm, pool (heated), sauna, spa (2), bbq, secure park, plygr, tennis, cots-fee. W ♦♦ $340 - $1,375, BC MC VI.

★★★☆ **Northcliffe**, (HU), 50 Duporth Ave, ☎ 07 5443 5912, fax 07 5443 9292, (Multi-stry), 39 units acc up to 6, (2 bedrm), [ensuite, shwr, bath, tlt, TV, video (38), clock radio, refrig, cook fac, micro, d/wash, lndry (in unit), blkts, linen, pillows], lift, dryer, pool-heated, sauna, spa, secure park, ☏, jetty, tennis (half court), cots-fee. D ♦♦ $110 - $130, ◊ $30, W ♦♦ $515 - $965.

★★★☆ **Paradis Pacifique**, (HU), Sixth Ave, 200m S of Cotton Tree PO, ☎ 07 5479 3400, fax 07 5479 3433, (Multi-stry gr fl), 14 units acc up to 6, (2 & 3 bedrm), [ensuite (14), shwr, bath, tlt, hairdry, tel, cable tv, video (14), clock radio, refrig, cook fac, micro, d/wash, lndry (in unit), blkts, linen, pillows], dryer, iron, pool-heated, bbq, secure park, cots. D ♦♦ $120, W $390.

★★★☆ **Sundeck Gardens**, (HU), Alexandra Pde, ☎ 07 5443 2797, fax 07 5443 2797, (Multi-stry), 24 units acc up to 4, [ensuite, shwr, bath, tlt, a/c, tel, TV, video-fee, clock radio, refrig, cook fac, micro, d/wash, ldry (in unit), blkts, linen, pillows], lift, pool, pool-heated, sauna, spa, bbq, secure park, cots-fee. D $76.50 - $143, W $535 - $1,145.

★★★☆ **Surfcomber on the Beach**, (HU), 1-6 Beach Pde, 200m SE from Cotton Tree, ☎ 07 5479 1474, fax 07 5479 1474, 8 units acc up to 6, (2 bedrm), [ensuite, heat, fan, tel, TV, video, clock radio, refrig, micro, d/wash, ldry, blkts, doonas, linen], w/mach, pool, bbq, secure park (undercover), cots-fee. RO ♦♦ $120 - $250, ♦♦ $460 - $1,070, ch con, weekly con, BC EFT MC VI.

★★★☆ **Trafalgar Towers**, (HU), 120 Duporth Ave, ☎ 07 5443 3288, fax 07 5443 9962, (Multi-stry), 42 units acc up to 6, (2 & 3 bedrm), [ensuite, shwr, bath, tlt, tel, cable tv, clock radio, cook fac, micro, d/wash, ldry (in unit), blkts, linen, pillows], lift, rec rm, pool (heated), sauna, spa, secure park, mooring-fee, ✆, tennis, cots-fee. D $120 - $185, W $465 - $1,310, BC MC VI.

★★★ **Harbourside Holiday Resort**, (HU), 48 David Low Way, ☎ 07 5448 4022, fax 07 5448 4283, 30 units acc up to 6, (2 bedrm), [shwr, tlt, c/fan, TV, clock radio (0), t/c mkg, refrig, cook fac, micro, ldry (in unit), linen reqd-fee], pool, bbq, boat park, ✆, tennis (half court), cots-fee. W $253 - $577.50, BC EFT MC VI.

★★★ **Kalua**, (HU), 5 Parker St, opposite beach, ☎ 07 5443 4914, fax 07 5443 1217, (Multi-stry gr fl), 23 units acc up to 6, (1, 2 & 3 bedrm), [ensuite (11), shwr, bath, tlt, tel, cable tv, refrig, cook fac, micro, d/wash, ldry (in unit), blkts, linen, pillows], lift, dryer, rec rm, pool, spa, bbq, secure park, tennis. W ♦♦ $300 - $1,200, BC MC VI.

★★☆ **Maroochy Sands**, (HU), Cnr Sixth Ave & Aerodrome Rd, ☎ 07 5443 1637, fax 07 5443 9387, (Multi-stry), 40 units acc up to 6, (2 & 3 bedrm), [shwr, tlt, heat, TV, clock radio, refrig, cook fac, micro, ldry (in unit), blkts, linen, pillows], lift, dryer, pool (heated), bbq, secure park, ✆, tennis (half court), cots-fee. D ♦♦ $85 - $95, ♦ $10, W ♦♦ $360 - $680, Min book applies, BTC MC VI.

★★☆ **Wun Palm**, (HU), Cnr Duporth Ave & Philipp St, 1km W of PO, ☎ 07 5443 4677, fax 07 5443 4158, 6 units acc up to 5, [shwr, spa bath (1), tlt, a/c-cool, c/fan, heat, tel, TV, video-fee, clock radio, refrig, cook fac, micro, elec frypan, toaster], pool, bbq, cots. D ♦♦ $72 - $99, W ♦♦ $350 - $522, ch con, AE BC DC MC VI, ♿.

★★ **Tallows Lodge**, (HU), 10 Memorial Ave, ☎ 07 5443 2981, fax 07 5443 7343, (2 stry gr fl), 8 units acc up to 6, (1 & 2 bedrm), [shwr, tlt, c/fan, TV, clock radio, refrig, cook fac, blkts, linen, pillows], ldry, iron, iron brd, bbq, ✆, cots. D ♦♦ $60 - $80, ♦ $10 - $14, W ♦♦ $275 - $700, AE BC DC MC.

★☆ **Maroochy River Bungalows**, (HF), David Low Way, ☎ 07 5448 4911, fax 07 5448 5373, 19 flats acc up to 5, (Studio), [shwr, tlt, c/fan, TV-fee, refrig, cook fac, linen reqd-fee], ldry, pool, bbq, ✆, tennis-fee, cots-fee. W $175 - $410, ch con.

Other Accommodation
Suncoast Backpackers Lodge, (Lodge), 50 Parker St, Alexandra Headland 4572, ☎ 07 5443 7544, 8 rms acc up to 8, [fan, blkts-fee, linen-fee], shwr, tlt, ldry-fee, dry rm-fee, rec rm, TV rm (cable TV), cook fac, t/c mkg shared, bbq (covered), courtesy transfer, ✆. RO ♦ $30 - $36, ♦♦ $34 - $40, ♦ $13, BC MC VI.

SUNSHINE COAST - MOOLOOLABA QLD 4557

Pop 6,818. (107km N Brisbane), See maps on page 417, ref D5. Harbour is base for Sunshine Coast's main prawning & fishing fleet and one of the safest anchorages on the eastern coast. Underwater World 'The Wharf' Tourist Complex. Boating, Bowls, Fishing, Golf, Scenic Drives, Surfing, Swimming.

Hotels/Motels

★★★☆ **Mooloolaba**, (M), 46 Brisbane Rd, ☎ 07 5444 2988, fax 07 5444 8386, (2 stry gr fl), 26 units (1 suite) [shwr, bath (2), spa bath (1), tlt, hairdry (24), a/c-cool, c/fan, heat, tel, TV, video (8), clock radio, t/c mkg (& Coffee), refrig, cook fac (4)], ldry-fee, dryer, pool, cots-fee, non smoking units (14). RO ♦ $78 - $115, ♦♦ $86 - $130, ♦ $12, Suite D $110 - $180, AE BC DC EFT MC VI.

★★★ **Motel Mediterranean**, (M), 197 Brisbane Rd, ☎ 07 5444 4499, fax 07 5444 4325, (2 stry gr fl) 18 units [shwr, tlt, a/c-cool, heat, tel, cable tv, clock radio, t/c mkg, refrig, mini bar], ldry, dryer, ⊠, pool, bbq, c/park (undercover) (6), cots. RO ♦ $55 - $104.50, ♦♦ $55 - $104.50, ♦ $7, AE BC DC MC VI.

★★★ **Twin Pines**, (M), 36 Brisbane Rd, ☎ 07 5444 2522, fax 07 5444 4645, (2 stry gr fl), 18 units [shwr, tlt, a/c-cool (18), a/c (8), heat (10), tel, TV, clock radio, t/c mkg, refrig, cook fac (8)], ldry, dryer, pool, cots-fee. RO ♦ $53 - $85, ♦♦ $58 - $90, ♦ $10, AE BC DC MC VI.

★★☆ **River Esplanade**, (M), 73 Brisbane Rd, ☎ 07 5444 3855, fax 07 5478 1365, 18 units [shwr, tlt, a/c-cool, fan, heat, tel (18), TV, clock radio, t/c mkg, refrig], ldry, pool, spa, bbq, cots, non smoking units (3). RO ♦ $45 - $89, ♦♦ $54 - $89, ch con, AE BC DC MC VI.

★★ **Kyamba Court**, (M), 94 Brisbane Rd, ☎ 07 5444 0202, fax 07 5444 8336, 6 units [shwr, tlt, a/c-cool, fan, c/fan, heat, tel, TV, t/c mkg, refrig], ldry, dryer, pool (salt water), spa, cook fac, bbq, c/park (undercover), jetty, non smoking units (3). RO ♦ $44 - $132, ♦♦ $44 - $132, ♦ $6.60, BC MC VI.

Self Catering Accommodation
★★★★☆ **Landmark Resort**, (HU), The Esplanade, ☎ 07 5444 5555, fax 07 5444 5055, 112 units acc up to 6, (Studio, 1, 2 & 3 bedrm), [ensuite (35), shwr, spa bath, tlt, hairdry, a/c, heat, tel, cable tv, video-fee, clock radio, refrig, cook fac, micro, d/wash (57), toaster, ldry, blkts, linen, pillows], dryer, iron, iron brd, rec rm, conf fac, pool-heated, sauna, spa, bbq, dinner to unit, secure park, gym, cots-fee. RO $120 - $330, W $770 - $2,310, AE BC DC EFT MC VI.

★★★★☆ **Outrigger Mooloolaba International Beach Res.**, (Apt), The Esplanade & Venning St, ☎ 07 5452 2600, fax 07 5452 2888, (Multi-stry), 198 apts acc up to 7, (1, 2 & 3 bedrm), [ensuite, shwr, spa bath, tlt, hairdry, a/c, tel, TV, movie, clock radio, refrig, cook fac, micro, d/wash (37), toaster, ldry, blkts, linen, pillows], lift, dryer, iron, iron brd, conf fac, ⊠, pool (1), pool indoor heated (1), sauna, spa, bbq (4), secure park, gym, cots-fee. D $198 - $715, W $1,001 - $4,760, AE BC DC JCB MC VI, ♿.

★★★★☆ **Riverdance Apartments**, (HU), 62 River Esplanade, ☎ 07 5444 3444, fax 07 5444 3322, (Multi-stry gr fl), 24 units acc up to 6, (2 & 3 bedrm), [ensuite, shwr, spa bath, tlt, hairdry, a/c (5), c/fan, heat, TV, video, clock radio, refrig, cook fac, d/wash, toaster, ldry, blkts, linen, pillows], lift, dryer, iron, iron brd, pool-heated (salt water), spa, bbq (covered), secure park, cots-fee. D $210 - $440, W $870 - $2,350, 9 units yet to be assessed, BC EFT MC VI.

★★★★☆ **Spinnaker Quays**, (HU), 101/105 Parkyn Pde, 300m E Underwater World, ☎ 07 5478 3899, fax 07 5478 3150, (Multi-stry gr fl), 18 units acc up to 6, (2 & 3 bedrm), [ensuite, shwr, bath, spa bath (1), tlt, tel, TV, video, clock radio, refrig, cook fac, micro, elec frypan, d/wash, ldry (in unit), blkts, linen, pillows], lift, dryer, pool-heated (salt water heated), spa, bbq (each unit), secure park, cots-fee. **W $645 - $1,860**, BC EFT MC VI.

Operator Comment: See advertisement on previous page.

★★★★☆ **The Caribbean**, (HU), 17 Brisbane Rd, 100m N of Underwater World, ☎ 07 5444 7311, fax 07 5444 8078, (Multi-stry gr fl), 62 units acc up to 5, [shwr, spa bath, tlt, hairdry, c/fan, heat, tel, cable tv, clock radio, refrig, cook fac, micro, d/wash, toaster, ldry (in unit), blkts, linen, pillows], lift, dryer, iron, iron brd, rec rm, ☒, pool-heated, wading pool, steam rm, bbq, rm serv, dinner to unit, secure park, gym. **D 👫 $145 - $220, W 👫 $700 - $1,540**, BC MC VI.

Operator Comment: Visit our website: www.caribbeanmooloolaba.com.au Email: caribbeanresort@bigpond.com

★★★★☆ **The Peninsular Beachfront Resort**, (HU), Cnr The Esplanade & Brisbane Rd, 200m SW of PO, ☎ 07 5444 4477, fax 07 5444 3544, (Multi-stry), 62 units acc up to 6, (1, 2 & 3 bedrm), [ensuite, shwr, bath, tlt, hairdry, tel, TV, video-fee, clock radio, refrig, cook fac, micro, d/wash, ldry (in unit), blkts, linen, pillows], lift, dryer, iron, ✕ (4), pool-heated, sauna, spa, bbq, rm serv, c/park (undercover), courtesy transfer, gym, tennis, cots-fee. **D $370 - $480, 🚹 $100, W $775 - $2,335**, BC MC VI.

★★★★☆ **Zanzibar Resort**, (HU), 47 The Esplanade, 500m NE from PO, ☎ 07 5444 5633, fax 07 5444 5733, 54 units acc up to 4, (1, 2 & 3 bedrm), [ensuite, spa bath, a/c-cool, heat, tel, cable tv-fee, video-fee, clock radio, t/c mkg, refrig, cook fac, micro, d/wash, ldry, blkts, linen], lift, w/mach, dryer, pool-heated, spa, bbq, secure park, gym, cots-fee, non smoking units (3). **RO $168 - $380**, Min book applies, BC EFT MC VI.

★★★★ **Beachside Mooloolaba**, (HU), 35 Brisbane Rd, ☎ 07 5478 3911, fax 07 5478 3203, (Multi-stry gr fl), 29 units acc up to 3, [shwr, bath, tlt, a/c (28), c/fan, tel, TV, video (21), refrig, cook fac, micro, elec frypan, ldry (in unit), blkts, linen, pillows], pool (salt water), spa, bbq, secure park, cots. **D 👫 $100 - $140, W 👫 $490 - $985**, BC EFT MC VI.

★★★★ **Malibu Mooloolaba**, (HU), 81 The Esplanade, ☎ 07 5444 1133, fax 07 5444 1280, (Multi-stry), 18 units acc up to 5, (2 bedrm), [shwr, spa bath, tlt, hairdry, heat, c/fan, tel, TV, refrig, cook fac, micro, toaster, blkts, linen, pillows], lift, iron, iron brd, pool (heated), spa (communal), bbq, secure park, cots-fee, non smoking units (2). **D $165 - $250, W $805 - $2,250**, AE BC DC EFT MC VI.

★★★★ **Mirra Chana**, (Apt), 60 Parkyn Pde, ☎ 07 5452 3000, fax 07 5452 3066, (Multi-stry), 13 apts acc up to 6, (3 bedrm), [ensuite, shwr, bath, spa bath, tlt, c/fan, TV, video, clock radio, refrig, cook fac, elec frypan, d/wash, toaster, ldry, blkts, linen, pillows], dryer, iron, iron brd, pool-heated (salt water), bbq, secure park. **W $800 - $1,750**, MC VI.

★★★★ **Nautilus Resort**, (HU), River Esplanade, ☎ 07 5444 3877, fax 07 5444 3977, (Multi-stry gr fl), 60 units acc up to 4, (1 & 2 bedrm), [shwr, spa bath, tlt, hairdry, a/c, c/fan, tel, cable tv, clock radio, refrig, micro, toaster, ldry (in unit), blkts, linen, pillows], lift, dryer, iron, iron brd, ☒, pool-heated, spa, bbq, rm serv, secure park, mini golf, gym, cots-fee. **D 👫 $120 - $165, 👫👫 $160 - $192, 🚹 $30**, AE BC DC MC VI, ♿.

★★★★ **Osprey Holiday Apartments**, (HU), Cnr The Esplanade & Buderim Ave, ☎ 07 5444 6966, fax 07 5444 7253, (Multi-stry gr fl), 50 units acc up to 6, (2 & 3 bedrm), [ensuite, shwr, bath, spa bath (4), tlt, c/fan, heat, tel, cable tv, clock radio, refrig, cook fac, micro, d/wash, ldry (in unit)], lift, dryer, pool-heated, spa, bbq, secure park, gym, cots-fee. **D 👫 $150, W 👫 $570 - $1,140**, Min book applies, BC MC VI.

★★★★ **Sailport Apartments**, (HU), Cnr River Esp & Hancock Lane, ☎ 07 5444 1844, fax 07 5444 6311, (Multi-stry gr fl), 28 units acc up to 6, (2 & 3 bedrm), [ensuite, shwr, bath, tlt, hairdry, a/c (12), c/fan, heat, tel, TV, video, clock radio, refrig, cook fac, micro, d/wash, ldry (in unit), blkts, linen, pillows], dryer, iron, pool-heated, spa, bbq, secure park, cots-fee. **D $180, W $690 - $1,650**, Min book applies, AE BC DC MC VI.

★★★★ **The Beach Club Resort**, (HU), Cnr Meta St & First Ave, 300m NW of PO, ☎ 07 5478 3000, fax 07 5444 3995, (Multi-stry gr fl), 74 units acc up to 4, [ensuite, shwr, tlt, hairdry, c/fan, heat, tel, cable tv, video, clock radio, refrig, cook fac, micro, elec frypan, d/wash, toaster, ldry (in unit), linen], lift, dryer, iron, iron brd, rec rm, sauna, spa, bbq, secure park (undercover), gym, cots-fee. **D 👫 $110 - $120, 🚹 $22, W 👫 $415 - $880, 🚹 $40**, AE BC EFT MC VI.

★★★☆ **84 The Spit**, (HU), 84 Parkyn Pde, 1km SE of PO, ☎ 07 5444 1642, fax 07 5444 8983, (Multi-stry), 20 units acc up to 6, (2 bedrm), [shwr, tlt, tel, TV, clock radio, t/c mkg, refrig, cook fac, micro, d/wash, ldry (in unit), blkts, linen, pillows], lift, dryer, pool-heated, secure park (undercover), cots-fee. **W $640 - $1,195**, Min book applies, BC MC VI.

★★★☆ **Aegean Mooloolaba**, (HU), 14 River Esplanade, 100m SE of PO, ☎ 07 5444 1255, fax 07 5444 1055, (Multi-stry), 23 units acc up to 5, (1 & 2 bedrm), [shwr, spa bath, tlt, hairdry, c/fan, tel, cable tv, video-fee, clock radio, refrig, cook fac, micro, d/wash, toaster, ldry (in unit), blkts, linen, pillows], lift, dryer, iron, iron brd, pool-heated, spa, freezer, bbq (covered), c/park (undercover), secure park, cots-fee. **D $143 - $242, W $605 - $1,595**, Min book all holiday times, BC EFT MC VI.

★★★☆ **Dockside**, (HU), Cnr Foote & Burnett Sts, 500m S of PO, ☎ 07 5478 2044, fax 07 5444 5288, (Multi-stry gr fl), 17 units acc up to 9, (2 & 3 bedrm), [ensuite (5), shwr, bath, spa bath (5), tlt, c/fan (3), tel, TV, video, clock radio (9), refrig, cook fac, micro, elec frypan, toaster, ldry (in unit), blkts, linen, pillows], dryer, pool-heated, spa, bbq, secure park, cots. **D $139 - $200, W $472 - $1,255**, Min book Christmas Jan and Easter, BC MC VI,
Operator Comment:
Visit our website on www.sunshinecoast.au.nu/dockside.htm

★★★☆ **Harbourview Apartments**, (HU), 13 Douglas St, 500m W of PO, ☎ 07 5444 0966, fax 07 5444 0966, (Multi-stry gr fl), 7 units acc up to 6, (2 & 3 bedrm), [ensuite (5), shwr, bath, tlt, fan, TV, refrig, cook fac, micro, d/wash, ldry (in unit), blkts, linen, pillows], dryer, iron, pool, c/park (undercover), cots-fee. **W $350 - $995.**

★★★☆ **Newport Beachside Apartments**, (HU), Cnr Parkyn Pde & River Esp, ☎ 07 5444 4833, fax 07 5444 6840, (Multi-stry), 49 units acc up to 7, (2 & 3 bedrm), [shwr, bath, tlt, c/fan, heat, tel, cable tv, clock radio, refrig, cook fac, micro, d/wash, ldry (in unit), blkts, linen, pillows], lift, dryer, pool-heated, sauna, spa, bbq, secure park, plygr, cots-fee. **D $270, W $700 - $1,975**, BC MC VI.

★★★☆ **Northwind Apartments**, (HU), 125 The Esplanade, ☎ 07 5444 3899, fax 07 5444 8233, (Multi-stry), 24 units acc up to 6, (1, 2 & 3 bedrm), [shwr, bath, tlt, c/fan, heat, tel, cable tv (23), video, clock radio, refrig, cook fac, micro, d/wash, ldry (in unit), blkts, linen, pillows], rec rm, pool-heated, sauna, spa, bbq, secure park, tennis (half court), cots-fee. **D 👥 $120 - $170, 👤 $35, RO 👥 $425 - $1,450**, Min book applies, BC MC VI.

★★★☆ **Pacific Mooloolaba**, (HU), 95 The Esplanade, ☎ 07 5444 4733, fax 07 5444 4059, (Multi-stry), 29 units acc up to 6, (1, 2 & 3 bedrm), [shwr, bath, tlt, c/fan, tel, cable tv, video-fee, clock radio, refrig, cook fac, micro, d/wash, ldry (in unit), blkts, linen, pillows], lift, rec rm, pool-heated, sauna, spa, bbq, secure park, tennis (half court), cots-fee. **D 👥 $145, W 👥 $560 - $1,475**, Min book Christmas Jan long w/ends and Easter, BC MC VI.

Comfort FLAG CHOICE HOTELS ★★★☆ **Sandcastles on the Beach Mooloolaba**, (SA), Cnr Parkyn Pde & River Esp, 400m SE of PO, ☎ 07 5478 0666, fax 07 5478 0063, (Multi-stry), 31 serv apts acc up to 4, [shwr, tlt, hairdry, a/c (26), c/fan, heat, tel, TV, movie, clock radio, refrig, cook fac, micro, elec frypan, ldry (in unit)], lift, dryer, pool-heated, spa, bbq, secure park, cots-fee. **D $129 - $196**, AE BC MC VI.

★★★☆ **Seaview**, (HU), 143 The Esplanade, ☎ 07 5444 3400, fax 07 5442 0298, (Multi-stry gr fl), 45 units acc up to 6, (1, 2 & 3 bedrm), [shwr, bath, tlt, fan, heat, tel, cable tv, clock radio, refrig, cook fac, micro, d/wash, ldry (in unit), blkts, linen, pillows], lift, dryer, rec rm, pool-heated, sauna, bbq, secure park, tennis (half court), cots-fee. **D 👥 $140 - $180, 👤 $20, W 👥 $650 - $1,490**, BC MC VI.

★★★☆ **Windward**, (HU), 137 Esplanade, ☎ 07 5444 1800, fax 07 5444 0038, (Multi-stry), 20 units acc up to 6, [ensuite, shwr, tlt, fan (14), c/fan (3), tel, cable tv, clock radio (17), refrig, cook fac, micro, d/wash, ldry (in unit), blkts, linen, pillows], lift, dryer, rec rm, pool-heated, sauna, bbq, secure park, tennis (half court), cots-fee. **W $450 - $1,350**, BC MC VI.

★★★ **Bayviews Apartments**, (HU), 9 Douglas St, 500m W of PO, ☎ 07 5444 0966, fax 07 5444 0966, (Multi-stry), 15 units acc up to 6, [shwr, bath, tlt, fan, TV, clock radio, refrig, cook fac, micro, elec frypan, d/wash, toaster, ldry (in unit), blkts, linen, pillows], dryer, iron, pool, c/park (undercover), cots-fee. **W $350 - $995.**

★★★ **Bellardoo**, (HU), Cnr Esplanade & Meta St, ☎ 07 5444 3241, fax 07 5444 6860, (Multi-stry gr fl), 27 units acc up to 6, (2 & 3 bedrm), [shwr, bath, tlt, fan, heat, tel, TV, clock radio, refrig, cook fac, micro (26), d/wash, ldry (in unit), linen reqd-fee], pool-heated (solar), bbq, cots-fee. **W $355 - $900**, Min book applies, BC MC VI.

SUNSHINE COAST - MUDJIMBA QLD 4564

Pop 4,350. Part of Marcoola, (118km N Brisbane), See maps on page 417, ref D4. Beach resort on the Sunshine Coast. Boating, Fishing, Golf, Scenic Drives, Surfing, Swimming.

Hotels/Motels

AAA TOURISM *Special Rates* ★★★★☆ **Novotel Twin Waters Resort**, (M), Resort, Ocean Dve, ☎ 07 5448 8000, fax 07 5448 8001, (2 stry gr fl), 366 units [shwr, bath (254), spa bath (112), tlt, hairdry, a/c, tel, TV, movie, radio, t/c mkg, refrig, mini bar, cook fac ltd, micro, pillows], ldry, iron, iron brd, rec rm, conf fac, ☒, pool, spa, bbq, 24hr reception, courtesy transfer, ✆, plygr, bush walking, bicycle, canoeing, golf, gym, tennis. **RO 👥 $200 - $380**, ch con, AE BC DC EFT JCB MC VI, ♿.
Operator Comment: See our display advertisement on following page.

Self Catering Accommodation

Santorini Twin Waters, (Apt), 13-17 Mudjimba Espl, ☎ 07 5450 6622, fax 07 5450 6733, 14 apts acc up to 7, (2 & 3 bedrm), [shwr, spa bath, tlt, a/c, tel, TV, video, clock radio, t/c mkg, refrig, cook fac, micro, d/wash, toaster, blkts, doonas, linen, pillows], w/mach, dryer, lounge firepl, pool-heated, bbq, cots, non smoking units. **D $220 - $250, W $560 - $1,330**, Min book applies, BC MC VI, (not yet classified).

SUNSHINE COAST - NOOSA HEADS QLD 4567

Pop 6,000. (145km N Brisbane), See maps on page 417, ref D4. Popular surfing beach on the Sunshine Coast. The Big Shell, House of Bottles. Boating, Bowls, Fishing, Golf, Sailing, Scenic Drives, Squash, Surfing, Swimming.

Hotels/Motels

★★★★☆ **Netanya Noosa**, (M), 75 Hastings St, ☎ 07 5447 4722, fax 07 5447 3914, (Multi-stry), 48 units [shwr, spa bath, tlt, hairdry, a/c, tel, TV, video, clock radio, refrig, cook fac ltd, micro (8)], lift, ldry, iron, iron brd, conf fac, pool-heated, sauna, spa, bbq, rm serv, secure park, gym, cots-fee. **D $195 - $555**, Min book applies, AE BC DC EFT MC VI.

★★★★☆ **Sheraton Noosa Resort**, (LH), Hastings St, entry on Noosa Pde, ☎ 07 5449 4888, fax 07 5449 2230, (Multi-stry gr fl), 140 rms (29 suites) [shwr, spa bath, tlt, hairdry, a/c, tel, TV, video, movie, t/c mkg, refrig, mini bar, micro, toaster], lift, ldry, iron, rec rm, lounge, conv fac, ☒, pool-heated, sauna, spa, rm serv, secure park, gym, cots, non smoking flr (3). **RO 👤 $250 - $410, 👥 $250 - $410, Suite D $344 - $544**, ch con, AE BC DC MC VI, ♿.

★★★☆ **Caribbean Noosa**, (M), 15 Noosa Pde, 200m to Hastings St☎ 07 5447 2247, fax 07 5447 2050, 16 units [shwr, tlt, a/c (16), c/fan, heat, tel, TV, video (16), clock radio, t/c mkg, refrig, cook fac ltd, micro (16)], ldry, pool-heated, bbq, c/park (undercover), mooring, jetty, cots. **RO 👥 $105 - $180, 👤 $10**, ch con, AE BC MC VI.

★★★☆ **Noosa Village**, (M), 10 Hastings St, ☎ 07 5447 5800, fax 07 5474 9282, 9 units [shwr, tlt, c/fan, TV, clock radio, t/c mkg, refrig, cook fac (2), micro (2), toaster], ⊠, c/park (undercover) (5), ☎, cots-fee. RO ♠ $88 - $160, ♠♠ $88 - $160, ♠ $15, AE BC DC EFT MC VI,

Operator Comment: Best value rates at Hastings Street's only Motel, located opposite Noosa Beach.

★★★ **Chez Noosa Resort**, (M), 263 David Low Way, 800m S of Noosa Junction, ☎ 07 5447 2027, fax 07 5447 2195, (2 stry gr fl), 28 units (1 bedrm), [ensuite, shwr, tlt, a/c (14), c/fan, tel, TV, clock radio, refrig, cook fac, micro, pillows], ldry-fee, dryer-fee, pool-heated (salt water heated), spa (gas heated), bbq, c/park (undercover), cots-fee. D ♠♠ $72 - $120, ♠ $15, ch con, BC MC VI.

Self Catering Accommodation

★★★★☆ **Castaway Cove**, (HU), David Low Way Marcus Beach, 5 km S of Noosa Heads PO, ☎ 07 5474 8890, fax 07 5474 8893, (Multi-stry), 25 units acc up to 10, (1, 2, 3 & 4 bedrm), [ensuite (25), shwr, bath, spa bath (16), tlt, c/fan, tel, TV, video, clock radio, CD (9), refrig, cook fac, micro, elec frypan, d/wash, toaster, ldry (in unit), blkts, linen, pillows], dryer, iron, iron brd, pool (salt water), spa, bbq, c/park (undercover), tennis, cots-fee. D $95 - $355, BC EFT MC VI.

★★★★☆ **Macquarie Lodge**, (Apt), 53 Banksia Ave, 500m N of PO, ☎ 07 5448 0822, fax 07 5448 0248, (Multi-stry gr fl), 35 apts acc up to 6, (1, 2 & 3 bedrm), [ensuite, shwr, bath, tlt, hairdry, c/fan, heat, tel, TV, video, clock radio, refrig, cook fac, micro, d/wash, ldry, blkts, linen, pillows], dryer, iron, pool-heated, spa, bbq, secure park, cots-fee. W $735 - $1,645, Min book applies, BC MC VI.

★★★★☆ **No 1 in Hastings Street**, (HU), Cnr Hastings St & Morwong Dve, ☎ 07 5449 2211, fax 07 5449 2001, (Multi-stry), 24 units acc up to 8, [shwr, bath, spa bath, tlt, a/c, fan, tel, TV, video, clock radio, t/c mkg, refrig, cook fac, micro, d/wash, ldry (in unit), blkts, linen, pillows], lift, dryer, pool-heated, sauna, spa, bbq, secure park, gym, cots-fee. D $242 - $396, Min book applies, AE BC DC EFT MC VI.

★★★★☆ **Noosa Blue Resort**, (Apt), 16 Noosa Dve, ☎ 07 5447 5699, fax 07 5447 5485, 63 apts acc up to 4, (1 bedrm), [shwr, spa bath, tlt, a/c, c/fan, cent heat, tel, cable tv, video, clock radio, t/c mkg, refrig, cook fac, micro, d/wash, toaster, ldry (in unit), blkts, doonas, linen, pillows], w/mach, dryer, conf fac, ⊠, pool-heated, sauna, spa, bbq, dinner to unit, secure park (undercover), cots. D ♠♠ $170 - $242, ♠ $11, ch con, AE BC DC EFT MC VI.

★★★★☆ **Noosa Crest**, (HU), 2 Noosa Dve, ☎ 07 5447 2412, fax 07 5447 2679, (2 stry gr fl), 39 units acc up to 6, (1, 2 & 3 bedrm), [shwr, bath, tlt, a/c-cool (11), c/fan, tel, TV, video, CD, refrig, cook fac, micro, d/wash, ldry (in unit), blkts, linen, pillows], pool (1 heated) (2), sauna, spa, bbq, c/park (undercover), boat park, tennis, cots-fee. D ♠♠ $179 - $429, Min book applies, AE BC DC MC VI.

★★★★☆ **Noosa Hill Resort**, (HU), 26 Noosa Dve, 100m fr PO, ☎ 07 5449 2644, fax 07 5449 2238, (Multi-stry), 34 units acc up to 6, (2 & 3 bedrm), [shwr, bath, spa bath (roof deck penthouse) (12), tlt, c/fan, heat, tel, TV, video, refrig, cook fac, micro, d/wash, ldry (in unit), blkts, linen, pillows], pool-heated, sauna, spa, bbq, secure park (under cover), car park, gym, tennis, cots-fee. W $803 - $1,870, BC MC VI.

★★★★☆ **Noosa Pacific on the Waterfront**, (HU), 24 Munna Cres Noosa Sound via, ☎ 07 5449 9444, fax 07 5449 9175, (Multi-stry gr fl), 32 units acc up to 4, (2 & 3 bedrm), [shwr, bath, tlt, c/fan, heat, tel, cable tv, video, refrig, cook fac, micro, d/wash, ldry (in unit), blkts, linen, pillows], lift, dryer, pool-heated, sauna, spa, bbq, secure park, gym, tennis, cots-fee. W $994 - $1,890, Min book applies, BC EFT MC VI.

★★★★☆ **Noosa Quays**, (HU), 4 Quamby Pl, 700m SW of Hastings St, ☎ 07 5449 2699, fax 07 5449 2247, (Multi-stry gr fl), 14 units acc up to 6, (2, 3 & 4 bedrm), [shwr, spa bath (13), tlt, hairdry, c/fan, heat, tel, cable tv, video (13), clock radio, refrig, cook fac, micro, d/wash, ldry (in unit), blkts, linen, pillows], lift, dryer, iron, conv fac, pool-heated, sauna, bbq, secure park, tennis (half court), cots-fee. D $700 - $2,000, Min book applies, BC MC VI.

★★★★☆ **Noosa Tropicana**, (HU), Cnr Noosa Pde & Munna Cres, Noosa Sound, ☎ 07 5449 0222, fax 07 5442 4350, (Multi-stry gr fl), 18 units acc up to 7, (2 & 3 bedrm), [shwr, spa bath, tlt, hairdry, c/fan, heat, tel, TV, video, clock radio, refrig, cook fac, micro, d/wash, ldry (in unit), blkts, linen, pillows], dryer, pool-heated, bbq, secure park, cots-fee. D $150 - $210, W $655, Min book applies, AE BC DC MC VI.

SECLUDED... ABSOLUTE BEACHFRONT

Nestled behind the dunes of Marcus Beach is Noosa's peaceful alternative... a stunning collection of comfortable, self-contained beach houses, villas, penthouses and apartments with pool, BBQ's, scenic bike trails, tennis and spas.

Castaway Cove - the perfect escape for families and couples alike with options for every budget.

AAAT ★★★★☆

David Low Way Marcus Beach Noosa Q 4573
Fax: 07 5474 8893 www.castawaycove.com
Ph: 07 **5474 8890**

CASTAWAY COVE NOOSA

Top position, close to river, beaches, shops and Noosa National Park

- 35 spacious 1, 2 & 3 bedroom fully self-contained apartments, all with both an ensuite and a bathroom
- A variety of views over Noosa Sound, Hastings Street and Laguna Bay
- Quiet and peaceful tropical setting with easy access to all of Noosa's main attractions
- 500m from the centre of Noosa, featuring great shopping, restaurants and a Cinema Complex

AAA Tourism ★★★★☆

MACQUARIE LODGE
NOOSA HEADS
LUXURY APARTMENTS
53 Banksia Avenue,
Noosa Heads, Qld., 4567
Ph: (07) 5448 0822
Fax: (07) 5448 0248
www.macquarielodge.com.au
Email: reception@macquarielodge.com.au

★★★★☆ **Picture Point Terraces**, (HU), 47 Picture Point Cres, ☎ 07 5449 2433, fax 07 5447 4002, (Multi-stry), 12 units acc up to 7, (1, 2 & 3 bedrm), [ensuite, shwr, bath, spa bath (12), tlt, hairdry, a/c, c/fan, tel, cable tv, video, clock radio, CD, refrig, cook fac, micro, elec frypan (6), d/wash, ldry (in unit), blkts, linen, pillows], pool-heated, sauna, spa, bbq, secure park, gym, cots-fee. **D $215 - $490, W $1,290 - $3,430**, Min book applies, BC EFT MC VI.

★★★★☆ **South Pacific Noosa Resort**, (Apt), 179 Weyba Rd, 2km W of Noosa Junction PO, ☎ 07 5473 1200, fax 07 5474 3200, (2 stry gr fl), 109 apts acc up to 6, (1, 2 & 3 bedrm), [ensuite, shwr, bath, spa bath, tlt, hairdry, a/c, heat, tel, cable tv, video, movie, clock radio, refrig, micro, elec frypan, d/wash, toaster, ldry (in unit), blkts, linen, pillows], iron, iron brd, rec rm, conf fac, ⊠, pool-heated, sauna, spa, steam rm, bbq, rm serv, tennis, cots-fee, non smoking units (109). **W $735 - $2,170**, ch con, AE BC DC MC VI.

Trouble-free travel tips - Jack
Check that the jack and spare wheel are on board and the jack works.

NOOSA TROPICANA

LUXURY HOLIDAY APARTMENTS
Features Include:
- 18 fully self contained and equipped 2 and 3 bedroom luxury apartments, 8 with own roof deck.
- Each with ensuite and bathroom, including spa bath.
- Designer kitchens with microwave and dishwasher.
- Spacious lounge and dining areas.
- Washing machine and dryer in every apartment.
- Swimming pool (heated), with spa area, and BBQ.
- Security undercover parking.

YOUR RESORT IN THE CENTRE OF NOOSA...
AAA TOURISM RATING ★★★★☆

140 Noosa Parade (Cnr. Munna Crescent), Noosa
Ph: (07) 5449 0222 - Fax: (07) 5442 4350   noosatropicana@ozemail.com.au

QUEENSLAND

★★★★☆ **The Emerald Noosa**, (HU), 42 Hastings St, ☎ 07 5449 6100, fax 07 5449 6196, (Multi-stry gr fl), 45 units acc up to 6, [shwr, spa bath, hairdry, a/c, c/fan, tel, cable tv, video, clock radio, refrig, cook fac, micro, elec frypan, d/wash, toaster, ldry (in unit)], lift, dryer, ⊠, pool-heated, sauna, spa, secure park, cots-fee. W $1,330 - $2,100, AE BC DC EFT MC VI.

★★★★☆ **The French Quarter**, (SA), 62 Hastings St, ☎ 07 5430 7100, fax 07 5474 8122, (Multi-stry gr fl), 119 serv apts acc up to 5, [shwr, spa bath, tlt, hairdry, a/c, tel, cable tv, movie (24 hrs), clock radio, refrig, cook fac, micro, elec frypan, ldry (in unit)], lift, dryer, iron, iron brd, ⊠, pool-heated, sauna, spa, c/park (undercover), cots-fee. D ♯ $200 - $360, ch con, AE BC DC MC VI.

★★★★ **# 2 Hastings Street**, (HU), 2 Hastings St, ☎ 07 5448 0777, fax 07 5448 0929, (Multi-stry gr fl), 13 units acc up to 4, (2 bedrm), [ensuite (13), shwr, bath (6), tlt, a/c, c/fan, tel, TV, video, clock radio, CD (4), refrig, cook fac, micro, d/wash, ldry (in unit), blkts, linen, pillows], dryer, iron, secure park, cots-fee. D $165 - $195, W $1,095 - $1,305, BC EFT MC VI.

★★★★ **At The Sound**, (SA), Previously Noosa Haven Motor Inn No children's facilities, 119 Noosa Parade, 2.1kms from Hastings St, ☎ 07 5449 9211, fax 07 5447 1331, (2 stry gr fl), 22 serv apts acc up to 5, (Studio), [shwr, spa bath (16), tlt, a/c, tel, TV, video, clock radio, t/c mkg, refrig, cook fac, micro, ldry, blkts, linen, pillows], dryer, iron, iron brd, pool, spa (13), bbq, 24hr reception, c/park (undercover). RO $450 - $550, AE BC DC MC VI.

★★★★ **Bali Hai Apartments**, (HU), 20 Edgar Bennett Ave, ☎ 07 5447 2381, fax 07 5474 5310, (Multi-stry), 11 units acc up to 6, (2 & 3 bedrm), [ensuite, shwr, bath, spa bath (4), tlt, hairdry, c/fan, heat, tel, TV, video, clock radio, CD, refrig, cook fac, micro, d/wash, ldry (in unit), blkts, linen, pillows], dryer, iron, pool-heated, spa, bbq, secure park, cots-fee. D $143 - $308, W $770 - $1,870, Min book applies, AE BC EFT MC VI.

★★★★ **Cloud Nine Luxury Apartments**, (HU), 39 Noosa Pde, 300m S of town centre, ☎ 07 5447 3400, fax 07 5449 2085, (2 stry gr fl), 7 units acc up to 6, (2 & 3 bedrm), [shwr, bath, spa bath (3), tlt, a/c (6), c/fan, tel, TV, refrig, cook fac, micro, d/wash, ldry (in unit), blkts, linen, pillows], dryer, iron, pool-heated (gas heated), sauna, spa, bbq, c/park (undercover), cots-fee. W $550 - $1,350, Min book applies, BC MC VI.

★★★★ **Culgoa Point Beach Resort**, (HU), Quamby Pl Noosa Sound via, ☎ 07 5447 5055, fax 07 5449 2925, (Multi-stry gr fl), 65 units acc up to 6, (2 & 3 bedrm), [shwr, bath, tlt, c/fan, heat, tel, cable tv, video, refrig, cook fac, micro, d/wash, ldry (in unit), blkts, linen, pillows], dryer, pool-heated, wading pool, sauna, spa, bbq (covered), c/park (undercover), tennis (half court), cots-fee. D $125 - $325, W $545 - $1,640, AE BC DC MC VI.

★★★★ **Fairshore Apartments**, (HU), 45 Hastings St, 2km N of PO, ☎ 07 5447 3444, fax 07 5447 2224, (Multi-stry gr fl), 29 units acc up to 6, (2 bedrm), [shwr, bath, tlt, a/c-cool, c/fan (29), tel, TV, video, t/c mkg, refrig, cook fac, micro, d/wash, linen, pillows], dryer, iron, rec rm, pool-heated, bbq, secure park, cots-fee. D $200 - $350, $380 - $600, W $2,600 - $4,050, AE BC DC MC VI.

★★★★ **Killara**, (HU), Cnr Grant St & Banksia Ave, ☎ 07 5447 2800, fax 07 5449 2257, (2 stry gr fl), 12 units acc up to 4, (1 & 2 bedrm), [shwr, bath (2), tlt, hairdry, a/c-cool, c/fan, heat, TV, video, clock radio, refrig, cook fac, micro, blkts, linen, pillows], ldry, dryer, iron, iron brd, pool-heated, spa, bbq, c/park (undercover), courtesy transfer, ✆, cots-fee. D $73 - $150, W $462 - $945, BC EFT MC VI.

★★★★ **Las Rias**, (HU), 8 Quamby Pl Noosa Sound, 2km N of PO, ☎ 07 5447 2799, fax 07 5474 5174, (Multi-stry gr fl), 20 units acc up to 6, (2 & 3 bedrm - Split level accommodation available.), [shwr, tlt, fan, tel, TV, video, clock radio, refrig, cook fac, micro, d/wash, ldry (in unit), blkts, linen, pillows], lift, dryer, pool-heated, sauna, spa, bbq, secure park, jetty, cots-fee. W $900 - $1,250, BC MC VI.

★★★★ **Maison la Plage**, (HU), 5 Hastings St, ☎ 07 5447 4400, fax 07 5447 4503, 21 units acc up to 7, [shwr, bath, tlt, c/fan, heat, tel, TV, video, clock radio, refrig, cook fac, micro, d/wash, blkts, linen, pillows], ldry, ✗, pool-heated (salt water heated), spa, bbq, secure park, cots-fee. D ♯ $175 - $320, BC MC VI.

★★★★ **Noosa Parade Holiday Inn**, (HU), Cnr Noosa Pde & Key Crt, ☎ 07 5447 4177, fax 07 5447 4441, (2 stry gr fl), 11 units acc up to 4, [shwr, tlt, a/c, c/fan, TV, video, clock radio, refrig, cook fac, micro], ldry, pool-heated, spa, bbq, c/park (undercover), cots-fee. RO ♯ $95 - $135, ♯ $95 - $135, ◊ $15, BC MC VI.

★★★★ **Picture Point Apartments**, (HU), 30 Edgar Bennett Ave, ☎ 07 5447 5255, fax 07 5447 5595, (Multi-stry gr fl), 12 units acc up to 6, (2 & 3 bedrm), [ensuite (9), shwr, bath (1), tlt, a/c (1), c/fan, heat, tel, TV, video, clock radio, refrig, cook fac, micro, d/wash, ldry (in unit), blkts, linen, pillows], dryer, pool-heated, sauna (4), spa (5), bbq, secure park. D $165 - $275, W $1,155 - $1,694, Min book applies.

★★★★ **Sandcastles**, (HU), 1 Hastings St, ☎ 07 5447 2730, fax 07 5447 2773, (Multi-stry), 14 units acc up to 6, (1 & 2 bedrm), [shwr, bath, tlt, a/c-cool, fan, heat, tel, TV, movie, clock radio, refrig, cook fac, d/wash], ldry, pool-heated, spa, bbq (covered), secure park, cots-fee. D $185 - $300, W $1,190 - $2,100, Min book applies, BC EFT MC VI.

★★★★ **Taralla Apartments**, (HU), 18 Edgar Bennett Ave, ☎ 07 5447 3195, fax 07 5448 0397, (2 stry), 8 units acc up to 6, [shwr, tlt, a/c-cool, fan, heat, tel, TV, clock radio, refrig, cook fac, micro, d/wash, ldry (in unit), blkts, linen, pillows], rec rm, pool-heated, spa, bbq, secure park. D ♯ $85 - $195, ◊ $15, W ♯ $450 - $1,200, Min book applies, BC MC VI.

★★★★ **The Noosa Apartments**, (HU), 45 Noosa Pde, ☎ 07 5447 5011, fax 07 5447 5722, 8 units acc up to 6, [shwr, spa bath, tlt, hairdry, c/fan, heat, tel, TV, video, clock radio, refrig, cook fac, micro, d/wash, ldry (dryer), blkts, linen, pillows], pool, spa, bbq, c/park (undercover), gym, cots-fee. **D $125 - $216, W $735 - $1,495**, BC MC VI.

★★★☆ **Hotel Laguna**, (HU), 6 Hastings St, ☎ 07 5447 3077, fax 07 5447 3806, (Multi-stry), 48 units acc up to 4, (Studio, 1 & 2 bedrm), [ensuite, shwr, tlt, a/c-cool, tel, TV, movie, clock radio, t/c mkg, refrig, cook fac (24), cook fac ltd (24), micro, d/wash (8), ldry (in unit) (24)], ldry, dryer, ⊠, pool-heated, wading pool, bbq, c/park (undercover), cots-fee. **D $110 - $330**, 24 units of a lower rating. AE BC DC MC VI.

★★★☆ **Le Court Villas**, (HU), 53-57 Noosa Pde, 600m to Hastings St, ☎ 07 5447 4522, fax 07 5447 2024, (2 stry), 8 units acc up to 6, (2 & 3 bedrm), [shwr, bath, tlt, a/c-cool (1), c/fan, heat, tel, TV, video, clock radio, CD (6), refrig, cook fac, micro, d/wash, ldry (in unit), blkts, linen, pillows], dryer, pool, pool-heated (solar), spa, bbq, c/park (undercover), cots-fee. **RO $78 - $250, W $550 - $1,320**, Min book applies, AE BC DC MC VI,
Operator Comment: Free call: 1800 255 779.

★★★☆ **Myuna Holiday Apartments**, (HU), 19 Katharina St, ☎ 07 5447 5588, fax 07 5449 2747, (Multi-stry gr fl), 13 units (Studio, 2 & 3 bedrm), [shwr, bath, tlt, c/fan, heat, TV, refrig, cook fac, micro, ldry (in unit), blkts, linen, pillows], rec rm, pool-heated, bbq, c/park (undercover), ✆, cots-fee. **D $70 - $130, W $460 - $985.**

★★★☆ **Noosa Harbour Resort**, (HU), Quamby Pl, Noosa Sound, ☎ 07 5447 4500, fax 07 5447 2151, (Multi-stry gr fl), 50 units acc up to 8, (1, 2 & 3 bedrm), [shwr, bath, tlt, heat, c/fan, tel, TV, video, refrig, cook fac, micro, d/wash, blkts, linen, pillows], w/mach, dryer, ⊠, pool-heated, sauna, spa, bbq, secure park, jetty, tennis (half court), cots-fee. **D ♦♦ $110 - $287, W $720 - $1,870**, weekly con, AE BC MC VI.

★★★☆ **Noosa International Resort**, (HU), Edgar Bennett Ave, ☎ 07 5447 4822, fax 07 5447 2025, (Multi-stry gr fl), 65 units acc up to 5, [ensuite, shwr, tlt, a/c, tel, TV, clock radio, t/c mkg, refrig, cook fac, d/wash, ldry (in unit)], dryer, rec rm, ⊠, pool-heated, sauna (2), spa (3), rm serv, dinner to unit, secure park, courtesy transfer (to beach), cots-fee. **D $135 - $195**, AE BC DC MC VI.

★★★☆ **Noosa Pacific 2**, (HU), 28 Munna Cres, Noosa Sound, ☎ 07 5449 9444, fax 07 5449 9175, (2 stry), 14 units acc up to 6, (2 & 3 bedrm), [shwr, bath, tlt, c/fan, heat, tel, cable tv, video, clock radio, refrig, cook fac, micro, d/wash, ldry (in unit), blkts, linen, pillows], dryer, pool-heated, sauna, spa, bbq, c/park (undercover), gym, tennis, cots-fee. **W $490 - $925**, Min book applies, BC EFT MC VI.

★★★☆ **Noosa Shores Resort**, (HU), 86 - 88 Noosa Pde, ☎ 07 5447 5766, fax 07 5447 2400, (Multi-stry), 25 units acc up to 6, (2 & 3 bedrm), [shwr, bath, tlt, c/fan, heat, tel, cable tv, clock radio, refrig, cook fac, micro, d/wash, ldry (in unit), blkts, linen, pillows], dryer, pool-heated, sauna, bbq, secure park, jetty. **RO $158 - $255, $785 - $1,650**, Min book applies, BC MC VI.

★★★☆ **Ocean Breeze Holiday Apartments**, (HU), 52 Hastings St, ☎ 07 5447 4977, fax 07 5447 2170, (Multi-stry gr fl), 64 units acc up to 6, [ensuite, shwr, tlt, a/c, fan, tel, TV, movie, clock radio, refrig, cook fac, d/wash, ldry (in unit), blkts, linen, pillows], dryer, rec rm, pool-heated, sauna, spa, bbq, secure park, tennis (half court), cots-fee. **D $155 - $300**, AE BC DC MC VI.

★★★☆ **Seahaven Beachfront Resort**, (SA), 13 Hastings St, ☎ 07 5447 3422, fax 07 5447 5260, (Multi-stry gr fl), 66 serv apts acc up to 7, [shwr, bath (50), spa bath (24), tlt, a/c, fan, tel, TV, movie, clock radio, refrig, cook fac, micro, d/wash (42), ldry (in unit) (24)], lift, ldry, ⊠ (evenings only), pool-heated (3), wading pool, sauna, spa (2), bbq, c/park (garage), gym, cots-fee. **D $115 - $425**, AE BC DC MC VI, ⅙.

★★★☆ **Sun Lagoon**, (HU), Quamby Pl, ☎ 07 5447 4833, fax 07 5447 5758, (Multi-stry), 27 units acc up to 6, (2 & 3 bedrm - Split level accommodation available.), [shwr, bath (6), tlt, c/fan, heat, tel, cable tv, clock radio, refrig, cook fac, micro, elec frypan, d/wash (26), ldry (in unit), blkts, linen, pillows], dryer, rec rm, pool, sauna, spa, bbq, mooring, cots-fee. **D $120 - $195, W $690 - $1,260**, AE BTC DC EFT MC VI.

★★★☆ **The Breakers on the Beach**, (HU), No children's facilities, Hastings St, ☎ 07 5447 5399, (Multi-stry gr fl), 6 units acc up to 2, [shwr, tlt, a/c, fan, heat, tel, TV, video, clock radio, refrig, cook fac, micro (3), d/wash, blkts, linen, pillows], ldry, c/park (undercover) (2). **D ♦♦ $195 - $335, W ♦♦ $1,365 - $2,345**, Min book applies, BC MC VI.

★★★ **Bottlebrush Holiday Townhouses**, (HU), 1 Bottlebrush Ave, 200m N of PO, ☎ 07 5447 3188, fax 07 5474 9978, (2 stry), 9 units acc up to 5, (2 bedrm - 1x1q3s. 8x1q2s), [shwr, bath (hip), tlt, c/fan, heat, TV, video, clock radio, refrig, cook fac, micro, d/wash, ldry (in unit), blkts, linen, pillows], dryer, iron, pool-heated (solar), secure park, cots-fee. **RO $79 - $100, W $550 - $856**, Min book applies.

★★★ **Saks on Hastings**, (HU), Hastings St, ☎ 07 5447 3444, fax 07 5447 2224, (Multi-stry gr fl), 9 units acc up to 4, [shwr, bath (hip), tlt, c/fan (8), heat, TV, clock radio, refrig, cook fac, d/wash, ldry (in unit), blkts, linen, pillows], iron, pool, sauna, spa, bbq, secure park, cots-fee. **D $90 - $200, W $600 - $1,400**, AE BC DC MC VI.

★★☆ **Jacaranda**, (HU), 12 Hastings St, ☎ 07 5447 4011, fax 07 5447 3410, (Multi-stry), 14 units acc up to 4, (1 bedrm), [shwr, tlt, a/c-cool, tel, TV, clock radio, refrig, cook fac, micro, blkts, linen, pillows], ldry, dryer, pool, bbq, c/park (undercover), cots-fee. **D $150 - $245**, BC EFT MC VI.

  (Studio Section), 14 rms acc up to 3, [shwr, tlt, a/c-cool, tel, TV, t/c mkg, refrig, blkts, linen], c/park (limited), cots-fee. **D $105 - $160**, Min book applies.

Bella Casa Noosa Apartments, (Apt), 40 Hastings St, ☎ 07 5473 5644, fax 07 5473 5688, 25 apts [shwr, tlt, a/c, tel, cable tv, video, clock radio, t/c mkg, refrig, cook fac, micro, d/wash, toaster, blkts, linen, pillows], lift, w/mach, dryer, pool-heated, spa, bbq, cots-fee. **D $185 - $243**, Min book applies, AE BC DC EFT MC VI, (not yet classified).

B&B's/Guest Houses

★★★★☆ **Noosa Valley Bed & Breakfast**, (B&B), No children's facilities, 84 Grays Rd, Weyba Downs 4562, 7km S of Noosa, ☎ 07 5471 1200, fax 07 5471 1200, 5 rms [ensuite, shwr, spa bath (1), tlt, a/c-cool, c/fan, heat, TV, video-fee, clock radio, refrig], ✕, pool (salt water), spa, bbq, c/park (undercover) (3). **BB ♦♦ $95 - $155**, Min book Christmas Jan long w/ends and Easter, BC MC VI.

★★★★☆ **Noosa Valley Manor Bed & Breakfast**, (B&B), No children's facilities, 115 Wust Rd, Doonan 4562, 8km W of PO, ☎ 07 5471 0088, fax 07 5471 0066, 4 rms [shwr, bath, tlt, hairdry, c/fan, heat, elec blkts, TV, video, clock radio, refrig, micro, ldry], dryer, iron, iron brd, TV rm, ✕, pool, spa, t/c mkg shared. **BB $145**, AE BC DC MC VI.

★★★★ **Villa Alba**, (B&B), 191 Duke Rd, Doonan, 15km SW of Noosa Heads, ☎ 07 5449 1900, fax 07 5449 1300, 4 rms [shwr, bath (sunken), tlt, c/fan, heat, TV, video, clock radio, CD, t/c mkg, refrig, cook fac ltd, micro, toaster], iron, iron brd, ✕, pool, bbq, secure park. **BB ♦♦ $122 - $185**, AE BC EFT MC VI.

SUNSHINE COAST - NOOSAVILLE QLD 4566

Pop 5,500. (150km N Brisbane), See maps on page 417, ref D4. Situated on the Noosa River. Boating, Fishing, Golf, Scenic Drives, Squash, Surfing, Swimming.

Hotels/Motels

★★★★ **Anchor Motel Noosa**, (M), Cnr Weyba Rd & Anchor St, 800m S of Noosa River, ☎ 07 5449 8055, fax 07 5449 8488, (2 stry gr fl), 19 units [shwr, tlt, hairdry, a/c, c/fan, heat, tel, cable tv, clock radio, t/c mkg, refrig, micro], ldry, dryer, pool-heated, spa, bbq (covered), c/park (undercover), cots-fee, non smoking rms (13). **RO ♦ $71 - $104, ♦♦ $71 - $104**, AE BC DC EFT MC VI, ⅙.

★★★ **Noosa Palm Tree**, (M), 233 Gympie Tce, 20m to Noosa River, ☎ 07 5449 7311, fax 07 5474 3246, (2 stry gr fl), 16 units [shwr, tlt, a/c (9), c/fan, TV, t/c mkg, refrig, cook fac (8)], ldry, pool, bbq, c/park (undercover), ✆, cots. **RO ♦ $50 - $100, ♦♦ $55 - $130, ◊ $5 - $10**, AE BC DC EFT MC VI.

★★☆ **Villa Ncosa**, (LMH), Mary St, ☎ 07 5449 7766, fax 07 5449 9944, (2 stry gr fl), 24 units [shwr, tlt, a/c, tel, TV, t/c mkg, refrig], conv fac, ⊠, pool, cots. **RO ♦ $49.50, ♦♦ $73.70, ◊ $5.50**, AE BC DC MC VI.

Self Catering Accommodation

★★★★☆ **Bermuda Villas**, (HU), 7-13 Howard St, 700m NE PO, ☎ 07 5449 8566, fax 07 5449 8577, (2 stry), 14 units acc up to 4, (2 bedrm), [ensuite, shwr, bath, tlt, hairdry, c/fan, heat, tel, TV, video, clock radio, refrig, cook fac, micro, elec frypan, d/wash, ldry (in unit), blkts, linen, pillows], dryer, pool, pool-heated, spa, bbq, secure park, car wash, cots-fee. **D $176 - $231, W $638 - $1,188**, AE BC DC EFT MC VI.

Trouble-free travel tips - **Tyre wear**

Check tyre treads for uneven wear and inspect tyre walls and tread for damage.

★★★★☆ **Noosa Lakes Resort**, (HU), 3 Hilton Tce, 1km W of P O, ☎ 07 5447 1400, fax 07 5447 1044, (2 stry gr fl), 188 units acc up to 4, [shwr, tlt, a/c, tel, TV, video, movie (hire), clock radio, t/c mkg, refrig, cook fac (94), cook fac ltd (94), micro, elec frypan, toaster], ldry, dryer, iron, iron brd, conv fac, pool, c/park (undercover), cots-fee. RO ♦ $115 - $145, ♦♦ $115 - $145, ♦ $15, AE BC DC EFT MC VI, ♿.

★★★★☆ **Noosa River Palms**, (HU), 137 Gympie Tce, ☎ 07 5474 2888, fax 07 5474 1833, (2 stry gr fl), 10 units acc up to 4, (1 & 2 bedrm), [shwr, tlt, a/c-cool, fan, c/fan, heat, TV, refrig, cook fac, micro, elec frypan, blkts, linen, pillows], ldry, pool-heated, bbq, c/park (undercover). RO ♦♦ $85, ♦ $10, W ♦♦ $390 - $450, BC EFT MC VI.

★★★★☆ **Noosa River Sandy Shores**, (HU), Previously Noosa River Motor Inn. 17 Albert Street, ☎ 07 5474 1122, fax 07 5474 9450, (Multi-stry), 10 units acc up to 4, (1 bedrm), [shwr, spa bath, tlt, hairdry, a/c, heat, c/fan, tel (STD), cable tv, video, clock radio, refrig, micro, elec frypan, d/wash, toaster, ldry, blkts, linen, pillows], lift, dryer, iron, iron brd, pool-heated, bbq, secure park. RO $85 - $110, ♦ $10, W $400 - $770, ♦ $70, BC EFT MC VI, ♿.

★★★★☆ **Outrigger Beach Resort**, (HU), 275 Gympie Tce, 1km E of PO, ☎ 07 5449 7040, fax 07 5449 7212, (Multi-stry gr fl), 37 units acc up to 6, (1, 2, 3 & 4 bedrm), [ensuite, shwr, bath, tlt, hairdry, a/c (35), c/fan, heat, tel, TV, video, clock radio, refrig, cook fac, micro, elec frypan, d/wash, ldry (in unit), blkts, linen, pillows], dryer, iron, iron brd, pool (3), pool-heated (2), sauna, spa (3), bbq (covered), c/park (undercover), gym, cots-fee, non smoking units (10). D ♦♦ $125 - $199, ♦ $15, W ♦♦ $600 - $1,000, ♦ $25, ch con, AE BC DC MC VI.

★★★★☆ **Portside Noosa Waters Resort**, (HU), Portside Crt (off Gibson Rd), ☎ 07 5449 9799, fax 07 5449 9373, (2 stry), 19 units acc up to 6, (2 & 3 bedrm), [ensuite, shwr, bath, tlt, a/c-cool (5), c/fan, heat, tel, TV, video, clock radio, refrig, cook fac, micro, elec frypan, d/wash, ldry (in unit), blkts, linen, pillows], dryer, pool-heated, spa, bbq, secure park, cots-fee. RO ♦ $100 - $200, BC EFT MC VI.

★★★★☆ **Sandy Beach Resort**, (HU), 173 Gympie Tce, 750m NW of PO, ☎ 07 5474 0044, fax 07 5474 0788, (2 stry), 20 units acc up to 6, (2 & 3 bedrm), [ensuite, shwr, bath (16), tlt, a/c (10), fan, heat, tel, cable tv, video, clock radio, CD (6), refrig, cook fac, micro, elec frypan, d/wash, toaster, ldry, blkts, linen, pillows], dryer, iron, iron brd, pool-heated, sauna, spa, bbq (covered), c/park (undercover) (25), cots-fee, non smoking units (10). W $650 - $795, BC CC EFT MC VI.

★★★★☆ **Sunset Cove Resort**, (HU), Robert St, 2km fr Hastings St, ☎ 07 5474 4477, fax 07 5474 4488, (Multi-stry gr fl), 10 units acc up to 6, (2 & 3 bedrm), [ensuite, shwr, bath, tlt, hairdry, a/c-cool (8), c/fan, heat, tel, cable tv, video, clock radio, CD, refrig, cook fac, micro, elec frypan, d/wash, toaster, ldry, blkts, linen, pillows], dryer, iron, iron brd, pool-heated, sauna, spa, bbq (covered), secure park, cots-fee. W $550 - $1,350, Min book applies, BC EFT MC VI.

★★★★☆ **The Entrance**, (HU), Gibson Rd, 1km W of PO. ☎ 07 5474 0366, fax 07 5442 4511, (2 stry gr fl), 37 units acc up to 6, [ensuite, shwr, bath (25), tlt, c/fan, tel, TV, video, clock radio, refrig, cook fac, micro, elec frypan, d/wash, toaster, ldry (in unit), blkts, linen, pillows], dryer, iron, iron brd, pool (1 heated) (3), bbq, c/park (garage), cots. RO $125 - $150, W $1,190 - $1,370, Min book applies, Min book Christmas and Jan, AE BC DC MC VI.

★★★★☆ **Twin Quays**, (HU), 3 Albert St, ☎ 07 5449 9093, fax 07 5474 4419, 32 units acc up to 6, [ensuite, shwr, bath (9), tlt, a/c-cool (20), c/fan, heat, tel, TV, video, clock radio, t/c mkg, refrig, cook fac ltd (16), micro, elec frypan (16), d/wash (16), toaster, ldry (16), blkts, linen, pillows], dryer (16), iron, iron brd, pool-heated (salt water), spa, bbq (covered), dinner to unit-fee, c/park (undercover), cots-fee. W $385 - $1,015, AE BC DC EFT MC VI.

★★★★☆ **Villa Aqua**, (HU), 134-136 Gympie Tce, 800m E of PO, ☎ 07 5474 2500, fax 07 5474 2511, (2 stry gr fl), 9 units acc up to 6, (2 & 3 bedrm), [ensuite, shwr, bath, spa bath (1), tlt, hairdry, a/c (7), c/fan, tel, TV, video, clock radio, CD, refrig, cook fac, micro, d/wash, ldry, blkts, linen, pillows], dryer, pool-heated (salt water), bbq, c/park (garage), cots-fee. D $165 - $300, W $670 - $1,690, BC MC VI.

★★★★ **Cayman Quays**, (HU), 100 Hilton Tce, ☎ 07 5449 7922, fax 07 5449 0842, (2 stry gr fl), 14 units acc up to 8, (2, 3 & 4 bedrm), [shwr, tlt, a/c (10), c/fan, tel, TV, video, refrig, cook fac, blkts, linen, pillows], ldry, pool-heated, spa, bbq, boat park, mooring, jetty, bicycle, canoeing, cots-fee. RO ♦♦ $70 - $130, W ♦♦ $425 - $880, BC EFT MC VI.

S
QUEENSLAND

★★★★ **Coco Bay Resort**, (HU), 287 Weyba Rd, ☎ 07 5449 0200, fax 07 5449 0411, (2 stry), 21 units acc up to 6, (2 & 3 bedrm), [shwr, bath, tlt, c/fan, tel, TV, video, clock radio, refrig, cook fac, micro, d/wash, ldry (in unit), blkts, linen, pillows], pool-heated, sauna, spa, bbq, c/park (undercover), cots-fee. **D** $155 - $235, **W** $560 - $1,190, BC MC VI.

★★★★ **Ivory Palms Resort**, (HU), 73 Hilton Tce, ☎ 07 5474 1688, fax 07 5474 1922, 75 units (1, 2 & 3 bedrm), [shwr, bath, spa bath (36), tlt, a/c-cool (45), c/fan, heat, tel, TV, clock radio, refrig, cook fac, micro, ldry (in unit)], conf fac, pool (one heated) (3), sauna, spa, bbq (covered), kiosk, secure park, tennis, cots-fee. **D** $120 - $165, **W** $520 - $1,215, AE BC DC MC VI.

★★★★ **Munna Beach**, (Apt), 291 Gympie Tce, ☎ 07 5449 7966, fax 07 5449 6249, (Multi-stry gr fl), 35 apts acc up to 6, (2 & 3 bedrm), [ensuite, shwr, bath, tlt (2), a/c-cool (on application), c/fan, heat, tel, cable tv, video, refrig, cook fac, micro, d/wash, ldry (in unit), blkts, linen, pillows], pool-heated, wading pool, sauna, bbq, c/park (undercover), cots-fee. **D** $125 - $240, **W** $560 - $1,430, AE BC DC EFT JCB MC VI.

★★★★ **Noosa Pelican Cove**, (HU), 229-231 Weyba Rd, 800m from PO, ☎ 07 5449 7177, fax 07 5449 7810, (2 stry gr fl), 11 units acc up to 5, [shwr, bath, tlt, c/fan, heat, tel, TV, video, refrig, cook fac, micro, d/wash (7), ldry (in unit), blkts, linen, pillows], dryer, iron, iron brd, pool-heated, spa, bbq (covered), c/park (undercover), cots-fee. **RO** ♦♦ $90 - $150, ♦ $15, ♦♦ $490 - $850, ♦ $70, BC EFT MC VI.

★★★★ **Noosa River Retreat**, (SA), No children's facilities, 243 Weyba Road, ☎ 07 5474 2811, fax 07 5474 2844, (2 stry), 20 serv apts acc up to 2, (Studio), [shwr, spa bath (10), tlt, a/c-cool, c/fan, tel, TV, clock radio, refrig, micro, toaster, blkts, linen, pillows], iron, iron brd, pool, spa, bbq. **RO** ♦♦ $65 - $140, DC EFT MC VI.

★★★★ **Noosa Riviera**, (HU), Cnr Noosa Pde & Munna Cres, 3 km NW of PO, ☎ 07 5474 1800, fax 07 5474 1650, (Multi-stry), 9 units acc up to 6, (2 & 3 bedrm), [shwr, bath (hip), spa bath (3), tlt, c/fan, tel, TV, video-fee, clock radio, refrig, micro, elec frypan, d/wash, ldry (in unit), blkts, linen, pillows], pool, bbq, c/park (undercover), cots-fee. **D** $110 - $130, **W** $580 - $880, AE BC MC VI.

★★★★ **Regatta Holiday Apartments**, (HU), 221-227 Gympie Tce, ☎ 07 5449 0522, fax 07 5449 0909, (Multi-stry gr fl), 24 units acc up to 8, (2 & 3 bedrm), [shwr, bath, tlt, hairdry (18), a/c-cool (5), c/fan, tel, TV, video, CD (20), refrig, cook fac, micro, d/wash, ldry (in unit), blkts, linen, pillows], dryer, pool-heated, bbq, secure park, cots-fee. **W** $599 - $1,300, AE BC DC MC VI.

★★★★ **Terrapin Apartments**, (HU), 15 The Cockleshell, 1km W of PO, ☎ 07 5449 8770, fax 07 5449 8110, (2 stry), 10 units acc up to 5, (2 bedrm), [ensuite, shwr, bath, tlt, heat, c/fan, tel, TV, video, clock radio, refrig, cook fac, micro, elec frypan, d/wash, toaster, ldry (in unit), blkts, linen, pillows], dryer, iron, iron brd, pool-heated, bbq (covered), c/park (undercover), cots-fee. **RO** $450 - $840, BC MC VI.

★★★☆ **Amalfi Resort Villas**, (HU), 11 Woorookool Pl, 2km W Noosaville, ☎ 07 5449 8095, fax 07 5449 8095, 2 units acc up to 4, [shwr, bath, tlt, c/fan, heat, TV, clock radio, refrig, cook fac, micro, elec frypan, d/wash (1), ldry (in unit), blkts, linen, pillows], dryer, pool-heated (solar), freezer, bbq, c/park (undercover), cots-fee. **D** ♦♦♦♦ $100 - $120, **W** ♦♦♦♦ $395 - $700, BC MC VI.

★★★☆ **Coral Beach Resort**, (HU), Robert St, 100m S of Noosa River, ☎ 07 5449 7777, fax 07 5449 7505, 45 units acc up to 6, (2 & 3 bedrm), [shwr, bath, tlt, c/fan, heat, tel, TV, video, clock radio, refrig, cook fac, micro, d/wash, ldry (in unit), blkts, linen, pillows], dryer, iron, pool-heated (3), sauna (2), spa (3), bbq, c/park (undercover), tennis, cots-fee. **D** $110 - $180, **W** $550 - $1,250, Min book applies, BC MC VI.

Medication and driving

Medication can effect your driving. Certain drugs can effect your mental alertness and/or co-ordination and therefore effect driving skills. Always check with your doctor the effect which any medication (over the counter or prescription) you are taking may have on your driving. There may be an alternative drug which will not affect your driving. It is best to avoid drinking alcohol while taking medication.

291 Gympie Tce NOOSAVILLE, QLD 4566
Phone: 1800 015 511
07 5449 7966
Fax: 07 5449 6249
email: munnabeachapts@altavista.net

AAA Tourism ★★★★

- Large 1, 2 & 3 bedroom fully self contained apartments.
- Private Balconies.
- Heated salt water Pool and Sauna.
- Picnic area with Free Barbecues.
- Extensive garden areas.
- Undercover Car & Boat parking with wash area.

221-227 Gympie Terrace Noosaville QLD 4566
Phone: (07) 5449 0522
Fax: (07) 5449 0909
Email: inquiries@regattaapartments.com.au
Internet: www.regattaapartments.com.au

Regatta overlooks the gentle ebb and flow of the magical Noosa River with its calm swimming beaches, 5 minutes away by road is the majestic Noosa surf.

Restaurants abound with a major shopping centre and boutique shopping all within walking distance while Hastings Street is only 5 minutes by car.

★★★☆ **Eumarella Shores**, (Cotg), Eumarella Rd Lake Weyba Downs, ☎ 07 5449 1738, 4 cotgs acc up to 4, (2 bedrm), [shwr, tlt, fan, heat, tel, TV, clock radio, refrig, ldry (in unit), blkts, linen, pillows], bbq, c/park (undercover), canoeing-fee. **RO** ♦♦ $105 - $165, Min book applies, BC MC VI.

★★★☆ **Islander Noosa Resort**, (HU), 187 Gympie Tce, 100m N of PO, ☎ 07 5449 7022, fax 07 5449 9358, (Multi-stry gr fl), 58 units acc up to 6, (2 & 3 bedrm), [ensuite (12), shwr, bath (49), tlt, a/c-cool, c/fan, tel, TV, video, clock radio, refrig, cook fac, micro, d/wash (56), ldry (in unit), blkts, linen, pillows], w/mach, dryer, iron, iron brd, rec rm, conv fac (seats 20-40), ✕ (7), pool-heated (1), sauna (2), spa (3), bbq (4), mini mart, c/park (undercover), gym, tennis (2), cots-fee. **RO** ♦♦♦♦ $135 - $210, ♦♦♦♦ $615 - $960, BC EFT MC VI, ⚘.

★★★☆ **Nautilus Noosa**, (HU), 124 Noosa Pde, ☎ 07 5449 9188, fax 07 5474 3421, (2 stry gr fl), 38 units acc up to 6, [shwr, bath, tlt, c/fan, heat, tel, TV, clock radio, refrig, cook fac, micro, ldry (in unit), blkts, linen, pillows], dryer, pool-heated, spa, bbq (covered), c/park (undercover), tennis, cots-fee. **D** $130 - $145, **W** $497 - $847, Min book applies, BC EFT MC VI.

★★★☆ **Nimbus**, (HU), 295 Weyba Rd, ☎ 07 5449 9333, fax 07 5449 0603, (2 stry gr fl), 39 units acc up to 6, [shwr, bath, tlt, c/fan, tel, cable tv, video, clock radio, refrig, cook fac, micro, elec frypan, d/wash (16), ldry (in unit), blkts, linen, pillows], pool (1 Gas Heated) (3), bbq, c/park (undercover) (29), boat park, secure park (10), cots-fee. **D** $115 - $195, **W** $485 - $1,285, BC MC VI.

★★★☆ **Noosa Gardens Riverside Resort**, (HU), 261 Weyba Rd, 1km NW of PO, 300m from Noosa River, ☎ 07 5449 9800, fax 07 5449 9472, 18 units acc up to 6, (2 bedrm - Split level accommodation available.), [shwr, bath, tlt (2), c/fan, heat, tel, TV, video, clock radio, refrig, cook fac, micro, d/wash, ldry (in unit), blkts, linen, pillows], dryer, pool (slt water/solar htd), wading pool, spa, bbq, c/park (undercover), cots-fee. **D** ♦♦♦♦ $110 - $140, **W** ♦♦♦♦ $434 - $805, BC EFT MC VI.

★★★☆ **Noosa Keys Resort**, (HU), 164 Noosa Pde, 2km N Hastings St, ☎ 07 5449 0333, fax 07 5449 0390, (2 stry gr fl), 24 units acc up to 6, (2 & 3 bedrm), [shwr, bath, tlt, tel, cable tv, video (24), clock radio, refrig, cook fac, micro, d/wash (7), ldry (in unit), blkts, linen, pillows], dryer, pool-heated, wading pool, spa, c/park (undercover), tennis, cots. **D** $100 - $140, **W** $450 - $900, ch con, BC EFT MC VI.

★★★☆ **Noosa Place Resort**, (HU), 272 Weyba Rd, ☎ 07 5449 8522, fax 07 5449 9023, (2 stry), 40 units acc up to 6, [shwr, bath, tlt, hairdry, fan, c/fan, tel, cable tv, video, clock radio, CD (28), t/c mkg, refrig, micro, elec frypan, d/wash, toaster, blkts, linen, pillows], w/mach, dryer, iron, iron brd, pool (saltwater) (3), pool-heated (gas heated) (1), spa (2), bbq (covered), c/park (undercover), tennis, cots-fee. **D** ♦♦♦♦ $165 - $200, ◊ $20 - $30, BC MC VI.

★★★☆ **Noosa Sound Holiday Resort**, (HU), 11 Munna Cres, ☎ 07 5449 8122, fax 07 5449 7678, (2 stry), 25 units acc up to 4, (2 bedrm), [shwr, bath, tlt, c/fan, heat, tel, TV, clock radio, refrig, cook fac, micro, ldry (in unit), blkts, linen, pillows], pool, bbq, c/park (undercover), tennis, cots-fee. **RO** ♦♦♦♦ $115 - $132, ♦♦♦♦ $374 - $759, Min book applies, BC EFT MC VI.

★★★☆ **Noosavillage River Resort**, (HU), 159 Gympie Tce, ☎ 07 5449 7698, fax 07 5449 0185, (2 stry), 25 units acc up to 4, (2 bedrm), [shwr, bath, tlt, a/c-cool (4), c/fan, heat, tel, cable tv, refrig, cook fac, micro, d/wash, ldry (in unit), blkts, linen, pillows], pool-heated, wading pool, sauna, spa, bbq, c/park (undercover), tennis. **D** $90 - $135, **W** $470 - $790, BC EFT MC VI.

★★★☆ **Pelican Beach Resort Noosa**, (HU), 13 James St, 3km W of Noosa Heads, ☎ 07 5449 0766, fax 07 5449 0220, 25 units acc up to 6, (2 bedrm - Split level accommodation available.), [shwr, bath, tlt, c/fan, tel, TV, video, clock radio, refrig, cook fac, micro, d/wash, ldry (in unit), blkts, linen, pillows], dryer, pool-heated, wading pool, sauna, spa, bbq (covered), c/park (undercover), plygr, gym, tennis (half court), cots-fee. **D** $100 - $125, Min book all holiday times, BC EFT MC VI.

★★★☆ **River Breeze Resort**, (HU), 16 James St, ☎ 07 5449 9216, fax 07 5449 9207, (2 stry gr fl), 8 units acc up to 4, [shwr, bath (3), tlt, a/c (2), c/fan, heat, tel (6), TV, video (2), clock radio, refrig, micro (5), elec frypan, d/wash (1), ldry (in unit), blkts, linen, pillows], pool, bbq, c/park (undercover), cots-fee. **D** $72.50 - $120, **W** $310 - $665, Min book applies, AE BC MC VI.

★★★☆ **Weyba Gardens Resort**, (HU), Lake Weyba Dve, 2.3km E of Noosa Heads PO, ☎ 07 5449 0277, fax 07 5449 0102, 40 units acc up to 5, [shwr, bath, tlt, hairdry (22), c/fan, heat, tel, cable tv, video, clock radio, refrig, cook fac, micro, d/wash (18), ldry (in unit)], dryer, pool (salt water), pool-heated (salt water), bbq, c/park (undercover), courtesy transfer (bus), cots-fee. **D** $110 - $130, **W** $390 - $865, BC EFT MC VI.

★★★☆ **Wolngarin**, (HU), 27 Munna Cres, Noosa Sound, 2km NW of PO, ☎ 07 5449 8755, fax 07 5447 1591, 22 units (2 bedrm), [shwr, bath, tlt, c/fan, heat, tel, TV, video-fee, clock radio, refrig, cook fac, micro, ldry (in unit), blkts, linen, pillows], pool-heated, wading pool (heated), spa, bbq (covered), c/park (undercover), tennis (half court), cots-fee. **D** $110 - $150, **W** $490 - $770, BC MC VI.

★★★ **Noosa Riverfront**, (HU), 277 Gympie Tce, ☎ 07 5449 7595, (2 stry), 7 units acc up to 4, (Studio & 2 bedrm), [shwr, tlt, fan, TV, refrig, cook fac, micro, blkts, linen, pillows], ldry, pool, bbq, c/park (undercover), cots. **D** ♦♦ $50 - $110, ◊ $10, **W** ♦♦ $320 - $720, BC EFT MC VI, ♿.

★★★ **Noosa Yallambee Holiday Apartments**, (HU), 219 Weyba Rd, ☎ 07 5449 8632, fax 07 5449 8632, (2 stry gr fl), 12 units acc up to 6, (1 & 2 bedrm - 1xd. 2xs), [shwr, tlt, c/fan, heat, TV, clock radio, refrig, cook fac, micro, ldry (in unit), blkts, linen, pillows], rec rm, pool-heated (solar), bbq, c/park (undercover), cots-fee. **RO** ♦♦ $60 - $90, ♦♦ $360 - $540, BC MC VI.

★★☆ **Regency Waterfront Motel**, (HU), 130 Gympie Tce, ☎ 07 5449 7139, fax 07 5442 4439, (2 stry), 14 units acc up to 7, [shwr, bath (2), tlt, c/fan (8), heat, TV, refrig, cook fac ltd (12), blkts, linen, pillows], ldry, pool, bbq, c/park (undercover), cots. **D** ♦♦ $55 - $105, ◊ $10, weekly con, BC MC VI.

Montpellier Villas Noosa, (Apt), 7 James St, ☎ 07 5455 5033, fax 07 5455 8022, (Multi-stry gr fl), 20 apts acc up to 4, (2 bedrm), [shwr, tlt, a/c, c/fan, tel, video, clock radio, refrig, cook fac, micro, d/wash, ldry, blkts, linen, pillows], w/mach, dryer, pool, spa, bbq, secure park, cots-fee, non smoking units (20). **D** ♦♦ $130 - $180, ◊ $15 - $20, **W** ♦♦ $700 - $1,225, Min book Christmas Jan and Easter, BC EFT MC VI, (not yet classified).

Rimini by the River, (HU), Resort, 7 Edward St, 500m N of PO, ☎ 07 5473 0000, fax 07 5473 0100, (2 stry), 19 units [shwr, tlt, hairdry, a/c, c/fan, tel, TV, video, movie, clock radio, cook fac], w/mach, dryer, pool-heated (saltwater), spa (heated), bbq (covered), cots-fee. **RO** $80 - $150, AE BC DC EFT MC VI, (not yet classified).

B&B's/Guest Houses
★★★★ **Noosa Country House B & B**, (B&B), No children's facilities, 93 Duke Rd, Noosa Valley, 1km N from cnr Duke & Noosa/Eumundi Rds, ☎ 07 5471 0121, fax 07 5471 0941, 4 rms [shwr, tlt, hairdry, a/c-cool, c/fan, fire pl, elec blkts, tel, TV, t/c mkg, refrig], ldry, dryer, lounge (TV), ✕, spa (heated), bbq, non smoking rms. **BB** ♦♦ $143 - $165, AE BC DC MC VI.

SUNSHINE COAST - PACIFIC PARADISE QLD 4564
Pop part of Marcoola (118km N Brisbane) See maps on page 417, ref D4. Adjacent to Mudjimba on the Sunshine Coast close to the beach.
Hotels/Motels
★★☆ **Pacific Paradise**, (M), 612 David Low Way, opposite Novotel Twin Waters Resort turnoff, ☎ 07 5448 7181, fax 07 5448 8584, 12 units [shwr, tlt, fan, heat, tel, TV, clock radio, t/c mkg, refrig, cook fac (1), toaster], ldry, pool (salt water), bbq, meals to unit (breakfast), cots-fee. **RO** ♦ $44, ♦♦ $49.50 - $77, ◊ $5.50 - $8.80, ch con, BC MC VI.

SUNSHINE COAST - PALMVIEW QLD 4553
Pop Nominal, (85km N Brisbane), See maps on page 417, ref D5. Tropical fruit growing area. Popular tourist attraction is the Ettamogah Pub. House of Herbs Opals Down Under, Suncoast Crayfish Farm, The Skin Thing Cedar Krafts.
Hotels/Motels
★★★ **Alacante**, (M), Ballantyne Ct, Exit 500m N of Caloundra turnoff, ☎ 07 5494 5357, 6 units [shwr, tlt, c/fan, TV, clock radio, t/c mkg, refrig, doonas]. **RO** ♦ $40 - $55, ♦♦ $50 - $66, ◊ $10 - $15, BC MC VI.

SUNSHINE COAST - PEREGIAN BEACH QLD 4573
Pop 2,950. Part of Coolum Beach, (136km N Brisbane), See maps on page 417, ref D4. Located on the Sunshine Coast. Boating, Bowls, Fishing, Golf, Scenic Drives, Surfing, Swimming.
Hotels/Motels
★★☆ **Peregian Motor Inn**, (M), Cnr Heron St & David Low Way, ☎ 07 5448 1110, fax 07 5448 2211, 20 units [shwr, tlt, fan, c/fan, heat, TV, clock radio, t/c mkg, refrig], pool (salt water), c/park (undercover) (6). **RO** ♦ $55 - $66, ♦♦ $55 - $100, BC MC VI.
Self Catering Accommodation
★★★★☆ **The Retreat Beachfront Resort**, (HU), 390 David Low Way, 2km N of Peregian village, ☎ 07 5448 1922, fax 07 5448 1057, (2 stry), 20 units acc up to 6, (3 bedrm - 20x1q4s), [ensuite, shwr, bath, tlt, c/fan, heat, tel, cable tv, clock radio, refrig, cook fac, micro, d/wash, ldry (in unit), blkts, linen, pillows], pool-heated, bbq, secure park, tennis, cots-fee. **W** $918 - $2,230, BC EFT MC VI.

Rates may change. Check before booking.

★★★★ **Calypso Sands**, (HU), Cnr David Low Way & Jabiru St, 1.3km S of Peregian Village, ☎ 07 5448 3399, fax 07 5448 3619, (2 stry), 14 units acc up to 4, (2 bedrm), [shwr, tlt, c/fan, tel, TV, video-fee, clock radio, refrig, cook fac, micro, elec frypan, toaster, ldry, blkts, linen, pillows], dryer, iron, iron brd, pool (saltwater/solar) (2), bbq (covered) (2), c/park (carport), cots-fee. **RO $90 - $150, W $370 - $810**, BC EFT MC VI.

Lake Weyba Cottages

★★★★ **Lake Weyba Cottages**, (Cotg), 79 Clarendon Rd, 4km W of Peregian, ☎ 07 5448 2285, fax 07 5448 2285, 4 cotgs [spa bath, a/c-cool, fan, heat (wood), TV, video, t/c mkg, refrig, cook fac ltd, micro, blkts, doonas, linen, pillows], ldry, bbq, bicycle, bowls, canoeing, cots, breakfast ingredients, non smoking property. **RO ♦ $60 - $100, ♦♦ $120 - $200, ◊ $25**, ch con, weekly con, Min book long w/ends, BC MC VI.

★★★☆ **Beachcomber Peregian Beach**, (HU), 384 David Low Way, 2km N of PO, ☎ 07 5448 1306, fax 07 5473 1331, (2 stry), 5 units acc up to 4, (1 & 2 bedrm), [shwr, tlt, fan, heat, TV, clock radio, refrig, micro, toaster, blkts, linen, pillows], ldry, w/mach, dryer, iron, iron brd, bbq, c/park (undercover). **D ♦♦ $88 - $126.50, ◊ $16.50, W ♦♦ $385 - $654.50**, BC MC VI.

★★★☆ **Glen Eden Beach Resort**, (HU), 388 David Low Way, ☎ 07 5448 1955, fax 07 5448 1677, (2 stry), 37 units acc up to 7, (2 & 3 bedrm), [shwr, bath, tlt, c/fan, heat, tel, TV, video-fee, clock radio, refrig, cook fac, micro, ldry (in unit), blkts, linen, pillows], rec rm, pool-heated, sauna, spa, bbq, kiosk, cots-fee. **D $115 - $170, W $504 - $1,190**, BC EFT MC VI.

★★★☆ **Lorikeet Lodge**, (HF), 31 Lorikeet Dve, 100m from beach, ☎ 07 5448 1315, fax 07 5448 3006, 7 flats acc up to 5, (1 & 2 bedrm), [shwr, tlt, fan, heat, TV, refrig, cook fac, blkts, linen, pillows], ldry, pool, bbq, c/park (undercover), ☎, cots, Pets on application. **D ♦♦ $75 - $125, W ♦♦ $375 - $685**, BC EFT MC VI.

★★★☆ **Ocean Shore Apartments**, (HU), 60 The Esplanade, 1km N of Peregian Shopping Centre, ☎ 07 5448 1511, fax 07 5448 2166, (2 stry gr fl), 7 units acc up to 5, (2 bedrm), [ensuite, shwr, bath, tlt, c/fan, TV, clock radio, refrig, cook fac, micro, elec frypan, d/wash, toaster, ldry (in unit), blkts, linen reqd-fee, pillows], iron, iron brd, pool, c/park (undercover), secure park, cots-fee. **W $360 - $920**, Min book applies.

★★★☆ **Peregian Court**, (HU), 380 David Low Way, ☎ 07 5448 1622, fax 07 5448 2302, (2 stry gr fl), 19 units acc up to 6, (1, 2 & 3 bedrm), [shwr, bath (1), tlt, c/fan, tel, TV, video, clock radio, refrig, cook fac, micro, d/wash (11), ldry (in unit), blkts, linen, pillows], pool-heated, sauna, bbq, c/park (undercover), plygr. **D ♦♦ $98 - $174, W ♦♦ $399 - $990**, BC MC VI.

★★★☆ **Sails Lifestyle Resort**, (HU), 43 Oriole Ave, 1.2km S of PO, ☎ 07 5448 1011, fax 07 5448 2882, 21 units acc up to 8, (2 & 3 bedrm), [shwr, bath (hip), tlt, a/c-cool (9), c/fan, tel, TV, movie, refrig, cook fac, micro, ldry (in unit), blkts, linen, pillows], dryer, iron, pool-heated, spa, bbq, c/park (undercover), cots-fee. **D $110 - $190, W $365 - $925**, BC MC VI.

★★★ **Hideaway Holiday Apartments**, (HU), 386 David Low Way, 2km N of PO, ☎ 07 5448 1006, fax 07 5448 3891, 4 units acc up to 4, (1 bedrm), [shwr, tlt, fan, heat, TV, clock radio, refrig, cook fac, blkts, linen, pillows], ldry, pool (salt water), bbq (gas), rm serv, meals to unit (cooked breakfast), c/park (undercover), cots-fee. **RO ♦♦ $80 - $105, ◊ $15**, AE BC EFT MC VI, ♿.

★★☆ **Surfedge**, (HF), 38 Lorikeet Dve, ☎ 07 5448 1511, (2 stry gr fl), 6 flats acc up to 6, (2 & 3 bedrm), [shwr, tlt, heat, TV, clock radio, cook fac, micro, linen reqd-fee], ldry, pool, bbq, c/park (undercover). **W ♦♦ $235 - $720**, Min book applies.

SUNSHINE COAST - SUNRISE BEACH QLD 4567

Pop Part of Noosa, (142km N Brisbane), See maps on page 417, ref E4. Satellite coastal suburb south of Noosa National Park.

Self Catering Accommodation

★★★★☆ **Aqua Promenade**, (HU), 1 Selene St. 3km S Noosa Heads, ☎ 07 5474 5788, fax 07 5474 5799, (Multi-stry gr fl), 12 units acc up to 6, [shwr, bath, tlt, hairdry, c/fan, tel, TV, video, refrig, cook fac, elec frypan, d/wash, ldry (in unit), blkts, linen, pillows], pool, bbq, secure park, cots-fee. **D $110 - $220, W $660 - $1,650**, BC DC MC VI.

★★★☆ **Beach Breakers**, (HU), 75 David Low Way, 3km S of PO, ☎ 07 5447 2829, fax 07 5447 5181, (2 stry), 25 units acc up to 4, (2 bedrm), [shwr, bath, tlt, hairdry, a/c (11), tel, TV, clock radio, refrig, cook fac, micro, elec frypan, d/wash (16), ldry (in unit), blkts, linen, pillows], pool-heated, spa, bbq (3), c/park (undercover), tennis. **RO $110 - $120, W $485 - $995**, BC EFT MC VI.

SUNSHINE COAST - SUNSHINE BEACH QLD 4567

Pop 5,600. Nominal, (142km N Brisbane), See maps on page 417, ref E4. Picturesque coastal suburb south of Noosa National Park.

Self Catering Accommodation

★★★★☆ **Andari**, (HU), 19-21 Belmore Tce, 8km E Hastings St, ☎ 07 5474 9996, fax 07 5474 9955, 9 units acc up to 6, (2 & 3 bedrm), [ensuite, shwr, bath, tlt, c/fan, tel, TV, video, refrig, cook fac, micro, elec frypan, d/wash, ldry (in unit), blkts, linen, pillows], dryer, iron, iron brd, pool, bbq-fee, secure park, cots-fee. **D $100 - $260, W $700 - $1,800**, AE BC DC MC VI.

★★★★☆ **Costa Nova**, (HU), 1 Belmore Tce, ☎ 07 5447 2709, fax 07 5474 9752, 16 units acc up to 6, (2 & 3 bedrm), [shwr, bath, tlt, c/fan, tel, cable tv (12), video, clock radio, CD, refrig, cook fac, micro, d/wash, ldry (in unit), blkts, linen, pillows], lift, pool-heated, spa, bbq, secure park, cots-fee. **D $165 - $475, W $900 - $3,300**, Min book applies, AE BC MC VI.

★★★★☆ **La Mer Sunshine**, (HU), 5 Belmore Tce, ☎ 07 5447 2111, fax 07 5449 2483, (Multi-stry), 19 units acc up to 5, (2 bedrm), [ensuite, shwr, bath, tlt, c/fan, tel, TV, video, clock radio, CD (19), refrig, cook fac, micro, d/wash, ldry (in unit), blkts, linen, pillows], lift, rec rm, pool-heated, bbq, c/park (garage), cots-fee. **D $124 - $253, W $769 - $1,680**, Min book applies, BC MC VI, ♿.

★★★★☆ **Sunshine Vista**, (HU), 45 Duke St, 2km S of Noosa Heads, ☎ 07 5447 2487, fax 07 5448 0670, (Multi-stry), 13 units acc up to 4, [shwr, spa bath, tlt, fan, c/fan, tel, TV, video (11), clock radio, refrig, cook fac, micro, d/wash, ldry (in unit), blkts, linen, pillows], lift, pool-heated (saltwater), spa, bbq, secure park, ☎. **RO $130 - $254, W $568 - $1,204**, BC MC VI.

★★★★ **Sundancer**, (HU), 11 Henderson St, ☎ 07 5449 2077, fax 07 5449 2074, (Multi-stry), 13 units acc up to 6, (2 & 3 bedrm), [shwr, bath, tlt, c/fan, tel, TV, video, clock radio, refrig, cook fac, micro, d/wash, ldry (in unit), blkts, linen, pillows], pool-heated, bbq. D ⓘ $91 - $264, W $637 - $1,988, Min book applies, AE BC BTC CC DC JCB MC MCH MP VI.

★★★★ **Sunseeker Lodge**, (HU), Cnr Ross Cres & Pilchers Gap, ☎ 07 5447 5344, fax 07 5447 5035, (2 stry gr fl), 20 units acc up to 4, (2 bedrm), [shwr, bath, tlt, c/fan, heat, tel, TV, video, radio, refrig, cook fac, micro, d/wash, ldry (in unit), blkts, linen], rec rm, pool-heated, sauna (2), spa, bbq, cots-fee. W $490 - $1,400, ⓛ占.

★★★☆ **Northgate Holiday Apartments**, (HU), 4 Solway Dve, ☎ 07 5449 2009, fax 07 5448 0474, (2 stry), 20 units acc up to 5, [shwr, tlt, c/fan, tel, TV, video, refrig, cook fac, micro, ldry (in unit), blkts, linen, pillows], pool, bbq, c/park (undercover), tennis (half court), cots-fee. RO $98 - $145, W $448 - $896, BC DC MC VI.

SUNSHINE COAST - TEWANTIN QLD 4565

Pop 26,050. (152km N Brisbane), See maps on page 417, ref D4.
Hotels/Motels
★☆ **Royal Mail Hotel**, (LH), 120 Poinciana Ave, ☎ 07 5447 1644, fax 07 5449 7516, (2 stry), 10 rms [basin, TV, t/c mkg, refrig], shwr, tlt, bathrm, lounge, ☒ (Mon to Sat), ☎. RO ⓘ $33, ⓘⓘ $44, ⓘ $5, AE BC MC VI.

End of Sunshine Coast Region

SURAT QLD 4417

Pop 400. (450km W Brisbane), See maps on page 414, ref D7.
★★★☆ **Cobb & Co Country Motel Surat**, (M), Previously Cobbs Camp Motel 47 Charlotte St, 500m S of PO, ☎ 07 4626 5533, fax 07 4626 5544, 8 units [shwr, tlt, hairdry, a/c, heat, tel, TV, movie, clock radio, t/c mkg, refrig, cook fac (2), toaster], iron, iron brd, dinner to unit, c/park (undercover), non smoking units (4). RO ⓘ $55, ⓘⓘ $65, ⓘ $5, AE BC DC EFT MC VI.

SURFERS PARADISE QLD

See Gold Coast Region.

TAMBO QLD 4478

Pop 400. (861km NW Brisbane), See maps on page 414, ref C7.
★★★★ **Tambo Mill Motel**, (M), Matilda Hwy, ☎ 07 4654 6466, fax 07 4654 6497, 12 units [shwr, tlt, hairdry, a/c, tel, TV, movie, clock radio, t/c mkg, refrig], ldry, dryer, ☒, pool (salt water), dinner to unit, c/park (undercover), cots. RO ⓘ $63 - $70, ⓘⓘ $76 - $83, ⓘ $13, ch con, AE BC DC MC VI, ⓛ占.

TAMBORINE MOUNTAIN QLD 4272

Pop 1,200. (81km S Brisbane), See maps on page 417, ref D8. Located in the Gold Coast Hinterland, amid beautiful rainforests.
★★★☆ **Bungunyah Manor**, (M), 160 Long Rd, Eagle Heights 4271, 300m from Gallery Walk, ☎ 07 5545 1044, fax 07 5545 2797, (2 stry gr fl), 16 units [shwr, tlt, fire pl, tel, TV, clock radio, t/c mkg, refrig], ldry, conv fac, ☒ (Mon - Sun), pool (1), sauna, spa, rm serv, tennis, cots. RO ⓘ $59 - $150, ⓘⓘ $59 - $150, AE BC BTC DC MC VI.
★★★☆ **Cedar Creek Lodges**, (M), Tamborine Mountain Rd, ☎ 07 5545 1468, fax 07 5545 2707, 30 units [shwr, tlt, a/c-cool (heat), tel, TV, clock radio, t/c mkg, refrig], conv fac, pool (saltwater), tennis (half court), cots. D ⓘⓘ $89, ⓘ $17, ch con, AE BC DC EFT MC VI.
   ★★★★ **(Creek Lodges)**, 10 units acc up to 4, (2 bedrm), [shwr, bath, spa bath, tlt, hairdry, c/fan, fire pl, tel, TV, t/c mkg, refrig, cook fac ltd, micro, d/wash, toaster, linen, pillows], iron, iron brd. D ⓘⓘ $215, ⓘ $17.
   ★★☆ **(Bush Lodges)**, 3 cabins [shwr, tlt, heat, TV, t/c mkg, refrig, cook fac, toaster, blkts, linen, pillows]. D ⓘⓘ $89, ⓘ $17.
★★★☆ **Tall Trees**, (M), 9 Eagle Heights Rd, ☎ 07 5545 1242, fax 07 5545 0055, 5 units [shwr, tlt, hairdry, fan, heat, elec blkts, tel, TV, clock radio, t/c mkg, refrig, toaster], ldry, bbq, cots-fee. RO ⓘ $65, ⓘⓘ $70, ⓘ $10, pen con, AE BC MC VI.
★★★ **St Bernards**, (LMH), 101 Alpine Tce, ☎ 07 5545 1177, fax 07 5545 2733, (2 stry gr fl), 24 units [shwr, tlt, fan, heat, TV, clock radio, t/c mkg, refrig], ldry, conv fac, ☒, pool, ☎, tennis, cots-fee. BLB ⓘ $59 - $69, ⓘⓘ $79 - $115, ch con, AE BC MC VI.
   ★☆ **(Hotel Section)**, 13 rms [basin], shwr, tlt, ☒, t/c mkg shared, refrig, cots-fee. BLB ⓘ $39 - $49, ⓘⓘ $59 - $79, ⓘ $20.

Self Catering Accommodation
★★★★★ **Lisson Grove - Cottages for Couples**, (Cotg), 274 - 280 Main Western Rd, ☎ 07 5545 1488, fax 07 5545 1188, 6 cotgs acc up to 12, [shwr, bath, spa bath, tlt, hairdry, a/c-cool, fan, fire pl, elec blkts, TV, video, clock radio, CD, t/c mkg, refrig, mini bar, micro, toaster], iron, iron brd. D ⓘⓘ $162 - $240.
★★★★★ **The Cottages-Mount Tamborine**, (Cotg), 23 Kootenai Dve, 2km W PO, ☎ 07 5545 2574, fax 07 5545 2591, 4 cotgs acc up to 4, [shwr, tlt, c/fan, heat, elec blkts, TV, video, clock radio, CD, t/c mkg, refrig, cook fac, micro, blkts, linen, pillows], ldry, dryer, iron, spa (3), bbq, c/park (undercover). BB ⓘⓘ $170, ⓘ $40, BC MC VI.
★★★★☆ **Mountain Edge Lodges & Cafe Kandinsky**, (Cotg), 387 Henri Robert Dve, ☎ 07 5545 3437, fax 07 5545 0971, 4 cotgs [shwr, bath (double) (2), spa bath (2), tlt, hairdry, c/fan, heat (wood fire), clock radio, CD, t/c mkg, refrig, cook fac ltd, micro, toaster], iron, iron brd, ☒, dinner to unit (by arrangement). BLB ⓘⓘ $169 - $219, ⓘⓘⓘⓘ $255 - $330, AE BC EFT MC VI.

★★★★☆ **The Polish Place**, (Cotg), 333 Main Western Rd, North Tamborine 4272, 3km S of PO, ☎ 07 5545 1603, fax 07 5545 1603, 5 cotgs (1 bedrm), [shwr, spa bath, tlt, fire pl, heat, TV, video, CD, refrig, cook fac, micro, ldry (in unit), blkts, linen, pillows], dryer, iron, ☒, c/park. BB ⓘⓘ $176 - $242, ⓘⓘ $990, AE BC DC MC VI,
Operator Comment:
Visit our website at: www.polishplace.com.au
★★★★★ **Tamborine Mountain Chalets**, (Cotg), No children's facilities, 112 Long Rd, Eagle Heights 4271, ☎ 07 5545 1132, fax 07 5545 1611, 6 cotgs [a/c-cool]. BB ⓘⓘ $149 - $200, RO ⓘⓘ $132 - $180, AE BC DC EFT JCB MC VI.

B&B's/Guest Houses
★★★★★ **Tamborine Mountain Bed & Breakfast**, (B&B), 19 Witherby Cres, 500m E Eagle Heights, ☎ 07 5545 3595, fax 07 5545 3322, 4 rms [shwr, tlt, a/c, TV, clock radio], ☒, c/park. BB ⓘ $70 - $120, ⓘⓘ $95 - $145, AE BC MC VI.
★★★★☆ **Barclay House**, (B&B), 724 Mainwestern Rd, 5km S of North Tamborine PO, ☎ 07 5545 4533, fax 07 5545 4534, (2 stry gr fl), 3 rms [ensuite, spa bath (2), fan, heat (elec), TV, video (dvd - avail), movie, t/c mkg, refrig], ldry, ☒, bbq, non smoking rms. BB ⓘⓘ $135 - $200, weekly con, AE BC DC MC VI.
★★★★☆ **Camelot Bed & Breakfast**, (B&B), 322 Main Western Rd, 500m N of Showgrounds, ☎ 07 5545 4380, fax 07 5545 4380, rms BB ⓘ $99 - $130, ⓘⓘ $120 - $160, BC EFT MC VI.
★★★★☆ **Christel & Tonys Chalet**, (B&B), 246 MacDonnell Rd, Eagle Heights 4271, 2km NE of Gallery Walk, ☎ 07 5545 1982, fax 07 5545 1982, (Multi-stry), 2 rms [ensuite, spa bath (1), fan, heat, doonas], lounge (TV, video), lounge firepl, ☒, BYO, non smoking property. BB ⓘ $75 - $95, ⓘⓘ $95 - $137, BC MC VI.
★★★★☆ **Cypress Cottage**, (B&B), (Farm), 103 Beacon Rd, North Tamborine, 1km W of PO, ☎ 07 5545 1573, fax 07 5545 2708, 1 rm (3 bedrm), [shwr, bath, tlt, hairdry, fire pl, elec blkts, tel, TV, video, CD, refrig, cook fac, micro, d/wash, toaster], c/park (undercover), non smoking property. BB ⓘ $100, ⓘⓘ $155, ⓘ $35.
★★★★☆ **Maz's on the Mountain**, (GH), 25 Eagle Heights Rd, ☎ 07 5545 1766, fax 07 5545 0271, 3 rms [shwr, spa bath, tlt, hairdry, c/fan, fire pl, elec blkts, TV, video, clock radio, t/c mkg, refrig], ldry, dryer, iron, iron brd, rec rm, pool-heated, spa, t/c mkg shared, bbq, rm serv, non smoking units (3). BB ⓘⓘ $95 - $175, BC CC MC VI.

★★★★☆ **Muscatels At Tamborine**, (B&B), No children's facilities, 161 Eagle Heights Rd, 2km W of Gallery Walk, ☎ 07 5545 3455, fax 07 5545 3655, (2 stry gr fl), 3 rms [shwr, bath (1), tlt, hairdry (3), fan, fire pl (log) (1), heat, TV, clock radio, t/c mkg], ldry, dryer, lounge, meals avail (evening), non smoking units. **BB ♦ $100 - $160, ♦♦ $120 - $195**, BC MC VI.

★★★★☆ **Sandiacre House**, (B&B), 45 Licuala Dve, 5km S of Nth Tamborine PO, ☎ 07 5545 3490, 2 rms [ensuite, fan, heat, elec blkts, doonas], lounge (TV), lounge firepl, t/c mkg shared, non smoking property. **BB ♦ $90 - $130, ♦♦ $110 - $130.**

★★★★☆ **Stonehaven Manor Bed & Breakfast**, (B&B), 79 Geissmann Dr, ☎ 07 5545 3462, fax 07 5545 2314, (2 stry gr fl), 4 rms (4 suites) [shwr, spa bath (double spa in room), tlt, hairdry, a/c-cool, fire pl, heat, TV, video, clock radio, t/c mkg, mini bar, pillows], iron brd, lounge firepl. **BB $139 - $165**, BC MC VI.

AAA TOURISM *Special Rates*
★★★★☆ **Woodleigh Homestead Cottages**, (B&B), 13 Munro Crt, Off Lahey Lookout Rd, ☎ 07 5545 3121, fax 07 5545 0693, 6 rms (2 suites) [shwr, tlt, hairdry, c/fan, heat, elec blkts, cable tv, clock radio, t/c mkg, refrig, micro, elec frypan, toaster, ldry], dryer, iron, iron brd, lounge (tv), pool, spa, bbq (covered), dinner to unit, secure park, cots, non smoking property. **BB ♦ $70 - $165, ♦♦ $98 - $165, Suite BB ♦♦ $140 - $150**, ch con, BC MC VI,
Operator Comment: Voted the most beautiful B&B on Mt Tamborine Stunning views only 20 min to Movieworld / Dreamworld Special 4 nights $325 dbl or Suite/spa $440.

★★★★ **Amber Lodge Bed & Breakfast**, (B&B), No children's facilities, 8 Wongawallan Rd, Eagle Heights 4271, 50m E Gallery Walk, ☎ 07 5545 3014, fax 07 5545 1631, (2 stry gr fl), 3 rms [shwr, tlt, hairdry, fire pl (log fire), heat, elec blkts, TV, t/c mkg, refrig], lounge, ✕, spa, bbq, non smoking rms. **BB ♦ $85 - $95, ♦♦ $95 - $125**, BC MC VI.

★★★★ **Cayambe View Bed & Breakfast**, (B&B), 20 Cayambe Crt, Eagle Heights 4271, ☎ 07 5545 4052, 3 rms [shwr, tlt, hairdry, heat, c/fan, elec blkts, TV, video, t/c mkg, refrig, cook fac ltd, micro, toaster], iron, iron brd, lounge, bbq-fee, non smoking units. **BB ♦♦ $95 - $120, ♦ $30 - $45.**

★★★★ **Gallery Hawk**, (B&B), 150 Long Rd, 80m S of Gallery Walk, ☎ 07 5545 2330, (2 stry gr fl), 4 rms [shwr, bath (1), spa bath (1), tlt, heat, elec blkts], dryer-fee, lounge, lounge firepl, ✕, t/c mkg shared, rm serv, non smoking flr (2), non smoking rms (4). **BB ♦♦ $120 - $145, ♦ $33**, AE BC MC VI.

★★★ **Eagle Heights Centre**, (B&B), 168 MacDonnell Rd Eagle Heights, 500m S of Eagle Heights Hotel, ☎ 07 5545 3903, fax 07 5545 2426, 8 rms [fan, heat, pillows], shwr, tlt, ldry, dryer, iron, iron brd, rec rm, lounge (TV), conf fac, ✕, pool-heated, sauna-fee, cook fac, t/c mkg shared, refrig, ✆, non smoking rms. **BLB ♦ $55, ♦♦ $90, ♦ $30**, ch con, BC MC VI.

★★★ **(Cottage Section)**, 3 cotgs acc up to 6, (2 bedrm), [shwr, tlt, heat, TV, t/c mkg, refrig, cook fac, toaster, blkts, linen, pillows], non smoking rms (2). **D $100 - $130.**

TANNUM SANDS QLD 4680

Pop 3,200. (520km N Brisbane), See maps on page 416, ref D7.
Hotels/Motels

★★★★ **Reef Adventureland Motor Inn**, (M), 64 Hampton Dve, ☎ 07 4973 8522, fax 07 4973 8691, (2 stry gr fl), 30 units (0 suites) [shwr, bath (2), tlt, a/c, c/fan, tel, cable tv, clock radio, t/c mkg, refrig, cook fac, micro, toaster], ldry, pool (salt water), spa, bbq, cots. **Suite D ♦ $87 - $98, ♦♦ $98 - $109, ♦ $11**, ch con, AE BC DC MC VI.

★★★☆ **Palm Valley**, (M), 22 Beach Ave. 300m SW Surf Life Saving Club, ☎ 07 4973 7512, fax 07 4973 9008, 20 units (2 bedrm), [shwr, tlt, a/c, c/fan, TV, movie, clock radio, t/c mkg, refrig, cook fac, micro, elec frypan, toaster], w/mach, iron, iron brd, bbq (covered), c/park (undercover), plygr, cots, non smoking rms. **BLB ♦ $55 - $60, ♦♦ $75 - $85, RO ♦ $50 - $55, ♦♦ $65 - $75, ♦ $5 - $10**, ch con, AE BC DC MC VI.

★★★☆ **Tannum on the Beach**, (M), 24 Ocean St, ☎ 07 4973 8911, fax 07 4973 8921, (2 stry gr fl), 14 units [shwr, tlt, a/c, c/fan, tel, TV, clock radio, t/c mkg, refrig, cook fac ltd (11), micro (11), toaster], ldry, w/mach, dryer, iron, pool (salt water), bbq (covered), c/park (undercover), cots-fee, non smoking rms. **RO ♦♦ $77, ♦ $11**, AE BC DC MC VI.

★★★ **Tannum Sands Hotel Motel**, (LMH), 34 Pacific Ave, ☎ 07 4973 7439, fax 07 4973 7131, 8 units [shwr, tlt, a/c, tel, TV, clock radio, t/c mkg, refrig, toaster], ldry, ✕, c/park (undercover), ✆, cots-fee. **RO ♦ $64.90, ♦♦ $75.90, ♦ $11**, ch con, AE BC MC VI.

B&B's/Guest Houses

★★★☆ **Tannum Sands Bed & Breakfast**, (B&B), Tannum Sands Rd, 5km W of beach, ☎ 07 4973 8889, fax 07 4973 8889, 3 rms [shwr, tlt, hairdry, a/c-cool, fire pl, clock radio], ldry, dryer, iron, iron brd, rec rm, TV rm, lounge (tv), ✕, t/c mkg shared, bbq, c/park (undercover), non smoking rms. **BB ♦ $55 - $65**, Dinner by arrangement. BC MC VI.

TARA QLD 4421

Pop 850. (300km SW Brisbane), See maps on page 414, ref D8.
★★ **Tara**, (LMH), Baddleys Rd, ☎ 07 4665 3410, fax 07 4665 3597, 12 units [shwr, tlt, a/c, elec blkts, tel, TV (12), radio, t/c mkg, refrig], ldry, conv fac, ☒ (Mon to Sat), dinner to unit (Mon to Sat), c/park (undercover), ☎, cots. **RO** ⚊ **$40**, ⚊⚊ **$50**, ⚊⚊⚊⚊ **$60**, ch con, fam con, BC EFT MC VI.

B&B's/Guest Houses
★★★★ **Wattle Downs**, (B&B), (Farm), 2325ha merino stud, grain, cattle & horse property, Leichhardt Hwy, The Gums, 125km N of Goondiwindi, 13km S of The Gums 190km W, ☎ 07 4665 9129, fax 07 4665 9179, 2 rms [fan, heat, elec blkts, TV (1), clock radio], dryer, lounge (TV), ☒, bbq, meals avail, c/park (undercover) (1). **D all meals** ⚊ **$132**, Dinner by arrangement.
★★★☆ **Grace Park**, (GH), (Farm), Neals Rd The Gums, 32km SW of PO, ☎ 07 4665 9101, or 07 4665 9104, fax 07 4665 9178, 3 rms [hairdry, fan, heat, elec blkts], shwr, tlt, rec rm, lounge (TV), ☒, t/c mkg shared, bbq, plygr. **D all meals** ⚊ **$132**, ⚊⚊ **$220**, Airstrip 1000m in length 900m above sea level.

TAROOM QLD 4420

Pop 650. (464km NW Brisbane), See maps on page 414, ref D7.

★★★ **Cattle Camp**, (M), Taroom St, ☎ 07 4627 3412, fax 07 4628 6188, 14 units [shwr, tlt, hairdry, a/c, tel, fax, TV, clock radio, t/c mkg, refrig], ldry, ☒ (Mon to Sat), pool (salt water), bbq, dinner to unit, c/park (undercover) (6), plygr, cots. **RO** ⚊ **$55**, ⚊⚊ **$66 - $68**, ⚊ **$11**, ch con, AE BC DC MC VI.

TEWANTIN QLD

See Sunshine Coast Region.

TEXAS QLD 4385

Pop 750. (320km SW Brisbane), See maps on page 414, ref E8.
Royal Hotel Motel, (LMH), 3 High St, ☎ 07 4653 1310, 8 units [shwr, tlt, a/c, TV, t/c mkg], ☒, cots. **RO** ⚊ **$22**, ch con, BC.
★★☆ **(Motel)**, units **RO** ⚊ **$46.20**, ⚊⚊ **$46.20**, ⚊ **$11**.

B&B's/Guest Houses
★★★☆ **Yellow Rose**, (B&B), 25 Moore St, opposite PO, ☎ 07 4653 1694, or 07 4653 1694, 6 rms [ensuite (4), shwr (4), tlt (4), a/c-cool (6), c/fan, elec blkts, TV (4), t/c mkg, refrig (4)], shwr, tlt, ldry, lounge (TV), ☒, cots. **BB** ⚊ **$60.50**, ⚊⚊ **$71.50**, ⚊ **$15**, **DBB** ⚊ **$85**, ⚊⚊ **$155**, ⚊ **$33**, ch con, BC MC VI.

THARGOMINDAH QLD 4492

Pop 200. Part of Cunnamulla, (991km W Brisbane), See maps on page 414, ref B8.
★★☆ **Bulloo River**, (LMH), Dowling St, ☎ 07 4655 3125, fax 07 4655 3136, 6 units [shwr, tlt, a/c, TV, t/c mkg, refrig], conv fac, ☒, courtesy transfer, ☎. **RO** ⚊ **$45**, ⚊⚊ **$52 - $58**, ch con.
★★ **Thargomindah Oasis**, (M), Dowling St, ☎ 07 4655 3155, fax 07 4655 3155, 6 units [shwr, tlt, a/c, TV, movie, clock radio, t/c mkg, refrig], ☒, bbq, ☎. **RO** ⚊ **$55**, ⚊⚊ **$55**, ⚊⚊⚊⚊ **$82.50**, AE BC MC VI.

THEODORE QLD 4719

Pop 500. (559km N Brisbane), See maps on page 416, ref B8.
★★★ **Theodore**, (LMH), The Boulevard, ☎ 07 4993 1244, fax 07 4993 1108, 11 units [shwr, tlt, a/c, fan, tel, TV, t/c mkg, refrig, ldry], ldry-fee, conv fac, ☒ (Mon to Sat), c/park (undercover), ☎, cots. **RO** ⚊ **$50**, ⚊⚊ **$66**, ⚊ **$11**, AE BC DC MC VI.
★☆ **(Hotel Section)**, (2 stry), 17 apts acc up to 6, [basin, a/c (17), fan], shwr, tlt, lounge (TV), t/c mkg shared, cots. **RO** ⚊ **$33**, ⚊⚊ **$44**, ⚊ **$8.80**.

THURSDAY ISLAND QLD 4875

Pop 2,500. (2817km NW Brisbane), See maps on page 414, ref B1.
★★★☆ **Jardine**, (M), Cnr Normanby St & Victoria Pde, 450m fr PO, ☎ 07 4069 1555, fax 07 4069 1470, (2 stry gr fl), 37 units [shwr, tlt, hairdry, a/c-cool, c/fan, tel, TV, clock radio, t/c mkg, refrig], ldry, conv fac, ☒, pool, rm serv, courtesy transfer, cots. **RO** ⚊ **$143**, ⚊⚊ **$176**, ⚊ **$30**, AE BC DC JCB MC VI, ♿.

Trouble-free travel tips - Hoses and belts
Inspect the condition of radiator hoses, heater hose fan and air conditioner belts.

TIN CAN BAY QLD 4580

Pop 1,800. (223km N Brisbane), See maps on page 417, ref D3. Located on an inlet behind Rainbow Beach.
★★★ **Sandcastle**, (M), Tin Can Bay Rd, ☎ 07 5486 4555, fax 07 5486 4594, 24 units [shwr, tlt, c/fan, tel, TV, clock radio, t/c mkg, refrig, elec frypan (18), toaster], ldry, conv fac, ☒ (Mon-Sat), pool, bbq, rm serv, dinner to unit. **RO** ⚊ **$50 - $53**, ⚊⚊ **$62**, ⚊ **$12**, BC MC VI.

Self Catering Accommodation
★★★★ **Dolphin Waters Holiday Apartments**, (Apt), 40-41 Esplanade, ☎ 07 5486 2600, fax 07 5486 2700, (2 stry), 10 apts acc up to 5, (1 & 2 bedrm), [shwr, tlt, a/c, c/fan, TV, video-fee, clock radio, refrig, micro, d/wash, toaster, ldry, blkts, linen, pillows], dryer, iron, iron brd, pool (saltwater), bbq, cots-fee. **D** ⚊⚊ **$95 - $140**, ⚊ **$11**, **W** ⚊⚊ **$430 - $830**, ⚊ **$42**, BC EFT MC VI, ♿.
★★ **Toolara General Store and Holiday Units**, (HF), 152 Toolara Rd, 2.5km SE of PO, ☎ 07 5486 4237, 4 flats acc up to 6, (2 bedrm), [shwr, tlt, c/fan, TV, clock radio, refrig, cook fac, elec frypan, toaster, blkts, linen reqd-fee, pillows], bbq, kiosk (closed Mondays), ☎, cots. **D** ⚊⚊ **$40 - $45**, ⚊ **$5**, **W** ⚊⚊ **$175 - $210**, ⚊ **$30 - $35**, EFT.

B&B's/Guest Houses
★★★★ **Seychelle Luxury Units**, (B&B), No children's facilities, 23 Bream St, ☎ 07 5486 2056, fax 07 5486 4855, 2 rms [shwr, tlt, a/c, c/fan, TV, video, clock radio, t/c mkg, refrig, cook fac, micro, elec frypan, toaster], ldry, dryer, bbq, c/park (undercover). **BB** ⚊⚊ **$100**, AE BC DC EFT MC VI.

TINAROO FALLS QLD 4872

Pop Nominal, (1765km N Brisbane), See maps on page 415, ref B3.
★☆ **Tinaroo Lakes**, (M), Palm St, 16km NE of Atherton PO, ☎ 07 4095 8200, fax 07 4095 8148, 8 units (1 suite) [shwr, bath (1), tlt, fan, TV, t/c mkg, refrig, cook fac (5)], ldry, dryer, pool (salt water), bbq, plygr, AE BC MC VI.

B&B's/Guest Houses
★★★★★ **Tinaroo Waters Birds & Barra**, (B&B), 61 Bluewater Drive, Tinaroo Waters, 3.5km N of Kairi, ☎ 07 4095 8425, fax 07 4095 8025, 1 rm (1 suite) [shwr, bath, tlt, hairdry, c/fan, elec blkts, clock radio, t/c mkg], bbq, non smoking property. **Suite BB** ⚊ **$60**, ⚊ **$60**, **Suite DBB** ⚊ **$82.50**, ⚊ **$82.50**, ch con, BC MC VI.

TOLGA QLD 4882

Pop 800. (1754km N Brisbane), See maps on page 415, ref B3.
★★★ **Corn Cob**, (M), Kennedy Hwy, 4km N of Atherton PO next to Tolga Park, ☎ 07 4095 4130, fax 07 4095 4563, 10 units [shwr, tlt, a/c-cool, c/fan, heat, tel, TV, t/c mkg, refrig, toaster], ldry, dryer, cots, non smoking units (5). **BLB** ⚊ **$45**, ⚊⚊ **$50**, ⚊ **$10**, AE BC DC MC VI.

B&B's/Guest Houses
Allawah Rural Retreat, (B&B), No children's facilities, Marnane Rd, ☎ 07 4095 4900, fax 07 4095 5350, 3 rms [ensuite (2), shwr (1), tlt (1), hairdry, c/fan, TV, radio, t/c mkg], ldry, bbq (covered). **BB** ⚊ **$75**, ⚊⚊ **$88**, **Unit BB $132**, **Unit D $700**, BC MC VI, (not yet classified).

TOOGOOLAWAH QLD 4313

Pop 850. (117km NW Brisbane), See maps on page 417, ref C5.
★★★ **Toogoolawah**, (M), 76 Brisbane Valley Hwy, On Highway at Toogoolawah, ☎ 07 5423 1144, 5 units [shwr, tlt, a/c, tel, TV, t/c mkg, refrig, toaster, ldry], bbq, meals to unit, non smoking flr (1). **RO** ⚊ **$40**, ⚊⚊ **$48**, AE BC DC MC VI.

TOOWOOMBA QLD 4350

Pop 83,350. (125km W Brisbane), See maps on page 417, ref B6. Queensland's largest inland city and centre of the Darling Downs.
★★★★ **Ambassador on Ruthven Motor Inn**, (M), 200 Ruthven St, 1.5k N of CBD, ☎ 07 4637 6800, fax 07 4637 6899, 18 units [shwr, bath (10), spa bath (1), tlt, hairdry, a/c, tel, TV, video (8), movie, clock radio, t/c mkg, refrig, mini bar, micro (1), toaster], ldry, dryer, iron, iron brd, ☒, rm serv, dinner to unit, c/park (undercover), cots-fee, non smoking units (6). **RO** ⚊ **$79**, ⚊⚊ **$89**, ⚊ **$10**, AE BC DC EFT MC VI, ♿.
★★★★ **Applegum Inn**, (M), 41 Margaret St, opposite Grammar School, ☎ 07 4632 2088, fax 07 4639 1334, 25 units (2 suites) [shwr, tlt, hairdry, a/c, heat, tel, TV, video, clock radio, t/c mkg, refrig, mini bar, cook fac (2), micro (2), elec frypan], ldry, iron, iron brd, ☒ (Mon-Sat), pool (salt water), bbq, rm serv, dinner to unit, c/park (undercover), cots-fee, non smoking units (18). **RO** ⚊ **$74.50 - $88**, ⚊⚊ **$79 - $98**, ⚊ **$11**, **Suite D $115 - $120**, ch con, AE BC DC MC MP VI.

★★★★ **Clifford Gardens**, (M), 316 James Street, 100m main Shop. Centre, ☎ 07 4633 1349, fax 07 4634 9022, 27 units (5 suites) [shwr, spa bath (1), tlt, hairdry, a/c, tel, TV, video, clock radio, t/c mkg, refrig, cook fac ltd, micro (5), elec frypan, toaster, ldry-fee], dryer-fee, iron, iron brd, conv fac, ✕, pool, bbq, rm serv, dinner to unit, c/park (9), secure park (5), cots. **RO ♦ $72, ♦♦ $83, ◊ $11, Suite RO $105 - $120**, ch con, AE BC DC EFT MC VI, ♿.

★★★★ **Country Gardens Motor Inn**, (M), 94 James St, 2km S/E of PO, ☎ 07 4632 3099, fax 07 4632 3920, 18 units (5 suites) [shwr, bath (2), spa bath (5), tlt, hairdry, a/c, tel, cable tv, video-fee, movie, clock radio, t/c mkg, refrig, mini bar, cook fac ltd, micro (7), elec frypan (4), toaster], ldry-fee, dryer-fee, iron, iron brd, pool-heated (salt water), spa, bbq (covered), rm serv, dinner to unit (Mon to Thurs), plygr, cots, non smoking units (16). **RO ♦ $77 - $88, ♦♦ $88 - $100, Suite D ♦♦ $95 - $120**, ch con, AE BC DC EFT MC VI, ♿.

★★★★ **Federal Hotel Motel**, (LMH), Cnr James & Geddes Sts, 800m SE of city centre, ☎ 07 4632 8686, or fax 07 4632 0900, 20 units [shwr, tlt, hairdry, a/c, tel, cable tv, clock radio, t/c mkg, refrig, micro (1)], ldry-fee, dryer-fee, conf fac, ⊠, ✕, bbq (covered)-fee, rm serv, dinner to unit, c/park (undercover), cots-fee, non smoking units (15). **RO ♦ $66 - $77, ♦♦ $77 - $88, ◊ $11**, AE BC DC EFT MC VI, ♿.

FLAG
FLAG CHOICE HOTELS

★★★★ **Glenfield Motor Lodge**, (M), 876 Ruthven St, Cnr Stenner St, ☎ 07 4635 4466, fax 07 4635 0911, 51 units (7 suites) [shwr, spa bath (2), tlt, hairdry, a/c, elec blkts, tel, cable tv, clock radio, t/c mkg, refrig, cook fac (7)], ldry, iron, iron brd, conv fac, ⊠ (Mon-Sat), pool, rm serv, dinner to unit, c/park (undercover), cots-fee, non smoking rms. **RO ♦ $90 - $121, ♦♦ $100 - $125, ◊ $11, Suite D ♦♦♦♦ $121**, AE BC DC MC MP VI, ♿.

Quality
FLAG CHOICE HOTELS

★★★★ **Grammar View Motor Inn**, (M), 39 Margaret St, ☎ 07 4638 3366, fax 07 4638 1976, (2 stry gr fl), 32 units [shwr, bath (2), tlt, hairdry, a/c, tel, cable tv, clock radio, t/c mkg, refrig, mini bar], ldry, ⊠, pool (salt water), rm serv, dinner to unit, cots-fee. **RO ♦ $97, ♦♦ $107, ◊ $10**, AE BC DC MC MP VI.

For Accommodation Booking information - see page 27

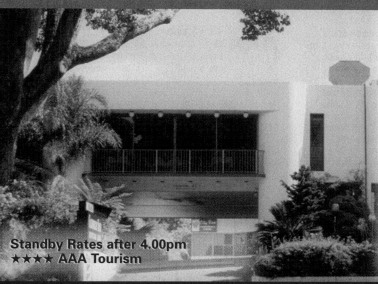

T

★★★★ **Great Divide Motor Inn**, (M), Cnr Warrego Hwy & Herries Street, 3km E of City Centre, ☎ 07 4639 6646, fax 07 4639 6755, (2 stry gr fl), 14 units (2 suites) [shwr, spa bath (4), tlt, hairdry, a/c, fan, tel, TV, video-fee, movie, clock radio, t/c mkg, refrig, mini bar, cook fac (2), micro (2), toaster], ldry, dryer, iron, iron brd, dinner to unit (4 days), cots-fee, non smoking units (12). RO ♦ $63 - $70, ♦♦ $75 - $83, ◊ $10, Suite RO ♦ $90 - $110, ♦♦ $90 - $110, AE BC DC EFT MC VI, ♿.

★★★★ **Highlander Motor Inn & Apartments**, (M), 226 James St, 800m SW of PO, ☎ 07 4638 4955, fax 07 4638 4977, 29 units (6 suites) [shwr, spa bath (12), tlt, hairdry, a/c, elec blkts, tel, TV, video, movie, clock radio, t/c mkg, refrig, mini bar, micro (14), toaster], ldry, dryer-fee, iron, iron brd, conv fac, ⊠, pool-heated, bbq, rm serv, dinner to unit, plygr, cots-fee, non smoking units (24). RO ♦ $70 - $80, ♦♦ $80 - $90, ◊ $10, Suite RO $90 - $100, AE BC DC EFT MC VI, ♿.

★★★★ **Murcure Hotel Burke & Wills Toowoomba**, (LH), 554 Ruthven St, ☎ 07 4632 2433, fax 07 4639 2002, (Multi-stry), 93 rms (4 suites) [shwr, bath (40), tlt, a/c, tel, TV, movie, clock radio, t/c mkg, refrig, mini bar], lift, ldry, iron, iron brd, conv fac, ⊠ (Mon to Sun), 24hr reception, rm serv, cots, non smoking flr (2). RO ♦ $132, ♦♦ $132, ◊ $18, Suite D $207, AE BC DC MC VI.

★★★★ **Park Motor Inn**, (M), 88 Margaret St, ☎ 07 4632 1011, fax 07 4638 1964, (2 stry gr fl), 47 units [shwr, tlt, hairdry, a/c-cool, tel, cable tv, clock radio, t/c mkg, refrig], ldry, dryer, iron, iron brd, conv fac, ⊠ (Mon to Sat), pool, bbq, rm serv, dinner to unit, cots-fee. RO ♦ $85 - $99, ♦♦ $95 - $109, ◊ $11, ch con, AE BC DC MC VI.

★★★★ **Shamrock**, (M), 604 Ruthven St, ☎ 07 4632 2666, fax 07 4639 4548, (2 stry gr fl), 32 units [shwr, spa bath (22), tlt, hairdry (22), a/c, tel, fax (22), cable tv (22), clock radio (22), t/c mkg, refrig], ⊠, dinner to unit. RO ♦ $65, ♦♦ $75, Unit 12 to 17 & 29 to 33 of a lower rating. AE DC VI.

★★★★ **Sunray Motor Inn**, (M), Cnr Bridge & McDougall Sts, close to airport, ☎ 07 4634 2200, fax 07 4634 6477, 19 units (0 suites) [shwr, spa bath (1), tlt, hairdry, a/c, fan (2), tel, TV, clock radio, t/c mkg, refrig, toaster], ldry, iron, iron brd, conf fac, pool, bbq (covered), dinner to unit, c/park (undercover), cots-fee, non smoking units (5). RO ♦ $71 - $76, ♦♦ $77 - $82, Suite D $108 - $120, AE BC BTC DC EFT MC MP VI.

★★★★ **Toowoomba**, (M), 2 Burnage St, located at top of Toowoomba range, ☎ 07 4631 8600, fax 07 4631 8660, 29 units [shwr, spa bath (1), tlt, a/c, tel, TV, movie, clock radio, t/c mkg, refrig, mini bar, cook fac (3)], ldry, iron, iron brd, conv fac, ⊠, pool, bbq, rm serv, dinner to unit, c/park (undercover), cots-fee. RO ♦ $70.20 - $110, ♦♦ $85 - $110, ◊ $11, ch con, fam con, Units 29 to 34 ★★★☆. AE BC DC MC MP VI.

★★★★ **Tuscany on Tor Motor Inn**, (M), Cnr Tor & Lendrum Sts, ☎ 07 4659 0000, fax 07 4659 0100, 10 units [shwr, spa bath (1), tlt, a/c, tel, cable tv, clock radio, t/c mkg, refrig, cook fac], ldry, pool, bbq, c/park (undercover), plygr, cots-fee, non smoking property. RO ♦ $85 - $95, ♦♦ $95 - $105, AE BC DC EFT MC MP VI.

★★★☆ **A Raceview Motor Inn**, (M), 52 Hursley Rd, opposite race course, ☎ 07 4634 6777, fax 07 4634 1160, (2 stry gr fl), 9 units (3 suites) [shwr, bath (2), tlt, a/c-cool (6), fan, heat, elec blkts, tel, TV, clock radio, t/c mkg, refrig, cook fac (4), micro (5), elec frypan, toaster], ldry, dryer, pool (salt water), dinner to unit, meals avail (breakfast), c/park (undercover), cots, non smoking rms (2). RO ♦ $50 - $70, ♦♦ $65 - $77, ◊ $5 - $11, Suite RO ♦♦ $70 - $93, AE BC DC MC VI.

★★★☆ **A Tudor Lodge**, (M), Cnr Scott & Cohoe Sts, ☎ 07 4638 1822, fax 07 4632 3601, (2 stry gr fl) 21 units [shwr, spa bath (4), tlt, hairdry, a/c, elec blkts, tel, fax, TV, video, movie, clock radio, t/c mkg, refrig, toaster], ldry, iron, iron brd, conv fac, ⊠ (Mon to Sat), pool, bbq, dinner to unit (Mon to Sat), cots-fee. RO ♦ $65 - $85, ♦♦ $75 - $95, ◊ $12, ch con, AE BC DC MC VI.

★★★☆ **Blue Violet Motor Inn**, (M), Cnr 31 Margaret & Mc Kenzie Sts, Close to St Vincent Hospital & Grammar School, ☎ 07 4638 1488, fax 07 4638 1654, 13 units [shwr, tlt, hairdry, a/c, heat, elec blkts, tel, fax, TV, movie, clock radio, t/c mkg, refrig, toaster], ldry, iron, iron brd, pool, dinner to unit, cots. RO ♦ $61, ♦♦ $70, ◊ $9, AE BC DC MC VI.

★★★☆ **Bridge Street Motor Inn**, (M), 291 Bridge St, near West St, close to St Andrews Hospital, ☎ 07 4634 3299, fax 07 4634 3060, 16 units (6 suites) [shwr, bath (6), tlt, a/c, fan, heat, elec blkts, tel, TV, movie, clock radio, t/c mkg, refrig, cook fac (6), micro (6), toaster], ldry, dryer, iron, iron brd, conv fac, pool (salt water), bbq, dinner to unit, c/park (undercover), plygr, tennis, cots-fee, non smoking rms (5). RO ♦ $58 - $63, ♦♦ $68 - $75, ◊ $11, Suite D ♦♦ $77 - $95, ch con, AE BC DC EFT MC VI.

★★★☆ **Colonial Motel Toowoomba**, (M), 730 Ruthven St, ☎ 07 4635 3233, fax 07 4636 1862, 24 units (3 suites) [shwr, bath (2), tlt, hairdry (21), a/c, fan (15), tel, TV, video (& free video library) (21), clock radio, t/c mkg, refrig, mini bar, ldry-fee], ⊠ (Mon to Fri), pool, bbq, dinner to unit, cots-fee. RO ♦ $69 - $76, ♦♦ $78 - $85, ◊ $10, Suite D $99 - $129, AE BC DC MC MP VI.

★★★☆ **Garden City Motor Inn**, (M), 718 Ruthven St, 2km fr city centre, ☎ 07 4635 5377, fax 07 4636 1731, 15 units [shwr, tlt, a/c, elec blkts, tel, TV, video-fee, movie, clock radio, t/c mkg, refrig, toaster], pool, dinner to unit (Mon-Thurs), cots-fee. RO ♦ $61 - $66, ♦♦ $69 - $75, ◊ $10, AE BC DC MC VI.

★★★☆ **Jacaranda Place Motor Inn**, (M), 794 Ruthven St, ☎ 07 4635 3111, fax 07 4635 3272, (2 stry gr fl), 19 units [shwr, spa bath (1), tlt, a/c, elec blkts, tel, cable tv (10 channels), clock radio, t/c mkg, refrig, cook fac (5)], ldry, dryer, pool, bbq, cots. RO ♦ $60 - $72, ♦♦ $72 - $83, ◊ $11, AE BC DC MC VI, ♿.

★★★☆ **James Street Motor Inn**, (M), Cnr James & Kitchener Sts, ☎ 07 4639 0200, fax 07 4639 0250, 31 units [shwr, tlt, a/c, tel, TV, movie, clock radio, t/c mkg, refrig], ldry, dryer, ⊠, pool-heated (solar), bbq, dinner to unit, plygr, cots-fee. RO ♦ $65, ♦♦ $75, ◊ $12, AE BC DC MC VI, ♿.

★★★☆ **Leichhardt Motor Inn**, (M), 682 Ruthven St, ☎ 07 4638 4644, fax 07 4638 4454, (2 stry gr fl), 24 units (1 & 2 bedrm), [shwr, spa bath (1), tlt, hairdry, a/c, elec blkts, tel, cable tv, clock radio, t/c mkg, refrig, toaster], ldry, iron, iron brd, pool, spa, bbq, dinner to unit, c/park (undercover) (6), cots, non smoking units (9). RO ♦ $69 - $75, ♦♦ $72 - $86, AE BC DC EFT MC VI.

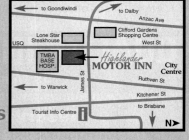
Rates may change. Check before booking.

★★★☆ **Motel Glenworth**, (M), 1 Margaret St, opp Weis Restaurant, ☎ 07 4638 1799, fax 07 4632 0919, 13 units [shwr, tlt, hairdry, a/c, elec blkts, tel, cable tv, clock radio, t/c mkg, refrig, toaster], ldry, dryer, iron, iron brd, c/park (undercover), cots-fee. **RO** ♦ **$62 - $72,** ♦♦ **$69 - $79,** ch con, AE BC DC MC VI.

★★★ **Allan Cunningham**, (M), 808 Ruthven St, ☎ 07 4635 5466, fax 07 4636 1564, 24 units [shwr, tlt, a/c, elec blkts, tel, TV, movie, clock radio, t/c mkg, refrig] ldry, ✉, pool, dinner to unit, c/park (undercover), cots-fee. **RO** ♦ **$55,** ♦♦ **$65,** ♦ **$10,** ch con, 4 units ★★★★. AE BC EFT MC VI.

 ★★★ **Coachman**, (M), 4 Burnage St, top of the Great Dividing Range, ☎ 07 4639 3707, fax 07 4639 4390, (2 stry gr fl), 22 units [shwr, tlt, hairdry, a/c, fan, heat, elec blkts, tel, TV, movie, clock radio, t/c mkg, refrig, toaster], ldry, dryer, pool, bbq, c/park (undercover) (5), cots. **RO** ♦ **$45 - $50,** ♦♦ **$55 - $60,** ♦ **$11,** Units 16 to 20 ★★☆. AE BC DC MC VI.

★★★ **Cosy**, (M), 195a West St, opposite Toowoomba Base Hospital, ☎ 07 4638 3900, fax 07 4632 2487, (2 stry gr fl), 11 units [shwr, tlt, heat, elec blkts, TV, clock radio, t/c mkg, refrig, micro (7), elec frypan (7), toaster (7), ldry-fee], ✆, plygr, cots-fee. **RO** ♦ **$51 - $63,** ♦♦ **$60 - $73,** ♦ **$11,** ch con, 4 units of a lower rating.

Cosy ...continued

★★ **(Budget Section)**, 9 units acc up to 2, [basin, heat-fee, TV, t/c mkg, refrig], shwr, tlt, ✆, plygr, cots-fee, non smoking rms (5). **RO** ♦ **$40,** ♦♦ **$50,** ♦ **$11,** ch con.

★★★ **Downs**, (M), 669 Ruthven St, Main street, ☎ 07 4639 3811, fax 07 4639 3806, 26 units [shwr, tlt, a/c (26), fan (2), heat (3), tel, TV, video, clock radio, t/c mkg, refrig, cook fac (4)], ldry, coffee shop, plygr, cots-fee. **RO** ♦ **$50 - $70,** ♦♦ **$56 - $75,** ch con, Units 3 to 15 ★★☆. Units 20 to 27 ★★★★. AE BC DC MC VI.

★★★ **Jefferys Rainforest**, (M), 864 Ruthven St South, ☎ 07 4635 5999, fax 07 4635 9823, 43 units [shwr, tlt, a/c, fan, heat, elec blkts, TV, clock radio (33), t/c mkg, refrig, cook fac], ldry, c/park (undercover), ✆, cots-fee. **RO** ♦ **$47 - $58,** ♦♦ **$49 - $63,** ♦ **$9,** ch con, Units 1 to 10 ★★. 30-43 ★★★☆. Light breakfast only available. BC EFT MC VI, ♿.

 ★★★ **Ruthven Street Motor Inn**, (M), 786 Ruthven St, ☎ 07 4636 1366, fax 07 4636 1911, (2 stry gr fl), 22 units [shwr, spa bath (2), tlt, a/c, elec blkts, tel, TV, movie, clock radio, t/c mkg, refrig, cook fac (2)], ldry, pool, bbq (covered), dinner to unit, c/park (undercover), cots-fee. **RO** ♦ **$55,** ♦♦ **$66,** ♦ **$11,** AE BC MC MCH VI.

★★★ **White Oaks**, (M), 12 Margaret St, ☎ 07 4639 2999, fax 07 4639 4718, 16 units (1 suite) [shwr, spa bath (1), tlt, a/c, fan, elec blkts, tel, cable tv, clock radio, t/c mkg, refrig, toaster], ldry, conf fac, pool, bbq, cots-fee. **RO** ♦ **$64,** ♦♦ **$75,** ♦ **$11,** Suite D **$120,** AE BC DC MC VI.

★★★ **Wilsonton Hotel**, (LMH), Richmond Dve, Wilsonton, adjacent airport & shopping centre, ☎ 07 4634 2033, fax 07 4633 1385, 21 units [shwr, tlt, a/c, heat, elec blkts, tel, TV, clock radio, t/c mkg, refrig], ldry, conv fac, ✉ (Mon - Sat). **RO** ♦ **$55,** ♦♦ **$66,** AE BC DC MC VI.

★★☆ **Clewleys**, (M), 683 Ruthven St, ☎ 07 4638 3466, (2 stry gr fl), 23 units [shwr, tlt, a/c (6), fan, heat, elec blkts (19), tel, TV, video, clock radio, t/c mkg, refrig, toaster], ldry, conv fac, ✉ (Mon to Sat, except P), pool-heated, spa, bbq, rm serv, dinner to unit, ✆, plygr, cots-fee, ch con, Units 5 to 10 ★★★. AE BC DC MC VI.

 ★★☆ **Flying Spur**, (M), 277 Taylor St, ☎ 07 4634 3237, fax 07 4633 2220, 16 units [shwr, tlt, a/c-cool, fan, heat (2), cent heat (9), elec blkts, tel, TV, clock radio, t/c mkg, refrig, cook fac (1), micro (6), toaster], ✕, pool, c/park (undercover), cots-fee. **BLB** ♦ **$46,** ♦♦ **$52 - $57,** ♦ **$11,** AE BC MC VI.

Asters on James Motor Inn, (M), 200 James St, 50m N of general hospital, ☎ 07 4659 5555, fax 07 4673 1955, (Multi-stry gr fl), 16 units (4 suites) [shwr, bath (1), spa bath (2), tlt, a/c, tel, cable tv, clock radio, t/c mkg, refrig, cook fac (4), micro (4), toaster], ldry, dinner to unit, c/park (undercover), cots-fee, non smoking units (12). **RO ╪ $75 - $85, ╪╪ $85 - $95, ◊ $14, Suite RO $85 - $130,** AE BC DC EFT MC VI, (not yet classified).

Villa Nova Motel, (M), Cnr Ruthven & South Sts, ☎ 07 4636 9200, fax 07 4636 9290, units [ensuite, spa bath, a/c, cent heat, tel, TV, video, clock radio, t/c mkg, refrig, micro, ldry], ⊠, pool indoor heated, dinner to unit, cots-fee, non smoking units (11). **RO ╪ $100, ╪╪ $115,** ch con, weekly con, AE BC DC EFT MC VI, (not yet classified).

Self Catering Accommodation
★★★★ Alhambra Units, (HU), 256 James St, 500m from RACQ Office, ☎ 07 4639 4155, fax 07 4639 4472, 11 units acc up to 5, (2 bedrm), [shwr, bath (hip), tlt, fan, heat, tel (ISD), TV, refrig, cook fac, micro, toaster, ldry (in unit), blkts, linen, pillows], iron (in unit), iron brd (in unit), secure park, cots. **D ╪╪ $66,** BC MC VI.

★★★★ Bridge Street Units, (HU), 293 Bridge St, near West St, ☎ 07 4634 3299, fax 07 4634 3060, 10 units acc up to 6, (2 bedrm), [shwr, bath (hip), tlt, a/c, fan, heat, elec blkts, tel, TV, movie, clock radio, refrig, cook fac, micro, ldry (in unit), blkts, linen, pillows], pool (salt water), bbq, dinner to unit, c/park (undercover), plygr, tennis, cots-fee. **D ╪ $68 - $75, ◊ $11, W ╪╪ $310 - $355, ◊ $35,** ch con, AE BC DC EFT MC VI.

★★★★ Jacaranda Place, (HU), 794 Ruthven St, ☎ 07 4635 3111, fax 07 4635 3272, 8 units acc up to 6, (1 & 2 bedrm), [shwr, bath (hip) (3), tlt, a/c, fan, tel, cable tv, clock radio, refrig, cook fac, micro, ldry (in unit), blkts, linen, pillows], pool, c/park (undercover), cots. **D ╪╪ $83 - $110, ◊ $11,** AE BC DC MC VI.

★★★☆ Apollo Lodge, (HU), 210 James St, near West St, ☎ 07 4632 1222, fax 07 4632 1343, 9 units acc up to 4, [shwr, tlt, a/c (2), fan (8), heat, elec blkts, tel, TV, refrig, cook fac, micro, ldry (in unit), blkts, linen, pillows], iron, c/park (garage). **D ╪╪ $60, ╪╪╪╪ $80,** BC MC VI.

★★★☆ Clewleys Country Haven, (Cotg), Iredale Rd, Withcott 4352, 12km E of Toowoomba, ☎ 07 4638 3466, 1 cotg acc up to 5, [shwr, spa bath (3), tlt, hairdry, fan, heat, tel, TV, clock radio, refrig, cook fac, micro (5), blkts, linen, pillows], ldry, rec rm, conv fac, pool (salt water), sauna, spa, bbq, plygr, tennis, cots-fee. **D ╪╪ $88 - $115.50, ◊ $11,** ch con, AE BC DC MC VI.

★★★☆ Clifford Park Holiday Motor Inn, (HU), 54 Hursley Rd, ☎ 07 4634 2222, fax 07 4634 2030, (2 stry gr fl), 20 units acc up to 8, [shwr, spa bath (2), tlt, fan, heat, tel, TV, clock radio, refrig, cook fac (16), micro (5), ldry (in unit) (11), blkts, linen, pillows], pool, bbq, c/park (undercover), tennis, cots, **D ╪ $49 - $69, ╪╪ $59 - $109, ◊ $12 - $15, W ╪╪ $225 - $695, ◊ $50,** BC MC VI.

★★★☆ White Oaks Lodge, (HU), 14 Margaret St, ☎ 07 4639 2999, fax 07 4639 4718, (2 stry), 16 units acc up to 6, (2 bedrm), [shwr, tlt, a/c, heat, cable tv, clock radio, refrig, cook fac, micro, blkts, linen, pillows], ldry, rec rm, pool, bbq, c/park (undercover), cots. **D $140 - $180, W $460 - $600,** AE BC DC MC VI.

Governor's Choice Winery & Cottage B&B, (Cotg), Beeghofee Rd, Westbrook, 19km W of Toowoomba PO, ☎ 07 4630 6101, fax 07 4630 6701, 2 cotgs [shwr, spa bath, tlt, fan, c/fan, heat, elec blkts, TV, video, clock radio, t/c mkg, refrig, cook fac, micro, d/wash, toaster, blkts, doonas, linen, pillows], lounge firepl, cafe, bbq, dinner to unit, breakfast ingredients, non smoking property. **D ╪ $80 - $90, ╪╪ $120 - $132, ◊ $40 - $80,** ch con, BC MC VI, (not yet classified).

Oakleigh Country Cottage, (Cotg), Lot 10 Bowtell Dve, Highfields, 19km N of Toowoomba at Highfields, ☎ 07 4696 7021, fax 07 4696 7284, 1 cotg [shwr, tlt, hairdry, fan, c/fan, heat (wood heater), elec blkts, TV, video, clock radio, t/c mkg, refrig, cook fac, micro, elec frypan, toaster], iron, iron brd, bbq, cots. **BB ╪╪ $110,** ch con, BC MC VI.

B&B's/Guest Houses
★★★★ Argyle, (B&B), Heritage, New England Hwy, Geham 4352, 20km N of Toowoomba, ☎ 07 4696 6301, fax 07 4696 6301, 5 rms [shwr, bath (1), tlt, fire pl (bedroom), cent heat, elec blkts], lounge firepl, ✕, t/c mkg shared, refrig, c/park (undercover), non smoking rms. **BB ╪ $65 - $75, ╪╪ $110 - $160,** BC MC VI.

★★★★ Inadale House, (B&B), 8 Inadale Crt, 6km SE of PO, ☎ 07 4635 2250, 3 rms [ensuite, hairdry, fire pl, elec blkts, tel, TV, clock radio, refrig, toaster], bathrm (private), lounge (private), non smoking suites (2). **BB ╪ $85, ╪╪ $115.**

★★★★ Jacaranda Grove Bed & Breakfast, (B&B), No children's facilities, 92 Tourist Rd, Minutes from CBD, ☎ 07 4635 8394, fax 07 4635 8394, 2 rms [shwr, tlt, hairdry, a/c, elec blkts, fax, t/c mkg, mini bar], lounge. **BB ╪ $95, ╪╪ $140 - $160,** BC DC MC VI.

★★★★ Lauriston House Bed & Breakfast, (B&B), 67 Margaret Street, 800m E of PO, ☎ 07 4632 4053, fax 07 4639 5526, 2 rms [shwr (2), spa bath (1), tlt (2), hairdry (2), elec blkts (2), TV (1), clock radio (2), t/c mkg (2)], ldry, pool, non smoking rms (2). **BB ╪╪ $120 - $145,** AE BC MC VI.

★★★★ Vacy Hall, (B&B), Classified by National Trust, Historic Inn. 135 Russell St, ☎ 07 4639 2055, fax 07 4632 0160, 12 rms (8 suites) [shwr (12), tlt (12), fire pl (8), cent heat, elec blkts, tel, TV, t/c mkg, refrig], ldry, meeting rm, ✕, rm serv, dinner to unit, cots. **BB ╪╪ $133 - $220, ◊ $55,** ch con, AE BC DC MC VI.

★★★☆ Moorlands, (GH), (Farm), A working cattle property. via Oakey on Cooyar Rd, 28km N Oakey, ☎ 07 4692 8215, fax 07 4692 8176, 1 rm [ensuite, hairdry, c/fan, elec blkts, clock radio, t/c mkg], ldry, lounge (TV), ✕, bbq, tennis, cots. **DBB ╪ $137, ◊ $137,** ch con, Airstrip.

★★★☆ Westaway Home Stay, (B&B), 12 Girrawheen St, 4 km SE of CBD, ☎ 07 4635 6931, fax 07 4635 6931, 3 rms [ensuite, shwr, bath, spa bath (portable), tlt, c/fan, heat, elec blkts, tel, clock radio, t/c mkg, refrig], shwr, tlt, ldry-fee, dryer, iron, iron brd, lounge (TV), cook fac, t/c mkg shared, bbq, rm serv, c/park (undercover), non smoking rms (1). **BB ╪ $65, ╪╪ $75.**

★★★ Mrs Bees Bed & Breakfast, (B&B), 11 Boulton Tce, 2km NW PO, ☎ 07 4639 1659, fax 07 4632 9834, 15 rms [heat, elec blkts, TV], ldry, ✕, ✆, cots. **BB ╪ $25 - $35, ╪╪ $50 - $75,** ch con, BC MC VI.

★★★ YWCA Gowrie House Hostel, (B&B), 112 Mary St, 1.3km NE PO, ☎ 07 4632 2642, (2 stry gr fl), 43 rms [heat], shwr, tlt, ldry, dryer, rec rm, lounge (TV), ✕, t/c mkg shared, refrig, ✆. **BB ╪ $25, ╪╪ $35 - $40,** ch con, ⅛⚲.

TORBANLEA QLD 4662
Pop 350. Part of Hervey Bay, (280km NW Brisbane), See maps on page 417, ref D1. Very small ex-mining community.

B&B's/Guest Houses
Torbanlea House, (B&B), 12 George St, 24km N of Maryborough, ☎ 07 4129 4981, 2 rms [fan, heat, elec blkts, TV], t/c mkg shared, refrig. **BB ╪ $45, ╪╪ $65,** (not yet classified).

TORQUAY QLD 4655
Pop Part of Hervey Bay, (299km N Brisbane), See maps on page 417, ref D1. Popular tourist area. Boating, Fishing, Swimming.

Self Catering Accommodation

★★★★☆ Jade Waters Luxury Apartments, (Apt), 407 The Esplanade, 100m N of PO, ☎ 07 4125 3611, fax 07 4125 4871, (Multi-stry), 16 apts acc up to 6, (2 bedrm), [shwr, tlt, a/c, fan, tel, TV, video, clock radio, t/c mkg, refrig, cook fac, micro, d/wash, toaster, doonas, linen, pillows], w/mach, dryer, pool, spa, bbq, rm serv, cots, non smoking units (8). **D ╪ $89 - $99, ╪╪ $89 - $99, ◊ $10,** ch con, AE BC DC EFT MC VI.

★★★★☆ La Mer Hervey Bay, (Apt), 396 Esplanade, 150m W of PO, ☎ 07 4128 3494, fax 07 4128 3616, 20 apts acc up to 6, (1 & 2 bedrm), [shwr, tlt, a/c, c/fan, tel, cable tv, clock radio, t/c mkg, refrig, cook fac, micro, d/wash, toaster, blkts, linen, pillows], w/mach, dryer, pool-heated, cots-fee. **D $80 - $140, W $370 - $900,** BC EFT MC VI.

TORRENS CREEK QLD 4816
Pop 12. (1661km NW Brisbane), See maps on page 414, ref C5. Situated on Torrens Creek. A small 'outback' township established around 1887.

Hotels/Motels
★☆ Exchange Hotel, (LMH), Flinders Hwy, ☎ 07 4741 7342, fax 07 4741 7342, (2 stry), 8 units [fan], shwr, tlt, bathrm, lounge, ⊠, pool-heated, spa, bbq. **RO ╪ $24.20, ╪╪ $36.30,** ch con.

★★★ (Motel Section), 5 units [shwr, tlt, a/c-cool, TV, clock radio, t/c mkg, refrig], ldry, pool-heated, spa, bbq (covered), ✆. **RO ╪╪ $60.50, ◊ $11.**

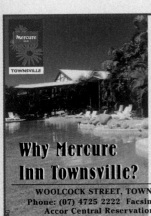

TOWNSVILLE QLD 4810

Pop 109,900. (1371km N Brisbane), See maps on page 415, ref D7. Capital of North Queensland boasting an average of 320 days of sunshine each year.

Hotels/Motels

★★★★☆ **Centra Townsville**, (LH), Flinders Mall, ☎ 07 4772 2477, fax 07 4721 1263, (Multi-stry), 158 rms (39 suites) [shwr, bath, tlt, hairdry, a/c, tel, cable tv, video-fee, clock radio, t/c mkg, refrig, mini bar, micro (32)], lift, ldry, iron, iron brd, conv fac, ⊠, pool, 24hr reception, rm serv, c/park (valet), ✆, bicycle, gym, cots, non smoking flr (7). **RO** ♦ **$220,** ♦♦ **$220,** ♦ **$33, Suite RO $231,** ch con, AE BC DC MC VI.

★★★★☆ **Jupiters Townsville Hotel & Casino**, (LH), Sir Leslie Thiess Dve, ☎ 07 4722 2333, fax 07 4772 3488, (Multi-stry), 192 rms (16 suites) [shwr, bath, tlt, hairdry, a/c, tel, TV, movie-fee, radio, t/c mkg, refrig, mini bar], lift, iron, iron brd, conf fac, ⊠, bar (6), pool, sauna, spa, 24hr reception, rm serv, gym, tennis, cots, non smoking flr (5). **RO** ♦♦ **$146,** AE BC DC JCB MC VI, ♿.

★★★★☆ **Reef International**, (M), 63 The Strand, ☎ 07 4721 1777, fax 07 4721 1779, (Multi-stry), 45 units (2 suites) [shwr, bath, tlt, hairdry, a/c, tel, TV, movie, clock radio, t/c mkg, refrig, mini bar], lift, ldry, iron, iron brd, conv fac, ⊠, pool, spa, bbq, 24hr reception, rm serv, dinner to unit, c/park (undercover), cots. **RO** ♦ **$130 - $145,** ♦♦ **$130 - $145,** ♦ **$15, Suite D $165,** ch con, AE BC DC MC VI, ♿.

★★★★☆ **Robert Towns**, (M), 261 Stanley St, ☎ 07 4771 6900, fax 07 4721 1492, (2 stry gr fl), 47 units (3 suites) [shwr, bath (3), tlt, hairdry, a/c-cool, tel, cable tv, t/c mkg, refrig, micro (13)], ldry, iron, iron brd, conv fac, ⊠, bar, pool (salt water), rm serv, gym, cots. **RO** ♦ **$120,** ♦♦ **$120, Suite RO $180,** AE BC DC MC VI.

★★★★☆ **Southbank Hotel & Convention Centre**, (M), 23 Palmer St, ☎ 07 4721 1474, fax 07 4721 2010, (Multi-stry), 98 units (4 suites) [shwr, bath (6), tlt, hairdry, a/c-cool, a/c, tel, cable tv, t/c mkg, refrig, mini bar], lift, ldry, conv fac, ⊠, pool (salt water), spa, 24hr reception, rm serv, c/park (undercover) (40), ✆, cots, non smoking rms (52). **RO** ♦ **$99 - $110,** ♦♦ **$99 - $110,** ♦ **$15, Suite D $135,** ch con, AE BC DC MC VI.

★★★★ **Aquarius on the Beach Townsville**, (Ltd Lic H), 75 The Strand, ☎ 07 4772 4255, fax 07 4721 1316, (Multi-stry), 100 rms [shwr, bath, tlt, hairdry, a/c-cool, cable tv, movie, clock radio, t/c mkg, refrig, micro], lift, ldry, iron, iron brd, conf fac, ⊠ (Mon-Sat), pool, 24hr reception, rm serv, cots, non smoking flr (2). **RO** ♦ **$126.50 - $137.50,** ♦♦ **$126.50 - $137.50,** ♦ **$11,** ch con, AE BC DC MC VI.

★★★★ **Mercure Inn Townsville**, (M), The Lakes, Woolcock St, ☎ 07 4725 2222, fax 07 4725 1384, (2 stry gr fl), 201 units [shwr, bath, tlt, a/c-cool, tel, TV, movie, clock radio, t/c mkg, refrig, mini bar, cook fac (75)], ldry, conv fac, ⊠, pool (salt water), spa, 24hr reception, rm serv, tennis (2), cots, non smoking rms (25). **RO** ♦ **$128 - $148,** ♦♦ **$128 - $148,** ♦ **$22,** AE BC DC JCB MC VI, ♿.

★★★★ **Ridgemont Executive Motel & Restaurant**, (M), 15 Victoria St, 500m fr PO, ☎ 07 4771 2164, fax 07 4772 1270, (2 stry gr fl), 24 units [shwr, tlt, hairdry, a/c, c/fan, tel, cable tv, radio, t/c mkg, refrig, mini bar, cook fac (14)], ldry, iron, iron brd, ⊠, pool (salt water), spa, bbq, rm serv, dinner to unit, cots. **RO** ♦ **$92 - $112,** ♦♦ **$92 - $112,** ♦ **$10,** AE BC DC MC VI.

★★★☆ **Beach House**, (M), 66 The Strand, ☎ 07 4721 1333, fax 07 4771 6893, (2 stry gr fl), 26 units [shwr, tlt, hairdry (6), a/c-cool, fan, c/fan, tel, TV, movie, clock radio, t/c mkg, refrig], ldry, dryer, iron, iron brd, ✕ (Mon-Sat), pool, dinner to unit (Mon - Sat), cots. **RO** ♦ **$66 - $71,** ♦♦ **$77,** ♦ **$11,** BC DC MC VI.

★★★☆ **Billabong Lodge**, (M), 96 Bowen Rd, Rosslea 4812, ☎ 07 4775 2055, fax 07 4779 1140, 29 units [shwr, tlt, a/c-cool, c/fan, tel, TV, video, clock radio, t/c mkg, refrig, cook fac ltd], ldry, pool, spa, bbq, dinner to unit (Mon to Fri), c/park (undercover), cots. **RO** ♦ **$66 - $70,** ♦♦ **$74 - $80,** ♦ **$10,** ch con, AE BC DC MC MP VI, ♿.

Rates may change. Check before booking.

★★★☆ **Castle Lodge Motel**, (M), Cnr Warburton, McKinley & Rose Sts, North Ward 4810, 500m from beach, ☎ 07 4721 2290, fax 07 4721 1716, (2 stry gr fl), 24 units [shwr, tlt, hairdry (12), a/c-cool, tel, TV, movie, clock radio, t/c mkg, refrig, mini bar, toaster (12)], ldry, dryer, iron, iron brd, ⊠ (Mon to Sat), pool, dinner to unit, c/park (undercover), cots. RO ♦ $91 - $102, ♦♦ $91 - $102, ch con, AE BC DC MC MP VI.

★★★☆ **Cedar Lodge**, (M), 214 Nathan St, Aitkenvale 4814, ☎ 07 4775 7800, fax 07 4775 7357, (2 stry gr fl), 25 units [shwr, tlt, a/c, tel, cable tv, clock radio, t/c mkg, refrig], ldry, conv fac, ⊠ (Mon to Sat), pool, bbq, rm serv, dinner to unit, cots-fee. RO ♦ $65 - $72, ♦♦ $65 - $80, ◊ $11, AE BC DC EFT MC VI.

★★★☆ **City Oasis Inn**, (M), 143 Wills St, ☎ 07 4771 6048, fax 07 4721 5076, (2 stry gr fl), 42 units (2 suites) [shwr, bath (19), spa bath (2), tlt, hairdry (20), a/c-cool, c/fan, tel, cable tv, clock radio, t/c mkg, refrig, mini bar (20), cook fac (12)], ldry, iron (20), iron brd (20), ⊠, pool (salt water), spa (2), bbq, rm serv, dinner to unit, plygr, cots. RO ♦ $95 - $169, ♦♦ $95 - $169, $16.50, 20 units ★★★★. AE BC DC MC VI.

★★★☆ **Colonial Rose**, (M), 23 Bowen Rd, Rosslea 4812, ☎ 07 4725 1422, fax 07 4779 9837, (2 stry), 35 units (1 suite) [shwr, bath, tlt, a/c-cool, c/fan, tel, TV, video, clock radio, t/c mkg, refrig], ldry, conv fac, ⊠ (Mon to Sat), pool (salt water), spa, rm serv, dinner to unit (Mon to Sat), cots-fee, non smoking rms. RO ♦♦♦ $78, AE BC DC MC VI, ♿.

★★★☆ **Historic Yongala Lodge**, (M), 11 Fryer St, North Ward 4810, 400m fr PO, ☎ 07 4772 4633, fax 07 4721 1074, (2 stry gr fl), 18 units (1 & 2 bedrm), [shwr, bath (2), tlt, hairdry, a/c-cool, c/fan, tel, TV, movie, clock radio, t/c mkg, refrig, cook fac (10), micro (10)], ldry, dryer, iron, iron brd, ⊠, pool (salt water), rm serv, dinner to unit, cots-fee. RO ♦ $79 - $109, ♦♦ $89 - $109, ◊ $15, ch con, AE BC DC EFT MC VI.

★★★☆ **Seagulls Resort**, (M), 74 The Esplanade, Belgian Gardens 4810, ☎ 07 4721 3111, fax 07 4721 3133, (2 stry gr fl), 70 units [shwr, tlt, hairdry, a/c-cool, c/fan, tel, TV, movie, clock radio, t/c mkg, refrig, cook fac (15)], ldry, iron, iron brd, conv fac, ⊠, pool (salt water), bbq, rm serv, dinner to unit, courtesy transfer, plygr, tennis (half court), cots-fee. RO ♦ $99 - $139, ♦♦ $99 - $139, ◊ $9 - $15, ch con, AE BC DC JCB MC VI, ♿.

★★★☆ **Shoredrive**, (M), 117 The Strand, ☎ 07 4771 6851, fax 07 4772 6311, (2 stry gr fl), 30 units [shwr, tlt, a/c-cool, c/fan, tel, cable tv, clock radio, t/c mkg, refrig], ldry, conv fac, ✗, pool, rm serv, cots-fee, non smoking units (3). RO ♦ $68, ◊ $10, BC MC VI.

★★★☆ **Summit Motel**, (M), 6 Victoria St Stanton Hill, ☎ 07 4721 2122, fax 07 4721 3986, (2 stry gr fl), 30 units [shwr, tlt, hairdry, a/c-cool, c/fan, tel, cable tv, movie, clock radio, t/c mkg, refrig, toaster], ldry, iron, iron brd, rec rm, conv fac, pool (salt water), rm serv, dinner to unit, c/park (undercover) (9), cots. RO ♦ $82, ♦♦ $82, ◊ $10, ch con, AE BC DC MC VI.

★★★☆ **Sundowner Chain Motor Inns**, (M), Previously Cluden Park Motor Inn. 147 Stuart Dr, Wulguru 4811, close to racecourse, ☎ 07 4778 4555, fax 07 4778 2154, (2 stry gr fl), 31 units [shwr, bath, tlt, hairdry, a/c, heat, tel, TV, video, clock radio, t/c mkg, refrig, cook fac (2), toaster], ldry, ⊠, bar, pool, bbq, rm serv, dinner to unit, c/park (undercover), cots-fee. RO ♦ $68 - $82.50, ♦♦ $68 - $82.50, ◊ $11, ch con, AE BC DC EFT MC VI, ♿.

★★★☆ **Townsville Plaza Hotel**, (LH), Cnr Flinders & Stanley Sts, ☎ 07 4772 1888, fax 07 4772 1299, (Multi-stry), 92 rms (6 suites) [shwr, tlt, a/c-cool, tel, cable tv, movie, clock radio, t/c mkg, refrig], lift, ldry, conv fac, ⊠, pool, sauna, spa, 24hr reception, ☎, cots-fee, non smoking rms (35). RO $99, Suite RO $125, ch con, No off street parking. AE BC DC MC VI.

★★★ **Aitkenvale**, (LMH), 224 Ross River Rd, ☎ 07 4775 2444, fax 07 4725 1417, (2 stry gr fl), 26 units (2 suites) [shwr, tlt, a/c-cool, a/c, tel, cable tv, movie, clock radio, t/c mkg, refrig, mini bar], ldry, ⊠, pool (salt water), rm serv, c/park (undercover), cots-fee. RO ♦ $60, ♦♦ $66 - $71, ◊ $11, Suite D $82, ch con, AE BC DC MC VI.

★★★ **Banjo Paterson Motor Inn**, (M), 72 Bowen Rd, Rosslea 4812, ☎ 07 4725 2333, fax 07 4725 1079, (2 stry gr fl), 25 units [shwr, tlt, a/c-cool, tel, fax (photocopy fac.), TV, movie, clock radio, t/c mkg, refrig, cook fac ltd-fee], ldry, conf fac, ⊠ (Mon-Sat), pool, 24hr reception, rm serv, dinner to unit, cots-fee, non smoking units (15). BB ♦ $61, ♦♦ $70 - $75, ◊ $11, ch con, AE BC DC MC VI.

Historic **Yongala Lodge**
AAAT ★★★☆

- *Licensed Greek & International Restaurant*
- *Motel Units (Some Heritage Style) ★★★☆*
- *Modern Self contained Units ★★★☆*
- *Adjacent to Beachfront (80metres) in quiet street*
- *Just a stroll to city heart (400metres);*
  Casino & major tourist attractions.

Unique Heritage Restaurant
11 Fryer St, North Ward,
Townsville, QLD 4810
Ph: (07) 4772 4633 • Fax: (07) 4721 1074
Email: info@historicyongala.com.au

TOWNSVILLE

This multi award winning resort is just 4 minutes from the CBD and set on 3 acres of tropical landscaped gardens that overlooks Cleveland Bay and Magnetic Island.

Seagulls
Resort on the Seafront

Reservation Freecall:
1800 079 929
Phone: (07) 4721 3111
Fax: (07) 4721 3133
Email: resort@seagulls.com.au
Web: www.seagulls.com.au

74 THE ESPLANADE, TOWNSVILLE

★★★ **Bessell Lodge**, (M), 38 Bundock St, Belgian Gardens 4810, ☎ 07 4772 5055, fax 07 4772 5949, (2 stry gr fl), 50 units [shwr, tlt, a/c-cool, fan, tel, TV, video (25), clock radio, t/c mkg, refrig], ldry, conv fac, ☒, pool, bbq, dinner to unit, cots. **BLB 🚹 $72, 🚹🚹 $82, 👤 $10**, AE BC DC MC VI.

Best Western

★★★ **Casino City Motor Inn**, (M), 100 Bowen Rd, Rosslea 4812, ☎ 07 4775 4444, fax 07 4775 4002, 17 units [shwr, tlt, hairdry, a/c-cool, c/fan (13), tel, TV, movie, clock radio, t/c mkg, refrig], ldry, dryer, iron, iron brd, ✕ (Mon to Fri), BYO, pool, dinner to unit (Mon to Fri), c/park (undercover), cots. **RO 🚹 $71, 🚹🚹 $79, 👤 $10**, AE BC DC EFT MC MP VI.

★★★ **Coolabah**, (M), 75 Bowen Rd, Rosslea 4812, ☎ 07 4779 2084, fax 07 4779 2087, 37 units [shwr, tlt, a/c-cool, c/fan, tel, TV, movie, clock radio, t/c mkg, refrig, cook fac (14)], ldry, dryer, ☒, pool (salt water), cots-fee. **RO 🚹 $53, 🚹🚹 $59 - $67, 👤 $9**, ch con, AE BC DC MC VI.

★★★ **Hi Roller**, (M), 36 Bowen Rd, Rosslea 4812, 5km S of PO, ☎ 07 4779 2179, fax 07 4779 2661, 34 units [shwr, tlt, a/c-cool, c/fan, tel, cable tv, clock radio, t/c mkg, refrig, micro (5)], ldry, dryer, ☒ (Sun-Frid), pool, bbq, rm serv, cots-fee, non smoking units (2). **RO 🚹 $55 - $65, 🚹🚹 $65 - $75, 👤 $11**, AE BC DC MC VI.

★★★ **Monte Carlo Motor Inn**, (M), 45 Bowen Rd, Mundingburra 4812, ☎ 07 4725 2555, fax 07 4725 1842, 52 units [shwr, bath (17), tlt, a/c-cool, c/fan, tel, TV, video, clock radio, t/c mkg, refrig, cook fac (4), micro (9)], ldry, conv fac, ☒ (Mon to Sat), pool (2), spa, c/park (undercover) (42), cots-fee. **RO 🚹 $66 - $80, 🚹🚹 $75 - $85, 👤 $12**, AE BC DC MC VI.

★★★ **Motel Palms**, (M), 44 Bowen Rd, Rosslea 4812, ☎ 07 4779 6166, fax 07 4775 5661, 26 units [shwr, tlt, a/c-cool, fan, c/fan, tel, TV, movie, clock radio, t/c mkg, refrig, toaster], ldry, dryer, pool, bbq, dinner to unit (Sun to Fri), cots. **RO 🚹 $57 - $59, 👤 $11**, ch con, 4 Self Contained Units are of a 3 plus Star Rating, AE BC DC MC VI.

★★★ **Raintree**, (M), Cnr Bowen Rd & Carmody St, ☎ 07 4775 3066, fax 07 4775 3120, (2 stry gr fl), 30 units [shwr, tlt, a/c, c/fan, tel, TV, movie, clock radio, t/c mkg, refrig], ldry, ☒ (Mon-Sat), pool, spa, rm serv, dinner to unit, cots-fee. **RO 🚹 $55, 🚹🚹 $72, 👤 $12**, ch con, AE BC DC MC VI, ♿.

★★★ **Spanish Lace Motor Inn**, (M), 106 Bowen Rd, Rosslea 4812, ☎ 07 4725 1510, fax 07 4775 6642, (2 stry gr fl), 25 units [shwr, tlt, a/c-cool, tel, TV, movie, clock radio, t/c mkg, refrig, cook fac ltd (4)], ldry, dryer, ☒ (Mon to Fri), pool, rm serv, dinner to unit, c/park (undercover), plygr. **BLB 🚹 $55, 🚹🚹 $64.90, 👤 $10**, ch con, AE BC DC MC VI.

★★☆ **A 1 Motel**, (M), 107 Bowen Rd, Rosslea 4812, ☎ 07 4779 3999, fax 07 4725 4404, 31 units [shwr, tlt, a/c-cool, tel, TV, clock radio, t/c mkg, refrig], ldry, ✕, pool, c/park (undercover). **RO 🚹 $55, 🚹🚹 $60, 👤 $8 - $10, Family Room of 4 RO 🚹🚹🚹🚹 $76**, ch con, fam con, AE BC DC EFT JCB MC MCH VI.

★★☆ **Adobi**, (M), 90 Abbott St, ☎ 07 4778 2533, 12 units [shwr, tlt, a/c-cool, c/fan, tel (6), TV, clock radio, t/c mkg, refrig, ldry], pool (salt water), bbq, cots-fee. **RO 🚹 $45, 🚹🚹 $50, 👤 $10**, ch con, pen con, AE BC DC MC VI.

★★☆ **Dalrymple**, (LMH), 310 Bayswater Rd, Garbutt 4814, ☎ 07 4779 6344, fax 07 4725 1087, 20 units [shwr, tlt, a/c-cool, tel, TV, movie, clock radio, t/c mkg, refrig], ldry, conv fac, ☒ (Mon-Sun), pool, c/park (undercover), cots-fee. **D 🚹 $55, 🚹🚹 $66 - $71, 🚹🚹🚹 $88, 👤 $16.50**, ch con, AE BC DC MC VI, ♿.

★★☆ **Hotel Allen**, (LMH), Cnr Gregory & Eyre Sts, North Ward 4810, ☎ 07 4771 5656, fax 07 4721 4129, (2 stry gr fl), 45 units (5 suites) [shwr, tlt, a/c-cool, tel, TV, t/c mkg, refrig], ☒, pool, ✆, cots. **RO 🚹 $67, 🚹🚹 $67, 👤 $10, Suite D $90 - $125**, AE BC DC MC VI.

★★☆ **Tropical Hideaway**, (M), 72 The Strand, 2km SW of PO, ☎ 07 4771 4355, fax 07 4771 4844, (2 stry gr fl), 29 units [shwr, tlt, a/c-cool, tel, TV, video-fee, clock radio, t/c mkg, refrig], ldry-fee, dryer-fee, iron, iron brd, ☒, bar, dinner to unit, cots-fee, non smoking units (5). **RO 🚹 $60, 🚹🚹 $65, 👤 $10**, ch con, AE BC DC EFT MC VI.

★★ **Midtown**, (LMH), 718 Sturt St, ☎ 07 4771 5121, fax 07 4771 6675, 21 units [shwr, tlt, a/c-cool, c/fan, tel, cable tv, clock radio, t/c mkg, refrig], ☒. **RO 🚹 $45, 🚹🚹 $57 - $60, 👤 $12**, AE BC DC EFT MC VI.

★★ **The Strand**, (M), 51 The Strand, ☎ 07 4772 1977, fax 07 4771 3029, (2 stry gr fl), 16 units [shwr, tlt, a/c-cool, c/fan, tel, TV, movie, clock radio, t/c mkg, refrig], ldry, dryer, pool, bbq, cots. **RO 🚹 $55 - $65, 🚹🚹 $62 - $75, 👤 $10**, ch con, pen con, Breakfast available. AE BC DC MC VI.

Self Catering Accommodation

★★★★☆ **Mariners North Apartments**, (HU), Mariners Dve The Strand, 800m N of PO, ☎ 07 4722 0777, fax 07 4722 0700, (Multi-stry gr fl), 40 units acc up to 6, (2 bedrm), [shwr, bath, tlt, a/c, c/fan, tel, TV, video, clock radio, refrig, cook fac, micro, elec frypan, d/wash, ldry (in unit), blkts, linen, pillows], lift, pool (salt water), bbq, c/park (undercover), tennis. **D $155, W $890**, Min book applies, AE BC DC MC VI.

★★★☆ **A & A Holiday Apartments**, (HU), 80 Mitchell St, North Ward 4810, ☎ 07 4721 1990, fax 07 4721 6708, 5 units acc up to 6, [shwr, bath, tlt, a/c-cool, c/fan, TV, clock radio, refrig, cook fac, micro, blkts, linen, pillows], ldry, dryer, pool (salt water), bbq, c/park (undercover), ✆, cots. **D 🚹🚹 $66 - $74.80, 🚹🚹🚹🚹 $82.50 - $94.60**, BC EFT MC VI.

★★★☆ **Bayside Holiday Apartments**, (HU), 102 The Strand, ☎ 07 4721 1688, fax 07 4724 1231, (Multi-stry gr fl), 9 units acc up to 6, (1 & 2 bedrm), [shwr, tlt, a/c-cool, c/fan, TV, clock radio, refrig, cook fac, micro, linen], ldry, dryer, pool (salt water), bbq, c/park (undercover), ✆, cots. **D 🚹🚹 $75, 👤 $15, W 🚹🚹 $455**, AE BC DC MC VI.

★★★☆ **Holiday Villa**, (HU), 89 Eyre St, North Ward 4810, ☎ 07 4772 4891, fax 07 4772 4891, 5 units acc up to 4, [shwr, tlt, a/c-cool-fee, c/fan, TV, clock radio, refrig, cook fac, blkts, linen, pillows], ldry, dryer, pool, bbq, c/park (undercover), cots. **D 🚹🚹 $66 - $80.30, 🚹🚹🚹🚹 $99 - $104.50**, BC MC VI.

★★★☆ **Palm Waters Holiday Villas**, (HU), Cnr Landsborough & Cook St, North Ward 4810, 1.5km N of Townsville PO, ☎ 07 4772 6011, fax 07 4772 6011, (2 stry), 13 units acc up to 6, (1 & 2 bedrm), [shwr, tlt, hairdry, a/c-cool, c/fan, tel, TV, clock radio, refrig, micro, toaster, ldry, blkts, linen, pillows], dryer, iron, iron brd, pool (saltwater), bbq, c/park (undercover), ✆, cots. **D 🚹🚹 $70 - $80, 👤 $5 - $11, W 🚹🚹 $396 - $484**, BC EFT MCH VI.

★★★☆ **The Villas Townsville**, (HU), 34 Bowen Rd, Rosslea 4812, ☎ 07 4775 7044, fax 07 4775 7277, (2 stry gr fl), 10 units acc up to 6, (1 & 2 bedrm), [shwr, bath (5), tlt, hairdry, a/c-cool, c/fan, tel (2), TV, clock radio, refrig, cook fac, micro, blkts, linen, pillows], ldry, iron, iron brd, pool, bbq, ✆, cots. **D 🚹🚹 $88 - $99, 👤 $5.50**, AE BC DC MC VI.

★★★☆ **Townsville Seaside Apartments**, (HU), 105 The Strand, ☎ 07 4721 3155, fax 07 4721 3089, (2 stry), 17 units acc up to 4, (Studio, 1 & 2 bedrm), [shwr, tlt, a/c-cool, c/fan, tel, TV, clock radio, refrig, cook fac, micro, ldry (in unit), blkts, linen, pillows], dryer, pool (salt water), spa, bbq, c/park (undercover), cots. **D 🚹🚹🚹🚹 $60.50 - $110, 👤 $19.80, W 🚹🚹🚹🚹 $385 - $638**, Min book applies, BC MC VI.

★★★ **Spanish Horseshoe**, (HU), 30 Rose St, North Ward 4810, ☎ 07 4772 1381, fax 07 4771 4887, 11 units acc up to 7, (1 & 2 bedrm), [shwr, bath, tlt, a/c-cool-fee, c/fan, TV, refrig, cook fac, blkts, linen, pillows], ldry, pool, bbq, c/park (undercover), ✆, cots. D ♦♦ $58 - $68, ◊ $9 - $10, W ♦♦ $348 - $408.

★★☆ **The Oasis**, (HU), 23 Cook St, ☎ 07 4721 1314, 7 units acc up to 4, (1 & 2 bedrm), [shwr, tlt, c/fan, TV, clock radio, t/c mkg, refrig, cook fac, ldry (in unit), blkts, linen, pillows], pool (salt water), c/park (undercover). D ♦ $35, ♦♦ $55, W $210 - $350.

Castle Hill Holiday Units, (HU), 44 Gregory St, 1km N of PO, ☎ 07 4772 3347, fax 07 4721 6497, (Multi-stry), 10 units acc up to 6, (1 & 2 bedrm), [shwr, tlt, a/c, fan, tel, TV, t/c mkg, refrig, cook fac, linen], ldry, pool, bbq, plygr, cots. D $66 - $99, ◊ $11, weekly con, AE BC MC VI, (not yet classified).

Port Of Call, 51 Ford St, Hermit Park 4812, 3km SW of Townsville PO, ☎ 07 4772 1507, fax 07 4772 1507, 12 cabins acc up to 3, [basin (10), shwr (3), tlt (3), a/c-cool, c/fan, TV, t/c mkg, refrig, cook fac], shwr, tlt, ldry, pool, c/park (undercover). RO ♦ $45 - $55, ♦♦ $60 - $80, ◊ $10.

B&B's/Guest Houses

★★★☆ **The Rocks Historic Guesthouse**, (B&B), 20 Cleveland Tce, 500m N of PO, ☎ 07 4771 5700, fax 07 4771 5711, 9 rms [shwr (3), tlt (3), fan, c/fan (7)], shwr (3), tlt (3), ldry, rec rm, lounge (tv), conv fac, ✗, spa (unheated), t/c mkg shared, bbq, cots, non smoking flr, non smoking rms (8). BB ♦ $79, ♦♦ $99, ch con, BC MC VI, ♿.

★★★ **Coral Lodge**, (B&B), 32 Hale St, 200m from city centre, ☎ 07 4771 5512, fax 07 4721 6461, (2 stry gr fl), 10 rms [shwr (2), tlt (2), a/c-cool, c/fan, tel, TV, refrig, cook fac (2), micro (3)], shwr (3), tlt (3), ldry, cook fac, t/c mkg shared, bbq, cots. BLB ♦♦ $60 - $75, ◊ $10, BC MC VI.

Other Accommodation

Adventurers Resort, (Lodge), Backpackers accommodation - YHA. 79 Palmer St, South Townsville 4810, 500m S of PO, ☎ 07 4721 1522, fax 07 4721 3251, (2 stry), 100 rms acc up to 16, [fan, refrig], shwr, tlt, ldry, dryer, iron, rec rm, lounge (TV), pool (salt water, rooftop), cook fac, c/park (undercover) (21), courtesy transfer, ✆. RO ♦ $16.50, ♦♦ $39.50, BC EFT MC VI.

Civic Guesthouse & Backpacker Inn, (Lodge), 262 Walker St, city centre, ☎ 07 4771 5381, fax 07 4721 4919, (2 stry gr fl), 27 rms [shwr (7), tlt (7), a/c-cool (14), fan, TV (2), refrig (24)], shwr, tlt, bathrm, ldry, dryer, rec rm, lounge (TV), cook fac, refrig, bbq, ✆. D ♦ $40 - $52, ♦♦ $43 - $57, No breakfast available. BC MC VI.

Reef Lodge, (Lodge), 4 Wickham St, 200m fr PO, ☎ 07 4721 1112, fax 07 4721 1405, (2 stry gr fl), 25 rms [a/c-cool-fee, fan, t/c mkg (13), refrig (13)], shwr, tlt, ldry, dryer, lounge (TV), cook fac, refrig, bbq, courtesy transfer, ✆. RO ♦ $37, ♦♦ $37, BC MC VI.

(Lodge Section), 3 rms acc up to 3, [shwr, tlt, a/c-cool-fee, c/fan, TV, t/c mkg, refrig, blkts, linen, pillows]. D ♦ $50, ♦♦ $50, ch con.

TRAVESTON QLD 4570

Pop Nominal, (153km N Brisbane), See maps on page 417, ref D4. Picturesque rural area inland from northern Sunshine Coast region. Bird Watching, Bush Walking, Horse Riding, Scenic Drives.

B&B's/Guest Houses

★★★★ **Banyandah Alpacas**, (B&B), (Farm), 50ha working alpaca stud, 1992 Old Noosa Rd, 15km NE of Cooroy, ☎ 07 5485 0890, fax 07 5485 0824, 2 rms [ensuite (2), elec blkts (1), TV, video, clock radio, t/c mkg, refrig, micro, doonas], iron, iron brd, lounge firepl, ✗, pool, bbq, c/park (undercover), courtesy transfer, gym, non smoking rms, Pets on application. BLB ♦ $60 - $66, ♦♦ $70 - $77, ◊ $10, ch con, Guest can bring own horse to ride.

Trouble-free travel tips - **Fluids**

Check all fluid levels and top up as necessary. Look at engine oil, automatic transmission fluid, radiator coolant (only check this when the engine is cold), power steering, battery and windscreen washers.

TRINITY BEACH QLD 4879

Pop 4,675. (1738km N Brisbane), See maps on page 415, ref C3. Part of Marlin Coast. Boating, Sailing, Wind Surfing.

Self Catering Accommodation

★★★★☆ **Coral Sands on Trinity Beach**, (HU), Cnr Trinity Beach Rd & Vasey Esp, 15km N of Cairns, ☎ 07 4057 8800, fax 07 4057 8811, (Multi-stry gr fl), 60 units acc up to 8, (1, 2 & 3 bedrm), [shwr, bath, tlt, a/c-cool, c/fan, tel, TV, clock radio, refrig, cook fac, micro, d/wash, ldry (in unit), blkts, linen, pillows], dryer, iron, ☒, pool (salt water), bbq, secure park, cots. D $160 - $314, W $1,120 - $2,198, AE BC DC MC VI.

★★★★☆ **Costa Royale Prestige Apartments**, (HU), 59 Vasey Esp, 10m from beach, ☎ 07 4057 8888, fax 07 4057 6577, (Multi-stry gr fl), 9 units acc up to 7, (2 & 3 bedrm - Split level accommodation available.), [shwr, bath, spa bath (9), tlt, a/c, c/fan, tel, TV, video, clock radio, refrig, cook fac, micro, d/wash, ldry (in unit), blkts, linen, pillows], lift, dryer, iron, pool (salt water), spa, bbq, secure park, cots-fee. D ♦♦♦♦ $185 - $300, W ♦♦♦♦ $1,260 - $1,645, ch con, AE BC DC MC VI.

★★★★ **(Townhouse Section)**, 7 units acc up to 6. D ♦♦♦♦ $120 - $165, W ♦♦♦♦ $805 - $1,120.

★★★★☆ **Marlin Cove Quest Resort**, (HU), 2 Keem St, 300m NW of Trinity Beach CBD, ☎ 07 4057 8299, fax 07 4057 8909, 99 units acc up to 7, (1, 2 & 3 bedrm), [ensuite, shwr, bath, tlt, hairdry (at reception), a/c, c/fan, tel, TV, clock radio, refrig, cook fac, micro, elec frypan, d/wash, toaster, ldry (in unit), blkts, linen, pillows], dryer, iron, iron brd, ✗, pool (salt water), sauna, spa, bbq (covered), c/park (undercover), plygr, gym, tennis, cots-fee. D $124 - $196, AE BC DC MC VI.

★★★★☆ **Roydon Beachfront Apartments**, (HU), 85 Vasey Esp, 20m W of beach, ☎ 07 4057 6512, fax 07 4055 6883, (Multi-stry gr fl), 19 units acc up to 8, (1, 2 & 3 bedrm), [ensuite, shwr, bath, tlt, hairdry, a/c-cool, c/fan, tel, TV, clock radio, refrig, cook fac, micro, d/wash, ldry (in unit), blkts, linen, pillows], lift, dryer, pool (salt water), bbq, c/park (undercover), courtesy transfer, cots-fee. RO ♦♦ $150 - $280, ◊ $20, ♦♦ $1,050 - $1,960, Min book applies, BC MC VI.

★★★★☆ **Seashells Holiday Apartments**, (HU), 53-55 Vasey St, ☎ 07 4057 8777, fax 07 4057 8833, (Multi-stry), 6 units acc up to 6, (2 & 3 bedrm), [ensuite, shwr, tlt, hairdry, a/c-cool, c/fan, tel, TV, clock radio, refrig, cook fac, micro, d/wash, toaster, ldry (in unit), blkts, linen, pillows], lift, dryer, iron, iron brd, pool, spa, bbq, c/park (undercover), secure park, tennis, cots-fee. D $210 - $269, BC CC MC VI.

★★★★ **Marlin Gateway Apartments**, (HU), 33 Trinity St, ☎ 07 4057 7600, fax 07 4057 7785, (2 stry gr fl), 16 units acc up to 8, (1, 2 & 3 bedrm), [shwr, bath, tlt, a/c-cool, fan, tel, TV, clock radio, refrig, cook fac, ldry (in unit) (5), blkts, linen, pillows], ldry, dryer, pool (salt water), bbq, c/park (undercover), courtesy transfer, cots-fee. D $121 - $1,015, AE BC DC MC VI.

★★★★ **On the Beach Holiday Apartments**, (HU), 49 Vasey Esp, 21km N of Cairns, ☎ 07 4057 7555, fax 07 4057 7622, (Multi-stry gr fl), 40 units acc up to 6, (1 & 2 bedrm), [shwr, bath, tlt, a/c-cool, c/fan (20), tel, TV, video-fee, clock radio, refrig, cook fac, micro, d/wash (20), toaster, ldry (in unit), blkts, linen, pillows], dryer, pool (salt water), spa, bbq, c/park (undercover) (19), secure park (21), cots-fee. D $141 - $180, W $749 - $1,190, AE BC DC MC VI.

★★★★ **Trinity Beach Club**, (HU), 19 Trinity Beach Rd, 15km N of Cairns PO, ☎ 07 4055 6776, fax 07 4055 6449, 33 units acc up to 4, (1 & 2 bedrm), [ensuite, shwr, tlt, a/c-cool, c/fan, tel, TV, clock radio, t/c mkg, refrig, cook fac, micro, toaster, blkts, linen, pillows], iron, iron brd, pool (saltwater), bbq (covered), c/park (carport), cots. D ♦♦ $80 - $125, ◊ $20, W ♦♦ $525 - $840, ◊ $140, BC CC MC VI.

★★★★ **Trinity Beach Pacific**, (HU), 56 Trinity Beach Rd, ☎ 07 4057 8666, (2 stry gr fl), 37 units acc up to 7, (Studio & 3 bedrm), [shwr, tlt, a/c, c/fan, tel, TV, clock radio, refrig, cook fac, micro, ldry (in unit), blkts, linen, pillows], dryer, iron, pool, bbq, c/park (undercover). D ♦♦ $94 - $185, W ♦♦ $590 - $1,165, AE BC DC JCB MC MP VI.

TRINITY BEACH QLD continued...

★★★☆ **Amaroo Trinity Beach Resort**, (HU), 92 Moore St, ☎ 07 4055 6066, fax 07 4057 7992, (Multi-stry gr fl), 38 units acc up to 4, (Studio), [shwr, tlt, a/c-cool, fan, tel, cable tv, clock radio, refrig, cook fac, micro, blkts, linen, pillows], lift, ldry, dryer, pool (salt water), spa, bbq (covered), c/park (undercover), courtesy transfer (pre-booking req), tennis, cots. D ⚤ $110 - $133, ♀ $18, W $660 - $800, AE BC DC EFT MC VI.

★★★☆ **The Palms**, (HU), 83 Moore St, ☎ 07 4055 6644, fax 07 4057 7122, (Multi-stry gr fl), 12 units acc up to 6, (1 & 2 bedrm), [shwr, tlt, a/c-cool, fan, tel, TV, clock radio, refrig, cook fac, micro, ldry (communal dryer), blkts, linen, pillows], pool, spa, bbq, c/park (undercover), courtesy transfer, cots-fee. D ⚤ $89 - $120, W ⚤ $574 - $742, ch con, Min book applies, BC MC VI.

★★★☆ **Tropical Holiday Units**, (HU), Cnr Trinity Beach Rd & Moore St, ☎ 07 4057 6699, fax 07 4057 6565, (Multi-stry gr fl), 42 units acc up to 6, (1 & 2 bedrm), [shwr, tlt, a/c-cool, fan, tel, cable tv, clock radio, refrig, cook fac, micro, ldry (in unit), blkts, linen, pillows], pool (salt water) (3), spa (3), bbq, c/park (undercover), courtesy transfer, cots-fee. D $96 - $160, W $576 - $960, ch con, Min book all holiday times, AE BC DC JCB MC VI.

★★★ **Casablanca Domes**, (HU), 47 Vasey Esp, ☎ 07 4055 6339, fax 07 4055 6319, 9 units acc up to 6, (1 & 2 bedrm), [shwr, bath (3), tlt, a/c-cool, c/fan, tel, TV, clock radio, refrig, cook fac, micro, blkts, linen, pillows], ldry, ✕, pool, bbq, cots. D ⚤ $65 - $80, ♀ $5, W ⚤ $390 - $560, Min book applies, AE BC DC MC VI.

★★★ **Tropic Sun Holiday Units**, (HU), 46 Moore Street, ☎ 07 4055 6619, fax 07 4057 6577, 4 units acc up to 4, (1 bedrm), [shwr, tlt, a/c-cool, fan, tel, TV, refrig, cook fac, micro, toaster, blkts, linen, pillows], ldry, dryer-fee, iron, iron brd, pool (salt water), bbq (covered), cots-fee. D ⚤ $65 - $85, ♀ $7.50, W ⚤ $395 - $545, ch con, AE BC DC MC VI.

B&B's/Guest Houses

★★★★★ **Absolute Beachfront Bed and Breakfast**, (B&B), No children's facilities, 6 Peacock St, ☎ 07 4055 6664, fax 07 4055 6179, (2 stry gr fl), 3 rms [shwr, tlt, hairdry, a/c-cool, fan, c/fan, tel (ISD), fax, TV, video-fee, clock radio, CD, t/c mkg, refrig, cook fac ltd, micro, toaster, ldry], iron, iron brd, TV rm, pool (saltwater), spa, secure park, ☎. BB ♀ $130 - $160, BC MC VI.

★★★★★ **Trinity on the Esplanade Bed & Breakfast**, (B&B), 21 Vasey Esp, 2km E of PO, ☎ 07 4057 6850, fax 07 4057 8099, (2 stry gr fl), 4 rms [ensuite, spa bath (2), a/c-cool, c/fan, tel, cable tv, radio, refrig, doonas], ldry, w/mach, dryer, t/c mkg shared, c/park (undercover). BLB ♀ $160 - $250, ⚤ $160 - $250, ♀ $35, Min book Christmas Jan and Easter, BC MC VI.

★★★☆ **Beach House Bed & Breakfast**, (B&B), 29 Moore St, 18km N Cairns, ☎ 07 4055 6304, fax 07 4055 6304, 2 rms [a/c-cool, c/fan, clock radio, t/c mkg], shwr, tlt, bathrm, ldry-fee, iron, iron brd. BB ♀ $50, ⚤ $75, ♀ $20, ch con.

★★★☆ **Tranquil Trinity**, (B&B), 154 Trinity Beach Rd, 19km N of Cairn PO, ☎ 07 4057 5759, 3 rms [shwr, tlt, a/c, c/fan, TV, t/c mkg, refrig], ldry-fee, pool (salt water), spa, courtesy transfer (airport)-fee. BLB ♀ $40 - $45, ⚤ $50 - $60, ♀ $10.

TUGUN QLD

See Gold Coast Region.

TULLY QLD 4854

Pop 2,500. (1577km N Brisbane) (44km Dunk Island), See maps on page 415, ref C5. Thriving sugar cane & banana growing area.

★★★ **Tully**, (M), Bruce Hwy, adjacent golf course 25km SW of Mission Beach, ☎ 07 4068 2233, fax 07 4068 2751, 22 units [shwr, tlt, a/c-cool, c/fan, tel, TV, movie, clock radio, t/c mkg, refrig, toaster], ✕, c/park (undercover), non smoking units (4). D ♀ $33 - $60.50, AE BC DC MC VI.

UNDARA VOLCANIC NATIONAL PARK

Pop Nominal, (1836km NW Brisbane), See maps on page 415, ref A5.

★★★☆ **Undara Lava Lodge**, (GH), Bush lodge in refurbished railway carriages. Turnoff 40km E of Mt Surprise, then 15km gravel rd, ☎ 07 4097 1411, fax 07 4097 1450, 25 rms shwr, tlt, bathrm, ldry, ✕, pool, t/c mkg shared, ☎, bush walking, cots, DBB ♀ $119.90, ch con, AE BC MC VI, ⛐.

WANDOAN QLD 4419

Pop 450. (405km NW Brisbane), See maps on page 414, ref D7. Quaint country town with new cultural centre.

★★☆ **Juandah Hotel/Motel**, (LMH), Royd St, ☎ 07 4627 4155, fax 07 4627 4394, 10 units [shwr, tlt, a/c, TV, t/c mkg, refrig], conv fac, ✕ (Fri & Sat), meals avail (counter meal Mon-Sat). RO ♀ $38.50, ⚤ $49.50, ♀ $11, ch con, AE BC MC VI.

WARWICK QLD 4370

Pop 10,950. (162km SW Brisbane), See maps on page 417, ref B8. Situated on the Condamine River, it is the second largest city on the fertile Darling Downs.

Hotels/Motels

★★★★☆ **McNevins Gunyah**, (M), Cnr New England Hwy & Glen Rd, ☎ 07 4661 5588, fax 07 4661 5588, 22 units [shwr, spa bath (9), tlt, a/c, heat, elec blkts, tel, TV, movie, clock radio, t/c mkg, refrig, toaster], ldry, w/mach, dryer, iron, iron brd, lounge, conv fac, ✕, bar, pool (salt water), spa, bbq, rm serv, dinner to unit, cots-fee. RO ♀ $66 - $82.50, ⚤ $82.50 - $104.50, ♀ $11 - $16.50, ch con, AE BC DC EFT MC MP VI.

★★★★ **Country Rose**, (M), Cnr Cunningham Hwy & Palmer Ave, ☎ 07 4661 7700, fax 07 4661 1591, 13 units [shwr, tlt, hairdry, a/c, elec blkts, tel, TV, movie, clock radio, t/c mkg, refrig, toaster], ldry, pool (salt water), spa, bbq, dinner to unit, cots, non smoking rms (4). RO ♀ $55 - $66, ⚤ $63 - $77, ♀ $11, AE BC DC EFT MC VI.

★★★★ **Village Motor Inn**, (M), 57 Victoria St, ☎ 07 4661 1699, fax 07 4661 1649, 14 units [shwr, tlt, a/c, elec blkts, tel, TV, movie, clock radio, t/c mkg, refrig, toaster], iron, iron brd, ✉ (Mon to Sat), pool (salt water), bbq, rm serv, cots-fee. RO ♀ $71 - $78, ⚤ $79 - $87, ♀ $10, AE BC DC EFT MC VI.

FLAG
FLAG CHOICE HOTELS

★★★☆ **Centre Point Mid City Motor Inn**, (M), 32 Albion St (New England Hwy), 500m N of PO, ☎ 07 4661 3488, fax 07 4661 8792, (2 stry gr fl), 19 units (3 suites) [shwr, bath (6), spa bath (1), tlt, hairdry, a/c, heat, elec blkts, tel, TV, movie, clock radio, t/c mkg, refrig, cook fac (1), micro (4), toaster], ldry, pool (salt water), bbq, dinner to unit, boat park, plygr, cots, non smoking rms (8). RO ♀ $57, ⚤ $68, ♀ $10, ch con, AE BC DC MC VI.

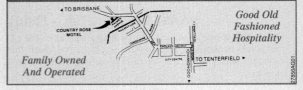

★★★☆ **Cherrabah Homestead Resort**, (M), Resort, Elbow Valley, 14km SW on Kilarney-Warwick Rd, ☎ 07 4667 9177, fax 07 4667 9186, 62 units [shwr, tlt, a/c, heat, tel (58), radio, t/c mkg, refrig, pillows], ldry, conv fac, ✕, pool, bush walking, canoeing, golf, tennis, cots. **BB ♦ $75, D all meals ♦ $145, DBB ♦ $100**, ch con, AE BC DC EFT MC VI.

  ★★★☆ **City View**, (M), Cnr Cunningham Hwy & Yangan Rd, 1.5km N of PO, ☎ 07 4661 5000, or 07 4661 8122, fax 07 4661 5000, 10 units [shwr, tlt, hairdry (5), a/c, c/fan, heat, elec blkts, tel, TV, movie, clock radio, t/c mkg, refrig, toaster], ldry, dinner to unit, cots-fee. **RO ♦ $56, ♦♦ $66 - $71, ◊ $10**, ch con, AE BC DC EFT MC MP VI.

★★★ **Abbey of the Roses**, (Ltd Lic H), Classified by National Trust, 8 Locke Street, 500m S of PO, ☎ 07 4661 9777, fax 07 4661 9790, (Multi-stry), 12 rms (2 suites) [shwr (2), bath (2), tlt (2), hairdry, heat, fan, elec blkts, tel (public), TV (3), video (2), clock radio, t/c mkg, refrig], iron (2), iron brd (2), rec rm, conf fac, ✕ (licensed), bbq, rm serv, plygr, tennis, non smoking units. **BB ♦ $80 - $100, ♦♦ $95 - $115, ◊ $15, Suite BB ♦ $100 - $120, ♦♦ $100 - $120**, AE BC MC VI.

 ★★★ **Buckaroo Motor Inn**, (M), 86 Wood St, ☎ 07 4661 3755, fax 07 4661 8099, 18 units [shwr, tlt, a/c, elec blkts, tel, TV, clock radio, t/c mkg, refrig, toaster], pool, dinner to unit (Mon to Fri), cots. **RO ♦ $50, ♦♦ $61 - $65, ◊ $9**, AE BC DC EFT MC MCH VI.

★★★ **Golden Harvest Motel**, (M), 71 Wood St, 1km W of PO, ☎ 07 4661 1810, fax 07 4667 0840, 17 units [shwr, tlt, a/c, tel, TV, clock radio, t/c mkg, refrig, toaster], iron, iron brd, cots. **RO ♦ $66, ♦♦ $77, ◊ $10**, AE BC DC EFT MC MP VI.

★★★ **Horse & Jockey**, (LMH), Cnr Palmerin & Victoria Sts, ☎ 07 4661 0600, fax 07 4661 4381, (2 stry gr fl), 32 units [shwr, a/c, tel, TV, t/c mkg, refrig], ✕. **RO ♦ $40 - $55, ♦♦ $50 - $70, ◊ $16.50**, 10 units ★★★. AE BC DC MC VI.

 ★★★ **Jackie Howe**, (M), Cnr Palmerin & Victoria Sts, ☎ 07 4661 2111, fax 07 4661 3858, 24 units [shwr, tlt, a/c, tel, TV, clock radio, t/c mkg, refrig, toaster], ldry, conf fac, ✕ (Mon to Sat), rm serv, dinner to unit, cots-fee. **RO ♦ $510, ♦♦ $61 - $64, ◊ $9**, ch con, AE BC DC MC VI.

★★★ **Warwick Homestead Motor Inn**, (M), 17 Albion St (New England Hwy), ☎ 07 4661 1533, fax 07 4661 8400, 18 units [shwr, bath (2), tlt, a/c, c/fan, tel, TV, clock radio, t/c mkg, refrig], ldry, ✕ (except public hols), pool, dinner to unit, boat park, plygr, cots-fee. **RO ♦ $55 - $70, ♦♦ $60 - $85, ◊ $7**, AE BC DC EFT JCB MC VI.

★★☆ **Alexander**, (M), Cnr Wood St & 5 Wentworth St, ☎ 07 4661 3888, fax 07 4661 5889, 18 units [shwr, tlt, a/c, elec blkts, tel, TV, movie, clock radio, t/c mkg, refrig], ldry, dryer, conf fac, ✕, rm serv, boat park, cots-fee, non smoking units (4). **RO ♦ $60, ♦♦ $65 - $70, ♦♦♦♦ $80**, AE BC DC EFT JCB MC MP VI.

Self Catering Accommodation

★★☆ **Braeside**, (Cotg), Cnr Crystal Mountain Rd & New England Hwy, Dalveen 4374, 28k S of PO, ☎ 07 4685 2339, fax 07 4685 2234, 2 cotgs acc up to 4, (2 bedrm), [shwr, tlt, hairdry, elec blkts, radio, t/c mkg, refrig, cook fac, micro, elec frypan, toaster, blkts, linen, pillows], iron, iron brd, c/park (undercover), tennis, cots. **D $50 - $100**.

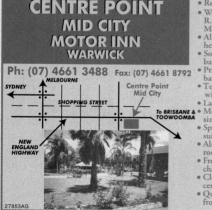

WHITSUNDAYS REGION

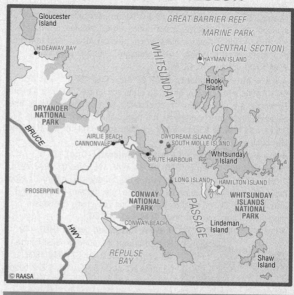

WHITSUNDAYS - AIRLIE BEACH QLD 4802

Pop 3,050. Part of Proserpine, (1125km N Brisbane). See maps on page 416, ref A1.

Hotels/Motels

★★★★☆ **Coral Sea Resort**, (M), 25 Oceanview Ave, 500m W of PO, ☎ 07 4946 6458, fax 07 4946 6516, (Multi-stry gr fl), 64 units [shwr, spa bath (45), tlt, a/c, fan, cent heat (56), movie, t/c mkg, refrig, ldry], conf fac, ✕ (2), pool, dinner to unit, cots-fee, non smoking units (55). **RO ♦ $51 - $270, ♦♦ $51 - $270, ◊ $27**, Min book applies, AE BC DC JCB MC VI.

(Apartment Section), 13 apts acc up to 6, (1, 2 & 3 bedrm), [a/c, fan, tel, TV, clock radio, t/c mkg, refrig, cook fac, d/wash, blkts, linen, pillows], w/mach (10), dryer (10). **D ♦ $216 - $490, ♦♦ $216 - $490**, (not yet classified).

★★★★ **Airlie Beach Hotel**, (LMH), cnr The Esplanade & Coconut Grove, ☎ 07 4964 1999, fax 07 4964 1988, (2 stry gr fl), 80 units [shwr, tlt, a/c-cool, tel, cable tv, t/c mkg, refrig, ldry], lift, pool (saltwater), cots-fee. **RO ♦ $72 - $187, ♦♦ $83 - $198**, ch con, AE BC DC EFT MC VI.

 ★★★☆ **Colonial Palms Motor Inn**, (M), Cnr Shute Harbour Rd & Hermitage Dve, 400m E of PO, ☎ 07 4946 7166, fax 07 4946 7522, (2 stry gr fl), 30 units [shwr, bath (hip) (17), tlt, a/c-cool, c/fan, tel, TV, movie, clock radio, t/c mkg, refrig, cook fac (8)], ldry, dryer, ✕ (Mon-Sun), pool (2), spa, rm serv, dinner to unit, c/park (undercover) (20), cots. **BLB ♦ $88 - $98, ♦♦ $98 - $108, RO ◊ $12**, ch con, AE BC DC JCB MC MP VI.

 ★★★ **Airlie Beach Motor Lodge**, (M), Lamond St, ☎ 07 4946 6418, fax 07 4946 5400, 9 units [shwr, tlt, a/c-cool, c/fan, TV, video, clock radio, t/c mkg, refrig, cook fac ltd, toaster], ldry, dryer, pool (salt water), sauna, bbq, c/park (undercover) (7), ☏, cots. **RO ♦♦ $79 - $99, ◊ $12 - $18**, AE BC DC MC VI.

★★☆ **The Islands Inn**, (M), Shute Harbour Rd, 3km SE of PO, ☎ 07 4946 6755, fax 07 4946 6755, (2 stry gr fl), 32 units [shwr, tlt, a/c-cool, c/fan (4), tel, TV, clock radio, t/c mkg, refrig, cook fac (4)], ldry, ✕, pool, spa, bbq, cots. **RO ♦ $55 - $65, ♦♦ $55 - $65, ◊ $5 - $10**, ch con, BC MC VI.

Self Catering Accommodation

★★★★☆ **Coral Sea Vista Apartments**, (HU), 5 Hermitage Drive, ☎ 07 4946 6088, fax 07 4946 6455, (Multi-stry), 12 units [shwr, tlt, hairdry, a/c-cool, c/fan, tel, radio, t/c mkg, refrig, cook fac], ldry-fee, dryer, pool, wading pool, spa, bbq, gym, cots. **RO ♦ $135 - $195, ♦♦ $135 - $195**, some units of a 4 star rating. Min book applies, BC MC VI.

 ★★★★ **Mediterranean Resorts**, (HU), 14 Golden Orchid Dve, 300m S main street, ☎ 07 4946 6391, fax 07 4946 5556, (Multi-stry), 19 units acc up to 8, (2 & 3 bedrm), [ensuite, shwr, tlt, a/c-cool, fan, tel, cable tv, clock radio, CD, refrig, cook fac, d/wash, ldry (in unit), blkts, linen, pillows], dryer, pool (2), spa, c/park (undercover), cots-fee. **D $154 - $307, W $970 - $2,027**, ch con, Min book all holiday times, AE BC DC MC VI.

★★★★☆ **Reefside Villas Whitsunday**, (HU), 12 Eshelby Dve, Whitsunday 4802, 2km NW of PO, ☎ 07 4946 4123, fax 07 4946 4124, (2 stry), 36 units acc up to 6, (2 & 3 bedrm), [ensuite (18), shwr, tlt, a/c-cool, tel, TV (satellite), clock radio, refrig, cook fac, micro, d/wash (6), toaster, ldry (in unit), blkts, linen, pillows], dryer, iron, iron brd, pool (salt water) (2), bbq, c/park (garage), cots-fee. D ♯♯ $120, W ♯♯ $700, ch con, BC DC MC VI.

★★★★ **Airlie Apartments**, (HU), 22 Airlie Cres, ☎ 07 4946 6222, fax 07 4946 4343, (2 stry gr fl), 15 units acc up to 6, (1, 2 & 3 bedrm), [shwr, tlt, a/c-cool, c/fan, TV, clock radio, refrig, cook fac, blkts, linen, pillows], ldry, w/mach, dryer, rec rm, pool, bbq, ☎, cots. D ♯♯ $81 - $116, ⚹ $11 - $17, W ♯♯ $504 - $742, ch con, some units of a 4 star rating. Min book applies, BC MC VI.

★★★★ **Airlie Cottage B&B In the Rainforest**, (Cotg), Lot 5, Timberland Rd, 3.6 km E of PO, ☎ 07 4946 6253, fax 07 4946 7276, 1 cotg acc up to 4, (2 bedrm), [shwr, tlt, hairdry, a/c, c/fan, TV, clock radio, t/c mkg, refrig, cook fac ltd, micro, elec frypan, toaster, ldry], iron, iron brd, TV rm, pool (saltwater), bbq (covered), breakfast ingredients, non smoking units. D ♯♯ $95 - $120.

★★★★ **Boathaven Lodge**, (HU), 440 Shute Harbour Rd, 400m S Town Centre, ☎ 07 4946 6421, fax 07 4946 4808, 12 units acc up to 5, (Studio, 1 & 2 bedrm), [shwr, tlt, a/c-cool, c/fan, TV, clock radio, refrig, cook fac, micro], ldry, dryer, pool, spa, bbq, c/park (undercover) (3), cots. D ♯♯ $85 - $105, ⚹ $20, W ♯♯ $595 - $735, ch con, Units 8 to 12 ★★☆, AE BC DC EFT MC VI.

★★★★ **Mango House Resort**, (HU), Cnr Shute Harbour Rd & Erromango Drive, 2km E of PO, ☎ 07 4946 4666, fax 07 494 6560, (2 stry gr fl), 19 units (12 suites) acc up to 7, [shwr, tlt, a/c-cool, c/fan, tel, TV, clock radio, t/c mkg, cook fac, micro, toaster, ldry], iron, pool (salt water), spa, bbq, c/park (undercover), cots. D ⚹ $93 - $132, ♯♯ $93 - $205, ⚹ $11, AE BC MC VI.

★★★★ **Whitsunday Vista Resort**, (SA), 1 Hermitage Dve, 700m SE of PO, ☎ 07 4946 7007, fax 07 4946 7786, 32 serv apts acc up to 8, (1, 2 & 3 bedrm Studio, 1, 2 & 3 bedrm), [shwr, tlt, hairdry, a/c-cool, c/fan, tel, cable tv, clock radio, refrig, cook fac, cook fac ltd, micro], ldry, dryer-fee, iron, ✗, pool (salt water), spa (1), bbq, c/park (undercover). D $145 - $250, W $875 - $1,610, 24 units yet to be assessed, AE BC MC VI.

★★★☆ **Whitsunday Terraces Resort**, (SA), Golden Orchid Dve, via Harper St, ☎ 07 4946 6788, fax 07 4946 7128, (Multi-stry), 63 serv apts acc up to 7, (Studio, 1 & 2 bedrm), [shwr, bath, spa bath (2), tlt, a/c, c/fan, tel, cable tv, clock radio, t/c mkg, refrig, cook fac, micro, toaster], ldry, dryer, conv fac, ✗, pool (2), spa (2), bbq, ☎, cots. D $125 - $193, AE BC DC MC VI.

★★★☆ **Whitsunday Wanderers Resort**, (HU), Resort, Shute Harbour Rd, ☎ 07 4946 6446, fax 07 4946 6761, (2 stry gr fl), 104 units acc up to 5, [shwr, tlt, a/c-cool, c/fan, cable tv, clock radio, t/c mkg, refrig, cook fac ltd, blkts, linen, pillows], ldry, conv fac, ✗ (Mon-Fri), pool, spa (2), bbq (covered), plygr, mini golf, gym. D ⚹ $98 - $148.50, ♯♯ $98 - $148.50, ⚹ $18, ch con, AE BC MC VI, ♿.

★★★ **Airlie Beach Motor Lodge**, (HU), Lamond St, ☎ 07 4946 6418, fax 07 4946 5400, (2 stry), 4 units acc up to 6, (2 bedrm), [shwr, bath (hip), tlt, a/c-cool, c/fan, TV, video, clock radio, refrig, cook fac, micro, ldry (in unit), blkts, linen, pillows], pool (salt water), sauna, bbq, c/park (undercover), ☎, cots. D $112 - $120, ⚹ $12 - $18, ch con, AE BC DC MC VI.

GOLDEN CHAIN

★★★ **Airlie Court Holiday Units**, (HU), 382 Shute Harbour Rd, ☎ 07 4946 6218, fax 07 4948 2999, (2 stry gr fl), 6 units acc up to 3, (Studio), [shwr, tlt, hairdry, a/c-cool, c/fan, cable tv, clock radio, refrig, cook fac, micro, blkts, linen, pillows], ldry, ✗, c/park (undercover). D ⚹ $66 - $115, ♯♯ $66 - $115, ⚹ $16.50, W $462 - $805, ch con, Min book applies, AE BC DC MC VI.

★★★ **McDowalls**, (HF), 32 Airlie Cres, ☎ 07 4946 6176, fax 07 4946 6059, (2 stry gr fl), 2 flats acc up to 7, (1 & 3 bedrm), [shwr, tlt, fan, TV, radio, refrig, cook fac, elec frypan, ldry (in unit), blkts, linen, pillows], cots. D ♯♯ $60, ⚹ $15, Min book applies.

★★★ **Rogers**, (HF), 265 Shute Harbour Rd, ☎ 07 4946 6224, fax 07 4946 6087, (2 stry gr fl), 5 flats acc up to 5, [shwr, tlt, a/c-cool, c/fan, TV, refrig, cook fac, micro, blkts, linen, pillows], ldry-fee, dryer-fee, c/park (undercover), security gates, cots-fee. D ♯♯ $66 - $77, ⚹ $11, W $418 - $495, Min book applies.

★★★ **Seaview Apartments**, (HU), 404 Shute Harbour Rd, 500m NW of PO, ☎ 07 4946 6911, fax 07 4946 5225, (2 stry gr fl), 7 units acc up to 5, (2 bedrm), [shwr, tlt, a/c-cool, c/fan, TV, clock radio, refrig, cook fac, micro, elec frypan, toaster, ldry, blkts, linen, pillows], dryer-fee, iron, iron brd, pool, bbq, c/park (undercover), ☎, cots. D ♯♯ $85, ⚹ $23, W ♯♯ $553, BC EFT MC VI.

★★★ **Sunlit Waters Studio Apartments**, (Apt), 20 Airlie Cres, Cnr Begley St, ☎ 07 4946 6352, fax 07 4946 6352, 5 apts acc up to 3, (Studio), [shwr, tlt, a/c-cool, c/fan, TV, refrig, cook fac, blkts, linen, pillows], ldry, dryer, pool, bbq, cots. D ♯♯ $65 - $85, ⚹ $15, W ♯♯ $420 - $581, ⚹ $107, BC MC VI.

★★★ **Whitehaven Beachfront**, (HU), 285 Shute Harbour Rd, ☎ 07 4946 5710, fax 07 4946 5711, (2 stry gr fl), 6 units acc up to 5, (Studio), [shwr, tlt, a/c-cool, c/fan, TV, clock radio, refrig, cook fac, blkts, linen, pillows], w/mach (in unit), cots. **D 👥 $72 - $95, +👤 $22, W 👥 $504 - $665, +👤 $115**, ch con, BC MC VI.

★★ **Airlie Island Traders**, (HU), Shute Harbour Rd, 2km E of PO, ☎ 07 4946 4056, fax 07 4946 5611, 9 units acc up to 6, (Studio & 1 bedrm), [shwr, tlt, a/c-cool, c/fan, TV, refrig, cook fac, micro, toaster, blkts, linen, pillows], w/mach-fee, dryer-fee, iron, iron brd, pool-heated (salt water), bbq (covered), c/park (carport) (5), 📞, plygr. **D 👥 $55 - $69, +👤 $15**, ch con, BC EFT MC VI.

Martinique Whitsunday, (SA), 18 Golden Orchid Dve, 500m SE of PO, ☎ 07 4948 0401, fax 07 4948 0402, (Multi-stry), 19 serv apts acc up to 6, (1, 2 & 3 bedrm), [shwr, spa bath (8), tlt, a/c, fan, TV, clock radio, t/c mkg, refrig, cook fac, micro, d/wash, blkts, doonas, linen, pillows], w/mach, dryer, pool, spa, bbq, cots-fee. **D 👤 $160, 👥 $160, +👤 $22**, weekly con, AE BC DC EFT MC VI, (not yet classified).

Seastar Apartments, (SA), 6A Orana St, 1km SW of PO, ☎ 07 4948 1188, fax 07 4948 2950, (Multi-stry), 20 serv apts acc up to 6, (2 & 3 bedrm), [shwr, tlt, a/c, fan, tel, TV, clock radio, t/c mkg, refrig, cook fac, micro, d/wash, blkts, linen, pillows], lift, w/mach, dryer, pool, spa (2), bbq, non smoking units (3). **D 👤 $99 - $145.50, 👥 $148.50 - $203.50, +👤 $16.50**, ch con, weekly con, BC MC VI, (not yet classified).

B&B's/Guest Houses

★★★★ **Airlie Waterfront B&B**, (B&B), Cnr Broadwater Ave & Marlin St, 500m N of PO, ☎ 07 4946 7631, or 07 4948 1300, fax 07 4948 1311, 3 rms (1 & 2 bedrm), [spa bath (2), a/c-cool, fan, tel, TV, clock radio, t/c mkg, refrig], pool, meals to unit, cots, non smoking units. **BLB 👤 $95, 👥 $125 - $139, +👤 $25**, ch con, weekly con, BC MC VI.

★★★★ **Whitsunday Moorings B & B**, (B&B), Previously Whitsunday Mooring Bed & Breakfast 37 Airlie Crescent, 300m S of Main Street, ☎ 07 4946 4692, fax 07 4946 4692, 2 rms (Studio), [shwr, tlt, hairdry, a/c, c/fan, TV, clock radio, t/c mkg, refrig, cook fac ltd, micro], ldry, iron, iron brd, pool. **BB 👤 $95, 👥 $105, +👤 $22**, AE BC MC VI.

WHITSUNDAYS - CANNONVALE QLD 4802

Pop 3,100. Part of Proserpine, (1122km N Brisbane), See maps on page 416, ref A1. Whitsunday tourist resort.

Hotels/Motels

FLAG
FLAG CHOICE HOTELS

★★★☆ **Club Crocodile Airlie Beach**, (M), Shute Harbour Rd, ☎ 07 4946 7155, fax 07 4946 6007, (Multi-stry gr fl), 160 units [shwr, bath (40), tlt, hairdry (40), a/c-cool, c/fan, tel, TV, clock radio, t/c mkg, refrig, mini bar (40)], lift, ldry, rec rm, conv fac, ⊠, pool, spa, bbq, rm serv, courtesy transfer, 📞, tennis, cots. **RO 👥 $66 - $77**, ch con, Units 123 to 161 ★★★★, AE BC DC EFT JCB MC VI, ♿.

★★☆ **Cannonvale Reef Gateway**, (LMH), Shute Harbour Rd, ☎ 07 4946 6588, fax 07 4946 7150, (2 stry gr fl), 24 units [shwr, tlt, a/c-cool, tel, TV, movie, radio, t/c mkg, refrig], ldry, dryer, conv fac, ⊠, pool, c/park (undercover), golf, cots. **RO 👤 $49.50, 👥 $60.50 - $66, 👥👤 $79.30, 👥👥 $92.40, +👤 $13.20**, ch con, Units 12A to 24 are ★★☆. AE BC DC EFT MC VI.

Self Catering Accommodation

★★★★☆ **Sailz Boutique Holiday Villas**, (HU), 24 Pandanus Drive, Whitsunday 4802, 2km S of Airlie Beach, ☎ 07 4946 5605, fax 07 4946 5688, 32 units acc up to 6, [shwr, bath, spa bath, tlt, a/c, c/fan, tel, TV, clock radio, refrig, cook fac, micro, d/wash, toaster, ldry (in unit), blkts, linen, pillows], dryer, iron, iron brd, pool (salt water), bbq (covered), c/park (undercover), cots-fee. **D $125 - $140, W $785 - $1,120**, ch con, BC MC VI.

★★★ **Orana Lodge Whitsunday**, (HU), 13 Beach Rd, ☎ 07 4946 7124, fax 07 4946 4944, (2 stry gr fl), 8 units acc up to 6, [shwr, tlt, a/c-cool, fan, c/fan, tel, TV, movie, clock radio, refrig, cook fac, elec frypan, blkts, linen, pillows], ldry, dryer-fee, iron, pool (salt water), bbq, 📞, cots. **D 👤 $49.50, 👥 $60**, AE BC MC VI.

★★★ **Paradise Court**, (HU), 181 Shute Harbour Rd, ☎ 07 4946 7139, fax 07 4946 7139, 8 units acc up to 4, (Studio), [shwr, tlt, a/c-cool, c/fan, tel, TV, video-fee, clock radio, t/c mkg, refrig, cook fac, micro, elec frypan, blkts, linen, pillows], ldry, pool, bbq, boat park, cots-fee. **D 👥 $66 - $88, +👤 $11, W 👥 $384 - $400**, Breakfast available. BC MC VI.

★★★ **Whitsunday Ocean View Apartments**, (HU), 48 Coral Esp (Beach Rd), ☎ 07 4946 6860, fax 07 4946 6778, (2 stry gr fl), 19 units acc up to 7, (Studio & 2 bedrm), [shwr, tlt, a/c-cool, fan, TV, refrig, cook fac, elec frypan, blkts, linen, pillows], ldry, dryer, iron, pool, bbq, c/park (undercover) (10), plygr, cots. **D 👥 $70, +👤 $15, W 👥 $490**, ch con, BC MC VI.

★★☆ **Whitsunday Palm Tree Lodge**, (HU), 14 Beach Rd, ☎ 07 4946 6461, (2 stry), 8 units acc up to 4, [shwr, tlt, a/c-cool, fan, TV, refrig, cook fac, micro (8), blkts, linen, pillows], ldry, pool, bbq, c/park (undercover), cots. **D 👥 $45 - $55, +👤 $10**.

Beach Court Holiday Villas, (HU), 24 Beach Rd, 500m fr PO, ☎ 07 4946 5316, fax 07 4946 7961, (Multi-stry gr fl), 20 units acc up to 8, (2 & 3 bedrm), [shwr, tlt, a/c, fan, tel, TV, clock radio, t/c mkg, refrig, cook fac, micro, d/wash, blkts, doonas, linen, pillows], w/mach, dryer, pool, spa (heated), bbq, cots-fee. **D ♦ $80 - $115, ♦♦ $100 - $135, ◊ $20**, ch con, weekly con, BC EFT MC VI, (not yet classified).

Other Accommodation

Reef Oceania Resort, 147 Shute Harbour Rd, ☎ 07 4946 6137, fax 07 4946 6846, 80 rms acc up to 5, [shwr, tlt, a/c-cool, c/fan, tel, TV, t/c mkg, refrig, cook fac], ldry-fee, ⊠, pool, bbq, courtesy transfer, cots. **BLB ♦ $5 - $14**, ch con, fam con, BC MC VI.

WHITSUNDAYS - DAYDREAM ISLAND QLD 4802

Pop Nominal, (1135km N Brisbane), See maps on page 416, ref A1. Tropical Great Barrier Reef Island (Whitsunday Group).

Hotels/Motels

★★★★ **Daydream Island Resort**, (M), Resort, Whitsunday Passage, via Shute Harbour, ☎ 07 4948 8488, fax 07 4948 8499, 17 units [shwr, spa bath, tlt, hairdry, a/c, tel, TV, movie, clock radio, t/c mkg, refrig, mini bar, ldry, pillows], iron, iron brd, rec rm, conv fac, night club, ⊠ (3), bar, bar, pool (2), sauna, spa (2), pool bar, 24hr reception, plygr, bush walking, gym, tennis (2), cots. **RO $460**, ch con, Tariff includes use of most non motorised water sports. Car storage available on mainland and transfers ex shute harbour included by arrangement. AE BC DC EFT JCB MC VI.

★★★★ **(Garden Section)**, Resort, 201 units [shwr, bath, tlt, hairdry, a/c, tel, TV, movie, clock radio, t/c mkg, refrig, mini bar], iron, iron brd, cots. **RO $290**.

★★★★ **(Oceanview Section)**, Resort, 80 units [shwr, bath, tlt, hairdry, a/c, tel, TV, movie, clock radio, t/c mkg, refrig, mini bar], iron, iron brd, cots. **RO $310**.

WHITSUNDAYS - HAMILTON ISLAND QLD 4803

Pop 1,500. Nominal, (1135km N Brisbane), See maps on page 416, ref A1. Located in the Whitsunday Passage.

Hotels/Motels

Reef View Hotel, (Ltd Lic H), Resort, Whitsunday Passage, via Shute Harbour, ☎ 07 4946 9999, fax 02 8353 8499, 363 rms (16 suites) [shwr, bath, spa bath (16), tlt, hairdry, a/c, c/fan, tel, TV, radio, t/c mkg, refrig, mini bar, pillows], ldry, iron, rec rm, conv fac, night club, ⊠, pool (6), spa, 24hr reception, rm serv, bush walking, mini golf, gym, squash (2), tennis (6), cots. **RO ♦ $347 - $416, ♦♦ $347 - $416, Suite RO $672 - $1,158**, AE BC DC EFT JCB MC VI, (Rating under review).

(Beachclub Resort), Resort, 60 units [shwr, bath, tlt, hairdry, a/c, c/fan, tel, TV, radio, CD, t/c mkg, refrig, mini bar], iron. **RO ♦ $486, ♦♦ $486**, (Rating under review).

(Coconut Palms Bungalows), Resort, 50 units [shwr, tlt, hairdry, a/c, c/fan, tel, TV, radio, t/c mkg, refrig, mini bar], iron, cots. **RO ♦ $277, ♦♦ $277**, (Rating under review).

(Whitsunday Holiday Apartments), Resort, 168 units [shwr, tlt, hairdry, a/c, c/fan, tel, TV, video, radio, t/c mkg, refrig, mini bar, cook fac, micro], iron, cots. **RO ♦♦ $324 - $502**, (Rating under review).

WHITSUNDAYS - HAYMAN ISLAND QLD 4801

Pop Nominal, (1125km N Brisbane), See maps on page 416, ref A1. Most northerly island of the Whitsunday Group.

Hotels/Motels

★★★★★ **Hayman**, (LH), Resort, via Shute Harbour Great Barrier Reef, Via Hamilton Island airport, Great Barrier Reef, ☎ 07 4940 1234, fax 07 4940 1567, 214 rms (33 suites) [shwr, bath, spa bath (44), tlt, hairdry, a/c, tel, TV, video, radio, t/c mkg, refrig, mini bar, pillows], rec rm, conv fac, night club, ⊠ (6), pool, sauna, spa, rm serv, bush walking, gym, cots. **BB ♦ $544.50 - $852.50, ♦♦ $544.50 - $852.50, Suite D $1,485 - $1,650**, ch con, AE BC DC MC VI.

WHITSUNDAYS - HIDEAWAY BAY QLD 4800

Pop Nominal, (1129km N Brisbane), See maps on page 416, ref A1.

Self Catering Accommodation

★★☆ **Montes Reef Resort**, (HU), 10km E of Bowen by sea. Gloucester Passage, 43km N of Proserpine by road, ☎ 07 4945 7177, fax 07 4945 7272, 9 units acc up to 6, [shwr, tlt, c/fan, TV, clock radio, refrig, cook fac, linen], ldry, ✕ (licensed), bbq, shop, tennis. **D ♦♦ $90 - $120, ◊ $15 - $20**, ch con, Access by 4WD. Courtesy 4WD pick up from Hydeaway Bay Caravan Park. (Prior arrangement necessary). 18km of unsealed road. BC MC VI.

WHITSUNDAYS - LONG ISLAND QLD 4800

Pop Nominal, (1125km N Brisbane), See maps on page 416, ref A1.

Hotels/Motels

★★★ **Club Crocodile Long Island**, (M), Resort, Via Shute Harbour, ☎ 07 4946 9400, fax 07 4946 9555, (2 stry gr fl), 86 units [shwr, bath (6), tlt, a/c-cool, c/fan, tel, TV, movie, radio, t/c mkg, refrig, pillows], ldry, rec rm, night club, ⊠, cafe, bar, pool (salt water), sauna, spa, ☎, bush walking, gym, tennis (2). **D all meals ♦ $341**, AE BC DC EFT MC VI.

★★★ **(Beachfront Units)**, Resort, (2 stry gr fl), 86 units [shwr, bath (6), tlt, a/c-cool, c/fan, tel, TV, movie, radio, t/c mkg, refrig]. **D all meals ♦ $297, ♦♦ $385**.

★★★ **(Garden Units)**, Resort, (2 stry gr fl), 54 units [shwr, tlt, a/c-cool, c/fan, tel, TV, movie, radio, t/c mkg, refrig]. **D all meals ♦ $265, ♦♦ $341**.

★★☆ **Palm Bay Hideaway**, (M), Resort, Via Shute Harbour, ☎ 07 4946 9233, fax 07 4946 9309, 6 units [shwr, tlt, c/fan, t/c mkg, refrig, pillows], ldry, lounge, ⊠, pool, spa, bbq, shop, bush walking. **RO ♦ $194, ♦♦ $284**, ch con, AE BC DC MC VI.

★★☆ **(Cabin Section)**, 8 cabins acc up to 6, [shwr, tlt, c/fan, t/c mkg, refrig, blkts, linen, pillows]. **RO ♦ $146, ♦♦ $224, ◊ $20**, ch con.

Self Catering Accommodation

Whitsunday Wilderness Lodge, Resort, No children's facilities, South Long Island, ☎ 07 3221 7799, fax 07 3221 7799, 10 cabins acc up to 2, [shwr, tlt, t/c mkg, refrig], ⊠, bbq. **D all meals ♦ $399**, Tariff includes helicopter transfers from Hamilton Island. BC MC VI, (not yet classified).

Kunapipi Springs Road, Whitsundays QLD 4800
Phone: +61 (07) 4947 7777 Fax: +61 (07) 4947 7770
Toll Free: 1800 812 626

LAGUNA QUAYS
RESORT
The Whitsundays
GREAT BARRIER REEF

26948ag

WHITSUNDAYS - PROSERPINE QLD 4800

Pop 3,250. (1099km N Brisbane), See maps on page 416, ref A1.
Centre of productive sugar cane farming area.

★★★★☆ **Laguna Quays Resort**, (Ltd Lic H), Resort, Kunapipi Springs
Rd, Repulse Bay, 26km S of Proserpine PO, ☎ 07 4947 7777,
fax 07 4947 7770, (Multi-stry gr fl), 60 rms (24 suites) [shwr, bath, spa
bath (24), tlt, hairdry, a/c, tel, TV, movie, radio, t/c mkg, refrig,
mini bar, pillows], lift, iron, iron brd, rec rm, conv fac, ✉, pool, sauna,
24hr reception, rm serv, ✆, plygr, bush walking, bicycle, golf, tennis,
cots. **RO $275, Suite D $305 - $395**, ch con, AE BC DC JCB MC VI.
Operator Comment: See our display advertisement above.

★★★★☆ **(Cascade Villas)**, (2 stry gr fl), 80 serv apts [shwr, bath,
tlt, a/c, c/fan, tel, TV, movie, clock radio, refrig, cook fac, micro,
d/wash, ldry (in unit)], dryer, cots. **D $300 - $365**, ch con.

★★★★☆ **(Club Villas)**, (2 stry gr fl), 15 serv apts [ensuite, shwr,
bath, tlt, a/c, c/fan, tel, TV, movie, clock radio, refrig, cook fac,
micro, d/wash, ldry (in unit)], dryer, c/park (undercover), cots.
D $300 - $365, ch con.

★★★★☆ **(Hillside Terraces)**, (Multi-stry gr fl), 36 serv apts [shwr,
bath, tlt, a/c, c/fan, tel, TV, movie, clock radio, refrig, cook fac,
micro, d/wash, ldry (in unit)], dryer, c/park (undercover), cots.
D $300 - $365, ch con.

★★★ **A & A**, (M), Main St, ☎ 07 4945 1888, fax 07 4945 2566, 14
units [shwr, tlt, a/c-cool, a/c, tel, TV, clock radio, t/c mkg, refrig], pool,
c/park (undercover), cots. **RO ♦ $50, ♦♦ $54, ◊ $11**, AE BC DC MC VI, ⚹.

★★★ **Proserpine Motor Lodge**, (M), 184 Main St, ☎ 07 4945 1788,
fax 07 4945 2898, (2 stry gr fl), 33 units [shwr, tlt, a/c-cool, tel, cable
tv, clock radio, t/c mkg, refrig], ldry, conv fac, ✉, pool, rm serv, c/park
(undercover) (20), cots-fee. **RO ♦ $59, ♦♦ $65, ◊ $5**, AE BC DC MC VI.

★★★ **Whitsunday Palms**, (M), Bruce Hwy, 1.5km S of PO,
☎ 07 4945 1868, fax 07 4945 3072, 6 units [shwr, tlt, a/c-cool, tel,
TV, clock radio, t/c mkg, refrig], bbq, dinner to unit, c/park (undercover),
cots-fee. **RO ♦ $50, ♦♦ $55 - $60, ◊ $10**, ch con, AE BC EFT MC VI.

★★☆ **Reef Gardens Motel**, (M), Bruce Hwy, 1.5km S of PO,
☎ 07 4945 1288, fax 07 4945 1288, 12 units [shwr, tlt, a/c-cool, fan,
tel, TV, clock radio, t/c mkg, refrig], pool, spa, bbq, dinner to unit,
c/park (undercover), plygr, cots-fee. **RO ♦ $47, ♦♦ $49 - $53, ◊ $11**,
Units 9 & 10 ★★★. AE BC EFT MC VI.

★★ **Anchor Motel Whitsunday**, (M), 32 Herbert St, 100m to town,
☎ 07 4945 1200, fax 07 4945 1200, 12 units [shwr, tlt, a/c-cool, fan,
TV, clock radio, t/c mkg, refrig], iron, dinner to unit,
c/park (undercover). **RO ♦ $38, ♦♦ $43, ◊ $7**, ch con.

WHITSUNDAYS - SHUTE HARBOUR QLD 4802

Pop Part of Proserpine, (1135km N Brisbane), See maps on page
416, ref A1. Whitsunday tourist resort, offering view of the
Whitsunday Passage islands.

★★★ **Coral Point Lodge**, (M), Harbour Ave, ☎ 07 4946 9500,
fax 07 4946 9469, (Multi-stry), 10 units [shwr, tlt, a/c-cool, c/fan, tel,
TV, clock radio, t/c mkg, refrig, cook fac (3)], ldry, ✗, cafe, pool,
c/park (undercover) (9), courtesy transfer. **RO ♦ $60 - $72, ♦♦ $70 -
$82, ◊ $10**, BC MC VI.

★★☆ **Shute Harbour**, (M), Shute Harbour Rd, 500m NW of Shute
Harbour Jetty, ☎ 07 4946 9131, fax 07 4946 9131, 12 units [shwr, tlt,
a/c-cool (9), a/c (3), c/fan, TV, t/c mkg, refrig,
cook fac (1), cook fac ltd (2), toaster (11)], ldry-fee, ✗, pool, rm serv,
dinner to unit, c/park. **RO ♦ $55 - $75, ♦♦ $65 - $85**, AE BC DC MC VI.

WHITSUNDAYS - SOUTH MOLLE ISLAND QLD 4741

Part of WHITSUNDAYS region. Pop Nominal, (1125km N Brisbane),
See maps on page 416, ref A1. Situated in the heart of Whitsunday
Passage. The island which covers 405ha, is 4km long & 2.4km wide.
National Park. Coral viewing, scuba diving, parasailing.

Hotels/Motels

★★★☆ **South Molle Island**, (M), Resort, Whitsunday Units, via Shute
Harbour, ☎ 07 4946 9433, fax 07 4946 9580, 44 units [shwr,
bath (38), tlt, a/c-cool, c/fan, tel, TV, clock radio, t/c mkg, refrig,
mini bar, pillows], ldry, dryer, iron, rec rm, night club, ✗, pool, wading
pool, spa, ✆, golf, gym, tennis (2). **D all meals ♦ $270, ♦♦ $430**,
ch con, AE BC DC EFT MC VI.

★★★ **(Beachcomber Units)**, Resort, 23 units [shwr, tlt, a/c-cool,
c/fan, tel, TV, clock radio, t/c mkg, refrig, mini bar], iron. **D all meals
♦ $292, ♦♦ $474**, ch con.

★★★ **(Golf Units)**, Resort, 20 units [shwr, tlt, a/c-cool, tel, TV,
clock radio, t/c mkg, refrig, mini bar], iron. **D all meals ♦ $226,
♦♦ $342**, ch con.

★★★ **(Reef Units)**, Resort, 62 units [shwr, tlt, a/c-cool, c/fan, tel,
TV, clock radio, t/c mkg, refrig, mini bar], iron. **D all meals ♦ $248,
♦♦ $386**, ch con.

★★☆ **(Family Units)**, Resort, 15 units [shwr, tlt, a/c-cool, c/fan,
tel, TV, clock radio, t/c mkg, refrig, mini bar], iron. **D all meals
♦♦♦♦ $496**, ch con.

End of Whitsundays Region

WILLOWBANK QLD 4306

Pop Part of Ipswich, (51km SW Brisbane), See maps on page 417,
ref C7. Outer satellite suburb of Ipswich.

Hotels/Motels

★★★ **Willowbank**, (M), Cnr Warwick & Coopers Rds, 11km SW of
Ipswich 1.5km S of Amberley A/F Base, ☎ 07 5464 3166,
fax 07 5464 3449, 21 units [shwr, tlt, a/c, fan, tel, TV, clock radio,
t/c mkg, refrig, cook fac], ldry, w/mach-fee, dryer, pool (salt water),
bbq, plygr, cots. **RO ♦ $61 - $66, ♦♦ $63 - $67, ◊ $11**, AE BC DC MC VI.

WINDORAH QLD 4481

Pop 100. (1,179km W Brisbane) See maps on page 414, ref B7. A
very small town surrounded by sand hills, wildflowers and bird life.
Fishing, Swimming.

Self Catering Accommodation

Cooper Cabins, 500m N of PO, ☎ 07 4656 3101, 4 cabins acc up to 4,
[shwr, tlt, heat, TV, refrig, cook fac, blkts, linen, pillows]. **D ♦♦ $60,
◊ $12**, (not yet classified).

Medication and driving

Medication can effect your driving. Certain drugs can effect your
mental alertness and/or co-ordination and therefore effect driving
skills.   Always check with your doctor the effect which any
medication (over the counter or prescription) you are taking may
have on your driving. There may be an alternative drug which will
not affect your driving. It is best to avoid drinking alcohol while
taking medication.

WINTON QLD 4735

Pop 1,150. (1433km NW Brisbane), See maps on page 414, ref B6. Lark Quarry (105km S of Winton) - dinosaur footprints. Home of Waltzing Matilda story. Birthplace of Qantas. Bowls, Gem Fossicking, Golf, Horse Racing, Scenic Drives, Swimming.

Hotels/Motels

★★☆ **Matilda Motel**, (M), 20 Oondooroo St, Centre of town, ☎ 07 4657 1433, fax 07 4657 1623, 20 units [shwr, tlt, a/c-cool, heat, tel, TV, movie (14), clock radio, t/c mkg, refrig, cook fac (1)], ldry, bbq, meals to unit, courtesy transfer, plygr, cots-fee. **RO** ┃ **$52.80**, ┃┃ **$60.50**, ◊ **$11**, ch con, Units 16 to 22 ★★★. AE BC DC MC VI.

★★☆ **Winton Outback**, (M), 95 Elderslie St, ☎ 07 4657 1422, fax 07 4657 1708, 10 units [shwr, tlt, a/c-cool, heat, tel, TV, movie, clock radio, t/c mkg, refrig, toaster], ldry, w/mach-fee, dryer-fee, bbq, c/park (undercover) (8). **RO** ┃ **$55**, ┃┃ **$60.50 - $61.60**, ◊ **$10**, AE BC DC EFT MC VI, ♿.

North Gregory Hotel/Motel, (M), 67 Elderslie St, 100m W of PO, ☎ 07 4657 1375, fax 07 4657 0106, 28 units [ensuite (14), bath (3), a/c-cool, fan, TV, t/c mkg (14), refrig (14), toaster (14)], conf fac, ⊠, dinner to unit, non smoking units (14). **BLB** ┃ **$33 - $55**, ┃┃ **$44 - $55**, ◊ **$15**, ch con, BC EFT MC VI, (not yet classified).

Self Catering Accommodation

★★★ **Banjos Motel & Cabins**, (SA), Cnr Manuka & Bostock Sts, ☎ 07 4657 1213, fax 07 4657 1213, 6 serv apts acc up to 5, [shwr, tlt, a/c-cool, heat, TV, movie, t/c mkg, refrig, cook fac (1), cook fac ltd (3), micro (2), toaster, blkts, linen, pillows], ldry-fee, pool (covered), bbq, dinner to unit, c/park (undercover), ☏, cots-fee, **RO** ┃ **$49.50 - $55**, ┃┃ **$55 - $60.50**, ◊ **$11**, ch con, Units 5 & 6 not rated. BC MC VI.

WONDAI QLD 4606

Pop 1,350. (241km NW Brisbane), See maps on page 417, ref B3. Produces a variety of grain crops, peanuts and beef cattle. Bowls, Fishing, Golf, Squash, Swimming.

Hotels/Motels

★★★ **Wondai Colonial**, (M), Bunya Hwy, ☎ 07 4168 5633, fax 07 4168 5770, 14 units [shwr, spa bath (1), tlt, a/c, tel, TV, movie, clock radio, t/c mkg, refrig], ldry, ⊠ (Mon-Sat), bar, pool, rm serv. **RO** ┃ **$55**, ┃┃ **$65**, ◊ **$10**, AE BC DC MC VI.

★☆ **Warana**, (LMH), McKenzie St, ☎ 07 4168 5366, 8 units [shwr, tlt, elec blkts, TV, t/c mkg, refrig], c/park (undercover). **RO** ┃ **$38.50**, ┃┃ **$49.50**, ◊ **$12.50**, BC MC.

WONGAWALLAN QLD 4210

Pop Nominal, (65km S Brisbane), See maps on page 417, ref D7. Located in northern section of Gold Coast Hinterland. Bush Walking, Scenic Drives.

B&B's/Guest Houses

★★★★★★ **Esconder Mountain Lodge**, (GH), No children's facilities, 200 Wongawallan Dve, Wongawallen 4210, ☎ 07 5561 7611, fax 07 5502 9761, 3 rms [shwr, tlt, a/c, TV, clock radio, refrig, mini bar], ldry, lounge (TV), ⊠, pool-heated (salt water), spa, t/c mkg shared, c/park (undercover), non smoking property, non smoking rms. **DBB** ┃┃ **$324**, AE BC DC MC VI.

WOODFORD QLD 4514

Pop 1,600. (70km NW Brisbane), See maps on page 417, ref D5. Small town between Caboolture and Kilcoy.

Hotels/Motels

★★★ **Woodford Country Motel**, (M), 77 Archer Street, 22Km N of Caboolture. ☎ 07 5496 1122, fax 07 5496 3480, 10 units [shwr, tlt, a/c, tel, TV, movie, clock radio, t/c mkg, refrig], iron, iron brd, rm serv, c/park (undercover). **RO** ┃ **$50 - $55**, ┃┃ **$55 - $66**, ◊ **$12.50**, BC MC VI, ♿.

B&B's/Guest Houses

★★★★ **Storeybrook Cottage**, (B&B), 71 Peterson Rd, 2km E of Woodford PO, ☎ 07 5496 1316, fax 07 5496 1332, (2 stry gr fl), 3 rms (1 suite) [shwr, spa bath (1), tlt, a/c-cool, c/fan (2), fire pl, elec blkts, TV, clock radio, t/c mkg, refrig, cook fac ltd, micro, ldry], ldry, dryer, iron, iron brd, cook fac, bbq-fee, dinner to unit, non smoking rms (4). **BB** ┃ **$60 - $80**, ┃┃ **$80 - $140**, ◊ **$30**, AE BC EFT MC VI.

★★★☆ **Cosy Dutch Retreat**, (B&B), 64 Curran St, D'Aguilar, 3km E of Woodford P 0, ☎ 07 5496 4848, fax 07 5496 4134, (2 stry gr fl), 4 rms [fan, elec blkts, TV, clock radio, pillows], bathrm (2), ldry, w/mach, dryer, ✗, spa, cook fac, t/c mkg shared, refrig, bbq, c/park (undercover) (3), cots, non smoking flr. **BB** ┃ **$40**, ┃┃ **$60**, ◊ **$15**, ch con, pen con.

WOODGATE QLD 4660

Pop 750. (352km N Brisbane), See maps on page 417, ref D1. Seaside resort adjacent to Woodgate National Park. Boat Ramp, Bowls, Bush Walking, Fishing, Scenic Drives, Swimming, Tennis.

Self Catering Accommodation

★★★★ **Shoreline Apartments**, (HU), 142 Esplanade, 50m W of Beach, ☎ 07 4126 8924, (2 stry gr fl), 6 units acc up to 6, (1 & 2 bedrm), [shwr, bath (3), tlt, c/fan, TV, clock radio, refrig, cook fac, micro, toaster, ldry (in unit), linen reqd-fee], iron, iron brd, bbq, c/park (undercover), cots. **D $45**, **W $220 - $450**, ch con, ♿.

★★★☆ **Woodgate Holiday Cottages**, (HU), Pepperina Ct, off 4th Ave, ☎ 07 4126 8888, 6 units acc up to 6, [shwr, bath (4), tlt, c/fan, heat, TV, clock radio, refrig, cook fac, micro, ldry (in unit), linen reqd-fee], pool (salt water), bbq (covered), c/park (undercover) (6), cots. **D** ┃┃ **$42 - $50**, ◊ **$5**, **W $220 - $455**, Min book applies, BC MC VI.

★★★ **Woodgate Lodge**, (HU), 83 Mackerel St (off Eleventh Ave), ☎ 07 4126 8924, 8 units acc up to 6, (2 bedrm), [shwr, bath, tlt, c/fan, TV, radio, refrig, cook fac, micro, ldry (in unit), linen reqd], iron, iron brd, bbq, c/park (undercover), boat park, cots. **D $40 - $50**, **W $180 - $385**.

★★☆ **Woodgate Hibiscus Holiday Units**, (HU), 139 Esplanade, beachfront, adjacent to PO, ☎ 07 4126 8709, fax 07 4126 8811, (2 stry gr fl), 8 units acc up to 6, (1 & 2 bedrm), [shwr, tlt, fan, TV, clock radio, refrig, cook fac, micro, linen reqd-fee], ldry, bbq, c/park (undercover). **D $40 - $70**, **W $200 - $450**.

WOOMBYE QLD 4559

Pop 800. (95km N Brisbane), See maps on page 417, ref D4. Centre of pineapple growing area. Thrill Hill Amusement Park & Waterslide.

Hotels/Motels

★★★☆ **Woombye Motor Inn**, (M), Old Bruce Hwy (Nambour Connection Rd), 2km N of Big Pineapple, ☎ 07 5442 1666, fax 07 5442 2373, (2 stry gr fl), 16 units [shwr, tlt, a/c, heat, tel, TV, clock radio], pool (salt water), c/park (undercover). **RO** ┃ **$55 - $70**, ┃┃ **$65 - $90**, ◊ **$10**, AE BC DC MC VI.

YANDINA QLD 4561

Pop 950. (115km N Brisbane), See maps on page 417, ref D4. Small township on the Bruce Hwy. Dunethin Rock Monolith Ginger Factory Bunya Park Wildlife Sanctuary located in grounds of Ginger Factory Fairhill Native Nursery & Botanical Gardens. Bowls, Gem Fossicking, Horse Riding.

B&B's/Guest Houses

★★★★☆ **Ninderry Manor Luxury Retreat**, (B&B), No children's facilities, 12 Karnu Drive, 7km E of Yandina, ☎ 07 5472 7255, fax 07 5446 7089, 3 rms [shwr, tlt, hairdry, c/fan, heat, TV (1), video (1), clock radio, CD (1), t/c mkg], ldry, dryer, iron (4), iron brd (4), TV rm, pool (salt water), bbq, dinner to unit, non smoking rms. **BB** ┃ **$95**, ┃┃ **$150**, AE BC DC MC VI.

YARRAMAN QLD 4614

Pop 800. (170km NW Brisbane), See maps on page 417, ref B5. Set amidst a range of forests. One of the closest towns to Palms National Park. Bush Walking, Horse Riding, Scenic Drives, Tennis.

Hotels/Motels

★★★ **Yarraman**, (M), D'Aguilar Hwy, ☎ 07 4163 8144, fax 07 4163 8665, 20 units [shwr, tlt, a/c, tel, TV, clock radio, t/c mkg, refrig], dinner to unit, c/park (undercover), non smoking units (7). **RO** ┃ **$49.50**, ┃┃ **$60.50**, ◊ **$10**, AE BC DC EFT JCB MC VI.

Trouble-free travel tips - **Tyre pressures**

Check tyre pressures and set them to the manufacturer's recommendation, including the spare.
The specifications can generally be found on the tyre placard located in either the glove box or on the front door frame.

YELARBON QLD 4388

Pop 200. (410km W Brisbane) See maps on page 414, ref D8. Small town in rural setting.

Hotels/Motels

★★☆ **Oasis Hotel Motel**, (LMH), Taloom St, 50km E of Goondiwindi, ☎ 07 4675 1230, fax 07 4675 1230, 3 units [shwr, tlt, a/c-cool, TV, clock radio, t/c mkg, refrig, toaster], dinner to unit. **RO 👤 $55, 👥 $55**, AE BC MC VI.

YEPPOON QLD 4703

Pop 8,800. (767km N Brisbane), See maps on page 416, ref C5. Large coastal resort on the shore of Keppel Bay. Gateway to Great Keppel Island. Largest shopping centre of the Capricorn Coast. Bowls, Bush Walking, Fishing, Golf, Horse Riding, Squash, Swimming, Tennis, Water Skiing.

Hotels/Motels

★★★★★ **Rydges Capricorn International Resort**, (LH), Resort, Capricorn Suites, Farnborough Rd, 8km N of PO, ☎ 07 4939 5111, fax 07 4939 5666, 7 rms [shwr, bath, hairdry, a/c-cool, tel, TV, movie, t/c mkg, mini bar, cook fac ltd (6), micro (6), pillows], ldry, rec rm, conv fac, ⊠, bar, pool, sauna, spa, 24hr reception, rm serv, c/park (undercover), courtesy transfer, bicycle, bowls, golf, mini golf, gym, tennis. **D $325 - $355**, ch con, AE BC DC JCB MC VI.

★★★★★ **(Junior Suites)**, 154 rms (135 suites) [shwr, bath, tlt, hairdry, a/c-cool, tel, TV, movie, t/c mkg, mini bar, cook fac ltd (29), micro (29)], rm serv, c/park (undercover), cots. **D $250 - $275**, ch con.

★★★★☆ **(Araucaria - Apartment Section)**, 49 units acc up to 5, (2 bedrm), [shwr, bath, tlt, a/c-cool, tel, TV, movie, clock radio, t/c mkg, refrig, cook fac, blkts, linen, pillows], ldry, dryer, c/park (undercover), cots. **RO 👥 $270 - $345**, ch con.

★★★★☆ **(Hotel Section)**, 56 rms [shwr, bath, tlt, hairdry, a/c-cool, tel, TV, movie, t/c mkg, mini bar], rm serv, c/park (undercover), cots. **RO 👥 $200.**

★★★☆ **Bayview Tower**, (M), Cnr Adelaide & Normanby Sts, ☎ 07 4939 4500, fax 07 4939 3915, (Multi-stry), 34 units [shwr, bath, tlt, hairdry, a/c-cool, tel, TV, video, clock radio, t/c mkg, refrig], lift, ldry, w/mach-fee, dryer-fee, conv fac, ⊠, pool, sauna, spa, ✆, cots-fee. **D 👥 $77 - $105, 👥👥 $99 - $126.50, 🧒 $5.50**, ch con, AE BC DC MC VI.

★★★ **Driftwood**, (M), 7 Todd Ave, ☎ 07 4939 2446, (2 stry gr fl), 9 units [shwr, bath, tlt, a/c (in all units), c/fan, TV, t/c mkg, refrig, cook fac, micro (9)], ldry, pool, bbq, c/park (undercover), cots. **RO 👥 $55 - $69**, BC MC VI.

Budget Motel Chain International

★★★ **Sail Inn**, (M), 19 James St, ☎ 07 4939 1130, fax 07 4839 1130, 9 units [shwr, tlt, a/c (9), TV, clock radio, t/c mkg, refrig, cook fac (3), toaster], bbq, c/park (undercover). **D 👥 $58 - $85, 🧒 $11**, AE BC MC MP VI.

★★★ **Tropical Nites**, (M), 34 Anzac Pde, ☎ 07 4939 1914, fax 07 4939 1914, 9 units [shwr, tlt, a/c, c/fan, TV, t/c mkg, refrig], pool. **RO 👥 $75 - $80, 🧒 $13**, ch con, AE BC MC VI.

★★★ **Yeppoon Surfside**, (M), 30 Anzac Pde, ☎ 07 4939 1272, fax 07 4939 1272, 12 units [shwr, tlt, a/c-cool, c/fan, heat (5), TV, t/c mkg, refrig, cook fac ltd, micro (1), elec frypan, toaster], ldry-fee, pool, bbq, rm serv, ✆, cots, non smoking units (5). **RO 👤 $50 - $60, 👥 $60 - $75, 🧒 $10**, AE BC DC EFT MC VI.

★☆ **The Strand**, (LMH), Cnr Normanby St & Anzac Pde, ☎ 07 4939 1301, (2 stry), 13 units [shwr, tlt, TV, t/c mkg, refrig], conv fac, pool, c/park (undercover). **RO 👤 $39, 👥 $49, 🧒 $5**, BC MC VI.

Self Catering Accommodation

★★★★ **Cooee Bay Holiday Resort**, (HU), 29-35 Melaleuca St, 3km S of PO, ☎ 07 4925 2100, fax 07 4925 2132, 27 units acc up to 4, (1 & 2 bedrm), [shwr, tlt, hairdry, a/c, fan, tel, TV, clock radio, t/c mkg, refrig, cook fac, micro, d/wash (3), blkts, linen, pillows], w/mach, dryer, iron, iron brd, conf fac, pool, bbq, meals to unit, plygr, cots-fee, non smoking units, ch con, weekly con, AE BC DC EFT MC VI.

★★★☆ **Blue Anchor Motel & Holiday Units**, (HU), 76 Whitman St, ☎ 07 4939 4288, fax 07 4939 4600, 8 units acc up to 6, (Studio), [shwr, tlt, a/c, c/fan, tel, TV, video, clock radio, refrig, cook fac, micro, elec frypan, toaster, blkts, linen, pillows], ldry, dryer, pool-heated (solar), bbq (covered), c/park (undercover), cots. **D 👤 $55 - $65, 👥 $66 - $80, 🧒 $11**, Breakfast available, AE BC EFT MC VI.

★★★ **Bay Vacationer**, (HU), 16 Anzac Pde, ☎ 07 4939 1213, (Multi-stry gr fl), 8 units acc up to 6, [shwr, tlt, a/c (2), TV, clock radio, refrig, cook fac, micro, ldry (in unit), blkts, linen, pillows], cots. **D $55 - $330, 🧒 $10 - $40**, ch con, BC MC VI.

★★★ **Como**, (HU), 32 Anzac Pde, beachfront, ☎ 07 4939 1594, (2 stry gr fl), 8 units acc up to 6, (1 & 2 bedrm), [shwr, tlt, a/c-cool (b/rs), fan, TV, clock radio, refrig, cook fac, blkts, linen, pillows], ldry, cots. **D 👥 $60 - $80, 🧒 $10**, Min book applies, AE BC MC VI.

★★★ **Kinka Lodge**, (HU), 1001 Scenic Hwy, Kinka Beach 4703, 13km S of Yeppoon, ☎ 07 4939 6205, fax 07 4939 6279, 6 units acc up to 4, [shwr, tlt, a/c-cool, fan, TV, refrig, cook fac, blkts, linen, pillows], ldry, pool, bbq, cots. **D 👤 $46, 👥 $53, W 👤 $230, 👥 $265**, ch con, BC MC VI, ♿.

★★★ **Seaspray Beachfront**, (HU), 45 Wattle Gr, Cooee Bay, 500m S of Information Centre, ☎ 07 4939 1421, fax 07 4939 1420, (2 stry gr fl), 8 units acc up to 6, (Studio & 1 bedrm), [shwr, tlt, fan, c/fan, heat (Oil Heater), TV, video, clock radio, refrig, cook fac, micro, blkts, linen, pillows], ldry, w/mach-fee, bbq, cots. **D 👥 $55 - $70, 🧒 $10 - $15**, weekly con, BC MC VI.

★★☆ **Tidewater Motel & Holiday Flats**, (HF), 7 Normanby St, ☎ 07 4939 1632, 8 flats acc up to 6, [shwr, tlt, c/fan, TV, cook fac ltd, elec frypan], ldry-fee, dryer-fee, pool-heated, c/park (undercover), cots. **RO 👤 $40, 👥 $45, 🧒 $10**, ch con, fam con, BC MC VI.

★★ **Gum Nut Glen**, (Cotg), Tanby Rd South, ☎ 07 4939 3988, 11 cotgs acc up to 6, [shwr, tlt, a/c, TV, clock radio, refrig, cook fac ltd, elec frypan, blkts, linen, pillows], ldry, dryer, rec rm, pool, bbq, plygr, tennis (half court). **D 👥 $50 - $70, 🧒 $7, W 👥 $350 - $448**, BC MC VI.

Villa Mar Colina, (HU), 34 Adelaide St, 1km E of PO, ☎ 07 4939 3177, fax 07 4939 3332, 10 units acc up to 8, (2 & 3 bedrm), [shwr, tlt, a/c, fan, tel, TV, clock radio, t/c mkg, refrig, cook fac, micro, d/wash, blkts, doonas, linen, pillows], w/mach, dryer, pool, cots-fee, non smoking units (2). **D 👤 $120, 👥 $130 - $145, 🧒 $15**, weekly con, Min book applies, BC MC VI, (not yet classified).

B&B's/Guest Houses

★★★★☆ **While Away Bed & Breakfast**, (B&B), 44 Todd Ave, ☎ 07 4939 5719, fax 07 4939 5577, 4 rms [shwr, tlt, hairdry, a/c, c/fan, clock radio], ldry, dryer, lounge (TV), ✕, t/c mkg shared, non smoking rms. **BB 👤 $65, 👥 $75 - $85**, MC VI, ♿.

YORKEYS KNOB QLD 4878

Pop 3,433. (1736km N Brisbane), See maps on page 415, ref C3. Part of Marlin Coast. Boating, Golf.

Self Catering Accommodation

★★★★★ **The York Beachfront Holiday Apartments**, (HU), 61 Sims Esplanade, 15km N of Cairns, ☎ 07 4055 8733, fax 07 4055 8744, 17 units acc up to 4, (1 bedrm), [ensuite, shwr, bath, tlt, hairdry, a/c, c/fan, tel, cable tv (1), video (2), clock radio, CD (1), t/c mkg, refrig, cook fac, micro, d/wash, toaster, ldry], dryer, iron, iron brd, pool (salt water), spa, bbq, cots-fee. **D 👥 $99 - $129, 🧒 $11, W 👥 $623 - $833, 🧒 $77**, pen con, AE BC DC EFT MC VI.

★★★★☆ **Golden Sands Beachfront Resort**, (HU), 12/14 Deauville Cl, 17km N Cairns, ☎ 07 4055 8033, fax 07 4055 8037, (Multi-stry gr fl), 30 units acc up to 6, (1 & 2 bedrm), [shwr, tlt, a/c-cool, c/fan, tel, cable tv, clock radio, refrig, cook fac, micro, ldry (in unit), blkts, linen, pillows], lift, dryer, rec rm, ⊠, pool (salt water), dinner to unit, c/park (undercover), tennis, cots-fee. **D $101 - $127**, AE BC DC MC VI.

★★★★☆ **Half Moon Bay Resort**, (HU), 101 Wattle St, ☎ 07 4055 8059, fax 07 4055 8282, (2 stry gr fl), 19 units acc up to 4, (1 bedrm), [shwr, bath, tlt, hairdry, a/c, c/fan, tel, TV, video-fee, clock radio, refrig, cook fac, micro, ldry (in unit), blkts, linen, pillows], dryer, iron, pool (salt water), spa, bbq, c/park (undercover), cots-fee. **D 👥 $95, W 👥 $595**, BC MC VI.

★★★ **Beach Front Lodge**, (HU), 45 Sims Esp, ☎ 07 4055 7322, fax 07 4055 7322, (2 stry gr fl), 5 units acc up to 5, (Studio & 2 bedrm), [shwr, bath, tlt, a/c-cool, fan, TV, clock radio, refrig, cook fac, ldry (in unit), blkts, linen, pillows], pool, bbq, c/park (undercover). **D $50 - $75**, ch con, BC MC VI.

★★★ **Villa Marine**, (HU), 8 Rutherford St, 16km N of Cairns, ☎ 07 4055 7158, fax 07 4055 8380, 9 units acc up to 5, (Studio, 1 & 2 bedrm), [shwr, tlt, a/c-cool, c/fan, TV, clock radio, refrig, cook fac, blkts, linen, pillows], ldry, pool, bbq. **RO 👥 $85, 👥 $500**, Min book applies, BC MC VI.

B&B's/Guest Houses

★★★★☆ **Green Tree Frog B&B**, (B&B), 9 Albion St, 1km S of PO, ☎ 07 4055 8188, (2 stry), 2 rms [a/c-cool, c/fan, TV (1), radio (1), micro, toaster, doonas], lounge (TV), pool, t/c mkg shared, refrig, bbq, dinner to unit, c/park. **BB 👤 $60.50, 👥 $71.50.**

YUNGABURRA QLD 4872

Pop 1,000. (1723km N Brisbane), See maps on page 415, ref B3. Located in the Tableland Lakes centre. Name is aboriginal for fig tree.

Hotels/Motels

★★★★ **Kookaburra Lodge**, (M), No facilities for children under 8, Cnr Oak St & Eacham Rd, off highway, ☎ 07 4095 3222, fax 07 4095 3222, 12 units [shwr, tlt, a/c, c/fan, TV, clock radio, t/c mkg, refrig], ldry, lounge, ✕, pool, ✆. **RO** ♦ **$72 - $88**, ♦♦ **$72 - $88**, AE BC DC MC VI.

★★★☆ **Curtain Fig Motel**, (M), 16 Gillies Hwy, 500m SE of PO, ☎ 07 4095 3168, fax 07 4095 2099, 6 units [shwr, tlt, a/c, fan, tel, TV, clock radio, t/c mkg, refrig], pool, cots-fee. **RO** ♦ **$66**, ♦♦ **$77**, ₪ **$16.50**, AE BC DC MC VI.

★★☆ **Lake Eacham**, (LH), Gillies Hwy, 11km E of Atherton PO, ☎ 07 4095 3515, fax 07 4095 3202, (2 stry gr fl), 32 rms [shwr, tlt, c/fan (21), TV, t/c mkg, refrig (21)], lounge (TV), conv fac, ✉, c/park (limited), ✆, cots, ch con, Units 6 to 11 and 26, 29, 30, 34, 35 are ★☆. AE BC DC MC VI.

Self Catering Accommodation

★★★★★ **Mt Quincan Crater Retreat**, 60ha farm property. No children's facilities, Peeramon Rd, 4km S of Yungaburra, ☎ 07 4095 2255, fax 07 4095 2255, 4 cabins acc up to 2, (1 bedrm), [ensuite, shwr (double), spa bath (double), tlt, hairdry, heat (wood fire), TV, video, clock radio, CD, t/c mkg, refrig, micro (convection), elec frypan, toaster, ldry, blkts, linen, pillows], iron, iron brd, breakfast ingredients. **D** ♦♦ **$170 - $210**, **W** ♦♦ **$1,150**, BC MC VI.

★★★★☆ **Emily Cottage**, (Cotg), 30 Oleander Drive, ☎ 07 4036 3212, fax 07 407157228, 1 cotg acc up to 4, [shwr, tlt, c/fan, cent heat, tel, TV, radio, CD, t/c mkg, refrig, cook fac, toaster], iron, iron brd, rm serv, ✆. **D $150**, Min book applies, BC MC VI.

★★★★ **Eden House Garden Cottages**, (Cotg), 20 Gillies Hwy, 500m N of PO, ☎ 07 4095 2312, fax 07 4095 3377, 6 cotgs [ensuite, spa bath, fan, heat (wood), TV, clock radio, t/c mkg, refrig, cook fac ltd, micro, blkts, linen, pillows], ldry, ✉, dinner to unit, non smoking property. **BLB** ♦ **$105 - $150**, ♦♦ **$105 - $150**, ₪ **$15**, weekly con, AE BC DC EFT MC VI.

★★★ **Chambers Wildlife Rainforest Lodge**, (HU), Eacham Close, Lake Eacham 4872, 5km E of PO, ☎ 07 4095 3754, fax 07 4095 3754, 7 units acc up to 8, [shwr, tlt, fan, heat, tel, TV, refrig, cook fac, micro, blkts, linen, pillows], ldry, bush walking, cots-fee. **D** ♦♦ **$280**, ♦♦ **$297**, Min book applies, BC MC VI.

★★☆ **Lakeside**, (HU), Tinaburra Dve, 3km N of PO, ☎ 07 4095 3563, 16 units acc up to 4, [shwr, tlt, c/fan, TV, video-fee, t/c mkg, refrig, cook fac, blkts, linen, pillows], ldry, w/mach-fee, dryer-fee, pool, bbq, cots-fee. **D $83**, **RO** ♦ **$67**, ♦♦ **$72**, ₪ **$10**, BC MC VI.

Crater Lakes Rainforest Cottages, (Cotg), Lot 1, Eacham Cl, 500m E of Lake Eacham ☎ 07 4095 2322, fax 07 4095 2233, 4 cotgs acc up to 2, (1 bedrm), [shwr, spa bath, tlt, c/fan, elec blkts, TV, clock radio, CD, t/c mkg, refrig, cook fac, micro, toaster, blkts, linen, pillows], iron, iron brd, cots. **D** ♦♦ **$150**, **W** ♦♦ **$910**, BC EFT MC VI, (not yet classified).

B&B's/Guest Houses

★★★★★ **Bonneterre Rural Retreat**, (B&B), 'La Terre' Denny Rd, 5km NW PO, ☎ 07 4095 3680, 1 rm (1 suite) [shwr, tlt, hairdry, fan, c/fan, heat (Fireplace), tel, TV, video, radio, t/c mkg, refrig, cook fac, micro, toaster], iron, iron brd, rm serv, cots, non smoking rms. **Suite D** ♦♦ **$235**, **Suite W** ♦♦ **$660**, ch con, Min book applies, BC MC VI.

★★★★★ **Bracken Ridge**, (B&B), Lot 65 Vance Cl, 16km NE of PO, ☎ 07 4095 3421, fax 07 4595 3461, 2 rms [shwr, spa bath, tlt, elec blkts, TV, clock radio, t/c mkg, refrig, micro], ldry, lounge (TV), bbq, c/park (undercover). **BB** ♦♦ **$140 - $200**, Min book applies, BC MC VI.
(**Cottage Section**), 1 cotg acc up to 6, (2 bedrm), [shwr, tlt, hairdry, c/fan (2), fire pl, heat, elec blkts, TV, clock radio, t/c mkg, refrig, cook fac, micro, toaster, ldry, blkts, linen, pillows], dryer, iron brd, pool-heated, spa, bbq (covered), c/park (undercover). **D** ♦♦ **$145 - $225**, ₪ **$20**, (not yet classified).

★★★★☆ **Gumtree Getaway**, (GH), (Farm), A working beef cattle breeding farm. Gillies Hwy, 800m W of PO, ☎ 07 4095 3105, 3 rms [shwr, bath, spa bath, tlt, fan, heat (Fire place), elec blkts, TV, clock radio, t/c mkg, refrig, toaster], ldry-fee, dryer-fee, pool-heated, spa, bbq, c/park (undercover). **BLB** ♦♦ **$118**, AE BC MC VI.

★★★★ **The Lavender Hill Rural Stay**, (B&B), 1 Favier Rd, Kairi 4872, 8km E of PO, ☎ 07 4095 8384, fax 07 4095 8084, 3 rms [shwr, bath, tlt, hairdry, TV, video, t/c mkg], ldry, iron, iron brd, TV rm, bbq, non smoking rms. **BB** ♦♦ **$90 - $120**.

★★★☆ **Banchory Gardens**, (B&B), 27 Bunya St, 250m W of Yungaburra PO, ☎ 07 4095 3147, fax 07 4095 3147, 1 rm [shwr, tlt, c/fan, heat, TV, clock radio, t/c mkg, refrig, toaster], iron, iron brd, c/park (undercover). **BLB** ♦ **$60**, ♦♦ **$70**, ₪ **$10**.

Ernie's holiday tip #25

All work and no play is very dull.

So take a holiday, learn to relax, reconnect with your family and get in touch with your inner nicer person again. Jump on our website today for some great new Aussie holiday ideas.

see australia
a national tourism initiative

Go on. Get out there.

www.seeaustralia.com.au

South Australia is the driest state in Australia. About two thirds of the state is near desert and more than 80 per cent of SA has an annual rainfall of less than 250 mm.

But South Australians see such things as a challenge to be overcome and the deep green of the world renown vineyards like the Barossa Valley underlines the success which has grown from their determination.

South Australia is extraordinary in its landscapes.

The Flinders Ranges have a rugged beauty which captures the mind and the eye. Colour takes on a new meaning when viewed against the grandeur of geological formations like Wilpena Pound in the Flinders Ranges.

The state is diverse, from the historic towns, galleries and scenery of the Adelaide Hills to the mystery of the changing hues of the Blue Lake at Mt Gambier.

Sheltered behind the coastal sand dunes where the Murray meets the sea at Lake Alexandrina, the waters of the Coorong National Park support one of Australia's most prolific bird sanctuaries. About 120 km south-west of Adelaide, Kangaroo Island is unique in its natural beauty and flora and fauna.

Coastal resort towns like Victor Harbour add to the pleasures of being beside the sea with attractions, which include a horse-drawn tram to Granite Island.

On the coast the climate is year round Mediterranean. In the north is a desert landscape which is most hospitable in winter. South Australia is an urban state with the majority of the population living in the capital Adelaide.

Adelaide is an easy to use, ordered city thanks to the planning and foresight of the first Surveyor - General, Colonel William Light.

The city centre lies within a circle of parks which give a feeling of space to this pleasant cosmopolitan capital.

The wines of South Australia extend into the crisp riesling and rich cabernet sauvignons of the Clare Valley and the wonderful shiraz of McLaren Vale in the striking Fleurieu Peninsula.

In the far south-east Coonawarra produces a great Australian Cabinet Sauvignon.

The Murray River is a mainstream for South Australian agriculture. After it crosses the Victorian border the river flows more than 2500km to the sea at Goolwa. Riverland centres like Renmark and Berri line its banks, flanked by vineyards, orchards and vegetable growing.

Tourism is a mainstay on the Murray and watersports, houseboats and cruising sternwheelers like the *Murray Princess* make the broad reaches of the mighty river's "Bottom End" a nationally attractive place to play.

To the north of Adelaide the Yorke and Eyre Peninsulas are popular with anglers.

Further north the outback opal town of Coober Pedy shelters in underground homes from the 40C deg heat of summer.

Care and preparation are essential in touring this region, particularly in summer.

SOUTH AUSTRALIA

Eye-catching SA presents extraordinary landscapes

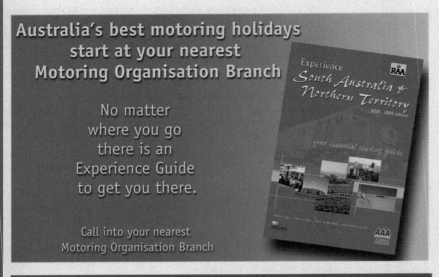
ADELAIDE SA 5000

Pop 1,079,200. See map on page 588, ref C4. Capital city of South Australia. Adelaide Botanic Gardens (approx 16ha), Adelaide Zoo, Adelaide Festival Centre, Art Gallery, Tandanya Aboriginal Centre, Old Adelaide Gaol, Adelaide Oval (tours and museum), Memorial Drive Tennis Courts and the Adelaide Aquatic Centre. Art Gallery, Boating, Bowls, Golf, Horse Racing, Rowing, Sailing, Scenic Drives, Swimming (Pool), Tennis, Trotting.

Hotels/Motels

★★★★★ **Hilton International Adelaide**, (LH), 233 Victoria Sq, ☎ 08 8217 2000, fax 08 8217 2001, (Multi-stry), 380 rms (10 suites) [ensuite, bath (361), spa bath (2), a/c, tel, TV, movie, clock radio, t/c mkg, refrig, mini bar], lift, ldry, conv fac, ✕, pool-heated, sauna, spa, rm serv, c/park (valet)-fee, gym, tennis, cots, non smoking flr (9). **RO ♦ $230 - $360, ♦♦ $230 - $360, Suite D $360 - $700**, AE BC DC JCB MC VI,

★★★★★ **Hyatt Regency Adelaide**, (LH), North Tce, ☎ 08 8231 1234, fax 08 8231 1120, (Multi-stry), 367 rms (21 suites) [ensuite, bath, spa bath (6), a/c, elec blkts, tel, cable tv, movie-fee, clock radio, t/c mkg, refrig, mini bar], lift, ldry, iron, iron brd, lounge, business centre, conv fac, night club, ✕, bar, pool-heated, sauna, spa, 24hr reception, rm serv, c/park (undercover)-fee, gym, cots, non smoking flr (5). **RO ♦ $300 - $360, ♦♦ $300 - $360, Suite D $700 - $2,000**, ch con, AE BC DC JCB MC VI,

★★★★★ **Radisson Playford Hotel Suite Adelaide**, (LH), 120 North Tce, ☎ 08 8213 8888, fax 08 8213 8833, (Multi-stry), 182 rms (64 suites) [ensuite, bath, spa bath (72), hairdry, a/c, cent heat, tel, TV, movie, clock radio, t/c mkg, refrig, mini bar, cook fac (72), micro, toaster], lift, ldry, w/mach, dryer, iron, iron brd, conf fac, ✕, pool indoor heated, sauna, rm serv, secure park, ☎, gym, cots, **RO ♦ $180 - $240, ♦♦ $180 - $240, Suite D $234 - $410**, AE BC DC MC VI,

★★★★★ **Stamford Plaza Adelaide**, (LH), 150 North Tce, ☎ 08 8461 1111, fax 08 8231 7572, (Multi-stry), 334 rms (21 suites) [ensuite, bath, spa bath (15), a/c, tel, TV, radio, t/c mkg, refrig, toaster], lift, iron, iron brd, conv fac, ✕, pool-heated, sauna, spa, rm serv, secure park-fee, gym, cots, non smoking flr (9). **RO ♦ $180 - $200, ♦♦ $180 - $200, ◊ $35, Suite D $280 - $1,030**, AE BC DC JCB MC VI,

★★★★☆ **Adelaide Barron Townhouse Motel**, (M), 164 Hindley St, ☎ 08 8211 8255, fax 08 8231 1179, (Multi-stry), 68 units [ensuite, bath, hairdry, a/c, tel, TV, movie, clock radio, t/c mkg, refrig, mini bar, toaster], lift, ldry, iron, iron brd, lounge, conv fac, ✕, pool-heated, sauna, bbq, 24hr reception, rm serv, dinner to unit, secure park (undercover), cots, non smoking rms (34). **BLB ♦ $127 - $181, ♦♦ $132 - $186, ◊ $18**, ch con, AE BC DC EFT JCB MC MP VI.

FLAG
FLAG CHOICE HOTELS

Rates may change. Check before booking.

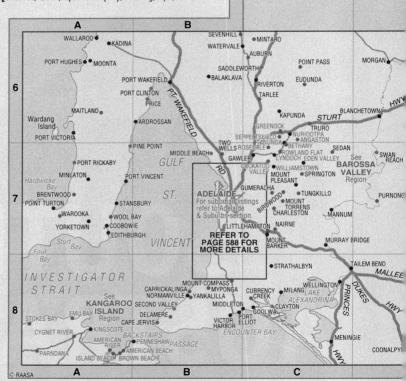

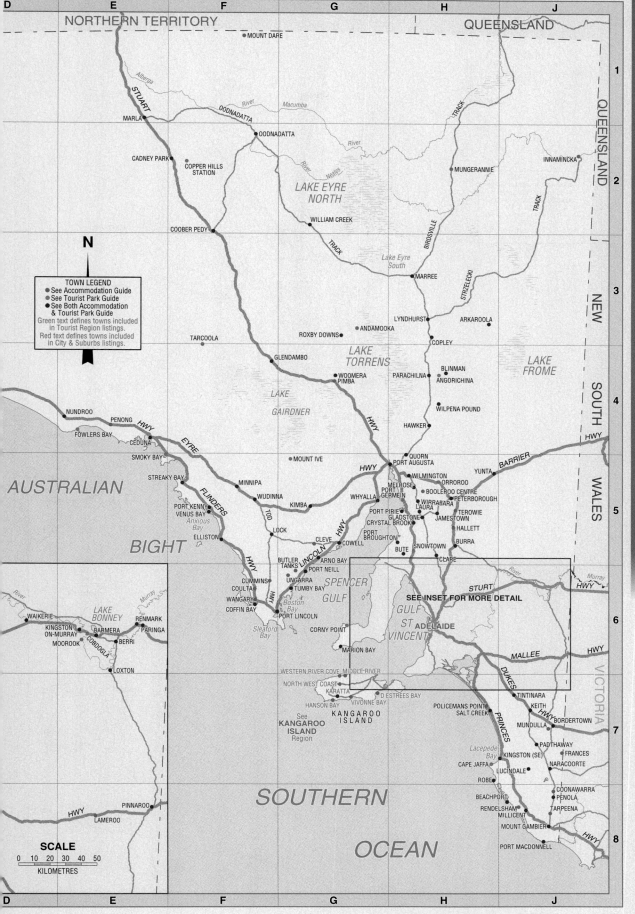

NORTHERN TERRITORY
QUEENSLAND

MOUNT DARE

STUART

MARLA

OODNADATTA

River

Macumba

CADNEY PARK

COPPER HILLS STATION

OODNADATTA

River

Neales

River

LAKE EYRE NORTH

MUNGERANNIE

INNAMINCKA

COOBER PEDY

WILLIAM CREEK

Lake Eyre South

TRACK

BIRDSVILLE

STRZELECKI

TRACK

N

TOWN LEGEND
● See Accommodation Guide
● See Tourist Park Guide
● See Both Accommodation
  & Tourist Park Guide
Green text defines towns included
in Tourist Region listings.
Red text defines towns included
in City & Suburbs listings.

MARREE

TARCOOLA

ROXBY DOWNS

ANDAMOOKA

LYNDHURST

ARKAROOLA

COPLEY

LAKE FROME

GLENDAMBO

LAKE TORRENS

WOOMERA
PIMBA

PARACHILNA

BLINMAN

ANGORICHINA

LAKE GAIRDNER

WILPENA POUND

NUNDROO

PENONG

HWY

HAWKER

HWY

FOWLERS BAY

CEDUNA

EYRE

SMOKY BAY

STREAKY BAY

FLINDERS

MINNIPA

WUDINNA

MOUNT IVE

QUORN
PORT AUGUSTA

WILMINGTON

ORROROO

YUNTA

BARRIER

HWY

AUSTRALIAN

PORT KENNY
VENUS BAY

Anxious Bay

ELLISTON

TOD

KIMBA

LOCK

HWY

MELROSE
PORT GERMEIN

WHYALLA

BOOLEROO CENTRE

PETERBOROUGH

WIRRABARA

LAURA

TEROWIE

PORT PIRIE
GLADSTONE

JAMESTOWN

CRYSTAL BROOK

HALLETT

BIGHT

LINCOLN

CLEVE

COWELL

PORT BROUGHTON

BUTE

SNOWTOWN

BURRA

BUTLER TANKS

ARNO BAY

PORT NEILL

CUMMINS

UNGARRA

TUMBY BAY

SPENCER GULF

CLARE

River

Murray

HWY

COULTA

WANGARY

COFFIN BAY

Boston Bay

PORT LINCOLN

SEE INSET FOR MORE DETAIL

STURT

LAKE BONNEY

WAIKERIE

RENMARK

KINGSTON-ON-MURRAY

BARMERA

PARINGA

Sleaford Bay

CORNY POINT

GULF ST VINCENT

ADELAIDE

MALLEE

HWY

MOOROOK

COBDOGLA

BERRI

MARION BAY

LOXTON

WESTERN RIVER COVE MIDDLE RIVER

DUKES

TINTINARA

KEITH

BORDERTOWN

VICTORIA

NORTH WEST COAST

KARATTA

D ESTREES BAY

POLICEMANS POINT
SALT CREEK

MUNDULLA

HANSON BAY

VIVONNE BAY

KANGAROO ISLAND

PRINCES

HWY

See KANGAROO ISLAND Region

PADTHAWAY

FRANCES

Lacepede Bay

KINGSTON (SE)

NARACOORTE

CAPE JAFFA

LUCINDALE

ROBE

COONAWARRA

PENOLA

PINNAROO

BEACHPORT

TARPEENA

RENDELSHAM
MILLICENT

SOUTHERN

LAMEROO

HWY

MOUNT GAMBIER

SCALE

0 10 20 30 40 50
KILOMETRES

OCEAN

PORT MACDONNELL

HWY

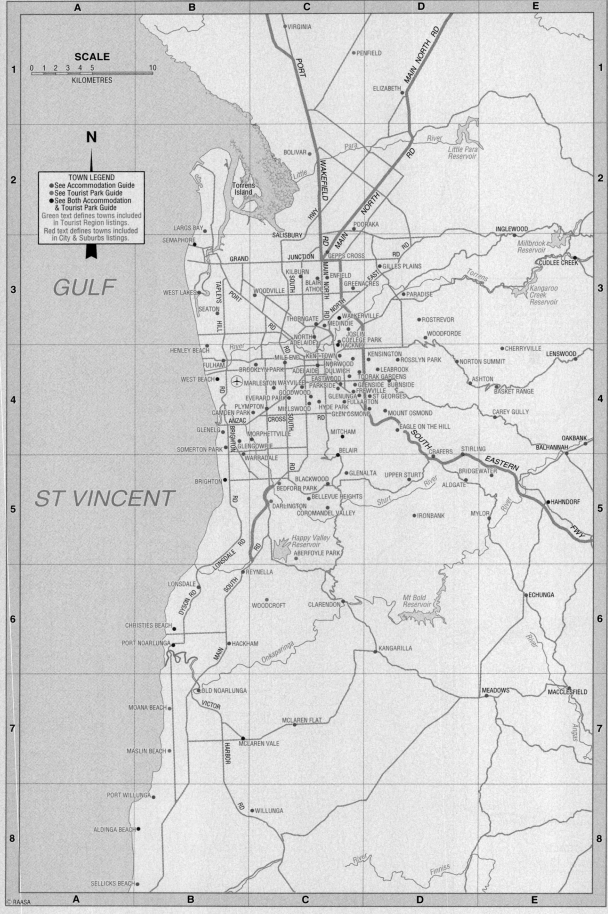

SCALE

0 1 2 3 4 5   10
KILOMETRES

N

TOWN LEGEND
● See Accommodation Guide
● See Tourist Park Guide
● See Both Accommodation
  & Tourist Park Guide
Green text defines towns included
in Tourist Region listings.
Red text defines towns included
in City & Suburbs listings.

GULF

ST VINCENT

VIRGINIA

PENFIELD

MAIN NORTH RD

PORT

ELIZABETH

WAKEFIELD

Para   River   Little Para Reservoir

BOLIVAR

Little

Torrens Island

NORTH

LARGS BAY

SEMAPHORE

SALISBURY

POORAKA

INGLEWOOD

Millbrook Reservoir

GRAND

JUNCTION

GEPPS CROSS

CUDLEE CREEK

KILBURN

ENFIELD

GILLES PLAINS

RD

WEST LAKES

WOODVILLE

SOUTH

BLAIR ATHOL

GREENACRES

East

Torrens

SEATON

THORNGATE

MEDINDIE

WALKERVILLE

PARADISE

Kangaroo Creek Reservoir

TAPLEYS

HILL

NORTH

JOSLIN

ROSTREVOR

WOODFORDE

HENLEY BEACH

River

RD

NORTH ADELAIDE

COLLEGE PARK

HACKNEY

KENT TOWN

KENSINGTON

ROSSLYN PARK

NORTON SUMMIT

CHERRYVILLE

LENSWOOD

FULHAM

PORT

BROOKLYN PARK

ADELAIDE

DULWICH

NORWOOD

LEABROOK

ASHTON

WEST BEACH

MARLESTON WAYVILLE

EASTWOOD

TOORAK GARDENS

BURNSIDE

BASKET RANGE

EVERARD PARK

PARKSIDE

GLENSIDE

GOODWOOD

GLENUNGA

FREWVILLE

ST GEORGES

CAMDEN PARK

PLYMPTON

MILLSWOOD

HYDE PARK

FULLARTON

CAREY GULLY

ANZAC

CROSS

SOUTH

GLEN OSMOND

MOUNT OSMOND

GLENELG

BRIGHTON

MORPHETTVILLE

MITCHAM

EAGLE ON THE HILL

OAKBANK

SOMERTON PARK

GLENGOWRIE

BELAIR

SOUTH

CRAFERS

STIRLING

BALHANNAH

WARRADALE

RD

EASTERN

BRIGHTON

BLACKWOOD

GLENALTA

UPPER STURT

River

BRIDGEWATER

HAHNDORF

BEDFORD PARK

ALDGATE

Sturt

BELLEVUE HEIGHTS

DARLINGTON

River

FWY

COROMANDEL VALLEY

IRONBANK

MYLOR

LONSDALE

RD

SOUTH

Happy Valley Reservoir

ABERFOYLE PARK

Mt Bold Reservoir

ECHUNGA

LONSDALE

DYSON RD

REYNELLA

CHRISTIES BEACH

WOODCROFT

CLARENDON

KANGARILLA

River

PORT NOARLUNGA

MAIN

HACKHAM

Onkaparinga

MEADOWS

MACCLESFIELD

OLD NOARLUNGA

MOANA BEACH

VICTOR

MCLAREN FLAT

Angas

MASLIN BEACH

HARBOR

MCLAREN VALE

PORT WILLUNGA

RD

WILLUNGA

ALDINGA BEACH

River

Finniss

SELLICKS BEACH

© RAASA

Back Forward Reload Home Search Netscape Images Print

Go To: http://www.southaustralia.com What's Related

WebMail Radio People Yellow Pages Download Calendar

WHEREVER YOU WANT TO GO IN SOUTH AUSTRALIA, START HERE.

The secret to getting your holiday off to the right start is being armed with all the best information.

If you have access to the internet, begin your South Australian holiday plans by visiting www.southaustralia.com

It's an up to date, simple to follow guide to South Australia's attractions.

The site offers information that's easy to skim plus the ability to search for in-depth detail like accommodation and special interest topics.

You can apply on-line for copies of all the regional 'Secrets' guides, and we'll post them to you.

If you are not an internet user, never fear. The South Australian Visitor and Travel Centre is just a phone call away.

Our experts will help you with all the information you need for a great South Australian holiday. Call them on 1300 655 276.

THE CHIFLEY
ON SOUTH TERRACE
ADELAIDE

★★★★☆ AAAT

RESERVATIONS:
1300 650 464

- Adjacent to extensive parklands and close to city CBD. 15 minutes to airport.
- 94 air-conditioned rooms including executive and junior suites and spa rooms.
- Undercover car parking.
- In-room dining services available 24 hours.
- Licensed Kurrajong restaurant & cocktail bar with open fireplace and lounge.
- TV, personal bar, direct dial phone, tea and coffee making facilities.
- Discounted rates for motoring club members.

Please mention this advertisement.

226 South Terrace, Adelaide SA 5000
Ph: (08) 8223 4355   Fax: (08) 8232 5997
www.chifleyhotels.com

16439AG

GDS BOOKING CODE: TH   ABN 65 065 297 403

★★★★☆ **Adelaide South Park Motel**, (M), Cnr South & West Tce, 2km SW of GPO, ☎ 08 8212 1277, fax 08 8212 3040, (Multi-stry), 98 units [ensuite, bath (28), spa bath (14), a/c, tel, TV, movie, clock radio, t/c mkg, refrig, mini bar], lift, ldry, conv fac, ✕, pool-heated, sauna, spa, rm serv, dinner to unit, gym, cots-fee, non smoking rms (51). **RO** � **$149,** ⟊ **$149,** ⟊ **$15**, ch con, AE BC DC EFT MC VI.

★★★★☆ **Hotel Richmond**, (LH), 128 Rundle Mall, ☎ 08 8223 4044, fax 08 8232 2290, 31 rms (7 suites) [ensuite, bath (31), hairdry, a/c, tel, TV, radio, t/c mkg, refrig], iron, iron brd, conf fac, ✕, rm serv, c/park-fee, ✆, cots, non smoking rms (16). **RO** ⟊ **$110 - $240,** ⟊ **$110 - $240,** ⟊ **$25**, 9 rooms ★★★. AE BC BTC DC EFT JCB MC VI.

★★★★☆ **Novotel Adelaide on Hindley**, (LH), Previously Hindley Parkroyal 65 Hindley St, ☎ 08 8231 5552, fax 08 8237 3800, (Multi-stry), 181 rms (41 suites) [ensuite, bath, hairdry, a/c, tel, fax (8), TV, video-fee, movie-fee, radio, t/c mkg, refrig, mini bar, cook fac (41)], lift, iron, iron brd, business centre, conf fac, ✕, pool-heated, sauna, spa, bicycle-fee, gym, non smoking flr (8). **RO** ⟊ **$192,** ⟊ **$192,** ⟊ **$27, Suite D $235**, ch con, AE BC JCB MC VI, ⟊.

★★★★☆ **The Chifley on South Terrace**, (LH), 226 South Tce, ☎ 08 8223 4355, fax 08 8232 5997, (Multi-stry gr fl), 94 rms (4 suites) [ensuite, bath (38), spa bath (4), hairdry, a/c, tel, TV, movie, clock radio, t/c mkg, refrig], lift, ldry, w/mach-fee, dryer-fee, iron, iron brd, business centre, ✕, pool, 24hr reception, rm serv, gym, cots-fee, non smoking rms (66). **RO** ⟊ **$150 - $181,** ⟊ **$150 - $181,** ⟊ **$27.50, Suite D $180 - $197**, ch con, AE BC DC EFT MC VI.

★★★★ **Adelaide Riviera Motel & Function Centre**, (M), 31 North Tce, 1km NW of PO, ☎ 08 8231 8000, fax 08 8212 2168, (Multi-stry), 84 units [ensuite, spa bath (16), hairdry, a/c, tel, TV, clock radio, t/c mkg, refrig, mini bar], lift, ldry, conf fac, ✕, rm serv, cots-fee, non smoking rms (21). **D** ⟊ **$121 - $170,** ⟊ **$121 - $170, RO** ⟊ **$22**, ch con, AE BC DC MC VI.

FLAG CHOICE *Hotels*

★★★★☆
AAA Tourism

ADELAIDE
South Park

Winner Flag Excellence
Award 1999
Qantas & Ansett
Frequent Flyer Points
Redeemable

Centrally located in the heart of Adelaide City

ADELAIDE SOUTH PARK
1 South Tce. ADELAIDE S.A. 5000
Ph: (08) 8212 1277 Fax: (08) 8212 3040
Email: sales@southpark.com.au www.southpark.com.au

16419AG

Coming to Adelaide?

Stay at the Adelaide Riviera, perfectly positioned on North Terrace, Adelaide's cultural boulevard. On business, or just sightseeing? Take advantage of our ideal location where everything is within easy reach. Want the comforts of home? Relax in our spacious suites or our executive spa suites. On a budget? Experience quality accommodation at economic prices. Planning an event? Our versatile function rooms cater for any occasion. Want more? Enjoy the informal surrounds of Cafe 31, our fully licensed restaurant. The Adelaide Riviera ... Just perfect for you.

16485AG

ADELAIDE RIVIERA
MOTEL & FUNCTION
CENTRE
31-34 North Terrace Adelaide SA 5000
Email: riviera@bigpond.com.au
Internet: www.adelaideriviera.com.au
Free call reservations 1800 061 300

★★★★ **Saville Park Suites Adelaide**, (LMH), 255 Hindley St, ☎ 08 8217 2500, fax 08 8217 2519, (Multi-stry), 141 units (Studio & 2 bedrm), [shwr, tlt, hairdry, a/c, tel, TV, video (4)-fee, movie (6), clock radio, CD (24), refrig, mini bar, cook fac], lift, ldry, w/mach (116), dryer (116), ☒, 24hr reception, secure park-fee, cots, non smoking units (96). **RO 👥 $125, 👥👥 $169**, ch con, AE BC DC MC VI.

★★★☆ **Centra Adelaide - Tower Wing**, (LH), 208 South Tce, ☎ 08 8223 2744, fax 08 8224 0519, (Multi-stry), 134 rms [ensuite, bath, hairdry, a/c, tel, TV, movie-fee, clock radio, t/c mkg, refrig, mini bar], lift, ldry, iron, iron brd, conf fac, ☒, pool, rm serv, cots, non smoking rms (78). **RO 👤 $121, 👥 $121, 🧒 $27.50**, ch con, AE BC DC JCB MC MP VI.

★★★☆ **(Parkside Wing)**, (2 stry gr fl), 60 units [ensuite, bath (13), a/c-cool, heat, tel, TV, video, movie-fee, clock radio, t/c mkg, refrig, mini bar], iron, iron brd, non smoking rms (34). **RO 👤 $104.50, 👥 $104.50, 🧒 $27.50**, ch con.

★★★☆ **Directors Studio Hotel**, (LH), 259 Gouger St, ☎ 08 8213 2500, fax 08 8213 2519, (Multi-stry), 58 rms [ensuite, bath (36), hairdry (36), a/c, tel, TV, clock radio, t/c mkg, refrig, mini bar (36), micro (36), doonas], lift, ldry-fee, rm serv, c/park (undercover) (20), cots, non smoking rms (24). **RO 👤 $83 - $100, 👥 $83 - $100, 🧒 $20**, AE BC DC MC VI.

★★★☆ **Grosvenor Vista Hotel**, (LH), 125 North Tce, ☎ 08 8407 8888, fax 08 8407 8866, (Multi-stry), 290 rms [ensuite, bath (25), a/c-cool (seasonal), tel, TV, clock radio, t/c mkg, refrig, mini bar], lift, ldry, lounge, conf fac, ☒, sauna, rm serv, secure park-fee, gym, cots, non smoking units (100). **RO 👤 $105 - $135, 👥 $105 - $135**, ch con, 16 rms ★★★★☆. Min book applies, AE BC DC EFT JCB MC VI.

★★★☆ **Strathmore Hotel**, (LH), 129 North Tce, 1km N of GPO, ☎ 08 8238 2900, fax 08 823 5475, (2 stry), 6 rms [ensuite, bath, hairdry, a/c, tel, TV, clock radio, t/c mkg, refrig], ☒ (Mon to Sat), rm serv, dinner to unit, c/park (undercover), 📞, non smoking rms (2). **RO 👤 $104.50 - $120, 👥 $104.50 - $120, 🧒 $10**, AE BC DC EFT MC VI.

GOLDEN CHAIN ★★★ **Adelaide Paringa Motel**, (M), 15 Hindley St, ☎ 08 8231 1000, fax 08 8231 6807, (Multi-stry), 45 units [ensuite, spa bath (9), a/c, elec blkts, tel, TV, clock radio, t/c mkg, refrig, mini bar], lift, rm serv, c/park (undercover), cots. **RO 👤 $88 - $150, 👥 $107 - $150, 🧒 $20**, ch con, AE BC DC EFT JCB MC MP VI, ♿.

Budget Motel Chain International ★★★ **Festival Lodge Motel**, (M), Entrance fr Bank St. 140 North Tce, 500m N of PO ☎ 08 8212 7877, fax 08 8211 8137, (Multi-stry), 44 units [ensuite, hairdry (4), a/c, elec blkts, tel, TV, movie, clock radio, t/c mkg, refrig], lift, ldry-fee, conf fac, ☒ (Thur to Sat), c/park (undercover)-fee, cots, non smoking rms (11). **BLB 👤 $90, 👥 $110, 🧒 $20**, AE BC DC EFT MC VI.

★★☆ **Adelaide City Park Motel**, (M), 471 Pulteney St, ☎ 08 8223 1444, fax 08 8223 1133, 18 units [ensuite, a/c, tel, TV, clock radio, t/c mkg, refrig, micro (avail), toaster], cots. **RO 👤 $64.90, 👥 $75.90 - $86.90, 🧒 $10**, ch con, AE BC DC MC VI.

★★☆ **City Central Motel**, (M), 23 Hindley St, ☎ 08 8231 4049, fax 08 8231 4804, (2 stry), 12 units [ensuite, a/c, fan, tel, TV, clock radio, t/c mkg, refrig, toaster], c/park-fee, cots-fee. **RO 👤 $59, 👥 $65, 👥👤 $82.50, 🧒 $10**, AE BC DC MC VI.

★★☆ **Motel Adjacent Casino**, (M), 25 Bank St, 750m NW of PO, ☎ 08 8231 8881, fax 08 8231 1021, (Multi-stry), 47 units [ensuite, a/c, tel, TV, clock radio, t/c mkg, refrig, toaster], lift, iron, iron brd, **RO 👤 $45 - $79, 👥 $79 - $89, 🧒 $15**, ch con, AE BC DC EFT MC VI.

ADELAIDE - SA continued...

★★☆ **Princes Arcade Motel**, (M), 262 Hindley St, ☎ 08 8231 9524, fax 08 8231 2671, (Multi-stry gr fl), 16 units [ensuite, hairdry (on request), a/c, elec blkts, tel, fax, TV, t/c mkg, refrig, toaster], ldry, iron (avail), iron brd (avail), cots-fee. RO ♦ $55 - $60, ♦♦ $70 - $80, ◊ $15, ch con, BC EFT MC VI.

★★ **Ambassadors Hotel**, (LH), 107 King William St, town centre, ☎ 08 8231 4331, fax 08 8231 5521, (Multi-stry), 30 rms [ensuite, bath (4), a/c, tel, TV, t/c mkg, refrig], lift, ldry, ✕ (licensed), cots. RO ♦ $55, ♦♦ $72, ◊ $20, ch con, AE BC DC EFT JCB MC VI.

★★ **Clarice Motel**, (M), 220 Hutt St, 1.5km from CBD, ☎ 08 8223 3560, fax 08 8224 0788, 6 units [ensuite, a/c-cool, heat, TV, t/c mkg, refrig], c/park (off street/limited). BLB ♦ $70, ♦♦ $70, ◊ $11, ch con, weekly con, AE BC DC EFT MC VI.

★ **(Private Hotel Section)**, 17 rms [ensuite (1), shwr (4), tlt (4), a/c-cool (4), c/fan (17), heat, TV], t/c mkg shared, cots-fee, BLB ♦ $43, ♦♦ $55, ◊ $11, ch con, weekly con, Min book applies.

★☆ **Brecknock Hotel**, (LH), 401 King William St, ☎ 08 8231 5467, fax 08 8410 1968, (2 stry), 8 rms [basin, a/c-cool (8), c/fan, heat, elec blkts], lounge (TV), conv fac, ✉, t/c mkg shared, refrig, bbq, c/park (limited), ☎. BLB ♦ $40, ♦♦ $55, ♦♦♦ $75, ◊ $15, ch con, AE BC DC EFT MC VI.

Austral Hotel, (LH), No children's facilities, 205 Rundle St, ☎ 08 8223 4660, fax 08 8223 4175, (2 stry), 14 rms [basin, t/c mkg], ✉, ☎. RO ♦ $35, ♦♦ $55, ♦♦♦ $70, ♦♦♦♦ $80, ◊ $20, AE BC EFT MC VI.

Kings Head Hotel, (LH), 357 King William St, cnr Sturt St, ☎ 08 8212 6657, fax 08 8231 2602, (2 stry), 8 rms [heat (avail)], ldry, lounge (TV), t/c mkg shared, refrig, ☎. RO ♦ $35, ♦♦ $45, ◊ $25, BC EFT MC VI.

Metropolitan Hotel, (LH), 46 Grote St, ☎ 08 8231 5471, fax 08 8231 0633, 26 rms ldry, ✕, ☎. RO ♦ $27.50, ♦♦ $44, ◊ $15, Key Deposit $10. AE BC DC EFT MC VI.

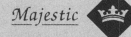 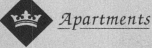

Self Catering Accommodation

★★★★☆ **Adelaide Parklands City Townhouse**, (Apt), No children's facilities, 5/376 South Tce, 1.5km SE of GPO, ☎ 08 8223 1832, fax 08 8223 1832, (2 stry), 1 apt acc up to 4, (3 bedrm), [shwr, bath, tlt (2), hairdry, a/c, tel, TV, video, clock radio (cassette), CD, t/c mkg, refrig, cook fac, micro, elec frypan, d/wash, toaster, ldry (in unit), blkts, linen, pillows], w/mach, dryer, iron, iron brd, bbq, secure park, non smoking units, **D ♦ $110, ♦♦ $120, ♦ $20, W ♦ $623, ♦♦ $693**, Min book applies, AE BC DC MC VI.

★★★★ **(McLaren St Section)**, No children's facilities, 1 cotg acc up to 4, (2 bedrm), [shwr, bath, tlt, hairdry, a/c, fan, c/fan, heat (elec/wood), tel, TV, video, clock radio, CD, t/c mkg, refrig, cook fac, micro, d/wash, blkts, doonas, linen, pillows], w/mach, dryer, c/park (2), non smoking property, **D ♦ $110, ♦♦ $120, ♦ $20, W ♦ $623, ♦♦ $693**, Security System, Min book applies.

★★★★☆ **East End Astoria Apartments**, (SA), 33 Vardon Ave, ☎ 08 8224 2400, fax 08 8224 0820, (2 stry gr fl), 32 serv apts acc up to 4, [shwr, bath (30), tlt, hairdry, a/c, tel, TV, video, clock radio, t/c mkg, refrig, cook fac, micro, toaster, blkts, linen, pillows], w/mach, dryer, iron, iron brd, cots-fee, non smoking rms (8), **D $163 - $218, W $966**, ch con, Min book long w/ends, AE BC DC EFT MC VI, ♦♦.

★★★★☆ **Franklin Central Apartments**, (SA), Previously Franklin Central Quest Inn, 36 Franklin St, 100m W of PO, ☎ 08 8221 7050, fax 08 8210 6333, (Multi-stry), 68 serv apts acc up to 5, (1, 2 & 3 bedrm), [shwr, tlt, hairdry, a/c, tel, TV, movie, clock radio, t/c mkg, refrig, cook fac, micro, d/wash, toaster, ldry, blkts, linen, pillows], w/mach, dryer, iron, iron brd, conf fac, ✗, rm serv, dinner to unit, c/park (limited), cots. **D $160 - $375**, ch con, AE BC DC EFT MC VI.

★★★★☆ **The Adelaide Ritz All Suites Hotel**, (SA), 88 Frome St, 600m NE of GPO, ☎ 08 8223 9000, fax 08 8223 9099, 58 serv apts acc up to 7, (1 bedrm2 bedrm3 bedrm Studio), [shwr, bath (10), spa bath (2), tlt, hairdry, a/c, tel, TV, movie, clock radio, t/c mkg, refrig, mini bar, cook fac ltd (16), micro, d/wash (29), toaster], ldry, w/mach (30), dryer (30), iron, iron brd, conf fac, ✗, rm serv, dinner to unit, secure park, non smoking rms (avail). **D $170 - $400**, AE BC DC MC VI.

★★★★ **Adelaide Regent Apartments**, (Apt), 177 Angas St, 700m SE of GPO, ☎ 1800 242 503, fax 08 8232 2583, (Multi-stry gr fl), 184 apts acc up to 5, (2 & 3 bedrm), [shwr, bath, tlt, tel, fax, TV, video, t/c mkg, refrig, cook fac, micro, toaster, ldry (in unit), blkts, doonas, linen, pillows], lift, w/mach, dryer, iron, iron brd, sauna, spa, secure park, gym, tennis, cots. **D $92.50 - $154, ♦ $16.50**, ch con, AE BC DC EFT MC VI.

★★★★ **Adelaide Terrace Apartments**, (Apt), 80 Sturt St, 500m W of GPO, ☎ 08 8294 5004, fax 08 8294 5004, (2 stry), 3 apts acc up to 4, (2 bedrm), [shwr, bath, tlt, hairdry, a/c-cool, heat, elec blkts, tel, TV, video (avail), clock radio, CD (2), t/c mkg, refrig, cook fac, micro, elec frypan, toaster, ldry (in unit), blkts, linen, pillows], w/mach, dryer, iron, iron brd, c/park (carport), cots, non smoking units. **D ♦♦ $140, ♦ $12, W ♦♦ $840, ♦ $72**, Min book applies, BC MC VI.

AAA TOURISM *Special Rates*
★★★★ **Apartments On The Park**, (SA), 274 South Tce, ☎ 08 8223 0500, fax 08 8223 0588, (Multi-stry gr fl), 62 serv apts (2 bedrm Studio), [shwr, bath (42), spa bath (2), tlt, a/c, heat, tel, TV, video-fee, clock radio, t/c mkg, refrig, cook fac, micro, toaster, ldry (individual)], iron, iron brd, rm serv, c/park (undercover), cots, non smoking units (35). **D ♦ $127.50 - $165, ♦♦ $127.50 - $165, ♦ $17**, ch con, Light breakfast available. AE BC DC MC VI, ♦♦.

★★★★ Treacles Row Cottages, (Cotg), 11 - 19 Gray St, 1km W of PO, ☎ 08 8299 9092, fax 08 8373 2114, 5 cotgs acc up to 6, (1 & 3 bedrm), [shwr, spa bath, tlt, a/c-cool, heat, tel, TV, video, clock radio, refrig, cook fac, micro, d/wash, toaster, blkts, linen, pillows], w/mach, dryer, breakfast ingredients, non smoking property. **D ♦♦ $165**, ♦ **$25**, Min book applies, AE BC DC MC VI.

★★★☆ Adelaide Old Terraces, (Cotg), Previously The Old Terrace 108 South Tce, 700m S of GPO, ☎ 08 8364 5437, fax 08 8364 6961, (2 stry), 1 cotg acc up to 7, (3 bedrm), [shwr (2), bath, tlt (2), a/c, fire pl, heat, elec blkts, tel, TV, video, clock radio, t/c mkg, refrig, cook fac, micro, toaster, blkts, doonas, linen, pillows], w/mach, dryer, iron, iron brd, cots, breakfast ingredients. **D ♦♦ $130**, ♦ **$40**, **W $770**, ch con, fam con, pen con, Min book applies, AE BC JCB MC VI.

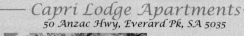

Trouble-free travel tips - Tyre wear
Check tyre treads for uneven wear and inspect tyre walls and tread for damage.

★★★☆ City Apartments, (HU), 25 Norman St, 500m W of PO, ☎ 08 8274 1222, fax 08 8272 7371, 6 units acc up to 6, (1, 2 & 3 bedrm), [shwr, bath, tlt, a/c, tel, TV, t/c mkg, refrig, cook fac, micro, d/wash, toaster, doonas], ldry, cots. **D ♦♦ $132 - $174.90**, AE BC DC MC VI.

★★★☆ (South Terrace), 366 South Tce, 6 units acc up to 4, (2 bedrm), [shwr, tlt, TV, clock radio, refrig, cook fac, micro, d/wash, blkts, linen, pillows], ldry, c/park (carport). **D ♦♦ $149.60**.

★★★☆ Florences Cottage, (Cotg), 14 Ely Pl, 800m E of GPO, ☎ 08 8364 5437, fax 08 8364 6961, (2 stry gr fl), 1 cotg acc up to 4, [shwr, tlt, hairdry, a/c-cool, fire pl, heat, elec blkts, tel, TV, video, clock radio, CD, t/c mkg, refrig, cook fac, micro, toaster, doonas, linen, pillows], w/mach, iron, iron brd, breakfast ingredients, non smoking property. **D ♦♦ $130**, ♦ **$45**, **W ♦♦ $770**, ch con, Min book applies, AE BC JCB MC VI.

★★★☆ Harriett's Cottage Accommodation, (Cotg), 31 Harriett St, 700m SE of GPO, ☎ 08 8271 6724, fax 08 8271 6724, 1 cotg acc up to 4, (2 bedrm), [shwr, tlt, evap cool, fan, c/fan, heat (elec), elec blkts, TV, clock radio, t/c mkg, refrig, cook fac, micro, toaster, blkts, doonas, linen, pillows], w/mach, dryer, cots-fee, non smoking property. **D ♦ $62 - $95**, ♦♦ **$62 - $95**, ♦ **$18 - $20**, **W ♦ $434**, ♦♦ **$434**, ♦ **$108**, ch con.

★★★☆ Kookaburra Cottage, (Cotg), 12 James St, ☎ 08 8299 9092, fax 08 8373 2114, 1 cotg acc up to 4, (1 bedrm), [shwr, tlt, a/c-cool, heat, tel, TV, video, clock radio, CD, refrig, cook fac, blkts, linen, pillows], w/mach, non smoking property, Pets on application. **D $120**, AE BC DC MC VI.

★★★☆ The Mansions Quest Inn, (SA), 21 Pulteney St, ☎ 08 8232 0033, fax 08 8223 4559, (Multi-stry), 52 serv apts acc up to 4, (1 bedrm Studio), [shwr, bath, tlt, a/c, tel, TV, video (3), movie, clock radio, t/c mkg, refrig, cook fac, micro, toaster], lift, ldry, ⊠, cafe, bar, sauna, spa, bbq, rm serv, c/park-fee, cots, non smoking property. **D ♦♦ $127 - $182**, ♦ **$17**, AE BC DC MC VI.

★★★☆ Wisteria Terrace, (Cotg), 26 Blackburn St, 900m SE of GPO, ☎ 08 8364 5437, fax 08 8364 6961, (2 stry gr fl), 1 cotg acc up to 7, (4 bedrm), [shwr, tlt, a/c, fan, c/fan, heat (elec/wood), elec blkts (4), tel, TV, video, clock radio, t/c mkg, refrig, cook fac, micro, toaster, blkts, doonas (4)], w/mach, dryer, lounge firepl, cots-fee, breakfast ingredients, non smoking property. **D ♦♦ $150**, ♦ **$45**, **W ♦♦ $910**, ch con, Min book applies, AE BC JCB MC VI.

ADELAIDE - ALDGATE SA 5154

Pop Part of Adelaide, (21km SE Adelaide), See map on page 588, ref D5. Located in the Adelaide Hills. The town which grew around the Aldgate Pump Hotel. The pump was installed for horses and bullocks and is still working today. Bush Walking, Scenic Drives.

B&B's/Guest Houses

★★★★★ **Chatsworth Manor Bed & Breakfast**, (B&B), No children's facilities, 3 Eton Rd, ☎ 08 8339 1455, fax 08 8339 1655, (2 stry), 2 rms [ensuite, spa bath, hairdry, a/c, elec blkts, tel, TV, video, movie, clock radio, CD, t/c mkg, refrig, mini bar], iron, iron brd, dinner to unit, non smoking rms, BLB ♦ **$150 - $235**, ♦♦ **$150 - $235**, AE BC DC EFT MC VI.

★★★★☆ **Arboury Manor**, (B&B), No children's facilities, 11 Nation Ridge Rd, 2km SE of PO, ☎ 08 8370 9119, fax 08 8370 9484, (2 stry gr fl), 4 rms [ensuite, hairdry, a/c, fan, cent heat, elec blkts, TV, video, clock radio, CD, t/c mkg, refrig, toaster], iron, iron brd, cook fac, bbq, meals avail, courtesy transfer, non smoking property. BB ♦♦ **$130 - $210**, AE BC DC MC VI.

★★★★☆ **Peacepoint Bed & Breakfast**, (B&B), 8 Arkaba Rd, 500m N of PO, ☎ 08 8370 8429, fax 08 8370 8429, 1 rm (1 suite) [ensuite, spa bath, hairdry, a/c, c/fan, heat, elec blkts, TV, clock radio, CD, t/c mkg, refrig, micro, toaster], w/mach, dryer, non smoking property. BB ♦ **$120 - $140**, ♦♦ **$125 - $160**, ♦ **$40**.

★★★★ **Aldgate Lodge Bed & Breakfast**, (B&B), 27 Strathalbyn Rd, 250m SE of PO, ☎ 08 8370 9957, fax 08 8370 9749, 3 rms (2 suites) [shwr, spa bath (double), tlt, a/c-cool (2), c/fan (2), heat, elec blkts, TV, video, clock radio, CD, t/c mkg, refrig, doonas], lounge (guest, log fire), non smoking property. BB ♦♦ **$125 - $190**, Min book long w/ends and Easter, BC MC VI.

★★★☆ **Chippings Cottage Bed & Breakfast**, (B&B), 32 Ludgate Hill Rd, 1km E PO, ☎ 08 8339 1008, fax 08 8339 1008, 1 rm [ensuite, a/c-cool, fire pl, heat, tel, TV, radio, t/c mkg, refrig], bbq. BB ♦ **$80**, ♦♦ **$90 - $100**, weekly con.

ADELAIDE - ALDINGA BEACH SA 5173

Pop 3,541. (43km S Adelaide), See map on page 588, ref B8. A small township situated on the Wine Coast. Boat Ramp, Boating, Fishing, Swimming, Vineyards, Wineries.

Self Catering Accommodation

★★★☆ **Aldinga Bay Holiday Village**, (HU), 209 The Esplanade, ☎ 08 8556 5019, fax 08 8556 5751, 20 units acc up to 12, (2 bedrm), [shwr, tlt, a/c, TV, refrig, cook fac, linen reqd-fee], ldry, w/mach-fee, dryer-fee, iron, iron brd, rec rm, pool-heated (solar), bbq, boat park, car wash, plygr, D **$71 - $120**, W **$435 - $765**, BC MC VI.

Cockleshell Cottage B&B, (Cotg), 10 Boomerang Ave, 45km SW of Adelaide, ☎ 08 8556 3722, fax 08 8556 3722, 1 cotg acc up to 5, (2 bedrm), [shwr, bath, tlt, a/c, c/fan (2), heat, elec blkts (4), TV, video, clock radio, t/c mkg, refrig, cook fac, micro, toaster, blkts, doonas (4), BB ♦ **$135**, ♦♦ **$135**, ♦ **$10**, D ♦ **$100**, ♦♦ **$100**, (not yet classified).

B&B's/Guest Houses

★★★★☆ **Illawarra Bed & Breakfast**, (B&B), 19 Morgan St, 2km SW of PO, ☎ 08 8557 7740, fax 08 8557 7740, (2 stry), 2 rms [ensuite, a/c-cool, heat, elec blkts, TV, clock radio, t/c mkg], lounge, bbq, meals avail, c/park. D **$145**.

★★★★☆ **Seadrift Point Bed & Breakfast**, (B&B), No children's facilities, 193 Esplanade, 1km E of PO, ☎ 08 8556 5342, 1 rm (1 suite) [ensuite, spa bath, hairdry, TV, video], BB ♦♦ **$150**, ♦ **$125**.

ADELAIDE - ASHTON SA 5137

Pop Part of Adelaide, (14km SE Adelaide), See map on page 588, ref D4. A small Adelaide Hills township within the fruit orchard districts which characterise this portion of the Mount Lofty Ranges. Scenic Drives, Vineyards, Wineries.

Self Catering Accommodation

 ★★★☆ **Abba Bed & Breakfast**, (HU), Lot A, Coach Rd, Situated on Adelaide Hill's Face, ☎ 08 8390 1172, fax 08 8390 1172, 1 unit acc up to 4, (1 bedrm), [shwr, tlt, a/c, fire pl, TV, video, clock radio, CD, refrig, cook fac, micro, doonas, linen, pillows], w/mach, spa (pool), c/park (carport), cots (avail). BB ♦♦ **$150 - $250**, ♦ **$75**, ♦♦ **$840**, Min book applies. BC MC VI.

Operator Comment: UBD Reference 133 B1 & 2. Visit our website on www.abba.com.au

ADELAIDE - BASKET RANGE SA 5138

Pop Part of Adelaide, (20km Adelaide), See map on page 588, ref E4. A small dormitory town for Adelaide in dramatic ridge country of the Adelaide Hills. While various aspects of agriculture have been pursued, fruit orchards are dominant. Scenic Drives.

Self Catering Accommodation

★★★★ **Bishops of Basket Range Cottages**, (Cotg), Adelaide-Lobethal Rd, 22km E of GPO, ☎ 08 8390 3469, fax 08 8390 3469, 2 cotgs acc up to 2, (1 bedrm), [shwr, spa bath (1), tlt, fan (1), c/fan (1), fire pl (1), heat, elec blkts, TV (1), radio, CD (1), refrig, cook fac (1), micro (1), blkts, doonas (1), linen, pillows], breakfast ingredients, non smoking rms. BLB ♦♦ **$80 - $180**, D **$80 - $180**, 1 cottage of a lower rating, Collect keys at Tetratheca Homestead, Adelaide - Lobethal Rd. Min book applies.

ADELAIDE - BELAIR SA 5052

Pop Part of Adelaide, (13km S Adelaide), See map on page 588, ref C5. A hills suburb of Adelaide. Golf, Horse Riding, Tennis.

Self Catering Accommodation

★★☆ **Uniting Church Accommodation**, (HU), Nunyara House Holiday Units. 5 Burnell Dve, ☎ 08 8278 1673, fax 08 8278 4117, 5 units acc up to 8, (1 bedrm), [bath (hip), tlt, c/fan, heat, TV, refrig, cook fac, linen reqd-fee], ldry, cots, non smoking property. D **$55**, W **$330**, BC MC VI.

ADELAIDE - BELLEVUE HEIGHTS SA 5050

Pop Part of Adelaide, (13km S Adelaide), See map on page 588, ref C5. A suburb of Adelaide.

B&B's/Guest Houses

★★★☆ **The Heights Bed & Breakfast**, (B&B), 38 Ridgehaven Dve, Adjacent to Flinders University & Hospital, ☎ 08 8277 8793, fax 08 8277 8793, (2 stry), 3 rms (Studio), [ensuite (1), hairdry (1), a/c, elec blkts, tel, clock radio], ldry-fee, w/mach-fee, dryer (avail)-fee, iron, iron brd, lounge (TV & video), pool, t/c mkg shared, bbq, meals avail (by arrangement), cots, non smoking rms. BLB ♦ **$45 - $65**, ♦♦ **$75 - $90**, ♦ **$45**, ch con, fam con, BC MC VI.

ADELAIDE - BLACKWOOD SA 5051

Pop Part of Adelaide, (13km S Adelaide), See map on page 588, ref C5. A hills suburb of Adelaide. Wittunga Botanic Gardens and Gamble Cottage Gardens. Golf, Tennis.

B&B's/Guest Houses

★★★★★ **Allessandro Maandini's Ryokan**, (B&B), 16 Brightview Ave, ☎ 0412 178 026, fax 08 8370 3507, 3 rms (3 suites) [ensuite, spa bath, hairdry, fan, heat, elec blkts, tel, TV, t/c mkg, refrig], sauna (1), bbq. BB ♦ **$150**, ♦♦ **$300**, BC MC VI.

ADELAIDE - BLAIR ATHOL SA 5084

Pop Part of Adelaide, (7km N Adelaide), See map on page 588, ref C3. A suburb of Adelaide.

Hotels/Motels

 ★★★★ **Sombrero Motel**, (M), 288-292 Main North Rd, ☎ 08 8269 3655, fax 08 8344 5642, (2 stry gr fl), 45 units [ensuite, bath (11), hairdry (35), a/c, elec blkts (on request), tel, TV, video (avail), movie, clock radio, t/c mkg, refrig, cook fac (9), toaster], ldry-fee, w/mach (8), dryer (8), iron, iron brd, conf fac, ✉ (Mon to Fri), pool-heated, sauna, spa, 24hr reception, rm serv, cots-fee, non smoking rms. D ♦ **$96 - $135**, ♦♦ **$101 - $145**, ♦ **$20**, ch con, AE BC DC JCB MC VI, &.

ADELAIDE - BRIDGEWATER SA 5155

Pop 3,735. (25km Adelaide), See map on page 588, ref E5. Small township in the Adelaide Hills. Scenic Drives, Vineyards, Wineries.

Self Catering Accommodation

★★★★☆ **St Githas Cottage**, (Cotg), 12 Rosewarne Cres, ☎ 08 8339 1264, 1 cotg acc up to 4, (1 bedrm), [shwr, spa bath, tlt, a/c-cool, fire pl, elec blkts, TV, clock radio, t/c mkg, refrig, mini bar, cook fac, ldry], w/mach, breakfast ingredients. D ♦♦ $140 - $150, ◊ $20, Min book applies.

ADELAIDE - BRIGHTON SA 5048

Pop Part of Adelaide, (13km SW Adelaide), See map on page 588, ref B5. A suburb of Adelaide. Croquet.

Hotels/Motels

★☆ **The Esplanade Hotel**, (LH), 135a Esplanade, ☎ 08 8296 7177, fax 08 8296 8943, (2 stry) 15 rms [ensuite (15), shwr, tlt (16), TV (16), t/c mkg], rec rm, ⊠, cots-fee. RO ♦ $33, ♦♦ $55, ◊ $7, 5 rooms of a lower rating. AE BC DC EFT MC VI.

ADELAIDE - BURNSIDE SA 5066

Pop Part of Adelaide, (8km E Adelaide), See map on page 588, ref D4. An eastern suburb of Adelaide. Waterfall Gully Reserve and Greenhill Recreation Park.

Self Catering Accommodation

★★★☆ **Azalea House Garden Apartment**, (Apt), No children's facilities, 27 Waterfall Gully Rd, ☎ 08 8379 5276, 1 apt acc up to 3, (1 bedrm), [shwr, tlt, a/c, heat, TV (2), clock radio, t/c mkg, refrig (2), cook fac, micro, elec frypan, toaster, blkts, linen, pillows], res liquor license, breakfast ingredients. D ♦♦ $132, W ♦♦ $539.

★★★☆ **Petts Wood Lodge Holiday Units**, (HU), 542 Glynburn Rd, 7km SE of GPO, ☎ 08 8331 9924, fax 08 8332 5139, 2 units acc up to 5, [shwr, tlt, hairdry, a/c-cool, heat, TV, clock radio, refrig, cook fac, cook fac ltd (1), micro, elec frypan, blkts, doonas, linen, pillows], bbq (covered), cots, non smoking property. BLB ♦ $95, ♦♦ $105, ◊ $25, ch con, BC MC VI.

ADELAIDE - CAMDEN PARK SA 5038

Pop Part of Adelaide, (8km SW Adelaide), See map on page 588, ref C4. A suburb of Adelaide.

Self Catering Accommodation

★★☆ **Moorstreet Holiday Units**, (HU), Collect keys from 75 Mooringe Ave. 2&4/75 Mooringe Ave, ☎ 08 8294 5841, fax 08 8350 0330, 2 units acc up to 4, (2 bedrm), [shwr, bath (hip), tlt, a/c-cool (1), a/c (1), heat, TV, clock radio, t/c mkg, refrig, cook fac, micro, toaster, ldry, blkts, linen, pillows], w/mach, dryer, iron, iron brd, c/park (carport). D ♦♦ $60, ◊ $15, W $315 - $630, Min book applies.

ADELAIDE - CAREY GULLY SA 5144

Pop Nominal, (26km Adelaide), See map on page 588, ref E4. A small township in the Adelaide Hills, where fine scenic drives can be enjoyed among country noted for vegetable market gardens and fruit orchards. Scenic Drives.

Self Catering Accommodation

★★★★ **Koolyangarra Bed & Breakfast**, (Cotg), Rangeview Dr, ☎ 08 8390 0238, fax 08 8390 0238, 1 cotg acc up to 4, (2 bedrm), [shwr, tlt, c/fan, heat (wood/pot belly), elec blkts, TV, clock radio, t/c mkg, refrig, cook fac ltd, micro, toaster, blkts, doonas, linen, pillows], iron, iron brd, meals to unit, D ♦♦ $125 - $145, ◊ $35, W ♦♦ $550, ◊ $250, BC MC VI.

★★★★ **Paddy Careys Barn**, (Cotg), Gully Rd, via Stirling, 5km NE of Stirling PO, ☎ 08 8390 3216, fax 08 8390 3216, 1 cotg acc up to 4, (2 bedrm), [shwr (2), bath (1), tlt (2), hairdry (1), fan, fire pl, heat, elec blkts, tel, TV, video, clock radio, CD, refrig, cook fac, micro, blkts, doonas, linen, pillows], ldry, dryer, iron, iron brd, spa, bbq, cots, breakfast ingredients, non smoking property. D ♦♦ $185, ◊ $40, W ♦♦ $750, ◊ $150, Min book applies, BC MC VI.

★ *Trouble-free travel tips* - **Fluids**

Check all fluid levels and top up as necessary. Look at engine oil, automatic transmission fluid, radiator coolant (only check this when the engine is cold), power steering, battery and windscreen washers.

ADELAIDE - CHERRYVILLE SA 5134

Pop Part of Adelaide, (22km Adelaide), See map on page 588, ref E4. A tiny settlement set attractively in a deep valley in the Adelaide Hills.

Self Catering Accommodation

★★★★☆ **The Cherryville Lofts**, (Cotg), No children's facilities, Cherryville Rd, ☎ 08 8390 1375, fax 08 8390 1375, (2 stry) 1 cotg acc up to 2, [shwr, spa bath, tlt, hairdry, a/c-cool, fire pl, heat, tel, TV, video, clock radio (cassette), CD, cook fac, micro, ldry, blkts, linen, pillows], iron, iron brd, rec rm, breakfast ingredients, non smoking property. BLB ♦♦ $150 - $165, Min book applies.

ADELAIDE - CHRISTIES BEACH SA 5165

Pop Part of Adelaide, (32km SW Adelaide), See map on page 588, ref B6. Outer suburb of Adelaide. Boating, Bowls, Fishing, Surfing, Swimming, Tennis.

Hotels/Motels

★★☆ **Christies Beach Hotel Motel**, (LMH), 12-30 Gulf View Rd, 1.2km S of PO, ☎ 08 8382 1166, fax 08 8326 1337, (2 stry gr fl) 20 units [ensuite, a/c, elec blkts, tel, TV, clock radio, t/c mkg, refrig], conv fac, ⊠, pool. RO ♦ $55, ♦♦ $62, ◊ $10, AE BC DC EFT MC VI.

ADELAIDE - CLARENDON SA 5157

Pop Part of Adelaide, (28km S Adelaide), See map on page 588, ref C6. Outer suburb of Adelaide. Bowls, Scenic Drives, Tennis, Vineyards, Wineries.

Hotels/Motels

★★★ **The Old Clarendon Winery**, (M), Millers Rd, off Grants Gully Rd, ☎ 08 8383 6166, fax 08 8383 6487, (Multi-stry), 25 units [ensuite, bath, a/c, elec blkts, tel, TV, clock radio, t/c mkg, refrig], ldry, conf fac, ⊠, cots-fee. RO ♦ $93.50 - $140, ♦♦ $93.50 - $140, ◊ $22 - $33, AE BC DC EFT MC VI, ⅊⅌.

Self Catering Accommodation

★★★★ **Little Hill Farm Cottage**, (Cotg), Lot 21, Clarendon Rd, 2km S of PO, ☎ 08 8383 6509, 1 cotg acc up to 4, (2 bedrm), [shwr, spa bath, tlt, fan, heat, TV, video, clock radio, CD, t/c mkg, refrig, cook fac, micro, toaster, blkts, linen, pillows], cots, breakfast ingredients. D ♦ $65, ♦♦ $130, fam con, Min book applies.

ADELAIDE - COLLEGE PARK SA 5069

Pop part of Adelaide (4.5km NE Adelaide). See map on page 588, ref C3. Inner suburb of Adelaide.

B&B's/Guest Houses

Possums Rest, (B&B), 8 Catherine St, 3km NE of GPO, ☎ 08 8362 5356, fax 08 8362 5356, 1 rm [ensuite (1), a/c, elec blkts, TV, clock radio, t/c mkg, refrig, toaster, doonas], pool, bbq, non smoking rms. BLB ♦♦ $95, (not yet classified).

ADELAIDE - COROMANDEL VALLEY SA 5051

Pop Part of Adelaide, (13km S Adelaide), See map on page 588, ref C5. Southern suburb of Adelaide. Scenic Drives, Vineyards, Wineries.

B&B's/Guest Houses

★★★★★ **Warrawee House Bed & Breakfast**, (B&B), No children's facilities, 177 Coromandel Pde, 2km S of PO, ☎ 08 8278 7391, fax 08 8278 2306, (2 stry) 3 rms (3 suites) [shwr, spa bath (2), tlt, hairdry, a/c, TV, refrig], pool, bbq, non smoking property. BB $160 - $210, 1 room of a lower rating, Min book applies, AE BC MC VI.

ADELAIDE - CRAFERS SA 5152

Pop 3,371. (16km SE Adelaide), See map on page 588, ref D5. First village to be settled in the Adelaide Hills which is set in attractive surroundings. Bush Walking, Golf, Scenic Drives.

B&B's/Guest Houses

★★★★☆ **Grand Mercure Hotel Mount Lofty House**, (GH), 74 Summit Rd, 1km N of PO, ☎ 08 8339 6777, fax 08 8339 5656, (Multi-stry gr fl), 29 rms [ensuite, bath, spa bath (6), hairdry, a/c, tel, TV, clock radio, t/c mkg, refrig, mini bar], iron, iron brd, lounge, conv fac, ⊠, pool-heated, rm serv, tennis, non smoking rms (29). RO ♦♦ $235 - $405, AE BC DC MC VI.

★★★☆ **Stordarlyn Bed & Breakfast**, (B&B), 30 Upper Sturt Rd, 2.2km SE of PO, ☎ 08 8339 4456, 2 rms [ensuite, spa bath (1), hairdry (1), fan, elec blkts, clock radio], spa (pool), bbq, dinner to unit, cots. **BB ♦ $85 - $90, ♦♦ $110 - $125**, ch con, 1 room of a lower rating.

ADELAIDE - DULWICH SA 5065

Pop Part of Adelade, (4km SE Adelaide), See map on page 588, ref C4. A suburb of Adelaide.

Self Catering Accommodation

★★★★ **Adelaide Oakford Apartments**, (Apt), 18 Stuart Rd, ☎ 08 8333 7400, fax 08 8332 7446, 23 apts (1 bedrm), [shwr, tlt, a/c, tel, refrig, cook fac, micro, d/wash, ldry], c/park (carport), cots. **D $93**, AE BC DC MC VI.

ADELAIDE - EAGLE ON THE HILL SA 5150

Pop Part of Adel, (12km SE Adelaide), See map on page 588, ref D4. Scenic lookout over the city of Adelaide, located at the top of the scarp which climbs from the Gully of Glen Osmond. It takes its name from the Eagle on the Hill Hotel.

Hotels/Motels

★★☆ **Eagle on the Hill Hotel Motel**, (LMH), Mt Barker Rd, ☎ 08 8339 2211, fax 08 8339 6922, 6 units [ensuite, a/c (3), heat, elec blkts, TV, clock radio, t/c mkg, refrig, toaster], ⊠, ☎, cots. **BLB ♦ $69.50, ♦♦ $75, ♀ $5**, AE BC DC EFT MC VI.

ADELAIDE - EASTWOOD SA 5063

Pop Part of Adelaide, (2km E Adelaide), See map on page 588, ref C4. Inner suburb of Adelaide.

Hotels/Motels

★★★ **Greenhill Lodge Motel**, (M), 204 Greenhill Rd, ☎ 08 8291 4200, fax 08 8272 9263, (2 stry gr fl), 52 units [ensuite, a/c, tel, TV, clock radio, t/c mkg, refrig], ldry, rec rm, ⊠ (Mon to Fri), bbq, cots, non smoking rms. **RO ♦ $60, ♦♦ $72, ♀ $12**, 3 units yet to be classified. BC EFT MC VI.

Self Catering Accommodation

★★★★ **North Adelaide Heritage Group**, (Cotg), 4 Markey St, 1km SE of Adelaide, ☎ 08 8272 1355, fax 08 8272 1355, 1 cotg acc up to 4, (2 bedrm), [shwr, bath, tlt, hairdry, a/c, c/fan, fire pl, heat, elec blkts, tel, fax (avail), TV, video (avail), radio, refrig, cook fac, micro, ldry, blkts, linen, pillows], w/mach, dryer, iron, cots, non smoking property. **D ♦♦ $140 - $175, ♀ $40**, ch con, AE BC DC JCB MC VI. *Operator Comment: For unique luxury apartment accm. See our award winning web site - www.adelaideheritage.com*

★★★★ **(Plum Cottage)**, 2 Markey St, 1 cotg acc up to 4, (2 bedrm), [shwr, bath, tlt, hairdry, a/c-cool, c/fan (bedroom), fire pl, heat, elec blkts, tel, fax (avail), TV, video (avail), clock radio, CD, refrig, cook fac, micro, ldry, blkts, linen, pillows], w/mach, dryer, iron, non smoking property. **D ♦♦ $140 - $175, ♀ $40**, ch con.

ADELAIDE - ELIZABETH SA 5112

Pop 26,400. (24km N Adelaide), See map on page 588, ref D1. Outer suburb of Adelaide.

Hotels/Motels

 ★★★☆ **Elizabeth Motor Inn**, (M), Cnr Main North & Ifould Rds, Elizabeth Park 5113, ☎ 08 8255 6555, fax 08 8255 6101, 30 units [ensuite, bath (7), a/c, elec blkts, tel, TV, clock radio, t/c mkg, refrig], ldry, w/mach, dryer, iron, iron brd, ⊠, pool, spa, cots-fee, non smoking units (14). **RO ♦ $85 - $120, ♦♦ $85 - $120, ♀ $11**, ch con, 2 units of a higher standard. AE BC DC MC VI, 𝄞⅃.

★★ **Downs Hotel Motel**, (LMH), 212 Midway Rd, ☎ 08 8255 3333, fax 08 8255 3373, 5 units [ensuite, a/c, TV, clock radio, t/c mkg, refrig], iron, ⊠, ☎, cots-fee. **BLB ♦ $45, ♦♦ $50, ♀ $10**, fam con, AE BC DC EFT MC VI.

ADELAIDE - ENFIELD SA 5085

Pop Part of Adelaide, (6km N Adelaide), See map on page 588, ref C3. A suburb of Adelaide.

Hotels/Motels

 ★★★★ **Adelaide Manhattan Motor Inn**, (M), 471 Main North Rd, ☎ 08 8262 2748, fax 08 8349 7619, (2 stry gr fl), 50 units [ensuite, bath (1), spa bath (10), a/c, elec blkts, tel, TV, clock radio, t/c mkg, refrig, cook fac (10), micro (6)], ldry, ⊠, pool, bbq, rm serv, cots-fee, non smoking units (16). **RO ♦ $85, ♦♦ $99 - $154, ♀ $15**, AE BC DC EFT MC VI, 𝄞⅃.

 ★★☆ **Motel Hoffmann**, (M), 393 Main North Rd, ☎ 08 8262 5115, fax 08 8260 2678, (2 stry gr fl), 16 units [ensuite, a/c, tel, TV, video (2), radio, t/c mkg, refrig], ldry, w/mach, dryer, cots. **RO ♦ $55, ♦♦ $66 - $82.50, ♀ $11**, ch con, fam con, pen con, 6 rooms ★★. AE BC DC MC MCH VI.

ADELAIDE - EVERARD PARK SA 5035

Pop Part of Adelaide, (4km S Adelaide), See map on page 588, ref C4. A suburb of Adelaide.

Self Catering Accommodation

★★★☆ **Capri Lodge Holiday Units**, (HU), 50 Anzac Hwy, ☎ 08 8297 1168, fax 08 8179 6222, (2 stry gr fl), 18 units acc up to 5, (1 & 2 bedrm), [shwr, bath (16), tlt, a/c (10), fan, heat, elec blkts, tel (18), TV, clock radio, refrig, cook fac, micro, ldry (1), blkts, linen, pillows], ldry, w/mach, dryer, cots. **D ♦♦ $62 - $74, ♀ $9**, BC EFT MC VI.

ADELAIDE - FREWVILLE SA 5063

Pop Part of Adelaide, (3km SE Adelaide), See map on page 588, ref C4. Suburb of Adelaide.

Hotels/Motels

 ★★☆ **Princes Highway Motel**, (M), 199 Glen Osmond Rd (Highway One), 3km SE of GPO, ☎ 08 8379 9253, fax 08 8379 0809, 25 units [ensuite, a/c, elec blkts, tel, TV, clock radio, t/c mkg, refrig], ldry, cots. **RO ♦ $44 - $52, ♦♦ $49 - $59, ♀ $10**, 9 units ★★★. AE BC DC JCB MC VI.

Self Catering Accommodation

★★★★ **Frewville Lodge Motor Inn**, (SA), Previously Tropicana Serviced Apartments 239 Glen Osmond Rd (Highway One), ☎ 08 8379 6027, fax 08 8379 6305, (2 stry gr fl), 14 serv apts acc up to 5, [ensuite, a/c, elec blkts (on request), tel, TV, t/c mkg, refrig, cook fac, micro], ldry. **D ♦♦ $49 - $88, ♀ $11**, ch con, AE BC DC EFT MC VI.

ADELAIDE - FULHAM SA 5024

Pop Part of Adelaide, (8km SW Adelaide), See map on page 588, ref B4. A suburb of Adelaide.

Hotels/Motels

★★ **Lockleys Hotel**, (LH), Henley Beach Rd, ☎ 08 8356 4822, fax 08 8235 2532, (2 stry), 12 rms [ensuite, a/c, TV, t/c mkg], ⊠, ☎. **D $55**, AE BC DC EFT MC VI.

ADELAIDE - FULLARTON SA 5063

Pop Part of Adelaide, (3km S Adelaide), See map on page 588, ref C4. A suburb of Adelaide.

Hotels/Motels

★★★☆ **Arkaba Motel**, (LMH), 150 Glen Osmond Rd,
☎ 08 8338 1100, fax 08 8338 1905, (Multi-stry gr fl), 29 units (5 suites) [shwr, spa bath (15), tlt, a/c, tel, TV, clock radio, t/c mkg, refrig], ⊠, cots. **RO** ♦♦ **$95,** ◊ **$30, Suite D $140 - $235,** 6 units ★★★★. BC MC VI.

★★★☆ **Keans Arkaba Court Motel**, (M), 232 Glen Osmond Rd (Highway One), 3.7km SE of PO, ☎ 08 8379 1645, fax 08 8338 2177, (Multi-stry gr fl), 21 units [ensuite, spa bath (10), a/c, tel, TV, movie, clock radio, t/c mkg, refrig], ldry, lounge (TV), pool, sauna, spa, dinner to unit, cots-fee. **RO** ♦ **$75,** ♦♦ **$85,** ◊ **$10,** ch con, 7 units ★★☆. AE BC DC MC VI.

★★★ **Fullarton Motor Lodge**, (M), 284 Glen Osmond Rd, 3km SE of PO, ☎ 08 8379 9797, fax 08 8338 2118, (2 stry gr fl), 20 units [ensuite, a/c, elec blkts, tel, TV, clock radio, t/c mkg, refrig, cook fac-fee], pool, rm serv, cots-fee. **RO** ♦ **$40,** ♦♦ **$40 - $50,** ◊ **$8 - $10,** BC MC VI.

★★★ **Sands Motel**, (M), 198 Glen Osmond Rd (Highway One), ☎ 08 8379 0066, fax 08 8379 0169, (2 stry gr fl), 20 units [ensuite, a/c, tel, TV, clock radio, t/c mkg, refrig, toaster], pool, cots-fee. **RO** ♦ **$50 - $55,** ♦♦ **$55 - $60,** ◊ **$11,** ch con, 5 rooms with 2.5 star rating, AE BC DC EFT MC VI.

Self Catering Accommodation

★★★ **Keans Arkaba Court Holiday Units**, (HU), 232 Glen Osmond Rd (Highway One), 3.7km SE of PO, ☎ 08 8379 1645, fax 08 8338 2177, 22 units acc up to 5, [shwr, bath, spa bath (5), tlt, a/c, tel, TV, movie, clock radio, refrig, cook fac, toaster, blkts, linen, pillows], ldry, pool, sauna, spa, cots-fee. **D $85 - $160,** ch con, AE BC DC MC VI.

ADELAIDE - GEPPS CROSS SA 5094

Pop Part of Adelaide, (10km N Adelaide), See map on page 588, ref C3. A suburb of Adelaide.

Hotels/Motels

★★★★☆ **Quality Inn Adelaide Manor**, (M), 574 Main North Rd, ☎ 08 8349 4999, fax 08 8349 4631, (2 stry gr fl), 46 units [ensuite, bath (8), spa bath (8), a/c, elec blkts, tel, cable tv, movie, clock radio, t/c mkg, refrig, micro (3)], w/mach-fee, dryer, iron, iron brd, conf fac, ⊠, pool, spa, cots-fee, non smoking rms (8), **RO** ♦ **$117 - $165,** ♦♦ **$117 - $165,** ◊ **$15,** ch con, AE BC DC MC VI, ♿.

ADELAIDE - GILLES PLAINS SA 5086

Pop Part of Adelaide, (10km NE Adelaide), See map on page 588, ref D3. A suburb of Adelaide.

Hotels/Motels

★★ **Highlander Hotel Motel**, (LMH), 647 North East Rd, ☎ 08 8261 5288, fax 08 8369 0643, 11 units [ensuite, a/c, elec blkts, TV, t/c mkg, refrig, toaster], ✗, cots-fee, non smoking rms (2). **BLB** ♦ **$70,** ♦♦ **$70,** ◊ **$5,** fam con, AE BC MC VI.

ADELAIDE - GLEN OSMOND SA 5064

Pop Part of Adelaide, (6km SE Adelaide), See map on page 588, ref D4. A suburb of Adelaide.

Hotels/Motels

★★☆ **Tollgate Motel**, (M), 20 Mount Barker Rd (Highway One), ☎ 08 8379 1651, fax 08 8379 1094, (2 stry gr fl), 37 units [ensuite, spa bath (1), a/c, elec blkts, tel, TV, t/c mkg, refrig, cook fac (3), toaster], ldry, pool. **RO** ♦ **$44 - $50,** ♦♦ **$47 - $75,** ◊ **$10,** ch con, 11 units ★★★. AE BC DC EFT MC VI.

ADELAIDE - GLENALTA SA 5052

Pop Part of Adelaide, (14km S Adelaide), See map on page 588, ref C5. A suburb of Adelaide.

B&B's/Guest Houses

★★★★ **Nottingham Way Bed & Breakfast**, (B&B), 2 Nottingham Way, ☎ 08 8278 7732, fax 08 8278 7732, (2 stry), 3 rms [shwr, tlt, a/c, fire pl, elec blkts, TV, video, clock radio, t/c mkg, refrig (1), micro (1), elec frypan (1), toaster (1)], lounge, spa, bbq, cots-fee, non smoking property. **BB** ♦ **$85 - $95,** ♦♦ **$125,** AE BC DC MC VI.

ADELAIDE - GLENELG SA 5045

Pop Part of Adelaide, (10km W Adelaide), See map on page 588, ref B4. Seaside suburb, site of the first mainland settlement at Holdfast Bay in 1836. Glenelg Art Gallery, HMS Buffalo Museum, Magic Mountain, the Old Gum Tree, Rodney Fox Shark Museum and Boomerang Arts & Crafts. Boating, Bowls, Croquet, Fishing, Sailing, Swimming.

Hotels/Motels

★★★★☆ **Stamford Grand Adelaide**, (LH), Moseley Sq, ☎ 08 8376 1222, fax 08 8376 1111, (Multi-stry), 241 rms (32 suites) [ensuite, bath, spa bath (15), hairdry, a/c, TV, movie, clock radio, t/c mkg, mini bar], lift, ldry, ⊠, pool-heated, sauna, spa, bbq, rm serv, c/park (undercover)-fee, gym, cots, non smoking flr (6). **RO** ♦ **$174 - $280,** ♦♦ **$174 - $280,** ◊ **$32.50, Suite D** ♦♦ **$280 - $655,** AE BC DC JCB MC VI, ♿.

(Serviced Apartment Section), 12 serv apts acc up to 6, (2 & 3 bedrm), [shwr, spa bath, tlt, a/c, TV, clock radio, t/c mkg, refrig, cook fac, micro, d/wash, toaster, ldry (3)], ldry (10), iron, iron brd, non smoking rms (3). **D $320 - $741,** (not yet classified).

★★★★ **Anzac Highway Motel**, (M), 626 Anzac Hwy, ☎ 08 8294 1344, fax 08 8295 1259, 34 units [ensuite, spa bath (7), hairdry, a/c, elec blkts, tel, TV, clock radio, t/c mkg, refrig, cook fac (3), micro (3), toaster], ldry-fee, lounge (cocktail), ✗ (Anzac's), bar (wine), pool, spa, bbq, rm serv, cots-fee, non smoking units (17), **RO** ♦ **$85 - $160,** ♦♦ **$85 - $160,** ◊ **$11,** AE BC DC EFT JCB MC MP VI, ♿.

★★★★ **Ensenada Motor Inn**, (M), 13 Colley Tce, ☎ 08 8294 5822, fax 08 8294 3393, (2 stry), 32 units [ensuite, a/c, elec blkts, tel, TV, video (22), clock radio, t/c mkg, refrig, mini bar, ldry], ldry, w/mach-fee, dryer-fee, iron, iron brd, rm serv, non smoking rms (21), **RO** ♦ **$109 - $125,** ♦♦ **$109 - $125,** ◊ **$15,** ch con, 10 units ★★★☆. AE BC DC EFT JCB MC MP VI.

★★★★ **Patawalonga Motor Inn**, (M), 13 Adelphi Tce, ☎ 08 8294 2122, fax 08 8295 7331, (2 stry gr fl), 50 units [ensuite, bath (5), spa bath (3), hairdry (25), a/c, elec blkts, tel, TV, clock radio, t/c mkg, refrig, mini bar, cook fac (3)], ldry, lounge, conv fac, ⊠, pool-heated, spa, rm serv, dinner to unit, cots, non smoking rms (4). **RO** ♦♦ **$99 - $242,** ◊ **$12,** ch con, 24 rms ★★★☆. AE BC DC EFT MC VI.

★★★☆ **Adelaide International Motel**, (M), 521 Anzac Hwy, 1km E of PO, ☎ 08 8294 2155, fax 08 8294 4881, (2 stry gr fl), 32 units [ensuite, bath (hip), spa bath (2), hairdry, a/c, tel, TV, radio, t/c mkg, refrig], ldry, conv fac, ⊠, pool, rm serv, dinner to unit, cots, non smoking units (10). **RO** ♦ **$68 - $78,** ♦♦ **$80 - $170,** ◊ **$13,** AE BC DC EFT MC VI.

★★★☆ **Atlantic Tower Motor Inn**, (M), 760 Anzac Hwy, ☎ 08 8294 1011, fax 08 8376 0964, (Multi-stry), 28 units [ensuite, bath (4), spa bath (3), hairdry (7), a/c, tel, TV, video (2), clock radio, t/c mkg, refrig, mini bar, micro (avail), toaster], lift, ldry-fee, iron (16), iron brd (16), rm serv, cots. **RO** ♦ **$84 - $165,** ♦♦ **$84 - $165,** AE BC DC EFT MC VI.

★★★☆ **Haven Marina Inn**, (M), 6 Adelphi Tce, ☎ 08 8294 1555, fax 08 8294 5773, (2 stry gr fl), 72 units [ensuite, bath (21), hairdry, a/c, fan (32), elec blkts, tel, cable tv, radio, t/c mkg, refrig, mini bar, cook fac (1)], ldry-fee, iron, iron brd, conv fac, ⊠, pool, sauna, rm serv. **RO** ♦ **$90 - $170,** ♦♦ **$90 - $170,** ◊ **$10,** ch con, 30 units of a 4 star rating, 4 units of a lower rating. AE BC DC EFT JCB MC VI.

Medication and driving

Medication can effect your driving. Certain drugs can effect your mental alertness and/or co-ordination and therefore effect driving skills. Always check with your doctor the effect which any medication (over the counter or prescription) you are taking may have on your driving. There may be an alternative drug which will not affect your driving. It is best to avoid drinking alcohol while taking medication.

★★★☆ **Taft Motor Inn**, (M), 18 Moseley St, ☎ 08 8376 1233, fax 08 8294 6977, (2 stry gr fl), 26 units [ensuite, bath (4), hairdry, a/c, elec blkts, tel, TV, video (4), clock radio, t/c mkg, refrig, cook fac (17), toaster], ldry, iron, pool, spa, bbq, rm serv, plygr, cots-fee. **RO** ♦ **$88 - $97**, ♦♦ **$89 - $102**, ♦ **$15**, ch con, 6 units of a 4 star rating. AE BC DC MC VI.

★★★☆ **(Serviced Apartments)**, 12 serv apts acc up to 4, (1 & 2 bedrm), [shwr, tlt, hairdry, a/c, elec blkts, tel, TV, clock radio, refrig, cook fac], ldry, iron. **D** ♦ **$105 - $115**, ♦♦ **$110 - $120**, ♦ **$15**.

★★★ **Bay Motel Hotel**, (LMH), 58 Broadway, ☎ 08 8294 4244, fax 08 8294 4821, (2 stry gr fl), 32 units [ensuite, bath (2), a/c, elec blkts, tel, TV, clock radio, t/c mkg, refrig], conv fac, ✉, ✗, ✆, cots-fee. **RO** ♦ **$66 - $105**, ♦♦ **$66 - $105**, ♦ **$10**, AE BC DC EFT MC MCH VI.

★★★ **Buffalo Motor Inn**, (M), 766 Anzac Hwy, cnr Durham St, ☎ 08 8294 6244, fax 08 8294 6656, (2 stry gr fl), 36 units [ensuite, bath, spa bath (3), a/c, elec blkts, tel, TV, clock radio, t/c mkg, refrig], cots. **RO** ♦ **$77 - $154**, ♦♦ **$88 - $154**, ♦ **$11**, ch con, AE BC DC EFT MC VI, ♿.

★★★ **Glenelg Motel**, (M), 41 Tapleys Hill Rd, ☎ 08 8295 7141, fax 08 8295 1113, 39 units [ensuite, spa bath (3), hairdry (38), a/c, elec blkts, tel (38), TV, clock radio, t/c mkg, refrig], ldry, w/mach-fee, dryer-fee, iron, iron brd, pool, spa, cots-fee. **RO** ♦ **$60 - $121**, ♦♦ **$60 - $121**, ♦ **$11**, ch con, Fresh rainwater available. Min book long w/ends and Easter, AE BC DC EFT MC VI.

★★★ **Watermark Glenelg**, (LMH), Previously St Leonards Hotel Motel 631 Anzac Hwy, cnr Adelphi Tce, ☎ 08 8294 2300, fax 08 8294 9360, (2 stry), 14 units [ensuite, a/c, elec blkts, tel, TV, clock radio, t/c mkg, refrig, micro, toaster], ldry, ✉, c/park (carport). **BLB** ♦ **$88**, ♦♦ **$99**, ♦ **$13.20**, AE BC DC EFT MC VI.

★★☆ **Norfolk Motor Inn**, (M), 71 Broadway, ☎ 08 8295 6354, fax 08 8295 6866, (2 stry gr fl), 20 units [ensuite, a/c, elec blkts, TV, clock radio, t/c mkg, refrig, toaster], iron (avail), iron brd (avail), bbq, ✆, cots, non smoking rms (20). **RO** ♦ **$60 - $70**, ♦♦ **$63 - $75**, ♦ **$10**, fam con, AE BC DC EFT MC MCH VI.

★☆ **Glenelg Jetty Hotel**, (LH), Previously St Vincent Hotel 28 Jetty Rd, ☎ 08 8294 4377, fax 08 8295 4412, (2 stry), 17 rms [basin, ensuite (7), a/c-cool (8), a/c (7), TV (10), clock radio (7), radio (3), t/c mkg (4), refrig (7)], ✉, t/c mkg shared, ✆, cots. **RO** ♦ **$35 - $55**, ♦♦ **$55 - $90**, 5 rms ★. AE BC DC EFT MC VI.

Self Catering Accommodation

★★★★ **Baybeachfront**, (HU), North Espl, ☎ 08 8294 9666, fax 08 8376 0933, 23 units acc up to 6, (1, 2 & 3 bedrm), [shwr, bath (1-hip 22), tlt, a/c, tel, TV, video (23), clock radio, refrig, cook fac, micro (23), blkts, doonas, linen, pillows], ldry, pool-heated (solar), spa, bbq (covered), plygr, cots. **D $82 - $200**, 3 strys, Min book applies, AE BC DC MC VI.

★★★★ **Bayswaterfront Holiday Units**, (HU), Adelphi Tce, ☎ 08 8294 9666, fax 08 8376 0933, 3 units acc up to 5, (2 bedrm), [shwr, tlt, hairdry, a/c, tel, TV, video, clock radio, refrig, cook fac, micro, d/wash, blkts, doonas, linen, pillows], ldry, cots. **D $92 - $150**, 3 strys, AE BC DC MC VI.

★★★★ **Bayview Holiday Units**, (HU), Anzac Hwy, ☎ 08 8294 9666, fax 08 8376 0933, (2 stry gr fl), 6 units acc up to 7, (2 bedrm), [shwr, bath (2), tlt, a/c, tel, TV, video (avail)-fee, clock radio, refrig, cook fac, micro, blkts, linen, pillows], ldry, c/park (undercover), cots. **D $77 - $136**, AE BC DC MC VI.

★★★★ **South Esplanade Apartment**, (Apt), Access via St Johns Row. Apt 26 & 34, 13 Sth Esplanade, 300m S of PO, ☎ 08 8326 3664, or a/h 08 8382 1278, 2 apts acc up to 6, (1 & 2 bedrm), [shwr, bath, tlt, hairdry, a/c, c/fan (1), tel, TV, video, clock radio, refrig, cook fac, micro, elec frypan, d/wash (1), toaster, doonas, linen, pillows], w/mach, dryer, iron, iron brd, c/park (carport). **D** ♦♦ **$80 - $150**, ♦ **$5**, Min book applies, AE BC DC MC VI.

★★★☆ **Alkoomi Holiday Units**, (HU), 7 North Esp, ☎ 08 8294 6624, fax 08 8294 8588, (Multi-stry), 18 units acc up to 7, (1, 2 & 3 bedrm), [shwr, tlt, a/c, tel, video-fee, clock radio, refrig, cook fac, micro, blkts, linen, pillows], ldry, bbq, cots, **D** ♦ **$60 - $110**, ♦♦ **$60 - $110**, ♦ **$10**, ch con, AE BC DC EFT JCB MC VI.

Ideally situated near Glenelg Beach, Shopping Centre, Tram direct to City, 30 units with cooking facilities including one and two bedroomed apartments all self contained plus motel suites. All units and apartments equipped with toasters, colour TV, fridge, phone, air cond, hairdryers and irons. Private showers some baths, swimming pool, spa, childs playground and pool, garden, BBQ, laundry facilities, 24 hour reception, courtesy pickup available.

Owned & operated by the Dal Zotto Family

1800 060 905

18 Moseley Street Glenelg Adelaide 5045

★★★☆ **Corfu Holiday Units**, (HU), Cnr Moseley & Kent Sts, ☎ 08 8295 2345, fax 08 8294 5666, (Multi-stry gr fl), 12 units acc up to 4, (2 bedrm), [shwr, tlt, a/c, tel, TV, clock radio, refrig, cook fac, micro, blkts, linen, pillows], ldry, **D $85 - $110**, Min book all holiday times, AE BC DC EFT MC VI.

★★★☆ **La Mancha Holiday Suites**, (HU), 8 Esplanade, ☎ 08 8295 2345, fax 08 8294 5666, (Multi-stry gr fl), 18 units acc up to 6, (1 & 2 bedrm), [shwr, tlt, a/c, tel, TV, clock radio, refrig, cook fac, micro, blkts, linen, pillows], ldry, cots, **D $80 - $149**, Min book all holiday times, AE BC DC MC VI.

★★★☆ **Moorings Holiday Apartments**, (Apt), 7 Patawalonga Frontage, ☎ 08 8295 6118, fax 08 8375 1620, (2 stry gr fl), 14 apts acc up to 5, (1 bedrm2 bedrm), [shwr, tlt, hairdry, a/c, elec blkts, tel, TV, movie, clock radio, refrig, cook fac, micro, blkts, linen, pillows], ldry, iron, bbq, c/park (undercover). **D ♦♦ $77 - $110**, ◊ **$16.50**, ch con, 3 units of a lower rating. BC EFT MC VI.

★★★☆ **Wambini Lodge Holiday Units**, (HU), 9 North Esp, ☎ 08 8295 4689, fax 08 8294 8588, (Multi-stry), 14 units acc up to 5, (2 bedrm), [shwr, tlt, a/c, elec blkts, tel, cable tv, video (avail)-fee, clock radio, refrig, cook fac, micro, blkts, linen, pillows], ldry-fee, bbq, cots, **D ♦ $68 - $114**, ♦♦ **$68 - $114**, ◊ **$12**, ch con, AE BC DC EFT MC VI.

★★★ **Glenelg Holiday Flats**, (HU), Coral Seaside Units, 2 South Esp, ☎ 08 8295 1952, fax 08 8294 7896, (Multi-stry gr fl), 8 units acc up to 5, (1 & 2 bedrm), [shwr, tlt, a/c, elec blkts, tel-fee, TV, video-fee, refrig, cook fac, blkts, linen, pillows], ldry, w/mach-fee, dryer-fee, iron (avail), iron brd (avail), ☎, cots. **D $77 - $160**, AE BC DC JCB MC VI.

Operator Comment: Visit us on www.glenelgholidayflats.com.au

★★★ **(Chevron Holiday Units)**, 12 Saltram Rd, 4 units acc up to 8, (2 & 3 bedrm), [shwr, bath, tlt, a/c, c/fan, elec blkts, TV, video-fee, refrig, cook fac, micro, blkts, linen, pillows], ldry, w/mach-fee, dryer-fee, iron, iron brd, cots. **D $99 - $135**, Keys to be collected from 2 South Esplanade.

★★★ **(Lake Holiday Units)**, George St, 8 units acc up to 7, (1 & 2 bedrm), [shwr, tlt, a/c, elec blkts, TV, video-fee, clock radio, refrig, cook fac, blkts, linen, pillows], w/mach, cots. **D $77 - $145**, Keys to be collected from 2 South Esplanade.

★★★ **Marco Polo Apartments**, (Apt), 18 Broadway, ☎ 08 8295 2345, fax 08 8294 5666, 30 apts acc up to 7, (1, 2 & 3 bedrm), [shwr, tlt, a/c, tel, TV, clock radio, refrig, cook fac, micro, blkts, linen, pillows], ldry, cots. **D $88 - $160**, Min book all holiday times, AE BC DC EFT MC VI.

★★★ **Sea Change**, (HU), 3 St Johns Row, ☎ 08 8356 3975, fax 08 8355 5373, 13 units acc up to 3, (1 bedrm), [shwr, tlt, a/c, elec blkts, TV, clock radio, t/c mkg, refrig, cook fac ltd, micro, blkts, doonas, linen, pillows], ldry, cots-fee, non smoking units (13). **D ♦ $60 - $80**, ♦♦ **$80 - $100**, ◊ **$10**, ch con, weekly con, Min book applies, BC MC VI.

★★☆ **Colley Motel**, (HU), Circa 1880. 22 Colley Tce, ☎ 08 8295 7535, fax 08 8350 0382, (2 stry gr fl), 8 units acc up to 5, [shwr, tlt, evap cool, heat, TV, refrig, cook fac, blkts, linen, pillows], c/park (limited), non smoking units. **D ♦ $55 - $60**, ♦♦ **$65 - $85**, BC MC VI.

★★☆ **South Pacific Holiday Units**, (HU), 16 Colley Tce, ☎ 08 8294 1352, (2 stry gr fl), 5 units acc up to 6, (1 & 2 bedrm), [shwr, bath (3), tlt, fan, heat, elec blkts, TV, refrig, cook fac, micro (1), blkts, linen, pillows], ldry, cots. **D ♦♦ $82.50 - $99**, ◊ **$11**, ch con, AE BC DC MC VI.

★★ **Seafront Holiday Units**, (HU), 6 South Esp, ☎ 08 8294 8940, 6 units acc up to 7, (1, 2 & 3 bedrm), [shwr, bath, tlt, fan (avail), heat, elec blkts, tel (1), TV, radio (avail), refrig, cook fac], iron, iron brd, cots. **D $45 - $160**, AE BC MC VI.

Sea Cottage, (Apt), 9A St Johns Row, 500m N of PO, ☎ 08 8356 3975, fax 08 8355 5373, 1 apt acc up to 7, (2 bedrm), [shwr, tlt, a/c, elec blkts, TV, clock radio, t/c mkg, refrig, cook fac, micro, ldry, blkts, doonas, linen, pillows], cots-fee, non smoking property, **D ♦ $100 - $132**, ♦♦ **$100 - $132**, ◊ **$10**, ch con, weekly con, Min book applies, BC MC VI, (not yet classified).

Maritimo Holiday Units, (HU), 15 Colley Tce, ☎ 08 8295 6780, fax 08 8295 6780, (2 stry gr fl), 10 units acc up to 6, (1 & 2 bedrm), [shwr, bath (7), tlt, a/c-cool (9), fan, heat, TV, refrig, cook fac, micro, blkts, linen, pillows], ldry, c/park (undercover). **D $50 - $176**, BC MC VI, (not yet classified).

B&B's/Guest Houses

★★★★☆ **Seaforth Hosted Accommodation**, (B&B), 20 Weewanda St, ☎ 08 8295 1226, fax 08 8295 1226, 1 rm [ensuite, bath, hairdry, a/c, c/fan, elec blkts, tel, TV, clock radio, t/c mkg, refrig], iron, iron brd, secure park, non smoking property. BB ♦ $130, ♦♦ $150, BC MC VI.

★★★★ **Away at the Bay**, (B&B), 12 St John's Row, ☎ 08 8294 8676, fax 08 8294 8881, 2 rms [ensuite, spa bath (2), hairdry, a/c, clock radio], lounge (TV), t/c mkg shared, bbq, non smoking rms. BB ♦ $130 - $150, ♦♦ $140 - $165, BC MC VI.

★★★★ **Water Bay Villa Bed & Breakfast**, (B&B), Circa 1910. 28 Broadway, 500m W of PO, ☎ 0412 221 724, fax 08 8294 8150, 1 rm [bath, hairdry, a/c, c/fan, fire pl, heat, elec blkts, t/c mkg], bathrm (private) (1), iron, iron brd, read rm, lounge (TV, video, stereo), bbq, c/park (carport), non smoking property. BB ♦ $170 - $180, ♦♦ $185 - $195, AE BC DC MC VI.

★★★☆ **Beresford Bed & Breakfast**, (B&B), 111 Brighton Rd, 1km W of PO, ☎ 08 8295 8533, fax 08 8294 4144, 1 rm (1 suite) [ensuite, a/c-cool, evap cool, cent heat, elec blkts, TV, video, clock radio, t/c mkg, refrig, micro, toaster], spa (heated), bbq, meals avail (by arrangement), secure park, cots, non smoking property. BB ♦♦ $120 - $130, BC MC VI.

★★★☆ **Glenelg Sea-Breeze**, (B&B), 2A First Ave, ☎ 08 8295 3791, 1 rm (2 bedrm), [shwr, tlt, heat, elec blkts, clock radio], ldry, iron, iron brd, lounge (TV/video), ✗, spa (heated), t/c mkg shared, secure park, bicycle (2A/2C). BB ♦ $77 - $100, ♦♦ $120 - $150, ⊖ $40.

Other Accommodation

★★★ **Glenelg Beach Resort**, (Lodge), 1-7 Moseley St, ☎ 08 8376 0007, fax 08 8376 0007, 1 rm acc up to 12, [ensuite (1), fan, heat, clock radio (15), refrig (27), cook fac (1), doonas, linen, pillows], ldry, rec rm, lounge (TV & Video), cafe (licensed), bar, spa, cook fac, refrig, courtesy transfer, ☎. BLB ♦ $20 - $50, ♦♦ $60 - $90, 3 storeys. BC EFT MC VI.

ADELAIDE - GLENGOWRIE SA 5044

Pop Part of Adelaide, (10km SW Adelaide), See map on page 588, ref B4. A suburb of Adelaide.

Hotels/Motels

★★★ **Morphett Arms Hotel**, (LH), 138 Morphett Rd, 8km SW of GPO, ☎ 08 8295 8371, fax 08 8295 3625, (2 stry) 11 rms [ensuite, a/c, cable tv, clock radio, t/c mkg, refrig], ✗. RO ♦ $35, ♦♦ $45, ⊖ $5, AE BC DC EFT MC VI.

ADELAIDE - GLENSIDE SA 5065

Pop Part of Adelaide, (4km SE Adelaide), See map on page 588, ref C4. A suburb of Adelaide.

Self Catering Accommodation

★★★★☆ **Village Apartments Burnside**, (Apt), 11 Sydney St, ☎ 08 8338 1212, fax 08 8338 2200, 4 apts acc up to 4, [shwr, spa bath, tlt, hairdry, a/c, tel, TV, video, clock radio, CD, t/c mkg, refrig, cook fac, micro, toaster, blkts, linen, pillows], w/mach, dryer, iron, iron brd, non smoking property. D $140 - $150, W $660 - $730, BC MC VI.

★★★★ **Adelaide Oakford Apartments**, (Apt), Flemington St. Check in at 18 Stuart Rd, Dulwich to collect keys. ☎ 08 8333 7400, fax 08 8332 7446, (2 stry) 14 apts acc up to 6, (3 bedrm), [shwr, bath, tlt, hairdry, a/c, tel, TV, video, clock radio, t/c mkg, refrig, cook fac, micro, elec frypan, d/wash, toaster, ldry, blkts, doonas, linen, pillows], w/mach, dryer, iron, iron brd, c/park (carport), cots. D $154 - $176, AE BC DC MC VI.

★★★★☆ **(Cedar Cres Section)**, Amber Woods, Cedar Cres, 3 apts acc up to 6, (3 bedrm), [shwr (2), tlt (2), a/c, fax, TV, video, clock radio, CD, refrig, cook fac, micro, elec frypan, d/wash, ldry, blkts, linen, pillows], w/mach, dryer, iron, iron brd, c/park (garage). D $220.

★★★★ **Glenside Apartments**, (Apt), 7/35-39 Sydney St, ☎ 08 8379 7276, fax 08 8338 3030, (2 stry gr fl) 17 apts acc up to 6, (1, 2 & 3 bedrm - 6x1q. 10x1q1t. 1x1q2t), [shwr, bath (11), tlt, a/c, heat, elec blkts, tel, TV, video, clock radio, refrig, cook fac, micro, d/wash (11), ldry, linen], w/mach, dryer, c/park (undercover), cots. D ♦♦ $88 - $125, ⊖ $7, AE BC MC VI.

★★★ **Renes Place Apartment**, (Apt), No children's facilities, 11 Cator St, ☎ 08 8379 5563, 1 apt acc up to 3, (Studio - 1x1d1s), [shwr, tlt, a/c, elec blkts, TV, clock radio, t/c mkg, refrig, cook fac, micro, elec frypan, toaster, blkts, linen, pillows], ldry, iron, iron brd. D ♦ $50, ♦♦ $80, ⊖ $20.

ADELAIDE - GLENUNGA SA 5064

Pop Part of Adelaide, (5km SE Adelaide), See map on page 588, ref C4. A suburb of Adelaide.

Hotels/Motels

★★★☆ **Adelaide Granada Motor Inn**, (M), 493 Portrush Rd, ☎ 08 8272 8211, fax 08 8272 8987, (2 stry gr fl), 55 units [shwr, spa bath (5), tlt, hairdry (15), a/c, tel, TV, clock radio, t/c mkg, refrig], ldry, w/mach-fee, dryer reqd, iron, iron brd, conv fac, ✗ (Mon - Sat only), pool indoor heated, spa, dinner to unit, cots. RO ♦ $54 - $141, ♦♦ $55 - $141, ch con, 11 units ★★★. AE BC DC MC MP VI, .

★★ **277 Motel**, (M), 277 Glen Osmond Rd (Highway One), ☎ 08 8379 9911, fax 08 8379 6628, (2 stry gr fl), 56 units [ensuite, a/c, elec blkts, tel, TV, t/c mkg, refrig, cook fac (30), ldry], ldry, w/mach-fee, dryer-fee, iron, iron brd, cots-fee. RO ♦ $46.20 - $52.80, ♦♦ $46.20 - $52.80, ⊖ $11, ch con, AE BC DC EFT MC MCH VI.

Self Catering Accommodation

★★★★ **Adelaide City Fringe Cottages**, (Apt), 135 Allinga Ave, ☎ 08 8338 2426, fax 08 8338 2426, 6 apts acc up to 5, (1 & 2 bedrm), [shwr, bath, tlt, a/c (ducted), elec blkts, tel, TV, video, clock radio, refrig, micro, toaster, ldry, blkts, linen, pillows], w/mach, dryer, iron, iron brd, bbq, c/park (carport), cots (avail). D ♦♦ $66 - $99, ⊖ $10, AE BC MC VI.

ADELAIDE - GOODWOOD SA 5034

Pop Part of Adelaide, (3km S Adelaide), See map on page 588, ref C4. A suburb of Adelaide.

Self Catering Accommodation

★★ **Affordable Accommodation**, (Apt), 49 Leader St, ☎ 08 8363 3413, fax 08 8363 0857, (2 stry), 3 apts acc up to 6, (2 bedrm), [shwr, tlt, TV, refrig, cook fac, blkts, linen, pillows], w/mach, c/park. D ♦♦ $45, ⊖ $10, W $250 - $300, ch con.

B&B's/Guest Houses

★★★☆ **Rose Villa Bed & Breakfast**, (B&B), 29 Albert St, ☎ 08 8271 2947, 1 rm [ensuite, a/c, elec blkts, TV, clock radio, t/c mkg], lounge, c/park. BB ♦ $95, ♦♦ $110.

ADELAIDE - HACKHAM SA 5163

Pop Part of Adelaide, (30km SW Adelaide), See map on page 588, ref B6. A southern suburb of Adelaide. Lakeside Leisure Park.

Hotels/Motels

★★★ **Mick O'Sheas Irish Pub Motel**, (M), Main South Rd, 3km N of PO, ☎ 08 8384 6944, fax 08 8326 2939, (2 stry gr fl), 12 units [ensuite, spa bath (3), hairdry, a/c, elec blkts, tel, TV, video, clock radio, t/c mkg, refrig, toaster], ✉, rm serv, dinner to unit, cots-fee. **D** $93.50 - $132, ⓥ $11 - $22, AE BC DC EFT MC VI, ♿.

ADELAIDE - HACKNEY SA 5069

Pop Part of Adelaide, (2km NE Adelaide), See map on page 588, ref C4. A suburb of Adelaide. Bowls, Squash, Tennis.

B&B's/Guest Houses

★★★★☆ **Fenners**, (B&B), 7 Athelney Ave, ☎ 08 8363 4436, fax 08 8363 4436, 1 rm [shwr, tlt, hairdry, a/c, c/fan, elec blkts, TV, video-fee, radio, CD, t/c mkg, refrig, mini bar, toaster], iron-fee, iron brd, bbq, secure park (by arrangement), non smoking rms. **BLB** ⓥ $100, ♦♦ $110, Closed July & August. BC MC VI.

ADELAIDE - HENLEY BEACH SA 5022

Pop Part of Adelaide, (10km W Adelaide), See map on page 588, ref B4. A coastal suburb of Adelaide. Boating, Fishing, Sailing, Swimming (Ocean).

Hotels/Motels

★ **Ramsgate Hotel**, (LH), 328 Seaview Rd, ☎ 08 8356 5411, fax 08 882350599, (2 stry), 10 rms [basin, TV (12)], lounge (TV), ✉ (Mon to Sat), t/c mkg shared. **RO** ♦♦♦♦ $40 - $60, ch con, AE DC EFT MC VI.

Self Catering Accommodation

★★★ **Allenby Court Holiday Units**, (HU), 405 Seaview Rd, ☎ 08 8235 0445, fax 08 8356 8479, (2 stry), 5 units (2 bedrm), [shwr, tlt, a/c-cool (3), a/c (2), heat (5), elec blkts, TV, clock radio, refrig, cook fac, micro, blkts, linen, pillows], w/mach, iron, iron brd, c/park (security gate). **D** ♦♦ $66 - $165, ⓥ $12, **W** ♦♦ $385 - $995, Min book applies, BC MC VI.

Seaview Holiday Apartments, (Apt), 192 Seaview Rd, 600m N of PO, ☎ 08 8356 3975, fax 08 8355 5373, 8 apts acc up to 8, (2 bedrm), [shwr, tlt, a/c, fan, elec blkts, TV, refrig, cook fac, micro, ldry, blkts, linen, pillows], w/mach, cots-fee, non smoking rms (6). **D** ⓥ $93 - $116, ♦♦ $93 - $116, ⓥ $93 - $116, weekly con, Min book applies, BC MC VI, (not yet classified).

B&B's/Guest Houses

★★★☆ **Australian Institute of Sport Del Monte**, (GH), 209 Esplanade, ☎ 08 8235 1447, fax 08 8353 5443, (2 stry), 20 rms [shwr, bath (6), spa bath (3), tlt, a/c, tel, TV (5), clock radio, refrig], ldry, lounge (TV), conf fac, ✗, t/c mkg shared, c/park (limited). **RO** ⓥ $70 - $85, ♦♦ $85 - $100, ♦♦♦ $100, ⓥ $20, ch con, No alcohol allowed on premises. BC MC VI.

★★★☆ **Meleden Villa Guest House**, (GH), 268 Seaview Rd, ☎ 08 8235 0577, fax 08 8235 0577, 4 rms [ensuite (2), a/c-cool, fan, heat, TV, clock radio, t/c mkg, refrig], bathrm (2), pool, ☎, cots, non smoking property. **BLB** $65 - $85, ch con, AE BC DC MC VI.

ADELAIDE - HYDE PARK SA 5061

Pop Part of Adelaide, (3km S Adelaide), See map on page 588, ref C4. A suburb of Adelaide.

Hotels/Motels

★★★ **Jasper Motor Inn**, (M), 17 Jasper St, 3.5km S of GPO, ☎ 08 8271 0377, fax 08 8271 1296, 30 units [ensuite, hairdry (19), heat, tel, TV, video-fee, clock radio, t/c mkg, refrig], ldry, w/mach-fee, dryer-fee, iron, iron brd, ✉ (Sun to Fri), cots-fee. **RO** ⓥ $77 - $98, ♦♦ $77 - $103, ⓥ $15, Split rating 6 units @ 2.5 star. AE BC DC EFT MC VI.

Self Catering Accommodation

★★★★ **Metro Luxury Serviced Apartments**, (Apt), 6 Macklin St, ☎ 08 8373 0083, fax 08 8373 3720, (2 stry gr fl), 12 apts acc up to 4, [shwr, bath, tlt, a/c, elec blkts (available), tel, TV, clock radio, refrig, cook fac, micro, toaster, doonas], c/park (undercover), cots (avail). **D** ♦♦ $80 - $105, ⓥ $10, ch con, AE BC DC MC VI.

★★★★ **(The Villa)**, 1 cotg acc up to 6, [shwr, bath (hip), tlt (2), a/c, elec blkts (available), tel, TV, cook fac, micro, d/wash, blkts, linen, pillows], w/mach, dryer, iron, c/park. **D** ♦♦ $140, ⓥ $10, ch con, fam con.

ADELAIDE - IRONBANK SA 5153

Pop Nominal, (22km SE Adelaide), See map on page 588, ref D5. A small town located in the Sturt River Valley possessing fine forests.

Self Catering Accommodation

★★★☆ **Wirra Birra Springs**, (Cotg), Coat Rd, ☎ 08 8388 2121, fax 08 8388 2121, 1 cotg acc up to 4, [shwr, tlt, hairdry, a/c, fire pl, elec blkts, tel, TV, video, clock radio, CD, t/c mkg, refrig, cook fac, micro, toaster, blkts, doonas, linen, pillows], iron, iron brd, bbq, c/park (covered), tennis, non smoking property, **D** ♦♦ $130, ⓥ $22, pen con, weekly con, AE BC DC MC VI.

★★★★ **(St Andrews)**, 1 apt acc up to 4, [shwr, bath, tlt, hairdry, a/c, c/fan, heat, elec blkts, tel, TV, video, clock radio, CD, t/c mkg, refrig, cook fac, micro, toaster, blkts, doonas, linen, pillows], iron, iron brd, bbq, tennis, **D** ♦♦ $145, ⓥ $45, weekly con, Min book applies.

★★★☆ **(Library Suite)**, 1 rm [shwr, tlt, hairdry, a/c, elec blkts, TV, video, clock radio, t/c mkg], bbq, tennis, **BB** ⓥ $120, ♦♦ $135, pen con, weekly con, Min book applies.

ADELAIDE - JOSLIN SA 5070

(7km NW Adelaide), See map on page 588, ref C3. A suburb of Adelaide.

B&B's/Guest Houses

★★★★ **Lambert House B&B**, (B&B), 31 Lambert Rd, ☎ 08 8363 7222, 2 rms [hairdry, fan, heat (elec), elec blkts, clock radio, ldry], bathrm, lounge (TV), t/c mkg shared (guests lounge), bicycle (2), tennis, **BB** ⓥ $80, ♦♦ $120, Rooms available for only one group at a time. AE BC MC VI.

ADELAIDE - KANGARILLA SA 5157

Pop Nominal, (33km SE Adelaide), See map on page 588, ref D6. Nestled in the Adelaide Hills, supporting local farming areas, near the states second largest reservoir, Mt Bold. Tennis.

Self Catering Accommodation

★★★★ **Aunt Amandas Cottage**, (Cotg), Peters Creek Rd, 3.5km S of PO, near McLaren Vale, ☎ 08 8383 7122, fax 08 8383 7179, 1 cotg acc up to 4, (2 bedrm), [shwr, bath, tlt, a/c-cool, fan, elec blkts, tel, TV, radio, t/c mkg, refrig, cook fac, toaster, ldry, blkts, linen, pillows], w/mach, iron, iron brd, lounge firepl, bbq, cots, breakfast ingredients, non smoking property, **D** ♦♦ $150, ⓥ $40, ch con, Min book applies, BC MC VI.

ADELAIDE - KENSINGTON SA 5068

Pop Part of Adelaide, (3km E Adelaide), See map on page 588, ref D4. Inner suburb of Adelaide.

Self Catering Accommodation

★★★ **Garden Court Apartments**, (Apt), 16 Jessie Rd, Kensington Park 5068, 300m E of PO, ☎ 08 8431 1120, fax 08 8431 3942, 2 apts acc up to 3, (1 bedrm), [shwr, tlt, a/c, fan, heat, tel, TV, clock radio, t/c mkg, refrig, cook fac, micro, elec frypan, toaster, blkts, linen, pillows], w/mach, iron, iron brd, c/park (carport), Pets on application. **D** $40 - $65, **W** $280 - $420.

★★★ **St George Apartments Kensington**, (Apt), Previously Kensington Apartments 79 High St, cnr Maesbury St, ☎ 08 8364 6030, fax 08 8364 2001, (2 stry gr fl), 4 apts acc up to 4, (2 bedrm), [shwr, bath (hip), tlt, a/c, tel, TV, video, clock radio, refrig, cook fac, micro, ldry], c/park (undercover), cots (avail). **D** ♦♦ $80 - $90, ⓥ $7, Min book applies, AE BC MC VI.

(Cottage Section), 1 cotg acc up to 6, (3 bedrm), [shwr, bath, tlt, a/c, tel, TV, video, clock radio, refrig, cook fac, micro, elec frypan, d/wash, ldry, blkts, linen, pillows], w/mach, dryer, iron, iron brd, c/park (carport). **D** $110 - $150, (not yet classified).

ADELAIDE - KENT TOWN SA 5067

Pop Part of Adelaide, (2km E Adelaide), See map on page 588, ref C4. Inner suburb of Adelaide.

Hotels/Motels

★★★★☆ **Royal Coach Motor Inn**, (M), 24 Dequetteville Tce, cnr Flinders St, ☎ 08 8362 5676, fax 08 8363 2180, (Multi-stry gr fl), 49 units [shwr, spa bath (5), tlt, hairdry, a/c, elec blkts, tel, TV, movie, clock radio, t/c mkg, refrig, mini bar], lift, ldry, w/mach, dryer, iron, iron brd, conv fac, conf fac, ✉, pool indoor heated, sauna, bbq, cots, non smoking units (37). **RO** ⓥ $121 - $203.50, ♦♦ $121 - $203.50, ⓥ $11, ch con, AE BC DC MC MP VI, ♿.

★★★☆ **Flinders Lodge Motel**, (M), 27 Dequetteville Tce, cnr Flinders St, ☎ 08 8332 8222, fax 08 8332 8590, (2 stry gr fl), 71 units (8 suites) [shwr, bath (4), spa bath (2), tlt, a/c, elec blkts, tel, TV, clock radio, t/c mkg, refrig, mini bar, cook fac (7)], ldry, ⌧, pool (salt water), bbq, rm serv, cots-fee, non smoking rms (50). **RO ♦ $90, ♦♦ $90, ◊ $11, Suite D $132 - $154**, ch con, 4 units of a higher rating. Min book long w/ends and Easter, AE BC DC EFT MC VI.

★★☆ **Adelaides Kent Town Lodge Motel**, (M), 22 Wakefield St, ☎ 08 8332 7571, fax 08 8364 0155, (Multi-stry gr fl), 40 units (2 bedrm), [shwr, tlt, a/c-cool, a/c (10), heat, tel, TV, clock radio, t/c mkg], lift, ldry (coin laundromat), iron, iron brd, lounge (TV), ⌧, pool (heated), sauna, spa, bbq, 24hr reception, cots, non smoking rms (8). **RO ♦ $44 - $66, ♦♦ $77 - $93, ◊ $11**, ch con, fam con, AE BC DC EFT JCB MC VI.

Self Catering Accommodation

★★★★ **Norwood Apartments**, (Apt), 7 Wakefield St, ☎ 08 8336 6555, fax 08 8336 6455, 3 apts acc up to 2, (1 bedrm), [shwr, tlt, a/c-cool (2), a/c (1), heat, tel, TV, video, radio, CD, t/c mkg, refrig, cook fac, micro, d/wash, toaster, ldry, blkts, linen, pillows], w/mach, dryer, iron, iron brd. **D $88**, Min book applies, AE BC DC MC VI.

★★★☆ **Georgia Mews Cottages**, (Cotg), 31 Wakefield St, ☎ 08 8362 0600, fax 08 8362 1317, 5 cotgs acc up to 5, (1 & 2 bedrm), [shwr, bath, tlt, a/c-cool, fan (2), c/fan (2), heat, tel, TV, clock radio, refrig, cook fac]. **BB ♦ $105, ♦♦ $110, ◊ $25**, ch con.

★★★ **Adelaide City Garden Apartments**, (Apt), 18 Flinders St, ☎ 08 8272 9122, fax 08 8272 0811, 4 apts acc up to 4, (1 & 2 bedrm), [shwr, tlt, c/fan, heat, TV, video (2), clock radio, CD (2), t/c mkg, refrig, cook fac, micro, toaster, blkts, linen, pillows], ldry, w/mach, dryer, iron, iron brd, bbq, cots. **D ♦♦ $65 - $85, ◊ $10**, ch con, Min book applies, AE BC DC MC VI.

B&B's/Guest Houses

★★★☆ **CWA Guest House**, (GH), 30 Dequetteville Tce, ☎ 08 8332 4166, (2 stry), 8 rms [a/c, elec blkts, TV, clock radio, t/c mkg, refrig, micro (avail), toaster], ldry, ☏, **BLB ♦ $61.20, ♦♦ $72.60 - $78.20**, BC MC VI, ♿.

ADELAIDE - KILBURN SA 5084

Pop Part of Adelaide, (8km N Adelaide), See map on page 588, ref C3. A suburb of Adelaide.

Hotels/Motels

★ **Blair Athol Hotel**, (LH), 414 Prospect Rd, ☎ 08 8262 3933, fax 08 8262 7390, (2 stry), 10 rms [ensuite, a/c, TV, t/c mkg], ⌧, refrig. **RO ♦ $30, ♦♦ $45, ◊ $10**, fam con.

ADELAIDE - LARGS BAY SA 5016

Pop Part of Adelaide, (18km NW Adelaide), See map on page 588, ref B2. A seaside suburb of Adelaide.

Hotels/Motels

★★★ **Largs Pier Motel Hotel**, (LMH), 198 Esplanade, ☎ 08 8449 5666, fax 08 8449 5190, 16 units [ensuite, a/c, tel, TV, clock radio, refrig], ldry, w/mach-fee, dryer-fee, ⌧, rm serv, cots-fee. **RO ♦ $70, ♦♦ $80, ◊ $11**, ATM, AE BC DC EFT MC VI.

★★☆ **(Hotel Section)**, (2 stry), 16 rms [ensuite, bath (3), a/c, tel, TV, clock radio, t/c mkg, refrig], lounge. **RO ♦ $65, ♦♦ $75, ◊ $11**.

ADELAIDE - LEABROOK SA 5068

Pop Part of Adelaide, (5km E Adelaide), See map on page 588, ref D4. A suburb of Adelaide.

B&B's/Guest Houses

★★★☆ **Leabrook Lodge**, (B&B), 314 Kensington Rd, 5km E of Adelaide, ☎ 08 8331 7619, fax 08 8364 4955, 3 rms [ensuite (2), tlt, hairdry, a/c], bathrm, lounge (TV), lounge firepl, bbq, c/park (garage). **BB ♦ $50 - $75, ♦♦ $75 - $90**, BC MC VI.

ADELAIDE - LONSDALE SA 5160

Pop Part of Adelaide, (28km SW Adelaide), See map on page 588, ref B6. Outer suburb of Adelaide.

Hotels/Motels

★★ **Lonsdale Hotel**, (LMH), Cnr Lindsay & Sherrifs Rd, ☎ 08 8381 3144, fax 08 8322 3594, 7 units [ensuite, a/c, elec blkts, tel, TV, clock radio, t/c mkg, refrig], ⌧, cots. **RO ♦ $54, ♦♦ $65, ◊ $6.50**, AE BC DC EFT MC VI.

ADELAIDE - MARLESTON SA 5033

Pop Part of Adelaide, (5km S Adelaide), See map on page 588, ref C4. A suburb of Adelaide.

Hotels/Motels

★★★ **Rex Hotel**, (LH), 172 Richmond Rd, ☎ 08 8443 8188, fax 08 8443 6892, (2 stry), 12 rms [ensuite, a/c, tel, TV, t/c mkg, refrig, toaster], ⌧, cots. **RO ♦ $50, ♦♦ $60, ◊ $12**, ch con, AE BC DC EFT MC VI.

ADELAIDE - MASLIN BEACH SA 5170

Pop 865. (42km S Adelaide) See map on page 588, ref B7. South Australia's first nude beach, within easy reach of the wineries of the Wine Coast. Art Gallery, Boating, Fishing (Beach), Surfing, Swimming (Beach).

B&B's/Guest Houses

★★★★☆ **Maslin House**, (B&B), Lot 52, Tuit Rd, 6km S of Main South Rd, ☎ 08 8556 5617, fax 08 8556 5617, (2 stry gr fl), 7 rms (1 suite) [ensuite, spa bath (1), hairdry, evap cool, heat, TV (2), video (1), clock radio, CD], ldry, lounge (TV), lounge firepl, ✕, spa, t/c mkg shared, refrig, bbq, c/park. **BB ♦ $110 - $130, ♦♦ $130, ◊ $60, Suite BB ♦♦ $290**, 2 rooms ★★★★★. AE BC MC VI.

ADELAIDE - MCLAREN FLAT SA 5171

Pop part of McLaren Vale. (38km S Adelaide) See map on page 588, ref C7. Located on the Fleurieu Peninsula.

Self Catering Accommodation

★★★★ **McLaren Ridge Log Cabin**, (Cotg), Lot 2 Whitings Rd, 8km NE of PO, ☎ 08 8383 0504, fax 08 8383 0504, 1 cotg acc up to 4, [shwr, spa bath, tlt, hairdry, a/c, c/fan, heat (wood), TV, clock radio, t/c mkg, refrig, cook fac, micro, toaster, blkts, doonas, linen, pillows], iron, iron brd, bbq. **D ♦♦ $140, ◊ $30, W ♦♦ $840, ◊ $70**, ch con, Min book applies, BC MC VI.

ADELAIDE - MCLAREN VALE SA 5171

Pop 1,473. (39km S Adelaide), See map on page 588, ref B7. Commercial centre of Southern Vales Wine district and central on the Fleurieu Peninsula. Bowls, Bush Walking, Fishing, Scenic Drives, Vineyards, Wineries.

Hotels/Motels

★★★☆ **McLaren Vale Motel**, (M), Cnr Main Rd & Caffrey St, 2km NW of PO, ☎ 08 8323 8265, fax 08 8323 9251, 25 units (5 suites) [shwr, spa bath (7), tlt, hairdry, a/c, elec blkts, tel, TV, clock radio, t/c mkg, refrig, toaster], ldry, iron (15), iron brd (15), conv fac, pool-heated (solar), sauna, spa, bbq, rm serv, cots-fee, non smoking units (7). **RO ♦ $75, ♦♦ $88 - $160, ◊ $13, Suite D $108 - $205**, ch con, 6 units of a 4.0 star rating, Min book long w/ends, AE BC DC JCB MC VI, ♿.

Self Catering Accommodation

★★★★ **Bev's Bear Cottage**, (Cotg), 2A Hardy Ave, ☎ 08 8323 9351, 1 cotg acc up to 4, (2 bedrm), [shwr, bath, tlt, a/c-cool, heat, elec blkts, TV, video, refrig, cook fac, ldry], w/mach, dryer, iron, c/park (garage), non smoking property. **D ♦♦ $120, ◊ $60, W $660**, Min book Christmas and Jan, AE BC DC JCB MC VI.

★★★★ **(Winnies Cottage)**, No children's facilities, 196 Main Rd, 1 cotg acc up to 16, [ensuite, spa bath, hairdry, a/c, heat (gas), elec blkts, TV, video, clock radio, t/c mkg, refrig, micro, elec frypan, toaster, ldry, blkts, doonas, linen, pillows], dryer, iron, iron brd, breakfast ingredients, non smoking property. **D ♦♦ $150, ◊ $75, W $770**.

★★★★ **Kidogo Cottage**, (Cotg), No children's facilities, Bayliss Rd, 4km W of PO, ☎ 08 8323 9774, fax 08 8323 9775, 1 cotg acc up to 2, (1 bedrm), [ensuite, hairdry, a/c-cool, fire pl, elec blkts, TV, video, clock radio (cassette), CD, t/c mkg, refrig, cook fac, micro, elec frypan, toaster, blkts, doonas, linen, pillows], pool-heated (solar), bbq, c/park (garage), breakfast ingredients. **D ♦♦ $110, W ♦♦ $650**.

B&B's/Guest Houses

★★★★☆ **Ashcroft Country Accommodation**, (B&B), Previously Ashcroft Bed & Breakfast Johnston Rd, 2.6km from PO, ☎ 08 8323 7700, fax 08 8323 7711, 5 rms [ensuite, hairdry, a/c-cool, heat, elec blkts, TV, clock radio, t/c mkg, refrig], ldry, w/mach, dryer, iron (avail), iron brd (avail), lounge, ✕ (on request), res liquor license, bbq, cots. **BB ♦♦ $130 - $150, ◊ $30**, BC MC VI.

★★★★☆ **Bellevue Bed & Breakfast**, (B&B), No children's facilities, 12 Chalk Hill Rd, 45km S of GPO, ☎ 08 8323 7929, fax 08 8323 7914, 2 rms [ensuite, hairdry, a/c, cent heat, elec blkts, TV, t/c mkg, refrig], w/mach, dryer, iron, iron brd, bbq, c/park (off street), non smoking property, **RO ♦♦ $120 - $160**, BC MC VI.

★★★★ **Villa Grenache Bed & Breakfast**, (B&B), Lot 29C Kangarilla Rd, McLaren Flat, ☎ 08 8383 0204, fax 08 8383 0204, 3 rms [ensuite (1), spa bath (1), hairdry, a/c, c/fan, elec blkts, TV, video, clock radio, CD, micro], bathrm (private) (2), lounge (TV), t/c mkg shared, refrig, bbq, c/park (undercover), non smoking rms, **BB ♦♦ $95 - $110, ◊ $65 - $90**, 1 room ★★★★☆. BC MC VI.

★★★☆ **McLaren Vale Bed & Breakfast**, (B&B), 56 Valley View Dve, ☎ 08 8323 9351, fax 08 8323 9948, 2 rms [c/fan, heat, elec blkts, clock radio], bathrm, lounge (TV & Video), t/c mkg shared, bbq, cots, non smoking property. **BB ♦ $65, ♦♦ $88**, AE BC DC JCB MC VI.

★★★☆ **Samarkand Bed & Breakfast**, (B&B), Branson Rd, 4km SE of PO, ☎ 08 8323 8756, fax 08 8323 8756, 1 rm (1 suite) [shwr, bath, tlt, evap cool, heat, elec blkts, TV, radio, t/c mkg, refrig, cook fac, micro, toaster], iron, iron brd, cots, non smoking property. **BB ♦ $100, ♦♦ $120, ◊ $45**, ch con, BC JCB MC VI.

★★★☆ **Southern Vales Bed & Breakfast**, (B&B), 13 Chalk Hill Rd, 1km NW of PO, ☎ 08 8323 8144, fax 08 8323 8144, 5 rms [ensuite (2), a/c-cool, cent heat, TV, video, doonas], bathrm (3), ldry, w/mach, dryer, iron, iron brd, lounge (TV, video, stereo), t/c mkg shared, refrig, bbq, non smoking property. **BB ♦♦ $95 - $105, ♦♦♦ $85 - $95**, AE BC MC VI.

Wirilda Creek Winery Cafe Bed & Breakfast, (GH), RSD 90, McMurtrie Rd, 2km SE of PO, ☎ 08 8323 9688, fax 08 8323 9260, 4 rms [ensuite (1), c/fan (1), heat, clock radio, t/c mkg], ldry, w/mach, dryer, iron, iron brd, bicycle-fee, cots, breakfast ingredients, non smoking rms. **D ♦♦ $95 - $115, ◊ $20**, ch con, Limited license cafe, daily for lunch, functions by arrangement.

ADELAIDE - MEDINDIE SA 5081

Pop Part of Adelaide, (3km E Adelaide), See map on page 588, ref C3. A suburb of Adelaide.

Hotels/Motels

★★★ **Scottys Motel**, (M), Cnr Nottage Tce & Main North Rd, ☎ 08 8269 1555, fax 08 8269 1199, (2 stry gr fl), 52 units [ensuite, a/c, elec blkts, tel, TV, clock radio, t/c mkg, refrig], ldry, ✕, pool, spa, rm serv, cots-fee, non smoking units (20). **RO ♦ $77, ♦♦ $88, ◊ $11**, ch con, AE BC DC EFT MC MCH VI.

ADELAIDE - MILE END SA 5031

Pop Part of Adelaide, (3km W Adelaide), See map on page 588, ref C4. A suburb of Adelaide.

Hotels/Motels

★★★ **City West Motel**, (M), 98B Henley Beach Rd, ☎ 08 8443 6449, fax 08 8234 6011, 12 units [ensuite, a/c, tel, TV, video, t/c mkg, refrig], cots. **RO ♦ $55, ♦♦ $55 - $75**, ch con, AE DC EFT MC VI.

ADELAIDE - MILLSWOOD SA 5034

Pop Part of Adelaide, (4km S Adelaide), See map on page 588, ref C4. A suburb of Adelaide.

Self Catering Accommodation

★★★ **Millswood Serviced Apartments**, (SA), 4 Malcolm St, ☎ 08 8271 4840, (2 stry gr fl), 6 serv apts acc up to 4, (2 bedrm), [shwr, tlt, a/c, c/fan, elec blkts, tel, TV, video (4), clock radio, t/c mkg, refrig, cook fac, micro, elec frypan, toaster], w/mach, dryer, iron, iron brd, c/park (garage), cots (avail). **D ♦♦ $85 - $95, ◊ $7**, AE BC MC VI.

ADELAIDE - MITCHAM SA 5062

Pop Part of Adelaide, (8km S Adelaide), See map on page 588, ref C4. A suburb of Adelaide, one of the first areas outside the city to be settled. Tennis.

Self Catering Accommodation

★★★ **Allisons Apothecary Bed & Breakfast**, (Cotg), 21 Albert St, Mitcham Village, 7.5km S of PO, ☎ 08 8271 1435, fax 08 8271 1435, 1 cotg acc up to 4, (2 bedrm), [shwr, spa bath, tlt, hairdry, a/c, heat, TV, video, clock radio, t/c mkg, refrig, cook fac ltd, toaster, blkts, doonas, linen, pillows], iron, iron brd, bbq, non smoking rms. **D ♦♦ $130, ◊ $65**, ch con, BC MC VI.

ADELAIDE - MORPHETTVILLE SA 5043

Pop Part of Adelaide, (9km SW Adelaide), See map on page 588, ref C4. A suburb of Adelaide. Morphettville Racecourse, the headquarters of South Australian horse racing, is alongside Anzac Highway. Horse Racing.

Hotels/Motels

 ★★★☆ **Morphettville Motor Inn**, (M), 444 Anzac Hwy, 6.4km SW of PO, ☎ 08 8294 8166, fax 08 8376 0280, (2 stry gr fl), 28 units [ensuite, a/c, elec blkts, tel, TV, clock radio, t/c mkg, refrig], ldry, conv fac, ✕ (Wed to Sat), pool-heated (solar), spa, rm serv, cots. **RO ♦ $77 - $88, ♦♦ $77 - $88, ◊ $10**, ch con, AE BC DC JCB MC MP VI, ♿.

ADELAIDE - MOUNT OSMOND SA 5064

Pop Part of Adelaide, (11km SE Adelaide), See map on page 588, ref D4. A suburb of Adelaide.

B&B's/Guest Houses

★★★☆ **Osmond Ridge Bed & Breakfast**, (B&B), 113 Mt Osmond Rd, ☎ 08 8379 9211, fax 08 8338 0926, 2 rms [spa bath (shared), a/c], w/mach, dryer, lounge (TV), pool (outdoor), t/c mkg shared, bbq. **BB ♦ $120, ♦♦ $140**, Min book applies, BC MC VI.

Mount Osmond House, (B&B), 115 Mt Osmond Rd, 2km N of Mt Osmond exit SE Freeway, ☎ 08 8379 7650, fax 08 8379 7650, 3 rms [ensuite (1), shwr (2), tlt (2), evap cool (1), c/fan (1), heat, elec blkts, tel, TV (2), cable tv (1), video (1), clock radio, micro, toaster, doonas], lounge (TV), ✕, pool-heated, spa, t/c mkg shared, refrig, c/park (undercover), cots, non smoking property. **BLB ♦ $80, ♦♦ $120, ◊ $20**, BC MC VI, (not yet classified).

ADELAIDE - MYLOR SA 5153

Pop Part of Adelaide, (27km SE Adelaide), See map on page 588, ref E5. A small Adelaide Hills township which has retained much of its early character. Warrawong Sanctuary.

Self Catering Accommodation

★★★ **Blue Wren Lodge**, (Cotg), No children's facilities, Stock Rd, 2km W of PO, ☎ 08 8388 5472, fax 08 8388 5472, 1 cotg acc up to 3, [shwr, bath (hip), tlt, a/c-cool, fan, fire pl, heat, TV, video, clock radio, CD, refrig, cook fac, ldry, blkts, linen, pillows], bbq, breakfast ingredients, non smoking property. **D ♦♦ $100, ◊ $20**, Children by negotiation. Pets by negotiation.

Warrawong Sanctuary Tent Cabins, Cnr Stock & William Rds, ☎ 08 8370 9197, fax 08 8370 8332, 15 cabins acc up to 5, [shwr, tlt, a/c, elec blkts, clock radio, t/c mkg, blkts, linen, pillows], rec rm, ✕, ✆, non smoking property, **D ♦ $137.50**, Tarrif includes 2 nature walks. AE BC MC VI.

ADELAIDE - NAIRNE SA 5252

Pop Nominal, (40km E Adelaide), See map on page 588, ref E4.

★★★☆ **Albert Mill Bed & Breakfast**, (B&B), 4 Junction Street, opp Millers Arms Hotel, ☎ 08 8388 6858, 2 Rooms, [ensuite, spa bath (1), hairdry, a/c, fire pl, elec blkts, TV, clock radio, t/c mkg, refrig, cook fac, toaster, blkts, linen, pillows], ✕ (Wed To Sun), dinner to unit (avail), breakfast ingredients. **D ♦♦ $85 - $150**, BC MC VI.

ADELAIDE - NORTH ADELAIDE SA 5006

Pop Part of Adelaide, (2km N Adelaide), See map on page 588, ref C3. A suburb of Adelaide.

Hotels/Motels

  ★★★★☆ **Adelaide Meridien**, (M), 21 Melbourne St, ☎ 08 8267 3033, fax 08 8239 0275, (Multi-stry gr fl), 95 units (40 suites) [bath (47), spa bath (3), hairdry, a/c, elec blkts, tel, cable tv, video (avail), clock radio, t/c mkg, refrig, cook fac (8)], lift, ldry, w/mach, dryer, iron, iron brd, conf fac, ✕, pool, sauna, spa (heated), rm serv, cots-fee, non smoking units (16). **RO ♦ $116 - $235, ◊ $33, Suite RO ♦ $116 - $155, ◊ $33**, ch con, 40 units ★★★☆. AE BC DC EFT JCB MC VI.

 ★★★★☆ **Old Adelaide Inn**, (M), 160 O'Connell St, ☎ 08 8267 5066, fax 08 8267 2946, (2 stry gr fl), 64 units [ensuite, bath, hairdry, a/c, elec blkts, tel, TV, video-fee, movie, clock radio, t/c mkg, refrig, mini bar], ldry, w/mach, dryer, iron, iron brd, conf fac, ✕, pool-heated, sauna, spa, 24hr reception, rm serv, cots, **RO ♦ $125 - $212, ♦♦ $125 - $212, ◊ $16.50**, 27 units yet to be classified. AE BC DC MC VI, ♿.

★★★★ **O'Connell Inn Motel**, (M), 197 - 199 O'Connell St, ☎ 08 8239 0766, fax 08 8239 0560, (Multi-stry), 24 units [shwr, bath, spa bath (14), tlt, a/c, tel, TV, movie, clock radio, t/c mkg, refrig, mini bar], lift, ldry, lounge, ☒, 24hr reception, rm serv, c/park (undercover) (7), cots. RO ♦ $115.50, ♦♦ $115.50, ◊ $16, AE BC DC MC MP VI, ﾋﾟ.

★★★★ **(Serviced Apartments Section)**, 4 serv apts acc up to 4, [shwr, bath, tlt, a/c, elec blkts, TV, refrig, cook fac, toaster], ldry, w/mach-fee, dryer-fee, iron, iron brd, cots. D ♦♦ $143, ◊ $16.50.

★★★☆ **Adelaide Regal Park Inn**, (M), 44 Barton Tce East, ☎ 08 8267 3222, fax 08 8239 0485, (2 stry gr fl), 37 units [shwr, tlt, a/c, tel, cable tv, clock radio, t/c mkg, refrig], ldry, w/mach, dryer, iron, iron brd, conv fac, ☒, pool-heated, rm serv, cots-fee, non smoking rms (32). RO ♦ $98 - $160, ♦♦ $105 - $160, ◊ $15, ch con, 16 units ★★☆. AE BC DC MC VI.

★★★☆ **Hotel Adelaide International**, (LH), 62 Brougham Pl, ☎ 08 8267 3444, fax 08 8239 0189, (Multi-stry), 140 rms (7 suites) [ensuite, bath, spa bath (7), hairdry, tel, TV, clock radio, t/c mkg, refrig], lift, lounge (tv), conv fac, ☒, pool, rm serv, cots, non smoking rms (31). RO ♦ $99 - $182, ♦♦ $99 - $182, ◊ $17 - $22, Suite D $160 - $264, ch con, 10 suites of a higher standard. Gambling machines & courtesy vehicle (Mon - Frid) available. AE BC DC MC VI, ﾋﾟ.

★★ **Princes Lodge Motel**, (M), 73 Lefevre Tce, ☎ 08 8267 5566, fax 08 8239 0787, (2 stry gr fl), 21 units [shwr, tlt, a/c-cool, heat, elec blkts, tel, TV, clock radio, t/c mkg, refrig], ldry, rec rm, bbq, cots. BLB ♦ $38.50 - $55, ♦♦ $55 - $66, ◊ $11, ch con, AE BC DC EFT MC VI.

Self Catering Accommodation

★★★★ **Fire Station Inn**, (SA), 78 Tynte St, 1.5km N of Adelaide, ☎ 08 8272 1355, fax 08 8272 1355, 1 serv apt acc up to 4, [shwr, bath, spa bath, tlt, hairdry, a/c, cent heat, tel, TV, clock radio, CD, t/c mkg, refrig, cook fac, micro, d/wash, toaster, blkts, doonas, linen, pillows], iron, iron brd, cots. D ♦♦ $220, ◊ $80, ch con, AE BC DC JCB MC VI.

Operator Comment: Imagine sleeping at a real Fire Station. www.adelaideheritage.com

★★★★ **(Loggia Suite)**, 39 George St, 3 serv apts acc up to 2, [shwr, bath, spa bath, tlt, hairdry, a/c, TV, clock radio, CD, t/c mkg, refrig, cook fac ltd, toaster, blkts, doonas, linen, pillows], iron, iron brd, c/park. D ♦♦ $220.

★★★★ **(Penthouse Residency)**, 80 Tynte St, 3 serv apts acc up to 6, [shwr, bath, tlt, hairdry, a/c, heat, tel, TV, video, clock radio, CD, t/c mkg, refrig, cook fac, micro, d/wash, toaster, blkts, linen, pillows], w/mach, dryer, iron, iron brd, spa, cots. D ♦♦ $330, ◊ $80, ch con.

★★★★ **Majestic Tynte Street Apartments**, (Apt), 82 Tynte St, ☎ 08 8223 0500, fax 08 8223 0588, (Multi-stry gr fl), 24 apts acc up to 2, [shwr, tlt, hairdry, a/c, elec blkts, tel, TV, clock radio, t/c mkg, refrig, cook fac, micro, toaster, ldry, blkts, linen, pillows], w/mach, dryer, iron, iron brd, secure park, cots, non smoking units (20). D ♦♦ $116, ◊ $17, ch con, pen con, AE BC DC MC VI, ﾋﾟ.

★★★★ **North Adelaide Heritage Group**, (SA), Office: 109 Glen Osmond Rd, Eastwood. Bishops Courtyard Apartment-82 Molesworth St. ☎ 08 8272 1355, fax 08 8272 1355, 1 serv apt acc up to 3, (2 bedrm), [shwr, bath, tlt, hairdry, fan, fire pl, heat, elec blkts, tel, fax (avail), cable tv, video (avail), clock radio, CD, refrig, cook fac, micro, blkts, linen, pillows], ldry, w/mach, dryer, iron, bbq, non smoking property. D ♦♦ $150 - $185, ◊ $40, Min book applies, AE BC DC JCB MC VI.

★★★★ **(141 Tynte St Section)**, Friendly Meeting Chapel, 1 cotg acc up to 2, (Studio), [shwr, spa bath, tlt, a/c, heat, tel (avail), fax (avail), TV, video (avail), clock radio, CD, refrig, cook fac, toaster, blkts, linen, pillows], cots, non smoking property. D ♦♦ $150 - $185.

★★★★ **(38 Melbourne St Section)**, Melbourne Street Mews, 1 cotg acc up to 4, (2 bedrm), [shwr (2), spa bath (2), tlt (2), hairdry, a/c, fan, heat, elec blkts, tel, fax (avail), TV, video (avail), CD, t/c mkg, refrig, cook fac, micro, toaster, blkts, linen, pillows], iron, iron brd, non smoking property. D ♦♦ $220, ♦♦♦♦ $280, ch con.

★★★★ **(69 Buxton St Section)**, Garden and Lofts Apartment, (2 stry), 1 serv apt acc up to 6, (3 bedrm), [shwr, bath, tlt, hairdry, a/c-cool, c/fan, fire pl, heat, elec blkts, tel, fax (avail), TV, video (avail), clock radio, CD, refrig, cook fac, micro, d/wash, blkts, linen, pillows], ldry, w/mach, dryer, iron, bbq, cots, non smoking property. D ♦♦ $150 - $195, ◊ $40.

★★★★ **(71 Buxton St Section)**, Musica Viva Apartment, 1 serv apt acc up to 3, (1 bedrm), [shwr, bath, tlt, hairdry, c/fan, fire pl, heat, elec blkts, tel, fax (avail), TV, video (avail), clock radio, CD, refrig, cook fac, micro, blkts, linen, pillows], ldry, w/mach, dryer, iron, bbq, cots, non smoking property. D ♦♦ $160 - $195, ◊ $40.

North Adelaide Heritage Group ...continued

★★★★ **(73 Buxton St Section)**, George Lowe Esq Apartment, 1 serv apt acc up to 4, (2 bedrm), [shwr, tlt, hairdry, c/fan, fire pl, elec blkts, tel, fax (avail), TV, video (avail), clock radio, CD, refrig, cook fac, micro, blkts, linen, pillows], ldry, w/mach, dryer, iron, bbq, cots, non smoking property. D ♦♦ $160 - $195, ◊ $40.

★★★★ **(75 Buxton St Section)**, Butlers Apartment, 1 serv apt acc up to 5, (2 bedrm), [shwr, bath, tlt, hairdry, c/fan, fire pl, heat, elec blkts, tel, fax (avail), TV, video (avail), clock radio, refrig, cook fac, micro, blkts, linen, pillows], w/mach, dryer, iron, bbq, cots, non smoking property. D ♦♦ $160 - $195, ◊ $40.

★★★★ **(91 Hill St Section)**, William Townhouse, (2 stry), 1 apt acc up to 5, (3 bedrm), [shwr (2), bath, spa bath, tlt (2), hairdry, a/c-cool, heat, elec blkts, tel, TV, radio (cassette), CD, t/c mkg, refrig, cook fac, micro, d/wash, toaster, blkts, linen, pillows], w/mach, dryer, iron, iron brd, c/park (carport). D ♦♦ $150 - $195, ◊ $40.

★★★☆ **(120 Sussex St Section)**, Sussex Cottage, 1 cotg acc up to 4, (2 bedrm), [shwr, bath, spa bath, tlt, hairdry, a/c, heat, elec blkts, tel, fax (avail), TV, video (avail), radio, CD, t/c mkg, refrig, cook fac, micro, ldry, blkts, linen, pillows], w/mach, dryer, iron, non smoking property. D ♦♦ $140 - $175, ◊ $40, ch con.

★★★☆ **(67 Buxton St Section)**, Paprika Cottage, 1 cotg acc up to 3, (2 bedrm), [shwr, bath, spa bath, tlt, hairdry, a/c, c/fan, heat, elec blkts, tel, fax (avail), TV, video (avail), clock radio (cassette), CD, t/c mkg, refrig, cook fac, micro, blkts, linen, pillows], iron, iron brd, bbq, cots, non smoking property. D ♦♦ $140 - $195, ch con.

(22 Chapel St), Chapel Cottage, 1 cotg acc up to 4, (2 bedrm), [shwr, bath, tlt, hairdry, a/c, fan, heat, elec blkts, tel (avail), fax (avail), TV, video (avail), clock radio, CD, refrig, cook fac, micro, blkts, linen, pillows], iron, cots, non smoking property. D ♦♦ $140 - $175, ◊ $40, ch con, (not yet classified).

★★★★ **Old Lion Apartments**, (Apt), 9 Jerningham St, 50m S of PO, ☎ 08 8223 0500, fax 08 8334 7788, (Multi-stry gr fl), 57 apts acc up to 7, (1, 2 & 3 bedrm), [ensuite, bath (40), a/c, elec blkts, tel, TV, video-fee, clock radio, t/c mkg, refrig, cook fac, micro, toaster, ldry, blkts, linen, pillows], w/mach, dryer, iron, iron brd, dinner to unit, secure park, cots, non smoking units (40). D ♦♦ $148 - $247, ◊ $17, W ♦♦ $1,036 - $1,729, ◊ $38.50 - $115.50, ch con, AE BC DC MC VI.

★★★★ **The Grand Apartments-North Adelaide**, (SA), 55 Melbourne St, ☎ 08 8267 8888, fax 08 8267 8899, (Multi-stry gr fl), 53 serv apts acc up to 4, [shwr, tlt, a/c, tel, TV, video, clock radio, t/c mkg, refrig, cook fac, micro, toaster, blkts, doonas, linen, pillows], w/mach, dryer, iron, iron brd, rec rm, conf fac, pool, sauna, spa, gym, cots (avail), D ♦♦ $93.50 - $143, ♦♦♦♦ $93.50 - $143, ◊ $5.50 - $16.50, W ♦♦ $654.50 - $1,001, ♦♦♦♦ $654.50 - $1,001, ◊ $38.50 - $115.50, AE BC DC EFT JCB MC VI.

★★★ **Aman & Gurny Lodge Apartments**, (Apt), Previously Gurny Lodge 190 Gover St, ☎ 08 8267 2500, 24 apts acc up to 6, (2 bedrm3 bedrm Studio), [shwr, tlt, a/c, tel, TV, clock radio, refrig, cook fac, micro, toaster, blkts, linen, pillows], ldry, iron, iron brd, bbq (covered), secure park, RO $65 - $105, fam con, 1 unit yet to be rated, AE BC DC EFT MC VI.

★★★ **Greenways Apartments**, (Apt), (Reception located at unit 16, first floor). 45 King William Rd, Cnr Kermode St, ☎ 08 8267 5903, fax 08 8267 1790, (Multi-stry gr fl), 25 apts acc up to 8, (1, 2 & 3 bedrm), [shwr, tlt, a/c-cool, heat, elec blkts, tel, TV, clock radio, refrig, cook fac, micro (10)], ldry, w/mach, dryer, iron, iron brd, c/park. D $75 - $188, BC EFT MC VI.

★★★ **Treacles at North Adelaide**, (Cotg), 84A Stanley St, ☎ 08 8299 9092, fax 08 8373 2114, 2 cotgs acc up to 2, (1 bedrm), [shwr, tlt, a/c-cool, heat, elec blkts, tel, TV, video, clock radio, t/c mkg, refrig, cook fac, micro, toaster, blkts, linen, pillows], w/mach, dryer, iron, iron brd, breakfast ingredients, non smoking property. D $140, Min book applies, AE BC MC VI.

★★★☆ **(Stanley Street Cottage Section)**, 1 cotg acc up to 2, [shwr, tlt, a/c, elec blkts, tel, TV, video, clock radio, t/c mkg, refrig, cook fac, micro, toaster, blkts, doonas, linen, pillows], w/mach, dryer, lounge firepl, cots-fee, breakfast ingredients. D ♦ $140, ♦♦ $140.

B&B's/Guest Houses

★★★★☆ **Seek & Share Bed & Breakfast**, (B&B), 112 Barnard St, ☎ 08 8239 0155, fax 08 8239 0125, 3 rms [ensuite, bath (1), spa bath (2), hairdry, a/c, heat, elec blkts, clock radio], ldry, w/mach, dryer, iron, iron brd, lounge (TV), pool, t/c mkg shared, refrig, bbq, non smoking rms. BLB ♦ $120 - $150, ♦♦ $155 - $195, Min book applies, BC MC VI.

ADELAIDE - NORTON SUMMIT SA 5136

Pop Part of Adelaide, (15km E Adelaide), See map on page 588, ref D4. A small township perched at the top of the steep Hills scarp east of Adelaide. Hornsell Gully Conservation Park, Marble Hill and Schoner Park Rose Garden. Bush Walking, Scenic Drives.

Self Catering Accommodation

★★★★ **Drysdale Bed & Breakfast**, (Cotg), Debneys Rd, ☎ 08 8390 1652, fax 08 8390 1652, 1 cotg acc up to 2, [ensuite, spa bath, a/c, heat, elec blkts, tel, TV, CD, refrig, cook fac, micro, blkts, linen], tennis, breakfast ingredients, non smoking property. **BLB ♦♦ $150.**

★★★★ **Norton Summit Holiday Cottage**, (Cotg), No children's facilities, 7 Crescent Dve, ☎ 08 8390 1329, fax 08 8390 1329, 1 cotg acc up to 2, [shwr, tlt, a/c, TV, clock radio, CD, t/c mkg, refrig, cook fac, micro, blkts, linen, pillows], bbq, breakfast ingredients, non smoking property. **BB ♦ $100, ♦♦ $125.**

★★★☆ **Morialta Cottage**, (Cotg), Colonial Dve, 1.5km E of PO, ☎ 08 8390 1111, 1 cotg acc up to 8, (3 bedrm), [shwr, tlt (2), c/fan, heat (slow combustion), refrig, cook fac, elec frypan, blkts, linen, pillows], w/mach, dryer, bbq, non smoking property. **D ♦♦ $110, ◊ $12,** Pool facilities available.

Other Accommodation

Fuzzies Farm Bunkhouse, (Bunk), Colonial Dve, 1.5km E of PO, ☎ 08 8390 1111, 1 bunkhouse acc up to 8, (Bunk Rooms), [c/fan (1), wood heat (slow combustion), blkts, linen, pillows], c/park. **D ♦ $12 - $15, ◊ $12 - $15.**

ADELAIDE - NORWOOD SA 5067

Pop Part of Adelaide, (3km E Adelaide), See map on page 588, ref C4. A suburb of Adelaide. Croquet.

Self Catering Accommodation

★★★★ **Norwood Apartments**, (Apt), 37 Donegal St, ☎ 08 8336 6555, fax 08 8336 4555, 5 apts acc up to 4, (2 bedrm), [shwr, bath (hip), tlt, a/c-cool (3), a/c (2), heat (3), elec blkts, tel, TV, video, clock radio, CD, t/c mkg, refrig, cook fac, micro, d/wash, toaster, ldry (in unit), blkts, linen, pillows], w/mach, dryer, iron, iron brd, bbq, c/park (carport). **D ♦♦ $110, ◊ $11, W ♦♦ $732, ◊ $77,** Min book applies, BC DC MC VI.

★★★★ **(Beulah Rd Cottage Section)**, 107 Beulah Rd, 1 cotg acc up to 6, (3 bedrm), [shwr, bath, tlt, evap cool, heat, elec blkts, tel, TV, video, clock radio, CD, t/c mkg, refrig, cook fac, micro, d/wash, toaster, ldry, blkts, linen, pillows], w/mach, dryer, iron, iron brd. **D ♦♦♦♦ $150, W ♦♦♦♦ $963.**

★★★★ **(William St Cottage Section)**, 129 William St, 1 cotg acc up to 4, (2 bedrm), [shwr, bath, tlt, a/c-cool, heat, elec blkts, tel, TV, video, clock radio, CD, t/c mkg, refrig, cook fac, micro, d/wash, toaster, ldry (in unit), blkts, linen, pillows], w/mach, dryer, iron, iron brd, c/park (carport), cots. **D ♦♦ $121, ◊ $11, W ♦♦ $809, ◊ $77,** ch con.

★★★★ **Norwood Bed & Breakfast**, (Apt), 6 Rosemont St, ☎ 08 8431 7097, 1 apt acc up to 4, (1 bedrm), [shwr, tlt, hairdry, a/c-cool, heat, elec blkts, tel, TV, video, clock radio, CD, t/c mkg, refrig, cook fac, micro, toaster, blkts, doonas, linen, pillows], w/mach, dryer, iron, iron brd, c/park (covered), breakfast ingredients. **D ♦♦ $100, ◊ $20, W ♦♦ $630, ◊ $140,** BC MC VI.

ADELAIDE - PARADISE SA 5075

Pop Part of Adelaide, (9km NE Adelaide), See map on page 588, ref D3. A suburb of Adelaide.

★★☆ **Paradise Hotel**, (LH), 700 Lower North East Rd, ☎ 08 8337 5055, fax 08 8337 1772, (2 stry), 10 rms [ensuite, a/c, TV, t/c mkg, refrig, toaster], ✉, ☏. **BLB ♦ $49.50, ♦♦ $49.50, ♦♦♦ $55, ♦♦♦♦ $60, ◊ $5,** AE BC DC EFT MC VI.

ADELAIDE - PARKSIDE SA 5063

Pop Part of Adelaide, (2km SE Adelaide), See map on page 588, ref C4. A suburb of Adelaide.

Hotels/Motels

★★★★☆ **Tiffins on the Park**, (M), 176 Greenhill Rd, cnr George St, ☎ 08 8271 0444, fax 08 8272 8675, (2 stry gr fl), 54 units (3 suites) [shwr, spa bath (6), tlt, hairdry, a/c, elec blkts, tel, fax, TV, video (2), movie, clock radio, t/c mkg, refrig, mini bar], ldry, w/mach-fee, dryer-fee, conv fac, ✉, cafe, pool-heated, sauna, bbq, rm serv, c/park (undercover) (6), cots, non smoking rms (4). **RO ♦ $105 - $135, ♦♦ $105 - $135, ◊ $15, Suite D $150,** AE BC DC EFT MC VI.

★★★ **Powells Court Motel**, (M), 2 Glen Osmond Rd, ☎ 08 8271 7033, fax 08 8271 1511, (Multi-stry gr fl), 16 units [shwr, bath (12), tlt, a/c, tel, TV, t/c mkg, refrig, cook fac], lift, ldry, iron, iron brd, cots, **RO ♦ $60, ♦♦ $65, ♦♦♦ $75, ♦♦♦♦ $85,** AE BC DC MC VI.

ADELAIDE - PLYMPTON SA 5038

Pop Part of Adelaide, (6km SW Adelaide), See map on page 588, ref C4. A suburb of Adelaide.

Hotels/Motels

★★★☆ **Adelaide Supercentre Motel**, (M), 540 Marion Rd, Plympton Park 5038, ☎ 08 8371 2899, fax 08 8371 2878, (2 stry gr fl), 32 units [ensuite, bath (10), a/c, elec blkts, tel, TV, clock radio, t/c mkg, refrig, toaster], ldry, conv fac, ✉, pool indoor heated-fee, sauna-fee, spa-fee, rm serv, gym-fee, tennis, cots, non smoking units (9). **RO ♦♦ $75, ◊ $12,** ch con, AE BC DC EFT MC MCH VI.

Self Catering Accommodation

★★★★ **Adelaide Sorrento-Meridien**, (SA), 201 Anzac Hwy, ☎ 08 8297 7122, fax 08 8297 5138, (Multi-stry gr fl), 30 serv apts [shwr, bath, tlt, a/c, elec blkts, tel, TV, clock radio, refrig, cook fac, micro, d/wash, toaster], lift, ldry, pool, cots-fee. **D $126.50 - $214.50,** 8 apartments ★★★☆. Complimentary breakfast first morning. AE BC DC EFT MC VI.

ADELAIDE - POORAKA SA 5095

Pop Part of Adelaide, (11km NNE Adelaide), See map on page 588, ref C2. A suburb of Adelaide.

Hotels/Motels

★★★☆ **Pooraka Motor Inn**, (M), 875 Main North Rd, 11km N of PO, ☎ 08 8349 6255, fax 08 8349 7559, (2 stry gr fl), 21 units [ensuite, spa bath (2), hairdry (12), a/c, elec blkts, tel, TV, clock radio, t/c mkg, refrig, toaster], ldry, iron, iron brd, ✉, bbq, cots-fee, non smoking rms (4). **RO ♦ $79 - $125, ♦♦ $79 - $125, ◊ $11,** ch con, 10 units ★★★☆. AE BC DC EFT MC VI, ⚐.

★★★ **Pavlos Motel**, (M), 859 Main North Rd, ☎ 08 8260 6655, fax 08 8349 7424, 31 units [ensuite, spa bath (1), a/c, elec blkts, tel, TV, clock radio, t/c mkg, refrig], ldry, ✉ (Mon to Sat), pool, bbq, cots-fee, non smoking units (2). **RO ♦ $68 - $78, ♦♦ $70 - $80, ◊ $11,** ch con, AE BC DC EFT MC VI, ⚐.

ADELAIDE - PORT NOARLUNGA SA 5167

Pop Part of Adelaide, (31km S Adelaide), See map on page 588, ref B6. Situated near the mouth of the Onkaparinga River, a popular beach destination with offshore reefs used by scuba divers. Boat Ramp, Boating, Bowls, Croquet, Fishing, Surfing, Swimming (Beach).

Hotels/Motels

★★★ **Port Noarlunga Motel**, (M), 39 Saltfleet St, ☎ 08 8382 1267, fax 08 8382 3332, 8 units [ensuite, a/c, elec blkts, TV, clock radio, t/c mkg, refrig], cots-fee, non smoking units (3). **RO ♦ $62, ♦♦ $67, ◊ $10,** BC MC VI.

Self Catering Accommodation

★★★★ **Port Noarlunga Coastview Motor Inn**, (Apt), 153 Esplanade, ☎ 08 8386 3311, fax 08 8386 3377, (2 stry gr fl), 15 apts acc up to 4, (Studio), [ensuite, a/c, elec blkts (on request), tel, fax, TV, video (avail)-fee, movie, clock radio, t/c mkg, refrig, toaster, blkts, linen, pillows], cafe (licensed), bbq, rm serv, meals to unit, non smoking units (3). **RO ♦♦ $88 - $99, ◊ $12,** AE BC DC MC VI.

B&B's/Guest Houses

★★★★☆ **Yandara By The Sea Bed & Breakfast**, (B&B), 6 Bunbury Rd, 2km S of PO, ☎ 08 8386 1236, fax 08 8386 1236, 1 rm [shwr, bath, tlt, evap cool, fan, heat, elec blkts, TV, video, clock radio, t/c mkg, refrig, micro], iron, iron brd, rec rm, breakfast rm, spa, bbq, secure park (undercover), non smoking units, **BB ♦ $80 - $105, ♦♦ $95 - $135.**

ADELAIDE - PORT WILLUNGA SA 5173

Pop Part of Adelaide, (46km S Adelaide), See map on page 588, ref B8. A coastal town on the Fleurieu Peninsula. Boating, Fishing, Swimming (Beach), Vineyards, Wineries.

Self Catering Accommodation

★★★★ **Anchor Cottage**, (Cotg), No children's facilities, ☎ 08 8557 8516, 1 cotg acc up to 2, (1 bedrm), [shwr, spa bath, tlt, hairdry, a/c, elec blkts, TV, video, CD, t/c mkg, refrig, cook fac, micro, d/wash, toaster, blkts, doonas, linen, pillows], iron, iron brd, lounge firepl, breakfast ingredients, non smoking property, **D ♦♦ $130 - $160,** BC MC VI.

★★★★☆ **(Shell Cottage)**, 1 cotg acc up to 2, (1 bedrm), [shwr, spa bath, tlt, hairdry, a/c, heat, elec blkts, TV, video (movies avail), CD, t/c mkg, refrig, cook fac, micro, elec frypan, d/wash, toaster, blkts, doonas, linen, pillows], w/mach, iron, iron brd. **D ♦♦ $130 - $160.**

Saltaire, (Cotg), 4 Marlin Rd, 1km W of PO, ☎ 08 8557 4452, fax 08 8557 4422, 1 cotg acc up to 4, (2 bedrm), [shwr, tlt, a/c, TV, video, clock radio, t/c mkg, refrig, cook fac, blkts, doonas, linen, pillows], w/mach, bbq, breakfast ingredients, non smoking property. D ♦♦ $100, ₵ $10, W ♦♦ $600, ₵ $50, ch con, Min book Christmas and Jan, (not yet classified).

ADELAIDE - REYNELLA SA 5161

Pop Part of Adelaide, (23km SW Adelaide), See map on page 588, ref B6. A southern suburb of Adelaide.

★★★★☆ **St Francis Winery Resort**, (M), Bridge St, ☎ 08 8322 2246, fax 08 8322 0921, (2 stry gr fl), 41 units [ensuite, spa bath (23), a/c, tel, clock radio, t/c mkg, refrig, mini bar, cook fac (6), ldry], iron, iron brd, ⊠, bar, pool indoor heated, sauna, 24hr reception, rm serv, ☏, cots-fee, non smoking units (20), RO ♦♦ $85 - $160, ₵ $12, AE BC DC EFT MC VI, ⚿.

ADELAIDE - ROSSLYN PARK SA 5072

Pop Part of Adelaide, (4km NE Adelaide), See map on page 588, ref D4. Inner suburb of Adelaide.

★★★★ **Mary Penfold Panorama Bed & Breakfast**, (B&B), 17 Mary Penfold Dve, ☎ 08 8332 6684, fax 08 8332 6684, (2 stry), 2 rms [shwr, spa bath, tlt, a/c, TV (1), video, t/c mkg, ldry], lounge, refrig, bbq. D ♦ $75, ♦♦ $100, ₵ $15.

ADELAIDE - ROSTREVOR SA 5073

Pop Part of Adelaide, (9km NE Adelaide), See map on page 588, ref D3. A suburb of Adelaide. Morialta Conservation Park. Bush Walking.

★★★★☆ **Marybank Farm Bed & Breakfast**, (B&B), No children's facilities, Montacute Rd, ☎ 08 8337 1282, fax 08 8336 1575, 2 rms (1 suite) [ensuite, bath, hairdry, a/c, c/fan, TV, clock radio, t/c mkg, refrig, cook fac ltd, micro, toaster, pillows], iron (avail), iron brd (avail), pool, breakfast ingredients, non smoking rms. D ♦♦ $154, W ♦♦ $847, AE BC MC VI.

ADELAIDE - SEATON SA 5023

Pop Part of Adelaide, (10km E Adelaide), See map on page 588, ref B3. A suburb of Adelaide.

Hotels/Motels

★★☆ **Links Hotel Motel**, (LMH), 346 Tapleys Hill Rd, ☎ 08 8356 3111, fax 08 8235 1860, 27 units [ensuite, bath (8), evap cool (4), a/c (23), elec blkts, tel, TV, clock radio, t/c mkg, refrig], ⊠, bbq, rm serv, cots-fee. RO ♦ $40 - $60, ♦♦ $60 - $70, ₵ $6 - $9, ch con, 9 rooms ★★☆, TAB, Sky & Keno, AE BC DC EFT MC VI.

ADELAIDE - SELLICKS BEACH SA 5174

Pop 712. (52km Adelaide), See map on page 588, ref B8. A small township located south of Adelaide. Swimming (Beach).

Self Catering Accommodation

★★★★ **Norbreck House**, (Apt), No children's facilities, 29 Esplanade, 1km S of PO, ☎ 08 8556 3539, fax 08 8556 3539, 1 apt acc up to 4, [shwr, tlt, hairdry, a/c, c/fan, heat, elec blkts, TV, video-fee, movie, clock radio, t/c mkg, refrig, cook fac, micro, elec frypan, toaster, blkts, linen, pillows], w/mach, dryer, iron, iron brd, pool-indoor (solar heated), sauna, spa, breakfast ingredients, non smoking property, D ♦♦ $125 - $155, ₵ $20 - $30, pen con, weekly con, Min book applies, BC MC VI.

B&B's/Guest Houses

★★★★☆ **Sellicks on the Sea Bed & Breakfast**, (B&B), 21 Esplanade, ☎ 08 8556 3273, 1 rm [shwr, tlt, a/c, TV, video, clock radio (cassette), t/c mkg, refrig, micro], bbq, non smoking rms. BB ♦♦ $105 - $135.

ADELAIDE - SEMAPHORE SA 5019

Pop Part of Adelaide, (15km NW Adelaide), See map on page 588, ref B3. A popular seaside suburb of Adelaide. Fort Glanville & Bower Cottage Arts and Crafts. Fishing (Beach), Swimming (Beach).

Hotels/Motels

★★ **Federal Hotel**, (LH), 25 Semaphore Rd, ☎ 08 8449 6866, fax 08 8449 6296, (2 stry), 13 rms [ensuite, a/c, TV, t/c mkg, refrig, toaster], ⊠, cots. RO ♦ $60, ♦♦ $70, ₵ $10, BC EFT MC VI.

Semaphore Hotel, (LH), 17 Semaphore Rd, ☎ 08 8449 4662, fax 08 8449 4626, (Multi-stry), 14 rms [basin (12), elec blkts, clock radio], rec rm, lounge (TV), lounge firepl, ⊠, cook fac, refrig. W ♦ $110, ♦♦ $143, RO ♦ $38.50, ♦♦ $55, ₵ $11, BC DC EFT MC VI, (not yet classified).

B&B's/Guest Houses

★★★☆ **Serendipity Bed & Breakfast**, (B&B), Cnr Esplanade & Union Sts, 500m N of PO, ☎ 08 8249 9924, 1 rm (1 suite) [ensuite, spa bath, hairdry, a/c, fan, heat, elec blkts, TV, video, clock radio (cassette), CD, t/c mkg, refrig, toaster], iron, iron brd, c/park. BLB ♦ $60 - $85, ♦♦ $100 - $125.

ADELAIDE - SOMERTON PARK SA 5044

Pop Part of Adelaide, (12km SW Adelaide), See map on page 588, ref B4. A suburb of Adelaide.

Self Catering Accommodation

★★★ **Aman Apartments**, (SA), 17 Phillips St, ☎ 08 8267 2500, fax 08 8239 2301, (2 stry gr fl), 6 serv apts acc up to 4, (2 bedrm), [shwr, tlt, a/c, fan, tel, TV, video-fee, clock radio, t/c mkg, refrig, cook fac, micro, toaster, blkts, doonas, linen, pillows], ldry, plygr, cots, D $75 - $105, AE BC DC EFT MC VI.

B&B's/Guest Houses

★★★★☆ **'Angove Villa' Bed & Breakfast**, (B&B), 14 Angove Rd, 1.6km S of Glenelg PO, ☎ 08 8376 6421, fax 08 8376 6170, 1 rm [ensuite (1), a/c, elec blkts, tel, TV, video, clock radio, CD, t/c mkg, refrig, doonas], c/park. BB ♦ $115 - $175, ♦♦ $115 - $175, AE BC DC MC VI.

★★★☆ **Forstens Bed & Breakfast**, (B&B), 19 King George Ave, ☎ 08 8298 3393, 2 rms [shwr, tlt, elec blkts, TV, clock radio, t/c mkg], c/park. BB ♦ $45, ♦♦ $60.

ADELAIDE - ST GEORGES SA 5064

Pop Part of Adelaide, (6km SE Adelaide), See map on page 588, ref D4. A suburb of Adelaide.

B&B's/Guest Houses

★★★★ **Kirkendale Bed & Breakfast**, (B&B), 16 Inverness Ave, ☎ 08 8338 2768, fax 08 8338 2760, 1 rm (2 bedrm), [shwr, tlt, a/c, c/fan, heat, elec blkts, TV, video, t/c mkg, refrig, cook fac ltd, toaster, doonas], bbq, non smoking property. BLB ♦♦ $90 - $110, ₵ $30, Min book Christmas Jan long w/ends and Easter, AE BC DC MC VI.

ADELAIDE - STIRLING SA 5152

Pop Part of Adelaide, (18km SE Adelaide), See map on page 588, ref D5. A suburb of Adelaide. Aptos Cruz Galleries and Stirling Parrot Farm. Scenic Drives, Vineyards, Wineries.

Self Catering Accommodation

★★★☆ **Coachmans Cottage**, (Cotg), 8 Orley Ave, ☎ 08 8370 8414, 1 cotg acc up to 3, (1 bedrm), [shwr, tlt, hairdry, heat, elec blkts, TV, clock radio, CD, refrig, cook fac, micro, blkts, linen, pillows], iron, breakfast ingredients, non smoking property. D ♦♦ $140, ₵ $50, ch con, BC MC VI.

★★☆ **Picodlla-Under Mt Lofty**, (Cotg), Nara Rd, 2.5km E of PO, ☎ 08 8339 3794, 1 cotg acc up to 6, (2 bedrm), [shwr, tlt, a/c, fire pl, heat, TV, radio, t/c mkg, refrig, cook fac, blkts, linen, pillows], ldry, w/mach, iron, breakfast ingredients. D ♦♦ $200 - $150, ₵ $15 - $35, W ♦♦ $350, ch con.

B&B's/Guest Houses

★★★★★ **Thorngrove Manor**, (B&B), 2 Glenside La, 3km NE of PO, ☎ 08 8339 6748, fax 08 8370 9950, (Multi-stry gr fl), 4 rms (3 suites) [shwr, bath, spa bath (3), tlt, a/c, fire pl (2), cent heat, elec blkts, tel, TV, video, clock radio (cassette), CD, t/c mkg, refrig, mini bar], iron, iron brd, lounge, spa (pool), rm serv, c/park (undercover). BB ♦♦ $506 - $1,072, 1 room of a lower rating, AE BC DC JCB MC VI.

★★★★☆ **Albemarle B&B**, (B&B), No children's facilities, 40 Avenue Rd, 1km E of PO, ☎ 08 8339 6019, 1 rm [ensuite, hairdry, a/c, elec blkts, clock radio, t/c mkg], w/mach, dryer, iron, iron brd, lounge (TV), non smoking property, BB ♦ $95, ♦♦ $135, pen con, BC MC VI.

★★★★☆ **The Orangerie Bed & Breakfast**, (B&B), No children's facilities, 4 Orley Ave, 350m NW of PO, ☎ 08 8339 5458, fax 08 8339 5912, 2 rms (1 & 2 bedrm - Suite.), [shwr, tlt, hairdry, fan, c/fan, cent heat, elec blkts, TV, video, clock radio, CD, t/c mkg, refrig, micro, elec frypan, toaster], ldry, w/mach, dryer, iron, iron brd, lounge firepl (1), pool (saltwater/solar heat), bbq, c/park (undercover), non smoking rms. BB ♦♦ $195, D ♦♦♦♦ $350, BC MC VI.

★★★☆ **Adelaide Hills Bed & Breakfast Accommodation**, (B&B), Previously Panorama Lodge Bed & Breakfast, 35 Garrod Cres, 500m NE of PO, ☎ 08 8339 1898, fax 08 8339 1898, 1 rm [shwr, tlt, hairdry, a/c, heat, elec blkts, TV, clock radio, t/c mkg, refrig, cook fac, micro, toaster], iron, iron brd, non smoking rms. BB ♦ $100, ♦♦ $110.

Other Accommodation

The Mount Lofty Railway Station Lodge, (Lodge), 2 Sturt Valley Rd, 800m from Stirling Main Street, ☎ 08 8339 7400, fax 08 8339 5560, 4 rms acc up to 6, [fan, fire pl (bedroom) (3), heat (elec/wood), cook fac ltd, micro, d/wash, toaster], shared fac (4), lounge (TV, video), conf fac, lounge firepl, ⊠, t/c mkg shared, refrig, non smoking rms. BLB ♦ $22 - $30, ♦♦ $50 - $75, BC MC VI, (not yet classified).

ADELAIDE - THORNGATE SA 5082

Pop Part of Adelaide, (5km N Adelaide), See map on page 588, ref C3. A suburb of Adelaide.

★★★★★ **Myoora Heritage Accommodation**, (B&B), No children's facilities, 4 Carter St, 3km N of GPO, ☎ 08 8344 2599, fax 08 8344 9575, 3 rms [ensuite, spa bath (2), a/c, TV, video, CD], pool, spa, tennis, **BB ♦♦ $180 - $290**, BC MC VI.

ADELAIDE - TOORAK GARDENS SA 5065

Pop Part of Adelaide, (3km E Adelaide), See map on page 588, ref C4. A suburb of Adelaide.

★★★★ **Adelaide's Toorak Gardens Serviced Apartments**, (Apt), 90 Grant Ave, ☎ 08 8338 6767, fax 08 8338 0499, 8 apts acc up to 4, (1 & 2 bedrm) [ensuite, a/c, tel, TV, video, clock radio, t/c mkg, refrig, cook fac, micro, blkts, linen, pillows], w/mach, dryer, iron, iron brd, c/park (undercover-3), cots, non smoking units (4). **D ♦♦ $75 - $110, ♦ $10,** AE BC DC MC VI.

ADELAIDE - UPPER STURT SA 5156

Pop Part of Adelaide, (13km SE Adelaide), See map on page 588, ref D5. Outer suburb of Adelaide, in the Adelaide Hills. Bush Walking, Golf.

B&B's/Guest Houses

★★★★ **Walmer House Bed & Breakfast**, (B&B), 22 Hilltop Dve, 1.5km SW of PO, ☎ 08 8339 1016, fax 08 8339 1016, 1 rm [ensuite, hairdry, heat, tel, TV, clock radio, t/c mkg, refrig, cook fac, micro, toaster], spa, bbq, meals avail (by arrangement), c/park. **BB ♦♦ $110 - $120,** pen con, BC MC VI.

★★★☆ **Canungra Bed and Breakfast**, (B&B), 24 Highwood Grove, ☎ 08 8370 1258, 1 rm [ensuite, hairdry, a/c, c/fan, elec blkts, TV, video, clock radio, CD, t/c mkg, refrig], iron (avail), iron brd (avail), spa (outside, heated), meals to unit, c/park (undercover), cots (avail), non smoking property. **BB ♦♦ $150,** Min book Christmas and Jan, BC MC VI.

ADELAIDE - WALKERVILLE SA 5081

Pop Part of Adelaide, (4km NE Adelaide), See map on page 588, ref C3. A suburb of Adelaide. Bowls, Tennis.

Self Catering Accommodation

★★★★ **Vale House Heritage Suites**, (Apt), enter via Harris Rd, No children's facilities, 69 Lansdowne Tce, within the Levi Park Caravan Park, ☎ 08 8344 2209, fax 08 8344 2209, 4 apts acc up to 2, [ensuite, hairdry, a/c, TV, video (avail), clock radio, refrig, cook fac, micro, toaster, blkts, linen, pillows], non smoking units, **D ♦♦ $95 - $110,** BC EFT MC VI.

★★★☆ **Adelaide Oakford Apartments**, (Apt), Check in at 18 Stuart Rd, Dulwich to collect keys. 147 Stephens Tce, ☎ 08 8333 7400, fax 08 8332 7446, 16 apts acc up to 4, (2 bedrm) [shwr, tlt, a/c, tel, TV, video-fee, refrig, cook fac, micro, d/wash, blkts, linen, pillows], **D $115 - $132,** AE BC DC MC VI.

ADELAIDE - WARRADALE SA 5046

Pop Part of Adelaide, (11km SW Adelaide), See map on page 588, ref B4. A suburb of Adelaide.

★★ **Warradale Hotel**, (LH), 234 Diagonal Rd, ☎ 08 8296 1019, fax 08 8377 1361, (2 stry) 10 rms [ensuite, a/c-cool (1), a/c (10), TV, t/c mkg, refrig], ⊠, ✆, cots. **D $70, RO ♦ $45, ♦♦ $55, ♦ $5,** fam con, AE BC EFT MC VI.

ADELAIDE - WEST BEACH SA 5024

Pop Part of Adelaide, (8km W Adelaide), See map on page 588, ref B4. A suburb of Adelaide. Boating, Fishing, Golf, Surfing, Swimming (Pool & Beach), Tennis.

Hotels/Motels

FLAG
FLAG CHOICE HOTELS

★★★☆ **Adelaide Aviators Lodge**, (M), 728 Tapleys Hill Rd, ☎ 08 8356 8388, fax 08 8353 2868, (2 stry gr fl), 30 units (1 suite) [shwr, bath (hip) (2), spa bath, tlt, a/c, elec blkts, tel, TV, video, clock radio, t/c mkg, refrig, mini bar, micro (2), elec frypan (2), toaster (2)], ldry, w/mach-fee, dryer-fee, iron, iron brd, conv fac, ⊠, bar, pool-heated, spa, bbq, rm serv, courtesy transfer, cots. **D ♦ $110 - $120, ♦♦ $120 - $135,** ch con, fam con, AE BC DC EFT JCB MC VI, ♿.

Self Catering Accommodation

★★★★☆ **Adelaide Shores Holiday Village**, (HU), Previously Marineland Village Holiday Villas Military Rd, 2km N of Glenelg PO, ☎ 08 8353 2655, fax 08 8353 3755, 29 units acc up to 6, (2 bedrm), [shwr, tlt, hairdry, a/c-cool, heat, cable tv, video, clock radio, refrig, cook fac, micro, toaster, ldry (in unit), blkts, linen, pillows], rec rm, pool-heated, bbq, plygr, tennis. **D ♦♦ $111, ♦ $15, W $777,** ch con, Min book Christmas Jan long w/ends and Easter, AE BC DC EFT MC VI.

★★★★☆ **(Holiday Unit Section)**, 32 units acc up to 4, (2 bedrm), [ensuite, a/c, TV, refrig, cook fac, micro, blkts, linen, pillows]. **D ♦♦ $87, ♦ $14, W ♦♦ $549,** ch con, ♿.

★★★☆ **Tuileries Holiday Apartments**, (HU), 13 Military Rd, West Beach 5024, ☎ 08 8353 3874, fax 08 8353 3874, (2 stry gr fl), 5 units acc up to 6, (1, 2 & 3 bedrm), [shwr, tlt, a/c-cool, heat, elec blkts, TV, refrig, cook fac, micro, blkts, linen, pillows], ldry, pool, bbq, c/park (undercover), cots, **RO $54 - $107,** Min book applies.

★★★ **Beachcomber Holiday Apartments**, (HU), 62 Seaview Rd, ☎ 08 8235 0354, fax 08 8356 8479, (2 stry gr fl), 5 units acc up to 5, (1 & 2 bedrm), [shwr, bath, tlt, c/fan, heat, elec blkts, TV, clock radio, refrig, cook fac, blkts, linen, pillows], ldry, c/park (undercover). **D ♦♦ $66 - $165, ♦ $12, W ♦♦ $385 - $995,** Min book applies, BC MC VI.

★★★ **Seavista Holiday Suites**, (HU), 52 Seaview Rd, ☎ 08 8356 3975, fax 08 8855 5373, (2 stry gr fl), 8 units acc up to 6, (1, 2 & 3 bedrm), [shwr, bath (4), tlt, a/c, heat, elec blkts, TV, refrig, cook fac, micro, blkts, linen, pillows], ldry, ✆, cots, **D $47 - $116,** Min book applies, BC MC VI.

★★★ **West Beach Townhouses**, (HU), 98 Seaview Rd, ☎ 08 8356 7245, (2 stry gr fl), 5 units acc up to 6, [shwr, bath, tlt, a/c, TV, refrig, cook fac, ldry, blkts, linen, pillows], cots. **D $60 - $90.**

★★☆ **Atlantic Holiday Units**, (HU), 68 Seaview Rd, ☎ 08 8376 1499, fax 08 8376 1161, 5 units acc up to 4, (1 & 2 bedrm), [shwr, tlt, fan, heat, elec blkts, TV, refrig, cook fac, elec frypan, toaster, blkts, linen, pillows], w/mach, iron, iron brd, c/park. **RO ♦♦ $210, ♦♦♦♦ $390,** Min book applies.

★★☆ **Beachside Holiday Units**, (HU), 90 Seaview Rd, ☎ 08 8356 5324, fax 08 8356 5324, 6 units acc up to 5, (2 bedrm), [shwr, bath (hip), tlt, c/fan, heat, elec blkts, TV, clock radio, refrig, cook fac, micro, blkts, linen, pillows], w/mach, bbq, c/park (undercover), cots, **D ♦ $11, $49.50 - $104.50, W $308 - $693,** ch con, Min book applies.

★★☆ **Holiday Palm Units**, (HU), 8 West Beach Rd, ☎ 08 8248 0010, fax 08 8248 2676, 6 units acc up to 5, (1 bedrm), [shwr, bath (3), tlt, hairdry, c/fan, elec blkts, TV, clock radio, refrig, cook fac, micro, elec frypan, blkts, linen, pillows], iron, iron brd, cots, **BLB $75,** Min book applies, BC MC VI.

★★☆ **Surfside Holiday Units**, (HU), 54 Seaview Rd, ☎ 08 8356 3339, 3 units acc up to 5, (2 bedrm), [shwr, bath (hip), tlt, a/c, elec blkts, TV, clock radio (3), refrig, cook fac, micro, blkts, linen, pillows], ldry, c/park. **D $45 - $80,** Min book applies.

Esplanade Apartments at West Beach, (HU), 80 Seaview Rd, ☎ 08 8353 0443, fax 08 8356 4478, (2 stry gr fl), 6 units acc up to 6, (2 bedrm), [shwr, tlt, a/c, elec blkts, TV, video, refrig, cook fac, micro, toaster, blkts, linen, pillows], ldry, bbq, c/park. **D ♦♦ $55 - $105,** (not yet classified).

Rates may change. Check before booking.

ADELAIDE - WEST LAKES SA 5021

Pop Part of Adelaide, (12km NW Adelaide), See map on page 588, ref B3. A lakeside suburb of Adelaide and home of Football Park. Boating, Fishing (Lake), Golf, Rowing, Squash, Swimming (Lake).

Hotels/Motels

★★★★☆ **Lakes Resort**, (LH), 141 Brebner Dve, ☎ 08 8356 4444, fax 08 8353 1212, (Multi-stry), 72 rms [ensuite, bath (35), spa bath (35), hairdry, a/c, heat, tel, TV, movie, clock radio, t/c mkg, refrig, mini bar], lift, ldry, iron, iron brd, lounge, conv fac, ☒, bar, pool, spa, steam rm, bbq, rm serv, bicycle, gym, cots-fee, non smoking rms (48). **RO 👫 $135 - $205, 🧍 $30**, ch con, AE BC DC EFT JCB MC VI, ♿.

ADELAIDE - WILLUNGA SA 5172

Pop 1,164. (44km S Adelaide), See map on page 588, ref C8. Small town on the Fleurieu Peninsula. James Bassett School, Old Court House & Police Station, Old Willunga Hill Geranium Nursery, Rondoro Clydesdale Stud, Rose Display Garden and wineries. Scenic Drives, Vineyards, Wineries.

Self Catering Accommodation

★★★★☆ **Tabandi 'The Awakening'**, (HU), (Farm), Lot 13, Range Rd, 2km SE of PO, ☎ 08 8556 7336, fax 08 8381 6098, 1 unit acc up to 14, [shwr, bath, tlt, a/c-cool, heat, tel, TV, video, movie, clock radio, t/c mkg, refrig, mini bar, cook fac, micro, d/wash, toaster, blkts, doonas, linen, pillows], w/mach, dryer, iron, bbq, c/park (garage). **D 👫 $189 - $279, 🧍 $28 - $80**, weekly con, AE BC DC MC VI.

★★★★ **Citrus Cottage B&B**, (Cotg), No children's facilities, Unit 3, 37 High St, ☎ 08 8554 3243, fax 08 8554 2438, 1 cotg acc up to 4, (2 bedrm), [shwr, bath, tlt, a/c, fire pl, elec blkts, TV, video, clock radio, CD, t/c mkg, refrig, cook fac, micro, toaster, blkts, doonas, linen, pillows], w/mach, iron, iron brd, breakfast ingredients, non smoking property. **D 👫 $150**, Min book applies, BC MC VI.

★★★☆ **Kurianda Accommodation**, (Cotg), Lot 5, Range Rd West, ☎ 08 8268 4471, fax 08 8345 4027, 1 cotg acc up to 7, (3 bedrm), [shwr, bath, tlt, a/c-cool, heat, TV, video, clock radio, refrig, cook fac, micro, toaster], ldry, w/mach, dryer, bbq, cots, breakfast ingredients. **D 🧍 $100 - $168, 👫 $100 - $168, 🧍 $27.50 - $42**, ch con.

★★★☆ **Normanton Peacock Farm Bed & Breakfast**, (Cotg), Lot 80, Norman Rd, 1km NW of PO, ☎ 08 8556 4051, fax 08 8556 4051, 1 cotg acc up to 2, (1 bedrm - split level.), [shwr, tlt, a/c, TV (2), video, clock radio, CD, t/c mkg, refrig, cook fac ltd, elec frypan, toaster, blkts, doonas, linen, pillows], w/mach, dryer, iron, iron brd, lounge firepl, bbq, c/park (garage), cots, breakfast ingredients, non smoking property. **D 👫 $126.50.**

★★★☆ **Weemilah Bed & Breakfast Cottage**, (Cotg), Lot 51, Delabole Rd, 3km SW of PO, ☎ 08 8556 2940, 1 cotg acc up to 4, (2 bedrm), [shwr, tlt, hairdry, a/c, wood heat, elec blkts, TV, video, clock radio, CD, t/c mkg, refrig, cook fac, micro, toaster, blkts, linen, pillows], iron, iron brd, bbq, c/park. **BLB 👫 $130, 🧍 $50**, ch con, BC MC VI.

The Dairy Bed and Breakfast, (Cotg), RSD 1627, Pottery Rd, 9km S of PO, ☎ 08 8556 7207, fax 08 8556 7290, 1 cotg acc up to 4, (2 bedrm), [shwr, spa bath, tlt, a/c, c/fan, heat (wood), elec blkts, tel, TV, video, clock radio, t/c mkg, refrig, cook fac, micro, toaster, doonas, linen, pillows], lounge firepl, bbq, non smoking property. **BLB 👫 $40**, BC MC VI, (not yet classified).

B&B's/Guest Houses

★★★★☆ **Bindarah Valley Bed and Breakfast**, (B&B), St John Tce East, 1.5km SW of PO, ☎ 08 8556 2819, fax 08 8556 2819, 1 rm [ensuite, hairdry, a/c-cool, c/fan, heat (slow combustion), elec blkts, radio (cassette), t/c mkg, refrig, micro, toaster], w/mach, iron, iron brd, bbq, meals to unit. **BLB 👫 $145, 🧍 $52**, AE BC MC VI.

★★★★☆ **Willunga House Bed & Breakfast**, (B&B), 1 St Peters Tce, 100m N of PO, ☎ 08 8556 2467, fax 08 8556 2465, 5 rms [ensuite (3), bath (2), a/c-cool (bedrooms), a/c, TV, clock radio], bathrm (2), lounge (open fire), pool-heated (solar), t/c mkg shared, non smoking property. **BB 🧍 $120 - $140, 👫 $140 - $160**, 2 rooms of a lower rating, BC MC VI.

ADELAIDE - WOODFORDE SA 5072

Pop Part of Adelaide, (11km ENE Adelaide), See map on page 588, ref D3.

★★★★★ **Adelong Lifestyle Accommodation**, (Cotg), No children's facilities, Norton Summit Rd, ☎ 08 8331 7485, fax 08 8361 2529, 3 cotgs acc up to 2, (1 bedrm), [ensuite, hairdry, a/c, tel, TV, video, clock radio, CD, refrig, cook fac, micro, ldry (in unit), blkts, linen, pillows], w/mach, dryer, sauna, spa (pool), c/park (carport), gym, breakfast ingredients, non smoking property, **D 👫 $330**, BC MC VI.

ADELAIDE - WOODVILLE SA 5011

Pop Part of Adelaide, (10km NW Adelaide), See map on page 588, ref C3. A suburb of Adelaide. The Brocas Historical Museum.

★★☆ **Lindy Lodge Motel**, (M), 445 Torrens Rd, Woodville Park 5012, ☎ 08 8268 2333, fax 08 8445 9023, (2 stry gr fl), 21 units [ensuite, bath (4), a/c, tel, TV, clock radio, t/c mkg, refrig], ldry-fee, conv fac, sauna, rm serv, cots. **RO 🧍 $58, 👫 $66, 🧍 $8**, AE BC DC MC VI.

End of Adelaide & Suburbs

ADELAIDE HILLS SA

See Birdwood, Charleston, Cudlee Creek, Gumeracha, Hahndorf, Inglewood, Lenswood, Littlehampton, Mt Barker, Mt Torrens, Oakbank.

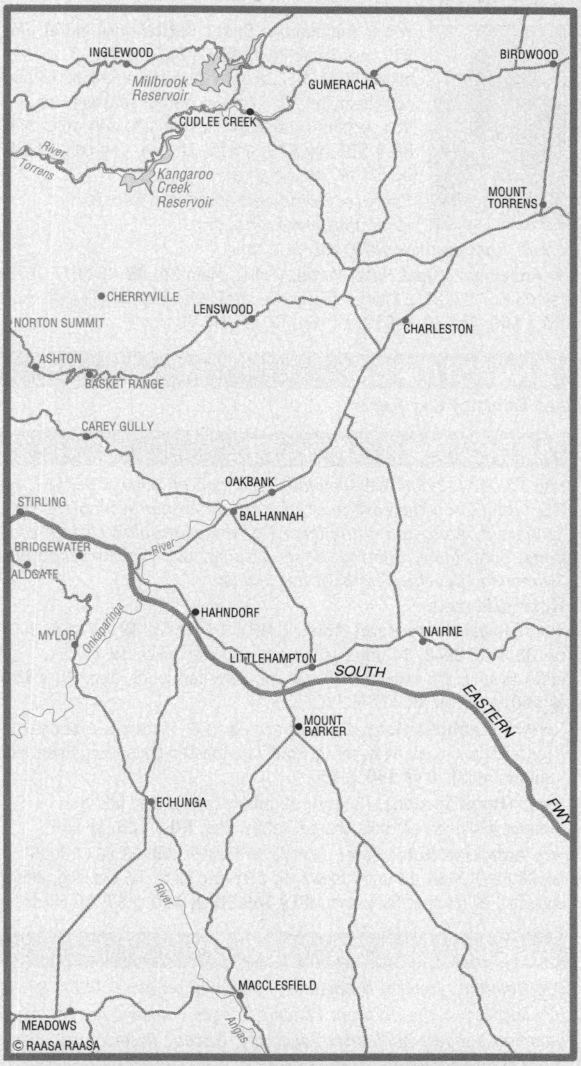

AMERICAN BEACH SA

See Kangaroo Island Region.

AMERICAN RIVER SA

See Kangaroo Island Region.

ANDAMOOKA SA 5722

Pop 471. (591km NNW Adelaide), See map on pages 586/587, ref G3. Once part of an inland sea, a unique township of miners homes, existing mainly on the production of opal, with a creekbed as the main street. Gem Fossicking.

Hotels/Motels

★★★ **Andamooka Dukes Bottlehouse Motel**, (M), 275 Opal Creek Blvd, ☎ 08 8672 7007, fax 08 8672 7062, 8 units [ensuite, a/c-cool, c/fan, cent heat, tel, TV, t/c mkg, refrig, toaster], ldry, bbq, c/park (undercover), non smoking rms. **RO** ♦ **$55**, ♦♦ **$72**, ◊ **$15**, ch con, pen con, AE BC DC EFT MC VI, ♿,

Operator Comment: Visit our website www.andamooka.au.com

Email andamookaopal@hotmail.com

★ **Andamooka Opal Hotel Motel**, (LMH), Main Rd, ☎ 08 8672 7078, fax 08 8672 7181, 11 units [shwr (6), a/c], ldry, lounge (TV), ☒, ☎. **RO** ♦ **$60**, ♦♦ **$70**, ◊ **$10**, ch con, BC EFT MC VI.

ANGASTON SA

See Barossa Valley Region.

ARDROSSAN SA 5571

Pop 1,008. (137km NW Adelaide), See map on pages 586/587, ref B6. Situated on the east coast of Yorke Peninsula overlooking Gulf St Vincent, Ardrossan is the largest of the peninsula's eastern coast ports. Boat Ramp, Boating, Bowls, Fishing, Golf, Sailing, Shooting, Swimming (Beach), Tennis, Water Skiing.

Hotels/Motels

★★☆ **Royal House Hotel Motel**, (LMH), 1 Fifth St, ☎ 08 8837 3007, fax 08 8837 3948, 14 units [shwr, tlt, a/c, elec blkts, TV, clock radio (avail), t/c mkg, refrig], rec rm, conv fac, pool, bbq. **RO** ♦ **$50**, ♦♦ **$60**, ◊ **$5**, AE BC EFT MC VI.

★★☆ **(Cabin Section)**, 9 cabins acc up to 8, (Studio & 1 bedrm), [ensuite, a/c-cool, heat, refrig, cook fac, toaster, blkts reqd, linen reqd, pillows reqd]. **D** ♦ **$50**, ◊ **$5**.

★☆ **(Hotel Section)**, (2 stry), 12 rms [a/c (4), elec blkts], lounge (TV), ☒, t/c mkg shared, refrig, bbq. **RO** ♦ **$25**, ♦♦ **$35**.

★★ **Ardrossan Motel Hotel**, (LMH), 36 First St, ☎ 08 8837 3008, fax 08 8837 3468, 11 units [shwr, tlt, a/c, elec blkts, TV, t/c mkg, refrig], conv fac, ☒ (Mon to Sat), cots. **RO** ♦ **$49.50**, ♦♦ **$60**, ◊ **$7**, BC EFT MC VI.

ARKAROOLA SA 5700

Pop Nominal, (682km N Adelaide), See map on pages 586/587, ref H3. Located in the northern Flinders Ranges adjacent to the Gammon Ranges. Mt Painter Sanctuary, Historic Reserve and Arkaroola Observatory. Bush Walking.

Hotels/Motels

★★☆ **Mawson Lodge**, (M), Situated in Arkaroola Wilderness Sanctuary, ☎ 08 8431 7900, fax 08 8431 7911, 20 units [ensuite, a/c, t/c mkg, refrig], ldry, lounge, ☒, pool, cots-fee. **RO** ♦ **$115.50**, ♦♦ **$115.50**, ◊ **$13.20**, ch con, AE BC EFT MC VI.

★★☆ **(Callitris Lodge)**, 10 units [ensuite, hairdry, a/c, elec blkts, t/c mkg, refrig], cots-fee. **RO** ♦♦ **$115.50**, ◊ **$13.20**, ch con.

★☆ **(Greenwood Lodge)**, 20 units [ensuite, a/c-cool, heat, t/c mkg], lounge (communal), refrig, cots-fee. **RO** ♦♦ **$53.90**, ◊ **$12**, ch con.

(Thomas Wing Section), 5 rms acc up to 2, [a/c-cool, heat (3), t/c mkg, blkts, linen, pillows], shared fac (3), ldry. **D** ♦♦ **$42.90**.

Self Catering Accommodation

★★☆ **Arkaroola Mt Painter Sanctuary Cottages**, (Cotg), Situated in the Arkaroola Wilderness Sanctuary, ☎ 08 8431 7900, fax 08 8431 7911, 2 cotgs acc up to 4, (2 bedrm), [shwr, tlt, c/fan, heat, refrig, cook fac, micro, blkts, linen, pillows], pool, cots. **D** **$108.90**, 1 cotg of a lower rating, AE BC EFT MC VI.

ARNO BAY SA 5603

Pop 400. (562km W Adelaide), See map on pages 586/587, ref G5. A popular seaside resort and original shipping port ideally situated midway between Port Lincoln and Whyalla. Boat Ramp, Boating, Bowls, Bush Walking, Bush Walking, Canoeing, Fishing, Golf, Sailing, Scenic Drives, Squash, Swimming (Beach & Creek), Tennis.

Hotels/Motels

Hotel Arno, (LH), Government Rd, On foreshore, ☎ 08 8628 0001, fax 08 8628 0150, (2 stry), 15 rms [elec blkts], lounge (TV), ☒ (Mon to Sat), t/c mkg shared, bbq (covered), cots-fee, **BLB** ♦ **$25**, ♦♦ **$40**, ♦♦♦♦ **$55**, fam con, BC EFT MC VI.

AUBURN SA 5451

Pop 331. (110km N Adelaide), See map on pages 586/587, ref C6. Small farming community. Art and craft galleries, the Police Station and Courtroom and wineries. Bowls, Croquet, Tennis, Vineyards, Wineries.

Hotels/Motels

★★☆ **Auburn Motel**, (M), Main North Rd, ☎ 08 8849 2125, fax 08 8849 2125, 8 units [ensuite, a/c-cool (4), c/fan, heat, elec blkts, TV, clock radio, t/c mkg, refrig], ☒, dinner to unit, cots-fee, **RO** ♦♦ **$45 - $55**, ◊ **$11**, AE BC DC EFT MC MCH VI.

Self Catering Accommodation

★★★★ **Dennis Cottage**, (Cotg), No children's facilities, St Vincent St, ☎ 08 8277 8177, fax 03 9696 6923, (2 stry), 1 cotg acc up to 4, (2 bedrm), [shwr, spa bath, tlt, a/c-cool, c/fan, fire pl, TV, video, clock radio, CD, refrig, cook fac, blkts, linen, pillows], w/mach, dryer, breakfast ingredients, **BB** ♦ **$160**, ♦♦ **$320**, Min book applies.

(Wild Olive Cottage), No children's facilities, (2 stry), 1 cotg acc up to 2, (1 bedrm), [shwr, spa bath, tlt, a/c, TV, video, CD, t/c mkg, refrig, cook fac, micro, blkts, linen, pillows], lounge firepl, breakfast ingredients, non smoking property, **D** ♦ **$180**, ♦♦ **$160 - $180**, Heritage & National Trust listed internal spiral staircase. (not yet classified).

★★★☆ **Pams Cottage**, (Cotg), Circa 1860. Elder St, 500m W of PO, ☎ 08 8849 2281, fax 08 8849 2281, 1 cotg acc up to 6, (2 bedrm), [shwr, bath, tlt, hairdry, a/c-cool, fan, heat, elec blkts, clock radio, CD, t/c mkg, refrig, cook fac, elec frypan, toaster, ldry (in unit), blkts, doonas, linen, pillows], w/mach, dryer, iron, iron brd, lounge firepl, bbq, cots, breakfast ingredients. **D** ♦♦ **$115**, ◊ **$80**, ch con, Min book applies, BC MC VI.

Stonehurst Country Style Bed & Breakfast, (Cotg), Cnr Main North Rd & Church St, ☎ 08 8849 2295, or 08 8523 5986, 1 cotg acc up to 6, (3 bedrm), [shwr (2), bath, tlt (2), fan, fire pl, elec blkts, radio (cassette), refrig, cook fac, toaster, blkts, doonas, linen, pillows], lounge, pool (salt water), breakfast ingredients, non smoking rms, **D** ♦♦ **$120**, ◊ **$55**.

B&B's/Guest Houses

★★★☆ **Daisy Manor Bed & Breakfast**, (B&B), 4 King St, ☎ 08 8849 2134, 1 rm [shwr, tlt, hairdry, fan (avail), heat, elec blkts, TV, CD, t/c mkg, refrig], non smoking rms. **BB** ♦ **$110**, ♦♦ **$120**, Surcharge for single Saturday night booking. Min book long w/ends and Easter, BC MC VI.

BALAKLAVA SA 5461

Pop 1,439. (93km N Adelaide), See map on pages 586/587, ref B6. Set on the banks of the River Wakefield and northern fringe of the Adelaide Plains, Balaklava is a large rural centre with the main activities being cereal growing, hay production and livestock. Centenary Hall and Urlwin Park.

Royal Hotel, (LH), 9 Edith Tce, 200m NW of PO, ☎ 08 8862 1607, fax 08 8862 2177, (2 stry), 10 rms [c/fan], lounge (TV), ☒ (Mon to Sat), t/c mkg shared, bbq, cots, non smoking property. **RO** ♦ **$30**, ♦♦ **$50**, fam con, pen con, BC EFT MC VI.

BALHANNAH SA 5242

Pop 900. (26km E Adelaide), See map on page 588, ref E4. A small town servicing the local orchard, agriculture and horse racing industries. Set in the valley of the Onkaparinga River, it was one of the early settlements in South Australia. Horse Racing, Scenic Drives, Tennis, Vineyards, Wineries.

★★★☆ **Tori Park Stud**, (Apt), Swamp Rd, 3km W of PO, ☎ 08 8388 4770, fax 08 8388 4771, 1 apt acc up to 2, (2 bedrm), [ensuite, spa bath, fan, heat (wood), elec blkts, TV, video, clock radio (cassette), CD, t/c mkg, refrig, cook fac, micro, ldry, doonas], ldry, w/mach, iron, iron brd, bbq, cots, breakfast ingredients. **D** ♦ **$110**, ♦♦ **$132 - $160**, ◊ **$66**, ch con, weekly con, Min book applies, BC MC VI.

BARMERA SA 5345

Pop 1,859. (220km NE Adelaide), See map on pages 586/587, ref E6. Situated on the shores of Lake Bonney, known as the centre of the Riverland the ideal holiday resort for the water-sport enthusiast. Boat Ramp, Boating, Bowls, Fishing, Golf, Greyhound Racing, Sailing, Squash, Swimming (Lake), Tennis, Water Skiing.

Hotels/Motels

FLAG
FLAG CHOICE HOTELS

★★★★ **Barmera Country Club Motel**, (M), Hawdon St, 1km N of PO, adjacent to hospital, ☎ 08 8588 2888, fax 08 8588 2785, 29 units (1 suite) [ensuite, spa bath (6), hairdry, a/c, c/fan (12), elec blkts, tel, cable tv, clock radio, t/c mkg, refrig, micro (1), elec frypan (2), toaster], ldry, w/mach, dryer, iron, iron brd, conv fac, conf fac, ☒, pool, spa, bbq, rm serv, c/park (undercover), plygr, tennis, cots. RO ╫ $89 - $120, ╫╫ $89 - $140, ◊ $15, Suite RO $130, ch con, AE BC DC EFT MC MP VI, ⚲.

★★★★ **Barmera Lake Resort Motel**, (M), Lakeside Dve, 2km NW of PO, Lake Bonney waterfront, ☎ 08 8588 2555, fax 08 8588 3169, 30 units [ensuite, a/c, c/fan, elec blkts, tel, TV, movie, clock radio, t/c mkg, refrig], ldry, w/mach, dryer-fee, iron, iron brd, conf fac, ☒, pool-heated (solar), bbq, rm serv, dinner to unit, c/park (carport), tennis. RO ╫ $66, ╫╫ $83, ◊ $11, 15 rooms ★★★☆. Min book long w/ends and Easter, AE BC DC EFT MC MCH VI.

★★★ **Barmera Hotel Motel**, (M), Barwell Ave, ☎ 08 8588 2111, fax 08 8588 1077, (2 stry), 20 units [ensuite, a/c, elec blkts (14), tel (15), TV, clock radio, t/c mkg, refrig]. RO ╫ $55, ╫╫ $60, ◊ $10, Min book long w/ends and Easter, AE BC MC VI.

★☆ **(Hotel Section)**, 36 units [ensuite (24), a/c (7)], conf fac, ☒, pool, rm serv, dinner to unit, cots. RO ╫ $40, ╫╫ $40, ◊ $10, 12 rooms list only.

(Motel Section), units RO ╫ $65, ╫╫ $70, ◊ $10.

Self Catering Accommodation

★★☆ **Loch Luna Eco-stay**, (HU), Morgan Rd, 16km W of PO, ☎ 08 8588 7210, fax 08 8588 7210, 1 unit acc up to 4, (2 bedrm), [shwr, tlt, a/c-cool, heat, TV, radio (cassette), CD, t/c mkg, micro, elec frypan, toaster, blkts, linen, pillows], iron, iron brd, bbq, c/park (carport), bicycle, canoeing. D ╫╫ $90, ◊ $35, Min book applies.

★★★★ **(Loch Luna Cottage)**, 1 cotg acc up to 3, (1 bedrm), [shwr, bath, tlt, a/c, TV, radio, t/c mkg, refrig, cook fac, micro, elec frypan, toaster, blkts, linen, pillows], iron, iron brd, bbq, c/park (carport), bicycle, canoeing. D ╫╫ $110, ◊ $35.

B&B's/Guest Houses

Berrinbo, (B&B), Section 234, Sturt Hwy, 4km E of PO, ☎ 0414 882 659, fax 08 8588 2088, 1 rm (2 bedrm), [shwr, tlt, hairdry, a/c, fan, elec blkts, tel, TV, video, clock radio, CD, t/c mkg, refrig, cook fac, micro, toaster, pillows], bbq, cots, non smoking property. BLB ╫ $60, ╫╫ $110, ◊ $30, BC MC VI, (not yet classified).

BAROSSA VALLEY REGION - SA

BAROSSA VALLEY - ANGASTON SA 5353

Pop 1,950. (84km NE Adelaide), See map on pages 586/587, ref C6. Set among the beatiful Barossa Range, not far from the heart of the Barossa. Collingrove Homestead, wineries, art and craft shops, Angas Park Dried Fruits and galleries. Vineyards, Wineries.

Hotels/Motels

Budget Motel Chain
International

★★★ **Vineyards Motel**, (M), Cnr Stockwell & Nuriootpa Rd, ☎ 08 8564 2404, fax 08 8564 2932, 22 units (1 suite) [ensuite, a/c-cool (14), a/c (7), heat, elec blkts, tel, TV, clock radio, t/c mkg, refrig, mini bar, toaster], ldry, pool-heated (solar), spa, bbq, rm serv, c/park (undercover), cots-fee, non smoking rms (6). RO ╫ $55, ╫╫ $55 - $88, ◊ $11, Suite RO $88 - $110, pen con, Min book long w/ends and Easter, AE BC DC EFT MC MCH VI,

Operator Comment: Email: vinmot@mail.mdt.net.au Web Site: www.mdt.net.au/~vinmot

★ **Baroosa Brauhaus**, (LH), Previously The Barossa Valley Hotel 41 Murray St, ☎ 08 8564 2014, (2 stry), 7 rms [elec blkts], lounge (TV), ☒, t/c mkg shared, refrig, ☎, cots. BLB ╫ $30, ╫╫ $55, AE BC DC EFT MC VI.

Self Catering Accommodation

★★★★☆ **Country Pleasures Bed & Breakfast**, (Cotg), 54-56 Penrice Rd, ☎ 08 8563 0754, fax 08 8563 3624, 2 cotgs acc up to 4, [shwr, spa bath, tlt, hairdry, a/c, wood heat (loung), elec blkts, TV, clock radio, t/c mkg, refrig, cook fac, micro, toaster, ldry, blkts, doonas, linen, pillows], w/mach, iron, iron brd, bbq, c/park (undercover), cots, breakfast ingredients. D ╫╫ $150, ╫╫╫╫ $230, ◊ $45, ch con, BC MC VI.

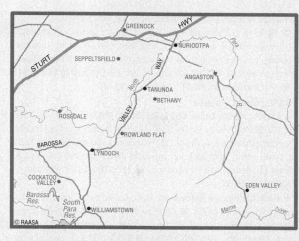

★★★★☆ **Strait Gate Cottage**, (Cotg), Stockwell Rd, Light Pass 5355, 3km W of Angaston, ☎ 08 8564 3397, fax 08 8564 3397, 1 cotg acc up to 2, (1 bedrm), [shwr, spa bath, tlt, hairdry, a/c, c/fan, heat, elec blkts, TV, clock radio, t/c mkg, refrig, cook fac, micro, toaster, blkts, doonas, linen, pillows], w/mach, dryer (on request), iron, iron brd, pool-indoor (solar, saltwater), bbq, c/park (garage on request). D ╫ $110 - $130, ╫╫ $125 - $145, W ╫ $700, ╫╫ $770, BC MC VI.

★★★★ **Angaston Upon the Hill**, (HU), Lot 6, Gawler Park Rd, ☎ 08 8272 2249, fax 08 8272 2249, 1 unit acc up to 4, [shwr, spa bath, tlt, hairdry, a/c, elec blkts, TV, video, clock radio, t/c mkg, refrig, cook fac, micro, toaster, blkts, doonas, linen, pillows], w/mach, dryer, iron, iron brd, bar, non smoking property. D ╫╫ $150 - $170, ◊ $55, W ╫╫ $780 - $700, ◊ $350, Min book applies, BC MC VI.

★★★★ **The Lilac Cottage**, (Cotg), 19 Moculta Rd, ☎ 08 8564 2635, fax 08 8564 2635, 1 cotg acc up to 6, (3 bedrm), [shwr, spa bath, tlt, a/c, fan, heat (wood), elec blkts, tel, TV, clock radio, CD, t/c mkg, refrig, cook fac, micro, blkts, doonas, linen, pillows], w/mach, dryer, bbq, c/park (undercover), breakfast ingredients, non smoking rms. D ╫ $130, ╫╫ $140 - $155, ◊ $40, ch con, weekly con, BC MC VI.

★★★☆ **Honey Room Bed & Breakfast Cottage**, (Cotg), Previously The Honey-Room Cottage L. Pumpas Rd, Eden Valley 5235, 12km S of PO, ☎ 08 8565 3256, fax 08 8565 3244, 1 cotg acc up to 3, [shwr, tlt, hairdry, evap cool (mobile), fan, heat (slow combustion), elec blkts, clock radio, CD, refrig, cook fac ltd, toaster, blkts, doonas, linen, pillows], iron, iron brd, bbq, BLB ╫╫ $125 - $165, ◊ $35, BC MC VI.

★★★☆ **Strathlyn Coach House**, (Cotg), Circa 1905. Nuriootpa Rd, 1km W of PO, Adjacent Saltram Winery, ☎ 08 8564 2430, 1 cotg acc up to 2, (1 bedrm), [shwr, bath, tlt, hairdry, a/c, c/fan, heat, elec blkts, TV, clock radio, t/c mkg, refrig, cook fac ltd, toaster, blkts, linen, pillows], w/mach, dryer, iron, iron brd, breakfast ingredients. D ╫╫ $175, BC MC VI.

★★★ **Fig Tree Cottage**, (Cotg), 92 Murray St, ☎ 08 8564 2635, fax 08 8564 2635, 1 cotg acc up to 4, (2 bedrm), [shwr, bath, tlt, hairdry, fan, heat, elec blkts, tel, TV, clock radio (2), CD, t/c mkg, refrig, cook fac, micro, elec frypan, toaster, blkts, linen, pillows], iron, iron brd, bbq, breakfast ingredients, non smoking property. D ╫╫ $130, ◊ $60, Min book applies, AE BC DC MC VI.

BAROSSA VALLEY - ANGASTON SA continued...

Wroxton Grange, (Apt), Flaxmans Valley Rd, 5km S of PO,
☎ 08 8565 3227, fax 08 8565 3227, 1 apt acc up to 2, (1 bedrm), [shwr, tlt, hairdry, a/c, fan, cent heat, elec blkts, TV, radio (cassette player), t/c mkg, refrig, cook fac, micro, toaster, blkts, linen, pillows], iron (on request), iron brd (on request), rec rm, c/park. D ⁑ $115 - $125, Min book applies, BC MC VI, (not yet classified).

B&B's/Guest Houses

★★★★☆ **Marble Lodge Bed & Breakfast**, (B&B), 21 Dean St, 100m S of PO, ☎ 08 8564 2478, fax 08 8564 2941, 2 rms (1 suite) [ensuite, spa bath, hairdry, a/c, fire pl (1), heat, elec blkts, tel, TV, clock radio, t/c mkg, refrig, mini bar], ldry, w/mach, dryer, iron, iron brd, lounge firepl (1), tennis, non smoking rms, BB ⁑ $170 - $195, Min book applies, BC MC VI.

★★★★ **Collingrove Homestead**, (GH), Owned by National Trust. Eden Valley Rd, 7km SE of PO, ☎ 08 8564 2061, fax 08 8564 3600, 2 rms [ensuite, hairdry, a/c-cool (1), fan (4), heat, elec blkts, tel (1), t/c mkg], ldry, lounge, spa, refrig. BB ⁎ $155, ⁑ $210, ◊ $72, 1 room of a lower rating. Dinner by prior arrangement. AE BC DC MC VI.

★★★★ **Hill House Bed & Breakfast**, (B&B), No children's facilities, Cnr Washington & Lindsay Sts, ☎ 08 8564 2023, fax 08 8564 2523, 2 rms [ensuite, fan, fire pl, heat, tel, TV, clock radio, CD, t/c mkg, refrig, pillows], lounge, non smoking rms. BB ⁑ $160 - $180, BC MC VI.

★★★★ **Hillview Guest House**, (GH), 12 Hill St West,
☎ 08 8564 2761, fax 08 8564 2508, 2 rms [ensuite, fan, heat, elec blkts, tel, TV, radio, t/c mkg, refrig], lounge, pool-heated, spa, bbq, meals avail, cots. BB ⁑ $170 - $190, BC MC VI.

BAROSSA VALLEY - BETHANY SA 5351

Pop Nominal, (74km Adelaide), See map on pages 586/587, ref C7. The Barossa's oldest German settlement founded in 1842 by 28 staunchly Lutheran German families. Scenic Drives, Vineyards, Wineries.

Self Catering Accommodation

★★★☆ **Bethany Cottages**, (Cotg), Nicolai Rd, ☎ 08 8563 3581, 2 cotgs acc up to 6, [shwr, bath, tlt, a/c-cool, c/fan, heat, elec blkts, clock radio, t/c mkg, refrig, cook fac, micro, elec frypan, toaster], bbq, breakfast ingredients, non smoking property. D ⁎ $100, ⁑ $120, ◊ $50, ch con, BC MC VI.

★★★☆ **Sonntag House**, (Cotg), Circa 1840. Bethany Rd,
☎ 08 8563 0775, fax 08 8524 7006, 1 cotg acc up to 5, (2 bedrm), [shwr, bath, tlt, hairdry, a/c-cool, fire pl, heat, elec blkts, TV, clock radio (cassette), CD, t/c mkg, refrig, cook fac, micro, toaster, ldry, doonas, linen, pillows], w/mach, dryer, iron, iron brd, cots, breakfast ingredients, non smoking property. D ⁑ $140 - $160, ◊ $40 - $55, ch con, BC MC VI, ⧖.

BAROSSA VALLEY - COCKATOO VALLEY SA 5351

Pop Nominal, (55km Adelaide), See map on pages 586/587, ref C7. A small settlement located in the outer region of the Barossa.

Self Catering Accommodation

★★★☆ **Enerby Farm Cottage**, (Cotg), Goldfields Rd, 5km S of PO, ☎ 08 8524 6297, fax 08 8524 7397, 1 cotg acc up to 4, (2 bedrm), [shwr, spa bath, tlt, hairdry, a/c, TV, clock radio, CD, t/c mkg, refrig, cook fac, micro, toaster, blkts, linen, pillows], iron, iron brd, lounge firepl, bbq, breakfast ingredients. D ⁑ $135 - $155, ◊ $50 - $55, BC MC VI.

The Miners Cottage, (Cotg), Goldfields Rd, ☎ 08 8524 6213, fax 08 8524 6650, 1 cotg acc up to 4, [shwr, bath, tlt, a/c, fire pl, CD, t/c mkg, refrig, cook fac ltd, elec frypan, toaster, blkts, linen, pillows], ldry, pool, bbq, breakfast ingredients. BLB ⁎ $70, ⁑ $154, AE BC MC VI.

B&B's/Guest Houses

★★★☆ **Kooringal Homestead**, (B&B), Yettie Rd, 3km SE of PO, ☎ 08 8524 6196, fax 08 8524 7317, 3 rms [ensuite, bath (1), hairdry (1), a/c-cool, c/fan, elec blkts, clock radio, t/c mkg, refrig, micro (1)], iron (1), iron brd (1), lounge (TV), ✗, bbq, cots (& highchair), non smoking property. BB ⁎ $110 - $130, ⁑ $120 - $140, ch con, additional meals by arrangmnt. Min book long w/ends, BC MC VI.

BAROSSA VALLEY - EDEN VALLEY SA 5235

Pop Part of Angaston, (70km NE Adelaide), See map on pages 586/587, ref C7. A picturesque town in the Barossa. Winery tours and tastings. Scenic Drives, Tennis, Vineyards, Wineries.

★★★☆ **Rushlea Homestead Bed & Breakfast**, (Cotg), Rushlea Rd, 1km from Hotel, ☎ 08 8564 1041, fax 08 8564 1259, 1 cotg acc up to 3, [shwr, tlt, evap cool, heat (elec/wood), elec blkts, TV, clock radio, t/c mkg, refrig, cook fac, toaster, ldry, blkts, doonas, linen, pillows], bbq, ✆, breakfast ingredients, non smoking rms. D ⁑ $110 - $140, ◊ $30.

BAROSSA VALLEY - GREENOCK SA 5360

Pop 451. (65km NE Adelaide), See map on pages 586/587, ref C6. An early settlement which served as a rural district near the northern edge of the Barossa. Tennis, Vineyards, Wineries.

Self Catering Accommodation

★★★☆ **Heavens Gate Serviced Apartments**, (SA), Branson Rd, 2km N of PO, ☎ 08 8562 8189, fax 08 8562 8189, 3 serv apts acc up to 3, (Studio), [shwr, tlt, a/c, elec blkts, TV, clock radio, t/c mkg, refrig, cook fac ltd, micro, elec frypan, toaster], ldry, w/mach, dryer, iron, pool, c/park (carport), breakfast ingredients, Pets on application. D ⁑ $110, ◊ $55, ch con.

★★★ **Sophies Cottage**, (Cotg), Frederick St, 200m W of PO, ☎ 08 8562 8084, fax 08 8562 8084, 1 cotg acc up to 2, [shwr, bath, tlt, hairdry, a/c, fire pl, elec blkts, refrig, cook fac, elec frypan, blkts, linen, pillows], ldry, w/mach, dryer, breakfast ingredients, non smoking property. D ⁑ $110 - $135, BC MC VI.

BAROSSA VALLEY - LYNDOCH SA 5351

Pop 957. (61km NE Adelaide), See map on pages 586/587, ref C7. Southern gateway to the Barossa. Bowls, Bush Walking, Gem Fossicking, Tennis, Vineyards, Wineries.

Hotels/Motels

★★★☆ **Barossa Park Motel**, (M), Barossa Valley Hwy,
☎ 08 8524 4268, fax 08 8524 4725, 34 units (1 suite) [shwr, tlt, a/c, elec blkts, tel, TV, clock radio, t/c mkg, refrig, mini bar, toaster], ldry-fee, rec rm, conf fac, ✉, pool, spa, bbq, rm serv, dinner to unit, plygr, cots-fee, non smoking units (10). RO ⁎ $81, ⁑ $90, ◊ $13, ch con, AE BC BTC DC EFT MC VI, ⧖.

Self Catering Accommodation

★★★★ **Applecroft Cottage**, (Cotg), Trial Hill Rd Pewsey Vale via, 6km E of PO, ☎ 08 8524 4536, fax 08 8524 5201, 1 cotg acc up to 2, (Studio), [ensuite, spa bath, hairdry, a/c, c/fan, wood heat (slow combustion), elec blkts, TV, clock radio, CD, t/c mkg, refrig, cook fac, micro, toaster, blkts, doonas, linen, pillows], iron, iron brd, bbq, c/park (carport), breakfast ingredients, non smoking property. D ⁑ $140, W ⁑ $600 - $700, pen con, Min book applies.

★★★★ **Barossa Country Cottages**, (Cotg), 55 Gilbert St, 500m W of PO, ☎ 08 8524 4426, fax 08 8524 4931, 2 cotgs acc up to 4, (2 bedrm), [shwr, bath, tlt, hairdry, a/c, TV, clock radio, t/c mkg, refrig, cook fac, micro, toaster, ldry, blkts, linen, pillows], w/mach, dryer, iron, iron brd, spa (shared), bbq (covered), bicycle, cots, breakfast ingredients, non smoking property, D ⁎ $115 - $140, ⁑ $115 - $140, ◊ $50 - $60, ch con, BC MC VI.

★★★★ **Bluebelle Cottage**, (Cotg), Circa 1938. 20 Barossa Valley Hwy, ☎ 08 8524 4825, fax 08 8524 4046, 1 cotg acc up to 6, (2 bedrm), [shwr, bath, spa bath (pool), tlt (2), hairdry, a/c, elec blkts, tel, TV, video, clock radio, t/c mkg, refrig, cook fac, micro, elec frypan, toaster, blkts, doonas, linen, pillows], iron, iron brd, lounge firepl, breakfast ingredients, non smoking property, Pets on application. D ⁑ $190, ◊ $65, W ⁑ $1,100, ◊ $400, pen con, Min book applies, AE BC MC VI.

★★★★ **Christabelle Cottage**, (Cotg), Circa 1849. 8 King St, 500m W of PO, ☎ 08 8524 4825, fax 08 8524 4046, (2 stry), 1 cotg acc up to 4, (1 bedrm), [shwr, bath, spa bath (pool), tlt, a/c, c/fan, elec blkts, tel, TV, video, clock radio, t/c mkg, refrig, cook fac, micro, elec frypan, toaster, ldry (in unit), blkts, linen, pillows], w/mach, dryer, iron, iron brd, lounge firepl, bbq, c/park (carport), breakfast ingredients. D ⁑ $190, ◊ $65, pen con, Min book applies, AE BC MC VI.

★★★☆ **Shiraz Cottage**, (Cotg), 14 Barossa Valley Way, 500m W of PO, ☎ 08 8524 5353, fax 08 8524 4993, 1 cotg acc up to 6, (3 bedrm), [shwr, spa bath, tlt, hairdry, a/c-cool, fan, heat, elec blkts, tel, TV, clock radio, refrig, cook fac, micro, toaster, ldry, blkts, pillows], w/mach, dryer, iron, iron brd, lounge firepl, breakfast ingredients, non smoking property. **D** ✿ $140 - $150, ◊ $40, **W** ✿ $750, ◊ $220, ch con, Min book long w/ends and Easter, AE BC JCB MC VI.

B&B's/Guest Houses

★★★★☆ **Glenfield Bed & Breakfast**, (B&B), Jollytown Rd, 2km NW of PO, ☎ 08 8524 5353, 1 rm [ensuite, bath, hairdry, fan, fire pl, heat, elec blkts, TV, clock radio, t/c mkg, refrig] ldry, lounge, non smoking property. **BB** ✿ $150, Min book long w/ends and Easter, AE BC JCB MC VI.

★★★★ **The Barossa Mud Manor**, (B&B), 31 Rushall Rd, ☎ 08 8524 4846, fax 08 8524 4789, 1 rm [ensuite, hairdry, a/c, fan, fire pl, elec blkts, TV, video, clock radio, refrig, micro, toaster], iron, iron brd, non smoking rms. **RO** ✿ $110 - $120, ◊ $600 - $650, AE BC MC VI.

BAROSSA VALLEY - NURIOOTPA SA 5355

Pop 3,321. (75km NE Adelaide), See map on pages 586/587, ref C6. Commercial centre of the Barossa. The town name comes from the aboriginal word meaning 'The Meeting Place'. Coulthard Reserve, Quilt & Craft Cottage, Strait Gate Lutheran Church and Wineries. Bowls, Bush Walking, Gem Fossicking, Squash, Swimming (Pool), Tennis, Vineyards, Wineries.

Hotels/Motels

★★★☆ **Nuriootpa Vine Inn**, (LMH), 14-22 Murray St, ☎ 08 8562 2133, fax 08 8562 3236, 18 units [ensuite, bath (6), spa bath (12), hairdry, a/c, elec blkts, tel, cable tv, clock radio, t/c mkg, refrig, mini bar, toaster], ldry, conv fac, ☒, pool-heated (solar), spa, cots-fee. **RO** ✿ $88, ✿✿ $104, ◊ $16, ch con, AE BC DC EFT MC VI, ♿.

★★★ **Nuriootpa Vine Court**, (M), Previously Top of the Valley Tourist Motel 49 Murray St, ☎ 08 8562 2133, fax 08 8562 3236, 18 units [ensuite, spa bath (1), hairdry, a/c, elec blkts, tel, TV, video, clock radio, t/c mkg, refrig, toaster], ldry, pool-heated (solar), spa, bbq (covered), cots-fee. **BLB** ✿ $71, ✿✿ $82, ◊ $16, ch con, AE BC DC EFT MC VI, ♿.

★★☆ **Barossa Gateway Motel**, (M), Kalimna Rd, 200m off Sturt Hwy, ☎ 08 8562 1033, fax 08 8562 1600, 17 units [ensuite, a/c (11), elec blkts, TV, clock radio, t/c mkg, refrig, doonas]. **RO** ✿✿ $53 - $64, ◊ $10, ch con, fam con, 4 rooms ★★★, AE BC DC MC VI.

Self Catering Accommodation

★★★★ **Barossa Valley Holiday Home**, (Cotg), 8 Kranz St, ☎ 08 8563 1234, fax 08 8563 1234, 1 cotg acc up to 6, (3 bedrm), [shwr, bath, tlt, hairdry, a/c, fire pl (combustion), heat, elec blkts, tel, TV, video, clock radio, CD, t/c mkg, refrig, cook fac, micro, d/wash, toaster, ldry, blkts, doonas, linen, pillows], w/mach, dryer, iron, iron brd, bbq, c/park (garage), breakfast ingredients. **BB** ✿✿ $132, ◊ $33, ✿✿ $540, ◊ $630, BC MC VI.

B&B's/Guest Houses

★★★★☆ **Kaesler Cottages**, (B&B), Barossa Valley Way, ☎ 08 8562 2711, fax 08 8562 2788, 3 rms [ensuite, spa bath, a/c, TV, clock radio, t/c mkg, refrig, doonas], rec rm, ☒, c/park. **BB** ✿✿ $160 - $180, ◊ $44, Min book applies, AE BC DC EFT MC VI.

★★★★☆ **Whirlwind Farm Bed & Breakfast**, (B&B), Samuel Rd, 3km W of PO, ☎ 08 8562 2637, fax 08 8562 4637, 2 rms [ensuite, hairdry, c/fan, wood heat (slow combustion) (1), elec blkts, TV, radio, refrig], ldry, iron (avail), iron brd (avail), t/c mkg shared, non smoking rms. **BB** ✿✿ $110 - $120, BC MC VI.

★★★☆ **Karawatha Guest House**, (GH), Greenock Rd, 3.5km W of PO, ☎ 08 8562 1746, 3 rms [ensuite, fan, heat, elec blkts, TV, t/c mkg, refrig], ldry, iron, pool, bbq, plygr, cots. **BB** ✿ $45 - $50, ✿✿ $70 - $90, ◊ $15, ch con.

Other Accommodation

Barossa Bunkhaus Travellers Hostel, (Bunk), Barossa Valley Hwy, 1.5km S of PO, ☎ 08 8562 2260, fax 08 8562 2260, 1 bunkhouse acc up to 12, (2 bedrm), [shwr (2), tlt (2), fire pl, radio, refrig, cook fac, micro, toaster, doonas, linen reqd-fee] ldry, lounge (TV), pool, bbq. **D** ✿ $15, ✿✿ $30, ◊ $15.

★★ **(Cottage Section)**, 1 cotg acc up to 4, [shwr, tlt, fan, fire pl, TV, radio, refrig, cook fac, micro, ldry, doonas, linen]. **D** ✿✿ $46, ◊ $9 - $10.

BAROSSA VALLEY - ROSEDALE SA 5350

Pop Nominal, (70km Adelaide), See map on pages 586/587, ref C7. Small settlement nestled on the banks of the North Para River, by the northern access to the Barossa.

★★☆ **Buckbury End Farm Cottage**, (Cotg), (Farm), Dahlenburg Rd, 1km S of PO, ☎ 08 8524 9035, 1 cotg acc up to 2, [shwr, tlt, fire pl, elec blkts, refrig, cook fac, toaster, blkts, linen, pillows]. **D** $75.

BAROSSA VALLEY - ROWLAND FLAT SA 5352

Pop Nominal, (67km NE Adelaide), See map on pages 586/587, ref C7. A small wine producing township in the Barossa, not far from Lyndoch. This area saw the genesis of the Barossa's wine industry and some of the early buildings survive in the vicinity. Vineyards, Wineries.

Hotels/Motels

AAA TOURISM *Special Rates* ★★★★☆ **Novotel Barossa Valley Resort**, (LH), Previously All Seasons Premier Barossa Valley Resort Golflinks Rd, ☎ 08 8524 0000, fax 08 8524 0100, (2 stry gr fl), 140 rms (2 bedrm Studio), [ensuite, bath, spa bath (9), hairdry, a/c, tel, TV, movie, clock radio, t/c mkg, refrig, mini bar, cook fac, micro, toaster], lift, ldry, w/mach, dryer, iron, iron brd, rec rm, conf fac, ☒, pool-heated, sauna, spa, rm serv, dinner to unit, plygr, gym, tennis, cots. **RO** ✿✿ $150 - $189, ◊ $40, Min book applies, AE BC DC EFT JCB MC VI.

B&B's/Guest Houses

★★★★☆ **Kirkala Estate**, (B&B), Kirkala Estate, Jacob Rd, 65km N of Adelaide, ☎ 08 8563 3812, fax 08 8563 3802, 4 rms [shwr, tlt, hairdry, a/c, c/fan (2), heat, elec blkts, t/c mkg, refrig], w/mach, iron (avail), iron brd (avail), lounge (3), bbq, dinner to unit (avail), non smoking rms. **BB** ✿ $155, ✿✿ $180, AE BC DC MC VI.

BAROSSA VALLEY - SEPPELTSFIELD SA 5355

Pop Nominal, (79km Adelaide), See map on pages 586/587, ref C6. Situated in the Barossa. B Seppelt & Sons, wine tastings and tours. Vineyards, Wineries.

Self Catering Accommodation

★★★☆ **Seppeltsfield Holiday Log Cabins**, (Log Cabin), Seppeltsfield Rd, ☎ 08 8562 8240, 8 log cabins acc up to 4, [shwr, spa bath (6), tlt, a/c, heat (6 slow combustion), TV, video-fee, clock radio (4), t/c mkg, refrig, cook fac (4), micro (4), toaster], sauna-fee, bbq, plygr. **D** ✿✿ $66 - $126.50, ◊ $22, ch con, Light breakfast available. Min book applies, BC MC VI.

B&B's/Guest Houses

★★★★★ **The Lodge Country House**, (GH), No children's facilities, Seppeltsfield Rd, town centre, ☎ 08 8562 8277, fax 08 8562 8344, 4 rms [ensuite, a/c, elec blkts], ldry, lounge (TV), ☒, pool (salt water), t/c mkg shared, refrig, bbq, c/park (undercover), ☎, tennis (lawn), non smoking rms. **BB** ✿✿ $310, **DBB** ✿✿ $420, AE BC DC MC VI.

★★★★☆ **The Workmans Cottage**, (B&B), Seppeltsfield Rd, 2km N of Seppelts Winery, ☎ 08 8562 8444, fax 08 8562 8555, 1 rm (1 suite) [hairdry, a/c-cool, wood heat (slow combustion), elec blkts, TV, t/c mkg, refrig, toaster], iron, iron brd, sauna, c/park (covered), non smoking property, **BB** ✿ $130, ✿✿ $140 - $150, AE BC DC MC VI.

BAROSSA VALLEY - TANUNDA SA 5352

Pop 3,087. (74km NE Adelaide), See map on pages 586/587, ref C7. One of the oldest towns in the Barossa. Barossa Historical Museum, Barossa Kiddypark, Art & Craft shops, Kaiserstuhl Conservation Park, The Keg Factory, Kev Rohrlach Collection, Menglers Hill Lookout, Norms Coolie Sheep Dog Performance, Story Book Cottage & Whacky Wood and wineries. Bowls, Golf, Swimming (Pool), Tennis, Vineyards, Wineries.

Hotels/Motels

FLAG
FLAG CHOICE HOTELS

★★★☆ **Barossa Motor Lodge**, (M), Murray St, 1km NE of PO, ☎ 08 8563 2988, fax 08 8563 3653, 40 units (2 suites) [ensuite, bath (2), hairdry, a/c, elec blkts, tel, TV, movie, clock radio, t/c mkg, refrig, mini bar], ldry, conv fac, ✉, pool, sauna, spa, bbq, rm serv, c/park (carport), tennis, cots-fee. **RO ♦ $87 - $96, ♦♦ $96 - $119, ◊ $11, Suite D ♦♦ $119 - $140,** ch con, AE BC DC MC VI, ♿.

★★★☆ **Barossa Weintal Resort**, (LMH), Murray St, 2km NE of PO, ☎ 08 8563 2303, fax 08 8563 2279, (2 stry gr fl), 40 units [ensuite, hairdry, a/c, elec blkts, tel, cable tv (5), clock radio, t/c mkg, refrig], ldry-fee, conv fac, ✉, pool-heated (solar), spa, bbq, rm serv, tennis, cots-fee. **RO ♦ $95.50 - $150, ♦♦ $104.50 - $150, ◊ $18,** 1 unit of a higher standard. AE BC DC EFT MC VI, ♿.

★★★ **Barossa Junction Motel**, (M), Rooms are converted railway carriages. Barossa Valley Way, 3.5km N of PO, ☎ 08 8563 3400, fax 08 8563 3660, 36 units (1 suite) [ensuite, bath (4), spa bath (2), a/c, elec blkts, tel, TV, clock radio, t/c mkg, refrig, toaster], iron brd, conv fac, ✉, BYO, pool indoor heated, spa (heat), bbq, rm serv, plygr, mini golf, tennis, cots-fee. **RO ♦ $69 - $126, ♦♦ $69 - $126, ◊ $16,** BC MC VI, ♿.

★★★ **The Valley Hotel**, (LMH), 73 Murray St, ☎ 08 8563 2039, fax 08 8563 3830, 5 units [ensuite, spa bath (1), hairdry, a/c, elec blkts, TV, clock radio, t/c mkg, refrig], ✉. **RO ♦♦ $77 - $99, ◊ $10 - $20,** AE BC DC EFT MC VI.

★★ **Tanunda Hotel**, (LH), 51 Murray St, ☎ 08 8563 2030, fax 08 8563 2165, (2 stry), 10 rms [basin, ensuite (6), a/c (6), fan (4), heat (10), elec blkts, TV (10), t/c mkg, refrig, toaster], ✉, c/park (limited), cots-fee. **RO ♦ $50 - $60, ♦♦ $60 - $70, ◊ $10,** ch con, 4 rms ★. Min book applies, AE BC DC EFT MC VI.

Self Catering Accommodation

★★★★☆ **Jewel of the Valley**, (House), 1 Elizabeth St, 160m N of PO, ☎ 1800 227 677, fax 08 8524 4993, 1 house acc up to 6, [shwr (2), spa bath (1), tlt (2), hairdry, a/c, fire pl (open/combustion), elec blkts, tel, TV (2), video, clock radio, t/c mkg, refrig, cook fac, micro, d/wash, toaster, blkts, doonas, linen, pillows], w/mach, dryer, iron, iron brd, bbq, c/park (carport). **D ♦♦ $190 - $210, ◊ $30 - $60,** ch con, Min book applies, AE BC DC JCB MC VI.

★★★★ **Byhurst at Tanunda**, (House), 3 Julius St, 500m E of PO, ☎ 08 8333 0010, fax 08 8332 6821, 1 house acc up to 6, (3 bedrm), [ensuite, shwr, bath (1), tlt, hairdry, a/c, fire pl, elec blkts, TV, clock radio, t/c mkg, refrig, cook fac, micro, ldry, doonas], iron, iron brd, bbq, c/park (garage), Pets on application. **BLB ♦♦ $110 - $145, ◊ $50 - $55,** ch con, Min book applies, BC MC VI.

★★★★ **Marananga Cottages**, (Cotg), No children's facilities, Seppeltsfield Rd, Marananga 5355, ☎ 08 8562 3277, fax 08 8562 4188, 1 cotg acc up to 2, (1 bedrm), [shwr, bath, tlt, a/c-cool, fire pl, TV, clock radio, refrig, micro, elec frypan, toaster, blkts, linen, pillows], w/mach, dryer, iron, iron brd, breakfast ingredients, non smoking property, **D ♦♦ $165, ◊ $55,** Min book applies.

★★★★ **(Country Suite)**, No children's facilities, 1 rm [ensuite, bath, a/c, elec blkts, TV, radio (cassette), t/c mkg, refrig, micro, toaster, pillows], breakfast ingredients, **BLB ♦♦ $135 - $150.**

★★★★ **Memory Lane Accommodation**, (Cotg), 27 John St, 200m NW of PO, ☎ 08 8524 6380, fax 08 8524 7006, (2 stry), 1 cotg acc up to 6, [shwr, spa bath, tlt, hairdry, a/c, fan, elec blkts, TV, radio, CD, t/c mkg, refrig, cook fac, micro, elec frypan, toaster, ldry, blkts, doonas, linen, pillows], w/mach, iron, iron brd, lounge firepl, bbq, c/park. **D ♦ $110, ♦♦ $140 - $160, ◊ $40,** ch con, fam con, pen con, Min book long w/ends and Easter, AE BC MC VI.

★★★★ **Merlot Cottage**, (Cotg), 1C Murray St, ☎ 08 8563 0577, fax 08 8563 0573, 1 cotg acc up to 2, (1 bedrm), [shwr, spa bath, tlt, a/c, wood heat, TV, clock radio, refrig, cook fac, micro, d/wash, toaster], breakfast ingredients, non smoking property. **D $160 - $210,** AE BC DC MC VI.

★★★★ **Miriams Cottage**, (Cotg), 22 College St, ☎ 08 8562 8103, fax 08 8562 8259, 1 cotg acc up to 6, (2 bedrm), [shwr, tlt, hairdry, a/c, heat, elec blkts, TV, video, clock radio, refrig, cook fac, micro, elec frypan, blkts, linen, pillows], w/mach, iron, iron brd, bbq, breakfast ingredients, non smoking property, **D ♦♦ $120 - $145, ◊ $40,** BC MC VI.

★★★☆ **Langmeil Cottages**, (SA), 89 Langmeil Rd, 1km NE of PO, ☎ 08 8563 2987, fax 08 8563 2987, 4 serv apts acc up to 3, [shwr, tlt, hairdry, a/c, elec blkts, TV, video (avail), clock radio, t/c mkg, refrig, cook fac], ldry, pool, sauna, spa (22 jet therapeutic), bbq, bicycle, non smoking property. **BLB ♦ $110 - $120, ♦♦ $145 - $160, ◊ $40,** BC MC VI.

★★★☆ **Normas Place Cottage**, (Cotg), 50 John St, 500m W of PO, ☎ 02 6257 9540, fax 02 6257 5531, 1 cotg acc up to 2, (1 bedrm), [shwr, bath, tlt, a/c, fire pl, tel, clock radio, refrig, cook fac, toaster, blkts, linen, pillows], w/mach, iron, iron brd, bbq, cots, breakfast ingredients. **BB ♦♦ $130, ◊ $20,** Min book all holiday times.

★★★☆ **The Dove Cote**, (Apt), 13 Edward St, 300m SE of PO, ☎ 08 8563 0335, 1 apt acc up to 2, (Studio), [shwr, spa bath, tlt, hairdry, a/c, elec blkts, TV, clock radio, t/c mkg, refrig, micro, elec frypan, toaster, ldry (in unit)], w/mach, dryer, iron, iron brd, breakfast ingredients, non smoking property. **D ♦♦ $120.**

★★★ **Naimanya Cottage**, (Cotg), Cnr Flaxmans Valley & Pohlners Rd, 13km SE of PO, ☎ 08 8565 3275, fax 08 8565 3275, 1 cotg acc up to 4, (2 bedrm), [shwr, tlt, fire pl, heat, elec blkts, TV, clock radio, t/c mkg, refrig, micro, elec frypan, toaster, blkts, linen, pillows], bbq, breakfast ingredients, non smoking property, **D ♦♦ $110, ◊ $45,** ch con.

★★★ **Tanunda Cottages**, (Cotg), 157 Murray St, 1km N of PO, ☎ 08 8563 0554, fax 08 8563 1482, 3 cotgs acc up to 6, (2 bedrm), [shwr, tlt, hairdry, a/c, fire pl, elec blkts, TV, clock radio, cook fac, blkts, linen, pillows], iron, iron brd, cots, breakfast ingredients. **D ♦♦ $120 - $140, ◊ $40 - $55,** ch con, Min book applies, BC MC VI.

★★★ **Treasured Memories Cottage**, (Cotg), 27 John St, 200m W of PO, ☎ 08 8524 6380, fax 08 8524 7006, 1 cotg acc up to 6, (3 bedrm), [shwr, bath, spa bath, tlt, a/c, heat (wood stove), TV, radio (cassette), t/c mkg, refrig, cook fac, micro, elec frypan, ldry, blkts, linen, pillows], w/mach, iron, iron brd, lounge firepl, bbq, c/park (carport), breakfast ingredients, non smoking property. **D ♦♦ $140, ◊ $40,** ch con, BC MC VI.

★★★ **Veritas Cottage**, (Cotg), Stelzer Rd, 2km NE of PO, ☎ 08 8562 3300, fax 08 8562 1177, 1 cotg acc up to 4, (2 bedrm), [shwr, bath, tlt, a/c-cool, heat (Pot Belly), elec blkts, TV, clock radio, t/c mkg, refrig, cook fac, toaster, ldry (in unit), blkts, linen, pillows], iron, iron brd, c/park (carport), cots, breakfast ingredients, non smoking property. **D ♦♦ $100, ◊ $45,** ch con, BC MC VI.

★★★ **Woodbridge Bed & Breakfast Cottage**, (Cotg), Gomersal Rd, 4km SW of PO, ☎ 08 8563 2059, fax 08 8563 2581, 1 cotg acc up to 6, (3 bedrm), [shwr, tlt, a/c, fan, heat (pot belly), elec blkts, TV, clock radio, refrig, cook fac, elec frypan, blkts, linen, pillows], w/mach, dryer, iron, bbq, tennis, breakfast ingredients. **D ♦♦ $125, ◊ $50,** BC MC VI.

Stonewell Cottages, (Cotg), Stonewell Rd, ☎ 08 8563 2019, fax 08 8563 3624, 3 cotgs acc up to 4, (1 & 2 bedrm), [shwr, spa bath, tlt, hairdry, a/c-cool, heat, wood heat, elec blkts, TV, t/c mkg, refrig, cook fac, micro, blkts, linen, pillows], iron, iron brd, bbq, cots, breakfast ingredients, **D $140 - $155,** Tariff includes use of row boat. BC MC VI.

B&B's/Guest Houses

★★★★★ **The Hermitage of Marananga**, (GH), Seppeltsfield Rd, 6km NW of PO, ☎ 08 8562 2722, fax 08 8562 3133, 11 rms [ensuite, spa bath (4), a/c, heat, elec blkts, tel, TV, video (avail) (1), clock radio, t/c mkg, refrig, mini bar, toaster, doonas], iron, iron brd, lounge (guest), ✉, pool, spa, bbq, cots. **BB ♦ $158 - $175, ♦♦ $195 - $245, ♦♦♦♦ $295, ◊ $50,** 5 rooms of a four plus star rating. Booking conditions apply. AE BC DC MC VI, ♿.

★★★★☆ **Lawley Farm Bed & Breakfast**, (B&B), (Farm), Krondorf Rd, ☎ 08 8563 2141, fax 08 8563 2141, 6 rms (2 suites) [ensuite, spa bath (2), a/c, fan (4), fire pl (3), elec blkts, tel, TV, clock radio, refrig, cook fac ltd (6), micro (1)], ldry, rec rm, conf fac, spa, bbq, c/park. **BB ♦ $101 - $120, ♦♦ $120 - $170, ◊ $21 - $42, Suite D $170,** 3 units ★★★★. AE BC MC VI.

★★★★ **Lanzerac Country Estate**, (B&B), Menge Rd, 1.5km E of PO, ☎ 08 8563 0499, fax 08 8563 3652, 7 rms [ensuite, spa bath (2), a/c (7), TV, clock radio, t/c mkg, refrig, pillows], bbq, c/park. **BB ♦ $135 - $150, ♦♦ $145 - $195, ◊ $40,** AE BC MC VI.

★★★★ **Paranook Bed & Breakfast**, (B&B), Circa 1899. No children's facilities, 6 Murray St, 200m S of PO, ☎ 08 8563 0208, fax 08 8563 0908, 1 rm [ensuite, hairdry, a/c, fire pl, elec blkts, tel, TV, video, radio (cassette), CD, t/c mkg, refrig], w/mach, dryer, iron, iron brd, pool-heated (solar), spa, non smoking rms. **BB ♦ $100, ♦♦ $150,** BC MC VI.

★★★☆ **Barossa House Bed & Breakfast**, (B&B), Barossa Valley Hwy, 3km N of PO, ☎ 08 8562 4022, fax 08 8562 4022, 3 rms [ensuite, hairdry, a/c-cool, heat, elec blkts, TV, clock radio, refrig], bbq, c/park (carport), non smoking rms. **BB ♦ $85, ♦♦ $99, ◊ $15,** AE BC MC VI.

Virginia House, (B&B), 20 Elizabeth St, 500m NW of PO, ☎ 08 8563 0577, fax 08 8563 0573, 2 rms (1 suite) [ensuite, spa bath, a/c, c/fan (1), fire pl (bedroom) (1), heat (elec/wood), elec blkts, TV, clock radio, t/c mkg, refrig, cook fac ltd (1), micro, toaster, doonas], lounge (TV), lounge firepl (1), non smoking property. **BB** ♥♥ **$140 - $190**, AE BC DC MC VI, (not yet classified).

BAROSSA VALLEY - WILLIAMSTOWN SA 5351

Pop 855. (48km NE Adelaide), See map on pages 586/587, ref C7. Set on the southern edge of the Barossa. Bush Walking, Gem Fossicking, Scenic Drives, Swimming (Pool), Tennis.

Self Catering Accommodation

★★★★☆ **Red Gum Retreat**, (Cotg), 68 Queen St, 500m N of PO, ☎ 08 8271 3323, 1 cotg acc up to 6, (3 bedrm), [shwr, bath, tlt, a/c, elec blkts, tel, TV, video, clock radio, CD, t/c mkg, refrig, cook fac, micro, toaster, ldry, blkts, doonas, linen, pillows], iron, iron brd, spa, breakfast ingredients, non smoking property. **D** ♥♥ **$150 - $200**, ◊ **$40**, ch con, BC DC MC VI.

★★★☆ **Treasured Memories Guest Accommodation**, (Cotg), Pine Vale Dve, 1km S of PO, ☎ 08 8524 6380, fax 08 8524 7006, 2 cotgs acc up to 2, [ensuite, bath, hairdry, a/c, elec blkts, TV, video, clock radio, t/c mkg, refrig], iron, iron brd, spa, bbq, c/park (undercover), non smoking rms. **BLB** ♥ **$100**, ♥♥ **$140 - $160**, ◊ **$40**, ch con, pen con, AE BC MC VI.

★★★☆ **Yallambee Cottage**, (Cotg), Springton Rd, 1.5km E of PO, ☎ 08 8524 6301, fax 08 8524 6301, 1 cotg acc up to 6, (3 bedrm), [shwr, bath, tlt (2), hairdry, fire pl, heat, elec blkts, TV, clock radio, t/c mkg, refrig, cook fac, toaster, blkts, linen, pillows], ldry, w/mach, iron, tennis, breakfast ingredients, non smoking property. **D $140 - $240**, ch con, fam con.

★★★ **Tungali Cottage**, (Cotg), Williamstown - Springton Rd, 10km SE of PO, ☎ 08 8524 6251, fax 08 8524 6315, 1 cotg acc up to 4, (2 bedrm), [shwr, tlt, a/c, fire pl, elec blkts, TV, radio, refrig, cook fac, ldry (in unit), blkts, linen, pillows], bbq, meals avail, cots, breakfast ingredients, non smoking property. **BLB** ♥ **$75**, ♥♥ **$100**, ◊ **$25**, ch con, BC MC VI.

B&B's/Guest Houses

★★★☆ **Thorn Fields Homestay Accommodation**, (B&B), Margaret St, 500m N of PO, ☎ 08 8524 6468, fax 08 8524 6468, (2 stry), 2 rms [shwr (2), bath (1), tlt (1), hairdry (1), a/c, c/fan, elec blkts, TV, clock radio, toaster], iron (1), iron brd (1), lounge, ✕, t/c mkg shared, refrig, bbq, **BLB** ♥♥ **$90 - $120**, ◊ **$45 - $60**, BC MC VI.

End of Barossa Valley Region

BEACHPORT SA 5280

Pop 443. (394km SE Adelaide), See map on pages 586/587, ref J8. Coastal town involved in the lobster fishing industry. Beachport Conservation Park, Woakwine Cutting, Old Wool and Grain Store and the Victoriana Museum. Boating, Bowls, Bush Walking, Fishing, Golf, Horse Riding, Sailing, Scenic Drives, Surfing, Swimming (Beach & Lake), Tennis, Water Skiing.

Hotels/Motels

★★★ **Beachport Motor Inn**, (M), Railway Tce, ☎ 08 8735 8070, fax 08 8735 8398, 13 units [ensuite, fan, heat, elec blkts, tel, TV, clock radio, t/c mkg, refrig, cook fac (5)], w/mach-fee, dryer-fee, iron, iron brd, bbq, non smoking rms (2), **RO** ♥ **$60 - $89**, ♥♥ **$65 - $89**, ◊ **$13**, ch con, AE BC DC EFT MC MCH VI.

B&B's/Guest Houses

★★★☆ **Bompas Hotel**, (PH), 3 Railway Tce, ☎ 08 8735 8333, fax 08 8735 8101, (2 stry), 8 rms [shwr (5), bath (hip) (3), tlt (5), fan (avail), heat, elec blkts, tel, TV, video-fee, clock radio, t/c mkg, refrig, toaster], ldry, ✕, cots-fee. **D $48 - $100**, BC DC EFT MC VI.

BERRI SA 5343

Pop 3,733. (235km NE Adelaide), See map on pages 586/587, ref E6. Located on the banks of the River Murray. Berri obtained its name from the aboriginal words 'Berri Berri' which means 'wide bend in the river'. Boating, Bowls, Croquet, Fishing, Golf, Greyhound Racing, Horse Racing, Horse Riding, Scenic Drives, Squash, Swimming (Pool & River), Tennis, Vineyards, Wineries, Water Skiing.

Hotels/Motels

★★★★☆ **Berri Resort Hotel**, (M), Riverview Dve, ☎ 08 8582 1411, fax 08 8582 2140, (2 stry gr fl), 51 units [ensuite, bath (11), hairdry, a/c, elec blkts, tel, cable tv, clock radio, t/c mkg, refrig], iron, iron brd. **RO** ♥ **$78 - $75**, ♥♥ **$88 - $85**, ◊ **$10**, ch con, AE BC DC EFT JCB MC MP VI, ♿.

Berri Resort Hotel ...continued
(Hotel Section), 25 units [ensuite (12), spa bath (2), hairdry, a/c, elec blkts, tel, cable tv, clock radio, t/c mkg, refrig], shared fac (13), iron, iron brd, conv fac, ✕, pool, bbq, rm serv, tennis, cots. **RO** ♥ **$98**, ♥♥ **$102**, ◊ **$10**, ch con, 12 rms ★★★★. (not yet classified).

★★★★ **Big River Motor Inn**, (M), Old Sturt Hwy, ☎ 08 8582 2688, fax 08 8582 3344, 30 units [ensuite, hairdry, a/c-cool, heat, elec blkts, tel, cable tv, clock radio, t/c mkg, refrig], iron, iron brd, ✕ (Mon to Sat), pool, bbq, dinner to unit, c/park (carport), car wash, golf-fee, cots, non smoking units (16). **RO** ♥ **$87**, ♥♥ **$96**, ◊ **$9**, AE BC DC EFT JCB MC MP VI, ♿.

★★★ **Glossop Motel**, (M), Old Sturt Hwy, 5km W of Berri, ☎ 08 8583 2379, fax 08 8583 2119, 11 units [ensuite, a/c, c/fan, elec blkts, tel, TV, clock radio, t/c mkg, refrig, toaster], ldry, w/mach, dryer, iron, iron brd, pool, bbq, c/park (undercover), plygr, cots, **RO** ♥ **$50**, ♥♥ **$55**, fam con, AE BC DC MC VI.

★★☆ **Berri Bridge Motel**, (M), 3 Worman St, ☎ 08 8582 1011, fax 08 8582 1083, 9 units [ensuite, a/c, elec blkts, tel, TV, clock radio, t/c mkg, refrig, toaster], iron (avail), iron brd (avail), pool. **RO** ♥ **$55**, ♥♥ **$66 - $82.50**, ◊ **$5 - $10**, AE BC DC EFT MC VI.

Self Catering Accommodation

★★★ **Linhayven Cottage**, (Cotg), Riverview Dve, 2.7km NE of PO, ☎ 08 8582 1917, fax 08 8582 3117, 1 cotg acc up to 6, (3 bedrm), [shwr, bath, tlt (2), a/c, c/fan, elec blkts, TV, video, clock radio, CD, t/c mkg, refrig, cook fac, micro, toaster, blkts, linen, pillows], w/mach, iron, iron brd, bbq, c/park (garage), jetty, non smoking property. **D $130 - $150**, **W $575 - $820**, Min book applies, BC MC VI.

Other Accommodation

Big River Holidays, (Hbt), Riverview Dve, 3km E of PO, ☎ 0429 672 392, 4 houseboats acc up to 12, [shwr, tlt, a/c-cool, fan, heat, TV, video, CD, refrig, cook fac, micro, blkts, linen, pillows], w/mach, ice box, bbq, c/park.

Swan Houseboats, (Hbt), Moorings southern bank, adjacent to bridge, ☎ 08 8582 3663, fax 08 8582 3077, 7 houseboats acc up to 8, [shwr, tlt, a/c, TV, video, refrig, cook fac, micro, d/wash, linen], w/mach, bbq, Small dogs at managements discretion. **W $810 - $1,960**, BC MC VI.

BETHANY SA

See Barossa Valley Region.

BIRDWOOD SA 5234

Pop 582. (44km E Adelaide), See map on pages 586/587, ref C7. A small rural township in the Mount Lofty Ranges, beside the upper reaches of the River Torrens. National Motor Museum. Scenic Drives.

Self Catering Accommodation

★★★☆ **Lavender Greene Country Cottage**, (Cotg), Cromer Rd, 3km NE of PO, ☎ 08 8568 5361, or 08 8568 5167, fax 08 8568 5361, 1 cotg acc up to 4, (1 bedrm), [shwr, tlt, hairdry, a/c-cool, TV, video, radio, t/c mkg, refrig, cook fac, elec frypan, toaster, blkts, doonas, linen, pillows], iron, iron brd, bbq, breakfast ingredients, non smoking property. **D** ♥ **$80**, ♥♥ **$95**, ◊ **$20**, ch con, pen con.

★★★☆ **The Elms at Birdwood**, (Cotg), Blocks Rd, 2.8 km E of PO, ☎ 08 8568 5287, fax 08 8568 5287, 1 cotg acc up to 3, [shwr, tlt, hairdry, heat, elec blkts, TV, clock radio, t/c mkg, refrig, micro, elec frypan, toaster, blkts, doonas, linen, pillows], iron, iron brd, spa (2 person), bbq, dinner to unit (by arrangement), cots. **D** ♥♥ **$135**, ◊ **$40**, BC MC VI.

★★★ **Birdwood Bed & Breakfast Cottages**, (Cotg), 38 Olivedale St (Main Rd), 1.5km E of PO, ☎ 08 8568 5444, fax 08 8568 2855, 3 cotgs acc up to 4, (1 bedrm2 bedrm), [spa bath (3), tlt, a/c-cool, heat (wood fire), elec blkts, TV, clock radio (cassette), t/c mkg, refrig, cook fac, micro (3), toaster, blkts, linen, pillows], breakfast ingredients. **D** ♥♥ **$140 - $160**, ◊ **$20**, ch con, MC VI.

B&B's/Guest Houses

★★★★ **Blumberg Mews Country Retreat**, (B&B), 7 Cromer Rd, 1km E of PO, ☎ 08 8568 5551, fax 08 8568 5551, (2 stry gr fl), 3 rms (1 suite) [shwr, bath (1), tlt, hairdry (3), c/fan, heat, elec blkts, TV, clock radio], ldry, lounge (TV, Video & Stereo), t/c mkg shared, bbq, meals avail (by arrangement), cots, non smoking rms. **BB** ♥ **$55**, ♥♥ **$132**, ◊ **$55**, ch con, BC MC VI.

★★★★★

Trouble-free travel tips - **Tools**

It pays to carry some basic tools for emergency roadside repairs, such as an adjustable spanner, phillips head and flat blade screwdrivers, pliers and a roll of masking tape.

BLANCHETOWN SA 5357

Pop 215. (133km NE Adelaide), See map on pages 586/587, ref D6. Holiday resort in the Riverland Region. Boating, Fishing, Golf, Swimming (River), Water Skiing.

Self Catering Accommodation

★★★☆ **Salters Station Cottage**, (Cotg), Paisley Rd, 4km NE of PO, ☎ 08 8289 0303, fax 08 8289 0303, 1 cotg acc up to 8, (3 bedrm), [shwr, tlt, a/c-cool, c/fan, heat, TV, clock radio, refrig, cook fac, elec frypan, toaster, ldry, linen reqd-fee, pillows reqd], w/mach, iron, bbq, c/park (carport), **D** ♦ **$30 - $35**, ♦♦ **$50 - $60**, ◊ **$20 - $25**, ch con.

★★★ **Bindmurra**, (Cotg), Swan Reach Rd, 5km from PO, ☎ 08 8540 5193, fax 08 8540 5373, 2 cotgs acc up to 8, [shwr, bath, tlt, a/c-cool (1), c/fan (1), fire pl, elec blkts, TV, video, clock radio, t/c mkg, refrig, cook fac, micro, toaster, ldry (1), blkts, doonas, linen, pillows], w/mach (1), iron (1), bbq, Pets on application. **D** ♦♦ **$66 - $85**, ◊ **$17 - $22**, **W $495 - $550**, ch con.

★★★ **Roonka River Front Cottages**, (Cotg), Blanchetown - Morgan Rd, 8km N of PO, ☎ 08 8540 5189, fax 08 8540 5189, 5 cotgs acc up to 6, (2 bedrm), [shwr, tlt, a/c, fire pl (3), heat (slow combustion) (2), elec blkts, TV, clock radio, refrig, cook fac, micro, elec frypan, toaster, linen reqd-fee], ldry, w/mach, dryer, spa (1), bbq, tennis, cots. **D $65 - $82**, AE BC MC VI.

B&B's/Guest Houses

★★★★☆ **Portee Station**, (PH), No children's facilities, 10km S of PO, ☎ 08 8540 5211, fax 08 8540 5016, 8 rms [ensuite, bath, elec blkts, tel, clock radio], lounge (TV), lounge firepl, res liquor license, t/c mkg shared, meals avail, c/park. **BB** ♦ **$149**, ♦♦ **$208**, ◊ **$104**, AE BC MC VI.

Other Accommodation

Shore to Please Houseboat, (Hbt), Sturt Hwy, Griffens Marina, 2km NE of PO, ☎ 08 8331 9248, fax 08 8331 9248, 1 houseboat acc up to 8, [shwr, tlt, heat, TV, video, refrig, cook fac, micro], bbq. **W $880 - $1,430**, Min book applies.

BLINMAN SA 5730

Pop Nominal, (502km N Adelaide), See map on pages 586/587, ref H4. Popular tourist venue in the Flinders Ranges, east of Parachilna Gorge. Bush Walking, Horse Riding, Scenic Drives.

Hotels/Motels

★ **North Blinman Hotel Motel**, (LMH), Mine Rd, ☎ 08 8648 4867, fax 08 8648 4621, 9 units [ensuite, a/c-cool, heat, t/c mkg, refrig], lounge, ☒, pool, bbq, cots. **RO** ♦ **$55**, ♦♦ **$85**, ◊ **$25**, ch con, AE BC EFT MC VI.

★ **(Hotel Section)**, 8 rms [ensuite, a/c, heat, t/c mkg, refrig], ☒, cots. **RO** ♦ **$55**, ♦♦ **$85**, ◊ **$25**, ch con.

BOOLEROO CENTRE SA 5482

Pop 295. (263km N Adelaide), See map on pages 586/587, ref H5. Deriving its name from the Aboriginal word for 'Place of Mud' Booleroo Centre is an early settlement town which remains as a support centre for mixed farming and agricultural pursuits. Bowls, Swimming (Pool).

Self Catering Accommodation

★★★ **Callum Brae Homestead**, (Cotg), off Booleroo to Orroroo Rd, 9km NE of PO, ☎ 08 8667 2162, 2 cotgs acc up to 22, (1 & 4 bedrm), [shwr, tlt, a/c (1), c/fan (1), fire pl (1), heat, TV, radio, refrig, cook fac, blkts, linen reqd-fee, pillows], ldry. **D** ♦♦ **$50**, ◊ **$25**, fam con.

BORDERTOWN SA 5268

Pop 2,235. (274km SE Adelaide), See map on pages 586/587, ref J7. Noted for its cereal growing, wool & fat stock. Bowls, Croquet, Golf, Horse Racing, Motor Racing, Scenic Drives, Swimming (Pool), Tennis.

Hotels/Motels

★★★ **Bordertown Dukes Motor Inn**, (M), Dukes Hwy, ☎ 08 8752 1177, fax 08 8752 2918, 34 units [ensuite, spa bath (3), hairdry (11), a/c-cool (4), a/c (30), heat (4), elec blkts, tel, TV, video-fee, clock radio, t/c mkg, refrig, mini bar], conf fac, ☒, pool, rm serv, tennis, cots-fee, non smoking rms (20). **RO** ♦ **$60 - $85**, ♦♦ **$69 - $94**, ◊ **$8**, fam con, 10 units of a 3 star plus rating. AE BC DC EFT MC MP VI, ♿.

GOLDEN CHAIN
BORDERTOWN
Dukes Motor Inn
34 Well appointed Units Fully Licensed Restaurant
For **RESERVATIONS** only phone 1800 088 109
ENQUIRIES: Ph (08) 8752 1177 Fax (08) 8752 2918

★★☆ **Bordertown Abode Parkland Motel**, (M), 105 Park Tce, 1km NW of PO, ☎ 08 8752 1622, fax 08 8752 1390, 15 units [ensuite, a/c, elec blkts, tel, TV, clock radio, t/c mkg, refrig, toaster], bbq, cots. **RO** ♦ **$50 - $66**, ♦♦ **$55 - $77**, ◊ **$5**, 5 rooms ★★. AE BC DC EFT MC VI.

★★☆ **Bordertown Motel**, (M), 25 Dukes Hwy, ☎ 08 8752 1444, fax 08 8752 2526, 30 units [ensuite, a/c-cool (20), a/c (10), heat (20), elec blkts, tel, TV, clock radio, t/c mkg, refrig], conv fac, ☒, pool, rm serv, plygr, cots-fee, non smoking units (10). **RO** ♦ **$44 - $57**, ♦♦ **$54 - $66**, ♦♦♦ **$59 - $70**, ◊ **$8**, AE BC EFT MC MCH VI.

★ **Bordertown Hotel**, (LH), 79 East Tce, ☎ 08 8752 1016, fax 08 8752 2691, (2 stry), 9 rms [a/c-cool, elec blkts], ☒, t/c mkg shared, cots-fee. **BLB** ♦ **$42**, ♦♦ **$62**, ◊ **$25**, ch con, AE BC EFT MC VI.

Self Catering Accommodation

★★★ **Dunalan Host Farm Cottage**, (Cotg), (Farm), Dukes Hwy, 18km E of PO, ☎ 08 8753 2323, fax 08 8753 2323, 1 cotg acc up to 10, (6 bedrm), [shwr (2), tlt (1), fan, TV, clock radio, refrig, cook fac, micro, toaster, doonas], lounge firepl (woodheater), bbq, cots-fee, breakfast ingredients, non smoking property, Dog & Cat - conditions apply. **D** ♦ **$55**, ♦♦ **$88**, ◊ **$35**, ch con.

BRENTWOOD SA 5575

Pop Nominal, (197km W Adelaide), See map on pages 586/587, ref A7. A small agricultural town situated on the lower Yorke Peninsula. Fishing, Horse Riding, Swimming (Sea).

Self Catering Accommodation

Get-Away Holidays, 1.6km SE of town centre, ☎ 08 8853 4201, fax 08 8553 4200, 5 cabins acc up to 5, [tlt (septic), refrig, cook fac, blkts reqd-fee, linen reqd-fee]. **W $784 - $889**, Min book applies.

★★ **(Hardwicke House)**, 4km SW of PO Hardwicke Bay, 1 cotg acc up to 8, (3 bedrm), [shwr, bath, tlt, fire pl, TV, refrig, cook fac, linen (queen bed)]. **D $52 - $70**, **W $364 - $490**.

★★ **(Sandalwood Park)**, 4km SE of PO, 1 cotg acc up to 8, (4 bedrm), [shwr, bath, tlt, fire pl, tel, TV, refrig, cook fac, linen (queen bed)]. **D $52 - $70**, **W $364 - $490**.

★ **(Paling Hut)**, Sturt Bay, 34km S of PO, 1 cotg acc up to 7, (3 bedrm), [shwr, bath, tlt, fire pl, tel, refrig, cook fac, linen (queen bed)]. **D $52 - $70**, **W $364 - $490**.

BURRA SA 5417

Pop 1,191. (156km N Adelaide), See map on pages 586/587, ref H5. Nestled in the Bald Hills Range, one of Australia's oldest mining towns. Bon Accord Mining Complex, Burra Mine Open Air Museum, Burra Smelting Works, Morphetts Enginehouse Museum, Hampton Village, Malowen Lowarth, Market Square Museum, Miners Dugouts, Peacocks Chimney Stack, Police Lock-Up & Stables, Powder Magazine, Redruth Gaol, Unicorn Brewery & Tourist Information Office on (08) 8892 2154. Art Gallery, Bowls, Golf, Horse Riding, Scenic Drives, Swimming (Pool), Tennis.

Hotels/Motels

★★★ **Burra Motor Inn**, (M), Market St, 400m N of PO, ☎ 08 8892 2777, fax 08 8892 2707, 20 units [shwr, tlt, a/c, elec blkts, tel, TV, movie, t/c mkg, refrig], ☒ (Mon to Sat), pool-indoor, spa, rm serv, dinner to unit, cots-fee. **RO** ♦ **$65**, ♦♦ **$75**, ◊ **$10**, 5 units ★★★☆. AE BC DC EFT MC VI, ♿.

Rates may change. Check before booking.

★ **Commercial Hotel**, (LH), 22 Commercial St, ☎ 08 8892 2010, fax 08 8892 2900, (2 stry), 8 rms [fan (2)], ldry, lounge (TV), ✉, t/c mkg shared, refrig, cots, non smoking rms. **BB ▮ $27.50, ▮▮ $44, ▮ $11**, AE BC EFT MC VI.

Self Catering Accommodation
★★★★ **Burra Heritage Cottages - Tivers Row**, (Cotg), 8-18 Truro St, ☎ 08 8892 2461, 6 cotgs acc up to 4, (2 bedrm), [shwr, tlt, fan, heat (open fire), elec blkts, TV, clock radio, refrig, cook fac, ldry, blkts, linen, pillows], w/mach, dryer, iron, cots, breakfast ingredients, **D ▮▮ $110, ▮ $30**, Min book long w/ends and Easter, AE BC MC VI.
★★★☆ **Burra View House Apartments & Cottages**, (Apt), 7 Mt Pleasant Rd, ☎ 08 8892 2648, fax 08 8892 2150, 2 apts acc up to 5, (1 bedrm2 bedrm), [shwr, bath (1), tlt, hairdry, fan, heat, elec blkts, TV, video (1), clock radio, t/c mkg, refrig, cook fac, micro, elec frypan, blkts, linen, pillows], ldry, w/mach, dryer, iron, lounge firepl, bbq, cots, non smoking property. **BLB ▮▮ $105, ▮ $25, D ▮▮ $95, ▮ $20**, Min book long w/ends and Easter, BC MC VI.
★★★ **(Coppervilla Cottage Section)**, 1 cotg acc up to 6, (3 bedrm), [shwr, bath, tlt, hairdry, fan, heat, elec blkts, TV, clock radio, t/c mkg, refrig, cook fac, micro, ldry, blkts, linen, pillows], w/mach, iron, bbq, cots, non smoking property. **BLB ▮▮ $105, ▮ $25, D ▮▮ $95, ▮ $20 - $25**, ch con.
★★★ **(Ellens Cottage Section)**, 1 cotg acc up to 4, (2 bedrm), [ensuite, bath, hairdry, fan, fire pl, elec blkts, TV, clock radio, t/c mkg, refrig, cook fac, micro, blkts, linen, pillows], w/mach, iron, cots, non smoking property. **BLB ▮▮ $105, ▮ $25, D ▮▮ $95, ▮ $20**, ch con.
★★★☆ **Morse Cottage**, (Cotg), 22 Chapel St, ☎ 08 8365 4170, fax 08 8278 2558, 1 cotg acc up to 6, (3 bedrm), [shwr, tlt, c/fan, fire pl, heat, tel, TV, video, clock radio, refrig, cook fac, micro, toaster, blkts, linen, pillows], ldry, iron, bbq. **D ▮▮ $75, ▮ $25**, ch con.
★★★ **Bon Accord Cottage**, (Cotg), West St, ☎ 08 8892 2519, fax 08 8892 2555, 1 cotg acc up to 8, (4 bedrm), [shwr, tlt, fan, fire pl, elec blkts, TV, radio, refrig, cook fac, micro, toaster, blkts, linen, pillows], w/mach, dryer, iron, bbq, cots, breakfast ingredients, non smoking property, **D ▮▮ $135, ▮ $25**, ch con, Min book long w/ends and Easter.
★★☆ **Paxton Square Cottages**, (Cotg), Kingston St, ☎ 08 8892 2622, fax 08 8892 2508, 32 cotgs acc up to 9, (1 & 2 bedrm), [shwr, tlt, fan, fire pl, heat, t/c mkg, refrig, cook fac, linen reqd-fee], ldry-fee, bbq-fee, cots. **D ▮▮ $41 - $63, ▮ $12**, ch con, BC MC VI, ♿.

BUTE SA 5560

Pop 275. (138km NW Adelaide), See map on pages 586/587, ref H5. Bute is on the plains in that indeterminate zone where the Yorke Peninsula and the Mid North merge.
Self Catering Accommodation
★★★☆ **Ashhurst Farm House**, (Cotg), Pine Flat Rd, 10km W of PO, ☎ 08 8821 4033, fax 08 8821 3455, 1 cotg acc up to 9, (4 bedrm), [shwr, bath, tlt, a/c-cool, fan, heat (combustion), TV, video, clock radio, refrig, cook fac, blkts, linen, pillows], w/mach, iron, bbq, c/park (garage), plygr, cots, breakfast ingredients, non smoking property, **D ▮▮ $80**, ch con.

BUTLER TANKS SA 5605

Pop Nominal, (579km NW Adelaide), See map on pages 586/587, ref G6. A small rural community. Tennis.
Self Catering Accommodation
★★ **Farmpak Holiday Cottage**, (Cotg), Mount Hill, ☎ 08 8688 0025, fax 08 8688 0068, 1 cotg acc up to 12, (3 bedrm), [shwr, bath, tlt, a/c-cool, fan, heat (open fire), tel, TV, video, clock radio, t/c mkg, refrig, cook fac, micro, toaster, blkts, linen, pillows], bbq, c/park. **D ▮▮ $35 - $54, ▮ $17 - $22**, BC MC VI.

CADNEY PARK SA 5723

Pop Nominal, (1010km Adelaide), See map on pages 586/587, ref F2. Located on the Stuart Hwy.
Hotels/Motels
★★★ **Cadney Homestead Motel**, (M), Stuart Hwy, 151km N of Coober Pedy, ☎ 08 8670 7994, fax 08 8670 7934, 6 units (1 bedrm - 4x1d1s. 2x1d2s), [shwr, tlt, a/c-cool, c/fan, heat, TV, t/c mkg, refrig, ldry-fee], ✕, pool, cots. **RO ▮ $91.50, ▮▮ $91.50, ▮ $6.50**, AE BC DC EFT MC VI.

CAPE JERVIS SA 5204

Pop Nominal, (108km S Adelaide), See map on pages 586/587, ref B8. A coastal township located on the southern tip of the Fleurieu Peninsula. Both passengers & cars can be accommodated on the Kangaroo Island Sealink which operates daily between Cape Jervis and Penneshaw. The journey takes approx 1 hour. Kangaroo Island Ferry Connections operate a passenger only ferry, daily between Cape Jervis and Penneshaw. The journey takes approx 30 minutes. Boat Ramp, Bush Walking, Fishing, Scenic Drives.
Self Catering Accommodation
★★★★ **Cape Jervis Holiday Units**, (HU), Lot 7 Flinders Dve, 1km E of ferry terminal, ☎ 08 8598 0229, fax 08 8598 0229, 5 units acc up to 5, (2 bedrm), [shwr, bath (hip), tlt, a/c, elec blkts, TV, clock radio, t/c mkg, refrig, cook fac, micro, toaster, doonas, linen, pillows], bbq, plygr, cots, breakfast ingredients. **D ▮▮ $105, ▮ $27, W ▮▮ $680**, ch con, BC MC VI, ♿.
B&B's/Guest Houses
★★★★☆ **Cape Jervis Station**, (B&B), Main Rd, 3km E of KI Ferry Terminal, ☎ 08 8598 0288, fax 08 8598 0278, 2 rms [ensuite, fan (2), c/fan (3), heat, TV, clock radio, mini bar], ldry, w/mach, dryer, iron, iron brd, rec rm, lounge firepl, ✉ (by arrangement), t/c mkg shared, refrig, bbq, golf (driving range), tennis. **BB ▮ $80, ▮▮ $110**, AE BC JCB MC VI.
★★★★☆ **(Pine Cottage Section)**, 1 cotg acc up to 4, (1 bedrm), [ensuite, a/c, elec blkts, TV, video, clock radio, refrig, mini bar, cook fac, micro, blkts, linen, pillows], ldry, w/mach, dryer, iron, iron brd, bbq, tennis. **D ▮ $90, ▮▮ $100, ▮▮▮ $120, ▮▮▮▮ $140**, fam con.
(Log Cabin Section), 1 log cabin acc up to 4, (1 bedrm), [ensuite, fan, heat, elec blkts, clock radio, refrig, cook fac, micro, blkts, linen, pillows], bbq, tennis. **D ▮ $45, ▮▮ $65, ▮▮▮ $80, ▮▮▮▮ $90**.
Cape Jervis Station, (B&B), Main Rd, ☎ 1300 130 974, fax 08 8598 0271, 1 rm (1 suite) [shwr, tlt, fan, heat, elec blkts, clock radio, t/c mkg, doonas, pillows], lounge (TV), meals avail, non smoking rms. **BB ▮ $90, ▮▮ $110**, AE BC MC VI, (not yet classified).
(Bunkhouse Section), 1 bunkhouse acc up to 8, [fan, fire pl, heat, t/c mkg, micro, elec frypan, toaster, doonas, linen, pillows], rec rm, lounge, cook fac, refrig, bbq. **RO ▮ $20, ▮ $10**.

CARRICKALINGA SA 5204

Pop 291. (79km Adelaide), See map on pages 586/587, ref B8. Coastal resort situated where the hills of the Fleurieu Peninsula meet the waters of Gulf St Vincent. Boating, Fishing, Scenic Drives, Surfing, Swimming (Beach).
Self Catering Accommodation
★★★☆ **Carrickalinga Retreat**, (Cotg), 29 Riverview Dve, ☎ 08 8337 2857, fax 08 8337 2857, 1 cotg acc up to 4, (2 bedrm), [shwr, tlt, hairdry, a/c, c/fan, elec blkts, tel, TV, video, clock radio, CD, t/c mkg, refrig, cook fac, micro, toaster, blkts, doonas, linen, pillows], w/mach, iron, iron brd, lounge firepl, bbq, breakfast ingredients, non smoking rms, **D ▮▮ $120, ▮ $60**.
★★★ **Carrickalinga Cove Apartments**, (HU), 5 Surf Ave, ☎ 08 8558 3330, fax 08 8558 2758, 7 units acc up to 6, (2 & 3 bedrm), [shwr, bath (3), tlt, a/c, elec blkts, TV, video (1), clock radio, refrig, cook fac, micro, d/wash (1), ldry (in unit) (3), linen reqd-fee], pool, spa, bbq, tennis (half court), **D ▮▮ $70 - $180, ▮ $10**, ch con, 3 units of a higher rating. BC MC VI.

CEDUNA SA 5690

Pop 2,753. (773km NW Adelaide), See map on pages 586/587, ref E4. Situated on the shores of Murat Bay, Ceduna is the focal point and business centre for the far west coast and the hub of a large cereal growing area. Old Schoolhouse National Trust Museum, Telecommunication Earth Station and Wittelbee Conservation Park. Boating, Bowls, Bush Walking, Fishing, Golf, Horse Racing, Horse Riding, Sailing, Squash, Surfing, Swimming (Beach), Tennis, Water Skiing, Wind Surfing.
Hotels/Motels

★★★ **Highway One Motel**, (M), Eyre Hwy, 2km NW of PO, ☎ 08 8625 2208, fax 08 8625 2866, 23 units [ensuite, tlt, a/c, fan, tel, cable tv, clock radio, t/c mkg, refrig, toaster], ldry, ✕ (Mon to Sat), dinner to unit, cots-fee, non smoking units (6). **RO ▮ $65 - $75, ▮▮ $70 - $80, ▮ $10**, 11 units ★★☆. AE BC DC EFT MC VI.

CEDUNA SA continued...

★★☆ Ceduna Foreshore Hotel Motel, (LMH), Cnr O'Loughlin Tce & South Tce, ☎ 08 8625 2008, fax 08 8625 3585, (2 stry gr fl), 42 units [ensuite, a/c, elec blkts, tel, cable tv (19), video-fee, clock radio, t/c mkg, refrig, toaster], ldry-fee, conv fac, ⊠, ✆, cots, non smoking rms (3). RO ♦ $60 - $80, ♦♦ $65 - $85, ◊ $8, ch con, 5 units ★★★. AE BC DC EFT MC VI.

★☆ (Hotel Section), 8 rms [basin, shwr (2), bath (1), tlt (2), a/c (2), elec blkts, tel (4), TV (3), t/c mkg, refrig (2), toaster], ldry-fee. RO ♦ $25 - $35, ♦♦ $29 - $37.

★★ Pine Grove Motel, (M), 49 McKenzie St, 500m E of PO, ☎ 08 8625 2201, fax 08 8625 3199, 25 units [ensuite, a/c, elec blkts, tel, TV, movie, t/c mkg, refrig, toaster], ldry-fee, ⊠, pool above ground, bbq, rm serv, dinner to unit, ✆, cots-fee. RO ♦ $55, ♦♦ $64, ◊ $6, AE BC DC EFT MC VI.

Self Catering Accommodation

Parkers Seaview Cottage Ceduna, (Cotg), Cnr Hill St & Seaview Tce, Thevenard, ☎ 08 8625 3272, 1 cotg acc up to 6, (3 bedrm), [shwr, tlt, a/c, elec blkts, TV, video, clock radio, t/c mkg, refrig, cook fac, micro, elec frypan, toaster, blkts, doonas, linen, pillows], w/mach, iron, iron brd, bbq, c/park. D ♦♦ $60 - $70, (not yet classified).

Decres Bay Beach Cabins, (Farm), Decres Bay Rd, 15km from Ceduna, ☎ 08 8625 3338, 2 cabins acc up to 4, [shwr, tlt, cook fac, blkts reqd, linen reqd-fee, pillows], bbq, Pets on application. D $40 - $45.

CHARLESTON SA 5244

Pop Nominal, (40km Adelaide), See map on pages 586/587, ref C7. This small community in gentle hill country near the headwaters of the Onkaparinga River was established early in the colony's history.

Self Catering Accommodation

★★★ Charley's Bed and Breakfast, (Cotg), 52 Onkaparinga Valley Rd, ☎ 08 8389 5112, fax 08 8389 5317, (2 stry), 1 cotg acc up to 4, [shwr, tlt, hairdry, heat, fan, c/fan, fire pl, TV, video, radio, t/c mkg, refrig, cook fac, micro, elec frypan, toaster, blkts, doonas, linen, pillows], spa (heated), bbq, meals to unit (by arrangement), plygr, cots. D ♦♦ $100 - $140, ◊ $40 - $50, W ♦♦ $500, ◊ $200, ch con, fam con, pen con, BC MC VI.

CLARE SA 5453

Pop 2,575. (135km N Adelaide), See map on pages 586/587, ref H5. Situated in a beautiful tree-clad valley, whose greatest industry is its wineries. Art Galleries, Bungaree Station, Geralka Rural Farm, Wineries and Wolta Wolta. Bowls, Bush Walking, Croquet, Golf, Horse Racing, Horse Riding, Scenic Drives, Squash, Swimming (Pool), Tennis, Vineyards, Wineries.

Hotels/Motels

★★★★☆ Clare Country Club Motel, (M), White Hut Rd, 1.5km NE of PO, ☎ 08 8842 1060, fax 08 8842 1042, 45 units (14 suites) [ensuite, spa bath, elec blkts, cable tv, clock radio, t/c mkg, refrig, mini bar, micro (15), elec frypan (15), toaster (15), doonas], ldry, w/mach-fee, dryer-fee, conf fac, ⊠, pool, sauna, spa, bbq, rm serv, tennis, cots, non smoking property. RO ♦ $121 - $132, ♦♦ $121 - $132, ◊ $16.50, ch con, AE BC DC MC VI, ⚹&.

★★★☆ Clare Central Motel, (M), 325 Main North Rd, 500m N of PO, ☎ 08 8842 2277, fax 08 8842 3563, 30 units [shwr, spa bath (7), tlt, a/c, elec blkts, tel, TV, clock radio, t/c mkg, refrig, mini bar, toaster], ldry, ⊠ (Mon to Sat), pool, rm serv, dinner to unit, cots. BLB ♦ $88 - $105, ♦♦ $97 - $132, ◊ $15, ch con, AE BC DC EFT MC VI, ⚹&.

★★★ Clare Valley Motel, (M), 74a Main North Rd, 2km S of PO, ☎ 08 8842 2799, fax 08 8842 3121, 33 units [shwr, spa bath (5), tlt, a/c-cool (22), a/c (10), heat, elec blkts, tel, TV, clock radio, t/c mkg, refrig, toaster], iron, iron brd, conf fac, ⊠ (Mon to Sat), bar, pool, cots (free or charge). RO ♦ $70 - $115, ♦♦ $80 - $115, ◊ $10, AE BC DC MC VI.

★★ Bentleys Hotel Motel, (M), 191 Main North Rd, ☎ 08 8842 1700, fax 08 8842 3474, (2 stry), 7 units [ensuite, a/c, elec blkts, TV, clock radio, t/c mkg, refrig]. RO ♦♦ $65, ◊ $10, AE BC EFT MC VI.

★ (Hotel Section), 10 units [shwr (7), tlt (7), a/c-cool, elec blkts, TV, clock radio, t/c mkg], cots. RO ♦ $35, ♦♦ $55 - $65, ◊ $10.

★ Taminga Hotel, (LH), Main St, ☎ 08 8842 2808, fax 08 8842 2461, (2 stry), 14 rms [basin, a/c-cool (3), elec blkts], ldry, lounge (TV), ⊠, non smoking rms. RO ♦ $20, ♦♦ $30, AE BC MC VI.

Clare Hotel, (LH), 244 Main St, ☎ 08 8842 2816, fax 08 8842 3592, (2 stry), 15 rms [basin, ensuite (6), a/c (6), heat, elec blkts, TV (6), t/c mkg (6), refrig (6)], shared fac (9), lounge (TV), ⊠, bbq, cots-fee. RO ♦ $21 - $60, ♦♦ $60, ◊ $12, ch con, 6 rms ★☆. AE BC DC MC VI.

Self Catering Accommodation

★★★★☆ Chaff Mill Village Holiday Apartments, (Apt), 310 Main North Rd, 500m N of PO, ☎ 08 8842 1111, fax 08 8842 1303, 6 apts acc up to 5, (1 bedrm 2 bedrm), [shwr, spa bath, tlt, hairdry, a/c, fire pl, elec blkts, TV, video, clock radio, t/c mkg, refrig, cook fac, micro, toaster, blkts, linen, pillows], ldry, bbq, c/park (undercover), non smoking units. D ♦♦ $148 - $178, ◊ $30 - $40, AE BC DC EFT MC VI.

★★★★ Brinkworth Country Lodge Bed & Breakfast, (Cotg), Main Rd Brinkworth, via, 29km NW of PO, ☎ 08 8379 0088, fax 08 8379 0068, 1 cotg acc up to 8, (3 bedrm), [shwr, bath, tlt (2), hairdry (2), a/c, fan, c/fan, fire pl, elec blkts, tel, TV, clock radio, t/c mkg, refrig, cook fac, micro, elec frypan, d/wash, toaster, ldry, blkts, doonas, linen, pillows], w/mach, iron, iron brd, spa, freezer, bbq, plygr, cots, non smoking property. D ♦ $135, ♦♦ $155, ◊ $78, ch con, fam con, pen con, Min book applies, BC MC VI.

★★★☆ Clare Valley Cabins, Hubbe Rd, 5km NE of PO, ☎ 08 8842 1155, fax 08 8842 1155, 8 cabins acc up to 6, (2 bedrm), [shwr, bath (7), tlt, a/c, fan, heat (combustion), TV, clock radio, refrig, cook fac, micro, toaster, linen reqd-fee], bbq, plygr, cots. D ♦♦ $66 - $77, ◊ $11, ch con, Min book long w/ends and Easter, BC MC VI.

★★★☆ Windmill Cottage, (Cotg), Lot 22, Scobie Rd, 6km W of PO, ☎ 08 8844 5175, fax 08 8844 5175, 1 cotg acc up to 4, (2 bedrm), [shwr, tlt, a/c-cool, fan, wood heat (slow combustion), elec blkts, TV, video, clock radio (cassette), CD, t/c mkg, refrig, cook fac, micro, elec frypan, toaster, blkts, doonas, linen, pillows], iron, iron brd, bbq, c/park (carport), breakfast ingredients, non smoking property, D ♦ $75, ♦♦ $105, ♦♦♦ $130, ♦♦♦♦ $155, ◊ $25, ch con, Collect keys from Medika Gallery, 16 Moore St, Blyth. Min book long w/ends and Easter, AE BC MC VI.

★★★ Croll Cottage, (Cotg), 23 Daly St, 700m NW of PO, ☎ 08 8842 3767, fax 08 8842 3948, 1 cotg acc up to 6, (3 bedrm), [shwr, bath, tlt, a/c, fan, heat, elec blkts, TV, clock radio, t/c mkg, refrig, cook fac, micro, toaster, ldry (in unit)], w/mach, dryer, iron, iron brd, lounge firepl, bbq, breakfast ingredients, D ♦ $80, ♦♦ $126, ◊ $40, ch con, BC MC VI.

★★★ Miss Nobels Cottage, (Cotg), Quarry Rd, ☎ 08 8843 4326, 1 cotg acc up to 7, (2 bedrm), [shwr, bath, tlt, c/fan, heat, elec blkts, tel, TV, radio, refrig, cook fac, blkts, linen, pillows], w/mach, iron, lounge firepl, bbq, cots, breakfast ingredients, non smoking property, Pets on application. D ♦♦ $95, ◊ $20, ch con.

★★★ Mundaworra Mews Cottages, (Cotg), Main North Rd, 7km N of PO, ☎ 08 8842 3762, fax 08 8842 3160, 4 cotgs acc up to 4, (1 & 2 bedrm), [shwr, tlt, c/fan, fire pl (2), wood heat (2), TV, clock radio, refrig, cook fac (1), cook fac ltd (3), toaster, blkts, linen, pillows], bbq, tennis, cots, breakfast ingredients, Pets on application. D ♦♦ $110 - $140, ◊ $30.

★★★ Springfarm Cottage, (Cotg), Springfarm Rd, 3km E of PO, ☎ 08 8842 1123, fax 08 8842 1123, 1 cotg acc up to 6, (3 bedrm), [shwr, tlt, fan, fire pl, elec blkts, clock radio, CD, refrig, cook fac, micro, toaster, blkts, doonas, linen, pillows], w/mach, iron, iron brd, bbq, plygr, cots, breakfast ingredients. D ♦♦ $130, ◊ $45, ch con.

Maggies Farm, (Cotg), Lot 1, Pt Section 427, 4km SW of PO, ☎ 08 8346 3953, fax 08 8346 3953, 1 cotg acc up to 6, [shwr, tlt, heat (wood), elec blkts, radio, t/c mkg, refrig, cook fac, micro, toaster, blkts, doonas, linen, pillows], w/mach, lounge firepl, bbq, breakfast ingredients, Pets on application. D ♦ $120 - $140, ♦♦ $120 - $140, ◊ $40 - $50, W ♦ $500 - $600, ♦♦ $500 - $600, ◊ $100 - $170, ch con, Min book applies, (not yet classified).

Wuthering Heights Cottages, (Cotg), Roach Rd, 5km N of PO, ☎ 08 8842 3196, fax 08 8842 1319, 3 cotgs acc up to 4, (2 bedrm), [shwr, tlt, a/c-cool, fan, heat, wood heat (2), elec blkts, clock radio, t/c mkg, refrig, cook fac, toaster, ldry (1)], iron, iron brd, lounge firepl (1), bbq, cots, breakfast ingredients, Pets on application. D ♦♦ $110, ◊ $25, ch con, 1 cotg ★★★. Min book long w/ends and Easter, BC MC VI, (not yet classified).

Bungaree Station, (Cotg), (Farm), Main North Rd, 12km N of PO, ☎ 08 8842 2677, fax 08 8842 3004, 6 cotgs acc up to 10, (3 bedrm4 bedrm Studio), [shwr, bath, tlt, fire pl, heat, tel (5), clock radio, refrig, cook fac, micro (2), blkts, linen, pillows], ldry, w/mach, dryer, iron, iron brd, lounge, conv fac, conf fac, pool, gym, cots, breakfast ingredients. **BB ♦ $44 - $55, ♦♦ $88 - $110, ◊ $44 - $55**, Tariff includes farm activities. AE BC DC MC VI.

B&B's/Guest Houses
★★★★ **Brice Hill Country Lodge**, (GH), Warenda Rd, 2km S of PO, ☎ 08 8842 2925, fax 08 8842 1116, 5 rms (1 bedrm2 bedrm), [ensuite, bath (1), spa bath, hairdry, a/c, c/fan, elec blkts, TV, video, clock radio, t/c mkg, refrig, micro, toaster, pillows], iron, iron brd, pool, bbq, non smoking units. **D ♦ $120 - $150, ♦♦ $150 - $180, ◊ $50**, Min book applies, AE BC DC MC VI.

★★★★ **Patly Hill Farm Guest House**, (GH), No children's facilities, St Georges Tce, Armagh, 4km NW of PO, ☎ 08 8842 3557, fax 08 8842 3389, (2 stry), 3 rms (3 suites) [shwr, tlt, c/fan, heat, elec blkts, TV, video, clock radio, t/c mkg, refrig], ldry, w/mach, dryer, iron, iron brd, rec rm, ✗, spa, steam rm, cook fac, bbq, c/park (undercover), non smoking rms, Pets on application. **BB ♦ $137.50, ♦♦ $165, ◊ $82.50**, 2 suites yet to be classified. Min book long w/ends and Easter.

★★★☆ **Clare Valley Palms Bed & Breakfast**, (B&B), 25 Victoria Rd, ☎ 08 8842 3911, fax 08 8842 3911, 3 rms [c/fan, wood heat, elec blkts, CD], shwr, tlt, lounge (TV & video), bbq, non smoking property. **BB ♦ $66, ♦♦ $132, ◊ $66**, AE BC DC JCB MC VI.

CLEVE SA 5640
Pop 738. (529km NW Adelaide), See map on pages 586/587, ref G5. The town was established as a service centre for the surrounding farming community, main products being barley, oats, sheep, cattle and pigs. Fauna Park, Old Council Chamber. Bowls, Bush Walking, Gem Fossicking, Golf, Horse Riding, Scenic Drives, Swimming (Pool), Tennis.

Hotels/Motels
★★ **Cleve Hotel Motel**, (LMH), Fourth St, 200m S of PO, ☎ 08 8628 2011, fax 08 8628 2409, 17 units [ensuite, a/c-cool, heat, elec blkts, tel, TV, t/c mkg, refrig, toaster], ldry, conv fac, ✗ (Mon to Sat), bbq (covered), rm serv, ✆, cots-fee. **RO ♦ $45, ♦♦ $55, ♦♦♦♦ $65, ◊ $10**, AE BC EFT MC VI.

COCKATOO VALLEY SA
See Barossa Valley Region.

COFFIN BAY SA 5607
Pop 343. (739km W Adelaide), See map on pages 586/587, ref F6. On one side the township is flanked by National Park and the other by a network of beaches and bays. Coffin Bay is also famous for its succulent oysters. Boating, Bowls, Bush Walking, Fishing (Rock, Surf & Boat), Golf, Sailing, Scenic Drives, Swimming (Pool & Beach), Tennis, Water Skiing.

Hotels/Motels
★★★ **Coffin Bay Hotel Motel**, (M), Shepperd Ave, 2km SW of PO, ☎ 08 8685 4111, fax 08 8685 4334, 8 units [ensuite, a/c, elec blkts, TV, t/c mkg, refrig, toaster], ldry, ✗, cots. **RO ♦ $65, ♦♦ $75, ◊ $10**, ch con, AE BC DC EFT MC VI.

Self Catering Accommodation
★★★★ **Sheoak Holiday Homes**, (HU), 257-259 The Esplanade, 1km W of Town Jetty, ☎ 08 8685 4314, fax 08 8346 0485, (2 stry gr fl), 3 units acc up to 10, [shwr, bath, spa bath (2), tlt, hairdry, TV, video, clock radio, t/c mkg, refrig, cook fac, micro, d/wash, toaster, doonas, pillows], w/mach, dryer, iron, iron brd. **D $110 - $160, ◊ $10**, weekly con.

★★★ **Alpine Holiday Units**, (HU), 337 Esplanade, 2km W of PO, ☎ 08 8685 4068, 3 units acc up to 5, [shwr, tlt, a/c-cool, heat, TV, video, refrig, cook fac, elec frypan, linen reqd-fee], ldry, w/mach, iron, bbq, c/park. **D $40 - $60, W $260 - $400.**

★★★ **Casuarina Holiday Units**, (HU), The Esplanade, ☎ 08 8685 4173, 4 units acc up to 5, (1 & 2 bedrm), [shwr, tlt, a/c, c/fan, TV, clock radio, refrig, cook fac, linen reqd-fee], ldry, bbq, cots. **D $45 - $60, W $275 - $395.**

★★★ **Kooringa Holiday Flats**, (HU), 83 Greenly Ave, ☎ 08 8685 4087, (2 stry gr fl), 6 units acc up to 5, (2 bedrm), [shwr, tlt, fan, heat, TV, clock radio, refrig, cook fac, ldry, blkts reqd-fee, linen reqd-fee, pillows reqd-fee], iron, rec rm, bbq. **D $45 - $70**, BC MC VI.

★★★ **Siesta Lodge Holiday Units**, (HU), 331 Esplanade, ☎ 08 8685 4001, fax 08 8685 5000, 6 units acc up to 7, (1, 2 & 3 bedrm), [shwr, tlt, a/c, TV, refrig, cook fac, micro, linen reqd-fee], ldry, rec rm, bbq, c/park (carport), tennis (half court), non smoking units. **D ♦♦ $49.50 - $61.50, ◊ $2.20 - $5.50**, BC MC VI.

★★ **Casuarina Cabins**, The Esplanade, ☎ 08 8685 4173, 4 cabins acc up to 4, [ensuite (2), shwr (external) (2), tlt (external) (2), evap cool (2), a/c (1), fan (2), c/fan (1), TV (2), refrig, cook fac, linen reqd-fee], ldry, bbq. **D $30 - $38, W $175 - $210**, 2 cabins of a lower rating.

B&B's/Guest Houses
★★★☆ **Open Shore Bed & Breakfast**, (B&B), Shelley Beach Rd, Dutton Bay West, 24km N of PO, ☎ 08 8685 4252, fax 08 8685 7252, (2 stry gr fl), 1 rm (1 suite) [shwr, tlt, a/c-cool, elec blkts, TV, clock radio, t/c mkg, refrig, cook fac], iron, iron brd, spa (pool), bbq, meals avail (on request), non smoking property (indoors), **BB ♦♦ $90, ◊ $40**, ch con.

COOBER PEDY SA 5723
Pop 2,491. (858km NW Adelaide), See map on pages 586/587, ref F2. Largest opal producing centre in Australia. Arckaringa Hills and Painted Desert, underground churches, mines and museums and numerous opal show rooms. Gem Fossicking, Golf, Horse Racing, Horse Riding, Motor Racing, Shooting, Swimming (Pool), Tennis.

Hotels/Motels
★★★☆ **Desert Cave Hotel**, (LH), Hutchison St, 200m N of PO, ☎ 08 8672 5688, fax 08 8672 5198, 50 rms [shwr, tlt, hairdry, a/c (31), tel, TV, movie, clock radio, t/c mkg, refrig, mini bar], iron, iron brd, lounge, conv fac, ✗, cafe, pool, sauna, spa, rm serv, gym, cots, non smoking rms (4). **RO ♦ $165, ♦♦ $165, ♦♦♦ $183, ◊ $16**, 19 units are underground. AE BC DC EFT JCB MC VI, 🐾&.

★★★ **Mud Hut Motel**, (M), St Nicholas St, ☎ 08 8672 3003, fax 08 8672 3004, 28 units [ensuite, a/c-cool, heat, tel, TV, clock radio, t/c mkg, refrig, cook fac (4), micro (4)], ldry, ✗, cots-fee. **RO ♦ $82, ♦♦ $94 - $132, ◊ $22**, ch con, 8 rooms yet to be rated. 🐾&.

★★★ **Opal Inn Hotel Motel**, (LMH), Hutchison St, 200m S of PO, ☎ 08 8672 5054, fax 08 8672 5501, (2 stry gr fl), 70 units [shwr, tlt, a/c, tel, TV, clock radio, t/c mkg, refrig], ldry, lounge, ✗, bbq, cots. **RO ♦ $82, ♦♦ $88, ◊ $6**, AE BC DC EFT MC VI.

★★ **(Budget Section)**, 12 units [shwr, tlt, a/c, tel (2), t/c mkg, refrig]. **RO ♦ $44, ♦♦ $52, ◊ $6.**

★☆ **(Hotel Section)**, 12 rms [a/c, t/c mkg, refrig]. **RO ♦ $33, ♦♦ $38.**

FLAG
FLAG CHOICE HOTELS™

★★★ **The Coober Pedy Experience Motel**, (M), Crowders Gully Rd, 500m E of PO, ☎ 08 8672 5777, fax 08 8672 5877, 10 units [shwr, tlt, fan, tel, TV, movie, t/c mkg, refrig, micro (8)], ldry, w/mach, dryer, iron, cots, non smoking property. **D ♦ $123, ♦♦ $123, ◊ $20**, ch con, Accommodation is underground. AE BC MC VI.

★★★ **The Underground Motel**, (M), Catacombe Rd, 1.5km N of PO, ☎ 08 8672 5324, fax 08 8672 5911, 8 units (2 suites) [shwr, tlt, fan, tel, TV, t/c mkg (2), refrig (2), micro (2)], ldry, cook fac, t/c mkg shared, refrig, bbq, c/park (undercover), plygr, cots, breakfast ingredients, Pets allowed. **BB ♦ $77, ♦♦ $93.50, ◊ $15 - $30, Suite BB ♦ $85, ♦♦ $105**, ch con, AE BC MC VI.

★★☆ **Lookout Cave Motel**, (M), Lot 1141 McKenzie Cl, 1.5km N of PO, ☎ 08 8672 5118, fax 08 8672 5228, 18 units [shwr, tlt, TV, clock radio, t/c mkg, refrig, toaster], c/park (undercover). **RO ♦ $77, ♦♦ $90, ◊ $20**, pen con, AE BC DC EFT MC VI.

★★ **Radekas Downunder Motel**, (M), Oliver St, 100m N of PO, ☎ 08 8672 5223, fax 08 8672 5821, 8 units [shwr, tlt, TV, clock radio, t/c mkg, refrig, toaster], cook fac, cots. **RO ♦ $77, ♦♦ $92, ◊ $10**, ch con, fam con, 1 unit of a higher standard. 6 rms are underground. AE BC EFT MC VI.

Self Catering Accommodation

Best Western
★★★ **Desert View Apartments**, (Apt), Shaw Pl, 1.5km NE of PO, ☎ 08 8672 3330, fax 08 8672 3331, 11 apts acc up to 7, (2 & 3 bedrm), [shwr, tlt, fan, heat (6), tel, TV, movie, refrig, cook fac, toaster, blkts, linen, pillows], ldry, pool, bbq, non smoking rms, **D ♦ $70, ♦♦ $91, ◊ $20**, ch con, Free local taxi service, AE BC MC VI.

B&B's/Guest Houses
The Opal Cave, (B&B), Fred & Wilma's Underground B&B. Hutchison St, 1km N of PO, ☎ 08 8672 5028, fax 08 8672 5208, 1 rm [shwr, tlt, fan, clock radio, t/c mkg, refrig, micro, toaster], lounge (TV), c/park. **BLB ♦ $80, ♦♦ $80, ◊ $15**, AE BC DC EFT MC VI, (not yet classified).

COOBER PEDY SA continued...

Umoona Opal Mine, (PH), Main St, ☎ 08 8672 5288, fax 08 8672 5731, 7 rms cook fac, t/c mkg shared, refrig. **RO** ⚥ **$15**, ⚥⚥ **$25**, ⚥ **$10**, ch con, Accommodation is underground. AE BC DC EFT MC VI.

Other Accommodation

Bedrock Bunkhouse, (Bunk), Hutchison St, 500m N of PO, ☎ 08 8672 5028, fax 08 8672 5208, 2 bunkhouses acc up to 112, [TV (1), blkts reqd-fee, linen reqd-fee, pillows reqd-fee], shwr (5G-10L), tlt (5G-10L), cook fac, refrig. **D** ⚥ **$15**, ⚥ **$15**, ch con, All accommodation is underground. AE BC DC EFT JCB MC VI.

(Unit Section), 1 unit acc up to 2, [shwr, tlt, TV, t/c mkg, refrig, cook fac, micro, toaster, blkts, linen, pillows], breakfast ingredients. **D** ⚥⚥ **$80**, ⚥ **$15**, (not yet classified).

COOBOWIE SA 5583

Pop Part of Edithburgh, (217km W Adelaide), See map on pages 586/587, ref A7. Located on the Yorke Peninsula originally known as Salt Creek. Boating, Croquet, Fishing, Swimming (Beach), Tennis.

Self Catering Accommodation

★★★ **Packards Retreat**, (Cotg), 4 Beach Rd, ☎ 08 8852 1229, 1 cotg acc up to 8, [shwr, bath, tlt, a/c, c/fan, tel, TV, video, clock radio, CD, t/c mkg, refrig, micro, toaster, ldry, blkts, doonas, linen, pillows], w/mach, iron, iron brd, bbq, c/park (carport), **D** ⚥⚥ **$95 - $145**, ⚥ **$15 - $30**, ch con.

★★☆ **The Shores Holiday Units**, (HU), 19 Anstey Tce, ☎ 08 8248 1531, 3 units acc up to 6, [shwr, tlt, a/c-cool (1), c/fan, heat, elec blkts, TV, clock radio, refrig, cook fac, micro (1), toaster, linen reqd], w/mach, iron. **D** $60 - $65, **W** $420, 1 unit ★★★.

★★ **Coobowie Lodge Holiday Units**, (HU), 67 Beach Rd, ☎ 08 8852 8211, 6 units acc up to 6, (1 & 2 bedrm), [shwr, tlt, TV, t/c mkg, refrig, cook fac, micro (5), toaster, linen reqd-fee], ldry, bbq, c/park. **D** $45 - $55, **W** $160 - $300, ch con, 3 units of a higher rating. Min book long w/ends and Easter, BC MC VI.

COONALPYN SA 5265

Pop 266. (162km SE Adelaide), See map on pages 586/587, ref D8. Located on the Dukes Hwy, Coonalpyn is a service centre for a fertile farming district. Bowls, Horse Riding, Scenic Drives, Swimming (Pool), Tennis.

Hotels/Motels

★☆ **Coonalpyn Hotel**, (LH), Dukes Hwy, ☎ 08 8571 1006, 13 rms [ensuite, bath (3), heat, elec blkts, t/c mkg], lounge (TV), ⊠. **BLB** ⚥ **$38.50**, ⚥⚥ **$49.50**, ⚥ **$11**, BC EFT MC VI.

COONAWARRA SA 5263

Pop Part of Penola, (381km SE Adelaide), See map on pages 586/587, ref J8. A noted wine region located between Naracoorte & Penola, produces full bodied grapes suited to dry red wines. Vineyards, Wineries.

Hotels/Motels

★★★★ **Chardonnay Lodge Motel**, (M), Riddoch Hwy, 1km S of PO, ☎ 08 8736 3309, fax 08 8736 3383, 24 units [ensuite, bath, hairdry, a/c, elec blkts, tel, TV, clock radio, t/c mkg, refrig, micro, toaster], ldry, w/mach, dryer, iron, iron brd, conf fac, ⊠, pool-heated (solar), rm serv, plygr, cots-fee. **BLB** ⚥ **$106**, ⚥⚥ **$115**, ⚥ **$22**, ch con, Min book long w/ends, AE BC DC EFT MC VI.

Self Catering Accommodation

★★★★☆ **Coonawarra Country Cottages**, (Cotg), Mary St, ☎ 08 8736 3304, fax 08 8736 3016, 1 cotg acc up to 2, (1 bedrm), [shwr, spa bath, tlt, a/c, heat (slow combustion) elec blkts, TV, clock radio, refrig, cook fac, micro, blkts, linen, pillows], w/mach, breakfast ingredients, **D** ⚥⚥ **$77**, ch con, AE BC MC VI.

★★★ **(Skinner Cottage)**, Mary St, 1 cotg acc up to 6, (2 bedrm), [shwr, tlt, a/c, fire pl, elec blkts, TV, clock radio, refrig, cook fac, micro, elec frypan, blkts, linen, pillows], w/mach, iron, iron brd, breakfast ingredients. **D** ⚥⚥ **$99**, ⚥ **$30**, ch con.

★★★ **(The Pickers Hut Cottage)**, Mary St, 1 cotg acc up to 4, (1 bedrm), [shwr, tlt, a/c, fan, fire pl, elec blkts, TV, clock radio, refrig, cook fac, micro, elec frypan, blkts, linen, pillows], breakfast ingredients. **D** ⚥⚥ **$75**, ⚥ **$20**, ch con.

★★★☆ **Coonawarra's Pyrus Cottage**, (Cotg), Helen St, ☎ 08 8736 3399, fax 08 8736 3208, 1 cotg acc up to 1, (1 bedrm), [shwr, tlt, a/c, wood heat (slow combustion), elec blkts, TV, clock radio, refrig, cook fac, micro, blkts, linen, pillows], w/mach, iron, iron brd, breakfast ingredients. **D** ⚥⚥ **$95**, ⚥ **$25**, BC MC VI.

★★★☆ **Murrays Cottages**, (Cotg), (Farm), Mulligans Rd, 17km NW of PO, ☎ 08 8736 3321, fax 08 8736 3040, 2 cotgs acc up to 6, (2 bedrm), [shwr, bath (hip), tlt, hairdry, a/c-cool, c/fan, elec blkts, tel, TV, clock radio (cassette), t/c mkg, refrig, cook fac, micro, toaster, blkts, linen, pillows], iron, iron brd, lounge firepl, bbq, golf (6 hole), tennis, cots, breakfast ingredients, non smoking property, Pets on application. **D** ⚥⚥ **$110**, ⚥ **$27.50**, ch con, Min book long w/ends and Easter, BC DC MC VI.

COPLEY SA 5732

Pop Nominal, (553km N Adelaide), See map on pages 586/587, ref H3. Located in the Flinders Ranges approximately halfway between Parachilna & Marree in undulating grazing country.

Hotels/Motels

Leigh Creek Hotel, (LH), Railway Tce, ☎ 08 8675 2281, fax 08 8675 2551, 12 rms [ensuite (1), a/c-cool, elec blkts], ⊠ (Mon-Sat), cots, **BLB** ⚥ **$37**, ⚥ **$20**, BC EFT MC VI.

COULTA SA 5607

Pop Nominal, (756km W Adelaide), See map on pages 586/587, ref F6. Grain crops & sheep grazing area, close to Marble Range, with easy access to nearby beaches.

B&B's/Guest Houses

★★★☆ **Wepowie Holiday Farm Bed & Breakfast**, (B&B), Gap Rd, 4km NE of PO, ☎ 08 8687 2063, fax 08 8687 2003, 2 rms [a/c (1), heat, elec blkts, TV (1), clock radio (1), radio (1)], lounge (TV & Video), bbq, meals avail (by arrangement), c/park. **BB** ⚥ **$35**, ⚥⚥ **$70**, ch con.

COWELL SA 5602

Pop 695. (487km NW Adelaide), See map on pages 586/587, ref G5. Seaside resort on the Eyre Peninsula. Airport adjacent to town. Museums and the Cowell Jade workshop. Boating, Bowls, Bush Walking, Fishing, Golf, Horse Riding, Sailing, Scenic Drives, Swimming (Beach), Tennis, Water Skiing.

Hotels/Motels

★★★ **Cowell Jade Motel**, (M), Lincoln Hwy, 1km N of PO, ☎ 08 8629 2002, fax 08 8629 2290, 21 units [shwr, tlt, a/c, elec blkts, TV, t/c mkg, refrig], bbq, rm serv, ✆, cots-fee, non smoking rms (4). **RO** ⚥ **$55 - $65**, ⚥⚥ **$63 - $75**, ⚥⚥⚥ **$73 - $85**, ⚥ **$5**, 10 rooms ★★☆, AE BC DC MC VI.

Self Catering Accommodation

★★★ **Cowell Holiday Units**, (HU), Third St, 200m SW of PO, ☎ 08 8629 6060, 3 units acc up to 6, (2 bedrm), [shwr, bath (hip) (2), tlt, a/c, TV, clock radio, t/c mkg, refrig, cook fac, micro, elec frypan, toaster, blkts-fee, linen-fee, pillows-fee], **D** ⚥⚥ **$55 - $70**, ⚥ **$5.50**, ch con, EFT.

B&B's/Guest Houses

★★★☆ **Schultz Farm Bed & Breakfast**, (B&B), (Farm), Schumann Rd, ☎ 08 8629 2194, 3 rms [clock radio], rec rm, lounge (TV), t/c mkg shared, refrig, plygr, non smoking property. **BB** ⚥⚥ **$45**, ch con, pen con.

CRYSTAL BROOK SA 5523

Pop 2,100. (198km N Adelaide), See map on pages 586/587, ref H5. The centre of a large cereal growing district and bulk handling of grain. Bowman Park and the Old Butchershop & Bakehouse Museum. Bowls, Bush Walking, Croquet, Golf, Horse Riding, Rock Climbing, Swimming (Pool), Tennis, Trotting.

Hotels/Motels

Crystal Brook Hotel, (LH), 47 Railway Tce, ☎ 08 8636 2023, fax 08 8636 2023, 14 rms [a/c (4), c/fan (5), heat (4), elec blkts (8), clock radio (5)], shwr, tlt, bathrm, lounge (TV), ⊠, t/c mkg shared, refrig. **RO** ⚥ **$25 - $30**, ⚥⚥ **$40 - $50**, fam con, AE BC EFT MC VI.

CUDLEE CREEK SA 5232

Pop Part of Adelaide, (30km Adelaide), See map on page 588, ref E3. Situated beside the Torrens River, it is surrounded by steep hill-sides near the eastern end of the Torrens Gorge. Gorge Wildlife Park and the Cudlee Creek Conservation Park. Bush Walking, Scenic Drives.

B&B's/Guest Houses

★★★ **Brookside Bed & Breakfast**, (B&B), Lobethal Rd, 2km E of PO, ☎ 08 8389 2384, 1 rm [ensuite, shwr, tlt, c/fan, fire pl, elec blkts, TV, video, clock radio, t/c mkg, refrig, cook fac, elec frypan], spa, bbq, c/park. **BB** ⚥ **$95**, ⚥⚥ **$120**, ⚥ **$25**, BC MC VI.

CUMMINS SA 5631

Pop 747. (683km NW Adelaide), See map on pages 586/587, ref F6. Located on the lower Eyer Peninsula. A centre for the surrounding rural area with industries including sheep, wheat, cattle & barley. Golf, Swimming (Pool), Tennis.

Hotels/Motels

★★ **Cummins Community Hotel**, (LH), 36 Railway Tce,
☎ 08 8676 2002, fax 08 8676 2495, (2 stry), 12 rms [basin (11), bath (1), a/c (5), fan, heat, elec blkts, TV, t/c mkg, refrig], conv fac, ⊠ (Mon to Sat), ☏. **RO ♦ $40, ♦♦ $55, ◊ $10**, AE BC EFT MC VI.

CURRENCY CREEK SA 5214

Pop Nominal, (83km Adelaide), See map on pages 586/587, ref C8. The little settlement was named after 'Currency Lass', which negotiated the Murray Mouth and then was the first vessel to explore the waterways here. Vineyards, Wineries.

Hotels/Motels

★★★★ **Currency Creek Winery Motel**, (M), Winery Rd, ☎ 08 8555 4013, fax 08 8555 4100, 6 units [ensuite, spa bath, a/c, elec blkts, tel, TV, clock radio, t/c mkg, refrig, cook fac, micro, toaster], ⊠, dinner to unit, cots, non smoking property. **RO ♦ $100 - $115, ♦♦ $100 - $115**, ch con, AE BC EFT MC VI.

DELAMERE SA 5204

Pop 946. (97km SW Adelaide), See map on pages 586/587, ref B8. A small township situated in hilly country astride the road to Cape Jervis. Eric Bonython Conservation Park and the Pig & Whistle Craft Cottage.

Self Catering Accommodation

★★★★ **Nowhere Else Cottage**, (Cotg), Main Cape Jervis Rd, 100m N of PO, ☎ 08 8598 0221, fax 08 8598 0221, 1 cotg acc up to 4, [shwr, bath, tlt, hairdry, a/c, TV, video, clock radio (cassette), CD, t/c mkg, refrig, cook fac, micro, toaster, blkts, doonas, linen, pillows], spa (4 person), breakfast ingredients, **D ♦♦ $145 - $165, ◊ $55, W ♦♦ $900, ◊ $385**, ch con, BC MC VI.

Southern Ocean Retreats, (Cotg), Range Rd, ☎ 08 8598 4169, cotgs (not yet classified).

★★★★ **(Deep Creek Homestead)**, Deep Creek Conservation Park Park Headquarters Rd, 1 cotg acc up to 8, (4 bedrm), [shwr (2), bath (1), tlt (2), hairdry, heat (slow combustion) (2), clock radio, refrig, cook fac, micro, elec frypan, toaster, blkts, linen, pillows], iron, iron brd, bbq, tennis, non smoking property. **D ♦♦ $125, ◊ $35**.

★★☆ **(Glenburn Cottage)**, Deep Creek Conservation Park Park Headquarters Rd, 1 cotg acc up to 10, (4 bedrm), [shwr, tlt, heat (slow combustion), clock radio, refrig, cook fac, micro, elec frypan, toaster, linen-fee], bbq, non smoking property. **D ♦♦ $70, ◊ $11**, ch con.

★★☆ **(Goondooloo Cottage)**, Blowhole Beach Rd, 1 cotg acc up to 6, (2 bedrm), [shwr, tlt, wood heat (slow combustion), clock radio, refrig, cook fac, elec frypan, toaster, linen reqd-fee], bbq, c/park. **D ♦♦ $70, ◊ $11**, ch con.

D'ESTREES BAY SA

See Kangaroo Island Region.

ECHUNGA SA 5153

Pop 435. (34km SE Adelaide), See map on page 588, ref E6. Small town, set amidst picturesque rolling hills in rich dairy area of the Adelaide Hills. Jupiter Creek Gold Diggings. Golf, Tennis.

Self Catering Accommodation

★★★★☆ **Hazelmere Homestead**, (Apt), Meadows Rd,
☎ 08 8388 8385, fax 08 8388 8385, (2 stry), 4 apts acc up to 7, (1 + 3 bedrm Studio), [shwr, bath (1), spa bath (1), tlt, hairdry, a/c, elec blkts, TV, video, clock radio, t/c mkg, refrig, cook fac, micro, elec frypan, toaster, blkts, linen, pillows], ldry, w/mach, dryer, iron, iron brd, pool-heated (solar), bbq, c/park (carport), non smoking property. **D ♦♦ $125 - $185, ◊ $35 - $72.50**, Min book long w/ends and Easter.

★★★★☆ **Wattlebark Cottage**, (Cotg), Pocock Rd, 6.7km SW of PO, ☎ 08 8388 8076, fax 08 8388 8763, 1 cotg acc up to 4, (2 bedrm), [shwr, spa bath, tlt, a/c, fire pl, elec blkts, TV, video, clock radio, refrig, cook fac, micro, d/wash, ldry, blkts, doonas, linen, pillows], w/mach, dryer, iron, bbq, breakfast ingredients, non smoking property. **D ♦♦ $190**, Min book applies, BC MC VI.

EDEN VALLEY SA

See Barossa Valley Region.

EDITHBURGH SA 5583

Pop 453. (222km W Adelaide), See map on pages 586/587, ref A7. A popular tourist and fishing town situated on the lower eastern coast of Yorke Peninsula. Edithburgh Museum & the Native Flora Reserve. Boat Ramp, Boating, Bowls, Croquet, Fishing, Golf, Horse Riding, Scenic Drives, Swimming (Pool & Beach), Tennis.

Hotels/Motels

★★★★ **Edithburgh Seaside Motel**, (LMH), Blanche St,
☎ 08 8852 6172, fax 08 8852 6047, 16 units (2 suites) [ensuite, hairdry (10), a/c, c/fan, elec blkts, tel, TV, clock radio, t/c mkg, refrig, cook fac ltd (2)], ldry, w/mach, dryer, iron (10), iron brd, c/park (undercover). **RO ♦♦ $66 - $72.60, ◊ $13.20, Suite RO ♦♦♦♦ $110 - $121**, 6 units ★★★. AE BC DC MC VI, ⚿.

★★★ **Troubridge Hotel Motel**, (LMH), Blanche St, ☎ 08 8852 6013, fax 08 8852 6323, (2 stry gr fl), 10 units [ensuite, hairdry, a/c, c/fan, heat, elec blkts, tel, TV, t/c mkg, refrig], ⊠. **RO ♦ $50 - $60, ♦♦ $60 - $70, ◊ $10**, AE BC DC EFT MC VI.

Self Catering Accommodation

★★★ **Anchorage Edithburgh Motel**, (HU), 25 O'Halloran Pde,
☎ 08 8852 6262, fax 08 8852 6147, 9 units acc up to 4, (2 bedrm), [shwr, tlt, fan, heat, elec blkts, tel, TV, clock radio, t/c mkg, refrig, cook fac, blkts, linen-fee, pillows], ldry, bbq, cots. **RO ♦ $45 - $75, ♦♦ $50 - $75, ◊ $6**, Boat washing facilities. AE BC DC MC VI.

★★★ **(Motel Section)**, 2 units [ensuite, fan, heat, elec blkts, tel, TV, clock radio, t/c mkg, refrig], non smoking rms (1). **RO ♦ $55 - $75, ♦♦ $60 - $75, ◊ $12**.

(Edithburgh Lodge), 1 cotg acc up to 16, (4 bedrm), [shwr (3), bath, tlt (3), heat, TV, radio, refrig, cook fac, linen reqd-fee], ldry, bbq, cots. **D $135, W $700**.

★★★ **Clan Ranald Holiday Units**, (HU), 1 George St, 400m NE of PO,
☎ 08 8852 6247, 2 units acc up to 4, (2 bedrm), [shwr, tlt, a/c, c/fan, TV, clock radio, refrig, cook fac, micro (2), toaster, linen reqd-fee], w/mach, bbq, c/park. **D $44 - $66**.

★★☆ **Edithburgh Lodge**, (Cotg), 24 O'Halloran Pde, ☎ 08 8852 6262, fax 08 8852 6147, 1 cotg acc up to 16, (4 bedrm), [shwr (3), bath, tlt (3), heat, TV, radio, refrig, cook fac, toaster, linen reqd-fee], bbq, cots. **D $80 - $165, W $500 - $770**.

★★☆ **Henrys Retreat Holiday Home**, (House), Cnr Anstey Tce & Henry St, 150m N of PO, ☎ 08 8326 5759, 1 house acc up to 7, (2 bedrm), [bath, tlt, fan, heat, TV, refrig, cook fac, micro, elec frypan, toaster, blkts reqd, linen reqd, pillows reqd], w/mach, c/park. **D ♦♦♦♦ $40 - $65, ◊ $5**, Min book long w/ends and Easter.

★★☆ **Ocean View Holiday Units**, (HU), O'Halloran Pde, ☎ 08 8852 6029, 10 units acc up to 6, (2 bedrm), [shwr, tlt, heat, TV, refrig, cook fac, linen reqd-fee], ldry, bbq, plygr, cots. **D $41 - $55, W $215 - $359**.

B&B's/Guest Houses

★★★★ **Marys Place Bed & Breakfast**, (B&B), 27 O'Halloran Pde,
☎ 08 8852 6410, fax 08 8852 6410, (2 stry gr fl), 2 rms [ensuite, bath, a/c, elec blkts, tel, TV, clock radio, t/c mkg, refrig], iron, iron brd, lounge (TV), bbq, non smoking rms. **BB ♦ $60, ♦♦ $100, ◊ $50**.

★★★ **Edithburgh House**, (GH), Edith St, ☎ 08 8852 6373, (2 stry), 6 rms [fan, heat, elec blkts, doonas], shared fac (3), ldry, lounge, ⊠, refrig, bbq (covered), c/park. **DBB ♦ $88, ♦♦ $176**, ch con, Min book applies, BC MC VI.

ELLISTON SA 5670

Pop 242. (639km W Adelaide), See map on pages 586/587, ref F5. Widely known for its scenic coastline, excellent fishing beaches & as a popular holiday resort. Talia Caves and Beaches. Boating, Fishing, Golf, Surfing, Swimming (Beach), Tennis.

Hotels/Motels

★★★ **Ellenliston Motel**, (M), Beach Tce, ☎ 08 8687 9028, fax 08 8687 9028, 3 units [ensuite, hairdry, c/fan, heat, elec blkts, tel, TV, clock radio, refrig, cook fac, micro, elec frypan], w/mach, iron (avail), iron brd (avail), bbq, cots. **RO ◊ $65, ♦♦ $70, ◊ $8.50**, ch con, AE BC MC VI.

★ **Elliston Hotel Motel**, (LMH), Beach Tce, ☎ 08 8687 9009, fax 08 8687 9037, 7 units [shwr, tlt, a/c (2), heat, elec blkts, TV, t/c mkg, refrig, cook fac (2), toaster], lounge, ⊠, cots. **D $40 - $50**, 2 rooms of a higher standard. BC EFT MC VI.

Self Catering Accommodation

★★☆ **Ellenliston Holiday Units**, (HU), Beach Tce, ☎ 08 8687 9028, fax 08 8687 9028, 2 units acc up to 6, (1 bedrm), [shwr, bath (hip), tlt, hairdry, c/fan, heat, TV, refrig, cook fac, micro, elec frypan, ldry, blkts, linen-fee, pillows], w/mach, iron (avail), iron brd (avail), cots. **D ◊ $49, ◊ $5.50**, ch con, AE BC MC VI.

EMU BAY SA

See Kangaroo Island Region.

EUDUNDA SA 5374

Pop 647. (106km NE Adelaide), See map on pages 586/587, ref C6. Set in rich wheat, sheep & dairying country. Bowls, Croquet, Golf, Swimming (Pool), Tennis.

Hotels/Motels

★☆ **Eudunda Hotel**, (LMH), 2 South Tce, ☎ 08 8581 1002, fax 08 8581 1002, 6 units [shwr, tlt, fan, heat, elec blkts, TV, radio, t/c mkg, refrig], ⊠, c/park (carport), cots, **RO** ♦ **$45**, ♦♦ **$55**, ◊ **$5**, AE BC EFT MC VI.

★ **Light Hotel**, (LH), 1 Bruce St, ☎ 08 8581 1298, (2 stry), 9 rms [elec blkts], ⊠, t/c mkg shared, bbq, c/park. **RO** ♦ **$25**, ♦♦ **$35**, ch con.

FLINDERS RANGES SA

See: Arkaroola, Blinman, Copley, Hawker, Parachilna, Quorn, Wilpena Pound.

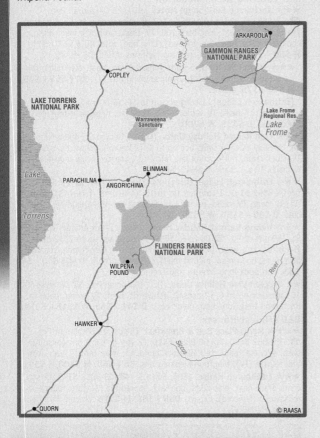

FRANCES SA 5262

Pop Nominal, (325km SE Adelaide), See map on pages 586/587, ref J7. Sheep and cattle farming area, practically on the Victorian border. Bowls, Tennis.

Self Catering Accommodation

★★★ **St Aubins Cottage**, (Cotg), (Farm), Danbys Rd, 10km W of PO, 40km N of Naracoorte, ☎ 08 8765 1051, fax 08 8765 1001, 1 cotg acc up to 12, (4 bedrm), [shwr, bath, tlt, a/c, elec blkts, tel, TV, radio, refrig, cook fac, toaster, doonas, linen reqd-fee], rec rm, pool, bbq, tennis, cots. **D $100 - $100, W $600**, BC MC VI.

★★★☆ **(Bed & Breakfast Section)**, 2 rms [TV, radio, refrig, pillows], lounge, pool, golf (9 hole), tennis, cots. **D all meals** ♦ **$95**, ♦♦ **$180**, ch con.

(Shearers Quarters), 1 bunkhouse acc up to 24, (Bunk Rooms), [elec blkts, TV, refrig, cook fac, toaster, blkts, linen-fee], ldry, rec rm, pool, bbq, tennis, cots. **D $60**, ◊ **$15 - $18**, Group bookings preferred for Shearers Quarters.

GAWLER SA 5118

Pop 13,835. (71km N Adelaide), See map on pages 586/587, ref C7. Western gateway to the Barossa Valley one of the first major settlements north of Adelaide. Clonlea Recreation Park, The Flower Waggon, Folk Museum, Gawler Visitor Centre and the Old Telegraph Station. Bowls, Bush Walking, Croquet, Golf, Greyhound Racing, Horse Racing, Horse Riding, Squash, Swimming (Pool & River), Tennis, Trotting.

Hotels/Motels

★★☆ **Prasads Gawler Motel**, (M), Cnr Main North Rd & Gawler By-Pass, 2km SW of PO, ☎ 08 8522 5900, fax 08 8522 5876, (2 stry gr fl), 104 units [shwr, bath (hip) (15), tlt, a/c-cool (40), a/c (60), heat (40), tel, TV, clock radio, t/c mkg, refrig], ldry, w/mach-fee, dryer-fee, iron (in laundry), iron brd (in laundry), conv fac, pool-indoor, plygr, tennis, cots. **RO** ♦ **$70**, ♦♦ **$80**, ◊ **$10**, ch con, AE BC DC MC VI.

Self Catering Accommodation

★★★ **Times Past Cottage**, (Cotg), 7A Fifth St, ☎ 08 8524 9169, or 08 8524 9169, fax 08 8524 9163, 1 cotg acc up to 4, (2 bedrm), [shwr, bath, tlt, fan, heat, elec blkts, TV, video, t/c mkg, refrig, cook fac, micro, toaster, blkts, doonas, linen, pillows], iron, iron brd, lounge firepl, bbq, ✆, breakfast ingredients, non smoking rms. **D** ♦♦ **$100**, ◊ **$30**, ch con.

B&B's/Guest Houses

★★★★ **Oxley Farm Bed & Breakfast**, (B&B), Fairlie Rd, Kangaroo Flat, 7km NW of PO, ☎ 08 8522 3703, fax 08 8522 3703, 4 rms [shwr, tlt, a/c, TV, clock radio, t/c mkg, refrig, toaster], spa, bbq, tennis (half court), cots, non smoking rms. **BB** ♦♦ **$130**, ◊ **$65**, ch con, BC MC VI.

★★★☆ **Eagle Foundry Bed & Breakfast**, (B&B), 23 King St, ☎ 08 8522 3808, fax 08 8522 3808, 2 rms [ensuite, a/c, c/fan, heat (pot belly), TV, radio, CD, refrig, cook fac (1)], spa (shared), bbq, c/park (carport) (2), non smoking rms. **BB** ♦♦ **$110 - $130**, ◊ **$30**, ch con, AE BC MC VI.

GLADSTONE SA 5473

Pop 643. (211km N Adelaide), See map on pages 586/587, ref H5. A large rural service town in the centre of a prosperous farming community. Old Gladstone Gaol. Bowls, Golf, Swimming (Pool), Tennis, Trotting.

Other Accommodation

Gladstone Gaol, (Lodge), Ward St, ☎ 08 8662 2200, fax 08 8662 2240, 48 rms acc up to 4, [blkts reqd, linen reqd, pillows reqd], rec rm, cook fac. **D** ♦ **$11**, ◊ **$11**.

GLENDAMBO SA 5710

Pop Nominal, (609km NW Adelaide), See map on pages 586/587, ref F4. Located on the Stuart Hwy, the second service centre north of Port Augusta.

Hotels/Motels

★★☆ **Glendambo Tourist Centre**, (LMH), Stuart Hwy, ☎ 08 8672 1030, fax 08 8672 1039, 60 units [shwr, tlt, a/c, TV, clock radio, t/c mkg, refrig, cook fac (2)], ldry, ⊠, pool, bbq, ✆, cots. **RO** ♦ **$72 - $82**, ♦♦ **$74 - $84**, ◊ **$12**, ch con, AE BC DC EFT MC VI, ♿.

GOOLWA SA 5214

Pop 3,018. (83km S Adelaide), See map on pages 586/587, ref C8. Historic town located at the mouth of the Murray River, on lake Alexandrina, it is now a popular fast growing tourist resort. The Cockle Train, Community Arts & Crafts, Goolwa Barrage, Goolwa National Trust Museum, Malleebaa Woolshed, Old Railway Superintendents Cottage and Signal Point. Boating, Bowls, Fishing, Golf, Horse Riding, Sailing, Surfing, Swimming (Pool, Beach & River), Tennis, Water Skiing.

Hotels/Motels

★★★☆ **Goolwa Central Motel**, (M), 30 Cadell St, ☎ 08 8555 1155, fax 08 8555 3827, (2 stry gr fl), 25 units [ensuite, spa bath (6), hairdry, a/c, elec blkts, tel, TV, clock radio, t/c mkg, refrig, mini bar, toaster], ldry-fee, rec rm, conv fac, ✉, pool, spa, rm serv, cots-fee. **BLB ♦ $97 - $130, ♦♦ $102 - $140, ◊ $12**, fam con, AE BC DC EFT MC VI.

★★★☆ **Goolwa Riverport Motel**, (M), Noble Ave, 3km NE of PO, ☎ 08 8555 5033, fax 08 8555 5022, 18 units [ensuite, spa bath (6), a/c, elec blkts, tel, TV, clock radio, t/c mkg, refrig, toaster], ldry, lounge, ✉, pool, bbq, rm serv, plygr, tennis, cots. **BLB ♦ $83 - $117, ♦♦ $83 - $117, ◊ $11**, Function Centre. AE BC DC EFT MC VI, ♿.

★★★ **South Lakes Motel**, (M), Barrage Rd, ☎ 08 8555 2194, fax 08 8555 2626, 20 units [ensuite, a/c, elec blkts, tel, TV, t/c mkg, refrig, cook fac, micro (10), toaster], iron (10), iron brd (10), ✉, rm serv, non smoking units (10). **RO ♦ $66, ♦♦ $77, ◊ $22**, AE BC EFT MC MCH VI.

Self Catering Accommodation

★★★★ **Casa Azzurro Cottage**, (Cotg), 2 Neighbour Ave, 2km SW of PO, ☎ 08 8178 0803, fax 08 8178 0803, (2 stry), 1 cotg acc up to 6, (3 bedrm), [shwr, bath, tlt, a/c, heat, TV, video, clock radio (cassette), t/c mkg, refrig, cook fac, micro, elec frypan, toaster, ldry (in unit), blkts, doonas, linen, pillows], w/mach, iron, iron brd, bbq, c/park. **D ♦♦ $100, ◊ $15**, ch con, Min book all holiday times.

★★★☆ **Foresters Lodge**, (Cotg), Property is a restored church. 1 Hay St, ☎ 08 8362 6229, 1 cotg acc up to 6, (2 bedrm), [shwr, tlt, a/c, c/fan, heat (pot belly), TV, video, clock radio, CD, t/c mkg, refrig (2), cook fac, micro, toaster, blkts, linen, pillows], w/mach, bbq, breakfast ingredients. **D ♦♦ $120 - $150, ◊ $35**, ch con.

★★★☆ **Holiday Cottages Goolwa**, (Cotg), 14 Hutchinson St, ☎ 08 8555 3601, fax 08 8555 3601, 3 cotgs acc up to 4, [shwr, tlt, a/c, elec blkts, TV, clock radio, t/c mkg, refrig, cook fac, toaster], pool, bbq, breakfast ingredients. **D ♦♦ $120, ◊ $27.50**, AE BC DC MC VI.

★★★☆ **Riverbank Lodge Cottage**, (Cotg), No children's facilities, 28 Edison St, 5km SE of PO, ☎ 08 8555 1331, fax 08 8555 1307, (2 stry), 1 cotg acc up to 6, (3 bedrm), [shwr (3), spa bath, tlt (3), a/c, fan, heat, elec blkts, TV (2), clock radio, CD, refrig, cook fac, micro, blkts, doonas, linen, pillows], ldry, w/mach, iron, iron brd, bbq, c/park (garage), jetty. **D ♦♦ $137.50, ◊ $16.50**, ch con, Min book applies.

★★★☆ **The Fleurieu Holiday Home**, (House), 53 Prince Alfred Pde, ☎ 08 8270 5250, 1 house acc up to 6, (3 bedrm), [shwr (2), spa bath, tlt (2), heat, elec blkts, TV, video, clock radio, t/c mkg, refrig, cook fac, elec frypan, toaster, ldry (in unit), linen reqd-fee], w/mach, iron, bbq, c/park (carport), jetty, non smoking property. **D $95 - $105, W $595 - $895**, Min book applies.

★★☆ **Goolayyahlee Beach House**, (House), 13 Eaton Ave, 3km W of PO, ☎ 08 8431 1120, fax 08 8431 3942, (2 stry), 1 house acc up to 7, (3 bedrm), [shwr, tlt (2), a/c-cool, fan, heat, TV, clock radio, t/c mkg, refrig, cook fac, micro, linen reqd], w/mach, iron, iron brd, rec rm, bbq, Pets on application. **D $40 - $75, W $280 - $520**, Power additional fee.

★★☆ **Narnu Pioneer Holiday Farm**, (Cotg), Cnr Monument Rd & Sidney Pde Hindmarsh Island, 5km SE of PO, ☎ 08 8555 2002, fax 08 8555 5272, 7 cotgs acc up to 12, (2, 3 & 4 bedrm), [shwr, bath (hip) (5), tlt, a/c-cool, fire pl (1), heat, wood heat (6), TV, refrig, cook fac, micro (4), toaster, ldry (1), blkts, linen reqd-fee, pillows], w/mach, bbq, tennis (half court), cots, **D ♦♦ $70 - $88, ◊ $8**, ch con, Farm activities included. BC MC VI.

B&B's/Guest Houses

★★★★☆ **Birks Harbour Bed & Breakfast**, (B&B), 138A Liverpool Rd, 2km E of PO, ☎ 08 8555 5393, fax 08 8555 5228, (2 stry gr fl), 3 rms [ensuite, spa bath (1), hairdry, a/c, fan, elec blkts, TV, video, clock radio, t/c mkg (communal), refrig], ldry, w/mach, dryer, iron, iron brd, bbq, cots. **BB ♦ $130 - $155, ♦♦ $135 - $160**, AE BC DC MC VI.

★★★★ **PS Goolwa**, (B&B), Paddlesteamer. Barrage Rd, ☎ 08 8555 5525, fax 08 8555 5525, (2 stry gr fl), 2 rms [heat, fan, elec blkts, TV, radio, t/c mkg], shwr, tlt, w/mach, dryer, bbq, non smoking rms (4). **BB ♦ $80, ♦♦ $150, ◊ $80**, AE BC DC MC VI.

★★☆ **Goolwa Cottage Bed & Breakfast**, (B&B), 3 Hays St, 100m S PO, ☎ 08 8555 1021, 1 rm (2 bedrm), [shwr, tlt, fan, heat, elec blkts, TV, radio, t/c mkg, pillows], c/park. **BB ♦♦ $78, ◊ $20**, ch con, pen con.

GREENOCK SA

See Barossa Valley Region.

GUMERACHA SA 5233

Pop 448. (37km E Adelaide), See map on pages 586/587, ref C7. Originally pronounced 'Umeracha' by the Aborigines, their description of a 'fine waterhole' which once existed near the town. The region relies on grazing, dairying & market gardening. The Toy Factory, home of The Big Rocking Horse, th largest rocking horse in the world and the Childhood Memories Museum. Scenic Drives.

Self Catering Accommodation

★★★★ **Vineyard Cottage**, (Cotg), Main Rd, 1km W of PO, ☎ 08 8389 1415, fax 08 8389 1877, 1 cotg acc up to 8, (3 bedrm), [shwr (2), bath (1), spa bath, tlt (2), c/fan, elec blkts, tel, TV, clock radio, t/c mkg, refrig, cook fac, d/wash, toaster, ldry, blkts, linen, pillows], w/mach, dryer, iron, lounge firepl, bbq, c/park (garage), breakfast ingredients, non smoking property, **D $95 - $145**, Min book applies, AE BC DC EFT MC VI.

HAHNDORF SA 5245

Pop 1,661. (28km E Adelaide), See map on page 588, ref E5. Settled in 1838 by Capt. Hahn. It was temporarily named Ambleside during the 1914/18 War. The town has now developed a character & charm of great appeal. Antique Clock Museum, Beerenberg, The Cedars, Craft Shops, Galleries, German Model Train Land, Lookouts and Totness Recreation Park. Bowls, Fishing, Golf, Horse Riding, Scenic Drives.

Hotels/Motels

★★★☆ **Hahndorf Inn Motor Lodge**, (M), 35a Main St, 300m S of PO, ☎ 08 8389 1415, fax 08 8388 1092, 19 units [ensuite, spa bath (2), hairdry, a/c, elec blkts, tel, TV, clock radio, t/c mkg, refrig, toaster], ldry, pool-heated, sauna, spa, rm serv, cots-fee, non smoking units (2). **RO ♦ $87 - $132, ♦♦ $87 - $132, ◊ $11**, AE BC DC EFT JCB MC VI.

★★★☆ **Hahndorf Old Mill Motel**, (M), 98 Main St, ☎ 08 8388 7888, fax 08 8388 7242, (2 stry gr fl), 22 units [ensuite, spa bath (18), hairdry, a/c (22), elec blkts, tel, TV, clock radio, t/c mkg, refrig, cook fac (18)], conv fac, rm serv, cots-fee. **RO ♦ $90 - $120, ♦♦ $90 - $165, ◊ $11**, ch con, AE BC DC EFT MC VI.

★★☆ **The Stables Restaurant & Inn**, (M), 74 Main Rd, ☎ 08 8388 7988, fax 08 8388 1152, 4 units [ensuite, spa bath, a/c, tel, TV, clock radio, t/c mkg, refrig, mini bar, toaster], ✉, non smoking property. **BLB ♦♦ $110 - $155**, AE BC MC VI.

Self Catering Accommodation

★★★★ **Hahndorf Cottages**, (Cotg), Mollens Cottage. 10 Mollens Rd, ☎ 08 8388 1897, fax 08 8391 5134, 1 cotg acc up to 4, (2 bedrm), [ensuite (1), shwr, bath (1), spa bath, tlt, hairdry, a/c-cool, c/fan, heat, elec blkts, TV, video, radio, t/c mkg, refrig, micro, toaster, ldry (in unit), blkts, linen, pillows], w/mach, dryer, iron, iron brd, bbq, breakfast ingredients, non smoking property. **D ♦♦ $155, ◊ $35**, Min book long w/ends and Easter, BC MC VI.

HAHNDORF SA continued...

Hahndorf Cottages ...continued

★★★★ **(Amber Cottage)**, 9 Auricht Rd, 1 cotg acc up to 2, (1 bedrm), [ensuite, spa bath, hairdry, a/c-cool, heat, elec blkts, TV, video, radio, t/c mkg, refrig, cook fac, micro, toaster, ldry, blkts, doonas, linen, pillows], w/mach, dryer, iron, iron brd. D ♦♦ $155, ch con.

★★★★ **(Ophelia Cottage)**, 34 Main St, 1 cotg acc up to 4, [shwr, tlt, hairdry, a/c, heat, elec blkts, TV, video, clock radio, CD, t/c mkg, refrig, cook fac ltd, micro, toaster, ldry, blkts, doonas, linen, pillows], w/mach, dryer, iron, iron brd, breakfast ingredients, non smoking rms. D ♦♦ $165, ◊ $35.

★★★☆ **Carinya Cottage**, (Cotg), Lot 54 Paechtown Rd, ☎ 08 8388 7266, fax 08 8388 7266, 1 cotg acc up to 5, (3 bedrm), [shwr, tlt, a/c, heat, elec blkts, TV, video, clock radio (cassette), CD, t/c mkg, refrig, cook fac (1), micro, d/wash (1), toaster, ldry (in unit), blkts, linen, pillows], w/mach, iron, iron brd, lounge firepl, bbq, c/park (carport), tennis, cots, non smoking property. D ♦♦ $90, ◊ $35, ch con, 1 apartment of a higher standard, BC MC VI.

★★★☆ **Elderberry Cottage**, (Cotg), Circa 1876. Mount Barker Rd, ☎ 08 8388 7997, fax 08 8388 1242, 1 cotg acc up to 4, (1 bedrm), [shwr, tlt, hairdry, a/c, fire pl, heat, elec blkts, TV, clock radio (cassette), t/c mkg, refrig, cook fac, micro, elec frypan, toaster, blkts, doonas, linen, pillows], ldry, w/mach, iron, iron brd, bbq, tennis, cots, breakfast ingredients, non smoking property. D ♦♦ $95, ◊ $15, ch con.

★★★ **Storison Cottages**, (Cotg), Classified by National Trust, 75 Main St, 30m N of PO, ☎ 08 8388 7247, fax 08 8388 7269, 2 cotgs acc up to 4, (2 bedrm), [shwr, bath, tlt, fan (1), heat, elec blkts, TV, video (1), t/c mkg, refrig, cook fac (1), micro (1), toaster, blkts, linen, pillows], c/park. D ♦♦ $85 - $95, ◊ $20, ch con, 1 cottage yet to be rated, BC MC VI.

HALLETT SA 5419

Pop Nominal, (189km N Adelaide), See map on pages 586/587, ref H5. The town has a backdrop Mount Bryan and the adjoining foothills. The area is well known for the many merino studs which have a reputation for quality livestock Australia wide.

B&B's/Guest Houses

★★★☆ **Tooralie Homestead and Lodge**, (B&B), (Farm), Mt Bryan East Rd, 11km E of PO, ☎ 08 8894 2067, fax 08 8894 2067, 3 rms [hairdry, c/fan, heat, elec blkts, clock radio], iron, iron brd, lounge (TV, video, stereo), lounge firepl, t/c mkg shared, plygr. BB ◊ $45 - $50, ♦♦ $50, BC MC VI.

★★☆ **(Lodge Section)**, 1 rm acc up to 19, [heat, micro, elec frypan, toaster, blkts, doonas, linen, pillows], lounge (TV), cook fac, t/c mkg shared, refrig. D ◊ $45, ◊ $45.

(Camp Ground Section), (Powered Site), [shwr (1G-1L), tlt (1G-1L), fire pl], pool, bbq (5), plygr. D $15.

HANSON BAY SA

See Kangaroo Island Region.

HAWKER SA 5434

Pop 345. (401km N Adelaide), See map on pages 586/587, ref H4. This township is the centre for a number of surrounding stations. many sightseers use it as headquarters for touring the Flinders Ranges. The town is situated on a plain, almost encircled by hills. Fred Teagues Museum. Bowls, Bush Walking, Golf, Horse Racing, Scenic Drives, Swimming (Solar Heated Pool), Tennis.

Hotels/Motels

★★☆ **Hawker Hotel Motel**, (LMH), Elder Tce, ☎ 08 8648 4102, fax 08 8648 4151, (2 stry) 20 units [shwr, tlt, a/c, heat, elec blkts, tel, TV, clock radio, t/c mkg, refrig], ldry, ⊠, bbq, rm serv, dinner to unit, cots. RO ◊ $60.50, ♦♦ $71.50, ◊ $11, ch con, AE BC DC EFT MC VI, ♿.

★☆ **(Hotel Section)**, 12 rms [a/c-cool (9), heat, TV (2), clock radio], dinner to unit. RO ◊ $33, ♦♦ $44 - $49.50, ◊ $11, ch con.

★★☆ **Outback Chapmanton Motor Inn**, (M), 1 Wilpena Rd, 500m NE of PO, ☎ 08 8648 4100, fax 08 8648 4109, 14 units [basin, shwr, tlt, a/c, tel, TV, clock radio, t/c mkg, refrig], ⊠, rm serv, dinner to unit, cots-fee. D ◊ $75, ♦♦ $80, ◊ $11, AE BC DC EFT MC VI.

Self Catering Accommodation

★★★ **Outback Chapmanton Holiday Units**, (HU), Arkaba Tce, ☎ 08 8648 4100, fax 08 8648 4109, 10 units acc up to 6, (2 bedrm), [shwr, tlt, a/c, TV, clock radio, cook fac, blkts, linen, pillows], ldry, cots-fee, D ◊ $75, ♦♦ $80, ◊ $11, Reception at Outback Chapmanton Motor Inn. AE BC DC EFT MC VI.

★★★ **Windana Cottages**, (HU), Previously Windana Holiday Units Quorn - Hawker Rd, 2km S of PO, ☎ 08 8648 4022, fax 08 8648 4283, 2 units acc up to 4, (2 bedrm), [shwr, tlt, a/c, heat, elec blkts, TV, refrig, cook fac, micro, blkts, linen (avail)], ldry. D ♦♦ $64, ◊ $10, ch con, AE BC DC MC VI.

★★☆ **Wonoka Cottage**, (Cotg), Leigh Creek Rd, 14km N of PO, ☎ 08 8648 4022, fax 08 8648 4283, 1 cotg acc up to 7, (2 bedrm), [shwr, tlt, a/c-cool, heat, TV, refrig, cook fac, micro, linen reqd-fee], cots. D ♦♦ $54, ◊ $10, ch con, Min book all holiday times, AE BC DC MC VI.

★★ **Merna Mora Holiday Units**, (HU), Parachilna Rd, 46km N of Hawker, ☎ 08 8648 4717, fax 08 8648 4712, 9 units acc up to 6, (1 & 2 bedrm), [shwr, bath (1), tlt, a/c-cool (7), fan (6), heat, clock radio, refrig, cook fac, micro, linen reqd-fee], ldry, cots. D ♦♦ $55, ◊ $11, ch con, Min book applies, BC MC VI.

★☆ **(Bunkhouse Section)**, 1 bunkhouse acc up to 10, [a/c-cool, heat], shwr (2G-2L), tlt (2G-2L), cook fac, refrig. D ◊ $15.

★☆ **Glen Lyle Cottage**, (Cotg), Glen Lyle Rd, 16km NE of PO, ☎ 08 8648 4022, fax 08 8648 4283, 1 cotg acc up to 8, (4 bedrm), [shwr, tlt, a/c-cool, heat, refrig, cook fac, micro, ldry, linen reqd-fee], bbq, D ♦♦ $50 - $72, ◊ $11, ch con, Min book all holiday times, BC MC VI.

★★★☆ **(Hillview Cottage)**, 1 cotg acc up to 4, (2 bedrm), [shwr, tlt, a/c, heat, elec blkts, TV, clock radio, t/c mkg, refrig, micro, elec frypan, toaster, blkts, doonas, linen-fee, pillows], w/mach, iron, iron brd, bbq, c/park. D ♦♦ $66 - $88, ◊ $6 - $11, ch con, Min book long w/ends and Easter.

Flinders Ranges Accommodation Booking Service, Emohruo Cabin Section, ☎ 08 8648 4022, fax 08 8648 4283, 1 cabin acc up to 4, (2 bedrm), [shwr, tlt, a/c, heat, clock radio, t/c mkg, refrig, cook fac, micro, blkts, linen reqd, pillows], w/mach, D ♦♦ $45, ◊ $12, ch con, AE BC DC MC VI, (not yet classified).

(Edeowie Shearer's Quarters), 1 rm acc up to 27, (Bunk Rooms), [shwr, bath, tlt, heat, refrig, cook fac ltd, micro, blkts, linen reqd-fee, pillows], w/mach. D ♦♦ $65, ◊ $12, ch con, Min book long w/ends and Easter, (not yet classified).

INGLEWOOD SA 5133

Pop 150. (25km Adelaide), See map on page 588, ref E3. A small, historic village in the Adelaide Hills, nestled in a valley surrounded by mountain range. Servicing the surrounding orchards and mixed farming community. Golf, Horse Riding, Scenic Drives.

B&B's/Guest Houses

★★★★☆ **Carramar Ridge Bed & Breakfast**, (B&B), Lot 746 Lower Hermitage Rd, Lower Hermitage, 2km N of PO, ☎ 08 8380 5661, fax 08 8380 5893, 2 rms (2 suites) [ensuite, hairdry, a/c, elec blkts, clock radio, t/c mkg, refrig], lounge (TV, CD & Video), pool, spa, bbq, non smoking rms. BB ♦♦ $180 - $220, Min book all holiday times, AE BC EFT MC VI.

★★★★ **Tally-Ho Lodge**, (GH), Millbrook Rd, 4km NE of PO, ☎ 08 8389 2377, fax 08 8389 2463, (2 stry), 4 rms [ensuite, shwr, tlt, a/c, elec blkts, clock radio], ⊠. BB ◊ $120, ♦♦ $153.

INNAMINCKA SA 5731

Pop Nominal, (1033km NNE Adelaide), See map on pages 586/587, ref J2. This is a small but important outback community in the State's far north-east, among the sprawling landscapes of the Strzelecki Desert. Memorials mark the place where Burke & Wills died.

Hotels/Motels

★☆ **Innamincka Hotel Motel**, (LMH), Main St, ☎ 08 8675 9901, fax 08 8675 9961, 4 units [ensuite, a/c, t/c mkg, refrig], ⊠, bbq, ☎. RO ◊ $45, ♦♦ $70, ♦♦♦ $90, ♦♦♦♦ $100, ◊ $10, AE BC MC VI.

(Bunkhouse Section), 1 bunkhouse acc up to 3, (Bunk Rooms), [blkts reqd-fee, linen reqd-fee, pillows reqd-fee], cook fac. RO ◊ $28, ♦♦ $45, ◊ $10.

Self Catering Accommodation

Bollards Lagoon Outback Accommodation, (Cotg), 180km S of Innamincka, ☎ 08 8091 3873, fax 08 8091 3866, 1 cotg acc up to 7, [shwr, bath, tlt, a/c-cool, fan, heat, t/c mkg, refrig, cook fac, ldry, doonas, linen], w/mach, iron, iron brd. D ♦♦ $88, W ♦♦ $462, (not yet classified).

Innamincka Trading Post Cabins, Main St, ☎ 08 8675 9900, 3 cabins acc up to 4, [ensuite, a/c, blkts, linen, pillows], cook fac, refrig, bbq, kiosk, shop, LPG, petrol, ice. D ◊ $44, ♦♦ $65, ◊ $15 - $25, ch con.

ISLAND BEACH SA

See Kangaroo Island Region.

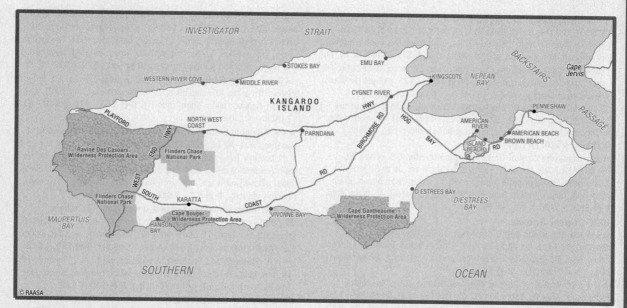

JAMESTOWN SA 5491

Pop 1,359. (206km N Adelaide), See map on pages 586/587, ref H5. A farming community and producer of wool, wheat, barley and meat. Railway Station & Goods Shed. Bowls, Croquet, Golf, Horse Racing, Horse Riding, Scenic Drives, Swimming (Pool), Tennis.

Hotels/Motels

★★☆ **Railway Hotel Motel**, (LMH), 32 Alexandra Tce, ☎ 08 8664 1035, fax 08 8664 1375, 9 units [ensuite, a/c, elec blkts, tel, TV, clock radio, t/c mkg, refrig, mini bar, toaster], ⊠, rm serv, cots-fee. **RO ♦ $55, ♦♦ $66,** ◊ **$6,** Bottleshop & gaming machines, AE BC DC MC VI.

★ **Commercial Hotel**, (LH), 35 Ayr St, ☎ 08 8664 1013, fax 08 8664 1140, (2 stry), 15 rms [basin (3), ensuite (3), a/c-cool (13), elec blkts, TV (1)], ⊠, refrig, c/park (limited), ✆, cots. **BLB ♦ $27.50, ♦♦ $50 - $55,** ◊ **$5,** BC EFT MC VI.

Jamestown Hotel, (LH), 79 Ayr St, 10m W of Town Hall, ☎ 08 8664 1387, fax 08 8664 1922, (2 stry), 9 rms [fan, elec blkts], rec rm, ⊠ (Mon to Sun), t/c mkg shared, bbq, ✆, cots (avail), non smoking rms (9). **BB ♦ $30, ♦♦ $45, BLB ♦ $20, ♦♦ $40,** fam con, BC EFT MC VI.

Self Catering Accommodation

★★★ **Jamestown Country Retreat Cabins**, Cnr Ayr & Bute Sts, ☎ 08 8664 0077, 5 cabins acc up to 4, [ensuite, a/c, elec blkts, TV, clock radio, refrig, cook fac, micro, blkts, linen, pillows]. **D ♦ $49.50, ♦♦ $55,** ◊ **$5.50,** AE BC MC VI.

KADINA SA 5554

Pop 3,536. (146km NNW Adelaide), See map on pages 586/587, ref A6. The largest town on the Yorke Peninsula. Once a thriving copper mining area, it is now the commercial centre for the surrounding districts. Banking & Currency Museum and the Yorke Peninsula Family History Group. Bowls, Croquet, Golf.

Hotels/Motels

★★★☆ **Kadina Gateway Motor Inn**, (M), Adelaide Rd, 1.5km E of PO, ☎ 08 8821 2777, fax 08 8821 1790, 20 units (1 suite) [ensuite, a/c, elec blkts, tel, cable tv, video (1), clock radio, t/c mkg, refrig, mini bar], ⊠ (Mon to Sat), pool, spa, bbq, rm serv, cots, **RO ♦ $78 - $80, ♦♦ $83 - $100,** ◊ **$11,** ch con, AE BC DC EFT MC VI, ⅃⅙.

★★★ **Kadina Village Motel**, (M), 28 Port Rd, ☎ 08 8821 1920, fax 08 8821 1102, 12 units [ensuite, a/c-cool, a/c (6), heat, elec blkts, TV, clock radio, t/c mkg, refrig], ldry, bbq, cots-fee, non smoking rms (5). **RO ♦ $50, ♦♦ $60,** ◊ **$11,** 3 units of a lower rating. AE BC DC EFT MC VI.

★☆ **Kadina Hotel**, (LH), 29 Taylor St, ☎ 08 8821 1008, fax 08 8821 3932, (2 stry), 5 rms [ensuite, shwr, bath (1), tlt, a/c, elec blkts, TV, clock radio, t/c mkg], ⊠ (Mon to Sat), refrig, cots. **BLB ♦ $44, ♦♦ $60,** ◊ **$20,** AE BC EFT MC VI.

★☆ **Wombat Hotel**, (LH), 19 Taylor St, ☎ 08 8821 1108, fax 08 8821 1425, (2 stry), 12 rms [a/c-cool (2), c/fan (9), elec blkts], lounge (TV), ⊠ (Mon to Sat), t/c mkg shared, refrig, cots. **BLB ♦ $20 - $25, ♦♦ $40 - $50,** ch con, AE BC EFT MC VI.

KANGAROO ISLAND REGION - SA

KANGAROO ISLAND - AMERICAN BEACH SA 5222

Pop Nominal, (137km SW Adelaide), See map on pages 586/587, ref A8.

★★☆ **White Crane Beach House**, (Cotg), 127 Esplanade, 9km W of Penneshaw, ☎ 08 8559 4201, 1 cotg acc up to 6, (2 bedrm), [shwr, bath, tlt (2), hairdry, c/fan, heat (slow combustion), TV, radio, t/c mkg, refrig, cook fac, micro, elec frypan, toaster], iron, c/park (carport), **D ♦♦ $55 - $68,** ◊ **$10,** Min book applies.

★★★★☆ **The Fig Tree Bed & Breakfast**, (B&B), No children's facilities, Leander Ave, 9km SW of Penneshaw, ☎ 08 8553 1054, fax 08 8553 1054, 3 rms [ensuite, c/fan, heat, elec blkts, TV, clock radio, t/c mkg, refrig, toaster, pillows], ldry, iron, cook fac, bbq (covered), **BLB ♦ $95, ♦♦ $112,** Communal kitchen includes micro, toaster, grill & refrig. BC MC VI.

KANGAROO ISLAND - AMERICAN RIVER SA 5221

Pop 300. (152km SW Adelaide), See map on pages 586/587, ref A8. This small hamlet situated on the edge of Eastern Cove is a great fishermans haven. Boating, Bush Walking, Canoeing, Fishing, Horse Riding, Water Skiing.

Hotels/Motels

AAA
TOURISM
Special Rates
★★★★ **Kangaroo Island Lodge**, (M), Scenic Rd, ☎ 08 8553 7053, fax 08 8553 7030, (2 stry gr fl), 38 units [ensuite, spa bath (2), a/c, elec blkts, tel, TV, video-fee, clock radio, t/c mkg, refrig, cook fac (6)], ldry, w/mach, dryer, iron, iron brd, conf fac, ⊠, pool, sauna, spa, rm serv, plygr, tennis, cots, **RO ♦ $127 - $157, ♦♦ $127 - $157,** ◊ **$24,** 10 rooms ★★★☆, AE BC DC EFT JCB MC VI, ⅃⅙.

★★★★ **Matthew Flinders Terraces Retreat**, (M), Previously Matthew Flinders Terraces Motel, Scenic Dr, ☎ 08 8553 7100, fax 08 8553 7250, 8 units (2 bedrm), [ensuite, bath (hip), hairdry, a/c, c/fan, heat, elec blkts, tel, TV, clock radio, t/c mkg, refrig, mini bar, toaster], ldry, ⊠, pool, spa, bbq, rm serv, dinner to unit, plygr, cots-fee. **RO ♦ $105, ♦♦ $125,** ◊ **$25,** AE BC DC MC VI.

Self Catering Accommodation

★★★ **Barbaree Cottage**, (Cotg), Pelican Lagoon, ☎ 08 8553 7190, 1 cotg acc up to 4, (2 bedrm), [shwr, tlt, fan, heat, TV, clock radio, CD, refrig, cook fac, micro, blkts, doonas, linen reqd-fee, pillows], ldry, w/mach, iron, iron brd, bbq. **D ♦♦ $95 - $100,** ◊ **$5 - $10,** Min book applies.

★★★ **Cooinda Holiday Village**, (HU), Bayview Rd, ☎ 08 8553 7063, fax 08 8553 7063, 4 units acc up to 4, (2 bedrm), [shwr, tlt, fan, heat, elec blkts, TV, clock radio, refrig, cook fac, blkts, linen, pillows], ldry, w/mach, iron, iron brd, bbq, c/park (carport), cots-fee. **D $82.50 - $93.50.**

★★★ **Riverview Cottage**, (Cotg), Government Rd, 4km S of PO, ☎ 08 8553 7169, fax 08 8553 7176, 1 cotg acc up to to 8, (3 bedrm), [shwr, bath, tlt, c/fan, heat, elec blkts, tel, TV, clock radio (cassette), t/c mkg, refrig, cook fac, micro, d/wash, toaster, ldry (in unit), blkts, linen, pillows], w/mach, iron, iron brd, bbq, cots. **D ♦♦ $77,** ◊ **$10,** ch con.

★★★ **Ulonga Lodge Holiday Units**, (HU), Scenic Dve, 1km S of PO, ☎ 08 8553 7171, fax 08 8553 7171, 5 units acc up to 6, (2 bedrm), [shwr, tlt, fan (5), heat, TV, clock radio, refrig, cook fac, linen reqd-fee], ldry, w/mach, iron, iron brd, bbq (covered), cots, **D** $75 - $100, BC MC VI.
    (Bed & Breakfast Section), 1 rm [fan, heat, TV, video, clock radio, CD, refrig, cook fac, micro], bbq, c/park. **BB ♦♦** $150, ◊ $25, (not yet classified).

★★☆ **Calico Cottage**, (Cotg), Scenic Dve, 200m E of PO, ☎ 08 8553 7054, fax 08 8553 7054, 1 cotg acc up to 8, (3 bedrm), [shwr, tlt, heat, elec blkts, TV, clock radio, refrig, cook fac, micro, elec frypan, toaster, blkts, linen reqd-fee, pillows], dryer, bbq, c/park. **D ♦♦** $45, ◊ $10, ch con.

★★☆ **Casuarina Coastal Units of Kangaroo Island**, 9 Ryberg Rd, ☎ 08 8553 7020, fax 08 8553 7020, 6 cabins acc up to 5, [ensuite, c/fan, heat, TV, clock radio, refrig, cook fac, micro, elec frypan, linen reqd-fee], ldry, w/mach, iron, iron brd, bbq (covered), ✆, plygr, cots. **D ♦♦** $50, ◊ $10, ch con, BC MC VI.

B&B's/Guest Houses
★★★★★ **The Kings Bed & Breakfast**, (B&B), Bayview Rd, ☎ 08 8553 7003, fax 08 8553 7277, 1 rm (1 suite) [ensuite, a/c-cool, c/fan, heat, TV, video, clock radio (cassette), CD, t/c mkg, refrig, pillows], bbq, c/park (carport). **BB ♦♦** $170.

★★★★☆ **Wanderers Rest of Kangaroo Island**, (GH), No children's facilities, Bayview Rd, 550m S of PO, ☎ 08 8553 7140, fax 08 8553 7282, (2 stry gr fl), 9 rms [ensuite, bath (hip), hairdry, c/fan, heat, elec blkts, fax, TV, clock radio, t/c mkg, refrig, mini bar], rec rm, lounge firepl, ⊠, pool-heated (solar), spa, bbq, non smoking units. **BB ♦** $162, **♦♦** $174, ◊ $43, AE BC DC EFT MC VI.

KANGAROO ISLAND - CYGNET RIVER SA 5223

Pop Nominal, (180km SW Adelaide), See map on pages 586/587, ref A8. A small rural community on Kangaroo Island, at the intersection of the Cygnet River and the Playford Hwy. Bush Walking, Fishing (River).

B&B's/Guest Houses
★★★☆ **Koala Lodge Bed & Breakfast**, (B&B), Playford Hwy, 13km SW Kingscote, ☎ 08 8553 9006, fax 08 8553 9006, 2 rms [ensuite, hairdry, a/c, elec blkts, TV, refrig, toaster, pillows], **BLB ♦** $88, **♦♦** $99, ◊ $22, BC MC VI.

KANGAROO ISLAND - D ESTREES BAY SA 5221

Pop Nominal, (177km SW Adelaide), See map on pages 586/587, ref G7. The establishment of a whaling station and the wrecks of many ships make this a interesting area that has seen a lot of history. Bush Walking, Fishing, Swimming (Sea).

Self Catering Accommodation
★★★ **MacGillivray Cottage**, (Cotg), Wheaton Rd, 32km S of PO, ☎ 08 8553 8244, fax 08 8553 8244, 1 cotg acc up to 4, (2 bedrm), [shwr, tlt, hairdry, fan, heat, TV, clock radio, t/c mkg, refrig, cook fac, micro, elec frypan, toaster, blkts, linen, pillows], bbq, cots, breakfast ingredients-fee, non smoking property. **D ♦♦** $66 - $88, ◊ $16.50 - $22, BC MC VI.

★★☆ **D'Estrees Lovering Beach House**, (HU), Beachfront Rd, ☎ 08 8553 8261, fax 08 8553 8261, 1 unit acc up to 8, (2 bedrm), [shwr, tlt, heat (slow combustion), elec blkts, tel, TV, clock radio, refrig, cook fac, micro, doonas, linen reqd-fee, pillows], bbq, cots. **D ♦♦** $60.50 - $77, ◊ $11, Min book applies.

Nautilus Lodge House, (House), D'Estrees Bay Rd, ☎ 08 8553 1140, fax 08 8553 1140, 1 house acc up to 10, (3 bedrm), [shwr, tlt, heat (slow combustion), clock radio, t/c mkg, refrig, cook fac, blkts, linen-fee, pillows], bbq. **D ♦♦** $70 - $100, ◊ $10, ch con, Western Red Cedar house with 12 volt electricity, Min book applies.

KANGAROO ISLAND - EMU BAY SA 5223

Pop Nominal, (142km SW Adelaide), See map on pages 586/587, ref A8. A popular destination situated on the north shore of Kangaroo Island. Fishing, Swimming (Beach).

Self Catering Accommodation
★★★★ **Loverings - Emu Bay**, (Cotg), 26 Hawthorn Ave, ☎ 08 8553 8261, fax 08 8553 8261, 1 cotg acc up to 8, (3 bedrm), [shwr, bath, tlt, tel, TV, clock radio, cook fac, micro, toaster, ldry, blkts, linen reqd-fee, pillows], w/mach, iron brd, bbq, c/park (garage), cots, non smoking property. **D ♦♦** $88 - $104.50, ◊ $11, Min book applies.

★★★☆ **Emu Bay Holiday Homes**, (HU), Lot 7 Bayview Rd, 500m W of beach, ☎ 08 8553 5241, fax 08 8553 5241, 3 units acc up to 10, (1 bedrm2 bedrm3 bedrm), [shwr, tlt, c/fan, heat, elec blkts, TV, clock radio, refrig, cook fac, micro, elec frypan, blkts, linen, pillows], ldry, iron, iron brd, plygr, cots, non smoking property, **D ♦♦** $80 - $90, ◊ $12, BC MC VI.

★★★★ **(Cabin Section)**, 4 cabins acc up to 6, (Studio, 1 & 2 bedrm), [shwr, tlt, c/fan (2), elec blkts, TV, refrig, cook fac, micro (2), elec frypan, toaster, blkts, linen, pillows], **D ♦♦** $55 - $70, ◊ $10 - $12, 2 cabins of a lower rating.

★★★ **Allambie Cottage & Wittow's Creek Rural Accom**, (Cotg), 6 Hawthorn Ave, ☎ 08 8559 4258, fax 08 8559 4258, 1 cotg acc up to 6, (3 bedrm), [shwr, tlt, wood heat (combustion), elec blkts, TV, clock radio (cassette), refrig, cook fac, micro, toaster, ldry (in unit), blkts, linen, pillows], w/mach, iron, iron brd, c/park (carport), cots, non smoking property, **D ♦♦** $77, ◊ $10, Min book applies.

★★★ **Wintersun Holiday House & Units**, (Cotg), Foreshore, ☎ 08 8553 5241, fax 08 8553 5241, 1 cotg acc up to 6, (3 bedrm), [shwr, tlt, fan, heat, TV, clock radio, t/c mkg, refrig, cook fac, micro, elec frypan, toaster, linen], bbq, c/park (carport). **D ♦♦** $90, ◊ $12.

★★★ **(Holiday Unit Section)**, 2 units acc up to 4, (2 bedrm), [shwr, tlt, fan, heat, TV, clock radio, t/c mkg, refrig, cook fac, micro, elec frypan, toaster, linen], c/park (carport). **D ♦♦** $80, ◊ $12.

★★☆ **Emu Bay Caravan Park Cabin**, Esplanade, ☎ 08 8553 2325, fax 08 8553 2325, 1 cabin acc up to 6, [ensuite, TV, t/c mkg, refrig, cook fac, micro, elec frypan, toaster, blkts reqd-fee, linen reqd-fee, pillows reqd-fee], tank water, bbq, Pets on application. **D ♦♦♦♦** $75, ◊ $12, Min book applies.

Birubi House, (House), 31 Hawthorn Ave, ☎ 08 8553 5238, fax 08 8553 5238, 1 house acc up to 8, (3 bedrm), [shwr, tlt, a/c, c/fan, heat (elec), tel, TV, video, clock radio, CD, t/c mkg, refrig, cook fac, micro, d/wash, toaster, blkts, doonas, linen reqd-fee, pillows], w/mach, dryer, iron, iron brd, bbq, cots, non smoking property. **D ♦♦** $130, ◊ $10, Min book applies, (not yet classified).

B&B's/Guest Houses
★★★★ **Merediths Beachside Bed & Breakfast**, (B&B), 500m N of Jetty, ☎ 08 8553 5381, fax 08 8553 5298, 1 rm (1 suite) [ensuite, wood heat (slow combustion), elec blkts, tel, TV, clock radio, t/c mkg, refrig, micro, elec frypan, toaster], iron, iron brd, bbq, c/park. **BB ♦♦** $125, ◊ $30.

KANGAROO ISLAND - HANSON BAY SA 5223

Pop Nominal, (204km Adelaide), See map on pages 586/587, ref G7. Situated on Kangaroo Island, near the southern boundary of Flinders Chase National Park. Bush Walking, Fishing, Swimming (Beach).

Self Catering Accommodation
★★★ **Hanson Bay Sanctuary Homestead**, (House), South Coast Rd, 4km E of Hanson Bay turn off, ☎ 08 8853 2603, fax 08 8853 2673, 1 house acc up to 10, [ensuite (2), shwr, tlt, c/fan, heat (slow combustion), t/c mkg, refrig, cook fac, micro, toaster, blkts, linen, pillows], rec rm, conf fac, lounge firepl, bbq, c/park (carport). **D ♦♦** $105 - $120, ◊ $17, ch con, BC MC VI.

★★☆ **Hanson Bay Sanctuary Holiday Units**, (HU), ☎ 08 8853 2603, fax 08 8853 2673, 6 units acc up to 5, (2 bedrm), [shwr, tlt, heat, refrig, cook fac, blkts, linen, pillows], ldry, bbq, cots. **D ♦♦** $105 - $120, ◊ $17, ch con, BC MC VI.

KANGAROO ISLAND - ISLAND BEACH SA 5222

Pop Nominal, (145km Adelaide), See map on pages 586/587, ref A8. A small hamlet situated on Eastern Cove, a haven for fishermen.

Self Catering Accommodation
★★★☆ **Kangaroo Island Beach House**, (Cotg), Lot 87 Flinders Gve, 17km SW of PO, ☎ 08 8271 2323, fax 08 8271 2323, 1 cotg acc up to 7, (3 bedrm), [shwr, tlt, hairdry, c/fan, heat, elec blkts, TV, video, clock radio, refrig, cook fac, micro, elec frypan, toaster, ldry, blkts, linen reqd-fee, pillows], w/mach, iron, bbq, c/park (carport), **D** $99 - $121, Dinghy available. Min book applies.

★★★☆ **Malibu Lodge** (Cotg), Lot 302 Borda Rd, 14km SW of PO, ☎ 08 8331 3059, fax 08 8364 3234, 1 cotg acc up to 8, (4 bedrm), [shwr, tlt, hairdry, c/fan, wood heat, elec blkts, tel, TV, video, clock radio, radio, CD, refrig, micro, toaster, ldry, blkts, doonas, pillows], w/mach, iron, No pets allowed. **D** $235 - $255, Min book applies.

★★★ **Bridgewater Park Nominees**, (Cotg), Lot 254, Willoughby Rd, Penneshaw 5222, ☎ 08 8339 1923, fax 08 8339 5799, 1 cotg acc up to 6, (3 bedrm), [shwr, tlt, hairdry, clock radio, refrig, cook fac, elec frypan, toaster, ldry (in unit), linen], iron, iron brd, bbq, c/park. **D $110 - $120**, Min book applies.

★★★ **Island Beach Cabins**, Lot 65, Island Beach Rd, 17km W of Penneshaw, ☎08 8382 0132, 2 cabins acc up to 5, (2 bedrm), [c/fan, wood heat, TV, clock radio, CD (cassette), refrig, cook fac, micro, elec frypan, toaster, linen reqd], bbq, **D $70 - $80**, Single night bookings not available.

★★★ **Kangaroo Island Beach Retreat**, (Cotg), 11 Nepean Dve, 19km W of Penneshaw, ☎ 08 8353 1335, fax 08 8353 1335, 1 cotg acc up to 4, (2 bedrm), [shwr, bath, tlt, hairdry, c/fan, heat (slow combustion), tel, TV, clock radio, t/c mkg, refrig, cook fac, micro, toaster, linen], iron, iron brd, bbq, c/park (double garage), cots, non smoking property. **D 👥 $80 - $100, 🧒 $22 - $28**, weekly con, Min book applies.

★★ **Careys Island Beach Cottages**, Government Rd, 15km W of PO, ☎ 08 8261 7646, fax 08 8553 7178, 4 cabins acc up to 5, (2 bedrm), [shwr, tlt, c/fan, heat (combustion), TV, clock radio, refrig, micro, elec frypan, toaster, linen reqd], ldry, w/mach, bbq, **D $60 - $85**, Min book applies.

B&B's/Guest Houses

★★★ **The Anchorage Bed & Breakfast**, (B&B), Willoughby Rd, 17km S of Penneshaw, ☎ 08 8553 7184, fax 08 8553 7033, 1 rm (Studio), [ensuite, fan, heat, TV, t/c mkg, refrig, cook fac, micro, elec frypan, toaster, doonas, pillows], bbq, c/park. **BLB 👤 $50 - $60, 👥 $70 - $80, 🧒 $20.**

KANGAROO ISLAND - KARATTA SA 5223

Pop Nominal, (200km SW Adelaide), See map on pages 586/587, ref G7. Located on the south coast of Kangaroo Island, known for the Kelly Caves and Outdoor Education School. Bush Walking.

Hotels/Motels

★★★★ **Kangaroo Island Wilderness Resort**, (M), 1 South Coast Rd, 95km SW of Kingscote, ☎ 08 8559 7275, fax 08 8559 7377, 5 units [ensuite, a/c, cable tv, video, clock radio, t/c mkg, refrig], ldry, w/mach-fee, dryer-fee, conf fac, ☒, bbq, ✆, non smoking property. **BB 👤 $130, 👥 $160, 🧒 $30**, ch con, AE BC DC EFT MC VI, ♿.

(Backpacker Section), 4 bunkhouses acc up to 4, [refrig, micro, toaster, blkts, linen, pillows], shwr (2G-2L), tlt (2G-2L), rec rm. **RO 👤 $33.**

Self Catering Accommodation

★★ **Wingara Farm House**, (Cotg), (Farm), Church Rd, 6km NW of Karatta, ☎ 08 8559 7222, fax 08 8559 7222, 1 cotg acc up to 12, [shwr, bath, tlt, heat, radio, refrig, cook fac, elec frypan, toaster, blkts, linen reqd-fee], ldry, c/park (undercover), cots. **D 👥 $60 - $80, 🧒 $5.**

KANGAROO ISLAND - KINGSCOTE SA 5223

Pop 1,450. (189km SW Adelaide), See map on pages 586/587, ref A8. Kangaroo Island's largest town and commercial centre. Situated on the north coast, offering views across Nepean Bay to the mainland. Galleries, Hope Cottage and the Old Mulberry Tree. Both passengers & cars can be accommodated on the Kangaroo Island Sealink which operates daily between Cape Jervis and Penneshaw. The journey takes approx 1 hour. Kangaroo Island Ferry Connections operate a passenger only ferry daily between Cape Jervis and Penneshaw. The journey takes approx 30 minutes. Kangaroo Island Fast Ferry operate a passenger only service daily (from September to April and Friday to Monday during May and June) between Glenelg and Kingscote. The journey takes approx 2 and a quarter hours. Boating, Bowls, Bush Walking, Fishing, Golf, Horse Racing, Horse Riding, Sailing, Squash, Swimming (Pool & Beach), Tennis.

Hotels/Motels

AAA TOURISM *Special Rates*

★★★☆ **Ozone Seafront Hotel**, (LMH), Previously Ozone Hotel Motel Commercial St, ☎ 08 8553 2011, fax 08 8553 2249, (2 stry gr fl), 37 units [ensuite, a/c, elec blkts, tel, TV, movie, clock radio, t/c mkg, refrig], ldry, w/mach-fee, dryer-fee, iron, iron brd, lounge, meeting rm, ☒, pool-heated (solar), sauna, spa, bbq, ✆, cots-fee. **RO 👤 $97 - $118.50, 👥 $97 - $118.50, 👤👤👤 $129.50, 🧒 $11**, 7 units ★★★. AE BC DC EFT JCB MC VI.

FLAG Flag Choice Hotels

★★★☆ **Wisteria Lodge Motel**, (M), 7 Cygnet Rd, ☎ 08 8553 2707, fax 08 8553 2200, (2 stry gr fl), 20 units [ensuite, spa bath (4), hairdry, a/c, elec blkts, tel, TV, video-fee, clock radio, t/c mkg, refrig, mini bar], ldry-fee, ☒, pool-heated (solar), spa, rm serv, plygr, tennis (half court), cots-fee. **RO 👤 $115 - $180, 👥 $130 - $180**, ch con, AE BC DC JCB MC VI, ♿.

★★★ **Ellsons Seaview Motel**, (M), Chapman Tce, 100m fr PO, ☎ 08 8553 2030, fax 08 8553 2368, 11 units [ensuite, hairdry, a/c, c/fan (6), elec blkts (6), tel, TV, clock radio, t/c mkg, refrig, toaster], ldry, w/mach-fee, dryer-fee, iron, iron brd (avail), lounge (shared), ☒, rm serv, cots-fee. **RO 👤 $88, 👥 $108, 🧒 $12**, AE BC DC EFT MC VI.

★★☆ **(Guest House Section)**, 6 rms [basin, heat, clock radio, t/c mkg, refrig, toaster], shared fac. **RO 👤 $46, 👥 $58, 🧒 $10.**

★★★ **The Island Resort Motel**, (M), 4 Telegraph Rd, ☎ 08 8553 2100, fax 08 8553 2747, 28 units [ensuite, spa bath (4), a/c-cool (13), c/fan (15), heat, elec blkts, tel, TV, clock radio, t/c mkg, refrig], rec rm, ☒, pool indoor heated, sauna, spa, bbq, cots (4). **BLB 👤 $93.50, 👥 $104.50 - $126.50**, ch con, fam con, AE BC BTC DC EFT JCB MC VI.

★★☆ **Queenscliffe Family Hotel**, (LH), 57 Dauncey St, ☎ 08 8553 2254, fax 08 8553 2291, (2 stry gr fl), 11 rms [ensuite, fan, heat, elec blkts, TV, clock radio, t/c mkg, refrig], ☒, ✆, cots. **BLB 👤 $55, 👥 $65, 👤👤👤 $75, 🧒 $5**, ch con, AE BC DC EFT MC VI.

Self Catering Accommodation

★★★★☆ **Acacia Apartments**, (Apt), 3 Rawson St, 1km N of PO, ☎ 08 8553 0088, fax 08 8553 0008, 10 apts acc up to 6, (1 bedrm2 bedrm), [shwr, spa bath (5), tlt, hairdry, a/c, tel, TV, video, clock radio, t/c mkg, refrig, cook fac, micro, elec frypan, toaster, blkts, linen, pillows], ldry, w/mach-fee, dryer-fee, iron, iron brd, conf fac, pool indoor heated, spa, bbq, plygr, cots, non smoking rms (8). **D 👥 $148 - $169, 🧒 $17 - $21**, Min book applies, AE BC DC MC VI, ♿.

★★★★ **Nepean Waters Getaway**, (Cotg), Emma Dve, 2km W of PO, ☎ 08 8231 0515, fax 08 8332 4659, 4 cotgs acc up to 6, (2 & 3 bedrm), [shwr, spa bath, tlt, hairdry, a/c, TV, video, clock radio, refrig, cook fac, micro, toaster, blkts, linen, pillows], ldry, w/mach, dryer, iron, iron brd, rec rm, freezer (communal), bbq (covered), ✆, plygr (cubby house), mini golf, cots, non smoking property, **D $155 - $180**, Min book applies, BC MC VI.

★★★☆ **The Folly Cottage**, (Cotg), Cnr Lovers La & Playford Hwy, 2.8km W of PO, ☎ 08 8553 2776, fax 08 8553 2881, 1 cotg acc up to 7, (2 bedrm), [shwr, bath, tlt, hairdry, c/fan, heat, elec blkts, tel, TV, video, clock radio, CD, t/c mkg, refrig, cook fac, micro, elec frypan, toaster, ldry (in unit), blkts, linen, pillows], w/mach, dryer, iron, iron brd, c/park (carport), cots-fee, Pets allowed. **D 👤👤👤👤 $80 - $100, 🧒 $15, W 👤👤👤👤 $504 - $630, 🧒 $90**, Min book Christmas Jan long w/ends and Easter.

★★★ **Graydon Holiday Lodge**, (HU), 16 Buller St, ☎ 08 8553 2713, fax 08 8553 3289, 7 units acc up to 6, (2 bedrm), [shwr, tlt, c/fan, heat, elec blkts, TV, clock radio, refrig, cook fac, blkts, doonas, linen, pillows], ldry, w/mach-fee, iron, iron brd, bbq (covered), c/park (carport), ✆, plygr, cots, **D 👥 $76 - $82, 🧒 $11**, ch con, Min book all holiday times, BC MC VI.

★★★ **Highgrove Cottage**, (Cotg), Emu Bay Rd, 9km W of PO, ☎ 08 8553 2600, 1 cotg acc up to 6, (2 bedrm), [shwr, tlt, heat, TV, radio (cassette), t/c mkg, refrig, cook fac, micro, elec frypan, toaster, blkts, linen, pillows], w/mach, iron, iron brd, bbq. **D 👥 $80, 🧒 $10**, Min book applies.

★★★ **Island Court Holiday Units**, (HU), 67-77 Cygnet Rd,
☎ 08 8553 2722, fax 08 8553 2657, 5 units acc up to 6, (1 & 2 bedrm),
[shwr, tlt, evap cool, heat, elec blkts, TV, video (avail), clock radio,
t/c mkg, refrig, cook fac, micro, elec frypan, toaster, blkts, linen, pillows],
iron, iron brd, bbq, courtesy transfer, plygr, bicycle, cots. D ♦ $60.50,
♦♦ $71.50, ◊ $13.20, ch con, pen con, AE BC MC VI.

★★★ **Kangaroo Island Holiday Village**, (HU), 9 Dauncey St,
☎ 08 8553 2225, fax 08 8553 2366, 11 units acc up to 5, (1 bedrm
Studio), [shwr, tlt, fan, heat, elec blkts, TV, clock radio, refrig, cook fac,
blkts, linen, pillows], ldry, w/mach, dryer, iron, iron brd, bbq, c/park
(boat/car), boat park, cots. D ♦ $77, ♦♦ $77, ◊ $13, ch con, AE BC MC VI.

★★★ **Nepean Bay Getaway**, (Cotg), Min-Oil Rd, 25km SE of PO,
☎ 08 8553 9181, fax 08 8553 9181, 1 cotg acc up to 10, (4 bedrm),
[shwr (2), bath, tlt (1), heat (slow combustion), tel, TV, clock radio,
refrig, cook fac, micro, elec frypan, toaster, ldry (in unit), doonas],
w/mach, dryer, iron, iron brd, bbq, c/park (carport), cots. D ♦♦ $50 -
$70, ◊ $10, Min book applies.

★★☆ **Brownlow Holiday Units**, (HU),
Third St, Brownlow 5223, 3km SW of
Kingscote, ☎ 08 8553 2293,
fax 08 8553 2293, 9 units acc up to 7,
[shwr, tlt, heat, TV, clock radio, t/c mkg,
refrig, cook fac, blkts, linen, pillows], ldry,
w/mach-fee, dryer-fee, bbq (covered), cots-fee, D ♦♦ $65, ◊ $10, BC MC VI.

★★☆ **Kegrah Cottage**, (Cotg), 19 Addison St, 1km N of PO,
☎ 08 8261 8481, fax 08 8367 5519, 1 cotg acc up to 9, (3 bedrm),
[shwr, bath, tlt, a/c, TV, video, clock radio, refrig, cook fac, micro, elec
frypan, toaster, ldry (in unit), blkts, linen reqd-fee, pillows], w/mach,
iron, iron brd, c/park. D ♦♦ $71.50, ◊ $11, ch con.

★★☆ **Morgans by the Sea**, (Cotg), 47 Chapman Tce, ☎ 08 8559 7236,
1 cotg acc up to 5, [shwr, bath, tlt, fan, fire pl, heat, tel, TV, clock
radio (cassette), t/c mkg, refrig, cook fac, micro, elec frypan, toaster,
ldry, blkts, linen reqd-fee, pillows], w/mach, iron, iron brd, c/park.
D ♦♦ $60 - $85, ◊ $5 - $10.

★★☆ **Parade Units**, (HU), The Parade,
Brownlow 5223, 3km SW of Kingscote,
☎ 08 8553 2394, fax 08 8553 2293, 7 units
acc up to 6, [shwr, tlt, heat, TV, clock
radio, refrig, cook fac, elec frypan, blkts,
doonas, linen, pillows], rec rm, bbq
(covered), cots-fee, non smoking units, D ♦♦ $65, ◊ $10, BC MC VI.

Dolphin Rise, (HU), Brownlow Rd, ☎ 08 8553 2688,
fax 08 8553 3005, 2 units acc up to 6, (3 bedrm), [ensuite, shwr, spa
bath, tlt, a/c, TV, clock radio, t/c mkg, refrig, cook fac, micro, toaster,
doonas, linen (by arrangement)-fee, pillows], w/mach, cots (by
arrangement), Pets on application. D $120, Min book applies,
(not yet classified).

Seashells K. Is, (HU), Cnr Emma Dr & Rapid Rise, 1km W of PO,
☎ 08 8553 2688, fax 08 8553 3005, 4 units acc up to 6, (3 bedrm),
[shwr, tlt, a/c, TV, clock radio, t/c mkg, refrig, cook fac, micro, d/wash,
toaster, doonas, linen, pillows], w/mach, dryer, bbq, cots (by
arrangement). D $120 - $140, Min book applies, (not yet classified).

Wishing Well House, Lot 3 Hundred of Menzies North Coast Rd, 11km
NW of PO, ☎ 08 8264 8102, fax 08 8263 3119, 1 cabin acc up to 2,
[ensuite, c/fan, heat, tel, TV, radio, t/c mkg, refrig, micro]. BB ♦♦ $95,
Min book applies, BC MC VI, (not yet classified).

B&B's/Guest Houses

★★★★★ **Correa Corner Bed & Breakfast**, (B&B), Second St,
☎ 08 8553 2498, fax 08 8553 2355, 3 rms (3 suites) [ensuite, hairdry,
a/c, heat (wood fire in winter), elec blkts, clock radio], lounge (TV,
Video & Stereo), res liquor license, t/c mkg shared, refrig, meals avail,
c/park. BB ♦ $160, ♦♦ $170 - $193, Resident wallabies. Airport
transfers available, BC MC VI.

★★★★☆ **Marlsie Bed & Breakfast**, (B&B), Lot 93 Minoil Rd Haines,
22km S of PO, ☎ 08 8553 9133, 1 rm [ensuite, hairdry, c/fan, heat,
elec blkts, tel, TV, video, clock radio, t/c mkg], c/park. BB ♦♦ $160.

★★★★ **Stanraer Homestead Bed & Breakfast**, (B&B), Wheatons Rd
McGillivray, 30km S of PO, ☎ 08 8553 8235, fax 08 8553 8226, 2 rms
[shwr (2), bath (2), tlt (2), hairdry, fan, heat, elec blkts, t/c mkg],
lounge (TV), ✕, meals avail (dinner), cots, non smoking rms. BB ♦♦ $130 -
$170, RO ♦♦ $120, ch con, BC.

★★★☆ **Yurara Homestead Bed & Breakfast**, (B&B), Margries Rd (off
Playford Hwy), 26km SW of PO, ☎ 08 8559 6143, fax 08 8559 6143,
2 rms [c/fan, heat, pillows], bathrm, lounge (TV), meals avail (by
arrangement), c/park. BLB ♦ $45, ♦♦ $90.

*Pop Nominal, (244km Adelaide), See map on pages 586/587, ref
G7. Located on the north western side of Kangaroo Island. Boating,
Fishing, Swimming.*

Self Catering Accommodation

★★★ **Middle River Homestead Cottages**, (Cotg), North Coast Rd,
☎ 08 8553 9119, fax 08 8553 9122, 3 cotgs acc up to 12, (3 & 4
bedrm), [shwr, bath, tlt, fan, c/fan (2), wood heat (slow combustion),
tel (1), clock radio, refrig, cook fac, micro, toaster, blkts, linen, pillows],
lounge firepl (2), cots, Dogs allowed by arrangement. D ♦♦ $120 - $140,
◊ $12, 1 cottage of a lower rating.

★★☆ **Middle River Heights Cottage**, (Cotg), North Coast Rd,
☎ 08 8559 3201, 1 cotg acc up to 8, (3 bedrm), [shwr, bath, tlt,
c/fan, heat (slow combustion), TV, radio (cassette), refrig, cook fac,
micro, elec frypan, toaster, linen reqd-fee], w/mach, iron, iron brd,
bbq, cots. D ♦♦ $60, ◊ $10, Min book applies.

*Pop Nominal, (241km Adelaide), See map on pages 586/587, ref
G7. Located on the north coast of Kangaroo Island at the mouth of
the Western River, a lovely spot where the Western River snakes
down to the beach, the area is backed by high cliffs.*

Self Catering Accommodation

★★★★ **Cape Forbin Wilderness Retreat**, Snug Cove Rd, 60km NW of
Parndana, ☎ 08 8559 3219, fax 08 8559 3219, 1 cabin acc up to 6, (3
bedrm), [shwr, tlt, heat, tel, CD, refrig, ldry, blkts, doonas, linen, pillows],
bbq. RO ♦♦ $154, ◊ $16.50, Solar power only. Min book applies, BC MC VI.

B&B's/Guest Houses

★★★☆ **Roo Lagoon Bed & Breakfast**, (B&B), Playford Hwy,
☎ 08 8559 3267, fax 08 8559 3267, 1 rm (1 bedrm), [shwr, tlt,
hairdry, fire pl, heat, t/c mkg, refrig, cook fac, micro, ldry, pillows],
w/mach, dryer, iron, iron brd, bbq, meals avail (by arrangement),
c/park (carport), breakfast ingredients. BB ♦♦ $110, DBB ♦♦ $170.

*Pop 150. (206km Adelaide), See map on pages 586/587, ref A8.
Located on Kangaroo Island, among sheep and cattle grazing areas
with some cereal crops, mainly oats. It is the main settlement
between Kingscote and the west coast. Bowls, Bush Walking,
Fishing, Golf, Horse Riding, Swimming, Tennis.*

Self Catering Accommodation

★★★ **Abbey Lodge**, (Apt), Lot 26 Rowland Hill Hwy, 500m S of PO,
☎ 08 8559 5072, 1 apt acc up to 8, (3 bedrm), [fan, heat, tel, TV,
clock radio, CD, cook fac, micro, ldry, blkts, doonas, linen, pillows], ✕,
secure park, non smoking property (inside), RO ♦♦ $100, ◊ $10, weekly con.

★★★ **Ficifolia Lodge Holiday Units**, (HU), Lot 45 Cook St,
☎ 08 8559 6104, fax 08 8559 6104, 3 units acc up to 6, (2 bedrm),
[shwr, tlt, hairdry, a/c, TV, video, clock radio, t/c mkg, refrig, cook fac,
micro, toaster, blkts, linen, pillows], iron, iron brd, bbq (undercover),
c/park (carport), ☎, cots, non smoking property, D ♦ $70, ♦♦ $84,
◊ $15, BC MC VI, ♿.

★★★ **Parndana Community Hotel Cabins**, Cook St, 300m E of PO,
☎ 08 8559 6071, fax 08 8559 6176, 2 cabins acc up to 6, (2 bedrm),
[shwr, tlt, a/c, elec blkts, TV, clock radio, t/c mkg, refrig, cook fac, micro,
toaster, blkts, linen, pillows], iron, ✉ (Mon to Sat), bbq, RO ♦♦ $77,
◊ $11, ch con, BC EFT MC VI.

★★ **Kellys Pioneer Bend Cottage**, (Cotg), Wetheralls Rd, 7km N of PO,
☎ 08 8559 2249, fax 08 8559 2249, 1 cotg acc up to 12, (4 bedrm),
[shwr, bath, tlt, fan, heat, elec blkts, TV, clock radio, t/c mkg, refrig,
cook fac, elec frypan, blkts, linen, pillows], ldry, w/mach, iron, bbq,
cots. D ♦ $55, ♦♦ $55, ◊ $5.50, Min book applies.

B&B's/Guest Houses

★★★★ **Lothlorien Homestead Bed & Breakfast**, (B&B), Lot 109
Seagers Rd, 22km SE of PO, ☎ 08 8553 8238, fax 08 8553 8238, 3 rms
[ensuite, heat, elec blkts, TV, clock radio, t/c mkg, ldry], lounge (video
& stereo), bbq, meals to unit (by arrangement), non smoking rms.
BB ♦ $99 - $148.50, ♦♦ $115 - $148.50, ◊ $65, BC MC VI.

★★★☆ **The Open House Bed & Breakfast**, (B&B), 70 Smith St,
☎ 08 8559 6113, fax 08 8559 6088, 4 rms [ensuite, c/fan (1),
wood heat, elec blkts], lounge (Stereo), t/c mkg shared, non smoking
rms. BB ♦ $93, ♦♦ $186, DBB ♦ $123, ♦♦ $246, ch con, BC MC VI.

KANGAROO ISLAND - PENNESHAW SA 5222

Pop 300. (10km American Beach) (127km SW Adelaide), See map on pages 586/587, ref B8. A small town and holiday resort across Backstairs Passage from the South Australian mainland. It is situated on the north east coast of Dudley Peninsula, and is the closest point to the mainland. Cape Willoughby Lighthouse, Christmas Cove, Frenchmans Rock and Penneshaw Maritime & Folk Museum. Boating, Fishing, Swimming, Tennis.

Hotels/Motels

★★★★ **Kangaroo Island Seafront Hotel**, (M), Previously Sorrento Resort Motel North Tce, ☎ 08 8553 1028, fax 08 8553 1204, (2 stry gr fl), 18 units [ensuite, hairdry (12), fan, heat, elec blkts, TV, clock radio, t/c mkg, refrig], ldry, iron brd (no irons in rooms) (12), rec rm, lounge (TV & video), conf fac, ✉, pool-heated, sauna, spa, bbq, dinner to unit, ✆, mini golf, tennis (half court), cots-fee, non smoking rms (4). D ♦♦ $120 - $155, ◊ $16.50, AE BC DC EFT MC VI.
Operator Comment: Completely refurbished Hotel. Stunning Ocean Views. www.seafront.com.au

Self Catering Accommodation

★★★★ **Baudin House**, (House), Cheopis St, 2km E of PO, ☎ 08 8553 1068, fax 08 8553 1068, (2 stry) 1 house acc up to 8, [shwr (2), tlt (2), hairdry, a/c, heat (combustion), TV, CD, t/c mkg, refrig, cook fac, micro, d/wash, toaster, doonas, linen, pillows], w/mach, dryer, iron, iron brd, cots (highchair). D ♦♦ $120 - $150, ◊ $20, Min book applies, BC MC VI.

★★★★ **Currawong Island Holiday**, (House), Lot 71 South Tce, 1km E of PO, ☎ 08 8332 5982, fax 08 8363 3880, (2 stry gr fl), 1 house acc up to 9, [shwr, spa bath, tlt, hairdry, a/c, c/fan, heat, elec blkts, tel, TV, video, clock radio, CD, t/c mkg, refrig, cook fac, micro, elec frypan, d/wash, toaster, ldry, blkts, doonas, linen reqd-fee, pillows], w/mach, iron, iron brd, bbq, c/park (carport). D ♦♦ $110, ◊ $11, W ♦♦ $770, ◊ $77, Min book applies, BC MC VI.

★★★★ **Dolphins Look-Out**, (House), 83 South Tce, 800m E of PO, ☎ 08 8373 2955, fax 08 8373 6175, 1 house acc up to 8, [shwr, bath, tlt, hairdry, a/c, c/fan, elec blkts, TV, video, clock radio, CD, refrig, cook fac, micro, elec frypan, toaster, ldry, blkts, doonas, linen, pillows], w/mach, dryer, iron, iron brd, freezer, bbq, c/park (covered). D ♦♦ $130, ♦♦♦♦ $150, ◊ $20, Min book applies.

★★★★ **Sheoaks Penneshaw**, (House), Lot 13 Trethewey Tce, 1.5km E of PO, ☎ 08 8322 7656, 1 house acc up to 6, (3 bedrm), [shwr (2), bath, tlt (2), c/fan, heat, elec blkts, TV, video, clock radio, CD, refrig, cook fac, micro, elec frypan, toaster, ldry, doonas, linen reqd-fee, pillows], w/mach, iron, iron brd, bbq, D ♦♦ $130, ◊ $20, Min book applies, AE BC MC VI.

★★★★ **The Penneshaw Beach House**, (Cotg), 131 Flinders Tce, 1km SE of PO, ☎ 08 8559 6129, fax 08 8559 5011, 1 cotg acc up to 7, (3 bedrm), [shwr, bath (hip), tlt, hairdry, a/c, elec blkts, TV, clock radio, refrig, micro, elec frypan, toaster, ldry, blkts, linen, pillows], w/mach, iron, iron brd, bbq, c/park. D ♦♦ $100, ◊ $10, Min book applies.

★★★☆ **Cape View Cottage**, (Cotg), Frenchmans Tce, ☎ 08 8553 1087, fax 08 8553 1087, 1 cotg acc up to 6, (3 bedrm), [shwr, tlt, heat, elec blkts, tel, TV, clock radio, refrig, cook fac, micro, blkts, linen, pillows], w/mach, bbq, cots-fee, D ♦♦ $65 - $80, ◊ $7, Min book applies, BC MC VI.

★★★☆ **Lonie Bay Cottage**, (Cotg), Lot 5 Pelican St, 1km E of PO, ☎ 08 8553 3053, 1 cotg acc up to 6, (3 bedrm), [shwr, bath, tlt, hairdry, fan, heat, tel, TV, clock radio, refrig, cook fac, micro, elec frypan, toaster, ldry, linen reqd-fee], w/mach, iron, iron brd, bbq, cots. D ♦♦♦♦ $65, ◊ $5.

★★★☆ **The Hideaway**, (Cotg), Christmas St, ☎ 08 8553 1230, fax 08 8553 1230, 1 cotg acc up to 6, (3 bedrm), [shwr, bath, hairdry, a/c-cool, fan, heat, tel, TV, video, clock radio, CD, t/c mkg, refrig, cook fac, micro, toaster, ldry, blkts, doonas, linen, pillows], w/mach, iron, iron brd, bbq, cots, non smoking property. D ♦♦ $75 - $90, ◊ $10, Min book applies.

★★★ **Bay Rainbow Beachfront Cottage**, (Cotg), Frenchmans Tce, ☎ 08 8278 8026, 1 cotg acc up to 4, (2 bedrm), [shwr, tlt, fan, heat, elec blkts, TV, clock radio, refrig, cook fac, micro, blkts, linen reqd-fee], w/mach, non smoking property, D ♦♦ $68, ◊ $10, Min book applies.

★★★ **Blue Wren Cottage**, (Cotg), Lot 133 Flinders Tce, ☎ 08 8553 1233, fax 08 8553 1190, 1 cotg acc up to 6, (3 bedrm), [shwr, tlt, TV, clock radio, refrig, cook fac, micro, toaster, linen], w/mach, iron, iron brd. D ♦♦ $75 - $85, ◊ $15, Min book applies.

★★★ **Butterfly Beachfront Cottage**, (Cotg), Lot 125 Frenchmans Tce, ☎ 08 8276 7993, fax 08 8276 7993, 1 cotg acc up to 4, (2 bedrm), [shwr, tlt, fan, heat, TV, clock radio, refrig, cook fac, micro, elec frypan, ldry, linen reqd-fee], w/mach, iron, non smoking property, D ♦♦ $60, ◊ $10, Min book applies.

★★★ **HG & BM Willson Cottages**, (Cotg), Frenchman's Tce, 1km SE of PO, ☎ 08 8553 1166, fax 08 8553 1166, 1 cotg acc up to 8, (3 bedrm), [shwr, bath, tlt, fan, heat, tel, TV, clock radio, refrig, cook fac, micro, elec frypan, toaster, ldry, blkts, linen, pillows], w/mach, iron, bbq, c/park. D ♦♦ $70, ◊ $12.50, ch con, Min book applies.

★★★ **Hog Bayview**, (House), Lot 73, South Tce, ☎ 08 8553 1142, fax 08 8553 1142, 1 house acc up to 7, (3 bedrm), [shwr, tlt, fan, heat (combustion w/heater), TV, clock radio, t/c mkg, refrig, cook fac, micro, toaster, blkts, doonas, linen, pillows], w/mach, bbq, cots (highchair), non smoking rms. D ♦♦ $70 - $100, ◊ $10, ch con.

★★★ **Tammar Holiday House**, (Cotg), 175 Karratta Tce, ☎ 08 8339 2047, fax 08 8339 7967, 1 cotg acc up to 6, (3 bedrm), [shwr, bath, tlt, fan, wood heat (slow combustion), TV, video, clock radio, CD, refrig, cook fac, micro, d/wash, blkts, linen, pillows], w/mach, dryer, iron, D ♦♦ $80 - $90, ◊ $10, Min book applies.

★★★ **Woodleigh Homestead KI Cottage**, (Cotg), Government Rd, 18km SE of PO, ☎ 08 8553 1087, fax 08 8553 1087, 1 cotg acc up to 11, (4 bedrm), [shwr (2), bath, tlt, a/c-cool, tel, TV, t/c mkg, refrig (2), cook fac, micro, elec frypan, toaster, ldry (in unit), blkts, linen reqd, pillows], w/mach, iron, iron brd, lounge firepl, bbq, c/park (carport), cots. D ♦♦♦♦ $80 - $85, ◊ $5, Min book applies, BC MC VI.

★★☆ **Charlie Bates Cottage**, (Cotg), 39 South Tce, 1.5km NW of PO, ☎ 08 8295 6480, fax 08 8294 5964, 1 cotg acc up to 5, [shwr, bath (hip), tlt, heat, elec blkts, tel, TV, video, clock radio, t/c mkg, refrig, micro, elec frypan, toaster, blkts, doonas, linen, pillows], w/mach, iron, iron brd, lounge firepl. D ♦♦ $70, ◊ $10, Min book applies.

★★☆ **Kangaroo Island Seafront Chalets and Cottages**, (HU), Previously Sorrento Alpine Village Holiday Units 49 North Tce, ☎ 08 8553 1028, fax 08 8553 1204, 9 units acc up to 6, (1, 2 & 3 bedrm), [shwr, bath (1), tlt, fan, heat, elec blkts, TV, clock radio, refrig, cook fac, blkts, linen, pillows], ldry, lounge (TV & video), pool-heated, sauna, spa, bbq, ✆, mini golf, tennis (half court), cots-fee. D ♦♦ $120 - $155, ◊ $16.50, 3 units ★★★☆. AE BC DC EFT MC VI.

★★ **Tuna & Trevally Cottages**, (Cotg), Frenchmans Tce, ☎ 08 8332 1083, 2 cotgs acc up to 6, (2 bedrm), [shwr, tlt, heat, TV, refrig, cook fac, micro, elec frypan, toaster], w/mach, D $55.

B&B's/Guest Houses

★★★★☆ **Seaview Lodge KI Bed & Breakfast**, (B&B), Willoughby Rd, 1km W of PO, ☎ 08 8553 1132, fax 08 8553 1183, 4 rms [ensuite (4), bath (1), a/c, fire pl (3), elec blkts, clock radio], lounge (TV, Video, CD Stereo), lounge firepl, t/c mkg shared, refrig, meals avail (by arrangement), c/park. BB ♦♦ $125 - $160, ◊ $80, BC MC VI.

★★★★☆ **The Lookout Bed & Breakfast**, (B&B), Cnr Willoughby & Ian Rds via, 10km E of PO, ☎ 08 8553 1048, fax 08 8553 1048, 2 rms [hairdry, a/c, c/fan, elec blkts, TV, video, clock radio, CD, t/c mkg, refrig, micro, toaster], ldry, w/mach, dryer, iron, iron brd, cook fac, non smoking property. BB ♦ $145, ♦♦ $145, ◊ $55, BC MC VI.

Other Accommodation

Kangaroo Island YHA, Previously Penguin Walk Youth Hostel 33 Middle Tce, ☎ 08 8553 1233, fax 08 8553 1190, 4 rms acc up to 6, (Bunk Rooms), [fan, heat, TV, refrig, cook fac, blkts, linen, pillows], shared fac. D ♦ $18, ♦♦ $44, ◊ $18, AE BC DC MC VI.

KANGAROO ISLAND - STOKES BAY SA 5223

Pop Nominal, (220km W Adelaide), See map on pages 586/587, ref A8. A small north shore town on Kangaroo Island.

Self Catering Accommodation

Dutton Park Beach Cottage, (Cotg), North Coast Rd, 6km W of TC, ☎ 08 8559 2253, fax 08 8559 2253, 1 cotg acc up to 9, (3 bedrm), [shwr, tlt, heat (slow combustion), refrig, cook fac, doonas, linen reqd-fee, pillows], bbq, cots, D ♦♦ $80, ◊ $10, Solar power only. Private beach. Min book applies.

K

SOUTH AUSTRALIA

KANGAROO ISLAND - VIVONNE BAY SA 5223

Pop Nominal, (177km SW Adelaide), See map on pages 586/587, ref G7. Small fishing town located on the South Coast of Kangaroo Island. Boating, Fishing, Swimming (Beach).

Self Catering Accommodation
★★★ **Blue Hills Farmstay Apartment Kangaroo Island**, (Apt), (Farm), Crabbs Rd, 14 km N of TC, ☎ 08 8559 4204, fax 08 8559 4204, 1 apt acc up to 4, (2 bedrm), [shwr, tlt, radio (cassette), t/c mkg, cook fac, micro, elec frypan, toaster, doonas, linen, pillows], ldry, w/mach, dryer, iron, iron brd, bbq, meals avail (by arrangement), cots, breakfast ingredients. D ♦♦ **$88**, ◊ **$11**, ch con.

★★★ **Green Gable Cottage**, (Cotg), Cnr Sunset Way & Flinders Rd, ☎ 08 8553 1233, fax 08 8553 1056, 1 cotg acc up to 4, (2 bedrm), [shwr, tlt, fan, heat, elec blkts, tel, radio (cassette), t/c mkg, refrig, cook fac, micro, toaster, linen], bbq, D ♦♦ **$75 - $85**, ◊ **$10 - $15**, Min book applies.

★★★ **Honeymyrtle Cottage**, (Cotg), 133 Crabb Rd, ☎ 08 8553 1233, fax 08 8553 1190, 1 cotg acc up to 6, (2 bedrm), [shwr, tlt, heat, refrig, cook fac, micro, blkts, linen reqd-fee, pillows], bbq, D ♦♦ **$60 - $70**, ◊ **$10**, ch con, Min book applies, AE BC DC MC VI.

★★★ **Tiki Holiday House**, (Cotg), off Jetty Rd, ☎ 08 8323 9331, fax 08 8323 9338, 1 cotg acc up to 8, (3 bedrm), [shwr, tlt, hairdry, fan (2), c/fan (2), heat (gas stove), video, clock radio, CD, refrig (2), cook fac, micro, elec frypan, toaster, blkts, doonas, linen-fee, pillows], iron, bbq, cots, D ♦♦ **$75**, ◊ **$10**, ch con, Min book applies.

★★★ **Vivonne Bay Island Getaway**, (House), Lot 14, Bayview Dr, ☎ 08 8558 2506, 1 house acc up to 8, (4 bedrm), [shwr, bath, tlt, hairdry, a/c, c/fan, TV, video, clock radio, t/c mkg, refrig, micro, toaster], iron, iron brd. D ◊ **$80**, ♦♦ **$80**, Min book applies.

★★☆ **Correa Cottage**, (Cotg), Dolphin Cres, ☎ 08 8553 1233, fax 08 8553 1190, 1 cotg acc up to 6, (2 bedrm), [shwr, tlt, hairdry, fan, heat, cable tv, clock radio, CD, refrig, cook fac, micro, linen reqd], iron, iron brd, bbq. D ♦♦♦♦ **$72.50**, ◊ **$11**, ch con, Min book applies, AE BC DC MC VI.

Honeyeaters Hideaway, (Cotg), Flinders Rd Harriet River Estate, ☎ 08 8331 9296, 1 cotg acc up to 4, [shwr, tlt, c/fan, wood heat, radio, CD, refrig, cook fac, micro, elec frypan, toaster, blkts, doonas, linen reqd-fee, pillows], bbq (gas). RO ♦♦ **$55**, ◊ **$5.50 - $11**.

KANGAROO ISLAND - WESTERN RIVER COVE SA 5220

Pop Nominal, (264km SW Adelaide), See map on pages 586/587, ref G7. Situated on the north coast of Kangaroo Island at the mouth of the Western River. Bush Walking, Fishing (River & Sea), Scenic Drives, Swimming.

Self Catering Accommodation
★★★★ **Western River Valley Cottages**, (HU), Western River Rd, 35km W of Parndana, ☎ 08 8559 3232, fax 08 8559 3202, 2 units acc up to 4, [shwr, bath (hip), tlt, a/c, heat (1), cable tv, clock radio, t/c mkg, refrig, mini bar, cook fac, micro, elec frypan, toaster, blkts, linen, pillows], iron, bbq, c/park. D ♦♦ **$100 - $130**, ◊ **$25**, AE BC DC MC VI.

B&B's/Guest Houses
★★★☆ **Gum Valley Retreat**, (GH), Previously Gum Valley Retreat Guest House 32km NW of Parndana PO, ☎ 08 8559 3207, fax 08 8559 3242, 7 rms [ensuite, hairdry, c/fan, heat (slow combustion), refrig], ldry, lounge, lounge firepl, ⊠, spa, t/c mkg shared, bbq, cots. BB ◊ **$99**, ♦♦ **$165**, ch con, BC MC VI.

End of Kangaroo Island Region

KAPUNDA SA 5373

Pop 1,980. (80km NE Adelaide), See map on pages 586/587, ref C6. This was the site of South Australias first major mining operation where copper was extracted from 1844 into the the 20th century. Copper Mine Site, Kapunda Mine Trail, Kapunda Museum, The Sheiks Camel and Donkey Farm and lookouts. Bowls, Bush Walking, Golf, Scenic Drives, Swimming (Pool), Tennis, Trotting.

Hotels/Motels
Sir John Franklin Hotel, (LH), Main St, ☎ 08 8566 3233, fax 08 8566 3873, (2 stry), 11 rms [basin, c/fan (2), elec blkts], ⊠, t/c mkg shared, cots. RO ◊ **$25**, ♦♦ **$55**, ◊ **$10**, BC EFT MC VI.

Self Catering Accommodation
★★★ **Blue Gum Retreat Cottage**, (Cotg), Greenock Kapunda Rd, 8km S of PO, ☎ 08 8563 4020, 1 cotg acc up to 2, (Studio), [shwr, bath, tlt, heat, TV, clock radio, t/c mkg, refrig, cook fac ltd, elec frypan, toaster, blkts, linen, pillows], iron, iron brd, bbq, cots, breakfast ingredients. D ♦♦ **$77 - $88**, ch con.

Kapunda Cottage, (Cotg), 27 Old Adelaide Rd, 750m SW of PO, ☎ 08 8337 6337, fax 08 8266 0502, 1 cotg acc up to 4, (2 bedrm), [shwr, tlt, fan, heat (elec/wood), elec blkts, TV, video, radio, t/c mkg, refrig, cook fac, micro, blkts, doonas, linen, pillows], breakfast ingredients, non smoking property. D ◊ **$60**, ◊ **$60**, ch con, weekly con, Min book applies, BC MC VI, (not yet classified).

B&B's/Guest Houses
★★★★☆ **Saint Christopher's Retreat**, (B&B), Bottom Old House Rd, 10km S of PO, ☎ 08 8525 2247, fax 08 8525 2608, 1 rm (1 suite) [ensuite, spa bath, a/c, heat (elec/wood), elec blkts, tel, TV, video, clock radio, CD, t/c mkg, refrig, cook fac, micro, doonas, blkts], sauna, bbq, non smoking suites, No pets allowed. Suite BB **$150**, weekly con, Min book applies, AE BC MC VI.

★★★★ **The Peppertrees Bed & Breakfast**, (B&B), 47 Clare Rd, 1km N of PO, ☎ 08 8566 2776, 2 rms (2 suites) [ensuite (1), a/c-cool, TV, clock radio, CD, t/c mkg, refrig], bathrm (1), meals avail, non smoking suites. Suite RO ♦♦ **$105**, ◊ **$30**, BC MC VI.

★★★☆ **Ford House Bed & Breakfast**, (GH), 80 Main St, ☎ 08 8566 2280, fax 08 8566 2280, (2 stry), 4 rms [ensuite, a/c-cool (3), a/c (1), heat, elec blkts, TV, clock radio, t/c mkg, refrig], lounge, ⊠. BB ◊ **$70**, ♦♦ **$90**, ◊ **$40**, BC MC VI.

KARATTA SA

See Kangaroo Island Region.

KEITH SA 5267

Pop 1,176. (227km SE Adelaide), See map on pages 586/587, ref J7. A commercial centre for the surrounding rural areas. Early Settlers Cottage, 1910 Congregational Church Building, Old Manse and Penny Farthing Coffee & Crafts. Bowls, Golf, Swimming (Pool), Tennis.

Hotels/Motels

★★★ **Keith Motor Inn**, (M), Dukes Hwy, 1km W of PO, ☎ 08 8755 1500, fax 08 8755 1928, 15 units [ensuite, hairdry, a/c, elec blkts, tel, TV, video, clock radio, t/c mkg, refrig, toaster], ldry-fee, ⊠, rm serv, cots-fee. RO ◊ **$75**, ♦♦ **$85**, ◊ **$10**, ch con, AE BC DC MC VI, ੯占.

★★☆ **Keith Hotel Motel**, (LMH), Makin St, ☎ 08 8755 1122, fax 08 8755 1411, 20 units [ensuite, a/c, elec blkts, tel, TV, clock radio, t/c mkg, refrig], lounge (TV), conv fac, ⊠, rm serv, ☎, cots. RO ◊ **$52**, ♦♦ **$59**, ◊ **$7**, ch con, pen con, AE BC DC EFT MC VI.

★★ **(Hotel Section)**, 8 rms [ensuite, bath (2), a/c, elec blkts, tel, TV, clock radio, t/c mkg, refrig]. RO ◊ **$46**, ♦♦ **$53**, ◊ **$7**, ch con, pen con.

Self Catering Accommodation
★★★★ **Pendleton Farm Retreat Cottages**, (Cotg), Eckerts Rd, 14km E of PO, ☎ 08 8756 7042, fax 08 8756 7067, 2 cotgs acc up to 7, (2 & 3 bedrm), [shwr, tlt, a/c-cool, elec blkts, clock radio, t/c mkg, refrig, cook fac, micro, elec frypan, toaster, blkts, linen, pillows], ldry, w/mach-fee, dryer-fee, iron, iron brd, lounge firepl, pool-heated (solar), bbq. D ♦♦ **$79.20 - $96.80**, ◊ **$8.80 - $11**, 1 Cottage of a lower rating. BC MC VI, ੯占.

B&B's/Guest Houses
★★★★ **Ashwood Park Bed & Breakfast**, (B&B), Lot 299 Park Tce, 1km E of PO, ☎ 08 8755 3114, fax 08 8755 3235, 1 rm (1 suite) [ensuite, spa bath, hairdry, fan, heat, elec blkts, clock radio (cassette), t/c mkg, ldry], iron, iron brd, lounge (TV & Video), meals avail (by prior arrangement). BB ◊ **$80**, ♦♦ **$135**, ♦♦♦ **$200**, ♦♦♦♦ **$250**, ◊ **$65**, ch con, AE DC.

KIMBA SA 5641

Pop 683. (477km NW Adelaide), See map on pages 586/587, ref G5. One of the larger towns on the highway across the Eyre Peninsula. The centre of a large wheat growing area. Bowls, Bush Walking, Gem Fossicking, Golf, Horse Racing, Horse Riding, Swimming (Pool), Tennis, Trotting.

Hotels/Motels
★★☆ **Kimba Community Hotel Motel**, (LMH), High St, ☎ 08 8627 2007, fax 08 8627 2310, (2 stry gr fl), 20 units [ensuite, a/c-cool, elec blkts, tel, TV, movie, clock radio, t/c mkg, refrig, toaster], ldry, conv fac, ⊠, bbq, c/park (limited), ☎, cots-fee, RO ◊ **$55 - $90**, ♦♦ **$65 - $100**, ♦♦♦ **$75 - $110**, ◊ **$8**, AE BC DC EFT MC VI, ੯占.

★★☆ **Kimba Motel Roadhouse**, (M), Eyre Hwy, 1km W of PO, ☎ 08 8627 2040, fax 08 8627 2092, 14 units [ensuite, bath (2), a/c-cool, heat, elec blkts, tel, TV, t/c mkg, refrig], ldry, w/mach-fee, dryer-fee, ⊠, bbq, rm serv, ☎, cots. RO ◊ **$50 - $60**, ♦♦ **$55 - $65**, ◊ **$10**, ch con, BC EFT MC VI.

KINGSCOTE SA

See Kangaroo Island Region.

KINGSTON (SE) SA 5275

Pop 1,425. (296km SE Adelaide), See map on pages 586/587, ref J7. Referred to as the 'Gateway to the South East'. A coastal town near the southern end of the Coorong, set on Lacepede Bay. Big Lobster, Cape Jaffa Lighthouse, Kingston National Trust Museum and The Woodhut. Boating, Bowls, Bush Walking, Fishing, Golf, Horse Riding, Sailing, Squash, Surfing, Swimming (Beach), Tennis, Water Skiing.

Hotels/Motels

★★★☆ **Lacepede Bay Motel**, (M), Cnr Hanson St & Marine Pde, ☎ 08 8767 2444, fax 08 8767 2044, (2 stry gr fl), 21 units [ensuite, a/c, tel, TV, clock radio, t/c mkg, refrig, mini bar (10), ldry-fee], ⊠, rm serv, dinner to unit, cots, non smoking rms (10). **RO ♦ $75 - $85, ♦♦ $75 - $85, ۇ $10**, AE BC DC MC VI, &.

★★★ **Kingston Lobster Motel**, (M), Princes Hwy, ☎ 08 8767 2322, fax 08 8767 2315, 25 units [shwr, tlt, a/c, elec blkts, tel, TV, video (avail), clock radio, t/c mkg, refrig], ⊠, pool, spa, rm serv, cots-fee, non smoking rms (11). **RO ♦ $73.70, ♦♦ $79.20, ۇ $8**, AE BC DC JCB MC VI, &.

★★☆ **Mobil 190 Mile Motel**, (M), Princes Hwy, 2km N of PO, ☎ 08 8767 2419, fax 08 8767 2419, 7 units [ensuite, shwr, tlt, a/c-cool, a/c, heat, elec blkts, TV, clock radio, t/c mkg, refrig, toaster, doonas (2)], ⊠, ♦, non smoking property. **BLB ♦ $60, ♦♦ $72, ♦♦♦ $84, ۇ $9**, fam con, AE BC DC EFT MC VI.

Self Catering Accommodation

★★☆ **Keilira Cottage**, (Cotg), Kingston - Bordertown Rd, 35km NE of PO, ☎ 08 8767 5055, fax 08 8767 5094, 1 cotg acc up to 6, (3 bedrm), [shwr, bath, tlt, wood heat, TV, t/c mkg, refrig, cook fac, toaster, ldry (in unit), blkts, linen, pillows], w/mach, iron, bbq, cots, breakfast ingredients, non smoking property. **D ♦♦ $75, ۇ $15**, ch con.

KINGSTON-ON-MURRAY SA 5331

Pop Part of Barmera, (210km NE Adelaide), See map on pages 586/587, ref E6. A small township on the Murray River, and site of a bridge across the river. Boating, Fishing, Swimming, Vineyards, Wineries, Water Skiing.

Other Accommodation

Golden Leisure Houseboats, (Hbt), ☎ 08 8588 1212, 4 houseboats acc up to 12, [shwr, tlt, a/c-cool, heat, TV, video, radio (cassette), CD, refrig, cook fac, micro, blkts, linen, pillows], w/mach (2), bbq. **High Season W $900 - $1,980, Low Season W $750 - $1,550.**

LAURA SA 5480

Pop 521. (223km N Adelaide), See map on pages 586/587, ref H5. A wheat, barley, sheep and cattle area in the southern Flinders Ranges. Bowls, Golf, Horse Racing, Tennis.

B&B's/Guest Houses

★★★☆ **Alder House Bed & Breakfast**, (B&B), 37 West Tce, 500m N of PO, ☎ 08 8663 2329, 2 rms [fire pl, elec blkts, pillows], lounge firepl, ✗, t/c mkg shared, non smoking rms. **BB ♦ $65, ♦♦ $85**, Min book applies.

LENSWOOD SA 5240

Pop Nominal, (32km Adelaide), See map on page 588, ref E4. A small town in the Adelaide Hills, closely involved with the area's fruit orchards.

Self Catering Accommodation

★★★ **Cloverhill Cottage**, (Cotg), Lobethal Rd, 2km NE of PO, ☎ 08 8389 6543, fax 08 8389 5244, (2 stry), 1 cotg acc up to 4, (2 bedrm), [shwr, tlt, a/c, fire pl, elec blkts, tel, TV, clock radio, t/c mkg, refrig, cook fac, micro, toaster, blkts, linen, pillows], ldry, w/mach, iron, iron brd, bbq, cots, breakfast ingredients, Pets on application. **D ♦♦ $100 - $120, ۇ $20**, ch con.

B&B's/Guest Houses

★★★★☆ **Villa Montebello**, (GH), Harris Rd, 4km SW of PO, ☎ 08 8389 8504, fax 08 8389 8114, (2 stry gr fl), 5 rms [spa bath (3), fire pl, heat, clock radio], ldry, lounge, conf fac, refrig, bbq. **BB ♦♦ $160 - $230**, 2 rms of a lower rating.

LITTLEHAMPTON SA 5250

Pop Part of Mount Barker, (35km Adelaide), See map on pages 586/587, ref C7. A small service town adjacent to Mount Barker, famous for its brickworks.

Self Catering Accommodation

★★★☆ **Liebelt House Cottage**, (Cotg), Junction Rd, 2km N of PO, ☎ 08 8391 2696, fax 08 8391 6864, 1 cotg acc up to 4, (1 bedrm), [shwr, tlt, hairdry, heat (open fire), elec blkts, TV, clock radio, CD, t/c mkg, refrig, cook fac, micro, toaster, blkts, doonas, linen, pillows], iron, iron brd, bbq (avail), cots, breakfast ingredients, non smoking property. **D ♦♦ $100 - $110, ۇ $20**, ch con.

LOCK SA 5633

Pop 219. (602km NW Adelaide), See map on pages 586/587, ref F5. Located in central Eyre Peninsula, Lock is an agricultural service town. Bowls, Golf, Horse Racing, Swimming (Pool), Tennis.

Hotels/Motels

Lock Hotel Motel, (LMH), Railway Tce, ☎ 08 8689 1181, 6 units [shwr, tlt, heat, elec blkts, t/c mkg, refrig], ldry, w/mach, dryer, rec rm, lounge (TV), ⊠ (Mon to Sat), c/park. **RO ♦ $25, ♦♦ $40.**

LOXTON SA 5333

Pop 7,288. (256km E Adelaide), See map on pages 586/587, ref E6. One of the largest riverland towns surrounded by vast areas of vineyards. Loxton Historical Village, Galleries, Lock 4, Craft Shops, Rotunda, the Tree of Knowledge and The Big Pelican. Boating, Bowls, Bush Walking, Fishing, Golf, Squash, Swimming (Pool & River), Tennis, Vineyards, Wineries, Water Skiing.

Hotels/Motels

★★★ **Loxton Community Hotel Motel**, (LMH), East Tce, ☎ 08 8584 7266, fax 08 8584 6850, 30 units [ensuite, bath (12), a/c, elec blkts, tel, TV, clock radio, t/c mkg, refrig, toaster], conv fac, ⊠, pool, bbq, rm serv, cots, non smoking units (2). **RO ♦ $69 - $74, ♦♦ $72 - $85, ۇ $11**, 12 units ★★★☆. AE BC DC EFT JCB MC VI, &. **(Hotel Section)**, 10 rms [ensuite, a/c, elec blkts, tel, TV, clock radio, t/c mkg], rm serv, cots. **RO ♦ $51 - $61, ♦♦ $72, ۇ $11**, (not yet classified).

B&B's/Guest Houses

★★★☆ **Briaken Park Bed & Breakfast**, (B&B), (Farm), 15km S of town centre, ☎ 08 8587 4326, fax 08 8587 4366, 2 rms [a/c-cool, heat, elec blkts, TV, video, radio (cassette), CD], ldry, w/mach, iron, iron brd, lounge firepl, spa, bbq, meals avail, c/park. **BB ♦ $60, ♦♦ $90**, Tariff includes farm activities. *Operator Comment: Be spoilt, enjoy good food, farm tours, bush walks. Flora & fauna abound.*

LUCINDALE SA 5272

Pop 249. (348km SE Adelaide), See map on pages 586/587, ref J7. Township at the centre of a rich farming district. Bowls, Golf, Tennis.

Self Catering Accommodation

★★★☆ **Petersville Host Farm**, (Cotg), (Farm), Thomas's Rd, Kingston (Se) 5275, 28km NW of Lucindale, ☎ 08 8767 5081, fax 08 8767 5081, 1 cotg acc up to 10, [shwr, bath, tlt, evap cool, heat, fire pl, TV, video (avail), clock radio, t/c mkg, refrig, cook fac, micro, toaster, ldry, blkts, doonas, linen, pillows], w/mach, iron, bbq, c/park (undercover). **BLB ♦♦ $85, ۇ $10**, ch con.

LYNDHURST SA 5732

Pop Nominal, (562km N Adelaide), See map on pages 586/587, ref H3. Historic old former railway town, at the start of the Strzelecki Track and on the way to Marree. It is also within sight of the far northern Flinders Ranges. Talc Alpha Rink Outback Art Gallery.

Hotels/Motels

★ **Lyndhurst Elsewhere Hotel**, (LH), 3 Short St, ☎ 08 8675 7781, fax 08 8675 7703, 9 rms [a/c-cool (5), fan (4), heat, clock radio (6)], ⊠, ♦. **RO ♦ $27.50, ♦♦ $44 - $66, ۇ $25**, BC EFT MC VI.

LYNDOCH SA

See Barossa Valley Region.

MACCLESFIELD SA 5153

Pop 400. (37km SE Adelaide), See map on page 588, ref E7. A small town nestled in the outer Adelaide Hills. Scenic Drives.

Self Catering Accommodation

★★★☆ **Mirrabooka Bed & Breakfast Cottage**, (Cotg), No children's facilities, Strathalbyn Rd, 3km SE of PO, ☎ 08 8388 9733, fax 08 8388 9467, 1 cotg acc up to 2, [shwr, spa bath, tlt, hairdry, a/c-cool, c/fan, elec blkts, clock radio, t/c mkg, refrig, cook fac ltd, elec frypan, toaster, blkts, doonas, linen, pillows], iron, iron brd, lounge firepl, non smoking property. **D ♦♦ $121, W ♦♦ $726.**

★★★ **Adelaide Hills Getaway Cottages**, (HU), 23-25 Venables St, 50m NE of PO, ☎ 08 8388 9295, 4 units acc up to 8, (1 bedrm4 bedrm), [shwr, bath (1), tlt, heat, elec blkts, TV, clock radio, t/c mkg, refrig, cook fac (3), micro (1), toaster, blkts, linen, pillows], iron, non smoking property. **D $60 - $120, W $350 - $650.**

MAITLAND SA 5573

Pop 1,066. (169km NW Adelaide), See map on pages 586/587, ref A6. Busy commercial centre located on the Yorke Peninsula, the centre of rich agricultural area. Maitland Public School Museum and St Johns Anglican Church. Bowls, Golf, Squash, Swimming (Pool), Tennis.

Self Catering Accommodation

★★★ **Eothen Farm**, (Cotg), Previously Eothen Farm Cottage Off Maitland to Balgowan Rd, 13km NW of PO, ☎ 08 8836 3210, fax 08 8836 3210, 1 cotg acc up to 8, (4 bedrm), [shwr, bath, tlt, a/c, fire pl, TV, clock radio, refrig, cook fac, micro, ldry, blkts, linen, pillows], w/mach, bbq, c/park (garage), cots, **D ♦ $13 - $40**, ch con, Min book applies.

MANNUM SA 5238

Pop 2,025. (84km E Adelaide), See map on pages 586/587, ref C7. Picturesque town overlooking the Murray River. Cactus Garden, Mary Ann Reserve and PS Marion. Boating, Bowls, Bush Walking, Croquet, Fishing, Golf, Horse Riding, Squash, Swimming (Pool & River), Tennis, Water Skiing.

Hotels/Motels

★★★ **Mannum Motel**, (M), 76 Cliff St, ☎ 08 8569 1808, fax 08 8569 1453, 26 units [shwr, tlt, hairdry (6), a/c, fan, elec blkts, tel, TV, clock radio, t/c mkg, refrig, cook fac (12), toaster], ldry, conv fac, ☒, pool, sauna, spa, bbq, tennis (half court), cots. **BLB ♦ $67 - $76, ♦♦ $76 - $89, ◊ $13.20**, ch con, AE BC DC EFT MC VI, ♿.

Self Catering Accommodation

★★★☆ **Fossil Farm Cottages**, (Cotg), Belvedere Rd, 5km W of PO, ☎ 08 8569 1558, 2 cotgs acc up to 6, (2 bedrm), [shwr, bath, tlt, hairdry, heat, elec blkts, TV, clock radio, t/c mkg, refrig, cook fac, micro (1), elec frypan, d/wash, toaster, blkts, doonas, linen, pillows], w/mach, iron, iron brd, bbq, c/park (carport) (1), breakfast ingredients. **D ♦♦ $110, ♦♦♦♦ $176**, ch con.

★★☆ **Mannum Holiday Village**, 30 Porter St Cowirra, 1.5km N of PO ☎ 08 8569 1179, 5 cabins acc up to 6, (2 bedrm), [shwr, tlt, a/c (2), refrig, cook fac, blkts reqd-fee, linen reqd-fee], bbq, kiosk, jetty. **D ♦♦ $40, ◊ $5.**

(Caravan Park Section), (10 pwr), bath (1), tank water, river water, shwr (2G-2L), tlt (1G-2L), bbq, Pets allowed on leash.
pwr-site D ♦♦ $12, ◊ $2.

B&B's/Guest Houses

★★★☆ **Mannaroo Farm Bed & Breakfast**, (B&B), East Front Rd, 12km NE of PO, ☎ 08 8569 1646, fax 08 8569 1646, 2 rms [shwr, bath, tlt, fan, fire pl, elec blkts, TV, clock radio, micro, pillows], lounge (TV). **BB ♦ $65, ♦♦ $100.**

★★★☆ **Mannum House Bed and Breakfast**, (B&B), 33 River Lane, 150m S of PO, ☎ 08 8569 2631, fax 08 8569 2633, (2 stry gr fl), 2 rms [ensuite, hairdry, a/c-cool, heat, c/fan, elec blkts, TV, clock radio, t/c mkg], ✕, meals avail, c/park. **BB ♦ $93.50, ♦♦ $115 - $130**, BC BTC MC VI.

Other Accommodation

Aurora Houseboats, (Hbt), Younghusband Rd, Kia Marina, 9km NE of PO, ☎ 08 9474 1846, fax 08 9331 3255, 1 houseboat acc up to 10, [shwr, tlt (2), hairdry, evap cool, heat, TV, video, t/c mkg, refrig, cook fac, micro, toaster, blkts, doonas, linen, pillows], w/mach. **W $795 - $1,345**, BC MC VI, (not yet classified).

Freedom Houseboats, (Hbt), Younghusband Rd, Kia Marina, 9km NE of PO, ☎ 08 9474 1846, fax 08 9331 3255, 1 houseboat acc up to 12, [shwr, tlt (2), hairdry, a/c-cool, heat, tel, TV, video, t/c mkg, refrig, cook fac, micro, toaster, blkts, doonas, linen, pillows], w/mach. **W $1,135 - $2,095**, BC MC VI, (not yet classified).

Nirvana Houseboat, (Hbt), River La, 1.5km S of PO, ☎ 08 9474 1846, fax 08 9331 3255, 1 houseboat acc up to 6, [shwr, tlt, evap cool, heat, tel, TV, video, t/c mkg, refrig, cook fac, micro, toaster, blkts, doonas, linen, pillows]. **W $695 - $995**, BC MC VI, (not yet classified).

Breeze Houseboat Holidays, (Hbt), Main St, ☎ 08 8569 2223, fax 08 8569 2223, 2 houseboats acc up to 10, [shwr, spa bath (1), tlt, tel (1), TV, video, radio, CD, refrig, cook fac, micro, d/wash (1), blkts, linen, pillows], ice box, canoeing-fee. **D $632 - $2,520**, AE BC DC MC VI.

Buccaneer Marine & Houseboats, (Hbt), Allambi Houseboat. 30 River La, 1km S of PO, ☎ 08 8569 2610, fax 08 8569 2910, 1 houseboat acc up to 10, (4 bedrm), [ensuite (2), tlt (2), a/c (ducted), heat, tel, TV, video, refrig, cook fac, micro, elec frypan, toaster, blkts, doonas, linen, pillows], w/mach, dryer, iron, iron brd, ice box, bbq, secure park, cots. **W $1,090 - $2,190**, BC MC VI.

(Vagabond Houseboat), 1 houseboat acc up to 10, (4 bedrm), [shwr, tlt (2), a/c-cool, heat, TV, video, radio, refrig, cook fac, micro, blkts, linen, pillows], w/mach, ice box, bbq. **W $1,180 - $1,990.**

Captain Cook Cruises - Murray Princess, (Cruiser), Previously Murray Princess Mooring at Mannum Wharf, ☎ 02 9206 1144, fax 02 9206 1178, 60 cruisers acc up to 3, (1 bedrm), [ensuite, a/c, elec blkts], lift, lounge, ☒, bar, sauna, spa, t/c mkg shared, c/park ($25 to $35). **D all meals ♦♦ $390 - $540, ♦♦ $925 - $1,285**, AE BC DC MC VI.

Galaxy Houseboat, (Hbt), 140 River La, 2km S of PO, ☎ 08 8569 2622, fax 08 8569 2872, 3 houseboats acc up to 12, [shwr (2), tlt (2), a/c-cool, heat, tel, TV, video, radio, CD, refrig, cook fac, micro, d/wash (1), blkts, linen, pillows], w/mach (2), ice box, bbq. **W $515 - $3,245**, BC MC VI.

Harmony Houseboats, (Hbt), River La, ☎ 08 8569 3032, fax 08 8569 3036, 2 houseboats acc up to 4, [a/c-cool, heat, tel, TV, video, radio, CD, refrig, cook fac, micro, d/wash, blkts, linen, pillows], ice box, bbq. **W $924 - $1,155**, Min book applies, BC MC VI.

Kia Magic Houseboat, (Hbt), Younghusband Rd, Kia Marina, 9km NE of PO, ☎ 08 8289 0117, fax 08 8288 7072, 1 houseboat acc up to 8, (3 bedrm), [shwr, tlt (2), a/c-cool, heat, TV, video, radio, CD, refrig, cook fac, blkts, linen, pillows], w/mach, ice box, bbq. **W $869 - $1,573.**

Kia Mist Houseboat, (Hbt), Younghusband Rd, Kia Marina, 9km NE of PO, ☎ 08 8389 7441, fax 08 8389 7441, 1 houseboat acc up to 12, (5 bedrm), [shwr (2), tlt (2), a/c-cool, heat, TV, video, refrig, cook fac, micro, d/wash, blkts, linen, pillows], w/mach, bbq. **W $1,595 - $2,475.**

Memories Houseboat, (Hbt), Younghusband Rd, Kia Marina, 9km NE of PO, ☎ 08 8569 2029, fax 08 8569 2029, 1 houseboat acc up to 8, (3 bedrm), [shwr (2), tlt (2), a/c-cool, heat, tel, TV, video, radio (cassette), CD, refrig, cook fac, micro, d/wash, toaster, blkts, linen, pillows], w/mach, ice box, bbq, **W $825 - $1,750**, ch con, Min book applies, BC MC VI.

Misty Houseboats, (Hbt), Younghusband Rd, Kia Marina, 9km NE of PO, ☎ 08 8251 3652, fax 08 8251 3652, 2 houseboats acc up to 12, (2 bedrm6 bedrm), [shwr, tlt, a/c-cool (1), heat, TV, video, CD (1), refrig, cook fac, micro (1), d/wash (1), ldry (in unit) (1), blkts, linen, pillows], w/mach (1), dryer (1), iron, iron brd, bbq, secure park, cots. **W $710 - $2,600**, Min book applies.

Sandinit Houseboat, (Hbt), Younghusband Rd, Kia Marina, 9km NE of PO, ☎ 08 8298 2462, 1 houseboat acc up to 8, [a/c-cool, heat, TV, video, radio, CD, refrig, cook fac, micro, blkts, linen, pillows], bbq. **W $990 - $1,650.**

Sharalyn-Too Houseboat, (Hbt), 66 River La, 500m SW of PO, ☎ 08 8569 1875, 3 houseboats acc up to 8, [shwr, tlt, a/c-cool, heat, TV, video, radio (cassette), CD, refrig, cook fac, micro, blkts, linen, pillows], bbq. **W $725 - $1,190.**

Tamba Houseboat, (Hbt), Younghusband Rd, Kia Marina, ☎ 08 8569 1175, fax 08 8569 1175, 1 houseboat acc up to 4, [shwr, spa bath (full size), tlt, a/c-cool, c/fan, heat, TV, video (movies avail), CD, t/c mkg, refrig, cook fac, micro, blkts, doonas, linen, pillows]. **D $810 - $1,290**, Min book applies.

Unforgettable Houseboats, (Hbt), 69 River La, ☎ 08 8569 2559, fax 08 8569 2822, 7 houseboats acc up to 12, (3,4,5 & 6 bedrm), [shwr, spa bath, a/c-cool (ducted), heat, TV, video, CD, refrig, cook fac, micro, d/wash, blkts, linen, pillows], w/mach, dryer, bbq. **W $1,090 - $2,925**, Child restraint fencing. Min book applies, AE BC DC EFT MC VI.

Wanderer Houseboat, (Hbt), Younghusband Rd, Kia Marina, 9km NE of PO, ☎ 08 8298 2122, fax 08 8298 2627, 1 houseboat acc up to 10, [shwr, tlt (2), a/c-cool, heat, TV, video, CD, refrig (2), cook fac, micro, blkts, linen, pillows], w/mach, bbq, shade. **W $990 - $1,760**, Min book applies.

MARION BAY SA 5575

Pop Nominal, (265km W Adelaide), See map on pages 586/587, ref G6. Located on the Yorke Peninsula the area is popular with fishermen. Boat Ramp, Boating, Fishing, Surfing, Swimming (Beach).

Self Catering Accommodation

★★★ **Marion Bay Holiday Villas**, (HU), Cnr Waratah & Templetonia Stst, 1km W of PO, ☎ 08 8278 5635, fax 08 8278 5635, 8 units acc up to 5, (1 & 2 bedrm), [shwr, tlt, a/c, TV, clock radio, refrig, cook fac, micro, elec frypan, toaster, linen reqd-fee] ldry, w/mach, iron, iron brd, bbq, cots, D ♥♥ **$94**, ▲ **$10**, ch con, BC MC VI, ⅄⅃.

★★★ **Marion Bay Seaside Apartments**, (HU), Lot 98, Stenhouse Bay Rd, ☎ 08 8339 1909, fax 08 8339 1910, 5 units acc up to 5, (2 bedrm), [shwr, tlt, a/c, cable tv, clock radio (cassette), refrig, cook fac, micro, elec frypan, toaster, linen], ldry, w/mach, bbq, D ♥♥♥♥ **$60 - $100**, ▲ **$10**, ch con, Min book applies, BC DC EFT MC VI.

MARLA SA 5723

Pop 243. (1099km NW Adelaide), See map on pages 586/587, ref E1. Located on the Stuart Hwy, a small town acting as a travellers service centre. Mintabie opal fields are 35km W (permit required to visit Mintabie, from Marla Police). Gem Fossicking, Swimming (Pool).

Hotels/Motels

★★☆ **Marla Travellers Rest Hotel Motel**, (LMH), Stuart Hwy, ☎ 08 8670 7001, fax 08 8670 7021, 49 units [ensuite, a/c, heat, tel (10), TV (20), t/c mkg], ldry, conv fac, ⊠, bbq, cots-fee. RO ▲ **$70 - $95**, ♥♥ **$70 - $95**, ▲ **$5**, AE BC DC EFT MC VI, ⅄⅃.

MEADOWS SA 5201

Pop 528. (35km SSE Adelaide), See map on page 588, ref E7. A small township with grazing and dairy farms, orchards and apiaries in the area. Historical Museum, Kuitpo State Forest, Paris Creek Pottery & Thimbella, Rose Meadow and the Silly Galah Gallery. Bowls, Tennis, Water Skiing.

Self Catering Accommodation

★★★★ **French-ip Cottage**, (Cotg), Cnr Goolwa Rd & Bald Hill Rd, 7km S of PO, ☎ 08 8536 6013, 1 cotg acc up to 4, (1 bedrm - split level.), [shwr, spa bath, tlt, a/c, heat (open fire), elec blkts, TV, video, clock radio, t/c mkg, refrig, cook fac ltd, micro, toaster, ldry (in unit), blkts, doonas, linen, pillows], dryer, iron, iron brd, bbq, c/park (carport), breakfast ingredients, non smoking property. D ♥♥ **$130**, ▲ **$65**.

★★★ **Chamel Fields Farm Stay**, (Cotg), Blackfellows Creek Rd, 6km S of Prospect Hill PO, ☎ 08 8556 7442, fax 08 8556 7442, 1 cotg acc up to 5, (2 bedrm), [shwr, bath, tlt, evap cool, heat (pot belly), elec blkts, TV, t/c mkg, refrig, cook fac, micro, elec frypan, toaster, blkts, doonas, linen, pillows], spa (outdoor), bbq, breakfast ingredients, non smoking property. D ♥♥ **$120 - $200**, ▲ **$40 - $80**, W ♥♥ **$660 - $1,000**, ▲ **$280 - $560**, ch con.

MELROSE SA 5483

Pop 205. (269km N Adelaide), See map on pages 586/587, ref H5. The oldest town in the Flinders Ranges nestled at the foot of Mt Remarkable. Town Heritage Walk, National Trust Police/Courthouse Complex, antiques, art & crafts, blacksmith shop, bushwalking, Heysen & Mawson Trail. Bowls, Bush Walking, Golf, Horse Riding, Tennis.

Self Catering Accommodation

★★★ **Melrose Holiday Units**, (HU), Whitbey St, ☎ 08 8666 2199, fax 08 8666 2299, 6 units acc up to 4, (2 bedrm), [shwr, bath (hip) (5), tlt, a/c, elec blkts, TV, radio, refrig, cook fac, blkts, linen, pillows], ldry, cots-fee. D ▲ **$60**, ♥♥ **$69**, ▲ **$16**, ch con, BC MC VI, ⅄⅃.

★★★ **Mount Remarkable Cottage**, (Cotg), Diocesan Rd, 4km N of PO, ☎ 08 8666 2171, 1 cotg acc up to 7, [shwr, tlt, hairdry, a/c, elec blkts, TV, clock radio, t/c mkg, refrig, cook fac, micro, toaster, blkts, doonas, linen, pillows], lounge firepl, bbq, c/park. D ♥♥ **$65**, ▲ **$10**, W ♥♥ **$350**, ▲ **$55**, AE BC DC EFT MC VI.

B&B's/Guest Houses

★★★★ **Bluey Blundstones Blacksmith Shop B&B**, (B&B), 30-32 Stuart St, ☎ 08 8666 2173, fax 08 8666 2173, 2 rms [ensuite (1), shwr, bath (1), tlt, hairdry, c/fan (1), heat, elec blkts, TV (1), t/c mkg, refrig], bathrm, ldry, bbq, non smoking rms, BB ▲ **$77**, ♥♥ **$95**, ▲ **$42**, ch con, 1 room of a lower rating, AE BC DC MC VI.

MENINGIE SA 5264

Pop 818. (152km SE Adelaide), See map on pages 586/587, ref C8. Small town situated on the shores of Lake Albert known as the Gateway to the Coorong. Boating, Bowls, Bush Walking, Canoeing, Croquet, Fishing, Golf, Sailing, Swimming (Lake & River), Tennis, Water Skiing.

Hotels/Motels

★★★ **Lake Albert Motel**, (M), 38 Princes Hwy, ☎ 08 8575 1077, fax 08 8575 1780, 12 units [ensuite, a/c, elec blkts, tel, TV, clock radio, t/c mkg, refrig], ⊠ (Mon-Sat), rm serv, dinner to unit, cots-fee. RO ▲ **$61**, ♥♥ **$71**, ▲ **$11**, ch con, AE BC DC MC VI.

 ★★ Meningies Waterfront Motel, (M), Princes Hwy, 2km N of PO, ☎ 08 8575 1152, fax 08 8575 0026, 10 units [ensuite, fan, heat, elec blkts, TV, t/c mkg, refrig], ldry, ⊠, bbq, cots. RO ▲ **$40 - $50**, ♥♥ **$45 - $55**, ▲ **$10**, ch con, Function Centre. AE BC DC EFT MC VI, ⅄⅃.

Meningie Hotel, (LH), 62 Princes Hwy, ☎ 08 8575 1007, fax 08 8575 1670, (2 stry), 8 rms [basin (7), a/c (3), c/fan, elec blkts], lounge (TV), ⊠, t/c mkg shared, refrig, ☎, cots. BLB ▲ **$30**, ♥♥ **$49.50**, ▲ **$15**, AE BC DC MC VI.

Self Catering Accommodation

★★★☆ **Mill Park Cottage**, (Cotg), Yumali Rd, 2km N of PO, ☎ 08 8575 6033, fax 08 8575 6033, 1 cotg acc up to 6, (3 bedrm), [shwr, spa bath, tlt, fan (avail), heat, elec blkts, tel, TV, clock radio, refrig, cook fac, toaster, ldry (in unit), blkts, linen, pillows], bbq, breakfast ingredients. D ♥♥ **$120**, ▲ **$25**.

★★★ **Sunset Lodge Cottage**, (Cotg), Princes Hwy, 34km S of PO, ☎ 08 8575 7035, fax 08 8575 7035, 1 cotg acc up to 10, (5 bedrm), [shwr (2), bath (1), tlt (2), a/c, heat (slow combustion), elec blkts, TV, clock radio, refrig, cook fac, toaster, blkts, linen, pillows], ldry, w/mach, bbq, non smoking property. BB ♥♥ **$82.50**, BLB ♥♥ **$77**, RO ▲ **$44**, ♥♥ **$66**, ▲ **$11 - $22**, ch con.

MIDDLETON SA 5213

Pop 395. (88km S Adelaide), See map on pages 586/587, ref C8. A small coastal township and centre for the surrounding agricultural district. A popular, quiet holiday destination, it has a renowned surfing beach. Fishing, Surfing, Swimming (Beach), Tennis, Vineyards, Wineries.

Self Catering Accommodation

★★★ **Wenton Farm Holiday Cottage**, (Cotg), Burgar Rd, 5km N of PO, ☎ 08 8555 4126, fax 08 8555 4126, 1 cotg acc up to 4, [shwr, tlt, a/c, elec blkts, TV, clock radio, t/c mkg, refrig, cook fac, micro, toaster, blkts, doonas, linen, pillows], bbq, D ♥♥ **$70 - $80**, ▲ **$5 - $10**, W ♥♥ **$420 - $480**, ▲ **$30 - $60**, ch con.

B&B's/Guest Houses

★★★★☆ **Seachange Bed & Breakfast**, (GH), No children's facilities, 48 Goolwa Rd, ☎ 08 8554 3243, fax 08 8554 2438, (2 stry), 3 rms [shwr, bath, tlt, hairdry, fan, heat, cent heat, elec blkts, fax, clock radio, doonas], ldry, w/mach, dryer, iron, iron brd, lounge (TV), lounge firepl, t/c mkg shared, refrig, non smoking property, BB ♥♥ **$170**, Third night free. Min book applies, BC MC VI.

★★★☆ **Warrawee Farmstay Bed & Breakfast**, (B&B), Old Telegraph Rd, 4km NW of PO, ☎ 08 8554 2496, fax 08 8554 2496, 3 rms [elec blkts], lounge (TV), ✗, t/c mkg shared, bbq, c/park (undercover). BB ▲ **$70**, ♥♥ **$105**, ch con, pen con, BC MC VI.

MIDDLE RIVER SA

See Kangaroo Island Region.

MILANG SA 5256

Pop 352. (73km SE Adelaide), See map on pages 586/587, ref C8. Located on the shores of Lake Alexandrina a popular holiday area. Historical Railway Station. Boating, Bowls, Fishing, Swimming (Lake), Tennis.

Hotels/Motels

★★★ **Milang Lakes Motel**, (M), 5 Daranda Tce, ☎ 08 8537 0090, fax 08 8537 0404, 12 units [shwr, tlt, a/c, elec blkts, tel, TV, clock radio, t/c mkg, refrig, cook fac (avail), micro (4), toaster], ldry, w/mach, iron, iron brd, bbq, non smoking units (12). BLB ▲ **$60**, ♥♥ **$66**, ▲ **$17**, ch con, BC MC VI.

MILLICENT SA 5280

Pop 5,118. (404km SE Adelaide), See map on pages 586/587, ref J8. The centre of a prosperous pastoral area and gateway to the pine forests of the South East. National Trust Museum, Millicent Art Gallery and the Tantanoola Caves. Bowls, Croquet, Golf, Horse Riding, Squash, Swimming (Lake), Tennis.

Hotels/Motels

★★★ **Diplomat Motel**, (M), 51 Mount Gambier Rd, ☎ 08 8733 2211, fax 08 8733 4134, 30 units [shwr, tlt, a/c, elec blkts, tel, TV, clock radio, t/c mkg, refrig], conf fac, ☒, pool, sauna, rm serv, plygr, cots-fee, non smoking units (2). **RO 👤 $55 - $66, 👥 $60.50 - $71.50, 🧒 $11**, ch con, fam con, 10 rms ★★★☆. AE BC DC EFT MC VI, ♿.

★★☆ **Somerset Hotel Motel**, (LMH), 2-4 George St, ☎ 08 8733 2888, fax 08 8733 2544, 21 units [shwr, tlt, a/c, elec blkts, tel, TV, t/c mkg, refrig], conf fac, ☒, meals to unit (by arrangement), ✆, cots-fee. **RO 👤 $33 - $60.50, 👥 $49.50 - $77, 🧒 $11**, 7 single rms not rated. AE BC EFT MC VI.

Millicent Motel, (M), 82 Mt Gambier Rd, ☎ 08 8733 1044, fax 08 8733 3905, 17 units (7 suites) [shwr, tlt, a/c, c/fan, heat (elec), elec blkts, tel, TV, clock radio, t/c mkg, refrig, toaster, doonas], ldry, ☒, bbq, meals to unit, ✆, plygr, cots-fee, non smoking rms (10). **BB 👤 $55 - $59, 👥 $59 - $69, 🧒 $10, Suite BB 👥 $99 - $120**, ch con, AE BC EFT MC VI, (not yet classified).

MINLATON SA 5575

Pop 796. (184km W Adelaide), See map on pages 586/587, ref A7. Commercial centre for the surrounding barley, wheat and grazing districts of the Yorke Peninsula. Captain Harry Butler Memorial, Galleries, Jollys Vintage Tractors & Engines and the National Trust Museum. Bowls, Golf, Tennis.

B&B's/Guest Houses

★★★☆ **Yurla Bed & Breakfast**, (B&B), 4 Main St, 400m N of PO, ☎ 08 8853 2213, fax 08 8853 2213, 3 rms [fan, heat, elec blkts], t/c mkg shared, meals avail (by arrangement), non smoking property. **BB 👤 $65 - $85, 👥 $115.**

MINNIPA SA 5654

Pop 191. (616km NW Adelaide), See map on pages 586/587, ref F5. Known as the gateway to the Gawler Ranges. Small service centre for the surrounding community, with the main crops being wheat and barley. Scenic Drives, Swimming (Pool).

Hotels/Motels

★★☆ **Minnipa Hotel Motel**, (LMH), Railway Tce, ☎ 08 8680 5005, fax 08 8680 5071, 8 units [ensuite, a/c, elec blkts, cable tv, video (1), movie, clock radio, t/c mkg, refrig, toaster], ldry, conv fac, ☒, rm serv, ✆, cots-fee. **RO 👤 $50 - $60, 👥 $65 - $74, 🧒 $8**, ch con, pen con, 2 units of a higher standard. AE BC DC EFT MC VI.

★☆ **(Hotel Section)**, 14 rms [basin (1), ensuite (1), a/c (1), c/fan, elec blkts, t/c mkg (2), refrig (4)]. **RO 👤 $26, 👥 $45, 🧒 $5**, ch con, pen con.

MINTARO SA 5415

Pop Nominal, (130km N Adelaide), See map on pages 586/587, ref C6. Located in the Mid North, near Clare. Martindale Hall and Mintaro Cellars. Scenic Drives, Vineyards, Wineries.

Self Catering Accommodation

★★★★☆ **Devonshire House**, (Apt), Heritage, Circa 1856. Burra St, ☎ 08 8843 9058, fax 08 8269 2876, 4 apts acc up to 4, (1 & 2 bedrm), [shwr, spa bath, tlt, a/c, fire pl, elec blkts, TV, video, clock radio, refrig, cook fac, micro, doonas], ldry, w/mach, dryer, iron, iron brd, bbq, ✆, breakfast ingredients. **D 👥 $135 - $155**, BC MC VI.

★★★★ **Blenheim Bed and Breakfast**, (House), Previously Blenheim Country House Leasingham Rd, ☎ 08 8843 0187, fax 08 8843 0177, 1 house acc up to 6, [shwr, bath, tlt, c/fan, heat, elec blkts, tel, TV, video, clock radio, CD, t/c mkg, refrig, cook fac, micro, elec frypan, d/wash, toaster, blkts, doonas, linen, pillows], w/mach, iron, iron brd, lounge firepl, breakfast ingredients. **D 👥 $150, 👥👤 $210, 👥👥 $240**, AE BC MC VI.

★★★★ **Mintaro Country Cottages**, (Cotg), Mintaro Rd, 2km S of PO, ☎ 0418 808 704, fax 08 8843 9085, 1 cotg acc up to 6, (2 bedrm), [shwr, tlt, a/c-cool, fan, fire pl, heat, tel, TV, refrig, cook fac, ldry (in unit), blkts, linen, pillows], bbq, cots, breakfast ingredients. **D 👥 $132, 🧒 $55**, ch con, Min book applies.

Mintaro Country Cottages ...continued

★★★☆ **(The Croft)**, 1 cotg acc up to 2, (1 bedrm), [shwr, tlt, a/c-cool, fan, fire pl, elec blkts, TV, video, clock radio, t/c mkg, refrig, cook fac, micro, elec frypan, toaster, blkts, linen, pillows], cots, breakfast ingredients. **D 👥 $132.**

(Peppertree Cottage), 1 cotg acc up to 6, (3 bedrm), [shwr, tlt, a/c-cool, fan, elec blkts, tel, TV, clock radio, t/c mkg, refrig, cook fac, micro, elec frypan, toaster, blkts, linen, pillows], lounge firepl, cots, breakfast ingredients. **D 👥 $132, 🧒 $55**, ch con, (not yet classified).

★★★☆ **Mintaro Hideaway**, (Apt), Circa 1856. Burra St, 200m SW of PO, ☎ 08 8843 9011, fax 08 8332 6062, 3 apts acc up to 4, (1 & 2 bedrm), [shwr, spa bath, tlt, a/c, heat (slow combustion), elec blkts, TV, video, clock radio, refrig, cook fac, micro, doonas], ldry, w/mach, dryer, iron, iron brd, bbq, c/park (undercover) (2), ✆, breakfast ingredients, non smoking property. **D 👥 $135 - $145, 🧒 $55**, 1 cottage of a higer standard. BC MC VI.

★★★☆ **Mintaro Pay Office Cottages**, (Cotg), Historic Accommodation. Hill St, ☎ 08 8843 9013, fax 08 8843 9013, 4 cotgs acc up to 6, [shwr, tlt, hairdry (1), a/c, fan, heat (open fire), elec blkts, TV, radio, refrig, cook fac, micro (1), blkts, linen, pillows], ldry, cots. **D 👥 $130, 🧒 $30**, BTC MC VI.

★★★☆ **Oldfields Colonial Accommodation**, (Cotg), Circa 1850. National Trust & State Heritage. No children's facilities, Young St, ☎ 08 8843 9038, 3 cotgs acc up to 4, (1 & 2 bedrm), [shwr, tlt, a/c (1), fan, fire pl (3), heat, elec blkts, TV, radio, t/c mkg, refrig, cook fac, toaster, ldry (in unit) (1), blkts, linen, pillows], w/mach (1), dryer (1), iron, breakfast ingredients. **D 👥 $125 - $150, 🧒 $80**, BC MC VI.

★★★ **Mintaro Heritage Accommodation**, (Cotg), The Old Post Office Residence, Circa 1884. 2 Burra St, ☎ 08 8843 9021, fax 08 8843 9292, 1 cotg acc up to 10, (4 bedrm), [shwr, bath, tlt (2), elec blkts, tel, TV, t/c mkg, refrig, cook fac, micro, toaster, ldry (in unit), blkts, linen, pillows], w/mach, iron, iron brd, lounge firepl, bbq, breakfast ingredients, non smoking rms, Pets on application. **D $100 - $330**, ch con, BC MC VI.

★★ **Millers House**, (Cotg), Cnr Young & Church Sts, 500m NW of PO, ☎ 08 8271 6601, fax 08 8274 1182, 1 cotg acc up to 8, (3 bedrm), [shwr, tlt, fire pl, elec blkts, clock radio, refrig, cook fac, blkts, linen, pillows], breakfast ingredients. **D $130 - $350**, ch con, Min book applies.

B&B's/Guest Houses

★★★★ **Mintaro Heritage Accommodation**, (B&B), The Old Manse, Circa 1859. No children's facilities, Cnr Hill & Stein Sts, 400m W of PO, ☎ 08 8843 9021, fax 08 8843 9292, 4 rms [ensuite (2), heat, elec blkts, TV, clock radio], shared fac (2), ldry, w/mach, dryer, iron, iron brd, lounge (TV), lounge firepl, spa, t/c mkg shared, bbq, non smoking rms. **BB 👤 $75 - $90, 👥 $115 - $145**, 2 rms ★★★☆. BC MC VI.

★★★☆ **Martindale Hall**, (B&B), Historic Building. Manoora Rd, 2km SE of PO, ☎ 08 8843 9088, fax 08 8843 9082, (2 stry), 6 rms [fan (avail), heat, elec blkts, t/c mkg], rec rm, lounge (video), ✕, t/c mkg shared, refrig, non smoking rms. **BB 👤 $71, 👥 $142, DBB 👤 $137 - $159, 👥 $274 - $318**, BC MC VI.

★★★☆ **Mintaro Mews Guest House**, (GH), Historic Building. No children's facilities, Burra St, ☎ 08 8843 9001, fax 08 8843 9002, (2 stry gr fl), 10 rms [ensuite, a/c (2), heat, elec blkts, clock radio, t/c mkg, refrig (7)], ldry, w/mach, dryer, iron, iron brd, lounge (TV & video), conv fac, ☒, pool indoor heated, spa, bbq, ✆. **BB 👤 $120, 👥 $135, 🧒 $40**, AE BC DC MC VI.

MOONTA SA 5558

Pop 2,723. (167km NW Adelaide), See map on pages 586/587, ref A6. Situated on the Yorke Peninsula, the town grew after the discovery of copper. The miners were mainly Cornishmen and their skills at building are still very much in evidence today. Hughes Pump House, Miners Cottage & Heritage Garden, Moonta Mines Public School Museum and Moonta Mines Tourist Railway. Boating, Bowls, Croquet, Fishing, Golf, Swimming (Beach & Pool).

Hotels/Motels

★★☆ **Moonta Bay Patio Motel**, (M), 196 Bay Rd, 2km W of PO, ☎ 08 8825 2473, fax 08 8825 2566, 18 units [ensuite, a/c, elec blkts, tel, TV, t/c mkg, refrig, doonas], iron (avail), iron brd (avail), ☒ (Mon to Sat), rm serv, cots-fee. **RO 👤 $66 - $71.50, 👥 $77 - $82.50, 🧒 $5.50 - $10.50**, Min book all holiday times, AE BC DC EFT MC VI.

★☆ **Cornwall Hotel**, (LH), 20 Ryan St, ☎ 08 8825 2304, fax 08 8825 2304, (2 stry), 10 rms [basin, a/c (5), c/fan (2), elec blkts, t/c mkg], lounge (TV), ☒, t/c mkg shared, refrig, cots. **BLB 👤 $29, 👥 $49, 👥👤 $69, 🧒 $16**, AE BC DC EFT MC VI.

Self Catering Accommodation

★★★★ **Cliff House Beachfront Villas**, (Apt), 2 Hughes Ave, 3km W of PO, ☎ 08 8825 3055, fax 08 8825 3112, 4 apts acc up to 8, [shwr (2), bath (2), spa bath (2), tlt (2), a/c, tel, cable tv, video, t/c mkg, refrig, micro, d/wash, doonas, linen, pillows], w/mach, dryer, **RO 👥 $160, 🧒 $10**, seasonal variation.

★★★★ **Moonta Heritage Cottages**, (Cotg), 74 George St, 1km W of Town Centre, ☎ 0417 890 573, fax 08 8642 2459, 1 cotg acc up to 4, [shwr, spa bath, tlt, a/c, c/fan, elec blkts, TV, video, clock radio, t/c mkg, refrig, cook fac, micro, toaster, blkts, doonas, linen, pillows], iron, iron brd, lounge firepl, bbq, c/park (garage), non smoking rms. D ♙♙ **$88 - $110**, ♙ **$44**, W ♙♙ **$495 - $550**, ♙ **$110**, Min book Christmas Jan long w/ends and Easter.

B&B's/Guest Houses
★★★★ **Peppertree Cottage**, (B&B), 85 Wallaroo Rd, 2km N of PO, ☎ 08 8825 2680, 1 rm [shwr, bath, tlt, hairdry, a/c, c/fan, elec blkts, TV, video, clock radio, t/c mkg, refrig, cook fac ltd, micro, toaster, doonas, pillows], iron, iron brd, cots, non smoking property.
BLB ♙ **$75 - $100**, ♙♙ **$100 - $110**, ♙ **$15**.

MOOROOK SA 5332

Pop 215. (221km E Adelaide), See map on pages 586/587, ref E6. Small settlement on the Murray River supported mainly by two citrus packaging factories. Bowls, Tennis.

Self Catering Accommodation
★★★★ **Orchard River Holidays**, (Cotg), Previously Orchard River Cottages, Main Loxton Road, 500m N of PO, ☎ 08 8583 9211, fax 08 8583 9211, 2 cotgs acc up to 6, (2 bedrm), [shwr, tlt, a/c, elec blkts, TV, video, clock radio, t/c mkg, refrig, cook fac, micro, toaster, ldry (in unit), blkts, linen, pillows], w/mach, iron, iron brd, bbq, plygr, tennis, cots, D ♙♙ **$77**, ♙ **$16.50**, Min book applies.
★★☆ **Yatco Holiday Cabins**, Loxton Rd, 5km S of PO, ☎ 08 8583 9247, fax 08 8583 9247, 2 cabins acc up to 6, [shwr, tlt, a/c, TV, refrig, cook fac, blkts, linen, pillows], bbq, Pets allowed. D ♙♙ **$45**, ♙ **$10**, ch con, fam con, Min book applies.

MORGAN SA 5320

Pop 446. (165km NE Adelaide), See map on pages 586/587, ref D6. Popular tourist area, the centre for local primary industries of wheat, sheep & fruit growing. Carmines Antiques, Glass Space Gallery, Port of Morgan Museum, Pumping Station & Water Filtration Plant. Boating, Bowls, Bush Walking, Fishing, Gem Fossicking, Golf, Shooting, Swimming (River), Tennis, Water Skiing.

Hotels/Motels
★ **Terminus Hotel Motel**, (LMH), Railway Tce, ☎ 08 8540 2006, fax 08 8540 2006, 6 units [ensuite, a/c, elec blkts, TV, t/c mkg, refrig], ☒, cots. RO ♙ **$45**, ♙♙ **$50**, ♙ **$10**, AE BC EFT MC VI, ♿.
Commercial Hotel, (LH), Railway Tce, ☎ 08 8540 2107, fax 08 8540 2044, (2 stry), 9 rms [a/c-cool, elec blkts], rec rm, lounge (TV), conf fac, ☒, cots. RO ♙ **$25**, ♙♙ **$50**, ♙ **$10**, fam con, BC EFT MC VI.

Other Accommodation
Houseboat Hire - Kanandah at Morgan, (Hbt), Koala Marina, ☎ 08 8338 2426, fax 08 8338 2426, 1 houseboat acc up to 12, (5 bedrm), [shwr, bath, tlt (2), a/c-cool, cent heat, tel, TV, video, movie, clock radio, t/c mkg, refrig, micro, d/wash, ldry, blkts, doonas, linen, pillows], w/mach, dryer. W **$1,350 - $2,350**, VI, (not yet classified).
Albatross Houseboat, (Hbt), 1km SE of PO, ☎ 08 8540 2257, 1 houseboat acc up to 8, [shwr, tlt, heat, TV, video, radio, refrig, cook fac, micro], bbq. W **$800 - $1,290**.
Why Not Houseboat, (Hbt), 200m SE of PO, ☎ 08 8532 5453, 1 houseboat acc up to 10, (4 bedrm), [shwr, tlt (2), a/c-cool, heat, TV, radio, CD, refrig, cook fac, micro, linen reqd-fee], bbq. W **$890 - $1,890**, Dinghy available.

MOUNT BARKER SA 5251

Pop 6,239. (35km E Adelaide), See map on pages 586/587, ref C7. The main town of the Adelaide Hills, among the first Hills settlements to be founded and now a large District Council centre. Bowls, Croquet, Golf, Swimming (Pool), Tennis.

Hotels/Motels
Hotel Barker, (LH), 22 Gawler St, ☎ 08 8391 1003, fax 08 8391 0390, 13 rms shwr, tlt, ☒, ☏. RO ♙ **$25**, ♙♙ **$40**, ♙ **$5**, BC EFT MC VI.

Self Catering Accommodation
★★★★ **Parkindula Cottage**, (Cotg), Lot 14 Wellington Rd, 3km SE of PO, ☎ 08 8389 7200, fax 08 8389 7524, 1 cotg acc up to 4, [shwr, bath, tlt, hairdry, a/c, TV, video, clock radio, CD, t/c mkg, refrig, cook fac, micro, toaster, blkts, doonas, linen, pillows], iron, iron brd, bbq, breakfast ingredients, non smoking property, D ♙♙ **$140**, ♙ **$30**, W ♙♙ **$650**, ch con, Min book applies.

★★★ **Willowbank Cottage**, (Cotg), Junction Rd, Littlehampton 5250, 1km N of PO, ☎ 08 8398 3364, 1 cotg acc up to 2, (1 bedrm), [shwr, tlt, fan, heat, elec blkts, TV, clock radio, t/c mkg, refrig, cook fac, elec frypan, toaster, blkts, linen, pillows], bbq, cots, breakfast ingredients. D ♙♙ **$95**.

MOUNT COMPASS SA 5210

Pop 310. (59km S Adelaide), See map on pages 586/587, ref B8. A small dairying community on the Fleurieu Peninsula. Bakehouse Gallery, Polana Deer Farm Park, Tooperang Rainbow Trout Farm and Mt Magnificent Farm. Art Gallery, Boating, Fishing, Golf.

Self Catering Accommodation
★★☆ **Compass Country Cabins**, Lot 8 Cleland Gully Rd, 3km S of PO, ☎ 08 8556 8425, 3 cabins acc up to 4, [shwr, tlt, a/c (2), TV, radio, refrig, cook fac ltd, micro, toaster, blkts, linen, pillows], w/mach (2), canoeing, Pets on application. D ♙♙ **$77 - $88**, ♙♙♙♙ **$88 - $110**, W ♙♙ **$300**.
★★☆ **Helgas Hideaway Cottage**, (Cotg), Cleland Gully Rd, ☎ 08 8556 8240, fax 08 8556 8240, 1 cotg acc up to 4, (2 bedrm), [shwr, tlt, hairdry, elec blkts, clock radio, t/c mkg, refrig, cook fac, toaster, blkts, linen, pillows], lounge firepl, bbq, c/park (carport), cots. D ♙♙ **$120**, ♙ **$10**.

MOUNT GAMBIER SA 5290

Pop 21,155. (30km Donovans) (439km SE Adelaide), See map on pages 586/587, ref J8. Modern city built on the slopes of an extinct volcano. The volcano has three craters, the main one containing the Blue Lake. The Crater Lakes and walking trails, Caves, Wineries, Museums, Lookouts and Galleries. Boating, Bowls, Bush Walking, Croquet, Fishing, Golf, Horse Racing, Horse Riding, Squash, Surfing, Swimming (Beach, Lake & Pool), Tennis, Trotting, Water Skiing.

Hotels/Motels
★★★★ **Commodore Motel**, (M), 1 Jubilee Hwy East, ☎ 08 8724 9666, fax 08 8725 8772, 53 units [shwr, spa bath (4), tlt, hairdry, a/c, elec blkts, tel, cable tv, video-fee, clock radio, t/c mkg, refrig, mini bar], ldry-fee, w/mach, dryer, iron, iron brd, conf fac, ☒, pool indoor heated, spa, rm serv, dinner to unit, cots, non smoking rms. RO ♙ **$80 - $125**, ♙♙ **$80 - $125**, ♙ **$10**, 21 rooms ★★★☆, AE BC DC EFT MC VI, ♿.

 ★★★★ **Mount Gambier International Motel**, (M), Millicent Rd, 5km NW of PO, ☎ 08 8725 9699, fax 08 8725 0843, 60 units [ensuite, bath (6), spa bath (3), hairdry, a/c, elec blkts, tel, TV, clock radio, t/c mkg, refrig], ldry-fee, conv fac, ☒, pool indoor heated, sauna, spa, rm serv, plygr, tennis, cots, non smoking units (21). RO ♙ **$91 - $112**, ♙♙ **$103 - $112**, ♙ **$12**, AE BC DC EFT MC MP VI.

 ★★★★ **Quality Inn Presidential**, (M), Jubilee Hwy West, 1km W of PO, ☎ 08 8724 9966, fax 08 8724 9975, 53 units [ensuite, bath, spa bath (29), hairdry, a/c, elec blkts, tel, TV, clock radio, t/c mkg, refrig, mini bar], ldry, iron, iron brd, conf fac, ☒, pool indoor heated, sauna, spa, cots, non smoking units (15), RO ♙ **$92**, ♙♙ **$107**, ♙ **$15**, ch con, AE BC DC MC MP VI, ♿.

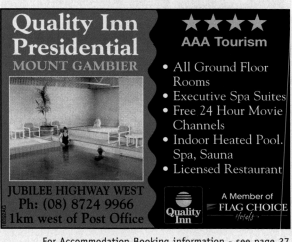

Quality Inn Presidential
MOUNT GAMBIER
★★★★ AAA Tourism
• All Ground Floor Rooms
• Executive Spa Suites
• Free 24 Hour Movie Channels
• Indoor Heated Pool. Spa, Sauna
• Licensed Restaurant

JUBILEE HIGHWAY WEST
Ph: (08) 8724 9966
1km west of Post Office
A Member of FLAG CHOICE Hotels

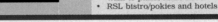

 ★★★★ **Southgate Motel**, (M), 175 Commercial St East, ☎ 08 8723 1175, fax 08 8723 1151, (2 stry gr fl), 52 units [ensuite, bath (23), spa bath (27), a/c, elec blkts, TV, video (27), clock radio, t/c mkg, refrig], ldry-fee, conf fac, ✕ (Mon to Sat), pool-heated, sauna, spa, rm serv, dinner to unit, cots-fee, non smoking rms (19). **RO** ╪ **$95 - $141,** ╫ **$106 - $152,** ╬ **$14,** ch con, AE BC DC EFT MC MP VI, 🅿☝.

 ★★★☆ **Arkana Motor Inn**, (M), 201 Commercial St East, 1.5km SE of PO, ☎ 08 8725 5823, fax 08 8725 6080, (2 stry gr fl), 20 units [ensuite, spa bath (1), hairdry, a/c-cool, heat, elec blkts, tel, cable tv, video-fee, clock radio, t/c mkg, refrig], pool indoor heated, spa, bbq, cots-fee, non smoking units (9). **RO** ╪ **$72 - $95,** ╫ **$77 - $105,** ╬ **$11,** AE BC DC EFT MC MP VI.

★★★☆ **(Terrace Apartments Section)**, 8 serv apts acc up to 5, (2 bedrm), [shwr, bath, spa bath, tlt, a/c-cool, heat, elec blkts, tel, cable tv, video-fee, clock radio, t/c mkg, refrig, cook fac, micro, ldry], pool indoor heated, spa, bbq, cots-fee. **RO** ╪ **$95,** ╫ **$120,** ╬ **$11.**

 ★★★☆ **Avalon Motel**, (M), 93 Gray St, 600m NE of PO, ☎ 08 8725 7200, fax 08 8725 9491, 22 units [ensuite, hairdry, a/c-cool (12), a/c (9), heat, elec blkts, tel, cable tv, clock radio, t/c mkg, refrig, mini bar, cook fac (1), micro (9), toaster], ldry-fee, iron, iron brd (16), pool indoor heated (solar), bbq, dinner to unit, plygr, cots-fee. **RO** ╪ **$55 - $60,** ╫ **$60 - $65,** ╬ **$12,** ch con, 6 units ★★★. AE BC DC EFT MC VI.

★★★☆ **(Serviced Apartment Section)**, 1 serv apt acc up to 8, (4 bedrm - 1x1d3twins), [shwr (2), tlt (2), a/c, elec blkts, TV, video, clock radio, t/c mkg, refrig, cook fac, micro, toaster, blkts, linen, pillows]. **D $110 - $180.**

★★★☆ **Lakes Resort Motel Mt Gambier**, (M), Previously Lakes Resort Mount Gambier Motel, 17 Lake Terrace West, ☎ 08 8725 5755, fax 08 8723 2710, 40 units [ensuite, spa bath (15), a/c, elec blkts, tel, TV, movie, clock radio, t/c mkg, refrig, mini bar (32)], ldry, w/mach-fee, dryer-fee, iron, iron brd, conf fac, ✕, pool indoor heated, sauna, spa, rm serv, gym, cots-fee. **RO** ╪ **$83 - $133,** ╫ **$89 - $140,** ╬ **$7,** ch con, 15 units ★★★★. AE BC DC MC VI.

 ★★★☆ **Mid City Motel**, (M), 15 Helen St, 100m SW of PO, ☎ 08 8725 7277, fax 08 8724 9650, 18 units [ensuite, hairdry, a/c, elec blkts, tel, TV, video-fee, t/c mkg, refrig, cook fac (9), toaster, ldry], iron, iron brd, bbq, cots-fee, non smoking units (4). **RO** ╪ **$65 - $125,** ╫ **$65 - $125,** ╬ **$11,** ch con, AE BC DC EFT MC VI.

 ★★★☆ **Motel Mt Gambier**, (M), 115 Penola Rd, 1.3km N of City, ☎ 08 8725 5800, fax 08 8725 8540, 32 units [ensuite, spa bath (1), a/c, elec blkts, tel, cable tv, movie, clock radio, t/c mkg, refrig, toaster], ldry-fee, ✕ (Mon-Fri), pool, bbq, rm serv, dinner to unit, cots-fee. **RO** ╪ **$54 - $61,** ╫ **$61 - $91,** ╬ **$11,** ch con, AE BC DC EFT MC MCH VI, 🅿☝.

 ★★★☆ **Red Carpet Motor Inn**, (M), 96 Jubilee Hwy East, 3km E of PO, ☎ 08 8725 4311, fax 08 8724 9659, (2 stry gr fl), 45 units [ensuite, hairdry, a/c, elec blkts, tel, TV, video-fee, clock radio, t/c mkg, refrig], ldry-fee, w/mach-fee, dryer-fee, ✕ (Mon to Sat), pool, spa, bbq, plygr, cots, non smoking units (21). **RO** ╪ **$80 - $99,** ╫ **$80 - $99,** ╬ **$11,** ch con, AE BC DC JCB MC MP VI.

 ★★★☆ **Silver Birch Motor Inn**, (M), Jubilee Hwy East, 1km E of PO, ☎ 08 8725 5122, fax 08 8724 9843, 42 units [ensuite, bath (6), spa bath (2), hairdry, a/c, elec blkts, tel, cable tv, video, clock radio, t/c mkg, refrig], ldry, iron, iron brd, conv fac, ✕ (Mon-Sat), pool indoor heated, bbq, rm serv, plygr, cots, non smoking units (4). **RO** ╪ **$88,** ╫ **$99,** ╬ **$11,** ch con, AE BC DC MC MP VI.

★★★☆ **The Barn Motel**, (M), Nelson Rd, 7km S of PO, ☎ 08 8726 8366, fax 08 8726 8333, 8 units [ensuite, a/c-cool, fan, elec blkts, tel, TV, video-fee, clock radio, t/c mkg, refrig], w/mach, dryer, iron, iron brd, cook fac, bbq, rm serv, plygr, tennis, cots, non smoking units, Pets on application. **BLB** ╪ **$65,** ╫ **$70,** ╬ **$5,** fam con, pen con, AE BC DC MC VI, 🅿☝.

★★★★☆ **(Apartment Section)**, 2 apts acc up to 6, (1 + 2 bedrm), [shwr, spa bath, tlt, hairdry, a/c-cool, elec blkts, tel, TV, video, clock radio, t/c mkg, refrig, cook fac, micro, toaster, linen], ldry, w/mach, dryer, iron, iron brd, non smoking units. **D** ╪ **$90 - $95,** ╫ **$115 - $120,** ╬ **$5 - $10,** fam con, pen con.

 ★★★ **Blue Lake Motel**, (M), Kennedy Ave, 2km E of TC, ☎ 08 8725 5211, fax 08 8725 5410, 24 units [ensuite, hairdry, a/c, elec blkts, tel, TV, clock radio, t/c mkg, refrig], ldry, w/mach-fee, dryer-fee, iron, iron brd, lounge, cook fac, cots-fee, non smoking rms (14). **RO** ╪ **$43 - $52,** ╫ **$51 - $62,** ╬ **$11,** ch con, 8 rooms ★★★. AE BC DC EFT MC MCH VI.

★★★ **Gambier Lodge-In Motel**, (M), 92 Penola Rd, 1.3km N of PO, ☎ 08 8725 1579, 4 units [ensuite, fan, heat, elec blkts, TV, clock radio, t/c mkg, refrig, toaster], non smoking rms (3). **RO** ╪ **$44,** ╫ **$49.50,** ╬ **$5.50,** BC MC VI.

 ★★★ **Grand Central Motel**, (M), 6 Helen St, 200m SW of PO, ☎ 08 8725 8844, fax 08 8725 8501, (2 stry gr fl), 23 units [ensuite, hairdry, a/c, elec blkts, tel, TV, video (avail), clock radio, t/c mkg, refrig, cook fac (1), micro (avail), toaster], ldry-fee, cots-fee, non smoking rms (11). **RO** ╪ **$52 - $54,** ╫ **$59 - $63,** ╬ **$9,** AE BC DC EFT MC VI.

★★★ **Le Cavalier Court Motel**, (M), 37 Bay Rd, 1km W of PO, ☎ 08 8725 9077, fax 08 8723 2711, 10 units [ensuite, a/c, elec blkts, tel, TV, video, clock radio, t/c mkg, refrig], ldry, w/mach, dryer, iron, iron brd, ✕ (Tues to Sun), rm serv, cots-fee, non smoking rms. **RO** ╪ **$44,** ╫ **$55,** ╬ **$11,** AE BC DC EFT MC VI.

★★★ **Mt Gambier Hotel**, (LH), 2 Commercial St, ☎ 08 8725 0611, fax 08 8723 1070, (2 stry), 15 rms [ensuite, spa bath, a/c, heat, tel, TV, video, clock radio, t/c mkg, refrig], ✕, cots. **RO** ╪ **$55,** ╫ **$65,** ╬ **$10,** AE BC DC EFT MC VI.

★★★ **Tower Motor Inn**, (M), 140 Jubilee Hwy West, 1.8km W of PO, ☎ 08 8724 9411, fax 08 8724 9973, 19 units [ensuite, a/c, elec blkts, tel, TV, video-fee, clock radio, t/c mkg, refrig, toaster], ldry, bbq, non smoking rms (4). **RO** ╪ **$55,** ╫ **$65,** ╬ **$11,** Min book long w/ends and Easter, AE BC DC EFT MC VI.

★★☆ **Jubilee Motor Inn**, (M), Jubilee Hwy East, 3km SE of PO, ☎ 08 8725 7444, fax 08 8723 0355, (2 stry gr fl), 35 units [ensuite, a/c, elec blkts, tel, TV, clock radio, t/c mkg, refrig, ldry-fee], ✕ (Mon-Sat), pool indoor heated, bbq, non smoking property. **RO** ╪ **$35 - $55,** ╫ **$35 - $55,** ╬ **$5,** Function Room. BC EFT MC VI.

★★☆ **Mt View Motel**, (M), 14 Davison St, 2km NE of PO, ☎ 08 8725 8478, fax 08 8725 6226, 9 units [ensuite, fan (4), heat, elec blkts, TV, clock radio, t/c mkg, refrig, cook fac (5), micro (4), toaster], bbq, rm serv, plygr, cots-fee, non smoking rms (4). **RO ∮ $39.60 - $42.90, ♯♯ $41.80 - $47.30, ◊ $8.80**, BC MC VI.

★☆ **The Halfway House Hotel Bellum Bellum**, (LH), Bay Rd, Mt Schank, 15km S of PO, ☎ 08 8738 5269, fax 08 8738 5289, 3 rms [ensuite, elec blkts, clock radio], ⊠ (Mon to Sat), bar, bbq, dinner to unit, non smoking property, **BLB ∮ $35, ♯♯ $45, ◊ $5**, Breakfast available. Gaming lounge. BC EFT MC VI.

Macs Hotel, (LH), 21 Bay Rd, 500m S of PO, ☎ 08 8725 2402, fax 08 8723 2647, (2 stry), 17 rms [heat (5), TV (15), clock radio (5), toaster], ⊠ (Mon to Sun), t/c mkg shared, refrig, cots. **RO ∮ $27, ♯♯ $38.50, ◊ $11**, AE BC DC EFT MC VI.

Self Catering Accommodation

★★★★☆ **Eliza Cottage**, (Cotg), Circa 1871. Cnr William & Wehl St South, 200m W of PO, ☎ 08 8725 0335, fax 08 8725 0335, 1 cotg acc up to 4, (1 bedrm), [shwr, spa bath, tlt, a/c-cool, c/fan, heat (gas), TV, video, clock radio, CD, refrig, cook fac, micro, elec frypan, toaster, blkts, linen, pillows], w/mach, dryer, c/park (carport), breakfast ingredients. **D ♯♯ $135, ◊ $25**, ch con, BC MC VI.

★★★★ **Clarendon Chalets**, (Chalet), Clarke Rd, 7km S of PO, ☎ 08 8726 8306, fax 08 8726 8344, (2 stry), 2 chalets acc up to 6, [ensuite, spa bath (3), a/c (2), c/fan (2), wood heat (slow combustion) (3), elec blkts (2), TV, video, clock radio, CD, t/c mkg, refrig, micro, elec frypan (1), toaster, blkts, doonas, linen, pillows], ldry, w/mach, dryer, iron, iron brd, bbq, ✆, bicycle, cots. **D $105 - $145**, Min book long w/ends and Easter, AE BC MC VI.

★★★☆ **Caradon House**, (HU), 15 Derrington St, 1.2km W of PO, ☎ 08 8725 2328, fax 08 8725 2328, 2 units acc up to 5, (2 bedrm), [shwr, tlt, hairdry, fan, heat (1), cent heat (gas) (1), elec blkts, TV, video (1), clock radio, t/c mkg, refrig, cook fac, micro, toaster, ldry, blkts, linen, pillows], w/mach-fee, dryer-fee, iron, iron brd, cots, non smoking property. **D ♯♯ $78, ◊ $10**, ch con, Surcharge for 3 nights or less.
Operator Comment: Spacious Quiet Comfortable
Web: home.austarnet.com.au/caradonhouse

B&B's/Guest Houses

★★★★☆ **Colhurst House Bed & Breakfast**, (B&B), 3 Colhurst Pl, ☎ 08 8723 1309, fax 08 8723 1238, (2 stry), 3 rms [ensuite, shwr, bath (hip) (1), tlt, fire pl, heat, elec blkts, tel, TV, clock radio], lounge firepl, t/c mkg shared, non smoking property. **BB ∮ $85 - $100, ♯♯ $105 - $125**, AE BC DC MC VI.

★★★★☆ **Worrolong Bed & Breakfast**, (B&B), Worrolong Rd, 11km E of PO, ☎ 08 8725 2256, fax 08 8725 2256, 1 rm [ensuite, spa bath, hairdry, fan, heat, TV, clock radio, t/c mkg, refrig], iron, iron brd, bbq, meals avail (by arrangement), c/park (undercover), non smoking rms. **BB ∮ $70, ♯♯ $90 - $99, ◊ $30**, ch con.

★★★★ **Ashlee House Bed & Breakfast**, (B&B), 61 Penola Rd, ☎ 08 8723 2150, fax 08 8723 2466, 2 rms [ensuite, hairdry, heat, elec blkts], lounge (TV), t/c mkg shared, non smoking rms. **BB ∮ $80, ♯♯ $120**, ch con, BC MC VI.

★★★★ **Berry Hill Bed & Breakfast**, (B&B), Cafpirco Rd, 7km W of PO, ☎ 08 8725 9912, fax 08 8725 9912, 2 rms [ensuite (1), a/c, elec blkts, TV, clock radio], bathrm (private) (1), lounge, meals avail (by arrangement), non smoking property. **BB ∮ $80, ♯♯ $100 - $120**, BC DC MC VI.

Other Accommodation

Blink Bonney Lodge, (Lodge), Wandilo Rd, 5km W of PO, ☎ 08 8723 0879, fax 08 8724 7776, 1 rm acc up to 12, (2 bedrm), [shwr, tlt, fan, wood heat (gas space), TV, video, refrig, cook fac, micro, blkts reqd-fee, linen reqd-fee, pillows reqd-fee], w/mach, c/park. **D ♯♯ $55, ◊ $15**, ch con, Diver's air & supplies available, AE BC MC VI.

MOUNT PLEASANT SA 5235

Pop 546. (55km E Adelaide), See map on pages 586/587, ref C7. A town located in the upper River Torrens Valley.

Self Catering Accommodation

★★☆ **Holmes Estate Cottage**, (Cotg), Burns Rd, 10km NE of PO, ☎ 08 8568 2319, fax 08 8568 2319, 1 cotg acc up to 4, [shwr, tlt, a/c-cool, heat, elec blkts, TV, refrig, cook fac, blkts, linen, pillows], breakfast ingredients, Pets on application. **D ♯♯ $80 - $95, ◊ $17.50 - $20**, AE BC BTC DC JCB MC VI.

Saunders Gorge Sanctuary, (Cotg), Walkers Flat Rd, 18km E of PO, ☎ 08 8569 3032, fax 08 8569 3036, 1 cotg acc up to 6, (2 bedrm), [shwr, tlt, a/c, heat (combustion), elec blkts, tel, video, radio (cassette), refrig, cook fac, micro, toaster, blkts, doonas, linen, pillows], bbq, c/park (garage), breakfast ingredients. **D ♯♯ $110, ◊ $20**, BC MC VI.
★★★ **(Cabin Section)**, 1 cabin acc up to 2, [shwr, tlt, heat, TV, video, radio, refrig, cook fac, blkts, doonas, linen, pillows], bbq, breakfast ingredients. **D ♯♯ $110**.

MOUNT TORRENS SA 5244

Pop Nominal, (46km E Adelaide), See map on pages 586/587, ref C7. A small rural township with many heritage buildings.

★★★★ **Fernwood Estate Bed & Breakfast Chalet**, (Chalet), No children's facilities, Mountview Rd, 1km NE of PO, ☎ 08 8389 4342, fax 08 8389 4464, 1 chalet acc up to 4, (Studio), [shwr, bath, tlt, a/c, heat (slow combustion), tel, TV, video, radio (cassette), t/c mkg, refrig, cook fac, micro, toaster, blkts, linen, pillows], bbq, breakfast ingredients, non smoking rms. **D $150**, AE BC EFT MC VI.

MUNDULLA SA 5270

Pop Nominal, (271km W Adelaide), See map on pages 586/587, ref J7. A small rural township located close to Bordertown.

Mundulla Bed & Breakfast, (B&B), 18 Nalang Rd, 200m S of PO, ☎ 08 8753 4133, fax 08 8758 2097, 3 rms [a/c-cool, heat (gas), elec blkts, tel, TV, CD, cook fac, micro, ldry, doonas, pillows], shared fac (3), w/mach, lounge (TV), refrig, bbq, non smoking rms. **D ∮ $100 - $110, ♯♯ $100 - $110, ◊ $40 - $45**, weekly con, Min book long w/ends, AE BC MC VI, (not yet classified).

MUNGERANNIE SA 5700

Pop Nominal, (878km N Adelaide), See map on pages 586/587, ref H2. A small Hotel and Roadhouse servicing travellers along the Birdsville Track.

Mungerannie Hotel, (LH), Birdsville Track, ☎ 08 8675 8317, fax 08 8675 8388, 9 rms [a/c-cool (6), heat], ⊠, bbq, ✆. **RO ∮ $38.50, ♯♯ $62**, ch con, AE BC MC VI.

MURRAY BRIDGE SA 5253

Pop 12,725. (78km ESE Adelaide), See map on pages 586/587, ref C7. A thriving town situated on the Murray River. First settled as a farming property in the 1850's, the town was eventually founded once a bridge spanned the river. Bowls, Bush Walking, Croquet, Fishing, Golf, Horse Racing, Sailing, Squash, Swimming (Pool & River), Tennis, Trotting, Vineyards, Wineries, Water Skiing.

Hotels/Motels

★★★☆ **Murray Bridge Motor Inn**, (M), 212 Adelaide Rd, 3km W of PO, ☎ 08 8532 1144, fax 08 8531 0313, 36 units [ensuite, a/c-cool (9), a/c (27), elec blkts, tel, cable tv (18), clock radio, t/c mkg, refrig, toaster], ldry, pool, plygr, non smoking rms (6). **RO** ♦ **$75**, ♦♦ **$84 - $99**, ۩ **$10**, ch con, 18 units ★★★. AE BC DC MC VI.

★★★ **Motel Greenacres**, (M), Princes Hwy, 5km E of PO, ☎ 08 8532 1090, fax 08 8532 5003, 18 units [ensuite, a/c, elec blkts, TV, t/c mkg, refrig, cook fac (8), toaster], ldry, w/mach-fee, dryer-fee, pool, bbq, rm serv, dinner to unit, plygr, cots-fee, non smoking units (3). **RO** ♦ **$49.50 - $60**, ♦♦ **$55 - $66**, ۩ **$10**, ch con, fam con, AE BC DC MC MCH VI.

★★★ **Murray Bridge Oval Motel**, (M), 4 LeMessurier St, 1km SW of PO, ☎ 08 8532 2388, fax 08 8531 1101, 12 units [ensuite, a/c, elec blkts, tel, TV, clock radio, t/c mkg, refrig], ldry, rm serv, c/park (undercover), cots, non smoking units (3). **RO** ♦ **$55 - $65**, ♦♦ **$66 - $77**, ۩ **$12**, fam con, Min book applies, AE BC DC EFT MC VI.

★★☆ **Olympic Pool Motel**, (M), 34 Standen St, 1km W of PO, ☎ 08 8532 2359, fax 08 8532 4194, 14 units [ensuite, a/c, heat, elec blkts, TV, clock radio, t/c mkg, refrig, toaster], ldry, w/mach, iron, iron brd, bbq, cots-fee. **RO** ♦ **$55**, ♦♦ **$64**, ۩ **$9**, AE BC DC EFT MC VI.

★☆ **Bridgeport Hotel**, (LH), 2 Bridge St, ☎ 08 8532 2002, fax 08 8531 0675, (2 stry), 21 rms [basin (10), ensuite (5), a/c (5), elec blkts, refrig (5)], lounge (TV), conv fac, ☒, t/c mkg shared, refrig. **BLB** ♦ **$27.50**, ♦♦ **$55 - $66**, ۩ **$27.50**, ch con, 5 rms ★★. AE BC DC EFT MC VI.

★☆ **Murray Bridge Hotel**, (LH), Sixth St, ☎ 08 8532 2024, fax 08 8531 0521, (2 stry), 8 rms [basin, shwr (4), tlt (5), a/c-cool (4), heat, elec blkts, TV (5), t/c mkg], lounge (TV), ☒, cots. **BB** ♦ **$27.50 - $35**, ♦♦ **$44 - $55**, ۩ **$13.20**, AE BC DC EFT MC VI.

Self Catering Accommodation

★★★★ **Treetops of Riverglades**, (Cotg), Torrens Rd, ☎ 08 8532 6483, fax 08 8531 0722, (2 stry), 1 cotg acc up to 2, (1 bedrm), [shwr (2), tlt (2), a/c-cool, fan, heat (combustion), TV, CD, refrig, cook fac, micro, blkts, linen, pillows], w/mach, canoeing, breakfast ingredients, non smoking property, **D** ♦♦ **$118**, ۩ **$43**, **W $630**, Min book applies.

★★★☆ **Hy-Am Home**, (Apt), 43 Parish Cres, ☎ 08 8532 1174, fax 08 8532 1174, 1 apt acc up to 6, (1 bedrm), [ensuite, a/c, elec blkts, TV, video, radio, refrig, cook fac, micro], w/mach, dryer, iron, bbq, plygr, cots, breakfast ingredients, non smoking property, Pets allowed. **BLB** ♦♦ **$75**, ۩ **$15**, ch con.

★★★☆ **(Bed & Breakfast Section)**, 2 rms [bath], cots, non smoking rms. **BB** ♦ **$25**, ۩ **$20**.

B&B's/Guest Houses

★★★☆ **Balcony Bed & Breakfast Guest House**, (GH), 6 Sixth St, ☎ 08 8531 1411, fax 08 8531 1477, (2 stry), 10 rms [ensuite (2), a/c (3), fan (avail), heat (avail), elec blkts, TV], lounge (TV & Video), t/c mkg shared, refrig, bbq, courtesy transfer, non smoking property, **BLB** ♦ **$20 - $30**, ♦♦ **$40 - $80**, ch con, fam con, 2 rooms ★★☆. Other meals by arrangement. BC MC VI.

★★★☆ **Childsdale Bed & Breakfast**, (B&B), Long Flat Rd, 4km SE of PO, ☎ 08 8531 1153, fax 08 8531 1649, 2 rms [ensuite, bath, hairdry, fan, fire pl (2), heat, elec blkts, TV, video, clock radio, t/c mkg, toaster], ldry, iron, iron brd, bbq, non smoking rms. **BB** ♦ **$80**, ♦♦ **$95**, BC MC VI.

Other Accommodation

Break Free Houseboat, (Hbt), Riverglen Marina, Jervois Rd, ☎ 08 8532 1986, fax 08 8532 1986, 1 houseboat acc up to 12, [shwr (2), tlt (2), a/c-cool, TV, refrig, cook fac, blkts, linen, pillows], bbq. **W $2,035 - $3,289**.

Cloud Nine Houseboat, (Hbt), Riverglen Marina, Jervois Rd, ☎ 08 8408 4204, 1 houseboat acc up to 7, [shwr (2), tlt (2), TV, video, CD, refrig, micro, d/wash, blkts, linen, pillows], w/mach, ice box, bbq. **W $1,155 - $2,090**.

France Australis Houseboat, (Hbt), Jervois Rd, Riverglen Marina, 10km S of PO, ☎ 08 8532 6639, fax 08 8532 6639, 1 houseboat acc up to 8, [shwr, tlt, a/c-cool, fan, heat, tel, TV, radio (cassette), CD, refrig, cook fac, micro, toaster, doonas, linen, pillows], ice box, bbq. **W $920 - $1,530**, Min book.

Huckleberry Houseboat, (Hbt), Jervois Rd, Riverglen Marina 10km S of PO, ☎ 08 8258 2448, 1 houseboat acc up to 12, [shwr, tlt, c/fan, heat, TV, radio, refrig, cook fac, linen], bbq. **W $700 - $1,200**.

Jubilee Line Houseboats, (Hbt), Long Island Marina, Roper Rd, ☎ 08 8364 6066, fax 08 8364 6061, 12 houseboats acc up to 12, [shwr, tlt, a/c-cool, heat, tel, TV, video, radio, refrig, cook fac, micro, blkts, linen, pillows], bbq. **D $390 - $2,490**, **W $290 - $1,490**.

Nomads Murray Bridge Backpackers Hostel, (Lodge), 1 McKay Rd, ☎ 08 8532 6994, fax 08 8531 3400, 1 rm (Bunk Rooms), [a/c, c/fan, heat, micro, toaster, doonas, linen], ldry, lounge (TV, video), lounge firepl, cook fac, t/c mkg shared, refrig, bbq, non smoking property. **BLB** ♦ **$18 - $22**, ♦♦ **$44**, ch con, BC EFT MC VI.

Porsha Houseboat, (Hbt), Riverglen Marina, Jervois Rd, ☎ 08 8532 1986, 1 houseboat acc up to 7, [shwr, tlt, TV, video, CD, refrig, micro, blkts, linen, pillows], bbq, **W $935 - $1,529**.

Reflection Houseboat, (Hbt), Riverglen Marina, Jervois Rd, ☎ 08 8391 6529, 1 houseboat acc up to 8, [shwr, tlt, heat, TV, video, radio (cassette), CD, cook fac, micro, blkts, linen, pillows], ice box, bbq. **W $770 - $1,540**.

Rivabella Houseboat, (Hbt), Riverglen Marina, Jervois Rd, ☎ 08 8333 0454, 1 houseboat acc up to 10, [shwr (2), spa bath, tlt (2), a/c-cool, refrig, cook fac, blkts, linen, pillows], bbq, **W $1,859 - $2,959**, Min book, AE DC MC VI.

Riverwren Houseboats, (Hbt), Riverglen Marina, Jervois Rd, ☎ 08 8532 1986, fax 08 8232 1986, 6 houseboats acc up to 6, [TV, video, CD, refrig, cook fac ltd, blkts, linen, pillows], ice box. **W $770 - $1,155**, Min book applies, BC MC VI.

Sky Houseboat, (Hbt), Long Island Marina, ☎ 08 8531 2132, 1 houseboat acc up to 6, [shwr, tlt, a/c (portable), heat, TV, video, CD, refrig, cook fac, micro], bbq. **W $715 - $990**.

Sun Seeka Houseboats, (Hbt), 220 Murray Dve, 5km N of PO, ☎ 08 8532 3313, 4 houseboats acc up to 10, [shwr, tlt, a/c-cool, heat, TV, video, radio, CD, refrig, cook fac, micro, blkts, linen, pillows]. **W $650 - $1,600**, Min book applies.

Takari Houseboat, (Hbt), Jervois Rd, Riverglen Marina, 10km S of PO, ☎ 08 8532 6639, fax 08 8532 6639, 1 houseboat acc up to 8, (3 bedrm), [shwr, tlt, a/c-cool, heat, tel, TV, video, radio (cassette), CD, t/c mkg, refrig, cook fac, micro, toaster, ldry, doonas, linen, pillows]. **W $920 - $1,530**, Min book.

MYPONGA SA 5202

Pop 154. (57km S Adelaide) See map on pages 586/587, ref B8. A small township which is in one of the State's most vital dairying regions.
Country Gates Cottage, (Cotg), Hindmarsh Tiers Rd, 9km SE of PO, ☎ 08 8554 7222, fax 08 8554 7277, 1 cotg acc up to 4, [shwr, spa bath, tlt, hairdry, fan, elec blkts, TV, video, clock radio, t/c mkg, refrig, cook fac, micro, elec frypan, toaster, blkts, doonas, linen, pillows], w/mach, dryer, iron, iron brd, c/park (carport), **D** ♦♦ **$132**, ۩ **$44**, BC MC VI, (not yet classified).

NAIRNE SA 5252

Pop Nominal, (41km E Adelaide), See map on pages 586/587, ref C7. Small town Located in the Adelaide Hills.
★★★★☆ **Albert Mill Bed and Breakfast**, (B&B), 4 Junction St, opp Millers Arms Hotel, ☎ 08 8388 6858, fax 08 8388 6155, 2 rms [ensuite, spa bath (1), hairdry, a/c, fire pl, elec blkts, TV, clock radio, t/c mkg, refrig, cook fac, toaster, doonas, pillows], ☒, dinner to unit (avail), breakfast ingredients. **D $98 - $158**, BC EFT MC VI.

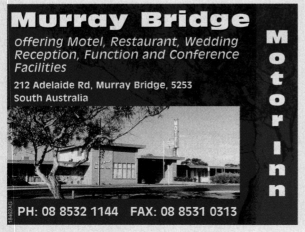

NARACOORTE SA 5271

Pop 4,711. (338km SE Adelaide), See map on pages 586/587, ref J7. Centre of thriving primary production area. Art Gallery, Bowls, Croquet, Golf, Horse Racing, Horse Riding, Scenic Drives, Squash, Swimming (Lake), Tennis, Vineyards, Wineries.

Hotels/Motels

 ★★★★ **Country Roads Motor Inn**, (M), 20 Smith St, 700m SW of PO, ☎ 08 8762 3900, fax 08 8762 3560, 22 units [ensuite, spa bath (2), hairdry, a/c-cool (6), a/c (16), heat (6), elec blkts, tel, cable tv, video, movie, clock radio, t/c mkg, refrig], iron, iron brd, bbq, dinner to unit, non smoking rms (18). RO ♦ $72 - $132, ♦♦ $80 - $145, ۅ $10, AE BC DC EFT MC VI, ௬&.

 ★★★★ **William MacIntosh Motor Lodge**, (M), Bordertown Rd (Adelaide Rd), 3km N of PO, opposite golf course, ☎ 08 8762 1644, fax 08 8762 1660, 30 units [ensuite, bath (2), spa bath (5), a/c, elec blkts, tel, cable tv, clock radio, t/c mkg, refrig, mini bar], ⊠, pool, rm serv, tennis, cots-fee. RO ♦ $87 - $115.50, ♦♦ $97 - $132, ۅ $12.10, 4 units yet to be classified. AE BC DC EFT MC VI, ௬&.

 ★★☆ **Belvedere Motel**, (M), 17 Fourth Ave, 2km S of PO, ☎ 08 8762 3655, fax 08 8762 3079, 13 units [ensuite, a/c-cool (5), a/c (8), elec blkts, tel, clock radio, t/c mkg, refrig, mini bar, toaster], conf fac, bbq, rm serv, cots-fee, non smoking rms (7). RO ♦ $39, ♦♦ $62 - $72, ۅ $8, AE BC DC EFT MC VI.

 ★★☆ **Motel Greenline**, (M), Bordertown Rd, 3.1km N of PO, ☎ 08 8762 2599, fax 08 8762 2180, 11 units [ensuite, a/c, elec blkts, tel, TV, movie, clock radio, t/c mkg, refrig, mini bar], ⊠, pool (seasonal), bbq, cots. RO ♦ $53 - $57, ♦♦ $61 - $65, ۅ $8, fam con, AE BC DC EFT MC MCH VI.

★★ **Commercial Hotel**, (LH), 20 Robertson St, 150m SE of PO, ☎ 08 8762 2100, fax 08 8762 3907, (2 stry), 9 rms [ensuite, a/c, elec blkts, TV, clock radio, t/c mkg, refrig, toaster], ⊠ (Mon to Sat), ✆, cots-fee. RO ♦ $38.50, ♦♦ $49.50, ۅ $10, AE BC DC EFT MC VI.

★ **Kincraig Hotel**, (LH), 158 Smith St, 400m W of PO, ☎ 08 8762 2200, fax 08 8762 1370, (2 stry), 26 rms [basin, elec blkts, t/c mkg], lounge (TV), ⊠ (Mon to Sat), cots-fee. RO ♦ $25, ♦♦ $40, ۅ $10, AE BC DC EFT MC VI.

★ **Naracoorte Hotel Motel**, (LMH), 73 Ormerod St, 150m E of PO, ☎ 08 8762 2400, fax 08 8762 0022, (2 stry), 18 units [basin, elec blkts], lounge (TV), ⊠, cots. RO ♦ $27, ♦♦ $47, ۅ $11, AE BC DC EFT MC VI.

★★☆ **(Motel Section)**, 14 units [ensuite, a/c, elec blkts, tel, TV, clock radio, t/c mkg, refrig, toaster], conf fac, ⊠, cots. RO ♦ $55, ♦♦ $60 - $66, ۅ $11, fam con.

Self Catering Accommodation

★★★★ **Mossville Manor B&B**, (HU), Blackwell Rd, 2.5km E of PO, ☎ 08 8762 1009, fax 08 8762 2080, 1 unit acc up to 6, (2 bedrm), [shwr, tlt, hairdry, a/c, fan, heat, tel, TV, video, clock radio, t/c mkg, refrig, cook fac, micro, toaster, blkts, doonas, linen, pillows], w/mach, iron, iron brd, rec rm, bbq, cots, non smoking units, Pets by arrangement. D ♦♦ $100, ۅ $20, ch con, Min book BC DC MC VI.

★★★★ **Naracoorte Cottages**, (Cotg), 192 Smith St, 1km W of PO, ☎ 08 8762 2906, fax 08 8762 3851, 1 cotg acc up to 8, (4 bedrm), [shwr (2), bath (1), tlt (2), a/c (2), heat (woodheater), elec blkts, TV, video, clock radio, CD, t/c mkg, refrig, cook fac, micro, toaster, ldry (in unit), blkts, linen, pillows], w/mach, iron, iron brd, bbq, c/park (garage), plygr, cots, breakfast ingredients, non smoking property, D ♦ $82, ♦♦ $121, ۅ $49.50, ch con, Min book long w/ends and Easter, AE BC MC VI.

★★★★ **(Handyside St Cottage)**, 1 cotg acc up to 6, (3 bedrm), [shwr (2), bath, tlt (2), a/c (2), heat (woodheater), elec blkts, TV, video, clock radio, CD, t/c mkg, refrig, cook fac, micro, toaster, blkts, linen, pillows], w/mach, iron, iron brd, bbq, cots, breakfast ingredients, non smoking property. D ♦ $82, ♦♦ $121, ۅ $49.50, ch con, Min book long w/ends.

★★★★ **Willowbrook Cottage B&B**, (Cotg), 3 Jenkins Tce, 1km E of PO, ☎ 08 8762 0259, fax 08 8762 0009, 1 cotg acc up to 6, (3 bedrm), [shwr, bath, tlt, hairdry, a/c, heat, TV, clock radio, t/c mkg, refrig, cook fac, micro, toaster, blkts, linen, pillows], w/mach, iron, iron brd, bbq, breakfast ingredients. D ♦♦ $100, ۅ $35, W ♦♦ $560, ch con, BC MC VI.

★★★☆ **The Shepherds Cave Apartment**, (Apt), Sandstone Ave, ☎ 08 8762 0246, fax 08 8762 0370, 1 apt acc up to 5, (2 bedrm), [shwr, tlt, fan, heat, elec blkts, TV, video, radio (cassette), CD, refrig, cook fac, blkts, linen, pillows], iron, pool, bbq, cots, breakfast ingredients. D ♦ $75, ♦♦ $100, ۅ $30.

★★★☆ **(Bed & Breakfast Section)**, 1 rm [ensuite, evap cool, c/fan, heat, elec blkts, radio, t/c mkg], ldry, lounge (TV). BB ♦ $70, ♦♦ $95.

★★★☆ **Wongary Farm Cottages**, (Cotg), (Farm), Ralphs Cottage. Concrete Bridge Rd, 25km SE of PO, ☎ 08 8762 3038, fax 08 8762 3394, 2 cotgs acc up to 8, (1 & 3 bedrm), [shwr, bath, spa bath (1), tlt, hairdry, a/c, heat (pot belly) (1), elec blkts, TV, clock radio, CD (1), t/c mkg, refrig, cook fac, micro, d/wash (1), toaster, ldry (1), blkts, linen, pillows], ldry (1), w/mach (1), dryer (1), iron (1), iron brd (1), lounge firepl (2), bbq, tennis, cots. D ♦♦ $120, ۅ $60, ch con, BC MC VI.

★★★ **Cave Park Cabins**, Caves Rd, 14km S of PO, ☎ 08 8762 0696, fax 08 8762 3180, 2 cabins acc up to 5, (2 bedrm), [shwr, tlt, a/c-cool, c/fan (1), heat, TV, clock radio, refrig, cook fac, micro, elec frypan, toaster, linen reqd-fee, pillows], bbq, cots. D ♦♦ $66, ۅ $11, ch con, BC MC VI.

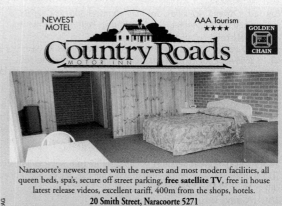

★★★ **Tynans View Bed & Breakfast Cottage**, (Cotg), Cnr Boddingtons Rd & Riddoch Hwy, 18km N of PO, ☎ 08 8765 3212, 1 cotg acc up to 6, (2 bedrm), [shwr, bath, tlt, a/c, fan (1), c/fan (1), wood heat (slow combustion), elec blkts, radio, refrig, cook fac, elec frypan, blkts, linen, pillows], bbq, cots, breakfast ingredients, non smoking property. D ♦♦ $105, ۞ $30, BC MC VI.

B&B's/Guest Houses
★★★★ **Tintagel Bed & Breakfast**, (B&B), Riddoch Hwy, 19km S of PO, ☎ 08 8764 7491, fax 08 8764 7491, 1 rm (1 suite) [shwr, bath, tlt, hairdry, a/c-cool, fan, heat, elec blkts, clock radio, t/c mkg, refrig, doonas], lounge (TV, Video & Stereo), bbq, meals avail, bush walking. BB ♦ $60, ♦♦ $98, ۞ $30, ch con, BC MC VI.
★★★☆ **Dartmoor Homestead Guest House**, (GH), 30 McLay St, 1km W of PO, ☎ 08 8762 0487, fax 08 8762 0481, 3 rms [ensuite (1), fan, heat, elec blkts, clock radio, t/c mkg], shared fac (2), ldry, w/mach, dryer, iron, lounge (TV, Video & Stereo), lounge firepl, bbq, meals avail (dinner), non smoking rms. BB ♦ $115 - $135, ♦♦ $175 - $196, ۞ $56, 1 rm ★★★★. BC MC VI.

NORMANVILLE SA 5204

Pop 513. (76km S Adelaide), See map on pages 586/587, ref B8. A popular holiday destination, great for fishing, boating & swimming.

Hotels/Motels
★★★★ **Paradise Wirrina Cove Resort**, (LMH), Cape Jervis Rd, 9km S of PO, ☎ 08 8598 4001, fax 08 8598 4037, 87 units (2 suites) [ensuite, bath, hairdry (20), a/c, elec blkts, tel, TV, movie, clock radio, t/c mkg, refrig], ldry, rec rm, conf fac, ⊠, pool indoor heated, sauna, spa, bbq, rm serv, plygr, golf, gym, tennis, cots. RO ♦ $195 - $220, ♦♦ $195 - $220, Suite D ♦♦ $250 - $400, ch con, 2 units ★★★★☆. AE BC BTC DC EFT JCB MC VI, ♪⛷.
★★★★ **(Executive Housing Section)**, 8 houses acc up to 6, (3 & 4 bedrm), [shwr, bath, spa bath (2), tlt, a/c, TV, clock radio, refrig, cook fac, micro, ldry, blkts, linen, pillows], w/mach, dryer, iron, iron brd, c/park (garage). D $250 - $300.
★★★☆ **(Apartment Section)**, 80 apts acc up to 6, (1, 2 & 3 bedrm), [shwr, bath, tlt, a/c, TV, t/c mkg, refrig, cook fac, micro, blkts, linen, pillows]. D $175 - $240.

B&B's/Guest Houses
★★★☆ **Normanville The Villager Bed & Breakfast**, (B&B), 95 Main St, ☎ 08 8558 2587, fax 08 8558 2587, 3 rms [ensuite (1), bath (1), hairdry (2), a/c, elec blkts, tel, clock radio (3)], shared fac (2), lounge (TV & Video), pool, t/c mkg shared, refrig, bbq, non smoking property. BB ♦ $42.50, ♦♦ $85, ch con.

NORTH WEST COAST SA

See Kangaroo Island Region.

NULLARBOR SA 5690

Pop Nominal, (1090km NW Adelaide), See map on pages 586/587, ref D4. Coastal town on the Eyre Hwy overlooking the Great Australian Bight.

FLAG
FLAG CHOICE HOTELS™

★★ **Nullarbor Hotel Motel**, (LMH), Eyre Hwy, ☎ 08 8625 6271, fax 08 8625 6261, 26 units [shwr, tlt, a/c-cool (6), a/c (20), heat, TV, movie, t/c mkg, refrig], ⊠, bbq, c/park (undercover), cots-fee. RO ♦ $76.50, ♦♦ $92, ۞ $16, AE BC DC EFT MC VI.

NUNDROO SA 5690

Pop Nominal, (936km NW Adelaide), See map on pages 586/587, ref E4.
★☆ **Nundroo Hotel Motel Inn**, (LMH), Eyre Hwy, ☎ 08 8625 6120, fax 08 8625 6107, 17 units [shwr, tlt, a/c, TV, t/c mkg, refrig], ldry, ⊠, pool, bbq, ✆, cots. RO ♦ $65, ♦♦ $75, ۞ $10, fam con, BC DC EFT MC VI.

NURIOOTPA SA

See Barossa Valley Region.

OAKBANK SA 5243

Pop 340. (32km Adelaide), See map on page 588, ref E4. Situated in the Adelaide Hills amongst rich beef, dairying and orchard producing region.

Self Catering Accommodation
★★★★☆ **Adelaide Hills Country Cottages**, (Cotg), Located on beef stud & apple growing property. Oakwood Rd, 3km N of PO, ☎ 08 8388 4193, fax 08 8388 4733, 5 cotgs acc up to 5, (2 bedrm), [shwr, bath, spa bath (4), tlt, a/c-cool (1), a/c (4), heat (combustion stove) (1), elec blkts, TV, video (2), clock radio (cassette), CD, refrig, cook fac, micro, ldry (3), blkts, linen, pillows], iron, iron brd, lounge firepl (4), bbq, breakfast ingredients, non smoking property. D ♦♦ $160 - $230, ۞ $60, 1 cotg yet to be assessed. Min book applies, BC MC VI.

Operator Comment: See our advertisement under Adelaide Hills.

OODNADATTA SA 5734

Pop 230. (1125km NNW Adelaide), See map on pages 586/587, ref F2. Small township in the Far North Region. The name derived from the aboriginal word meaning 'Flower of the Mulga'.
Transcontinental Hotel, (LH), ☎ 08 8670 7804, fax 08 8670 7804, 6 rms [a/c-cool, ldry], ✗, bbq, c/park. RO ♦ $35, ♦♦ $65, BC MC VI.

PADTHAWAY SA 5271

Pop 218. 218, (291km SE Adelaide), See map on pages 586/587, ref J7. A small township set in an expanding vineyard and winery area, first settled in the 1840's.

Self Catering Accommodation
★★☆ **Russells Camp Cottage**, (Cotg), Kingston (SE) Rd, 24km NW of PO, ☎ 08 8757 3061, fax 08 8757 3060, 1 cotg acc up to 6, (2 bedrm), [shwr, bath, tlt, a/c, radio, cook fac, elec frypan, toaster, blkts, linen, pillows], w/mach, dryer, iron, pool, bbq, tennis. BLB ♦♦ $100, ۞ $25.
★★★☆ **(Bed & Breakfast Section)**, 1 rm (1 suite) [ensuite, bath, a/c, heat, elec blkts, TV, t/c mkg, refrig], lounge, bbq. BLB ♦ $90.

B&B's/Guest Houses
★★★ **Padthaway Estate - Historic Homestead**, (GH), Classified by National Trust, Riddoch Hwy, ☎ 08 8765 5039, fax 08 8765 5097, (2 stry), 6 rms [basin, fan, heat, elec blkts, tel], rec rm, lounge (TV), ✗, tennis, non smoking property. BB ♦ $150, ♦♦ $220, 2 rms ★★☆. Function centre available. AE BC DC MC VI.

PARINGA SA 5340

Pop 588. (261km Adelaide), See map on pages 586/587, ref E6. A small rural settlement in the heart of the Riverland region.

Hotels/Motels
★★ **Paringa Hotel Motel**, (LMH), Sturt Hwy, town centre, ☎ 08 8595 5005, fax 08 8595 5378, 19 units [ensuite, a/c, elec blkts, tel, TV, clock radio, t/c mkg, refrig], ldry, w/mach, dryer, iron, iron brd, ⊠, rm serv, ✆, cots. RO ♦ $32, ♦♦ $38, ۞ $10, ch con, AE BC DC EFT MC VI.

Self Catering Accommodation
★★★★ **Mundic Grove Cottages**, (Cotg), Sturt Hwy, 1.5km E of PO, ☎ 08 8595 5116, fax 08 8595 5116, 2 cotgs acc up to 7, (3 & 4 bedrm), [shwr, tlt, a/c, c/fan, TV, video, clock radio, refrig, cook fac, micro, toaster, blkts, linen, pillows], w/mach, iron, bbq, c/park (carport), jetty, cots, non smoking property. D ♦♦ $55, ۞ $12.50, ch con, 1 cottage ★★★☆.

Other Accommodation
Houseboat Holidays, (Hbt), Lock 5 Rd, Marina, 3km SW of PO, ☎ 0418 842 741, fax 08 8586 4434, 3 houseboats acc up to 8, (3 & 4 bedrm), [shwr, tlt, a/c-cool, heat, TV, video, CD, refrig, cook fac, micro, doonas, linen, pillows], w/mach, ice box, bbq, W $990 - $1,485, Min book all holiday times.
Warriuka Houseboats, (Hbt), Lock 5 Rd, Lock 5 Marina, ☎ 08 8595 5324, fax 08 8595 5324, 8 houseboats acc up to 12, [shwr, tlt, a/c-cool (8), TV, video, radio (cassette), CD (4), refrig, cook fac, micro, blkts, linen, pillows], bbq. W $700 - $2,420, BC MC VI.

PARNDANA SA

See Kangaroo Island Region.

PENNESHAW SA

See Kangaroo Island Region.

PENOLA SA 5277

Pop 1,147. (388km SE Adelaide), See map on pages 586/587, ref J8. Service town for the local pastoral & forestry industries. Bowls, Croquet, Golf, Swimming (Pool), Tennis, Vineyards, Wineries.

Hotels/Motels

GOLDEN CHAIN

★★★☆ **Coonawarra Motor Lodge Motel**, (M), 114 Church St, ☎ 08 8737 2364, fax 08 8737 2543, 12 units [ensuite, bath (11), a/c, elec blkts, tel, TV, video-fee, clock radio, t/c mkg, refrig], ldry, ⊠ (Thur to Tues), pool-heated (solar), plygr, cots-fee, non smoking units (5). RO ♦ $80, ♦♦ $90 - $95, ♦♦♦ $99, ۞ $15, ch con, AE BC DC MC VI.
★★ **Prince of Wales Hotel Motel**, (LMH), 58 Church St, ☎ 08 8737 2402, fax 08 8737 2189, 10 units [ensuite, a/c (2), heat, elec blkts, TV, t/c mkg, refrig], ⊠, ✆, cots-fee. BLB ♦ $45, ♦♦ $65, ۞ $10, BC EFT MC VI.

Self Catering Accommodation

★★★★ **Cobb & Co Cottages**, (Cotg), 2 Portland St, 150m E of PO, ☎ 08 8737 2526, fax 08 8737 2926, 3 cotgs acc up to 4, (2 bedrm), [shwr, spa bath, tlt, a/c, elec blkts, TV, clock radio (cassette), CD, refrig, cook fac, micro, ldry (in unit), blkts, linen, pillows], w/mach, iron, iron brd, bbq, c/park (undercover), cots-fee, breakfast ingredients, **D** †† **$115**, ⚥ **$30**, ch con, BC DC MC VI, ♨⚕.

★★★★ **Mirnat Bed and Breakfast**, (Cotg), Bott Rd, Kalangadoo, 31km SW of PO, ☎ 08 8739 3278, fax 08 8739 3008, 1 cotg acc up to 4, (2 bedrm), [shwr, bath, tlt, hairdry, fire pl, elec blkts, tel, TV, clock radio, t/c mkg, refrig, cook fac, micro, toaster, ldry, doonas, linen, pillows], w/mach, iron, iron brd, bbq, breakfast ingredients. **D** †† **$115 - $125**, ⚥ **$25 - $30**, Min book applies.

★★★★ **Naomis Villa**, (Cotg), 20 Riddoch St, ☎ 08 8736 3309, fax 08 8736 3383, 1 cotg acc up to 7, (2 bedrm), [shwr, bath, spa bath (pool), tlt, fan, heat, TV, video, radio, refrig, cook fac, ldry, blkts, linen, pillows], w/mach, dryer, iron, cots, breakfast ingredients, **D** †† **$149 - $159**, ⚥ **$40**, ch con, Min book long w/ends, BC DC EFT MC VI.

★★★☆ **Jessies Penola Cottage**, (Cotg), Cnr Clark & Scott Sts, 1km W of PO, ☎ 08 8737 2630, 1 cotg acc up to 4, (2 bedrm), [shwr, tlt, fan, fire pl, heat, elec blkts, TV, clock radio, t/c mkg, refrig, micro, elec frypan, blkts, doonas, linen, pillows], w/mach, breakfast ingredients, non smoking property. **D** †† **$100 - $110**, ⚥ **$20**, ch con.

★★★☆ **Julian Court Apartments**, (Apt), 1/13 Julian St, 200m E of PO, ☎ 08 8762 3038, fax 08 8762 3394, 2 apts acc up to 5, (2 bedrm), [shwr, bath, tlt, hairdry, a/c, elec blkts, TV, clock radio, t/c mkg, cook fac, micro, toaster, blkts, linen, pillows], iron, breakfast ingredients. **D** †† **$110**, ⚥ **$55**, ch con, Min book applies, BC MC VI, *Operator Comment: Private - spacious - central and easy! www.seol.net.au/wongary/*

★★★☆ **Moerlong Serviced Apartment**, (SA), Old Kalangadoo Rd, 19km SW of PO, ☎ 08 8739 3030, 1 serv apt acc up to 2, (1 bedrm), [shwr, tlt, a/c, fire pl, heat, elec blkts, TV, clock radio, refrig, cook fac, micro, blkts, linen, pillows], bbq, breakfast ingredients, non smoking units. **D** † **$50**, †† **$80**, ⚥ **$20**, ch con, BC MC VI.

★★★☆ **Sarahs Cottage**, (Cotg), Check in and collect keys at Chardonnay Lodge. 24 Julian St West, ☎ 08 8736 3309, fax 08 8736 3383, 1 cotg acc up to 2, (1 bedrm), [shwr, spa bath, tlt, a/c, fire pl, elec blkts, TV, video, radio, refrig, cook fac, micro, toaster, blkts, linen, pillows], ldry, iron, c/park (carport), breakfast ingredients, **D** †† **$142 - $149**, Min book long w/ends, BC DC EFT MC VI.

★★★ **Great Escapes South East**, (Cotg), Ulva Cottage. 33 Riddoch St, ☎ 08 8737 2250, fax 08 8737 2075, 1 cotg acc up to 4, (2 bedrm), [shwr, bath (hip), tlt, a/c, fire pl, TV, video, clock radio, t/c mkg, refrig, cook fac, toaster, blkts, linen, pillows], ldry, w/mach, dryer, iron, c/park. **D** †† **$90**, ⚥ **$22**, BC MC VI.

★★☆ **(Miss Thompsons Cottage)**, 1 cotg acc up to 10, (4 bedrm), [shwr, tlt, fire pl, TV, video, radio, refrig, cook fac, blkts, linen, pillows], w/mach, dryer, sauna. **D** †† **$85**, ⚥ **$20**.

★★★ **Susies Bed & Breakfast Cottage**, (Cotg), 110 Church St, 1km N of PO, ☎ 08 8737 2122, fax 08 8737 2820, 1 cotg acc up to 6, (2 bedrm), [shwr, tlt, a/c, heat, elec blkts, TV, video, clock radio, t/c mkg, refrig, cook fac, micro, toaster, ldry (in unit), blkts, doonas, linen, pillows], iron, iron brd, bbq-fee, ☎, breakfast ingredients. **D** † **$80**, †† **$90**, ⚥ **$25**, **W** †† **$450**, ⚥ **$110**, AE BC DC MC VI.

B&B's/Guest Houses

★★★☆ **Heywards Royal Oak Hotel**, (B&B), 31 Church St, ☎ 08 8737 2322, fax 08 8737 2825, (2 stry), 9 rms [heat, elec blkts, TV, clock radio, t/c mkg], lounge (TV & video), ⊠, bbq, ☎, non smoking rms. **BLB** † **$35**, †† **$50 - $72**, BC EFT MC VI.

★☆ **(Hotel Section)**, 4 rms [basin, heat, elec blkts, TV, clock radio, t/c mkg]. **BLB** † **$35**.

★★★☆ **Penolas Old Rectory Bed & Breakfast**, (B&B), 5 Bowden St, 400m SE of PO, ☎ 08 8737 2684, fax 08 8737 2064, 2 rms [shwr, spa bath (1), tlt, fan, heat, elec blkts, clock radio], lounge (TV), t/c mkg shared, bbq, non smoking property. **BB** † **$50**, †† **$90**, BC MC VI.

Other Accommodation

McKays Trek Inn, (Lodge), 38 Riddoch St, ☎ 08 8723 0032, fax 08 8723 2477, 1 rm acc up to 24, (Bunk Rooms), [fan, cent heat, t/c mkg, micro, doonas, linen reqd-fee], lounge (TV & Video), cook fac, refrig, bbq, c/park (limited), non smoking property. **BLB** † **$18**, ⚥ **$18**, BTC DC MC VI.

Pop 2,138. (235km N Adelaide), See map on pages 586/587, ref H5. An historic railway town, on the edge of the Flinders Ranges. Bowls, Golf, Scenic Drives, Swimming (Pool), Tennis.

Hotels/Motels

★★★☆ **Peterborough Motor Inn**, (M), 25 Queen St, ☎ 08 8651 2078, fax 08 8651 2428, 27 units [ensuite, spa bath (1), hairdry, a/c, elec blkts, tel, TV, clock radio, t/c mkg, refrig], ldry, ⊠, pool, rm serv, cots, non smoking units (13). **RO** † **$65 - $115**, †† **$75 - $115**, ⚥ **$11**, fam con, 1 unit of a higher rating. AE BC DC EFT MC VI, ♨⚕.

★★★☆ **Railway Hotel Motel**, (LMH), 221 Main St, ☎ 08 8651 2427, fax 08 8651 2132, 5 units [ensuite, spa bath (1), hairdry, a/c, tel, TV, clock radio, refrig], iron, iron brd, ⊠, rm serv, ☎, cots. **RO** † **$60.50 - $77**, †† **$66 - $77**, ⚥ **$5.50**, AE BC DC EFT MC VI.

★ **(Hotel Section)**, 16 rms [ensuite (2), a/c (5), c/fan, elec blkts, TV (5), t/c mkg (2), refrig (2)], lounge (TV), t/c mkg shared, refrig. **RO** † **$27.50**, †† **$38.50**, †† **$49.50**, ⚥ **$55**, 5 rooms of a higher standard.

★★★ **Peterborough Hotel Motel**, (LMH), 195 Main St, ☎ 08 8651 2006, fax 08 8651 2205, 9 units [ensuite, hairdry (5), a/c, elec blkts, TV, clock radio, t/c mkg, refrig], iron (5), iron brd (5), ⊠, ☎, cots-fee. **RO** † **$58**, †† **$63**, ⚥ **$11**, AE BC DC EFT MC MCH VI.

B&B's/Guest Houses

Amelia Park, (B&B), Hwy 56, Hwy 56, 10km E of Peterborough, ☎ 08 8651 3177, fax 08 8651 3177, 1 rm [shwr, tlt, hairdry, fan, heat, elec blkts, TV, clock radio, t/c mkg], w/mach-fee, iron, iron brd, lounge (TV), Pets allowed outside only and restrained. **BB** † **$70**, †† **$105 - $110**, ⚥ **$15**. BC MC VI, (not yet classified).

Saint Cecilia Hotel, (PH), Callary St, ☎ 08 8651 2654, (2 stry), 20 rms [elec blkts, doonas], bathrm, ldry, lounge (TV), lounge firepl, ⊠, t/c mkg shared, refrig, cots. **BB** † **$44**, Minimum of 2 people by reservation. Min book applies, AE BC MC VI.

Pop 645. (243km E Adelaide), See map on pages 586/587, ref E8. A modern town situated in low undulating country, 5km from the Victorian border. Bowls, Bush Walking, Croquet, Golf, Swimming (Pool), Tennis.

Hotels/Motels

★★★ **Pinnaroo Motel**, (M), Mallee Hwy, ☎ 08 8577 8261, fax 08 8577 8240, 14 units [ensuite, a/c-cool, heat, elec blkts, tel, TV, video-fee, clock radio, t/c mkg, refrig, toaster], rm serv, cots. **RO** † **$52**, †† **$64**, ⚥ **$10**, ch con, AE BC DC MC VI.

Self Catering Accommodation

★★★☆ **Wattle Farm**, (Cotg), Venning Rd, 8km N of PO, ☎ 08 8577 8305, fax 08 8577 8530, 1 cotg acc up to 6, (3 bedrm), [shwr (2), bath, tlt, a/c, fan, tel, TV, clock radio, t/c mkg, refrig, cook fac, toaster, ldry (in unit), blkts, doonas, linen, pillows], w/mach, iron, iron brd, lounge firepl, bbq, c/park (carport), breakfast ingredients, non smoking property. **D** †† **$77 - $110**, ch con.

B&B's/Guest Houses

★★★☆ **Alcheringa Homestead**, (B&B), Bordertown Rd, 25km S of PO, ☎ 08 8576 6171, fax 08 8576 6171, 3 rms [shwr (2), bath (1), tlt (2), fan, elec blkts], w/mach, lounge (TV & Radio), t/c mkg shared, meals avail. **BB** † **$60**, †† **$85**, ⚥ **$35**, **DBB** † **$77**, †† **$121**, ch con.

Pop Nominal, (117km N Adelaide), See map on pages 586/587, ref C6. Situated in the Mid North Region.

★★★★ **Old Immanuel College Bed & Breakfast**, (B&B), Robertstown Rd, ☎ 08 8581 1552, fax 08 8581 1552, 3 rms [ensuite (1), shwr (2), tlt (2), elec blkts, t/c mkg], lounge, non smoking rms. **BB** † **$85**, †† **$120**.

Pop Part of Warooka, (247km W Adelaide), See map on pages 586/587, ref A7. Small fishing port located on the coast. Boating, Fishing, Swimming (Beach).

Cables Holiday House, (Cotg), Section 363, North Coast Rd, 2.5km W of PO, ☎ 08 8552 6725, fax 08 8552 6725, 1 cotg acc up to 7, (3 bedrm), [a/c, fan, TV, video, t/c mkg, refrig, cook fac, toaster, blkts, linen (main bed only), pillows], w/mach, c/park. **D** †† **$80 - $90**, (not yet classified).

PORT AUGUSTA SA 5700

Pop 14,595. (305km NNW Adelaide), See map on pages 586/587, ref H5. Known as the 'Crossroads of the North', it is an important city at the head of Spencer Gulf. Roads from Adelaide, the Flinders Ranges, Alice Springs, Perth and Whyalla all intersect here. ETSA Augusta Power Stations, Galleries, Lookouts, Museums, Royal Flying Doctor Services base, School of the Air and Wadlata Outback Centre. Boating, Bowls, Croquet, Fishing, Golf, Greyhound Racing, Horse Racing, Horse Riding, Sailing, Squash, Swimming (Beach & Pool), Tennis, Trotting.

Hotels/Motels

★★★★ **Augusta Westside Motel**, (M), 3 Loudon Rd, 1km W of PO, ☎ 08 8642 2488, fax 08 8641 0722, 20 units [ensuite, a/c, c/fan, elec blkts, tel, cable tv, video-fee, clock radio, t/c mkg, refrig, mini bar, toaster], ldry-fee, w/mach-fee, dryer-fee, iron, iron brd, pool, bbq, rm serv, dinner to unit, plygr, cots-fee, non smoking units (9). **RO** ♦ **$92 - $145,** ♦♦ **$98 - $145,** ◊ **$6,** pen con, AE BC DC EFT JCB MC VI.

★★★★ **Pastoral Hotel Motel**, (LMH), 17 Stirling Rd, 1km S of PO, ☎ 08 8642 2818, fax 08 8641 0948, 13 units [ensuite, bath (1), hairdry, a/c, tel, TV, clock radio, t/c mkg, refrig, toaster], ldry-fee, w/mach, dryer, iron (avail), iron brd (avail), ⊠ (Mon to Sat), bar, rm serv, dinner to unit (Mon to Sat), ✆, non smoking units (7). **BLB** ♦ **$82,** ♦♦ **$88,** ◊ **$20,** pen con, AE BC DC EFT MC VI.

★★★☆ **Myoora Motel**, (M), Eyre Hwy, 3km NW of PO, ☎ 08 8642 3622, fax 08 8642 2857, 21 units [ensuite, hairdry (18), a/c, tel, TV, t/c mkg, refrig, toaster], iron (18), iron brd (18), ⊠ (Mon to Sat), bbq, dinner to unit, cots. **RO** ♦ **$66 - $60,** ♦♦ **$74 - $70,** ◊ **$12,** AE BC DC EFT JCB MC MP VI, ♿.

★★★☆ **Pt Augusta Hi-Way One Motel**, (M), Highway One, ☎ 08 8642 2755, fax 08 8641 0588, 45 units [ensuite, hairdry, a/c, elec blkts, tel, cable tv, clock radio, t/c mkg, refrig], ldry, iron, ⊠ (Mon to Sat), pool-heated (solar), bbq, rm serv, cots-fee. **RO** ♦ **$66 - $104,** ♦♦ **$74 - $112,** ◊ **$8,** ch con, 14 units ★★★. AE BC DC EFT MC VI, ♿.

★★★☆ **Standpipe Golf Motor Inn**, (M), Cnr Eyre & Stuart Hwys, 2.1km N of PO, ☎ 08 8642 4033, fax 08 8641 0571, (2 stry gr fl), 87 units [ensuite, spa bath (1), a/c, c/fan (12), elec blkts, tel, TV, video (4), clock radio, t/c mkg, refrig, toaster], ldry, w/mach-fee, dryer-fee, conf fac, ⊠, pool, bbq, rm serv, cots-fee, non smoking units (84). **RO** ♦ **$87,** ♦♦ **$92,** ♦♦♦ **$109,** ◊ **$16,** fam con, AE BC DC EFT MC VI, ♿.

★★★ **Acacia Ridge Motor Inn**, (M), 33 Stokes Tce, 2km NW of PO, ☎ 08 8642 3377, fax 08 8642 4323, 47 units [ensuite, bath (hip) (22), a/c, elec blkts, tel, cable tv, video (avail), clock radio, t/c mkg, refrig], ldry, w/mach-fee, dryer-fee, iron (avail), iron brd (avail), conf fac, ⊠ (Mon to Sat), pool, bbq, cots-fee, non smoking units (12). **RO** ♦ **$58 - $65,** ♦♦ **$65 - $73,** ◊ **$11,** 15 units ★★★☆ and 8 units of a lower rating. AE BC DC EFT MCH VI.

★★☆ **Hotel Flinders**, (LMH), 39 Commercial Rd, ☎ 08 8642 2544, fax 08 8641 0589, (2 stry gr fl), 30 units [ensuite, bath (1), a/c, tel, TV, clock radio, t/c mkg, refrig], lounge, conf fac, ⊠ (Mon to Sat), dinner to unit, c/park (limited), ✆, cots-fee. **RO** ♦ **$49.50,** ♦♦ **$66,** ◊ **$11,** AE BC EFT MC VI, ♿.

(Backpacker Section), 3 rms acc up to 3, [a/c, TV, refrig, blkts, linen, pillows], shared fac. **D** ♦ **$16.50,** ◊ **$16.50.**

★★☆ **Motel Pampas**, (M), 76 Stirling Rd, 2km E of PO, ☎ 08 8642 3795, fax 08 8641 1126, 8 units [ensuite, hairdry, a/c-cool, heat, TV, clock radio, t/c mkg, refrig, micro, toaster], ✗, dinner to unit, ✆, non smoking property. **RO** ♦ **$55,** ♦♦ **$66,** ◊ **$11,** BC MC VI.

★★☆ **Motel Poinsettia**, (M), 24 Burgoyne St, 3km N of PO, ☎ 08 8642 2411, fax 08 8641 0822, 23 units [ensuite, a/c, tel, TV, video-fee, clock radio, t/c mkg, refrig, toaster], ldry, w/mach-fee, bbq, rm serv, dinner to unit (Mon to Sat), cots. **RO** ♦ **$55,** ♦♦ **$60.50,** ◊ **$5,** AE BC EFT MC VI.

★★ **Port Augusta East Motel**, (M), Highway One, 5km E of PO, ☎ 08 8641 1008, fax 08 8641 0571, 15 units [ensuite, a/c, elec blkts, tel, TV, clock radio, t/c mkg, refrig, toaster], bbq, cots-fee, non smoking units (5). **RO** ♦ **$54,** ♦♦ **$59,** ♦♦♦♦ **$80,** ◊ **$16,** AE BC DC EFT MC VI.

Northern Hotel Port Augusta, (LH), 4 Tassie St, 200m N of PO, ☎ 08 8642 2522, fax 08 8642 3143, (2 stry), 28 rms [ensuite (4), a/c (12)], ✗, ✆, cots, non smoking rms. **BLB** ♦ **$25 - $45,** ♦♦ **$35 - $50,** ◊ **$5,** BC EFT MC VI.

Other Accommodation

Nuttbush Retreat Lodge, (Lodge), Eyre Hwy, Pandurra Station, 40km W of PO, ☎ 08 8643 8941, fax 08 8643 8906, 30 rms acc up to 8, [a/c (30), c/fan (10), doonas, linen, pillows], rec rm, lounge (TV), ⊠, res liquor license, pool, t/c mkg shared, refrig, tennis. **D** ♦ **$33,** ♦♦ **$55,** AE BC MC VI.

PORT BROUGHTON SA 5522

Pop 681. (170km N Adelaide), See map on pages 586/587, ref H5. A coastal holiday resort on the Yorke Peninsula. Boating, Bowls, Fishing, Golf, Swimming (Beach), Tennis.

★★☆ **Port Broughton Sunnyside Hotel Motel**, (LMH), 17 Bay St, ☎ 08 8635 2100, fax 08 8635 2353, 19 units [shwr, tlt, a/c, elec blkts, tel, TV, clock radio, t/c mkg, refrig], conv fac, ⊠, pool, rm serv, ✆, cots. **RO** ♦ **$55 - $95,** ♦♦ **$60.50 - $95,** ♦♦♦ **$71.50 - $95,** ◊ **$5,** Breakfast available, AE BC EFT MC VI.

★ **Port Broughton Hotel**, (LH), 2 Bay St, ☎ 08 8635 2004, fax 08 8635 2117, (2 stry), 8 rms [a/c-cool (5), c/fan (2), heat], lounge (TV), ⊠, t/c mkg shared, ✆, cots, non smoking rms. **BLB** ♦ **$35,** ♦♦ **$45,** ch con, BC EFT MC VI.

PORT ELLIOT SA 5212

Pop 1,203. (82km S Adelaide), See map on pages 586/587, ref B8. A tourist resort set on picturesque Horseshoe Bay, on the Fleurieu Peninsula. Boating, Bowls, Fishing, Gem Fossicking, Horse Riding, Sailing, Surfing, Swimming (Beach), Tennis, Water Skiing.

Hotels/Motels

★★★☆ **The Strand Inn**, (M), 7 The Strand, ☎ 08 8554 2067, fax 08 8554 3066, (2 stry gr fl), 15 units [ensuite, bath (3), spa bath (2), a/c, elec blkts, tel, TV, clock radio, t/c mkg, refrig], ldry, ⊠ (Mon-Sat), pool, bbq, rm serv, cots-fee, non smoking property. **RO** ♦ **$80 - $140,** ♦♦ **$80 - $140,** ◊ **$12.50,** 1 room of a higher standard. 2 rooms of a lower rating, AE BC DC MC VI.

Self Catering Accommodation

★★★★☆ **LJ Hooker Holiday Accommodation**, (Apt), Seaspell Apartment. 10 Basham Pde, 300m E of PO, ☎ 08 8552 1944, fax 08 8552 5075, (2 stry gr fl), 1 apt acc up to 16, (4 bedrm), [shwr (3), spa bath (1), tlt (3), a/c-cool, fan, heat, elec blkts, TV, video, clock radio, CD, t/c mkg, refrig, cook fac, micro, d/wash, toaster, ldry (in unit), blkts, doonas, linen, pillows], w/mach, dryer, iron, iron brd, sauna, bbq, c/park (garage), cots, non smoking property, **W $950 - $2,650,** $200 bond. Min book applies.

★★★★☆ **Southcoast Retreat**, (Cotg), Resort, 2A The Strand, ☎ 08 8552 5744, fax 08 8396 1833, (2 stry gr fl), 1 cotg acc up to 8, (3 bedrm), [shwr (2), spa bath, tlt (2), a/c, c/fan, elec blkts, TV (2), video, clock radio (cassette), CD, refrig, cook fac, micro, elec frypan, toaster, ldry, doonas, linen reqd-fee, pillows], w/mach, dryer, iron, iron brd, **W $550 - $1,200,** Min book applies.

★★★☆ **Heathfield Estate**, (House), 30 Waterport Rd, ☎ 0407 604 337, fax 08 8554 3292, 1 house acc up to 16, (8 bedrm), [shwr, bath, tlt, a/c, fan, elec blkts, tel, TV, video, t/c mkg, refrig, cook fac, micro, d/wash, toaster, ldry, blkts, linen, pillows], w/mach, iron, iron brd, pool (salt water), spa, bbq, c/park (garage), non smoking property, **W $1,600 - $4,500,** Min book applies.

★★★ **R & R Country Cottage**, (Cotg), Crows Nest Rd, 9km N of PO, ☎ 08 8554 6556, fax 08 8554 6553, 1 cotg acc up to 4, [shwr, tlt, a/c, fan, TV, video, CD, t/c mkg, refrig, cook fac, micro, elec frypan, toaster, blkts, pillows], tank water, w/mach, iron, iron brd, bbq, non smoking property. **D $99, W $495**, Min book applies.

★★☆ **Adare Caravan Park & Holiday Units**, (Cotg), Devona Cottages. 2 Mason St, ☎ 08 8552 1657, fax 08 8552 1657, 2 cotgs acc up to 6, (2 bedrm3 bedrm), [shwr, tlt, heat, elec blkts, TV, clock radio, refrig, cook fac, micro, linen reqd], w/mach, iron, iron brd, bbq, non smoking property, **D ♦♦ $55, ◊ $3.30, W ♦♦ $330, ◊ $19.80**, Min book applies, BC MC VI.

★★☆ **Dodd & Page Accommodation**, (HU), Dolphins Court Holiday Units. Strangways Tce, Horseshoe Bay 500m E of PO, ☎ 08 8554 2029, fax 08 8554 2993, (2 stry gr fl), 9 units acc up to 6, (1, 2 & 3 bedrm), [shwr, bath, tlt, fan, heat, TV, refrig, cook fac, micro (7), linen reqd], ldry, cots (avail), non smoking units (6). **W $280 - $680**, Min book Christmas Jan and Easter.

★★☆ **Horseshoe Apartments**, (HU), 4-6 The Strand, cnr Freeling St, ☎ 08 8554 2029, fax 08 8554 2993, 16 units acc up to 6, (1 & 2 bedrm), [shwr, bath (hip), tlt, fan, heat, TV, refrig, cook fac, micro, blkts, pillows], w/mach, iron, bbq, c/park (undercover). **D $50 - $400**, Min book.

★★☆ **Rosetta Cottage**, (Cotg), 3 Rosetta Tce, ☎ 08 8388 6296, fax 08 83913399, 1 cotg acc up to 6, (2 bedrm), [shwr, tlt, heat (slow combustion), TV, video, micro, ldry, linen reqd-fee], w/mach, bbq, plygr, cots, non smoking property. **D $65 - $100, W $360 - $650**, Min book all holiday times.

Tarooki B&B, (Apt), 13 Charteris St, ☎ 08 8554 2886, fax 08 8554 2796, 1 apt acc up to 4, (2 bedrm), [shwr, bath (1), tlt, c/fan, heat (elec), elec blkts, TV, video, clock radio, t/c mkg, refrig, cook fac, micro, toaster, blkts, doonas, linen, pillows], w/mach, bbq. **BB ♦ $100, ♦♦ $140, ◊ $10**, BC MC VI, (not yet classified).

B&B's/Guest Houses

★★★☆ **Thomas Henry's**, (B&B), 8 Charteris St, 400m S of PO, ☎ 08 8554 3388, fax 08 8554 3388, 6 rms [c/fan, heat (combustion/oil), elec blkts], lounge (guest), res liquor license, meals avail (dinner), non smoking property. **BB ♦ $99, ♦♦ $115.50**, BC MC VI.

★★★☆ **Trafalgar House Accommodation**, (B&B), No children's facilities, 25 The Strand, ☎ 08 8554 3888, fax 08 8554 3888, 4 rms (1 suite) [ensuite (1), hairdry (2), fan, heat, elec blkts, clock radio, cook fac (1)], t/c mkg shared, bbq, non smoking property. **BB ♦ $85, ♦♦ $90 - $120, ◊ $20, Suite D ♦♦ $120**, BC MC VI.

(Cottage Section), 1 cotg acc up to 4, (2 bedrm), [shwr, tlt, a/c, fan, c/fan, elec blkts, TV, clock radio, t/c mkg, refrig, cook fac, micro, toaster, blkts, linen-fee, pillows], w/mach, iron, iron brd, bbq, non smoking property. **D $95 - $120, W $400 - $600**, (not yet classified).

PORT HUGHES SA 5558

Pop Part of Moonta, (171km NW Adelaide), See map on pages 586/587, ref A6. Popular fishing resort on the Yorke Peninsula. Boating, Fishing.

Self Catering Accommodation

★★★ **Cabarita Holiday Homes**, (HU), 45 Randolph St, ☎ 08 8825 2981, fax 08 8825 2981, 3 units acc up to 6, (2 & 3 bedrm), [shwr, bath (1), tlt, a/c, heat, elec blkts, TV, radio, t/c mkg, refrig, cook fac, micro, elec frypan, toaster, ldry (in unit), linen reqd-fee], iron, iron brd, bbq, c/park (carport) (2), cots, non smoking units. **D $50 - $85**, BC MC VI.

★★★★☆ **(Bed & Breakfast Section)**, 47 South Tce, 2 rms [ensuite, hairdry, elec blkts, clock radio, refrig], spa, t/c mkg shared, bbq, non smoking rms. **BB ♦♦ $120 - $135**.

★★★ **Maji**, (HU), 20 Minnie Tce, ☎ 08 8825 2251, 1 unit acc up to 7, (4 bedrm), [shwr (2), bath, tlt (2), a/c, TV, clock radio (avail), refrig, cook fac, micro, doonas], w/mach, iron, iron brd, bbq, non smoking property. **D ♦♦♦♦ $110, ◊ $10**.

PORT LINCOLN SA 5606

Pop 11,345. (692km W Adelaide), See map on pages 586/587, ref F6. Located at its southern tip, Port Lincoln is Eyre Peninsula's second largest city. Boating, Bowls, Croquet, Fishing, Golf, Greyhound Racing, Horse Racing, Horse Riding, Sailing, Squash, Surfing, Swimming (Beach), Tennis, Vineyards, Wineries, Water Skiing.

Hotels/Motels

★★★★ **Limani Motel**, (M), 50 Lincoln Hwy, 1km N of PO, ☎ 08 8682 2200, fax 08 8682 6602, (Multi-stry gr fl), 22 units [ensuite, spa bath (1), hairdry, a/c, elec blkts, tel, cable tv, video-fee, clock radio, t/c mkg, refrig, cook fac (4), micro-fee, toaster], w/mach-fee, dryer-fee, iron, iron brd, c/park (undercover). **BLB ♦ $100 - $145, ♦♦ $105 - $145, ♦♦♦ $115 - $140, ♦♦♦♦ $126 - $140, ◊ $15**, fam con, AE BC DC EFT MC VI, ⅙.

★★★☆ **First Landing Motel**, (M), 11 Shaen St, 2km N of PO, ☎ 08 8682 2344, fax 08 8683 0470, 8 units [ensuite, hairdry, a/c, elec blkts, tel, TV, video, clock radio, t/c mkg, refrig], cots. **RO ♦ $62 - $68, ♦♦ $69 - $75, ◊ $10**, 4 rooms ★★★, Min book long w/ends and Easter, AE BC DC MC MCH VI.

★★★☆ **Hilton Motel**, (M), 13 King St, beachfront, 2km SE of PO, ☎ 08 8682 1144, fax 08 8682 3786, (2 stry gr fl), 39 units [ensuite, spa bath (8), a/c, elec blkts, tel, cable tv, clock radio, t/c mkg, refrig], ldry, w/mach, dryer, iron, iron brd, conf fac, ⊠ (Mon to Sat), rm serv, cots-fee. **RO ♦ $60 - $90, ♦♦ $65 - $150, ◊ $8**, ch con, 18 rooms ★★★★, Min book long w/ends and Easter, AE BC DC EFT MC VI.

★★★ **Blue Seas Motel**, (M), 7 Gloucester Tce, 900m NW of PO, ☎ 08 8682 3022, fax 08 8682 6932, (Multi-stry gr fl), 15 units [ensuite, a/c, elec blkts, tel, TV, video-fee, movie, clock radio, t/c mkg, refrig, toaster], ldry, w/mach-fee, dryer-fee, iron, iron brd, dinner to unit, c/park (carport) (4), cots-fee. **RO ♦ $55 - $65, ♦♦ $65 - $75, ◊ $11**, AE BC DC EFT MC VI,
Operator Comment: Central location with Panoramic Harbour Views.

★★★ **Navigators Motel**, (M), Cnr Lincoln Hwy & Normandy Pl, 1km NE of PO, ☎ 08 8682 4633, fax 08 8683 4045, (2 stry gr fl), 11 units [ensuite, spa bath (5), a/c, elec blkts, tel, cable tv, video (5), clock radio, t/c mkg, refrig, mini bar (5)], ⊠ (Mon-Sat), rm serv, dinner to unit, cots. **BLB ♦ $65 - $88, ♦♦ $75 - $98, ◊ $10**, ch con, 5 rooms ★★★★. AE BC DC MC VI.

★★★ **Peninsula Motel**, (M), 12-14 Tasman Tce, 1km NE of PO, ☎ 08 8682 2033, fax 08 8682 6951, (Multi-stry), 41 units [ensuite, a/c, elec blkts, tel, cable tv (25), clock radio, t/c mkg, refrig, cook fac (3), elec frypan (8), toaster], ldry, w/mach-fee, dryer-fee, iron, ⊠ (Mon to Sat), cots. **RO ♦ $55 - $88, ♦♦ $66 - $99, ◊ $11**, ch con, 13 rooms ★★★☆, AE BC DC EFT MC VI.

★★ **Boston House (Motel)**, (M), Lincoln Hwy, 4.5km N of PO, ☎ 08 8682 1872, 4 units [heat, elec blkts, TV, t/c mkg, refrig], cots-fee. **RO ♦ $33, ♦♦ $44, ◊ $10**.

Self Catering Accommodation

★★★★ **Lincoln Cove Accommodation Apartments**, (Apt), 1 Bridge Cres, ☎ 08 8683 0495, fax 08 8683 0495, (2 stry), 2 apts acc up to 6, (3 bedrm), [shwr, spa bath, tlt, c/fan, heat, elec blkts, TV, clock radio, t/c mkg, refrig, cook fac, micro, elec frypan, d/wash, toaster, ldry (in unit), linen], w/mach, dryer, iron, iron brd, c/park (garage), **D $100 - $140**, Min book applies, BC MC VI.

★★★★ **Mc Kechnie Springs Farmstay**, (Cotg), 1905 McFarlane Rd, Greenpatch, 15km NW of PO, ☎ 08 8684 5057, fax 08 8684 5057, 1 cotg acc up to 5, (2 bedrm), [shwr, bath, tlt, hairdry, fan, fire pl, elec blkts, TV, video, clock radio, CD, refrig, cook fac, micro, toaster, doonas, linen, pillows], w/mach, dryer, iron, iron brd, lounge, bbq, meals to unit (min. 4 persons), cots, breakfast ingredients, non smoking rms, Pets on application. **D ♦♦ $90, ♦♦♦ $100, ♦♦♦♦ $110, ◊ $10, W ♦♦ $540, ♦♦♦ $600, ♦♦♦♦ $660, ◊ $60**, German & English library available. Min book applies,
Operator Comment: www.enneking.net
email: enneking@camtech.net.au

★★★☆ **(Woolshed Cottage)**, 1 cotg acc up to 11, (4 bedrm), [shwr, bath, tlt, hairdry, fan, fire pl, elec blkts, TV, video, clock radio, refrig, cook fac, micro, toaster, blkts, doonas, linen, pillows], w/mach, dryer, iron, iron brd, lounge, freezer, bbq, meals avail (min. 4 persons), cots, breakfast ingredients, non smoking rms, Pets on application. **D ♦ $35, ♦♦ $50, ♦♦♦ $60, ♦♦♦♦ $70, ◊ $10, W ♦ $210, ♦♦ $300, ♦♦♦ $360, ♦♦♦♦ $420, ◊ $60**, German & English library available. Min book applies.

★★★★ **Port Lincoln Marina Townhouses**, (Apt), Unit 8-19B Island Dr, ☎ 08 8682 2222, fax 08 8683 1650, 8 apts acc up to 6, [shwr (2), bath (6), spa bath, tlt (2), a/c, c/fan, elec blkts, TV, video (avail) (1), movie (Pay TV), clock radio, t/c mkg, refrig, cook fac, micro, d/wash, toaster, blkts, doonas, linen, pillows], w/mach, dryer, iron, iron brd, c/park (garage). **D $155, W $700 - $1,085**, AE BC DC MC VI.

★★★★ **The Marina Hotel & Apartments**, (Apt), 13 Jubilee Dr, ☎ 08 8682 6141, fax 08 8682 6702, (Multi-stry), 11 apts acc up to 9, [shwr, bath, spa bath (5), tlt (2), hairdry, a/c, c/fan, elec blkts, tel, cable tv, clock radio, t/c mkg, refrig, mini bar, cook fac, micro, toaster, blkts, doonas, linen, pillows], w/mach, dryer, iron, iron brd, ⊠, bbq, non smoking units. **D ♦♦ $100 - $140, ◊ $15 - $20**, AE BC DC EFT MC VI.

★★★☆ **Harbourview Apartments**, (Apt), 30 Lincoln Hwy, Spalding Lodge, 1.5km N of PO, ☎ 08 8682 4477, (Multi-stry), 2 apts acc up to 5, (2 bedrm), [shwr, bath (hip), tlt, a/c, elec blkts, tel, TV, video, clock radio, t/c mkg, refrig, cook fac, micro, elec frypan (1), toaster, blkts, linen, pillows], ldry, w/mach-fee, dryer-fee, iron, iron brd, pool, c/park (carport), cots. **D $77 - $85**, BC MC VI.

PORT LINCOLN SA continued...

★★★ **Lincoln Cove Villas**, (Apt), Previously San Pan Apartments, 42 Parnkalla Ave, Lincoln Cove, ☎ 08 8683 0657, fax 08 8683 3165, 3 apts acc up to 6, (2 & 3 bedrm), [shwr, bath (2), tlt, a/c, heat, TV, clock radio, refrig, cook fac, micro, elec frypan, toaster, blkts, linen, pillows], ldry, w/mach, dryer, c/park (garage). **D** $80 - $120, One unit designed specifically for disabled persons. ♿

★★★ **Sorrento Lodge**, (HU), 8 Lincoln Hwy, 1km NE of PO, ☎ 08 8682 2033, fax 08 8682 6951, (Multi-stry gr fl), 12 units acc up to 5, (1 & 2 bedrm), [shwr, tlt, a/c, elec blkts, tel, TV, t/c mkg, refrig, cook fac, micro (4), elec frypan, toaster], ldry, ⊠ (Mon to Sat), cots. **RO ♦ $71.50, ♦♦ $82.50, ◊ $11**, ch con, AE BC DC EFT MC VI.

★★★ **The Yardarm B & B Holiday Unit**, (HU), 14 Telford Ave, 1km W of PO, ☎ 08 8683 0984, fax 08 8683 3621, 1 unit acc up to 3, (Studio), [ensuite, c/fan, heat, elec blkts, TV, video, clock radio, t/c mkg, refrig, cook fac, micro, toaster, blkts, doonas, linen, pillows], ldry, iron, iron brd, breakfast ingredients, non smoking units. **D ♦♦ $75 - $90, ◊ $12.**

Port Lincoln Cabin Park, Cnr London & Stevenson St, ☎ 08 8683 4884, fax 08 8682 2727, 7 cabins acc up to 5, (1 & 2 bedrm), [shwr, spa bath, tlt, a/c, elec blkts, TV, video-fee, clock radio, t/c mkg, refrig, cook fac, micro, toaster, blkts, linen, pillows], bbq-fee, non smoking property. **D** $38 - $90, ◊ $10, **W** $266 - $630, ◊ $70, Min book applies, AE BC DC EFT MC VI, (not yet classified).

B&B's/Guest Houses

★★★★☆ **Abeona Cottage Bed & Breakfast**, (B&B), 13 Para St, 2km N of PO, ☎ 08 8682 2344, fax 08 8683 0470, 1 rm (2 bedrm), [ensuite, bath, hairdry, a/c, elec blkts, tel, TV, video, radio (cassette), CD, t/c mkg, micro, toaster, pillows], lounge firepl. **BLB ♦ $95 - $115, ♦♦ $115 - $135, ◊ $20**, Min book long w/ends and Easter, AE BC DC MC MCH VI.

★★★★☆ **Port Lincoln Bed & Breakfast**, (B&B), 2 Power Tce, 3km S of PO, ☎ 08 8682 3550, fax 08 8682 1044, (2 stry), 1 rm (1 suite) [ensuite, spa bath, hairdry, a/c, elec blkts, TV, clock radio, t/c mkg, refrig, toaster], w/mach, bbq, non smoking units. **BB ♦ $85 - $95, ♦♦ $95 - $130.**

★★★★☆ **Swanmore Bed & Breakfast**, (B&B), 12 Adelphi Tce, 2km S of PO, ☎ 08 8682 2776, fax 08 8683 3660, (2 stry), 2 rms [ensuite, bath (1), hairdry, a/c (2), c/fan, heat, elec blkts, cable tv (1), video, clock radio (cassette), CD (1), t/c mkg, refrig, cook fac (1), micro (3), toaster, pillows], ldry, w/mach, dryer (shared), iron, iron brd, lounge (TV & Video), bbq, c/park. **BLB ♦ $80, ♦♦ $90, ◊ $10.**

★★★☆ **Island Towers Bed & Breakfast**, (B&B), 9 Island Dr, 1.5km SE from town centre, ☎ 08 8683 3677, 1 rm [ensuite, hairdry, heat, TV, video (movies), clock radio, t/c mkg, refrig, mini bar, toaster], ldry, w/mach-fee, dryer-fee, iron, iron brd, bbq. **BLB ♦ $90, ♦♦ $100, ◊ $20**, AE BC DC MC VI.

★★★☆ **Willtrees Bed & Breakfast**, (B&B), Lincoln Hwy, 5km N of PO, ☎ 08 8684 3570, fax 08 8684 3570, 1 rm [ensuite, a/c-cool, c/fan, fire pl, elec blkts, TV, clock radio, t/c mkg], c/park (undercover), non smoking property. **BB ♦ $50, ♦♦ $80.**

Pilkarra Lodge, (B&B), 1 New West Rd, 1km NW of PO, ☎ 08 8683 3040, fax 08 8683 1109, 1 rm [shwr, tlt, c/fan (1), heat (elec/gas/wood), elec blkts, tel, TV, video, clock radio, cook fac, ldry, doonas], lounge firepl, ✗, t/c mkg shared, refrig, bbq, breakfast ingredients, non smoking property. **D ♦ $220, ♦♦ $220, ◊ $70**, BC DC MC VI, (not yet classified).

Pop 677. (467km SE Adelaide), See map on pages 586/587, ref J8. The town is noted for its $1.2 million breakwater which shelters the largest rock lobster fishing fleet in the State. Boating, Bowls, Bush Walking, Fishing, Golf, Surfing, Swimming (Beach), Tennis.

Hotels/Motels

★★ **Seaview Motel & Holiday Units**, (M), 77 Sea Pde, ☎ 08 8738 2243, 7 units [ensuite, heat, elec blkts, TV, clock radio, t/c mkg, refrig, cook fac (2), toaster], ldry, bbq, cots-fee. **RO ♦ $38.50, ♦♦ $44 - $49.50, ◊ $5.50**, BC EFT MC VI.

★★☆ **(Holiday Unit Section)**, 4 units acc up to 4, (1 & 2 bedrm), [ensuite, heat, elec blkts, TV, clock radio, refrig, cook fac, micro, linen reqd-fee], cots-fee. **D** $44 - $49.50.

Self Catering Accommodation

★★★ **Meybook Cottage**, (Cotg), 12 Bookey St, 479km SE of Adelaide, ☎ 08 8724 8667, 1 cotg acc up to 5, [shwr, tlt, fan, heat, elec blkts, TV, video, clock radio, t/c mkg, refrig, cook fac, micro, toaster, blkts, doonas, linen, pillows], lounge firepl (slow combustion), c/park. **D ♦ $70, ♦♦ $85, ◊ $20**, ch con, weekly con.

Pop 510. (608km NW Adelaide), See map on pages 586/587, ref G6. Located on the western shores of Spencer Gulf on the Eyre Peninsula. Bowls, Fishing, Golf, Swimming (Beach), Tennis, Water Skiing.

Hotels/Motels

Port Neill Hotel, (LH), 7 Peake Tce, ☎ 08 8688 9006, fax 08 8688 9096, (2 stry), 5 rms [ensuite (1), TV (1), cable tv (1), refrig (1), cook fac (1)], lounge (TV), ⊠, t/c mkg shared, **♦. BLB ♦ $25, ♦♦ $50, ◊ $25**, ch con, BC EFT MC VI.

Self Catering Accommodation

★★ **Henleys Holiday Flats**, (HU), 1 Gill St, ☎ 08 8688 9001, fax 08 8688 9001, 4 units acc up to 6, [shwr, tlt, a/c, TV, clock radio, refrig, cook fac, ldry, linen reqd], cots. **D** $50, **W** $335.

Pop 15,114. (229km NNW Adelaide), See map on pages 586/587, ref H5. South Australia's first provincial city, a thriving industrial and commercial centre. Boating, Bowls, Bush Walking, Croquet, Fishing, Golf, Greyhound Racing, Horse Racing, Horse Riding, Sailing, Squash, Swimming (Beach & Pool), Tennis, Trotting, Water Skiing.

Hotels/Motels

FLAG
FLAG CHOICE HOTELS

★★★☆ **John Pirie Motor Inn**, (M), Main Rd, ☎ 08 8632 4200, fax 08 8632 3959, 34 units [ensuite, bath (7), spa bath (7), hairdry, a/c, elec blkts, tel, cable tv, clock radio, t/c mkg, refrig, mini bar], ldry, iron, iron brd, ⊠, pool, bbq, rm serv, cots, non smoking rms (14). **RO ♦ $89, ♦♦ $89, ◊ $15**, ch con, 7 units ★★★★. AE BC DC MC VI, ♿.

Budget
Motel
Chain
International

★★★ **Travelway Motel**, (M), 149 Gertrude St, CBD, ☎ 08 8632 2222, fax 08 8633 0440, 29 units [ensuite, a/c, elec blkts, tel, TV, video-fee, clock radio, t/c mkg, refrig, mini bar], ldry, conv fac, ⊠ (Mon to Sat), pool, bbq, rm serv, plygr, cots, Pets on application. **RO ♦ $62, ♦♦ $70, ♦♦♦ $80, ◊ $10**, AE BC DC EFT MC MCH VI.

★★☆ **Abbacy Motel**, (M), 46 Florence St, ☎ 08 8632 3701, fax 08 8633 0896, 10 units [shwr, tlt, hairdry, a/c, elec blkts, tel, TV, movie, clock radio, t/c mkg, refrig, toaster], ⊠, rm serv, cots-fee. **RO ♦ $49.50, ♦♦ $55, ◊ $6**, AE BC DC MC VI.

Hotel Newcastle, (LH), 18 Main Rd, ☎ 08 8632 3925, fax 08 8632 3925, (2 stry), 9 rms [a/c, heat, elec blkts], lounge (TV), t/c mkg shared, **♦**, cots. **BLB ♦ $25, ♦♦ $40**, ch con, EFT.

Self Catering Accommodation

★★★★ **Cabin Park Port Pirie**, 137 Main Rd, 1km E of PO, ☎ 08 8633 2666, fax 08 8633 1677, 31 cabins acc up to 6, [ensuite, spa bath (3), hairdry, a/c, elec blkts, TV, video (3), clock radio, refrig, cook fac, micro, toaster, blkts, linen, pillows], ldry, w/mach-fee, dryer-fee, iron, iron brd, **♦. D ♦♦ $55 - $93.50, ◊ $11**, AE BC DC EFT MC VI.

★★★★ **Sampsons Cottage**, (Cotg), Classified by National Trust, No children's facilities, 66 Ellen St, ☎ 08 8632 2272, 1 cotg acc up to 6, (2 bedrm), [shwr, spa bath, tlt, hairdry, a/c, fire pl, elec blkts, TV, video, radio, refrig, cook fac, micro, d/wash, toaster, blkts, linen, pillows], w/mach, dryer, iron, iron brd, bbq, breakfast ingredients, non smoking property. **D ♦ $90 - $95, ♦♦ $95 - $100, ◊ $28.**

★★★★ **The Old Schoolhouse Cottage**, (Cotg), 122 Three Chain Rd, ☎ 08 8632 2272, 1 cotg acc up to 6, (3 bedrm), [shwr, bath, spa bath, tlt, hairdry, a/c, c/fan, fire pl (bedroom), elec blkts, TV (2), video, clock radio, refrig, cook fac, micro, toaster, blkts, linen, pillows], w/mach, dryer, iron, iron brd, bbq, breakfast ingredients, non smoking property. **D ♦♦ $95 - $100, ◊ $28.**

Pop 313. (198km W Adelaide), See map on pages 586/587, ref A6. Popular tourist town situated on the west coast of Yorke Peninsula on Spencer Gulf, overlooking Wardang Island. Boating, Bowls, Fishing, Golf, Sailing, Swimming (Beach), Tennis, Water Skiing.

★★☆ **Bayview Holiday Units**, (HU), 29 Davis Tce, 500m N of PO, ☎ 08 8834 2082, fax 08 8834 2082, 9 units acc up to 8, (1, 2 & 3 bedrm), [shwr, tlt, a/c-cool (3), TV, clock radio, refrig, cook fac, micro, linen reqd-fee], ldry, w/mach, bbq. **D** $35 - $60.

Pop 458. (181km W Adelaide), See map on pages 586/587, ref A7. Popular holiday resort set on a sweeping bay on the Yorke Peninsula. Boating, Bowls, Fishing, Golf, Swimming (Beach), Tennis, Water Skiing.

Hotels/Motels

★ **Ventnor Hotel**, (LH), Main St, ☎ 08 8853 7036, 2 rms **♦**, cots. **RO** $44, BC EFT MC VI.

Self Catering Accommodation

★★★★ **Port Vincent Holiday Cabins**, 12 Main St, 100m NW of PO, ☎ 08 8853 7411, fax 08 8853 7422, 8 cabins acc up to 4, (2 bedrm) [shwr, bath (hip), tlt, a/c, c/fan, heat, elec blkts, TV, clock radio, t/c mkg, refrig, cook fac, micro, toaster, blkts, linen, pillows], ldry-fee, dryer-fee, iron, iron brd, bbq, boat park, cots. **D ♦♦ $66 - $82.50, ◊ $11,** ch con, Min book long w/ends and Easter, EFT.

★★★ **Port Vincent Fishermans Retreat**, (HU), Parsons St, ☎ 08 8853 7057, 5 units acc up to 6, (2 bedrm), [shwr, tlt, a/c (4), c/fan, heat, TV, refrig, cook fac, micro, elec frypan, toaster, linen reqd-fee], w/mach, iron, iron brd, bbq, boat park, cots (highchair). **D $50 - $85**, Private courtyards, Min book Christmas Jan and Easter.

★★ **Alma Cottage**, (Cotg), 2 Alma St, ☎ 08 8854 2126, fax 08 8854 2103, 1 cotg acc up to 6, (2 bedrm), [shwr, tlt, TV, refrig, cook fac, micro, ldry, linen reqd], w/mach, c/park (garage), **D ♦♦♦♦ $50, ◊ $2,** Min book long w/ends and Easter.

★☆ **Gulf View Holiday Units**, (HU), McPharlin Ave, ☎ 08 8853 7018, (2 stry gr fl), 6 units acc up to 5, (2 & 3 bedrm), [shwr, tlt, heat, refrig, cook fac, blkts reqd, linen reqd], ldry, w/mach-fee, bbq-fee, cots. **D $30 - $45, W $150 - $250**, Min book school holidays and Easter.

PORT WAKEFIELD SA 5550

Pop 512. (96km NW Adelaide), See map on pages 586/587, ref B6. Historic township located at the head of Gulf St Vincent. Boating, Bowls, Croquet, Fishing, Golf, Swimming (Pool), Tennis.

 ★★☆ **Port Wakefield Motel**, (M), Main Rd, ☎ 08 8867 1271, fax 08 8867 1271, 9 units [ensuite, a/c-cool (5), a/c (4), heat, elec blkts, TV, t/c mkg, refrig], ldry, plygr, cots. **RO ♦ $50, ♦♦ $60, ◊ $5,** AE BC DC MC MCH VI.

PURNONG SA 5238

Pop Nominal, (121km E Adelaide), See map on pages 586/587, ref D7. A quiet township overlooking the Murray River which was originally the centre of a huge pastoral run. Boating, Fishing, Sailing, Swimming (River), Water Skiing.

Nankuri Houseboat, (Hbt), Purnong Rd, Mannum 5238, ☎ 08 8250 1370, fax 08 8250 1370, 1 houseboat acc up to 6, (2 bedrm), [shwr, tlt, c/fan, heat, TV, video, CD, refrig, cook fac, micro, blkts, doonas, linen, pillows], spa, ice box, bbq, secure park, cots. **W $803 - $1,278**, (not yet classified).

Wirraway Houseboats, (Hbt), Mannum to Purnong Rd, ☎ 08 8570 4273, 4 houseboats acc up to 12, [shwr, tlt, a/c-cool (3), heat, TV, video, radio, CD (2), refrig, cook fac, blkts, linen, pillows], bbq. **W $450 - $1,680**, BC MC VI.

QUORN SA 5433

Pop 1,389. (334km N Adelaide), See map on pages 586/587, ref H5. Old railway town nestled in a valley, amidst the colourful Flinders Ranges. Bowls, Bush Walking, Golf, Horse Racing, Horse Riding, Scenic Drives, Swimming (Pool), Tennis.

Hotels/Motels

★★★ **Flinders Ranges Motel**, (M), Previously The Mill Motel Quorn 2 Railway Tce, 200m SE of PO, ☎ 08 8648 6016, fax 08 8648 6279, 12 units [ensuite, a/c, heat, elec blkts, TV, clock radio, t/c mkg, refrig, toaster], ✉, cots-fee. **RO ♦ $74, ♦♦ $84, ◊ $12,** ch con, AE BC DC MC VI.

★☆ **Transcontinental Hotel**, (LH), 15 Railway Tce, ☎ 08 8648 6076, fax 08 8648 6759, 19 rms [fan (6), elec blkts], lounge, ✉, t/c mkg shared, refrig, ☎, non smoking rms. **BLB ♦ $32, ♦♦ $54 - $60, ♦♦♦ $65,** fam con, EFT.

Self Catering Accommodation

★★★ **Blossoms Cottage**, (Cotg), Railway Tce, Bruce, 25km SE of PO, ☎ 08 8648 6344, fax 08 8648 6994, 1 cotg acc up to 8, (2 bedrm), [shwr, tlt, hairdry, fire pl, elec blkts, TV, clock radio, refrig, cook fac, micro, toaster, blkts, linen, pillows], iron, bbq, breakfast ingredients. **D ♦♦ $150, ◊ $25,** ch con, Min book applies.

Pichi Richi Park Lodge, (HU), Quorn Rd, 20km N of Port Augusta, ☎ 08 8648 6075, fax 08 8648 6904, 2 units acc up to 6, [shwr, tlt, a/c, elec blkts, TV, video, t/c mkg, refrig, cook fac, micro, toaster, doonas, linen, pillows], w/mach-fee, iron-fee, iron brd, bbq, dinner to unit (by arrangement), ☎, Pets on application. **D ♦♦ $55, ◊ $20, W ♦♦ $330, ◊ $120,** BC MC VI, (not yet classified).

B&B's/Guest Houses

★★★☆ **Bruce Railway Station Hosted Accom**, (B&B), Railway Tce, Bruce, 25km SE of PO, ☎ 08 8648 6344, fax 08 8648 6994, 3 rms [evap cool, c/fan, heat, elec blkts, clock radio], bathrm (private), lounge (TV & video), lounge firepl, non smoking rms. **DBB ♦ $135, ♦♦ $250,** BC MC VI.

Other Accommodation

Andu Lodge, (Bunk), 12 First St, ☎ 08 8648 6655, fax 08 8648 6898, 1 bunkhouse acc up to 62, (Bunk Rooms) [shwr, bath, tlt, a/c-cool, heat, tel, TV, video, radio, refrig, cook fac, micro, toaster (communal), ldry, blkts, doonas, linen, pillows], tlt, w/mach, dryer, iron, iron brd, rec rm, TV rm, ✗, cook fac, t/c mkg shared, bbq, ☎. **D $18 - $26,** ch con, BC MC VI.

RENDELSHAM SA 5280

Pop Nominal, (398km SE Adelaide), See map on pages 586/587, ref J8. A small town on the Beachport to Millicent Road.

★★★☆ **The Cottage at Whispering Pines Farm**, (Cotg), Lot 10, Varcoe Rd, 1.2km S of PO, ☎ 08 8735 4211, fax 08 8735 4354, (2 stry), 1 cotg acc up to 2, (1 bedrm), [shwr, spa bath, tlt, heat (slow combustion), t/c mkg, refrig, cook fac, toaster, blkts, linen, pillows], ldry, bbq, breakfast ingredients. **D ♦♦ $90 - $110, ◊ $25.**

RENMARK SA 5341

Pop 4,256. (256km NE Adelaide), See map on pages 586/587, ref E6. Renmark is a modern community with a large commercial and business centre. Boating, Bowls, Bush Walking, Fishing, Golf, Horse Riding, Sailing, Squash, Swimming, Tennis, Vineyards, Wineries, Water Skiing.

Hotels/Motels

 ★★★☆ **Citrus Valley Best Western Motel**, (M), 210 Renmark Ave, 1km W of PO, ☎ 08 8586 6717, fax 08 8586 4080, 25 units [ensuite, hairdry (4), a/c (some), elec blkts, tel, cable tv, clock radio, t/c mkg, refrig, mini bar, toaster], ldry, w/mach-fee, dryer-fee, iron, iron brd, ✉ (Mon to Sat), pool, rm serv, meals to unit, c/park (undercover), plygr, cots-fee. **RO ♦ $75 - $90, ♦♦ $80 - $99, ◊ $15,** ch con, 6 rooms of a 2.5 star rating, Min book long w/ends and Easter, AE BC DC EFT JCB MC MP VI.

★★★☆ **Renmark Hotel Motel**, (LMH), Murray Ave, ☎ 08 8586 6755, fax 08 8586 6186, (Multi-stry), 37 units [ensuite, bath (hip) (9), a/c, elec blkts, tel, TV, clock radio, t/c mkg, refrig, mini bar], lift, conf fac, ✉, dinner to unit, cots. **RO ♦ $69 - $115, ♦♦ $81 - $126, ◊ $11.50,** ch con, AE BC DC EFT MC VI.

★★☆ **(Hotel Section)**, 29 rms [basin, ensuite, bath (1), a/c, elec blkts, tel, TV, clock radio, t/c mkg, refrig], dinner to unit. **RO ♦ $45, ♦♦ $57, ◊ $11.50,** ch con.

 ★★★☆ **Ventura Motel**, (M), 234 Renmark Ave, ☎ 08 8586 6841, fax 08 8586 5795, 15 units [ensuite, a/c, fan (4), c/fan (6), elec blkts, tel, TV, video-fee, clock radio, t/c mkg, refrig], ldry, w/mach, dryer, iron, iron brd, pool, bbq, rm serv, cots-fee. **RO ♦ $66, ♦♦ $75, ◊ $9,** AE BC DC EFT MC VI.

 ★★★ **Renmark Country Club Motel**, (M), Sturt Hwy, 8km SW of PO, ☎ 08 8595 1401, fax 08 8595 1771, 39 units (3 suites) [ensuite, hairdry, a/c-cool, heat, elec blkts, tel, TV, video-fee, clock radio, t/c mkg, refrig, mini bar, toaster], ldry, conv fac, ✉ (Mon to Sat), pool, rm serv, c/park (undercover), golf, tennis, cots-fee. **RO ♦ $84, ♦♦ $90, ◊ $11, Suite D ♦♦ $98, ◊ $11,** 7 units ★★★★. AE BC DC MC MP VI.

★★☆ **Fountain Gardens Motel**, (M), Renmark Ave, ☎ 08 8586 6899, fax 08 8586 6890, 22 units [ensuite, a/c-cool, heat, elec blkts, tel, TV, video-fee, clock radio, t/c mkg, refrig], pool, bbq, rm serv, c/park (undercover), plygr, cots. **RO ♦ $60.50 - $69.30, ◊ $11,** ch con, AE BC MC VI.

Self Catering Accommodation

Wilkadene Cottage, (Cotg), Wilkadene Homestead, Wilkinson Rd, Murtho 5340, 19km NE of PO, ☎ 08 8595 8188, fax 08 8595 8191, 1 cotg acc up to 6, [shwr, tlt, hairdry, a/c-cool, heat (combustion), tel, TV, video, clock radio, t/c mkg, refrig, cook fac, micro, toaster, blkts, doonas, linen, pillows], w/mach, iron, iron brd, bbq, tennis, breakfast ingredients, Pets on application. **D $580 - $979**, Punt with motor. Kayaks & bush bikes for hire. BC MC VI, (not yet classified).

Willows and Waterbirds Cottage, (Cotg), 41 Murray Ave, 1km E of PO, ☎ 08 8586 6704, 1 cotg acc up to 8, (3 bedrm), [a/c-cool, fire pl, heat, tel, TV, video, refrig, cook fac, micro, ldry, linen reqd], w/mach, iron, bbq, c/park (carport). **D ♦♦ $80 - $90, ◊ $10,** ch con, Min book applies.

Other Accommodation

Above Renmark Houseboats, (Hbt), Wilkadene Homestead, Wilkinson Rd, Murtho 5340, 19km NE of PO, ☎ 08 8595 8188, fax 08 8595 8191, 3 houseboats acc up to 12, [shwr, tlt, hairdry, a/c-cool, heat, TV, video, clock radio (1), t/c mkg, refrig, cook fac, micro, d/wash (3), toaster, blkts, doonas, linen, pillows], w/mach, iron (3), iron brd (1), bbq, Pets on application. **D $840 - $1,800,** BC MC VI, (not yet classified).

Chowilla Station Shearers Quarters, (Bunk), Chowilla Station, 48km N of PO, ☎ 08 8595 8048, fax 08 8595 8048, 1 bunkhouse acc up to 25, (Bunk Rooms), [H & C (3), t/c mkg, refrig (3), pillows], shwr, tlt. **D $50, ◊ $10,** ch con, Min book applies.

RENMARK continued...

Cocktails & Dreams Houseboats, (Hbt), ☎ 08 8586 4598, fax 08 8586 4598, 2 houseboats acc up to 12, [shwr (2), tlt (2), a/c-cool, heat, tel, TV, video, CD, refrig, cook fac, micro, d/wash, blkts, linen, pillows], w/mach, bbq, shade. **W $980 - $2,550.**

Liba Liba Houseboats, (Hbt), Jane Eliza Landing, 2km NE of PO, ☎ 08 8586 6734, fax 08 8586 4520, 19 houseboats acc up to 12, [shwr, tlt, a/c-cool, fan, heat, TV, video, radio (cassette), CD (4), refrig, cook fac, micro, blkts, linen, pillows], w/mach (13), ice box, bbq, Pets at managements discretion. **W $407 - $2,145, BC MC VI.**

Magnum Houseboats-Renmark, (Hbt), 1 Lookout Dve, Paringa 5340, ☎ 08 8595 5217, fax 08 8595 5425, 6 houseboats acc up to 12, [shwr, spa bath (1), tlt, a/c-cool, heat, TV, video, radio (cassette), CD, refrig, cook fac, d/wash (3), ldry, blkts, linen, pillows], ldry, w/mach, bbq. **W $715 - $3,100, BC MC VI.**

RIVERLAND SA

See: Barmera, Berri, Blanchetown, Kingston-on-Murray, Loxton, Moorook, Morgan, Paringa, Renmark, Waikerie.

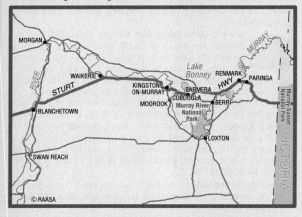

RIVERTON SA 5412

Pop 757. (96km N Adelaide), See map on pages 586/587, ref C6. Noted for grain growing, cattle, fat lambs, sheep and wool production. Bowls, Golf, Horse Riding, Swimming (Pool), Tennis.

Hotels/Motels

★ **Hotel Central**, (LH), Torrens Rd, ☎ 08 8847 2314, fax 08 8847 2314, (2 stry), 6 rms [doonas], rec rm, conv fac, ⊠ (Mon to Sat), t/c mkg shared, refrig, bbq. **RO ♦ $28, ♦♦ $45, BC EFT MC VI.**

Riverton Hotel, (LH), 27 Torrens Rd, ☎ 08 8847 2303, fax 08 8847 2523, 9 rms [elec blkts], ✕ (licensed), t/c mkg shared, cots-fee, non smoking property. **BLB ♦ $33, ♦♦ $44 - $55, ♦ $10,** ch con, AE BC EFT MC VI.

B&B's/Guest Houses

Riverton Railway Station, (B&B), Hannaford Rd, ☎ 08 8847 2051, fax 08 8847 2714, 5 rms [ensuite, spa bath, a/c, TV (1), clock radio, t/c mkg], lounge (TV), conf fac, ✕, bbq, non smoking property. **BB ♦ $100 - $150, ♦♦ $110 - $170, ♦ $25,** ch con, BC MC VI, (not yet classified).

ROBE SA 5276

Pop 730. (341km SE Adelaide), See map on pages 586/587, ref H7. Situated on Guichen Bay & known as the Centre of the South East, Robe has reliedlargely on its crayfishing industry for many years. CSIRO Research Centre, Historical Interpretation Centre, Little Dip Conservation park, Narraburra Woolshed, Old Customs House and Wilsons at Robe. Boating, Bowls, Bush Walking, Fishing (Beach, Rock & Surf), Golf, Sailing, Squash, Surfing, Swimming (Beach), Tennis, Vineyards, Wineries, Water Skiing.

Hotels/Motels

★★★★ **Boat Haven Motel**, (M), Cnr Hagen & Smillie Sts, ☎ 08 8768 2588, fax 08 8768 2490, 20 units [shwr, tlt, heat, elec blkts, tel, TV, clock radio, t/c mkg, refrig, toaster], ldry, w/mach, dryer, iron (10), iron brd (10), ⊠, bbq, rm serv, cots, non smoking property. **RO ♦ $66 - $100, ♦♦ $66 - $120, ♦ $15,** pen con, 11 rooms 3.5 stars. AE BC BTC DC EFT MC VI.

★★★★ **Lake View Motel**, (M), Cnr Tobruk Ave & Lakeside Tce, 2km E of PO, ☎ 08 8768 2100, fax 08 8768 2184, 5 units [ensuite, spa bath (1), a/c, tel, TV, movie, t/c mkg, refrig, micro, toaster], ldry, bbq, rm serv, plygr, non smoking units. **RO ♦♦ $69 - $132, ♦ $11,** ch con, pen con, AE BC DC EFT MC VI.

★★★☆ **Melaleuca Motel**, (M), 20 Smillie St, 200m S of PO, ☎ 08 8768 2599, fax 08 8768 2629, 5 units [ensuite, hairdry, a/c, elec blkts, tel, TV, video-fee, clock radio, t/c mkg, refrig, toaster], ldry, bbq, cots, non smoking units (3). **RO ♦♦ $65 - $85, ♦ $15,** ch con, AE BC DC EFT MC VI.

★★★ **Guichen Bay Motel**, (M), Victoria St, ☎ 08 8768 2001, fax 08 8768 2684, 17 units [ensuite, bath (hip) (1), heat, elec blkts, tel, TV, video-fee, clock radio, t/c mkg, refrig, mini bar (5), cook fac ltd (1)], lounge, ⊠, pool, spa, bbq, rm serv, cots-fee, non smoking property. **RO ♦ $50 - $77, ♦♦ $55 - $85, ♦ $11,** ch con, AE BC DC EFT MC VI.

★★★ **Harbour View Motel**, (M), 2 Sturt St, ☎ 08 8768 2148, fax 08 8768 2155, (2 stry), 14 units [ensuite, bath (4), spa bath (2), a/c (4), fan, heat, elec blkts, tel, TV, clock radio, t/c mkg, refrig, cook fac (3), toaster], ldry, conf fac, bbq, plygr, cots, non smoking property. **RO ♦ $50 - $60, ♦♦ $60 - $150, ♦ $5 - $10,** 5 rooms of 4 star rating. Executive room $120-$150. AE BC MC VI.

★★★ **Robe Hotel**, (LH), Mundy Tce, ☎ 08 8768 2077, fax 08 8768 2495, (2 stry), 11 rms [basin (3), ensuite (8), bath (7), spa bath (1), c/fan (8), heat (8), elec blkts, TV, t/c mkg, refrig (8)], ldry, w/mach, dryer, iron (avail), iron brd (avail), meeting rm, ⊠, ☎, cots-fee. **RO ♦ $35 - $65, ♦♦ $50 - $130, ♦ $10,** 3 rms of a lower rating. Min book long w/ends and Easter, AE BC DC EFT MC VI.

★★★ **Robetown Motor Inn**, (M), 14 Main St, ☎ 08 8768 2185, fax 08 8768 2678, 14 units [ensuite, a/c (6), elec blkts, tel, TV, video-fee, clock radio, t/c mkg, mini bar, toaster], ldry, pool indoor heated, spa, bbq, c/park (carport) (6), cots-fee. **RO ♦ $55 - $65, ♦♦ $71 - $90, ♦ $12,** Min book Christmas and Jan, AE BC DC EFT MC VI.

★★☆ **Caledonian Inn Hotel Motel**, (M), Victoria St, ☎ 08 8768 2029, fax 08 8768 2636, (2 stry), 4 units [ensuite, heat, elec blkts, TV, clock radio, refrig, cook fac ltd, micro, elec frypan], iron (avail), iron brd (avail), conf fac, cots. **BLB ♦♦ $110, ♦ $22,** ch con, AE BC EFT MC VI.

★☆ **(Hotel Section)**, Circa 1859. (2 stry), 7 rms lounge (TV), ⊠, t/c mkg shared, ☎, cots. **BLB ♦ $33, ♦♦ $55, ♦ $22,** ch con.

Self Catering Accommodation

★★★★★ **White Sails Apartments**, (Apt), 14 Lake Rd, ☎ 08 8768 2812, 2 apts acc up to 2, (1 bedrm), [ensuite, bath, hairdry, a/c-cool, tel, TV, video, clock radio, CD, t/c mkg, refrig, micro, d/wash, toaster, ldry, blkts, linen, pillows], w/mach, dryer, iron, iron brd, bbq, c/park (garage), non smoking property, D **$190 - $275**, BC MC VI.

★★★★☆ **Cricklewood Cottage**, (Cotg), 24 Woolundry Rd, 2km E of PO, ☎ 08 8768 2137, fax 08 8768 2180, 1 cotg acc up to 4, [shwr, bath, tlt (2), hairdry, c/fan, heat, elec blkts, tel, TV, video, clock radio, t/c mkg, refrig, cook fac, micro, elec frypan, d/wash, toaster, ldry, blkts, doonas, linen, pillows], w/mach, iron, iron brd, bbq, cots (avail), breakfast ingredients, non smoking property, D ♥♥ **$130**, ♦ **$25**, BC MC VI.

★★★★☆ **Lake View Apartments**, (Apt), Cnr Tobruk Ave & Lakeside Tce, 2km E of PO, ☎ 08 8768 2100, fax 08 8768 2184, (2 stry), 11 apts acc up to 4, (Studio & 2 bedrm), [ensuite, spa bath (2), a/c (avail), fan, heat, tel, video-fee, movie, refrig, cook fac, blkts, linen-fee, pillows], ldry, plygr, non smoking units. D ♥♥ **$69 - $220**, ♦ **$11**, ch con, pen con, 4 units ★★★★☆, AE BC DC EFT MC VI.

★★★★ **Beachside Cottage**, (Cotg), 26 The Esplanade, ☎ 08 8768 2812, 1 cotg acc up to 4, (2 bedrm), [shwr, tlt, hairdry, fan, heat, tel, TV, video, clock radio, CD, refrig, cook fac, micro, toaster, ldry, blkts, linen, pillows], w/mach, dryer, iron, bbq, non smoking property, D ♥♥ **$155 - $240**, ♦ **$33**, BC MC VI.

★★★★ **Melaleuca Holiday Apartments**, (HU), 20 Smillie St, 150m S of PO, ☎ 08 8768 2599, fax 08 8768 2629, 12 units acc up to 6, (1 & 2 bedrm), [shwr, bath (5), spa bath (4), tlt, hairdry, a/c, fan, elec blkts, tel, TV, video-fee, refrig, cook fac, blkts, linen, pillows], ldry, w/mach, dryer, iron (4), iron brd (4), cots. D **$75 - $130**, W **$500 - $800**, 5 units ★★★☆. AE BC DC MC VI.

★★★☆ **Bowman Cottages**, (HU), Previously Bowman Stone Holiday Units 22 Smillie St, ☎ 08 8768 2236, 2 units acc up to 6, (1 & 2 bedrm), [shwr, bath, tlt, heat, elec blkts, TV, clock radio, refrig, cook fac, micro, linen], w/mach, bbq, cots. D **$65 - $100**, W **$380 - $700**, Built of stone.

★★★☆ **Criterion Cottage**, (Cotg), 1 Bagot St, ☎ 08 8768 2137, fax 08 8768 2180, 1 cotg acc up to 4, (2 bedrm), [shwr, bath, tlt, hairdry, fan, elec blkts, TV, clock radio (cassette), t/c mkg, refrig, cook fac, toaster, ldry, blkts, doonas, linen, pillows], w/mach, iron, iron brd, lounge firepl, c/park (undercover), breakfast ingredients. D ♥♥ **$125 - $145**, ♦ **$25**, BC MC VI.

★★★☆ **Flinders Rest Holiday Units**, (HU), 17 Powell Ave, ☎ 08 8725 2086, fax 08 8725 2086, 2 units acc up to 6, (2 bedrm), [shwr, bath (hip), tlt, hairdry, c/fan, heat, elec blkts, TV, video, clock radio, refrig, cook fac, micro, elec frypan, ldry (in unit), doonas, linen, pillows], w/mach, iron, iron brd, bbq, cots. D **$65 - $100**, W **$430 - $680**.

★★★☆ **Robe Links Units**, (HU), Davenport St, 1km SW of PO, ☎ 08 8768 6206, fax 08 8768 6206, 2 units acc up to 6, (3 bedrm), [ensuite, c/fan, heat, TV, video, clock radio, refrig, cook fac, micro, elec frypan, toaster, ldry, blkts, linen, pillows], w/mach, iron, iron brd, bbq, c/park (garage), non smoking units. D **$85 - $150**, W **$550 - $850**.

★★★☆ **Robe Nampara Cabins**, 28 Laurel Tce, ☎ 08 8768 2264, fax 08 8768 2091, 7 cabins acc up to 6, (2 bedrm), [ensuite, fan, heat, elec blkts, TV, clock radio, refrig, cook fac, micro, elec frypan, blkts, linen reqd-fee, pillows], ldry, w/mach-fee, iron, iron brd, bbq, plygr, non smoking rms, D ♥♥ **$55 - $85**, ♦ **$10**, W **$385 - $595**, ch con, BC MC VI.

★★★☆ **Wilsons at Robe - Cottage Accommodation**, (Cotg), Christmas Tree Cottage. Smillie St, 500m E of PO, ☎ 08 8768 2459, fax 08 8768 2459, 1 cotg acc up to 4, (2 bedrm), [shwr, bath, tlt, heat (slow combustion), TV, video, refrig, cook fac, micro, toaster, ldry (in unit), blkts, linen, pillows], w/mach, BLB ♥♥ **$130**, ♦ **$25**, ch con, AE BC DC MC VI.

★★★ **(Victoria Cottage)**, Victoria St, 1 cotg acc up to 4, (2 bedrm), [shwr, tlt, fire pl, elec blkts, TV, video, refrig, cook fac, micro, ldry, blkts, linen, pillows], w/mach, c/park (carport), breakfast ingredients. BLB ♥♥ **$120**, ♦ **$25**, ch con.

★★★ **Campbell Stone Holiday Units**, (HU), 26 Smilie St, ☎ 08 8768 2932, 4 units acc up to 6, (2 & 3 bedrm), [shwr, bath, tlt, fire pl (4), heat, elec blkts, TV, video, clock radio, refrig, cook fac, micro (4), linen-fee], w/mach, bbq (covered), cots. D **$65 - $100**.

★★★ **Cornerstone Cottage**, (Cotg), Smillie St, ☎ 08 8768 2137, fax 08 8768 2180, 1 cotg acc up to 6, (3 bedrm), [shwr, tlt, wood heat, elec blkts, TV, clock radio, t/c mkg, refrig, cook fac, toaster, doonas, linen, pillows], w/mach, iron, iron brd, c/park. D ♥♥ **$110 - $130**, ♦ **$25**, BC MC VI.

★★★ **Green Gables Units**, (HU), 26 O'Byrne Ave, ☎ 08 8768 2600, fax 08 8768 2353, 2 units acc up to 6, [shwr, bath, tlt, c/fan, heat, TV, video, clock radio, refrig, cook fac, micro, elec frypan, toaster, linen], w/mach, iron, iron brd, bbq, c/park (carport). D **$80 - $120**, W **$460 - $740**.

ROBE continued...

★★★ **Robe Lake Vista Holiday Units**, (HU), 2 O'Hallaron St, ☎ 08 8768 2113, 6 units acc up to 5, [ensuite, heat, TV, refrig, cook fac, linen], ldry, bbq. **D $50 - $80.**

★★★ **Tobruk Cottage**, (Cotg), 1 Tobruk Ave, ☎ 0408 308 559, 1 cotg acc up to 6, (2 bedrm), [shwr, bath, tlt, fan, heat, TV, clock radio, t/c mkg, refrig, cook fac, micro, elec frypan, toaster, blkts, linen, pillows], w/mach, iron, iron brd, bbq, c/park. **D $50 - $85**,
Operator Comment: Pretty cottage fenced safely for children in large garden setting. Ample parking for boat & vehicles, two minutes walk to beach, shops & galleries.

★★★ **Walker & Ottoson Accommodation**, (Cotg), Outrigger Surf Holiday House. Adam Lindsay Gordon Dve, 2.5km W of PO, ☎ 08 8768 2600, fax 08 8768 2353, 1 cotg acc up to 8, (3 bedrm), [shwr, tlt (2), hairdry, c/fan, heat, TV, video, radio (cassette), CD, refrig, cook fac, micro, ldry, linen reqd], w/mach, iron, iron brd, bbq, c/park. **D $75 - $130, W $545 - $860.**

(Villa San Danci (Upstairs Apartment)), 15 Wrattonbully Rd, 1 apt acc up to 4, (2 bedrm), [shwr, spa bath, tlt, a/c, elec blkts, tel, TV, video, clock radio, CD, t/c mkg, refrig, cook fac, micro, d/wash, toaster, blkts, doonas, linen, pillows], w/mach, dryer, bbq, non smoking property. **D 👥 $225 - $375, 🧍 $30**, Min book Christmas Jan and Easter, (not yet classified).

★★☆ **Bushland Cabins**, Cnr Main Rd & Nora Creina Rd, 1km E of PO, ☎ 08 8768 2386, 8 cabins acc up to 6, [ensuite, c/fan, heat, TV, refrig, cook fac, micro (5), toaster, blkts reqd-fee, linen reqd-fee], w/mach, iron, iron brd, bbq (2), shade, Pets allowed on leash. **D $49 - $70, W $294 - $462**, BC MC VI, ♿.

★★☆ **(Caravan Park Section)**, (6 pwr), town water, tank water, shwr (2G-2L), tlt (2G-2L), taps (6), ldry, w/mach-fee, sink, bbq, LPG, Pets allowed on leash. **pwr-site D 👥 $15, 🧍 $4, un-pwr-site D 👥 $13, 🧍 $4**, , ch con.

(Bunkhouse Section), 2 bunkhouses acc up to 3, [heat, TV, refrig, cook fac, toaster, blkts-fee, linen-fee], shwr, tlt. **D 👤 $15, 🧍 $15.**

Sunrise Apartments, (Apt), 15 Lakeside Cres, 1km SE of PO, ☎ 0428 838 784, (2 stry), 2 apts acc up to 6, (3 bedrm), [shwr, spa bath, tlt, a/c, c/fan, cent heat, elec blkts, TV, video, clock radio, t/c mkg, refrig, cook fac, micro, toaster, blkts, doonas, linen, pillows], w/mach, dryer, bbq, cots, non smoking property. **D $122 - $160, W $850 - $1,100**, Min book Christmas and Jan, (not yet classified).

B&B's/Guest Houses

★★★★☆ **Ann's Place Bed & Breakfast**, (B&B), 2 Royal Circus, 500m W of PO, ☎ 08 8768 2262, fax 08 8768 2111, 4 rms [ensuite, bath (1), spa bath (3), hairdry, a/c, tel, TV, clock radio, t/c mkg], iron, iron brd, bbq, c/park. **BB 👥 $138 - $148**, AE BC DC MC VI.

★★★★ **Robe House Bed & Breakfast**, (B&B), 1A Hagen St, 1km W of PO, ☎ 08 8768 2770, fax 08 8768 2770, 4 rms (2 suites) [ensuite, fan, fire pl (2), heat, elec blkts, TV, clock radio (cassette), t/c mkg, refrig, cook fac, toaster], ldry, w/mach, dryer, bbq, c/park. **BLB 👤 $65 - $75, 👥 $90 - $140, 🧍 $20**, AE BC MC VI.

ROSEDALE SA

See Barossa Valley Region.

ROWLAND FLAT SA

See Barossa Valley Region.

ROXBY DOWNS SA 5725

Pop 3,025. (580km NNW Adelaide), See map on pages 586/587, ref G3. Roxby Downs was built to service the mine operations.

★★★☆ **Roxby Downs Motor Inn**, (M), Cnr Richardson Pl & Arcoona St, ☎ 08 8671 0311, fax 08 8671 0470, (2 stry gr fl), 52 units [ensuite, a/c, elec blkts, tel, cable tv, clock radio, t/c mkg, refrig, mini bar, toaster], ldry, conv fac, ☒, pool-heated, spa, rm serv, cots. **RO 👤 $110, 👥 $110, 🧍 $24.20**, ch con, fam con, AE BC DC EFT MC VI, ♿.

SALT CREEK SA 5264

Pop Nominal, (212km SE Adelaide), See map on pages 586/587, ref H7. A small coastal town on the Coorong Set. Boating, Bush Walking, Fishing, Scenic Drives.

★★☆ **Gemini Downs Holiday Units**, (HU), Highway One, 3km N of Town, ☎ 08 8575 7013, fax 08 8575 7067, 4 units acc up to 6, (2 bedrm), [shwr, tlt, fan, TV, refrig, cook fac, linen reqd-fee]. **D 👥 $40 - $55, 🧍 $8 - $10**, ch con, Min book long w/ends and Easter, BC MC VI.

> *Trouble-free travel tips* - **Tyre pressures**
>
> Check tyre pressures and set them to the manufacturer's recommendation, including the spare.
> The specifications can generally be found on the tyre placard located in either the glove box or on the front door frame.

SEDAN SA 5353

Pop Nominal, (97km NE Adelaide), See map on pages 586/587, ref C7. A small rural town on the River Murray Plains servicing the surrounding rural community. Tennis.

Yookamurra Sanctuary, (Bunk), Tariff includes Bush walking, nocturnal walks, and bird watching tours. No arrival before 4pm. Pipeline Rd, 24km NE of PO, ☎ 08 8562 5011, fax 08 8562 5023, 20 bunkhouses [a/c-cool, blkts, linen, pillows], shared fac (4), ldry, w/mach, ☒, bbq, ✆, non smoking property. **D all meals 👤 $125, 🧍 $125**, ch con, BC MC VI.

SEPPELTSFIELD SA

See Barossa Valley Region.

SEVENHILL SA 5453

Pop Nominal, (106km N Adelaide), See map on pages 586/587, ref B6. An historic settlement in the Clare Valley. Vineyards, Wineries.

Self Catering Accommodation

★★★☆ **Rosella Cottages**, (Cotg), Main North Rd, ☎ 08 8843 4281, fax 08 8843 4281, 3 cotgs acc up to 9, (2 bedrm), [shwr, tlt, a/c (2), fan (1), c/fan (2), heat (wood fire), elec blkts, TV, clock radio, refrig, cook fac, micro (1), blkts, linen, pillows], w/mach (2), bbq, cots, breakfast ingredients, non smoking property. **D 👥 $121, 🧍 $22**, ch con, 1 cottage ★★☆. Min book long w/ends and Easter, BC MC VI.

Stringy Brae Cottages, (Cotg), Sawmill Rd, Scenic Drive 18, ☎ 08 8843 4313, fax 08 8843 4319, 2 cotgs acc up to 4, (1 bedrm), [shwr, tlt, a/c, fan, wood heat (slow combustion), elec blkts, TV, clock radio, refrig, cook fac, blkts, linen, pillows], bbq, breakfast ingredients. **D $121.**

Trestrail Cottage, (Cotg), No children's facilities, Sawmill Rd, ☎ 08 8842 3794, 1 cotg acc up to 2, (1 bedrm), [bath, tlt, hairdry, a/c-cool, wood heat (slow combustion), elec blkts, radio, CD, refrig, cook fac, micro, toaster, blkts, linen, pillows], iron, iron brd, breakfast ingredients. **D 👥 $109 - $115, 🧍 $20.**

B&B's/Guest Houses

★★★★☆ **Thorn Park Country House**, (GH), College Rd, via Clare, 7km S of PO, ☎ 08 8843 4304, fax 08 8843 4296, 6 rms [ensuite, bath (1), hairdry, a/c, fan, heat, elec blkts, tel (3), TV (3), video (2), refrig], ldry, lounge (TV), ☒, t/c mkg shared, bbq, non smoking rms. **BB 👤 $195, 👥 $290**, AE BC DC MC VI.

SPRINGTON SA 5235

Pop 220. (62km E Adelaide), See map on pages 586/587, ref C7. An historic township noted for its wine production.

★★★ **The Dairy Cottage**, (Cotg), Williamstown Rd, 1.3km SW of PO, ☎ 08 8568 2218, fax 08 8568 2298, 1 cotg acc up to 2, (1 bedrm), [shwr, spa bath (6 person), tlt, a/c-cool, c/fan, heat (combustion), TV, video, radio, refrig, cook fac ltd, micro, blkts, linen, pillows], bbq, breakfast ingredients, non smoking rms. **D 👥 $130, 🧍 $40.**

STANSBURY SA 5582

Pop 520. (197km E Adelaide), See map on pages 586/587, ref A7. Holiday town, situated on the east coast of Yorke Peninsula. Boating, Bowls, Fishing, Golf, Horse Riding, Swimming (Beach), Tennis.

Hotels/Motels

★★★ **Stansbury Holiday Motel**, (M), Adelaide Rd, ☎ 08 8852 4455, fax 08 8852 4111, 16 units [shwr, spa bath (1), tlt, a/c-cool (8), a/c (8), heat, elec blkts, TV, clock radio, t/c mkg, refrig, cook fac (9), micro (9), toaster (9)], ldry, pool, bbq, rm serv, dinner to unit, plygr. **RO 👤 $66 - $74, 👥 $76 - $84, 🧍 $5 - $10, Suite D 👥 $142**, AE BC DC EFT MC VI.

★★ **Oyster Court Motel**, (M), Cnr South & West Tce, ☎ 08 8852 4136, fax 08 8852 4136, 11 units [shwr, tlt, fan, heat, elec blkts, TV, radio, refrig, cook fac], ldry, pool, bbq (covered), plygr, cots-fee. **RO 👤 $49.50 - $66, 👥 $60.50 - $66, 🧍 $12**, BC MC VI.

Self Catering Accommodation

★★☆ **Stansbury Villas Holiday Units**, (HU), Adelaide Rd, ☎ 08 8852 4282, fax 08 8852 4417, 4 units acc up to 6, [shwr, tlt, fan, heat, elec blkts, TV, refrig, cook fac, micro (3), elec frypan, toaster, linen reqd-fee], ldry, cots. **D 👥 $50 - $55, 🧍 $5**, ch con.

★★☆ **Willow Holiday Cabins**, 3 Pioneer St, ☎ 08 8852 4303, 4 cabins acc up to 6, [ensuite (1), fan, heat, TV, clock radio, refrig, cook fac, linen reqd], ldry, w/mach, bbq, cots. **D $25 - $35.**

Oyster Bay Holiday House, (House), 2 Annie Watt St, ☎ 08 8852 4250, 1 house acc up to 10, [shwr, tlt, a/c, elec blkts, TV, video, clock radio, t/c mkg, refrig, cook fac, micro, doonas, pillows], w/mach, iron, iron brd, bbq. **D 👥 $70, 🧍 $5**, Min book applies, (not yet classified).

STOKES BAY SA

See Kangaroo Island Region.

STRATHALBYN SA 5255

Pop 2,623. (52km SE Adelaide), See map on pages 586/587, ref C8. Situated on the banks of the Angas River. Bowls, Bush Walking, Fishing, Golf, Greyhound Racing, Horse Racing, Horse Riding, Sailing, Scenic Drives, Swimming (Pool), Tennis, Trotting, Water Skiing.

Hotels/Motels

★★★ **Victoria on the Park Hotel Motel**, (LMH), 16 Albyn Tce, ☎ 08 8536 2202, fax 08 8536 2469, 10 units [shwr, spa bath (5), tlt, a/c, tel, TV, clock radio, t/c mkg, refrig, toaster], iron, iron brd, ⊠, c/park (undercover), cots-fee. **BLB** ♦♦ **$93.50 - $132,** ◊ **$22,** ch con, AE BC DC EFT JCB MC VI.

Robin Hood Hotel, (LH), 18 High St, ☎ 08 8536 2608, 6 rms [elec blkts], lounge (TV), cots. **RO** ♦ **$30,** ♦♦ **$50,** ◊ **$18.**

Self Catering Accommodation

★★★ **The Railway Cottages**, (Cotg), 3 & 5 Parker Ave, 500m E of PO, ☎ 0407 601 692, fax 08 8536 4910, 2 cotgs acc up to 6, (3 bedrm), [shwr, bath, tlt, fan, heat (slow combustion), elec blkts, TV, clock radio, CD, t/c mkg, refrig, cook fac, micro, toaster, blkts, linen, pillows], ldry, w/mach, iron, breakfast ingredients, non smoking property. **BB** ♦ **$110,** ♦♦ **$120 - $140,** ◊ **$35 - $40,** ch con, BC MC VI.

B&B's/Guest Houses

★★★★ **Hamilton House Bed & Breakfast**, (B&B), 23 Commercial Rd, 150m N of PO, ☎ 08 8536 4275, 2 rms [ensuite, c/fan (1), heat, elec blkts, clock radio], lounge (TV), ✕, non smoking property. **BB** ♦ **$75 - $80,** ♦♦ **$95 - $105,** BC MC VI.

★★★☆ **Watervilla House Bed & Breakfast**, (B&B), No children's facilities, 2 Mill St, 50m N of PO, ☎ 08 8536 4099, fax 08 8536 4099, 6 rms [c/fan (1), heat, elec blkts, clock radio], bathrm (2), lounge (TV), t/c mkg shared, bbq, meals avail, c/park (carport). **BB** ♦ **$110,** ♦♦ **$132,** AE BC DC MC VI.

STREAKY BAY SA 5680

Pop 957. (713km NW Adelaide), See map on pages 586/587, ref F5. A picturesque coastal resort, fishing and service centre for the surrounding rural community on the west coast. Boating, Bowls, Fishing, Golf, Horse Racing, Surfing, Swimming (Pool & Beach), Tennis.

Hotels/Motels

★★★ **Streaky Bay Community Hotel Motel**, (LMH), 35 Alfred Tce, ☎ 08 8626 1008, fax 08 8626 1630, (2 stry gr fl), 23 units [shwr, tlt, a/c (4), elec blkts, tel, TV, movie, clock radio, t/c mkg, refrig], ldry, conf fac, ⊠, ✆, cots-fee, non smoking units (8). **RO** ♦ **$22 - $99,** ♦♦ **$33 - $99,** ♦♦♦ **$44 - $82.50,** ◊ **$11,** 7 units ★★☆. AE BC DC EFT MC VI, ♿.
★★☆ **(Hotel Section)**, 14 rms [basin, ensuite (9), spa bath (1), a/c (3), fan (6), heat (9), elec blkts, tel (9), TV (9), clock radio (9), t/c mkg, refrig (9)], cots-fee. **RO** ♦ **$55 - $71.50,** ♦♦ **$66 - $82.50,** ♦♦♦ **$77 - $93.50,** ◊ **$11,** 1 rm of a higher standard and 5 rms of a lower rating.

★★☆ **Streaky Bay Motel**, (M), 7 Alfred Tce, ☎ 08 8626 1126, fax 08 8626 1126, 10 units [shwr, tlt, a/c, c/fan, elec blkts, tel, TV, refrig, cook fac], ldry, bbq, cots. **RO** ♦ **$60 - $66,** ♦♦ **$66,** ◊ **$12,** AE BC DC EFT MC VI, ♿.

Budget Motel Chain International

B&B's/Guest Houses

★★★☆ **Headland House Bed & Breakfast**, (B&B), No children's facilities, 5 Flinders Dve, 500m NE of PO, ☎ 08 8626 1315, 2 rms [hairdry, c/fan, heat, elec blkts, clock radio, t/c mkg, pillows], ldry, w/mach, lounge (TV & Video), refrig, bbq, Pets on application. **BB** ♦ **$65 - $80,** ♦♦ **$75 - $90,** ◊ **$38 - $45,** Min book applies.

TAILEM BEND SA 5260

Pop 1,600. (99km SE Adelaide), See map on pages 586/587, ref C8. Situated on the banks of the Murray River at the 'Big Bend', from from which the town derived its name. Boating, Bowls, Fishing, Golf, Sailing, Squash, Swimming (River), Tennis.

Hotels/Motels

★★★ **Motel River Bend**, (M), 39 Princes Hwy, S of PO, ☎ 08 8572 3633, fax 08 8572 3633, 13 units [shwr, bath (1), tlt, a/c-cool (6), a/c (7), heat (6), elec blkts, tel, TV, clock radio, t/c mkg, refrig, toaster], cots-fee. **RO** ♦ **$50,** ♦♦ **$55,** ◊ **$12,** AE BC DC EFT MC VI.

Self Catering Accommodation

★★★☆ **Tilbrook House Bed & Breakfast**, (Cotg), 6 First Ave, ☎ 08 8572 3099, 1 cotg acc up to 4, [shwr, bath, tlt, fan, fire pl, elec blkts, TV, radio, t/c mkg, refrig, cook fac, toaster, ldry, blkts, doonas, linen, pillows], bbq, non smoking property. **D** ♦ **$75,** ♦♦ **$90,** ◊ **$40,** ch con, weekly con.

TANUNDA SA

See Barossa Valley Region.

TARCOOLA SA 5710

Pop Nominal, (733km NW Adelaide), See map on pages 586/587, ref F4. Historic gold mining town at the junction of the Trans Australian and Alice Springs railway lines.
Wilgena Hotel, (LH), Railway Tce, ☎ 08 8672 2042, fax 08 8672 2048, 7 rms [a/c (6), heat (avail)], rec rm, ⊠. **RO** ♦ **$40,** ♦♦ **$50.**

TARLEE SA 5411

Pop 200. (81km N Adelaide), See map on pages 586/587, ref C6. Small service town for an area noted for grain crops, cattle, fat lambs, sheep and wool.

Self Catering Accommodation

★★★☆ **Ryelands Farm Retreat**, (Cotg), (Farm), Ryelands Rd, 8km E of PO, ☎ 08 8528 5262, fax 08 8528 5262, 1 cotg acc up to 6, (3 bedrm), [shwr, bath, tlt, hairdry, a/c-cool, fan, elec blkts, TV, clock radio, t/c mkg, refrig, cook fac, ldry, blkts, linen, pillows], iron, lounge, lounge firepl, bbq, c/park (carport), non smoking rms (bedrooms). **D** ◊ **$70,** ◊ **$10,** ch con.

B&B's/Guest Houses

★★★★ **Tarlee Antiques Guest House**, (GH), Main North Rd, ☎ 08 8528 5328, fax 08 8528 5326, 4 rms [shwr, tlt, a/c, c/fan, heat, elec blkts, TV, clock radio, t/c mkg, refrig, doonas], ⊠, spa (shared), rm serv, ✆, non smoking property, Lap dogs under control. **RO** ♦ **$65,** ♦♦ **$75,** BC MC VI.

★★★☆ **Elizabeth Henry House**, (B&B), Circa 1900. 86 Gilbert St, 300m N of PO, ☎ 08 8528 5309, 3 rms [shwr, bath, tlt, hairdry, a/c-cool, fan (2), fire pl, heat, elec blkts, TV, video, clock radio (avail), t/c mkg], iron, iron brd, meals avail (on request), non smoking property. **BB** ♦ **$55,** ♦♦ **$70,** **DBB** ♦ **$71.50,** ♦♦ **$99,** ch con.

TARPEENA SA 5277

Pop 443. (416km SE Adelaide), See map on pages 586/587, ref J8. A small township close to the Victorian Border, in the heart of pine forest country. Fairy Tale Park.

Hotels/Motels

Pines Hotel, (LH), 24 Penola Rd, ☎ 08 8739 6287, 3 rms [ensuite, fan (avail), elec blkts], ldry, w/mach, dryer, ⊠ (Mon to Sat), plygr. **BLB** ♦ **$25 - $27.50,** ♦♦ **$40 - $45,** ◊ **$10,** AE BC DC EFT MC VI.

TEROWIE SA 5421

Pop 226. (221km N Adelaide), See map on pages 586/587, ref H5. Located in an agricultural & pastoral area in the Mid North. Scenic Drives.

Hotels/Motels

★★ **Terowie Motel**, (M), Barrier Hwy, ☎ 08 8659 1082, fax 08 8659 1084, 6 units [shwr, tlt, a/c, heat, elec blkts, tel, TV, radio, t/c mkg, refrig], ✕, rm serv, c/park (undercover), cots. **RO** ♦ **$28 - $33,** ♦♦ **$36 - $40,** ◊ **$5,** AE BC DC EFT MC MCH VI.

TINTINARA SA 5266

Pop 316. (191km SE Adelaide), See map on pages 586/587, ref J7. A well established farming, grazing and small manufacturing Community surrounded by 10 conservation parks. Tintinara Homestead & Tolmer Rock. Bowls, Golf, Swimming (Pool), Tennis.

Hotels/Motels

★ **Tintinara Hotel**, (LH), 41 Becker Tce, ☎ 08 8757 2008, fax 08 8757 2393, (2 stry) 10 rms [ensuite, fan, elec blkts, t/c mkg], ⊠ (Mon to Sat), cots. **RO** ♦ **$33,** ♦♦ **$50,** ◊ **$5,** EFT.

Self Catering Accommodation

★★★☆ **O'Deas Bed & Breakfast Cottage**, (Cotg), Dukes Hwy, 3.8km S of PO, ☎ 08 8756 5018, fax 08 8756 5018, 1 cotg acc up to 4, (2 bedrm), [shwr, bath, tlt, fan, fire pl, elec blkts, tel, TV, clock radio, CD, t/c mkg, refrig, cook fac, micro, toaster, ldry, blkts, linen, pillows], w/mach, iron, iron brd, bbq, cots, breakfast ingredients, non smoking property, Pets on application. **D** ♦♦ **$95 - $125,** ◊ **$45,** ch con, fam con, BC MC VI.

TRURO SA 5356

Pop 150. See map on pages 586/587, ref C6. Located on the Sturt Highway at the point where the Ranges are about to drop away to the River Murray plains.

Hotels/Motels

★★★ **Truro Weighbridge Motel**, (M), Moorundie St, ☎ 08 8564 0400, fax 08 8564 0422, 5 units [ensuite, a/c, TV, clock radio, t/c mkg, refrig, toaster], ⊠ (Thur-Tues), c/park. **BLB** ♦ **$40,** ♦♦ **$60,** AE BC DC EFT MC VI.

TUMBY BAY SA 5605

Pop 1,147. (646km NW Adelaide), See map on pages 586/587, ref G6. Scenic town situated on the western shores of Spencer Gulf. Boating, Bowls, Croquet, Fishing, Golf, Horse Racing, Sailing, Scenic Drives, Squash, Swimming (Beach), Tennis, Water Skiing.

Hotels/Motels

★★★ **Tumby Bay Marina Motel**, (M), 4 Berryman St, 2km S of PO, ☎ 08 8688 2311, fax 08 8688 1988, 15 units (3 suites) [ensuite, a/c-cool (11), c/fan, heat, elec blkts, tel, TV, video-fee, clock radio, t/c mkg, refrig, toaster], conf fac, ⊠ (Open on demand), pool (seasonal), bbq, rm serv, boat park (trailer), cots. **RO ♦ $45 - $75, ♦♦ $50 - $85,** ▯ $8, ch con, 2 rooms of a lower rating, AE BC DC EFT MC VI.

★☆ **Seabreeze Hotel**, (LH), Tumby Bay Tce, ☎ 08 8688 2362, fax 08 8688 2722, (2 stry), 12 rms [bath (1), a/c (2), fan (5), heat, elec blkts, TV (3)], ldry, lounge (TV), conv fac, ⊠ (Mon to Sat), c/park (limited), ✆, cots. **RO ♦ $19, ♦♦ $27, ♦♦♦ $46,** ch con, BC EFT MC VI.

★ **Tumby Bay Hotel**, (LH), 1 North Tce, ☎ 08 8688 2005, fax 08 8688 2005, (2 stry), 8 rms [basin, heat (2), clock radio (3)], lounge (TV), ⊠ (Mon to Sat), t/c mkg shared, refrig, ✆, cots. **RO ♦ $19, ♦♦ $29 - $35,** ch con, AE BC DC EFT MC VI.

Self Catering Accommodation

★★★ **Tumby Bayside Holiday Units**, (HU), 2 Yaringa Ave, ☎ 08 8688 2087, fax 08 8688 2087, 16 units acc up to 8, (1 & 2 bedrm Studio), [shwr, tlt, a/c-cool (3), a/c (13), fan (8), heat (3), elec blkts (16), TV, video (8), clock radio, refrig, cook fac, micro, toaster, blkts, doonas, linen (4 supplied - 12 fee), pillows], ldry, w/mach-fee, dryer-fee, iron, iron brd, bbq, c/park (carport), plygr, cots. **D ♦♦ $55 - $65, ♦♦♦ $60 - $85,** Holiday surcharge applies, BC MC VI, ⚹.

Hillview Country Retreat, (Cotg), Sect-10c Hd of Stockes, Ungarra 5607, 7km S of PO, 24km NW of Tumby Bay, ☎ 08 8688 8008, 1 cotg acc up to 8, (3 bedrm), [shwr, tlt, fan, heat (elec/wood), elec blkts, TV, clock radio, t/c mkg, refrig, cook fac, ldry, blkts, doonas, linen, pillows], bbq, non smoking property, Pets on application. **D ♦ $50, ♦♦ $50,** ▯ $10, ch con, weekly con, (not yet classified).

TUNGKILLO SA 5236

Pop Nominal, (55km E Adelaide), See map on pages 586/587, ref C7.

Self Catering Accommodation

★★★☆ **Sunnybrook B&B**, (Cotg), Mannum Rd, 1.5km W of PO, ☎ 08 8568 2159, fax 08 8568 2159, 2 cotgs acc up to 2, (1 bedrm), [shwr, spa bath, tlt, a/c-cool (1), a/c (1), heat (gas) (2), elec blkts, t/c mkg, refrig, cook fac, micro, elec frypan, toaster, blkts, linen, pillows], bbq, breakfast ingredients, non smoking property. **D ♦♦ $140,** BC MC VI.

Forget-me-not Cottage, (Cotg), Mannum Rd, 1.6km W of PO, ☎ 08 8568 2011, fax 08 8568 1739, 1 cotg acc up to 2, (Studio), [ensuite, spa bath, hairdry, a/c, elec blkts, TV, video, clock radio, CD, t/c mkg, refrig, cook fac, micro, elec frypan, toaster, ldry, doonas, linen, pillows], iron, iron brd, ⊠, bbq, cots, breakfast ingredients, non smoking property, Pets on application. **D ♦♦ $145 - $165,** ▯ $50 - $60, AE BC MC VI, (not yet classified).

B&B's/Guest Houses

★★★★☆ **Marengo Hame Bed & Breakfast**, (B&B), Mannum Rd, 1.6km W of PO, ☎ 08 8568 2011, fax 08 8568 1739, 2 rms [bath (1), spa bath (2), hairdry, a/c-cool (2), c/fan, heat, elec blkts, TV, video (2), CD (2), t/c mkg, refrig, mini bar], res liquor license, meals avail, non smoking property. **BB ♦♦ $140 - $160,** ch con, 1 rm of a lower rating, Chef on site. Children by arrangement. AE BC MC VI.

TWO WELLS SA 5501

Pop 519. (40km N Adelaide), See map on pages 586/587, ref B7. District noted for hot-house tomato cultivation. Early settlers gained their water from a couple of wells, hence the town's name.

★★ **Two Wells Motel**, (M), 116 Old Port Wakefield Rd, ☎ 08 8520 2210, fax 08 8520 3022, (2 stry gr fl), 10 units [shwr, tlt, a/c, elec blkts, TV, clock radio, t/c mkg, refrig, toaster], pool, bbq, cots. **RO ♦ $49.50, ♦♦ $60,** ▯ $15, ch con, BC DC MC VI.

VICTOR HARBOR SA 5211

Pop 10,184. (83km S Adelaide), See map on pages 586/587, ref B8. Situated on the shores of picturesque Encounter Bay, Victor Harbor is now a thriving holiday resort. A causeway leads to Granite Island just offshore. The Bluff, craft shops, galleries, Horse Tramway, Greenhills Adventure Park, Old Customs & Station Masters House, SA Whale Centre and Urimbirra Wildlife Park. Boating, Bowls, Croquet, Fishing, Golf, Scenic Drives, Surfing, Swimming, Tennis.

Hotels/Motels

★★★★☆ **Whalers Inn Resort**, (M), Franklin Pde, 3km SW of PO, ☎ 08 8552 4400, fax 08 8552 4240, 32 units [ensuite, spa bath (18), a/c, elec blkts, tel, TV, video (avail), clock radio, t/c mkg, refrig, micro (18), toaster], ldry, iron, iron brd, conf fac, ⊠, cafe, bar, pool (1), pool-heated (1), bbq, dinner to unit, tennis, cots. **BLB ♦ $99 - $159.50, ♦♦ $99 - $159.50,** Min book applies, AE BC DC EFT MC VI.

★★★★☆ **(Serviced Apartment Section)**, (2 stry gr fl), 14 serv apts acc up to 6, (3 bedrm), [shwr, spa bath, tlt, a/c, c/fan, elec blkts, tel, fax, TV, clock radio, t/c mkg, refrig, cook fac, micro, d/wash, toaster], ldry, w/mach, dryer, iron, iron brd, conf fac, bbq, ✆, cots. **BLB $176 - $302.50.**

★★★☆ **Hotel Victor**, (LH), Albert Pl, town centre, ☎ 08 8551 5100, fax 08 8551 5150, (2 stry), 33 rms [ensuite, spa bath (1), a/c, tel, fax, TV, clock radio, t/c mkg, refrig, mini bar, cook fac (1), micro (1), toaster], lounge, conf fac, ⊠, dinner to unit, ✆, cots. **RO ♦ $83 - $88, ♦♦ $94 - $187,** ▯ $11, ch con, fam con, 2 rms of a higher standard, AE BC DC EFT MC VI.

★★★☆ **Wintersun Motel**, (M), 119 Hindmarsh Rd, ☎ 08 8552 3533, fax 08 8552 3412, (2 stry gr fl), 20 units [ensuite, hairdry (10), a/c, elec blkts, tel, TV, clock radio, t/c mkg, refrig, cook fac (2), toaster], ldry-fee, w/mach, dryer, iron (in laundry), iron brd (in laundry), cots-fee. **RO ♦ $60 - $77, ♦♦ $71.50 - $93.50,** ▯ $15, ch con, Min book long w/ends and Easter, AE BC EFT MC VI, ⚹.

★★★ **Apollon Motor Inn**, (M), 15 Torrens St, ☎ 08 8552 2777, fax 08 8552 2701, (2 stry gr fl), 32 units [ensuite, a/c, elec blkts, tel, TV, clock radio, t/c mkg, refrig, mini bar (on request)], iron (on request), iron brd (on request), rec rm, lounge, conv fac, ⊠, pool indoor heated, spa, rm serv, dinner to unit, cots-fee, non smoking rms (6). **RO ♦ $65 - $90, ♦♦ $80 - $110,** ▯ $10, AE BC DC EFT MC VI.

★★★ **City Motel**, (M), 51 Ocean St, ☎ 08 8552 2455, fax 08 8552 5583, 15 units [ensuite, hairdry, a/c, elec blkts, tel, TV, clock radio, t/c mkg, refrig, cook fac (2), micro (2), toaster], ldry, w/mach-fee, dryer-fee, iron (avail), iron brd, bbq, rm serv, cots-fee, non smoking property. **RO ♦ $66 - $99, ♦♦ $77 - $99,** ▯ $11, fam con, Min book all holiday times, AE BC DC MC VI.

★★★ **Kerjancia Motor Lodge**, (M), 141 Hindmarsh Rd, ☎ 08 8552 2900, fax 08 8552 2246, (2 stry), 12 units [ensuite, a/c-cool, fan, heat, elec blkts, tel, TV, clock radio, t/c mkg, refrig, cook fac, micro, toaster], ldry, w/mach, dryer, iron (in laundry), iron brd (in laundry), pool-heated (solar), spa, bbq, cots. **RO ♦ $60 - $70, ♦♦ $72 - $85,** ▯ $11, Min book Christmas Jan long w/ends and Easter, AE BC MC VI.

★★★ **Ocean Crest Motel**, (M), 117 Mentone Rd, 3km E of PO, ☎ 08 8552 3233, fax 08 8552 4293, 10 units [ensuite, a/c-cool, heat, elec blkts, TV, video (1), clock radio, t/c mkg, refrig, micro (4)], ldry, pool, spa, cook fac, bbq, dinner to unit, non smoking rms (4), **RO ♦ $55 - $65, ♦♦ $60 - $75, ♦♦♦♦ $80 - $95,** ch con, Min book Christmas Jan long w/ends and Easter, AE BC DC MC VI.

★★☆ **Bayview Victor Motel Inn**, (M), 17 Hindmarsh Rd, ☎ 08 8552 1755, fax 08 8552 3223, (2 stry gr fl), 36 units [shwr, tlt, a/c, tel, TV, clock radio, t/c mkg, refrig], ldry, ⊠ (Tue-Sun), pool (In-ground), spa (heated), rm serv, dinner to unit (Tues-Sun), cots (avail). **RO ♦ $65 - $110, ♦♦ $65 - $110,** ▯ $10, ch con, Min book long w/ends, AE BC DC EFT MC VI.

★★☆ **Family Inn Motel**, (M), 300 Pt Elliott Rd, 2km NE of PO, ☎ 08 8552 1941, fax 08 8552 8645, (2 stry gr fl), 18 units (2 bedrm), [ensuite, a/c (10), fan, heat, elec blkts, TV, clock radio, t/c mkg, refrig, cook fac (4), toaster], ldry, rec rm, conv fac, pool, bbq, plygr, tennis (half court), cots. **D $82.50 - $99, RO ♦ $49.50 - $60.50, ♦♦ $60.50 - $71.50,** ▯ $11, BC MC VI.

★ **Grosvenor Hotel**, (LH), Previously Grosvenor Junction Hotel 40 Ocean St, ☎ 08 8552 1011, fax 08 8552 7274, (2 stry), 30 rms [basin, elec blkts, t/c mkg], lounge (TV), ✗, c/park (limited), ✆, plygr, cots. **BLB ♦ $30, ♦♦ $55,** ▯ $10, Min book school holidays and Easter, AE BC DC EFT MC VI.

Self Catering Accommodation

★★★★ **Hermsen Beach House**, (Cotg), 17 Bartel Boulevard, ☎ 08 8391 2445, 1 cotg acc up to 8, [shwr, bath, tlt, hairdry, a/c, c/fan, TV, video, clock radio, CD, t/c mkg, refrig, cook fac, micro, d/wash, toaster, blkts, doonas, linen, pillows], w/mach, dryer, iron, iron brd. **D ♦♦♦ $79 - $187.80, W $550 - $1,100,** Min book applies.

★★★★ **Settlers Cottage**, (Cotg), Franklin Pde, 3km SW of PO, ☎ 08 8552 4400, fax 08 8552 4240, 1 cotg acc up to 2, [shwr, spa bath, tlt, a/c, elec blkts, tel, fax, TV, clock radio, t/c mkg, refrig, cook fac, micro, blkts, linen, pillows], ldry, w/mach, dryer, iron, iron brd, conf fac, ⊠, cafe, bar, pool (salt water/seasonal), bbq, ✆, tennis-fee, cots, non smoking property. **D $136 - $162,** AE BC DC EFT MC VI.

WHALERS INN RESORT

AAA Tourism ★★★★☆

Spectacular Waterfront Location with sweeping ocean views nestled at the foot of the Bluff in fully landscaped gardens

THREE STYLES OF LUXURY ACCOMMODATION AT REASONABLE RATES
- *Beautifully appointed motel-style units* • *Deluxe Studios*
- *Fully self-contained 1-3 Bedroom Apartments*

Double Spa Bath in most units
2 Swimming pools
Award-winning Restaurant

Tennis Court
Conference Facilities
Guests private BBQ lawn area

Ph: (08) 8552 4400   Fax: (08) 8552 4240

Address: 121 Franklin Parade, Encounter Bay, Victor Harbor SA 5211
Email: Whalers@granite.net.au   Web site: www.whalers.com.au

★★★☆ **Adare Caravan Park & Holiday Units**, (HU), The Drive, ☎ 08 8552 1657, fax 08 8552 1657, 2 units acc up to 6, (2 & 3 bedrm), [shwr, tlt, fan, heat, elec blkts, TV, clock radio, t/c mkg, refrig, cook fac, micro, linen reqd-fee], ldry, w/mach, iron, iron brd, non smoking property, **D** ♦ **$55**, ⊕ **$3.30**, **W** ♦♦ **$330**, ⊕ **$19.80**, Min book applies, BC MC VI.

★★★☆ **Blue Seas Holiday Apartments**, (HU), 27 Esplanade, 500m W of PO, ☎ 08 8552 1033, fax 08 8552 1207, (2 stry gr fl), 4 units acc up to 6, (2 bedrm3 bedrm), [shwr, bath (hip), tlt, hairdry, a/c, elec blkts, TV, clock radio, refrig, cook fac, micro, ldry (2), blkts, linen reqd-fee, pillows], w/mach, iron, c/park (carport). **D $90 - $130**, **W $295 - $785**, Min book all holiday times.

★★★☆ **Hautbois Cottage**, (Cotg), Newland Hill, 5km SW of PO, ☎ 08 8552 2353, fax 08 8552 2353, 1 cotg acc up to 6, (2 bedrm), [shwr, bath, tlt, c/fan, heat, TV, video, clock radio, CD, t/c mkg, refrig, cook fac, micro, toaster, ldry (in house), blkts, linen, pillows], w/mach, iron, iron brd, lounge firepl, bbq, c/park (garage). **D** ♦♦ **$120 - $165**, ⊕ **$25 - $42**, ch con, Min book applies.

★★★☆ **Lakeside Getaway House**, (House), 42 Lakeside Circ, 5km W of PO, ☎ 08 8552 3935, 1 house acc up to 4, (2 bedrm), [shwr, tlt, c/fan, heat, tel, TV, video, clock radio, t/c mkg, refrig, cook fac, micro, elec frypan, toaster, blkts, doonas, linen, pillows], w/mach, iron, iron brd, bbq, c/park (carport), non smoking property. **D** ♦♦ **$110**, ⊕ **$12**, ch con, Min book applies, BC MC VI.

★★★☆ **Pinhigh Lodge Holiday Units**, (HU), Inman Valley Rd, 3km W of PO, ☎ 08 8552 5124, fax 08 8552 4874, 5 units acc up to 4, (2 bedrm), [shwr, bath, tlt, a/c, elec blkts, TV, clock radio, refrig, cook fac, micro, blkts, linen, pillows], ldry, w/mach, dryer, iron, iron brd, bbq (covered), c/park (carport), car wash, ✆, plygr, cots-fee, non smoking units, **D $60 - $110**, ch con, Min book Christmas and Jan, BC MC VI.

★★★ **Smugglers Inn**, (SA), 16 Crozier Rd, 300m SW of PO, ☎ 08 8551 5227, fax 08 8551 5222, (2 stry gr fl), 20 serv apts acc up to 4, [shwr, spa bath (1), tlt, hairdry, a/c, elec blkts, tel, TV, video (avail)-fee, clock radio, t/c mkg, refrig, cook fac ltd, micro, toaster, blkts, linen, pillows], ldry, iron (avail), iron brd (avail), ☒ (Tue-Sat), cots-fee. **RO** ♦ **$77 - $145**, ♦♦ **$94 - $145**, ⊕ **$22**, ch con, fam con, AE BC DC EFT MC VI.

Morgan Park Bed & Breakfast, (Apt), 1 Shetland Crt, 5km N of PO, ☎ 08 8552 9151, fax 08 8552 9151, 1 apt [shwr, spa bath, tlt, a/c, fan, heat, tel, TV, video, clock radio, t/c mkg, refrig, cook fac ltd, micro, ldry, blkts, doonas, linen, pillows], lounge, bbq, non smoking property. **BLB** ♦ **$85 - $95**, ♦♦ **$110 - $140**, ⊕ **$35**, ch con, weekly con, (not yet classified).

B&B's/Guest Houses

★★★★☆ **Avalon**, (B&B), No children's facilities, Tjilbruke Dve, Encounter Bay, 7km S of PO, ☎ 08 8552 7588, fax 08 8552 7933, 2 rms (2 suites) [ensuite, bath (1), spa bath (1), hairdry, cent heat, elec blkts, TV, clock radio, t/c mkg, refrig, cook fac ltd (communal), micro (communal), toaster, pillows], iron (avail), iron brd (avail), lounge, ✕, dinner to unit (on request), c/park (carport), non smoking property. **D** ♦♦ **$130 - $140**, BC MC VI.

★★★★☆ **Bartrells Bed & Breakfast**, (B&B), No children's facilities, 47 Rapid Dve, 2km N of PO, ☎ 08 8552 7758, fax 08 8552 7768, 2 rms [ensuite, a/c, c/fan, elec blkts, clock radio, t/c mkg], ldry, w/mach, dryer, lounge (TV & Video), bbq, meals avail, non smoking rms. **BB** ♦ **$110**, ♦♦ **$126.50**, AE BC MC VI.

★★★★☆ **Parkfield Lodge Bed & Breakfast**, (B&B), 66 Rapid Dve, 600m Sth of McCracken Country Club, ☎ 08 8552 7270, fax 08 8552 8386, (2 stry), 3 rms [ensuite (2), a/c-cool, heat, elec blkts, clock radio, CD, t/c mkg], bathrm (private) (1), w/mach, dryer, lounge (TV), refrig, bbq, meals avail (on request), non smoking rms. **BB ♦ $65, ♦♦ $100 - $130**, BC MC VI.

★★★★ **Avoca-Victor Harbor**, (B&B), 2 Emma Ct, McCracken Estate, ☎ 08 8552 8112, fax 08 8552 8112, 2 rms (2 suites) [ensuite, bath, hairdry, a/c, elec blkts, TV, video, clock radio, t/c mkg, refrig, toaster], iron, iron brd, read rm, lounge, non smoking units. **Suite BB ♦ $90 - $110, ♦♦ $120, ◊ $50 - $60**.

★★★☆ **Annies House Bed & Breakfast**, (B&B), 26 Sturt St, 500m W of PO, ☎ 08 8552 6092, fax 08 8552 6092, 2 rms [ensuite (1), bath, hairdry, fan, fire pl, heat, elec blkts, tel, TV, video, radio, CD, t/c mkg], iron, iron brd, lounge (TV), c/park (undercover), non smoking rms. **BB ♦ $60 - $70, ♦♦ $100 - $110**, ch con, fam con, pen con, *Operator Comment: 'Open fires, 4 poster bed. Stopover for Kangaroo Island. On the Fleurieu Way'.*

★★★☆ **Villa Victor Bed & Breakfast**, (B&B), 59 Victoria St, 500m W of PO, ☎ 08 8552 4258, fax 08 8552 4258, 4 rms [ensuite (1), heat, elec blkts, TV, clock radio], shared fac (2), ldry, w/mach, t/c mkg shared, bbq (covered), non smoking property. **BB ♦ $65, ♦♦ $75 - $95, ◊ $25**, ch con, BC MC VI.

★★★☆ **Yelki By The Sea**, (B&B), 66 Franklin Pde, ☎ 08 8552 1999, fax 08 8552 1333, 4 rms [ensuite (2), bath (2), hairdry (2), fan (2), c/fan (2), heat, elec blkts, tel (2), TV (2), clock radio, refrig (2), micro (1)], ldry, w/mach, dryer, iron, iron brd, lounge (TV), ✕, t/c mkg shared, bbq, meals avail (by arrangement), non smoking rms. **BB ♦ $60 - $80, ♦♦ $90 - $120, ◊ $60**, BC MC VI.

★★★ **Anchorage at Victor Harbor Seafront Hotel**, (GH), 23-23 Flinders Pde, ☎ 08 8552 5970, fax 08 8552 1970, (2 stry gr fl), 22 rms [basin, ensuite (16), spa bath (7), a/c (7), TV (13), t/c mkg (10), refrig (10)], shared fac (6), lounge (TV), conf fac, ⊠, t/c mkg shared (12), c/park. **BLB ♦ $40 - $140, ♦♦ $65 - $140, ◊ $17**, 9 rms ★★★☆. AE BC DC EFT MC VI.

VIVONNE BAY SA

See Kangaroo Island Region.

WAIKERIE SA 5330

Pop 1,748. (175km NE Adelaide), See map on pages 586/587, ref D6. The Waikerie district is the largest citrus growing area in Australia. The town is also known for its world renowned gliding conditions. Boating, Bowls, Croquet, Fishing, Golf, Horse Riding, Scenic Drives, Swimming (Pool & River), Tennis, Vineyards, Wineries, Water Skiing.

Hotels/Motels
★★★ **Kirriemuir Motel & Cabins**, (M), Ian Oliver Dr, 1km SE of PO, ☎ 08 8541 2488, fax 08 8541 3313, 10 units [ensuite, spa bath (3), hairdry (3), a/c, elec blkts, tel, TV, video-fee, clock radio, t/c mkg, refrig, toaster], bbq, tennis (half court), cots-fee. **RO ♦ $72 - $100, ♦♦ $82 - $110, ◊ $12 - $15**, 3 units of a higher standard. Other accommodation styles available, AE BC DC EFT MC VI, ♿.

★★☆ **Waikerie Hotel Motel**, (LMH), McCoy St, ☎ 08 8541 2999, fax 08 8541 3104, (2 stry), 16 units [ensuite, a/c, elec blkts, tel, TV, clock radio, t/c mkg, refrig], conf fac, ⊠. **RO ♦ $55, ♦♦ $66, ♦♦♦ $77**, ch con, 6 rooms ★★★, Min book long w/ends and Easter, AE BC DC EFT MC VI.
★★ **(Hotel Section)**, 19 rms [ensuite (4), a/c, elec blkts, tel, TV, clock radio, t/c mkg, refrig]. **RO ♦ $49.50, ♦♦ $60.50, ♦♦♦ $71.50**.

Self Catering Accommodation
★★★☆ **Jo's Bed & Breakfast Cottage**, (Cotg), Cnr West Rd & The Avenue, 2km W of PO, ☎ 08 8541 3491, fax 08 8541 3491, 1 cotg acc up to 4, [shwr, tlt, a/c, cable tv, clock radio, t/c mkg, refrig, micro, toaster], iron, iron brd, bbq, breakfast ingredients, non smoking property. **D ♦ $71.50, ♦♦ $82.50, ◊ $5.50 - $16.50**, ch con, pen con, BC VI.

★★★ **Riversleigh Lagoon Cottage**, (Cotg), Renmark Rd, 17km NW of PO, ☎ 08 8543 2273, fax 08 8543 2256, 1 cotg acc up to 4, (1 bedrm), [shwr, tlt, a/c-cool, fire pl, TV, refrig, cook fac, linen reqd], bbq. **W $400**, Min book applies.

B&B's/Guest Houses
★★ **C J Duncan Bed & Breakfast**, (B&B), No children's facilities, Lot 409, Nitschke Rd, 16km E of PO off Sturt Hwy, ☎ 08 8589 3083, 1 rm [ensuite, a/c-cool, heat, TV], bbq, meals avail, c/park. **BLB ♦ $50 - $55, ♦♦ $55**.

Other Accommodation
Green & Gold Houseboats, (Hbt), 1.5km N of PO, ☎ 08 8541 2001, fax 08 8541 4005, 7 houseboats acc up to 12, [shwr, spa bath (1), tlt, a/c-cool (7), heat (6), TV (7), video (7), radio, CD (6), refrig, cook fac, micro (6), d/wash (3), linen reqd], w/mach (6), bbq. **W $490 - $3,045**, 3 houseboats built specifically for wheelchair access. Min book applies, BC MC VI.

Jensta Houseboat, (Hbt), Riverfront, 1.5km N of PO, ☎ 08 8541 2757, fax 08 8541 2123, 3 houseboats acc up to 10, [shwr, tlt, a/c-cool, heat, radio (cassette), refrig, cook fac, micro (3), linen reqd], w/mach (3), ice box, bbq. **W $800 - $1,540**.

WALLAROO SA 5556

Pop 2,465. (157km NW Adelaide), See map on pages 586/587, ref A6. Thriving tourist centre & major country port on the Yorke Peninsula. Boating, Bowls, Croquet, Fishing, Golf, Horse Riding, Swimming (Beach & Pool), Tennis.

Hotels/Motels
★★★ **Sonbern Lodge Motel**, (M), 18 John Tce, opposite railway station, ☎ 08 8823 2291, fax 08 8823 3355, 8 units [ensuite, a/c, elec blkts, tel, TV, clock radio, t/c mkg, refrig], rec rm, ⊠, bbq, cots-fee, non smoking units (4). **RO ♦ $62, ♦♦ $78, ◊ $15**, ch con, AE BC DC EFT MC VI.
★★★ **(Lodge Section)**, (2 stry), 9 rms [ensuite (4), a/c-cool (2), a/c (4), fan, heat, elec blkts, TV (4)], ldry, lounge (TV), t/c mkg shared, refrig. **RO ♦ $26 - $43, ♦♦ $41 - $59, ◊ $15**, ch con.

★★ **Anglers Inn Hotel Motel**, (LMH), 9 Bagot St, ☎ 08 8823 2545, 20 units [shwr, tlt, a/c, elec blkts, TV, radio (20), t/c mkg, refrig, toaster], conv fac, ⊠, bbq, rm serv, ☎, cots (available). **RO ♦ $50, ♦♦ $60, ◊ $11**, ch con, fam con, BC EFT MC VI.

Self Catering Accommodation
★★★★ **The Macs Beachfront Villas**, (HU), 9 Jetty Rd, 1.5km W of PO, ☎ 08 8823 2137, fax 08 8823 3622, 6 units acc up to 5, (1 & 2 bedrm), [shwr, spa bath (1), tlt, a/c, TV, clock radio, refrig, cook fac, micro, toaster, ldry (in unit), blkts, linen, pillows], w/mach, dryer, iron, iron brd, c/park (carport). **D $130 - $145**, Min book applies, AE BC DC MC VI.

★★★ **Riley Village**, (HF), Woodforde Dve, North Beach township, 6km N of PO, ☎ 08 8823 2057, fax 08 8823 3507, 6 flats (2 bedrm), [shwr, tlt, a/c, fan, heat, TV, clock radio, refrig, cook fac, micro, doonas, linen reqd-fee, pillows], bbq. **D ♦♦♦♦ $60 - $80**, Min book Christmas Jan long w/ends and Easter, BC MC VI.

WANGARY SA 5607

Pop Nominal, (692km W Adelaide), See map on pages 586/587, ref F6. A small township located close to Mount Dutton. Tennis. See also Coffin Bay & Port Lincoln.

Mt Dutton Bay Shearers Quarters Cottage, (Cotg), circa 1875, Woolshed Dve, Mt Dutton Bay, 2km W of PO, ☎ 08 8685 4031, fax 08 8685 4031, 1 cotg acc up to 6, [shwr, bath, tlt, fan, c/fan, fire pl (2), heat, TV, radio, t/c mkg, refrig, cook fac, toaster, blkts, doonas, linen reqd-fee, pillows], iron (avail), iron brd (avail), conf fac, bbq, cots, breakfast ingredients. **D ♦ $70 - $90, ♦♦ $90 - $110, ◊ $20, W ♦ $490 - $630, ♦♦ $630 - $790, ◊ $140**, ch con, BC MC VI.
(Backpacker Section), 1 rm acc up to 36, (Bunk Rooms), [c/fan (4), radio, blkts reqd-fee, linen reqd-fee, pillows reqd-fee], shwr (6), tlt (8), iron, iron brd, rec rm, cook fac, t/c mkg shared, refrig. **D ♦ $15, ◊ $15**, ch con, ♿.

WAROOKA SA 5577

Pop 236. (215km W Adelaide), See map on pages 586/587, ref A7. Small township located in southern Yorke Peninsula. Though small, it serves a wide area of agricultural country. Scenic Drives.

Hotels/Motels
★★☆ **Warooka Hotel Motel**, (LMH), Main St, ☎ 08 8854 5001, fax 08 8854 5002, 7 units [shwr, tlt, a/c-cool, heat, TV, t/c mkg, refrig], ⊠ (Mon to Sat), c/park (undercover). **RO ♦ $50, ♦♦ $60, ♦♦♦ $65**, AE BC DC EFT MC VI.

Self Catering Accommodation
★★☆ **Peesey Park Cottage**, (Cotg), Warooka - Yorketown Rd, 11km E of PO, ☎ 08 8852 1770, fax 08 8852 1770, 1 cotg acc up to 7, (3 bedrm), [shwr, bath, tlt, a/c-cool, c/fan, elec blkts, TV, video, clock radio, t/c mkg, refrig, cook fac, elec frypan, toaster, blkts, doonas, linen, pillows], iron, lounge firepl, bbq, cots, breakfast ingredients, **D ♦ $65, ♦♦ $95, ◊ $25**, ch con, fam con, weekly con.

WATERVALE SA 5452

Pop Nominal, (118km N Adelaide), See map on pages 586/587, ref B6. Situated in the Clare Valley. Bowls, Tennis, Vineyards, Wineries.

★★★★☆ **Ethel's Cottage**, (Cotg), Main North Rd, Leasingham, 2km S of Watervale PO, ☎ 08 8342 0406, fax 08 8342 0406, 1 cotg acc up to 6, [shwr, bath, tlt, hairdry, a/c, fire pl (2), elec blkts, tel, TV, video, clock radio, CD, t/c mkg, refrig, cook fac, micro, d/wash, toaster, blkts, doonas, linen, pillows], w/mach, dryer, iron, iron brd, bbq, c/park (undercover), cots (avail), breakfast ingredients, **BB ♦♦ $145, ◊ $60**, ch con, BC MC VI.

★★★ **Battunga Bed & Breakfast Cottages**, (Cotg), Skilly Rd, 2km W of PO, ☎ 08 8843 0120, fax 08 8843 0129, 4 cotgs acc up to 4, (1 & 2 bedrm), [shwr, tlt, c/fan, heat (slow combustion), clock radio, refrig, micro, elec frypan, toaster, blkts, linen, pillows], conv fac, bbq, breakfast ingredients, non smoking property. D ♦♦ $120 - $130, ◊ $30, ch con.

★★★ **Watervale Retreat**, Lot 4 Saint Vincent Rd, 1.5km W of town centre, ☎ 08 8843 0070, fax 08 8843 0070, 4 cabins acc up to 6, [ensuite, bath (3), TV, refrig, cook fac, micro, toaster, doonas, linen-fee, pillows], bbq. D ♦ $71.50, ◊ $5.50 - $11, Deposit required, BC MC VI.

★★☆ **Watervale Cottage**, (Cotg), Previously Watervale Cottage Vineyard Bed & Breakfast, Cnr Sheoak & St Vincents Rds, ☎ 0429 193 622, fax 08 8468 6994, 1 cotg acc up to 6, (3 bedrm), [shwr, tlt, elec blkts, TV, t/c mkg, refrig, cook fac, toaster, blkts, linen, pillows], iron, iron brd, c/park (garage), breakfast ingredients, non smoking property. D $150, ch con, BC MC VI.

WELLINGTON SA 5259

Pop Part of Tailem Bend, (105km S Adelaide), See map on pages 586/587, ref C8. Historically significant town situated on the Murray where it enters Lake Alexandrina. Boating, Fishing, Scenic Drives, Swimming (River).

★★☆ **Wellington Courthouse Bed & Breakfast**, (B&B), Circa 1864. Mason Rd, ☎ 08 8572 7330, fax 08 8572 7139, 2 rms [fan, heat, elec blkts, TV, clock radio, t/c mkg, refrig], cafe, cots-fee, BB ♦ $65, ♦♦ $110, ◊ $30, Outside bathroom. BC MC VI.

WESTERN RIVER COVE SA

See Kangaroo Island Region.

WHYALLA SA 5600

Pop 24,700. (380km NNW Adelaide), See map on pages 586/587, ref G5. The Gateway to the Eyre Peninsula. Boating, Bowls, Croquet, Fishing, Golf, Greyhound Racing, Horse Racing, Sailing, Squash, Swimming (Beach & Pool), Tennis, Trotting.

Hotels/Motels

FLAG
FLAG CHOICE HOTELS

★★★★ **Derhams Foreshore Motor Inn**, (M), Watson Tce, 1km SW of PO, ☎ 08 8645 8877, fax 08 8645 2549, (2 stry gr fl), 40 units [ensuite, bath (1), hairdry, a/c, elec blkts, tel, cable tv, video, clock radio, t/c mkg, refrig, mini bar], ldry-fee, iron, iron brd, conv fac, ⊠, pool, bbq, rm serv, plygr, tennis, cots, non smoking rms (14). RO ♦ $95 - $115, ♦♦ $95 - $115, ◊ $15, ch con, fam con, 12 rooms of a ★★★★, AE BC DC MC VI.

(Serviced Apartment Section), 1 serv apt acc up to 4, (2 bedrm), [shwr, bath, tlt, hairdry, a/c, heat, elec blkts, tel, TV, video-fee, clock radio, t/c mkg, refrig, mini bar, cook fac ltd, micro, elec frypan, toaster, blkts, linen, pillows]. D $180, (not yet classified).

★★★☆ **Alexander Motor Inn**, (M), 99 Playford Ave, ☎ 08 8645 9488, fax 08 8645 2211, (2 stry gr fl), 40 units (1 bedrm2 bedrm), [ensuite, spa bath (1), hairdry, a/c, elec blkts, tel, TV, movie, clock radio, t/c mkg, refrig, mini bar], ldry-fee, iron, iron brd, conv fac, ⊠, pool, bbq, rm serv, dinner to unit, plygr, cots-fee, non smoking rms (6). RO ♦ $87, ♦♦ $92, ♦♦♦♦ $109, ◊ $16, ch con, AE BC DC EFT MC MP VI.

Best Western

★★★☆ **Westland Hotel Motel**, (LMH), 100 McDouall Stuart Ave, Whyalla Norrie 5608, ☎ 08 8645 0066, fax 08 8645 1656, (2 stry), 55 units [ensuite, spa bath (4), hairdry (20), a/c (55), elec blkts, tel, TV, movie, clock radio, t/c mkg, refrig, mini bar], ldry-fee, conv fac, ⊠, pool, sauna, spa, bbq, rm serv, dinner to unit, gym, cots. RO ♦ $71 - $107, ♦♦ $71 - $107, ◊ $5.50, ch con, 4 rms ★★★★. AE BC DC EFT MC MP VI, 🛆.

★★★★ **(Motel Section)**, 36 units [ensuite, spa bath (6), hairdry, a/c, elec blkts, tel, TV, movie, clock radio, t/c mkg, refrig, mini bar], ldry-fee, iron, iron brd, ⊠, sauna, spa, c/park (covered), cots, non smoking units (5). RO ♦ $98 - $107, ♦♦ $98 - $107, ◊ $11, ch con, 🛆.

Budget Motel Chain International

★★★ **Airport Whyalla Motel**, (M), Lincoln Hwy, 3km W of PO, ☎ 08 8645 2122, fax 08 8645 5753, 11 units [ensuite, a/c, elec blkts, tel, cable tv (5), clock radio, t/c mkg, refrig], bbq, non smoking units (7). RO ♦ $62 - $65, ♦♦ $67 - $70, ♦♦♦♦ $76, ◊ $10, fam con, AE BC DC EFT MC MCH VI.

★★★ **Whyalla Country Inn Motel**, (M), 95 Playford Ave, ☎ 08 8645 0588, fax 08 8645 2003, (2 stry gr fl), 20 units [ensuite, a/c, tel, TV, video (avail), movie, clock radio, t/c mkg, refrig, mini bar], ldry, iron (avail), iron brd (avail), conv fac, ⊠, bbq, rm serv, dinner to unit, cots-fee, non smoking units (7). RO ♦ $55 - $75, ♦♦ $60 - $75, ◊ $10, ch con, fam con, AE BC DC MC VI.

★★☆ **Hotel Eyre**, (LH), Cnr Playford Ave & Elliott St, ☎ 08 8645 7188, fax 08 8645 8650, (2 stry), 15 rms [ensuite, a/c, heat, TV, t/c mkg, refrig], TV rm, ⊠, bbq, cots-fee. RO ♦ $35, ♦♦ $45, ◊ $5, TAB, Keno, Gaming machines & Sky Channel, AE BC DC EFT MC VI.

★★ **Spencer Hotel**, (LH), Forsyth St, ☎ 08 8645 8411, fax 08 8645 1743, (2 stry), 28 rms [ensuite, a/c, elec blkts, TV, t/c mkg, refrig], lounge (TV), conf fac, ⊠ (Mon to Sat), ☏, cots-fee. RO ♦ $33 - $30, ♦♦ $44, ◊ $11, ch con, AE BC DC MC VI.

★☆ **Bayview Hotel**, (LH), 11 Forsyth St, ☎ 08 8645 8544, fax 08 8644 0145, (2 stry), 15 rms [ensuite, a/c, elec blkts, cable tv, t/c mkg, refrig, toaster], ldry-fee, lounge, conf fac, ⊠ (6 days), c/park (limited). RO ♦ $33, ♦♦ $55, ◊ $10, ch con, AE BC DC EFT MC VI.

★ **Lord Gowrie Hotel**, (LH), 10 Gowrie Ave, ☎ 08 8645 8955, fax 08 8645 1611, (2 stry), 9 rms [ensuite, a/c-cool, heat, tel, TV, radio, t/c mkg, refrig], ⊠ (Mon to Sat), c/park. RO ♦ $33, ♦♦ $44, BC EFT MC VI.

Sundowner Motel Hotel, (LMH), Lincoln Hwy, ☎ 08 8645 7688, fax 08 8645 2488, 24 units [ensuite, a/c, elec blkts, tel, TV, video (1), radio, t/c mkg, refrig], lounge (TV), ⊠, bar, pool, bbq, rm serv, ☏, cots. RO ♦ $44, ♦♦ $48, ♦♦♦ $57, ◊ $10, fam con, Function Centre, Gaming lounge, ATM. AE BC DC EFT MC VI, (not yet classified).

Self Catering Accommodation

★★★☆ **Red Gum Cottage**, (Cotg), 65 Wileman St, 3km W of PO, ☎ 0419 213 853, 1 cotg acc up to 6, [shwr, bath, tlt, a/c, heat, elec blkts, TV, video, clock radio, CD, t/c mkg, refrig, micro, elec frypan, toaster, blkts, linen, pillows], non smoking property. BLB ♦ $77, ♦♦ $88, ◊ $11, ch con, AE BC MC VI.

Playford Apartments, (HU), 100 Playford Ave, ☎ 08 8645 0588, fax 08 8645 2003, 8 units acc up to 4, [shwr, tlt, a/c, cent heat, TV, video, clock radio, t/c mkg, refrig, cook fac, micro, toaster, blkts, linen], w/mach, dryer, pool, bbq, cots, non smoking units (5). D ♦ $85, ♦♦ $95, ◊ $10, AE BC DC MC VI, (not yet classified).

WILLIAMSTOWN SA

See Barossa Valley Region.

WILMINGTON SA 5485

Pop 250. (294km N Adelaide), See map on pages 586/587, ref H5. Formerly known as Beautiful Valley, located at the northern end of Mt Remarkable National Park in the Flinders Ranges. Bowls, Bush Walking, Croquet, Golf, Tennis.

Hotels/Motels

Wilmington Hotel, (LH), Main St, ☎ 08 8667 5154, fax 08 8667 5233, (2 stry), 17 rms [basin, a/c (6), elec blkts, t/c mkg], ⊠, cots. RO ♦ $25, ♦♦ $45, ◊ $15, ch con, BC EFT MC VI.

B&B's/Guest Houses

★★☆ **Wilmington Bed & Breakfast Lodge**, (B&B), 31 Maria Tce, ☎ 08 8667 5323, 7 rms [bath, a/c, heat, TV (3)], ldry, breakfast rm, t/c mkg shared, c/park (undercover) (3), non smoking rms. BLB ♦ $32 - $56, ♦♦ $50 - $56, ◊ $12, BC MC VI.

WILPENA POUND SA 5434

Pop Nominal, (481km N Adelaide), See map on pages 586/587, ref H4. Part of the Flinders Ranges National Park. Wilpena Pound, the greatest single formation in the Flinders, is completely surrounded by mountains. Other places of interest are Sacred Canyon - aboriginal carvings - and Stokes Hill Lookout. Bush Walking.

Hotels/Motels

★★★★ **Wilpena Pound Resort**, (M), Wilpena Pound, ☎ 08 8648 0004, fax 08 8648 0028, 60 units [ensuite, a/c, elec blkts, TV, movie, clock radio, t/c mkg, refrig, cook fac (10), micro (10)], ldry, lounge, ⊠, pool, bbq, cots, non smoking units (26). RO ♦ $93.50, ♦♦ $107.80, ◊ $13.20, ch con, 26 units ★★★☆ and 10 units ★★☆. AE BC DC EFT MC VI, 🛆.

Self Catering Accommodation

★★★★ **Rawnsley Park Station**, (HU), Previously Rawnsley Park Holiday Units Wilpena Rd, 21km S of Wilpena Pound, ☎ 08 8648 0030, fax 08 8648 0013, 27 units acc up to 6, (1, 2 & 3 bedrm), [shwr, tlt, a/c-cool, heat, heat, TV, clock radio, refrig, cook fac, micro, blkts, doonas, linen (19) reqd-fee, pillows], ldry (2), bbq, non smoking property. D ♦♦ $70 - $85, ◊ $14 - $20, ch con, 12 units ★★★☆. Min book all holiday times, AE BC DC EFT MC VI.

WILPENA SOUND SA continued...

★★★☆ **Arkaba Station Cottage**, (Cotg), Wilpena Rd, 35km S of Wilpena Pound, ☎ 08 8648 0004, fax 08 8648 4195, 1 cotg acc up to 6, (2 bedrm), [shwr, tlt, a/c, c/fan, heat, elec blkts, TV, video, clock radio, CD, refrig, cook fac, micro, ldry, blkts, linen, pillows], w/mach, bbq, D ♦♦ $140, ◊ $15, ch con, Min book applies, BC MC VI.

Willow Springs, Willow Springs Station, Hawker 5434, 71km NE of Hawker, ☎ 08 8648 4022, fax 08 8648 4283, 1 cabin acc up to 5, [shwr, tlt, heat (open fire), refrig (gas), cook fac ltd, blkts reqd, linen reqd, pillows reqd], D ♦♦ $35 - $47, ◊ $6, ch con, Solar powered lighting, Min book applies, AE BC DC MC VI, (not yet classified).

(Jackeroos' Cottage), 1 cotg acc up to 5, [shwr, tlt, fan, heat (open fire lounge), t/c mkg, refrig, cook fac ltd, toaster, blkts, linen-fee, pillows], D ♦♦ $65 - $91, ◊ $13, ch con, Generated power only 6.30am to 10.30pm. Min book applies, (not yet classified).

(Manager's Residence), 1 rm acc up to 17, [shwr, bath, tlt, fan, heat (combustion), t/c mkg, refrig, cook fac, toaster, ldry, blkts, doonas, linen-fee, pillows], D ♦♦ $65 - $143, ◊ $13, ch con, Minimum number of 8 people per booking at all times. Generated power only 6.30am to 10.30pm. 12 volt lighting. Min book applies, (not yet classified).

(Overseers' Cottage), 1 cotg acc up to 4, [shwr, tlt, fan, heat, t/c mkg, refrig (gas), cook fac ltd, blkts, doonas, linen-fee, pillows], D ♦♦ $65 - $78, ◊ $13, ch con, Generated power only 6.30am to 10.30pm. 12 volt lighting. Min book applies, (not yet classified).

(Shearers Quarters), 1 rm acc up to 20, [shwr, tlt, heat (open fire), t/c mkg, refrig, cook fac ltd, blkts, linen-fee, pillows], w/mach, D ♦♦ $65 - $143, ◊ $13, ch con, Minimum number of 8 persons per booking at all times. Generated power only 6.30am to 10.30pm. Min book applies, (not yet classified).

WIRRABARA SA 5481

Pop 292. (242km N Adelaide), See map on pages 586/587, ref H5. Located in the Flinders Ranges, Wirrabara - an aboriginal name meaning 'Creek with big trees'. Bowls, Bush Walking, Golf, Tennis.

Hotels/Motels

Wirrabara Hotel, (LH), High St, town centre, ☎ 08 8668 4162, fax 08 8668 4133, 5 rms [a/c (4), heat (avail), elec blkts], lounge (TV), ✗, c/park. **BLB** ♦ $30, ♦♦ $45, ch con, BC MC VI.

Self Catering Accommodation

★★★ **Taralee Orchards**, (Cotg), Forest Rd, 12km W of Wirrabara, ☎ 08 8668 4343, fax 08 8668 4344, 1 cotg acc up to 5, [shwr, bath, tlt, fan, c/fan, heat, elec blkts, TV, video, clock radio, t/c mkg, refrig, cook fac, micro, toaster, blkts, doonas, linen, pillows], iron (avail), iron brd, bbq, c/park (carport). cots. D ♦♦ $72 - $83, ◊ $11 - $17, W ♦♦ $420, ◊ $70, ch con.

B&B's/Guest Houses

★★★☆ **Wirrabara Heritage Bed & Breakfast**, (B&B), 70 West Tce, 50m S of PO, ☎ 08 8668 4018, 5 rms [c/fan, heat, elec blkts, TV, clock radio, t/c mkg, refrig (4)], lounge (TV, Video & Stereo), bbq, c/park (carport), cots, non smoking rms. **BB** ♦ $37, ♦♦ $65, ◊ $20, **BLB** ♦ $32, ♦♦ $55, ◊ $15, ch con, fam con, AE BC MC VI.

WOOL BAY SA 5575

Pop Part of Stansbury, (209km W Adelaide), See map on pages 586/587, ref A7. Tiny outport for handling grain on the Yorke Peninsula. Boating, Fishing, Swimming (Beach).

★★ **Wool Bay Holiday Units**, (HU), Lot 7, Esplanade, ☎ 08 8852 8284, 6 units acc up to 6, [shwr, tlt, fan, heat, TV, refrig, cook fac, micro, linen reqd-fee], ldry, w/mach (1), dryer, bbq, cots, D $45, W $280, Min book long w/ends and Easter.

WOOMERA SA 5720

Pop 1,810. (502km NNW Adelaide), See map on pages 586/587, ref G4. Established in 1947 as launch base for experimental rockets and space craft. Now residential support centre for Joint Defence Facility. Bowls, Swimming (Pool), Tennis.

★★ **Woomera Eldo Hotel**, (LH), Kotara Cres, ☎ 08 8673 7867, fax 08 8673 7226, (2 stry), 158 rms [shwr (22), tlt (22), a/c, tel (52), TV (95), cable tv (2), clock radio (95), refrig], ldry, conv fac, ✗, bbq, c/park (undercover), ✎, cots-fee. **RO** ♦ $32.50 - $70, ♦♦ $66 - $77, ♦♦♦ $99 - $115.50, ♦♦♦♦ $134 - $154.50, ch con, 136 units list only. 136 units use unisex share bathroom facilities. AE BC DC EFT MC VI.

WUDINNA SA 5652

Pop 573. (578km NW Adelaide), See map on pages 586/587, ref F5. Growing service centre to surrounding agricultural community. Bowls, Golf, Horse Riding, Scenic Drives, Squash, Swimming (Pool), Tennis.

★★★ **Gawler Ranges Motel**, (M), Eyre Hwy, ☎ 08 8680 2090, fax 08 8680 2184, 23 units (2 bedrm), [ensuite, a/c, tel, TV, movie (9), clock radio, t/c mkg, refrig, toaster], ✉, pool-indoor, spa, bbq, rm serv, dinner to unit, cots, non smoking units. **RO** ♦ $58 - $119, ♦♦ $67 - $119, ◊ $9, 6 units ★★☆ and 8 units ★★. AE BC DC MC VI.

★★ **Wudinna Hotel Motel**, (LMH), 19 Burton Tce, ☎ 08 8680 2019, fax 08 8680 2030, 22 units [shwr, tlt, a/c, fan (avail), elec blkts, TV, clock radio, t/c mkg, refrig, toaster], ✉, bbq, ✎, cots. **RO** ♦ $43, ♦♦ $54, ◊ $8, 8 rooms yet to be rated. AE BC DC EFT MC VI.

YANKALILLA SA 5203

Pop 532. (72km S Adelaide), See map on pages 586/587, ref B8. A quaint rural town that outlooks mrolling hills that meet the nearby sea. Bowls, Golf, Tennis, Vineyards, Wineries.

★★★★ **Meander Cottage**, (Cotg), 161 Main Rd, 1km W of PO, ☎ 08 8558 3139, fax 08 8558 2021, 1 cotg acc up to 4, (2 bedrm), [shwr, spa bath, tlt, a/c-cool, c/fan, fire pl, TV, clock radio (cassette), CD, refrig, cook fac, micro, blkts, linen, pillows], w/mach, bbq, breakfast ingredients, non smoking property, D ♦ $140, ♦♦ $140, ◊ $60, ch con, BC MC VI.

★★★★ **Rose Cottage Bed & Breakfast Cottage**, (Cotg), Lot 2, Smith Hill Rd, 3.5km NE of PO, ☎ 08 8558 3399, fax 08 8558 3399, 1 cotg acc up to 6, (3 bedrm), [shwr, tlt, hairdry, a/c, c/fan, heat (slow combustion), elec blkts, TV, video, clock radio (cassette), CD, t/c mkg, cook fac, micro, toaster, blkts, linen, pillows], w/mach, iron, iron brd, bbq, breakfast ingredients, non smoking property, Pets on application. D ♦♦ $100 - $130, ◊ $55, ch con, Min book long w/ends and Easter.

★★★☆ **Highview Cottage**, (Cotg), Range Rd, Parawa, 14km S of PO, ☎ 08 8598 5224, 1 cotg acc up to 5, (2 bedrm), [shwr, bath, tlt, fan, heat, elec blkts, TV, radio, t/c mkg, refrig, cook fac, micro, toaster, ldry (in unit), blkts, linen, pillows], w/mach, iron, cots, breakfast ingredients, non smoking property. D ♦♦ $95, ◊ $25, Min book applies.

★★★☆ **Sleepy Hollow Farm Cottage**, (Cotg), Woodvale Rd, 4.5km E of PO, ☎ 08 8558 3190, fax 08 8558 3770, 1 cotg acc up to 6, (3 bedrm - split level.), [shwr, tlt, hairdry, a/c-cool, heat, elec blkts, TV, video, clock radio (cassette), t/c mkg, refrig, cook fac, micro, toaster], w/mach, dryer, iron, iron brd, bbq (covered), cots, breakfast ingredients, non smoking property. D ♦♦ $99 - $110, ◊ $22, ch con, Farm animals. AE BC DC JCB MC VI.

★★★ **Blacklock Nominees Cottage**, (Cotg), Mary MacKillop Schoolhouse Cottage. 48 Main Rd, 400m E of PO, ☎ 08 8558 3200, 1 cotg acc up to 6, (3 bedrm), [shwr, bath, tlt, hairdry, c/fan, fire pl, heat, elec blkts, TV, video, radio, t/c mkg, refrig, cook fac, micro, toaster, ldry (in unit), blkts, linen, pillows], w/mach, breakfast ingredients. D ♦♦ $100, ◊ $30, W ♦♦ $600, ◊ $180, AE BC MC VI.

★★★ **Camelid Cottage**, (Cotg), Lot 91 Main South Rd, Wattel Flat ☎ 0414 340 904, 1 cotg acc up to 6, [shwr, tlt, hairdry, c/fan, heat, elec blkts, tel, cable tv, video, clock radio, CD, t/c mkg, refrig, cook fac, micro, toaster, blkts, doonas, linen, pillows], iron, iron brd, lounge firepl, cots (avail), Small pet by negotiation. D ♦ $85, ♦♦ $120, ◊ $30, ch con, BC MC VI.

YORKETOWN SA 5576

Pop 738. (230km W Adelaide), See map on pages 586/587, ref A7. Centre of one of the very earliest pastoral settlements on the Yorke Peninsula. Bowls, Golf, Horse Racing, Horse Riding, Tennis.

★★ **Melville Hotel Motel**, (LMH), 1 Minlaton Rd, ☎ 08 8852 1019, fax 08 8852 1110, 6 units [ensuite, shwr, tlt, a/c-cool, a/c, heat, elec blkts, TV, clock radio, t/c mkg, refrig], ✉, bbq, c/park. **RO** ♦ $44, ♦♦ $52, ◊ $9, AE BC DC EFT MC VI.

YUNTA SA 5440

Pop 150. (312km NNE Adelaide), See map on pages 586/587, ref H5. Once the focal point of local mining activities. Yunta is now the centre of surrounding pastoral interests. Aboriginal rock carvings located nearby. Golf.

Yunta Hotel, (LH), Barrier Hwy, town centre, ☎ 08 8650 5002, fax 08 8650 5006, 11 rms [fan, elec blkts, TV, video (3), t/c mkg], ldry, lounge (TV), ✉, **RO** ♦ $33, ♦♦ $49.50, ◊ $7, fam con, Deposit on confirmed bookings. BC EFT MC VI.

C loser than you think and so diverse it will surprise you – that's Tasmania, Australia's island State. A short hop from Melbourne or Sydney, Tasmania offers great contrast with the mainland or 'big island'. Enjoy a few rounds of golf, sample Tasmania's award-winning cool climate wines, spend your time shopping for the art and craft for which Tasmania is famous, or explore Tasmania's many gardens, which are at their best clothed in spring bloom or autumnal splendour.

Hire a car and discover Tasmania's hidden secrets. There are many little towns and villages tucked away just awaiting exploration. Take a back road, wander country lanes and stay in accommodation unlike any other.

Start your stay in Hobart, the second oldest Australian city after Sydney. Mellow sandstone buildings line the waterfront. Once warehouses, they are now galleries, craft shops and restaurants. Join the locals at a pavement café and soak up the atmosphere of this small but stylish city. Launceston, Tasmania's second city, is a stately matron, her streets lined by Victorian and Edwardian mansions.

Launceston is the gateway to Tasmania's premier wine growing region – the Tamar Valley. Here you will find vineyard after vineyard, where a warm sun and gentle rain provide the perfect growing environment for Tasmania's acclaimed cool climate wines.

Vineyards can also be found along Tasmania's east coast and around Hobart. Tasmania produces award winning cheeses, succulent grass-fed beef and wonderful fruit and vegetables. Tasmanian crisp apples and summer's mouth-watering raspberries are renowned.

Head west to a land apart, where wild rivers flow and vast wilderness of temperate rainforest covers mile after mile. Stay in Strahan, a quaint and secluded fishing village nestled serenely in Macquarie Harbour, and take a scenic flight to best appreciate the extent of the region's dramatic beauty.

Further north, Cradle Mountain rises majestically over Dove Lake on the edge of the Cradle Mountain-Lake St Clair National Park. The mountain is the single most famous icon of Tasmanian tourism. Alternatively, venture out of Hobart or Launceston along the east coast. This is a region of pristine white beaches washed by a turquoise sea. Locals call this the sunshine coast – and with good reason, as the sun shines on average 300 days a year.

Visit Freycinet National Park to see stunning Wineglass Bay. Further north are the Bay of Fires, Mt William and Douglas Aspley national parks. Take the ferry to Maria Island National Park, one of Tasmania's three former penal settlements.

Tasmania's Midlands offers historic towns and villages, many dating back to the State's days as a penal settlement.

Last century when the state was called Van Diemens Land, it was the final destination for thousands of convicts, the dregs of British society, sent to a land at the end of the world.

Their legacy remains today in the penal settlements at Port Arthur, Sarah Island and Maria Island. Visit these sites, still evocative today of their past brutality.

More than 30 per cent of Tasmania is protected wilderness, marine and nature reserves or forest, much of it granted World Heritage Area status.

Tasmania is also one of the best freshwater fishing places in the world - grab your rod and stalk the wily trout.

TASMANIA
Let Tasmania surprise you

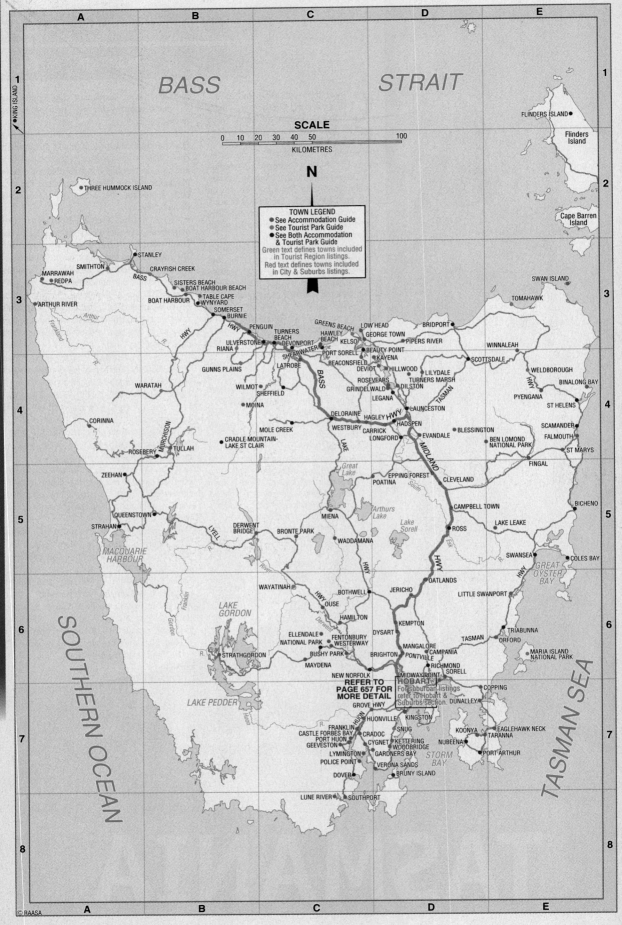

BASS STRAIT

SCALE

0 10 20 30 40 50 100
KILOMETRES

N

TOWN LEGEND
● See Accommodation Guide
● See Tourist Park Guide
● See Both Accommodation
   & Tourist Park Guide
Green text defines towns included
in Tourist Region listings.
Red text defines towns included
in City & Suburbs listings.

KING ISLAND

THREE HUMMOCK ISLAND

FLINDERS ISLAND

Flinders
Island

Cape Barren
Island

STANLEY
SMITHTON
CRAYFISH CREEK
MARRAWAH
REDPA
ARTHUR RIVER
SISTERS BEACH
BOAT HARBOUR BEACH
BOAT HARBOUR
TABLE CAPE
WYNYARD
SOMERSET
BURNIE
PENGUIN
TURNERS BEACH
ULVERSTONE
DEVONPORT
RIANA
SHEARWATER
LATROBE
GUNNS PLAINS
WARATAH
WILMOT
SHEFFIELD
MOINA
DELORAINE
MOLE CREEK
WESTBURY
CARRICK
LONGFORD
CRADLE MOUNTAIN-
LAKE ST CLAIR

SWAN ISLAND
TOMAHAWK
BRIDPORT
GREENS BEACH
LOW HEAD
HAWLEY BEACH
GEORGE TOWN
KELSO
PIPERS RIVER
PORT SORELL
BEAUTY POINT
WINNALEAH
BEACONSFIELD
KAYENA
SCOTTSDALE
DEVIOT
HILLWOOD
LILYDALE
WELDBOROUGH
ROSEVEARS
TURNERS MARSH
BINALONG BAY
GRINDELWALD
DILSTON
PYENGANA
LEGANA
ST HELENS
LAUNCESTON
HADSPEN
EVANDALE
BLESSINGTON
HAGLEY
SCAMANDER
BEN LOMOND
NATIONAL PARK
FALMOUTH
ST MARYS

CORINNA
ROSEBERY
TULLAH
ZEEHAN
QUEENSTOWN
STRAHAN
DERWENT
BRIDGE
BRONTE PARK
WADDAMANA
MIENA

EPPING FOREST
POATINA
CLEVELAND
CAMPBELL TOWN
ROSS
LAKE LEAKE
FINGAL
BICHENO
SWANSEA
COLES BAY

Great
Lake

Arthurs
Lake

Lake
Sorell

GREAT
OYSTER
BAY

MACQUARIE
HARBOUR

WAYATINAH
BOTHWELL
OUSE
HAMILTON
ELLENDALE
NATIONAL PARK
FENTONBURY
WESTERWAY
BUSHY PARK
MAYDENA
STRATHGORDON
NEW NORFOLK

JERICHO
OATLANDS
LITTLE SWANPORT
DYSART
KEMPTON
TRIABUNNA
ORFORD
MANGALORE
TASMAN
PONTVILLE
CAMPANIA
MARIA ISLAND
NATIONAL PARK
BRIGHTON
RICHMOND
SORELL
MIDWAY POINT
HOBART
COPPING
DUNALLEY

LAKE
GORDON

LAKE PEDDER

REFER TO
PAGE 657 FOR
MORE DETAIL

For suburban listings
refer to Hobart &
Suburbs section

GROVE HWY
HUONVILLE
KINGSTON
FRANKLIN
CASTLE FORBES BAY
SNUG
KOONYA
EAGLEHAWK NECK
PORT HUON
CRADOC
TARANNA
GEEVESTON
CYGNET
KETTERING
NUBEENA
LYMINGTON
WOODBRIDGE
PORT ARTHUR
GARDNERS BAY
POLICE POINT
VERONA SANDS
STORM
BAY
DOVER
BRUNY ISLAND
LUNE RIVER
SOUTHPORT

SOUTHERN OCEAN

TASMAN SEA

© RAASA

HOBART TAS 7000

Pop 128,603. See map on page 657, ref B3, INCLUDES: NORTH HOBART, SOUTH HOBART, WEST HOBART. Capital city of Tasmania, and the second oldest capital in the Commonwealth. Boat Ramp, Boating, Rock Climbing, Rowing, Sailing, Swimming (Aquatic Centre), Tennis.

Hotels/Motels

★★★★☆ **Hobart Vista Hotel**, (LH), 156 Bathurst St, 600m fr GPO, ☎ 03 6232 6255, fax 03 6234 7884, (Multi-stry), 140 rms (13 suites) [shwr, bath, spa bath (13), tlt, heat, elec blkts, tel, TV, movie, clock radio, t/c mkg, refrig], lift, ldry, lounge, conv fac, ⊠, bar, rm serv, cots, non smoking flr (2). **RO** ♦ **$140**, ♦♦ **$140**, ◊ **$40**, **Suite RO** ♦♦ **$249**, ch con, AE BC DC EFT JCB MC VI, ♿.

★★★★☆ **Hotel Grand Chancellor**, (LH), 1 Davey St, 200m S of GPO, ☎ 03 6235 4535, fax 03 6223 8175, (Multi-stry), 234 rms (12 suites) [shwr, bath, tlt, hairdry, a/c, cent heat, tel, TV, movie, clock radio, t/c mkg, refrig, mini bar], lift, iron, iron brd, conv fac, ⊠, bar, pool indoor heated, sauna, 24hr reception, rm serv, c/park (undercover), gym, cots. **RO** ♦ **$260 - $290**, ♦♦ **$260 - $290**, ◊ **$35**, **Suite RO** ♦♦ **$395 - $650**, ch con, AE BC DC JCB MC VI, ♿.

★★★★ **Hadleys Hotel**, (LH), 34 Murray St, 200m W of GPO, ☎ 03 6223 4355, fax 03 6224 0303, (Multi-stry), 65 rms (3 suites) [shwr, bath, tlt, heat, elec blkts, tel, TV, movie, clock radio, t/c mkg, refrig, mini bar], lift, conv fac, ⊠, cots, non smoking rms (17). **RO** ♦♦ **$100 - $150**, ◊ **$15**, **Suite D** ♦♦ **$180 - $200**, ch con, AE BC DC MC VI.

Trouble-free travel tips - Lights

Check the operation of all lights. If you are pulling a trailer of caravan make sure turning indicators and brake lights are working.

★★★★ **Oakford on the Pier**, (LH), Previously Oakford on Elizabeth Pier, Elizabeth St Pier, 500m S of GPO, ☎ 03 6220 6600, fax 03 6224 1277, 56 rms [shwr, tlt, hairdry, a/c-cool, fan, heat, tel, TV, video-fee, clock radio, t/c mkg, refrig, cook fac, micro, pillows], w/mach, dryer, conf fac, ⊠, sauna, cots-fee, non smoking rms. **RO** ♦ **$170 - $195**, ♦♦ **$170 - $195**, AE BC DC MC VI, ♿. *Operator Comment: Fully self-contained apartments featuring panoramic water views.*

★★★★ **Quest Waterfront Hobart**, (M), 3 Brooke St, 300m S of GPO, ☎ 03 6224 8630, fax 03 6224 8633, (Multi-stry), 34 units (10 suites) [shwr, spa bath, tlt, a/c, cent heat, tel, clock radio, t/c mkg, refrig, cook fac ltd (24)], ldry, meals avail, c/park (limited), secure park (6), cots, non smoking rms (25). **RO** ♦ **$115 - $148**, ♦♦ **$115 - $148**, **Suite RO** **$170 - $192**, ch con, AE BC DC MC VI, ♿.

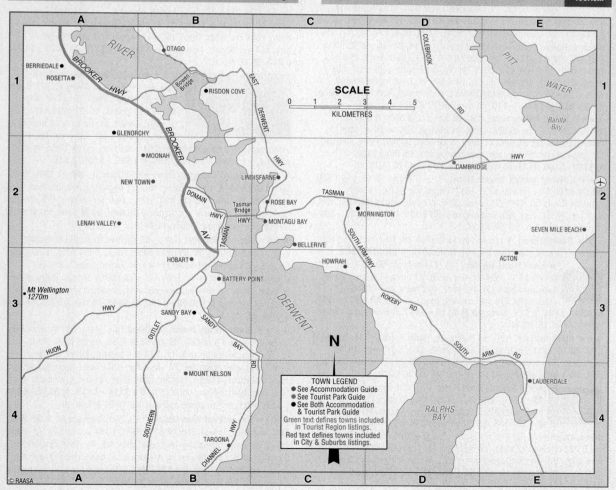

HOBART & SUBURBS – TASMANIA

★★★★ **Rydges Hobart**, (LH), c1850-1900. Cnr Argyle & Lewis Sts, North Hobart 7002, 1km N of GPO, ☎ 03 6231 1588, fax 03 6231 1916, (2 stry gr fl), 63 rms (63 suites) [shwr, bath, spa bath (3), tlt, elec blkts, tel, fax, TV, movie, t/c mkg, refrig, mini bar, cook fac, micro], ldry, conf fac, ⊠, bar, pool-heated, sauna, spa, 24hr reception, rm serv, cots, non smoking suites (32). **RO** ♦♦ **$135 - $180,** ◊ **$27.50, Suite D** ♦ **$155 - $275,** ch con, AE BC DC JCB MC VI.

★★★★ **Salamanca Inn**, (LH), 10 Gladstone St, 500m S of GPO, ☎ 03 6223 3300, fax 03 6223 7167, (Multi-stry), 60 rms (60 suites) [shwr, spa bath (2), tlt, fan, cent heat, tel, TV, clock radio, t/c mkg, refrig, cook fac], lift, ldry, conv fac, ⊠, pool indoor heated, spa, 24hr reception, rm serv, c/park (undercover), cots. **RO** ♦ **$150,** ♦♦ **$150,** ◊ **$25,** ch con, AE BC DC MC VI, ₤₤.

★★★★ **(Apartment Section)**, 8 apts (2 bedrm), [shwr, spa bath (4), tlt, fan, cent heat, tel, TV, clock radio, t/c mkg, refrig, cook fac, d/wash], w/mach, dryer. **D** ♦ **$240,** ♦♦ **$240,** ◊ **$25,** ch con.

★★★★ **The Old Woolstore Apartment Hotel**, (LH), 1 Macquarie St, 250m S of GPO, ☎ 03 6235 5355, fax 03 6234 9954, (Multi-stry), 59 rms (59 suites) [shwr, bath, tlt, heat, tel, TV, clock radio, t/c mkg, refrig, mini bar], lift, ldry, 24hr reception, rm serv, c/park. **RO** ♦ **$146 - $160,** ♦♦ **$146 - $160,** ◊ **$25,** ch con, AE BC DC MC VI, ₤₤.

★★★★☆ **(Apartment Section)**, 59 units acc up to 6, (1, 2 & 3 bedrm), [ensuite, heat, tel, TV, cable TV, video, clock radio, CD, t/c mkg, refrig, cook fac, micro, d/wash], w/mach, dryer, c/park. **RO** ♦ **$173 - $185,** ♦♦ **$173 - $185,** ₤₤.

★★★☆ **Argyle Motor Lodge**, (M), Cnr Argyle & Lewis Sts, 2km N of GPO, ☎ 03 6234 2488, fax 03 6234 2292, (2 stry gr fl), 36 units [shwr, bath (3), spa bath (2), tlt, hairdry (26), heat, elec blkts, tel, TV, clock radio, t/c mkg, refrig, cook fac (10), toaster], ldry, iron (26), iron brd (26), bar, rm serv, cots-fee. **RO** ♦ **$81 - $98,** ♦♦ **$88 - $102,** ◊ **$15, Suite D** $132, ch con, 22 rooms ★★★★. AE BC DC MC VI.

★★★☆ **Fountainside Motor Inn**, (M), Cnr Brooker Hwy & Liverpool St, 500m N of GPO, ☎ 03 6234 2911, fax 03 6231 0710, (Multi-stry), 42 units [shwr, tlt, heat, elec blkts, tel, TV, video-fee, clock radio, t/c mkg, refrig], lift, ldry, ⊠, 24hr reception, rm serv, cots-fee. **RO** ♦ **$89 - $109,** ♦♦ **$89 - $109,** ◊ **$15,** ch con, 14 units of a lower rating. AE BC DC EFT MC VI.

★★★☆ **Hobart Macquarie Motor Inn**, (LH), 167 Macquarie St, 500m S of GPO, ☎ 03 6234 4422, fax 03 6234 4273, (Multi-stry), 104 rms [shwr, bath, tlt, heat, elec blkts, tel, TV, clock radio, radio, t/c mkg, refrig, mini bar], lift, ldry, rec rm, conf fac, ⊠, pool indoor heated, sauna, 24hr reception, c/park (limited, undercover), cots, non smoking flr (3). **BLB** ♦♦ **$120,** ◊ **$30,** ch con, AE BC DC VI.

★★★☆ **Hobart Midcity Hotel**, (LH), 96 Bathurst St, 500m N of GPO, ☎ 03 6234 6333, fax 03 6231 0898, (Multi-stry), 107 rms [shwr, bath, tlt, heat, elec blkts, tel, TV, cable TV (free), clock radio, t/c mkg, refrig, mini bar], lift, ldry, conv fac, rm serv, cots, non smoking rms (50). **RO** ♦ **$120,** ♦♦ **$120 - $148,** ◊ **$17,** ch con, 30 rooms ★★★★. AE BC DC MC VI.

★★★☆ **Montgomery's Private Hotel**, (LH), 9 Argyle St, 85m E of GPO, ☎ 03 6231 2660, fax 03 6231 4817, (Multi-stry gr fl), 14 rms [ensuite, heat, tel, TV, clock radio, radio, t/c mkg, refrig, doonas], ldry, conf fac, ✕, ⊠, cots, non smoking rms. **RO** ♦ **$79 - $89,** ♦♦ **$89 - $99,** ch con, weekly con, BC EFT MC VI.

(YHA Backpackers), 6 rms acc up to 8, shwr, tlt, ldry, iron, iron brd, lounge (TV), ✕, cook fac, t/c mkg shared, refrig. **RO** $18 - $21.

★★★☆ **Motel Mayfair**, (M), 17 Cavell St, ☎ 03 6231 1188, fax 03 6231 2554, (2 stry gr fl), 23 units (3 suites) [shwr, bath, spa bath (3), tlt, heat, elec blkts, tel, TV, video, clock radio, t/c mkg, refrig], ldry, cots-fee. **RO** ♦ **$77 - $93,** ♦♦ **$88 - $104,** ◊ **$15, Suite RO** ♦♦ **$115 - $137,** 8 rooms of a higher rating. AE BC DC MC VI.

★★★ **Black Buffalo**, (LH), 14 Federal St, North Hobart 7002, 3km N of GPO, ☎ 03 6234 7711, fax 03 6231 0802, 11 rms [shwr, bath, tlt, cent heat, elec blkts, tel, TV, radio, t/c mkg, refrig], iron, conv fac, ⊠, cots. **RO** ♦ **$65,** ♦♦ **$75,** ◊ **$10,** ch con, AE BC DC MC VI.

★★★ **Marquis Hotel Motel**, (LH), 209 Brisbane St, ☎ 03 6234 3541, fax 03 6234 3141, (2 stry), 11 rms [shwr, tlt, heat, elec blkts, TV, t/c mkg, refrig], ✆, cots. **RO** ♦ **$71.50,** ♦♦ **$82 - $88,** ◊ **$11,** ch con, AE BC EFT MC MCH VI.

★★★ **Waratah**, (LH), 272 Murray St, 1km N of GPO, ☎ 03 6234 3685, fax 03 6231 2365, (2 stry), 18 rms (1 suite) [shwr, tlt, fan, heat (elec), elec blkts, tel, TV, radio, refrig (3)], ⊠, t/c mkg shared, bbq, ✆, cots-fee, non smoking rms (7). **BB** ♦ **$55,** ♦♦ **$70,** ◊ **$30,** ch con, AE BC DC EFT MC VI.

★★ **Alabama**, (LH), Classified by National Trust, 72 Liverpool St, 250m N of GPO, ☎ 03 6234 3737, (Multi-stry), 9 rms [heat, elec blkts, TV, t/c mkg], ldry, ⊠. **RO** ♦ **$35,** ♦♦ **$50,** ◊ **$10,** ch con, weekly con, AE BC MC VI.

★★ **The Welcome Stranger**, (LH), Cnr Davey & Harrington Sts, ☎ 03 6223 6655, fax 03 6224 1093, 10 rms [shwr, tlt, heat, elec blkts, tel, TV, t/c mkg], ldry, lounge (TV), ⊠ (Mon to Sat), refrig, c/park (limited). **BLB** ♦ **$64,** ♦♦ **$75,** ◊ **$12,** ch con, AE BC DC MC VI.

★☆ **Brunswick**, (LH), 67 Liverpool St, 250m N of GPO, ☎ 03 6234 4981, fax 03 6234 4981, 20 rms [heat, elec blkts, TV, t/c mkg], lounge (TV), ⊠ (Mon to Sat), c/park (limited), cots. **BLB** ♦ **$35,** ♦♦ **$50,** ch con, BC MC VI.

★☆ **Globe**, (LH), 178 Davey St, 2km S of GPO, ☎ 03 6223 5800, (2 stry), 12 rms [heat, elec blkts, t/c mkg], lounge (TV), ✕, ✆. **BB** ♦ **$30,** ♦♦ **$40,** ◊ **$10,** ch con, AE BC DC MC VI.

★☆ **Theatre Royal Hotel Hobart**, (LH), 31 Campbell St, 500m S of PO, ☎ 03 6234 6925, fax 03 6234 6356, (2 stry), 8 rms [ensuite (2), heat, elec blkts, TV (3), clock radio, t/c mkg, refrig, toaster, doonas], ldry, conf fac, ⊠, ✆, non smoking rms (2). **BLB** ♦ **$45 - $60,** ♦♦ **$65 - $100,** ◊ **$15,** ch con, 2 rooms ★★★. AE BC DC EFT MC VI.

Self Catering Accommodation

★★★★★ **Moorilla Estate Vineyard Chalets**, (Apt), 655 Main Rd, Berriedale 7011, 12km N of Hobart PO, ☎ 03 6277 9900, fax 03 6249 4093, (2 stry gr fl), 4 apts acc up to 4, (1 & 2 bedrm), [shwr, spa bath, tlt, a/c, tel, cable TV, clock radio, radio, t/c mkg, refrig, cook fac, micro, d/wash, toaster, blkts, linen, pillows], conf fac, ⊠, bbq, dinner to unit, secure park, plygr, cots, non smoking property. **D** ♦ **$240,** ♦♦ **$240,** ◊ **$30, W** ♦ **$1,512,** ♦♦ **$1,512,** ◊ **$189,** AE BC DC MC VI, ₤₤.

★★★★ **Abbey Apartments**, (HU), 101 Campbell St, 500 mt NE of Bathurst St PO, ☎ 03 6234 3197, fax 03 6234 3197, (gr fl), 2 units acc up to 4, [ensuite, fan, heat, elec blkts, TV, video, clock radio, t/c mkg, refrig, cook fac, micro, ldry, blkts, doonas, linen], w/mach, dryer, cots-fee, non smoking rms (bedrooms). **D** ♦ **$75 - $95,** ♦♦ **$75 - $95,** ch con, weekly con, Min book applies, BC MC VI.

★★★★ **Corinda**, (Cotg), 17 Glebe St, 1km N of GPO, ☎ 03 6234 1590, fax 03 6234 2744, (2 stry), 3 cotgs acc up to 3, (1 bedrm), [shwr, spa bath (1), tlt, heat (elec/wood), elec blkts, TV, clock radio, t/c mkg, refrig, cook fac, blkts, linen, pillows], w/mach, dryer, cots-fee, breakfast ingredients, non smoking units. **D** ♦ **$170,** ♦♦ **$170 - $190,** ◊ **$30,** BC DC MC VI.

★★★★ **Davey Place Holiday Town Houses**, (HU), 31-34 Davey Pl, 326 Davey St, South Hobart 7004, 2km S of GPO, ☎ 03 6234 6065, fax 03 6234 1374, (2 stry), 4 units acc up to 5, (2 bedrm), [shwr, tlt, fan, heat, elec blkts, tel, TV, video, radio, t/c mkg, refrig, mini bar, cook fac, micro, blkts, linen, pillows], w/mach, dryer, bbq, cots. **D** ♦ **$95 - $105,** ◊ **$15.**

★★★★ **Feltham Cottage**, (Cotg), 33 Feltham St, ☎ 03 6293 1347, fax 03 6293 1347, 1 cotg acc up to 2, (1 bedrm), [shwr, tlt, heat (elec) elec blkts, TV, radio, CD, t/c mkg, refrig, cook fac, micro, blkts, doonas, linen, pillows], w/mach, non smoking property. **BB** ♦♦ **$154, RO** ♦♦ **$132,** weekly con, Min book applies, BC MC VI.

★★★★ **Fuchsia Cottage**, (Cotg), 65 Wentworth St, South Hobart 7004, 3km S of GPO, ☎ 03 6234 8351, fax 03 6234 8351, 1 cotg acc up to 6, (3 bedrm), [shwr, tlt, heat (elec/wood), elec blkts, TV, clock radio, t/c mkg, refrig, cook fac, micro, blkts, doonas, linen, pillows], w/mach, dryer, c/park (undercover), cots, breakfast ingredients, non smoking property. **D** ♦ **$135 - $160,** ♦♦ **$135 - $160,** ◊ **$33,** Min book applies, BC MC VI.

★★★★ **Quest Trinity House - A Quest Inn**, (Apt), 149 Brooker Ave, Glebe 7000, 2km S of CBD, ☎ 03 6236 9656, fax 03 6236 9655, (gr fl), 29 apts acc up to 8, (1, 2, 3 & 4 bedrm), [shwr, tlt, fan, heat (elec), elec blkts, tel, TV, video-fee, clock radio, t/c mkg, refrig, cook fac, micro, d/wash, toaster, blkts, linen, pillows], w/mach, dryer, bbq, cots, non smoking units (10). **D** ♦ **$114 - $143,** ♦♦ **$132 - $165,** ◊ **$17,** Min book Christmas and Jan, AE BC DC EFT MC VI.

★★★★ **The Jackson Town House**, (HU), 194 Macquarie St, 800m W of GPO, mob 0417 369 042, fax 03 6249 5573, 1 unit acc up to 4, (2 bedrm), [shwr, spa bath, tlt, hairdry, heat, elec blkts, tel, TV, video, clock radio, t/c mkg, refrig, cook fac, micro, d/wash, blkts, linen, pillows], w/mach, dryer, non smoking units. **D** ♦ **$135,** ♦♦ **$135,** weekly con, No car parking on property, Min book applies, AE BC DC MC VI.

★★★☆ **Barrack Street Colonial Cottage**, (Cotg), c1830. 55 Barrack St, 500m W of Bathurst St GPO, ☎ 03 6224 1054, fax 03 6224 1754, (2 stry), 1 cotg acc up to 2, (1 bedrm), [shwr, spa bath, tlt, heat (elec/wood), elec blkts, TV, radio, t/c mkg, refrig, cook fac, blkts, linen, pillows], w/mach, cots, breakfast ingredients, Pets on application. **D ♦ $77, ♦♦ $154**, weekly con.

★★★☆ **Cascade Hotel**, (HU), 22 Cascade Rd, South Hobart 7004, 3km S of GPO, ☎ 03 6223 6385, fax 03 6223 6332, (2 stry gr fl), 4 units acc up to 4, (1 & 2 bedrm), [shwr, tlt, heat, elec blkts, tel, TV, cable TV, clock radio, radio, t/c mkg, refrig, cook fac, micro, blkts, linen, pillows], ldry, ⊠, cots. **D ♦ $65, ♦♦ $75 - $85, ◊ $12, W ♦ $385 - $450, ♦♦ $440 - $500**, ch con, BC MC VI.

★★★ **Domain View Apartments**, (HU), 352 Argyle St, 1km N of GPO, ☎ 03 6234 1181, (2 stry gr fl), 3 units acc up to 6, (1 & 3 bedrm), [shwr, bath, tlt, fan, heat, elec blkts, tel, TV, video, radio, refrig, cook fac, micro, toaster, ldry, blkts, linen, pillows], cots, non smoking units. **D ♦♦ $75, ◊ $10**, weekly con.

B&B's/Guest Houses

★★★★☆ **Islington**, (B&B), Classified by National Trust, c1840. No children's facilities, 321 Davey St, 1.5km fr GPO, ☎ 03 6223 3900, fax 03 6224 3167, (2 stry gr fl), 8 rms [ensuite, heat, elec blkts, tel, TV, clock radio, radio], lounge, pool, t/c mkg shared, non smoking property. **BLB ♦ $80 - $105, ♦♦ $150 - $172**, AE BC DC MC VI.

[FLAG — FLAG CHOICE HOTELS]

★★★★☆ **Macquarie Manor**, (B&B), 172 Macquarie St, ☎ 03 6224 4999, fax 03 6224 4333, 18 rms [ensuite, heat, elec blkts, tel, TV, video (6), clock radio, t/c mkg, refrig], ldry, meeting rm, breakfast rm, c/park (limited), cots, non smoking rms (18). **BB ♦♦ $154 - $203.50, ◊ $33**, ch con, AE BC DC MC VI, ♿.

★★★★☆ **The Elms of Hobart**, (B&B), Classified by National Trust, 452 Elizabeth St, North Hobart 7000, 1.5km N of GPO, ☎ 03 6231 3277, fax 03 6231 3276, (2 stry gr fl), 6 rms [ensuite, spa bath (2), heat (elec/wood), elec blkts, tel, TV, clock radio, t/c mkg], lounge, lounge firepl, breakfast rm, ✗, c/park. **BB ♦ $120 - $145, ♦♦ $145 - $190, ◊ $40**, AE BC DC MC VI.

★★★★ **Crows Nest Bed & Breakfast**, (B&B), 2 Liverpool Cres, West Hobart 7000, 1.5km W of GPO, ☎ 03 6234 9853, fax 03 6234 9853, 2 rms [ensuite, heat, elec blkts, tel, TV, t/c mkg, refrig, micro], ldry, bbq, breakfast ingredients, non smoking property. **BLB ♦ $65 - $75, ♦♦ $85 - $100**, BC MC VI.

★★★★ **Harringtons of Hobart**, (B&B), No children's facilities, 102 Harrington St, 2km W of GPO, ☎ 03 6234 9240, fax 03 6234 9270, 10 rms [ensuite, a/c, heat, elec blkts, tel, TV, clock radio, t/c mkg, refrig, ldry], conf fac, c/park (limited off site), non smoking property. **D $121, Suite D $143**, weekly con, AE BC DC EFT MC VI.

★★★★ **Lapoinya Lodge B&B**, (B&B), 9 Lapoinya Rd, Fern Tree 7054, 8km SW of South Hobart PO, ☎ 03 6239 1005, fax 03 6239 1005, 2 rms [ensuite (2), fan, heat (elec/wood), elec blkts, TV, video, clock radio, t/c mkg, refrig, doonas], ldry, ✗, bbq, non smoking rms. **BB $110 - $120**, weekly con, AE BC DC MC VI.

★★★★ **Tasmania Heritage Accommodation**, (B&B), Previously Masonic Club of Tasmania 181 Macquarie St, 1km W of GPO, ☎ 03 6223 5231, fax 03 6223 3201, (2 stry), 8 rms (Bunk Rooms), [ensuite (6), heat, tel, TV, video, clock radio, t/c mkg, refrig, micro, toaster], lift, shared fac (2), ldry, conf fac, ✗, rm serv, secure park, cots, non smoking property. **BLB ♦ $65, ♦♦ $115 - $135, ◊ $10**, 2 bunk rooms not rated. AE BC DC EFT MC VI.

★★★★ The Lodge on Elizabeth, (B&B), Classified by National Trust, 249 Elizabeth St, 1km N of GPO, ☎ 03 6231 3830, fax 03 6234 2566, 13 rms [ensuite, spa bath (6), fan, heat, elec blkts, tel, TV, radio, t/c mkg], ldry, conv fac (limited), cots, non smoking rms (2). **BLB** ♦ $90 - $124, ♦♦ $110 - $135, ♀ $25, ch con, AE BC DC MC VI.

★★★★ Wellington Lodge, (B&B), Classified by National Trust, 7 Scott St, 1km N of GPO, ☎ 03 6231 0614, fax 03 6234 1551, (2 stry gr fl), 4 rms [ensuite (2), fire pl, heat, elec blkts, TV, clock radio, t/c mkg], bathrm (2), lounge (guest), ✗, non smoking property. **BB** ♦ $80 - $90, ♦♦ $90 - $110, ♀ $32, BC MC VI.

Other Accommodation

Narrara Backpackers, (Lodge), 88 Goulburn St, 1km W of PO, ☎ 03 6231 3191, fax 03 6231 3160, 20 rms [heat, doonas], ☎. **RO** ♦ $20, ♀ $20.

New Sydney Hotel & Backpacker Inn, 87 Bathurst St, ☎ 03 6234 4516, fax 03 6236 9965, 7 rms lounge (TV), ✗, cook fac, t/c mkg shared, refrig. **RO** ♦ $18, AE BC DC MC VI.

Ocean Child Hotel, 86 Argyle St, ☎ 03 6234 6730, 8 rms acc up to 5, [heat, doonas-fee, linen], ldry, lounge (TV), ✗, cook fac, t/c mkg shared, refrig, ☎. **RO** ♦ $16, ♦♦ $33, BC MC VI.

Transit Centre Backpackers, 1st floor, Redline Coaches, 199 Collins St, ☎ 03 6231 2400, fax 03 6231 2400, 8 rms acc up to 8, [micro], shwr (4G-4L), tlt (4G-4L), ldry, lounge (TV), cook fac, t/c mkg shared, refrig, ☎. **RO** ♦ $17, BC MC VI.

HOBART - ACTON TAS 7170

Pop Part of Lauderdale, (18km E Hobart), See map on page 657, ref E3, Country residential area.

Self Catering Accommodation

★★★★☆ Acton Cottage, (Cotg), 47 Everton Plc, ☎ 03 6248 1210, fax 03 6248 1217, 1 cotg acc up to 2, (1 bedrm), [shwr, tlt, fan, cent heat, elec blkts, TV, clock radio, t/c mkg, refrig, cook fac, blkts, linen, pillows], w/mach, lounge firepl, bbq, breakfast ingredients, non smoking property. **D** ♦♦ $160.

HOBART - BATTERY POINT TAS 7004

Pop Part of Hobart, (1km S Hobart), See map on page 657, ref B3, One of the best examples of old Hobart. Many of the buildings and homes are as they were in the 1830s.

Hotels/Motels

★★★★ Lenna of Hobart, (LH), Classified by National Trust, 20 Runnymede St, ☎ 03 6232 3900, fax 03 6224 0112, (Multi-stry gr fl), 50 rms (5 suites) [shwr, bath, tlt, hairdry, heat, elec blkts, tel, cable TV, clock radio, t/c mkg, refrig, mini bar], lift, ldry, conf fac, ✗, bar, 24hr reception, rm serv, cots, non smoking rms (40). **RO** ♦ $170 - $195, ♦♦ $170 - $195, ♀ $30, Suite **RO** ♦♦ $220 - $245, AE BC DC JCB MC VI.

★★★☆ Blue Hills, (M), 96a Sandy Bay Rd, ☎ 03 6223 1777, fax 03 6223 3995, (2 stry gr fl), 26 units [shwr, tlt, hairdry, heat (4), cent heat (22), elec blkts, tel, TV, cable TV, radio, t/c mkg, refrig, mini bar, cook fac (4)], ldry, iron, iron brd, rm serv (breakfast service), c/park (limited), cots-fee, non smoking units. **RO** ♦ $90, ♦♦ $100 - $110, ♀ $15, ch con, AE BC DC EFT MC VI.

★★☆ Prince of Wales, (LH), 55 Hampden Rd, ☎ 03 6223 6355, fax 03 6223 2311, (2 stry), 10 rms [shwr, tlt, cent heat, elec blkts, TV, clock radio, t/c mkg], ldry, ⊠ (6 days, smoke free), non smoking rms. **BB** ♦ $70 - $80, ♦♦ $81 - $97, ♀ $17, ch con, AE BC EFT MC VI.

★★ Shipwrights Arms Hotel, (LH), 29 Trumpeter St, ☎ 03 6223 5551, fax 03 6224 8048, (2 stry), 4 rms [heat, clock radio], lounge (TV), ⊠, t/c mkg shared, refrig, bbq, ☎, non smoking rms. **BLB** ♦ $40 - $50, ♦♦ $60 - $70, AE BC DC EFT MC VI.

Self Catering Accommodation

★★★★ Avon Court, (HU), 4 Colville St, ☎ 03 6223 4837, fax 03 6223 7207, (2 stry gr fl), 10 units acc up to 6, (2 bedrm), [shwr, bath, tlt, fan, heat, elec blkts, tel, TV, radio, t/c mkg, refrig, cook fac, micro, blkts, linen, pillows], ldry, cots-fee. **D** ♦ $92 - $106, ♦♦ $106 - $136, ♀ $25 - $28, ch con, BC MC VI.

★★★★ Battery Point Boutique Accommodation, (Apt), 27-29 Hampden Rd, 2km SW of PO, ☎ 03 6224 2244, fax 03 6224 2243, (2 stry gr fl), 3 apts acc up to 3, (2 bedrm), [shwr, tlt, heat, elec blkts, tel, TV, clock radio, t/c mkg, refrig, cook fac, micro, blkts, linen, pillows], w/mach, breakfast ingredients, non smoking rms. **D** ♦♦ $155, ♀ $35, BC MC VI.

★★★★ Coopers Cottage, (Cotg), 44A Hampden Rd, 1km S of Hobart GPO, ☎ 03 6223 8255, 1 cotg acc up to 3, (1 bedrm), [shwr, tlt, heat (gas), elec blkts, tel, TV, video, clock radio, radio, t/c mkg, refrig, cook fac, blkts, linen, pillows], w/mach, dryer, breakfast ingredients, non smoking property. **D** ♦♦ $135, BC MC VI.

★★★★ The Grand Old Duke, (HU), Classified by National Trust, c1850, 31 Hampden Rd, ☎ 03 6224 1606, fax 03 6224 1282, 1 unit acc up to 3, (1 bedrm), [shwr, bath, tlt, heat (elec/wood), elec blkts, tel, TV, clock radio, t/c mkg, refrig, cook fac, blkts, linen, pillows], cots, non smoking property. **D** ♦ $150 - $165, ♦♦ $150 - $165, ♀ $35, AE BC DC EFT MC VI.

★★★☆ Crelin Lodge, (HU), 1 Crelin St, ☎ 03 6223 1777, fax 03 6223 3995, (2 stry gr fl), 4 units acc up to 5, (1 & 2 bedrm), [shwr, bath, tlt, heat (off peak), elec blkts, TV, radio, t/c mkg, refrig, cook fac, micro, blkts, linen, pillows], ldry, cots-fee. **D** ♦ $90, ♦♦ $90, ♀ $15, **W** ♦ $190, ♦♦ $590, ♀ $80, AE BC DC EFT MC VI.

★★★☆ Knopwood Apartment, (HU), 6 Knopwood St, ☎ 03 6223 2290, 1 unit acc up to 6, (3 bedrm), [shwr, tlt, heat, elec blkts, TV, radio, t/c mkg, refrig, cook fac, blkts, linen, pillows], w/mach, dryer, cots-fee. **D** ♦♦ $77, ♀ $22.

★★★☆ Quince Cottage, (Cotg), 45 Arthur Circus, 500m E of PO, ☎ 03 6223 7895, fax 03 6223 7015, 1 cotg acc up to 5, (2 bedrm), [shwr (2), tlt (2), heat (elec/wood), tel, TV, clock radio, t/c mkg, refrig, cook fac, blkts, linen, pillows], w/mach, dryer, plygr, cots. **D** $110, **W** $450 - $700, Min book applies, AE BC DC EFT MC VI.

★★★☆ St Ives Motel Apartments, (SA), 67 St Georges Tce, ☎ 03 6224 1044, fax 03 6223 8774, (Multi-stry gr fl), 38 serv apts [shwr, tlt, heat, tel, TV, movie, radio, t/c mkg, refrig, mini bar, cook fac], ldry, cots. **RO** ♦ $89 - $129, ♦♦ $89 - $129, ♀ $16, AE BC DC EFT JCB MC VI.

★★★ Portsea Terrace, (HU), 62 Montpelier Ret, ☎ 03 6234 1616, fax 03 6223 1638, (2 stry gr fl), 9 units acc up to 4, (1 & 2 bedrm), [shwr, tlt, fan, heat, elec blkts, TV, clock radio, t/c mkg, refrig, cook fac, blkts, linen, pillows], ldry, cots, breakfast ingredients. **D** ♦ $83 - $88, ♦♦ $105 - $110, ♦♦♦♦ $130 - $140, ch con, AE BC DC MC VI.

B&B's/Guest Houses

★★★★☆ Ascot of Battery Point, (B&B), c1915. No children's facilities, 6 Colville St, ☎ 03 6224 2434, fax 03 6224 3324, (2 stry gr fl), 2 rms [ensuite, hairdry, heat, elec blkts, tel, TV, clock radio, t/c mkg], iron, lounge (TV), ✗, refrig, non smoking property. **BB** ♦ $110 - $120, ♦♦ $140 - $165, ♀ $35, AE BC DC MC VI.

★★★★☆ Barton Cottage, (B&B), Classified by National Trust, c1837. 72 Hampden Rd, ☎ 03 6224 1606, fax 03 6224 1282, (2 stry gr fl), 7 rms [ensuite, hairdry, a/c-cool, heat, elec blkts, TV, clock radio, t/c mkg, refrig], iron, iron brd, breakfast rm, c/park (limited), ☎, cots, non smoking rms. **BB** ♦ $100 - $110, ♦♦ $130 - $150, ♀ $35, AE BC DC EFT MC VI.

★★★★☆ Battery Point Manor, (B&B), Classified by National Trust, c1834, 15 Cromwell St, ☎ 03 6224 0888, fax 03 6224 2254, 8 rms (1 suite) [ensuite, a/c, tel, TV, clock radio, t/c mkg], lounge (TV), breakfast rm (views of harbour), cots-fee, non smoking property. **BB** ♦ $75 - $125, ♦♦ $95 - $175, ♀ $35, ch con, AE BC DC MC VI.

★★★★☆ **Colville Cottage**, (B&B), Classified by National Trust, c1877. 32 Mona St, ☎ 03 6223 6968, fax 03 6224 0500, 6 rms [shwr, tlt, a/c (4), fan, heat (2), elec blkts, TV, radio, t/c mkg, refrig, doonas], lounge, breakfast rm, ✗, c/park (limited), non smoking property. BB ♦ $46 - $136, ♦♦ $136 - $155, ◊ $35, BC MC VI.

★★★★☆ **Gattonside Heritage Accommodation**, (B&B), 51-53 Sandy Bay Rd, 1km S of Hobart GPO, ☎ 03 6224 1200, fax 03 6224 0207, 8 rms [ensuite, spa bath, heat (elec), elec blkts, tel, TV, video, clock radio, t/c mkg, refrig], ldry, ✗, non smoking property. BB ♦ $135 - $155, ♦♦ $145 - $195, ◊ $40, Min book applies, AE BC DC EFT MC VI, ⚷&.

★★★★☆ **Jarem Waterfront Guest House**, (B&B), 8 Clarke Ave, ☎ 03 6223 8216, fax 03 6224 8443, 3 rms [ensuite, heat, elec blkts, tel, TV, clock radio, cook fac ltd], ldry, ✗, t/c mkg shared, refrig, bbq, meals avail, c/park (undercover), non smoking rms. BLB ♦ $56 - $83, ♦♦♦ $54 - $83, BC DC MC VI.

★★★★ **Battery Point Bed & Breakfast**, (B&B), 74 Hampden Rd, 3km NE of Hobart GPO, ☎ 03 6223 3124, fax 03 622231456, 2 rms (2 suites) [ensuite, fan, heat (elec), elec blkts, TV (all rooms), video, clock radio, doonas], ldry, breakfast rm, ✗, t/c mkg shared, refrig, bbq, non smoking rms. BB ♦ $99 - $115, ♦♦ $121 - $143, BC EFT MC VI.

★★★★ **Battery Point Guest House**, (B&B), 7 McGregor St, via Kelly St, ☎ 03 6224 2111, fax 03 6224 3648, (2 stry gr fl), 5 rms (1 suite) [ensuite, spa bath (1), fire pl, heat (floor/off peak), tel (direct dial), TV, clock radio, t/c mkg, refrig (2)], lounge (TV), breakfast rm, cots-fee. BB ♦ $105 - $115, ♦♦ $135 - $144, ◊ $27.50 - $36, Suite D $145 - $190, ch con, 1unit of a higher rating. Min book Christmas Jan and Easter, AE BC MC VI.

★★★☆ **Battery Point Homestay**, (B&B), 9 Mona St, 4km S of Hobart GPO, ☎ 03 6223 4614, fax 03 6224 8603, 1 rm (2 bedrm), [shwr, tlt, fan, heat (elec/wood), tel, TV, video, clock radio, radio, t/c mkg, refrig, cook fac ltd, micro, doonas, pillows], ldry, ✗, bbq, plygr, cots, non smoking property. BB ♦♦ $120, ◊ $20, ch con, weekly con, BC MC VI.

★★★☆ **Cromwell Cottage**, (B&B), Classified by National Trust, c1873. 6 Cromwell St, ☎ 03 6223 6734, fax 03 6224 1282, (2 stry gr fl), 5 rms [ensuite, heat, elec blkts, TV, clock radio, t/c mkg, refrig], breakfast rm. BB ♦ $110, ♦♦ $130, ◊ $30, AE BC DC EFT MC VI.

HOBART - BELLERIVE TAS 7018

Pop Part of Hobart, (5.5km E Hobart), See map on page 657, ref C2, Located on Hobart's pretty Eastern Shore. World Series Cricket Tests held at Bellerive Oval. Boat Ramp, Boating, Canoeing, Golf, Sailing, Squash.

Self Catering Accommodation
★★★★ **Bellerive Heritage Cottage**, (Cotg), 29 Alma St, 1km S of PO, mob 0408 122 122, fax 02 6245 0708, 1 cotg acc up to 4, (1 bedrm), [shwr, tlt, a/c, cent heat, TV, clock radio, t/c mkg, refrig, cook fac, ldry, blkts, doonas, linen, pillows], bbq, cots-fee, breakfast ingredients, non smoking property. D ♦ $100 - $120, ♦♦ $100 - $120, ◊ $15 - $20, ch con, weekly con, BC MC VI.

★★★ **Ashwood Park Holiday Units**, (HU), 1 Church St, ☎ 03 6244 4278, 3 units acc up to 5, (1 & 2 bedrm), [shwr, tlt, fan, heat (elec), elec blkts, tel, TV, clock radio, t/c mkg, refrig, cook fac, micro, blkts, linen, pillows], w/mach, c/park (undercover), cots-fee, non smoking property. D ♦ $59 - $65, ♦♦ $60 - $66, ◊ $10, ch con, BC MC VI.

HOBART - BERRIEDALE TAS 7011

Pop Part of Glenorchy, (9km N Hobart), See map on page 657, ref A1, Home to Moorilla Estate Vineyard. Boating, Canoeing, Sailing, Tennis.

Hotels/Motels

★★★ **Highway Village Motor Inn**, (M), 897 Brooker Hwy, ☎ 03 6272 6721, fax 03 6273 1061, (2 stry gr fl), 40 units [shwr, tlt, cent heat, elec blkts, tel, TV, movie, radio, t/c mkg, refrig], ldry, conv fac, ✗, bbq, rm serv, plygr, tennis, cots. RO ♦ $53 - $77, ♦♦ $64 - $99, ◊ $12, ch con, 20 rooms ★★☆. AE BC DC MC MP VI.

Self Catering Accommodation
★★★☆ **Tudor Holiday Village**, (HU), 889 Brooker Hwy, 10Km N of Hobart, ☎ 03 6272 2649, fax 03 6273 1061, 21 units acc up to 6, (2 bedrm), [shwr, tlt, heat, elec blkts, tel, TV, radio, t/c mkg, refrig, cook fac, ldry, blkts, linen, pillows], ✗, plygr, tennis, cots, Pets on application. D ♦♦ $97 - $126, ◊ $16, W ♦ $560, ♦♦ $665, ◊ $77, ch con, AE BC DC MC MP VI.

HOBART - GLENORCHY TAS 7010

Pop Part of Glenorchy, (7km N Hobart), See map on page 657, ref A1, Retail outlets located along the Main Road. Home to Derwent Entertainment Centre. Tolosa Park Reserve. Elwick Racecourse, KGV Football Park. Royal Showgrounds. Tasmanian Transport Museum. Inter-City Bicycle Path-from Glenorchy to Hobart. Bowls, Greyhound Racing, Horse Racing, Squash, Swimming (Pool), Tennis, Trotting.

Hotels/Motels

★★★☆ **Balmoral Motor Inn**, (M), 511 Brooker Hwy, ☎ 03 6272 5833, fax 03 6272 1077, (2 stry gr fl), 31 units [shwr, tlt, heat, elec blkts, tel, TV, cable TV, clock radio, t/c mkg, refrig, mini bar, cook fac (2)], ldry, conv fac, ✗, bar, rm serv, cots. RO ♦ $100, ♦♦ $100, ◊ $10, ch con, 11 Rooms of a Lower Rating. AE BC DC JCB MC VI.

★★★☆ **Martin Cash Motor Lodge**, (M), 238 Main Rd, ☎ 03 6272 5044, fax 03 6273 0725, (2 stry gr fl), 27 units (4 suites) [shwr, spa bath (1), tlt, hairdry, heat, elec blkts, tel, TV, radio, t/c mkg, refrig], ldry, bbq, rm serv, plygr, cots. RO ♦ $90, ♦♦ $90, ◊ $10, Suite RO $100, ch con, AE BC DC MC VI.

Self Catering Accommodation
★★★ **Northside Holiday Villas**, (HU), 9B McGough St, ☎ 03 6272 4472, fax 03 6272 3837, 13 units acc up to 8, (2 & 4 bedrm), [shwr, tlt, heat, elec blkts, tel, TV, radio, refrig, cook fac, micro, blkts, linen, pillows], w/mach, cots, non smoking units, Pets on application. D ♦ $61 - $85, ♦♦ $65 - $95, ◊ $15 - $20, W ♦♦ $395 - $495, ◊ $66 - $100, ch con, AE BC MC VI.

HOBART - HOWRAH TAS 7018

Pop Part of Hobart, (8.5km E Hobart), See map on page 657, ref C3, Residential area with picturesque views of the River Derwent and Mount Wellington. Close to popular beaches. Boating, Swimming.

Hotels/Motels
★★☆ **Shoreline Hotel**, (LH), 10 Shoreline Dve, ☎ 03 6247 9504, fax 03 6247 9266, 11 rms [shwr, tlt, heat, elec blkts, tel, TV, clock radio, t/c mkg, refrig], conv fac, ✗, rm serv, cots. BLB ♦ $60, ♦♦ $70, ◊ $15, ch con, AE BC DC MC VI.

Self Catering Accommodation
★★★★ **Cottage on the Rocks**, (HU), 1 Corinth St, 12km E of Hobart, ☎ 03 6247 9372, fax 03 6247 3359, 1 unit acc up to 2, (1 bedrm), [shwr, tlt, a/c, cent heat, elec blkts, TV, clock radio, radio, t/c mkg, refrig, cook fac, blkts, linen, pillows], w/mach, dryer, bbq, breakfast ingredients, non smoking property. D ♦ $120, ♦♦ $120, W ♦ $560, ♦♦ $560, Min book applies, BC MC VI.

★★★ **Silwood Park Holiday Unit**, (HU), 7 Silwood Ave, ☎ 03 6244 4278, 1 unit acc up to 5, (2 bedrm), [shwr, tlt, fan, heat (elec floor), elec blkts, tel, TV, radio, t/c mkg, refrig, cook fac, micro, blkts, linen, pillows], cots-fee, non smoking property. D ♦ $59, ♦♦ $60, ◊ $10, ch con, BC MC VI.

Trouble-free travel tips - **Hoses and belts**
Inspect the condition of radiator hoses, heater hose fan and air conditioner belts.

HOBART - LAUDERDALE TAS 7021

Pop 2,509. (18km E Hobart), See map on page 657, ref E4, Beachside residential area. Swimming (Beach).

★★★ **Kirra Guest House**, (HU), 3 Kirra Rd, 12km S of Hobart Airport, ☎ 03 6248 6359, fax 03 6248 6359, (gr fl), 2 units acc up to 4, (1 bedrm), [shwr, tlt, heat (elec), TV, radio, t/c mkg, refrig, cook fac, ldry, blkts, linen, pillows], c/park. **D** ♦ $55 - $65, ♦♦ $65 - $70, ⊕ $16.50 - $25, **W** ♦ $320 - $360, ♦♦ $395 - $430, ch con.

HOBART - LENAH VALLEY TAS 7008

Pop Part of Hobart, (3km N Hobart), See map on page 657, ref A2, Lovely suburb with many historic properties. Lady Franklin Gallery.

Hotels/Motels

★★★☆ **Valley Lodge**, (M), 11 Augusta Rd, ☎ 03 6228 0125, fax 03 6228 3387, (Multi-stry gr fl), 23 units [shwr, bath (some), tlt, hairdry, heat, elec blkts, tel, TV, cable TV (25 channel), clock radio, t/c mkg, refrig, mini bar], ldry, conv fac, bbq, rm serv, cots. **RO** ♦ $65 - $97, ♦♦ $65 - $97, ⊕ $13, ch con, AE BC DC MC VI.

Self Catering Accommodation

★★★☆ **Greenway House**, (HU), 2a Greenway Ave, 500m S of PO, ☎ 03 6228 6023, fax 03 6278 7024, (gr fl), 1 unit acc up to 6, (3 bedrm), [shwr, tlt, fan (1), heat (elec), elec blkts, TV, video, clock radio, radio, t/c mkg, refrig, cook fac, blkts, linen], w/mach, bbq, non smoking property. **D** ♦ $93, ♦♦ $93, ⊕ $11, ch con, weekly con.

HOBART - LINDISFARNE TAS 7015

Pop Part of Hobart, (5km NE Hobart), See map on page 657, ref C2, Residential area overlooking the River Derwent. Boat Ramp, Boating, Canoeing, Rowing, Sailing.

Hotels/Motels

★★★☆ **Beltana Hotel**, (LH), 160 East Derwent Hwy, ☎ 03 6243 8677, fax 03 6243 8308, (2 stry), 24 rms (1 suite) [ensuite, heat (elec), elec blkts, TV, clock radio, t/c mkg, refrig, toaster, ldry] conf fac, ✉, ✆, cots-fee, non smoking rms. **BLB** ♦ $60, ♦♦ $72 - $76, ⊕ $15, ch con, AE BC DC EFT MC VI.

★★★ **Lindisfarne Motor Inn**, (M), 103 East Derwent Hwy, ☎ 03 6243 8666, fax 03 6243 5820, 21 units [shwr, bath (8), tlt, hairdry, heat (8), cent heat (13), elec blkts, tel, TV, clock radio, t/c mkg, refrig, cook fac (1), toaster], ldry, ✉, rm serv, cots. **RO** ♦ $60 - $75, ♦♦ $66 - $85, ⊕ $13 - $16.50, ch con, AE BC BTC DC EFT MC MCH VI.

Self Catering Accommodation

★★★★ **Apex**, (HU), 18 Wellington Rd, ☎ 03 6243 8594, fax 03 6243 8787, (2 stry gr fl), 7 units acc up to 5, (2 bedrm), [shwr, bath, tlt, heat, elec blkts, tel, TV, radio, t/c mkg, refrig, cook fac, blkts, linen, pillows], w/mach, cots-fee. **D** ♦ $88, ♦♦ $88, ⊕ $11, Min book applies.

★★★★ **Majestic View**, (HU), 49 Karoola Rd, 4km NE of Hobart, ☎ 0419 361 194, (gr fl), 1 unit acc up to 4, (1 bedrm), [fan, cent heat, elec blkts, TV, video, clock radio, t/c mkg, refrig, cook fac, blkts, linen, pillows], w/mach, dryer, pool-heated, bbq, breakfast ingredients, non smoking property. **D** ♦♦ $130, ⊕ $30, AE BC MC VI.

★★★☆ **Emily Cottage**, (Cotg), 32 Wellington St, 4km NE of Hobart GPO, ☎ 0419 361 194, fax 03 6243 0201, 1 cotg acc up to 6, (4 bedrm), [shwr, tlt, fan, heat (elec), elec blkts, tel, TV, clock radio, t/c mkg, refrig, cook fac, blkts, linen, pillows], w/mach, dryer, bbq, cots, breakfast ingredients, non smoking property. **D** ♦♦ $140, ⊕ $30, Min book applies, AE BC MC VI.

B&B's/Guest Houses

★★★★☆ **Orana House**, (B&B), 20 Lowelly Rd, ☎ 03 6243 0404, fax 03 6243 9017, 10 rms (4 suites) [ensuite, spa bath (3), heat, elec blkts, clock radio, t/c mkg], lounge (TV), ✗, refrig, cots-fee, non smoking property. **BB** ♦ $80 - $125, ♦♦ $105 - $140, ⊕ $45, AE BC MC VI.

Medication and driving

Medication can effect your driving. Certain drugs can effect your mental alertness and/or co-ordination and therefore effect driving skills. Always check with your doctor the effect which any medication (over the counter or prescription) you are taking may have on your driving. There may be an alternative drug which will not affect your driving. It is best to avoid drinking alcohol while taking medication.

HOBART - MONTAGU BAY TAS 7018

See map on page 657, ref C2, (4.9 km NE of Hobart). Residential area with views of the river Derwent and Mount Wellington.

★★★☆ **City View Motel**, (LMH), 30 Tasman Hwy, 5km fr Hobart City Centre, ☎ 03 6243 8388, fax 03 6243 8155, 30 units [ensuite, fan, heat (elec), elec blkts, tel, TV, clock radio, t/c mkg, refrig], ldry, conf fac, bbq, cots, non smoking rms. **BLB** ♦ $80 - $95, ♦♦ $80 - $95, ⊕ $28, ch con, Minium booking Dec 29 to Jan 02, AE BC DC EFT MC VI.

HOBART - MOONAH TAS 7009

Pop Part of Hobart, (4.5km N Hobart), See map on page 657, ref B2, Residential and commercial area with many retail outlets and cafes. 10 Pin Bowling, Bowls.

★☆ **Carlyle Hotel**, (LH), 232 Main Rd, Derwent Park 7009, ☎ 03 6272 0299, fax 03 6273 1290, (2 stry), 17 rms [shwr, tlt, heat, elec blkts, TV, t/c mkg], ✉, cots. **RO** ♦ $44, ♦♦ $66, AE BC DC MC VI.

HOBART - MORNINGTON TAS 7018

Pop Part of Hobart, (7.5km E Hobart), See map on page 657, ref C2, Residential area with many commercial retail outlets.

★★☆ **The Mornington Inn Hotel Motel**, (M), 322 Cambridge Rd, ☎ 03 6244 3855, fax 03 6244 6399, (2 stry gr fl), 8 units [shwr, tlt, cent heat, elec blkts, TV, radio, t/c mkg, refrig], conv fac, ✉, c/park. **RO** ♦ $55, ♦♦ $65, ♦♦♦ $75, ch con, fam con, Min book applies, AE BC DC MC VI.

HOBART - MOUNT NELSON TAS 7007

Pop Part of Hobart, (6km SW Hobart), See map on page 657, ref B4, Residential area with magnificient views of the Derwent Estuary. Historic signal station and aboriginal memorial.

Self Catering Accommodation

★★★★ **Crawfords B&B**, (Apt), 178 Nelson Rd, 2km S from Sandy Bay PO, ☎ 03 6225 3751, fax 03 6225 2307, 1 apt acc up to 4, (1 bedrm), [shwr, tlt, heat (elec/gas), elec blkts, TV, clock radio, CD, t/c mkg, refrig, cook fac, blkts, linen, pillows], bbq, breakfast ingredients. **BLB** ♦ $85, ♦♦ $95, ⊕ $20, ch con, weekly con.

B&B's/Guest Houses

★★★ **The Signalmans B & B**, (B&B), 685 Nelson Rd, ☎ 03 6223 1215, fax 03 6223 1537, 1 rm (1 bedrm), [shwr, tlt, heat, elec blkts, TV, radio, t/c mkg, refrig, micro, pillows], ldry, bbq, c/park. **BLB** ♦ $66, ♦♦ $77.

HOBART - NEW TOWN TAS 7008

Pop Part of Hobart, (2.5km N Hobart), See map on page 657, ref B2, Lovely suburb with many quaint old homes. Runnymede House (c1836).

Hotels/Motels

★★★ **Hobart Tower**, (M), 300 Park St, ☎ 03 6228 0166, fax 03 6278 1056, (2 stry gr fl), 47 units [shwr, tlt, heat, elec blkts, tel, TV, movie (videos), radio, t/c mkg, refrig], ldry, cots. **RO** ♦ $57 - $68, ♦♦ $62 - $72, ⊕ $15, ch con, AE BC DC MC VI.

★★ **Waterfront Lodge**, (M), Previously Marina 153 Risdon Rd, Moonah 7009, 6km N of GPO, ☎ 03 6228 4748, fax 03 6228 1945, 27 units [shwr, tlt, heat, elec blkts, TV, radio, t/c mkg, refrig], ldry, pool-heated (solar), bbq, cots, non smoking property. **D** $65, **RO** ♦ $39, ♦♦ $49, 15 rooms of a lower rating, AE BC DC EFT MC VI, ♿.

(Hostel Section), 5 rms [heat, t/c mkg, refrig, micro, doonas], ldry, lounge (TV), bbq, ✆, non smoking property. **D** ♦ $15, ♦♦ $30.

Self Catering Accommodation

★★★★ **Railway Cottage**, (Cotg), 62 Bellevue Pde, 5km N of PO, ☎ 03 6223 6734, fax 03 6224 1282, 1 cotg acc up to 5, (2 bedrm), [shwr, tlt, heat, elec blkts, tel, TV, clock radio, t/c mkg, refrig, cook fac, micro, toaster, ldry, doonas, pillows], w/mach, cots, non smoking property. **D** ♦♦ **$160 - $220**, ◊ **$35**, **W** ♦♦ **$550 - $750**, ◊ **$250**, AE BC DC EFT MC VI.

★★★★ **Wendover Colonial Accommodation**, (HU), c1828, 10 Wendover Pl, ☎ 03 6278 2066, fax 03 6278 2329, (2 stry gr fl), 4 units acc up to 4, (1 & 2 bedrm), [shwr, bath, spa bath (1), tlt, heat (elec), cent heat, elec blkts, tel, fax, TV, clock radio, t/c mkg, refrig, cook fac (3), micro, blkts, linen, pillows], ldry, lounge firepl, cots-fee, breakfast ingredients, non smoking units. **BB** ♦ **$135 - $214**, ♦♦ **$150 -$229**, $52, AE BC DC MC VI.

★★★☆ **Graham Court Apartments**, (HU), 15 Pirie St, ☎ 03 6278 1333, fax 03 6278 1087, (2 stry gr fl), 21 units acc up to 8, (1, 2 & 3 bedrm), [shwr, tlt, heat, elec blkts, tel, video-fee, radio, t/c mkg, refrig, cook fac, micro, blkts, linen, pillows], ldry, bbq, plygr, cots-fee. **D** ♦♦ **$79 - $122**, ◊ **$12 - $20**, ch con, weekly con, AE BC DC MC VI, ㏙.

Other Accommodation

Adelphi Court YHA, 17 Stoke St, ☎ 03 6228 4829, fax 03 6278 2047, 25 rms acc up to 5, [heat, linen], rec rm, lounge (TV), cook fac, t/c mkg shared, refrig, bbq, c/park. **RO** ♦ **$20 - $63**, BC MC VI.

HOBART - OTAGO TAS 7017

Pop Part of Hobart, (12.7km N Hobart), See map on page 657, ref B1, On Eastern Shore north of Risdon Cove.

★★★★ **Otago Cottage**, (HU), 19 Restdown Dr, 15km N of Hobart, ☎ 03 6273 3922, fax 03 6273 3923, 1 unit acc up to 6, (3 bedrm), [shwr, spa bath, tlt, heat (elec), elec blkts, TV, video (video library), clock radio, CD, t/c mkg, refrig, cook fac, blkts, linen, pillows], w/mach, bbq, cots-fee. **D** ♦♦ **$143**, ◊ **$33**, ch con, weekly con, BC DC MC VI.

HOBART - RISDON COVE TAS 7017

Pop Part of Hobart, (11km N Hobart), See map on page 657, ref B1, Historic settlement site and birdlife sanctuary.

★★★★ **Saracen's Head Inn**, (B&B), 727 East Derwent Hwy, 3km N of Lindisfarne PO, ☎ 03 6243 0669, fax 03 6243 0631, (2 stry), 3 rms [ensuite (2), heat (elec/wood), elec blkts, TV, clock radio], bathrm (1), ldry, ✕, t/c mkg shared, refrig, cots, non smoking property. **BB** ♦ **$95**, ♦♦ **$108**, ◊ **$25**, ch con, BC MC VI.

HOBART - ROSE BAY TAS 7015

Pop Part of Hobart, (3.5km NE Hobart), See map on page 657, ref C2, Residential area with superb views of the river Derwent and Mount Wellington.

★★★★ **Roseneath**, (B&B), 20 Kaoota Rd, ☎ 03 6243 6530, fax 03 6243 0518, 4 rms [ensuite (1), cent heat, elec blkts, clock radio], ldry, rec rm, lounge (TV), lounge firepl, pool-heated (solar), t/c mkg shared, refrig, bbq, c/park (undercover), non smoking property. **BLB** ♦ **$85 - $95**, ♦♦ **$115**, AE BC DC VI.

★★★★☆ **(Suite Section)**, 1 unit acc up to 2, (1 bedrm), [ensuite, heat, elec blkts, tel, t/c mkg, refrig, cook fac, micro, blkts, linen, pillows]. **D** ♦ **$95**, ♦♦ **$115**.

HOBART - ROSETTA TAS 7010

Pop Part of Glenorchy, (8km N Hobart), See map on page 657, ref A1, Modern residential area. Bicycle (Path), Rowing, Sailing.

★★★★☆ **Undine**, (B&B), 6 Dodson St, ☎ 03 6273 3600, fax 03 6273 3900, (2 stry), 6 rms [ensuite, fan, heat, elec blkts, TV, clock radio], ldry, rec rm, pool indoor heated (2), t/c mkg shared, refrig, bbq, cots, non smoking property. **BB** ♦ **$99**, ♦♦ **$132**, ◊ **$33**, ch con, AE BC BTC DC MC VI.

HOBART - SANDY BAY TAS 7005

Pop Part of Hobart, (1.5km S Hobart), See map on page 657, ref B3, Picturesque suburb of Hobart. Speciality fashion and gift shops. Home to Australia's first Casino. Boating, Canoeing, Sailing, Squash, Swimming, Wind Surfing.

Hotels/Motels

FLAG
FLAG CHOICE HOTELS™

★★★★☆ **Wrest Point Hotel Casino**, (LH), 410 Sandy Bay Rd, Derwent River frontage, ☎ 03 6225 0112, fax 03 6225 3909, (Multi-stry), 197 rms (13 suites) [shwr, tlt, hairdry, a/c, elec blkts, tel, TV, movie, clock radio, t/c mkg, refrig, mini bar, toaster], lift, iron, iron brd, conv fac, ✕, bar, pool indoor heated, sauna, spa, bbq, rm serv, mini golf, gym, tennis, cots. **RO** ♦ **$197 - $264**, ♦♦ **$242 - $264**, **Suite D** ♦♦ **$330**, ch con, AE BC DC MC VI, ㏙.

★★★☆ **(Motor Inn Section)**, (Multi-stry), 81 units [shwr, tlt, hairdry, heat, elec blkts, tel, TV, movie, radio, t/c mkg, refrig, mini bar], lift, iron, iron brd, c/park. **RO** ♦ **$127 - $131**, ♦♦ **$127 - $131**, ch con.

★★★★ **Mayfair Plaza Motel**, (M), 236 Sandy Bay Rd, 500m S PO, ☎ 03 6220 9900, fax 03 6224 5255, 17 units [a/c, heat, tel, cable TV, radio, t/c mkg, refrig, toaster], ldry, ✕, dinner to unit, c/park (undercover), non smoking property. **D** ♦ **$99 - $149**, ♦♦ **$99 - $149**, ◊ **$10**, AE BC DC EFT MC VI.

★★★☆ **Sandy Bay Motor Inn**, (M), 429 Sandy Bay Rd, ☎ 03 6225 2511, fax 03 6225 4354, (Multi-stry gr fl), 33 units [shwr, tlt, heat, elec blkts, tel, TV, movie, radio, t/c mkg, refrig], ldry, rec rm, sauna, spa, bbq, c/park (undercover), cots. **RO** ♦ **$88**, ♦♦ **$99**, ◊ **$16**, ch con, AE BC DC MC VI.

Operator Comment: Member Discounts apply to above rates.

★★ **Dr Syntax**, (LH), 139 Sandy Bay Rd, ☎ 03 6223 6258, fax 03 6224 0132, (2 stry), 7 rms [shwr, bath, tlt, heat, elec blkts, TV, clock radio, t/c mkg, refrig], iron, ✕, cots-fee. **RO** ♦ **$49**, ♦♦ **$65**, ◊ **$19**, ch con, Light breakfast only available, AE BC MC VI.

Self Catering Accommodation

★★★★ **Grosvenor Court**, (HU), 42 Grosvenor St, ☎ 03 6223 3422, fax 03 6223 6344, (Multi-stry gr fl), 17 units acc up to 6, (1 & 2 bedrm), [shwr, tlt, heat, tel, TV, movie, radio, t/c mkg, refrig, cook fac, micro, blkts, linen, pillows], ldry, bbq, plygr, cots. **D** ♦♦ **$89 - $120**, ◊ **$20**, ch con, BC MC VI.

★★★★ **Mount Pleasant Mews**, (Cotg), c1835. No children's facilities, 32 Maning Ave, ☎ 03 6225 1467, fax 03 6225 0514, (2 stry), 1 cotg acc up to 2, (1 bedrm), [shwr, bath, tlt, heat, elec blkts, TV, clock radio, t/c mkg, refrig, cook fac, blkts, linen, pillows], w/mach, dryer, breakfast ingredients, non smoking property. **D** ♦♦ **$174**, ♦♦ **$174**, ◊ **$15**, BC MC VI.

★★★★ **Woolmers Inn**, (HU), 123 Sandy Bay Rd, ☎ 03 6223 7355, fax 03 6223 1981, (2 stry gr fl), 36 units acc up to 5, (1 & 2 bedrm), [shwr, bath, tlt, heat, tel (ISD), TV, cable TV, video, radio, t/c mkg, refrig, cook fac, micro, blkts, linen, pillows], ldry, non smoking property. **D** ♦♦ **$124 - $154**, ◊ **$16.50**, ch con, AE BC DC MC VI, ㏙.

★★★☆ **Hobart Horizon**, (HU), 23 Wayne Ave, 5km S of Hobart, ☎ 03 6225 1235, 1 unit acc up to 4, (1 & 2 bedrm), [heat, elec blkts, TV, video, clock radio, t/c mkg, refrig, cook fac, d/wash, ldry], cots. **BLB** ♦ **$80**, ♦♦ **$100**, ◊ **$25**, ch con, weekly con.

★★☆ **Flinders Apartments**, (HU), 2-4 Flinders Lane, ☎ 03 6234 6882, 2 units acc up to 3, (1 bedrm), [shwr (over bath), bath, tlt, heat, elec blkts, TV, clock radio, t/c mkg, refrig, cook fac, blkts, linen, pillows], w/mach, dryer, iron, c/park (undercover). **D** ♦ **$68**, ♦♦ **$68**, ◊ **$13**, weekly con.

B&B's/Guest Houses

★★★★☆ **Honeymoon House**, (B&B), 17 Gregory St, ☎ 03 6224 2900, fax 03 6224 2911, 3 rms [ensuite, spa bath, heat, elec blkts, clock radio, refrig, doonas], iron, iron brd, lounge (TV), breakfast rm, t/c mkg shared, non smoking property. **BB** ♦♦ **$140 - $154**, AE BC DC MC VI.

★★★★ **26 Red Chapel**, (B&B), 26 Red Chapel Ave, ☎ 03 6225 1512, (2 stry gr fl), 1 rm [shwr, tlt, heat (elec), tel, TV, radio, clock radio, t/c mkg], refrig, non smoking rms. **BLB** ♦ **$120 - $140**, ♦♦ **$140 - $155**, BC DC MC VI.

★★★★ **Amberley House**, (B&B), c1897. 391 Sandy Bay Rd, ☎ 03 6225 1005, fax 03 6225 0639, (2 stry gr fl), 5 rms [ensuite, spa bath (1), heat, elec blkts, TV, radio, t/c mkg, refrig], breakfast rm, non smoking property. **RO** ♦ **$104 - $124**, ♦♦ **$104 - $134**, AE BC MC VI.

★★★★ **Clydesdale Heritage Accommodation**, (B&B), 292 Sandy Bay Rd, 5km S of Hobart, ☎ 03 6223 7289, fax 03 6223 2465, (2 stry gr fl), 7 rms [ensuite, spa bath (2), heat (elec/wood), elec blkts, tel, TV, clock radio, t/c mkg, refrig, toaster], ldry, breakfast rm, bbq, plygr, cots, non smoking rms. **BLB** ♦♦ **$126 - $146**, ◊ **$50**, AE BC DC MC VI.

★★★★ **Merre Bes**, (B&B), c1884, 24 Gregory St, ☎ 03 6224 2900, fax 03 6224 2911, 5 rms [ensuite, spa bath (2), fan, heat, elec blkts, tel, fax, TV, clock radio, t/c mkg], ldry, lounge (TV), ✕, refrig, bbq, cots. **BB** ♦ **$90**, ♦♦ **$110 - $154**, ◊ **$30**, ch con, AE BC DC MC VI.

★★★☆ **Alexandra on Battery**, (B&B), 3 Sonning Cres, 2km SW of PO, ☎ 03 6225 2574, fax 02 6225 3522, (2 stry gr fl), 1 rm (1 suite) [ensuite, heat (elec), elec blkts, TV, video, clock radio, t/c mkg, refrig, micro], ldry, bbq, cots-fee. **BB** ♦ **$80**, ♦♦ **$90**, ch con, BC MC VI.

HOBART - SEVEN MILE BEACH TAS 7170

Pop 947. Part of Hobart, (16km E Hobart), See map on page 657, ref E2, Popular summer destination and residential area. Boat Ramp, Bush Walking, Fishing, Golf, Horse Riding, Swimming.

★★★☆ **The Pines Resort**, (SA), 78 Surf Rd, 20km E of Hobart, ☎ 03 6248 6222, fax 03 6248 6628, 20 serv apts (2 bedrm), [shwr, bath, tlt, heat, elec blkts, tel, TV, radio, t/c mkg, refrig, cook fac, blkts, linen, pillows], ldry, rec rm, conv fac, ✕, pool-heated (solar), sauna, spa, bbq, dinner to unit, plygr, tennis, cots. **RO** ♦ **$135 - $145**, ♦♦ **$135 - $145**, ◊ **$22**, ch con, AE BC DC MC VI, ㏙.

HOBART - TAROONA TAS 7053

Pop Part of Hobart, (10km S Hobart), See map on page 657, ref B4, Residential area overlooking the River Derwent.

★★★★☆ **Hillgrove Colonial Accommodation**, (HU), c1840. 269 Channel Hwy, ☎ 03 6227 9043, fax 03 6227 8337, 1 unit acc up to 3, (Ensuite Site), [shwr, bath, tlt, fire pl, heat, elec blkts, tel (direct dial), TV, clock radio, radio, refrig, cook fac, blkts, linen, pillows], ldry, cots-fee, breakfast ingredients. **D ǂ $88, ǂǂ $110, ◊ $22**, ch con, weekly con, BC MC VI.

End of Hobart & Suburbs

ARTHUR RIVER TAS 7330

Pop 109. (448km NW Hobart), See map on page 656, ref A3, Popular fishing village. Scenic river cruises and rainforest. Boat Ramp, Boating, Bush Walking, Canoeing, Fishing, Horse Riding, Swimming.

Self Catering Accommodation

★★★☆ **Alert Cottage**, (Cotg), 16 Davidson St, 16km S of Marrawah PO, ☎ 03 6457 1340, fax 03 6457 1340, 1 cotg acc up to 6, (3 bedrm), [shwr, tlt, heat (elec/wood), elec blkts, TV, video, radio, t/c mkg, refrig, cook fac, micro, ldry, blkts, linen, pillows], bbq, cots, Pets on application. **D ǂ $55, ǂǂ $65, ◊ $10**, ch con.

★★★☆ **Arthur River Holiday Units**, (HU), 4 Gardiner St, ☎ 03 6457 1288, fax 03 6457 1288, 3 units acc up to 6, (1, 2 & 3 bedrm), [shwr, tlt, fan, heat (elec/wood), elec blkts, TV, radio, t/c mkg, refrig, cook fac, blkts, doonas, linen, pillows], w/mach, dryer, bbq, shop, plygr, cots. **D ǂ $55 -$66, ǂǂ $66 - $88, ◊ $22, W ǂ $350 - $425, ǂǂ $425 - $560, ◊ $77**, ch con.

★★★☆ **Ocean View Holiday Cottage**, (Cotg), 300 Gardner St, 18km S of Marrawah, ☎ 03 6452 1278, fax 03 6452 1278, (gr fl), 1 cotg acc up to 6, (3 bedrm), [shwr, tlt, heat (elec/wood), elec blkts, tel, TV, video, radio, t/c mkg, refrig, cook fac, blkts, linen, pillows], w/mach, bbq, c/park (undercover), plygr, cots. **D ǂ $60 - $70, ǂǂ $65 - $80, ◊ $10 - $15, W ǂ $350 - $400, ǂǂ $350 - $425, ◊ $20 - $40**, Min book applies.

★★★☆ **Sunset Holiday Villas**, (HU), 23 Gardiner St, ☎ 03 6457 1197, fax 03 6457 1197, 2 units acc up to 8, (2 bedrm), [shwr, tlt, fan, heat (elec), elec blkts, TV, clock radio, t/c mkg, refrig, cook fac, blkts, linen, pillows], w/mach, bbq (undercover), cots, non smoking units. **D ǂ $55, ǂǂ $70, ◊ $15, W ǂ $340, ǂǂ $420, ◊ $70**, ch con, BC MC VI.

BEACONSFIELD TAS 7270

Pop 1,719. (245km N Hobart), See map on page 656, ref C4, Historic township located at the head of the Tamar river. Once the site of the State's biggest gold mine where mining operations have begun again.

★★☆ **Holiday Lodge**, (LH), Clarence Point Rd, Clarence Point 7270, 12km N of Beaconsfield ☎ 03 6383 4188, fax 03 6383 4188, (2 stry gr fl), 9 rms [ensuite (5), heat, elec blkts, t/c mkg], ldry, lounge (TV, video), ✕, sauna, spa, bbq, plygr, cots. **BB ǂ $45 - $55, ǂǂ $60 - $75, ◊ $12**, AE BC EFT MC VI.

BEAUTY POINT TAS 7270

Pop 1,498. (238km N Hobart), See map on page 656, ref C3, Popular fishing and aquatic centre.

Hotels/Motels

★★★ **Beauty Point Motor Hotel**, (LH), 116 Flinders St, 500m S of PO, ☎ 03 6383 4363, fax 03 6383 4730, 9 rms [shwr, tlt, heat, elec blkts, tel, cable TV, clock radio, t/c mkg, refrig], ldry, conf fac, ✕, rm serv, plygr, cots-fee. **RO ǂ $55, ǂǂ $66, ◊ $10**, AE BC DC EFT MC VI.

★★★ **Tamar Cove**, (M), Flinders St, 1.5km S of PO, ☎ 03 6383 4375, fax 03 6383 4759, 10 units [shwr, tlt, elec blkts, TV, t/c mkg, refrig], ldry, ✕, pool-heated (inground), bbq, rm serv, plygr, cots. **RO ǂ $54, ǂǂ $65, ǂǂǂǂ $86, ◊ $10**, ch con, fam con, AE BC MC VI.

★★ **Riviera**, (LH), Lenborough St, 1km NW of PO, ☎ 03 6383 4153, fax 03 6383 4315, (2 stry) 9 rms [shwr, tlt, heat, elec blkts, TV, t/c mkg, refrig], ldry, ✕, bbq, cots. **BLB ǂ $50, ǂǂ $60**, ch con, BC VI.

B&B's/Guest Houses

★★★★☆ **Pomona Bed & Breakfast**, (B&B), 77 Flinders St, 2km S of PO, ☎ 03 6383 4073, fax 03 6383 4074, 2 rms [ensuite, bath (1), cent heat, elec blkts, TV, clock radio, CD, t/c mkg, refrig], lounge firepl, ✕, spa, bbq, non smoking property. **BB ǂ $80, ǂǂ $105 - $120, ◊ $40**, BC MC VI.

★★★★☆ **(Cottage Section)**, 1 cotg acc up to 3, (1 bedrm), [shwr, spa bath, tlt, a/c, elec blkts, TV, video, clock radio, t/c mkg, cook fac, micro, d/wash, toaster, ldry, blkts, doonas, linen, pillows], w/mach, lounge firepl, bbq, breakfast ingredients, non smoking property. **BLB ǂǂ $140 - $160, ◊ $30 - $40.**

BEN LOMOND NATIONAL PARK

Pop Nominal, (254km N Hobart), See map on page 656, ref E4, Popular ski fields. Bird Watching.

Creek Inn on Ben Lomond, (LH), Alpine Village, ☎ 03 6372 2444, fax 03 6372 2444, 6 rms [shwr, tlt, heat, t/c mkg, refrig (1), cook fac (1)], conv fac, ✕, bbq, cots. **BLB ǂ $110 - $150, ǂǂ $110 - $150**, Min book applies, BC MC VI.

(Ben Lomond Ski Chalet), 6 rms [shwr (2), tlt (2), cook fac ltd], dry rm, lounge, t/c mkg shared, refrig. **D ǂ $25 - $35**, fam con.

BICHENO TAS 7215

Pop 705. (182km NE Hobart), See map on page 656, ref E5, One of Tasmania's most popular holiday resorts. Centre and home port of important fishing industry. Sea charters and boat cruises.

Hotels/Motels

★★★ **Beachfront**, (M), Tasman Hwy, 500m W of PO, ☎ 03 6375 1111, fax 03 6375 1130, 46 units (1 suite) [shwr, bath, tlt, heat, elec blkts, tel, TV, video, t/c mkg, refrig], ldry, conv fac, ✕, pool-heated (solar), bbq, rm serv, plygr, cots, non smoking rms (5). **RO ǂ $95, ǂǂ $95, ◊ $15, Suite D ǂ $120**, ch con, 14 rooms of a higher rating. AE BC DC EFT VI.

★★★ **Silver Sands Resort**, (LH), Burgess St, 1km N of PO, ☎ 03 6375 1266, 35 rms [shwr, spa bath (1), tlt, heat, elec blkts, tel, TV, t/c mkg, refrig], ldry, conv fac, ✕, pool, rm serv, plygr, cots. **RO ǂ $40 - $70, ǂǂ $50 - $85, ◊ $12**, ch con, 8 rooms ★★. AE BC DC MC VI.

★★★ **Wintersun Gardens Motel**, (M), 35 Gordon St, 8 km N of PO, ☎ 03 6375 1225, fax 03 6375 1606, 10 units [tlt, hairdry, heat, elec blkts, TV, clock radio, t/c mkg, mini bar, ldry], pool, bbq, plygr. **RO ǂ $72 - $83, ǂǂ $77 - $94, ◊ $16**, ch con, 3 rooms ★★★☆. BC MC VI, ⚅.

★★★ **(Unit Section)**, 1 unit (2 bedrm), [shwr, tlt, heat, elec blkts, TV, clock radio, t/c mkg, refrig, cook fac, micro]. **D ǂǂ $116, ◊ $16**, ch con.

Self Catering Accommodation

★★★★ **Bicheno Berrie Retreat**, (HU), Tasman Hwy, 4km N of PO, ☎ 03 6375 1481, fax 03 6375 1554, (2 stry), 3 units acc up to 14, (2 bedrm), [shwr, tlt, hairdry, fan, heat (elec/wood), elec blkts, TV, video (ext video library), clock radio, t/c mkg, refrig, cook fac, micro, blkts, doonas, linen, pillows], w/mach, iron, iron brd, bbq, cots, breakfast ingredients. **D ǂǂ $98 - $135, ◊ $20 - $30**, ch con, 1 unit of a lower rating. BC EFT MC VI.

★★★★ **Bicheno Gaol Cottages**, (HU), Classified by National Trust, Cnr Burgess & James Sts, 200m E of PO, ☎ 03 6375 1430, fax 03 6375 1866, 3 units acc up to 10, (1 & 2 bedrm), [shwr, tlt, heat (elec/wood), TV, clock radio, t/c mkg, refrig, cook fac, blkts, linen, pillows], ✕, bbq, cots, breakfast ingredients, non smoking units. **D ǂǂ $128 - $143, ◊ $28**, ch con, 1 unit of a lower rating. BC MC VI.

★★★★ **Coombend Cottages**, (Cotg), Tasman Hwy, 16km S of Bicheno PO, ☎ 03 6257 8256, or 03 6257 8881, fax 03 6257 8484, 2 cotgs acc up to 6, (2 & 3 bedrm), [shwr, tlt, heat (wood & electric), elec blkts, TV, radio, refrig, cook fac, blkts, linen, pillows], w/mach, bbq, dinner to unit, c/park (undercover), cots, breakfast ingredients. **D $100 - $144**, ch con, AE BC MC VI.

★★★★ **Dolly's Haven**, (HU), 20 Tasman Hwy, 1km N of PO, ☎ 03 6375 1671, fax 03 6375 1671, 1 unit acc up to 2, (1 bedrm), [shwr, tlt, hairdry, fan, heat (elec), elec blkts, TV, video, clock radio, CD, t/c mkg, refrig, cook fac, ldry, blkts, linen, pillows], bbq, breakfast ingredients, non smoking property. **D ǂ $75 - $85, ǂǂ $85 - $110, ◊ $20.**

★★★★ **Forest Ridge Country Retreat**, (Log Cabin), Tasman Hwy, 10km N of PO, ☎ 03 6375 1565, fax 03 6375 1565, 1 log cabin acc up to 6, (3 bedrm), [shwr, bath, tlt, heat (elec/wood), TV, radio, t/c mkg, refrig, cook fac, blkts, linen, pillows], w/mach, dryer, bbq, c/park (undercover), cots, breakfast ingredients, non smoking units. **D ǂ $93.50, ǂǂ $127, ◊ $27.50, W ǂǂ $605 - $715**, ch con, BC MC VI.

★★★★ **Greenlawn Cottage**, (Cotg), 'Greenlawn', Tasman Hwy, 6km S of PO, ☎ 03 6375 1114, or 0418 561 395, 1 cotg acc up to 6, (2 bedrm), [shwr, spa bath, tlt, heat (elec/wood), elec blkts, TV, radio, t/c mkg, refrig, cook fac, micro, ldry, blkts, doonas, linen, pillows], bbq, c/park (undercover), tennis, cots, breakfast ingredients, non smoking property. **D ǂǂ $148, ◊ $38.50**, ch con, BC MC VI.

★★★★ **Sandpiper Ocean Cottages**, (HU), 18546 Tasman Highway, 8 km from Bicheno, ☎ 03 6375 1122, fax 03 6375 1122, 3 units acc up to 18, (2 bedrm), [heat, fan, heat (wood fires), TV, video, clock radio, t/c mkg, refrig, cook fac, micro, ldry, blkts, doonas, linen], w/mach, dryer, bbq, c/park. **BB ǂ $95 - $115, ǂǂ $95 - $115, ◊ $20**, Minimum booking Sep 1 to Ap 30, BC MC VI.

★★★★ **Sea the Sunrise Holiday Unit**, (HU), 17 Allen St, 600m N of PO, ☎ 03 6375 1493, fax 03 6375 1880, 1 unit acc up to 6, (2 bedrm), [shwr, tlt, fan, heat, tel, TV, clock radio, radio, t/c mkg, refrig, cook fac, ldry, blkts, linen, pillows], bbq, non smoking property. D ♦ $55, ♦♦ $110 - $120, ◊ $50, Min book applies.

★★★☆ **Apsley Holiday Unit**, (HU), 42 Rosedale Rd, 4.5km N of PO, ☎ 03 6375 1682, fax 03 6375 1682, (gr fl), 1 unit acc up to 4, (1 bedrm), [shwr, tlt, fan, heat (elec), elec blkts, TV, clock radio, radio, t/c mkg, refrig, cook fac, micro, blkts, linen, pillows], w/mach, bbq, non smoking units, Pets on application. D ♦ $70 - $80, ♦♦ $70 - $80, ◊ $15, weekly con, Min book Christmas and Jan, BC MC VI.

 ★★★☆ **Bicheno Hideaway**, (Cotg), 179 Harveys Farm Rd, 3km S of PO, ocean frontage, ☎ 03 6375 1312, fax 03 6375 1700, 3 cotgs acc up to 5, (1 & 2 bedrm), [shwr, tlt, heat, TV, CD (for hire), cook fac, ldry, linen, pillows], bbq, bicycle (for hire), cots. D ♦ $75, ♦♦ $118, ◊ $22, ch con, weekly con, BC DC MC VI.

★★★☆ **Bicheno Holiday Village**, (HU), The Esplanade, 500m E of PO, ☎ 03 6375 1171, fax 03 6375 1144, (2 stry gr fl), 20 units acc up to 8, (1, 2, 3 & 4 bedrm), [shwr, tlt, heat, elec blkts, TV, video-fee, t/c mkg, refrig, cook fac, blkts, doonas, linen, pillows], w/mach, rec rm, ⊠, pool-heated, plygr, tennis, cots-fee. D ♦ $90 - $150, ♦♦ $90 - $150, ◊ $15, ch con, AE BC DC MC VI.

FLAG
FLAG CHOICE HOTELS ★★★☆ **Diamond Island**, (HU), Tasman Hwy, 2.5km N of PO, ☎ 03 6375 1161, fax 03 6375 1349, (2 stry gr fl), 15 units acc up to 6, (1 & 2 bedrm), [shwr, spa bath (4), tlt, heat, elec blkts, tel, TV, video-fee, radio, t/c mkg, refrig, cook fac, blkts, linen, pillows], rec rm, conv fac, ⊠ (Mon to Sat), pool-heated, bbq, tennis, cots. D ♦ $77 - $154, ♦♦ $88 - $165, ◊ $22, Free penguin rookery tours. AE BC DC MC VI, &.

★★ **Seaview Accommodation Centre**, (HU), 29 Banksia St, 1km NW of PO, ☎ 03 6375 1247, fax 03 6375 1155, 6 units acc up to 6, (2 bedrm), [shwr, tlt, heat, TV, t/c mkg, refrig, cook fac, micro, linen], rec rm, plygr, cots, non smoking units. D ♦♦ $50 - $60, ◊ $6 - $8, ch con, 2 units ★★★. EFT, &.

(Hostel Section), 6 rms acc up to 10, [linen-fee], shwr, tlt, lounge (TV), ⊠, t/c mkg shared. D ♦ $13.

B&B's/Guest Houses

★★★★ **Anchlia Waterfront Cottage**, (B&B), 2 Murray St, ☎ 03 6375 1225, fax 03 6375 1606, (2 stry), 1 rm (2 bedrm), [shwr, tlt, heat, elec blkts, TV, clock radio, t/c mkg, refrig], ldry. BB ♦♦ $160, BC MC MCH VI.

(Penguin Nook), 1 unit acc up to 2, [shwr, tlt, heat, elec blkts, TV, clock radio, t/c mkg, refrig, cook fac, micro, blkts, linen, pillows]. D ♦♦ $135, (not yet classified).

★★★★ **Campbells at Bicheno**, (B&B), 24 Harvey's Farm Rd, 500m S of PO, ☎ 03 6375 1829, fax 03 6375 1829, 1 rm (Studio), [ensuite, fan, heat (elec), elec blkts, TV, video, clock radio, t/c mkg, refrig, cook fac ltd], ldry, spa, bbq, cots, non smoking property. BB ♦♦ $132, ch con.

★★★★ (Unit Section), 1 unit acc up to 6, (2 bedrm), [shwr, tlt, fan, heat (elec), elec blkts, TV, video, clock radio, t/c mkg, refrig, cook fac, blkts, linen, pillows], w/mach, dryer, bbq, cots, breakfast ingredients, non smoking property. D ♦♦ $110, ◊ $15, ch con.

★★★★ **Fleurs by the Sea**, (B&B), 25 Tribe St, 750m W of PO, ☎ 03 6375 1851, fax 03 6375 1851, 4 rms (4 suites) [ensuite (3), spa bath (1), fan, heat, elec blkts, TV, clock radio, t/c mkg, refrig], bathrm (1), ldry, breakfast rm, pool indoor heated, plygr, tennis, cots, non smoking property. BB ♦♦ $110 - $132, ◊ $27.50, ch con, BC MC VI.

★★★★ **Old Tram Rd Bed & Breakfast**, (B&B), 3 Old Tram Rd, 500m NE of PO, ☎ 03 6375 1555, fax 03 6375 1555, (gr fl), 2 rms [ensuite, heat (elec/wood), elec blkts, TV, video (1), clock radio, radio, t/c mkg, refrig], ⊠, cots, Pets on application. BB ♦ $75 - $85, ♦♦ $105 - $115, ◊ $15, weekly con.

Other Accommodation

Bicheno Backpackers Hostel, 11 Morrison St, ☎ 03 6375 1651, fax 03 6375 1651, 4 rms acc up to 5, ldry, lounge (TV), cook fac, t/c mkg shared, refrig. RO ♦ $15.

BINALONG BAY TAS 7216

Pop 204. (263km NE Hobart), See map on page 656, ref E4, Popular coastal holiday destination overlooking Bay of Fires.

★★★★ **Binalong Bay Character Cottages**, (HU), Main Rd, 11km E of St Helens, ☎ 03 6376 8262, fax 03 6376 8261, 6 units acc up to 8, (1, 2 & 3 bedrm), [shwr, tlt, heat (wood & Hydro Heat), elec blkts, TV, video, clock radio, refrig, cook fac, micro, doonas, linen-fee, pillows], w/mach, bbq, c/park. D ♦ $66, ♦♦ $88, ◊ $22, ch con.

BLESSINGTON TAS 7212

Pop 207. (120km N Hobart), See map on page 656, ref D4, Farming countryside. Bush Walking, Fishing.

★★★ **Old Whisloca Cottage**, (Cotg), Blessington Rd (C401), ☎ 03 6390 6262, fax 03 6390 6296, 1 cotg acc up to 6, (1 bedrm), [shwr, tlt, heat (elec/wood), elec blkts, TV, clock radio, t/c mkg, refrig, cook fac, micro, blkts, doonas, linen, pillows], w/mach, bbq, c/park (undercover), tennis, cots, Pets on application. D ♦♦ $70, ◊ $15, ch con.

BOAT HARBOUR TAS 7321

Pop 389. (387km NW Hobart), See map on page 656, ref B3, Pretty rural setting within close proximity to Boat Harbour Beach.

Self Catering Accommodation

★★★★ **Killynaught Spa Cottages**, (Cotg), 17266 Bass Hwy, 1km E of PO, ☎ 03 6445 1041, fax 03 6445 1556, 5 cotgs acc up to 4, (1 & 2 bedrm), [shwr, spa bath, tlt, hairdry, heat (elec/wood), elec blkts, TV, clock radio, t/c mkg, refrig, cook fac, doonas, linen, pillows], w/mach, dryer, ☏, breakfast ingredients. D ♦ $140 - $150, ♦♦ $140 - $150, ◊ $33, ch con, AE BC JCB MC VI.

★★★☆ **Country Garden Cottages**, (Cotg), (Farm), 15 Port Rd, 2km fr PO, ☎ 03 6445 1233, fax 03 6445 1019, 4 cotgs acc up to 4, (1 & 2 bedrm), [shwr, tlt, elec blkts, TV, radio, t/c mkg, refrig, cook fac, micro, blkts, linen, pillows], ldry, bbq, cots. D ♦♦ $88 - $99, ◊ $11, ch con, weekly con, Breakfast available, BC MC VI.

B&B's/Guest Houses

★★★★ **Cape View Guest House**, (B&B), 64 Strawberry Lane, 3km W of PO, ☎ 03 6445 1273, fax 03 6445 1273, (2 stry gr fl), 2 rms (1 suite) [ensuite, spa bath (1), fan, heat (elec), elec blkts, clock radio, t/c mkg, refrig, ldry], lounge (TV/video), bbq, non smoking property, Pets on application. BB ♦ $70, ♦♦ $95 - $120, ◊ $30, ch con.

★★★★ **Killynaught Homestead (Apartments)**, (B&B), 17266 Bass Hwy, 1km E of PO, ☎ 03 6445 1041, fax 02 6445 1556, 1 rm (1 suite) [shwr, spa bath, tlt, hairdry, heat (elec/wood), elec blkts, TV, clock radio, t/c mkg, refrig, micro, doonas], ☏, breakfast ingredients. Suite D ♦♦ $122 - $125, AE BC JCB MC VI.

★★★★☆ **(Holiday Unit Section)**, 1 unit acc up to 4, (2 bedrm), [shwr, spa bath, tlt, hairdry, heat (elec/wood), elec blkts, TV, video, clock radio, CD, t/c mkg, refrig, cook fac, micro, doonas, linen, pillows], w/mach, dryer, ☏, breakfast ingredients. D ♦♦ $166 - $170, ◊ $33.

BOAT HARBOUR BEACH TAS 7321

Pop Nominal, (392km NW Hobart), See map on page 656, ref B3, Attractive holiday resort with beautiful sheltered beaches.

Hotels/Motels

 ★★★☆ **Boat Harbour Beach Resort**, (M), The Esplanade, 5km fr PO, ☎ 03 6445 1107, fax 03 6445 1027, 24 units [shwr, tlt, heat, elec blkts, tel, TV, radio, t/c mkg, refrig], ldry, rec rm, conv fac, ⊠, bar, pool indoor heated, sauna, spa, bbq, rm serv, plygr, cots. RO ♦ $69 - $103, ♦♦ $79 - $115, ◊ $15, ch con, Bottleshop.

 ★★★ **Boat Harbour Beach Seaside Garden**, (M), The Esplanade, 1km W of PO, ☎ 03 6445 1111, 4 units [shwr, tlt, heat, elec blkts, TV, clock radio, t/c mkg, refrig, toaster], ✕ (BYO), bbq, rm serv, cots-fee. RO ♦ $65, ♦♦ $70, ◊ $10, ch con, AE BC DC MC MCH VI.

★★★ **(Unit Section)**, 2 units acc up to 5, (2 bedrm), [shwr, tlt, heat, TV, clock radio, refrig, cook fac, micro, blkts, linen, pillows]. D ♦♦ $88 - $99, ◊ $10, ch con.

Other Accommodation

Boat Harbour Beach Backpackers, Strawberry Lane, ☎ 03 6445 1273, 4 rms acc up to 16, [heat (wood), micro, linen-fee], ldry, lounge, cook fac, refrig, bbq, kiosk, courtesy transfer, non smoking property. RO ♦ $15, ♦♦ $38, ch con.

BOTHWELL TAS 7030

Pop 396. (73km NW Hobart), See map on page 656, ref C6, Beautiful historic village on the banks of the Clyde River and centred around the lovely tree-studded Queen's Park. Home of the Australasian Golf Museum.

Self Catering Accommodation

★★★☆ **Highland House**, (HU), Historic Site, 'Nant', ☎ 03 6259 5506, fax 03 6259 3061, 1 unit acc up to 9, (5 bedrm), [shwr, tlt, heat (wood), elec blkts, TV, clock radio, t/c mkg, refrig, cook fac, micro, blkts, doonas, linen, pillows], w/mach, cots, breakfast ingredients. D ♦ $50 - $60, ♦♦ $85 - $90, ◊ $25 - $30, W ♦ $400 - $450, ♦♦ $500 - $550, ◊ $100 - $125, BC MC VI.

BOTHWELL TAS continued...

★★★ **Meadsfield**, (HU), Ouse Rd, 10km N of PO, ☎ 03 6259 5524, (2 stry), 1 unit acc up to 5, (2 bedrm), [shwr, tlt, heat (wood), clock radio, t/c mkg, refrig, cook fac, blkts, linen, pillows], w/mach, bbq, plygr, cots, breakfast ingredients. **D** ⸙ **$30**, ⸙⸙ **$70**, ch con.

B&B's/Guest Houses
★★★☆ **Bothwell Grange Guest House**, (B&B), c1836. No children's facilities, Alexander St, opposite PO, ☎ 03 6259 5556, fax 03 6259 5788, (2 stry), 7 rms [shwr, tlt, heat, elec blkts, clock radio, ldry (service-fee)], lounge (TV, video), ✕, t/c mkg shared, refrig, ☎, non smoking property. **BLB** ⸙⸙ **$108 - $112**, Dinner by arrangement, AE BC DC MC VI.

BRIDPORT TAS 7262

Pop 1,234. (280km N Hobart), See map on page 656, ref D3, Popular holiday destination and fishing port overlooking Anderson Bay.

Hotels/Motels

★★★☆ **Bridport Bay Inn**, (LMH), Previously Bridport Motor Inn, 105 Main St, 400m W of PO, ☎ 03 6356 1238, fax 03 6356 1267, 6 units [shwr, bath, tlt, elec blkts, tel, TV, radio, t/c mkg, refrig], ldry, ✕, plygr, cots. **RO** ⸙ **$64 - $69**, ⸙⸙ **$74 - $77**, ⸙ **$15**, ch con, AE BC DC MC VI.
★★★☆ **(Unit Section)**, 4 units acc up to 4, (2 bedrm), [shwr, tlt, elec blkts, tel, TV, radio, t/c mkg, refrig, cook fac]. **D** ⸙⸙ **$86 - $92**, ⸙ **$15**.

Self Catering Accommodation
★★★★ **Bridport Resort**, (HU), 35 Main St, 1km S of PO, ☎ 03 6356 1789, fax 03 6356 1732, 16 units acc up to 8, (1, 2 & 3 bedrm), [shwr, spa bath, fan, heat (elec), TV, video, clock radio, t/c mkg, refrig, cook fac, blkts, linen, pillows], w/mach, dryer, conv fac, ✕, bar, pool-indoor, spa (heated), bbq, tennis, cots. **D** ⸙⸙ **$120 - $128**, ⸙⸙⸙⸙ **$145 - $155**, ch con, AE BC DC EFT MC VI, ♿.
★★★★ **Platypus Park Country Retreat**, (HU), Ada St, 2km E of PO, ☎ 03 6356 1873, fax 03 6356 0173, 5 units acc up to 6, (1 & 2 bedrm), [shwr, spa bath (1), tlt, hairdry, heat (elec/wood), elec blkts, TV, clock radio, CD (1), t/c mkg, refrig, cook fac (4), micro, ldry, blkts, doonas, linen, pillows], dryer, spa, bbq, cots, breakfast ingredients, non smoking units. **D** ⸙⸙ **$75 - $148**, ⸙ **$15 - $25**, weekly con, 2 units yet to be rated. AE BC MC VI.
★★★☆ **Bridport Indra Holiday Units**, (HU), 53 Westwood St, 1km N of PO, ☎ 03 6356 1196, fax 03 6356 1332, 8 units acc up to 6, (2 bedrm), [shwr, tlt, hairdry, heat, elec blkts, TV, clock radio, t/c mkg, refrig, cook fac, micro, blkts, linen, pillows], w/mach, bbq, c/park (undercover), plygr, cots-fee. **D** ⸙ **$55 - $72**, ⸙⸙ **$66 - $77**, ⸙ **$11**, **W** ⸙ **$345 - $423**, ⸙⸙ **$345 - $423**, ⸙ **$77**, ch con, Light breakfast available, BC EFT MC VI.

B&B's/Guest Houses
★★★★ **Bridaire Bed & Breakfast**, (B&B), 22 Frances St, 500m S of PO, ☎ 03 6356 1438, fax 03 6356 1438, 4 rms [ensuite (3), spa bath (2), heat, elec blkts, TV (2), t/c mkg (2)], bathrm (1), ldry, lounge (TV), ✕, t/c mkg shared, bbq, cots, non smoking rms. **BLB** ⸙ **$45 - $55**, ⸙⸙ **$60 - $80**, ch con, BC MC VI.

Other Accommodation
Bridport Seaside Lodge, 47 Main St, 500m SE of PO, ☎ 03 6356 1585, 8 rms acc up to 4, [blkts, linen-fee], shwr, tlt, cook fac, t/c mkg shared, refrig, bbq, non smoking rms. **RO** ⸙ **$28 - $34**, ⸙⸙ **$42 - $45**, ⸙ **$19**, ch con.

BRIGHTON TAS 7030

Pop Nominal, (26km N Hobart), See map on page 656, ref D6, Brighton was an early 19th century garrison town and staging post on the Hobart-Launceston main road. Bonorong Wildlife Park.

★★☆ **Brighton Hotel Motel**, (LMH), Midland Hwy, 1km S of PO, ☎ 03 6268 1201, fax 03 6268 1264, 7 units [shwr, tlt, heat, elec blkts, TV, radio, t/c mkg, refrig], ldry, ✕, cots. **BLB** ⸙ **$50**, ⸙⸙ **$70**, ⸙ **$17**, ch con.

BRONTE PARK TAS 7140

Pop 117. (148km NW Hobart), See map on page 656, ref C5, Former Hydro Electric Commission village now developed into a holiday and leisure village. Bush Walking, Fishing.

Hotels/Motels

★★☆ **Bronte Park Highland Village**, (LH), Marlborough Hwy, 500m E of PO, ☎ 03 6289 1126, fax 03 6289 1109, 12 rms (1 suite) [shwr, tlt, heat (elec), elec blkts, TV (5), clock radio, t/c mkg, refrig], ldry, lounge (TV), conv fac, ✕, ✉, ☎, plygr, cots-fee, non smoking rms (6). **RO** ⸙ **$60 - $70**, ⸙⸙ **$80 - $90**, ⸙ **$20**, ch con, 5 rooms of a higher rating. Trout fishing gear hire and licences. AE BC DC EFT MC VI.
★★☆ **(Holiday Unit Section)**, 7 units acc up to 10, (2, 3 & 4 bedrm), [shwr, tlt, heat (elec/wood), elec blkts, TV (1), clock radio (2), t/c mkg, refrig, cook fac, ldry, blkts, linen, pillows], c/park (undercover) (7), non smoking units (4), Pets on application. **D** ⸙⸙ **$100 - $140**, ⸙ **$25.30**, ch con, weekly con, Emily Cottage a four star rating.

B&B's/Guest Houses
★★★★☆ **London Lakes Fly Fishing Lodge**, (B&B), 'London Lakes' (C173), 4km E of PO, ☎ 03 6289 1159, fax 03 6289 1122, (2 stry gr fl), 5 rms [ensuite, heat], lounge (TV), ✕, c/park. **D all meals $495 - $1,133**, Tariff includes trout fishing gear and licences.

BRUNY ISLAND

Pop 520. (25km S Hobart), See map on page 656, ref D7, Almost two distinct islands connected by a narrow isthmus. North Bruny comprises pastoral and lightly timbered land whilst South Bruny is hilly and heavily timbered.

Hotels/Motels
★★ **Hotel Bruny**, (LH), Main Rd, Alonnah 7150, ☎ 03 6293 1148, 2 rms [shwr, tlt, heat, elec blkts, TV, clock radio, t/c mkg, refrig], ✕, c/park. **RO** ⸙ **$50**, ⸙⸙ **$70**, ⸙ **$10**, BC MC VI.

Self Catering Accommodation
★★★★☆ **St Clairs**, (HU), No children's facilities, 8km S of Alonnah PO, ☎ 03 6293 1300, 1 unit acc up to 2, (1 bedrm), [shwr, tlt, fan, heat (elec/gas), elec blkts, tel, TV, video, clock radio, t/c mkg, refrig, cook fac, blkts, linen, pillows], w/mach, spa, bbq (gas), meals avail (dinner), breakfast ingredients (full), non smoking property. **D** ⸙⸙ **$165**, **W** ⸙⸙ **$900**, Tariff include use of boat & fishing gear, AE BC DC JCB MC VI.
★★★★ **Alonnah Retreat**, (HU), 31 William Carte Dr, Alonnah 7150, 400m S of Alonnah PO, ☎ 03 6229 3721, 1 unit acc up to 8, (4 bedrm), [shwr, tlt, fan, heat (wood), TV, video, clock radio, t/c mkg, refrig, cook fac, blkts, linen, pillows], w/mach, bbq, plygr, cots, non smoking property. **D** ⸙ **$55**, ⸙⸙ **$66**, ⸙ **$22**, **W** ⸙ **$330**, ⸙⸙ **$385**, ⸙ **$100**, ch con, Min book applies, AE BC DC MC VI.
★★★★ **Inala Country Accommodation**, (Cotg), 250ha property, 320 Cloudy Bay Rd, Lunawanna 7150, 9km S of Alonnah PO, ☎ 03 6293 1217, fax 03 6293 1217, 1 cotg acc up to 7, (3 bedrm), [shwr, bath, tlt, heat, elec blkts, TV, video, clock radio, t/c mkg, refrig, cook fac, micro, blkts, linen, pillows], w/mach, dryer, lounge firepl, bbq, meals avail, cots, non smoking units. **D** ⸙ **$121**, ⸙⸙ **$121**, ⸙ **$22**, ch con.
★★★★ **Mavista Spa Cottages**, (Cotg), 500m SE of PO, ☎ 03 6293 1347, fax 03 6293 1347, (2 stry), 3 cotgs acc up to 8, (1, 2 & 3 bedrm), [shwr, spa bath, tlt, heat (elec/wood), elec blkts, TV, radio, t/c mkg, refrig, cook fac, blkts, linen, pillows], w/mach, dryer, bbq, meals avail, c/park (undercover), cots-fee, non smoking units. **D** ⸙ **$110**, ⸙⸙ **$120 - $145**, ⸙ **$45**, **W** ⸙⸙ **$720 - $870**, ch con, Dinner by arrangement.
★★★★ **Morella Island Retreats**, (HU), 46 Adventure Bay Rd, ☎ 03 6293 1131, fax 03 6293 1137, 4 units acc up to 8, (1, 2 & 3 bedrm), [shwr, bath (1), tlt, fan, heat (elec/wood), TV, video (1), clock radio, t/c mkg, refrig, cook fac, blkts, doonas, linen, pillows], w/mach, dryer, bbq, plygr, cots. **D** ⸙⸙ **$130 - $220**, ⸙ **$15**, ch con, 1 unit ★★★☆, AE BC DC EFT MC VI.
★★★★ **Sea Rise Cottage**, (Cotg), Daniels Bay, Lunawanna 7150, 7km S of Alonnah PO, ☎ 03 6293 1255, fax 03 6293 1266, 1 cotg acc up to 6, (3 bedrm), [shwr, spa bath, tlt, heat (elec/wood), elec blkts, TV, video, t/c mkg, refrig, cook fac, micro, blkts, linen, pillows], w/mach, dryer, bbq, cots (highchair), non smoking property. **D** ⸙ **$99**, ⸙⸙ **$110**, ⸙ **$16.50**, **W** ⸙⸙ **$660**, ⸙ **$99**, ch con, BC MC VI.
★★★☆ **Barnes Bay Villa**, (HU), 315 Missionary Rd, Barnes Bay 7150, ☎ 03 6260 6287, fax 03 6260 6287, 1 unit acc up to 5, (1 bedrm), [shwr, tlt, fan, heat, elec blkts, TV, video, radio, t/c mkg, refrig, cook fac, micro, blkts, linen, pillows], w/mach, bbq, cots. **D** ⸙ **$80 - $90**, ⸙⸙ **$80 - $90**, ⸙ **$15**, ch con, weekly con, Min book applies.
★★★☆ **Cloudy Bay Cabin**, (HU), 1000 ha farm, 20km S of Alonnah, ☎ 03 6293 1171, fax 03 6293 1171, 1 unit acc up to 6, (2 bedrm), [shwr, tlt, heat (wood), TV, radio, t/c mkg, refrig, cook fac, blkts, linen, pillows]. **D** ⸙⸙ **$95**, ⸙ **$12**, **W** ⸙⸙ **$570**, ⸙ **$72**, Min book applies.
★★★☆ **Mill Cottage**, (Cotg), 338 Cloudy Bay Rd, Lunawanna 7150, 9.5km S of Alonnah PO, ☎ 03 6293 1217, fax 03 6293 1217, 1 cotg acc up to 7, (3 bedrm), [shwr, tlt, heat (elec/wood), elec blkts, TV, video, radio, t/c mkg, refrig, cook fac, micro, blkts, linen, pillows], w/mach, bbq, meals avail, cots, non smoking units, Pets on application. **D** ⸙ **$105**, ⸙⸙ **$105**, ⸙ **$22**, ch con, ♿.
★★★ **Christopher Lumsden Cottage**, (Cotg), c1906. Main Rd, Great Bay 7150, ☎ 03 6239 6547, (2 stry), 1 cotg acc up to 9, (3 bedrm), [shwr, tlt, heat, elec blkts, tel, TV, clock radio, t/c mkg, refrig, cook fac, blkts, linen, pillows], w/mach, lounge firepl, bbq, cots, Pets on application. **D** ⸙ **$82.50**, ⸙ **$11**, **W** ⸙ **$450**, ch con, Min book applies.
★★☆ **Coolangatta Cottage**, (Cotg), Cloudy Bay Rd, Lunawanna 7150, ☎ 03 6293 1164, 1 cotg acc up to 5, (2 bedrm), [shwr, tlt, heat, TV (colour), t/c mkg, refrig, cook fac, blkts, doonas, linen, pillows], w/mach, bbq, cots, Pets on application. **D $60**, **W $300**, ch con.

B&B's/Guest Houses

★★★★ **Active Holidays Kelly's Lookout**, (B&B), 212 Main Rd, Dennes Point 7150, ☎ 03 6260 6466, fax 03 6260 6456, 3 rms [ensuite (2), spa bath (1), heat (elec/wood), TV, radio, t/c mkg, pillows], bathrm (1), ✉ (seafood), cafe, bbq, c/park. **BB ♦ $110 - $132, ♦♦ $132 - $154, ◊ $33**, ch con.

Other Accommodation

Lumeah YHA, Lumeah Rd, Adventure Bay 7150, ☎ 03 6293 1265, 3 rms acc up to 8, [heat (2), linen-fee], ldry, lounge (TV), cook fac, t/c mkg shared, refrig, bbq, cots, non smoking rms. **RO ♦ $17 - $63**, ch con.

BURNIE TAS 7320

Pop 20,000. (326km NW Hobart), See map on page 656, ref B3, Burnie is built on the shores of Emu Bay and combines a unique blend of history, natural beauty and industry.

Hotels/Motels

★★★★ **Beachfront Voyager Motor Inn**, (M), 9 North Tce, 500m fr PO, ☎ 03 6431 4866, fax 03 6431 3826, (2 stry gr fl), 41 units (1 suite) [shwr, bath, spa bath (1), tlt, hairdry, heat, elec blkts, tel, TV, movie (24 hours), clock radio, t/c mkg, mini bar], ldry, iron brd, conv fac, ✉ (a la carte), bar, rm serv, cots, non smoking rms (20). **RO ♦ $110, ♦♦ $110**, ch con, AE BC DC MC VI.

★★★☆ **Burnie Town House**, (LH), 139 Wilson St, 250m from PO, ☎ 03 6431 4455, fax 03 6431 1026, (Multi-stry), 56 rms [shwr, bath, tlt, heat (elec), elec blkts, tel, TV, video, clock radio, t/c mkg, refrig], lift, ldry, conf fac, ✉, bar (cocktail & Irish), rm serv, cots, non smoking rms (19). **RO ♦ $115, ♦♦ $115, ◊ $15**, ch con, 19 rooms ★★★. AE BC DC EFT MC MP VI.

★★★☆ **Ocean View Motel**, (M), 253 Bass Hwy, Cooee 7320, 4km W of Burnie, ☎ 03 6431 1925, fax 03 6431 1753, (2 stry gr fl), 11 units (1 & 2 bedrm) [shwr, tlt, elec blkts, tel (direct dial), TV, video-fee, clock radio, t/c mkg, refrig, cook fac, pillows], ldry, pool indoor heated (closed winter), bbq, car wash, cots-fee. **RO ♦ $70, ♦♦ $77, ◊ $13**, ch con, BC EFT MC MCH VI.

★★★☆ **Wellers Inn**, (M), 36 Queen St, 1.5km W of PO, ☎ 03 6431 1088, fax 03 6431 6480, 24 units (2 suites) [shwr, tlt, hairdry, heat, elec blkts, tel, TV, movie, clock radio, t/c mkg, mini bar], ldry, conf fac, ✉, spa, rm serv, cots, non smoking rms. **RO ♦ $104, ♦♦ $104**, ch con, AE BC DC MC VI.

★★★★ **(Unit Section)**, 9 units acc up to 4, (1 bedrm), [shwr, spa bath (4), tlt, hairdry, heat, elec blkts, tel, TV, video, movie, radio, t/c mkg, mini bar, cook fac (4), cook fac ltd (5)]. **D ♦ $132 - $148, ♦♦ $132 - $148.**

★★★ **Burnie Motor Lodge**, (M), 12-16 Bass Hwy, Wivenhoe 7320, 2km E of Burnie CBD, ☎ 03 6431 2466, fax 03 6431 4798, (gr fl), 30 units [shwr, tlt, heat (elec), elec blkts, tel, TV, clock radio, t/c mkg, refrig], ldry, ✉, pool, rm serv, c/park. **RO ♦ $74, ♦♦ $88, ◊ $22**, ch con, AE BC EFT JCB MC VI.

Self Catering Accommodation

★★★★ **Apartments Down Town**, (HU), 52 Alexander St, 500m S of PO, ☎ 03 6432 3219, fax 03 6431 8844, (2 stry gr fl), 9 units acc up to 6, (1, 2 & 3 bedrm), [shwr, spa bath (3), heat (elec), elec blkts, tel, TV, clock radio, t/c mkg, refrig, cook fac, micro, linen], w/mach, dryer, breakfast ingredients. **D ♦ $99, ♦♦ $110**, AE BC DC MC VI.

★★★★ **The Duck House**, (Cotg), 26-28 Queen St, 1km W of PO, ☎ 03 6431 1712, 2 cotgs acc up to 6, (3 bedrm), [shwr, bath, tlt, a/c-cool, a/c (1), heat, elec blkts, tel (1), fax (1), TV, video, clock radio, t/c mkg, refrig, cook fac, micro, blkts, doonas, linen, pillows], w/mach, dryer (1), c/park (garage) (1), cots, breakfast ingredients, non smoking property. **D ♦ $85, ♦♦ $105.**

★★★☆ **West Beach Villas**, (HU), 43A North Tce, 1km NW of PO, ☎ 03 6431 5708, fax 03 6431 5710, (2 stry gr fl), 8 units acc up to 4, (2 bedrm), [shwr, bath, tlt, fan, heat, elec blkts, tel, TV, clock radio, t/c mkg, refrig, cook fac, micro, blkts, linen, pillows], ldry, bbq, cots-fee. **D ♦ $66 - $77, ♦♦ $77 - $99, ◊ $22 - $27.50**, BC EFT MC VI, ♿.

B&B's/Guest Houses

★★★★☆ **Glen Osborne House**, (B&B), 9 Aileen Cres (off Mount St), 1km SE of PO, ☎ 03 6431 9866, fax 03 6431 4354, (2 stry gr fl), 6 rms [ensuite, spa bath (1), cent heat, elec blkts, tel, TV, clock radio, CD, t/c mkg, refrig], lounge, breakfast rm, cots-fee. **BB ♦ $88, ♦♦ $121 - $132**, AE BC DC MC VI.

★★★★ **Baird's**, (B&B), 22 Cunningham St, 1km S of PO, ☎ 03 6431 9212, fax 03 6431 9797, 3 rms [ensuite (2), a/c, cent heat, elec blkts, TV, video, clock radio], bathrm (1), ldry, ✉, spa, t/c mkg shared, refrig, bbq, ☎. **BB ♦ $93.50, ♦♦ $121**, AE BC DC MC VI.

BUSHY PARK TAS 7140

Pop 329. (54km W Hobart), See map on page 656, ref C6, Bushy Park is now experiencing a revival of hop growing which previously had its heyday prior to the 1960s.

★★★★ **Hawthorn Lodge**, (B&B), Glenora Rd (B62), ☎ 03 6286 1311, fax 03 6286 2001, 2 rms [ensuite, heat (wood), elec blkts], lounge (TV), ✗, t/c mkg shared, c/park. **BB ♦ $97, ♦♦ $116**, BC MC VI.

CAMPANIA TAS 7026

Pop 232. (34km N Hobart), See map on page 656, ref D6, Located in picturesque farming area with many historic properties. Fishing.

★★★☆ **Campania House**, (B&B), Estate Rd, 3km E of PO, ☎ 03 6260 4281, fax 03 6260 4493, 7 rms (1 suite) [ensuite (1), heat (gas), elec blkts, ldry], shared fac (4), lounge (TV), ✗, t/c mkg shared, refrig, bbq, meals avail, cots. **BB ♦ $90, ♦♦ $135, ◊ $30**, ch con.

★★★☆ **Elmshurst**, (B&B), (Farm), Cnr Estate & White Kangaroo Rds, 4.2km E of PO, ☎ 03 6260 4209, 2 rms [shwr, tlt, heat, elec blkts, t/c mkg], ldry, lounge (TV), ☎. **BB ♦ $60, ♦♦ $80.**

CAMPBELL TOWN TAS 7210

Pop 879. (132km N Hobart), See map on page 656, ref D5, Historic township situated on the banks of Elizabeth River. Centre of fine wool industry. Bowls, Golf, Swimming (Pool), Tennis.

Self Catering Accommodation

★★★★ **Elizas Cottage**, (Cotg), 'Winton' Valleyfield Rd, 13km NW of Campbell Town, ☎ 03 6381 1221, fax 03 6381 1407, 1 cotg acc up to 4, (2 bedrm), [shwr, bath, tlt, heat (elec/wood), elec blkts, TV, clock radio, t/c mkg, refrig, cook fac, blkts, linen, pillows], w/mach, dryer, bbq, cots, breakfast ingredients. **BB ♦♦ $120, ◊ $25**, ch con.

★★★☆ **Lake Yalleena Holiday Cabin**, (HU), 35km E of Campbell Town, ☎ 03 6376 1869, fax 03 6376 1869, 2 units acc up to 5, (2 bedrm), [shwr, tlt, heat (wood), elec blkts, TV, clock radio, t/c mkg, refrig, cook fac, micro, blkts, linen, pillows], w/mach, non smoking units. **D $100 - $130.**

★★★ **The Broadwater on Macquarie**, (Cotg), 'Barton', 2464 Macquarie Rd, 27km W of PO, ☎ 03 6398 5114, fax 03 6398 5170, 1 cotg acc up to 6, (1 bedrm), [shwr, tlt, heat (wood), elec blkts, TV, clock radio, t/c mkg, refrig, cook fac, blkts, doonas, linen, pillows], w/mach, bbq, c/park. **D ♦ $105, ◊ $20**, Dinghy avail.

B&B's/Guest Houses

★★★★☆ **Foxhunters Return**, (B&B), c1834. 132 High St, 500m S of PO, ☎ 03 6381 1602, fax 03 6381 1545, (2 stry gr fl), 7 rms [ensuite (6), cent heat, TV, clock radio, t/c mkg, refrig], bathrm (1), conf fac, lounge firepl, ✗, bbq, cots-fee, non smoking property. **BLB ♦ $90, ♦♦ $120, ◊ $30**, 1 room ★★★★. AE BC DC MC VI.

★★★★ **The Grange**, (B&B), Midlands Hwy, 300m N of PO, ☎ 03 6381 1686, fax 03 6381 1536, (2 stry gr fl), 5 rms [ensuite, heat (elec), elec blkts, clock radio], lounge (TV), conv fac, t/c mkg shared, ☎, cots, non smoking rms. **BLB ♦ $82.50, ♦♦ $110, ◊ $22**, ch con, AE BC MC VI.

★★★☆ **The Gables**, (B&B), 35 High St, 1km N of PO, ☎ 03 6381 1347, fax 03 6381 1347, 3 rms [hairdry, heat, elec blkts, tel, TV], lounge, ✗, t/c mkg shared, bbq, meals avail, Pets allowed. **BLB ♦ $85, ♦♦ $93.50, ◊ $22**, ch con, AE BC JCB MC VI.

★★★★ **(Holiday Cottage Section)**, 3 cotgs acc up to 4, (1 bedrm), [shwr, tlt, heat, elec blkts, TV, clock radio, refrig, cook fac, micro, blkts, linen, pillows], w/mach, dryer, meals avail, breakfast ingredients. **BLB ♦♦ $105, ◊ $22**, ch con.

CARRICK TAS 7291

Pop 325. (203km N Hobart), See map on page 656, ref D4, Historic village with many stately homes and buildings.

★★★☆ **Hawthorn Villa**, (B&B), Classified by National Trust, c1873, Cnr Old Bass Hwy & Bishopsbourne Rd, ☎ 03 6393 6150, fax 03 6393 1610, (2 stry), 3 rms [ensuite, heat, t/c mkg], lounge (TV), ✗, bbq, cots. **BB ♦ $60, ♦♦ $95, ◊ $35**, ch con.

★★★ **(Carriage House Section)**, 4 units acc up to 3, (1 bedrm), [shwr, tlt, heat (wood), elec blkts, TV, clock radio, refrig, cook fac, blkts, linen, pillows], breakfast ingredients. **BB ♦ $60, ♦♦ $95, ◊ $35**, ch con.

CASTLE FORBES BAY TAS 7116

Pop 507. (53km SW Hobart), See map on page 656, ref C7, Fruit growing area (apples).
★★★★ **Camellia Cottage at Maple Hill**, (B&B), 119 Crowthers Rd, 53km SW fr Hobart PO, ☎ 03 6297 1528, fax 03 6297 1528, 1 rm [ensuite, heat (elec/wood), elec blkts, TV, clock radio, t/c mkg, refrig], ldry, bbq, non smoking property. **BB ♦ $85, ♦♦ $85.**
★★★☆ **Castle Forbes Bay House**, (B&B), Meredith Rd, ☎ 03 6297 1995, fax 03 6297 1995, 2 rms [heat, elec blkts, clock radio, t/c mkg], bathrm (2), ldry, lounge (TV), breakfast rm, bbq, meals avail, c/park. **BB ♦ $50, ♦♦ $75, ◊ $25, BC MC VI.**

CLEVELAND TAS 7211

Pop Nominal, (148km N Hobart), See map on page 656, ref D5, Historic village once a coaching stop between Hobart and Launceston.
★★★★ **St Andrews Inn**, (B&B), Midland Hwy, 10km N of Campbell Town, ☎ 03 6391 5525, fax 03 6391 5525, (2 stry), 2 rms [ensuite (2), heat (elec), elec blkts, tel, clock radio], lounge (TV/video), conf fac, ⊠, t/c mkg shared, refrig, bbq, non smoking rms. **BB ♦ $88, ♦♦ $110, ◊ $22, BC DC MC VI.**

COLES BAY TAS 7215

Pop 118. (206km NE Hobart), See map on page 656, ref E5, Popular holiday destination and fishing township. The town is dominated by the jagged pink granite peaks of Freycinet National Park.
Hotels/Motels
★★★★ **Freycinet Lodge**, (M), 2km fr Coles Bay PO, ☎ 03 6257 0101, fax 03 6257 0278, 60 units [shwr, spa bath (17), tlt, hairdry, heat, t/c mkg, refrig, cook fac (21)], ldry, rec rm, conv fac (hire), ⊠, bbq, plygr, bicycle, tennis, cots-fee. **RO ♦ $185, ♦♦ $185, ◊ $35,** Min book applies, AE BC DC VI, ♿.
Self Catering Accommodation
★★★★ **Churinga Farm Cottages**, (Cotg), 55ha farm and bushland property. Coles Bay Rd, 12km N of PO, ☎ 03 6257 0190, 5 cotgs acc up to 6, (1 & 2 bedrm), [shwr, tlt, heat (wood), elec blkts, TV, t/c mkg, refrig, cook fac, blkts, linen, pillows], w/mach, dryer, bbq, plygr, cots, Pets on application. **D ♦ $75 - $85, ♦♦ $90 - $130, ◊ $15,** Min book applies, BC MC VI.
★★★★ **Coles Bay Retreat**, (HU), 29 Jetty Rd, 500m N of PO, ☎ 0418 132 538, fax 03 6333 0135, (2 stry), 1 unit acc up to 7, (3 bedrm), [shwr, spa bath, tlt, heat (elec), elec blkts, TV, clock radio, radio, t/c mkg, refrig, cook fac, blkts, linen, pillows], w/mach, bbq, non smoking property. **D $90 - $200,** Min book applies.
★★★★ **Freycinet Cottages - Swan River**, (Cotg), Swanwick Dve, 7km N of Coles Bay PO, ☎ 03 6257 0370, 1 cotg acc up to 6, (3 bedrm), [shwr, tlt, heat (wood), TV, clock radio, t/c mkg, refrig, cook fac, blkts, linen, pillows], w/mach, bbq, cots. **D ♦♦ $75 - $85, ◊ $10.**
★★★★ **Jessies Cottage**, (HU), 7 Esplanade East, 50m E of PO, ☎ 03 6257 0143, 2 units acc up to 4, (1 & 2 bedrm), [shwr, tlt, heat (elec), elec blkts, TV, video, clock radio, radio, refrig, cook fac, micro, doonas, linen, pillows], w/mach, dryer, bbq, cots. **D ♦♦ $90 - $160,** Min book applies.
★★★★ **Three Peaks Units**, (HU), 60 Freycinet Dve, 500m N of PO, ☎ 03 6257 0333, fax 03 6257 0333, 3 units acc up to 6, (1, 2 & 3 bedrm), [shwr, tlt, hairdry, heat (elec/wood), elec blkts, TV, video, clock radio, t/c mkg, refrig, cook fac, micro], w/mach, dryer, bbq, cots. **D ♦ $85, ♦♦ $85 - $115, ◊ $25,** ch con.
★★★☆ **Coles Bay Waterfronters**, (HU), 3 Florence St, 2km NE of PO, ☎ 03 6257 0146, 2 units acc up to 5, (2 & 3 bedrm), [shwr, tlt, heat (elec), elec blkts (2), TV, clock radio (1), t/c mkg, refrig, cook fac, ldry (in unit), blkts, doonas, linen (Unit 1)-fee, pillows], cots, non smoking units (2). **D ♦ $68 - $88, ♦♦ $68 - $88, ◊ $12,** ch con.
★★★☆ **Freycinet Villas**, (HU), Bradley Dr, 1km E of PO, ☎ 03 6257 0320, fax 03 6257 0320, 2 units acc up to 6, (3 bedrm), [shwr, tlt, heat (elec), elec blkts, TV, video, t/c mkg, refrig, cook fac, ldry, blkts, linen, pillows], bbq, cots. **D ♦♦ $95 - $110, ◊ $10,** Min book applies, BC EFT MC VI.
★★★ **Gum Nut Cottage**, (Cotg), Cnr Freycinet Dr & Jetty Rd, ☎ 03 6257 0320, fax 03 6257 0320, 1 cotg acc up to 5, (2 bedrm), [shwr, bath, tlt, heat (wood), elec blkts, TV, video, clock radio, t/c mkg, refrig, cook fac, blkts, linen, pillows], w/mach, bbq, cots. **D ♦ $70 - $85, ♦♦ $70 - $85, ◊ $10,** ch con, weekly con, Min book applies, BC MC VI.
Other Accommodation
Freycinet Backpackers, 2352 Coles Bay Rd (C302), 4km W of PO, ☎ 03 6257 0100, fax 03 6257 0270, 24 rms [doonas-fee], lounge, cook fac, t/c mkg shared, refrig, non smoking rms. **D ♦ $16.50, ◊ $13.50.**

COPPING TAS 7174

Pop Nominal, (51km E Hobart), See map on page 656, ref D7, Gateway to Marion Bay.
★★★★ **Beach Breaks - Marion Bay**, (HU), 357 Marion Bay Rd, Bream Creek 7175, 8km N of Dunalley PO, ☎ 03 6253 5476, fax 03 6253 6081, 1 unit acc up to 4, (2 bedrm), [shwr, tlt, heat (elec), elec blkts, TV, video, clock radio, radio, t/c mkg, refrig, cook fac, micro, blkts, doonas, linen, pillows], w/mach, bbq, breakfast ingredients. **D ♦♦ $120, ◊ $25,** weekly con, BC MC VI.

CORINNA TAS 7321

Pop 5. (450km NW Hobart), See map on page 656, ref A4, The Western Explorer links the town with Marrawah to the North and Zeehan to the South. Accommodation available. Bush Walking, Fishing.
★★ **Pieman Retreat Cabins**, (HU), ☎ 03 6446 1170, fax 03 6446 1180, 3 units acc up to 6, (2 bedrm), [shwr, tlt, refrig, cook fac, blkts-fee, linen-fee, pillows-fee], bbq, kiosk, cots. **D $70 - $115.**
(Camping Ground), tank water. **D ♦♦ $7, ◊ $3.50,** ch con.

PIEMAN RIVER CRUISES & RETREAT CABINS

Sea eagles soaring, mirror images of natures paradise on the beautiful Pieman River. The 60 year old Arcadia II Cruises majestically out of the historically goldmining township of Corinna. The time gone by of the 1880's lives on for your enjoyment with river cruising, cabin accommodation, bushwalking, fishing, fossicking, canoeing & rafting. Corinna a memorable experience. Call now for booking on (03) 6446 1170, or any travel agent. Sailing at 10:30AM, returning at 2:30PM (winter sailings by appointment and no cruise Christmas day).

*Call now for booking on (03) 6446 1170, or any travel agent
Fax: (30) 6446 1180*

CRADLE MOUNTAIN-LAKE ST CLAIR

Pop 321 (Cradle Valley), (284km NW Hobart), See map on page 656, ref B4, World Heritage Area covering an area of 161,108ha of scenic rugged mountain peaks and alpine moorland.
★★★☆ **Cradle Mountain Highlanders**, (HU), Cradle Mountain Rd, ☎ 03 6492 1116, fax 03 6492 1188, 4 units acc up to 6, (1 & 2 bedrm), [spa bath (2), heat (wood/gas), elec blkts, TV, clock radio, t/c mkg, refrig, cook fac, blkts, linen, pillows], ldry, cots, breakfast ingredients. **D ♦ $95, ♦♦ $147 - $168, ◊ $22 - $27,** ch con, 2 units of a higher rating. BC MC VI.
Cradle Mountain Wilderness Village, (Cotg), Cradle Mountain Rd, 45Km SW of Sheffield, ☎ 03 6492 1018, fax 03 6492 1076, (gr fl), 25 cotgs acc up to 6, (1 bedrm2 bedrm), [fire pl, heat, tel, TV, cable TV, clock radio, radio, t/c mkg, refrig, micro, toaster, blkts, doonas, linen, pillows], w/mach, dryer, lounge firepl, ✕, ✕, ⊠, res liquor license, t/c mkg shared, bbq, petrol, ☎, cots-fee, non smoking units (25). **D ♦ $160 - $170, ♦♦ $160 - $170, ◊ $30,** ch con, BC MC VI, (not yet classified).
Waldheim Cabins, Cradle Mountain, ☎ 03 6492 1110, fax 03 6492 1120, 8 cabins acc up to 8, [heat (wood/gas), cook fac ltd (gas)], shared fac. **D ♦♦ $60.50 - $82.50, ◊ $20.90,** ch con, No pets or firearms permitted.

CRADOC TAS 7109

Pop Nominal, (50km S Hobart), See map on page 656, ref C7, Agricultural area.
B&B's/Guest Houses
★★★★ **Squirrels in the Park**, (B&B), Rowes Rd, 9km S of Huonville PO, ☎ 03 6266 3291, fax 03 6266 3791, 2 rms [heat (elec), elec blkts, clock radio, t/c mkg, refrig], bathrm (2), ldry, lounge (TV/Video), ✕, bbq, cots, non smoking property, Pets on application. **BB ♦ $50, ♦♦ $85 - $90, ◊ $25,** ch con, BC MC VI, ♿.
Other Accommodation
Huon Valley Balfes Hill YHA Hostel, 4 Sandhill Rd, ☎ 03 6295 1551, fax 03 6295 0875, 10 rms acc up to 4, ldry, rec rm, lounge (TV), cook fac, t/c mkg shared, refrig. **RO ♦ $16, ◊ $16,** ch con, BC MC VI.

Rates may change. Check before booking.

CYGNET TAS 7112

Pop 924. (54km S Hobart), See map on page 656, ref C7, Centre of a large fruit growing district, also noted for its deep sheltered harbour. Cygnet also offers Wineries, Pottery, Woodturning and a Wildlife Park.

Hotels/Motels

★★★ **Howard Cygnet Central**, (LH), Mary St, 200m fr PO, ☎ 03 6295 1244, 2 rms [shwr, tlt, heat, elec blkts, TV, t/c mkg, refrig], plygr. **BLB ∮ $37.50, ♦♦ $55, ◊ $10**, ch con, BC MC VI.

Cygnet Hotel, (LH), 14 Mary St, 500m N of PO, ☎ 03 6295 1267, (2 stry), 7 rms [heat, elec blkts], ldry, lounge (TV), ✕, t/c mkg shared, c/park. **RO ∮ $20 - $30, ♦♦ $45 - $55**, ch con, BC MC VI.

Self Catering Accommodation

★★★☆ **Paradise Lodge**, (HU), 51 Chuter St, Deep Bay, 5km S of Cygnet PO, ☎ 03 6225 1235, fax 0419 184 385, 1 unit acc up to 5, (3 bedrm), [fan, heat, elec blkts, TV, t/c mkg, refrig, cook fac], ldry, bbq, c/park (undercover), mooring, cots. **BLB ∮ $80, ♦♦ $100, ◊ $25**, ch con, weekly con.

★★★ **Arundel Cottage**, (Cotg), 643 Silver Hill Rd, Glaziers Bay 7112, 6.5km W of Cygnet PO, ☎ 03 6295 1577, 1 cotg acc up to 4, (2 bedrm), [shwr, tlt, heat (elec), elec blkts, TV, clock radio, t/c mkg, refrig, cook fac, micro, blkts, linen, pillows], w/mach, bbq, c/park (undercover), non smoking units. **D ♦♦ $75, ◊ $10, W ♦♦ $350**, Min book applies.

B&B's/Guest Houses

★★★☆ **Cygnet Guest House**, (B&B), 89 Mary St, 100m S of PO, ☎ 03 6295 0080, fax 03 6295 1905, 4 rms [heat (elec), elec blkts, clock radio, t/c mkg], bathrm (3), lounge (TV), ✕, coffee shop, non smoking property. **BB ♦♦ $95 - $105**, AE BC EFT MC VI.

★★★☆ **Leumeah Lodge**, (B&B), 2km S of PO, ☎ 03 6295 0980, (2 stry), 5 rms [heat (elec/wood), elec blkts, tel, TV, video, clock radio, t/c mkg], shared fac (2), lounge (TV), ✕, bbq, non smoking rms. **BB ∮ $82.50, ♦♦ $93.50**, BC MC VI.

★★★★ **(Holiday Unit Section)**, 1 unit acc up to 4, (2 bedrm), [shwr, tlt, fan, heat (elec), TV, video, clock radio, t/c mkg, refrig, cook fac, blkts, linen, pillows], w/mach, bbq, breakfast ingredients (Continental), non smoking units. **D ∮ $110, ♦♦ $110, ◊ $25**, ch con.

DELORAINE TAS 7304

Pop 2,168. (228km NW Hobart), See map on page 656, ref C4, Picturesque old town on the Meander River with spectacular views of the Western Tiers. Centre of a large agricultural district. Many of the historic buildings date back to the 1830s.

Hotels/Motels

★★★ **Mountain View Country Inn**, (M), 144 Emu Bay Rd, 1.5km W of PO, ☎ 03 6362 2633, fax 03 6362 3232, 24 units [shwr, tlt, heat, elec blkts, tel, TV, radio, t/c mkg, refrig], ldry, conv fac, ✕ (Mon to Sat), bbq, rm serv, plygr, cots. **RO ∮ $80 - $90, ♦♦ $80 - $90, ◊ $15**, ch con, AE BC DC MC VI.

Self Catering Accommodation

★★★☆ **Bentley Cottage**, (Cotg), Classified by National Trust, c1879. 'Bentley', 1519 Mole Creek Rd, Chudleigh 7304, 15km fr Deloraine, ☎ 03 6363 6131, fax 03 6363 6131, 1 cotg acc up to 5, (2 bedrm), [shwr, tlt, heat (elec/wood), elec blkts, TV, radio, t/c mkg, refrig, cook fac, micro, blkts, linen, pillows], w/mach, ✕, dinner to unit, cots-fee, breakfast ingredients. **D ∮ $72, ♦♦ $88, ◊ $17**.

★★★☆ **Tier View Cottage**, (Cotg), 125 Emu Bay Rd, 1km NW of PO, ☎ 03 6362 2377, fax 03 6362 2120, 1 cotg acc up to 4, (2 bedrm), [shwr, tlt, heat (elec/wood), elec blkts, TV, radio, t/c mkg, refrig, cook fac, micro, blkts, linen, pillows], w/mach, dryer, cots, breakfast ingredients, Pets on application. **D ∮ $82.50, ♦♦ $82.50, ◊ $16.50**, ch con, weekly con, AE BC DC MC VI.

★★★☆ **Western Creek Retreat**, (HU), 760 Western Creek Rd, Western Creek 7304, 24km W of PO, ☎ 03 6363 1399, fax 03 6363 1420, 1 unit acc up to 6, (3 bedrm), [shwr, tlt, fan, heat (elec), elec blkts, TV, video, clock radio, t/c mkg, refrig, cook fac, linen, pillows], ldry, bbq, cots-fee, breakfast ingredients, non smoking units, Pets on application. **D ∮ $99, ♦♦ $99, ◊ $25**, ch con, BC EFT MC VI.

B&B's/Guest Houses

★★★★☆ **Arcoona**, (B&B), Classified by National Trust, c1892. East Barrack St, 500m E of PO, ☎ 03 6362 3443, fax 03 6362 3228, (2 stry gr fl), 7 rms (1 suite) [ensuite, hairdry, fan, heat, elec blkts, tel, TV, radio, t/c mkg, refrig], rec rm, ✕ (Lic. Tues to Sun), bbq, non smoking property. **BB ∮ $130, ♦♦ $130 - $170, ◊ $45, Suite BB ♦♦ $190**, AE BC DC MC VI.

★★★★☆ **Calstock Country Guest House**, (B&B), c1838, Lake Hwy, 1km W of PO, ☎ 03 6362 2642, fax 03 6362 2635, 5 rms (1 suite) [ensuite (4), spa bath (2), heat (elec), TV, radio, doonas], bathrm (1), lounge (TV) (2), ✕, t/c mkg shared, refrig, bbq, non smoking property. **BB ♦♦ $255 - $295, ◊ $60**, weekly con, Min book applies, BC MC VI.

★★★★ **Bonney's Inn**, (B&B), c1830, 19 West Pde, 500m S of PO, ☎ 03 6362 2974, fax 03 6362 4087, (2 stry), 6 rms (1 suite) [ensuite (5), hairdry, heat, elec blkts, TV, clock radio], bathrm (1), ldry, lounge (TV/bar facilities), ✕, t/c mkg shared, refrig, non smoking property. **BB $95 - $152**, AE BC EFT MC VI.

★★★★ **Liffey Falls Lodge**, (B&B), 1363 Bogan Rd, Golden Valley 7304, 18km S of Deloraine PO, ☎ 03 6369 5363, (2 stry), 2 rms [ensuite, fan, heat (elec), elec blkts, tel, TV, clock radio, t/c mkg, refrig], ldry, ✕, bbq, meals avail (evenings only), cots, non smoking rms, Pets on application. **BB ∮ $85, ♦♦ $95, ◊ $20, RO ∮ $80, ♦♦ $90, ◊ $15**, ch con, BC MC VI.

★★★★ **Villarett Cottage**, (B&B), 739 Railton Rd, Moltema 7304, 18km NW of Deloraine, ☎ 03 6368 1214, fax 03 6368 1214, 1 rm (2 bedrm), [shwr, tlt, heat (wood), elec blkts, TV, t/c mkg], meals avail, non smoking units. **BB ∮ $85, ◊ $20**, ch con, BC DC MC VI.

★★★☆ **Bonneys Farm**, (B&B), 76 Archer St, 4km W of PO, ☎ 03 6362 2122, fax 03 6362 3566, 1 rm [shwr, tlt, heat, elec blkts, TV, radio, t/c mkg, refrig, pillows], ldry, dryer, ✕, cots-fee. **RO ∮ $50, ♦♦ $70, ◊ $15**, BC MC VI.

★★★ **(Holiday Unit Section)**, 3 units acc up to 6, (2 & 3 bedrm), [shwr, tlt, heat, elec blkts, TV, radio, t/c mkg, refrig, cook fac, blkts, linen, pillows], w/mach. **D ∮ $50 - $60, ♦♦ $70 - $80, ◊ $12 - $15, W ∮ $300 - $370, ♦♦ $440 - $510, ◊ $84 - $105**, 1 unit ★★★☆.

★★★☆ **Bowerbank Mill Cottages**, (B&B), c1853, Meander Valley Hwy, 2km E of PO, ☎ 03 6362 2628, fax 03 6362 3586, (2 stry), 3 rms (1 suite) [shwr, tlt, heat (elec/wood), elec blkts, TV, radio, t/c mkg, refrig, cook fac ltd (2), pillows], ldry, bbq, meals avail, cots, non smoking suites. **BB ∮ $115.50, ♦♦ $148.50, ◊ $33**, AE BC MC VI.

★★★☆ **Highland Rose B&B**, (B&B), No children's facilities, 47 West Church St, 500m NW of PO, ☎ 03 6362 2634, 2 rms [ensuite (1), fan, heat, elec blkts, TV, clock radio, doonas], bathrm (1), ldry, lounge (TV), breakfast rm, t/c mkg shared, refrig, bbq, non smoking property. **BB ∮ $75 - $85, ♦♦ $90 - $100**, weekly con, BC MC VI.

Other Accommodation

Highview Lodge YHA, 8 Blake St, ☎ 03 6362 2996, 5 rms acc up to 10, ldry, cook fac, t/c mkg shared, refrig. **RO ∮ $14 - $32**, ch con.

DERWENT BRIDGE TAS 7140

Pop 117. (164km NW Hobart), See map on page 656, ref B5, This small township is named for the bridge which spans the Derwent closest to its source. Lake St Clair Wilderness cruises.

Hotels/Motels

★☆ **Derwent Bridge Wilderness Hotel**, (LH), Lyell Hwy, 500m NW of PO, ☎ 03 6289 1144, fax 03 6289 1173, 7 rms [ensuite (2), heat, elec blkts, t/c mkg], ldry, conf fac, ✕, ☏, cots. **RO ♦♦ $85 - $105, ◊ $12.50**, ch con, AE BC DC MC VI.

Self Catering Accommodation

★★★☆ **Derwent Bridge Chalets**, (HU), Lyell Hwy, 500m E of Lake St Clair junction, ☎ 03 6289 1000, fax 03 6289 1230, (2 stry gr fl), 6 units acc up to 8, (1, 2 & 3 bedrm), [shwr, bath, spa bath (2), tlt, hairdry, heat (elec/wood/gas), elec blkts, radio, CD, t/c mkg, refrig, cook fac, micro, blkts, doonas, linen, pillows], w/mach, dryer, bbq, c/park (undercover), cots, breakfast ingredients. **D ∮ $120 - $160, ♦♦ $135 - $194, ◊ $33**, ch con, 3 chalets of a higher rating. AE BC DC MC VI.

DEVIOT TAS 7251

Pop 473. (233km N Hobart), See map on page 656, ref D4, Riverside township on the western banks of the Tamar River. Boat Ramp, Boating, Bush Walking, Fishing, Sailing, Wind Surfing.

B&B's/Guest Houses

★★★★ **Norfolk Reach**, (B&B), 84 Motor Rd, 5km N of Exeter PO, ☎ 03 6394 7681, fax 03 6394 7681, 4 rms [ensuite, heat (elec/wood), cent heat, elec blkts, tel, TV, radio, refrig (2)], ldry, lounge (TV/video), conf fac, ✕, ✕, res liquor license, t/c mkg shared, refrig, bbq, c/park. **BB ∮ $60, ♦♦ $88 - $92, ◊ $40**, BC VI, ♿.

DEVONPORT TAS 7310

Pop 25,000. (278km NW Hobart), See map on page 656, ref C3, A major city nestled between the Mersey and Forth Rivers and the largest town on the northern coastline. Home port for the Bass Strait vehicular ferry Spirit of Tasmania. Devonport Airport, scenic flights. Bowls, Golf, Greyhound Racing, Horse Racing, Scenic Drives, Squash, Swimming (Pool), Tennis, Trotting.

Hotels/Motels

★★★★ **Gateway Inn (Innkeepers)**, (LH), 16 Fenton St, 1km W of PO, Located in central CBD, ☎ 03 6424 4922, fax 03 6424 7720, (Multi-stry gr fl), 64 rms [shwr, bath, tlt, heat, elec blkts, tel, TV, cable TV, clock radio, t/c mkg, refrig, mini bar], lift, ldry, conv fac, ⊠, cafe, bar, rm serv, cots. **RO ♦ $98 - $132, ♦♦ $108 - $148, ♀ $17**, ch con, AE BC DC JCB MC VI.

★★★★ **Sunrise Motor Inn**, (M), 140 North Fenton St, 2km NW of PO, ☎ 03 6424 8411, fax 03 6424 8329, (2 stry gr fl), 33 units [shwr, spa bath (2), tlt, hairdry, a/c (24), heat (9), elec blkts, tel, TV, video, clock radio, t/c mkg, refrig, mini bar, cook fac (2), ldry], conf fac, ⊠ (Mon to Thursday), plygr, cots, non smoking rms (27). **RO ♦ $109 - $153, ♦♦ $120 - $164, ♀ $19**, ch con, 9 rooms ★★★☆. AE BC DC EFT JCB MC MP VI.

★★★☆ **Argosy Motor Inn**, (LH), 221 Tarleton St, 2km E of PO, ☎ 03 6427 8872, fax 03 6427 9819, (2 stry gr fl), 37 rms [shwr, spa bath (16), tlt, heat, fan, elec blkts, tel, TV, video (16), clock radio, t/c mkg, refrig], ldry, conf fac, ⊠, rm serv, dinner to unit, cots. **RO ♦ $80 - $110, ♦♦ $85 - $116, ♀ $16**, ch con, 16 rooms ★★★★. AE BC DC MC VI.

★★☆ **Edgewater Motor Inn**, (M), 2 Thomas St, East Devonport 7310, ☎ 03 6427 8441, fax 03 6427 8290, 29 units [shwr, tlt, heat, elec blkts, TV, t/c mkg, refrig], ⊠, ✆, cots-fee. **D ♦ $49 - $59, ♦♦ $59 - $69, ♀ $11**, Min 2 night booking Riverfront rooms. BC MC VI.

★★ **Hotel Formby**, (LH), 82 Formby Rd, opposite PO, ☎ 03 6424 1601, fax 03 6424 8123, 23 rms [ensuite (11), heat, elec blkts, tel (11), TV], ⊠, t/c mkg shared, cots-fee. **BB ♦ $30 - $55, ♦♦ $40 - $75, ♀ $20**, ch con, 11 rooms ★☆. AE BC DC MC VI.

Self Catering Accommodation

★★★★☆ **Elsie Cottage**, (Cotg), c1890. No children's facilities, 150 David St, 3km from PO, mob 0413 028 438, fax 03 6243 0595, 1 cotg acc up to 4, (2 bedrm), [shwr, bath, tlt, hairdry, heat, elec blkts, tel, TV, clock radio, t/c mkg, refrig, cook fac, micro, blkts, linen, pillows], w/mach, dryer, iron, lounge firepl, bbq, plygr, breakfast ingredients, non smoking units. **D ♦ $130 - $140, ♦♦ $130 - $140, ♀ $35**, BC MC VI.

★★★★ **Barclay Lodge**, (SA), 112 North Fenton St, 1km N of PO, ☎ 03 6424 4722, fax 03 6423 1019, 19 serv apts acc up to 5, (1 & 2 bedrm), [shwr, spa bath (1), tlt, heat (elec), elec blkts, tel, TV, video-fee, clock radio, t/c mkg, refrig, blkts, linen, pillows], ldry, rec rm, pool indoor heated, bbq, rm serv (b'fast), plygr, tennis (half court), cots. **RO ♦ $75 - $130, ♦♦ $86 - $140, ♀ $17**, ch con, 6 units ★★★☆. AE BC DC EFT MC VI.

★★★★ **Devonport Historic Cottages**, (Cotg), c1883, 66 Wenvoe St, ☎ 03 6424 1560, fax 03 6424 2090, 1 cotg acc up to 4, (2 bedrm), [shwr, bath, tlt, heat (elec/wood), elec blkts, TV, video, clock radio, t/c mkg, refrig, cook fac, micro, blkts, linen, pillows], w/mach, dryer, bbq, cots, breakfast ingredients. **D ♦♦ $139 - $149, ♀ $38**, ch con.

★★★★ **Trelawney by the Sea**, (HU), 6 Chalmers Lane, 3km NW of PO, ☎ 03 6424 3263, fax 03 6424 3263, 1 unit acc up to 5, (2 bedrm), [shwr, tlt, fan, heat, elec blkts, TV, video, radio, t/c mkg, refrig, cook fac], ldry, lounge (TV), spa (outdoor), bbq, meals avail, bicycle (2), cots-fee, breakfast ingredients, Small pets allowed. **BB ♦ $90, ♦♦ $100 - $120**, ch con.

★★★☆ **Daisy Cottages**, (Cotg), 16 Mersey Main Rd, 4.6km S of PO, ☎ 03 6424 2267, fax 03 6427 2944, 2 cotgs acc up to 4, (2 bedrm), [shwr, bath, tlt, heat (elec/wood), elec blkts, TV, clock radio, refrig, cook fac, micro, blkts, linen, pillows], w/mach, bbq, breakfast ingredients. **D ♦♦ $98, ♀ $22**, ch con, BC VI.

★★★☆ **Glasgow Lodge**, (HU), 59 George St, 1km N of PO, ☎ 03 6424 1480, fax 03 6424 8436, 12 units acc up to 6, (2 bedrm), [shwr, tlt, heat, fan, elec blkts, TV, clock radio, t/c mkg, refrig, cook fac, blkts, linen, pillows], w/mach, bbq, c/park (garage), ✆, plygr, cots-fee. **D ♦ $77 - $83, ♦♦ $94 - $99, ♀ $22**, ch con, Light breakfast available. AE BC BTC DC MC MCH VI.

★★★☆ **Keswick by the River**, (HU), 2 James St, 1.5km N of PO, ☎ 03 6424 3745, 1 unit (1 suite) acc up to 2, [shwr, tlt, heat (elec/gas), elec blkts, TV, clock radio, radio, t/c mkg, refrig, cook fac, ldry, blkts, linen, pillows], breakfast ingredients, non smoking units. **Suite RO ♦♦ $100 - $110**.

★★★☆ **Mersey Bluff Lodge**, (SA), 247 William St, 1km N of PO, ☎ 03 6424 5289, fax 03 6424 2998, 14 serv apts acc up to 6, (1 & 2 bedrm), [shwr, bath, tlt, hairdry, heat (elec), elec blkts, tel (24hr direct dial), fax (modem sockets), TV, clock radio, t/c mkg, refrig, cook fac, micro, blkts, linen, pillows], ldry, bbq, plygr, cots, breakfast ingredients, non smoking rms. **RO ♦ $78 - $83, ♦♦ $89 - $99, ♀ $18**, ch con, AE BC DC EFT MC VI.

B&B's/Guest Houses

★★★★☆ **Birchmore of Devonport**, (B&B), 8-10 Oldaker St, 500m S of PO, ☎ 03 6423 1336, fax 03 6423 1338, (2 stry gr fl), 6 rms (1 suite) [ensuite, hairdry, fan, cent heat, elec blkts, tel, fax, TV, video, clock radio, t/c mkg, refrig, mini bar], ldry, meeting rm, breakfast rm, bbq, cots, non smoking property. **BB ♦ $99 - $110, ♦♦ $99 - $110, ♀ $20, Suite D $110**, AE BC DC MC VI.

★★★★☆ **Ochill Manor**, (B&B), c1880, 27 Old Kindred Rd, Forth 7310, 10km W of Devonport, ☎ 03 6428 2660, fax 03 6428 2330, 3 rms [ensuite, hairdry, cent heat, elec blkts, video, radio, CD, t/c mkg], lounge (TV), lounge firepl, non smoking property. **BB ♦ $100, ♦♦ $134 - $150, ♀ $35**, AE BC MC VI.

(Thomas Jacob Spa Cottage), c1880, 1 cotg acc up to 2, (1 bedrm), [shwr, tlt, hairdry, heat, elec blkts, TV, radio, t/c mkg, refrig, cook fac, blkts, linen, pillows], ldry, spa, breakfast ingredients, non smoking property. **D ♦♦ $150, ♀ $35, W ♦♦ $450**, Min book applies, (not yet classified).

★★★★ **Macfie Manor**, (B&B), 44 MacFie St, 500m S of PO, ☎ 03 6424 1719, fax 03 6424 8766, (2 stry), 6 rms [ensuite, hairdry, heat, heat, elec blkts, tel, TV, clock radio, t/c mkg, refrig], breakfast rm, non smoking property. **BB ♦ $84, ♦♦ $94, ♀ $25**, AE BC DC MC VI.

★★★★ **(Unit Section)**, 1 unit acc up to 2, (1 bedrm), [shwr, bath, tlt, heat, tel, TV, t/c mkg, refrig, cook fac, blkts, linen, pillows], breakfast ingredients, non smoking units. **D ♦ $110, ♦♦ $110**.

★★★★ **Rannoch House**, (B&B), No facilities for children under 2. 5 Cedar Ct, East Devonport 7310, ☎ 03 6427 9818, fax 03 6427 9181, (2 stry), 5 rms (1 suite) [ensuite, hairdry, heat, heat, elec blkts, TV, clock radio, t/c mkg, refrig], lounge, breakfast rm, tennis, non smoking property. **BB ♦ $90, ♦♦ $110 - $130**, ch con, BC MC VI.

★★★★ **Riverview Lodge**, (B&B), 18 Victoria Pde, 850m N of PO, ☎ 03 6424 7357, fax 03 6423 6026, (2 stry gr fl), 10 rms [ensuite (7), hairdry, heat, elec blkts, TV, clock radio], shared fac (2), ldry, lounge (TV), breakfast rm, t/c mkg shared, refrig, bbq, ✆, plygr, cots-fee. **BB ♦ $50 - $65, ♦♦ $60 - $85, ♀ $25**, ch con, 3 rooms of a 3.5 star rating. AE BC DC EFT JCB MC VI, ♿.

★★★☆ **The Wattles**, (B&B), Pumping Station Rd, Forth 7310, 9km W of Devonport, ☎ 03 6428 2242, (2 stry gr fl), 2 rms [shwr, tlt, heat (1), elec blkts, tel, TV (1), t/c mkg (1), refrig, micro], ldry, bbq, cots. **BB ♦ $45, ♦♦ $70, ♀ $20**, ch con.

Other Accommodation

MacWright House YHA, 115 Middle Rd, ☎ 03 6424 5696, fax 03 6424 9952, 9 rms acc up to 8, ldry, cook fac, t/c mkg shared, refrig. **RO ♦ $12 - $21.50**, ch con.

Tasman House Backpackers, 114 Tasman St, ☎ 03 6423 2335, 39 rms [heat, linen-fee], ldry, rec rm, lounge (TV), cook fac, t/c mkg shared, refrig, bbq, c/park. **RO ♦♦ $11 - $37**.

DILSTON TAS 7252

Pop 304. (216km N Hobart), See map on page 656, ref D4, Originally a staging post on the overland route from Launceston to George Town.

★★★★☆ **Riverbank Cottages**, (HU), 1325 East Tamar Hwy, 13 km N of Launceston PO, ☎ 03 6328 1555, fax 03 6328 1117, 3 units acc up to 3, (1 bedrm), [spa bath (1), fan, heat, elec blkts, tel, TV, video, radio, CD, t/c mkg, refrig, cook fac, toaster, blkts, linen, pillows], ldry, w/mach, dryer, bbq, tennis, breakfast ingredients, non smoking property. **BLB ♦♦ $130 - $160, ♀ $25**, AE BC DC EFT MC VI.

DOVER TAS 7117

Pop 570. (82km S Hobart), See map on page 656, ref C7, Popular holiday retreat located on the shores of picturesque Port Esperance. Main industries are fruit growing, fishing and Atlantic Salmon fish farms. Scenic cruises on Port Esperance to Salmon farms. Boat Ramp, Boating, Fishing, Golf, Swimming.

Hotels/Motels
★★ **Dover Hotel**, (LMH), Main Rd, 1km S of PO, ☎ 03 6298 1210, fax 03 6298 1504, 7 units [heat (elec), clock radio, t/c mkg], ⊠, cots. RO ╪ $42, ╪╪ $54, ◊ $11, ch con, BC EFT MC VI.

★★★ **(House Section)**, 1 unit acc up to 7, (2 bedrm), [shwr, tlt, heat (elec), tel, TV, clock radio, t/c mkg, refrig, cook fac, blkts, linen, pillows], ldry, cots. RO ╪ $90, ╪╪ $90, ◊ $18.50, ch con.

★★★ **(Motel Section)**, 5 units [shwr, tlt, heat (elec), TV, clock radio, t/c mkg, refrig, cook fac (3)], ldry, cots. RO ╪ $42.50, ╪╪ $66.50, ◊ $18, ch con.

Self Catering Accommodation
★★★★ **Driftwood Holiday Cottages**, (Cotg), Bay View Rd, 500m S of PO, ☎ 03 6298 1441, fax 03 6298 1401, 6 cotgs acc up to 6, (1, 2 & 3 bedrm), [shwr, tlt, cent heat, elec blkts, tel, TV, clock radio, t/c mkg, refrig, cook fac, micro, blkts, linen, pillows], ldry, bbq, cots, non smoking property. D ╪╪ $130, ╪╪╪ $165, ╪╪╪╪ $200, ch con, AE BC DC MC VI.

★★★ **Smugglers Rest**, (HU), Previously 3 Island Holiday Apartments. Station Rd, ☎ 03 6298 1396, fax 03 6298 1396, 4 units acc up to 6, (1 & 2 bedrm), [shwr, tlt, fan, heat, elec blkts, TV, video-fee, radio, t/c mkg, refrig, cook fac, blkts, doonas, linen, pillows], ldry-fee, bbq, cots. D ╪ $50 - $60, ╪╪ $60.50 - $71.50, ◊ $11.

B&B's/Guest Houses
★★★★ **Dover Bayside Lodge**, (B&B), Bayview Rd, 500m S of PO, ☎ 03 6298 1788, fax 03 6298 1788, 6 rms [ensuite (5), heat (elec), elec blkts, TV, clock radio, t/c mkg, refrig, cook fac ltd], bathrm (1), ✕, bbq, meals avail, ☏, non smoking property. BLB ╪ $73 - $98, ╪╪ $25 - $98, ◊ $20, ch con, weekly con, BC MC VI, ⌕&.

★★★☆ **Annes Old Rectory**, (B&B), Huon Hwy, 500m N of PO, ☎ 03 6298 1222, (2 stry gr fl), 2 rms [fan, heat, elec blkts], ldry-fee, lounge (TV), ✕, t/c mkg shared, meals avail, non smoking property. BB ╪ $53, ╪╪ $68 - $72, ◊ $30, ch con.

★★★☆ **Riseley Cottage**, (B&B), 170 Narrows Rd, Strathblane 7116, 7km S of PO, ☎ 03 6298 1630, fax 03 6298 1815, 2 rms [ensuite, heat (elec/wood), elec blkts, clock radio, ldry], lounge (TV/video), ✕, t/c mkg shared, refrig, cots, non smoking property. BB ╪ $75, ╪╪ $95, ◊ $30, ch con, BC MC VI.

DUNALLEY TAS 7177

Pop 286. (59km E Hobart), See map on page 656, ref D7, Dunalley stands on the narrow isthmus connecting the Forestier Peninsula. Bush Walking, Fishing, Golf, Surfing.

B&B's/Guest Houses
★★★★ **Potters Croft**, (B&B), Arthur Hwy, 3km NE of PO, water frontage, ☎ 03 6253 5469, fax 03 6253 5651, 2 rms [ensuite, heat (elec), TV, video, clock radio, t/c mkg, refrig, micro, toaster], ldry, bbq, meals avail, plygr, cots-fee, breakfast ingredients, non smoking property. BLB ╪ $80 - $95, ╪╪ $90 - $116, ◊ $25, D $400 - $560, weekly con, BC BTC MC VI.

★★★☆ **(Holiday Unit Section)**, 1 cotg acc up to 5, (2 bedrm), [shwr, tlt, heat (elec/pot belly), elec blkts, TV, video, clock radio, t/c mkg, refrig, cook fac, micro, blkts, linen, pillows], w/mach, bbq, cots-fee, breakfast ingredients, Pets on application. D ╪ $80 - $95, ╪╪ $90 - $116, ◊ $25, W $400 - $560, ch con, fam con, weekly con.

DYSART TAS 7030

Pop Nominal, (40km N Hobart), See map on page 656, ref D6, Pastoral and agricultural area.

Self Catering Accommodation
Woodfield Lodge, (HU), 160 Harbachs Rd, ☎ 03 6268 6187, fax 03 6268 6375, 4 units acc up to 7, (2 bedrm), [shwr, tlt, heat, t/c mkg, refrig, cook fac, micro, blkts-fee, linen-fee, pillows-fee], ldry, bbq, plygr, cots. RO ╪╪ $44, ◊ $5.50, ch con.

Trouble-free travel tips - **Hoses and belts**
Inspect the condition of radiator hoses, heater hose fan and air conditioner belts.

EAGLEHAWK NECK TAS 7179

Pop 84. (78km SE Hobart), See map on page 656, ref E7, Narrow isthmus of only a few hundred metres wide connects the peninsulas. Noted for its unique coastal formations and little town named 'Doo Town'.

Hotels/Motels

★★★ **Penzances Pirates Bay Motel**, (M), Blowhole Rd, 'Doo Town', ☎ 03 6250 3272, fax 03 6250 3519, 10 units [shwr, tlt, heat, elec blkts, tel, TV, radio, t/c mkg, refrig], ⊠, bbq, plygr, cots. RO ╪ $65, ╪╪ $80, ╪╪╪ $95, ╪╪╪╪ $110, ◊ $15, ch con, AE BC BTC EFT MC MCH VI.

★★☆ **Lufra Country Hotel**, (LH), Pirates Bay Road, ☎ 03 6250 3262, fax 03 6250 3460, (2 stry gr fl), 27 rms [shwr, bath, tlt, heat, elec blkts, TV, t/c mkg, ldry (guest)], ⊠, cots-fee. BLB ╪ $60.50, ╪╪ $77, ◊ $22, ch con, AE BC DC EFT MC VI.

Self Catering Accommodation
★★★☆ **The Neck Beach House**, (HU), 423 Pirates Bay Dve, ☎ 03 6250 3541, fax 03 6250 3541, 1 unit acc up to 6, (2 bedrm), [shwr, tlt, heat (wood), elec blkts, TV, video, radio, t/c mkg, refrig, cook fac, micro, blkts, linen, pillows], w/mach, c/park (garage), cots-fee, breakfast ingredients. D ╪╪ $90 - $110, ╪╪╪ $120 - $150, ◊ $15, weekly con, Min book applies.

B&B's/Guest Houses

★★★★☆ **Osprey Lodge Beachfront B&B**, (B&B), 14 Osprey Rd, 53km SE of Sorell, ☎ 03 6250 3629, fax 03 6250 3031, 2 rms [ensuite, heat (elec), elec blkts, TV, clock radio, t/c mkg, refrig], ldry, bbq, non smoking property. BB ╪ $125, ╪╪ $160 - $180, ◊ $45, ch con, Min book applies, AE BC DC MC VI.

★★★★☆ **Wunnamurra Waterfront B&B**, (B&B), 21 Osprey Rd, ☎ 03 6250 3145, fax 03 6250 3145, 2 rms [ensuite, heat (elec/wood), elec blkts, tel, CD, t/c mkg, refrig (1)], lounge firepl, cots, non smoking property. BB ╪ $80, ╪╪ $100 - $120, ch con, BC MC VI.

ELLENDALE TAS 7140

Pop 465. (75km N Hobart), See map on page 656, ref C6, Picturesque village nestled at the foothills of Mount Field National Park. Once the centre of a hop and small fruit growing industry.

★★★★ **Hopfield Cottages**, (Cotg), Ellendale Rd, 500m W of PO, ☎ 03 6288 1223, fax 03 6288 1207, 3 cotgs acc up to 6, (1, 2 & 3 bedrm), [shwr, bath, tlt, heat (elec/wood), elec blkts, TV, radio, t/c mkg, refrig, cook fac, micro, blkts, doonas, linen, pillows], w/mach, dryer, bbq, meals avail, cots-fee, breakfast ingredients. D ╪ $90, ╪╪ $99 - $120, ◊ $20, ch con, weekly con.

EPPING FOREST TAS 7211

Pop Nominal, (160km N Hobart), See map on page 656, ref D5, A small community on main Highway between Hobart and Launceston.

★★★★ **Rose Cottage B&B**, (B&B), 23 Barton Rd, 200m W of Caltex Road House, ☎ 03 6391 5569, fax 03 6391 5654, 3 rms [ensuite, heat (elec/wood), clock radio, t/c mkg], lounge (TV/Video), ✕, bbq, meals avail (dinner), c/park. BB ╪ $70, ╪╪ $95, BC MC VI.

EVANDALE TAS 7212

Pop 1,033. (199km N Hobart), See map on page 656, ref D4, One of Tasmania's best preserved historic villages with buildings dating back to the 1820s and streetscapes reminiscent of the Victorian era.

Self Catering Accommodation
★★★★ **Bees Nees Cottage**, (Cotg), c1840. 26 Russell St, 200m E of PO, ☎ 03 6391 8772, fax 03 6391 8783, 1 cotg acc up to 5, (3 bedrm), [shwr, tlt, heat (elec/wood), elec blkts, tel, TV, video, clock radio, CD, t/c mkg, refrig, cook fac, micro, blkts, linen, pillows], w/mach, bbq, cots, breakfast ingredients, Pets on application. D ╪ $110, ╪╪ $220, ◊ $22, ch con, BC MC VI.

★★★★ **The Stables**, (HU), 5 Russell St, 50m E of PO, ☎ 03 6391 8048, fax 03 6391 8047, 3 units acc up to 4, (1 bedrm), [shwr, tlt, heat (electric), elec blkts, TV, clock radio, t/c mkg, refrig, cook fac, micro, blkts, linen, pillows], ldry, bbq, non smoking units. D ╪ $60, ╪╪ $120, BC MC VI.

★★★☆ **Greg & Jills Place**, (HU), 35 Collins St, 500m E of PO, ☎ 03 6391 8248, fax 03 6391 8248, 2 units acc up to 3, (1 bedrm), [shwr, tlt, heat, elec blkts, TV, clock radio, t/c mkg, refrig, cook fac, blkts, linen, pillows], w/mach, bbq, cots, breakfast ingredients, non smoking units. D ╪ $50, ╪╪ $75, ◊ $10, ch con, weekly con, AE BC DC MC VI.

EVANDALE TAS continued...

B&B's/Guest Houses

★★★★ **Harland Rise**, (B&B), White Hills Rd, 3km NE of PO, ☎ 03 6391 8283, (2 stry gr fl), 2 rms [shwr, tlt, heat (electric), elec blkts, clock radio, CD], ldry, lounge (TV), lounge firepl, ✗, t/c mkg shared, refrig, non smoking property. **BB** ♦ **$65**, ♦♦ **$90**, ◊ **$35**, ch con.

★★★★ **Strathmore**, (B&B), Classified by National Trust, c1826. 868 Nile Rd, 8.7km S of Evandale PO, ☎ 03 6398 6213, fax 03 6398 6273, (2 stry gr fl), 3 rms [shwr (3), tlt (3), heat (electric), elec blkts, TV, t/c mkg, refrig], ldry, conv fac, bbq, tennis, non smoking property. **BB** ♦ **$150**, ♦♦ **$150**, ch con, BC MC VI.

★★★★ **(Holiday Unit Section)**, 2 units acc up to 4, (1 bedrm), [shwr, tlt, fire pl, elec blkts, TV, t/c mkg, refrig, cook fac, blkts, linen, pillows], cots. **BB** ♦♦ **$150**, **W** ♦♦ **$900**, ch con.

★★★☆ **Solomon Cottage**, (B&B), Classified by National Trust, c1836. 1 High St, opposite PO, ☎ 03 6391 8331, 1 rm [shwr, tlt, fire pl, elec blkts, TV, clock radio, t/c mkg, refrig], ldry, lounge, conv fac, bbq, tennis (plexi-pave), cots, non smoking property. **D** ♦♦ **$105**, ◊ **$25**, ch con.

FALMOUTH TAS 7215

Pop 80. (230km NE Hobart), See map on page 656, ref E4, Seaside township located on the East Coast.

★★☆ **The White Sands Resort**, (HU), Previously Cray Drop In Iron House Point, ☎ 03 6372 2228, fax 03 6372 2226, 27 units acc up to 10, (2 & 3 bedrm), [shwr, tlt, heat, elec blkts, TV, refrig, cook fac, blkts, linen, pillows], w/mach, conv fac, ✉, bar (Lic.), pool, spa, bbq, c/park (undercover), plygr, golf, cots-fee. **D** ♦♦ **$55 - $80**, ◊ **$5 - $10**, ch con, 13 rooms ★★☆, Trout fishing-private lake. Bottleshop. BC EFT MC VI.

FENTONBURY TAS 7140

Pop Nominal, (68km W Hobart), See map on page 656, ref C6, Peaceful country area close to Mt Field National Park and Russell Falls.

★★★★ **Hamlet Downs**, (B&B), c1862. 50 Gully Rd, 3.5km N of Westerway PO, ☎ 03 6288 1212, fax 03 6288 1258, 3 rms [ensuite (1), heat (elec/wood), elec blkts, TV, video, t/c mkg], ✗ (home grown produce), bbq, plygr, cots, non smoking property. **BB** ♦ **$60 - $80**, ♦♦ **$80 - $110**, ◊ **$28**, ch con, weekly con, BC MC VI.

FINGAL TAS 7214

Pop 392. (197km NE Hobart), See map on page 656, ref E4, Originally a gold mining town. Local industries are farming, sawmilling and coal mining. Bush Walking, Canoeing, Fishing, Golf, Rock Climbing.

★★★☆ **Glenesk B&B**, (HU), 9 Talbot St, ☎ 03 6374 2195, fax 03 6374 2195, 1 unit acc up to 6, (2 bedrm), [shwr, tlt, heat (elec/wood), elec blkts, TV, t/c mkg, refrig, cook fac, blkts, linen, pillows], w/mach, cots, breakfast ingredients, non smoking units. **D** ♦ **$45**, ♦♦ **$85**, ◊ **$10**, weekly con.

FLINDERS ISLAND TAS 7255

Pop 924. (175km NNE Launceston), See map on page 656, ref E1, Ideal holiday spot for the adventurous. Known for its beautiful beaches, bays and unique wildlife with excellent fishing and bushwalks.

Hotels/Motels

★★ **Flinders Island Interstate Hotel**, (LMH), Patrick St, Whitemark 7255, ☎ 03 6359 2114, fax 03 6459 2250, (2 stry), 10 units [ensuite (8), heat (elec), elec blkts, TV (9)], ldry, lounge (TV), ✉, t/c mkg shared, refrig, cots. **BB** ♦ **$47 - $60**, ♦♦ **$60 - $90**, ch con, BC MC VI.

Self Catering Accommodation

★★★☆ **Boat Harbour Beach House**, (HU), 404ha property. 45km NW of Whitemark PO, ☎ 03 6359 6510, 1 unit acc up to 8, (3 bedrm), [shwr, tlt, heat (gas), tel, TV, radio, t/c mkg, refrig, cook fac, blkts, linen, pillows], w/mach, bbq, cots. **D** ♦ **$75**, ♦♦ **$75**, ◊ **$10**, **W** ♦ **$525**, ♦♦ **$525**, ◊ **$70**, ch con, Min book applies.

★★★☆ **Bucks at Lady Barron**, (HU), Franklin Pde, Lady Barron 7255, 1km fr Lady Barron PO, ☎ 03 6223 3055, fax 03 6223 3099, 1 unit acc up to 6, (3 bedrm), [shwr, tlt, fan, heat (elec/gas/wood), elec blkts, tel (local only), TV, video, radio, CD, t/c mkg, refrig, cook fac, blkts, doonas, linen, pillows], w/mach, iron, iron brd, bbq, cots, breakfast ingredients, non smoking units. **D** ♦♦ **$90**, ◊ **$15**, ch con, Min book applies.

★★★☆ **Bulloke**, (HU), Butter Factory Rd, Whitemark 7255, ☎ 03 6359 9709, fax 03 6359 9709, 1 unit acc up to 6, (3 bedrm), [shwr, tlt, heat (elec), tel, TV, video, radio, t/c mkg, refrig, cook fac (gas), micro, blkts, linen, pillows], w/mach, dryer, iron, bbq (wood/gas), cots. **D** ♦ **$50**, ♦♦ **$75**, ◊ **$15**, ch con.

★★★☆ **Carnsdale Host Farm**, (HU), Melrose Rd, Memana 7255, 28km E of Whitemark PO, ☎ 03 6359 9718, 1 unit acc up to 9, (4 bedrm), [shwr, tlt, fan, heat (wood fire), elec blkts, tel, TV, t/c mkg, refrig, cook fac (elec), micro, doonas, linen, pillows], w/mach, bbq, meals avail, plygr, cots. **D** ♦♦ **$80**, ◊ **$15**.

★★★☆ **Echo Hills**, (HU), Madeleys Rd, Lackrana 7255, 25km fr Whitemark PO, ☎ 03 6359 6509, fax 03 6359 6559, 2 units acc up to 8, (3 bedrm), [shwr, tlt, fire pl, elec blkts, tel, TV, radio, t/c mkg, refrig, cook fac (gas), blkts, doonas, linen, pillows], w/mach, dryer, bbq, cots, breakfast ingredients. **D** ♦♦ **$88**, ♦ **$12**, **W** ♦♦ **$420 - $465**, ◊ **$60 - $72**, ch con.

★★★☆ **Felicitys Cottage**, (Cotg), Original fisherman's cottage. Holloway St, Lady Barron 7255, 400m W of PO, ☎ 03 6359 3641, 1 cotg acc up to 6, (2 bedrm), [shwr, tlt, fan, heat (wood), tel, TV, video, t/c mkg, refrig, cook fac (gas), micro, blkts, linen, pillows], w/mach, dryer, iron, bbq, cots-fee. **D** ♦ **$80**, ♦♦ **$80**, ◊ **$10**.

★★★☆ **Lady Barron Holiday House**, (HU), 24km S of Whitemark PO, ☎ 03 6359 3555, fax 03 6359 3555, 1 unit acc up to 6, (3 bedrm), [shwr, tlt, heat (wood), elec blkts, tel, TV, radio, t/c mkg, refrig, cook fac, blkts, linen, pillows], w/mach, bbq, cots. **D** ♦♦ **$70 - $80**, ◊ **$15**, **W** ♦♦ **$420 - $480**, ◊ **$90**, ch con.

★★★☆ **Leafmoor Cottage**, (Cotg), 3.5km W of PO, ☎ 03 6359 3517, fax 03 6359 3517, 1 cotg acc up to 6, (4 bedrm), [shwr, tlt, heat (wood), elec blkts, tel, TV, video, radio, t/c mkg, refrig, cook fac, micro, blkts, linen, pillows], w/mach, dryer, bbq, cots, breakfast ingredients. **D** ♦♦ **$70 - $90**, ◊ **$20**, ch con.

★★★☆ **Lisas Cottage**, (Cotg), Lees Rd, Memana 7255, ☎ 03 6359 6530, fax 03 6359 6530, 1 cotg acc up to 6, (3 bedrm), [shwr, tlt, heat (wood), elec blkts, tel, TV, radio, t/c mkg, refrig, cook fac, blkts, linen, pillows], ldry, bbq, plygr, cots. **D** ♦♦ **$70**, ◊ **$10**, ch con, Min book applies.

★★★☆ **Seaview Cottage**, (Cotg), (Farm), 5km S of PO, ☎ 03 6359 2011, 1 cotg acc up to 4, (2 bedrm), [shwr, tlt, heat (elec/wood), tel, TV, radio, t/c mkg, refrig, cook fac, blkts, doonas, linen, pillows], w/mach, dryer, bbq, cots. **D** ♦♦ **$66**, ◊ **$6**, Min book applies.

★★★☆ **Yaringa**, (Cotg), Holloway St, Lady Barron 7255, ☎ 03 6359 4522, 3 cotgs acc up to 6, (2 bedrm), [shwr, tlt, fan, heat, TV, radio, t/c mkg, refrig, cook fac, blkts, doonas, linen, pillows], w/mach, bbq, plygr, cots. **D** ♦ **$82.50**, ♦♦ **$82.50 - $104.50**, ch con.

★★★ **Bellnacroft**, (HU), Coast Rd, Lady Barron 7255, 1km SW of Lady Barron PO, ☎ 03 6359 3554, fax 03 6359 3554, 1 unit acc up to 2, (1 bedrm), [shwr, tlt, fan, heat (elec/wood), tel, clock radio, radio, t/c mkg, refrig, cook fac, blkts, linen, pillows], w/mach, bbq, non smoking property. **D** ♦♦ **$99**, Min book applies, BC MC VI.

★★★ **Oakridge Holiday Home**, (HU), Killiecrankie Bay, 45km N of Whitemark PO, ☎ 03 6359 2160, 1 unit acc up to 6, (3 bedrm), [shwr (2), tlt (2), heat (elec/wood), elec blkts, radio, t/c mkg, refrig, cook fac, blkts, linen, pillows], w/mach, bbq, cots. **D** ♦♦ **$65**, ◊ **$10**, ch con.

Elvstan Beach Cottage, (HU), 2/7 Esplanade, Whitemark 7255, 5km NW of Whitemark PO, ☎ 03 6359 2008, fax 03 6359 2009, 1 unit acc up to 5, (3 bedrm), [shwr, tlt, heat (elec/wood), tel, TV, clock radio, t/c mkg, refrig, cook fac, blkts, linen, pillows], w/mach, cots, breakfast ingredients, non smoking property, Pets allowed. **D** ♦ **$85**, ♦♦ **$85**, weekly con, (not yet classified).

★★★ **(2 Bowman St Section)**, 1 unit acc up to 4, (2 bedrm), [shwr, tlt, heat, tel, TV, clock radio, t/c mkg, refrig, cook fac, blkts, linen, pillows], breakfast ingredients. **D** **$55**, **W** **$300**.

B&B's/Guest Houses

★★★☆ **Holloway Haven**, (B&B), "Butley", Whitemark 7255, ☎ 03 6359 4530, fax 03 6359 4530, 2 rms [shwr, tlt, heat (elec), elec blkts, TV, radio, t/c mkg, refrig, cook fac, ldry, pillows], bathrm (1), bbq, c/park. **BLB** ♦ **$120**, ♦♦ **$120**, Min book applies.

★★★☆ **Partridge Farm**, (B&B), Badger Corner, 9km W of Lady Barron, ☎ 03 6359 3554, 1 rm [shwr, spa bath, tlt, cent heat, tel, TV, CD, t/c mkg, refrig, micro], ldry, bbq, meals avail, non smoking rms. **BLB** ♦♦ **$115.50**, Min book applies.

★★★★ **(Retreat)**, 1 unit acc up to 2, (1 bedrm), [shwr, tlt, fan, heat (wood), tel, TV, clock radio, CD, t/c mkg, refrig, cook fac, micro, doonas, linen, pillows], bbq, meals avail, non smoking property. **D** ♦♦ **$115.50**, ◊ **$22**.

★★★★ **(Top House)**, 1 unit acc up to 6, (3 bedrm), [heat (wood), tel, TV, radio, clock radio, CD, t/c mkg, refrig, cook fac, linen, pillows], w/mach, bbq, meals avail, plygr, cots, non smoking property, Pets on application. **D** ♦♦ **$121**, ◊ **$22**.

FRANKLIN TAS 7113

Pop 462. (46km SW Hobart), See map on page 656, ref C7, Located on the western bank of the Huon River. Franklin has still maintained its 19th century river port authenticity. Location of Wooden Boat Building School.

Self Catering Accommodation

★★★★ **Whispering Spirit**, (HU), 253 Swamp Rd, 3.5km from PO, ☎ 03 6266 3341, fax 03 6266 3342, 1 unit acc up to 3, (1 bedrm), [shwr, tlt, fan, heat (elec/wood), elec blkts, TV, video, clock radio, radio, t/c mkg, refrig, cook fac, blkts, linen, pillows], w/mach, bbq, plygr, breakfast ingredients, non smoking units. D ▪ $70 - $85, ▪▪ $85 - $95, ⚬ $20, W ▪ $450 - $550, ▪▪ $500 - $600, ⚬ $100, ch con, BC MC VI.

B&B's/Guest Houses

★★★★☆ **Franklin Lodge**, (B&B), No children's facilities, Main Rd, 500m S of PO, ☎ 03 6266 3506, fax 03 6266 3731, (2 stry gr fl), 4 rms [ensuite, spa bath (1), heat, elec blkts, TV, radio, t/c mkg (1), refrig (bar)], lounge, ✗, t/c mkg shared, refrig, bbq. BB ▪ $117 - $130, ▪▪ $126 - $162, ⚬ $45.

GARDNERS BAY TAS 7112

Pop 387. (57km S Hobart), See map on page 656, ref C7, Small wine growing district. Bush Walking, Horse Riding.

B&B's/Guest Houses

★★★★☆ **Hartzview Vineyard Homestead**, (B&B), 50ha working farm, vineyard & wine centre. 70 Dillons Rd, ☎ 03 6295 1623, fax 03 6295 1723, (2 stry gr fl), 1 rm (3 bedrm), [shwr, tlt, heat (elec/wood), cent heat, elec blkts, tel, TV, video, clock radio, t/c mkg, refrig, cook fac, pillows], w/mach, dryer, bbq, meals avail, cots-fee, breakfast ingredients, non smoking units. D ▪▪ $130 - $160, ⚬ $30, ch con, AE BC MC VI.

GEEVESTON TAS 7116

Pop 826. (61km S Hobart), See map on page 656, ref C7, Geeveston today is a small community still involved in the timber industry and fruit growing. The massive swamp gums at the entrance to Geeveston symbolise the landscape and forests. Bowls, Bush Walking, Canoeing, Fishing, Golf, Tennis.

B&B's/Guest Houses

★★★☆ **Cambridge House**, (B&B), Heritage, c1870, Huon Hwy, 500m S of PO, ☎ 03 6297 1561, (2 stry), 3 rms [fan, heat (elec), elec blkts, clock radio, doonas], ldry, lounge (TV/video), lounge firepl, breakfast rm, t/c mkg shared, refrig, bbq, cots, non smoking property. BLB ▪ $55 - $65, ▪▪ $70 - $85, ⚬ $20, ch con, weekly con, BC MC VI.

★★★☆ **Hemmerton Homestead**, (B&B), 40 Fourfoot Rd, 1.5km NW of Geeveston, ☎ 03 6297 1518, fax 03 6297 1518, 3 rms [heat (elec/wood), elec blkts, TV, t/c mkg, ldry], bathrm, bbq, meals avail, c/park (undercover), non smoking rms. BB ▪ $55 - $60, ▪▪ $80 - $90, ch con.

GEORGE TOWN TAS 7253

Pop 5,592. (250km N Hobart), See map on page 656, ref C3, One of Australia's oldest towns, George Town saw rapid development during the 1950's to house workers and service expanding industry at nearby Bell Bay. Boat Ramp, Boating, Bowls, Golf, Swimming (Beach).

Hotels/Motels

FLAG
FLAG CHOICE HOTELS™

★★★★ **The Pier**, (LMH), 5 Elizabeth St, 1km NE of PO, ☎ 03 6382 1300, fax 03 6382 2085, 16 units [shwr, tlt, heat, elec blkts, tel, TV, clock radio, t/c mkg, refrig], cots. RO ▪▪ $110, ⚬ $15, AE BC MC VI, ♿.

★★★★ **(Unit Section)**, (2 stry gr fl), 8 units acc up to 4, (1 & 2 bedrm), [shwr, tlt, heat, elec blkts, tel, TV, clock radio, refrig, cook fac, micro, blkts]. D ▪▪ $130, ⚬ $15, ch con.

★★☆ **(Hotel Section)**, (2 stry), 5 rms [shwr (3), tlt (3), heat, elec blkts, tel (2), TV, clock radio, t/c mkg, refrig]. RO ▪▪ $55 - $110, 2 rooms ★★★★.

★★☆ **Central Court Apartments**, (M), 30 Main Rd, 1km fr PO, ☎ 03 6382 2155, fax 03 6382 2177, 16 units (1 & 2 bedrm), [shwr, tlt, heat, elec blkts, tel, TV, radio, t/c mkg, refrig, cook fac, pillows], ldry, bbq, plygr, cots. D ▪ $55 - $65, ▪▪ $65 - $100, ch con, 8 rooms of a higher rating. BC VI.

★☆☆☆☆

Trouble-free travel tips - **Tools**

It pays to carry some basic tools for emergency roadside repairs, such as an adjustable spanner, phillips head and flat blade screwdrivers, pliers and a roll of masking tape.

Self Catering Accommodation

★★★ **Pilot Station**, (HU), 5km N of George Town PO, ☎ 03 6382 1143, fax 03 6382 1143, 3 units acc up to 8, (3 & 4 bedrm), [shwr, tlt, heat (elec/wood), TV, video, clock radio, radio, t/c mkg, refrig, cook fac, blkts, linen, pillows], w/mach, bbq, breakfast ingredients, non smoking property, Pets on application. D ▪ $44 - $66, ▪▪ $55 - $88, ⚬ $22 - $33, ch con.

B&B's/Guest Houses

★★★☆ **Nannas Cottage**, (B&B), Classified by National Trust, c1835. 'The Grove' 25 Cimitiere St, 500m NW of PO, ☎ 03 6382 1336, fax 03 6382 3352, 1 rm (1 bedrm), [shwr, tlt, heat (electric), elec blkts, TV, radio, t/c mkg, refrig, cook fac], ✗, bbq, cots, non smoking rms. BB ▪ $60, ▪▪ $75 - $85, ⚬ $20, ch con, BC MC VI.

Other Accommodation

Travellers YHA Hostel, 4 Elizabeth St, ☎ 03 6382 3261, 5 rms acc up to 7, ldry, cook fac, t/c mkg shared, refrig. RO ▪ $18 - $50, ch con, BC MC VI.

GRINDELWALD TAS 7277

Pop 658. (219km N Hobart), See map on page 656, ref D4, Authentic Swiss-style village, nestled in the rolling hills of the Tamar Valley. Canoeing, Golf.

Hotels/Motels

AAA
TOURISM
Special Rates

★★★★ **Grindelwald Resort**, (LH), Waldhorn Dve, 6km N of Legana PO, ☎ 03 6330 0400, fax 03 6330 1607, (2 stry gr fl), 30 rms (3 suites) [shwr, bath, spa bath (5), tlt, heat, elec blkts, tel, TV, clock radio, refrig, mini bar], ldry, rec rm, conv fac, ✗, pool indoor heated, sauna, spa, bbq, shop (village), plygr, bicycle, golf, gym, tennis, cots, non smoking rms (14). BLB ▪ $140, ▪▪ $140, ⚬ $22, Suite BLB ▪ $179 - $215, ▪▪ $179 - $215, ⚬ $22, ch con, Lake for paddle boats & canoes, AE BC DC MC VI, ♿.

★★★★ **(Holiday Unit Section)**, 27 units acc up to 6, (1 & 2 bedrm), [shwr, tlt, elec blkts, tel, TV, radio, t/c mkg, refrig, cook fac, micro, blkts, doonas, linen, pillows], w/mach, dryer. BLB ▪ $160, ▪▪ $160, ▪▪▪ $189, ▪▪▪▪ $189, ch con.

GROVE TAS 7109

Pop 745. (32km SW Hobart), See map on page 656, ref C7, Suburb of Huonville.

B&B's/Guest Houses

★★★★☆ **Grove Manor**, (B&B), Crabtree Rd, 7km N of Huonville, ☎ 03 6266 4227, fax 03 6266 4223, 3 rms [ensuite, fire pl, cent heat, elec blkts, doonas], lounge, ✗, t/c mkg shared, bbq, meals avail, non smoking property. BB ▪ $120, ▪▪ $145 - $160, ⚬ $25.

HADSPEN TAS 7290

Pop 1,730. (193km N Hobart), See map on page 656, ref D4, Located on the South Esk River this small township was established in the early 1820s. Buildings of historic interest include Entally House, Red Feather Inn, Hadspen Gaol and Church. Boat Ramp, Boating, Swimming, Water Skiing.

Hotels/Motels

Budget Motel Chain
International

★★★ **Rutherglen**, (M), Old Bass Hwy, 1km NW of PO, ☎ 03 6393 6307, fax 03 6393 6885, (2 stry gr fl), 20 units [shwr, bath, tlt, heat (elec), elec blkts, tel, TV, clock radio, t/c mkg, refrig], ldry, conv fac, ✗ (6 days), pool indoor heated (seasonal), sauna, spa, bbq, tennis, cots. RO ▪ $68, ▪▪ $79, ch con, AE BC DC MC VI.

HAGLEY TAS 7292

Pop 153. (213km N Hobart), See map on page 656, ref C4, Early colonial village.

B&B's/Guest Houses

★★★★☆ **Hagley House**, (B&B), Classified by National Trust, Station Lane (C507), ☎ 03 6392 2366, (2 stry gr fl), 6 rms [ensuite, heat, elec blkts, radio, t/c mkg], lounge (TV), tennis, non smoking property. BB ▪▪ $138.

★★★☆ **Beveridges Stables**, (B&B), Original stables c1854. 119 Beveridges Lane, 2km NW of PO, ☎ 03 6393 1203, fax 03 6392 2278, (2 stry gr fl), 2 rms (2 suites) [shwr, tlt, heat (wood), elec blkts, TV, radio, t/c mkg, refrig, cook fac, micro], ldry, bbq, cots, non smoking property. BB ▪ $97, ▪▪ $120, ⚬ $27, ch con, BC MC VI.

HAMILTON TAS 7140

Pop 150. (74km NW Hobart), See map on page 656, ref C6,
Located on the Clyde River this historic township still retains many
of its colonial buildings which date back to the beginning of settlement.

Hotels/Motels
★★ **Hamilton Inn**, (LH), Classified by National Trust, Tarleton St, 1km
S of PO, ☎ 03 6286 3204, fax 03 6286 3281, (Multi-stry), 11 rms
[ensuite (7), heat, elec blkts, TV (4), radio, t/c mkg (4), refrig (4)],
lounge (TV), ⊠, cots-fee. **BB** ≆ **$35 - $50**, ≆≆ **$55 - $80**, ≈ **$6 - $16**,
ch con, 4 rooms list only. BC MC VI.

Self Catering Accommodation
★★★★ **McCauleys Cottage**, (Cotg), c1840. Main Rd, Enquire at
Jackson's Emporium, ☎ 03 6286 3258, fax 03 6249 8877, (2 stry gr fl),
1 cotg acc up to 5, (2 bedrm), [shwr, bath, tlt, heat, elec blkts, TV, video,
clock radio, t/c mkg, refrig, cook fac, blkts, doonas, linen, pillows],
w/mach, dryer, lounge firepl, bbq, plygr, cots, breakfast ingredients.
D ≆ **$165**, ≆≆ **$165**, ≈ **$35**, AE BC BTC MC VI.

★★★★ **Over-The-Back Lakeside Accommodation**, (Cotg), 'Curringa'
Lyell Hwy, 4km W of PO, ☎ 03 6286 3332, fax 03 6286 3350, 1 cotg
acc up to 7, (2 bedrm), [shwr, bath, tlt, fire pl, elec blkts, TV, radio,
t/c mkg, refrig, cook fac, micro, blkts, doonas, linen, pillows], w/mach,
dryer, bbq, cots-fee. **D** ≆≆ **$145**, ≈ **$20**, ch con, Firearms not permitted.

★★★★ **Overington's**, (HU), c1836, Arthur St, Enquire at Jackson's
Emporium, ☎ 03 6286 3258, fax 03 6249 8877, (2 stry gr fl), 1 unit
acc up to 8, (4 bedrm), [shwr, bath, tlt, heat (wood heater), cent heat,
elec blkts, TV, clock radio, t/c mkg, refrig, cook fac, blkts, doonas,
linen, pillows], w/mach, dryer, cots, breakfast ingredients. **D** ≆ **$160**,
≆≆ **$160**, ≈ **$25**, AE BC BTC MC VI.

★★★☆ **Hamiltons Historic Cottages**, (Cotg), c1835-45. 'Uralla' Main Rd,
200m N of PO, ☎ 03 6286 3270, 4 cotgs acc up to 5, (1 & 2 bedrm),
[shwr, tlt, fan, fire pl, heat, elec blkts, video-fee, clock radio, t/c mkg,
refrig, cook fac, blkts, linen, pillows], w/mach, bbq, cots-fee, breakfast
ingredients. **D** ≆ **$70**, ≆≆ **$100**, ≈ **$30**, W ≆≆ **$500 - $550**, ch con.

B&B's/Guest Houses
★★★★ **The Old Schoolhouse**, (B&B), c1856. Lyell Hwy, ☎ 03 6286 3292,
fax 03 6286 3369, (2 stry gr fl), 3 rms [ensuite, hairdry, fan,
heat (elec), elec blkts, TV, video, clock radio, CD, t/c mkg], ldry,
lounge firepl, ✕, refrig, meals avail, non smoking property. **BB** ≆ **$99**,
≆≆ **$132**, ≈ **$44**, No facilities for children under 10, BC EFT MC VI.

　★★★☆ **(Principal Cottage)**, 1 cotg acc up to 6, (2 bedrm), [shwr,
tlt, hairdry, fan, heat (elec/wood), elec blkts, TV, clock radio, t/c mkg,
refrig, cook fac, micro, blkts, linen, pillows], ldry, bbq, cots-fee,
breakfast ingredients. **D** ≆≆ **$132**, ≈ **$27.50**, ch con.

HAWLEY BEACH TAS 7307

Pop 420. (266km NW Hobart), See map on page 656, ref C3, Where
housing and the native environment complement each other,
Hawley is a popular holiday spot.

★★★★ **Larooma Cottages**, (HU), Larooma Rd, 2.5km N of Port Sorell PO,
☎ 03 6428 6754, fax 03 6428 6829, 3 units acc up to 8, (1, 2 & 4 bedrm),
[shwr, spa bath (1), tlt, heat (elec/wood), elec blkts, tel, TV, video,
clock radio, CD, t/c mkg, refrig, cook fac, blkts, linen, pillows], w/mach,
bbq, plygr, cots-fee, breakfast ingredients (on request), Pets on application.
D ≆ **$120**, ≆≆ **$135**, ≈ **$22**, W ≆≆ **$750 - $975**, BC EFT MC VI.

★★★ **Hawley Beach Court Villas**, (HU), 16 Dumbleton St,
☎ 03 6428 6744, fax 03 6428 6744, 6 units acc up to 6, (1 & 2 bedrm),
[shwr, tlt, heat, elec blkts, TV, radio, t/c mkg, refrig, cook fac, blkts,
linen, pillows], w/mach, bbq, cots. **D** ≆≆ **$60**, ch con.

HILLWOOD TAS 7252

Pop 350. (233km N Hobart), See map on page 656, ref D4,
Important fruit growing centre. Strawberry Farm and Orchard.
Aviation flights. Local Restaurant. Boat Ramp, Scenic Drives.

B&B's/Guest Houses
★★★☆ **Hillwood Bed & Breakfast**, (B&B), 7 Jacques Rd, 26km N of
Launceston, 24km S of George Town, ☎ 03 6394 8208,
fax 03 6394 8208, 2 rms [ensuite (1), shwr (1), tlt (1), heat,
elec blkts, radio, t/c mkg, doonas], lounge (TV), ✕, bbq. **BLB** ≆ **$50 -**
$70, ≆≆ **$70 - $80**, ≈ **$15.20**, ch con, Dinner by arrangement.

★★★☆ **The Welsh Dragon B&B**, (B&B), 10 Burton St, 1km from PO,
☎ 03 6394 8423, 1 rm [heat (elec), elec blkts, tel, TV, video,
clock radio, radio, doonas], bathrm (2), ldry, ✕, t/c mkg shared, bbq,
cots, non smoking property. **BB** ≆ **$75 - $85**, ≆≆ **$75 - $85**, ≈ **$20**,
ch con, weekly con.

HUONVILLE TAS 7109

Pop 1,524. (38km SW Hobart), See map on page 656, ref C7, Principal
producer of apples and pears in Tasmania. Jet boat rides on the Huon.

Hotels/Motels
★★ **Grand Hotel**, (LH), 2 Main Rd, ☎ 03 6264 1004, fax 03 6464 2301,
(2 stry), 18 rms [elec blkts], lounge (TV), ✕ (lic.), t/c mkg shared,
refrig, cots. **BLB** ≆ **$27.50**, ≆≆ **$40**, ≈ **$10**, BC MC VI.

B&B's/Guest Houses
★★★★ **Constables**, (B&B), 12 Crofton Crt, 1km E of PO, ☎ 03 6264 1691,
fax 03 6264 2002, 1 rm (1 suite) [ensuite, fan, heat (elec), elec blkts,
clock radio], lounge (TV/Video), ✕, bbq, non smoking property, Pets
on application. **BB** ≆ **$65**, ≆≆ **$95**, ch con, AE BC MC VI.

JERICHO TAS 7030

Pop 60. (71km N Hobart), See map on page 656, ref D6, Located
in pastoral and agricultural area with hisoric features.

★★★★ **Commandants Cottage**, (Cotg), Classified by National Trust,
c1842. Park Farm, ☎ 03 6254 4115, fax 03 6254 4137, 1 cotg acc up
to 9, (4 bedrm), [shwr, tlt, heat (floor), elec blkts, TV, t/c mkg, refrig,
cook fac, micro, blkts, linen, pillows], w/mach, dryer, lounge firepl,
plygr, tennis, cots, breakfast ingredients. **D** ≆ **$88**, ≆≆ **$110**, ≈ **$33**,
W ≆ **$528**, ≆≆ **$660**, ≈ **$198**, AE BC MC VI.

★★★ **Rosehill Quarters**, (HU), 'Rosehill' 486 Lower Marshes Rd, 5km
W of PO, ☎ 03 6254 4141, fax 03 6254 4100, 1 unit acc up to 6, (2
bedrm), [shwr, tlt, heat (elec/wood), elec blkts, TV, radio, t/c mkg,
refrig, cook fac, blkts, linen, pillows], w/mach, breakfast ingredients.
D ≆ **$80**, ≆≆ **$105**, ≈ **$30**, weekly con.

KAYENA TAS 7270

Pop 614. (238km N Hobart), See map on page 656, ref D4, Located
35km north of Launceston, close to the West Tamar River with
spectacular views. Batman Bridge (5km).

★★★★☆ **Tamar River Retreat**, (B&B), Kayena Rd, ☎ 03 6394 7030,
fax 03 6394 7030, 4 rms (1 bedrm), [ensuite, spa bath (1), heat,
elec blkts, TV (2), clock radio, refrig (2), cook fac ltd (2), micro (2)],
lounge (TV), ✕, t/c mkg shared, refrig, bbq, meals avail, non smoking
property. **BB** ≆ **$55 - $77**, ≆≆ **$88 - $110**, BC MC VI.

KEMPTON TAS 7030

Pop 342. (49km N Hobart), See map on page 656, ref D6,
Charming and well preserved colonial town first settled in the 1820s.

★★★★ **Wilmot Arms Inn**, (B&B), Classified by National Trust, Main
Rd, 500m N of PO, ☎ 03 6259 1272, fax 03 6259 1396, (2 stry), 4 rms
[ensuite (2), fire pl, cent heat, elec blkts, radio], ldry, breakfast rm,
t/c mkg shared, bbq, meals avail, non smoking rms. **BB** ≆ **$80**, ≆≆ **$100**,
≈ **$25**, ch con, AE BC MC VI.

KETTERING TAS 7155

Pop 295. (37km S Hobart), See map on page 656, ref D7, Marina's
and terminal for the Bruny Island vehicular ferry which crosses
between Kettering and Roberts Point on North Bruny.

Hotels/Motels
★★ **Oyster Cove Inn**, (LH), Ferry Rd, ☎ 03 6267 4446, (2 stry),
10 rms [heat, elec blkts], lounge (TV), conf fac, ⊠, t/c mkg shared,
cots-fee. **BLB** ≆ **$38**, ≆≆ **$65**, ≆≆≆≆ **$100**, AE BC DC MC VI.

Self Catering Accommodation
★★★★ **Herons Rise Vineyard**, (Cotg), Saddle Rd (B68), 1km W of
PO, ☎ 03 6267 4339, 2 cotgs acc up to 4, (Studio & 2 bedrm),
[shwr, bath, tlt, fan, heat (solar/wood), elec blkts, TV, radio, CD,
t/c mkg, refrig, cook fac, blkts, linen, pillows], meals avail, plygr,
cots-fee, breakfast ingredients, non smoking units. **D** ≆ **$100**,
≆≆ **$110 - $125**, ≈ **$20**.

B&B's/Guest Houses
★★★★☆ **Anstey Barton**, (B&B), 82 Ferry Rd, 1km SE of PO,
☎ 03 6267 4199, fax 03 6267 4433, (2 stry gr fl), 3 rms [ensuite,
heat (elec/wood), cent heat, tel, clock radio, radio, ldry],
lounge (TV/video), ✕, bar, bbq, rm serv, c/park. **DBB** ≆ **$300**, ≆≆ **$600**,
≈ **$300**, AE BC MC VI.

★★★★ **The Old Kettering Inn**, (B&B), c1894. 58 Ferry Rd, 1km E of
PO, ☎ 03 6267 4426, fax 03 6267 4884, 1 rm (1 suite) [ensuite, heat,
elec blkts, TV, radio, t/c mkg, refrig, doonas], lounge (TV/video),
lounge firepl, bbq, non smoking rms. **BB** ≆ **$85**, ≆≆ **$98**, ≈ **$25 - $30**.

KING ISLAND TAS 7256

Pop 1,762. See map on page 656, ref A1, King Island is about 110,000 hectares in area and ranges from sandy beaches to pockets of rain forest. From the air the island resembes a patchwork quilt of various greens.

Hotels/Motels

★★★☆ **Boomerang by the Sea**, (M), Golf Club Rd, Currie 7256, 500m from PO, ☎ 03 6462 1288, fax 03 6462 1607, (gr fl) 16 units [shwr, tlt, hairdry, heat, elec blkts, TV, video-fee, clock radio, t/c mkg, refrig], ldry, ⊠, bbq. BLB ♦ $77 - $88, ♦♦ $99 - $132, ♀ $17, AE BC DC EFT MC VI.

★★★☆ **King Island Gem Motel**, (M), 95 Main St, Currie 7256, 1.5km N of PO, ☎ 03 6462 1260, fax 03 6462 1563, 10 units [shwr, tlt, cent heat, tel, TV, clock radio, t/c mkg, refrig], ldry, bbq, rm serv, courtesy transfer, cots. BLB ♦ $70 - $90, ♦♦ $90 - $110, ♀ $16.50, ch con, BC MC VI.

★★★☆ **(A-Frame Holiday Homes)**, (2 stry), 3 units acc up to 6, (3 bedrm), [shwr, tlt, heat, TV, radio, t/c mkg, refrig, cook fac, blkts, doonas, linen, pillows], w/mach. D ♦ $110, ♦♦ $110, ♀ $20, W ♦ $660, ♦♦ $660, ♀ $120, ch con.

★★★ **Parers**, (LH), 7 Main St, Currie 7256, ☎ 03 6462 1633, fax 03 6462 1655, 13 rms [shwr, tlt, heat, tel, TV, video, t/c mkg], ⊠, cots. BLB ♦ $66 - $77, ♦♦ $88 - $110, ♀ $11 - $33, ch con, 1 room yet to be rated. AE BC DC EFT MC VI.

Self Catering Accommodation

★★★★☆ **Shannon Coastal Cottage**, (HU), Previously Shannon Cottages Charles St, Currie 7256, 3km N of PO, ☎ 03 6462 1370, fax 03 6462 1370, 1 unit acc up to 6, (2 bedrm), [shwr, tlt, heat (gas), elec blkts, tel, fax, TV, video, radio, t/c mkg, refrig, cook fac, micro, blkts, linen, pillows], w/mach, dryer, spa, breakfast ingredients, non smoking property, Pets on application. D ♦♦ $143, ♦♦♦♦ $152.90, ♀ $33, ch con, Min book applies. BC MC VI.

★★★★ **Baudins Cottages & Restaurant**, (Cotg), The Esplanade, Naracoopa 7256, 25km E of Currie PO, ☎ 03 6461 1110, fax 03 6461 1110, 4 cotgs acc up to 6, (1 & 2 bedrm), [spa bath (1), heat (elec), elec blkts, TV, video, clock radio, CD, t/c mkg, refrig, cook fac, doonas, linen, pillows], ldry, ⊠ (Lounge Bar), bbq, cots, breakfast ingredients (Continental). D ♦ $99 - $121, ♦♦ $110 - $154, ♀ $39, ch con, Min book applies. AE BC MC VI.

★★★★ **Wave-Watcher**, (HU), Lot 18, Beach Rd, Currie 7256, 800m SW of PO, ☎ 03 6462 1517, fax 03 6462 1517, (2 stry gr fl), 2 units acc up to 3, (1 bedrm), [shwr, tlt, fan, cent heat, elec blkts, TV, video, t/c mkg, refrig, cook fac, blkts, linen, pillows], w/mach, bbq, courtesy transfer, cots, breakfast ingredients. D ♦ $120, ♦♦ $148, ♀ $32, Min book applies, AE BC MC VI.

★★★☆ **Naracoopa Holiday Units**, (HU), 25km E of Currie, ☎ 03 6461 1326, fax 03 6461 1326, 2 units acc up to 7, (Studio & 2 bedrm), [shwr, tlt, heat (gas), TV, radio, t/c mkg, refrig, cook fac (gas), blkts, linen, pillows], ldry, rec rm, bbq, cots-fee. D ♦ $68, ♦♦ $90, ♀ $22, ch con, Min book applies.

★★★☆ **St. Andrews-King Island**, (HU), Netherby Rd, Currie 7256, 500m S of Currie PO, ☎ 03 6462 1490, fax 03 6462 1621, 1 unit acc up to 6, (3 bedrm), [spa bath, heat (wood), tel, TV, video, radio, t/c mkg, refrig, cook fac, micro, blkts, linen, pillows], w/mach, dryer, bbq, cots, Pets on application. D ♦ $110, ♦♦ $110, ♀ $22, ch con.

★★★ **Gullhaven**, (HU), 11 Huxley St, Currie 7256, ☎ 03 6462 1560, fax 03 6462 1453, 1 unit acc up to 8, (4 bedrm), [shwr, tlt, elec blkts, TV, video, refrig, cook fac, micro, blkts, linen, pillows], w/mach, iron, cots. D ♦ $40, ♦♦ $72, ♀ $25, ch con.

B&B's/Guest Houses

★★★☆ **Yarra Creek Host Farm**, (B&B), 49 Bold Head Rd, Yarra Creek, 27km SE of Currie PO, ☎ 03 6461 1276, fax 03 6461 1076, 2 rms [shwr (private bathroom), tlt, heat, tel, refrig], ldry, lounge (TV), ✕, t/c mkg shared, bbq, meals avail, cots, non smoking rms. BB ♦ $77, ♦♦ $90, ch con.

★★★ **King Island Colonial Lodge**, (B&B), 13 Main St, Currie 7256, 150m N of Currie PO, ☎ 03 6462 1066, fax 03 6462 1067, (2 stry), 6 rms [heat (elec), elec blkts, clock radio, t/c mkg, refrig, ldry], lounge (TV), c/park. BLB ♦ $57, ♦♦ $67.

★★★ **King Island Holiday Village**, (B&B), Blue Gum Dr, Grassy 7256, ☎ 03 6461 1177, fax 03 6461 1387, 10 rms [heat, elec blkts], lounge (TV), t/c mkg shared, refrig, c/park. BLB ♦ $40 - $209, ♦♦ $80 - $209, ♀ $28 - $85, BC DC MC VI.

★★★★ **(Holiday Unit Section)**, 7 units acc up to 6, (2 & 3 bedrm), [spa bath (5), fan, heat, elec blkts, TV, video, clock radio, CD, t/c mkg, refrig, cook fac, blkts, linen, pillows], w/mach, dryer, bbq, cots-fee, breakfast ingredients. D ♦ $110, ♦♦ $110 - $209, ♀ $28 - $64, 1 unit ★★★★☆.

KINGSTON TAS 7050

Pop 12,907. (12km S Hobart), See map on page 656, ref D7, Now a major residential area and administrative centre for the Kingborough Municipality.

Hotels/Motels

★★★☆ **Welcome Inn**, (M), Kingston View Dve, 2km W of PO, ☎ 03 6229 4800, fax 03 6229 3454, 20 units [shwr, spa bath (4), tlt, heat, tel, TV, t/c mkg, refrig], ldry, conv fac, ⊠, sauna, spa, rm serv, cots. RO ♦♦ $80 - $100, ♀ $11, ch con, AE BC EFT MC VI.

★★★ **Kingston Beach Motel**, (M), 31 Osborne Espl, Kingston Beach 7050, 500m S of PO, ☎ 03 6229 8969, fax 03 6229 8969, 4 units [ensuite, fan, heat (elec), elec blkts, TV, clock radio, t/c mkg, refrig, cook fac, micro, doonas], ldry, bbq, cots. RO ♦ $65, ♦♦ $75 - $95, ♀ $15, ch con, weekly con.

Self Catering Accommodation

★★★☆ **On The Beach**, (HU), 38 Osborne Esp, Kingston Beach 7050, 500m S of PO, ☎ 03 6229 3096, fax 03 6229 3096, 1 unit acc up to 4, (1 bedrm), [shwr, tlt, fan, heat (elec), elec blkts, TV, clock radio, CD, t/c mkg, refrig, cook fac, micro, blkts, linen, pillows], ldry, bbq, non smoking property. D ♦ $70, ♦♦ $80, ♀ $15, ch con, weekly con, BC MC VI.

★★★☆ **Recreation Cottage**, (Cotg), 4 Recreation St, Kingston Beach 7050, 500m S of PO, ☎ 03 6229 1940, 1 cotg acc up to 4, (2 bedrm), [shwr, tlt, heat (elec), elec blkts, TV, radio, t/c mkg, refrig, cook fac, blkts, linen, pillows], w/mach, cots, breakfast ingredients, non smoking property. D ♦ $60 - $70, ♦♦ $75 - $85, ♀ $15, ch con, weekly con.

B&B's/Guest Houses

★★★☆ **Tranquilla**, (B&B), 30 Osborne Esp, 500m S of PO, ☎ 03 6229 6282, fax 03 6229 6282, 2 rms [fan, heat, elec blkts, TV, clock radio, t/c mkg, refrig, cook fac (1), toaster (1)], bathrm, ldry, cots. RO ♦ $70, ♦♦ $80, ♀ $20, ch con.

KOONYA TAS 7187

Pop 229. (93km SE Hobart), See map on page 656, ref D7, Small township overlooking Norfolk Bay. Once an important outpost for timber milling.

Self Catering Accommodation

★★★★ **Cascades**, (Cotg), No children's facilities, 533 Main Rd, 5km fr Taranna, ☎ 03 6250 3873, fax 03 6250 3013, 4 cotgs acc up to 2, (1 bedrm), [shwr, tlt, fan, fire pl, elec blkts, TV, clock radio, t/c mkg, refrig, cook fac, blkts, doonas, linen, pillows], breakfast ingredients. D ♦ $95 - $122, ♦♦ $104 - $132, ♀ $16 - $22.

B&B's/Guest Houses

Norfolk Bayview Bed & Breakfast, (B&B), RA111 Nubeena Rd, 1.11km W of Arthur Hwy, ☎ 03 6250 3855, fax 03 6250 3855, (gr fl), 4 rms [elec blkts, doonas], lounge firepl, breakfast rm, t/c mkg shared, cots, non smoking rms. BB ♦♦ $55 - $65, BC EFT MC VI, (not yet classified).

Other Accommodation

Seaview Lodge, (Bunk), 96ha property, 732 Nubeena Back Rd, Located on the (C343) via the Main Rd, ☎ 03 6250 2766, 1 bunkhouse acc up to 70, [micro, blkts, linen-fee, pillows], shwr (6), tlt (6), rec rm, conv fac, lounge firepl, ✕, cook fac, t/c mkg shared, refrig, bbq, meals avail, plygr, cots, Pets on application. RO ♦ $16.50, ♦♦ $38.50, ch con, BC MC VI.

LAKE LEAKE TAS 7210

Pop 241. (168km NE Hobart), See map on page 656, ref E5, Best known for its trout fishing and game farm. Scenic Drives.

Hotels/Motels

★★ **Lake Leake Chalet**, (LH), c1912. Lake Leake Hwy, via Campbell Town, ☎ 03 6381 1329, fax 03 6381 1329, 6 rms [heat, elec blkts], ldry, lounge (TV), t/c mkg shared, bbq, plygr. BLB ♦ $38, ♦♦ $55, ♦♦♦♦ $70, ch con.

Self Catering Accommodation

★★★ **Currawong Lakes Evansville**, (HU), Long Marsh Rd, via Campbell Town, ☎ 03 6381 1148, fax 03 6381 1148, 4 units acc up to 6, (2 bedrm), [shwr, tlt, heat (wood), clock radio, t/c mkg, refrig, cook fac, blkts, linen, pillows], w/mach, bbq, cots-fee. D ♦ $80, ♦♦ $80, ♀ $40, ch con.

LATROBE TAS 7307

*Pop 2,551. (273km NW Hobart), See map on page 656, ref C4,
Officially the 'Platypus Capital of the World', Latrobe is the ideal base
for the eco-tourist Warrawee Forest Reserve.*

Hotels/Motels

★★★☆ **Latrobe Motel**, (M), 1 Palmers Rd, 1km N of PO,
☎ 03 6426 2030, fax 03 6426 2060, 6 units [shwr, tlt,
heat, elec blkts, TV, radio, t/c mkg, refrig, cook fac (2)],
ldry, bbq, cots. RO ♦ $55, ♦♦ $65, ◊ $10, ch con, AE BC
DC EFT MC VI.

★★★☆ **Lucas**, (LH), Classified by National Trust, 46 Gilbert St,
☎ 03 6426 1101, (2 stry), 9 rms [ensuite (4), spa bath (1), heat,
elec blkts, tel, TV, refrig], ldry, lounge (TV), ⊠, c/park. BLB ♦♦ $110,
D ♦♦ $90, 4 rooms ★★★★.

★ **Mackeys Royal**, (LH), 161 Gilbert St, ☎ 03 6426 1142, (2 stry),
13 rms [heat, elec blkts, refrig], ldry, lounge (TV), ⊠ (Tues to Sun),
t/c mkg shared, cots. RO ♦ $27.50, ♦♦ $33, ◊ $11, ch con, BC MC VI.

Self Catering Accommodation

★★★☆ **Colonial Cottage of Latrobe**, (Cotg), Platypus Creek Cottage.
c1869. 11 Hamilton St, 500m fr PO, ☎ 03 6426 2717, fax 03 6426 2733,
1 cotg acc up to 4, (2 & 3 bedrm), [shwr, tlt, heat (elec/wood), elec blkts,
TV, radio, t/c mkg, refrig, cook fac, blkts, linen, pillows], w/mach, dryer,
bbq, cots, breakfast ingredients. D ♦ $90, ♦♦ $137.50, ◊ $33, W ♦ $550,
♦♦ $770, ◊ $231.

B&B's/Guest Houses

★★★★ **Lucinda**, (B&B), Classified by National Trust, c1891, 17 Forth St,
☎ 03 6426 2285, 5 rms [ensuite, spa bath (1), hairdry, heat, elec blkts,
TV, clock radio, t/c mkg], lounge, bar, non smoking rms. BB ♦ $85,
♦♦ $95 - $120, ◊ $25, ch con, AE BC DC MC VI.

LAUNCESTON TAS 7250

*Pop 66,747. (198km N Hobart), See map on page 656, ref D4,
Founded in 1805, Launceston is Australia's third oldest city.*

Hotels/Motels

★★★★☆ **Country Club Casino**, (LH), Country Club Ave,
Prospect Vale 7250, 8km SW of Launceston, ☎ 03 6335 5777,
fax 03 6335 5788, (Multi-stry gr fl) 104 rms (16 suites)
[shwr, spa bath (12), tlt, a/c, cent heat, tel, TV, movie,
clock radio, t/c mkg, refrig], lift, rec rm, conv fac, ⊠, bar,
pool indoor heated, sauna, spa, bbq, rm serv, golf, gym, squash, tennis,
cots. RO ♦ $255 - $275, ♦♦ $255 - $275, ◊ $30, Suite D ♦♦ $339 - $439,
ch con, AE BC DC MC VI.

★★★★☆ **Novotel Launceston**, (LH), 29 Cameron St, 300m E of PO,
☎ 03 6334 3434, fax 03 6331 7347, (Multi-stry), 162 rms (7 suites)
[shwr, bath, spa bath (2), tlt, hairdry, cent heat, tel, TV, movie, clock
radio, t/c mkg, refrig, mini bar], lift, ldry, iron, iron brd, conf fac, ⊠,
24hr reception, rm serv, c/park (undercover), cots, non smoking rms
(136). RO ♦ $164, ♦♦ $164, ◊ $33, Suite RO ♦♦ $249 - $459, AE BC DC
JCB MC VI, Partial Access

★★★★ **Coach House Motor Inn**, (M), 10
York St, 1km E of PO, ☎ 03 6331 5311,
fax 03 6334 1305, (Multi-stry gr fl), 31 units
(2 suites) [shwr, bath, tlt, hairdry, heat,
elec blkts, tel, TV, radio, t/c mkg, refrig, mini bar, toaster], ldry, iron,
iron brd, ⊠, bar, rm serv, cots, non smoking rms (12). RO ♦ $103 - $113,
♦♦ $103 - $113, ◊ $11, Suite RO ♦ $123, ♦♦ $123, ch con, 14 rooms
of a 3.5 star rating, AE BC DC MC MP VI.

★★★★ **Colonial Motor Inn**, (LH), Classified by National Trust,
c1847. 31 Elizabeth St, 1km S of PO, ☎ 03 6331 6588,
fax 03 6334 2765, (Multi-stry gr fl), 64 rms (2 suites)
[shwr, tlt, heat, elec blkts, tel, TV, movie, t/c mkg,
refrig], ldry, conv fac, ⊠, bar, rm serv, cots, non smoking rms (48).
RO ♦ $99 - $145, ♦♦ $99 - $145, ◊ $25, Suite RO ♦♦ $155 - $235,
ch con, AE BC DC MC VI.

★★★★ **Commodore Regent Motor Inn**, (M), 13 Brisbane St,
1km E of PO, ☎ 03 6331 4666, fax 03 6331 5707, (2 stry
gr fl), 43 units [shwr, tlt, heat, elec blkts, tel, TV, movie,
clock radio, t/c mkg, mini bar], ldry, ⊠, rm serv, cots.
RO ♦ $109, ♦♦ $129, ◊ $15, ch con, AE BC DC VI.

★★★★ **(Unit Section)**, 2 units acc up to 4, (2 bedrm), [shwr, tlt,
heat, elec blkts, tel, TV, movie, clock radio, t/c mkg, refrig, cook fac,
blkts, linen, pillows]. D ♦♦♦♦ $140.

Launceston International Hotel
LAUNCESTON

29 Cameron Street
Launceston TAS 7250
Phone: 03 6334 3434 Fax: 03 6331 7347
Email: res.launceston@dohertyhotels.com.au

AAA TOURISM
★★★★☆

(Refer to listing under Novotel
Launceston - name change to
Launceston International 01/02/01)

★★★★ **Country Club Villas**, (LH), 10 Casino Rise, Prospect Vale 7250,
8km SW of Launceston, ☎ 03 6343 1744, fax 03 6344 9943, 65 rms
(65 suites) [shwr, spa bath (24), tlt, hairdry, fire pl (4), heat, elec blkts,
tel, TV, clock radio, t/c mkg, refrig, cook fac (18), cook fac ltd (40),
micro (40)], ldry, conv fac, ⊠, bar, pool indoor heated, sauna, spa,
24hr reception, plygr, golf, tennis, cots, non smoking rms (16).
RO ♦♦ $150, ♦♦♦♦ $182, Suite RO ♦♦ $280, ch con, 4 suites yet to be
rated. AE BC DC MC VI.

★★★★ **(Cottage Section)**, 8 cotgs acc up to 6, (2 & 3 bedrm), [shwr,
tlt, heat, elec blkts, tel, TV, clock radio, t/c mkg, refrig, cook fac, blkts,
linen, pillows], w/mach, dryer. D $195 - $238, ch con.

★★★★ **Great Northern**, (LH), 3 Earl St, 1km NE of PO,
☎ 03 6331 9999, fax 03 6331 3712, (Multi-stry),
114 rms (2 suites) [shwr, bath, tlt, heat, elec blkts,
tel, TV, movie, radio, t/c mkg, refrig, mini bar], lift,
ldry, conv fac, ⊠ (5 days), rm serv (limited), cots, non smoking
flr (3). RO ♦ $85, ♦♦ $85, ◊ $15, Suite RO ♦♦ $135, ch con, AE BC
DC MC VI, ♦&.

★★★★ **Prince Albert Inn**, (M), Classified by National
Trust, c1855. 22 Tamar St, 500m fr PO, ☎ 03 6331 7633,
fax 03 6334 1579, (Multi-stry), 22 units [shwr, spa bath (11),
tlt, a/c (12), heat, elec blkts, tel, TV, t/c mkg, mini bar],
ldry, cots-fee, non smoking property. RO ♦♦ $148.50 - $184.80, ◊ $22, ♦&.

★★★☆ **Abel Tasman Airport Motor Inn**, (M), 303 Hobart Rd,
Kings Meadows 7249, 4.5km S of Launceston, ☎ 03 6344 5244,
fax 03 6343 1930, 42 units [shwr, tlt, hairdry, fan, heat,
elec blkts, tel, TV, cable TV (free), radio, t/c mkg, refrig,
toaster], ldry, iron, rec rm, conv fac, ⊠, rm serv, plygr, cots-fee.
BLB ♦ $85, ♦♦ $90, D $150, ch con, AE BC DC MC VI.

★★★☆ **Balmoral Motor Inn**, (M), 19 York St, 500m SE
of PO, ☎ 03 6331 8000, fax 03 6334 1870, (Multi-stry),
36 units [shwr, tlt, heat, elec blkts, tel, TV, video,
clock radio, t/c mkg, refrig, mini bar], lift, ldry, iron,
iron brd, conv fac, ⊠ (Mon to Sat), rm serv, cots. BLB ♦ $78 - $124,
♦♦ $94 - $141, ◊ $24, RO ♦ $70 - $115, ♦♦ $78 - $123, ◊ $15,
ch con, AE BC DC MC VI, ♦&.

★★★☆ **Elphin Villas**, (M), 29A Elphin Rd, 500m E of PO,
☎ 03 6334 2233, fax 03 6334 2045, 12 units [shwr, bath, tlt, hairdry (8),
heat, elec blkts, tel, TV, clock radio, CD (8), t/c mkg, refrig, micro],
ldry, cots. BLB ♦♦ $132 - $155, ◊ $28, BC MC VI, ♦&.

★★★★ **(Holiday Unit Section)**, 8 units acc up to 7, (Studio & 3
bedrm), [shwr, bath, spa bath (1), tlt, hairdry, heat, elec blkts, tel, TV,
clock radio, refrig, cook fac, blkts, linen, pillows]. BLB ♦♦ $132 - $185,
◊ $28, Suite BLB ♦♦ $218.

★★★☆ **Olde Tudor Motor Inn**, (M), Westbury Rd, Prospect Vale 7250, 6km
SW of Launceston, ☎ 03 6344 5044, fax 03 6344 1774, 42 units [shwr, spa
bath, tlt, heat, elec blkts, tel, TV, cable TV, radio, t/c mkg, refrig], ldry,
conv fac, ⊠ (Mon to Sat), pool indoor heated, sauna, bbq, rm serv, plygr,
tennis (half court), cots. RO ♦♦ $104, ◊ $27, AE BC DC EFT MC VI.

★★★☆ **(Unit Section)**, 8 units (1 & 2 bedrm), [shwr, tlt, heat,
elec blkts, tel, TV, radio, t/c mkg, refrig, cook fac, pillows], w/mach,
dryer. D ♦♦ $126, ◊ $27, ch con.

★★★☆ **Parklane**, (M), 9 Brisbane St, 1km E of PO, ☎ 03 6331 4233, fax 03 6334 0694, 23 units (2 suites) [shwr, bath, tlt, heat, elec blkts, tel, TV, radio, t/c mkg, refrig, toaster], ldry, spa, rm serv, cots. **RO** ♦ **$66 - $71.50**, ♦♦ **$77 - $82.50**, ◊ **$11, Suite RO** ♦♦ **$99 - $110**, ch con, AE BC DC MC VI.

★★★☆ **(City Court Villas)**, 18 units acc up to 5, [shwr, bath, spa bath (2), tlt, heat, elec blkts, tel, TV, radio, t/c mkg, refrig, cook fac, blkts, linen, pillows], c/park. **D** ♦ **$82.50 - $93.50**, ♦♦ **$82.50 - $93.50**, ◊ **$11 - $16.50**, **W** ♦ **$517 - $539**, ♦♦ **$517 - $539**, ch con.

★★★☆ **Penny Royal Watermill**, (M), Classified by National Trust, 147 Paterson St, 1.5km W of PO, ☎ 03 6331 6699, fax 03 6334 4282, (Multi-stry gr fl), 33 units [shwr, tlt, heat, elec blkts, tel, TV, radio, t/c mkg, refrig, mini bar], ldry, conv fac, ⊠, bar, rm serv, cots. **RO** ♦♦ **$127**, ◊ **$30**, ch con, AE BC DC MC VI.

★★★☆ **(Holiday Unit Section)**, (2 stry gr fl), 33 units acc up to 10, (1 & 4 bedrm), [shwr, tlt, heat, elec blkts, tel, TV, radio, t/c mkg, refrig, cook fac, blkts, linen, pillows], c/park. **D** ♦♦ **$126**, ◊ **$30**, ch con.

★★★☆ **Sandors On The Park**, (LH), 3 Brisbane St, 1km NE of PO, ☎ 03 6331 2055, fax 03 6334 3910, (2 stry), 70 rms [shwr, bath, tlt, hairdry, a/c-cool, elec blkts, tel, fax, TV, movie, radio, t/c mkg, refrig], ldry, iron, iron brd, conv fac, ⊠, bar (cafe/bistro), rm serv, cots. **RO** ♦ **$75 - $90**, ♦♦ **$80 - $95**, ◊ **$15**, ch con, AE BC DC MC VI.

 ★★★☆ **The Old Bakery Inn**, (M), Classified by National Trust, c1870. Cnr York & Margaret Sts, ☎ 03 6331 7900, fax 03 6331 7756, (2 stry gr fl), 24 units (1 suite) [shwr, tlt, heat, elec blkts, tel, TV, radio, t/c mkg, refrig, mini bar, cook fac (2)], ldry, ⊠ (Mon to Sat), rm serv, cots, non smoking property. **RO** ♦ **$120 - $130**, ♦♦ **$120 - $130**, ◊ **$25**, ch con, AE BC DC MC VI.

★★★ **Hotel Tasmania**, (LH), 191 Charles St, 500m S of PO, ☎ 03 6331 7355, fax 03 6331 2414, (2 stry), 25 rms [shwr, tlt, fan, heat (9), cent heat (16), elec blkts, tel, TV, t/c mkg, refrig], ⊠, cots. **BLB** ♦ **$50 - $55**, ♦♦ **$64 - $70**, ◊ **$15**, ch con, BC EFT MC VI.

★★★ **Mews**, (M), Classified by National Trust, 89 Margaret St, 2km SW of PO, ☎ 03 6331 2861, fax 03 6331 2861, 6 units [shwr, tlt, fan, heat, elec blkts, TV, clock radio, t/c mkg, refrig], ⬎. **BLB** ♦ **$55 - $60**, ♦♦ **$68 - $75**.

 ★★★ **Riverside Hotel Motel**, (LMH), 407 West Tamar Hwy, Riverside 7250, 4.5km NW of Launceston, ☎ 03 6327 2522, fax 03 6327 3709, (2 stry), 27 units [shwr, tlt, heat, elec blkts, tel, TV, movie, radio, t/c mkg, refrig], ldry, ⊠, rm serv, cots, non smoking rms (4). **BLB** ♦ **$95**, ♦♦ **$95**, ◊ **$15**, ch con, AE BC DC MC VI.

★★★ **(Unit Section)**, 10 units [shwr, bath, tlt, heat, elec blkts, tel, TV, movie, radio, t/c mkg, refrig, micro, pillows]. **BLB** ♦ **$100**, ♦♦ **$100**, ◊ **$15**, ch con.

★★★ **Village Family Motor Inn**, (M), Westbury Rd, 5km SW of Launceston, ☎ 03 6343 1777, fax 03 6343 1574, 24 units [shwr, tlt, heat, elec blkts, tel, TV, radio, t/c mkg, refrig], ldry, rec rm, conv fac, pool indoor heated, sauna, spa, rm serv, courtesy transfer, plygr, cots. **BLB** ♦♦ **$99**, ◊ **$30**, ch con, AE BC DC MC VI.

★★★☆ **(Holiday Unit Section)**, (2 stry gr fl), 10 units acc up to 5, (2 bedrm), [shwr, tlt, heat, elec blkts, tel, TV, clock radio, t/c mkg, refrig, cook fac, blkts, linen, pillows], c/park. **D** ♦♦ **$125**, ◊ **$30**, ch con.

 ★★☆ **Archers Manor**, (LH), 17 Alanvale Rd, Newnham 7248, 2km N of Launceston, ☎ 03 6326 3600, fax 03 6324 6313, 12 rms [ensuite, heat (elec), elec blkts, tel, TV, clock radio, t/c mkg, refrig, micro], ldry, conv fac, ⊠, cots. **RO** ♦ **$75**, ♦♦ **$85**, ◊ **$17**, ch con, AE BC BTC DC EFT MC VI.

★★★ **(Apartment Section)**, 38 apts acc up to 6, (1, 2 & 3 bedrm), [shwr, tlt, heat (elec), tel, TV, t/c mkg, refrig, cook fac, micro, blkts, linen, pillows], w/mach, dryer, cots. **D** ♦ **$99 - $150**, ♦♦ **$99 - $150**.

Batman Fawkner Inn, (LH), 35 Cameron St, 300m fr PO, ☎ 03 6331 7222, fax 03 6331 7158, (2 stry), 38 rms [shwr, bath (5), tlt, heat (electric), elec blkts, tel, TV, clock radio, t/c mkg, refrig], conf fac, ⊠ (4 days), c/park (undercover) (6), non smoking rms (5). **RO** ♦ **$38 - $50**, ♦♦ **$71 - $85**, ◊ **$10**, ch con, AE BC DC EFT MC VI.

Sportsman Hall, (LH), Classified by National Trust, 252 Charles St, 500m N of Hospital, ☎ 03 6331 3968, 6 rms [heat, elec blkts, refrig, ldry], lounge (TV), ⊠, t/c mkg shared, cots-fee. **BLB** ♦ **$30**, ♦♦ **$50**, **RO** ♦ **$12**.

Self Catering Accommodation

★★★★☆ **Elphin Gardens**, (SA), 47 Elphin Rd, 1km E of PO, ☎ 03 6334 5988, fax 03 6334 5588, (2 stry gr fl), 8 serv apts acc up to 7, (Studio, 1, 2 & 3 bedrm), [shwr, bath, spa bath (1), tlt, heat, elec blkts, tel, TV, video, clock radio, CD, t/c mkg, refrig, mini bar, cook fac, micro, d/wash, blkts, linen, pillows], ldry, c/park (undercover), cots-fee, breakfast ingredients. **BLB** ♦♦ **$186 - $228**, ◊ **$40**, ch con, Min book Christmas and Jan.

★★★★ **Adina Place**, (HU), 50 York St, 1km E of PO, ☎ 03 6331 6866, fax 03 6331 2822, (Multi-stry gr fl), 30 units acc up to 5, (1 & 2 bedrm), [shwr, spa bath (8), tlt, heat (elec), elec blkts, tel, TV, cable TV, t/c mkg, refrig, cook fac, blkts, linen, pillows], lift, ldry, bbq, cots. **D** ♦ **$95 - $105**, ♦♦ **$95 - $120**, ◊ **$17**, ch con, 8 rooms of a lower rating. AE BC DC MC VI.

★★★★ **Alices Cottages**, (Cotg), Classified by National Trust, c1840, Office: 129 Balfour St, ☎ 03 6334 2231, fax 03 6334 2696, 4 cotgs acc up to 2, (1 bedrm), [shwr, bath, tlt, heat, elec blkts, TV, radio, t/c mkg, refrig, cook fac, blkts, linen, pillows], w/mach, dryer, lounge firepl, breakfast ingredients. **D** ♦♦ **$154 - $157**.

★★★★ **Alices Spa Hideaways**, (Cotg), No children's facilities, Office: 129 Balfour St, ☎ 03 6334 2231, fax 03 6334 2696, 7 cotgs acc up to 6, (1 & 2 bedrm), [shwr, spa bath, tlt, heat (elec/wood), elec blkts, TV, video (on request), clock radio, CD, t/c mkg, refrig, cook fac, micro, d/wash, blkts, linen, pillows], w/mach, dryer, lounge firepl, breakfast ingredients, Pets on application. **D** ♦♦ **$187 - $220**, ◊ **$55**.

★★★★ **Bass Villas**, (Villa), 1 Casino Rise, Prospect Vale 7250, Next to Country Club Casino, ☎ 03 6344 7259, fax 03 6344 1127, 3 villas acc up to 6, (2 bedrm), [tel, TV, ldry], c/park (undercover). **D** ♦♦ **$110**, ♦♦♦♦ **$160**, ◊ **$30**, ch con, BC MC VI.

★★★★ **Brickfields Terrace**, (Cotg), c1889. 68 Margaret St, 2km S of PO, ☎ 03 6331 0963, fax 03 6331 7778, (2 stry gr fl), 1 cotg acc up to 4, (2 bedrm), [shwr, tlt, hairdry, heat (wood/off peak/elec), elec blkts, tel, TV, clock radio, radio, t/c mkg, refrig, cook fac, micro, blkts, linen, pillows], w/mach, dryer, cots, breakfast ingredients, non smoking property. **D** ♦ **$132**, ♦♦ **$144 - $158**, ◊ **$37 - $41**, AE BC DC MC VI.

★★★★ **Cottages on the Park**, (Cotg), c1890. 35 Cimitiere St, 500m E of PO, ☎ 03 6334 2238, fax 03 6334 5061, 2 cotgs acc up to 5, (2 bedrm), [shwr, bath, tlt, hairdry, heat (wood), elec blkts, tel, TV, video, clock radio, CD, t/c mkg, refrig, cook fac, micro, doonas, linen, pillows], w/mach, dryer, cots, breakfast ingredients, non smoking units, Pets on application. **D** ♦ **$110 - $120**, ♦♦ **$145 - $159**, ◊ **$38.50**, ch con, AE BC MC VI.

★★★★ **York Mansions**, (HU), Classified by National Trust, c1840. No children's facilities, 9 York St, 675m SE of GPO, ☎ 03 6334 2933, fax 03 6334 2870, (Multi-stry gr fl), 5 units acc up to 6, (2 & 3 bedrm), [shwr, bath, spa bath (some), tlt, hairdry, fire pl, heat, elec blkts, tel, TV, clock radio, t/c mkg, refrig, cook fac, micro, blkts, doonas, linen, pillows], w/mach, dryer, iron, bbq, breakfast ingredients. **D** ♦ **$178 - $226**, ♦♦ **$178 - $226**, ◊ **$55**, AE BC DC MC VI.

★★★☆ **Apartments 1930 Style**, (HU), 70 Penquite Rd, Newstead 7250, 3km E of Launceston, ☎ 03 6344 6953, fax 03 6344 6953, 2 units acc up to 5, (1 & 2 bedrm), [shwr, bath (1), tlt, heat (elec/gas), elec blkts, TV, clock radio, t/c mkg, refrig, cook fac, micro, blkts, linen, pillows], ldry, bbq, cots, Pets on application. **D** ♦ **$55 - $60**, ♦♦ **$60 - $72**, ◊ **$15**, **W** ♦ **$330 - $396**, ♦♦ **$360 - $432**, ◊ **$90**, ch con.

★★★☆ **Clarke Holiday House**, (Cotg), 19 Neika Ave, 2km SW of PO, ☎ 03 6334 2237, 1 cotg acc up to 6, (3 bedrm), [shwr, bath, tlt, fan, heat (elec/off peak), elec blkts, TV, radio, refrig, cook fac, micro, blkts, linen, pillows], w/mach, bbq, plygr, cots. **D** ♦ **$35 - $40**, ♦♦ **$40 - $50**, ◊ **$7 - $10**, ch con.

★★★☆ **Glebe Cottages**, (Cotg), Classified by National Trust, 14A Cimitiere St, 1km NE of PO, ☎ 03 6334 3688, fax 03 6334 0934, (2 stry gr fl), 2 cotgs acc up to 6, (2 & 3 bedrm), [shwr, bath, spa bath, tlt, a/c-cool, a/c, fire pl, heat (elec/wood), elec blkts, TV, radio, t/c mkg, refrig, cook fac, micro, blkts, linen, pillows], w/mach, dryer, cots, Pets on application. **D** ♦ **$92**, ♦♦ **$103**, ◊ **$28**, ch con, AE BC VI.

★★★☆ **Highbury**, (HU), c1856, 97 Arthur St, 600m E of PO, ☎ 03 6331 8767, fax 03 6391 9181, 6 units acc up to 4, (1 & 2 bedrm), [shwr, tlt, heat (elec), elec blkts, TV, clock radio, t/c mkg, refrig, cook fac, blkts, linen, pillows], w/mach, dryer. **D** ♦ **$85 - $95**, ♦♦ **$95 - $120**, ◊ **$15**, ch con, weekly con.

LAUNCESTON TAS continued...

★★★☆ **Tamar River Villas**, (HU), 23 Elouera St, Riverside 7250, 3km NW of Launceston, ☎ 03 6327 1022, fax 03 6327 2626, (2 stry gr fl), 20 units [shwr, bath, tlt, heat, elec blkts, tel, fax, cable TV, movie, radio, t/c mkg, refrig, cook fac], ldry, conv fac, bbq, rm serv, plygr, cots. **RO** ♦ **$99.70**, ◊ **$11.50**, ch con, AE BC DC JCB MC MP VI, ⚷&.

★★★☆ **(Apartment Section)**, 10 units acc up to 6, (2 bedrm), [shwr, tlt, heat, elec blkts, tel, cable TV, movie (free), radio, t/c mkg, refrig, cook fac, blkts, linen, pillows]. **D** ♦♦ **$125.60**, ◊ **$11.50**, ch con.

★★★ **Aberdeen Court Motel**, (HU), 35 Punchbowl Rd, 4.5km S of Launceston, ☎ 03 6344 5811, fax 03 6343 2533, (2 stry gr fl), 26 units acc up to 6, (1 & 2 bedrm), [shwr, tlt, heat (elec), elec blkts, tel, TV, clock radio, t/c mkg, refrig, cook fac, blkts, linen, pillows], ldry, plygr, cots, non smoking units (14). **D** ♦ **$84 - $102**, ♦♦ **$95 - $135**, ◊ **$11**, ch con, AE BC DC MC VI, ⚷&.

★★★ **Charlton Lodge**, (HU), 14 Charlton St, Norwood 7250, 6km SE of Launceston PO, ☎ 03 6343 1752, (2 stry), 1 unit acc up to 4, (2 bedrm), [shwr, tlt, fan, heat, elec blkts, TV, radio, t/c mkg, refrig, cook fac, blkts, linen, pillows], w/mach, bbq, plygr, non smoking units. **D** ♦♦ **$50**, ◊ **$10**, ch con.

★★★ **North Lodge Motel**, (HU), 7 Brisbane St, 1km S of PO, ☎ 03 6331 9966, fax 03 6334 2810, (2 stry gr fl), 26 units acc up to 9, (1, 2 & 3 bedrm), [shwr, tlt, heat (elec), elec blkts, tel, TV, clock radio, t/c mkg, refrig, cook fac, blkts, linen, pillows], ldry, cots. **D** ♦ **$84 - $102**, ♦♦ **$95 - $135**, ◊ **$11**, ch con, AE BC DC MC VI.

B&B's/Guest Houses

★★★★★ **Werona Five Star Accommodation**, (B&B), 33 Trevallyn Rd, 700m N of Kings Bridge, ☎ 03 6334 2272, fax 03 6334 2277, 6 rms [ensuite, spa bath, a/c, cent heat, elec blkts, tel, TV, clock radio, t/c mkg, refrig], rec rm, lounge, ✕, non smoking property. **RO** ♦ **$132 - $198**, ♦♦ **$154 - $220**, AE BC DC EFT MC VI.

★★★★☆ **Edenholme Grange**, (B&B), c1881. 14 St Andrews St, 1.5km S of PO, ☎ 03 6334 6666, fax 03 6334 3106, (2 stry gr fl), 6 rms (2 suites) [ensuite, spa bath (3), a/c (2), heat (elec), elec blkts, tel, TV, clock radio, t/c mkg, cook fac (3)], ldry, lounge firepl, ✕, refrig, bbq, non smoking property. **BB** ♦ **$120 - $130**, ♦♦ **$156 - $172**, ◊ **$52**, **Suite BB** ♦♦ **$176 - $198**, AE BC DC JCB MC VI.

★★★★☆ **(Settler's Cottage)**, 1 cotg acc up to 6, (2 bedrm), [ensuite (1), shwr, spa bath, tlt, heat (elec), elec blkts, TV, clock radio, t/c mkg, refrig, cook fac, micro, blkts, linen, pillows], ldry, cots-fee, breakfast ingredients, non smoking property. **D** ♦ **$176 - $198**, ♦♦ **$126 - $198**.

★★★★☆ **The Turret House**, (B&B), 41 West Tamar Rd, 1.5km NNW of PO, ☎ 03 6334 7033, fax 03 6331 6091, 3 rms [ensuite, cent heat, elec blkts, tel, TV, clock radio, t/c mkg, refrig], lounge, ✕, non smoking property. **BB** ♦ **$95**, ♦♦ **$130**, AE BC MC VI.

★★★★☆ **Waratah on York**, (B&B), c1862. 12 York St, 1km E of PO, ☎ 03 6331 2081, fax 03 6331 9200, (2 stry gr fl), 9 rms [ensuite, spa bath (6), hairdry, heat (elec), tel, TV, clock radio, t/c mkg, refrig, doonas], iron, iron brd, lounge (fireplace), ✕ (breakfast only), non smoking property. **BLB** ♦♦ **$156 - $208**, AE BC DC MC VI.

★★★★ **'Airlie' of Launceston**, (B&B), Classified by National Trust, c1888. 138 St John St, 1km S of PO, ☎ 03 6334 2162, fax 03 6331 1029, (2 stry), 5 rms (1 suite) [ensuite, fan, heat, elec blkts, TV, radio, t/c mkg, refrig (4)], ✕, non smoking property. **BB** ♦ **$75**, ♦♦ **$95**, ◊ **$20**, BC MC VI.

★★★★ **Ashton Gate**, (B&B), Classified by National Trust, c1880. 32 High St, 1km E of PO, ☎ 03 6331 6180, fax 03 6334 2232, 8 rms (1 suite) [ensuite, spa bath (1), hairdry, heat, cent heat, elec blkts, TV, clock radio, t/c mkg, refrig, doonas], ldry, lounge (TV/video), ✕, non smoking property. **BB** ♦ **$90 - $110**, ♦♦ **$120 - $145**, **Suite BB** ♦♦ **$155**, AE BC DC EFT JCB MC VI.

★★★★ **Highfield House**, (B&B), Classified by National Trust, c1860. 23 Welman St (Cnr Elizabeth St), 500m fr PO, ☎ 03 6334 3485, fax 03 6334 3492, (2 stry gr fl), 5 rms [ensuite, fan, heat, elec blkts, TV, clock radio, t/c mkg], lounge (open fire), breakfast rm, refrig, non smoking property. **BB** ♦ **$115**, ♦♦ **$146**, ◊ **$52**, AE BC DC MC VI.

★★★★ **Jennifer's Bed & Breakfast**, (B&B), 12 St Andrews St, West Launceston 7250, 2km N of PO, ☎ 03 6331 5954, 1 rm [shwr, tlt, heat, elec blkts, radio, t/c mkg, refrig, toaster, doonas], lounge (TV), bbq, non smoking property. **BB** ♦ **$70**, ♦♦ **$80**, ◊ **$15**.

★★★★ **Kilmarnock House**, (B&B), Classified by National Trust, Heritage, c1905. 66 Elphin Rd, 1.5km E of PO, ☎ 03 6334 1514, fax 03 6334 4516, (2 stry gr fl), 10 rms [ensuite, heat, elec blkts, tel, TV, clock radio, t/c mkg, refrig, cook fac], ldry, cots-fee, non smoking property. **BB** ♦ **$85**, ♦♦ **$110**, ◊ **$25**, ch con, BC MC VI.

★★★★ **The Edwardian**, (B&B), c1906. 227 Charles St, 200m fr PO, ☎ 03 6334 7771, fax 03 6334 7771, 1 rm [shwr, tlt, hairdry, heat, elec blkts, TV, clock radio, t/c mkg, refrig], ldry, breakfast ingredients, non smoking suites. **BB** ♦ **$100**, ♦♦ **$105**, No car parking on property, AE BC MC VI.

★★★★ **(Holiday Unit Section)**, 2 units acc up to 4, (1 bedrm), [shwr, tlt, hairdry, heat, elec blkts, TV, clock radio, t/c mkg, refrig, cook fac, blkts, doonas, linen, pillows], breakfast ingredients, non smoking units. **D** ♦ **$100**, ♦♦ **$125**, ◊ **$25**.

★★★★ **The Maldon**, (B&B), c1855. 32 Brisbane St, ☎ 03 6331 3211, fax 03 6334 4641, (2 stry gr fl), 12 rms [ensuite, heat, elec blkts, tel, TV, radio, t/c mkg, refrig, toaster], cots. **BB** ♦ **$77**, ♦♦ **$88 - $99**, ◊ **$16.50**, **Suite D** **$99**, ch con, AE BC DC MC VI.

★★★☆ **Hillview House**, (B&B), Classified by National Trust, 193 George St, 500m fr PO, ☎ 03 6331 7388, (2 stry gr fl), 9 rms [ensuite, heat, elec blkts, TV, clock radio, t/c mkg], ✕, c/park. **BB** ♦ **$65**, ♦♦ **$90 - $105**, ◊ **$30**, AE BC MC VI.

★★★☆ **Rose Lodge**, (B&B), 270 Brisbane St, 500m W of PO, ☎ 03 6334 0120, fax 03 6334 7147, (2 stry), 5 rms [ensuite, heat, elec blkts, TV, t/c mkg, refrig], ✕, cots, non smoking rms. **BB** ♦ **$60.50**, ♦♦ **$77**, ch con.

★★★☆ **Windmill Hill Tourist Lodge**, (B&B), Classified by National Trust, 22 High St, 1km E of PO, ☎ 03 6331 9337, fax 03 6334 3292, (2 stry), 8 rms [ensuite (4), heat, elec blkts, TV, radio, t/c mkg, refrig], bathrm (1), ldry, lounge (TV), ✕, cots. **BB** ♦ **$75 - $95**, ♦♦ **$85 - $95**, ◊ **$20**, AE BC MC VI.

Other Accommodation

Launceston Backpackers, 103 Canning St, ☎ 03 6334 2327, fax 03 6331 6091, 25 rms [blkts, linen, pillows], shared fac (2), ldry, TV rm, cook fac, ☎, non smoking rms. **RO** ♦ **$15.50**, BC MC VI.

LEGANA TAS 7277

Pop 6,115. (213km N Hobart), See map on page 656, ref D4, Residential and important fruit growing district. Swimming.

B&B's/Guest Houses

★★★★ **Freshwater Point**, (B&B), Classified by National Trust, 56 Nobelius Dve, 4km E of PO, ☎ 03 6330 2200, fax 03 6330 2030, 2 rms [shwr, bath, tlt, heat, elec blkts, radio, t/c mkg], ldry, lounge (TV), ✕, pool-heated, bbq, meals avail, jetty, cots, non smoking rms. **BLB** ♦♦ **$130**, BC MC VI.

★★★★ **(Holiday Unit Section)**, 3 units acc up to 4, (1 & 2 bedrm), [shwr, tlt, heat (elec/wood), elec blkts, TV, clock radio, t/c mkg, refrig, cook fac, micro, blkts, linen, pillows], breakfast ingredients. **D** ♦♦ **$155**.

LILYDALE TAS 7268

Pop 333. (244km N Hobart), See map on page 656, ref D4, Known as Tasmania's 'country garden' with wonderful reserves. Walking track to Mount Arthur offers wonderful panoramic views of the Lalla district and Pipers River Valley. Bush Walking, Swimming (Pool).

B&B's/Guest Houses

★★★★ **Falls Farm**, (B&B), 231 Golconda Rd, 2.5km NW of PO, ☎ 03 6395 1598, fax 03 6395 1598, 1 rm [ensuite, heat (elec), elec blkts, TV, video, clock radio, t/c mkg, refrig, micro, ldry], ldry, ✕, t/c mkg shared, bbq, meals avail (evening only), c/park. **BLB** ♦♦ **$90 - $110**, ♦♦♦♦ **$110 - $130**, ◊ **$20**, Meals by arrangement, BC MC VI.

★★★★ **Plovers Ridge Country Retreat**, (B&B), 132 Lalla Rd, 2km SE of PO, ☎ 03 6395 1102, fax 03 6395 1107, 2 rms (Studio & 2 bedrm), [shwr, tlt, heat (elec/wood fire), elec blkts, TV, radio, t/c mkg, refrig, cook fac (2)], bbq, meals avail, cots-fee. **BB** ♦ **$95**, ♦♦ **$123**, BC MC VI.

LITTLE SWANPORT TAS 7190

Pop Nominal, (107km NE Hobart), See map on page 656, ref E6, Small holiday retreat located on the East Coast. Bush Walking.

Self Catering Accommodation

★★★ **Gumleaves**, (HU), 166ha bushland. Swanston Rd, ☎ 03 6244 8147, fax 03 6244 7560, 4 units acc up to 7, (2 bedrm), [shwr, bath (hip), tlt, heat, t/c mkg, refrig, cook fac, micro, blkts, linen, pillows], w/mach, bbq, plygr, mini golf, cots. **D** ♦ **$90**, ♦♦ **$100**, ◊ **$15**, ch con, BC MC VI.

(Family Cabins), 3 units acc up to 8, (3 bedrm), [shwr, tlt, heat, t/c mkg, refrig, cook fac, micro, blkts, linen, pillows], bbq, plygr, cots. **D** ♦ **$90**, ♦♦ **$100**, ◊ **$15**, ch con.

(Hostel Section), rms [blkts, linen reqd], shwr, tlt, rec rm, cook fac. **RO** ♦ **$22**, ch con.

LONGFORD TAS 7301

Pop 2,829. (188km N Hobart), See map on page 656, ref D4, Situated on the South Esk and Macquarie rivers, Longford was first settled in 1813 and is one of the oldest towns in Northern Tasmania.

Self Catering Accommodation

★★★★☆ **The Old Chapel**, (Cotg), Classified by National Trust, c1846, 107 Wellington St, 500m S of PO, ☎ 03 6391 1319, fax 03 6391 1318, 1 cotg acc up to 2, (1 bedrm), [shwr, bath, tlt, hairdry, fan, heat (elec/wood), elec blkts, TV, video, clock radio, CD, t/c mkg, refrig, cook fac ltd, micro, blkts, doonas, linen, pillows], ldry, bbq, meals avail, breakfast ingredients. **BB** ♦♦ **$121, BLB** ♦ **$121**, weekly con, BC MC VI.

★★★★☆ **(Cottage Section)**, Classified by National Trust, c1897, (2 stry), 1 cotg acc up to 6, (3 bedrm), [shwr (2), bath, tlt, fan, heat (elec/wood)], TV, video, clock radio, CD, t/c mkg, refrig, cook fac, d/wash, ldry, blkts, linen, pillows], bbq, cots (highchair avail), breakfast ingredients. **BLB** ♦ **$132**, ♦♦ **$132**, ⬡ **$33**, ch con, weekly con.

★★★★ **Brickendon Historic & Farm Cottages**, (Cotg), Classified by National Trust, Woolmers Lane, via Wellington St, ☎ 03 6391 1251, fax 03 6391 2073, (Multi-stry gr fl), 5 cotgs acc up to 6, (1 & 3 bedrm), [ensuite (1), shwr, bath, tlt, heat (elec/wood), elec blkts, TV, radio, t/c mkg, refrig, cook fac, blkts, doonas, linen, pillows], w/mach, bbq, cots, breakfast ingredients, Pets on application. **D** ♦♦ **$99 - $143**, ⬡ **$27.50 - $33**, ch con.

★★★★ **Salem Chapel**, (Cotg), No children's facilities, 589 Pateena Rd, 10km N of PO, ☎ 03 6391 2212, fax 03 6391 2212, 1 cotg acc up to 2, (1 bedrm), [shwr, tlt, heat (elec), elec blkts, TV, clock radio, CD, t/c mkg, refrig, cook fac, blkts, linen, pillows], w/mach, bbq, meals avail, breakfast ingredients. **D** ♦ **$125**, ♦♦ **$125**, BC MC VI.

★★★★ **The Old Rosary**, (Cotg), c1830. Longford Hall, 2km SW of PO, ☎ 03 6391 1662, fax 03 6391 1077, (2 stry), 1 cotg acc up to 4, (2 bedrm), [shwr, tlt, heat (floor), elec blkts, TV, clock radio, t/c mkg, refrig, cook fac, blkts, linen, pillows], breakfast ingredients. **BB** ♦♦ **$143**, ♦♦♦ **$181.50**, ♦♦♦♦ **$222.20**, ch con, weekly con, Min book applies.

★★★★ **Woolmers Estate**, (Cotg), Woolmers La, 5km S of PO, ☎ 03 6391 2230, fax 03 6391 2270, 3 cotgs acc up to 6, (2 & 3 bedrm), [fan, heat, elec blkts, tel, TV, clock radio, t/c mkg, refrig, cook fac, blkts, linen, pillows], w/mach, ⊠ (Lunch only), bbq, cots. **D** ♦ **$138**, ♦♦ **$138 - $143**, ⬡ **$33**, ch con, 1 cottage ★★★☆. AE BC DC MC VI.

★★★☆ **Kingsley House Olde World Accommodation**, (HU), Wellington St, ☎ 03 6391 2318, (2 stry gr fl), 6 units acc up to 5, (1 & 3 bedrm), [shwr, tlt, fire pl, elec blkts, TV, t/c mkg, refrig, cook fac, blkts, linen, pillows], ldry-fee, dryer, bbq, plygr, cots-fee. **D** ♦ **$60**, ♦♦ **$100**, ⬡ **$30**, ch con.

B&B's/Guest Houses

★★★★☆ **Ringley Cottage Romance Revisited**, (B&B), c1856. 16 Union St, ☎ 03 6391 2305, fax 03 6391 1608, 1 rm [shwr, tlt, heat (elec), elec blkts, TV, video, clock radio, t/c mkg, refrig, micro], lounge firepl, non smoking property. **BB** ♦ **$100**, ♦♦ **$120**.

★★★★☆ **The Racecourse Inn**, (B&B), Classified by National Trust, c1840, No children's facilities, 114 Marlborough St, 1.2km S of PO, ☎ 03 6391 2352, fax 03 6391 2430, (2 stry gr fl), 5 rms [ensuite, spa bath (1), hairdry, a/c (3), heat, elec blkts, TV, radio, t/c mkg], lounge, ✕, non smoking property. **BB** ♦ **$105 - $138**, ♦♦ **$132 - $175**, ⬡ **$35 - $52**, Dinner by arrangement. AE BC DC MC VI.

LOW HEAD TAS 7253

Pop 454. (261km N Hobart), See map on page 656, ref C3, Coastal town located near George Town noted for its marine activities.

★★★ **Belfont Cottages**, (Cotg), c1881. 178 Low Head Rd, ☎ 03 6382 1399, fax 03 6382 1304, 2 cotgs acc up to 4, (2 bedrm), [shwr, tlt, heat (elec/wood), elec blkts, TV, clock radio, t/c mkg, refrig, cook fac, blkts, doonas, linen, pillows], w/mach, cots-fee, breakfast ingredients. **D** ♦ **$121**, ♦♦ **$121**, ⬡ **$33**, ch con, BC DC MC VI.

LUNE RIVER TAS 7109

Pop Nominal, (108km SW Hobart), See map on page 656, ref C8, Location of Australia's southernmost haven for gem collectors.

B&B's/Guest Houses

★★★ **Lune River Cottage**, (B&B), 7 Lune River Rd, 7Km from Southport Turnoff, ☎ 03 6298 3107, 3 rms [heat, elec blkts], lounge (TV), t/c mkg shared, refrig, bbq, meals avail, cots-fee. **BB** ♦ **$45**, ♦♦ **$75**, ch con.

Other Accommodation

Lune River YHA, Main Rd, ☎ 03 6298 3163, 3 rms acc up to 8, cook fac. **RO** ♦ **$14**, ch con.

LYMINGTON TAS 7109

Pop Nominal, (59km S Hobart), See map on page 656, ref C7, Picturesque countryside at the mouth of the Huon River. The Lymington Lace Agate can sometimes be found at Drip Beach, an area to which it is unique. At nearby Poverty Point, an abundance of Gondwanan fossils along foreshore.

★★★★☆ **Beaupre Cottage**, (Cotg), 3 Cygnet Coast Rd, 8km S of Cygnet PO, ☎ 03 6295 1542, fax 03 6295 1543, 1 cotg acc up to 2, (1 bedrm), [fan, heat, elec blkts, tel, TV, clock radio, t/c mkg, refrig, cook fac, blkts, linen, pillows], w/mach, dryer, bbq, meals avail, non smoking property. **BB** ♦ **$195**, ♦♦ **$210**, BC MC VI.

MANGALORE TAS 7030

Pop Nominal, (28km N Hobart), See map on page 656, ref D6, Small rural community.

★★★★ **Oakwood B&B**, (B&B), Heritage, 1125 Midland Hwy, 4km N of Brighton PO, ☎ 03 6268 1273, 1 rm (1 suite) [ensuite, heat (elec), elec blkts, TV, radio, t/c mkg, refrig, cook fac ltd, doonas], non smoking property. **BB** ♦ **$85**, ♦♦ **$100**, ch con, weekly con, BC MC VI.

MARRAWAH TAS 7330

Pop 371. (464km NW Hobart), See map on page 656, ref A3, The most westerly town in Tasmania, located in a rich dairy farming district.

★★★☆ **Glendonald Cottage**, (Cotg), R.A. 79, Arthur River Rd, 2.6km S of Marrawah, ☎ 03 6457 1191, fax 03 6457 1191, 1 cotg acc up to 5, (2 bedrm), [heat (elec/wood), elec blkts, tel, TV, clock radio, t/c mkg, refrig, cook fac, blkts, doonas, linen, pillows], w/mach, dryer, c/park (undercover). cots. **D** ♦ **$55**, ♦♦ **$80**, ⬡ **$17.50**, ch con, BC MC VI.

MAYDENA TAS 7140

Pop 381. (86km W Hobart), See map on page 656, ref C6, 'The Big Tree', the tallest known hardwood in the world, is located in this area. Toll gate at Maydena before entering the Gordon River Road.

Self Catering Accommodation

★★☆ **Tyenna Valley Lodge**, (HU), Junee Rd, 200m N of PO, ☎ 03 6288 2293, fax 03 6288 2166, 2 units acc up to 10, (4 bedrm), [shwr (2), tlt (2), heat (woodheater), t/c mkg, refrig, cook fac, blkts, linen, pillows], ldry, ⊠, plygr, breakfast ingredients ($6 per person), ch con, BC MC VI.

(The Lodge), 6 rms acc up to 2, [heat, blkts, linen, pillows], shwr (2), tlt (2), ldry, lounge (communal), cook fac, t/c mkg shared, refrig, non smoking rms. **BB** ♦♦ **$60 - $65**, ch con.

MIDWAY POINT TAS 7171

Pop 2,591. (24km E Hobart), See map on page 656, ref D6, Residential area. Long causeways cross both arms of Pitt Water.

Hotels/Motels

★★★☆ **Pittwater Haven**, (M), 17 Tasman Hwy, 2km S of Sorell, ☎ 03 6265 2693, fax 03 6265 2639, (gr fl), 3 units [ensuite, heat (elec), elec blkts, TV, clock radio, t/c mkg, refrig (bar)], c/park. **RO** ♦ **$80 - $90**, ♦♦ **$80 - $90**, ch con, BC EFT MC VI.

B&B's/Guest Houses

★★★★ **Reflections**, (B&B), 13 Southern Dve, 5km S of Sorell, ☎ 03 6265 2410, fax 03 6265 2429, 3 rms [ensuite (2), hairdry, heat, elec blkts, TV, clock radio, t/c mkg, refrig (1)], bathrm (1), ldry, lounge (TV), ✕, cots. **BLB** ♦ **$60 - $65**, ♦♦ **$90 - $130**, ch con, BC MC VI.

MIENA TAS 7030

Pop 49. (138km NW Hobart), See map on page 656, ref C5, Popular fishing retreat located at the southern end of the Great Lake.

Hotels/Motels

★★★ **Central Highlands Lodge**, (LH), Haddens Bay, ☎ 03 6259 8179, fax 03 6259 8351, 10 rms [ensuite, heat (elec/floor), elec blkts, TV], ⊠, c/park. **DBB** ♦ **$195**, ♦♦ **$300**, ch con, Open Aug 1 to Apr 30.

★★☆ **Great Lake Hotel**, (LH), Cnr Lake & Marlborough Hwy, 3km W of PO, ☎ 03 6259 8163, 6 rms [shwr, tlt, heat, elec blkts, TV, t/c mkg, refrig], ldry, lounge (TV), ⊠, bbq, rm serv, cots. **BLB** ♦ **$66**, ♦♦ **$77**, ⬡ **$11**, ch con.

★★★ **(Holiday Unit Section)**, 3 units acc up to 4, (2 bedrm), [shwr, tlt, heat, elec blkts, refrig, cook fac], breakfast ingredients. **D $110**, ch con.

MOINA TAS 7306

*Pop Nominal, (321km NW Hobart), See map on page 656, ref B4,
Close to Cradle Mountain-Lake St Clair National Park.*

Self Catering Accommodation

★★★★ **High Country Green Gable**, (HU),
Cnr Cradle Mt & Cethana Rd, 32km fr Sheffield,
☎ 03 6492 1318, fax 03 6492 1326,
8 units acc up to 6, (1, 2 & 3 bedrm),
[shwr, bath (3), spa bath (1), tlt, heat (elec),
elec blkts, tel (5), TV, clock radio, t/c mkg,
refrig, cook fac (7), micro, blkts, linen,
pillows], ldry, ⊠ (In-house only), bbq, meals avail, cots-fee, breakfast
ingredients, non smoking units. D ♦ $112 - $168, ♦♦ $112 - $168,
◊ $25, BC MC VI.

B&B's/Guest Houses

★★★★☆ **Lemonthyme Lodge**, (B&B), Cradle Valley, (C132), 10km fr
Moina, ☎ 03 6492 1112, fax 03 6492 1113, 18 rms (18 suites) [shwr,
bath (7), spa bath (11), tlt, heat (11), heat (wood) (11), tel (4),
TV (4), CD (4), t/c mkg, refrig, mini bar], ldry, conv fac, ⊠, bbq,
c/park. RO ♦♦ $210 - $299, 4 units ★★★★★. AE BC DC MC VI.
  ★★★☆ **(Cabin Section)**, 5 units acc up to 6, (2 bedrm), [shwr, tlt,
heat (wood), refrig, cook fac, blkts, linen, pillows], plygr, cots.
D ♦♦ $225, ◊ $35, ch con.
  ★★★ **(Lodge Section)**, (2 stry), 8 rms shared fac (2), t/c mkg shared.
RO ♦ $99, ♦♦ $110, ch con.
  ★★★☆ **Cradle Chalet**, (B&B), Previously Cradle Country Chalet 1422
Cradle Mountain Rd, ☎ 03 6492 1401, fax 03 6492 1144, 4 rms
(Studio), [ensuite, heat (elec), elec blkts, TV, clock radio, t/c mkg,
refrig, pillows], ldry, ⊠, non smoking rms. D ♦♦ $132, BC MC VI.
  ★★★★☆ **(Chalet Section)**, 4 rms (Studio), [ensuite, spa bath (2),
hairdry, heat (elec), elec blkts, TV, video (2), clock radio, CD (2), t/c mkg,
refrig, doonas, pillows], non smoking suites. D ♦♦ $168 - $188.

MOLE CREEK TAS 7304

*Pop 249. (227km NW Hobart), See map on page 656, ref C4,
Located in an important forestry area. Starting point for tours into
the Great Western Tiers and limestone caves.*

Hotels/Motels

★★ **Mole Creek Hotel**, (LH), Main Rd, ☎ 03 6363 1102, 9 rms
[ensuite (1), heat, elec blkts, TV (8)], lounge (TV), ⊠, t/c mkg shared,
cots. BLB ♦ $30, ♦♦ $55, BC MC VI.

Self Catering Accommodation

★★★★ **Blackwood Park Cottages**, (Cotg),
Alum Cliffs Rd, ☎ 03 6363 1208, 2 cotgs
acc up to 6, (2 & 3 bedrm), [shwr, bath, tlt,
heat (woodheater), cent heat, elec blkts, TV,
t/c mkg, refrig, cook fac, blkts, linen,
pillows], cots, breakfast ingredients,
non smoking property. D ♦♦ $96 - $110, ◊ $22.50 - $27.50.
★★★☆ **Alum Cliffs Homestead**, (HU), Mersey Hill Rd, 5km E of PO,
☎ 03 6363 6149, 1 unit acc up to 6, (3 bedrm), [shwr, tlt,
heat (elec/wood), elec blkts, TV, clock radio, t/c mkg, refrig, cook fac,
blkts, linen, pillows], w/mach, bbq, cots-fee, breakfast ingredients.
D ♦ $65, ♦♦ $70, ◊ $15, ch con.
★★★☆ **Mole Creek Holiday Village**, (HU), 1876 Mole Creek Rd, 4km E
of PO, ☎ 03 6363 6124, fax 03 6363 6166, 6 units acc up to 6, (1 & 2
bedrm), [shwr, tlt, heat (elec), elec blkts, TV, clock radio, t/c mkg, refrig,
cook fac, blkts, linen, pillows], ldry, rec rm, ✕, bbq, dinner to unit, cots-fee.
D ♦ $71, ♦♦ $84 - $122, ◊ $11 - $17, weekly con, AE BC DC MC VI.
★★★☆ **Rosewick Cottage**, (Cotg), Alum Cliff Rd, 4km E of PO,
☎ 03 6363 1354, fax 03 6363 1354, 1 cotg acc up to 5, (3 bedrm),
[shwr, bath, tlt, heat (wood), elec blkts, TV, t/c mkg, refrig, cook fac,
micro, blkts, linen, pillows], w/mach, iron, cots, breakfast ingredients.
D ♦ $60, ♦♦ $65, ◊ $15, ch con.

B&B's/Guest Houses

★★★★ **Mole Creek Guest House**, (B&B), 100 Pioneer Dve, 200m W of PO,
☎ 03 6363 1399, fax 03 6363 1420, (2 stry), 5 rms (1 suite) [ensuite (5),
heat, elec blkts, TV, t/c mkg], lounge (TV), ⊠ (Wed to Sun), bbq, cots-fee,
non smoking rms. BB ♦ $90, ♦♦ $110, ◊ $40, AE BC DC EFT MC VI.
★★★☆ **Blue Wren Hideaway**, (B&B), No children's facilities, 36 South
Mole Creek Rd, 4km N of PO, ☎ 03 6363 1483, fax 03 6363 1393,
4 rms [ensuite (3), heat (elec/wood), elec blkts, TV, t/c mkg, refrig,
ldry], shared fac (1), lounge (guest), ✕, sauna, spa, meals
avail (evening only), c/park. BB ♦ $35, ♦♦ $70 - $95, BC MC VI.

NATIONAL PARK TAS 7140

*Pop 203. (73km W Hobart), See map on page 656, ref C6, Gateway
to Mount Field National Park and Russell Falls. Bush Walking.*

Hotels/Motels

★☆ **National Park Hotel**, (LH), Gordon River Rd, 400m past Mt. Field
entrance, ☎ 03 6288 1103, fax 03 6288 1042, 7 rms [heat, elec blkts],
lounge (TV), lounge firepl, bar. BB ♦ $37.50, ♦♦ $60.

Self Catering Accommodation

★★★ **Russell Falls Holiday Cottages**, (HU), Lake Dobson Rd, 8km W
of PO, ☎ 03 6288 1198, 4 units acc up to 6, (1 & 2 bedrm), [shwr, tlt,
heat (gas), elec blkts, TV, clock radio, t/c mkg, refrig, cook fac, blkts,
doonas, linen, pillows], w/mach, bbq, Pets on application. D ♦ $55,
♦♦ $66, ◊ $13, ch con, weekly con, BC MC VI.

Other Accommodation

Mount Field National Park YHA, Main Rd, ☎ 03 6288 1369, 5 rms acc
up to 6, cook fac, t/c mkg shared, refrig. RO ♦ $16 - $36, ch con.

NEW NORFOLK TAS 7140

*Pop 9,000. (33km W Hobart), See map on page 656, ref C6, This
lovely town boasts many historic buildings and churches. Jet boat
rides on the Derwent River.*

Hotels/Motels

★★☆ **Amaroo**, (M), Cnr Lyell Hwy & Pioneer Ave, 600m NE of PO,
☎ 03 6261 2000, 29 units (3 suites) [shwr, tlt, heat, elec blkts, tel,
TV, clock radio, t/c mkg, refrig], ldry, conv fac, ⊠ (Mon to Sat),
rm serv, plygr. RO ♦ $55, ♦♦ $66, ◊ $10, ch con, AE BC DC MC VI.
★☆ **Bush Inn**, (LH), 49 Montagu St, 500m NW of PO, ☎ 03 6261 2011,
(2 stry gr fl), 20 rms [heat, elec blkts], ldry, lounge (TV), ⊠ (Mon to Sat),
t/c mkg shared, bbq, cots. BB ♦ $33, ♦♦ $55, ◊ $25, ch con, BC DC VI.

B&B's/Guest Houses

★★★★☆ **Glen Derwent**, (B&B), Classified
by National Trust, c1820. 44 Hamilton Rd,
2km NW of PO, ☎ 03 6261 3244,
fax 03 6261 3770, (2 stry gr fl), 4 rms
(1 suite) [ensuite, bath, heat, elec blkts, tel,
TV, radio], lounge, ✕, res liquor license,
pool-heated, meals avail, non smoking rms.
BB ♦ $122 - $130, ♦♦ $142 -$182, ◊ $44 - $47, AE BC DC MC VI,
*Operator Comment: " A Hobart alternative. We invite you to
experience a unique combination of convict built history,
modern facilities and friendly personal service".*
  ★★★★ **(Cottage Section)**, 2 cotgs acc up to 5, (1 & 2 bedrm),
[shwr, bath (1), tlt, heat, tel, TV, radio, refrig, cook fac, blkts, linen,
pillows], meals avail, non smoking units. D ♦ $110, ♦♦ $130, ◊ $35,
Breakfast available.
★★★★ **Denmark Hill**, (B&B), Classified by National Trust, c1830.
43 Black Hills Rd, Magra 7140, 4km NE of New Norfolk PO,
☎ 03 6261 3313, fax 03 6261 3313, 1 rm [shwr, tlt, heat, elec blkts,
TV, radio, t/c mkg, refrig], non smoking property. BLB ♦ $80 - $90,
♦♦ $90 - $100, BC MC VI.

★★★★ **Rosies Inn**, (B&B), No children's
facilities, 5 Oast St, ☎ 03 6261 1171,
fax 03 6261 3872, (2 stry gr fl), 13 rms
(5 suites) [ensuite, spa bath (1), hairdry,
heat, elec blkts, TV, clock radio, t/c mkg,
refrig], lounge (2), conf fac, ✕, non
smoking property. BLB ♦ $80, ♦♦ $90,
◊ $40, Suite BLB ♦ $110, ♦♦ $110 - $130, 5 rooms of a higher
standard. AE BC MC VI.
★★★★ **Saints 'N' Sinners Colonial B&B**, (B&B), 93 High St, 300m E
of PO, ☎ 03 6261 1877, fax 03 6261 2955, (2 stry gr fl), 5 rms
[ensuite, heat (elec/wood), elec blkts, TV (2), clock radio, t/c mkg (2),
doonas], TV rm, lounge (TV), ✕, cafe (Lic./BYO), t/c mkg shared, refrig,
non smoking property. BB ♦ $90, ♦♦ $100 - $120, ◊ $40, weekly con,
BC MC VI.
★★★★ **Tynwald - Willow Bend Estate**, (B&B), Classified by National Trust,
c1830. Lyell Hwy (A10), 2km S of PO, ☎ 03 6261 2667, fax 03 6261 2040,
(Multi-stry gr fl), 6 rms [ensuite (3), heat, elec blkts, clock radio],
bathrm (2), lounge (TV), conf fac, ⊠ (Mon to Sun), pool (outdoor, solar
heat), spa (1), t/c mkg shared, bbq, plygr, tennis, non smoking property.
BB ♦♦ $150 - $176, BC MC VI.
  ★★★★ **(Cottage Section)**, The Granary c1822. (2 stry), 1 cotg acc
up to 3, [shwr, tlt, heat (off peak/wood), cent heat, elec blkts, TV,
radio, t/c mkg, refrig, cook fac, blkts, linen, pillows], breakfast ingredients,
non smoking units. D ♦♦ $150 - $176.
★★☆ **Old Colony Inn**, (B&B), c1835. 21 Montagu St, 500m S of PO,
☎ 03 6261 2731, 1 rm (1 suite) [shwr, tlt, heat (gas), elec blkts, TV,
t/c mkg], meals avail, non smoking property. BB ♦♦ $80, ch con, BC MC VI.

NUBEENA TAS 7184

Pop 229. (108km SE Hobart), See map on page 656, ref D7, Nubeena is the largest town on the Tasman Peninsula. Popularly known for its great surf at Roaring Beach and White Beach.

Self Catering Accommodation

★★★★ **White Beach Holiday Villas**, (HU), 309 White Beach Rd, 5km S of PO, ☎ 03 6250 2152, fax 03 6250 2578, 7 units acc up to 6, (1 & 2 bedrm), [shwr, spa bath (1), tlt, hairdry, fan, heat, elec blkts, TV, clock radio, t/c mkg, refrig, cook fac, micro, ldry, blkts, linen, pillows], w/mach, bbq, plygr, cots, non smoking units. **D ‖ $76 - $115, ‖‖ $76 - $115, ◊ $12 - $15,** ch con, 3 units ★★★★. AE BC DC EFT MC MCH VI, 🐾.

★★★☆ **Fairway Resort**, (HU), 1583 Nubeena Rd, 1km N of PO, ☎ 03 6250 2171, fax 03 6250 2605, 13 units acc up to 9, (1, 2 & 3 bedrm), [shwr, tlt, heat, elec blkts, TV, clock radio, t/c mkg, refrig, cook fac, toaster, blkts, linen, pillows], ldry, pool indoor heated, spa, bbq, ✆, plygr, golf, tennis (half court), cots-fee. **D ‖ $102 - $124, ‖‖ $102 - $124, ◊ $20,** ch con, BC MC VI.

★★★ **(Motel Section)**, 6 units [shwr, tlt, heat, elec blkts, TV, clock radio, t/c mkg, toaster]. **RO ‖‖ $94 - $112, ◊ $20,** ch con.

★★★ **Parkers** (HU) Main Rd, 50m W of PO, ☎ 03 6250 2138, 3 units acc up to 5, (2 bedrm), [shwr, tlt, heat, elec blkts, TV, t/c mkg, refrig, cook fac, micro, blkts, linen, pillows], ldry, bbq, cots. **D ‖ $40, ‖‖ $60, ◊ $12.**

OATLANDS TAS 7120

Pop 545. (84km N Hobart), See map on page 656, ref D6, Pretty historic town located on the Lake Dulverton foreshore.

Self Catering Accommodation

★★★☆ **Currajong Cottages**, (Cotg), 10km N of PO, ☎ 03 6255 2150, fax 03 6255 2150, 1 cotg acc up to 6, (3 bedrm), [shwr, tlt, heat (elec/woodheater), elec blkts, TV, clock radio, t/c mkg, refrig, cook fac, micro, blkts, doonas, linen, pillows], w/mach, lounge firepl, cots (portacot), breakfast ingredients. **D ‖‖ $90, ◊ $25.**

B&B's/Guest Houses

★★★★ **Oatlands Lodge**, (B&B), 92 High St, 250m NW of PO, ☎ 03 6254 1444, fax 03 6254 1444, (2 stry), 3 rms [ensuite, fire pl (lounge), heat, elec blkts, t/c mkg], lounge (TV), ✗, non smoking rms. **BB ‖ $85, ‖‖ $110, ◊ $35,** AE BC MC VI.

ORFORD TAS 7190

Pop 502. (81km NE Hobart), See map on page 656, ref E6, An attractive holiday retreat located on the Prosser River. Excellent walking tracks.

Hotels/Motels

★★★☆ **The Eastcoaster Resort**, (LH), Louisville Point Rd, 4km N of PO, ☎ 03 6257 1172, fax 03 6257 1564, (2 stry gr fl), 48 rms (15 suites) [shwr, tlt, heat, elec blkts, tel, TV, clock radio, t/c mkg, refrig, cook fac], ldry, rec rm, conv fac, ✗, pool indoor heated, sauna, spa, bbq, plygr, mini golf, squash, tennis, cots-fee. **RO ‖ $77 - $88, ‖‖ $88 - $110, ◊ $27.50,** ch con, BC MC VI.

★★★☆ **(Holiday Unit Section)**, 10 units acc up to 6, (1 & 2 bedrm), [shwr, spa bath (7), tlt, heat, tel, TV, t/c mkg, refrig, cook fac, blkts, linen, pillows]. **D ‖‖ $110 - $140, ◊ $27.50,** ch con.

★★★ **Island View**, (M), Tasman Hwy, ☎ 03 6257 1114, fax 03 6257 1534, 6 units [shwr, tlt, heat (elec), elec blkts, TV, clock radio, t/c mkg, refrig, toaster], bbq, cots-fee. **RO ‖ $59, ‖‖ $72, ◊ $16,** ch con, AE BC DC MC MCH VI.

★★ **Blue Waters**, (M), Tasman Hwy, 200m S of PO, ☎ 03 6257 1102, fax 03 6257 1261, 18 units [shwr, tlt, heat, elec blkts, cable TV, t/c mkg, refrig], ldry, ✗, bbq, ✆, plygr, cots. **RO ‖ $44, ‖‖ $66, ◊ $10,** ch con, 5 rooms - list only. AE BC BTC EFT MC VI.

Self Catering Accommodation

★★★★★ **Cottages on the Bay**, (Cotg), Louisville Point Rd, ☎ 03 6257 1172, fax 03 6257 1564, 3 cotgs acc up to 4, (2 bedrm), [shwr, tlt, a/c, elec blkts, tel, TV, clock radio, t/c mkg, refrig, cook fac, micro, d/wash, toaster, blkts, linen, pillows], conf fac, ✗, pool indoor heated, spa, bbq, plygr, non smoking property. **D ‖‖ $180, ◊ $60,** BC EFT MC VI.

★★★★★ **Orford Riverside Cottages**, (Cotg), Old Convict Rd, 1km S of PO, ☎ 03 6257 1655, fax 03 6257 1655, 4 cotgs acc up to 8, (1, 2 & 3 bedrm), [ensuite (3), shwr, spa bath (4), tlt, a/c (3), elec blkts, tel (office only), TV, video (free movies), clock radio, t/c mkg, refrig, cook fac, micro, d/wash (3), blkts, linen, pillows], baby bath, w/mach, dryer, bbq (gas) (4), jetty (ramp), cots (highchair), non smoking units. **D ‖‖ $110 - $154, ◊ $27,** ch con, weekly con, 1 unit of a lower rating. Free use of dinghy & outboard, AE BC DC EFT MC VI.

★★★★ **Miranda Cottage**, (Cotg), Tasman Hwy, 500m NE of PO, ☎ 03 6257 1248, fax 03 6257 1248, 1 cotg acc up to 4, (2 bedrm), [shwr, tlt, fire pl, heat (elec), elec blkts, TV, video, clock radio, t/c mkg, refrig, cook fac, micro, blkts, linen, pillows], w/mach, dryer, bbq, tennis, cots, breakfast ingredients. **D ‖ $70, ‖‖ $85, ◊ $25,** ch con, weekly con.

★★★★ **Spring Beach Holiday Villas**, (HU), Rheban Rd, 5km SE of PO, ☎ 03 6257 1440, fax 03 6257 1440, 5 units acc up to 6, (2 bedrm), [shwr, tlt, heat (wood), elec blkts, TV, clock radio, t/c mkg, refrig, cook fac, micro, blkts, linen, pillows], w/mach, bbq, plygr, mini golf, tennis, cots. **D ‖‖ $99 - $125, ◊ $16.50 - $25,** ch con, weekly con, BC MC VI.

★★☆ **Prosser**, (HU), Cnr Charles St & Tasman Hwy, ☎ 03 6257 1427, (gr fl), 5 units acc up to 4, (2 bedrm), [shwr, tlt, fire pl, heat, elec blkts, TV, t/c mkg, refrig, cook fac, blkts, doonas, linen, pillows], ldry, dryer, bbq, cots. **D ‖‖‖‖ $85, ◊ $10, W ‖‖‖‖ $360, ◊ $30,** 2 units ★★.

★★☆ **Sea Breeze**, (HU), Cnr Rudd Ave & Walpole St, 2km E of PO, ☎ 03 6257 1375, fax 03 6257 1375, 3 units acc up to 5, (2 bedrm), [shwr, tlt, heat, elec blkts, TV, t/c mkg, refrig, cook fac, linen], ldry, bbq, cots. **D ‖ $40 - $45, ‖‖ $55 - $60, ◊ $7,** AE BC MC VI.

B&B's/Guest Houses

★★★★ **Orford's Shalom**, (B&B), Homestyle B&B. 50 Tasman Hwy, 200m fr PO, ☎ 03 6257 1175, 3 rms [ensuite, spa bath (1), heat (elec), elec blkts, tel, TV, clock radio, t/c mkg, refrig], bbq, c/park. **BLB ‖ $30 - $50, ‖‖ $60 - $95, ◊ $20,** AE BC DC MC VI.

OUSE TAS 7140

Pop 158. (88km NW Hobart), See map on page 656, ref C6, Small township located between Hamilton and Wayatinah. Visitors may enjoy the round trip from Ouse via Wayatinah, Liapootah, Tarraleah and Tungatinah, Bronte Lagoon returning through Dee and Osterley.

Self Catering Accommodation

★★★☆ **Rosecot**, (HU), 'Millbrook', Victoria Valley Rd, ☎ 03 6287 1222, fax 03 6287 1222, 1 unit acc up to 6, (3 bedrm), [shwr, tlt, heat (wood), elec blkts, TV, radio, refrig, cook fac, micro, blkts, linen, pillows], w/mach, dryer, bbq, cots, breakfast ingredients. **D ‖ $77, ‖‖ $99, ◊ $28,** ch con, weekly con, Min book Christmas and Jan.

★★★☆ **Sassa-Del-Gallo**, (HU), Main Rd, 200m N of PO, ☎ 03 6287 1289, fax 03 6287 1289, 1 unit acc up to 6, (3 bedrm), [shwr, tlt, heat (elec/wood), elec blkts, TV, clock radio, t/c mkg, refrig, cook fac, micro, blkts, linen, pillows], w/mach, bbq, cots, breakfast ingredients. **D ‖ $55, ‖‖ $70, ◊ $20,** ch con.

PENGUIN TAS 7316

Pop 2,876. (296km NW Hobart), See map on page 656, ref B3, Residential area and major producer of vegetables. Named after the fairy penguins still evident in rookeries along the coast. Bowls, Bush Walking, Fishing, Golf, Horse Riding, Squash, Swimming, Tennis.

Self Catering Accommodation

★★★☆ **Watercress Valley Farm**, (Cotg), Browns Lane, 3km S of PO, ☎ 03 6437 1145, fax 03 6437 1308, 1 cotg acc up to 2, (1 bedrm), [shwr, tlt, heat, elec blkts, TV, radio, t/c mkg, refrig, cook fac, blkts, linen, pillows], ldry, breakfast ingredients. **D ‖ $77, ‖‖ $88, W ‖ $330, ‖‖ $385.**

B&B's/Guest Houses

★★★☆ **Inglenook**, (B&B), 360 Bass Hwy, Sulphur Creek 7316, 5km W of Penguin, ☎ 03 6435 4134, fax 03 6435 4665, 4 rms [ensuite (1), heat, elec blkts], bathrm (1), ldry, lounge (TV), ✗, t/c mkg shared, refrig, bbq, cots-fee, non smoking property. **BB ‖ $45 - $50, ‖‖ $60 - $70,** ch con, BC MC VI.

★★★ **Mabroonca**, (B&B), 196 Main St (Scenic Hwy), 1km E of PO, ☎ 03 6437 2147, 2 rms [ensuite (1), elec blkts, tel], ldry, lounge (TV), t/c mkg shared, refrig, meals avail, cots, non smoking property. **BB ‖ $30, ‖‖ $50,** ch con.

PIPERS RIVER TAS 7252

Pop 381. (246km N Hobart), See map on page 656, ref D3, Rural farming and wine growing district producing wines acknowledged as among the best in Australia. Of historic interest is the Graveyard at St Alban's church. Horse Riding, Tennis, Vineyards, Wineries (Tamar Valley).

B&B's/Guest Houses

★★★☆ **Wildflower Cottage**, (B&B), 16 Seascape Dr, 10km N of PO, ☎ 03 6382 6268, fax 03 6382 6293, (gr fl), 1 rm [heat (elec), elec blkts, TV, clock radio, radio, t/c mkg, refrig, ldry, doonas], bathrm (1), bbq, dinner to unit, golf (club)-fee, non smoking rms (1). **BLB ‖ $66, ‖‖ $88, ◊ $17.**

POATINA TAS 7302

Pop 120. (166km N Hobart), See map on page 656, ref D5, Located on a plateau at the foothills of the Great Western Tiers 20 minutes from the Great Lake.

★★★ **Poatina Chalet**, (M), Gordon St, ☎ 03 6397 8290, fax 03 6397 8370, 13 units (1 suite) [shwr, tlt, heat, elec blkts, tel, fax, TV, video, clock radio, t/c mkg, refrig, cook fac (1)], ✗, bbq, shop, petrol, c/park (undercover), plygr, golf, tennis, cots. BLB ♦ $80, ♦♦ $85, Suite RO ♦♦ $93, ch con, AE BC MC VI.

POLICE POINT TAS 7116

Pop Nominal. (80km S Hobart), See map on page 656, ref C7, Coastal settlement overlooking the Huon River.

★★★☆ **Huon Charm Waterfront Cottage**, (Cotg), 525 Esperance Coast Rd, Desolation Bay, ☎ 03 6297 6314, fax 03 6297 6314, 1 cotg acc up to 4, (2 bedrm), [shwr, tlt, heat (elec/wood), elec blkts, TV, video, t/c mkg, refrig, cook fac, micro, blkts, linen, pillows], w/mach, bbq, non smoking property. D ♦♦ $90 - $100, ◊ $25, W ♦♦ $540 - $600, ◊ $130 - $150, ch con, AE BC MC VI.

★★★☆ **Huon Delight**, (Cotg), 582 Esperance Coast Rd, ☎ 03 6297 6336, fax 03 6297 6336, 1 cotg acc up to 2, (1 bedrm), [shwr, tlt, heat, elec blkts, TV, video, radio, t/c mkg, refrig, cook fac, micro, blkts, linen, pillows], w/mach, bbq, cots, non smoking property. D ♦♦ $75 - $85, W ♦♦ $450 - $510, ch con.

PONTVILLE TAS 7030

Pop 1,125. (27km N Hobart), See map on page 656, ref D6, Mid 19th century garrison town with convict bridge spanning the Jordan River.

Self Catering Accommodation

★★★★ **The Barracks**, (Cotg), Classified by National Trust, c1845. Midlands Hwy, 2km N of Brighton PO, ☎ 03 6268 1665, fax 03 6268 1011, (2 stry gr fl), 3 cotgs acc up to 4, (2 bedrm), [shwr, tlt, fan, heat (elec/wood), TV, clock radio, radio, t/c mkg, refrig, cook fac, blkts, linen, pillows], w/mach, cots, breakfast ingredients. D ♦ $124, ♦♦ $124, ◊ $29.

B&B's/Guest Houses

★★★☆ **The Sheiling**, (B&B), c1819, 2 Rifle Range Rd, 2.5km fr Brighton PO, ☎ 03 6268 1951, fax 03 6268 0535, (2 stry), 2 rms (1 suite) [shwr, bath, tlt, fire pl, heat, elec blkts, tel, TV, video, clock radio, t/c mkg, refrig, mini bar, doonas], ldry, lounge (TV), ✗, bbq, c/park. BB ♦ $75 - $85, ♦♦ $95 - $105, ◊ $38.50.

PORT ARTHUR TAS 7182

Pop 168. (99km SE Hobart), See map on page 656, ref D7, Sited on the Tasman Peninsula, Port Arthur is Australia's best known historic site. Bush Walking, Golf, Swimming.

Hotels/Motels

★★★☆ **Fox & Hounds Motor Inn**, (LH), Arthur Hwy, 2km N of PO, ☎ 03 6250 2217, fax 03 6250 2590, (2 stry gr fl), 28 rms [shwr, spa bath (1), tlt, heat, elec blkts, tel, TV, movie, t/c mkg, refrig], ldry, conv fac, ✗, bbq, rm serv, plygr, tennis, cots. RO ♦ $90 - $104, ♦♦ $96 - $120, ◊ $17, ch con, AE BC DC MC VI.

★★★☆ **(Holiday Unit Section)**, 10 units acc up to 4, (2 bedrm), [shwr, tlt, elec blkts, tel, TV, movie, clock radio, t/c mkg, refrig, cook fac, blkts, linen, pillows]. D ♦♦ $128, ♦♦♦♦ $168, ch con.

★★★☆ **Port Arthur Motor Inn**, (LH), Safety Cove Rd, 500m W of PO, ☎ 03 6250 2101, fax 03 6250 2417, 35 rms [shwr, tlt, heat, elec blkts, tel, TV, clock radio, t/c mkg, refrig, mini bar], ldry, conv fac, ✗, dinner to unit, cots. RO ♦ $100, ♦♦ $110, ◊ $22, ch con, 2 rooms of a higher rating. AE BC DC MC VI.

Self Catering Accommodation

★★★★ **Port Arthur Villas**, (HU), 52 Safety Cove Rd, 1km SE of PO, ☎ 03 6250 2239, fax 03 6250 2589, 9 units acc up to 6, (1 & 2 bedrm), [shwr, tlt, heat (elec/off peak), elec blkts, tel, TV, clock radio, t/c mkg, refrig, cook fac, micro, blkts, doonas, linen, pillows], ldry, dryer, bbq, plygr, cots, Pets on application. D ♦♦ $88 - $115, ◊ $20 - $25, ch con, 3 units of a lower rating. AE BC DC EFT MC VI.

★★★☆ **Port Arthur Holiday World**, (Cotg), Arthur Hwy, Next to PO, ☎ 03 6250 2262, fax 03 6250 2513, 18 cotgs acc up to 8, (1, 2 & 3 bedrm), [shwr, tlt, heat, elec blkts, TV, radio, t/c mkg, refrig, cook fac, blkts, linen, pillows], ldry, bbq, plygr (beach), cots. D ♦♦ $90 - $112, ◊ $17, AE BC DC MC VI, ♿.

B&B's/Guest Houses

★★★★ **Andertons Accommodation**, (B&B), Remarkable Cave Rd, 3km SE of PO, Carnarvon Bay, ☎ 03 6250 2378, fax 03 6250 2378, (2 stry) 1 rm [shwr, bath, tlt, heat (elec/wood), elec blkts, TV, video, clock radio, t/c mkg], bbq, non smoking rms. BLB ♦ $55, ♦♦ $70 - $80, ♦♦♦♦ $110 - $120.

Operator Comment: Don't be disappointed, book 2 nights.

★★★☆ **(Holiday Unit Section)**, 1 unit acc up to 4, (2 bedrm), [shwr, tlt, heat (elec/wood), elec blkts, TV, radio, t/c mkg, refrig, cook fac, micro, blkts, linen, pillows], bbq, breakfast ingredients. BLB ♦ $50 - $55, ♦♦ $60 - $70, ♦♦♦♦ $80 - $90, ch con.

★★★★ **Sea Change Safety Cove**, (B&B), 425 Remarkable Cave Rd, 4km S of PO, ☎ 03 6250 2719, fax 03 6250 2115, 2 rms [ensuite, bath (1), heat (elec), elec blkts, TV, clock radio, t/c mkg, refrig], ldry, bbq, non smoking property. BB ♦ $88, ♦♦ $112, BC DC MC VI,

Operator Comment: Web-site www.safetycove.com Email rex@safetycove.com Breathtaking location surrounded by water. Stunning views of Tasman Island Cape Pillar and Safety Cove beach. 35 world class walks fishing horse riding golf kayaking Historic Site. Time for a SEA CHANGE.

★★★★ **(Unit Section)**, 1 unit acc up to 5, (2 bedrm), [shwr, tlt, fan, heat (elec/wood), elec blkts, TV, video, radio, t/c mkg, refrig, cook fac, doonas, linen, pillows], ldry, bbq, breakfast ingredients, non smoking property. D ♦♦ $128, ◊ $32, ch con, weekly con.

Other Accommodation

Roseview YHA, c1920, 27 Champ St, ☎ 03 6250 2311, 8 rms acc up to 8, ldry, cook fac, t/c mkg shared, refrig. RO ♦ $17 - $55, ch con, BC MC VI.

PORT HUON TAS 7116

Pop 507. (58km S Hobart), See map on page 656, ref C7, Popular residential and holiday area. Scenic river cruises. Access to Hartz Mountains National Park. Extensive Sports Centre including heated pool, communal spa, sauna, squash courts. Boating, Fishing.

Hotels/Motels

★★★☆ **Kermandie Lodge (Motel)**, (M), Main Rd, ☎ 03 6297 1110, fax 03 6297 1710, 8 units [shwr, tlt, hairdry, heat (elec), elec blkts, tel, TV, video (on request)-fee, radio, t/c mkg], ldry, conv fac, ✗, bbq, plygr, cots, non smoking rms. RO ♦ $77, ♦♦ $86, ◊ $22, ch con, AE BC DC MC VI.

★★★☆ **(Villa Unit Section)**, 9 rms (1 & 2 bedrm), [shwr, tlt, hairdry, heat, elec blkts, tel, TV, clock radio, t/c mkg, refrig, cook fac], non smoking units. D ♦ $88, ♦♦ $105, ◊ $22, ch con.

★★☆ **(Hotel Section)**, (2 stry), 10 rms [shwr, tlt, heat (elec), elec blkts, t/c mkg], non smoking rms. RO ♦ $55, ♦♦ $75, ◊ $22, ch con.

PORT SORELL TAS 7307

Pop 788. (264km NW Hobart), See map on page 656, ref C3, Port Sorell is a quiet, friendly hamlet rich in history offering a wide range of accommodation.

Hotels/Motels

★★★★ **Shearwater Cottages Motel**, (M), 7-9 The Boulevard, 100m S of PO, ☎ 03 6428 6895, fax 03 6428 6895, 6 units (Studio), [shwr, tlt, heat, elec blkts, TV, clock radio, t/c mkg, refrig, cook fac ltd, micro], ldry, bbq, ☎, golf, cots-fee, non smoking units (3). RO ♦ $70 - $80, ♦♦ $85 - $95, ◊ $15, AE BC BTC DC MC VI.

B&B's/Guest Houses

★★★★ **Appleby Creek Lodge**, (B&B), 55 Springfield Park, 5km W of PO, ☎ 03 6428 7222, (2 stry gr fl), 3 rms [ensuite (2), heat, elec blkts, clock radio], bathrm (1), ldry, lounge (TV), ✗, t/c mkg shared, refrig, bbq, cots-fee, non smoking rms. BB ♦ $40 - $55, ♦♦ $55 - $75, ◊ $15, ch con.

★★★★ **Hiller's Haven**, (B&B), 54 Rice St, 1.5km E of PO, ☎ 03 6428 7580, 3 rms [ensuite, fan, heat (elec), elec blkts, TV, clock radio, t/c mkg, refrig, toaster], bbq, cots, non smoking property. BLB ♦♦ $60 - $65, ch con, BC MC VI.

★★★☆ **(Unit Section)**, 1 unit acc up to 4, (2 bedrm), [shwr, tlt, fan, heat (elec), elec blkts, TV, clock radio, radio, t/c mkg, refrig, cook fac, micro, blkts, linen-fee, pillows], w/mach, bbq, cots (& highchair), non smoking property. D ♦♦ $60 - $65, ◊ $10, W ♦♦ $360, ◊ $60, ch con.

★★★★ **Newcroft**, (B&B), 39 Sunhaven Dve, 2km W of PO, ☎ 03 6428 6835, fax 03 6428 6835, 2 rms [shwr, tlt, heat, elec blkts, radio, t/c mkg], ldry, lounge (TV), bbq, cots, non smoking rms. BLB ♦ $40, ♦♦ $65, ◊ $25, ch con.

PYENGANA TAS 7216

Pop 300. (282km N Hobart), See map on page 656, ref E4, With an early history of tin mining, nearby townships of Lottah and Goulds Country successfully turned to agriculture, dairy farming, cheese making and forestry. Bush Walking, Gem Fossicking.

★★ **St Columba Falls**, (LH), 3km SW of PO, ☎ 03 6373 6121, fax 03 6373 6178, 7 rms [heat], shared fac (2), ⊠, ☎. RO ♦ $30, ♦♦ $40, ⏃ $10.

QUEENSTOWN TAS 7467

Pop 3,368. (258km W Hobart), See map on page 656, ref B5, Queenstown today is a combination of historic buildings surrounded by the naked hills of the copper mines. Gateway to the Franklin-Gordon Wild Rivers National Park. Bowls, Bush Walking, Fishing, Golf, Squash, Swimming (Pool), Tennis.

Hotels/Motels

★★★☆ **Westcoaster Motor Inn**, (LH), Batchelor St, 1km N of PO, ☎ 03 6471 1033, fax 03 6471 2421, (2 stry gr fl), 60 rms (2 suites) [shwr, tlt, heat, elec blkts, tel, TV, clock radio, t/c mkg, refrig], ldry, ⊠, rm serv, c/park (undercover), cots. RO ♦ $95, ♦♦ $95, ⏃ $20, AE BC DC MC VI, ♿.

★★★ **Queenstown Motor Lodge**, (M), 54 Orr St, ☎ 03 6471 1866, fax 03 6471 2413, (2 stry gr fl), 24 units [shwr, tlt, fan, heat, elec blkts, tel, TV, radio, t/c mkg, refrig], ldry, ✗, ⊠, bar, rm serv, plygr, cots. RO ♦ $81, ♦♦ $96, ♦♦♦ $111, ch con, AE BC DC JCB MC VI.

★★★ **The Gold Rush Motor Inn**, (M), Batchelor St, ☎ 03 6471 1005, fax 03 6471 1084, (gr fl), 26 units [shwr, bath, tlt, heat, elec blkts, tel, TV, t/c mkg, refrig, cook fac (3)], ldry, ⊠, rm serv, cots-fee. RO ♦ $75 - $99, ♦♦ $75 - $99, ⏃ $16.50, AE BC DC JCB MC VI, ♿.

★★☆ **Silver Hills**, (M), Penghana Rd, 1km N of PO, ☎ 03 6471 1755, fax 03 6471 1452, (2 stry gr fl), 56 units [shwr, tlt, heat, elec blkts, tel, TV, radio, t/c mkg, refrig, cook fac (2)], ldry, ⊠, rm serv, cots. RO ♦ $77, ♦♦ $88, ⏃ $12, ch con, AE BC DC MC VI.

★★ **Mount Lyell Motor Inn**, (LH), 1 Orr St, 100m fr PO, ☎ 03 6471 1888, fax 03 6471 2598, (2 stry gr fl), 40 rms [shwr, tlt, heat, elec blkts, heat, t/c mkg, refrig (30)], ldry, ⊠ (evenings only), rm serv, cots-fee. RO ♦ $44, ♦♦ $49.50, ⏃ $22, AE BC DC EFT MC VI.

★☆ **Commercial**, (LH), Driffield St, 500m SW of PO, ☎ 03 6471 1511, 6 rms [shwr, tlt, heat, elec blkts, TV, cable TV, radio, t/c mkg, refrig], ldry, ⊠ (Nightly), ☎. BLB ♦ $38, ♦♦ $66, ch con.

Mountain View Holiday Lodge, (M), 1 Penghana Rd, 500m N of PO, ☎ 03 6471 1163, fax 03 6471 1306, 27 units [shwr, tlt, heat, elec blkts, TV, t/c mkg, refrig], ldry, ✗ (Mon to Sat), bbq, plygr, cots-fee. ch con, AE BC MC MCH VI, (Rating under review).

(**Backpack Section**), 7 rms acc up to 4, [heat, cook fac (communal), blkts reqd-fee, linen reqd-fee], lounge (Tv), t/c mkg shared, refrig. D ♦ $14, ch con.

Self Catering Accommodation

★★★★ **Comstock Cottage**, (Cotg), 45 McNamara St, 500m S of PO, ☎ 03 6471 2154, fax 03 6471 2430, 1 cotg acc up to 6, (2 bedrm), [shwr, tlt, a/c-cool, heat (elec), elec blkts, TV, video, clock radio, t/c mkg, refrig, cook fac, blkts, linen, pillows], w/mach, dryer, breakfast ingredients, non smoking property. D ♦ $99 - $132, ♦♦ $99 - $132, ⏃ $25, ch con, BC MC VI.

★★★ **Pioneer's Retreat**, (HU), 1 Batchelor St, 1km N of PO, ☎ 03 6471 3033, fax 03 6471 3011, (2 stry gr fl), 12 units acc up to 6, (2 bedrm), [shwr, tlt, heat (elec), elec blkts, tel, TV, clock radio, t/c mkg, refrig, cook fac, blkts, linen, pillows], w/mach, bbq, plygr, cots, non smoking units (4). D ♦ $70, ♦♦ $110, ⏃ $15, ch con, AE BC BTC DC MC VI.

B&B's/Guest Houses

★★★★ **Penghana**, (B&B), 32 The Esplanade, ☎ 03 6471 2560, fax 03 6471 1535, (2 stry), 5 rms [ensuite (4), a/c-cool, heat (elec/wood), elec blkts, TV, clock radio], bathrm (1), ✗, t/c mkg shared, refrig, cots, non smoking rms. BB ♦♦ $110 - $140, ch con, AE BC DC MC VI.

REDPA TAS 7330

Pop 370. (464km NW Hobart) See map on page 656, ref A3, Located in a rich dairy farming district.

★★★☆ **Rest-A-While Holidays**, (HU), RA 27192, Bass Hwy, 6km E of Marrawah PO, ☎ 03 6457 1272, 1 unit acc up to 6, (3 bedrm), [shwr, tlt, heat (wood), elec blkts, TV, clock radio, t/c mkg, refrig, cook fac, blkts, linen, pillows], w/mach, dryer, bbq, plygr, cots, Pets on application. D ♦ $40 - $45, ♦♦ $65 - $70, ⏃ $20, W ♦ $240 - $270, ♦♦ $390 - $420, ⏃ $120, ch con, fam con, pen con, BC MC VI.

RICHMOND TAS 7025

Pop 754. (27km NE Hobart), See map on page 656, ref D6, An olde world village where the past is reflected in the perfectly preserved buildings. Golf.

Hotels/Motels

★★★☆ **Richmond Arms Hotel**, (LH), 42 Bridge St, 100m fr PO, ☎ 03 6260 2109, fax 03 6260 2623, (2 stry gr fl), 4 rms (1 & 2 bedrm), [shwr, tlt, heat, elec blkts, TV, clock radio, t/c mkg, refrig, cook fac ltd], ldry, lounge (TV), ⊠, dinner to unit, ☎, cots, non smoking rms. RO ♦ $70, ♦♦ $95, ⏃ $25, ch con, BC EFT MC VI.

Self Catering Accommodation

★★★★ **Daisy Bank Cottages**, (Cotg), c1830, 625ha farm. 'Daisy Bank' Middle Tea Tree Rd, 1.5km NW of PO, ☎ 03 6260 2390, fax 03 6260 2635, (2 stry), 2 cotgs acc up to 4, (1 bedrm), [shwr, spa bath (1), tlt, fan, heat (wood), elec blkts, TV, clock radio, radio, t/c mkg, refrig, cook fac, micro, blkts, doonas, linen, pillows], ldry, bbq, cots-fee, breakfast ingredients. D ♦ $120, ♦♦ $120, ⏃ $20, BC MC VI.

★★★★ **Hollyhock Cottage**, (Cotg), c1830. 3 Percy St, 200m W of PO, ☎ 03 6260 1079, fax 03 6260 1078, 1 cotg acc up to 2, (1 bedrm), [shwr, spa bath, tlt, heat (elec/wood), elec blkts, TV, clock radio, CD, t/c mkg, refrig, cook fac, micro, blkts, linen, pillows], w/mach, bbq, breakfast ingredients, non smoking property. D ♦♦ $140, AE BC MC VI.

★★★★ **Red Brier Cottage**, (Cotg), 15 Bridge St, 250m W of PO, ☎ 03 6260 2349, 1 cotg acc up to 4, (2 bedrm), [shwr, spa bath, tlt, fan, heat (wood), TV, video, clock radio, t/c mkg, refrig, cook fac, micro, blkts, linen, pillows], w/mach, dryer, cots-fee, breakfast ingredients, non smoking units. D ♦ $138, ♦♦ $138, ⏃ $33, W ♦ $828, ♦♦ $828, ch con, AE BC MC VI.

★★★★ **Richmond Colonial Accommodation**, (Cotg), Bridge & Percy Sts, ☎ 03 6260 2570, fax 03 6260 2570, 5 cotgs acc up to 6, (1, 2 & 3 bedrm), [shwr, tlt, elec blkts, TV, video, clock radio, t/c mkg, refrig, cook fac, micro, blkts, linen, pillows], w/mach, ☎, plygr, cots, breakfast ingredients, non smoking property. D ♦ $100 - $120, ♦♦ $120 - $145, ⏃ $33, ch con, 1 cottage yet to be rated, AE BC DC EFT MC VI.

★★★★ **Richmond Cottages**, (Cotg), Classified by National Trust, c1835. 12 Bridge St, 500m W of PO, ☎ 03 6260 2561, fax 03 6239 9597, (gr fl), 2 cotgs acc up to 6, (1 & 3 bedrm), [shwr, spa bath (1), tlt, heat (elec/wood), elec blkts, TV, radio, t/c mkg, refrig, cook fac, blkts, linen, pillows], w/mach, plygr, cots-fee, breakfast ingredients. D ♦♦ $149.60, ⏃ $33, ch con, BC MC VI.

★★★☆ **Laurel Cottage**, (Cotg), c1830, 9 Wellington St, ☎ 03 6260 2397, fax 03 6260 2536, 1 cotg acc up to 4, (2 bedrm), [heat (elec/wood), elec blkts, TV, radio, t/c mkg, refrig, cook fac, micro, blkts, linen, pillows], w/mach, cots, breakfast ingredients. D ♦ $105, ♦♦ $122, ⏃ $22, ch con, BC MC VI.

★★★ **Richmond Coachman's Rest**, (HU), 30 Bridge St, 300m W of PO, ☎ 03 6260 2729, 1 unit acc up to 4, (Studio), [shwr, tlt, heat (elec), elec blkts, TV, clock radio, t/c mkg, refrig, cook fac, ldry, blkts, linen, pillows], bbq, cots, non smoking units, Pets on application. D ♦ $65, ♦♦ $65 - $75, ⏃ $12, ch con, BC MC VI.

B&B's/Guest Houses

★★★★☆ **Millhouse on the Bridge**, (B&B), c1853. No children's facilities, 2 Wellington St, ☎ 03 6260 2428, fax 03 6260 2148, (Multi-stry), 4 rms [ensuite (3), heat (wood), cent heat, TV, clock radio, t/c mkg, ldry-fee], bathrm (1), lounge (TV), breakfast rm (air cond), res liquor license, refrig, bbq, meals avail, non smoking rms. BB ♦ $135 - $160, ♦♦ $135 - $160, ⏃ $50, 1 room ★★★★. BC MC VI.

★★★★☆ **Prospect House**, (B&B), c1830. 1384 Richmond Rd, 1km W of PO, ☎ 03 6260 2207, fax 03 6260 2551, (2 stry gr fl), 11 rms [ensuite, hairdry, heat, elec blkts, tel, TV, clock radio, t/c mkg, refrig], ldry, conv fac, ⊠, rm serv, cots-fee. RO ♦ $121, ♦♦ $132, AE BC DC MC VI, ♿.

★★★★ **Hatchers Richmond Manor**, (B&B), 40ha farm property & apricot orchard. 73 Prossers Rd, 750m fr PO, ☎ 03 6260 2622, fax 03 6260 2744, 7 rms (2 suites) [ensuite, spa bath (6), a/c, heat (open log fire) (4), elec blkts, tel, TV, video, clock radio, t/c mkg, refrig, cook fac (4)], ldry, ✗, pool indoor heated, meals avail, plygr, cots, non smoking rms. BB ♦♦ $85 - $95, Suite RO ♦♦ $125 - $160, 4 rooms of a higher rating.

★★★★ **(Holiday Unit Section)**, 1 cotg acc up to 5, (2 bedrm), [shwr, spa bath, tlt, a/c, elec blkts, tel, TV, video, clock radio, t/c mkg, refrig, cook fac, micro, blkts, linen, pillows], w/mach, pool indoor heated, bbq, plygr, cots. BB ♦ $95 - $125, ♦♦ $125 - $160, ⏃ $15.

RICHMOND TAS continued...

★★★★ **Mrs Curries House**, (B&B), 4 Franklin St, ☎ 03 6260 2766, fax 03 6260 2110, (2 stry gr fl), 4 rms [ensuite (3), heat (elec/wood), elec blkts, tel, clock radio, t/c mkg, refrig, cook fac ltd, micro], bathrm (1), ldry, lounge (TV), ✕, plygr, non smoking rms. BB ♦ **$96**, ♦♦ **$110**, ♦♦♦ **$132**, ch con, AE BC DC MC VI.

★★★★ **Richmond Barracks**, (B&B), 16 Franklin St, ☎ 03 6260 2453, fax 03 6260 2373, 2 rms [ensuite, hairdry, heat, elec blkts, TV, clock radio, t/c mkg, refrig], lounge, lounge firepl, ✕, bar, bbq, non smoking rms. BB ♦ **$88**, ♦♦ **$121**, BC MC VI.

★★★☆ **Richmond Antiques Bed & Breakfast**, (B&B), 2 Edward St, ☎ 03 6260 2601, fax 03 6260 2601, 2 rms [ensuite (1), fan, heat (elec), elec blkts, TV, clock radio, t/c mkg, refrig, cook fac ltd, doonas], bathrm (1), non smoking rms. BLB ♦ **$75 - $85**, ♦♦ **$85 - $95**, ♦ **$20**, ch con, weekly con, BC EFT MC VI.

★★★☆ **Richmond Country B&B**, (B&B), 472 Prossers Rd, 6km NE of PO, ☎ 03 6260 4238, fax 03 6260 4423, 2 rms [shwr, tlt, heat, elec blkts], lounge (TV), t/c mkg shared, cots-fee, non smoking property. BLB ♦ **$65**, ♦♦ **$85**, ♦ **$25**, ch con.

ROSEBERY TAS 7470

Pop 1,637. (303km NW Hobart), See map on page 656, ref B4, A major mining town on the West Coast with over 100 strong years in mining.

Hotels/Motels

★★☆ **Plandome**, (LH), Agnes St, 100m N of PO, ☎ 03 6473 1351, fax 03 6473 1351, (2 stry), 13 rms [ensuite (4), heat, elec blkts, TV (5), t/c mkg (5), refrig (5)], lounge (TV), ✕ (Mon to Sat), cots. RO ♦ **$27.50 - $52.80**, ♦♦ **$41.80 - $63.80**, ♦ **$11**, ch con, EFT.

Self Catering Accommodation

★★★☆ **Miners Cottages**, (Cotg), 14 Karlson St, 500m NW of PO, ☎ 03 6473 1796, fax 03 6473 1808, 2 cotgs acc up to 6, (2 bedrm), [shwr, bath, tlt, heat (wood), elec blkts, TV, video, clock radio, t/c mkg, refrig, cook fac, micro, blkts, linen, pillows], w/mach, dryer, plygr, cots, breakfast ingredients, Pets on application. D ♦ **$65 - $70**, ♦♦ **$90 - $100**, ♦ **$25 - $30**, W ♦ **$300 - $330**, ♦♦ **$420 - $450**, ♦ **$120 - $150**, ch con.

B&B's/Guest Houses

★★★☆ **Mount Black Lodge**, (B&B), Hospital Rd, 750m N of PO, ☎ 03 6473 1039, fax 03 6473 1918, 9 rms [heat, cook fac, ldry], TV rm, ✕. BLB ♦ **$49.50**, ♦♦ **$66 - $85**, BC MC VI, ⚭⚬.

(Hostel Section), 3 rms acc up to 8. RO ♦ **$18**, ♦ **$18**.

ROSEVEARS TAS 7277

Pop 157. (218km N Hobart), See map on page 656, ref D4, Historic shipbuilding area. Waterbird Trust Haven.

Self Catering Accommodation

★★★★ **Conmel Cottage**, (Cotg), No children's facilities, 125 Rosevears Dve, 4km N of Legana PO, ☎ 03 6330 1466, fax 03 6330 1466, 1 cotg acc up to 2, (1 bedrm), [shwr, tlt, heat, elec blkts, tel, TV, clock radio, t/c mkg, refrig, cook fac, blkts, linen, pillows], w/mach, dryer, bbq, breakfast ingredients, non smoking property. D ♦ **$95**, ♦♦ **$105**.

B&B's/Guest Houses

★★★★ **Tamar House**, (B&B), 85 Rosevears Dve, 3km N of Legana PO, ☎ 03 6330 1744, fax 03 6330 2035, 3 rms (1 suite) [ensuite, heat, elec blkts, TV, radio, t/c mkg, refrig], ldry, rec rm, ✕, spa (pool), bbq, meals avail, non smoking rms. BB ♦ **$86**, ♦♦ **$95 - $116**, ♦ **$28**, Suite D ♦♦ **$110 - $128**, BC MC VI.

ROSS TAS 7209

Pop 275. (122km N Hobart), See map on page 656, ref D5, Situated on the banks of the Macquarie River, this district is famous for producing superfine merino wool. Fishing, Swimming (Pool).

Hotels/Motels

★★★ **Man O Ross Hotel**, (LH), Classified by National Trust, c1835. Church St, 182m S of PO, ☎ 03 6381 5240, fax 03 6381 5423, (2 stry), 9 rms [heat, elec blkts], ldry, lounge (TV), conv fac, ✕, bar, t/c mkg shared, meals avail, cots. RO ♦ **$40 - $60**, ♦♦ **$60 - $80**, ♦ **$5**, ch con, BC MC VI.

Self Catering Accommodation

★★★★ **Somercotes Estate**, (HU), c1823. Historic working farm & gardens. 4km S of PO, ☎ 03 6381 5231, fax 03 6381 5356, 4 units acc up to 4, (1 & 2 bedrm), [shwr, tlt, heat (elec/wood), elec blkts, TV, clock radio, t/c mkg, refrig, cook fac, blkts, linen, pillows], ldry, bbq, meals avail, cots, breakfast ingredients. D ♦ **$120**, ♦♦ **$150**, ♦ **$35**, ch con, AE BC DC MC VI.

★★★☆ **Colonial Cottages of Ross**, (Cotg), c1830-80. Office:12 Church St, ☎ 03 6381 5354, fax 03 6343 6005, 4 cotgs acc up to 6, (1, 2 & 3 bedrm), [shwr, bath (2), tlt, heat (wood), elec blkts, TV, clock radio, t/c mkg, refrig, cook fac, blkts, linen, pillows], w/mach, lounge firepl, bbq, cots-fee, breakfast ingredients, non smoking units (1). D ♦♦ **$130 - $144**, ♦ **$25 - $30**, ch con, weekly con, BC MC VI.

B&B's/Guest Houses

★★★☆ **Ross Bakery Inn**, (B&B), Classified by National Trust, 15 Church St, 250m N of PO, ☎ 03 6381 5246, fax 03 6381 5360, (2 stry), 4 rms [shwr, tlt, heat (elec), elec blkts, TV, video, t/c mkg], conf fac, lounge firepl, ✕, coffee shop, non smoking property. BLB ♦ **$69**, ♦♦ **$109**, ♦ **$25**, ch con, AE BC JCB MC VI.

SCAMANDER TAS 7215

Pop 430. (236km NE Hobart), See map on page 656, ref E4, Pretty coastal town offering excellent beaches for water sports and fishing, and uninterrupted coastline to Beaumaris.

Hotels/Motels

 ★★★☆ **Scamander Beach Resort Hotel**, (LH), Tasman Hwy, 100m fr PO, ☎ 03 6372 5255, fax 03 6372 5428, (Multi-stry gr fl), 57 rms [shwr, tlt, heat, elec blkts, tel, TV, t/c mkg, refrig], lift, ldry, conv fac, ⊠, pool, sauna, spa, bbq, rm serv, plygr, cots. RO ♦ **$70 - $100**, ♦♦ **$70 - $100**, ♦ **$15**, ch con, AE BC DC MC VI.

 ★★★ **Surfside**, (LH), Tasman Hwy, 5km N of Scamander, ☎ 03 6372 5177, fax 03 6372 5322, 11 rms [shwr, tlt, heat, elec blkts, tel, TV, radio, t/c mkg, refrig], ⊠, rm serv, cots-fee, non smoking rms (2). RO ♦ **$61**, ♦♦ **$77**, ♦ **$38**, ch con, fam con, BC DC EFT MC VI.

Self Catering Accommodation

★★★★ **Blue Seas**, (HU), Wattle Dve, 500m N of PO, ☎ 03 6372 5211, fax 03 6372 5393, (2 stry gr fl), 14 units acc up to 6, (1 & 2 bedrm), [shwr, tlt, hairdry, fan, heat, elec blkts, TV, t/c mkg, refrig, cook fac, blkts, linen, pillows], ldry, rec rm, pool-indoor (heated), spa, bbq, plygr, cots. D ♦ **$45 - $55**, ♦♦ **$80**, ♦ **$20**, ch con, AE BC DC EFT MC VI.

★★★ **Carmens Inn Holiday Units**, (HU), 4 Pringle St, 200m W of PO, ☎ 03 6372 5160, fax 03 6372 5160, 6 units acc up to 7, (1 & 2 bedrm), [shwr, tlt, heat, elec blkts, TV, video, t/c mkg, refrig, cook fac, blkts, linen, pillows], ldry, bbq, plygr, cots. D ♦ **$35 - $55**, ♦♦ **$45 - $75**, ♦ **$15**, ch con, pen con, weekly con, ⚭⚬.

★★★ **Pelican Sands**, (HU), 157 Scamander Ave, 500m N of PO, ☎ 03 6372 5231, fax 03 6372 5340, 14 units acc up to 7, (1 & 2 bedrm), [shwr, tlt, heat, elec blkts, TV, t/c mkg, refrig, cook fac, blkts, linen, pillows], ldry, pool-heated (solar), bbq, plygr, cots, Pets allowed outside. D ♦ **$20 - $60**, ♦♦ **$95**, ♦ **$15**, ch con, weekly con, Deposit required, AE BC DC MC VI.

B&B's/Guest Houses

★★★★☆ **Bensons**, (B&B), Tasman Hwy, 3km N of Scamander, ☎ 03 6372 5587, fax 03 6372 5610, (2 stry), 3 rms (1 suite) [ensuite, heat (wood)], ldry, lounge (TV), ✕, t/c mkg shared, refrig, bbq, meals avail, ☎. BB ♦♦ **$132 - $176**, BC MC VI.

SCOTTSDALE TAS 7260

Pop 2,000. (263km NE Hobart), See map on page 656, ref D4, Centre of a rich agricultural, dairy and forestry district.

Hotels/Motels

★★★★ **Anabels of Scottsdale**, (M), Classified by National Trust, 46 King St, 600m of PO, ☎ 03 6352 3277, fax 03 6352 2144, 6 units (1 bedrm), [shwr, bath (1), tlt, heat (electric), elec blkts, tel, TV, clock radio, t/c mkg, refrig, cook fac ltd (3)], ⊠ (Tues to Sat), rm serv, breakfast ingredients ($7 per person). D ♦ **$88**, ♦♦ **$99**, ♦ **$15**, AE BC DC MC VI.

★★☆ **Kendalls Scottsdale Hotel Motel**, (M), 18 George St, 500m NE of PO, ☎ 03 6352 2510, fax 03 6352 3545, 18 units [shwr, tlt, heat, elec blkts, TV, cable TV, radio, t/c mkg, refrig], conv fac, ⊠, cots. RO ♦ **$43**, ♦♦ **$54**, ♦ **$12**, ch con, BC MC VI.

Self Catering Accommodation

★★★★ **Belle Cottage**, (Cotg), 80 King St, 900m W of PO, ☎ 03 6352 2144, fax 03 6352 2144, 1 cotg acc up to 4, (2 bedrm), [shwr, tlt, heat, elec blkts, tel (local), TV, clock radio, t/c mkg, refrig, cook fac, d/wash, toaster, ldry, blkts, doonas, linen, pillows], w/mach, lounge firepl, c/park (undercover), breakfast ingredients, non smoking property. BLB ♦ **$99**, ♦♦ **$110**, ♦ **$15**, AE BC DC EFT MC VI.

★★★★ **Kames Cottage**, (Cotg), Tighnabruaich Farm, 461 Bridport Rd, 2.5km fr Scottsdale, ☎ 03 6352 2760, 1 cotg acc up to 2, (1 bedrm), [shwr, tlt, fan, heat, elec blkts, tel, TV, radio, t/c mkg, refrig, cook fac, blkts, linen, pillows], ldry, bbq, meals avail, breakfast ingredients. D ♦ $85, ♦♦ $95, BC MC VI.

B&B's/Guest Houses

★★★★ **Beulah of Scottsdale**, (B&B), Heritage, c1879, 9 King St, 200m E of PO, ☎ 03 6352 3723, (2 stry), 4 rms [ensuite, fan, heat (elec), elec blkts, TV (2), clock radio], ✕, t/c mkg shared, refrig, non smoking rms. BB ♦ $70 - $80, ♦♦ $90 - $130, ch con.

Other Accommodation

Bellows Accommodation, 65 King St, ☎ 03 6352 2263, fax 03 6352 2263, 4 rms acc up to 12, [heat (elec), TV, linen, pillows], ldry, res liquor license, cook fac, t/c mkg shared, refrig, bbq, breakfast ingredients, non smoking rms. D $22, RO ♦♦ $49.50, BC JCB MC VI.

SHEARWATER TAS 7307

Pop 610. (261 km N of Hobart). See map on page 656, ref C3, Shearwater is the Central Business District for the Port Sorell and Hawley Beach areas with the Rubicon Estuary as the common feature.

★★★☆ **Shearwater Country Club**, (LH), Shearwater Blvd, 1km N of PO, ☎ 03 6428 6205, fax 03 6428 6786, (2 stry gr fl), 26 rms [shwr, tlt, heat, elec blkts, tel, TV, video, radio, t/c mkg, refrig, cook fac], ldry, conv fac, ✕ (Daily - Lunch & Tea), pool-heated, sauna, bbq, plygr, golf, gym, squash, tennis, cots. RO ♦ $77 - $110, ♦♦ $88 - $121, ◊ $13.20, ch con, AE BC DC MC VI.

★★★★ **(Holiday Unit Section)**, (2 stry gr fl), 23 units acc up to 9, (1 & 2 bedrm), [shwr, spa bath (8), tlt, cent heat, tel, TV, video, radio, t/c mkg, refrig, cook fac, micro, blkts, doonas, linen, pillows], ldry. D ♦♦ $126.50 - $150.50, ◊ $22, ch con, 8 units ★★★★☆.

SHEFFIELD TAS 7306

Pop 992. (273km NW Hobart), See map on page 656, ref C4, Historic town of murals depicting history of area, scenic countryside, forests, waterfalls and rugged mountain gorges. Nearby to picturesque Lake Barrington, Roland and Pioneer Settlement, Gowrie Park.

Hotels/Motels

★★★★ **Kentish Hills Retreat Motel**, (M), Cnr West Nook Rd & Main Rd, 600m W of PO, ☎ 03 6491 2484, fax 03 6491 2550, 8 units [ensuite, spa bath (1), heat (elec), elec blkts, tel, TV, video, clock radio, t/c mkg, refrig, cook fac], ldry, cots-fee, non smoking rms. RO ♦ $71.50 - $82.50, ♦♦ $88 - $132, ch con, AE BC DC EFT MC VI, ⅃&.

★★★ **Sheffield Country Motor Inn**, (M), 51-53 Main St, 100m W of PO, ☎ 03 6491 1800, fax 03 6491 1966, (2 stry gr fl), 8 units [shwr, tlt, heat, elec blkts, tel, TV, t/c mkg, refrig, mini bar, cook fac (2)], ldry, cots. RO ♦ $58, ♦♦ $68, ◊ $16, ch con, AE BC DC EFT MC VI.

★☆ **Sheffield Hotel**, (LH), 38 Main St, 50m fr PO, ☎ 03 6491 1130, fax 03 6491 2286, 5 rms [heat, elec blkts, TV, refrig], ldry, lounge, ✕, t/c mkg shared, bbq, rm serv, c/park. BLB ♦ $30, ♦♦ $50, ◊ $10, ch con, EFT.

Self Catering Accommodation

★★★★ **Silver Ridge Retreat**, (Cotg), 55ha farm property. Rysavy Rd (C136), 11km S of Sheffield PO, ☎ 03 6491 1727, fax 03 6491 1925, 9 cotgs acc up to 6, (2 bedrm), [shwr, spa bath (3), tlt, heat (woodheater), radio, t/c mkg, refrig, cook fac, micro, blkts, linen, pillows], ldry, conf fac, ✕, pool indoor heated, bbq, cots. D ♦ $110 - $180, ♦♦ $110 - $180, ◊ $25, ch con, 3 units of a lower rating. AE BC DC JCB MC VI.

SHEFFIELD TAS *continued...*

★★★☆ **Carinya Farm Accommodation**, (HU), 63 Staverton Rd, Roland 7306, 9km SW of Sheffield PO, ☎ 03 6491 1593, fax 03 6491 1256, (2 stry), 2 units acc up to 8, (1 & 2 bedrm), [shwr, tlt, heat (elec/wood), elec blkts, TV, radio, t/c mkg, refrig, cook fac, micro, blkts, linen, pillows], ldry, bbq, meals avail, plygr, cots-fee, non smoking units. **D ‖ $85, ‖‖ $92, ◊ $20**, ch con, Breakfast available, BC VI.

★★★☆ **Helvetia Retreat**, (HU), Tylers Rd, 6km S of PO, ☎ 03 6491 1806, 2 units acc up to 5, (Studio), [shwr, tlt, heat (elec/wood), TV, clock radio, t/c mkg, refrig, cook fac, blkts, linen, pillows], w/mach, non smoking units. **D ‖ $68, ‖‖ $68, ◊ $18**, ch con, ⚿.

★★★☆ **Minnow Cabins Accommodation**, 324 Lower Beulah Rd, 13km E of PO, ☎ 03 6491 1903, fax 03 6491 1903, 2 cabins acc up to 4, (2 bedrm), [shwr, tlt, heat, TV, clock radio, t/c mkg, refrig, cook fac, toaster, blkts, doonas, linen, pillows], ldry, w/mach, bbq, c/park (undercover), cots-fee, non smoking property. **D ‖ $40 - $45, ‖‖ $80 - $85, ◊ $25 -$30, W ‖ $250 - $300, ‖‖ $450 - $500, ◊ $100 - $110**, ch con, BC MC VI.

★★★☆ **The Granary**, (Cotg), 575 Staverton Rd 14km SW of Sheffield PO, ☎ 03 6491 1689, fax 03 6491 1367, (2 stry gr fl), 6 cotgs acc up to 10, (1, 2, 3 & 4 bedrm), [shwr, bath, tlt, heat (wood/gas), elec blkts, TV, video, radio, t/c mkg, refrig, cook fac, blkts, linen, pillows], w/mach, rec rm, conv fac, sauna, spa, bbq, plygr, mini golf, gym, cots. **D ‖ $73 - $96, ‖‖ $88 - $116, ◊ $30, W ‖ $438 - $576, ‖‖ $528 - $696, ◊ $180**, ch con, 3 units of a higher rating. BC MC VI.

★★★☆ **White Hawk**, (HU), 2033 Main Rd, 3km fr PO, ☎ 03 6491 1644, fax 03 6491 1644, (2 stry gr fl), 2 units acc up to 12, (2 bedrm), [shwr, tlt, heat, TV, clock radio, t/c mkg, refrig, cook fac, blkts, linen, pillows], bbq, cots, non smoking units. **D ‖ $55 - $65, ‖‖ $65 - $85, ◊ $15 - $25**, Breakfast available, AE BC JCB MC VI.

★★★ **Gowrie Park Wilderness Cabins**, (HU), Weindorfers, Gowrie Park 7306, 14km S of Sheffield, ☎ 03 6491 1385, fax 03 6491 1848, 4 units acc up to 6, (2 bedrm), [heat (elec), elec blkts, TV, clock radio, t/c mkg, refrig, cook fac, blkts, linen, pillows], ldry, conv fac, ⊠, bbq, meals avail, ✆, plygr, cots, non smoking units (4), Pets on application. **D ‖ $66, ‖‖ $66, ◊ $11**, ch con, BC MC VI.

★★★ **Kentish Cottage**, (Cotg), 620 West Kentish Rd, West Kentish 7306, 7km W of PO, ☎ 0418 538 227, 1 cotg acc up to 4, (2 bedrm), [fan, heat (elec/wood), elec blkts, tel, TV, radio, t/c mkg, refrig, cook fac, micro, d/wash, ldry, blkts, doonas, linen, pillows], bbq, cots, breakfast ingredients, non smoking rms, Pets on application. **D ‖ $55, ‖‖ $85, ◊ $15**, ch con, weekly con.

★★★ **Paradise Cottage**, (Cotg), 29ha farm property. 75 Jeffries Rd, Paradise 5075, 5km SW of PO, ☎ 03 6491 1626, fax 03 6491 1626, 3 cotgs acc up to 6, (2 bedrm), [shwr, tlt, heat, elec blkts, TV, radio, t/c mkg, refrig, cook fac, micro (2), blkts, linen, pillows], w/mach, dryer, bbq, plygr, cots-fee. **D ‖ $45, ‖‖ $60 - $70, ◊ $15**, ch con, 1 unit of a lower rating. BC MC VI.

★★★ **Sheffield Pioneer Holiday Units**, (HU), 3 Pioneer Cres, 100m fr PO, ☎ 03 6491 1149, fax 03 6491 1102, 2 units acc up to 10, (5 bedrm), [shwr, tlt, heat, TV, radio (1), t/c mkg, refrig, cook fac, micro, blkts, linen, pillows], w/mach, dryer, bbq, c/park (undercover), cots-fee, non smoking units. **D ‖‖ $65 - $75, ◊ $15**, ch con, BC MC VI.

B&B's/Guest Houses

★★★★☆ **Atherfield**, (B&B), 241 Jeffries Rd, 7km S of PO, ☎ 03 6491 1996, fax 03 6491 1996, 2 rms [ensuite, heat, elec blkts, clock radio], ldry, rec rm, lounge (TV/video), lounge firepl, ✕, t/c mkg shared, refrig, meals avail, ✆, non smoking property. **BB ‖ $85, ‖‖ $110, ◊ $55**, AE BC DC JCB MC VI.

★★★★ **Acacia**, (B&B), 113 High St, 1km N of PO, ☎ 03 6491 2482, fax 03 6491 2553, 3 rms [ensuite (1), heat, elec blkts, TV, clock radio], bathrm (2), ldry, lounge firepl, ✕, t/c mkg shared, refrig, bbq, meals avail, non smoking rms. **BB ‖ $45 - $50, ‖‖ $75 - $95, ◊ $27 - $35**, ch con, AE BC MC VI.

★★★★ **Badgers Host Farm**, (B&B), Nook Rd, 3km NW of PO, ☎ 03 6491 1816, fax 03 6491 2488, 3 rms [shwr, tlt, heat, elec blkts, tel, t/c mkg], ldry, lounge (TV), ✕, refrig, meals avail, cots, non smoking rms, **BB ‖ $110, ‖‖ $110, ◊ $55**, ch con, AE BC MC VI.

★★★★ **Cradle Vista Guest House**, (B&B), 978 Staverton Rd (C140) via (C141), 17km fr Sheffield, ☎ 03 6491 1129, fax 03 6491 1930, 4 rms [ensuite (3), heat (elec/wood), elec blkts, clock radio], bathrm (1), ldry, lounge (TV), lounge firepl, ✕, t/c mkg shared, refrig, meals avail, non smoking property. **BB ‖ $100, ‖‖ $120**, BC MC VI.

★★★★ **Glencoe Farm Guest House**, (B&B), Main Rd, Barrington 7306, 8km NW of Sheffield, ☎ 03 6492 3267, fax 03 6492 3267, 4 rms [ensuite, heat, elec blkts, radio], ldry, lounge (TV), ✕, t/c mkg shared, refrig, meals avail, cots-fee, non smoking rms, Pets on application. **BB ‖ $75 - $83, ‖‖ $106 - $114, ◊ $75**, ch con, AE BC DC MC VI.

★★★☆ **Gnome Home**, (B&B), (Farm), 499 Staverton Rd (C140), 14km SW of Sheffield PO, ☎ 03 6491 1560, fax 03 6491 1307, 4 rms [ensuite (1), spa bath (1), heat, elec blkts, TV], shared fac (3), ldry, lounge (TV), ✕, t/c mkg shared, refrig, non smoking rms. **BB ‖ $40 - $55, ‖‖ $70 - $95**, ch con.

Other Accommodation

Mount Roland Recreation Centre, Weindorfers, Gowrie Park 7306, 14km S of Sheffield, ☎ 03 6491 1385, fax 03 6491 1848, 34 rms [blkts, linen-fee], shared fac (4), ldry, conv fac, lounge firepl, ⊠, cook fac, t/c mkg shared, refrig, bbq, plygr, non smoking rms, Pets on application. **RO ‖ $11**, ch con, BC MC VI.

SISTERS BEACH TAS 7321

Pop 241. (398km NW Hobart), See map on page 656, ref B3, Small holiday resort with coastal views and white sandy beaches.

★★★☆ **Tasman Buray Holiday Cottages**, (Cotg), ☎ 03 6445 1147, 3 cotgs acc up to 6, (3 bedrm), [shwr, bath, tlt, heat, TV, radio, t/c mkg, refrig, cook fac, blkts, linen, pillows], w/mach, plygr, Pets on application. **D ‖ $70, ◊ $10**, ch con, weekly con.

★★☆ **Birdland Holiday Cottages**, (Cotg), 7 Banksia Ave, ☎ 03 6445 1471, 3 cotgs acc up to 6, (2 & 3 bedrm), [shwr, tlt, heat (elec/wood), elec blkts, radio, TV, t/c mkg, refrig, cook fac], w/mach, bbq, plygr, cots. **D ‖‖ $55, ◊ $6**, ch con, 1 cottage ★★★.

SMITHTON TAS 7330

Pop 3,495. (413km NW Hobart), See map on page 656, ref A3, Rich agricultural distict in vegetable processing, timber milling, dairy farming and fishing industry. Administrative centre of the region.

Hotels/Motels

★★★★ **Tall Timbers**, (M), Scotchtown Rd, 2km S of PO, ☎ 03 6452 2755, fax 03 6452 2742, 59 units [shwr, tlt, hairdry, fan, heat, elec blkts, tel, TV, radio, t/c mkg, refrig, mini bar], ldry, rec rm, conv fac, ⊠, bar, bbq, plygr, tennis, cots. **RO ‖ $80 - $130, ‖‖ $90 - $143, ◊ $16.50 - $27**, AE BC DC EFT MC VI, ⚿.

★★☆ **Bridge Hotel**, (LMH), Montagu Rd, 500m W of PO, ☎ 03 6452 1389, fax 03 6452 2709, (2 stry gr fl), 38 units [shwr, tlt, heat (14), cent heat (24), elec blkts, tel (24), TV (26), movie, radio (24), t/c mkg (26), refrig (24)], ldry, lounge (TV), conv fac, ✕, ⊠, bar (gaming mach etc), rm serv, cots. **RO ‖ $35 - $70, ‖‖ $45 - $90**, ch con.

Self Catering Accommodation

★★★★ **Eixel Cottage**, (Cotg), 1430 South Rd, Lileah 7330, 14km S of Smithton, ☎ 03 6456 4143, fax 03 6456 4143, 1 cotg acc up to 7, (3 bedrm), [shwr, tlt, heat (wood), elec blkts, TV, video, clock radio, t/c mkg, refrig, cook fac, blkts, linen, pillows], w/mach, dryer, breakfast ingredients. **D ‖ $55, ‖‖ $110, ◊ $25**, ch con, BC MC VI.

★★★☆ **Millfarm Cottage**, (Cotg), West Rd, Roger River 7330, 15km SW of Smithton, ☎ 03 6456 5118, fax 03 6456 5118, 1 cotg acc up to 7, (2 bedrm), [shwr, tlt, fan, heat (elec/wood), elec blkts, tel, TV, video, clock radio, t/c mkg, refrig, cook fac, micro, blkts, linen, pillows], w/mach, dryer, pool-indoor, bbq, c/park (undercover), plygr, cots, breakfast ingredients, Pets on application. **D ‖ $90 - $100, ‖‖ $90 - $100, ◊ $20**, ch con, BC MC VI.

Rosie's, (HU), 42A Goldie St, 500m NE of PO, ☎ 03 6452 2660, fax 03 6452 2779, 1 unit acc up to 5, (2 bedrm), [shwr, tlt, heat (elec/wood), elec blkts, TV, clock radio, radio, t/c mkg, refrig, cook fac, blkts, linen, pillows], w/mach, dryer, bbq, cots, breakfast ingredients, non smoking units. **D ‖ $132, ‖‖ $132, ◊ $30**, BC MC VI, (not yet classified).

B&B's/Guest Houses

★★★★ **Christies Corner**, (B&B), 46 Goldie St, 500m E of PO, ☎ 03 6452 3132, fax 03 6452 3132, 2 rms [heat (elec), elec blkts, clock radio, t/c mkg, refrig], bathrm, lounge (TV), ✕, meals avail, cots, non smoking property. **BB ‖ $66, ‖‖ $88, ◊ $22**, ch con, BC MC VI.

SOMERSET TAS 7322

Pop Part of Wynyard Muni, (333km NW Hobart), See map on page 656, ref B3, Situated on the Cam River at the junction of Bass and Murchison Hwys.

★★★☆ **Murchison Lodge Motor Inn**, (M), 9 Murchison Hwy, 1km E of PO, ☎ 03 6435 1106, fax 03 6435 2778, (2 stry gr fl), 30 units (1 suite) [shwr, tlt, heat, elec blkts, tel, TV, clock radio, t/c mkg, refrig], conv fac, ⊠ (Mon to Sat), bbq, dinner to unit, plygr, cots, non smoking rms (19). **RO ‖ $95, ‖‖ $95, ◊ $19.50**, AE BC DC JCB MC VI.

SORELL TAS 7172

Pop 1,732. (26km E Hobart), See map on page 656, ref D6, Gateway to the East Coast and Port Arthur.

B&B's/Guest Houses

★★★★ **Blue Bell Inn**, (B&B), c1829. 26 Somerville St, 100m W of PO, ☎ 03 6265 2804, fax 03 6265 3880, (2 stry), 5 rms [ensuite (4), spa bath (ensuite) (1), elec blkts], bathrm (1), lounge (TV, video), lounge firepl, cots, non smoking property. **BB ♦ $80 - $95, ♦♦ $95 - $110, ◊ $25,** AE BC MC VI.

★★★★ **Sorell Colonial Cottages 'The Barracks'**, (B&B), 31-33 Walker St, 350m from PO, ☎ 03 6265 2804, fax 03 6265 2805, 5 rms (2 suites) [ensuite, spa bath (2), heat (elec), elec blkts, TV, clock radio (2), t/c mkg, refrig, doonas], ldry, bbq, cots-fee, non smoking rms. **BB ♦ $88 - $110, ♦♦ $99 - $121, ◊ $30, Suite BB ♦♦ $121,** ch con, weekly con, AE BC MC VI.

★★★☆ **Cherry Park Estate**, (B&B), 114 Pawleena Rd, 2km N of PO, ☎ 03 6265 2271, fax 03 6265 3971, (2 stry), 4 rms [ensuite (1), fan (1), heat (elec), elec blkts, TV (4), video, clock radio, t/c mkg, refrig (3)], shared fac (3), ldry, ✕, bbq, cots, non smoking rms. **BB ♦ $65 - $85, ♦♦ $75 - $95, ◊ $16.50 - $30,** ch con, 1 room of a higher rating. AE BC MC VI.

SOUTHPORT TAS 7109

Pop 304. (101km S Hobart), See map on page 656, ref C8, Southport is one of the oldest towns in this area and is now primarily a seaside resort with some farming and fishing activity.

★★★☆ **Southern Forest Bed & Breakfast**, (B&B), Kent St, 500m NW of PO, ☎ 03 6298 3306, fax 03 6298 3306, 3 rms [fan, cent heat, radio, CD], bathrm (2), ✕, t/c mkg shared, refrig, cots, non smoking rms. **BB ♦ $45 - $50, ♦♦ $75 - $85,** ch con.

★★★☆ **The Jetty House**, (B&B), Main Rd, Southport Centre, ☎ 03 6298 3139, fax 03 6298 3139, 2 rms [cent heat, video, doonas], lounge, ✕, t/c mkg shared, bbq, plygr, non smoking property, Pets on application. **BB ♦ $55 - $60, ♦♦ $80 - $90, ◊ $30,** ch con, weekly con.

ST HELENS TAS 7216

Pop 2,000. (253km NE Hobart), See map on page 656, ref E4, St Helens is the largest town on the East Coast. Popular resort with magnificent coastal scenery and peaceful unspoilt beaches.

Hotels/Motels

★★★☆ **Anchor Wheel**, (M), 61 Tully St, 1km N of PO, ☎ 03 6376 1358, fax 03 6376 2009, 7 units [shwr, tlt, hairdry, heat, elec blkts, tel, TV, t/c mkg, refrig, mini bar], ldry, ⊠ (Mon-Sat), bbq, rm serv (b'fast), cots. **RO ♦ $44 - $55, ♦♦ $49.50 - $66, ◊ $11,** ch con, AE BC DC JCB MC VI.

★★★ **Bayside Inn**, (LMH), 2 Cecilia St, 500m S of PO, ☎ 03 6376 1466, fax 03 6376 1656, 27 units [shwr, bath, tlt, hairdry (6), heat, elec blkts, tel, TV, radio, t/c mkg, mini bar], ldry, conf fac, ⊠, pool indoor heated, rm serv, cots. **RO $58 - $115,** ch con, fam con, AE BC DC MC MCH VI, ♿.

★★☆ **(Poolside Rooms)**, 15 units [shwr, bath, tlt, heat, elec blkts, tel, TV, radio, t/c mkg, refrig]. **RO ♦ $55 - $65, ♦♦ $65 - $80, ◊ $11.**

(Budget Family Units), 12 units (1 & 2 bedrm), [shwr, tlt, heat, elec blkts, tel, TV, radio, t/c mkg, refrig, micro, toaster]. **RO ♦ $40 - $50, ♦♦ $50 - $60, ◊ $11.**

Self Catering Accommodation

★★★★ **Homelea Accommodation**, (HU), 16-18 Tasman Hwy, 1.5km S of PO, ☎ 03 6376 1601, fax 03 6376 2701, 1 unit acc up to 7, (2 bedrm), [shwr, spa bath, tlt, a/c, heat (Heat Pump), TV, video, clock radio, t/c mkg, refrig, cook fac, blkts, linen, pillows], w/mach, plygr, cots, non smoking property (inside), Pets allowed. **D ♦♦ $85 - $95, ◊ $15,** ch con, Min book applies.

★★★★ **Kellraine**, (HU), 72 Tully St, 1km N of PO, ☎ 03 6376 1169, fax 03 6376 1169, 14 units acc up to 6, (1, 2 & 3 bedrm), [shwr, tlt, heat (elec), elec blkts, TV, video, clock radio, t/c mkg, refrig, cook fac, micro, blkts, linen, pillows], w/mach, bbq, boat park, cots. **D ♦ $35, ♦♦ $40, ◊ $10 - $15,** ch con, BC MC VI, ♿.

★★★☆ **Cockle Cove Beachfront**, (SA), 234 St Helens Point Rd (C851), 7km S of St Helens, ☎ 03 6376 3036, fax 03 6376 3226, 2 serv apts acc up to 4, (1 bedrm), [shwr, tlt, heat, elec blkts, TV, video, clock radio, t/c mkg, refrig, cook fac, micro, ldry, blkts, doonas, linen, pillows], w/mach (2), iron, cots-fee, breakfast ingredients (on request)-fee. **D ♦ $45 - $55, ♦♦ $50 - $60, ◊ $15,** ch con, weekly con, BC MC VI.

★★★☆ **Halcyon Grove**, (HU), 16 Halcyon Gr, 2km S of PO, ☎ 03 6376 1424, fax 03 6376 1424, (Multi-stry), 11 units acc up to 6, (1 & 2 bedrm), [shwr, tlt, heat (elec), elec blkts, TV, clock radio, t/c mkg, refrig, cook fac, ldry], boat park, plygr, cots. **D ♦♦ $50 - $70, ◊ $10,** ch con, BC EFT MC VI, ♿.

★★★☆ **Queechy Cottages**, (Cotg) Cnr Jason St & Tasman Hwy, 1km S of PO, ☎ 03 6376 1321, fax 03 6376 1652, 18 cotgs acc up to 6, (1, 2 & 3 bedrm), [shwr, tlt, heat, elec blkts, TV, clock radio, refrig, cook fac, micro, blkts, linen, pillows], w/mach, ⊠, bbq, boat park, plygr, tennis (half court), non smoking units (17). **D ♦ $72 - $90, ♦♦ $72 - $90, ◊ $18 - $19.20,** ch con, BC MC VI.

★★★ **Daisy House Accommodation**, (HU), 36 A&B Quail St, 250m S of PO, ☎ 03 6376 1815, fax 03 6376 2466, 2 units acc up to 7, (3 bedrm), [shwr, bath, tlt, heat, heat (elec), elec blkts, TV, clock radio, t/c mkg, refrig, cook fac, micro, blkts, doonas, linen, pillows], w/mach, bbq (1), cots-fee, non smoking units. **D ♦♦ $45 - $50, ◊ $10, W ♦♦ $315 - $350,** ch con, 1 unit ★★, BC DC EFT MC VI.

★★☆ **Corraleau**, (HU), 22 Tasman Hwy, 1km S of PO, ☎ 03 6376 1363, fax 03 6376 1363, 7 units acc up to 6, (1 & 2 bedrm), [shwr, tlt, heat (elec/wood), elec blkts, TV, t/c mkg, refrig, cook fac, blkts, linen, pillows], w/mach, bbq, boat park, plygr, cots. **D ♦♦ $45 - $65, ◊ $15,** ch con, BC EFT MC VI.

B&B's/Guest Houses

★★★★☆ **Warrawee**, (B&B), Tasman Hwy, 3km S of PO, ☎ 03 6376 1987, fax 03 6376 1012, 7 rms (2 suites) [ensuite, spa bath (2), heat, elec blkts, TV (8), video (3), clock radio, t/c mkg], lounge (TV), breakfast rm, ✕, bbq, non smoking rms. **BB ♦ $90, ♦♦ $128 - $160, Suite BB ♦♦ $192, ◊ $52,** AE BC MC VI.

★★★☆ **(Cottage Section)**, 1 cotg acc up to 8, (3 bedrm), [shwr, bath, tlt, TV, video, refrig, cook fac, micro, ldry, blkts, linen, pillows], non smoking units, Pets on application. **D ♦ $95, ♦♦ $95, ◊ $20,** Min book applies.

★★★★ **Cecilia House**, (B&B), 78 Cecilia St, 500m N of PO, ☎ 03 6376 1723, fax 03 6376 2355, 3 rms [ensuite, heat (electric), elec blkts], lounge (TV), ✕, non smoking property. **BB ♦ $72, ♦♦ $94.**

★★★★ **Wybalenna Guest House**, (B&B), c1909. Tasman Hwy, 2km S of PO, ☎ 03 6376 1611, fax 03 6376 2612, 5 rms [ensuite, fire pl, heat, elec blkts, TV, radio, t/c mkg], lounge, breakfast rm, ✕, refrig, non smoking property. **BB ♦ $120, ♦♦ $145, ◊ $50,** BC MC VI.

★★★☆ **Artnor Lodge**, (B&B), 71 Cecilia St, 100m N of PO, ☎ 03 6376 1234, fax 03 6376 1234, 6 rms [ensuite (2), heat, elec blkts, TV (5), t/c mkg, refrig], ldry, rec rm (table tennis), lounge (TV), bbq, cots. **BB ♦ $35 - $50, ♦♦ $50 - $75, ◊ $15,** ch con.

Other Accommodation

St Helens YHA, 5 Cameron St, ☎ 03 6376 1661, 4 rms acc up to 8, ldry, cook fac, t/c mkg shared, refrig. **RO ◊ $16 - $50,** ch con.

ST MARYS TAS 7215

Pop 580. (217km NE Hobart), See map on page 656, ref E4, Situated at the headwaters of the South Esk River.

Hotels/Motels

★☆ **St Marys Hotel**, (LH), Main St, ☎ 03 6372 2181, (2 stry) 14 rms [heat, elec blkts], lounge (TV-Sky Channel), t/c mkg shared, ☏. **BLB ♦ $33, ♦♦ $55, ◊ $13, RO ♦ $27.50, ♦♦ $44, ◊ $8,** ch con.

B&B's/Guest Houses

★★★★☆ **Addlestone House B & B**, (B&B), 19 Gray Rd, 500m S of hotel, ☎ 03 6372 2783, fax 03 6372 2889, 2 rms [ensuite, fan, heat, elec blkts, clock radio, t/c mkg, micro, toaster, ldry, doonas], lounge (TV), t/c mkg shared, refrig, bbq, cots. **BB ♦ $66 - $70, ♦♦ $77 - $81,** BC MC VI.

STANLEY TAS 7331

Pop 600. (411km NW Hobart), See map on page 656, ref A3, A fishing port and historic town, Stanley has changed little since the days of the early settlers. Many of the original buildings, including Highfield House, have been restored to their former glory.

Hotels/Motels

★★★★ **Stanley Village**, (M), 15/17 Wharf Rd, 500m W of PO, ☎ 03 6458 1404, fax 03 6458 1403, (2 stry gr fl), 8 units [shwr, spa bath (4), tlt, heat, elec blkts, tel, TV, video, movie, clock radio, t/c mkg, refrig, mini bar], ldry, ⊠, cots. **RO ♦ $90 - $120, ♦♦ $100 - $140,** AE BC DC EFT MC VI.

★★★☆ **Stanley Motel**, (M), Dovecote Rd, 1.5km W of PO, ☎ 03 6458 1300, fax 03 6458 1448, 18 units [shwr, spa bath (1), tlt, fan, heat, elec blkts, tel, TV, radio, t/c mkg, refrig], ldry, conv fac, ⊠, rm serv, cots. **RO ♦ $85 - $110, ♦♦ $95 - $130, ◊ $15,** ch con, AE BC DC EFT MC VI, ♿.

★★★☆ **(Dovecote Cottages)**, 6 units acc up to 5, (Studio & 2 bedrm), [shwr, bath, tlt, fan, heat, elec blkts, tel, TV, radio, t/c mkg, refrig, cook fac, blkts, linen, pillows]. **D ♦ $100 - $120, ♦♦ $110 - $120, ◊ $15, W ♦♦ $520 - $700,** ch con, ♿.

★☆ **Union**, (LH), 19 Church St, 100m NW of PO, ☎ 03 6458 1161, (Multi-stry), 10 rms [elec blkts, t/c mkg], ldry, lounge (TV), ✕, cots. **RO ♦ $30, ♦♦ $50,** ch con.

Self Catering Accommodation

★★★★★ **Beachside Retreat West Inlet**, (HU), No facilities for children under 5, 253 Stanley Hwy, The Peninsula, 2.5km S of Stanley, ☎ 03 6458 1350, fax 03 6458 1350, 1 unit acc up to 6, (3 bedrm), [shwr, spa bath (1), tlt, hairdry, cent heat, elec blkts, tel, TV, video, clock radio, t/c mkg, refrig, mini bar, cook fac, micro, d/wash, doonas, linen, pillows], ldry, iron, bbq, car wash, non smoking property. D $140 - $156, $40, weekly con, Light breakfast available, BC MC VI.

(Eco-Cabin Section), No facilities for children under 5. 2 cabins acc up to 2, (1 bedrm), [shwr, tlt, heat (gas), elec blkts, TV, clock radio, t/c mkg, refrig, mini bar, cook fac, doonas, linen, pillows], ldry, bbq, non smoking property. D $128 - $148, weekly con, Min book applies, (not yet classified).

★★★★☆ **The Town House-Stanley**, (Cotg), 4 Church St, ☎ 03 6458 1485, fax 03 6458 1455, 1 cotg acc up to 8, (4 bedrm), [shwr, tlt, fan, heat (elec), elec blkts, tel, TV, video, clock radio, radio, t/c mkg, refrig, cook fac, micro, blkts, linen, pillows], w/mach, dryer, bbq, cots, breakfast ingredients, Pets on application. D $135, $20, BC MC VI.

★★★★ **Abbey's Cottage**, (Cotg), c1850. 1 Marshall St, 400m N of PO, ☎ 03 6458 1186, fax 03 6458 1290, 1 cotg acc up to 6, (3 bedrm), [shwr, bath, tlt, hairdry, fan, heat, elec blkts, tel, TV (2), video, clock radio, radio, CD, t/c mkg, refrig, cook fac, micro, blkts, doonas, linen, pillows], w/mach, dryer, cots, breakfast ingredients, non smoking property. BB $144, $25, BC EFT MC VI.

★★★★ **Abbey's on the Terrace**, (Cotg), 34 Alexander Terrace, 150m S of PO, ☎ 03 6458 1186, fax 03 6458 1290, 1 cotg acc up to 4, (2 bedrm), [shwr, bath, tlt, hairdry, fan, heat, elec blkts, tel, TV, video, clock radio, radio, CD, t/c mkg, refrig, cook fac, micro, blkts, doonas, linen, pillows], w/mach, dryer, cots, breakfast ingredients, non smoking property. BB $144, $25, BC EFT MC VI.

★★★★ **Bayside Colonial Cottage**, (Cotg), Classified by National Trust, 4 Alexander Tce, 500m S of PO, ☎ 03 6458 1209, fax 03 6458 1209, 1 cotg acc up to 4, (2 bedrm), [shwr, tlt, heat (elec/wood), elec blkts, TV, clock radio, radio, t/c mkg, refrig, cook fac, blkts, linen, pillows], w/mach, dryer, breakfast ingredients, non smoking property. D $100 - $120, $100 - 120, $30, W $600, $600, $150.

★★★★ **Captain's Cottage**, (Cotg), 30 Alexander Tce, ☎ 03 6458 3230, fax 03 6458 3237, (2 stry gr fl), 1 cotg acc up to 6, (3 bedrm), [shwr, bath, tlt, hairdry, heat (elec/wood), elec blkts, TV (2), video, radio, CD, t/c mkg, refrig, cook fac, micro, blkts, doonas, linen, pillows], w/mach, dryer, cots, breakfast ingredients. D $152, $30, W $700 - $800, ch con, BC MC VI.

★★★★ **Gateforth Cottages**, (Cotg), Historic working farm c1841. Gateforth Farm, 12km SE of Stanley, ☎ 03 6458 3230, fax 03 6458 3237, 3 cotgs acc up to 7, (2 & 3 bedrm), [shwr, bath, spa bath (1), tlt, hairdry, fan, heat (elec/wood), elec blkts, tel, TV, video (3), radio, CD, t/c mkg, refrig, cook fac, micro, blkts, linen, pillows], w/mach, dryer, bbq, meals avail, plygr, cots-fee, breakfast ingredients. D $134 - $152, $29, W $700, ch con, Min book Christmas Jan and Easter, BC MC VI.

★★★★ **Ride Cottage**, (Cotg), 12 Pearse St, 500m NW of PO, ☎ 03 6458 1137, 1 cotg acc up to 4, (2 bedrm), [shwr, tlt, heat (elec/wood), elec blkts, TV, radio, t/c mkg, refrig, cook fac, d/wash, blkts, linen, pillows], w/mach, cots, non smoking units. D $75, $80, $20, W $500, $500, $650, $70, ch con.

★★★★ **Touchwood**, (Cotg), 33 Church St, 200m NW of PO, ☎ 03 6458 1348, fax 03 6458 1348, 2 cotgs acc up to 8, (1 & 3 bedrm), [shwr (3), bath (1), tlt (3), heat, elec blkts, TV, clock radio, refrig, mini bar, cook fac, blkts, linen, pillows], ldry, elec blkts, cots, breakfast ingredients, non smoking property. D $138, $29, W $520 - $720, $120, ch con, 1 unit ★★★☆. AE BC DC EFT MC VI.

★★★☆ **Anthonys at Highfield**, (HU), Green Hills Rd, 1.5km NW of PO, ☎ 03 6458 1245, fax 03 6458 1286, 1 unit acc up to 6, (4 bedrm), [shwr, tlt, heat, elec blkts, TV, t/c mkg, refrig, cook fac, blkts, linen, pillows], w/mach, c/park (garage), breakfast ingredients, non smoking units. D $44, $88, $22.

★★★ **Pol and Pen**, (HU), 8 Pearse St, ☎ 03 6458 1186, fax 03 6458 1290, 2 units acc up to 4, (2 bedrm), [shwr, tlt, fan, heat (wood), elec blkts, TV, radio, t/c mkg, refrig, cook fac, micro, blkts, linen, pillows], w/mach, iron, c/park (undercover), cots-fee. D $75, $10, BC EFT MC VI.

★★★ **The Retreat**, (HU), 13 Wharf Rd, ☎ 03 6458 1109, fax 03 6458 1109, 1 unit acc up to 2, (1 bedrm), [shwr, tlt, heat (elec), elec blkts, TV, clock radio, t/c mkg, refrig, cook fac, blkts, linen, pillows], w/mach, dryer, breakfast ingredients. D $90, $90.

B&B's/Guest Houses

★★★★☆ **Hanlon House**, (B&B), 6 Marshall St, 200m N of PO, ☎ 03 6458 1149, fax 03 6458 1257, (2 stry gr fl), 5 rms (1 suite) [ensuite, spa bath (1), hairdry, heat (log fires/gas), elec blkts, tel, clock radio], ldry, lounge (TV/Video) (2), ✗, t/c mkg shared, refrig, meals avail (lunch & dinner), non smoking property. BB $100, $125 - $165, $33, ch con, AE BC MC VI.

★★★★ **Philately House**, (B&B), 11-13 Church St, Next door to PO, ☎ 03 6458 1109, fax 03 6458 1109, 1 rm (Studio), [shwr, tlt, heat (wood), elec blkts, TV, video, clock radio, t/c mkg, refrig, cook fac ltd, ldry], bbq, BLB $80 - $90, $90 - $100, $25, ch con, MC VI.

★★★★ **Rosebank Cottage Collection**, (B&B), Brooks Rd, 10km S of Stanley, ☎ 03 6452 2660, fax 03 6452 2779, 1 rm (1 bedrm), [shwr, spa bath, tlt, heat (floor), elec blkts, TV, radio, t/c mkg, refrig, toaster], ldry, bbq, cots. BLB $132, $30, BC MC VI.

★★★★ **(Cottage Section)**, 2 cotgs acc up to 6, (1 & 2 bedrm), [shwr, bath (1), spa bath (1), tlt, heat, elec blkts, TV, clock radio, t/c mkg, refrig, cook fac, micro, blkts, linen, pillows], lounge firepl, breakfast ingredients. D $132 - $143, $30.

★★★★ **Stanley Guest House**, (B&B), 27 Main Rd, 450m NW of PO, ☎ 03 6458 1488, 3 rms [ensuite (1), heat (elec/wood), elec blkts, clock radio], shared fac (family room) (1), lounge (TV), t/c mkg shared, refrig, non smoking rms. BB $75 - $98, $80 - $110, $25, BC MC VI.

★★★★ **The Old Cable Station**, (B&B), West Beach Rd, 7km W of PO, ☎ 03 6458 1312, fax 03 6458 2009, 4 rms [ensuite, spa bath (1), hairdry, heat, elec blkts, TV, clock radio, t/c mkg], ✗, refrig, non smoking rms. BLB $110 - $140, $30, BC MC VI.

★★★☆ **Myrtle Brook**, (B&B), 4ha organic property. 10km S Stanley, (C221), ☎ 03 6458 3174, fax 03 6458 3174, 2 rms [shwr, tlt, heat, elec blkts], lounge (TV), ✗, t/c mkg shared, non smoking rms, Pets on application. BB $50, $85, ch con.

STRAHAN TAS 7468

Pop 597. (300km W Hobart), See map on page 656, ref A5, Situated on the Macquarie Harbour, Strahan's major industries include fishing, aquaculture and forestry.

Hotels/Motels

★★★☆ **The Strahan Village**, (M), The Esplanade, ☎ 03 6471 7191, fax 03 6471 7389, 63 units [shwr, tlt, tel, TV, radio, t/c mkg, refrig, ldry], lounge firepl, ✗, bar, plygr. RO $94, $94, $29, AE BC DC EFT MC VI, &.

★★★★ **(Strahan Village)**, Cottages & Terraces, 44 units (7 suites) [shwr, spa bath (10), tlt, heat, elec blkts, TV, radio, t/c mkg, refrig, cook fac ltd (7), micro (7)], ldry, iron, iron brd, ✗, ✆, cots. RO $148, $148, $29.

★★ **(Hamers Hotel)**, 18 rms [heat, elec blkts, TV], ✗, t/c mkg shared, ✆, BB $53, $73, $29.

Self Catering Accommodation

★★★★ **Castaway Holiday Apartments**, (HU), Reception: Cnr Harvey & Herbert Sts, 500m N of PO, ☎ 03 6471 7400, fax 03 6471 7580, 6 units acc up to 6, (2 bedrm), [shwr, tlt, fan, heat (elec), elec blkts, TV, clock radio, radio, t/c mkg, refrig, cook fac, blkts, linen, pillows], ldry, bbq, ✆, plygr, cots-fee, non smoking property. D $55 - $95, $55 - $95, $20, ch con, BC EFT MC VI, &.

Castaway Holiday Apartments ...continued

★★★★ **(Chalet Section)**, 1 unit acc up to 6, (3 bedrm), [ensuite (1), shwr, tlt, heat (elec/wood), elec blkts, TV, clock radio, t/c mkg, refrig, cook fac, blkts, linen, pillows], w/mach, dryer, bbq, cots-fee, non smoking property. **D ♦ $135, ♦♦ $135, ◊ $20**, ch con.

★★★ **(Shoalhaven Chalet)**, 1 cotg acc up to 3, (Studio), [ensuite, heat (elec), elec blkts, TV, clock radio, t/c mkg, refrig, cook fac ltd, blkts, linen, pillows], bbq, breakfast ingredients, non smoking property. **D ♦ $50 - $75, ♦♦ $50 - $75, ◊ $15**, weekly con.

★★★★ **Kitty's Place**, (HU), Innes St, ☎ 03 6471 7666, fax 03 6471 7660, 5 units acc up to 5, (1 & 2 bedrm), [shwr, spa bath (2), tlt, heat (elec), elec blkts, TV, clock radio, t/c mkg, refrig, cook fac, ldry, blkts, linen, pillows], cots, non smoking units. **D ♦ $55 - $99, ♦♦ $66 - $132, ◊ $27.50**, BC EFT MC VI, ⓕ&.

★★★★ **Macquarie Cottage**, (Cotg), c1890, 5 Reid St, 800m N of PO, ☎ 03 6471 7028, fax 03 6471 7663, 1 cotg acc up to 5, (2 bedrm), [shwr, bath, tlt, hairdry, heat (elec/wood), elec blkts, tel (local only), TV, clock radio, t/c mkg, refrig, cook fac, blkts, doonas, linen, pillows], w/mach, dryer, iron, iron brd, lounge firepl, cots, breakfast ingredients. **D ♦ $130, ♦♦ $160, ◊ $30**, ch con, BC MC VI.

★★★★ **McIntosh Cottages**, (Cotg), c1898. 18 Harvey St, ☎ 03 6471 7358, fax 03 6471 7074, 2 cotgs acc up to 6, (1 & 2 bedrm), [shwr, bath (1), tlt, hairdry, heat (elec/woodheater), elec blkts, TV, clock radio, t/c mkg, refrig, cook fac, micro, blkts, linen, pillows], ldry, cots-fee, breakfast ingredients. **D ♦ $110, ♦♦ $154 - $160, ◊ $35.20**, ch con.

★★★★ **Renison Cottage**, (Cotg), 34-58 Harvey St, 1.5km E of PO, ☎ 03 6471 7390, fax 03 6471 7076, 3 cotgs acc up to 4, (1 & 2 bedrm), [shwr, tlt, fan, heat (gas), elec blkts, TV, video, clock radio, t/c mkg, refrig, cook fac, micro, blkts, doonas, linen, pillows], ldry, bbq, cots-fee, breakfast ingredients. **D ♦ $165 - $180, ♦♦ $165 - $180, ◊ $38**, ch con, BC MC VI, ⓕ&.

★★★★ **Risby House**, (HU), 1 Vivian St, 2km E of PO, ☎ 03 6471 7572, fax 03 6471 7340, 1 unit acc up to 7, (3 bedrm), [shwr, tlt, fan, heat (gas, elec), elec blkts, tel, TV, video, clock radio, CD, t/c mkg, refrig, mini bar, blkts, linen, pillows], w/mach, dryer, bbq, cots, breakfast ingredients, non smoking property. **D ♦ $144, ♦♦ $144, ◊ $33**, ch con, AE BC EFT MC VI.

★★★★ **The Piners Loft**, (HU), Esplanade, 3km E of PO, ☎ 03 6471 7390, fax 03 6471 7076, (2 stry), 1 unit acc up to 7, (3 bedrm), [shwr, tlt, fan, heat, elec blkts, TV, video, clock radio, t/c mkg, refrig, cook fac, blkts, linen, pillows], w/mach, dryer, read rm, cots, breakfast ingredients. **D ♦ $195, ♦♦ $195, ◊ $38**, ch con, BC MC VI.

★★★☆ **Cape Horn Accommodation**, (HU), 3 Frazer St, 50m W of PO, ☎ 03 6471 7169, fax 03 6471 7169, 2 units acc up to 4, (1 bedrm), [ensuite, heat (elec), elec blkts, TV, clock radio, radio, t/c mkg, refrig, cook fac (1), cook fac ltd (1), micro], ldry, bbq, non smoking units. **RO ♦ $55 - $85, ♦♦ $65 - $85, ◊ $20**, ch con, Light breakfast available, ⓕ&.

★★★☆ **Gordon Gateway Chalet**, (HU), Grining St, 1km NE of PO, ☎ 03 6471 7165, fax 03 6471 7588, 12 units acc up to 6, (1 & 2 bedrm), [shwr, bath (2), tlt, fan, heat (elec), elec blkts, TV, t/c mkg, refrig, cook fac, doonas, linen, pillows], ldry, bbq, ✆, plygr, cots. **RO ♦♦ $100 - $195**, ch con, 2 chalets of a higher rating, ⓕ&.

★★★☆ **Greengate Cottages**, (Cotg), 21 Meredith St, 2km NW of PO, ☎ 03 6471 7456, fax 03 6471 2507, 2 cotgs acc up to 5, (2 bedrm), [shwr, tlt, heat, elec blkts, TV, clock radio, t/c mkg, refrig, cook fac, micro, blkts, linen, pillows], w/mach, bbq (portable), c/park (undercover), cots, Pets on application. **D ♦♦ $66 - $82.50, ◊ $16.50**, ch con.

★★★☆ **Gull Cottage**, (HU), Office: Esplanade, 500m W of PO, ☎ 03 6471 7227, fax 03 6471 7765, 1 unit acc up to 4, (2 bedrm), [shwr, bath, tlt, heat, elec blkts, TV, radio, refrig, cook fac, blkts, linen, pillows], w/mach, dryer, bbq, cots. **D ♦ $60, ♦♦ $75, ◊ $20**, ch con, weekly con.

★★★☆ **Harbour Views**, (HU), 1 Charles St, 700m from PO, ☎ 0438 584 143, fax 03 6471 7766, 2 units acc up to 4, (1 & 2 bedrm), [shwr, tlt, heat, elec blkts, TV, t/c mkg, refrig, cook fac ltd (1), blkts, linen, pillows], cots, breakfast ingredients. **BLB ♦♦ $60 - $85, ◊ $10 - $15**, ch con, BC MC VI.

GOLDEN CHAIN ★★★☆ **Sailors Rest**, (Cotg), 14-16 Harvey St, 400m N of PO, ☎ 03 6471 7237, fax 03 6471 7837, 8 cotgs acc up to 8, (1, 2 & 3 bedrm), [shwr, bath, tlt, hairdry, heat (elec/wood), elec blkts, TV, video, clock radio, CD, t/c mkg, refrig, cook fac, blkts, linen, pillows], w/mach, dryer, bbq, cots, non smoking units. **D ♦♦ $80 - $100, ◊ $22**, ch con, BC EFT MC VI.

★★★☆ **Sharonlee Strahan Villas**, (HU), Previously Sharonlee Andrew St, 1km W of PO, ☎ 03 6471 7224, fax 03 6471 7375, 15 units acc up to 6, (1 & 2 bedrm), [shwr, tlt, heat, elec blkts, TV, radio, t/c mkg, refrig, cook fac, micro, blkts, linen, pillows], ldry, rec rm, bbq, c/park (undercover), plygr, cots-fee. **D ♦ $65 - $124, ◊ $27**, ch con, AE BC DC MC VI.

★★★☆ **Strahan Colonial Cottages**, (Cotg), Reid St, 1km E of PO, ☎ 03 6471 7612, fax 03 6471 1513, 4 cotgs acc up to 4, (1 & 2 bedrm), [shwr, spa bath, tlt, fire pl, heat, elec blkts, TV, clock radio, t/c mkg, refrig, cook fac, blkts, linen, pillows], w/mach, dryer, bbq, breakfast ingredients. **D ♦♦ $195, ◊ $35**, ch con, 2 units ★★★★. BC MC VI.

★★★ **Regatta Point**, (HU), Esplanade, 2km E of PO, ☎ 03 6471 7103, fax 03 6471 7366, 8 units acc up to 6, (2 bedrm), [shwr, tlt, heat, elec blkts, TV, radio, t/c mkg, refrig, cook fac, blkts, linen, pillows], ldry, ⊠, bbq, plygr, cots. **D ♦ $60 - $120, ◊ $20**.

Cedar Heights, (Apt), 7 Meredith St, ☎ 03 6471 7717, fax 03 6471 7817, (gr fl), 1 apt [shwr, spa bath, tlt, heat (elec), elec blkts, TV, video, clock radio, t/c mkg, refrig, micro, toaster, blkts, doonas, linen, pillows], w/mach, bbq, cots, non smoking units (1). **BLB ♦ $55 - $70, ♦♦ $60 - $85, ◊ $15**, BC MC VI, (not yet classified).

B&B's/Guest Houses

★★★★★ **Ormiston House**, (B&B), c1899, Esplanade, 500m W of PO, ☎ 03 6471 7077, fax 03 6471 7007, 5 rms [ensuite, spa bath (1), a/c-cool, cent heat, elec blkts, tel, TV, t/c mkg], lounge firepl, ⊠, non smoking property. **BB ♦♦ $180 - $235**, AE BC DC EFT MC VI.

★★★★☆ **Franklin Manor**, (B&B), c1896. The Esplanade, ☎ 03 6471 7311, fax 03 6471 7267, 18 rms [ensuite, spa bath (2), hairdry, fire pl (2), heat (elec), elec blkts, tel, TV, video (4), t/c mkg, refrig, cook fac (2)], iron, iron brd, lounge (2), ✗, ⊠, cots. **BB ♦ $135 - $229, ♦♦ $130 - $239, ◊ $38 - $48**, AE BC BTC DC MC VI.

★★★★☆ **Risby Cove**, (B&B), Risby Cove, Esplanade, 1 km E of PO, ☎ 03 6471 7572, fax 03 6471 7340, (2 stry gr fl), 4 rms (3 suites) [ensuite, spa bath (3), hairdry, heat (elec), elec blkts, tel, TV, clock radio, t/c mkg, refrig, mini bar, cook fac ltd, ldry], lounge (TV), conf fac, ⊠, non smoking rms. **BLB ♦♦ $124 - $156, ◊ $33, Suite BLB ♦♦ $145 - $178, ◊ $33**, ch con, AE BC EFT MC VI, ⓕ&.

★★★★ **Strahan Central**, (B&B), 1 Harold St, ☎ 03 6471 7612, fax 03 6471 7513, 4 rms [ensuite, bath, hairdry, heat (elec/wood), elec blkts, clock radio, t/c mkg, refrig], iron, iron brd, lounge (TV), cafe (Lic.), cots, breakfast ingredients. **BB ♦♦ $100 - $165**, AE BC DC EFT JCB MC VI.

★★★ **Cozy Pines**, (B&B), Lot 5, Lynch St, 500m S of P, ☎ 03 6471 7423, 1 rm (Studio), [shwr, tlt, heat (wood), elec blkts, TV, clock radio, t/c mkg, refrig, cook fac, micro, pillows], bbq, cots, non smoking rms. **BLB ♦ $50 - $70, ♦♦ $55 - $75, ◊ $15**, ch con.

★★★ **Strahan Wilderness Lodge**, (B&B), Ocean Beach Rd, 2.5km NW of PO, ☎ 03 6471 7142, fax 03 6471 7147, 5 rms [bath, elec blkts], lounge (TV), pool indoor heated, spa, t/c mkg shared, bbq, cots-fee. **BLB ♦ $40 - $50, ♦♦ $45 - $60, ◊ $15**, BC MC VI.

★★★ **(Bay View Cottages & Cabins)**, 5 units acc up to 6, (1, 2 & 3 bedrm), [shwr, bath (some), tlt, hairdry, heat, elec blkts, TV, clock radio, refrig, cook fac, micro (some), blkts, doonas, linen, pillows], bbq, breakfast ingredients. **D ♦ $55 - $70, ♦♦ $60 - $85, ◊ $20**.

Other Accommodation

Strahan YHA, Harvey St, ☎ 03 6471 7513, fax 03 6471 7255, 20 rms acc up to 10, ldry, cook fac, t/c mkg shared, refrig. **RO ♦ $17 - $70**.

STRATHGORDON TAS 7139

Pop 72. (158km W Hobart), See map on page 656, ref B6, Strathgordon was developed to service the Hydro Electric schemes in the Gordon and Pedder region. The lakes combined hold 37 times the volume of water in Sydney Harbour.

★★ **Lake Pedder Chalet**, (LH), Gordon River Rd, ☎ 03 6280 1166, fax 03 6280 1145, 68 rms (1 suite) [shwr, tlt, fan, heat, elec blkts, t/c mkg], ldry, lounge (TV), lounge firepl, ⊠ (Mon to Sun), pool-heated, bbq, squash, tennis, cots-fee. **RO ♦ $55 - $88, ♦♦ $72 - $99, ◊ $11 - $16.50, Suite RO ♦ $121, ♦♦ $144**, ch con, 1 room of a higher standard, BC MC VI.

SWAN ISLAND 7255

See map on page 656, ref E3, Swan Island is the first in a chain of Bass Strait islands stretching to Wilson's Promontory in Victoria. The island offers a rich diversity of plant and wildlife, water activites and unspoilt sparkling beaches and diving.

★★★ **Swan Island Retreat**, (B&B), ☎ 03 6357 2211, 3 rms [shwr, tlt, radio, t/c mkg, refrig, cook fac], w/mach, bbq, meals avail, cots. **D ♦♦ $110, ◊ $55**.

$

TASMANIA

SWANSEA TAS 7190

Pop 550. (137km NE Hobart), See map on page 656, ref E5, This charming seaside town is steeped in history and nestles on the magnificent blue waters of the Great Oyster Bay.

Hotels/Motels

GOLDEN CHAIN ★★★ **Swansea Motor Inn**, (M), 1 Franklin St, 500m E of PO, ☎ 03 6257 8102, fax 03 6257 8811, 28 units [shwr, tlt, heat, elec blkts, tel, TV, clock radio, t/c mkg, refrig, toaster], ldry, rm serv, cots. RO ♦ $55 - $90, ♦♦ $55 - $90, ◊ $15, ch con, 10 rooms ★★☆. AE BC DC MC VI.

★★★ **Swansea Waterloo Inn Motel**, (LMH), 1A Franklin St, ☎ 03 6257 8577, fax 03 6257 8397, (Multi-stry gr fl), 28 units [ensuite, spa bath (5), heat (elec), elec blkts, tel, TV, clock radio, t/c mkg, refrig], ldry, conf fac, c/park. RO ♦ $85 - $150, ♦♦ $85 - $150, AE BC DC MC VI.

★☆ **Swan Inn**, (LH), 1B Franklin St, 500m E of PO, ☎ 03 6257 8899, 6 rms [shwr, tlt, heat, elec blkts, TV, t/c mkg, refrig], conv fac, ⊠, bbq, cots. RO ♦♦ $55, ◊ $12.

Self Catering Accommodation

★★★★☆ **Piermont Resort**, (Cotg), Tasman Hwy, 3km S of PO, ☎ 03 6257 8131, fax 03 6257 8422, 6 cotgs acc up to 6, (1 & 2 bedrm), [shwr, spa bath (3), tlt, fan, heat (elec/wood), elec blkts, tel, TV, video, clock radio, t/c mkg, refrig, cook fac, blkts, linen, pillows], w/mach, dryer, conf fac, pool, bbq, tennis, breakfast ingredients, non smoking units (4). BB $195, AE BC DC MC VI.

★★★★ **Lester Cottages**, (Cotg), 42 Gordon St, 1km S of PO, ☎ 03 6257 8105, fax 03 6257 8425, (2 stry gr fl), 4 cotgs acc up to 6, (1 & 2 bedrm), [shwr, tlt, fan, fire pl (1), heat (elec/wood), elec blkts, TV, radio, t/c mkg, refrig, cook fac, blkts, linen, pillows], w/mach, bbq, plygr, cots-fee, breakfast ingredients, non smoking units. D ♦ $93.50 - $132, ♦♦ $93.50 - $132, ◊ $22, W ♦♦ $550 - $660, ch con, BC MC VI.

★★★★ **Scarecrow Cottage**, (Cotg), c1860. 22 Noyes St, 400m SW of PO, ☎ 03 6334 3860, or 03 6257 8065, 1 cotg acc up to 5, (2 bedrm), [shwr, tlt, elec blkts, TV, t/c mkg, refrig, cook fac, micro, blkts, linen, pillows], w/mach, dryer, lounge firepl, breakfast ingredients. D ♦♦ $140 - $160, ◊ $22 - $24, W ♦♦ $840 - $960, ch con, BC MC VI.

★★★★ **Tubby & Padman Cottage Living**, (HU), 20 Franklin St, ☎ 03 6257 8901, fax 03 6257 8901, 4 units acc up to 4, (1 & 2 bedrm), [shwr, spa bath (3), tlt, heat, elec blkts, TV, clock radio, t/c mkg, refrig, cook fac, micro, toaster, blkts, doonas, linen], ldry, w/mach, dryer, lounge firepl, bbq, breakfast ingredients, non smoking property. BLB ♦ $110 - $120, ♦♦ $145 - $155, BC DC MC VI.

★★★★ **Wagners Cottages**, (Cotg), c1860. Tasman Hwy, 2km S of PO, ☎ 03 6257 8494, fax 03 6257 8267, 4 cotgs acc up to 4, (1 & 2 bedrm), [shwr, spa bath (3), tlt, fire pl, heat (elec/wood), elec blkts, TV, radio, CD, t/c mkg, refrig, cook fac, doonas, linen, pillows], w/mach, cots, breakfast ingredients. D ♦♦ $112 - $178, ◊ $34, ch con, AE BC MC VI.

★★★☆ **Kabuki by the Sea**, (Cotg), 'Rocky Hills' Tasman Hwy, 12km S of PO, ☎ 03 6257 8588, fax 03 6257 8588, 5 cotgs acc up to 4, (1 & 2 bedrm), [shwr, tlt, cent heat, elec blkts, t/c mkg, refrig, cook fac, micro, blkts, linen, pillows], ⊠, meals avail, breakfast ingredients. D ♦ $110, ♦♦ $132, ◊ $40, ch con, AE BC DC MC VI.

B&B's/Guest Houses

FLAG
FLAG CHOICE HOTELS

★★★★☆ **Meredith House**, (B&B), c1853. 15 Noyes St, 300m SW of PO, ☎ 03 6257 8119, fax 03 6257 8123, (2 stry) 7 rms (1 suite) [ensuite, bath (1), spa bath (1), heat, elec blkts, tel, TV, clock radio, t/c mkg, refrig, mini bar], ldry, lounge firepl, ✕, bbq, meals avail, cots, non smoking property. BB ♦ $110 - $115, ♦♦ $146 - $160, ◊ $52, Suite BB ♦♦ $170 - $192, ch con, AE BC DC JCB MC VI.

★★★★☆ **(Meredith Mews)**, (gr fl), 4 rms [shwr, spa bath (3), tlt, heat, elec blkts, tel, TV, clock radio, t/c mkg, refrig, mini bar, cook fac ltd], ldry, ✕, bbq, meals avail, cots-fee, non smoking property. BB ♦♦ $146 - $192, ◊ $52, ch con.

★★★★ **Braeside Cottage**, (B&B), 21 Julia St, 500m S of PO, ☎ 03 6257 8008, fax 03 6257 8889, 2 rms (2 suites) [ensuite, fan, heat (elec), elec blkts, TV, clock radio, t/c mkg, refrig], breakfast rm, ✕, pool-heated (solar), cots, non smoking rms. Suite BB ♦ $104 - $110, ♦♦ $124 - $132, BC MC VI.

★★★★ **Freycinet Waters**, (B&B), No facilities for children under 14, 16 Franklin St, Next to PO, ☎ 03 6257 8080, fax 03 6257 8075, (gr fl), 3 rms [ensuite, elec blkts, TV, clock radio, t/c mkg, refrig], lounge, breakfast rm, non smoking property. BB ♦ $88, ♦♦ $100, ◊ $28, AE BC DC MC VI.

★★★★ **Redcliffe House**, (B&B), 13569 Tasman Hwy, 1.5km N of PO, ☎ 03 6257 8667, fax 03 6257 8667, (2 stry gr fl), 3 rms [ensuite, fire pl (1), elec blkts, TV, t/c mkg], ldry, read rm, breakfast rm, cots-fee, non smoking rms. BB ♦ $85 - $100, ♦♦ $95 - $125, ◊ $30, ch con, AE BC MC VI.

★★★★ **Schouten House**, (B&B), c1846. 1 Waterloo Rd, ☎ 03 6257 8564, fax 03 6257 8767, (2 stry), 4 rms [ensuite, heat, elec blkts, TV, clock radio, t/c mkg, refrig], conf fac, lounge firepl, ⊠, bar, non smoking rms. BB ♦♦ $120 - $145, ◊ $30, AE BC DC MC VI.

AAA TOURISM Special Rates ★★★★ **Swansea Cottages & Sherbourne Lodge**, (B&B), 43 Franklin St, 600m N of PO, ☎ 03 6257 8328, fax 03 6257 8502, 5 rms [ensuite, bath (2), spa bath (1), hairdry, heat, elec blkts, TV, clock radio, t/c mkg, refrig, micro, ldry, doonas], res liquor license, bbq, cots-fee, non smoking rms. BLB ♦ $88 - $165, ♦♦ $88 - $165, ◊ $33, ch con, AE BC DC MC VI.

★★★★ **(Cottage Section)**, 6 cotgs (1, 2 & 3 bedrm), [shwr, spa bath (1), tlt, hairdry, fire pl (4), heat, elec blkts, TV, video-fee, clock radio, t/c mkg, refrig, cook fac, micro, d/wash, doonas, linen, pillows], w/mach, dryer, iron, bbq, cots-fee, non smoking rms. D ♦ $121 - $187, ♦♦ $121 - $187, ◊ $33, ch con, Breakfast available. ♦&.

★★★★ **Swansea Ocean Villas & Amos House**, (B&B), 3 Maria St, 300m N of PO, ☎ 03 6257 8656, fax 03 6257 8656, 7 rms [ensuite, heat (elec), elec blkts, TV, clock radio, t/c mkg, refrig], ✕, ⊠, non smoking rms. AE BC DC EFT MC VI.

★★★★ **(Villa Section)**, 8 units acc up to 6, (1 & 2 bedrm), [shwr, tlt, hairdry, heat (elec/wood), elec blkts, TV, clock radio, t/c mkg, refrig, cook fac, micro, blkts, linen, pillows], w/mach, dryer, ⊠, cots, non smoking units. D ♦♦ $105 - $176, ◊ $27.50 - $33.

★★★☆ **Oyster Bay Guest House**, (B&B), 10 Franklin St, 50m S of PO, ☎ 03 6257 8110, fax 03 6257 8703, (2 stry), 9 rms [ensuite, heat (elec/wood), elec blkts, clock radio, t/c mkg], ldry, lounge (TV), conf fac, ⊠, bbq, plygr, cots, non smoking rms. BB ♦ $45 - $80, ♦♦ $75 - $106, ◊ $40, ch con, AE BC DC EFT MC VI.

Other Accommodation

Swansea YHA, 5 Franklin St, ☎ 03 6257 8367, 4 rms acc up to 6, ldry, cook fac, t/c mkg shared, refrig. RO ♦ $16 - $50, ch con.

TABLE CAPE TAS 7325

Pop 436. (350km NW Hobart), See map on page 656, ref B3, Prominent headland offering spectacular views of beautiful beaches and coastline for hundreds of kilometres.

★★★★ **Skyescape**, (B&B), 'Skye', 282 Tollymore Rd, 7.8km NW of PO, ☎ 03 6442 1876, fax 03 6442 4118, 2 rms (2 suites) [ensuite, spa bath, heat (elec), elec blkts, tel, TV, clock radio, t/c mkg, refrig, ldry (service)], ✕, bbq, meals avail, non smoking suites. BB ♦♦ $180 - $250, BC MC VI.

TARANNA TAS 7180

Pop 157. (88km SE Hobart), See map on page 656, ref D7, Overlooking Norfolk Bay. Tasmanian Devil Park.

Self Catering Accommodation

★★★★ **Mason's Cottages**, (HU), Arthur Hwy, 8km N of Port Arthur, ☎ 03 6250 3323, fax 03 6250 3088, 3 units acc up to 5, (2 bedrm), [shwr, tlt, heat (elec), elec blkts, TV, clock radio, t/c mkg, refrig, cook fac, blkts, linen, pillows], ldry, bbq, cots, breakfast ingredients, non smoking units (2). D ♦ $70, ♦♦ $70, ◊ $10.

B&B's/Guest Houses

AAA TOURISM Special Rates ★★★★ **Norfolk Bay Convict Station**, (B&B), 5862 Arthur Hwy, ☎ 03 6250 3487, fax 03 6250 3487, 5 rms [ensuite (2), hairdry, a/c, elec blkts, clock radio], lounge, breakfast rm, res liquor license, t/c mkg shared, bbq, cots, non smoking property. BB ♦ $50 - $70, ♦♦ $70 - $140, ◊ $30 - $50, ch con, BC MC VI.

Other Accommodation

Norfolk Bay Houseboats, (Hbt), Little Norfolk Bay, 11km N of Port Arthur, ☎ 03 6250 3499, fax 03 6250 3499, 2 houseboats acc up to 8, (1 & 3 bedrm), [shwr, tlt, heat (gas), TV, video, radio, CD (1), t/c mkg, refrig, blkts, linen, pillows], cook fac, bbq, non smoking property. D $180 - $1,220, Insurance bond, BC MC VI.

THREE HUMMOCK ISLAND TAS 7330

See map on page 656, ref A2, The island lies off the North West tip of Tasmania in Bass Strait in the path of the 'Roaring Forties'.
Eagle Hill Lodge, (HU), ☎ 03 6452 1554, fax 03 6452 1554, 1 unit acc up to 10, (3 bedrm), [shwr, tlt, heat (elec/wood), radio, t/c mkg, refrig, cook fac, blkts, linen, pillows], ldry, bbq, cots, non smoking property.
D ⋔ $49.50 - $60.50, ⋔⋔ $88 - $104.50, ◊ $44 - $55, W ⋔ $231 - $242, ⋔⋔ $539 - $583, ◊ $223.30 - $236.50, ch con, EFT, (not yet classified).

TRIABUNNA TAS 7190

Pop 924. (88km NE Hobart), See map on page 656, ref E6, Fishing port on Spring Bay and centre of a large wood chipping industry.
Hotels/Motels
★★★ **Tandara Motor Inn,** (LH), Tasman Hwy, 500m N of PO, ☎ 03 6257 3333, fax 03 6257 3155, 26 rms [shwr, tlt, cent heat, elec blkts, tel, TV, clock radio, t/c mkg, refrig], ldry, conf fac, ⊠ (3-6 days), pool, bbq, dinner to unit, plygr, cots-fee. **RO ⋔ $55, ⋔⋔ $66, ⋔⋔⋔ $77,** AE BC DC MC VI.

Other Accommodation
Triabunna YHA, 12 Spencer St, ☎ 03 6257 3439, fax 03 6257 3439, 8 rms acc up to 9, ldry, cook fac, t/c mkg shared, refrig. **RO ⋔ $16 - $18,** ch con.

TULLAH TAS 7321

Pop 718. (330km NW Hobart), See map on page 656, ref B4, Located in mountainous country with heavily timbered sections.
Hotels/Motels
★★★ **Tullah Lakeside Chalet,** (M), Farrell St, ☎ 03 6473 4121, fax 03 6473 4130, 36 units [shwr, tlt, heat, t/c mkg], ldry, ⊠, refrig, ✆, canoeing, cots, non smoking rms. **RO ⋔ $85 - $99, ⋔⋔ $85 - $99,** 18 rooms ★★. AE BC DC MC VI.

Self Catering Accommodation
★★★☆ **Tullah Lakeside Cottage,** (HU), 6 Meredith St, ☎ 03 6473 4165, fax 03 6473 4177, 1 unit acc up to 6, (2 bedrm), [shwr, bath, tlt, heat, elec blkts, TV, video, clock radio, t/c mkg, refrig, cook fac, micro, blkts, doonas, linen, pillows], w/mach, dryer, bbq, c/park (undercover), Pets on application. **D ⋔ $60, ⋔⋔ $70, ◊ $15, W ⋔ $400, ◊ $100.**
★★★ **Wombat Lodge,** (HU), Murchison Hwy, 'The Bush Nook', 1.5km N of PO, ☎ 03 6473 4252, (2 stry gr fl), 1 unit acc up to 5, (1 bedrm), [shwr, tlt, heat (elec), elec blkts, TV, video, t/c mkg, refrig, mini bar, cook fac, blkts, doonas, linen, pillows], w/mach, bbq, c/park. **D ⋔ $60, ⋔⋔ $60, ◊ $10.**

TURNERS BEACH TAS 7315

Pop 905. (296km NW Hobart), See map on page 656, ref C3, Popular seaside holiday resort. Boat Ramp, Boating, Fishing, Swimming.
Self Catering Accommodation
★★★★ **Sea-Forth Holiday Apartments,** (HU), 58-60 Susan St, 6km E of Ulverstone PO, ☎ 03 6428 3334, fax 03 6428 3747, 5 units acc up to 6, (2 & 3 bedrm), [shwr, tlt, heat (elec), elec blkts, TV, video, clock radio, t/c mkg, refrig, cook fac, blkts, linen, pillows], w/mach, bbq, cots, non smoking rms (5). **D ⋔ $118 - $132, ⋔⋔ $118 - $132, ◊ $15 - $20, W ⋔ $708 - $792, ⋔⋔ $708 - $792, ◊ $90 - $120,** BC MC VI.

★★★☆ **Delaney Park Holiday Villas,** (HU), Lethborg Ave, ☎ 03 6428 2552, fax 03 6428 2434, 14 units acc up to 6, (2 bedrm), [shwr, tlt, heat, elec blkts, TV, video, t/c mkg, refrig, cook fac, micro, doonas], ldry, bbq, car wash, ✆, plygr, cots-fee, Pets on application. **D ⋔ $66 - $120, ⋔⋔ $66 - $120, ◊ $15, W ⋔ $396 - $580, ⋔⋔ $396 - $580, ◊ $90,** BC MC VI, ♿.

TURNERS MARSH TAS 7267

Pop 355. (220km N Hobart), See map on page 656, ref D4, A small rural community just north of Launceston.
★★★☆ **Nirvana,** (B&B), 951 Pipers River Rd, 16km NE of Launceston, ☎ 03 6395 4160, fax 03 6395 4160, 3 rms [ensuite, heat (elec/wood), elec blkts, TV, radio, ldry], ✗, t/c mkg shared, bbq, meals avail (evenings), non smoking rms. **BB ⋔ $55, ⋔⋔ $98.**

ULVERSTONE TAS 7315

Pop 9,792. (297km NW Hobart), See map on page 656, ref C3, Situated on the banks of the River Leven. The hinterland behind Ulverstone provides spectacular scenery while the sunny beaches on the coastline are a popular holiday destination.
Hotels/Motels

★★★☆ **Bass & Flinders Motor Inn,** (M), 49 - 51 Eastlands Dve, 1km E of PO, ☎ 03 6425 3011, fax 03 6425 4936, 11 units [shwr, tlt, heat, elec blkts, tel, TV, clock radio, t/c mkg, refrig], ldry, conv fac, ⊠ (Mon to Sat), bbq, rm serv, plygr, cots, non smoking rms (9). **RO ⋔ $100, ⋔⋔ $100, ◊ $15,** ch con, AE BC DC MC VI.

★★★☆ **The Lighthouse,** (LH), 33 Victoria St, 150m E of PO, ☎ 03 6425 1197, fax 03 6425 1219, (2 stry) 27 rms (1 suite) [shwr, bath, tlt, heat, elec blkts, tel, TV, clock radio, t/c mkg, refrig], conv fac, ⊠, sauna, spa, bbq, gym, cots. **RO ⋔ $115, ⋔⋔ $15,** AE BC DC MC VI.

★★★ **Beachway,** (M), Heathcote St, 1km E of PO, ☎ 03 6425 2342, fax 03 6425 5798, 28 units [shwr, tlt, heat, elec blkts, TV, radio, t/c mkg, refrig], ldry, conv fac, ⊠ (Tues to Sat), pool, cots-fee. **RO ⋔ $52, ⋔⋔ $60, ◊ $16,** ch con, AE BC DC MC VI.

★★★ **Ulverstone Waterfront Inn,** (M), 2 Tasma Pde, 1km W of PO, ☎ 03 6425 1599, fax 03 6425 5973, 25 units (2 suites) [shwr, spa bath (2), tlt, heat, elec blkts, tel, TV, clock radio, t/c mkg, refrig, mini bar], ldry, ⊠ (Mon to Sat), cafe, bar (cocktail), bbq, rm serv, plygr, cots, non smoking rms. **RO ⋔ $50 - $55, ⋔⋔ $55 - $60, Suite RO ⋔⋔ $94,** ch con, 6 Rooms of a higher rating. AE BC DC MC VI.

★★☆ **Furners,** (LH), Classified by National Trust, 42 Reibey St, 30m NW of PO, ☎ 03 6425 1488, fax 03 6425 5933, (2 stry) 15 rms [shwr, tlt, heat, elec blkts, TV, clock radio], conv fac, ⊠, t/c mkg shared, cots. **BB ⋔ $83.50, ⋔⋔ $83.50, ◊ $22,** ch con, BC MC VI.

Self Catering Accommodation
★★★☆ **Willaway Motel Apartments,** (HU), 2 Tucker St, 1km NE of PO, ☎ 03 6425 2018, fax 03 6425 6783, 8 units acc up to 6, (2 bedrm), [shwr, tlt, heat, elec blkts, TV, clock radio, t/c mkg, refrig, cook fac, blkts, linen, pillows], ldry, bbq, plygr, cots. **D ⋔ $60, ⋔⋔ $80, ◊ $20,** ch con, weekly con, AE BC DC JCB MC VI.
★★★ **Brigadoon Holiday Units,** (HU), 4 Moore St, West Ulverstone 7315, 500m W of PO, ☎ 03 6425 1697, fax 03 6425 4065, 15 units acc up to 6, (1 & 2 bedrm), [shwr, tlt, heat (elec), elec blkts, TV, clock radio, t/c mkg, refrig, cook fac, micro, blkts, linen, pillows], ldry, pool-indoor (solar heated), bbq, ✆, cots, Pets on application. **D ⋔ $65 - $70, ⋔⋔ $80 - $90, ◊ $11,** weekly con, BC MC VI.

B&B's/Guest Houses
★★★★☆ **Boscobel of Ulverstone,** (B&B), 27 South Rd, 1km W of PO, ☎ 03 6425 1727, fax 03 6425 1727, 3 rms [ensuite, spa bath (1), hairdry, fire pl, heat (elec), elec blkts, TV (2), clock radio, t/c mkg], iron, iron brd, lounge, ✗, pool-indoor, refrig, bbq, non smoking rms. **BB ⋔ $85 - $100, ⋔⋔ $100 - $150,** BC MC VI.
★★★★ **Ocean View,** (B&B), 1 Victoria St, 1km NE of PO, ☎ 03 6425 5401, fax 03 6425 5401, (2 stry gr fl), 6 rms (1 suite) [ensuite, spa bath (1), heat, elec blkts, clock radio, t/c mkg], lounge (TV), breakfast rm, refrig, cots, non smoking property. **BB ⋔ $72 - $95, ⋔⋔ $106 - $130, ◊ $35 - $40, Suite BB ⋔⋔ $146,** ch con, BC MC VI, ♿.

★★★★ **Westella,** (B&B), Classified by National Trust, c1865, 'Westella House' Westella Dve, 2km E of PO, ☎ 03 6425 6222, fax 03 6425 6276, (2 stry), 3 rms [ensuite (2), elec blkts, TV, clock radio], ldry, lounge (TV), lounge firepl, breakfast rm, t/c mkg shared, refrig, bbq, meals avail, plygr, non smoking property. **BB ⋔ $89 - $99, ⋔⋔ $122 - $132, ◊ $28,** ch con, BC MC VI.

VERONA SANDS TAS 7112

Pop 155. (70km S Hobart), See map on page 656, ref D7, Coastal town and popular holiday destination with pleasant beaches at Verona Sands, Randalls Bay and Eggs and Bacon Bay. Boat Ramp, Boating, Bowls, Fishing, Sailing, Swimming, Tennis.
Self Catering Accommodation
★★★ **Verona Sands Holiday Units,** (HU), 5693 Channel Hwy, 17km W of Cygnet, ☎ 03 6297 8177, fax 03 6297 8299, 4 units acc up to 6, (2 bedrm), [shwr, tlt, heat (elec), elec blkts, TV, clock radio, t/c mkg, refrig, cook fac, blkts, doonas, linen, pillows], ldry, bbq, plygr, cots. **D ⋔ $50, ⋔⋔ $60, ◊ $5 - $10, W ⋔ $300, ⋔⋔ $350,** ch con, AE BC MC VI.

WADDAMANA TAS 7030

(110km N Hobart), See map on page 656, ref C5, Former Hydro Electric Village, situated on the banks of the Ouse River. Acclaimed Geographical Centre, Power Museum. Bush Walking, Fishing, Horse Riding.
Self Catering Accommodation
★★★ **Waddamana Village Holiday Accommodation,** (HU), ☎ 03 6259 6158, 4 units acc up to 8, (3 bedrm), [shwr, tlt, heat (elec/wood), radio, t/c mkg, refrig, cook fac, blkts-fee, linen-fee], rec rm, conv fac, ✗, bbq, plygr, tennis. **D ⋔ $50, ⋔⋔ $65, ◊ $15.**
(Bunkhouse Section), 3 bunkhouses acc up to 20, (Bunk Rooms), [heat, blkts reqd, linen reqd], shwr, tlt, conv fac, ✗, cook fac, bbq.

WESTBURY TAS 7303

Pop 1,280. (216km NW Hobart), See map on page 656, ref C4, Quaint village graced with the charm of yesteryear. White House, Fitzpatrick's Inn, Pearns Steam World, St Andrews Church, Westbury Maze, Village Green, Shows Tractor Shed, The Old Bakehouse, Culzean Gardens. Bowls, Squash, Swimming, Tennis.

Self Catering Accommodation

★★★★ **Gingerbread Cottages**, (Cotg), c1880. 52 William St, 200m S of PO, ☎ 03 6393 1140, fax 03 6393 1140, 1 cotg acc up to 2, (1 bedrm), [shwr, tlt, fan, heat, elec blkts, TV, video, clock radio, radio, t/c mkg, refrig, cook fac, micro, blkts, doonas, linen, pillows], w/mach, dryer, dinner to unit, breakfast ingredients, non smoking units. **D ♦ $125, ♦♦ $125, W ♦ $787, ♦♦ $787**, AE BC MC VI.

★★★☆ **Cluan Homestead (The Manager's Residence)**, (HU), (Farm), 462 Cluan Rd, 10km S of Westbury, ☎ 03 6393 1549, fax 03 6393 2003, 1 unit acc up to 6, (3 bedrm), [shwr, bath, tlt, heat (elec/wood), elec blkts, TV, clock radio, t/c mkg, refrig, cook fac, doonas, linen, pillows], w/mach, dryer, bbq, tennis, cots. **BB ♦♦ $80, ♦ $22**, ch con.

★★★☆ **Egmont**, (Cotg), Classified by National Trust, c1838. Birralee Rd, 4km N of PO, ☎ 03 6393 1164, fax 03 6393 1164, 1 cotg acc up to 8, (4 bedrm), [shwr, tlt, heat (elec/wood), elec blkts, TV, t/c mkg, refrig, cook fac, blkts, linen, pillows], w/mach, plygr, cots. **D ♦ $66, ♦♦ $88, ♦ $16.50**, ch con.

B&B's/Guest Houses

★★★★ **The Olde Coaching Inn**, (B&B), 54 William St, 200m S of PO, ☎ 03 6393 2100, fax 03 6393 2100, 2 rms [ensuite, heat (elec/wood), elec blkts, TV, radio], ldry, ✗, cook fac, t/c mkg shared, refrig, cots. **BLB ♦ $75, ♦♦ $85, ♦ $15**, ch con, AE BC MC VI.

★★★☆ **Fitzpatricks Inn**, (B&B), Bass Hwy, ☎ 03 6393 1153, fax 03 6393 1153, 4 rms [ensuite, heat, elec blkts, TV, clock radio, t/c mkg], cots. **BLB ♦ $35 - $40, ♦♦ $70**, BC MC VI.

WESTERWAY TAS 7140

Pop 161. (65km W Hobart), See map on page 656, ref C6, Situated on the picturesque Tyenna River. Mount Field National Park (8km).

Self Catering Accommodation

★★★☆ **Tyenna Retreat**, (Cotg), 1587 Gordon River Rd, 200m E of PO, ☎ 03 6288 1552, 1 cotg acc up to 4, (2 bedrm), [shwr, tlt, heat, TV, clock radio, refrig, cook fac, micro, toaster, ldry, blkts, doonas, linen, pillows], w/mach, lounge firepl, bbq, cots-fee, breakfast ingredients, non smoking property. **BLB ♦ $75 - $95, ♦♦ $75 - $95, ♦ $25**.

WILMOT TAS 7310

Pop 285. (312km NW Hobart), See map on page 656, ref C4, Small township located in picturesque countryside. Fishing, Golf, Tennis.

Self Catering Accommodation

★★★☆ **Wilmot Accommodation Units**, (HU), Main Rd, 50m fr PO, ☎ 03 6492 1156, fax 03 6492 1156, 2 units acc up to 4, (1 bedrm), [heat (elec), elec blkts, TV, clock radio, t/c mkg, refrig, cook fac, micro, blkts, linen, pillows], ldry, bbq, c/park (undercover), ✆, plygr, cots-fee, breakfast ingredients, non smoking rms. **D ♦♦ $85**, EFT.

B&B's/Guest Houses

★★★☆ **Jacquies**, (B&B), Main Rd, 50m S of PO, ☎ 03 6492 1117, fax 03 649 2117, 5 rms [ensuite, heat, elec blkts, TV, clock radio, refrig], lounge (guest), ✗, res liquor license, ✆, non smoking rms (4). **BB ♦ $55, ♦♦ $70, ♦ $55**, EFT.

WINNALEAH TAS 7265

Pop 152. (310km NE Hobart), See map on page 656, ref E4, A small farming community. Bush Walking.

Other Accommodation

Merlinkei Farm YHA, Racecourse Rd, ☎ 03 6354 2152, fax 03 6354 1000, 3 rms acc up to 9, [micro], ldry, cook fac, t/c mkg shared, refrig. **RO ♦ $15 - $35**, ch con, BC MC VI.

WOODBRIDGE TAS 7162

Pop 253. (40km S Hobart), See map on page 656, ref D7, Small coastal township. Marine Studies Centre. Boat Ramp, Fishing, Sailing, Swimming.

Self Catering Accommodation

★★★☆ **Honeywood Cottage**, 72 Pullens Rd, 1.5km N of PO, ☎ 03 6267 4654, 1 cabin acc up to 4, (2 bedrm), [shwr, tlt, heat (elec/wood), elec blkts, tel, TV, clock radio, t/c mkg, refrig, cook fac, blkts, linen, pillows], w/mach, dryer, bbq, cots, breakfast ingredients (1st night only), non smoking rms. **D ♦ $65, ♦♦ $65 - $80, ♦ $30 - $45**, BC MC VI.

B&B's/Guest Houses

★★★★ **Geebin Vineyard**, (B&B), 3729 Channel Hwy, Birchs Bay 7162, 3km S of Woodbridge PO, ☎ 03 6267 4750, fax 03 6267 5090, 2 rms (2 suites) [ensuite, fan, heat (elec), radio, t/c mkg, refrig, ldry, pillows], lounge, ✗ (living area), bbq, meals avail, non smoking property. **BLB ♦ $85, ♦♦ $95**.

★★★★ **Orchard Lea Guest House**, (B&B), 11 Weedings Way, 1km S of PO, ☎ 03 6267 4108, fax 03 6267 4797, 2 rms [ensuite, heat, elec blkts, TV, video, clock radio, radio, t/c mkg], lounge (TV), ✗, refrig, bbq, non smoking property. **BB ♦ $85 - $100, ♦♦ $95 - $110, ♦ $20 - $25**, AE BC MC VI.

★★★★ **The Old Woodbridge Rectory**, (B&B), 15 Woodbridge Hill Rd, 200m E of PO, ☎ 03 6267 4742, fax 03 6267 4746, 2 rms [ensuite, heat (elec), elec blkts, radio, t/c mkg], lounge (TV), ✗, bbq, non smoking rms. **BB ♦ $96, ♦♦ $120, ♦ $40**, AE BC MC VI, ♿.

WYNYARD TAS 7325

Pop 4,509. (345km NW Hobart), See map on page 656, ref B3, Nestled beneath picturesque Table Cape at the mouth of the Inglis River. Centre of a prosperous farming district. Scenic flights and airport for Burnie. Scenic flights and airport for Burnie. Boat Ramp, Boating, Bowls, Bush Walking, Fishing, Golf, Horse Riding, Sailing, Scenic Drives, Squash, Swimming, Tennis.

Hotels/Motels

★★★☆ **The Waterfront Wynyard Motor Inn**, (M), 1 Goldie St, 1km E of PO, adjacent to the Wharf, ☎ 03 6442 2351, fax 03 6442 3749, (gr fl) 25 units [shwr, tlt, heat (elec), elec blkts, tel, TV, clock radio, t/c mkg, refrig], ldry, conv fac, ✗, rm serv, cots. **RO ♦ $67, ♦♦ $84**, 12 rooms ★★★. AE BC DC MC VI.

★★ **Inglis River**, (LMH), 10 Goldie St, 1km E of PO, ☎ 03 6442 2344, fax 03 6442 1172, (2 stry), 20 units [shwr, tlt, heat, elec blkts, TV, clock radio, t/c mkg], ✗, ✆, cots. **RO ♦ $40, ♦♦ $50, ♦ $5**, ch con, BC EFT MC VI.

Self Catering Accommodation

★★★★ **Leisure Ville Holiday Units**, (HU), 145 Old Bass Hwy, 3km E of PO, ☎ 03 6442 2291, fax 03 6442 3058, 9 units acc up to 8, (2 bedrm), [shwr, bath, tlt, heat, elec blkts, TV, radio, t/c mkg, refrig, cook fac, micro, blkts, linen, pillows], w/mach, rec rm, pool indoor heated, spa, tennis. **D ♦ $75 - $79, ♦♦ $88 - $114, ♦ $14 - $15**, ch con, BC EFT MC VI.

★★★☆ **Gutteridge Court**, (HU), 5/22 Goldie St, 400m N of PO, ☎ 03 6442 2886, 1 unit acc up to 6, (2 bedrm), [shwr, tlt, fan, heat (elec), elec blkts, TV, clock radio, t/c mkg, refrig, cook fac, micro, blkts, linen, pillows], w/mach, bbq, c/park (undercover), cots-fee, breakfast ingredients, non smoking rms. **D ♦ $65, ♦♦ $80, ♦ $15**, ch con.

★★★ **Alcheringa**, (HU), 450 Preolenna Rd, Flowerdale 7325, 10km W of Wynyard PO, ☎ 03 6445 4255, 1 unit acc up to 4, (2 bedrm), [shwr, tlt, heat, elec blkts, TV, radio, t/c mkg, refrig, cook fac, micro, blkts, linen, pillows], w/mach, dryer, iron, bbq, cots. **D ♦ $45, ♦♦ $65, ♦ $10**, ch con.

B&B's/Guest Houses

★★★★ **Alexandria**, (B&B), c1905. 1 Table Cape Rd, 1.4km N of PO, ☎ 03 6442 4411, fax 03 6442 4424, 5 rms [ensuite, fan, heat, elec blkts, TV, clock radio, t/c mkg, refrig], ldry, ✗ (booking essential), pool-heated (summer), bbq, cots, non smoking property. **BLB ♦ $88 - $99, ♦♦ $110 - $120, ♦ $30**, ch con, AE BC DC MC VI.

ZEEHAN TAS 7469

Pop 1,132. (296km NW Hobart), See map on page 656, ref A5, Once a properous silver mining town, rejuvenated with the opening of the Renison Bell tin mine. Pioneer Memorial Museum. Coastal fishing at Trial Harbour and Granville Harbour. Bush Walking, Gem Fossicking, Golf, Tennis.

Hotels/Motels

★★★☆ **Heemskirk Motor Hotel**, (M), Main St, 1.5km SE of PO, ☎ 03 6471 6107, fax 03 6471 6694, (2 stry gr fl), 33 units [shwr, tlt, heat, elec blkts, tel, TV, clock radio, t/c mkg, refrig, cook fac (1)], ldry, iron, iron brd, ✗, rm serv, cots. **RO ♦ $85, ♦♦ $90, ♦ $15**, ch con, AE BC DC MC VI

★ *Trouble-free travel tips* - **Tyre pressures**

Check tyre pressures and set them to the manufacturer's recommendation, including the spare.

The specifications can generally be found on the tyre placard located in either the glove box or on the front door frame.

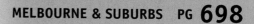
Victoria is a Jigsaw of things to do and see which can be arranged into an endless combination of options to suit all age groups and interests.

In essence, this is the attraction of a state which can be crossed from the crashing surf of the Great Ocean Road, to the lazy course of the meandering Murray in an easy days drive. Each of the states regions has its own special appeal, all linked by excellent roads. The State Tourism Signing Program incorporates accredited Information Centres and directional signs in a world class system which makes touring Victoria easier and safer. Regional touring is growing strong, and now cosmopolitan Melbourne is flaunting its unique lifestyle and attitude as an intriguing segment in the Victorian Jigsaw. Cool jazz, sophisticated cafes, international art, brilliant architecture, busy, world class shopping centres, fine food and style, style, style - with a sense of humour - challenge established perceptions of Victoria's capital. Experience Victoria and -

• Driving around Port Phillip Bay on a 199 km Bay tour which combines vistas of one of the world's great bays with 264 kilometres of beaches, picturesque headlands, attractions and constantly changing natural beauty.

• Less than two hours drive from Melbourne via either the Calder, Western or Hume, Northern and McIvor Highways, Victoria's Goldfields region retains the character and charm of the gold rush period.

• The Great Ocean Road is one of the world's most breath-taking coastal driving experiences.

• The Goulburn Murray Waters region is home to some of Victoria's most interesting towns, great expanses of untouched bushland and a wide range of activities.

• The inland oasis of the Grampians in the heart of Western Victoria has been 400 million years in the making. The Grampians seem torn from the ground in steep craggy slopes, cliffs and giddy rock formations, beloved of rock-climbers.

• The Lakes and Wilderness area, in the eastern corner of Victoria, has a huge diversity of things to do and see. Where else can visitors bask on the beach one day and snow ski the next, in between exploring extensive waterways and unique national parks?

• Legends, Wine and High Country Region is as diversified as its title suggests. North-east Victoria is heritage in the Australian legendary tradition. Bushrangers like Ned Kelly and Mad Dog Morgan are part of the local folklore.

• An hour from Melbourne, on the International Airport side, Macedon Ranges and Spa Country represents one of Victoria's most accessible and enticing regions.

• As the lively heart of the Murray Outback Region, Mildura could also be described as a front door to the Outback. The region stretches along Australia's greatest river, the border between Victoria and New South Wales, also acting as a last, luscious, feast of irrigated oasis before the northern banks give way to the arid vastness of the continental interior.

• Touring the Gippsland Discovery Region opens up a part of Victoria filled with things to do and see and peppered with interesting touring on good bitumen roads. There is the opportunity for interesting diversions to natural wonders like Wilson's Promontory, which contains 50,000 unspoilt hectares of native flora and fauna, at the southern most part of mainland Australia.

• A popular attraction is Phillip Island, home of the Little Penguins and Koala Conservation Centre.

• The Yarra Valley, Dandenongs, and The Ranges Region offer marvellous diversity to visitors . . . forest walks, mountain vistas, famous vineyards, cosy places to stay, unique shopping experiences, diverse restaurants, bistros and tea rooms, grand and gracious gardens exhibiting native and exotic flora in abundance, a brand of hospitality unique to the region.

• Victoria has extensive high country and alpine regions, offering outstanding experience in all seasons. The 280 km Great Alpine Road is a mountain-top high for people who love to drive.

VICTORIA
Enjoy the Victoria experience

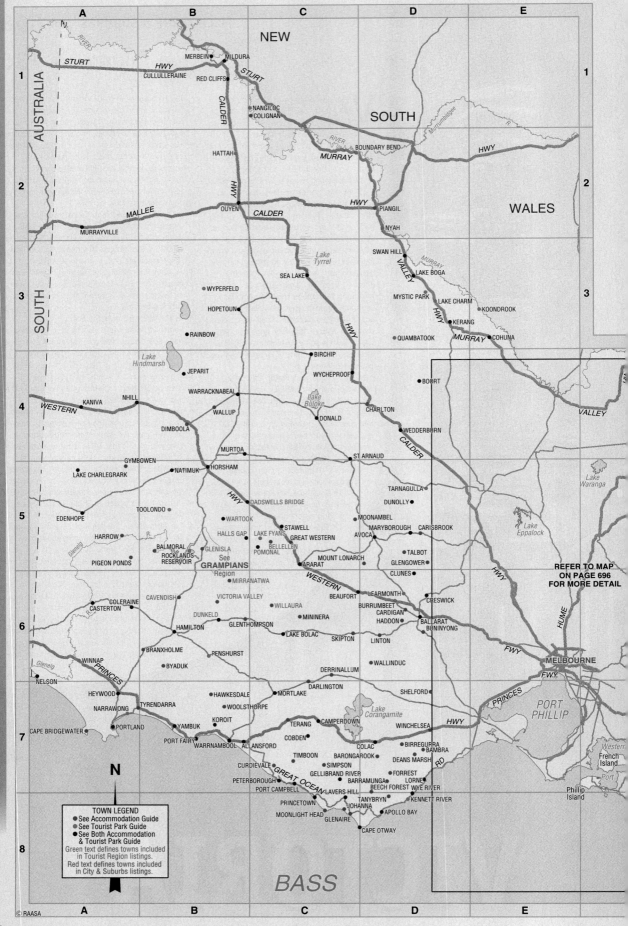

NEW

SOUTH

WALES

AUSTRALIA

SOUTH

BASS

TOWN LEGEND
● See Accommodation Guide
● See Tourist Park Guide
● See Both Accommodation
   & Tourist Park Guide
Green text defines towns included
in Tourist Region listings.
Red text defines towns included
in City & Suburbs listings.

N

REFER TO MAP
ON PAGE 696
FOR MORE DETAIL

© RAASA

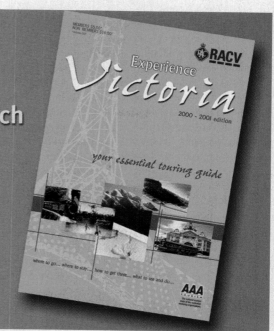

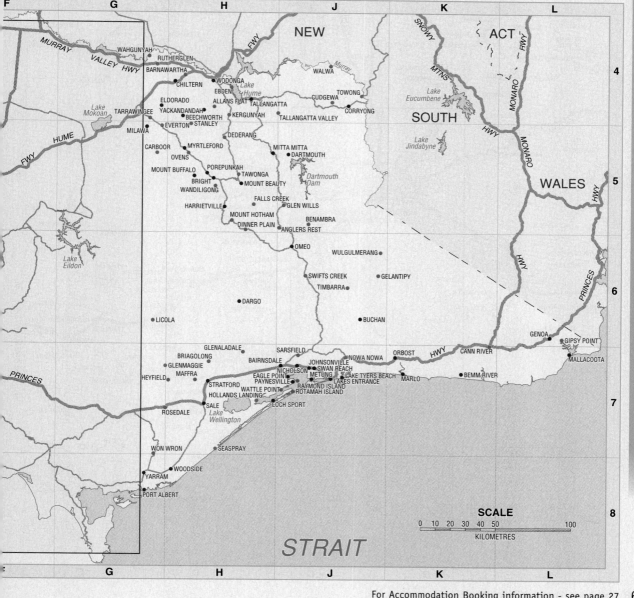

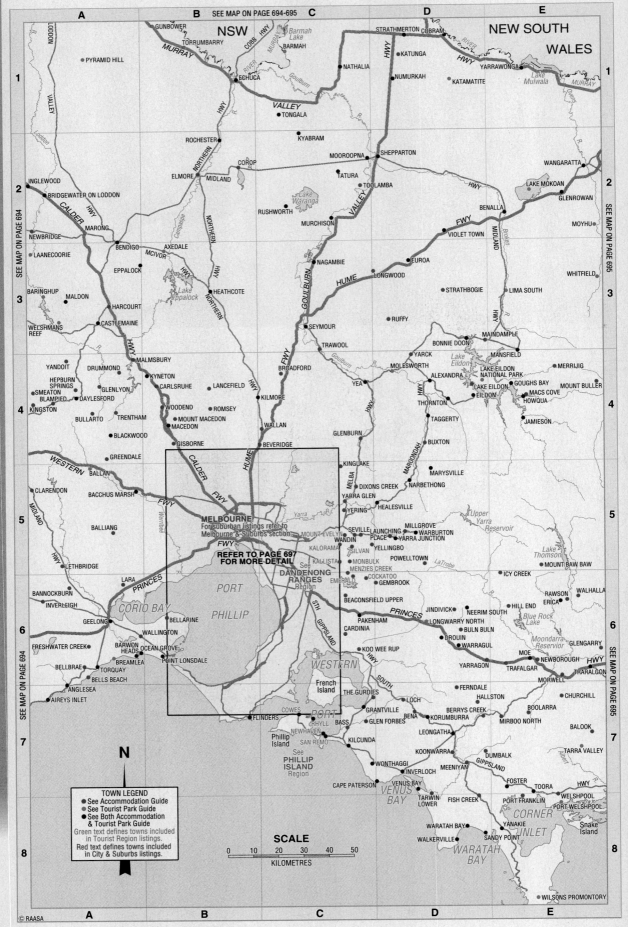

SEE MAP ON PAGE 694-695

NSW

NEW SOUTH

WALES

SEE MAP ON PAGE 694

SEE MAP ON PAGE 695

REFER TO PAGE 697
FOR MORE DETAIL

MELBOURNE
For suburban listings refer to
Melbourne & Suburbs section

DANDENONG
RANGES
Region

See
PHILLIP
ISLAND
Region

N

TOWN LEGEND
● See Accommodation Guide
● See Tourist Park Guide
● See Both Accommodation
  & Tourist Park Guide
Green text defines towns included
in Tourist Region listings.
Red text defines towns included
in City & Suburbs listings.

SCALE
0   10   20   30   40   50
KILOMETRES

© RAASA

Rates may change. Check before booking.

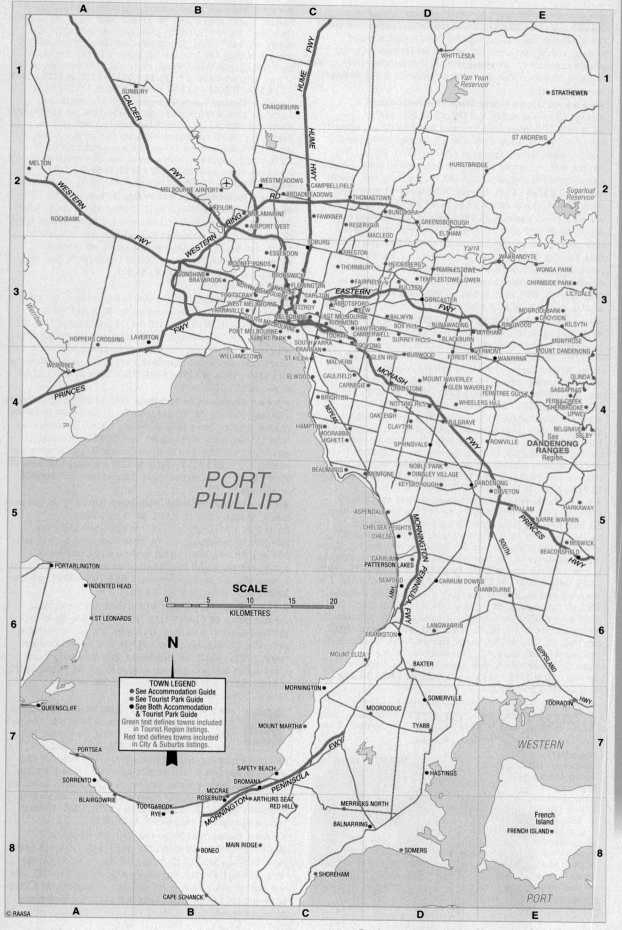

PORT
PHILLIP

SCALE

0   5   10   15   20
KILOMETRES

N

TOWN LEGEND
● See Accommodation Guide
● See Tourist Park Guide
● See Both Accommodation
   & Tourist Park Guide
Green text defines towns included
in Tourist Region listings.
Red text defines towns included
in City & Suburbs listings.

© RAASA

MELBOURNE VIC 3000

Pop 3,400,000. See map on page 697, ref C3. Capital city of Victoria. Termed the Garden City, with 815ha set aside as parks, gardens and reserves. See also Carlton, East Melbourne, North Melbourne, Parkville, Port Melbourne, South Melbourne & West Melbourne.

Hotels/Motels

★★★★★ **All Seasons Premier Grand Hotel Melbourne**, (LH), Heritage, 33 Spencer St, 1km S of GPO, ☎ 03 9611 4567, fax 03 9611 4655, (Multi-stry), 118 rms [shwr, bath (90), spa bath, tlt, hairdry, a/c, tel, TV, movie, clock radio, CD, t/c mkg, refrig, mini bar, cook fac, micro, d/wash, toaster, ldry (in unit) (20)], lift, ldry, iron, iron brd, read rm, meeting rm, ✉, pool indoor heated, sauna, spa, bbq, 24hr reception, rm serv, secure park (80), ✆, gym, cots, non smoking rms (55). **D** ♦ **$228 - $325**, Minimum booking all Melbourne major events/$150 surcharge applies, AE BC DC EFT JCB MC VI, ⌘&.

★★★★★ **Crown Towers**, (LH), 8 Whiteman St, Southbank 3006, 1km S of GPO, ☎ 03 9292 6666, fax 03 9292 6600, (Multi-stry), 484 rms (119 suites) [shwr, spa bath, tlt, hairdry, a/c, tel, fax, cable tv, movie, radio, t/c mkg, refrig, mini bar], lift, iron, iron brd, lounge, business centre, conf fac, ✉, cafe, bar (cocktail), pool indoor heated, spa, 24hr reception, rm serv, c/park (undercover), ✆, gym, tennis, cots, non smoking flr (7). **RO** ♦ **$630**, ♦♦ **$630**, ⊙ **$55**, Suite RO **$1,000 - $2,000**, ch con, AE BC DC JCB MC VI, ⌘&.

★★★★★ **Grand Hyatt Melbourne**, (LH), 123 Collins St, 750m SE of GPO, ☎ 03 9657 1234, fax 03 9650 4685, (Multi-stry), 547 rms (26 suites) [shwr, bath, spa bath (26), tlt, hairdry, a/c, tel, fax (49), TV, video (26), movie, radio, CD (30), t/c mkg, refrig, mini bar], lift, lounge, business centre, conf fac, ✉, pool indoor heated, sauna (2), spa, 24hr reception, rm serv, c/park (undercover)-fee, ✆, gym-fee, tennis, cots, non smoking rms (400). **RO** ♦ **$270 - $630**, ♦♦ **$270 - $630**, ⊙ **$55**, Suite D **$630 - $840**, ch con, AE BC DC JCB MC VI, ⌘&.

★★★★★ **Hotel Sofitel**, (LH), 25 Collins St, 1.1km E of GPO, ☎ 03 9653 0000, fax 03 9650 4261, (Multi-stry), 363 rms (52 suites) [shwr, bath, tlt, hairdry, a/c, tel, TV, video (avail), movie, clock radio, t/c mkg, refrig, mini bar, toaster], lift, iron, iron brd, business centre, conf fac, ✉, 24hr reception, rm serv, c/park (undercover)-fee, ✆, gym, cots, non smoking flr (10). **RO** ♦ **$308**, ♦♦ **$308**, ⊙ **$45**, Suite RO **$435 - $1,760**, ch con, AE BC DC JCB MC VI, ⌘&.

★★★★★ **Le Meridien at Rialto Melbourne**, (LH), 495 Collins St, 850m SW of GPO, ☎ 03 9620 9111, fax 03 9614 1219, (Multi-stry), 242 rms (10 suites) [shwr, bath, spa bath (6), tlt, hairdry, a/c, tel, fax (30), TV, video (30), movie, clock radio, CD (30), t/c mkg, refrig, mini bar, toaster], lift, iron, iron brd, business centre, conf fac, ✉, pool indoor heated, sauna, spa, 24hr reception, rm serv, c/park (garage)-fee, ✆, gym, cots, non smoking flr (5). **RO** ♦ **$425 - $505**, ♦♦ **$425 - $505**, ⊙ **$50**, Suite D **$700 - $1,030**, ch con, AE BC DC EFT JCB MC VI, ⌘&.

★★★★★ **Park Hyatt Melbourne**, (LH), 1 Parliament Sq, Melbourne 3002, off Parliament Pl, ☎ 03 9224 1234, fax 03 9224 1200, (Multi-stry), 240 rms (23 suites) [shwr, bath (190), spa bath (50), tlt, hairdry, a/c, fire pl (29), tel, TV, movie, clock radio, t/c mkg, refrig, mini bar], lift, iron, iron brd, lounge, business centre, conf fac, ✉, bar, pool indoor heated, sauna, spa, 24hr reception, rm serv, c/park (undercover)-fee, ✆, gym, tennis-fee, cots, non smoking rms (186). **RO** ♦♦ **$295 - $315**, ⊙ **$50**, Suite RO **$565 - $4,400**, AE BC DC EFT JCB MC VI, ⌘&.

★★★★★ **Rockmans Regency Hotel**, (Ltd Lic H), Cnr Exhibition & Lonsdale Sts, 900m NE of GPO, ☎ 03 9662 3900, fax 03 9663 4297, (Multi-stry), 185 rms (20 suites) [shwr, bath, spa bath (20), tlt, hairdry, a/c, tel, TV, video (20), movie, clock radio, t/c mkg, refrig, mini bar, toaster], lift, iron, iron brd, business centre, conf fac, ✉, bar (cocktail), pool indoor heated, sauna, spa, 24hr reception, rm serv, ✆, gym, cots, non smoking flr (6). **RO** ♦ **$225 - $375**, ♦♦ **$225 - $375**, ⊙ **$30**, Suite D **$485 - $1,450**, ch con, AE BC DC EFT JCB MC VI, ⌘&.

★★★★★ **Sheraton Towers Southgate**, (LH), 1 Southgate Ave, Southbank 3006, 1.6km S of GPO, ☎ 03 9696 3100, fax 03 9690 5889, (Multi-stry), 385 rms (12 suites) [shwr, bath, spa bath (13), tlt, hairdry, a/c, tel, TV, movie, clock radio, t/c mkg, refrig, mini bar, doonas], lift, iron, iron brd, lounge, business centre, conf fac, ✉, bar (cocktail), pool indoor heated, sauna, spa, 24hr reception, rm serv, c/park (valet)-fee, gym. **RO** ♦ **$479 - $693**, ♦♦ **$479 - $693**, Suite RO **$1,007 - $2,500**, ch con, AE BC DC JCB MC VI, ⌘&.

★★★★★ **The Westin Melbourne on Regent Place**, (LH), 205 Collins St, ☎ 03 9635 2222, fax 03 9635 2333, (Multi-stry), 262 rms (2 suites) [shwr, bath (256), spa bath (12), tlt, hairdry, a/c, tel, cable tv, movie, clock radio, t/c mkg, refrig, mini bar], lift, iron, iron brd, business centre, conf fac, ✉, pool (lap - heated), sauna, spa (heated), steam rm, 24hr reception, rm serv, c/park (valet)-fee, ✆, gym, cots, non smoking rms (218). **RO** **$248 - $1,023**, AE BC DC EFT JCB MC VI, ⌘&.

★★★★★ **The Windsor**, (LH), Classified by National Trust, 103 Spring St, 950m E of GPO, opposite Parliament House, ☎ 03 9633 6000, fax 03 9633 6001, (Multi-stry), 180 rms (20 suites) [shwr, bath, tlt, hairdry, a/c, tel, TV, video (20), movie, clock radio, CD (8), t/c mkg, refrig, mini bar], lift, iron, iron brd, business centre, conf fac, ✉, 24hr reception, rm serv, c/park (undercover)-fee, ✆, cots, non smoking rms. **RO** ♦ **$299 - $381**, ♦♦ **$299 - $381**, ⊙ **$55**, Suite D **$463 - $1,306**, ch con, AE BC DC JCB MC VI.

★★★★☆ **Bayview on the Park Hotel**, (LH), 52 Queens Rd, Melbourne 3004, 4km S of GPO, ☎ 03 9243 9999, fax 03 9243 9800, (Multi-stry), 203 rms (9 suites) [shwr, bath, tlt, hairdry, a/c, tel, TV, movie, clock radio, t/c mkg, refrig, mini bar], lift, conf fac, ✉, bar (cocktail), pool-heated, spa, bbq, 24hr reception, rm serv, ✆, gym, cots-fee, non smoking flr (2). **RO** ♦ **$130 - $200**, ♦♦ **$130 - $200**, ⊙ **$35**, Suite RO **$250 - $300**, ch con, Minium booking applies Grand Prix weekend. AE BC DC MC VI, ⌘&.

★★★★☆ **Carlton Crest Hotel (Melbourne)**, (Ltd Lic H), 65 Queens Rd, Melbourne 3004, 4.5km SE of GPO, ☎ 03 9529 4300, fax 03 9521 3111, (Multi-stry), 374 rms [shwr, bath (339), spa bath (40), tlt, hairdry, a/c, tel, TV, movie, clock radio, t/c mkg, refrig, mini bar], lift, ldry, iron, iron brd, business centre, conf fac, ✉, pool-heated, sauna, spa, 24hr reception, rm serv, c/park (undercover), ✆, gym, cots, non smoking units (147). **BB** ♦ **$160 - $265**, ♦♦ **$160 - $265**, ⊙ **$35**, ch con, AE BC DC JCB MC VI, ⌘&.

★★★★☆ **Centra Melbourne**, (LH), Cnr Flinders & Spencer Sts, opposite casino, ☎ 03 9629 5111, fax 03 9629 5624, (Multi-stry), 384 rms (13 suites) [shwr, bath, tlt, hairdry, a/c, tel, TV, movie-fee, clock radio, t/c mkg, refrig, mini bar], lift, iron, iron brd, business centre, conf fac, ✉ (2), bar, pool-heated, 24hr reception, rm serv, c/park (valet)-fee, gym, cots, non smoking flr (6). **RO** ♦ **$196 - $272**, ♦♦ **$196 - $272**, ⊙ **$33**, Suite D **$545 - $1,090**, ch con, AE BC DC JCB MC MP VI, ⌘&.

Clarion
FLAG CHOICE HOTELS

★★★★☆ **Clarion Suites Pacific Internat'l Melbourne**, (LH), Previously Pacific International Suites 471 Lt Bourke St, 500m W of GPO, ☎ 03 9607 3000, fax 03 9642 3822, (Multi-stry), 150 rms (150 suites) [shwr, bath, spa bath (10), tlt, hairdry, a/c, tel, TV, movie-fee, clock radio, t/c mkg, refrig, mini bar, cook fac ltd, micro, d/wash (10), toaster], lift, ldry, iron, iron brd, business centre, conf fac, ✉, bar (cocktail), sauna, spa, 24hr reception, rm serv, c/park (valet), ✆, gym, cots, non smoking suites (60). **RO** ♦ **$270 - $330**, ♦♦ **$270 - $330**, ⊙ **$20**, Minimum booking all Melbourne major events, AE BC DC MC VI, ⌘&.

★★★★☆ **Duxton Hotel Melbourne**, (LH), 328 Flinders St, ☎ 03 9250 1888, fax 03 9250 1877, (Multi-stry), 350 rms (6 suites) [shwr, bath, spa bath (2), tlt, hairdry, a/c, tel, TV, movie, t/c mkg, refrig, mini bar], lift, iron, iron brd, conf fac, ✉, bar (cocktail), 24hr reception, rm serv, c/park (valet), gym, non smoking rms. **RO** ♦ **$125 - $295**, ♦♦ **$125 - $295**, ⊙ **$23**, Suite BLB **$410**, Surcharge applies during special events, AE BC DC MC VI.

Melbourne

Two Ideal Bases for your Many Memorable Excursions...

...centrally located for your ideal holidays

TWIN BRIDGE TOURIST PARK

AAAT ★★★★

Gateway to: Melbourne City, Dandenong Ranges & Phillip Island

BIG4 HOLIDAY PARKS

370 Frankston-Dandenong Rd Dandenong Victoria 3175
Melways ref: 95 C9

Both Twin Bridge Tourist Park and Frankston Holiday Village provide luxury holiday units, shady quiet parks, wide range of accommodation, many BBQs, recreation facilities and playgrounds.
Plus public transport to Melbourne.

Frankston Pool

Frankston HOLIDAY VILLAGE

Frankston Holiday Village, ideally located to Mornington Peninsula wineries, beaches, Phillip Island Penguins & Koalas

AAAT ★★★★☆   **2 Robinsons Road, Frankston Victoria 3199**
Melways ref: 102 G10

Reservations...

Internet: www.twinbridgetouristpark.com.au
Internet: www.frankstonholidayvillage.com.au

Dandenong: 1800 648 346
Frankston: 1800 623 491

HOTEL GRAND CHANCELLOR
MELBOURNE

• In the heart of the city • Walk to the Theatres, Cinema Chinatown and Shopping • Lobby, Bar and Coffee Shop • Restaurants • Heated Roof Top Pool and Sauna
• **Discount Rates for Auto Club members**

Free Call 1800 331 006

131 Lonsdale Street, Melbourne, Victoria 3000
Ph No: 03 9656 4000
Fax No: 03 9662 3479

WINNER 2000 VICTORIAN TOURISM AWARDS

2000 Victorian Awards Winner for Best Superior Accommodation

reshgc@hgcmelbourne.com.au
www.hotelchancellor.com.au

11817AG

★★★★☆ **Grand Mercure Hotel Melbourne**, (Ltd Lic H), 321 Flinders La, 500m S of GPO, ☎ 03 9629 4088, fax 03 9629 4066, (Multi-stry), 58 rms (58 suites) [shwr, bath, tlt, hairdry, a/c, tel, TV, video (avail), movie, clock radio, t/c mkg, refrig, mini bar, micro, toaster], lift, ldry, iron, iron brd, conf fac, ⊠, bar (cocktail), sauna, 24hr reception, rm serv, c/park (valet)-fee, gym, cots, non smoking flr (6). **D $263**, AE BC DC JCB MC VI, ♿.

AAA TOURISM Special Rates ★★★★☆ **Hotel Grand Chancellor (Melbourne)**, (LH), 131 Lonsdale St, 850m NE of GPO, ☎ 03 9656 4000, fax 03 9662 3479, (Multi-stry), 160 rms [shwr, bath, spa bath (5), tlt, hairdry, a/c, tel, fax (30), TV, movie, clock radio, t/c mkg, refrig, mini bar], lift, iron, iron brd, conf fac, ⊠, cafe, pool-heated, sauna, 24hr reception, rm serv, c/park (undercover)-fee, ☏, cots, non smoking rms (40). **RO 👤 $143 - $235, 👥 $143 - $235, ➕ $20 - $25**, ch con, AE BC DC JCB MC MP VI.

FLAG CHOICE HOTELS · METRO INNS ★★★★☆ **Metro Hotel & Suites Bank Place**, (Ltd Lic H), 20 Bank Place, ☎ 03 9604 4321, fax 03 9604 4300, (Multi-stry), 59 rms (1 suite) (Studio & 1 bedrm), [shwr, tlt, hairdry, a/c, tel, TV, movie, clock radio, t/c mkg, refrig, mini bar, cook fac ltd, micro, d/wash, toaster, ldry], lift, iron, iron brd, ⊠, 24hr reception, rm serv, dinner to unit, cots, non smoking flr (5). **D $130 - $240**, AE BC DC EFT MC VI.

★★★★☆ **Novotel Melbourne on Collins**, (LH), 270 Collins St, ☎ 03 9667 5800, fax 03 9667 5805, (Multi-stry), 323 rms [shwr, bath, tlt, hairdry, a/c, tel, TV, movie, clock radio, t/c mkg, refrig, mini bar], lift, conf fac, ⊠, bar (cocktail), pool indoor heated, sauna, spa, 24hr reception, rm serv, ☏, gym, cots, non smoking flr (5). **RO 👥 $241, ➕ $32**, ch con, AE BC DC EFT JCB MC VI.

★★★★☆ **Parkroyal on St Kilda Road**, (LH), 562 St Kilda Rd, 4.2km S of GPO, ☎ 03 9529 8888, fax 03 9525 1242, (Multi-stry), 220 rms (2 suites) [shwr, bath, spa bath (2), tlt, hairdry, a/c, tel, TV, movie-fee, clock radio, t/c mkg, refrig, mini bar], lift, ldry, iron, iron brd, lounge, business centre, conf fac, ⊠, sauna, spa, 24hr reception, rm serv, c/park (undercover), gym, cots, non smoking flr (7). **RO 👥 $198 - $225**, ch con, AE BC DC EFT JCB MC MP VI, ♿.

★★★★☆ **Premier Swanston Hotel**, (LH), 195 Swanston St, 200m NE of GPO, ☎ 03 9663 4711, fax 03 9663 8191, (Multi-stry), 200 rms (44 suites) [shwr, bath, tlt, hairdry, a/c, tel, TV, video (44), movie, clock radio, CD, t/c mkg, refrig, mini bar, micro, toaster], lift, iron, iron brd, business centre, conf fac, ⊠, cafe, bar, pool indoor heated, spa, 24hr reception, rm serv, c/park (garage)-fee, ☏, cots, non smoking flr (4). **RO 👤 $175 - $219, 👥 $175 - $219, ➕ $44, Suite RO 👤 $208 - $263, 👥 $208 - $263, ➕ $44**, ch con, Vehicle access off Lt Bourke St. AE BC DC EFT JCB MC VI, ♿.

★★★★☆ **Radisson Hotel on Flagstaff Gardens**, (LH), 380 William St, ☎ 03 9322 8000, fax 03 9322 8888, (Multi-stry), 184 rms (6 suites) [shwr, spa bath (5), tlt, hairdry, a/c, tel, TV, movie, clock radio, t/c mkg, refrig, mini bar], lift, iron, iron brd, business centre, ⊠, spa, steam rm, rm serv, c/park (limited), gym, non smoking rms (40). **RO 👥 $179 - $299, ➕ $33**, ch con, Minium booking applies on all Melbourne major events, AE BC DC JCB MC VI, ♿.

★★★★☆ **Royce on St Kilda Road**, (LH), 379 St Kilda Rd, Melbourne 3004, 1.3km S of GPO, ☎ 03 9677 9900, fax 03 9677 9922, (Multi-stry gr fl), 71 rms [shwr, spa bath (18), tlt, hairdry, a/c, tel, TV, movie, clock radio, t/c mkg, refrig, mini bar], lift, iron, iron brd, conf fac, ⊠, 24hr reception, rm serv, c/park (valet), ☏, gym, cots, non smoking rms (30). **RO 👤 $204, 👥 $204**, ch con, AE BC DC EFT JCB MC VI, ♿.

41212AG

THE CHIFLEY
OFF LITTLE BOURKE APARTMENT HOTEL
MELBOURNE
★★★★☆ AAAT

RESERVATIONS: 1300 650 464

• Superb location in the heart of Chinatown.
• Surrounded by restaurants, theatres and Melbourne's attractions.
• Stylishly designed, new, self-contained apartment style accommodation.
• Indoor lap pool and gym.
• Innovative Asian restaurant and bar.

GDS BOOKING CODE: TH

ABN 77 003 142 489

11-17 Cohen Place, MELBOURNE VIC 3000 Ph: (03) 9662 3422 Fax: (03) 9662 3433 www.chifleyhotels.com

★★★★☆ **Savoy Park Plaza**, (LH), 630 Lt Collins St, 1km SW of GPO, opposite Spencer St railway station, ☎ 03 9622 8888, fax 03 9622 8877, (Multi-stry), 162 rms (5 suites) [shwr, bath, tlt, hairdry, a/c, tel (& voice mail), fax (& data points), TV (Satellite TV), video-fee, clock radio, t/c mkg, refrig, mini bar], lift, conf fac, ✉, cafe, bar (cocktail), 24hr reception, rm serv, c/park-fee, gym, cots, non smoking flr (6). **RO** ∦ **$170**, ∦∦ **$170**, ch con, AE BC DC MC VI, ⅄⅃.

★★★★☆ **Stamford Plaza Melbourne**, (LH), 111 Lt Collins St, 600m E of GPO, ☎ 03 9659 1000, fax 03 9659 0999, (Multi-stry), 283 rms (283 suites) [shwr, spa bath, tlt, hairdry, a/c, tel, TV, video-fee, movie, clock radio, t/c mkg, refrig, mini bar, cook fac, micro, d/wash, toaster], lift, ldry, iron, iron brd, lounge, conf fac, ✉, bar (cocktail), pool indoor heated, sauna, spa, 24hr reception, rm serv, c/park (valet)-fee, ✆, gym, cots, non smoking suites (230). **Suite D $251 - $873**, ch con, AE BC DC JCB MC VI, ⅄⅃.

★★★★☆ **The Chifley off Little Bourke**, (LH), 11 Cohen Pl, ☎ 03 9662 3422, fax 03 9662 3433, (Multi-stry), 78 rms (42 suites) [shwr, bath (48), spa bath (30), tlt, hairdry, a/c, cable tv, movie, clock radio, t/c mkg, refrig, mini bar, cook fac, micro, toaster, ldry, doonas], lift, w/mach, dryer, iron, iron brd, business centre, conf fac, ✉, pool indoor heated, 24hr reception, secure park (undercover) (7)-fee, gym, cots-fee, non smoking flr (4). **RO** ∦ **$164 - $212**, ∦∦ **$164 - $212**, ∮ **$27.50**, **Suite RO** ∦∦ **$186 - $241**, ∮ **$27.95**, ch con, Minimum booking all Melbourne major events, AE BC DC EFT MC VI, ⅄⅃.

★★★★☆ **The Sebel Suites St Kilda Road**, (LH), Previously Sebel on St Kilda Road, 348 St Kilda Rd, Melbourne 3004, 2.3km S of GPO, ☎ 03 9685 3000, fax 03 9685 2999, (Multi-stry), 127 rms (Studio, 1 & 2 bedrm), [shwr, bath, tlt, hairdry, a/c, tel, TV, movie, clock radio, t/c mkg, mini bar, cook fac, micro, d/wash, toaster, ldry], lift, w/mach, iron, iron brd, conf fac, ✉, pool indoor heated, sauna (commual), spa, 24hr reception, rm serv, c/park (valet), ✆, gym, non smoking flr (6). **RO** ∦ **$159 - $215**, ∦∦ **$159 - $265**, ∮ **$25**, AE BC DC JCB MC VI.

★★★★ **All Seasons Crossley Hotel**, (LH), 51 Lt Bourke St, 850m NE of GPO, ☎ 03 9639 1639, fax 03 9639 0566, (Multi-stry), 88 rms (4 suites) [shwr, bath, spa bath (4), tlt, hairdry, a/c, tel, TV, movie, t/c mkg, refrig, mini bar, cook fac (4), micro (40)], lift, iron, iron brd, ✉, bar (cocktail), sauna (1), 24hr reception, rm serv, c/park (valet)-fee, cots, non smoking rms (30). **RO** ∦ **$169 - $189**, ∦∦ **$169 - $189**, ∮ **$32**, **Suite RO** ∦∦ **$299**, ch con, AE BC DC EFT JCB MC VI.

★★★★ **All Seasons Paragon Hotel**, (LH), 600 Lt Bourke St, 200m E of Docklands Stadium, ☎ 03 9672 0000, fax 03 9672 0123, (Multi-stry), 120 rms [shwr, bath (hip), tlt, hairdry, a/c, tel, TV, movie, clock radio, t/c mkg, refrig, mini bar], lift, iron, iron brd, business centre (40 Private offices), conf fac, ✕, 24hr reception, rm serv (incl liquor), c/park-fee, gym, cots, non smoking rms (56). **RO** ∦ **$152 - $172**, ∦∦ **$152 - $172**, ∮ **$35**, AE BC DC JCB MC VI, ⅄⅃.

★★★★ **Causeway Inn on the Mall**, (Ltd Lic H), 327 Bourke St Mall, located in The Causeway, off the Bourke St Mall, ☎ 03 9650 0688, fax 03 9650 0711, (Multi-stry), 82 rms [shwr, tlt, hairdry, a/c, cent heat, elec blkts, tel, TV, movie, clock radio, t/c mkg, refrig, mini bar], lift, ldry, conf fac, bar (cocktail), 24hr reception, rm serv, cots, non smoking rms (28). **BLB** ∦ **$155 - $195**, ∦∦ **$155 - $195**, ch con, No car parking available. AE BC DC EFT JCB MC VI.

★★★★ **Gateway Suites Melbourne**, (LH), 1 William St, 1.1km SW of GPO, ☎ 03 9296 8888, fax 03 9296 8880, (Multi-stry), 130 rms [shwr, bath (110), tlt, hairdry, a/c, tel, TV, movie, clock radio, t/c mkg, refrig, mini bar, cook fac (84), micro, d/wash (84), ldry (in unit) (84)], lift, iron, iron brd, ✉, pool indoor heated, 24hr reception, rm serv, dinner to unit, c/park (undercover)-fee, non smoking rms (90). **RO** ∦ **$175 - $215**, ∦∦ **$175 - $215**, ∮ **$22**, AE BC DC MC VI.

★★★★ **Holiday Inn on Flinders Melbourne**, (LH), Cnr Spencer St & Flinders La, 100m S of Spencer St railway station, ☎ 03 9629 4111, fax 03 9629 4300, (Multi-stry), 202 rms (14 suites) [shwr, bath, spa bath (7), tlt, hairdry, a/c, tel, TV, movie, clock radio, t/c mkg, refrig, mini bar], lift, ldry, iron, iron brd, business centre, conf fac, ✉, bar (cocktail), pool-heated, sauna, 24hr reception, rm serv, c/park (valet) (40)-fee, courtesy transfer, gym, non smoking flr (5). **Suite RO** ∦ **$200 - $260**, ∦∦ **$200 - $260**, ∮ **$27.50**, ch con, 16 rooms of a lower rating. Minium bookings Grand Prix Weekend, AE BC DC EFT JCB MC VI, ⅄⅃.

★★★★ **Mercure Hotel Melbourne**, (LH), 13 Spring St, 1km E of GPO, ☎ 03 9205 9999, fax 03 9205 9905, (Multi-stry), 164 rms (4 suites) [shwr, bath, spa bath (4), tlt, hairdry, a/c, tel, TV, movie, clock radio, t/c mkg, refrig, mini bar], lift, iron, iron brd, conf fac, ✉ (& bar), bar, 24hr reception, rm serv, c/park (limited), ✆, cots, non smoking flr (6). **D $172 - $215**, ch con, AE BC DC JCB MC VI.

★★★★ **Rydges Melbourne**, (LH), 186 Exhibition St, 750m NE of GPO, ☎ 03 9662 0511, fax 03 9663 6988, (Multi-stry), 363 rms (66 suites) [shwr, bath (349), spa bath (56), tlt, hairdry, a/c, tel, TV, movie, clock radio, t/c mkg, refrig, mini bar], lift, conf fac, night club, ✉, cafe (2), bar (2), pool-heated, sauna, 24hr reception, rm serv, c/park (undercover), ✆, cots, non smoking flr (9). **RO** ∦ **$192**, ∦∦ **$192**, ∮ **$27.50**, ch con, AE BC DC JCB MC VI.

★★★★ **Saville Park Suites Melbourne**, (Ltd Lic H), 333 Exhibition St, 1km N of GPO, ☎ 03 9668 2500, fax 03 9663 8811, (Multi-stry), 144 rms (144 suites) [shwr, bath, tlt, hairdry, a/c, tel, TV, video-fee, movie, clock radio, CD (60), t/c mkg, refrig, mini bar, cook fac, d/wash, toaster, ldry (in unit)], lift, iron, iron brd, conf fac, ✉, pool indoor heated, sauna, 24hr reception, rm serv, cots, non smoking rms (72). **D $187 - $330**, ch con, AE BC DC JCB MC MP VI, ⅄⅃.

★★★☆ **All Seasons Welcome Hotel**, (LH), 265 Lt Bourke St, 200m E of GPO, ☎ 03 9639 0555, fax 03 9639 1179, (Multi-stry), 328 rms [shwr, bath (hip), tlt, hairdry, a/c, tel, TV, movie, clock radio, t/c mkg, refrig, micro (100), toaster], lift, ldry, iron, iron brd, business centre, conf fac, ✉, cafe, bar (cocktail), pool-heated, spa, 24hr reception, ✆, cots, non smoking flr (4). **RO** ∦ **$136 - $170**, ∦∦ **$136 - $170**, ∮ **$33**, ch con, No car parking at property, AE BC DC EFT JCB MC VI, ⅄⅃.

★★★☆ **Astoria City Travel Inn**, (M), 288 Spencer St, 500m N of Spencer St railway station, ☎ 03 9670 6801, fax 03 9670 3034, (Multi-stry), 36 units [shwr, bath (hip) (3), tlt, hairdry, a/c-cool, heat, tel, TV, movie, clock radio, t/c mkg, refrig, micro (15), toaster (15)], dryer, iron, iron brd, pool (salt water), bbq, 24hr reception, c/park (limited), ✆, cots, non smoking units (15). **RO** ∦ **$98**, ∦∦∦ **$150**, ch con, Light breakfast only available. AE BC DC MC VI.

City Limits
MOTEL ▪ STUDIO APARTMENTS

Situated in the "Entertainment District" of Melbourne we are minutes walk to all major theatres, Chinatown, Cinemas, Restaurants & Shopping precincts.

The Casino, M.C.G, tennis centre & major hospitals are easily accessible. All our rooms are air conditioned with ensuite & kitchenette.

20-22 Little Bourke Street, Melbourne
Ph: (03) 9662 2544
Fax: (03) 9662 2287
Toll Free: 1800 808 651
www.citylimits.com.au
Email: res@citylimits.com.au

★ ★ ★ *AAA Tourism*

*S*ituated next to the new Crown Casino, Melbourne Convention and Exhibition Centres, Hotel Enterprize is a newly refurbished Three Star Hotel in the CBD Rooms offer ensuites with excellent appointments, air conditioning, heating, Mini Bar, TV, FREE in-house movies and tea/coffee facilities, while there is an excellent restaurant and bar for entertaining. We also provide complimentary transfers to CBD areas and undercover parking

Hotel Enterprize

HOTEL ENTERPRIZE PTY. LTD.
44 Spencer Street, Melbourne 3000. Australia.
Telephone (03) 9629 6991 Fax (03) 9614 7963

The Victoria Hotel
MELBOURNE

Superb City Centre Location
Comfortable
Value for Money
★★★ AAA Tourism
Special Rates for Motoring
Association Members

Reservations
Toll Free
1800 331 147

215 Little Collins St, Melbourne, 3000
Ph: (03) 9653 0441 Fax: (03) 9650 9678
Email: stay@victoriahotel.com.au
www.victoriahotel.com.au

CABANA COURT MOTEL
APARTMENTS

46 Park St, St Kilda   AAAT ★★★☆

★ Self contained
  SERVICED APARTMENTS
★ Fully equipped kitchenette
★ One & Two bedroom
★ Close to CBD & major
  tourist attractions
★ 2 mins from beach, away
  from traffic
★ Tram to City at door

Ph: (03) 9534 0771   Fax: (03) 9525 3484

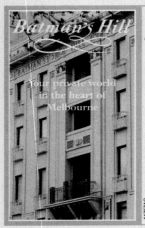

Batman's Hill

Your private world in the heart of Melbourne

Just minutes from our front door

you will find Spencer Street Railway Station, Sky Bus Terminus and the Free City Circle Tram
We are located within walking distance of the Melbourne Exhibition and Convention Centres, Crown Casino and Entertainment Complex and the "Docklands" precinct including the Colonial Stadium. The new direct tram route linking all major sporting venues is at our door Benefit from the close proximity to the best shopping, fine dining and theatres whilst enjoying our personal service and quality facilities

66-70 Spencer Street Melbourne Victoria 3000 Australia
Tel: 61 3 9614 6344 Fax: 61 3 9614 1189 Toll Free 1800 335 308
Email: res@batmanshill.com.au   Web: www.batmanshill.com

AAAT
★★★☆

AAA
TOURISM
Special Rates

FLAG

★★★☆ City Limits Motel, (M), 20 Lt Bourke St, 1km E of GPO, ☎ 03 9662 2544, fax 03 9662 2287, (Multi-stry), 32 units [shwr, bath, tlt, hairdry, a/c, heat, elec blkts, tel, TV, clock radio, t/c mkg, refrig, cook fac ltd, micro, toaster], lift, ldry, iron, iron brd, c/park (limited) (16), cots. **BLB** ♦ **$116 - $136,** ♦♦ **$116 - $136,** ♦♦♦ **$136 - $156,** ♦♦♦♦ **$156 - $176,** ◊ **$20,** ch con, AE BC DC EFT MC MP VI.

  ★★★☆ The Batmans Hill Hotel, (LH), 66 Spencer St, opposite Spencer St railway station, ☎ 03 9614 6344, fax 03 9614 1189, (Multi-stry), 86 rms [shwr, bath (13), tlt, hairdry, a/c, tel, TV, movie-fee, clock radio, t/c mkg, refrig, mini bar], lift, iron, iron brd, ⊠, 24hr reception, c/park (limited) (12)-fee, ✆, cots, non smoking flr (2). **RO** ♦ **$139.50 - $157.50,** ♦♦ **$139.50 - $157.50,** ◊ **$22,** ch con, AE BC DC JCB MC VI.

★★★ Hotel Enterprize, (Ltd Lic H), 44 Spencer St, 1.2km SW of GPO, ☎ 03 9629 6991, fax 03 9614 7963, (Multi-stry), 210 rms [shwr (100), bath (11), tlt (100), hairdry (50), a/c-cool (100), a/c (14), cent heat, tel, TV, movie, clock radio (100), t/c mkg (100), refrig, micro (50)], lift, ldry, lounge, ⊠, 24hr reception, c/park (limited), ✆, cots. **RO** ♦ **$89,** ♦♦ **$99,** ch con, AE BC DC JCB MC VI.

★★★ Hotel Ibis, (LH), 21 Therry St, 100m E of Queen Victoria Market, ☎ 03 9639 2399, fax 03 9639 1988, (Multi-stry), 250 rms [shwr, bath (hip) (90), tlt, hairdry, a/c, tel, cable tv, movie-fee, clock radio, t/c mkg, refrig, micro (90), toaster], lift, ldry, iron, iron brd, conf fac, ⊠, 24hr reception, c/park (30)-fee, ✆, cots, non smoking rms (150). **RO** ♦ **$109 - $186,** ♦♦ **$109 - $186,** ◊ **$27.50,** ch con, AE BC DC EFT JCB MC VI, ♿.

Before you travel

Before a trip have your vehicle serviced and checked over to ensure reliable motoring. There are some checks you can make yourself, generally the procedure can be found in the vehicle owners manual.

KIMBERLEY GARDENS
HOTEL AND APARTMENTS

- 4½ star airconditioned luxury apartments
- 1, 2, 3 bedroom Apartments & Studios
- Indoor Heated Pool, Spa and Gym
- Business Centre with Internet
- 24 hour Reception - personalised service
- Security entrance and parking
- Restaurant, Cafe and Bar
- Close to CBD, Beach, and all major attractions
- Direct dial, Fax, and Modem access
- Function and Conference facilities
- Short or long term stay
- Corporate or leisure
- Foxtel & Free Videos

9526 3888
FREECALL
1800 646 406

FLAG
HOTELS·INNS·RESORTS·APARTMENTS

www.kimberleygardens.com.au
441 Inkerman St, St Kilda East, Vic 3183
See our listing under St Kilda

FREE SOFT DRINK ON ARRIVAL

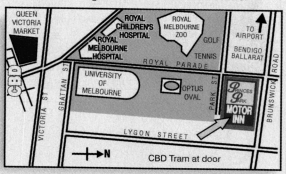

MELBOURNE'S
Princes Park MOTOR INN

When we say that we enjoy a great position ... we mean it!
Ideally located on the way in from the Airport ... on the edge of Marvellous Melbourne.

CBD Tram at door

Motel Features

◆ 24 Hour Reception
◆ Non-Smoking Rooms available
◆ Foxtel Satellite T.V
◆ Free Off-Street parking - some undercover
◆ Fax & Photocopying
◆ Guest Laundry

◆ Remote Control TV
◆ Individually controlled heating
◆ Direct dial STD/ISD phones
◆ Modem ports and Voicemail
◆ Iron and ironing boards
◆ Tea & coffee making facilities
◆ Safety deposit boxes

◆ In-House movies
◆ Airconditioning
◆ Queen Size beds
◆ Heated towel racks
◆ Electric Blankets
◆ Hair Dryers

And More

◆ In addition to our motel rooms we also offer:
◆ Suites with Spa baths
◆ Family rooms with:
◆ Full kitchens
◆ Full-sized baths
◆ Microwave ovens
◆ Balconies overlooking Princes Park
◆ 28 Renovated rooms of ★★★★ AAAT rating

FREECALL RESERVATION
1800 33 7770
24 HOUR RECEPTION

Best Western

Princes Park
MOTOR INN

Old Fashioned Hospitality

AAAT ★★★☆

Website: www.princesparkmotorinn.com.au
Email: enquiry@princespark.com.au

Corner Royal Parade & Park Street
Carlton North, Melbourne, Victoria, 3054

Fax: (03) 9388 1011 Ph: (03) 9388 1000

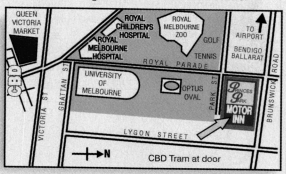

VICTORIA – MELBOURNE & SUBURBS

MELBOURNE continued...

★★★ **The Victoria Hotel**, (LH), 215 Lt Collins St, 250m E of GPO, ☎ 03 9653 0441, fax 03 9650 9678, (Multi-stry), 462 rms [basin (116), shwr (346), tlt (346), hairdry (346), a/c (414), fan (48), heat (48), tel, TV, radio, t/c mkg, refrig], lift, ldry, iron (63), iron brd (63), conf fac, ✉, bar (cocktail), 24hr reception, c/park (undercover)-fee, ✆, cots. RO ♦ $55 - $155, ♦♦ $75 - $155, ♦♦♦ $96 - $162, ch con, 116 rooms ★★☆. AE BC DC JCB MC VI.

★★☆ **City Square Motel**, (M), 67 Swanston St, 500m SE of GPO, ☎ 03 9654 7011, fax 03 9650 7107, (Multi-stry), 24 units [shwr, bath (18), tlt, a/c, tel, TV, clock radio, t/c mkg, refrig, toaster], lift, ldry, lounge, cots. RO ♦ $79 - $105, ♦♦ $105, ⬟ $10, ch con, AE BC DC JCB MC VI.

★ **Exford Hotel**, (LH), 199 Russell St, cnr Lt Bourke St, ☎ 03 9663 2697, fax 03 9663 2248, 31 rms shwr (12), tlt (12), w/mach (3), dryer (3), lounge (TV, video), cook fac, refrig, ✆. RO ♦ $19-$32, ♦♦ $38-$64, No breakfast available. BC EFT MC VI.

Self Catering Accommodation

★★★★☆ **Apartments of Melbourne**, (Apt), Manhattan, 57 Flinders La, ☎ 03 9820 1000, fax 03 9820 0900, (Multi-stry), 54 apts acc up to 6, (1, 2 & 3 bedrm), [shwr, bath, spa bath (8), tlt, a/c, tel, TV, video, clock radio, CD, refrig, cook fac, micro, d/wash, toaster, ldry (in unit), blkts, doonas, linen, pillows], lift, iron, conf fac, pool (heated), spa, c/park (limited), gym, cots-fee, non smoking flr. D $165 - $693, AE BC DC EFT MC VI.

★★★★☆ **(400 St Kilda Rd Section)**, Botanica, 43 apts acc up to 6, (1, 2 & 3 bedrm), [shwr, bath, tlt, a/c, tel (direct dial), TV, video, clock radio, CD, refrig, cook fac, micro, toaster, blkts, doonas, linen, pillows], iron, iron brd, secure park, cots-fee, breakfast ingredients, non smoking flr (1). D $165 - $693.

 Medina

★★★★☆ **Medina Grand Melbourne**, (Apt), 189 Queen St, ☎ 03 9934 0000, fax 03 9602 1187, (Multi-stry), 155 apts acc up to 6, (Studio, 1, 2 & 3 bedrm), [shwr, bath, tlt, hairdry, a/c, tel, cable tv, movie-fee, clock radio, CD, t/c mkg, refrig, cook fac (135), cook fac ltd (20), micro, d/wash, toaster, ldry (in unit) (135), blkts, linen, pillows], lift, iron, iron brd, conf fac, ✕, pool indoor heated, sauna, 24hr reception, rm serv, c/park-fee, ✆, gym, cots, non smoking rms (123). D $160 - $550, AE BC DC MC VI, ♿.

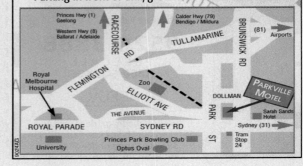

★★★★☆ **Pacific International Apartments**, (Apt), 318 Lt Bourke St, 20m NE of GPO, ☎ 03 9664 2000, fax 03 9663 1977, (Multi-stry gr fl), 31 apts acc up to 4, (Studio, 1 & 2 bedrm), [shwr, bath, tlt, hairdry, a/c, tel (direct dial), TV, video (avail), t/c mkg, refrig, cook fac, elec frypan, d/wash (5), blkts, linen, pillows], lift, ldry, iron, iron brd, ☎, cots, non smoking rms (22). **D $160 - $249**, Minimum booking all Melbourne major events, AE BC DC EFT JCB MC VI.

★★★★☆ **Quest on Bourke**, (Apt), Previously Mansion on Bourke Apartment Hotel, 155 Bourke St, 300m E of Bourke St Mall, ☎ 03 9631 0400, fax 03 9631 0500, (Multi-stry), 63 apts acc up to 4, (Studio, 1 & 2 bedrm), [shwr, spa bath, tlt, hairdry, a/c, tel, cable tv, movie, clock radio, CD, t/c mkg, cook fac, micro, d/wash (51), toaster], lift, w/mach, dryer, iron, iron brd, conf fac, ⊠, gym, cots. **RO $167 - $261**, AE BC DC JCB MC VI.

★★★★☆ **Quest on William**, (Apt), 172 William St, 500m W of GPO, ☎ 03 9605 2222, fax 03 9605 2233, (Multi-stry), 62 apts acc up to 5, (1 & 2 bedrm), [shwr, bath, tlt, hairdry, a/c, cent heat, tel, TV, clock radio, t/c mkg, refrig, cook fac, micro, d/wash, toaster, ldry (in unit)], lift, iron brd, cots. **D $198**, AE BC DC MC VI.

★★★★☆ **Saville on Russell**, (Apt), 222 Russell St, 500m NE of GPO, ☎ 03 9915 2500, fax 03 9915 2599, 220 apts acc up to 5, (Studio, 1 & 2 bedrm), [shwr, tlt, hairdry, a/c, tel, TV, movie-fee, clock radio, CD, t/c mkg, refrig, mini bar, cook fac, micro, toaster, ldry (in unit), blkts, linen, pillows], lift, w/mach, dryer, iron, iron brd, conf fac, ⊠, pool indoor heated, sauna, spa, rm serv (24hr), dinner to unit, secure park (undercover), ☎, cots, non smoking flr (9). **BB ⸙ $195 - $320, ⸙⸙ $195 - $390, ⸙ $48**, ch con, AE BC DC EFT MC VI, ⟨⟩.

★★★★ **Darling Towers Executive Apartments**, (Apt), 23 Queens Rd, ☎ 03 9867 5200, fax 03 9866 8215, 37 apts acc up to 4, (2 bedrm), [shwr, bath, tlt, a/c-cool, heat, elec blkts, clock radio, refrig, cook fac, micro, d/wash, ldry (in unit), blkts, linen, pillows], lift. **D $242, W $1,463**, AE BC DC EFT JCB MC VI.

★★★★ **Fairfax Quest House**, (Apt), 392 Lt Collins St, 800m SW of GPO, ☎ 03 9642 1333, fax 03 9642 4607, (Multi-stry), 37 apts acc up to 6, (Studio, 1, 2 & 3 bedrm), [ensuite (12), shwr, bath (15), tlt, evap cool (2), a/c (35), heat, tel, TV, video, clock radio, refrig, cook fac, micro, d/wash, toaster, ldry (in unit), blkts, doonas, linen, pillows], lift, iron, iron brd, cots. **D $155 - $299**, 10 apartments ★★★☆. Minimum booking all Melbourne major events, AE BC DC JCB MC VI.

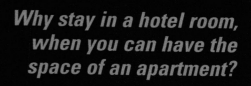

Rates may change. Check before booking.

★★★★ **Oakford Gordon Place**, (Apt), Classified by National Trust, 24 Lt Bourke St, 900m E of GPO, ☎ 03 9663 2888, fax 03 9639 1537, 82 apts acc up to 4, (1 & 2 bedrm), [shwr, bath, tlt, hairdry, a/c, tel, cable tv, video-fee, clock radio, t/c mkg, refrig, mini bar, cook fac, micro (74), d/wash (59), toaster, ldry (in unit) (28)], lift, ldry, iron, iron brd, ✗, pool-heated, sauna, spa, 24hr reception, c/park (undercover)-fee, gym, cots-fee. **D ♦♦ $174 - $217, ♦ $22**, AE BC DC JCB MC VI.

★★★★ **Oakford Gordon Towers**, (Apt), 43 Lonsdale St, 1km N of PO, ☎ 03 9663 3317, fax 03 9663 1095, (Multi-stry), 54 apts acc up to 4, (1 & 2 bedrm), [shwr, bath (6), spa bath (12), tlt, hairdry, a/c, tel, cable tv, clock radio, t/c mkg, refrig, mini bar, cook fac ltd, micro, d/wash (12), toaster, ldry, blkts, linen, pillows], lift, iron, iron brd, conf fac, ✗, bar (cocktail), bar, pool indoor heated, sauna, spa, bbq, 24hr reception, meals to unit (Tues to Sat), gym, cots, non smoking units (18). **D ♦♦ $217 - $275**, AE BC DC JCB MC VI.

★★★★ **Oakford on Collins**, (Apt), 182 Collins St, 500m SE of GPO, ☎ 03 9639 1811, fax 03 9639 2423, (Multi-stry), 54 apts acc up to 6, (1 & 2 bedrm), [shwr, bath (43), spa bath (8), tlt, hairdry, a/c, tel, TV, video (40), clock radio, CD (40), t/c mkg, refrig, cook fac ltd, micro, d/wash (11), toaster, ldry (in unit) (11), blkts, linen, pillows], lift, ldry, w/mach (11), dryer (11), iron, iron brd, spa (heated), 24hr reception, gym, cots, non smoking rms (12). **D ♦♦ $190, ♦♦♦♦ $243**, No car parking available. Minimum booking all Melbourne major events. AE BC DC MC VI.

AAA TOURISM Special Rates
★★★★ **Punt Hill Serviced Apartments**, (Apt), 267 Flinders La, ☎ 03 9650 1299, fax 03 9650 4409, (Multi-stry), 60 apts acc up to 5, (Studio, 1 & 2 bedrm), [shwr, bath, tlt, hairdry, a/c, cent heat, elec blkts, tel, TV, video-fee, movie, clock radio, refrig, cook fac, micro, d/wash (40), toaster, blkts, linen, pillows], lift, ldry, iron, iron brd, 24hr reception, rm serv (limited), c/park (undercover)-fee, cots-fee. **D $162 - $191**, Minium booking applies all Melbourne major events, AE BC DC MC VI.

The newly renovated Birches Serviced Apartments are located in fashionable East Melbourne, renowned for its beautiful parks and gardens, architecture and quiet tree-lined streets.

The ideal alternative to inner city hotel accommodation.

BIRCHES SERVICED APARTMENTS

Within walking distance to:

- Central Business District
- Melbourne Cricket Ground
- Melbourne Park National Tennis Centre
- Crown Casino at Southbank
- Stage and Film theatres
- Internationally renowned restaurants
- Bridge Rd Fashion Warehouses
- Docklands Colonial Stadium

Features & Services:

- Superior service
- 1 & 2 bedroom newly renovated Apartments with new fully equipped kitchens
- New ensuite bathrooms and queen size beds
- Complimentary security on-site parking
- Cable T.V.

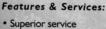 AAA Tourism ★★★★

160 Simpson St, (Cnr Albert St), East Melbourne, 3002 Australia

Telephone - 03 9417 2344
Fax - 03 9417 5872

Email - birches@mikka.net.au
Internet - www.birches.com.au
Freecall - 1800 651 623

THE HOTEL Y

Australian and Victorian Tourism Award Winner

location comfort style

The Hotel Y offers a range of accommodation
24 hour reception • Cafe Y • Discount parking
Guest kitchen & laundry • Tour desk

489 Elizabeth St Melbourne 3000
Tel 9329 5188   Fax 9329 1469
Email hotely@ywca.net   www.ywca.net

Discover the winning difference

B&B's/Guest Houses

 AAA TOURISM *Special Rates* **Comfort** FLAG CHOICE HOTELS™ ★★★☆ **Comfort Inn Pacific International Terrace**, (PH), Previously Pacific International Terrace Inn, 16 Spencer St, 1.4km SW of GPO, ☎ 03 9621 3333, fax 03 9621 1922, (Multi-stry), 93 rms [ensuite, a/c, cent heat, tel, TV, clock radio, t/c mkg, refrig], lift, ldry, lounge, conf fac, ⊠, c/park-fee, ✆, cots. BLB ♦ $124 - $138, ♦♦ $124 - $138, ⚱ $16.50, ch con, AE BC DC JCB MC MP VI.

AAA TOURISM *Special Rates* ★★★ **Charsfield on St Kilda Road**, (B&B), Previously Charsfield Bed & Breakfast, 478 St Kilda Rd, Melbourne 3004, 50m from St Kilda Rd PO, ☎ 03 9866 5511, fax 03 9867 2277, (2 stry gr fl), 46 rms [ensuite (19), heat, TV], rec rm, conf fac, ✕, t/c mkg shared, 24hr reception, ✆, cots, non smoking property. BLB ♦ $75 - $140, ♦♦ $75 - $140, ⚱ $15, ch con, AE BC DC EFT MC VI.
★★★ **The Hotel Y**, (PH), 489 Elizabeth St, 300m N of GPO, ☎ 03 9329 5188, fax 03 9329 1469, (Multi-stry), 60 rms [shwr, tlt, a/c-cool (36), a/c (37), heat, tel (49), clock radio, t/c mkg (49), cook fac ltd (2), micro (2), toaster (2)], lift, ldry, lounge (TV), conf fac, cook fac, refrig, ✆, cots, non smoking property. RO ♦ $77 - $99, ♦♦ $93 - $115, ♦♦♦ $104 - $126, ⚱ $16.50, 23 rooms of a lower rating. AE BC DC EFT MC VI.

GREAT VALUE & COMFORT JUST 5 MINS FROM MELBOURNE'S CBD!

Choose from economy or ensuite rooms with TV.
All tariffs include our delicious full breakfast.

- 24 hr reception
- Free parking
- Laundry
- TV, lounge & games room

 **MIAMI MOTOR INN**

Daily Rates:

Single	$44-78
Twin/Double	$66-96
Triple	$90-120

13 Hawke St West Melbourne Melbourne Victoria 3003
Tel: 03 9329 8499 Fax: 03 9328 1820 Toll Free: 1800 132 333
Email: desk@themiami.com.au Website: www.themiami.com.au

COMFORT AND GREAT VALUE JUST 20 MINUTES FROM MELBOURNE CBD

LUXURY HOLIDAY CABINS
- 2 Doubles, 1 single, 2 ensuites
- 2-bedroom cabins with ensuite

CRYSTALBROOK HOLIDAY CENTRE

Phone (03) 9844 3637

182 Warrandyte Road, Doncaster East. 3109

Fax: (03) 9844 3342

Email: crystalbrook@iphonemail.net.au

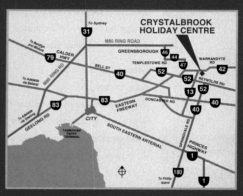

CRYSTALBROOK HOLIDAY CENTRE

★★ **Kingsgate**, (PH), 131 King St, 750m W of GPO, ☎ 03 9629 4171, fax 03 9629 7110, (Multi-stry gr fl), 225 rms [basin (150), shwr (76), tlt (76), a/c-cool (76), cent heat, tel (76), TV (76), t/c mkg (76), refrig (76)], lift, ldry, lounge (TV), ✉ (Mon to Sat), cafe, 24hr reception, ☎, cots. RO ♦ $79 - $105, ♦♦ $99 - $132, ♦ $20 - $26, ch con, 76 rooms ★★★, AE BC DC EFT MC VI.

★ **City Centre Private Hotel**, (PH), 22 Lt Collins St, 1km E of GPO, ☎ 03 9654 5401, fax 03 9650 7256, (Multi-stry), 36 rms [heat, t/c mkg, refrig (30)], bathrm (1G-1L), ldry, lounge (TV), cook fac, refrig, c/park-fee, ☎. RO ♦ $19.50 - $52, ♦♦ $40 - $70, ♦♦♦ $70, ♦ $11, Key Deposit $10, BC EFT MC VI.

Other Accommodation

Albert Park Manor Boutique Hotel Motel, (Lodge), 405 St Kilda Rd, Melbourne 3004, ☎ 03 9821 4486, fax 03 9821 4496, (Multi-stry gr fl), 20 rms [shwr (14), spa bath (3), tlt (14), c/fan, heat, tel, TV, clock radio, t/c mkg, refrig], ldry, c/park (10), cots, non smoking units (10). D ♦ $76 - $153, ♦♦ $76 - $153, ♦ $20, ch con, No breakfast available, AE BC BTC DC MC VI.

Carlton Hotel, (Lodge), 197 Bourke St, 400m E of PO, ☎ 03 9650 2734, fax 03 9650 5474, (2 stry), 29 rms [shwr (6G-6L), tlt (6G-6L), heat, blkts, linen, pillows], ldry, rec rm, lounge (TV), ✕, cook fac, refrig, ☎. RO ♦ $16 - $33, ♦♦ $49, AE BC DC MC VI.

Hotel Spencer, (Lodge), 475 Spencer St, West Melbourne 3003, 1km N of Spencer St railway station, ☎ 03 9329 7755, fax 03 9329 1133, (Multi-stry), 25 rms [basin (2), ensuite (5), shwr (5), tlt (5), heat], ldry, lounge (TV), ✉, cook fac, t/c mkg shared, refrig, c/park (limited), courtesy transfer, ☎, non smoking property. RO ♦ $16 - $80, ♦♦ $40 - $80, ♦ $10, ch con, AE BC DC EFT MC VI.

Toad Hall Guesthouse Hotel, (Lodge), 441 Elizabeth St, 300m N of GPO, ☎ 03 9600 9010, fax 03 9600 9013, (Multi-stry), 39 rms [basin, ensuite (10), refrig, blkts, linen, pillows], shwr (10G/L), tlt (10G/L), ldry, lounge (cable TV), ✕, cook fac, bbq, c/park-fee, ☎, non smoking property. D ♦ $25 - $60, ♦♦ $60 - $90, ♦ $25 - $30, No breakfast available. BC EFT MC VI.

MELBOURNE - ABBOTSFORD VIC 3067

Pop Part of Melbourne, (5km E Melbourne), See map on page 697, ref C3.

Hotels/Motels

★★★ **Abbotsford Inn**, (LMH), Rear 48 Hoddle St,
☎ 03 9417 2316, fax 03 9419 7981, (2 stry), 25 units
(1 suite) [shwr, spa bath (2), tlt, a/c, tel, TV, video (2),
clock radio, t/c mkg, refrig, toaster], ldry, dryer-fee,
⊠ (Thursday & Friday), bbq, c/park (15), non smoking units (17).
BLB ♦ $104.50 - $126.50, ♦♦ $115.50 - $137.50, ◊ $11, Minimum
booking all Melbourne major events, AE BC DC EFT MC VI.

MELBOURNE - AIRPORT WEST VIC 3042

Pop Part of Melbourne, (17km NW Melbourne), See map on page 697, ref B2.

Hotels/Motels

★★★ **Skyways International**, (LMH), 113 Matthews Ave,
☎ 03 9338 1300, fax 03 9338 1744, 18 units [shwr, bath, tlt, a/c, tel,
TV, clock radio, t/c mkg, refrig], conf fac, ⊠, 24hr reception, ✆, non
smoking units (9). BLB ♦ $105, ♦♦ $115, Light breakfast only available.
AE BC DC EFT MC VI.

MELBOURNE - ALBERT PARK VIC 3206

*Pop 6,468. (3km S Melbourne), See map on page 697, ref C3.
Inner residential, recreational suburb and tourist precinct. Home of
the Australian Formula 1.*

Hotels/Motels

★★ **Hotel Victoria**, (LH), Cnr Kerferd Rd & Beaconsfield Pde,
☎ 03 9690 3666, fax 03 9699 9570, (Multi-stry), 27 rms [shwr (7),
bath (10), spa bath (2), tlt (17), cent heat, tel (17), TV (17),
clock radio (17), t/c mkg, refrig (17)], conf fac, ⊠, c/park (limited), ✆.
D $65 - $165, 10 rooms ★. AE BC DC MC VI.

B&B's/Guest Houses

★★★★☆ **The Avoca Albert Park**, (B&B), 98 Victoria Ave,
☎ 03 9696 9090, fax 03 9696 9092, 3 rms [ensuite, hairdry, a/c-cool,
c/fan, heat, elec blkts, TV, clock radio, t/c mkg, refrig], lounge (TV,
cd player, video), lounge firepl, non smoking property. BB ♦ $125 - $135,
♦♦ $150 - $160, 1 room ★★★★. AE BC DC MC VI.

★★★★ **Jackson's on Middle Park**, (B&B), 404 Richardson St, Middle
Park 3206, near cnr Fraser St, ☎ 03 9534 7615, fax 03 9534 7615,
2 rms [shwr, spa bath, tlt, hairdry, fan, heat, elec blkts, TV, video,
clock radio, t/c mkg, refrig], iron, iron brd, non smoking property.
BB ♦ $120, ♦♦ $140, AE BC DC MC VI.

MELBOURNE - ASPENDALE VIC 3195

*Pop Part of City of Kingston, (27km SE Melbourne), See map on
page 697, ref D5. Seaside suburb of Melbourne. Golf, Swimming (Bay), Tennis.*

Hotels/Motels

★★★ **Aspendale Shore Motel**, (M), 31 Nepean Hwy, 1km S of Mordialloc
railway station, ☎ 03 9580 6140, fax 03 9580 6005, (2 stry gr fl),
10 units [shwr, a/c, elec blkts, cable tv, t/c mkg, refrig], ldry, bbq, car wash,
cots. RO ♦ $82.50 - $88, ♦♦ $88 - $98, ◊ $10, AE BC DC EFT MC VI.

MELBOURNE - BALWYN VIC 3103

*Pop Part of City of Boroondara, (13km E Melbourne), See map on
page 697, ref D3. A suburb of Melbourne. Bowls, Squash, Swimming
(Pool), Tennis.*

B&B's/Guest Houses

Bellevue Bed and Breakfast, (B&B), 32 Columba St, Balwyn North 3104,
☎ 03 9859 4492, 1 rm [shwr, tlt, a/c, heat, elec blkts, TV, video, clock
radio, t/c mkg, refrig, micro, d/wash, toaster], iron, iron brd. BLB ♦ $75,
♦♦ $90, ◊ $20 - $30, (not yet classified).

MELBOURNE - BEACONSFIELD VIC 3807

*Pop 751. (47km SE Melbourne), See map on page 697, ref E5.
Small residential town on the fringe of the metropolitan area. Bush
Walking, Golf, Horse Riding, Scenic Drives, Squash, Tennis.*

Hotels/Motels

★★★☆ **Melaleuca Lodge**, (M), Cnr Princes Hwy & Brunt Rd,
2km E of PO, ☎ 03 9796 1044, fax 03 9796 1865, 21 units
[shwr, spa bath (2), tlt, a/c, elec blkts, tel, TV, clock radio,
t/c mkg, refrig, toaster], ldry, conf fac, pool, bbq, cots-fee,
non smoking units (7). RO ♦ $71 - $77, ♦♦ $77 - $82.50, ch con,
AE BC DC EFT MC VI.

★★★ **Beaconsfield Lodge**, (M), 1 Souter St, 500m E of PO,
☎ 03 9707 1454, fax 03 9707 2581, 12 units (2 bedrm),
[shwr, tlt, fan, heat, elec blkts, tel, TV, clock radio, t/c mkg,
refrig], cots-fee, non smoking units (9). RO ♦ $65 - $70,
♦♦ $70 - $75, AE BC DC MC MCH VI.

MELBOURNE - BEAUMARIS VIC 3193

*Pop Part of Melbourne, (22km SE Melbourne), See map on page
697, ref C5. Bayside suburb of Melbourne. Bowls, Sailing, Swimming
(Bay), Tennis.*

Hotels/Motels

★★★☆ **Beaumaris Bay Motel**, (M), 31 Bodley St, 200m N of PO,
☎ 03 9589 6044, fax 03 9589 5976, (2 stry gr fl), 28 units [shwr,
spa bath (4), tlt, hairdry, a/c, elec blkts, tel, cable tv, video, clock radio, t/c mkg,
refrig, mini bar], ldry, ⊠ (Mon to Sat), bar (cocktail), rm serv, cots.
RO ♦ $110 - $150, ♦♦ $110 - $150, ◊ $10, ch con, AE BC DC EFT MC MP VI.

MELBOURNE - BERWICK VIC 3806

Pop 16,868. (42km SE Melbourne), See map on page 697, ref E5. An outer south eastern residential suburb. Bowls, Squash, Tennis.

B&B's/Guest Houses

★★★★☆ **Berwick Garden B & B**, (B&B), 101 Buchanan Rd, 3km N of PO, ☎ 03 9707 2525, fax 03 9794 0675, 1 rm [ensuite, hairdry, elec blkts, TV, video, clock radio, t/c mkg], lounge, lounge firepl, c/park. **BB** ♦ **$90,** ♦♦ **$130.**

MELBOURNE - BLACKBURN VIC 3130

Pop 24,662. (19km E Melbourne), See map on page 697, ref D3. Residential suburb in the outer metropolitan area. Bowls, Squash, Swimming, Tennis.

Hotels/Motels

★★★★☆ **Elizabethan Lodge Conference Centre**, (M), 604 Middleborough Rd, ☎ 03 9898 9551, fax 03 9890 8230, (2 stry gr fl), 39 units [shwr, spa bath, tlt, hairdry, a/c, elec blkts, tel, TV, video (avail), movie, clock radio, t/c mkg, refrig, mini bar, cook fac (1)], ldry, iron, iron brd, conf fac, ⊠, pool indoor heated, sauna, spa, bbq, 24hr reception, rm serv, gym, tennis, cots. **RO** ♦ **$135 - $225,** ♦♦ **$135 - $225,** ♦ **$10,** ch con, AE BC DC MC MP VI.

Self Catering Accommodation

★★★★ **Bethbiri Brook**, (HU), 7 Jeffery St, ☎ 03 9878 6142, fax 03 9878 6600, 1 unit acc up to 4, (1 bedrm), [shwr, tlt, hairdry, a/c, cent heat, elec blkts, TV, clock radio, t/c mkg, refrig, cook fac, micro, toaster, blkts, doonas, linen, pillows], ldry, iron, iron brd, bbq, non smoking property. **BB** ♦ **$100,** ♦♦ **$115,** ♦ **$30, RO** ♦ **$90,** ♦♦ **$95,** ♦ **$20,** Breakfast available. AE BC MC VI.

B&B's/Guest Houses

★★★★☆ **Treetops Bed & Breakfast**, (B&B), 16 Linum St, 2km SW of PO, ☎ 03 9877 2737, fax 03 9894 3279, 2 rms [ensuite, hairdry, a/c-cool, c/fan, heat, elec blkts, tel, TV, video (1), clock radio, CD, t/c mkg, refrig, micro, toaster], iron, iron brd, pool-heated (solar), spa, bbq. **BLB** ♦ **$90 - $110,** ♦♦ **$110 - $130,** ♦ **$20,** AE BC DC MC VI.

MELBOURNE - BOX HILL VIC 3128

Pop 27,232. (16km E Melbourne), See map on page 697, ref D3. Residential suburb in the outer metropolitan area.

Hotels/Motels

AAA
TOURISM
Special Rates

★★★★ **The Tudor - Box Hill**, (M), 1101 Whitehorse Rd (Maroondah Hwy), 500m E of PO, ☎ 03 9898 9581, fax 03 9890 2238, 46 units (8 suites) [shwr, bath, spa bath (14), tlt, hairdry, a/c, elec blkts, tel, TV, video-fee, clock radio, t/c mkg, refrig, mini bar], ldry, iron, lounge, conf fac, ⊠, pool-heated, sauna, spa, 24hr reception, rm serv, gym, cots, non smoking units (7). **RO** ♦ **$105 - $146,** ♦♦ **$105 - $146,** AE BC DC MC VI, ⅋⅃.

★★★☆ **Box Hill Motel**, (M), 177 Station St, 2.5km S of PO, ☎ 03 9808 3622, fax 03 9808 3622, 21 units [shwr, tlt, hairdry, a/c, elec blkts, tel, TV, video-fee, clock radio, t/c mkg, refrig, toaster], ldry, pool, cots. **RO** ♦ **$77,** ♦♦ **$82 - $88,** ♦ **$10 - $15,** ch con, AE BC DC MC VI.

★★★ **Maroondah Motel**, (M), 768 Whitehorse Rd (Maroondah Hwy), 500m W of PO, ☎ 03 9890 0517, fax 03 9890 9344, (2 stry gr fl), 21 units (2 suites) [shwr, tlt, hairdry, a/c, elec blkts, tel, TV, video-fee, clock radio, t/c mkg, refrig, cook fac (2), micro (13), toaster], ldry, c/park (carport) (12), cots, non smoking units (3). **RO** ♦ **$71.50,** ♦♦ **$77 - $88,** ♦ **$11 - $15, Suite D $99 - $140,** AE BC DC MC VI.

The Tudor Box Hill

1101 Whitehorse Rd
Box Hill 3128

Tel (03) 9898 9581
Fax (03) 9890 2238

Email: enquiries@thetudor.com.au
Website www.thetudor.com.au

- Centrally located, walking to Box Hill station
- Cnr Simpson Rd and Whitehorse Road
- 4 star rooms, spa suite, family suites, serviced apartments
- 24 hour reception, cable TV
- Indoor heated pool, sauna, spa, gym.

BOX HILL MOTEL
177 Station Street Box Hill South
Ph/Fax (03) 9808 3622

- • **Quiet, modern units**
- • **Non smoking rooms**
- • **Easy tram & train access to city**
- • **All ground floor units**

MELWAYS MAP 61 C4

Self Catering Accommodation

★★★★ **The Tudor Serviced Town Houses & Apartments**, (Apt), 1101 Whitehorse Rd (Maroondah Hwy), ☎ 03 9898 6665, (2 stry gr fl), 22 apts acc up to 6, (1, 2 & 3 bedrm), [shwr, bath, tlt, hairdry, a/c, heat, elec blkts, tel, cable tv, video-fee, clock radio, refrig, cook fac, d/wash, toaster, ldry (in unit), blkts, linen, pillows], pool-indoor, c/park (garage), cots-fee. **D $120 - $205,** AE BC DC MC VI.

MELBOURNE - BRIGHTON VIC 3186

Pop Part of Melbourne, (10km S Melbourne), See map on page 697, ref C4. Bayside suburb of Melbourne. Bowls, Croquet, Golf, Squash, Swimming (Bay, Pool), Tennis.

Hotels/Motels

★★★★☆ **Brighton Savoy Motel**, (M), 150 The Esplanade, ☎ 03 9592 8233, fax 03 9592 3384, (Multi-stry gr fl), 60 units [shwr, bath, spa bath (13), tlt, hairdry (13), a/c, tel, cable tv-fee, clock radio, t/c mkg, refrig], lift, ldry, iron, iron brd, conf fac, ⊠, sauna, spa, bbq, 24hr reception, rm serv, c/park (undercover), ✆, gym, cots-fee. **RO** ♦ **$137 - $159,** ♦♦ **$137 - $159,** ♦ **$10,** ch con, AE BC DC EFT JCB MC VI, ⅋⅃.

B&B's/Guest Houses

★★★★☆ **Clairbank Bed & Breakfast**, (B&B), 14 Pine St, ☎ 03 9592 6539, 1 rm (1 suite) [shwr, bath, tlt, hairdry, fan, heat, elec blkts, TV, clock radio, CD, t/c mkg]. **BB** ♦ **$75 - $85,** ♦♦ **$135 - $150.**

★★★★ **Brighton on Sussex**, (B&B), 9 Sussex St, ☎ 03 9530 5838, fax 03 9533 3368, 1 rm (Studio), [shwr, tlt, c/fan, heat, cable tv, clock radio, CD, t/c mkg, refrig, cook fac ltd, micro, elec frypan, toaster, blkts, doonas, linen, pillows], pool-heated, bbq, breakfast ingredients, non smoking property. **BLB** ♦♦ **$110 - $150,** ♦ **$30,** BC MC VI.

★★★☆ **Warringa B & B - Rene Phipps Enterprises**, (B&B), 28 Cole St, ☎ 03 9596 2907, (2 stry), 2 rms [bath, hairdry, a/c-cool, c/fan, heat, elec blkts, clock radio], pool, non smoking units (8). **RO** ♦ **$68 - $86,** ♦♦ **$78 - $110,** ♦ **$15,** BC MC VI.

MELBOURNE - BROADMEADOWS VIC 3047

Pop Part of Melbourne, (17km N Melbourne), See map on page 697, ref C2. Industrial area on the outskirts of Melbourne. Squash, Swimming (Pool).

Hotels/Motels

★★★ **Penthouse Hotel**, (LMH), Cnr Barry Rd & Maffra St, ☎ 03 9309 3211, fax 03 9309 4528, 16 units [shwr, bath (1), tlt, a/c, tel, TV, clock radio, t/c mkg, refrig, toaster], conf fac, ⊠, ✆. **BLB** ♦ **$70,** ♦♦ **$70,** ♦ **$10,** Light breakfast only available. AE BC DC EFT MC VI.

MELBOURNE - BRUNSWICK VIC 3056

Pop Part of Melbourne, (6km N Melbourne), See map on page 697, ref C3. Inner residential & light industrial area. Croquet, Squash, Swimming (Pool), Tennis.

Hotels/Motels

GOLDEN CHAIN

★★★★ **Brunswick Tower Motel**, (M), 188 Moreland Rd, ☎ 03 9383 4002, fax 03 9383 4099, (2 stry gr fl), 38 units [shwr, tlt, hairdry (19), a/c, tel, TV, clock radio, t/c mkg, refrig], ldry, ⊠ (Wed to Sat). **RO** ♦ **$82.50,** ♦♦ **$93.50,** ♦ **$10 - $20,** AE BC EFT MC VI.

★★★☆ Princes Park Motor Inn, (M), Cnr Royal Pde & Park St, 3km N of GPO, opposite Princes Park, ☎ 03 9388 1000, fax 03 9388 1011, (2 stry gr fl), 70 units [shwr, bath (20), spa bath (2), tlt, hairdry, a/c, elec blkts, tel, cable tv, movie, clock radio, t/c mkg, refrig, cook fac (28), micro (28)], ldry, iron, iron brd, 24hr reception, c/park (undercover) (50), cots-fee, non smoking units (21). **RO** ┆ **$119 - $135**, ┆┆ **$124 - $135**, ┆ **$113**, ch con, 28 units ★★★★, AE BC DC EFT MC VI.
Operator Comment: See our advert in Melbourne City.

★★★ Parkville Motel, (M), 759 Park St, 500m S of PO, ☎ 03 9388 1500, fax 03 9387 3384, 20 units [shwr, tlt, a/c, tel, cable tv, clock radio, t/c mkg, refrig], ldry, cots. **RO** ┆ **$80**, ┆┆ **$90**, ┆ **$10**, AE BC DC EFT MC VI.

Self Catering Accommodation
★★★★ Ye Oxley Lodge, (Apt), 793 Park St, 600m S of PO, ☎ 03 9388 0055, fax 03 9388 0293, (2 stry gr fl), 15 apts acc up to 3, (1 bedrm), [shwr, bath, tlt, a/c, elec blkts, tel, TV, clock radio, t/c mkg, refrig, cook fac, micro, toaster, blkts, linen, pillows], ldry, c/park (limited undercover), non smoking units. **D** ┆ **$85 - $110**, ┆┆ **$85 - $110**, ┆ **$16**, Minimum booking all major Melbourne events, BC MC VI.

★★★ Parkville Place Apartments & Motor Inn, (Apt), 124 Brunswick Rd, ☎ 03 9387 8477, fax 03 9387 8556, 23 apts acc up to 2, (Studio), [shwr, tlt, a/c, elec blkts, tel, TV, video-fee, refrig, cook fac ltd, micro, toaster, blkts, linen, pillows], ldry, c/park (limited undercover), cots-fee, non smoking property. **D** ┆ **$75 - $85**, ┆┆ **$85 - $95**, ┆ **$15**, **W** **$490 - $700**, ch con, BC EFT MC MCH VI.

MELBOURNE - BULLEEN VIC 3105
Pop Part of Melbourne, (15km NE Melbourne), See map on page 697, ref D3. Residential area set amid undulating hills. Tennis.
Hotels/Motels
★★★ Manningham Hotel, (LMH), 1 Thompsons Rd, 2.4km SW of PO, ☎ 03 9850 5555, fax 03 9850 2888, 12 units [shwr, tlt, hairdry, a/c, elec blkts, tel, TV, clock radio, t/c mkg, refrig, toaster], conf fac, ⊠. **RO** ┆ **$71**, ┆┆ **$85**, ┆ **$12**, Light breakfast only available. AE BC DC EFT MC VI.

MELBOURNE - BUNDOORA VIC 3083
Pop 6,464. (18km NE Melbourne), See map on page 697, ref D2. Suburb of Melbourne. Bowls, Golf, Tennis.
Hotels/Motels
★★★☆ Parkside Inn Motel, (M), 1045 Plenty Rd, directly opposite Latrobe University, ☎ 03 9467 3344, fax 03 9467 5462, (2 stry gr fl), 18 units [shwr, bath (1), spa bath (2), tlt, a/c, elec blkts, tel, cable tv, video (11), clock radio, t/c mkg, refrig, cook fac (1)], conf fac, dinner to unit (Mon to Thur), cots. **RO** ┆┆ **$76 - $87**, ┆ **$11**, 7 units ★★☆. AE BC DC EFT MC VI.

Other Accommodation
Chisholm College, (Lodge), Only available in university breaks. Kingsbury Dve, On Latrobe University Campus, ☎ 03 9479 2899, (2 stry), 22 rms [heat], shwr (6), tlt (4), ldry, rec rm, read rm, lounge (TV, video), ✗, cook fac, refrig, bbq, kiosk, ☏. **D** ┆ **$12.50**, ┆┆ **$16**, **W** ┆ **$82.25**, ┆┆ **$101.50**.

MELBOURNE - BURWOOD VIC 3125
Pop 14,875. (14km E Melbourne), See map on page 697, ref D4. Residential eastern suburb.
Hotels/Motels
★★★ Burwood East Motel, (M), 355 Blackburn Rd, Burwood East 3151, 50m S of Burwood Hwy, ☎ 03 9803 8211, fax 03 9887 8080, 23 units [shwr, tlt, a/c, elec blkts, tel, TV, clock radio, t/c mkg, refrig, toaster], ldry, pool, bbq, cots-fee. **RO** ┆ **$77**, ┆┆ **$77**, ┆ **$11**, AE BC DC EFT MC VI.

Self Catering Accommodation
★★★★☆ Ningana B & B, (Cotg), 7 O'Grady St, Burwood East 3151, ☎ 03 9802 6902, fax 03 9802 1487, 1 cotg acc up to 4, (Studio), [shwr, tlt, hairdry, a/c, elec blkts, tel, TV, video, clock radio, t/c mkg, refrig, cook fac, micro, toaster, blkts, linen, pillows], w/mach, iron, iron brd, spa, bbq, non smoking property. **BB** ┆ **$90**, ┆┆ **$98 - $125**, ┆ **$20**, BC MC VI.

MELBOURNE - CAMBERWELL VIC 3124
Pop Part of City Boroondara, (9km E Melbourne), See map on page 697, ref D3. Inner residential suburb.
B&B's/Guest Houses
★★★☆ Herb & Lolas B & B, (B&B), 16 Fordham Ave, ☎ 03 9836 1618, fax 03 9888 6522, 1 rm [shwr, bath, tlt, hairdry, fan, heat, clock radio], lounge (TV, Video), lounge firepl, t/c mkg shared, non smoking property. **BLB** ┆ **$60**, ┆┆ **$80 - $90**.

★★★☆ Springfields Homestay, (B&B), 4 Springfield Ave, ☎ 03 9809 1681, 2 rms [hairdry, fan, heat, elec blkts, clock radio], ldry-fee, lounge (TV), t/c mkg shared, cots, non smoking property. **BB** ┆ **$65**, ┆┆ **$95**, ┆ **$30**, ch con.

★★★☆ Toad Hall - Frog Hollow B & B, (B&B), 34 Fordham Ave, Cnr Carramar Ave, ☎ 03 9830 5620, (2 stry), 1 rm [shwr, bath, tlt, hairdry, a/c, elec blkts, TV, clock radio, t/c mkg, refrig], lounge. **BB** ┆ **$50**, ┆┆ **$95**, Other meals by arrangement.

MELBOURNE - CARLTON VIC 3053
Pop Part of Melbourne, (3km N Melbourne), See map on page 697, ref C3. Inner suburb of Melbourne. Bowls, Swimming (Pool).
Hotels/Motels

★★★★ Downtowner on Lygon, (M), 66 Lygon St, 1.4km N of GPO, Cnr Queensberry St, ☎ 03 9663 5555, fax 03 9662 3308, (Multi-stry), 98 units (2 suites) [shwr, bath (36), spa bath (35), tlt, hairdry, a/c, tel, cable tv, movie, clock radio, t/c mkg, refrig, mini bar, cook fac (2), micro (6), toaster], lift, ldry, iron, iron brd, conf fac, ⊠ (Mon to Sat), bar (cocktail), 24hr reception, rm serv, dinner to unit, c/park (undercover) (45), cots. **RO** ┆ **$149**, ┆┆ **$149**, ┆ **$22**, Suite **D** **$209**, ch con, AE BC DC EFT MC VI.
Operator Comment: See our advert on following page.

★★★★ Rydges Carlton Melbourne, (Ltd Lic H), 701 Swanston St, ☎ 03 9347 7811, fax 03 9347 8225, (Multi-stry), 107 rms (8 suites) [shwr, bath (44), tlt, hairdry, a/c, tel, TV, movie, clock radio, t/c mkg, refrig, mini bar], lift, ldry, iron, iron brd, business centre, conf fac, ⊠, pool-heated (solar), sauna, spa, bbq, 24hr reception, rm serv, secure park, cots. **RO** ┆ **$140 - $240**, ┆┆ **$140 - $240**, ┆ **$27.50**, ch con, AE BC DC MC VI.

★★★★ Travel-Inn Hotel, (M), Cnr Grattan & Drummond Sts, 1.8km N of GPO, ☎ 03 9347 7922, fax 03 9347 1424, (Multi-stry), 100 units [shwr, bath (1), spa bath (26), tlt, hairdry, a/c, tel, TV, movie, clock radio, t/c mkg, refrig], lift, ldry, iron, iron brd, conf fac, ⊠, bar (cocktail), pool, bbq, 24hr reception, rm serv, dinner to unit, secure park, ☏, cots, non smoking flr (2). **RO** ┆ **$145 - $176**, ┆┆ **$145.20 - $176**, ┆ **$22**, ch con, AE BC DC EFT MC VI.

★★★ Elizabeth Tower Motel, (M), 792 Elizabeth St, 1.7km N of GPO, ☎ 03 9347 9211, fax 03 9347 0396, (Multi-stry), 100 units (6 suites) [shwr, bath (96), tlt, hairdry, a/c, tel, TV, clock radio, t/c mkg, refrig, mini bar], lift, ldry, conf fac, ⊠, bar (cocktail), pool, 24hr reception, rm serv, c/park (limited), cots. **RO** ┆ **$137 - $175**, ┆┆ **$137 - $175**, ┆ **$20**, Suite **D** **$145 - $195**, ch con, AE BC DC JCB MC VI.

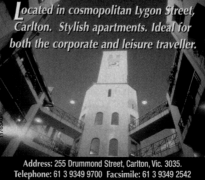
For Accommodation Booking information - see page 27

★★★ **Lygon Lodge**, (M), 220 Lygon St, 1.8km N of GPO, ☎ 03 9663 6633, fax 03 9663 7297, (Multi-stry), 40 units [shwr, bath (23), spa bath (1), tlt, hairdry, a/c, tel, TV, clock radio, t/c mkg, refrig, cook fac (10), toaster], lift, ldry, iron, iron brd, ⊠, 24hr reception, c/park (undercover) (36), cots. D ♯♯ $110 - $165, AE BC EFT MC VI.

Self Catering Accommodation
★★★★ **Carlton Clocktower Apartments**, (Apt), 255 Drummond St, ☎ 03 9349 9700, fax 03 9349 2542, (Multi-stry), 28 apts acc up to 6, (1 & 2 bedrm), [shwr, bath, tlt, hairdry, a/c, heat, tel, TV, video-fee, clock radio, t/c mkg, refrig, cook fac, micro, d/wash, toaster, ldry (in unit), blkts, linen, pillows], lift, w/mach, dryer, iron, iron brd, c/park (undercover), cots. D $171 - $198, Breakfast pack available, AE BC DC EFT MC VI.

★★★★ **Lygon Quest Lodgings**, (Apt), 700 Lygon St, Carlton North 3054, 3.1km N of GPO, ☎ 03 9345 3888, fax 03 9349 1250, (Multi-stry gr fl), 26 apts (1 & 2 bedrm), [shwr, bath, tlt, hairdry, a/c, tel, clock radio, t/c mkg, refrig, cook fac, micro, d/wash, toaster, ldry (in unit), blkts, linen, pillows], w/mach, dryer, iron, iron brd, non smoking units. D ♯♯ $125.40 - $148.50, ♯♯♯♯ $154 - $181.50, Breakfast Pack available, AE BC DC JCB MC VI.

★★★★ **Oakford on Lygon**, (Apt), 2 Finlay Pl, 2km N of GPO, ☎ 03 8341 4773, fax 03 8341 4799, (Multi-stry), 53 apts acc up to 5, (Studio, 1 & 2 bedrm), [shwr, bath, tlt, hairdry, a/c, heat, tel, cable tv-fee, movie-fee, clock radio, t/c mkg, refrig, mini bar, cook fac, micro, d/wash, toaster, ldry (in unit) (48), blkts, linen, pillows], lift, w/mach, dryer, iron, iron brd, c/park (undercover) (22), cots, non smoking flr (3). D ⓪ $22, $159 - $225, ch con, AE BC DC MC VI.

★★★ **The Drummond Apartments**, (Apt), 371 Drummond St, ☎ 03 9486 1777, fax 03 9482 2649, (2 stry gr fl), 10 apts acc up to 2, (Studio & 1 bedrm), [shwr, bath (4), tlt, hairdry, fan, heat, tel, TV, clock radio, refrig, cook fac, toaster, blkts, linen, pillows], ldry, w/mach, dryer, iron, iron brd, c/park (carport). D $115.50 - $126.50, AE BC DC MC VI.

MELBOURNE - CARNEGIE VIC 3163
Pop Part of Melbourne, (14km SE Melbourne), See map on page 697, ref D4. Older suburb of Melbourne. Bowls, Swimming (Pool), Tennis.
Hotels/Motels
★★★☆ **Carnegie Motor Inn**, (M), 1102 Dandenong Rd (Princes Hwy), ☎ 03 9568 5422, fax 03 9563 1348, 10 units [shwr, tlt, hairdry, a/c, elec blkts, tel, cable tv, clock radio, t/c mkg, refrig, toaster], ldry, iron, iron brd, pool-heated (solar), spa, bbq, cots. RO $93 - $104, ch con, AE BC DC EFT MC VI.

★★★☆ **(Holiday Flat Section)**, (2 stry gr fl), 8 flats acc up to 6, (1 & 2 bedrm), [shwr, bath (4), tlt, hairdry, a/c-cool (1), a/c (7), heat, elec blkts, tel, cable tv, clock radio, refrig, cook fac, micro, elec frypan, toaster, blkts, linen, pillows], ldry, iron, iron brd. D $104 - $165.

MELBOURNE - CARRUM DOWNS VIC 3201

Pop 2,350. Part City of Frankston, (37km S Melbourne), See map on page 697, ref D6. Outer suburb, close to Frankston Bayside.
Hotels/Motels

 ★★★☆ **Carrum Downs Motel**, (M), 1325 Frankston-Dandenong Rd, 2km SW of PO, ☎ 03 9786 8355, fax 03 9786 8078, 12 units [shwr, spa bath (3), tlt, a/c, elec blkts, tel, TV, video-fee, clock radio, t/c mkg, refrig, toaster], ldry, pool, bbq, plygr, cots, non smoking units (1).
BLB ♥ $68 - $91, ◊ $11, ch con, fam con, AE BC EFT MC VI.

 ★★★ **Kingston Lodge Motel**, (M), 1165 Frankston-Dandenong Rd, 200m SW of PO, ☎ 03 9782 1292, fax 03 9782 0823, 31 units [shwr, spa bath (4), tlt, a/c, elec blkts, tel, TV, video-fee, clock radio, t/c mkg, refrig, toaster], ldry, pool, bbq, dinner to unit, cots. **BLB ♥ $68 - $89, ◊ $10**, ch con, BC EFT MC VI.

MELBOURNE - CARRUM VIC 3197

Pop Part of City of Frankston, (32km SE Melbourne), See map on page 697, ref D5. Bayside suburb of Melbourne. Golf, Sailing, Swimming (Beach), Tennis.
B&B's/Guest Houses

★★★☆ **B&B at Mac's - Carrum**, (B&B), 49 Valetta St, 200m E of railway station, ☎ 03 9772 1435, 2 rms [shwr, bath, tlt, hairdry, heat, elec blkts], lounge (TV, video, stereo), bbq, non smoking property.
BB ◊ $45, ♥ $75.

MELBOURNE - CAULFIELD VIC 3162

Pop Part of City of Glen Eira, (11km SE Melbourne), See map on page 697, ref C4. Suburb of Melbourne. Bowls, Croquet, Tennis.
B&B's/Guest Houses

★★★★ **Lord Lodge at Caulfield**, (B&B), No children's facilities, 30 Booran Rd, ☎ 03 9572 3969, fax 03 9571 5310, 3 rms [ensuite (2), shwr (1), tlt (1), fire pl (3), cent heat, elec blkts, clock radio], lounge (TV, video, cd), lounge firepl, t/c mkg shared, bbq.
BB ◊ $105 - $125, ♥ $120 - $155, AE BC DC MC VI.

MELBOURNE - CHADSTONE VIC 3148

Pop Part of City of Monash, (14km E Melbourne), See map on page 697, ref D4. Residential suburb in the metropolitan area.
Hotels/Motels

★★★ **Matthew Flinders Hotel**, (LMH), Previously Zagames of Chadstone, 667 Warrigal Rd, ☎ 03 9568 8004, fax 03 9568 6853, (2 stry gr fl), 21 units [shwr, tlt, a/c, tel, TV, clock radio, t/c mkg, refrig, toaster], ldry, ⊠ (Tues to Sat), ✆, cots. **BLB ◊ $88, ♥ $88, ◊ $16.50**, Light breakfast only available. AE BC DC EFT MC VI.

MELBOURNE - CHELSEA VIC 3196

Pop Part of Melbourne, (30km SE Melbourne), See map on page 697, ref D5. Bayside suburb of Melbourne. Bowls, Sailing, Swimming (Bay), Tennis.
Self Catering Accommodation

 ★★★★☆ **Beachstay B & B Cottages**, (Cotg), 3 Kelvin Gve, ☎ 03 9776 2989, fax 03 9500 2269, 1 cotg acc up to 5, (3 bedrm), [shwr, spa bath, tlt, hairdry, a/c-cool, fan, cent heat, TV, video, clock radio, t/c mkg, refrig, cook fac, micro, elec frypan, d/wash, toaster, ldry, blkts, doonas, linen, pillows], w/mach, dryer, iron, iron brd, lounge firepl, pool-heated (solar, salt), non smoking property, Pets on application. **D ♥ $80 - $160, ◊ $30, W $600 - $1,050**, ch con, Min book all holiday times, AE BC MC VI.
Operator Comment: A world of luxury within this spacious cottage, set in formal gardens with in/outdoor pool. Romantic escape/Family holiday 100m to beach. www.beachstay.com

★★★ **Bay Beach Cottage**, (HU), 12 Berwen St, ☎ 03 9772 5274, 1 unit acc up to 4, (2 bedrm), [shwr, tlt, fan, heat, TV, video, clock radio, t/c mkg, refrig, cook fac, micro, toaster, doonas, linen, pillows], w/mach, iron, iron brd, bbq. **D ♥ $80 - $160, ◊ $30, W ♥ $500 - $1,000, ◊ $150 - $210**, ch con, Min book Christmas Jan and Easter, BC MC VI.

★★★ **Chelsea Gardens Caravan Park**, (HU), 100 Broadway, 3 km E of PO, ☎ 03 9772 2485, fax 03 9776 2059, 4 units acc up to 2, [ensuite, hairdry, a/c, elec blkts, TV, clock radio, refrig, cook fac, micro, toaster, blkts, linen, pillows], ldry, pool, bbq-fee. **D ◊ $68 - $73**, AE BC EFT MC VI.

MELBOURNE - CHIRNSIDE PARK VIC 3116

Pop Part of Yarra Ranges, (35km E Melbourne), See map on page 697, ref E3. Outer eastern suburb. Bowls, Golf, Tennis, Vineyards, Wineries.
Self Catering Accommodation

★★★★ **Colensay Park**, (Cotg), (Farm), 415 Edward Rd, 4.1km N of Chirnside Park shopping centre, ☎ 03 9735 3265, fax 03 9735 3476, 1 cotg acc up to 4, (1 bedrm), [shwr, bath, tlt, hairdry, a/c-cool, c/fan, heat (wood fire), elec blkts, TV, clock radio, t/c mkg, refrig, cook fac, micro, toaster, blkts, doonas, linen, pillows], lounge (tv, cd player), bbq, breakfast ingredients, non smoking rms. **D ♥ $165, ◊ $75, W ♥ $550 - $670, ◊ $325.**

B&B's/Guest Houses

★★★★☆ **The Cottage at the Old Wood**, (B&B), 12 Cherry Hill Way, ☎ 03 9739 6311, fax 03 9739 7556, 1 rm (Studio), [shwr, bath, tlt, a/c-cool, c/fan, heat, elec blkts, TV, video, clock radio, refrig, cook fac, micro, toaster], iron, iron brd, c/park (undercover), non smoking property. **BB ◊ $90 - $130, ♥ $100 - $160**, BC MC VI.

MELBOURNE - CLAYTON VIC 3168

Pop Part of City of Monash, (21km E Melbourne), See map on page 697, ref D4. Residential area. Location of Monash University and Monash Medical Centre. Bowls, Swimming (Pool), Tennis.
Hotels/Motels

★★★★ **Clayton - Monash Motor Inn**, (M), 1790 Dandenong Rd (Princes Hwy), 500m S of Monash University, ☎ 03 9544 0911, fax 03 9543 3638, (2 stry gr fl), 16 units [shwr, tlt, hairdry, a/c, elec blkts, tel, cable tv, video-fee, clock radio, t/c mkg, refrig, toaster], ldry, iron, iron brd, dinner to unit, cots, non smoking units (5). **RO ♥ $105 - $115, ◊ $10**, ch con, AE BC DC MC VI.

Self Catering Accommodation

★★★★ **Clayton - Monash Serviced Apartments**, (Apt), 1790 Dandenong Rd, ☎ 03 9544 0911, fax 03 9543 3638, 8 apts acc up to 4, (1 & 2 bedrm), [shwr, bath, tlt, hairdry, fan (cooling) (4), heat, elec blkts, tel, cable tv, video-fee, clock radio, refrig, cook fac, micro, elec frypan, toaster, blkts, linen, pillows], ldry, iron, iron brd, cots, non smoking units (3). **D $145 - $195, W $910 - $1,225**, AE BC DC MC VI.

Sharing the roads - Trucks and cars

Trucks are different from cars. They take up more road space than cars, especially when turning, and are slower to accelerate, turn and reverse. Here are some hints in sharing our roads safely with trucks:

• Don't cut in on trucks. Because trucks need a greater braking distance than cars, truck drivers leave more space in front of them when approaching a red light or stop sign than a car.

• Allow extra time and space to overtake trucks. You will need about 1.5 kilometres of clear road space to pass a truck.

• Don't pass a left-turning truck on the inside. Trucks sometimes need more than one lane to turn tight corners, so watch for a truck swinging out near intersections.

• Be patient - follow at a safe distance. Truck drivers may not see you because of blind spots, particularly if you travel right behind them.

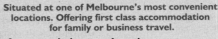

MELBOURNE - COBURG VIC 3058

Pop Part of City of Darebin, (9km N Melbourne), See map on page 697, ref C3. An inner residential suburb - Olympic pool and Merri Creek Environmental Walking Trail.
Operator Comment: See display advertisement on opposite page.

Hotels/Motels

★★★☆ **Coburg Motor Inn**, (M), 726 Sydney Rd (Hume Hwy), ☎ 03 9350 1855, fax 03 9350 3799, (2 stry gr fl), 26 units [shwr, tlt, hairdry, a/c, elec blkts, tel, TV, video-fee, clock radio, t/c mkg, refrig, cook fac ltd (5)], ldry, w/mach, iron, iron brd, pool, c/park (undercover) (15), cots-fee, non smoking units (9). RO ♦ $74 - $95, ♦♦ $85 - $95, ♦♦♦♦ $99 - $128, ◊ $11, ch con, AE BC DC EFT MC MCH VI.

★★★ **Coburg Coach House Motel**, (M), 846 Sydney Rd (Hume Hwy), 1.6km N of PO, ☎ 03 9350 2844, fax 03 9350 1255, (2 stry gr fl), 27 units [shwr, tlt, hairdry (15), a/c, elec blkts, tel, TV, video, clock radio, t/c mkg, refrig], ldry, conf fac, ☒ (Mon to Sat), pool, rm serv, cots-fee. RO ♦ $66, ♦♦ $72, ◊ $9, fam con, AE BC DC EFT MC VI.

★★★ **Disabled Motorists Motel Units**, (M), 2A Station St, 100m N of Moreland railway station, ☎ 03 9386 0413, fax 03 9386 0413, 2 units [shwr, tlt, a/c, elec blkts, tel, TV, clock radio, t/c mkg, refrig, toaster]. D ♦ $60, ♦♦ $75, ◊ $10, BC MC VI, ♿.

MELBOURNE - CRAIGIEBURN VIC 3064

Pop 12,900. (21km N Melbourne), See map on page 697, ref C1. Industrial suburb on the outskirts of metropolitan area.

Hotels/Motels

★★ **Motel Melbourne**, (M), 280 Hume Hwy, ☎ 03 9308 1248, fax 03 9305 7096, 18 units [shwr, tlt, a/c, elec blkts, tel, TV (16), clock radio (14), t/c mkg, refrig], ldry, cots-fee. RO ♦♦ $60.50 - $66, ♦♦♦ $77, ♦♦♦♦ $88.50, ch con, Light breakfast only available. AE BC DC EFT MC VI.

MELBOURNE - CRANBOURNE VIC 3977

Pop 24,750. (48km SE Melbourne), See map on page 697, ref E6. Outer metropolitan area. Bowls, Golf, Greyhound Racing, Horse Riding, Squash, Swimming (Indoor Pool), Tennis, Trotting.

Hotels/Motels

★★★★ **Mahogany Park**, (M), 110 Sladen St, ☎ 03 5996 8555, fax 03 5996 1865, 30 units (30 suites) [shwr, tlt, hairdry, a/c, elec blkts, tel, TV, clock radio, t/c mkg, refrig, mini bar, cook fac ltd, micro, toaster], ☒ (Mon to Sat), rm serv, cots, non smoking rms (19). Suite D ♦ $88, ♦♦ $99, ◊ $11, AE BC DC EFT MC VI, ♿.

★★★★ **The Terrace Motel at Cranbourne**, (LMH), Cnr Sth Gippsland Hwy & Camms Rd, ☎ 03 5996 3366, fax 03 5996 7717, (2 stry gr fl), 26 units [shwr, bath (8), spa bath (12), tlt, hairdry, a/c, tel, TV, video, clock radio, t/c mkg, refrig], ldry, ☒, rm serv, cots-fee. RO ♦ $100 - $130, ♦♦ $100 - $160, ◊ $10, ch con, AE BC DC EFT MC VI.

★★ **Fourth Furlong**, (M), 1449 South Gippsland Hwy, opposite racecourse, ☎ 03 5996 7500, fax 03 5995 0034, 16 units [shwr, spa bath (2), tlt, hairdry, a/c-cool (4), fan, heat, elec blkts, TV, clock radio, t/c mkg, refrig, toaster], ldry, cots. RO ♦ $60, ♦♦ $66, ◊ $10, ch con, AE BC DC MC VI.

MELBOURNE - CROYDON VIC 3136

Pop 49,450. (33km E Melbourne), See map on page 697, ref E3. Located at the foot of Mount Dandenong. Bowls, Golf, Swimming (Pool), Tennis.

Hotels/Motels

★★★★ **Victoria House Motor Inn**, (M), 331 Maroondah Hwy, 2km NW of PO, ☎ 03 9725 1955, fax 03 9725 1778, (2 stry gr fl), 20 units [shwr, spa bath (9), tlt, hairdry, a/c, elec blkts, tel, TV, clock radio, t/c mkg, refrig, mini bar, cook fac ltd (1), micro (5), toaster], ldry, iron, iron brd, conf fac, ☒, bbq, rm serv, non smoking units (4). RO ♦ $109 - $213, ♦♦ $109 - $213, AE BC DC EFT MC VI, ♿.

★★★ **Dorset Gardens**, (LMH), 335 Dorset Rd, 1.5km E of PO, ☎ 03 9725 6211, fax 03 9725 3177, (2 stry gr fl), 45 units [shwr, bath (36), tlt, a/c, elec blkts, tel, TV, clock radio, t/c mkg, refrig], conf fac, night club (Sat), ☒, rm serv, bowls, tennis, cots. RO ♦ $80, ♦♦ $80, ch con, AE BC DC EFT MC VI.

★★ **Croydon Hotel**, (LMH), 47 Maroondah Hwy, 3km W of PO, ☎ 03 9870 9344, fax 03 9879 6118, 8 units [shwr, tlt, a/c, TV, t/c mkg, refrig, toaster], ☒, ☎. RO ♦ $55, ♦♦ $60, AE BC DC EFT MC VI.

MELBOURNE - DANDENONG VIC 3175

Pop Part of Melbourne, (32km SE Melbourne), See map on page 697, ref D5. Residential & light industrial suburb. Bowls, Croquet, Squash, Swimming (Pool), Tennis.

Hotels/Motels

★★★★ **Quality Inn Imperial**, (M), Previously Imperial Inn, 124 Princes Hwy, 1km W of PO, ☎ 03 9706 8611, fax 03 9706 7595, (2 stry gr fl), 47 units [shwr, spa bath (22), tlt, hairdry, a/c, elec blkts, tel, TV, video, movie, clock radio, t/c mkg, refrig, mini bar], iron, iron brd, conf fac, ☒, pool indoor heated, sauna-fee, spa, 24hr reception, rm serv, cots, non smoking units (20). RO ♦ $100 - $159, ♦♦ $100 - $219, ◊ $15, ch con, AE BC DC EFT MC MP VI.

★★★ **Dandenong Motel**, (M), 147 Princes Hwy, 1.6km W of PO, ☎ 03 9794 0599, fax 03 9706 7489, (2 stry gr fl), 33 units [shwr, spa bath (2), tlt, hairdry (14), a/c, elec blkts, tel, TV, video (avail), clock radio, t/c mkg, refrig, toaster], ldry, pool, bbq, cots-fee, non smoking units (11). RO ♦ $73 - $108, ♦♦ $73 - $108, ◊ $11, 14 units ★★★☆. AE BC DC EFT MC VI.

Self Catering Accommodation

★★★★☆ **Dandenong Quest Inn**, (Apt), Cnr Princes Hwy & James St, opposite High School, ☎ 03 9797 2200, fax 03 9797 2299, (2 stry gr fl), 34 apts acc up to 6, (Studio, 1 & 2 bedrm), [shwr, bath, tlt, hairdry, a/c, elec blkts, tel, TV, movie, clock radio, refrig, cook fac, micro, d/wash, toaster, ldry (in unit), blkts, linen, pillows], iron, iron brd, conf fac, pool, bbq (covered), cots-fee, non smoking rms (3). **D $132 - $173**, Breakfast available. AE BC DC EFT MC VI.

MELBOURNE - DINGLEY VILLAGE VIC 3172

Pop 8,882. (28km SE Melbourne), See map on page 697, ref D5. Suburb of Melbourne. Golf, Tennis.

Hotels/Motels

★★★☆ **Dingley International Motor Inn**, (M), 334 Boundary Rd, ☎ 03 9551 8411, fax 03 9551 8659, 55 units [shwr, bath, spa bath (6), tlt, hairdry, a/c, tel, TV, movie, clock radio, t/c mkg, refrig, mini bar], ldry, iron, iron brd, conf fac, ☒, pool, sauna, spa, 24hr reception, rm serv, ☏, gym, cots, non smoking units (11). **RO ♦ $143 - $204, ♦♦ $143 - $204, ◊ $10**, 20 units ★★★★. AE BC DC EFT MC VI, ♿.

MELBOURNE - DONCASTER VIC 3108

Pop Part of City of Manningham, (17km NE Melbourne), See map on page 697, ref D3. Residential eastern suburb.

Hotels/Motels

★★★★☆ **Beau Monde International Hotel**, (M), 934 Doncaster Rd, Doncaster East 3109, 600m W of Doncaster East PO, ☎ 03 9841 9744, fax 03 9841 8339, (2 stry gr fl), 35 units [spa bath, a/c-cool, cable tv (Pay TV), mini bar], lift, ldry, ☒, 24hr reception, rm serv (24 hour), c/park (undercover). **RO ♦ $132, ♦♦ $132 - $143**, AE BC DC EFT MC VI, ♿.

★★★★ **Donview Heights Motel**, (M), 855 Doncaster Rd, 1.8km E of Doncaster Shoppingtown, ☎ 03 9840 1444, fax 03 9840 1010, (2 stry gr fl), 34 units (12 suites) [shwr, spa bath (12), tlt, hairdry, a/c, tel, cable tv, clock radio, t/c mkg, refrig, mini bar, cook fac (3), micro (3), toaster (3)], ldry, lounge, conf fac, bar (cocktail), bbq, 24hr reception, rm serv, cots, non smoking units (6). **RO ♦ $99 - $130, ♦♦ $99 - $130, ◊ $20, Suite D $110 - $150**, ch con, AE BC DC EFT MC VI, ♿.

★★★ **Shoppingtown Hotel**, (LMH), 13 Williamsons Rd, opposite Doncaster Shoppingtown, ☎ 03 9848 6811, fax 03 9840 1718, (2 stry gr fl), 8 units [shwr, tlt, hairdry, a/c, tel, cable tv, clock radio, t/c mkg, refrig, toaster], conf fac, ☒. **BLB ♦ $77 - $82.50, ♦♦ $82.50 - $88**, Light breakfast only available. AE BC DC EFT MC VI.

MELBOURNE - DOVETON VIC 3177

(34km SE Melbourne), See map on page 697, ref E5. Residential south eastern suburb of Melbourne.

Hotels/Motels

★★★ **Prince Mark Motor Inn**, (M), 4 Power Rd, 100m off Princes Hwy, ☎ 03 9794 7580, fax 03 9793 2878, (2 stry gr fl), 25 units [shwr, spa bath (1), tlt, a/c, heat, elec blkts, cable tv, clock radio, t/c mkg, toaster], cots, non smoking units (3). **DBB $82 - $93, RO ♦ $63, ♦♦ $71 - $74, ◊ $11**, ch con, AE BC DC EFT MC VI.

MELBOURNE - EAST MELBOURNE VIC 3002

Pop Part of Melbourne, (2km E Melbourne), See map on page 697, ref C3. Inner suburb of Melbourne.

Hotels/Motels

★★★★★ **Hilton on the Park Melbourne**, (LH), 192 Wellington Pde, 2.2km E of GPO, ☎ 03 9419 2000, fax 03 9419 2001, (Multi-stry), 403 rms (38 suites) [shwr, bath, spa bath (5), tlt, hairdry, a/c, tel, TV, movie, clock radio, CD (38), t/c mkg, refrig, mini bar], lift, conf fac, ☒, bar (cocktail), pool-heated, sauna, spa, 24hr reception, rm serv, c/park (undercover)-fee, ☏, gym, cots, non smoking flr (10). **RO ♦ $255 - $385, ♦♦ $300 - $430, ◊ $45, Suite RO $485 - $1,650**, ch con, AE BC DC JCB MC VI, ♿.

Haven   FLAG   FLAG CHOICE HOTELS   METRO INNS

★★★★☆ **Metro Hotel & Suites Melbourne**, (Ltd Lic H), 133 Jolimont Rd, 1.7km E of GPO, ☎ 03 9663 4321, fax 03 9650 1833, (Multi-stry), 136 rms [shwr, bath (70), tlt, hairdry, a/c, tel, TV, movie, clock radio, t/c mkg, refrig, mini bar, cook fac (70), micro, toaster], lift, ldry, iron, iron brd, ☒, pool-heated, spa, 24hr reception, rm serv (limited), c/park (undercover)-fee, ☏, gym, cots, non smoking flr (4). **RO ♦ $119 - $250, ♦♦ $300, ◊ $25**, ch con, AE BC DC EFT JCB MC VI.

★★★★ Magnolia Court Boutique Hotel, (M), 101 Powlett St, 2.8km E of GPO, ☎ 03 9419 4222, fax 03 9416 0841, (Multi-stry gr fl), 26 units (4 suites) [shwr, bath (hip) (24), tlt, hairdry, a/c, elec blkts, tel, TV, video, clock radio, t/c mkg, refrig, cook fac (3), micro (3)], ldry, c/park (limited), cots, non smoking units (23). **RO ♦♦ $128 - $170, ♦ $17, Suite D ♦ $128 - $203, ♦♦ $128 - $203, ♦ $17**, ch con, AE BC DC MC VI.

★★★ The George Powlett, (M), 30 Powlett St, 2.4km E of GPO, ☎ 03 9419 9488, fax 03 9419 0806, (Multi-stry gr fl), 45 units [shwr, bath (hip) (33), tlt, a/c-cool, heat, tel, TV, clock radio, t/c mkg, refrig, cook fac ltd, micro, toaster], ldry, c/park (limited), cots, non smoking units (17). **RO ♦ $96.80, ♦♦ $104.50, ♦ $16.50**, ch con, Light Breakfast only, AE BC DC EFT MC VI.

★★★ Treasury Motor Lodge, (M), 179 Powlett St, 2.4km E of GPO, 200m E of Fitzroy Gardens, ☎ 03 9417 5281, fax 03 9416 0893, (2 stry gr fl), 21 units [shwr, bath, tlt, hairdry (13), a/c, elec blkts, tel, cable tv, clock radio, t/c mkg, refrig, micro (13), elec frypan (13)], c/park (limited), cots-fee. **RO ♦ $130 - $150, ♦♦ $130 - $150, ♦ $12**, ch con, AE BC DC MC VI.

Self Catering Accommodation

★★★★ Birches Boutique Apartments, (Apt), 160 Simpson St, 2.7km E of GPO, ☎ 03 9417 2344, fax 03 9417 5872, (Multi-stry gr fl), 22 apts acc up to 4, (1 bedrm), [shwr, bath, tlt, hairdry, a/c, tel, cable tv, video-fee, clock radio, t/c mkg, refrig, cook fac, micro, toaster, blkts, linen, pillows], ldry, sauna, bbq, secure park, cots-fee. **D ♦ $125 - $155, ♦ $20**, ch con, Light Breakfast available, AE BC DC MC VI.

Operator Comment: See our display advertisement under Melbourne.

★★★★ City Edge Serviced Apartments, (Apt), 92 Albert St, W off Hoddle St, ☎ 03 9419 3433, fax 03 9419 8733, (Multi-stry), 19 apts acc up to 4, (1 bedrm - 15q.), [shwr, bath (14), tlt, hairdry, a/c, tel, TV, video-fee, clock radio, t/c mkg, refrig, cook fac, micro, toaster, blkts, linen, pillows], ldry, w/mach-fee, dryer-fee, c/park (limited), cots. **D ♦ $114 - $200, ♦ $20, W $721 - $1,000**, ch con, AE BC DC EFT MC VI.

★★★★ Knightsbridge Apartments, (Apt), 101 George St, 2.5km E of GPO, ☎ 03 9419 1333, fax 03 9486 0861, (Multi-stry gr fl), 26 apts acc up to 4, (Studio & 2 bedrm), [shwr, bath, tlt, hairdry, a/c, heat, tel, TV, video-fee, clock radio, t/c mkg, refrig, cook fac ltd, micro, toaster, blkts, linen, pillows], ldry, w/mach, dryer, iron, iron brd, c/park (limited), cots-fee. **D $135 - $175**, ch con, Breakfast available. AE BC DC MC VI.

Operator Comment: See our display advertisement opposite.

★★★☆ Albert Heights Executive Apartments, (Apt), 83 Albert St, 1.5km E of PO, ☎ 03 9419 0955, fax 03 9419 9517, (Multi-stry gr fl), 34 apts acc up to 4, (1 bedrm), [shwr, bath (30), tlt, hairdry, a/c, tel, cable tv, video-fee, clock radio, t/c mkg, refrig, cook fac ltd, micro, toaster, blkts, linen, pillows], lift, ldry, w/mach, dryer, iron, iron brd, pool-heated, spa, c/park (limited), cots. **D ♦ $125 - $156, ♦♦ $125 - $156, ♦ $20**, ch con, Light breakfast available. AE BC DC EFT MC VI,

Operator Comment: See our ad under Melbourne, visit our website:- www.albertheights.com.au

★★★☆ The East Melbourne Apartment Hotel, (Apt), 25 Hotham St, 2.5km E of GPO, ☎ 03 9412 2555, fax 03 9412 2567, (Multi-stry gr fl), 38 apts acc up to 4, (Studio), [shwr, tlt, a/c, tel, TV, clock radio, refrig, cook fac ltd, micro, toaster, blkts, linen, pillows], ldry, w/mach, dryer, iron, iron brd, c/park (limited), cots. **D ♦ $121 - $176, ♦♦ $121 - $176, ♦ $15 - $22**, Breakfast available. AE BC DC MC VI.

★★★ Eastern Town House, (Apt), 90 Albert St, 2.6km NE of GPO, ☎ 03 9418 6666, fax 03 9415 1502, (Multi-stry gr fl), 51 apts acc up to 4, (Studio & 1 bedrm), [shwr, bath (10), spa bath (4), tlt, hairdry (15), a/c, elec blkts, tel, TV, clock radio, t/c mkg, refrig, cook fac ltd, micro, ldry, blkts, linen, pillows], lift, ldry, dryer, iron, iron brd, cafe, dinner to unit, c/park (25), cots-fee. **D $109 - $150, ♦ $20**, ch con, AE BC DC EFT MC VI.

★★★ Punt Hill Serviced Apartments, (Apt), 60 Gipps St, ☎ 03 9650 1299, fax 03 9650 4409, (Multi-stry gr fl), 17 apts (1 & 2 bedrm), [shwr, bath (5), tlt, hairdry, a/c, elec blkts, tel, TV, video-fee, clock radio, refrig, cook fac, micro, toaster, blkts, linen, pillows], ldry, w/mach, dryer, iron, iron brd, c/park. **D $128 - $162**, Minium booking applies all Melbourne major events. AE BC DC MC VI.

B&B's/Guest Houses

★★★☆ Georgian Court, (GH), 21 George St, 2.7km E of GPO, ☎ 03 9419 6353, fax 03 9416 0895, (2 stry gr fl), 31 rms [ensuite (17), hairdry (17), a/c (10), fan, heat, TV, clock radio, t/c mkg, refrig], ldry, lounge (TV, video), spa (2), ☎, cots, non smoking property. **BLB ♦ $73.70 - $95.70, ♦♦ $84.70 - $128.70, ♦ $22**, ch con, 14 rooms ★★★. AE BC DC MC VI.

MELBOURNE - ELTHAM VIC 3095

Pop Part of Melbourne, (24km NE Melbourne), See map on page 697, ref D2. Outer residential & commercial area of Melbourne in a semi rural area on Diamond Creek and Yarra River. Bowls, Swimming (Pool), Tennis.

Hotels/Motels

★★★★☆ Eltham Gateway Motel, (M), 1339 Main Rd, 2.4km E of PO, ☎ 03 9431 1666, fax 03 9439 7846, (2 stry gr fl), 37 units (10 suites) [shwr, bath (19), spa bath (17), tlt, hairdry, a/c, elec blkts, tel, TV, movie, clock radio, t/c mkg, refrig, mini bar, cook fac (4), micro (5)], ldry, iron, iron brd, conf fac, ☒, bbq, 24hr reception, rm serv, cots, non smoking units (10). **RO ♦♦ $98 - $200, ♦ $15, Suite D $150 - $200**, ch con, AE BC DC EFT MC VI, ♿.

★★★★ Flag Inn Eltham, (M), 1450 Main Rd, 3.4km E of PO, ☎ 03 9437 1122, fax 03 9437 1108, 19 units [shwr, spa bath (8), tlt, hairdry, a/c, elec blkts, tel, TV, movie, clock radio, t/c mkg, refrig, toaster], ldry, iron, iron brd, conf fac, ☒ (Mon to Thurs), pool, bbq (covered), rm serv, cots, non smoking units (6). **RO ♦ $88 - $182, ♦♦ $94 - $182, ♦ $11**, ch con, AE BC DC EFT MC MP VI, ♿.

Self Catering Accommodation

★★★★ Eltham Garden Retreat, (Cotg), 70B John St, 1km S of PO, ☎ 03 9439 9010, fax 03 9439 9010, 2 cotgs acc up to 4, (1 & 2 bedrm), [shwr, tlt, hairdry, fan, heat, elec blkts, tel, TV, video, clock radio, t/c mkg, refrig, cook fac, toaster, blkts, doonas, linen, pillows], iron, iron brd, bbq, cots, breakfast ingredients, non smoking property. **BB ♦ $120, ♦♦ $140**, ch con, BC MC VI.

★★★ **Sheringa Farm**, (Cotg), 185 Flat Rock Rd, Kangaroo Ground 3097,
☎ 03 9718 2370, fax 03 9718 2370, 1 cotg acc up to 4, (2 bedrm),
[shwr, tlt, fan, heat, elec blkts, TV, clock radio, CD, refrig, cook fac ltd,
elec frypan, toaster, blkts, doonas, linen, pillows], iron, iron brd,
spa (heated), bbq, breakfast ingredients. D ♀♀ $100, ♀ $30, W $450,
Min book long w/ends.

MELBOURNE - ELWOOD VIC 3184

*Pop Part of City of Port Phillip, (9km S Melbourne), See map on
page 697, ref C4. Bayside inner residential suburb. Bowls, Croquet,
Golf, Sailing, Swimming (Bay), Tennis.*

Self Catering Accommodation

★★★★ **47 Shelley Street**, (House), 47 Shelley St, ☎ 03 9531 3980,
fax 03 9531 3980, 1 house acc up to 4, (2 bedrm), [shwr, bath, tlt,
hairdry, a/c-cool, cent heat, tel, fax, TV, video, clock radio, t/c mkg,
refrig, cook fac, micro, d/wash, toaster, ldry, doonas, linen, pillows],
w/mach, iron, iron brd. D ♀♀ $110 - $250, ♀ $25 - $50, W ♀♀ $440 -
$1,300, ♀ $50 - $100, Min book school holidays and Easter.

MELBOURNE - ESSENDON VIC 3040

*Pop Part of Melbourne, (10km NW Melbourne), See map on page 697,
ref C3. Residential & light industrial suburb. Site of original Melbourne
Airport. Bowls, Croquet, Golf, Squash, Swimming (Pool), Tennis.*

Hotels/Motels

★★★★ **Essendon Motor Inn**, (M), 93 Bulla Rd, Essendon
North 3041, ☎ 03 9374 2433, fax 03 9374 1516,
25 units [shwr, spa bath (4), tlt, hairdry, a/c, elec blkts,
tel, TV, video-fee, clock radio, t/c mkg, refrig], ldry, iron,
iron brd, ☒ (Mon to Fri), bar (cocktail), pool, sauna, spa,
bbq, rm serv, courtesy transfer, plygr, cots-fee. RO ♀ $105 - $160,
♀♀ $115 - $160, ♀ $11, ch con, AE BC DC EFT MC MP VI, ⛓.

★★★☆ **Alexander Motor Inn**, (M), 980 Mt Alexander Rd,
200m W of PO, ☎ 03 9374 1255, fax 03 9379 8784, (2 stry
gr fl), 40 units [shwr, spa bath (2), tlt, hairdry, a/c, elec blkts,
tel, TV, clock radio, t/c mkg, refrig], ldry, conf fac, night club (Fri),
☒ (Mon to Fri), 24hr reception, rm serv, cots-fee. RO ♀ $110 - $150,
♀♀ $115.50 - $159.50, ♀ $11, 10 units ★★★. AE BC DC EFT MC VI.

Alexander Motor Inn...continued
★★★☆ **(Apartment Section)**, 3 apts acc up to 6, (1 & 2 bedrm),
[shwr, tlt, hairdry, a/c, elec blkts, tel, TV, clock radio, CD, t/c mkg,
refrig, cook fac, micro, toaster, ldry (in unit), blkts, linen, pillows],
w/mach, c/park (carport). D ♀♀ $143, ♀♀♀♀ $198, ♀ $11.

Self Catering Accommodation

★★★★ **Alexandria's Bed & Breakfast**, (Cotg), 22 Daisy St,
☎ 03 9386 7571, fax 03 9386 7571, 1 cotg acc up to 6, (3 bedrm),
[ensuite (2), shwr, bath (1), tlt, a/c-cool, heat, elec blkts, tel, cable tv,
clock radio, t/c mkg, refrig, cook fac, micro, toaster, ldry, blkts, linen,
pillows], iron, iron brd, bbq, non smoking property. BB ♀ $77, ♀♀ $99,
♀ $25, ♀ $462, ♀♀ $594, pen con.

B&B's/Guest Houses

★★★☆ **Amelia Bed & Breakfast**, (B&B), 41 Amelia Ave,
☎ 03 9379 4258, fax 03 9379 4258, 2 rms [ensuite (1), shwr, tlt,
hairdry (1), fan, c/fan (1), heat, cent heat, elec blkts (1), TV (1),
clock radio, t/c mkg], iron, iron brd, lounge (TV, cd player).
BB ♀ $75 - $85, ♀♀ $95 - $120, ♀ $20.

MELBOURNE - FAIRFIELD VIC 3078

Pop Part of Melbourne, (7km NE Melbourne), See map on page 697, ref C3. Residential & light industrial suburb. Bowls.

Hotels/Motels

★★★☆ **Jika International Motor Inn**, (M), 551 Heidelberg Rd, ☎ 03 9481 2822, fax 03 9489 8819, (2 stry gr fl), 48 units (4 suites) [shwr, bath (38), spa bath (4), tlt, hairdry, a/c, elec blkts, tel, TV, video (avail), clock radio, t/c mkg, refrig, mini bar (9), cook fac ltd (2), micro (2)], ldry, ⌧ (Mon to Sat), bar (cocktail), sauna, 24hr reception, rm serv, ✆, cots, non smoking units (5). D $121 - $165, Suite D $137 - $165, ch con, 9 units ★★★★. AE BC DC EFT MC VI,

Operator Comment: For full details visit our Website at www.jika.com.au

Self Catering Accommodation

★★★★ **Alphington Quest Lodging**, (Apt), 35 Coate Ave, Alphington 3078, 500m SE of PO, ☎ 03 9488 1188, fax 03 9482 2649, (2 stry), 19 apts acc up to 6, (1 & 2 bedrm), [shwr, bath, tlt, hairdry, a/c-cool, fan, heat, tel, TV, video-fee, clock radio, refrig, cook fac, micro, d/wash, toaster, ldry (in unit), blkts, linen, pillows], iron, iron brd, cots. D $128 - $148, Light breakfast available. AE BC DC EFT MC VI.

MELBOURNE - FAWKNER VIC 3060

Pop Part of Melbourne, (12km N Melbourne), See map on page 697, ref C2. Residential & light industrial suburb.

Hotels/Motels

★★★☆ **Fawkner Airport Motor Inn & Serviced Apart**, (M), 1164 Sydney Rd (Hume Hwy), opposite Fawkner Memorial Park, ☎ 03 9359 1011, fax 03 9359 1722, (2 stry gr fl), 18 units [shwr, bath (hip), spa bath (2), tlt, hairdry, a/c, elec blkts, tel, cable tv, t/c mkg, refrig, cook fac (5)], ldry, courtesy transfer (airport), cots-fee, non smoking units (9). RO ♦ $74 - $130, ♦♦ $80 - $130, ◊ $8, AE BC DC EFT MC MCH VI.

★★★☆ **Hume Villa Motor Inn**, (M), 1324 Sydney Rd (Hume Hwy), ☎ 03 9357 1522, fax 03 9359 6114, (2 stry), 23 units [shwr, spa bath (5), tlt, hairdry, a/c, tel, cable tv, video-fee, clock radio, t/c mkg, refrig, cook fac (2)], ldry, ✗ (Mon to Thur), BYO, c/park (undercover), courtesy transfer, cots-fee. RO ♦ $98 - $170, ♦♦ $98 - $170, ◊ $10, ch con, AE BC DC EFT MC VI.

★ **Motel Formule 1**, (M), 1401 Sydney Rd (Hume Hwy), ☎ 03 9357 2623, fax 03 9357 2693, (Multi-stry gr fl), 103 units [shwr, tlt, a/c, TV], t/c mkg shared-fee, refrig, ✆, non smoking units (43). RO ♦ $59, ♦♦ $59, ◊ $59, Light breakfast only available. AE BC DC MC VI, ♿.

MELBOURNE - FERNTREE GULLY VIC 3156

Pop Part of City of Knox, (33km E Melbourne), See map on page 697, ref E4. Outer eastern suburb at the foot of the Dandenong ranges. Bowls, Bush Walking, Scenic Drives, Swimming, Tennis.

Hotels/Motels

★★★☆ **Ferntree Gully Motor Inn**, (M), 1132 Burwood Hwy, ☎ 03 9758 0111, fax 03 9758 0150, (2 stry gr fl), 34 units [shwr, spa bath (2), tlt, a/c, tel, cable tv, clock radio, t/c mkg, refrig], ldry, conf fac, ⌧, sauna, spa, gym, cots. RO ♦ $99 - $150, ◊ $11, ch con, AE BC DC EFT MC VI.

B&B's/Guest Houses

★★★★☆ **The Villa Renaissance**, (GH), No children's facilities, 75 Underwood Rd, ☎ 03 9752 2169, fax 03 9758 0551, (2 stry gr fl), 3 rms [ensuite, bath (1), hairdry, a/c (2), c/fan (2), heat, elec blkts, TV, video, clock radio, CD (2), t/c mkg, refrig, mini bar, toaster, doonas], rec rm, lounge (TV, cd player), lounge firepl, ✗, spa (heated), bbq, gym. DBB ♦ $300, ♦♦ $400, Bookings essential.

MELBOURNE - FITZROY VIC 3065

Pop Part of Melbourne, (4km N Melbourne), See map on page 697, ref C3. Older inner residential suburb.

Hotels/Motels

★★★★☆ **Metropole Hotel Apartments**, (Ltd Lic H), 44 Brunswick St, ☎ 03 9411 8100, fax 03 9411 8200, (Multi-stry gr fl), 60 rms [shwr, spa bath (9), tlt, hairdry, a/c, tel, TV, t/c mkg, refrig, cook fac (23), micro (49), d/wash (23), toaster], lift, ldry, iron, iron brd, conf fac, ⌧, pool-heated, 24hr reception, dinner to unit, c/park (garage), gym, cots, non smoking units (36). D ♦♦ $135 - $325, ◊ $20, W $1,250 - $2,950, ch con, Minimum booking major events, AE BC DC MC VI.

Self Catering Accommodation

★★★★☆ **Royal Gardens Apartments**, (Apt), 8 Royal La, ☎ 03 9419 9888, fax 03 9416 0451, (Multi-stry gr fl), 70 apts acc up to 6, (1, 2 & 3 bedrm), [shwr, bath, tlt, hairdry, heat, tel, TV, video-fee, clock radio, refrig, cook fac, d/wash, toaster, ldry (in unit), blkts, linen, pillows], iron, iron brd, pool-heated (solar), spa, bbq, c/park (undercover). D $175.95 - $299.10, Breakfast available. AE BC DC EFT MC VI.

★★★★ **55 Webb St**, (Apt), 55 Webb St, ☎ 03 9417 7876, fax 03 9417 7803, (2 stry), 1 apt acc up to 3, (1 bedrm), [shwr, bath (hip), tlt, hairdry, c/fan, heat, elec blkts, cable tv, video, clock radio, refrig, cook fac, micro, toaster, blkts, linen, pillows], ldry, iron, iron brd, lounge firepl, bbq, c/park (garage). D ♦♦ $140, ◊ $20, W ♦♦ $900, ◊ $100, AE BC DC MC VI.

B&B's/Guest Houses

★★★★☆ Slatterys Nth Fitzroy B & B, (B&B), 41 Rae St, Fitzroy North 3068, ☎ 03 9489 1308, (2 stry), 1 rm (1 suite) [shwr, tlt, hairdry, a/c-cool, cent heat, elec blkts, tel, TV, video, refrig, micro], iron, iron brd, c/park. BB ⚲ $85, ⚲⚲ $110.

★★★★ King Boutique Accommodation, (B&B), c1852. 122 Nicholson St, opposite Exhibition Building & museum, ☎ 03 9417 1113, fax 03 9417 1116, (Multi-stry), 3 rms [shwr, bath (1), tlt, a/c (bedroom) (1), heat, clock radio, t/c mkg, refrig, mini bar], lounge (TV, video, cd), non smoking property. BB ⚲⚲ $140 - $180, BC EFT MC VI.

Other Accommodation

The Nunnery, (Lodge), Classified by National Trust, 116 Nicholson St, ☎ 03 9419 8637, fax 03 9417 7736, (2 stry), 22 rms [heat, blkts, linen, pillows], shwr (10), tlt (14), bathrm (2), ldry, lounge (TV), lounge firepl, cook fac, refrig, bbq, ☎. BLB ⚲ $20 - $50, ⚲⚲ $50 - $90.

MELBOURNE - FLEMINGTON VIC 3031

Pop Part of Melbourne, (5km W Melbourne), See map on page 697, ref C3. Inner residential & light industrial suburb. Flemington racecourse is famous for the Melbourne Cup horse race, which is run on the first Tuesday in November.

Hotels/Motels

★☆ Racecourse Flemington Motel Hotel, (LMH), Cnr Epsom & Ascot Vale Rds, opposite Flemington racecourse, ☎ 03 9376 3700, fax 03 93765438, (2 stry gr fl), 21 units [shwr, tlt, fan, heat, elec blkts, tel, TV, t/c mkg, refrig], ⊠ (Mon to Sat), ☎. RO ⚲ $70, ⚲⚲ $82.50, ⚲ $20, ch con, Light breakfast only available. AE BC DC MC VI.

Self Catering Accommodation

★★★★☆ Quest Flemington, (Apt), Cnr Smithfield & Epsom Rds, 4km E of GPO, ☎ 03 9371 2200, fax 03 9371 2299, (Multi-stry), 48 apts acc up to 7, (1, 2 & 3 bedrm), [shwr, tlt, a/c, tel, TV, video-fee, clock radio, t/c mkg, refrig, cook fac, micro, d/wash, toaster, ldry (in unit), blkts, linen, pillows], iron, iron brd, conf fac, pool, bbq, plygr, tennis, cots, non smoking units (32). D ⚲⚲ $159 - $170, ⚲⚲⚲ $174 - $237, ⚲ $17, Breakfast available. AE BC DC EFT MC VI.

MELBOURNE - FOOTSCRAY VIC 3011

Pop Part of Melbourne, (7km W Melbourne), See map on page 697, ref C3. Western light industrial & older residential suburb.

Hotels/Motels

★★★★ Footscray Motor Inn & Serviced Apartments, (M), 90 Droop St, ☎ 03 9687 6877, fax 03 9689 1286, 30 units [shwr, spa bath (7), tlt, hairdry, a/c, c/fan, elec blkts, tel, cable tv, video, clock radio, refrig], ldry, iron, iron brd, ⊠ (Mon to Fri), bar (cocktail), 24hr reception, rm serv, cots-fee. RO ⚲ $115 - $154, ⚲⚲ $120 - $154, ⚲ $15, ch con, AE BC DC EFT MC VI, ⚲⚲.

★★★★ (Apartment Section), 9 apts acc up to 3, (Studio & 1 bedrm), [shwr, bath (4), spa bath (5), tlt, hairdry, a/c, c/fan, elec blkts, tel, cable tv, clock radio, t/c mkg, refrig, cook fac ltd, micro, toaster, blkts, linen, pillows], ldry, iron, iron brd, rm serv. D ⚲ $135 - $154, ⚲⚲ $135 - $154, W $770 - $847.

★★★★ The Plough Hotel, (LH), 333 Barkly St, 300m W of PO, ☎ 03 9687 2070, fax 03 9396 1085, 11 rms [shwr, tlt, hairdry, a/c, elec blkts, TV, clock radio, t/c mkg, refrig], ldry, lounge, conf fac, ⊠, cots, non smoking units. BLB ⚲ $98 - $108, ⚲⚲ $98 - $108, ⚲ $10, AE BC DC EFT MC VI.

★★★ Palm Motel, (M), 50 Geelong Rd (Princes Hwy), 200m W of PO, ☎ 03 9689 2288, fax 03 9687 5640, (2 stry gr fl), 37 units [shwr, tlt, a/c, tel, TV, clock radio (53), t/c mkg, refrig], cots. RO ⚲ $75, ⚲⚲ $75, ⚲ $10, AE BC DC EFT MC VI.

★★☆ Mid Gate Motor Lodge, (M), 76 Droop St, ☎ 03 9689 2300, fax 03 9689 2334, (2 stry gr fl), 25 units [shwr, tlt, a/c-cool, heat, tel, TV, clock radio, t/c mkg, refrig], ldry, c/park (carport) (9), non smoking units (8). RO ⚲ $77, ⚲⚲ $82, ⚲ $15, ch con, 7 units ★★★. AE BC DC MC VI.

MELBOURNE - FOREST HILL VIC 3131

Pop 13,531. (20km E Melbourne), See map on page 697, ref D3. Suburb of Melbourne. Swimming (Pool), Tennis.

Hotels/Motels

FLAG
FLAG CHOICE HOTELS

★★★★☆ The Canterbury, (M), 330 Canterbury Rd, Cnr Springvale Rd, ☎ 03 9878 4111, fax 03 9878 4199, (Multi-stry gr fl), 40 units (5 suites) [shwr, bath (20), spa bath (15), tlt, hairdry, a/c, elec blkts, tel, cable tv, video (avail), clock radio, t/c mkg, refrig, mini bar, micro (5), toaster (5)], ldry, w/mach (5), dryer (5), iron, iron brd, lounge, conf fac, ⊠, bar (cocktail), rm serv, ☎, gym, cots-fee, non smoking units (27). RO ⚲⚲ $175 - $195, ⚲ $20, Suite D ⚲⚲ $200 - $350, ⚲ $20, ch con, AE BC DC EFT MC VI, ⚲⚲.

Self Catering Accommodation

★★★★☆ Park Avenue Executive Accommodation, (Apt), 305 Canterbury Rd, 700m E of Forest Hill Shopping Centre, ☎ 03 9807 5777, fax 03 9807 5677, 15 apts acc up to 6, (1, 2 & 3 bedrm), [shwr, spa bath, tlt, hairdry, a/c-cool, cent heat, elec blkts, tel, cable tv (Pay TV), video, clock radio, t/c mkg, refrig, cook fac, micro, d/wash, toaster, ldry (in unit), blkts, linen, pillows], iron, iron brd, c/park (garage), cots, non smoking units (6). D $120 - $190, W $840 - $1,330, Central booking office: 2 Hamilton Pl, Mt Waverley 3149, AE BC DC EFT MC VI.

B&B's/Guest Houses

★★★☆ Glenmore Homestyle Accommodation, (B&B), 46 Husband Rd, ☎ 03 9893 3333, 2 rms [evap cool, fan, heat, elec blkts, clock radio, t/c mkg, refrig, micro, toaster], lounge (TV), bbq, cots. BB ⚲ $55 - $77, ⚲⚲ $61 - $89, ⚲ $10 - $22, ch con, Other meals by arrangement.

MELBOURNE - FRANKSTON VIC 3199

Pop 43,993. (41km S Melbourne), See map on page 697, ref D6. Bayside commerce centre servicing the Mornington Peninsula. Information Centre, 54 Playne St, Ph 03 9781 5244. Boating, Bowls, Bush Walking, Croquet, Fishing, Golf, Horse Riding, Sailing, Scenic Drives, Swimming (Beach, Pool), Tennis, Water Skiing.

Hotels/Motels

AAA
TOURISM
Special Rates

COUNTRY
COMFORT

★★★★ Country Comfort Frankston, (M), Previously The Ambassador Frankston. 325 Nepean Hwy, ☎ 03 9781 4488, fax 03 9781 4785, (2 stry gr fl), 66 units (2 suites) [shwr, spa bath (53), tlt, hairdry, a/c, tel, TV, movie, clock radio, t/c mkg, refrig, mini bar (37)], ldry, conf fac, ⊠, bar (cocktail), pool, sauna, spa, bbq, 24hr reception, rm serv, c/park (undercover), ☎, plygr, cots-fee, non smoking units (19). RO ⚲ $104.50 - $253, ⚲⚲ $104.50 - $253, ⚲ $11, Suite D $253 - $330, ⚲ $16.50, ch con, AE BC DC EFT JCB MC VI.

★★★★ (Apartment Section), 33 apts acc up to 5, (2 bedrm), [shwr, bath, spa bath (17), tlt, hairdry, a/c, c/fan, tel, TV, movie, clock radio, refrig, cook fac ltd, micro, elec frypan, toaster, blkts, linen, pillows], iron, iron brd, bbq, cots-fee. D ⚲⚲⚲⚲ $132 - $176, ⚲ $11, W $495 - $715, 17 apartments ★★★☆.

Operator Comment: See our display advertisement on following page.

GOLDEN
CHAIN

★★★☆ Frankston Colonial Motor Inn, (M), 406 Nepean Hwy, 600m N of PO, ☎ 03 9781 5544, fax 03 9781 5886, (2 stry gr fl), 30 units [shwr, bath (hip) (24), spa bath (5), tlt, hairdry (12), a/c, elec blkts, tel, TV, video-fee, clock radio, t/c mkg, refrig, mini bar (8), toaster], ldry, iron (12), iron brd (12), ⊠ (Mon to Sat), pool, spa, bbq, cots-fee, non smoking units (7). D ⚲ $80 - $110, ⚲⚲ $80 - $154, ⚲⚲⚲ $90 - $154, ch con, AE BC DC EFT MC MP VI.

 ★★★☆ **Frankston Motel**, (M), Cnr Frankston-Flinders Rd & Bartlett St, 3.6km S of PO, ☎ 03 9783 8224, fax 03 5971 4375, 24 units [shwr, tlt, a/c, elec blkts, tel, TV, video-fee, clock radio, t/c mkg, refrig, toaster], ldry, pool, bbq, dinner to unit, tennis, cots, non smoking rms (4). **BLB** ♦ **$62 - $66**, ♦♦ **$72 - $77**, ◊ **$11**, AE BC DC MC MCH VI.

 ★★★☆ **The Frankston International Motel**, (M), Cnr Nepean Hwy & O'Grady St, 600m N of PO, ☎ 03 9781 3444, fax 03 9781 3738, (2 stry gr fl), 44 units [shwr, bath, spa bath (40), tlt, hairdry, a/c, tel, TV, movie, clock radio, t/c mkg, refrig, mini bar], ldry, conf fac, ⊠ (Mon to Sat), bar (cocktail), 24hr reception, rm serv, c/park (undercover) (30), cots. **RO** ♦ **$97 - $275**, ♦♦ **$97 - $275**, ◊ **$10**, 20 units ★★★. Public Holidays $10 extra, AE BC DC EFT MC MCH MP VI, ♿.

★★★ **(Apartment Section)**, 1 apt acc up to 4, (2 bedrm), [shwr, tlt, a/c, tel, TV, movie, clock radio, refrig, cook fac, micro, toaster, ldry (in unit), blkts, linen, pillows], iron, iron brd. **D** ♦♦ **$109 - $119**, ◊ **$10**.

 ★★ **Beach Motor Inn**, (M), 9 Beach St, 500m N of PO, ☎ 03 9783 6222, fax 03 9781 4176, (2 stry gr fl), 32 units [shwr, spa bath (2), tlt, a/c-cool (15), a/c (17), heat (15), elec blkts, tel, TV, clock radio, t/c mkg, refrig, cook fac (1), toaster], ldry, bbq, cots, non smoking rms (6). **RO** ♦ **$64 - $83**, ♦♦ **$72 - $83**, ◊ **$10**, ch con, 6 units ★★★. AE BC DC MC MCH VI.

Self Catering Accommodation
★★★ **Abbey Apartments**, (HF), 337A Nepean Hwy, ☎ 03 5975 2130, fax 03 5976 2491, 12 flats acc up to 4, (2 bedrm), [shwr, bath (hip), tlt, hairdry, fan, heat, elec blkts, TV, clock radio, refrig, cook fac, micro, toaster, ldry (in unit), blkts, doonas, linen, pillows], w/mach, iron, iron brd, cots. **D $90 - $120**, **W $495 - $565**, BC MC VI.

B&B's/Guest Houses
★★★★ **The Oaks Bed and Breakfast**, (B&B), 20 Victoria Pde, 1km SE of PO, ☎ 03 9783 5746, 2 rms [ensuite (1), shwr (1), spa bath (1), tlt (1), hairdry, evap cool, heat, elec blkts, TV, clock radio, CD (1), t/c mkg, refrig, micro (1), toaster, doonas], iron, iron brd, bbq, cots, non smoking property. **BB** ♦ **$90 - $140**, ♦♦ **$140 - $200**, weekly con, 1 room ★★★★☆.

MELBOURNE - GLEN IRIS VIC 3146

Pop Part of City of Boroondara, (11km SE Melbourne), See map on page 697, ref D4. Suburb of Melbourne. Bowls, Swimming (Pool), Tennis.

Self Catering Accommodation
★★★★ **Astonby**, (HU), 24 Hazeldine Rd, ☎ 03 9885 5278, fax 03 9885 5278, 1 unit acc up to 4, (1 bedrm), [shwr, tlt, hairdry, a/c, fan, heat, tel, TV, video, clock radio, refrig, cook fac, micro, elec frypan, toaster, blkts, linen, pillows], w/mach, iron, iron brd, bbq, non smoking property. **D** ♦♦ **$95**, ◊ **$10**, Min book applies.

B&B's/Guest Houses
★★★★☆ **Staughton Bed & Breakfast**, (B&B), Unit 2, 67 Staughton Rd, ☎ 03 9889 4372, fax 03 9889 9712, (2 stry), 1 rm [shwr, bath, tlt, hairdry, a/c, fan, heat, elec blkts, clock radio, t/c mkg], iron, iron brd, lounge (TV), bbq, non smoking property. **BB** ♦ **$90 - $100**, ♦♦ **$120 - $140**, ch con, Minimum booking all Melbourne major events, BC MC VI.

MELBOURNE - GLEN WAVERLEY VIC 3150

Pop Part of City of Monash, (23km SE Melbourne), See map on page 697, ref D4. Residential suburb.

Hotels/Motels
 ★★★★☆ **Novotel Glen Waverley**, (LH), 285 Springvale Rd, ☎ 03 8561 2345, fax 03 8561 2350, (Multi-stry), 200 rms (8 suites) [shwr, bath, spa bath (46), tlt, hairdry, a/c, tel, cable tv, movie-fee, clock radio, t/c mkg, refrig, mini bar], lift, iron, iron brd, business centre, conf fac, ⊠, bar (cocktail), pool indoor heated, sauna, 24hr reception, rm serv, dinner to unit, secure park (undercover) (100), gym, non smoking flr (5). **RO** ♦ **$122 - $253**, ♦♦ **$122 - $253**, ◊ **$32**, **Suite RO** ♦ **$249 - $290**, ♦♦ **$249 - $290**, ◊ **$32**, ch con, AE BC DC EFT JCB MC VI, ♿.

★★★★ **The Waverley Inn**, (M), Cnr Springvale Rd & Kingsway, 300m S of PO, ☎ 03 9560 3311, fax 03 9561 4075, 65 units [shwr, bath (4), spa bath (27), tlt, hairdry, a/c, elec blkts, tel, TV, video-fee, clock radio, t/c mkg, refrig, mini bar], ldry, conf fac, ✉, 24hr reception, rm serv, cots. **RO** ♦ **$99 - $245**, ♦♦ **$119 - $245**, ♦ **$17**, AE BC DC EFT MC VI.

Self Catering Accommodation

★★★★☆ **Park Avenue Executive Accommodation**, (Apt), 11 Graham St, 400m N of Syndal railway station, ☎ 03 9807 5777, fax 03 9807 5677, 3 apts acc up to 6, (3 bedrm), [shwr, bath, tlt, hairdry, a/c-cool, cent heat, tel, cable tv, video, clock radio, refrig, cook fac, micro, d/wash, toaster, ldry (in unit), blkts, linen, pillows], iron, iron brd, c/park (garage), cots. **D $130 - $190, W $910 - $1,330**, Central booking office: 2 Hamilton Pl, Mt Waverley 3149, AE BC DC MC VI.

MELBOURNE - GREENSBOROUGH VIC 3088

Pop part of Melbourne, (20km NE Melbourne). See map on page 697, ref D2. An outer residential and commercial area, situated along the Plenty River.

Greensborough Motor Inn

GOLDEN CHAIN

AAA Tourism ★★★★

• 24 Ground floor units • Spa suites with full size double spas
• Family rooms • No smoking rooms available
• Swimming pool

Bookings Freecall: 1800 807 782
Phone: (03) 9434 7000 Fax: (03) 9434 6492
Cnr Greensborough Road & Torbay Street, Macleod, 3805

See listing under "Macleod"

11492AG

MELBOURNE - HALLAM VIC 3803

Pop 7,647. (37km SE Melbourne), See map on page 697, ref E5. Outer residential suburb. Tennis.

Hotels/Motels

★★★☆ **Abode Thomas Lodge**, (M), 218 Princes Hwy, ☎ 03 9703 1255, fax 03 9796 5343, 15 units [shwr, tlt, hairdry (8), a/c, heat, elec blkts, tel, TV, clock radio, t/c mkg, refrig, doonas], iron, iron brd, cots-fee, non smoking units (7). **RO** ♦ **$87 - $98**, ♦♦ **$87 - $98**, ♦ **$14**, ch con, AE BC DC EFT MC VI.

MELBOURNE - HAMPTON VIC 3188

Pop Part of Melbourne, (14km S Melbourne), See map on page 697, ref C4. Bayside suburb of Melbourne. Bowls, Fishing, Swimming, Tennis.

Self Catering Accommodation

Park Avenue Executive Accommodation, (Apt), 18 Small St, 200m S of railway station, ☎ 03 9807 5777, fax 03 9807 5677, 2 apts acc up to 5, (2 bedrm), [shwr, bath, tlt, hairdry, a/c-cool, cent heat, tel, cable tv, video, clock radio, t/c mkg, refrig, cook fac, micro, ldry (in unit), blkts, linen, pillows], iron, iron brd, c/park (garage), cots-fee. **D** ♦♦♦♦ **$120 - $190, W** ♦♦♦♦ **$840 - $1,330**, Central booking office: 2 Hamilton Pl, Mt Waverley 3149, AE BC DC MC VI, (Rating under review).

MELBOURNE - HARKAWAY VIC 3806

Pop Part of City of Casey, (46km SE Melbourne), See map on page 697, ref E5. A rural, outer south eastern suburb. Scenic Drives, Tennis.

Self Catering Accommodation

★★★☆ **Chadwick Cottage Bed & Breakfast**, (Cotg), 68 Chadwick Rd, 4km from Berwick, ☎ 03 9796 8439, fax 03 8790 4276, 1 cotg acc up to 4, (2 bedrm), [shwr, bath, tlt, hairdry, fan, heat, elec blkts, tel, TV, video, radio, t/c mkg, refrig, cook fac, micro, toaster, blkts, linen, pillows], iron, iron brd, cots. **D** ♦ **$55 - $85**, ♦♦ **$110 - $130**, ♦ **$35 - $45**, BC MC VI.

MELBOURNE - HAWTHORN VIC 3122

Pop Part of City of Boroondara, (6km E Melbourne), See map on page 697, ref C3. Older inner residential suburb.

Hotels/Motels

★★★★ **Glenferrie Hotel**, (LH), 324 Burwood Rd, 200m S of Town Hall, ☎ 03 9818 6530, fax 03 9818 5988, (Multi-stry), 16 rms [shwr, spa bath, tlt, hairdry, a/c, tel, TV, radio, t/c mkg, refrig, mini bar], iron, iron brd, ✉, rm serv, cots, non smoking rms (6). **RO** ♦ **$145**, ♦♦ **$145**, AE BC DC EFT JCB MC VI.

FLAG
FLAG CHOICE HOTELS

★★★☆ **California Motel**, (M), 138 Barkers Rd, opp Xavier College, ☎ 03 9818 0281, fax 03 9819 6845, (2 stry gr fl), 79 units [shwr, bath (hip) (8), spa bath (2), tlt, hairdry, a/c, elec blkts, tel, TV, clock radio, t/c mkg, refrig, cook fac (3), toaster], ldry, iron, iron brd, conf fac, ✉, pool, bbq, 24hr reception, rm serv, plygr, cots-fee, non smoking units (22). **RO** ♦ **$100 - $125**, ♦♦ **$120 - $150**, ♦ **$20**, fam con, AE BC BTC DC EFT JCB MC MP VI.

★★☆ **Whitehorse Inn**, (LH), 5 Burwood Rd, 100m W of PO, ☎ 03 9818 4991, fax 03 9819 6146, (2 stry), 5 rms [shwr, tlt, a/c, heat, TV, clock radio, t/c mkg, refrig, toaster], conf fac, ✉, ☎, **BLB** ♦ **$99**, ♦♦ **$99**, ♦ **$20**, Light breakfast only available. AE BC DC EFT MC VI.

Self Catering Accommodation

AAA
TOURISM
Special Rates

★★★★☆ **Hawthorn Gardens Serviced Apartments**, (Apt), 750 Toorak Rd, Hawthorn East 3123, 350m E of South Eastern Fwy, ☎ 03 9822 7699, fax 03 9822 5287, (2 stry gr fl), 28 apts acc up to 6, (2 & 3 bedrm), [shwr, bath, tlt, hairdry, a/c, heat, elec blkts, tel, cable tv, video, clock radio, t/c mkg, refrig, cook fac, micro, toaster, ldry (in unit), blkts, linen, pillows], iron, iron brd, c/park (garage), cots-fee, non smoking units (12). **D** ♦ **$129 - $170**, ♦ **$11 - $22, W** ♦♦ **$770 - $875**, ♦ **$55 - $110**, Breakfast available. AE BC DC EFT MC VI,

Operator Comment: Please visit our website at www.hawthorngardens.com.au

B&B's/Guest Houses

★★★★☆ **Honeyeater Lodge**, (B&B), No children's facilities, 3 Xavier Ave, 200m E of Xavier College, ☎ 03 9819 0772, fax 03 9819 0873, (2 stry), 3 rms [ensuite, spa bath (1), hairdry, a/c, elec blkts, TV, clock radio, t/c mkg, refrig], ldry, lounge (TV, video, stereo), lounge firepl, pool-heated, bbq, non smoking property. **BB** ♦ **$132 - $170**, ♦♦ **$140 - $205**, AE BC DC MC VI.

MELBOURNE - HEIDELBERG VIC 3084

Pop Part of City of Darebin, (14km NE Melbourne), See map on page 697, ref D3. Residential north eastern suburb, including parklands and the Yarra River.

B&B's/Guest Houses

★★☆ **Oakenfold**, (B&B), Cnr Hawdon & Brown St, ☎ 03 9459 1135, 1 rm (1 suite) [shwr, tlt, hairdry, a/c-cool, fan, cent heat, TV, clock radio, t/c mkg, refrig, micro, toaster], iron, iron brd, cots. **BB** ♦ **$80**, ♦♦ **$95**, ♦ **$15**, ch con.

MELBOURNE - HIGHETT VIC 3190

Pop Part of Melbourne, (16km SE Melbourne), See map on page 697, ref C4. Light industrial and residential suburb, close to Southland shopping centre. Swimming (Pool), Tennis.

Hotels/Motels

★★★★☆ **Buckingham Motor Inn**, (M), 1130 Nepean Hwy, 1km N of Southland Shopping Centre, ☎ 03 9555 0011, fax 03 9555 0044, (2 stry gr fl), 66 units [shwr, bath (7), spa bath (5), tlt, hairdry, a/c, elec blkts, tel, cable tv, clock radio, t/c mkg, refrig, toaster], ldry, conf fac, ⊠, pool, sauna, spa, 24hr reception, rm serv, ✆, cots-fee, non smoking units (22). **RO** ♦ **$130 - $170**, ♦♦ **$141 - $170**, ◊ **$14**, AE BC DC EFT MC VI, ⅙⅙.

*Operator Comment: Homely garden setting, 3km from popular bay beaches, surrounded by sand belt golf courses. Shopping tours arranged. www.thebuckingham.com.au
e-mail: contact@thebuckingham.com.au*

(Apartment Section), 3 apts acc up to 6, (2 & 3 bedrm), [shwr, bath, tlt, a/c, elec blkts, tel, cable tv, video, clock radio, refrig, cook fac, micro, d/wash, toaster], c/park (carport). **D $206 - $240**, **W $1,040 - $1,200**, (Rating under review).

MELBOURNE - HOPPERS CROSSING VIC 3029

Pop 29,485. (31km SW Melbourne), See map on page 697, ref A3. Modern outer residential suburb, near Werribee township.

Hotels/Motels

★★★★ **Monte Villa Motor Inn**, (M), 78 Old Geelong Rd, 2km E of PO, ☎ 03 9748 7700, fax 03 9748 7451, (2 stry gr fl), 37 units [shwr, spa bath (23), tlt, hairdry, a/c, elec blkts, tel, TV, video-fee] clock radio, t/c mkg, refrig], ldry, iron, iron brd, conf fac, ⊠, pool indoor heated, sauna, spa, rm serv, cots. **RO** ♦ **$79.20 - $95.70**, ♦♦ **$79.20 - $95.70**, ◊ **$11**, ch con, AE BC DC MC VI.

MELBOURNE - HURSTBRIDGE VIC 3099

Pop 3,100. Part of Melbourne, (33km NE Melbourne), See map on page 697, ref E2. Outer suburb, north of Melbourne. Bowls, Tennis.

B&B's/Guest Houses

★★★★☆ **Bluehaven Bed & Breakfast**, (B&B), 762 Heidelberg - Kinglake Rd, ☎ 03 9718 1811, fax 03 9718 1811, (2 stry gr fl), 3 rms [ensuite (2), shwr, bath (1), tlt, hairdry, a/c, cent heat, elec blkts, clock radio, doonas], lounge (TV, video), lounge firepl, t/c mkg shared, bbq, non smoking property. **BB** ♦ **$93.50**, ♦♦ **$110**, AE BC MC VI.

★★★★☆ **Goulds Farm**, (B&B), (Farm), 30 Hildebrand Rd, ☎ 03 9714 8289, fax 03 9714 8708, 1 rm (1 suite) [ensuite, hairdry, fan, c/fan, cent heat, tel, TV, t/c mkg, refrig, micro, elec frypan, toaster], iron, iron brd, pool-heated (solar heated), non smoking property. **BB** ♦ **$88**, ♦♦ **$120**, ch con, weekly con, BC DC MC VI.

★★★★ **(Holiday Unit Section)**, 1 unit acc up to 4, (2 bedrm), [shwr, tlt, hairdry, a/c, c/fan, cent heat, elec blkts, tel, TV, video, t/c mkg, refrig, cook fac ltd, micro, toaster, blkts, doonas, linen, pillows], ldry, iron, iron brd, bbq, breakfast ingredients. **BB** ♦♦ **$130**, ◊ **$40**, weekly con.

MELBOURNE - KEILOR VIC 3036

Pop Part of Melbourne, (19km NW Melbourne), See map on page 697, ref B2. Outer residential suburb.

Hotels/Motels

★★★☆ **Keilor Motor Inn**, (M), 765 Old Calder Hwy, ☎ 03 9336 3011, fax 03 9336 4982, 25 units (2 suites) [shwr, spa bath (2), tlt, hairdry (18), a/c, heat, elec blkts, tel, TV, video (avail), clock radio, t/c mkg, refrig, cook fac ltd (1), toaster], ldry, conf fac, courtesy transfer, cots, non smoking units (10). **RO** ♦ **$82 - $126**, ♦♦ **$87 - $135**, ◊ **$11**, **Suite D $120 - $135**, 11 units ★★★. AE BC DC EFT MC MP VI.

MELBOURNE - KEW VIC 3101

Pop Part of City of Boroondara, (7km E Melbourne), See map on page 697, ref C3. Older residential eastern suburb. Art Gallery, Bowls, Golf, Tennis.

Hotels/Motels

★★★★ **Beaumont Hotel**, (M), 7 Studley Park Rd, 100m W of Kew Junction, ☎ 03 9853 2722, fax 03 9853 3773, (2 stry gr fl), 46 units [shwr, bath, spa bath (10), tlt, hairdry, a/c, tel, TV, clock radio, t/c mkg, refrig, mini bar], iron, iron brd, lounge, conf fac, ⊠, spa, 24hr reception, rm serv, c/park (undercover), cots, non smoking units (38). **RO $139 - $270**, AE BC DC JCB MC VI.

★★★☆ **Pathfinder Motel & Chez Marie Restaurant**, (M), Cnr Burke & Cotham Rds, 2.6km E of PO, ☎ 03 9817 4551, fax 03 9817 5680, (2 stry gr fl), 24 units [shwr, tlt, a/c-cool, heat, elec blkts, tel, TV, video-fee, clock radio, t/c mkg, refrig, mini bar, cook fac (3), micro (3)], ldry, ⊠ (Mon to Sat), pool, rm serv, dinner to unit, cots-fee. **RO** ♦ **$87 - $121**, ♦♦ **$98 - $121**, ◊ **$11**, AE BC DC EFT MC MP VI.

Self Catering Accommodation

★★★★★ **Park Avenue Executive Accommodation**, (Apt), Previously Park Avenue Serviced Apartments. 104 Walpole St, 800m N of PO, ☎ 03 9807 5777, fax 03 9807 5677, (2 stry), 11 apts acc up to 6, (2 bedrm3 bedrm), [shwr, spa bath (4), tlt, hairdry, a/c, cent heat, elec blkts, tel, cable tv, video, clock radio, CD, refrig, cook fac, micro (convection), elec frypan, d/wash, toaster, ldry (in unit), blkts, linen, pillows], iron, iron brd, bbq, secure park (undercover), cots, non smoking units (3). **D $150 - $290**, **W $1,050 - $2,030**, Central booking office: 2 Hamilton Pl, Mt Waverley 3149, AE BC DC EFT MC VI.

★★★★☆ **(85 Peel St Section)**, (Multi-stry), 4 apts acc up to 6, (2 & 3 bedrm), [shwr, bath, tlt, hairdry, a/c-cool, heat, tel, cable tv, video, clock radio, refrig, cook fac, micro, d/wash, toaster, ldry (in unit), blkts, linen, pillows], iron, iron brd, secure park (undercover), cots. **D $115 - $200**, **W $805 - $1,400**.

★★★★☆ **Quest Kew - A Quest Inn**, (Apt), 19-21 Walpole St, ☎ 03 9854 7201, fax 03 9853 7301, (Multi-stry gr fl), 36 apts acc up to 6, (2 & 3 bedrm), [shwr, bath, tlt, hairdry, a/c, tel, TV, clock radio, t/c mkg, refrig, cook fac, micro, d/wash, toaster, ldry (in unit), blkts, linen, pillows], w/mach, dryer, iron, iron brd, pool-heated, bbq, secure park, cots-fee, non smoking units (6). **D $182 - $231**, AE BC DC EFT MC VI.

MELBOURNE - KEYSBOROUGH VIC 3175

Pop 11,334. (32km SE Melbourne), See map on page 697, ref D5. Residential suburb. Bowls, Golf, Tennis.

Hotels/Motels

★★★ **Keysborough Hotel**, (LMH), Cnr Cheltenham & Corrigan Rds, ☎ 03 9798 2055, fax 03 9798 8608, (2 stry gr fl), 15 units [shwr, tlt, hairdry, a/c, TV, clock radio, t/c mkg, refrig], ⊠, plygr, cots-fee. **RO** ♦ **$71**, ♦♦ **$71**, ◊ **$28**, AE BC DC EFT MC VI.

MELBOURNE - KILSYTH VIC 3137

Pop Part of Yarra Ranges, (36km E Melbourne), See map on page 697, ref E3. Outer eastern suburb situated at the foot of Mt Dandenong. Bowls, Bush Walking, Golf, Horse Riding, Scenic Drives, Tennis.

Hotels/Motels

★★★ **Linley Estate**, (M), 723 Mt Dandenong Rd, 1.5km SE of PO, ☎ 03 9728 1511, fax 03 9728 1496, 30 units (1 suite) [shwr, bath (1), tlt, a/c, elec blkts, tel, TV, clock radio, t/c mkg, refrig, mini bar], ldry, rec rm, conf fac, pool-heated (solar), sauna, spa, tennis, cots-fee. **RO** ♦ **$93.50**, ♦♦ **$93.50**, ◊ **$15**, ch con, AE BC DC MC VI, ⅙⅙.

MELBOURNE - KOOYONG VIC 3144

Pop Nominal, (8km SE Melbourne), See map on page 697, ref C3. Inner suburb.

B&B's/Guest Houses

★★★★ **Carlisle Bed & Breakfast**, (B&B), 400 Glenferrie Rd, ☎ 03 9822 4847, fax 03 9822 6637, 2 rms [ensuite (1), shwr, bath (1), tlt, hairdry, fan, cent heat, elec blkts, clock radio], lounge (TV, video, cd), t/c mkg shared, refrig, bbq, non smoking property. **BB** ♦♦ **$130 - $150**, ch con, Minimum booking all Melbourne major events. BC DC MC VI.

MELBOURNE - LANGWARRIN VIC 3910

Pop 13,000. (45km SE Melbourne), See map on page 697, ref D6. Outer suburb of Melbourne. Bush Walking, Golf, Tennis.

B&B's/Guest Houses

★★★☆ **Hemerton Homestead Retreat**, (B&B), 30 Nirvana Cl, ☎ 03 9789 9318, 3 rms [hairdry, heat, elec blkts, clock radio], ldry, lounge (TV, video, stereo), lounge firepl, t/c mkg shared. **BB** ♦ **$50 - $65**, ♦♦ **$99**, Other meals by arrangement.

MELBOURNE - LAVERTON VIC 3028

Pop Part of Melbourne, (18km SW Melbourne), See map on page 697, ref B3. Outer residential suburb. Nearby Point Cook is RAAF base - and museum.

Hotels/Motels

★★★ **Club Laverton**, (M), 15 Aviation Rd, 200m NE of Pt Cook turnoff, ☎ 03 9369 1811, fax 03 9369 1201, (2 stry gr fl), 30 units [shwr, tlt, a/c, tel, TV, video-fee, clock radio, t/c mkg, refrig, toaster], ldry, lounge, conf fac, ⊠, dinner to unit, ✆. RO ♦ $88, ♦♦ $88, ◊ $11, AE BC DC MC VI.

★★☆ **Westside Hotel Motel**, (LMH), Cnr Fitzgerald & Leakes Rds, Laverton North 3026, 1.6km N of PO, ☎ 03 9369 2300, fax 03 9369 2899, (2 stry gr fl), 12 units [shwr, tlt, a/c, TV, clock radio, t/c mkg, refrig, toaster], ldry, conf fac, ⊠, ✆, cots. BLB $75, Light breakfast only available. AE BC DC EFT MC VI.

MELBOURNE - LILYDALE VIC 3140

Pop 9,502. (39km E Melbourne), See map on page 697, ref E3. Rapidly growing suburb on the Maroondah Hwy. Bowls, Bush Walking, Fishing, Golf, Horse Riding, Scenic Drives, Shooting, Swimming (Pool, River), Tennis.

Hotels/Motels

★★★☆ **Billanook Country Inn Motel**, (M), 420 Main St (Maroondah Hwy), 500m E of PO, ☎ 03 9735 3000, fax 03 9735 1838, 26 units [shwr, spa bath (4), tlt, hairdry, a/c, elec blkts, tel, TV, movie, clock radio, t/c mkg, refrig], ldry, ⊠ (Mon to Sat), pool indoor heated, sauna, spa, bbq, rm serv (Mon to Sat), cots-fee. RO ♦ $75 - $140, ♦♦ $85 - $140, AE BC DC EFT MC VI, 🐾.

 ★★★☆ **Lilydale Motor Inn**, (M), 474 Maroondah Hwy, 1km E of PO, ☎ 03 9735 5222, fax 03 9739 5922, (2 stry gr fl), 45 units [shwr, spa bath (4), tlt, hairdry, a/c, elec blkts, tel, TV, clock radio, t/c mkg, refrig, toaster], ldry, conf fac, ⊠ (Mon to Sat), pool, bbq, rm serv, ✆, plygr, cots-fee, non smoking units (22). RO ♦ $70 - $85, ♦♦ $80 - $95, ◊ $10, AE BC DC EFT MC MP VI, 🐾.

B&B's/Guest Houses

★★★☆ **Lillydale Herb Farm**, (B&B), No children's facilities, 61 Mangans Rd, ☎ 03 9735 0486, 2 rms [shwr, bath (1), tlt, fire pl (1), heat, TV, clock radio, t/c mkg, refrig, toaster], ⊠ (Thurs to Sat), pool (salt water), spa, bbq, tennis. BB ♦ $102, ♦♦ $132, AE BC DC EFT MC VI.

MELBOURNE - MACLEOD VIC 3085

Pop Part of Melbourne, (16km NE Melbourne), See map on page 697, ref D2. Suburb of Melbourne.

Hotels/Motels

 ★★★★ **Greensborough Motor Inn**, (M), Cnr Greensborough Rd & Torbay St, ☎ 03 9434 7000, fax 03 9434 6492, 24 units [shwr, spa bath (6), tlt, a/c, elec blkts, tel, TV, video-fee, clock radio, t/c mkg, refrig, toaster], ldry, iron, iron brd, pool, rm serv, cots-fee, non smoking units (5). RO ♦ $99, ♦♦ $99, ◊ $14, AE BC DC EFT MC MP VI.

MELBOURNE - MALVERN VIC 3144

Pop 43,396. (10km SE Melbourne), See map on page 697, ref C4. Large residential suburb with many parks and gardens.

Hotels/Motels

★★ **Evancourt Motel**, (M), 1015 Dandenong Rd, 1km E Caulfield Racecourse, ☎ 03 9572 4733, fax 03 9572 4895, 38 units [ensuite (10), a/c-cool (10), c/fan (10), heat, TV (7), video (avail), clock radio (2), t/c mkg (10), refrig (3), micro (3), pillows], shwr, tlt, ldry, w/mach-fee, dryer-fee, lounge (Cable TV), cook fac, t/c mkg shared, secure park (16), ✆, cots (avail), non smoking property. RO ♦ $49 - $69, ♦♦ $66 - $79, ◊ $11 - $16, ch con, fam con, pen con, BC DC EFT MC VI, 🐾.

MELBOURNE - MELBOURNE AIRPORT VIC 3045

Pop Part of Melbourne, (19km NW Melbourne), See map on page 697, ref B2. International Airport for Victoria.

Hotels/Motels

★★★★ **Centra Melbourne Airport**, (LH), 1 Centre Rd, 400m E of terminal building, ☎ 03 9933 5111, fax 03 9330 3230, (Multi-stry), 202 rms [shwr, bath, tlt, hairdry, a/c, tel, TV, movie-fee, clock radio, t/c mkg, refrig, mini bar], lift, ldry, iron, iron brd, business centre, conf fac, ⊠, bar (cocktail), pool, 24hr reception, rm serv, courtesy transfer, ✆, gym, cots, non smoking rms (135). RO ♦ $142 - $250, ♦♦ $142 - $250, ◊ $33, ch con, AE BC DC EFT JCB MC MP VI.

Hilton Melbourne Airport, (LH), Arrival Dve, ☎ 03 8336 2000, fax 03 8336 2001, (Multi-stry), 276 rms (4 suites) [ensuite, bath, a/c, tel, cable tv, movie, t/c mkg, refrig, mini bar, toaster (16), doonas], lift, lounge, conf fac, ⊠, pool indoor heated, sauna, spa, 24hr reception, rm serv, dinner to unit, secure park (undercover), cots, non smoking flr (3). RO ♦ $179 - $229, ♦♦ $179 - $229, ◊ $45, Suite RO ♦♦ $309 - $359, ◊ $45, ch con, AE BC DC EFT JCB MC VI, (not yet classified).

MELBOURNE - MELTON VIC 3337

Pop 30,300. (39km W Melbourne), See map on page 697, ref A2. Outer residential suburb. Bowls, Golf, Greyhound Racing, Horse Riding, Squash, Swimming (Reservoir), Tennis.

Hotels/Motels

 ★★★ **Melton Motel**, (M), 344 High St, 50m W of PO, ☎ 03 9743 5599, fax 03 9746 9510, 18 units [shwr, tlt, hairdry, a/c, elec blkts, tel, TV, clock radio, t/c mkg, refrig], ldry, cots, non smoking units (6). RO ♦ $77 - $88, ♦♦ $88 - $130, ◊ $10, ch con, AE BC DC MC VI.

MELBOURNE - MENTONE VIC 3194

Pop Part of Melbourne, (22km SE Melbourne), See map on page 697, ref C5. Bayside suburb. Bowls, Sailing, Swimming (Bay, Pool), Tennis.

Hotels/Motels

★★★ **Mentone Hub Inn**, (M), 200 Nepean Hwy, 1km E of PO, Cnr Warrigal Rd, ☎ 03 9584 4222, fax 03 9583 0723, (2 stry gr fl), 48 units [shwr, bath (hip) (35), spa bath (8), tlt, a/c, elec blkts, tel, TV, clock radio, t/c mkg, refrig], ldry, conf fac, ⊠ (Mon to Sat), 24hr reception, rm serv, c/park (undercover) (30), cots, non smoking units (3). **RO ♦ $99 - $140, ♦♦ $104 - $140, ◊ $12**, ch con, AE BC DC MC VI.

Deluxe, Spa, Family and Standard Rooms
• Close to Beach, New Shopping Complex and Transport
• 25 Minutes from Heart of the City
• Function/Wedding Facilities
• 24 Hour Reception • Fully Licensed Restaurant
200 Nepean Highway, Mentone VIC 3194
www.mentonehub.com.au
Phone: (03) 9584 4222   Fax: (03) 9583 0723

MELBOURNE - MITCHAM VIC 3132

Pop 11,322. (22km E Melbourne), See map on page 697, ref D3. Outer eastern residential suburb. Bowls, Tennis.

Hotels/Motels

★★★★☆ **Manor Motor Inn**, (M), 669 Maroondah Hwy, 1.8km E of PO, ☎ 03 9872 4200, fax 03 9872 4472, (2 stry gr fl), 36 units [shwr, bath, spa bath (2), tlt, hairdry, a/c, tel, TV, clock radio, t/c mkg, refrig, mini bar], business centre, conf fac, ⊠, bar (cocktail), 24hr reception, rm serv, c/park (undercover), ✆, cots, non smoking suites (20). **RO ♦ $160 - $210, ♦♦ $160 - $210, ◊ $15**, AE BC DC EFT MC VI.

MELBOURNE - MONTROSE VIC 3765

Pop 7,651. (36km E Melbourne), See map on page 697, ref E3. Outer eastern residential suburb. Tennis.

B&B's/Guest Houses

★★★★☆ **Goodwood Bed and Breakfast**, (B&B), 833 Mt Dandenong Rd, 1km W of PO, mob 0419 875 699, fax 03 9761 8950, 1 rm (1 suite) [shwr, spa bath, tlt, hairdry, a/c, heat, elec blkts, TV, video, clock radio, CD, t/c mkg, refrig, micro, toaster], pool (solar heated), bbq, cots, non smoking property. **BB ♦ $90 - $100, ♦♦ $139 - $154, ◊ $20**, ch con, BC MC VI.

★★★★☆ **Lea-Lodge**, (B&B), Roslyn St, ☎ 03 9761 9183, fax 03 9761 9183, (2 stry gr fl), 2 rms [shwr, tlt, hairdry, a/c-cool, cent heat, TV, video, clock radio, CD], lounge (TV, video, CD player), pool (salt water), spa (heated), t/c mkg shared, bbq, non smoking property. **BB ♦ $121, ♦♦ $143**, Dinner by arrangement, BC EFT MC VI.

MELBOURNE - MOONEE PONDS VIC 3039

Pop Part of Melbourne, (7km NW Melbourne), See map on page 697, ref C3. Residential suburb and home of the Moonee Valley Racecourse. Horse Racing, Swimming (Pool).

Self Catering Accommodation

★★★☆ **Moonee Valley Views**, (Apt), 81 Wilson St, ☎ 03 9373 3777, fax 03 9373 3715, (Multi-stry gr fl), 13 apts acc up to 6, (2 & 3 bedrm), [shwr, bath, tlt, a/c-cool, cent heat, tel, TV, video, clock radio, refrig, cook fac, micro, d/wash, toaster, ldry (in unit), blkts, linen, pillows], c/park (garage), cots-fee. **D ♦ $135, ♦♦ $160, ◊ $10, W ♦♦ $945**, AE BC DC EFT MC VI.

MELBOURNE - MOORABBIN VIC 3189

Pop Part of Melbourne, (15km S Melbourne), See map on page 697, ref C4. Residential & light industrial area. Bowls, Golf, Horse Riding, Swimming (Pool), Tennis.

Hotels/Motels

★★★ **Sandbelt Club Hotel**, (LMH), Cnr South & Bignell Rds, 1.6km E of PO, ☎ 03 9555 6899, fax 03 9553 3757, 25 units [shwr, tlt, a/c, TV, clock radio, t/c mkg, refrig, toaster], ldry, iron brd, conf fac, ⊠, ✆, cots, non smoking units (4). **BLB $71 - $99**, AE BC DC EFT MC VI, ⌂⅄.

MELBOURNE - MOUNT ELIZA VIC 3930

Pop 15,716. (47km S Melbourne), See map on page 697, ref D6. Residential area & holiday resort with good beaches. Bowls, Swimming (Bay), Tennis.

Hotels/Motels

★★★ **Norwood House Receptions**, (M), 1198 Nepean Hwy, 3km SW of PO, ☎ 03 5975 7977, fax 03 5975 1249, (2 stry gr fl), 15 units (2 suites) [shwr, spa bath (4), tlt, hairdry, a/c, elec blkts, tel, TV, video (avail), clock radio, t/c mkg, refrig, cook fac (1), toaster], iron, iron brd, conf fac, pool, bbq, dinner to unit, plygr. **RO ♦ $49.50 - $75, ♦♦ $55 - $99, Suite RO ♦♦ $132, ◊ $10**, AE BC DC EFT MC VI.

Self Catering Accommodation

★★★☆ **Ro-Onda Enterprises**, (Cotg), 75 Oakbank Rd, 5km SW of PO, ☎ 03 5975 9766, 1 cotg acc up to 3, (1 bedrm), [shwr, tlt, hairdry, c/fan, heat, elec blkts, TV, clock radio, t/c mkg, refrig, cook fac, toaster, blkts, linen, pillows], iron, iron brd, bbq, cots, breakfast ingredients, non smoking property. **BB ♦ $85 - $95, ♦♦ $100 - $110, ◊ $20**, ch con.

★★★ **Eastern View Cottage**, (Cotg), (Farm), 1 Shotton Rd, 5km S of PO, off Nepean Hwy, ☎ 03 5975 0828, fax 03 5975 0872, 1 cotg acc up to 7, (2 bedrm), [shwr, tlt, c/fan, elec blkts, TV, video, clock radio, t/c mkg, refrig, cook fac ltd, micro, elec frypan, toaster, blkts, doonas, linen, pillows], w/mach, dryer, iron, iron brd, lounge firepl, bbq, plygr, cots. **BB ♦♦ $120, W ♦♦ $350 - $600, RO ♦♦ $100**, ch con, Breakfast by arrangement. Min book long w/ends and Easter.

B&B's/Guest Houses

★★★★☆ **Daubel Lodge**, (B&B), Cnr Canadian Bay Rd & Spero Ave, ☎ 03 9787 9476, fax 03 9787 9576, (2 stry), 3 rms [shwr, bath (1), tlt, hairdry, a/c-cool, cent heat, elec blkts, clock radio, ldry], w/mach, dryer, lounge (TV, video, cd, stereo), lounge firepl, pool, t/c mkg shared, bbq. **BB ♦ $80 - $140, ♦♦ $110 - $160**, BC EFT MC VI.

★★★★ **Merksgrove**, (B&B), No children's facilities, 11 Jacksons Rd, 1.5km N of Mt Eliza Village, ☎ 03 9775 2059, fax 03 9775 4639, 2 rms [ensuite, hairdry, a/c (1), fan, heat, elec blkts, clock radio, t/c mkg], lounge (TV, video, cd), lounge firepl, non smoking property. **BB ♦ $90 - $105, ♦♦ $100 - $110**, AE BC MC VI.

★★★☆ **Bareena Lodge Bed & Breakfast**, (B&B), No children's facilities, 25 Bareena Dve, 1.5km NE of Mt Eliza Village PO, ☎ 03 9787 6859, fax 03 9787 6859, (2 stry gr fl), 3 rms [ensuite, shwr, spa bath (1), tlt, fan, heat, TV, clock radio, t/c mkg, refrig, toaster], lounge (TV, video), pool, spa, tennis. **BB ♦ $100 - $130, ♦♦ $95 - $135, ◊ $35 - $40**, BC MC VI.

MELBOURNE - MOUNT WAVERLEY VIC 3149

Pop Part of City of Monash, (19km SE Melbourne), See map on page 697, ref D4. Residential eastern suburb. Bowls, Golf, Swimming (Pool), Tennis.

Hotels/Motels

★★★★☆ **Bruce County Motor Inn**, (M), 445 Blackburn Rd, ☎ 03 9803 5411, fax 03 9887 9284, (2 stry gr fl), 39 units (7 suites) [shwr, bath (12), spa bath (12), tlt, hairdry, a/c, tel, cable tv, clock radio, t/c mkg, refrig, mini bar], ldry, iron, iron brd, conf fac, ⊠, bar (cocktail), pool, sauna, spa, 24hr reception, rm serv (24 hour), cots. **RO ♦ $165, ♦♦ $170.50, ◊ $22**, ch con, AE BC DC EFT MC VI.

Trouble-free travel tips **- Tools**

It pays to carry some basic tools for emergency roadside repairs, such as an adjustable spanner, phillips head and flat blade screwdrivers, pliers and a roll of masking tape.

Self Catering Accommodation

★★★★☆ Park Avenue Executive Accommodation, (Apt), Previously Park Avenue Serviced Apartments. 14 Lang Rd, 2km SW of PO, ☎ 03 9807 5777, fax 03 9807 5677, 12 apts acc up to 6, (1 & 2 bedrm), [shwr, bath, tlt, hairdry, a/c-cool, cent heat, tel, cable tv, video, clock radio, t/c mkg, refrig, cook fac, micro, d/wash, toaster, ldry (in unit), blkts, linen, pillows], iron, iron brd, c/park (garage), cots, non smoking units (6). D $110 - $170, Central booking office: 2 Hamilton Pl, Mt Waverley 3149, AE BC DC MC VI.

MELBOURNE - MULGRAVE VIC 3170

(23km SE Melbourne), See map on page 697, ref D4. Residential suburb.

Hotels/Motels

★★★ Mulgrave Court Motor Inn, (M), Previously Springvale Motor Inn. 5 Harcourt Ave, ☎ 03 9547 2233, fax 03 9547 0605, (2 stry gr fl), 25 units [shwr, tlt, hairdry, a/c-cool, heat, elec blkts, tel, cable tv, clock radio, t/c mkg, refrig, toaster], ldry, cots-fee. RO ♦ $71.50, ♦♦ $71.50 - $77, ◊ $11, AE BC DC MC VI.

★★★☆ (Apartment Section), (2 stry), 1 apt acc up to 8, (2 bedrm), [shwr, bath, tlt, hairdry, a/c-cool, heat, elec blkts, tel, cable tv, clock radio, t/c mkg, refrig, cook fac, micro, toaster, ldry (in unit), blkts, linen, pillows], iron, iron brd. D ♦♦♦♦ $165, ◊ $11.

MELBOURNE - NARRE WARREN VIC 3805

Pop 18,947. (42km E Melbourne), See map on page 697, ref E5. Growing outer south eastern suburb.

B&B's/Guest Houses

★★★★☆ Narre Green Hills, (B&B), 112 Bailey Rd, Narre Warren North 3804, 2km E of PO, ☎ 03 9796 8452, fax 03 9796 8003, 1 rm [shwr, bath, tlt, hairdry, a/c, elec blkts, TV, clock radio, t/c mkg, refrig, micro, toaster], lounge (CD player), lounge firepl. BB ♦ $95, ♦♦ $110 - $130, BC MC VI,

Operator Comment: "Country setting with beautiful views. Close to Berwick & D'nong Ranges".

MELBOURNE - NOBLE PARK VIC 3174

Pop 9,259. (28km SE Melbourne), See map on page 697, ref D5. Location of RACV'S Headquarters - 550 Princes Hwy, and residential & light industrial suburb. Swimming (Pool), Tennis.

Hotels/Motels

★★★★ Sandown Heritage Motor Inn, (M), 433 Princes Hwy, ☎ 03 9548 0866, fax 03 9548 0533, 16 units [shwr, spa bath (3), tlt, hairdry, a/c, elec blkts, tel, TV, video-fee, clock radio, t/c mkg, refrig], ✕ (Mon to Thur), pool-heated (solar), rm serv (Mon to Thur), cots-fee, non smoking rms (7). RO ♦ $95 - $140, ♦♦ $97 - $155, ◊ $15, AE BC DC EFT JCB MC MP VI.

★★★★ Sandown Regency Motor Inn, (M), 477 Princes Hwy, ☎ 03 9548 3444, fax 03 9548 2520, (2 stry gr fl), 37 units [shwr, spa bath (36), tlt, hairdry, a/c, tel, cable tv, clock radio, t/c mkg, refrig], iron, iron brd, conf fac, ✕ (Sat - Thur), pool-heated (solar), 24hr reception, rm serv, ✆, cots-fee, non smoking rms (20). RO ♦ $98 - $148.50, ♦♦ $98 - $148.50, ch con, AE BC DC EFT MC VI.

★★★ The Sandown Park Hotel, (LMH), Cnr Corrigan Rd & Princes Hwy, opposite Springvale Crematorium, ☎ 03 9546 5755, fax 03 9546 7720, 14 units [shwr, tlt, a/c, elec blkts, tel, TV, clock radio, t/c mkg, refrig, toaster], ✉, rm serv. RO ♦ $77, ♦♦ $77, ◊ $22, ch con, AE BC EFT MC VI.

MELBOURNE - NORTH MELBOURNE VIC 3051

Pop Part of Melbourne, (2km N Melbourne), See map on page 697, ref C3. Inner suburb of Melbourne. Swimming (Pool), Tennis.

Hotels/Motels

★★★★☆ The Chifley on Flemington Melbourne, (LH), 5 Flemington Rd, 1.6km N of GPO, ☎ 03 9329 9344, fax 03 9328 4870, (Multi-stry gr fl), 225 rms (9 suites) [shwr, bath, spa bath (11), tlt, hairdry, a/c, tel, cable tv, clock radio, t/c mkg, refrig, mini bar, micro (9)], lift, ldry, iron, iron brd, conf fac, ✉, coffee shop, bar (cocktail), pool-heated, sauna, 24hr reception, rm serv, c/park (undercover), ✆, gym, cots, non smoking rms (113). RO ♦ $136 - $200, ♦♦ $136 - $200, ◊ $15, ch con, AE BC DC EFT JCB MC VI.

★★★☆ Marco Polo Inn, (M), Cnr Harker St & Flemington Rd, 2.4km NE of GPO, ☎ 03 9329 1788, fax 03 9329 9950, (2 stry), 70 units [shwr, bath (51), spa bath (8), tlt, a/c, tel, TV, movie, clock radio, t/c mkg, refrig], lift, ldry, conf fac, ✉, bar (cocktail), pool, sauna, 24hr reception, rm serv, ✆, cots-fee, non smoking units (13). RO ♦ $98 - $198, ♦♦ $108 - $198, ◊ $10, ch con, AE BC DC MC VI.

★★★ Arden Motel, (M), Office hours strictly 7.30am to 10pm. 15 Arden St, 1.8km NE of GPO, ☎ 03 9329 7211, fax 03 9329 5574, (Multi-stry), 61 units [shwr, bath (10), spa bath (2), tlt, hairdry, a/c, elec blkts, tel, TV, clock radio, t/c mkg, refrig, cook fac (10), micro, toaster], ldry, bbq, c/park (carport), cots. BLB ♦ $83 - $88, ♦♦ $83 - $88, ◊ $18 - $20, ch con, AE BC DC MC VI, &.

Self Catering Accommodation

★★★☆ Abbeville Apartments, (Apt), 205 Flemington Rd, ☎ 03 9397 8549, fax 03 9397 2279, 4 apts acc up to 6, (1 & 2 bedrm), [shwr, tlt, hairdry, a/c, fan, heat, tel, TV, video, clock radio, CD, refrig, cook fac, micro, ldry (in unit), blkts, linen, pillows], w/mach, dryer, iron, iron brd. D ♦♦ $125 - $200, ◊ $15, AE BC DC MC VI.

★★★ Punt Hill Serviced Apartments, (Apt), 113 Flemington Rd, 2.3km N of GPO, ☎ 03 9650 1299, fax 03 9650 4409, (Multi-stry gr fl), 17 apts acc up to 4, (Studio, 1 & 2 bedrm), [shwr, tlt, a/c-cool, heat, elec blkts, tel, TV, video-fee, clock radio, refrig, cook fac, micro, toaster, blkts, linen, pillows], ldry, w/mach-fee, dryer-fee, iron, iron brd, c/park (undercover) (10), cots. D $118 - $162, Min book. applies all Melbourne major events, AE BC DC MC VI.

B&B's/Guest Houses

★★★ Queensberry Hill YHA, (PH), 78 Howard St, 1.5km NW of GPO, ☎ 03 9329 8599, fax 03 9326 8427, (Multi-stry gr fl), 26 rms [ensuite (9), c/fan (9), cent heat, t/c mkg (9)], lift, ldry, read rm, lounge (TV), ✉, cook fac, t/c mkg shared, refrig, bbq, c/park (undercover), ✆, non smoking rms. RO ♦ $55 - $65, ♦♦ $62 - $78, ♦♦♦ $72 - $85, ◊ $12, ch con, BC MC VI, &.

(Dormitory Section), 57 rms acc up to 8, (Bunk Rooms), [cent heat, linen reqd-fee]. RO ♦ $20 - $21, ◊ $20, ch con.

Other Accommodation

YHA Victoria, (Lodge), 76 Chapman St, 500m SE of PO, ☎ 03 9328 3595, fax 03 9329 7863, (Multi-stry), 54 rms [heat, linen], shwr (7G-7L), tlt (7G-7L), ldry, lounge (TV, video), cook fac, refrig, bbq, ✆. D ♦ $20 - $25, RO ♦ $21 - $29, BC MC VI.

MELBOURNE - NOTTING HILL VIC 3168

Pop Part of Melbourne, (20km E Melbourne), See map on page 697, ref D4. Residential area, adjacent to Monash University. Tennis.

Hotels/Motels

★★★★☆ **Gateway on Monash Motor Inn**, (M), 630 Blackburn Rd, ☎ 03 9561 4455, fax 03 9561 7544, (2 stry gr fl), 30 units (4 suites) [shwr, spa bath, tlt, hairdry, a/c, c/fan, heat, elec blkts, tel, TV, movie, clock radio, t/c mkg, refrig, mini bar], ldry, iron, iron brd, ✕ (Mon to Sun), bar (cocktail), pool-heated (salt water heated), sauna, spa, 24hr reception, rm serv, gym, cots, non smoking units (18). **RO** ♦ **$121 - $175.50**, ♦♦ **$121 - $170.50**, ◊ **$22**, Suite D ♦♦♦♦ **$242**, ◊ **$22**, AE BC DC MC VI.

★★★★☆ **(Apartment Section)**, 3 apts acc up to 6, (2 bedrm), [shwr, spa bath, tlt, hairdry, a/c, c/fan, cent heat, elec blkts, tel, TV, video, movie, clock radio, t/c mkg, refrig, mini bar, cook fac, micro, d/wash, toaster, ldry (in unit), blkts, linen, pillows], iron, iron brd. **D** ♦♦♦♦ **$242**, ◊ **$22**.

Self Catering Accommodation

★★★☆ **Monash Serviced Apartments**, (Apt), Cnr Clayton & Ferntree Gully Rds, 3km N of PO, ☎ 03 9568 6411, fax 03 9569 4960, (Multi-stry), 10 apts acc up to 6, (2 bedrm), [shwr, tlt, hairdry, a/c-cool, cent heat, elec blkts, tel, TV, clock radio, refrig, cook fac, micro, d/wash, toaster, ldry, blkts, linen, pillows], iron, iron brd, bbq, plygr. **D** ♦ **$140 - $200**, ♦♦ **$140 - $200**, ◊ **$51**, Min book applies, AE BC DC MC MP VI.

B&B's/Guest Houses

★★★★☆ **Cameo House**, (B&B), 78 Westerfield Dve, 1.5km NE of Monash University, ☎ 03 9562 1212, fax 03 9560 4675, 3 rms [shwr, spa bath (1), tlt, hairdry, a/c, c/fan, heat, elec blkts, cable tv (2), video (1), clock radio, t/c mkg, refrig, micro, toaster], lounge, non smoking property. **BLB** ♦ **$105**, ♦♦ **$135 - $160**, AE BC DC MC VI.

MELBOURNE - NUNAWADING VIC 3131

Pop 8,711. (21km E Melbourne), See map on page 697, ref D3. Residential eastern suburb. Golf, Swimming (Indoor Pool), Tennis.

Hotels/Motels

★★★☆ **Nunawading Motor Inn**, (M), Cnr Whitehorse Rd & Goodwin St, 1.5km W of PO, ☎ 03 9877 6511, fax 03 9894 2739, (2 stry gr fl), 32 units [shwr, bath (27), spa bath (5), tlt, hairdry, a/c, elec blkts, tel, TV, video-fee, clock radio, t/c mkg, refrig, mini bar, cook fac ltd (6), micro (6)], ldry, iron, iron brd, conf fac, ✕ (Sun to Thurs), pool, bbq, cots-fee. **RO** ♦ **$83 - $154**, ♦♦ **$83 - $154**, ◊ **$5**, AE BC DC MC VI.
Operator Comment: See our display advertisement opposite.

★★★ **Burvale Hotel**, (LMH), Cnr Springvale Rd & Burwood Hwy, 2.4km S of PO, ☎ 03 9802 1111, fax 03 9803 6778, 27 units [shwr, tlt, a/c, tel, TV, clock radio, t/c mkg, refrig, toaster], ldry, iron, iron brd, ✕, ✆, cots. **RO** ♦ **$59.95**, ♦♦ **$59.95**, ◊ **$10**, ch con, AE BC DC EFT MC VI.

Self Catering Accommodation

★★★☆ **Birds, Trees, Suburbia**, (Cotg), 7 Meringer Crt, 1.6km NE of PO, ☎ 03 9874 6553, 1 cotg acc up to 6, (3 bedrm), [ensuite, shwr, tlt, hairdry, fan, c/fan, heat, elec blkts, tel, TV, clock radio, t/c mkg, refrig, cook fac, micro, d/wash, ldry, blkts, linen, pillows], w/mach, dryer, bbq, non smoking property. **D** ♦ **$75**, ♦♦ **$105**, ◊ **$27.50**.

★★★ **(Holiday Unit Section)**, 1 unit acc up to 6, (2 bedrm), [shwr, spa bath, tlt, fan, heat, elec blkts, TV, clock radio, refrig, cook fac ltd, micro, elec frypan, blkts, linen, pillows]. **D** ♦ **$75**, ♦♦ **$105**, ◊ **$27.50**.

MELBOURNE - OAKLEIGH VIC 3166

(16km E Melbourne), See map on page 697, ref D4. Residential, light industrial suburb. Bowls, Golf, Squash, Swimming (Pool), Tennis.

Hotels/Motels

★★★★ **The Chadstone Motor Inn**, (M), 1350 Dandenong Rd (Princes Hwy), 200m S of Chadstone Shopping Centre, ☎ 03 9568 6277, fax 03 9569 6250, (2 stry gr fl), 20 units [shwr, tlt, hairdry, a/c, elec blkts, tel, TV, video, clock radio, t/c mkg, refrig, toaster], conf fac, meals to unit, meals avail, cots. **RO** ♦ **$104 - $115**, ♦♦ **$104 - $115**, ◊ **$10**, AE BC DC EFT JCB MC VI.

★★★☆ **(Apartment Section)**, 3 apts acc up to 6, (2 bedrm), [shwr, bath, tlt, hairdry, a/c, heat, elec blkts, tel, TV, video, clock radio, t/c mkg, refrig, cook fac, micro, toaster, ldry, blkts, linen, pillows], w/mach, dryer, iron, iron brd, bbq, c/park (garage). **D $160 - $195**.

★★★☆ **Lamplighter Motel**, (M), 1440 Dandenong Rd (Princes Hwy), 1km NE of PO, ☎ 03 9568 6411, fax 03 9569 4960, (2 stry gr fl), 25 units [shwr, tlt, hairdry, a/c, elec blkts, tel, cable tv, clock radio, t/c mkg, refrig, toaster], iron, iron brd, ✕, spa, bbq, rm serv, cots-fee, non smoking units (4). **RO** ♦♦ **$106**, ◊ **$20**, ch con, AE BC DC MC MP VI.
Operator Comment: See our display advertisement under Melbourne. www.austpacinns.com.au

★★★☆ **The Oakleigh Motel**, (M), 1650 Dandenong Rd, Oakleigh East 3166, ☎ 03 9544 3566, fax 03 9544 9781, 31 units [shwr, tlt, a/c, elec blkts, TV, clock radio, t/c mkg, refrig], ✕, pool, bbq, ✆, cots-fee, non smoking units (20). **RO** ♦ **$66**, ♦♦ **$66 - $77**, ◊ **$10**, ch con, Light breakfast only available. AE BC DC EFT MC VI.

★★★ **Chadstone Executive Motel**, (M), 1362 Dandenong Rd (Princes Hwy), 1km NW of PO, ☎ 03 9569 6945, fax 03 9568 8416, 18 units [shwr, bath (5), spa bath (1), tlt, a/c-cool, heat, elec blkts, tel, cable tv, video (avail), clock radio, t/c mkg, refrig, micro, elec frypan, toaster], ldry, rec rm, conf fac, bbq, cots. **RO** ♦ **$85**, ♦♦ **$100**, ◊ **$10**, AE BC DC EFT MC MCH VI.

★★☆ **Chadstone Centre Motel**, (M), 1330 Dandenong Rd (Princes Hwy), 1.7km NW of PO, opposite Chadstone shopping centre, ☎ 03 9568 2955, fax 03 9569 4136, 30 units [shwr, tlt, a/c, elec blkts, tel, TV, clock radio, t/c mkg, refrig], ldry, conf fac, cots-fee. **RO** ♦♦ **$77**, ◊ **$10**, 8 units ★★. AE BC DC MC VI.

Self Catering Accommodation

★★★☆ **Lamplighter Apartments**, (Apt), 810 Warrigal Rd, 1km E of PO, ☎ 03 9568 6411, fax 03 9569 4960, (2 stry gr fl), 7 apts acc up to 6, (3 & 4 bedrm), [hairdry, a/c, heat, tel, TV, clock radio, t/c mkg, refrig, cook fac, micro, d/wash, toaster, ldry (in unit), blkts, linen, pillows], iron, iron brd, c/park (carport), cots-fee. **D** ♦ **$140 - $200**, ♦♦ **$140 - $200**, ◊ **$10 - $20**, AE BC DC MC MP VI.

Trouble-free travel tips - Lights

Check the operation of all lights. If you are pulling a trailer of caravan make sure turning indicators and brake lights are working.

MELBOURNE - PARKVILLE VIC 3052

Pop Part of Melbourne, (3km N Melbourne), See map on page 697, ref C3. Inner suburb of Melbourne. Golf, Tennis.

Hotels/Motels

FLAG
FLAG CHOICE HOTELS

★★★☆ **Ramada Inn**, (M), 539 Royal Pde, 4.1km N of GPO, ☎ 03 9380 8131, fax 03 9388 0519, (2 stry gr fl), 41 units [shwr, spa bath (1), tlt, hairdry, a/c, elec blkts, tel, TV, clock radio, t/c mkg, refrig], ldry, ✉, BYO, dinner to unit, cots-fee. **RO** ♦ **$105 - $130**, ♦♦ **$110 - $165**, ◊ **$11**, AE BC DC EFT MC VI.

Budget Motel Chain International

★★★☆ **The Park Squire Motor Inn**, (M), 94 Flemington Rd, 2.5km NW of GPO, ☎ 03 9329 6077, fax 03 9326 6576, (2 stry), 24 units [shwr, tlt, a/c, elec blkts, tel, TV, clock radio, t/c mkg, refrig], ldry, c/park (undercover), cots, non smoking units (3). **RO** ♦ **$93 - $103**, ♦♦ **$93 - $110**, ◊ **$10**, AE BC DC EFT MC VI.

★★★ **(Apartment Section)**, (Multi-stry) 18 apts acc up to 5, (1 bedrm), [shwr, bath, tlt, a/c, elec blkts, tel, TV, clock radio, t/c mkg, refrig, cook fac, micro, blkts, linen, pillows]. **D** **$105 - $148**, **W** **$655 - $959**.

Quality
FLAG CHOICE HOTELS

Quality Hotel Laureate, (M), Previously Park Avenue Quality Hotel 441 Royal Pde, 3.6km N of GPO, ☎ 03 9380 9222, fax 03 9387 6846, (Multi-stry gr fl), 90 units [shwr, bath, tlt, a/c, cent heat, tel, TV, clock radio, t/c mkg, refrig, toaster (27)], lift, ldry, conf fac, ✉, coffee shop, bar (cocktail), pool, 24hr reception, ☎, cots. **BLB** ♦ **$88**, ♦♦ **$93.50**, ◊ **$5**, ch con, AE BC DC MC VI, (Rating under review).

MELBOURNE - PATTERSON LAKES VIC 3197

Pop 2,910. (32km SE Melbourne), See map on page 697, ref D5. Residential development based on a lakes system. Boating, Canoeing, Sailing, Water Skiing.

B&B's/Guest Houses

★★★★☆ **Comcentre**, (B&B), 55 Palm Beach Dve, ☎ 03 9776 1914, fax 03 9773 3510, (Multi-stry), 3 rms (1 suite) [ensuite, spa bath, a/c, heat, tel, TV, video, clock radio, t/c mkg (1), refrig (1), micro (1), toaster (1), ldry], conf fac, lounge firepl, ✉, pool-heated, sauna, spa, t/c mkg shared, refrig, bbq, secure park, jetty, tennis. **BB** ♦♦ **$140 - $180**, **Suite BB** ♦♦ **$360 - $520**, BC MC VI.

MELBOURNE - PORT MELBOURNE VIC 3207

Pop 7,769. (5km SW Melbourne), See map on page 697, ref C3. Inner suburb of Melbourne.

Self Catering Accommodation

★★★★☆ **Station Pier Condominiums**, (Apt), 15 Beach St, opposite Station Pier, ☎ 03 9647 9666, fax 03 9646 3539, 55 apts acc up to 6, (1 & 2 bedrm), [shwr, spa bath, tlt, hairdry, a/c, tel, cable tv, movie, clock radio, t/c mkg, refrig, cook fac, micro, d/wash, toaster, ldry (in unit), blkts, linen, pillows], w/mach, dryer, iron, iron brd, conf fac, ✉, pool-heated, sauna, spa, bbq, 24hr reception, rm serv, plygr, gym, tennis, cots-fee. **D** **$170 - $240**, **W** **$980 - $1,330**, AE BC DC EFT MC MP VI.

MELBOURNE - PRAHRAN VIC 3181

Pop 42,664. (6km SE Melbourne), See map on page 697, ref C3. Inner residential suburb of Melbourne. Bowls, Squash, Swimming (Heated Pool), Tennis.

Self Catering Accommodation

★★★★☆ **Quest Windsor**, (Apt), 111 Punt Rd, ☎ 03 9520 3333, fax 03 9520 3344, (Multi-stry), 50 apts (1, 2 & 3 bedrm), [shwr, tlt, hairdry, a/c, tel, TV, video-fee, clock radio, t/c mkg, refrig, cook fac, micro, d/wash, toaster, ldry (in unit), blkts, linen, pillows], lift, iron, iron brd, conf fac, sauna, spa, secure park, gym, cots. **D** **$120 - $243**, AE BC DC EFT JCB MC VI.

AAA
TOURISM
Special Rates

★★★ **Punt Hill Serviced Apartments**, (Apt), 6 Williams Rd, 7km from CBD, ☎ 03 9650 1299, fax 03 9650 4409, (Multi-stry gr fl), 47 apts acc up to 5, (1 & 2 bedrm), [shwr, bath, tlt, a/c, elec blkts, tel, TV, video-fee, clock radio, refrig, cook fac, toaster, blkts, linen, pillows], ldry, w/mach-fee, dryer-fee, iron, iron brd, c/park (limited), cots. **D** **$103 - $135**, Minium booking applies all Melbourne major events. AE BC DC MC VI.

MELBOURNE - PRESTON VIC 3072

(10km N Melbourne), See map on page 697, ref C3. Large residential and light industrial suburb.

Hotels/Motels

★★★☆ **Bell Motor Inn**, (M), Cnr Bell & Patterson Sts, ☎ 03 9480 2099, fax 03 9484 0356, (2 stry gr fl), 33 units [shwr, spa bath (4), tlt, hairdry (4), a/c, elec blkts, tel, cable tv, clock radio, t/c mkg, refrig, cook fac ltd, micro], ldry, conf fac, ✉ (Mon to Thurs), pool-heated (solar), 24hr reception, cots-fee, non smoking units. **RO** ♦ **$113.30 - $181.50**, ♦♦ **$113.30 - $181.50**, ◊ **$16.50**, ch con, AE BC DC MC VI, ♿.

Other Accommodation

The Terrace Inn, (Lodge), 418 Murray Rd, 800m NW of PO, ☎ 03 9470 1006, fax 03 9470 3446, 38 rms acc up to 8, (Bunk Rooms), [ensuite (15), heat, cent heat, refrig], shwr, tlt, bathrm, ldry, rec rm, lounge (TV), cook fac, refrig, bbq, c/park (limited), ☎. **RO** ♦ **$15.40 - $30.80**, ♦♦ **$41.80**, ◊ **$3.20**, ch con, fam con, Key deposit $20. BC EFT MC VI.

MELBOURNE - RESERVOIR VIC 3073

Pop Part of Melbourne, (14km N Melbourne), See map on page 697, ref C2. Residential suburb north of Melbourne.

Hotels/Motels

Best Western

★★★☆ **Mahoneys Motor Inn**, (M), Cnr Mahoneys Rd & Wilson Blvd, 4km E of Hume Hwy, ☎ 03 9462 1966, fax 03 9462 1147, (2 stry gr fl), 27 units [shwr, bath (14), spa bath (12), tlt, hairdry, a/c, elec blkts, tel, TV, video-fee, movie, clock radio, t/c mkg, refrig, toaster], ldry, conf fac, ✉, rm serv, dinner to unit, c/park (undercover) (12), cots-fee. **RO** ♦ **$100 - $136**, ♦♦ **$100 - $136**, ◊ **$10**, ch con, AE BC DC EFT JCB MC MP VI, ♿.

MELBOURNE - RICHMOND VIC 3121

Pop Part of Melbourne, (3km E Melbourne), See map on page 697, ref C3. Location of the Melbourne Cricket Ground.

Hotels/Motels

★★★★☆ **Rydges Riverwalk Melbourne**, (LH), Cnr Bridge Rd & River St, 1km E of PO, ☎ 03 9246 1200, fax 03 9246 1222, 62 rms [shwr, bath, tlt, hairdry, a/c, tel, TV, movie, clock radio, t/c mkg, refrig, mini bar], lift, iron, iron brd, business centre, conf fac, ⊠, bar (cocktail), bbq, 24hr reception, rm serv, secure park, cots, non smoking flr (1). **RO** ♦ **$163 - $250**, ♦♦ **$163 - $250**, ◊ **$27.50 - $38.50**, ch con, AE BC DC EFT JCB MC VI.

★★★★☆ **(Apartment Section)**, 32 apts acc up to 4, (Studio, 1 & 2 bedrm), [shwr, bath, spa bath (1), tlt, a/c, tel, TV, movie, clock radio, refrig, mini bar, cook fac, micro, d/wash, ldry (in unit), blkts, linen, pillows], lift, w/mach, dryer, iron, iron brd, business centre, conf fac, ⊠, bbq, 24hr reception, rm serv, secure park, cots. **D** ♦♦ **$210 - $338**, ◊ **$27.50 - $38.50**.

Self Catering Accommodation

★★★★ **Tozer Terrace**, (Cotg), 27 Union St, ☎ 03 9415 1159, 1 cotg acc up to 5, (2 bedrm), [shwr, tlt, c/fan, cent heat, tel, TV, clock radio, refrig, cook fac, d/wash, toaster, ldry, blkts, doonas, linen, pillows], w/mach, dryer, non smoking property. **BB** ♦♦ **$190 - $250**, ◊ **$20**, ♦♦ **$900 - $1,500**, ◊ **$140**, BC MC VI.

★★★ **Richmond Lodge**, (Apt), 37 Buckingham St, 500m N of PO, ☎ 03 9428 0237, fax 03 9428 1032, (2 stry gr fl), 10 apts acc up to 7, (Studio, 2 & 3 bedrm), [shwr, tlt, hairdry, a/c, elec blkts, tel, TV, video-fee, clock radio, t/c mkg, refrig, cook fac ltd, micro, toaster, blkts, doonas, linen, pillows], ldry, w/mach-fee, dryer-fee, iron, iron brd. **D** **$100 - $161**, **W** **$550 - $1,100**, AE BC DC EFT JCB MC MP VI.

B&B's/Guest Houses

★★★★ **Villa Donati**, (B&B), 377 Church St, ☎ 03 9428 8104, (2 stry), 3 rms [ensuite, bath (1), hairdry, a/c-cool, fan, cent heat, elec blkts, TV, clock radio, t/c mkg, refrig], lounge (cd player), non smoking property. **BB** ♦ **$120 - $130**, ♦♦ **$140 - $150**, AE BC DC EFT MC VI.

  ★★★ **Richmond Hill Hotel**, (PH), 353 Church St, ☎ 03 9428 6501, fax 03 9427 0128, (2 stry), 46 rms [ensuite (27), heat, TV, clock radio, t/c mkg, refrig (15)], ldry, lounge (TV), conf fac, bar, c/park (limited), ↙, non smoking property. **BLB** ◊ **$75 - $105**, ♦♦ **$85 - $120**, ◊ **$28**, AE BC DC EFT MC VI.

(Lodge Section), (Multi-stry gr fl), 17 rms acc up to 6, (Bunk Rooms), [blkts, linen, pillows], ldry, lounge (TV), cook fac, ✆, **RO** ♦ **$22 - $44**, ♦♦ **$54**.

MELBOURNE - RINGWOOD VIC 3134

Pop 43,000. (25km E Melbourne), See map on page 697, ref E3. Residential outer eastern suburb. Croquet, Golf, Swimming (Pool), Tennis.

Hotels/Motels

 ★★★★ **Ringwood Lake Motor Inn**, (M), 327 Maroondah Hwy, 1km E of Clock Tower, ☎ 03 9870 7799, fax 03 9879 5802, 21 units [shwr, bath (9), spa bath (9), tlt, hairdry, a/c, tel, TV, clock radio, t/c mkg, refrig, mini bar], ldry, iron, iron brd, ⊠ (Mon to Thu), pool-heated (solar), rm serv, dinner to unit, cots-fee, non smoking units (5). **RO** ♦ **$107 - $168**, ♦♦ **$107 - $168**, ◊ **$11**, ch con, AE BC DC EFT MC VI, ♿.

  ★★★☆ **Sundowner Chain Motor Inns**, (M), 346 Maroondah Hwy, 2.1km E of Clock Tower, ☎ 03 9870 4344, fax 03 9870 3421, (2 stry gr fl), 35 units [shwr, bath (34), spa bath (9), tlt, hairdry, a/c, elec blkts, tel, TV, video, movie, clock radio, t/c mkg, refrig, mini bar (23), toaster], ldry, iron, iron brd, conf fac, ⊠, bar (cocktail), pool, sauna, spa, bbq, rm serv, cots-fee, non smoking units (17). **RO** ♦ **$83.50 - $199**, ♦♦ **$88 - $199**, ◊ **$11**, ch con, Min book long w/ends, AE BC DC EFT MC VI.

 ★★★ **Motel Ringwood**, (M), 442 Maroondah Hwy, 3km E of PO, ☎ 03 9870 3222, fax 03 9870 3445, 15 units [shwr, tlt, hairdry, a/c, elec blkts, tel, TV, video-fee, movie, clock radio, t/c mkg, refrig], ldry, bbq, plygr, non smoking units (10). **RO** ♦ **$70 - $76**, ♦♦ **$75 - $80**, ◊ **$11**, ch con, AE BC DC EFT MC MCH VI.

B&B's/Guest Houses

★★★★ **Hazelwood House**, (B&B), 44 Holland Rd, Ringwood East 3135, ☎ 03 9870 9817, 1 rm (1 suite) [ensuite, bath, hairdry, evap cool, cent heat, TV, video, clock radio, t/c mkg, refrig, micro, toaster], iron, iron brd, bbq, non smoking property. **BB** ♦ **$85 - $100**, ♦♦ **$130 - $170**, pen con, Min book long w/ends and Easter, BC MC VI.

MELBOURNE - ROWVILLE VIC 3178

Pop Part of City of Knox, (30km SE Melbourne), See map on page 697, ref E4. Outer south eastern residential suburb. Tennis.

Hotels/Motels

 ★★★★ **Quality Inn Knox**, (M), 1233 Stud Rd, ☎ 03 9764 5050, fax 03 9764 5148, 31 units (2 suites) [shwr, bath (2), spa bath (12), tlt, hairdry, a/c, elec blkts, tel, cable tv, video, clock radio, t/c mkg, refrig, mini bar], ldry, iron, iron brd, conf fac, ⊠, bar (cocktail), sauna, spa, rm serv, plygr, cots, non smoking units (12). **RO** ♦ **$108 - $189**, ♦♦ **$108 - $230**, ◊ **$15**, ch con, AE BC DC EFT MC MP VI.

MELBOURNE - SEAFORD VIC 3198

Pop 9,815. (35km SE Melbourne), See map on page 697, ref D6. Bayside residential suburb. Boating, Bowls, Fishing, Horse Riding, Sailing, Scenic Drives, Swimming (Beach), Tennis, Water Skiing.

Hotels/Motels

★★ **Seaford**, (LMH), 362 Frankston - Dandenong Rd, 2.4km E of PO, ☎ 03 9786 5999, fax 03 9785 3254, (2 stry gr fl), 16 units [shwr, tlt, a/c, elec blkts, TV, t/c mkg, refrig], ⊠, ✆, **BLB** ♦ **$55**, ♦♦ **$55**, ◊ **$5**, AE BC DC EFT MC VI.

MELBOURNE - SOUTH MELBOURNE VIC 3205

Pop Part of Melbourne, (3km S Melbourne), See map on page 697, ref C3. A suburb of Melbourne. Boating, Bowls, Fishing, Golf, Squash, Swimming (Bay), Tennis.

Hotels/Motels

★★★☆ **Centra St Kilda Road**, (LH), Cnr St Kilda Rd & Park St, 2.4km S of GPO, ☎ 03 9209 9888, fax 03 9690 1603, (Multi-stry), 226 rms [shwr, bath, tlt, hairdry, a/c, tel, TV, movie-fee, clock radio, t/c mkg, refrig, mini bar], lift, ldry, iron, iron brd, conf fac, ⊠, pool, c/park (garage), cots, non smoking flr (9). **RO** ♦ **$110 - $142**, ♦♦ **$110 - $142**, ◊ **$33**, ch con, AE BC DC EFT JCB MC MP VI.

★★★☆ **City Park Hotel**, (M), 308 Kingsway, 2km S of GPO, ☎ 03 9686 0000, fax 03 9699 9224, (Multi-stry), 44 units [shwr, bath, spa bath (13), tlt, hairdry, a/c, tel, TV, movie, clock radio, t/c mkg, refrig, mini bar], lift, iron, iron brd, ⊠, 24hr reception, rm serv, c/park (undercover), cots, non smoking flr (2). **RO** ♦ **$110 - $180**, ♦♦ **$110 - $180**, ♦ **$10**, ch con, 18 units ★★★★. AE BC DC MC MP VI, ⅃&.

★★★ **Kingsway Motel**, (M), Cnr Park St & Eastern Rd, 1.5km S of GPO, ☎ 03 9699 2533, fax 03 9696 2341, (Multi-stry), 40 units [shwr, bath (5), tlt, a/c, tel, TV, clock radio, t/c mkg, refrig, toaster], lift, ✆, cots. **D $115 - $135**, ch con, AE BC DC MC VI.

Self Catering Accommodation

★★★★☆ **Quest South Melbourne**, (Apt), 21 Park St, 2km S of GPO, ☎ 03 9685 8888, fax 03 9685 8880, (Multi-stry gr fl), 11 apts acc up to 7, (1, 2 & 3 bedrm), [shwr, spa bath, tlt, hairdry, a/c, tel, TV, video, clock radio, t/c mkg, refrig, micro, d/wash, toaster, ldry, blkts, linen, pillows], w/mach, dryer, iron, iron brd, secure park (undercover), cots, non smoking property. **D $165 - $259**, AE BC DC EFT JCB MC VI.

MELBOURNE - SOUTH YARRA VIC 3141

Pop Part of Melbourne, (5km SE Melbourne), See map on page 697, ref C3. Exclusive inner Melbourne suburb. Rowing, Tennis.

Hotels/Motels

★★★★★ **The Hotel Como**, (Ltd Lic H), 630 Chapel St, Cnr Toorak Rd, ☎ 03 9825 2222, fax 03 9824 1263, 107 rms (107 suites) [shwr, spa bath (90), tlt, hairdry, a/c, tel, fax, TV, video-fee, clock radio, CD, t/c mkg, refrig, mini bar, cook fac (50), d/wash (19), toaster, doonas], lounge (TV), conf fac, ⊠, bar (cocktail), pool indoor heated, sauna, spa, bbq, 24hr reception, rm serv, c/park (valet), courtesy transfer, gym, cots, non smoking flr (2). **Suite D $570 - $1,270**, ch con, AE BC DC JCB MC VI, ⅃&.

★★★ **Albany Motel**, (M), 1 Millswyn St, Cnr Toorak Rd, 500m S of Botanical Gardens, ☎ 03 9866 4485, fax 03 9820 9419, (2 stry gr fl), 70 units [shwr, bath (70), tlt, hairdry (5), a/c, heat, tel, TV, t/c mkg, refrig], lift, ldry, ✕ (Mon to Fri), BYO, sauna, cook fac, cots. **RO** ♦ **$80 - $115**, ♦♦ **$85 - $120**, ♦♦♦ **$100 - $130**, AE BC DC MC VI.

★★★ **Hotel Saville**, (M), 5 Commercial Rd, 500m E of Alfred Hospital, ☎ 03 9867 2755, fax 03 9820 9726, (Multi-stry), 35 units [shwr, tlt, hairdry (22), a/c, tel, TV, clock radio, t/c mkg, refrig], lift, iron, iron brd, conf fac, ⊠ (Mon to Fri), 24hr reception, rm serv, cots, non smoking units (7). **RO** ♦ **$110**, ♦♦ **$121**, ♦♦♦ **$132**, ch con, Min book. applies Grand Prix, Melbourne Cup & Australian Open. AE BC DC EFT JCB MC MP VI.

★★★ **St James Motel**, (M), 35 Darling St, 350m N of PO, ☎ 03 9866 4455, fax 03 9820 4059, (2 stry), 15 units [shwr, tlt, a/c, tel, TV, clock radio, t/c mkg, refrig, micro, toaster], ldry, c/park (limited, garage), cots. **RO** ♦ **$61 - $77**, ♦♦ **$66 - $82**, ♦ **$10**, AE BC DC MC VI.

Self Catering Accommodation

★★★★★ **Manor House**, (Apt), 36 Darling St, 200m N of Punt Rd, ☎ 03 9867 1266, fax 03 9867 4613, 40 apts acc up to 5, (1, 2 & 3 bedrm), [shwr, bath (32), tlt, hairdry, heat, elec blkts, tel, fax, TV, video, movie, clock radio, CD, refrig, mini bar, cook fac, micro, d/wash, ldry (in unit), blkts, linen, pillows], iron, iron brd, conf fac, pool indoor heated, spa, c/park (undercover), gym, cots. **D ♦♦ $150 - $355**, ♦ **$30**, Light breakfast available. ⅃&.

★★★ **(23 Avoca St Section)**, 20 apts acc up to 2, (Studio), [shwr, tlt, heat, tel, TV, clock radio, refrig, cook fac, blkts, linen, pillows], ldry, c/park (undercover) (8). **D $100**, **W $665**, Light breakfast available.

★★★ **(27 Avoca St Section)**, 3 apts acc up to 5, (2 bedrm), [shwr, tlt, tel, TV, clock radio, refrig, cook fac, micro, blkts, linen, pillows], ldry, c/park (undercover), cots. **D ♦♦♦♦ $140 - $170**, ♦ **$30**.

★★★★★ **South Yarra Hill Suites**, (Apt), 14 Murphy St, 100m N of PO, ☎ 03 9868 8222, fax 03 9820 1724, (Multi-stry gr fl), 37 apts acc up to 4, (1 & 2 bedrm), [shwr, bath, spa bath, tlt, hairdry, a/c, tel, fax, cable tv, movie, clock radio, refrig, cook fac, micro, d/wash, ldry (in unit) (20)], lounge, conf fac, 24hr reception, rm serv, c/park (undercover) (20), cots. **D $256 - $381**, AE BC DC JCB MC VI.

★★★★★ **(274 Domain Rd Section)**, (Multi-stry), 20 apts acc up to 4, (1 & 2 bedrm), [shwr, bath, tlt, hairdry, a/c, tel, fax, cable tv, movie, clock radio, refrig, cook fac, micro, d/wash, ldry (in unit), blkts, linen, pillows], lift, iron, iron brd, pool-heated (salt water heated), sauna, spa, rm serv, c/park (15), gym, cots. **D $256 - $381**.

 ★★★★☆ **Medina Executive South Yarra**, (Apt), 52 Darling St, ☎ 03 9926 0000, fax 03 9866 4869, (Multi-stry gr fl), 61 apts acc up to 5, (1 & 2 bedrm), [shwr, bath, tlt, hairdry, a/c, elec blkts, tel, TV, movie, clock radio, CD, t/c mkg, refrig, cook fac, micro, d/wash, toaster, ldry (in unit), blkts, doonas, linen, pillows], lift, iron, iron brd, rec rm, lounge, pool indoor heated, steam rm, gym, cots, non smoking units (50). **D $170 - $285**, Light breakfast available. Min book applies, AE BC DC MC VI.

 ★★★★☆ **Oakford South Yarra Mews**, (Apt), 9 Balmoral St, next to Prahran Market, ☎ 03 9823 8888, fax 03 9823 8899, (2 stry gr fl), 40 apts acc up to 6, (1, 2 & 3 bedrm), [shwr, tlt, a/c, heat, tel, cable tv, video-fee, radio, t/c mkg, refrig, cook fac, micro, d/wash, ldry (in unit), blkts, linen, pillows], w/mach, dryer, cots. **D ♦♦ $152 - $325**, ♦ **$22**, AE BC DC MC VI.

★★★★☆ **Quest South Yarra Mews**, (Apt), 1 Park La, ☎ 03 9867 5400, fax 03 9867 5399, (2 stry), 14 apts acc up to 6, (3 bedrm), [shwr, spa bath, tlt, hairdry, a/c, tel, TV, video-fee, clock radio, refrig, cook fac, micro, d/wash, toaster, ldry (in unit), blkts, linen, pillows], iron, iron brd, secure park, cots. **D $191 - $303**, AE BC DC EFT JCB MC VI, ⅃&.

★★★★☆ **Quest on Chapel**, (Apt), 651 Chapel St, ☎ 03 9826 3466, fax 03 9826 3622, (Multi-stry), 46 apts acc up to 4, (1 & 2 bedrm), [shwr, bath, tlt, hairdry, a/c, tel, TV, video, clock radio, t/c mkg, refrig, cook fac, micro, d/wash, toaster, ldry (in unit), blkts, linen, pillows], lift, w/mach, dryer, iron, iron brd, sauna, spa (heated), gym, cots-fee. **D ♦♦ $209 - $242**, ♦ **$16.50**, **W ♦♦ $1,155 - $1,386**, ♦ **$115.50**, Min booking Christmas/Jan & all major events. AE BC DC EFT MC VI.

 ★★★★ **Oakford Ultimate**, (Apt), Cnr Cromwell Cres & Surrey Rd Nth, ☎ 03 9823 8888, fax 03 9823 8899, (2 stry), 25 apts acc up to 6, (2 & 3 bedrm), [shwr, bath, tlt, hairdry, a/c, cent heat, tel, TV, video-fee, refrig, cook fac, micro, d/wash, toaster, ldry (in unit), blkts, linen, pillows], iron, iron brd, bbq, secure park, cots. **D ♦♦ $140 - $210**, ♦ **$22**, Breakfast available, Minimum booking all Melbourne major events, AE BC DC MC VI.

AAA TOURISM *Special Rates*

★★★★ **Punt Hill Serviced Apartments**, (Apt), 470 Punt Rd, ☎ 03 9650 1299, fax 03 9650 4409, (2 stry gr fl), 21 apts acc up to 4, (1 bedrm), [shwr, bath, tlt, hairdry, a/c-cool, heat, elec blkts, tel, TV, video-fee, clock radio, refrig, cook fac, micro, toaster, blkts, linen, pillows], ldry, iron, iron brd, cots. **D $121**, Minium booking applies all Melbourne major events, AE BC DC MC VI.

★★★☆ **(Northampton Tce Section)**, 8 apts acc up to 4, (2 bedrm), [shwr, bath, tlt, hairdry, a/c, elec blkts, tel, TV, clock radio, refrig, cook fac, micro, d/wash, toaster, ldry (in unit), blkts, linen, pillows], w/mach, dryer, iron, iron brd, tennis, cots. **D $192**.

★★★ **(813 Punt Rd Section)**, 6 apts acc up to 4, (1 & 2 bedrm), [shwr, bath, tlt, hairdry, heat, tel, TV, clock radio, refrig, cook fac, toaster, blkts, linen, pillows], w/mach, dryer (shared), iron, iron brd, cots. **D $162**.

★★★★ **Punt Hill Serviced Apartments**, (Apt), 25 apts acc up to 4, (Studio & 1 bedrm), [shwr, tlt, hairdry, a/c-cool, heat, tel, TV, clock radio, refrig, cook fac, micro, toaster, blkts, linen, pillows], ldry, c/park (limited), cots. **D ♦♦ $132 - $214**, ⚹ **$11**, Minium booking applies all Melbourne major events, AE BC DC MC VI.

★★★★ **Sovereign Serviced Apartments**, (Apt), 218 Toorak Rd, ☎ 03 9804 8044, fax 03 9824 1317, (Multi-stry gr fl), 12 apts acc up to 6, (2 & 3 bedrm), [shwr, bath, tlt, hairdry, a/c-cool, cent heat, tel, TV, video, clock radio, CD, refrig, cook fac, micro, d/wash, toaster, ldry (in unit), blkts, linen, pillows], lift, iron, iron brd, c/park (garage), cots-fee, non smoking property. **D ♦♦♦♦ $295 - $325**, ⚹ **$25**, Min book applies, AE BC DC MC VI.

★★★ **Apartments of Melbourne**, (Apt), Toorak, 238 Toorak Rd, ☎ 03 9820 1000, fax 03 9820 0900, (Multi-stry), 12 apts acc up to 4, (1 bedrm), [shwr, bath, tlt, tel, TV, clock radio, refrig, cook fac, micro, toaster, blkts, linen, pillows], c/park (limited). **D $99 - $203**, AE BC DC MC VI.

★★★★ **(274a Domain Rd Section)**, Wilshire Heights, (Multi-stry gr fl), 16 apts acc up to 4, (1 bedrm), [shwr, bath, tlt, tel, TV, clock radio, refrig, cook fac, micro, d/wash, toaster, blkts, linen, pillows], lift, ldry, secure park, gym. **D $99 - $170**.

★★★☆ **(275 Domain Rd Section)**, Domain Hill, (Multi-stry), 12 apts acc up to 6, (2 bedrm), [shwr, bath, tlt, fan, c/fan, heat, tel, TV, video-fee, refrig, cook fac, micro, toaster, ldry (in unit), blkts, linen, pillows], c/park (carport), cots-fee. **D $132 - $203**, ⚹&.

★★★ **(49 Tivoli Rd Section)**, Tivoli, 12 apts acc up to 6, (2 bedrm), [shwr, bath, tlt, tel, TV, clock radio, refrig, cook fac, micro, d/wash, toaster, ldry (in unit), blkts, linen, pillows], secure park. **D $132 - $203**, ⚹&.

★★★ **Aston Apartments**, (HU), 42 Powell St, 100m S of PO, ☎ 03 9866 2953, fax 03 9867 8685, (Multi-stry), 12 units acc up to 3, (1 bedrm), [shwr, bath, tlt, a/c-cool, heat, elec blkts, tel, TV, clock radio, refrig, cook fac, micro, toaster, blkts, linen, pillows], ldry, pool, sauna, spa, cots-fee. **D ♦♦ $95 - $110**, ⚹ **$15**, **W ♦♦ $560 - $665**, ⚹ **$105**, AE BC MC VI.

★★★ **(45 Albion St Section)**, (Multi-stry), 6 units acc up to 4, (2 bedrm), [shwr, bath, tlt, a/c-cool, heat, tel, TV, clock radio, refrig, cook fac, micro, d/wash, toaster, ldry (in unit), blkts, linen, pillows], c/park (undercover). **D ♦♦♦♦ $150 - $175**, ⚹ **$15**, **W ♦♦♦♦ $840 - $980**, ⚹ **$105**.

★★★ **(51 Davis Ave Section)**, (Multi-stry gr fl), 12 units acc up to 2, (1 bedrm), [shwr, bath, tlt, a/c, heat, tel, TV, clock radio, refrig, cook fac, micro, d/wash, toaster, blkts, linen, pillows], ldry, pool, sauna, spa, c/park (undercover), cots-fee. **D ♦♦ $95 - $110**, ⚹ **$15**, **W ♦♦ $560 - $665**, ⚹ **$105**.

★★★ **(6 Powell St Section)**, (Multi-stry), 12 units acc up to 2, (1 bedrm), [shwr, bath, tlt, a/c-cool, heat, elec blkts, tel, TV, clock radio, refrig, cook fac, micro, d/wash, toaster, blkts, linen, pillows], ldry, cots-fee. **D ♦♦ $95 - $110**, ⚹ **$15**, **W ♦♦ $560 - $665**, ⚹ **$105**.

★★★ **(85 Caroline St Section)**, (Multi-stry), 18 units acc up to 2, (1 bedrm), [shwr, bath, tlt, a/c-cool, heat, tel, TV, clock radio, refrig, cook fac, micro, toaster, blkts, linen, pillows], ldry, cots-fee. **D ♦♦ $95 - $110**, ⚹ **$15**, **W ♦♦ $560 - $665**, ⚹ **$105**.

★★☆ **(49 Davis St Section)**, (Multi-stry gr fl), 12 apts acc up to 4, (2 bedrm), [shwr, bath, tlt, tel, TV, refrig, cook fac, micro, blkts, linen, pillows], ldry, c/park. **D ♦♦♦♦ $150 - $175**, ⚹ **$15**, **W ♦♦♦♦ $840 - $980**, ⚹ **$105**.

★★★ **Darling Towers Executive Apartments**, (Apt), 32 Darling St, 100m N of station, ☎ 03 9867 5200, fax 03 9866 8215, (Multi-stry), 14 apts acc up to 2, (1 bedrm), [shwr, tlt, a/c-cool, heat, elec blkts, tel, TV, clock radio, t/c mkg, refrig, cook fac, micro, toaster], ldry, iron, iron brd, c/park (carport) (8), cots-fee. **D $77 - $94**, **W $539 - $616**, AE BC DC EFT JCB MC VI.

Darling Towers Executive Apartments . . . cont

★★★★ **(30 Murphy St Section)**, (Multi-stry gr fl), 36 apts acc up to 4, (1 & 2 bedrm), [shwr, bath, tlt, fan, heat, elec blkts, tel, TV, video, clock radio, t/c mkg, refrig, cook fac, micro, d/wash, toaster, blkts, linen, pillows], iron, iron brd. **D $264, W $1,617**.

★★★★ **(47-49 Caroline St Section)**, 18 apts acc up to 6, (1, 2 & 3 bedrm), [shwr, bath, tlt, a/c-cool, heat, elec blkts, tel, clock radio, t/c mkg, refrig, cook fac, micro, d/wash, toaster, blkts, linen, pillows], iron, iron brd, c/park. **D $176 - $380, W $1,120 - $2,520**.

★★★★ **(88 Park St Section)**, 3 units acc up to 5, (2 bedrm), [shwr, bath, tlt, a/c-cool, heat, elec blkts, tel (direct dial), TV, video, clock radio, t/c mkg, refrig, micro, d/wash, toaster, ldry (in unit), blkts, linen, pillows], iron, iron brd, pool (lap), gym. **D $275, W $1,694**.

★★★ **(22 Darling St Section)**, (Multi-stry gr fl), 15 apts acc up to 5, (2 bedrm), [shwr, bath, tlt, hairdry, a/c-cool, heat, elec blkts, tel, TV, clock radio, t/c mkg, refrig, cook fac, micro, d/wash, toaster, ldry (in unit), blkts, linen, pillows], iron, iron brd, c/park. **D $187, W $1,155**.

★★★ **(43 Caroline St Section)**, 36 apts acc up to 2, (1 bedrm), [shwr, bath, tlt, a/c-cool, heat, tel, TV, video, clock radio, refrig, cook fac, micro, toaster, blkts, linen, pillows]. **D $176, W $1,120**.

★★★ **(65 Tivoli Rd Section)**, (Multi-stry gr fl), 12 apts acc up to 3, (1 bedrm), [shwr, bath, tlt, heat, elec blkts, tel, TV, clock radio, t/c mkg, refrig, cook fac, micro, toaster, blkts, linen, pillows], ldry, iron, iron brd. **D $94, W $616**.

★★★ **(99 Osborne St Section)**, 9 apts acc up to 3, (1 bedrm), [shwr, bath, tlt, elec blkts, tel, clock radio, t/c mkg, refrig, cook fac, micro, toaster, ldry (in unit), blkts, linen, pillows], iron, iron brd, c/park. **D $110, W $728**.

(30 Davis St Section), 7 apts acc up to 2, (1 bedrm), [shwr, tlt, elec blkts, tel, clock radio, t/c mkg, refrig, cook fac, micro, toaster, ldry (in unit), blkts, linen, pillows], iron, iron brd, c/park. **D $110, W $728**, (Rating under review).

(41 Walsh St Section), 10 apts acc up to 3, (1 bedrm), [shwr, bath, tlt, elec blkts, tel, clock radio, t/c mkg, refrig, cook fac, micro, toaster, ldry (in unit), blkts, linen, pillows], iron, iron brd, c/park. **D $143, W $924**, (Rating under review).

(49 Osborne St Section), (Multi-stry gr fl), 7 apts acc up to 3, (1 bedrm), [shwr, bath, tlt, heat, tel, TV, clock radio, t/c mkg, refrig, cook fac, micro, toaster, ldry (in unit), blkts, linen, pillows], iron, iron brd, c/park. **D $110, W $728**, (Rating under review).

★★★ **South Yarra Gardens**, (Apt), 283 Domain Rd, Cnr Darling St, ☎ 03 9820 0266, fax 03 9820 4059, 18 apts acc up to 2, (Studio), [shwr, tlt, a/c, elec blkts, tel, TV, clock radio, refrig, cook fac, micro, toaster], ldry, iron, secure park (undercover). **RO ♦ $66 - $87**, ♦♦ **$72 - $92**, ⚹ **$10**, AE BC DC MC VI.

★★★ **South Yarra Place**, (Apt), 41 Margaret St, 400m E of Alfred Hospital, ☎ 03 9867 6595, (Multi-stry gr fl), 18 apts acc up to 6, (Studio, 1 & 2 bedrm), [shwr, tlt, a/c, heat, tel, TV, clock radio, t/c mkg, refrig, cook fac, toaster, blkts, doonas, linen, pillows], ldry, bbq, c/park. **D $71.50 - $165**, AE BC DC EFT MC VI.

B&B's/Guest Houses

★★★★ **Balmoral of Melbourne**, (B&B), 783 Punt Rd, ☎ 03 9866 4449, fax 03 9866 4449, 1 rm [shwr, bath, tlt, hairdry, fan, cent heat, elec blkts, TV, clock radio, CD, t/c mkg], lounge, c/park. **BLB ♦ $95 - $125**, ♦♦ **$115 - $145**, Front bedroom not listed or rated.

★★ **Claremont Budget 'Bed & Breakfast' Accom**, (B&B), 189 Toorak Rd, 50m E of South Yarra railway station, ☎ 03 9826 8000, fax 03 9827 8652, (Multi-stry), 81 rms [fan, heat, TV, refrig (8)], ldry, ✕, t/c mkg shared, c/park (limited), ✆, cots, non smoking rms (10). **BLB ♦ $53 - $62**, ♦♦ **$63 - $74**, ⚹ **$10**, ch con, AE BC DC EFT MC VI.

MELBOURNE - SPRINGVALE VIC 3171

Pop 27,605. (26km SE Melbourne). See map on page 697, ref D4. Residential south eastern suburb.

Hotels/Motels

★★☆ **Waltzing Matilda**, (LMH), Cnr Springvale & Heatherton Rds, ☎ 03 9546 1333, fax 03 9558 5713, (2 stry gr fl), 17 units [shwr, bath, tlt, a/c, tel, TV, clock radio, t/c mkg, refrig, toaster], ldry, ✕, rm serv, c/park (limited), ✆, non smoking units (6). **RO ♦ $71.50**, ⚹ **$15**, Light breakfast only available. AE BC DC EFT MC VI.

MELBOURNE - ST ANDREWS VIC 3761

Pop 350. (43km NE Melbourne), See map on page 697, ref E2. Rural district, close to Kinglake. Tennis.

B&B's/Guest Houses

★★★★☆ **Adams of North Riding Restaurant**, (B&B), No children's facilities, 1726 Heidelberg-Kinglake Rd, ☎ 03 9710 1461, fax 03 9710 1541, 2 rms [ensuite, spa bath, hairdry, a/c, c/fan, cent heat, elec blkts, TV, clock radio, t/c mkg, refrig, mini bar, doonas], lounge (cd player, stereo), ☒ (Thur to Sun), non smoking property. **BB ♨ $155, DBB ♨ $315**, Dinner by arrangement - Mon to Wed, AE BC DC EFT MC VI.

★★★★ **Indarra Bed & Breakfast**, (B&B), 50 Tarra Pl, 4km E of PO, off Buttermans Track ☎ 03 9710 1191, fax 03 9710 1191, 2 rms (1 suite) [shwr, tlt, hairdry, c/fan, cent heat, TV, clock radio, CD, t/c mkg, refrig, cook fac ltd, micro, toaster, doonas], pool (salt water), sauna, spa (heated), bbq, cots, non smoking property. **BB ♨ $100 - $130**, ch con.

MELBOURNE - ST KILDA VIC 3182

Pop Part of City of Port Phillip, (5km S Melbourne), See map on page 697, ref C4. Inner residential suburb and tourist precinct. Boat Ramp, Boating, Bowls, Sailing, Squash, Swimming (Bay), Water Skiing.

Hotels/Motels

★★★★☆ **Novotel St Kilda**, (Ltd Lic H), No children's facilities, 16 The Esplanade, ☎ 03 9525 5522, fax 03 9525 5678, (Multi-stry), 209 rms (6 suites) [shwr, bath, spa bath (49), tlt, hairdry, a/c, tel, TV, movie, clock radio, t/c mkg, refrig, mini bar], lift, ldry, iron, iron brd, conf fac, ☒, pool-heated (salt water), sauna, spa, 24hr reception, rm serv, c/park (undercover), gym, cots, non smoking flr (4). **RO ♦ $172 - $297, ♨ $172 - $297, ◊ $43, Suite D $422 - $572**, AE BC DC JCB MC VI, ♿.

★★★★ **Kimberley Gardens**, (M), 441 Inkerman St, St Kilda East 3183, ☎ 03 9526 3888, fax 03 9525 9691, (2 stry gr fl), 41 units (11 suites) [shwr, spa bath (14), tlt, hairdry, a/c, elec blkts, tel, cable tv, video, clock radio, t/c mkg, refrig, cook fac (11), micro (11), d/wash (11), toaster (11)], lift, ldry, business centre, ☒ (Sun to Thur), pool indoor heated, spa, bbq, 24hr reception, rm serv, gym, cots. **RO ♦ $200 - $275, ♨ $200 - $275, ◊ $20**, ch con, AE BC DC MC VI, ♿.

★★★★☆ **(Serviced Apartment Section)**, (2 stry), 6 apts acc up to 6, (2 & 3 bedrm), [shwr, bath, spa bath, tlt, a/c, tel, cable tv, video, clock radio, refrig, cook fac, micro, d/wash, toaster, ldry (in unit), blkts, linen, pillows], w/mach, dryer, conf fac, secure park. **D $250 - $385, W $1,350**.

★★★☆ **Cabana Court Motel**, (M), 46 Park St, St Kilda West 3182, 200m N of PO, ☎ 03 9534 0771, fax 03 9525 3484, (2 stry gr fl), 16 units (16 suites) [shwr, bath, tlt, hairdry, a/c, elec blkts, tel, TV, clock radio, t/c mkg, refrig, cook fac, micro, toaster], ldry, iron, iron brd, cots. **RO ♦ $99 - $120, ♨ $99 - $120, ◊ $15**, ch con, AE BC DC MC VI.

★★★☆ **Cosmopolitan Motor Inn**, (M), 6 Carlisle St, 200m E of Luna Park, ☎ 03 9534 0781, fax 03 9534 8262, (Multi-stry gr fl), 78 units [shwr, bath (25), spa bath (26), tlt, hairdry, a/c, cent heat, tel, TV, video (avail), movie, clock radio, t/c mkg, refrig, cook fac ltd (25), toaster (25), ldry], lift, conf fac, ☒, cafe, 24hr reception, rm serv, c/park (undercover), ✆, cots, non smoking units (24). **BLB ♦ $120 - $130, ♨ $120 - $130, ◊ $14**, ch con, AE BC DC EFT MC VI.

★★★☆ **(Apartment Section)**, (Multi-stry gr fl), 7 apts acc up to 4, (1 bedrm), [shwr, tlt, hairdry, a/c, tel, video (avail), movie, clock radio, refrig, cook fac, blkts, linen, pillows], ldry. **RO ♦ $145, ♨ $145, ◊ $16**, ch con.

★★★☆ **Crest on Barkly Hotel Melbourne**, (LMH), 47 Barkly St, 100m E of St Kilda junction, ☎ 03 9537 1788, fax 03 9534 0609, (Multi-stry), 60 units [shwr, bath, tlt, hairdry, a/c, elec blkts, tel, TV, clock radio, t/c mkg, refrig], lift, ldry, iron, iron brd, conf fac, ☒, sauna, 24hr reception, rm serv, cots. **RO ♦ $109 - $157, ♨ $109 - $157, ◊ $15**, ch con, AE BC DC MC VI.

★★★ **Charnwood Motor Inn**, (M), 3 Charnwood Rd, 4 Km SE of City, ☎ 03 9525 4199, fax 03 9525 4587, (Multi-stry), 20 units [shwr, bath (2), tlt, a/c, elec blkts, tel, TV, clock radio, t/c mkg, refrig, toaster], 24hr reception, c/park (undercover), cots-fee, non smoking units (2). **RO ♦ $77 - $83, ♨ $83 - $99, ◊ $11**, ch con, AE BC DC EFT MC VI.

★★ **Bayside St Kilda**, (M), 63 Fitzroy St, 400m E of St Kilda beach, ☎ 03 9525 3833, fax 03 9534 8131, (2 stry) 40 units [ensuite, fan, heat, TV, t/c mkg, refrig], 24hr reception, ✆, cots, non smoking rms (4). **BLB ♦ $60 - $70, ♨ $72 - $85, ◊ $10**, ch con, AE BC DC EFT MC VI.

★★ **Carlisle Lodge Motel**, (M), 32 Carlisle St, 400m E of PO, ☎ 03 9534 0316, (2 stry gr fl), 18 units [shwr, bath (2), tlt, a/c-cool, heat, TV, t/c mkg, refrig, cook fac (3), toaster], ✆, cots. **RO ♦ $82, ♨ $82**, ch con, No breakfast available, AE BC DC MC VI.

Self Catering Accommodation

★★★★☆ **Apartments of Melbourne**, (Apt), Maddison, 157 Fitzroy St, ☎ 03 9820 1000, fax 03 9820 0900, (Multi-stry) 41 apts acc up to 7, (1, 2 & 3 bedrm), [shwr, bath (39), tlt, hairdry, a/c, c/fan, tel, TV, video-fee, movie, clock radio, CD, t/c mkg, refrig, cook fac, micro, d/wash, toaster, ldry (in unit), blkts, doonas, linen, pillows], lift, iron, iron brd, secure park, cots-fee, non smoking units (8). **D $143 - $522**, AE BC DC EFT MC VI.

★★★★ **Barkly Quest Lodgings**, (Apt), 180 Barkly St, 600m SW of PO, ☎ 03 9525 5000, fax 03 9525 3618, 23 apts acc up to 4, (1 bedrm), [shwr, bath, tlt, hairdry, a/c, heat, elec blkts, tel, TV, video (avail), clock radio, t/c mkg, refrig, cook fac, micro, toaster, ldry (in unit)], blkts, linen, pillows], w/mach, dryer, iron, iron brd, bbq, secure park, cots. **D $94 - $116, W $658**, Light breakfast available. AE BC DC EFT MC VI.

★★★★ **Royal Albert Apartments**, (Apt), 12 Acland St, ☎ 03 9536 8988, fax 03 9536 8989, (Multi-stry gr fl), 22 apts acc up to 6, (1 & 2 bedrm), [shwr, spa bath (6), tlt, hairdry, a/c, tel, TV, video, clock radio, refrig, cook fac, micro, d/wash, toaster, ldry (in unit), blkts, doonas, linen, pillows], lift, iron, iron brd, pool, secure park, cots. **D ♨ $154 - $220, ♨♨ $264, ◊ $33, W $970.20 - $1,578.50**, AE BC DC EFT MC VI.

★★★★ **St Kilda Quest Inn**, (Apt), 1 Eildon Rd, 300m N of PO, ☎ 03 9593 9500, fax 03 9525 4571, (Multi-stry), 48 apts acc up to 5, (Studio, 1 & 2 bedrm), [shwr, tlt, a/c, heat, tel, TV, video, clock radio, t/c mkg, refrig, cook fac, micro, d/wash, toaster, ldry (in unit), blkts, linen, pillows], lift, w/mach, dryer, iron, iron brd, pool-heated (solar), secure park, gym, cots. **D $132 - $190, W $833 - $1,197**, Minimum booking all Melbourne major events, AE BC DC MC VI.

S

MELBOURNE & SUBURBS – VICTORIA

★★★ **Redan Quest Lodgings**, (Apt), 25 Redan St, St Kilda East 3183, 1km N of PO, ☎ 03 9529 7595, fax 03 9521 2269, (Multi-stry), 41 apts acc up to 3, (Studio), [shwr, tlt, c/fan, cent heat, tel, TV, video (avail), clock radio, refrig, cook fac ltd, micro, toaster, blkts, linen, pillows], ldry, c/park (undercover), cots. D $78 - $105, Light breakfast available. AE BC DC MC VI.

★★★ **Warwick Beachside**, (HU), 363 Beaconsfield Pde, 200m W of Yacht Club, ☎ 03 9525 4800, fax 03 9537 1056, (Multi-stry gr fl), 64 units acc up to 5, (Studio, 1 & 2 bedrm), [shwr, tlt, fan, heat, tel, TV, movie, refrig, cook fac, micro (38), toaster, blkts, linen, pillows], ldry, w/mach-fee, dryer-fee, bbq, security gates. D $65 - $125, W $350 - $690, 17 units ★★★. AE BC EFT MC VI.

B&B's/Guest Houses

★★★★☆ **Keslan Hall**, (B&B), 57 Blessington St, ☎ 03 9593 9198, fax 03 9593 9812, (2 stry), 2 rms [ensuite, bath (1), hairdry, a/c-cool, fan, heat, elec blkts, TV, clock radio, t/c mkg], iron, iron brd, lounge (CD). BB ♦ $130, ♦♦ $155 - $165, ◊ $30, Minimum booking all Melbourne major events, AE BC DC MC VI.

★★★☆ **Robinsons by the Sea**, (B&B), 335 Beaconsfield Pde, St Kilda West 3182, ☎ 03 9534 2683, fax 03 9534 2683, (2 stry gr fl), 5 rms [hairdry, fan, fire pl (1), heat, elec blkts, TV, clock radio, t/c mkg, doonas], lounge (TV, cd player), spa. BB $135 - $185, AE BC DC MC VI.

★★★☆ **Victoria House International**, (B&B), 57 Mary St, St Kilda West 3182, 150m NW of St Kilda West PO, ☎ 03 9525 4512, fax 03 9525 3024, (2 stry gr fl), 2 rms [hairdry, cent heat, elec blkts, TV, clock radio, t/c mkg, refrig (1), cook fac (1)], lounge, non smoking property. BB ♦ $110, ♦♦ $120, Other meals by arrangement.

★★★ **Tolarno Boutique Hotel**, (PH), 42 Fitzroy St, 50m N of PO, ☎ 03 9537 0200, fax 03 9534 7800, (Multi-stry), 34 rms (4 suites) [shwr, bath (2), tlt, hairdry, a/c-cool (18), c/fan (16), heat, tel, TV, video (avail), clock radio, t/c mkg, refrig, cook fac (4), micro (4)], iron, iron brd, conf fac, bbq, non smoking rms. RO ♦♦ $130 - $160, Suite RO $180 - $260, ◊ $20, Light breakfast only, Minimum booking all Melbourne major events, AE BC DC EFT MC VI.

Other Accommodation

Olembia Private Hotel, (Lodge), 96 Barkly St, ☎ 03 9537 1412, fax 03 9537 1600, (2 stry gr fl), 21 rms [basin, cent heat], shwr (5G/L), tlt (6G/L), ldry, lounge (TV), cook fac, t/c mkg shared, refrig, bbq, c/park (limited), ✆, cots, non smoking property. RO ♦ $48, ♦♦ $70, AE BC MC VI.

Oslo Private Hotel, (Lodge), 38 Grey St, 150m fr PO, ☎ 03 9525 4498, fax 03 9530 0018, 90 rms [ensuite (4), heat, blkts, linen, pillows], shwr (15G/L), tlt (14G/L), lounge (TV), cook fac, refrig, ✆. RO ♦ $14 - $44, ♦♦ $50 - $70, ◊ $15, AE BC EFT MC VI.

St Kilda Coffee Palace Backpackers Inn, (Lodge), 24 Grey St, ☎ 03 9534 5283, fax 03 9593 9166, (Multi-stry), 48 rms [ensuite (12), cable tv, linen, pillows], shwr (12G/L), tlt (15G/L), ldry, lounge (TV), cafe (Internet), cook fac, refrig, bbq, c/park (limited), courtesy transfer, ✆. D ♦ $15 - $20, ◊ $15 - $20, BC MC VI.

MELBOURNE - SUNBURY VIC 3429

Pop 22,150. (40km N Melbourne), See map on page 697, ref A1. Picturesque residential town on Jacksons Creek. Bowls, Golf, Horse Riding, Squash, Swimming (Pool), Tennis.

Hotels/Motels

★★★☆ **Sunbury Motor Inn Motel**, (M), Cnr Ligar St & Gap Rd, 900m W of PO, ☎ 03 9740 4000, fax 03 9740 4888, 13 units [shwr, spa bath (1), tlt, a/c, elec blkts, tel, TV, video-fee, clock radio, t/c mkg, refrig, toaster], ldry, non smoking units (7). RO ♦ $77 - $99.50, ♦♦ $93.50 - $121, ◊ $16.50, AE BC DC EFT MC VI, ♿.

B&B's/Guest Houses

★★★☆ **Country Rose Lodge**, (B&B), Closed Jun & Jul. 46 Jackson St, ☎ 03 9740 7508, (2 stry), 3 rms [a/c-cool (1), c/fan (2), cent heat, elec blkts, clock radio], rec rm, lounge (TV, video, cd), t/c mkg shared, bbq, non smoking property. D ♦ $89, ♦♦ $99, ◊ $22, AE BC MC VI.

★★★ **The Bluegum Suite**, (B&B), 6 O'Malley Crt, ☎ 03 9744 3172, fax 03 8601 2222, 2 rms [shwr, tlt, heat, elec blkts, TV, radio, t/c mkg, refrig, toaster], c/park (carport), non smoking property. BLB ♦♦ $55 - $65, ch con.

MELBOURNE - SUNSHINE VIC 3020

Pop Part of Melbourne, (13km W Melbourne), See map on page 697, ref B3. Industrial suburb.

Hotels/Motels

★★☆ **Sunshine Motor Inn**, (M), 608 Ballarat Rd (Western Hwy), 800m from Western Ring Road, ☎ 03 9363 1899, fax 03 9363 5645, (2 stry gr fl), 41 units [shwr, tlt, hairdry, a/c, elec blkts, tel, movie, clock radio, t/c mkg, refrig, mini bar (30)], iron (30), iron brd (30), conf fac, ✉, pool, 24hr reception, rm serv, cots-fee, non smoking units (9). BLB ♦ $104 - $120, ♦♦ $104 - $120, ◊ $10, ch con, 13 units ★★★, 6 units ★★★★. AE BC DC EFT MC VI.

★★ **West City Motel**, (M), 610 Ballarat Rd (Western Hwy), ☎ 03 9360 5230, fax 03 9363 3262, 34 units [shwr, tlt, a/c, elec blkts, TV, t/c mkg, refrig], ldry, cots-fee. RO ♦ $65, ♦♦ $65, ◊ $11, BC MC VI.

MELBOURNE - SURREY HILLS VIC 3127

Pop Part of City of Whitehorse, (14km E Melbourne). See map on page 697, ref D3. A residential suburb, particularly noted for its many parks and gardens and tree-lined streets.

B&B's/Guest Houses

★★★★ **Chestnut Cottage**, (B&B), 15 Chestnut St, ☎ 03 9808 6644, fax 03 9808 6633, 1 rm [shwr, tlt, a/c, fan, elec blkts, TV, video, clock radio, t/c mkg, refrig, toaster], pool-heated (solar), non smoking property. BLB ♦ $75 - $95, ♦♦ $110 - $130, *Operator Comment: Charming, modern cottage separated from the main residence and situated in a tranquil garden. See www.chestnutcottage.com.au*

MELBOURNE - TEMPLESTOWE LOWER VIC 3107

(19km NE Melbourne), See map on page 697, ref D3. Residential suburb. Fishing, Tennis.

Self Catering Accommodation

★★★★ **Jimon's**, (HU), 40 Ironbark Dve, 14Kms E of CBD, ☎ 03 9850 9775, fax 03 9850 9775, 2 units acc up to 5, (1 & 2 bedrm), [shwr, tlt, c/fan, heat, TV, video, clock radio, t/c mkg, refrig, cook fac ltd, micro, elec frypan (1), blkts, doonas, linen, pillows], ldry, w/mach, pool-heated, bbq, plygr, cots, non smoking property. D ♦ $70 - $90, ♦♦ $75 - $95, ◊ $12.50 - $15, W ♦ $385 - $490, ♦♦ $420 - $525, ◊ $87.50 - $105, ch con, 1 unit ★★★☆.

MELBOURNE - TEMPLESTOWE VIC 3106

Pop Part of City of Manningham, (19km NE Melbourne), See map on page 697, ref D3. Suburb of Melbourne situated in Yarra Parklands area.

B&B's/Guest Houses

★★★☆ **Kookaburra Corner**, (B&B), 19 Unwin St, ☎ 03 9846 3800, fax 03 9846 3391, 2 rms [hairdry, c/fan (1), cent heat, elec blkts, TV, clock radio], lounge (TV, video, cd), t/c mkg shared. BB ♦ $75, ♦♦ $90, ◊ $30, ch con.

MELBOURNE - THOMASTOWN VIC 3074

Pop 23,812. (17km N Melbourne), See map on page 697, ref C2. Light industrial outer northern suburb. Swimming (Pool).

Hotels/Motels

★★ **The Excelsior Hotel Motel**, (LMH), 82 Mahoneys Rd, ☎ 03 9460 3666, fax 03 9460 5612, (2 stry gr fl), 14 units [shwr, tlt, a/c, elec blkts, TV, t/c mkg, refrig], ldry, ✕, ☎. RO ♦ $75, ♦♦ $75 - $90, ◊ $15, Light breakfast only available. AE BC DC EFT MC VI.

MELBOURNE - THORNBURY VIC 3071

Pop Part of Melbourne, (9km N Melbourne), See map on page 697, ref C3. Residential suburb of Melbourne. Bowls, Swimming (Pool).

Hotels/Motels

 ★★★☆ **Flag Inn St Georges**, (M), Previously St Georges Motor Inn 334 St Georges Rd, ☎ 03 9416 8233, fax 03 9416 9707, (2 stry gr fl), 28 units [shwr, spa bath (3), tlt, hairdry (11), a/c, elec blkts, tel, cable tv, video-fee, movie, clock radio, t/c mkg, refrig], ldry, conf fac, ✕, rm serv, cots-fee. D ♦ $120 - $175, ♦♦ $120 - $175, ch con, AE BC DC EFT JCB MC MP VI, ₰₠.

MELBOURNE - TOORAK VIC 3142

Pop Part of Melbourne, (7km SE Melbourne), See map on page 697, ref C3. Exclusive inner Melbourne suburb known for its shops, bars and restaurants. Bowls, Rowing.

B&B's/Guest Houses

 ★★★★☆ **Flag Heritage Toorak Manor**, (PH), Previously Toorak Manor, 220 Williams Rd, opposite Hawksburn Station, ☎ 03 9827 2689, fax 03 9824 2830, (2 stry gr fl), 18 rms [shwr, tlt, a/c, cent heat, elec blkts, tel, TV, clock radio, mini bar, doonas], lounge, non smoking rms (5). BLB ♦♦ $145 - $200, AE BC DC MC VI.

MELBOURNE - TULLAMARINE VIC 3043

Pop Part of Melbourne, (21km NW Melbourne), See map on page 697, ref B2. International airport. Freeway runs from the airport to Flemington Rd.

Hotels/Motels

 ★★★★ **Tullamarine Airport Motor Inn**, (M), 265 Mickleham Rd, 4km E of Melbourne Airport, ☎ 03 9338 3222, fax 03 9338 3818, (2 stry gr fl), 69 units [shwr, bath, spa bath (21), tlt, hairdry, a/c, elec blkts, tel, cable tv-fee, movie, clock radio, t/c mkg, refrig], ldry, iron, iron brd, conf fac, ✕, bar (cocktail), pool, spa, 24hr reception, rm serv, courtesy transfer, ☎, tennis, cots-fee. RO ♦ $124, ♦♦ $136, ◊ $14, AE BC DC EFT MC VI.

★★★☆ **Ciloms Airport Lodge**, (M), 398 Melrose Dve, 1.5km E of International airport terminal, ☎ 03 9335 2788, fax 03 9335 4388, (Multi-stry gr fl), 81 units (1 suite) [shwr, bath (20), spa bath (10), tlt, hairdry, a/c, elec blkts, tel, TV, video, clock radio, t/c mkg, refrig], ldry, iron, iron brd, conf fac, ✕ (Mon to Sat), bar (cocktail), pool indoor heated, sauna, spa, bbq, 24hr reception, rm serv, courtesy transfer, ☎, gym, cots, non smoking units (2). BLB ♦♦ $121, ♦♦♦ $131, Suite D $220, 32 units ★★★★. AE BC DC EFT MC VI, ₰₠.

★★ **Gladstone Park Hotel**, (LMH), Mickleham Rd, adjacent to Gladstone Park shopping centre, ☎ 03 9338 3723, fax 03 9338 6969, (2 stry gr fl), 13 units [shwr, tlt, a/c, TV, clock radio, t/c mkg, refrig, toaster], ldry, conf fac, ✕, ☎. BLB ♦ $65, ♦♦ $75, ♦♦♦ $85, ch con, Light breakfast only available. AE BC DC EFT MC VI.

MELBOURNE - VERMONT VIC 3133

Pop 22,396. (17km E Melbourne), See map on page 697, ref D3. Suburb of Melbourne. Tennis.

Self Catering Accommodation

★★★☆ **AA Relocation & Holiday Homes**, (House), 3 Cantley La, ☎ 03 9873 3060, fax 03 9874 3141, 1 house acc up to 6, (3 bedrm), [ensuite (1), shwr, bath, tlt, hairdry, fan, cent heat, elec blkts, tel, TV, video, clock radio, refrig, cook fac, micro, elec frypan, d/wash, toaster, ldry, blkts, doonas, linen, pillows], w/mach, dryer, iron, iron brd, lounge, lounge firepl, bbq, c/park (carport), non smoking property. W $770 - $945, Min book applies.

AA Relocation & Holiday Homes . . . cont

★★★★☆ **(Cottage Section)**, (2 stry gr fl), 1 cotg acc up to 6, (3 bedrm), [ensuite (1), shwr, bath, tlt, hairdry, c/fan, heat, tel (local calls), TV, video, clock radio, refrig, cook fac, micro, elec frypan, d/wash, toaster, blkts, doonas, linen, pillows], w/mach, dryer, iron, iron brd. W $770 - $945, Min book applies.

B&B's/Guest Houses

★★★★☆ **Benriana Bed & Breakfast**, (B&B), 81 Terrara Rd, Vermont South 3133, ☎ 03 9800 2210, fax 03 9800 2210, 2 rms [shwr, bath (1), tlt, hairdry (1), c/fan, cent heat, TV, clock radio, t/c mkg, refrig], lounge (cd), lounge firepl, ✕. BB ♦ $95 - $105, ♦♦ $130 - $150, ◊ $85 - $95, BC MC VI.

MELBOURNE - WANTIRNA VIC 3152

Pop Part of City of Knox, (26km E Melbourne), See map on page 697, ref E4. Residential eastern suburb. Squash, Tennis.

Hotels/Motels

★★★★ **Hotel Cavalier**, (M), Previously Cavalier Motor Inn 343 Stud Rd, Wantirna South 3152, ☎ 03 9801 9733, fax 03 9887 1359, (2 stry gr fl), 39 units (20 suites) [shwr, spa bath (5), tlt, hairdry, a/c, elec blkts, tel, TV, clock radio, t/c mkg, refrig, cook fac (4), micro (4)], ldry, iron (20), iron brd (20), conf fac, pool, sauna, spa, bbq, cots-fee, non smoking units (12). RO ♦ $100 - $150, ♦♦ $100 - $150, ◊ $10, ch con, 19 units ★★★☆. AE BC DC EFT MC VI, ₰₠.

★★★☆ **King Village Resort**, (M), 137 Mountain Hwy, ☎ 03 9801 6044, fax 03 9800 3550, (2 stry gr fl), 60 units (2 suites) [shwr, bath (16), spa bath (6), tlt, hairdry, a/c, elec blkts, tel, TV, clock radio, t/c mkg, refrig, cook fac ltd (16), micro (16), ldry (in unit) (16)], ldry, iron, iron brd, conf fac, ✕, pool, 24hr reception, rm serv, ☎, cots. RO ♦ $119 - $129, ♦♦ $119 - $129, ◊ $12, Suite D ♦ $149 - $179, ♦♦ $149 - $179, ◊ $12, ch con, AE BC DC EFT MC VI, ₰₠.

B&B's/Guest Houses

★★★★ **Litande**, (B&B), Closed May 1 to Jul 30, 27 White Rd, Wantirna South 3152, ☎ 03 9801 4117, fax 03 9801 4117, (2 stry), 1 rm [shwr, tlt, hairdry, a/c, c/fan, cent heat, elec blkts, TV, video, clock radio, t/c mkg, refrig], ldry, iron, iron brd, bbq. BLB ♦ $90, ♦♦ $90 - $100, ◊ $15 - $20.

MELBOURNE - WARRANDYTE VIC 3113

Pop Part of City of Manningham, (29km E Melbourne), See map on page 697, ref E3. Residential outer eastern suburb, situated on the Yarra River. Bush Walking, Canoeing, Scenic Drives, Squash, Tennis.

Self Catering Accommodation

★★★★ **Kembla Cottage**, (Cotg), 36 Tills Dve, ☎ 03 9844 2301, fax 03 9844 4013, 1 cotg acc up to 2, (1 bedrm), [shwr, tlt, hairdry, fan, heat, elec blkts, clock radio, refrig, cook fac ltd, micro, elec frypan, toaster, blkts, doonas, linen, pillows], iron, iron brd, lounge (TV, video, cd player), pool, bbq, tennis, breakfast ingredients, non smoking property. BB ♦♦ $150, BC MC VI.

B&B's/Guest Houses

★★★★ **Warrandyte Goldfields Bed & Breakfast**, (B&B), Cnr Yarra & Whipstick Gully Rd, ☎ 03 9844 0666, fax 03 9844 2199, (2 stry), 5 rms [ensuite, spa bath (1), a/c-cool (3), a/c (1), c/fan, cent heat, elec blkts, TV, clock radio], ldry, lounge (TV, cd player), t/c mkg shared, bbq. BB ♦ $88, ♦♦ $99 - $130, ◊ $20, ch con, BC MC VI.

MELBOURNE - WERRIBEE VIC 3030

Pop 23,461. (32km SW Melbourne), See map on page 697, ref A4. Residential township, on the outer fringe of the metropolitan area. The Werribee Zoo is located on the remaining farmland of Werribee Park, a historic mansion with splendid gardens and parkland. Boating, Fishing, Golf, Horse Racing, Shooting, Swimming.

Hotels/Motels

 ★★★★ **Best Western Werribee Motor Lodge**, (M), 6 Tower Rd, ☎ 03 9741 9944, fax 03 9742 4709, (2 stry gr fl), 20 units [shwr, spa bath (3), tlt, hairdry, a/c, elec blkts, tel, TV, movie, clock radio, t/c mkg, refrig, toaster], ldry-fee, iron, iron brd, pool, bbq, plygr, cots-fee, non smoking units (15). RO ♦ $98 - $130, ♦♦ $108 - $155, ◊ $12, AE BC DC EFT MC MP VI, ₰₠.

W

MELBOURNE & SUBURBS – VICTORIA

Best Western Werribee Motor Lodge . . . *continued*

★★★★ **(Apartment Section)**, (2 stry gr fl), 6 apts acc up to 4, (2 bedrm), [shwr, tlt, a/c-cool, heat, elec blkts, tel, TV, movie, clock radio, t/c mkg, refrig, cook fac, elec frypan, toaster, blkts, linen, pillows], ldry-fee, iron, iron brd. **D ♦♦♦♦ $175, ◊ $12.**

★★★ **Werribee Park Motor Inn**, (M), 112 Duncans Rd, 1km E of PO, ☎ 03 9741 7222, fax 03 9741 8553, 20 units [shwr, spa bath (2), tlt, hairdry, a/c, elec blkts, tel, TV, video-fee, clock radio, t/c mkg, refrig, toaster], iron, iron brd, pool, spa, bbq, plygr, cots-fee, non smoking units (7). **RO ♦ $75 - $107, ♦♦ $85 - $130, ◊ $10,** ch con, AE BC DC EFT MC MCH VI.

MELBOURNE - WEST MELBOURNE VIC 3003

Pop Part of Melbourne, (2km W Melbourne), See map on page 697, ref C3. Inner suburb of Melbourne.

Hotels/Motels

★★★ **Flagstaff City Motor Inn**, (M), 45 Dudley St, 1.8km NW of GPO, ☎ 03 9329 5788, fax 03 9329 8559, (2 stry) 39 units [shwr, bath (10), tlt, hairdry, a/c-cool, cent heat, elec blkts, tel, TV, clock radio, t/c mkg, refrig, micro (16), toaster], ldry, spa, 24hr reception, c/park (limited), cots-fee. **RO ♦ $102 - $160, ♦♦ $112 - $160, ◊ $15,** ch con, AE BC DC EFT MC VI.

B&B's/Guest Houses

★★ **Miami Motor Inn**, (PH), 13 Hawke St, 2.1km NW of GPO, ☎ 03 9329 8499, fax 03 9328 1820, (Multi-stry gr fl), 86 rms [basin, ensuite (32), c/fan (32), cent heat, TV (32), t/c mkg (32), refrig (32)], ldry, lounge (TV, video), c/park (limited undercover), ✆, cots-fee. **BB ♦ $44 - $78, ♦♦ $66 - $98, ◊ $15 - $20,** ch con, 32 rooms ★★★. BC EFT MC VI.

MELBOURNE - WESTMEADOWS VIC 3049

Pop Part of Melbourne, (17km NW Melbourne), See map on page 697, ref C2. Outer residential north western suburb. Tennis.

Hotels/Motels

AAA TOURISM *Special Rates*

★★★★ **Airport Motel & Convention Centre**, (M), Previously Airport Motel 33 Ardlie St, 1km N of Tullamarine Fwy, ☎ 03 9333 2200, fax 03 9333 2696, 103 units (1 suite) [shwr, spa bath (31), tlt, hairdry, a/c, elec blkts, tel, TV, clock radio, t/c mkg, refrig, mini bar], ldry, iron, iron brd, rec rm, conf fac, ✕, bar, pool-heated, spa, bbq-fee, 24hr reception, rm serv, courtesy transfer, cots, non smoking units (40). **RO $108 - $144,** ch con, AE BC DC EFT MC VI, ⅊.

★★★★ **(Apartment Section)**, (2 stry), 3 apts acc up to 2, (1 bedrm), [shwr, tlt, a/c, heat, elec blkts, tel, TV, clock radio, t/c mkg, refrig, mini bar, cook fac, elec frypan, toaster, ldry, blkts, linen, pillows], iron, iron brd, cots. **D $108 - $144.**

MELBOURNE - WHEELERS HILL VIC 3150

Pop Part of City of Monash, (26km SE Melbourne), See map on page 697, ref D4. Residential suburb. Tennis.

Hotels/Motels

★★★★☆ **Wheelers Hill International Motor Inn**, (M), 242 Jells Rd, ☎ 03 9561 3900, fax 03 9561 8672, (2 stry gr fl), 40 units (9 suites) [shwr, bath (8), spa bath (15), tlt, hairdry, a/c, tel, TV, video (avail), movie, clock radio, t/c mkg, refrig, mini bar], ldry, iron, iron brd, conf fac, ✕, bar (cocktail), pool, spa, 24hr reception, rm serv, cots-fee, non smoking units (4). **RO ♦ $173 - $206, ♦♦ $173 - $206, ◊ $22, Suite D $190 - $206,** ch con, AE BC DC EFT MC VI, ⅊.

MELBOURNE - WHITTLESEA VIC 3757

Pop 1,750. (40km N Melbourne), See map on page 697, ref D1. Agricultural and pastoral township. Whittlesea Show (Nov). Bowls, Golf, Squash, Swimming (Pool), Tennis.

B&B's/Guest Houses

★★★★ **Stonehaven Cottage**, (B&B), 145 Holts Rd, 7km NW of PO, ☎ 03 9716 1055, 1 rm [ensuite, elec blkts, TV, video, CD, refrig, cook fac ltd, micro, toaster], w/mach, lounge firepl, bbq. **BLB ♦ $50, ♦♦ $90 - $100,** Dinner by arrangement.

★★★ **Hiltonvale Homestead**, (GH), 485 Wallan Rd, 5.2km NE of PO, ☎ 03 9716 2744, 4 rms [elec blkts, TV, clock radio, refrig, cook fac ltd, micro, toaster], ldry, lounge, lounge firepl, sauna, spa, breakfast ingredients. **BLB ♦ $55, ♦♦ $77, ◊ $33,** 1 room ★★☆.

MELBOURNE - WILLIAMSTOWN VIC 3016

Pop 10,408. (13km W Melbourne), See map on page 697, ref B4. Bayside residential suburb. Bowls, Croquet, Swimming (Pool, Beach), Tennis.

Self Catering Accommodation

★★★★☆ **Quest Williamstown**, (Apt), 1 Syme St, ☎ 03 9393 5300, fax 03 9393 5350, (2 stry gr fl), 40 apts acc up to 5, (Studio, 1 & 2 bedrm), [shwr, bath, tlt, hairdry, a/c, tel, TV, video, clock radio, t/c mkg, refrig, cook fac, micro, d/wash, toaster, ldry (in unit), blkts, linen, pillows], lift, iron, iron brd, cots. **D $152.90 - $198, W $970.02 - $1,247.40,** Breakfast available. AE BC DC EFT MC VI, ⅊.

B&B's/Guest Houses

★★★★ **Heathville House**, (B&B), 171 Aitken St, ☎ 03 9397 5959, fax 03 9397 5959, 4 rms [hairdry, fan, fire pl, cent heat, elec blkts, clock radio], lounge (TV, video, cd), t/c mkg shared, non smoking property. **BB ♦ $85 - $110, ♦♦ $105 - $140, ◊ $40,** AE BC DC MC VI.

MELBOURNE - WONGA PARK VIC 3115

Pop 1,750. (36km NE Melbourne), See map on page 697, ref E3. Outer residential area. Swimming (River), Tennis, Vineyards, Wineries.

B&B's/Guest Houses

★★★★☆ **A Tudor Manor**, (B&B), 55 Jumping Creek Rd, ☎ 03 9722 2699, fax 03 9822 8994, (2 stry), 3 rms [shwr, spa bath (1), tlt, hairdry, a/c, fan, cent heat, TV, video, clock radio], rec rm, sauna, t/c mkg shared, bbq, cots-fee, non smoking property. **BB ♦ $125 - $150, ♦♦ $145 - $185, ◊ $20 - $30,** ch con, Min book Christmas Jan long w/ends and Easter, AE BC MC VI.

★★★★ **Jacqui & Johns Bed & Breakfast**, (B&B), 3 Inverbervie Crt, ☎ 03 9722 1775, fax 03 9722 1796, 2 rms [ensuite, hairdry, c/fan, heat, elec blkts, clock radio], lounge (TV, video), t/c mkg shared, refrig. **BB ♦ $60, ♦♦ $100,** AE BC MC VI.

MELBOURNE - YARRAVILLE VIC 3013

Pop Part of Melbourne, (9km W Melbourne), See map on page 697, ref B3. A suburb of Melbourne.

Self Catering Accommodation

★★★★☆ **Yarravillas**, (Apt), 357 Williamstown Rd, 6km W Melbourne GPO, ☎ 03 9314 6602, fax 03 9314 6679, 2 apts acc up to 5, (3 bedrm), [shwr, bath, tlt, hairdry, a/c-cool, heat, elec blkts, tel, TV, video, clock radio, CD, t/c mkg, refrig, cook fac, micro, d/wash, toaster, ldry (in unit), blkts, linen, pillows], iron, iron brd, bbq, secure park, non smoking units. **D ♦♦ $150, ◊ $20, W ♦♦♦♦ $990,** ch con, Min book applies, BC MC VI.

End of Melbourne and Suburbs

AIREYS INLET VIC 3231

Pop 750. (119km SW Melbourne), See map on page 696, ref A7. Seaside holiday resort. Historic lighthouse, Angahook Forest Park. Boating, Bush Walking, Fishing, Scenic Drives, Surfing, Swimming (Beach).

Hotels/Motels

★★★★ **Lightkeepers Inn Motel**, (M), 64 Great Ocean Rd, 400m S of PO, ☎ 03 5289 6666, fax 03 5289 6806, 20 units [shwr, spa bath (3), tlt, hairdry (12), a/c, elec blkts, tel, TV, video, clock radio, t/c mkg, refrig, micro (10), toaster], ldry, iron (13), iron brd (13), conf fac, pool-heated (solar), spa, bbq, cots-fee, non smoking units (6). **RO ♦ $69 - $155, ◊ $15,** 8 units ★★★. AE BC DC EFT MC VI, ⅊.

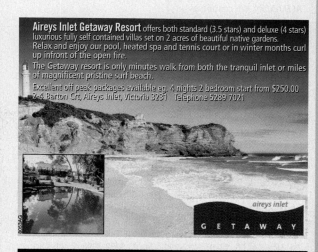
Self Catering Accommodation

★★★★☆ **Aireys-on-Aireys**, (Villa), 19 Aireys St, ☎ 03 5289 6844, fax 03 5289 6884, (2 stry), 4 villas acc up to 6, (2 & 3 bedrm), [shwr, spa bath, tlt, hairdry, a/c, heat (wood), tel, TV, video, clock radio, refrig, cook fac, micro, elec frypan, d/wash, toaster, ldry, blkts, linen, pillows], iron, iron brd, bbq, c/park (carport). **D $115 - $235, W $775 - $1,340**, Min book applies, BC MC VI.

★★★★☆ **Split Point Cottages**, (Cotg), 40 Hopkins St, 1km N of PO, ☎ 03 5289 6566, fax 03 5289 6500, 4 cotgs acc up to 5, (2 bedrm), [shwr, tlt, hairdry, heat, elec blkts, TV, video, clock radio, refrig, cook fac, micro, elec frypan, toaster, blkts, doonas, linen, pillows], ldry, w/mach-fee, dryer, iron, iron brd, spa (heated), bbq, tennis, cots, non smoking property. **D $121 - $154, W $847 - $990**, Min book all holiday times, BC EFT MC VI.

★★★☆ **Aireys Inlet Getaway**, (HU), 4 Barton Crt, ☎ 03 5289 7021, fax 03 5289 7021, 8 units acc up to 8, (2 & 3 bedrm), [shwr, spa bath, tlt, fan, fire pl, heat, elec blkts, TV, video, CD, refrig, cook fac, micro, ldry (in unit), doonas, linen], pool, spa, bbq (covered), tennis, cots. **D ♦♦♦♦ $45 - $235, W ♦♦♦♦ $650 - $1,600**, 3 units ★★★★, Min book Christmas Jan long w/ends and Easter, BC MC VI.

★★★☆ **The Glen Farm Cottages**, (Cotg), Hartleys Rd, via Bambra Rd, ☎ 03 5289 6306, fax 03 5289 6306, 4 cotgs acc up to 7, (2 & 3 bedrm - mudbrick.), [shwr, bath (1), tlt, a/c, heat (wood), TV, video, CD, refrig, cook fac, micro, elec frypan, toaster, linen reqd-fee], w/mach, bbq (gas), ☏, tennis. **D $135 - $175**, BC MC VI.

★★☆ **Lightkeepers Cottages**, (Cotg), Federal St, adjacent to lighthouse, ☎ 03 5289 6306, fax 03 5289 6306, 2 cotgs acc up to 6, (2 & 3 bedrm), [shwr, bath, tlt, heat, elec blkts, TV, video, radio, CD, refrig, cook fac, micro, toaster, blkts, doonas, linen, pillows], ldry, lounge firepl, bbq. **D $165 - $175, W $850 - $910**, BC MC VI.

B&B's/Guest Houses

★★★★☆ **Aireys by the Light**, (B&B), No children's facilities, 2 Federal St, 200m SW of Lighthouse, ☎ 03 5289 6134, fax 03 5289 6535, 3 rms [ensuite, shwr, spa bath (1), tlt, hairdry, a/c, cent heat, elec blkts, TV, clock radio, t/c mkg, refrig], ldry. **BB ♦ $121 - $187, ♦♦ $143 - $198**, BC EFT MC VI,

Operator Comment: Absolute Ocean Frontage. 200 metres from Lighthouse.

★★★★☆ **Lorneview Bed & Breakfast**, (B&B), 677 Great Ocean Rd, Eastern View 3231, 350m E of memorial archway, 5.8km W of PO, ☎ 03 5289 6430, 2 rms [ensuite, hairdry, a/c, c/fan, heat, elec blkts, TV, video, clock radio, CD, t/c mkg, refrig, toaster], rec rm, bbq, non smoking property. **BLB ♦♦ $100 - $150**, AE BC MC VI.

★★★★ **Aireys - River Bend**, (B&B), 7B River Rd, ☎ 03 5289 7137, fax 03 5289 7052, (2 stry), 1 rm [ensuite, hairdry, c/fan, heat, elec blkts, TV, clock radio], ldry, w/mach, dryer, bbq, non smoking property. **BB ♦♦ $100 - $130, ◊ $20**, BC MC VI.

★★★★ **(Holiday Unit Section)**, (2 stry), 1 unit acc up to 4, (2 bedrm), [shwr, bath, tlt, hairdry, fan, heat (wood), elec blkts, TV, video, clock radio, t/c mkg, cook fac ltd, micro, elec frypan, toaster], bbq, breakfast ingredients, non smoking property. **D ♦♦ $120 - $165, ◊ $20**.

★★★★ **Inlet Hideaway**, (B&B), 34 Hopkins St, 600m SE of PO, ☎ 03 5289 7471, (2 stry), 2 rms [shwr, tlt, c/fan, heat, elec blkts, clock radio, refrig], lounge (TV), t/c mkg shared, non smoking property. **BB ♦♦♦ $90 - $130**, BC EFT MC VI.

Pop 1,850. (130km NE Melbourne), See map on page 696, ref D4. Gateway to Fraser National Park. Boating, Bowls, Bush Walking, Fishing, Golf, Horse Riding, Sailing, Scenic Drives, Shooting, Squash, Swimming (Pool, Lake, River), Tennis, Water Skiing.

Hotels/Motels

★★★ **Alexandra Motor Inn**, (M), 76 Downey St (Maroondah Hwy), 600m W of PO, ☎ 03 5772 2077, fax 03 5772 2614, 16 units [shwr, tlt, a/c, elec blkts, tel, TV, video-fee, clock radio, t/c mkg, refrig], ldry, bbq. **RO ♦ $58, ♦♦ $68 - $70, ◊ $11**, ch con, AE BC DC EFT MC VI.

★★★ **Alexandra Redgate Motel**, (M), Cnr Rose & Nihil Sts, 1km SW of PO, ☎ 03 5772 1777, fax 03 5772 2808, 20 units [shwr, spa bath (1), tlt, a/c-cool, heat, elec blkts, tel, TV, t/c mkg, refrig], rec rm, conf fac, ✉, bbq, cots-fee, non smoking rms (14). **RO ♦ $55 - $65, ♦♦ $65 - $80, ◊ $19.20**, 6 units ★★☆. AE BC DC EFT MC VI.

ALEXANDRA VIC continued...

★☆ **Shamrock Hotel**, (LH), 80 Grant St, 200m S of PO, ☎ 03 5772 1015, fax 03 5772 2585, (2 stry), 9 rms [basin (4), evap cool, elec blkts, t/c mkg, refrig, toaster, doonas], ⊠, bbq, \. **BLB** ╫ **$25**, ╫╫ **$45**, Light breakfast only available. BC EFT MC VI.

★ **Mt Pleasant Hotel**, (LH), 90 Grant St, 300m W of PO, ☎ 03 5772 1083, (2 stry), 13 rms [basin, elec blkts, refrig (1), toaster, doonas], ⊠, t/c mkg shared, \. **BLB** ╫ **$25**, ◊ **$15**, ch con, Light breakfast only available. BC EFT MC VI.

Self Catering Accommodation
★★★★☆ **Crystal Creek Cottages**, (Cotg), 566 Crystal Creek Rd, 10.5km SW of PO, ☎ 03 5772 291, fax 03 5772 1048, 1 cotg acc up to 4, (2 bedrm), [shwr, spa bath, tlt, hairdry, a/c, c/fan, cent heat, elec blkts, TV, video, clock radio, CD, refrig, cook fac, micro, d/wash, toaster, doonas, linen, pillows], iron, iron brd, lounge firepl, c/park (carport), breakfast ingredients, non smoking property. **BB** ╫╫ **$130 - $210**, ◊ **$50**, **W $900**, AE BC DC MC VI.

★★★★ **Athlone Country Cottages**, (Cotg), Lake Eildon National Park Rd, 5km E of PO, ☎ 03 5772 2992, fax 03 5772 2992, 2 cotgs acc up to 4, (2 bedrm), [shwr, tlt, hairdry, c/fan, fire pl, elec blkts, TV, video, radio, CD, refrig, cook fac, micro, toaster, blkts, doonas, linen, pillows], ldry, w/mach, iron, iron brd, lounge firepl, pool, bbq, c/park (undercover), tennis, cots, breakfast ingredients. **BB** ╫╫ **$155**, ◊ **$30**, **W $900**, Dinner by arrangement. BC MC VI.

★★★★ **Idlewild Park Farm Accommodation**, (Cotg), 5545 Maroondah Hwy, 5km NE of PO, ☎ 03 5772 1178, fax 03 5772 1203, 1 cotg acc up to 4, (2 bedrm), [shwr, spa bath, tlt, hairdry, a/c, c/fan, heat (wood & elec), elec blkts, TV, video, clock radio, refrig, cook fac, micro, linen], iron, bbq, c/park (carport), tennis, cots, non smoking property, Pets on application. **D** ╫╫ **$120 - $150**, ◊ **$15**.

★★★★ **Sherntarl Lodge**, (Cotg), 894 Maintongoon Rd, 10km NE of PO, extension of Endicott Rd, ☎ 03 5772 1637, fax 03 5772 2423, 1 cotg acc up to 6, (2 bedrm), [shwr, tlt, heat, elec blkts, TV, video, clock radio, CD, refrig, cook fac, micro, elec frypan, linen reqd-fee], pool-heated (solar), bbq, plygr, tennis, non smoking property. **D** ╫╫ **$100**, ◊ **$16**, **W** ╫╫ **$600 - $700**, ◊ **$112**, ch con.

★★★ **Maybole Cottage**, (Cotg), 399 Maintongoon Rd, 5km NE of PO, ☎ 03 5772 1690, 1 cotg acc up to 5, (2 bedrm), [shwr, bath, tlt, hairdry, a/c-cool, fan, heat, elec blkts, clock radio, CD, refrig, cook fac, toaster, ldry, blkts, doonas, linen, pillows], w/mach, rec rm, lounge firepl, bbq, c/park (garage). **D** ╫╫ **$125**, ◊ **$25**, **W** ╫╫ **$450 - $550**.

B&B's/Guest Houses
★★★★☆ **Mittagong Homestead**, (B&B), 462 Spring Creek Rd, 11.5 km NW of PO, ☎ 03 5772 2250, fax 03 5772 2425, 2 rms [ensuite (1), shwr, tlt, cent heat, elec blkts, clock radio, t/c mkg, doonas], ldry, lounge (TV), pool-heated (solar), sauna, refrig, bbq, tennis. **BB** ╫╫ **$150 - $165**, ◊ **$44**, Other meals by arrangement. Min book long w/ends and Easter, AE BC MC VI.

★★★★ **(Cottage Section)**, 3 cotgs acc up to 4, (1 & 2 bedrm), [shwr, spa bath, tlt, hairdry, c/fan, heat (wood), elec blkts, TV, video, clock radio, CD, t/c mkg, refrig, cook fac, micro, toaster, ldry (in unit) (2), blkts, doonas, linen, pillows], bbq, breakfast ingredients. **BB** ╫╫ **$160 - $220**, ◊ **$45**, **W $850**, Dinner by arrangement.

★★★★☆ **Pendaven Country House**, (GH), No children's facilities, 159 Halls Flat Rd, 3km S of PO, ☎ 03 5772 2452, fax 03 5772 2493, (2 stry), 6 rms [ensuite, bath (5), c/fan, heat, elec blkts, TV, clock radio, t/c mkg, refrig, mini bar], lounge (TV, cd player), lounge firepl, ⊠, pool-heated (solar), sauna, spa. **BB** ╫ **$100**, Group bookings only. BC MC VI, ⟲.

★★★★☆ **Stonelea Country Estate**, (GH), Previously Stonelea. Connellys Creek Rd, Acheron 3714, 10km S of PO, ☎ 03 5772 2222, fax 03 5772 2210, 47 rms [ensuite, bath, hairdry (27), a/c-cool (27), a/c (20), c/fan (27), heat, tel, t/c mkg, refrig, mini bar, cook fac (3), doonas], iron, iron brd, lounge (TV), conf fac, ⊠, bar (cocktail), pool indoor heated, sauna, spa, bowls, golf (18 hole), gym, tennis. **DBB** ╫╫ **$295 - $350**, ◊ **$88**, AE BC EFT MC VI.

★★★★☆ **The Old Convent Alexandra**, (B&B), 32 Downey St, ☎ 03 5772 3220, fax 03 9879 3155, 3 rms (2 suites) [ensuite (2), shwr (1), tlt, a/c, clock radio, doonas], lounge (TV, video), ✗, spa (1), t/c mkg shared, refrig, non smoking property. **BB** ╫ **$105**, ╫╫ **$145**, ◊ **$22**, **Suite BB $145**, AE BC EFT MC VI.

Pop Part of Wodonga, (315km NE Melbourne), See map on pages 694/695, ref H4. Agricultural and dairying district. Fishing, Scenic Drives, Vineyards, Wineries.
Hotels/Motels
★★★ **Colonial Inn Guest Rooms**, (M), Osbornes Flat Rd, 9km NE of Yackandandah, ☎ 02 6027 1530, fax 02 6027 1530, 4 units [shwr, tlt, hairdry (2), a/c-cool, heat, elec blkts, TV, clock radio, t/c mkg, refrig, toaster, doonas], bbq, cots-fee, non smoking rms (4). **BLB** ╫ **$50 - $60**, ╫╫ **$60 - $70**, ◊ **$20**, ch con, Dinner by arrangement. BC MC VI.

Pop 550. (245km SW Melbourne), See map on pages 694/695, ref B7. Agricultural & pastoral district, situated on the Hopkins river. Fishing, Scenic Drives, Swimming, Tennis.
Self Catering Accommodation
★★ **Mt Pleasant Farm Holidays**, (Cotg), (Farm), 9709 Princes Hwy, ☎ 03 5565 1266, fax 03 5565 1606, 1 cotg acc up to 6, (2 bedrm), [shwr, tlt, heat, elec blkts, TV, refrig, cook fac, micro, elec frypan, linen reqd-fee], ldry. **D** ╫╫ **$55**, ◊ **$16.50**, ch con.
B&B's/Guest Houses
★★★☆ **Lanaud B & B Farmstay**, (B&B), 160 ha beef and sheep grazing property. Dry Lake Rd, 3 km NW of PO, ☎ 03 5565 1549, fax 03 5565 1549, 4 rms [shwr, bath, tlt, heat, elec blkts, TV (1), clock radio, t/c mkg (1), refrig (1)], bbq, cots. **BB** ╫ **$30 - $33**, ╫╫ **$71.50 - $110**, ◊ **$22 - $27.50**, ch con, 1 room ★★★★. BC EFT MC VI.

Pop Part of Omeo, (446km NE Melbourne), See map on pages 694/695, ref J5. Situated on the banks of the Cobungra River, popular area for experienced canoeists. Bush Walking, Fishing, Gold Prospecting.
Self Catering Accommodation
Blue Duck Inn Hotel & Holiday Cabins, (HU), Previously Blue Duck Inn Hotel & Holiday Cabins. Limited facilities. Omeo Hwy, 30km N of Omeo, ☎ 03 5159 7220, fax 03 5159 7212, 7 units acc up to 8, (1 & 3 bedrm), [shwr, bath (1), tlt, fire pl, refrig, cook fac, doonas, linen], ⊠, bbq, plygr. **D** ╫╫ **$65**, Generated power. BC MC VI.

Pop 2,000. (109km SW Melbourne), See map on page 696, ref A7. Popular beachside resort. Bowls, Bush Walking, Fishing, Golf, Hangliding, Horse Riding, Scenic Drives, Surfing, Swimming (Beach), Tennis.
Hotels/Motels
★★★★ **Anglesea Motor Inn**, (M), Previously Anglesea Homestead Motor Lodge, 109 Great Ocean Rd, 400m SW of PO, ☎ 03 5263 3888, fax 03 5263 2593, 16 units [shwr, tlt, a/c, elec blkts, tel, TV, movie, clock radio, t/c mkg, refrig, toaster], pool, spa, cots, non smoking property. **RO** ╫ **$90 - $175**, ╫╫ **$100 - $209**, ◊ **$20**, Min book Christmas Jan and Easter, BC EFT MC VI.

Self Catering Accommodation
★★★★ **Anglesea Cottage Accommodation**, (Cotg), Resort, 49 Harvey St, 500m to Surf Beach & River, ☎ 03 5289 6272, 2 cotgs acc up to 6, (3 bedrm), [shwr, spa bath, tlt, hairdry, fan, heat, elec blkts, tel, TV, video, clock radio, CD, refrig, cook fac, micro, elec frypan, toaster, ldry, blkts, doonas, linen, pillows], w/mach, dryer, iron, iron brd, bbq, c/park (carport), cots. **D** ╫╫ **$110 - $187**, ◊ **$22 - $33**, **W** ╫╫ **$770 - $1,500**, ◊ **$77 - $115**, Min book school holidays and Easter, AE BC DC MC VI.

★★★☆ **Roadknight Cottages**, (Cotg), 26 Great Ocean Rd, 2.5km SW of PO, ☎ 03 5263 1820, fax 03 5263 3573, (2 stry), 8 cotgs acc up to 6, (2 bedrm), [shwr, tlt, hairdry, fan, c/fan, heat (wood), TV, video, clock radio, refrig, cook fac ltd, micro, elec frypan, toaster, blkts, doonas, linen, pillows], ldry, w/mach, dryer, spa, bbq, \. **D** ╫╫╫ **$110 - $143**, ◊ **$11**, **W** ╫╫╫ **$660 - $990**, ◊ **$66**, Min book Christmas Jan long w/ends and Easter, AE BC MC VI.

★★★☆ **Surfcoast Spa Resort Anglesea**, (HU), 105 Great Ocean Rd, ☎ 03 5263 3363, fax 03 5263 2687, 33 units acc up to 6, (Studio, 1 & 2 bedrm), [shwr, spa bath (12), tlt, a/c, elec blkts, tel, TV, movie, t/c mkg, refrig, cook fac (5), cook fac ltd (28), blkts, linen, pillows], ldry, rec rm, conf fac, pool-indoor, spa, bbq-fee, tennis, cots, non smoking property. **RO** ╫╫ **$90 - $250**, ◊ **$20**, 13 units ★★☆. AE BC DC EFT MC VI.

★★☆ **First Red-Holiday Cottage**, (Cotg), 58 Camp Rd, 1km N of PO, ☎ 03 5263 3267, 1 cotg acc up to 4, (1 bedrm), [shwr, tlt, hairdry, fan, heat, elec blkts, TV, video-fee, clock radio, t/c mkg, refrig, cook fac ltd, micro, elec frypan, toaster, ldry, blkts, linen-fee, pillows], iron, iron brd, bbq. D ♦♦ $60 - $90, ◊ $10, W ♦♦ $360 - $600, ch con, AE BC MC VI.

★★☆ **Maroo Park**, (Cotg), 1230 Great Ocean Rd, 3km NE of PO, ☎ 03 5263 2889, fax 03 5263 1387, 9 cotgs acc up to 6, (2 bedrm), [shwr, spa bath (2), tlt, TV, clock radio, refrig, cook fac ltd, micro, elec frypan, toaster, blkts reqd-fee, doonas reqd-fee, linen reqd-fee], lounge firepl, pool-heated (solar), spa, bbq, plygr, golf (Pitch & Putt), tennis, Pets allowed. D ♦♦ $85 - $165, ◊ $25, ch con, AE BC DC MC VI.

B&B's/Guest Houses

★★★★☆ **The Point Anglesea**, (B&B), 145 - 147 Great Ocean Rd, ☎ 03 5263 3738, fax 03 5263 3739, (2 stry), 4 rms [shwr, spa bath (3), tlt, hairdry, a/c, elec blkts, cable tv, video, clock radio, CD, refrig], lounge, lounge firepl, t/c mkg shared, c/park (undercover). BB ◊ $175 - $210, ♦♦ $175 - $210, AE BC DC MC VI.

★★★★ **Anglesea Rivergums Bed & Breakfast**, (B&B), 10 Bingley Pde, 100m W of PO, ☎ 03 5263 3066, fax 03 5263 3066, 1 rm [ensuite, hairdry, a/c, fan, cent heat, elec blkts, TV, video, clock radio, CD, t/c mkg, refrig, micro], iron, iron brd, bbq, c/park (carport), non smoking rms. BLB ♦♦ $90 - $120, ◊ $10 - $20, BC MC VI.

★★★★ **Thornton Heath**, (B&B), 33 Pickworth Dve, 2.4km W of bridge, off Noble St, ☎ 03 5263 2542, fax 03 5263 2546, 2 rms [shwr, tlt, hairdry, fan, heat, elec blkts, TV, video, clock radio], lounge (TV), t/c mkg shared, refrig. BB ◊ $80, ♦♦♦ $110, AE BC MC VI.

APOLLO BAY VIC 3233

Pop 1,000. (187km SW Melbourne), See map on pages 694/695, ref D8. Popular beachside resort. Boating, Bowls, Bush Walking, Fishing, Golf, Hangliding, Sailing, Surfing, Swimming (Beach, River), Tennis, Water Skiing.

Hotels/Motels

FLAG
FLAG CHOICE HOTELS

★★★★ **Apollo International**, (M), 37 Great Ocean Rd, 50m N of PO, ☎ 03 5237 6100, fax 03 5237 6066, (2 stry gr fl), 24 units [shwr, spa bath (6), tlt, hairdry, a/c, c/fan, elec blkts, tel, TV, video-fee, t/c mkg, refrig, toaster], ldry, pool, spa, bbq, cots-fee. RO ◊ $93.50 - $176, ♦♦ $110 - $176, ◊ $17, ch con, AE BC DC MC MP VI, ♿.

★★★★ **Coastal Motel**, (M), 171 Great Ocean Rd, 100m N of PO, ☎ 03 5237 6681, fax 03 5237 6134, 15 units [shwr, bath (4), spa bath (4), tlt, a/c, fire pl (gas log) (4), elec blkts, tel, cable tv, clock radio, t/c mkg, refrig, cook fac (4), micro (10), toaster], ldry, spa, bbq-fee, cots-fee, non smoking units (7). RO ◊ $66, ♦♦ $66 - $165, ◊ $15, fam con, 4 units ★★★☆, AE BC EFT MC VI.

★★★★ **The Lighthouse Keeper's Inn**, (M), 175 Great Ocean Rd, 875m N of PO, ☎ 03 5237 6278, fax 03 5237 7843, (2 stry), 5 units [shwr, bath (hip) (1), tlt, hairdry, a/c-cool (2), fan (3), heat, elec blkts, TV, clock radio, t/c mkg, refrig, toaster], ldry, iron, iron brd, ☏, non smoking property. RO ◊ $80 - $150, ♦♦ $102 - $150, ◊ $15, ch con, BC EFT MC VI.

GOLDEN CHAIN

★★★☆ **Apollo Bay Beachfront Motel**, (M), 163 Great Ocean Rd, 600m N of PO, ☎ 03 5237 6437, fax 03 5237 7197, 10 units [shwr, tlt, hairdry, c/fan, heat, elec blkts, tel, TV, video-fee, clock radio, t/c mkg, refrig, cook fac ltd, elec frypan, toaster], ldry, iron, iron brd, bbq-fee, c/park (undercover), cots-fee. RO ◊ $79 - $189, ♦♦ $79 - $189, ◊ $12, AE BC DC MC VI.

Operator Comment: See our display advertisement ad on following page.

★★★★ **(Apartment Section)**, 3 apts acc up to 3, (Studio), [shwr, tlt, hairdry, c/fan, heat, elec blkts, tel, TV, video-fee, clock radio, t/c mkg, refrig, cook fac, micro, toaster, blkts, linen, pillows], ldry, iron, iron brd, c/park (undercover). D ◊ $98 - $240, ♦♦ $98 - $240, ◊ $12.

Best Western

★★★☆ **Apollo Bay Motel**, (M), 2 Moore St, 300m N of PO, ☎ 03 5237 7577, fax 03 5237 7042, 12 units [shwr, tlt, c/fan, heat, elec blkts, tel, cable tv, clock radio, t/c mkg, refrig, mini bar, toaster], ldry, rec rm, lounge, pool, sauna, spa, bbq, cots. RO ◊ $90 - $155, ♦♦ $95 - $155, ◊ $15, AE BC DC MC MP VI.

★★★★ **(Holiday Flat Section)**, (2 stry gr fl), 14 flats acc up to 6, (1, 2 & 3 bedrm), [shwr, bath (hip), tlt, c/fan, heat, elec blkts, tel, cable tv, clock radio, refrig, mini bar, cook fac, micro, blkts, linen, pillows], ldry. D $115 - $285.

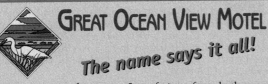

 ★★★☆ **Waterfront Motor Inn**, (M), 173 Great Ocean Rd, 150m N of PO, ☎ 03 5237 7333, fax 03 5237 7533, (2 stry gr fl), 12 units [shwr, spa bath (6), tlt, hairdry, elec blkts, tel, TV, clock radio, t/c mkg, refrig, cook fac (5), micro (5), toaster], ldry, cots, non smoking units (3). RO ♦ $77 - $198, ♦♦ $89 - $198, ◊ $14, ch con, 6 units ★★★★, Min book Christmas Jan long w/ends and Easter, AE BC DC EFT MC VI, ⓕ.

★★★★ **(Apartment Section)**, 2 apts acc up to 5, (2 bedrm), [shwr, tlt, hairdry, a/c, elec blkts, tel, TV, clock radio, t/c mkg, refrig, cook fac, micro, toaster]. D ♦ $105 - $280.

★★★☆ **Whitecrest Resort**, (M), Great Ocean Rd, 13km NE of PO, ☎ 03 5237 0228, fax 03 5237 0245, (2 stry), 11 units [shwr, tlt, heat, elec blkts, tel, TV, clock radio, t/c mkg, refrig, mini bar, micro, elec frypan, toaster], conf fac, lounge firepl, ⊠, bbq, non smoking property. RO ♦♦ $135, ◊ $45, ch con, AE BC DC EFT MC VI.

 ★★★ **Motel Marengo**, (M), 26 Great Ocean Rd, Marengo 3233, 2km S of PO, ☎ 03 5237 6808, fax 03 5237 6902, 14 units [shwr, spa bath (4), tlt, a/c (4), heat, elec blkts, tel, TV, video-fee, clock radio, t/c mkg, refrig, cook fac ltd, micro, elec frypan, toaster], ldry, pool-heated (solar), spa, bbq, cots. RO ♦♦ $60.50 - $154, ◊ $6.60 - $12, 4 units ★★★★. AE BC DC MC VI, ⓕ.

 ★★★ **Skenes Creek Lodge**, (M), 61 Great Ocean Rd, Skenes Creek 3233, 6.8km NE of PO, ☎ 03 5237 6918, fax 03 5237 6918, 24 units [shwr, tlt, c/fan, heat, elec blkts, TV, clock radio, t/c mkg, refrig, micro, toaster, doonas], ⊠, bbq, rm serv, ☎, cots. RO ♦ $50 - $88, ♦♦ $65 - $143, ◊ $11, 4 units ★★☆. AE BC EFT MC VI, ⓕ.

 ★★☆ **Great Ocean View Motel**, (M), 1 Great Ocean Rd, 500m S of PO, ☎ 03 5237 6527, fax 03 5237 7049, 10 units [shwr, tlt, fan, heat, elec blkts, tel, TV, clock radio, t/c mkg, refrig, toaster], bbq, cots-fee. RO ♦ $70 - $170, ♦♦ $70 - $170, ◊ $15, BC MC VI.

★★ **Bay Pine Motel & Guest House**, (M), 3 Murray St, 800m N of PO, ☎ 03 5237 6732, fax 03 5237 7562, 11 units [shwr, bath (3), tlt, c/fan (3), heat, elec blkts, TV, clock radio, t/c mkg, refrig], ldry, lounge (TV), ✕ (seasonal), ☎, cots. RO ♦ $45 - $75, ♦♦ $65 - $95, ♦♦♦♦ $92 - $130, ch con, BC MC VI.

★★ **(Guest House Section)**, 6 rms [shwr (2), bath (1), tlt (2), heat, elec blkts], t/c mkg shared. D ♦ $18 - $45, ♦♦ $44 - $66, ch con.

Self Catering Accommodation

 ★★★★☆ **Otway Paradise Cottages**, (Cotg), 935 Barham River Rd, 10km NW of PO, ☎ 03 5237 7102, fax 03 5237 7103, 5 cotgs acc up to 8, (Studio, 2 & 3 bedrm), [shwr, bath, tlt, hairdry, a/c, elec blkts, clock radio, CD, t/c mkg, refrig, cook fac, micro, toaster, ldry (in unit) (3), blkts, linen, pillows], iron, iron brd, bbq, ☎. D ♦ $120 - $135, ◊ $20 - $30, ch con, 2 cottages ★★★★, Minimum booking w/ends, public & school holidays. AE BC EFT MC VI.

★★★★☆ **Rayville Boat Houses**, (HU), 9-13 Noel St, 500m SE of PO, ☎ 03 5237 6381, fax 03 5237 7822, (2 stry gr fl), 10 units acc up to 7, (1, 2 & 3 bedrm), [shwr, spa bath, tlt, hairdry, c/fan, heat, elec blkts, TV, video, clock radio, CD, t/c mkg, refrig, cook fac, micro, d/wash, toaster, blkts, doonas, linen, pillows], ldry, w/mach, dryer, iron, iron brd, bbq, c/park (carport), cots, non smoking property. D ♦♦ $110 - $230, ◊ $10 - $20, W ♦♦ $750 - $1,610, ◊ $60, Min book all holiday times, BC EFT MC VI.

★★★★☆ **Top O' the Town**, (Apt), 3 Cartwright St, 600m S of PO, ☎ 03 5237 6762, fax 03 5237 6762, 1 apt acc up to 4, (2 bedrm), [shwr, spa bath, tlt, hairdry, c/fan, heat, elec blkts, TV, video, clock radio, CD, refrig, cook fac, micro, elec frypan, d/wash, toaster, ldry, blkts, doonas, linen, pillows], w/mach, dryer, iron, iron brd, sauna, bbq. **D ♦♦ $120 - $150, ♦ $20, W ♦♦ $750 - $1,050, ♦ $280**, Min book Christmas Jan long w/ends and Easter, BC MC VI,
Operator Comment: Magnificent views from all rooms of town, ocean and hills from this luxury apartment which has every amenity for a self catering holiday.

★★★★☆ **Valkei Villas**, (Villa), 9 Great Ocean Rd, Marengo 3233, 2km W of Shopping Centre, ☎ 03 5237 7538, fax 03 5237 7595, (2 stry gr fl), 4 villas acc up to 6, (3 bedrm), [shwr, spa bath, tlt, hairdry, evap cool, fan, heat, elec blkts, tel (local), TV, video, clock radio, CD, t/c mkg, refrig, cook fac, micro, elec frypan, toaster, ldry (in unit), blkts, linen, pillows], iron, iron brd, lounge firepl, bbq, c/park (carport), cots. **D ♦♦ $140 - $200, ♦ $30 - $40**, Min book Christmas Jan long w/ends and Easter, BC MC VI.

★★★★ **Apollo Bay Colonial Cottages**, (Cotg), Cnr Great Ocean Rd & Telford St, Marengo 3233, ☎ 03 5237 6511, fax 03 5237 6511, 6 cotgs acc up to 6, (2 & 3 bedrm), [shwr, spa bath, tlt, heat, elec blkts, tel (local), TV, clock radio, CD, refrig, cook fac, micro, ldry (in unit), blkts, linen, pillows], lounge firepl, bbq, c/park (carport), cots. **D $143 - $242, W $770 - $1,540**, Min book applies, BC MC VI.

★★★★ **Bayview Apartments**, (HU), 46 Noel St, 300 W of PO, ☎ 03 5237 6263, fax 03 5222 2955, (2 stry), 3 units acc up to 5, (2 bedrm), [ensuite, shwr, spa bath, tlt, hairdry, c/fan, heat, elec blkts, TV, video, clock radio, CD, refrig, cook fac, micro, toaster, ldry, blkts, linen, pillows], bbq, c/park (garage), non smoking property. **D $100 - $240, W $500 - $1,400**, Min book applies, BC MC VI.

★★★★ **Beachcomber Motel & Apartments**, (Apt), 15 Diana St, 450m W of PO, ☎ 03 5237 6290, fax 03 5237 7474, 7 apts acc up to 5, (Studio & 2 bedrm), [shwr, bath (1), spa bath (4), tlt, a/c, heat (wood fire - 4), elec blkts, tel, TV, video-fee, clock radio, refrig, cook fac (2), cook fac ltd (5), micro, blkts, linen, pillows], ldry, bbq, cots-fee, non smoking units (3). **D ♦ $66 - $145, ♦♦ $72 - $170, ♦ $11**, AE BC EFT MC VI.

★★★ **(Motel Section)**, 9 units [shwr, tlt, fan, heat, elec blkts, tel (8), TV, video-fee, clock radio, t/c mkg, refrig, toaster, doonas], ldry, bbq, cots-fee. **RO ♦ $40 - $88, ♦♦ $50 - $88, ♦ $8**, Light breakfast only available.

★★★★ **Beacon Point Motel Lodges**, (Cotg), 270 Skenes Creek Rd, 8km NE of PO, ☎ 03 5237 6218, fax 03 5237 6196, 18 cotgs acc up to 5, (1 & 2 bedrm), [shwr, tlt, hairdry, c/fan, heat, elec blkts, TV, video, clock radio, CD, t/c mkg, refrig, cook fac, micro, ldry (in unit), blkts, doonas, linen, pillows], w/mach, iron, iron brd, lounge firepl, spa, bbq, ☎, tennis, cots. **D ♦♦ $115 - $190, ♦ $20, W ♦♦ $730 - $1,045**, Light breakfast available. AE BC EFT MC VI.

★★★★ **But 'n' Ben**, (Cotg), 28 Harrison St, Marengo 3233, 2.5km W of PO, ☎ 03 5237 6682, fax 03 5237 6682, 1 cotg acc up to 4, (2 bedrm), [shwr, bath, tlt, hairdry, fan, c/fan, heat, elec blkts, TV, video, clock radio, CD, refrig, cook fac, micro, toaster, ldry (in unit), blkts, linen, pillows], w/mach, iron, iron brd, bbq, c/park (carport), cots. **D ♦♦ $90 - $110, ♦ $15 - $20, W $500 - $800**, Breakfast available. Min book all holiday times, AE BC MC VI.

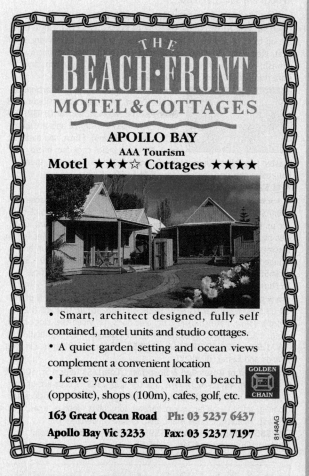

★★★★ **Chris's Beacon Point Restaurant & Villas**, (HU), 280 Skenes Creek Rd, 9km NE of PO, ☎ 03 5237 6411, fax 03 5237 6930, 6 units acc up to 4, (2 bedrm - split level.), [shwr, spa bath, tlt, hairdry, c/fan, heat, elec blkts, TV, video, clock radio, CD, refrig, cook fac, micro, d/wash, toaster, ldry (in unit), blkts, linen, pillows], w/mach, dryer, iron, iron brd, ⊠, cots. **D $200 - $265**, AE BC DC MC VI.

★★★★ **Reef View Holiday Apartments on the Coast**, (Apt), Cnr Great Ocean Rd & Ocean Park Dve, Seabrook 3028, ☎ 03 9395 1859, or 03 5237 7917, (2 stry) 2 apts acc up to 6, (2 bedrm + 3 bedrm), [shwr, spa bath, tlt, heat, TV, clock radio, cook fac, micro, toaster, ldry, blkts, linen, pillows], dryer, pool indoor heated, sauna, bbq, cots, non smoking property. **D** ♦♦ **$150 - $220, W** ♦♦ **$750 - $1,600**, Min book Christmas and Jan.

★★★★ **The Nelson Palms Holiday Villas**, (HF), Unit 1/1 Pascoe St, 150m SW of PO, ☎ 03 5237 6755, fax 03 5237 6755, (2 stry), 1 flat acc up to 4, (2 bedrm), [shwr, spa bath, tlt, hairdry, fan, c/fan, elec blkts, TV, video, clock radio, refrig, cook fac ltd, micro, elec frypan, toaster, ldry (in unit), blkts, doonas, linen], w/mach, iron, iron brd, lounge firepl (gas log), bbq, c/park (garage), cots. **D $137.50 - $175, W $655 - $1,331**, 1 unit only included in rating. Booking office: 26 Murray St. BC MC VI.

★★★☆ **Bayside Gardens**, (HU), 219 Great Ocean Rd, 1.2km N of PO, ☎ 03 5237 6248, fax 03 5237 6248, 10 units acc up to 4, (1 & 2 bedrm), [shwr, bath (hip) (2), tlt, elec blkts, TV, video-fee, clock radio, refrig, cook fac, blkts, linen, pillows], ldry, lounge firepl (7), bbq, ☏. **D $71.50 - $126.50, W $440 - $1,050**, Min book Christmas Jan long w/ends and Easter, BC MC VI.

★★★☆ **Bed of Roses Bed & Breakfast**, (Cotg), 53 Nelson St, 500m W of Police Stn, ☎ 03 5237 7149, fax 03 5237 7149, 1 cotg acc up to 5, (2 bedrm), [shwr, tlt, c/fan, heat, elec blkts, TV, video, clock radio, t/c mkg, refrig, cook fac, micro, toaster, ldry, blkts, doonas, linen, pillows], w/mach, lounge firepl, bbq, c/park (undercover). **D** ♦♦ **$85 - $150,** ♦ **$15, W** ♦♦ **$595 - $1,050,** ♦ **$105**, ch con, Min book Christmas and Jan, BC MC VI.

★★★☆ **Paradise Court Villas**, (HU), Resort, 20 Murray St, 1km N of PO, ☎ 03 5237 6133, 5 units acc up to 6, (2 bedrm), [shwr, bath (hip) tlt, hairdry (5), c/fan (5), heat, elec blkts, TV, clock radio, refrig, cook fac, micro (5), toaster, ldry (in unit), blkts, doonas, linen, pillows], w/mach, iron, iron brd, bbq-fee, cots. **D $65 - $143.30, W $350 - $1,045**, Booking Office: 26 Murray St, Min book Christmas Jan long w/ends and Easter, BC EFT MC VI.

★★★☆ **Petticoat Beach Cottage**, (Cotg), 5810 Great Ocean Rd, Skenes Creek 3233, 7km NE of PO, ☎ 03 5237 6789, 1 cotg acc up to 4, (1 bedrm), [shwr, tlt, hairdry, fan, heat, elec blkts, TV, video, clock radio, CD, t/c mkg, refrig, cook fac ltd, micro, elec frypan, toaster, blkts, doonas, linen, pillows], iron, bbq, cots, breakfast ingredients. **BLB** ♦♦ **$100 - $135,** ♦ **$10 - $20**, ch con, BC MC VI.

★★★☆ **Seafarers Motel Lodge**, (HU), Great Ocean Rd, 4.6km NE of PO, ☎ 03 5237 6507, fax 03 5237 7061, 12 units acc up to 5, (2 bedrm), [shwr, tlt, elec blkts, TV, video-fee, clock radio, refrig, cook fac, micro, toaster, blkts, linen, pillows], ldry, lounge firepl, bbq, kiosk, ☏, cots. **D** ♦♦ **$108 - $140,** ♦ **$20, W** ♦♦ **$715 - $1,080,** ♦ **$100**, ch con, Light breakfast available. Min book school holidays and Easter, BC MC VI.

★★★☆ **(Studio Units Section)**, 7 units acc up to 3, (Studio), [shwr, tlt, heat, elec blkts, TV, video-fee, clock radio, refrig, cook fac, micro, toaster, blkts, linen, pillows], cots. **D** ♦♦ **$90 - $119,** ♦ **$20, W** ♦♦ **$595 - $840**, ch con, ♿.

★★★☆ **The Coach Houses**, (Cotg), Cnr Great Ocean & Old Coach Rds, Skenes Creek 3233, 6km NE of PO, ☎ 03 5237 6535, fax 03 5237 6535, 4 cotgs acc up to 6, (2 & 3 bedrm), [shwr, bath (2), spa bath (2), tlt, hairdry, fan, heat (wood - 3), elec blkts, TV, video, clock radio, CD, t/c mkg, refrig, cook fac, micro, d/wash (2), toaster, ldry (in unit), blkts, linen, pillows], w/mach, dryer, iron, iron brd, bbq, c/park (carport) (1), cots, non smoking property. **D** ♦♦ **$99 - $165,** ♦ **$16.50 - $22, W $616 - $731**, 2 cottages ★★★★. Min book all holiday times.

★★★ **Marriners Lodge**, (HF), Unit 1, 11 Martin St, 250m NE of PO, ☎ 03 5460 4612, 1 flat acc up to 6, (2 bedrm), [shwr, tlt, hairdry, heat, elec blkts, TV, video, refrig, cook fac, micro, elec frypan, ldry (in unit), linen reqd], w/mach, iron, iron brd, bbq, c/park (carport). **D $60 - $110, W $350 - $700**.

★★★ **Otway Lodge**, (HF), 23 Pascoe St, 200m W of PO, ☎ 03 5237 6263, fax 03 5237 7385, (2 stry gr fl), 6 flats acc up to 10, (1, 2 & 3 bedrm), [shwr, bath (2), spa bath (4), tlt, heat, TV, refrig, cook fac, elec frypan, ldry (in unit) (3), doonas, linen], ldry (3), bbq, c/park (carport) (3), cots. **D $50, W $275 - $1,050**, BC MC VI.

★★★ **Rannock Holiday Flats**, (HF), 9 Cawood St, 500m N of PO, ☎ 0417 553 968, fax 03 5237 6518, 2 flats acc up to 5, (2 bedrm), [shwr, bath (hip), tlt, heat, elec blkts, TV, video (1), refrig, cook fac, elec frypan, linen reqd-fee], ldry, bbq, c/park (carport). **D $72 - $105, W $495 - $732**, ch con, Min book Christmas Jan long w/ends and Easter.

★★☆ **Grandview Holiday Flats**, (HF), 1 McLennan St, 900m NW of PO, ☎ 03 5237 6461, 8 flats acc up to 6, (1 & 2 bedrm), [shwr, tlt, hairdry, fan, heat, elec blkts, TV, clock radio, refrig, cook fac, micro, blkts, doonas, linen, pillows], ldry, w/mach, iron, bbq, cots. **D $55 - $120**, Min book Christmas Jan long w/ends and Easter, BC MC VI.

Rates may change. Check before booking.

B&B's/Guest Houses

★★★★☆ **Captain's at the Bay**, (B&B), No facilities for children under 15. Cnr Pascoe & Whelan Sts, 500m NW of PO, ☎ 03 5237 6771, fax 03 5237 7337, (2 stry gr fl), 7 rms [shwr, spa bath (3), tlt, hairdry, a/c, elec blkts, tel, TV, video, CD, t/c mkg, refrig, mini bar, doonas], lounge, ☒ (by arrangement), non smoking property. **BB** ♥♥ **$165 - $210**, ⏸ **$165**, 1 unit ★★★☆. Minimum booking holiday times & weekends, AE BC DC EFT MC VI.

★★★★☆ **Claerwen Retreat**, (GH), 480 Tuxion Rd, 6.km N of PO, ☎ 03 5237 7064, fax 03 5237 7054, 4 rms [shwr, tlt, hairdry, cent heat, elec blkts, TV, video, t/c mkg], ldry, iron, iron brd, lounge (cd player, stereo), lounge firepl, pool (salt water), spa, refrig, tennis, non smoking property. **BB** ♦ **$145 - $176**, ♥♥ **$154 - $198**, ch con, AE BC DC EFT JCB MC VI.

★★★★ **(Cottage Section)**, 2 cotgs acc up to 6, (3 bedrm), [shwr, tlt, hairdry, c/fan (2), cent heat, elec blkts, TV, video, clock radio, CD, t/c mkg, refrig, cook fac (2), cook fac ltd (2), micro, toaster, blkts, linen, pillows], ldry, w/mach, dryer, iron, iron brd, lounge firepl (2), pool (saltwater), spa, bbq, tennis, non smoking property. **D $198 - $297**, 2 studio cottages not listed or rated, Min book applies.

★★★★☆ **Triggers Place**, (B&B), 48 Cawood St, 2km N of PO, ☎ 03 5237 7652, fax 03 5237 7652, (2 stry) 1 rm [ensuite, c/fan, heat, elec blkts, tel, cable tv, video, clock radio, cook fac ltd, toaster, ldry-fee, doonas], lounge firepl, ✗, t/c mkg shared, refrig, bbq, c/park (undercover), non smoking property. **BB** ♦ **$50 - $100**, ♥♥ **$80 - $140**, ⏸ **$30 - $50**, ch con, Min book Christmas and Jan, AE BC DC MC VI.

★★★★ **Greenacres Country House by the Sea**, (GH), Cnr Great Ocean Rd & Nelson St, 150m S of PO, opposite golf course, ☎ 03 5237 6309, fax 03 5237 6891, (2 stry), 17 rms [shwr, tlt, hairdry (5), c/fan (13), heat, elec blkts, tel, TV, clock radio, t/c mkg, refrig], ldry, conf fac, ☒, bar (cocktail), spa, bbq, c/park (limited), tennis, cots-fee, non smoking rms. **BLB** ♦ **$60 - $210**, ♥♥ **$60 - $220**, ⏸ **$30**, ch con, 4 rooms ★★★. Min book Christmas Jan long w/ends and Easter, AE BC DC EFT MC VI.

★★☆ **(Motel Section)**, 9 units [shwr, tlt, heat, elec blkts, tel, TV, clock radio, t/c mkg, refrig]. **BLB** ♦ **$50 - $110**, ♥♥ **$60 - $110**, ⏸ **$30**, ch con.

★★★★ **Paradise Devonshire Tea Gardens**, (B&B), Barham River Rd, 7.7km W of PO, ☎ 03 5237 6939, fax 03 5237 6499, 1 rm [ensuite, spa bath, hairdry, elec blkts, TV, video, clock radio, t/c mkg, refrig, toaster], iron, iron brd, non smoking property. **BB** ♥♥ **$90 - $110**.

★★★★ **Spindrift Bed & Breakfast**, (B&B), 2 Marengo Cres, 2km S of PO, ☎ 03 5237 7410, fax 03 5237 7410, 2 rms [ensuite, hairdry, fan, heat, elec blkts, TV, clock radio, doonas], lounge (TV, video, cd), t/c mkg shared, refrig, bbq, cots, non smoking property. **BLB** ♦ **$60 - $80**, ♥♥ **$90 - $120**, ⏸ **$15 - $20**, ch con, BC MC VI.

★★★★ **Stewart's Bed & Breakfast**, (B&B), 2 Tuxion Rd, 1.3km NW of PO, ☎ 03 5237 6447, fax 03 5237 6447, 3 rms [ensuite, spa bath (2), fan, heat, elec blkts, cable tv (1), video (1), doonas], lounge (Cable TV, video, cd), t/c mkg shared, refrig, non smoking property. **BB** ♥♥ **$130 - $170**, ⏸ **$50**, ch con, Min book Christmas Jan and Easter, AE BC MC VI.

★★★☆ **Arcady Homestead**, (B&B), (Farm), 925 Barham River Rd, 9.8km W of PO, ☎ 03 5237 6493, fax 03 5237 6493, 4 rms [elec blkts, doonas], lounge (tv, video, cd player), cots, non smoking property. **BB** ♦ **$45**, ⏸ **$45**, ch con, Dinner by arrangement. AE.

★★★☆ **Crystal Waters Guest House**, (B&B), 4 Joyce St, 1.5km N of PO, ☎ 03 5237 7129, fax 03 5237 7501, (2 stry), 4 rms [hairdry, c/fan, elec blkts, TV, clock radio], lounge (TV), spa, t/c mkg shared, refrig, non smoking property. **BB $80 - $130**.

★★★ **Wongarra Heights**, (B&B), (Farm), No facilities for children under 13. 65 Sunnyside Rd, Wongarra 3221, 12km NE of Apollo Bay, ☎ 03 5237 0257, (2 stry gr fl), 5 rms [elec blkts, doonas], lounge (TV, stereo), lounge firepl, refrig, bbq, non smoking property. **BB** ♦ **$60**, ♥♥ **$100**, ⏸ **$30**, AE BC MC VI.

ARARAT VIC 3377

Pop 6,900. (203km W Melbourne), See map on pages 694/695, ref C5. Centre of major tourist areas, Mt Cole State Forest & The Grampians. Langi Morgala Museum featuring the Mooney collection of Aboriginal Artifacts. Greenhill Lake provides water sport activities. Art Gallery, Bowls, Bush Walking, Croquet, Fishing, Golf, Horse Racing, Scenic Drives, Swimming, Tennis, Trotting, Vineyards, Wineries.

Hotels/Motels

★★★☆ **Ararat Colonial Lodge & Pyrenees Restaurant**, (M), 6 Ingor St, 100m N of PO, ☎ 03 5352 4644, fax 03 5352 3385, 19 units [shwr, tlt, a/c-cool, heat, elec blkts, tel, TV, video-fee, clock radio, t/c mkg, refrig], ✗, BYO, pool, bbq, dinner to unit, cots-fee, non smoking units (2). **RO** ♦ **$83 - $103**, ♥♥ **$93 - $103**, ⏸ **$12**, ch con, AE BC DC EFT MC MP VI, ⅃⅁.

★★★☆ **Statesman Motor Inn**, (M), Western Hwy, 1.2km NW of PO, ☎ 03 5352 4111, fax 03 5352 4125, 19 units [shwr, spa bath (6), tlt, hairdry, a/c, heat, elec blkts, tel, TV, video (avail), clock radio, t/c mkg, refrig, mini bar, toaster], iron, iron brd, ☒, rm serv, cots-fee, non smoking units (7). **RO** ♦ **$77 - $88**, ♥♥ **$88 - $99**, ⏸ **$11**, ch con, AE BC DC EFT MC MP VI, ⅃⅁.

★★★ **Ararat Central Motel**, (M), 249 Barkly St, 550m E of PO, ☎ 03 5352 4444, fax 03 5352 4992, 22 units [shwr, tlt, a/c, elec blkts, tel, TV, clock radio, t/c mkg, refrig], pool, cots-fee, non smoking units (2). **RO** ♦ **$54**, ♥♥ **$65**, ⏸ **$10**, Min book all holiday times, AE BC EFT MC MCH VI.

★★★ **Mount Ararat Motor Inn**, (M), 367 Barkly St, 1.6km E of PO, ☎ 03 5352 2521, fax 03 5352 2521, 9 units [shwr, tlt, a/c-cool (9), a/c (3), heat, elec blkts, TV, clock radio, t/c mkg, refrig, micro, toaster], bbq, dinner to unit, c/park (undercover), cots-fee, non smoking units (3). **RO** ♦ **$55**, ♥♥ **$60**, ⏸ **$11**, AE BC DC EFT MC VI.

★★ **Chalambar Motel**, (M), 132 Lambert St (Western Hwy), 1.8km N of PO, ☎ 03 5352 2430, fax 03 5352 2430, 10 units [shwr, tlt, a/c, elec blkts, TV, clock radio, t/c mkg, refrig], ldry, cots-fee. **RO** ♦ **$37.40**, ♥♥ **$44**, ⏸ **$6**, fam con, BC MC VI.

Self Catering Accommodation

★★★★☆ **Ararat Holiday Homes**, (House), 26 Banfield St, 600m NW of PO, ☎ 03 5352 3862, fax 03 5352 3862, 2 houses acc up to 8, (2 & 3 bedrm), [shwr, bath, tlt, a/c-cool, heat, elec blkts, tel, TV, video, clock radio, CD, refrig, cook fac, micro, d/wash, toaster, ldry, blkts, linen, pillows], w/mach, dryer, iron, iron brd, bbq, c/park (carport), breakfast ingredients. **D** ♥♥ **$120 - $145**, ⏸ **$30 - $40**, **W** ♥♥ **$600 - $850**, ⏸ **$100**, Dinner by arrangement. ⅃⅁.

ARARAT VIC continued...

★★★★☆ **Westgate Vineyard Country House**, (House), RMB 1124 Westgate Rd, ☎ 03 5356 2394, fax 03 5356 2594, 1 house acc up to 10, (4 bedrm), [shwr (3), tlt (3), hairdry, c/fan, heat, elec blkts, tel (local), TV, video, clock radio, refrig, cook fac, micro, d/wash, toaster, ldry, blkts, doonas, linen, pillows], w/mach, dryer, iron, iron brd, lounge firepl, bbq, breakfast ingredients. D ♦♦ $135, ♦ $35, weekly con, Min book all holiday times, BC MC VI, ⚡♿.

★★★☆ **Crochan Self Contained**, (HU), RMB 2528 Moyston Rd, 7km W of PO, ☎ 03 5352 4797, fax 03 5352 4797, 1 unit acc up to 6, (2 bedrm), [shwr, tlt, hairdry, a/c-cool, c/fan, TV, clock radio, t/c mkg, refrig, cook fac, micro, toaster, ldry (in unit), blkts, linen, pillows], w/mach, iron, iron brd, lounge firepl, bbq, c/park (carport), plygr, tennis, cots, non smoking units. D ♦ $45 - $60, ♦♦ $65 - $75, ♦ $25 - $30, ch con, AE BC MC VI.

★★★☆ **Gorrinn Pastoral Co**, (Cotg), (Farm), RMB 3590 Western Hwy, 12km E of PO, ☎ 03 5352 1225, fax 03 5352 1225, 1 cotg acc up to 10, (5 bedrm), [shwr, bath, tlt, TV, clock radio, refrig, cook fac, micro, ldry, linen reqd-fee], lounge firepl, bbq. D $88 - $192.50.

★★★ **Acacia Caravan Park**, (HF), 6 Acacia Ave, 1km N of PO, off Western Hwy, ☎ 03 5352 2994, fax 03 5352 1733, 3 flats acc up to 5, (1 bedrm), [shwr, tlt, a/c-cool, heat, elec blkts, TV, clock radio, refrig, cook fac, toaster, linen reqd-fee], ldry, pool-heated (solar), bbq (covered), plygr. D ♦♦ $55 - $66, ♦ $5.50, ch con, Min book long w/ends, BC MC VI.

ARTHURS SEAT VIC 3936

Pop part of Dromana (68km S Melbourne), See map on page 697, ref C8. Bush Walking. Inland from Dromana on the Mornington Peninsula.

B&B's/Guest Houses

★★★★★ **Arthurs Superb Views & Luxury Accommodation**, (B&B), No children's facilities, 10 Nestle Crt, 4km E of Dromana PO, ☎ 03 5981 8400, fax 03 5981 8500, (2 stry) 2 rms [ensuite, spa bath, hairdry, a/c, TV, clock radio, CD, t/c mkg, refrig], non smoking property. BB ♦♦ $190 - $360, BC EFT MC VI.

AVOCA VIC 3467

Pop 950. (185km NW Melbourne), See map on pages 694/695, ref D5. An agricultural township at foot of Pyrenees Ranges. Bowls, Bush Walking, Fishing (River), Gold Prospecting, Golf, Horse Racing, Horse Riding, Scenic Drives, Shooting, Squash, Swimming (Pool, River), Tennis, Vineyards, Wineries.

Hotels/Motels

 ★★★ **Avoca Motel**, (M), Previously Motel Avoca 159 High St (Sunraysia Hwy), 200m N of PO, ☎ 03 5465 3464, fax 03 5465 3613, 12 units [shwr, spa bath (2), tlt, hairdry, a/c, elec blkts, tel, TV, clock radio, t/c mkg, refrig, toaster], ldry, bbq, cots-fee. RO ♦ $65 - $110, ♦♦ $77 - $110, ♦ $12, ch con, BC EFT MC VI.

★★★ **Pyrenees Motel**, (M), Cnr Pyrenees & Sunraysia Hwys, 100m S of PO, ☎ 03 5465 3693, fax 03 5465 3584, 7 units [shwr, tlt, a/c-cool, heat, elec blkts, TV, clock radio, t/c mkg, refrig, toaster], bbq. RO ♦ $50, ♦♦ $60, ♦ $15, ch con, AE BC DC EFT MC VI.

Self Catering Accommodation

★★★☆ **Rock Brook**, (Cotg), (Farm), 168 Gordon Rd, Bung Bong 3465, 16km E Avoca PO, ☎ 03 5460 5454, 1 cotg acc up to 2, (1 bedrm), [shwr, bath (hip), tlt, hairdry, a/c-cool, elec blkts, TV, video, radio, refrig, cook fac, toaster, ldry, blkts, linen, pillows], lounge firepl. D $95, W $500, Dinner available by arrangement.

B&B's/Guest Houses

★★★★ **Young's Bed & Breakfast**, (B&B), 237 High St, 1km N of PO, ☎ 03 5465 3147, fax 03 5465 3147, 1 rm [ensuite, spa bath, hairdry, evap cool, c/fan, heat, elec blkts, clock radio, t/c mkg], ldry, lounge (TV, video, stereo), bbq, tennis, non smoking rms. BB ♦♦ $90 - $100.

★★★★ **(Arcadia Cottage Section)**, 1 cotg acc up to 2, (Studio), [shwr, tlt, hairdry, evap cool, c/fan, heat, TV, clock radio, t/c mkg, refrig, cook fac, toaster, blkts, linen, pillows], ldry, w/mach, dryer, bbq, tennis, cots, breakfast ingredients. BB ♦♦ $90 - $100.

★★★☆ **Avoca Heritage School**, (B&B), No children's facilities, 124 Rutherford St, ☎ 03 5465 3691, (2 stry gr fl), 3 rms [ensuite (1), elec blkts, TV, clock radio, t/c mkg], lounge (TV), lounge firepl, t/c mkg shared, refrig, bbq, non smoking property. BB ♦ $80 - $90, ♦♦ $95 - $105.

BACCHUS MARSH VIC 3340

Pop 11,300. (53km W Melbourne), See map on page 696, ref A5. Fruit growing, dairying & pastoral town, adjacent to the Werribee River. Bowls, Bush Walking, Golf, Horse Riding, Swimming (Pool), Tennis, Vineyards, Wineries.

Hotels/Motels

 ★★★☆ **Bacchus Marsh Avenue Motel**, (M), 272 Main St, 1km E of PO, ☎ 03 5367 3766, fax 03 5367 7589, 10 units [shwr, tlt, hairdry, a/c, elec blkts, tel, TV, clock radio, t/c mkg, refrig, toaster], iron, iron brd, conf fac, pool, plygr, cots. RO ♦ $72 - $88, ♦♦ $77 - $88, ♦ $13, AE BC DC EFT MC MCH VI.

★★★ **(Cottage Section)**, 1 cotg acc up to 6, (2 bedrm), [shwr, spa bath, tlt, hairdry, a/c, elec blkts, TV, clock radio, t/c mkg, refrig, cook fac, micro, toaster, ldry], iron, iron brd. D ♦ $95 - $165, ♦♦ $126 - $165, ♦ $15.

Other Accommodation

Sunnystones, (Bunk), Previously Sunnystones Bences Rd, 7.7km NE of PO, via Buckleys Rd, off Gisborne Rd, ☎ 03 5367 1984, fax 03 5367 1984, 10 bunkhouses acc up to 10, (Bunk Rooms), [shwr (7), tlt (7), linen reqd-fee], rec rm, lounge (TV, video), lounge firepl. D all meals ♦ $35, ch con, Self catering D $18. Minium booking - 20 people.

BAIRNSDALE VIC 3875

Pop 10,900. (282km E Melbourne), See map on pages 694/695, ref J7. Supply point for East Gippsland. Centre for wool growing, dairying, agricultural & timber industries. Tourist centre for the beautiful Gippsland Lakes. Tourist Information Centre, 240 Main St, 03 5152 3444 & 03 5152 6444. Boating, Bowls, Bush Walking, Croquet, Fishing (River), Golf, Horse Racing, Horse Riding, Sailing, Scenic Drives, Swimming (Pool, River), Tennis, Water Skiing. See also Eagle Point, Paynesville, Sarsfield & Wattle Point.

Hotels/Motels

 ★★★★ **Colonial Motor Inn Bairnsdale**, (M), 335 Main St (Princes Hwy), 1.5km SW of PO, ☎ 03 5152 1988, fax 03 5152 1987, 14 units [shwr, bath (1), spa bath (1), tlt, hairdry, a/c, elec blkts, tel, cable tv, video, movie, clock radio, t/c mkg, refrig, micro (3), toaster], iron, iron brd, pool, sauna, spa, bbq, cots-fee, non smoking units (4). RO $92 - $125, ♦ $11, AE BC DC EFT MC MP VI.

 ★★★☆ **Mitchell Motor Inn**, (M), 295 Main St (Princes Hwy), 1km SW of PO, ☎ 03 5152 5012, fax 03 5152 5660, (2 stry gr fl), 38 units (2 bedrm), [shwr, bath (3), spa bath (4), tlt, a/c, elec blkts, tel, TV, video-fee, movie, clock radio, t/c mkg, refrig, mini bar, cook fac ltd (3), toaster], ldry, ⊠ (Mon to Sat), pool, bbq, rm serv, cots-fee, non smoking units (5). RO ♦ $85 - $120, ♦♦ $90 - $140, ♦ $12, AE BC DC EFT MC MP VI.

 ★★★ **Bairnsdale Kansas City Motel**, (M), 310 Main St (Princes Hwy), 300m N of railway station, ☎ 03 5152 6266, fax 03 5152 5309, 20 units [shwr, tlt, hairdry, a/c-cool, cent heat, elec blkts, tel, TV, video, clock radio, t/c mkg, refrig], ldry, pool, spa (heated), plygr, cots. RO ♦ $66 - $95.90, ♦♦ $70.40 - $82.50, ♦ $10, ch con, AE BC DC EFT MC MP VI.

 ★★★ **Bairnsdale Main Motel**, (M), 544 Main St (Princes Hwy), 2.9km SW of PO, ☎ 03 5152 5000, fax 03 5152 1688, 17 units [shwr, tlt, a/c, elec blkts, tel, TV, movie, clock radio, t/c mkg, refrig], ldry, pool, bbq, dinner to unit, boat park, car wash, plygr, cots-fee, non smoking units (9). RO ♦ $55 - $65, ♦♦ $65 - $75, ♦ $10, ch con, AE BC DC EFT MC MP VI.

★★★ **Bairnsdale Motor Inn**, (M), 598 Main St (Princes Hwy), 3.4km SW of PO, ☎ 03 5152 3004, fax 03 5152 2544, 33 units [shwr, spa bath (2), tlt, a/c, heat, elec blkts, tel, TV, clock radio, t/c mkg, refrig, mini bar (17), toaster (17)], ldry, iron (17), iron brd (17), ✉ (Mon to Sat), pool-heated (solar), bbq, plygr, cots, non smoking units (3). **RO** ╫ **$80 - $135**, ╫╫ **$86 - $135**, ╫ **$11**, ch con, 16 units ★★☆, AE BC DC EFT MC VI.

★★★ **Flag Heritage Riversleigh Country Hotel**, (Ltd Lic H), Previously The Riversleigh Country Hotel, 1 Nicholson St, 150m NE of PO, ☎ 03 5152 6966, fax 03 5152 4413, (2 stry gr fl) 20 rms [ensuite, spa bath (2), a/c (5), c/fan, heat, elec blkts, tel, TV, clock radio, t/c mkg, refrig, mini bar, doonas], conf fac, ✉ (Mon to Sat), pool, spa, non smoking rms. **RO** ╫ **$88 - $126.50**, ╫╫ **$115 - $148.50**, ╫ **$11**, AE BC DC EFT MC VI.

★★★ **Riverhill Motor Inn**, (M), 45 Main St (Princes Hwy), 350m E of PO, ☎ 03 5153 1551, fax 03 5153 0249, 17 units [shwr, tlt, a/c-cool (10), a/c (7), heat, elec blkts, tel, cable tv, video-fee, clock radio, t/c mkg, refrig, toaster], ldry, conf fac, pool-heated (solar), bbq, meals avail (breakfast), boat park, trailer park, cots-fee, non smoking units (7). **RO** ╫ **$60 - $80**, ╫ **$14 - $20**, AE BC DC EFT MC MP VI.

★★★ **Tanjil Motor Inn**, (M), 384 Main St (Princes Hwy), 1.3km SW of PO, ☎ 03 5152 6677, fax 03 5152 6677, 20 units [shwr, bath (2), spa bath (1), tlt, hairdry, a/c, elec blkts, tel, cable tv, video-fee, t/c mkg, refrig, toaster], iron, iron brd, pool, bbq, dinner to unit (Mon-Thurs), cots-fee. **RO** ╫ **$62 - $85**, ╫╫ **$72 - $145**, ╫ **$12**, 6 units yet to be rated. AE BC DC EFT MC MP VI, ♿.

★★★ **Town Central Motel**, (M), 164 Nicholson St, 500m SW of PO, ☎ 03 5152 3084, fax 03 5152 1995, 11 units [shwr, tlt, a/c-cool (9), cent heat, elec blkts, tel, TV, movie, clock radio, t/c mkg, refrig, cook fac (2), toaster], ldry, bbq, cots-fee, non smoking units (4). **RO** ╫ **$55 - $62**, ╫╫ **$62 - $105**, ╫ **$10**, AE BC DC EFT MC MCH VI.

★★ **Bairnsdale Wander Inn Motel**, (M), 620 Main St (Princes Hwy), 3.7km SW of PO, ☎ 03 5152 6477, fax 03 5152 3402, 16 units [shwr, tlt, a/c, elec blkts, tel, TV, clock radio, t/c mkg, refrig], ✕, ✕, BYO, pool, bbq, cots-fee. **RO** ╫ **$47 - $50**, ╫╫ **$55 - $58**, ╫ **$8**, AE BC DC EFT MC VI.

★★ **Travelana Motel**, (M), 49 Main St (Princes Hwy), 300m E of PO, ☎ 03 5152 3200, fax 03 5152 5928, 14 units [shwr, tlt, a/c-cool (12), a/c (2), heat, elec blkts, tel (10), TV, clock radio, t/c mkg, refrig], cots, non smoking units (4). **RO** ╫ **$53 - $55**, ╫╫ **$58 - $62**, ch con, AE BC DC MC MCH VI.

Self Catering Accommodation

★★★★ **Bayview Lodge**, (Cotg), 300 Morrisons La, Bairnsdale East 3875, 9km E of PO, ☎ 03 5153 0476, fax 03 5153 0476, 1 cotg acc up to 5, (2 bedrm), [shwr, tlt, hairdry, a/c-cool, c/fan, heat (wood), elec blkts, TV, video, clock radio, CD, cook fac, micro, elec frypan, toaster, ldry (in unit), blkts, doonas, linen, pillows], w/mach, dryer, iron, iron brd, spa, bbq, jetty, canoeing, golf (pitch n putt). **D** ╫╫ **$137**, ╫ **$25**, **W** ╫╫ **$959**, ╫ **$150**, ch con.

★ **Bush Hide Away Log Cabins**, (Log Cabin), 140 Waterholes Rd, Granite Rock 3875, 14km N of Bairnsdale, off Omeo Hwy, ☎ 03 5156 8448, 4 log cabins acc up to 6, (2 bedrm), [shwr, tlt, heat, TV, refrig, cook fac ltd, linen reqd], pool (seasonal), bbq, cots. **D** **$44 - $60**, 2 electric powered cabins ★★. All cabins have hand pumped water, gas lighting-2, Min book applies.

B&B's/Guest Houses

★★★★☆ **Dalfruin**, (B&B), 18 McCulloch St, ☎ 03 5153 1443, fax 03 5152 6578, 2 rms [shwr, bath, tlt, hairdry, a/c-cool, a/c, cent heat, elec blkts, t/c mkg], lounge (TV, video), non smoking property. **BB** ╫ **$110**, ╫╫ **$130**, AE BC MC VI.

★★★★☆ **Tara House Bed & Breakfast**, (B&B), 37 Day St, 1.1 Km N of Hospital, ☎ 03 5153 2253, fax 03 5153 2426, 3 rms [ensuite, bath (1), hairdry, c/fan, heat, elec blkts, clock radio], lounge (TV, DVD), lounge firepl, t/c mkg shared, bbq, non smoking property. **BB** ╫ **$100**, ╫╫ **$115 - $135**, Min book long w/ends and Easter, BC MC VI.

★★★☆ **Peaceful Waters**, (B&B), No children's facilities, 56 Robb St, 1km SE of bridge, ☎ 03 5153 0736, fax 03 5153 0040, 3 rms [shwr, tlt, hairdry, c/fan, cent heat, elec blkts, clock radio], iron, iron brd, lounge (TV, cd player), spa, t/c mkg shared, bbq, jetty, non smoking property. **BB** ╫ **$90 - $115**, ╫╫ **$110 - $125**, 1 unit ★★★★, BC MC VI.

BALLARAT VIC 3350

Pop 64,850. (113km W Melbourne), See map on pages 694/695, ref D6. Includes: DELECOMBE, SEBASTOPOL, WARRENHEIP, WENDOUREE. Victoria's largest inland provincial city. Visitor Information Centre, 39 Sturt St, 03 5332 2694. Art Gallery, Boating, Bowls, Croquet, Fishing, Golf, Greyhound Racing, Horse Racing, Rowing, Sailing, Scenic Drives, Squash, Swimming, Tennis, Trotting. See also Buninyong & Cardigan.

Hotels/Motels

★★★★☆ **Ballarat Lodge**, (M), 613 Main Rd, 500m W of Sovereign Hill, ☎ 03 5331 3588, fax 03 5333 3042, 71 units [shwr, bath (60), spa bath (8), tlt, hairdry, a/c, c/fan (4), tel, TV, clock radio, t/c mkg, refrig, mini bar], ldry, iron, iron brd, business centre, conf fac, ✉ (Sun to Mon), pool (solar heated), bbq, 24hr reception, rm serv (incl liquor), dinner to unit, c/park (carport) (18), ☏, tennis (royal)-fee, cots, non smoking units (27). **BB** ╫ **$125 - $165**, ╫╫ **$140 - $180**, ╫ **$10**, Min book long w/ends, AE BC DC EFT MC VI.

★★★★☆ **Menzies Motor Inn & Apartments**, (M), 7 Humffray St, 30m W of Bakery Hill PO, ☎ 03 5331 3277, fax 03 5332 3855, 24 units [shwr, spa bath (15), tlt, hairdry, a/c, elec blkts, tel (direct dial), clock radio, t/c mkg, refrig, micro, toaster], ldry, w/mach-fee, dryer-fee, iron, iron brd, ✉, bar, rm serv, cots-fee, breakfast ingredients, non smoking property. **BLB** ╫ **$100 - $155**, ╫╫ **$120 - $210**, ╫ **$15**, Partial Disabled facilities, Min book long w/ends and Easter, AE BC DC EFT MC VI, ♿.

★★★★ **(Apartment Section)**, 4 apts acc up to 4, (1 bedrm - 4 divided, 4 interconnecting), [shwr, spa bath, tlt, a/c, elec blkts, tel (direct dial), TV, video, clock radio, t/c mkg, refrig, cook fac ltd, micro, d/wash (4), toaster, blkts, linen, pillows], ldry, iron, iron brd, lounge, rm serv, cots-fee, breakfast ingredients. **D** ╫╫ **$155 - $175**, ╫ **$20**.

★★★★☆ **Mercure Inn Ballarat**, (M), 1845 Sturt St, 6km W of PO, ☎ 03 5334 1600, fax 03 5334 2540, (2 stry gr fl), 76 units [shwr, bath (8), spa bath (40), tlt, a/c, elec blkts, tel, TV, movie, clock radio, t/c mkg, refrig, mini bar, cook fac (8)], ldry, iron, iron brd, conf fac, ✉, bar (cocktail), pool-heated, sauna, spa, bbq, 24hr reception, rm serv, tennis, cots, non smoking units (40). **RO** ╫ **$84 - $129**, ╫╫ **$84 - $129**, ╫╫╫╫ **$106 - $151**, ch con, AE BC DC EFT MC VI, ♿.

SUMMER

AUTUMN

Ballarat. For all seasons.

WINTER

SPRING

For al fresco dining and picnics at Lake Wendouree, a trip to Sovereign Hill or historic Her Majesty's Theatre, visit Ballarat, in any season. Stop by our Information Centre at 39 Sturt Street, Ballarat, or phone **1800 44 66 33** for information and bookings.

Ballarat*eureka!
www.ballarat.com

★★★★☆ **The Ansonia**, (Ltd Lic H), 32 Lydiard St South, 50m S of PO, ☎ 03 5332 4678, fax 03 5332 4698, 20 rms (1 suite) [shwr, bath, tlt, hairdry, c/fan, heat, tel, TV, video (avail), clock radio, CD (1), doonas], iron, iron brd, lounge (CD), conf fac, lounge firepl, ☒, t/c mkg shared, non smoking property. **RO 🚹 $135 - $210, 🚹🚹 $135 - $210**, AE BC DC MC VI.

GOLDEN CHAIN ★★★★ **Ambassador Motor Inn**, (M), 1759 Sturt St (Western Hwy), 5km W of PO, opposite golf course, ☎ 03 5334 1505, fax 03 5334 2134, 22 units [shwr, bath (hip) (1), spa bath (9), tlt, hairdry, a/c-cool (13), a/c (9), cent heat (13), elec blkts, tel, cable tv, video-fee, clock radio, t/c mkg, refrig, mini bar, cook fac (3), toaster, ldry], iron, iron brd, ☒ (Mon to Sat), pool, bbq, plygr, cots-fee, non smoking units (11). **RO 🚹 $70 - $101, 🚹🚹 $79 - $113, 🚹 $11**, ch con, AE BC DC EFT MC MP VI.

Trouble-free travel tips - **Jack**

Check that the jack and wheel are on board and the jack works.

★★★★ **Barkly Motor Lodge**, (M), 45 Main Rd, 900m SE of PO, ☎ 03 5331 8838, fax 03 5331 8787, (2 stry gr fl), 25 units (2 suites) [shwr, bath (14), spa bath (10), tlt, hairdry, a/c, elec blkts, tel, TV, movie, clock radio, t/c mkg, refrig, mini bar, micro (4), toaster], iron, iron brd, conf fac, ⊠, rm serv, cots-fee, non smoking units (8). **D** ╪ **$83.50,** ╫ **$93.50, Suite D** ╪ **$104.50 - $115.50,** ╫ **$115.50 - $126.50,** AE BC DC EFT MC MP VI.

★★★★ **Central City Motor Inn Ballarat**, (M), 16 Victoria St, ☎ 03 5333 1775, fax 03 5332 9437, (2 stry gr fl), 15 units [shwr, spa bath (4), tlt, a/c, elec blkts, tel, TV, movie, t/c mkg, refrig, mini bar, micro, toaster], iron, iron brd, pool indoor heated, bbq, cots-fee, non smoking units (4). **D** ╫ **$99 - $131, RO** ╪ **$86 - $105,** ◊ **$11,** AE BC DC EFT MC MP VI, ⅃⅄.

★★★★ **Sovereign Hill Lodge**, (M), Magpie St, adjacent to gold mining township, ☎ 03 5333 3409, fax 03 5333 5861, 14 units [shwr, spa bath (4), tlt, hairdry (8), a/c-cool, cent heat, elec blkts, tel, TV, clock radio, t/c mkg, refrig, toaster], ldry, iron, iron brd, rec rm, ⊠, bar (cocktail), cook fac, bbq, 24hr reception, ☏, cots-fee. **BLB** ╪ **$81 - $139,** ╫ **$90 - $139,** ◊ **$10 - $12,** ch con, 6 units ★★★. AE BC DC EFT MC VI.

★★★★ **Sovereign Park Motor Inn**, (M), 223 Main Rd, 600m N of Sovereign Hill, ☎ 03 5331 3955, fax 03 5333 4066, 49 units [shwr, spa bath (15), tlt, hairdry, a/c, elec blkts, tel, TV, video-fee, movie, clock radio, t/c mkg, refrig, toaster], ldry, iron, iron brd, business centre, conf fac, ⊠, cafe, pool indoor heated, sauna, spa, bbq, rm serv, gym, tennis (half court), cots-fee, breakfast ingredients, non smoking units (10). **BLB** ╪ **$80 - $105,** ╫ **$90 - $115,** ◊ **$10,** AE BC DC EFT MC MP VI, ⅃⅄.
(Apartment Section), apts [shwr, tlt, hairdry, a/c, heat, tel, TV, video, refrig, cook fac, micro, toaster, ldry, blkts, linen, pillows], w/mach, dryer, plygr. **D** ╪ **$80 - $155,** ◊ **$10,** (not yet classified).

★★★★ **The Victoriana Motor Inn**, (M), 214 Victoria St (Western Hwy), 2km E of PO, ☎ 03 5333 3577, fax 03 5333 3580, 20 units (1 suite) [shwr, spa bath (13), tlt, hairdry, a/c, elec blkts, tel, TV, video-fee, clock radio, t/c mkg, refrig, mini bar, toaster], ldry, iron, iron brd, cots, non smoking units (6). **RO** ╪ **$87 - $105,** ╫ **$98 - $134,** ◊ **$11,** AE BC DC EFT JCB MC MP VI.

★★★☆ **Alfred Motor Inn**, (M), 1843 Sturt St (Western Hwy), 5.9km W of PO, ☎ 03 5334 1607, fax 03 5334 1273, 19 units [shwr, tlt, a/c-cool, heat, elec blkts, tel, cable tv, video-fee, clock radio, t/c mkg, refrig, toaster], ldry, pool (salt water), bbq, plygr, cots-fee, non smoking units (8). **RO** ╪ **$60 - $67,** ╫ **$70 - $78,** ◊ **$11,** AE BC DC EFT MC MCH VI.

★★★☆ **Bakery Hill Motel**, (M), Cnr Humffray & Victoria Sts, 800m E of PO, ☎ 03 5333 1363, fax 03 5333 2335, (2 stry gr fl), 14 units [shwr, bath (3), tlt, hairdry, a/c, elec blkts, tel, TV, video-fee, movie, clock radio, t/c mkg, refrig, mini bar], ldry, cots-fee, non smoking units (6). **RO** ╪ **$88 - $124,** ╫ **$99 - $124,** ◊ **$12,** AE BC DC EFT MC MP VI, ⅃⅄.

★★★☆ **Ballarat Mid City Motor Inn**, (M), 19 Doveton St North, 200m NW of PO, ☎ 03 5331 1222, fax 03 5333 4494, (2 stry gr fl), 71 units (3 suites) [shwr, bath (18), tlt, hairdry, a/c, elec blkts, tel, TV, clock radio, t/c mkg, refrig, mini bar, toaster], ldry, iron (41), iron brd (41), conf fac, ⊠ (Mon to Sat), pool-heated, sauna, rm serv, cots-fee, non smoking rms (8). **D $100 - $122,** 3 units ★★★★. AE BC DC EFT MC MP VI.

★★★☆ **Ballarat Woodmans Hill Motor Inn**, (M), Melbourne Rd East (Western Hwy), Ballarat East 3352, 6km E of PO, ☎ 03 5334 7202, or 03 5334 7324, fax 03 5334 7883, 16 units (2 bedrm), [shwr, tlt, a/c-cool, heat, elec blkts, tel, TV, video-fee, clock radio, t/c mkg, refrig, toaster], ldry, bbq, meals avail, car wash, plygr, cots, non smoking units (8). **RO** ♦ $50 - $80, ♦♦ $60 - $85, ♦ $10, AE BC DC EFT MC MP VI.

★★★☆ **Gold Sovereign Motor Inn**, (M), 422 Learmonth Rd, Wendouree 3355, 7.5km NW of PO, ☎ 03 5339 3161, fax 03 5338 1059, 30 units [shwr, spa bath (5), tlt, hairdry, a/c, heat, elec blkts, tel, cable tv, video-fee, clock radio, t/c mkg, refrig, mini bar, toaster], ldry, iron, iron brd, conf fac, ⊠, pool, bbq, rm serv, dinner to unit, plygr, cots-fee, non smoking units (14). **RO** ♦ $69 - $120, ♦♦ $80 - $130, ♦ $11, ch con, AE BC DC EFT MC MP VI, ♿.

★★★☆ **Park View Motor Inn**, (M), 1611 Sturt St, 3.9km W of PO, ☎ 03 5334 1001, fax 03 5334 2202, (2 stry gr fl), 46 units [shwr, spa bath (17), tlt, a/c, cent heat, elec blkts, tel, TV, clock radio, t/c mkg, refrig], ldry, pool, cots-fee, non smoking rms (21). **RO** ♦ $71.50 - $93.50, ♦♦ $77 - $99, ♦ $11, AE BC DC MC MP VI.

★★★☆ **Peppinella Motel**, (M), 102 Smythes Rd (Glenelg Hwy), Delacombe 3356, 5km SW of PO, ☎ 03 5335 9666, fax 03 5335 9929, 15 units [shwr, tlt, hairdry, a/c, heat, elec blkts, tel, cable tv, movie, clock radio, t/c mkg, refrig, micro (3), toaster], ldry, iron, iron brd, pool-heated (solar), spa, bbq (covered), plygr, cots-fee, non smoking units (12). **RO** ♦ $55 - $75, ♦♦ $69 - $75, ♦ $11, AE BC DC EFT MC MCH VI.

★★★☆ **Sundowner Chain Motor Inns**, (M), 312 Main Rd, 500m N of Sovereign Hill, ☎ 03 5331 7533, fax 03 5332 2853, (2 stry gr fl), 25 units [shwr, bath (4), spa bath (2), tlt, hairdry, a/c, elec blkts, tel, cable tv, clock radio, t/c mkg, refrig, mini bar], ldry, iron, iron brd, ⊠ (Mon to Sat), pool indoor heated, spa, rm serv, cots-fee, non smoking units (12). **RO** ♦ $93 - $145.50, ♦♦ $98.50 - $145.50, ♦ $11, ch con, Min book long w/ends and Easter, AE BC DC EFT JCB MC MP VI, ♿.

★★★ **Begonia City Motor Inn**, (M), 244 Albert St (Midland Hwy), Sebastopol 3356, 250m S of Sebastopol PO, ☎ 03 5335 5577, fax 03 5335 5583, 17 units [shwr, spa bath (3), tlt, hairdry (6), a/c, elec blkts, tel, TV, video-fee, clock radio, t/c mkg, refrig, cook fac ltd (2), micro (4), toaster], pool, bbq, cots, non smoking units (6). **RO** ♦ $65 - $86, ♦♦ $86 - $108, ♦ $15, 3 units ★★★☆, AE BC DC EFT MP VI.

★★★ **Eureka Lodge Motel**, (M), 119 Stawell St South, 3.2km E of PO, ☎ 03 5331 1900, fax 03 5331 5266, 17 units [shwr, tlt, a/c-cool (5), a/c (12), heat, elec blkts, tel, TV, video, movie, radio, t/c mkg, refrig, toaster], ldry, bbq, cots, non smoking units (5). **BLB** ♦ $50 - $67, ♦♦ $62 - $67, ♦ $10, AE BC DC EFT MC VI.

★★★ **Kryal Castle**, (M), 121 Forbes Rd, Warrenheip 3352, ☎ 03 5334 7388, fax 03 5334 7422, 15 units [shwr, spa bath, tlt, hairdry, heat, elec blkts, tel, TV, clock radio, t/c mkg, refrig], ldry, conf fac, ⊠, plygr, cots. **BLB** ♦ $110, ♦♦ $125 - $215, ♦ $55, ch con, Tariff includes entrance to Castle, AE BC DC MC VI.

★★★ **Miners Retreat Motel**, (M), 604 Eureka St, 100m E of Eureka Stockade, ☎ 03 5331 6900, fax 03 5331 6944, 20 units [shwr, tlt, fan, cent heat, elec blkts, tel, TV, video-fee, clock radio, t/c mkg, refrig, toaster], ✕, bbq, dinner to unit, plygr, cots, non smoking units (10). **BLB** ♦ $52, ♦♦ $62 - $64, ♦ $11, AE BC DC EFT MC MCH VI.

★★★ **(Park Cabin Section)**, 4 cabins acc up to 6, [shwr, tlt, a/c, TV, clock radio, t/c mkg, refrig, cook fac ltd, micro, toaster, blkts, linen, pillows], non smoking units. **BLB** ♦ $57, ♦♦ $62 - $67, ♦ $11.

★★★ **The Arch Motel**, (M), 1853 Sturt St (Western Hwy), 1.6 km W of The Arch, 6.1km W of PO, ☎ 03 5334 1464, 11 units [shwr, bath (1), tlt, a/c, elec blkts, TV, clock radio, t/c mkg, refrig, cook fac (1), toaster], ldry. **RO** ♦ $48, ♦♦ $55 - $66, ♦ $12, 3 units ★★, BC MC VI.

★★★ **The Avenue Motel**, (M), 1813 Sturt St (Avenue of Honour), 5.5km W of PO, ☎ 03 5334 1303, fax 03 5343 3365, 24 units [shwr, tlt, a/c-cool, cent heat, elec blkts, tel, TV, video-fee, clock radio, t/c mkg, refrig, toaster], ldry, pool, bbq, non smoking units (12). **RO** ♦ $63 - $78, ♦♦ $70 - $78, ♦ $12, AE BC DC EFT MC MP VI.

★★☆ **City Oval**, (LMH), Cnr Pleasant & Mair Sts, 2.4km W of PO, opposite City Oval, ☎ 03 5332 1155, fax 03 5333 4459, 8 units [shwr, tlt, fan, heat, elec blkts, tel, TV, t/c mkg, refrig, toaster], ⊠, ✆, cots-fee. BLB ⏽ $53, ⏽⏽ $64, ⏽ $11, BC MC VI.

★★☆ **George Hotel**, (LH), 27 Lydiard St North, 50m N of PO, ☎ 03 5333 4866, fax 03 5333 4818, (Multi-stry), 17 rms [basin, shwr (6), tlt (6), c/fan (2), heat, TV (6), clock radio, t/c mkg (6)], lounge (TV), conf fac, meeting rm, night club (Fri & Sat), ⊠ (Tues to Sat), bar, t/c mkg shared, refrig, c/park (limited), ✆, cots, non smoking rms (17). BLB ⏽ $35 - $50, ⏽⏽ $50 - $75, ⏽ $15, ch con, AE BC DC EFT MC VI.

★★☆ **Melesa Motor Inn**, (M), Melbourne Rd (Western Hwy), 6.9km E of PO, ☎ 03 5334 7303, fax 03 5334 7281, 12 units [shwr, tlt, a/c-cool (6), fan (6), cent heat, elec blkts, tel, TV, video-fee, clock radio, t/c mkg, refrig, toaster], ldry, bbq, cots, non smoking units (4). RO ⏽ $53, ⏽⏽ $64, ⏽ $11, 4 units of a higher rating, AE BC DC EFT MC MCH VI.

Ballarat

★★☆ **Motel Ballarat**, (M), Melbourne Rd (Western Hwy), 6.7km E of PO, ☎ 03 5334 7234, fax 03 5334 7500, 14 units [shwr, tlt, a/c-cool (10), fan (4), heat, elec blkts, tel, TV, video-fee, movie, clock radio, t/c mkg, refrig, toaster], ldry, pool above ground (summer), dinner to unit, plygr, cots, non smoking units (5). BLB ⏽ $42 - $55, ⏽⏽ $53 - $66, ⏽⏽⏽⏽ $75 - $99, ⏽ $11, 4 units ★★★. AE BC DC EFT MC MCH VI.

★☆ **Criterion Hotel Ballarat**, (LH), 18 Doveton St South, 500m SW of PO, ☎ 03 5331 1451, fax 03 5331 5520, (2 stry), 22 rms [basin, elec blkts, refrig (3)], lounge (TV), conf fac, ⊠, t/c mkg shared, refrig, ✆, plygr (indoor), non smoking rms. BLB ⏽ $25 - $30, ⏽⏽ $40 - $50, ⏽ $10, ch con, BC EFT MC VI.

Balwaren Motel, (M), Melbourne Rd (Western Hwy), 6.3km E of PO, ☎ 03 5334 7444, fax 03 5334 8002, 14 units [shwr, bath (1), tlt, fan, cent heat, elec blkts, tel, TV, clock radio, t/c mkg, refrig, cook fac (1), toaster], ldry, ✕, BYO, bbq, plygr, tennis, cots. BLB ⏽ $55 - $66, ⏽⏽ $66 - $77, ⏽ $11, ch con, BC EFT MC VI, (Rating under review).

The Views Motor Inn.Bar.Cafe, (LMH), Previously Lake View 22 Wendouree Pde, 1.5km W of PO, ☎ 03 5331 4592, fax 03 5331 4326, (2 stry), 12 units [shwr, tlt, hairdry, a/c-cool, heat (6), cent heat (12), elec blkts, tel, cable tv, video, clock radio, t/c mkg, refrig, toaster], ldry, conf fac, ⊠, c/park (undercover), cots-fee. RO ⏽ $55 - $69, ⏽⏽ $66 - $80, ⏽ $10 - $11, ch con, AE BC DC EFT MC VI, (Rating under review).

Self Catering Accommodation

★★★★☆ **Abena's Ballarat B & B**, (Cotg), 210 Grant St, 400m S of PO, ☎ 03 5331 9834, fax 03 5332 4244, 1 cotg acc up to 6, (3 bedrm), [shwr, bath, tlt, c/fan, cent heat, tel (local), TV, video, clock radio, CD, t/c mkg, refrig, cook fac, micro, elec frypan, d/wash, toaster, ldry, blkts, linen, pillows], w/mach, dryer, bbq, secure park, cots. D ⏽⏽ $110 - $150, ⏽ $13, Min book school holidays and Easter, BC MC VI.

★★★★☆ **Quest Colony Operations**, (Apt), 674 Melbourne Rd, Ballarat 3352, 6km E of PO, ☎ 03 5334 7788, fax 03 5334 7834, 28 apts acc up to 6, (1, 2 & 3 bedrm), [ensuite (18), shwr, tlt, hairdry, a/c, tel, TV, video, clock radio, t/c mkg, refrig, cook fac, micro, d/wash, toaster, ldry (in unit), blkts, linen, pillows], w/mach, dryer, iron, iron brd, conf fac, ⊠ (Mon to Sat), pool indoor heated, bbq, rm serv, tennis, cots. D $132 - $198, Breakfast available, AE BC DC EFT MC VI.
★★★★ **(Motel Section)**, 16 units [shwr, spa bath (4), tlt, hairdry, a/c, tel, TV, clock radio, t/c mkg, refrig], iron, iron brd, rm serv. RO ⏽⏽ $94.50, ⏽ $15, ⏽⏽.

★★★★☆ **Serenity Tranquility Therapy Centre**, (Cotg), Health retreat. 115 Winter St, 2.5km SW of PO, ☎ 03 5336 1343, fax 03 5336 1729, 2 cotgs acc up to 6, (2 & 3 bedrm), [shwr, spa bath (3), tlt, hairdry, a/c-cool, c/fan, heat (log fire), elec blkts, tel, cable tv, video, CD, refrig, cook fac, micro, d/wash, toaster, blkts, linen, pillows], ldry, w/mach, bbq, breakfast ingredients, non smoking units, Pets on application. BB ⏽ $82.50, ⏽⏽ $148.50, ⏽ $22, Meals by arrangement. BC EFT MC VI.

★★★★☆ **Yarrowee Cottage**, (Cotg), 711 Morres St, 3km E of PO, ☎ 03 5331 5558, fax 03 5331 5600, 1 cotg acc up to 5, (2 bedrm), [shwr, spa bath, tlt, hairdry, a/c, elec blkts, TV, video, clock radio, CD, t/c mkg, refrig, cook fac, micro, elec frypan, toaster, blkts, linen], iron, iron brd, bbq, breakfast ingredients. D ⏽⏽ $130, ⏽ $10, Min book long w/ends.

★★★★ **Ballarat City Apartments**, (Apt), 225 Lydiard St North, 600m N of PO, ☎ 03 5332 6992, fax 03 5338 7878, (2 stry gr fl), 5 apts acc up to 4, (1 & 2 bedrm), [shwr, spa bath, tlt, hairdry, a/c (1), c/fan, heat, elec blkts, TV, video, clock radio, CD, t/c mkg, refrig, cook fac ltd (3), micro (3), elec frypan (3), toaster, blkts, linen, pillows], cots-fee. D ♥♥ $88 - $143, ◊ $16, 2 units ★★★, Min book long w/ends and Easter, AE BC MC VI.

★★★★ **Ballarat Heritage Homestay**, (Cotg), Wilton House, 177 Victoria St, ☎ 03 5332 8296, fax 03 5331 3358, 1 cotg acc up to 6, (3 bedrm), [shwr (2), bath, tlt (2), hairdry, cent heat, elec blkts, TV, video, clock radio, CD, refrig, cook fac, micro, ldry, blkts, linen, pillows], w/mach, dryer, lounge firepl, bbq, non smoking property. D ♥♥ $160 - $165, ◊ $30, W ♥♥ $760, ch con, AE BC DC MC VI.

★★★★☆ **(187 Victoria St Section)**, Kingsley Place, 1 cotg acc up to 6, (3 bedrm), [shwr (2), spa bath, tlt (2), hairdry, fan, cent heat, elec blkts, tel (local), TV, video, clock radio, CD, refrig, cook fac, micro, elec frypan, d/wash, toaster, ldry, blkts, doonas, linen, pillows], w/mach, dryer, lounge firepl, bbq, non smoking property. D ♥♥ $160 - $175, ◊ $30, W ♥♥ $840, ch con.

★★★★ **(404 Havelock St Section)**, Ravenswood, 1 cotg acc up to 6, (3 bedrm), [shwr, bath, tlt, hairdry, heat, elec blkts, tel (local), TV, video, clock radio, CD, refrig, cook fac, micro, ldry, blkts, linen, pillows], w/mach, lounge firepl, bbq, c/park (undercover), non smoking property. D ♥♥ $135 - $165, ◊ $15 - $30, W ♥♥ $640.

★★★★ **Ballarat Spa Cottages**, (Cotg), 8 Doveton Cres, 400m N of PO, ☎ 03 5339 9779, fax 03 5332 4482, 1 cotg acc up to 4, (2 bedrm), [shwr, spa bath, tlt, hairdry, fan, cent heat, elec blkts, tel (local), TV, video, clock radio, refrig, cook fac ltd, micro, elec frypan, toaster, ldry (in unit), doonas, linen, pillows], w/mach, dryer, iron, iron brd, bbq, c/park (garage), breakfast ingredients, non smoking property. BLB ♥♥ $130, ◊ $20, W ♥♥ $650, ◊ $100, ch con, Min book long w/ends and Easter, BC MC VI.

★★★★ **Harrowfield House**, (Cotg), 106 Ripon St South, ☎ 03 5344 8302, fax 03 5344 8307, 1 cotg acc up to 6, (3 bedrm), [shwr, spa bath, tlt, hairdry, fan, cent heat, elec blkts, tel, TV, video, clock radio, CD, refrig, cook fac, micro, d/wash, toaster, ldry (in unit), blkts, linen, pillows], w/mach, iron, iron brd, bbq, c/park (undercover), cots. D ♥♥ $129 - $159, ◊ $17 - $24, W ♥♥ $760 - $880, ◊ $95 - $135, pen con, AE BC DC MC VI,

Operator Comment: Centrally located, romantic heritage cottage. Phone for brochure or www.pchost.com/cardigan

★★★★ **Hermiston Retreat**, (HU), Cnr Chisholm & Ligar Sts, 2km N of PO, ☎ 03 5332 6880, fax 03 5332 6880, 1 unit acc up to 4, (1 bedrm), [shwr, tlt, hairdry, a/c-cool, fan, heat, elec blkts, TV, clock radio, refrig, cook fac, micro, elec frypan, toaster, blkts, linen, pillows], ldry, iron, iron brd, sauna-fee, bbq, c/park (garage), cots-fee, non smoking property. BB ♥♥ $90, RO ♥♥ $80, ◊ $20, Min book long w/ends and Easter,

Operator Comment: Beautiful garden setting, close to Town Centre and all attractions.

★★★★ **Magpie Views**, (Cotg), 14 Magpie St, ☎ 03 5331 9979, 1 cotg acc up to 4, (2 bedrm), [shwr, tlt, hairdry, a/c-cool, fan, heat, elec blkts, tel (local), video, clock radio, CD, t/c mkg, refrig, cook fac, micro, elec frypan, ldry, blkts, linen, pillows], w/mach, dryer, iron, iron brd, bbq, non smoking property. D ♥♥ $135, ◊ $30, W $745, Min book applies.

★★★★ **Quest Mews Townhouse Apartments**, (Apt), 603 Main Rd, 1km NW of PO, ☎ 03 5333 7781, fax 03 5334 7834, (2 stry), 9 apts acc up to 5, (2 bedrm), [shwr, bath, tlt, hairdry, a/c, tel, TV, video, clock radio, t/c mkg, refrig, cook fac, micro, d/wash (6), ldry (in unit), blkts, linen, pillows], w/mach, dryer, iron, iron brd, bbq, cots-fee. D ◊ $117 - $130, ◊ $15, Breakfast available. AE BC DC EFT MC VI.

★★★☆ **Mopoke Gully - Accommodation**, (Cotg), 404B Havelock St, 1.2km NE of PO, ☎ 03 5331 1668, 1 cotg acc up to 2, (1 bedrm), [shwr, tlt, hairdry, evap cool, fan, heat, elec blkts, TV, clock radio, CD, refrig, cook fac ltd, micro, elec frypan, toaster, blkts, linen, pillows], ldry, w/mach, dryer, iron, iron brd, lounge firepl, bbq, non smoking property. D $100 - $125, W $480, Min book long w/ends and Easter.

★★★☆ **Ripon Cottage**, (Cotg), 413 Ripon St, 2.5km SW of PO, ☎ 03 5331 7217, fax 03 5332 1113, 1 cotg acc up to 6, (3 bedrm), [shwr, bath, tlt, hairdry, fan, cent heat, elec blkts, TV, video, CD, cook fac, micro, elec frypan, blkts, linen, pillows], w/mach, iron, iron brd, bbq, cots, breakfast ingredients, non smoking property. D ♥♥ $90, ◊ $20, W $510 - $990, ch con, AE BC MC VI.

★★★ **Gloriette**, (Cotg), 107 Lyons St Sth, ☎ 03 5332 3100, 1 cotg acc up to 5, (2 bedrm), [shwr, bath, tlt, fan, cent heat, elec blkts, tel (local), TV, clock radio, refrig, cook fac, micro, d/wash, toaster, blkts, linen, pillows], ldry, w/mach, c/park (carport). D ♥♥ $90 - $100, ◊ $10, W $375 - $450, Min book applies.

★★★ **Lake Terrace Apartments**, (Apt), 20 Wendouree Pde, 1.5km W of PO, ☎ 03 5332 1812, fax 03 5332 1813, (Multi-stry gr fl), 10 apts acc up to 6, (1 & 2 bedrm), [shwr, tlt, a/c, elec blkts, tel, TV, video-fee, clock radio, refrig, cook fac, micro, toaster, blkts, linen, pillows], ldry, w/mach, dryer, bbq, cots-fee. D ◊ $55 - $79, ♥♥ $69 - $94, ◊ $10 - $11, AE BC DC EFT MC VI.

BALLARAT VIC continued...

B&B's/Guest Houses

★★★★☆ **Ballara Cottage Bed & Breakfast**, (B&B), 315 Finch St, Central Ballarat ☎ 03 5331 6216, fax 03 5331 3187, (2 stry), 1 rm [shwr, tlt, hairdry, c/fan, heat, elec blkts, TV, video, clock radio, CD, t/c mkg, refrig, micro, toaster], bbq, c/park (garage), cots. **BB** ♦♦ **$110 - $125**, ◊ **$20 - $30**.

★★★★☆ **Blythewood Grange Conference Centre**, (GH), Cnr Morgan & Grant Sts, Sebastopol 3356, ☎ 03 5335 8133, fax 03 5336 1550, (2 stry gr fl), 59 rms (4 suites) [shwr, bath (2), tlt, cent heat, elec blkts, tel, TV, clock radio, t/c mkg, doonas], rec rm, lounge (TV, cd), conf fac, lounge firepl, ✕, pool indoor heated, sauna, spa (heated), bbq, gym, tennis, non smoking property. **BLB** ♦ **$75**, ♦♦ **$130**, **DBB** ♦ **$120 - $150**, ♦♦ **$210 - $230**, AE BC DC MC VI, &.

★★★★☆ **Bodlyn Bed & Breakfast**, (B&B), 9 Errard St Nth, 500m W of PO, ☎ 03 5332 1318, fax 03 5332 2899, 3 rms [ensuite, bath (2), spa bath (1), hairdry, fan, cent heat, elec blkts, clock radio], lounge (TV, cd player), t/c mkg shared, refrig, non smoking property. **BB** ♦ **$80 - $100**, ♦♦ **$120**, BC MC VI.

★★★★ **A Special Occasion**, (B&B), 812 Macarthur St, 3km N of PO, ☎ 03 5333 3600, fax 03 5333 7030, (2 stry), 1 rm [shwr, spa bath, tlt, fan, heat, elec blkts, TV, video, clock radio, CD, t/c mkg, refrig, mini bar, micro], secure park, non smoking property. **BB** ♦ **$94 - $105**, ♦♦ **$99 - $110**, ch con, Min book long w/ends and Easter, AE BC MC VI.

★★★★ **Al Hayatt**, (B&B), 800 Mair St, 900m W of PO, ☎ 03 5332 1396, (2 stry gr fl), 2 rms [ensuite (1), shwr, tlt, hairdry, fan, cent heat, elec blkts, clock radio], lounge (TV, video), t/c mkg shared, bbq, c/park. **BB** ♦ **$80**, ♦♦ **$105**, ◊ **$40**.

★★★★ **Braeside Garden Cottages**, (B&B), 3 Albion St, 900m W of Sovereign Hill, ☎ 03 5331 7659, fax 03 5331 7659, 2 rms [ensuite, spa bath (1), hairdry, a/c, elec blkts, TV, video, clock radio, CD (1), refrig, micro (1)], c/park (undercover) (1). **BB** ♦♦ **$130**, ◊ **$15**, ch con, BC MC VI,

Operator Comment: Visit us on the web at www.ballarat.com/braeside.htm

★★★★ **Eilean Donan Bed and Breakfast**, (B&B), Children by arrangement. 3 Karingal Park Dve, Ballarat 3352, 8km SW of PO, off Glenelg Hwy, ☎ 03 5342 4699, fax 03 5342 4665, 2 rms [ensuite (1), bath (1), hairdry, a/c, fan, heat, elec blkts], lounge (TV, video, stereo), t/c mkg shared, bbq, non smoking property. **BB** ♦ **$75 - $85**, ♦♦ **$85 - $95**, 1 room ★★★★☆, Min book long w/ends and Easter, BC MC VI.

★★★☆ **Woodside**, (B&B), No children's facilities, 120 Fisken Rd, Mount Helen 3350, 9.8km SE of PO, ☎ 03 5341 3451, 2 rms [shwr (2), tlt (1), hairdry, fan, heat, elec blkts], lounge (TV, video, cd), t/c mkg shared, non smoking rms. **BB** ♦ **$50**, ♦♦ **$80**.

★★★ **Ballarat Bed & Breakfast**, (GH), Wandella c1865, 202 Dawson St Sth, 750m SW of PO, ☎ 03 5333 7046, fax 03 5333 4106, (2 stry), 13 rms [ensuite (1), a/c-cool (1), heat, elec blkts, tel, clock radio, t/c mkg, micro (communal)], lounge (TV), t/c mkg shared, refrig (3), non smoking property. **BLB** ♦ **$22 - $33**, ♦♦ **$49 - $60**, ◊ **$22**, ch con, BC MC VI.

★★★ **Eastern Station Guest House**, (GH), 81 Humffray St Nth, 1km N of PO, ☎ 03 5338 8722, fax 03 5338 8723, (2 stry), 8 rms [fan, heat, clock radio, micro, toaster, doonas], ldry, w/mach, lounge (TV, cd), lounge firepl, ✕, bar (Fri night), cook fac, t/c mkg shared, refrig, bbq, ✆, cots, non smoking property. **RO** ♦ **$33**, ♦♦ **$55**, ◊ **$10**, BC EFT MC VI.

★☆ **Tawana Lodge**, (PH), Classified by National Trust, 128 Lydiard St North, 400m N of PO, adjacent to Railway Station, ☎ 03 5331 3461, (Multi-stry), 22 rms [shwr (12), tlt (12), c/fan (12), heat (12), elec blkts, TV (12), clock radio (12), t/c mkg (12), refrig (12)], lounge (TV), conf fac, ✉ (Mon to Sat), ✆, cots-fee. **RO** ♦ **$29.70 - $58.30**, ♦♦ **$44 - $69.30**, ◊ **$12**, BC MC VI.

Other Accommodation

AAA TOURISM *Special Rates*

Sovereign Hill Lodge, (Lodge), Magpie St, adjacent to gold mining township, ☎ 03 5333 3409, fax 03 5333 5861, 22 rms acc up to 10, (Bunk Rooms - 4x2bunks.), [ensuite (4), cent heat, blkts, linen reqd-fee, pillows], shwr (10G-11L), tlt (10G-11L), rec rm, lounge (TV), lounge firepl, cook fac, t/c mkg shared, refrig, bbq, ✆. **RO** ♦ **$18.50 - $21.50**, ◊ **$18.50 - $21.50**, Group meals by arrangement. AE BC DC EFT MC VI.

BALLIANG VIC 3340

Pop Nominal, (61km NW Melbourne), See map on page 696, ref A5. Pastoral district situated between the You Yangs and the Brisbane Ranges. Bush Walking, Scenic Drives.

B&B's/Guest Houses

★★★★ **Ripley Park**, (B&B), Gilmores Rd, ☎ 03 5369 4222, fax 03 5369 4256, 1 rm [shwr, tlt, c/fan, heat, elec blkts, clock radio, t/c mkg], lounge (TV, video, cd). **BB** ♦ **$95 - $110**, ♦♦ **$115 - $125**, ◊ **$45**, Other meals by arrangement. AE.

★★★ **(Cottage Section)**, 1 cotg acc up to 4, (2 bedrm), [shwr, bath, tlt, c/fan, elec blkts, TV, clock radio, t/c mkg, refrig, micro, elec frypan, toaster, blkts, linen, pillows], lounge firepl, bbq. **BB** ♦ **$95 - $110**, ♦♦ **$115 - $125**, ◊ **$54**, Other meals by arrangement.

BALMORAL VIC 3407

Pop 214. (320km W Melbourne), See map on pages 694/695, ref B5. Small agricultural township near Rocklands Spillway. Access to the western end of the Grampians & Black Range. Bowls, Bush Walking, Fishing, Golf, Sailing, Scenic Drives, Swimming (Pool), Tennis, Water Skiing.

Hotels/Motels

★ **Western Hotel**, (LH), 20 Glendinning St, ☎ 03 5570 1268, fax 03 5570 1312, 6 rms [basin (2), elec blkts], ✉, ✆. **BLB** ♦ **$25**, ♦♦ **$35 - $40**, ◊ **$10**, BC EFT MC VI.

Self Catering Accommodation

★★★ **Thistledome**, (Cotg), Cnr Harrow Rd & Railway St, 800m NW of PO, ☎ 03 5570 1206, fax 03 5570 1206, 1 cotg acc up to 10, (3 bedrm), [shwr, tlt, evap cool, TV, clock radio, refrig, cook fac, micro, elec frypan, toaster, ldry (in unit), doonas, linen reqd-fee, pillows], w/mach, iron, iron brd, lounge firepl, bbq, c/park (carport). **D** ♦♦♦♦ **$55**, ◊ **$13.20**, BC EFT MC VI.

★★ **Crofton Cottage**, (Cotg), (Farm), Harrow Rd, 7.3km W of PO, ☎ 03 5570 1293, 1 cotg acc up to 10, (5 bedrm), [shwr, bath, tlt, heat, elec blkts, TV, clock radio, refrig, cook fac, micro, toaster, ldry, blkts, doonas, linen, pillows], w/mach, iron, lounge firepl, bbq, tennis. **D $80**, **W $400**.

B&B's/Guest Houses

★★★☆ **Benwerrin Host Farm**, (B&B), (Farm), Glendinning Rd, 17km SE of PO, ☎ 03 5574 3255, 2 rms [hairdry, fan, heat, elec blkts, clock radio, doonas], lounge (TV, video, cd), t/c mkg shared, bbq. **BB** ♦ **$100**, ◊ **$100**, Dinner by arrangement. Tariff includes farm activities.

BALNARRING VIC 3926

Pop 1,950. (71km SE Melbourne), See map on page 697, ref D8. A residential and holiday township, overlooking Westernport Bay. Bowls, Swimming (Beach), Tennis.

Hotels/Motels

★★★★ **Balnarring Village Motor Inn**, (M), 3055 Frankston - Flinders Rd, 100m S of PO, ☎ 03 5983 5222, fax 03 5983 2549, 16 units [shwr, bath (1), spa bath (2), tlt, hairdry, a/c, elec blkts, tel, TV, video, clock radio, t/c mkg, refrig, micro (6), toaster], ldry, iron, iron brd, bbq (covered), dinner to unit, plygr, cots-fee, non smoking units (8). **RO** ♦ **$78 - $125**, ♦♦ **$88 - $125**, ◊ **$11**, ch con, AE BC DC EFT MC VI, &.

Rates may change. Check before booking.

B&B's/Guest Houses

★★★★☆ **Arundel Farm B & B**, (B&B), No children's facilities, 26 Bittern - Dromana Rd, 3km NE of Balnarring Village, ☎ 03 5983 2536, fax 03 5983 2588, 3 rms [ensuite, bath (hip) (1), spa bath (1), hairdry, c/fan, heat, elec blkts, TV (2)], rec rm, lounge (TV), lounge firepl, spa (heated), t/c mkg shared, refrig, bbq, gym, non smoking property. **BB ♦♦ $140 - $160**, Dinner by arrangement. BC MC VI.

★★★ **Warrawee Homestead Restaurant**, (GH), Children by arrangement. No children's facilities, Cnr Warrawee & Stanley Rds, 1.2km W of PO, ☎ 03 5983 1729, fax 03 5983 5199, 4 rms [ensuite, spa bath (2), heat, elec blkts, clock radio], lounge (TV), lounge firepl, ✕ (weekends & summer), t/c mkg shared, refrig, non smoking property. **BB ♦ $120, ♦♦ $160**, AE BC DC MC VI.

★★★ **(Cottage Section)**, 1 cotg acc up to 2, [shwr, bath, tlt, hairdry, fan, heat (wood), elec blkts, TV, video, clock radio, refrig, cook fac ltd, micro, blkts, linen, pillows], iron, iron brd. **D ♦♦ $180.**

BALOOK VIC 3971

Pop Nominal, (198km SE Melbourne), See map on page 696, ref E7. Small hamlet nestled high in the Strzelecki Ranges. Tarra Valley & Bulga National Parks. Bush Walking, Scenic Drives.

B&B's/Guest Houses

★★★☆ **Tarra - Bulga Guest House**, (GH), Grand Ridge Rd, 50m W of Tarra-Bulga National Park Visitors Centre, ☎ 03 5196 6141, fax 03 5196 6141, 11 rms [cent heat, elec blkts, doonas], ldry, rec rm, lounge (TV, video), ✕, t/c mkg shared, cots, non smoking property. **BB ♦♦ $85, DBB ♦ $130, ♦ $130**, ch con, BC MC VI.

BAMBRA VIC 3241

Pop 50. (126km SW Melbourne), See map on pages 694/695, ref D7. Small settlement in a sheep & dairying district. Bush Walking, Horse Riding, Scenic Drives.

Self Catering Accommodation

★★★★ **Countrywide Cottages**, (Cotg), 1205 Deans Marsh Rd, ☎ 03 5288 7399, fax 03 5288 7406, 2 cotgs acc up to 8, (2 & 3 bedrm), [shwr, tlt, c/fan, elec blkts, TV, clock radio, t/c mkg, refrig, cook fac, micro, toaster, blkts, doonas, linen, pillows], w/mach, lounge firepl, bbq, cots, non smoking property. **D ♦♦ $80 - $160, ♦ $10 - $20, W ♦♦ $480 - $960, ♦ $60 - $120**, ch con, Min book Christmas Jan long w/ends and Easter.

BANNOCKBURN VIC 3331

Pop 900. (90km SW Melbourne), See map on page 696, ref A6. Sheep & wheat farming district. Bowls, Golf, Tennis.

B&B's/Guest Houses

★★★☆ **The Station Retreat**, (B&B), Heritage, Railway Station, 1 Geelong Rd, ☎ 03 5281 1667, (2 stry), 3 rms [hairdry, elec blkts, TV, video, clock radio, refrig, cook fac, micro, toaster, doonas], iron, lounge (video), lounge firepl, bbq, non smoking property. **BLB ♦ $76, ♦♦ $109**, BC MC VI.

BARMAH VIC 3639

Pop 250. (239km N Melbourne), See map on page 696, ref C1. Barmah State Forest - Victoria's largest stand of red gum. Boating, Bush Walking, Fishing, Scenic Drives, Shooting, Swimming (Lake), Water Skiing.

Other Accommodation

Belinda Lodge, (Bunk), (Farm), Back Rd, 3.6km SE of PO, ☎ 03 5869 3244, 2 bunkhouses acc up to 14, (Bunk Rooms), [shwr, tlt, a/c, heat, elec blkts, blkts, doonas, linen, pillows], ldry, rec rm, lounge (TV), t/c mkg shared, refrig, bbq, cots. **RO ♦ $20, ♦ $20**, ch con.

BARNAWARTHA VIC 3688

Pop 450. (277km NE Melbourne), See map on pages 694/695, ref H4. Centre of a rich agricultural district. Scenic Drives, Vineyards, Wineries.

B&B's/Guest Houses

★★★★☆ **Koendidda Country House**, (B&B), c1855. No children's facilities, Pooleys Rd, 4km E of Hume Fwy, off Yackandandah Rd, ☎ 02 6026 7340, fax 02 6026 7300, (2 stry), 5 rms (1 suite) [ensuite, bath (1), hairdry, a/c-cool, c/fan, cent heat, elec blkts, clock radio], lounge (TV, video, cd), t/c mkg shared, refrig, non smoking property. **BB $210 - $260**, Dinner by arrangement. AE BC DC MC VI.

BARONGAROOK VIC 3249

Pop Part of Colac, (158km SW Melbourne), See map on pages 694/695, ref D7. Pastoral and saw milling district.

Self Catering Accommodation

★★★★☆ **Otway Vineyard Cottages**, (Cotg), 20 Hoveys Rd, 12km S of PO, ☎ 03 5233 8400, fax 03 5233 8409, 3 cotgs acc up to 5, (1 & 2 bedrm), [shwr, spa bath, tlt, a/c, heat, elec blkts, TV, video, CD, t/c mkg, refrig, cook fac, micro, toaster, ldry, blkts, doonas, linen, pillows], w/mach, dryer, bbq, c/park (carport), cots-fee, non smoking property. **D ♦♦ $88 - $132, ♦ $22 - $33, W ♦♦ $550 - $880, ♦ $110**, Children by arrangement, Min book applies, BC MC VI.

BARRAMUNGA VIC 3249

Pop Nominal, (191km SW Melbourne), See map on pages 694/695, ref D7. Small township in the Otway Ranges, north of Apollo Bay. Bush Walking, Scenic Drives.

Self Catering Accommodation

★★★ **Barramunga - Cabins**, Upper Gellibrand Rd, 900m S of Barramunga, ☎ 03 5236 3302, fax 03 5236 3302, 3 cabins acc up to 12, (2 & 3 bedrm), [shwr, tlt, c/fan, heat, TV, radio, refrig, cook fac, micro, linen], w/mach, bbq, cots. **D ♦♦ $160, ♦ $20, W $650 - $800**, Min book applies, BC MC VI.

★★★ **Top of the Otways**, (Cotg), 1130 Forrest-Apollo Bay Rd, 11.3km S of Forrest, ☎ 03 5236 6494, 1 cotg acc up to 5, (2 bedrm), [shwr, tlt, hairdry, a/c-cool, fan, heat (wood), elec blkts, TV, video, clock radio, refrig, cook fac, micro, elec frypan, toaster, blkts, linen, pillows], ldry, cots, non smoking property, Pets on application. **D ♦♦ $77 - $99, ♦ $11, W $385 - $550.**

BARWON HEADS VIC 3227

Pop 1,914. (95km SW Melbourne), See map on page 696, ref A6. Seaside resort on western side of Barwon River estuary. Bowls, Bush Walking, Fishing, Golf, Surfing, Swimming (Beach), Tennis.

Hotels/Motels

★★☆ **Barwon Heads Hotel**, (LH), Cnr Ewing Blyth Dve & Bridge Rd, adjacent bridge & beach, ☎ 03 5254 2201, fax 03 5254 2182, (2 stry), 7 rms [shwr, bath (4), spa bath (1), tlt, c/fan, heat, elec blkts, TV, clock radio, t/c mkg, refrig], conf fac, ✉, ✆, cots. **RO ♦♦ $70 - $100**, ch con, AE BC DC EFT MC VI.

Self Catering Accommodation

★★★★ **Tobermory B&B**, (Cotg), 16 Bridge Rd, 200m W of PO, ☎ 03 5255 4444, fax 03 5255 4744, 1 cotg acc up to 9, (3 bedrm), [shwr, tlt, hairdry, c/fan, heat, elec blkts, TV, video, clock radio, CD, t/c mkg, refrig, cook fac, micro, d/wash, toaster, ldry, blkts, doonas, linen, pillows], w/mach, dryer, iron, iron brd, lounge firepl, bbq, c/park (undercover), cots, breakfast ingredients, non smoking property. **BLB $190**, Min book applies, AE BC DC EFT MC VI.

★★★ **Village Park Cottages**, (Cotg), 1 - 7 Geelong Rd, 600m N of PO, ☎ 03 5244 3336, fax 03 5244 3336, 4 cotgs acc up to 6, (2 & 3 bedrm), [shwr, spa bath (2), tlt, hairdry, fan, heat (log fire), elec blkts, TV, video, clock radio, CD, refrig, cook fac, micro, toaster, ldry (in unit) (2)], ldry, iron, bbq, cots. **D ♦♦ $80 - $160, ♦ $10 - $20, W ♦♦ $490 - $1,120**, ch con, 1 cottage ★★★☆, 1 cottage of a 4 star rating, Min book all holiday times.

B&B's/Guest Houses

★★★★☆ **River-Tree Retreat**, (B&B), 37 Carr St, 1.3km N of PO, ☎ 03 5254 3030, fax 03 5254 3044, 1 rm [shwr, bath, tlt, hairdry, fan, heat, elec blkts, tel, TV, clock radio, t/c mkg, refrig, toaster], c/park (undercover), non smoking property. **BB ♦ $110 - $130, ♦♦ $130 - $150**, *Operator Comment: "A restful romantic B&B with your own front entry door, dining and sitting areas, TV & bathroom. www.babs.com.au/rivertree".*

BASS VIC 3991

Pop Nominal, (111km SE Melbourne), See map on page 696, ref C7. A dairying township, also one of the earliest settlements in Victoria. Scenic Drives, Swimming (Beach), Tennis.

Self Catering Accommodation

★★★★ **Randwick Cottage**, (Cotg), No children's facilities, Soldiers Rd, 2.2km N of PO, ☎ 03 5678 2392, 1 cotg acc up to 4, (2 bedrm), [shwr, bath, tlt, hairdry, a/c, c/fan, heat (wood), elec blkts, TV, video, clock radio, refrig, cook fac, micro, toaster, blkts, doonas, linen, pillows], iron, iron brd, bbq, breakfast ingredients. **BB ♦♦ $120, ♦ $33.**

BAXTER VIC 3911

Pop 1,178. (47km S Melbourne), See map on page 697, ref D6. Rural township close to Frankston.

Hotels/Motels

★★ **Baxter Tavern Hotel Motel**, (LMH), Baxter-Tooradin Rd, ☎ 03 5971 2207, fax 03 5971 2407, 6 units [shwr, tlt, a/c, heat, TV, video (avail), clock radio, refrig, toaster], ⊠, ✆. BLB ∮ $60, ♦♦ $66, ◊ $10, Light breakfast only available. AE BC DC EFT MC VI.

BEACONSFIELD UPPER VIC 3808

Pop 1,300. (50km SE Melbourne), See map on page 696, ref C6. Fruit growing district on fringe of metropolitan area. Bush Walking, Golf, Horse Riding, Scenic Drives, Tennis.

Self Catering Accommodation

★★★☆ **Ttekceba**, (Cotg), 120 A'Beckett Rd, ☎ 03 5944 3636, 1 cotg acc up to 4, (2 bedrm), [shwr, tlt, hairdry, tel, TV, video, CD, refrig, cook fac, micro, elec frypan, blkts, linen, pillows], lounge firepl, pool, sauna, breakfast ingredients. BB ♦♦ $120 - $200, ◊ $60 - $100.

B&B's/Guest Houses

★★★★☆ **Farthings of Fernhill Bed & Breakfast**, (B&B), Children by arrangement. 546 Salisbury Rd, 2km E of PO, ☎ 03 5944 3116, fax 03 5944 3116, 1 rm [hairdry, a/c, heat, elec blkts, TV, clock radio, refrig, ldry, doonas], lounge (TV), lounge firepl, t/c mkg shared, bbq, non smoking property. BB ∮ $80, ♦♦ $120, Other meals by arrangement.

★★★★☆ **Yuulong Bed & Breakfast**, (B&B), 574 Salisbury Rd, 2km E of PO, ☎ 03 5944 3440, fax 03 5944 3440, 1 rm [ensuite, hairdry, a/c, c/fan, fire pl, heat, elec blkts, TV, clock radio, CD, t/c mkg, refrig, micro, toaster], bbq, non smoking property. BB ♦♦ $160 - $200, Dinner by arrangement. Min book all holiday times, BC MC VI.

★★★★ **(Cottage Section)**, 1 cotg acc up to 2, (1 bedrm), [shwr, bath, tlt, hairdry, c/fan, heat, elec blkts, TV, clock radio, CD, refrig, cook fac, micro, toaster, blkts, linen, pillows], iron, iron brd, lounge firepl, breakfast ingredients. BB ♦♦ $130 - $180, W ♦♦ $700 - $900.

BEAUFORT VIC 3373

Pop 1,050. (158km W Melbourne), See map on pages 694/695, ref C6. Centre of a rich pastoral region. Boating, Bowls, Bush Walking, Croquet, Fishing, Gold Prospecting, Golf, Rock Climbing, Scenic Drives, Shooting, Squash, Swimming (Lake, Pool), Tennis, Water Skiing.

Hotels/Motels

★★★ **Beaufort Motel**, (M), 18 Neill St (Western Hwy), 400m E of PO, ☎ 03 5349 2297, fax 03 5349 2297, 10 units [shwr, tlt, fan (5), c/fan (5), heat, elec blkts, TV, video-fee, clock radio, t/c mkg, refrig, toaster], lounge, bbq, dinner to unit, plygr, cots-fee, non smoking units (2). RO ∮ $50 - $55, ♦♦ $60 - $66, ◊ $11, AE BC DC MC MCH VI.

BEECH FOREST VIC 3237

Pop Nominal, (187km SW Melbourne), See map on pages 694/695, ref D7. Small settlement, centre of a rich potato & timber district, noted for the beauty of the mountain scenery. Scenic Drives.

Hotels/Motels

★★ **Beech Forest**, (LMH), Main Rd, 200m E of Information Centre, ☎ 03 5235 9220, 4 units [shwr, tlt, heat, elec blkts, TV, t/c mkg, refrig], ⊠, bbq. BLB ∮ $40, ♦♦ $65, ◊ $6, ch con, BC EFT MC VI.

BEECHWORTH VIC 3747

Pop 2,950. (271km NE Melbourne), See map on pages 694/695, ref H4. Historic gold mining town, founded in 1852, is today the principal municipal town of the Ovens District. Many of its fine old buildings have been classified by the National Trust, including the government buildings on Ford Street, the Powder Magazine and Tanswells Hotel. Boating, Bowls, Croquet, Fishing, Gem Fossicking, Golf, Horse Riding, Scenic Drives, Swimming (Pool), Tennis, Water Skiing.

Hotels/Motels

★★★☆ **Armour Motor Inn**, (M), 1 Camp St, 130m SE of PO, ☎ 03 5728 1466, fax 03 5728 2257, (2 stry gr fl), 20 units [shwr, tlt, hairdry, a/c-cool, heat, elec blkts, tel, TV, video-fee, clock radio, t/c mkg, refrig, toaster, doonas], iron, iron brd, pool, sauna, spa, cots-fee. RO ∮ $84 - $108, ♦♦ $86 - $111, ◊ $12, BC EFT MC VI, ♿.

★★★☆ **Beechworth Motor Inn**, (M), 54 Sydney Rd, 1.3km N of PO, ☎ 03 5728 1301, fax 03 5728 2007, 10 units [shwr, tlt, hairdry, a/c-cool, cent heat, elec blkts, tel, TV, movie, clock radio, t/c mkg, refrig, toaster], pool, bbq, c/park (carport), plygr, cots, Pets allowed. RO ∮ $64 - $75, ♦♦ $68 - $78, ◊ $12, ch con, Min book long w/ends and Easter, AE BC DC EFT MC VI.

★★★☆ **Carriage Motor Inn**, (M), Cnr Camp & Finch Sts, 200m NW of PO, ☎ 03 5728 1830, fax 03 5728 1489, 27 units [shwr, spa bath (1), tlt, hairdry, a/c-cool, c/fan, heat, elec blkts, tel, TV, clock radio, t/c mkg, refrig, mini bar, toaster], ldry, ⊠ (Tues to Sat), pool, dinner to unit, plygr, cots-fee, non smoking units (23). RO ∮ $66 - $75, ♦♦ $75 - $140, ◊ $12, AE BC DC MC VI.

★★★☆ **Golden Heritage Motor Inn**, (M), 51 Sydney Rd, 1.2km N of PO, ☎ 03 5728 1404, fax 03 5728 2119, 10 units [shwr, tlt, hairdry (8), a/c, c/fan, heat, elec blkts, tel, TV, clock radio, t/c mkg, refrig, mini bar], ldry, iron, iron brd, pool, bbq, plygr, cots-fee, non smoking units (5). D $140 - $180, RO ∮ $68 - $82, ♦♦ $75 - $82, ◊ $12, AE BC DC EFT MC VI.

★★★ **La Trobe at Beechworth**, (LH), Albert Rd, 1km E of PO, ☎ 03 5720 8050, fax 03 5720 8051, (Multi-stry gr fl), 77 rms (4 suites) [shwr (33), spa bath (6), tlt (33), hairdry (33), a/c-cool (20), a/c (17), heat (57), cent heat (20), tel, TV, movie (20), clock radio, t/c mkg, refrig, mini bar], lift, iron (6), iron brd (6), business centre, conf fac, ⊠ (Wed to Sun), pool-heated (solar), sauna, spa, bbq, ✆, tennis, cots-fee, non smoking property. BLB ∮ $65, ♦♦ $80 - $165, ◊ $25, Suite BLB $180, ch con, Minimum booking Christmas/Jan, Easter, Wangaratta Jazz & Celtic festivals, AE BC DC EFT JCB MC VI, ♿.

★★☆ **(Cottage Section)**, 5 cotgs acc up to 6, (3 bedrm), [shwr, tlt, a/c-cool (1), heat, TV, t/c mkg, refrig, cook fac, micro, toaster, ldry, blkts, linen, pillows], w/mach, dryer (3), bar, non smoking property. D $100 - $150.

(Lodge Section), 3 rms acc up to 32, [heat], ldry, w/mach, dryer, lounge (TV, video), cook fac, t/c mkg shared, refrig, non smoking property. D $450 - $550.

★★★ **Newtown Park Motel**, (M), 38 Bridge Rd (Wangaratta Rd), 1.4km SW of PO, ☎ 03 5728 2244, fax 03 5728 3344, 14 units [shwr, bath (hip), tlt, a/c, elec blkts, tel, TV, video-fee, clock radio, t/c mkg, refrig], ldry-fee, cots, non smoking units (4). **RO** ♦ **$54 - $80**, ♦♦ **$64 - $80**, ◊ **$12**, ch con, AE BC DC MC MCH VI.

★☆ **Tanswells Commercial Hotel**, (LH), Classified by National Trust, 50 Ford St, 100m SW of PO, ☎ 03 5728 1480, fax 03 5728 1160, (2 stry), 13 rms [basin, cent heat, t/c mkg], lounge (TV), ⊠, ✆. **BLB** ♦ **$30 - $40**, ♦♦ **$50 - $60**, ♦♦♦♦ **$70**, BC EFT MC VI.

Self Catering Accommodation

★★★★☆ **Country Charm Swiss Cottages**, (Cotg), No children's facilities, 22 Malakoff Rd, 1.5km S of PO, ☎ 03 5728 2435, fax 03 5728 2435, 5 cotgs acc up to 4, (1 & 2 bedrm) [shwr, spa bath, tlt, hairdry, a/c, c/fan (3), elec blkts, TV, video (avail), clock radio, CD, refrig, cook fac ltd, micro, toaster, blkts, linen, pillows], ldry, lounge firepl, bbq, c/park (carport), breakfast ingredients, non smoking property. **BB** ♦♦ **$149 - $199**, ◊ **$66**, ♦♦ **$780 - $850**, ◊ **$220**, Minimum booking weekends, school holidays & Easter, AE BC MC VI.

★★★★ **Mrs Doig's Cottage**, (Cotg), 11 William St, 5 Minute walk to shops, ☎ 03 5728 1169, 1 cotg acc up to 8, (4 bedrm) [shwr, bath, tlt, hairdry, evap cool, c/fan, cent heat, elec blkts, TV, video, clock radio, t/c mkg, refrig, cook fac, micro, toaster, ldry, blkts, linen, pillows], w/mach, iron, iron brd, lounge firepl (gas coal), bbq, cots, non smoking property. **D** ♦♦ **$110 - $120**, ◊ **$30**, **W** ♦♦ **$660**, ◊ **$180**, ch con.

★★★ **Woolshed Cabins**, Cnr Chiltern & McFeeters Rds, 5km NW of PO, 1.5km E of Woolshed Falls, ☎ 03 5728 1035, 4 cabins acc up to 5, (2 bedrm) [shwr, bath (hip) (3), tlt, hairdry, evap cool, c/fan, heat, elec blkts, TV, video (avail), clock radio, t/c mkg, refrig, cook fac, toaster, blkts, doonas, linen reqd-fee, pillows], bbq, cots. **D** ♦♦ **$68**, ◊ **$11**, ch con, fam con, AE BC MC VI.

B&B's/Guest Houses

★★★★☆ **Apple Tree Cottage Bed & Breakfast**, (B&B), 16 Frederick St, 1km N of PO, ☎ 03 5728 1044, fax 03 5728 1044, 2 rms [ensuite, hairdry, fan, heat, elec blkts, TV, CD, t/c mkg], iron, iron brd, lounge (TV, video, cd), non smoking property. **BB** ♦♦ **$110**, AE BC MC VI.

★★★★☆ **Beechworth House**, (B&B), 5 Dingle Rd, 1km E of PO, ☎ 03 5728 2817, fax 03 5728 2737, (2 stry gr fl), 5 rms [ensuite (5), bath (1), spa bath (2), hairdry, a/c-cool (1), a/c (3), heat, elec blkts, TV, clock radio, CD (2)], iron, iron brd, lounge, lounge firepl, t/c mkg shared, refrig, non smoking property. **BB** ♦♦ **$132 - $165**, **D** ♦ **$110**, Dinner by arrangement, Children by arrangement, BC MC VI.

Operator Comment: Make your stay in historic Beechworth a special occasion. Enjoy superb views, guest sitting room with open fire, quiet gardens & delicious cooked breakfast. A perfect stopover between Sydney & Melbourne. www.beechworth.com/bhouse/

★★★★☆ **Kinross Guest House**, (B&B), c1858. 34 Loch St, 400m NE of PO, ☎ 03 5728 2351, fax 03 5728 3333, 5 rms [ensuite, hairdry, a/c (lounge, dining), c/fan, fire pl, heat, elec blkts, TV, clock radio, t/c mkg, doonas], lounge (cd), lounge firepl, refrig, non smoking property. **BB** ♦ **$130**, ♦♦ **$160**, Dinner by arrangement. BC EFT MC VI.

★★★★ **Barnsley House**, (B&B), 5 John St, 800m S of PO, ☎ 03 5728 1037, fax 03 5728 1098, 4 rms [ensuite (3), shwr (1), bath (1), spa bath (1), tlt (1), hairdry, fan, fire pl (3), cent heat, elec blkts, TV, clock radio], iron, iron brd, lounge (TV, video, cd), lounge firepl, res liquor license, non smoking property. **BB** ♦ **$95 - $135**, ♦♦ **$115 - $155**, Dinner by arrangement. Min book long w/ends and Easter, BC MC VI.

★★★★ **Beechworth Gorge Walk Guest House**, (GH), 10 Last St, ☎ 03 5728 2867, fax 03 5728 2867, 3 rms [ensuite, hairdry, a/c, elec blkts, TV, clock radio, t/c mkg, doonas], lounge (TV, video), lounge firepl, spa, refrig, bbq, cots, non smoking property. **BB** ♦ **$85**, ♦♦ **$105**, ch con, BC MC VI.

★★★★ **Beechworth's Rose Cottage Accommodation**, (B&B), c1876. 42 Camp St, 180m NW of PO, ☎ 03 5728 1069, fax 03 5728 1069, 4 rms [ensuite (2), shwr (2), tlt (2), hairdry, evap cool, c/fan, fire pl (2), heat, elec blkts, TV, video, clock radio, t/c mkg, micro, toaster, doonas], ldry, lounge, ✕, spa, refrig. **BB** ♦ **$121**, ♦♦ **$121 - $143**, ◊ **$88**, ch con, BC MC VI.

★★★★☆ **(Cottage Section)**, (2 stry gr fl), 1 cotg acc up to 5, (2 bedrm) [ensuite (1), shwr, spa bath, tlt, hairdry, evap cool, c/fan, elec blkts, TV, video, clock radio, CD, t/c mkg, refrig, cook fac, micro, toaster, ldry, blkts, doonas, linen, pillows], w/mach, iron, iron brd, lounge firepl, c/park (undercover), breakfast ingredients. **BB** ♦ **$121**, ♦♦ **$121 - $143**, ◊ **$88**, ch con.

★★★★ **The Bank Restaurant**, (B&B), 86 Ford St, adjacent to PO, ☎ 03 5728 2223, fax 03 5728 2883, (2 stry gr fl), 4 rms [ensuite, hairdry, c/fan, heat, TV, clock radio, CD, t/c mkg, refrig, mini bar, toaster], iron, iron brd, ⊠, non smoking property. **BLB** ♦♦ **$160**, AE BC DC EFT MC VI.

★★★☆ **Alba Country Rose Private B & B**, (B&B), 30 Malakoff Rd, 1.5km SW of PO, ☎ 03 5728 1107, fax 03 5728 1107, 2 rms [ensuite, bath (1), hairdry, a/c-cool, fan, heat, elec blkts, TV, clock radio, t/c mkg, refrig, micro, toaster], iron, iron brd. **BLB** ♦ **$70**, ♦♦ **$90**, ◊ **$20**, ch con.

Other Accommodation

The Old Priory, (Lodge), c1886, 8 Priory La, ☎ 03 5728 1024, fax 03 5728 2035, 20 rms [fan, heat, clock radio (7)], rec rm, lounge (TV), conf fac, lounge firepl, ✕, t/c mkg shared, bbq (covered), ✆. **BLB** ♦ **$35**, ♦♦ **$65**, ch con, fam con.

★★★ **(Bed & Breakfast Section)**, 2 rms [ensuite, bath (hip), c/fan, fire pl (1), heat, elec blkts, TV, t/c mkg, refrig, toaster]. **BB** ♦♦ **$90**.

(Dormitory Section), (2 stry gr fl), 4 bunkhouses acc up to 30, [heat]. **BB** ♦ **$30**, ch con, Full catering available for groups.

BELGRAVE VIC

See Dandenong Ranges Region.

BELLARINE VIC 3221

Pop Part of Portarlington, (100km SW Melbourne), See maps on page??12, ref B6. Situated on Bellarine Peninsula.

B&B's/Guest Houses
★★★★☆ **Views End**, (B&B), 265 Scotchmans Rd, ☎ 03 5253 1695, fax 03 5253 1205, 2 rms [ensuite, bath (1), c/fan, heat, elec blkts, TV, clock radio], lounge, t/c mkg shared, bbq, non smoking rms, Dogs allowed. **BB** ♦ **$121 - $154**, ♦♦ **$145 - $198**, Other meals by arrangement. AE BC MC VI.

BELLBRAE VIC 3228

Pop 133. (97km SW Melbourne), See map on page 696, ref A6. Rural settlement close to Torquay and fine surf beaches. Bells Beach Surfing Championship (Easter). Golf, Horse Riding, Scenic Drives, Tennis.

Hotels/Motels

★★☆ **Bellbrae Motel**, (M), 20 School Rd, 5km W of Torquay, ☎ 03 5261 3777, fax 03 5261 3777, 5 units [shwr, tlt, a/c-cool, fan, heat, elec blkts, TV, clock radio, t/c mkg, refrig, toaster], bbq, cots-fee, non smoking units (3). **RO** ♦ **$63 - $85**, ♦♦ **$68 - $90**, ♦ **$11**, ch con, AE BC DC EFT MC MCH VI.

Self Catering Accommodation
★★★★ **Cedars Great Ocean Road Cottages**, (Cotg), 545 Great Ocean Rd, ☎ 03 5261 3844, fax 03 5261 3844, 3 cotgs acc up to 6, (1 & 2 bedrm), [shwr, spa bath (2), tlt, a/c-cool, c/fan, fire pl, heat (wood), TV, video, clock radio, refrig, micro, toaster, ldry, blkts, linen, pillows], iron, iron brd, pool-indoor, spa. **D** ♦♦ **$121 - $187**, ♦ **$22**, BC MC VI.

★★★ **Glen Fiddich Cabins**, (Cotg), 125 Eaglepoint Rd, 5.5km SW of Great Ocean Rd, off Gundrys Rd, ☎ 03 5266 1442, 4 cotgs acc up to 6, (2 & 3 bedrm), [shwr, bath (hip), tlt, fire pl, TV, video, clock radio, refrig, cook fac, micro, toaster, ldry, linen reqd-fee], bbq, plygr, canoeing, tennis, cots. **D** **$85 - $110**, **W** **$595 - $750**.

B&B's/Guest Houses
★★★☆ **Merriview Bed and Breakfast**, (B&B), 1675 Hendy Main Rd, 9km NW of Torquay, ☎ 03 5266 2130, fax 03 5266 2130, 2 rms [spa bath (1), hairdry, heat, elec blkts, clock radio], ldry, lounge (TV, video, cd player), t/c mkg shared, bbq, non smoking property. **BB** ♦ **$50 - $70**, ♦♦ **$90 - $110**, ♦ **$20 - $40**, ch con, Other meals by arrangement. AE BC MC VI.

BELLS BEACH VIC 3228

Pop Nominal, See map on page 696, ref A6. Rural settlement with fine surf beaches - close to Torquay Bells Beach Surfing Championship (Easter).

Self Catering Accommodation
★★★☆ **Bells Holiday Cottages**, (Cotg), 35 Dunloe Crt, ☎ 03 5261 5243, 3 cotgs acc up to 4, (2 bedrm), [shwr, tlt, heat, TV, video-fee, clock radio, t/c mkg, refrig, cook fac, micro, toaster, blkts, doonas, linen, pillows], w/mach, iron, iron brd, lounge firepl, bbq, cots-fee. **D** ♦♦ **$100 - $120**, ♦ **$10 - $15**, **W** ♦♦ **$600 - $700**, ♦ **$60 - $99**, Min book Christmas Jan long w/ends and Easter, BC MC VI.

BEMM RIVER VIC 3889

Pop Nominal, (441km E Melbourne), See map on pages 694/695, ref K7. Small East Gippsland coastal fishing town. Boating, Bush Walking, Fishing, Sailing, Scenic Drives.

Self Catering Accommodation
★★★ **Cosy Nook Flats**, (HF), Sydenham Pde, 1.1km E of hotel, ☎ 03 5158 4231, fax 03 5158 4231, 7 flats acc up to 8, (1, 2 & 3 bedrm), [shwr, tlt, heat, elec blkts, TV, movie, refrig, cook fac, toaster], ldry, rec rm, bbq, plygr, cots. **RO** ♦♦ **$48.50**, ♦ **$15.80**, **W** ♦♦ **$308**, ch con, BC EFT MC VI.

★★☆ **Alcheringa Lodge**, (HF), 43 Sydenham Pde, 500m E of hotel, ☎ 03 5158 4233, 5 flats acc up to 10, (2, 3 & 4 bedrm), [shwr, tlt, heat, elec blkts, TV, refrig, cook fac, toaster, blkts, linen], ldry, bbq, boat park. **D** ♦♦ **$38 - $47**, ♦ **$15**, **W** **$266 - $560**, ch con, Min book all holiday times.

★★ **(Cabin Section)**, 5 cabins acc up to 5, (2 bedrm), [heat, refrig, cook fac, blkts reqd, linen reqd, pillows], ldry, w/mach. **D** ♦♦ **$22 - $29**, ♦ **$11**, **W** **$154 - $275**, ch con.

★★ **Roses Holiday Units**, (HU), Sydenham Inlet Rd, 400m N of hotel, ☎ 03 5158 4210, 5 units acc up to 6, (Studio, 1 & 2 bedrm), [shwr, tlt, fan, heat, TV, refrig, cook fac, blkts, linen, pillows], ldry, bbq. **D** ♦♦ **$40 - $45**, **W** **$320**, ch con.

BENA VIC 3946

Pop Nominal, (104km SE Melbourne), See map on page 696, ref D7. Dairying district. Bush Walking, Scenic Drives.

B&B's/Guest Houses
★★★☆ **Benaway B & B**, (B&B), 810 Anderson Inlet Rd, 4km S of PO, ☎ 03 5657 2268, fax 03 5657 2303, (2 stry), 3 rms [shwr, tlt, hairdry, heat, elec blkts, TV, clock radio, t/c mkg, refrig, micro, doonas], lounge (Cable TV, cd), bbq, breakfast ingredients, non smoking property. **BLB** ♦ **$45 - $55**, ♦♦ **$90 - $95**, ♦ **$40 - $50**, AE BC MC VI.

★★★ **(Cottage Section)**, No children's facilities, 1 cotg acc up to 2, [ensuite, hairdry, fan, heat, elec blkts, cable tv, clock radio, CD, refrig, cook fac ltd, micro, toaster, blkts, linen, pillows], breakfast ingredients, non smoking units. **D** **$90 - $95**.

BENALLA VIC 3672

Pop 8,600. (196km NE Melbourne), See map on page 696, ref E2. Centre of rich agricultural & pastoral area. Home of Australias' largest Gliding Centre. Tourist Information Centre, 14 Mair St, 03 5762 1749. Art Gallery, Boating, Bowls, Fishing, Golf, Horse Racing, Horse Riding, Sailing, Scenic Drives, Shooting, Swimming, Tennis.

Hotels/Motels
★★★★ **Glider City Motel**, (M), Cnr Old Sydney Rd & Witt St, 1.5km NE of PO, ☎ 03 5762 3399, fax 03 5762 5822, 13 units [shwr, spa bath (2), tlt, hairdry, a/c, heat, elec blkts, tel, TV, video (avail), clock radio, t/c mkg, refrig], ldry, iron, iron brd, pool, bbq, dinner to unit, cots, non smoking units (4). **RO** ♦ **$65 - $80**, ♦♦ **$75 - $100**, ♦ **$11**, AE BC DC EFT MC VI, ⚹&.

★★★☆ **Avondel Motor Inn**, (M), 21 Bridge St West (Midland Hwy), 800m SW of PO, ☎ 03 5762 3677, fax 03 5762 3943, 17 units [shwr, tlt, hairdry, a/c, elec blkts, tel, TV, video (9), clock radio, t/c mkg, refrig, toaster], iron, iron brd, pool, bbq, dinner to unit, cots-fee, non smoking units (8). **BLB** ♦ **$70 - $83**, ♦♦ **$80 - $96**, ♦ **$11**, ch con, AE BC DC EFT MC MP VI.

★★★☆ **Benalla Motor Inn**, (M), 48 Bridge St West (Midland Hwy), 1.1km SW of PO, ☎ 03 5762 4088, fax 03 5762 4539, 20 units [shwr, tlt, a/c, elec blkts, tel, cable tv, clock radio, t/c mkg, refrig, mini bar, toaster], ldry, pool indoor heated, spa, dinner to unit, plygr, cots-fee, non smoking units (8). **RO** ♦ **$70 - $80**, ♦♦ **$80 - $87**, ♦ **$11**, ch con, AE BC DC EFT MC VI, ⚹&.

★★★☆ **Rose City Motor Inn**, (M), Cnr Midland Hwy & Faithful St, 1.8km SW of PO, ☎ 03 5762 2611, fax 03 5762 2611, 24 units [shwr, tlt, hairdry (18), a/c, elec blkts, tel, TV, video-fee, movie, clock radio, t/c mkg, refrig, toaster (18)], iron (18), iron brd (18), rec rm, ⊠, pool, bbq, rm serv, plygr, cots, non smoking units (6). **RO** ♦ **$50 - $65**, ♦♦ **$65 - $75**, ♦ **$10**, 6 units ★★☆. AE BC BTC DC EFT MC VI.

★★★☆ **Top of the Town Motel**, (M), 136 Bridge St East, 600m NE of PO, ☎ 03 5762 4866, fax 03 5762 4573, 22 units [shwr, spa bath (3), tlt, hairdry, a/c, elec blkts, tel, TV, video-fee, clock radio, t/c mkg, refrig, toaster], ldry, iron, iron brd, pool, bbq, cots-fee, non smoking units (13). **RO** ♦ **$68 - $104**, ♦♦ **$79 - $104**, ♦ **$12**, ch con, AE BC DC EFT MC MP VI, ⚹&.

★★★ **Benalta Family Inn Motel**, (M), 27 Bridge St West (Midland Hwy), 900m SW of PO, ☎ 03 5762 5600, fax 03 5762 5656, 10 units [shwr, tlt, a/c, elec blkts, tel, TV, video (avail), clock radio, t/c mkg, refrig], pool, bbq, c/park (carport), cots-fee, non smoking units (3). **RO** ♦ **$44,** ♦♦ **$55,** ◊ **$11,** ch con, AE BC DC MC MCH VI.

★★★ **Motel Haven**, (M), Old Hume Hwy, 2.6km NE of PO, ☎ 03 5762 1722, fax 03 5762 5603, 10 units [shwr, bath (hip) (7), tlt, a/c-cool (1), a/c (9), heat (1), elec blkts, tel, TV, clock radio, t/c mkg, refrig], pool, bbq, dinner to unit, plygr, cots. **RO** ♦ **$42 - $57,** ♦♦ **$52 - $57,** ◊ **$11,** ch con, AE BC DC EFT MC MCH VI.

Self Catering Accommodation

★★★☆ **Executive Hideaway**, (SA), 71 Samaria Rd, 2km E of PO, ☎ 03 5762 4055, fax 03 5762 5770, 16 serv apts (1 bedrm2 bedrm), [shwr, tlt, hairdry, a/c, heat, elec blkts, tel, TV, video-fee, clock radio, t/c mkg, refrig, cook fac ltd, micro, toaster, ldry (in unit)], iron, iron brd, ⊠ (Mon to Sat), pool (salt water), bbq, dinner to unit, plygr, cots-fee, non smoking units (9). **RO** ♦ **$74 - $132,** ♦♦ **$91 - $132,** ◊ **$20,** ch con, AE BC DC EFT JCB MC MP VI.

B&B's/Guest Houses

★★★★ **Belmont Bed & Breakfast**, (B&B), 80 Arundel St South, 800m S of PO, ☎ 03 5762 6575, 3 rms [ensuite (2), shwr (1), tlt (1), hairdry, fan, fire pl, cent heat, elec blkts, TV, video (avail), clock radio, t/c mkg], lounge (cd player), spa, refrig, cots. **BB** ♦ **$88 - $125,** ♦♦ **$125,** ch con, BC MC VI.

★★★★ **Yaridni Host Farm**, (B&B), (Farm), Yarrawonga Rd, 13km off Old Sydney Rd, ☎ 03 5764 1273, fax 03 5764 1352, 2 rms [ensuite (1), shwr (1), spa bath (1), tlt (1), a/c, c/fan, cent heat, elec blkts, clock radio], ldry, rec rm, lounge (TV, video, cd), lounge firepl, non smoking property. **BB** ♦ **$85 - $100,** ♦♦ **$110 - $125,** ch con, Other meals by arrangement. AE BC MC VI.

BENAMBRA VIC 3900

Pop 262. (437km E Melbourne), See map on pages 694/695, ref J5. A small pastoral & agricultural farming district. Bush Walking, Fishing, Scenic Drives, Swimming (River), Tennis.

★ **Benambra**, (LH), Gibbo Rd, 50m S of PO, ☎ 03 5159 9214, fax 03 5159 9233, 7 rms [elec blkts], lounge (TV, video), ⊠, bbq, ✎. **BB** ♦ **$24 - $28,** ◊ **$19, RO** ♦ **$22,** BC EFT MC VI.

BENDIGO VIC 3550

Pop 59,950. (150km NW Melbourne), See map on page 696, ref A2. Includes: EAGLEHAWK, EPSOM, GOLDEN SQUARE, JUNORTOUN, KANGAROO FLAT, MAIDEN GULLY, WHITE HILLS. Historical gold mining city & marketing centre. 'Talking Trams' Tourist Information Centre, 26 High St, 03 5447 1383. Bowls, Croquet, Golf, Greyhound Racing, Horse Racing, Swimming, Tennis, Trotting. See also Marong.

Hotels/Motels

★★★★☆ **All Seasons International Motor Inn**, (M), 171 McIvor Hwy, 3km E of fountain, ☎ 03 5443 8166, fax 03 5441 5221, (2 stry gr fl), 71 units (3 suites) [shwr, bath (3), spa bath (27), tlt, hairdry, a/c, elec blkts, tel, TV, video (avail), movie, clock radio, t/c mkg, refrig, mini bar, cook fac ltd (3), micro (3), toaster], lift, ldry, iron, iron brd, conf fac, ⊠, bar (cocktail), pool indoor heated, sauna (9), spa, bbq, 24hr reception, rm serv, ✎, plygr, gym, cots-fee, non smoking units (32). **RO** ♦ **$115 - $180,** ♦♦ **$125 - $180,** ◊ **$16.50, Suite D $180,** AE BC DC MC VI, ♿.

★★★★ **Alexandra Place**, (M), 200 McCrae St, 1.1km N of fountain, ☎ 03 5441 6088, fax 03 5441 8073, (2 stry gr fl), 18 units [shwr, spa bath (2), tlt, hairdry, a/c, elec blkts, tel, cable tv, clock radio, t/c mkg, refrig], ldry, c/park (undercover), cots, non smoking units (10). **RO** ♦ **$80 - $135,** ♦♦ **$90 - $135,** ◊ **$11,** Minimum booking Easter, Swap meet weekend & Elmore Field Days. AE BC DC EFT MC VI, ♿.

★★★★ **Auld Goldfields Motor Inn (Bendigo)**, (M), 308 High St, Golden Square 3555, 2km S of fountain, ☎ 03 5441 7797, fax 03 5441 3732, 11 units [shwr, spa bath (4), tlt, hairdry, a/c, elec blkts, tel, TV, movie, clock radio, t/c mkg, refrig, toaster], iron, iron brd, bbq, cots-fee, non smoking units (11). **RO** ♦ **$70 - $110,** ♦♦ **$82 - $150,** ◊ **$10,** AE BC DC EFT MC VI, ♿.

★★★★ **Barclay 'On View' Motor Inn**, (M), 181 View St (Calder Hwy), 350m N of fountain, opposite Queen Elizabeth Oval, ☎ 03 5443 9388, fax 03 5443 9705, (2 stry gr fl), 30 units [shwr, tlt, hairdry, a/c, elec blkts, tel, video (avail), movie, clock radio, t/c mkg, refrig, toaster], ldry, conf fac, sauna, spa, bbq, gym, non smoking units (27). **RO** ♦ **$78 - $95,** ♦♦ **$95 - $110,** ◊ **$12,** AE BC DC EFT MC VI.

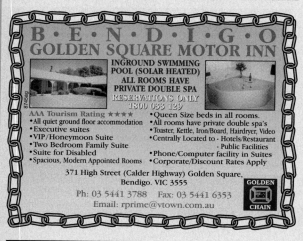

 ★★★★ Bendigo Colonial Motor Inn, (M), 483 High St (Calder Hwy), Golden Square 3555, 3.9km S of Bendigo PO, ☎ 03 5447 0122, fax 03 5447 9529, 34 units (4 suites) [shwr, spa bath (6), tlt, hairdry, a/c, elec blkts, tel, cable tv, video-fee, clock radio, t/c mkg, refrig, mini bar, toaster], ldry, iron, iron brd, conf fac, ✉ (Mon to Sat), bar (cocktail), pool indoor heated, sauna, spa, bbq (covered), rm serv, cots-fee, non smoking units (8). **RO ♦ $110 - $180, ♦♦ $120 - $180, ♦ $12, Suite RO ♦♦ $155 - $190, ♦ $12 - $14**, AE BC DC EFT JCB MC MP VI, ♿.

 ★★★★ Bendigo Haymarket Motor Inn, (M), 5 McIvor Rd, 600m NE of fountain, ☎ 03 5441 5654, fax 03 5441 5655, 14 units [shwr, spa bath (3), tlt, hairdry, a/c, elec blkts, tel, cable tv, video-fee, clock radio, t/c mkg, refrig], iron, iron brd, pool, bbq, cots-fee, non smoking units (10). **RO ♦ $84 - $140, ♦♦ $95 - $140, ♦ $10**, AE BC DC EFT MC VI, ♿.

 ★★★★ Cathedral Motor Inn, (M), 96 High St (Calder Hwy), 500m S of fountain, ☎ 03 5442 5333, fax 03 5442 5195, 31 units [shwr, spa bath (3), tlt, hairdry, a/c, elec blkts, tel, cable tv, video-fee, clock radio, t/c mkg, refrig, toaster], ldry, conf fac, bbq, dinner to unit, cots-fee, non smoking units (7). **RO ♦ $95 - $125, ♦♦ $105 - $135, ♦ $10**, AE BC DC EFT MC MP VI, ♿.

 ★★★★ Golden Reef Motor Inn, (M), 186 McIvor Hwy, 3.1km E of fountain, ☎ 03 5441 1000, fax 03 5441 1001, 26 units [shwr, spa bath (6), tlt, hairdry (6), a/c, elec blkts, tel, TV, video-fee, clock radio, t/c mkg, refrig, mini bar, toaster], iron, iron brd, pool-heated (solar), spa, dinner to unit, cots-fee, non smoking units (2). **RO ♦ $85 - $110, ♦♦ $95 - $120, ♦ $10**, Minimum booking long weekends, Easter, swap meets and Elmore field days, AE BC DC EFT MC VI, ♿.

 ★★★★ Golden Square Motor Inn, (M), 371 High St (Calder Hwy), Golden Square 3555, 2.5km S of fountain, ☎ 03 5441 3788, fax 03 5441 6353, 12 units [shwr, spa bath, tlt, hairdry, a/c, elec blkts, tel, TV, video, clock radio, t/c mkg, refrig, toaster], iron, iron brd, pool-heated (solar), cots-fee, non smoking units (4). **RO ♦♦ $84 - $120, ♦ $11**, ch con, pen con, AE BC DC MC MP VI, ♿.

 ★★★★ Heritage Motor Inn, (M), 259 High St (Calder Hwy), 1.7km S of fountain, ☎ 03 5442 2788, fax 03 5442 2873, 24 units [shwr, spa bath (2), tlt, hairdry, a/c, elec blkts, tel, TV, movie, clock radio, t/c mkg, refrig], ldry, iron, iron brd, ✗ (Mon to Thu), BYO, pool-heated (solar), spa, dinner to unit, cots-fee, non smoking units (6). **RO ♦ $85 - $110, ♦♦ $95 - $125, ♦ $10**, AE BC DC EFT JCB MC MP VI, ♿.

 ★★★★ Julie-Anna Inn, (M), 268 Napier St (Midland Hwy), 1.6km N of fountain, opposite Lake Weeroona, ☎ 03 5442 5855, fax 03 5441 6032, 33 units (1 suite) [shwr, spa bath (18), tlt, hairdry, a/c, elec blkts, tel, cable tv, video (18), clock radio, t/c mkg, refrig, mini bar], ldry, iron, iron brd, lounge, ✉ (Mon to Sat), pool, sauna (1), spa, rm serv, cots, non smoking units (20). **RO ♦ $110 - $155, ♦♦ $120 - $200, ♦ $11, Suite D $198**, AE BC DC EFT MC MP VI, ♿.

 ★★★☆ Allara Motor Lodge, (M), 569 Napier St (Midland Hwy), White Hills 3550, 5km N of fountain, ☎ 03 5448 4700, fax 03 5448 4699, 15 units (2 bedrm), [shwr, tlt, hairdry, a/c-cool, heat, elec blkts, tel, TV, clock radio, t/c mkg, refrig, mini bar], ldry, pool, bbq, dinner to unit (Mon to Thurs), tennis (half court), cots, non smoking units (3). **RO ♦♦ $90 - $110, ♦ $12 - $22**, AE BC DC EFT MC MP VI.

 ★★★☆ Bendigo Gateway Motel, (M), 401 Eaglehawk Rd (Loddon Valley Hwy), Eaglehawk 3556, 5 km NW of fountain, ☎ 03 5446 9688, fax 03 5446 9017, 19 units [shwr, tlt, hairdry, a/c, elec blkts, tel, TV, video (avail), clock radio, t/c mkg, refrig, mini bar], ldry, bbq, rm serv, dinner to unit (Mon to Fri), cots-fee, non smoking units (8). **RO ♦ $62 - $85, ♦♦ $72 - $105, ♦ $12**, ch con, pen con, AE BC DC EFT MC MP VI.

 ★★★☆ Bendigo Motor Inn, (M), 232 High St (Calder Hwy), Kangaroo Flat 3555, 6.5km S of fountain, ☎ 03 5447 8555, fax 03 5447 0720, (2 stry gr fl), 32 units [shwr, bath (4), tlt, a/c, elec blkts, tel, TV, video-fee, movie, clock radio, t/c mkg, refrig], ldry, ✉ (Tues to Sat), pool, sauna, spa, bbq, plygr, cots-fee, non smoking units (5). **RO ♦ $64 - $86, ♦♦ $75 - $86, ♦ $11**, ch con, AE BC DC EFT MC MP VI.

★★★☆ **Bendigo National Motor Inn**, (M), 186 High St (Calder Hwy), opposite Central Deborah Gold Mine, ☎ 03 5441 5777, fax 03 5441 5890, (2 stry gr fl), 24 units (1 suite) [shwr, spa bath (2), tlt, hairdry (2), a/c, elec blkts, tel, TV, movie, clock radio, t/c mkg, refrig, mini bar, toaster], ldry, iron, iron brd, conf fac, ⊠, pool, spa, bbq, dinner to unit, cots-fee. **RO 👤 $82 - $100, 👥 $93 - $100, 🧍 $16, Suite RO $140 - $220**, AE BC DC EFT MC MP VI, ♿.

★★★☆ **Central Deborah Motor Inn**, (M), 177 High St (Calder Hwy), 1km S of fountain, ☎ 03 5443 7488, fax 03 5441 2180, (2 stry gr fl), 26 units [shwr, spa bath (3), tlt, hairdry, a/c, elec blkts, tel, cable tv, video-fee, clock radio, t/c mkg, refrig, mini bar], ldry, iron, iron brd, ⊠ (Mon to Sat), spa, rm serv, cots-fee, non smoking units (13). **P 👤 $82.50 - $100, RO 👥 $95.70 - $111.50, 🧍 $11**, ch con, AE BC DC EFT MC MP VI, ♿.

★★★☆ **Homestead Motor Inn**, (M), 508 High St (Calder Hwy), Golden Square 3555, 4km S of fountain, ☎ 03 5447 7455, fax 03 5447 0826, 24 units (1 suite) [shwr, spa bath (1), tlt, hairdry, a/c, heat, elec blkts, tel, TV, video-fee, clock radio, t/c mkg, refrig, mini bar, cook fac ltd (1), toaster], ldry, iron, iron brd, pool-heated (solar), spa, bbq, rm serv, dinner to unit, cots, non smoking units (8). **RO 👤 $79, 👥 $89 - $165, 🧍 $12**, ch con, Min book all holiday times, AE BC DC MC MP VI.

★★★☆ **(Holiday Unit Section)**, 4 units acc up to 7, (2 bedrm), [shwr, tlt, hairdry, a/c-cool, heat, elec blkts, tel, TV, video-fee, clock radio, refrig, cook fac, micro, ldry (in unit), blkts, linen, pillows], iron, iron brd, c/park (carport). **D 👤👤👤👤 $150 - $210, W 👤👤👤👤 $560 - $1,500**, ch con.

★★★☆ **Lakeview Motor Inn**, (M), 286 Napier St (Midland Hwy), 1.5km N of PO, opposite Lake Weeroona, ☎ 03 5442 3099, fax 03 5443 4309, 33 units [shwr, spa bath, tlt, hairdry, a/c, elec blkts, tel, TV, clock radio, t/c mkg, refrig], ldry, conf fac, ⊠ (Mon to Sat), pool, spa, bbq, rm serv, dinner to unit (Mon to Sat), cots, non smoking units (6). **RO 👤 $88 - $98, 👥 $98 - $108, 🧍 $10**, AE BC DC MC MP VI.

★★★☆ **Tea House Motor Inn**, (M), 280 Napier St (Midland Hwy), 1.2km N of fountain, opposite Lake Weeroona, ☎ 03 5441 7111, fax 03 5441 6755, 20 units [shwr, spa bath (2), tlt, a/c, elec blkts, tel, cable tv, video-fee, clock radio, t/c mkg, refrig, toaster], ldry, pool-heated, spa, bbq, cots, non smoking units (9). **RO 👤 $70 - $85, 👥 $80 - $120, 🧍 $10**, 8 units ★★★★. AE BC DC MC MCH VI, ♿.

★★★☆ **(Holiday Flat Section)**, 4 flats acc up to 5, (2 bedrm), [shwr, tlt, a/c, heat, elec blkts, tel, cable tv, clock radio, t/c mkg, refrig, cook fac, micro, toaster, blkts, linen, pillows], ldry, cots-fee. **D 👥 $96 - $135, 🧍 $10.**

★★★ **Bendigo Budget Oval Motel**, (M), 194 Barnard St, 300m N of fountain, ☎ 03 5443 7211, fax 03 5441 6898, (2 stry gr fl), 27 units [shwr, tlt, hairdry, a/c-cool, cent heat, elec blkts, tel, TV, video-fee, clock radio, t/c mkg, refrig, toaster], ldry, conf fac, bbq, rm serv (incl liquor), dinner to unit, plygr, cots-fee, non smoking units (20). **RO 👤 $50 - $69, 👥 $62 - $69, 🧍 $11**, ch con, AE BC DC EFT MC MCH VI.

★★★ **Golden Hills Motel**, (M), 145 Marong Rd (Calder Hwy), 3.3km NW of fountain, ☎ 03 5443 1333, fax 03 5441 7077, 21 units [shwr, bath (1), spa bath (1), tlt, a/c, elec blkts, tel, TV, clock radio, t/c mkg, refrig, toaster], conf fac, ⊠, pool, bbq, dinner to unit, plygr, cots, non smoking rms (3). **RO 👤 $49.50 - $99, 👥 $60.50 - $99, 🧍 $11**, ch con, pen con, AE BC DC EFT MC MCH MP VI.

★★★ **McIvor Motor Inn**, (M), 45 McIvor Rd (McIvor Hwy), 1.2km E of fountain, ☎ 03 5443 8444, fax 03 5442 5686, 20 units [shwr, tlt, a/c, heat, elec blkts, tel, TV, video (avail), clock radio, t/c mkg, refrig, toaster], conf fac, ✕ (Thur to Sat), BYO, pool, rm serv, dinner to unit, cots. **RO 👤 $49.50 - $88, 👥 $66 - $88, 🧍 $11**, ch con, AE BC DC EFT MC MP VI.

★★★ **Sandhurst Motor Inn**, (M), 211 High St (Calder Hwy), Kangaroo Flat 3555, 6.4km S of fountain, ☎ 03 5447 8855, fax 03 5447 8128, 18 units [shwr, tlt, a/c, elec blkts, tel, cable tv, clock radio, t/c mkg, refrig, mini bar, toaster], ldry, pool, bbq, cots, non smoking units (6). **RO 👤 $71 - $110, 👥 $77 - $120, 🧍 $11**, AE BC DC EFT MC MP VI.

★★★ **Shamrock Hotel Bendigo**, (LH), Classified by National Trust, Cnr Pall Mall & Williamson St, 100m N of fountain, ☎ 03 5443 0333, fax 03 5442 4494, (Multi-stry), 30 rms (2 suites) [basin (7), shwr (23), bath (2), spa bath (3), tlt (23), a/c (18), fan, heat, tel, TV, clock radio, t/c mkg, refrig], lift, ldry, lounge, conf fac, ⊠, ☎, cots-fee. **D $70 - $145, Suite D $180**, 10 rooms ★★☆. AE BC DC MC VI.

★★★ **Welcome Stranger Motel & Function Centre**, (M), 56 Mackenzie St West, Golden Square 3555, 2.9km SW of fountain, ☎ 03 5443 6266, fax 03 5443 9779, 17 units (1 suite) [shwr, tlt, a/c, elec blkts, tel, TV, clock radio, t/c mkg, refrig], conf fac, pool, dinner to unit, cots-fee, non smoking units (7). **RO 👤 $54 - $99, 👥 $65 - $99, 🧍 $11**, AE BC DC MC VI.

★★☆ **Calder Motel**, (M), 296 High St (Calder Hwy), Kangaroo Flat 3555, 7km S of fountain, ☎ 03 5447 7411, fax 03 5447 7720, 12 units [shwr, tlt, a/c, elec blkts, TV, clock radio, t/c mkg, refrig, toaster], ldry, pool, bbq, dinner to unit, plygr, cots, non smoking units (7). **RO 👤 $40 - $65, 👥 $50 - $65, 🧍 $11**, ch con, AE BC EFT MC VI, ***Operator Comment: First Motel from Melb. On Calder Hwy. Opposite Lansell Plaza shopping centre. Package deals available. Seniors Card welcome.***

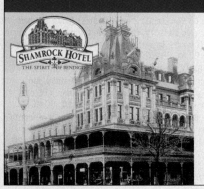

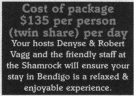

BENDIGO VIC continued...

★★☆ City Centre Motel, (M), 26 Forest St, 200m NW of fountain, ☎ 03 5443 2077, fax 03 5443 2996, (2 stry gr fl), 20 units [shwr, tlt, a/c, elec blkts, tel, TV, t/c mkg, refrig, toaster], cots-fee. **RO ♦ $49 - $69, ♦♦ $58 - $69, ♦♦♦♦ $75 - $86, ◊ $11**, 8 units ★★★. AE BC DC EFT MC VI.

★★ Brougham Arms Hotel & Motel, (LMH), 150 Williamson St, 600m SE of fountain, ☎ 03 5442 3555, 6 units [shwr, tlt, a/c, elec blkts, TV, clock radio, t/c mkg, refrig, toaster], ✉, ☎. **BLB ♦ $49, ♦♦ $60, ◊ $10**, Light breakfast only available. BC MC VI.

★★ The Elm Motel, (M), 454 High St (Calder Hwy), Golden Square 3555, 3.5km S of fountain, ☎ 03 5447 7522, 15 units [shwr, tlt, a/c, elec blkts, tel (12), TV, clock radio, t/c mkg, refrig], cots-fee, non smoking units (4). **RO ♦ $49 - $68, ♦♦ $58 - $68, ◊ $11**, ch con, AE BC DC MC VI.

Self Catering Accommodation

★★★★☆ Ascot Park Gardens, (Cotg), 66 Taylor St, Epsom 3551, 7.1km N of fountain, on Barnadown - Fosterville Rd, ☎ 03 5448 4334, fax 03 5448 4332, 1 cotg acc up to 4, (2 bedrm), [shwr, spa bath, tlt (3), hairdry, c/fan, heat, elec blkts, TV, video, clock radio, t/c mkg, refrig, cook fac, micro, elec frypan, d/wash, toaster, ldry, blkts, linen, pillows], w/mach, dryer, iron, iron brd, pool, bbq, c/park (carport), cots, breakfast ingredients, non smoking property. **BB ♦♦ $120, ◊ $25, W $650 - $720**, ch con.

★★★★☆ Nanga Gnulle, (Cotg), No children's facilities, 40 Harley St, 4.2km SE of fountain, off Strathfieldsaye Rd, ☎ 03 5443 7891, fax 03 5442 3133, 1 cotg acc up to 2, (1 bedrm), [ensuite, spa bath, hairdry, c/fan, heat, elec blkts, TV, video, clock radio, CD, t/c mkg, refrig, cook fac, micro, toaster, ldry], w/mach, iron, iron brd, breakfast ingredients, non smoking property. **BB ♦ $110 - $120, ♦♦ $145 - $170**, BC MC VI.

★★★★☆ Quest Bendigo, (Apt), 489 High St, Golden Square 3555, 4km S of fountain, ☎ 03 5447 0822, fax 03 5447 9722, (2 stry gr fl), 37 apts acc up to 6, (1, 2 & 3 bedrm), [shwr, bath, tlt, hairdry, a/c, tel, TV, video, clock radio, t/c mkg, refrig, cook fac, micro, d/wash, toaster, ldry (in unit), blkts, linen, pillows], w/mach, dryer, iron, iron brd, conf fac, pool (solar heated s/water), bbq, cots, non smoking units (6). **D ♦♦ $126 - $175, ◊ $17, W ♦♦ $575 - $1,190, ◊ $120**, Breakfast pack available. Minimum booking long weekends and swap meets. AE BC DC EFT MC VI, ♿.

★★★★ Green Hedges, (Cotg), 2 Reserve St, Eaglehawk 3556, ☎ 03 5446 8685, fax 03 5446 8685, 1 cotg acc up to 4, (2 bedrm), [shwr, spa bath, tlt, hairdry, a/c, fan, heat, elec blkts, TV, video, clock radio, CD, t/c mkg, refrig, cook fac, toaster], c/park (carport), non smoking property. **D ♦♦ $95 - $125, ◊ $20**.

★★★★ Trent House, (Cotg), 95 Baxter St, ☎ 03 5449 3937, fax 03 5449 3937, 1 cotg acc up to 4, (2 bedrm), [shwr, spa bath, tlt, hairdry, a/c, heat, elec blkts, TV, video, clock radio, CD, t/c mkg, refrig, cook fac ltd, toaster, ldry, blkts, doonas, linen, pillows], w/mach, iron, iron brd, breakfast ingredients, non smoking property. **BB ♦♦ $120 - $145, ◊ $25**, AE BC DC MC VI.

★★★ 420 High Holiday Units, (HU), 420 High St, Golden Square 3555, 2.8km S of fountain, ☎ 03 5447 0261, 6 units acc up to 6, (1 & 2 bedrm), [shwr, tlt, a/c, heat, elec blkts, TV, video-fee, clock radio, refrig, cook fac, micro, elec frypan, toaster, ldry (in unit), blkts, linen, pillows], iron, iron brd, bbq, c/park (carport), cots. **D $68 - $145, W $385 - $550**, Min book long w/ends and Easter, BC MC VI.

★★★ Bendigo Holiday Flats, (HF), 24 Nolan St, 1.3km N of fountain, ☎ 03 5441 3598, 6 flats acc up to 5, (1 bedrm), [shwr, tlt, a/c, elec blkts, TV, video-fee, clock radio, refrig, cook fac, toaster, blkts, linen, pillows], ldry, w/mach, dryer-fee, cots, non smoking property. **D ♦♦ $60 - $80, ◊ $11, W ♦♦ $400 - $450, ◊ $49 - $77**, ch con, Min book all holiday times, BC MC VI.

★★★ Navron, (HF), 466 High St (Calder Hwy), Golden Square 3555, 3km S of fountain, ☎ 03 5447 7669, or 03 5444 4613, fax 03 5444 4099, 7 flats acc up to 6, (1 bedrm), [shwr, tlt, a/c-cool, heat, elec blkts, cable tv, clock radio, t/c mkg, refrig, cook fac, toaster, ldry (in unit), blkts, linen, pillows], w/mach, iron, iron brd, bbq, c/park (carport), cots. **D ♦♦ $60 - $80, ◊ $11**, Light breakfast available.

★★ A-Line Holiday Village, (HU), 5615 Calder Hwy, Kangaroo Flat 3555, 4.2km S of Kangaroo Flat PO, ☎ 03 5447 9568, (2 stry gr fl), 7 units acc up to 6, (2 bedrm), [shwr, bath, tlt, a/c-cool, heat, elec blkts, TV, refrig, cook fac, toaster, blkts, linen, pillows], ldry, w/mach-fee, dryer-fee, pool, bbq-fee. **D ♦♦ $55, ◊ $8**, BC MC VI.

B&B's/Guest Houses

★★★★☆ Antoinette's Bed & Breakfast, (B&B), Not suitable for children. 179 Wattle St, 900m NW of fountain, ☎ 03 5442 3609, fax 03 5442 3613, 1 rm (1 suite) [ensuite, hairdry, a/c, cent heat, elec blkts, clock radio, t/c mkg, refrig], lounge (TV, video, stereo), bbq. **BB ♦ $95 - $110, ♦♦ $105 - $125**, AE BC MC VI.

★★★★☆ Benlee Bendigo, (B&B), 160 Durstons Rd, Maiden Gully 3551, 7.9km W of fountain, ☎ 03 5449 6510, fax 03 5449 6138, 1 rm [ensuite, hairdry, evap cool, c/fan, heat, TV, clock radio], lounge (cd, stereo), t/c mkg shared, non smoking rms. **BB ♦ $95, ♦♦ $100**.

★★★★☆ Cathedral Terrace Bed & Breakfast, (B&B), 81 Wattle St, 300m SE of fountain, ☎ 03 5441 3242, fax 03 5443 3335, 2 rms [ensuite, bath (1), hairdry, a/c-cool, fan, cent heat, elec blkts, TV, clock radio, t/c mkg], lounge (TV, video, cd), refrig, c/park (undercover), non smoking property. **BB ♦♦ $130 - $150**, BC EFT MC VI.

★★★★☆ Greystanes Manor, (GH), No children's facilities, 57 Queen St, ☎ 03 5442 2466, fax 03 5442 2447, (2 stry), 7 rms [ensuite, a/c, fire pl (3), cent heat, elec blkts, tel, TV, clock radio], lounge, conf fac, ✗, t/c mkg shared, non smoking rms. **BLB $125 - $145**, AE BC DC MC VI.

★★★★☆ Jubilee Villa, (B&B), c1887. 170 McCrae St, 400m N of fountain, ☎ 03 5442 2920, fax 03 5442 2580, 1 rm (1 suite) [shwr, spa bath, tlt, c/fan, heat, elec blkts, TV, clock radio, t/c mkg, refrig, micro], bbq, non smoking property. **BB ♦ $85, ♦♦ $120 - $145**, Minimum booking Easter & swap meet weekends, AE BC DC MC VI.

★★★★☆ Lynnevale Lodge, (B&B), 83 Cahills Rd, Mandurang 3551, 8km S of fountain, ☎ 03 5439 3635, fax 03 5439 3635, 3 rms [ensuite, hairdry, evap cool, cent heat, clock radio], lounge (TV, video, cd), lounge firepl, spa (heated), t/c mkg shared, refrig, bbq. **BB ♦ $95, ♦♦ $110**, Dinner by arrangement. Min book long w/ends and Easter, BC MC VI.

★★★★☆ Marlborough House Bendigo, (B&B), 115 Wattle St, 900m W of fountain, ☎ 03 5441 4142, fax 03 5441 4142, (2 stry gr fl), 6 rms [ensuite, a/c, cent heat, elec blkts, clock radio, doonas], lounge (TV, cd), lounge firepl, ✉, BYO, t/c mkg shared. **BB ♦ $77 - $88, ♦♦ $137.50 - $154**, 1 room ★★★★. Dinner by arrangement. BC MC VI.

★★★★☆ The Cottages Bendigo, (B&B), Cnr Niemann & Anderson Sts, ☎ 03 5441 5613, fax 03 5444 4313, 2 rms [shwr, tlt, hairdry, a/c, c/fan, TV, video, clock radio, CD, refrig, cook fac ltd, doonas], iron, iron brd, non smoking property. **BB ♦ $75, ♦♦ $110 - $135, ◊ $15**, BC MC VI.

★★★★ Caradon House, (B&B), 80 Victoria St, Eaglehawk 3556, 100m E of Eaglehawk PO, ☎ 03 5446 3981, fax 03 5446 3980, (2 stry), 4 rms [ensuite, a/c-cool, cent heat, elec blkts, clock radio], ldry, rec rm, read rm, lounge, t/c mkg shared, refrig, non smoking rms. **BB ♦ $75 - $95, ♦♦ $95 - $135, ◊ $55 - $65**, Dinner by arrangement. AE BC DC EFT MC VI.

★★★★ Gardena, (B&B), 176 Williamson St, 900m E of fountain, ☎ 03 5443 0551, fax 03 5443 0551, 2 rms (2 suites) [shwr, spa bath, tlt, hairdry, c/fan, fire pl, elec blkts, TV, clock radio, t/c mkg, refrig, micro, toaster], pool, c/park (carport), breakfast ingredients, non smoking property. **BLB ♦ $77, ♦♦ $110**, BC MC VI.

★★★★ Landonia, (B&B), 87 Mollison St, 900m N of fountain, ☎ 03 5442 2183, fax 03 5442 2183, 1 rm [ensuite, hairdry, fan, cent heat, elec blkts, clock radio, t/c mkg, refrig], lounge (TV, cd), lounge firepl, non smoking property. **BB ♦ $80, ♦♦ $110**, BC MC VI.

★★★★ Napier Rose B & B, (B&B), 440 Napier St, 3.1km N of fountain, ☎ 03 5443 3719, fax 03 5443 3899, 1 rm [shwr, bath, tlt, c/fan, cent heat, TV, clock radio, t/c mkg, refrig], lounge firepl. **BB ♦ $120, ♦♦ $150**, BC MC VI.

Operator Comment: See our web site at:
www.bwc.com.au/sites/napierrose

★★★☆ **Skye Glen Llama Farm**, (B&B), Clearing Crt, Mandurang 3551, 9.1km S of fountain, off Nankervis Rd, ☎ 03 5439 3054, fax 03 5441 5051, 2 rms [shwr, tlt, hairdry, elec blkts], iron, iron brd, lounge (TV, video), cook fac, refrig, bbq. **BB ♦ $60 - $70, ♦♦ $85 - $100,** ◊ **$25,** ch con, *Operator Comment: Rustic stone cottage retreat now avail. For details see www.skyeglen.bendigo.net.au*

★★★☆ **Whistle Inn**, (B&B), 213 Allingham St, Kangaroo Flat 3555, 5.6km S of fountain, ☎ 03 5447 8685, fax 03 5447 8685, 2 rms [spa bath, hairdry, a/c, c/fan, heat, elec blkts, TV, video, radio, CD, t/c mkg, refrig, micro], lounge firepl, bbq. **BB ♦ $55, ♦♦ $95,** ch con.

Other Accommodation
Central City Caravan Park, (Lodge), 362 High St (Calder Hwy), Golden Square 3555, 2.5km S of fountain, ☎ 03 5443 6937, fax 03 5443 6937, 6 rms acc up to 4, (Bunk Rooms), [linen reqd], shwr (4L/G), tlt (4L/G), ldry, w/mach-fee, dryer-fee, lounge (TV), pool, cook fac, t/c mkg shared, refrig, bbq-fee, kiosk, ✆, plygr. **D ♦ $15,** ◊ **$15,** BC EFT MC VI.
Ironbark Riding Centre, (Lodge), Lot 2 Watson St, ☎ 03 5448 3344, fax 03 5448 3787, 6 rms acc up to 5, [shwr, tlt, heat, elec blkts, clock radio, t/c mkg, refrig, toaster, blkts, linen, pillows], bbq, ✆. **D ♦♦ $44,** ◊ **$11,** ch con, fam con, Catering available. BC MC VI.

BERRYS CREEK VIC 3953

Pop Nominal, (145km SE Melbourne), See map on page 696, ref D7. Grazing country with fertile river flats. Bush Walking, Scenic Drives.
Self Catering Accommodation
★★ **Greycotes Stud**, (Cotg), (Farm), RMB 5855 Strzlecki Hwy, 16km NE of Leongatha, entry via Mossvale Park, ☎ 03 5668 8227, 1 cotg acc up to 8, (3 bedrm), [shwr, bath (hip), tlt, fan, heat, elec blkts, TV, video, radio, refrig, cook fac, micro, elec frypan, toaster, ldry], w/mach, lounge firepl, bbq, cots. **D $65 - $100, W $350 - $450.**

BEVERIDGE VIC 3753

Pop 340. (42km N Melbourne), See map on page 696, ref C4. Small rural township situated north of Melbourne. Horse Riding, Tennis.
B&B's/Guest Houses
★★★☆ **The Hunters Tryst**, (B&B), No children's facilities, Old Hume Hwy, ☎ 03 9745 2309, fax 03 9745 2309, (2 stry gr fl), 3 rms [shwr, spa bath (1), tlt, elec blkts, clock radio], lounge (TV), ⊠, ✆, non smoking rms (3). **BB ♦ $50 - $60, ♦♦ $80 - $100,** ◊ **$20,** AE BC DC EFT MC VI.

BIRCHIP VIC 3483

Pop 800. (319km NW Melbourne), See map on pages 694/695, ref C4. Small town in wool & wheat growing area. Home of the 'Mallee Bull'. Bowls, Fishing, Golf, Squash, Swimming (Pool), Tennis.
Hotels/Motels
★★★ **Birchip Motel & Caravan Park**, (M), Sunraysia Hwy, 1km W of PO, opposite High School, ☎ 03 5492 2566, fax 03 5492 2566, 5 units [shwr, tlt, a/c, elec blkts, tel, TV, clock radio, t/c mkg, refrig], ldry, pool, dinner to unit, plygr, cots, non smoking units (2). **RO ♦ $55, ♦♦ $66,** ◊ **$11,** BC EFT MC VI.

BIRREGURRA VIC 3242

Pop 400. (134km SW Melbourne), See map on pages 694/695, ref D7. Small agricultural township in a pastoral district. Bowls, Golf, Scenic Drives, Tennis.
B&B's/Guest Houses
★★★★ **Elliminook Bed & Breakfast**, (B&B), Classified by National Trust, No facilities for children under 12. 585 Warncoort Rd, 500m NW of PO, ☎ 03 5236 2080, fax 03 5236 2423, 4 rms [ensuite (3), shwr (1), spa bath (1), tlt (1), hairdry, c/fan (3), fire pl (2), cent heat, elec blkts, TV (2), clock radio, t/c mkg (2)], lounge (TV, stereo), lounge firepl, t/c mkg shared, tennis, non smoking property. **BB ♦ $99 - $143, ♦♦ $121 - $176,** BC DC MC VI.
★★★☆ **Gannawarra Host Farm**, (B&B), (Farm), 585 Dunlops Rd, 6.4km SW of PO, off Ennis Rd, ☎ 03 5236 2131, 2 rms [cent heat, elec blkts, doonas], ldry, lounge (TV). **BB ♦ $44,** ◊ **$44, D all meals ♦ $77,** ◊ **$77,** ch con, Pets allowed by arrangement.

Trouble-free travel tips - **Hoses and belts**
Inspect the condition of radiator hoses, heater hose fan and air conditioner belts.

BLACKWOOD VIC 3458

Pop 300. (85km NW Melbourne), See map on page 696, ref A4. Holiday resort known for its mineral springs. Bush Walking, Fishing, Gem Fossicking, Gold Prospecting, Horse Riding, Scenic Drives, Swimming (River), Tennis.
Hotels/Motels
★★ **Blackwood Hotel**, (LMH), Martin St, opposite PO, ☎ 03 5368 6501, fax 03 5368 6848, 3 units [shwr, tlt, heat, elec blkts, TV, t/c mkg, refrig, toaster], ⊠, ✆. **BLB ♦♦ $60,** ◊ **$12,** ch con, BC EFT MC VI.
Self Catering Accommodation
★★★★ **Woodbine Cottage**, (Cotg), 11 Simmons Reef Rd, 200m SW of PO, ☎ 03 5368 6770, fax 03 5368 6773, 1 cotg acc up to 6, (3 bedrm), [shwr, spa bath, tlt, a/c, elec blkts, tel, TV, video, radio, CD, t/c mkg, refrig, cook fac, micro, toaster, ldry, blkts, doonas, linen, pillows], w/mach, dryer, iron, iron brd, lounge firepl, bbq, c/park (undercover), cots, breakfast ingredients. **BB $135 - $225, $900,** BC MC VI.

BLAIRGOWRIE VIC 3942

Pop 1,948. (85km S Melbourne), See map on page 697, ref A8. Bayside resort. Boating, Bush Walking, Fishing, Sailing, Scenic Drives, Swimming (Bay), Water Skiing.
Hotels/Motels
★★★ **Moodys Motel**, (M), 2867 Point Nepean Rd, 300m W of PO, ☎ 03 5988 8463, fax 03 5988 8314, (2 stry gr fl), 9 units [shwr, bath (hip) (3), spa bath (1), tlt, hairdry, a/c, heat, elec blkts, tel, TV, video (avail), t/c mkg, refrig, micro (1), toaster], ldry, bbq, cots-fee, non smoking units (3). **RO ♦ $50 - $140,** ch con, pen con, AE BC EFT MC VI.
Self Catering Accommodation
★★★★ **Arcady Cottage**, (Cotg), 110 Canterbury Jetty Rd, 2km SE from Blairgowrie, ☎ 03 5984 2413, fax 03 5984 0452, 1 cotg acc up to 6, (3 bedrm), [shwr, bath, tlt, c/fan, heat, elec blkts, tel (local), TV, video, clock radio, CD, t/c mkg, refrig, cook fac, micro, elec frypan, d/wash, toaster, ldry, blkts, doonas, linen, pillows], w/mach, iron, iron brd, lounge firepl (gas log), bbq, c/park (undercover), breakfast ingredients, non smoking property. **D $220, W $660 - $1,200,** Min book all holiday times, AE BC DC MC VI.
★★★★ **Daisy Cottage Bed & Breakfast**, (Cotg), 21 Foam Ave, ☎ 03 5984 4431, fax 03 5984 5840, 2 cotgs acc up to 4, (2 bedrm), [shwr, tlt, hairdry, fan, heat, tel (portable), TV, video, clock radio, CD, refrig, cook fac, micro, ldry, blkts, linen, pillows], w/mach, iron, iron brd, bbq, breakfast ingredients, non smoking property. **BLB ♦ $100, ♦♦ $140,** ◊ **$35,** ch con, Min book Christmas Jan and Easter.
★★★★ **Hidden Treasure at Pirates Bay**, (Cotg), 15 Knox Rd, ☎ 03 5988 0126, fax 03 5988 0126, (2 stry), 1 cotg acc up to 4, (1 bedrm), [shwr, tlt, a/c, c/fan, wood heat, TV, video, clock radio, CD, t/c mkg, refrig, cook fac ltd, micro, toaster, blkts, doonas, linen, pillows], iron, iron brd, bbq, c/park (carport), breakfast ingredients. **D ♦♦ $150,** ◊ **$25,** ch con.

BLAMPIED VIC 3364

Pop Nominal, (121km NW Melbourne), See map on page 696, ref A4. Farming & grazing district.
Other Accommodation
Rutherford Park - Country Retreat, (Lodge), Kangaroo Hills Rd, off Kooroocheang Rd, ☎ 03 5345 7457, fax 03 534 5459, 38 rms acc up to 8, [shwr, tlt, cent heat, linen reqd-fee], ldry, rec rm, lounge (TV), conf fac, t/c mkg shared, refrig, bbq (covered), tennis. **D all meals ♦ $60 - $150,** ◊ **$60 - $150,** ch con, Group accommodation only.

BONEO VIC 3939

Pop Part of Rosebud, (83km S Melbourne), See map on page 697, ref B8. Grazing & agricultural district on Mornington Peninsula. Golf, Horse Riding, Tennis.
B&B's/Guest Houses
★★★☆ **Cheringa Hideaway**, (B&B), 171 Maxwell Rd, 10km S of Arthurs Seat, ☎ 03 9568 6411, fax 03 9569 4960, 2 rms [shwr, tlt, hairdry, heat, elec blkts, tel, TV, video, clock radio, t/c mkg, refrig], iron, iron brd. **BB ♦♦ $160,** AE BC DC MC VI.

BONNIE DOON VIC 3720

Pop 322. (179km NE Melbourne), See maps on page??12, ref D3. Situated on shore of Lake Eildon. Boat Ramp, Boating, Bowls, Bush Walking, Fishing (Lake), Golf, Horse Riding, Sailing, Scenic Drives, Shooting, Swimming (Lake), Tennis, Water Skiing.

Hotels/Motels

★★☆ **Lakeland Resort Hotel**, (LMH), Cnr Maroondah Hwy & Hutchinsons Rd, overlooking Lake Eildon, ☎ 03 5778 7335, fax 03 5778 7268, 12 units [shwr, bath (1), spa bath (1), tlt, a/c, heat, elec blkts, TV, clock radio, t/c mkg, refrig, toaster], ldry, ☒, pool, spa (heated), ✆, plygr. **BLB ♦ $55, ♦♦ $70**, ch con, AE BC DC EFT MC VI.

★★ **Bonnie Doon Motor Inn**, (M), Maroondah Hwy, adjacent to PO, 1km W of bridge, ☎ 03 5778 7390, fax 03 5778 7790, (2 stry gr fl), 15 units [shwr, tlt, a/c, elec blkts, TV, video-fee, clock radio, t/c mkg, refrig, cook fac (1), micro (1), toaster], cafe, bbq, cots. **RO ♦ $45 - $60, ♦♦ $60 - $70, ◊ $11**, AE BC DC EFT MC VI.

Self Catering Accommodation

★★★ **Bonnie Doon Holiday Apartments**, (HU), Maroondah Hwy, on shore of Lake Eildon, ☎ 03 5778 7445, fax 03 5778 7616, 9 units acc up to 12, (Studio, 1 & 4 bedrm), [shwr, tlt, a/c, TV, refrig, cook fac ltd, micro (9), blkts, linen, pillows], ldry, ☒ (seasonal), bbq. **D ♦ $33 - $44, ♦♦ $49.50 - $220, ◊ $13.20**, BC MC VI.

B&B's/Guest Houses

★★★ **Starglen Lodge**, (GH), (Farm), Star of the Glen Rd, 10km N of PO, Glen Creek Rd, ☎ 03 5778 7312, fax 03 5778 7603, 20 rms [shwr, tlt, fan, heat, elec blkts, t/c mkg, refrig (15)], ldry, rec rm, lounge (TV, video), conf fac, lounge firepl, ☒, ☒, pool, sauna, spa, bbq, tennis, cots. **BB ♦ $65, ◊ $65, DBB ♦ $90, ◊ $90**, ch con, AE BC DC MC VI.

(**Bunkhouse Section**), 2 bunkhouses acc up to 30, (Bunk Rooms), [a/c, heat, blkts reqd, linen reqd, pillows reqd], lounge, cook fac, refrig. **D ♦ $15 - $25, ◊ $15 - $25**, Minimum booking - 10 people.

Other Accommodation

Lake Eildon Houseboat Hire, (Hbt), Kennedy's Point, off Maintongoon Rd, 3km S of PO, ☎ 03 5778 7747, fax 03 5778 7747, 3 houseboats acc up to 10, (3 bedrm), [shwr, tlt, heat, TV, video, radio (cassette), refrig, cook fac, micro, toaster, linen reqd], bbq. **W $825 - $2,970**, Security bond - $600 to $1000. Min book Christmas Jan and Easter, BC MC VI.

BOOLARRA VIC 3870

Pop 550. Nominal, (174km SE Melbourne), See map on page 696, ref E7. Dairying district in the foothills of the Strzelecki Ranges. Bowls, Bush Walking, Scenic Drives, Tennis.

B&B's/Guest Houses

★★★★ **Twelve Mile Peg B&B**, (B&B), 1550 Darlimurla Rd, 2.4km W of PO, ☎ 03 5169 6337, fax 03 5169 6685, 1 rm (1 suite) (1 bedrm), [ensuite, shwr, bath, tlt, hairdry, evap cool, heat, elec blkts, TV, clock radio, t/c mkg, refrig, cook fac ltd, micro, toaster], lounge (TV, stereo), bar, bbq, non smoking rms. **BB ♦♦ $85, ◊ $30**, ch con.

BOORT VIC 3537

Pop 800. (254km NW Melbourne), See maps on page??11, ref D4. Situated on shore of Lake Boort. Boating, Bowls, Bush Walking, Croquet, Fishing, Golf, Horse Riding, Sailing, Scenic Drives, Shooting, Swimming (Pool), Tennis, Trotting, Water Skiing.

Hotels/Motels

★★★ **Lake Boort Motel**, (M), Lakeside Dve, ☎ 03 5455 2106, fax 03 5444 2106, 10 units [shwr, tlt, a/c, elec blkts, tel, TV, video-fee, radio, t/c mkg, refrig], ✗, pool, bbq, dinner to unit, cots-fee. **RO ♦ $60.50 - $66, ♦♦ $71.50 - $77, ◊ $11**, AE BC MC VI.

BRANXHOLME VIC 3302

Pop 100. (314km W Melbourne), See maps on page??11, ref B6. Agricultural & pastoral district. Bush Walking, Fishing, Horse Riding, Scenic Drives, Swimming, Tennis.

Self Catering Accommodation

★★☆ **Treasland Groves**, (Cotg), RMB 2210 Condah-Coleraine Rd, ☎ 03 5578 6388, fax 03 5578 6399, (2 stry gr fl), 1 cotg acc up to 6, (5 bedrm), [shwr (2), bath (1), tlt (2), heat (2), elec blkts, TV (2), t/c mkg, refrig, cook fac, micro, toaster, ldry, blkts, linen, pillows], w/mach, dryer, iron, iron brd. **D $120 - $175**, BC MC VI.

B&B's/Guest Houses

★★★★ **Arrandoovong Homestead**, (B&B), (Farm), Children by prior arrangement. Chrome Rd, 3km N of PO, ☎ 03 5578 6221, fax 03 5578 6249, (2 stry), 2 rms [shwr, tlt, fan, elec blkts, clock radio, t/c mkg], lounge (TV, stereo), lounge firepl, bbq. **BB ♦ $120, ♦♦ $125 - $155**, Dinner by arrangement. BC VI.

BRIAGOLONG VIC 3860

Pop 500. (249km E Melbourne), See maps on page??11, ref H7. Agricultural township specializing in the production of honey and fruit growing.

B&B's/Guest Houses

★★★★☆ **Redgum Gully**, (B&B), No children's facilities, Lot 3 Boundary Rd, 3km NE of PO, off Victoria St, ☎ 03 5145 5755, fax 03 5145 5766, 2 rms [ensuite, hairdry, a/c, elec blkts, tel, TV, movie, clock radio, t/c mkg, refrig], iron brd, res liquor license, bbq, non smoking property. **BB ♦ $70 - $90, ♦♦ $105 - $130, ◊ $40 - $55**, Dinner by arrangement. Min book Christmas Jan and Easter, BC MC VI.

BRIDGEWATER ON LODDON VIC 3516

Pop 300. (188km NW Melbourne), See maps on page??12, ref A2. Popular water sports town on the bank of the Loddon River. Water Wheel Flour Mill. Boating, Bowls, Fishing, Golf, Swimming (Pool, River), Tennis, Water Skiing.

Hotels/Motels

★★★ **Riverside Motel**, (M), Cnr Calder Hwy & Arnold Rd, ☎ 03 5437 3200, fax 03 5437 3200, 12 units [shwr, bath (hip) (2), tlt, a/c-cool, heat, elec blkts, TV, clock radio, t/c mkg, refrig, cook fac (2), toaster], bbq, cots-fee. **BLB ♦ $52 - $75, ♦♦ $62 - $75, ◊ $12 - $15**, AE BC DC MC MCH VI.

BRIGHT VIC 3741

Pop 1,900. (312km NE Melbourne), See maps on page??11, ref H5. Includes: Freeburgh. Gateway to the Victorian Alps. Art Gallery, Bowls, Bush Walking, Croquet, Fishing (River), Gold Prospecting, Golf, Hang gliding, Horse Riding, Scenic Drives, Snow Skiing, Swimming (River), Tennis. See also Harrietville, Porepunkah & Wandiligong.

Hotels/Motels

★★★★☆ **Bright Chalet**, (Ltd Lic H), 113 Delany Ave (Great Alpine Rd), 2km E of PO, ☎ 03 5755 1833, fax 03 5755 2187, (2 stry gr fl), 25 rms [shwr, bath (hip) (15), spa bath (6), tlt, hairdry, a/c-cool, cent heat, tel, cable tv, video-fee, clock radio, t/c mkg, refrig, micro (6), doonas], conf fac, ☒, bar (cocktail), pool-heated, rm serv, ✆, plygr, bicycle (Fee)-fee, ski hire, tennis, cots, non smoking property. **BB ♦♦ $135, ◊ $15**, ch con, AE BC DC EFT MC VI.

AAA TOURISM *Special Rates* ★★★★ **Barrass's John Bright Motor Inn**, (M), 10 Wood St, 200m N of PO, ☎ 03 5755 1400, fax 03 5750 1455, 20 units [shwr, bath (12), spa bath (2), tlt, a/c, elec blkts, tel, TV, video-fee, clock radio, t/c mkg, refrig, toaster], ldry, dry rm, pool-heated (solar), spa, bbq, dinner to unit, car wash, cots-fee, non smoking units (12). **RO ♦ $85 - $145, ♦♦ $85 - $145, ◊ $15**, Booking conditions apply, BC EFT MC VI.

★★★★ **Bright Avenue Motor Inn**, (M), 87 Delany Ave (Great Alpine Rd), 1.7km E of PO, ☎ 03 5755 1911, fax 03 5750 1105, 13 units [shwr, spa bath (3), tlt, a/c-cool (5), a/c (8), fire pl (3), heat, elec blkts, tel, TV, video (12), clock radio, t/c mkg, refrig, cook fac], ldry, dry rm, pool, spa, bbq, cots, non smoking units (13). **BLB** ♦ **$72 - $130,** ♦♦ **$77 - $130,** ♦ **$12,** ch con, AE BC DC MC VI.

★★★★ **High Country Motor Inn**, (M), 13 Gavan St (Great Alpine Rd), 1.4km NW of PO, ☎ 03 5755 1244, fax 03 5755 1575, 32 units [shwr, bath (hip) (15), spa bath (5), tlt, hairdry, a/c, fire pl, elec blkts, tel, TV, video-fee, movie, clock radio, t/c mkg, refrig, cook fac (5)], ldry, iron, iron brd, dry rm, lounge, conf fac, ✉ (Mon to Sat), bar (cocktail), pool, sauna, spa, bbq, rm serv, plygr, cots-fee, non smoking units (24). **RO** ♦♦ **$89 - $112,** ♦ **$10,** AE BC DC EFT JCB MC VI, ♿.

★★★☆ **Bright Colonial Inn Motel**, (M), 54 Gavan St (Great Alpine Rd), 400m N of PO, ☎ 03 5755 1633, fax 03 5750 1377, 18 units [shwr, tlt, hairdry, a/c-cool, heat, elec blkts, tel, TV, video-fee, movie, clock radio, t/c mkg, refrig, toaster], ldry, iron, iron brd, dry rm, pool (solar heated), bbq, car wash, plygr, cots-fee, non smoking units (7). **RO** ♦ **$66 - $79,** ♦♦ **$77 - $88,** ♦ **$13,** ch con, AE BC DC EFT MC MP VI.

★★★ **Acacia Motor Lodge**, (M), 85 Gavan St (Great Alpine Rd), 300m N of PO, ☎ 03 5755 1441, fax 03 5755 1441, (2 stry), 12 units [shwr, spa bath (2), tlt, a/c, c/fan (2), heat, elec blkts, tel, TV, video-fee, clock radio, t/c mkg, refrig, cook fac (2), micro, toaster], ldry, dry rm, pool, bbq. **RO** ♦ **$66 - $80,** ♦♦ **$77 - $125,** ♦ **$15,** AE BC MC VI.

★★★ **Bright Central Motel Lodge**, (M), 2 Ireland St, opposite PO, ☎ 03 5755 1074, fax 03 5755 1074, 7 units [shwr, tlt, a/c, heat, elec blkts, TV, clock radio, t/c mkg, refrig, micro (4), toaster]. **RO** ♦ **$55 - $100,** ♦♦ **$65 - $110,** ch con, BC MC VI.

★★★ **(Bed & Breakfast Section)**, (2 stry gr fl), 9 rms [basin, shwr (5), tlt (5), a/c-cool, heat, elec blkts, TV (2)], ldry, dry rm, rec rm, lounge (TV, video), ✉ (Group bookings only), cook fac, t/c mkg shared, refrig. **BB** ♦ **$45 - $55,** ♦ **$30 - $35,** ch con.

★★★ **Bright Motor Inn**, (M), 1 Delany Ave (Great Alpine Rd), 700m E of PO, ☎ 03 5750 1433, fax 03 5755 1382, 26 units [ensuite, bath (1), a/c, heat, elec blkts, TV, video-fee, clock radio, t/c mkg, refrig, micro (9), toaster], ldry, rec rm, ✉, bar (Cocktail), pool (solar), spa (heated), bbq, ✆, cots, non smoking units (2). **RO** ♦ **$50 - $65,** ♦♦ **$60 - $75,** ♦ **$10,** ch con, BC MC VI,

Operator Comment: Visit our Alpine Valleys Wine Bar at www.brightmotorinn.brightvic.com

★★★ **Ovens Valley Motor Inn**, (M), Cnr Great Alpine Rd & Ashwood Ave, 1.9km W of PO, ☎ 03 5755 2022, fax 03 5755 1371, 24 units [shwr, tlt, a/c-cool, heat, elec blkts, tel, TV, clock radio, t/c mkg, refrig, toaster], ldry, dry rm, ✉, pool, spa, bbq, tennis, cots-fee. **RO** ♦ **$60 - $85,** ♦♦ **$75 - $95,** ♦ **$15,** ch con, AE BC DC MC VI.

Operator Comment: See our display advertisement on following page.

★★★ **Riverbank Park Motel**, (M), 69 Gavan St (Great Alpine Rd), 300m N of PO, ☎ 03 5755 1255, fax 03 5755 1476, (2 stry gr fl), 24 units [shwr, tlt, a/c-cool, heat, elec blkts, tel, TV, video-fee, clock radio, t/c mkg, refrig, mini bar, toaster], ✉ (Tue to Sat), pool, bbq, rm serv, dinner to unit, plygr, cots-fee. **RO** ♦ **$72 - $78,** ♦♦ **$88 - $100,** ch con, AE BC DC EFT MC MP VI.

★★☆ **Elm Lodge**, (M), 2 Wood St, 250m N of PO, ☎ 03 5755 1144, fax 03 5755 2206, 16 units [shwr, bath (1), spa bath (1), tlt, cent heat, elec blkts, TV, clock radio, t/c mkg, refrig], ldry, dry rm, ⊠, pool, bbq, c/park (carport) (5), cots, non smoking rms (5). RO ⚄ $43 - $55, ⚄⚄ $54 - $110, ⚄ $13, ch con, 5 units ★★. BC EFT MC MCH VI.

★★ **The Star**, (LMH), 91 Great Alpine Rd, 300m NE of PO, ☎ 03 5755 1277, fax 03 5755 1000, (2 stry gr fl), 30 units [shwr, tlt, a/c-cool, heat, elec blkts, TV, t/c mkg, refrig, toaster], conf fac, ⊠, ☏ (2), cots. RO ⚄ $38.50 - $44, ⚄⚄ $55 - $66, ⚄ $10, AE BC DC EFT MC VI.

★ **Alpine Hotel**, (LMH), 7 Anderson St, 200m NE of PO, opposite clock tower, ☎ 03 5755 1366, fax 03 5755 2325, (2 stry gr fl), 24 units [shwr, bath (8), tlt, a/c-cool, cent heat, elec blkts, TV, t/c mkg, refrig, toaster], ldry, dry rm, ⊠, ☏, cots. RO ⚄ $30 - $35, ⚄⚄ $45 - $55, ⚄ $10, 6 units ★★☆. AE BC DC EFT MC VI.

Self Catering Accommodation

★★★★☆ **Chestnut Tree Holiday Units - Bright**, (HF), 154 Delany Ave (Great Alpine Rd), 2.4km E of PO, ☎ 03 9374 1233, fax 03 9374 1233, 10 flats acc up to 5, (2 bedrm), [shwr, spa bath (3), tlt, hairdry, evap cool, fan, heat, elec blkts, cable tv, video, clock radio, refrig, cook fac, micro, elec frypan, toaster, blkts, linen, pillows], ldry, dry rm, pool, bbq (covered), c/park (carport), ☏, plygr, golf (chipping green), tennis, cots, non smoking units. D $85 - $143, W $490 - $1,001, ch con, fam con, Min book all holiday times, BC MC VI.

★★★★☆ **Westwood Lodge**, (HU), 8 Wood St, 300m W of PO, ☎ 03 5755 1465, 2 units acc up to 5, (2 bedrm), [shwr, tlt, hairdry, a/c, elec blkts, TV, clock radio, t/c mkg, refrig, cook fac, micro, toaster, blkts, linen, pillows], ldry, w/mach, dryer, bbq, cots, non smoking units. D ⚄⚄ $85 - $130, ⚄ $12 - $17, W ⚄⚄ $525 - $910, ⚄ $55 - $85, Breakfast available. BC MC VI.

★★★★ **Alice Alpine**, (HU), 1 Lewis Cl, 400m S of PO, ☎ 03 5756 2094, 1 unit acc up to 5, (2 bedrm), [shwr, bath, tlt, a/c, c/fan, heat, elec blkts, TV, video, clock radio, CD, refrig, cook fac, micro, toaster, ldry (in unit), blkts, doonas, linen, pillows], w/mach, dryer, iron, iron brd, bbq, c/park (garage), cots, non smoking property. D $100.

★★★★ **Alinga-Longa Lodge**, (HU), 12 Gavan St (Great Alpine Rd) 12 Gavan St (G, 1.4km W of PO, ☎ 03 5755 1073, 6 units acc up to 6, (2 bedrm), [shwr, tlt, hairdry, a/c, c/fan, elec blkts, TV, video, clock radio, refrig, cook fac, micro, elec frypan, toaster, blkts, linen, pillows], ldry, dry rm, pool, bbq (covered), plygr, bicycle, cots. D ⚄⚄ $77 - $140, ⚄ $11 - $16.50, W $440, AE BC DC MC VI.

★★★★ **Autumn Grove Holiday Units**, (HU), 57 Delany Ave (Great Alpine Rd), 1.3km E of PO, ☎ 03 5750 1750, fax 03 5750 1605, 4 units acc up to 7, (1, 2 & 3 bedrm), [shwr, bath (1), spa bath (3), tlt, a/c, elec blkts, TV, video, clock radio, refrig, cook fac, micro, elec frypan, d/wash, toaster, ldry (in unit), blkts, linen, pillows], w/mach, dryer, iron, iron brd, bbq, c/park (carport), plygr, cots. D ⚄⚄ $95 - $170, ⚄ $15 - $20, Min book all holiday times, AE BC MC VI.

★★★★ **Delany Lodge**, (HU), 90 Delany Ave (Great Alpine Rd), 1.7km E of PO, ☎ 03 5755 1900, 5 units acc up to 6, (2 & 3 bedrm), [shwr, spa bath (3), tlt, a/c, elec blkts, TV, video, clock radio, refrig, cook fac, micro, elec frypan, toaster, ldry (in unit), blkts, doonas, linen, pillows], dry rm, pool-heated (solar), spa, bbq, c/park (undercover), plygr, cots. D ⚄⚄ $85 - $145, ⚄ $10 - $15, W $420 - $995, AE BC DC MC VI.

★★★★ **(Cottage Section)**, 1 cotg acc up to 6, (3 bedrm), [shwr, bath, tlt, a/c, elec blkts, TV, video, clock radio, refrig, cook fac, micro, elec frypan, toaster, ldry (in unit), blkts, doonas, linen, pillows], c/park (garage). D ⚄⚄ $95 - $120, ⚄ $10 - $15, W $650 - $1,200.

★★★★ **Mystic Valley Cottages**, (HU), 9 Mystic La, 2km SE of PO, ☎ 03 5750 1502, fax 03 5750 1502, 5 units acc up to 4, (1 & 2 bedrm), [shwr, bath (hip), tlt, hairdry, a/c, heat, elec blkts, TV, video, clock radio, refrig, cook fac, micro, toaster, ldry (in unit), blkts, linen, pillows], w/mach, iron, iron brd, pool-heated (solar), spa, bbq, plygr, tennis, cots, non smoking units. D ♦♦ $82 - $105, ♦ $10, W ♦♦ $420 - $880, ♦ $45, BC MC VI.

★★★★ **Panorama Holiday Units**, (HU), 54 Coronation Ave, 1.1km SE of PO, ☎ 03 5755 1315, 4 units acc up to 5, (2 bedrm), [shwr, tlt, a/c, heat, elec blkts, TV, video (available), clock radio, refrig, cook fac, micro, elec frypan, toaster, ldry (in unit), blkts, doonas, linen, pillows], iron, iron brd, bbq, plygr, cots. D $70 - $120, W $420 - $720, BC MC VI.

★★★★ **The Silver Birches**, (Cotg), 16 Gavan St (Great Alpine Rd), 1.3km NW of PO, ☎ 03 5755 1047, fax 03 5755 1047, 10 cotgs acc up to 5, (2 bedrm), [shwr, tlt, a/c, elec blkts, tel, TV, video (avail), clock radio, t/c mkg, refrig, cook fac, micro, toaster, ldry (in unit), blkts, doonas, linen, pillows], w/mach, dryer, iron, iron brd, dry rm, pool, bbq (covered), c/park (carport), cots. D $77 - $145, BC MC VI.

★★★★ **Tudor Village**, (Cotg), 1 Racecourse Rd, 2.4km SE of PO, ☎ 03 5755 2088, fax 03 5755 2128, 6 cotgs acc up to 5, (2 bedrm), [shwr, tlt, a/c, elec blkts, tel, TV, video, clock radio, t/c mkg, refrig, cook fac, micro, toaster, ldry (in unit), blkts, doonas, linen, pillows], w/mach, dryer, iron, iron brd, dry rm, pool, bbq, c/park (carport), cots, non smoking property. D $95 - $150, W $550 - $1,050, AE BC MC VI.

AAA TOURISM *Special Rates* ★★★★ **Willow Dene**, (HF), 25 Toorak Rd, 900m N of PO, ☎ 03 5755 2191, fax 03 5755 2191, 5 flats acc up to 6, (2 bedrm), [shwr, tlt, a/c, heat, elec blkts, TV, video, clock radio, t/c mkg, refrig, cook fac, micro, elec frypan, toaster, blkts, linen, pillows], ldry, w/mach, dryer, dry rm, bbq (covered), c/park (carport), ☎, plygr, cots, non smoking units (2). D ♦♦ $69 - $91, ♦ $12, W $434 - $1,037, ch con, BC MC VI, ♿.

★★★☆ **Aspens Springs**, (Cotg), (Farm), Roberts Creek Rd, 4km NE of PO, ☎ 03 5756 2400, fax 03 5756 2190, 1 cotg acc up to 10, (4 bedrm), [shwr, bath, tlt, a/c-cool, c/fan, elec blkts, TV, video, clock radio, refrig, cook fac, micro, elec frypan, d/wash, toaster, ldry (in unit), blkts, doonas, linen, pillows], iron, iron brd, rec rm, lounge firepl, bbq, c/park (carport), cots, non smoking property. D ♦♦♦♦ $130, ♦ $27.50, W $655 - $840, Min book applies.

★★★☆ **Bright - All Seasons**, (HU), 28 Toorak Rd, 700m N of PO, ☎ 03 5755 2303, fax 03 5755 2303, (2 stry), 2 units acc up to 5, (2 bedrm), [shwr, bath (hip) (1), tlt, hairdry, a/c, heat, elec blkts, TV, video, clock radio, refrig, cook fac, micro, elec frypan, toaster, ldry (in unit) (2), blkts, doonas, linen, pillows], w/mach, dryer, iron, iron brd, bbq, c/park (carport) (1), cots, non smoking property. D ♦♦ $65 - $85, ♦ $5 - $10, W ♦♦ $425 - $565, ♦ $35 - $70, Min book applies, BC MC VI.

★★★☆ **Ellenvale Holiday Units**, (HU), 68 Delany Ave (Great Alpine Rd), 1.4km E of PO, ☎ 03 5755 1582, fax 03 5755 1582, 8 units acc up to 5, (2 bedrm), [shwr, tlt, a/c, elec blkts, TV, video (avail), clock radio, refrig, cook fac, micro, elec frypan, toaster, blkts, linen, pillows], ldry, pool-heated (solar), spa (Indoor), bbq (covered), c/park (carport), plygr, tennis, cots, non smoking units. D ♦♦ $66 - $110, ♦ $11, W ♦♦ $385 - $715, ♦ $33, ch con, Min book all holiday times, BC MC VI.

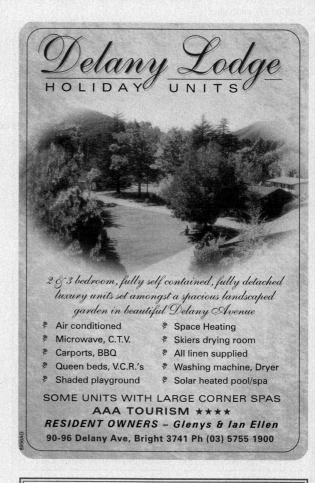

★★★☆ **Forest Lodge Holiday Chalets**, (HF), 34 Coronation Ave, 1km SE of PO, ☎ 03 5755 1583, 9 flats acc up to 6, (1 & 2 bedrm), [shwr, tlt, hairdry, c/fan, cent heat, elec blkts, TV, clock radio, refrig, cook fac, micro, toaster, blkts, linen, pillows], ldry-fee, pool-heated (solar), spa, bbq, plygr, tennis (half court), cots. D ♦♦ $70 - $110, ♦ $10, W $390 - $750, Min book all holiday times, BC MC VI.

★★★☆ **Goldfield Flats**, (HF), 55 Gavan St (Great Alpine Rd), 700m NW of PO, ☎ 03 5750 1295, fax 03 5750 1145, 5 flats acc up to 5, (2 bedrm), [shwr, tlt, a/c-cool (1), a/c (4), fan, heat, elec blkts, TV, video (avail), clock radio, refrig, cook fac, micro, toaster, blkts, linen, pillows], ldry, bbq, plygr, cots, non smoking property. D ♦♦ $60 - $100, ♦ $10 - $15, W $295 - $700, ch con, Min book Christmas Jan and Easter, BC MC VI.

★★★☆ **Grevillea Gardens**, (HF), 4 Gavan St (Great Alpine Rd), 1.6km W of PO, ☎ 03 5755 1375, fax 03 5755 1375, 7 flats acc up to 5, (2 bedrm), [shwr, tlt, a/c-cool, heat, elec blkts, TV, video, clock radio, refrig, cook fac, micro, toaster, ldry (in unit), blkts, linen, pillows], w/mach, iron, iron brd, dry rm, pool, spa (heated), bbq, c/park (carport), plygr, tennis (half court). D ♦♦ $60 - $110, ♦ $11, W ♦♦ $360 - $770, ♦ $77, ch con, Min book all holiday times, AE BC EFT MC VI.

★★★☆ **Highland Valley Holiday Units**, (HU), 14 Gavan St (Great Alpine Rd), 1.3km W of PO, ☎ 03 5755 1631, fax 03 5750 1139, 4 units acc up to 5, (2 bedrm), [shwr, bath (hip), tlt, hairdry, a/c, fan, heat, elec blkts, TV, video, clock radio, t/c mkg, refrig, cook fac, micro, toaster, ldry (in unit), blkts, linen, pillows], w/mach, dryer, iron, iron brd, pool (salt water), bbq, plygr, cots. D ♦♦ $75 - $150, ♦ $12 - $20, W $480 - $900, AE BC DC MC VI.

★★★★★ **(Porcellato Lane Section)**, 1 cotg acc up to 8, [ensuite, shwr, spa bath, tlt, hairdry, a/c, heat, elec blkts, tel, TV, video, clock radio, CD, t/c mkg, refrig, cook fac, micro, d/wash, toaster, ldry (in unit), blkts, linen, pillows], w/mach, dryer, iron, iron brd, lounge firepl, bbq, c/park (carport), cots, non smoking property. D ♦♦ $120 - $265, ♦ $20, W $840 - $1,855, ch con.

★★★☆ **Karnu Cottages**, (HU), Back Porepunkah Rd, 2.6km NW of PO, ☎ 03 5755 1261, fax 03 5755 1819, 10 units acc up to 8, (1, 2 & 3 bedrm), [shwr, tlt, hairdry, fan, heat, elec blkts, TV, video-fee, clock radio, t/c mkg, refrig, cook fac, micro, toaster, blkts, doonas, linen, pillows], ldry-fee, dry rm, rec rm, pool-heated (& toddlers), bbq, c/park (carport), golf, tennis, cots, non smoking property. D $70 - $190, W $420 - $1,140, 1 unit ★★★★☆. BC MC VI.

★★★☆ **Pioneer Garden Cottages**, (Cotg), Cnr Cobden St & Pioneer La, 800m SE of PO, ☎ 03 5755 1233, fax 03 5750 1960, 9 cotgs acc up to 8, (1, 2 & 3 bedrm), [shwr, bath (3), tlt, evap cool (3), fan, c/fan (6), heat, elec blkts, TV, clock radio, refrig, cook fac, micro, toaster, blkts, linen, pillows], ldry, w/mach-fee, dryer-fee, dry rm, bbq, c/park (carport), plygr, cots. D $55 - $134, W $312 - $794, BC MC VI.

★★★ **Adina Lodge**, (HF), 1 Ashwood Ave, 1.9km W of PO, ☎ 03 5755 1531, fax 03 5755 1531, 6 flats acc up to 5, (2 bedrm), [shwr, tlt, fan, heat, elec blkts, TV, video (avail), clock radio, refrig, cook fac ltd, micro, toaster, blkts, linen, pillows], ldry-fee, pool-heated (solar), bbq, plygr, cots. D ♦♦ $55 - $120, ♦ $11 - $16.50, W $330 - $720, ch con, BC MC VI.

★★★ **Carawatha Gardens**, (HF), 54 Delany Ave (Great Alpine Rd), 1.3km E of PO, ☎ 03 5755 1414, fax 03 5755 2200, 5 flats acc up to 5, (2 bedrm), [shwr, tlt, hairdry, fan, heat, elec blkts, TV, clock radio, refrig, cook fac, micro, elec frypan, toaster, blkts, linen, pillows], ldry, w/mach-fee, dryer-fee, dry rm, bbq, plygr, cots. D ♦♦ $65 - $75, ♦ $10, W $380 - $480, Min book all holiday times, BC MC VI.

VICTORIA

★★★ **Cedar Holiday Units Bright**, (HU), 40 Bakers Gully Rd, 400m S of PO, ☎ 03 5755 1554, fax 03 5755 1254, (2 stry gr fl), 6 units acc up to 7, (1 & 2 bedrm), [shwr, tlt, hairdry, fan, c/fan, cent heat, elec blkts, TV, video, clock radio, refrig, cook fac (5), cook fac ltd (1), micro, elec frypan (1), toaster, blkts, doonas, linen, pillows], ldry, bbq, cots, non smoking units. D ♦♦ $60 - $95, ⋒ $10, W ♦♦ $385 - $680, ⋒ $40, ch con, Min book applies, BC MC VI.
Operator Comment: New owners. Spacious refurbished units in a quiet area with creek frontage, only 400 metres from Post Office.

★★★ **Country Park Holiday Lodge**, (Cotg), 6 Mystic La, 2km SE of PO, ☎ 03 5755 1670, 2 cotgs acc up to 6, (2 bedrm), [shwr, bath, tlt, fan, heat, elec blkts, TV, clock radio, refrig, cook fac, micro, elec frypan, toaster, ldry (in unit), blkts, linen, pillows], c/park (carport), cots. D ♦♦♦ $70 - $110, ⋒ $5 - $10, W ♦♦♦ $420 - $620, ⋒ $20 - $35, ch con.

★★★ **Romany Lodge Holiday Flats**, (HF), 51 Delany Ave (Great Alpine Rd), 1.3km E of PO, ☎ 03 5750 1409, 3 flats acc up to 5, (2 bedrm), [shwr, tlt, a/c, elec blkts, TV, refrig, cook fac, micro, elec frypan, toaster, blkts, linen, pillows], ldry, w/mach, dryer, bbq. D ♦♦ $44 - $55, ⋒ $11, W $264 - $330, ch con, Min book all holiday times, BC MC VI.

★★★ **Tandara Flats**, (HF), Cnr Coronation Ave & Hawthorn La, 800m SE of PO, ☎ 03 5755 1093, 4 flats acc up to 5, (2 bedrm), [shwr, bath (hip), tlt, heat, elec blkts, TV, clock radio, refrig, cook fac, toaster, ldry, blkts, linen reqd, pillows], w/mach, bbq, c/park (carport). D $50 - $70, W $320 - $420.

★★★ **View Hill**, (HF), 64 Delany Ave (Great Alpine Rd), 1.4km E of PO, ☎ 03 5755 1235, 9 flats acc up to 4, (1 & 2 bedrm), [shwr, bath (hip) (5), tlt, c/fan (4), heat, elec blkts, TV, refrig, cook fac, toaster, blkts, linen, pillows], ldry, w/mach, dryer, bbq (covered), c/park (carport). D ♦♦ $55 - $77, ⋒ $10, W $330 - $550, BC VI.

B&B's/Guest Houses

★★★★☆ **Eucalypt Mist**, (B&B), 152A Delany Ave (Great Alpine Rd), 1.8km E of Information Centre, ☎ 03 5755 1336, fax 03 5755 1336, (2 stry), 1 rm [ensuite, hairdry, a/c, elec blkts, clock radio, t/c mkg, ldry], lounge (TV, video, cd), lounge firepl, refrig, bbq, non smoking rms. BB ⋒ $75 - $85, ♦♦ $105 - $130, BC MC VI.

★★★★☆ **Oastlers of Bright**, (B&B), 4 Cindy Crt, 1km W of PO, ☎ 03 5750 1357, fax 03 5750 1357, (Multi-stry gr fl), 1 rm [ensuite, hairdry, fan, heat, elec blkts, TV, clock radio, t/c mkg], lounge (TV, video), non smoking property. BB ♦♦ $130, Dinner by arrangement.

★★★★☆ **The Mine Managers House**, (B&B), 30 Coronation Ave, 900m SE of Clock Tower, ☎ 03 5755 1702, fax 03 5755 1702, 2 rms [ensuite, hairdry, c/fan, heat, elec blkts, clock radio, t/c mkg], iron, iron brd, lounge (tv.cd), lounge firepl, non smoking property. BB ♦♦ $125.

★★★☆ **Bright Alps Guest House**, (GH), 83 Delany Ave (Great Alpine Rd), 1.6km E of PO, ☎ 03 5755 1197, fax 03 5755 1197, 13 rms [fan, heat, elec blkts], dry rm, rec rm, lounge (TV, video), BYO, t/c mkg shared, refrig, bbq (covered), ✆, ski hire, non smoking rms. BB ⋒ $33 - $50, ♦♦ $66 - $77, ⋒ $20, ch con, BC MC VI, ⛞⛏.

★★★ **(Holiday Flat Section)**, 1 flat acc up to 5, (2 bedrm), [shwr, tlt, a/c-cool, heat, elec blkts, TV, refrig, cook fac, toaster, blkts, linen, pillows], w/mach, non smoking units. D ♦♦ $55 - $77, ⋒ $10, W $330 - $550.

(Group Accommodation Section), 5 rms acc up to 3, [heat, elec blkts, blkts, linen, pillows], TV rm, cook fac, t/c mkg shared, refrig. D ⋒ $20 - $25, ⋒ $20 - $25.

★★★☆ **Germantown Lodge**, (B&B), No children's facilities, Tawonga Rd, 6km E of PO, ☎ 03 5755 2360, 2 rms [shwr, bath, tlt, hairdry, a/c-cool, elec blkts, TV, video, doonas], lounge firepl. BB ⋒ $55, ♦♦ $85, Other meals by arrangement.

Other Accommodation

Bright Hikers, (Lodge), 4 Ireland St, ☎ 03 5750 1244, fax 03 5750 1246, 6 rms acc up to 8, (Bunk Rooms - 1x2bunk, 1x3bunk, 1x4bunk.), [shwr (2G-2L), tlt (2G-2L), heat], ldry, rec rm, lounge (TV, video), cook fac, bbq, c/park. D ⋒ $17 - $27, ♦♦ $37, AE BC DC JCB MC VI.

Coach House Holiday Flats, (Lodge), 100 Gavan St (Great Alpine Way), 200m E of PO, ☎ 03 5755 1475, fax 03 5755 2230, 19 rms acc up to 6, (1 & 2 bedrm), [shwr, tlt, a/c (9), heat, TV, t/c mkg, refrig, toaster, blkts, linen, pillows], ldry, dry rm, ✗ (BYO), bbq, ✆, ski hire, cots. D ♦♦ $66, ⋒ $14, AE BC DC EFT MC VI.

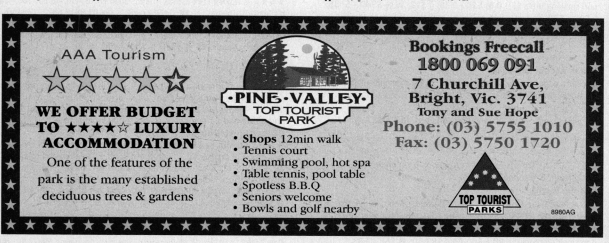

BROADFORD VIC 3658

Pop 2,350. (75km N Melbourne), See map on page 696, ref C4. Agricultural and industrial town on Sunday Creek - off Hume Hwy. Bowls, Golf, Swimming (Pool), Tennis.

Hotels/Motels

★★★ **Sugarloaf Motel**, (M), Cnr High & Short Sts, 500m N of PO, ☎ 03 5784 1069, fax 03 5784 1010, 12 units [shwr, tlt, a/c, elec blkts, tel, TV, clock radio, t/c mkg, refrig, toaster], bbq, cots-fee.
RO ⧫ **$49.50 - $60.50**, ⧫⧫ **$60.50 - $71.50**, ⧫ **$11**, BC MC VI, ⅃&.

BUCHAN VIC 3885

Pop 400. (359km E Melbourne), See map on pages 694/695, ref J6. Historic township, now a prominent farming and timber milling town, situated on the Buchan River, nestled in the foothills of the Victorian Alps. Cave tours conducted daily - Entrance fee. Bush Walking, Canoeing, Fishing, Golf, Horse Riding, Scenic Drives, Shooting, Swimming (Pool, River), Tennis.

Hotels/Motels

★★★ **Buchan Motel**, (M), off Main St, 500m NW of PO, ☎ 03 5155 9201, fax 03 5155 9201, 8 units [shwr, tlt, evap cool, heat, elec blkts, tel, TV, video-fee, clock radio, t/c mkg, refrig], ✕ (by arrangement), bbq, cots. **RO** ⧫ **$50 - $60**, ⧫⧫ **$61 - $71**, ⧫ **$12 - $13.20**, ch con, AE BC MC VI.

★★★ **Sherrington Motel**, (M), Basin Rd, 700m NE of PO, ☎ 03 5155 9262, 1 unit [shwr, tlt, a/c-cool, heat, elec blkts, TV, t/c mkg, refrig, micro, toaster]. **RO** ⧫ **$55**, ⧫⧫ **$70**, ⧫ **$15**, Light breakfast only available. BC MC VI.

Self Catering Accommodation

★★★☆ **Buchan Valley Log Cabins**, (Cotg), Main Rd, 650m N of PO, ☎ 03 5155 9494, fax 03 5155 9494, 4 cotgs acc up to 6, (2 bedrm - log.), [shwr, tlt, c/fan (lounge), heat, elec blkts, TV, clock radio, refrig, cook fac, micro, toaster, ldry (in unit), blkts, linen, pillows], conf fac, bbq, plygr, golf (pitch n putt), tennis (half court), cots (avail), non smoking units (2). **D** ⧫⧫ **$70 - $95**, ⧫ **$18**, **W** ⧫⧫ **$380 - $535**, ⧫ **$95 - $99**, ch con, Light breakfast available. Min book long w/ends and Easter, BC MC VI,

Operator Comment: Adjacent Buchan Caves - See our website www.buchanlogcabins.com.au

Other Accommodation

Buchan Lodge, (Lodge), Children under 14 by arrangement, Saleyard Rd, 500m NW of PO, ☎ 03 5155 9421, fax 03 5155 9421, 3 rms [TV, video (avail), linen reqd], shwr (4G/L), tlt (4G/L), ldry, lounge, cook fac, t/c mkg shared, refrig, bbq, non smoking rms. **BLB** ⧫ **$17**, ⧫ **$17**.

BULLARTO VIC 3461

Pop 100. (106km NW Melbourne), See map on page 696, ref A4. Agricultural & farming township.

Hotels/Motels

★★★ **Pine Cone Motel**, (M), 966 Daylesford - Trentham Rd, 9km E of Daylesford, ☎ 03 5348 5522, 5 units [shwr, tlt, heat, elec blkts, TV, clock radio, t/c mkg, refrig, cook fac (1)], bbq, dinner to unit, cots-fee, non smoking property. **RO** ⧫ **$60.50 - $82.50**, ⧫⧫ **$66 - $88**, ⧫ **$16.50 - $22**, BC EFT MC VI.

Self Catering Accommodation

★★ **Lightwood Farm**, (Cotg), (Farm), 76 Orrs Rd, 3km N of General Store, ☎ 03 5348 5503, 1 cotg acc up to 12, (4 bedrm), [shwr, bath, tlt, hairdry, heat (wood), elec blkts, tel, TV, clock radio, refrig, cook fac, micro, elec frypan, toaster, ldry, linen reqd-fee], w/mach, dryer, iron, iron brd, lounge firepl, bbq, cots. **D** **$90**, **W** **$360 - $400**.

BULN BULN VIC 3821

Pop Part Baw Baw Shire, (112km SE Melbourne), See map on page 696, ref D6. Rural township north of Warragul. Bush Walking, Scenic Drives, Tennis.

B&B's/Guest Houses

Bunurong Bed and Breakfast, (B&B), (Farm), RMB 6335 Stolls Rd, 7.5km NE of Primary School, ☎ 03 5626 6289, 1 rm [shwr, tlt, heat, elec blkts], ldry, lounge, t/c mkg shared, bbq, cots. **BB** ⧫⧫ **$100**, ⧫ **$65**, (Rating under review).

BUNINYONG VIC 3357

Pop 1,800. (124km W Melbourne), See map on pages 694/695, ref D6. Historic mining and agricultural town, located on the Midland Hwy. Victoria's first inland settlement. Bowls, Bush Walking, Golf, Scenic Drives, Tennis.

Self Catering Accommodation

★★★★ **Ballarat Coach House**, (Cotg), 102 Somerville St, 1.5km SE of PO, ☎ 03 5341 3615, fax 03 5341 3615, 1 cotg acc up to 6, (2 bedrm), [shwr, tlt, heat, elec blkts, TV, video, clock radio, CD, refrig, cook fac, micro, d/wash, toaster, blkts, linen, pillows], bbq, plygr, tennis, cots, breakfast ingredients. **D** ⧫⧫ **$132**, ⧫ **$22**, **W** **$550**, ch con.

B&B's/Guest Houses

★★★★☆ **Nandana**, (B&B), No children's facilities, Hogarths Rd, 4km E of PO, off Yendon No 2 Rd, ☎ 03 5341 2223, fax 03 5341 2223, 1 rm (1 suite) [ensuite, spa bath, hairdry, a/c, elec blkts, TV, clock radio, CD, t/c mkg, refrig], lounge firepl, bbq, c/park (carport), non smoking property. **BB** ⧫ **$90 - $110**, ⧫⧫ **$100 - $125**, ⧫ **$20**, Min book long w/ends and Easter, AE BC MC VI.

★★★★ **Mt Buninyong Bed & Breakfast**, (B&B), Previously Beautiful Mt Buninyong Bed & Breakfast Hogarths Rd, 3km E of PO, ☎ 03 5341 3595, 1 rm (1 suite) [ensuite, hairdry, fan, heat, elec blkts, TV, clock radio, t/c mkg, refrig], G, lounge, non smoking property. **BB** ⧫ **$75**, ⧫⧫ **$95**.

BUXTON VIC 3711

Pop 350. (100km NE Melbourne), See map on page 696, ref D4. Small farming township, on the Maroondah Hwy, at the foot of Mt Cathedral. Trout hatchery. Bush Walking, Fishing, Horse Riding, Scenic Drives, Swimming (River), Tennis.

Self Catering Accommodation

★★★★ **Little Dene Garden Cottages**, (Cotg), 69 Williams La, 5km S of PO, ☎ 03 5774 7504, fax 03 5774 7504, 2 cotgs acc up to 4, (2 bedrm), [shwr, tlt, hairdry, fan, heat (wood), elec blkts, TV, clock radio, t/c mkg, refrig, cook fac, micro, toaster, doonas, linen], ldry, dry rm, bbq, plygr, tennis, cots, breakfast ingredients, non smoking property. **BB** ⧫⧫ **$120 - $140**, ⧫ **$30**, Min book long w/ends, BC MC VI.

B&B's/Guest Houses

★★★★☆ **Howen Park Estate**, (B&B), Open Fri to Mon. 40 Batchelor La, off South Cathedral La, ☎ 03 9817 6861, fax 03 9817 6822, (2 stry), 2 rms [ensuite, hairdry, a/c, c/fan, elec blkts, clock radio], ldry, rec rm, lounge (TV, video), lounge firepl, pool indoor heated, t/c mkg shared, refrig, bbq, tennis. **BB** ⧫⧫ **$175**, ⧫ **$50**, AE BC MC VI.

BYADUK VIC 3301

Pop Nominal, (320km W Melbourne), See map on pages 694/695, ref B6. Located on Scotts Creek in an agricultural and grazing district. The area is noted for its extensive caves, extinct volcanos, lava flows and unique stone fences. Golf, Swimming (Pool), Tennis.

B&B's/Guest Houses

★★★☆ **Glenira Bed & Breakfast**, (B&B), (Farm), c1890. No children's facilities, Old Crusher Rd, 3.5km N of PO, off Port Fairy-Hamilton Rd, ☎ 03 5578 7213, fax 03 5578 7222, 3 rms [ensuite (1), hairdry, fan, elec blkts, clock radio], lounge (TV, billiards), lounge firepl, t/c mkg shared, refrig, c/park (undercover), non smoking property. **BB** ⧫ **$80**, ⧫⧫ **$90**, 1 room ★★★★, Other meals by arrangement. BC MC VI.

CAMPERDOWN VIC 3260

Pop 3,150. (193km W Melbourne), See map on pages 694/695, ref C7. Attractive town at the foot of Mt Leura. Boating, Bowls, Croquet, Fishing, Golf, Horse Racing, Sailing, Scenic Drives, Squash, Swimming (Pool, Lake), Tennis, Water Skiing.

Hotels/Motels

★★★☆ **A Cascade Motel**, (M), 311 Manifold St (Princes Hwy), 1km W of PO, ☎ 03 5593 1144, fax 03 5593 2393, 20 units [shwr, spa bath (1), tlt, hairdry (12), a/c-cool, c/fan (2), cent heat, elec blkts, tel, TV, video-fee, clock radio, t/c mkg, refrig, mini bar], ldry, cook fac, refrig, bbq, cots-fee, non smoking units (5). **RO** ⧫ **$55 - $95**, ⧫⧫ **$65 - $110**, ⧫ **$10**, 8 units ★★★, AE BC DC EFT JCB MC MCH MP VI, ⅃&.

★★★☆ **AAA Manifold Motor Inn**, (M), 295 Manifold St (Princes Hwy), 900m W of PO, ☎ 03 5593 2666, fax 03 5593 3042, 15 units [shwr, spa bath (1), tlt, hairdry, c/fan, heat, elec blkts, tel, cable tv, clock radio, t/c mkg, refrig, mini bar, toaster], iron, iron brd, rec rm, bbq, dinner to unit, cots-fee, non smoking units (3). **RO** ⧫ **$75 - $99**, ⧫⧫ **$86 - $115**, ⧫ **$12**, ch con, AE BC DC EFT MC MP VI.

★★★ **Amble-Inn Motel**, (M), 71 Manifold St (Princes Hwy), 700m E of PO, ☎ 03 5593 1646, fax 03 5593 1646, 14 units [shwr, tlt, a/c-cool (13), heat, elec blkts, TV, clock radio, t/c mkg, refrig], ldry, bbq, dinner to unit, plygr, cots. **RO** ♦ $44 - $50, ♦♦ $55 - $62, ◊ $10, ch con, 6 units ★★☆, AE BC DC EFT MC MP VI.

★ **Commercial Hotel**, (LH), 115 Manifold St (Princes Hwy), 200m SE of PO, ☎ 03 5593 1187, fax 03 5593 1637, (2 stry) 14 rms [elec blkts], lounge (TV), ⊠, t/c mkg shared, refrig, ✆. **BB** ♦ $30, ♦♦ $50, ch con, Light breakfast only available. AE BC DC EFT MC VI.

Self Catering Accommodation

★★★★☆ **A Historic Camperdown Mill**, (Apt), 3 Curdie St, 500m E of PO, ☎ 03 5593 2200, fax 03 5593 1637, (Multi-stry gr fl), 3 apts acc up to 6, (2 & 3 bedrm), [shwr, spa bath, tlt, hairdry, fan, heat, elec blkts, TV, video, clock radio, CD, t/c mkg, refrig, cook fac, micro, d/wash, toaster, ldry, blkts, linen, pillows], w/mach, dryer, iron, iron brd, ⊠ (weekends), res liquor license, bbq, breakfast ingredients. **BLB** ♦♦ $90 - $130, ◊ $40 - $45, **W** ♦♦ $500 - $560, ◊ $245 - $280, AE BC MC VI.

★★☆ **Lake Purrumbete Cottages**, (Cotg), (Farm), Purrumbete Estate Rd, 10.2km SE of PO, ☎ 03 55938282a/h, fax 03 5593 8282, 1 cotg acc up to 6, (2 bedrm), [shwr, bath, tlt, c/fan, heat, elec blkts, TV, clock radio, CD, t/c mkg, refrig, cook fac, micro, toaster, blkts, linen], lounge firepl, bbq. **D** ♦♦ $90, ◊ $20, **W** ♦♦ $420, ◊ $60, ch con, BC MC VI.

★★★ **(Uncle Bobs Cottage)**, (Farm), 1 cotg acc up to 4, (1 bedrm), [shwr, bath, tlt, fan, heat, elec blkts, TV, video, clock radio, t/c mkg, refrig, cook fac, micro, toaster, blkts, doonas, linen], bbq. **D** ♦♦ $80, ◊ $10, **W** ♦♦ $420, ◊ $60.

CANN RIVER VIC 3890

Pop 250. (451km E Melbourne), See map on pages 694/695, ref K7. Small town at the junction of Princes & Cann Valley Hwys. Bush Walking, Fishing, Scenic Drives, Tennis.

Hotels/Motels

★★★☆ **Cann River Hop Inn Motor Inn**, (M), Monaro Hwy, ☎ 03 5158 6331, fax 03 5158 6491, 12 units [shwr, tlt, a/c-cool, heat, elec blkts, tel, TV, clock radio, t/c mkg, refrig, toaster], pool-heated (solar), bbq, cots-fee, non smoking property. **RO** ♦ $58 - $70, ♦♦ $68 - $80, ◊ $9, BC EFT MC VI.

★★★☆ **Cann Valley Motel**, (M), Princes Hwy, 200m E of bridge, ☎ 03 5158 6300, fax 03 5158 6472, 10 units [shwr, bath (hip) (1), spa bath (2), tlt, a/c, elec blkts, tel, TV, video, clock radio, t/c mkg, refrig, toaster], ldry, bbq, dinner to unit, cots-fee, non smoking units (4). **RO** ♦ $44 - $75, ♦♦ $50 - $85, ◊ $8 - $11, AE BC DC EFT MC MCH VI, ⚹&.

★★☆ **Motel Cann River**, (M), Princes Hwy, 100m E of bridge, ☎ 03 5158 6255, fax 03 5158 6363, 6 units [shwr, tlt, a/c-cool, fan, heat, elec blkts, TV, t/c mkg, refrig], cots-fee, non smoking units (3). **BLB** ♦ $45 - $50, ♦♦ $48 - $55, ◊ $10, BC MC VI.

CAPE BRIDGEWATER VIC 3306

Pop Nominal, (405km W Melbourne), See map on pages 694/695, ref A7. Popular surf fishing and surfing beach on Bridgewater Bay. Boating, Bush Walking, Fishing, Scenic Drives, Surfing, Swimming.

Self Catering Accommodation

★★★★ **Cockles on the Beach Cape Bridgewater Accomm**, (Cotg), RMB 4432 Bridgewater Rd, ☎ 03 5529 5206, fax 03 5529 5206, 1 cotg acc up to 5, (2 bedrm), [shwr, bath (hip), tlt, heat, elec blkts, tel (local), TV, video, clock radio, CD, t/c mkg, refrig, cook fac, micro, toaster, ldry, blkts, doonas, linen, pillows], w/mach, dryer, iron, iron brd, bbq, cots, non smoking property. **D** ♦♦ $120, ◊ $20, **W** $700 - $1,000, ch con, Min book Christmas Jan long w/ends and Easter.

★★★★ **Discovery Bay Cottage**, (Cotg), Kennedys Rd, ☎ 03 5526 5201, 1 cotg acc up to 6, (2 bedrm), [shwr, spa bath, tlt, hairdry, heat (wood), tel (local), TV, video, clock radio, CD, refrig, cook fac, micro, elec frypan, toaster, ldry, blkts, doonas, linen, pillows], w/mach, iron, iron brd, bbq, c/park (carport), non smoking property. **D** ♦♦ $130, ◊ $20, Min book applies.

B&B's/Guest Houses

★★★★ **Berry's by the Bay**, (B&B), Closed July, RMB 4382 Flinders St, ☎ 03 5526 7122, 2 rms [ensuite, hairdry, heat, elec blkts, TV (1), clock radio, micro], lounge (TV, video, stereo), t/c mkg shared, bbq, non smoking property. **BLB** ♦ $90, ♦♦ $100 - $110, ◊ $25, Min book Christmas Jan long w/ends and Easter, BC MC VI,
Operator Comment: Check our website for photos: www.greatoceanroad.nu/berrysbythebay

★★★★ **Cape Bridgewater Sea View Lodge**, (GH), RMB 4370 Bridgewater Rd, ☎ 03 5526 7276, (2 stry), 5 rms [ensuite, bath (2), spa bath (1), heat, elec blkts, clock radio], ldry, lounge (TV, video), cook fac, t/c mkg shared, refrig, cots. **BB** ♦ $70 - $100, ♦♦ $95 - $125, ◊ $25, Min book Christmas Jan and Easter, AE BC DC MC VI.

Other Accommodation

Cape Bridgewater Holiday Camp, (Lodge), Cape Bridgewater Rd, ☎ 03 5526 7267, 6 rms acc up to 6, [blkts reqd, linen reqd], ldry, rec rm, conf fac, cook fac, refrig, bbq, plygr. **D** ♦ $18.70, ◊ $18.70, ch con.
(Cabin Section), 4 cabins acc up to 10, [shwr, tlt, a/c (1), heat, clock radio, refrig, cook fac, blkts, linen, pillows]. **D** $66.
(Church Building Section), 1 bunkhouse acc up to 16, [blkts reqd, linen reqd], cook fac, refrig. **D** ♦ $18.70, ◊ $18.70, Mimimum booking - 16 people.

National Trust of Australia (Victoria), (Lodge), St Peters' Church - c1884. Bridgewater Lakes Rd, ☎ 03 5526 7271, fax 03 5526 7271, 4 rms acc up to 6, [shwr, tlt, fan, heat, tel (local), refrig, cook fac, micro, toaster, ldry, linen reqd], w/mach, dryer, iron, iron brd, lounge firepl, bbq. **D** ♦♦♦♦ $75 - $85, ◊ $10.

CAPE OTWAY VIC 3233

Pop Nominal, (229km SW Melbourne), See map on pages 694/695, ref C8. Small farming settlement. Bush Walking, Scenic Drives.

Self Catering Accommodation

★★★★☆ **Cape Otway Cottages**, (Cotg), 615 Hordern Vale Rd, Hordern Vale 3238, 7km S of Great Ocean Rd, ☎ 03 5237 9256, fax 03 5237 9263, 4 cotgs acc up to 8, (1 & 2 bedrm), [shwr, bath (1), spa bath (3), tlt, hairdry, evap cool, c/fan, heat (wood), elec blkts, TV, video, clock radio, CD, refrig, cook fac, ldry (wmach, dryer, iron), doonas, linen, pillows], bbq, Pets allowed. **D** ♦♦ $140 - $190, ◊ $30, **W** ♦♦ $785 - $1,175, ◊ $150, 3 cottages of a 4.5 star rating & 1 cottage of a 4 star rating, Min book applies, AE BC DC EFT MC VI.

★★★★ **Cape Otway Log Cabins**, 760 Lighthouse Rd, 27km S of Apollo Bay, ☎ 03 5237 9290, fax 03 5237 9290, 3 cabins (1 & 2 bedrm), [evap cool, c/fan, heat (gas), elec blkts, TV, video, clock radio, t/c mkg, refrig, cook fac, micro, toaster, blkts, doonas, linen, pillows], ldry, lounge firepl, ✗, c/park (undercover), non smoking property, Pets on application. **D** ♦♦ $145 - $180, ◊ $20 - $25, **W** ♦♦ $950 - $1,210, ◊ $175 - $210, ch con, Min book Christmas Jan long w/ends and Easter, BC MC VI.

★★☆ **Cape Otway Light Station**, (Cotg), Otway Lighthouse Rd, 34km SW of Apollo Bay, ☎ 03 5237 9240, fax 03 5237 9245, 4 cotgs acc up to 12, (1 & 4 bedrm), [shwr, tlt, heat, elec blkts, TV, video, t/c mkg, refrig, cook fac, micro, toaster, blkts, doonas, linen, pillows], ldry, w/mach, lounge firepl, bbq, cots-fee. **D** ♦♦ $115 - $180, ◊ $25, **W** ♦♦ $745 - $1,185, ◊ $75, 2 cottages ★★★, Min book applies, AE BC DC EFT MC VI.

Other Accommodation

Cape Otway Bunkhouses, (Lodge), 150 Bracks Access, ☎ 03 5237 9272, fax 03 5237 9246, 2 rms acc up to 16, (Bunk Rooms), [fan, refrig, cook fac, toaster, blkts, linen reqd, pillows], shwr (2G-2L), tlt (2G-2L), lounge (TV, video), lounge firepl, ✗, t/c mkg shared, bbq-fee, non smoking property. **D** ♦ $15 - $25.

CAPE PATERSON VIC 3995

Pop 600. Part of Wonthaggi, (140km SE Melbourne), See map on page 696, ref D7. Small seaside holiday resort. Boat Ramp, Bush Walking, Fishing (Surf), Scenic Drives, Surfing, Swimming (Rock Pool).

Self Catering Accommodation

★★★ **Ibis Inn**, (Cotg), (Farm), Cape Paterson Rd, ☎ 03 5672 2555, fax 03 5672 2555, (2 stry gr fl), 2 cotgs acc up to 5, (Studio & 1 bedrm), [shwr, tlt, fan, heat, elec blkts, TV, radio, CD, t/c mkg, refrig, cook fac ltd, micro, toaster, blkts, linen, pillows], ldry, w/mach, iron, iron brd, bbq, cots, breakfast ingredients, non smoking property. **BB** ♦♦ **$100**, ◊ **$20**, **W $280 - $500**, ch con, Min book Christmas Jan long w/ends and Easter, AE BC MC VI.

★★ **Surfside Flats (Cape Paterson)**, (HF), 6 Cape Paterson Rd, 200m N of beach, ☎ 03 5674 4521, 4 flats acc up to 5, (1 bedrm), [shwr, tlt, heat, TV, refrig, cook fac, toaster, blkts, linen reqd-fee, pillows], ldry, w/mach, bbq. **D** ♦♦ **$55**, ◊ **$11**, **W $264 - $550**, ch con, BC MC VI.

CAPE SCHANCK VIC 3939

Pop Nominal, (92km S Melbourne), See map on page 697, ref B8. Scenic seaside region, 15km south of Rosebud. Golf, Horse Riding, Scenic Drives, Tennis.

Hotels/Motels

★★★★ **The Shearwater Cape Schanck Resort**, (M), Boneo Rd, 12km S of Rosebud PO, ☎ 03 5950 8000, fax 03 5950 8111, (2 stry), 48 units [shwr, bath, tlt, a/c, tel, TV, clock radio, t/c mkg, refrig, toaster], ldry, conf fac, ⊠, pool, sauna, spa, kiosk, ✆, golf-fee, tennis. **BB** ♦♦ **$200**, ♦♦♦♦ **$435**, ch con, AE BC DC MC VI.

★★★★☆ **(Terrace Suites Section)**, 4 apts acc up to 4, (2 bedrm), [shwr, bath, tlt, a/c, tel, TV, video, clock radio, refrig, cook fac, micro, blkts, linen, pillows], ldry. **BB $400 - $440**.

B&B's/Guest Houses

★★★★☆ **Cape Schanck Lodge B & B**, (B&B), No children's facilities, 134 Cape Schanck Rd, ☎ 03 5988 6395, fax 03 5988 6395, 2 rms [ensuite, hairdry, fan, heat, elec blkts, clock radio, t/c mkg, refrig], lounge (TV, video, cd player), pool, non smoking property. **BB $120 - $150**, BC MC VI.

★★★★ **The Grange at Cape Schanck Conference Centre**, (GH), 41 Trent Jones Dve, in the southern section of the golf course, ☎ 03 5988 2333, fax 03 5988 6100, (Multi-stry gr fl), 9 rms [shwr, spa bath (1), tlt, a/c, tel, TV, video (avail), clock radio, t/c mkg], iron, iron brd, rec rm, lounge, conf fac, ✗, bbq, ✆, golf, non smoking units. **BB** ♦ **$220 - $299**, ♦♦ **$220 - $299**, BC VI.

★★★★☆ **(Condominium Section)**, 12 apts acc up to 6, [shwr, spa bath (4), tlt, a/c, tel, TV, video, clock radio, t/c mkg, refrig, cook fac, d/wash], iron, iron brd, lounge (tv, video), non smoking units. **D $280 - $465**.

★★ **Cape Schanck Lighthouse**, (B&B), Previously Australia Pacific Lighthouses Cape Schanck Rd, 16kms from Rosebud. ☎ 03 9568 6411, or fax 03 5988 6251, 2 rms [heat, elec blkts, toaster], ldry, w/mach-fee, dryer-fee, iron, lounge (tv), t/c mkg shared, bbq. **BB** ♦♦ **$90**, AE BC DC MC VI.

Other Accommodation

Ace Hi Riding Ranch, (Lodge), Boneo Rd, 10km S of Rosebud PO, ☎ 03 5988 6262, fax 03 5988 6698, 13 rms acc up to 8, [shwr, tlt, c/fan, heat, TV, refrig, cook fac, micro, toaster, linen reqd-fee], ldry, ✗, BYO, bbq-fee, kiosk, ✆, plygr. **D** ♦♦ **$60**, ◊ **$20**, ch con, BC EFT MC VI.

(Group Accommodation Section), Limited facilities. 9 rms acc up to 8, [blkts reqd, linen reqd, pillows reqd], shwr (2G-2L), tlt (1G-1L), cook fac, refrig. **D** ♦ **$16.50**, ◊ **$16.50**, Catering by arrangement - minimum 40 people. Self catering - minimum 12 people.

CARBOOR VIC 3678

Pop Nominal, (254km NE Melbourne), See map on pages 694/695, ref G5. A small town in the farming and wine producing district.
★★☆ **Dawn View Cottage**, (Cotg), Carboor-Everton Rd, 23km SE of Milawa, ☎ 03 5729 5520, fax 03 5729 5559, 1 cotg acc up to 6, (3 bedrm), [shwr, bath, tlt, hairdry, a/c-cool, fan, heat, elec blkts, TV, clock radio, refrig, cook fac, micro, toaster, ldry (in unit), blkts, linen, pillows], w/mach, dryer, iron, iron brd, bbq, breakfast ingredients. **BLB** ♦♦ **$99**, ◊ **$11**.

CARDIGAN VIC 3352

Pop 200. Part of Ballarat, (128km W Melbourne), See map on pages 694/695, ref D6. Farming, pastoral & dairying district.

FLAG
FLAG CHOICE HOTELS

★★★☆ **Cardigan Lodge Motel**, (M), Avenue of Honour, 14.8km W of Ballarat PO, ☎ 03 5344 8302, fax 03 5344 8307, 27 units (1 suite) [shwr, tlt, hairdry (17), a/c-cool, heat, elec blkts, tel, TV, video (avail), clock radio, t/c mkg, refrig, mini bar (17), micro (2), toaster], ldry, iron, iron brd, rec rm, conf fac, ⊠, pool-heated, bbq, rm serv, plygr, cots-fee, non smoking units (3). **RO** ♦ **$78 - $88**, ♦♦ **$88 - $98**, ◊ **$11**, **Suite D $130 - $145**, ch con, AE BC DC EFT MC VI.

CARDINIA VIC 3978

Pop Nominal, (65km SE Melbourne), See map on page 696, ref C6. Township located in a rich agricultural and dairying distric.

B&B's/Guest Houses

★★★☆ **Cardinia Country Lodge**, (GH), Previously Jasons Country House 75 Bould Rd, off Cardinia Rd, ☎ 03 5998 8111, (Multi-stry gr fl), 7 rms [ensuite (3), heat, elec blkts, clock radio], lounge (TV), conf fac, ⊠, t/c mkg shared, bbq, non smoking property. **BB** ♦ **$80**, ♦♦ **$120**, ◊ **$50**, 3 rooms ★★★★, Dinner by arrangement, AE BC DC EFT MC VI.

CARISBROOK VIC 3464

Pop 600. (159km NW Melbourne), See map on pages 694/695, ref D5. Farming community located 8km east of Maryborough, on the Pyrenees Hwy. Bowls, Bush Walking, Fishing, Scenic Drives.

Hotels/Motels

★★★ **Carisbrook Country Retreat**, (M), Pyrenees Hwy, 8km E of Maryborough PO, ☎ 03 5464 2334, 4 units [shwr, tlt, a/c-cool, heat, elec blkts, TV, clock radio, t/c mkg, refrig, toaster], ldry, dinner to unit. **RO** ♦ **$47 - $57**, ♦♦ **$57 - $67**, ◊ **$10**, ch con, AE BC MC VI.

Self Catering Accommodation

★★★☆ **Lochinver**, (Cotg), (Farm), Maldon Rd, 3km NE of PO, ☎ 03 5464 2356, fax 03 5464 1255, 1 cotg acc up to 2, (1 bedrm), [shwr, tlt, a/c, heat (wood), TV, video (avail), clock radio, refrig, cook fac, toaster, blkts, linen, pillows], bbq, non smoking property. **D $95, W $550**, Meals available by arrangement. Min book applies.

★★★☆ **(Cottage)**, 1 cotg acc up to 4, (3 bedrm), [shwr, tlt, elec blkts, TV, video, clock radio, refrig, cook fac, micro, toaster, ldry, blkts, linen, pillows], w/mach, iron, iron brd, lounge firepl, bbq, non smoking property. **D $130, W $700**, Other meals by arrangement.

CARLSRUHE VIC 3444

Pop Part of Kyneton, (80km NW Melbourne), See map on page 696, ref B4. Situated on the Campaspe River, in an agricultural and pastoral district. Fishing (River).

Self Catering Accommodation

★★★☆ **West Rock Farm**, (Cotg), 124 Three Chain Rd, 1km E of Calder Hwy, ☎ 03 5422 2636, fax 03 5422 3504, 1 cotg acc up to 6, (3 bedrm), [shwr, tlt, a/c, heat, elec blkts, tel, TV, video, CD, refrig, cook fac, micro, elec frypan, toaster, ldry, blkts, doonas, linen, pillows], w/mach, dryer, iron, iron brd, lounge firepl, bbq, c/park (carport), breakfast ingredients. **BB** ♦♦ **$110 - $165**, BC MC VI.

★★★★ **(Farmhouse Section)**, 1 cotg acc up to 10, (5 bedrm), [shwr, bath, tlt, a/c, heat, elec blkts, tel, TV, video, clock radio, CD, refrig, cook fac, micro, d/wash, toaster, ldry, blkts, linen, pillows], w/mach, dryer, iron, iron brd, lounge firepl, pool, c/park (carport), breakfast ingredients. **BB** ♦♦ **$110 - $165**, Min book applies.

CASTERTON VIC 3311

Pop 1,750. (352km W Melbourne), See map on pages 694/695, ref A6. Centre of large pastoral district. Bowls, Bush Walking, Gem Fossicking, Golf, Horse Racing, Scenic Drives, Shooting, Swimming (Pool), Tennis.

Hotels/Motels

★★★☆ **Albion**, (LMH), Henty St, ☎ 03 5581 1092, fax 03 5581 2287, 12 units [shwr, spa bath (2), tlt, a/c, tel, TV, clock radio, t/c mkg], ⊠. **RO** ♦ **$53 - $73**, ♦♦ **$62 - $82**, ◊ **$9**, AE BC EFT MC VI, ⌂.

★★☆ **Casterton Motel**, (M), 29 Mt Gambier Rd (Glenelg Hwy), 1.9km W of PO, ☎ 03 5581 1317, fax 03 5568 1283, 7 units [shwr, tlt, fan, heat, elec blkts, tel (5), TV, movie, clock radio, t/c mkg, refrig, cook fac (1)], pool, bbq. **RO** ♦ **$45**, ♦♦ **$55**, ◊ **$12**, ch con, AE BC DC EFT MC VI.

Self Catering Accommodation

★★★☆ **The Bluff Holiday Farm**, (Cotg), Kilmoc Rd, 22km SW of PO, off Casterton - Dartmoor Rd, ☎ 03 5581 1784, fax 03 5581 2508, 1 cotg acc up to 6, (2 bedrm), [shwr, bath, tlt, a/c-cool, heat, elec blkts, TV, video, refrig, cook fac, micro, toaster, blkts, linen, pillows], bbq, c/park (garage), plygr. **D** ♦♦♦ **$80**, ◊ **$15 - $20**, **W $380**, Min book long w/ends and Easter.

★★ **Satimer Merino Stud**, (Cotg), (Farm), Satimer Rd, 23km NE of PO, ☎ 03 5579 8558, 1 cotg acc up to 12, (5 bedrm), [shwr, bath, tlt, heat, TV, clock radio, refrig, cook fac, linen reqd] ldry, c/park (carport), tennis, cots. **D $60 - $100, W $400.**

B&B's/Guest Houses

★★★☆ **Glen-Aron House**, (B&B), 77 Jackson St, 1km W of PO, ☎ 03 5581 2350, 2 rms [heat, elec blkts, clock radio], lounge (TV), lounge firepl, t/c mkg shared. **BB** ♦ **$50**, ♦♦ **$80**, AE.

Pop 6,700. (119km NW Melbourne), See map on page 696, ref A3. Once a famous gold mining town in the 1850's, now a properous industrial rural city and rail junction. Art & Craft Show (Queens Birthday Weekend in June). Art Gallery, Boating, Bowls, Bush Walking, Croquet, Fishing, Gold Prospecting, Golf, Horse Riding, Sailing, Scenic Drives, Shooting, Swimming (Pool, Lake, River), Tennis, Water Skiing.

Hotels/Motels

★★★★ **Castlemaine Colonial Motel**, (M), 252 Barker St (Midland Hwy), 200m N of PO, ☎ 03 5472 4000, fax 03 5470 5347, 15 units [shwr, bath (hip) (2), spa bath (2), tlt, hairdry, a/c, elec blkts, tel, TV, video-fee, t/c mkg, refrig], cots-fee, non smoking units (8). **RO** ♦ **$79 - $130**, ♦♦ **$89 - $130**, ◊ **$14**, AE BC DC MC VI.

★★★★ **(Class on Colonial Section)**, 5 units [shwr, spa bath, tlt, hairdry, a/c, fan, c/fan (3), heat, elec blkts, TV, video, clock radio, t/c mkg, refrig, micro], iron, iron brd, rm serv, non smoking property. **RO $170**, Min book long w/ends and Easter.

★★★☆ **Castle Motel**, (M), 1 Duke St (Melbourne Rd), 400m E of PO, ☎ 03 5472 2433, fax 03 5472 4011, 21 units [shwr, tlt, hairdry, a/c, elec blkts, tel, cable tv, clock radio, t/c mkg, refrig], iron, conf fac, pool, spa, dinner to unit, plygr, cots-fee, non smoking units (8). **RO** ♦ **$77 - $90**, ♦♦ **$88 - $118**, ◊ **$10**, AE BC DC MC VI.

★★☆ **Campbell St Motor Lodge**, (M), Classified by National Trust, 33 Campbell St, 300m NE of PO, ☎ 03 5472 3477, fax 03 5472 4597, (2 stry gr fl), 14 units (1 suite) [shwr, bath (3), tlt, a/c (7), heat, elec blkts, tel, TV, t/c mkg, refrig, cook fac (1)], ldry-fee, ✆, cots-fee. **RO** ♦ **$58 - $65**, ♦♦ **$76 - $85**, ◊ **$10**, Suite **D $120**, AE BC DC MC VI.

Self Catering Accommodation

★★★ **Inverness Park Bed & Breakfast**, (Cotg), 1725 Pyrenees Hwy (Maryborough Rd), ☎ 03 5470 5078, 1 cotg acc up to 2, (1 bedrm), [shwr, bath, tlt, heat, TV, clock radio, refrig, cook fac, micro, blkts, linen, pillows], breakfast ingredients. **BB** ♦ **$55**, ♦♦ **$79**.

★★★ **Sage Cottage Fryerstown**, (Cotg), 25 Castlemaine St, Fryerstown 3451, 10 mins from Castlemaine, ☎ 03 5473 4322, 1 cotg acc up to 4, (2 bedrm), [shwr, bath (hip), tlt, hairdry, evap cool, fan, heat, elec blkts, TV, clock radio, refrig, cook fac ltd, micro, toaster, blkts, doonas, linen, pillows], ldry, w/mach, bbq, cots, breakfast ingredients, non smoking property. **BB** ♦♦ **$90 - $115**, ◊ **$20**, ch con.

★★★ **The Hermitage Castlemaine**, (HU), No children's facilities, Blakeley Rd, ☎ 03 5472 2008, fax 03 5470 5638, (2 stry), 1 unit acc up to 4, (2 bedrm), [shwr, tlt, a/c-cool, fan, heat, TV, video, refrig, cook fac ltd, micro, elec frypan, toaster, blkts, linen, pillows], breakfast ingredients, non smoking property. **D** ♦♦ **$90**, ◊ **$25**.

B&B's/Guest Houses

★★★★ **Coach and Rose**, (B&B), No children's facilities, 68 Mostyn St, 400m SE of PO, ☎ 03 5472 4850, fax 03 5472 4850, 4 rms [shwr, tlt, c/fan, heat, elec blkts, clock radio], rec rm, lounge (TV, stereo), lounge firepl, t/c mkg shared, refrig, bbq. **BB** ♦ **$85 - $100**, ♦♦ **$105 - $120**, AE BC MC VI.

★★★★ **The Yellow House B & B/Gallery**, (B&B), 95 Lyttleton St, ☎ 03 5472 3368, fax 03 5472 3368, (2 stry gr fl), 3 rms [ensuite, cent heat, elec blkts, clock radio], lounge (TV), bbq, non smoking property. **BLB** ♦♦ **$100 - $140**, Min book long w/ends and Easter, BC MC VI.

★★★★ **Wisteria House**, (B&B), c1874. 256 Barker St, ☎ 03 5470 6604, fax 03 5472 1024, 3 rms [shwr, bath (2), tlt, hairdry, fan, cent heat, elec blkts, clock radio, micro (1), doonas], lounge (TV, cd), lounge firepl, t/c mkg shared, refrig, non smoking property. **BB** ♦ **$95 - $105**, ♦♦ **$135 - $155**, BC MC VI.

★★★☆ **Ambri Bed & Breakfast**, (B&B), No children's facilities, 6 Brown St, 1km SW of PO, ☎ 03 5472 4025, 2 rms [shwr, bath, tlt, cent heat, elec blkts, clock radio, t/c mkg, refrig], rec rm, lounge (TV, video), pool, c/park (carport), non smoking property. **BB** ♦ **$50**, ♦♦ **$85**.

★★★☆ **Clevedon Manor**, (B&B), 260 Barker St, ☎ 03 5472 5212, fax 03 5472 5212, 5 rms [ensuite (2), shwr (3), spa bath (2), tlt (5), hairdry, cent heat, elec blkts, clock radio, t/c mkg, refrig (communal)], lounge (TV), pool, bbq, non smoking property. **BB** ♦ **$77**, ♦♦ **$100 - $120**, ch con, pen con, BC MC VI.

★★★☆ **Green Gables of Castlemaine**, (B&B), 94 Hargraves St, 350m NE of PO, ☎ 03 5472 2482, 4 rms [shwr (3), bath (2), tlt (3), heat, elec blkts], rec rm, lounge (TV, CD player), lounge firepl, t/c mkg shared, cots (avail). **BB** ♦ **$55 - $65**, ♦♦ **$95 - $105**, BC MC VI.

★★★☆ **Midland Private Hotel**, (PH), Classified by National Trust, No children's facilities, 2 Templeton St, ☎ 03 5472 1085, (2 stry), 20 rms [heat (10), elec blkts], lounge (TV), lounge firepl, refrig, ✆, non smoking property. **BB** ♦ **$60 - $70**, ♦♦ **$88 - $110**, ◊ **$60 - $70**, Bookings essential. AE BC DC MC VI.

★★★☆ **Montrose Bed & Breakfast**, (B&B), 11 Merrifield St, 2km N of PO, ☎ 03 5472 1197, 1 rm (1 suite) [ensuite, hairdry, a/c, heat, elec blkts, t/c mkg], lounge (TV, stereo), lounge firepl, refrig, bbq, non smoking rms. **BB** ♦♦ **$80**, ch con.

Other Accommodation

★★ **Old Castlemaine Gaol**, (Lodge), Accommodation in gaol cells. Bowden St, ☎ 03 5470 5311, fax 03 5470 5097, (2 stry gr fl), 60 rms (Bunk Rooms - 55x1bunk. - 2x1d1s. - 1x1d1bunch.), [fan, doonas], rec rm, conf fac, bar, t/c mkg shared, bbq, ✆, non smoking property. **BLB** ♦ **$55**, **DBB** ♦ **$77**, AE BC DC EFT MC VI.

Yarramalong Waler Stud, (Bunk), 295 Rilens Rds, Muckleford 3451, 10km W of PO, ☎ 03 5470 5802, 3 bunkhouses acc up to 8, (Bunk Rooms), [ensuite (1), a/c-cool (1), blkts reqd, linen reqd], tank water, rec rm, lounge (TV, video), lounge firepl, cook fac, refrig, bbq. **D $60**, ch con.

Pop 120. (315km W Melbourne), See map on pages 694/695, ref B6. Situated on the Wannon River. Bush Walking, Fishing, Tennis.

Self Catering Accommodation

★★★★ **South Mokanger Farm Cottages**, (Cotg), (Farm), Mountain Duck & Stoneycroft, Mokanger Rd, 8.3km E of PO, off Dunkeld-Cavendish Rd, ☎ 03 5574 2398, fax 03 5574 2307, 2 cotgs acc up to 8, (2 & 4 bedrm), [shwr, bath (1), tlt, hairdry, fan (1), c/fan (1), heat, elec blkts, TV, video, clock radio, CD, refrig, cook fac, micro, elec frypan, toaster, ldry, blkts, linen, pillows], w/mach, dryer (1), lounge firepl, pool, bbq, cots. **D** ♦♦ **$105 - $120**, ◊ **$15**, **W** ♦♦ **$630 - $720**, ◊ **$75**, Breakfast available, BC MC VI.

(Shearers Quarters), 4 bunkhouses acc up to 2, [heat, blkts, linen, pillows]. **D** ♦ **$15**, ◊ **$15**, Let only with Stoneycroft cottage.

CHARLTON VIC 3525

Pop 1,100. (254km NW Melbourne), See map on pages 694/695, ref D4. Situated on banks of the Avoca River.

★★★☆ **Foundry Palms Motel**, (M), 86 High St (Calder Hwy), 100m E of PO, ☎ 03 5491 1911, fax 03 5491 1911, 12 units [shwr, tlt, a/c, elec blkts, tel, TV, clock radio, t/c mkg, refrig, toaster], spa (heated), bbq, dinner to unit, non smoking units (4). **RO** ♦ **$49 - $54**, ♦♦ **$55 - $65**, ◊ **$10**, AE BC DC MC MCH MP VI.

★★☆ **Charlton Motel**, (M), Calder Hwy, 600m E of PO, ☎ 03 5491 1600, fax 03 5491 1650, 25 units [shwr, spa bath (4), tlt, a/c, heat, elec blkts, tel, TV, clock radio, t/c mkg, refrig, mini bar (17)], conf fac, ⊠, pool, sauna, bbq, plygr, gym, tennis (half court), cots-fee. **RO** ♦ **$55 - $70**, ♦♦ **$60 - $75**, ◊ **$11**, ch con, AE BC DC EFT MC VI.

★★★ **Vale of Avoca**, (B&B), c1879, Cnr Calder & Borung Hwys, ☎ 03 5491 1999, fax 03 5491 2345, (2 stry), 3 rms [shwr, tlt, a/c (2), fan (1), heat, elec blkts, TV, clock radio, t/c mkg, refrig], rec rm, lounge (TV, video, cd), ✕ (Sat), BYO, non smoking property. **BB** ♦ **$63 - $77**, ♦♦ **$72 - $88**, ch con, 2 rooms yet to be rated, Meals by arrangement, BC EFT MC VI.

CHILTERN VIC 3683

Pop 1,100. (274km NE Melbourne), See map on pages 694/695, ref H4. Historic town in an agricultural and pastoral district.

★★★☆ **Chiltern Colonial Motor Inn**, (M), 1 Main St, 800m E of PO, ☎ 03 5726 1788, fax 03 5726 1131, 14 units [shwr, tlt, hairdry, a/c, elec blkts, tel, TV, clock radio, t/c mkg, refrig, toaster], ldry, ⊠, bbq, rm serv, dinner to unit, meals avail (dinner to unit), cots-fee, non smoking units (5). **RO** ♦ **$61 - $72**, ♦♦ **$72 - $83**, ◊ **$11**, AE BC DC EFT MC MP VI.

★★★☆ **The Mulberry Tree Restaurant**, (HU), 28 Conness St, ☎ 03 5726 1277, 1 unit acc up to 2, (1 bedrm), [shwr, tlt, fan, fire pl, heat, elec blkts, tel (local), TV, clock radio, t/c mkg, refrig, cook fac, micro, toaster, blkts, linen, pillows], non smoking property. **BB** ♦ **$95**, ♦♦ **$125**, Dinner by arrangement.

Chiltern Colonial Motor Inn

Wineries, Antiques, Box Ironbark National Park, Historic Towns, National Trust Buildings.

Historic Chiltern Fine Food and Wine

Quality Accommodation

Phone: (03) 5726 1788 / 5726 1706 Fax: (03) 5726 1131

CHURCHILL VIC 3842

Pop 4,900. (158km SE Melbourne), See map on page 696, ref E7. Satellite city of the Latrobe Valley.

Hotels/Motels

★★ **Churchill Hotel Motel**, (LMH), Cnr Monash Way & Balfour Pl, 200m S of PO, ☎ 03 5122 1808, or 03 5122 1919, fax 03 5122 1302, 5 units [shwr, tlt, heat, elec blkts, tel, TV, radio, t/c mkg, refrig, cook fac (1), toaster], ldry, ⊠. **RO** ♦ **$44**, ♦♦ **$55**, ◊ **$44**, ch con, Light breakfast only available. AE BC DC MC VI.

CLARENDON VIC 3352

Pop Nominal, (114km W Melbourne), See map on page 696, ref A5.

★★★★ **Swallowvale Properties**, (Cotg), Blue Bridge Rd, ☎ 03 5341 7777, 1 cotg acc up to 6, (3 bedrm), [ensuite, shwr, bath, tlt, c/fan, heat, tel (local), TV, clock radio, CD, t/c mkg, refrig, cook fac, toaster, ldry, blkts, doonas, linen, pillows], iron, iron brd, spa (heated), bbq, c/park (carport), golf (driving range), tennis. **D** ♦♦ **$120**, ♦♦♦♦ **$240**, **W** ♦♦ **$640**, ♦♦♦♦ **$1,270**, BC MC VI.

CLUNES VIC 3370

Pop 850. (150km NW Melbourne), See map on pages 694/695, ref D6. One of the first towns where gold was discovered in Victoria.

★★☆ **Clunes Motel**, (M), 46 Talbot Rd, 800m W of PO, ☎ 03 5345 3092, fax 03 53453943, 6 units [shwr, tlt, hairdry (3), a/c-cool (6), fan, heat, elec blkts, TV, t/c mkg, refrig, toaster], bbq, meals to unit, non smoking rms (2). **RO** ♦ **$45**, ♦♦ **$55**, ◊ **$10**, AE BC MC VI.

★★★★☆ **Keebles of Clunes**, (B&B), No facilities for children under 12. 114 Bailey St, 200m E of PO, ☎ 03 5345 3220, fax 03 5345 3200, (2 stry), 6 rms [shwr, spa bath (1), tlt, hairdry, c/fan (4), heat, elec blkts], rec rm, lounge, lounge firepl, ⊠, t/c mkg shared, non smoking property. **BB** ♦ **$99 - $132**, ♦♦ **$154 - $209**, **DBB** ♦ **$137.50 - $170.50**, ♦♦ **$231 - $286**, BC MC VI.

COBDEN VIC 3266

Pop 1,400. (208km SW Melbourne), See map on pages 694/695, ref C7. Centre of rich dairy country, originally known as Lovely Banks.

★★ **Parlours Cobden Motel Food & Auto Care**, (M), 1236 Camperdown Rd, 1km NE of PO, ☎ 03 5595 1140, fax 03 5595 1146, 8 units [shwr, bath (hip) (1), tlt, heat, elec blkts, TV, clock radio, t/c mkg, refrig, toaster], ✕, BYO, ☎, cots-fee. **RO** ♦ **$49.50**, ♦♦ **$60**, ◊ **$11**, BC EFT MC MCH VI.

★★★★ **Grand Central B&B Cobden**, (B&B), 30 Victoria St, 300m SW of PO, ☎ 03 5595 1208, fax 03 5595 1546, 7 rms [shwr, spa bath (2), tlt, hairdry, a/c (4), c/fan (3), heat (3), TV, clock radio, t/c mkg, refrig, mini bar, toaster], ldry, bbq, cots, non smoking property. **BLB** ♦♦ **$100 - $165**, ◊ **$20**, ch con, AE BC EFT MC VI.

★★★★ **Heytesbury House**, (B&B), 33 Parrott St, 300m S of PO, ☎ 03 5595 1886, fax 03 5595 1944, 4 rms [ensuite (2), shwr, bath (2), spa bath (1), tlt, hairdry, fan (1), c/fan (3), heat, elec blkts, TV (2), cable tv (1), video, clock radio, CD (3), refrig], iron, iron brd, lounge (TV, video), t/c mkg shared, bbq, c/park (undercover), non smoking rms. **BB** ♦ **$105**, ♦♦ **$130 - $165**, Dinner by arrangement. AE BC DC MC VI.

★★★★ **(Cottage Section)**, 1 cotg acc up to 4, (2 bedrm), [ensuite (2), bath, spa bath, hairdry, c/fan, heat, elec blkts, TV, video, clock radio, t/c mkg, refrig, cook fac, ldry, blkts, linen, pillows], breakfast ingredients. **BB** ♦ **$105**, ♦♦ **$200**.

COBRAM VIC 3644

Pop 3,850. (251km N Melbourne), See map on page 696, ref D1. Centre of a district producing wheat, wool, dairying, tobacco, citrus fruits and tomatoes. Boating, Bowls, Fishing, Golf, Scenic Drives, Shooting, Swimming (Pool, River Beach), Tennis, Trotting, Water Skiing.

★★★★ **The Charles Sturt Motor Inn**, (M), 31 Mookarii St, 500m NE of PO, ☎ 03 5872 2777, fax 03 5871 1255, (2 stry gr fl), 18 units [shwr, spa bath (2), tlt, hairdry, a/c, c/fan, elec blkts, tel, cable tv, video-fee, clock radio, t/c mkg, refrig, toaster], ldry, pool-heated (solar), spa, bbq, cots-fee. **RO** ♦ **$79.20 - $101.20**, ◊ **$11**, AE BC DC EFT MC VI, ♿.

★★★ **Cobram Colonial Motor Inn**, (M), Cnr Murray Valley Hwy & William St, 1km SE of PO, ☎ 03 5872 1866, fax 03 5872 1929, 20 units [shwr, bath (hip) (5), tlt, a/c, elec blkts, tel, TV, clock radio, t/c mkg, refrig, cook fac (1), toaster], ldry, pool, spa, bbq, dinner to unit, cots, non smoking units (6). **RO** ♦ **$55**, ♦♦ **$65**, ◊ **$13**, AE BC DC EFT MC VI.

★★★ **Regency Court Motel**, (M), 1 Main St, 300m W of PO, ☎ 03 5872 2488, fax 03 5871 1425, 12 units [shwr, tlt, a/c, elec blkts, tel, TV, video, clock radio, t/c mkg, refrig, toaster], pool-heated (solar), bbq, dinner to unit (Mon to Fri), cots-fee. **RO** ♦ **$71.50 - $85.80**, ♦♦ **$77 - $85.80**, ◊ **$13**, ch con, AE BC DC MC MP VI.

★★☆ **Cobram Classic Motel**, (M), Cnr Murray Valley Hwy & Station St, 700m S of PO, ☎ 03 5872 1633, fax 03 5871 1121, 25 units [shwr, tlt, a/c, elec blkts, tel, TV, clock radio, t/c mkg, refrig], rec rm, conf fac, pool, bbq, cots-fee, non smoking units (5). **RO** ♦ **$55 - $65**, ♦♦ **$65 - $82**, ◊ **$15**, ch con, AE BC DC MC VI.

★★★★☆ **RACV Club Cobram**, (HF), Campbell Rd, 2km E of PO, ☎ 03 5872 2467, fax 03 5872 2795, 20 flats acc up to 6, (2 bedrm), [shwr, tlt, hairdry, a/c, elec blkts, TV, video-fee, movie, clock radio, refrig, cook fac, micro, elec frypan, toaster, ldry, blkts, linen, pillows], w/mach, dryer, rec rm, pool, bbq, c/park (carport), ☎, plygr, bicycle-fee, tennis, cots-fee. **D** ♦♦ **$100 - $135**, ◊ **$11 - $14**, **W** ♦♦ **$630 - $800**, ◊ **$77 - $98**, ch con, AE BC DC EFT MC VI.

COCKATOO VIC

See Dandenong Ranges Region.

COHUNA VIC 3568

Pop 2,000. (270km N Melbourne), See map on pages 694/695, ref E3. Dairying & agricultural town situated on Murray Valley Hwy, adjacent Gunbower Creek. Boating, Bowls, Bush Walking, Croquet, Fishing, Golf, Horse Riding, Scenic Drives, Shooting, Swimming (Pool, River), Tennis, Water Skiing.

Hotels/Motels

★★★ **Cohuna Motor Inn**, (M), Murray Valley Hwy, 1.6km N of PO, ☎ 03 5456 2974, or 03 5456 2547, 13 units [shwr, tlt, a/c-cool, heat, elec blkts, tel, TV, clock radio, t/c mkg, refrig, toaster], pool, bbq, cots, non smoking units (3). **RO** ⚹ $50 - $55, ⚹⚹ $60 - $70, ⚹ $12, ch con, AE BC DC EFT MC VI.

★★☆ **Cohuna Hotel**, (LMH), 39 King George St (Murray Valley Hwy), 200m E of PO, ☎ 03 5456 2604, fax 03 5456 4522, 12 units [shwr, tlt, a/c, elec blkts, TV, t/c mkg, refrig, toaster], ldry, ✉, ☎, cots. **RO** ⚹ $55, ⚹⚹ $60 - $65, ⚹ $10, AE BC DC EFT MC VI.

★☆ **(Hotel Section)**, (2 stry), 16 rms [shwr, tlt, fan, heat, elec blkts], t/c mkg shared, refrig. **RO** ⚹ $35, ⚹⚹ $40 - $50, ⚹ $10.

COLAC VIC 3250

Pop 9,800. (148km SW Melbourne), See map on pages 694/695, ref D7. Centre of the South-Western District. Boating, Bowls, Bush Walking, Croquet, Fishing (Lake), Golf, Horse Racing, Sailing, Scenic Drives, Shooting, Swimming (Heated Pool), Tennis, Water Skiing.

Hotels/Motels

★★★★ **Baronga Motor Inn**, (M), 35 Murray St East (Princes Hwy), 600m E of PO, ☎ 03 5231 2100, fax 03 5232 1354, 28 units [shwr, bath (hip) (4), spa bath (4), tlt, hairdry, a/c, heat, elec blkts, tel, TV, video-fee, clock radio, t/c mkg, refrig, toaster], iron, iron brd, ✉ (Mon to Sat), pool, bbq, dinner to unit (Mon to Sat), plygr, cots-fee, non smoking units (9).
RO ┆ $68.20 - $90.20, ┆┆ $79.20 - $102.30, ┆ $11, ch con, AE BC DC MC MP VI.

★★★☆ **Flag Inn Colac Mid City**, (M), Previously Colac Mid City Motel 289 Murray St (Princes Hwy), 500m W of PO, ☎ 03 5231 3333, fax 03 5231 1979, (2 stry gr fl), 30 units [shwr, bath (5), spa bath (1), tlt, hairdry, a/c-cool (7), a/c (23), heat (7), elec blkts, tel, cable tv (23), video (avail), clock radio, t/c mkg, refrig, mini bar, cook fac (2), toaster], ldry, iron, iron brd, conf fac, ✉, pool, rm serv, cots, non smoking units (25). **RO** ┆ $65 - $104, ┆┆ $75 - $104, AE BC DC EFT JCB MC VI, ⅙.

★★★ **Colac Central Hotel-Motel**, (LMH), Previously Colac Hotel Motel 10 Murray St (Princes Hwy), adjacent PO, ☎ 03 5231 5777, fax 03 5231 5020, 20 units [ensuite, a/c, heat, elec blkts, tel, TV, clock radio, t/c mkg, refrig, toaster], ✉. **RO** ┆ $55 - $60, ┆┆ $65 - $70, ┆ $10, AE BC DC EFT MC VI.

★★ **(Hotel Section)**, 15 rms [a/c (6), fan, heat, elec blkts, TV, t/c mkg, refrig, toaster]. **RO** ┆ $35 - $40, ┆┆ $45 - $50, ┆ $10.

★★★ **Otway Gate Motel**, (M), 52 Murray St East (Princes Hwy), 800m E of PO, ☎ 03 5231 3244, fax 03 5231 3244, 18 units [shwr, bath (hip) (2), tlt, a/c, elec blkts, tel, TV, video-fee, clock radio, t/c mkg, refrig, mini bar], ldry, ✉ (Mon to Sat), dinner to unit (6 nights), plygr, cots-fee, non smoking units (7). **RO** ┆ $52 - $57, ┆┆ $63 - $68, ┆ $11, ch con, 6 units ★★★, AE BC DC MC VI.

Self Catering Accommodation

★★★ **Bogandeena Studio**, (Cotg), 75 Colac - Lavers Hill Rd, Elliminyt 3249, 4km S of PO, ☎ 03 5231 5273, 1 cotg acc up to 5, (Studio), [shwr, tlt, hairdry, fan, heat, TV, clock radio, CD, refrig, cook fac ltd, micro, toaster, blkts, linen, pillows], iron, iron brd, bbq, cots, breakfast ingredients, non smoking property. **D** ┆ $45 - $70, ┆┆ $80, ┆ $25, ch con, BC EFT MC VI.

B&B's/Guest Houses

★★★★ **Wanawong**, (B&B), 950 Colac - Lavers Hill Rd, Barongarook 3249, 12km S of PO, ☎ 03 5233 6215, fax 03 5233 8258, 1 rm [shwr, bath, tlt, c/fan, heat, elec blkts, clock radio, t/c mkg, refrig, micro], lounge (TV, stereo, piano), lounge firepl, bbq, tennis, non smoking property. **BB** ┆ $60 - $100, ┆┆ $95 - $100.

★★★★ **Balnagowan**, (B&B), 3 - 21 Stodart St, 2.8km NW of PO, ☎ 03 5232 2044, fax 03 5232 2318, (2 stry), 3 rms [ensuite, heat, elec blkts, TV, clock radio], conf fac, t/c mkg shared, refrig. **BB** ┆ $93.50 - $99, Dinner by arrangement. AE BC MC VI.

★★★☆ **The Elms Bed & Breakfast**, (B&B), 14 Gellibrand St, ☎ 03 5231 5112, 2 rms [fan, heat, elec blkts, TV, video, clock radio, doonas], non smoking property. **BB** ┆ $45, ┆┆ $85, ┆ $45.

★★★☆ **The Prince of Wales Guest House**, (GH), 2 Murray St East (Princes Hwy), 600m E of PO, ☎ 03 5231 3385, fax 03 5231 3385, 3 rms [clock radio], lounge (TV), lounge firepl, bbq, non smoking property. **BB** ┆ $33, ┆┆ $66, Other meals by arrangement. AE BC MC VI.

COLERAINE VIC 3315

Pop 1,100. (325km W Melbourne), See map on pages 694/695, ref A6. Situated in the Wannon Valley. Bowls, Croquet, Fishing, Gem Fossicking, Golf, Horse Racing, Scenic Drives, Swimming (Pool), Tennis.

Hotels/Motels

★☆ **National**, (LH), 70 Whyte St (Glenelg Hwy), 100m E of PO, ☎ 03 5575 2064, fax 03 5575 2064, (2 stry), 18 rms [elec blkts], lounge (TV), ✉, t/c mkg shared, cots. **BLB** ┆ $25, ┆┆ $45, ┆ $10 - $20.

Self Catering Accommodation

Pemberley Lodge, (House), 25 Whyte St, 1km E of PO, ☎ 03 5579 1220, or 03 5575 2364, fax 03 5579 1220, 1 house acc up to 8, (4 bedrm), [evap cool, fan, heat, elec blkts, TV, video, refrig, cook fac, micro, toaster, ldry, blkts, doonas, linen, pillows], baby bath, w/mach, secure park, cots. **D** ┆ $60, ┆ $10, (not yet classified).

Other Accommodation

Melville Forest Partnership, (Lodge), Previously Melville Forest Farm Stay (Farm), Coleraine-Cavendish Rd, 18km E of PO, ☎ 03 5575 8229, fax 03 5575 8267, 9 rms acc up to 20, (Bunk Rooms), [elec blkts, doonas, linen reqd-fee, pillows], lounge (TV, video), conf fac, lounge firepl, cook fac, t/c mkg shared, refrig, bbq, cots. **D** ┆ $15, ┆ $15.

COLIGNAN VIC 3494

Pop 896. (529km NW Melbourne), See map on pages 694/695, ref C1. Citrus, avocado & almond growing district on the banks of the Murray River. Hattah-Kulkyne National Park (8km), a bird watchers mecca.

★★★ **Hattah - Kulkyne Wilderness Lodge**, (HF), Kulkyne Way, 48km SE of Mildura, ☎ 03 5029 1572, fax 03 5029 1844, 4 flats acc up to 6, (2 bedrm), [shwr, tlt, evap cool, heat, elec blkts, TV, video, clock radio, t/c mkg, refrig, cook fac, micro, elec frypan, ldry (in unit), blkts, linen, pillows], w/mach, iron, iron brd, bbq, c/park (carport), plygr, cots, non smoking units. **D** ┆┆ $71.50, ┆ $8.25, BC MC VI.

COROP VIC 3559

Pop Nominal, (160km N Melbourne), See map on page 696, ref B2. Irrigation area - grain crops, sheep & cattle grazing. Boat Ramp.

Curumbene, (Lodge), (Farm), 138 Darrigans Rd, 5.5km SE of PO, near Lake Cooper, ☎ 03 5484 8236, fax 03 5484 8226, 11 rms acc up to 12, [ensuite (9), blkts reqd, linen reqd], ldry, rec rm, lounge (TV, video), ✗, pool-heated (solar), t/c mkg shared, refrig, bbq, canoeing, tennis. **D all meals** ┆ $35, ┆ $35, ch con, Minimum booking - 35 people. Tariff includes seasonal farm activities.

CORRYONG VIC 3707

Pop 1,200. (425km NE Melbourne), See map on pages 694/695, ref J4. Victorian Gateway to the Snowy Mountains. Burrowa-Pine Mountain National Park. Bowls, Bush Walking, Fishing (Trout, Murray Cod), Gold Prospecting, Golf, Scenic Drives, Snow Skiing, Squash, Swimming (Pool, River), Tennis.

Hotels/Motels

★★★ **Corryong Country Inn**, (M), 7 Towong Rd (Murray Valley Hwy), 300m E of PO, ☎ 02 6076 1333, fax 02 6076 1905, 9 units [shwr, bath (6), spa bath (2), tlt, a/c, heat, elec blkts, tel, TV, clock radio, t/c mkg, refrig], ldry, lounge, ✗, bar (cocktail), cots-fee, non smoking property. **RO** ┆ $66 - $77, ┆┆ $84 - $105, ┆ $13, AE BC DC EFT MC VI, ⅙.

★★ **Pinnibar Motel**, (M), 74 Towong Rd (Murray Valley Hwy), 600m E of PO, ☎ 02 6076 1766, fax 02 6076 2008, 18 units [shwr, tlt, a/c-cool, heat, elec blkts, tel, TV, clock radio, t/c mkg, refrig, toaster], ldry, ✗ (by prior arrangement), pool, bbq, plygr, cots-fee. **D** ┆ $49.50, ┆┆ $60.50, ┆ $11, 3 units ★★★. AE BC EFT MC VI, ⅙.

★☆ **Corryong Hotel**, (LMH), 54 Towong Rd (Murray Valley Hwy), 500m E of PO, ☎ 02 6076 1004, 12 units [shwr, tlt, a/c (6), fan, heat, TV, t/c mkg, refrig], ldry, ✗, c/park (carport) (6), ✆, cots. **BLB** ┆ $40, ┆┆ $50, ┆ $10, ch con, AE BC EFT MC VI.

B&B's/Guest Houses

★★★★ **Jardine Cottage**, (B&B), 23 Jardine St, 50m N of PO, ☎ 02 6076 1318, fax 02 6076 1318, (2 stry gr fl), 4 rms [ensuite, spa bath (2), a/c, c/fan, heat, elec blkts, clock radio], lounge (TV, video, cd), ✗, t/c mkg shared, refrig, cots, non smoking property. **BB** ┆ $85 - $95, ┆┆ $95 - $115, ┆ $20, ch con, BC MC VI.

COWES VIC

See Phillip Island Region.

CRESWICK VIC 3363

Pop 2,350. (130km NW Melbourne), See map on pages 694/695, ref D6. Historic gold mining town at the base of Creswick State Forest. Dinosaur Park, Koala Park, St George Lake, Timber Industry Training Centre, School of Forestry. Bowls, Bush Walking, Fishing, Gold Prospecting, Golf, Scenic Drives, Swimming (Pool, Lake), Tennis.

★★★ **Creswick Motel**, (M), Cnr Cushing Ave & Albert St (Midland Hwy), 700m N of PO, ☎ 03 5345 2400, fax 03 5345 2400, 10 units (2 bedrm), [shwr, tlt, heat, elec blkts, tel, TV, clock radio, t/c mkg, refrig, toaster], bbq, dinner to unit, plygr, cots-fee, non smoking units (3). **BLB** ┆ $55 - $60, ┆┆ $68 - $74, ┆ $11, AE BC DC EFT MC MCH VI.

Self Catering Accommodation

★★★★ **Rossmore Cottage**, (Cotg), 12 Bald Hills Rd, ☎ 03 5345 2759, fax 03 5345 2127, 1 cotg acc up to 4, [shwr, spa bath, tlt, hairdry, fan, elec blkts, TV, video, clock radio, CD, t/c mkg, refrig, cook fac, micro, toaster, blkts, doonas, linen, pillows], iron, iron brd, lounge firepl, bbq, non smoking property. **D** $100 - $170, **W** $650, BC MC VI.

★★★ **Hillview Hostfarm**, (Cotg), (Farm), 33ha beef grazing and cropping property. Spittle Rd, 4km N of PO, off Australasia Dve, ☎ 03 5345 2690, fax 03 5345 2690, 1 cotg acc up to 6, (1 bedrm), [shwr, tlt, fan, heat (wood), elec blkts, TV, video, clock radio, refrig, cook fac, micro, elec frypan, toaster, ldry, linen reqd], iron, iron brd, bbq, cots. **D** $63 - $74, **W** $370 - $405.

B&B's/Guest Houses
★★★★ **Belfield Creswick**, (B&B), c1880. No children's facilities, 53 Clunes Rd, 1.2km N of PO, ☎ 03 5345 2605, fax 03 5345 2605, 2 rms [ensuite (1), shwr (1), tlt (1), hairdry, fire pl, cent heat, elec blkts, TV, clock radio], lounge (cd), t/c mkg shared, refrig, non smoking property. **BB** ♦ **$95**, ♦♦ **$120**, Dinner by arrangement. BC MC VI.

★★★★ **Old Gold Bank**, (B&B), 99 Albert St, 200m S of PO, ☎ 03 5345 2291, fax 03 5333 1565, (2 stry gr fl), 3 rms [shwr, bath (1), spa bath (1), tlt, hairdry, fire pl, elec blkts, clock radio, t/c mkg (shared)], lounge (TV, cd), lounge firepl, non smoking property. **BB** ♦ **$70 - $110**, ♦♦ **$100 - $140**, ◊ **$30**.

CUDGEWA VIC 3705
Pop Nominal, (412km NE Melbourne), See map on pages 694/695, ref J4.
Self Catering Accommodation
★★★ **Elmstead B & B**, (Cotg), (Farm), Ashstead Park La, ☎ 02 6077 4324, fax 02 6077 4324, 1 cotg acc up to 4, (Studio), [shwr, bath (hip), tlt, c/fan, heat (wood), elec blkts, TV, clock radio, t/c mkg, refrig, micro, elec frypan, toaster, blkts, linen, pillows], bbq, breakfast ingredients, non smoking property. **BB** ♦ **$50**, ♦♦ **$75**, ◊ **$15**, ch con.

★ **(Arthur's Cottage Section)**, 1 cotg acc up to 5, (2 bedrm), [shwr, bath (hip), tlt, heat (wood), radio, refrig (gas), cook fac, doonas, linen reqd, pillows]. **D** ♦♦ **$75**, ◊ **$5**, Solar lighting.

CURDIEVALE VIC 3268
Pop Part of Timboon, (249km SW Melbourne), See map on pages 694/695, ref C7. Small township on the Curdies River, in a dairying district.
★★ **Boggy Creek Pub**, (LH), Timboon - Curdievale Rd, 50m E of Curdies River bridge, ☎ 03 5566 5223, 4 rms [shwr, tlt, heat, elec blkts, TV, t/c mkg, refrig, toaster], ⊠, ☏. **BLB** ♦ **$50**, ♦♦ **$80 - $110**, BC EFT MC VI.

DADSWELLS BRIDGE VIC
See Grampians Region.

DANDENONG RANGES REGION - VIC

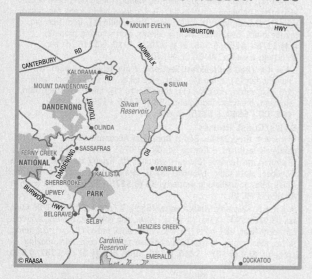

DANDENONG RANGES - BELGRAVE VIC 3160
Pop Part of Yarra Ranges, (39km E Melbourne), See map on page 697, ref E4. Home of world famous Puffing Billy. The MET train service connects with Puffing Billy.
Self Catering Accommodation
★★★★ **Foxes Hollow Cottage-Style Spa Apartments**, (Apt), 48 Edward St, ☎ 03 9751 1438, fax 03 9751 2030, 3 apts acc up to 6, (1 & 3 bedrm), [shwr, spa bath, tlt, hairdry, fan, heat, elec blkts, tel, TV, video (1), clock radio, refrig, cook fac, micro, toaster, ldry (in unit), blkts, doonas, linen, pillows], w/mach, dryer, iron, iron brd, c/park (carport), breakfast ingredients. **D** ♦♦ **$140 - $230**, ◊ **$40**, **W** ♦♦♦♦ **$900 - $1,120**, 1 apartment ★★★★☆, AE BC DC EFT MC VI.

★★★☆ **Pinetree Cottage**, (Cotg), 11 Marama Rd, Belgrave Heights 3160, ☎ 03 9754 2745, 1 cotg acc up to 4, (1 bedrm), [shwr, bath, tlt, hairdry, a/c-cool, fan, heat, elec blkts, TV, video, refrig, cook fac, micro, elec frypan, toaster, ldry, blkts, linen, pillows], w/mach, dryer, iron, iron brd, bbq, cots, breakfast ingredients, non smoking property. **BB** ♦♦ **$95 - $115**, ◊ **$20**, **W** ♦♦ **$380 - $440**.

B&B's/Guest Houses
★★★★☆ **Garden Heights**, (B&B), 73 Lockwood Rd, Belgrave Heights 3160, 4.6km S of PO, ☎ 03 9754 5308, 1 rm (1 suite) [shwr, bath, tlt, fan, heat, elec blkts, clock radio, t/c mkg, refrig, cook fac ltd, micro, toaster, ldry-fee, doonas], lounge (TV, video), c/park (undercover), non smoking property. **BB** ♦♦ **$95 - $150**, ch con.

★★★☆ **Rose-A-Lee Manor**, (B&B), 6 Talbot Ave, 700m S of Burwood Hwy, ☎ 03 9754 4473, fax 03 9754 1414, (2 stry), 3 rms (1 suite) [ensuite (1), spa bath (1), hairdry, a/c, heat, elec blkts, TV, video (1), clock radio, CD, t/c mkg, refrig (1), micro], lounge, spa (heated), non smoking property. **BB** ♦ **$120 - $132**, ♦♦ **$150 - $165**, ◊ **$50 - $55**, **Suite BB** ♦♦ **$220**, ch con, 1 suite ★★★★☆. AE BC MC VI.

★★★☆ **Wonderland Pottery Bed & Breakfast**, (B&B), No children's facilities, 85 Terrys Ave, ☎ 03 9754 4547, fax 03 9754 4573, 2 rms [shwr, spa bath, tlt, hairdry, fan, c/fan, heat, clock radio, doonas], lounge (TV, video, cd), t/c mkg shared, bbq, non smoking property. **BB** ♦ **$70 - $95**, ♦♦ **$85 - $120**, BC MC VI.

DANDENONG RANGES - COCKATOO VIC 3781
Pop 2,800. (52km E Melbourne), See map on page 696, ref C6. Located on Cockatoo Creek between Emerald & Gembrook. Bowls, Bush Walking, Scenic Drives.
Self Catering Accommodation
★★★★ **Cockatoo Cottages**, (Cotg), 380 Woori Yallock Rd, ☎ 03 5968 9383, fax 03 5968 9383, 2 cotgs (1 bedrm), [shwr, spa bath, tlt, hairdry, a/c-cool, heat, elec blkts, TV, video, clock radio, CD, refrig, cook fac ltd, micro, toaster, blkts, doonas, linen, pillows], iron, iron brd, lounge firepl, pool above ground, bbq, plygr, non smoking units (1). **D** ♦♦ **$125 - $195**, BC MC VI.

B&B's/Guest Houses
 ★★★★☆ **Whistle-Stopover**, (B&B), 11 Doonaha Rd, ☎ 03 5968 8208, fax 03 5968 8278, 1 rm [ensuite, spa bath, hairdry, heat, TV, CD, t/c mkg, refrig], pool, non smoking property. **BB** ♦ **$100**, ♦♦ **$150**, ch con, Twin room not included in listing. AE BC DC MC VI.

★★★★☆ **(Cottage Section)**, (2 stry gr fl), 1 cotg acc up to 8, (3 bedrm), [ensuite (1), shwr, spa bath, tlt, hairdry, a/c, c/fan, elec blkts, TV, video, CD, t/c mkg, refrig, cook fac, micro, elec frypan, d/wash, toaster, blkts, doonas, pillows], iron, iron brd, cots, breakfast ingredients, non smoking property. **BB** ♦♦ **$220**, ◊ **$60**, ch con.

DANDENONG RANGES - EMERALD VIC 3782

*Pop 4,650. (49km E Melbourne), See map on page 696, ref C6.
Destination of world famous Puffing Billy. Art Gallery, Bowls, Bush
Walking, Fishing, Golf, Scenic Drives, Swimming (Pool, Lake), Tennis.*

Self Catering Accommodation

★★★★☆ **Glenview Retreat**, (Cotg), No children's facilities, 48
Fernglade Dr, 45km SE Melbourne, ☎ 03 5968 5399, fax 03 5968 5399,
2 cotgs acc up to 2, (Studio), [shwr, spa bath, tlt, hairdry, c/fan, heat,
TV, video, clock radio, t/c mkg, refrig, cook fac ltd, micro, elec frypan,
toaster, blkts, linen, pillows], iron, bbq, non smoking property.
D $120 - $170, W $750 - $900, BC MC VI.

★★★★ A **Timbertop Lodge**, (Cotg), 3 Silvan Crt, 5km S of PO,
☎ 03 5968 5476, 2 cotgs acc up to 6, (2 bedrm - mudbrick), [shwr,
spa bath, tlt, hairdry, a/c-cool, c/fan, TV, video, clock radio, CD,
t/c mkg, refrig, cook fac, micro, toaster, blkts, linen, pillows],
non smoking property. **BB ♛♛ $140 - $190, ♛ $30**, ch con, BC MC VI,
*Operator Comment: Unique mud brick lodge
www.timbertop.dandenong-ranges.net.au*

★★★★ **Fernglade Lodge**, (Cotg), 49 Fernglade Dve, 7km E of PO,
☎ 03 5968 2228, fax 03 5968 2233, 1 cotg acc up to 13, (4 bedrm),
[ensuite (1), shwr, bath, tlt, c/fan, cent heat, tel, TV, video, clock radio,
t/c mkg, refrig, cook fac, micro, toaster, ldry (in unit), blkts, doonas,
linen, pillows], w/mach, iron, iron brd, lounge firepl, bbq, non smoking
property. **BB ♛♛ $80 - $140, ♛ $20, W $600 - $900**, ch con, BC MC VI.

★★★★☆ **(Bed & Breakfast Section)**, 11 Caroline Cres, 2 rms [spa
bath, evap cool, fan, heat, elec blkts, tel, video, clock radio, t/c mkg,
refrig, cook fac ltd, micro, toaster, doonas], ldry, conf fac, lounge firepl,
bbq, non smoking property. **BB ♛♛ $80 - $140, ♛ $20, W $600 - $900.**

★★★★ **Tarramena Country Accommodation**, (HU), 3 Kitty Lane,
Clematis 3782, ☎ 03 5968 6075, fax 03 5968 2227, 1 unit acc up to
6, (2 bedrm), [shwr, spa bath, tlt, hairdry, heat, elec blkts, TV, video,
clock radio, CD, refrig, cook fac, micro, toaster, ldry, blkts, doonas,
linen, pillows], iron, iron brd, bbq, cots, breakfast ingredients, non
smoking property. **BB ♛♛ $150 - $190, ♛ $20**, BC MC VI.

B&B's/Guest Houses

★★★★☆ **The Nook**, (B&B), 50 Lakeside Dve, 2km N of PO, adjacent
to lake, ☎ 03 5968 4080, 2 rms [ensuite, hairdry, cent heat, elec blkts,
TV, video (1), clock radio, t/c mkg, refrig (1)], non smoking rms.
BB ♛ $75 - $100, ♛♛ $110 - $130.

★★★ **Emerald Golf & Country Resort**, (GH), 48 Lakeside Dve,
☎ 03 5968 4211, fax 03 5968 4949, 6 rms [ensuite, hairdry, heat,
elec blkts, tel, TV, clock radio, t/c mkg], ldry, ☒, bar (cocktail), golf,
tennis, non smoking rms (6). **RO ♛ $77, ♛♛ $88, ♛ $15**, ch con, AE BC
DC EFT MC VI.

★★ **(Clubhouse Section)**, 7 rms [heat, elec blkts, t/c mkg]. **RO ♛ $44,
♛♛ $55, ♛ $15.**

Other Accommodation

Emerald Hostel, (Lodge), Lakeview Crt, 2.5km fr PO, ☎ 03 5968 4086,
8 rms [ensuite (3), heat], ldry, w/mach, dryer, rec rm, lounge (TV, video),
cook fac, refrig, bbq, ☏. **D ♛ $15, ♛ $15.**

DANDENONG RANGES - FERNY CREEK VIC 3786

*Pop 1,761. (37km E Melbourne), See map on page 697, ref E4.
Scenic township situated in the Dandenong Ranges.*

B&B's/Guest Houses

★★★★☆ **A Forest View Country House**, (B&B), 16 Clarke Rd,
☎ 03 9755 2502, fax 03 9755 1779, 1 rm (1 suite) [ensuite, hairdry,
a/c-cool, cent heat, elec blkts, clock radio, t/c mkg, refrig, micro,
toaster], lounge (TV, video, cd), lounge firepl, bbq, non smoking suites.
BB ♛ $85 - $135, ♛♛ $95 - $155, Children by arrangement
Other meals by arrangement, BC MC VI.
Operator Comment: See our display advertisement top right.

★★★★☆ **Shannon House**, (B&B), No children's facilities, 238 Mt
Dandenong Tourist Rd, 200m N of PO, ☎ 03 9755 1711, fax 03 9755 1711,
2 rms [ensuite, spa bath, hairdry, heat (gas log), elec blkts, TV, video,
clock radio, t/c mkg, mini bar], lounge (TV, video, cd), non smoking
property. **BB ♛♛ $130 - $260**, Other meals by arrangement. AE BC MC VI.

Before you travel

Before a trip have your vehicle serviced and checked over to
ensure reliable motoring. There are some checks you can make
yourself, generally the procedure can be found in the vehicle
owners manual.

DANDENONG RANGES - KALLISTA VIC 3791

*Pop 1,659. (44km NE Melbourne), See map on page 696, ref C5.
Picturesque township in the heart of the Dandenongs. Bush Walking,
Scenic Drives, Tennis.*

B&B's/Guest Houses

★★★★☆ **Katrina Lodge**, (B&B), 76
Sassafras Creek Rd, ☎ 03 9755 3375,
fax 03 9755 3194, (2 stry gr fl), 3 rms
[shwr, bath (1), spa bath (2), tlt, hairdry,
heat, elec blkts, TV, CD, t/c mkg (1), refrig (1),
cook fac ltd (1), micro (1), toaster (1)],
iron, iron brd, lounge firepl (1), t/c mkg shared, refrig, bbq,
non smoking property. **BB ♛♛ $130 - $275**, BC MC VI,
*Operator Comment: Romantic escape offering superb forest
views. See us on www.katrina.com.au*

★★★☆ **Burrowye Bed & Breakfast**, (B&B), 3 Owen St, ☎ 03 9755 2028,
2 rms [hairdry, cent heat, elec blkts], lounge, lounge firepl, spa (heated),
t/c mkg shared, refrig, bbq, non smoking rms. **BB $100 - $200**, Dinner
by arrangement. BC MC VI.

DANDENONG RANGES - KALORAMA VIC 3766

*Pop 1,194. (40km E Melbourne), See map on page 696, ref C5.
Situated in the Dandenong Ranges. Art Gallery, Bush Walking, Golf,
Horse Riding, Scenic Drives, Tennis.*

Hotels/Motels

Villa Toscano, (M), 13 Barbers Rd, 1km SE of PO, ☎ 03 9728 1298,
fax 03 9728 5484, (2 stry gr fl), 7 units [shwr, spa bath (3), tlt,
cent heat, tel, TV, t/c mkg, refrig], lounge, conf fac, ☒ (Fri & Sat),
pool, sauna, cots-fee. **RO ♛ $88 - $132, ♛♛ $99 - $275, ♛ $22,**
ch con, AE BC DC EFT MC VI,

Self Catering Accommodation

★★★★☆ **Gumbirra Bed & Breakfast**, (Cotg), 68 Inverness Rd,
☎ 03 9761 9656, fax 03 9728 8268, (2 stry), 1 cotg acc up to 5,
(3 bedrm), [shwr, bath, spa bath, tlt, hairdry, fan, c/fan, cent heat,
elec blkts, TV, video, clock radio, CD, t/c mkg, refrig, cook fac, micro,
d/wash, toaster, ldry (in unit), blkts, linen, pillows], iron, iron brd,
lounge firepl, bbq, breakfast ingredients, non smoking property.
D ♛♛ $175 - $250, ♛ $45, W ♛♛ $700 - $910, ♛ $315, ch con,
1 cottage ★★★★☆. AE BC DC MC VI.

★★★★ **(Bed & Breakfast Section)**, 2 rms [shwr, spa bath, tlt,
hairdry, fan (1), c/fan (1), heat, elec blkts, TV, video, clock radio, CD,
t/c mkg, refrig, cook fac (1), cook fac ltd (1), micro, toaster], iron,
iron brd, breakfast ingredients. **BB ♛♛ $135 - $200, ♛ $45,
♛♛ $700 - $840, ♛ $315**, ch con.

B&B's/Guest Houses

★★★★☆ **Grey Gables Bed & Breakfast Accommodation**, (B&B), No
children's facilities, 3 Grange Rd, ☎ 03 9761 8609, fax 03 9728 8033,
(2 stry), 3 rms [ensuite (2), shwr, spa bath, tlt, hairdry, fan, heat, elec blkts,
TV, video, clock radio, t/c mkg, refrig], lounge (cd, stereo), lounge firepl
(gas), bbq, non smoking property. **BB ♛♛ $175 - $270**, 1 room ★★★★.
AE BC EFT MC VI.

★★★★☆ **Kalorama Holly Lodge**, (B&B), 7 Erith La, ☎ 03 9728 6064,
fax 03 9761 9907, 2 rms (1 suite) [shwr, spa bath, tlt, hairdry, a/c-cool,
fan, cent heat, elec blkts, tel, TV, video, clock radio, CD, t/c mkg, refrig,
micro, elec frypan, toaster], bbq, dinner to unit, cots, non smoking
property. **BLB ♛♛ $97 - $210, ♛ $20, Suite BLB ♛♛ $77 - $187, ♛ $20,**
ch con, BC MC VI.

★★★★☆ **Rosehill Lodge**, (B&B), Kalorama Tce, ☎ 03 9761 8889, fax 03 9761 8889, 2 rms (2 suites) [ensuite, hairdry, fan, heat, elec blkts, tel, clock radio, t/c mkg], lounge (TV, video, cd), lounge firepl (1), bbq, non smoking property. **BB ♦ $150, ♦♦ $150**, Dinner by arrangement. AE DC.

★★★★☆ **Tanglewood Chalet**, (B&B), 18 Erith La, ☎ 03 9728 1542, fax 03 9728 1542, 1 rm (1 suite) [ensuite, spa bath, hairdry, fan, heat, elec blkts, t/c mkg, refrig, toaster], lounge (TV, video, cd), lounge firepl (gas), non smoking property. **BB ♦♦ $165 - $255**, BC MC VI.

DANDENONG RANGES - MENZIES CREEK VIC 3159

Pop Part of Yarra Ranges, (45km E Melbourne), See map on page 696, ref C6. Small settlement in the Dandenong Ranges. Puffing Billy Museum. Bush Walking, Scenic Drives.

Self Catering Accommodation

★★★★ **Glovalley**, (Apt), 18 School Rd, ☎ 03 9754 2484, fax 03 9754 1985, 1 apt acc up to 4, (2 bedrm), [shwr, tlt, hairdry, heat (wood), elec blkts, TV, video, clock radio, CD, t/c mkg, refrig, cook fac ltd, toaster, blkts, linen, pillows], w/mach, bbq, non smoking property. **BB ♦♦ $142 - $160, ◊ $60**, AE BC DC MC VI.

★★★★ **(Cottage Section)**, 4 cotgs acc up to 9, (2 bedrm), [shwr, bath, spa bath, tlt, hairdry, a/c-cool, heat, elec blkts, TV, video, clock radio, CD, t/c mkg, refrig, cook fac, micro, elec frypan (1), d/wash (1), toaster, blkts, doonas, linen, pillows], ldry, w/mach, iron, iron brd, lounge firepl. **D $192 - $220, W $750 - $1,050**, ch con, 1 cottage ★★★☆.

B&B's/Guest Houses

★★★☆ **Kharwa Homestay Bed & Breakfast**, (B&B), 174 Belgrave - Gembrook Rd, off service road, ☎ 03 5968 3926, 1 rm (1 suite) [shwr, tlt, evap cool, c/fan, heat, elec blkts, TV, clock radio, t/c mkg, refrig], lounge, cots-fee. **BB ♦ $50, ♦♦ $85, ◊ $25**, ch con.

DANDENONG RANGES - MONBULK VIC 3793

Pop 3,839. (47km E Melbourne), See map on page 696, ref C5. Small township in the heart of the Dandenongs. Vegetable, fruit & tulip growing district. Bowls, Bush Walking, Fishing, Horse Riding, Scenic Drives, Swimming (Pool), Tennis.

Self Catering Accommodation

★★★★☆ **Eaglehammer Cottages**, (Cotg), 440 Old Emerald Rd, ☎ 03 9756 7700, fax 03 9756 7444, 3 cotgs acc up to 2, [shwr, spa bath, tlt, hairdry, a/c, c/fan, elec blkts, TV, video (avail), clock radio, CD, t/c mkg, refrig, cook fac ltd, micro, d/wash, toaster, blkts, doonas, linen, pillows], iron, iron brd, conf fac, lounge firepl, res liquor license, pool (salt water), bbq, dinner to unit, ☎, breakfast ingredients. **D $176 - $308**, Min book Christmas Jan long w/ends and Easter, AE BC DC EFT MC VI.

★★★★ **Spring Waters Retreat**, (Cotg), 210 Monbulk Rd, 1.5km W of PO, ☎ 03 9756 6332, fax 03 9756 6332, 1 cotg acc up to 8, (3 bedrm), [ensuite (1), shwr, bath, tlt, heat, elec blkts, TV, video, clock radio, CD, refrig, cook fac, micro, elec frypan, d/wash, toaster, ldry, blkts, doonas, linen, pillows], w/mach, iron, iron brd, lounge firepl, bbq, cots, breakfast ingredients. **D ♦♦ $130 - $170, ◊ $40**, ch con, BC MC VI.

Other Accommodation

Camp Waterman, (Lodge), 25 McCarthy Rd, 4km N of PO, off Monbulk-Silvan Rd, ☎ 03 9756 6120, fax 03 9756 7979, 13 rms acc up to 8, [heat, linen reqd], shwr, tlt, rec rm, lounge (TV, video), bbq, ☎, non smoking rms. **D all meals ♦ $38.50, ◊ $38.50**, ch con, Minimum booking - 35 people.

(Rita Roberts Lodge), 3 rms acc up to 10, [heat, linen reqd], shwr, tlt, lounge (TV, video), cook fac, refrig. **D ♦ $50, ◊ $16.50**, ch con.

DANDENONG RANGES - MOUNT DANDENONG VIC 3767

Pop 1,149. (43km E Melbourne), See map on page 697, ref E4. Situated in the Dandenongs. Art Gallery, Bush Walking, Golf, Horse Riding, Scenic Drives, Tennis.

Self Catering Accommodation

★★★★ **Adeline**, (Cotg), No children's facilities, Cnr Mt Dandenong Tourist & Toorak Rds, ☎ 03 9751 2484, fax 03 9751 2784, 2 cotgs acc up to 2, (1 bedrm), [shwr, spa bath, tlt, a/c-cool, fan, heat, elec blkts, tel, TV, video (avail), clock radio, refrig, cook fac (1), cook fac ltd (1), blkts, linen, pillows], lounge, lounge firepl, bbq, breakfast ingredients. **BB ♦♦ $135 - $200**, BC MC VI.

★★★★ **Gumbirra Bed & Breakfast**, (Cotg), 1 Summerlea Rd, ☎ 03 9761 9656, fax 03 9728 8268, 1 cotg acc up to 6, (3 bedrm), [ensuite (1), shwr, spa bath (2), tlt, fan, cent heat, TV (2), video (2), CD, t/c mkg, refrig, cook fac, micro (2), ldry (in unit), blkts, linen, pillows], iron, iron brd, breakfast ingredients, non smoking property. **BB ♦♦ $155 - $400, ♦ $45, ♦♦ $840 - $910, ♦ $315**, ch con, AE BC DC MC VI.

B&B's/Guest Houses

★★★★★ **Linden Gardens Mount Dandenong**, (B&B), No children's facilities, 1383 Mt Dandenong Tourist Rd, 200m fr William Ricketts Sanctuary, ☎ 03 9751 1103, fax 03 9751 2241, (Multi-stry gr fl), 3 rms (3 suites) [ensuite, spa bath, hairdry, a/c-cool, cent heat, elec blkts, TV, video, clock radio, CD, t/c mkg, refrig, mini bar], iron, iron brd, bbq, non smoking property. **BB $225 - $355**, AE BC DC EFT MC VI.

★★★★☆ **Attic House Bed and Breakfast**, (B&B), No children's facilities, 1438 Mt Dandenong Tourist Rd, 1km N of PO, ☎ 03 9751 1397, fax 03 9751 2889, (2 stry gr fl), 3 rms [ensuite, spa bath (2), hairdry, c/fan, heat, elec blkts, TV, clock radio, t/c mkg], lounge (CD, stereo, video), refrig, non smoking property. **BB ♦ $122 - $250, ♦♦ $122 - $250, ♦ $75**, Dinner by arrangement. AE BC EFT MC VI,

Operator Comment: A simply outstanding B & B. Web: www.attichouse.com.au

★★★★☆ **Penrith Country House Retreat**, (B&B), Children by arrangement. 1413 Mt Dandenong Tourist Rd, Enter off Fordyce Rd, ☎ 03 9751 2391, fax 03 9751 2391, (2 stry gr fl), 4 rms [ensuite, spa bath (2), hairdry, a/c-cool, heat, elec blkts, TV, video (2), clock radio, t/c mkg, refrig, doonas], iron, iron brd, lounge (TV, cd), lounge firepl, pool, bbq. **BB ♦♦ $110 - $245**, AE BC DC MC VI.

★★★★☆ **Tavlock Retreat B & B**, (B&B), Toorak Rd, 1km N of PO, enter off Mt Dandenong Tourist Rd, ☎ 03 9751 2336, fax 03 9751 2336, 2 rms [ensuite, bath (1), spa bath (1), hairdry, a/c-cool, cent heat, elec blkts, clock radio], lounge (TV, CD player), t/c mkg shared, bbq, non smoking property. **BB ♦♦ $145 - $180**, Dinner by arrangement. AE BC DC MC VI.

★★★★ **Fern N Chestnut**, (B&B), No children's facilities, 1434 Mt Dandenong Tourist Rd, ☎ 03 9751 1064, fax 03 9751 1064, 4 rms (3 suites) [ensuite, spa bath, hairdry, fan, heat, elec blkts, TV, video, clock radio, radio (cassette) (1), CD (3), t/c mkg, refrig, doonas], lounge firepl (3), non smoking property. **BB ♦♦ $132**, AE BC MC VI.

DANDENONG RANGES - MOUNT EVELYN VIC 3796

Pop 7,995. (45km E Melbourne), See map on page 696, ref C5. Outer eastern residential suburb, situated on Olinda Creek. Tennis.

★★★★☆ **Quality Inn York on Lilydale Resort**, (M), Previously York on Lilydale Resort Cnr York & Swansea Rds, 3km SW of PO, ☎ 03 9736 4000, fax 03 9723 9922, (2 stry gr fl), 40 units [shwr, spa bath, tlt, hairdry, a/c, elec blkts, tel, TV, movie, clock radio, t/c mkg, refrig, toaster], ldry, conf fac, ⊠ (Thurs to Sat), bar (cocktail), pool-heated (solar), bbq, 24hr reception, rm serv, courtesy transfer, ☏, tennis, cots. **BLB ♦♦ $90 - $140, ♦ $12**, ch con, AE BC DC EFT MC MP VI.

DANDENONG RANGES - OLINDA VIC 3788

Part of DANDENONG RANGES region. Pop 1,358. (45km E Melbourne), See map on page 697, ref E4. Small township located at the top of Mt Dandenong. Bush Walking, Golf, Scenic Drives, Swimming (Pool).

Self Catering Accommodation

★★★★☆ **A Cottage in the Forest at Olinda**, (Cotg), 452 Mt Dandenong Tourist Rd, 600m S of PO, ☎ 03 9751 1700, fax 03 9751 2030, 1 cotg acc up to 3, [shwr, spa bath, tlt, hairdry, fan, c/fan, fire pl, cent heat, elec blkts, tel, TV, video, clock radio, t/c mkg, refrig, cook fac, micro, toaster, doonas, linen, pillows], iron, cots (avail). **D ♦♦ $230 - $265, ♦ $40, W $1,200 - $1,500**, AE BC DC EFT MC VI.

★★★★☆ **Aarcadia Cottages**, (Cotg), No children's facilities, 190 Falls Rd, 400m N of PO, off Monash Ave, ☎ 03 9751 1017, fax 03 9751 1817, 3 cotgs acc up to 2, (Studio & 1 bedrm), [shwr, spa bath, tlt, hairdry, a/c-cool (2), fan, c/fan (2), heat (wood), elec blkts, TV, video, clock radio, CD, t/c mkg, refrig, cook fac, micro, toaster, ldry, blkts, linen, pillows], iron, iron brd, bbq, c/park (undercover), breakfast ingredients, non smoking units. **BB ♦♦ $175 - $285**, BC MC VI.

★★★★☆ **Coach House Cottage**, (HU), 1564 Mt Dandenong Tourist Rd, ☎ 03 9751 1601, or 03 9751 2067, fax 03 9751 2995, (2 stry gr fl), 2 units acc up to 4, (1 & 2 bedrm), [shwr, spa bath (1), tlt, hairdry, a/c-cool (1), TV, video (1), clock radio, t/c mkg, refrig, cook fac, micro (1), d/wash (1), toaster, blkts, linen, pillows], iron, iron brd, lounge firepl, bbq, breakfast ingredients. **BB ♦♦ $137.50 - $275, ♦ $100**, ch con, BC EFT MC VI.

Operator Comment: Romantic, luxurious atmosphere with 4 poster bed, spa & breathtaking views. Stroll to restaurants, antique shops, galleries & local attractions.

★★★★☆ **Minack Cottage**, (Cotg), 20 Everest Cres, ☎ 03 9751 1196, 1 cotg acc up to 2, (1 bedrm), [shwr, bath (hip), tlt, hairdry, fan, heat, elec blkts, TV, video, clock radio, CD, t/c mkg, refrig, cook fac ltd, micro, toaster, blkts, linen, pillows], w/mach, dryer, iron, iron brd, lounge firepl, spa (heated), c/park (carport), breakfast ingredients, non smoking property. **D $150 - $240, W $600 - $750**, BC MC VI.

Operator Comment: Your cottage is set in beautiful gardens promising complete privacy & seclusion. 300m to restaurants & galleries. Mid week specials.

★★★★☆ **Port Phillip Penthouse**, (Apt), 9 Sunset Ave, 1km W of PO, ☎ 03 9751 1883, or 03 9751 2250, fax 03 9751 2254, (2 stry), 2 apts acc up to 4, (1 bedrm), [shwr, spa bath, tlt, hairdry, a/c-cool, heat, elec blkts, tel, TV, video, clock radio, CD, refrig, cook fac, micro, toaster, blkts, linen, pillows], iron, iron brd, c/park (1), breakfast ingredients, non smoking property. **BB ♦♦ $165 - $286, ♦ $45 - $50**, AE BC MC VI.

★★★★ **Annie Roe's**, (Cotg), 4 Monash Ave, ☎ 03 9751 1752, fax 03 9751 1377, 2 cotgs acc up to 2, (Studio), [shwr, spa bath (1), tlt, hairdry, a/c-cool, heat, elec blkts, TV, video (1), clock radio, CD, t/c mkg, refrig, cook fac ltd (1), micro, toaster, doonas, linen, pillows], bbq, breakfast ingredients, non smoking property. **BB ♦♦ $110 - $297**, BC MC VI.

Operator Comment: Million $$$ views. Walking distance to restaurants & shops. www.annieroes.citysearch.com.au

★★★★☆ **(Apartment Section)**, (2 stry), 1 apt acc up to 2, (1 bedrm), [shwr, spa bath, tlt, hairdry, a/c-cool, heat, elec blkts, TV, clock radio, CD, t/c mkg, refrig, cook fac ltd, micro, toaster, blkts, linen, pillows], breakfast ingredients, non smoking property. **D ♦♦ $143 - $214.50**.

★★★★ **Baytree House**, (Cotg), 11 Ida Gve, ☎ 03 9751 1836, fax 03 9751 2265, 1 cotg acc up to 6, (3 bedrm), [shwr, spa bath, tlt, hairdry, cent heat, elec blkts, TV, video, clock radio, refrig, cook fac, micro, toaster, ldry, blkts, doonas, linen, pillows], w/mach, dryer, iron, iron brd, lounge firepl, bbq, c/park (carport), breakfast ingredients, non smoking property. **BB ♦♦ $150 - $220, ♦ $20 - $50**, BC DC MC VI.

★★★★ **Cambridge Cottages**, (Cotg), 182 Falls Rd, Cnr Williams Rd, 2km E of PO, ☎ 03 9751 1178, fax 03 9751 2433, 2 cotgs acc up to 3, (Studio), [shwr, spa bath, tlt, hairdry, a/c, fan, heat, elec blkts, TV, video, clock radio, CD, refrig, cook fac ltd, micro, toaster, ldry, blkts, doonas, linen, pillows], iron, iron brd, bbq, breakfast ingredients, non smoking property. **BB ♦♦ $130 - $240, ♦ $50**, ch con, AE BC MC VI.

★★★★ **Candlelight Cottages**, (Cotg), 7 Monash Ave, 500m N of PO, ☎ 03 9751 2464, fax 03 9751 2464, 1 cotg acc up to 2, (1 bedrm), [shwr, spa bath, tlt, hairdry, a/c-cool, fan, cent heat, elec blkts, TV, video, clock radio, CD, t/c mkg, refrig, cook fac, micro, toaster, blkts, linen, pillows], iron, iron brd, lounge firepl, cots, breakfast ingredients, non smoking property. **BB ♦♦ $165 - $270, ♦ $40**, AE BC DC MC VI.

★★★★ **Forest Glade Olinda**, (Cotg), 82 Olinda-Monbulk Rd, 1km S of PO, ☎ 03 9751 2627, fax 03 9751 2040, (2 stry), 3 cotgs acc up to 2, (1 bedrm), [shwr, spa bath, tlt, hairdry, evap cool, cent heat, TV, video, CD, t/c mkg, refrig, cook fac ltd, micro, toaster], w/mach, dryer, iron, iron brd, lounge firepl, bbq, breakfast ingredients, non smoking property. **BB ♦♦ $175 - $260, ♦ $40**, AE BC MC VI.

★★★★ **Henty's Bed & Breakfast**, (Cotg), 228 Ridge Rd, ☎ 03 9737 0896, fax 03 9737 0895, 2 cotgs acc up to 2, (Studio), [shwr, spa bath, tlt, hairdry, a/c, elec blkts, tel, TV, video, clock radio, CD, t/c mkg, refrig, cook fac, toaster, blkts, doonas, linen, pillows], ldry, w/mach, dryer, lounge firepl, breakfast ingredients, non smoking property. **BB ♦♦ $130 - $200**, BC MC VI.

★★★☆ **Como Cottage Accommodation**, (Cotg), 1465 Mt Dandenong Tourist Rd, ☎ 03 9751 2264, fax 03 9751 2263, 4 cotgs acc up to 4, (1 & 2 bedrm), [shwr, bath (2), spa bath (4), tlt, hairdry, a/c (3), heat, elec blkts, TV, video, CD, t/c mkg, refrig, cook fac, blkts, doonas, linen, pillows], iron, lounge firepl, bbq, breakfast ingredients. BB ♛ $150 - $250, ⚲ $50, 2 cottages ★★★★. AE BC EFT MC VI,

Operator Comment: Enchanting Victorian style, private, self-contained cottages. Great views, walking distance to Olinda village. Visit our website: www.comocottages.com 20% discount midweek and multi-night.

B&B's/Guest Houses

★★★★☆ **A Country House**, (B&B), 13 Warwick Farm Rd, ☎ 03 9755 1783, fax 03 9755 3335, 1 rm [shwr, spa bath (2), tlt, fire pl, heat, elec blkts, TV, t/c mkg], lounge, non smoking property. BB ♛ $121 - $247, ♛ $170 - $265, 1 room ★★★★. BC MC VI.

★★★★☆ **The Loft in the Mill**, (B&B), 1 Harold St, 200m NW of PO, off Mt Dandenong Tourist Rd, ☎ 03 9751 1700, fax 03 9751 2030, (2 stry gr fl), 8 rms [ensuite, spa bath (6), a/c (6), heat, TV, clock radio, refrig, micro (3), toaster, doonas], ldry. BB ♛ $96 - $265, ⚲ $40, ch con, AE BC DC EFT MC VI.

★★★★ **(Apartment Section)**, 1 apt acc up to 4, (1 bedrm), [shwr, spa bath, tlt, a/c-cool, fan, heat, TV, clock radio, refrig, cook fac ltd, micro, d/wash, toaster, blkts, doonas, linen, pillows], ldry. D ♛ $170 - $265, ⚲ $40, ch con, Breakfast available.

★★★★ **Delvin Manor**, (B&B), Children by arrangement, 25 Monash Ave, ☎ 03 9751 1800, fax 03 9751 1829, (2 stry), 4 rms [ensuite (3), shwr, bath (1), tlt, cent heat, elec blkts], lounge (TV, video), lounge firepl, t/c mkg shared, refrig, non smoking property. BB ♛ $99 - $132, Other meals by arrangement. AE BC MC VI.

Arcadia Cottages

188-190 Falls Road,
Olinda,
"Heart of the Dandenongs"
Ph: 03 9751 1017
Mob: 0417 367 299
Fax: 03 9751 1817
AAA Tourism Rating ★★★★☆

Award–winning enchanting cottages hidden in acres of fragrant rambling gardens with ponds. Enjoy leafy views from large spas or hot tub. Cathedral ceilings with secret lofts. Soaring windows and conservatories of dappled sunlight. Rich furnishings create a stylish atmosphere.

500m to restaurants. We adjoin National Parks and Rhododendron Gardens.

Age "52 Goodweekends," Ch9 "Postcards" and "Getaway's Aus. Ten Most Romantic."

www.arcadiacottages.com.au
Email: arcadia@arcadiacottages.com.au

12724AG

The Cottage has a large oval spa, open fire.

A Cottage In The Forest

The most totally private old world cottage in the Dandenongs, nestled into native forest with spectacular gum trees and massive tree ferns.
Walk to two villages.

Ph (03) 9751 1700
Free Call: 1800 64 55 64

Reception at 1 Harold Street, Olinda Village
Operated by Loft In The Mill

12740AGB

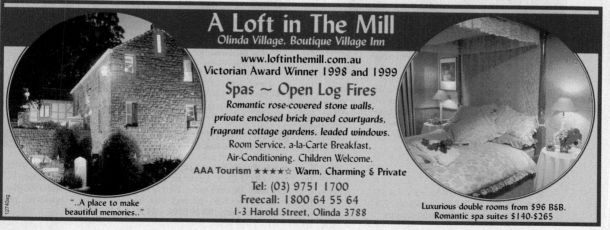

A Loft in The Mill
Olinda Village, Boutique Village Inn

www.loftinthemill.com.au
Victorian Award Winner 1998 and 1999

Spas ~ Open Log Fires
Romantic rose-covered stone walls, private enclosed brick paved courtyards, fragrant cottage gardens, leaded windows.
Room Service, a-la-Carte Breakfast,
Air-Conditioning. Children Welcome.
AAA Tourism ★★★★☆ Warm, Charming & Private

Tel: (03) 9751 1700
Freecall: 1800 64 55 64
1-3 Harold Street, Olinda 3788

"..A place to make beautiful memories.."

12740ag

Luxurious double rooms from $96 B&B.
Romantic spa suites $140-$265

DANDENONG RANGES - SASSAFRAS VIC 3787

Pop 1,495. (42km E Melbourne), See map on page 697, ref E4. Small township, located in the Dandenong Ranges. Bowls, Bush Walking, Croquet, Scenic Drives.

Self Catering Accommodation

★★★★☆ **A Cottage Amidst Tranquility**, (Cotg), 81 The Crescent, 2.9km S of PO, ☎ 03 9755 1773, fax 03 9755 2729, 4 cotgs acc up to 2, (Studio), [shwr, spa bath, tlt, hairdry, a/c, elec blkts, TV, video, clock radio, CD, refrig, cook fac, blkts, doonas, linen, pillows], ldry, dryer, iron, iron brd, lounge firepl, breakfast ingredients. BB ♦♦ **$190 - $330**, ⓦ **$40**, AE BC DC MC VI.

★★★★☆ **(Bed & Breakfast Section)**, 3 rms [ensuite, hairdry, heat, elec blkts, TV, video (1), clock radio, refrig (1), cook fac ltd (1), micro (1), doonas], lounge firepl, refrig, non smoking rms. BB ♦♦ **$130 - $245**, ⓦ **$30**.

★★★★☆ **Chudleigh Park of Sassafras**, (Cotg), 6 Chudleigh Cres, 300m W of PO, ☎ 03 9755 2320, fax 03 9755 2320, 3 cotgs acc up to 2, [shwr, spa bath, tlt, hairdry, a/c-cool, heat (gas log), TV, video, clock radio, t/c mkg, refrig, cook fac, cook fac ltd (2), micro, blkts, doonas, linen, pillows], ldry, coffee shop, bbq, breakfast ingredients, non smoking property. D ♦♦ **$175 - $255**, BC EFT MC VI.

★★★★☆ **Foxgloves at Sassafras**, (Cotg), 1 Gwenneth Cres, 1km SE of PO, ☎ 03 9755 3332, fax 03 9755 3331, 1 cotg acc up to 2, (1 bedrm), [shwr, spa bath, tlt, hairdry, a/c-cool, fan, heat (gas log), elec blkts, TV, video, clock radio, CD, refrig, cook fac ltd, micro, elec frypan, toaster, ldry (in unit), blkts, doonas, linen, pillows], w/mach, iron, iron brd, bbq, breakfast ingredients, non smoking property. BB ♦♦ **$165 - $245**, Min book long w/ends and Easter, BC MC VI,

Operator Comment: Ideal romantic retreat for two. Luxury and cleanliness assured.

★★★★☆ **Moulton Park Cottages**, (Cotg), Children by arrangement. 2 Cooloongatta Rd, ☎ 03 9755 2114, fax 03 9755 2005, 2 cotgs (1 bedrm), [shwr, spa bath, tlt, hairdry, fan, heat, elec blkts, TV, video, clock radio, CD, t/c mkg, refrig, cook fac, micro, toaster, blkts, linen, pillows], iron, iron brd, lounge firepl, bbq, bicycle, cots, breakfast ingredients. BB ♦♦ **$160**, BC MC VI.

★★★★☆ **Wicklow Heights Cottage**, (Cotg), 273 Mt Dandenong Tourist Rd, ☎ 03 9751 2404, fax 03 9754 5858, 1 cotg acc up to 4, (2 bedrm), [shwr, spa bath, tlt, hairdry, a/c, cent heat, elec blkts, tel (local), TV, video, clock radio, t/c mkg, refrig, cook fac, micro, elec frypan, toaster, ldry, blkts, doonas, linen, pillows], w/mach, dryer, iron, iron brd, lounge firepl, bbq, cots, non smoking property. D ♦♦ **$120 - $220**, ⓦ **$60**, W **$700 - $1,000**, ch con, BC MC VI.

B&B's/Guest Houses

★★★★ **Fleurbaix B & B**, (B&B), 286 Mt Dandenong Tourist Rd, ☎ 03 9755 1185, fax 03 9755 1185, 1 rm [ensuite, spa bath, hairdry, fan, heat (gas log), cent heat, elec blkts, TV, video, clock radio, CD, t/c mkg, refrig, doonas], non smoking property. BB ♦♦ **$100 - $242**, AE BC DC MC VI.

★★★★ **(Cottage Section)**, 1 cotg (Studio), [shwr, spa bath, tlt, hairdry, heat (wood), elec blkts, TV, video, clock radio, CD, t/c mkg, refrig, cook fac ltd, micro, elec frypan, toaster, blkts, doonas, linen, pillows], iron, iron brd, breakfast ingredients. BB ♦♦ **$100 - $242**.

Charma, (B&B), 75 The Crescent, 2.8km S of PO, ☎ 03 9751 1496, fax 03 9755 1491, (2 stry), 2 rms [shwr, bath (1), tlt, hairdry, fan, fire pl (1), heat, elec blkts, tel, TV, video, t/c mkg, refrig, cook fac (1), micro, toaster], lounge, bbq, cots, non smoking rms. BB ♦ **$121**, ♦♦ **$143 - $165**, ⓦ **$44**, ch con, AE BC MC VI, (Rating under review).

DANDENONG RANGES - SELBY VIC 3159

Pop Part of Yarra Ranges, (41km E Melbourne), See map on page 697, ref E4. Township in Dandenong Ranges. Bush Walking, Horse Riding.

★★★★☆ **Selby's Serendipity Homestay**, (B&B), 11 Horizon Rd, 2.2km S of general store, off Temple Rd, ☎ 03 9754 4820, fax 03 9754 4820, 2 rms (1 suite) [shwr, tlt, hairdry, a/c, heat, tel, TV, video, clock radio, CD, t/c mkg, refrig, cook fac, micro, elec frypan, doonas], cots, non smoking rms. BB ♦ **$75 - $120**, ♦♦ **$100 - $185**, ⓦ **$40 - $50**, ch con, BC MC VI.

DANDENONG RANGES - SHERBROOKE VIC 3789

Pop 570. (42km NE Melbourne), See map on page 697, ref E4.

Hotels/Motels

★★★ **Poets Lane Motel**, (M), 13 Sherbrooke Rd, Cnr Poets La, adjacent to Sherbrooke Forest, ☎ 03 9755 2044, fax 03 9755 2089, 21 units (5 suites) [shwr, spa bath (5), tlt, hairdry (3), a/c-cool, a/c (3), c/fan, heat, elec blkts, tel, TV, video-fee, clock radio, t/c mkg, refrig, micro (3), toaster (3)], iron brd, conf fac, courtesy transfer, ✆, non smoking units. RO **$69 - $115**, Suite RO **$139 - $239**, 3 suites ★★★★. AE BC DC EFT MC VI.

Self Catering Accommodation

★★★★☆ **Cottages of Sherbrooke**, (Cotg), 35 Sherbrooke Lodge Rd, ☎ 03 9755 1912, 2 cotgs acc up to 6, (1 & 2 bedrm), [shwr, bath (2), spa bath (1), tlt, hairdry, fan, heat, elec blkts, cable tv, video, clock radio, CD, t/c mkg, refrig, cook fac, micro, d/wash (1), toaster, ldry (in unit) (1), blkts, doonas, linen, pillows], bbq, breakfast ingredients, non smoking property. D ♦ **$160 - $180**, ♦♦ **$160 - $180**.

DANDENONG RANGES - SILVAN VIC 3795

Pop 792. (48km E Melbourne), See map on page 696, ref C5.

★★★ **Wandin Valley Cottage**, (Cotg), 12 Foch Rd, ☎ 03 9737 9373, fax 03 9737 9373, 1 cotg acc up to 6, (2 bedrm), [shwr, tlt, heat, elec blkts, TV, clock radio, CD, t/c mkg, refrig, cook fac, micro, toaster, blkts, doonas, linen, pillows], iron, iron brd, breakfast ingredients, non smoking property. BB ♦♦ **$100 - $155**, ⓦ **$22**, BC MC VI.

DANDENONG RANGES - UPWEY VIC 3158

Pop 6,790. (36km E Melbourne), See map on page 697, ref E4. Residential area situated in the Dandenong Ranges. Bush Walking, Scenic Drives, Tennis.

B&B's/Guest Houses

★★★★☆ **A Dandenong Ranges Retreat - Talanoa**, (B&B), 6 Day St, 1.2km NE of PO, ☎ 03 9752 5407, fax 03 9752 5457, (2 stry gr fl), 2 rms (2 suites) [ensuite (1), shwr, spa bath (1), tlt, hairdry, evap cool (1), a/c (1), c/fan, cent heat, elec blkts, TV (1), clock radio, CD, t/c mkg, refrig, cook fac ltd, micro], lounge (TV, video, stereo), lounge firepl, bbq, c/park (undercover), cots, non smoking property. **BLB** ♦♦ **$90 - $160,** ♦ **$40,** ♦♦ **$610 - $750,** ch con, Dinner by arrangement. BC MC VI.

★★★★☆ **Mast Gully Gardens**, (B&B), 20 Dealbata Rd, ☎ 03 9752 5275, fax 03 9752 6952, 1 rm (1 suite) [shwr, bath, tlt, hairdry, evap cool, cent heat, elec blkts, TV, video, clock radio, CD, t/c mkg, refrig, toaster], iron, iron brd, bbq, non smoking property. **BLB** ♦ **$90 - $110,** ♦♦ **$110 - $130,** AE BC DC MC VI.

End of Dandenong Ranges Region

DARGO VIC 3862

Pop Nominal, (323km E Melbourne), See map on pages 694/695, ref H6. Agricultural district. Fuel available limited hours. Bush Walking, Fishing, Gold Prospecting, Scenic Drives, Shooting, Swimming (River), Tennis.

Self Catering Accommodation

★ **Dargo Mill Tavern**, (Cotg), Lower Dargo Rd, 1.5km S of general store, ☎ 03 5140 1280, fax 03 5140 1280, 3 cotgs acc up to 12, (3 & 4 bedrm), [shwr, bath (1), tlt (external), heat (gas), t/c mkg, cook fac, toaster, doonas, linen, pillows], ldry, w/mach, dryer, ⊠, cots. **D** ♦ **$30,** ♦♦ **$55,** ♦ **$30,** ch con, 2 cottages not listed or rated, Breakfast available, BC EFT MC VI.

B&B's/Guest Houses

★★★☆ **Dargo Valley Winery & Wine Bar Restaurant**, (B&B), Lower Dargo Rd, 500m S of PO, ☎ 03 5140 1228, fax 03 5140 1388, 1 rm [ensuite, fan, heat, clock radio], ldry, lounge (TV), ⊠, t/c mkg shared, refrig, bbq, cots, non smoking rms. **BB** ♦ **$45,** ♦♦ **$60,** ch con, AE BC DC VI,

Operator Comment: Take a step back in time. A great place to relax & sample country hospitality. Enjoy our winery & licensed restaurant. Package deals available.

(Bunkhouse Section), 1 bunkhouse acc up to 6, [ensuite, shwr, fan, TV, clock radio, t/c mkg, refrig, toaster, blkts, linen, pillows]. **BB** ♦ **$35,** **D** ♦ **$20.**

DARLINGTON VIC 3271

Pop 440. (209km W Melbourne), See map on pages 694/695, ref C7. Located in an area noted for wool and beef production. Scenic Drives, Swimming (River), Tennis.

Hotels/Motels

★☆ **Elephant Bridge Hotel**, (LH), Classified by National Trust, Hamilton Hwy, ☎ 03 5597 9231, (2 stry), 5 rms [elec blkts, clock radio (3)], ⊠, t/c mkg shared, bbq, ☎. **BB** ♦ **$30,** ♦♦ **$60,** BC EFT MC VI.

DARTMOUTH VIC 3701

Pop 514. (424km NE Melbourne), See map on pages 694/695, ref J5. Established in 1972 to build dam and small power station. Rather isolated but offering attractive recreational facilities, the 180m wall is Australia's highest. Boating, Bush Walking, Fishing, Golf, Horse Riding, Sailing, Scenic Drives, Tennis. See also Mitta Mitta.

Hotels/Motels

★★☆ **Rainbow Lodge Motel**, (M), Banimboola Rd, 100m W of PO, ☎ 02 6072 4233, fax 02 6072 4220, 24 units [shwr, tlt, a/c-cool (14), a/c (10), heat, elec blkts, TV, clock radio, t/c mkg, refrig, toaster], ldry, pool, sauna, spa, bbq, cots, non smoking rms (8). **RO** ♦ **$55 - $65,** ♦♦ **$60 - $70,** ♦ **$10.50,** ch con, 8 units ★★★. BC DC MC VI.

Self Catering Accommodation

★★☆ **Dartmouth Alpine Retreat**, (Cotg), 1 Murtagh Pl, ☎ 02 6072 4511, fax 02 6072 4293, 10 cotgs acc up to 8, (3 bedrm), [shwr, bath (8), tlt, c/fan, heat, elec blkts, TV, refrig, cook fac, elec frypan, toaster, ldry, blkts, linen, pillows], w/mach, cots-fee. **D** **$80 - $140,** AE BC DC EFT MC VI.

DAYLESFORD VIC 3460

Pop 3,300. (109km NW Melbourne), See map on page 696, ref A4. Area known as the spa centre of Australia with some 20 mineral springs with in 10km of the town. Bowls, Bush Walking, Fishing, Golf, Scenic Drives, Swimming (Pool, Lake), Tennis.

Hotels/Motels

★★★★ **The Lakes Motel Daylesford**, (M), 1 King St, 250m S of PO, ☎ 03 5348 2763, fax 03 5348 2763, 4 units [shwr, tlt, hairdry, a/c, elec blkts, TV, clock radio, t/c mkg, refrig, micro (1), toaster], non smoking units (4). **RO** ♦ **$90 - $110,** ♦ **$25 - $35,** BC MC VI.

★★★☆ **Central Springs Inn**, (M), Classified by National Trust, Cnr Camp & Howe Sts, ☎ 03 5348 3134, or 03 5348 3388, fax 03 5348 3967, (2 stry gr fl), 26 units [elec blkts, tel, TV, clock radio], conf fac, ⊠, bar (cocktail), sauna-fee, spa-fee, bbq. **RO** ♦ **$71.50,** ♦♦ **$104.50,** ♦ **$27.50,** AE BC DC EFT MC VI.

★★★☆ **Royal Hotel Daylesford**, (LH), Cnr Vincent & Albert Sts (Midland Hwy), 200m N of PO, ☎ 03 5348 2205, fax 03 5348 3987, (2 stry), 10 rms [shwr, spa bath (7), tlt, hairdry, a/c (4), c/fan, cent heat, elec blkts, tel, TV, clock radio, t/c mkg, refrig, toaster], ldry, ⊠, c/park. **BLB** ♦ **$75 - $190,** ♦♦ **$100 - $195,** ♦ **$30,** AE BC EFT MC VI.

★★★ **Daylesford Motel**, (M), 54 Albert St (Midland Hwy), 600m W of PO, ☎ 03 5348 2029, fax 03 5348 2029, 10 units [shwr, tlt, fan, heat, elec blkts, TV, clock radio, t/c mkg, refrig, toaster], c/park (carport) (8), cots-fee. **RO** ♦ **$54 - $70,** ♦♦ **$66 - $77,** ♦ **$13,** ch con, BC MC VI.

★ **Walshs Daylesford Hotel**, (LH), 2 Burke Sq, ☎ 03 5348 2335, fax 03 5348 1083, (2 stry), 9 rms [heat, elec blkts], lounge (TV), ⊠, t/c mkg shared, refrig, ☎. **BLB** ♦ **$30 - $55,** Light breakfast only available.

Self Catering Accommodation

★★★★☆ **Blue Poppy Cottage**, (Cotg), 71 West St, ☎ 03 5348 3577, fax 03 5348 3577, 1 cotg acc up to 4, (2 bedrm), [shwr, bath, tlt, hairdry, c/fan, heat, elec blkts, tel (local), TV, video, CD, refrig, cook fac, micro, toaster, ldry (in unit), blkts, doonas, linen, pillows], iron, iron brd, lounge firepl, bbq, c/park (carport), cots (avail), non smoking property. **D** ♦♦ **$120 - $180,** ♦ **$30,** W **$630.**

★★★☆ **Court House Villas**, (Apt), 11 Camp St, 500m NE of PO, ☎ 03 5348 1592, fax 03 5348 1593, (2 stry), 9 apts acc up to 4, (2 bedrm), [shwr, spa bath, tlt, hairdry, c/fan, heat, elec blkts, tel (local), TV, video, clock radio, CD, t/c mkg, refrig, cook fac, micro, d/wash, toaster, ldry (in unit), doonas, linen, pillows], w/mach, dryer, iron, iron brd, pool indoor heated (saltwater), spa (heated), steam rm, bbq (covered), ✆. D ♦♦ **$150 - $220**, ⏢ **$25 - $40**, AE BC DC EFT MC VI.

★★★★ **Daylesford Lake Villas**, (Cotg), 110 West St, 700m W of PO, ☎ 03 5348 3722, fax 03 5348 3777, (2 stry gr fl), 2 cotgs acc up to 5, (Studio & 2 bedrm), [shwr, spa bath, tlt, hairdry, a/c, heat (wood), cent heat, elec blkts, TV, video, clock radio, refrig, cook fac, micro, d/wash, toaster, doonas, linen, pillows], iron, iron brd, bbq, c/park (carport) (1), non smoking property. D ♦♦ **$215 - $230**, ⏢ **$50**, W ♦♦ **$1,040 - $1,120**, ⏢ **$77.50**, Min book long w/ends, AE BC DC MC VI.

★★★★ **Forget-Me-Not Garden Cottages**, (Cotg), 9 Stanhope St, 1km E of PO, ☎ 03 5348 3507, fax 03 5348 1941, 1 cotg acc up to 2, (1 bedrm), [shwr, spa bath, tlt, hairdry, fan, heat, elec blkts, TV, video, clock radio, CD, refrig, micro, elec frypan, toaster, blkts, linen, pillows], ldry, iron, iron brd, lounge firepl, bbq, breakfast ingredients, non smoking property. BB ♦♦ **$120 - $170**, BC MC VI.

★★★★ **Gloriette**, (Cotg), 7 Camp St, 600m NE of PO, ☎ 03 5348 1498, 1 cotg acc up to 8, (4 bedrm), [shwr (2), bath (hip), tlt (2), hairdry, a/c (lounge), c/fan (lounge), heat, elec blkts, tel (local), TV, clock radio, refrig, cook fac, micro, d/wash, toaster, ldry, blkts, linen, pillows], iron, iron brd, lounge firepl, bbq, c/park (carport), cots. D ♦♦ **$125**, W **$495 - $715**, ch con, Min book applies, BC MC VI.

★★★★ **Lake Cottage**, (Cotg), 31 Leggatt St, ☎ 03 9596 8801, (Multi-stry gr fl), 1 cotg acc up to 6, (3 bedrm), [shwr, bath, tlt, hairdry, fan, cent heat, elec blkts, tel ((local calls)), TV, video, clock radio, CD, refrig, cook fac, micro, elec frypan, d/wash, toaster, ldry, blkts, doonas, linen, pillows], w/mach, dryer, iron, iron brd, lounge firepl, bbq, c/park (carport). D **$200**, W **$1,400**, Min book applies.

★★★★ **Possum Cottage on the Lake**, (Cotg), 33 Leggatt St, 1km S of PO, ☎ 03 5348 3173, 1 cotg acc up to 6, (3 bedrm), [ensuite, shwr, bath, tlt, hairdry, fan, heat, elec blkts, tel (local), TV, video, clock radio, CD, refrig, cook fac, micro, toaster, ldry, blkts, linen, pillows], w/mach, iron, iron brd, lounge firepl, bbq, cots, breakfast ingredients. BLB ♦♦♦ **$140 - $400**, **$900**, AE BC DC EFT MC VI.

★★★★ **Tahara Cottage**, (Cotg), 41 Leggatt St, 1km S of PO, ☎ 03 5348 1255, fax 03 5348 3606, (2 stry gr fl), 1 cotg acc up to 6, (2 bedrm), [shwr, bath, tlt, hairdry, fan, heat, elec blkts, tel, TV, video, clock radio, CD, refrig, cook fac, micro, toaster, ldry, blkts, doonas, linen, pillows], w/mach, iron, iron brd, lounge firepl, bbq, non smoking property. D **$190**, W **$800**, Min book applies.

★★★★ **Tarascon Village**, (Cotg), 530 Porcupine Ridge Rd, 8.5km NE of PO, ☎ 03 5348 7773, fax 03 5348 7888, (2 stry gr fl), 6 cotgs acc up to 8, (2 & 4 bedrm), [shwr, bath (1), spa bath (2), tlt, hairdry, heat (5), video, clock radio, CD, t/c mkg, refrig, cook fac (1), cook fac ltd (5), micro, d/wash (1), toaster, blkts, doonas, linen, pillows], ldry, iron, iron brd, conf fac, lounge firepl (1), ✉, spa, bbq, golf (Par 3), non smoking property. BLB ♦♦ **$176 - $220**, ⏢ **$33 - $44**, ♦♦ **$550 - $880**, ⏢ **$220**, Studio unit not rated. BC MC VI.

★★★☆ **Bergamo**, (Apt), 51 Woolnoughs Rd Porcupine Ridge via, Daylesford 3461, 9.5km NE of PO, ☎ 03 5348 7572, (2 stry gr fl), 2 apts acc up to 4, (Studio & 2 bedrm), [shwr, tlt, hairdry, a/c (1), fan (1), heat, TV, video, clock radio (1), CD, t/c mkg, refrig, cook fac (1), cook fac ltd (1), micro, elec frypan (1), toaster, ldry (in unit) (1), doonas, linen, pillows], iron, iron brd, lounge firepl, bbq, c/park (carport), breakfast ingredients, non smoking property. BB ♦♦ **$90 - $175**, ⏢ **$25**, 1 apartment ★★★★.

★★★☆ **Burnt Hill Farm**, (Cotg), (Farm), Brandy Hot Rd, Egastown 3461, 7.6km W of Daylesford, off Basalt Rd, ☎ 03 5348 2069, fax 03 5348 2069, 1 cotg acc up to 9, (3 bedrm), [shwr, bath, tlt, hairdry, fan, heat (pot belly), elec blkts, TV, video, refrig, cook fac, micro, elec frypan, toaster, ldry, linen reqd-fee], iron, iron brd, lounge firepl, bbq, cots. D ♦♦ **$80 - $370**, ⏢ **$40**, W **$520 - $640**.

★★★☆ **Porcupine Ridge Estate**, (Cotg), (Farm), Porcupine Ridge Rd, Daylesford 3461, 14km N of PO, ☎ 03 5348 7602, or 03 5348 7815, fax 03 5348 7816, 1 cotg acc up to 4, (2 bedrm), [shwr, spa bath, tlt, TV, clock radio, CD, refrig, cook fac, micro, toaster, blkts, linen, pillows], lounge firepl, bbq, tennis, breakfast ingredients. BB ♦♦ **$260**, ⏢ **$50**, AE MC VI.

★★★ **(Cottage Section)**, 2 cotgs acc up to 2, (1 bedrm), [shwr, spa bath, tlt, fire pl, heat, TV, clock radio, CD, refrig, cook fac, micro, toaster, blkts, linen, pillows], bbq, breakfast ingredients. BB ♦♦ **$180**.

★★★☆ **Wombat Flat Cottages**, (Cotg), 9 Jubilee Lake Rd, 800m S of PO, ☎ 03 5348 2651, fax 03 5348 3833, 2 cotgs acc up to 4, (2 bedrm), [shwr, spa bath, tlt, hairdry, fan, heat, elec blkts, TV, video, clock radio, t/c mkg, refrig, cook fac, micro, toaster, ldry, blkts, doonas, linen, pillows], w/mach, dryer (1), iron, iron brd, lounge firepl, bbq, cots, breakfast ingredients. BLB ♦♦ **$120 - $165**, ⏢ **$15**, ♦♦ **$600**, ⏢ **$105**, 1 cottage ★★★★, Min book all holiday times, BC MC VI.

★★★ **Lake Top Cottage**, (Cotg), 2 Tessiers Rd, ☎ 03 5224 1744, 1 cotg acc up to 5, (3 bedrm), [shwr, bath, tlt, fan, elec blkts, tel (local), TV, clock radio, refrig, cook fac, micro, toaster, ldry, doonas, linen, pillows], ldry, iron, iron brd, c/park (carport). D ♦♦ **$95 - $120**, W ♦♦ **$400 - $450**, BC MC VI.

★★★ **Oaktree Cottage (Daylesford)**, (Cotg), 2 Central Springs Rd, 1.1km E of PO, ☎ 03 5348 1255, fax 03 5348 3606, 1 cotg acc up to 2, (1 bedrm), [shwr, bath, tlt, fan, heat, elec blkts, TV, video, clock radio, CD, refrig, cook fac, micro, toaster, ldry (in unit), blkts, doonas, linen, pillows], w/mach, iron, iron brd, non smoking property. D **$120**, W **$500** Min book applies, AE BC DC EFT MC VI.

★★★ **Trewhella Farm**, (Cotg), 50 Cantillons Rd, Musk 3461, 10km E of Daylesford, ☎ 03 9808 4489, fax 03 9808 4489, 1 cotg acc up to 6, (3 bedrm), [shwr, bath (hip), tlt, c/fan, heat, tel, TV, video, clock radio, refrig, cook fac, micro, elec frypan, toaster, ldry, blkts, doonas, linen, pillows], w/mach, iron, iron brd, bbq, cots, non smoking property. D ♦♦ **$88 - $110**, ⏢ **$11**, W ♦♦ **$440 - $550**, ⏢ **$55**.

★★★ **Willowbrook Cottages**, (Cotg), 319 Trentham Rd, Daylesford 3461, 4.8km E of PO, ☎ 03 5348 2219, fax 03 9427 0788, 7 cotgs acc up to 6, (2 bedrm), [shwr, bath (hip), tlt, fan, c/fan, elec blkts, TV, video, clock radio, CD, refrig, cook fac, micro, toaster, blkts, doonas, linen, pillows], rec rm, lounge firepl, pool (saltwater), bbq, tennis, breakfast ingredients. D ♦♦ **$120 - $297**, ⏢ **$55**, W **$858**, Pets welcome by arrangement. Min book applies, BC MC VI,

Operator Comment: www.willowbrookcottages.com Families & Pets most welcome.

★★☆ **Wattleglen Cottage**, (Cotg), 1549 Ballan Rd, 2.5km S of PO, ☎ 03 5348 1255, fax 03 5348 3606, 1 cotg acc up to 6, (3 bedrm), [shwr, bath, tlt, c/fan, heat, elec blkts, tel (local), TV, video, clock radio, CD, refrig, micro, toaster, blkts, doonas, linen, pillows], w/mach, dryer, iron, iron brd, lounge firepl. D **$160**, W **$700**, Min book applies, AE BC DC EFT MC VI.

B&B's/Guest Houses

★★★★☆ **Ambleside on the Lake**, (B&B), No children's facilities, 15 Leggatt St, 700m SW of PO, overlooking Lake Daylesford, ☎ 03 5348 2691, fax 03 5348 4532, 3 rms [ensuite, hairdry, fan, heat, elec blkts, clock radio, t/c mkg], iron, iron brd, lounge (TV, video,cd), lounge firepl, non smoking property. **BB** ♦ **$110 - $170,** ♦♦ **$175 - $215,** ◊ **$55,** Min book long w/ends, AE BC DC MC VI,

Operator Comment: Absolute lake frontage, stunning views and Gourmet breakfast. Gift vouchers,"Special Occasion" & "Massage" Packages available.

★★★★☆ **Barbara's on Bridport**, (B&B), 4 Bridport St, 500m N of PO, ☎ 03 5348 2448, fax 03 5348 2630, 2 rms [ensuite, hairdry, fan, cent heat, elec blkts, clock radio], lounge (TV, cd), lounge firepl, t/c mkg shared, non smoking property. **BB** ♦ **$95 - $165,** ♦♦ **$115 - $190,** AE BC MC VI.

★★★★☆ **La Piccola Pensione**, (B&B), 75 Vincent St Nth, 1km N of PO, ☎ 03 5348 4014, fax 03 5348 4014, (2 stry gr fl), 2 rms [ensuite, bath (1), spa bath (1), hairdry, a/c-cool, heat, elec blkts, TV, video, clock radio, CD, t/c mkg, refrig], bbq, non smoking property. **BB** ♦♦ **$100 - $150,** Min book applies, BC MC VI.

★★★★☆ **Lake House Restaurant & Accommodation**, (GH), King St, 600m S of PO, overlooking Lake Daylesford, ☎ 03 5348 3329, fax 03 5348 3995, 22 rms [shwr, bath (14), tlt, a/c (12), c/fan, heat, elec blkts, tel, cable tv, clock radio, t/c mkg, refrig (21), mini bar, doonas], iron, iron brd, lounge (TV), conf fac, lounge firepl, ⊠, pool, sauna, spa, ☎, tennis, non smoking property. **BB** ♦♦ **$235 - $360,** **DBB** ♦♦ **$355 - $505,** AE BC DC MC VI.

★★★★☆ **Paganetti's Country House**, (B&B), 80 Patterson St, 1.5km S of PO, ☎ 03 5348 3892, fax 03 5348 4262, (2 stry gr fl), 3 rms [ensuite (2), shwr (1), bath, tlt (1), hairdry, cent heat, elec blkts, clock radio], iron, iron brd, lounge (TV), lounge firepl, spa, t/c mkg shared, bbq. **BB** ♦ **$60 - $180,** ♦♦ **$120 - $190,** 1 room ★★★★. BC MC VI.

★★★★ **(Cottage Section)**, 1 cotg acc up to 2, (1 bedrm), [shwr, spa bath, tlt, hairdry, a/c, heat, elec blkts, TV, video, clock radio, CD, refrig, cook fac ltd, micro, elec frypan, blkts, linen, pillows], lounge firepl, bbq, breakfast ingredients. **BB** ♦♦ **$200 - $250.**

AAA
TOURISM
Special Rates

★★★★☆ **Pendower House**, (B&B), No children's facilities, 10 Bridport St, 500m N of PO, ☎ 03 5348 1535, fax 03 5348 1545, 3 rms [ensuite, hairdry, cent heat, elec blkts], lounge (TV, cd player), lounge firepl, t/c mkg shared, refrig, bbq, non smoking property. **BB** ♦ **$110 - $150,** ♦♦ **$150 - $195,** AE BC DC MC VI.

★★★★ **The Station Guest House**, (GH), 15 Raglan St, ☎ 03 5348 1591, fax 03 5348 1459, 8 rms [ensuite, bath (5), hairdry, cent heat, elec blkts, TV, clock radio], lounge (cableTV, video, stereo), conf fac, spa (heated), t/c mkg shared, refrig, bbq, ☎, plygr, non smoking property. **BLB** ♦ **$65 - $95,** ♦♦ **$105 - $165,** ◊ **$30,** ch con, Dinner by arrangement. Min book applies, BC MC VI.

★★★☆ **(Homestead Section)**, 4 rms [hairdry, fire pl (2), cent heat, clock radio], lounge (cable TV, video), lounge firepl, cook fac, non smoking rms. **BLB** ♦ **$70 - $100,** ♦♦ **$105 - $165.**

★★★☆ **Highdale House Bed & Breakfast**, (B&B), 8 Malmsbury Rd (Midland Hwy), 1km N of PO, ☎ 03 5348 4012, (2 stry), 2 rms [shwr, bath, tlt, hairdry, c/fan, heat, elec blkts, doonas], lounge (TV, video, cd), t/c mkg shared, bbq, bicycle, non smoking property. **BB** ♦♦ **$121 - $143,** BC MC VI.

★★★☆ **Rose of Daylesford**, (B&B), 58 Raglan St (Midland Hwy), 700m NE of PO, ☎ 03 5348 1482, fax 03 5348 4884, 4 rms [ensuite (2), spa bath (3), hairdry, fire pl (in bedrooms), heat, elec blkts, clock radio, t/c mkg], lounge (TV, video, cd). **BB** ♦♦ **$88 - $198,**

Operator Comment: Budget Accommodation available, ideal for singles or groups. $38.00 mid week, $45.00 Sat nt only. www.netconnect.com.au/~tulku_r

★★★ **35 Hill Street**, (B&B), 35 Hill St, 700m NE of PO, ☎ 03 5348 3878, fax 03 5348 2883, 3 rms [fan, fire pl (1), cent heat, elec blkts, doonas], lounge (TV, stereo), lounge firepl, spa, t/c mkg shared, bbq. **BB** ♦ **$55,** ♦♦ **$88.**

Other Accommodation

Boomerang Holiday Ranch, (Lodge), (Farm), Ranch Rd, 1.9km W of PO, ☎ 03 5348 2525, fax 03 5348 2525, 10 rms acc up to 4, (Bunk Rooms), [cent heat, linen reqd], ldry, rec rm, lounge (TV), t/c mkg shared, refrig, bbq, plygr. **D** all meals ♦ **$95,** ◊ **$95,** ch con, Group accommodation - tariff includes farm activities. BC MC VI.

(Bunkhouse Section), 2 bunkhouses acc up to 16, [linen reqd]. **D** all meals ♦ **$95,** ◊ **$95,** ch con, Group accommodation - tariff includes farm activities.

DEANS MARSH VIC 3235

Pop 80. (132km SW Melbourne), See map on pages 694/695, ref D7. Agricultural township. Tennis.

Self Catering Accommodation

★★★☆ **Cootamundra Retreat**, (Cotg), (Farm), 70 Bambra Cemetery Rd, off Deans Marsh - Lorne Rd, ☎ 03 9584 1325, or 03 9570 3095, 1 cotg acc up to 5, (3 bedrm), [ensuite, shwr, bath (hip), tlt, heat (wood), TV, video, clock radio, refrig, cook fac, micro, toaster, ldry, linen reqd], bbq, c/park (carport). **D** **$90 - $100, W** **$500 - $600.**

★★★☆ **King Parrot Holiday Cabins**, (Cotg), Dunse Trk, Pennyroyal 3235, 8km S of PO, off Pennyroyal Valley Rd, ☎ 03 5236 3372, fax 03 5236 3332, (2 stry gr fl), 6 cotgs acc up to 10, (1, 2, 3 & 4 bedrm - mudbrick.), [shwr, bath (2), tlt, a/c (1), c/fan, heat, TV, video, clock radio, CD, refrig, cook fac (1), cook fac ltd, micro, toaster, ldry (in unit) (1)], ldry, conf fac, bbq, c/park (carport), cots. **D** **$135 - $176,** ch con, 1 cabin ★★★★, Min book applies, BC MC VI.

★★★ **Farm Cottage Holidays**, (Cotg), 225 Pennyroyal Valley Rd, ☎ 03 5236 3249, or 03 5236 3445, 4 cotgs acc up to 8, (2 & 3 bedrm), [shwr, bath, spa bath (1), tlt, c/fan, heat (wood), elec blkts, TV, video, clock radio, refrig, cook fac, micro, toaster, doonas, linen reqd-fee, pillows], w/mach, bbq, plygr, Pets allowed. **D** ♦♦ **$60 - $100,** ◊ **$20,** ch con.

★★★ **Hidden Valley Holiday Cabins**, 65 Pennyroyal Station Rd, ☎ 03 5236 3424, 5 cabins acc up to 6, [shwr, tlt, heat, TV, video, refrig, cook fac, ldry, blkts, linen, pillows], rec rm, bbq, plygr, golf (Chip & Putt). **D** **$50 - $100.**

★★★ **Pennyroyal Raspberry Farm**, (Cotg), 115 Division Rd, Murroon 3243, 10km SW of Deans Marsh, ☎ 03 5236 3238, 2 cotgs acc up to 2, [shwr, tlt, heat, wood heat (gas) (1), elec blkts, clock radio, refrig, cook fac, micro (1), toaster, blkts, linen, pillows], lounge firepl (1), bbq, non smoking property. **BB** ♦ **$80,** ♦♦ **$90.**

★★★ **Pennyroyal Valley Cottages**, (Cotg), Pennyroyal Valley Rd, 7km S of PO, ☎ 03 5236 3201, fax 03 5236 3271, 3 cotgs acc up to 16, (3, 4 & 5 bedrm), [shwr, tlt, heat (wood), CD, refrig, cook fac, micro, toaster, ldry (in unit), linen reqd-fee], bbq, golf, tennis. **D** ◊ **$16.50 - $35,** Min book applies.

DEDERANG VIC 3691

Pop Part of Wodonga, (352km NE Melbourne), See map on pages 694/695, ref H5. Pastoral township on Kiewa Valley Hwy.

Self Catering Accommodation

★★★★ **Edelweiss Cottage B & B**, (Cotg), Speers La, 5km N of General Store, off Kiewa Valley Hwy, ☎ 02 6028 9335, fax 03 6028 9089, 1 cotg acc up to 5, (2 bedrm), [shwr, tlt, hairdry, c/fan, heat (wood), elec blkts, TV, video, clock radio, CD, refrig, cook fac, micro, toaster, ldry, blkts, doonas, linen, pillows], w/mach, iron, iron brd, bbq, breakfast ingredients. **BB** ♦♦ **$85 - $95,** ◊ **$20.**

DERRINALLUM VIC 3325

Pop 250. (180km W Melbourne), See map on pages 694/695, ref C6. Small township in a dairy & grazing district. Boating, Bowls, Bush Walking, Fishing, Tennis, Water Skiing.

Hotels/Motels
★★☆ **Mt Elephant Hotel Motel**, (LMH), Main St (Hamilton Hwy), 300m E of PO, ☎ 03 5597 6641, fax 03 5597 6812, 7 units [shwr, tlt, fan, heat, elec blkts, TV, clock radio, t/c mkg, refrig, toaster], conf fac, ⊠. **BLB ⋔ $35, ⋔⋔ $55, ⋒ $10**, BC EFT MC VI.

B&B's/Guest Houses
★★★☆ **The Elms Restaurant**, (B&B), 2 Main St, ☎ 03 5597 6517, 2 rms [heat, elec blkts, clock radio], lounge (TV, cd player), lounge firepl, ✕, BYO, t/c mkg shared, bbq, c/park (undercover), non smoking property. **BB ⋔ $70, ⋔⋔ $99**, BC MC VI.

DIMBOOLA VIC 3414

Pop 1,550. (335km NW Melbourne), See map on pages 694/695, ref B4. An agricultural township on the banks of the Wimmera River, often referred to as 'The Gateway to the Little Desert'. Little Desert National Park (4km S), Rowing Regatta (Nov). Boating, Bowls, Bush Walking, Fishing, Golf, Sailing, Scenic Drives, Shooting, Swimming (Pool, River), Tennis, Water Skiing.

Hotels/Motels
★★★☆ **Motel Dimboola**, (M), Horsham Rd, 1.7km E of PO, ☎ 03 5389 1177, fax 03 5389 1030, 18 units [shwr, tlt, a/c, elec blkts, tel, TV, video-fee, clock radio, t/c mkg, refrig, toaster], ldry, rec rm, pool, cook fac, bbq, dinner to unit, car wash, plygr, cots-fee, non smoking units (6). **RO ⋔ $50 - $56, ⋔⋔ $62 - $68, ⋒ $13**, ch con, 4 units ★★★. AE BC DC EFT MC MP VI.

★☆ **Victoria Hotel**, (LH), Cnr Victoria & Wimmera Sts, 500m N of PO, ☎ 03 5389 1630, fax 03 5389 2050, (2 stry), 12 rms [basin (3), elec blkts, clock radio (8)], lounge (TV), ⊠, t/c mkg shared, refrig, ✆, non smoking rms. **BLB ⋔ $32, ⋔⋔ $47**, BC EFT MC VI.

Self Catering Accommodation

★★★ **Little Desert Log Cabins & Cottage**, Horseshoe Bend Rd, 4km S of PO, ☎ 03 5389 1122, fax 03 5389 1128, 1 cabin acc up to 4, (2 bedrm), [shwr, tlt, hairdry, a/c-cool, heat, elec blkts, TV, clock radio, refrig, cook fac, micro, blkts, doonas, linen, pillows], rec rm, pool, bbq, breakfast ingredients, non smoking units. **BLB ⋔⋔ $70 - $80, ⋒ $10**, ch con, BC MC VI.

★★★ **(Cottage Section)**, 1 cotg acc up to 6, (2 bedrm), [shwr, tlt, a/c-cool, c/fan, heat (wood), elec blkts, TV, clock radio, refrig, cook fac, micro, toaster, ldry (in unit), blkts, linen], bbq, breakfast ingredients, non smoking units. **BLB ⋔⋔ $80 - $90, ⋒ $10**.

★★★ **Riverside Host Farm**, (Farm), Riverside Rd, on banks of Wimmera River, 4km SW of PO, ☎ 03 5389 1550, 1 cabin acc up to 4, (1 bedrm), [shwr, tlt, fan, heat, TV, clock radio, refrig, cook fac, toaster, blkts, doonas, linen, pillows], ldry, iron, bbq, plygr. **D $77, W $484**.

B&B's/Guest Houses
★★★★ **Wimmera Gums**, (B&B), 8 School St, 1.3km NE of PO, ☎ 03 5389 1207, fax 03 5389 1207, (2 stry gr fl), 3 rms [ensuite (2), shwr, spa bath (1), tlt, hairdry, a/c-cool, c/fan, heat, elec blkts, clock radio, t/c mkg, refrig, doonas], lounge (TV, video, cd), bbq, non smoking property. **BB ⋔ $75 - $90, ⋔⋔ $105 - $125**, Dinner by arrangement.

DINNER PLAIN VIC 3898

Pop 400. (460km E Melbourne), See map on pages 694/695, ref H5. Building of Snowgum Village commenced in 1986 and is Australia's only 'Freehold' Alpine ski resort. Bush Walking, Fishing, Horse Riding, Rock Climbing, Scenic Drives, Tennis.

Self Catering Accommodation
★★★★ **Mayford at Dinner Plain**, (Chalet), Lot 2481 Halter La, 150m S of Village Square, ☎ 03 5159 6696, fax 03 5159 6690, (2 stry), 1 chalet acc up to 10, (3 bedrm), [ensuite, shwr, bath, tlt, c/fan, cent heat, TV, video, clock radio, refrig, cook fac, micro, elec frypan, d/wash, toaster, ldry, doonas, linen], w/mach, dryer, iron, dry rm, spa (heated), bbq, non smoking property. **Low Season D $250, High Season G $1,400, High Season W $2,780**, Minimum booking Easter & winter, BC MC VI.

★★★ **Bullumwaal**, (Cotg), Big Muster Dve, ☎ 03 5159 6696, fax 03 5159 6690, (2 stry gr fl), 1 cotg acc up to 13, (5 bedrm), [shwr, bath, tlt, cent heat (2), TV, video, CD (& sound system), refrig, cook fac, micro, elec frypan, d/wash, toaster], ldry, c/park (garage). **High Season W $2,720, Low Season W $1,975, W $2,220**, BC MC VI.

★★★ **Crystal Creek Resort Chalets**, (Chalet), Big Muster Dve, ☎ 1800 354 555, fax 03 5159 6500, (2 stry), 11 chalets acc up to 6, [shwr, tlt, fire pl, heat, TV, video (avail), refrig, cook fac, micro, elec frypan, toaster, ldry (in unit), blkts, linen, pillows], dry rm, ⊠ (seasonal), pool, sauna, spa, tennis (half court). **High Season D $715 - $1,760, Low Season D $285**, Min book applies, AE BC DC MC VI.

B&B's/Guest Houses
★★★★ **Crystal Creek Resort**, (GH), Big Muster Dve, ☎ 03 5159 6422, fax 03 5159 6500, (2 stry gr fl), 13 rms (2 bedrm - 3x1d2s.), [shwr, tlt, cent heat, TV, movie, t/c mkg, refrig, doonas], ldry, dry rm, lounge, conf fac, ⊠ (seasonal), pool, sauna, spa, ✆, tennis (half court), cots-fee, non smoking property. **D ⋔ $132 - $220, W ⋔⋔ $616 - $1,078**, AE BC EFT MC VI, ⅋⅂.

★★★★ **Wildflowers House**, (GH), 962 Halter La, ☎ 03 5159 6400, fax 03 5159 6515, 3 rms [shwr, tlt, hairdry, cent heat, doonas], dry rm, lounge (TV, video, CD player), lounge firepl, t/c mkg shared, non smoking property. **BB ⋔⋔ $160 - $180**, BC MC VI.

★★★☆ **High Plains Lodge**, (GH), Big Muster Dve, ☎ 03 5159 6455, fax 03 5159 6405, (2 stry gr fl), 18 rms [ensuite, cent heat, cable tv, t/c mkg, refrig, ldry, doonas], dry rm, rec rm, lounge (stereo), ⊠, spa, bbq, ✆, cots. **High Season BB ⋔⋔ $220, Low Season BB ⋔⋔ $120**, Min book applies, AE BC EFT MC VI.

Other Accommodation
Currawong Lodge at Dinner Plain, (Lodge), Big Muster Dve, ☎ 03 5159 6452, fax 03 9593 6568, (2 stry), 7 rms acc up to 6, (Bunk Rooms), [shwr, tlt, cable tv, doonas, linen, pillows], ldry, dry rm, rec rm, lounge (CD player), lounge firepl, spa (heated), cook fac, t/c mkg shared, refrig, ✆. **High Season BLB ⋔ $55 - $80, ⋒ $55 - $80, Low Season BLB ⋔ $30 - $60, ⋒ $30 - $60**, ch con, BC MC VI.

DIXONS CREEK VIC 3775

Pop Part of Yarra Glen, (62km NE Melbourne), See map on page 696, ref C5. A small wine growing district situated in the Yarra valley. Scenic Drives, Vineyards, Wineries.

Self Catering Accommodation
★★★★☆ **Leafield Cottages**, (Cotg), 1923 Melba Hwy, 10.3km N of Yarra Glen PO, ☎ 03 5965 2356, fax 03 5965 2555, 3 cotgs acc up to 5, (Studio & 2 bedrm), [shwr, tlt, hairdry, a/c (2), c/fan (1), heat (wood, gas), elec blkts, TV, video (avail), clock radio, CD, t/c mkg, refrig, cook fac, micro, toaster, blkts, linen, pillows], ldry, iron, iron brd, pool (salt water), bbq, c/park (carport) (1), gym (mini), breakfast ingredients, non smoking property. **BB ⋔⋔ $165**, 1 cottage ★★★★. BC MC VI.

★★★ **A Yarra Valley Conference Centre**, (Cotg), 2164 Melba Hwy, 14km N of Yarra Glen PO, ☎ 03 5965 2397, fax 03 5965 2025, 9 cotgs acc up to 12, (3 bedrm), [shwr, tlt, c/fan, heat, elec blkts, TV, clock radio, refrig, cook fac, micro, toaster, blkts, doonas, linen, pillows], ldry, conf fac, pool-heated, sauna, spa, bbq, courtesy transfer, golf (practice net)-fee, tennis, breakfast ingredients. **D ⋔ $60**, ch con, Min book applies.

★★★ **(Lodge Section)**, 3 rms acc up to 16, [ensuite (8), heat, elec blkts, clock radio, blkts, linen, pillows], lounge (TV). **D ⋔ $60**, ch con, Self catering available.

B&B's/Guest Houses
★★★★★ **Amethyst Lodge**, (B&B), 139 Wills Rd, 8.5km N of Yarra Glen PO, ☎ 03 5965 2559, or 03 5965 2558, fax 03 5965 2559, 4 rms (2 suites) [shwr, spa bath (2), tlt, hairdry, a/c, elec blkts, TV, video (2), t/c mkg, refrig], spa (heated), bbq, non smoking property. **BB ⋔ $132 - $165, ⋔⋔ $143 - $176, Suite BB ⋔ $154 - $187, ⋔⋔ $165 - $198**, Min book applies, AE BC DC EFT MC VI.

DONALD VIC 3480

Pop 1,400. (286km NW Melbourne), See map on pages 694/695, ref C4. Situated on the banks of the Avon River. Agricultural Museum. Boating, Bowls, Croquet, Fishing, Golf, Horse Racing, Horse Riding, Scenic Drives, Shooting, Swimming (Pool, Lake, River), Tennis, Water Skiing.

Hotels/Motels

★★★★ **Donald Motor Lodge**, (M), Cnr Borung & Sunraysia Hwys, 150m W of PO, ☎ 03 5497 1700, fax 03 5497 1799, 12 units [shwr, tlt, a/c, elec blkts, tel, TV, clock radio, t/c mkg, refrig, cook fac (4), toaster], ldry, bbq, cots-fee, non smoking units (2). **RO ⋔ $68, ⋔⋔ $75, ⋒ $10**, AE BC DC EFT MC VI, ⅋⅂.

★★★ **Motel Avon**, (M), 3 Woods St (Sunraysia Hwy), 200m W of PO, ☎ 03 5497 1488, fax 03 5497 1488, 7 units [shwr, tlt, a/c-cool, heat, elec blkts, tel, TV, clock radio, t/c mkg, refrig], ldry, cots-fee, non smoking rms (1). **RO ⋔ $50, ⋔⋔ $55 - $58, ⋒ $11**, AE BC EFT MC MCH VI.

Self Catering Accommodation
★★★ **Peppertree Cottage**, (Cotg), (Farm), Depot Rd, 12.6km W of PO, off Sheephills Rd, ☎ 03 5498 6265, fax 03 5498 6265, 3 cotgs acc up to 10, (2, 3 & 4 bedrm), [shwr, bath (2), tlt, a/c (1), c/fan (2), heat, elec blkts, TV, video, clock radio, refrig, cook fac, micro, elec frypan, d/wash, ldry, blkts, linen, pillows], w/mach, iron, iron brd, lounge firepl, bbq, cots. **D ♦♦ $110, ◊ $22**, ch con.

DROMANA VIC 3936

Pop 5,078. (68km S Melbourne), See map on page 697, ref C7. Popular bayside beach at the foot of Arthur's Seat. Dolls Museum. Information Centre, Nepean Hwy, 03-5987 3078. Art Gallery, Boating, Bowls, Fishing, Sailing, Scenic Drives, Swimming (Beach), Tennis, Water Skiing.

Hotels/Motels
★★☆ **Blue Dolphin Motor Lodge**, (M), 21 Nepean Hwy, Safety Beach 3936, 1km W of PO, ☎ 03 5987 2311, 15 units [shwr, spa bath (3), tlt, a/c (4), c/fan, heat, elec blkts, TV, video-fee, clock radio, t/c mkg, refrig, toaster], bbq, cots-fee. **RO ♦ $40 - $90, ♦♦ $50 - $100, ◊ $10**, BC EFT MC VI.

★★ **Dromana Beach Motel**, (M), 91 Point Nepean Rd, 1km NE of PO, ☎ 03 5987 1837, fax 03 5981 9438, 8 units [shwr, tlt, c/fan, heat, elec blkts, TV, video-fee, clock radio, t/c mkg, refrig, toaster], pool-heated (solar, salt water), cots-fee, non smoking units (4). **RO ♦ $55 - $90, ♦♦ $65 - $100, ◊ $17**, ch con, pen con, AE BC EFT MC MCH VI.

Self Catering Accommodation
★★★☆ **Lurnea Bed & Breakfast**, (Apt), 15 Manna St, ☎ 03 5987 1216, 1 apt acc up to 4, (2 bedrm), [shwr, tlt, hairdry, heat, elec blkts, TV, t/c mkg, refrig, cook fac, micro, elec frypan, toaster, ldry, blkts, doonas, linen, pillows], ldry, w/mach, bbq, breakfast ingredients, non smoking property. **BB ♦♦ $100 - $120, ◊ $30 - $40**, ch con.

★★★☆ **The Studio Bed and Breakfast**, (Cotg), Glassonby, 190 Purves Rd, Arthurs Seat 3936, 2.1km S of Arthurs Seat, ☎ 03 5989 6267, fax 03 5975 9564, 1 cotg acc up to 4, (1 bedrm), [shwr, tlt, hairdry, c/fan, heat (wood), elec blkts, TV, clock radio, CD, refrig, cook fac, micro, elec frypan, toaster, blkts, doonas, linen, pillows], ldry, bbq, breakfast ingredients, non smoking property. **BB ♦♦ $160 - $175, ◊ $25, ♦ $85 - $100, ♦♦ $790 - $900**.

B&B's/Guest Houses
★★★★ **Heritage Bayview House**, (B&B), No children's facilities, 215 Palmerston Ave, 1km E of PO, ☎ 03 5987 3785, fax 03 5987 3897, 2 rms [shwr, spa bath (1), tlt, hairdry, cent heat, elec blkts, t/c mkg], pool (lap-salt water). **BB ♦♦ $220 - $280**.

★★★★ **Pennyroyal by the Bay Bed & Breakfast**, (B&B), 15 McCulloch St, ☎ 03 5981 0590, 3 rms [ensuite, spa bath (1), hairdry, c/fan, elec blkts, TV, clock radio, t/c mkg], ldry, refrig, non smoking property. **BB ♦ $80, ♦♦ $95 - $120**, Min book long w/ends.

DROUIN VIC 3818

Pop 4,800. (97km SE Melbourne), See map on page 696, ref D6. An agricultural, pastoral & dairying township. Bowls, Bush Walking, Croquet, Fishing, Golf, Scenic Drives, Shooting, Swimming (Pool), Tennis.

Hotels/Motels

★★★ **Drouin Motor Inn**, (M), 275 Princes Way (Old Princes Hwy), 1.5km W of PO, ☎ 03 5625 3296, fax 03 5625 3488, 14 units [shwr, spa bath (1), tlt, hairdry, a/c-cool, fan, heat, elec blkts, tel, TV, clock radio, t/c mkg, refrig], dinner to unit, plygr. **RO ♦ $65 - $71, ♦♦ $75 - $81, ◊ $11**, ch con, AE BC DC EFT MC VI.

★★ **Robin Hood Inn - Drouin**, (LMH), 30 Princes Way, 6.1km W of PO, ☎ 03 5625 4884, 10 units [ensuite, fan, heat, elec blkts, TV, clock radio (6), t/c mkg, refrig, toaster], ⊠ (Mon to Sat), bar (2), ✆. **RO ♦ $40, ♦♦ $60 - $70, ♦♦♦ $75**, AE BC DC EFT MC VI.

Self Catering Accommodation
★★★★ **Berry Farm Cottages**, (Cotg), 315 Fisher Rd, 11km W of PO, ☎ 03 5628 7627, fax 03 5628 7627, 2 cotgs acc up to 6, (1 bedrm), [shwr, tlt, fan, heat, elec blkts, clock radio, t/c mkg, refrig, cook fac, micro, ldry-fee, blkts, doonas, linen, pillows], ⊠, bbq, dinner to unit, breakfast ingredients, non smoking property. **D ♦ $90, ♦♦ $145**, ch con, BC EFT MC VI.

B&B's/Guest Houses
★★★★☆ **Parnassus Private Guest House**, (GH), Camp Hill Rd, 7.7km NE of PO, off Buln Buln Rd, ☎ 03 5626 8522, 5 rms [shwr, spa bath (1), tlt, hairdry, c/fan, heat, elec blkts, TV, t/c mkg, refrig], iron, iron brd, ⊠, bar, pool, spa, non smoking property. **BB ♦ $90, ♦♦ $135 - $145, ◊ $40**, Dinner by arrangement. AE BC MC VI.

DRUMMOND VIC 3461

Pop Part of Daylesford, (107km NW Melbourne), See map on page 697, ref A4. Mining and agricultural township on main Malmsbury - Daylesford Rd. Bush Walking, Scenic Drives.

Self Catering Accommodation
★★★★☆ **Drummond Park Cottages**, (Cotg), No children's facilities, 1555 Malmsbury - Daylesford Rd, 15km N of Daylesford, ☎ 03 5423 9196, fax 03 5423 9332, (2 stry gr fl), 2 cotgs acc up to 4, (2 bedrm), [shwr, spa bath, tlt, hairdry, c/fan, heat, elec blkts, TV, video (& DVD), clock radio, CD, t/c mkg, refrig, cook fac, micro, d/wash, toaster, ldry (in unit), blkts, doonas, linen, pillows], w/mach, dryer, iron, iron brd, lounge firepl (gas log), bbq, golf (9 hole), breakfast ingredients, non smoking property. **BB ♦♦ $190 - $225, ◊ $80**, BC MC VI.

★★★ **Springbank Farm B & B**, (Cotg), (Farm), 115 Pudding Bag Rd, ☎ 03 5423 9200, fax 03 5423 9295, 1 cotg acc up to 6, (3 bedrm), [shwr, bath, tlt, hairdry, evap cool, heat, elec blkts, CD, refrig, cook fac, micro, toaster, ldry, blkts, linen, pillows], w/mach, iron, iron brd, lounge firepl, bbq, cots, breakfast ingredients, Pets on application. **BB ♦♦ $80, ◊ $40, ♦♦♦♦ $480**, ch con, Tariff includes some farm activities.

B&B's/Guest Houses
★★★★ **Cliston Farm**, (B&B), (Farm), Daylesford - Malmsbury Rd, 4km W of school, ☎ 03 5423 9155, fax 03 5423 9155, 2 rms [ensuite, bath (1), hairdry, c/fan, heat, elec blkts, clock radio, doonas], lounge (TV, video, cd), t/c mkg shared. **D all meals ♦ $145, ◊ $145**, ch con.

★★★★ **(Cottage Section)**, 1 cotg acc up to 6, (3 bedrm), [shwr, tlt, hairdry, c/fan, heat, elec blkts, TV, video, clock radio, t/c mkg, refrig, cook fac, micro, d/wash, toaster, ldry, blkts, doonas, linen, pillows], w/mach, iron, iron brd, bbq, c/park (carport). **D ♦♦♦♦ $145, ◊ $22, W ♦♦♦♦ $650, ◊ $110**, Meals by arrangement.

DUMBALK VIC 3956

Pop Nominal, (153km SE Melbourne), See map on page 697, ref D7. Dairy farming district. Scenic Drives.

Self Catering Accommodation
★★★☆ **Trelawney Cottage**, (Cotg), (Farm), Milford Rd, 10km N of PO, ☎ 03 5664 5430, fax 03 5664 5430, 1 cotg acc up to 6, (3 bedrm), [shwr, bath, tlt, evap cool, fan, elec blkts, TV, clock radio, refrig, cook fac, micro, toaster, ldry, blkts, linen, pillows], w/mach, dryer, iron, iron brd, lounge firepl, bbq, c/park (carport), cots. **D ♦♦ $110, W ♦♦ $550 - $660**, ch con, Min book applies.

DUNKELD VIC

See Grampians Region.

DUNOLLY VIC 3472

Pop 650. (174km NW Melbourne), See map on pages 694/695, ref D5. Centre of a farming, grazing & agricultural district, once a rich gold mining town. Boating, Bowls, Fishing, Golf, Swimming (Pool), Tennis, Water Skiing.

Hotels/Motels
★★★ **Golden Triangle Motel**, (M), Maryborough-Dunolly Rd, 1km S of PO, ☎ 03 5468 1166, fax 03 5468 1166, 7 units [shwr, tlt, a/c, elec blkts, TV, clock radio, t/c mkg, refrig, toaster], non smoking property. **RO ♦ $46 - $50, ♦♦ $60 - $65, ◊ $10**, BC MC VI.

EAGLE POINT VIC 3878

Pop 350. (293km E Melbourne), See map on pages 694/695, ref J7. Picturesque lakeside village. Boating, Bowls, Fishing, Golf, Horse Riding, Sailing, Scenic Drives, Swimming (Lake, River), Water Skiing.

Self Catering Accommodation
★★★★ **Old Nats**, (Cotg), 245 Lake Victoria Rd, 2km S of Bairnsdale-Paynesville Rd, ☎ 03 5156 6420, fax 03 5156 6420, 1 cotg acc up to 4, (2 bedrm), [shwr, tlt, c/fan, heat (wood), TV, video, radio, refrig, cook fac ltd, micro, elec frypan, toaster, blkts, linen, pillows], bbq, c/park (carport), breakfast ingredients. **BB ♦♦ $70 - $80, D ◊ $10**, ch con, BC MC VI.

★★★ **Leeward Cove Holiday Units**, (HF), 1553 Bay Rd, ☎ 03 5156 6297, 4 flats acc up to 6, (2 bedrm), [shwr, bath (hip), tlt, c/fan, heat, elec blkts, TV, clock radio, refrig, cook fac, micro, toaster, blkts, linen, pillows], w/mach, bbq, jetty. **D $50 - $70, W $300 - $500**.

ECHUCA VIC 3564

*Pop 10,000. (201km N Melbourne), See map on page 696, ref B1.
Popular tourist city on the banks of the Murray River, home of the
river boats. Boating, Bowls, Bush Walking, Croquet, Fishing, Golf,
Horse Racing, Horse Riding, Sailing, Scenic Drives, Shooting,
Swimming (Pool, River), Tennis, Trotting, Water Skiing.*

Hotels/Motels

★★★★ **Campaspe Lodge at the Echuca Hotel**, (LMH), 571 High St,
☎ 03 5482 1087, fax 03 5480 2275, 6 units (1 suite) [shwr, bath (5),
tlt, hairdry, a/c, TV, clock radio, t/c mkg, cook fac (1), micro (1),
toaster, ldry (in unit) (2)], iron, iron brd, ✉, ✆. RO ♦ $77, ♦♦ $100,
Light breakfast only. AE BC DC EFT MC VI.

★★★★ **Georgian Motor Lodge**, (M), 373-375 High St, 200m S of PO,
☎ 03 5480 9313, fax 03 5480 9048, 21 units [shwr, spa bath (7), tlt,
a/c, heat, elec blkts, tel, cable tv, video, clock radio, refrig, toaster, ldry],
pool (salt water), bbq, dinner to unit, plygr, cots, non smoking units (10).
RO ♦ $65 - $130, ♦♦ $85 - $130, ◊ $10, pen con, AE BC DC EFT MC VI.

★★★★ **Nirebo Motel**, (M), 251 Hare St,
100m NW of PO, ☎ 03 5482 2033,
fax 03 5482 5322, (2 stry gr fl), 42 units
[shwr, spa bath (3), tlt, hairdry, a/c, elec blkts,
tel, cable tv, video-fee, clock radio, t/c mkg, refrig, micro (14), toaster],
iron, iron brd, rec rm, ✉ (Mon to Fri), pool, sauna, spa (heated),
dinner to unit (Mon to Fri), cots-fee, non smoking units (30).
RO ♦ $110 - $130, ♦♦ $110 - $130, ◊ $15, AE BC DC EFT JCB MC MP VI.

★★★★ **Paddle Wheel Motel**, (M), 385 High St, 500m S of PO,
☎ 03 5482 3822, fax 03 5480 6689, (2 stry gr fl), 31 units
[shwr, spa bath (9), tlt, hairdry, a/c, elec blkts, tel, cable tv,
clock radio, t/c mkg, refrig, toaster], iron, iron brd, pool-heated
(solar), spa, bbq, cots-fee, non smoking units (16). RO ♦ $63 - $120,
♦♦ $65 - $135, ◊ $10, 12 units ★★★. AE BC DC EFT MC VI.

★★★★ **Port of Echuca Motor Inn**, (M), 465 High St,
200m W of PO, ☎ 03 5482 5666, fax 03 5482 5682,
(2 stry gr fl), 62 units [shwr, bath (hip) (2), spa bath (27),
tlt, hairdry, a/c, elec blkts, tel, TV, video, clock radio, t/c mkg,
refrig, mini bar, toaster], ldry, iron, iron brd, conf fac,
✉ (Mon to Sat), bar (cocktail), pool, spa, bbq, rm serv, ✆, gym, cots,
non smoking units (17). RO ♦ $126.50 - $159.50, ♦♦ $137.50 - $159.50,
◊ $16, Min book all holiday times, AE BC DC EFT MC MP VI.

★★★☆ **All Rivers Motor Inn**, (M), 115 Northern Hwy,
4.4km SW of PO, ☎ 03 5482 5677, fax 03 5480 6098,
31 units [shwr, spa bath (2), tlt, hairdry, a/c, c/fan, elec blkts,
tel, TV, video, clock radio, t/c mkg, refrig, mini bar,
cook fac (1), toaster], ldry, iron, iron brd, ✉ (Mon to Sat),
bar (cocktail), pool, bbq, rm serv, plygr, cots, non smoking units (10).
RO ♦ $82 - $126, ♦♦ $88 - $137, ◊ $11, AE BC DC EFT MC MP VI, ♿.

★★★☆ **Pevensey Motor Lodge**, (M), 365 High St, 500m S
of water tower, ☎ 03 5482 5166, fax 03 5480 6913,
20 units [shwr, spa bath (1), tlt, hairdry (3), a/c, elec blkts,
tel, cable tv, video-fee, clock radio, t/c mkg, refrig, toaster],
ldry, pool (salt water), bbq, cots-fee, non smoking units (13). RO ♦ $82 - $120,
♦♦ $89 - $120, ◊ $12, AE BC DC EFT MC MP VI, ♿.

★★★☆ **Philadelphia Motor Inn**, (M), 340 Ogilvie Ave
(Murray Valley Hwy), 3.4km S of PO, ☎ 03 5482 5700,
fax 03 5482 6961, 24 units [shwr, bath (hip) (4), spa
bath (2), tlt, a/c, c/fan, elec blkts, tel, TV, clock radio, t/c mkg,
refrig, mini bar, toaster], conf fac, ✉ (Tue to Sat), pool (inground),
bbq, rm serv, plygr, cots-fee, non smoking units (8). RO ♦ $81 - $120,
♦♦ $88 - $120, ◊ $10, ch con, AE BC DC EFT JCB MC MP VI, ♿.

★★★☆ **Riverboat Lodge Motor Inn**, (M), 476 High St,
200m W of PO, ☎ 03 5482 5777, fax 03 5482 6279, (2 stry
gr fl), 19 units [shwr, spa bath-fee, tlt, a/c, elec blkts, tel,
video-fee, clock radio, t/c mkg, refrig, toaster],
pool-heated (solar), cots-fee, non smoking units (5). RO ♦ $82 - $109,
♦♦ $93 - $115, ◊ $15, AE BC DC EFT MC VI, ♿.

★★★ **Big River Motel**, (M), 317 High St, 1.5km S of PO,
☎ 03 5482 2522, fax 03 5480 2223, (2 stry gr fl),
15 units [shwr, tlt, a/c, heat (10), elec blkts, TV, clock
radio, t/c mkg, refrig, toaster], ldry, pool above ground,
bbq, cots, non smoking units (3). D ♦ $50 - $75, ♦♦ $60 - $85, ◊ $15,
AE BC DC EFT MC MCH VI.

*Operator Comment: Simply the best value for money
accommodation in the main street of Echuca. (High St.)*

★★★ **Caledonian Hotel Motel Echuca**, (LMH), 110 Hare St, 400m S of PO,
☎ 03 5482 2100, fax 03 5482 2764, (2 stry gr fl), 14 units [shwr,
bath (7), spa bath (7), tlt, hairdry, a/c, tel, TV, clock radio, t/c mkg,
refrig, toaster], ✗, ✉ (Mon to Sat), cots-fee. RO ♦ $60 - $95,
♦♦ $75 - $95, ◊ $10, ch con, AE BC DC EFT MC VI, ♿.

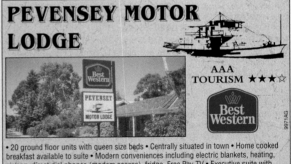

★★★ **Campaspe Motor Inn**, (M), 305 Ogilvie Ave (Murray Valley Hwy), 2.5km S of PO, on the banks of the Campaspe River, ☎ 03 5482 3900, fax 03 5480 7230, 14 units [shwr, tlt, a/c, elec blkts, TV, clock radio, t/c mkg, refrig, toaster], ldry, pool, bbq, ✆, plygr, cots, non smoking units (5).
RO ♦ $50 - $80, ♦♦ $60 - $100, ⊕ $12, AE BC DC MC VI.

★★★ **Echuca Motel**, (M), 268 Ogilvie Ave (Murray Valley Hwy), 2.5km S of PO, ☎ 03 5482 2899, fax 03 5482 2721, 22 units [shwr, tlt, a/c-cool, heat, elec blkts, tel, TV, clock radio, t/c mkg, refrig, toaster], ldry, pool (solar), bbq, c/park (carport), cots-fee. RO ♦ $55 - $60, ♦♦ $60 - $70, ⊕ $10, ch con, BC MC VI.

★★★ **Echuca River Gum Motor Inn**, (M), 85 Northern Hwy, 4.3km S of PO, ☎ 03 5482 4244, fax 03 5480 6670, 35 units [shwr, spa bath (2), tlt, a/c, elec blkts, tel, TV, clock radio, t/c mkg, refrig, toaster], pool, bbq, plygr, tennis, cots-fee. RO ♦ $55 - $110, ♦♦ $77 - $120, ⊕ $10, AE BC DC EFT MC VI.

★★★ **Fountain Motel**, (M), 77 Northern Hwy, 4km S of PO, ☎ 03 5482 3200, fax 03 5480 2093, 13 units [shwr, spa bath (1), tlt, a/c, elec blkts, tel, TV, clock radio, t/c mkg, refrig, toaster], conf fac, pool, bbq, dinner to unit (Sun to Thur), plygr, cots-fee, non smoking units (4).
RO ♦ $45 - $105, ♦♦ $55 - $105, ⊕ $11, AE BC DC MC MCH VI.

★★★ **Settlement Motor Inn**, (M), 405 High St, opposite water tower, ☎ 03 5482 4777, fax 03 5482 4780, (2 stry gr fl), 34 units [shwr, tlt, a/c, elec blkts, tel, cable tv, clock radio, t/c mkg, refrig, toaster], pool, spa, bbq, cots, non smoking units (12). RO ♦ $82 - $96, ♦♦ $89 - $96, ⊕ $10, Min book long w/ends and Easter, AE BC DC EFT MC MP VI, ♿.

★★★ **The Old Coach Motor Inn**, (M), 288 Ogilvie Ave (Murray Valley Hwy), 2.7km S of PO, ☎ 03 5482 3155, fax 03 5482 6568, 19 units [shwr, spa bath (3), tlt, a/c, elec blkts, tel, cable tv, movie, clock radio, t/c mkg, refrig, micro (1), toaster], pool-heated (solar), spa, bbq, non smoking units (6). RO ♦ $55 - $80, ♦♦ $65 - $115, ⊕ $10, 5 units ★★★☆. AE BC DC EFT MC MCH VI.

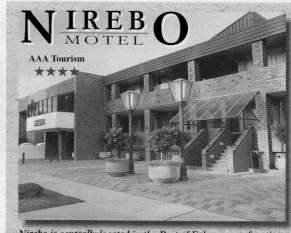

Indulge yourself!

★★ Highstreet Motel, (M), 439 High St, 200m SW of PO, ☎ 03 5482 1013, fax 03 5482 1013, 11 units [shwr, tlt, a/c, c/fan, elec blkts, TV, video-fee, clock radio, t/c mkg, refrig, micro (1)], c/park (carport), ⬧, cots-fee, non smoking units (3). **RO** ⬧ **$50 - $62**, ⬧⬧ **$62 - $70**, ⬧ **$10**, AE BC DC EFT MC MCH VI.

★ American Hotel, (LH), Cnr Hare & Heygarth Sts, 100m N of PO, ☎ 03 5482 5044, fax 03 5480 2178, (2 stry), 9 rms [basin (3), c/fan, elec blkts], lounge (TV), ⬧ (Mon to Sat), t/c mkg shared, refrig, ⬧, cots. **RO** ⬧ **$30**, ⬧⬧ **$50**, Light breakfast only available. AE BC EFT MC VI.

★ Pastoral Inn Hotel Motel, (LMH), 100 Sturt St, 1km SE of PO, opp railway station, ☎ 03 5482 1812, fax 03 5480 6898, 15 units [shwr, tlt, a/c, elec blkts, TV, clock radio, t/c mkg, refrig, toaster], ⬧, ⬧, cots-fee. **RO** ⬧ **$45 - $55**, ⬧⬧ **$55 - $65**, ⬧ **$10**, BC EFT MC VI.

Self Catering Accommodation
★★★☆ Echuca Sunshine Villas, (HU), Cnr Hovell & Leichardt Sts, 1.7km SE of PO, ☎ 03 5480 6931, fax 03 5482 2900, 4 units acc up to 7, (1, 2 & 3 bedrm), [shwr, tlt, hairdry, a/c, elec blkts, TV, clock radio, refrig, cook fac, micro, toaster, ldry (in unit), blkts, linen, pillows], iron, iron brd, pool-heated (solar), bbq, c/park (carport), cots. **D** **$55 - $135**, **W** **$330 - $840**, BC MC VI.

★★★ Echuca Holiday Flats, (HF), 105 Sutton St, 1.1km E of PO, ☎ 03 5480 6350, fax 03 5480 6350, 4 flats acc up to 5, (1 & 2 bedrm), [shwr, tlt, a/c-cool, c/fan, heat, elec blkts, TV, clock radio, refrig, cook fac, micro, toaster, linen reqd-fee], ldry, pool, bbq, cots. **D** ⬧⬧ **$50 - $60**, weekly con, BC MC VI.

★★★ Riverside Holiday Village, (HU), 134 Pianta Rd, 9km W of PO, off Murray Valley Hwy, ☎ 03 5482 4829, fax 03 5482 4829, 10 units acc up to 10, (2 & 3 bedrm), [shwr, tlt, a/c, fan (4), c/fan (6), heat (4), elec blkts, TV, video-fee, clock radio, refrig, cook fac, micro, toaster, linen reqd-fee], ldry, w/mach, dryer-fee, pool (salt water), bbq, c/park (carport), ⬧, plygr, jetty, canoeing-fee, tennis, cots. **D** ⬧⬧ **$66 - $130**, **W** ⬧⬧ **$462 - $910**, ⬧ **$77**, ch con, pen con, Min book long w/ends and Easter, BC MC VI.

★★ River Village Motel & Holiday Units, (HU), 310 Bangerang Rd, 5km E of PO, ☎ 03 5480 6039, fax 03 5483 5333, 16 units (1 & 2 bedrm), [shwr, tlt, evap cool, heat, TV, clock radio (12), t/c mkg, refrig, cook fac ltd, micro, toaster, blkts, linen, pillows], ldry, w/mach-fee, dryer-fee, conf fac, pool, bbq, ⬧, plygr, tennis, cots-fee. **D** ⬧ **$66 - $82.50**, ⬧⬧ **$66 - $82.50**, ⬧ **$11**, Min book Christmas Jan long w/ends and Easter, AE BC EFT MC MCH VI.

B&B's/Guest Houses

★★★★☆ **Coriander Bed & Breakfast**, (B&B), No children's facilities, 7260 Northern Hwy, 8km S of PO, ☎ 03 5480 1254, fax 03 5480 1254, 4 rms [shwr, tlt, hairdry, a/c-cool, c/fan, cent heat, elec blkts, CD], lounge (TV, video), ✕, spa (heated), t/c mkg shared, bbq. **BB 👥 $120**, Dinner by arrangement, BC MC VI.

★★★★☆ **Echuca Hideaway**, (B&B), No children's facilities, 718 Stratton Rd, 10km S of PO, ☎ 03 5482 6742, fax 03 5480 0467, 3 rms [ensuite (private), hairdry, a/c, elec blkts, clock radio], rec rm, lounge (TV, video, stereo), pool (salt water), t/c mkg shared, refrig, bbq, c/park (undercover). **BB $100 - $120**, Dinner by arrangement. BC MC VI.

★★★★☆ **Etan House**, (B&B), 11 Connelly St, ☎ 03 5480 7477, fax 03 5480 7466, 4 rms [ensuite, bath (2), hairdry, a/c-cool, fire pl (bedroom) (1), cent heat, elec blkts], lounge (TV, cd), lounge firepl, pool, cook fac, t/c mkg shared, bbq, tennis, non smoking property. **BB 👤 $120, 👥 $130 - $165**, BC MC VI.

★★★★☆ **Murray House Bed & Breakfast**, (B&B), No children's facilities, 55 Francis St, 700m S of water tower, ☎ 03 5482 4944, fax 03 5480 6432, 5 rms [shwr, tlt, hairdry, evap cool, fan, heat, elec blkts, TV, clock radio], lounge (TV, video, cd), non smoking property. **BB 👥 $180 - $220**, BC MC VI.

★★★ **(Cottage Section)**, 1 cotg acc up to 4, (2 bedrm), [shwr, tlt, a/c-cool, heat, elec blkts, TV, clock radio, t/c mkg, refrig, cook fac, toaster, blkts, linen, pillows]. **D $110 - $145, W $550.**

★★★★☆ **River Gallery Inn**, (B&B), c1865. No children's facilities, 578 High St, 205m NW of PO, ☎ 03 5480 6902, fax 03 5480 6902, (2 stry gr fl), 8 rms [ensuite, bath (2), spa bath (5), hairdry, a/c, fire pl (7), elec blkts, TV, clock radio, t/c mkg, refrig], 📞, non smoking property. **BLB 👥 $145 - $210**, BC MC VI.

★★★★ **Elinike Guest Cottages**, (B&B), 209 Latham Rd, 9km W of PO, ☎ 03 5480 6311, fax 03 5480 6506, (2 stry), 3 rms [shwr, bath (1), spa bath (2), tlt, hairdry, a/c-cool (2), a/c (1), heat (wood), TV, clock radio, CD, t/c mkg, refrig, micro (2)], non smoking property. **BB 👤 $125 - $140, 👥 $160 - $180**, Dinner by arrangement. Min book Christmas and Jan, AE BC MC VI.

★★★☆ **Buffalo Bend**, (B&B), Cnr Murray Valley Hwy & McDonald Rd, 12km E of Echuca, ☎ 03 5859 2200, fax 03 5859 2200, 4 rms [evap cool, c/fan, elec blkts, clock radio], lounge (TV, video, cd, piano), lounge firepl, ☒, t/c mkg shared, refrig, bbq, non smoking property. **BB 👤 $70, 👥 $97, 👤 $20 - $25**, BC MC VI.

★★★☆ **Echuca Gardens Bed & Breakfast**, (B&B), 103 Mitchell St, 2km E of PO, ☎ 03 5480 6522, (2 stry) 3 rms [a/c-cool (2), c/fan, heat, elec blkts, TV], lounge (TV, video, stereo), lounge firepl, sauna, spa, t/c mkg shared. **BB** ♦ **$50 - $90**, ♦♦ **$85 - $130**, BC MC VI. *Operator Comment: Selected and featured on National TV. Magnificent water gardens, murals, hand painted rooms, live piano, international room, quiet central location overlooking state forest. Simply the best! Phone for brochure or www.echucagardens.com*

★★★ **Steam Packet Inn**, (B&B), Classified by National Trust, Murray Esp, 800m NW of PO, ☎ 03 5482 3411, fax 03 5482 3408, (2 stry gr fl), 10 rms [ensuite, a/c-cool (5), a/c (4), c/fan, heat (6), elec blkts, tel, TV, clock radio, t/c mkg, refrig], lounge (TV), BYO, cots. **BB** ♦ **$95**, ♦♦ **$112**, ch con, AE BC DC MC VI.

Other Accommodation
Echuca Gardens Hostel, (Lodge), 103 Mitchell St, 900m E of Water Tower, ☎ 03 5480 6522, 6 rms [c/fan, heat, video, linen], shwr, tlt, w/mach, lounge (TV), sauna, spa, cook fac, refrig, bbq, c/park (limited), bicycle. **D** ♦ **$18 - $21.50**, ◊ **$18 - $21.50**, BC MC VI.

Magic Murray Houseboats, (Hbt), 100 Chanter St, Moama 2731, Mooring at Maidens Inn Holiday Park, ☎ 03 5480 6099, fax 03 5480 6690, 3 houseboats acc up to 8, [shwr, tlt, heat, TV, radio, t/c mkg, refrig, cook fac, micro, linen], bbq, cots. **W** **$814 - $3,960**, Security deposit - $400 to $1000, BC MC VI.

Rich River Houseboats, (Hbt), Riverboat Dock, moored at Riverboat Dock, 500m NW of PO, ☎ 03 5480 2444, fax 03 5482 6993, 5 houseboats acc up to 12, (3 & 5 bedrm), [shwr, tlt, heat, TV, video, radio, refrig, cook fac, micro, d/wash (4), doonas, linen reqd-fee, pillows], bbq, secure park. **D** **$140 - $560**, **W** **$870 - $2,670**, Security deposit - $400 to $1000. Provisions provided - fee. Min book applies, BC MC VI.

EDENHOPE VIC 3318

Pop 800. (412km W Melbourne), See map on pages 694/695, ref A5. Sheep & grain growing district. Boating, Bowls, Fishing, Golf, Swimming (Lake), Tennis, Water Skiing. See also Lake Charlegrark.
Hotels/Motels
★★☆ **Edenhope Motor Inn**, (M), 157 Elizabeth St (Wimmera Hwy), 1.1km W of PO, ☎ 03 5585 1369, fax 03 5585 1867, 13 units [shwr, tlt, hairdry (6), a/c, elec blkts, tel, TV, video (avail), clock radio, t/c mkg, refrig, toaster], ldry, ✉ (Mon to Sat), dinner to unit (Mon to Sat), cots. **RO** ♦ **$55**, ♦♦ **$61.60**, ◊ **$10.90**, AE BC DC EFT MC VI.

EILDON VIC 3713

Pop 700. (138km NE Melbourne), See map on page 696, ref D4. Situated below the wall of Lake Eildon. Trout Hatchery, Visitor Information Centre, Main St, 03 5774 2909. Boating, Bowls, Bush Walking, Fishing, Golf, Horse Riding, Sailing, Scenic Drives, Shooting, Swimming (Pool), Tennis, Water Skiing.
Hotels/Motels
★★★ **Eildon Lake Motel**, (M), 2 Girdwood Pde, 100m SW of PO, ☎ 03 5774 2800, fax 03 5774 2800, (2 stry gr fl), 12 units [shwr, tlt, a/c, elec blkts, TV, video (avail), radio, t/c mkg, refrig, toaster], pool, bbq, cots. **RO** ♦ **$55 - $66**, ♦♦ **$65 - $80**, ◊ **$11**, ch con, AE BC DC EFT MC VI.

★★★ **Eildon Parkview Motor Inn**, (M), Hillside Ave, 100m N of PO, ☎ 03 5774 2165, fax 03 5774 2155, 12 units [shwr, tlt, a/c, elec blkts, tel, TV, video-fee, radio, t/c mkg, refrig, cook fac (3), toaster], ldry, bbq, dinner to unit, boat park, cots. **RO** ♦ **$60 - $66**, ♦♦ **$73 - $78**, ◊ **$12**, AE BC DC EFT MC VI.

FERNLEIGH COTTAGES & LODGE

- 4 self-contained Miner Cottages
- 5 bedrooms Country Lodge
- Salt pool
- Tennis Court
- Basketball
- Volleyball
- Pony rides
- Yabbying
- 2 BBQ's
- Colour TV

Goughs Bay on Lake Eildon Ph/Fax (03) 5777 3531

★★☆ **Golden Trout**, (LMH), Riverside Dve, 200m S of PO, ☎ 03 5774 2508, fax 03 5774 2429, (2 stry gr fl), 30 units [shwr, tlt, a/c (14), fan (16), heat, elec blkts, TV, radio, t/c mkg, refrig, toaster, doonas], rec rm, conf fac, ⊠, sauna, spa, bbq, gym, cots-fee. BLB ♠♠ $60 - $75, 14 units ★★. BC EFT MC VI.

Self Catering Accommodation

★★★☆ **Alrima Flats**, (HF), 11 High St, 300m E of PO, ☎ 03 5774 2529, 1 flat acc up to 5, (2 bedrm), [shwr, tlt, a/c, elec blkts, TV, clock radio, refrig, cook fac, micro, ldry (in unit), blkts, linen, pillows], w/mach, bbq (covered), c/park (carport), boat park, non smoking property. D ♠♠ $55 - $77, ◊ $8 - $10, W ♠♠ $280 - $465, ◊ $55, ch con, ♠⅄.

★★★☆ **Rudawe Lodge**, (House), 279 Taylor Bay Rd, 5km NW of PO, ☎ 03 9428 3622, fax 03 9428 3610, (2 stry gr fl), 1 house acc up to 18, (5 bedrm), [shwr (3), tlt (3), a/c, heat, tel, cable tv, video, clock radio, CD, t/c mkg, refrig, cook fac, micro, toaster, ldry, doonas, linen reqd, pillows], rec rm, lounge firepl, spa, bbq, c/park (carport). D $320 - $495.

★★★ **Silverwater Holiday Flats**, (HF), 4 South Cres, 900m W of PO, ☎ 03 5774 2050, fax 03 5774 2050, 9 flats acc up to 6, (1 & 2 bedrm), [shwr, bath (hip), tlt, hairdry, a/c-cool (1), evap cool (8), heat, elec blkts, TV, refrig, cook fac, micro (1), toaster, doonas, linen reqd, pillows], ldry, w/mach, pool, bbq, plygr, tennis, cots. D ♠♠ $55 - $72, ◊ $7 - $11, W $330 - $500, 1 cottage ★★★☆. BC MC VI.

B&B's/Guest Houses

★★★★★ **Eucalypt Ridge Private Country Retreat**, (GH), Open weekends only. No facilities for children under 16. Skyline Rd, ☎ 03 5774 2033, fax 03 5774 2610, 4 rms [ensuite, hairdry, a/c, cent heat, tel, doonas], lounge (TV, video, cd), tennis, non smoking property. D all meals ♠ $600, ♠♠ $1,200, Min book applies, AE BC DC MC VI.

★★★☆ **Stoanco Maranatha**, (B&B), 208 Snobs Creek Rd, 8km W of PO, ☎ 03 5774 2773, fax 03 5774 2773, 3 rms [fan, heat, elec blkts], ldry, lounge (TV, video, cd), t/c mkg shared, refrig, bbq, cots-fee. BB ♠ $50 - $60, ♠♠ $85 - $95, ch con, BC MC VI.

ELDORADO VIC 3746

Pop Nominal, (256km NE Melbourne), See map on pages 694/695, ref G4. Old gold mining area, situated on the banks of Reedy Creek. Goldmining Dredge Museum. Bush Walking, Gem Fossicking, Horse Riding, Scenic Drives, Shooting, Tennis.

Self Catering Accommodation

★★★ **Wirra Wolla**, (Cotg), (Farm), Cemetery La, 5km S of PO, ☎ 03 5725 1666, fax 03 5725 1829, 1 cotg acc up to 5, (2 bedrm - mudbrick.), [shwr, bath, tlt, hairdry, a/c-cool, fan, heat (wood), TV, video (avail), refrig, cook fac, micro, elec frypan, blkts, linen, pillows], w/mach, iron, iron brd, bbq (wood), Pets on application. D $60 - $70.

ELMORE VIC 3558

Pop 650. (161km N Melbourne), See map on page 696, ref B2. Agricultural town situated along the Campaspe River. Bowls, Fishing (River), Golf, Horse Riding, Shooting, Swimming (Pool, River), Tennis.

Hotels/Motels

★★ **Victoria Hotel-Motel Elmore**, (LMH), Railway Pl (Northern Hwy), opposite PO, ☎ 03 5432 6002, fax 03 5432 6002, 6 units [shwr, tlt, a/c, elec blkts, TV, t/c mkg, refrig, toaster], ldry, ⊠ (Mon to Sat), ♠. RO ♠ $45, ♠♠ $55, ◊ $11, ch con, AE BC EFT MC VI.

EMERALD VIC

See Dandenong Ranges Region.

EPPALOCK VIC 3551

Pop Part of Bendigo, (137km N Melbourne), See map on page 696, ref A3. Popular lakeside resort for all aquatic sports. Boating, Bush Walking, Fishing, Sailing, Scenic Drives, Swimming (Lake), Water Skiing.

Hotels/Motels

★★ **Lake Eppalock Hotel - Motel**, (LMH), Sunset Dve, on Kimbolton Pool, ☎ 03 5439 2533, fax 03 5439 2555, 16 units [shwr, tlt, a/c, elec blkts, tel, TV, clock radio, t/c mkg, refrig], conf fac, ⊠, ♠. BLB ♠ $45 - $60, ♠♠ $60 - $70, ◊ $15, ch con, BC EFT MC VI.

Other Accommodation

Melbourne Girls College Council, (Lodge), Ryans Rd, Redesdale 3444, off Twin Rivers Rd, ☎ 03 5439 2513, fax 03 5439 2668, 3 rms acc up to 8, [fan, heat, blkts reqd, linen reqd, pillows reqd], ldry, rec rm, lounge (TV), cook fac, bbq, bicycle-fee, canoeing, golf (9 hole). D ♠♠ $40, ◊ $10, ch con, fam con.

(Cabin Section), 4 cabins acc up to 8, [ensuite (3), fan, heat, blkts reqd, linen reqd, pillows reqd]. D ♠♠ $40, ◊ $10, ch con.

ERICA VIC 3825

Pop 271. (169km E Melbourne), See map on page 696, ref E6. Agricultural township & timber-milling centre. Scenic Drives.

Hotels/Motels

★ **Erica Hotel**, (LMH), Walhalla Rd, 200m S of PO, ☎ 03 5165 3252, fax 03 5165 3603, 7 units [shwr, tlt, heat, elec blkts, TV, t/c mkg, refrig, toaster], ⊠. RO ♠ $40, ♠♠ $50, ◊ $10, BC EFT MC VI.

EUROA VIC 3666

Pop 2,700. (151km NE Melbourne), See map on page 696, ref D3. Rich agricultural district. Secondary industries include sawmilling, joinery, clay products and building materials. Forlonge Memorial, 13km S, commemorates the introduction of the fine wool Saxony Merino sheep to the district from Tasmania by pioneer Mrs Eliza Forlonge in 1835. Farmers Arms Museum, Kirkland Ave, International Shearing Championships (Oct). Bowls, Bush Walking, Croquet, Fishing (River), Golf, Horse Riding, Scenic Drives, Shooting, Squash, Swimming (Pool, River), Tennis.

Hotels/Motels

★★★☆ **Jolly Swagman Motor Inn**, (M), Cnr Hart & Clifton Sts (Old Hume Hwy), 1km S of PO, ☎ 03 5795 3388, fax 03 5795 3352, 14 units [shwr, tlt, hairdry, a/c, elec blkts, tel, TV, video-fee, movie, clock radio, t/c mkg, refrig], iron, iron brd, pool, bbq, cots, non smoking units (5). RO ♠ $74 - $81, ♠♠ $80 - $90, ◊ $10, AE BC DC EFT MC MP VI.

★★★ **Castle Creek Motel**, (M), 53 Clifton St (Old Hume Hwy), 1km S of PO, ☎ 03 5795 2506, fax 03 5795 2549, 17 units [shwr, tlt, a/c, elec blkts, tel, TV, video-fee, clock radio, t/c mkg, refrig, toaster], ldry, pool, bbq, non smoking units (6). RO ♠ $52 - $55, ♠♠ $57 - $67, ◊ $10, AE BC DC EFT MC MCH VI,

Operator Comment: Pets & horses welcome by arrangement. Website castlecreekmotel.com

★★☆ **Euroa Motel**, (M), Hume Hwy, 1.6km N of PO, ☎ 03 5795 2211, 11 units [shwr, bath (hip) (2), tlt, a/c, fan (8), elec blkts, tel (3), TV, movie, clock radio, t/c mkg, refrig], pool, bbq, dinner to unit, cots-fee. RO ♠ $44 - $55, ♠♠ $55 - $60, ◊ $11, ch con, AE BC DC MC VI.

Self Catering Accommodation

★★★☆ **High Lane Farm**, (Cotg), Strathbogie Rd, 8km E of Old Hume Hwy, ☎ 03 5795 1344, fax 03 5795 1202, 1 cotg acc up to 8, (4 bedrm), [ensuite, shwr, tlt, a/c, c/fan, heat, elec blkts, TV, video, clock radio, CD, refrig, cook fac, micro, elec frypan, d/wash, toaster, ldry, blkts, doonas, linen, pillows], w/mach, iron, iron brd, lounge firepl, bbq, c/park (carport), cots, non smoking property. D ♠♠♠♠ $120 - $154, ◊ $15 - $16.50, W $500 - $770.

Operator Comment: "Enjoy the unique experience of a thoroughbred horse stud. Magnificent views."

B&B's/Guest Houses

★★★★ **Camerons by the Falls**, (B&B), No children's facilities, The Falls, 6km E of Hume Fwy, ☎ 03 5798 5291, fax 03 5798 5437, 2 rms [ensuite (1), shwr (1), tlt (1), hairdry, evap cool, c/fan, heat, elec blkts, TV (1), video (1), clock radio (1), t/c mkg], lounge (TV, video, cd), lounge firepl, pool, tennis, non smoking rms. BB ♠♠ $120 - $150, 1 room ★★★★☆. Dinner by arrangement. BC MC VI.

★★★☆ **Forlonge Bed & Breakfast**, (B&B), 76 Anderson St, 500m E of PO, ☎ 03 5795 2460, fax 03 5795 1020, 1 rm (1 suite) [shwr, bath, tlt, hairdry, a/c, fan, heat, elec blkts, clock radio, t/c mkg, refrig, micro, toaster, ldry], lounge (TV, video, cd), bbq, tennis, non smoking property. Suite BB ♦ $95 - $150, ♦♦ $120 - $240, Dinner by arrangement. BC MC VI.

★★★☆ **Tegwani House Bed & Breakfast**, (B&B), 33 Hunter St, 1km N of PO, ☎ 03 5795 1171, fax 03 5795 1171, 3 rms [fan, c/fan (2), elec blkts, radio], ldry, lounge (TV, cd player), pool-heated, t/c mkg shared, refrig, bbq, c/park (undercover), tennis, non smoking rms (2). BB ♦ $50, ♦♦ $80.

FALLS CREEK VIC 3699

Pop Part of Mount Beauty, (375km NE Melbourne), See map on pages 694/695, ref H5. Winter skiing area controlled by the Alpine Resorts Commission. Rocky Valley and Pretty Valley dams nearby. Park entry fees apply during winter. Boating, Bush Walking, Fishing (Stream, Lake), Horse Riding, Scenic Drives, Snow Skiing, Swimming (Lake), Tennis, Water Skiing.

Self Catering Accommodation

★★★☆ **Falls Creek Country Club**, (Apt), 7 Bogong High Plains Rd, ☎ 03 5758 3391, fax 03 5758 3481, (Multi-stry gr fl), 59 apts acc up to 10, (Studio, 1, 2 & 3 bedrm), [shwr, bath (11), spa bath (26), tlt, cent heat, tel, TV, video-fee, clock radio, refrig, cook fac, micro, d/wash (12), blkts, linen, pillows], lift, ldry, conf fac, ✆, ski hire. **High Season D ♦♦ $150 - $300, Low Season D ♦♦ $85 - $95**, 16 apartments ★★★★☆. AE BC MC VI.

★★★☆ **Koki Alpine Resort Falls Creek Vic**, (HF), 1 Arlberg St, ☎ 03 5758 3518, fax 03 5758 3541, (2 stry gr fl), 12 flats acc up to 8, (1, 2 & 4 bedrm), [shwr, tlt, cent heat, tel, TV, clock radio, refrig, cook fac, micro, d/wash, toaster, doonas, linen, pillows], ldry, dry rm, lounge, pool indoor heated, sauna, spa, ski hire. **Low Season D ♦ $36 - $69, High Season W ♦ $200 - $677**, AE BC DC EFT MC VI.

   (Lodge Section), 11 rms [shwr, tlt, cent heat, t/c mkg, refrig, doonas], cook fac. **Low Season D ♦ $44, High Season W ♦ $416 - $540, Low Season P ◊ $11.**

★★★ **Les Chalets Booking Service**, (HF), 5 Slalom St, ☎ 03 5758 3256, (Multi-stry gr fl), 25 flats acc up to 12, (1, 2, 3 & 4 bedrm), [shwr, tlt, cent heat, TV, video, clock radio, refrig, cook fac, micro, d/wash (11), linen], ldry, dry rm, cots. **High Season W $480 - $4,600, Low Season W $230 - $1,000**, Security deposit - $300.

Naarilla Alpine Flats, (HF), 3 Parallel St, ☎ 03 5758 3231, fax 02 6027 1862, (2 stry), 2 flats acc up to 6, (2 bedrm), [shwr, bath (hip), tlt, cent heat, TV, clock radio, refrig, cook fac, micro, toaster, blkts, linen, pillows], ldry, dry rm, ski hire, cots. **D ♦♦ $70, ◊ $12, W $400 - $2,300**, BC MC VI, (Rating under review).

Kilimanjaro Flats, (HF), Open snow season only. 3 Arlberg St, ☎ 03 5758 3242, fax 03 5758 3590, (Multi-stry), 8 flats acc up to 8, (Studio, 1, 2 & 3 bedrm), [shwr, spa bath (2), tlt, cent heat, tel (2), TV, clock radio, refrig, cook fac, micro, elec frypan, d/wash (2), ldry (in unit) (2), blkts, linen, pillows], ldry, dry rm, ✆. **W $780 - $3,920.**

B&B's/Guest Houses

★★★★☆ **Summit Ridge Alpine Lodge**, (GH), 8 Schuss St, ☎ 03 5758 3800, fax 03 5758 3833, (Multi-stry gr fl), 17 rms [shwr, bath, tlt, hairdry, cent heat, TV, clock radio, refrig], ldry, dry rm, rec rm, ✖, sauna, spa, ✆, non smoking property. **Low Season BLB ♦ $72, ◊ $72, High Season DBB ♦ $110 - $230, ◊ $110 - $230**, ch con, AE BC DC EFT MC VI.

★★★★ **Karelia Alpine Lodge**, (GH), 9 Parallel St, ☎ 03 5758 3278, fax 03 5758 3644, (Multi-stry), 16 rms [shwr, tlt, cent heat, TV (6), video (1), clock radio, refrig (9), mini bar (9), doonas], ldry, dry rm, rec rm, lounge (TV, video), lounge firepl, ✖, bar (cocktail), sauna, spa, t/c mkg shared, ✆. **Low Season BB ♦ $46 - $78, ◊ $46 - $78, High Season DBB ♦ $120 - $260, ◊ $130 - $220**, ch con, AE BC MC VI.

★★★☆ **Attunga Alpine Lodge**, (GH), No facilities for children under 6 in guest house section. 10 Arlberg St, ☎ 03 5758 3255, fax 03 5758 3309, (2 stry gr fl), 11 rms [shwr, tlt, hairdry, cent heat, elec blkts, TV, movie, clock radio, t/c mkg (3), refrig (3), mini bar (3), doonas], ldry-fee, dry rm, lounge, lounge firepl, ✖, bar (cocktail), pool indoor heated, sauna, spa, t/c mkg shared, bbq, ✆, non smoking property. **High Season BB ♦ $100 - $250, ♦♦ $100 - $190, Low Season BB ♦ $85 - $110, ♦♦ $99 - $135, High Season BB ♦ $585 - $1,410, ◊ $585 - $1,215**, AE BC DC MC VI.

   ★★★☆ **(Holiday Flat Section)**, 5 flats acc up to 8, (2 & 3 bedrm), [shwr, tlt, hairdry, cent heat, elec blkts, TV, clock radio, refrig, cook fac, micro, elec frypan, d/wash, toaster, blkts, doonas, linen, pillows]. **High Season D $350 - $875, Low Season D $125 - $185, High Season W $1,675 - $4,600**, Min book applies.

★★★☆ **Falls Creek Hotel**, (GH), Previously Falls Creek Motel Closed Oct 11 to Dec 26. 23 Falls Creek Rd, ☎ 03 5758 3282, fax 03 5758 3296, (Multi-stry), 24 rms [shwr, bath (2), tlt, hairdry, cent heat, tel, TV, movie, clock radio, t/c mkg, refrig], ldry, lounge (TV, video), ✖, pool indoor heated, sauna, spa, bbq, ski hire, cots. **Low Season BLB ♦ $50, ♦♦ $100, ◊ $20, High Season DBB ♦ $140 - $300, ◊ $120 - $255**, ch con, AE BC EFT MC VI.

★★★ **Cooroona Alpine Lodge**, (GH), 24 Slalom St, ☎ 03 5758 3244, fax 03 5758 3414, (2 stry gr fl), 13 rms [shwr, tlt, hairdry, cent heat, TV, movie, clock radio], ldry, dry rm, lounge (TV, video), lounge firepl, ✖, sauna, t/c mkg shared, bbq, ✆, non smoking rms. **High Season BB ♦ $65 - $145, Low Season BB ♦ $44, ♦♦ $88, ◊ $44, High Season DBB ♦ $95 - $175, ♦♦ $190 - $350, ◊ $95 - $140**, ch con, AE BC DC MC VI.

★★★ **Feathertop Alpine Lodge**, (GH), Ski Lodge. 14 Parallel St, ☎ 03 5758 3232, fax 03 5758 3514, (Multi-stry gr fl), 10 rms [shwr, tlt, cent heat, doonas], ldry, dry rm, lounge, ✖, bar, pool indoor heated, sauna, t/c mkg shared, ✆. **DBB ♦ $95 - $185**, AE BC MC VI.

★★★ **Lakeside Lodge**, (GH), Ski Lodge. Open snow season only. 14 Schuss St, ☎ 03 9761 8466, fax 03 9761 8477, (Multi-stry gr fl), 16 rms [shwr, tlt, cent heat], ldry, dry rm, rec rm, lounge (TV, video), ✖, sauna, spa, t/c mkg shared, refrig, ✆, cots, non smoking rms. **BB ♦ $65 - $155, ◊ $50 - $135, W ♦ $395 - $990, ◊ $290 - $850**, ch con, AE BC DC EFT MC VI.

★★★ **Pretty Valley Alpine Lodge**, (GH), Ski Lodge. 10 Slalom St, ☎ 03 5758 3210, fax 03 5758 3493, (2 stry), 26 rms [shwr, tlt, cent heat, TV (6), doonas], ldry, dry rm, lounge, lounge firepl, ✖, bar, pool-heated, sauna, spa, t/c mkg shared, ✆, ski hire. **High Season D all meals ♦ $160 - $210, ♦ $800 - $1,300**, AE BC DC MC VI.

★★★ **Ski Club of Victoria**, (GH), Nelse Lodge. 17 Slalom St, ☎ 03 5758 3263, or 03 9826 0428, fax 03 5758 3688, (2 stry gr fl), 12 rms [shwr, tlt, cent heat, elec blkts, clock radio, doonas], ldry, dry rm, lounge (TV, video), ✖, bar, pool indoor heated, sauna, spa, t/c mkg shared, bbq, ✆. **Low Season BB ♦ $66, ◊ $66, High Season D ♦ $137.50 - $165, ◊ $137.50 - $165, High Season W ♦ $1,083.50 - $1,221**, AE BC DC EFT MC VI.

   ★★★☆ **(Apartment Section)**, 1 apt acc up to 10, (3 bedrm), [ensuite (1), shwr, bath (hip) (1), tlt, tel, TV, video, clock radio, refrig, cook fac, micro, d/wash]. **High Season W $3,630 - $5,500.**

Diana Lodge, (GH), Ski Lodge. 6 Falls Creek Rd, ☎ 03 5758 3214, fax 03 5758 3523, (Multi-stry gr fl), 16 rms [shwr, tlt, hairdry (6), cent heat, TV (9), t/c mkg (9), refrig, doonas], ldry, dry rm, lounge (TV, video), ✖, BYO, spa, t/c mkg shared, refrig, ✆, cots. **High Season D all meals ♦ $127 - $240, ◊ $85 - $160, ♦ $893 - $1,680, ◊ $595 - $1,120**, ch con, AE BC MC VI, (Rating under review).

Halleys Lodge, (GH), Ski Lodge. Open snow season only. 11 Slalom St, ☎ 03 5758 3363, fax 03 5758 3259, (Multi-stry), 21 rms [shwr, tlt, cent heat], lounge (TV, video), ✖, pool indoor heated, sauna, spa, t/c mkg shared, ski hire. **DBB ♦ $496 - $896**, ch con, AE BC DC EFT MC VI, (Rating under review).

Silver Ski Lodge & Restaurant, (GH), Open snow season only. 1 Sitzmark St, ☎ 03 9755 1528, fax 03 9755 1833, (Multi-stry), 31 rms [shwr, tlt, cent heat, doonas], dry rm, lounge (TV), ✖, bar (cocktail), sauna, spa, t/c mkg shared, ✆. **DBB ♦ $70 - $120, ◊ $70 - $120, ♦ $420 - $920, ◊ $420 - $920**, ch con, (Rating under review).

Other Accommodation

Viking Alpine Lodge, (Lodge), Ski Lodge. 13 Parallel St, ☎ 03 5758 3247, fax 03 5758 3483, (Multi-stry), 15 rms [shwr, tlt, cent heat, clock radio, doonas], ldry, dry rm, lounge (TV, video), cook fac, t/c mkg shared, refrig, bbq, ✆, ski hire. **High Season D ♦ $45 - $90, ◊ $45, Low Season D ♦♦ $65, ◊ $22**, ch con, AE BC DC EFT MC VI.

FERNDALE VIC 3821

Pop Nominal, (101km SE Melbourne), See map on page 696, ref D7. Dairying district in the Strzelecki Ranges. Bush Walking, Scenic Drives.

B&B's/Guest Houses

★★★☆ **Clearview Farm**, (B&B), Van Ess Rd, 28km S of Warragul, ☎ 03 5626 4263, fax 03 5626 4263, 4 rms (1 suite) [spa bath, cent heat, elec blkts], lounge (TV, video), ✖, spa-fee, t/c mkg shared, non smoking rms. **BB ♦ $77, ♦♦ $110 - $121**, 1 suite ★★★★. Dinner by arrangement. AE BC MC VI.

   ★★★ **(Cottage Section)**, 2 cotgs acc up to 6, (2 & 3 bedrm), [shwr, bath (1), tlt, heat (pot belly), elec blkts, TV, video (1), clock radio, CD, refrig, cook fac, micro, ldry, linen]. **G $264 - $407, W $462 - $627.**

   (Group Accommodation Section), 2 bunkhouses acc up to 8, (Bunk Rooms), [shwr, tlt, elec blkts, clock radio, t/c mkg, linen, pillows]. **BB ♦♦ $121, ◊ $44.**

FERNY CREEK VIC

See Dandenong Ranges Region.

FISH CREEK VIC 3959

Pop Nominal, (167km SE Melbourne), See map on page 696, ref D8. Small farming community. Bowls, Scenic Drives, Tennis.

Hotels/Motels

★★ **The Fishy Pub**, (LMH), Old Waratah Rd, 300m S of PO, ☎ 03 5683 2404, fax 03 5683 2550, 9 units [shwr, tlt, a/c, TV, clock radio, t/c mkg, refrig, toaster], ✉, ✆, cots. **RO ♦ $50 - $55, ♦♦ $66 - $88, ◊ $15**, ch con, BC EFT MC VI.

B&B's/Guest Houses

★★★★ **Milkwood**, (B&B), Previously Pamalby B & B 660 Harding Lawson Rd, 20 min to Prom Gate, ☎ 03 5683 2449, fax 03 5683 2446, 1 rm [shwr, tlt, hairdry, fan, heat, elec blkts, TV, clock radio, t/c mkg, refrig, cook fac ltd, micro, toaster], c/park (carport). **BB ♦♦ $120**.

★★★ **(Cottage Section)**, 1 cotg acc up to 2, (1 bedrm), [shwr, tlt, hairdry, fan, heat, elec blkts, TV, clock radio, t/c mkg, refrig, cook fac, micro, toaster, blkts, linen, pillows], breakfast ingredients. **BB ♦♦ $105**.

FLINDERS VIC 3929

Pop 500. (89km S Melbourne), See map on page 696, ref B7. Popular beach resort. Fishing, Golf, Scenic Drives, Surfing, Swimming (Beach), Tennis.

Hotels/Motels

★★★☆ **Flinders Cove Motor Inn**, (M), 32 Cook St, 300m E of PO, ☎ 03 5989 0666, fax 03 5989 0906, (2 stry gr fl), 25 units [shwr, tlt, hairdry, a/c, elec blkts, tel, TV, movie, clock radio, t/c mkg, refrig, toaster], iron, iron brd, conf fac, ✉, pool indoor heated, sauna, spa, rm serv, cots-fee, non smoking units (11). **RO ♦ $99 - $119, ♦♦ $99 - $119, ◊ $10**, AE BC DC EFT JCB MC MP VI, ♿.

★★☆ **Flinders Hotel**, (LMH), Cnr Cook & Wood Sts, 300m E of PO, ☎ 03 5989 0201, fax 03 5989 0878, 8 units [shwr, tlt, a/c, elec blkts, tel, TV, clock radio, t/c mkg, refrig, toaster], conf fac, ✉, cots. **BLB ♦ $70 - $110, ♦♦ $85 - $110**, Min book long w/ends and Easter, AE BC DC EFT MC VI.

Self Catering Accommodation

★★★★☆ **Nazaaray**, (Cotg), 25ha beef grazing property, 266 Meakins Rd, 10km W of Flinders, off Boneo Rd, ☎ 03 9585 1138, fax 03 9585 1140, (2 stry) 1 cotg acc up to 8, (3 bedrm), [shwr, tlt, hairdry, a/c, fan, heat, elec blkts, tel, TV, video, clock radio, CD, refrig, cook fac, micro, d/wash, ldry, doonas, linen, pillows], iron, iron brd. **D ♦♦ $140, ◊ $50, W $840 - $1,925**, ch con, BC MC VI.

★★★☆ **Flinders Bed & Breakfast**, (Cotg), 94 Cook St, ☎ 03 5989 0301, fax 03 5989 0301, 1 cotg acc up to 4, (Studio), [shwr, tlt, hairdry, c/fan, heat, elec blkts, TV, clock radio, CD, refrig, cook fac, toaster, ldry (in unit), blkts, linen, pillows], iron, iron brd, bbq, tennis, breakfast ingredients, non smoking property. **BB ♦♦ $105 - $140**, ch con.

B&B's/Guest Houses

★★★★☆ **Samburu**, (B&B), No children's facilities, 75 Eastern Grey Rise, 14km W of Flinders, off Meakins Rd, ☎ 03 5989 0093, fax 03 5989 0053, 2 rms [ensuite, hairdry, c/fan, heat, t/c mkg, refrig, mini bar], lounge (TV, video, cd), lounge firepl, bbq, non smoking property. **BB ♦♦ $130 - $145**, AE BC MC VI.

★★★★ **(Birdcage)**, 1 unit acc up to 2, (Studio), [shwr, spa bath, tlt, a/c, refrig, cook fac, micro, toaster], lounge (TV, cd player), bbq. **BB ♦♦ $120 - $180, ♦♦ $700 - $850**.

★★★★ **Cipriani's Flinders Country Inn**, (B&B), 165 Wood St (Frankston - Flinders Rd), ☎ 03 5989 0933, fax 03 5989 0059, (2 stry), 2 rms [ensuite (1), shwr, bath (1), tlt, hairdry, c/fan, heat], lounge (TV, video, cd), lounge firepl, ✗, BYO, t/c mkg shared. **BB ♦ $100, ♦♦ $165**, ch con, BC MC VI.

★★★★ **Fulbry Manor**, (B&B), 1827 Mornington-Flinders Rd, 6km N of PO, ☎ 03 5989 0295, fax 03 5989 0290, 1 rm [shwr, tlt, hairdry, a/c-cool, cent heat, elec blkts, clock radio], lounge (TV, video, cd), t/c mkg shared, bbq, non smoking property. **BB ♦♦ $120**, BC MC VI.

★★★★ **(Holiday Unit Section)**, 1 unit acc up to 6, (3 bedrm), [shwr, tlt, hairdry, a/c-cool, cent heat, TV, video, t/c mkg, refrig, cook fac, micro, toaster, ldry (in unit), blkts, linen, pillows], iron, iron brd, breakfast ingredients. **BB ♦♦ $165, ◊ $60, W $900**.

FORREST VIC 3236

Pop 371. (158km SW Melbourne), See map on pages 694/695, ref D7. Small farming & sawmilling township. Bush Walking, Fishing, Scenic Drives, Shooting, Swimming (River), Tennis.

Self Catering Accommodation

★★★★ **Forrest Ti Tree Cottages**, (Cotg), 5 Grant St, Otway Ranges, ☎ 03 5236 6427, fax 03 5236 6427, 2 cotgs acc up to 6, (3 bedrm), [shwr, spa bath, tlt, c/fan, heat (wood), elec blkts, video, clock radio, t/c mkg, refrig, cook fac, toaster, ldry, blkts, doonas, linen, pillows], w/mach, dryer, iron, iron brd, lounge firepl, breakfast ingredients, Pets on application. **D ♦♦ $110, ◊ $35, W ♦♦ $700 - $800**, Min book applies.

B&B's/Guest Houses

★★★★ **Rhyders Bed & Breakfast**, (B&B), 99 Grant St, 1km S of PO, ☎ 03 5236 6556, 2 rms [shwr, tlt, heat, TV, clock radio, t/c mkg, refrig, micro, toaster], bbq, non smoking units, Pets allowed. **BB ♦ $60, ♦♦ $100, ◊ $35**, ch con.

★★★ **The Forrest Country Guesthouse**, (GH), 16 Grant St (Colac - Apollo Bay Rd), 200m N of PO, ☎ 03 5236 6446, fax 03 5236 6446, 7 rms [ensuite, bath, heat], lounge (CD player), lounge firepl, sauna, bbq, plygr, non smoking rms. **BB ♦ $60, ♦♦ $105**, ch con, Dinner by arrangement. BC MC VI.

FOSTER VIC 3960

Pop 1,050. (175km SE Melbourne), See map on page 696, ref E7. Dairy farming area. Boating, Bowls, Bush Walking, Fishing, Golf, Horse Riding, Sailing, Scenic Drives, Shooting, Swimming, Tennis, Water Skiing.

Hotels/Motels

★★★☆ **Foster Motel**, (M), South Gippsland Hwy, ☎ 03 5682 2022, fax 03 5682 2898, 29 units [shwr, spa bath (2), tlt, hairdry, a/c, elec blkts, tel, TV, video-fee, clock radio, CD (4), t/c mkg, refrig, mini bar (4), toaster], ldry, iron, iron brd, rec rm, ✉, pool, sauna, spa, plygr, cots-fee. **RO ♦ $94 - $150, ♦♦ $104 - $160, ◊ $12**, ch con, 4 units ★★★★. AE BC DC JCB MC MP VI, ♿.

★★☆ **Wilsons Promontory Motel**, (M), 26 Station Rd, 200m SE of PO, ☎ 03 5682 2055, fax 03 5682 1064, 19 units [shwr, bath (1), tlt, a/c, elec blkts, tel, TV, clock radio (11), t/c mkg, refrig, toaster], cots-fee, non smoking units (5). **RO ♦ $55 - $75, ♦♦ $65 - $85, ◊ $10**, BC EFT MC VI.

Self Catering Accommodation

★★★★ **Ripplebrook by the Prom**, (Cotg), 30 Powells Rd, 10km SW of PO, ☎ 03 5687 1224, fax 03 5687 1225, 1 cotg acc up to 2, (1 bedrm), [shwr, tlt, hairdry, fan, heat, TV, clock radio, CD, t/c mkg, refrig, cook fac, micro, toaster, doonas, linen, pillows]. **D $90 - $120**, Min book Christmas Jan long w/ends and Easter, BC MC VI.

★★★☆ **Stockyard Creek Cottage**, (Cotg), (Farm), McGleads Rd, 2km NW of PO, off Gardiners Rd, ☎ 03 5682 2493, fax 03 5682 2524, 2 cotgs acc up to 6, (2 bedrm), [shwr, bath (1), tlt, a/c (1), heat (wood), elec blkts, TV, CD (1), refrig, cook fac, micro, toaster, ldry (in unit), blkts, linen, pillows]. **D $70 - $120, W $350 - $700**, BC MC VI.

★★★ **Warrawee Holiday Units**, (HU), 38 Station Rd, 200m SE of PO, ☎ 03 5689 1242, (2 stry gr fl), 5 units acc up to 5, (2 bedrm), [shwr, bath (hip), tlt, c/fan, heat (wood), elec blkts, TV, clock radio, refrig, cook fac, toaster, ldry (in unit), blkts, linen, pillows], iron, iron brd, bbq, plygr, cots. **D** ♯♯ **$80**, ◊ **$15 - $25, W $420 - $700**, ch con, Min book long w/ends and Easter.

Rose Cabin, (HU), 21 Victory Ave, 300m N of PO, ☎ 03 5682 2628, 1 unit acc up to 2, (Studio), [shwr, tlt, heat, elec blkts, radio, refrig, toaster]. **D** ♯ **$30**, ♯♯ **$60**, (Rating under review).

B&B's/Guest Houses

★★★★☆ **Larkrise Pottery & Farm**, (B&B), RMB 3216 Fish Creek/Foster Rd, 3.4km SW of PO, ☎ 03 5682 2953, fax 03 5682 2953, 2 rms [ensuite, hairdry, evap cool, fan, heat (wood), elec blkts, micro], lounge (TV, cd), t/c mkg shared, refrig, bbq, c/park (carport), non smoking property. **BB** ♯ **$90**, ♯♯ **$120**, Dinner by arrangement.

★★★★ **Hillcrest Farmhouse B & B**, (B&B), 175 Ameys Track, 3.2km NE of PO, off South Gippsland Hwy, ☎ 03 5682 2769, fax 03 5682 2101, 2 rms [ensuite (1), shwr (1), bath (1), tlt (2), hairdry, fan, heat, elec blkts, clock radio], lounge (TV, cd player), lounge firepl, t/c mkg shared (in lounge). **BB** ♯ **$75**, ♯♯ **$110**, 1 room ★★★★☆, Dinner by arrangement. AE BC MC VI.

★★★☆ **Aruma Projects**, (B&B), 20 Maines Way, 3 km SW of PO, off Fish Creek - Foster Rd, ☎ 03 5682 1715, or 03 5682 1716, (2 stry), 2 rms [hairdry, fan, heat, elec blkts, clock radio], lounge (TV, video, cd), t/c mkg shared, refrig, cots, non smoking property. **BB** ♯ **$75**, ♯♯ **$95**, ◊ **$45 - $75**, BC MC VI.

FRENCH ISLAND VIC 3921

Pop 75. (64km S Melbourne), See map on page 697, ref E8. Situated in Westernport Bay - accessible by passenger ferry from Cowes or Stony Point. Ferry departs Stony Point 8am & 9am, 4pm & 5pm (Mon - Fri). Peninsula Charter Services 03 5979 3722. Car access only by barge from Corinella but is not recommended for tourists. For island tours contact French Island Roadlines 03-5980 1241. Bush Walking, Fishing.

B&B's/Guest Houses

★★★ **Tortoise Head - French Island**, (GH), 10 Tankerton Rd, 200m E of Tankerton jetty, ☎ 03 5980 1234, or 03 9889 3807, fax 03 5980 1222, (2 stry gr fl), 9 rms [ensuite (4), doonas], lounge (stereo, cd player), conf fac, ✗, BYO, t/c mkg shared, courtesy transfer, cots. **BB** ♯ **$65**, ◊ **$65**, ch con, Property is solar powered. Meals by arrangement. BC MC VI.

FRESHWATER CREEK VIC 3216

Pop 50. (85km SW Melbourne), See map on page 696, ref A6. Agricultural township. Horse Riding, Tennis.

Self Catering Accommodation

★★★ **Fresh Water Creek Cottages**, (Cotg), 815 Pettavel Rd, off Blackgate Rd, 6.9km SW of General Store, ☎ 03 5264 5296, fax 03 5264 5296, 4 cotgs acc up to 6, (1 & 2 bedrm), [shwr, bath, spa bath (1), tlt, a/c, heat, elec blkts, TV, clock radio, refrig, cook fac, cook fac ltd (1), ldry (in unit) (3), blkts, linen, pillows], sauna (1), spa, plygr, tennis, cots. **D** ♯♯ **$115**, **W $500 - $800**, 1 cottage ★★★★. AE BC MC VI.

GEELONG VIC 3220

Pop 125,400. (72km SW Melbourne), See map on page 696, ref A6. Includes: BELMONT, CORIO, DRUMCONDRA, GEELONG NORTH, GEELONG WEST, GROVEDALE, LEOPOLD, MOOLAP, MT DUNEE. The second largest city in Victoria and a modern seaport. Geelong Otway Tourism, Bay end of Moorabool St, 03 5222 2900 or 03 5223 2399. Boating, Bowls, Bush Walking, Fishing, Golf, Greyhound Racing, Horse Racing, Sailing, Scenic Drives, Shooting, Squash, Surfing, Swimming (Beach, Pool), Tennis, Trotting, Water Skiing. See also Lara.

Hotels/Motels

AAA *TOURISM Special Rates* ★★★★ **Abbotswood Motor Inn**, (M), 308 High St (Princes Hwy), Belmont 3216, 1.5km W of Belmont PO, ☎ 03 5243 0122, fax 03 5243 0791, 19 units [shwr, spa bath (4), tlt, hairdry (8), a/c, c/fan (3), elec blkts, tel, TV, video (8), movie, clock radio, t/c mkg, refrig, cook fac ltd (3), toaster], ldry, iron, iron brd, conf fac, ✗ (licensed), pool indoor heated, bbq, rm serv, dinner to unit, plygr, tennis, cots-fee, non smoking units (6). **RO** ♯ **$67 - $110**, ♯♯ **$72 - $132**, ◊ **$15**, 4 units ★★★☆. AE BC DC MC VI.

★★★★ **Mercure Hotel Geelong**, (M), Cnr Gheringhap & Myers Sts, 500m S of PO, ☎ 03 5221 6844, fax 03 5221 5814, 142 units (3 suites) [shwr, tlt, hairdry, a/c, tel, cable tv, movie, clock radio, t/c mkg, refrig, mini bar], lift, ldry, iron, iron brd, conf fac, ✉, pool, sauna, spa, 24hr reception, rm serv, ✆, cots, non smoking flr (4). **RO** ♯ **$137**, ♯♯ **$137**, ◊ **$33**, ch con, AE BC DC EFT JCB MC VI.

 ★★★★ **Quality Inn Parkside**, (M), 68 High St, Belmont 3216, 400m SW of Barwon River, ☎ 03 5243 6766, fax 03 5243 6987, (Multi-stry), 36 units [shwr, bath (hip) (6), spa bath (3), tlt, hairdry, a/c, heat, elec blkts, tel, TV, video-fee, clock radio, t/c mkg, refrig, mini bar (23), micro (8), toaster], lift, ldry, iron, iron brd, conf fac, ✉, pool-heated, bbq, rm serv, cots-fee, non smoking units (12). **RO** ♯ **$75 - $150**, ◊ **$11**, AE BC DC EFT MC VI.

★★★★ **Rose Garden Motor Inn**, (M), 14 Settlement Rd (Princes Hwy), Belmont 3216, ☎ 03 5241 9441, fax 03 5241 9563, 15 units [shwr, spa bath (5), tlt, hairdry, a/c, elec blkts, tel, TV, clock radio, t/c mkg, refrig, micro (13), toaster], ldry, iron, iron brd, pool, bbq, rm serv, dinner to unit, c/park (carport) (5), plygr, cots-fee, non smoking units (11). **RO** ♯ **$72**, ♯♯ **$86 - $115**, AE BC DC EFT MC VI.

 ★★★☆ **Admiralty Motor Inn**, (M), 66 McKillop St, 500m SW of city centre, ☎ 03 5221 4288, fax 03 5221 4044, (2 stry gr fl), 40 units (4 suites) [shwr, spa bath (4), tlt, hairdry, a/c, fire pl (3), elec blkts, tel, TV, t/c mkg, refrig, cook fac (2), micro (2)], ldry, conf fac, pool (salt water), cots-fee, non smoking units (13). **RO** ♯♯ **$97 - $195**, ◊ **$12**, Suite RO ♯ **$130 - $195**, ♯♯ **$130 - $195**, AE BC DC EFT MC MP VI.

 ★★★☆ **Geelong Motor Inn & Serviced Apartments**, (M), Cnr Princes Hwy & Kooyong Rd, 1.5km N of PO, ☎ 03 5222 4777, fax 03 5223 1493, (2 stry gr fl), 18 units (1 suite) [shwr, bath (1), spa bath (2), tlt, hairdry (10), a/c, elec blkts, tel, TV, clock radio, t/c mkg, refrig, toaster], ldry, conf fac, ✉ (Mon to Sat), pool indoor heated, spa, rm serv, cots-fee. **RO** ♯ **$90 - $100**, ♯♯ **$101 - $110**, ◊ **$11**, 6 units ★★★★. AE BC DC MC MP VI.

★★★☆ **(Apartment Section)**, (Multi-stry gr fl), 9 apts acc up to 5, (1 & 2 bedrm), [shwr, tlt, a/c-cool, heat, tel, TV, clock radio, refrig, cook fac, blkts, linen, pillows]. **D** ♯♯ **$100 - $170**, ◊ **$10**.

 ★★★☆ **Hacienda Geelong Motel**, (M), 15 Mt Pleasant Rd, Belmont 3216, 2.8km S of Geelong PO, ☎ 03 5243 5844, fax 03 5241 9613, (2 stry gr fl), 12 units [shwr, tlt, hairdry, a/c, elec blkts, tel, TV, video-fee, clock radio, t/c mkg, refrig, cook fac (1)], iron, iron brd, pool, bbq, cots-fee, non smoking units (5). **RO** ♯ **$66 - $93.50**, ♯♯ **$77 - $93.50**, ◊ **$12**, AE BC DC JCB MC MP VI.

  ★★★☆ **Sundowner Chain Motor Inns**, (M), 13 The Esplanade, 1km N of PO, ☎ 03 5222 3499, fax 03 5221 8912, (2 stry gr fl), 35 units [shwr, spa bath (6), tlt, hairdry, a/c, elec blkts, tel, TV, clock radio, t/c mkg, refrig, mini bar, toaster], ldry, iron, iron brd, conf fac, ✉, pool, sauna, rm serv, cots-fee, non smoking units (12). **RO** ♯ **$94 - $175**, ♯♯ **$105 - $175**, ◊ **$11**, ch con, Min book long w/ends, AE BC DC EFT MC MP VI, ⚒.

 ★★★ **Aristocrat Waurnvale Motel**, (M), 90 Princes Hwy, Waurn Ponds 3216, 800m W of Anglesea turnoff, ☎ 03 5241 8211, fax 03 5241 8283, 10 units [shwr, spa bath (4), tlt, hairdry (4), a/c (4), c/fan (10), heat, elec blkts, tel, TV, video-fee, clock radio, t/c mkg, refrig], iron (4), iron brd (4), pool (heated), bbq, cots-fee, non smoking units (3). **RO** ♯ **$56 - $74**, ♯♯ **$67 - $81**, ◊ **$12**, 4 units ★★★★. AE BC DC EFT MC VI.

★★★ **Bay City (Geelong) Motel**, (M), 231 Malop St, 500m E of PO, ☎ 03 5221 1933, fax 03 5221 7101, 18 units [shwr, tlt, a/c, elec blkts, tel, TV, clock radio, t/c mkg, refrig], ✗, BYO, cots-fee. **RO** ♯ **$72 - $94**, ♯♯ **$77 - $94**, ◊ **$12**, ch con, AE BC DC MC VI.

 ★★★ **Colonial Lodge Motel**, (M), 57 Fyans St, 200m SE of Kardinia Park football ground, ☎ 03 5223 2266, fax 03 5229 1141, 10 units [shwr, tlt, hairdry, a/c-cool, heat, elec blkts, tel, TV, video-fee, clock radio, t/c mkg, refrig], ldry, iron, iron brd, cots-fee, non smoking units (5). **RO** ♯ **$56 - $61**, ♯♯ **$66 - $72**, ◊ **$10**, ch con, AE BC DC EFT MC VI.

 ★★★ **Flag Inn Eastern Sands**, (M), Previously Eastern Sands Motel 1 Bellerine St, 200m E of PO, ☎ 03 5221 5577, fax 03 5221 7775, (2 stry gr fl), 25 units [shwr, tlt, hairdry, a/c, elec blkts, tel, TV, clock radio, t/c mkg, refrig], ✉, dinner to unit, c/park (carport) (15), cots-fee. **RO** ♯ **$82 - $125**, ♯♯ **$92 - $125**, ◊ **$14**, AE BC DC MC MP VI.

★★★ **Golden Palms Motel**, (M), 234 Torquay Rd (Surfcoast Hwy), Grovedale 3216, 3km SW of Belmont PO, ☎ 03 5243 1077, fax 03 5243 3045, 13 units [shwr, tlt, a/c (9), c/fan (4), heat (4), elec blkts, tel, TV, video-fee, clock radio, t/c mkg, refrig, toaster], ldry, bbq, dinner to unit, plygr, cots. **RO** ♦ **$55 - $82,** ♦♦ **$70 - $92,** ◊ **$15,** AE BC DC EFT MC VI.

★★★ **Grovedale Motel**, (M), 142 Torquay Rd (Surfcoast Hwy), Grovedale 3216, 2km S of Belmont PO, ☎ 03 5243 3264, fax 03 5243 8532, 12 units [shwr, tlt, a/c-cool (4), a/c (8), heat (4), elec blkts, tel, TV, clock radio, t/c mkg, refrig], bbq, plygr, cots-fee, non smoking units (5). **RO** ♦ **$64 - $83,** ♦♦ **$75 - $90,** ◊ **$15,** AE BC EFT MC VI.

★★★ **Huntsman Innkeepers Motor Inn**, (M), 9 Aberdeen St, 1km W of City Centre, ☎ 03 5221 2177, fax 03 5222 2941, (2 stry gr fl), 36 units [shwr, tlt, a/c-cool, heat, elec blkts, tel, TV, video (avail), clock radio, t/c mkg, refrig], ldry, ⊠ (Mon to Sat), bar (cocktail), pool, sauna, spa, rm serv, cots-fee, non smoking units (12). **RO** ♦ **$65 - $89,** ♦♦ **$76 - $89,** ◊ **$15,** ch con, AE BC DC EFT MC MP VI.

★★★ **Kiloran Motel**, (M), Princes Hwy, Waurn Ponds 3216, 7km SW of Geelong City Centre, ☎ 03 5243 6333, fax 03 5241 9199, 14 units [shwr, tlt, hairdry, a/c, fan (3), elec blkts, tel, TV, clock radio, t/c mkg, refrig, cook fac (5), micro (6), toaster], ldry, pool, bbq, boat park, cots, non smoking units (4). **RO** ♦ **$54 - $60,** ♦♦ **$65 - $77,** ◊ **$11,** AE BC EFT MC VI.

★★★ **Parkwood Motel**, (M), Cnr Shannon Ave & Ballarat Rd, Geelong North 3215, 3.2km NW of PO, opposite Geelong Golf Club, ☎ 03 5278 5477, fax 03 5278 5477, (2 stry gr fl), 12 units [shwr, tlt, fan, cent heat, tel, TV, clock radio, t/c mkg, refrig], pool, bbq, plygr, cots-fee. **RO** ♦ **$55 - $62,** ♦♦ **$66 - $72,** ◊ **$13,** ch con, AE BC DC EFT MC VI.

★★★ **Rippleside Park Motor Inn**, (M), 67 Melbourne Rd, Drumcondra 3220, Cnr Bell Pde, ☎ 03 5278 2017, fax 03 5278 8244, 13 units [shwr, tlt, hairdry, fan, heat, elec blkts, tel, TV, radio, t/c mkg, refrig], meals avail (breakfast), non smoking rms (7). **RO** ♦ **$55 - $77,** ♦♦ **$63.80 - $77,** ◊ **$11,** ch con, AE BC EFT MC VI.

★★★ **Shannon Motor Inn**, (M), 285 Shannon Ave, Newtown 3220, 1.5km W of PO, ☎ 03 5222 4355, fax 03 5222 4276, 18 units [shwr, spa bath (1), tlt, a/c, elec blkts, tel, TV, video-fee, clock radio, t/c mkg, refrig, micro-fee, toaster], ldry, bbq, cots-fee. **RO** ♦ **$65 - $99,** ♦♦ **$76 - $150,** ◊ **$11,** AE BC DC MC VI.

★★★☆ **(Holiday Unit Section)**, 4 units acc up to 5, (2 bedrm), [shwr, bath, tlt, a/c-cool, fan, heat, elec blkts, tel, TV, video, clock radio, refrig, cook fac, micro, elec frypan, toaster, ldry (in unit), blkts, doonas, linen, pillows], c/park (garage). **D $132 - $150, W $605 - $750.**

★★☆ **Kangaroo Motel**, (M), 16 The Esplanade South, 1km N of City Centre, ☎ 03 5221 4022, fax 03 5221 4892, (2 stry gr fl), 10 units [shwr, tlt, a/c-cool, heat, elec blkts, tel, TV, clock radio, t/c mkg, refrig], ldry, ⊠ (Tue to Sun), cots-fee. **RO** ♦ **$55 - $60,** ♦♦ **$68 - $75,** ◊ **$10,** ch con, BC MC MP VI.

★★☆ **The Ponds Hotel Motel**, (LMH), Princes Hwy, Waurn Ponds 3216, 4.2km W of Belmont PO, ☎ 03 5243 1244, fax 03 5244 2575, 15 units [shwr, tlt, heat, elec blkts, tel, TV, clock radio, t/c mkg, refrig, toaster], ldry, ⊠, ☏, cots-fee. **RO** ♦ **$60,** ♦♦ **$66 - $70,** ◊ **$10,** Light breakfast only available. AE BC DC EFT MC VI.

★★ **Motel Corio Bay**, (M), 292 Princes Hwy, Corio 3214, ☎ 03 5275 1489, fax 03 5275 5950, (2 stry gr fl), 24 units [shwr, tlt, a/c, elec blkts, tel, TV, video-fee, clock radio, t/c mkg, refrig, toaster], cots-fee. **RO** ♦ **$58,** ♦♦ **$69,** ◊ **$11,** AE BC DC MC VI.

★★ **Peninsula**, (LMH), 195 Queenscliff Rd (Bellarine Hwy), Newcomb 3219, 5km SE of PO, ☎ 03 5248 2606, fax 03 5248 1700, 10 units [shwr, tlt, a/c, elec blkts, tel, TV, radio, t/c mkg, refrig], ⊠, plygr. **RO** ♦ **$55,** ♦♦ **$66,** ◊ **$5.50,** ch con, AE BC DC EFT MC VI.

★ **Jokers on Ryrie**, (LH), Cnr Ryrie & Yarra Sts, 300m E of City Centre, ☎ 03 5229 1104, fax 03 5229 1135, (2 stry), 10 rms [basin (1)], lounge (TV), ⊠, t/c mkg shared, c/park (limited), ☏. **RO** ♦ **$40 - $55,** ♦♦ **$55 - $65,** ch con, BC EFT MC VI.

Self Catering Accommodation

★★★★ **Barwon Valley Lodge**, (HU), 99 Barrabool Rd, Belmont 3216, 3km S of Geelong PO, overlooking Barwon River, ☎ 03 5244 2111, fax 03 5244 3377, 15 units acc up to 6, (2 bedrm), [shwr, bath, tlt, a/c-cool, heat, elec blkts, tel, TV, video, clock radio, refrig, cook fac, micro, toaster, ldry (in unit), blkts, linen, pillows], pool, spa, bbq, plygr, tennis, cots, non smoking property. **D ♦ $88 - $115.50, ♦♦ $104.50 - $132, ◊ $16.50**, ch con, AE BC DC MC VI.

★★★★ **Hyatt Apartments**, (Apt), 63 Fyans St, 200m SE of Kardinia Park /Shell Stadium, ☎ 03 5274 9192, fax 03 5274 9192, 3 apts acc up to 6, (2 bedrm), [shwr, tlt, a/c-cool, fan, heat, elec blkts, tel, TV, clock radio, refrig, micro, elec frypan, d/wash, toaster, ldry (in unit), blkts, linen, pillows], c/park (garage). **D $77 - $154**, Breakfast available, AE BC DC EFT MC VI.

★★★ **Costa Verde Geelong**, (HU), 621 Torquay Rd (Surfcoast Hwy), Mount Duneed 3221, 10km S of Geelong PO, ☎ 03 5264 1243, fax 03 5264 1508, 9 units acc up to 6, (2 bedrm), [shwr, bath (hip), tlt, hairdry, a/c, elec blkts, tel, TV, video (avail), clock radio, refrig, cook fac, toaster, blkts, linen, pillows], ldry, iron, pool, spa, kiosk, plygr. **D ♦♦ $72 - $99, ◊ $11, W $422 - $594**, Min book Christmas Jan long w/ends and Easter, BC EFT MC VI.

★★★ **Seamist Holiday Apartments Geelong**, (HU), 62 Western Beach Rd, ☎ 03 5222 2447, fax 03 5221 7988, 10 units acc up to 4, (1 bedrm), [shwr, bath (hip), tlt, a/c, heat, elec blkts (double beds), TV, clock radio, refrig, cook fac, micro, elec frypan, toaster, blkts, linen, pillows], ldry, ✆, cots. **D ♦♦ $77 - $97, ◊ $11**, ch con, AE BC DC EFT MC VI.

★★★ **Warren Crest Self Contained Units**, (HU), 206 Myers St, 800m SE of Geelong GPO, ☎ 03 5278 2667, fax 03 5278 2667, (2 stry gr fl), 6 units acc up to 4, (Studio), [shwr, tlt, heat, elec blkts, tel, TV, clock radio, refrig, cook fac, micro, toaster, ldry (in unit), blkts, linen, pillows], iron, iron brd, c/park (carport), non smoking units (6). **D ♦♦ $82.50 - $105, ◊ $11, W ♦♦ $440 - $550, ◊ $66**, pen con, BC MC VI.

Nireeda Apartments on Clare, (Apt), 1 Clare St, ☎ 03 5221 0566, 13 apts acc up to 6, (Studio, 2 & 3 bedrm), [shwr, tlt, tel, TV, clock radio, t/c mkg, refrig, cook fac, micro, toaster, doonas, linen, pillows], ldry, w/mach, dryer, secure park, non smoking property. **D ♦♦ $115 - $145, ◊ $15**, (not yet classified).

B&B's/Guest Houses

★★★★☆ **Lilydale House Home Hosting**, (B&B), 100 Dog Rocks Rd, off Midland Hwy, 12km NW of PO, ☎ 03 5276 1302, fax 03 5276 1026, 3 rms [shwr, bath (1), tlt, a/c, elec blkts, clock radio, t/c mkg] lounge (TV, stereo, video), lounge firepl, ✕ (licensed), ✉, pool, refrig, bbq, meals avail, non smoking property. **BB ♦ $95 - $105, ♦♦ $135 - $145**, ch con, AE BC MC VI.

★★★★ **Duneed Guest House**, (B&B), 369 Boundary Rd, Grovedale 3216, 4km S of Belmont PO, ☎ 03 5264 1436, 3 rms [ensuite, c/fan, heat (wood), elec blkts, clock radio], lounge (TV, cd player), t/c mkg shared, refrig, non smoking property. **BB ♦ $60, ♦♦ $70 - $80**, Min book long w/ends and Easter.

★★★☆ **Ardara House**, (GH), 4 Aberdeen St, Geelong West 3218, 550m W of City Centre, ☎ 03 5229 6024, fax 03 5229 6180, 7 rms [hairdry, cent heat, elec blkts], ldry, lounge (TV, video), t/c mkg shared, refrig, ✆. **BB ♦ $50, ♦♦ $90**.

★★★☆ **Willowra House B & B**, (B&B), 34 Mc Killop St, ☎ 03 5229 8790, fax 03 5229 8790, 2 rms [ensuite, hairdry, fan, cent heat, TV, video, clock radio, CD, refrig, micro], iron, iron brd, lounge, ✕, t/c mkg shared, cots, non smoking property. **BB ♦ $50 - $70, ♦♦ $95 - $105, ◊ $30, ♦ $420, ♦♦ $650**, ch con.

Pop Nominal, (399km E Melbourne), See map on pages 694/695, ref J6. Small agricultural settlement. Bush Walking, Scenic Drives, Tennis.

Self Catering Accommodation

★★ **Sykes Karoonda Park**, (Cotg), (Farm), Gelantipy Rd, 40km N of Buchan, ☎ 03 5155 0220, fax 03 5155 0308, 5 cotgs acc up to 8, (2 bedrm), [shwr, bath (1), tlt, heat, elec blkts, clock radio (4), refrig, cook fac, micro (1), elec frypan (2), toaster, linen reqd-fee], ldry, rec rm, lounge firepl (2), pool-heated (solar), bbq, kiosk, ✆, tennis. **D ♦ $22, $75**, Min book school holidays and Easter, BC MC VI.

★★ **(Motel Section)**, 2 units [shwr, tlt, heat, elec blkts, clock radio, t/c mkg, refrig]. **DBB ♦ $50, ◊ $50**.

(Bunkhouse Section), 6 bunkhouses acc up to 14, (2 & 3 bedrm), [shwr, tlt, refrig, cook fac, linen reqd-fee], t/c mkg shared. **D ♦ $20 - $22, ◊ $20 - $22**.

Pop Nominal, (169km SW Melbourne), See map on pages 694/695, ref C7. Quiet farming & forestry village in the heart of the Otway Ranges. Bush Walking, Fishing, Scenic Drives, Shooting.

Self Catering Accommodation

★★★ **Gellibrand River Valley Cabins**, (Cotg), 20 Gellibrand Valley Rd, 5.2km W of PO, ☎ 03 5235 8242, 2 cotgs acc up to 5, (2 bedrm), [shwr, tlt, heat (wood), TV, refrig, cook fac, micro, elec frypan, blkts, linen, pillows], ldry. **D $77 - $99, W $500 - $600**, No trail bikes or firearms.

★★☆ **Otway Pastoral**, (Cotg), 'Wonga' Wonga Rd, 6km W of PO, ☎ 03 5235 8377, fax 03 5235 8377, 1 cotg acc up to 8, (3 bedrm), [shwr, bath, tlt, heat (wood & gas), elec blkts, TV, video, clock radio, refrig, cook fac, micro, elec frypan, toaster, ldry, doonas, linen reqd], iron. **D ♦♦ $95 - $130, ◊ $20, W ♦♦ $480 - $780, ◊ $120**, ch con, Min book Christmas Jan long w/ends and Easter.

Pop 700. (63km E Melbourne), See map on page 696, ref D6. Potato growing district. Bush Walking, Scenic Drives, Tennis.

Hotels/Motels

★★ **The Ranges Hotel**, (LMH), Main St, 300m E of PO, ☎ 03 5968 1220, fax 03 5968 1436, 4 units [shwr, tlt, heat, elec blkts, TV, clock radio, t/c mkg, refrig, toaster], ✉ (Thurs to Sun), bbq, ✆, cots. **BLB ♦ $60, ♦♦ $80, ◊ $15**, Light breakfast only available. AE BC DC MC VI.

Self Catering Accommodation

★★★★ **Alkira Farm Cottages**, (Cotg), (Farm), 2427 Gembrook-Launching Place Rd, adjacent to Gilwell Park, 7.4km NE of PO, ☎ 03 5968 1484, fax 03 5968 1907, 2 cotgs acc up to 6, (2 bedrm), [shwr, bath (hip), tlt, hairdry, fan, heat, elec blkts, TV, video, clock radio, CD, t/c mkg, refrig, cook fac, d/wash, toaster, blkts, doonas, linen, pillows], ldry, w/mach, dryer, iron, iron brd, lounge firepl, spa (heated), bbq, non smoking property. **D $130 - $310, W $810 - $1,400**, Breakfast available, AE BC DC MC VI.

B&B's/Guest Houses

★★★★☆ **Brilynbrook Country Accommodation**, (B&B), (Farm), No children's facilities, 3065 Launching Place Rd, 1km N of PO, ☎ 03 5968 1938, fax 03 5968 1197, 1 rm (2 bedrm), [shwr, bath, tlt, hairdry, c/fan, elec blkts, TV, video, clock radio, t/c mkg], iron, iron brd, lounge firepl (wood heater), bbq, cots, non smoking property, Horses allowed. BB ♠♠ $130 - $230, ♦ $50, Other meals by arrangement, BC MC VI.

★★★★ **(Units Section)**, (2 stry), 2 units acc up to 4, (1 bedrm), [shwr, spa bath (1), tlt, hairdry, a/c, elec blkts, TV, video, clock radio, t/c mkg, refrig, cook fac, micro, toaster, ldry, blkts, doonas, linen, pillows], w/mach, dryer, iron, iron brd, breakfast ingredients. BB ♠♠ $130 - $230, ♦ $25.

GENOA VIC 3891

Pop Nominal, (518km E Melbourne), See map on pages 694/695, ref L6. Grazing & farming district. Bush Walking, Fishing, Scenic Drives, Swimming (River), Tennis.

Hotels/Motels

★ **Genoa Hotel**, (LMH), Cnr Princes Hwy & Old Princes Hwy, opposite PO, ☎ 03 5158 8222, 10 units [shwr, tlt, heat, elec blkts, TV, t/c mkg, refrig, toaster], lounge, ⊠, bbq, boat park, cots-fee. BLB ♦ $35, ♠♠ $45, ♦ $7.50, ch con, BC EFT MC VI.

Self Catering Accommodation

★★★ **Coopracambra Cottage**, (Cotg), Wangarabell Rd, 18km NW of PO, ☎ 03 5158 8277, fax 03 5158 8277, 2 cotgs acc up to 6, (2 & 3 bedrm), [shwr, tlt, heat (wood), TV, video, radio, refrig, cook fac, ldry, blkts, doonas, linen, pillows], w/mach, iron, iron brd, bbq. D ♠♠ $60, ♦ $5, W $420, Solar power.

GIPSY POINT VIC 3891

Pop Part of Orbost, (521km E Melbourne), See map on pages 694/695, ref L6. Small fishing resort near Mallacoota Inlet. Boat Ramp, Boating, Bush Walking, Fishing, Scenic Drives, Swimming.

Self Catering Accommodation

★★★★★ **Gipsy Point Luxury Lakeside Apartments**, (Apt), Waterfront Section, Gipsy Point Rd, adjacent to jetty, ☎ 03 5158 8200, fax 03 5158 8308, 6 apts acc up to 2, (1 bedrm), [ensuite, spa bath, hairdry, a/c, elec blkts, tel (direct dial), TV, video, clock radio, CD, refrig, mini bar, cook fac, micro, d/wash, toaster, ldry (in unit), blkts, linen, pillows], iron, iron brd, pool-heated, bbq, jetty, canoeing, non smoking property. D $145 - $185, W $790 - $1,190, Breakfast available Not suitable for children under 8 yrs, Min book Christmas Jan long w/ends and Easter, AE BC DC EFT MC VI.

Operator Comment: Luxury lakeside accommodation set in landscaped gardens w/pool, waters edge Mallacoota Lakes and Croajingalong National Park. See our ad under Mallacoota.

★★★★☆ **(Lakeview Section)**, 4 apts acc up to 4, (1 & 2 bedrm), [ensuite, hairdry, a/c, c/fan, heat (wood), elec blkts, tel, TV, video, clock radio, refrig, mini bar, cook fac, micro, d/wash, toaster, ldry (in unit), blkts, linen, pillows], iron, iron brd, non smoking property. D $130 - $220, W $690 - $1,390, Breakfast available. Min book Christmas Jan long w/ends and Easter.

B&B's/Guest Houses

★★★★ **Gipsy Point Lodge**, (GH), McDonald St, Mallacoota Lakes, ☎ 03 5158 8205, fax 03 5158 8225, 7 rms [ensuite, c/fan, heat, elec blkts, clock radio, doonas], ldry, rec rm, lounge, ⊠, t/c mkg shared, refrig, ✆, jetty, tennis, non smoking rms. DBB ♦ $120, ♦ $120, BC MC VI.

★★★ **(Holiday Flat Section)**, 3 flats acc up to 5, (1 & 2 bedrm), [shwr, bath (1), tlt, fan, heat, elec blkts, TV, refrig, cook fac, micro, elec frypan, toaster, blkts, doonas, linen, pillows], bbq, non smoking units. D $70 - $100, W $440 - $630.

GISBORNE VIC 3437

Pop 3,600. Part of Macedon Ranges, (51km NW Melbourne), See map on page 696, ref B4. A pleasant tourist town, with elm-lined streets. Bowls, Bush Walking, Fishing (River), Golf, Horse Riding, Scenic Drives, Squash, Swimming (Pool), Tennis.

★★★ **Gisborne Motel**, (M), 106 Sheedy Rd, 2km E of PO, ☎ 03 5428 2414, fax 03 5428 2949, 13 units [shwr, tlt, a/c-cool, heat, elec blkts, tel, TV, movie, clock radio, t/c mkg, refrig, toaster], ✕, bbq, dinner to unit, plygr, cots, non smoking units (7). RO ♦ $59 - $84, ♠♠ $74 - $84, ♦ $15, AE BC DC MC VI.

GLEN FORBES VIC 3990

Pop Nominal, (106km SE Melbourne), See map on page 696, ref C7. Small grazing district nestled at the foothills Beside the Bass River, off the Bass Hwy.

B&B's/Guest Houses

★★★★☆ **Coorie Doon Country Retreat**, (B&B), 1205 Dalyston-Glen Forbes Rd, 10km E off Bass Hwy, ☎ 03 5678 8451, 3 rms [shwr, spa bath (1), tlt, hairdry, heat, elec blkts, clock radio, doonas], lounge (TV, video, cd), lounge firepl, t/c mkg shared, refrig, non smoking property. BB ♠♠ $120 - $150, 1 room ★★★★. Dinner by arrangement. Children by arrangement, AE BC DC MC VI.

GLENISLA VIC

See Grampians Region.

GLEN WILLS VIC 3898

Pop Nominal, (467km NE Melbourne), See map on pages 694/695, ref J5. Old gold mining district situated in rugged country on the Omeo Hwy. Bush Walking, Canoeing, Fishing, Snow Skiing, Swimming (River).

Self Catering Accommodation

★★ **Glen Wills**, (Cotg), Omeo Hwy, 52km N of Omeo, ☎ 03 5159 7254, fax 03 5159 7254, 1 cotg acc up to 15, (5 bedrm), [shwr (2), tlt (3), radio, refrig, cook fac, linen], lounge firepl, spa, bbq, tennis. D ♠♠ $70, ♦ $15, Meals by arrangement.

GLENAIRE VIC 3238

Pop Nominal, (216km SW Melbourne), See map on pages 694/695, ref C8. Small settlement on Great Ocean Road. Bush Walking, Scenic Drives.

Self Catering Accommodation

★★★☆ **Glenaire Cottages**, (Log Cabin), 3440 Great Ocean Rd, 35km W of Apollo Bay, ☎ 03 5237 9237, fax 03 5237 9269, 4 log cabins acc up to 6, (2 bedrm), [shwr, spa bath (2), tlt, a/c (2), c/fan, fire pl, elec blkts, TV, video, clock radio, CD, refrig, cook fac, micro, d/wash, toaster, ldry (in unit), blkts, doonas, linen, pillows], iron, iron brd, bbq, c/park (carport), Pets allowed - fee. D ♠♠ $110 - $237.50, ♦ $20 - $35, W ♠♠ $745 - $1,125, ♦ $140 - $245, 2 cottages ★★★★☆, Min book applies, BC MC VI.

Operator Comment: See our sensational views, location & facilities at www.glenaire.net

GLENALADALE VIC 3864

Pop Nominal, (295km E Melbourne), See map on pages 694/695, ref H7. Farming & timber district. Bush Walking, Canoeing, Fishing, Gem Fossicking, Scenic Drives, Swimming.

Other Accommodation

Coonawarra Farm Resort, (Bunk), Dargo Rd, 3km N of Iguana Creek bridge, ☎ 03 5157 6315, fax 03 5157 6200, 4 bunkhouses acc up to 26, (Bunk Rooms), [cent heat, linen reqd], shwr (8G-8L), tlt (8G-10L), ldry, w/mach, dry rm, rec rm, lounge (TV), conf fac, pool, cook fac, bbq (covered), LPG, ✆, plygr, tennis, D ♦ $27.50 - $38.50, ♦ $27.50 - $38.50, ch con, ♿.

(Cabin Section), 5 cabins acc up to 8, (2 & 3 bedrm), [shwr, tlt, heat, TV, refrig, cook fac, toaster, linen reqd]. D ♦ $38.50 - $50, ♦ $38.50 - $62.50, ch con.

(Lodge Section), 12 rms acc up to 8, (Bunk Rooms), [shwr (9), tlt (9), TV (2), refrig (1), linen reqd], dry rm, rec rm, lounge (TV, video), cook fac, bbq (covered). D ♦ $33 - $55, ♦ $33 - $55, ch con.

GLENBURN VIC 3717

Pop Part of Yea, (83km NE Melbourne), See map on page 696, ref C4. Small agricultural town in dairying and wool growing district. Convenient to Yarra Valley wineries and Healesville Sanctuary Bush Walking, Fishing, Horse Riding, Scenic Drives.

Self Catering Accommodation

★★★★☆ **Erimbali Country Cottage**, (Cotg), 820 Break-O-Day Rd, 9km N of Glenburn, ☎ 03 5780 2341, fax 03 5780 2238, 1 cotg acc up to 6, (3 bedrm), [shwr, bath, tlt, hairdry, c/fan, heat, TV, video, clock radio, CD, t/c mkg, refrig, cook fac, micro, d/wash, toaster, ldry (in unit), blkts, doonas, linen, pillows], iron, iron brd, bbq, c/park (garage), breakfast ingredients, non smoking property. BB ♦ $70, ♠♠ $150, Dinner by arrangement. BC MC VI.

GLENBURN VIC continued...

B&B's/Guest Houses

★★★☆ **Dixons Bed & Breakfast**, (B&B), 1042 Break O Day Rd, ☎ 03 5780 2471, fax 03 9415 7457, 4 rms [ensuite (1), shwr (1), bath (1), tlt (1), ldry, doonas], w/mach, dryer, lounge (TV), conf fac, lounge firepl, ✗, res liquor license, t/c mkg shared, refrig, bbq, secure park (undercover), ☎. BB ∮ $70, ∮∮ $110 - $132, ⋔ $60, ch con, Meals by arrangement, AE BC DC MC VI.

Operator Comment: Exp. Country Life at its best. Visit Judy & Brian Dixon at www.dixons.au.com

★★★ **(Cottage Section)**, 1 cotg acc up to 4, (2 bedrm), [shwr, tlt, TV, t/c mkg, refrig, cook fac, toaster, blkts, doonas, linen, pillows], lounge firepl, breakfast ingredients. BB ∮ $70, ∮∮ $110, ⋔ $60, ∮ $300, ∮∮ $400, ⋔ $100.

GLENGARRY VIC 3854

Pop Nominal, (174km E Melbourne), See map on page 696, ref E6. Small Central Gippsland township.

B&B's/Guest Houses

★★★★ **Railglen B & B**, (B&B), 25 Main St, 9km N of Traralgon, ☎ 03 5192 4222, fax 03 5192 4903, 2 rms [shwr, spa bath (1), tlt, hairdry, a/c-cool, c/fan, heat, elec blkts, TV, clock radio, t/c mkg, refrig, toaster], iron, iron brd, ✗ (Tue to Sat), bbq, cots, non smoking property. BB ∮ $80 - $90, ∮∮ $90 - $100, ⋔ $20, AE BC DC EFT MC VI.

GLENGOWER VIC 3370

Pop Nominal, (160km NW Melbourne), See map on pages 694/695, ref D5. Grazing district on Middle Creek.

Self Catering Accommodation

★★★ **Lodge Glengower**, (Cotg), (Farm), Castlemaine Rd, 10km NE of Clunes PO, ☎ 03 5476 6227, 1 cotg acc up to 9, (3 bedrm), [shwr, tlt, a/c-cool, fan, heat, TV, clock radio, refrig, cook fac, elec frypan, ldry (in unit), blkts, doonas, linen, pillows], w/mach, pool, bbq, c/park (carport). D $110, W $550, Meals by arrangement.

GLENLYON VIC 3461

Pop Part of Daylesford, (114km NW Melbourne), See map on page 696, ref A4. Small farming community. Bush Walking, Scenic Drives.

Self Catering Accommodation

★★★ **Loddon Valley View Cottages**, (Cotg), RMB 3701 Daylesford-Malmsbury Rd, ☎ 03 5348 7538, fax 03 5348 7538, 2 cotgs acc up to 6, (1 & 3 bedrm), [shwr, bath (hip), tlt, a/c-cool (1), fan (1), c/fan (1), heat (wood), elec blkts, TV, video, clock radio, CD, refrig, cook fac (1), cook fac ltd (1), micro, elec frypan, d/wash (1), toaster, blkts, doonas, linen], w/mach, spa (heated), bbq. D ∮∮ $100 - $135, ⋔ $20 - $50, W $550 - $700, Min book Christmas Jan long w/ends and Easter, BC DC MC VI.

GLENROWAN VIC 3675

Pop 350. (220km NE Melbourne), See map on page 696, ref E2. Scene of the last stand & capture of Ned Kelly. Kelly Museum. Tourist Information Centre, 03 5766 2367. Boating, Fishing, Scenic Drives, Swimming, Vineyards, Wineries, Water Skiing.

Hotels/Motels

★★★ **Glenrowan Kelly Country Motel**, (M), 44 Gladstone St, 100m N of PO, ☎ 03 5766 2202, fax 03 5766 2022, 8 units [shwr, bath (hip), tlt, evap cool, heat, elec blkts, TV, clock radio, t/c mkg, refrig], ldry, pool, bbq, dinner to unit, c/park (carport), plygr, cots-fee. RO ∮ $47 - $58, ∮∮ $56 - $67, ⋔ $11, ch con, pen con, AE BC DC EFT MCH VI.

GLENTHOMPSON VIC 3293

Pop 170. (211km W Melbourne), See map on pages 694/695, ref B6. Agricultural and pastoral community. Swimming (Pool), Tennis.

Self Catering Accommodation

★★★☆ **Cherrymount Retreat**, (Cotg), (Farm), Cherrymount La, off Caramut Rd, 5.5km S of PO, ☎ 03 5577 4396, fax 03 5577 4318, 1 cotg acc up to 6, (3 bedrm), [shwr, tlt, a/c, heat, elec blkts, tel, TV, video, clock radio, refrig, cook fac, elec frypan, toaster, blkts, doonas, linen, pillows], tennis. BB ∮∮ $90, D all meals ∮ $90, ⋔ $90, ch con, Tariff includes farm activities.

(Shearers Quarters Section), 5 bunkhouses acc up to 2, [heat, video (avail), micro, blkts, linen reqd-fee], bathrm, lounge (TV, cd player), lounge firepl (wood), pool, cook fac. D ∮ $20, ⋔ $20.

GOUGHS BAY VIC 3723

Pop Part of Mansfield, (204km NE Melbourne), See map on page 696, ref E4. Situated on shore of Lake Eildon. Boat Ramp, Boating, Bush Walking, Fishing, Horse Riding, Sailing, Scenic Drives, Swimming (Lake), Water Skiing.

Self Catering Accommodation

★★★ **Fernleigh Resort**, (Cotg), Goughs Bay Rd, ☎ 03 5777 3531, fax 03 5777 3531, 4 cotgs acc up to 8, (Studio & 3 bedrm), [shwr, tlt, hairdry, fan, heat, TV, refrig, cook fac (1), cook fac ltd, toaster, linen], pool, bbq (covered), plygr, tennis. D ∮∮ $80 - $100, ⋔ $24, ch con,

Operator Comment: See our ads under Eildon and Mansfield.

(Lodge Section), Group accommodation only. 5 rms acc up to 6, [heat, TV, refrig, cook fac, blkts reqd-fee, linen reqd-fee, pillows reqd], lounge, ✗. D ∮ $20, ⋔ $13 - $20, ch con, minimum booking applies.

Other Accommodation

Ahoy High Country Houseboats, (Hbt), 2 Hills Rd, ☎ 03 5777 3899, fax 03 5777 3899, 4 houseboats acc up to 12, (3 & 4 bedrm), [shwr, tlt, TV, CD (4), refrig, cook fac, micro (4), blkts reqd, linen reqd, pillows reqd], bbq. D $250, W $800 - $3,410, Security deposit - $600. BC MC VI.

GRAMPIANS REGION - VIC

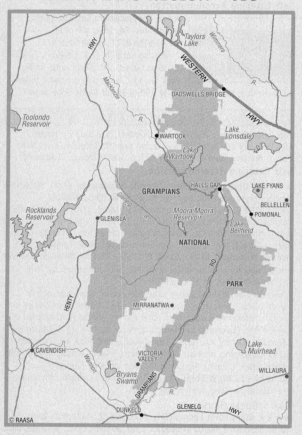

© RAASA

GRAMPIANS - DADSWELLS BRIDGE VIC 3385

Pop 228. (271km NW Melbourne), See map on pages 694/695, ref B5. Entrance to the Northern end of Grampians.

Hotels/Motels

★★★ **Dadswells Bridge Motel Hotel**, (M), Western Hwy, ☎ 03 5359 5251, fax 03 5359 5302, 13 units [shwr, tlt, a/c-cool (2), a/c (11), heat (2), elec blkts, tel, TV, video-fee, clock radio, t/c mkg, refrig], lounge, ✉, pool, bbq, cots. RO ∮ $40 - $65, ∮∮ $48 - $85, ⋔ $12. BC EFT MC VI.

Self Catering Accommodation

★★☆ **Mt Zero Log Cabins**, (Log Cabin), Dadswell Bridge - Laharum Rd, 3km W of Western Hwy, ☎ 03 5384 3226, 7 log cabins acc up to 6, (1 & 2 bedrm), [shwr, tlt, a/c-cool, c/fan (5), fire pl, heat, TV, video (avail), clock radio, cook fac ltd, micro, elec frypan, toaster, doonas, linen reqd-fee, pillows], ldry, w/mach, pool, bbq, plygr, tennis, cots. D ∮∮ $58 - $95, ⋔ $12, ch con, Min book Christmas Jan long w/ends and Easter, BC MC VI.

GRAMPIANS - DUNKELD VIC 3294

Pop 450. (257km W Melbourne), See map on pages 694/695, ref B6. Southern gateway to the Grampians National Park.

Hotels/Motels

★★★★ **Royal Mail Hotel**, (LMH), Parker St (Glenelg Hwy), 200m NW of PO, ☎ 03 5577 2241, fax 03 5577 2577, 25 units [shwr, spa bath (5), tlt, hairdry, a/c (22), c/fan (3), heat, elec blkts, tel, TV, clock radio, t/c mkg, refrig, cook fac (1)], ldry, lounge, conf fac, ☒, pool, spa, bbq, dinner to unit, ☎. RO ⅋ $82.50 - $115, ⅋⅋ $99 - $140, ⅋ $22, ch con, AE BC DC EFT MC VI, ⅋⅋.

Self Catering Accommodation

★★★★ **'Aquila' Mt Abrupt Eco Lodges**, (HU), Manns Rd, 6 km NW of PO, ☎ 03 5577 2582, fax 03 5577 2582, (Multi-stry gr fl), 4 units acc up to 6, (2 bedrm), [evap cool, heat, cable tv, video-fee, radio, t/c mkg, refrig, cook fac, blkts, doonas, linen, pillows], conf fac, lounge firepl, bbq, ☎, cots, breakfast ingredients, non smoking property. D ⅋⅋ $165 - $220, ⅋ $20, W ⅋⅋ $1,000 - $1,400, ⅋ $120, Minimum booking weekends & public holidays, AE BC DC MC VI.

★★★★ **Mt Sturgeon Cottages**, (Cotg), Cavendish Rd, 5km W of PO, ☎ 03 5577 2241, fax 03 5577 2577, 8 cotgs acc up to 4, (1 & 2 bedrm), [shwr, tlt, hairdry, heat, elec blkts, clock radio, refrig, cook fac ltd, micro, elec frypan, toaster, blkts, linen, pillows], ldry, lounge firepl, bbq. D ⅋⅋ $116 - $160, ⅋ $22, Reception at Royal Mail Hotel. AE BC DC EFT MC VI, ⅋⅋.

★★★☆ **Southern Grampians Cottages**, (Log Cabin), 35 Victoria Rd, 1km N of PO, ☎ 03 5577 2457, fax 03 5577 2489, 8 log cabins acc up to 5, (1 & 2 bedrm), [shwr, spa bath (3), tlt, a/c-cool (2), fan, heat, elec blkts, TV, video, clock radio, CD (3), refrig, cook fac, micro, blkts, linen, pillows], ldry, lounge firepl (3), bbq, plygr, cots. DBB ⅋⅋ $570 - $960, D ⅋⅋ $90 - $185, ⅋ $10, W ⅋ $90, ch con, 4 log cabins ★★★★, BC EFT MC VI.

B&B's/Guest Houses

★★★★ **Grampians View Bed and Breakfast**, (B&B), 70 Macarthur St, 2kn N of PO, ☎ 03 5577 2450, fax 03 5577 2626, 3 rms [shwr, tlt, c/fan, cent heat, TV, clock radio, t/c mkg, refrig], iron, iron brd, non smoking property. BB ⅋ $70, ⅋⅋ $95, BC MC VI.

★★★ **Dunkeld Lodge**, (B&B), Wills St, 800m W of Police Station, ☎ 03 5577 2584, 4 rms [fan, heat, elec blkts, clock radio], lounge (TV, video), lounge firepl, t/c mkg shared, bbq, ☎, cots. BB ⅋ $40, ⅋⅋ $55 - $65, ⅋ $25, ch con.

Other Accommodation

Grampians Retreat & Field Studies Centre, (Lodge), Wright's Rd, 5km N of PO, ☎ 03 5577 2657, 12 rms acc up to 10, [ensuite (3), blkts reqd, linen reqd], shwr (2G-2L), tlt (2G-2L), rec rm, ☓, cook fac, refrig, bbq, ☎. RO ⅋ $20.50, ch con, fam con, Minimum booking - 25 people.

GRAMPIANS - GLENISLA VIC 3314

Pop Nominal, (330km W Melbourne), See map on pages 694/695, ref B5.

B&B's/Guest Houses

★★★★☆ **Glenisla**, (B&B), Classified by National Trust, (Farm), c1870, Henty Hwy, 40km N of Cavendish, ☎ 03 5380 1532, fax 03 5380 1566, 3 rms [shwr, tlt, hairdry, fan, heat, elec blkts, radio, t/c mkg, refrig], ldry, lounge (TV, video), bbq, courtesy transfer, non smoking rms. BB ⅋ $96, ch con, Tariff includes farm activities. Dinner by arrangement.

GRAMPIANS - HALLS GAP VIC 3381

Pop 250. (262km NW Melbourne), See map on pages 694/695, ref B5. Unique tourist centre in the valley between the rugged peaks of the Grampians National Park.

Hotels/Motels

 ★★★★ **Halls Gap Colonial Motor Inn**, (M), Grampians Rd, 500m S of PO, ☎ 03 5356 4344, fax 03 5356 4442, 53 units [shwr, spa bath (35), tlt, hairdry, a/c-cool, heat, elec blkts, tel, TV, video-fee, clock radio, t/c mkg, refrig, mini bar, toaster], ldry, conf fac, ☒, pool-heated, bbq, rm serv, cots-fee. D ⅋⅋ $98 - $118, ⅋ $10, 17 units ★★★☆, AE BC DC EFT JCB MC VI.

 ★★★☆ **Grampians Motel**, (M), Dunkeld Rd, 3km S of PO, ☎ 03 5356 4248, fax 03 5356 4491, 29 units [shwr, spa bath (2), tlt, hairdry, a/c-cool, heat, elec blkts, tel, TV, video-fee, clock radio, t/c mkg, refrig, mini bar, toaster], ldry, iron, iron brd, rec rm, pool, bbq, tennis, cots-fee, non smoking units (9). RO ⅋ $69 - $90, ⅋⅋ $79 - $115, ⅋ $12, ch con, BC DC EFT MC VI, ⅋⅋.

 ★★★☆ **Halls Gap Kookaburra Lodge**, (M), 24 Heath St, 100m E of PO, ☎ 03 5356 4395, fax 03 5356 4490, 14 units [shwr, tlt, hairdry, a/c-cool, heat, elec blkts, tel, TV, clock radio, t/c mkg, refrig, toaster], ldry, iron, iron brd, bbq, cots, non smoking units (12). RO ⅋ $65 - $80, ⅋⅋ $75 - $100, ⅋ $12, AE BC DC MC VI, ⅋⅋.

 ★★★☆ **Halls Gap Motel**, (M), Grampians Rd, 600m S of PO, ☎ 03 5356 4209, fax 03 5356 4308, 10 units [shwr, tlt, hairdry, a/c-cool, heat, elec blkts, tel, TV, video-fee, clock radio, t/c mkg, refrig, toaster], iron, iron brd, bbq, dinner to unit, cots-fee, non smoking units (4). RO ⅋ $58 - $95, ⅋⅋ $69 - $95, ⅋ $12, AE BC DC MC MCH VI.

 ★★★☆ **Mountain View Motor Inn and Holiday Lodges**, (M), Ararat Rd, 4.1km E of PO, ☎ 03 5356 4364, fax 03 5356 4262, 13 units [shwr, spa bath (1), tlt, hairdry, a/c-cool, fire pl (1), heat, elec blkts, tel, video-fee, clock radio, t/c mkg, refrig, cook fac ltd (1), toaster], ldry, iron, iron brd, pool, spa, bbq, dinner to unit (Sun to Thurs), plygr, tennis, cots, non smoking rms (11). RO ⅋ $75 - $155, ⅋⅋ $85 - $155, ⅋ $11, AE BC DC EFT MC VI.

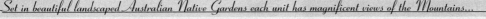

★★★ **Grand Canyon Motel**, (M), Grampians Rd, 700m NE of PO, ☎ 03 5356 4280, fax 03 5356 4336, 24 units [shwr, bath (9), spa bath (2), tlt, a/c-cool, heat, elec blkts, tel, TV, clock radio, t/c mkg, refrig], ⊠ (seasonal), pool, bbq, cots-fee, non smoking rms (2). **RO ♦ $55 - $88, ♦♦ $72 - $11, ◊ $15**, ch con, BC EFT MC MCH MP VI.

★★ **Grampians Gardens Caravan Park & Motel**, (M), Cnr Ararat & Stawell Rds, 2.8km NE of PO, ☎ 03 5356 4244, fax 03 5356 4244, 4 units [shwr, tlt, a/c, elec blkts, TV, video-fee, t/c mkg, refrig, cook fac (1), cook fac ltd (3), micro, toaster], ldry, pool, bbq. **BLB ♦ $56 - $68, ♦♦ $68 - $80, ◊ $10**, Light breakfast only available. BC DC MC VI.

Self Catering Accommodation

★★★★★ **Boroka Downs**, (HU), No children's facilities, Birdswing Rd, 7km SE of PO, ☎ 03 5356 6243, fax 03 5356 6343, 5 units acc up to 2, (1 bedrm), [shwr, spa bath, tlt, hairdry, a/c, c/fan, elec blkts, tel, TV, video, clock radio, t/c mkg, refrig, mini bar, cook fac, micro, elec frypan, d/wash, toaster, ldry, blkts, doonas, linen, pillows], w/mach, dryer, iron, iron brd, lounge firepl, bbq, c/park (carport), non smoking property. **D $275 - $325, W $1,470 - $2,065**, AE BC DC EFT MC VI.

★★★★★ **Heatherlie Cottages Halls Gap**, (Cotg), No children's facilities, 3 Flatrock Rd, 900m NE of PO, ☎ 03 5358 2921, 4 cotgs acc up to 2, (1 bedrm), [shwr, spa bath, tlt, hairdry, a/c, c/fan, heat, elec blkts, tel, clock radio, CD, t/c mkg, refrig, cook fac, micro, d/wash, toaster, ldry (in unit), blkts, doonas, linen, pillows], w/mach, dryer, iron, iron brd, lounge (TV, video), lounge firepl, bbq, non smoking units (4). **D ♦♦ $165 - $220, W ♦♦ $1,000 - $1,100**, BC MC VI.

★★★★★ **Marwood Villas**, (HU), No children's facilities, Mt Zero Rd, ☎ 03 5356 4231, fax 03 5356 4513, 6 units acc up to 2, (Studio), [ensuite, spa bath, hairdry, a/c, elec blkts, tel, TV, video, clock radio, refrig, cook fac, micro, elec frypan, d/wash, toaster, ldry (in unit), blkts, linen, pillows], w/mach, lounge firepl, ✉, bbq, non smoking units. **BB ♦♦ $245 - $350**, AE BC DC JCB MC VI.

★★★★☆ **Halls Gap Holiday Villas**, (Cotg), Lot 8 High Rd, ☎ 03 5356 4457, fax 03 5356 4670, 1 cotg acc up to 2, (1 bedrm), [shwr, spa bath, tlt, a/c-cool, heat, elec blkts, cable tv, video, clock radio, CD, t/c mkg, refrig, cook fac, micro, elec frypan, d/wash, toaster, blkts, linen, pillows], iron, iron brd, bbq. **D $180 - $250, W $945 - $1,260**.

★★★★☆ **Mackeys Peak Holiday Units**, (HU), No children's facilities, Rosea St, 300m S of PO, ☎ 03 5358 1850, fax 03 5358 1850, 4 units acc up to 2, (1 bedrm), [shwr, spa bath, tlt, hairdry, a/c-cool, c/fan, heat, elec blkts, TV, video, clock radio, CD, refrig, cook fac, micro, toaster, ldry (in unit), blkts, doonas, linen, pillows], w/mach, iron, iron brd, lounge firepl, bbq, breakfast ingredients. **D ♦♦ $121 - $165**, BC MC VI.

★★★★ **Acacia Rise Holiday Units**, (Cotg), Wirilda Crt, 3km E of PO, ☎ 03 5356 4547, or 03 9379 3722, fax 03 9379 9072, 1 cotg acc up to 6, (3 bedrm), [shwr, tlt, a/c-cool, heat, cable tv, video, clock radio, t/c mkg, cook fac, micro, toaster, ldry, blkts reqd, doonas, linen reqd-fee, pillows reqd], lounge firepl, pool, spa, bbq, non smoking property. **D ♦♦ $135 - $145, ♦ $15**, BC EFT MC VI.

★★★★ **Boronia Peak Holiday Villas**, (HU), Cnr Grampians & Tandara Rds, 1.4km S of PO, ☎ 03 5356 4500, fax 03 5356 4503, 13 units acc up to 12, (1, 2 & 3 bedrm), [shwr, spa bath (10), tlt, a/c (4), c/fan, heat, elec blkts, TV, video, clock radio, CD, refrig, cook fac, micro (5), toaster, ldry (in unit), blkts, linen, pillows], w/mach, rec rm, lounge firepl (6), bbq, ✆, plygr, cots, breakfast ingredients. **D ♦♦ $110 - $275, ♦ $16.50**, BC MC VI.

★★★★ **Grampians Blue**, (House), Scott Rd, 2km S of PO, ☎ 03 5382 6023, 1 house acc up to 8, (3 bedrm), [a/c, heat, elec blkts, TV, video, clock radio, cook fac, micro, toaster, ldry, blkts, doonas, linen reqd-fee, pillows], w/mach, bbq, cots, non smoking property. **D ♦♦♦♦ $790 - $900, $130 - $170**, Min book applies.

★★★★ **Grampians Pinnacle Haven Cottage**, (Cotg), Royston Rd, 1.5km S of PO, 1st left off Young Rd, ☎ 03 5356 4342, fax 03 5356 4342, 1 cotg acc up to 7, (3 bedrm), [shwr (double), spa bath (double), tlt, hairdry, a/c (lounge), c/fan (lounge), heat, tel (local), TV, video, clock radio, refrig, cook fac, micro, elec frypan, toaster, ldry, linen reqd-fee], w/mach, dryer, iron, iron brd, bbq, cots, non smoking property. **D ♦♦ $130 - $140, ♦ $20 - $130, W ♦♦ $790 - $900, ♦ $100 - $150**, Min book school holidays and Easter, BC MC VI.

★★★★ **Grampians Wonderland Cabins**, (HU), Ellis St, 1km S of PO, off Hill St, ☎ 03 5356 4264, fax 03 5356 4264, 6 units acc up to 4, (2 bedrm - split level.), [shwr, bath, tlt, hairdry, a/c-cool (5), a/c (1), c/fan, heat (wood), elec blkts, TV, video, clock radio, refrig, cook fac, micro, toaster, ldry (in unit), blkts, linen, pillows], w/mach, bbq (covered), cots (avail), non smoking property. **D ♦♦ $104 - $145, ♦ $33**, ch con, BC MC VI.

★★★★ **Halls Gap Log Cabins**, (HU), Dunkeld Rd, 1.5km S of PO, ☎ 03 5356 4256, fax 03 5356 4559, 12 units acc up to 6, (1 & 2 bedrm), [shwr, bath (8), spa bath (4), tlt, hairdry, heat (wood), elec blkts, TV, video, clock radio, refrig, cook fac, micro, toaster, blkts, linen, pillows], ldry, w/mach, pool, bbq (covered), c/park (carport), ✆, plygr, cots. **D ♦♦ $105 - $140, ♦ $22**, ch con, Min book all holiday times, BC EFT MC VI.

Treat yourself to a peaceful retreat or romantic getaway

Experience luxury accommodation nestled in the heart of the Grampians. Enjoy the glow of a crackling fire and bushwalks in the fresh mountain air. Mountain bikes, in house movies – everything you could wish for and more available to ensure ultimate relaxation and enjoyment.

Features
• In house movies • In house CD's
• Wide Verandahs • Video
• CD Player • Quality Cookware, Crockery, Cutlery • Large Spa

Postal Address:
92 Scott Road, Halls Gap

Telephone:
(03) 5382 5821 or 0417 595 099

Halls Gap
Pinnacle Retreat

Perhaps the hardest thing will be leaving to go home!

Grampians Pioneer Cottages

AAA Tourism ★★★☆

WINNER 2000 VICTORIAN TOURISM AWARDS

Winner for Unique Accommodation

Experience one of our uniquely built cottages.
• Stone Cottage • Mudbrick cottage
• Redbrick Cottage • Redgum Log Cottage

Cosy open log fire - Peaceful - Majestic Mountain views
& - *Disabled Facilities*

Tel/ Fax (03) 5356 4402
Birdswing Rd. Box 15, Halls Gap 3381.
www.grampians.net.au/pioneer

Grampians View COTTAGES & FLATS

HALLS GAP   AAAT ★★★

Relax on 6 acres of native gardens with picturesque mountain views.
The ideal place to enjoy our peace of the Grampians.

TWO BEDROOM COTTAGES ★★★★

1 & 2 BEDROOM UNITS ★★★ and ★★★☆

All air conditioned, have excellent TV reception, video players, Queen size beds and full kitchens. Cottages also have wood fires, ducted airconditioning and washing machines.

INDOOR HEATED POOL
Tennis Court, Basketball, Playground, BBQs

email: gramview@netconnect.com.au
web: grampiansview.com.au

Ph (03) 5356 4444 Stawell Road, Halls Gap, VIC 3381

Pinnacle HOLIDAY LODGE

Heath Street, Halls Gap 3381 Tel: (03) 5356 4249 Fax: (03) 5356 4482
E-mail: info@pinnacleholiday.com.au Web: www.pinnacleholiday.com.au

Tranquillity in the heart of Halls Gap awaits you at the 'Pinnacle'. Centrally located yet quietly secluded, offering excellent facilities for your enjoyment.
After a day exploring the Grampians relax in our indoor heated pool & spa. Why not have a hit on our plexipave tennis court? Maybe unwind in the bush with a picnic hamper beside Stony Creek, or just spend some time browsing at the specialty shops.

All this without leaving the Lodge's spacious native garden surroundings.

• 1 & 2 Bedroom S/C Units
• Laundries/BBQs
• Disabled Units
• Conference/Function Room

• Executive s/c Units (spa)
• Deluxe Motel Suites (Spa)
• Seniors Card Welcome (Conditions Apply)

CALL TOLL FREE FOR RESERVATIONS: 1800 819 283

★★★★ **Halls Gap Pinnacle Retreat**, (Cotg), 9 Scott Rd, 2.2km S of PO, ☎ 03 5382 5821, fax 03 5382 1600, 1 cotg acc up to 10, (3 bedrm), [shwr, tlt, a/c, heat, elec blkts, TV, video, clock radio, CD, t/c mkg, refrig, cook fac, micro, toaster, ldry, blkts, doonas, linen reqd-fee, pillows], w/mach, dryer, lounge firepl, bbq, bicycle, non smoking property. **D ♦♦ $130, ♦ $20, W ♦♦ $780, ♦ $140**, ch con, Min book applies.

★★★★ **Holiday Heights**, (Cotg), Lot 1, 46 Scott Rd, ☎ 03 5352 2818, 1 cotg acc up to 6, (3 bedrm), [shwr, spa bath (double), tlt, hairdry, a/c, c/fan, heat, elec blkts, TV, video, clock radio, CD, refrig, cook fac, elec frypan, ldry, blkts, linen, pillows], w/mach, dryer, iron, iron brd, bbq. **D ♦♦ $121, ♦ $11.**

★★★★ **Mountain View Motor Inn and Lodge**, (Cotg), Ararat Rd, 4.1km E of PO, ☎ 03 5356 4364, fax 03 5356 4262, 6 cotgs acc up to 6, (1 & 2 bedrm), [shwr, spa bath (3), tlt, hairdry, a/c-cool (4), a/c (2), fire pl (6), heat (4), elec blkts, video-fee, clock radio, refrig, cook fac, micro, elec frypan, toaster, ldry (in unit), blkts, linen, pillows], w/mach, pool, spa, bbq, plygr, tennis, cots, non smoking units. **D ♦♦ $132 - $209, ♦ $11, W ♦♦ $914 - $1,430**, Min book applies, AE BC DC EFT MC VI.

★★★★ **Park Gate Resort**, (HF), Grampians Rd, 1.3km NE of PO, ☎ 03 5356 4215, fax 03 5356 4472, 24 flats acc up to 6, (1 & 2 bedrm), [shwr, spa bath (2), tlt, hairdry (4), c/fan (4), heat, elec blkts, TV, video (2), clock radio, CD (2), refrig, cook fac, micro, toaster, linen (13) reqd-fee], ldry, iron, rec rm, pool, bbq, c/park (carport), ☎, plygr, tennis, cots. **D ♦♦ $75 - $148.50, ♦ $11.50 - $16.50**, ch con, 2 flats ★★★★☆. BC EFT MC VI.

★★★★ **The Lodges Accommodation**, (Cotg), Grampians Rd, 400m S of PO, ☎ 03 5358 3196, fax 03 5358 3196, (2 stry), 1 cotg acc up to 4, (1 bedrm), [shwr, spa bath, tlt, evap cool, heat, elec blkts, TV, video, clock radio, CD, refrig, cook fac, micro, toaster, ldry, blkts, doonas, linen, pillows], w/mach, iron, iron brd, lounge firepl, breakfast ingredients. **D ♦♦ $150 - $195, ♦ $25 - $40, W ♦♦ $900, ♦ $175 - $280**, BC MC VI.

★★★☆ **Grampians Getaway**, (HU), Cnr Halls Gap - Ararat Rd & Trajul Rd, 5km E of PO, ☎ 03 5356 4448, fax 03 5356 4461, (2 stry gr fl), 6 units acc up to 6, (3 bedrm), [shwr, bath, spa bath, tlt, c/fan, heat (wood), elec blkts, TV, video, clock radio, CD, refrig, cook fac, micro, toaster, ldry (in unit), blkts, linen, pillows], w/mach, iron, iron brd, bbq, bicycle, canoeing, cots. **D ♦♦ $110 - $167, ♦ $24, W ♦♦ $640 - $994**, ch con, Minimum booking weekends & school holidays, BC MC VI.

★★★☆ **Grampians Pioneer Cottages**, (Cotg), Birdswing Rd, 9.2km E of PO, ☎ 03 5356 4402, fax 03 5356 4402, (2 stry gr fl), 4 cotgs acc up to 8, (2 & 3 bedrm), [shwr, tlt, hairdry, evap cool, elec blkts, TV, video (avail), clock radio, t/c mkg, refrig, cook fac, micro, toaster, ldry, blkts, doonas, linen reqd-fee, pillows], w/mach, iron, iron brd, lounge firepl, bbq, non smoking property. **D ♦♦ $105 - $132, ♦ $22**, ch con, ♿.

★★★☆ **Mount Dryden Country Charm**, (Cotg), (Farm), Greenhole Rd, 15km N of Halls Gap PO, ☎ 03 5356 4212, fax 03 5356 4613, 1 cotg acc up to 8, (2 bedrm), [shwr, tlt, evap cool, fan, heat, elec blkts, TV, clock radio, CD, t/c mkg, refrig, cook fac, micro, toaster, ldry, blkts, doonas, linen, pillows], w/mach, iron, iron brd, lounge firepl, bbq, non smoking property. **D ♦♦ $100 - $110, ♦ $20, W ♦♦ $450 - $600, ♦ $60**, ch con, *Operator Comment: www.grampians.org.au/mountdryden*

★★★☆ **Pinnacle Holiday Lodge**, (HF), Heath St, 50m E of PO, ☎ 03 5356 4249, fax 03 5356 4482, 24 flats acc up to 6, (1 & 2 bedrm), [shwr, bath (hip) (20), spa bath (2), tlt, hairdry (2), a/c, c/fan, heat, elec blkts, tel, TV, video-fee, clock radio, refrig, micro, elec frypan, toaster, linen], ldry, conf fac, pool indoor heated, spa, bbq, plygr, tennis, cots. **D ♦♦ $80 - $155, ♦ $15**, ch con, AE BC DC MC VI, ♿.

★★★★ **(Motel Section)**, 6 units [shwr, spa bath, tlt, hairdry, a/c, heat, elec blkts, tel, TV, video (2), clock radio, CD (2), refrig, toaster], iron, iron brd, non smoking units. **RO ♦ $22, $120 - $203**, ch con.

★★★ **Banksia Cottage Halls Gap**, (Cotg), Lot 13 Tandara Rd, ☎ 03 5358 3703, 1 cotg acc up to 7, (2 bedrm), [shwr, bath (hip), tlt, a/c, heat, cable tv, clock radio, refrig, cook fac, micro, elec frypan, toaster, ldry (in unit), linen reqd-fee], w/mach, bbq, cots. **D $85, W $595**, Min book applies.

★★★ **Country Lane Cottage - Halls Gap**, (Cotg), Cnr Wattletree & High Rds, 2.5km E of PO, ☎ 03 5382 3669, fax 03 5382 0600, 1 cotg acc up to 8, (2 bedrm), [shwr, spa bath, tlt, c/fan, heat, cable tv, video, clock radio, CD, refrig, cook fac, micro, toaster, ldry (in unit), linen reqd-fee], w/mach, dryer, iron, bbq. **D ♦♦ $110, ♦ $15, W ♦♦ $660, ♦ $90**, Min book applies.

AAA TOURISM *Special Rates*

★★★ **Grampians View Cottages & Flats**, (HF), Stawell Rd, 2.7km NE of PO, ☎ 03 5356 4444, fax 03 5356 4655, 10 flats acc up to 5, (2 bedrm), [shwr, tlt, a/c, elec blkts, TV, video, clock radio, refrig, cook fac, micro, toaster, linen, pillows], ldry, w/mach, pool-indoor, tennis. **D ♦♦ $100 - $130, ♦ $10**, ch con, 2 flats ★★★☆, BC EFT MC VI.

★★★★ **(Grampians View Cottages & Flats)**, 4 cotgs acc up to 5, (1 & 2 bedrm), [shwr, bath (hip) (2), tlt, a/c-cool, elec blkts, TV, video, clock radio, refrig, cook fac, micro, toaster, linen, pillows], ldry, w/mach, pool indoor heated, bbq-fee, plygr, tennis, cots. **D ♦♦ $75 - $105, ♦ $10**, ch con.

★★★ **Halls Haven Holiday Units**, (HU), Stawell Rd, 3.5km NE of PO, ☎ 03 5356 4304, or 03 5356 4418, 10 units acc up to 5, (1 & 2 bedrm), [shwr, tlt, a/c, heat, elec blkts, TV, video-fee, clock radio, refrig, cook fac, micro, elec frypan, toaster, linen reqd-fee], ldry, w/mach, pool-heated, bbq, ☏, plygr, bicycle, tennis, cots. **D $52 - $87, W $340 - $560**, BC MC VI.

★★★★ **(Cottage Section)**, 1 cotg acc up to 6, (2 bedrm), [shwr, spa bath, tlt, a/c, heat (gas log), elec blkts, TV, video, clock radio, refrig, cook fac, micro, toaster, blkts, linen, pillows]. **D ♦♦ $120 - $140**, ♦ **$10, W $840 - $1,050**, ch con.

★★★ **Kingsway Holiday Flats**, (HF), Grampians Rd, 1.1km S of PO, ☎ 03 5356 4202, fax 03 5356 4625, 7 flats acc up to 5, (1 & 2 bedrm), [shwr, bath (hip) (4), tlt, a/c-cool, fan, heat, elec blkts, TV, clock radio, refrig, cook fac ltd, micro, elec frypan, toaster, linen reqd-fee], ldry, bbq, plygr, cots. **D ♦♦ $58 - $70, ♦♦♦♦ $70 - $98, W $390 - $590**, pen con, seasonal variation, Min book school holidays and Easter.

★★★ **Noonameena**, (Cotg), Cnr Grampians Tourist Rd & Glen St, 600m S of PO, ☎ 03 5341 7520, 1 cotg acc up to 5, (2 bedrm), [shwr, bath, tlt, fire pl, heat, elec blkts, TV, clock radio, refrig, cook fac, micro, toaster, ldry, linen reqd], w/mach, bbq. **D $75 - $95, W $450 - $490**, Min book applies.

★★★ **Sundial Holiday Units**, (HU), Dunkeld Rd, 1km S of PO, ☎ 03 5356 4422, 2 units acc up to 5, (2 bedrm), [shwr, bath, tlt, a/c, heat, elec blkts, TV, clock radio, refrig, cook fac, micro, elec frypan, toaster, ldry (in unit), linen reqd-fee], w/mach, bbq, cots. **D ♦♦ $55 - $85**, ♦ **$10, W $350 - $475**, ch con, Min book school holidays and Easter.

★★☆ **Grampians Farm**, (Cotg), Stawell Rd, 5.5km NE of PO, ☎ 03 5356 4267, fax 03 5356 4267, 1 cotg acc up to 4, (2 bedrm), [shwr, tlt, evap cool, fan, fire pl, heat, elec blkts, tel, TV, radio, refrig, cook fac, toaster, ldry, blkts, doonas, linen, pillows], bbq, Pets allowed. **D $90 - $100**.

★★ **Rocky Glen Cottage**, (Cotg), Cnr Pinnacle & High Rds, 2.8km S of PO, ☎ 03 5356 4670, (2 stry), 1 cotg acc up to 7, (3 bedrm), [shwr, tlt, fan, heat, elec blkts, TV, video, clock radio, refrig, cook fac, micro, elec frypan, toaster, ldry, doonas], w/mach, iron, bbq, c/park (carport). **D ♦♦ $110 - $120, W $600**.

Grampians Holiday Retreat, (House), 18 Warren Rd, ☎ 03 5358 4350, fax 03 5358 4350, 2 houses acc up to 12, (4 bedrm), [shwr, tlt, evap cool (1), c/fan (1), heat, elec blkts, TV, video, clock radio, t/c mkg, cook fac, micro, toaster, blkts, doonas, pillows], w/mach, dryer, lounge firepl (1), bbq, c/park (undercover), non smoking property. **D $130 - $150, W $750 - $850**, (not yet classified).

B&B's/Guest Houses

★★★☆ **Mountain Grand Guest House**, (GH), Main Rd, 200m S of PO, ☎ 03 5356 4232, fax 03 5356 4254, 13 rms [ensuite, spa bath (1), a/c, elec blkts, clock radio, t/c mkg], lounge (TV, video), conf fac, ⊠, bar (cocktail), ☎, non smoking property. **BB** ♦♦ **$108**, ♦ **$44, DBB** ♦♦ **$176**, ♦ **$70**, ch con, Min book all holiday times, BC EFT MC VI.

Other Accommodation

Tandara Lutheran Camp, (Lodge), Tandara Rd, ☎ 03 5356 4253, fax 03 5356 4220, 11 rms acc up to 7, [blkts reqd, linen reqd, pillows reqd], ldry, lounge (TV, video), cook fac, refrig, bbq (covered), ☎, plygr, non smoking rms. **D all meals** ♦ **$33 - $38**, ch con, Minimum booking - 30 people.

★★ **(Tandara Cottage)**, 1 cotg acc up to 8, (3 bedrm), [shwr, tlt, a/c-cool, heat (wood & gas), TV, refrig, cook fac, micro, elec frypan, toaster, ldry (in unit), blkts, linen reqd-fee, pillows reqd-fee], w/mach, bbq. **D $69 - $87.**

YHA Victoria, (Lodge), Cnr Buckler St & Grampians Rd, ☎ 03 5356 4544, fax 03 5356 4543, 10 rms [heat], shwr, tlt, ldry, lounge (TV, video), lounge firepl, cook fac, refrig, bbq, ☎. **D** ♦ **$40**, ♦♦ **$45**, ♦♦♦ **$62**, BC MC VI.

(Dormitory Section), 10 rms acc up to 4, [heat], shwr, tlt, cook fac, refrig. **D** ♦ **$18 - $23**, ♦ **$18 - $23**, ch con.

GRAMPIANS - LAKE FYANS VIC 3381

See display advertisement on facing page.

GRAMPIANS - MIRRANATWA VIC 3294

Pop Nominal, (227km W Melbourne), See map on pages 694/695, ref B6. Agricultural district at the northern end of the Victoria Valley, in the Grampians.

★★★ **Barrahead Partnership**, (Cotg), (Farm), Mirranatwa School Rd, 400m W of school hall, ☎ 03 5574 0204, fax 03 5574 0204, 1 cotg acc up to 6, (3 bedrm), [shwr, bath, tlt, fan, heat (wood), elec blkts, TV, clock radio, refrig, cook fac, micro, toaster, ldry, blkts, linen reqd, pillows], w/mach, dryer, iron, iron brd, bbq, cots. **BB $75, W$430.**

GRAMPIANS - POMONAL VIC 3381

Pop Nominal, (248km NW Melbourne), See map on pages 694/695, ref C5. On Eastern slopes of Grampians.

★★★★ **Grampians Country Cottages**, (Cotg), 10km S of PO, ☎ 03 5354 2516, fax 03 5354 2513, 2 cotgs acc up to 6, (2 bedrm), [shwr, bath (hip), tlt, hairdry, a/c, elec blkts, TV, video, clock radio, CD, t/c mkg, refrig, cook fac, micro, d/wash, toaster, ldry (in unit), doonas, linen reqd-fee, pillows], w/mach, dryer, iron, iron brd, lounge firepl, bbq, cots. **D** ♦♦ **$84 - $120**, ♦ **$15**, ch con, Breakfast available. BC MC VI, *Operator Comment: Real peace and quiet. Luxury accommodation close to Halls Gap.*

★★★☆ **Grampians Sunrise Holiday Units**, (HU), Halls Gap Rd, 300m N of PO, ☎ 03 5356 6300, 6 units acc up to 6, (2 bedrm), [shwr, tlt, hairdry, c/fan, heat, elec blkts, TV, video, clock radio, refrig, cook fac, micro, toaster, ldry (in unit), blkts, linen reqd-fee, pillows], w/mach, iron, iron brd, rec rm, pool-heated (solar), bbq, plygr, cots. **D** ♦♦ **$70 - $85**, ♦ **$12**, **W** ♦ **$420 - $510**, ♦ **$72**, ch con, BC MC VI.

★★★ **Sarah Jane Cottage**, (Cotg), (Farm), Lake Fyans Rd, 3.6km NE of PO, ☎ 03 5332 9896, 1 cotg acc up to 6, (2 bedrm), [shwr, tlt, heat, elec blkts, TV, clock radio, refrig, cook fac, micro, toaster, blkts, linen reqd, pillows], ldry, cots. **D $70, W $350**, Min book applies.

GRAMPIANS - VICTORIA VALLEY VIC 3294

Pop Part of Dunkeld, (274km W Melbourne), See map on pages 694/695, ref B6.

★★★☆ **Bona Vista Host Farm**, (Cotg), (Farm), Victoria Valley Rd, 15.9km N of Public Hall, 28km N of Dunkeld, ☎ 03 5574 0225, fax 03 5574 0213, 1 cotg acc up to 8, (3 bedrm), [shwr, bath, tlt, hairdry, fan, heat, elec blkts (some), TV, clock radio, refrig, cook fac, micro, elec frypan, toaster, ldry, blkts, doonas, linen reqd, pillows], w/mach, iron, iron brd, lounge firepl, bbq, c/park (carport), plygr, cots, non smoking property, Pet allowed by prior arrangement. **D $90, W $450**, Tariff includes seasonal farm activities.

GRAMPIANS - WARTOOK VIC 3401

Pop 105. (295km NW Melbourne), See map on pages 694/695, ref B5. Small settlement in a picturesque valley at the western entrance to the Grampians National Park.

★★★☆ **Happy Wanderer Holiday Resort**, (Log Cabin), RMB 7364 Grampians Rd, ☎ 03 5383 6210, fax 03 5383 6350, 9 log cabins acc up to 6, [shwr, tlt, hairdry, a/c-cool, heat, elec blkts, TV, clock radio, refrig, cook fac, micro, d/wash (2), linen reqd-fee], ldry, w/mach-fee, dryer-fee, iron, pool-heated (solar), bbq, ☎, plygr, golf (9 hole), tennis. **D** ♦♦ **$56 - $106**, ♦ **$17**, **W** ♦♦ **$336 - $742**, ♦ **$102 - $119**, ch con, 2 units ★★★★☆, Min book all holiday times, BC MC VI.

★★★ **Chinaman's Lodge**, (Cotg), Roses Gap Rd, 7km E off Grampians Rd, ☎ 03 5383 6203, fax 03 5383 6347, (2 stry gr fl), 1 cotg acc up to 8, (4 bedrm), [shwr, tlt, c/fan, heat, elec blkts, TV, video, radio, refrig, cook fac, ldry (in unit), doonas, linen, pillows], w/mach, iron, iron brd, bbq. **D** ♦♦ **$100 - $120**, ♦ **$15**, Min book applies, BC MC VI.

★★☆ **(Chinaman's Lodge)**, 1 unit acc up to 8, (Studio), [shwr, tlt, fire pl (1), heat, elec blkts, TV, refrig, cook fac, doonas, linen, pillows], bbq, canoeing. **D** ♦ **$35 - $38.50**, ♦♦ **$70 - $80**, **W** ♦♦ **$300 - $495**, ch con.

★★★ **Emu Holiday Park**, (Cotg), Rosebrook-Glenisla Rd, ☎ 03 5383 6304, fax 03 5383 6319, 2 cotgs acc up to 7, (2 bedrm), [shwr, tlt, a/c, c/fan, heat (wood & gas), elec blkts, clock radio, refrig, cook fac, micro, linen reqd-fee], ldry, w/mach-fee, dryer-fee, bbq, plygr. **D** ♦♦ **$80 - $90**, ♦ **$12**, **W** ♦♦ **$480 - $580**, ♦ **$72**, ch con, BC EFT MC VI.

★★★ **The Grelco Run**, (Cotg), RMB 7353 Schmidt Rd, Brimpaen 3401, 15km W of Wartook, off Wartook-Brimpaen Rd, ☎ 03 5383 9221, fax 03 5383 9222, (2 stry gr fl), 2 cotgs acc up to 6, (2 & 3 bedrm), [shwr, tlt, hairdry (2), a/c, heat, elec blkts, TV, video, clock radio, CD, refrig, cook fac, micro, toaster, blkts, doonas, linen, pillows], iron, iron brd, bbq, bicycle, breakfast ingredients, non smoking property. **BB** ♦ **$66 - $71.50**, ♦ **$66 - $71.50**, ch con, 1 cottage ★★★★. BC MC VI.

★★ **Wartook Rise**, (HU), Northern Grampians Rd, ☎ 03 5383 6260, (2 stry gr fl), 2 units acc up to 12, (3 bedrm), [shwr, tlt, c/fan, heat (wood), TV, refrig, cook fac ltd, micro, elec frypan, toaster, blkts reqd-fee, linen reqd-fee], bbq, ☎, cots. **D** ♦♦ **$70**, ♦ **$12**, ch con.

B&B's/Guest Houses

★★★★ **Wartook Gardens**, (B&B), Mt Victory Rd, ☎ 03 5383 6200, fax 03 5383 6240, 3 rms [ensuite (1), shwr, bath (2), tlt, hairdry, a/c-cool, c/fan, heat (underfloor), elec blkts, clock radio, doonas], lounge (TV, video, cd), pool-heated (solar), t/c mkg shared, bbq, non smoking rms (3). **BB** ♦ **$80**, ♦♦ **$100**, 1 room ★★★★☆. Dinner by arrangement. BC MC VI.

GRAMPIANS - WILLAURA VIC 3379

Pop 300. (240km W Melbourne), See map on pages 694/695, ref C6. A small township in farming district of western Victoria.

★★★☆ **Greenvale Homestead**, (House), (Farm), RMB 415 Wickliffe - Willaura Rd, 9.3km N of Wickliffe, off Glenelg Hwy, ☎ 03 5354 1343, fax 03 5354 1341, 1 house acc up to 22, [shwr, bath (3), spa bath (1), tlt, elec blkts, TV, video (1), clock radio, refrig, cook fac, micro, d/wash (1), toaster, ldry, blkts reqd, linen reqd-fee, pillows reqd], lounge firepl, bbq, tennis, non smoking property. **D** ♦ **$50.**

★★★☆ **Hawksview**, (Cotg), (Farm), off Mafeking Rd Mafeking via, 33.3km NW of PO, off Dunkeld - Moyston Rd, ☎ 03 5354 6244, fax 03 5354 6244, 1 cotg acc up to 6, (2 bedrm), [shwr, bath, tlt, c/fan, heat (wood fire), elec blkts, tel, TV, radio, refrig, cook fac, micro, toaster, ldry, blkts, linen, pillows], c/park (carport), cots, non smoking property. **D** ♦♦ **$100**, ♦ **$15**, **W $500 - $600**, Tariff includes some seasonal farm activities. Meals by arrangement.

★★★ **Kerillo**, (Cotg), off Mafeking Rd, 33.3km NW of PO, off Dunkeld - Moyston Rd, ☎ 03 5354 6244, 1 cotg acc up to 4, (2 bedrm), [shwr, tlt, heat (wood), radio, refrig, cook fac, blkts, linen, pillows]. **D** ♦♦ **$100**, ♦ **$15**, **W $500 - $600**, Meals by arrangement. Min book applies.

★★★ **Thermopylae Enterprises**, (Cotg), (Farm), Miners Cottage, Mafeking Rd, 25km NW of PO, off Dunkeld - Moyston Rd, ☎ 03 5354 6245, fax 03 5354 6257, 1 cotg acc up to 10, (5 bedrm), [shwr, tlt (2), a/c, fire pl, heat, elec blkts, TV, clock radio, refrig, cook fac, micro, toaster, ldry (in unit), linen reqd-fee], bbq, tennis, cots. **D $120 - $264**, **W $720 - $1,540**, Tariff includes farm activities. AE BC DC MC VI.

★★☆ **(Shearers Quarters)**, 1 cotg acc up to 12, [shwr (2), tlt (2), a/c, fire pl, elec blkts, TV, clock radio, refrig, cook fac, micro, toaster, ldry, blkts, linen reqd-fee, pillows], bbq. **D $120 - $264, W $720 - $1,540.**

End of Grampians Region

GRANTVILLE VIC 3984

Pop 400. (100km SE Melbourne), See map on page 696, ref C7. Small township on the shore of Westernport Bay. Boating, Fishing, Sailing, Shooting, Swimming (Beach), Tennis.

B&B's/Guest Houses
★★★★☆ **The Heath B & B**, (B&B), 1705 Bass Hwy, ☎ 03 5678 8500, fax 03 5678 8769, 4 rms [shwr, tlt, hairdry, c/fan, cent heat, elec blkts, TV, clock radio], rec rm (TV, video), lounge (CD player), pool (solar), spa (heated), bbq, golf (12 hole pitch & putt), non smoking property. **BB ♦ $70 - $90, ♦ $110 - $132**, Min book long w/ends, BC MC VI.

GREAT WESTERN VIC 3377

Pop 250. (219km W Melbourne), See map on pages 694/695, ref C5. Famous for its wines for over 100 years. Vineyards, Wineries.

Hotels/Motels
★★☆ **Great Western Hotel Motel**, (LMH), Western Hwy, 100m SE of PO, ☎ 03 5356 2270, fax 03 5356 2435, 8 units [shwr, tlt, hairdry (6), a/c-cool, heat, elec blkts, TV, clock radio, t/c mkg, refrig, toaster], ⊠, ☎, cots. **RO ♦ $40, ♦♦ $45, ♦ $10**, ch con, AE BC EFT MC VI.

GREENDALE VIC 3341

Pop Nominal, (67km W Melbourne), See map on page 696, ref A4. Agricultural district situated on Dales Ck. Scenic Drives.

Self Catering Accommodation
★★★★ **Greendale Country House**, (Cotg), No children's facilities, Lot 90 Shuter Ave, ☎ 03 5368 7215, fax 03 5368 7378, 1 cotg acc up to 4, (2 bedrm), [shwr, spa bath, tlt, hairdry, fan, heat, elec blkts, TV, video, clock radio, CD, t/c mkg, refrig, cook fac ltd, micro, toaster, ldry (in unit), blkts, doonas, linen, pillows], w/mach, iron, iron brd, lounge firepl, bbq, c/park (carport), breakfast ingredients, non smoking property. **BB ♦♦ $160 - $195, ♦ $56.25 - $80**, Min book Christmas Jan long w/ends and Easter, BC MC VI.

GYMBOWEN VIC 3401

Pop Nominal, (353km W Melbourne), See map on pages 694/695, ref A5. Agricultural district. Rock Climbing, Tennis.

Self Catering Accommodation
★★ **Duffholme Cabins and Museum**, (Cotg), Natimuk - Goroke Rd, 10km W of Natimuk, ☎ 03 5387 4246, 1 cotg acc up to 7, (2 bedrm), [shwr, bath, tlt, evap cool, fan, heat (wood), elec blkts, TV, clock radio, refrig, cook fac, micro, elec frypan, toaster, blkts, linen, pillows]. **D ♦♦ $44, ♦ $22**, ch con.
(Bunkhouse Section), 3 bunkhouses acc up to 6, (Bunk Rooms), [blkts reqd, linen reqd], shwr, tlt. **D ♦ $6, ♦ $6**, ch con.

HALLS GAP VIC

See Grampians Region.

HALLSTON VIC 3953

Pop Nominal, (150km SE Melbourne), See map on page 696, ref D7. Dairy farming area.

B&B's/Guest Houses
Hallston Forrest Trail Riders Station, (GH), Grand Ridge Rd, ☎ 03 5668 5287, fax 03 5668 5289, 8 rms [cent heat, pillows], shwr, tlt, lounge (TV, video), ✗, t/c mkg shared, refrig, ☎. **BB ♦ $45, ♦ $45**, (not yet classified).

HAMILTON VIC 3300

Pop 9,250. (290km W Melbourne), See map on pages 694/695, ref B6. Centre of one of the finest wool producing areas in the world. Tourist Bureau, Lonsdale St, 03 5572 3746. Art Gallery, Boating, Bowls, Croquet, Fishing, Golf, Horse Racing, Rowing, Sailing, Scenic Drives, Shooting, Swimming (Pool, River), Tennis, Trotting, Water Skiing.

Hotels/Motels

★★★★ **Botanical Motor Inn**, (M), Cnr Thompson & French Sts, 300m S of PO, ☎ 03 5572 1855, fax 03 5571 1419, 32 units [shwr, spa bath (6), tlt, hairdry, a/c, elec blkts, tel, TV, video, clock radio, t/c mkg, refrig, mini bar, ldry], conf fac, ⊠ (open 7 days), pool, rm serv, cots-fee, non smoking units (13). **RO ♦ $96 - $132, ♦♦ $107 - $143, ♦ $11**, ch con, AE BC DC EFT MC MP VI, ♿.

★★★★ **Quality Inn Grange Burn**, (M), Previously Grange Burn Motor Inn, 142 Ballarat Rd (Glenelg Hwy), 2.7km E of PO, ☎ 03 5572 5755, fax 03 5571 2295, 31 units (2 suites) [shwr, spa bath (10), tlt, hairdry, a/c, elec blkts, tel, cable tv, clock radio, t/c mkg, refrig, mini bar, cook fac (2), micro (2), toaster], ldry, iron, iron brd, lounge, business centre, conf fac, ⊠ (Mon to Sat), pool, spa, rm serv, cots-fee, non smoking units (11). **RO ♦ $105 - $111, ♦♦ $116 - $121, Suite RO ♦ $152, ♦♦ $163, ♦ $11**, AE BC DC EFT MC VI, ♿.

★★★☆ **Bandicoot Motor Inn**, (M), 152 Ballarat Rd (Glenelg Hwy), 3.2km E of PO, ☎ 03 5572 1688, fax 03 5572 5443, 26 units [shwr, tlt, hairdry, a/c, elec blkts, tel, TV, video-fee, clock radio, t/c mkg, refrig, mini bar, toaster], ldry, iron, iron brd, ⊠, bbq, cots-fee, non smoking units (9). **RO ♦ $66, ♦♦ $77, ♦ $16.50**, ch con, AE BC DC EFT MC VI, ♿.

★★★☆ **Goldsmith Motel**, (M), 30 Goldsmith St, 300m NE of PO, ☎ 03 5572 4347, fax 03 5571 1841, 15 units [shwr, tlt, hairdry, a/c, c/fan, elec blkts, tel, cable tv, video-fee, clock radio, t/c mkg, refrig, mini bar, micro (3), toaster], iron, iron brd, bbq, rm serv, cots-fee. **RO ♦ $85, ♦♦ $87 - $92, ♦ $12**, ch con, AE BC DC EFT MC MP VI, ♿.

★★★☆ **Hamilton Lakeside**, (M), 24 Ballarat Rd (Glenelg Hwy), 1.5km E of PO, ☎ 03 5572 3757, fax 03 5572 4010, 10 units [shwr, bath, tlt, hairdry, a/c, heat, elec blkts, tel, TV, video-fee, clock radio, t/c mkg, refrig, cook fac, toaster], bbq, c/park (carport), cots-fee. **RO ♦ $62 - $73, ♦♦ $71 - $82, ♦ $11**, AE BC DC EFT MC MCH MP VI.

★★★☆ **Lonsdale Motor Inn**, (M), 110 Lonsdale St (Glenelg Hwy), 700m NE of PO, ☎ 03 5572 4055, fax 03 5571 1367, 15 units [shwr, bath (hip) (2), tlt, hairdry, a/c, elec blkts, tel, cable tv, video-fee, clock radio, t/c mkg, refrig, mini bar, toaster], iron, iron brd, ⊠ (Mon to Sat), pool-heated (solar), bbq, rm serv, cots-fee, non smoking units (6). **RO ♦ $83, ♦♦ $92, ♦ $12**, ch con, AE BC DC EFT MC MP VI, ♿.

★★★ **George Hotel Motel Hamilton**, (LMH), 213 Gray St, 600m NE of PO, ☎ 03 5572 1844, fax 03 5571 2282, 25 units [shwr, tlt, a/c-cool (11), a/c (14), heat, elec blkts, tel, TV, movie, clock radio, t/c mkg, refrig, toaster], conf fac, ⊠, cots, non smoking units (3). **BLB** ⋔ **$50 - $55,** ⋔ **$61 - $66,** ◊ **$10,** ch con, 11 units ★★. AE BC DC EFT JCB MC VI.

★★★ **Hamilton Town House Motel on Shakespeare**, (M), Previously The Town Lodge, 27 Shakespeare St, 800m N of PO, ☎ 03 5571 2517, fax 03 5571 2517, 9 units [shwr, tlt, hairdry, a/c, elec blkts, TV, clock radio, t/c mkg, refrig, toaster], cots, non smoking units (4). **BLB** ⋔ **$55,** ⋔ **$66,** ◊ **$11,** pen con, AE BC DC EFT MC VI.

★★★ **Lenwin on the Lake Motor Inn**, (M), 2 Riley St, 1.5km E of PO, ☎ 03 5571 2733, fax 03 5572 3817, 12 units [shwr, spa bath (1), tlt, a/c (11), c/fan, elec blkts, tel, TV, clock radio, t/c mkg, refrig, toaster], cots-fee. **RO** ⋔ **$55 - $115,** ◊ **$11,** ch con, AE BC DC EFT MC MCH VI.

★★☆ **Caledonian Hotel Motel**, (LMH), 153 Thompson St (Glenelg Hwy), 500m NE of PO, ☎ 03 5572 1055, fax 03 5571 1218, 14 units [shwr, tlt, a/c, elec blkts, tel, TV, clock radio, t/c mkg, refrig], ldry, ⊠, cots, non smoking units (4). **RO** ⋔ **$52,** ⋔ **$62,** ◊ **$10,** ch con, AE BC DC EFT MC MP VI.

B&B's/Guest Houses

★★★★ **Hewlett House**, (B&B), c1876. 36 Gray St, 100m SW of PO, ☎ 03 5572 2494, fax 03 5572 5395, (2 stry gr fl), 2 rms [ensuite, spa bath (1), fan, cent heat, elec blkts, TV, t/c mkg, doonas], lounge, lounge firepl, cots, non smoking property. **BB** ⋔ **$93.50,** ⋔ **$140,** ch con, AE BC MC VI.

★★★☆ **Acton Lodge Bed & Breakfast**, (B&B), (Farm), Strathkellar Rd, 8km E of PO, ☎ 03 5572 5818, fax 03 5572 5818, (2 stry), 3 rms [ensuite (1), hairdry, cent heat, elec blkts, clock radio, t/c mkg], rec rm, lounge (TV), lounge firepl, non smoking property. **BB** ⋔ **$44 - $55,** ⋔ **$88 - $99,** ◊ **$38.50 - $44,** ch con, 1 room ★★★★. Dinner by arrangement.

★★★☆ **Mourilyan**, (B&B), 22 Pope St, ☎ 03 5572 4989, fax 03 5572 4748, 2 rms [shwr, bath, tlt, fan, cent heat, doonas], rec rm, lounge (TV, video), t/c mkg shared, refrig, non smoking property. **BB** ⋔ **$75,** ⋔ **$100,** ◊ **$40 - $45,** ch con, AE BC DC MC VI.

Other Accommodation

Peppercorn Lodge, (Lodge), 10 Ballarat Rd (Glenelg Hwy), 1.5km E of PO, ☎ 03 5571 9046, 20 rms acc up to 4, [basin, heat, t/c mkg, ldry, blkts reqd-fee, linen reqd-fee], iron, iron brd, lounge (TV), cook fac, refrig, bbq, ✆. **D** ⋔ **$16.50,** ⋔ **$27.50,** ⋔⋔ **$33,** ⋔⋔⋔ **$44,** ch con, Catering by arrangement.

HARCOURT VIC 3453

Pop 400. (123km NW Melbourne), See map on page 696, ref A3. A horticultural township, famed for its apples & pears. Located on Calder Hwy, adjacent to Barkers Creek. Bowls, Bush Walking, Fishing (Lake, River), Golf, Scenic Drives, Swimming, Tennis.

Hotels/Motels

★★★ **Harcourt Motel**, (M), 96 Calder Hwy, 150m N of PO, ☎ 03 5474 2104, fax 03 5474 2306, 14 units [shwr, tlt, a/c-cool (5), c/fan (9), heat, elec blkts, tel, TV, clock radio, t/c mkg, refrig], ⊠, rm serv, dinner to unit, cots-fee. **RO** ⋔ **$48 - $68,** ⋔ **$57 - $68,** ◊ **$11,** ch con, 5 units ★★. AE BC DC MC MCH VI.

Self Catering Accommodation

★★★ **Tintooki Cottage**, (Cotg), Cnr Calder Hwy & Fogartys Gap Rd, 5km N of PO, ☎ 03 5474 2205, 1 cotg acc up to 8, (4 bedrm - 2x1q,1x2s,1xbunks), [shwr, tlt, TV, radio, refrig, cook fac, toaster, blkts, linen, pillows], lounge firepl, pool above ground, bbq, breakfast ingredients. **BLB** ⋔ **$90,** ◊ **$25,** **RO** ⋔ **$75,** ◊ **$20,** BC MC VI.

B&B's/Guest Houses

★★★ **Ayron & Dan Teed**, (B&B), Solar power. 'Penrhos' 3100 Calder Hwy, 4.8km S of Harcourt, ☎ 03 5474 2415, (2 stry), 1 rm [shwr, tlt, fan, heat (wood), CD, t/c mkg], lounge (TV), cots, non smoking property. **BB** ⋔ **$85,** ◊ **$20,** ch con, Other meals by arrangement.

HARRIETVILLE VIC 3741

Pop Part of Bright, (332km NE Melbourne), See map on pages 694/695, ref H5. A picturesque town at the foot of the Victorian Alps. Bush Walking, Fishing (Trout), Scenic Drives, Snow Skiing.

Hotels/Motels

★★ **Snowline Hotel**, (LMH), Great Alpine Rd, 100m S of PO, ☎ 03 5759 2524, fax 03 5759 2698, 16 units [shwr, tlt, heat, elec blkts, TV, t/c mkg, doonas], ⊠, ✆. **RO** ⋔ **$44,** ⋔ **$66 - $100,** ◊ **$11,** BC EFT MC VI.

Self Catering Accommodation

★★★★☆ **Pick & Shovel Cottage**, (Cotg), 1 Pick & Shovel Rise, 1km S of PO, ☎ 03 5759 2627, fax 03 5759 2627, 1 cotg acc up to 6, (2 bedrm), [shwr, bath, tlt, hairdry, a/c, fan, fire pl, heat, tel, TV, video, clock radio, CD, t/c mkg, refrig, cook fac, micro, elec frypan, d/wash, toaster, ldry, blkts, linen, pillows], w/mach, dryer, iron, iron brd, pool (salt/solar heated), bbq, c/park (carport), cots, breakfast ingredients. **BB** ⋔ **$110 - $130,** ◊ **$20,** ⋔ **$750,** ◊ **$40,** ch con, BC MC VI,

Operator Comment:
See our web site at: www.pickandshovel.com.au

★★☆ **Cas-Bak Flats**, (HU), Great Alpine Rd, 50m N of PO, ☎ 03 5759 2531, fax 03 5759 2720, 12 units acc up to 7, (1 & 2 bedrm), [shwr, tlt, heat, elec blkts, TV, refrig, cook fac ltd, elec frypan, blkts, linen, pillows], ldry, w/mach, dryer, dry rm, rec rm, pool, sauna, bbq, c/park (carport) (6), plygr. **D** ⋔ **$55,** ⋔ **$75,** ◊ **$25,** **W** **$380 - $720,** Min book all holiday times, AE BC DC MC VI.

★★ **Fishermans Haven**, (HF), Great Alpine Rd, 700m N of PO, ☎ 03 9720 1663, 1 flat acc up to 6, (2 bedrm), [shwr, tlt, heat (wood), TV, refrig, cook fac ltd, micro, elec frypan, toaster, linen reqd], ldry, bbq. **W** **$180 - $400.**

B&B's/Guest Houses

★★★★ **Lavender Hue**, (B&B), Great Alpine Rd, 2km N of PO, ☎ 03 5759 2588, fax 03 5759 2606, (2 stry), 1 rm (1 suite) [shwr, bath, tlt, hairdry, c/fan, cent heat, elec blkts, TV, clock radio, t/c mkg, refrig, micro, toaster], iron, iron brd. **BB** ⋔ **$231,** Min book applies.

★★★ **Feathertop Chalet**, (GH), Bon Accord Track, off Great Alpine Rd, ☎ 03 5759 2688, fax 03 5759 2690, (2 stry gr fl), 36 rms [ensuite (30), cent heat], ldry, dry rm, rec rm, lounge (TV, microwave), conf fac, ⊠, pool indoor heated, sauna, t/c mkg shared, bbq, ✆, plygr, mini golf, ski hire, squash, tennis, cots-fee. **DBB** ⋔ **$55,** ◊ **$55,** ch con, BC MC VI.

★★★ **Harrietville Hotel Motel**, (GH), Previously Alpine Lodge Inn Great Alpine Rd, 500m N of PO, ☎ 03 5759 2525, fax 03 5759 2766, 26 rms [shwr, tlt, heat, elec blkts, TV, t/c mkg, refrig, cook fac ltd (1), micro (1)], ldry, dry rm, lounge (TV, video), ⊠, pool, spa, bbq, ✆, ski hire. **RO** ⋔ **$35 - $50,** ⋔ **$60 - $75,** ◊ **$15,** ch con, AE BC DC MC VI.

HARROW VIC 3317

Pop 200. (378km W Melbourne), See map on pages 694/695, ref A5. Pastoral township on the Glenelg River. Canoeing, Fishing, Golf, Swimming (River), Tennis.

Self Catering Accommodation

★★★☆ **Nerrinyerie Cottage**, (Cotg), (Farm), Harrow - Edenhope Rd, 10km W of PO, ☎ 03 5588 1216, fax 03 5588 1260, 1 cotg acc up to 5, (3 bedrm), [shwr, tlt, hairdry, fan, heat, elec blkts, TV, clock radio, refrig, cook fac, elec frypan, toaster, ldry (in unit), blkts, doonas, linen, pillows], w/mach, dryer, iron, iron brd, bbq, cots. **D** ⋔ **$82.50,** **W** **$440,** Light breakfast available.

HASTINGS VIC 3915

Pop 5,900. (61km S Melbourne), See Melbourne map, ref D7. Natural deepwater harbour, which houses a large fishing fleet. Information Centre, Frankston Flinders Rd, 03 5979 3333. Boat Ramp, Boating, Bowls, Fishing, Golf, Horse Riding, Sailing, Swimming (Pool), Tennis.

★★★★ **Hastings Harbour View Motor Inn**, (M), 126 Marine Pde, 1km N of PO, ☎ 03 5979 3333, fax 03 5979 3206, 30 units [shwr, bath (hip) (6), spa bath (7), tlt, a/c, c/fan, elec blkts, tel, TV, clock radio, t/c mkg, refrig, mini bar, cook fac (2), toaster], ldry, iron, iron brd, conf fac, ✉ (Mon to Sat), pool, bbq (covered), dinner to unit (Mon to Sat), gym, cots-fee, non smoking units (8). **RO ♦ $90 - $135, ♦♦ $95 - $135, ♦ $12, AE BC DC MC VI,** ♿.

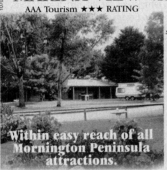

HAWKESDALE VIC 3287

Pop Nominal, (296km W Melbourne), See map on pages 694/695, ref B7. Pastoral and dairying district.

★★★☆ **Banuke Pastoral Co**, (Cotg), (Farm), Woolsthorpe - Heywood Rd, 7km SEof township, ☎ 03 5560 7293, fax 03 5560 7293, 1 cotg acc up to 5, (2 bedrm), [shwr, tlt, fan, heat, elec blkts, TV, clock radio, refrig, cook fac, toaster], ldry, blkts, doonas, linen, pillows], iron, iron brd, lounge firepl, bbq, breakfast ingredients. **BB ♦♦ $75, ♦ $10,** ch con, fam con.

HEALESVILLE VIC 3777

Pop 6,350. (61km E Melbourne), See map on page 696, ref D5. Nestling at the foot of the mountains on the Watts River. Healesville Sanctuary is Victoria's major park of Australian Fauna. RACV Country Club - golf course for RACV Club members and their guests. Bowls, Bush Walking, Canoeing, Fishing, Golf, Greyhound Racing, Horse Riding, Scenic Drives, Swimming (River), Tennis, Vineyards, Wineries.

Hotels/Motels

★★★★ **Yarra Gables Motel**, (M), 55 Maroondah Hwy, 1km SW of information centre, ☎ 03 5962 1323, fax 03 5962 6321, 5 units [shwr, spa bath (2), tlt, hairdry, a/c, elec blkts, tel, TV, video (3), clock radio, t/c mkg, refrig, micro, toaster], ldry, iron, iron brd, cots. **RO ♦ $99 - $140, ♦♦ $99 - $140, ♦ $15, AE BC DC MC VI,** ♿.

★★★ **Healesville Maroondah View Motel**, (M), 1 McKenzie Ave, 3km E of PO, ☎ 03 5962 4154, fax 03 5962 3782, 10 units [shwr, tlt, a/c, heat, elec blkts, TV, clock radio, t/c mkg, refrig, toaster], ✗, pool, cots (avail), non smoking units (5). **RO ♦ $60 - $75, ♦♦ $70 - $75, ♦ $15, AE BC MC MCH VI.**

★★★ **Healesville Motor Inn**, (M), 45 Maroondah Hwy, 1.7km SW of PO, ☎ 03 5962 5188, fax 03 5962 1661, 14 units [shwr, spa bath (2), tlt, a/c, elec blkts, tel, TV, video-fee, clock radio, t/c mkg, refrig, toaster], ldry, bbq, plygr, cots-fee, non smoking units (5). **RO ♦ $57 - $135, ♦♦ $75 - $140, ♦ $15,** ch con, AE BC DC EFT MC VI, ♿.

★★☆ **Sanctuary House Healesville**, (M), 326 Badger Creek Rd, 400m N of Sanctuary, ☎ 03 5962 5148, fax 03 5962 5392, 12 units [shwr, tlt, a/c-cool, heat, elec blkts, TV, clock radio, t/c mkg, refrig], ldry, rec rm, lounge, ✗, BYO, pool, sauna, spa-fee, ☎, tennis (half court), cots-fee. **RO ♦ $50 - $60, ♦♦ $65 - $80,** ch con, AE BC DC EFT MC VI.

Self Catering Accommodation

★★★★☆ **Villa Australis**, (Cotg), 939 Don Rd, 10km S of PO, ☎ 03 5962 4260, fax 03 5962 6077, 1 cotg acc up to 2, (1 bedrm), [shwr, bath, tlt, hairdry, fan, heat (wood), elec blkts, TV, clock radio, t/c mkg, refrig, cook fac, micro, toaster, blkts, doonas, linen, pillows], iron, iron brd, pool, bbq, breakfast ingredients, non smoking property. **BB ♦♦ $180, W ♦♦ $800,** BC MC VI.

★★★★ **Sanctuary Park Cottages**, (Cotg), 85 Badger Ave, ☎ 03 5962 6240, fax 03 5962 2904, 4 cotgs acc up to 8, (1, 2 & 3 bedrm), [shwr, spa bath, tlt, hairdry, c/fan, clock radio, refrig, cook fac, micro, toaster, ldry (in unit), blkts, linen, pillows], iron, iron brd, lounge (tv, video, cd player), lounge firepl, pool, bbq, plygr. **D ♦♦ $140, ♦ $20,** ch con, BC MC VI.

★★★☆ **Toolebewong Cottage B & B**, (Cotg), 120 Toolebewong Rd, ☎ 03 5962 3437, 1 cotg acc up to 5, (3 bedrm), [shwr, spa bath, tlt, hairdry, a/c-cool, heat, elec blkts, TV, video, clock radio, CD, t/c mkg, refrig, cook fac, micro, toaster, blkts, doonas, linen, pillows], iron, lounge firepl, bbq, breakfast ingredients. **BB ♦♦ $130 - $170, ♦ $33, W $600 - $800,** ch con, AE BC MC VI.

B&B's/Guest Houses

★★★★☆ **Wide Horizons Bed & Breakfast**, (B&B), No children's facilities, 19 Juliet Cres, 2km E of PO, ☎ 03 5962 4119, fax 03 5962 4571, 3 rms [ensuite, a/c, elec blkts, clock radio, t/c mkg], lounge (TV, video, cd), lounge firepl, refrig, non smoking property. **BB ♦ $110, ♦♦ $121 - $143**, Dinner by arrangement. AE BC JCB MC VI.

★★★☆ **Brentwood Bed & Breakfast**, (B&B), 506 Myers Creek Rd, 7km N of PO, ☎ 03 5962 5028, fax 03 5962 4749, (2 stry gr fl), 3 rms [shwr, tlt, evap cool, heat, elec blkts, clock radio, t/c mkg, refrig], lounge (TV, video), bbq, non smoking property. **BB ♦ $75, ♦♦ $110**, Dinner by arrangement.

★★★☆ **Healesville Therapy Centre & The Retreat**, (B&B), 95 Rogers Rd, 8km N of PO, off Chum Creek Rd, ☎ 03 5962 4502, fax 03 5962 6304, 1 rm (1 suite) [shwr, tlt, heat, elec blkts, TV, clock radio, t/c mkg, refrig, micro, toaster], pool-heated, bbq, non smoking property. **BB ♦ $60 - $65, ♦♦ $100**, BC MC VI.

★★★☆ **Strathvea Guest House**, (GH), No children's facilities, Myers Creek Rd, 9.5km N of PO, ☎ 03 5962 4109, fax 03 5962 3939, 8 rms [shwr (4), tlt (4), heat, elec blkts, clock radio, doonas], lounge, lounge firepl, ✗, t/c mkg shared, refrig, non smoking rms. **BB ♦♦ $121 - $154**, AE BC MC VI.

Other Accommodation

Cranbrook Lodge, (Lodge), No alcohol. 7 Westmount Rd, 1.1km NW of PO, ☎ 03 5962 4208, fax 03 5962 1045, 22 rms [basin (2), ensuite (2), cent heat, elec blkts], ldry, lounge, conf fac, ✗, ✆, cots, non smoking property. **BB ♦ $40, ♦♦ $62**, ch con, pen con.

HEATHCOTE VIC 3523

Pop 1,550. (109km N Melbourne), See map on page 696, ref B3. Agricultural town on the banks of the McIvor Creek. Lake Eppalock nearby. Boating, Bowls, Bush Walking, Fishing (River, Lake), Golf, Horse Racing, Horse Riding, Sailing, Swimming (Pool, Lake), Tennis, Vineyards, Wineries, Water Skiing.

Hotels/Motels

★★★ **Heathcote Motor Inn**, (M), 257 High St (Northern Hwy), 1km N of PO, ☎ 03 5433 2655, fax 03 5433 2655, 10 units [shwr, tlt, a/c, elec blkts, TV, clock radio, t/c mkg, refrig, toaster], pool, bbq, cots. **RO ♦ $55 - $65, ♦♦ $66 - $77, ◊ $11 - $16.50**, AE BC DC EFT MC VI.

★★ **The Commercial Hotel Heathcote**, (LMH), 139 High St (Northern Hwy), ☎ 03 5433 2944, fax 03 5433 3249, (2 stry gr fl), 8 units [shwr, tlt, a/c, elec blkts, TV, clock radio, t/c mkg, refrig, cook fac (1), toaster], ldry, ✗, cots. **BLB ♦ $45, ♦♦ $60, ◊ $15**, Light breakfast only available. BC EFT MC VI.

Self Catering Accommodation

★★★★☆ **Carronshore Farm**, (Cotg), Northern Hwy, Tooborac 3604, 5.4 km N of PO, ☎ 03 5433 5217, fax 03 5433 5217, (2 stry gr fl), 1 cotg acc up to 10, (4 bedrm), [shwr (3), bath, tlt (2), c/fan, heat, elec blkts, tel (local), TV, video, clock radio, CD, t/c mkg, refrig, mini bar, cook fac, micro, d/wash, toaster, ldry, blkts, doonas, linen, pillows], w/mach, lounge firepl, bbq, c/park (undercover), tennis, non smoking property. **D ♦♦ $125, W $600**, AE BC MC VI.

B&B's/Guest Houses

★★★★☆ **Argyle Lodge**, (B&B), No children's facilities, 52 Newlans La, 5km S of PO, ☎ 03 5433 3413, fax 03 5433 3413, 2 rms (2 suites) [ensuite, bath (1), spa bath (1), hairdry, a/c-cool (1), a/c (1), c/fan, heat, elec blkts, TV, video, clock radio, CD, t/c mkg, micro], lounge (TV, stereo), lounge firepl, bbq, non smoking property. **BB ♦ $70 - $95, ♦♦ $115 - $145**, Other meals by arrangement. BC MC VI.

★★★★☆ **Emeu Inn Restaurant & Bed & Breakfast**, (B&B), 187 High St, ☎ 03 5433 2668, fax 03 5433 4022, 3 rms [shwr, spa bath (2), tlt, hairdry, a/c, fire pl (1), TV, clock radio], lounge (cd), ✗, t/c mkg shared, secure park, non smoking property, pets allowed. **BB ♦♦ $155, ◊ $35**, AE BC DC EFT MC VI.

Fayes Fawlty Towers, (GH), 9 Hunter Pl, ☎ 03 5433 2409, fax 03 5433 2794, (2 stry), 5 rms [evap cool, fan, heat, clock radio, micro], ldry, w/mach-fee, dryer-fee, lounge (TV, video, cd), ✗, pool (salt water), cook fac, t/c mkg shared, refrig, bbq, squash-fee, cots, non smoking property. **D ♦ $45, ♦♦ $55, ◊ $20**, ch con, Breakfast available. AE BC MC VI.

★★★ **(Holiday Unit Section)**, 1 unit acc up to 5, (2 bedrm), [shwr, bath, tlt, c/fan, heat, TV, video, clock radio, refrig, cook fac, micro, elec frypan], ldry, w/mach-fee, dryer-fee, bbq. **D ♦♦ $70, ◊ $20**.

HEPBURN SPRINGS VIC 3461

Pop 750. (114km NW Melbourne), See map on page 696, ref A4. A rural tourist town famous for health-giving mineral springs. The Spa Centre of Australia. Bowls, Bush Walking, Fishing, Golf, Horse Riding, Scenic Drives, Tennis.

Hotels/Motels

★★★★ **Hepburn Springs Motor Inn**, (M), 105 Main Rd, 100m N of PO, ☎ 03 5348 3234, fax 03 5348 3207, (2 stry gr fl), 18 units [shwr, spa bath (2), tlt, hairdry, a/c-cool (15), c/fan (5), cent heat, elec blkts, tel, TV, clock radio, t/c mkg, refrig, toaster], ldry, bbq, cots, non smoking units (5). **RO ♦ $79 - $110, ♦♦ $90 - $150, ◊ $15**, AE BC DC EFT MC VI, ♿.

★★★ **Springs Hotel**, (LMH), Cnr Main Rd & Tenth St, 200m N of PO, ☎ 03 5348 2202, fax 03 5348 2506, 10 units [shwr, tlt, a/c-cool, c/fan, heat, elec blkts, tel, TV, clock radio, t/c mkg, refrig, doonas], ⊠, bbq, non smoking units (2). **BLB ♦ $115 - $240, ♦♦ $125 - $250, ◊ $35**, AE BC DC EFT MC VI.

★★ **(Hotel Section)**, (2 stry), 14 rms [basin (2), shwr (10), tlt (10), heat, elec blkts, tel, clock radio (8), t/c mkg (4), doonas], lounge (TV), t/c mkg shared, ✆, **BLB ♦ $75 - $105, ♦♦ $85 - $115, ◊ $35**.

Self Catering Accommodation

★★★★ **Poolway Cottages**, (Cotg), Cnr Borsa Cres & Sixth St, ☎ 03 5348 1049, fax 03 5348 1049, 6 cotgs acc up to 4, (2 bedrm), [shwr, spa bath, tlt, hairdry, a/c-cool, c/fan, heat, elec blkts, TV, video, clock radio, CD, refrig, cook fac, micro, doonas, linen, pillows], w/mach, dryer, iron, iron brd, lounge firepl, bbq. **D ♦♦ $150 - $380, ◊ $25, W $550 - $850**, ch con, BC MC VI, ♿.

★★★★ **St Andrews Homestead**, (Cotg), 27 Second St, ☎ 03 5348 1255, fax 03 5348 3606, 3 cotgs acc up to 6, (3 bedrm), [shwr, spa bath (2), tlt, a/c (2), cent heat (1), elec blkts, refrig, micro, toaster, ldry (1), doonas, linen, pillows], iron, iron brd, lounge (TV, video, cd player), bbq, non smoking property. **D ♦♦ $140 - $160, W ♦♦♦♦ $240 - $340**, BC MC VI.

★★★ **(Studio Section)**, 2 cotgs acc up to 2, [shwr, tlt, fan, heat, elec blkts, refrig, cook fac ltd, micro, toaster, doonas, linen, pillows], iron, iron brd, lounge (TV), non smoking property. **D ♦♦ $105**.

★★★★ **Swiss Mount Villas**, (Cotg), 5 Swiss Mount Ave, 500m S of PO, ☎ 03 5348 3722, fax 03 5348 4336, 5 cotgs acc up to 4, (1 & 2 bedrm), [shwr, spa bath, tlt, hairdry, a/c, fan, heat (wood), cent heat, elec blkts, TV, video, clock radio, refrig, cook fac, micro, toaster, doonas, linen, pillows], iron, iron brd, bbq. **D ♦♦ $165 - $220, ◊ $12.50 - $42.50, W ♦♦ $910 - $1,210, ◊ $50**, Min book long w/ends, AE BC DC MC VI.

★★★☆ **Heritage House (Hepburn Springs)**, (Cotg), 21 Spa Ave, 1.1km NW of PO, ☎ 03 9579 0764, 1 cotg acc up to 14, (4 bedrm) [shwr (2), bath, tlt (2), c/fan, heat, tel (local), TV, video, refrig, cook fac, micro, elec frypan, toaster, blkts, doonas, linen, pillows], w/mach, dryer, iron, iron brd, bbq, non smoking property. **RO ♦♦ $70 - $100, ◊ $35 - $50, W $875 - $980**, ch con
Operator Comment: Centrally located to attractions & eateries.
www.travelaustralia.com.au/heritage

★★★ **Four Seasons Cottages**, (HF), 8 Forest Ave, adjacent to Mineral ☎ 03 5348 1221, fax 03 5348 4333, 4 flats acc up to 4, (1 & 2 bedrm), [shwr, tlt, hairdry, fan, heat, elec blkts, TV, video, clock radio, refrig, cook fac, toaster, blkts, linen, pillows], ldry, cots, non smoking property. **D ♦♦ $100, ◊ $20, W ♦♦ $380 - $450**, AE BC DC EFT MC VI.

★★★★ **(Cottage Section)**, 3 cotgs acc up to 6, (3 bedrm), [shwr, bath, tlt, hairdry, fan, heat (wood & gas), elec blkts, tel (local), TV, video, clock radio, CD, refrig, cook fac, blkts, linen, pillows], ldry, bbq, cots. **D ♦♦ $150, ◊ $20, W $550 - $700**.

★★★ **Linga Longa Cosy Cottages**, (Cotg), 112 Main Rd, ☎ 03 5348 3317, fax 03 5348 3317, 6 cotgs acc up to 10, (1, 2 & 5 bedrm), [shwr, bath, spa bath (2), tlt, fan, heat, elec blkts, TV, refrig, cook fac (1), cook fac ltd (5), micro (1), blkts, linen, pillows], ldry, lounge firepl, bbq, breakfast ingredients. **D ♦♦ $82.50 - $122, ◊ $20 - $45**.

★★★ **Lulworth Holiday Cottages**, (Cotg), 5 Forest Ave, ☎ 03 5476 4428, fax 03 5476 4428, 8 cotgs acc up to 6, (2 bedrm), [shwr, bath (3), tlt, a/c, c/fan, TV, video, refrig, cook fac, micro, toaster, ldry, blkts, linen, pillows], iron, bbq, ✆, non smoking property. **W $440 - $605**.

★★★ **Nina Springs Spa Suites**, (HU), 122 Main Rd, 100m N of PO, ☎ 03 5348 2782, fax 03 5348 2782, 2 units acc up to 4, [shwr, spa bath (2), tlt, a/c-cool, heat, elec blkts, TV, video, clock radio, refrig, cook fac, micro, toaster, blkts, linen, pillows], ldry, iron, bbq. **BLB ♦♦ $90 - $120, ◊ $25**.

★★★ **Ninth Street Cottage**, (Cotg), 4 Ninth St, opposite PO, ☎ 03 5348 3033, fax 03 5348 3033, 1 cotg acc up to 6, (3 bedrm), [shwr, bath, tlt (2), hairdry, a/c-cool, heat (wood & gas), TV, video (avail), clock radio, CD, refrig, cook fac, micro, toaster, blkts, linen, pillows], iron, iron brd, bbq, non smoking property. **D $110 - $275, W $495 - $650**, AE BC MC VI.

B&B's/Guest Houses

★★★★☆ **Beethams of Hepburn Springs**, (B&B), 9B Tenth St, ☎ 03 5348 1632, fax 03 5348 1988, 5 rms [ensuite, spa bath (2), hairdry, a/c-cool, c/fan, cent heat, elec blkts, TV, video (2), clock radio, t/c mkg, refrig], iron, iron brd, non smoking property. **BB ♦ $115 - $200, ♦♦ $140 - $250, ⑤ $65 - $80**, 2 rooms yet to be rated, Minimum booking Swiss/Italian Festa, long weekends & Easter, AE BC DC MC VI.

★★★★☆ **Lauristina Bed & Breakfast**, (B&B), No children's facilities, 44 Main Rd, 1km S of PO, ☎ 03 5348 3175, fax 03 5348 1845, 2 rms [ensuite, hairdry, fan, cent heat, elec blkts], lounge (cd player), lounge firepl, t/c mkg shared, non smoking rms. **BB ♦ $120 - $175, ♦♦ $140 - $195**, BC MC VI.

★★★★☆ **Perini Country House**, (B&B), 4 Eighth St, 117km W of PO, ☎ 03 5348 1620, fax 03 5348 1620, 3 rms [ensuite, hairdry, cent heat, elec blkts], lounge (TV, cd, stereo), lounge firepl, t/c mkg shared, non smoking property. **BB ♦♦ $155 - $375**, Dinner by arrangement. AE BC DC EFT MC VI.

★★★★ **Bellinzona Country House**, (GH), 77 Main Rd, 200m S of PO, ☎ 03 5348 2271, fax 03 5348 3838, 24 rms [ensuite, bath (3), spa bath (2), hairdry, cent heat, elec blkts, tel, TV, t/c mkg], rec rm, lounge (TV), conf fac, ✉, pool indoor heated, sauna, spa, bbq, gym (ltd facilities), squash. **DBB ♦ $185 - $205, ♦♦ $285 - $320**, AE BC DC MC VI.

★★★★ **Cloverhill - Hepburn Springs**, (GH), 16 Forest Ave, ☎ 03 5348 3498, fax 03 5348 3498, (2 stry gr fl), 5 rms [ensuite, hairdry, heat, elec blkts, TV, clock radio, t/c mkg, refrig, toaster], lounge (TV), sauna, spa, bbq. **BB ♦ $110 - $132, ♦♦ $121 - $164**, AE BC DC MC VI.

★★★★ **(Holiday Unit Section)**, (2 stry gr fl), 4 units acc up to 3, (1 bedrm), [shwr, tlt, hairdry, a/c-cool, fan, heat, elec blkts, TV, video-fee, clock radio, CD, refrig, cook fac, micro, toaster, blkts, linen, pillows], ldry, sauna, spa, bbq, breakfast ingredients. **BB ♦ $110 - $143, ♦♦ $132 - $176**, Min book long w/ends.

★★★★ **Dudley House**, (GH), c1908. No facilities for children under 16. 101 Main Rd, Opposite PO, ☎ 03 5348 3033, fax 03 5348 3033, 4 rms [ensuite (3), shwr, bath (1), tlt, hairdry, heat, elec blkts, clock radio], lounge (TV, cd player, video), lounge firepl, ✉, t/c mkg shared, refrig, non smoking property. **BB ♦ $105, ♦♦ $140 - $197.50**, Dinner by arrangement. AE BC MC VI.

★★★☆ **Truro Homestead**, (GH), (Farm), 871 Daylesford-Newstead Rd, Franklinford 3461, 15.5km N of Daylesford PO, ☎ 03 5476 4207, 2 rms [shwr, bath, tlt, evap cool, fan, heat, elec blkts, clock radio], ldry, lounge (TV, video), meals to unit (dinner avail), cots. **BB ♦♦ $95 - $130**.

★★★ **Liberty House**, (GH), 20 Mineral Springs Cres, ☎ 03 5348 2809, fax 03 5348 2809, (2 stry gr fl), 7 rms [basin, elec blkts], lounge, lounge firepl, ✗, cots. **DBB ♦ $125, ♦♦ $250**, ch con, BC EFT MC VI.

★★★ **The Hepburn Chalet**, (GH), 78 Main Rd, 250m S of PO, ☎ 03 5348 2344, fax 03 5348 1228, (2 stry gr fl), 24 rms [basin, shwr (3), bath (hip) (3), tlt (3), heat, elec blkts], rec rm, lounge (TV, cd), ✉, spa, t/c mkg shared, refrig, c/park (carport) (16). **BB ♦ $60 - $160**, AE BC DC EFT MC VI.

HEYFIELD VIC 3858

Pop 1,600. (206km E Melbourne), See map on pages 694/695, ref H7. Timber & agricultural town on the banks of the Thompson River. Boating, Bowls, Bush Walking, Fishing, Golf, Horse Riding, Scenic Drives, Shooting, Swimming (Pool, Lake), Tennis.

Hotels/Motels

★★★ **Broadbents Motor Inn**, (M), Rosedale Rd, 1.4km S of PO, ☎ 03 5148 2434, fax 03 5148 2688, 10 units [shwr, tlt, heat, elec blkts, tel, TV, clock radio, t/c mkg, refrig], pool, bbq (covered), cots. **RO ♦ $55 - $57.20, ♦♦ $68.20 - $71.50, ⑤ $8.80**, ch con, AE BC MC VI.

Self Catering Accommodation

★★★ **Abington Bed & Breakfast**, (Cotg), Coghlans La, ☎ 03 5148 2430, 1 cotg acc up to 4, (1 & 2 bedrm), [shwr, tlt, a/c-cool, heat, clock radio, cook fac, blkts, linen, pillows], breakfast ingredients. **BB ♦ $50, ♦♦ $80, ⑤ $30**, ch con.

★★ **(Holiday Flat Section)**, 1 flat acc up to 4, (2 bedrm), [shwr, tlt, fan, heat, video, clock radio, refrig, cook fac ltd, blkts, linen, pillows], breakfast ingredients. **BB ♦ $45, ♦♦ $70, ⑤ $30**, ch con.

HEYWOOD VIC 3304

Pop 1,300. (348km W Melbourne), See map on pages 694/695, ref A7. Agricultural & grazing township, situated on the Princes Hwy, adjacent to Fitzroy River. Bowls, Golf, Scenic Drives, Tennis.

Hotels/Motels

★★★ **Heywood Motor Inn**, (M), 42 Portland Rd (Princes Hwy), 1.2km S of PO, ☎ 03 5527 1703, fax 03 5527 1387, 16 units [shwr, tlt, a/c-cool (12), fan, heat, elec blkts, tel (12), TV, clock radio, t/c mkg, refrig, micro (1), toaster], ✗, BYO, cots, non smoking units (6). **RO ♦ $46, ♦♦ $52 - $55, ⑤ $10**, AE BC DC EFT MC VI.

HILL END VIC 3825

Pop Nominal, (145km E Melbourne), See map on page 696, ref E6. Timber & dairying district.

B&B's/Guest Houses

★★★☆ **Tanjam**, (B&B), (Farm), Russell Creek Rd, ☎ 03 5635 4307, fax 03 5635 4307, 2 rms [bath, a/c, heat, doonas], lounge (TV, video), t/c mkg shared. **BB ♦♦ $55, ⑤ $27.50**, ch con, pen con, Farm activities included in tariff.

HOPETOUN VIC 3396

Pop 650. (399km NW Melbourne), See map on pages 694/695, ref B3. Situated on the west bank of Yarriambiack Creek. Boating, Bowls, Fishing, Golf, Horse Riding, Sailing, Shooting, Swimming (Pool, Lake), Tennis, Water Skiing.

Hotels/Motels

★★ **Hopetoun Hotel Motel**, (LMH), 16 Austin St, 200m NW of PO, ☎ 03 5083 3070, fax 03 5083 3070, 13 units [shwr, tlt, a/c, elec blkts, TV, clock radio, t/c mkg, refrig, toaster], ✉ (Mon to Sat). **RO ♦ $45, ♦♦ $55**, BC EFT MC VI.

HORSHAM VIC 3400

Pop 12,600. (301km NW Melbourne), See map on pages 694/695, ref B5. Progressive city, gateway to the Northern Grampians, located close to the Little Desert and Mount Arapiles Tooan State Park. Located halfway between Melbourne & Adelaide on the Western Hwy it is a popular stopover point. Wimmera River and a number of lakes are nearby. Horsham Rural City Visitor Centre, 20 O'Callaghan Pde, 03 5382 1832 or Freecall 1800 633 218. Abseiling, Art Gallery, Bicycle, Boating, Bowls, Bush Walking, Canoeing, Croquet, Fishing, Golf, Greyhound Racing, Horse Racing, Horse Riding, Rock Climbing, Rowing, Sailing, Scenic Drives, Shooting, Swimming (Pool, Lake), Tennis, Trotting, Water Skiing.

Hotels/Motels

  ★★★★ **Country City Motor Inn**, (M), 11 O'Callaghan Pde, 700m S of PO, ☎ 03 5382 5644, fax 03 5382 5435, 12 units [shwr, spa bath (1), tlt, hairdry, a/c, elec blkts, tel, cable tv, video-fee, clock radio, t/c mkg, refrig, mini bar, toaster], ldry, iron, iron brd, pool, cots-fee, non smoking units (3). **RO ♦ $91 - $108, ♦♦ $101 - $128, ⑤ $10**, AE BC DC EFT JCB MC MP VI.

 ★★★★ **Golden Grain Motor Inn**, (M), 6 Dimboola Rd (Western Hwy), 400m NW of PO, ☎ 03 5382 4741, fax 03 5382 0151, 36 units (2 suites) [shwr, spa bath (13), tlt, hairdry, a/c, elec blkts, tel, TV, video-fee, clock radio, t/c mkg, refrig, mini bar, toaster], ldry, rec rm, conf fac, pool indoor heated, spa (heated)-fee, bbq, cots-fee. **RO ♦ $95, ♦♦ $106 - $140, ⑤ $10, Suite RO $150**, AE BC DC EFT MC MP VI.

  ★★★★ **Horsham Mid City Court**, (M), 14 Darlot St, 250m W of PO, ☎ 03 5382 5400, fax 03 5382 5947, 17 units [shwr, spa bath (2), tlt, hairdry, a/c, elec blkts, tel, cable tv, video-fee, clock radio, t/c mkg, refrig, mini bar], meeting rm, pool indoor heated, spa-fee, cots-fee, non smoking units (5). **RO ♦ $93 - $115, ♦♦ $103 - $135**, AE BC DC EFT MC MP VI, ⚬.

 ★★★☆ **Commodore Major Mitchell Motor Inn**, (M), 109 Firebrace St, 400m S of PO, ☎ 03 5382 0125, fax 03 5382 0149, (2 stry gr fl), 35 units [shwr, tlt, hairdry, evap cool, heat, elec blkts, tel, TV, video-fee, clock radio, t/c mkg, refrig, mini bar], iron, iron brd, ✉ (Mon to Sat), rm serv, cots-fee, non smoking units (21). **RO ♦ $74 - $94, ♦♦ $74 - $95, ⑤ $14**, ch con, AE BC DC JCB MC MP VI.

★★★☆ **May Park Motor Lodge**, (M), Cnr Darlot & Baillie Sts, 350m W of PO, ☎ 03 5382 4477, fax 03 5381 1477, 23 units [shwr, spa bath (2), tlt, hairdry, evap cool, heat, elec blkts, tel, TV, video-fee, movie, clock radio, t/c mkg, refrig, mini bar, toaster], ldry, iron, iron brd, rec rm, pool indoor heated, spa-fee, bbq, car wash, cots-fee, non smoking units (7). RO ∮ $95 - $107, ♦♦ $107 - $129, ◊ $11, AE BC DC EFT MC MP VI.

★★★☆ **Town House Motel Horsham**, (M), 31 Roberts Ave, 100m S of PO, ☎ 03 5382 4691, fax 03 5381 1436, (2 stry gr fl), 19 units [shwr, spa bath (3), tlt, hairdry, a/c, heat, elec blkts, tel, TV, video-fee, clock radio, t/c mkg, refrig, toaster], ldry, iron, iron brd, pool, bbq, cots-fee, non smoking units (7). RO ∮ $95 - $107, ♦♦ $107 - $129, ◊ $11, ch con, AE BC DC EFT MC MP VI.

★★★☆ **Westlander Motel**, (M), Western Hwy, 2.7km S of PO, ☎ 03 5382 0191, fax 03 5382 4866, (2 stry gr fl), 39 units [shwr, spa bath (8), tlt, hairdry (25), a/c, elec blkts, tel, TV, video-fee, clock radio, t/c mkg, refrig], ldry, iron (8), iron brd (8), rec rm, conf fac, ⊠ (Mon to Sat), pool indoor heated, spa-fee, bbq, rm serv, plygr, non smoking units (24). RO ∮ $67 - $106, ♦♦ $76 - $129, ◊ $10, 8 units ★★★★, 15 units ★★★, AE BC DC MC MP VI.

★★★ **Darlot Motor Inn**, (M), 47 Stawell Rd (Western Hwy), 1.5km S of PO, ☎ 03 5381 1222, fax 03 5382 1440, 15 units [shwr, tlt, a/c, elec blkts, tel, TV, video-fee, clock radio, t/c mkg, refrig, toaster], meeting rm, pool (solar heated), bbq, plygr, cots-fee, non smoking units (2). RO ∮ $45 - $50, ♦♦ $50 - $55, ◊ $11, ch con, AE BC DC EFT MC VI.

★★★ **Glynlea Motel**, (M), 26 Stawell Rd (Western Hwy), 1.7km S of PO, ☎ 03 5382 0145, fax 03 5382 1260, 17 units [shwr, tlt, hairdry, a/c, elec blkts, tel, TV, video-fee, clock radio, t/c mkg, refrig, toaster], iron, iron brd, pool, bbq, plygr, cots, non smoking units (7). RO ∮ $48.40, ♦♦ $59.40 - $61.60, ◊ $8.80, ch con, AE BC DC EFT MC MCH VI.

★★★ **Horsham Motel**, (M), 5 Dimboola Rd (Western Hwy), 500m W of PO, ☎ 03 5382 5555, fax 03 5381 1710, 20 units [shwr, bath (1), tlt, a/c, elec blkts, tel, TV, video-fee, clock radio, t/c mkg, refrig, toaster], iron, iron brd, cots-fee, non smoking units (7). RO ∮ $50 - $52.80, ♦♦ $61 - $63.80, ◊ $11, ch con, AE BC DC EFT MC MCH VI.

★★★ **Olde Horsham Motor Inn**, (M), Western Hwy, 3.7km SE of PO, ☎ 03 5381 0033, fax 03 5382 4233, 18 units [shwr, tlt, hairdry (6), a/c, elec blkts, tel (direct dial), TV, movie, clock radio, t/c mkg, refrig, mini bar, toaster], pool, bbq, cots-fee, non smoking units (1). RO ∮ $70 - $100, ♦♦ $80 - $110, ◊ $11, ch con, 6 units ★★★★, AE BC DC EFT MC VI.

★★☆ **Majestic Motel**, (M), 56 Stawell Rd (Western Hwy), 1.5km S of PO, ☎ 03 5382 0144, fax 03 5381 1960, 21 units [shwr, tlt, a/c-cool (2), a/c (19), heat (2), elec blkts, tel, TV, video-fee, clock radio, t/c mkg, refrig, toaster], iron, iron brd, ⊠ (Mon to Sat), pool indoor heated, bbq, plygr, cots, non smoking units (6). RO ∮ $44, ♦♦ $55 - $57, ◊ $8, AE BC DC EFT MC MCH MP VI.

★★☆ **Smerdon Lodge Motel**, (M), 42 Dimboola Rd (Western Hwy), 700m NW of PO, ☎ 03 5382 3122, fax 03 5381 1787, 21 units [shwr, tlt, hairdry (6), a/c, elec blkts, tel, TV, video-fee, clock radio, t/c mkg, refrig], iron (6), iron brd (6), pool (salt water), bbq, cots-fee, non smoking units (5). RO ∮ $46 - $52, ♦♦ $53 - $61, ◊ $8, ch con, 6 units ★★★, AE BC DC EFT MC VI

Operator Comment: Mention this listing and receive a free continental breakfast.

★★ **Wheatfields Motor Inn**, (M), 71 Stawell Rd (Western Hwy), 2.1km S of PO, ☎ 03 5382 4555, fax 03 5381 0483, 10 units [shwr, tlt, a/c, elec blkts, tel, TV, clock radio, t/c mkg, refrig], cots-fee, non smoking units (1). RO ∮ $50.60 - $61.60, ♦♦ $61.60 - $77, ◊ $11, AE BC DC MC VI.

★ **Royal Hotel**, (LH), 132 Firebrace St, 350m S of PO, ☎ 03 5382 1255, fax 03 5381 1939, (2 stry), 28 rms [basin], lounge (TV), ⊠, t/c mkg shared, refrig, c/park (limited), ☏. BLB ∮ $27.50, ♦♦ $44, ◊ $20, ch con, BC MC VI.

Self Catering Accommodation

★★★★☆ **Sylvania Park**, (Cotg), Lubeck Rd, Drung 3400, 10km E of Horsham, ☎ 03 5382 2811, fax 03 5382 5409, 2 cotgs acc up to 10, [shwr, bath, tlt, hairdry, a/c-cool (1), c/fan (2), elec blkts, tel, TV, video, clock radio, CD, t/c mkg, refrig, cook fac, micro, elec frypan, d/wash, toaster, blkts, linen, pillows], ldry, w/mach, dryer, iron, iron brd, bbq, cots, breakfast ingredients. BB ♦♦ $132, ◊ $55, ch con, AE BC MC VI.

B&B's/Guest Houses

★★★★☆ **Banksia Hill**, (B&B), Hutchinsons Rd, Quantong 3405, 15km W of PO, off Wimmera Hwy, ☎ 03 5384 0264, fax 03 5384 0384, 2 rms [ensuite, hairdry, a/c-cool, c/fan, heat, elec blkts, TV, clock radio, t/c mkg, refrig, micro, doonas], pool, bbq, non smoking property. **BB ♦ $80**, ♦♦ **$100**, Other meals by arrangement. AE BC DC MC VI, ƛɛ.

★★★★ **Horsham House**, (B&B), 27 Roberts Ave, ☎ 03 5382 5053, fax 03 5382 6779, (2 stry gr fl), 2 rms [ensuite, bath (1), a/c, TV, video, clock radio, t/c mkg, refrig, micro], rec rm, bbq, non smoking property. **BB ♦ $75 - $100, ♦♦ $85 - $110**.

★★★★ **(Cottage Section)**, 1 rm [shwr, spa bath, tlt, a/c, TV, video, clock radio, t/c mkg, refrig, toaster, pillows], non smoking property. **D $110 - $120**.

★★★☆ **Garrett's Bed & Breakfast**, (B&B), No children's facilities, Cnr Landy & Rose Sts, ☎ 03 5382 3928, (2 stry), 2 rms [hairdry, a/c-cool, c/fan, heat, elec blkts, clock radio], lounge (TV, cd), pool-heated (solar), t/c mkg shared, refrig, bbq, non smoking property. **BB ♦ $70 - $75, ♦♦ $95 - $100**.

★★★☆ **Stronsay Bed & Breakfast**, (B&B), No children's facilities, 24 Plozzas Rd, Haven 3401, 4km S of PO, ☎ 03 5382 6247, fax 03 5382 6247, 2 rms [hairdry, heat, elec blkts, clock radio], lounge (TV, video, cd), lounge firepl, pool, t/c mkg shared, bbq, cots, non smoking property. **BB ♦ $85**, ♦♦ **$105**, AE BC DC MC VI.

★★★★ **(Mudbrick Cottage)**, 1 rm (1 suite) [shwr, tlt, hairdry, fan, heat, elec blkts, clock radio, t/c mkg, refrig, micro], lounge (TV), lounge firepl, non smoking property. **BB ♦ $85, ♦♦ $105**.

HOWQUA VIC 3722

Pop Part of Mansfield, (208km NE Melbourne), See map on page 696, ref E4. Located in a picturesque valley on the shore of Lake Eildon. Boating, Bush Walking, Fishing, Sailing, Scenic Drives, Swimming (Lake).

Self Catering Accommodation

★★★★ **Howqua Country Retreat**, (Chalet), No children's facilities, Mansfield - Jamieson Rd, 23km S of Mansfield, ☎ 03 5777 3725, fax 03 5777 3725, 4 chalets acc up to 2, (1 bedrm), [shwr, spa bath, tlt, hairdry, a/c-cool, heat (wood), elec blkts, TV, video, clock radio, CD, refrig, cook fac, micro, toaster, blkts, doonas, linen, pillows], pool-heated, bbq, bicycle, tennis. **D $195**, Breakfast available. BC MC VI.

★★★★ **(Cottage Section)**, 4 cotgs acc up to 2, (1 bedrm), [shwr, spa bath, tlt, hairdry, a/c-cool, heat (wood), elec blkts, TV, video, clock radio, CD, refrig, cook fac, micro, toaster, ldry (in unit) (3), blkts, doonas, linen, pillows], bbq. **D $135**, Breakfast available.

★★★☆ **Howqua Lakeside Lodge**, (Cotg), Government Rd, ☎ 03 5777 3588, fax 03 5777 3713, 1 cotg acc up to 10, (3 bedrm), [shwr, bath (hip), tlt, hairdry, a/c, TV, video, CD, refrig, cook fac, micro, elec frypan, toaster, ldry, doonas, linen reqd, pillows reqd], w/mach, iron, iron brd, lounge firepl, bbq, cots. **W $750 - $1,100**, Min book Christmas Jan long w/ends and Easter, BC EFT MC VI.

★★★☆ **Kallarroo Lakefront Homes**, (HU), Mansfield-Jamieson Rd, 28km S of Mansfield, ☎ 03 9877 4176, (2 stry gr fl), 2 units acc up to 10, (3 bedrm), [shwr (3), bath, tlt (2), a/c-cool, heat, tel, TV, CD, refrig, cook fac, micro, d/wash, toaster, ldry, linen reqd], w/mach, rec rm, lounge firepl, bbq, c/park (carport), jetty. **D $200, W $600 - $1,400**, Min book Christmas and Jan.

★★★ **Hillside Howqua**, (Cotg), Mansfield - Woods Point Rd, ☎ 03 5777 3522, 2 cotgs acc up to 4, (2 bedrm), [shwr, tlt, a/c, elec blkts, TV, clock radio, refrig, cook fac ltd, micro, toaster, blkts, doonas, linen, pillows], ldry, w/mach, dryer, iron, bbq, cots, non smoking property. **D ♦♦ $85 - $100, ◊ $15, W $570, ◊ $90**, ch con, Min book long w/ends and Easter, BC MC VI.

B&B's/Guest Houses

★★★★ **Howqua Dale Gourmet Retreat**, (GH), Howqua River Rd, 25km SE of Mansfield, ☎ 03 5777 3503, fax 03 5777 3896, 6 rms [shwr, tlt, hairdry, heat, doonas], lounge (cd player), conf fac, lounge firepl, pool-heated (solar), t/c mkg shared, refrig, tennis. **D all meals ♦ $385, ◊ $385**, AE BC DC MC VI.

ICY CREEK VIC 3833

Pop Nominal, (124km E Melbourne), See map on page 696, ref E6. Small mountain fishing resort. Bush Walking, Fishing (River, Dam), Gold Prospecting, Horse Riding, Scenic Drives, Shooting, Snow Skiing.

Self Catering Accommodation

★☆ **Christmas Pines Mountain Retreat**, (Farm), 91a Willow Grove Rd, 11km SE of Noojee, ☎ 03 5621 0174, fax 03 5621 0127, 9 cabins acc up to 6, (1 bedrm), [shwr, tlt, heat (wood), refrig, cook fac ltd, micro, toaster, blkts (5) reqd, linen (5) reqd], ldry, w/mach, rec rm, lounge, conf fac, bbq, kiosk. **D $44, ♦♦ $55, ◊ $22**, ch con, 4 cabins ★★, BC MC VI.

INDENTED HEAD VIC 3223

Pop 450. (109km SW Melbourne), See map on page 697, ref A6. Small seaside resort. Boating, Fishing, Golf, Horse Riding, Sailing, Scenic Drives, Shooting, Swimming (Beach), Tennis, Water Skiing.

Self Catering Accommodation

★★☆ **Wallerang Holiday Flats**, (HF), 297 The Esplanade, ☎ 03 5452 1081, 2 flats acc up to 5, (2 bedrm), [shwr, bath (1), tlt, refrig, cook fac, micro, linen reqd], ldry, cots. **W $302.50 - $440**.

INGLEWOOD VIC 3517

Pop 700. (195km NW Melbourne), See map on page 696, ref A2. Old goldmining township, now the centre of a farming district. Bowls, Golf, Scenic Drives, Swimming (Pool), Tennis.

Hotels/Motels

★★☆ **Inglewood Motel & Caravan Park**, (M), 196 Calder Hwy, 1km N of PO, ☎ 03 5438 3232, fax 03 5438 3232, 8 units [shwr, tlt, c/fan, heat, TV, clock radio, t/c mkg, refrig, cook fac (1), toaster], ldry, bbq, ✆, cots, Pets allowed on leash. **BLB ♦ $44, ♦♦ $55, ◊ $11**, ch con, pen con, Light breakfast only available. BC MC VI, ƛɛ.

INVERLEIGH VIC 3321

Pop 300. (98km SW Melbourne), See map on page 696, ref A6. Pastoral township, located on the Leigh & Barwon Rivers. Golf, Tennis.

Self Catering Accommodation

★★★ **Barunah Plains**, (Cotg), (Farm), 4484 Hamilton Hwy, 18km W of PO, ☎ 03 5287 1234, fax 03 5287 1234, 2 cotgs acc up to 8, (3 & 4 bedrm), [shwr, bath (hip), tlt, heat, TV, refrig, cook fac, micro, elec frypan (1), toaster, ldry, blkts, doonas, linen, pillows], lounge firepl, golf, tennis. **D $132**, ch con.

(Lodge Section), 15 rms acc up to 4, [shwr, tlt, c/fan, heat, micro, blkts, doonas, linen, pillows], ldry, lounge (TV, video), lounge firepl, cook fac, refrig, bbq, ✆, golf, tennis. **D ♦ $29.70, ◊ $16.50**, ch con, Minimum booking - 16 people.

INVERLOCH VIC 3996

Pop 2,450. (143km SE Melbourne), See map on page 696, ref D7. A wool growing, grazing & dairying township, situated on Anderson's Inlet, also a popular seaside resort. Boating, Bowls, Fishing, Golf, Horse Riding, Sailing, Scenic Drives, Surfing, Swimming (Beach), Tennis, Water Skiing.

Hotels/Motels

★★★ **Inverloch Central Motor Inn**, (M), 32 A'Beckett St, 100m W of PO, ☎ 03 5674 3500, fax 03 5674 3526, 10 units [shwr, spa bath (2), tlt, hairdry, a/c, elec blkts, tel, TV, clock radio, t/c mkg, refrig]. **RO ♦ $66 - $93.50, ♦♦ $82.50 - $132, ◊ $13**, AE BC DC EFT MC VI.

★★★ **Inverloch Motel**, (M), Bass Hwy, 1.2km N of PO, ☎ 03 5674 3100, fax 03 5674 1268, 10 units [shwr, tlt, c/fan, cent heat, elec blkts, tel, TV, video-fee, clock radio, t/c mkg, refrig, mini bar, toaster], bbq, boat park, plygr, cots-fee, non smoking units (2). **RO ♦ $48 - $63, ♦♦ $58 - $75, ◊ $11**, AE BC DC EFT MC VI.

Self Catering Accommodation

★★★★ **The Reefs Apartments**, (Apt), 20 William St, 100m S of PO, ☎ 03 5674 2255, fax 03 5674 2704, (2 stry gr fl), 3 apts acc up to 6, (2 bedrm), [shwr, spa bath, tlt, c/fan, heat, elec blkts, TV, video, clock radio, refrig, cook fac, micro, elec frypan, d/wash, ldry (in unit), linen reqd-fee], iron, iron brd, pool, spa, bbq, c/park (garage), cots. **D $110 - $140, W $450 - $950**, Min book Christmas and Jan.

★★★ **Sand Castle Cabin Park**, Closed 15 Jul to 15 Sep, 14 Cuttriss St, ☎ 03 5674 2203, 3 cabins acc up to 5, (1 bedrm), [shwr, bath (hip), tlt, fan, heat, elec blkts, TV, refrig, cook fac, micro, toaster, blkts, doonas, linen reqd-fee, pillows], ldry, w/mach, rec rm, bbq, plygr. D ♦♦ **$55 - $65**, ♦ **$8**, W **$330 - $450**, ch con.

★★★ **(External En-suite Section)**, 2 cabins acc up to 5, [shwr (external), tlt (external), heat, radio, refrig, cook fac, toaster, linen reqd-fee]. D ♦♦ **$40**, ♦ **$5**, W **$280**, ch con.

★★★ **South Kolora**, (Cotg), (Farm), Oban Cottage. Korumburra/Kongwak Rd, 3km N of PO, ☎ 03 5674 1305, fax 03 5674 2332, 1 cotg acc up to 6, (2 bedrm), [shwr, bath (hip), tlt, hairdry, fan, heat, elec blkts, TV, video, clock radio, refrig, cook fac, micro, elec frypan, ldry (in unit), doonas, linen reqd-fee], w/mach, iron, iron brd, bbq, tennis, cots. D **$85 - $110**, W **$360 - $495**.

(Bonshaw Cottage), 1 cotg acc up to 10, (5 bedrm), [shwr, bath (hip), tlt, hairdry, fan, heat, elec blkts, TV, video, clock radio, refrig, cook fac, micro, elec frypan, d/wash, ldry (in unit), doonas, linen reqd-fee], w/mach, iron, iron brd, spa, bbq. D **$90 - $125**, W **$385 - $660**, (Rating under review).

★★ **Eagles Nest Cottage by the Sea**, (Cotg), 190 Surf Pde, ☎ 03 5674 2255, fax 03 5674 2704, 1 cotg acc up to 4, (2 bedrm), [shwr, tlt, c/fan, heat, TV, clock radio, refrig, cook fac, micro, toaster, doonas, linen reqd, pillows], w/mach, iron, iron brd, lounge firepl, bbq. D **$110**, W **$550 - $700**.

B&B's/Guest Houses

★★★★☆ **Hill Top House**, (B&B), No children's facilities, Lower Tarwin Rd, 4km E of PO, ☎ 03 5674 3514, fax 03 5674 3514, (2 stry gr fl), 2 rms [ensuite, hairdry, fan, heat, elec blkts, clock radio], lounge (TV, cd), t/c mkg shared, bbq, non smoking property. BB ♦ **$82.50**, ♦♦ **$100 - $110**, Other meals by arrangement. BC MC VI.

★★★★☆ **Sandymount B & B**, (B&B), No children's facilities, 25 Sandymount Ave, 600m SW of PO, ☎ 03 5674 1325, fax 03 5674 3270, (2 stry), 3 rms [shwr, bath (1), spa bath (2), tlt, hairdry, c/fan, heat, elec blkts, TV, clock radio, t/c mkg], non smoking property. BB ♦ **$99 - $140**, ♦♦ **$145 - $165**, AE BC MC VI.

JAMIESON VIC 3723

Pop 250. (237km NE Melbourne), See map on page 696, ref E4. Peaceful fishing retreat. Boating, Bush Walking, Fishing (Lake, River), Sailing, Scenic Drives, Swimming (Lake, River), Tennis, Water Skiing.

Hotels/Motels

★★☆ **Jamieson Lakeside Hotel Motel**, (LMH), Eildon Rd, 3km W of PO, ☎ 03 5777 0515, fax 03 5777 0555, 14 units [shwr, bath (2), tlt, heat, elec blkts, t/c mkg, refrig, toaster], ldry, ⊠, pool, ✆, plygr, tennis. BLB ♦ **$30**, ♦♦ **$55**, ♦ **$10**, ch con, BC EFT MC VI.

★★ **Court House**, (LMH), 25 Perkins St, diagonally opposite PO, ☎ 03 5777 0503, fax 03 5777 0527, (2 stry gr fl), 19 units [shwr, tlt, heat, elec blkts, t/c mkg (shared)], ldry, w/mach, dryer, lounge (TV), ⊠, bbq, ✆, plygr, cots. BLB ♦ **$35**, ♦♦ **$60**, ♦ **$11 - $16.50**, ch con, AE BC EFT MC VI.

Self Catering Accommodation

★★★★ **Jamieson Valley Retreat**, (Cotg), Licola Rd, 4.1km E of Brewery Bridge, ☎ 03 5777 0510, fax 03 5777 0510, 4 cotgs acc up to 6, (2 bedrm), [shwr, tlt, hairdry, heat (wood), elec blkts, TV, clock radio, t/c mkg, refrig, cook fac, micro, ldry, blkts, doonas, linen, pillows], w/mach, dryer, lounge firepl, bbq, cots, non smoking units (2). D ♦ **$80 - $100**, ♦♦ **$80 - $100**, ♦ **$20 - $25**, W ♦ **$500 - $700**, ♦♦ **$500 - $700**, ♦ **$100 - $150**, ch con.

★★★★ **The Jamieson Cottages**, (Cotg), 40 Brown St, 100m NE of PO, ☎ 03 5777 0670, 4 cotgs acc up to 6, (2 bedrm), [shwr, bath (hip) (3), tlt, hairdry, c/fan, heat, elec blkts, TV, clock radio, refrig, cook fac, micro, elec frypan, toaster, ldry (in unit), blkts, doonas, linen, pillows], w/mach, iron, bbq, c/park (carport), cots, non smoking units (2). D ♦♦ **$98**, ♦ **$20**, W ♦♦ **$637**, ♦ **$140**, ch con, BC MC VI.

★★★ **Berrington Holiday Units**, (HU), Cobham & Grey Sts, 100m S of PO, ☎ 03 5777 0518, fax 03 5777 0518, 3 units acc up to 6, (2 bedrm), [shwr, tlt, fan, heat, elec blkts, TV, clock radio, refrig, cook fac, micro, toaster, doonas, linen, pillows], ldry, w/mach, bbq, c/park (carport), cots, non smoking property. D **$65 - $120**.

★★★ **Emerald Park**, (HF), (Farm), Licola Rd, 2.5 km E of PO, ☎ 03 5777 0569, fax 03 5777 0569, 4 flats acc up to 6, (2 bedrm), [shwr, tlt, fan, heat, TV, clock radio, refrig, cook fac, micro, ldry (in unit), doonas, linen reqd-fee], w/mach, bbq (covered), plygr, cots. D ♦♦ **$65**, ♦ **$10**, W ♦♦ **$390**, ♦ **$60**, ch con.

Twin River Cabins, Chenery St, 400m N of PO, ☎ 03 5777 0582, 6 cabins acc up to 6, [fire pl, refrig, cook fac ltd, toaster, linen reqd], shwr (2G-2L), tlt (2G-2L), ldry, w/mach, bbq. D **$38.50 - $49.50**, W **$242 - $291.50**.

B&B's/Guest Houses

★★★ **Duck Inn Jamieson**, (B&B), 39 Bank St, 300m W of PO, ☎ 03 5777 0554, fax 03 5777 0811, 3 rms [ensuite, hairdry, heat, elec blkts, t/c mkg, refrig, doonas], ✗, BYO, non smoking property. BB ♦ **$65 - $85**, ♦♦ **$80 - $100**, BC MC VI.

JEPARIT VIC 3423

Pop 400. (372km NW Melbourne), See map on pages 694/695, ref B4. Agricultural town in the Wimmera wheat belt, on the banks of the Wimmera River. Jeparit is situated near Lake Hindmarsh, Victoria's largest freshwater lake. It provides a welcome retreat during hot Wimmera weather. Jeparit is Aboriginal for 'home of small birds'. Boating, Bowls, Fishing, Golf, Sailing, Scenic Drives, Shooting, Swimming (Lake, River), Tennis, Water Skiing.

Hotels/Motels

★★ **Hopetoun House**, (LMH), 31 Roy St, 200m S of PO, ☎ 03 5397 2051, 3 units [shwr, tlt, a/c-cool, heat, elec blkts, TV, t/c mkg, refrig, toaster], ldry, ⊠ (Mon to Sat), bbq, ✆. BLB ♦♦ **$45**, BC EFT MC VI.

★☆ **Hindmarsh**, (LH), 50 Roy St, 100m E of PO, ☎ 03 5397 2041, (2 stry), 10 rms [elec blkts, clock radio], lounge (TV), ⊠, t/c mkg shared, refrig, bbq, ✆, cots. BB ♦ **$30**, ♦♦ **$45**, ch con, BC EFT MC VI.

JINDIVICK VIC 3818

Pop Nominal, (116km E Melbourne), See map on page 696, ref D6. Small township located in an agricultural & dairying district.

B&B's/Guest Houses

★★★★☆ **Broughton Lodge**, (B&B), 125 Palmer Rd, ☎ 03 5628 5235, fax 03 5628 5235, 2 rms [ensuite, hairdry, cent heat, elec blkts, tel, TV, video, clock radio, t/c mkg, refrig, toaster, ldry], iron, iron brd, ✆. BB ♦ **$85 - $110**, ♦♦ **$170 - $220**, BC MC VI.

★★★★ **Jindivick Gardens**, (GH), No children's facilities, Jacksons Tk, 500m E of store, ☎ 03 5628 5319, fax 03 5628 5280, 3 rms [ensuite, hairdry, cent heat, elec blkts], ldry, lounge, t/c mkg shared, refrig, bbq, non smoking property. BB ♦♦ **$132**, DBB ♦♦ **$180**, pen con, Min book applies.

JOHANNA VIC 3238

Pop 251. (209km SW Melbourne), See map on pages 694/695, ref C8. A dairying area in the Otway Ranges. Bush Walking, Fishing, Scenic Drives, Tennis.

Self Catering Accommodation

★★★★ **Blue Johanna Cottages**, (Apt), 225 Blue Johanna Rd, 5km SE of Lavers Hill PO, ☎ 03 5237 4224, fax 03 5237 4224, 2 apts acc up to 2, (Studio & 1 bedrm), [shwr, spa bath, tlt, hairdry, c/fan, heat (wood), elec blkts, TV, video, clock radio, t/c mkg, refrig, cook fac, micro, toaster, blkts, doonas, linen, pillows], ldry, w/mach, iron, iron brd, bbq, breakfast ingredients. **BB $120 - $170, W $700 - $850**, Min book Christmas and Jan, BC MC VI.

★★★★ **(Bed & Breakfast Section)**, (2 stry gr fl), 2 rms [ensuite (1), shwr (1), tlt (1), heat, elec blkts, TV, clock radio, t/c mkg, refrig, toaster]. **BLB ♦♦ $60 - $120.**

★★★★ **Boomerang Cabins**, Great Ocean Rd, 35km W of Apollo Bay, ☎ 03 5237 4213, fax 03 5237 4213, 3 cabins acc up to 4, (2 bedrm), [shwr, spa bath, tlt, hairdry, a/c, fan, c/fan, heat, elec blkts, video, CD, refrig, cook fac, micro, toaster, ldry, blkts, linen, pillows], lounge firepl, bbq. **D $140 - $215, ♦ $30**, Min book Christmas Jan and Easter, AE BC EFT MC VI.

★★★★ **Johanna Bluegum Holiday Cabins**, 575 Blue Rd, ☎ 03 5237 4255, fax 02 5237 4255, 2 cabins acc up to 5, (1 & 2 bedrm), [shwr, spa bath, tlt, hairdry, fan, heat, elec blkts, TV, video, clock radio, CD, t/c mkg, refrig, cook fac, micro, toaster, ldry, blkts, linen, pillows], iron, iron brd, bbq, c/park (garage). **D ♦♦ $120 - $175, ♦ $25**, Min book long w/ends and Easter, BC MC VI.

★★★★ **Johanna River Farm and Cottages**, (Cotg), 420 Blue Rd, 4km S off Great Ocean Rd, ☎ 03 5237 4219, 4 cotgs acc up to 6, (1 & 2 bedrm), [shwr, spa bath (1), tlt, hairdry (1), heat (wood), elec blkts, cable tv (1), video, clock radio, CD, refrig, cook fac, micro, toaster, ldry, blkts, linen, pillows], bbq, ☏. **D $110 - $180, W $650 - $850**, Min book applies, BC MC VI.

★★★★ **Johanna Seaside Cottages**, (Cotg), (Farm), Red Johanna Rd, ☎ 03 5237 4242, fax 03 5237 4200, 4 cotgs acc up to 8, (2 & 3 bedrm), [shwr, spa bath (4), tlt, hairdry, fan, heat, elec blkts, TV, video, clock radio, CD, refrig, cook fac, micro, elec frypan, d/wash, ldry, blkts, linen, pillows], pool indoor heated, bbq, tennis, cots. **D ♦♦ $115 - $200, W ♦♦ $820 - $1,550**, 1 cottage ★★★☆, BC MC VI.

★★★☆ **(Farmhouse Section)**, 1 cotg acc up to 10, (4 bedrm), [shwr, bath, tlt (2), hairdry, heat, elec blkts, TV, video, clock radio, refrig, cook fac, micro, d/wash, toaster, ldry, blkts, linen, pillows], lounge firepl, bbq, cots. **D ♦♦ $110 - $160, ♦ $105 - $160, W $787 - $1,386.**

★★★☆ **Glow Worm Cottages**, (Cotg), 70 Stafford Rd, off Red Johanna Rd, ☎ 03 5237 4238, fax 03 5237 4297, 4 cotgs acc up to 8, (1 & 3 bedrm), [shwr, bath (hip) (3), tlt, hairdry (2), c/fan, heat (wood), elec blkts, TV, video, clock radio, CD, refrig, cook fac, micro, toaster, ldry (in unit), blkts, linen, pillows], iron, iron brd, spa, bbq, cots. **D ♦♦ $90 - $175, ♦ $20, W $355 - $995**, Min book applies, AE BC DC EFT JCB MC VI.

B&B's/Guest Houses

★★★ **Iona Seaview Farm**, (B&B), Blue Johanna Rd, ☎ 03 5237 4254, fax 03 5237 4266, 1 rm [heat (wood), TV, video, clock radio, t/c mkg, refrig, micro, toaster], bbq. **BB ♦ $55, ♦♦ $65 - $70, ♦ $10**, ch con, AE BC MC VI.

★★★ **(Cottage Section)**, 1 cotg acc up to 5, (2 bedrm), [shwr, bath, tlt, c/fan, heat (wood), elec blkts, video, CD, refrig, cook fac, micro, toaster], iron, iron brd, bbq, c/park (carport). **D ♦♦ $95 - $100, ♦ $7.50**, ch con.

JOHNSONVILLE VIC 3902

Pop 925. (301km E Melbourne), See map on pages 694/695, ref J7. Located on the Princes Hwy. Boating, Fishing, Swimming.

Self Catering Accommodation

★★★ **Bream Lodge**, (HF), Princes Hwy, ☎ 03 5156 4281, fax 03 5156 4281, 6 flats acc up to 6, (1 & 2 bedrm), [shwr, tlt, fan, heat, elec blkts, TV, clock radio, refrig, cook fac, micro, toaster, doonas], ldry, bbq, ☏, cots. **D ♦♦ $60 - $72, ♦ $20, W $360 - $650**, BC MC VI.

KALLISTA VIC

See Dandenong Ranges Region.

KALORAMA VIC

See Dandenong Ranges Region.

KANIVA VIC 3419

Pop 750. (412km NW Melbourne), See map on pages 694/695, ref A4. Farming township. Little Desert National Park. Bird Watching, Boating, Bowls, Bush Walking, Golf, Gym, Scenic Drives, Shooting, Squash, Swimming (Pool), Tennis.

Hotels/Motels

★★★ **Kaniva Colonial Motor Inn**, (M), 134 Commercial St (Western Hwy), 800m E of PO, ☎ 03 5392 2730, fax 03 5392 2730, 13 units [shwr, tlt, a/c, elec blkts, tel, cable tv, clock radio, t/c mkg, refrig], conf fac, ✕, dinner to unit, cots-fee, non smoking units (4). **RO ♦ $61, ♦♦ $72, ♦ $11**, BC DC MC VI.

★★★ **Kaniva Midway Motel**, (M), 14 Commercial St (Western Hwy), 500m W of PO, ☎ 03 5392 2515, fax 03 5392 2774, 12 units [shwr, tlt, hairdry, a/c-cool, fan, heat, elec blkts, tel, TV, clock radio, t/c mkg, refrig, toaster], ldry, ✕, BYO, dinner to unit, plygr, cots, non smoking units (2). **RO ♦ $48, ♦♦ $55 - $60, ♦ $10**, AE BC DC MC MCH VI.

B&B's/Guest Houses

★★★☆ **Parlawidgee Holiday Farm**, (GH), (Farm), No children's facilities, Edenhope Rd, 11.6km SE of PO, ☎ 03 5392 2613, fax 03 5392 2666, 2 rms [hairdry, c/fan, heat, elec blkts, clock radio], ldry, lounge (TV, video), t/c mkg shared, non smoking property. **D all meals ♦ $75, ♦ $75**, Tariff includes farm activities.

KATUNGA VIC 3640

Pop Part of Numurkah, (214km N Melbourne), See map on page 696, ref D1. Located in dairying district. Tennis.

Self Catering Accommodation

★★★ **Glenarron Farms**, (Cotg), (Farm), Hutchins La, 4.6km S of PO, off Numurkah - Katunga Rd, ☎ 03 5864 6246, 2 cotgs acc up to 8, (2 & 3 bedrm), [shwr, tlt, fan, heat, elec blkts, TV, clock radio, refrig, cook fac, micro, toaster, ldry, blkts, linen, pillows], bbq, c/park (carport), cots. **D ♦♦ $66 - $88, ♦ $16.50**, ch con.

KERANG VIC 3579

Pop 3,900. (278km N Melbourne), See map on pages 694/695, ref D3. Located on the Murray Valley Hwy, adjacent to the Loddon River. Ibis viewing centre, Boating, Bowls, Bush Walking, Croquet, Fishing, Golf, Horse Racing, Horse Riding, Sailing, Scenic Drives, Shooting, Swimming (Pool, Lake, River), Tennis, Water Skiing.

Hotels/Motels

★★★ **Downtown Motor Inn**, (LMH), 77 Wellington St, 400m W of PO, ☎ 03 5452 1911, fax 03 5450 3290, 10 units [shwr, spa bath (1), tlt, a/c-cool, heat, elec blkts, tel, TV, clock radio, t/c mkg, refrig, mini bar, toaster], ldry, conf fac, ✕ (Mon to Sat), cots. **RO ♦ $60 - $65, ♦♦ $70 - $75, ♦ $10**, ch con, AE BC DC EFT MC VI.

★★★ **Kerang Valley Resort**, (M), Previously Motel Kerang, 76 Bendigo Rd, 1km S of PO, ☎ 03 5452 1311, fax 03 5452 1490, 31 units [shwr, spa bath (3), tlt, hairdry, a/c, c/fan (3), elec blkts, tel, TV, clock radio, t/c mkg, refrig, toaster], iron, iron brd, rec rm, conf fac, ✕, pool, dinner to unit, plygr, cots-fee, non smoking units (2). **D $120 - $130, RO ♦ $55 - $65, ♦♦ $64 - $130**, ch con, pen con, AE BC DC EFT MC MP VI.

★★★ **Motel Loddon River**, (M), Murray Valley Hwy, 900m W of PO, ☎ 03 5452 2511, fax 03 5452 2083, 12 units [shwr, tlt, evap cool (9), a/c (3), c/fan, heat, elec blkts, tel, TV, clock radio, t/c mkg, refrig, toaster], bbq, cots, non smoking units (9). **RO ♦ $50, ♦♦ $60 - $64, ♦ $9**, AE BC DC EFT MC MCH VI.

KERGUNYAH VIC 3691

Pop Nominal, (330km NE Melbourne), See map on pages 694/695, ref H4. Situated in the Kiewa Valley. Fishing.

Self Catering Accommodation

★★★ **Wyuna of Kergunyah**, (HU), RMB 1184 Gundowring Rd, Wodonga 3691, ☎ 02 6027 5290, fax 02 6027 5290, 4 units acc up to 5, (1 & 2 bedrm), [shwr, tlt, a/c, heat, elec blkts, TV, clock radio, refrig, cook fac, blkts, linen, pillows], w/mach (2), iron, iron brd, rec rm, ✕, pool, bbq, plygr. **D $60 - $70, W $320 - $360**, BC MC VI.

KILCUNDA VIC 3995

Pop 300. (117km S Melbourne), See map on page 696, ref C7. Small seaside township with extensive open beaches. Fishing, Hangliding, Tennis.

Hotels/Motels

★☆ **Ocean View**, (LMH), Bass Hwy, adjacent to PO, ☎ 03 5678 7245, 6 units [shwr, tlt, heat, elec blkts, TV, t/c mkg, refrig, toaster], ☒, cots-fee. **RO** ♦ **$30 - $40**, ♦♦ **$45 - $55**, ♦♦♦ **$60 - $70**, ch con, Light breakfast only available. BC MC VI.

B&B's/Guest Houses

★★★★☆ **Ocean Walk Bed & Breakfast**, (B&B), 8 Gilbert St, ☎ 03 5678 7419, fax 03 5678 7419, 3 rms [ensuite, bath (1), spa bath (1), hairdry, a/c, elec blkts, TV, clock radio], lounge (TV), t/c mkg shared, non smoking property. **BB** ♦♦ **$110 - $140**, BC MC VI.

KILMORE VIC 3764

Pop 2,700. (60km N Melbourne), See map on page 696, ref C4. Residential & light industrial town on the Northern Hwy. Whitburgh Cottage Pioneer Museum, Bowls, Golf, Horse Racing, Swimming, Tennis, Trotting.

Hotels/Motels

★★★ **Kestrel Motor Inn**, (M), 99 Powlett St, 1km S of PO, ☎ 03 5782 1457, fax 03 5781 1515, 12 units [shwr, tlt, a/c, elec blkts, tel, TV, clock radio, t/c mkg, refrig, toaster], ldry, pool, bbq, plygr, cots-fee. **RO** ♦ **$53**, ♦♦ **$64**, AE BC EFT MC VI.

★★ **Kilmore Country Motel**, (M), 95 Sydney St, 900m N of PO, ☎ 03 5782 1346, 12 units [shwr, tlt, heat, elec blkts, TV, clock radio, t/c mkg, refrig], bbq. **RO** ♦ **$50 - $55**, ♦♦ **$50 - $55**, ch con, BC EFT MC VI.

Self Catering Accommodation

★★★★ **Bindley House**, (Cotg), Cnr Powlett & Piper Sts, 50m N of Police Station, ☎ 03 5781 1142, fax 03 5781 1142, 2 cotgs acc up to 4, (Studio), [shwr, spa bath, tlt, a/c, elec blkts, TV, video, clock radio, CD, t/c mkg, refrig, cook fac, micro, elec frypan, toaster, blkts, doonas, linen, pillows], lounge firepl, bbq, breakfast ingredients. **BB** ♦ **$95**, ♦♦ **$125**, ♦ **$20**, Meals by arrangment. AE BC DC MC VI.

★★★★ **Brackley Cottage**, (Cotg), 165 Diggings Rd, 11km fr PO, ☎ 03 5781 0904, 1 cotg acc up to 4, [ensuite (1), shwr, spa bath (1), tlt, a/c-cool, fan, heat, elec blkts, tel, TV, clock radio, t/c mkg, refrig, cook fac, toaster, blkts, linen, pillows], w/mach, lounge firepl, breakfast ingredients, Pets on application. **D** ♦♦ **$130**, ♦ **$50**, **W** ♦♦ **$430**, ♦ **$100**.

★★★☆ **Laurel Hill Cottage B&B**, (Cotg), 12 Melrose Dve, ☎ 03 5782 1630, fax 03 5782 2591, 1 cotg acc up to 4, (2 bedrm), [shwr, spa bath, tlt, hairdry, cent heat, elec blkts, TV, video, clock radio, CD, refrig, cook fac, micro, toaster, blkts, linen, pillows], ldry, bbq. **D** ♦♦ **$120**, ♦ **$20**, BC MC VI.

KINGLAKE VIC 3763

Pop 700. (54km NE Melbourne), See map on page 696, ref C5. Township located in agricultural district, near the Kinglake National Park. Art Gallery, Bush Walking, Horse Riding, Scenic Drives.

Hotels/Motels

Kinglake National Park Hotel Motel, (LMH), Main Rd, 100m N of PO, ☎ 03 5786 1230, 6 units [shwr, tlt, hairdry, heat, TV, clock radio (2), t/c mkg, refrig, toaster], conf fac, ☒. **BLB** ♦ **$40 - $50**, ♦♦ **$50 - $75**, ♦ **$20**, ch con, BC EFT MC VI, (Rating under review).

B&B's/Guest Houses

★★★★ **Lamon Farm**, (B&B), No children's facilities, 3555 Mt Slide Rd (Healesville - Kinglake Rd), 6.6km W of Melba Hwy, ☎ 03 5786 1684, fax 03 5786 2130, (2 stry gr fl), 3 rms [ensuite, hairdry, c/fan, cent heat, elec blkts, clock radio, t/c mkg, doonas], lounge (TV, video, cd), lounge firepl, refrig, bbq, non smoking property, Pets allowed. **BB** ♦ **$140**, ♦♦ **$154**, Other meals by arrangement. AE BC DC MC VI.

★★★★ **(Cottage Section)**, 1 cotg acc up to 2, (1 bedrm), [shwr, spa bath, tlt, hairdry, fan, heat, elec blkts, TV, video, clock radio, CD, t/c mkg, refrig, cook fac ltd, micro, toaster, blkts, linen, pillows], breakfast ingredients. **BB** ♦♦ **$198**.

★★★☆ **Heatherbrae Homestead**, (B&B), 3715 Mount Slide Rd, 800 m E of PO, ☎ 03 5786 2058, fax 03 5786 2058, 2 rms [hairdry, fan, heat, elec blkts, clock radio], lounge (TV, video, cd player), lounge firepl, spa (heated), bbq, non smoking rms. **BB** ♦ **$85**, **D** ♦♦ **$125**, Dinner by arrangement.

KINGSTON VIC 3364

Pop Nominal, (140km NW Melbourne), See map on page 696, ref A4. Farming township in agricultural and grazing district. Tennis.

Self Catering Accommodation

★★★★ **Kirkside Cottages**, (Cotg), 1 Church Pde, 600m N of PO, ☎ 03 5345 6252, fax 03 5345 6200, 3 cotgs acc up to 5, (2 bedrm), [shwr, spa bath, tlt, hairdry, heat (wood & gas), elec blkts, TV, video (avail), clock radio, CD, refrig, cook fac, toaster, ldry, blkts, linen, pillows], iron, iron brd, lounge firepl, bbq. **BLB** ♦♦ **$155 - $225**, ♦ **$25**, Meals by arrangement. Pets welcome. AE BC EFT MC VI.

★★★★ **Laurel Bank Cottages**, (Cotg), Victoria Rd, 1.5km SE of PO, ☎ 03 5345 7343, fax 03 5345 7343, 2 cotgs acc up to 2, (1 bedrm), [shwr, tlt, hairdry, fan, heat, elec blkts, TV, clock radio, t/c mkg, refrig, cook fac, toaster, blkts, linen, pillows], lounge firepl, bbq, c/park (carport), breakfast ingredients, non smoking property. **BB** ♦♦ **$120 - $140**, Min book long w/ends and Easter, BC MC VI.

KOO WEE RUP VIC 3981

Pop 1,100. (70km SE Melbourne), See map on page 696, ref C6. Rich agricultural and dairying district, holding a Potato Festival early March. Bowls, Swimming (Pool), Tennis.

Hotels/Motels

★★☆ **Koo Wee Rup Motel**, (M), Previously Koowee Motel 132-138 Station St, ☎ 03 5997 1880, fax 03 5997 1139, 9 units [shwr, tlt, a/c, heat, elec blkts, TV, t/c mkg, refrig], ✆, cots-fee. **RO** ♦ **$44 - $66**, ♦♦ **$55 - $66**, ♦ **$13**, ch con, Light breakfast only available. AE BC MC VI.

KOONWARRA VIC 3954

Pop Nominal, (147km SE Melbourne), See map on page 696, ref D7. Tiny township located in a rich dairy farming district. Bush Walking, Golf, Scenic Drives, Tennis.

B&B's/Guest Houses

★★★★☆ **Lyre Bird Hill Winery & Guest House**, (B&B), No children's facilities, Inverloch Rd, 3.8km SW of PO, ☎ 03 5664 3204, fax 03 5664 3206, 3 rms [ensuite, hairdry, heat, elec blkts, clock radio], lounge (TV, video, cd), lounge firepl, t/c mkg shared, refrig, bbq, non smoking property. **BB** ♦ **$85**, ♦♦ **$130 - $150**, Dinner by arrangement. AE BC DC MC VI.

KOROIT VIC 3282

Pop 1,000. (280km W Melbourne), See map on pages 694/695, ref B7. Historic township with areas classified by the National Trust. Close to Tower Hill State Game Reserve & extinct volcano. An extensive potato, onion & dairying area. Bowls, Croquet.

Hotels/Motels

★ **Koroit Hotel**, (LH), Cnr Commercial Rd & High St, opposite PO, ☎ 03 5565 8201, fax 03 5565 8203, (2 stry), 10 rms [basin (5), hairdry, pillows], shwr, tlt, ✆. **BLB** ♦ **$30**, ch con, EFT.

Self Catering Accommodation

★★★ **Yangery Cottages**, (Cotg), 807 Tower Hill Rd, Yangery 3283, 5km SE of PO, ☎ 03 5565 9377, fax 03 5565 9017, 2 cotgs acc up to 5, (2 bedrm), [shwr, bath, tlt, c/fan, heat, elec blkts, TV, clock radio, t/c mkg, refrig, cook fac, micro, toaster, doonas, linen, pillows], w/mach, iron, iron brd, lounge firepl, bbq, cots (avail), breakfast ingredients. **D** ♦♦ **$90**, ♦ **$20**, **W** ♦♦ **$385 - $600**, ♦ **$140**, ch con.

B&B's/Guest Houses

★★☆ **The Olde Courthouse Inn**, (GH), 100 Commercial Rd, opposite PO, ☎ 03 5565 8346, fax 03 5565 8146, 8 rms [elec blkts], bathrm, lounge (TV), lounge firepl, t/c mkg shared. **BB** ♦ **$53.90 - $93.50**, ♦ **$53.90 - $93.50**, ch con, Dinner by arrangement. BC MC VI.

KORUMBURRA VIC 3950

Pop 2,750. (119km SE Melbourne), See map on page 696, ref D7. Dairy farming area. Bowls, Croquet, Fishing, Golf, Horse Riding, Scenic Drives, Shooting, Swimming (Pool), Tennis.

Hotels/Motels

★★★ **Coal Creek Motel**, (M), South Gippsland Hwy, opposite Coal Creek Historical Park, ☎ 03 5655 1822, fax 03 5655 1464, 25 units [shwr, spa bath (1), tlt, a/c, elec blkts, tel, TV, video-fee, clock radio, t/c mkg, refrig], conf fac, ☒ (Wed to Sat), pool, bbq, rm serv, plygr, cots-fee, non smoking units (8). **RO** ♦ **$60**, ♦♦ **$74**, ♦ **$10**, AE BC DC EFT MC VI.

Self Catering Accommodation

★★★ **Quilters Barn**, (Apt), 155 Fitzgeralds Rd, Arawata 3951, 11km N of Korumburra, ☎ 03 5659 8271, fax 03 5659 8209, 1 apt (2 bedrm), [shwr, tlt, hairdry, heat, elec blkts, TV, clock radio, t/c mkg, refrig, cook fac ltd, micro, toaster, blkts, linen, pillows], bbq, non smoking property. **BLB ♦ $55 - $70, ♦♦ $100 - $110, ◊ $20 - $30**, Other meals by arrangement. BC EFT MC VI.

★★☆ **White Law Cottage**, (Cotg), (Farm), Sullivans Rd, 5km SW of PO, ☎ 03 5655 1410, fax 03 5655 1410, 1 cotg acc up to 6, (3 bedrm), [shwr, bath, tlt, fan, heat, elec blkts, TV, video, clock radio, refrig, cook fac, toaster, blkts, linen, pillows], iron, lounge firepl, cots, breakfast ingredients. **BB ♦♦ $105, ◊ $25.**

B&B's/Guest Houses

★★★★ **Pindari**, (B&B), (Farm), No children's facilities, 9170 South Gippsland Hwy, Ruby via, 8km SE of PO, ☎ 03 5662 2005, fax 03 5662 2005, 1 rm [ensuite, heat, elec blkts, clock radio], lounge (TV, video, cd), lounge firepl, pool-indoor, t/c mkg shared, refrig, bbq, tennis. **BB ♦ $66, ♦♦ $132.**

★★★★ **(Cottage Section)**, 1 cotg acc up to 4, (2 bedrm), [ensuite, bath, hairdry, heat (wood), elec blkts, TV, clock radio, refrig, cook fac, micro, elec frypan, toaster, blkts, linen, pillows], breakfast ingredients. **BB ♦ $66, ◊ $66.**

KYABRAM VIC 3620

Pop 5,750. (200km N Melbourne), See map on page 696, ref C2. Fauna Park town. Boating, Bowls, Croquet, Fishing, Golf, Sailing.

Hotels/Motels

★★★★ **Kyabram Motor Inn**, (M), 364 Allan St, 500m E of PO, ☎ 03 5852 2111, fax 03 5852 2912, 16 units [shwr, tlt, hairdry (9), a/c-cool, heat, elec blkts, tel, TV, video (avail), clock radio, t/c mkg, refrig, toaster], iron (9), iron brd (9), pool, bbq, dinner to unit (Mon to Sat), c/park (carport) (9), cots, non smoking units (6). **RO ♦ $60 - $70, ♦♦ $75 - $95, ◊ $10**, 7 units ★★★. AE BC DC EFT MC VI.

★★★☆ **Country Roads Motor Inn Kyabram**, (M), 363 Allan St, 450m E of PO, ☎ 03 5852 3577, fax 03 5852 3564, 14 units [shwr, tlt, hairdry, a/c-cool, heat, elec blkts, tel, TV, video (avail), clock radio, t/c mkg, refrig], bbq, dinner to unit (Mon to Thurs), cots, non smoking units (5). **RO ♦ $58 - $82, ♦♦ $68 - $82, ◊ $9**, AE BC DC EFT MC VI

Operator Comment: Also available a fully S.C. 2 br B&B, set in an 80yr old home. www.kyabram.net.au

★★ **Commercial Hotel**, (LMH), 217 Allan St, 250m E of PO, ☎ 03 5852 1005, 8 units [shwr, tlt, a/c-cool, heat, elec blkts, TV, t/c mkg, refrig, toaster], ⊠, ✆, cots. **BLB ♦ $40, ♦♦ $45, ◊ $10**, BC EFT MC VI.

KYNETON VIC 3444

Pop 3,750. Part of Macedon Ranges, (84km NW Melbourne), See map on page 696, ref B4. Located on Calder Hwy, adjacent to Campaspe River, centre of a rich agricultural and pastoral district with several secondary industries. Bowls, Bush Walking.

Hotels/Motels

★★ **Central Highlands Motor Inn**, (M), 104 High St (Old Calder Hwy), 900m S of PO, ☎ 03 5422 2011, fax 03 5422 7470, 10 units [shwr, tlt, fan, heat, elec blkts, tel, TV, clock radio, t/c mkg, refrig, toaster], res liquor license, bbq, cots-fee. **RO ♦ $44 - $49, ♦♦ $55 - $59, ◊ $11**, AE BC DC MC VI.

★★ **Kyneton Motel**, (M), 101 Piper St, 1.25km NW of PO, ☎ 03 5422 1098, fax 03 5422 1098, 9 units [shwr, spa bath (1), tlt, fan, heat, elec blkts, TV, clock radio, t/c mkg, refrig, toaster, doonas], plygr, cots-fee. **RO ♦ $47 - $51, ♦♦ $55 - $59, ◊ $13**, ch con, AE BC DC MC VI.

Self Catering Accommodation

★★★★ **Pipers Retreat**, (Apt), Rear 30 Piper St, ☎ 03 5422 3745, fax 03 5422 6460, 1 apt acc up to 4, (2 bedrm), [shwr, spa bath, tlt, hairdry, c/fan, heat, TV, radio, t/c mkg, refrig, cook fac, elec frypan, d/wash, toaster, ldry (in unit), blkts, doonas, linen, pillows], w/mach, dryer, iron, iron brd, coffee shop, breakfast ingredients. **BB ♦♦ $150 - $170, ◊ $25 - $50, W $450 - $700**, AE BC MC VI.

★★★☆ **Kyneton Bushland Resort**, (Cotg), 252 Edgecombe Rd, 4km N of PO, ☎ 03 5422 0888, fax 03 5422 3289, 55 cotgs acc up to 6, (2 & 3 bedrm), [shwr, spa bath (12), tlt, a/c, c/fan (11), elec blkts, tel, TV, video, clock radio, refrig, cook fac (38), cook fac ltd (17), micro, elec frypan (17), d/wash, toaster, ldry (in unit), blkts, doonas, linen, pillows], w/mach, dryer, iron, iron brd, rec rm, lounge, conf fac, pool indoor heated, sauna, spa, bbq, ✆, plygr, bicycle, canoeing, squash, tennis, cots. **D $110 - $155, W $440 - $990**, Min book applies, BC EFT MC VI.

B&B's/Guest Houses

★★★★☆ **Kinsale Waters Country Retreat**, (B&B), 206 Premier Mine Rd Tylden via, 6km S of PO, ☎ 03 5422 3911, fax 03 9650 2218, 2 rms [ensuite, spa bath, hairdry, fan, heat, elec blkts, TV, video, clock radio, t/c mkg, refrig], lounge (cd), lounge firepl. **BB $130**, BC MC VI.

★★★★☆ **Kyneton Country House**, (B&B), Classified by National Trust, 66 Jennings St, 800m W of PO, ☎ 03 5422 3556, fax 03 5422 3556, (2 stry), 3 rms [ensuite, bath (hip) (2), hairdry, cent heat, clock radio, doonas], iron, iron brd, lounge (TV, stereo), lounge firepl, t/c mkg shared, non smoking property. **BB ♦ $125 - $155, ♦♦ $135 - $185, ◊ $20 - $75, DBB ♦ $155 - $210, ♦♦ $195 - $295**, Dinner by arrangement, AE BC DC JCB MC VI.

Operator Comment: Visit our website www.babs.com.au/kyneton, or phone 03 5422 3556.

★★★★ **Bringalbit**, (B&B), (Farm), 512 Sidonia Rd, Sidonia via, 14.7km NE of PO, ☎ 03 5423 7223, fax 03 5423 7223, 2 rms [shwr, tlt, hairdry, evap cool (1), heat, elec blkts, TV (1), clock radio, t/c mkg, refrig (1)], lounge (TV, stereo, cd), lounge firepl. **BB ♦ $70 - $80, ♦♦ $115 - $140, ◊ $35**, Other meals by arrangement, AE BC DC MC VI.

★★★★ **(Woolshed Hill House Section)**, 1 cotg acc up to 9, (4 bedrm), [ensuite (2), shwr, bath, tlt, hairdry, fan, heat, TV, video, clock radio, t/c mkg, refrig, cook fac, micro, elec frypan, d/wash, toaster, ldry (in unit), blkts, linen, pillows], w/mach, dryer, iron, iron brd, bbq, cots, breakfast ingredients. **BLB ♦♦ $150, ◊ $55**, ch con, Other meals by arrangement.

★★★★ **Moorville at Kyneton**, (B&B), 1 Powlett St, ☎ 03 5422 6466, fax 03 5422 6460, 3 rms [ensuite (2), shwr (1), tlt (1), hairdry, fan, heat], ldry, lounge (TV, video, cd), lounge firepl, pool-indoor (summer), t/c mkg shared, refrig, tennis. **BB ♦ $100, ♦♦ $130 - $155**, Dinner by arrangement, AE BC MC VI.

★★★☆ **Kyneton Ridge Estate**, (B&B), No children's facilities, 90 Blackhill School Rd, 8km fr PO, ☎ 03 5422 7377, fax 03 5422 3747, 3 rms [ensuite (1), spa bath (1), hairdry, c/fan, heat, elec blkts, TV (1), video (1), clock radio, CD (1), refrig (1)], lounge (TV, cd), lounge firepl, t/c mkg shared, bbq, non smoking property. **BB ♦ $100 - $120, ♦♦ $120 - $165**, 1 room ★★★★☆. BC MC VI.

LAKE BOGA VIC 3584

Pop 450. (320km N Melbourne), See map on pages 694/695, ref D3. On the shores of the lake, located on Murray Valley Hwy. Tours of Bests Winery available. Bowls, Fishing, Horse Riding, Sailing, Scenic Drives, Swimming (Lake), Tennis, Vineyards, Wineries, Water Skiing.

Hotels/Motels

★★★ **Catalina Motel**, (M), Murray Valley Hwy, ☎ 03 5037 2790, 8 units [shwr, tlt, a/c, heat, elec blkts, TV, clock radio, t/c mkg, refrig, micro (1), toaster], ldry, conf fac, ⊠, bbq, c/park (carport), non smoking units (2). **RO ♦ $45 - $49.50, ♦♦ $55 - $66, ◊ $10 - $11**, ch con, BC MC VI.

★★☆ **Aquatic Lodge**, (M), Murray Valley Hwy, ☎ 03 5037 2103, fax 03 5037 2111, 32 units [shwr, tlt, hairdry (8), a/c-cool, heat, elec blkts, tel (8), TV, clock radio (8), radio (24), t/c mkg, refrig, toaster], ldry, conf fac, ⊠ (seasonal), pool, bbq, rm serv, plygr, cots-fee. **RO ♦ $40, ♦♦ $45 - $50, ◊ $10**, 8 units ★★★☆. BC MC VI.

B&B's/Guest Houses

★★★☆ **Burrabliss Farms**, (B&B), Lakeside Dve, off Murray Valley Hwy, ☎ 03 5037 2527, fax 03 5037 2808, 2 rms [hairdry, a/c-cool, heat, elec blkts, clock radio], lounge (TV, cd player), t/c mkg shared, bbq. **BB ♦ $60 - $70, ♦♦ $85 - $95**, Dinner available. BC MC VI.

LAKE BOLAC VIC 3351

Pop 250. (182km W Melbourne), See map on pages 694/695, ref C6. Agricultural and pastoral community at north end of Lake Bolac.-. Boating, Bowls, Fishing, Golf, Sailing, Scenic Drives, Squash, Swimming (Pool, Lake), Tennis, Water Skiing.

Hotels/Motels

Country Haven

★★★ **Lake Bolac Motel**, (M), Glenelg Hwy, 500m W of PO, ☎ 03 5350 2218, 7 units [shwr, tlt, fan (1), c/fan (6), heat, elec blkts, TV, clock radio, t/c mkg, refrig, cook fac (1)]. **RO ♦ $50, ♦♦ $60, ◊ $11**, ch con, BC MC VI.

B&B's/Guest Houses

★★★★ **Lakeview B & B**, (B&B), No facilities for children under 14. Glenelg Hwy, 3km E of PO, ☎ 03 5350 2240, fax 03 5350 2240, 2 rms [c/fan, heat, elec blkts, TV, clock radio], lounge (TV, video, cd), lounge firepl, spa, t/c mkg shared, bbq. **BB ♦ $70, ♦♦ $100 - $110**, Other meals by arrangement. BC MC VI.

LAKE CHARLEGRARK VIC 3412

Part of GRAMPIANS region. Pop Nominal, (381km NW Melbourne), See map on pages 694/695, ref A5. Situated in agricultural and pastoral district. Fishing, Swimming (Lake), Tennis, Water Skiing.

Self Catering Accommodation
★ **Lake Charlegrark Cottages**, (Cotg), Edenhope-Kaniva Rd, 80km W of Horsham, ☎ 03 5386 6281, fax 03 5386 6281, 3 cotgs acc up to 9, (1, 2 & 5 bedrm), [shwr, bath (1), tlt, a/c-cool (2), evap cool (1), heat, TV, clock radio (1), refrig, cook fac (1), cook fac ltd (2), elec frypan, ldry (in unit) (1), doonas, linen reqd, pillows], ldry, bbq. **D** ♦♦ **$40 - $50,** ◊ **$10, W $250 - $300,** 1 cottage ★★.

LAKE EILDON VIC 3713

Pop Nil, (138km NE Melbourne), See map on page 696, ref D4. Lake Eildon, covering an area of 138 sq kms, is Victoria's largest inland boating resort.

Other Accommodation
Eildon Starline Houseboats, (Hbt), Moored at Goughs Bay, Goughs Bay 3723, ☎ 03 5775 1797, fax 03 5779 1285, 3 houseboats acc up to 12, (1, 3 & 4 bedrm), [shwr, tlt, heat, TV (2), radio, CD (2), refrig, cook fac, micro, toaster, blkts reqd, linen reqd, pillows reqd], bbq. **W $660 - $2,860,** Security deposit $300 to $650, BC MC VI.

Howqua Houseboat Holidays, (Hbt), Mansfield-Jamieson Rd, Howqua 3722, 27km S of Mansfield, ☎ 03 5777 3588, fax 03 5777 3713, (2 stry), 1 houseboat acc up to 12, (4 bedrm), [shwr, tlt, TV, video, CD, refrig, cook fac, micro, blkts reqd-fee, linen reqd-fee, pillows reqd-fee], bbq. **W $2,170 - $3,850,** Security deposit - $1000. BC EFT MC VI.

Lake Eildon Holiday Boats Pty Ltd, (Hbt), Boat Harbour, Eildon 3713, 2km N of PO, ☎ 03 5774 2107, fax 03 5774 2613, 25 houseboats acc up to 10, (2, 3 & 4 bedrm), [shwr, tlt, heat, refrig, cook fac, blkts reqd, linen reqd]. **W $699 - $5,445,** Security deposit - $300 to $1000. BC MC VI.

Peppin Point Houseboats, (Hbt), Peppin Dve, Bonnie Doon 3720, 9km S of PO, off Maintongoon Rd, ☎ 03 5778 7338, fax 03 5778 7551, 11 houseboats acc up to 10, (3 & 4 bedrm), [shwr, tlt, heat (5), TV, video, radio (cassette), refrig, cook fac, micro, blkts reqd-fee, linen reqd-fee, pillows reqd-fee], spa (1), bbq. **W $440 - $4,400,** Security bond - $600 to $1000. Min book all holiday times, BC EFT MC VI.

LAKE TYERS BEACH VIC 3909

Pop 350. (331km E Melbourne), See map on pages 694/695, ref J7. Picturesque submerged river valley. Excellent fishing available.
★★☆ **Sunrise Holiday Flats**, (HF), 559 Lake Tyers Beach Rd, Cnr Gully Rd, ☎ 03 5156 5669, 3 flats acc up to 4, (1 & 2 bedrm), [shwr, tlt, hairdry, fan, heat, elec blkts, TV, clock radio, refrig, cook fac, micro, elec frypan, toaster, linen reqd-fee], ldry, bbq, cots. **D $25 - $70, W $140 - $450,** Min book Christmas Jan and Easter.

★★★★ **Airdrie Ocean View Bed and Breakfast**, (B&B), 19 Cross St, 9km E of Lakes Entrance, ☎ 03 5156 5640, (2 stry gr fl), 2 rms [ensuite (1), shwr, spa bath, tlt, hairdry, a/c, c/fan, heat, elec blkts, TV, video, clock radio, CD, t/c mkg, refrig, toaster, doonas], iron, iron brd, bbq, non smoking property. **BB** ♦♦ **$120 - $160,** 1 room ★★★★☆.

LAKES ENTRANCE VIC 3909

Pop 5,250. (319km E Melbourne), See map on pages 694/695, ref J7. Fishing & tourist port at entrance to Gippsland Lakes.

Hotels/Motels
★★★★ **Abel Tasman Motor Lodge**, (M), 643 Esplanade (Princes Hwy), 1.6km E of PO, ☎ 03 5155 1655, fax 03 5155 1603, (2 stry gr fl), 11 units [shwr, spa bath (1), tlt, hairdry, a/c, elec blkts, tel, cable tv, video, movie, clock radio, t/c mkg, refrig, cook fac ltd (9), micro, toaster], ldry, pool-heated (solar), bbq (covered), cots-fee, non smoking units. **RO** ♦ **$72 - $165,** ♦♦ **$72 - $165,** ◊ **$15,** ch con, BC EFT MC VI.

★★★★ **(Apartment Section)**, 5 apts acc up to 6, (2 & 3 bedrm), [ensuite (1), shwr, bath, spa bath (1), tlt, hairdry, a/c (1), fan, heat, elec blkts, TV, video, clock radio, t/c mkg, cook fac, micro, elec frypan, d/wash, ldry (in unit), blkts, doonas, linen], iron, iron brd, non smoking units (3). **D** ♦ **$115 - $310,** ♦♦ **$115 - $310,** ◊ **$15,** Min book applies.

★★★★ **Banjo Paterson Motor Inn**, (M), 131 Esplanade (Princes Hwy), 500m W of PO, ☎ 03 5155 2933, fax 03 5155 2855, 22 units [shwr, spa bath (6), tlt, hairdry, a/c, elec blkts, tel, TV, video (avail), clock radio, t/c mkg, refrig, mini bar, ldry], iron, iron brd, ⊠, pool-heated (solar, salt water), bbq, rm serv, cots, non smoking rms. **RO** ♦ **$98 - $185,** ♦♦ **$115 - $185,** ◊ **$15,** AE BC DC EFT JCB MC MP VI.

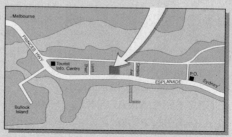

Rates may change. Check before booking.

★★★★ **Bellevue Quality Inn**, (M), 191 Esplanade (Princes Hwy), 200m W of PO, ☎ 03 5155 3055, fax 03 5155 3429, (2 stry gr fl), 32 units [shwr, spa bath (8), tlt, hairdry, a/c, elec blkts, tel, TV, video (avail), movie, clock radio, t/c mkg, refrig, mini bar, toaster], ldry, conf fac, ✕, bar (cocktail), pool-heated (solar), pool indoor heated, sauna, spa, bbq, boat park, courtesy transfer, ✆, plygr, jetty, cots-fee, non smoking units (16). **RO** ♦ $110 - $210, ♦♦ $130 - $230, ♦ $16.50, AE BC DC EFT MC MP VI, ♿.

★★★★ **(Apartment Section)**, (Multi-stry gr fl), 12 apts acc up to 5, (2 bedrm), [shwr, tlt, hairdry, c/fan, heat, elec blkts, tel, TV, video, movie, clock radio, refrig, cook fac, micro, d/wash, toaster, ldry (in unit), blkts, linen, pillows]. **D** ♦ $140 - $230, ♦♦ $140 - $230, ♦ $16.50.

★★★★ **Coastal Waters**, (M), 635 Esplanade (Princes Hwy), 350m E of footbridge, ☎ 03 5155 1792, fax 03 5155 1052, 12 units [shwr, spa bath (8), tlt, hairdry, a/c, tel, TV, video, clock radio, t/c mkg, refrig, mini bar], ldry, pool-heated (salt water heated), bbq, cots, non smoking suites. **RO** ♦ $105 - $187, ♦♦ $105 - $187, ♦ $11 - $22, ch con, AE BC DC MC MP VI.

★★★★ **Sand Bar Motel Lakes Entrance**, (M), 637 Esplanade (Princes Hwy), 1.5km E of PO, ☎ 03 5155 2567, fax 03 5155 2900, 10 units [shwr, tlt, hairdry, a/c, elec blkts, tel, cable tv, clock radio, t/c mkg, refrig, toaster], ldry, iron, iron brd, pool-heated (solar), spa (heated)-fee, bbq, cots-fee, non smoking units (9). **RO** ♦ $60 - $110, ♦♦ $66 - $110, ♦ $12, AE BC DC EFT MC VI.

★★★☆ **Albatross Motor Inn**, (M), 661 Esplanade (Princes Hwy), 400m E of Footbridge, ☎ 03 5155 1779, fax 03 5155 3781, 11 units [shwr, tlt, hairdry, a/c, elec blkts, tel, TV, video-fee, clock radio, t/c mkg, refrig, toaster], iron, iron brd, pool-heated (solar), bbq, dinner to unit, boat park, cots-fee, non smoking units (8). **RO** ♦ $48 - $94, ♦♦ $48 - $135, ♦ $15, ch con, 3 units of a higher rating. AE BC DC EFT MC MP VI.

★★★☆ **Cunningham Shore Motel**, (M), 639 Esplanade (Princes Hwy), 1.5km E of PO, ☎ 03 5155 2960, fax 03 5155 4969, 10 units [shwr, spa bath (1), tlt, a/c, elec blkts, tel, TV, video-fee, clock radio, t/c mkg, refrig, micro (2), toaster, ldry], pool-heated (solar), spa-fee, bbq, cots-fee, non smoking units (7). **RO** ♦ $65 - $165, ♦♦ $69 - $165, ♦ $16.50, ch con, AE BC DC EFT MC VI, ♿.

★★★☆ **George Bass Motor Inn**, (M), Princes Hwy, 2.2km W of PO, ☎ 03 5155 1611, fax 03 5155 2491, 40 units [shwr, spa bath (3), tlt, hairdry (4), a/c, elec blkts, tel, TV, video-fee, clock radio, t/c mkg, refrig], ldry, ✕, pool (salt water), plygr, cots-fee. **RO** ♦ $70 - $95, ♦♦ $79 - $104, ♦ $10, ch con, 1 unit ★★★★. AE BC DC EFT JCB MC MP VI.

★★★☆ **Golden Beach Motor Inn**, (M), 607 Esplanade (Princes Hwy), 1.1km E of PO, ☎ 03 5155 1666, fax 03 5155 2328, (2 stry gr fl), 29 units [shwr, tlt, a/c, elec blkts, tel, TV, clock radio, t/c mkg, refrig], ✕ (BYO), pool, bbq, non smoking units (10). **RO** ♦ $50 - $99, ♦♦ $55 - $99, ♦ $11, ch con, 9 units ★★★☆. AE BC DC EFT MC VI.

★★★☆ **Lakes Waterfront Motel & Holiday Cottages**, (M), 10 Princes Hwy, 2.3km E of PO, ☎ 03 5155 2841, fax 03 5155 2399, 7 units [shwr, bath (hip), tlt, hairdry, a/c, elec blkts, tel, TV, clock radio, t/c mkg, refrig, cook fac, micro, elec frypan, toaster], ldry, iron, iron brd, pool (solar heated), bbq, c/park (undercover), plygr, cots, non smoking rms (6). **RO** ♦ $50 - $95, ♦♦ $55 - $95, ♦ $10, AE BC DC EFT MC MCH VI.

★★★☆ **(Cottage Section)**, 3 cotgs acc up to 4, (2 bedrm), [shwr, bath (hip), tlt, hairdry, a/c, elec blkts, tel, TV, clock radio, refrig, cook fac, micro, elec frypan, toaster, blkts, linen, pillows], bbq, non smoking rms (2). **D** $90 - $125, **W** $450 - $875.

★★★☆ **Sherwood Lodge Motor Inn**, (M), 151 Esplanade (Princes Hwy), 450m W of PO, ☎ 03 5155 1444, fax 03 5155 2401, 24 units [shwr, bath (10), spa bath (6), tlt, hairdry, a/c-cool, cent heat, elec blkts, tel, TV, video-fee, clock radio, t/c mkg, refrig, toaster], ldry, iron, iron brd, pool-heated (solar), spa, bbq, plygr, cots-fee, non smoking units (4). **BLB** ♦ $89 - $156, ♦♦ $89 - $156, ♦ $16, AE BC DC MC VI.

★★★ **Bamboo Motor Inn**, (M), 167 Esplanade (Princes Hwy), 300m W of PO, ☎ 03 5155 1551, fax 03 5155 4430, 18 units [shwr, tlt, hairdry, a/c, elec blkts, tel, TV, clock radio, t/c mkg, refrig, cook fac ltd (8), micro, toaster], bbq, cots-fee, non smoking units (4). **RO** ♦ $40 - $85, ♦♦ $45 - $90, ♦ $7 - $10, ch con, BC MC VI.

★★★ **Lakes Central Hotel**, (LMH), 321 - 333 Esplanade (Princes Hwy), 100m E of PO, ☎ 03 5155 1977, fax 03 5155 1841, (2 stry gr fl), 16 units [shwr, tlt, a/c, elec blkts, tel, TV, movie, clock radio, t/c mkg, refrig, cook fac (4), toaster], ldry, ✕, pool, spa, bbq, cots-fee. **RO** ♦ $49.50 - $77, ♦♦ $55 - $93.50, ch con, AE BC DC EFT MC VI.

★★★ Lakeside Motel, (M), 164 Marine Pde, 250m W of PO, ☎ 03 5155 1811, fax 03 5155 1811, 27 units [shwr, bath (hip) (6), tlt, fan, heat, elec blkts, tel (21), TV, clock radio, t/c mkg, refrig, cook fac (11), toaster], ldry, bbq, plygr, jetty, cots-fee, non smoking units. **RO** ♦ $40 - $88, ♦♦ $42 - $88, ♦ $11.

★★★ Pelican at Lakes Motel, (M), 171 Esplanade (Princes Hwy), 500m W of PO, ☎ 03 5155 1277, fax 03 5155 1101, 27 units [shwr, bath (11), tlt, hairdry, fan, heat, elec blkts, tel, TV, video-fee, clock radio, t/c mkg, refrig, micro (3), toaster], ldry, iron, iron brd, ⊠ (Mon to Fri), pool-heated (solar), bbq, cots-fee, non smoking units (13). **RO** ♦ $40 - $70, ♦♦ $50 - $95, ♦ $11 - $15, ch con, AE BC EFT MC VI.

★★☆ Glenara Hotel, (LMH), 221 Esplanade (Princes Hwy), 200m W of PO, ☎ 03 5155 1555, fax 03 5155 2872, (2 stry gr fl), 70 units [shwr, bath (26), tlt, fan (7), c/fan (63), heat, elec blkts, tel (58), TV, video-fee, clock radio, t/c mkg, refrig], ldry, rec rm, conf fac, ⊠, bar (cocktail), pool (salt water), rm serv, ☎, cots. **RO** ♦ $38.50 - $66, ♦♦ $55 - $110, ♦ $11, AE BC DC EFT MC VI.

★★☆ The Esplanade Motel, (M), 251 Esplanade (Princes Hwy), 100m W of PO, ☎ 03 5155 1933, fax 03 5155 1024, 40 units [shwr, bath (hip) (2), tlt, fan, heat, elec blkts (30), tel, TV, t/c mkg, refrig, cook fac (3), toaster, doonas (6)], ldry, pool-heated (solar), spa, bbq, boat park, car wash, cots-fee, non smoking units (6). **RO** ♦ $35 - $95, ♦♦ $40 - $125, ♦ $6 - $12, ch con, pen con, AE BC DC EFT MC VI.

★★ Blue Horizon Motel, (M), Princes Hwy, 2.2km W of PO, ☎ 03 5155 1216, 13 units [shwr, tlt, a/c-cool (10), fan (2), c/fan (1), heat, elec blkts, TV, clock radio, t/c mkg, refrig], ldry, pool, bbq, cots. **D** ♦♦ $50, ♦ $10, **W** $350 - $735, **RO** ♦ $40 - $85, ♦♦ $44 - $85, ♦ $10, AE BC DC MC VI.

★★★ (Holiday Flat Section), 2 flats acc up to 3, (1 bedrm), [shwr, tlt, a/c-cool, heat, elec blkts, TV, clock radio, refrig, cook fac, toaster, blkts, linen, pillows]. **D** ♦♦ $50, ♦ $10, **W** $350 - $665.

★★ Lakes Seaview Motel, (M), 12 New St, 3.7km E of PO, ☎ 03 5155 1318, 11 units [shwr, bath (hip) (1), tlt, c/fan, heat, elec blkts, TV, clock radio (5), radio (6), t/c mkg, refrig, cook fac (1), toaster], bbq, plygr. **RO** ♦ $33 - $60, ♦♦ $40 - $80, ♦♦♦♦ $60 - $110, ♦ $11, BC MC VI.

Self Catering Accommodation

★★★★☆ Southern Cross Holiday Apartments, (HF), 21 Roadknight St, 1.4km E of PO, ☎ 03 5155 2647, fax 03 5155 1593, 7 flats acc up to 8, (1 & 2 bedrm), [shwr, tlt, hairdry, a/c, c/fan, elec blkts, TV, video, clock radio, t/c mkg, refrig, cook fac, micro, elec frypan, toaster, ldry (in unit), blkts, linen, pillows], w/mach, dryer, iron, iron brd, pool-heated (solar), bbq, plygr, cots, non smoking units (3). **D** $65 - $228, **W** $390 - $1,495, BC MC VI.

★★★★ Allambi Holiday Flats, (HF), 34 Carpenter St, 600m N of footbridge, ☎ 03 5155 1199, (2 stry gr fl), 7 flats acc up to 5, (1 & 2 bedrm), [shwr, tlt, hairdry, a/c, elec blkts, TV, video-fee, clock radio, refrig, cook fac, micro, elec frypan, toaster, ldry (in unit), blkts, doonas, linen, pillows], iron, iron brd, rec rm, spa-fee, bbq, c/park (carport), cots. **D** $60 - $190, **W** $320 - $972, Min book all holiday times, BC MC VI.

★★★★ Black Swan Motor Inn Motel & Apartments, (HU), Cnr Esplanade (Princes Hwy) & Clarkes Rd, 1.9km E of PO, ☎ 03 5155 1913, fax 03 5155 4500, 10 units acc up to 6, (Studio, 1 & 2 bedrm), [shwr, tlt, hairdry, a/c, c/fan, heat, elec blkts, tel (direct dial), TV, video-fee, clock radio, refrig, cook fac, micro, toaster, blkts, linen, pillows], ldry, pool-heated (solar/salt water), bbq, plygr, cots-fee. **D** $50 - $175, **W** $330 - $1,225, Breakfast available. Min book all holiday times, BC MC VI.

★★★★ Footbridge Holiday Apartments, (HF), Cnr Stock St & Esplanade, 1.2km E of PO, 100m E of footbridge, ☎ 03 5155 2882, 2 flats acc up to 6, (2 bedrm), [shwr, tlt, hairdry, a/c, c/fan, elec blkts, TV, video, clock radio, refrig, cook fac, micro, elec frypan, toaster, ldry (in unit), blkts, linen, pillows], w/mach, dryer, iron, iron brd, bbq, boat park, cots. **D** $60 - $150, Min book Christmas Jan and Easter, BC MC VI.

★★★★ Fountain Court, (HF), 6 Lake St, 150m N of PO, ☎ 03 5155 1949, fax 03 5155 1949, 8 flats acc up to 6, (2 bedrm), [shwr, tlt, hairdry, c/fan, heat, elec blkts, TV, video (avail), movie, clock radio, t/c mkg, refrig, cook fac, micro, toaster, ldry (in unit), blkts, linen, pillows], w/mach, iron, iron brd, rec rm, pool-heated (solar), spa, bbq, boat park, plygr, tennis (half court), cots, non smoking units (4). **D** $66 - $150, **W** $375 - $1,100, Min book school holidays and Easter, BC MC VI.

★★★★ Lakes Entrance Country Cottages, (Cotg), Lot 2 Colquhoun Rd, 6km N of PO, ☎ 03 5155 4314, fax 03 5155 1446, 7 cotgs acc up to 6, (2 bedrm), [shwr, tlt, hairdry, c/fan, heat, elec blkts, TV, movie, clock radio, refrig, cook fac, micro, elec frypan, toaster, blkts, linen, pillows], ldry, pool-heated (solar), bbq, tennis, cots, non smoking property. **D** ♦♦ $65 - $132, ♦ $11, ch con, BC MC VI.

★★★★ Lazy Acre Log Cabins, (Log Cabin), 35 Roadknight St, 500m E of footbridge, ☎ 03 5155 1323, fax 03 5155 1212, 9 log cabins acc up to 8, (2 & 3 bedrm), [shwr, bath (hip) (8), tlt, c/fan, heat, elec blkts, TV, video, clock radio, refrig, cook fac, micro, toaster, ldry (in unit), blkts, doonas, linen, pillows], w/mach, iron, iron brd, pool, spa-fee, plygr, cots, non smoking property. **W** $420 - $913, ch con, pen con, AE BC MC VI, ♦☝.

★★★★ Lookout Holiday Units, (Apt), 25 Lookout Rd, 2km W of PO, ☎ 03 5155 1381, 2 apts acc up to 6, (2 bedrm), [shwr, tlt, heat, elec blkts, TV, refrig, cook fac, micro, elec frypan, toaster, ldry, doonas, linen, pillows], w/mach, bbq. **D** $60 - $110, **W** $300 - $750, Min book applies.

VICTORIA   L

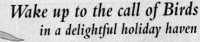
★★★★ **Ocean Breeze Units**, (HU), Cnr Eastern Beach Rd & Merrangbauer St, 2.8km E of PO, ☎ 03 5155 1369, fax 03 5155 1369, 7 units acc up to 6, (2 bedrm), [shwr, tlt, fan, heat, elec blkts, TV, video-fee, clock radio, refrig, cook fac, micro, toaster, blkts, linen, pillows], ldry, w/mach-fee, dryer-fee, rec rm, pool-heated (solar), spa, bbq (covered), plygr, cots. D ♥♥ $60 - $140, ⓘ $10, W $350 - $1,000, BC MC VI.

★★★★ **Tambo Lodge**, (HF), Princes Hwy, Kalimna West 3909, 9km W of PO, ☎ 03 5156 3215, fax 03 5156 3332, 4 flats acc up to 4, (2 bedrm), [shwr, tlt, hairdry, a/c-cool (2), c/fan, heat, elec blkts, TV, video (2), clock radio, t/c mkg, refrig, cook fac ltd, micro, elec frypan, toaster, blkts, doonas, linen, pillows], ldry, iron, iron brd, rec rm, pool-heated (solar), spa-fee, bbq (covered), plygr, tennis, non smoking property. D $65 - $145, W $330 - $895, Light breakfast available. BC MC VI.

★★★★ **(Cottage Section)**, 3 cotgs acc up to 6, (2 & 3 bedrm), [shwr, tlt, hairdry, a/c (1), c/fan, heat, elec blkts, TV, video, clock radio, t/c mkg, refrig, cook fac, micro, elec frypan, toaster, ldry (in unit), blkts, doonas, linen, pillows], w/mach, dryer, iron, iron brd, non smoking property. D $110 - $170, W $550 - $1,155, Light breakfast available.

★★★☆ **(Holiday Unit Section)**, 3 units acc up to 2, (Studio), [shwr, tlt, hairdry, c/fan, heat, elec blkts, TV, video-fee, clock radio, t/c mkg, refrig, micro, elec frypan, toaster, blkts, linen, pillows], ldry, non smoking property. D $55 - $95, W $275 - $595, Light breakfast available.

★★★★ **Whiters Holiday Village**, (HU), Cnr Roadknight & Whiters Sts, 2km E of PO, ☎ 03 5155 1343, fax 03 5155 4038, 22 units acc up to 6, [shwr, bath (hip) (2), tlt, a/c, TV, video (16), clock radio, t/c mkg, refrig, cook fac, micro, d/wash, toaster, ldry (in unit), blkts, doonas, linen, pillows], w/mach, dryer, iron, iron brd, rec rm, conf fac, pool-heated (solar), spa, bbq (covered), ☏, plygr, tennis, non smoking property. D ♥♥ $112 - $190, ⓘ $17 - $29, ch con, Min book all holiday times, AE BC EFT MC VI.

★★★☆ **Anchorage Holiday Flats**, (HF), 7 Roadknight St, 200m N of footbridge, ☎ 03 5155 1368, fax 03 5155 1368, 8 flats acc up to 6, (1 & 2 bedrm), [shwr, bath (hip), tlt, hairdry, fan, heat, elec blkts, TV, video (8), clock radio, refrig, cook fac, micro, elec frypan, toaster, ldry (1), linen], ldry, pool-heated, bbq, c/park (carport), plygr, cots, non smoking units. D ♥♥ $55 - $150, ⓘ $10, W $330 - $1,150, Min book Christmas Jan and Easter, AE BTC DC EFT MC VI.

★★★☆ **Beachcomber Holiday Flats**, (HF), 605 Esplanade (Princes Hwy), 1km E of PO, ☎ 03 5155 2754, 5 flats acc up to 6, (1 & 2 bedrm), [shwr, tlt, a/c (3), c/fan (2), heat, elec blkts, TV, clock radio, refrig, cook fac, micro, elec frypan, toaster, ldry (in unit), linen reqd-fee], bbq, plygr, cots, non smoking units (1). D ♥♥ $45 - $100, ⓘ $5 - $10, W $245 - $770, 2 flats ★★★. Min book long w/ends, BC MC VI.

★★★☆ **Beachwalk Holiday Units**, (HU), Eastern Beach Rd, 3km E of PO, ☎ 03 5155 1414, 3 units acc up to 2, (1 bedrm), [shwr, tlt, fan, heat, elec blkts, TV, video, clock radio, refrig, cook fac, micro, toaster, ldry (in unit), blkts, linen, pillows], bbq, cots. D $50 - $90, W $300 - $690, Min book school holidays and Easter, Min book long w/ends.

★★★☆ **Emmanuel Holiday Apartments**, (HF), 90 Marine Pde, 450m W of PO, ☎ 03 5155 2600, fax 03 5155 2401, (2 stry gr fl), 8 flats acc up to 7, (2 bedrm), [shwr, bath, tlt, hairdry, a/c, heat, elec blkts, tel, TV, video, clock radio, t/c mkg, refrig, cook fac, micro, toaster, ldry (in unit), blkts, linen, pillows], w/mach, dryer, iron, iron brd, pool-heated (solar), spa, bbq, cots. D ♥♥ $114 - $216, ⓘ $10, W $475 - $1,351, Min book all holiday times, AE BC DC MC VI.

★★★☆ **Heyfield Motel Flats**, (HF), 115 Esplanade (Princes Hwy), 550m W of PO, ☎ 03 5155 1711, fax 03 5155 4054, 13 flats acc up to 6, (1 & 2 bedrm), [shwr, tlt, heat, elec blkts, TV, video-fee, clock radio, refrig, cook fac (9), cook fac ltd (4), micro, toaster, blkts, linen, pillows], ldry, bbq, c/park (carport) (4), plygr, cots. D ♯♯ $40 - $95, ◊ $7, W $270 - $780, 4 units ★★★. BC MC VI.

★★★☆ **Hybiscus Lodge**, (HF), 132 Marine Pde, 500m W of PO, ☎ 03 5155 1768, fax 03 5155 1768, 10 flats acc up to 5, (1 & 2 bedrm), [shwr, tlt, hairdry, c/fan, heat, elec blkts, TV, video, clock radio, t/c mkg, refrig, cook fac, micro, toaster, ldry (in unit), blkts, linen, pillows], w/mach, iron, iron brd, pool-heated (solar), sauna, boat park, plygr, jetty. D ♯♯ $55 - $135, W ♯♯ $340 - $1,050, Min book school holidays and Easter, BC MC VI.

★★★☆ **Lakes Jakaranda Holiday Flats**, (HF), 59 Church St, 1.1km E of PO, ☎ 03 5155 1511, 6 flats acc up to 5, (2 bedrm), [shwr, tlt, c/fan, heat, elec blkts, TV, clock radio, refrig, cook fac, micro, elec frypan, toaster, linen], w/mach, iron, iron brd, bbq, c/park (carport) (3), cots, non smoking units (2). D ♯♯ $55 - $121, ◊ $11, W $308 - $847, Min book all holiday times, BC MC VI.

★★★☆ **Ocean Bridge Quality Units**, (HF), 6 Roadknight St, ☎ 03 5155 2735, fax 03 5155 2735, 10 flats acc up to 6, (1 & 2 bedrm), [shwr, bath (hip) (8), tlt, fan, heat, elec blkts, TV, clock radio, refrig, cook fac, micro, elec frypan, toaster, ldry (in unit), blkts, linen, pillows], w/mach, iron, iron brd, pool-heated (solar), bbq, plygr. RO ♯♯ $55 - $170, ◊ $15 - $25, W $300 - $1,200, BC MC VI.

★★★☆ **Paradise Holiday Flats**, (HF), 89 Lake Bunga Beach Rd, 4.8km E of PO, ☎ 03 5155 2934, fax 03 5155 2938, (2 stry gr fl), 9 flats acc up to 6, (1 & 2 bedrm), [shwr, tlt, a/c (5), fan, heat, elec blkts, TV, video, clock radio, refrig, cook fac, micro, toaster, ldry (in unit) (3), blkts, doonas, linen, pillows], ldry, rec rm, pool-heated (solar), spa-fee, bbq, ✆, plygr, cots, non smoking units (2). D $60 - $150, W $250 - $950, 3 flats ★★★★. Min book all holiday times, AE BC DC JCB MC VI.

★★★★☆ **(Villa Unit Section)**, 2 apts acc up to 4, (2 bedrm), [shwr, tlt, hairdry, a/c, elec blkts, TV, video, clock radio, refrig, cook fac, micro, d/wash, toaster, ldry, blkts, linen, pillows], w/mach, dryer, iron, iron brd, lounge (TV, video,), spa, c/park (garage), secure park, non smoking units (1). D ♯♯ $125 - $200, W ♯♯ $500 - $1,200.

★★★☆ **Sandpiper Holiday Apartments**, (Apt), 15 Roadknight St, ☎ 03 5155 2323, fax 03 5155 4953, (2 stry gr fl), 8 apts acc up to 6, (Studio, 1, 2 & 3 bedrm), [shwr, bath (hip), tlt, hairdry, c/fan, heat, elec blkts, TV, video, clock radio, refrig, cook fac, micro, toaster, ldry (in unit), blkts, linen, pillows], w/mach, iron, iron brd, pool-heated (solar), spa (heated), bbq, bicycle, cots. D ♯♯ $60 - $110, ◊ $10 - $15, W $385 - $765, ◊ $105, ch con, Min book all holiday times, AE BC DC MC VI.

★★★☆ **Summer Dream Court**, (HU), Cnr Myer & Church Sts, 200m N of footbridge, ☎ 03 5155 1321, fax 03 5155 4665, 9 units acc up to 8, (1, 2 & 3 bedrm), [shwr, bath (hip) (3), tlt, hairdry, fan, heat, elec blkts, TV, video-fee, clock radio, refrig, cook fac, micro (4), toaster, blkts, linen (available) reqd-fee, pillows], ldry, w/mach-fee, dryer-fee, bbq, plygr, cots. D $45 - $150, W $290 - $1,050, BC MC VI.

★★★☆ **Town Centre Holiday Apartments**, (HU), 13 Orme St, 200m N of PO, ☎ 03 5155 2395, 3 units acc up to 5, (2 bedrm), [shwr, tlt, hairdry, a/c, elec blkts, TV, video-fee, clock radio, t/c mkg, refrig, cook fac, micro, elec frypan, toaster, ldry (in unit), blkts, linen, pillows], w/mach, iron, iron brd, bbq, plygr, cots. D $48 - $115, W $300 - $770, BC MC VI.

★★★ **Beaches Family Holiday Units**, (HF), 671 Esplanade (Princes Hwy), 1.8km E of PO, ☎ 03 5155 1274, fax 03 5155 1408, 14 flats acc up to 7, (1, 2 & 3 bedrm), [shwr, bath (hip) (4), tlt, hairdry, fan, heat, elec blkts, tel, TV, video (5), clock radio, refrig, cook fac, micro (10), toaster, blkts, linen, pillows], ldry, pool-heated (solar, salt water), spa, bbq, plygr, cots (2), non smoking units (5). D $40 - $137.50, W $200 - $950, 4 units ★★★☆. BC MC VI

Operator Comment: "Fully Self Contained Units at Cabin Prices". www.lakes-entrance.com/beaches

★★★ **Bellbrae Cottages**, (Cotg), 161 Ostlers Rd, 5.5km NE of PO, continuation of Myer St, ☎ 03 5155 2319, fax 03 5155 2207, 12 cotgs acc up to 8, (1 bedrm), [shwr, tlt, heat, elec blkts, TV, movie, radio, refrig, cook fac, micro, toaster, linen reqd-fee], ldry, rec rm, pool-heated (solar), bbq (covered), golf (9 hole), tennis, cots. D $63.50 - $89, W $404 - $606, BC MC VI.

★★★ **Bonito Flats**, (HF), 36 Carpenter St, 500m N of footbridge, ☎ 03 5156 5550, 3 flats acc up to 5, (2 bedrm), [shwr, tlt, heat, TV, clock radio, refrig, cook fac, micro, elec frypan, toaster, ldry (in unit), linen reqd-fee], bbq, cots, non smoking property. D $50 - $100, W $275 - $650.

★★★ **Conifer Court Holiday Units**, (HU), 42 Myer St, 1.3km E of PO, ☎ 03 5155 1791, 9 units acc up to 5, (1 & 2 bedrm), [shwr, tlt, a/c, fan, elec blkts, TV, clock radio, refrig, cook fac, micro, elec frypan, toaster, linen reqd-fee], ldry, pool-heated (solar), spa-fee, bbq (covered), plygr, cots. D ♯♯ $55 - $110, ◊ $11, W $352 - $924, Min book Christmas Jan and Easter.

Before you travel

Before a trip have your vehicle serviced and checked over to ensure reliable motoring. There are some checks you can make yourself, generally the procedure can be found in the vehicle owners manual.

★★★ **Kalimna Woods**, (Cotg), Kalimna Jetty Rd, 1.8km W of PO, ☎ 03 5155 1957, fax 03 5155 1957, 8 cotgs acc up to 4, (1 & 2 bedrm), [shwr, spa bath (4), tlt, hairdry, a/c-cool (4), fan, fire pl (5), heat, elec blkts, TV, video, clock radio, CD, t/c mkg, refrig, cook fac (5), cook fac ltd (3), micro, elec frypan, toaster, blkts, doonas, linen, pillows], ldry, w/mach, dryer, bbq, non smoking units (5). **D** $70 - $210, **W** $300 - $1,470, Breakfast available, BC MC VI.

★★★ **Killara Holiday Flats**, (HF), 23 Princes Hwy, 2.6km E of PO, ☎ 03 5155 1220, 5 flats acc up to 6, (2 bedrm), [shwr, tlt, a/c, elec blkts, TV, clock radio, refrig, cook fac, micro, elec frypan, toaster, linen reqd-fee], ldry, w/mach, dryer-fee, bbq, plygr, cots, non smoking units. **D** $50 - $120, **W** $210 - $820, Min book Christmas Jan long w/ends and Easter.

★★★ **Lakes Entrance Sea Vista Flats**, (HU), 54 Merrangbauer Rd, 3.6km E of PO, ☎ 03 5155 1495, fax 03 5155 1495, 2 units acc up to 7, (2 bedrm), [shwr, tlt, heat, elec blkts, TV, clock radio, refrig, cook fac, micro, toaster, linen reqd-fee], ldry-fee, w/mach, dryer, pool-heated (solar), bbq (covered), c/park (carport), plygr, cots. **D ♦♦** $50 - $100, **W ♦♦** $300 - $840, Min book all holiday times.

★★★ **Roma Holiday Units**, (HU), 280 Marine Pde, ☎ 03 5155 1897, 2 units acc up to 5, (2 bedrm), [shwr, tlt, c/fan, heat, elec blkts, TV, video, clock radio, refrig, cook fac, micro, toaster, ldry (in unit), blkts, linen, pillows], w/mach, iron, iron brd, bbq, plygr. **W** $250 - $600.

★★☆ **El Torito Flats & Caravan Park**, (HF), 35 Church St, 900m E of PO, ☎ 03 5155 1606, fax 03 5155 2100, 12 flats acc up to 8, (1, 2 & 3 bedrm), [shwr, tlt, a/c (8), heat, elec blkts, TV, clock radio (8), refrig, cook fac, micro (8), toaster, linen reqd-fee], pool. **D** $45 - $205, **W** $270 - $1,435, 5 flats ★★★.

B&B's/Guest Houses

★★★★☆ **Deja-Vu Lakes Entrance Bed & Breakfast**, (B&B), No facilities for children under 16. 17 Clara St, ☎ 03 5155 4330, fax 03 5155 3718, (Multi-stry), 6 rms [ensuite, spa bath, hairdry, heat, elec blkts, TV, clock radio, t/c mkg, refrig], lounge (TV, cd), bbq, non smoking property. **BB ♦** $105, **♦♦** $160 - $210, AE BC DC VI.

★★★★☆ **Lou's B & B**, (B&B), 37 Esplanade (Princes Hwy), 700m W of PO, ☎ 03 5155 2732, fax 03 5155 2746, 1 rm [shwr, tlt, hairdry, a/c, elec blkts, TV, video, clock radio, CD, t/c mkg, refrig, micro, doonas], c/park (garage), non smoking rms, Pets on application. **BB ♦** $65 - $110, **♦♦** $85 - $130, AE BC DC MC VI.

Operator Comment: EXTREMELY COMFORTABLE and WELL APPOINTED. FRIENDLY DOGS WELCOME.

★★★★☆ **(Holiday Unit Section)**, 1 unit acc up to 3, (1 bedrm), [shwr, bath, tlt, hairdry, a/c, elec blkts, TV, video, clock radio, CD, refrig, cook fac ltd, micro, elec frypan, toaster, blkts, doonas, linen, pillows], w/mach, dryer, iron, iron brd, non smoking units, Pets on application. **BB ♦** $65 - $110, **♦♦** $85 - $130.

★★★★☆ **The Gables Bed and Breakfast**, (B&B), No facilities for children under 15. 1 Creighton St, ☎ 03 5155 2699, fax 03 5155 2559, (2 stry), 3 rms [ensuite, hairdry, a/c, elec blkts], rec rm, lounge (TV, Video, CD player), lounge firepl, pool, spa, t/c mkg shared, bbq, gym, non smoking property. **BB ♦** $115, **♦♦** $145, BC MC VI.

★★★★ **Goldsmith's in the Forest**, (B&B), No children's facilities, Harrisons Tk, 10km N of PO, ☎ 03 5155 2518, 4 rms [ensuite, a/c-cool (4), c/fan, heat, elec blkts, clock radio, t/c mkg (communal), refrig (communal)], lounge (cd player), lounge firepl, non smoking property. **BB ♦** $95, **♦♦** $130, Dinner by arrangement.

Other Accommodation

Fraser Island Resort, (Lodge), 3km W of Lakes Entrance on Gippsland Lakes, ☎ 03 5156 3256, fax 03 5156 3344, 11 rms acc up to 6, [ensuite (2), elec blkts, blkts, linen, pillows], ldry, rec rm, lounge (TV, video, cd player), conf fac, lounge firepl, pool, cook fac, t/c mkg shared, bbq, plygr, canoeing-fee, golf, tennis. **D ♦ $48 - $135, ◊ $48 - $135**, Minimum 4 adults - maximum 38 persons. Meals by arrangement. Transport from Lakes Entrance included. AE BC DC MC VI.

Lakes Main Caravan Park, (Lodge), 7 Willis St, 2.4km E of PO, ☎ 03 5155 2365, 7 rms [shwr (3G-3L), tlt (3G-3L), a/c-cool, heat], ldry, lounge (TV), cook fac, refrig, bbq, kiosk, ☏. **D ♦ $11 - $22**, BC MC VI.

Riviera Backpackers, (Lodge), 3 Clarkes Rd, 3km E of PO, ☎ 03 5155 2444, fax 03 5155 4558, 17 rms [heat, blkts, linen, pillows], ldry, rec rm, read rm, lounge (TV), pool, cook fac, refrig, bbq, kiosk, ☏. **D ♦ $17 - $21, ◊ $17 - $21**, AE BC DC MC VI.

LANCEFIELD VIC 3435

Pop 1,150. (66km N Melbourne), See map on page 696, ref B4. Agricultural township. Bush Walking, Scenic Drives.

Hotels/Motels

★★★☆ **Centrevic Motor Inn**, (M), 50 Main Rd, 800m SE of PO, ☎ 03 5429 1777, fax 03 5429 1533, 20 units [shwr, bath (1), tlt, hairdry, a/c-cool, elec blkts, tel, TV, video-fee, clock radio, t/c mkg, refrig, mini bar], iron, iron brd, conf fac, ☒, pool, sauna, spa, bbq, rm serv, dinner to unit, tennis, cots. **RO ♦♦ $72 - $93, ◊ $15**, ch con, AE BC DC EFT MC VI, ♿.

Self Catering Accommodation

★★★★☆ **Parkside at Lancefield Country Cottage**, (Cotg), 308 Parks Rd, 4km SW of PO, ☎ 03 5429 1787, fax 03 5429 1787, 1 cotg acc up to 4, (2 bedrm), [shwr, spa bath, tlt, hairdry, fan, elec blkts, video, clock radio, refrig, cook fac, micro, toaster, ldry, blkts, linen, pillows], iron, iron brd, lounge firepl, bbq, breakfast ingredients, non smoking property. **BB ♦♦ $160, ◊ $90**, Min book applies.

B&B's/Guest Houses

★★★★☆ **Glen Erin Vineyard Retreat**, (GH), Roachford Rd, 4km W of PO, ☎ 03 5429 1041, fax 03 5429 2053, 24 rms [shwr, bath, spa bath (4), tlt, hairdry, a/c, cent heat, elec blkts, tel, TV, video (avail) (3), clock radio, t/c mkg, mini bar, doonas], iron, iron brd, rec rm, lounge, conf fac, ☒, pool-heated (salt water/solar), spa (heated), bbq, rm serv (licensed), plygr, gym, tennis, cots, non smoking property. **BB ♦♦ $253 - $306**, ch con, AE BC DC EFT JCB MC VI.

★★★★ **Fairways**, (GH), 55 Golfhouse La, 3.9km N of PO, ☎ 03 5429 1903, 6 rms [shwr, tlt, a/c (2), c/fan, heat, elec blkts, doonas], lounge (TV, video, stereo), lounge firepl, ☒ (Fri to Sun), pool-heated, spa, cook fac, t/c mkg shared, c/park (carport) (4). **BB ♦♦ $120 - $150**, Other meals by arrangement. AE MC VI.

LARA VIC 3212

Pop 7,350. (60km SW Melbourne), See map on page 696, ref A6. Farming community, situated at the foot of the You Yangs. Bush Walking, Scenic Drives.

B&B's/Guest Houses

★★★★☆ **Laras Bed & Breakfast Penny Royal**, (B&B), 25 West Gateway, ☎ 03 5282 2813, fax 03 5282 2578, (2 stry gr fl), 2 rms [shwr, tlt, hairdry, a/c-cool (1), c/fan (1), heat, TV, video, clock radio, t/c mkg, refrig, micro, toaster], lounge (TV, CD player), pool (salt water), bbq, plygr, gym (1), cots. **BB ♦ $110, ♦♦ $143, ◊ $22**, AE BC EFT MC VI.

LAUNCHING PLACE VIC 3139

Pop 1,550. Part of Yarra Ranges, (65km E Melbourne), See map on page 696, ref D5. Dairying district, located on the Warburton Hwy. Logs were floated from here to the sawmills downstream, hence the name Launching Place. Bush Walking, Fishing, Horse Riding, Scenic Drives, Swimming (River), Tennis.

Self Catering Accommodation

★★★★ **Hill N Dale Farm Cottage**, (Cotg), 1284 Don Rd, 8.5km N of Warburton Hwy, ☎ 03 5967 3361, fax 03 5967 3408, 4 cotgs acc up to 6, (1 & 2 bedrm), [shwr, spa bath, tlt, hairdry, a/c-cool, heat (wood), elec blkts, TV, video, clock radio, CD, t/c mkg, refrig, cook fac, micro, toaster, ldry (in unit) (3), blkts, linen, pillows], w/mach, dryer, lounge firepl, bbq, plygr, breakfast ingredients. **BB ♦♦ $154, ◊ $22**, ch con, BC MC VI.

Operator Comment: Close to Yarra Valley wineries, Pets welcome. Web -: www.aussieholidays.com/hill

LAVERS HILL VIC 3238

Pop 251. (235km SW Melbourne), See map on pages 694/695, ref C8. Centre of a dairy farming, timber and potato growing district. Bush Walking, Fishing, Scenic Drives.

Hotels/Motels

★★★☆ **Otway Junction Motor Inn**, (M), 4730 Great Ocean Rd, at the junction of Beech Forest Rd, ☎ 03 5237 3295, fax 03 5237 3273, 8 units [shwr, tlt, a/c-cool, cent heat, elec blkts, tel (direct dial), TV, clock radio, t/c mkg, refrig], ☒, c/park (undercover), cots. **RO ♦ $77 - $110, ♦♦ $88 - $121, ◊ $11**, AE BC EFT MC VI.

B&B's/Guest Houses

★★★★ **Melba Gully Cottage Flower Farm**, (B&B), Previously Cottage Flower Farm, 20 Melba Gully Rd, 3 km W of PO, ☎ 03 5237 3208, fax 03 5237 3208, (2 stry), 2 rms [ensuite, c/fan], lounge (TV, video, CD player), lounge firepl, t/c mkg shared, non smoking rms, Pets on application. **BB ♦ $70 - $90, ♦♦ $90 - $150**, BC MC VI.

LEONGATHA VIC 3953

Pop 4,150. (134km SE Melbourne), See map on page 696, ref D7. Dairy farming area. Bowls, Croquet, Golf, Horse Riding, Scenic Drives, Squash, Swimming (Pool), Tennis.

Hotels/Motels

★★★ **Leongatha Motel**, (M), 18 Turner St, 300m N of PO, ☎ 03 5662 2375, fax 03 5662 4479, 28 units [shwr, tlt, cent heat, elec blkts, tel, TV, video-fee, clock radio, t/c mkg, refrig], ldry, conf fac, cots-fee. **RO ♦ $52 - $65, ♦♦ $62 - $80, ◊ $12**, AE BC DC EFT MC VI.

★★★ **Opal Motel**, (M), South Gippsland Hwy, 1.6km S of PO, ☎ 03 5662 2321, fax 03 5662 2501, 13 units [shwr, tlt, heat, elec blkts, tel, TV, clock radio, t/c mkg, refrig], bbq, dinner to unit (Mon to Thurs), plygr, cots-fee. **RO ♦ $55 - $65, ♦♦ $66 - $75, ◊ $15**, ch con, AE BC DC MC MCH VI.

Self Catering Accommodation

★★★ **Araucaria Cottages**, (Cotg), (Farm), 167 South Gippsland Hwy, ☎ 03 5662 3205, fax 03 5662 3205, 3 cotgs acc up to 5, (2 bedrm), [shwr, tlt, heat (gas), elec blkts, TV, refrig, cook fac, micro, toaster, blkts, linen, pillows], w/mach, lounge firepl (1), bbq (covered), cots, non smoking property. **D ♦ $70, ♦♦ $90, ◊ $20, W $350**, ch con, Cotg No. 3 ★★★☆. Min book Christmas Jan long w/ends and Easter.

B&B's/Guest Houses

★★★★ **Clair De Lune Vineyard**, (B&B), Closed Mon & Thurs, No children's facilities, Lot 1 Sth Gippsland Hwy, Kardella South 3950, 7km SE of Korumburra, ☎ 03 5655 1032, 2 rms [ensuite, c/fan, heat, elec blkts, TV, clock radio, t/c mkg], iron-fee, iron brd, lounge, bbq, non smoking property. **BB ♦♦ $90**.

★★★★ **Moondani House - Bushland Retreat**, (B&B), 535 Rougheads Rd, Leongatha South 3825, ☎ 03 5664 3259, fax 03 5664 3259, (2 stry), 1 rm (1 suite) [shwr, tlt, a/c, TV, video, clock radio, t/c mkg, refrig, micro, toaster], bbq, tennis. **BB ♦♦ $95, ◊ $15**, ch con, BC MC VI.

★★★☆ **El Jaradeno**, (B&B), 3 Johnson St, 1km S of PO, ☎ 03 5662 2647, fax 03 5662 5888, (2 stry), 3 rms [hairdry, heat, elec blkts, clock radio, refrig, micro], rec rm, lounge (TV, video), conf fac, res liquor license, bar, t/c mkg shared, bbq, c/park (undercover), non smoking property. **BB ♦ $55, ♦♦ $96, ◊ $48**.

★★★☆ **Kardella Classic Carriages**, (GH), 15 Barnes Rd, Kardella South 3950, 6km W of PO, ☎ 03 5662 2107, 2 rms [shwr, tlt, hairdry, heat, clock radio, t/c mkg, refrig, micro, elec frypan, toaster, ldry], iron, lounge (TV, video), bbq. **BB ♦ $55 - $65, ♦♦ $65 - $80**, ch con.

LETHBRIDGE VIC 3332

Pop 400. (99km SW Melbourne), See map on page 696, ref A5. Pastoral town. Scenic Drives, Tennis, Vineyards, Wineries.

Other Accommodation

Moranghurk Farm Accommodation, (Lodge), Classified by National Trust, (Farm), Midland Hwy, 4.7km N of School, ☎ 03 5331 4899, fax 03 5333 2083, 11 rms acc up to 8, (Bunk Rooms), [blkts reqd, linen reqd], lounge, cook fac, refrig, bbq. **D ♦ $12.50 - $20, ◊ $12.50 - $20**, ch con, Minimum booking - 15 people, ♿.

★★★★★ Trouble-free travel tips - Lights

Check the operation of all lights. If you are pulling a trailer of caravan make sure turning indicators and brake lights are working.

LICOLA VIC 3858

Pop Nominal, (256km E Melbourne), See map on pages 694/695, ref G6. Old timber town, now owned by the Lions Club of Victoria, used as a holiday camp for children. Bush Walking, Fishing, Horse Riding, Scenic Drives, Shooting, Swimming (River).

Other Accommodation

Camp Welcola, (Lodge), Situated within the Alpine National Park. Self catering group accommodation. Tamboritha Rd, 11km N of PO, ☎ 03 5176 2240, fax 03 5174 7126, 16 rms acc up to 52, (Bunk Rooms), [blkts reqd, linen reqd, pillows reqd], shwr (3G-4L), tlt (3G-4L), rec rm, cook fac, refrig, bbq, National Park regulations prohibit all pets & firearms. **D ╫ $11, ╻ $11**, ch con, Generated power only. Minimum booking - 10 people.

LINTON VIC 3360

Pop 400. (168km W Melbourne), See map on pages 694/695, ref D6. Small farming township on Springdallah Creek. Bowls, Tennis.

Self Catering Accommodation

★★★☆ Sundew Country Cabins, Pittong Rd, 6km NW of PO, ☎ 03 5368 1969, fax 03 5368 2033, 2 cabins acc up to 2, (1 bedrm), [shwr, tlt, hairdry, a/c-cool, heat, elec blkts, video, clock radio, CD, refrig, cook fac, micro, toaster, blkts, linen, pillows], iron, iron brd, spa (heated), bbq, breakfast ingredients. **BB ╫ $190.**

LOCH VIC 3945

Pop 200. (102km SE Melbourne), See map on page 696, ref D7. Dairy farming area. Bowls, Tennis.

B&B's/Guest Houses

★★★★ Tallwood Lodge, (GH), No children's facilities, Henrys Rd, off South Gippsland Hwy, 5km W of PO, ☎ 03 5659 6336, fax 03 5659 6336, 4 rms [ensuite, c/fan, heat, elec blkts, clock radio, t/c mkg], lounge (TV, stereo), conf fac, refrig, bbq, non smoking property. **BB ╻ $50 - $60, ╫ $100 - $120**, Dinner by arrangement.

LOCH SPORT VIC 3851

Pop 800. (272km E Melbourne), See map on pages 694/695, ref H7. Small coastal holiday town. Gippsland Lakes Coastal Park. Boat Ramp, Boating, Bowls, Bush Walking, Fishing (Lake, Surf), Golf, Sailing, Scenic Drives, Swimming, Tennis, Water Skiing, Wind Surfing.

Hotels/Motels

★★ Loch-Sport Motel, (M), National Park Rd, 2.4km E of PO, ☎ 03 5146 0488, 13 units [shwr, tlt, a/c, elec blkts, TV, t/c mkg, refrig, cook fac (4), toaster (4)], ldry, ⊠, bbq, dinner to unit, ╲, cots. **RO ╻ $50, ╫ $75, ╻ $10**, ch con, Min book Christmas Jan and Easter, BC MC VI.

Self Catering Accommodation

★★★ Marina Beach Accommodation, (Cotg), Victoria St, 250m E of Marina, ☎ 03 5146 0243, fax 03 5146 0243, (2 stry gr fl), 4 cotgs acc up to 6, (3 bedrm), [shwr, tlt, heat, TV, clock radio, CD, refrig, cook fac ltd, micro, toaster, blkts, doonas, linen, pillows], bbq, c/park (carport). **D ╫╫╫╫ $82 - $104, ╻ $13**, ch con, BC EFT MC VI.

LONGWOOD VIC 3665

Pop 250. (140km N Melbourne), See map on page 696, ref D3. Agricultural township in pastoral district on Nine Mile Creek. Golf, Squash, Tennis.

Self Catering Accommodation

★★★★ Stringybarks, (Cotg), Ruffy Rd, 8km SE of PO, ☎ 03 5798 5544, 1 cotg acc up to 6, (3 bedrm), [ensuite (3), shwr, tlt, hairdry, evap cool, c/fan, heat, elec blkts, tel, TV, video, clock radio, CD, t/c mkg, refrig, cook fac, micro, elec frypan, toaster, blkts, doonas, linen, pillows], iron, iron brd, bbq, breakfast ingredients. **BB ╫ $80 - $170, ╻ $40**, BC DC MC VI.

★★★ Maygars Cottage, (Cotg), Longwood-Mansfield Rd, 1.5km E of Hume Fwy, ☎ 03 5798 5417, (2 stry gr fl), 1 cotg acc up to 6, (3 bedrm), [shwr, tlt, evap cool, heat (wood), TV, clock radio, t/c mkg, refrig, cook fac, blkts, doonas, linen, pillows], bbq. **D ╫ $105, ╻ $18**, Breakfast available. BC MC VI.

LORNE VIC 3232

Pop 1,100. (140km SW Melbourne), See map on pages 694/695, ref D7. Popular tourist resort on the Great Ocean Road. Lorne State Park is 3,700 ha of Otway Ranges, the forest contains several rivers, waterfalls & gorges, many species of animals & birds can be seen in the fern gullies. Bowls, Fishing, Golf, Scenic Drives, Surfing, Swimming, Tennis.

Hotels/Motels

★★★★ Lorne Coachman Inn, (M), 1 Deans Marsh Rd, 700m N of PO, ☎ 03 5289 2244, fax 03 5289 2475, (Multi-stry gr fl), 19 units [shwr, spa bath (4), tlt, a/c, heat, tel, TV, video-fee, t/c mkg, refrig, mini bar, micro, toaster], ldry, iron, iron brd, bbq, c/park (undercover) (12), non smoking units (8). **RO ╻ $75 - $160, ╫ $85 - $160, ╻ $10 - $15**, AE BC DC EFT JCB MC MP VI, ╱&.

★★★★ Lorne Main Beach Motor Inn, (M), 3 Bay St, ☎ 03 5289 1199, fax 03 5289 1690, (2 stry gr fl), 34 units [shwr, spa bath, tlt, hairdry, a/c, heat, tel, TV, video, clock radio, t/c mkg, refrig, mini bar, cook fac ltd, micro, toaster], ldry, conf fac, bar (cocktail), cots-fee, non smoking units (12). **RO ╫ $125 - $265, ╻ $20**, Min book Christmas Jan long w/ends and Easter, AE BC DC JCB MC MP VI, ╱&.

★★★☆ Sandridge Motel, (M), 128 Mountjoy Pde (Great Ocean Rd), 150m W of PO, ☎ 03 5289 2180, fax 03 5289 2722, (2 stry gr fl), 21 units [shwr, bath (hip) (4), tlt, hairdry, a/c, elec blkts, tel, TV, video, movie, clock radio, t/c mkg, refrig, toaster], ldry, cots, non smoking units (15). **RO ╻ $75 - $185, ╫ $75 - $185, ╻ $15**, 5 units ★★★★, AE BC DC EFT MC VI.

★★★ Anchorage Motel, (M), 32 Mountjoy Pde (Great Ocean Rd), 500m N of PO, ☎ 03 5289 1891, fax 03 5289 1891, (2 stry gr fl), 10 units [shwr, tlt, a/c, heat, elec blkts, tel, TV, clock radio, t/c mkg, refrig, cook fac], ldry, pool, spa, bbq, cots-fee. **RO ╻ $65 - $140, ╫ $75 - $140, ╻ $10**, ch con, Min book Christmas Jan long w/ends and Easter, AE BC DC MC VI.

★★★★ (Villa Section), (2 stry), 4 units acc up to 4, (2 bedrm), [shwr, spa bath (2), tlt, a/c, elec blkts, tel, TV, video, cook fac, micro, d/wash, ldry, blkts, linen, pillows]. **D $90 - $255, W $580 - $1,870**, Min book Christmas Jan long w/ends and Easter.

★★★ Ocean Lodge Motel, (M), 6 Armytage St, 1km S of PO, ☎ 03 5289 1330, fax 03 5289 1380, 12 units [shwr, tlt, hairdry, fan, heat, elec blkts, TV, clock radio, t/c mkg, refrig, micro, toaster], ldry, lounge, bbq (covered)-fee, ╲, tennis, cots-fee, non smoking units (12). **RO ╻ $75 - $120, ╫ $85 - $130, ╻ $10**, ch con, Breakfast not available. BC EFT MC VI.

★★★☆ (Apartment Section), 6 apts acc up to 4, (1 & 2 bedrm - split level), [shwr, tlt, hairdry, a/c, c/fan, TV, clock radio, t/c mkg, refrig, cook fac ltd, micro, d/wash, toaster, blkts, doonas, linen, pillows], ldry, iron, iron brd, c/park (carport), non smoking units (6). **D $110 - $210.**

★★ Lorne Hotel, (LH), 176 Mountjoy Pde (Great Ocean Rd), 750m S of PO, ☎ 03 5289 1409, fax 03 5289 2200, (2 stry), 19 rms [shwr, tlt, c/fan, heat, elec blkts, TV, t/c mkg, refrig, toaster], conf fac, night club (Summer only), ⊠, ╲, cots-fee. **RO $90 - $150**, AE BC DC EFT MC VI.

★★★ (Holiday Units Section), 4 units acc up to 6, (2 bedrm), [shwr, tlt, heat, elec blkts, TV, t/c mkg, refrig, cook fac, micro, toaster, ldry (in unit), blkts, doonas, linen, pillows], w/mach, dryer, iron. **D ╫ $160 - $190.**

Rates may change. Check before booking.

The Sandridge Lorne

ROOMS WITH A VIEW

Sandridge Motel is located in the heart of Lorne on the ocean front.

With fantastic ocean views, private balconies and all the requirements to make your stay a memorable one.

Suit your needs and budget with a choice of very comfortable Standard, Executive and Deluxe rooms.

Sandridge Motel
is the perfect holiday destination or travelling stop over

'Deluxe Rooms' shown on two bedroom Photos

Corner Mountjoy Parade and William Street, Lorne.
ph: 03 5289 2180 fax: 03 5289 2722
email: enquiries@sandridgemotel.com.au
website: www.sandridgemotel.com.au

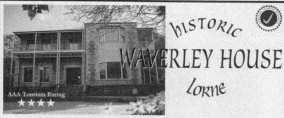

hIstoric WAVERLEY HOUSE Lorne

AAA Tourism Rating ★★★★

• Newly renovated historic home
• Exclusive, well appointed self-contained studio apartments
• Magnificent old-world character and charm
• Ideal central location near beaches, river, shops & restaurants
• Spas available

CNR GREAT OCEAN ROAD & WAVERLEY AVE, LORNE
ENQUIRIES: PHONE (03) 5289 2044
POSTAL: WAVERLEY HOUSE, PO BOX 60, LORNE 3232

GREAT OCEAN ROAD COTTAGES
LORNE

AAA Tourism Rating ★★★☆

• Highly rated, superb self-contained, air-conditioned cottages.
• Central Lorne, with views.
• Near beaches, bushwalking, shops, restaurants, etc.
• Peaceful bush setting

10 Erskine Ave., Lorne.
Ph: (03) 5289 1070
Mail: PO Box 60, Lorne, 3232
Special Midweek Rates - Low Season

Backpackers' budget accommodation also available.

ANCHORAGE MOTEL & VILLAS

MOTEL-Comfortable self contained, air conditioned units, Pool, Heated Spa, BBQ in quiet garden setting.
VILLAS-2 b/r with ocean views, full kitchens, air conditioned, private balconies, laundry, all linen supplied, spas available.

LORNE OCEAN SUN APARTMENTS

New 2/3 bedroom fully self contained apartments with air conditioning, private balconies, spa, lock-up garages, ocean views, 2 bathrooms, laundry. 100metres to shops, beach, restaurants. All linen supplied. All you want to see & do is right outside your door!

ALL ENQUIRIES PHONE: 03 52 891 891   FAX: 03 52 892 988

Self Catering Accommodation

★★★★☆ **Cumberland Lorne Resort**, (Apt), 150 Mountjoy Pde (Great Ocean Rd), 100m S of PO, ☎ 03 5289 2400, fax 03 5289 2256, 99 apts acc up to 6, (1 & 2 bedrm), [ensuite (12), shwr, spa bath, tlt, hairdry, heat, elec blkts, tel, TV, movie, clock radio, refrig, cook fac, micro, d/wash, toaster, ldry (in unit), blkts, linen, pillows], iron, rec rm, conf fac, ✉, pool indoor heated, sauna, spa, rm serv, meals to unit, c/park (undercover), gym, squash, tennis, cots. **D $210 - $395**, AE BC DC EFT MC VI.

★★★★ **Allenvale Farm Cottages**, (Cotg), 150 Allenvale Rd, Allenvale 3232, 2km SW of PO, ☎ 03 5289 1450, fax 03 5289 1450, 5 cotgs acc up to 5, (2 & 3 bedrm), [shwr, bath (hip) (1), tlt, fan, heat (wood & gas), elec blkts, TV, video, clock radio, refrig, cook fac, toaster, blkts, doonas, linen, pillows], ldry, bbq, cots. **D $99 - $220, W $660 - $1,500**, Min book Christmas Jan and Easter, BC DC MC VI.

ALLENVALE COTTAGES LORNE

One of the great Ocean Road's most delightful secrets, these award winning 2 & 3 bedr'm cottages are found in a tranquil garden setting beside the beautiful St. George River in the Otways.
Wildlife, waterfalls and bushwalks right at your doorstep with magnificent beaches and all Lorne offers just three minutes away.
Golf, restaurants, fishing and simple pleasures. Historic Allenvale. With log fires, BBQ, linen and breakfast hampers provided.
Special midweek rates during low season.

FOR INFORMATION & BOOKINGS CALL 03 5289 1450

Lemonade Creek Cottages
LORNE

A ★
A ★
A ★
T ★

Nestled on 44 acres, surrounded by gardens, wildlife and temperate rainforest in Lorne's Angahook State Park. Secluded, yet a mere 7 minutes to beaches, shops, restaurants and the Great Ocean Road.

Just the thing for guests seeking peace and quiet or for romancing couples looking for that somewhere special. You will feel you've stepped back in time, relaxing in your own century old farm house, with high ceilings, Victorian open fire and welcoming verandahs, yet with the conveniences of a fully equipped kitchen, bathroom, central heating, air-conditioning, TV and VCR. Tennis and basketball court. Also Double spas, heated pool. Three Cottages 4.5 stars

Some guests choose to sit back and soak up the scenic charms, while others choose to walk from their cottage to the beautiful Erskine Falls, then take a streamside walk along the Erskine River into Lorne itself, past fern fringed pools, rocky gorges, thick fern groves and rippling water courses.

Easy day trips from your cottage, include the Twelve Apostles and Ballarat's Sovereign Hill.

Our guests continue to praise Lemonade Creek Cottages, by judging them the finest cottages available. With this in mind we offer a money back guarantee, if on arrival your expectations are not met. (All linen provided).

690 Erskine Falls Road, Lorne, Victoria 3232.
Telephone: (03) 5289 2600

Lorne Bush House Cottages

The newly built Bush House cottages offer a delightful blend of bush and sea.

Just 5 minutes from the cafés, boutiques and surfing beaches of Lorne, the 5 two-storey self-contained cottages offer peace and privacy on 43 acres of natural bush.

Perfect for a romantic getaway with double spa, wood fire, expansive deck and private BBQ or just a bit of peace to relax and unwind.

AAA TOURISM ★★★★
Telephone: (03) 5289 2477
Web: www.greatoceanrd.org.au/lornebushcott

★★★★ **Lemonade Creek Cottages Lorne**, (Cotg), 690 Erskine Falls Rd, 6.7km NW of PO, ☎ 03 5289 2600, fax 03 5289 2600, 6 cotgs acc up to 5, (1 & 2 bedrm), [shwr, bath (hip) (3), tlt, hairdry, a/c-cool, cent heat, TV, video, clock radio, refrig, cook fac, toaster, doonas, linen, pillows], ldry, lounge firepl, pool-heated, bbq, tennis, cots, non smoking property. **D** $110 - $245, 3 cottages ★★★★☆. BC MC VI.

★★★★ **Lorne Bush House Cottages**, (Cotg), 1860 Deans Marsh Rd, 5km N of PO, ☎ 03 5289 2477, fax 03 5289 1992, (2 stry gr fl), 5 cotgs acc up to 5, (2 bedrm), [shwr, spa bath, tlt, hairdry, a/c, c/fan, heat (wood), elec blkts, TV, video, clock radio, CD (avail), refrig, cook fac, micro, toaster, blkts, linen, pillows], ldry, w/mach, dryer, bbq, plygr, cots. **D** ♦♦ $140 - $220, 👤 $25 - $35, **W** $960 - $1,600, ch con, Min book all holiday times, BC EFT MC VI.

★★★★ **Lorne Ocean Sun Apartments**, (Apt), 14 Smith St, 500m N of PO, ☎ 03 5289 1891, fax 03 5289 2988, (2 stry), 6 apts acc up to 6, (2 & 3 bedrm), [ensuite, shwr, spa bath, tlt, a/c, elec blkts, TV, video, clock radio, t/c mkg, refrig, cook fac, micro, d/wash, toaster, ldry, blkts, doonas, linen, pillows], w/mach, dryer, iron, iron brd, c/park (garage), cots-fee. **D** ♦♦ $90 - $300, **W** ♦♦ $600 - $2,100, Min book Christmas Jan long w/ends and Easter, AE BC DC EFT MC VI.

★★★★ **Waverley House**, (Apt), Cnr Waverley Ave & Great Ocean Rd, 700m N of PO, ☎ 03 5289 2044, fax 03 5289 2508, (2 stry gr fl), 7 apts acc up to 5, (Studio & 2 bedrm), [shwr, spa bath (5), tlt, hairdry, fan, heat, elec blkts, TV, video, clock radio, CD, t/c mkg, refrig, cook fac ltd, micro, elec frypan, toaster, blkts, linen, pillows], ldry, w/mach, dryer, bbq, cots, breakfast ingredients, non smoking units. **BB** ♦♦ $110 - $220, $215 - $300, AE BC DC MC VI.

★★★☆ **Erskine Falls Cottages**, (Cotg), Cora-Lynn Crt, off Erskine Falls Rd, 4.3km NW of PO, ☎ 03 5289 2666, fax 03 5289 2247, 8 cotgs acc up to 7, (2 & 3 bedrm), [shwr, tlt, a/c-cool, c/fan, heat (wood fire), elec blkts, TV, clock radio, refrig, cook fac, micro, d/wash (1), toaster, ldry (in unit) (1), blkts, linen, pillows], ldry, iron, iron brd, cafe, pool-heated (solar), spa, bbq, ✆, plygr, mini golf, tennis. **D** $125 - $220, **W** $780 - $1,540, $780 - $1,540, 4 units ★★★★, Breakfast available. Min book all holiday times, BC EFT MC VI.

★★★★ **(Holiday Unit Section)**, (2 stry), 4 units acc up to 4, (1 bedrm), [shwr, tlt, fan, fire pl, TV, clock radio, refrig, cook fac, micro, toaster, blkts, linen, pillows], cafe, spa, mini golf. **D** $110 - $190, **W** $645 - $1,330.

★★★☆ **Great Ocean Road Cottages**, (Cotg), 10 Erskine Ave, 600m N of PO, ☎ 03 5289 1070, fax 03 5289 2508, 10 cotgs acc up to 5, (Studio), [shwr, tlt, hairdry, a/c, c/fan (6), elec blkts, TV, video, clock radio, refrig, cook fac ltd, micro, toaster, blkts, doonas, linen, pillows], ldry, w/mach, dryer, bbq, ✆, cots, non smoking property. **D** ♦♦ $115 - $200, $20 - $30, ch con, Min book Christmas Jan long w/ends and Easter, AE BC DC MC VI.

★★★ **Yurara Holiday Flats**, (HF), 3 Doble St, 1.7km N of PO, ☎ 03 5289 1800, fax 03 5289 1381, 3 flats acc up to 4, (2 bedrm), [shwr, bath (hip) (1), tlt, fan, heat, elec blkts, TV, clock radio, refrig, cook fac, micro, toaster, blkts, linen reqd, pillows], ldry, w/mach, cots. **D** ♦♦ $80 - $135, 👤 $15, **W** ♦♦ $550 - $900, 👤 $70, Min book all holiday times.

VICTORIA

B&B's/Guest Houses

★★★★☆ **Chatby Lane**, (B&B), 4 Howard St, 1 km N of PO, ☎ 03 5289 1616, fax 03 5289 2041, 6 rms [ensuite, spa bath (6), hairdry, a/c (6), heat (1), elec blkts, tel, TV, video, clock radio, t/c mkg, refrig, cook fac ltd (6), micro (6), toaster, doonas], ldry-fee, iron, iron brd, conf fac, bbq, cots, non smoking property. **BLB ♦ $85 - $185, ♦♦ $85 - $185**, Min book all holiday times, BC EFT MC VI.

★★★★☆ **(Apartment Section)**, 3 apts (1 & 2 bedrm), [shwr, tlt, hairdry, a/c, elec blkts, tel, TV, video, clock radio, t/c mkg, refrig, cook fac, micro, toaster, blkts, doonas, linen, pillows], ldry, c/park (undercover) (2), cots. **D ♦♦ $110 - $225, ◊ $20, W ♦♦ $600 - $1,400, ◊ $100 - $200**, Min book all holiday times.

★★★★ **Ravenswood Bed & Breakfast**, (B&B), 70 Smith St, 150m W of PO, ☎ 03 5289 2655, fax 03 5289 2755, (2 stry gr fl), 3 rms (1 suite) [shwr, bath (1), spa bath (2), tlt, hairdry, a/c (1), c/fan (2), cent heat, elec blkts, TV, video, clock radio, t/c mkg, refrig, toaster], non smoking property. **BB ♦♦ $170 - $240, ◊ $50**, BC MC VI.

★★★★ **Stanmorr Bed & Breakfast**, (B&B), No facilities for children under 12. Cnr William & Otway Sts, 400m W of PO, ☎ 03 5289 1530, fax 03 5289 2805, 5 rms [ensuite, spa bath (5), hairdry (5), c/fan, fire pl (gas coal) (4), heat, elec blkts, TV, video, clock radio, t/c mkg, refrig (2)], lounge (TV), t/c mkg shared, refrig. **BB ♦♦ $125 - $225**, Twin room not listed or rated. Min book Christmas Jan long w/ends and Easter, AE BC DC EFT MC VI.

★★★☆ **Erskine House**, (GH), Mountjoy Pde, ☎ 03 5289 1209, fax 03 5289 1185, 82 rms [elec blkts, t/c mkg, refrig], lounge (TV & openfires), ✕, bar, bowls, tennis, cots. **BB ♦ $70 - $155, ♦♦ $115 - $195**, ch con, AE BC DC MC VI.

★★★ **Lorne Chalet**, (GH), Group Accommodation. Closed 31st May - 1 Sept. 4 Smith St, 200m NW of PO, ☎ 03 5289 1241, fax 03 5289 1005, (2 stry gr fl), 36 rms [shwr, tlt, heat, t/c mkg, refrig], rec rm, ✕, BYO, pool, spa, ✆, cots-fee, non smoking property. **BB ♦ $76 - $92, ♦♦ $121 - $154**, ch con, Min book applies, BC EFT MC VI.

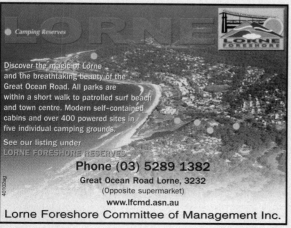
Other Accommodation

Great Ocean Road Backpackers, (Lodge), 10 Erskine Ave, 600m N of PO, ☎ 03 5289 1809, fax 03 5289 2508, 4 rms acc up to 10, (Bunk Rooms - 1x2bunk. - 1x3bunk.), [c/fan (1), heat, micro], ldry, cook fac, refrig, bbq. **D ♦ $18 - $32, ♦♦ $42 - $70**, AE BC DC MC VI.

MACEDON VIC 3440

Pop 1,250. (58km NW Melbourne), See map on page 696, ref B4. Small township on the slopes of the Great Dividing Range. Art Gallery, Bush Walking, Golf, Horse Riding, Rock Climbing, Scenic Drives, Tennis.

Hotels/Motels

★★★ **Black Forest Motel**, (M), Black Forest Dve, 1km W of PO, ☎ 03 5426 1600, fax 03 5426 2186, 14 units [shwr, tlt, fan, heat, elec blkts, tel, TV, clock radio, t/c mkg, refrig], bbq, cots, non smoking units (5). **RO ♦ $50 - $60, ♦♦ $60 - $70, ◊ $10**, AE BC DC MC VI.

MACS COVE VIC 3722

Pop Part of Mansfield, (202km NE Melbourne), See map on page 696, ref E4. Small settlement on shore of Lake Eildon. Boating, Fishing, Horse Riding, Sailing, Scenic Drives, Swimming (Lake), Water Skiing.

Self Catering Accommodation

★★★★☆ **Willowlake Restaurant & Cottages**, (Cotg), 16 Willowlake Dve, 20km SE of Mansfield, ☎ 03 5777 3814, fax 03 5777 3814, 4 cotgs [shwr, spa bath, tlt, hairdry, a/c-cool, c/fan, heat, elec blkts, TV, video, CD, t/c mkg, refrig, micro, elec frypan, toaster], iron, iron brd, lounge firepl, ✕, pool, bbq, bicycle, breakfast ingredients. **BB ♦♦ $190 - $210**, BC EFT MC VI.

★★★★☆ **(All Seasons Section)**, 1 cotg acc up to 4, (2 bedrm), [ensuite, spa bath, hairdry, a/c, c/fan, elec blkts, TV, video, CD, t/c mkg, refrig, cook fac, micro, elec frypan, toaster, blkts, doonas, linen, pillows], w/mach, iron, iron brd, lounge firepl, bbq, c/park (carport). **D ♦♦ $165 - $190, ◊ $15**.

MAFFRA VIC 3860

Pop 4,050. (220km E Melbourne), See map on pages 694/695, ref H7. Centre of a rich agricultural, pastoral & irrigation area, situated on the Macalister River. Bowls, Bush Walking, Croquet, Fishing, Golf, Horse Riding, Scenic Drives, Shooting, Swimming (Pool), Tennis.

Hotels/Motels

★★★ **Maffra Motor Inn**, (M), 184 Johnson St, 500m E of PO, ☎ 03 5147 2111, fax 03 5141 1450, 18 units [shwr, tlt, a/c, elec blkts, tel, TV, clock radio, t/c mkg, refrig], ldry, pool-heated (solar), spa, bbq, cots-fee, non smoking units (18). **RO ♦ $60.50, ♦♦ $71.50, ◊ $11**, AE BC DC MC VI.

★ **Metropolitan Hotel**, (LH), 97 Johnson St, opposite PO, ☎ 03 5147 1809, fax 03 5141 1551, (2 stry), 9 rms [elec blkts], lounge (TV), ✕, t/c mkg shared, refrig, c/park. **BLB ♦ $20, ♦♦ $35, ◊ $15**, ch con, BC EFT MC VI.

B&B's/Guest Houses

★★★★☆ **Powerscourt Country House**, (GH), c1859. RMB 6095 Maffra - Stratford Rd, 4.2km W of Princes Hwy, ☎ 03 5147 1897, fax 03 5147 1431, 5 rms [ensuite, bath, hairdry, fire pl (4), cent heat, elec blkts, doonas], lounge (TV, video), ✕. **BB ♦ $108 - $140, ♦♦ $140 - $180, DBB ♦ $139 - $193, ◊ $135 - $155**, AE BC DC EFT MC VI.

MAIN RIDGE VIC 3928

Pop 530. (74km S Melbourne), See map on page 697, ref C8. Rural area located in central lower Mornington Peninsula. Art Gallery, Bowls, Bush Walking, Horse Riding, Scenic Drives, Tennis.

Self Catering Accommodation

★★★☆ **Woodgate Bed & Breakfast**, (Apt), RMB 6182 Arthur Seat Rd, ☎ 03 5989 2639, (2 stry), 1 apt acc up to 2, (Studio), [shwr, tlt, a/c-cool, c/fan, heat, elec blkts, TV, CD, t/c mkg, refrig, micro, elec frypan, toaster, blkts, pillows], bbq, c/park (undercover), breakfast ingredients. **D ♦♦ $150, ◊ $30**.

★★★ **Summerhill Farm Bed & Breakfast**, (Cotg), 264 Barkers Rd, ☎ 03 5989 6077, fax 03 5989 6077, 1 cotg acc up to 2, (1 bedrm), [shwr, bath, tlt, hairdry, fan, heat (wood), elec blkts, TV, video, clock radio, CD, t/c mkg, refrig, cook fac ltd, micro, blkts, doonas, linen, pillows], breakfast ingredients. **BB ♦ $90 - $100, ♦♦ $110 - $120**.

MAINDAMPLE VIC 3721

Pop Nominal, (186km NE Melbourne), See map on page 696, ref D3. Agricultural district situated on the Maroondah Hwy. A former gold mining area. Fishing, Scenic Drives.

Hotels/Motels

★★☆ **Bridge Inn Hotel Maindample**, (LMH), RMB 6325 Maroondah Hwy, ☎ 03 5778 7281, fax 03 5778 7281, 12 units [shwr, tlt, a/c, elec blkts, TV, clock radio, t/c mkg, refrig, toaster, ldry], ✕, bbq, ✆, cots, non smoking units (4). **BLB** ╫ $40, ╫╫ $60, ╫ $10, ch con, Light breakfast only, BC EFT MC VI.

MALDON VIC 3463

Pop 1,250. (137km NW Melbourne), See map on page 696, ref A3. First Notable Town - classified by the National Trust in 1966. Mt Tarrengower Lookout offers unrestricted views over the surrounding district. Beehive Chimney (30 metres high) is the only one of any size remaining on a goldfield. The main shopping centre still retains the wooden verandah construction of the 1850's. Bowls, Bush Walking, Croquet, Fishing, Golf, Scenic Drives, Swimming (Pool), Tennis.

Hotels/Motels

GOLDEN CHAIN

★★★ **Maldon's Eaglehawk Motel**, (M), 35 Reef St, 1.5km NE of PO, ☎ 03 5475 2750, fax 03 5475 2914, 11 units [shwr, bath, tlt, a/c, elec blkts, tel, TV, video-fee, clock radio, t/c mkg, refrig, mini bar, toaster], ldry, conf fac, pool, bbq, cots-fee, non smoking property. **RO** ╫ $77 - $90, ╫╫ $88 - $99, ╫ $13.20, AE BC DC MC VI.

★★★ **Porcupine Township**, (M), Pioneer Village. Cnr Bendigo & Allans Rds, ☎ 03 5475 1000, fax 03 5475 1001, 8 units (2 suites) [shwr, bath, tlt, c/fan, heat, elec blkts, TV, clock radio, t/c mkg, refrig, toaster], ✕, pool. **BLB** ╫ $75 - $85, ╫╫ $85 - $95, ╫ $15, **Suite BLB** ╫╫ $110 - $120, ╫ $15, Light breakfast only available. AE BC MC VI.

Self Catering Accommodation

★★★★☆ **Cornflowers at the Barn B & B**, (Cotg), 64 Main St, 200m E of PO, ☎ 03 5475 2015, fax 03 5475 2015, (2 stry), 1 cotg acc up to 2, (1 bedrm), [shwr, bath, tlt, hairdry, a/c-cool, c/fan, heat, elec blkts, TV, video, clock radio, CD, t/c mkg, refrig, cook fac, micro, elec frypan, toaster, ldry (in unit), blkts, doonas, linen, pillows], w/mach, dryer, iron, iron brd, bbq, non smoking property. **BB** ╫╫ $150 - $176, Dinner by arrangement. BC MC VI.

★★★★ **Fairbank House**, (Cotg), 9 Ireland St, 700m NE of PO, ☎ 03 5475 1094, fax 03 5475 1880, 1 cotg acc up to 6, (3 bedrm), [shwr, spa bath, tlt, hairdry, c/fan, cent heat, elec blkts, tel, TV, video, t/c mkg, refrig, cook fac, micro, elec frypan, d/wash, toaster, ldry, blkts, linen, pillows], w/mach, dryer, iron, iron brd, lounge firepl, bbq, c/park (garage), non smoking property. **D** ╫╫ $125 - $150, ╫ $40, **W** ╫╫ $740, ╫ $115, ch con, Central booking office: 60 Main St, BC EFT MC VI.

★★★★ **Hardys B & B**, (Cotg), 113 High St, ☎ 03 5475 1027, 1 cotg acc up to 4, (2 bedrm), [shwr, bath, tlt, a/c-cool, heat (wood), elec blkts, TV, video, clock radio, CD, refrig, cook fac ltd, micro, elec frypan, toaster, blkts, linen, pillows], ldry, w/mach, dryer, bbq, breakfast ingredients, non smoking property. **BB** ╫╫ $90, ╫ $30, ch con.

★★★★ **Peppercorn Cottage**, (Cotg), 5 Phoenix St, ☎ 03 5475 1778, 1 cotg acc up to 5, [shwr, spa bath, tlt, fan, c/fan, heat, elec blkts, TV, video, clock radio, t/c mkg, refrig, cook fac, micro, elec frypan, toaster, ldry, blkts, linen], w/mach, iron, iron brd, lounge firepl, c/park (carport), breakfast ingredients, non smoking property. **BLB** ╫╫ $100 - $115, ╫ $30, ch con, BC MC VI.

★★★★ **The Cottage Thalgarrah**, (Cotg), Lot 13 Baringhup Rd, 2km W of PO, ☎ 03 5475 2649, fax 03 5475 2649, 1 cotg acc up to 2, (1 bedrm), [shwr, tlt, hairdry, fan, c/fan, heat, elec blkts, TV, video, clock radio, CD, t/c mkg, refrig, mini bar, cook fac, micro, elec frypan, toaster, blkts, linen], ldry, bbq, breakfast ingredients, non smoking property. **D** $95 - $115, **W** $450 - $495.

★★★★ **Witbank Cottage**, (Cotg), 11 Reef St, ☎ 03 5475 1094, fax 03 5475 1880, 1 cotg acc up to 7, (4 bedrm), [shwr, spa bath, tlt, hairdry, a/c-cool, c/fan, cent heat, elec blkts, TV, video, clock radio, CD, t/c mkg, refrig, cook fac, micro, d/wash, toaster, ldry, blkts, doonas, linen, pillows], w/mach, dryer, iron, iron brd, lounge firepl, bbq, c/park (carport). **D** ╫╫ $125 - $150, ╫ $40, **W** ╫╫ $740, ╫ $115, ch con, Minimum booking Easter, long w/ends & folk festival. BC EFT MC VI.

★★★☆ **Dabb & Co Rose Cottage**, (Cotg), 16 Adair St, ☎ 03 5475 1094, fax 03 5475 1880, 1 cotg acc up to 4, (2 bedrm), [shwr, bath, tlt, fan, heat, elec blkts, TV, clock radio, t/c mkg, refrig, cook fac, micro, elec frypan, toaster, ldry, blkts, linen, pillows], w/mach, dryer, iron, iron brd, lounge firepl, c/park (undercover), non smoking property. **D** ╫╫ $90 - $115, ╫ $30, **W** ╫╫ $515, ╫ $80, ch con, Central booking office: 60 Main St, BC EFT MC VI.

★★★☆ **Hales Cottage**, (Cotg), Previously Heritage Cottages of Maldon. 18 Church St, 900m N of PO, ☎ 03 5475 1094, fax 03 5475 1880, 1 cotg acc up to 4, (2 bedrm), [shwr, spa bath, tlt, hairdry, a/c-cool, fan, heat, elec blkts, TV, video, clock radio, CD, t/c mkg, refrig, cook fac, micro, elec frypan, toaster, ldry, blkts, doonas, linen, pillows], w/mach, dryer, iron, iron brd, lounge firepl, bbq, non smoking property. **D** ╫╫ $100 - $135, ╫ $30, **W** ╫╫ $590, ╫ $95, ch con, Central booking office: 60 Main St, BC EFT MC VI.

★★★☆ **Maldons Bluegum Cottage**, (Cotg), 14 Church St, 800m N of PO, ☎ 03 5475 1094, fax 03 5475 1880, 1 cotg acc up to 6, (3 bedrm), [shwr, bath, tlt, hairdry, a/c-cool, fan, heat, elec blkts, TV, video, clock radio, CD, refrig, cook fac, micro, toaster, ldry, blkts, linen, pillows], iron, lounge firepl, bbq, c/park (undercover), cots-fee. **D** ╫╫ $95 - $125, ╫ $25, **W** ╫╫ $540, ╫ $80, ch con, Central booking office: 60 Main St, BC EFT MC VI.

★★★☆ **Nuggetty Cottages**, (Cotg), Bradford Rd (Nuggetty Rd), 3km N of PO, ☎ 03 5475 2472, fax 03 5475 2472, 1 cotg acc up to 5, (2 bedrm - stone.), [shwr, tlt, hairdry, fan, heat (wood), elec blkts, TV, video, clock radio, CD, t/c mkg, refrig, cook fac, micro, elec frypan, toaster, blkts, doonas, linen, pillows], bbq, breakfast ingredients, non smoking property. **BB** ╫╫ $100 - $120, ╫ $30.

★★★ **Maldon Holiday Cottages**, (Cotg), Sells La, 4.5km SW of PO, off Newstead Rd, ☎ 03 5475 2927, fax 03 5475 1515, 3 cotgs acc up to 6, (1 & 2 bedrm), [shwr, bath (2), tlt, hairdry, fan, heat, TV, clock radio, t/c mkg, refrig, cook fac, toaster, blkts, doonas, linen, pillows], ldry, w/mach, dryer, iron, iron brd, bbq, cots, Pets accepted subject to conditions. **D** ╫ $40, ╫╫ $60, ╫ $20, **W** ╫╫ $310, ╫ $100, ch con, 1 cottage ★★★☆.

B&B's/Guest Houses

★★★★☆ **Mount Hawke of Maldon**, (B&B), No children's facilities, 24 Adair St, 500m N of PO, ☎ 03 5475 1192, fax 03 5475 1192, 3 rms [ensuite, hairdry, c/fan, cent heat, elec blkts], lounge (TV, cd), lounge firepl, t/c mkg shared, non smoking property. **BB** ╫ $85, ╫╫ $120, Dinner by arrangement. Min book long w/ends, BC EFT MC VI.

★★★★ **Calder House**, (B&B), 44 High St, diagonally opposite PO, ☎ 03 5475 2912, fax 03 5475 1884, (2 stry gr fl), 4 rms [ensuite (3), shwr (1), bath, tlt (1), hairdry, a/c, heat, elec blkts], lounge (TV, video, cd), lounge firepl, ⊠ (Fri to Sun), t/c mkg shared. BB ♦ $88 - $110, ♦♦ $110 - $132, ◊ $22, BC DC MC VI.

★★★★ **Wattle Gum Cottage**, (B&B), Castlemaine - Maldon Rd, 7km SE of PO, ☎ 03 5475 1113, 1 rm [ensuite, c/fan, heat (wood), elec blkts, TV, clock radio, CD, t/c mkg, refrig, toaster], non smoking property. BB ♦ $55 - $65, ♦♦ $70 - $90.

Operator Comment: "Midweek Specials 3 nights for price of 2".

★★★☆ **Alick's Lead**, (B&B), Lisle's Gully Rd, off Parkins Reef Rd, ☎ 03 5475 1068, 1 rm [ensuite, hairdry, a/c, elec blkts, TV, video, radio, t/c mkg, refrig, micro, toaster], c/park (carport), non smoking property. BLB ♦♦ $80, pen con, BC MC VI.

Operator Comment: Studio Flat in park-like garden. BBQ Facilities. URL:http://users.netcon.net.au/cmwarn

★★★☆ **Palm House**, (B&B), 2 High St, 500m SW of PO, ☎ 03 5475 2532, fax 03 5475 1877, 4 rms [fan, heat, elec blkts, clock radio], lounge (TV, video, cd), lounge firepl, t/c mkg shared, bbq, cots, non smoking property. BB ♦♦ $90, ◊ $33, Min book long w/ends and Easter.

 ★★★ **(Cottage Section)**, 1 cotg acc up to 4, (1 bedrm), [shwr, tlt, a/c-cool, heat, elec blkts, TV, clock radio, refrig, cook fac, micro, toaster, blkts, linen, pillows], breakfast ingredients. BB ♦ $52, ♦♦ $100, ◊ $33.

Gowar Homestead, (B&B), Lot 6 Castlemaine Rd Gowar via, 5km E of PO, ☎ 03 5475 1090, fax 03 5475 1600, 4 rms [ensuite, hairdry, fan, heat], lounge (TV), t/c mkg shared, bbq, non smoking property. BB ♦ $45 - $55, ♦♦ $75 - $105, (Rating under review).

Other Accommodation

Victorian Blue Light Youth Camps, (Lodge), Open weekends and school holidays. Phoenix St, 1km SE of PO, ☎ 03 5475 2033, fax 03 5475 2117, (2 stry gr fl), 9 rms [shwr, bath (hip), tlt, heat, TV (avail), clock radio, t/c mkg, refrig, cook fac ltd, toaster, blkts, doonas, linen, pillows], rec rm, conv fac, bbq (covered), ☎ RO ♦ $30, ♦♦ $60, ◊ $30, ch con, Light breakfast available. BC MC VI.

MALLACOOTA VIC 3892

Pop 1,000. (542km E Melbourne), See map on pages 694/695, ref L7. One of Victoria's best & most popular fishing resorts. Overlooking the entrance to Mallacoota Inlet, there are many BBQ areas, some accessible only by boat. Boating, Bowls, Bush Walking, Fishing, Golf, Sailing, Scenic Drives, Surfing, Swimming (Beach, Lake, River), Tennis, Water Skiing.

Hotels/Motels

★★★☆ **Mallacoota Motor Inn**, (M), 15 Maurice Ave, 400m W of PO, ☎ 03 5158 0544, fax 03 5158 0980, (2 stry), 8 units [shwr, tlt, hairdry, c/fan, heat, elec blkts, TV, clock radio, t/c mkg, refrig, micro, toaster], iron, iron brd, bbq, ☎, plygr, cots, non smoking units (3). RO ♦ $65 - $99, ♦♦ $65 - $105, ◊ $10 - $15, ch con, AE BC EFT MC VI.

★★★☆ **Silver Bream Motel and Self Contained Flats**, (M), Previously Silver Bream Motel Suites & Flats, 32 Maurice Ave, 100m W of PO, ☎ 03 5158 0305, fax 03 5158 0322, 6 units [shwr, tlt, c/fan, heat, elec blkts, TV, video-fee, clock radio, t/c mkg, refrig], ldry, bbq, c/park (carport), boat park, plygr, cots, non smoking units (6). RO ♦ $50 - $88, ♦♦ $60 - $99, ◊ $11 - $16.50, ch con, pen con, BC EFT MC VI.

 ★★★☆ **(Holiday Flat Section)**, 4 flats acc up to 4, (2 bedrm), [shwr, tlt, hairdry, c/fan, heat, elec blkts, TV, video-fee, clock radio, t/c mkg, refrig, cook fac ltd, micro, elec frypan, toaster, blkts, linen, pillows], ldry, w/mach, dryer, non smoking units. D $330 - $770, ch con, pen con.

★★☆ **Mallacoota Hotel Motel**, (LMH), 51 Maurice Ave, 50m S of PO, ☎ 03 5158 0455, fax 03 5158 0453, (2 stry gr fl), 21 units [shwr, tlt, a/c, heat, elec blkts, tel, TV, clock radio, t/c mkg, refrig, cook fac ltd (6), toaster], conf fac, ⊠, pool, bbq, cots-fee. RO ♦ $49.50 - $60.50, ♦♦ $55 - $77, ◊ $11, ch con, AE BC DC EFT MC VI.

Self Catering Accommodation

★★★★ **Gowings (Mallacoota)**, (HF), 8 Dorron Ave, 100m N of PO, ☎ 03 5158 0401, fax 03 5158 0401, (2 stry gr fl), 16 flats acc up to 5, (1 & 2 bedrm), [shwr, bath (hip), tlt, hairdry, heat, TV, clock radio, refrig, cook fac, elec frypan (some), toaster, ldry (in unit), blkts, linen, pillows], rec rm, pool-heated (solar), bbq, boat park, jetty, cots. D $66 - $143, W $357 - $935, AE BC DC EFT MC VI.

★★★★ **Grevillea Grove (Mallacoota)**, (Apt), 32 Bruce St, ☎ 03 5158 0223, fax 03 5158 0223, 4 apts acc up to 5, (1 & 2 bedrm), [shwr, tlt, hairdry, heat, elec blkts, TV, video-fee, clock radio, refrig, cook fac, micro, toaster, ldry (in unit), doonas, linen-fee], iron, iron brd, boat park, cots. D ♦♦ $50 - $90, ♦♦♦♦ $60 - $110, ◊ $10, W ♦♦ $280 - $600, ♦♦♦♦ $380 - $750, BC MC VI.

★★★★ **Mallacoota Court**, (HF), 90 Bastion Point Rd, 400m S of PO, ☎ 03 5158 0508, fax 03 5158 0180, 4 flats acc up to 6, (2 bedrm), [shwr, tlt, fan, heat, elec blkts, TV, video, clock radio, refrig, cook fac, micro, toaster, ldry (in unit), blkts, doonas, linen, pillows], w/mach, iron, iron brd, bbq, c/park (carport), boat park, cots. D $70, W $420, BC MC VI.

★★★★ **Melaleuca Grove Holiday Units**, (HU), Cnr Genoa & Mirrabooka Rds, 2km W of PO, ☎ 03 5158 0407, fax 03 5158 0407, 6 units acc up to 5, (2 bedrm), [shwr, bath, tlt, fan, fire pl, heat, elec blkts, TV, video-fee, clock radio, t/c mkg, refrig, cook fac, micro, elec frypan, toaster, ldry (in unit), blkts, linen, pillows], w/mach, iron, iron brd, bbq, c/park (carport), boat park, ☎, plygr, cots. D $50 - $100, W $320 - $700, Breakfast available. Min book Christmas Jan and Easter, AE BC DC EFT JCB MC VI.

★★★☆ **Adobe (Mudbrick) Holiday Flats**, (HF), 17 Karbeethong Ave, 4km NW of PO, ☎ 03 5158 0329, 7 flats acc up to 6, (1 & 2 bedrm - mudbrick.), [shwr, bath (2), tlt, hairdry, heat (wood), elec blkts, TV, video-fee, clock radio, refrig, cook fac, elec frypan, toaster, linen reqd-fee], ldry, bbq, boat park, plygr, cots. D ♦♦♦♦ $40 - $70, ◊ $12, W ♦♦♦♦ $230 - $450, ◊ $84, Pets welcome.

Operator Comment: Pets can come inside with Mum & Dad. Lots of visible wildlife. Well worth a visit, also with overseas friends.See main ad.

 ★★★☆ **(Cottage Section)**, 1 cotg acc up to 6, (3 bedrm), [shwr, bath, tlt, hairdry, heat (wood), elec blkts, TV, clock radio, refrig, cook fac, elec frypan, toaster, ldry, linen reqd-fee], cots. D ♦♦♦♦ $40 - $70, ◊ $12, W ♦♦♦♦ $230 - $450, ◊ $84.

Seatbelts save lives

No one knows when a crash will occur and unless everyone in the car is properly restrained, there is a chance of unnecessary injury.

Even low-speed crashes can cause serious injury if people are not safely restrained, this highlights the need to wear those belts at all times, from the very start of every trip.

Get into the habit of not starting the car until all passengers are properly restrained.

Remember half of all crashes occur within five kilometres of home.

★★★ **Ballymena Holiday Units**, (HU), 10 Bruce St, 400m W of PO, ☎ 03 5158 0258, fax 03 5158 0607, 5 units acc up to 5, (1 & 2 bedrm), [shwr, tlt, fan, heat, elec blkts, TV, clock radio, refrig, cook fac, micro, toaster, blkts, linen, pillows], ldry, bbq, boat park, jetty, cots. **D $50 - $90, W $280 - $600.**

★★★ **Banksia Mudbrick Flats**, (HF), 11 Banksia Pde, 1.3km NW of PO, ☎ 03 5158 0044, 3 flats acc up to 6, (2 bedrm - mudbrick.), [shwr, tlt, heat, TV, clock radio, refrig, cook fac, toaster, linen reqd], ldry, iron, iron brd, bbq, cots, non smoking units (2). **D $70 - $110, W $490 - $770.**

★★★ **Blue Waters Holiday Cottages**, (Cotg), Karbeethong Ave, 4km NW of PO, ☎ 03 5158 0261, fax 03 5158 0963, 4 cotgs acc up to 2, (1 bedrm), [shwr, tlt, heat, elec blkts, TV, clock radio, refrig, cook fac, micro, toaster, linen reqd-fee], ldry, bbq, non smoking units (2). **D $60 - $70, W $215 - $495**, 1 cottage ★★★★. BC MC VI.

★★★ **Bruces Flats**, (HF), Cnr Dorron Ave & Fairhaven Dve, 200m N of PO, ☎ 03 5158 0190, fax 03 5158 0849, 3 flats acc up to 5, (2 bedrm), [shwr, tlt, heat, elec blkts, TV, clock radio, refrig, cook fac, micro, ldry (in unit), linen reqd-fee], bbq, jetty, cots. **D $40 - $90, W $275 - $760**, BC MC VI.

★★★ **Harbour Lights**, (HF), 88 Betka Rd, 200m S of PO, ☎ 03 5158 0246, 7 flats acc up to 6, (Studio & 1 bedrm), [shwr, tlt, hairdry, heat, elec blkts, TV, clock radio, refrig, cook fac, micro, elec frypan, toaster, linen reqd-fee], ldry, w/mach, dryer, bbq, c/park (carport), boat park, plygr, cots. **D $40 - $60, W $266 - $610**, Pets welcome. AE BC MC VI.

★★★ **Mallacoota Luxury Town Houses**, (HU), 36 Maurice Ave, ☎ 03 5158 0266, fax 03 5158 0536, (2 stry) 3 units acc up to 6, (2 bedrm), [shwr, bath, tlt, heat, TV, refrig, cook fac, micro, d/wash, ldry (in unit), doonas, linen reqd-fee, pillows], w/mach, iron, iron brd, c/park (undercover). **D $70 - $110, W $400 - $750.**

★★☆ **Cape Howe Wilderness Lodge**, Access by ferry from Karbeethong jetty. Maxwells Rd, On eastern shore of Inlet, ☎ 03 5158 0352, fax 03 5158 0919, 10 cabins acc up to 6, (1 & 2 bedrm), [shwr, tlt, fan, heat, clock radio, refrig, cook fac ltd, blkts, linen, pillows], ldry, w/mach, rec rm, bbq, shop (seasonal), ☎, jetty, canoeing, cots. **D $70 - $125**, Generated power.

★★☆ **Mallamaurice**, (HF), 2 Maurice Ave, 500m W of PO, ☎ 03 5158 0432, 4 flats acc up to 5, (2 bedrm), [shwr, tlt, fan, heat, TV, clock radio, refrig, cook fac, micro, elec frypan, toaster, linen reqd], ldry, w/mach, pool, bbq, c/park (carport), boat park. **D $40 - $85, W $210 - $560.**

B&B's/Guest Houses

★★★☆ **Mareeba Lodge**, (B&B), No children's facilities, 59 Mirrabooka Rd, 1.6km NW of PO, ☎ 03 5158 0378, (2 stry gr fl), 3 rms [fan, heat, elec blkts], ldry, lounge (TV), t/c mkg shared, refrig, bbq. **BB ♦ $50 - $60, ♦♦ $60 - $80.**

Other Accommodation

Karbeethong Lodge, (Lodge), No children's facilities, 16 Schnapper Point Dve, 4km N of PO, ☎ 03 5158 0411, fax 03 5158 0081, 11 rms [ensuite (8), c/fan, elec blkts, blkts, doonas, linen, pillows], shwr, tlt (outside), ldry, lounge, lounge firepl, cook fac, t/c mkg shared, refrig, bbq, ☎, jetty. **D $85 - $150**, BC MC VI.

Mallacoota Hotel Motel, (Lodge), 51 Maurice Ave, 50m S of PO, ☎ 03 5158 0455, fax 03 5158 0453, 4 rms [shwr, tlt, heat, doonas, linen reqd-fee], lounge (TV), ⊠, pool, cook fac, refrig, bbq, ☎. **D ♦ $10 - $18**, ch con, AE BC DC EFT MC VI, ⚹⚘.

MALMSBURY VIC 3446

Pop 500. (97km NW Melbourne), See map on page 696, ref A4. Small township on the Calder Highway. Fishing (Reservoir), Horse Riding.

Hotels/Motels

★★☆ **Malmsbury Hotel**, (LMH), Mollison St (Calder Hwy), ☎ 03 5423 2322, fax 03 5423 2322, 7 units [shwr, spa bath (4), tlt, fan, heat, elec blkts, tel, TV, clock radio (4), t/c mkg, refrig, toaster, doonas], ⊠. **RO ♦ $44 - $60, ♦♦ $60 - $82.50, ◊ $11**, ch con, Light breakfast only available, AE BC DC EFT MC VI.

Self Catering Accommodation

★★★★ **Hopewell Cottage**, (Cotg), Ross St, ☎ 03 5423 2470, fax 03 5423 2145, 1 cotg acc up to 6, (3 bedrm), [shwr (2), tlt (2), fan, heat, elec blkts, TV, clock radio, refrig, cook fac, micro, toaster, ldry, blkts, doonas, linen, pillows], w/mach, iron, iron brd, lounge firepl, breakfast ingredients, non smoking property. **BB ♦ $80, ♦♦ $120, ◊ $40.**

B&B's/Guest Houses

★★ **Malmsbury Cottage**, (B&B), 53 Mollison St (Calder Hwy), ☎ 03 5423 2432, 3 rms [elec blkts, video, doonas], lounge (TV), ✗, BYO, t/c mkg shared, refrig. **BB ♦ $45, ◊ $45**, Other meals by arrangement. BC MC VI.

MANSFIELD VIC 3722

Pop 2,500. (183km NE Melbourne), See map on page 696, ref E4. The centre of a large grazing district. Boating, Bowls, Bush Walking, Fishing, Golf, Horse Riding, Scenic Drives, Shooting, Swimming (Pool), Tennis. See also Bonnie Doon, Goughs Bay, Howqua, Macs Cove, Maindample & Merrijig.

Hotels/Motels

★★★☆ **Mansfield Valley Motor Inn**, (M), Cnr Maroondah Hwy & Elvin St, 600m W of PO, ☎ 03 5775 1300, fax 03 5775 1693, 23 units [shwr, bath (2), spa bath (4), tlt, hairdry, a/c, elec blkts, tel, TV, video-fee, clock radio, t/c mkg, refrig, mini bar], ldry, dry rm, conf fac, ⊠ (Mon to Thurs), pool, sauna, bbq, cots-fee, non smoking units (9). **RO ♦ $66 - $100, ♦♦ $77 - $120, ◊ $15 - $20**, ch con, 6 units ★★★★. Minimum booking at Easter & weekends during snow season, AE BC DC EFT MC VI.

Rates may change. Check before booking.

MANSFIELD VALLEY MOTOR INN

cnr Elvins St and Maroondah Hwy
Mansfield Vic 3722
Tel: (03) 5775 1300

11626AG

AAA
T O U R I S M
Special Rates

★★★ **Alzburg Inn**, (M), 39 Malcolm St, 800m S of PO, ☎ 03 5775 2367, fax 03 5775 2719, (2 stry gr fl), 58 units (4 suites) [shwr, spa bath (4), tlt, hairdry, a/c, c/fan (4), heat, tel, cable tv, video (4), movie, clock radio, t/c mkg, refrig, cook fac (34), micro (34), d/wash (4), toaster, ldry (in unit) (4), doonas], ldry, dry rm, rec rm, conf fac, ⊠, pool-heated, sauna, spa, bbq (covered), ☎, plygr, ski hire, tennis, cots-fee, non smoking suites (4). **High Season BB ♦♦ $114, ◊ $35, Low Season RO ♦♦ $84, ◊ $20, Suite High Season BB ♦♦ $190, ◊ $35, Suite Low Season RO ♦♦ $160, ◊ $20**, ch con, 4 suites ★★★★, Min book Christmas Jan long w/ends and Easter, AE BC DC EFT MC VI.

B udget Motel Chain *International*

★★★ **Mansfield Motel**, (M), 3 Highett St (Midland Hwy), 200m N of PO, ☎ 03 5775 2377, fax 03 5775 2632, 21 units [shwr, bath (hip), tlt, hairdry (8), a/c-cool, heat, elec blkts, tel, TV, video-fee, clock radio, t/c mkg, refrig, toaster], ldry, dry rm, pool, bbq, c/park (carport), car wash, plygr, cots, non smoking units (7). **RO ♦ $59 - $80, ♦♦ $65 - $80, ◊ $11 - $16.50**, pen con, Minium bookings weekends, long weekends, Easter, and snow season. AE BC DC EFT MC MCH VI.

★★ **Travellers Lodge Mansfield**, (M), 116 High St, 250m W of PO, ☎ 03 5775 1800, fax 03 5775 2396, 6 units [shwr, tlt, a/c-cool (3), c/fan (3), heat, elec blkts, TV, clock radio, t/c mkg, refrig], ldry, dry rm, cook fac, bbq, non smoking units (6). **RO ♦♦ $70 - $80, ◊ $11**, No breakfast available. BC EFT MC VI.

★ **Commercial Hotel**, (LH), 83 High St (Maroondah Hwy), 100m E of PO, ☎ 03 5775 2046, fax 03 5779 1476, (2 stry), 6 rms [basin (2), fan, elec blkts], ⊠, ☎. **BLB ♦ $30, ♦♦ $50**, ch con, Light breakfast only available.

★ **Delatite Hotel**, (LH), 95 High St (Maroondah Hwy), opposite PO, ☎ 03 5775 2004, fax 03 5775 1824, (2 stry), 14 rms [basin (8), elec blkts], ⊠, t/c mkg shared, refrig, ☎. **BLB ♦ $27.50, ◊ $27.50**, ch con, BC EFT MC VI.

Mansfield Hotel, (LH), 86 High St (Maroondah Hwy), 50m E of PO, ☎ 03 5775 2101, fax 03 5775 2032, (2 stry), 9 rms [shwr (2), tlt (2), elec blkts], ⊠, t/c mkg shared, ☎. **BLB ♦ $25, ◊ $25**, ch con, AE BC DC EFT MC VI, (Rating under review).

Self Catering Accommodation

★★★★☆ **Burnt Creek Cottages**, (Cotg), Lot 8 O'Hanlons Rd, 13km SW of Mansfield, ☎ 03 5775 3067, fax 03 5775 3169, 4 cotgs acc up to 6, (2 bedrm), [shwr, bath (hip) (1), spa bath (2), tlt, hairdry, a/c, c/fan, heat (wood), elec blkts, TV, video, clock radio, CD, refrig, cook fac, micro, toaster, ldry (in unit), blkts, doonas, linen, pillows], w/mach, dryer, iron, iron brd, pool, bbq, bicycle, tennis. **D ♦♦ $120 - $160, ◊ $20 - $30**, ch con, Breakfast available. Min book applies, BC MC VI.

1160 6AG

ALZBURG INN RESORT & CONFERENCE CENTRE, MANSFIELD

Located in the heart of Victoria's magnificent High Country at the foot of Mt. Buller and within easy reach of Lake Eildon, the historical building, dating back to 1891 was originally Our Lady of Mercy Convent. Surrounded by picturesque gardens and lawn areas, the Resort blends the old and new with 54 comfortable motel units and 4 luxury 2 and 3 bedroom spa suites.

RESORT FACILITIES:
Motel and Spa Suite Accommodation, 5 Function Rooms with extensive Conference Facilities.
• Fully Licensed Dining Room • Disco & Karaoke bar • Poolside bar
• Solar Heated Swimming Pool & Spa with banana lounges, tables, chairs & umbrellas on large grass area • Sauna & Spa • Two Floodlit Tennis Courts • Games Room & Children's Playground & Covered Sandpit
• Volleyball & Basketball • Covered Picnic tables & Free Gas BBQs.

SUMMER PACKAGES AVAILABLE:
Getaway Weekends • Kids are Free • Group Packages including Murder Mystery Weekends, Overnight Car Rallies and Trivia Weekends.

WINTER PACKAGES & TOURS:
Self Drive All-up Packages including Ski Hire, Lift Tickets, Accommodation & Meals.

COACH TOURS FROM MELBOURNE:
Inclusive of Luxury Coach Transportation, Ski hire, Lift Tickets, Accommodation, Meals & Entrance Fees to Mt Buller. Day Coach Tours to Mt Buller for skiers or sightseers depart daily during the Ski Season from Melbourne for groups and individuals.

Alzburg Inn Resort & Conference Centre
39 Malcolm Street, Mansfield, Victoria, 3722
FREECALL 1800 033 023
or (03) 5775 2367 fax (03) 5775 2719
Website: www.alzburg.com.au   www.alzburginnresort.com.au
Email: info@alzburg.com.au

★★★★ **Alpine Country Cottages**, (Cotg), 5 The Parade, 1.2km SE of PO, off Mt Buller Rd, ☎ 03 5775 1694, fax 03 5775 1866, 4 cotgs acc up to 4, (1 & 2 bedrm), **[**shwr, spa bath, tlt, a/c-cool, a/c (2), c/fan, heat, elec blkts, TV, video, clock radio, CD, refrig, cook fac, micro (2), elec frypan, toaster, blkts, linen, pillows**]**, iron, iron brd, bbq, c/park (carport) (3), ✆, cots, non smoking property. **BB 👥 $150 - $165, 👤 $40**, ch con, Min book long w/ends and Easter, AE BC EFT MC VI, ♿.

★★★★ **Greenvale Holiday Units**, (HU), 30 Greenvale La, off Mt Buller Rd, 2.7km E of PO, ☎ 03 5775 2842, fax 03 5775 2842, 4 units acc up to 6, (Studio & 2 bedrm), **[**shwr, bath (1), tlt, hairdry, fan, c/fan, heat, elec blkts, TV, video (1), movie, clock radio, refrig, cook fac ltd, micro, elec frypan, toaster, linen, pillows**]**, ldry, bbq, plygr, cots. **D 👤 $60, 👥 $75 - $150, 👤 $20**, ch con.

★★★★ **Ovata Mansfield**, (Cotg), (Farm), Lot 1 Old Tolmie Rd, 12km NE of PO, ☎ 03 9379 0401, fax 03 9324 3668, (2 stry gr fl), 1 cotg acc up to 6, (3 bedrm), **[**shwr, bath (hip), hairdry, a/c-cool, fan, heat (wood), elec blkts, TV, video, clock radio, CD, t/c mkg, refrig, cook fac, micro, toaster, ldry (in unit), blkts, linen, pillows**]**, iron, iron brd, pool, bbq, cots, non smoking property. **D $185 - $230, W $1,100**, Min book applies, BC MC VI.

★★★★ **Wollondilly**, (Cotg), Monkey Gully Rd, 10km W of PO, ☎ 03 9435 4746, fax 03 9435 4746, (2 stry gr fl), 1 cotg acc up to 8, (3 bedrm), **[**shwr, bath, tlt, hairdry, c/fan, heat, TV, video, CD, t/c mkg, refrig, cook fac, micro, d/wash, toaster, ldry, blkts, linen, pillows**]**, w/mach, dryer, iron, iron brd, lounge firepl, c/park (carport), cots, non smoking property. **D $150 - $250, W $1,250 - $1,400.**

★★★★ **Wombat Hills**, (Cotg), 55 Lochiel Rd, Barwite 3722, off Old Tolmie Rd, 17.8km NE of PO, ☎ 03 5776 9507, fax 03 5776 9507, 3 cotgs acc up to 6, (Studio & 3 bedrm), **[**shwr, bath (1), spa bath (2), tlt, hairdry, a/c, fan (1), c/fan (2), heat, elec blkts, TV, video, clock radio, CD, refrig, mini bar, cook fac, micro, elec frypan, toaster, ldry (in unit) (1), blkts, doonas, linen, pillows**]**, iron, iron brd, lounge firepl, bbq, c/park (carport) (1), tennis, cots-fee, breakfast ingredients, non smoking units (3). **D 👥 $145 - $180, 👤 $20**, ch con, Other meals by arrangement. AE BC DC EFT MC VI.

★★★☆ **Banjo's Accommodation**, (HU), Cnr Mt Buller Rd & Greenvale La, 2.5km E of PO, ☎ 03 5775 2335, fax 03 5775 2335, 8 units acc up to 5, (Studio & 2 bedrm), **[**shwr, bath (2), tlt, hairdry (2), a/c, c/fan, heat, elec blkts (2), TV, video (6), clock radio, refrig, cook fac, micro, toaster, ldry (in unit) (2), blkts, doonas, linen, pillows**]**, w/mach (2), iron brd, dry rm, pool, bbq, c/park (carport) (2), plygr, tennis, cots, non smoking property. **D 👥 $77 - $125, 👤 $16.50**, ch con, 2 units ★★★★, Light breakfast available, AE BC MC VI.

★★★☆ **Mansfield Country Resort**, (Cotg), Banumum Rd, 14km SW of PO, ☎ 03 5775 2679, fax 03 5775 2642, 15 cotgs acc up to 6, (2 bedrm), **[**shwr, tlt, a/c-cool, heat, elec blkts, TV, video-fee, clock radio, refrig, cook fac, micro, elec frypan, toaster, ldry (in unit), blkts, linen, pillows**]**, w/mach, dryer, iron, iron brd, rec rm, pool, sauna, spa, bbq, kiosk, petrol, c/park (carport), ✆, plygr, canoeing, mini golf, gym, squash, tennis, cots. **D 👥 $110, 👤 $22.50, W $450 - $825**, Min book applies, BC MC VI.

★★★☆ **Mary's Place**, (HU), 32 Somerset Cres, 800m N of PO, ☎ 03 5775 1928, fax 03 5775 1928, 1 unit acc up to 4, (2 bedrm), **[**fan, heat, elec blkts, TV, clock radio, t/c mkg, refrig, cook fac ltd, micro, elec frypan, toaster, blkts, doonas, linen, pillows**]**, iron, iron brd, dry rm, bbq, c/park (carport), cots, breakfast ingredients. **BLB 👥 $90, 👤 $30**, ch con, weekly con

Operator Comment: Quiet, cosy spacious hideaway with beautiful garden. Rural view towards Mt Buller yet close to town centre.

★★★ **Lara Cottage**, (Cotg), (Farm), Hearns Rd, off Mt Buller Rd, via Hearns La, 19km E of PO, ☎ 03 5777 5536, fax 03 5777 5536, 1 cotg acc up to 6, (2 bedrm), [shwr, tlt, evap cool, c/fan, heat, elec blkts, TV, clock radio, refrig, cook fac, micro, toaster, ldry], w/mach, iron, iron brd, bbq. **D ♦ $55**, ♦ **$25**, **W $600**, ch con, BC MC VI.

Operator Comment: Relax in an original farm cottage after a day of activities in the High Country of Mansfield, Mt Buller, Lakes Eildon and Nillahcootie.

★★☆ **Delancy Tourism Partnership**, (Cotg), (Farm), Delatite La, off Jamieson Rd, 13km SE of PO, ☎ 03 5777 3518, fax 03 5777 3986, 1 cotg acc up to 6, (3 bedrm), [shwr, bath, tlt, heat, elec blkts, TV, refrig, cook fac, micro, toaster, ldry, doonas], w/mach, iron, iron brd, lounge firepl, bbq. **D $120 - $160**.

★★ **Black Horse Park**, (Cotg), 2 Desmonds Rd, Booroolite 3722, 20km SE of PO, off Hearns La, ☎ 03 5777 5530, fax 03 5777 5530, 3 cotgs acc up to 12, (2 & 3 bedrm), [shwr, tlt, hairdry, fan (2), heat (2), TV (1), video (1), clock radio (1), refrig, cook fac, micro (1), toaster, ldry (in unit) (1), blkts, doonas, linen, pillows], lounge firepl (2), bbq, plygr, Horses allowed. **D $110 - $330**, **W $670 - $1,650**, Meals by arrangement.

B&B's/Guest Houses

★★★☆ **Craigmont Bed & Breakfast**, (B&B), 1 Hollams Rd, 9km S of PO, ☎ 03 5775 1337, fax 03 5775 1337, 3 rms [ensuite (1), spa bath (1), hairdry, a/c-cool, c/fan, heat, elec blkts, clock radio, t/c mkg], lounge (TV), res liquor license, bbq, non smoking rms (3). **BB ♦ $88 - $110**, ♦♦ **$110 - $132**, 1 room ★★★★☆, BC MC VI.

★★★☆ **Highton Manor Country House**, (B&B), 140 Highton La, 3km SE of PO, ☎ 03 5775 2700, fax 03 5779 1305, (2 stry), 6 rms [ensuite (4), shwr (1), bath (1), spa bath (1), tlt (1), hairdry (3), a/c (1), heat, elec blkts, clock radio, t/c mkg (1), refrig (1)], lounge (TV), lounge firepl, ✗, BYO, pool, t/c mkg shared, refrig, bbq, non smoking property.
BB ♦ $185 - $350, ♦♦ **$200 - $365**, AE BC EFT MC VI.

★★☆ **(Motel Section)**, 5 units [shwr, bath (hip), tlt, a/c, elec blkts, TV, clock radio, t/c mkg, refrig, toaster], non smoking units. **BB ♦ $95**, ♦♦ **$110**, ♦ **$55**, ch con.

★★★☆ **Merrilea Guest House**, (GH), 22 Kidston Pde, 1.7km SW of PO, ☎ 03 5775 1148, fax 03 5775 1148, (2 stry gr fl), 4 rms [ensuite (2), shwr, bath (1), tlt, a/c (1), fan, heat, elec blkts, TV], ldry, dry rm, rec rm, lounge, t/c mkg shared, refrig, bbq, ☎. **BB ♦ $30 - $55**, ch con, BC MC VI.

★★★☆ **The Magnolia Mansfield**, (GH), 190 Mt Buller Rd, ☎ 03 5775 2963, fax 03 5775 2963, (2 stry gr fl), 4 rms [ensuite (3), shwr (1), bath (1), tlt (1), a/c (2), cent heat, clock radio], lounge, lounge firepl, ✗, t/c mkg shared, non smoking property. **BB ♦ $90 - $110**, ♦♦ **$135 - $165**, BC MC VI.

Other Accommodation

Mansfield Backpackers Inn, (Lodge), 112 High St, 250m W of PO, ☎ 03 5775 1800, fax 03 5775 2396, 8 rms [shwr (2G-2L), tlt (2G-2L), cent heat, doonas, linen, pillows], dry rm, lounge (TV, video), cook fac, refrig, bbq, non smoking property. **RO ♦ $17 - $22**, ♦ **$17 - $22**, BC EFT MC VI, ♿.

Mansfield Farm Accommodation, (Bunk), (Farm), McLeod La, off Tolmie Rd, 5.8km NE of PO, ☎ 03 5775 2084, fax 03 5775 2084, 1 bunkhouse acc up to 16, (Bunk Rooms), [fire pl (1), elec blkts, micro, blkts reqd], shwr (2G-2L), tlt (2G-2L), dry rm, lounge, lounge firepl, cook fac, refrig, bbq. **D ♦ $30**, ♦ **$30**, ch con.

Stumphill, (Bunk), (Farm), Mansfield - Benalla Rd (Midland Hwy), Barjarg 3721, 16km NW of PO, ☎ 03 5775 4227, fax 03 5776 4306, 1 bunkhouse acc up to 25, (7 bedrm), [a/c-cool, heat, micro, blkts reqd, linen reqd], lounge (TV), cook fac, refrig, bbq (covered), tennis. **D ♦ $22**, ♦ **$22**, ch con.

(Lodge Section), 2 bunkhouses acc up to 12, (2 bedrm), [shwr, tlt, a/c-cool, heat, TV, refrig, cook fac, micro, d/wash (1), toaster, blkts reqd, linen reqd], bbq. **D ♦ $22**, ♦ **$22**, ch con.

Wairere, (Bunk), (Farm), Fielding La, off Boorolite-Chapel Hill Rd, 16km SE of PO, ☎ 03 5777 3541, fax 03 5777 3705, 1 bunkhouse acc up to 20, (4 bedrm), [heat (wood), radio (cassette), micro, toaster, linen reqd], ldry, w/mach, dryer, dry rm, lounge (TV), lounge firepl, cook fac, refrig, bbq (covered). **D ♦ $10 - $15**, ♦ **$10 - $15**, BC MC VI.

Pop 300. (396km E Melbourne), See map on pages 694/695, ref K7. Small fishing & coastal holiday resort. Boating, Bush Walking, Fishing, Horse Riding, Sailing, Scenic Drives, Surfing, Swimming (Beach, River), Tennis, Water Skiing.

Hotels/Motels

★★★☆ **The Marlo Hotel**, (LH), Bed & Breakfast style property. 17 Argyle Pde, ☎ 03 5154 8201, fax 03 5154 8493, 3 rms [shwr, spa bath (2), tlt, hairdry (2), TV, clock radio], ✗, ☎, non smoking rms (3). **BLB ♦ $90 - $130**, ♦♦ **$90 - $130**, BC EFT MC VI.

Self Catering Accommodation

★★★☆ **AA Relocation & Holiday Homes**, (House), Jetty Rd, 200m E of jetty, ☎ 03 9873 3060, (2 stry), 1 house acc up to 8, (4 bedrm), [shwr, tlt, hairdry, heat, tel (local), TV, video, clock radio, refrig, cook fac, micro, elec frypan, d/wash, linen reqd-fee], ldry, lounge firepl, non smoking property. **W $750 - $1,050**.

★★★ **Brodribb River Rainforest Cabins**, Healeys Rd, 3km NE of PO, ☎ 03 5154 8223, fax 03 5154 8223, 3 cabins acc up to 6, (2 bedrm), [shwr, tlt, evap cool, TV, radio, refrig, cook fac ltd, micro, d/wash, toaster, blkts, doonas, linen, pillows], ldry, w/mach, iron, iron brd, lounge firepl, bbq, c/park (carport), plygr, cots, non smoking property, **D ♦♦♦♦ $99**, ♦ **$11**, Min book applies, ♿.

★★★ **Marlo Motel**, (Apt), 6 Argyle Pde, ☎ 03 5154 8226, fax 03 5154 8463, 12 apts acc up to 6, [shwr, bath, tlt, heat, elec blkts, TV, clock radio, refrig, cook fac, toaster, blkts, doonas, linen, pillows], ldry, bbq (BBQ area)-fee, ☎. **D ♦♦ $60.50 - $93.50**, ♦ **$11**, ch con, Min book applies, BC MC VI, ♿.

★★☆ **Tabbara Lodge Marlo**, (HU), 1 Marlo Rd, 500m N of PO, ☎ 03 5154 8231, 4 units acc up to 5, (1 bedrm), [shwr, tlt, c/fan, heat, elec blkts, TV, video, clock radio, refrig, cook fac, micro, elec frypan, blkts, doonas, linen, pillows], ldry, pool (salt water), spa, bbq (covered), boat park, plygr, cots. **D $48 - $80**, **W $285 - $560**, ch con, Light breakfast available. BC MC VI.

★★★ **(Cottage Section)**, 71 Marine Pde, 1 cotg acc up to 7, (3 bedrm), [shwr, bath, tlt, heat, elec blkts, tel, TV, video, clock radio, refrig, cook fac, micro, elec frypan, blkts, linen, pillows], ldry, bbq, cots. **D $65 - $96**, **W $390 - $680**.

★☆ **Cape Conran Coastal Park**, Yeerung Rd, 19km E of PO, ☎ 03 5154 8438, 8 cabins acc up to 8, [shwr, tlt, heat (pot belly), refrig, cook fac ltd, micro, toaster, blkts reqd, linen reqd, pillows reqd], ldry, bbq, ice, ☎. **D ♦♦♦♦ $73 - $110**, ♦ **$14 - $16**, **W ♦♦♦♦ $440 - $670**, ♦ **$85 - $99**, ch con, Coastal Park location restricts facilities.

(Lodge Section), 3 rms acc up to 17, [shwr, tlt, heat (pot belly), refrig, cook fac, d/wash, toaster, blkts reqd, linen reqd, pillows reqd], bbq. **D $140 - $220**, **W $885 - $1,320**, Minimum booking - 10 people.

Pop 7,400. (164km NW Melbourne), See map on pages 694/695, ref D5. Old gold mining town located on the Pyrenees Hwy.

★★★☆ **Bristol Hill Motor Inn**, (M), 1 High St (Pyrenees Hwy), 1km W of PO, ☎ 03 5461 3833, fax 03 5460 4944, 17 units [shwr, spa bath (2), tlt, hairdry, a/c, elec blkts, tel, TV, video, clock radio, t/c mkg, refrig, mini bar, toaster], iron, iron brd, ✗ (Mon to Sat), bar (cocktail), pool, spa, bbq, rm serv (Mon to Sat), cots-fee. **RO ♦ $77 - $110**, ♦♦ **$82.50 - $121**, ♦ **$11**, ch con, 5 units ★★★★. AE BC DC EFT MC VI, ♿.

★★★☆ **Golden Country Caratel**, (M), 134 Park Rd, 1.6km N of PO, ☎ 03 5461 2344, fax 03 5460 5166, 10 units [shwr, tlt, hairdry, a/c, elec blkts, tel, TV, video-fee, clock radio, t/c mkg, refrig, toaster], ldry, iron, iron brd, rec rm, pool-heated (solar), bbq, plygr. **RO ♦ $64 - $80**, ♦♦ **$75 - $80**, ♦ **$12**, ch con, Min book long w/ends and Easter, AE BC DC EFT MC MP VI, ♿.

★★★ **Dorojon Motel**, (M), 1 Primrose St, 1.6km E of PO, ☎ 03 5461 1555, fax 03 5461 1866, 11 units [shwr, tlt, a/c, elec blkts, tel, TV, movie, clock radio, t/c mkg, refrig], ✕, pool, bbq, dinner to unit, plygr, cots-fee. **RO ⬩ $42 - $49.50, ⬩⬩ $52 - $60.50, ⬩⬩⬩ $70 - $82.50**, AE BC EFT MC VI.

★★★ **Junction Motel Maryborough**, (M), 2 High St (Pyrenees Hwy), 1km W of PO, ☎ 03 5461 1744, fax 03 5461 4908, 16 units [shwr, tlt, a/c, elec blkts, tel, TV, radio, t/c mkg, refrig, toaster], pool, bbq, cots-fee, non smoking units (9). **RO ⬩ $60 - $65, ⬩⬩ $70 - $110, ⬩ $11**, ch con, AE BC DC EFT MC VI.

★★★ **The Highlanders Haven**, (M), 72 Sutton Rd, 1.7km E of PO, ☎ 03 5460 4122, fax 03 5460 4122, 12 units [shwr, tlt, a/c-cool (3), a/c (9), heat (3), elec blkts, TV, clock radio, t/c mkg, refrig], ldry, conf fac, c/park (undercover) (6), cots, non smoking rms (6). **BLB ⬩ $44, ⬩⬩ $55, ⬩ $11**, BC MC VI.

★★☆ **Wattle Grove Motel**, (M), 65 Derby Rd (Ballarat Rd), 1.6km S of PO, ☎ 03 5461 1877, fax 03 5461 1877, 11 units [shwr, tlt, hairdry, a/c, elec blkts, tel, TV, clock radio, t/c mkg, refrig, toaster], ✕, BYO, bbq, dinner to unit, plygr, cots-fee. **RO ⬩ $49 - $55, ⬩⬩ $55 - $61, ⬩ $8**, ch con, AE BC DC EFT MC MCH VI.

★ **Bull & Mouth Hotel**, (LH), 119 High St, opposite PO, ☎ 03 5461 1002, (2 stry), 9 rms [shwr (3), tlt (3), elec blkts, t/c mkg], ✕ (Wed to Sat), ✆. **RO ⬩ $27.50 - $38.50, ⬩⬩ $38.50 - $49.50, ⬩⬩⬩ $49.50 - $60.50**, BC EFT MC VI.

Self Catering Accommodation

★★★ **Davoren Bed and Breakfast**, (Cotg), 376 Majorca Rd, 4km S of PO, ☎ 03 5461 2934, 1 cotg acc up to 3, (Studio - mudbrick & stone.), [ensuite, hairdry, fan, elec blkts, TV, t/c mkg, refrig, cook fac ltd, micro, elec frypan, toaster], lounge firepl, bbq. **BLB ⬩ $50, ⬩⬩ $80, ⬩ $35**, ch con.

B&B's/Guest Houses

★★★★☆ **Bella's Country House (c 1887)**, (B&B), 39 Burns St, 500m SE of PO, ☎ 03 5460 5574, fax 03 5460 5574, 4 rms [ensuite, bath (1), hairdry, a/c-cool (lounge only), fan, fire pl (2), cent heat, elec blkts, clock radio], lounge (TV, video, cd), lounge firepl, t/c mkg shared, refrig, non smoking property. **BB ⬩⬩ $110 - $165, ⬩ $33**, AE BC DC MC VI.

★★★☆ **Eany Farm**, (B&B), 178 Talbot Rd, Majorca 3465, 10km SE of PO, ☎ 03 5464 7267, 3 rms [c/fan (1), heat, elec blkts (1)], rec rm, lounge (cd player), lounge firepl, t/c mkg shared, cots, non smoking property. **BB ⬩ $60, ⬩⬩ $100**, ch con, BC MC VI.

★★★☆ **Maryborough Guest House B & B**, (GH), 44 Goldsmith St, 680m NW of PO, ☎ 03 5460 5808, 6 rms [hairdry, evap cool, c/fan (6), heat, cent heat, clock radio, doonas], lounge (TV, video), tennis, non smoking property. **BB ⬩ $60 - $65, ⬩⬩ $93 - $104**, ch con, Other meals by arrangement.

MARYSVILLE VIC 3779

Pop 650. (97km E Melbourne), See map on page 696, ref D5. Popular tourist resort with many walking tracks radiating from the town. Steavenson Falls, the tallest waterfall in Victoria at 84 metres is floodlit at night. Bowls, Bush Walking, Fishing, Golf, Horse Riding, Scenic Drives, Snow Skiing, Swimming (Pool), Tennis.

Hotels/Motels

★★★★☆ **The Cumberland Marysville**, (Ltd Lic H), 34 Murchison St, 100m W of PO, ☎ 03 5963 3203, fax 03 5963 3458, (2 stry gr fl), 43 rms [shwr, bath (9), spa bath (4), tlt, hairdry (16), a/c-cool, heat, elec blkts, tel, TV, clock radio, t/c mkg, refrig, mini bar (16)], ldry, dry rm, rec rm, lounge, conf fac, ✕, bar (cocktail), pool, sauna, spa, bbq, gym, tennis, cots, non smoking rms (5). **BB ⬩ $125, ⬩⬩ $190, DBB ⬩ $135 - $175, ⬩⬩ $220 - $260**, ch con, 18 rooms ★★★★. AE BC DC EFT MC VI, ⬩⬩.

★★★☆ **Scenic Bed & Breakfast Motel**, (M), Resort, 16 Darwin St, 400m W of PO, ☎ 03 5963 3247, fax 03 5963 4232, 10 units [shwr, tlt, hairdry, a/c-cool, heat, elec blkts, TV, t/c mkg, refrig, micro, toaster], ldry, ✕, bbq, cots, non smoking units. **BLB ⬩ $55 - $85, ⬩⬩ $69 - $99, ⬩ $16 - $26**, Min book long w/ends and Easter, AE BC EFT MC VI.

★★★ **Keppel's Hotel Marysville**, (LMH), Previously Marysville Hotel Motel, 42 Murchison St, 200m W of PO, ☎ 03 5963 3207, fax 03 5963 3566, (2 stry gr fl), 24 units [shwr, bath (5), tlt, hairdry, a/c, elec blkts, tel, TV, clock radio, t/c mkg, refrig], lounge, conf fac, ✕, pool, ✆, cots-fee, non smoking units (4). **RO ⬩ $55 - $66, ⬩⬩ $60.50 - $77, ⬩ $11**, BC EFT MC VI.

★★★ **Tower Motel**, (M), 33 Murchison St, 100m W of PO, ☎ 03 5963 3225, (2 stry gr fl), 17 units [shwr, tlt, a/c-cool, heat, elec blkts, tel, TV, t/c mkg, refrig], pool, bbq, plygr, cots, non smoking units (5). **RO ⬩ $69 - $82, ⬩⬩ $69 - $82, ⬩ $10**, ch con, BC DC MC VI.

★★☆ **Crossways Motel**, (M), 4 Woods Point Rd, 150m N of PO, ☎ 03 5963 3290, fax 03 5963 4445, 6 units [shwr, tlt, a/c, heat, elec blkts, TV, clock radio, t/c mkg, refrig, toaster], conf fac, ✕, cots-fee, non smoking units (3). **RO ⬩ $55 - $65, ⬩⬩ $60 - $70, ⬩ $10 - $15**, ch con, AE BC DC MC VI.

Self Catering Accommodation

★★★★☆ **Blackwood Cottages**, (Cotg), 38 Falls Rd, 300m S of PO, ☎ 03 5963 3333, fax 03 5963 3430, 9 cotgs acc up to 5, (2 bedrm), [shwr, tlt, hairdry, a/c-cool, c/fan, heat, elec blkts, TV, video-fee, clock radio, t/c mkg, refrig, cook fac, micro, d/wash (2), toaster, ldry (6), blkts, linen, pillows], ldry, w/mach, iron, iron brd, dry rm, bbq, c/park (carport), car wash, ✆, plygr, tennis, cots, non smoking property. **D ⬩⬩ $95 - $130, ⬩ $28**, ch con, Light breakfast available. AE BC DC EFT JCB MC VI.

★★★★ **Dalrymples Guest Cottages**, (Cotg), 18 Falls Rd, 300m S of PO, ☎ 03 5963 3416, fax 03 5963 3325, 4 cotgs [shwr, spa bath (2), tlt, hairdry, c/fan (1), fire pl, heat, elec blkts, TV, CD, t/c mkg, refrig, micro, toaster], bbq, breakfast ingredients. **BLB 👥 $132 - $165**, Other meals available. BC MC VI.

★★★★ **Melina Cottage**, (Cotg), 1120 Buxton Rd, 400m N of PO, ☎ 0419 103 834, 1 cotg acc up to 4, (2 bedrm), [shwr, tlt, hairdry, heat, elec blkts, TV, video, clock radio, t/c mkg, refrig, cook fac, micro, toaster, ldry (in unit), blkts, doonas, linen, pillows], w/mach, dryer, iron, iron brd, lounge firepl, non smoking property. **D 👥 $95 - $110, 👤 $15, W $630**, pen con, Min book long w/ends.

★★★☆ **Anastasia's Cottages**, (Cotg), 47 Lyell St, 800m SW of PO, ☎ 03 9543 6848, (2 stry), 1 cotg acc up to 6, (3 bedrm), [shwr, spa bath, tlt, c/fan, heat, elec blkts, tel, TV, clock radio, refrig, cook fac, micro, ldry (in unit), blkts, doonas, linen, pillows], lounge firepl, bbq, non smoking property. **D $120 - $170, W $700 - $750**, ch con, Minimum booking weekends & all holiday times.

★★★☆ **Barree Holiday Cottages**, (Cotg), 1 McLean St, 600m SW of PO, ☎ 03 5963 3287, fax 03 5963 3287, 2 cotgs acc up to 4, (2 bedrm - Mudbrick), [shwr, spa bath, tlt, c/fan, heat, elec blkts, TV, video, clock radio, refrig, cook fac, micro, toaster, ldry (in unit), blkts, doonas, linen, pillows], bbq (covered), cots-fee, non smoking property. **D 👥 $90 - $110, 👤 $20, W $550 - $650**, ch con.

★★★☆ **Fruit Salad Farm Garden Cottages**, (Cotg), Aubrey - Cuzens Dve, 1km W of PO, ☎ 03 5963 3232, 5 cotgs acc up to 13, (Studio, 1, 2 & 3 bedrm), [shwr, bath (hip) (4), spa bath (1), tlt, c/fan (1), fire pl, heat, elec blkts, TV, video-fee, clock radio, refrig, cook fac (3), cook fac ltd (2), micro (3), toaster, blkts, doonas, linen, pillows], ldry, w/mach, dryer, ☒, bbq, cots, breakfast ingredients. **BB 👥 $95 - $125, 👤 $25 - $30**, ch con, AE BC DC EFT MC VI.

★★★ **Amber View Lodges**, (Cotg), 3 Racecourse Rd, 600m N of PO, ☎ 03 5963 7214, fax 03 5963 7242, 2 cotgs acc up to 5, (2 bedrm), [shwr, tlt, a/c-cool, heat, elec blkts, TV, video (avail), clock radio, refrig, cook fac, micro, toaster, ldry (in unit), blkts, doonas, linen, pillows], w/mach, iron, bbq, c/park (carport), plygr, cots. **D $60 - $100, W $360 - $620**, BC MC VI.

★★★ **Rose Cottage Marysville**, (Cotg), 9 Settlers Way, 650m N of PO, ☎ 03 5963 7214, fax 03 5963 7242, (2 stry), 1 cotg acc up to 11, (4 bedrm), [shwr, spa bath, tlt, a/c, c/fan, heat, elec blkts, tel, TV, video, clock radio, refrig, cook fac, micro, toaster, ldry (in unit), blkts, linen, pillows], w/mach, iron, iron brd, bbq, non smoking property. **D $180 - $200, W $800 - $930**, Min book applies, BC MC VI.

B&B's/Guest Houses

★★★★☆ **Kerami House**, (GH), Children by arrangement. 7 Kerami Cres, 700m E of PO, ☎ 03 5963 3260, fax 03 5963 3525, (2 stry), 4 rms [ensuite, spa bath (1), hairdry, a/c, cent heat, elec blkts, clock radio, doonas], lounge (TV, stereo), lounge firepl, t/c mkg shared, refrig, non smoking rms. **BB 👥 $132 - $180, DBB 👥 $195 - $290**, Dinner by arrangement. BC MC VI.

★★★★ **Marylands Country House**, (GH), 22 Falls Rd, 500m S of PO, ☎ 03 5963 3204, fax 03 5963 3251, (2 stry gr fl), 62 rms [ensuite, spa bath (14), hairdry, c/fan, cent heat, tel, TV, clock radio, t/c mkg, doonas], ldry, iron, iron brd, rec rm, lounge (TV), conf fac, ☒, bar (cocktail), pool indoor heated, sauna, spa, t/c mkg shared, refrig, bbq, bicycle, gym, tennis, cots. **BB 👤 $159, 👥 $213, 👤 $100, DBB 👤 $203, 👥 $296, 👤 $130**, ch con, AE BC DC EFT MC VI.

★★★★ **Maryton Park B&B Country Cottages**, (B&B), Maryton La, 5km N of PO, ☎ 03 5963 3242, fax 03 5963 3752, 7 rms [shwr, tlt, fan, cent heat, elec blkts, radio, CD, t/c mkg, refrig, toaster], lounge (TV), bbq. **BB 👤 $80 - $100, 👥 $95 - $120**, Other meals by arrangement. BC JCB MC VI.

M
VICTORIA

Mountain Lodge Maryville Guest House

• Set in 2.5 hectares of gardens and bushland

• Superb dining (both traditional and a la carte)

• Good value for your money

• Brochure available

32 KINGS ROAD, MARYSVILLE, 3779 PH: (03) 5963 3270

★★★☆ **Mary Lyn Fifty & Over Holiday Resort**, (GH), 35 Lyell St, 500m SW of PO, ☎ 03 5963 3206, fax 03 5963 3510, (Multi-stry gr fl), 75 rms [shwr, tlt, c/fan, cent heat, elec blkts, tel], lift, ldry, w/mach, dryer, rec rm, lounge (TV), ✕, BYO, pool indoor heated, spa, t/c mkg shared, refrig, bowls, tennis. **D all meals ♦ $133 - $138, ♦♦ $240 - $250, W ♦ $798 - $833, ♦♦ $1,428 - $1,484**, BC MC VI.

★★★☆ **Mountain Lodge Marysville**, (GH), 32 Kings Rd, 650m S of PO, ☎ 03 5963 3270, fax 03 5963 4078, 24 rms [basin, shwr (21), tlt (21), heat (26), elec blkts, clock radio (8)], ldry, rec rm, lounge (TV), conf fac, ✕, BYO, pool (salt water), t/c mkg shared, refrig, bbq, tennis, cots-fee. **DBB ♦ $83 - $93, W ♦ $510 - $530, ◊ $510 - $530**, ch con, BC MC VI.

★★★☆ **Nanda Binya Lodge**, (GH), 29 Woods Point Rd, 900m E of PO, ☎ 03 5963 3433, fax 03 5963 3465, 6 rms [ensuite, bath (2), heat, t/c mkg, refrig, micro (1), doonas], ldry, dry rm, lounge (TV, video, stereo), lounge firepl, sauna, spa (heated), bbq, cots, non smoking rms. **BLB ♦♦ $70 - $115, ◊ $27**, ch con, Dinner by arrangement. AE BC MC VI.

★★☆ **Cathedral Mountain Christian Centre**, (GH), No alcohol. 975 Buxton Rd, "El Kanah", 2km N of PO, ☎ 03 5963 3229, fax 03 5963 3650, (2 stry gr fl), 30 rms [basin (20), ensuite (2), cent heat, elec blkts], ldry, rec rm, lounge (TV, video), conf fac, lounge firepl, ✕, t/c mkg shared, bbq, ✆, plygr, tennis, cots, non smoking property. **BLB ♦ $44, ♦♦ $66, D all meals ♦ $66, ♦♦ $110**, ch con, BC MC VI, ♿.

McCRAE VIC 3938

Pop 1,221. (74km S Melbourne), See map on page 697, ref B8. Popular peninsula tourist suburb. McCrae Homestead, erected in 1844, classified by the National Trust and open during holiday times. Boating, Fishing, Sailing, Swimming (Beach), Water Skiing.

B&B's/Guest Houses
★★★★☆ **Morning Glory Bed & Breakfast**, (B&B), No children's facilities, 93 Cinerama Cres, 5.5 km SE of Dromana PO, ☎ 03 5986 8744, fax 03 5986 1544, 2 rms [ensuite, bath (1), hairdry, fan, heat, elec blkts, clock radio], ldry, iron, iron brd, lounge (TV, video, cd), lounge firepl, t/c mkg shared, bbq, non smoking property. **BB ♦ $90 - $100, ♦♦ $110 - $130**, AE BC MC VI.

MEENIYAN VIC 3956

Pop 400. (151km SE Melbourne), See map on page 696, ref D7. Dairy farming area. Bowls, Golf, Swimming, Tennis.

Self Catering Accommodation
★★★ **The Bush Haven Cottage**, (Cotg), Tarwin Lower Rd, 3km W of PO, ☎ 03 5664 7237, 1 cotg acc up to 6, (3 bedrm), [shwr, tlt, c/fan, heat (wood), elec blkts, TV, clock radio, refrig, cook fac, toaster, blkts, linen, pillows], w/mach, bbq, breakfast ingredients, non smoking property. **BB ♦ $45, ♦♦ $85 - $100, ◊ $20**, ch con.

MENZIES CREEK VIC

See Dandenong Ranges Region.

MERBEIN VIC 3505

Pop 1,750. (570km NW Melbourne), See map on pages 694/695, ref B1. Citrus growing district on the banks of the Murray River. Boating, Bowls, Croquet, Fishing, Golf, Rowing, Sailing, Scenic Drives, Swimming (Pool, River), Tennis, Vineyards, Wineries, Water Skiing.

Hotels/Motels
★★★ **Merbein Motor Inn**, (M), 42 Box St, 300m NW of PO, ☎ 03 5025 3276, 10 units [shwr, tlt, a/c, elec blkts, tel, TV, clock radio, t/c mkg, refrig, toaster], cots. **RO ♦ $45 - $49, ♦♦ $54 - $60, ◊ $11**, ch con, BC MC MCH VI.

★★☆ **Merbein Hotel**, (LH), 89 Game St, 200m S of PO, ☎ 03 5025 2704, fax 03 5025 2809, (2 stry), 20 rms [basin, evap cool (15), elec blkts, TV (6), t/c mkg], ldry, conf fac, ✕ (Mon to Sat), bar, bbq, ✆. **BLB ♦ $27.50, ♦♦ $38.50, ◊ $11**, ch con, AE BC EFT MC VI.

Self Catering Accommodation
★★★★ **Glenbar Cottage**, (Cotg), Lot 1 Wentworth Rd, 4km N of PO, ☎ 03 5025 1239, 1 cotg acc up to 4, (2 bedrm), [shwr, bath (hip), tlt, hairdry, evap cool, c/fan, heat, TV, video, clock radio, t/c mkg, refrig, cook fac ltd, micro, toaster, blkts, doonas, linen, pillows], iron, iron brd, bbq, cots, breakfast ingredients, non smoking property. **BB ♦♦ $80, ◊ $10, W ♦♦ $350, ◊ $50**.

Other Accommodation
Sundreamer Houseboats, (Hbt), Paschendale Ave, 8km NW of PO, on S bank of Murray River, ☎ 03 5025 3538, 1 houseboat acc up to 10, (5 bedrm), [shwr, tlt, evap cool, heat, TV, radio, refrig, cook fac, micro, blkts, linen, pillows], w/mach, bbq. **W $1,400 - $2,000**, Security deposit - $400.

MERRICKS NORTH VIC 3926

Pop Part of Balnarring, (123km SE Melbourne), See map on page 697, ref C8. Mainly rural area situated on the Mornington Peninsula.

Hillingdon at Tussie Mussie Farm, (B&B), 206 Bittern-Dromana Rd, ☎ 03 5989 7348, fax 03 5989 7530, 3 rms (1 suite) [ensuite, spa bath (1), hairdry, a/c-cool, heat, elec blkts, tel, TV, clock radio, CD, t/c mkg, refrig], lounge firepl, bbq, tennis. **BB ♦♦ $150 - $240**, BC MC VI, (Rating under review).

MERRIJIG VIC 3723

Pop Nominal, (203km NE Melbourne), See map on page 696, ref E4. At foot of Mt Buller. Bush Walking, Fishing, Horse Riding, Scenic Drives, Swimming (River).

Hotels/Motels

AAA TOURISM *Special Rates*
★★★★ **Pinnacle Valley Resort**, (Ltd Lic H), 1 Mimosa Dve, 5.5km E of Mirimbah general store, ☎ 03 5777 5788, fax 03 5777 5736, (Multi-stry gr fl), 39 rms (3 suites) [shwr, bath (13), spa bath (7), tlt, hairdry, a/c, tel, TV, movie, clock radio, t/c mkg, refrig, mini bar, doonas], ldry, dry rm, rec rm, conf fac, ✕, pool-heated (solar), sauna, spa, bbq, ✆, mini golf, gym, ski hire, tennis, cots-fee. **D $125 - $250**, AE BC EFT MC VI.

★★★☆ **(Chalet Section)**, (2 stry gr fl), 17 chalets acc up to 6, (3 bedrm), [shwr, tlt, hairdry, a/c, cent heat, tel, TV, clock radio, t/c mkg, refrig, cook fac ltd, micro, toaster, blkts, doonas, linen, pillows], ldry-fee, cots-fee. **D $245 - $330**.

★★☆ **Arlberg Merrijig Motel Resort**, (M), Mt Buller Rd, ☎ 03 5777 5633, fax 03 5777 5780, 42 units [shwr, tlt, a/c, c/fan, heat, TV, movie, t/c mkg, refrig, cook fac ltd (1), micro (1), doonas], dry rm, rec rm, conf fac, ✕ (seasonal), pool-heated (solar), spa, bbq, ✆, ski hire, tennis, cots. **RO ♦ $65 - $95, ♦♦ $65 - $95, ◊ $15 - $20**, ch con, BC EFT MC VI.

★★☆ **Merrijig Motor Inn Resort**, (M), Mt Buller Rd, ☎ 03 5777 5702, fax 03 5777 5790, 23 units [shwr, tlt, cent heat, elec blkts (double bed only), TV, t/c mkg, refrig, cook fac (14), toaster, doonas], ldry, dry rm, lounge (TV), ✕, pool, sauna-fee, spa-fee, bbq, ✆, ski hire, tennis. **RO ♦ $55 - $90, ♦♦ $70 - $110, ◊ $10 - $25**, BC EFT MC VI, ♿.

Self Catering Accommodation
★★★★★ **Buttercup Cottage**, (Cotg), 271 Buttercup Rd, ☎ 03 5777 5591, fax 03 5777 5905, 1 cotg acc up to 4, (2 bedrm), [shwr, spa bath, tlt, hairdry, a/c, c/fan, elec blkts, cable tv, video, clock radio, CD, t/c mkg, refrig, cook fac, micro, d/wash, toaster, ldry, blkts, doonas, linen, pillows], iron, iron brd, lounge firepl, bbq, non smoking property. **BB ♦♦ $175, ◊ $55, W ♦♦ $1,050, ◊ $330**, ch con, Min book Christmas Jan long w/ends and Easter, AE BC MC VI.

★★★★ **(Guest House)**, 1 unit acc up to 4, (2 bedrm), [shwr, spa bath, tlt, hairdry, a/c-cool, heat, elec blkts, cable tv, video, clock radio, t/c mkg, refrig, cook fac, micro, toaster, blkts, doonas, linen, pillows], ldry, iron, iron brd, bbq, c/park (carport). **BB ♦♦ $145, ◊ $45, W ♦♦ $870, ◊ $270, RO ♦♦ $125, ◊ $40**, ch con.

B&B's/Guest Houses
★★★★ **Timbertop House B&B and Private Accomm**, (B&B), No children's facilities, 2057 Mt Buller Rd, 1km E of Timbertop bridge, ☎ 03 5777 5880, fax 03 5777 5983, (2 stry gr fl), 4 rms [ensuite, bath (2), spa bath (1), hairdry, a/c-cool, cent heat, elec blkts, t/c mkg, refrig], lounge (TV, cd player), bbq, non smoking property. **BB $159.50 - $192.50**, AE BC EFT MC VI.

★★★☆ **(Unit Section)**, No children's facilities, (2 stry), 1 unit acc up to 4, (2 bedrm), [shwr, tlt, hairdry, a/c-cool, cent heat, elec blkts, TV, t/c mkg, refrig, cook fac, micro, d/wash, ldry, blkts, linen, pillows], non smoking property. **D $192.50**.

★★★☆ **Brumby's Run**, (GH), No facilities for children under 12. Buttercup Rd, off Mt Buller Rd, 6km NE of school, ☎ 03 5777 5768, fax 03 5777 5981, 5 rms [heat, elec blkts, doonas], lounge (TV, video, stereo), t/c mkg shared, non smoking property. **BB ♦ $60, ♦♦ $110 - $125**, Dinner available. BC MC VI.

★★★☆ **Highlander Lodge**, (B&B), No facilities for children under 12. 4 Summit View Crt, off Alpine Ridge Dve, ☎ 03 5777 5511, fax 03 5777 5912, (Multi-stry), 4 rms [ensuite (2), hairdry, heat, elec blkts, clock radio, doonas], ldry, dry rm, lounge (TV, video, cd), spa, cook fac, t/c mkg shared, refrig, bbq, non smoking rms. **BB ♦ $45 - $50**, BC MC VI.

★★ **The Dunlops Merrijig Lodge**, (GH), Mt Buller Hwy, ☎ 03 5777 5590, fax 03 5777 5290, 14 rms [ensuite (2), cent heat, doonas], dry rm, rec rm, lounge (TV, video), pool, sauna, spa, t/c mkg shared, bbq. **BB ♦ $35, ◊ $35**, ch con, BC MC VI.

METUNG VIC 3904

Pop 500. (314km E Melbourne), See map on pages 694/695, ref J7. Small tourist resort, situated on Lake King. Boating, Bowls, Fishing, Sailing, Swimming (Lake), Tennis, Water Skiing.

Self Catering Accommodation

AAA
TOURISM
Special Rates

★★★★☆ **McMillans of Metung**, (Cotg), 155 Metung Rd, ☎ 03 5156 2283, fax 03 5156 2375, 11 cotgs acc up to 11, (1, 2, 3 & 4 bedrm), [shwr, bath, spa bath (4), tlt, a/c, c/fan, TV, video, clock radio, refrig, cook fac, micro, d/wash, ldry (in unit), blkts, linen, pillows], rec rm, conf fac, pool-heated, bbq, c/park (carport), ☏, jetty, gym, tennis, cots. **D ♦♦ $95 - $185, ◊ $25**, ch con, Min book Christmas Jan long w/ends and Easter, BC MC VI.

★★★★☆ **Slipway**, (HU), 50 Metung Rd, ☎ 03 5156 2469, fax 03 5156 2761, (2 stry), 6 units acc up to 8, (3 bedrm), [shwr, spa bath, tlt, c/fan, heat, tel, TV, video, CD, cook fac, micro, d/wash, ldry (in unit), blkts, linen, pillows], iron, lounge firepl, c/park (garage), jetty. **D $168 - $264**, Min book all holiday times.

★★★★☆ **Terrazas Del Lago**, (Cotg), Cnr Metung Rd & Nicholas Ave, 1.5km E of PO, ☎ 03 5156 2666, fax 03 5156 2677, (2 stry gr fl), 10 cotgs acc up to 1, (1, 2, 3 & 5 bedrm), [shwr, bath, spa bath (2), tlt, hairdry, a/c-cool (3), fan, heat (wood), elec blkts, TV, video, clock radio, t/c mkg, refrig, cook fac, micro, elec frypan, d/wash, toaster, ldry (in unit), blkts, linen, pillows], iron, iron brd, conf fac, pool-heated (solar), spa (heated), bbq, ☏, plygr, cots-fee, non smoking units (9). **D ♦♦ $90 - $200**, Min book Christmas Jan long w/ends and Easter, BC EFT MC VI.

★★★★ **Metung Marina Views**, (Cotg), 35 Reserve Rd, 1km N of PO, ☎ 03 9707 2402, fax 03 9707 2402, 1 cotg acc up to 9, (3 bedrm), [ensuite, shwr, spa bath, tlt, hairdry, c/fan, heat, TV, video, clock radio, refrig, cook fac, micro, d/wash, toaster, ldry, blkts, doonas, linen reqd, pillows], w/mach, dryer, iron, iron brd, bbq, c/park (undercover), non smoking property. **D ♦♦ $75 - $100, ◊ $15**, ch con, Min book applies.

★★★★ **The Moorings**, (Apt), Metung Rd, ☎ 03 5156 2750, fax 03 5156 2755, (2 stry gr fl), 33 apts acc up to 6, (1, 2 & 3 bedrm), [shwr, bath (21), tlt, a/c (15), heat, elec blkts (4), cable tv, clock radio, t/c mkg, refrig, cook fac, micro, d/wash, toaster, ldry (in unit), blkts, linen, pillows], iron, iron brd, pool, pool indoor heated, spa, bbq, mooring, tennis, cots-fee. **D $135 - $305**, AE BC DC EFT MC VI.

★★★★ **(Motel Section)**, (2 stry gr fl), 7 units [shwr, spa bath (2), tlt, hairdry, a/c, cable tv, clock radio, t/c mkg, refrig, toaster], ldry. **RO ♦ $115 - $140, ♦♦ $115 - $140**.

★★★☆ **The Pelican Perch**, (HU), 7 Smiths Way, 1.5km E of PO, off Nicholas Ave, ☎ 03 5156 2519, fax 03 5156 2519, 1 unit acc up to 2, (Studio), [shwr, tlt, hairdry, heat, elec blkts, TV, video, clock radio, refrig, cook fac ltd, micro, elec frypan, toaster, blkts, linen, pillows], iron, bbq, c/park (carport), non smoking units. **D $90 - $120, W $500 - $800**, Min book Christmas Jan long w/ends and Easter.

Operator Comment: Completely private, fabulous boat and water views

★★★ **Arendell Holiday Units**, (HU), 30 Mairburn Rd, ☎ 03 5156 2507, fax 03 5156 2507, 6 units acc up to 6, (1 & 2 bedrm), [shwr, bath (hip) (5), tlt, c/fan, heat, TV, clock radio, refrig, cook fac, micro, toaster, linen reqd-fee], ldry, w/mach (4), dryer (3), pool, bbq, plygr, cots. **D $55 - $120, W $350 - $840**.

★★★ **Maeburn Cottages**, (Cotg), 33 Mairburn Rd, 1km W of PO, ☎ 03 5156 2736, 4 cotgs acc up to 4, (2 bedrm), [shwr, bath (hip) (1), tlt, fan, heat, TV, clock radio, refrig, cook fac, micro, elec frypan, toaster, ldry (in unit)], iron, iron brd, bbq, boat park. **D $66 - $95, W $396 - $570**, Dogs welcome.

★★ **Akora Flats**, (HU), 51 Stirling Rd, 1km N of PO, ☎ 03 5156 2320, fax 03 5156 2320, 4 units acc up to 5, (2 bedrm), [shwr, tlt, heat, TV, clock radio, refrig, cook fac, micro, toaster, blkts, linen reqd-fee, pillows], ldry, bbq, plygr, Pets allowed by prior arrangement. **D $50 - $90, W $240 - $600**, Min book Christmas Jan long w/ends and Easter.

METUNG VIC continued...

B&B's/Guest Houses

★★★★☆ **Bancroft Bay Apartments**, (GH), No facilities for children under 12. 28 Main Rd, 300m S of PO, ☎ 03 5156 2216, fax 03 5156 2216, (2 stry gr fl), 8 rms (3 suites) [shwr, tlt, hairdry, a/c, elec blkts, TV, clock radio, t/c mkg, refrig, micro (2), doonas], ldry, cafe, mooring, ☎. **D** ♦♦ **$85 - $140**, ⚲ **$20**, Breakfast available, AE BC MC VI.

★★★★☆ **Beecroft's Clovelly of Metung B & B**, (B&B), 5 Essington Cl, 500m N of PO, ☎ 03 5156 2428, fax 03 5156 2424, 3 rms [ensuite, spa bath, hairdry, c/fan, heat, elec blkts, clock radio], lounge (TV), t/c mkg shared, non smoking property. **BB** ♦ **$114**, ♦♦ **$143**, ⚲ **$50**.

Other Accommodation

Metung Cruiser, (Cruiser), Metung Rd, ☎ 03 5156 2208, fax 03 5156 2291, 14 cruisers acc up to 10, [shwr, tlt, heat (8), TV (6), radio, refrig, cook fac, blkts reqd-fee, doonas reqd, linen reqd-fee]. **D $350**, Security deposit - $500 to 750.

Riviera Nautic, (Cruiser), 185 Metung Rd, at entrance to Chinamans Creek, 1.3km N of PO, ☎ 03 5156 2243, fax 03 5156 2404, 6 cruisers acc up to 10, [shwr, tlt, radio, refrig, cook fac, blkts, linen, pillows]. **W $1,450 - $3,420**, Security deposit $300. BC EFT MC VI.

(Cruising Yacht Section), 16 yachts acc up to 8, [shwr, tlt, radio, refrig, cook fac, blkts, linen, pillows]. **W $1,600 - $3,250**, Security deposit $300.

MILAWA VIC 3678

Pop 270. (237km NE Melbourne), See map on pages 694/695, ref G5. Centre of farming & wine producing district. Bowls, Scenic Drives, Squash, Tennis, Vineyards, Wineries.

Hotels/Motels

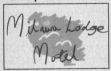

★★★ **Milawa Lodge Motel**, (M), Snow Rd, ☎ 03 5727 3326, fax 03 5727 3799, 10 units [shwr, tlt, a/c, elec blkts, tel, TV, clock radio, t/c mkg, refrig], ldry, ⊠ (bookings preferred), BYO, pool, spa, bbq, cots. **RO** ♦ **$70 - $75**, ♦♦ **$75 - $80**, ⚲ **$10**, ch con, AE BC DC MC VI.

MILDURA VIC 3500

Pop 24,150. (557km NW Melbourne), See map on pages 694/695, ref B1. Includes: IRYMPLE. Citrus, dried fruit & wine producing district, in the heart of Sunraysia. Tourist Information Centre 180 - 190 Deakin Ave, 03 5021 4424. Art Gallery, Boating, Bowls, Bush Walking, Croquet, Fishing, Golf, Horse Racing, Horse Riding, Rowing, Sailing, Scenic Drives, Shooting, Squash, Swimming (Pool, River), Tennis, Trotting, Vineyards, Wineries, Water Skiing. See also Buronga, Colignan, Merbein, Nangiloc & Red Cliffs.

Hotels/Motels

★★★★☆ **Mildura Inlander Sun Resort**, (M), 373 Deakin Ave, 2.6km SW of PO, ☎ 03 5023 3823, fax 03 5023 7610, 87 units [shwr, spa bath (15), tlt, hairdry, a/c, TV, movie, clock radio, t/c mkg, refrig, mini bar, cook fac ltd (9)], ldry, iron, iron brd, conf fac, ⊠, bar (cocktail), pool, spa (heated), bbq, 24hr reception, rm serv, plygr, gym, tennis, cots-fee, non smoking units (30). **RO** ♦ **$99 - $205**, ♦♦ **$104 - $205**, ⚲ **$12**, AE BC DC EFT MC VI.

★★★★ **Boulevard Motor Inn**, (M), 385 Deakin Ave, 2.7km SW of PO, ☎ 03 5023 5023, fax 03 5022 1675, (2 stry gr fl), 48 units [shwr, spa bath (1), tlt, hairdry, evap cool, heat, elec blkts, tel, cable tv, video-fee, movie, clock radio, t/c mkg, refrig], ldry, iron, iron brd, conf fac, ⊠, bar (cocktail), pool, AE BC DC MC MP VI.

★★★★ **Chaffey International Motor Inn**, (M), 244 Deakin Ave, 1.4km SW of PO, ☎ 03 5023 5833, fax 03 5021 1972, (2 stry gr fl), 33 units [shwr, spa bath (8), tlt, hairdry, a/c-cool, heat, tel, cable tv, video, clock radio, t/c mkg, refrig, mini bar, cook fac (1)], ldry, iron, iron brd, conv fac, ⊠ (Mon to Sat), pool, spa, rm serv, plygr, cots, non smoking units (25). **RO** ♦ **$94 - $172**, ♦♦ **$99 - $172**, ⚲ **$11**, AE BC DC EFT MC MP VI, ♿.

★★★★ **City Colonial Motor Inn**, (M), 24 Madden Ave, 100m NE of PO, ☎ 03 5021 1800, fax 03 5023 4520, (2 stry gr fl), 14 units [shwr, spa bath (3), tlt, hairdry, a/c, elec blkts, tel, cable tv, video-fee, clock radio, t/c mkg, refrig, toaster], ldry, pool-heated (solar), bbq, dinner to unit (Tues to Sun), cots-fee. **RO** ♦ **$68 - $85.80**, ♦♦ **$77 - $103.40**, ⚲ **$10**, ch con, AE BC DC EFT MC MP VI, ♿.

★★★★ **Commodore Motor Inn - Mildura**, (M), Cnr Deakin Ave & Seventh St, 150m SE of railway station, ☎ 03 5023 0241, fax 03 5021 1585, (2 stry gr fl), 58 units [shwr, spa bath (12), tlt, hairdry, evap cool (14), a/c (30), heat, elec blkts, tel, TV, video (12), clock radio, t/c mkg, refrig, mini bar (44)], ldry, iron (44), iron brd (44), ⊠ (Mon to Sat), pool, bbq, rm serv, cots-fee, non smoking units (29). **RO** ♦ **$65 - $121**, ♦♦ **$75 - $121**, ⚲ **$10**, ch con, 14 units ★★★☆, AE BC DC EFT MC VI

Operator Comment: Refer to main advertisement.

★★★★ **Early Australian Motor Inn**, (M), 453 Deakin Ave, 75m N of Centre Plaza, ☎ 03 5021 1011, fax 03 5021 2929, (2 stry gr fl), 16 units [shwr, spa bath (9), tlt, hairdry, a/c, c/fan (6), tel, cable tv, video (avail), clock radio, t/c mkg, refrig, mini bar], iron, iron brd, ⊠ (Mon to Sat), pool, rm serv, cots-fee, non smoking units (5). **RO** ♦ **$98 - $108**, ♦♦ **$108 - $118**, ♦♦♦ **$118 - $128**, ♦♦♦♦ **$128 - $138**, AE BC DC EFT MC MP VI.

★★★☆ **7th Street Motel**, (M), 153 Seventh St, opposite railway station, ☎ 03 5023 1796, fax 03 5023 7691, 11 units (2 suites) [shwr, tlt, hairdry, a/c, c/fan (10), elec blkts, cable tv, clock radio, t/c mkg, refrig, micro, toaster], ldry, iron, iron brd, pool, bbq, c/park (carport) (9), ☎, cots, non smoking units (7). **RO** ♦ **$65 - $85**, ♦♦ **$80 - $120**, ♀ **$12 - $15**, AE BC DC EFT MC VI.
Operator Comment: Reservations 1800 152050. 7thstreet.com.au

★★★☆ **Central Motel Mildura**, (M), Cnr Tenth St & Madden Ave, 500m SW of PO, ☎ 03 5021 1177, fax 03 5021 3280, (2 stry gr fl), 26 units [shwr, spa bath (2), tlt, a/c, elec blkts, tel, cable tv, video-fee, clock radio, t/c mkg, refrig, cook fac (2), toaster], ldry, ✗, pool, rm serv, dinner to unit, c/park (carport), cots, non smoking units (11). **BLB** ♦ **$80**, ♦♦ **$88**, ♀ **$11**, AE BC DC MC MP VI.

★★★☆ **City Gate Motel**, (M), 89 Seventh St, 700m SE of railway station, ☎ 03 5022 1077, fax 03 5021 1438, 22 units [shwr, bath, spa bath (1), tlt, hairdry, a/c, elec blkts, tel, TV, video-fee, movie, clock radio, t/c mkg, refrig, toaster], ldry, pool, spa, bbq, dinner to unit, cots, non smoking units (3). **RO** ♦ **$64 - $72**, ♦♦ **$72 - $90**, ♀ **$12**, ch con, AE BC DC MC VI.

★★★☆ **Mid City Plantation Motel**, (M), 145 Deakin Ave, 500m SW of PO, ☎ 03 5023 0317, fax 03 5023 2552, (2 stry gr fl), 22 units [shwr, spa bath (2), tlt, hairdry, evap cool (20), a/c (2), heat, elec blkts, tel, TV, clock radio, t/c mkg, refrig, toaster], ldry, iron, iron brd, ✗, pool, bbq, c/park (carport) (12), cots-fee, non smoking units (8). **RO** ♦ **$59 - $99**, ♦♦ **$66 - $132**, ♀ **$12**, AE BC DC EFT MC VI.

★★★☆ **Mildura All Seasons Motor Inn**, (M), Previously New Wheatlands Motel, 433 Deakin Ave, 150m N of Centre Plaza, ☎ 03 5023 3266, fax 03 5023 5455, (2 stry gr fl), 22 units [shwr, tlt, hairdry, a/c, elec blkts, tel, TV, video-fee, clock radio, t/c mkg, refrig], ldry, iron, iron brd, pool, bbq, dinner to unit, c/park (carport), plygr, cots-fee, non smoking units (8). **RO** ♦ **$55 - $85**, ♦♦ **$62 - $92**, ♀ **$11**, AE BC DC EFT MC VI.

★★★☆ **Mildura Grand Hotel**, (LH), Seventh St, opp railway station, ☎ 03 5023 0511, fax 03 5022 1801, (2 stry gr fl), 101 rms (8 suites) [shwr, bath (hip) (24), spa bath (11), tlt, hairdry (63), a/c, tel, TV, movie, clock radio, t/c mkg, refrig, mini bar (63)], lift, ldry, lounge, conf fac, ✉ (Mon to Sat), pool-heated (solar), sauna, spa, 24hr reception, rm serv, c/park (limited), ☎, cots. **BB** ♦ **$77 - $110**, ♦♦ **$110 - $143**, ♀ **$22, Suite BB $176 - $462**, ch con, 38 rooms ★★☆, 3 suites ★★★★☆, AE BC DC EFT JCB MC VI, ₰.

★★★☆ **Mildura Motor Inn**, (M), 376 Deakin Ave, 350m N of Centre Plaza, ☎ 03 5023 7377, fax 03 5023 7065, (2 stry gr fl), 26 units [shwr, spa bath (7), tlt, hairdry, a/c, c/fan (12), elec blkts, tel, cable tv, video-fee, clock radio, t/c mkg, refrig, mini bar (63)], ldry, iron, iron brd, conf fac, ✉, bar (cocktail), pool, spa, bbq, rm serv, cots-fee, non smoking units (10). **RO** ♦ **$90 - $165**, ♦♦ **$95 - $175**, ♀ **$11**, 5 units ★★★★. AE BC DC EFT JCB MC MP VI, ₰.

★★★☆ **Mildura Park Motel**, (M), 250 Eighth St, 1.4km W of Deakin Ave, ☎ 03 5023 0479, fax 03 5022 1651, (2 stry gr fl), 28 units [shwr, bath (hip) (14), tlt, hairdry (21), evap cool (14), a/c (14), heat (14), elec blkts, tel, TV, video-fee, clock radio, t/c mkg, refrig, toaster], ldry, iron brd (21), conf fac, bar, pool, bbq, c/park (carport) (14), trailer park, cots-fee, non smoking units (11). **RO** ♦ **$46 - $92**, ♦♦ **$49 - $99**, ♀ **$11**, ch con, 4 units ★★☆. AE BC DC EFT MC MCH VI
Operator Comment: Off highway, genuine quiet place to sleep, park garden setting.

★★★☆ **Mildura Plaza Motor Inn**, (M), 836 Fifteenth St (Calder Hwy), opposite Centre Plaza, ☎ 03 5021 1155, fax 03 5021 1844, (2 stry gr fl), 24 units [shwr, spa bath (5), tlt, hairdry, a/c, elec blkts, tel, cable tv, video-fee, clock radio, t/c mkg, refrig], ldry, iron, iron brd, conf fac, pool-heated (solar), spa, bbq, dinner to unit (Sun to Thur), cots-fee, non smoking units (8). **RO** ♦ **$76 - $106**, ♦♦ **$87 - $117**, ♀ **$11**, ch con, AE BC DC EFT JCB MC MP VI, ₰.

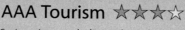

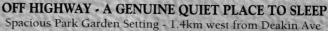

Aarinda Retreat

*A*ccommodation for 2 to 6 people, you have complete privacy, your own swimming pool, bbq & outdoor furniture in a pleasant garden setting. Short stroll to all shopping (7 days), restaurants, hotel and transport.

Friendliness, Cleanliness, Comfort and Every Convenience

Aabrinderlea Cottage

A cottage in a garden, shady trees, swimming pool, BBQ & outdoor furniture.

Free Call 1800 637 269

3 Elizabeth Avenue, Mildura, 3500

Ph: 03 5023 2601 Fax: 03 5021 3094

Resident Owners: Dorithe & Ron Dowson

Mildura Holiday Houseboats

Drift, dream and discover ...

...the delight and magic of the Murray and Darling Rivers, in luxury, space and comfort

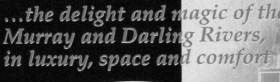

Fully self-contained with:
- Microwave • Dishwasher • Colour TV • VCR
- CD Player • Two Large Fridges • Heating
- Ducted Air Conditioning • Linen • Two way radio
- 2-10 Berth • Diesel 12 Volt / 240 V Power
- Gas • BBQ • Shady canopy on top deck.

PO Box 249, Mildura, Vic. 3502

Tel: (03) 5021 4414   Fax: (03) 5021 1453

Toll Free: 1800 800 842

★★★☆ **Murray View Motel**, (M), 82 Seventh St, 800m SE of railway station, ☎ 03 5021 1200, fax 03 5021 1199, (2 stry gr fl), 10 units [shwr, bath (hip) (3), tlt, hairdry, a/c, elec blkts, tel, cable tv, video-fee, clock radio, t/c mkg, refrig], ldry, iron, iron brd, pool-heated (solar), bbq, dinner to unit (Mon-Fri), cots, non smoking units (6). **RO** ♦ **$63 - $110**, ♦♦ **$68 - $120**, ♦ **$11**, ch con, AE BC DC EFT MC VI.

★★★☆ **Orana Motor Inn**, (M), 2101 Calder Hwy, Irymple 3498, 3km SE of Mildura Plaza, ☎ 03 5024 5903, fax 03 5024 5903, 12 units [shwr, tlt, hairdry, a/c, elec blkts, tel, TV, movie, clock radio, t/c mkg, refrig, toaster], ldry, iron, iron brd, pool, bbq, dinner to unit, c/park (carport), plygr, cots, non smoking units (8). **RO** ♦ **$47 - $70**, ♦♦ **$54 - $70**, ♦ **$11**, pen con, AE BC DC EFT MC MCH VI.

★★★☆ **River City Motel**, (M), Cnr San Mateo Ave & Fifteenth St, 200m SE of Centre Plaza, ☎ 03 5023 5177, fax 03 5021 2155, 16 units [shwr, tlt, a/c, elec blkts, tel, TV, clock radio, t/c mkg, refrig, toaster], ldry, pool, spa, bbq, cots-fee, non smoking units (5). **RO** ♦ **$66**, ♦♦ **$71.50**, ♦ **$11**, AE BC DC MC VI.

★★★☆ **Sandors Motor Inn - Mildura**, (M), 179 Deakin Ave, 800m SW of PO, ☎ 03 5023 0047, fax 03 5022 2395, (2 stry gr fl), 30 units [shwr, bath (hip) (15), tlt, hairdry (21), a/c, heat, elec blkts, tel, TV, video (9)-fee, clock radio, t/c mkg, refrig, mini bar, toaster], ldry, iron (21), iron brd (21), conf fac, ✕, bar (cocktail), pool, sauna-fee, spa, bbq, rm serv, cots, non smoking units (8). **RO** ♦ **$93 - $98**, ♦♦ **$100 - $105**, ♦ **$10**, ch con, 8 units ★★★★. AE BC DC MC MP VI.

★★★☆ **Sunland Motel**, (M), 232 Deakin Ave, 1.3km SW of PO, ☎ 03 5022 1466, fax 03 5022 1756, (2 stry gr fl), 34 units [shwr, bath (hip) (14), tlt, hairdry (20), evap cool (26), a/c (8), heat, elec blkts, tel, cable tv, video-fee, clock radio, t/c mkg, refrig], ldry, ✕ (Sat), pool, bbq, car wash, cots, non smoking units (11). **RO** ♦ **$60 - $75**, ♦♦ **$65 - $85**, ♦ **$15**, 14 units ★★★☆. AE BC EFT MC VI.

★★★☆ **The New Deakin Motor Inn**, (M), 413 Deakin Ave, 300m N of Centre Plaza, ☎ 03 5023 0218, fax 03 5021 3193, 25 units [shwr, bath (2), spa bath (1), tlt, hairdry (21), a/c, elec blkts, tel, TV, video-fee, clock radio, t/c mkg, refrig, toaster], ldry, rec rm, ✕, pool, sauna-fee, spa-fee, bbq, dinner to unit, plygr, gym, cots, non smoking units (10). **RO** ♦ **$60 - $125**, ♦♦ **$66 - $175**, ♦ **$10 - $15**, ch con, AE BC DC EFT MC VI.

★★★ **Cottonwood Motel**, (M), 326 Deakin Ave, 2.4km SW of PO, ☎ 03 5023 5166, fax 03 5021 1534, 31 units [shwr, tlt, a/c, elec blkts, tel, TV, movie, clock radio, t/c mkg, refrig], ldry, ✕ (Mon to Sat), pool, bbq, rm serv, non smoking units (13). **RO** ♦ **$55 - $60.50**, ♦♦ **$66 - $71.50**, ♦ **$15**, ch con, AE BC DC EFT MC VI.

★★★ **Mildura Golf Club Inc**, (M), Twelfth St Extension, 2.9km W of PO, ☎ 03 5023 3966, fax 03 5023 1751, 40 units (4 suites) [shwr, tlt, a/c-cool, heat, elec blkts, tel, TV, clock radio, t/c mkg, refrig, toaster], ldry, conf fac, ✕, pool, sauna, spa, bbq, rm serv, c/park (carport), golf-fee, cots. **RO $60.50, Suite D $71.50 - $104.50**, ch con, 20 units ★★★☆, AE BC DC MC VI.

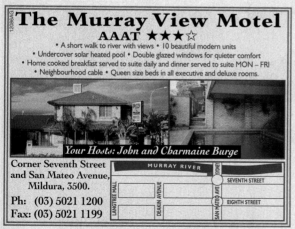

★★★ **Sunraysia Motel & Holiday Apartments**, (M), 441 Deakin Ave, 100m N of Centre Plaza, ☎ 03 5023 0137, fax 03 5022 2638, 12 units [shwr, tlt, hairdry, a/c, elec blkts, tel, TV, video, clock radio, t/c mkg, refrig, mini bar, toaster], ldry, pool, bbq, dinner to unit, plygr, cots, non smoking units (5). **RO** ♦ **$44 - $59**, ♦♦ **$52 - $69**, ♦ **$10**, ch con, AE BC DC EFT MC MCH VI, ♿.

★★★☆ **(Apartment Section)**, 4 apts acc up to 6, (1 & 2 bedrm), [shwr, bath (1), tlt, a/c, elec blkts, tel, TV, video-fee, clock radio, refrig, cook fac, elec frypan, toaster, blkts, linen, pillows], cots. **D $65 - $125, W $390 - $825**, pen con.

★★★ **Three States Motel**, (M), 847 Fifteenth St, 50m NW of Centre Plaza, ☎ 03 5023 3735, or 03 5023 7310, fax 03 5023 3735, 10 units [shwr, tlt, hairdry, a/c, elec blkts, tel, TV, video-fee, clock radio, t/c mkg, refrig, toaster], ldry, pool, spa, bbq, dinner to unit, c/park (carport), plygr, tennis (half court), cots-fee, non smoking units (8). **RO** ♦ **$46 - $68**, ♦♦ **$55 - $77**, ♦ **$10**, pen con, 2 units ★★★☆, AE BC DC EFT MC MCH VI.

★★☆ **Irymple Community Motel/Hotel**, (LMH), Cnr Karadoc Ave & Calder Hwy, Irymple 3498, 7.6km S of Mildura PO, ☎ 03 5024 5506, fax 03 5024 5952, 12 units [shwr, tlt, a/c, elec blkts, tel, TV, clock radio, t/c mkg, refrig, toaster], conf fac, ✕, c/park (carport), cots. **BLB** ♦ **$42**, ♦♦ **$48**, ♦ **$11**, Light breakfast only available. AE BC EFT MC VI.

★★☆ **Kar-Rama Motor Inn**, (M), 153 Deakin Ave, 600m SW of PO, ☎ 03 5023 4221, fax 03 5021 3334, (2 stry gr fl), 34 units [shwr, tlt, a/c, elec blkts, tel, TV, clock radio, t/c mkg, refrig], ldry, pool, bbq, c/park (undercover), cots-fee, non smoking units (4). **RO** ♦ **$46 - $70**, ♦♦ **$54 - $82**, ♦ **$10**, pen con, AE BC DC EFT MC MCH VI.

★★☆ **Vineland Motel**, (M), 363 Deakin Ave, 2.5km SW of PO, ☎ 03 5023 4036, fax 03 5023 2642, 12 units [shwr, tlt, evap cool, c/fan (1), heat, elec blkts, TV, clock radio, t/c mkg, refrig, toaster], pool, bbq, c/park (carport), ☏, cots, non smoking units (4). **RO** ♦ **$50 - $63**, ♦♦ **$55 - $80**, ♦ **$14**, AE BC DC EFT MC VI.

Self Catering Accommodation

★★★★☆ **Aabrinderlea**, (Cotg), 3 Elizabeth Ave, 300m SW of Centre Plaza, ☎ 03 5023 2601, fax 03 5021 3094, 1 cotg acc up to 2, (1 bedrm), [ensuite, hairdry, evap cool, heat, elec blkts, TV, video, clock radio, refrig, cook fac, micro, d/wash, toaster, ldry (in unit), blkts, linen, pillows], w/mach, iron, iron brd, pool, bbq, c/park (carport), ☏, non smoking property. **D** ♦♦ **$73 - $94, W** ♦♦ **$435 - $539**, BC MC VI.

★★★★☆ **Aaden Holiday Apartments**, (HF), 293 Cureton Ave, 2.2km W of PO, ☎ 03 5022 1526, fax 03 5021 4321, 4 flats acc up to 6, (2 bedrm), [shwr, tlt, hairdry, a/c, heat, elec blkts, tel (local), TV, video, clock radio, refrig, cook fac, micro, toaster, blkts, linen, pillows], w/mach, iron, iron brd, bbq, c/park (carport), cots, non smoking property. **D** ♦♦ **$65 - $85**, ♦ **$5 - $6, W** ♦♦ **$403 - $515**, ♦ **$39**, Min book applies, BC MC VI.

★★★★☆ **Aarinda Holiday Flats**, (HF), 3 Elizabeth Ave, 300m SW of Centre Plaza, ☎ 03 5023 2601, fax 03 5021 3094, 4 flats (2 bedrm), [shwr, tlt, hairdry, heat, elec blkts, TV, video, clock radio, refrig, cook fac, micro, toaster, ldry (in unit), blkts, linen, pillows], w/mach, pool, bbq, c/park (carport), ☏, cots, non smoking property. **D** ♦♦ **$73 - $94**, ♦ **$13 - $15, W $435 - $638**, BC MC VI.

★★★★☆ **Aarinda Retreat**, (Cotg), 22 Elizabeth Ave, 300m SW of Centre Plaza, ☎ 03 5023 2601, fax 03 5021 3094, 1 cotg acc up to 6, (3 bedrm), [shwr, bath, tlt, hairdry, evap cool, c/fan, heat, elec blkts, TV, video, clock radio, refrig, cook fac, micro, d/wash (3), toaster, ldry (in unit), blkts, linen, pillows], w/mach, dryer, iron, iron brd, lounge firepl, pool, bbq, c/park (carport), cots, non smoking property. **D** ♦♦ **$132 - $143**, ♦ **$16 - $28, W $539 - $968**, BC MC VI.

★★★★☆ **Callistemon Holiday Flats**, (HF), Cnr Ninth St & Olive Ave, 700m W of PO, ☎ 03 5023 8975, fax 03 5023 1975, 4 flats acc up to 5, (2 bedrm), [shwr, tlt, hairdry, evap cool, heat, elec blkts, tel (local), TV, video, clock radio, refrig, cook fac, micro, elec frypan, toaster, ldry (in unit), blkts, linen, pillows], w/mach, dryer, iron, iron brd, bbq, c/park (carport), cots, non smoking property. **D $70 - $120, W $420 - $630**, AE BC MC VI.

CARN COURT
Holiday Apartments

The perfect family holiday in an ideal location, relaxing and informal in your own space. It's a short walk to Mildura Centre Plaza shops, restaurants, take aways and sports centre. Opposite Tavern Hotel with Pokies. You will be transferred from coach and airport if required. There is public transport at door and courtesy buses to Clubs. We offer large modern 1 & 2 bedroom, fully self contained, heated & air conditioned units with colour TV and Video •Microwave • All linen supplied • Electric Blankets • Laundry • Large lawn area with fenced swimming pool, Barbecue, Covered Parking, Security lights and Gold phone • Moderate tariff.

Resident owners: Fred and Gwen Simmons

AAA TOURISM
★★★★✈

Free Call 1800 066 675 • Phone: 03 5023 6311 • Fax: 03 5021 3283
826 15th Street, Mildura • PO Box 2148 Mildura, Victoria 3502

Aarinda *Holiday Apartments*

HIGHLY RECOMENDED
AAA TOURISM
★★★★★

*E*njoy a quiet, relaxing holiday in *"home away from home"* comfort. Five modern, well furnished, spacious, fully self-contained one and two bedroom apartments. The units are situated in one acre of tranquil gardens and shady trees.

*I*deally located, close to Mildura Centre Plaza (7 days), Bakeries, Several Restaurants, Take-Aways, Tavern Hotel and Public Transport. **Resident owners:** Dorithe & Ron Dowson

Free Call 1800 637 269 • Phone: 03 5023 2601 • Fax: 03 5021 3094
3 Elizabeth Avenue, Mildura, Victoria 3500

MILDURA and DEAKIN HOLIDAY PARK

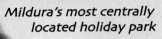

AAA Tourism ★★★★☆

Mildura's most centrally located holiday park

• Featuring the finest range of cabin style holiday accommodation in the district including AAA Tourism rated ★★★★ deluxe holiday units with some designed for wheelchair access.

• Opposite Mildura Centre Plaza Shopping Complex (Open 7 days) this quiet family park is within walking distance to the Gateway Tavern Bistro, the famous Hudak's Bakery and Mc Donalds.

• Swimming Pool

OUR PRIDE IS YOUR GUARANTEE

• Free BBQs

• Our park is beautifully shaded with all modern amenities including new drive through ensuite sites.

• Enquire about our special winter and off peak rates

**Sturt Highway
(Near 15th Street)
PO Box 3181
Mildura, VIC 3502
Fax (03) 50222729**

*Your hosts
Neil and Lyn Saunders*

Email:admin@mildura-deakin.com.au

TOLL FREE 1800 060 705

www.mildura-deakin.com.au

★★★★☆ **Camellia Court Holiday Apartments**, (Apt), 169 Cureton Ave, 1.5km N of PO, ☎ 03 5021 1834, fax 03 5029 1723, 3 apts acc up to 6, (2 & 3 bedrm), [shwr, tlt, hairdry, evap cool, heat, elec blkts, tel (local), cable tv, video, clock radio, refrig, cook fac, micro, d/wash (1), toaster, ldry (in unit), blkts, linen, pillows], w/mach, dryer, iron, iron brd, pool-heated (solar), spa, bbq, c/park (carport), cots. **D $80 - $96, W $482 - $590**, AE BC DC MC VI.

★★★★☆ **Carn Court Holiday Apartments**, (HF), Cnr Fifteenth St (Calder Hwy) & San Mateo Ave, 250m SE of Centre Plaza, ☎ 03 5023 6311, fax 03 5021 3283, 8 flats acc up to 7, (1 & 2 bedrm), [shwr, bath (1), tlt, hairdry, a/c-cool, c/fan (2), heat, elec blkts, tel, TV, video, clock radio, refrig, cook fac, micro, elec frypan, toaster, ldry (in unit), blkts, linen, pillows], w/mach, iron, iron brd, pool, bbq, c/park (carport), ☎, plygr, cots. **D ⋔⋔ $68 - $75, ⋔ $11, W $390 - $650**, Min book all holiday times, BC MC VI.

★★★★☆ **Murrayland Holiday Apartments**, (Apt), 757 Fifteenth St (Calder Hwy), 400m SE of Centre Plaza, ☎ 03 5025 5000, fax 03 5025 5050, 10 apts acc up to 8, (2 & 3 bedrm), [shwr, bath (2), tlt, hairdry, evap cool, heat, elec blkts, tel, cable tv, video-fee, clock radio, refrig, cook fac, micro, elec frypan, toaster, ldry (in unit), blkts, linen, pillows], w/mach, dryer, iron, iron brd, pool-heated, spa, bbq, c/park (carport), plygr, tennis (half court), cots. **D ⋔⋔ $85 - $95, ⋔ $15 - $20**, ch con, BC EFT MC VI.

★★★★☆ **Sunraysia Resort**, (HU), 300 Tenth St, 2.2km W of PO, ☎ 03 5022 2511, fax 03 5023 7819, (2 stry gr fl), 72 units acc up to 6, (2 bedrm), [shwr, bath, spa bath (62), tlt, hairdry, a/c, c/fan, elec blkts, tel, cable tv, video-fee, clock radio, t/c mkg, refrig, cook fac ltd, micro, elec frypan, d/wash, toaster, ldry (in unit) (31), blkts, doonas, linen, pillows], ldry, w/mach, iron, iron brd, rec rm, lounge, pool-heated (solar/shaded), pool indoor heated, sauna, spa, bbq, c/park (carport) (31), ☎, plygr, bowls, mini golf, tennis, cots. **D $100 - $175, W $630 - $1,045**, ch con, BC EFT MC VI.

★★★★ **Acacia Holiday Apartments & Cabins**, (HU), 761 Fifteenth St (Calder Hwy), 450m SE of Centre Plaza, ☎ 03 5023 3855, fax 03 5023 3855, 9 units acc up to 8, (1, 2 & 3 bedrm), [shwr, tlt, hairdry, evap cool, heat, elec blkts, cable tv, clock radio, refrig, cook fac, micro, toaster, blkts, linen, pillows], ldry, w/mach, dryer, iron, iron brd, rec rm, pool, bbq, c/park (carport) (4), car wash, plygr, tennis (half court), cots, non smoking units (5). **D $64 - $139, W $379 - $1,004**, AE BC DC EFT MC VI.

★★★☆ **(Park Cabin - En-suite Section)**, 6 cabins acc up to 6, [shwr, tlt, hairdry (3), a/c (3), heat, elec blkts, cable tv, clock radio, refrig, cook fac, micro, toaster, blkts, linen, pillows]. **D $51 - $66, W $299 - $433**.

★★★★ **Green Patch Holidays**, (Apt), 884 Fifteenth St, 250m NW of Centre Plaza, ☎ 03 5023 3784, fax 03 5023 0035, 3 apts acc up to 6, (2 bedrm), [shwr, bath, tlt, hairdry, a/c, heat, elec blkts, TV, video, clock radio, refrig, cook fac, micro, toaster, blkts, linen, pillows], ldry, w/mach, dryer, iron, iron brd, bbq, c/park (carport), cots. **D ♦♦ $77 - $121, W ♦♦ $462 - $693**, BC MC VI.

★★★★ **Kalimna Lodge**, (House), 4 Kalimna Dve, ☎ 03 5023 3266, fax 03 5023 5455, 1 house acc up to 6, (3 bedrm), [ensuite, hairdry, evap cool, heat, elec blkts, tel, TV, video, clock radio, t/c mkg, refrig, cook fac, micro, elec frypan, toaster, ldry, blkts, pillows], w/mach, iron, iron brd, bbq, c/park. **D ♦♦ $85 - $135, ♦ $10 - $20, W ♦♦ $525 - $970, ♦ $70 - $140**, BC MC VI.

★★★★ **Kookaburra Village**, (Cotg), 265 Tenth St, 1.5km NW of PO, ☎ 03 5022 1323, fax 03 5022 1858, 19 cotgs acc up to 7, (1, 2 & 3 bedrm), [shwr, bath, tlt, evap cool, heat, elec blkts, cable tv, video, clock radio, refrig, cook fac, micro, toaster, ldry (in unit), blkts, doonas, linen, pillows], w/mach, iron, iron brd, pool, bbq, c/park (carport), ✆, plygr, cots-fee. **D $75 - $140, W $357 - $882**, BC MC VI.

★★★★ **Landura**, (HF), 226 Deakin Ave, 1.3km SW of PO, ☎ 03 5023 0674, fax 03 5023 0627, (2 stry), 3 flats acc up to 7, (1, 2 & 3 bedrm), [shwr, bath, tlt, hairdry, evap cool, heat, cable tv, clock radio, refrig, cook fac, micro, toaster, ldry (in unit), blkts, doonas, linen, pillows], w/mach, iron, iron brd, pool-heated (solar), bbq, c/park (carport), cots. **D ♦♦ $75, ♦ $10, W ♦♦ $500**, pen con.

★★★☆ **Albatross Holiday Villas**, (HF), 30 Olive Ave, 600m W of PO, ☎ 03 5023 0542, fax 03 5023 0542, 4 flats acc up to 6, (2 & 3 bedrm), [shwr, tlt, hairdry, a/c-cool, heat, elec blkts, TV, clock radio, refrig, cook fac, micro, toaster, ldry (in unit), blkts, linen, pillows], w/mach, iron, iron brd, rec rm, pool, bbq, c/park (carport), cots, Pets allowed. **D $350 - $580**, Min book all holiday times.

★★★☆ **Mildura Greensview Holiday Homes**, (HF), 428 Eleventh St, 2.5km W of PO, ☎ 03 5021 4654, fax 03 5021 2459, 9 flats acc up to 6, (2 & 3 bedrm), [shwr, bath (6), tlt, evap cool, heat, elec blkts, TV (6), cable tv (3), video (4), clock radio, refrig, cook fac, micro, toaster, ldry (in unit), blkts, linen, pillows], w/mach, pool, bbq, c/park (carport), ✆, plygr, cots. **D $77 - $165, W $440 - $830**, BC MC VI.

★★★ **Colonial Court Holiday Flats**, (HF), Cnr Chaffey Ave & Eighth St, 700m NW of PO, ☎ 03 5022 2430, fax 03 5022 2537, 3 flats acc up to 6, (2 bedrm), [shwr, bath (hip), tlt, evap cool, heat, elec blkts, TV, clock radio, refrig, cook fac, micro, toaster, ldry (in unit), blkts, linen, pillows], w/mach, iron, iron brd, c/park (carport), cots, non smoking units (1). **D $70 - $90, W $385 - $615**.

★★★ **Sandpiper Villas on Walnut Ave**, (HF), 274 Walnut Ave, 2.3km W of PO, ☎ 03 5021 1900, fax 03 5021 3323, 4 flats acc up to 5, (2 bedrm), [shwr, tlt, a/c-cool, heat, TV, clock radio, refrig, cook fac, toaster, ldry (in unit), blkts, linen, pillows], w/mach, iron, iron brd, pool, bbq, c/park (carport), cots. **D** $72 - $82, ♿.

B&B's/Guest Houses
★★★★☆ **Riverview B & B**, (B&B), 115 Seventh St, 200m SE of railway station, ☎ 03 5023 8975, fax 03 5023 1975, 2 rms [ensuite, hairdry, a/c-cool, c/fan, heat, elec blkts, TV, clock radio], lounge (TV, video, cd), t/c mkg shared, bbq, non smoking property. **BB** ♦ $72 - $85, ♦♦ $85 - $110, AE BC MC VI.

Other Accommodation
Amaroo Houseboats, (Hbt), Murray River Chaffey Bridge, ☎ 03 5021 1858, fax 03 5021 1858, 1 houseboat acc up to 10, (3 bedrm), [shwr, tlt, evap cool, TV, video, refrig, cook fac, micro, doonas, linen, pillows], bbq. **W** $1,090 - $1,956, Security deposit - $200 & Bond $300, BC MC VI.
Mildura Holiday Houseboats, (Hbt), Hugh King Dve, 800m upstream from bridge, ☎ 03 5021 4414, fax 03 5021 1453, 4 houseboats acc up to 10, (3 bedrm), [shwr, tlt, a/c-cool, heat, TV, radio, CD, refrig, cook fac, micro, blkts, linen, pillows], bbq, cots. **W** $1,017 - $2,409, Security deposit - $200 & Bond $300. BC MC VI.
Riverqueen, (Hbt), Bruces Bend Marina, 8km E of PO, ☎ 03 5023 2955, fax 03 5023 2955, 4 houseboats acc up to 10, (3 & 4 bedrm), [shwr, tlt, evap cool, heat, tel, TV, video, CD, refrig, cook fac, micro, blkts, linen, pillows]. **W** $575 - $2,750, Security deposit - $300 to $600.
Riviera Motel, (Lodge), 157 Seventh St, opposite railway station, ☎ 03 5023 3696, fax 03 5023 3696, (2 stry gr fl), 12 rms [shwr, tlt, a/c, elec blkts, TV, video-fee, clock radio, t/c mkg, refrig, blkts, linen, pillows], ldry, cook fac, refrig, bbq. **D** ♦ $20, ♦ $20, **W** ♦ $100, ♦ $100, ch con, BC MC VI.
Sunseeker Houseboats, (Hbt), Bruces Bend Marina, 8km E of PO, ☎ 03 5025 1101, fax 03 5025 3321, 2 houseboats (3 bedrm), [shwr, tlt, evap cool, heat, tel, TV, radio, refrig, cook fac, micro, blkts, linen, pillows], bbq. **W** $781 - $2,189, Security deposit - $300.

MILLGROVE VIC 3799
Pop 1,700. Part of Yarra Ranges, (74km E Melbourne), See map on page 696, ref D5.
★★★★ **Millwaters Retreat**, (HU), Previously Tranquility Villas, 30 River Rd, 3.2km W of Warburton PO, ☎ 03 5966 5459, fax 03 5966 5088, 2 units acc up to 2, (Studio & 1 bedrm), [shwr, spa bath, tlt, hairdry, a/c-cool, c/fan, heat (wood), elec blkts, TV, video (1), clock radio, CD, t/c mkg, refrig, cook fac, micro, toaster, ldry (in unit) (1), blkts, linen, pillows], bbq, breakfast ingredients. **BB** ♦♦ $150 - $165, 1 cottage ★★★★☆, BC MC VI.

MININERA VIC 3351
Pop Nominal, (207km W Melbourne), See map on pages 694/695, ref C6.
★★★★ **Menenia Pastoral Co**, (B&B), c1881 homestead on a sheep grazing & cereal growing property. Delacombe Way, ☎ 03 5350 6536, fax 03 5350 6591, 2 rms [ensuite (1), shwr (1), bath (1), tlt (1), hairdry, fan, cent heat, elec blkts, clock radio, t/c mkg], lounge (TV, stereo), lounge firepl, bbq. **BB** ♦ $90, ♦♦ $115 - $130, 1 room ★★★☆. Other meals by arrangement. BC MC VI.

MIRBOO NORTH VIC 3871
Pop 1,250. (156km SE Melbourne), See map on page 696, ref E7. Dairy farming & potato growing area.
★★ **Mirboo North Hotel**, (LMH), 70 Ridgway, ☎ 03 5668 1552, fax 03 5668 2051, 6 units [shwr, tlt, heat, TV, clock radio, refrig, toaster], ⊠. **BLB** ♦ $49.50, ♦♦ $55, ♦ $11, Light breakfast only available. BC EFT MC VI.

Self Catering Accommodation
★★★★ **Campbell Homestead**, (Cotg), (Farm), RMB 5620 Twomeys Rd Mardan Via, 6.5km SW of PO, ☎ 03 5664 1282, fax 03 5664 1282, 1 cotg acc up to 8, (4 bedrm), [shwr, bath, tlt (2), hairdry, fan, TV, clock radio, refrig, cook fac, micro, elec frypan, toaster, ldry, blkts, linen, pillows], lounge, lounge firepl, dinner to unit, tennis, cots, breakfast ingredients, non smoking property. **BB** ♦♦ $100 - $120, ♦ $50 - $70, ch con, BC MC VI.
★★★☆ **Strathmore Cottage B&B**, (Cotg), Mardan Rd, 3km S of PO, ☎ 03 5668 1571, 1 cotg (2 bedrm), [ensuite, shwr, tlt, hairdry, a/c, elec blkts, TV, video, clock radio, t/c mkg, refrig, cook fac, toaster, ldry, blkts, linen, pillows], w/mach, iron, iron brd, lounge (tv), bbq, tennis, breakfast ingredients. **BB** ♦ $40 - $70, ♦♦ $70, ♦ $30, ch con.
★★★☆ **(Bed & Breakfast Section)**, 1 rm [ensuite, hairdry, elec blkts, clock radio, t/c mkg], lounge (TV). **BB** ♦ $44, ♦♦ $77.

★★★ **Koomerang Park**, (HF), Old Thorpdale Rd, 4km N of PO, ☎ 03 5668 1221, fax 03 5668 1221, 1 flat acc up to 2, (1 bedrm), [shwr, tlt, fan, heat, elec blkts, TV, clock radio, refrig, cook fac, micro, toaster, blkts, linen, pillows], ldry, iron, iron brd, c/park (carport). **D** ♦♦ $50 - $65, ch con.

B&B's/Guest Houses
★★★★ **Piralillia Park**, (B&B), (Farm), No children's facilities, 115 Dickies Hill Rd, ☎ 03 5668 2045, fax 03 5668 2045, 2 rms [ensuite, c/fan, heat, elec blkts, clock radio, t/c mkg], lounge (TV, video), lounge firepl. **BB** ♦♦ $95.

MIRRANATWA VIC
See Grampians Region.

MITTA MITTA VIC 3701
Pop 514. (406km NE Melbourne), See map on pages 694/695, ref H5, at the junction of the Mitta River & Snowy Creek.
★★★☆ **Wonjeena Hodgkins Farm House**, (HU), Scrubby Creek Rd, 4km NW of PO, ☎ 02 6072 3505, 1 unit acc up to 4, (Studio), [shwr, tlt, hairdry, a/c-cool, c/fan, heat, elec blkts, TV, video, clock radio, refrig, cook fac, micro, elec frypan, toaster, ldry, blkts, linen, pillows], w/mach, dryer, iron, iron brd, bbq, plygr. **D** ♦♦ $60, ♦ $10.

MOE VIC 3825
Pop 15,500. (134km SE Melbourne), See map on page 696, ref E6. The city of Moe is situated in the Latrobe Valley on the Princes Hwy.
 ★★★★ **Moe Motor Inn**, (M), 3 Fowler St, 200m S of railway station, ☎ 03 5127 1166, fax 03 5127 8436, (2 stry gr fl), 30 units (2 suites) [shwr, spa bath (2), tlt, a/c, elec blkts, tel, TV, video-fee, movie, clock radio, t/c mkg, refrig, toaster], iron, iron brd, conf fac, pool-heated (seasonal), spa, bbq, dinner to unit, cots, non smoking units (12). **RO** ♦ $76 - $85, ♦♦ $86 - $95, ♦ $12, ch con, AE BC DC EFT JCB MC MP VI.
★★★★ **(Apartment Section)**, Breakfast available, (2 stry gr fl), 2 apts acc up to 4, (2 bedrm), [shwr, spa bath, tlt, a/c, elec blkts, TV, video-fee, clock radio, t/c mkg, refrig, cook fac, micro, d/wash, toaster, ldry, blkts, linen, pillows]. **D** ♦♦ $110 - $170, ♦ $12 - $50, **W** $605 - $825.

 ★★★☆ **The Park Motor Inn**, (M), 98 Narracan Dve (Old Princes Hwy), 1.8km E of PO, ☎ 03 5127 3344, fax 03 5127 3650, 28 units [shwr, spa bath (1), tlt, a/c, c/fan (10), elec blkts, tel, TV, movie, clock radio, t/c mkg, refrig, mini bar], ldry, pool, rm serv, dinner to unit, cots-fee, non smoking units (9). **RO** ♦ $66 - $82.50, ♦♦ $77 - $110, ♦ $13.20, pen con, AE BC DC EFT MC MP VI.

MONBULK VIC
See Dandenong Ranges Region.

Trouble-free travel tips - **Windscreen wipers**
Check the operation of windscreen wipers and washers. Replace windscreen wiper rubbers if they are not cleaning the windscreen properly.

MOONAMBEL VIC 3478

Pop Part of Avoca, (211km NW Melbourne), See map on pages 694/695, ref C5. Farming & wine growing district situated on Mountain Creek.

Self Catering Accommodation

★★★ **Summerfield Vineyards**, (HU), RMB 4355 Main Rd, 400m W of PO, ☎ 03 5467 2264, fax 03 5467 2380, 6 units acc up to 6, (2 bedrm), [shwr, tlt, c/fan, heat, elec blkts, TV, clock radio, t/c mkg, refrig, cook fac, toaster, doonas, linen, pillows], bbq, breakfast ingredients. **BLB ♦♦ $99 - $143, ♦ $27.50**, ch con, Min book long w/ends and Easter, BC MC VI.

B&B's/Guest Houses

★★★★ **Warrenmang Vineyard Resort**, (PH), Mountain Creek Rd, 3km W of PO, ☎ 03 5467 2233, fax 03 5467 2309, (2 stry gr fl), 26 rms [shwr, tlt, hairdry (7), a/c (8), c/fan (12), heat, elec blkts, t/c mkg, refrig, mini bar, doonas], lounge, conf fac, lounge firepl, ⊠, bar (cocktail), pool, spa, bbq (covered), ⚲, tennis. **DBB ♦ $155 - $225, ♦ $155 - $225**, 12 cottages ★★★☆. AE BC EFT MC VI.

MOONLIGHT HEAD VIC 3238

Pop Nominal, (230km SW Melbourne). See map on pages 694/695, ref C8. Situated close to the Port Campbell National Park.

★★★★☆ **Moonlight Retreat**, (Cotg), Moonlight Head Rd, ☎ 03 5237 5277, fax 03 5237 4297, 2 cotgs acc up to 6, (1 & 3 bedrm), [shwr, spa bath, tlt, evap cool (1), a/c (1), c/fan, heat, elec blkts, tel, TV, video, clock radio, t/c mkg, refrig, cook fac, micro, d/wash, toaster, ldry, blkts, doonas, linen, pillows], w/mach, dryer, lounge firepl, bbq, c/park (carport), cots-fee, non smoking property. **D $155 - $275, ♦ $35 - $65, W $895 - $1,365, ♦ $175 - $275**, 1 cottage ★★★★★, Min book applies, AE BC DC JCB MC VI

Operator Comment: Views of 12 Apostles. PETS VERY WELCOME. www.greatoceanrd.com

MOOROODUC VIC 3933

Pop Part of Melbourne, (55km SE Melbourne), See map on page 697, ref D7. Small peninsula township. Golf, Horse Riding, Scenic Drives.

★★★★☆ **Kenilworth Park Alpaca Stud**, (Cotg), No children's facilities, 305 Bungower Rd, ☎ 03 5978 8534, fax 03 5978 8035, 1 cotg acc up to 2, (1 bedrm), [shwr, tlt, hairdry, a/c, heat, elec blkts, TV, video, clock radio, t/c mkg, refrig, cook fac ltd, micro, toaster, blkts, doonas, linen, pillows], ldry, w/mach, dryer, iron, iron brd, lounge firepl, bbq, breakfast ingredients, non smoking property. **BB ♦♦ $110 - $150**, Dinner by arrangement, AE BC DC MC VI

Operator Comment: Quiet farm setting, new cottage. Unique animals, fishing in dams.

★★★★☆ **Nedlands Farm**, (Cotg), No children's facilities, 500 Old Moorooduc Rd, Tuerong 3933, ☎ 03 5974 4160, fax 03 5974 4161, 1 cotg acc up to 4, (2 bedrm), [shwr, tlt, hairdry, a/c, c/fan, elec blkts, tel, TV, video, clock radio, CD, refrig, cook fac, micro, d/wash, toaster, ldry (in unit), blkts, linen, pillows], w/mach, dryer, iron, iron brd, lounge firepl, bbq, c/park (carport), breakfast ingredients, non smoking property. **D $220**, BC MC VI.

★★★★ **Gooseberry Hill Olive Grove**, (Cotg), 170 Graydens Rd, 500m E of Devil Bend Reservoir spillway, ☎ 03 5978 8227, fax 03 5978 8227, 1 cotg acc up to 4, (2 bedrm), [shwr, tlt, hairdry, a/c (lounge), c/fan, heat, TV, video, clock radio, CD, refrig, cook fac, micro, elec frypan, d/wash, toaster, ldry (in unit), blkts, doonas, linen, pillows], w/mach, iron, iron brd, bbq, cots, breakfast ingredients, non smoking property, Dogs allowed at mgrs discretion. **BB ♦ $130, ♦♦ $160, ♦ $30**, ch con, Min book applies, BTC MC VI.

MOOROOPNA VIC 3629

Pop 5,260. (187km N Melbourne), See map on page 696, ref C2. Fruit Salad City on the Goulburn River irrigation scheme.

★★★☆ **Rodney Motor Inn**, (M), 146 McLennan St (Midland Hwy), 250m W of water tower, ☎ 03 5825 3188, fax 03 5825 3200, (2 stry gr fl), 20 units [shwr, spa bath (3), tlt, a/c, elec blkts, tel, TV, clock radio, t/c mkg, refrig, mini bar, toaster], ldry, pool, spa, dinner to unit (Mon to Sat), cots-fee. **RO ♦ $77 - $100, ♦♦ $86 - $115, ♦ $10**, ch con, 5 units ★★★★. AE BC DC EFT MC MP VI, ⚲.

★★ **Cricketers Arms**, (LMH), McLennan St (Midland Hwy), 200m W of water tower, ☎ 03 5825 2066, fax 03 5825 3714, 6 units [shwr, tlt, a/c, elec blkts, TV, t/c mkg, refrig, toaster], ⊠ (Mon to Sat), ⚲. **RO ♦ $44, ♦♦ $55, ♦ $10**, ch con, AE BC DC EFT MC VI.

★★ **Mid Park Motel & Caravan Park**, (M), Previously Mid-Park 220 McLennan St (Midland Hwy), 1km W of PO, ☎ 03 5825 2706, fax 03 5825 2706, 5 units [shwr, tlt, c/fan, heat, elec blkts, TV, clock radio, refrig, cook fac ltd, micro (1)], ldry, pool, bbq (covered), ⚲, plygr, tennis (half court). **RO ♦♦ $55, ♦ $8**, ch con, BC EFT MC VI.

MORNINGTON VIC 3931

Pop 14,149. (55km S Melbourne), See map on page 697, ref C7. One of the oldest & best known communities on the Peninsula.

Hotels/Motels

★★★☆ **Brooklands of Mornington**, (M), 101 Tanti Ave, 700m N of PO, ☎ 03 5975 1166, fax 03 5975 9989, 36 units [shwr, spa bath (14), tlt, hairdry (11), a/c, c/fan (23), elec blkts, tel, TV, clock radio, t/c mkg, refrig, mini bar (11)], ldry, iron, iron brd, conf fac, ⊠, bar, rm serv, dinner to unit, cots-fee, non smoking units (4). **D $90 - $175**, 11 units ★★★★. AE BC DC MC VI.

★★★ **Mornington Motel**, (M), 334 Main St, 1km SE of PO, ☎ 03 5975 3711, fax 03 5975 3772, 12 units [shwr, tlt, a/c-cool (heat & cool), a/c, elec blkts, tel, TV, clock radio, t/c mkg, refrig, toaster], ldry, pool, bbq, cots, non smoking units (12). **BLB ♦ $75 - $95, ♦♦ $75 - $95, ♦ $15**, Light breakfast only available. AE BC DC EFT MC VI.

★★★ **Ranch Motel**, (M), 65 Bentons Rd, enter off Bentons Rd, 2.4km S of PO, ☎ 03 5975 4022, fax 03 5976 2082, 13 units (3 suites) [shwr, spa bath (2), tlt, a/c-cool, heat, elec blkts, tel, TV, clock radio, t/c mkg, refrig, cook fac (2), micro (2), toaster], ldry, pool, spa, bbq, cots, non smoking units (5). **RO ♦ $60 - $95, ♦♦ $65 - $95, ♦ $11**, ch con, AE BC DC EFT MC VI.

★★★ **The Royal Hotel Mornington**, (LH), 770 Esplanade, 1km SW of PO, ☎ 03 5975 5466, fax 03 5975 9115, (2 stry), 9 rms (2 suites) [shwr (6), tlt (6), a/c (6), heat (3), tel (8), TV, clock radio, t/c mkg, refrig, doonas], conf fac, ⊠, cots. **D $80 - $135**, AE BC DC EFT MC VI.

Self Catering Accommodation

★★★★ **Bath at Mills**, (HU), 14 Bath St, 1.2km W of PO, ☎ 03 5977 0576, fax 03 5977 0576, 1 unit acc up to 3, (1 bedrm), [shwr, tlt, hairdry, a/c-cool, c/fan, heat, elec blkts, TV, video, clock radio, CD, t/c mkg, refrig, cook fac, micro, toaster, linen, pillows], w/mach, dryer, iron, iron brd, spa, bbq, cots, breakfast ingredients, non smoking property. **BB ♦♦ $150, $20**.

★★★★ **Canterbury by the Bay**, (Cotg), Unit 2, 5 Canterbury St, 700m NW of PO, ☎ 03 5974 3136, 1 cotg acc up to 4, (2 bedrm), [shwr, tlt, hairdry, a/c-cool, c/fan, heat, elec blkts, TV, video, clock radio, CD, t/c mkg, refrig, cook fac, micro, elec frypan, d/wash, toaster, ldry, blkts, linen, pillows], w/mach, dryer, iron, iron brd, bbq, c/park (garage), non smoking property. **D ♦♦ $120, ♦ $11, W ♦♦ $840, ♦ $77**, Min book applies, BC MC VI.

★★★★ **Fish Cottage**, (Cotg), 12 Neptune St, ☎ 03 5977 1308, fax 03 5976 1512, 1 cotg acc up to 4, (2 bedrm), [shwr, bath, tlt, hairdry, a/c, heat (wood), elec blkts, tel, TV, video, clock radio, CD, refrig, cook fac, micro, elec frypan, toaster, ldry, blkts, linen, pillows], iron, iron brd, bbq, c/park (carport), non smoking property. **D ♦♦ $120 - $140, ♦ $20**, BC MC VI.

★★★★ **Rosemont on the Beach**, (HU), Unit 5, 799 The Esplanade, Entry off Cook St, ☎ 03 9596 6922, (2 stry), 1 unit acc up to 4, (2 bedrm), [shwr, tlt, hairdry, fan, heat (gas & wood), elec blkts, tel, TV, video, CD, refrig, cook fac, micro, d/wash, ldry, blkts, linen, pillows], w/mach, dryer, iron, iron brd, bbq, c/park (carport). **D ♦♦ $140 - $165, ♦ $25**.

B&B's/Guest Houses

★★★★ **Barkly House**, (B&B), 44 Barkly St, ☎ 03 5977 0957, fax 03 5973 4135, (2 stry gr fl), 3 rms [ensuite (1), shwr, bath (1), spa bath (1), tlt, hairdry, c/fan (2), fire pl (1), cent heat, elec blkts, clock radio, t/c mkg, refrig], lounge (TV, video, cd), lounge firepl, bbq, non smoking property. **BB ♦ $75 - $100, ♦♦ $150 - $200, ♦ $50 - $70**, AE BC EFT JCB MC VI.

MORTLAKE VIC 3272

Pop 1,000. (232km W Melbourne), See map on pages 694/695, ref C7. Pastoral & agricultural township founded as a village in 1838. Located at the foot of Mt Shadwell on a rich volcanic plain. Bowls, Gem Fossicking, Golf, Horse Racing, Scenic Drives, Squash, Swimming (Pool), Tennis.

Hotels/Motels

★★★☆ **The Stables Motel**, (LMH), 128 Dunlop St, Rear of Mt Shadwell Hotel, ☎ 03 5599 2019, fax 03 5599 2728, (2 stry gr fl), 5 units [shwr, spa bath (1), tlt, hairdry, a/c, elec blkts, tel, TV, video (avail), t/c mkg, refrig, mini bar, toaster], ldry, conf fac, ⊠ (Mon to Sat), bbq, rm serv. **RO 👤 $66.50, 👥 $82.50, 🧍 $16**, ch con, AE BC DC EFT MC VI.

B&B's/Guest Houses

★★★☆ **Rockgrove Homestead**, (B&B), 1376ha sheep & cattle grazing & Golden Retriever breeding property. RMB 3276 Hamilton Hwy, 18 km E of PO, ☎ 03 5597 9235, fax 03 5597 9235, 2 rms [heat, elec blkts, clock radio, cook fac ltd], lounge (TV), t/c mkg shared, bbq, tennis, non smoking property. **BB 👤 $55, 👥 $95, 🧍 $40**, ch con.

MORWELL VIC 3840

Pop 13,850. (150km SE Melbourne), See map on page 696, ref E6. Properous town near the La Trobe Valley's second major open cut. Boating, Bowls, Bush Walking, Croquet, Fishing, Golf, Horse Riding, Sailing, Scenic Drives, Shooting, Swimming (Pool, Lake), Tennis, Water Skiing.

Hotels/Motels

★★★☆ **Cedar Lodge Motor Inn**, (M), 1 Maryvale Cres, 1km S of PO, adjacent to Court House, ☎ 03 5134 5877, fax 03 5133 7434, 27 units [shwr, tlt, a/c, tel, TV, video-fee, clock radio, t/c mkg, refrig, mini bar], ⊠ (Mon to Sat), bbq, dinner to unit (Mon to Sat), cots-fee, non smoking units (15). **RO 👤 $63 - $70, 👥 $73 - $85, 🧍 $10**, ch con, AE BC DC MC MP VI.

★★★☆ **Coal Valley Motor Inn**, (M), 141 Princes Hwy, 600m W of PO, ☎ 03 5134 6211, fax 03 5134 8453, (2 stry gr fl), 40 units [shwr, spa bath (3), tlt, hairdry (9), a/c-cool, heat, elec blkts, tel, TV, video-fee, movie, clock radio, t/c mkg, refrig, mini bar, micro-fee, toaster], conf fac, ⊠ (Mon to Fri), pool (summer), spa (summer), Pets on application. **RO 👤 $75 - $120, 👥 $85 - $120, 🧍 $10**, AE BC DC MC MP VI.

★★★☆ **Del Spana Motor Inn**, (M), Cnr Church & Buckley Sts, 200m N of PO, ☎ 03 5134 4155, fax 03 5134 2265, (2 stry gr fl), 40 units [shwr, bath (17), spa bath (2), tlt, hairdry, a/c-cool (11), a/c (36), heat, elec blkts, tel, TV, video-fee, clock radio, t/c mkg, refrig, cook fac (2)], ldry, ⊠ (Mon to Fri), pool, sauna, rm serv, meals to unit (Mon to Fri), cots-fee. **RO 👤 $55 - $66, 👥 $70 - $80, 🧍 $15**, ch con, 15 units ★★★. Units 1, 21, 22, 23, 24, 25, 26 not listed or rated. AE BC DC EFT MC VI.

★★★☆ **Farnham Court Motel and Restaurant**, (M), Princes Hwy, 1.8km E of PO, ☎ 03 5134 6544, fax 03 5134 6878, 33 units [shwr, spa bath (3), tlt, hairdry (23), a/c, cent heat, tel, TV, clock radio, t/c mkg, refrig, mini bar], iron (23), iron brd (23), conf fac, ⊠ (Mon to Sat), sauna, rm serv, cots-fee. **RO 👤 $62 - $79, 👥 $68 - $85, 🧍 $6**, fam con, Units 11 to 20 ★★☆. AE BC DC MC MP VI.

★★★☆ **Hazelwood Motor Inn**, (M), 259 Princes Dve, 450m E of PO, ☎ 03 5134 4222, fax 03 5134 3823, (2 stry gr fl), 24 units [shwr, tlt, a/c, elec blkts, tel, TV, video, clock radio, t/c mkg, refrig, mini bar], ldry, ⊠ (Mon to Sat), pool-heated, spa, rm serv, dinner to unit (Mon to Sat), cots, non smoking units (16). **RO 👤 $74 - $79.20, 👥 $82.50 - $88, 🧍 $10**, ch con, AE BC DC EFT MC MP VI.

★★★ **Mid Valley Motel**, (M), 14 Chickerell St, 3.5km E of PO, ☎ 03 5133 7155, fax 03 5134 8535, 13 units [shwr, tlt, a/c, elec blkts, tel, TV, video-fee, clock radio, t/c mkg, refrig, cook fac (1), micro-fee, toaster], ldry, conf fac, cots, non smoking units (4). **RO 👤 $45, 👥 $55, 🧍 $10**, AE BC DC MC MCH VI.

★★★ **Morwell Southside Motel**, (M), 7 Maryvale Cres, 1km SW of PO, ☎ 03 5134 8266, fax 03 5134 8363, 14 units [shwr, spa bath (1), tlt, c/fan, heat, elec blkts, tel, TV, video-fee, clock radio, t/c mkg, refrig, mini bar], ldry, bbq, cots. **RO 👤 $48 - $55, 👥 $56 - $64, 🧍 $9**, AE BC DC EFT MC VI,
Operator Comment: Freecall 1800 358 266, Web site - www.morwellsouthside.com.au

★★★ **Parkside Motel & Reception Centre**, (M), 245 Princes Hwy, 300m E of PO, ☎ 03 5134 3366, fax 03 5133 9091, (2 stry gr fl), 18 units [shwr, tlt, a/c-cool, c/fan (5), cent heat, elec blkts, tel, TV, video-fee, clock radio, t/c mkg, refrig], ldry, ⊠ (Mon to Sat), rm serv, cots-fee, non smoking units (6). **RO 👤 $44 - $48, 👥 $56 - $59, 🧍 $10**, AE BC DC MC VI.

★☆ **The Merton Rush Hotel**, (LH), Cnr Princes Hwy & Collins St, 200m W of PO, ☎ 03 5134 2633, (2 stry), 10 rms [shwr, tlt, heat, elec blkts, clock radio, t/c mkg, refrig], ⊠, 📞. **RO 👤 $38.50, 👥 $49.50, 🧍 $11**, ch con, BC DC MC VI.

Self Catering Accommodation

★★★☆ **Morwell Serviced Apartments**, (Apt), 13 Maryvale Cres, 1km SW of PO, ☎ 03 5134 8266, fax 03 5134 8363, 4 apts acc up to 8, (2 bedrm), [shwr, bath (3), tlt, heat, elec blkts, video, clock radio, refrig, cook fac, micro, toaster, ldry, blkts, linen, pillows]. **D 👤 $42 - $100, 👥 $44 - $105, 🧍 $5**, Min book applies, AE BC DC EFT MC VI.

B&B's/Guest Houses

★★★☆ **Eden Park B & B**, (B&B), Cnr Wilkan Dve & Loriel Crt, Hazelwood North 3840, 9km SE of Princes Fwy, ☎ 03 5166 1398, fax 03 5166 1595, 3 rms [hairdry, fan, cent heat, elec blkts], lounge (TV, video), refrig, c/park (carport), plygr, non smoking property. **BB 👤 $70, 👥 $90**, ch con, BC MC VI.

(Cottage Section), 1 cotg acc up to 4, (2 bedrm), [shwr, tlt, c/fan, heat, elec blkts, clock radio, t/c mkg, refrig, cook fac, micro, elec frypan, toaster, ldry, blkts, linen, pillows], w/mach, iron, iron brd, lounge (TV), breakfast ingredients. **D $100, W $450**, (Rating under review).

MOUNT BAW BAW VIC 3833

Pop Nominal, (157km E Melbourne), See map on page 696, ref E5. Popular winter snow resort. Bush Walking, Scenic Drives, Snow Skiing.

Self Catering Accommodation

★★ **Cascade Ski Apartments**, (Apt), Alpine Village, ☎ 03 9755 2438, 9 apts acc up to 12, (1 & 3 bedrm), [shwr, tlt, heat, TV, refrig, cook fac, micro, toaster, doonas, linen reqd-fee], dry rm, spa (outdoor). **High Season D $130 - $390, High Season W $580 - $1,650.**

MOUNT BEAUTY VIC 3699

Pop 1,650. (344km NE Melbourne), See map on pages 694/695, ref H5. Includes: TAWONGA SOUTH. Gateway to the Kiewa Hydro-Electric Scheme, the ski slopes of Falls Creek & the vast Bogong High Plains. Boating, Bowls, Bush Walking, Fishing (Trout Streams), Golf, Horse Riding, Scenic Drives, Snow Skiing, Swimming (Pool, Lake, River), Tennis, Water Skiing.

Hotels/Motels

★★★ **Bogong Moth Motel**, (M), 172 Kiewa Valley Hwy, Tawonga South 3698, 2km NE of PO, ☎ 03 5754 4644, fax 03 5754 4621, 8 units [shwr, tlt, a/c-cool, heat, elec blkts, TV, clock radio, t/c mkg, refrig, toaster, doonas], dry rm, bbq, dinner to unit, plygr, cots. **RO 👤 $55 - $80, 👥 $65 - $90, 🧍 $10 - $15**, ch con, AE BC DC MC VI.

★★★ **Snowgum Motel**, (M), Kiewa Valley Hwy, Tawonga South 3698, 700m NW of PO, ☎ 03 5754 4508, fax 03 5754 1544, 12 units [shwr, bath, tlt, a/c-cool, cent heat, elec blkts, tel, TV, clock radio, t/c mkg, refrig, toaster], dry rm, pool, bbq, cots. **RO 👤 $65 - $85, 👥 $75 - $120, 🧍 $15 - $35**, AE BC DC EFT MC VI.

★★☆ **Meriki Motel**, (M), Tawonga Cres, Adjacent hospital, off Kiewa Valley Hwy, ☎ 03 5754 4145, fax 03 5754 4145, 10 units [shwr, tlt, a/c, heat, elec blkts, TV, clock radio, t/c mkg, refrig, toaster, doonas], dry rm, pool (salt water), bbq, 📞, plygr, cots, non smoking units (5). **RO 👤 $49.50 - $66, 👥 $62 - $88, 🧍 $15**, ch con, AE BC DC EFT MC MCH VI.

★★ **Allamar Motor Inn**, (M), Ranch Rd, Tawonga South 3698, 3.2km NW of PO, ☎ 03 5754 4365, fax 03 5754 4365, 10 units [shwr, tlt, a/c-cool, heat, elec blkts, TV, clock radio, t/c mkg, refrig, toaster], ldry, dry rm, bbq, c/park (carport), plygr, tennis (floodlit). **RO 👤 $45 - $50, 👥 $65 - $80, 🧍 $10**, ch con, BC MC VI.

Trouble-free travel tips - **Windscreen wipers**

Check the operation of windscreen wipers and washers. Replace windscreen wiper rubbers if they are not cleaning the windscreen properly.

Kiewa Country Cottages

Mount Beauty

Your Retreat to Tranquility

Experience our four magnificent alpine seasons, relax and enjoy our bubbling stream, tall trees, abundant birdlife and mountain views from your private verandah. Our cottages are pined lined, warm & cosy with fully equipped kitchen, laundry and drying area.

One or two bedroom, Queen sized beds. Treat yourself to our spa suite with sun deck and wood heater. 3 acre bush creek setting with pool, BBQs picnic areas and playground.

Resident owners: Phone (03) 5754 4004 Fax (03) 5754 1255
www.netc.net.au/Region1/kiewa.html
PO Box 95 Mount Beauty Vic. 3699

12339AG

Self Catering Accommodation

★★★★☆ **Dreamers**, (Chalet), Kiewa Valley Hwy, Tawonga South 3698, 1km N of PO, ☎ 03 5754 1222, fax 03 5754 1333, (2 stry gr fl), 5 chalets acc up to 4, (Studio & 2 bedrm), [shwr, bath (1), spa bath (4), tlt, hairdry, a/c, c/fan, heat, elec blkts, tel, TV, video, clock radio, CD, refrig, cook fac, micro, d/wash, toaster, blkts, doonas, linen, pillows], ldry, conf fac, lounge firepl, pool-heated (inground), spa, bbq, non smoking property. **D** ♦♦ **$150 - $230,** ⦿ **$30, W** ♦♦ **$930 - $1,500,** ⦿ **$180**, Min book applies, AE BC MC VI.

★★★★☆ **(Cottage Section)**, Kangaroo, No children's facilities, (2 stry gr fl), 1 cotg acc up to 2, (2 bedrm), [shwr, spa bath, tlt, a/c, c/fan, tel, TV, video, CD, cook fac, micro, ldry (in unit), blkts, linen, pillows], lounge firepl, bbq. **D** ♦♦ **$280, W** ♦♦ **$1,800**, Min book applies.

★★★★ **Montana Holiday Cottages**, (HU), 3 Allamar Crt, Tawonga South 3698, 2km N of PO, ☎ 03 5754 4962, fax 03 5754 4962, 2 units acc up to 8, (3 bedrm), [shwr, bath, tlt, a/c, c/fan, elec blkts, TV, clock radio, refrig, cook fac, micro, toaster, ldry (in unit), doonas, linen reqd-fee], dry rm, bbq. **D** **$85 - $370, W $340 - $820**, Min book Christmas Jan long w/ends and Easter, BC MC VI.

★★★☆ **Kiewa Country Cottages**, (Cotg), Simmonds Creek Rd, Tawonga South 3698, 1km W of PO, ☎ 03 5754 4004, fax 03 5754 1255, 7 cotgs acc up to 6, (1 & 2 bedrm), [shwr, spa bath (1), tlt, hairdry, c/fan, cent heat, elec blkts, TV, video (1)-fee, clock radio, refrig, cook fac, micro, elec frypan, toaster, ldry (in unit), blkts, linen, pillows], dry rm, pool, bbq, plygr, cots. **D $70 - $190, W $360 - $815**, 1 cottage ★★★★, BC MC VI.

★★★ **Alpenhorn Holiday Flats**, (HU), Kiewa Valley Hwy, Tawonga South 3698, 1.8km NW of PO, ☎ 03 5754 4133, (2 stry gr fl), 5 units acc up to 6, (1 & 2 bedrm), [shwr, tlt, fan, cent heat, elec blkts, TV, CD (1), refrig, cook fac, micro, elec frypan, toaster, doonas, linen], ldry, dry rm, pool, bbq, cots. **D $65 - $210**, BC MC VI.

★★★ **Snow View Holiday Units**, (HU), Simmonds Creek Rd, Tawonga South 3698, 1km W of PO, ☎ 03 5754 4733, fax 03 5754 4657, 8 units acc up to 5, (2 bedrm), [shwr, bath (hip), tlt, heat, TV, video (avail), clock radio, refrig, cook fac, micro, elec frypan, toaster, doonas, linen, pillows], ldry, dry rm, pool, spa, bbq, c/park (carport), ☎, plygr, cots. **D $80 - $120,** ⦿ **$10, W $350 - $630**, BC MC VI.

★★★ **The Carvers Log Cabins**, (HU), 16 Buckland St, Tawonga South 3698, 2.2km NW of PO, ☎ 03 5754 4863, fax 03 5754 4863, 5 units acc up to 6, (3 bedrm), [shwr, bath, tlt, a/c-cool, heat, elec blkts, TV, clock radio, refrig, cook fac, micro, toaster, ldry (in unit), blkts, linen, pillows], w/mach, iron, iron brd, dry rm, bbq, plygr, cots. **D $115 - $138, W $397 - $937**, AE BC DC MC VI.

★★☆ **Mt Beauty Caravan Park & Holiday Centre**, (HU), Kiewa Valley Hwy, Tawonga South 3698, 800m NW of PO, ☎ 03 5754 4396, fax 03 5754 4877, 12 units acc up to 5, (Studio), [shwr, tlt, fan, heat, TV, refrig, cook fac ltd, micro (6), toaster, linen], ldry, dry rm, TV rm, spa, bbq (covered)-fee, c/park (carport), ☎, plygr, mini golf, tennis, cots. **D** ♦♦ **$60 - $88,** ⦿ **$11, W $360 - $484**, ch con, Minimum booking Easter & weekends in Aug, BC MC VI.

B&B's/Guest Houses

★★★★☆ **Braeview Bed & Breakfast**, (B&B), No children's facilities, 4 Stewarts Rd, Tawonga South 3698, 1.5km SW of PO, ☎ 03 5754 4746, fax 03 5754 4757, 4 rms [ensuite, spa bath (3), hairdry, a/c-cool, heat, elec blkts, cable tv, clock radio], ldry, lounge (TV, video, cd), lounge firepl, spa (heat), t/c mkg shared, bbq, non smoking property. **BB** ♦ **$60 - $90,** ♦♦ **$110 - $148.50**, BC MC VI.

★★★★ **Janes Bed & Breakfast**, (B&B), 40 Tawonga Cres, ☎ 03 5754 4036, fax 03 5754 4036, 3 rms [ensuite (1), shwr (2), bath (1), tlt (2), hairdry, a/c (2), c/fan, elec blkts, cable tv, clock radio], ldry, lounge (TV, video, cd), t/c mkg shared, c/park (undercover), non smoking property. **BB** ♦ **$50 - $60,** ♦♦ **$100 - $120,** ⦿ **$25**, BC MC VI.

★★★★ **(Cottage Section)**, 1 cotg acc up to 6, (3 bedrm), [shwr, tlt, hairdry, a/c, fan, heat, elec blkts, cable tv, video, clock radio, refrig, cook fac, micro, d/wash, toaster, ldry, blkts, doonas, linen, pillows], iron, iron brd, dry rm, bbq. **D $100, W $500 - $600**.

★★★☆ **Mt Beauty Homestay Holidays**, (B&B), 1 Buckland St, Tawonga South 3698, 2.1km NW of PO, ☎ 03 5754 1301, fax 03 5754 4777, (2 stry), 2 rms [hairdry, a/c-cool, fan, heat, elec blkts, doonas], ldry, lounge (TV, video, cd), t/c mkg shared, bbq. **BB** ♦ **$45 - $50,** ♦♦ **$85 - $100**.

★★★ **(Holiday Unit Section)**, 1 unit acc up to 4, (1 bedrm), [shwr, tlt, hairdry, fan, heat, elec blkts, TV, video, refrig, cook fac, micro, blkts, doonas, linen, pillows], ldry, bbq. **D** ♦♦ **$100 - $110,** ⦿ **$10, W** ♦♦ **$450 - $600**.

★★★☆ **The Valley View Lodge Motel Mt Beauty**, (GH), Allamar Crt, Tawonga South 3698, 2.2km NW of PO, ☎ 03 5754 1033, fax 03 5754 4567, (2 stry gr fl), 11 rms [shwr, tlt, evap cool, c/fan, heat, elec blkts, TV, movie, t/c mkg], ldry, dry rm, lounge, ⊠, pool, spa, ☎. **BB** ♦ **$75 - $100,** ♦♦ **$85 - $100,** ⦿ **$15 - $25**, ch con, BC MC VI.

MOUNT BUFFALO VIC 3745

Pop 527. (333km NE Melbourne), See map on pages 694/695, ref H5. Mt Buffalo National Park encompasses the entire plateau. The scenery is spectacular and there are 100km of walking and horse riding trails. Winter cross country skiing centre. Bush Walking, Fishing, Horse Riding, Rock Climbing, Scenic Drives, Snow Skiing, Swimming.

B&B's/Guest Houses

★★★☆ **Mt Buffalo Chalet**, (GH), Mount Buffalo Rd, Mt Buffalo National Park, ☎ 03 5755 1500, fax 03 5755 1892, (Multi-stry gr fl), 97 rms [basin, shwr (72), bath (19), tlt (72), cent heat, t/c mkg], ldry, dry rm, rec rm, lounge (TV), conf fac, ⊠, ✕, bar (cocktail), pool, sauna, spa, ☎, bicycle, canoeing-fee, gym, ski hire, tennis, cots-fee. **D $128 - $224**, ch con, AE BC DC EFT MC VI

Operator Comment: What can we say? Our visitors book overflows with comments like 'Beautiful Food & Hospitality', 'Great Staff' and 'Love the Walks'. If you haven't been recently (or at all), we look forward to welcoming you soon.

MOUNT BUFFALO VIC continued...

★★★ **Mount Buffalo Lodge**, (GH), Mount Buffalo National Park, Cresta, ☎ 03 5755 1988, fax 03 5750 1194, (2 stry gr fl), 12 rms [shwr, tlt, cent heat, t/c mkg], ldry, dry rm, lounge (TV, video), conf fac, ☒, bar (cocktail), bbq, ✆, ski hire, cots-fee. **DBB $89 - $109**, ch con, BC DC MC VI

Operator Comment: In summer relax & enjoy alpine wildflower walks, bubbling streams & a great range of activities. In winter, the magic of fresh snow, snow play and skiing create a special experience for your whole family.

(Bunkhouse Section), 1 bunkhouse (Bunk Rooms), [cent heat, blkts reqd, linen reqd], shwr, tlt, cook fac, refrig. **D $22 - $32**, ch con.

(Lodge Section), 8 rms acc up to 4, (Bunk Rooms), [cent heat, t/c mkg, blkts, linen, pillows], shwr ((2L-2G)), tlt ((2L-2G)), ldry, dry rm. **DBB $73 - $83**, ch con.

MOUNT BULLER VIC 3723

Pop Part of Mansfield, (246km NE Melbourne), See map on page 696, ref E4. Winter skiing area controlled by the Alpine Resorts Commission. Resort has 75km of ski runs and trails. Bush Walking, Scenic Drives, Snow Skiing.

Hotels/Motels

AAA
TOURISM
Special Rates

★★★★☆ **Mt Buller Chalet Hotel**, (LH), Summit Rd, ☎ 03 5777 6566, fax 03 5777 6455, (Multi-stry), 65 rms (4 suites) [shwr, bath, spa bath (3), tlt, hairdry, cent heat, tel, TV, movie, clock radio, t/c mkg, refrig, mini bar, cook fac (5)], ldry, iron, iron brd, dry rm, lounge, conf fac, ☒, bar (cocktail), pool indoor heated, sauna, spa, 24hr reception, rm serv, ✆, gym, ski hire, squash. **High Season BB ♦♦ $170 - $500, Suite BB $220 - $1,900**, ch con, AE BC DC EFT MC VI.

★★★ **Abom**, (LH), Summit Rd, ☎ 03 5777 6091, fax 03 5777 6041, 10 rms [shwr, tlt, cent heat, TV, clock radio, t/c mkg, refrig, doonas], ldry, dry rm, ☒ (seasonal), spa, ✆, cots-fee. **High Season BB ♦ $55 - $75, ◊ $55 - $75**, ch con, AE BC DC EFT MC VI.

★★★ **Arlberg Hotel Mt Buller**, (LH), 189 Summit Rd, 600m W of Village Square, ☎ 03 5777 6260, fax 03 5777 6298, (Multi-stry), 51 rms (6 suites) [shwr, bath (36), spa bath (3), tlt, cent heat, TV, movie, t/c mkg, refrig, cook fac (6), doonas], dry rm, rec rm, ✕, ☒ (seasonal), 24hr reception, ✆, ski hire, cots-fee, non smoking rms (2). **BLB ♦♦ $90 - $200, ◊ $10 - $60, Suite D $130 - $520**, Minimum weekend booking during snow season, AE BC DC EFT MC VI.

Self Catering Accommodation

Breathtaker All Suite Hotel, (HU), Previously Breathtaker Ski Lodge Ski Lodge. Open snow season only. 8 Breathtaker Rd, 350m W of PO, ☎ 03 5777 6377, fax 03 5777 6312, (Multi-stry), 33 units acc up to 8, (1, 2 & 3 bedrm Studio), [shwr, spa bath (4), tlt, hairdry, cent heat, tel, TV, video (5), movie, clock radio, refrig, cook fac (18), cook fac ltd (10), micro (28), blkts, doonas, linen, pillows], ldry, dry rm, rec rm, lounge (TV), business centre, conf fac, ☒, cafe, bar (cocktail), sauna, spa, ✆. **High Season W $1,470 - $6,895**, AE BC DC EFT MC VI, (Rating under review).

B&B's/Guest Houses

★★★★ **Pension Grimus**, (GH), Open snow season only. 224 Breathtaker Rd, 400m W of Village Square, ☎ 03 5777 6396, fax 03 5777 6127, (Multi-stry), 19 rms (4 suites) [ensuite, spa bath, hairdry, cent heat, tel, TV, video, clock radio (2), t/c mkg, refrig, cook fac (4), micro (4), d/wash (4), doonas], ldry, iron, iron brd, dry rm, rec rm, lounge (TV), ☒, bar (cocktail), sauna, spa, bbq, ✆, ski hire, cots. **BB ♦ $160 - $530, ♦♦ $160 - $530, Suite D $400 - $1,700**, ch con, AE BC MC VI.

★★★ **Duck Inn Mt Buller**, (GH), 18 Goal Post Rd, Mount Buller Village, ☎ 03 5777 6326, fax 03 5777 6385, (2 stry), 16 rms [ensuite (14), cent heat, doonas], dry rm, lounge (TV, video), lounge firepl, ☒, sauna, t/c mkg shared, ✆, ski hire, non smoking property. **BB ♦ $70, ♦♦ $90**, ch con, AE BC EFT MC VI,

Operator Comment: Mt.Buller's best kept secret - Traditional B & B. Open year round.

★★★ **Ski Club of Victoria**, (GH), Ivor Whitaker Lodge - Open snow season only. 32 Summit Rd, adjacent to medical centre, ☎ 03 9826 0428, fax 03 5777 6722, (Multi-stry), 19 rms (1 bedrm), [ensuite, cent heat, clock radio, doonas], dry rm, rec rm (games room), TV rm (for children), lounge (TV, video), ☒, sauna, t/c mkg shared, bbq, ✆, cots, non smoking rms. **High Season DBB ♦ $125 - $150, ◊ $95 - $120, W ♦ $625 - $750, ◊ $475 - $600**, ch con, AE BC DC EFT MC VI.

Other Accommodation

Ski Club of Victoria, (Lodge), Kandahar Lodge - Open snow season only. off Summit Rd, ☎ 03 9826 0428, fax 03 9827 3259, (Multi-stry), 16 rms [ensuite (1), cent heat, linen reqd], ldry, dry rm, lounge (TV, video), cook fac, t/c mkg shared, refrig, bbq, ✆, cots, non smoking property. **High Season D ♦♦ $60 - $70, High Season W ♦♦ $470 - $520**, ch con, AE BC DC MC VI.

Ski-Lib Alpine Club Co-Operative Inc, (Lodge), 2 Goal Post Rd,
☎ 03 9801 5134, 18 rms [basin, ensuite (4), cent heat], ldry, dry rm,
lounge (TV, video, stereo), lounge firepl, sauna, cook fac, t/c mkg shared,
refrig, bbq, ✆, cots. **High Season D ♦ $60 - $155, High Season W ♦ $395 -
$483,** ◊ **$395 - $483,** BC MC VI.

MOUNT DANDENONG VIC

See Dandenong Ranges Region.

MOUNT EVELYN VIC

See Dandenong Ranges Region.

MOUNT HOTHAM VIC 3741

*Pop Part of Bright, (373km NE Melbourne), See map on pages
694/695, ref H5. Small alpine village controlled by the Alpine
Resorts Commission. Bush Walking, Gold Prospecting, Hangliding,
Scenic Drives, Snow Skiing.*

Hotels/Motels

★★ **Snowbird Inn**, (LH), Great Alpine Rd, ☎ 03 5759 3503,
fax 03 5759 3696, (Multi-stry), 25 rms [shwr, tlt, cent heat, t/c mkg,
doonas], dry rm, TV rm, ⊠, sauna, spa (heated), ✆, ski hire. **DBB ♦ $60 -
$145,** AE BC DC EFT MC VI.

Self Catering Accommodation

★★★★☆ **Hotham Central Reservations**, (Apt), White Crystal
Apartments, Great Alpine Rd, ☎ 03 5759 4444, fax 03 5759 3083,
(2 stry) 34 apts acc up to 12, (Studio, 1, 2 & 3 bedrm), [shwr, spa
bath, tlt, hairdry, cent heat, tel (local), TV, video, clock radio, CD,
t/c mkg, refrig, cook fac, micro, d/wash, toaster, ldry (in unit) (25),
doonas, linen, pillows], iron, iron brd, dry rm, ⊠, cots-fee. **D $180 -
$907, W $630 - $9,790,** Min book applies, AE BC DC EFT MC VI.

★★★★ **Alpine Haven**, (HF), Alpine Rd, ☎ 03 5759 3522,
fax 03 5759 3683, (Multi-stry), 8 flats acc up to 12, (Studio, 1, 2 & 3
bedrm), [shwr, bath (4), tlt, fire pl (4), cent heat, cable tv, video, clock
radio, CD, refrig, cook fac, micro, d/wash (5), toaster, ldry (in unit) (4),
blkts, linen, pillows], ldry, dry rm, ✆, ski hire. **W $1,260 - $3,805,**
2 flats ★★☆. AE BC DC MC VI.

★★★☆ **Arlberg Hotham**, (Apt), Open snow season and summer
vacation periods only. Great Alpine Rd, ☎ 03 5759 3618,
fax 03 5759 3605, (Multi-stry), 164 apts acc up to 8, (Studio, 1, 2 & 3
bedrm), [shwr, bath (hip), tlt, cent heat, TV, video, clock radio (60),
refrig, cook fac, micro, toaster, blkts, doonas, linen, pillows], lift, ldry,
dry rm, rec rm, ⊠, pool indoor heated, sauna, spa, shop, ✆. **W $1,485 -
$3,960,** AE BC MC VI.

★★★ **Fountains**, (HF), Alpine Rd, ☎ 03 5759 3522, fax 03 5759 3683,
(Multi-stry gr fl), 10 flats acc up to 8, (2 & 3 bedrm), [shwr, bath, tlt,
hairdry, fire pl (1), cent heat, TV, video, clock radio, CD, refrig, cook fac,
micro, d/wash, toaster, ldry (in unit) (5), blkts, linen, pillows], ldry,
dry rm. **D $2,570 - $3,410,** AE BC DC MC VI.

★★★ **Hotham 1750**, (HF), Alpine Rd, ☎ 03 5759 3522,
fax 03 5759 3683, (Multi-stry gr fl), 12 flats acc up to 10, (Studio & 3
bedrm), [shwr, bath, tlt, fire pl (7), heat, TV, video (12), clock radio,
refrig, cook fac, micro, d/wash, toaster, ldry (in unit) (9), blkts, linen,
pillows], dry rm. **D $1,470 - $3,935,** AE BC DC MC.

★★★ **Lawlers Apartments**, (HF), Great Alpine Rd, ☎ 03 5759 3606,
fax 03 5759 3111, 26 flats acc up to 15, (1, 2, 3 & 4 bedrm), [shwr,
spa bath (4), tlt, fire pl (5), cent heat, tel (2), TV, video (26), radio (14),
refrig, cook fac, micro, d/wash, ldry (in unit), linen reqd], dry rm,
⊠ (seasonal), sauna (2), ✆. **D $140, W $675 - $2,304,** AE BC EFT MC VI.

MOUNT LONARCH VIC 3468

*Pop Nominal, (170km NW Melbourne), See map on pages 694/695,
ref D5. A small grazing, agricultural and fruit growing district.*

B&B's/Guest Houses

★★★ **Mt Lonarch Gallery**, (B&B), (Farm), RMB 4246 Beaufort Rd,
15km NW of Lexton PO, ☎ 03 5466 2258, fax 03 5466 2258, 4 rms
[fan, heat, elec blkts, clock radio], ldry, lounge (TV, video), t/c mkg
shared, non smoking rms. **BB ♦ $45, ♦♦ $85,** ◊ **$40,** ch con, AE BC DC
EFT MC VI.

Before you travel

Before a trip have your vehicle serviced and checked over to
ensure reliable motoring. There are some checks you can make
yourself, generally the procedure can be found in the vehicle
owners manual.

MOUNT MACEDON VIC 3441

*Pop 700. (61km NW Melbourne), See map on page 696, ref B4.
Township lies in a secluded valley below the summit of the mount.
Bowls, Bush Walking, Golf, Horse Riding, Scenic Drives.*

Hotels/Motels

★★ **Mountain Inn**, (LH), 694 Mt Macedon Rd, 100m N of PO,
☎ 03 5426 1755, fax 03 5426 4036, (2 stry gr fl), 9 rms [basin (2),
shwr (3), tlt (3), heat, elec blkts, TV (3), clock radio (3), t/c mkg (3),
refrig (3), toaster (3)], lounge (TV), ⊠, t/c mkg shared, refrig, ✆,
tennis. **BLB ♦ $50 - $55, ♦♦ $65 - $105,** AE BC DC EFT MC VI.

Self Catering Accommodation

★★★★ **Ballantrae Mews**, (Cotg), 750 Mt Macedon Rd, ☎ 03 5426 2078,
fax 03 5426 3478, 1 cotg acc up to 2, (Studio), [shwr, bath (hip), tlt,
hairdry, fan, heat, elec blkts, TV, video, CD, t/c mkg, refrig, cook fac,
micro, elec frypan, ldry, blkts, linen, pillows], iron, iron brd, breakfast
ingredients, non smoking property. **D ♦♦ $110.**

★★★★ **Braeside Mt Macedon**, (Cotg), Young children restricted by
unfenced dam. 47 Taylors Rd, 1.7km SE of PO, ☎ 03 5426 1762,
fax 03 5426 1762, 1 cotg acc up to 6, [ensuite (1), shwr, bath, tlt,
heat, elec blkts, TV, video, refrig, cook fac, micro, d/wash, toaster, ldry,
blkts, doonas, linen, pillows], w/mach, dryer, iron, iron brd, lounge firepl,
bbq, non smoking property. **BB ♦ $100, ♦♦ $140,** Dinner by arrangement,
BC MC VI.

B&B's/Guest Houses

★★★★☆ **Blue Ridge Inn**, (GH), Cnr Mt Macedon & Falls Rds, 5km N
of PO, ☎ 03 5427 0220, fax 03 5427 0337, (2 stry gr fl), 8 rms [shwr,
tlt, c/fan, cent heat, tel, TV, t/c mkg, refrig, mini bar], lounge, conf fac,
lounge firepl, ✗, res liquor license, dinner to unit, non smoking property.
BB ♦ $176 - $242, ♦♦ $198 - $264, DBB ♦ $220 - $286, ♦♦ $286 - $352,
pen con, AE BC DC EFT MC VI, ⚹⚹.

★★★★☆ **Horley Bed & Breakfast**, (B&B), 148 Alton Rd, 2km NW of PO,
☎ 03 5426 2448, fax 03 5426 2448, (2 stry), 2 rms [shwr, bath (1),
spa bath (1), tlt, hairdry, fan, heat, TV, clock radio, t/c mkg, refrig],
iron, iron brd, lounge (cd player), lounge firepl, cots (avail). **BB ♦ $65,
♦♦ $120 - $130,** ch con.

★★★★ **Mariah Vale**, (B&B), 515 Barringo Rd, 6.8km SE of PO,
☎ 03 5426 1281, 1 rm [shwr, tlt, hairdry, a/c, c/fan, heat, elec blkts,
clock radio], lounge (TV), lounge firepl, bbq, c/park (undercover), non
smoking property. **BB ♦ $75, ♦♦ $120,** ch con.

MOUNT MARTHA VIC 3934

*Pop 7,386. (63km S Melbourne), See map on page 697 ref C7.
Residential area and seaside resort. Many vantage points offer
excellent views of bays and headlands. Boating, Bush Walking,
Fishing, Horse Riding, Sailing, Scenic Drives, Shooting, Swimming
(Bay), Tennis, Water Skiing.*

Self Catering Accommodation

★★★★ **Cottage by the Sea Mt Martha**, (Cotg), 1 Smith St,
☎ 03 5988 4839, fax 03 5988 4839, 1 cotg acc up to 6, (3 bedrm),
[shwr, bath, tlt, hairdry, fan, heat, elec blkts, tel (local), TV, video,
clock radio, CD, refrig, cook fac, micro, elec frypan, toaster, ldry (in unit),
blkts, doonas, linen, pillows], w/mach, dryer, iron, iron brd, bbq,
c/park (carport), breakfast ingredients, non smoking property. **BB ♦♦ $125,**
◊ **$55,** ch con, BC MC VI.

★★★★ **Marlin Cottage Guest Wing**, (Apt), 8 Wattle Ave,
☎ 03 5974 4900, fax 03 5974 1959, 1 apt acc up to 4, (2 bedrm),
[shwr, tlt, hairdry, a/c, elec blkts, TV, video, clock radio, CD, t/c mkg,
refrig, cook fac, micro, toaster, blkts, doonas, linen, pillows], w/mach,
iron, iron brd, bbq, cots, non smoking property. **D ♦♦ $115 - $145,** ◊ **$50,
W ♦♦ $700 - $1,000,** ◊ **$300,** ch con, BC MC VI.

★★★☆ **Kacey - el**, (Cotg), 54 Glamorgan Cres, ☎ 03 5974 1208,
1 cotg acc up to 6, (2 bedrm), [shwr, tlt, hairdry, fan, heat, elec blkts,
TV, video, refrig, cook fac, micro, elec frypan, toaster, blkts,
linen, pillows], w/mach, iron, iron brd, bbq, c/park (undercover), cots,
breakfast ingredients. **BLB ♦ $60, ♦♦ $95,** ◊ **$35, W ♦♦ $500 - $600,** ch con.

B&B's/Guest Houses

★★★★☆ **Glynt by the Sea**, (GH), No children's facilities, 16 Bay Rd,
☎ 03 5974 1216, fax 03 5974 2546, 6 rms (6 suites) [bath, hairdry,
cent heat, TV, video (avail), clock radio, t/c mkg, refrig, doonas], iron,
iron brd, lounge (and conservatory), ⊠, tennis, non smoking property.
D ♦ $250 - $400, ♦♦ $300 - $450, AE BC DC MC VI.

MOUNT MARTHA VIC continued...

★★★★ **Mount Martha Bed & Breakfast by the Sea**, (B&B), 538 Esplanade, ☎ 03 5974 1019, fax 03 5974 1022, 2 rms [ensuite, spa bath (1), fire pl, cent heat, TV, video, clock radio, t/c mkg, refrig, toaster, ldry], lounge firepl, res liquor license, bar, bbq, c/park (undercover), ☎, plygr, cots-fee, non smoking property. **BB** ♦ **$80 - $100**, ♦♦ **$160 - $200**, ◊ **$80**, ch con, Min book applies, AE BC DC MC VI.

★★★★ **Seppelt House**, (B&B), 10 Seppelt Ave, ☎ 03 5974 3594, 4 rms (1 suite) [shwr, tlt, a/c, c/fan, cent heat, tel, clock radio, t/c mkg, refrig, toaster], lounge (TV), bbq, non smoking property. **BB** ♦ **$65**, ♦♦ **$115 - $130**, Other meals by arrangement. ⚹.

★★★★ **(Holiday Unit Section)**, 2 units acc up to 6, (2 bedrm), [shwr, tlt, hairdry, a/c, c/fan, tel, TV, clock radio, t/c mkg, refrig, cook fac (1), cook fac ltd (1), micro, elec frypan (1), toaster, blkts, linen, pillows], ldry, w/mach, iron, iron brd. **D $100**, ⚹.

★★★★ **Woodland by the Bay**, (B&B), 24 Alexandrina Rd, 2km S of PO, ☎ 03 5974 8924, fax 03 5974 8922, 1 rm [shwr, bath, tlt, hairdry, c/fan, elec blkts, TV, video, clock radio, toaster], ldry, lounge (TV, video, cd), t/c mkg shared, refrig, bbq, non smoking property. **BB** ♦ **$90**, ♦♦ **$130 - $140**, ◊ **$65 - $90**.

MURCHISON VIC 3610

Pop 650. (150km N Melbourne), See map on page 696, ref C2. River Bank Garden Town. Bowls, Bush Walking, Fishing, Golf, Horse Riding, Scenic Drives, Shooting, Swimming (Pool, River), Tennis.

Hotels/Motels

★★★ **Murchison Motel**, (M), High Rd, 1.6km E of PO, ☎ 03 5826 2488, fax 03 5826 2488, 8 units [shwr, tlt, a/c-cool, heat, elec blkts, TV, clock radio, t/c mkg, refrig], lounge, ✕, BYO, pool, bbq, cots-fee, non smoking units (8). **RO** ♦ **$38.50 - $44**, ♦♦ **$49.50 - $60.50**, ◊ **$11**, ch con, BC MC VI.

MURRAYVILLE VIC 3512

Pop 250. (563km NW Melbourne), See map on pages 694/695, ref A2. Agricultural township. Bowls, Bush Walking, Golf, Horse Riding, Scenic Drives, Shooting, Swimming (Pool), Tennis.

Hotels/Motels

★★ **Murrayville**, (LMH), Mallee Hwy, 100m N of PO, ☎ 03 5095 2120, 8 units [shwr, tlt, a/c-cool, heat, elec blkts, TV, clock radio, t/c mkg, refrig, toaster], ✕, bbq, ☎. **BLB** ♦ **$40**, ♦♦ **$50**, BC EFT MC VI.

MURTOA VIC 3390

Pop 850. (304km NW Melbourne), See map on pages 694/695, ref B4. Located on the shore of Lake Marma, pastoral wheat growing area. Boating, Bowls, Fishing, Golf, Horse Racing, Squash, Swimming (Pool), Tennis.

Hotels/Motels

★★ **Railway Hotel**, (LMH), 2 Comyn St, 600m N of PO, ☎ 03 5385 2241, 1 unit [shwr, tlt, c/fan, heat, elec blkts, TV, clock radio, t/c mkg, refrig, toaster], ldry, ✕, ☎, non smoking units. **BLB** ♦ **$44**, ♦♦ **$55**, ◊ **$15**, ch con, BC DC EFT MC VI.

MYRTLEFORD VIC 3737

Pop 2,700. (280km NE Melbourne), See map on pages 694/695, ref H5. Important centre for tobacco growing, dairying, beef cattle & hops. Located on the Ovens Hwy, at the junction of the Ovens & Buffalo rivers. Bowls, Bush Walking, Croquet, Fishing (Trout), Golf, Scenic Drives, Squash, Swimming, Tennis. See also Ovens.

Hotels/Motels

★★★☆ **Golden Leaf Motor Inn**, (M), 186-188 Great Alpine Rd, 700m W of PO, ☎ 03 5752 1566, fax 03 5751 1260, 24 units [shwr, spa bath (1), tlt, hairdry, a/c, c/fan (16), heat, elec blkts, tel, TV, video-fee, clock radio, t/c mkg, refrig, toaster], iron, iron brd, dry rm, ✕ (Mon to Sat), pool-heated (solar), spa-fee, bbq, rm serv, cots-fee. **RO** ♦ **$66 - $85**, ♦♦ **$72 - $105**, ◊ **$10**, AE BC DC EFT MC MP VI.

★★★☆ **Myrtleford Country Motel**, (M), 258 Great Alpine Rd, 1.4km W of PO, ☎ 03 5752 1438, fax 03 5752 1256, 18 units [shwr, tlt, hairdry (10), a/c-cool (2), a/c (16), heat, elec blkts, tel, TV, clock radio, t/c mkg, refrig, toaster], iron (10), iron brd (10), bbq (covered), c/park (carport), cots, non smoking units (18). **RO** ♦ **$55 - $77**, ♦♦ **$55 - $80**, ◊ **$11**, ch con, 8 units ★★★, AE BC DC EFT MC MP VI.

★★★ **The Railway Hotel - Motel Myrtleford**, (LMH), Standish Street Motel, 101 Standish St, 400m N of PO, ☎ 03 5752 1583, fax 03 5752 2134, 14 units [shwr, tlt, a/c, heat, elec blkts, tel, TV, t/c mkg, refrig, toaster, ldry], ✕, bbq, dinner to unit, c/park (carport) (9), cots. **RO** ♦ **$55**, ♦♦ **$66**, ◊ **$11**, ch con, AE BC DC EFT MC VI, ⚹.

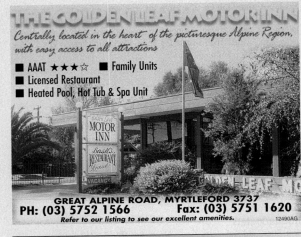
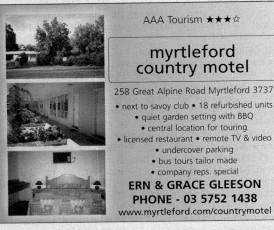
NAGAMBIE VIC 3608

Pop 1,350. (126km N Melbourne), See map on page 696, ref C3. Agricultural and pastoral township, situated on Lake Nagambie. The annual Boxing Day Regatta is a leading rowing feature. Tourist Bureau, Goulburn Valley Hwy, 03-5794 2647. Boat Ramp, Boating, Bowls, Croquet, Fishing, Golf, Rowing, Sailing, Scenic Drives, Swimming (Pool, Lake), Tennis, Vineyards, Wineries, Water Skiing.

Hotels/Motels

★★★★ **Nagambie Motor Inn & Conference Centre**, (M), 185 High St (Goulburn Valley Hwy), 1km S of PO, ☎ 03 5794 2833, fax 03 5794 2138, 18 units [shwr, bath (1), spa bath (4), tlt, hairdry, a/c, elec blkts, tel, TV, clock radio, t/c mkg, refrig, cook fac, toaster], ldry, conf fac, pool, spa, bbq, dinner to unit, cots-fee, breakfast ingredients (supplied). **BLB** ♦ **$66 - $88**, ♦♦ **$77 - $110**, ◊ **$11 - $13**, AE BC DC EFT MC VI.

★★★☆ **Centretown Motel Nagambie**, (M), 266 High St (Goulburn Valley Hwy), 200m S of PO, ☎ 03 5794 2511, fax 03 5794 1590, 16 units [shwr, tlt, hairdry, a/c, c/fan, elec blkts, tel, TV, video (avail), clock radio, t/c mkg, refrig, toaster], ldry, iron, iron brd, pool, bbq, cots, non smoking units (6). **RO** ♦ **$55**, ♦♦ **$67 - $71**, ◊ **$12**, AE BC DC EFT MC VI.

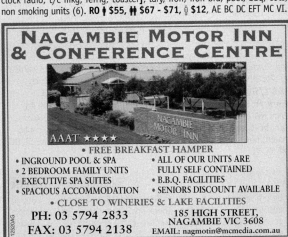

★★★ **Nagambie Lake Motel**, (M), 271 High St (Goulburn Valley Hwy), 150m S of PO, ☎ 03 5794 2300, fax 03 5794 2300, 6 units [shwr, tlt, hairdry, a/c, elec blkts, TV, clock radio, t/c mkg, refrig, toaster], ldry, cots, non smoking units (2). RO ♦ $50, ♦♦ $58 - $62, ♦ $12, ch con, AE BC MC VI.

★★☆ **Nagambie Goulburn Highway**, (M), 143 High St (Goulburn Valley Hwy), 1.5km S of PO, ☎ 03 5794 2681, fax 03 5794 2919, 10 units [shwr, tlt, evap cool, c/fan, heat, TV, clock radio, refrig], ldry, pool, bbq, plygr, tennis, cots-fee. RO ♦ $46 - $50, ♦♦ $49 - $55, ♦ $10, ch con, Light breakfast only available. AE BC DC MC VI.

★★☆ **Nagambie Lakes Country Resort**, (M), RMB 2290 Goulburn Weir Rd, 8km N of PO, off Goulburn Valley Hwy, ☎ 03 5794 7221, fax 03 5794 7388, 4 units [shwr, tlt, a/c, heat, elec blkts, TV, t/c mkg, refrig, cook fac, toaster], ldry, bbq, plygr, golf (pitch'n'putt), tennis, cots. BLB ♦♦ $66, ♦♦♦♦ $77, Min book Christmas and Jan, BC MC VI.

★★☆ **(Holiday Flat Section)**, 6 flats (Studio), [shwr, tlt, c/fan, heat, TV, refrig, cook fac, micro, linen reqd-fee, pillows]. D $66 - $77.

NARBETHONG VIC 3778

Pop Nominal, (84km NE Melbourne), See map on page 696, ref D5. Tiny settlement in the Acheron Valley. Bush Walking, Fishing, Horse Riding, Scenic Drives.

Hotels/Motels
★★☆ **Black Spur Motel & Caravan Park**, (M), 262 Maroondah Hwy, 1.6km S of PO, ☎ 03 5963 7153, 5 units [shwr, tlt, fan, heat, elec blkts, TV, clock radio, t/c mkg, refrig], ldry, pool above ground, bbq, plygr, mini golf, cots. RO ♦ $70, ♦ $10, AE BC MC VI.

Self Catering Accommodation
★★★★☆ **Woodlands of Narbethong**, (Cotg), Manby Rd, 700m W of Maroondah Hwy, ☎ 03 5963 7150, fax 03 9459 7664, 1 cotg acc up to 4, (2 bedrm), [shwr, bath, tlt, hairdry, fan, cent heat, elec blkts, tel (local), TV, video, clock radio, CD, refrig, cook fac, micro, elec frypan, d/wash, ldry, blkts, doonas, linen, pillows], iron, iron brd, lounge firepl, spa (heated), bbq, breakfast ingredients, non smoking property. BB ♦♦ $192 - $265, ♦ $98 - $123, W $1,430 - $1,595, Min book applies, BC MC VI.

★★★ **Blue Views Holiday Units**, (HF), 635 Maroondah Hwy, Adjacent supermarket, ☎ 03 5963 7214, fax 03 5963 7242, 4 flats acc up to 6, (2 bedrm), [shwr, tlt, heat, elec blkts, TV, video, clock radio, refrig, cook fac, toaster, blkts, doonas, linen, pillows], w/mach, spa, bbq, plygr, ski hire. D $60 - $100, W $360 - $620, BC MC VI.

B&B's/Guest Houses
★★★★☆ **Abbey Green B & B Cottages**, (B&B), 629 Maroondah hwy, ☎ 03 5963 7226, fax 03 5963 7199, 2 rms [shwr, spa bath, tlt, hairdry, a/c, elec blkts, TV, CD, micro], non smoking property. BB ♦♦ $165 - $385, Dinner by arrangement, Min book applies, BC MC VI.

★★★★ **St Fillan Bed & Breakfast**, (B&B), No children's facilities, 723 Maroondah Hwy, opposite Marysville turn off, ☎ 03 5963 7126, 2 rms [shwr, spa bath, tlt, a/c, cent heat (1), elec blkts, TV, radio (1), t/c mkg, refrig, toaster], lounge firepl (1), bbq, non smoking property. BB ♦♦ $165, BC MC VI.

★★★☆ **The Hermitage Narbethong**, (B&B), Classified by National Trust, Children bookings by arrangement, 161 Maroondah Hwy, ☎ 03 5963 7120, fax 03 5963 7133, 7 rms [ensuite (3), shwr (3), tlt (4), heat, elec blkts, doonas], ldry, lounge (TV), t/c mkg shared, bbq. BB ♦ $65 - $75, ♦♦ $130 - $150, ♦ $65 - $75, Dinner by arrangement, BC EFT MC VI.

★★★ **(Cottage Section)**, Classified by National Trust, 2 cotgs acc up to 6, (1 & 3 bedrm), [shwr, bath (2), tlt, c/fan (2), cent heat, elec blkts, t/c mkg, refrig, cook fac, toaster, blkts, doonas, linen, pillows], lounge. BB ♦♦ $130 - $170, ♦ $65 - $85.

NATHALIA VIC 3638

Pop 1,450. (241km N Melbourne), See map on page 696, ref C1. Agricultural & dairy farming township, on the Murray Valley Hwy located adjacent to Broken Creek. Boating, Bowls, Fishing, Golf, Scenic Drives, Shooting, Swimming (Pool, River), Tennis, Water Skiing.

Hotels/Motels
★★★ **Nathalia Motel**, (M), Murray Valley Hwy, 200m S of Bridge, ☎ 03 5866 2615, fax 03 5866 2829, 13 units [shwr, spa bath (1), tlt, a/c, elec blkts, tel, TV, clock radio (8), radio, t/c mkg, refrig, toaster], ldry, pool, bbq, plygr, cots. D ♦♦♦♦ $75 - $85, RO ♦ $47 - $50, ♦♦ $58 - $65, ♦ $10, Min book Christmas Jan long w/ends and Easter, AE BC DC EFT MC VI.

NATIMUK VIC 3409

Pop 500. (323km W Melbourne), See map on pages 694/695, ref B5. Agricultural township on the Wimmera Hwy, located adjacent to Natimuk Creek. Boating, Bowls, Fishing, Golf, Rock Climbing, Swimming (Lake, River), Tennis, Water Skiing.

Hotels/Motels
★☆ **National Hotel**, (LH), 65 Main St (Wimmera Hwy), ☎ 03 5387 1300, (2 stry), 6 rms [basin (4), elec blkts, clock radio], lounge (TV, video), ☒, t/c mkg shared. RO ♦ $20, ♦ $20, ch con, BC EFT MC VI.

★★★ **(Holiday Unit Section)**, 5 units acc up to 6, (2 bedrm), [shwr, tlt, a/c, heat, elec blkts, TV, t/c mkg, refrig, cook fac ltd, micro, toaster, blkts, linen, pillows], bbq (covered), c/park. D ♦♦ $60, ♦ $5 - $10, ch con.

Other Accommodation
Tims Place Horsham-Arapiles Travellers Hostel, (Lodge), Asplins Rd, Quantong 3405, 8km E of PO, ☎ 03 5384 0236, fax 03 5384 0236, 6 rms [a/c-cool, c/fan, heat, t/c mkg, blkts, doonas, linen, pillows], shwr, tlt, bathrm, ldry, w/mach, lounge (TV, video, stereo), cook fac, refrig, bbq, non smoking property, Pets allowed. BLB ♦ $23.

NEERIM SOUTH VIC 3831

Pop 500. (116km E Melbourne), See map on page 696, ref D6. Rich dairying & agricultural district. Bowls, Bush Walking, Fishing, Gold Prospecting, Scenic Drives, Swimming (Pool), Tennis.

Self Catering Accommodation
★★★ **Blerick**, (Cotg), 55 McDougal Rd, 1km E of PO, ☎ 03 5628 1498, (2 stry gr fl), 1 cotg acc up to 6, (2 bedrm), [shwr, bath, tlt, hairdry, fan, heat, elec blkts, TV, clock radio, CD, t/c mkg, refrig, cook fac, micro, toaster, doonas, linen, pillows], iron, iron brd, lounge firepl, bbq, plygr, cots, non smoking property. D ♦♦ $66 - $88, ♦ $22, W $460, ch con, pen con, Breakfast available. Min book long w/ends and Easter, BC MC VI.

NELSON VIC 3292

Pop 200. (423km W Melbourne), See map on pages 694/695, ref A6. Situated at mouth of Glenelg River, popular holiday resort. National Park. Boating, Fishing, Scenic Drives, Swimming (River, Beach), Tennis, Water Skiing.

Hotels/Motels
★★★ **Motel Black Wattle**, (M), Mt Gambier Rd, 50m W of Glenelg River bridge, ☎ 08 8738 4008, fax 08 8738 4292, 14 units [shwr, tlt, hairdry, heat, elec blkts, tel, TV, clock radio, t/c mkg, refrig], ldry, ☒, bbq, cots. D ♦♦♦♦ $105, RO ♦ $65, ♦♦ $72, ♦♦♦♦ $85, BC MC VI.

★★ **Pinehaven Chalet Motel**, (M), Main Rd, 100m E of Glenelg River bridge, ☎ 08 8738 4041, 8 units [shwr, tlt, fan, heat, elec blkts, TV, clock radio, t/c mkg, refrig, toaster, doonas], bbq, cots. RO ♦ $35 - $50, ♦♦ $45 - $60, ♦ $10, AE BC DC EFT MC VI.

Self Catering Accommodation
★★★ **Casuarina Cabins**, North Nelson Rd, 1km N of Glenelg River bridge, ☎ 08 8738 4105, 7 cabins acc up to 5, [shwr, tlt, fan, c/fan (3), heat, elec blkts, TV, clock radio, refrig, cook fac ltd, micro, toaster, blkts reqd-fee, linen reqd-fee, pillows reqd-fee], ldry, w/mach-fee, dryer-fee, bbq, plygr, No dogs allowed. D ♦ $50, ♦ $4.50, BC EFT MC VI.

B&B's/Guest Houses
★★★☆ **Nelson Cottage**, (GH), Cnr Kellett & Sturt Sts, ☎ 08 8738 4161, fax 08 8738 4161, 6 rms [elec blkts, micro], lounge (TV), lounge firepl, t/c mkg shared, refrig, bbq, cots. BB ♦ $35, ♦♦ $66, ch con, BC MC VI.

NEWBOROUGH VIC 3825

Pop Part of Moe, (137km SE Melbourne), See map on page 696, ref E6. Residential area in the Latrobe Valley.

Self Catering Accommodation
★★★★ **Brigadoon Bed & Breakfast**, (Cotg), 106 Haunted Hills Rd, 4km E of Moe PO, ☎ 03 5127 2656, fax 03 5127 5056, 5 cotgs (1 & 2 bedrm), [shwr, bath, spa bath (4), tlt, hairdry, fan, heat, elec blkts, TV, video, CD, refrig, cook fac (3), cook fac ltd (2), toaster, blkts, linen, pillows], lounge firepl, bbq, breakfast ingredients, non smoking property. D $131, W $722, 1 cottage of a lower rating. Min book long w/ends, BC MC VI.

NEWBRIDGE VIC 3551

Pop 100. (171km NW Melbourne), See map on page 696, ref A2. Agricultural district on Loddon River. Fishing (River), Scenic Drives, Swimming, Tennis, Vineyards, Wineries.

★★★☆ **Brewery Farm**, (B&B), Catto La, off Newbridge - Bridgewater Rd, ☎ 03 5438 7282, fax 03 5438 7412, 3 rms [hairdry], lounge (TV, radio, video), lounge firepl, t/c mkg shared, bbq, tennis. BB ♦ $48, ♦♦ $88, ch con.

(Jackaroo Quarters), 3 rms [blkts, linen, pillows]. ♦ $20, ♦ $20, ch con.

NEWHAVEN VIC

See Phillip Island Region.

NHILL VIC 3418

Pop 1,900. (373km NW Melbourne), See map on pages 694/695, ref A4. Home of the Mallee Fowl. Centre of Little Desert & Big Desert National Parks region. Location of the only Mallee Fowl aviary in the world - situated in a natural setting at Whimpeys Desert Lodge, 16km S of township. (Open daily 9.30am to 4.30pm) - admission fee. Bowls, Bush Walking, Fishing, Golf, Horse Racing, Horse Riding, Scenic Drives, Shooting, Swimming (Pool), Tennis.

Hotels/Motels

 ★★★ **Motel Wimmera**, (M), 103 Victoria St (Western Hwy), 1.1km SW of PO, ☎ 03 5391 1444, fax 03 5391 2177, 12 units [shwr, tlt, a/c-cool, heat, elec blkts, tel, TV, clock radio, t/c mkg, refrig, toaster], bbq, cots-fee. **RO** ♦ **$44**, ♦♦ **$55**, ◊ **$10**, AE BC DC MC MCH VI.

★★★ **Nhill Oasis Motel**, (M), 21 Dimboola Rd (Western Hwy), 1.6km E of PO, ☎ 03 5391 1666, fax 03 5391 1363, 16 units [shwr, tlt, a/c, elec blkts, tel, TV, clock radio, t/c mkg, refrig], ldry, ✗ (Mon to Fri), BYO, bbq, dinner to unit (Mon to Fri), cots-fee. **RO** ♦ **$44**, ♦♦ **$55**, ◊ **$11**, BC EFT MC VI.

 ★★★ **Zero Inn**, (M), 31 Nelson St (Western Hwy), 800m E of PO, ☎ 03 5391 1622, fax 03 5391 1552, (2 stry gr fl), 28 units [shwr, bath, tlt, a/c-cool, heat, elec blkts, tel, TV, clock radio, t/c mkg, refrig], ✗ (Mon to Fri), pool, rm serv, cots-fee. **D** **$68**, ch con, AE BC DC MC VI.

★★ **Motel Halfway Nhill**, (M), Western Hwy, 2.3km E of PO, ☎ 03 5391 1888, fax 03 5391 1277, 9 units [shwr, tlt, a/c, elec blkts, TV, clock radio, t/c mkg, refrig, toaster], cots-fee. **RO** ♦ **$42**, ♦♦ **$53**, ◊ **$11**, ch con, pen con, AE BC DC EFT MC VI.

★ **Commercial Hotel**, (LH), 105 Nelson St (Western Hwy), opposite PO, ☎ 03 5391 1500, fax 03 5391 1485, (2 stry), 12 rms [basin (9), elec blkts], lounge (TV), ✗, t/c mkg shared, c/park. **BLB** ♦ **$20**, ♦♦ **$34**, ch con, BC EFT MC VI.

Other Accommodation

Little Desert Tours, (Lodge), Nhill - Harrow Rd, Winiam 3418, 16km S of Nhill, ☎ 03 5391 5232, fax 03 5391 5217, 16 rms acc up to 4, (Bunk Rooms), [elec blkts, blkts, linen, pillows], ldry, rec rm, conf fac, ✗, bbq-fee, ☏. **BLB** ♦ **$26 - $28.60**, ◊ **$26 - $28.60**, **DBB** ♦ **$41 - $48.40**, ◊ **$41 - $48.40**, ch con, Group bookings only. BC MC VI.

(Units Section), 12 rms [ensuite, bath, heat, elec blkts, blkts, linen, pillows], lounge, t/c mkg shared, refrig. **BLB** ♦ **$38.50 - $55**, ♦♦ **$50.30 - $70**, **DBB** ♦ **$70 - $77**, ♦♦ **$100 - $116**, ch con.

NICHOLSON VIC 3882

Pop 750. (295km E Melbourne), See map on pages 694/695, ref J7. Located on Princes Hwy, adjacent to Nicholson River. Boating, Fishing, Scenic Drives, Swimming (River), Tennis.

★★☆ **Retreat Hotel**, (LMH), 929 Princes Hwy, on bank of Nicholson River, ☎ 03 5156 8250, fax 03 5156 8879, 9 units [shwr, bath, tlt, a/c-cool, heat, elec blkts, TV, clock radio, t/c mkg, refrig, toaster], ✗, cots-fee. **RO** ♦ **$50**, ♦♦ **$55 - $60**, ◊ **$10**, ch con, AE BC DC EFT MC VI.

NUMURKAH VIC 3636

Pop 3,150. (217km N Melbourne), See map on page 696, ref D1. Business centre of a wide irrigation district. Bowls, Fishing, Golf, Shooting, Swimming (Pool), Tennis.

Hotels/Motels

 ★★★☆ **El Toro Motel**, (M), Cnr Melville & Brenion Sts, 300m S of PO, ☎ 03 5862 1966, fax 03 5862 1453, (2 stry gr fl), 14 units [shwr, spa bath (1), tlt, hairdry, a/c, elec blkts, TV, video-fee, clock radio, t/c mkg, refrig], conf fac, BYO, pool (salt water), bbq-fee, cots-fee. **RO** ♦ **$45 - $93.50**, ♦♦ **$55 - $93.50**, ◊ **$11**, AE BC DC EFT MC MP VI.

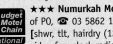 ★★★ **Numurkah Motel**, (M), 46 Tocumwal Rd, 500m N of PO, ☎ 03 5862 1922, fax 03 5862 1106, 16 units [shwr, tlt, hairdry (12), a/c, fan, elec blkts, tel, TV, video-fee, clock radio, t/c mkg, refrig, cook fac ltd (1), toaster], pool, bbq, plygr, cots-fee. **RO** ♦ **$42 - $48**, ♦♦ **$53 - $59**, ◊ **$11**, AE BC DC EFT MC VI.

Self Catering Accommodation

★★☆ **Brookfield Historic Farm**, (Cotg), RMB 4478 Brookfield Rd, off Kellys Rd, 4km S of PO, ☎ 03 5862 2353, fax 03 5862 2353, 1 cotg acc up to 8, (2 bedrm), [shwr, bath, tlt, fan, heat, elec blkts, TV, clock radio, refrig, cook fac, micro, elec frypan, toaster, linen], lounge firepl, bbq (covered), cots. **D** **$65**, **W** **$400**.

OCEAN GROVE VIC 3226

Pop 11,300. (97km SW Melbourne), See map on page 696, ref A6. Residential area, popular seaside resort with good surf beaches. On the eastern side of Barwon River estuary, overlooking Bass Strait. Boating, Bowls, Bush Walking, Fishing, Golf, Horse Riding, Sailing, Scenic Drives, Surfing, Swimming (Beach, Lake, River), Tennis, Water Skiing.

Hotels/Motels

 ★★★☆ **Boat Ramp Motel**, (M), 14 Guthridge St, 1km NW of PO, ☎ 03 5255 2018, fax 03 5256 2110, 9 units [shwr, bath (hip) (6), tlt, hairdry, a/c-cool (7), a/c (2), heat, elec blkts, tel, TV, clock radio, t/c mkg, refrig, toaster], ldry, pool, spa, bbq, boat park, plygr, tennis, cots, non smoking units (3). **RO** ◊ **$72 - $110**, ♦♦ **$77 - $115**, ◊ **$17**, AE BC DC EFT MC MCH VI.

★★★☆ **(Holiday Flat Section)**, 3 flats acc up to 6, (2 bedrm), [shwr, bath, tlt, a/c-cool (1), a/c (2), heat, elec blkts, tel, TV, clock radio, refrig, cook fac, micro, toaster, linen reqd-fee]. **D** **$120 - $160**, **W** ♦♦♦♦ **$500 - $1,000**, ◊ **$100**.

★★★☆ **Ocean Grove Gardens Motel**, (M), 17 Lake Ave, 2km W of PO, ☎ 03 5256 1199, fax 03 5256 1966, 12 units [shwr, spa bath (1), tlt, hairdry, c/fan, heat, elec blkts, tel, TV, video-fee, clock radio, t/c mkg, refrig, micro, toaster], ldry, pool, bbq, tennis, cots, non smoking units (5). **RO** ◊ **$68 - $88**, ♦♦ **$88 - $150**, ◊ **$15**, ch con, AE BC DC EFT MC VI.

 ★★★☆ **Ocean Grove Motor Inn**, (M), 64 Wallington Rd, 1km NW of PO, ☎ 03 5256 2555, fax 03 5256 2206, 17 units [shwr, bath (hip) (5), spa bath (2), tlt, hairdry (11), a/c, elec blkts, tel, TV, video-fee, clock radio, t/c mkg, refrig, cook fac ltd, micro, toaster], ldry, pool, spa, bbq, plygr, cots-fee, non smoking units (2). **RO** ◊ **$66 - $150**, ♦♦ **$66 - $150**, ◊ **$15**, ch con, AE BC DC EFT MC VI, ⚲.

★★☆ **(Holiday Unit Section)**, 4 units acc up to 4, (1 bedrm), [shwr, tlt, a/c, TV, clock radio, refrig, cook fac ltd, toaster, blkts, linen, pillows], c/park (carport). **D** ♦♦ **$66 - $88**, ◊ **$11**.

★★ **Ocean Grove Collendina Motel Hotel**, (LMH), Bonnyvale Rd, ☎ 03 5255 1122, fax 03 5256 2860, 10 units [shwr, tlt, fan, heat, elec blkts, TV, clock radio, t/c mkg, refrig, toaster], conf fac, pool, sauna, bbq, ✆, squash, tennis, cots-fee. D $100 - $132, AE BC EFT MC VI.

Self Catering Accommodation

★★★★☆ **Ti-Tree Village**, (Cotg), 34 Orton St, 500m W of PO, ☎ 03 5255 4433, fax 03 5255 4433, 16 cotgs acc up to 6, (1 & 2 bedrm), [shwr, spa bath (8), tlt, hairdry, c/fan, fire pl, elec blkts, TV, video, clock radio, refrig, cook fac, micro, toaster, blkts, linen, pillows], ldry, rec rm, res liquor license, bbq, ✆, plygr, cots. D ♦♦ $120 - $205, ♦ $10, W ♦♦ $850 - $1,380, ◊ $105 - $140, ch con, 8 cottages ★★★★, Min book Christmas Jan long w/ends and Easter, BC EFT MC VI.

★★★★ **The Terrace Lofts Bed & Breakfast**, (HU), 92 The Terrace, 100m E of PO, ☎ 03 5255 4167, fax 03 5256 1101, (2 stry), 4 units acc up to 6, (2 bedrm), [shwr, spa bath (1), tlt, hairdry, c/fan, heat (wood), elec blkts, TV, video, clock radio, CD, refrig, cook fac, micro, toaster, blkts, doonas, linen, pillows], ldry, bbq, breakfast ingredients, non smoking property. BB ♦♦ $125 - $200, BC MC VI.

★★☆ **Ocean Grove Collendina Motel Hotel**, Bonnyvale Rd, ☎ 03 5255 1122, fax 03 5256 2860, 7 cabins acc up to 6, (1 & 2 bedrm), [shwr, bath, tlt, fan, heat, TV, clock radio, refrig, cook fac, toaster, blkts, linen, pillows], conf fac, pool, sauna, bbq, c/park (carport), squash, tennis. D $90 - $120, AE BC EFT MC VI.

B&B's/Guest Houses

★★★★☆ **Ocean House B & B**, (B&B), 86 President Ave, 200m W of PO, ☎ 03 5255 2740, fax 03 5255 2740, 2 rms [heat, elec blkts, clock radio], lounge (TV, cd player), pool, spa, refrig. BB ♦ $100 - $120, ♦♦ $120 - $140, ◊ $35 - $50, Min book Christmas Jan and Easter.

OLINDA VIC

See Dandenong Ranges Region.

OMEO VIC 3898

Pop 300. (415km E Melbourne), See map on pages 694/695, ref J6. Centre of a rich grazing district producing fine Hereford cattle. Old gold mining area & several historic buildings in the town. Stepping off point for skiers to Mt Hotham. Bowls, Bush Walking, Canoeing, Fishing (River), Gold Prospecting, Golf, Horse Riding, Scenic Drives, Swimming (Pool, River), Tennis. See also Anglers Rest, Benambra, Glen Wills & Swifts Creek.

Hotels/Motels

★★★ **Colonial Motel Omeo**, (M), Day Ave, 50m W of PO, ☎ 03 5159 1388, 4 units [shwr, tlt, c/fan, heat, elec blkts, TV, clock radio, refrig, cook fac ltd, toaster, doonas], ldry, bbq. RO ♦ $55 - $80, ♦♦ $70 - $85, ◊ $10, ch con, BC MC VI.

★★★ **Omeo Motel**, (M), Park St, 700m E of PO, ☎ 03 5159 1297, fax 03 5159 1297, 11 units [shwr, spa bath (2), tlt, a/c (2), heat, elec blkts, tel, TV, clock radio, t/c mkg, refrig, toaster], ldry, ✕ (Mon to Sat), dinner to unit (Mon to Sat), plygr, cots. RO ♦ $40 - $65, ♦♦ $50 - $85, ◊ $10, BC EFT MC VI.

Self Catering Accommodation

★★★★ **Cobungra View Holiday Units**, (HU), Lot 12 Fox Crt, Cobungra 3898, 23km W of PO, ☎ 03 5159 1467, 3 units acc up to 10, (3 bedrm), [shwr, tlt, c/fan, heat, TV, clock radio, refrig, cook fac, micro, toaster, ldry (in unit), blkts, doonas, linen, pillows], iron, iron brd, dry rm, spa, bbq, c/park (carport), cots. D $125 - $350, W $490 - $1,155, BC MC VI.

★★★☆ **Livingstone Holiday Units**, (HU), Omeo Hwy, 1.8km NE of PO, ☎ 03 5159 1308, fax 03 5159 1308, 4 units acc up to 4, (2 bedrm), [shwr, tlt, cent heat, TV, video (avail), clock radio, refrig, cook fac, toaster, blkts, linen, pillows], ldry, bbq, non smoking units (1). D ♦♦ $65 - $75, ◊ $15, ch con, BC MC VI.

★★★ **(Cabin Section)**, 2 cabins acc up to 2, [shwr, tlt, heat, elec blkts, TV, refrig, micro, toaster, blkts, linen, pillows], non smoking units. D ♦♦ $55 - $60.

B&B's/Guest Houses

★★★★ **Omeo Snug as a Bug**, (GH), Great Alpine Rd, 350m W of PO, ☎ 03 5159 1311, fax 03 5159 1517, (2 stry gr fl), 4 rms [shwr, tlt, heat, video (avail), clock radio], ldry, rec rm, lounge (TV), lounge firepl, t/c mkg shared, bbq, cots. BLB ♦ $55, ♦♦ $66, ◊ $33, BC MC VI.

★★★★ **The Omeo Golden Age Motel**, (PH), Great Alpine Rd, 250m W of PO, ☎ 03 5159 1344, fax 03 5159 1305, (2 stry gr fl), 15 rms [shwr, bath (12), spa bath (2), tlt, hairdry, heat, elec blkts, tel, TV, clock radio, t/c mkg, refrig, doonas], ✕, ✆, cots-fee. BLB ♦ $60, ♦♦ $88 - $125, ◊ $12 - $16.50, ch con, AE BC DC EFT MC VI.

★★★☆ **The Manse**, (B&B), Great Alpine Rd & Day Ave, 200m E of PO, ☎ 03 5159 1441, fax 03 5159 1441, 4 rms [ensuite, cent heat, elec blkts], ldry, lounge (TV, video, cd player), t/c mkg shared. BB ♦ $60 - $70, ♦♦ $80 - $100, ◊ $20, BC MC VI, ⚥⅄.

ORBOST VIC 3888

Pop 2,150. (381km E Melbourne), See map on pages 694/695, ref K7. Business centre on the Snowy River. Maize, beans and other vegetables are grown on the rich river flats claimed to be the most fertile in Australia. Dairying, grazing and timber are important. Bowls, Bush Walking, Canoeing, Fishing, Golf, Scenic Drives, Squash, Swimming (Pool, River), Tennis.

Hotels/Motels

 ★★★☆ **Orbost Country Roads Motor Inn**, (M), 94 Salisbury St, 700m E of PO, ☎ 03 5154 2500, fax 03 5154 3036, 14 units [shwr, tlt, a/c-cool, heat, elec blkts, tel, TV, video-fee, clock radio, t/c mkg, refrig], ldry, pool, bbq, dinner to unit, cots-fee, non smoking units (5). RO ♦ $62 - $73, ♦♦ $68 - $79, ◊ $11, AE BC DC MC VI, ⚥⅄.

★★★ **Countryman Motor Inn**, (M), Cnr Salisbury & Livingstone Sts, 700m E of PO, ☎ 03 5154 1311, fax 03 5154 2950, 23 units [shwr, spa bath (7), tlt, hairdry (6), a/c, elec blkts, tel, TV, video, clock radio, t/c mkg, refrig, mini bar (7)], iron, iron brd, ✕. RO ♦ $49, ♦♦ $55, ◊ $10, 7 units ★★★☆. Min book all holiday times, AE BC DC EFT MC VI.

★★☆ **Orbost Motel Lodge**, (M), Irvines Rd, 1.6km E of Snowy River bridge, ☎ 03 5154 1122, fax 03 5154 1604, 22 units [shwr, tlt, heat, elec blkts, tel, TV, clock radio, t/c mkg, refrig, toaster], ldry, conf fac, cots, non smoking rms (13). RO ♦ $45, ♦♦ $55, ◊ $7, BC EFT MC VI.

 ★★☆ **Snowy River Lodge Motel**, (M), Princes Hwy, Newmerella 3886, 4.2km W of Snowy River bridge, ☎ 03 5154 1242, fax 03 5154 1177, 11 units [shwr, tlt, a/c, fan, heat, elec blkts, TV, clock radio, t/c mkg, refrig, cook fac ltd (5), toaster], bbq (undercover), dinner to unit, plygr, cots. RO ♦ $42 - $47, ♦♦ $50 - $55, ◊ $9, AE BC MC MCH VI.

★ **Commonwealth**, (LH), 159 Nicholson St, 200m N of PO, ☎ 03 5154 1077, fax 03 5154 2066, (2 stry), 23 rms [basin (17), ensuite (1), TV (1), doonas], lounge (cable TV), ✕ (Mon to Sat), t/c mkg shared, refrig, ✆. BLB ♦ $27.50, ♦♦ $38.50, ♦♦♦ $44, ch con, Light breakfast only available, BC MC VI.

ORBOST VIC continued...

Self Catering Accommodation

★★★ **Casa - Mia Park**, (Cotg), Warrens Rd, Newmerella 3886, 3.5km W of Snowy River bridge, ☎ 03 5154 1503, fax 03 5154 1503, 1 cotg acc up to 4, (1 bedrm), [shwr, tlt, hairdry, fan, heat (wood), elec blkts, TV, clock radio, t/c mkg, refrig, toaster, doonas, linen, pillows], ldry, bbq, cots, breakfast ingredients. **BLB** ♦♦ **$75**, ◊ **$10 - $20**, **W $420 - $450**.

★★☆ **Coringle Holiday Flats**, (HF), 73 Stanley St, 1km NE of PO, ☎ 03 5154 1153, 2 flats acc up to 8, (2 bedrm), [shwr, bath (1), tlt, fan, heat, elec blkts, TV, video, clock radio, t/c mkg, refrig, cook fac, micro, toaster, blkts, doonas, linen, pillows], ldry, w/mach, iron, iron brd, bbq. **D $60**, **W $300**.

★★☆ **(Park Unit Section)**, 1 ▣ acc up to 2, [shwr, tlt, heat, TV, CD, refrig, cook fac, toaster, blkts, doonas, linen, pillows]. **D $50**, **W $250**.

★★☆ **Snowy River WilderNest Retreat**, (Cotg), (Farm), Buchan Rd, 29km N of PO, on bank of Snowy River, ☎ 03 5154 1923, 2 cotgs acc up to 12, (3 & 4 bedrm), [shwr, tlt, refrig, cook fac, doonas, linen, pillows], ldry, w/mach, lounge firepl, bbq, c/park (carport). **D $99 - $132**, **W $693 - $924**, ch con, Meals by arrangement. Solar lighting & gas appliances - 1, gas lighting & appliances - 1.

B&B's/Guest Houses

★★★ **Killarney Bed & Breakfast**, (B&B), (Farm), No children's facilities, Duggans Rd, 1.5km N of golf course, ☎ 03 5154 1804, fax 03 5154 1804, 3 rms [ensuite, shwr (1), tlt (1), hairdry, c/fan, heat, clock radio, t/c mkg], lounge (TV, video, cd), lounge firepl. **BB** ♦♦ **$45 - $70**, Dinner by arrangement.

★★★ **Kuna Kuna Farm Holidays**, (B&B), (Farm), Cnr Buchan & Birkins Rds, 8.7km W of Snowy River bridge, ☎ 03 5154 1825, fax 03 5154 2685, 2 rms [hairdry, fan, heat, elec blkts, clock radio, doonas], lounge (TV, video, cd), lounge firepl. **BB** ♦♦ **$85**, ch con.

★★★☆ **Riverview Rural Retreat**, (B&B), 15 Irvines Rd, 2km E of Snowy River bridge, ☎ 03 5154 2411, fax 03 5154 1949, 2 rms [hairdry, fan, heat, elec blkts, TV (1), clock radio], ldry, lounge (TV, video, stereo), t/c mkg shared, bbq, non smoking property. **BB** ♦ **$50**, ♦♦ **$85**, ◊ **$40**, ch con, BC MC VI.

OUYEN VIC 3490

Pop 1,250. (452km NW Melbourne), See map on pages 694/695, ref B2. Pastoral area and an important wheat town. A highway & rail junction. Boating, Bowls, Bush Walking, Croquet, Golf, Horse Riding, Scenic Drives, Shooting, Swimming (Pool), Tennis, Trotting, Water Skiing.

Hotels/Motels

★★★ **Hilltop Motel**, (M), 20 Calder Hwy, 500m S of railway station, ☎ 03 5092 1410, fax 03 5092 1103, 10 units [ensuite, shwr, tlt, a/c, elec blkts, tel, TV, video-fee, clock radio, t/c mkg, refrig, toaster], bbq, dinner to unit, plygr, cots, non smoking units (5). **RO** ♦ **$55 - $66**, ♦♦ **$63 - $72**, ◊ **$9**, EFT.

★★★ **Mallee View**, (M), 14 Hughes St (Mallee Hwy), 200m E of PO, ☎ 03 5092 2195, fax 03 5092 2197, 7 units [shwr, spa bath (1), tlt, a/c-cool (2), a/c (5), c/fan, heat, elec blkts, tel, TV, video, clock radio, t/c mkg, refrig], bbq, cots. **BLB** ♦ **$55**, ♦♦ **$60**, ◊ **$8**, AE BC DC EFT MC VI.

★★★ **Ouyen Motel**, (M), Cnr Calder & Mallee Hwys, 200m E of PO, ☎ 03 5092 1397, fax 03 5092 1600, 18 units [shwr, tlt, a/c-cool, heat, elec blkts, tel, cable tv, clock radio, t/c mkg, refrig, mini bar, toaster], pool, plygr. **RO** ♦ **$52 - $63**, ♦♦ **$63 - $75**, AE BC DC MC MP VI.

★☆ **Victoria Hotel**, (LH), 22 Rowe St, 150m SE of PO, ☎ 03 5092 1550, (2 stry), 33 rms [basin (6), shwr (1), tlt (1), fan, elec blkts], rec rm, lounge (TV), conf fac, ⊠, t/c mkg shared, ✆, cots. **BB** ♦ **$25 - $27**, ♦♦ **$40 - $42**, ch con, BC VI.

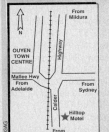

Hilltop Motel

Built 1994

20 Calder Highway
OUYEN VIC 3490

- *Family rooms*
- *Queen size beds available*
- *Tea, coffee and toaster facilities*
- *Evening meals delivered to rooms*
- *Non smoking rooms available*
- *Night bell*
- *Eftpos*
- *Playground*
- *Easy walk to shops & restaurants*

Quality accommodation at affordable prices

Ph: (03) 5092 1410   Fax: (03) 5092 1103

OVENS VIC 3738

Pop 1,500. (289km NE Melbourne), See map on pages 694/695, ref H5. Located on Ovens Hwy between Myrtleford & Bright. Important centre for tobacco growing, beef cattle & hops. Bush Walking, Fishing, Golf, Hangliding, Scenic Drives, Swimming, Tennis.

Hotels/Motels

★★ **Happy Valley Hotel**, (LH), Great Alpine Rd, 4km E of Myrtleford PO, ☎ 03 5751 1628, 6 rms [basin (1), elec blkts, doonas], lounge (TV), ⊠, ✆, cots. **BLB** ♦ **$35**, ♦♦ **$55**.

B&B's/Guest Houses

★★★★☆ **Rosewhite House**, (B&B), No children's facilities, Carrolls Rd, Rosewhite 3737, 6.8km NE of Great Alpine Rd, ☎ 03 5753 5300, fax 03 5753 5239, (2 stry), 3 rms [ensuite, hairdry, a/c, elec blkts, TV, clock radio, doonas], ldry, iron, iron brd, spa (heated), cook fac, t/c mkg shared, refrig, bbq, c/park (undercover), non smoking rms. **BB** ♦ **$121**, ♦♦ **$159.50**, Other meals by arrangement. BC MC VI.

★★★ **Happy Valley Bed & Breakfast**, (B&B), Happy Valley Rd, 4.2km NE of general store, ☎ 03 5752 1308, fax 03 5752 1308, 3 rms ldry, lounge (TV, cd player), lounge firepl, t/c mkg shared, refrig, bbq. **BB** ♦ **$55**, ♦♦ **$90**.

Other Accommodation

Valley Homestead, (Lodge), Great Alpine Road, 10km E of Myrtleford PO, ☎ 03 5752 2187, fax 03 5752 1408, 26 rms [shwr, bath (hip), tlt, heat, TV (2), refrig (2), cook fac ltd (2), micro (2), blkts, doonas, linen, pillows], dry rm, rec rm, lounge (TV), conf fac, lounge firepl, ⊠, pool-heated, spa, t/c mkg shared, bbq, ✆, tennis, cots. **D all meals** ♦ **$55.25 - $77**, ch con, Min book applies, AE BC DC MC VI.

PAKENHAM VIC 3810

Pop 9,500. (56km SE Melbourne), See map on page 696, ref C6. Growing south eastern residential suburb, located on the Princes Hwy.
★★ **Pakenham Park Motel**, (M), 14 Toomuc Valley Rd, 2.5km NW of PO, ☎ 03 5941 2785, fax 03 5940 2965, 6 units [shwr, tlt, c/fan (6), heat, elec blkts, TV, t/c mkg, refrig, toaster, doonas]. **BLB** ♦ **$45**, ♦♦ **$55 - $60**, ◊ **$12**, ch con, Light breakfast only available. BC MC VI.

PAYNESVILLE VIC 3880

Pop 2,650. (299km E Melbourne), See map on pages 694/695, ref J7. Lakeside resort between Lake King & Lake Victoria. Car ferry available to Raymond Island. Boat Ramp, Boating, Bowls, Fishing, Golf, Horse Riding, Sailing, Scenic Drives, Swimming (Lake), Tennis, Water Skiing, Wind Surfing.

Hotels/Motels

★★★☆ **Mariners Cove Resort**, (M), The Esplanade, on canals adjacent to McMillan Straits, ☎ 03 5156 7444, fax 03 5156 7069, 15 units [shwr, spa bath (2), tlt, a/c, elec blkts, tel, TV, movie, clock radio, t/c mkg, refrig, toaster], ldry, bbq, jetty, cots. **RO** ♦ **$75 - $120**, ♦♦ **$85 - $135**, ◊ **$10 - $11**, AE BC DC EFT MC VI.

★★★ **(Holiday Flat Section)**, (2 stry), 8 flats acc up to 6, (1 & 2 bedrm), [shwr, tlt, c/fan, heat, elec blkts, tel, video, clock radio, refrig, cook fac, micro, toaster, ldry (in unit), blkts, linen, pillows]. **RO** ♦♦ **$110 - $145**, ◊ **$15 - $20**.

Self Catering Accommodation

★★★★ **Captains Cove**, (Apt), 13 Mitchell St, ☎ 03 5156 7223, fax 03 5156 0952, (2 stry gr fl), 18 apts acc up to 6, [shwr, tlt, a/c, elec blkts, TV, video, clock radio, refrig, cook fac, micro, d/wash, toaster, ldry (in unit), blkts, doonas, linen, pillows], w/mach, dryer, iron, iron brd, pool indoor heated, bbq, c/park (carport), mooring, tennis. **D** ♦♦ **$80 - $200**, ◊ **$11**, **W** ♦♦ **$560 - $1,400**, ◊ **$77**, BC MC VI.

★★★★ **Merindah Holiday Cottages**, (Cotg), 90 Jones Rd, ☎ 03 5156 6519, fax 03 5156 0857, 2 cotgs acc up to 6, (Studio & 2 bedrm), [shwr, tlt, a/c, c/fan, TV, video, clock radio, refrig, cook fac, micro, blkts, doonas, linen, pillows], iron, iron brd, bbq, non smoking property, Pets welcome. **D $90 - $160**, **W $725 - $1,000**, ch con, Min book applies, BC MC VI, ⅏.

Operator Comment: Wheel in shower, secluded farm near town, www.merindah.com.au

★★★ **Maddisons Holiday Units**, (HU), 2 Fort King Pl, 2.1km N of PO, ☎ 03 5156 6766, 1 unit acc up to 6, (2 bedrm), [shwr, bath (hip), tlt, a/c, TV, clock radio, refrig, cook fac, elec frypan, toaster, ldry (in unit), linen reqd], lounge firepl, c/park (carport), jetty, non smoking property. **W $370 - $650**.

★★★ **Mariners Quay**, (HU), 9 King St, 800m NE of PO, water frontage, ☎ 03 5156 6766, (2 stry) 3 units acc up to 6, (2 & 3 bedrm), [shwr, bath, tlt, c/fan, heat, TV, video, clock radio, refrig, cook fac, micro, d/wash, toaster, ldry (in unit), blkts, linen reqd, pillows], w/mach, dryer, iron, iron brd, bbq, jetty. W $550 - $950, BC MC VI.

★★★ **Sunlake Gardens**, (HU), Toonalook Pde, 300m W of PO, ☎ 03 5156 6261, 12 units acc up to 6, (2 & 3 bedrm), [shwr, tlt, hairdry, heat, elec blkts, TV, clock radio, refrig, cook fac, linen reqd-fee], ldry, dryer-fee, rec rm, pool indoor heated, sauna-fee, spa-fee, bbq, c/park (carport) (4), plygr, mini golf, tennis. D $44 - $143, W $251 - $825, 3 units ★★☆. Min book Christmas Jan long w/ends and Easter, BC MC VI.

B&B's/Guest Houses

★★★☆ **The Crowes Nest Bed & Breakfast**, (B&B), 39 Langford Pde, ☎ 03 5156 6699, 3 rms [hairdry, c/fan (2), elec blkts, clock radio], lounge (TV), t/c mkg shared. BB ♦ $55, ♦♦ $95, BC MC VI.

Other Accommodation

Crystal Cruisers, (Cruiser), 54 Slip Rd, ☎ 03 5156 6971, 15 cruisers acc up to 10, [shwr, tlt, heat (4), TV (5), video (2), radio, refrig (14), cook fac, blkts reqd, linen reqd, pillows reqd]. W $880 - $3,300, Security deposit - $350 to $400. BC MC VI.

PETERBOROUGH VIC 3270

Pop 210. (262km W Melbourne), See map on pages 694/695, ref C7. Tiny fishing resort at the mouth of the Curdies River. Ocean road by-passes the town centre. Viewpoint overlooks the river mouth. Boating, Bush Walking, Fishing, Golf, Sailing, Scenic Drives, Surfing, Swimming (Beach, River), Tennis.

Hotels/Motels

★★★ **Peterborough Motel**, (M), 9 Irvine St, 150m S of bridge, ☎ 03 5598 5251, fax 03 5598 5251, 12 units [shwr, tlt, hairdry, a/c, elec blkts, TV, clock radio, t/c mkg, refrig, micro (2)], ldry, pool-heated (solar), spa-fee, bbq (covered), cots, non smoking units (4). RO ♦ $55 - $80, ♦♦ $65 - $100, ⊙ $12 - $16, ch con, AE BC EFT MC MCH VI.

★★ **Schomberg Inn**, (LMH), Great Ocean Rd, Adjacent to bridge, ☎ 03 5598 5285, fax 03 5598 5260, 8 units [shwr, tlt, heat, elec blkts, TV, clock radio (4), radio (4), t/c mkg, refrig], ⊠, bbq, ✆, cots-fee. RO ♦ $50 - $75, ♦♦ $55 - $75, ⊙ $10, BC EFT MC VI.

Self Catering Accommodation

★★★ **Stillwater Cottages**, (HU), RMB 4277 Timboon Rd, ☎ 03 5598 5349, fax 03 5598 5349, (2 stry gr fl), 2 units acc up to 6, (2 bedrm), [shwr, tlt, c/fan, heat, TV, clock radio, t/c mkg, refrig, cook fac, micro, elec frypan, toaster, ldry, blkts, doonas, linen, pillows], w/mach, bbq, cots. D ♦♦ $90 - $110, ⊙ $10, Breakfast available, Min book Christmas Jan long w/ends and Easter, BC EFT MC VI, ⚿.

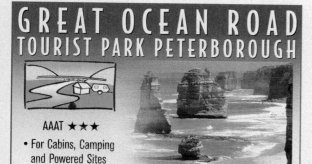
Medication and driving

Medication can effect your driving. Certain drugs can effect your mental alertness and/or co-ordination and therefore effect driving skills. Always check with your doctor the effect which any medication (over the counter or prescription) you are taking may have on your driving. There may be an alternative drug which will not affect your driving. It is best to avoid drinking alcohol while taking medication.

© RAASA

PHILLIP ISLAND - COWES VIC 3922

Part of PHILLIP ISLAND region. Pop 3,050. (137km S Melbourne), See map on page 696, ref C7. Popular tourist town & administrative centre of Phillip Island. Coastal walks. Penguins, Seals & Koalas. Boating, Bowls, Croquet, Fishing, Golf, Horse Riding, Scenic Drives, Surfing, Swimming (Beach), Tennis. See also Newhaven, Rhyll & San Remo.

Hotels/Motels

Best Western

★★★★☆ **Banfields**, (M), 192 Thompson Ave, 1.1km S of PO, ☎ 03 5952 2486, fax 03 5952 3056, 34 units [shwr, spa bath (4), tlt, hairdry, a/c-cool (13), a/c (21), heat (13), elec blkts, tel, TV, video, clock radio, t/c mkg, refrig, toaster], ldry, iron (20), iron brd (20), conf fac, ⊠, pool-heated, bbq, rm serv, plygr, cots-fee, non smoking units (24). RO ♦ $71 - $169, ♦♦ $87 - $169, ⊙ $12, 14 units ★★★☆. AE BC DC EFT JCB MC MP VI.

★★★★ **Arthur Phillip Motor Inn Phillip Island**, (M), Cnr Thompson Ave & Redwood Dve, 1.1km S of PO, ☎ 03 5952 3788, fax 03 5952 3748, 12 units [shwr, spa bath (4), tlt, hairdry, a/c, elec blkts, tel, TV, video-fee, clock radio, t/c mkg, refrig, micro (3), toaster], ldry, non smoking units. RO ♦ $72 - $149, ♦♦ $79 - $159, ⊙ $10, AE BC EFT MC VI.

★★★★ **Coachman Motel and Holiday Units**, (M), 51 Chapel St, 200m E of PO, ☎ 03 5952 1098, fax 03 5952 1283, 12 units [shwr, spa bath (10), tlt, a/c-cool (10), fan (6), heat, elec blkts, tel, TV, video (9)-fee, clock radio, t/c mkg, refrig, cook fac ltd (6), micro (10), toaster, doonas], ldry, pool-heated, spa, bbq, plygr, cots-fee. RO ♦ $58 - $121, ♦♦ $64 - $154, ⊙ $11 - $16.50, ch con, 7 units ★★★☆. BC DC MC VI.

Operator Comment: See advertisement on following page.

★★★☆ **(Holiday Unit Section)**, 8 units (2 bedrm), [shwr, spa bath (2), tlt, a/c (2), fan (2), heat, elec blkts, tel (2), TV, video (2)-fee, clock radio, refrig, cook fac, micro, d/wash (2), toaster, ldry (in unit) (2), doonas, linen, pillows], cots-fee. W $385 - $1,320, 2 units ★★★★.

AAA TOURISM Special Rates

★★★★ **The Continental Phillip Island**, (M), 5-8 Esplanade, ☎ 03 5952 2316, fax 03 5952 1878, (Multi-stry gr fl), 67 units [shwr, bath (53), spa bath (19), tlt, hairdry (53), a/c-cool (15), a/c (38), heat, tel, TV, clock radio, t/c mkg, refrig], ldry, iron (53), iron brd (53), rec rm, conf fac, ⊠, bar, pool, bbq, rm serv, ✆, squash, cots-fee. RO ♦ $84 - $110, ♦♦ $84 - $110, ⊙ $17, 14 units ★★★. AE BC DC JCB MC VI, ⚿.

Operator Comment: See advertisement on following page.

★★★★ **The Tropicana Motor Inn**, (M), 22 Osbourne Ave, 500m W of PO, ☎ 03 5952 1874, fax 03 5952 2272, 18 units (1 suite) [shwr, bath (1), spa bath (8), tlt, hairdry (18), a/c, elec blkts, tel, TV, video-fee, clock radio, t/c mkg, refrig, mini bar, toaster], ldry, rec rm, conf fac, ✕ (seasonal), pool-heated, bbq, plygr, cots-fee, non smoking units (7). **RO** ♦ $58 - $130, ♦♦ $58 - $138, ◊ $10 - $15, Suite D $100 - $190, 5 units ★★★☆, AE BC DC EFT MC VI, ♿.

★★★☆ **Kaloha Motel**, (M), Resort, Cnr Chapel & Steele Sts, 500m E of PO, ☎ 03 5952 2179, fax 03 5952 2723, (2 stry gr fl), 34 units [shwr, spa bath (14), tlt, hairdry (6), a/c, c/fan, heat, tel, TV, video, clock radio, t/c mkg, refrig, cook fac ltd (18), toaster (21)], ldry, ✕, pool-heated (solar), spa-fee, bbq (covered)-fee, plygr, cots-fee. **RO** ♦ $65 - $150, ♦♦ $65 - $150, ◊ $15 - $20, ch con, 10 units ★★★★. Min book Christmas Jan long w/ends and Easter, AE BC DC MC VI, ♿.

★★★ **(Apartment Section)**, (2 stry gr fl), 3 apts acc up to 7, (2 & 4 bedrm), [shwr, bath (1), spa bath (2), tlt, a/c-cool, fan, heat, TV, clock radio, refrig, cook fac, micro, blkts, linen, pillows], bbq, cots-fee. **D** ♦♦ $85 - $160, ◊ $15 - $20, **W** $500 - $1,000.

 ★★★☆ **Seahorse Motel At Phillip Island**, (M), Previously Seahorse Motel 29 Chapel St, 200m E of PO, ☎ 03 5952 2269, fax 03 5952 3775, (2 stry gr fl), 12 units [shwr, tlt, hairdry, a/c, c/fan (8), elec blkts, tel, TV, video-fee, clock radio, t/c mkg, refrig, toaster], ldry, iron, iron brd, bbq, plygr, cots-fee, non smoking units (6). **RO** ♦ $55 - $155, ♦♦ $64 - $165, ◊ $12 - $18, 4 units ★★★★, AE BC DC MC MCH VI, ♿.

★★★☆ **(Apartment Section)**, 12 apts acc up to 6, (1 & 2 bedrm), [shwr, tlt, a/c, c/fan (10), heat, elec blkts, tel, TV, clock radio, refrig, cook fac (5), cook fac ltd (7), micro, elec frypan, blkts, linen, pillows]. **D** $75 - $165, 2 apartments ★★★★, ♿.

★★☆ **Glen Isla Motel**, (M), 234 Church St, 1.8km W of PO, ☎ 03 5952 2822, fax 03 5952 2822, (2 stry gr fl), 6 units [shwr, tlt, fan, heat, elec blkts, TV, refrig, cook fac, micro, toaster], ldry, pool-heated (solar), bbq, non smoking property. **RO** ♦ $55 - $99, ♦♦ $60 - $110, ◊ $10, ch con, Light breakfast only available. Min book Christmas Jan and Easter, AE BC MC VI.

★★☆ **Holiday Island Motel**, (M), 349 Church St, 2km W of PO, ☎ 03 5952 2285, fax 03 5952 1103, (2 stry gr fl), 25 units [shwr, tlt, heat (8), cent heat (17), elec blkts, TV, radio, t/c mkg, refrig, cook fac (9)], ldry, ✕ (Seasonal), pool, bbq, ✎, plygr, tennis, cots-fee. **RO** ♦♦ $55 - $82.50, ◊ $11, ch con, 6 units ★★★. AE BC DC EFT MC VI.

Self Catering Accommodation

★★★★★ **Cottages for Two**, (Cotg), No children's facilities, 226 Settlement Rd, ☎ 03 5952 2426, fax 03 5952 6300, 6 cotgs acc up to 2, (Studio), [shwr, spa bath, tlt, a/c, c/fan, heat (gas log), elec blkts, cable tv, video, clock radio, CD, t/c mkg, refrig, cook fac, micro, d/wash, toaster, ldry (in unit), doonas, linen, pillows], w/mach, dryer, iron, iron brd, bbq, c/park (undercover), non smoking property. **D** ♦♦ $140 - $180, ◊ $25 - $35, **W** ♦♦ $800 - $1,080, BC EFT MC VI.

★★★★☆ **Abaleigh on Lovers Walk**, (Apt), 6 Roy Crt, 400m E of PO, ☎ 03 5952 5649, fax 03 5952 2057, (2 stry gr fl), 4 apts acc up to 8, (Studio, 1, 2 & 3 bedrm), [shwr, spa bath (3), tlt, hairdry, c/fan, elec blkts, TV, video (2), clock radio, CD, t/c mkg, refrig, cook fac, micro, d/wash (2), toaster, ldry, blkts, doonas, linen, pillows], w/mach, dryer, iron, iron brd, lounge firepl (gas log), bbq, c/park (carport), breakfast ingredients. **BB** ♦ $140 - $190, ♦♦ $155 - $225, ◊ $45, BC MC VI.

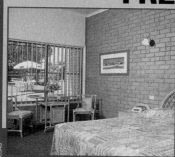

★★★★☆ **Elizabeth Cove Cottage**, (Cotg), 5 The Esplanade via Harris Rd, Ventnor 3922, ☎ 03 5956 8801, fax 03 5956 8801, 1 cotg acc up to 4, (2 bedrm), [shwr, spa bath, tlt, hairdry, c/fan, heat, TV, video, clock radio, CD, t/c mkg, refrig, cook fac, micro, toaster, ldry, blkts, doonas, linen, pillows], w/mach, iron, iron brd, lounge firepl, bbq, breakfast ingredients. D ♦♦ $130 - $150, ◊ $35, Minimum booking at special events, *Operator Comment: Romantic retreat, f/shore frontage, safe swimming beach.* http://home.waterfront.net.au/~ecove

★★★★☆ **Quest Phillip Island**, (Apt), Previously Bass Apartments Cnr Bass Ave & Chapel St, 200m E of PO, ☎ 03 5952 2644, fax 03 5952 2377, (Multi-stry gr fl), 32 apts acc up to 6, (2 & 3 bedrm), [shwr, bath (28), spa bath (4), tlt, hairdry, a/c, tel, cable tv, video-fee, clock radio, t/c mkg, refrig, cook fac, micro, d/wash, toaster, ldry (in unit), blkts, linen, pillows], w/mach, dryer, iron, iron brd, conf fac, pool-heated, spa (heated), bbq, cots, non smoking property. D $180 - $220, Minimum booking school holidays & all major events, AE BC DC EFT MC VI.

★★★★☆ **Rothsaye on Lovers Walk Bed & Breakfast**, (Cotg), 2 Roy Crt, 400m E of PO, ☎ 03 5952 2057, fax 03 5952 2057, 3 cotgs acc up to 2, (Studio), [shwr, tlt, hairdry, a/c, c/fan, heat, elec blkts, TV, clock radio, CD, t/c mkg, refrig, cook fac, micro, toaster, ldry (in unit), blkts, doonas, linen, pillows], w/mach, dryer, iron, iron brd, bbq, breakfast ingredients. BB ♦ $110 - $155, ♦♦ $130 - $170, ◊ $35 - $40, BC MC VI.

★★★★ **Alexanders on Church**, (Cotg), Cnr Church St & Alexander Ave, 500m W of PO, ☎ 03 5952 3345, 1 cotg acc up to 6, (3 bedrm), [shwr, bath, tlt, hairdry, fan, heat, elec blkts, TV, clock radio, CD, t/c mkg, refrig, cook fac, micro, toaster, ldry (in unit), blkts, linen], w/mach, iron, iron brd, lounge firepl, bbq, c/park (carport), breakfast ingredients, non smoking property. BB ♦♦ $165 - $198, ◊ $33 - $38, W ♦♦ $1,155 - $1,375, ◊ $190 - $220, BC MC VI.

★★★★ **Cowes Cottages**, (Cotg), Children by arrangement. 100 Church St, 250m W of PO, ☎ 03 5952 5199, fax 03 5952 3045, 1 cotg acc up to 4, (2 bedrm), [shwr, tlt, hairdry, a/c-cool, fan, heat, elec blkts, TV, video, CD, t/c mkg, refrig, cook fac, micro, ldry, blkts, doonas, linen, pillows], w/mach, iron, iron brd, bbq, c/park (carport), cots, breakfast ingredients. BB ♦♦ $125 - $165, ◊ $10 - $20, W ♦♦ $790 - $1,050, ◊ $70 - $140, Minium booking applies Public holidays, School holidays and Special events. Min book school holidays and Easter, AE BC DC MC VI.

★★★★ **Phillip Island Cottages**, (Cotg), 21 Osbourne Ave, ☎ 03 5952 3068, fax 03 5952 3068, 5 cotgs acc up to 8, (1, 2 & 3 bedrm), [shwr, tlt, heat, elec blkts, TV, clock radio, refrig, cook fac, micro, elec frypan, blkts, linen, pillows], w/mach-fee, iron, bbq, cots. D ♦♦ $70 - $95, ♦ $10 - $20, W $450 - $950, Light breakfast available. Min book applies, AE BC MC VI.

★★★★ **The Anchor and Waves Apartments**, (Apt), 1 The Esplanade, 2km NE of PO, ☎ 03 5952 1351, fax 03 5952 3144, (Multi-stry gr fl), 54 apts acc up to 4, [shwr, spa bath, tlt, hairdry, a/c, heat, tel, TV, video-fee, clock radio, t/c mkg, refrig, cook fac ltd, micro, toaster, blkts, doonas, linen, pillows], ldry, conf fac, ✉, bbq, plygr, cots-fee. D ♦ $159.50, ♦♦ $159.50, ♦ $11, Min book long w/ends, AE BC DC MC VI.

★★★★ **Ventnor Views**, (HU), No children's facilities, 9 Ventnor Blvd, 10km S of PO, ☎ 03 5956 8624, fax 03 5956 8770, (2 stry), 1 unit acc up to 2, (1 bedrm), [shwr, bath, tlt, a/c, fan, heat, elec blkts, TV, video, clock radio, t/c mkg, refrig, cook fac, micro, elec frypan, toaster, blkts, linen, pillows], non smoking property. D $90 - $145, W $550 - $770.

★★★☆ **Dixon Lodge**, (HU), 68 Walton St, ☎ 03 5952 2108, fax 03 5952 2246, 2 units acc up to 6, (2 bedrm), [shwr, bath, tlt, a/c (2), elec blkts, TV, clock radio, refrig, cook fac, micro, elec frypan, toaster, ldry (in unit), linen reqd-fee], w/mach, iron, iron brd, bbq, c/park (garage), cots. D ♦♦ $93 - $105, ♦ $11, BC MC VI. **Operator Comment: Our units have fully fenced private gardens and lock-up garages.**

★★★ **(Cottage Section)**, 1 cotg acc up to 8, (3 bedrm), [shwr, bath, tlt, a/c, heat, TV, clock radio, refrig, cook fac, micro, toaster, ldry (in unit), linen reqd-fee], w/mach, iron, iron brd, bbq, cots. D ♦♦ $93 - $105, ♦ $11.

★★★☆ **Mistiblue Bed & Breakfast**, (Apt), 5 Ventnor Blvd, Ventnor 3922, ☎ 03 5956 8759, fax 03 5956 8754, (2 stry gr fl), 3 apts acc up to 4, (Studio & 1 bedrm), [shwr, tlt, a/c (1), fan, heat, elec blkts, TV, video, CD, refrig, cook fac ltd (2), micro, toaster, ldry (in unit) (1), doonas, linen, pillows], ldry, w/mach, iron (1), iron brd, bbq, breakfast ingredients, non smoking property. BB ♦♦ $99, ♦ $25 - $50, 1 apartment of a three star rating. BC MC VI.

★★★☆ **(Bed & Breakfast Section)**, 1 rm [ensuite, hairdry, fan, heat, TV, CD, t/c mkg, refrig, micro, toaster]. BB ♦♦ $99.

★★★☆ **Park View Holiday Units**, (HU), 2 Park St, 700m E of PO, ☎ 03 5952 1496, fax 03 5952 6496, 9 units acc up to 7, (2 & 3 bedrm), [shwr, tlt, fan, heat, elec blkts, TV, video-fee, clock radio, refrig, cook fac, micro, elec frypan, toaster, ldry (in unit), doonas, linen reqd-fee], w/mach, iron, iron brd, rec rm, pool-heated (solar), bbq, plygr, cots. D $72 - $138, W $385 - $950.

★★★ **Hobsons Holiday Lodge**, (Cotg), 189 Thompson Ave, ☎ 03 5952 5088, fax 03 5952 5088, 1 cotg acc up to 8, (3 bedrm), [shwr, bath, tlt, fan, heat, TV, video, clock radio, refrig, cook fac, micro, toaster, ldry, blkts, doonas, linen, pillows], w/mach, iron, iron brd. D ♦♦ $80 - $110, ♦ $5 - $10, W $400 - $1,000.

★★★ **McHaffies Lodge**, (HF), 4 McHaffie Dve, 1.3km W of PO, ☎ 03 5952 1140, 4 flats acc up to 6, (3 bedrm), [shwr, bath, tlt, a/c-cool, heat, TV, clock radio, refrig, cook fac, toaster, ldry (in unit), linen reqd-fee], w/mach, c/park (garage). D ♦♦ $60, ♦ $5 - $10, W $300 - $550, ch con.

★★★ **Sheerwater Holiday Units**, (HU), 32 Beach St, 600m W of PO, ☎ 03 5952 2528, fax 03 5952 3107, 11 units acc up to 6, (1 & 2 bedrm), [shwr, tlt, fan (2), c/fan (9), heat, elec blkts, TV, clock radio, refrig, cook fac, micro, toaster, blkts, linen, pillows], w/mach, iron, pool-heated (solar), sauna-fee, bbq, cots-fee. D ♦♦ $72 - $120, ♦ $6 - $10, W ♦♦ $440 - $825, ♦ $36 - $55, BC MC VI.

★★★ **Smiths Beach Cottages**, (Cotg), 17 Barramundi Ave, Smiths Beach Via, ☎ 03 5952 5702, fax 03 5952 5702, 4 cotgs acc up to 6, (3 bedrm), [shwr, bath, tlt, a/c, TV, video, clock radio, t/c mkg, refrig, cook fac, micro, toaster, ldry (in unit), linen reqd-fee], w/mach, iron, iron brd, bbq, c/park (carport). D $160 - $200, W $750 - $1,100, BC MC VI.

The Green Garden Gate, (HU), 202 Thompson Ave, ☎ 03 5952 2628, 1 unit acc up to 8, (2 bedrm), [shwr, tlt, hairdry, a/c, fan, heat, elec blkts, TV, video, clock radio, refrig, cook fac, micro, toaster, blkts, doonas, linen, pillows], ldry, w/mach, bbq, c/park (undercover), non smoking property. D ♦♦ $75 - $125, ♦ $15 - $30, W ♦♦ $350, ♦ $105 - $175, BC MC VI, (not yet classified).

B&B's/Guest Houses

★★★★ **Chicory Dock**, (B&B), 25 Cadogan Ave, Ventnor 3922, 9.5km W of Cowes PO, ☎ 03 5956 8808, fax 03 5956 8808, 1 rm [ensuite, spa bath, hairdry, a/c, c/fan, heat (gas log), elec blkts, TV, video, clock radio, CD, t/c mkg, refrig, cook fac ltd, micro, toaster], bbq, c/park (carport). BB ♦ $85 - $100, ♦♦ $110 - $125, AE BC MC VI.

★★★★☆ **Cliff Top Country House**, (B&B), 1 Marlin St, Smiths Beach, ☎ 03 5952 1033, fax 03 5952 1423, (2 stry gr fl), 8 rms (1 suite) [ensuite, bath (1), spa bath (2), hairdry, fan, cent heat, elec blkts, TV (5), clock radio], lounge (TV, stereo), lounge firepl, bbq, gym, non smoking property. BB ♦♦ $187 - $264, 2 rooms ★★★★. Dinner by arrangement. AE BC DC EFT MC VI.

★★★★☆ **Genesta House Bed & Breakfast**, (B&B), 18 Steele St, 400m E of PO, ☎ 03 5952 3616, fax 03 5952 3616, 4 rms [ensuite, a/c, elec blkts, TV, clock radio], lounge (TV), spa (saltwater - heated), bbq, non smoking property. BB ♦ $85 - $100, ♦♦ $110 - $135, AE BC MC VI.

★★★★☆ **Holmwood Guesthouse**, (GH), Cnr Chapel & Steele Sts, ☎ 03 5952 3082, fax 03 5952 3083, 3 rms [shwr, bath (hip) (1), tlt, hairdry, a/c-cool, fan, heat, elec blkts, TV, clock radio, CD, t/c mkg, doonas], lounge (TV), lounge firepl, ⊠, refrig, breakfast ingredients, non smoking property. **BB 👤 $115, 👥 $150, 👤 $55**, ch con, pen con, 2 cottages yet to be rated, Other meals by arrangement. AE BC DC MC VI

Operator Comment: Visit our new self contained cottage at www.holmwoodguesthouse.com.au

★★★★☆ **Narrabeen Guest House**, (GH), No children's facilities, 16 Steele St, ☎ 03 5952 2062, fax 03 5952 3670, 5 rms [ensuite (3), shwr (1), tlt (1), hairdry, heat, elec blkts, TV], lounge, lounge firepl, ⊠, t/c mkg shared, refrig, non smoking property. **BB 👤 $110 - $145, 👥 $115 - $155, DBB 👤 $150 - $175, 👥 $210 - $250**, 2 rooms ★★★☆. AE BC DC JCB MC VI.

★★★★☆ **The Castle - Villa by the Sea**, (B&B), 7 Steele St, ☎ 03 5952 1228, fax 03 5952 3926, (2 stry), 5 rms [ensuite, spa bath, hairdry, c/fan, heat, elec blkts, TV, clock radio, t/c mkg, doonas], lounge (TV), lounge firepl, ⊠, bar (cocktail), refrig, bbq, 📞. **BB 👤 $100 - $250, 👥 $155 - $390, 👤 $55 - $99**, AE BC DC MC VI.

★★★★☆ **Ventnor House**, (B&B), 61 Grossard Point Rd, Ventnor 3922, 8km W of PO, ☎ 03 5956 8320, fax 03 5956 8663, 4 rms [ensuite, hairdry, a/c, heat, elec blkts, TV, clock radio], ldry, lounge (TV, video), pool-heated (solar), t/c mkg shared, bbq, tennis (half court), non smoking property. **BB 👤 $110, 👥 $140, 👤 $50**, Minimum booking Super Bikes & Grand Prix weekends, BC MC VI, ♿.

★★★★ **Aljara**, (B&B), 170 Thompson Ave, 1km N of PO, ☎ 03 5952 2155, fax 03 5952 5763, 3 rms [ensuite, hairdry, elec blkts, TV, clock radio, t/c mkg], lounge (TV, CD player), refrig, bbq, cots-fee, non smoking property. **BB 👤 $60 - $85, 👥 $85 - $100, 👤 $15**, ch con, BC MC VI.

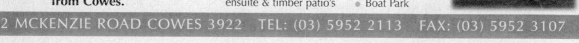

★★★★ **Dumfries Park B & B**, (B&B), 223 Church St, 1.2km W of PO, ☎ 03 5952 2820, fax 03 5952 2820, 3 rms [ensuite, hairdry, heat, TV, video, clock radio], bbq, secure park, non smoking property. **BB** ♦ **$90**, ♦♦ **$120**.

★★★★ **First Class Bed & Breakfast**, (B&B), Lot 1 Ventnor-Nobbies Rd, Ventnor 3922, 6km SW f PO, 6 rms [ensuite, heat, elec blkts, TV (3), clock radio], lounge (TV, video), non smoking property. **BB** ♦ **$88**, ♦♦ **$110 - $165**, ♦ **$44**, ch con, Other meals by arrangement. AE BC DC MC VI

Operator Comment: Superb panoramic ocean views, close to all attractions. www.penguins.org.au/first/

★★★★ **Manildra Bed & Breakfast**, (B&B), Cnr The Esplanade & Shalfleet Ave, Ventnor 3922, 9.2km SW of PO, ☎ 03 5956 8400, fax 03 5956 8400, 3 rms [shwr, bath (1), tlt, heat, elec blkts, TV, radio, t/c mkg, cook fac (1)], bbq, non smoking rms. **BB** ♦ **$65 - $70**, ♦♦ **$110 - $120**, ♦ **$25**, ch con, 1 room ★★★☆. BC MC VI.

★★★★ **Otira on Needle's Eye**, (B&B), RMB 1165 Ventnor Beach Rd, 7.5km W of PO, ☎ 03 5956 8294, fax 03 5956 8741, (2 stry gr fl), 3 rms [shwr, bath (1), tlt, fan, heat, clock radio], lounge (TV, stereo), t/c mkg shared, tennis. **BB** ♦ **$80**, ♦♦ **$120 - $140**, Dinner by arrangement. BC MC VI.

★★★★ **Penguin Hill Country House**, (B&B), No facilities for children under 5. Cnr Backbeach & Ventnor Rds, 12km SW of PO, ☎ 03 5956 8777, 3 rms [ensuite (2), shwr (1), tlt (1), hairdry, fan, heat, elec blkts, clock radio], lounge (TV, video, stereo), t/c mkg shared, non smoking property. **BB** ♦♦ **$120**, Other meals by arrangement. AE BC MC VI.

★★★★ **The Rookery**, (B&B), 4 Cadogan Ave Ventnor Via, 10km S of PO, ☎ 03 5956 8637, (2 stry gr fl), 1 rm [ensuite, hairdry, heat, elec blkts, TV, clock radio, t/c mkg], ldry, iron, bbq, non smoking property. **BB** ♦♦ **$95 - $120**.

★★★☆ **Cowes Bed & Breakfast**, (B&B), 1 Charmandene Crt, 700m E of PO, ☎ 03 5952 5146, fax 03 5952 5846, (2 stry gr fl), 2 rms [ensuite, hairdry, a/c, c/fan, heat], lounge (TV, video, CD), lounge firepl, spa, t/c mkg shared, bbq. **BB** ♦ **$90 - $150**, ♦♦ **$90 - $150**, ♦ **$20**, Minimum booking special events, BC MC VI.

Operator Comment: Private access to beach, stroll to shops & restaurants. www.nex.net.au/users/cowesbb

★★★ **Rhylston Park Historic Homestead**, (B&B), 190 Thompson Ave, 1km S of PO, ☎ 03 5952 2730, fax 03 5952 2705, 4 rms [shwr (2), bath (2), tlt (2), heat, elec blkts], lounge (TV), t/c mkg shared, refrig, non smoking property. **BB** ♦♦ **$111 - $122**, ♦ **$28 - $33**, ch con, Min book long w/ends.

Other Accommodation
Amaroo Caravan Park, (Lodge), Cnr Church St & Osborne Rd, 400m SW of PO, ☎ 03 5952 2548, fax 03 5952 3620, 4 rms [shwr (4G-4L), tlt (4G-4L), blkts, doonas, linen, pillows], ldry, rec rm, pool above ground, cook fac, refrig, bbq, kiosk, ☎, bicycle-fee. **D** ♦ **$16 - $19**, ♦ **$16 - $19**, BC DC MC VI.

Koala Park Resort Motel, (Lodge), Phillip Island Tourist Rd, 4.8km SE of PO, ☎ 03 5952 2176, fax 03 5952 2298, 18 rms acc up to 8, [shwr, tlt, heat, elec blkts, TV, clock radio (14), t/c mkg, refrig, toaster], pool, bbq, plygr, tennis, cots. **RO** ♦ **$60 - $70**, ♦♦ **$60 - $105**, ♦ **$11**, Meals by arrangement, BC MC VI.

PHILLIP ISLAND - NEWHAVEN VIC 3925

Pop 1,100. (122km S Melbourne), See map on page 696, ref C7. Small tourist village. Located on the island side of the 640 metre bridge linking Phillip Island to the mainland. Boating, Bowls, Fishing, Sailing, Scenic Drives, Surfing, Swimming (Berach), Tennis, Water Skiing.

Hotels/Motels
 ★★★ **Bridge Motel Newhaven**, (M), 31 Forrest Ave, 700m N of bridge, ☎ 03 5956 7218, fax 03 5956 7218, 9 units [shwr, spa bath (1), tlt, a/c-cool, heat, elec blkts, TV, clock radio, t/c mkg, refrig], bbq, dinner to unit. **RO** ♦ **$50 - $127**, ♦♦ **$58 - $127**, ♦ **$11 - $15**, AE BC EFT MC MCH VI.

★★ **Sea Breeze Motel**, (M), 40 Forrest Ave, 700m W of bridge, ☎ 03 5956 7387, 6 units [shwr, tlt, fan, heat, elec blkts, TV, t/c mkg, refrig, cook fac (2), toaster], bbq. **RO** ♦ **$50 - $77**, ♦♦ **$55 - $77**, ♦ **$15**, ch con, Light breakfast only available. BC MC VI.

Self Catering Accommodation
★★☆ **Sea Breeze Motel**, (HF), 40 Forrest Ave, 700m W of bridge, ☎ 03 5956 7387, 2 flats acc up to 5, (2 bedrm), [shwr, tlt, fan, heat, elec blkts, TV, refrig, cook fac ltd, toaster, blkts, linen, pillows], bbq. **D $70 - $100**, **W $450 - $700**, Min book Christmas Jan long w/ends and Easter, BC MC VI.

B&B's/Guest Houses
★★★★☆ **Banksia Park Estate**, (B&B), Phillip Island Rd, ☎ 03 5956 7796, fax 03 5956 6683, (2 stry gr fl), 4 rms [shwr, spa bath (1), tlt, hairdry, a/c (1), fan, cent heat, elec blkts, clock radio, refrig (1), cook fac ltd (1), micro (1)], ldry, lounge (TV, video, cd), lounge firepl, pool-heated (solar), t/c mkg shared, tennis. **BB** ♦ **$60 - $90**, ♦♦ **$100 - $180**, ♦ **$30 - $50**, Min book Christmas Jan long w/ends and Easter, BC MC VI.

★★★★☆ **Watani Waters by the Bay Phillip Island**, (B&B), No children's facilities, 9 Cleeland St, ☎ 03 5956 6300, fax 03 5956 6301, (2 stry gr fl), 4 rms [shwr, tlt, hairdry, a/c (1), c/fan, heat, elec blkts, TV, video, clock radio, t/c mkg, refrig, cook fac ltd], lounge (TV, video, cd), bbq, non smoking property. **BB** ♦♦ **$154 - $176**, ♦ **$55**, AE BC DC EFT JCB MC VI.

★★★★ **Beachfront Lodge Bed & Breakfast**, (B&B), Closed May 10 to Sep 15, 47 Forrest Ave, ☎ 03 5956 7360, fax 03 5956 7361, 2 rms [ensuite, hairdry, c/fan, heat, elec blkts, TV, clock radio, ldry], iron, iron brd, lounge (video), cook fac, t/c mkg shared, refrig, bbq, non smoking property. **BLB** ♦ **$65 - $95**, ♦♦ **$95 - $130**, ♦ **$40 - $95**, Minimum booking Christmas/Jan, Easter, Grand Prix and Super Bike Races.

★★★★ **The Rocks Waterfront Retreat**, (GH), 5 Phillip Island Tourist Rd, ☎ 03 5956 7371, fax 03 5956 6540, 4 rms [shwr, spa bath, tlt, a/c, tel, TV, video, clock radio, t/c mkg, refrig, toaster], conf fac, ✉, pool (saltwater), bbq. **BLB** ♦ **$90 - $150**, ♦♦ **$150 - $250**, Minimum booking all major events and school holidays, AE BC DC EFT JCB MC VI.

Other Accommodation
Anglicare Discovery Centre, (Lodge), 60 Forrest Ave, ☎ 03 5956 7202, fax 03 5956 7184, (2 stry gr fl), 23 rms [shwr (10), tlt (10), heat, linen reqd], ldry, rec rm, lounge (TV), conf fac, cook fac, t/c mkg shared, refrig, bbq, ☎, plygr. **D** ♦ **$16.50 - $36**, ♦ **$16.50 - $36**, ch con.

PHILLIP ISLAND - RHYLL VIC 3923

Pop 400. (140km S Melbourne), See map on page 696, ref C7. Site of the first settlement in 1801. Tall local stone monument near the jetty records on a tablet of Woolamai granite the early history & discovery of Phillip Island. Boating, Bowls, Bush Walking, Fishing, Golf, Horse Riding, Sailing, Scenic Drives, Swimming (Beach), Tennis, Water Skiing.

Self Catering Accommodation
★★★★ **Moonthalie**, (HU), 45 Lock Rd, ☎ 03 5956 9443, fax 03 5956 9468, 3 units acc up to 2, (Studio & 1 bedrm), [hairdry, a/c (2), fan (1), elec blkts, TV, clock radio, t/c mkg, refrig, micro, elec frypan, toaster, doonas], ldry, w/mach, dryer, bbq, breakfast ingredients, non smoking property. **BLB** ♦♦ **$145**, ♦ **$60**, Min book long w/ends.

★★★★ **The Gatehouse Cottage**, (Cotg), 34 Walton St, ☎ 03 5956 9406, fax 03 5956 9426, 2 cotgs acc up to 2, (1 bedrm), [shwr, bath (hip), spa bath (1), tlt, hairdry, fan, c/fan, heat, elec blkts, TV, video (1), radio, CD, refrig, cook fac, ldry, blkts, linen, pillows], iron, iron brd, bbq, c/park (carport), breakfast ingredients, non smoking property. **BB** ♦♦ **$160 - $195**, 1 cottage ★★★★☆. Min book applies, BC MC VI.

VICTORIA

P

★★★☆ **Coleshill Lodge**, (HF), 51 Rhyll - Newhaven Rd, ☎ 03 5956 9304, fax 03 5956 9304, 6 flats acc up to 4, (2 bedrm), [shwr, tlt, heat, elec blkts, TV, video-fee, clock radio, t/c mkg, refrig, cook fac, micro, toaster, linen], ldry, bbq, cots. **D** ♦ **$66 - $99**, ♦♦ **$66 - $110**, ♦ **$11 - $16.50**, AE BC MC VI.

PHILLIP ISLAND - SAN REMO VIC 3925

Pop 650. (121km S Melbourne), See map on page 696, ref C7. Mainland fishing village & centre of a dairying district. Base for Bass Strait commercial fishing fleet. Boating, Bowls, Bush Walking, Fishing, Sailing, Squash, Surfing, Swimming (Beach), Tennis.

Hotels/Motels

★★★☆ **Quays Motel**, (M), Phillip Island Rd, 600m N of PO, ☎ 03 5678 5555, fax 03 5678 5889, 12 units [shwr, spa bath (2), tlt, hairdry, a/c, elec blkts, tel, TV, clock radio, t/c mkg, refrig, toaster], ldry, iron, iron brd, cots-fee, non smoking units (8). **RO** ♦♦ **$73 - $143**, ♦ **$11**, AE BC DC MC MP VI.

★★★☆ **San Remo Motor Inn**, (M), 43 Back Beach Rd, 200m E of PO, ☎ 03 5678 5380, fax 03 5678 5416, 13 units (1 suite) [shwr, spa bath (3), tlt, hairdry, a/c, c/fan, elec blkts, tel, TV, video-fee, clock radio, t/c mkg, refrig, micro (1), elec frypan (1)], ldry, iron, iron brd, pool-heated (solar), bbq, plygr, cots-fee. **RO** ♦ **$49 - $132**, ♦♦ **$60 - $138**, ♦ **$11 - $17**, **Suite RO** ♦♦♦♦ **$105 - $149**, ♦ **$11 - $17**, ch con, AE BC DC MC MCH VI.

Operator Comment: Inquire about our special off peak rates including a cooked breakfast.

★★★ **San Remo Hotel**, (LMH), 145 Marine Pde, ☎ 03 5678 5352, fax 03 5678 5381, 6 units [shwr, tlt, a/c-cool, heat, elec blkts, TV, clock radio, t/c mkg, refrig, toaster], ldry, conf fac, ✕, **℄. RO** ♦ **$55 - $125**, ♦♦ **$65 - $135**, ♦ **$10**, pen con, Min book long w/ends, AE BC DC EFT MC VI.

B&B's/Guest Houses

★★★★ **Quarter Deck B & B**, (B&B), 20 Genista St, 800m E of PO, ☎ 03 5678 5485, fax 03 5678 5545, (2 stry gr fl), 3 rms [shwr, bath, spa bath (2), tlt, hairdry, fan, cent heat, elec blkts, TV, video (2), clock radio, t/c mkg, refrig, cook fac ltd, micro (2), toaster, ldry], w/mach (1), dryer, iron, iron brd, bbq. **BB** ♦ **$80**, ♦♦ **$125**, ♦ **$60**, ch con, 1 room ★★★★☆, BC MC VI.

End of Phillip Island Region

PIANGIL VIC 3597

Pop 530. (379km NW Melbourne), See map on pages 694/695, ref D2. Citrus fruit, vineyard & market garden district. Fishing, Golf, Swimming (River).

★★★☆ **Renewan Vineyard**, (B&B), Murray Valley Hwy, 1km S of Mallee Hwy Junction, ☎ 03 5030 5525, fax 03 5030 5695, 2 rms [evap cool, c/fan, heat, doonas], lounge (TV, video, cd), lounge firepl, pool-heated (solar), spa (heated), non smoking property. **BB** ♦♦ **$99**, ♦ **$66**, Dinner by arrangement. BC MC VI.

PIGEON PONDS VIC 3407

Pop Nominal, (359km W Melbourne), See map on pages 694/695, ref A5. Grazing district.

★★★ **Yetholm Host Farm**, (Cotg), (Farm), McFarlanes La, 16km W of Balmoral - Harrow Rd, ☎ 03 5570 4237, fax 03 5570 4202, 1 cotg acc up to 10, (6 bedrm), [shwr, bath, tlt, a/c, c/fan, elec blkts, TV, clock radio, t/c mkg, refrig, cook fac, micro, elec frypan, toaster, ldry (in unit), doonas, linen, pillows], w/mach, iron, iron brd, lounge firepl, bbq, c/park (carport), tennis, cots. **D $90 - $100**, **W $425 - $500**.

POINT LONSDALE VIC 3225

Pop 1,742. (101km SW Melbourne), See map on page 696, ref B6. Picturesque township on the far tip of the Bellarine Peninsula, overlooking Bass Strait & the rip at Port Phillip Heads. Bowls, Fishing, Horse Riding, Sailing, Scenic Drives, Surfing, Swimming (Beach), Tennis. See also Queenscliff.

Hotels/Motels

★★★ **Point Lonsdale Motel**, (M), 4 Kirk Rd, 100m N of PO, ☎ 03 5258 2970, fax 03 5258 2050, (2 stry gr fl), 10 units [shwr, tlt, fan, heat, elec blkts, TV, video-fee, clock radio, t/c mkg, refrig, cook fac (1), micro (avail), toaster], ldry, lounge (TV), bbq. **RO** ♦ **$72 - $118**, ♦♦ **$78 - $145**, ♦ **$15 - $25**, ch con, Light breakfast only available. AE BC DC MC VI.

Queenscliff

Beacon Resort QUEENSCLIFF

GOLDEN CHAIN

AAAT ★★★★ MOTEL

WINNER

SEE FULL LISTING UNDER "QUEENSCLIFF"

RESERVATIONS ☎ 1800 351 152

★★☆ **Lighthouse Resort Motel**, (M), 31 Point Lonsdale Rd, 200m SE of PO, ☎ 03 5258 1142, fax 03 5258 4223, (2 stry gr fl), 20 units [shwr, tlt, heat, elec blkts, TV, clock radio, t/c mkg, refrig], ldry-fee, rec rm, lounge, conf fac, ✕ (seasonal), pool, spa, bbq, **℄**, tennis, cots, non smoking property. **RO** ♦ **$70 - $130**, ♦♦ **$78 - $135**, ch con, Min book Christmas Jan long w/ends and Easter, AE BC DC EFT MC VI.

Self Catering Accommodation

★★★★ **Bailey Bed & Breakfast**, (Cotg), 22 Bailey St, ☎ 03 5250 2523, 1 cotg acc up to 5, (2 bedrm), [shwr, bath, tlt, hairdry, fan, heat, elec blkts, TV, video, clock radio, CD, t/c mkg, refrig, cook fac, micro, toaster, ldry, blkts, doonas, linen, pillows], dryer, iron, iron brd, bbq, c/park (carport), cots, breakfast ingredients, non smoking property. **BLB** ♦♦ **$130**, ♦ **$15**, **W $450 - $1,200**.

★★★☆ **(Studio Section)**, 1 cotg acc up to 2, (Studio), [ensuite, hairdry, heat, TV, refrig, cook fac ltd, micro, doonas, linen, pillows], w/mach, iron, iron brd, bbq, breakfast ingredients, non smoking property. **BLB** ♦♦ **$100**.

★★★★ **Lonsdale Villas**, (Villa), 87 Bellarine Hwy, 1km NW of PO, ☎ 03 5258 4533, fax 03 5258 4597, (2 stry gr fl), 18 villas acc up to 6, (Studio, 2 & 3 bedrm), [shwr, spa bath, tlt, a/c (5), c/fan, heat (wood), TV, video (5), movie, clock radio, CD (5), refrig, cook fac, micro, d/wash (5), toaster, ldry (in unit), doonas, linen, pillows], w/mach, dryer, iron, iron brd, bbq, c/park (carport) (13), **℄**, cots. **D** ♦♦ **$95 - $264**, ♦♦♦♦ **$180 - $280**, ♦ **$22 - $44**, **W $495 - $2,500**, 5 villas ★★★☆. 5 villas ★★★★☆. Breakfast available. Min book Christmas Jan long w/ends and Easter, AE BC EFT MC VI.

B&B's/Guest Houses

★★★☆ **Terminus Bed & Breakfast**, (B&B), No children's facilities, 31 Point Lonsdale Rd, 200m S of PO, ☎ 03 5258 1142, fax 03 5258 4223, (2 stry gr fl), 8 rms [shwr, spa bath (1), tlt, heat, elec blkts, TV, video (2), clock radio, t/c mkg, refrig, micro (2)], ldry-fee, rec rm, lounge, conf fac, ✕ (seasonal), BYO, pool, spa, **℄**, tennis, non smoking property. **BB** ♦♦ **$130 - $200**, Min book Christmas Jan long w/ends and Easter, AE BC DC EFT MC VI.

POMONAL VIC

See Grampians Region.

POREPUNKAH VIC 3740

Pop 450. (304km NE Melbourne), See map on pages 694/695, ref H5. Agricultural township on the Ovens River, near the junction of the Buckland River. Turn off to Mt Buffalo National Park. Art Gallery, Bush Walking, Fishing (Trout), Gold Prospecting, Golf, Hangliding, Horse Riding, Rock Climbing, Scenic Drives, Snow Skiing, Swimming (River).

Hotels/Motels

★★★ **Buffalo Motel**, (M), Great Alpine Rd, 2km W of roundabout, ☎ 03 5756 2242, fax 03 5756 2242, 20 units [shwr, tlt, a/c-cool, heat, elec blkts, TV, clock radio, t/c mkg, refrig], bbq, cots-fee. **RO** ♦ **$56 - $68**, ♦♦ **$63 - $80**, ♦ **$13**, BC EFT MC MCH VI.

Self Catering Accommodation

★★★ **Alpine Park Holiday Flats**, (HF), Great Alpine Rd, 2.8km W of PO, ☎ 03 5756 2334, 10 flats acc up to 5, (1 bedrm), [shwr, bath (hip) (8), tlt, heat, elec blkts, TV, movie, clock radio, refrig, cook fac (8), cook fac ltd (2), micro, ldry (in unit) (4), blkts, linen, pillows], ldry, dry rm, bbq, plygr, cots, non smoking property. **D** ♦♦ **$55 - $77**, ♦ **$11**, **W** ♦♦ **$308 - $630**, ch con, BC MC VI.

★★★ **Pine Ridge Holiday Village Porepunkah**, (HF), Great Alpine Rd, 500m E of bridge, ☎ 03 5756 2282, fax 03 5756 2282, 8 flats acc up to 5, (2 bedrm), [shwr, tlt, evap cool, heat, elec blkts, TV, clock radio, refrig, cook fac, micro, ldry (in unit), blkts, linen, pillows], bbq, c/park (carport), cots. **D** $60 - $115, **W** $378 - $605, pen con, Min book all holiday times, BC MC VI.

★★★ **Restaway Holiday Units**, (HU), Great Alpine Rd, 1km W of bridge, ☎ 03 5756 2322, fax 03 5756 2790, 9 units acc up to 6, (Studio & 2 bedrm), [shwr, tlt, a/c (1), fan, heat, elec blkts, TV, clock radio, refrig, cook fac, micro, toaster, linen, pillows], ldry, rec rm, pool, bbq (undercover), plygr, cots, non smoking units. **D ♯♯** $66 - $88, ♀ $11, **W ♯♯** $462 - $610, ♀ $61.50 - $80, BC MC VI.

★★☆ **Falls View Lodge**, (HF), Cnr Mt Buffalo Rd & Sykes La, 6km SW of PO, ☎ 03 5756 2485, fax 03 5756 2485, 5 flats acc up to 7, (2 bedrm), [shwr, tlt, c/fan, heat, elec blkts, TV, video, refrig, cook fac ltd, micro, toaster, doonas, linen reqd-fee], ldry, dry rm, pool (salt water), cots.
D ♯♯ $50, ♀ $25, **W ♯♯♯♯** $400 - $500, ♀ $80, ch con, Minimum booking Easter & snow season.

B&B's/Guest Houses

★★★★ **Buckland Valley Bed & Breakfast**, (B&B), No children's facilities, Buckland Valley Rd, 10.8km S of PO, ☎ 03 5756 2656, fax 03 5756 2656, (2 stry), 3 rms [ensuite, elec blkts, doonas], lounge, lounge firepl, t/c mkg shared, refrig, non smoking property. **BLB ♯** $77, **♯♯** $110, AE BC MC VI.

★★★★ **Sugar Maples Dinner & Doona**, (B&B), Harris Lane, 4km W of PO, ☎ 03 5756 2919, fax 03 5756 2919, (2 stry), 3 rms [ensuite (2), shwr (1), bath (2), tlt (1), c/fan (2), heat, clock radio (2), doonas], lounge (TV, video), lounge firepl (2), ✉, spa, t/c mkg shared, refrig, non smoking property. **BLB ♯** $70 - $120, **♯♯** $100 - $135, Minimum booking Christmas/Jan, Easter & autumn festival, BC MC VI.

PORT ALBERT VIC 3971

Pop 250. (229km SE Melbourne), See map on pages 694/695, ref G8. An historical maritime town - the port is the oldest in Gippsland. Maritime Museum. Boat Ramp, Bush Walking, Fishing, Sailing, Scenic Drives.

★★★★ **Port Albert Holiday Homes**, (Cotg), Tarraville Rd, 1km N of PO, ☎ 03 5183 2677, fax 03 5183 2677, 6 cotgs acc up to 7, (1, 2 & 3 bedrm), [shwr, tlt, a/c, heat, elec blkts, TV, video (3), clock radio, refrig, cook fac, micro, toaster, blkts, linen, pillows], ldry, bbq, boat park, non smoking property. **D** $88 - $178, **W** $440 - $780, Min book all holiday times, BC EFT MC VI.

PORT CAMPBELL VIC 3269

Pop 300. (249km W Melbourne), See map on pages 694/695, ref C7. Popular holiday resort with spectacular coastal scenery. Port Campbell National Park. Boating, Bush Walking, Fishing, Sailing, Scenic Drives, Surfing, Swimming (Beach), Tennis.

Hotels/Motels

★★★★ **Great Ocean Road Motor Inn**, (M), 10 Great Ocean Rd, 500m N of PO, ☎ 03 5598 6522, fax 03 5598 6523, 14 units [shwr, spa bath (5), tlt, hairdry, evap cool, fan, heat, elec blkts, tel, TV, video, clock radio, t/c mkg, refrig, micro, toaster], ldry, iron, bar, bbq, cots, non smoking units (10).
RO ♯ $105 - $175, **♯♯** $120 - $175, ♀ $15, Min book Christmas Jan long w/ends and Easter, AE BC DC JCB MC VI, ♿.

★★★☆ **Port Campbell Motor Inn**, (M), 12 Great Ocean Rd, 400m NE of PO, ☎ 03 5598 6222, fax 03 5598 6418, 16 units [shwr, spa bath (3), tlt, hairdry, a/c (3), c/fan, heat, elec blkts, tel, TV, video-fee, clock radio, t/c mkg, refrig, cook fac (1)], ldry reqd, pool, bbq (covered), cots, non smoking units (5). **RO ♯** $75 - $145, **♯♯** $85 - $145, ♀ $15, AE BC DC EFT MC MP VI.

Operator Comment: See advertisement on opposite page.

★★★ **Loch Ard Motor Inn**, (M), Lord St (Great Ocean Rd), opposite PO, ☎ 03 5598 6328, fax 03 5598 6433, 9 units [shwr, tlt, hairdry, c/fan, heat, elec blkts, TV, clock radio, t/c mkg, refrig, toaster], bbq, cots-fee. **RO ♯** $78 - $120, **♯♯** $88 - $120, ♀ $12, Light breakfast only available. AE BC DC EFT MC VI.

★★★ **(Apartment Section)**, 7 apts acc up to 7, (Studio), [shwr, bath (1), spa bath (1), tlt, hairdry, c/fan, heat, TV, video (2), clock radio, refrig, cook fac ltd, micro, toaster, blkts, linen, pillows].
D $98 - $148, ♀ $12, Light breakfast available.

★★★ **Southern Ocean Motor Inn**, (M), Lord St (Great Ocean Rd), 100m S of PO, ☎ 03 5598 6231, fax 03 5598 6471, 28 units [shwr, spa bath (3), tlt, hairdry, fan, heat, elec blkts, tel, TV, movie, clock radio, t/c mkg, refrig], ldry, ✉, rm serv, cots-fee. **RO ♯** $95 - $160, ♀ $12, 8 units ★★★☆. AE BC DC EFT JCB MC MP VI.

★★☆ **Port O'Call Accommodation House**, (M), Great Ocean Rd, ☎ 03 5598 6206, or 03 5598 6366, fax 03 5598 6032, 6 units [shwr, tlt, fan, heat, elec blkts, TV, clock radio, t/c mkg, refrig, cook fac ltd (2), micro (2), toaster, doonas], ldry (limited fac. 5-6pm), bbq. **RO ♯** $45 - $80, **♯♯** $60 - $80, ♀ $10, Light breakfast only available. BC EFT MC VI.

Self Catering Accommodation

★★★★ **Daysy Hill Country Cottages**, (Cotg), RMB 7353 Timboon-Port Campbell Rd, 1.8km N of PO, ☎ 03 5598 6226, fax 03 5598 6566, 5 cotgs acc up to 6, (1 & 2 bedrm), [shwr, bath (3), spa bath (2), tlt, a/c-cool, c/fan, fire pl (2), heat, elec blkts, TV, video-fee, clock radio, refrig, cook fac, micro, toaster, ldry, blkts, linen, pillows], bbq, ☏.
D ♯♯ $115 - $140, **W ♯♯** $805 - $980, ♀ $84, AE BC DC EFT MC VI.

★★★★ **(Cottage Suites)**, 4 units acc up to 2, [shwr, spa bath (2), tlt, a/c-cool, fire pl (2), heat, elec blkts, TV, video-fee, refrig, cook fac ltd, micro, toaster, ldry, doonas, linen, pillows], bbq, ☏. **D ♯♯** $110 - $140.

★★★☆ **Port Campbell Park View Units**, (Apt), 2A Desaily St, 50m N of PO, ☎ 03 5598 6445, fax 03 5598 6370, 2 apts acc up to 4, (1 & 2 bedrm), [shwr, tlt, c/fan, heat, elec blkts, TV, video (avail), clock radio, t/c mkg, refrig, cook fac ltd, micro, toaster, blkts, linen, pillows], bbq, non smoking property. D ♦♦ $75 - $110, ♦♦♦♦ $100 - $150, W $700 - $980, BC MC VI.

★★★ **Beacon Cottage**, (Cotg), 10 Cairns St, 200m W of PO, ☎ 03 5598 6328, 1 cotg acc up to 6, (3 bedrm), [shwr, tlt, hairdry, heat, elec blkts, TV, video, clock radio, refrig, cook fac, micro, toaster, ldry, blkts, doonas, linen, pillows], bbq. D ♦♦ $98 - $125, ◊ $10, AE BC DC EFT MC MP VI.

★★★ **Eastern Reef Accommodation**, (Cotg), Lot 1 Cobden - Port Campbell Rd, 1km E of PO, ☎ 03 5598 6561, (2 stry gr fl), 2 cotgs acc up to 6, (2 bedrm), [shwr, tlt, hairdry, a/c-cool, heat, elec blkts, TV, clock radio, t/c mkg, refrig, cook fac ltd, micro, elec frypan, toaster, blkts, doonas, linen, pillows], iron, iron brd, bbq, cots. D ♦♦ $80 - $135, ◊ $10 - $20, W $500 - $1,200, ch con, Min book long w/ends and Easter, BC MC VI.

Bayview Villas, (HU), Unit 2, 4 Tregea St, ☎ 03 5598 6582, fax 03 5261 5567, 1 unit acc up to 4, [shwr, spa bath, tlt, a/c, TV, video, radio, t/c mkg, cook fac, micro, d/wash, toaster, ldry, blkts, doonas, linen, pillows], c/park (undercover), non smoking property. D ♦♦ $130 - $180, ◊ $10, BC MC VI, (not yet classified).

B&B's/Guest Houses

★★★★☆ **Port Campbell Shearwater Haven**, (B&B), 12 Pleasant Dve, ☎ 03 5598 6532, fax 03 5598 6302, 2 rms [ensuite, hairdry, cent heat, elec blkts, clock radio, t/c mkg, refrig, micro, toaster], lounge (TV, video, cd), bbq. BB ♦ $80 - $100, ♦♦ $120 - $140, BC EFT MC VI.

★★★☆ **Port Campbell Bed & Breakfast**, (B&B), 2619 Cobden Rd, 1km N of PO, ☎ 03 5598 6260, fax 03 5598 6504, 3 rms [ensuite, hairdry, heat, TV, clock radio, t/c mkg, refrig, micro, toaster], lounge (TV), non smoking property. BLB ♦ $55 - $71.50, ♦♦ $82.50 - $110, ◊ $16.50 - $22, BC MC VI.

★★★☆ **Sea Breeze Bed & Breakfast**, (B&B), 13 Ocean Rd, 1km E of PO, ☎ 03 5598 6469, fax 03 5598 4669, 1 rm [hairdry, c/fan, heat, elec blkts, TV, clock radio, t/c mkg, refrig, toaster]. BLB ♦ $40 - $80, ♦♦ $50 - $150, AE BC EFT MC VI.

★★★ **Port Bayou**, (B&B), 52 Lord St, ☎ 03 5598 6403, 1 rm [shwr, tlt, hairdry, heat, elec blkts, TV, clock radio, t/c mkg, refrig, toaster], c/park (carport), non smoking property. BLB ♦ $55 - $90, ♦♦ $55 - $90, ◊ $5 - $10, ch con, BC EFT MC VI.

PORT FAIRY VIC 3284

Pop 2,650. (291km W Melbourne), See map on pages 694/695, ref B7. One of Victoria's earliest settlements. Tourist Information 03-5568 2682. Boating, Bowls, Fishing, Golf, Sailing, Scenic Drives, Squash, Surfing, Swimming (Beach), Tennis, Water Skiing.

Hotels/Motels

★★★★ **Ashmont Motor Inn**, (M), 47 Bank St, 700m E of PO, ☎ 03 5568 1588, fax 02 5568 3199, 14 units [shwr, spa bath (4), tlt, hairdry, a/c, elec blkts, tel, cable tv, video (4), clock radio, t/c mkg, refrig, mini bar, cook fac ltd (8), micro, toaster], ldry, iron, iron brd, dinner to unit (Mon to Fri), cots, non smoking units (3). RO ♦ $95 - $110, ♦♦ $105 - $155, ◊ $20, AE BC DC EFT JCB MC VI, *Operator Comment: New luxury motel. Spacious and beautifully appointed rooms.*

 FLAG FLAG CHOICE HOTELS

★★★★ **Seacombe House Motor Inn**, (M), 22 Sackville St, diagonally opposite PO, ☎ 03 5568 1082, fax 03 5568 2323, (2 stry gr fl), 21 units [shwr, bath (2), tlt, hairdry, a/c (14), heat, elec blkts, tel, TV, video (avail), clock radio, t/c mkg, refrig], ldry, iron, iron brd, rm serv, cots-fee, non smoking units (12). RO ♦ $104 - $145, ♦♦ $115 - $155, ◊ $15, 3 units ★★★, AE BC DC MC VI.

★★★★ **(Historic Cottage Section)**, Classified by National Trust, 3 units (1 & 2 bedrm), [shwr, spa bath, tlt, hairdry, a/c, fire pl, elec blkts, tel, TV, video-fee, clock radio, t/c mkg, refrig, micro (2), elec frypan, toaster], ldry, iron, iron brd. RO ◊ $165 - $225, ♦♦ $165 - $225, ◊ $25.

★★★ **(Private Hotel Section)**, Classified by National Trust, (2 stry), 9 rms [ensuite (3), spa bath (1), fan (1), cent heat, elec blkts, tel (1), t/c mkg (3), refrig (3)], ldry, iron (1), iron brd (1), lounge (TV), t/c mkg shared, non smoking property. BB ♦ $45 - $160, 1 room of ★★★☆.

★★★ **Central Motel Port Fairy**, (M), Previously Lady Julia Percy Motel 56 Sackville St, 100m N of PO, ☎ 03 5568 1800, fax 03 5568 2258, (2 stry gr fl), 19 units [shwr, bath (1), tlt, fan, heat, tel, TV, video (avail), clock radio, t/c mkg, refrig, toaster], bar, bbq, non smoking rms (available). RO ♦ $65 - $95, ♦♦ $75 - $95, ◊ $15, ch con, AE BC EFT MC VI, /♿.

 Budget Motel Chain International

★★★ **Killarney Hotel Motel**, (LMH), Princes Hwy, Killarney 3283, 10km E of PO, ☎ 03 5568 7290, fax 03 5568 7388, 3 units [shwr, tlt, c/fan, heat, elec blkts, tel, TV, clock radio, t/c mkg, refrig, toaster], ⊠, ✆, non smoking units (2). RO ♦ $47 - $62, ♦♦ $55 - $70, ◊ $10, AE BC EFT MC VI.

★★★ **Port Fairy Motel**, (M), 124 Princes Hwy, 1.9km N of PO, ☎ 03 5568 1735, fax 03 5568 1735, 10 units [shwr, tlt, a/c (8), fan (2), heat (2), elec blkts, tel, TV, clock radio, t/c mkg, refrig, micro, toaster], bbq, dinner to unit, cots, non smoking units. RO ♦ $50 - $70, ♦♦ $55 - $85, ◊ $12, ch con, 2 units ★★★. AE BC MC VI.

 Budget Motel Chain International

★★☆ **Learnean Anchorage Motel**, (M), 115 Princes Hwy, 1.8km N of PO, ☎ 03 5568 1145, fax 03 5568 1145, 5 units [shwr, tlt, a/c, elec blkts, TV, video-fee, clock radio, refrig, cook fac ltd, toaster], ldry, pool, bbq (covered)-fee, ✆, plygr, tennis (half court), cots-fee. RO ♦♦ $75 - $99, ◊ $15 - $17, ch con, BC MC VI.

★★☆ **Port Fairy - Caledonian Inn Hotel Motel**, (LMH), Cnr Bank & James St, 300m NW of PO, ☎ 03 5568 1044, fax 03 5568 1144, 12 units [shwr, tlt, heat, elec blkts, tel, TV, clock radio, t/c mkg, refrig, toaster], ⊠, ✆, cots. RO ♦ $65 - $85, ◊ $10, AE BC DC EFT MC VI.

★★ **Royal Oak Hotel Port Fairy**, (LH), 9 Bank St, ☎ 03 5568 1018, fax 03 5568 2922, (2 stry), 6 rms [basin (5), elec blkts, clock radio], ⊠, t/c mkg shared, ✆. BLB ♦ $25, ♦♦ $50, ◊ $10, AE BC DC EFT MC VI.

Self Catering Accommodation

 FLAG FLAG CHOICE HOTELS

★★★★★ **Flag Heritage Hearns Cottage Suites**, (Apt), Previously Hearn's Cottage Suites, 54 Bank St, ☎ 03 5568 2388, fax 03 5568 2521, (2 stry gr fl), 3 apts acc up to 2, (1 bedrm), [shwr, spa bath, tlt, hairdry, a/c, tel, TV, video, clock radio, CD, t/c mkg, refrig, cook fac, micro, elec frypan, d/wash, toaster, ldry (in unit), blkts, doonas, linen, pillows], iron, iron brd, non smoking property. D $190 - $220, W $1,190 - $1,380, AE BC DC EFT MC VI.

★★★★ **(Motel Section)**, (2 stry), 4 units [shwr, tlt, hairdry, a/c, tel, TV, video, clock radio, CD, t/c mkg, refrig, cook fac ltd, micro, toaster, doonas], iron, iron brd, non smoking property. RO ♦♦ $160.

★★★★☆ **Boathouse Holiday House**, (Apt), 2A Hanley Crt, ☎ 03 5562 3185, fax 03 5561 2670, (Multi-stry gr fl), 1 apt acc up to 8, (3 bedrm), [shwr, spa bath, tlt, hairdry, a/c, heat, elec blkts, tel (local), TV, video, clock radio, CD, t/c mkg, refrig, cook fac, micro, d/wash, toaster, ldry, doonas, linen, pillows], w/mach, dryer, iron, iron brd, bbq, c/park (carport). **D $180 - $260, W $1,100 - $2,000**, AE BC MC VI.

★★★★☆ **Johansson's Perch**, (Apt), 43 Gipps St, 200m E of PO, ☎ 03 5568 2378, 2 apts acc up to 6, (3 bedrm), [ensuite, shwr, spa bath, tlt, hairdry, a/c, heat, elec blkts, TV, video, clock radio, t/c mkg, refrig, cook fac, micro, d/wash, toaster, blkts, doonas, pillows], w/mach, dryer, iron, iron brd, bbq, c/park (garage), non smoking property. **D †† $175, ⚲ $45**, Min book Christmas Jan and Easter, BC MC VI.

★★★★☆ **(Bed & Breakfast Section)**, (Multi-stry), 1 rm (1 bedrm), [ensuite, hairdry, a/c, elec blkts, TV, clock radio, t/c mkg, refrig], non smoking property. **BLB †† $130.**

★★★ **(Cottage Section)**, 1 cotg acc up to 2, (1 bedrm), [shwr, tlt, hairdry, fan, heat, TV, clock radio, t/c mkg, refrig, cook fac, micro, toaster, ldry, blkts, linen, pillows], w/mach, dryer, iron, iron brd, bbq, non smoking property. **D †† $110.**

★★★★☆ **Lagoons Bay Holiday Accommodation**, (Apt), 2575 Princes Hwy, Gateway 250m W of Water Tower, mob 0402 096 905, 1 apt acc up to 4, (2 bedrm), [shwr, tlt, hairdry, fan, heat, elec blkts, TV, video, clock radio, CD, t/c mkg, refrig, cook fac, micro, elec frypan, d/wash, toaster, ldry, blkts, doonas, linen, pillows], w/mach, dryer, iron, iron brd, bbq, non smoking property. **D $100 - $165, W $650 - $1,100**, Breakfast available. Min book Christmas Jan long w/ends and Easter.

★★★★☆ **Riverhaven Holiday Unit Port Fairy**, (HU), Unit 1, 73 Gipps St, ☎ 03 5568 1082, fax 03 5568 2323, 1 unit acc up to 4, (2 bedrm), [shwr, spa bath, tlt, a/c, c/fan, elec blkts, TV, video, refrig, cook fac, micro, elec frypan, d/wash, toaster, ldry, blkts, linen, pillows], iron, bbq. **D †† $140 - $240, ⚲ $20, W †† $850, ⚲ $50**, AE BC DC MC VI,

Operator Comment: River frontage, scenic & peaceful with shared private jetty. Short stroll to beaches, town & historic wharf. RELAX, REVITALISE & RENEW.

★★★★☆ **The Constable Cottage at Port Fairy**, (Cotg), 11 Cox St, 20m SW of PO, ☎ 03 5568 2390, 1 cotg acc up to 6, (3 bedrm), [shwr, spa bath, tlt, hairdry, fan, fire pl (master bedroom), heat, elec blkts, tel (local), TV, video, clock radio, CD, t/c mkg, refrig, cook fac, micro, d/wash, toaster, ldry, doonas, linen, pillows], w/mach, dryer, iron, iron brd, bbq, c/park (garage), cots, non smoking property. **D †† $150, ⚲ $10, W $900.**

★★★★☆ **The Penthouse Port Fairy**, (Apt), 2A Ritchie St, 2km N of PO, ☎ 03 5562 3185, fax 03 5561 2670, (2 stry), 1 apt acc up to 6, (3 bedrm), [shwr, spa bath, tlt, hairdry, a/c, fan, heat, tel, TV, video, radio, CD, t/c mkg, refrig, cook fac, micro, d/wash, toaster, ldry, doonas, linen, pillows], w/mach, dryer, iron, iron brd, bbq, cots. **D $250, W $1,500 - $2,500**, Minimum booking Christmas/Jan & weekends, AE BC MC VI.

★★★★ **Bluestone Bay Port Fairy**, (Cotg), 2579 Princes Hwy, 3.5km W of PO, mob 0417 592 678, 1 cotg acc up to 10, (4 bedrm), [shwr, spa bath (1), tlt, c/fan, TV, video, clock radio, CD, refrig, cook fac, micro, d/wash, toaster, doonas, linen, pillows], iron, iron brd, lounge firepl. **D $150 - $250, W $800 - $1,650**, Min book all holiday times.

★★★★ **Clonmara Bed & Breakfast**, (Cotg), 106 Princes Hwy, ☎ 03 5568 2595, fax 03 5568 2595, 1 cotg acc up to 2, (1 bedrm), [shwr, spa bath, tlt, hairdry, fan, heat, elec blkts, TV, clock radio, t/c mkg, refrig, micro, toaster], iron, iron brd, res liquor license, cots, non smoking property. **BB ‡ $95 - $110, †† $110 - $150**, BC MC VI.

Operator Comment: Romantic and cosy with old world charm. www.users.bigpond.com/clonmara

★★★★ **Cottages of the Port**, (Cotg), Coach House Cottage. 56A Gipps St, ☎ 03 5568 7345, fax 03 5568 7345, (2 stry gr fl), 1 cotg acc up to 2, (1 bedrm), [shwr, bath, tlt, hairdry, fan, heat, elec blkts, TV, video, clock radio, CD, t/c mkg, refrig, cook fac, micro, toaster, ldry (in unit), doonas, linen, pillows], w/mach, dryer, iron, iron brd, lounge firepl, bbq, cots, non smoking property. **D $110 - $160, W $650 - $950**, Breakfast available.

★★★★ **(Railway Cottage)**, 1 cotg acc up to 6, (2 bedrm), [shwr, bath, tlt, hairdry, fan, heat, elec blkts, TV, video, t/c mkg, refrig, cook fac, micro, toaster, ldry, doonas, linen, pillows], w/mach, dryer, iron, iron brd, lounge firepl, bbq, cots, non smoking property. **D $110 - $160, W $650 - $1,200.**

★★★★ **Kilkarlen at Killarney**, (HU), 228 Survey La, Killarney 3283, off Rocks Rd, 9km E of PO, ☎ 03 5568 7258, fax 03 5568 7298, 1 unit acc up to 4, (2 bedrm), [shwr, bath, tlt, hairdry, fan, heat, elec blkts, TV, video, clock radio, CD, t/c mkg, refrig, cook fac, micro, toaster, ldry, blkts, doonas, linen, pillows], w/mach, dryer, iron, iron brd, bbq, non smoking units. **BB †† $120 - $135, ⚲ $50**, ch con, BC MC VI,

Operator Comment: All you hear in the mornings are magpies and the ocean.

★★★★ **(Bed and Breakfast Section)**, 1 rm [ensuite, fan, heat, elec blkts, TV, clock radio, CD, t/c mkg, refrig, micro, toaster], non smoking rms. **BB †† $95 - $105**, ch con.

★★★★ **Matilda Cottage Port Fairy**, (Cotg), 19 Cox St, 100m S of PO, ☎ 03 5568 2700, 1 cotg acc up to 5, (3 bedrm), [shwr, bath, tlt, heat, elec blkts, TV, video, clock radio, CD, t/c mkg, refrig, cook fac, micro, toaster, blkts, linen, pillows], w/mach, dryer, iron, bbq, non smoking property. **D †† $132 - $165, ⚲ $22 - $35, W $715 - $880**, Min book all holiday times, BC MC VI.

★★★★ **Moorings on Moyne**, (Apt), 69A Gipps St, 200m N of PO, ☎ 03 5561 4690, (2 stry gr fl), 1 apt acc up to 6, (3 bedrm), [shwr, bath, tlt, hairdry, fan, heat, elec blkts, TV, video, clock radio, refrig, cook fac, micro, toaster, ldry (in unit), blkts, linen, pillows], bbq, cots. **D $120 - $150, W $750 - $1,200**, Min book Christmas and Jan.

★★★★ **Myndarra Shepherds Cottage**, (Cotg), (Farm), Porters Rd, Orford 3284, 26km NW of PO, off Hamilton Rd, ☎ 03 5568 9201, 1 cotg acc up to 6, (3 bedrm), [shwr, bath, tlt, fan, c/fan, elec blkts, tel, clock radio, CD, refrig, cook fac, micro, toaster, ldry, blkts, linen, pillows], iron, iron brd, lounge firepl, bbq, cots. **D $95 - $160, W $400 - $750**, Breakfast available. Dinner by arrangement.

★★★★ **Port Fairy Colonial Cottages**, (Cotg), Nivani, No children's facilities, 27 Regent St, ☎ 03 5568 1234, fax 03 5568 2966, 1 cotg acc up to 4, (2 bedrm), [shwr, bath, tlt, fan, heat, elec blkts, TV, video, clock radio, CD, refrig, cook fac, micro, elec frypan, ldry, blkts, linen, pillows], dryer, iron, iron brd, bbq. **D †† $110 - $130, ⚲ $12.50, W $550 - $1,000.**

★★★★ **(49 Regent St Section)**, Swyn-Y-Mor, No children's facilities, 1 cotg acc up to 5, (3 bedrm), [shwr, bath, tlt, fan, heat, elec blkts, TV, video, clock radio, CD, refrig, cook fac, micro, elec frypan, ldry, blkts, linen, pillows], dryer, iron, iron brd, bbq. **D †† $110 - $130, ⚲ $12.50, W $550 - $1,000.**

★★★★ **Sandy Cove**, (Cotg), 129 Beach St, ☎ 03 5568 1904, fax 03 5568 2526, (2 stry), 1 cotg acc up to 8, (3 bedrm), [ensuite, shwr, bath, tlt, a/c, heat, elec blkts, TV, video, clock radio, t/c mkg, refrig, cook fac, micro, elec frypan, d/wash, toaster, ldry, doonas, linen, pillows], w/mach, dryer, iron, iron brd, non smoking property. **D $220, W $1,200 - $1,900.**

★★★★ **Skye Beachfront Retreat**, (HU), 72 Griffith St, 1km NE of PO, ☎ 03 5568 1181, (2 stry), 1 unit acc up to 5, (2 bedrm), [shwr, tlt, hairdry, fan, heat, elec blkts, TV, video, clock radio, refrig, cook fac, micro, ldry (in unit), blkts, doonas, linen, pillows], iron, iron brd, bbq, cots. **D $110 - $185, W $750 - $1,300**, Min book Christmas and Jan.

★★★★ **(Apartment Section)**, (2 stry gr fl), 2 apts acc up to 8, (2 & 3 bedrm), [ensuite (1), shwr, bath (1), tlt, hairdry, evap cool, heat, fan (1), elec blkts, tel (local) (1), TV, video, clock radio, CD, refrig, cook fac, micro, d/wash, toaster, ldry (in unit), blkts, doonas, linen, pillows], dryer (1), iron, iron brd, bbq. **D $110 - $258, W $750 - $1,800.**

★★★★ **The Dockside Boathouse**, (Apt), 6/25 Gipps St, ☎ 03 5562 3185, fax 03 5561 2670, (2 stry), 1 apt acc up to 6, (2 bedrm), [shwr, spa bath, tlt, a/c, heat, elec blkts, tel (local), TV, video, clock radio, CD, t/c mkg, refrig, cook fac, micro, d/wash, toaster, ldry, doonas, linen, pillows], w/mach, dryer, iron, iron brd, c/park (carport). **D $150 - $228, W $1,000 - $1,600**, Minimum booking Christmas/Jan & weekends, AE BC MC VI.

★★★☆ **Belfast Cottages**, (Cotg), 5 Thistle Pl, 1.5km W of PO, ☎ 03 5568 1350, fax 03 5568 1379, 2 cotgs acc up to 4, (1 bedrm), [shwr, bath (hip), tlt, hairdry, c/fan, heat, elec blkts, TV, video, clock radio, t/c mkg, cook fac, micro, toaster, ldry, blkts, linen, pillows], w/mach, iron, iron brd, plygr, cots. **D †† $80 - $100, ⚲ $15, W †† $480 - $600, ⚲ $90 - $100**, Min book all holiday times, BC MC VI.

★★★☆ **Garden Pavillions**, (HU), 11 Tieman St, 1km N of PO, ☎ 03 5568 1045, 3 units acc up to 2, (Studio), [shwr, spa bath, tlt, hairdry, c/fan, heat, elec blkts, TV, video, clock radio, refrig, micro, elec frypan, toaster, blkts, doonas, linen, pillows], iron, iron brd, bbq. **D $100 - $110.**

★★★ **Eastern Beach Holiday Units**, (HF), Cnr Griffith St & Bourne Ave, 1.3km NE of PO, ☎ 03 5568 1117, (2 stry gr fl), 6 flats acc up to 5, (2 bedrm), [shwr, bath (hip), tlt, heat, elec blkts, TV, clock radio, refrig, cook fac, micro, toaster, blkts, linen reqd-fee, pillows], ldry, bbq, plygr, cots. **W $400 - $770,** Min book all holiday times, BC MC VI.

★★★ **Maison Hannah**, (Cotg), 177 Griffith St, 1.5km NE of PO, ☎ 03 5568 1583, 1 cotg acc up to 7, (3 bedrm), [shwr, bath, tlt, c/fan, heat, elec blkts, TV, video, clock radio, refrig, cook fac, micro, toaster, ldry, blkts, linen, pillows], iron, iron brd, bbq. **D ♦♦ $70 - $90, ♦ $15 - $25, W $450 - $800.**

★★★ **Mungala Holiday Flats**, (HF), 192 Griffith St, 1.9km NE of PO, ☎ 03 5568 1118, fax 03 5568 1178, (2 stry), 5 flats acc up to 6, (1, 2 & 3 bedrm), [shwr, bath (hip) (2), tlt, heat, elec blkts, TV, clock radio, refrig, cook fac, elec frypan, linen reqd], ldry, bbq, c/park (carport), plygr, cots. **D $75 - $140, W $350 - $1,200,** Min book all holiday times, BC MC VI.

★★★ **Tandara-on-Sea**, (HU), 190 Griffith St, 1.9km NE of PO, ☎ 03 5568 1852, 1 unit acc up to 5, (2 bedrm), [shwr, bath (hip), tlt, heat, TV, clock radio, refrig, cook fac, micro, toaster, ldry (in unit), blkts, linen reqd, pillows], iron, iron brd, c/park (carport), cots, non smoking property. **D ♦♦ $70, ♦ $10,** ch con.

★★★ **Terrace Holiday Flats**, (HF), Cnr Griffith St & Hughes Ave, 1km NE of PO, ☎ 03 5568 2889, fax 03 5568 2889, (2 stry), 5 flats acc up to 6, (2 bedrm), [shwr, bath, tlt, heat, elec blkts, TV, video, refrig, cook fac, micro, toaster, ldry (in unit), linen reqd], c/park (carport), cots. **D $75 - $115.**

★★★ **Whalers Cottages**, (Cotg), Cnr Whalers Dve & Regent St, 600m N of PO, ☎ 03 5568 1488, fax 03 5568 1488, 2 cotgs acc up to 5, (2 bedrm), [shwr, bath, tlt, heat, elec blkts, TV, video, clock radio, refrig, cook fac, micro, elec frypan, ldry (in unit), doonas, linen reqd], cots. **D $90 - $120, W $550 - $900,** Minimum booking folk festival weekend.

★★☆ **Abavest**, (HF), Bourne Ave, 1.3km NE of PO, ☎ 03 5568 7206, 3 flats acc up to 6, (2 bedrm), [shwr, tlt, c/fan, heat, elec blkts, TV, video, clock radio, refrig, cook fac, micro, toaster, ldry (in unit), blkts, linen reqd-fee], w/mach, iron, iron brd, non smoking property. **D $65 - $120, W $345 - $635,** Min book Christmas and Jan.

★★ **Riverside Cottages**, (Cotg), 41 Gipps St, 400m SE of PO, ☎ 03 5529 2253, 2 cotgs acc up to 4, (Studio & 1 bedrm), [shwr, bath (1), tlt, fan, heat, TV, clock radio, refrig, cook fac, elec frypan (2), toaster, blkts, linen reqd, pillows], ldry, iron (2), mooring, cots. **D $60 - $120, W $420 - $600.**

B&B's/Guest Houses

★★★★☆ **Cherry Plum Cottage**, (B&B), No children's facilities, 37 Albert Rd, 2km N of PO, ☎ 03 5568 2433, fax 03 5568 3006, 1 rm [ensuite, hairdry, c/fan, heat, TV, clock radio, CD, t/c mkg, refrig, micro, toaster], iron, iron brd, bbq (under-cover). **BB ♦ $90, ♦♦ $90 - $110.**

★★★★ **Gobles Mill House**, (B&B), Classified by National Trust, No children's facilities, 75 Gipps St, 500m NE of PO, ☎ 03 5568 1118, fax 03 5568 1178, (Multi-stry), 6 rms [ensuite, hairdry, heat, elec blkts, TV (1)], lounge, lounge firepl, t/c mkg shared, refrig, non smoking property. **BB ♦ $95 - $175, ♦♦ $110 - $175,** BC MC VI.

★★★★ **King George Cottage Bed & Breakfast**, (B&B), 22 Gipps St, 1km S of PO, ☎ 03 5568 2229, fax 03 5568 3004, 3 rms [ensuite, bath (1), fan, heat, cent heat, elec blkts, tel, TV, clock radio, micro, toaster, doonas], ldry, lounge (TV), lounge firepl, t/c mkg shared, refrig, non smoking property. **BLB $100 - $150,** BC MC VI.

★★★★ **Kingsley Bed & Breakfast**, (B&B), 71 Cox St, 500m W of PO, ☎ 03 5568 1269, fax 03 5568 2069, 2 rms [ensuite (1), shwr, bath (1), tlt, hairdry, c/fan, cent heat, elec blkts, clock radio], lounge (TV, cd, fireplace), t/c mkg shared, refrig. **BB ♦ $60, ♦♦ $90 - $95,** 1 room ★★★★☆. BC MC VI.

★★★★ **Lough Cottage**, (B&B), 216 Griffith St, 2km NE of PO, ☎ 03 5568 1583, fax 03 5568 1583, 1 rm [hairdry, heat, elec blkts, clock radio, t/c mkg, refrig], ldry, lounge (TV), bbq. **BB ♦ $60, ♦♦ $85.**

★★★★ **Oscars Waterfront Boutique Hotel**, (B&B), 41B Gipps St, 400m E of PO, ☎ 03 5568 3022, fax 03 5568 3042, 5 rms [ensuite, heat, elec blkts, TV, clock radio, refrig, doonas], conf fac, lounge firepl, t/c mkg shared, non smoking property. **BB ♦♦ $220 - $275,** BC MC VI.

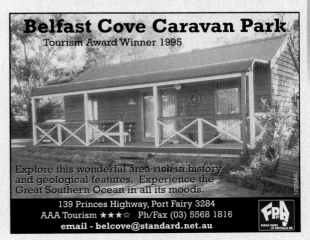

★★★★ Shearwater House Bed & Breakfast, (B&B), No facilities for children under 12, 53 Gipps St, 200m E of PO, ☎ 03 5568 1081, fax 03 5568 2981, (2 stry gr fl), 5 rms [ensuite, bath (1), hairdry, cent heat, elec blkts, TV], lounge (cd), lounge firepl, t/c mkg shared, non smoking property. BB ♦ $100 - $120, ♦♦ $121 - $155, Min book long w/ends and Easter, AE BC DC MC VI.

★★★★ Talara House, (B&B), Classified by National Trust,Heritage, No children's facilities, 549 Princes Hwy, 2km W of PO, ☎ 03 5568 2575, (2 stry gr fl), 3 rms [ensuite (1), shwr (2), bath (2), tlt (2), heat, elec blkts], lounge (TV, cd), t/c mkg shared, non smoking property. BB ♦ $104.50, ♦♦ $137.50, Min book long w/ends and Easter, BC MC VI.

★★★★ The Boathouse on Moyne, (B&B), 19 Gipps St, ☎ 03 5568 2608, fax 03 5568 2740, 2 rms [ensuite (1), shwr, tlt, hairdry, fan, heat, elec blkts, clock radio], ldry, lounge (TV, stereo), cook fac, t/c mkg shared, refrig, bbq, non smoking property. BLB ♦ $70, ♦♦ $95 - $100, BC MC VI.

★★★★ The Douglass Bed & Breakfast, (B&B), 85 Gipps St, 600m NE of PO, ☎ 03 5568 1016, fax 03 5568 1888, 6 rms [ensuite, hairdry, heat, elec blkts, TV, clock radio, t/c mkg]. BB ♦ $95 - $160, ♦♦ $110 - $160, ch con, BC MC VI.

★★★ (Holiday Flat Section), 1 flat acc up to 4, (Studio), [shwr, tlt, hairdry, a/c, elec blkts, TV, clock radio, cook fac, toaster, doonas, linen, pillows]. D ♦♦ $120, ♦ $40, W $800.

★★★★ The Old Market Inn, (B&B), No children's facilities, 51 William St, ☎ 03 5568 2221, (2 stry), 2 rms [ensuite (1), shwr (1), bath (1), tlt (1), clock radio], lounge, lounge firepl, t/c mkg shared, refrig, non smoking property. BB ♦♦ $120 - $130, BC MC VI.

★★★☆ Boodcarra, (B&B), 2100 Princes Hwy, 5km W of PO, ☎ 03 5568 2829, 5 rms [heat, elec blkts], ldry, lounge (TV, video, stereo), lounge firepl, bbq, non smoking property. BB ♦♦ $85 - $125, Other meals by arrangement, BC MC VI.

★★★☆ Hanley House, (B&B), 14 Sackville St, 100m S of PO, ☎ 03 5568 2709, 2 rms [shwr, bath (1), tlt, heat, elec blkts], lounge (TV), lounge firepl, t/c mkg shared. BB ♦ $70 - $80, ♦♦ $95, ♦ $30, ch con.

★★★ Port Fairy Merrijig Inn, (GH), Classified by National Trust, 1 Campbell St, ☎ 03 5568 2324, fax 03 5568 2436, (2 stry gr fl), 8 rms [shwr, bath (2), tlt, a/c-cool (5), fan (4), cent heat, elec blkts, TV (4), clock radio, doonas], lounge (TV), lounge firepl, ⊠, t/c mkg shared, refrig. BB ♦ $95, ♦♦ $95 - $165, 4 rooms ★★★★. BC EFT MC VI.

Other Accommodation

YHA Victoria, (Lodge), Classified by National Trust, 8 Cox St, 150m E of PO, ☎ 03 5568 2468, fax 03 5568 2302, 9 rms [heat, linen reqd-fee], shwr (4G-4L), tlt (4G-4L), ldry, lounge (TV), cook fac, t/c mkg shared, refrig, bbq, c/park. D ♦ $16, ch con, BC MC VI, ♿.

(Unit Section), 8 rms [shwr, tlt, heat, linen reqd-fee]. D ♦ $19, ♦♦ $18, ch con.

PORT FRANKLIN VIC 3964

Pop Nominal, (188km SE Melbourne), See map on page 696, ref E8. A small settlement situated on Corner Inlet, close to Foster & Wilsons Promontory.

★★★★ Franklin Cottage, (Cotg), 6 South St, 11km SE of Foster PO, ☎ 03 5686 2452, 1 cotg acc up to 8, (3 bedrm), [shwr, bath, tlt, hairdry, fan, heat, elec blkts, TV, video, clock radio, t/c mkg, refrig, cook fac, micro, toaster, ldry, blkts, doonas, linen, pillows], w/mach, iron, iron brd, bbq, cots, non smoking property. D ♦♦ $75, ♦ $10, Min book applies.

PORTARLINGTON VIC 3223

Pop 2,400. (103km SW Melbourne), See map on page 697, ref A5. Pastoral, agricultural and seaside township with sheltered beaches. Mill Museum. Boat Ramp, Boating, Bowls, Croquet, Fishing, Golf, Sailing, Swimming (Bay, Pool), Tennis, Water Skiing.

Hotels/Motels

★★★☆ Portarlington Beach Motel, (M), 153 Newcombe St, 1km E of PO, ☎ 03 5259 3801, fax 03 5259 3993, 14 units [shwr, tlt, hairdry, a/c, elec blkts, tel, TV, video-fee, clock radio, t/c mkg, refrig, micro, toaster], ldry, pool-heated, spa, bbq, rm serv, cots-fee. RO ♦ $66 - $96, ♦♦ $70 - $96, ♦ $15, ch con, AE BC DC MC VI, ♿..

Self Catering Accommodation

★★★★☆ Ardrossan Bed & Breakfast, (HU), 2435 Geelong-Portarlington Rd, Bellarine 3221, ☎ 03 5259 3252, fax 03 5259 3787, 1 unit acc up to 4, (2 bedrm), [shwr, tlt, hairdry, a/c-cool, heat, elec blkts, TV, clock radio, refrig, cook fac, micro, elec frypan, toaster, ldry, blkts, doonas, linen, pillows], w/mach, dryer, iron, iron brd, bbq, tennis, breakfast ingredients, non smoking property. D ♦♦ $90 - $120, ♦ $15 - $25.

★★★★ Ballawein Country Cottage, (Cotg), 60 Greenhills Rd, off Church Rd, ☎ 03 5259 2232, 1 cotg acc up to 5, (2 bedrm), [shwr, tlt, c/fan, heat, elec blkts, TV, video, refrig, cook fac, micro, elec frypan, toaster, ldry, blkts, doonas, linen, pillows], bbq, cots, Pets on application. D ♦♦ $100 - $120, ♦ $10 - $25, W $460 - $770, Breakfast available.

★★★ Carrick-by-the-Sea, (Cotg), c1856. 30 The Esplanade, 1km E of PO, ☎ 03 5259 2567, fax 03 5259 2936, 1 cotg acc up to 2, (1 bedrm), [shwr, bath, tlt, heat, elec blkts, tlt (local), TV, clock radio, CD, cook fac, ldry, blkts, linen, pillows], lounge firepl, bbq, breakfast ingredients. D $175.

★★★ Portarlington Swimming Pool, (HF), 86-110 Smythe St, ☎ 03 5259 2910, 10 flats acc up to 8, (2 & 3 bedrm), [shwr, tlt, heat, TV, refrig, cook fac, toaster, ldry (in unit), linen reqd], conf fac, pool indoor heated, sauna, spa, bbq-fee, tennis. D $71.50 - $121.

PORTLAND VIC 3305

Pop 9,650. (362km W Melbourne), See map on pages 694/695, ref A7. First permanent settlement in Victoria - 1834. Only deep sea port between Melbourne and Adelaide. Boating, Bowls, Bush Walking, Croquet, Fishing, Golf, Horse Riding, Sailing, Scenic Drives, Shooting, Surfing, Swimming (Pool, Beach, River), Tennis, Water Skiing. See also Cape Bridgewater, Narrawong & Tyrendarra

Hotels/Motels

★★★★ Hotel Bentinck, (Ltd Lic H), Cnr Bentinck & Gawler Sts, 800m W of PO, ☎ 03 5523 2188, fax 03 5523 7011, (Multi-stry), 9 rms (1 suite) [shwr, spa bath (8), tlt, a/c, fire pl (3), elec blkts, tel, cable tv, clock radio, t/c mkg, refrig, mini bar], iron, iron brd, ⊠, rm serv, dinner to unit, ☎. BLB ♦ $154 - $198, ♦♦ $154 - $198, ♦ $18.70, AE BC DC EFT MC MP VI.

★★ (Motel Section), 15 units [shwr, tlt, heat, elec blkts, TV, clock radio, t/c mkg, refrig], ☎, cots-fee. RO ♦ $49.50, ♦♦ $57, ♦ $8.80.

★★★★ Victoria Lodge Motor Inn, (M), 155 Percy St, 500m N of PO, ☎ 03 5523 5966, fax 03 5523 1132, 15 units [shwr, bath (4), spa bath (7), tlt, hairdry, a/c, elec blkts, tel, TV, video-fee, clock radio, t/c mkg, refrig], cots-fee, non smoking units (5). RO ♦ $74 - $132, ♦♦ $77 - $132, ♦ $11, Apartments not listed or rated. AE BC DC JCB MC MP VI, ♿.

★★★★ Whalers Rest Motor Inn, (M), 8 Henty Hwy, 4km N of PO, ☎ 03 5523 4077, fax 03 5521 7641, 13 units [shwr, bath (2), spa bath (1), tlt, hairdry, a/c, elec blkts, tel, TV, movie, clock radio, t/c mkg, refrig, toaster], ldry, iron, iron brd, pool above ground, bbq, dinner to unit, plygr, cots-fee, non smoking units (5). RO ♦♦ $80 - $105, ♦ $10, AE BC DC EFT MC MP VI.

★★★☆ Grosvenor Motel, (M), 206 Hurd St, 1.6km N of PO, ☎ 03 5523 2888, fax 03 5521 7277, 14 units [shwr, tlt, hairdry, a/c, elec blkts, tel, TV, video-fee, clock radio, t/c mkg, refrig], ldry, conf fac, bbq, dinner to unit, plygr, cots-fee, non smoking units (6). RO ♦ $60 - $80, ♦♦ $65 - $85, ♦ $10, AE BC DC EFT MC MP VI,

Operator Comment: When you need a quiet location, a decent shower, a good night sleep and a hearty home cooked meal in our licenced Dining Room look for our signs on the Highway into town, and take the first left after the 60km sign.

★★★☆ The Richmond Henty Hotel, (LMH), 101 Bentinck St, 500m SE of PO, ☎ 03 5523 1032, fax 03 5523 5954, (Multi-stry gr fl), 41 units [shwr, tlt, hairdry, a/c-cool, cent heat, tel, cable tv, video, clock radio, t/c mkg, refrig], iron, iron brd, conf fac, ⊠, pool-heated, plygr, cots-fee. RO ♦ $97.90 - $130, ♦♦ $97.90 - $130, ♦ $14.30 - $17, AE BC DC EFT MC MP VI.

★★★ Admella Motel, (M), 5 Otway Crt, 300m N of PO, ☎ 03 5523 3347, fax 03 5523 3589, 10 units [shwr, tlt, fan, heat, elec blkts, tel, TV, video, clock radio, t/c mkg, refrig, toaster], ldry, bbq, cots. RO ♦ $49, ♦♦ $57, ♦ $9, ch con, AE BC DC EFT MC MCH VI.

★★★ **Mariner Motel**, (M), 196 Percy St, 800m N of PO,
☎ 03 5523 2877, fax 03 5523 4614, 12 units [shwr, tlt, heat,
elec blkts, tel, TV, video-fee, clock radio, t/c mkg, refrig, toaster], bbq,
cots-fee. RO ∮ $49 - $59, ∮∮ $55 - $70, ∮ $5, AE BC DC MC VI.

★★★ **Melaleuca Motel**, (M), 25 Bentinck St, 1.1km SE
of PO, ☎ 03 5523 3397, fax 03 5523 5813, 16 units
[shwr, tlt, heat, elec blkts, tel, TV, video (avail), clock radio,
t/c mkg, refrig, cook fac ltd (1), micro (1), toaster], ldry
⊠ (Mon to Sat), bbq, cots-fee. RO ∮ $66 - $77, ∮∮ $71.50 - $88,
6 rooms ★★★☆. AE BC DC EFT MC VI.

★★★ **William Dutton Motel**, (M), Cnr Percy & Otway
Sts, 300m N of PO, ☎ 03 5523 4222, fax 03 5523 5786,
(2 stry gr fl), 29 units [shwr, tlt, a/c-cool, heat, elec blkts,
tel, TV, video, movie, clock radio, t/c mkg, refrig, toaster],
cots-fee, non smoking units (10). RO ∮ $55 - $65, ∮∮ $60 - $76, ∮ $11,
AE BC DC EFT MC MCH VI.

Self Catering Accommodation

★★★★ **Arbour Potter's Cottage**, (Cotg), RMB 2448 Nelson Rd, Gorae
West Via, 10km NW of Portland, ☎ 03 5526 5265, fax 03 5526 5250,
1 cotg acc up to 2, (1 bedrm), [shwr, tlt, hairdry, heat, elec blkts, TV,
video, clock radio, CD, refrig, cook fac, micro, toaster, blkts, linen,
pillows], lounge firepl, bbq, non smoking property. BB ∮∮ $85, ∮∮ $500.

★★★★ **Gawler by the Sea**, (Apt), 1st Floor, 2 Gawler St, 1km SE of PO,
☎ 03 5521 7242, fax 03 5521 7242, (2 stry), 1 apt acc up to 4, (2
bedrm), [shwr, spa bath, tlt, hairdry, a/c, elec blkts, TV, radio, t/c mkg,
refrig, cook fac, micro, toaster, ldry (in unit), blkts, linen, pillows],
iron, iron brd, breakfast ingredients. BB ∮∮ $130, ∮ $15, Min book
Christmas Jan long w/ends and Easter, AE BC EFT MC VI.

★★★★ **Julia Cottage**, (Cotg), 74 Julia St, 600m SW of PO,
☎ 03 5523 6004, fax 03 5526 7155, 1 cotg acc up to 4, (2 bedrm),
[shwr, bath, tlt, hairdry, evap cool, heat, elec blkts, tel (local), TV,
t/c mkg, refrig, cook fac, micro, toaster, ldry, blkts, doonas, linen,
pillows], w/mach, dryer, iron, iron brd, breakfast ingredients, non
smoking property. BLB ∮∮ $100, ∮ $15, ∮∮ $500 - $700, Min book
Christmas Jan long w/ends and Easter,

*Operator Comment: Ideally located for leisurely strolls to
restaurants, shops, theatre, beaches and harbour.*

★★★★ **The Finials**, (Cotg), 39 Henty St, 200m SW of PO,
☎ 03 5523 2226, fax 03 5523 2226, 3 cotgs acc up to 6, (Studio, 2 &
3 bedrm), [shwr, spa bath (1), tlt, heat (2), cent heat (1), TV, video,
clock radio, t/c mkg, refrig, cook fac (2), cook fac ltd (1), micro,
toaster, blkts, doonas, linen, pillows], ldry, w/mach, dryer, bbq-fee,
c/park (undercover) (2), cots, non smoking property. D ∮ $90 - $100,
∮∮ $90 - $110, ∮ $20 - $30, W ∮ $500 - $700, ∮∮ $630 - $700,
∮ $140, ch con, 1 unit ★★★, BC MC VI.

★★★★ **Tram Retreat B & B**, (Cotg), Crowes Rd, 6km N of PO,
☎ 03 5523 2679, 1 cotg acc up to 2, (1 bedrm), [shwr, tlt, fan, heat,
elec blkts, TV, video, clock radio, t/c mkg, refrig, cook fac, micro, toaster,
blkts, linen, pillows], res liquor license, pool, bbq, c/park (undercover),
cots, breakfast ingredients, non smoking property. BLB ∮ $80, ∮∮ $100,
∮ $10, Min book long w/ends, BC MC VI.

★★★ **Allestree Beach Holiday Units**, (HU), 53 Fergusons Rd,
Allestree 3305, 7km NE of PO, off Dutton Way, ☎ 03 5529 2431,
fax 03 5529 2431, 11 units acc up to 8, (2 bedrm), [shwr, tlt, heat,
elec blkts, TV, clock radio, refrig, cook fac, micro, linen reqd-fee], ldry,
rec rm, lounge, bar, bbq, ✆, plygr, cots. D $66 - $99, ∮ $6 - $9, W $396 -
$594, Breakfast available. BC EFT MC VI.

★★★ **Bonnie View Farm Holidays**, (Log Cabin), Pennys Rd, Heathmere 3305,
off Henty Hwy, 12km N of Portland PO, ☎ 03 5529 2313, fax 03 5529 2313,
2 log cabins acc up to 6, (2 bedrm), [shwr, tlt, heat, TV, clock radio, refrig,
cook fac, toaster, blkts, doonas, linen, pillows], ldry, bbq. D ∮∮ $65, ∮ $6.

★★★ **Centreport Units**, (HF), Cnr Bentinck & Tyers Sts, 300m E of PO,
☎ 03 5523 1882, (2 stry), 5 flats acc up to 6, (1 & 2 bedrm), [shwr, tlt,
hairdry, heat, elec blkts, TV, clock radio, refrig, cook fac, micro, toaster,
ldry (in unit), blkts, linen, pillows], w/mach, dryer, iron, iron brd,
c/park (carport), cots. D ∮∮ $105, ∮ $22, W $440 - $1,050, BC MC VI.

Cape Nelson Lightstation, (Cotg), Cape Nelson Lighthouse Rd, Cape
Nelson 3305, 13km S of Portland, ☎ 03 5523 5100, fax 03 5523 5166,
2 cotgs acc up to 8, (1 & 4 bedrm), [shwr, tlt, fire pl, elec blkts, TV,
video, t/c mkg, refrig, cook fac, micro, toaster], ⊠, cots-fee, breakfast
ingredients, non smoking property. BLB ∮∮ $80 - $100, ∮ $20 - $30,
W ∮∮ $510 - $780, ∮ $130 - $190, ch con, Min book Christmas and
Jan, AE BC DC EFT JCB MC VI, (not yet classified).

VICTORIA HOUSE
AAAT ★★★★
HERITAGE PRIVATE HOTEL
Fine Accommodation

5-7 Tyers Street, Portland Vic. 3305
PHONE: (03) 5521 7577

B&B's/Guest Houses

★★★★☆ **Burswood Homestead Bed &
Breakfast**, (B&B), Classified by National
Trust, 15 Cape Nelson Rd, 1.8km S of PO,
☎ 03 5523 4686, fax 03 5523 7141,
(2 stry gr fl), 5 rms [ensuite, hairdry, fan,
heat, elec blkts, tel, TV, clock radio],
lounge, lounge firepl, t/c mkg shared, courtesy transfer, cots-fee, non
smoking property. BB ∮ $105 - $140, ∮∮ $145 - $220, ∮ $70, ch con,
Single room not listed or included in rating. AE BC DC MC VI.

*Operator Comment: Be our special guest and enjoy a releaxing
stay in the gracious 19th century bluestone mansion of
Edward Henty, Victoria's founding settler, nestled within 12
acres of historic gardens.*

★★★★☆ **Lorelei Bed & Breakfast**, (B&B), 53 Gawler St, 500m SW of
PO, ☎ 03 5523 4466, fax 03 5523 4477, 5 rms [ensuite, shwr,
bath (hip) (1), spa bath (4), tlt, hairdry, a/c, elec blkts, TV, clock radio,
t/c mkg, refrig], iron, iron brd, rec rm, bbq, cots, non smoking rms (5).
BB ∮ $120, ∮∮ $130, ∮ $25, BC EFT MC VI.

★★★★ **Portland Inn**, (B&B), Heritage,
c1840, 4 Percy St, 800m S of PO,
☎ 03 5523 2985, 2 rms [shwr, bath (1),
tlt, hairdry, fan, cent heat, elec blkts, clock
radio], lounge (TV, video, cd, games),
t/c mkg shared, non smoking property.
BB ∮ $95, ∮∮ $110, ∮ $20, BC MC VI.

★★★★ **Victoria House Portland**, (PH), Classified by National Trust, 5
Tyers St, 200m NE of PO, ☎ 03 5521 7577, fax 03 5523 6300, (2 stry
gr fl), 8 rms [ensuite, bath (2), hairdry, fan, heat, elec blkts, tel, TV,
clock radio, t/c mkg, refrig], ldry, lounge (cd), lounge firepl, cots-fee,
non smoking property. RO ∮ $100, ∮∮ $110, ∮ $20, AE BC DC EFT MC VI.

★★★☆ **Whalers Cottage**, (B&B), c1890, 12 Whalers Crt,
☎ 03 5521 7522, fax 03 5521 7522, 4 rms [hairdry, fan, fire pl (2),
heat, elec blkts, clock radio], ldry, lounge (TV, cd), lounge firepl,
t/c mkg shared, refrig, cots, non smoking property. BB ∮∮ $80 - $120,
∮ $10, BC MC VI.

PORTSEA VIC 3944

Pop 749. (97km S Melbourne), See map on page 697, ref A7.
Situated at the termination of the Nepean Hwy, noted for its
excellent beaches. Boating, Bush Walking, Fishing (Ocean, Bay),
Golf, Surfing, Swimming (Beach), Tennis, Water Skiing.

Self Catering Accommodation

★★★★☆ **Portsea Village Resort**, (HU), Previously Synergy Resort
Management. 3765 Point Nepean Rd, ☎ 03 5984 8484,
fax 03 5984 4686, (Multi-stry), 30 units acc up to 8, (1, 2 & 3 bedrm),
[shwr, spa bath, tlt, hairdry, c/fan, heat, tel, cable tv, video, clock radio,
CD, t/c mkg, refrig, cook fac, micro, d/wash, toaster, ldry (in unit),
blkts, doonas, linen, pillows], conf fac, ⊠, bar, pool-heated (salt water
heated), pool indoor heated, sauna, spa, bbq, c/park (undercover), ✆,
gym, squash, tennis, cots. D $195 - $540, W $1,365 - $3,780,
Min book Christmas Jan long w/ends and Easter, AE BC DC EFT MC VI.

B&B's/Guest Houses

★★★★☆ **Peppers Delgany**, (PH), Classified by National Trust, Point Nepean Rd, 500m W of shopping centre, ☎ 03 5984 4000, fax 03 5984 4022, (Multi-stry), 32 rms (17 suites) [shwr, bath, spa bath (13), tlt, hairdry, a/c, cent heat, tel, TV, video-fee, movie, clock radio, t/c mkg, refrig, mini bar], lift, iron, iron brd, rec rm, lounge, conf fac, ⊠, pool-heated, sauna, spa, 24hr reception, gym, tennis. **RO** ♦♦ **$297 - $434**, ch con, AE BC DC EFT MC VI.

Other Accommodation

The Portsea Camp, (Bunk), 3704 Point Nepean Rd, ☎ 03 5984 2333, fax 03 5984 1676, 4 bunkhouses acc up to 42, (Bunk Rooms), [shwr, tlt, refrig (2), blkts, linen, pillows], ldry, cook fac, bbq, BC MC VI.

POWELLTOWN VIC 3797

Pop Part of Yarra Ranges, (80km E Melbourne), See map on page 696, ref D5. Small township in timber milling area.

★★★★ **Millview Cottage**, (Cotg), No children's facilities, 23 Yarra St, 600m SW of PO, ☎ 03 5966 7280, fax 03 5966 7280, 1 cotg acc up to 6, (3 bedrm), [shwr, tlt, hairdry, a/c-cool (lounge), heat, elec blkts, tel, TV, video, radio, CD, refrig, cook fac, micro, toaster, ldry, blkts, linen, pillows], w/mach, iron, iron brd, bbq, breakfast ingredients, non smoking property. **D** ♦♦ **$140**, ◊ **$25**, **W** ♦♦ **$650**, BC EFT MC VI.

PRINCETOWN VIC 3269

Pop Part of Port Campbell, (230km SW Melbourne), See map on pages 694/695, ref C8. Small settlement on the mouth of the Gellibrand River. Port Campbell National Park. Bush Walking, Scenic Drives.

Hotels/Motels

★★★☆ **Twelve Apostles Motel & Country Retreat**, (M), RMB 1435 Booringa Rd, Port Campbell 3269, off Great Ocean Rd, ☎ 03 5598 8277, fax 03 5598 8215, 13 units [shwr, tlt, hairdry, a/c, heat, tel, TV, movie, clock radio, t/c mkg, refrig, micro (4), toaster], iron, iron brd, rec rm, ⊠, pool indoor heated, bbq, dinner to unit, plygr, cots. **RO** ♦ **$66 - $110**, ♦♦ **$77 - $110**, ◊ **$11**, ch con, AE BC DC EFT MC VI.

Operator Comment: We are the closest accommodation to the Twelve Apostles & a multi award winning country retreat. Offering a successful blend of motel, B & B and farm stay with truly Australian hospitality. See our ad under Port Campbell.

Self Catering Accommodation

★★★★ **Glenample**, (Cotg), (Farm), Princetown - Simpson Rd, 900m N of Great Ocean Rd, ☎ 03 5598 8237, fax 03 5598 8234, 2 cotgs acc up to 8, (4 bedrm), [shwr, bath, tlt, hairdry, a/c-cool, heat, elec blkts, TV, video, refrig, cook fac, micro, d/wash (1), toaster, ldry, blkts, linen, pillows], bbq. **D** ♦♦ **$90**, ◊ **$20**, **W** ♦♦ **$560 - $630**, ◊ **$100**.

Operator Comment: Our 900 ha. Farm stretches along the Great Ocean Rd opposite the famous 12 Apostles. Come and enjoy the best of both worlds while staying in one of our secluded farm Cottages.

★★★☆ **Apostles Coastal Retreat**, (Cotg), 1455 Booringa Rd, Port Campbell 3269, off Great Ocean Road, ☎ 03 5598 8277, fax 03 5598 8215, 1 cotg acc up to 8, (3 bedrm), [shwr, tlt, hairdry, a/c-cool, TV, video, clock radio, refrig, cook fac, micro, toaster, ldry, blkts, linen, pillows], lounge firepl, bbq, c/park (garage). **D** ♦♦ **$121 - $176**, **W $770 - $1,150**, Min book Christmas Jan long w/ends and Easter, AE BC DC EFT MC VI.

★★★ **Clifton Lodge**, (Cotg), RMB 1450 Great Ocean Rd, 1.8km NW of bridge, ☎ 03 5598 8128, 5 cotgs acc up to 6, (1 & 2 bedrm), [shwr, tlt, heat, TV, refrig, cook fac, toaster, blkts, linen, pillows], ldry, rec rm, bbq. **D $60 - $80**, **W $360 - $560**, Breakfast by arrangement. BC MC VI.

★★★ **Mackas Family Farm**, (HU), (Farm), 2310 Princetown Rd, 3.8km N of Great Ocean Rd, ☎ 03 5598 8261, fax 03 5598 8201, 2 units acc up to 6, (Studio), [shwr, bath, tlt, heat, clock radio, refrig, cook fac, micro, blkts, linen, pillows], ldry, bbq, cots. **D** ♦♦ **$93.50**, ◊ **$16.50**.

★★★ **Toogoolawah Cottage Retreat**, (Cotg), Latrobe Rd, 6km N of PO, ☎ 03 5598 8222, fax 03 5598 8287, 1 cotg acc up to 2, (1 bedrm), [shwr, tlt, c/fan, heat, elec blkts, TV, video (avail), clock radio, refrig, cook fac, micro, toaster, ldry, blkts, doonas, linen, pillows], iron, iron brd, bbq, **D** ♦♦ **$66 - $88**, Breakfast available. BC MC VI.

★★ **Princetown Cottages**, (Cotg), Great Ocean Rd, 2km E of PO, ☎ 03 5598 8103, 2 cotgs acc up to 4, (2 bedrm), [shwr, tlt, heat, clock radio, refrig, cook fac, micro, toaster, blkts, doonas, linen, pillows], bbq, cots. **D $60 - $80**.

B&B's/Guest Houses

★★★★ **Arabella Country House**, (B&B), 7219 Great Ocean Rd, 6km E of PO, ☎ 03 5598 8169, fax 03 5598 8186, 4 rms [shwr (4), bath (3), spa bath (1), tlt, hairdry, heat, elec blkts, TV, clock radio], dryer, iron, iron brd, ✗, t/c mkg shared, bbq. **BB** ♦ **$95 - $110**, ◊ **$20 - $35**, BC MC VI.

QUEENSCLIFF VIC 3225

Pop 3,850. (103km SW Melbourne), See map on page 697, ref A7. Popular seaside resort. Fort Queenscliff was established in 1882 as a permanent defence over the entrance to Port Phillip Bay. The fort is classified by the National Trust and is now a school for Army Officers. A vehicle and passenger ferry operates between Queenscliff and Sorrento. For enquiries ph 03 5258 3244. Boating, Bowls, Bush Walking, Croquet, Fishing, Golf, Horse Riding, Sailing, Scenic Drives, Surfing, Swimming (Beach), Tennis, Water Skiing. See also Point Lonsdale.

Hotels/Motels

GOLDEN CHAIN

★★★★ **Beacon Resort Motel**, (M), 78 Bellarine Hwy, 3.5km W of PO, opposite Point Lonsdale Rd junction, ☎ 03 5258 1133, fax 03 5258 1152, 9 units [shwr, tlt, hairdry, a/c, elec blkts, tel, TV, video (avail), clock radio, t/c mkg, refrig, toaster], ldry, iron, iron brd, rec rm, pool indoor heated, bbq (covered)-fee, car wash, ☏, plygr, tennis, cots-fee, non smoking units (9). **RO** ♦ **$95 - $135**, ♦♦ **$100 - $135**, ◊ **$20**, AE BC DC EFT MC VI.

★★★★ **(Beacon Holiday Units)**, 5 units acc up to 5, (2 bedrm), [shwr, tlt, heat, elec blkts, tel, TV, video (avail), clock radio, refrig, cook fac, micro, toaster, blkts, linen, pillows], iron, iron brd, non smoking units. **D $90 - $125**, ◊ **$15 - $20**.

★★★★ **Vue Grand Hotel**, (Ltd Lic H), 46 Hesse St, opposite PO, ☎ 03 5258 1544, fax 03 5258 3471, (Multi-stry gr fl), 32 rms [shwr, spa bath (7), tlt, hairdry, cent heat, tel, TV, clock radio, CD, t/c mkg], ldry, iron, iron brd, rec rm, lounge (TV), conf fac, ⊠, bar (cocktail), pool indoor heated, spa, refrig, bbq, ☏, gym, cots-fee. **BB** ♦ **$137.50**, ♦♦ **$231**, **DBB** ♦ **$187**, ♦♦ **$324.50**, ch con, AE BC DC MC VI.

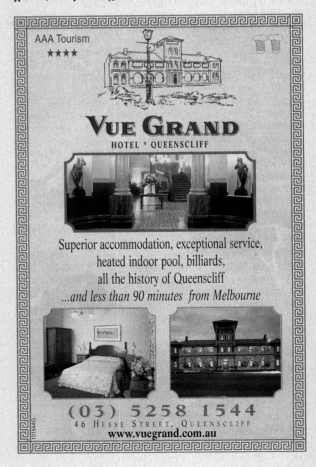

★★★★ **Wyuna Motor Inn**, (M), 32 Hesse St, 60m NE of PO, ☎ 03 5258 4540, fax 03 5258 4636, (2 stry gr fl), 36 units [shwr, spa bath, tlt, hairdry, a/c, elec blkts, tel, TV, clock radio, t/c mkg, refrig, cook fac (1), micro (1)], ldry, iron, iron brd, conf fac, ⊠, cots-fee, non smoking units (3). **RO** ♦ **$99 - $132,** ♦♦ **$99 - $132,** ♦♦♦♦ **$150 - $198,** ch con, Min book long w/ends and Easter, AE BC DC EFT MC VI, ⅋.

★★★☆ **Ozone Hotel**, (Ltd Lic H), c1881, 42 Gellibrand St, 100m SE of PO, ☎ 03 5258 1011, fax 03 5258 3712, (Multi-stry), 20 rms [shwr, bath (2), spa bath (1), tlt, hairdry, heat, elec blkts, tel, TV (8), clock radio, t/c mkg], iron, iron brd, lounge, conf fac, ✕, ⊠, refrig, bbq, ☎. **BB** ♦ **$137.50,** ♦♦ **$154 - $220,** ◊ **$66, DBB** ♦ **$195 - $290,** ♦♦ **$220 - $418,** ◊ **$110,** ch con, AE BC DC MC VI.

★★☆ **Queenscliff Hotel**, (Ltd Lic H), Classified by National Trust, 16 Gellibrand St, 200m NE of PO, ☎ 03 5258 1066, fax 03 5258 1899, (2 stry), 21 rms [basin (6), fire pl (6), elec blkts], ldry, lounge, lounge firepl, ⊠ (Wed - Sun), t/c mkg shared, refrig. ☎. **DBB** ♦ **$120 - $209,** AE BC DC MC VI.

Queenscliffe - Point Lonsdale

Lighthouse Resort Motel   Terminus Bed and Breakfast
• Romantic, Historic Bed & Breakfast Rooms
• Restaurant
• Conference Facilities   **31 Point Lonsdale Road**
• Pool, Tennis Court
• Modern Motel   **Tel (03) 5258 1142**
• Opposite the Beach   **Fax (03) 5258 4223**

Self Catering Accommodation

★★★★ **Historic Gordon Terrace**, (House), c1890, 36 Stokes St, 250m S of PO, ☎ 03 5231 5335, fax 03 5231 5335, (2 stry), 1 house acc up to 4, (2 bedrm), [shwr, bath, tlt, hairdry, fan, heat, elec blkts, TV, clock radio, CD, t/c mkg, refrig, cook fac, micro, elec frypan, toaster, ldry, blkts, linen, pillows], w/mach, iron, iron brd, bbq, breakfast ingredients. D ♦♦ $110 - $190, ۩ $25, W $650 - $1,200, ch con, Min book Christmas Jan long w/ends and Easter.

★★★★ **Suma Park Cottages**, (Cotg), 2135 Bellarine Hwy, 4.5km W of PO, ☎ 03 5258 3507, fax 03 5258 3602, 10 cotgs acc up to 6, (2 bedrm), [ensuite, shwr, tlt, tel, TV, clock radio, t/c mkg, refrig, cook fac ltd, micro, blkts, linen, pillows], rec rm, conf fac, pool-indoor, bbq, tennis. D ♦♦ $90 - $110, ♦♦♦♦ $150 - $185, ۩ $30, ch con, Meals by arrangement. BC DC MC VI.

★★★ **Queenscliff Seaside Cottages**, (Cotg), No facilities for children under 10yrs. 96 Hesse St, ☎ 03 5258 1934, 2 cotgs acc up to 4, (2 bedrm), [shwr, bath (1), spa bath (1), tlt, fan, heat, TV, radio, refrig, cook fac, micro, toaster, ldry (in unit), doonas, linen, pillows], iron, iron brd, lounge firepl (1), bbq, bicycle. D ♦♦ $150, ۩ $25, W $754, Min book applies, BC MC VI.

★★☆ **Riptide Motel**, (HF), 31 Flinders St (Bellarine Hwy), 1.2km SW of PO, ☎ 03 5258 1675, 9 flats acc up to 4, (1 & 2 bedrm), [shwr, tlt, heat, elec blkts, TV, refrig, cook fac, blkts, linen, pillows], ldry, cots. D $66 - $99, W $310 - $590, BC MC VI.

★★ **Springs Caravan Park**, 4 powered tourist sites available. 54 Bellarine Hwy, 4km SW of PO, entrance off Wards Rd, ☎ 03 5258 1895, 2 cabins acc up to 5, [tlt (1), fan, heat, TV, refrig, cook fac, micro, elec frypan, linen reqd], ldry. D $50 - $60.

B&B's/Guest Houses

★★★★☆ **Banks at Queenscliffe**, (B&B), 78A Hesse St, 130m SW of PO, ☎ 03 5258 4326, fax 03 5258 4362, 3 rms (3 suites) [shwr, bath (2), tlt, hairdry, c/fan, heat, elec blkts, clock radio, t/c mkg], ldry, w/mach, dryer, lounge (TV, video), lounge firepl, non smoking property. BB ♦ $120 - $140, ♦♦ $145 - $180, ۩ $45 - $55, ch con, fam con, Min book Christmas Jan long w/ends and Easter, AE BC DC EFT MC VI.

Operator Comment: Luxury accommodation with a splash of decadence. www.tourvic.com.au/Accommodation/banks

★★★★☆ **The Pilot's House Bed & Breakfast**, (B&B), c1876. 50 Gellibrand St, 240m S of PO, ☎ 03 5258 4171, fax 03 5258 4163, 3 rms [ensuite, bath (1), hairdry, fan, cent heat, elec blkts, TV, video, clock radio, ldry], lounge (cd), lounge firepl, t/c mkg shared, refrig, bbq, c/park (garage), non smoking property. BB ♦ $120 - $130, ♦♦ $140 - $150, ۩ $44, Min book long w/ends and Easter, BC MC VI.

★★★★ **Kia-Ora Cottage**, (B&B), No children's facilities, 38 Gellibrand St, 200m SE of PO, ☎ 03 5258 1122, fax 03 5258 1833, 4 rms [ensuite, spa bath (1), cent heat, elec blkts, clock radio], lounge (TV), t/c mkg shared, refrig. BB ♦ $80 - $155, ♦♦ $90 - $165, 1 unit ★★★☆. AE BC MC VI.

Trouble-free travel tips - Tyre wear

Check tyre treads for uneven wear and inspect tyre walls and tread for damage.

★★★★ **Leyton Gables**, (B&B), 35 King St, ☎ 03 5258 3452, 4 rms [ensuite, bath (1), spa bath (2), hairdry, c/fan, heat, elec blkts, TV, clock radio, t/c mkg, refrig], lounge (TV, video), pool (solar heated), bbq, non smoking property. BB ♦ $90 - $125, ♦♦ $100 - $135, ۩ $25, ch con, AE BC MC VI.

★★★★ **Maytone by the Sea**, (GH), Cnr Stevens St & The Esplanade, 1km SW of PO, ☎ 03 5258 4059, fax 03 5258 4071, (2 stry gr fl), 11 rms [ensuite (8), bath (5), c/fan, heat, elec blkts, clock radio, t/c mkg, refrig], lounge (TV), spa (2), t/c mkg shared, non smoking property. BB ♦♦ $110 - $154, ch con, 3 units ★★★☆. Other meals by arrangement. AE BC MC VI.

★★★★ **Seaview House**, (GH), 86 Hesse St, 200m S of PO, ☎ 03 5258 1763, fax 03 5258 4772, (2 stry), 14 rms [ensuite, bath (1), a/c-cool, cent heat, elec blkts, TV, video (10), clock radio, t/c mkg], lounge (TV), ⊠, cots, non smoking property. BLB ♦ $82.50 - $148, ♦♦ $98 - $170, ۩ $20, BC MC VI.

★★★☆ **Queenscliff Lavender Farm**, (B&B), 6 McDonald Rd, 5.5km W of PO, ☎ 03 5258 3389, 1 rm [shwr, tlt, cent heat, TV, radio, refrig, toaster], bbq. BLB ♦ $105, ♦♦ $105.

★★☆ **The Queenscliff Inn**, (GH), 59 Hesse St, 50m S of PO, ☎ 03 5258 4600, fax 03 525883737, (2 stry), 11 rms [heat, elec blkts], bathrm, lounge, lounge firepl, cook fac, non smoking property. BB ♦ $55, ♦♦ $99, ۩ $16, ch con, AE BC DC EFT MC VI.

RAINBOW VIC 3424

Pop 650. (404km NW Melbourne), See map on pages 694/695, ref B3. Farming township in Mallee scrub area. Boating, Bowls, Croquet, Fishing, Golf, Sailing, Scenic Drives, Shooting, Swimming (Pool, Lake), Tennis, Water Skiing.

Hotels/Motels

★★★ **Rainbow Motor Lodge Pot of Gold**, (M), 68-70 Taverner St, 400m SE of PO, ☎ 03 5395 1060, fax 03 5395 1585, 9 units [shwr, tlt, hairdry, a/c-cool, heat, elec blkts, tel, TV, clock radio, t/c mkg, refrig, cook fac (2), toaster], ldry, cots. RO ♦ $47 - $49, ♦♦ $57 - $59, ۩ $10, ch con, AE BC DC EFT MC MCH VI.

RAWSON VIC 3825

Pop 300. (173km E Melbourne), See map on page 696, ref E6. Scenic mountain township close to Thomson Dam, Walhalla & Mt St Gwinear. Bush Walking, Scenic Drives, Snow Skiing, Squash, Swimming, Tennis.

Hotels/Motels

★★☆ **Rawson Village**, (M), Pinnacle Dve, 200m N of PO, ☎ 03 5165 3200, fax 03 5165 3377, 20 units [shwr, tlt, a/c-cool (8), heat, elec blkts, tel (17), TV, clock radio, t/c mkg, refrig], ldry, dry rm, conf fac, ⊠, cots-fee. BB ♦ $60, ♦♦ $88, ۩ $24, ch con, BC MC VI.

(Donnelly & Cornderrk Lodges), 31 rms [basin, heat, elec blkts, t/c mkg], lounge (TV). BB ♦ $44, ♦♦ $66, ۩ $24, ch con.

(Silvan & Cardinia Hostels), 20 rms [shwr, tlt, heat, elec blkts], lounge, t/c mkg shared. RO ♦ $17, ۩ $17, ch con, Minimum booking - 15 people.

RAYMOND ISLAND VIC 3880

Pop 320. (303km E Melbourne), See map on pages 694/695, ref J7. Island situated across McMillan Strait from Paynesville. Served by a free vehicular ferry on a quarter hourly basis. Boat Ramp, Boating, Bush Walking, Fishing, Sailing, Scenic Drives, Swimming (Lake), Water Skiing.

Self Catering Accommodation

★★★★ **Currawong Cottage**, (Cotg), 27 Currawong Cl, 2km NE of Paynesville PO, ☎ 03 5156 7226, fax 03 5156 7226, 1 cotg acc up to 4, (2 bedrm), [shwr, tlt, hairdry, fan, heat, TV, video, clock radio, CD, t/c mkg, refrig, cook fac, micro, blkts, doonas, linen, pillows], w/mach, dryer, iron, iron brd, bbq, jetty, non smoking property. D ♦ $65, ♦♦ $95, ۩ $12, ch con.

★★☆ **Swan Cove Holiday Flats**, (HF), 390 Centre Rd, Off Gravelly Point Rd, ☎ 03 5156 6716, (2 stry), 2 flats acc up to 5, (2 bedrm), [shwr, tlt, fan, heat, elec blkts, TV, clock radio, refrig, cook fac, micro, elec frypan, toaster, blkts, linen reqd-fee, pillows], ldry, w/mach, bbq, mooring, cots. D $55 - $82.50, W $330 - $550.

The Cottage Raymond Island, (Cotg), 27 Seventh Pde, ☎ 03 5657 2268, fax 03 5657 2303, 1 cotg acc up to 6, (3 bedrm), [shwr, tlt, fan, heat (gas), TV, clock radio, t/c mkg, refrig, cook fac, micro, toaster, blkts, doonas, linen, pillows], w/mach, bbq, non smoking property. **D** $90 - $100, **W** $500 - $600, Min book applies, BC MC VI, (not yet classified).

Other Accommodation

Espas Arts Resort & Budget Group Facility, (Lodge), Group accommodation. Lot 2 Eighth Ave, ☎ 03 5156 7275, fax 03 5156 0983, 6 rms acc up to 10, (2 bedrm), [shwr, tlt, heat, blkts, linen reqd-fee, pillows], rec rm, lounge (TV), conf fac, ⊠, pool-heated (solar), jetty, non smoking property. **D** ♦♦ $80, ♦ $20, ch con, Min book Christmas Jan and Easter, BC MC VI, ♿.

RED CLIFFS VIC 3496

Pop 2,550. (541km NW Melbourne), See map on pages 694/695, ref B1. Citrus, dried fruit & wine producing district. Boating, Bowls, Bush Walking, Croquet, Fishing, Golf, Horse Riding, Scenic Drives, Shooting, Swimming (Pool, River), Tennis, Vineyards, Wineries, Water Skiing.

Hotels/Motels

★★★☆ **Red Cliffs Colonial Motor Lodge**, (M), Calder Hwy, 350m NW of PO, ☎ 03 5024 1060, fax 03 5024 3000, (2 stry gr fl), 18 units [shwr, spa bath (5), tlt, hairdry (5), a/c, elec blkts, tel, cable tv, movie, clock radio, t/c mkg, refrig, mini bar, micro (3), toaster], iron (5), iron brd (5), pool, bbq, dinner to unit, cots-fee, non smoking units (6). **RO** ♦ $55 - $94, ♦♦ $66 - $127, ♦ $10, ch con, 5 units ★★★★. AE BC DC EFT MC MP VI, ♿.

★★★ **Big Lizzie Motor Inn**, (M), 133 Jacaranda St (Calder Hwy), 1km S of PO, ☎ 03 5024 2691, fax 03 5024 2691, 24 units [shwr, spa bath (4), tlt, hairdry (4), a/c, elec blkts, tel, TV, clock radio, t/c mkg, refrig, cook fac (4), toaster], ldry, iron (4), iron brd (4), pool (salt water), bbq, cots, non smoking units (20). **RO** ♦ $50 - $80, ♦♦ $60 - $95, ♦ $11, 4 units ★★★☆, AE BC DC MC VI, ♿.

B&B's/Guest Houses

★★★☆ **Mirrabinda**, (B&B), Buloke St, 4km NE of PO, off Cocklin Ave, ☎ 03 5024 1520, fax 03 5024 3354, 3 rms [ensuite (1), spa bath (1), a/c-cool (2), evap cool (1), c/fan (1), heat, clock radio, t/c mkg, refrig, micro (2)], lounge (TV), pool, bbq. **BLB** ♦ $44, ♦♦ $55, pen con.

RED HILL VIC 3937

Pop 2,576. (74km S Melbourne), See map on page 697, ref C8. Small fruit growing district on the Mornington Peninsula. Art Gallery, Bush Walking, Horse Riding, Tennis.

Self Catering Accommodation

★★★★★ **Azimuth Country Estate**, (Cotg), Previously Azimuth B & B. 426 Arthurs Seat Rd, ☎ 03 5989 2807, fax 03 5981 4010, 3 cotgs acc up to 2, (1 bedrm), [shwr, spa bath, tlt, hairdry, a/c, heat, elec blkts, tel, fax, TV, video, clock radio, CD, t/c mkg, refrig, mini bar, cook fac, micro, d/wash, toaster, ldry (in unit), blkts, linen, pillows], w/mach, dryer, iron, iron brd, lounge firepl (2), pool (salt water), bbq, tennis, breakfast ingredients. **BB** $250 - $350, **W** $1,555, Dinner by arrangement. BC DC EFT MC VI.

★★★★ **Ellisfield Farm**, (Cotg), 109 McIlroys Rd, 2.2km E of Mornington - Flinders Rd, ☎ 03 5989 2008, fax 03 5989 2804, 1 cotg acc up to 2, (Studio), [shwr, tlt, hairdry, fan, c/fan, heat (wood), elec blkts, TV, video, clock radio, refrig, cook fac, micro, toaster, blkts, doonas, linen, pillows], ldry, iron, iron brd, bbq, breakfast ingredients, non smoking property. **BB** ♦♦ $125 - $145, ♦♦ $560, BC MC VI.

★★★★ **Wendy Fleetwood Meadowood**, (HU), Beaulieu Rd, Red Hill South 3937, ☎ 03 5989 2368, fax 03 5989 3080, 1 unit acc up to 4, (2 bedrm), [shwr, bath, tlt, hairdry, fan, c/fan, heat (wood), elec blkts, TV, video, clock radio, CD, t/c mkg, refrig, micro, elec frypan, toaster, blkts, doonas, linen, pillows], ldry, w/mach, dryer, iron, iron brd, bbq, tennis, breakfast ingredients. **BB** ♦♦ $135 - $165, ch con, Dinner by arrangement.

★★★☆ **Tallowood Cottage**, (Cotg), 92 Donaldsons Rd, 3km fr general store, ☎ 03 5989 2165, fax 03 5989 3036, 1 cotg acc up to 6, (3 bedrm), [shwr, bath, tlt, hairdry, fan, heat, elec blkts, TV, video, clock radio, CD, t/c mkg, refrig, cook fac, micro, toaster, blkts, doonas, linen, pillows], iron, iron brd, lounge firepl, bbq, breakfast ingredients, non smoking property. **BB** ♦♦ $120 - $140, ♦ $55.

B&B's/Guest Houses

★★★★★ **Lindenderry**, (PH), 142 Arthurs Seat Rd, off Red Hill Rd, ☎ 03 5989 2933, fax 03 5989 2936, (2 stry gr fl), 40 rms [ensuite, spa bath (16), hairdry, a/c, fire pl (5), elec blkts, tel, TV, clock radio, t/c mkg, refrig, mini bar], iron, iron brd, rec rm, lounge, conf fac, ⊠, bar (cocktail), pool-heated, sauna, spa, gym, tennis, cots. **BB** ♦♦ $340 - $495, **DBB** ♦♦ $470 - $625, AE BC DC MC VI.

★★★★☆ **Glenvale Bed & Breakfast**, (B&B), 160 Shoreham Rd, Red Hill South 3937, 300m N of PO, ☎ 03 5989 2625, fax 03 5989 2759, 2 rms [shwr, tlt, hairdry, heat, elec blkts, TV, clock radio, t/c mkg, refrig, toaster], lounge, bbq, cots, non smoking property. **BLB** ♦ $80 - $100, ♦♦ $95 - $120, Min book long w/ends and Easter.

★★★★☆ **Orchard Luxury Accommodation**, (B&B), 45 Thomas Rd, Red Hill South 3937, 3km SW of Red Hill South PO, ☎ 03 5989 3152, fax 03 5989 3153, 3 rms [ensuite, spa bath, hairdry, c/fan, heat, elec blkts, TV, video, clock radio, t/c mkg, refrig], cots, non smoking property. **BB** ♦♦ $120 - $180, BC EFT MC VI.

Operator Comment: Quiet beautiful setting; close to restaurants, wineries, galleries, golf and beaches. Book by email: orchard@cdi.com.au www.the-orchard.com.au

★★★★☆ **Rosebank Cottage**, (B&B), No children's facilities, 144 Red Hill Rd, ☎ 03 5989 2870, 2 rms [ensuite, hairdry, fan, heat, clock radio, t/c mkg (1), refrig (1), micro (1)], lounge (TV, video, cd), lounge firepl, non smoking property. **BB** ♦ $100, ♦♦ $140, BC MC VI.

★★★★☆ **Rosehill Bed & Breakfast**, (B&B), 125 Shoreham Rd (Station Rd), Red Hill South 3937, 200m S of PO, ☎ 03 5989 3110, fax 03 5989 3110, 2 rms [ensuite, bath (1), hairdry, fan, heat, elec blkts, clock radio], lounge (TV, CD, Video), lounge firepl, t/c mkg shared, refrig, bbq. **BB** ♦ $90, ♦♦ $120 - $140, BC MC VI.

★★★★ **Langdons of Red Hill**, (B&B), Previously Pickle Cottage. No children's facilities, 52-54 Arthurs Seat Rd, Red Hill South 3937, ☎ 03 5989 2965, fax 03 5989 2355, 4 rms [ensuite, c/fan, cent heat, radio], lounge (cd player), lounge firepl, res liquor license, t/c mkg shared, refrig, bbq, non smoking property. **BLB** ♦♦ $132 - $160, BC MC VI.

★★★★ **Ridgefield Country House**, (B&B), Children by arrangement. 97 Stanleys Rd, ☎ 03 5989 2116, (2 stry gr fl), 3 rms [ensuite, bath (1), a/c-cool (1), fan, heat, elec blkts, t/c mkg], lounge (TV), lounge firepl, bbq. **BB** ♦♦ $75 - $85, ♦♦ $125 - $140, Dinner by arrangement. Min book all holiday times, BC MC VI.

★★★☆ **Red Hill Retreat**, (B&B), 81 William Rd, 3.2km W of recreation reserve, ☎ 03 5989 2035, fax 03 5989 2427, 2 rms [ensuite, hairdry, a/c (1), fan, heat (wood) (1), elec blkts, TV, video, clock radio, CD (1), t/c mkg, refrig, micro], lounge (TV), bbq, non smoking property. **BB** ♦ $120, ♦♦ $180 - $200, ♦ $50, 1 room ★★★★☆. AE BC DC EFT MC VI.

RHYLL VIC

See Phillip Island Region.

ROBINVALE VIC 3549

Pop 1,750. (470km NW Melbourne), See map on pages 52/53, ref B5. Grape, citrus fruit & vegetable growing area, on Murray River. Euston Weir & Lock 15 (3km downstream). Boating, Bowls, Bush Walking, Fishing, Golf, Greyhound Racing, Scenic Drives, Shooting, Swimming (Pool, River), Tennis, Vineyards, Wineries, Water Skiing.

Hotels/Motels

★★★ **Motel Robinvale**, (M), 112 Bromley Rd (Murray Valley Hwy), 500m W of PO, ☎ 03 5026 3090, fax 03 5026 4306, 14 units [shwr, tlt, a/c-cool (2), evap cool (12), heat, elec blkts, tel, TV, video-fee, clock radio, t/c mkg, refrig, toaster], iron, iron brd, ✗, BYO, pool, bbq, dinner to unit, plygr, cots-fee. **RO** ♦ $44 - $46, ♦♦ $55 - $57, ♦ $11 - $13, AE BC DC EFT MC VI.

★★☆ **Homestyle Motel**, (M), 36 Ronald St, 500m E of PO, ☎ 03 5026 3513, 6 units [shwr, tlt, a/c-cool, heat, elec blkts, tel, TV, clock radio, t/c mkg, refrig, toaster], ldry, bbq, dinner to unit, cots-fee, non smoking units (3). **RO** ♦ $44, ♦♦ $55, ♦♦♦♦ $88, ♦ $11, AE BC MC VI.

ROCHESTER VIC 3561

Pop 2,550. (179km N Melbourne), See map on page 696, ref B2. Situated on Northern Hwy, adjacent Campaspe River. Boating, Bowls, Fishing (River), Golf, Horse Riding, Sailing, Scenic Drives, Shooting, Squash, Swimming (Pool, Lake, River), Tennis, Water Skiing.

Hotels/Motels

★★★ **Rochester Motel**, (M), 24 Echuca Rd (Northern Hwy), 400m W of PO, ☎ 03 5484 1077, fax 03 5484 1078, 14 units [shwr, spa bath (2), tlt, hairdry (2), a/c, elec blkts, tel, TV, video (avail), clock radio, t/c mkg, refrig, micro (2), toaster], pool, bbq, dinner to unit (Mon to Thurs), plygr, cots-fee, non smoking units (6). **RO** ♦♦ $59, ♦ $13, fam con, 2 units ★★★★. AE BC DC EFT MC MCH VI.

ROCHESTER VIC continued...

Other Accommodation

Kimbob, (Bunk), 968 Middleton Rd, Bamawm 3561, 22km SW of Echuca, ☎ 03 5486 5252, 10 bunkhouses acc up to 80, (Bunk Rooms), [linen reqd], rec rm, TV rm, cook fac, refrig, bbq (covered)-fee, plygr. **D ♦ $17.50 - $32, ◊ $17.50 - $32**, Meals by arrangement.

(Camping Section), Limited facilities. (18 pwr), tank water, shwr (4G-4L), tlt (5G-5L), ldry, w/mach, LPG, Pets allowed by prior arrangement. **pwr-site D ♦♦ $12, ◊ $2, un-pwr-site D $5.**

ROMSEY VIC 3434

Pop 2,350. Part of Macedon Ranges, (61km N Melbourne), See map on page 696, ref B4. A small township located in an agricultural district. Bowls, Golf, Squash, Tennis.

B&B's/Guest Houses

★★★★ Morn Moot Bed & Breakfast Farm, (B&B), 100 Crooked Rd, 3km N of PO, ☎ 03 5429 5901, 2 rms [hairdry (1), heat, elec blkts, clock radio, t/c mkg, refrig (1), toaster (1), ldry], iron (1), iron brd (1), lounge (TV), cook fac, bbq, plygr, cots. **BB ♦ $50, ♦♦ $80.**

★★★★ Romsey Gardens Bed & Breakfast, (B&B), 10 Garden Pl, 1.5km S of PO, ☎ 03 5429 5337, fax 03 5429 6152, 2 rms [ensuite, hairdry, fan, heat, elec blkts, TV, video, clock radio, t/c mkg, refrig], iron, iron brd, bbq, non smoking property. **BLB ♦ $82, ♦♦ $93 - $104**, BC MC VI

Operator Comment: Brochure available.
Email: compacct@netcon.net.au
Home Page: http://users.netcon.net.au/compacct

ROSEBUD VIC 3939

Pop 13,275. (77km S Melbourne), See map on page 697, ref B8. Popular bayside resort & residential area. Boating, Bowls, Fishing, Golf, Horse Riding, Sailing, Swimming (Pool, Beach), Tennis, Water Skiing. See also Boneo & Tootgarook.

Hotels/Motels

★★★★ The Admiral, (M), 799 Point Nepean Rd, 800m E of PO, ☎ 03 5986 8933, fax 03 5982 2558, (2 stry gr fl), 12 units [shwr, spa bath (2), tlt, hairdry, a/c, elec blkts, tel, TV, video, clock radio, t/c mkg, refrig, cook fac (2), toaster], ldry, iron, iron brd, bbq, cots, non smoking property. **RO ♦ $76 - $96, ♦♦ $88 - $145, ◊ $12**, AE BC DC EFT MC MP VI.

★★★ Bayview Motor Inn, (M), 1795 Point Nepean Rd, 4km W of PO, Cnr Truemans Rd, ☎ 03 5981 1333, fax 03 5981 2970, (2 stry gr fl), 21 units [shwr, spa bath (7), tlt, hairdry, a/c (12), c/fan, elec blkts, tel, TV, video-fee, clock radio, t/c mkg, refrig, cook fac (1), toaster], ldry, pool-heated (solar), bbq, rm serv, cots. **RO ♦ $85 - $115, ♦♦ $85 - $115, ◊ $10**, ch con, AE BC DC MC VI.

★★☆ Copper Lantern Motel, (M), 1571 Point Nepean Rd, Rosebud West 3940, 1km W of PO, ☎ 03 5986 2220, fax 03 5986 2220, 10 units [shwr, spa bath (1), tlt, c/fan, heat, elec blkts, TV, video-fee, clock radio, t/c mkg, refrig, micro (2), toaster], ☒, spa, bbq, non smoking units (4). **RO ♦ $55 - $121, ♦♦ $61 - $121, ◊ $10**, ch con, BC EFT MC VI.

Self Catering Accommodation

★★★★☆ Nepean Country Club, (Apt), Browns Rd, 4.9km S of PO, West of Boneo Rd, ☎ 03 5986 9800, fax 03 5986 9700, 77 apts acc up to 8, (1 & 2 bedrm), [shwr, spa bath (15), tlt, a/c, elec blkts, tel, TV, video, clock radio, refrig, cook fac, micro, d/wash, toaster, ldry (in unit), blkts, linen, pillows], rec rm, conf fac, ☒, pool (outdoor), pool indoor heated, spa, bbq-fee, plygr, golf, mini golf, gym, squash, tennis. **D ♦♦ $121 - $214.50, ◊ $13.20**, AE BC DC EFT MC VI.

★★★☆ (Motel Section), 32 units [shwr, spa bath, tlt, c/fan, heat, tel, TV, video, clock radio, refrig, micro, toaster], ldry. **RO ♦ $121, ♦♦ $121.**

★★★★☆ Seacove on the Beach, (Apt), 910 Point Nepean Rd, 100m N of PO, ☎ 03 5986 4365, fax 03 5986 7980, 1 apt acc up to 5, (2 bedrm), [shwr, tlt, hairdry, fan, heat, elec blkts, TV, video, clock radio, CD, refrig, cook fac, micro, toaster, ldry, blkts, doonas, linen, pillows], iron, iron brd, pool-heated (Solar), spa, bbq, c/park (carport), non smoking property. **D ♦♦ $125 - $245, ◊ $30 - $55, W ♦♦ $685 - $1,700, ◊ $110 - $150**, Min book Christmas and Jan, AE BC MC VI.

★★★★ Amberlee Four Star Family Holidays, (HU), 306 Jetty Rd, 4km S of PO, ☎ 03 5982 2122, fax 03 5981 2567, (2 stry), 5 units acc up to 6, [shwr, spa bath, tlt, c/fan, heat, refrig, cook fac, micro, toaster, blkts reqd-fee, linen reqd-fee, pillows reqd-fee]. **D ♦♦ $57 - $119, ◊ $25 - $30**, ch con, BC MC VI.

★★★ Rosebud by the Bay, (HU), 3/757 Point Nepean Rd, 700m E of pier, ☎ 03 5986 1433, fax 03 5986 2232, 1 unit acc up to 5, (2 bedrm), [shwr, tlt, hairdry, evap cool, fan, heat, elec blkts, TV, video, clock radio, CD, t/c mkg, refrig, cook fac, micro, elec frypan, toaster, ldry, blkts, doonas, linen, pillows], w/mach, iron, iron brd, plygr, cots. **D ♦♦ $50, W $350 - $945**, Min book Christmas Jan and Easter, BC MC VI.

★★★ Beachside Apartments Rosebud, (HU), 860 Point Nepean Rd, 400m E of PO, ☎ 03 5986 1433, fax 03 5986 2232, 3 units acc up to 5, (2 bedrm), [shwr, tlt, hairdry, fan, heat, elec blkts, TV, clock radio, t/c mkg, refrig, cook fac, micro, elec frypan, toaster, blkts, doonas, linen, pillows], w/mach, iron, iron brd, pool, bbq-fee, cots. **W $350 - $945**, Min book Christmas Jan and Easter, BC MC VI.

★★☆ Dixey Court Holiday Flats, (HF), 7 Chatfield Ave, Rosebud West 3940, 2.8km W of PO, ☎ 03 5986 5208, 6 flats acc up to 5, (2 bedrm), [shwr, tlt, fan, heat, TV, clock radio, refrig, cook fac, toaster, linen reqd-fee], ldry, iron, iron brd, bbq. **D $66 - $130, W $264 - $572.**

B&B's/Guest Houses

★★★★ 4th Ave B&B, (B&B), 115 Fourth Ave, 2km SW of PO, ☎ 03 5986 6663, 1 rm (3 bedrm), [ensuite (1), shwr, bath, tlt, hairdry, c/fan, heat, TV, video, clock radio, t/c mkg, refrig, cook fac, micro, elec frypan, d/wash, toaster, ldry, pillows], w/mach, dryer, iron, iron brd, bbq, cots, breakfast ingredients, non smoking property. **BB ♦ $60 - $90, ♦♦ $90 - $120, ◊ $60 - $90**, ch con.

★★★☆ Inglewood Bed & Breakfast, (B&B), 268 Jetty Rd, ☎ 03 5986 1552, fax 03 5986 1552, 2 rms (1 suite) [shwr, tlt, hairdry, fan, c/fan, heat, elec blkts, clock radio, t/c mkg], lounge (TV). **BB ♦ $70, ♦♦ $100, Suite BB ♦♦ $120**, AE BC MC VI.

★★★☆ Tapestry House, (B&B), 6 Morgan St, 1km E of PO, ☎ 03 5986 4119, fax 03 5981 2424, 2 rms [a/c, c/fan, elec blkts, clock radio, t/c mkg, refrig, micro, toaster], lounge (TV, video, cd), spa, bbq, non smoking property. **BB ♦ $90, ♦♦ $132, ♦♦♦♦ $198**, AE BC MC VI.

ROSEDALE VIC 3847

Pop 1,154. (187km E Melbourne), See map on pages 694/695, ref G7. Centre of an agricultural & pastoral district, on the La Trobe River. Holey Plains State Park. Bowls, Fishing, Golf, Scenic Drives, Squash, Swimming (Pool), Tennis.

Hotels/Motels

★★★ Coach-Lamp Motel, (M), Princes Hwy, 400m W of PO, ☎ 03 5199 2301, fax 03 5199 2862, 10 units [shwr, tlt, a/c, elec blkts, tel, TV, video-fee, clock radio, t/c mkg, refrig, toaster], ✕ (BYO), dinner to unit, plygr, cots-fee. **RO ♦ $40 - $45, ♦♦ $46 - $54, ◊ $9**, ch con, AE BC DC MC VI.

★★☆ Rosedale Motel, (M), Princes Hwy, 500m W of PO, ☎ 03 5199 2555, fax 03 5199 2406, 14 units [shwr, tlt, a/c, elec blkts, tel, TV, clock radio, t/c mkg, refrig], ldry, dinner to unit, cots-fee. **RO ♦ $36 - $39.60, ♦♦ $42 - $46.20, ◊ $8 - $8.80**, ch con, pen con, BC MC VI.

ROTAMAH ISLAND VIC 3880

Pop Nominal, (282km E Melbourne), See map on pages 694/695, ref J7. Island situated between Lake Victoria and Ninety Mile Beach. Boating, Bush Walking, Fishing, Sailing, Swimming.

Other Accommodation

Rotamah Island Bird Observatory, (Lodge), Solar power within National Park. ☎ 03 5156 6398, fax 03 5156 6398, 5 rms acc up to 16, [shwr (2), tlt (2), linen reqd], tank water, lounge, t/c mkg shared, refrig, bbq, non smoking property. **D all meals ♦ $71.50, ◊ $71.50**, ch con, National Park regulations prohibit all pets and firearms. Self catering by arrangement.

RUFFY VIC 3666

Pop Part of Euroa, (134km NE Melbourne), See map on page 696, ref D3. Situated near Strathbogie Ranges in Granite Boulder Country. Bush Walking, Fishing, Scenic Drives, Shooting, Swimming.

Self Catering Accommodation

★★★★ Binnum Cottage, (Cotg), 'Frithwood' RMB 2607 McLean's La, ☎ 03 5790 4312, fax 03 5790 4213, 1 cotg acc up to 3, (2 bedrm), [shwr, tlt, hairdry, fan, c/fan, heat, elec blkts, TV, video, clock radio, refrig, cook fac, micro, elec frypan, toaster, ldry (in unit), blkts, doonas, linen, pillows], w/mach, iron, iron brd, bbq, c/park (carport), breakfast ingredients, non smoking property. **BB ♦♦ $115, ◊ $20**, BC MC VI.

RUSHWORTH VIC 3612

Pop 1,000. (163km N Melbourne), See map on page 696, ref C2. Gold & Iron Bark Country. Boating, Bowls, Bush Walking, Fishing, Gold Prospecting, Golf, Horse Riding, Motor Racing, Sailing, Scenic Drives, Shooting, Swimming (Pool, Lake, River), Tennis, Water Skiing.

Hotels/Motels

★★★ **Rushworth Motel**, (M), 4 School St, ☎ 03 5856 1090, fax 03 5856 1090, 8 units [shwr, tlt, hairdry, a/c, elec blkts, TV, clock radio, t/c mkg, refrig, micro, toaster], pool, bbq. **RO ♦ $55, ♦♦ $61 - $64, ♦ $11**, AE BC MC VI.

Other Accommodation

Lake Waranga Caravan Park & Holiday Camp, (Lodge), 98 Waranga Basin Rd, 5km N of PO, ☎ 03 5856 1243, fax 03 5856 1243, 12 rms [ensuite (2), blkts reqd, linen reqd, pillows], ldry, lounge (TV, video), lounge firepl, pool, cook fac, t/c mkg shared, refrig, bbq, kiosk, ✆, plygr, canoeing. **D ♦ $13.50 - $17, ♦ $13.50 - $17**, ch con, Catering by arrangement. Minimum booking - 20 people, AE BC MC VI, ♿.

RUTHERGLEN VIC 3685

Pop 1,900. (274km NE Melbourne), See map on pages 694/695, ref G4. The hub of Victoria's North-East Wineries. Boating, Bowls, Bush Walking, Fishing, Golf, Rowing, Scenic Drives, Shooting, Swimming (Pool), Tennis, Vineyards, Wineries, Water Skiing. See also Corowa & Wahgunyah.

Hotels/Motels

★★★★ **The Vineyards at Tuileries**, (M), Drummond St, 700m W of PO, ☎ 02 6032 9033, fax 02 6032 8296, 5 units [shwr, spa bath, tlt, hairdry, a/c, elec blkts, tel, TV, video, clock radio, t/c mkg, refrig, mini bar, micro], iron, iron brd, lounge, conf fac, ✉ (Mon to Sun), res liquor license, pool-heated, bbq, rm serv, tennis, non smoking units (5). **BB ♦ $165, ♦♦ $165, ♦ $20**, AE BC DC EFT MC VI.

★★★★ **Walkabout Motel**, (M), 15 Moodemere St (Murray Valley Hwy), 750m W of PO, ☎ 02 6032 9572, fax 02 6032 8187, 9 units [shwr, spa bath (3), tlt, hairdry, a/c, fire pl (1), elec blkts, tel, TV, video, clock radio, t/c mkg, refrig, toaster, ldry], iron, iron brd, pool above ground, spa, bbq, dinner to unit, plygr, cots, non smoking units. **RO ♦ $59 - $82, ♦♦ $72 - $120, ♦ $16**, AE BC DC MC VI.

★★★★ **Wine Village Motor Inn**, (M), 217 Main St (Murray Valley Hwy), 600m W of PO, ☎ 02 6032 9900, fax 02 6032 8125, 16 units [shwr, spa bath (1), tlt, hairdry, a/c, elec blkts, tel, cable tv, clock radio, t/c mkg, refrig, mini bar, toaster], ldry, iron, iron brd, pool, bbq, plygr, cots-fee, non smoking units (12). **RO ♦ $75 - $88, ♦♦ $82 - $98, ♦ $11**, Minimum booking may apply, AE BC DC EFT MC VI, ♿.

★★★☆ **Motel Woongarra**, (M), Cnr Drummond & Main Sts (Murray Valley Hwy), 600m W of PO, ☎ 02 6032 9588, fax 02 6032 9951, 12 units [shwr, tlt, a/c, elec blkts, tel, TV, video, clock radio, t/c mkg, refrig, toaster], ldry, pool, bbq, plygr, cots-fee, non smoking units (6). **RO ♦ $49.50 - $77, ♦♦ $60.50 - $77, ♦ $11**, AE BC DC MC MCH VI.

★★★☆ **Rutherglen Motor Inn**, (M), 10 Moodemere St (Murray Valley Hwy), 1km W of PO, ☎ 02 6032 9776, fax 02 6032 9495, 15 units [shwr, tlt, a/c-cool, heat, elec blkts, tel, TV, video-fee, clock radio, t/c mkg, refrig, mini bar, toaster], ldry, pool, bbq, dinner to unit, plygr, cots, non smoking units (10). **RO ♦ $55 - $88, ♦♦ $66 - $99, ♦ $16.50**, ch con, AE BC DC EFT MC VI.

★★★ **Poachers Paradise Hotel Pty Ltd**, (M), 97 Murray St, 800m W of PO, ☎ 02 6032 7373, fax 03 6032 7374, 10 units [spa bath (2), hairdry, a/c, heat, elec blkts, TV, clock radio, t/c mkg, refrig, toaster], ldry, iron, cots, non smoking units (10). **BLB ♦♦ $80, ♦ $11**, BC EFT MC VI, ♿.

★★ **Star Hotel Rutherglen**, (LMH), 105 Main St (Murray Valley Hwy), ☎ 02 6032 9625, fax 02 6032 8081, 6 units [shwr, tlt, a/c, TV, clock radio, t/c mkg, refrig, toaster], ✉, ✆. **RO ♦ $30, ♦♦ $50, ♦ $20**, ch con.

Self Catering Accommodation

★★★★ **'Cuddle Doon' Cottages Rutherglen**, (Cotg), 13 Hunter St, 750m NE of PO, ☎ 02 6032 7107, 1 cotg acc up to 4, (2 bedrm), [shwr, spa bath, tlt, hairdry, a/c, c/fan (1), heat, elec blkts, TV, video, clock radio, CD, refrig, cook fac, micro, blkts, linen, pillows], iron, iron brd, bbq, non smoking property. **D ♦♦ $143 - $165, ♦ $20 - $25**, Min book applies, BC MC VI.

B&B's/Guest Houses

★★★★ **A Country Experience**, (B&B), Classified by National Trust, Previously Mt Ophir (Farm), Mount Ophir Estate, Stillards Lane, 5.7km SE of PO, off Chiltern Rd, ☎ 02 6032 8920, fax 02 6032 9911, 7 rms [spa bath (suite) (7), a/c (1), fan, heat, elec blkts], w/mach, lounge, lounge firepl, t/c mkg shared, non smoking property. **BB ♦♦ $180 - $500, ♦ $90 - $110, DBB ♦♦ $290 - $645, ♦ $145 - $165**, ch con, pen con, 3 rooms ★★★☆. BC MC VI.

★★★☆ **(Gatehouse Cottage Section)**, Classified by National Trust, 1 cotg acc up to 12, (4 bedrm), [ensuite (2), shwr, tlt, evap cool, c/fan, heat, TV, clock radio, cook fac, micro, toaster, ldry, blkts, linen, pillows], lounge firepl, bbq, cots. **D $150 - $450, W $1,200**, ch con, Min book applies.

★★★★ **Cannobie Country House**, (B&B), Cnr Jacks Rd & Grahams La, 3km W of PO, ☎ 02 6032 9524, fax 02 6032 9524, 2 rms [ensuite (1), shwr (1), bath (1), tlt (1), heat, elec blkts, radio], lounge (tv, video), t/c mkg shared, bbq, tennis. **BB ♦ $95, ♦♦ $143, ♦ $28**, Dinner by arrangement. BC MC VI.

★★★★ **Carlyle House Rutherglen**, (B&B), No children's facilities, 147 High St, 100m SW of PO, ☎ 02 6032 8444, fax 02 6032 7119, 6 rms (1 suite) (Studio), [shwr, tlt, a/c, fan (2), c/fan (4), heat, elec blkts, clock radio], iron, iron brd, lounge (TV, video, cd), lounge firepl, t/c mkg shared, refrig, non smoking property. **BB ♦ $110, ♦♦ $130 - $155, Suite BB ♦ $145, ♦♦ $185**, 1 suite & 1 room ★★★★☆. Studios yet to be rated. Min book long w/ends, AE BC EFT MC VI.

★★★★ **Country Cottage Accommodation**, (B&B), 2 Moodemere St, ☎ 02 6032 8328, fax 02 6032 7328, 3 rms (1 & 3 bedrm - cottages), [ensuite, a/c-cool, heat (gas), elec blkts, TV, clock radio, t/c mkg, refrig, mini bar, micro, toaster, ldry (1)], pool, bbq, non smoking property. **BB ♦ $55, ♦♦ $90, ♦ $50**, ch con, BC MC VI.

★★★★ **Holroyd Bed & Breakfast**, (B&B), 28 Church St, 500m S of PO, ☎ 02 6032 8218, fax 02 6032 7511, 2 rms [ensuite (1), shwr (1), bath (1), tlt (1), hairdry, a/c-cool, evap cool, c/fan, heat, elec blkts], lounge (cable TV, video, CD), t/c mkg shared, non smoking property. **BB ♦♦ $100 - $130**, Min book long w/ends, BC MC VI.

★★★★ **Lake Moodemere Homestead**, (B&B), (Farm), Cnr Murray Valley Hwy & Moodemere Rd, 6.2km W of PO, ☎ 02 6032 8650, fax 02 6032 8118, 3 rms [hairdry, a/c-cool (lounge), c/fan, heat, elec blkts], ldry, lounge (TV, video, cd), lounge firepl, t/c mkg shared. **BB ♦ $110, ♦♦ $140, ♦ $110**, BC MC VI.

★★★☆ **Greenmount B & B**, (B&B), Mia Mia Rd, 14.4km E of PO, ☎ 02 6026 7237, 3 rms [ensuite (1), evap cool, c/fan, heat, elec blkts, clock radio], lounge (TV, stereo). **BB ♦ $50, ♦ $50**.

RYE VIC 3941

Pop 7,284. (85km S Melbourne), See map on page 697, ref B8. A popular bayside community with good beaches. Boating, Bowls, Fishing, Golf, Horse Riding, Sailing, Surfing, Swimming (Beach), Tennis, Water Skiing. See also Rosebud & Tootgarook.

Self Catering Accommodation

★★★★ **St Andrews by the Sea**, (House), 5 Moana Crt, 7km S of PO, ☎ 0414 926 446, 1 house acc up to 6, (2 bedrm), [shwr, bath, tlt, hairdry, heat, TV, video, clock radio, refrig, cook fac, micro, elec frypan, d/wash, toaster, blkts, doonas, linen, pillows], w/mach, dryer, iron, iron brd, lounge firepl, bbq. **D ♦♦ $150, ♦ $25, W ♦♦ $900, ♦ $160**, Min book Christmas and Jan, BC MC VI.

B&B's/Guest Houses

★★★★★ **Acacia Rye**, (B&B), No children's facilities, 32 Bethany Cl, 2.5km S of Yacht Club, ☎ 03 5985 8820, fax 03 5985 1377, 2 rms [ensuite, spa bath, hairdry, a/c, elec blkts, tel, TV, video, clock radio, CD], lounge, lounge firepl (gas log), pool-heated (solar), spa, t/c mkg shared, refrig, bbq, non smoking property. **BB ♦♦ $195 - $245**, Min book Christmas Jan long w/ends and Easter, BC MC VI.

★★★★☆ **Hilltonia Homestead**, (B&B), Lot B1 Browns Rd, ☎ 03 5985 2654, fax 03 5985 2684, 1 rm [shwr, spa bath, tlt, hairdry, a/c, c/fan, heat, elec blkts, TV, video, clock radio, CD, t/c mkg, refrig, mini bar, micro], rec rm, pool-heated (solar), bbq (covered), tennis, non smoking property. **BB ♦♦ $180 - $210**, AE BC DC EFT MC VI.

★★★★☆ **Rumdoodle Retreat**, (B&B), 26 Horners La, 1km W of PO, via Minimurra Rd, ☎ 03 5985 1114, fax 03 5985 8497, 2 rms (1 suite) [shwr, spa bath (1), tlt, hairdry, a/c-cool, c/fan, cent heat, elec blkts, TV, video (avail), clock radio, CD, t/c mkg, refrig, toaster, doonas], spa (heated), non smoking suites. BB ♦♦ $190 - $220, Other meals by arrangement. AE BC JCB MC VI.

★★★★☆ **Weeroona**, (B&B), 26 Creedmore Dve, ☎ 03 5985 3946, fax 03 5985 2761, 7 rms (7 suites) [ensuite, spa bath (4), hairdry, a/c, elec blkts, TV, video, CD, t/c mkg, refrig, cook fac, micro], iron, iron brd, bbq, non smoking property. BB ♦♦ $187, ch con, BC EFT MC VI.

Westbrook by the Bay, (B&B), 11 Stratheden Crt, 500m E of Blairgowrie PO, ☎ 03 5985 2644, fax 03 5985 2644, 3 rms [cent heat, elec blkts, TV], lounge (TV, cd player), pool indoor heated-fee, sauna, t/c mkg shared, bbq, non smoking rms. BB ♦ $95 - $130, ♦♦ $130 - $150, ◊ $95 - $130, (Rating under review).

SAFETY BEACH VIC 3936

Pop 1,400. (70km S Melbourne), See map on page 697, ref C7. Small bayside location, derives its name from the safe children's beach. Boating, Fishing, Swimming (Beach), Water Skiing.

Self Catering Accommodation

★★★★ **The Valley Resort Mt Martha Valley**, (Apt), Country Club Dve, ☎ 03 5987 3535, fax 03 5981 0878, 9 apts acc up to 4, (1 & 2 bedrm), [shwr, spa bath, tlt, hairdry, a/c, TV, clock radio, t/c mkg, refrig, cook fac ltd, micro, blkts], ⊠, pool, bbq, golf, tennis. D $170 - $205, AE BC DC EFT MC VI.

B&B's/Guest Houses

★★★★☆ **Stroud House**, (B&B), 16 Berry Crt, ☎ 03 5988 4962, 2 rms (1 suite) [ensuite, hairdry, a/c (in lounge), c/fan, heat, elec blkts, clock radio, t/c mkg, refrig, micro, doonas], lounge (cable TV, cd, video), lounge firepl (gas log), bbq, c/park (undercover), non smoking property. Suite BLB ♦♦ $95 - $130, ◊ $15.

★★★★ **Bluestone Homestead**, (B&B), Pickings Rd, ☎ 03 5981 4073, 2 rms [ensuite, hairdry, c/fan, cent heat, elec blkts, TV, clock radio, t/c mkg, refrig], lounge (TV, video, cd), lounge firepl, pool, bbq, non smoking property. BB ♦♦ $100, ch con, BC DC MC VI.

★★★☆ **Palms on Waters Edge**, (B&B), 152 Marine Dve, ☎ 03 5981 0129, 1 rm [shwr, tlt, hairdry, fan, cent heat, elec blkts, TV, clock radio, t/c mkg, refrig, micro, toaster], iron, iron brd, bbq. BLB ♦♦ $70 - $95, Min book Christmas Jan long w/ends and Easter.

SALE VIC 3850

Pop 13,350. (214km E Melbourne), See map on pages 694/695, ref H7. Located at the junction of Princes & South Gippsland Hwys. Administration centre for Victoria's off shore oil & natural gas fields. RAAF base. Boating, Bowls, Bush Walking, Croquet, Fishing, Golf, Greyhound Racing, Horse Racing, Sailing, Scenic Drives, Shooting, Swimming (Pool), Tennis, Water Skiing.

Hotels/Motels

★★★★ **Aspen Motor Inn**, (M), 342 York St (Princes Hwy), 400m E of PO, ☎ 03 5144 3888, fax 03 5143 1530, 23 units [shwr, tlt, hairdry, a/c, elec blkts, tel, TV, video (13), clock radio, t/c mkg, refrig, mini bar, micro-fee], iron, iron brd, dinner to unit, cots-fee, non smoking units (10). RO ♦ $74 - $96, ♦♦♦ $79 - $99, ◊ $11, AE BC DC JCB MC MP VI.

★★★★ **The King Avenue Motor Inn**, (M), 20 Princes Hwy, 1.9km NE of PO, ☎ 03 5143 2222, fax 03 5143 2000, (2 stry gr fl), 33 units (1 suite) [shwr, spa bath (5), tlt, hairdry, a/c, elec blkts, tel, TV, video-fee, clock radio, t/c mkg, refrig, mini bar, cook fac (1), micro (1)], ldry, iron, iron brd, ⊠, bar (cocktail), rm serv, dinner to unit, cots-fee, non smoking units (14). RO ♦ $149 - $240, ♦♦ $161 - $240, ◊ $16, ch con, AE BC DC MC VI.

★★★★ **The Princeton Motor Lodge & Convention Centre**, (M), 25 Princes Hwy, 1.9km NE of PO, ☎ 03 5144 6599, fax 03 5144 5166, (2 stry gr fl), 30 units [shwr, spa bath (2), tlt, a/c, elec blkts, tel, TV, video-fee, clock radio, t/c mkg, refrig], iron, iron brd, conf fac, ⊠, sauna-fee, squash-fee, cots-fee. RO ♦ $115 - $155, ♦♦ $126 - $155, ◊ $16, ch con, AE BC DC EFT MC VI, ♿.

★★★☆ **Riverstay**, (LMH), 1 Princes Hwy, 2km W of PO, ☎ 03 5144 3222, fax 03 5144 3401, 30 units [shwr, tlt, a/c, elec blkts (on request), tel, TV, video (5), clock radio, t/c mkg, refrig], iron (20), iron brd (20), conf fac, ⊠, bbq, dinner to unit, plygr, cots-fee, non smoking units (12). RO ♦ $40 - $65, ♦♦ $55 - $76, ◊ $10, ch con, 10 units ★★★, AE BC DC EFT MC VI.

★★★☆ **Sale Hacienda International Motor Inn**, (M), Cnr Princes Hwy & Raymond St, 500m S of PO, ☎ 03 5144 1422, fax 03 5144 4704, (2 stry gr fl), 54 units [shwr, tlt, hairdry (54), a/c, elec blkts, tel, TV, clock radio, t/c mkg, refrig, mini bar], ldry, iron, iron brd, conf fac, ⊠ (Mon to Sat), pool, rm serv, cots-fee, non smoking units (44). RO ♦ $76 - $84, ♦♦ $92 - $98, ◊ $14, ch con, AE BC DC EFT MC MP VI.

★★★ **Ace Swan Motel**, (M), 386 York St (Princes Hwy), 1.6km NE of PO, ☎ 03 5144 3096, fax 03 5144 3096, 16 units [shwr, tlt, a/c, c/fan (4), elec blkts, tel, TV, video-fee, clock radio, t/c mkg, refrig, cook fac (1), micro], bbq, plygr, cots-fee, non smoking units (8). RO ♦ $50 - $60, ♦♦ $60 - $70, ◊ $11, ch con, AE BC MC VI.

★★★ **Captain's Lodge Intl Motel & VIP Restaurant**, (M), 46 Princes Hwy, 2.4km W of PO, ☎ 03 5144 3766, fax 03 5143 1311, 30 units [shwr, tlt, hairdry, a/c, elec blkts, tel, TV, clock radio, t/c mkg, refrig], ldry, ⊠, pool, rm serv, ☏, plygr, cots-fee, non smoking units (20). RO ♦ $50 - $85, ♦♦ $50 - $95, pen con, 15 units ★★★☆, AE BC DC JCB MC VI.

★★★ **Midtown Motor Inn Sale**, (M), Cnr York (Princes Hwy) & Bond Sts, 600m SE of PO, ☎ 03 5144 1444, fax 03 5143 1001, (2 stry gr fl), 58 units [shwr, tlt, a/c, elec blkts, tel, TV, video-fee, clock radio, t/c mkg, refrig], ldry, ⊠, pool, rm serv, plygr, cots-fee, non smoking units (20). RO ♦ $67.10 - $73.70, ♦♦ $73.70 - $85.80, ◊ $13.20, ch con, AE BC DC JCB MC MP VI.

★★★ **Sale Motel**, (M), Cnr York (Princes Hwy) & Stawell Sts, 500m N of Lake Guthridge, ☎ 03 5144 2744, fax 03 5143 3122, (2 stry gr fl), 12 units (1 suite) [shwr, spa bath (1), tlt, a/c (5), fan (7), heat, elec blkts, tel, TV, video-fee, clock radio, t/c mkg, refrig, cook fac (1), micro (1), toaster], cots-fee. RO ♦ $52 - $60, ♦♦ $63 - $68, ◊ $10, Suite RO ♦♦ $108, ◊ $10, ch con, Breakfast available. AE BC DC MC MCH VI.

Self Catering Accommodation

★★★ **Swan Historic Miners Cottage**, (Cotg), 101 Pearson St, ☎ 03 5144 3866, fax 03 5144 3866, 1 cotg acc up to 6, (2 bedrm), [shwr, bath, spa bath, tlt, hairdry, fan, heat, elec blkts, TV, clock radio, t/c mkg, refrig, cook fac, micro, toaster, ldry (in unit), blkts, doonas, linen, pillows], w/mach, iron, iron brd, lounge firepl. D ♦♦ $95 - $135, ◊ $11, AE BC MC VI.

★★★ **The Creek Bed & Breakfast**, (Cotg), 51 York St, ☎ 03 5144 4426, fax 03 5144 2613, 1 cotg acc up to 6, (3 bedrm), [fan, heat, elec blkts, TV, clock radio, t/c mkg, refrig, cook fac, micro, toaster, ldry], lounge firepl, breakfast ingredients. **BB** ♯♯ **$95 - $105**, ◊ **$40**, AE BC MC VI.

B&B's/Guest Houses

★★★★ **Bon Accord Bed & Breakfast & Tea Rooms**, (B&B), c1860 homestead, 153 Dawson St, ☎ 03 5144 5555, fax 03 5144 5555, 5 rms [ensuite (3), hairdry, heat, clock radio], lounge (TV, video), bbq. **BB** ♦ **$121**, ♯♯ **$154**, 2 rooms ★★★☆. Other meals by arrangement. AE BC DC MC VI.

★★★★ **The Creek Bed & Breakfast**, (B&B), 3 Foster St (Princes Hwy), opposite Information Centre, ☎ 03 5144 4426, fax 03 5144 2613, 2 rms [ensuite (1), shwr, tlt, hairdry, fire pl (1), heat, elec blkts, clock radio], lounge (TV, cd), t/c mkg shared, refrig. **BB $130, D $95 - $160**, AE BC MC VI.

SAN REMO VIC

See Phillip Island Region.

SANDY POINT VIC 3959

Pop Nominal, (201km SE Melbourne), See map on page 696, ref D8. Surf beach, situated on Waratah Bay. Boating, Fishing, Sailing, Surfing, Swimming (Pool, Beach), Tennis, Water Skiing.

Self Catering Accommodation

★★★☆ **Doonagatha**, (Cotg), (Farm), Sandy Point Rd, ☎ 03 5687 1356, fax 03 5687 1356, 1 cotg acc up to 8, (5 bedrm), [shwr, bath (hip), tlt, hairdry, fan, heat, elec blkts, tel, TV, video, clock radio, t/c mkg, refrig, cook fac, micro, elec frypan, toaster, blkts, linen-fee, pillows], w/mach, iron, iron brd, lounge firepl, bbq, c/park (garage), cots. **D** ♯♯ **$100 - $130**, ◊ **$10, W $700 - $900**, Min book Christmas Jan long w/ends and Easter.

★★★ **Iluka Holiday Cottages - Sandy Point**, (Cotg), Cnr Manuka & Anderson Sts, ☎ 03 5682 2761, fax 03 5682 2761, 4 cotgs acc up to 6, (2 bedrm), [shwr, bath (hip), tlt, heat (wood), TV, video, clock radio, refrig, cook fac, micro, toaster, ldry (in unit), doonas, linen reqd-fee], bbq, cots. **W $400 - $735**, Min book Christmas Jan and Easter.

SARSFIELD VIC 3875

Pop Nominal, (298km E Melbourne), See map on pages 694/695, ref J7. Situated on the Great Alpine Rd between Bairnsdale and Bruthen. Scenic Drives.

★★★★ **Allitra**, (B&B), 225 Duncan Rd, 16km NE of Bairnsdale, ☎ 03 5156 8885, fax 03 5156 8885, 1 rm (1 suite) [shwr, tlt, fan, heat, elec blkts, TV, video (avail), clock radio, t/c mkg, refrig, micro], bbq, non smoking property. **BB** ♦ **$55**, ♯♯ **$70**, ◊ **$20**.

SASSAFRAS VIC

See Dandenong Ranges Region.

SEA LAKE VIC 3533

Pop 700. (362km NW Melbourne), See map on pages 694/695, ref C3. Centre of wheat growing, sheep & cattle raising area. Green Lake - 10.5km S on Birchip Rd. Croquet, Golf, Horse Riding, Scenic Drives, Swimming (Pool), Tennis.

★★ **Motel Thisledome**, (M), Calder Hwy, 1km S of PO, ☎ 03 5070 1252, 16 units [shwr, tlt, a/c, elec blkts, TV, t/c mkg, refrig], ✕ (Mon to Thurs), BYO, pool, plygr, cots-fee. **RO** ♦ **$49.50**, ♯♯ **$60.50**, ◊ **$7**, ch con, AE BC DC MC VI.

SELBY VIC

See Dandenong Ranges Region.

SEVILLE VIC 3139

Pop 1,600. Part of Yarra Ranges, (50km NE Melbourne), See map on page 696, ref C5. Centre of a large area producing berry fruits. Vineyards, Wineries.

Self Catering Accommodation

★★★★ **Merrigum Cottage**, (Cotg), (Farm), c1903, Douthie Rd, Seville East 3139, 6.5km SE of PO, ☎ 03 5964 8462, fax 03 5964 8550, 1 cotg acc up to 4, (2 bedrm), [shwr, bath, tlt, hairdry, a/c, fan, heat, elec blkts, TV, video, clock radio, CD, refrig, cook fac, micro, elec frypan, toaster, ldry, blkts, doonas, linen, pillows], w/mach, dryer, iron, iron brd, lounge firepl, bbq, non smoking property. **BB $150 - $185**, ◊ **$25, W** ♯♯ **$700**, ◊ **$50**.

★★★☆ **Zamira Cottage**, (Cotg), 631 Victoria Rd, Victoria Rd, ☎ 03 5964 3110, fax 03 5964 3110, 1 cotg acc up to 4, (2 bedrm), [shwr, bath, tlt, hairdry, fan, heat, elec blkts, tel, TV, video, clock radio, cook fac, ldry, blkts, doonas, linen, pillows], w/mach, dryer, iron, iron brd, lounge firepl, pool indoor heated, bbq, c/park (carport). **BB** ♯♯ **$140**, ◊ **$40, W** ♯♯ **$700**, ◊ **$200**, ch con.

SEYMOUR VIC 3660

Pop 6,300. (98km N Melbourne), See map on page 696, ref C3. Centre of rich agricultural and pastoral area on Goulburn River. Puckapunyal military camp is 11km SW - Tank Museum. Bowls, Fishing, Golf, Horse Racing, Scenic Drives, Shooting, Swimming (Pool), Tennis.

Hotels/Motels

 ★★★☆ **New Crossing Place Motel**, (M), 53 Emily St (Old Hume Hwy), 1.4km W of PO, ☎ 03 5792 2800, fax 03 5792 1212, 16 units (1 suite) [shwr, spa bath (1), tlt, hairdry, a/c, elec blkts, tel, cable tv, video-fee, clock radio, CD (4), t/c mkg, refrig, micro, toaster], ldry, iron, iron brd, pool, bbq, plygr, cots-fee, non smoking units (2). **RO** ♦ **$63 - $73**, ♯♯ **$74 - $84**, ◊ **$9, Suite RO $95 - $109**, AE BC DC EFT JCB MC MP VI.

 ★★★☆ **Wattle Motel**, (M), 9 Emily St (Old Hume Hwy), 1.6km SW of PO, ☎ 03 5792 2411, fax 03 5792 2427, 15 units [shwr, bath (hip) (2), tlt, hairdry, a/c, elec blkts, tel, TV, video-fee, movie, clock radio, t/c mkg, refrig, cook fac (2), micro (3), toaster], ldry, pool, bbq, plygr, cots-fee, non smoking units (5). **RO** ♦ **$62 - $79**, ♯♯ **$73 - $79**, ◊ **$11**, 4 units ★★★. AE BC DC EFT JCB MC MP VI.

 ★★★ **Coach & Bushmans Inn**, (M), 66 Emily St (Old Hume Hwy), 1.4km W of PO, ☎ 03 5799 3744, fax 03 5799 1162, 17 units [shwr, bath (15), tlt, a/c, elec blkts, tel, cable tv, video-fee, clock radio, t/c mkg, refrig, cook fac (4), toaster], ldry, iron, iron brd, pool, bbq, cots-fee. **RO** ♦ **$79.50**, ♯♯ **$89**, ch con, AE BC DC EFT MC MP VI.

★★☆ **Seymour Motel**, (M), Goulburn Valley Hwy, 3.2km N of PO, ☎ 03 5792 1500, fax 03 5792 1600, 17 units [shwr, tlt, a/c-cool, heat, elec blkts, tel (10), TV, clock radio, t/c mkg, refrig, toaster], ✕, pool, bbq, dinner to unit, plygr, cots. **RO** ♦ **$45**, ♯♯ **$55**, ◊ **$8**, ch con, AE BC MC VI.

 Auto Lodge Motor Inn, (M), 22 Emily St (Old Hume Hwy), 1.4km W of PO, ☎ 03 5792 1700, fax 03 5792 1700, 14 units [shwr, tlt, a/c, heat, elec blkts, tel, TV, clock radio, t/c mkg, refrig, toaster], pool, cook fac, bbq, plygr, cots-fee, non smoking units (5). **RO** ♦ **$49 - $59**, ♯♯ **$73**, ♯♯♯♯ **$10**, ch con, AE BC DC EFT MC MCH VI, (Rating under review).

SHELFORD VIC 3329

Pop Nominal, (139km W Melbourne), See map on pages 694/695, ref D7. Small country township.

Self Catering Accommodation

★★★☆ **Golden Leigh Bed & Breakfast**, (Cotg), Closed Jun 1 to Aug 31, 110 Thomson St, 100m SW of PO, ☎ 03 5281 3287, fax 03 5281 3287, (2 stry), 1 cotg acc up to 4, (Studio), [shwr, tlt, c/fan, heat, TV, video, clock radio, refrig, cook fac ltd, micro, elec frypan, toaster, blkts, linen, pillows], cots, breakfast ingredients, non smoking property. **D** ♦ **$45**, ♯♯ **$88, W** ♦ **$250**, ♯♯ **$500**, ch con, Ground floor unit not rated, BC MC VI.

SHEPPARTON VIC 3630

Pop 31,950. (182km N Melbourne), See map on page 696, ref D2. City on the Goulburn River. Shepparton International Village - Australia's first National Aboriginal Museum. Art Gallery, Boating, Bowls, Croquet, Fishing, Golf, Greyhound Racing, Scenic Drives, Squash, Swimming (Pool), Tennis, Trotting, Water Skiing.

Hotels/Motels

 ★★★★☆ **Parklake Motor Inn**, (M), 481 Wyndham St (Goulburn Valley Hwy), 800m S of PO, ☎ 03 5821 5822, fax 03 5821 0894, (2 stry gr fl), 79 units (6 suites) [shwr, bath (10), spa bath (25), tlt, hairdry, a/c, elec blkts, tel, cable tv, video (24), clock radio, t/c mkg, refrig, mini bar, cook fac (3), micro (14), d/wash (2), toaster (14), ldry (in unit) (2)], ldry, iron, iron brd, conf fac, ✕, bar (cocktail), pool indoor heated, sauna-fee, spa, 24hr reception, rm serv, plygr, gym, cots-fee, non smoking units (10). **RO** ♦ **$104.50 - $165**, ♯♯ **$115.50 - $176**, ◊ **$10, Suite D $188.10 - $297**, ch con, AE BC DC JCB MC MP VI, ♿.

S
VICTORIA

★★★★ **Courtyard Motor Inn**, (M), 58 Wyndham St (Goulburn Valley Hwy), 950m N of PO, ☎ 03 5831 2355, fax 03 5831 2748, (2 stry gr fl), 25 units [shwr, spa bath (10), tlt, hairdry, a/c, elec blkts, tel, TV, video (avail) (1), movie, clock radio, t/c mkg, refrig, mini bar, toaster], ldry, pool, spa, bbq, plygr, cots, non smoking units (13). D ♦♦ $81.40 - $97.90, ♦♦♦ $92, ◊ $11, ch con, AE BC DC EFT MC VI.

★★★★ **Flag Inn Big Valley Shepparton**, (M), Previously Big Valley Motor Inn - Chantelles 564 Wyndham St (Goulburn Valley Hwy), 1.6km S of PO, ☎ 03 5821 3666, fax 03 5821 7706, 29 units [shwr, bath (4), spa bath (2), tlt, hairdry (26), a/c, elec blkts, tel, TV, movie, clock radio, t/c mkg, refrig, mini bar, toaster], ldry, conf fac, ⊠ (Mon to Sat), pool, bbq, rm serv, cots-fee, non smoking units (9). RO ♦ $72 - $125, ♦♦ $85 - $125, ◊ $11, ch con, 12 units ★★★☆. AE BC DC EFT MC MP VI.

★★★★ **Paradise Lakes Motel Resort**, (M), 7685 Goulburn Valley Hwy, Shepparton South 3630, 6.6km S of PO, ☎ 03 5823 1800, fax 03 5823 1819, 26 units [shwr, spa bath (6), tlt, hairdry, a/c, elec blkts, tel, TV, video (avail), movie, clock radio, t/c mkg, refrig, mini bar, toaster], ldry, pool, spa, bbq, dinner to unit (Mon to Thu), plygr, cots. RO ♦ $70.40 - $115, ♦♦ $81.40 - $115, ◊ $11, ch con, AE BC DC EFT MC VI, ♿.

★★★★ **Pines Country Club Motor Inn**, (M), 103 Numurkah Rd (Goulburn Valley Hwy), 2.4km N of PO, ☎ 03 5831 2044, fax 03 5831 2024, 20 units [shwr, spa bath (5), tlt, hairdry, a/c, elec blkts, tel, cable tv, video (avail), clock radio, t/c mkg, refrig], ldry, iron, iron brd, conf fac, ⊠ (Mon to Sat), bar (cocktail), pool, spa, bbq, rm serv, plygr, cots, non smoking units (9). RO ♦ $100 - $110, ♦♦ $110 - $130, ◊ $10, ch con, AE BC DC EFT JCB MC MP VI, ♿.

★★★★ **Sherbourne Terrace**, (LMH), 109 Wyndham St (Goulburn Valley Hwy), 500m N of PO, ☎ 03 5821 4977, fax 03 5821 6887, (2 stry gr fl), 57 units [shwr, spa bath (12), tlt, hairdry, a/c, elec blkts, tel, TV, movie, clock radio, t/c mkg, refrig, mini bar], ldry, iron, iron brd, conf fac, ⊠, bar, pool, sauna, spa, rm serv, cots-fee, non smoking units (14). RO ♦ $93 - $137, ♦♦ $104 - $148, ◊ $11, ch con, AE BC DC EFT MC MP VI, ♿.

★★★★ **Tirana Motor Inn**, (M), 33 Wyndham St (Goulburn Valley Hwy), 1.2km N of PO, ☎ 03 5831 1766, fax 03 5831 2226, 24 units [shwr, spa bath (6), tlt, a/c, elec blkts, tel, TV, movie, clock radio, t/c mkg, refrig, toaster], ldry, conf fac, pool (salt water), spa, bbq, cots, non smoking units (8). RO ♦ $73.70, ♦♦ $83.60 - $85.80, ch con, AE BC DC EFT MC VI, ♿.

★★★☆ **Country Home Motor Inn**, (M), 11 Wyndham St (Goulburn Valley Hwy), 1.4km N of PO, ☎ 03 5821 7711, fax 03 5821 7667, 15 units [shwr, tlt, hairdry, a/c, elec blkts, tel, TV, video (avail), movie, clock radio, t/c mkg, refrig, toaster], pool, bbq, dinner to unit, cots-fee, non smoking units (5). RO ♦ $63 - $69, ♦♦ $69 - $77, ◊ $11, ch con, AE BC DC EFT MC MP VI.

★★★☆ **Peppermill Inn**, (LMH), 7900 Goulburn Valley Hwy, Kialla 3631, 4.6km S of PO, ☎ 03 5823 1800, fax 03 5823 1855, (2 stry gr fl), 26 units [shwr, spa bath (6), tlt, hairdry, a/c, elec blkts, tel, TV, clock radio, t/c mkg, refrig, toaster], ldry, conf fac, ⊠, pool, sauna, spa (heated), ✆, plygr, gym, cots-fee. RO ♦ $72 - $94, ♦♦ $81 - $105, ◊ $11, AE BC DC EFT JCB MC MP VI, ♿.

SHEPPARTON - MOOROOPNA
Rodney
MOTOR INN
• Continental Breakfast inclusive weekdays
• Luxury Units with Spas
• 2 br Family Units
• Disabled Facilities
• Pool & Spa
• Special RACV Member Rates

ALL MAJOR CORPORATE & CREDIT CARDS ACCEPTED

Phone: (03) 5825 3188
Fax: (03) 5825 3200
146 McLennan St, Mooroopna 3629

★★★☆ **Shepparton Belltower**, (M), 587 Wyndham St (Goulburn Valley Hwy), 400m S of Victoria Lake, ☎ 03 5821 8755, fax 03 5831 3232, 19 units [shwr, tlt, hairdry, a/c, elec blkts, tel, TV, video-fee, clock radio, t/c mkg, refrig, toaster], iron, iron brd, pool, spa, bbq, dinner to unit (Mon to Thurs), cots-fee, non smoking units (4). RO ♦ $55 - $70, ♦♦ $75 - $85, ◊ $15, 5 units ★★★. AE BC DC EFT MC MCH VI, ♿.

★★★☆ **The Bel-Air Motor Inn**, (M), 630 Wyndham St (Goulburn Valley Hwy), 2.3km S of PO, ☎ 03 5821 4833, fax 03 5831 2231, 30 units [shwr, tlt, hairdry (20), a/c, elec blkts, tel, TV, video-fee, clock radio, t/c mkg, refrig, mini bar], ldry, ⊠ (Tue to Sun), pool, sauna-fee, spa-fee, bbq, plygr, cots, non smoking units (5). RO ♦ $63 - $69, ♦♦ $69 - $77, ◊ $11, AE BC DC EFT MC VI.

★★★☆ **The Carrington Shepparton**, (M), 505 Wyndham St (Goulburn Valley Hwy), 900m S of PO, ☎ 03 5821 3355, fax 03 5821 3734, (2 stry gr fl), 28 units [shwr, bath (1), spa bath (5), tlt, hairdry, a/c, elec blkts, tel, cable tv, clock radio, t/c mkg, refrig, mini bar, cook fac (1), d/wash (1), toaster], ldry, iron, iron brd, conf fac, ⊠ (Mon to Sat), bar (cocktail), pool, cots, non smoking units (11). RO ♦ $88 - $143, ♦♦ $108 - $170, ◊ $10, 11 units ★★★★, AE BC DC EFT MC MP VI.

★★★☆ **Wyndhamere Motel**, (M), 65 Wyndham St (Goulburn Valley Hwy), 900m N of PO, ☎ 03 5821 3088, fax 03 5831 1923, 26 units [shwr, spa bath (6), tlt, hairdry, a/c, elec blkts, tel, cable tv, video (avail), clock radio, t/c mkg, refrig, toaster], ldry, iron, iron brd, conf fac, ⊠ (Mon to Sat), pool, bbq, rm serv, plygr, cots-fee. RO ♦ $88 - $118, ♦♦ $96 - $118, ◊ $10, ch con, AE BC DC EFT MC MP VI.

★★★ **Overlander Hotel Motel**, (LMH), 97 Benalla Rd (Midland Hwy), 2.4km E of PO, ☎ 03 5821 5622, fax 03 5831 2629, 30 units [shwr, tlt, hairdry, a/c, elec blkts, tel, TV, clock radio, t/c mkg, refrig, toaster], ldry, conf fac, ⊠, pool (salt water), plygr, cots-fee. RO ♦ $60 - $65, ♦♦ $65 - $70, ◊ $10, AE BC DC EFT MC VI.

★★★ **Tudor House Motor Inn**, (M), 64 Wyndham St (Goulburn Valley Hwy), 900m N of PO, ☎ 03 5821 8411, fax 03 5822 1319, 22 units [shwr, tlt, hairdry, a/c, elec blkts, tel, TV, video, clock radio, t/c mkg, refrig, toaster], ldry, pool, cots-fee, non smoking units (4). RO ♦ $59 - $64, ♦♦ $74 - $79, ◊ $15, ch con, AE BC DC EFT MC MCH VI, ♿.

★★☆ **Apex Motel**, (M), Goulburn Valley Hwy, 2.8km N of PO, ☎ 03 5821 4472, 16 units [shwr, tlt, a/c-cool (8), a/c (8), heat (8), elec blkts, TV, video-fee, clock radio, t/c mkg, refrig], rec rm, pool, bbq. RO ♦ $40 - $44, ♦♦ $46 - $50, ◊ $10, AE BC DC EFT MC VI.

★★☆ **Maude's on the Green**, (M), Golf Link Dve, 5km NW of PO, ☎ 03 5821 2155, fax 03 5831 3045, (2 stry gr fl), 11 units [shwr, tlt, a/c-cool, heat, elec blkts, tel, TV, clock radio, t/c mkg, refrig, toaster], conf fac, bbq, golf, cots-fee, non smoking units (3). RO ♦ $55, ♦♦ $66, ◊ $11, AE BC EFT MC VI.

★★ **Four Corners Motel & Caravan Park**, (M), Goulburn Valley Hwy, Congupna 3633, 9.4km N of Shepparton PO, ☎ 03 5829 9404, fax 03 5829 9404, 6 units [shwr, tlt, a/c, heat, elec blkts, TV, clock radio, t/c mkg, refrig, cook fac ltd (2), toaster, doonas (3)], ldry, pool, bbq, plygr. RO ♦ $40, ♦♦ $45, ◊ $5, pen con, Min book long w/ends and Easter, BC MC VI.

★★ **Victoria Hotel Shepparton**, (LH), Cnr Wyndham & Fryers Sts, 100m N of PO, ☎ 03 5821 9955, fax 03 5831 1961, (2 stry), 37 rms [basin (13), shwr (24), bath (2), tlt (24), a/c (24), c/fan (3), tel (24), TV, clock radio, t/c mkg, refrig, toaster (24)], conf fac, ⊠, ✆, cots. BLB ♦ $31.90 - $53.90, ♦♦ $41.80 - $64.90, ◊ $8 - $15, Light breakfast only available, AE BC DC EFT MC VI.

★☆ **Terminus Hotel**, (LH), 212 High St (Midland Hwy), 600m E of PO, ☎ 03 5821 2147, fax 03 5831 6139, (2 stry gr fl), 9 rms [basin (7), shwr (2), tlt (2), a/c-cool (2), c/fan (5), heat (2), elec blkts, TV (2), t/c mkg (2), refrig (2)], lounge (TV), ⊠ (Mon to Sat), ✆. BLB ♦ $27.50 - $38.50, ♦♦ $44 - $55, ◊ $10, ch con, 2 rooms ★★. AE BC DC MC VI.

The Carrington Manor, (M), 497 Wyndham St, 800m S of PO, ☎ 03 5821 3355, fax 03 5821 3734, (2 stry), 6 units (2 suites) [ensuite, bath (1), spa bath (2), a/c, fire pl (2), elec blkts, tel, cable tv, clock radio, t/c mkg, refrig], conf fac, pool indoor heated, sauna, dinner to unit, c/park (undercover), non smoking property. RO $145 - $250, Suite RO $400, AE BC DC EFT MC VI, (not yet classified).

Self Catering Accommodation

★★★☆ **Central Shepparton Apartments**, (Apt), 3 Maude St, 1.4km N of PO, ☎ 03 5821 4482, fax 03 5821 4482, 6 apts acc up to 4, (1 & 2 bedrm), [shwr, tlt, hairdry, a/c-cool, heat, TV, video, clock radio, CD, refrig, cook fac, micro, toaster, ldry, blkts, doonas, linen, pillows], w/mach, iron, iron brd, c/park (carport), non smoking property. D ♦♦ $85 - $140, ♦ $12 - $20, W ♦♦ $325 - $450, ♦ $40 - $160, ch con, Min book applies, BC.

Operator Comment: Plus 3br cottage close to town and lake. www.ozemail.com.au/~shepapartments

SHERBROOKE VIC

See Dandenong Ranges Region.

SHOREHAM VIC 3916

Pop 250. (79km S Melbourne), See map on page 697, ref C8. Small township located on the western side of Western Port Bay. Boating, Bush Walking, Fishing (Rock, Beach), Golf, Scenic Drives, Surfing, Tennis.

Self Catering Accommodation

★★★★ **Le Pavillon**, (Cotg), 1 Pine Gve, ☎ 03 5989 8433, (2 stry gr fl), 1 cotg acc up to 6, (3 bedrm), [shwr, bath (hip), tlt, hairdry, heat, TV, video, clock radio, CD, refrig, cook fac, micro, d/wash, toaster, ldry, blkts, linen, pillows], bbq, breakfast ingredients, non smoking property. BB ♦♦ $150, ♦ $62.50, ch con.

B&B's/Guest Houses

★★★★☆ **The Outlook Shoreham**, (B&B), No children's facilities, 9 Nelson St, 1.5km SE of PO, ☎ 03 5989 8532, fax 03 5989 8800, 3 rms [ensuite, bath (1), spa bath (1), hairdry, a/c-cool (1), a/c (1), c/fan (2), heat, elec blkts, TV, video, clock radio, CD, t/c mkg, refrig, micro, toaster], bbq, non smoking property. BB ♦ $120 - $132, ♦♦ $165 - $198, D ♦ $55, pen con, Dinner by arrangement. BC MC VI.

SILVAN VIC

See Dandenong Ranges Region.

SIMPSON VIC 3266

Pop 220. (172km SW Melbourne), See map on pages 694/695, ref C7. Centre of a large soldier settlement area. Bowls, Fishing, Motor Racing, Scenic Drives, Tennis.

B&B's/Guest Houses

★★★☆ **Bignold**, (B&B), (Farm), Timboon - Colac Rd, 9km N of PO, ☎ 03 5594 6233, 2 rms [heat, doonas], lounge (TV, video), cots. BB ♦ $35 - $38.50, ♦♦ $60 - $66, ch con.

SKIPTON VIC 3361

Pop 450. (167km W Melbourne), See map on pages 694/695, ref C6. Located on Mount Emu Creek, grazing & pastoral town. 1,562ha property - Mooramong Historic Homestead - located 10km NW of town. Bowls, Fishing, Golf, Swimming (Pool).

Self Catering Accommodation

★★ **National Trust of Australia (Victoria)**, (Cotg), Classified by National Trust, (Farm), Glenelg Hwy, 12km NW of PO, turnoff 4km W of PO, ☎ 03 5340 6556, or 03 5340 6558, fax 03 5340 6558, 1 cotg acc up to 8, (3 bedrm), [shwr, bath, tlt, a/c-cool, heat (wood), elec blkts, refrig, cook fac, toaster, doonas, linen reqd], ldry, lounge firepl, pool, bbq, tennis, cots. D ♦♦♦♦ $85, ♦ $20, ch con, No bookings 20-30th of Dec.

(Shearers Quarters), 10 bunkhouses acc up to 2, (Bunk Rooms), [heat, blkts reqd, linen reqd], cook fac, refrig, bbq, cots. D ♦ $16.50, ch con.

SMEATON VIC 3364

Pop Part of Creswick, (140km NW Melbourne), See map on page 696, ref A4. Farming and grazing district situated just north of Birch Creek. Bowls, Tennis.

Self Catering Accommodation

★★★★ **Tuki**, (Cotg), Newstead - Castlemaine Rd, Stoney Rises, 8km N of Smeaton, ☎ 03 5345 6233, fax 03 5345 6377, 6 cotgs acc up to 2, (1 bedrm), [shwr, spa bath (4), tlt, hairdry, TV, video, clock radio, CD (2), refrig, micro (4), linen, pillows], conv fac, lounge firepl, ☒, dinner to unit, breakfast ingredients. D ♦♦ $130, ♦ $35, W ♦♦ $528 - $648, 2 units ★★★☆. Dinner by arrangement. Min book applies, BC DC EFT MC VI.

B&B's/Guest Houses

★★★★ **Abergeldie Bed & Breakfast**, (B&B), (Farm), Ballarat - Newstead Rd, 500m N of town, ☎ 03 5345 6223, fax 03 5345 6223, 3 rms [ensuite (2), bath (1), hairdry, heat, elec blkts], lounge, t/c mkg shared, bbq. BB ♦♦ $120 - $180, Dinner by arrangement. AE BC DC MC VI.

★★★★ **(Cottage Section)**, 1 rm (1 bedrm), [shwr, tlt, hairdry, heat (wood), elec blkts, TV, clock radio, CD, t/c mkg, refrig], lounge firepl, bbq. BB ♦♦ $120 - $200.

SOMERVILLE VIC 3912

Pop 7,050. (50km SE Melbourne), See map on page 697, ref D7. Residential area located in horticultural & fruit growing district.

B&B's/Guest Houses

★★★☆ **Bangunya Bed and Breakfast**, (B&B), No children's facilities, 989 Frankston-Flinders Rd, 800m N of PO, ☎ 03 5977 7338, fax 03 5977 7338, (2 stry), 3 rms [hairdry, heat (1), cent heat (2), elec blkts, TV (1), video (avail), t/c mkg (2)], lounge, lounge firepl, spa (heated), bbq, non smoking property. BB ♦ $77, ♦♦ $110 - $132, Dinner by arrangement. BC MC VI.

SORRENTO VIC 3943

Pop 1,161. (90km S Melbourne), See map on page 697, ref A7. Popular seaside resort, near the site of the first Victorian settlement by Collins at Sullivans Bay. Snorkelling with dolphins and seals. A vehicle and passenger ferry operates between Sorrento and Queenscliff. For enquiries ph 03-5258 3244. Boat Ramp, Boating, Bowls, Fishing, Golf, Sailing, Swimming (Beach), Tennis.

Hotels/Motels

★★★ **Hotel Sorrento**, (LH), 5 Hotham Rd, 150m N of PO, ☎ 03 5984 2206, fax 03 5984 3424, (2 stry), 10 rms (10 suites) [shwr, spa bath (1), tlt, hairdry, c/fan, heat, elec blkts, tel, TV, clock radio, t/c mkg, refrig], ldry, ✕, cots-fee, non smoking rms (10). BLB ♦♦ $110 - $190, ♦ $25, AE BC DC EFT MC VI.

Self Catering Accommodation

★★★★☆ **Killarney Cottage**, (Cotg), 4 Richard St, off St Pauls Rd, ☎ 03 5984 1970, fax 03 5984 5415, 1 cotg acc up to 6, (3 bedrm), [ensuite, shwr, bath, tlt, hairdry, c/fan, cent heat, tel (local), TV, video, clock radio, CD, refrig, cook fac, micro, d/wash, toaster, blkts, doonas, linen, pillows], w/mach, dryer, iron, iron brd, lounge firepl, bbq, c/park (carport), cots, non smoking property, Pets on application. RO ♦♦ $160, W $850 - $1,800, ch con, Min book Christmas Jan long w/ends and Easter, BC DC MC VI.

★★★★ **Sorrento on the Park**, (Apt), 15 Hotham Rd, 200m N of PO, ☎ 03 5984 4777, fax 03 5984 4198, (2 stry gr fl), 12 apts acc up to 6, (Studio & 2 bedrm), [shwr, bath (hip) (6), spa bath (6), tlt, hairdry, c/fan, heat, elec blkts, tel, TV, video, clock radio, t/c mkg, refrig, cook fac ltd, micro, d/wash (4), toaster, blkts, linen, pillows], ldry, iron, iron brd, conf fac, bbq, bicycle-fee, cots. D $130 - $275, AE BC DC EFT MC VI.

★★★☆ **(Motel Section)**, (2 stry gr fl), 6 units [shwr, tlt, hairdry, c/fan, heat, elec blkts, tel, TV, video, clock radio, t/c mkg, refrig, toaster], iron, iron brd. D $130 - $195.

★★★☆ **Palm Cottage**, (Cotg), 6 Hiskens St, ☎ 0408 997 795, 1 cotg acc up to 8, (4 bedrm), [shwr, bath (hip), tlt, hairdry, fan (6), heat, elec blkts (6), tel (local), TV, clock radio, refrig, cook fac, micro, toaster, ldry (in unit), blkts, doonas, linen, pillows], w/mach, dryer, iron, iron brd, lounge firepl, bbq, c/park (carport), cots. D ♦♦ $130, ♦ $55, ch con, Min book applies, BC MC VI.

B&B's/Guest Houses

★★★★☆ **Bilinga**, (B&B), 105 Hotham Rd, 1.2km SW of PO, ☎ 03 5984 5530, fax 03 5984 0868, 1 rm [ensuite, hairdry, c/fan, cent heat, elec blkts, clock radio, t/c mkg, doonas], lounge (TV, video, stereo), non smoking property. **BB ♕♕ $145**, AE BC DC MC VI.

★★★★☆ **(Cottage Section)**, 2 cotgs acc up to 5, (2 bedrm), [shwr, tlt, hairdry, a/c, c/fan, heat (wood), elec blkts, TV, video, clock radio, CD, t/c mkg, refrig, cook fac, micro, d/wash, toaster, blkts, doonas, linen, pillows], iron, iron brd, bbq, c/park (carport) (1), breakfast ingredients, non smoking property. **BB ♕♕ $145 - $185, ◊ $40.**

★★★★☆ **Dougal's Guest House**, (GH), 212 Ocean Beach Rd, ☎ 03 5984 0712, fax 03 5984 0712, (2 stry), 4 rms [ensuite, hairdry, heat, elec blkts, clock radio], lounge (TV, cd), lounge firepl, t/c mkg shared, refrig, non smoking property. **BB ♕♕ $155 - $175**, BC MC VI.

★★★★☆ **Eastcliff Cottage**, (B&B), No children's facilities, 881 Melbourne Rd, ☎ 03 5984 0668, fax 03 5984 0667, 3 rms [ensuite, spa bath, hairdry, a/c-cool (1), fan (2), heat, TV, video (avail), clock radio, t/c mkg, refrig], ldry, w/mach, dryer, iron, iron brd, res liquor license, bbq, non smoking property. **BB ♕♕ $165 - $199.50**, pen con, AE BC DC EFT MC VI.

★★★★☆ **Tower House Resort Sorrento**, (B&B), No facilities for children under 15. 3395 Point Nepean Rd, 200m N of PO, ☎ 03 5984 1343, fax 03 5984 1341, 2 rms (1 suite) [ensuite, spa bath (2), hairdry, a/c, elec blkts, TV, clock radio, t/c mkg, refrig], iron, iron brd, lounge, lounge firepl, pool (salt water), spa (heated), ✆, tennis, non smoking property. **BB ♕ $170 - $270, ♕♕ $190 - $290**, Min book Christmas Jan long w/ends and Easter, AE BC DC MC VI.

★★★★ **Tamasha House**, (B&B), No children's facilities, 699 Melbourne Rd, 1km SE of PO, ☎ 03 5984 2413, fax 03 5984 0452, 2 rms [ensuite, heat, elec blkts, clock radio], ldry, lounge (TV, video, stereo), t/c mkg shared, non smoking property. **BB ♕ $110, ♕♕ $150**, AE BC DC JCB MC VI.

★★★☆ **Carmel Bed & Breakfast**, (B&B), 142 Ocean Beach Rd, ☎ 03 5984 3512, fax 03 5984 0146, 4 rms (2 suites) [ensuite (2), shwr (1), bath (1), tlt (1), hairdry, fan, fire pl (1), cent heat, elec blkts, TV, clock radio, t/c mkg, refrig, doonas], bbq, non smoking property. **BLB ♕ $115, ♕♕ $145, ♕♕♕ $165**, AE BC DC EFT MC VI.

★★★ **(Holiday Flat Section)**, 2 flats acc up to 4, (1 bedrm), [shwr, tlt, fan, heat, cent heat (1), elec blkts, TV, clock radio, t/c mkg, cook fac, toaster, blkts, linen, pillows], w/mach (1), iron, iron brd, bbq, non smoking property. **D $145, W $880 - $1,250**, ch con, fam con.

★★★ **Oceanic-Whitehall**, (GH), 231 Ocean Beach Rd, 1km SW of PO, ☎ 03 5984 4166, fax 03 5984 3369, (2 stry gr fl), 34 rms [basin, ensuite (5), spa bath (5), fire pl (9), heat], ldry, rec rm, lounge (TV), conf fac, pool (salt water), t/c mkg shared, bbq, ✆, tennis, cots. **BB ♕ $60 - $180, ♕♕ $70 - $180, ◊ $25 - $35**, Min book Christmas and Jan, AE BC DC MC VI.

★★☆ **(Motel Section)**, 20 units [shwr, tlt, fan, heat, TV, clock radio, t/c mkg, refrig, toaster], ldry, conf fac, pool (salt water), bbq, cots. **BB ♕ $90 - $125, ♕♕ $100 - $135, ◊ $25 - $35.**

Other Accommodation

Sorrento YHA Backpackers, (Lodge), 3 Miranda St, 600m SW of PO, ☎ 03 5984 4323, fax 03 5984 2430, 6 rms (Bunk Rooms), [basin, ensuite (2), shwr (4), tlt (4), wood heat, doonas, linen, pillows], lounge (TV), cook fac, t/c mkg shared, refrig, bbq, kiosk, ✆, non smoking property. **D ♕ $18 - $23, ◊ $18 - $23**, AE BC EFT JCB MC VI, ♿.

ST ARNAUD VIC 3478

Pop 2,650. (245km NW Melbourne), See map on pages 694/695, ref C4. Rich agricultural & pastoral centre, founded as a gold-mining village in 1858. Panoramic views from View Point & Wilson's Hill. Boating, Bowls, Bush Walking, Croquet, Fishing, Golf, Horse Racing, Horse Riding, Scenic Drives, Shooting, Swimming (Pool, Lake), Tennis, Trotting.

Hotels/Motels

★★★ **Motel St Arnaud**, (M), 5 Ballarat Rd (Sunraysia Hwy), 1.6km SE of PO, ☎ 03 5495 1755, fax 03 5495 1646, 17 units [shwr, tlt, a/c, heat, elec blkts, tel, TV, video (avail), clock radio, t/c mkg, refrig], ldry, ✗ (Tue to Sun), BYO, bar, bbq, dinner to unit, cots-fee, non smoking units (6). **RO ♕ $51, ♕♕ $61, ◊ $10**, ch con, AE BC DC EFT MC MP VI.

★★★ **St Arnaud Country Road Inn**, (M), Cnr Bendigo & Ballarat Rds, 1.1km SE of PO, ☎ 03 5495 2255, fax 03 5495 2253, 14 units [shwr, tlt, a/c-cool, heat, elec blkts, tel, TV, video-fee, clock radio, refrig], bbq, dinner to unit, cots-fee. **RO ♕ $53 - $60, ♕♕ $62 - $70, ◊ $8**, ch con, AE BC DC MC VI.

★★☆ **Kings Avenue Motel**, (M), 17 Kings Ave (Sunraysia Hwy), 600m E of PO, ☎ 03 5495 1186, fax 03 5495 1186, 5 units [shwr, tlt, hairdry, a/c-cool, heat, elec blkts, TV, video, clock radio, t/c mkg, refrig, toaster, ldry], cots, non smoking units (2). **RO ♕ $45, ♕♕ $50 - $55, ◊ $10**, ch con, AE BC MC VI.

★★ **Botanical Hotel**, (LH), 11 Napier St (Sunraysia Hwy), 200m E of PO, ☎ 03 5495 1336, fax 03 5495 3178, (2 stry), 5 rms [basin (4), elec blkts], lounge (TV), conf fac, ✗ (Tue to Sat), t/c mkg shared, refrig, ✆, non smoking rms. **BLB ♕ $35, ♕♕ $50**, ch con, Light breakfast only available. BC EFT MC VI.

★★ **The Victoria of St Arnaud Motor Inn**, (M), Previously Old Victorian Inn. 123 Napier St (Sunraysia Hwy), 200m W of PO, ☎ 03 5495 3244, 5 units [shwr, tlt, a/c, TV, clock radio, t/c mkg, refrig, toaster], sauna, spa, bbq, cots-fee. **RO ♕ $40, ♕♕ $45, ◊ $5**, BC DC EFT MC VI.

B&B's/Guest Houses

★★★ **Hush of Kellane B & B**, (B&B), 38 Millett St, 1km SW of PO, ☎ 03 5495 1618, fax 03 5495 2825, 2 rms [hairdry, c/fan, heat, elec blkts, clock radio], lounge (TV, stereo, piano), t/c mkg shared, refrig. **BB ♕ $60 - $65, ♕♕ $75 - $85, ◊ $40**, ch con, BC MC VI.

★★★☆ **The Old Post Office Bed & Breakfast**, (B&B), No children's facilities, 2 Napier St, ☎ 03 5495 2313, fax 03 5495 2313, (2 stry), 2 rms [ensuite, hairdry, a/c (1), fan, heat, elec blkts, clock radio], lounge (TV, Stereo), lounge firepl, ✗ (Thur to Mon), BYO, t/c mkg shared, bbq. **BB ♕ $95 - $100, ♕♕ $100 - $110**, BC MC VI.

STANLEY VIC 3747

Pop 200. (299km NE Melbourne), See map on pages 694/695, ref H5. Agricultural and fruit growing district on the northern slopes of the Dingle Ranges.

B&B's/Guest Houses

★★★★☆ **Indigo Inn**, (B&B), Wallace St, 100m E of general store, ☎ 03 5728 6502, fax 03 5728 6502, 2 rms [ensuite, hairdry, c/fan (1), heat, elec blkts, TV, video (1)], lounge, lounge firepl, bar, spa (heated), t/c mkg shared, bbq, non smoking rms (1). **BB ♕♕ $141 - $161**, Dinner by arrangement. BC MC VI.

STAWELL VIC 3380

Pop 6,250. (233km NW Melbourne), See map on pages 694/695, ref C5. Pastoral, goldmining & industrial town. Stawell Grampians Information Centre, Western Hwy, 03-5358 2314. Bowls, Bush Walking, Croquet, Fishing, Golf, Horse Racing, Horse Riding, Scenic Drives, Shooting, Swimming (Pool), Tennis, Trotting.

Hotels/Motels

★★★★ **Diamond House Heritage Restaurant & Motor Inn**, (M), 24 Seaby St, 1.1km SE of PO, ☎ 03 5358 3366, fax 03 5358 4826, 10 units [shwr, tlt, hairdry, a/c, heat, elec blkts, tel, TV, video (avail), clock radio, t/c mkg, refrig, mini bar, toaster], conf fac, ✗ (Mon to Sat), bbq, rm serv (Mon to Sat), cots, non smoking units (4). **RO ♕ $60 - $88, ♕♕ $72 - $99, ◊ $16 - $22**, AE BC DC EFT MC VI.

★★★★ **Magdala Motor Lodge**, (M), Western Hwy, 2km W of Tourist Information Centre, ☎ 03 5358 3877, fax 03 5358 4176, 28 units [shwr, spa bath (7), tlt, a/c, elec blkts, tel, TV, video-fee, clock radio, t/c mkg, refrig], ldry, ✗ (Mon to Sat), pool indoor heated, spa, rm serv (Mon to Sat), golf (6 hole), tennis, cots-fee, non smoking units (10). **RO ♕ $79 - $105, ♕♕ $92 - $118, ◊ $13**, AE BC DC EFT JCB MC MP VI, ♿.

★★★☆ **Flag Inn Goldfields**, (M), Previously Goldfields Motor Inn Western Hwy, 500m E of Tourist Information Centre, ☎ 03 5358 2911, fax 03 5358 2090, 23 units [shwr, bath (2), tlt, a/c, elec blkts, tel, TV, video (avail), clock radio, t/c mkg, refrig, mini bar, cook fac (5), toaster (5)], conf fac, ✗ (Mon to Sat), bar (cocktail), pool, bbq, rm serv, plygr, cots-fee. **RO ♕ $70 - $120**, AE BC DC EFT MC MP VI.

★★★☆ **Hi-Way Eight Motor Inn**, (M), 28 Longfield St (Western Hwy), 200m W of Tourist Information Centre, ☎ 03 5358 2411, fax 03 5358 2411, 17 units [shwr, tlt, hairdry, a/c, elec blkts, tel, TV, movie, clock radio, t/c mkg, refrig], ldry, ✗, BYO, pool, spa (heated)-fee, bbq, dinner to unit, plygr, gym, cots-fee. **RO ♕ $55 - $66, ♕♕ $66 - $77, ◊ $11**, ch con, AE BC DC EFT MC VI.

★★★☆ **Motel Stawell**, (M), 21 Longfield St (Western Hwy), 300m W of Tourist Information Centre, ☎ 03 5358 2041, fax 03 5358 5160, 16 units [shwr, tlt, a/c-cool (11), a/c (5), heat (11), elec blkts, tel, TV, video-fee, clock radio, t/c mkg, refrig], ldry, ✕, pool above ground (solar heat), bbq, plygr, cots-fee, non smoking units (3). **BB ♦ $50 - $60, ♦♦ $60 - $70**, AE BC EFT MC MCH VI, ♿.

★★★ **Central Park Motel**, (M), 3 Seaby St, 900m SW of PO, ☎ 03 5358 2417, fax 03 5358 5130, 11 units [shwr, bath (1), tlt, a/c (4), c/fan (2), heat (2), elec blkts, tel, TV, clock radio, t/c mkg, refrig], bbq, plygr, cots, non smoking units (4). **RO ♦ $46, ♦♦ $57**, AE BC EFT MC VI.

★★★ **Coorrabin Motor Inn**, (M), 7 Longfield St (Western Hwy), 600m W of Tourist Information Centre, ☎ 03 5358 3933, fax 03 5358 3933, 10 units [shwr, tlt, a/c, elec blkts, tel, TV, movie, clock radio, t/c mkg, refrig, toaster], spa (heated), cots, non smoking units (3). **RO ♦ $44 - $55, ♦♦ $55 - $66, ♦ $11**, AE BC DC EFT MC MP VI, ♿.

★★☆ **London Motor Inn**, (M), 10 Horsham Rd (Western Hwy), 1.1km W of Tourist Information Centre, ☎ 03 5358 2200, fax 03 5358 5111, 24 units [shwr, tlt, a/c, elec blkts, tel, TV, video-fee, clock radio, t/c mkg, refrig, toaster], conf fac, ✕, pool, bbq, dinner to unit, plygr, cots. **RO ♦ $45 - $55, ♦♦ $55 - $65, ♦♦♦♦ $65 - $85**, 7 units ★★★. AE BC DC MC MP VI.

Self Catering Accommodation

★★★☆ **Old Coongee Homestead**, (Cotg), (Farm), Kirkella Rd, 6.4km NE of PO, off Navarre Rd, ☎ 03 5358 1507, fax 03 5358 4399, 1 cotg acc up to 8, (3 bedrm), [shwr, tlt, hairdry, fan, fire pl (1), heat, elec blkts, tel, TV, video, clock radio, CD, refrig, cook fac, micro, elec frypan, d/wash, toaster, ldry, blkts, linen reqd-fee, pillows], w/mach, dryer, iron, iron brd, lounge firepl, spa (double), bbq, c/park (carport), plygr, cots. **D ♦♦ $125, ♦ $10 - $25**, Min book applies.

★★★ **Stawell Holiday Cottages**, (Cotg), Errington Rd, 2km NW of PO, ☎ 03 5358 2868, fax 03 5358 2868, 6 cotgs acc up to 6, (2 bedrm), [shwr, tlt, a/c, TV, clock radio, refrig, cook fac, toaster, blkts, doonas, linen reqd-fee, pillows], ldry, w/mach, dryer, pool (Salt water), bbq, ✆, plygr, cots. **D ♦♦ $66 - $77, ♦ $11**, ch con, Min book long w/ends, BC MC VI.

B&B's/Guest Houses

★★★★☆ **Bellellen Homestead**, (B&B), Stawell - Jallukar Rd, Bellellen 3381, 11.3km SW of Stawell PO, ☎ 03 5358 4800, fax 03 5358 3542, 3 rms [hairdry, a/c, cent heat, elec blkts, cable tv, clock radio], lounge (TV, video, cd player), lounge firepl, bar (cocktail), spa (heated), t/c mkg shared, bbq. **BB ♦ $70 - $140, ♦♦ $140**, Min book long w/ends and Easter, BC EFT MC VI.

★★★★☆ **Wayfarer House Bed & Breakfast**, (B&B), 30 Patrick St, 300m NE of PO, ☎ 03 5358 2921, fax 03 5358 2921, 3 rms [ensuite, spa bath (2), hairdry, a/c-cool, fan, fire pl, heat, elec blkts, clock radio], lounge (TV, stereo), lounge firepl, t/c mkg shared, refrig. **BB ♦ $90 - $140, ♦♦ $120 - $140**, BC MC VI.

★★★ **Natural-way Therapeutic Massage**, (B&B), RMB 2013 Bullocky Mary Rd, off Pomonal Rd, 7km S of PO, ☎ 03 5358 3896, fax 03 5358 3896, (2 stry), 1 rm [ensuite, a/c-cool, heat, elec blkts, t/c mkg, refrig], lounge (TV, stereo, video), spa, bbq. **BB ♦ $50, ♦♦ $77, ♦ $28**, BC MC VI.

Pop 1,350. (232km E Melbourne), See map on pages 694/695, ref H7. Rich dairying & pastoral area. The town is located adjacent to the Avon River. Bowls, Fishing, Gem Fossicking, Horse Riding, Scenic Drives, Swimming (Pool), Tennis. See also Hollands Landing.

Hotels/Motels

★★★ **Stratford Motel**, (M), Princes Hwy, 100m S of PO, ☎ 03 5145 6500, fax 03 5145 6008, 11 units [shwr, spa bath (1), tlt, a/c (1), c/fan, heat, elec blkts, TV, video-fee, clock radio, t/c mkg, refrig, cook fac (1), toaster], ✕, bbq, c/park (carport), cots-fee, non smoking units (4). **RO ♦ $49 - $55, ♦♦ $55 - $75, ♦ $11**, BC EFT MC VI.

Self Catering Accommodation

★★★ **Woolenook Accommodation**, (Cotg), 201 Redbank Rd, 2.8km E of PO, ☎ 03 5145 6576, 1 cotg acc up to 5, (2 bedrm - rock), [shwr, tlt, fan, TV, clock radio, t/c mkg, refrig, cook fac, micro, toaster, blkts, linen, pillows], iron, iron brd, lounge firepl, cots, breakfast ingredients. **BB ♦ $15**, Min book applies, AE.

Pop Nominal, (49km NE Melbourne), See map on page 697, ref E1. Small settlement located in agricultural district, close to Kinglake National Park. Bush Walking, Scenic Drives.

Self Catering Accommodation

★★★☆ **Strathewen Hills**, (Cotg), (Farm), 1090 Strathewen Rd, Adjacent to Public Hall, ☎ 03 9714 8464, fax 03 9714 8464, 1 cotg acc up to 4, (2 bedrm), [shwr, bath, tlt, a/c-cool, heat (open fire), elec blkts, TV, video, clock radio, refrig, cook fac, micro, toaster, ldry (in cottage), blkts, linen, pillows], iron, iron brd, bbq, breakfast ingredients. **BB ♦ $65, ♦♦ $120, ♦ $50**, ch con.

Pop 450. (238km N Melbourne), See map on page 696, ref D1. Agricultural area with cheese production as its major industry. Bowls, Fishing, Golf, Shooting, Swimming (Pool, River), Tennis, Water Skiing.

Hotels/Motels

★★☆ **Matilda Motor Inn**, (M), Murray Valley Hwy, 200m W of PO, ☎ 03 5874 5303, 12 units [shwr, tlt, a/c-cool (3), a/c, elec blkts, tel, TV, clock radio, t/c mkg, refrig], plygr. **RO ♦ $45, ♦♦ $50 - $52, ♦ $11**, ch con, BC DC EFT MC VI.

Pop 9,400. (336km N Melbourne), See map on pages 694/695, ref D3. Located on the banks of the Murray River. It is the site of Australia's first heritage museum, the Swan Hill Pioneer Settlement and Sound & Light Show. Tyntynder & Murray Downs Historic Homesteads. Military & Clock Museums. Pheasant & Angora goat farms nearby. Development & Information Centre 306 Campbell St, Ph 03 5032 3033. Boating, Bowls, Croquet, Fishing, Golf, Horse Racing, Sailing, Scenic Drives, Squash, Swimming (Pool, River), Tennis, Vineyards, Wineries.

Hotels/Motels

★★★★ **Burke & Wills Motor Inn Swan Hill**, (M), 370 Campbell St, 500m S of PO, ☎ 03 5032 9788, fax 03 5033 1104, (2 stry gr fl), 18 units (2 bedrm), [shwr, spa bath (11), tlt, hairdry, a/c, c/fan (7), elec blkts, tel, TV, movie, clock radio, t/c mkg, refrig, mini bar], iron, iron brd, conf fac, ⊠ (Mon to Sat), pool-heated (solar), spa, bbq, rm serv, cots-fee. **RO ♦ $90 - $95, ♦♦ $101 - $111, ♦ $11**, AE BC DC MC MP VI.

★★★★ **Lady Augusta Motor Inn**, (M), 375 Campbell St, 700m S of PO, ☎ 03 5032 9677, fax 03 5032 9573, (2 stry gr fl), 24 units [shwr, bath (4), spa bath (3), tlt, hairdry, a/c, elec blkts, tel, cable tv, movie, clock radio, t/c mkg, refrig, mini bar], iron, iron brd, conf fac, ⊠ (Mon to Sat), bar (cocktail), pool-heated, sauna, spa, rm serv, cots-fee. **RO ♦ $98 - $145, ♦♦ $110 - $145, ♦ $12**, AE BC DC EFT MC MP VI.

★★★★ **Murray Downs Golf & Country Club Motor Inn**, (M), Murray Downs Dve Murray Downs NSW via, 4.7km E of PO, ☎ 03 5033 1966, fax 03 5033 1268, 50 units [shwr, spa bath (7), tlt, hairdry, a/c, c/fan, elec blkts, tel, cable tv, movie, clock radio, t/c mkg, refrig, mini bar], ldry, iron, iron brd, conf fac, pool, spa, bbq, plygr, golf, tennis, cots. **RO ♦ $89 - $165, ♦♦ $105 - $165, ♦ $20**, AE BC DC EFT MC VI, ♿.

Safety first for younger cyclists

It's a sad fact of life that young cyclists are one of the high-risk groups on our roads, so it is vital that parents put safety first when their children start riding bicycles.

Only when parents are sure of a child's ability to handle traffic should they allow the child to take to the roads.

The best way to check that children are safe riding on the road is to go for a ride with them - a sort of road test, but without the child necessarily knowing it's a test.

If children are to ride to school, check out a safe route between home and school and familiarise the children with the route and any special problems. Helmets are now mandatory.

★★★★ Sundowner Chain Motor Inns, (M), 405 Campbell St (Murray Valley Hwy), 800m S of PO, ☎ 03 5032 2726, fax 03 5032 9109, (2 stry gr fl), 62 units (2 suites) [shwr, spa bath (13), tlt, hairdry, a/c, elec blkts, tel, cable tv (austar), clock radio, CD (3), t/c mkg, refrig, mini bar], iron, iron brd, rec rm, conf fac, ⊠ (Mon to Sat), pool (salt water), pool indoor heated, sauna, spa, bbq, rm serv, plygr, mini golf, gym, squash, tennis (half court), cots-fee, non smoking units (29). **RO ♦ $92 - $197.50, ♦♦ $100 - $197.50, ◊ $11**, ch con, Min book Easter June long w/ends Christmas, AE BC DC JCB MC MP VI, ₤&.

★★★★ Travellers Rest Motor Inn, (M), 110 Curlewis St, 200m NW of PO, ☎ 03 5032 9644, fax 03 5033 1127, (2 stry gr fl), 20 units [shwr, spa bath (2), tlt, hairdry, a/c, c/fan, elec blkts, tel, cable tv, movie, clock radio, t/c mkg, refrig, mini bar], iron, iron brd, pool, spa (heated), cots, non smoking units (8). **RO ♦ $87 - $100, ♦♦ $97 - $110, ◊ $10**, AE BC DC EFT MC MP VI.

★★★☆ Australian Settlers Motor Inn Swan Hill, (M), 354 Campbell St, 500m S of PO, ☎ 03 5032 9277, fax 03 5032 3643, 15 units [shwr, spa bath (1), tlt, a/c, elec blkts, tel, TV, video-fee, clock radio, t/c mkg, refrig, mini bar], iron, iron brd, pool, spa, bbq, dinner to unit, plygr, cots, non smoking units (6). **RO ♦ $70 - $86, ♦♦ $85 - $95, ◊ $11**, AE BC DC EFT MC MP VI, ₤&.

★★★☆ Lazy River Motor Inn, (M), Murray Valley Hwy, 1.6km N of PO, ☎ 03 5032 2123, fax 03 5032 2125, 35 units [shwr, tlt, a/c, elec blkts, tel, TV, clock radio, t/c mkg, refrig, toaster], ldry, conf fac, ✕ (by arrangement), pool, bbq, dinner to unit, car wash, cots. **RO ♦ $49 - $56, ♦♦ $56 - $64, ♦♦♦ $64 - $72, ♦♦♦♦ $70 - $78, ◊ $8**, 12 units ★★☆. AE BC DC EFT MC MCH VI.

★★★☆ Paddle Steamer Motel Holiday Resort, (M), Murray Valley Hwy, 3.2km S of PO, ☎ 03 5032 2151, fax 03 5032 2251, 19 units [shwr, bath (2), tlt, hairdry, evap cool (17), a/c (2), heat, elec blkts, tel, TV, clock radio, t/c mkg, refrig, cook fac ltd (2), toaster], ldry, iron, iron brd, ⊠ (Tue to Sat), pool, cook fac, bbq, plygr, cots-fee, non smoking units (4). **RO ♦ $34 - $44, ♦♦ $44 - $65, ◊ $10**, ch con, BC DC EFT MC VI.

★★★ Campbell Motor Inn, (M), 396 Campbell St, 700m S of PO, ☎ 03 5032 4427, fax 03 5032 9110, (2 stry gr fl), 26 units [shwr, spa bath (1), tlt, a/c, c/fan (8), elec blkts, tel, cable tv, clock radio, t/c mkg, refrig, mini bar, toaster], ldry, iron, iron brd, ⊠ (Mon to Sat), pool, bbq, rm serv, plygr, cots-fee, non smoking units (12). **RO ♦ $77 - $120, ♦♦ $88 - $120, ◊ $11**, ch con, AE BC DC EFT MC MP VI.

★★★ Jane Eliza Motor Inn, (M), 263 Campbell St, 300m S of PO, ☎ 03 5032 4411, fax 03 5033 1022, (2 stry gr fl), 40 units [shwr, tlt, a/c, elec blkts, tel, TV, clock radio, t/c mkg, refrig, toaster], ldry, pool indoor heated, spa, bbq, cots. **RO ♦ $60 - $88, ♦♦ $60 - $95, ◊ $11**, ch con, 6 units ★★★☆, AE BC DC EFT MC VI.

★★★ Murray River Motel, (M), Previously Motel Murray River 481 Campbell St (Murray Valley Hwy), 1.6km S of PO, ☎ 03 5032 2217, fax 03 5032 2257, 17 units [shwr, tlt, a/c, elec blkts, tel, TV, clock radio, t/c mkg, refrig, cook fac (1), micro (1), toaster], pool-heated, bbq, cots, non smoking units (4). **RO ♦ $52 - $59, ♦♦ $60 - $72, ◊ $11**, AE BC DC EFT MC VI.

★★★ Oasis Hotel Motel, (LMH), 287 Campbell St, 400m S of PO, ☎ 03 5032 2877, fax 03 5032 9401, (2 stry gr fl), 22 units [shwr, bath (hip) (4), tlt, a/c, elec blkts, tel, TV, clock radio, t/c mkg, refrig, toaster], conf fac, ⊠, pool, bbq, non smoking units (1). **RO ♦ $51 - $62, ♦♦ $62 - $72, ◊ $11**, AE BC DC EFT MC VI.

★★★ Paruna Motel, (M), 386 Campbell St, 600m S of PO, ☎ 03 5032 4455, fax 03 5032 4964, 16 units [shwr, spa bath (2), tlt, a/c-cool, heat, elec blkts, tel, TV, movie, clock radio, t/c mkg, refrig, mini bar], ldry, pool, bbq, dinner to unit (Mon-Fri), plygr, cots. **RO ♦ $56 - $75, ♦♦ $66 - $100**, AE BC DC EFT MC MCH MP VI.

★★★ Sun Centre Motel, (M), 491 Campbell St (Murray Valley Hwy), 1.7km S of PO, ☎ 03 5032 4466, fax 03 5032 4467, 18 units [shwr, tlt, a/c, elec blkts, tel, TV, video-fee, clock radio, refrig], ldry, pool, bbq, dinner to unit, cots, non smoking units (2). **RO ♦ $55 - $75, ♦♦ $65 - $75, ◊ $11**, AE BC DC EFT MC MCH VI.

★★☆ Pioneer Motor Inn, (M), 421 Campbell St (Murray Valley Hwy), 1km S of PO, ☎ 03 5032 2017, fax 03 5033 1387, (2 stry gr fl), 30 units [shwr, tlt, a/c, elec blkts, tel, TV, video-fee, clock radio, t/c mkg, refrig, toaster], conf fac, ⊠, pool, bbq, rm serv, plygr, cots-fee. **RO ♦♦ $50, ◊ $15**, 3 units ★★★. AE BC BTC DC MC VI.

Self Catering Accommodation

★★★☆ Hill Top Resort, (HF), Murray Valley Hwy, 5km NW of PO, ☎ 03 5033 1515, fax 03 5033 1533, 16 flats acc up to 4, (Ensuite SiteStudio), [shwr, tlt, a/c, elec blkts, tel, TV, t/c mkg, refrig, cook fac ltd, toaster, blkts, linen, pillows], ldry, w/mach, rec rm, ✕, pool (salt water), bbq, kiosk, c/park (carport), plygr, tennis, cots-fee. **D ♦ $55 - $65, ♦♦ $65 - $75, ◊ $14 - $15**, ch con, BC EFT MC VI.

★★★☆ **Jacaranda Holiday Units**, (HU), 179 Curlewis St, 800m S of PO, ☎ 03 5032 9077, fax 03 5032 3730, 13 units acc up to 6, (1 & 2 bedrm), [shwr, tlt, a/c-cool (4), a/c (10), heat, elec blkts, tel, TV, video (avail), clock radio, refrig, cook fac], ldry, w/mach, pool, bbq, plygr, cots, non smoking units (4). **D ♦♦ $57 - $68, ◊ $10, W ♦♦ $360 - $399, ◊ $56**, Min book long w/ends and Easter, BC EFT MC VI.

★★★☆ **Pioneer City Caravan Park**, (HF), Murray Valley Hwy, 1km N of PO, ☎ 03 5032 4372, fax 03 5032 1531, 18 flats acc up to 6, (1 & 2 bedrm), [shwr, tlt, evap cool (8), heat, elec blkts (4), TV, refrig, cook fac, micro (9), linen reqd-fee], ldry, w/mach-fee, dryer-fee, iron-fee, rec rm, pool, bbq, ☏, plygr, golf (6 hole), tennis, non smoking units (4), Pets allowed at managers discretion. **D $50 - $90, W $300 - $540**, ch con, Min book all holiday times.

SWAN REACH VIC 3903

Pop 226. (304km E Melbourne), See map on pages 694/695, ref J7. Situated on the banks of the Tambo River. Boating, Fishing, Scenic Drives, Swimming, Tennis.

Hotels/Motels

★★ **Tambo River Hotel Motel**, (LMH), Princes Hwy, adjacent to river, ☎ 03 5156 4222, fax 03 5156 4779, 16 units [shwr, bath (hip), tlt, a/c, elec blkts, TV, clock radio, t/c mkg, refrig], ldry, ⊠, bbq (covered), cots-fee. **BLB ♦ $38 - $55, ♦♦ $50 - $65, ◊ $15**, ch con, BC EFT MC VI.

Self Catering Accommodation

★★★ **Tambo Park Cottages**, (Cotg), Bruthen Rd, 700m N of PO, ☎ 03 5156 4440, fax 03 5156 4440, 5 cotgs acc up to 6, (2 bedrm), [shwr, spa bath (1), tlt, c/fan, heat, elec blkts, TV, clock radio, refrig, cook fac, micro, blkts, doonas, linen, pillows], w/mach, bbq (covered), c/park (carport), plygr, cots. **D ♦♦ $66 - $93.50, ◊ $16.50 - $22.20, W ♦♦ $275 - $687.50, ◊ $99 - $154**, ch con, BC MC VI.

SWIFTS CREEK VIC 3896

Pop 250. (383km E Melbourne), See map on pages 694/695, ref J6. Situated on the Omeo Hwy, on the lower slopes of the Great Dividing Range. Bowls, Bush Walking, Fishing, Gold Prospecting, Golf, Horse Riding, Scenic Drives, Shooting, Squash, Swimming (Pool), Tennis.

Self Catering Accommodation

★★★☆ **The Miners Cottages Accommodation**, (Cotg), Cassilis Rd, 5km NW of PO, ☎ 03 5159 4205, fax 03 5159 4205, 2 cotgs acc up to 6, (2 bedrm), [shwr, tlt, hairdry, a/c-cool, heat (wood), elec blkts, TV, video, clock radio, refrig, cook fac, micro, toaster, ldry (in unit), blkts, doonas, linen, pillows], dryer, iron, iron brd, pool above ground, bbq. **D ♦♦ $110, ◊ $20, W ♦♦ $570, ◊ $120**, ch con, BC EFT MC VI.

TAGGERTY VIC 3714

Pop Part of Alexandra, (111km NE Melbourne), See map on page 696, ref D4. Situated at the foot of Mt Cathedral, on Maroondah Hwy, a farming district. Bush Walking, Fishing, Golf, Rock Climbing, Scenic Drives, Swimming (River), Tennis.

Self Catering Accommodation

Mount Cathedral Lodge Holiday Resort, Maroondah Hwy, ☎ 03 5774 7382, fax 03 5774 7421, 8 cabins acc up to 7, [shwr, tlt, cook fac (5), blkts reqd, linen reqd], dry rm, rec rm, TV rm, pool, cook fac, bbq, ☏. **D ♦♦♦♦ $66, ◊ $22**, ch con, Group catering-minimum 20 people (daily all meals-$44 per person).

B&B's/Guest Houses

★★★★☆ **Willowbank at Taggerty**, (B&B), No children's facilities, 29 Coomb St, ☎ 03 5774 7503, fax 03 5774 7633, 3 rms [ensuite, bath (2), hairdry, c/fan, cent heat, elec blkts, TV, CD, t/c mkg, refrig, cook fac (1), toaster], ldry, lounge firepl, ⊠ (Thu to Sun), bbq, non smoking property. **BB ♦ $88 - $99, ♦♦ $160 - $176**, AE BC MC VI.

★★★★ **Darrowby Deer Farm**, (B&B), No children's facilities, Maroondah Hwy, ☎ 03 5774 7454, fax 03 5774 7454, 1 rm (1 suite) [ensuite, hairdry, c/fan, heat, elec blkts, clock radio, t/c mkg, refrig, toaster], lounge (TV, video, stereo). **BB ♦ $90 - $95, ♦♦ $100 - $120, ◊ $50, DBB ♦ $130 - $135, ♦♦ $175 - $195**, Dinner by arrangement. BC MC VI.

Other Accommodation

Riverland Lodge, (Lodge), Group accommodation only. 3370 Maroondah Hwy, ☎ 03 5774 7270, 14 rms acc up to 12, (Bunk Rooms), [blkts reqd, linen reqd, pillows], rec rm, pool, cook fac, refrig, bbq, tennis. **D ♦ $15, ◊ $15**, Full catering available. Minimum booking - 30 people.

TALBOT VIC 3371

Pop 350. (167km NW Melbourne), See map on pages 694/695, ref D5. Old gold mining area. Historic Post Office. Bowls, Bush Walking, Gem Fossicking, Gold Prospecting, Golf, Scenic Drives, Swimming (Pool), Tennis.

Hotels/Motels

★☆ **Court House Hotel**, (LMH), Camp St, opposite PO, ☎ 03 5463 2204, 5 units [shwr, tlt, heat, elec blkts, TV, clock radio, t/c mkg, refrig, toaster], ⊠ (Fri to Sat), dinner to unit (Mon to Sat), cots. **BLB ♦ $45, ♦♦ $55, ◊ $15**, ch con, Light breakfast only available. BC EFT MC VI.

Self Catering Accommodation

★★★ **Cherokee Park Exotic Getaway**, (Cotg), 50 Whittles Rd, ☎ 03 5463 2301, fax 03 5463 2301, 4 cotgs acc up to 8, (2 & 3 bedrm), [shwr, tlt, hairdry, c/fan (2), fire pl, elec blkts, TV, clock radio, refrig, cook fac, micro, toaster, blkts, doonas, linen, pillows], spa, bbq, plygr. **D $104, W $650**, ch con, BC MC VI.

B&B's/Guest Houses

★★★★ **Bull & Mouth Restaurant**, (GH), Ballaarat St, 300m E of PO, ☎ 03 5463 2325, fax 03 5463 2122, 6 rms [ensuite, hairdry, a/c-cool (3), c/fan (2), heat, elec blkts, clock radio, t/c mkg, refrig], ⊠. **BLB ♦♦ $90 - $110**, AE BC EFT MC VI.

TALLANGATTA VIC 3700

Pop 950. (346km NE Melbourne), See map on pages 694/695, ref H4. Tourist township relocated at its present site in 1956, because of the extension of Lake Hume. Beef, dairy cattle & softwood plantations are the main industries. Boat Ramp, Boating, Bowls, Bush Walking, Fishing, Golf, Horse Riding, Sailing, Scenic Drives, Shooting, Squash, Swimming (Lake, River), Tennis, Water Skiing. See also Tallangatta Valley.

Hotels/Motels

★★★ **Tallangatta Motor Inn**, (M), 1 Akuna Ave, 100m W of PO, ☎ 02 6071 2208, fax 02 6071 2502, 20 units [shwr, tlt, hairdry, a/c-cool, heat, elec blkts, tel, TV, clock radio, t/c mkg, refrig, toaster], spa, bbq, cots. **RO ♦ $46, ♦♦ $53, ◊ $9**, 7 units ★★☆. AE BC DC EFT MC VI.

★ **Victoria Hotel**, (LH), Cnr Banool Rd & Akuna Ave, opposite PO, ☎ 02 6071 2672, fax 02 6071 3672, (2 stry gr fl), 11 rms [basin, elec blkts], ⊠. **BLB ♦♦ $35, ◊ $10**, ch con, BC MC VI.

Self Catering Accommodation

★★☆ **Bing Ventures**, (Cotg), (Farm), Omeo Hwy, 24km S of PO, ☎ 02 6071 7276, fax 02 6071 7276, 1 cotg acc up to 6, (3 bedrm), [shwr, bath, tlt, evap cool, fan, heat, elec blkts (1), TV (1), refrig, cook fac, micro, ldry, linen reqd], bbq, cots. **W $200 - $424**, Min book school holidays and Easter.

★★ **(Homestead Section)**, 2 flats acc up to 3, (1 bedrm), [shwr, bath (1), tlt, evap cool (1), c/fan, heat, elec blkts, TV, refrig, cook fac, micro, linen reqd], ldry, cots. **D $45 - $83, W $270 - $385**.

Other Accommodation

Tooma Host Farm, (Lodge), 4202 Tallangatta Valley Rd, 24km E of PO, ☎ 02 6072 5555, fax 02 6072 5306, 21 rms acc up to 12, (Bunk Rooms), [blkts reqd-fee, linen reqd-fee], ldry, rec rm, lounge (TV, video, cd), pool above ground, t/c mkg shared, refrig, bbq, ☏, plygr. **BB ♦ $8.80 - $27.50, ◊ $8.80 - $27.50, D all meals ♦ $9.90 - $71.50, ◊ $9.90 - $71.50**, ch con, ♿.

TALLANGATTA VALLEY VIC 3701

Pop Nominal, (386km NE Melbourne), See map on pages 694/695, ref J4. Agricultural and pastoral district 40km SE of Tallangatta. Fishing, Golf, Scenic Drives, Tennis.

B&B's/Guest Houses

★★★☆ **Waterfall Creek**, (GH), 60ha ecofriendly organic red deer property. Waterfall Creek Rd, 38km SE of PO, off Tallangatta Valley Rd, ☎ 02 6071 0210, fax 02 6071 0210, 4 rms [cent heat], ldry, lounge, t/c mkg shared, bbq, non smoking property. **DBB** ♦ **$99 - $132**, ♦♦ **$187 - $200**.

TANYBRYN VIC 3249

Pop Nominal, (187km SW Melbourne), See map on pages 694/695, ref D8. Small town situated near the Otway Ranges.

Self Catering Accommodation

★★★ **Meadows Farm Tanybryn**, (Cotg), 1240 Wild Dog Rd, 22km N of Apollo Bay, ☎ 03 5237 6634, 1 cotg acc up to 6, (2 bedrm), [shwr, tlt, heat (wood), CD, refrig, cook fac, micro, toaster, ldry, blkts, doonas, linen, pillows], w/mach, iron, iron brd, bbq. **D** ♦♦ **$70 - $90**, ♦ **$10**, **W** ♦♦ **$400 - $580**, ♦ **$70**, Minimum booking applies Nov 1 to May 1.

TARRAWINGEE VIC 3746

Pop Nominal, (245km NE Melbourne), See map on pages 694/695, ref G4. Agricultural district on the Ovens River. Golf, Tennis.

B&B's/Guest Houses

★★★☆ **Carinya House Bed & Breakfast**, (B&B), Beechworth Rd, 500m off Great Alpine Rd, ☎ 03 5725 1704, (2 stry gr fl), 4 rms [ensuite (2), fan, heat, elec blkts], lounge (TV), t/c mkg shared. **BB** ♦ **$75 - $90**, ♦♦ **$100 - $120**, 2 rooms ★★★★. Dinner by arrangement. BC MC VI.

TARWIN LOWER VIC 3956

Pop 200. (166km SE Melbourne), See map on page 696, ref D7. Beef, dairy cattle & sheep area, close to Phillip Island, Coal Creek & Wilson's Promontory. Boating, Bowls, Bush Walking, Canoeing, Fishing, Tennis, Water Skiing.

Hotels/Motels

★★★ **Tarwin River Motel**, (M), 19 River Dve, 500m W of PO, ☎ 03 5663 5220, 5 units [shwr, tlt, hairdry, c/fan, heat, elec blkts, TV, clock radio, t/c mkg, refrig, toaster]. **RO** ♦ **$72**, ♦♦ **$90**, ♦ **$6**, Light breakfast only available.

Self Catering Accommodation

★★ **Boggabri**, (Cotg), (Farm), 240 McBurnies & Boags Rd, off Walkerville Rd, 20km SE of PO, ☎ 03 5663 2225, fax 03 5663 2225, 1 cotg acc up to 6, (2 bedrm), [shwr, bath, tlt, fan, heat, elec blkts, TV, clock radio, refrig, cook fac, micro, elec frypan, linen reqd], ldry, w/mach, iron brd, bbq, cots. **D $85, W $300 - $425**.

TATURA VIC 3616

Pop 2,850. (168km NE Melbourne), See map on page 696, ref C2. Water Wheel Country. Bowls, Fishing, Golf, Horse Racing, Horse Riding, Shooting, Squash, Swimming (Pool), Tennis.

Hotels/Motels

★★★ **Whim-Inn Motel**, (M), Cnr Hogan St & Dhurringile Rd, 1km E of PO, ☎ 03 5824 1155, fax 03 5824 2822, 12 units [shwr, tlt, a/c, elec blkts, tel, TV, video-fee, clock radio, t/c mkg, refrig, micro (3), toaster], ⊠ (Group bookings only), bbq, plygr, cots-fee. **RO** ♦ **$65**, ♦♦ **$71 - $76**, ♦ **$11**, AE BC DC MC VI.

TERANG VIC 3264

Pop 1,850. (216km W Melbourne), See map on pages 694/695, ref C7. Old established township, centre of a dairying & mixed farming area. District was subdivided as part of the Soldier Settlement Scheme. Bowls, Croquet, Fishing, Golf, Horse Racing, Scenic Drives, Swimming (Pool), Tennis, Trotting.

Hotels/Motels

★★★ **Dalvue Motel**, (M), Princes Hwy, opposite Police Station, ☎ 03 5592 1566, fax 03 5592 1900, 11 units [shwr, tlt, a/c (10), fan (1), heat, elec blkts, tel, TV, clock radio, t/c mkg, refrig], bbq, dinner to unit, cots. **RO** ♦ **$58 - $75**, ♦♦ **$68 - $85**, ♦ **$12**, ch con, AE BC DC MC VI.

★★★ **Terang Motor Inn**, (M), Princes Hwy, 1.6km W of PO, ☎ 03 5592 1260, fax 03 5592 1268, 12 units [shwr, tlt, a/c (6), c/fan (6), heat, elec blkts, TV, clock radio, t/c mkg, refrig, micro (1)], ldry, bbq, cots-fee, non smoking units (3). **RO** ♦ **$45 - $66**, ♦♦ **$60 - $88**, ♦ **$15**, AE BC DC MC VI.

B&B's/Guest Houses

★★★☆ **Lyndhurst Bed & Breakfast**, (B&B), No children's facilities, 140 High St, ☎ 03 5592 2042, 4 rms [hairdry, fan, heat, elec blkts, clock radio], lounge (TV, video), t/c mkg shared, non smoking property. **BB** ♦ **$60 - $65**, ♦♦ **$80 - $110**, pen con, BC DC MC VI.

THE GURDIES VIC 3984

Pop Part of Lang Lang, (90km SE Melbourne), See map on page 696, ref C7. Small township overlooking Western Port Bay, located on Bass Hwy. Boating, Fishing, Swimming (Beach).

Self Catering Accommodation

★★★ **Ramsay's Vin Rose**, (HU), St Helier Rd, 400m off Bass Hwy, ☎ 03 5997 6531, fax 03 5997 6158, 4 units acc up to 6, (2 bedrm), [shwr, tlt, a/c, elec blkts, TV, clock radio, refrig, cook fac, micro (1), toaster, linen reqd-fee], w/mach (1), rec rm, bbq, cots. **D $90 - $110, W $330 - $385**, Min book Christmas Jan long w/ends and Easter, BC MC VI.

THORNTON VIC 3712

Pop 316. (127km NE Melbourne), See map on page 696, ref D4. Situated on the banks of the Goulburn River. Trout hatchery. Boating, Bush Walking, Fishing, Golf, Horse Riding, Scenic Drives, Swimming. See also Alexandra & Eildon.

Hotels/Motels

★★☆ **Rubicon Hotel**, (LMH), 1362 Taggerty Rd (Goulburn Valley Hwy), 200m SE of PO, ☎ 03 5773 2251, fax 03 5773 2437, 22 units (6 suites) [shwr, tlt, a/c, heat, cable tv, clock radio (16), t/c mkg, refrig], ldry, ⊠, ✆. **BLB** ♦ **$50 - $61**, ♦♦ **$66 - $77**, ♦ **$20**, 12 suites ★★. BC EFT MC VI.

TIMBARRA VIC 3885

Pop Nominal, (398km E Melbourne), See map on pages 694/695, ref J6. Grazing & timber district. Swimming (River).

Self Catering Accommodation

Glendoone, (Cotg), No electricity. Timbarra Rd, 41km N of Buchan, ☎ 03 5155 9323, fax 03 5155 9323, 1 cotg acc up to 6, (2 bedrm), [shwr, bath (hip), tlt, heat, refrig, cook fac, linen], bbq. **D $55 - $80**.

TIMBOON VIC 3268

Pop 700. (230km W Melbourne), See map on pages 694/695, ref C7. Centre of a noted dairying, wool growing & timber milling district. Bowls, Golf, Swimming (Pool), Tennis.

Hotels/Motels

★★ **Timboon Hotel**, (LMH), 85 Curdievale Rd, 100m N of PO, ☎ 03 5598 3021, 7 units [shwr, tlt, fan, heat, elec blkts, TV, clock radio, t/c mkg, refrig, toaster], ⊠ (Wed to Sun), cots-fee. **BLB** ♦ **$38.50**, ♦♦ **$44 - $55**, ♦ **$7.50**, Light breakfast only available. BC MC VI.

Self Catering Accommodation

★★★★ **Willow Glen Cottages**, (Cotg), Timboon - Cobden Rd Scotts Creek Via, 6km E of Timboon, ☎ 03 5595 9277, fax 03 5595 9277, 1 cotg acc up to 5, (2 bedrm), [shwr, bath (hip), tlt, hairdry, a/c, c/fan, heat, elec blkts, TV, clock radio, t/c mkg, refrig, cook fac ltd, micro, elec frypan, toaster, blkts, linen, pillows], iron, iron brd, spa, bbq, non smoking property. **BLB** ♦♦ **$85 - $105**, ♦ **$15**, **W** ♦♦ **$450 - $735**, ♦ **$70 - $105**, Min book Christmas Jan and Easter.

★★★☆ **Curdies Holiday Farm**, (Cotg), (Farm), 330 Clovers Rd, 10km SW of PO, off Curdievale Rd, ☎ 03 5598 3260, fax 03 5598 3260, 1 cotg acc up to 8, (4 bedrm), [shwr (2), bath, tlt (2), hairdry, fan, heat, elec blkts, TV, video, clock radio, refrig, cook fac, micro, elec frypan, toaster, ldry, blkts, doonas, linen], iron, iron brd, bbq, c/park. **D $50 - $110**, Min book Christmas Jan long w/ends and Easter.

★★★ **Inglenook Cottage Industries**, (Cotg), (Farm), H Robilliards Rd, 7km SW of PO, via N Robilliards Rd, ☎ 03 5598 3250, fax 03 5598 3752, 1 cotg acc up to 8, (3 bedrm), [shwr, bath, tlt (2), hairdry, fan, heat, elec blkts, clock radio, CD, t/c mkg, refrig, cook fac, micro, toaster, ldry (in cottage), blkts, linen, pillows], iron, iron brd, bbq, plygr, Dogs allowed by arrangement. **D** ♦♦ **$95**, ♦ **$25**, BC MC VI.

Inglenook Cottage Industries ...continued
★★★☆ **(Bed & Breakfast Section)**, 1 rm [shwr, tlt, hairdry, fan, heat, elec blkts, TV, clock radio, CD, t/c mkg, refrig, cook fac ltd, micro, elec frypan, toaster, pillows], lounge. **BB 👤 $65, 👥 $95, 🧒 $30**, Dinner by arrangement.

★★★ **Ridgewood Heights**, (Cotg), RMB 5158 Cobden - Port Campbell Rd, ☎ 03 5598 7327, fax 03 5598 7337, 2 cotgs acc up to 9, (3 bedrm), [shwr, bath, tlt, hairdry (1), fan, heat, elec blkts, TV, video, clock radio, refrig, cook fac, micro, toaster, ldry (in unit), blkts, doonas, linen, pillows], iron, iron brd, bbq, cots, non smoking property. **D 👥 $88 - $132, 🧒 $16.50**, 1 cottage ★★★★, BC MC VI.

★★★ **Timboon Railway Cottage**, (Cotg), 1 Barrett St, 400m W of PO, ☎ 03 5598 3612, fax 03 5598 3612, 1 cotg acc up to 6, (3 bedrm), [shwr, bath, tlt, heat, elec blkts, TV, clock radio, refrig, cook fac, micro, toaster, ldry (in unit), blkts, linen, pillows], dryer, iron, non smoking property. **BLB 👥 $60 - $80, 🧒 $15**, ch con, Min book Christmas Jan and Easter.

TONGALA VIC 3621

Pop 1,170. (220km N Melbourne), See map on page 696, ref C1. The Friendly Town. Irrigation & dairying area. Bowls, Fishing, Golf, Scenic Drives, Squash, Swimming (Pool), Tennis.

Hotels/Motels

★★ **Tongala**, (LMH), 70 Mangan St, 250m W of PO, ☎ 03 5859 0204, fax 03 5859 0931, 9 units [shwr, tlt, a/c-cool, heat, TV, clock radio (6), t/c mkg, refrig, toaster], ⊠ (Mon to Sat), 📞. **BLB 👤 $45 - $55, 👥 $55 - $66, 🧒 $10**, ch con, Light breakfast only available. BC MC VI.

TOOLAMBA VIC 3614

Pop Nominal, (171km N Melbourne), See map on page 696, ref C2. Small township west of the Goulburn River.

B&B's/Guest Houses

★★★☆ **Waramanga**, (B&B), 1275 Craven Rd, ☎ 03 5826 6376, or 03 5826 6238, fax 03 5826 6376, 4 rms [ensuite (1), shwr, spa bath, tlt, hairdry, a/c-cool (3), fan, elec blkts, TV, clock radio, t/c mkg], tlt, iron, iron brd, lounge (TV, video, cd), pool, refrig, bbq, c/park (undercover), tennis. **BB 👤 $95, 👥 $115, 🧒 $50**, Dinner by arrangement. Min book long w/ends, BC MC VI.

TOORA VIC 3962

Pop 550. (188km SE Melbourne), See map on page 696, ref E7. A dairying & agricultural district, situated between scenic mountain forests and tranquil ocean bays. Agnes Falls. Boating, Bowls, Bush Walking, Fishing, Scenic Drives, Swimming (Pool), Tennis.

Hotels/Motels

★★★ **Tooralodge Motel**, (M), South Gippsland Hwy, 500m W of PO, ☎ 03 5686 2666, fax 03 5686 2710, 14 units [shwr, spa bath (1), tlt, heat, elec blkts, tel, TV, video-fee, clock radio, t/c mkg, refrig, mini bar, toaster], ⊠, dinner to unit, boat park, cots. **RO 👤 $70 - $80, 👥 $80 - $100, 🧒 $10**, pen con, AE BC DC EFT MC VI.

B&B's/Guest Houses

★★★★ **Gumnuts Weaving Gallery**, (B&B), No children's facilities, 265 Silcocks Hill Rd, 3km N of PO, ☎ 03 5686 2621, 2 rms [shwr, tlt, heat, elec blkts, clock radio], lounge (TV, stereo, video). **BB 👤 $55, 👥 $100**, Other meals by arrangement. BC MC VI.

★★★★ **Miranda Farmhouse**, (B&B), 5208 South Gippsland Hwy, 2 kms E of PO, ☎ 03 5686 2557, fax 03 5686 2557, 3 rms [shwr, tlt, hairdry, fire pl (1), elec blkts, clock radio, t/c mkg, refrig], lounge (TV). **BB 👤 $65 - $70, 👥 $100 - $110**, 1 room ★★★☆. Dinner by arrangement. BC DC MC VI.

TOOTGAROOK VIC 3941

Pop 2,410. (82km SW Melbourne), See map on page 697, ref B8. Bayside suburb. Boating, Bowls, Fishing, Golf, Horse Riding, Sailing, Swimming (Beach), Tennis, Water Skiing.

Hotels/Motels

★★☆ **Rosebud Motel**, (M), 1869 Point Nepean Rd, 4.5km W of Rosebud PO, ☎ 03 5985 2041, fax 03 5985 6626, 12 units [shwr, tlt, fan, heat, elec blkts, TV, movie, clock radio, t/c mkg, refrig], pool, bbq, plygr, cots. **RO 👤 $50 - $90, 👥 $55 - $95, 🧒 $10**, BC MC VI.

★★☆ **Rye Motel**, (M), 1929 Point Nepean Rd, 4.9km W of Rosebud PO, ☎ 03 5985 2002, fax 03 5985 8033, 14 units [shwr, tlt, a/c-cool (2), c/fan, heat, elec blkts, TV, video-fee, clock radio, t/c mkg, refrig, micro (7), toaster], ldry, spa, bbq, plygr, cots. **RO 👤 $55 - $88, 👥 $55 - $88, 🧒 $11**, ch con, AE BC MC MCH VI.

Self Catering Accommodation

★★★★★ **Truemans Cottage**, (Cotg), 59 Truemans Rd, 4.5km SW of Rosebud PO, ☎ 03 9562 1434, fax 03 9562 0814, 1 cotg acc up to 6, (3 bedrm), [shwr, bath, tlt, hairdry, a/c, heat, elec blkts, tel (local), TV, video, clock radio, CD, t/c mkg, refrig, cook fac, micro, elec frypan, d/wash, toaster, ldry, blkts, doonas, linen, pillows], iron, iron brd, bbq, bicycle, cots, breakfast ingredients, non smoking property. **D 👥 $165 - $175, 🧒 $48, W $730 - $1,485**, ch con, BC DC MC VI.

★★★ **Elandra Holiday Flats**, (HF), 1971 Point Nepean Rd, 2km E of Rye PO, ☎ 03 5985 3701, 3 flats acc up to 6, (1 & 2 bedrm), [shwr, tlt, fan, heat, elec blkts, TV, refrig, cook fac, elec frypan, toaster, blkts, doonas, linen, pillows], ldry, w/mach, dryer, bbq, cots. **D 👤 $35 - $60, 👥 $40 - $70, 🧒 $15, W $200 - $650.**

★★☆ **Blanche Court Motel**, (HU), 1959 Point Nepean Rd, Rye 3941, 1.5km E of Rye PO, ☎ 03 5985 2917, 8 units acc up to 4, (1 & 2 bedrm), [shwr, spa bath (1), tlt, heat, TV, refrig, cook fac (7), cook fac ltd (1), micro (4), toaster, blkts, linen, pillows], ldry, bbq, 📞, cots. **D 👥 $50 - $130, 🧒 $16.50, W $240 - $800**, ch con, AE BC MC VI.

TORQUAY VIC 3228

Pop 6,000. (95km SW Melbourne), See map on page 696, ref A6. Attractive holiday and residential township, with fine sandy beaches. Bells Beach Surfing Championship (Easter). Boat Ramp, Boating, Bowls, Bush Walking, Fishing (Surf), Golf, Hangliding, Horse Riding, Sailing, Squash, Surfing, Swimming (Beach), Tennis, Water Skiing.

Hotels/Motels

Best Western

★★★★ **Surf City Motel**, (M), 35 The Esplanade, 400m SE of PO, ☎ 03 5261 3492, fax 03 5361 4032, 16 units [shwr, bath (2), spa bath (4), tlt, a/c, elec blkts, tel, TV, video-fee, clock radio, t/c mkg, refrig, mini bar], ⊠, pool-heated (solar), spa, rm serv, cots. **RO 👤 $89 - $155, 👥 $96 - $155, 🧒 $15**, 2 units ★★★☆, AE BC DC EFT MC MCH MP VI.

GOLDEN CHAIN

★★★☆ **Torquay Tropicana Motel**, (M), Cnr Surfcoast Hwy & Grossmans Rd, 1km N of PO, ☎ 03 5261 4399, fax 03 5261 4431, 18 units [shwr, spa bath (4), tlt, hairdry (4), a/c, elec blkts, tel, TV, video-fee, clock radio, t/c mkg, refrig, cook fac ltd (4), micro, toaster], ldry, rec rm, pool, spa, bbq, cots. **RO 👤 $88 - $121, 👥 $99 - $150, 🧒 $11**, AE BC DC EFT MC VI.

★★★ **Torquay Hotel Motel**, (LMH), 36 Bell St, 800m S of PO, start of Great Ocean Rd, ☎ 03 5261 6046, fax 03 5261 4065, 10 units [shwr, tlt, hairdry, a/c, heat, elec blkts, tel, TV, clock radio, t/c mkg, refrig, toaster], ⊠, rm serv (breakfast avail), non smoking units (10). **RO 👤 $75 - $110, 👥 $75 - $140, 🧒 $15**, Min book Christmas Jan and Easter, AE BC DC MC VI.

Trouble-free travel tips - **Lights**

Check the operation of all lights. If you are pulling a trailer of caravan make sure turning indicators and brake lights are working.

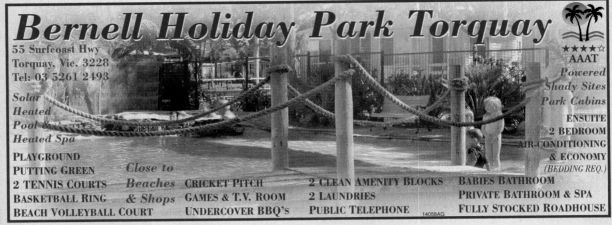

Bernell Holiday Park Torquay

55 Surfcoast Hwy
Torquay, Vic. 3228
Tel: 03 5261 2493

★★★★☆
AAAT
Powered
Shady Sites
Park Cabins
ENSUITE
2 BEDROOM
AIR-CONDITIONING
& ECONOMY
(BEDDING REQ.)

*Solar
Heated
Pool &
Heated Spa*

PLAYGROUND
PUTTING GREEN
2 TENNIS COURTS
BASKETBALL RING
BEACH VOLLEYBALL COURT

*Close to
Beaches
& Shops*

CRICKET PITCH
GAMES & T.V. ROOM
UNDERCOVER BBQ's

2 CLEAN AMENITY BLOCKS
2 LAUNDRIES
PUBLIC TELEPHONE

BABIES BATHROOM
PRIVATE BATHROOM & SPA
FULLY STOCKED ROADHOUSE

14058AG

Self Catering Accommodation

★★★★☆ **Ocean Vista B & B**, (House), 48 Cowrie Rd, ☎ 03 5261 9826, fax 03 9583 6355, (2 stry), 1 house acc up to 6, (3 bedrm), [shwr, bath, tlt, hairdry, a/c-cool, c/fan, heat, tel (local), cable tv, video, clock radio, CD, t/c mkg, refrig, cook fac (1), micro, d/wash, ldry, blkts, linen, pillows], w/mach (1), dryer, iron, iron brd, lounge firepl, bbq, c/park (garage), non smoking rms. **BLB ♦♦ $90 - $135**, Min book applies, BC MC VI.
Operator Comment: Ocean views, CLS Beach, Shops. Accom 1 to 17. Ideal for families & conference groups.
(Unit Section), 2 units acc up to 6, (1 & 2 bedrm), [shwr, tlt, evap cool (1), fan, c/fan, heat, TV, video, refrig, cook fac, cook fac ltd (1), micro, toaster, ldry (1), blkts, linen, pillows], w/mach, iron (1), iron brd (1), bbq, non smoking rms. **D ♦♦ $60 - $95, ♦ $10 - $20, W ♦♦ $360 - $650, ♦ $70 - $120**, (not yet classified).

★★★★☆ **Torquay Townhouses**, (HU), 578 Anderson St, ☎ 03 5261 9715, fax 03 5261 9716, (2 stry gr fl), 1 unit acc up to 6, (3 bedrm), [ensuite, shwr, bath, tlt, a/c, c/fan, heat, elec blkts, tel, fax, TV, video, clock radio, CD, t/c mkg, refrig, cook fac, micro, d/wash, toaster, ldry (in unit), blkts, linen, pillows], w/mach, dryer, iron, iron brd, bbq, c/park (garage), non smoking property. **D ♦♦ $125 - $160, ♦ $20, W $700 - $1,500**, ch con, Min book applies, BC MC VI.

★★★★ **Bundanoon Beach Houses**, (HU), Cnr Price & Pride Sts, ☎ 03 5261 2141, 3 units acc up to 6, (2 bedrm), [hairdry, a/c, heat, elec blkts, TV, video, clock radio, t/c mkg, refrig, cook fac, micro, toaster, ldry, blkts, doonas, linen, pillows], ldry, w/mach, lounge firepl, spa, bbq, c/park (undercover). **D $120 - $230, W $700 - $1,500**.

★★★★ **Surfcoast Retreat**, (HU), 15 Aquarius Ave, 2Km NE of PO, ☎ 03 5261 3025, fax 03 5261 3045, (2 stry gr fl), 2 units acc up to 6, (2 bedrm), [shwr, tlt, fan, heat, TV, video, clock radio, refrig, cook fac, micro, toaster, ldry, linen], bar, spa, bbq, plygr, tennis, non smoking property. **D ♦♦ $80, ♦ $20, W $500 - $700**, ch con, pen con, Min book Christmas Jan long w/ends and Easter, AE BC JCB MC VI.
(Cottage Section), (2 stry), 2 cotgs acc up to 4, (3 bedrm), [shwr, spa bath, tlt, heat, TV, video, clock radio, t/c mkg, refrig, cook fac, micro, elec frypan, d/wash, toaster, ldry, blkts, doonas, linen, pillows], w/mach, dryer, iron, iron brd, bbq, c/park (garage), cots, non smoking property. **D ♦♦ $110 - $125, ♦ $20, W $600 - $1,400**, ch con, Min book Christmas Jan long w/ends and Easter.

★★★☆ **Amikos at Torquay**, (Cotg), Previously Torquay Bed & Breakfast 17 Anderson St, 300m S of PO, ☎ 03 5261 4732, fax 03 9379 8645, 1 cotg acc up to 5, (2 bedrm), [shwr, tlt, hairdry, heat, elec blkts, TV, clock radio, t/c mkg, refrig, cook fac ltd, micro, toaster], iron, iron brd, lounge firepl, non smoking property, Pets welcome. **D ♦ $40 - $75, ♦♦ $60 - $110, ♦ $10 - $40**, Min book Christmas Jan and Easter, AE BC MC VI.

★★★ **Torquay Country Retreat**, (Cotg), (Farm), 135 Briody Dve, 3.2km NW of PO, ☎ 03 5261 3144, fax 03 5261 3144, 1 cotg acc up to 4, (2 bedrm), [shwr, tlt (external), a/c-cool, heat, clock radio, refrig, cook fac, micro, blkts, linen, pillows], rec rm, tennis. **BB ♦♦ $139, ♦ $30**, ch con.

B&B's/Guest Houses

★★★★☆ **Potters Inn**, (B&B), 40 Bristol Rd, 100m W of PO, ☎ 03 5261 4131, fax 03 5261 4131, 2 rms [ensuite, bath (1), elec blkts], lounge (TV, video, cd), t/c mkg shared, non smoking property. **BB ♦ $60, ♦♦ $85**, AE BC MC VI.

★★★★☆ **Pride of Torquay B & B**, (B&B), Previously Torquay Beach B & B, 6 Pride St, 1km S of PO, ☎ 03 5261 4127, fax 03 5261 3904, (2 stry), 2 rms [shwr, tlt, hairdry, a/c, c/fan, elec blkts, clock radio], ldry, t/c mkg shared, refrig, bbq, non smoking property. **BB ♦ $90 - $120, ♦♦ $120 - $150**, Dinner by arrangement. Min book Christmas Jan long w/ends and Easter, AE BC BTC MC VI.

★★★★ **Ocean Manor Bed & Breakfast**, (B&B), 3 Glengarry Dve, 2km N of PO, ☎ 03 5261 3441, fax 03 5261 9140, (2 stry), 1 rm (1 suite) [hairdry, a/c, c/fan, cent heat, elec blkts, TV, video, clock radio, t/c mkg, refrig, micro, toaster], non smoking property. **Suite BLB ♦♦ $110 - $120**, Min book Christmas Jan long w/ends and Easter, BC MC VI.

★★★★ **Ocean Road Retreat**, (B&B), 101 Sunset Strip, Jan Juc 3228, ☎ 03 5261 2971, fax 03 5261 2971, 4 rms (1 suite) [ensuite (3), shwr (1), spa bath (3), tlt (1), a/c-cool (2), c/fan (3), heat (wood) (1), TV, video, clock radio, CD, t/c mkg, refrig, micro (3), toaster (1)]. **BB ♦♦ $120 - $195**, BC MC VI.

★★★★ **Seawyns Bed & Breakfast**, (B&B), 21 Torquay Blvd, Jan Juc 3228, 3km SW of PO, ☎ 03 5261 3474, fax 03 5261 3474, (2 stry), 1 rm (1 suite) [shwr, bath, tlt, hairdry, a/c, elec blkts, TV, video, clock radio, t/c mkg, refrig, cook fac, micro, toaster], ldry, bbq. **BLB ♦ $85, ♦♦ $120**, ch con, Min book Christmas Jan long w/ends and Easter, BC MC VI.

★★★★ **Tracks Bed - Breakfast**, (B&B), 12 Carnoustie Ave, Jan Juc 3228, ☎ 03 5261 5514, fax 03 5261 5514, 2 rms [shwr, tlt, hairdry, heat, elec blkts, TV, clock radio, t/c mkg, refrig, micro, toaster, doonas], iron, iron brd, non smoking property. **BB ♦ $80, ♦♦ $100 - $110**, Min book Christmas Jan and Easter.

★★★☆ **Just Junes B & B**, (B&B), 12 Casino Crt, ☎ 03 5261 3771, 2 rms [shwr, bath, tlt, fan, heat, elec blkts, radio, t/c mkg], lounge (TV, stereo, video), refrig, c/park (undercover), non smoking property. **BB ♦ $60 - $70, ♦♦ $85 - $95**.

Other Accommodation

Bells Beach Backpackers, (Lodge), 51 Surfcoast Hwy, ☎ 03 5261 7070, fax 03 5261 3879, (Multi-stry gr fl), 5 rms acc up to 6, (Bunk Rooms), [c/fan, heat], ldry, rec rm, lounge (TV, video, stereo), cook fac, bbq, non smoking property. **D ♦ $20, ♦♦ $50**, Key Deposit $10. AE BC DC EFT MC VI, 🖾.
(Holiday Flat Section), 1 flat acc up to 6, [shwr, tlt, heat, elec blkts, TV, clock radio, refrig, cook fac, blkts, linen]. **D $100, W $600**.

TOWONG VIC 3707

Pop Part of Corryong, (436km NE Melbourne), See map on pages 694/695, ref J4. A small pastoral township in the Murray River. Burrowa-Pine Mountain National Park. Bush Walking, Fishing (Trout, Murray Cod), Scenic Drives, Snow Skiing, Swimming (River), Tennis.

Self Catering Accommodation

★★★ **Snowy Mountain Holidays**, (Cotg), Sullivan St, off Tumbarumba Rd, ☎ 02 6076 8252, fax 02 6076 2175, 2 cotgs acc up to 6, (1 bedrm), [shwr, bath (hip) (1), tlt, fan, heat, TV, radio, refrig, cook fac, micro, ldry, blkts, linen, pillows], bbq. **D ♦ $70, ♦ $12**.

TRAFALGAR VIC 3824

Pop 2,250. (122km SE Melbourne), See map on page 696, ref E6. Dairying and pastoral district in Central Gippsland. Bowls, Golf.

B&B's/Guest Houses

★★★★ **Windrush Cottage**, (B&B), No children's facilities, RMB 3220 Sunny Creek Rd, 7km S of PO, ☎ 03 5634 7668, (2 stry gr fl), 2 rms [ensuite, bath (1), hairdry, a/c (1), heat, elec blkts, clock radio], lounge, lounge firepl, t/c mkg shared, non smoking property. **BB ♦ $80 - $110, ♦♦ $100 - $132**, Dinner available. AE BC MC VI.

Other Accommodation

Delhuntie Park, (Lodge), Cemetery Rd, 3km E of PO, off Princes Hwy, ☎ 03 5633 1688, fax 03 5633 1683, 6 rms acc up to 15, [heat (wood), cook fac, blkts reqd-fee, linen reqd-fee, pillows reqd-fee], bbq, plygr, canoeing. **D $88 - $180, W $440 - $900**, VI.

VICTORIA

T

TRARALGON VIC 3844

Pop 19,000. (164km E Melbourne), See map on page 696, ref E6. Expanding Latrobe Valley city on the main Gippsland railway, supported by pastoral, agricultural & timber industries. Bowls, Croquet, Fishing, Golf, Greyhound Racing, Horse Racing, Scenic Drives, Swimming, Tennis, Trotting.

Hotels/Motels

★★★★ **Latrobe Motel & Convention Centre**, (M), Princes Hwy, 3.6km W of PO, ☎ 03 5174 2338, fax 03 5174 9576, (2 stry gr fl), 25 units [shwr, spa bath (14), tlt, hairdry, a/c, elec blkts, tel, TV, video-fee, movie, clock radio, t/c mkg, refrig, mini bar], ldry, iron, iron brd, rec rm, conf fac, ⊠ (Mon to Sat), bar (cocktail), pool, spa, rm serv, gym, tennis, cots-fee. **RO ♦ $120 - $150, ♦♦ $130 - $160, ◊ $15**, AE BC DC EFT MC VI.

★★★☆ **(Trans Eastern Section)**, 36 units (7 suites) [shwr, spa bath (6), tlt, hairdry, a/c, elec blkts, tel, TV, video-fee, clock radio, t/c mkg, refrig, mini bar], iron, iron brd, pool, spa, rm serv, gym, tennis. **RO ♦ $70 - $130, ◊ $15, Suite D $125 - $140.**

★★★☆ **Century Inn**, (M), Previously Victorianos Motor Inn. Cnr Princes Hwy & Airfield Rd, 6.5km W of PO, ☎ 03 5176 1822, fax 03 5176 1910, 12 units [shwr, tlt, a/c-cool, heat, elec blkts, tel, TV, t/c mkg, refrig, toaster], conf fac, ⊠, pool, cots. **D $85**, ch con, 5 units not rated. AE BC DC MC VI.

★★★☆ **Connells Motel**, (M), 144 Princes Hwy, 1km W of PO, ☎ 03 5174 5221, fax 03 5174 5222, (2 stry gr fl) 14 units [shwr, tlt, a/c, elec blkts, tel, TV, video-fee, clock radio, t/c mkg, refrig, toaster], dinner to unit, cots-fee, non smoking units (10). **RO ♦ $54, ♦♦ $60 - $70, ◊ $11**, AE BC DC EFT MC VI.

 ★★★☆ **Governor Gipps Motor Inn**, (M), 59 Argyle St (Princes Hwy), 500m E of PO, ☎ 03 5174 5382, fax 03 5174 3888, (2 stry gr fl), 22 units [shwr, spa bath (2), tlt, hairdry, a/c, elec blkts, tel, TV, video, clock radio, t/c mkg, refrig, mini bar, toaster], iron, iron brd, conf fac, ⊠, pool, spa, rm serv, cots. **RO ♦ $70 - $110, ♦♦ $73 - $110, ◊ $10**, 24 hour cancellation notice, AE BC DC EFT JCB MC MP VI.

(Apartment Section), 2 apts **D ♦ $135 - $160, ◊ $10**, (not yet classified).

 ★★★☆ **Murphy's Motor Inn**, (M), Previously The Angus McMillan Motel Princes Hwy, 3.4km E of PO, ☎ 03 5174 2381, fax 03 5174 2389, 32 units [shwr, spa bath (4), tlt, a/c (24), heat (8), elec blkts, tel, TV, video-fee, clock radio, t/c mkg, refrig, cook fac (4), toaster, ldry], pool, sauna, cots-fee, non smoking units (16). **RO ♦ $45 - $90, ♦♦ $45 - $90, ◊ $10**, 8 units ★★★☆. 8 units ★★★★. AE BC DC EFT MC VI.

★★★☆ **Strzelecki Motor Lodge**, (M), 54 Argyle St (Princes Hwy), 600m E of PO, ☎ 03 5174 6322, fax 03 5174 6113, (2 stry gr fl), 23 units [shwr, tlt, a/c-cool, heat, elec blkts, tel, cable tv, video-fee, clock radio, t/c mkg, refrig], iron, iron brd, conf fac, ⊠ (Mon to Sat), pool, rm serv, cots-fee, non smoking units (8). **RO ♦ $85 - $120, ◊ $10**, AE BC DC EFT JCB MC MP VI.

 ★★★☆ **Sundowner Chain Motor Inns**, (M), 40 Princes Hwy, 400m SW of PO, ☎ 03 5174 7277, fax 03 5174 0793, (2 stry gr fl), 31 units (1 suite) [shwr, spa bath (1), tlt, a/c, elec blkts, tel, TV, video-fee, clock radio, t/c mkg, refrig, mini bar, toaster], iron, iron brd, conf fac, ⊠, cots-fee, non smoking units (12). **RO ♦ $73 - $116, ♦♦ $78 - $116, ◊ $11**, ch con, AE BC DC EFT MC MP VI.

 ★★★ **City Gardens Motel Traralgon**, (M), 80 Argyle St (Princes Hwy), 1km E of PO, ☎ 03 5174 6066, fax 03 5174 4434, (2 stry gr fl), 13 units [shwr, tlt, a/c-cool, heat, elec blkts, tel, TV, clock radio, t/c mkg, refrig], cots, non smoking units (2). **RO ♦ $50, ♦♦ $63 - $65, ♦♦♦♦ $80**, AE BC DC EFT MC MCH VI.

★★★ **Motel Traralgon**, (M), Cnr Lodge Dve & Princes Hwy, 2.6km W of PO, ☎ 03 5174 2241, fax 03 5174 2242, 22 units [shwr, spa bath (2), tlt, a/c, heat, elec blkts, tel, TV, clock radio, t/c mkg, refrig], dinner to unit, cots. **RO ♦ $38.50, ♦♦ $55 - $71.50, ◊ $10**, ch con, AE BC MC VI.

★ **Grand Junction**, (LH), Cnr Franklin St & Princes Hwy, 400m S of PO, ☎ 03 5174 6011, fax 03 5176 2130, (2 stry), 10 rms [basin, shwr, tlt, a/c, elec blkts, TV, t/c mkg, refrig], ⊠, ✆, cots. **RO ♦ $35, ♦♦ $45, ◊ $4**, No car parking available. AE BC MC VI.

Self Catering Accommodation

★★★★ **Creek Cottage Bed & Breakfast**, (HU), 14 George St, 500m E of PO, ☎ 03 5174 4367, fax 03 5174 4367, (2 stry gr fl), 3 units acc up to 6, (Studio, 1 & 2 bedrm), [ensuite, bath (1), spa bath (2), hairdry, a/c (2), c/fan, heat (1), elec blkts, TV, video (3), clock radio, refrig, cook fac (1), micro, elec frypan (1), toaster, ldry, blkts, doonas, linen, pillows], iron, iron brd, bbq, breakfast ingredients, non smoking property. **BLB ♦ $85 - $110, ♦♦ $95 - $120, ◊ $40**, ch con, BC MC VI.

TRAWOOL VIC 3660

Pop Part of Seymour, (100km N Melbourne), See map on page 696, ref C3. Agricultural & dairying district. Fishing, Scenic Drives, Swimming (River).

Hotels/Motels

★★★☆ **Trawool Valley Resort**, (LMH), Goulburn Valley Hwy, 13km SE of Seymour, ☎ 03 5792 1444, fax 03 5792 1643, (2 stry), 20 units [shwr, bath (hip), spa bath (13), tlt, hairdry, a/c, elec blkts, tel, TV, clock radio, t/c mkg, refrig, mini bar, toaster], ldry, iron, iron brd, rec rm, conf fac, ⊠ (Sat only), pool indoor heated, sauna, spa, bbq, plygr, squash, tennis, cots-fee. **RO ♦ $77 - $150, ♦♦ $105 - $350, ◊ $35**, ch con, AE BC DC EFT MC VI.

★★★ **(Motel Section)**, 7 units [shwr, bath (hip), tlt, hairdry, a/c, fan, c/fan, heat, elec blkts, tel, TV, clock radio, t/c mkg, refrig, mini bar, toaster], iron, iron brd, cots-fee. **D $140 - $180.**

B&B's/Guest Houses

★★★★☆ **Rosehill Cottages and Licensed Cafe**, (B&B), Goulburn Valley Hwy, ☎ 03 5799 1595, fax 03 5799 1467, 2 rms [ensuite, hairdry, c/fan, heat (wood), elec blkts, TV, video, clock radio, CD, t/c mkg, refrig, micro, doonas], iron, iron brd, non smoking property. **BB ♦ $100, ♦♦ $130 - $160, ◊ $35**, AE BC DC EFT MC VI.

★★★☆ **Schoolhouse Gallery**, (B&B), 5570 Goulburn Valley Hwy, 1.5km E of Trawool Bridge, ☎ 03 5792 3118, 2 rms [shwr, spa bath (1), tlt, hairdry, fan, elec blkts, radio, t/c mkg], lounge (TV), bbq, non smoking rms (2). **BB ♦ $80, ♦♦ $95**, BC MC VI.

TRENTHAM VIC 3458

Pop 650. (100km NW Melbourne), See map on page 696, ref A4. Close to historic gold mining area & mineral springs. Bowls, Fishing, Golf, Horse Riding, Shooting, Swimming (Pool), Tennis.

Self Catering Accommodation

★★★★ **Feldspar Cottage Bed & Breakfast**, (Cotg), 11 Falls Rd, 2km W of PO, ☎ 03 5424 1821, fax 03 5424 1884, 1 cotg acc up to 4, (1 bedrm), [shwr, bath, tlt, hairdry, c/fan, heat, elec blkts, TV, video, clock radio, CD, t/c mkg, refrig, cook fac, toaster, blkts, doonas, linen, pillows], iron, iron brd, bbq, breakfast ingredients, non smoking property. **BB ♦♦ $130 - $180, ◊ $30, W $600 - $770**, Min book applies, BC MC VI.

★★★☆ **Blue Mount Accommodation**, (Cotg), Kearneys Rd, Newbury 3458, 800m off Trentham-Blackwood Rd, 7km S of PO, ☎ 03 5424 1296, 1 cotg acc up to 2, (1 bedrm), [shwr, tlt, hairdry, c/fan, heat, elec blkts, TV, video, CD, t/c mkg, refrig, cook fac, micro, toaster, blkts, doonas, linen, pillows], ldry, w/mach, dryer, iron, iron brd, bbq, breakfast ingredients, non smoking property. **BB ♦♦ $140 - $150, W ♦♦ $600 - $700**, BC MC VI.

★★★ **Trentham Guest Accommodation**, (Cotg), 37 Market St, 50m S of PO, ☎ 0419 324 367, 1 cotg acc up to 4, (2 bedrm), [shwr, bath, tlt, hairdry, heat, TV, video, CD, cook fac, micro, toaster, ldry, blkts, doonas, linen, pillows], w/mach, dryer, iron, iron brd, lounge firepl, c/park (carport), non smoking property. **D $120 - $175**, Min book applies.

★★☆ **Kattemingga**, (HU), Beaches La, Newbury 3458, 8km S of Trentham, off Blackwood - Trentham Rd, ☎ 03 5424 1415, fax 03 5424 1609, 6 units acc up to 3, (Studio), [shwr, tlt, heat, t/c mkg, refrig, cook fac, blkts, linen, pillows], conf fac, spa, bbq, ✆, tennis. **D ♦ $85 - $120, ♦♦ $104 - $137, ◊ $16.50.**

(Lodge Section), 9 rms acc up to 24, [ensuite (2), heat, t/c mkg (2), blkts, linen, pillows], lounge (tv), cook fac, refrig, ✆. **D ♦ $35, ◊ $35**, ch con.

B&B's/Guest Houses

★★★★☆ **Wattlefield Bed & Breakfast**, (B&B), 130 McGiffords Rd, 14km E of Trentham PO, ☎ 03 5424 8561, fax 03 5424 8563, 2 rms [ensuite, hairdry, heat, elec blkts, clock radio, t/c mkg], lounge (TV, cd), lounge firepl, bbq. **BB ♦♦ $125 - $150**, Min book long w/ends, BC MC VI.

★★★★ **Lisieux B & B and Writers Retreat**, (B&B), RMB 580 Newtons La Fern Hill Via, ☎ 03 5424 1401, fax 03 5424 1051, 2 rms (1 suite) [shwr, tlt, hairdry, fan (1), c/fan (1), fire pl (1), heat, elec blkts, TV, video, CD, t/c mkg, refrig, micro (1), toaster], bbq, non smoking property. **BB ♦♦ $140 - $180**, Min book long w/ends and Easter, BC MC VI.

★★★☆ **The Cosmopolitan Trentham**, (B&B), Classified by National Trust, Cnr Cosmo Rd & High St, ☎ 03 5424 1616, fax 03 5424 1616, (2 stry gr fl), 6 rms [ensuite (2), heat, elec blkts, TV (2)], ldry, lounge (TV, video, cd), lounge firepl. **BB ♦ $70, ♦♦ $125**, BC MC VI.

TYABB VIC 3913

Pop 1,250. (56km S Melbourne), See map on page 697, ref D7. Small township in an agricultural & fruit growing district.

Hotels/Motels

★★★ **Peninsula Motor Inn**, (M), Cnr Mornington -Tyabb Rd & Stuart Rd, 600m W of town centre, ☎ 03 5977 4431, fax 03 5977 3208, (2 stry gr fl), 34 units [shwr, spa bath (2), tlt, hairdry (2), a/c, tel, TV, clock radio, t/c mkg, refrig], ldry, rec rm, lounge, conf fac, ⊠, pool indoor heated, sauna, spa, bbq, rm serv, dinner to unit, cots-fee, non smoking units (2). **RO** ♦ **$71.50 - $99**, ♦♦ **$77 - $99**, ◊ **$11**, AE BC DC EFT MC VI.

TYRENDARRA VIC 3285

Pop 880. (338km SW Melbourne), See map on pages 694/695, ref A7. Small township on the Fitzroy River near Portland. Boating, Fishing, Horse Riding, Swimming.

Self Catering Accommodation

★★★ **Gran's Cottage**, (Cotg), (Farm), RMB 7070, 600m N of PO, ☎ 03 5529 5361, 1 cotg acc up to 4, (2 bedrm), [shwr, bath, tlt, hairdry, fan, heat, elec blkts, TV, clock radio, refrig, cook fac, micro, elec frypan, ldry, blkts, doonas, linen, pillows], bbq, breakfast ingredients, non smoking property. **D** ♦♦ **$70**, ◊ **$15**, **W $300**.

UPWEY VIC

See Dandenong Ranges Region.

VENUS BAY VIC 3956

Pop 400. (165km SE Melbourne), See map on page 696, ref D7. Coastal hideaway featuring 22km of magnificent sandy surf beach, patrolled over the summer months. Cape Liptrap Coastal Park and Anderson Inlet with wildlife in abundance. Bird Watching, Boating, Bush Walking, Fishing, Surfing, Swimming.

Self Catering Accommodation

★★★ **Inlet View Accommodation**, (HU), 723 Lees Rd, ☎ 03 5663 7344, 2 units acc up to 8, (1 & 3 bedrm), [shwr, tlt, hairdry, c/fan, heat, TV, clock radio, t/c mkg, refrig, cook fac, toaster, blkts, linen, pillows], ldry, w/mach, dryer, pool, bbq, cots, breakfast ingredients. **BB** ♦♦ **$80**, ◊ **$25**, ch con.

★★★ **Jupiter Lodge Holiday Apartments**, (Apt), 192 Jupiter Blvd, ☎ 03 9306 5298, fax 03 9306 5711, (2 stry gr fl), 2 apts acc up to 6, (3 bedrm), [c/fan, heat, TV, video, clock radio, refrig, cook fac, micro, elec frypan, toaster, ldry (in unit), blkts, doonas, linen reqd-fee, pillows], w/mach, iron, iron brd, bbq, c/park (undercover), non smoking property. **D $105 - $115, W $670 - $750**, Min book Christmas and Jan, BC MC VI.

B&B's/Guest Houses

★★★★☆ **Te Kiteroa Bed & Breakfast**, (B&B), 43 Louis Rd, ☎ 03 5663 7437, fax 03 5663 7737, 3 rms [shwr, tlt, hairdry, c/fan, heat, elec blkts, TV (2), video (2), clock radio], lounge (TV, video), t/c mkg shared, bbq, non smoking property. **BB** ♦♦ **$121**, BC MC VI, ♿.

★★★★ **Sundowner Lodge Guest House & Restaurant**, (GH), No children's facilities, 128 Inlet View Rd, ☎ 03 5663 7099, fax 03 5663 7674, (2 stry), 4 rms [ensuite, hairdry, c/fan, heat, TV, clock radio], ldry, ⊠, spa, t/c mkg shared, refrig, bbq, non smoking property. **BB** ♦ **$77 - $88**, ♦♦ **$109 - $120**, BC EFT MC VI.

VICTORIA VALLEY VIC

See Grampians Region.

VIOLET TOWN VIC 3669

Pop 600. (169km NE Melbourne), See map on page 696, ref D2. Small farming community. Northern foothills of the Strathbogie Ranges closeby. Bowls, Bush Walking, Golf, Scenic Drives, Shooting, Swimming, Tennis.

Self Catering Accommodation

★★ **Rivendell Rural Retreat**, (Cotg), Solar power. Seebers Rd, Marraweeney 3669, 14km E of PO, ☎ 03 5790 8516, 1 cotg acc up to 6, (2 bedrm), [shwr, tlt, heat (wood), refrig (gas), cook fac, blkts, doonas, linen, pillows], bbq. **D** ♦♦ **$71.50**, ◊ **$11**, **W $429**.

WAHGUNYAH VIC 3687

Pop 700. (283km NE Melbourne), See map on pages 694/695, ref G4. Situated on the bank of Murray River. Bowls, Fishing, Golf, Scenic Drives, Swimming (River), Tennis, Vineyards, Wineries. See also Corowa & Rutherglen.

Hotels/Motels

★★★☆ **Wahgunyah Motel**, (M), 59 Victoria St, 800m SW of PO, ☎ 02 6033 1322, fax 02 6033 1243, 7 units [shwr, tlt, hairdry, a/c, fan, elec blkts, tel, TV, video-fee, movie, clock radio, t/c mkg, refrig, toaster], ldry, iron, iron brd, bbq, dinner to unit, cots-fee, non smoking units (2). **RO** ♦ **$54 - $82.50**, ♦♦ **$82.50 - $86**, ◊ **$16 - $22**, AE BC DC MC VI.

★★★ **Motel Riverside Wahgunyah**, (M), Short St, 300m SE of PO, ☎ 02 6033 1177, fax 02 6033 1177, 10 units [shwr, tlt, a/c-cool, heat, elec blkts, tel, TV, clock radio, t/c mkg, refrig, toaster], ldry, bbq, cots (avail)-fee. **BLB** ♦ **$62 - $70**, ♦♦ **$68 - $78**, ◊ **$20**, ch con, 4 units ★★☆. BC MC VI.

WALHALLA VIC 3825

Pop 28. (180km E Melbourne), See map on page 696, ref E6. Historic gold mining town, situated on Stringer's Creek. Museum, Long Tunnel Mine, Spetts Cottage, Windsor House, Old Bank Vault, cemetery. Bush Walking, Scenic Drives.

B&B's/Guest Houses

★★★★ **Walhalla's Star Hotel**, (GH), Main Rd, 150m N of PO, ☎ 03 5165 6262, fax 03 5165 6261, (2 stry gr fl), 12 rms [ensuite, c/fan, heat, elec blkts, clock radio, CD], lounge, conf fac, ⊠, t/c mkg shared, cots, non smoking property. **BLB** ♦ **$149 - $181**, ♦♦ **$149 - $181**, ◊ **$15**, Min book long w/ends and Easter, AE BC DC MC VI, ♿.

★★★ **Walhalla's Federation House**, (B&B), Open weekends only. No children's facilities, Church Hill Rd, 500m E of PO, ☎ 03 9803 9365, fax 03 9803 9365, 4 rms **BB** ♦ **$65**, ♦♦ **$110**, ◊ **$65**, Other meals by arrangement.

WALKERVILLE VIC 3959

Pop 722. (188km SE Melbourne), See map on page 696, ref D8. Situated on Waratah Bay. Boating, Bush Walking, Fishing, Sailing, Scenic Drives, Surfing, Swimming (Beach).

Self Catering Accommodation

★★★ **N & M Freeman**, (Cotg), 820 Walkerville Rd, ☎ 03 5663 2339, 1 cotg acc up to 6, (3 bedrm), [shwr, bath, tlt, heat, elec blkts, TV, clock radio, refrig, cook fac, micro, elec frypan, d/wash, toaster, ldry, blkts, doonas, pillows], w/mach, iron, iron brd, lounge firepl, bbq (wood fire), cots. **D $82.50 - $93.50, W $440 - $660**, Minimum booking Christmas/Jan, Easter & all weekends.

★★★ **Yaringa Farm & Seaside Cottage**, (Cotg), Bayside Dve, ☎ 03 5663 2291, fax 03 5663 2317, 2 cotgs acc up to 4, (2 bedrm), [shwr, bath (hip), tlt, heat, tel (1), TV, video (1), radio, refrig, cook fac, micro, ldry (in unit) (1), blkts, linen, pillows], bbq. **D $100 - $120, W $600 - $1,000**.

B&B's/Guest Houses

★★★★ **Jindalee Lodge**, (GH), Cape Liptrap Rd, ☎ 03 5663 2336, fax 03 5663 2323, 4 rms [ensuite, heat, elec blkts, doonas], bbq. **BB** ♦♦ **$110 - $120**, Facilities available for self catering.

WALLAN VIC 3756

Pop 3,100. (47km N Melbourne), See map on page 696, ref C4. A pastoral district presently enjoying a rapid commuter development.

Self Catering Accommodation

★★★★ **Luxury Cedar Farm Cottages**, (Cotg), Lot 4 Hadfield Rd West, Wallan East 3756, ☎ 03 5783 1342, fax 03 5783 1342, 4 cotgs acc up to 6, (Studio & 2 bedrm), [shwr, bath (1), tlt, a/c, c/fan, TV, clock radio, t/c mkg, refrig, cook fac, micro, toaster, ldry (4), blkts, doonas, linen, pillows], w/mach (1), lounge firepl, bbq, plygr, Pets on application. **D** ♦♦ **$105**, ◊ **$11**.

WALLINDUC VIC 3351

Pop Part of Ballarat, (167km W Melbourne), See map on pages 694/695, ref D6. Grazing & pastoral community. Bush Walking, Gold Prospecting, Scenic Drives, Tennis.

Self Catering Accommodation
★★★ **Naringal**, (Cotg), (Farm), 1300ha sheep & cattle property. Ballarat - Lismore Rd, 8.2km SW of Pitfield Junction, ☎ 03 5596 5122, fax 03 5596 5148, 1 cotg acc up to 6, (2 & 3 bedrm), [shwr, tlt, heat, elec blkts, TV, video, clock radio, refrig, cook fac, micro, toaster, ldry (in unit), blkts, linen, pillows], lounge firepl, bbq, breakfast ingredients. **D $100 - $125, W $500 - $700,** Tariff includes farm activities.

(Shearers Quarters), 10 bunkhouses acc up to 4, (Bunk Rooms), [blkts reqd, linen reqd], lounge (stereo), cook fac, t/c mkg shared, refrig, bbq. **D $125 - $600.**

WALLINGTON VIC 3221

Pop Part of Geelong, (90km SW Melbourne), See map on page 696, ref A6. Small settlement in the centre of the Bellarine Peninsula. Scenic Drives.

B&B's/Guest Houses
★★★☆ **Cottage Garden Bed & Breakfast**, (B&B), 395 Grubb Rd, ☎ 03 5250 2620, fax 03 5250 2620, (2 stry), 3 rms [ensuite (1), bath (1), c/fan, heat, elec blkts, clock radio, doonas], lounge (TV, stereo), t/c mkg shared. **BB ♦ $70, ♦♦ $90 - $105,** 1 room ★★★★. BC MC VI.

WALLUP VIC 3401

Pop Nominal, (341km NW Melbourne), See map on pages 694/695, ref B4. Farming district in the Wimmera.

Self Catering Accommodation
★★★☆ **Glenwillan Homestead**, (Cotg), Cnr Borung Hwy & Blue Ribbon Nth Rd, ☎ 03 5398 9224, fax 03 5398 9224, 1 cotg acc up to 12, (5 bedrm), [shwr (2), tlt (2), hairdry, fan, heat, tel (local), TV, clock radio, t/c mkg, refrig, cook fac, micro, toaster, ldry, blkts, doonas, linen, pillows], w/mach, iron, iron brd, lounge firepl, bbq, cots, non smoking property. **D ♦ $40, ♦ $40,** ch con, Meals by arrangement. Min book applies, BC MC VI.

WALWA VIC 3709

Pop 309. (433km NE Melbourne), See map on pages 694/695, ref J4. Agricultural & pastoral district, situated on the Murray Valley Hwy, adjacent Murray River. Burrowa-Pine Mountain National Park. Information centre - guided sight seeing tours available. Bush Walking, Canoeing, Fishing (Trout, Murray Cod), Golf, Scenic Drives, Swimming (River), Tennis.

Hotels/Motels
★★★ **Upper Murray Holiday Resort**, (M), Murray River Rd, 4.5km SW of PO, ☎ 02 6037 1226, fax 02 6037 1228, 4 units [shwr, tlt, hairdry, a/c, elec blkts, TV, video, clock radio, t/c mkg, refrig, toaster, doonas], rec rm, conf fac, ✉, pool, bbq, ✆, plygr, canoeing-fee, tennis, cots. **BLB ♦♦ $65 - $70, ♦ $15,** Light breakfast only available. AE BC EFT JCB MC VI.
★☆ **Walwa Hotel**, (LH), Murray River Rd, ☎ 02 6037 1310, fax 02 6037 1310, 6 rms [basin, c/fan, elec blkts], ✉ (Daily), t/c mkg shared, bbq, cots. **BLB ♦ $22, ♦ $22,** BC EFT MC VI.

Self Catering Accommodation
★★★★ **Upper Murray Holiday Resort**, (Cotg), Murray River Rd, 4.5km SW of PO, ☎ 02 6037 1226, fax 02 6037 1228, (2 stry gr fl), 16 cotgs acc up to 6, (2 bedrm), [shwr, bath (3), spa bath (12), tlt, hairdry (4), a/c, heat (wood), elec blkts, TV, video, clock radio, t/c mkg, refrig, cook fac, micro, toaster, ldry (in unit), blkts, doonas, linen, pillows], iron, iron brd, rec rm, conf fac, ✉, pool, bbq, ✆, plygr, canoeing-fee, tennis, cots. **D ♦♦ $110 - $150, ♦ $15,** 4 cottages ★★★☆. AE BC EFT JCB MC VI.

WANDILIGONG VIC 3744

Pop Nominal, (318km NE Melbourne), See map on pages 694/695, ref H5. Old mining township at the junction of Growler & Morses Creeks. Bush Walking, Fishing (River, Creek), Gold Prospecting, Scenic Drives.

Self Catering Accommodation
★★★★☆ **Knox Farm Bed & Breakfast**, (HU), School Rd, 200m E of PO, 5 minutes from Bright, mob 0417 367 494, fax 03 5755 1178, 1 unit acc up to 2, [shwr, spa bath, tlt, hairdry, a/c-cool, cent heat, TV, video, clock radio, CD, t/c mkg, refrig, cook fac ltd, micro, toaster, ldry (in unit), blkts, doonas, linen, pillows], w/mach, iron, iron brd, bbq, c/park (carport), breakfast ingredients. **D ♦♦ $120 - $150, W ♦♦ $700,** Min book Christmas Jan and Easter.

Camp Wandiligong, School Rd, 6km S of Bright PO, ☎ 03 5755 1848, fax 03 5750 1401, 6 cabins acc up to 16, [blkts reqd-fee, linen reqd-fee], shwr, tlt, ldry, rec rm, bbq, ✆, cots. **D ♦ $14.50, ♦ $14.50,** ch con, Catering available - fee.

WANDIN VIC 3139

Pop Part of Yarra Ranges, (48km E Melbourne), See map on page 696, ref C5. Picturesque rural area in the Dandenong Ranges.

Self Catering Accommodation
★★★★☆ **Katandra Gardens**, (Cotg), 49 Hunter Rd, 1km W of Beenak Rd, ☎ 03 5964 4523, fax 03 5964 4605, 2 cotgs acc up to 2, (1 bedrm), [shwr, tlt, hairdry, a/c-cool, heat, elec blkts, TV, clock radio, t/c mkg, refrig, cook fac, micro, toaster, blkts, doonas, linen, pillows], lounge (TV, cd player), bbq, breakfast ingredients, non smoking property. **D ♦♦ $140, ♦ $30, W ♦♦ $700, ♦ $140,** BC MC VI.
★★★★☆ **(Bed & Breakfast Section)**, 1 rm (1 suite) [shwr, spa bath, tlt, hairdry, fan, heat, elec blkts, TV, video, clock radio, t/c mkg, micro, toaster, doonas]. **BB ♦♦ $160.**

WANGARATTA VIC 3677

Pop 15,550. (237km NE Melbourne), See map on page 696, ref E2. Situated at the junction of the Ovens & King Rivers, on the Hume Hwy. Rich agricultural & dairying district. Name is Aboriginal for 'camping place of cormorants' Tobacco, hops & maize grown nearby, cherries, passion fruit & orange groves in the Warby Ranges. North East Tourism, Hume Hwy, 03 5721 5711. Bowls, Croquet, Fishing, Gem Fossicking, Golf, Greyhound Racing, Horse Racing, Scenic Drives, Shooting, Swimming (Pool, River), Tennis, Trotting.

Hotels/Motels

FLAG
FLAG CHOICE HOTELS™

★★★★☆ **Gateway Wangaratta**, (M), 29 Ryley St, 600m SW of PO, ☎ 03 5721 8399, fax 03 5721 3879, (2 stry), 60 units [shwr, bath (21), spa bath (35), tlt, hairdry, a/c, elec blkts, tel, TV, movie, clock radio, t/c mkg, refrig, mini bar, toaster], lift, ldry, iron, iron brd, conf fac, ✉, bar (cocktail), pool-heated, sauna, spa, rm serv, c/park (undercover), ✆, cots-fee, non smoking rms (21). **RO ♦ $94 - $160, ♦♦ $104 - $160, ♦ $10,** AE BC DC EFT MC MP VI, ⛨.
★★★★ **Hermitage Motor Inn**, (M), 7 Cusack St, 400m SW of PO, ☎ 03 5721 7444, fax 03 5722 1812, (2 stry gr fl), 18 units [shwr, tlt, hairdry, a/c, elec blkts, tel, TV, video (avail), clock radio, t/c mkg, refrig, mini bar, toaster], iron, iron brd, pool, bbq, dinner to unit (Mon to Sat), cots, non smoking units. **RO ♦ $82 - $99, ♦♦ $94 - $110, ♦ $12,** AE BC DC MC MP VI, ⛨.

★★★★ **Warby Lodge Motor Inn**, (M), 55 Ryley St, 300m SW of PO, ☎ 03 5721 8433, fax 03 5721 9533, (2 stry gr fl), 30 units [shwr, spa bath (6), tlt, hairdry, a/c, elec blkts, tel, cable tv, clock radio, t/c mkg, refrig, mini bar, toaster], ldry, iron, iron brd, pool-heated (solar), bbq, rm serv, dinner to unit, cots, non smoking units (10). RO ♦ $79.50 - $95, ♦♦ $87.50 - $110, ♦♦♦ $115 - $125, ◊ $10, ch con, AE BC DC EFT JCB MC MP VI, ⌂.

★★★☆ **Advance Motel Wangaratta**, (M), Old Hume Hwy, 1.3km NE of PO, ☎ 03 5721 9100, fax 03 5721 9647, (2 stry gr fl), 25 units [shwr, bath (hip) (2), spa bath (3), tlt, hairdry (3), a/c, elec blkts, tel, cable tv, clock radio, t/c mkg, refrig, mini bar], ldry, pool, spa, bbq, cots, non smoking units (12). RO ♦ $76 - $118, ♦♦ $87 - $125, ◊ $10, AE BC DC EFT MC VI, ⌂.

★★★☆ **Merriwa Park Motel**, (M), 56 Ryley St, 300m SW of PO, ☎ 03 5721 5655, fax 03 5721 5478, (2 stry gr fl), 28 units [shwr, tlt, hairdry, evap cool (14), a/c (14), heat, elec blkts, tel, TV, video (avail), clock radio, t/c mkg, refrig, toaster], ldry, iron (14), iron brd (14), conf fac, pool, bbq, rm serv, plygr, cots, non smoking units (7). RO ♦ $58 - $68, ♦♦ $62 - $78, AE BC DC EFT MC MP VI, ⌂.

★★★☆ **(Apartment Section)**, 10 apts acc up to 5, (1 & 2 bedrm), [shwr, spa bath (1), tlt, hairdry, a/c, elec blkts, tel, TV, video (avail), clock radio, t/c mkg, refrig, cook fac, micro, toaster, ldry (in unit), blkts, linen, pillows], w/mach, c/park (carport), non smoking units (4). D $72 - $120.

★★★☆ **Wangaratta Motor Inn**, (M), 6 Roy St East, 700m SW of PO, ☎ 03 5721 5488, fax 03 5721 5805, 28 units [shwr, tlt, a/c, elec blkts, tel, TV, video-fee, clock radio, t/c mkg, refrig, toaster], ldry, iron (15), iron brd (15), ⌧ (Tues to Sat), pool, bbq, cots-fee, non smoking units (10). RO ♦ $55 - $75, ♦♦ $67 - $87, ◊ $11, 13 units ★★★. AE BC DC EFT MC MP VI.

★★★ **El-Portego Motel**, (M), 52 Ryley St, 400m SW of PO, ☎ 03 5721 6388, fax 03 5721 6132, 17 units [shwr, tlt, hairdry, a/c-cool, heat, elec blkts, tel, cable tv, clock radio, t/c mkg, refrig, toaster], pool, bbq, cots-fee. RO ♦ $57 - $69, ♦♦ $67 - $79, ◊ $10, AE BC DC EFT MC VI.

★★★ **Millers Cottage Motel**, (M), Cnr Great Alpine Rd & Old Hume Hwy, 900m NE of PO, ☎ 03 5721 5755, fax 03 5721 5755, 14 units [shwr, tlt, hairdry (9), a/c-cool (7), a/c (7), heat, elec blkts, tel, TV, video-fee, clock radio, t/c mkg, refrig, toaster], ldry, pool, bbq, dinner to unit (Mon to Fri), plygr, cots-fee, non smoking units (3). RO ♦ $44 - $85, ♦♦ $52 - $85, ◊ $11, 6 units ★★☆. AE BC DC MC MCH VI,
Operator Comment: Good value accommodation including refurbished rooms, executive suite & economy rooms. Quiet rear units in garden setting with pool, BBQ & play area. Off-peak packages available including accommodation, breakfast & discount vouchers to local attractions.

★★★ **Wangaratta North Family Motel**, (M), Old Hume Hwy, Wangaratta North 3678, 5.3km NE of PO, ☎ 03 5721 2624, fax 03 5722 4020, 12 units [shwr, tlt, a/c-cool, heat, elec blkts, tel, TV, clock radio, t/c mkg, refrig, cook fac (6), micro (3), doonas], ldry, bbq, meals avail, c/park (carport), cots-fee, non smoking rms (3), Pets on application. RO ♦ $46 - $57, ♦♦♦ $55 - $66, ◊ $11, AE BC DC EFT MC MCH VI.

(Backpacker Section), 3 rms acc up to 10, (Bunk Rooms), [fan, heat (gas & wood), doonas, pillows], rec rm, lounge (TV), cook fac, t/c mkg shared, refrig, meals avail, courtesy transfer. D ♦ $18, ◊ $18, Breakfast available.

★★☆ **Billabong Motel**, (M), 12 Chisholm St, 100m S of PO, ☎ 03 5721 2353, 7 units [a/c-cool, c/fan, cent heat, elec blkts, TV, clock radio, t/c mkg, refrig], bbq, c/park (carport) (4), ✆, cots-fee. RO ♦ $30 - $35, ♦♦ $42 - $50, ◊ $8, ch con.

★ **(Guest House Section)**, 7 rms [a/c-cool, c/fan, cent heat, TV, clock radio, t/c mkg, refrig], shwr, tlt, ✆. RO ♦ $25 - $30, ♦♦ $40 - $42, ◊ $8.

★★☆ **Central Wangaratta Motel**, (M), 11 Ely St, 100m S of PO, ☎ 03 5721 2188, fax 03 5721 2945, 10 units [shwr, tlt, evap cool, fan, heat, elec blkts, TV, clock radio, t/c mkg, refrig], ldry, bbq, cots-fee. RO ♦ $44 - $55, ♦♦ $55 - $66, ◊ $11, BC EFT MC VI.

★★☆ **Crana Motel**, (M), 93 Tone Rd, 2.3km SW of PO, ☎ 03 5721 4469, fax 03 5721 4469, 8 units [shwr, tlt, hairdry (4), a/c-cool (3), a/c (5), heat, elec blkts, TV, clock radio, t/c mkg, refrig, micro (4)], iron (4), iron brd (4), dinner to unit (Mon to Thurs), cots. RO ♦ $45 - $53, ♦♦ $53 - $62, ◊ $12, AE BC DC EFT MC MCH VI.

★★☆ **Pinsent Hotel**, (LH), 20 Reid St, 150m S of PO, ☎ 03 5721 2183, fax 03 5721 9405, (2 stry), 11 rms [shwr, tlt, a/c, heat, elec blkts, TV, t/c mkg, refrig, toaster], ☒, ☎. BLB ♦ $50, ♦♦ $70, ♦♦♦ $85, ◊ $15, ch con, AE BC DC MC VI.

★★ **North Eastern Hotel Wangaratta**, (LMH), 1 Spearing St, opposite railway station, ☎ 03 5721 3741, fax 03 5722 3024, 4 units [shwr, tlt, fan, heat, TV, t/c mkg, refrig, toaster], ldry, ☒, bbq, ☎. BB ♦ $32, ♦♦ $48, RO ♦ $27, ♦♦ $43, Light breakfast only available. BC EFT MC VI.

B&B's/Guest Houses

★★★★☆ **Warby Range Homestead B & B**, (B&B), RMB 8720 Warby Range Rd, Wangaratta 3678, 10km SW of PO, ☎ 03 5725 7238, fax 03 5725 7218, 1 rm (1 suite) [ensuite, hairdry, c/fan, heat, elec blkts, clock radio, t/c mkg, refrig, mini bar, micro], w/mach, iron, iron brd, lounge (TV, video, cd), lounge firepl, bbq, cots, non smoking property. BB ♦ $100 - $110, ♦♦ $130 - $140, Min book long w/ends and Easter, AE BC DC MC VI.

★★★☆ **The Pelican Bed & Breakfast**, (B&B), 160ha cattle & horse stud. Oxley Flats Rd via, Wangaratta 3678, continuation of Faithfull St, 6km SE of Wangaratta, ☎ 03 5727 3240, (2 stry), 3 rms [evap cool (1), fan (1), c/fan (1), heat, elec blkts, clock radio], lounge (TV, video), t/c mkg shared, non smoking property. BB ♦ $65, ♦♦ $100, ◊ $35, ch con, Dinner by arrangement. BC MC VI.

WARATAH BAY VIC 3959

Pop 722. (201km SE Melbourne), See map on page 696, ref D8. Scenic coastal area. Boating, Bush Walking, Fishing, Sailing, Scenic Drives, Surfing, Swimming.

Self Catering Accommodation

★★★ **Sabrelyn Park Farm Holidays**, (Cotg), (Farm), Savages Rd, Waratah North 3959, 12km S of Fish Creek, off Wilsons Promontory Rd, ☎ 03 5683 2298, fax 03 5683 2298, 1 cotg acc up to 9, (4 bedrm), [shwr, bath (hip), tlt, c/fan, heat (wood), TV, video (avail), radio, cook fac, micro, linen reqd-fee], ldry, bbq, plygr, cots. D $80 - $150, W $350 - $700, ch con, Meals by arrangement.

B&B's/Guest Houses

★★★★☆ **Waratah Park Country House**, (GH), Thomson Rd (off Walkerville- fish Creek Rd), 11.6km S of Fish Creek, ☎ 03 5683 2575, fax 03 5683 2275, (2 stry gr fl), 6 rms [ensuite, spa bath, hairdry, heat, elec blkts, TV, clock radio, t/c mkg, refrig], lounge, conf fac, ☒, bar, bbq, c/park. BB ♦ $156, DBB ♦ $230 - $290, ch con, AE BC MC VI.

★★★★ **Taigh-Na-Mara Bed & Breakfast**, (B&B), No children's facilities, Cnr Waratah & Savages Rds, Waratah North 3959, 8km S of Fish Creek, ☎ 03 5683 2408, fax 03 5683 2408, 2 rms [shwr, bath, tlt, fan, heat, clock radio, t/c mkg, refrig], rec rm, lounge (TV, stereo), bbq (covered). BB ♦ $55, ♦♦ $110, ◊ $55.

WARBURTON VIC 3799

Pop 2,450. Part of Yarra Ranges, (77km E Melbourne), See map on page 696, ref D5. Sawmilling & farming township with mountains rising on three sides. Trout & blackfish are plentiful. Fern gullies & tall forests are other attractions. 'Riverslide' on river near caravan park. Art Gallery, Bowls, Bush Walking, Canoeing, Fishing, Golf, Horse Riding, Scenic Drives, Swimming, Tennis. See also Yarra Junction.

Hotels/Motels

★★★ **Motel Won Wondah**, (M), Donna Buang Rd, 1.6km E of PO, ☎ 03 5966 2059, fax 03 5966 2274, (2 stry gr fl), 11 units [shwr, tlt, fan, heat, elec blkts, TV, video-fee, clock radio, t/c mkg, refrig, toaster], ldry, ☒, bbq, cots-fee, non smoking property. RO ♦ $75, ♦♦ $85, ◊ $10, AE BC MC VI.

★★☆ **Mt Victoria Motel**, (M), 18 Park Rd, 1.2km E of PO, ☎ 03 5966 2037, fax 03 5966 9311, (2 stry gr fl), 19 units [shwr, bath (2), tlt, a/c-cool, heat, elec blkts, TV, clock radio, t/c mkg, refrig, micro (2)], ldry, rec rm, lounge, conf fac, lounge firepl, ☒, bbq, ☎, tennis, cots. RO ♦ $55 - $65, ♦♦ $75 - $80, ◊ $10, ch con, 4 units ★★★, AE BC MC VI.

Self Catering Accommodation

★★★★ **Ferny Glade**, (Cotg), Wellington Rd, 1km S of PO, ☎ 03 9707 2612, fax 03 9707 2612, 1 cotg acc up to 6, (3 bedrm), [shwr (2), bath (2), tlt, a/c, c/fan, heat (wood), tel (local), TV, video, clock radio, CD, refrig, cook fac, micro, linen reqd, doonas, linen, pillows], bbq, non smoking property. D ♦♦ $120, ◊ $20, W $650, ◊ $100.

Operator Comment: Romantic, tranquil bush setting. Close to main street & g/course. www.babs.com.au/fernyglade

★★★★ **Forget Me Not Cottage**, (Cotg), 18 Brett Rd, ☎ 03 5966 5805, fax 03 5966 9177, 3 cotgs acc up to 2, (Studio), [shwr, bath (1), tlt, hairdry, c/fan, heat (wood), TV, video, clock radio (2), CD, t/c mkg, refrig, cook fac (2), cook fac ltd (1), micro, elec frypan (1), d/wash (1), toaster, ldry (in unit) (2), doonas, linen, pillows], iron, iron brd, spa, bbq, breakfast ingredients. BB ♦♦ $150 - $280, 1 cotg ★★★☆, 1 cotg ★★★★★ (Mondos). BC MC VI.

★★★★ **Yumbara Mountain Retreat**, (Cotg), 245 Hazelwood Rd, Warburton East 3799, 8km NE of PO, off Woods Point Rd, ☎ 03 5966 5315, fax 03 5966 5315, (2 stry gr fl), 1 cotg acc up to 4, (2 bedrm - mudbrick.), [shwr, bath, tlt, hairdry, fan, heat (wood), elec blkts, TV, video, clock radio, CD, refrig, cook fac, micro, elec frypan, toaster, blkts, doonas, linen, pillows], ldry, bbq, c/park (carport), breakfast ingredients, non smoking property. BB ♦♦ $120 - $140, ◊ $20.

★★★☆ **Arrabri Lodge**, (Cotg), (Farm), Woods Point Rd, Warburton East 3799, 5.5km E of PO, ☎ 03 5966 2202, fax 03 5966 2290, 1 cotg acc up to 8, (3 bedrm), [shwr, bath, tlt, hairdry, fan, heat, elec blkts, TV, video, clock radio, CD, refrig, cook fac, micro, d/wash, toaster, ldry (in unit), blkts, doonas, linen, pillows], iron, pool, bbq, ☎, plygr, mini golf, tennis. D ♦♦♦♦ $95 - $140, ◊ $10, W $550 - $850, ch con, Tariff includes farm activities. BC MC VI.

(Bunkhouse Section), 11 rms acc up to 6, (Bunk Rooms), [cent heat, TV, video (avail), CD (avail), micro, linen reqd], shwr, tlt, ldry, lounge, cook fac, bbq. D ♦ $25, ◊ $25, ch con.

(Lodge Section), 25 rms acc up to 8, (Bunk Rooms), [ensuite (4), a/c-cool, cent heat, linen reqd-fee], ldry, dry rm, rec rm, lounge (TV, video), conf fac, ☒, BYO, t/c mkg shared, refrig, bbq, cots. D all meals ♦ $37.50 - $55, ◊ $37.50 - $55, ch con, Tariff includes farm activities.

B&B's/Guest Houses

★★★★☆ **Marion Park Gardens Bed & Breakfast**, (B&B), No children's facilities, 189 Woods Point Rd, Warburton East 3799, 3km E of PO, ☎ 03 5966 5579, (2 stry), 2 rms [shwr, spa bath, tlt, hairdry, c/fan, cent heat, elec blkts, TV, video (avail), clock radio, CD, t/c mkg, refrig], res liquor license, non smoking rms. BB ♦ $90 - $125, ♦♦ $120 - $155, AE BC MC VI.

Operator Comment: Email: info@marionparkgardens.com.au www.marionparkgardens.com.au

★★★★☆ **St Lawrence Bed & Breakfast Warburton**, (B&B), Cnr Brett & Richards Rds, ☎ 03 5966 5649, fax 03 5966 5007, 3 rms [ensuite, hairdry, fan, fire pl (2), heat, elec blkts, clock radio], lounge (TV, video, cd), res liquor license, t/c mkg shared, refrig, bbq, non smoking property. BB ♦♦ $130 - $160, BC MC VI, ♿.

★★★★ **Magnolia Country Retreat**, (B&B), 33 Blackwood Ave, 1.3km NE of PO, off Dammans Rd, ☎ 03 5966 9469, 2 rms [shwr, bath, tlt, hairdry, fan, heat, elec blkts], lounge (TV, CD player), t/c mkg shared. BB ♦ $100, ♦♦ $130.

★★★★ **Warburton Grange Conference Centre**, (GH), 3185 Warburton Hwy, 2.1km W of PO, ☎ 03 5966 9166, fax 03 5966 9310, 21 rms [shwr, spa bath (3), tlt, cent heat, tel, TV, clock radio], rec rm, lounge (TV, video, cd), conf fac, meeting rm, lounge firepl, ☒ (Sat to Sun), t/c mkg shared, bbq, cots, non smoking property. BB ♦ $120 - $170, ♦♦ $175 - $220, BC VI.

★★★★ **Warburton Health Resort**, (GH), Holiday centre for health management - no facilities for children under 16. Yuonga Rd, off Donna Buang Rd, ☎ 03 5954 7000, fax 03 5954 7001, (Multi-stry), 40 rms [shwr, tlt, a/c (2), c/fan, cent heat, tel, TV, clock radio, t/c mkg (2)], lift, ldry, rec rm, lounge, conf fac, ☒, pool indoor heated, sauna, spa, t/c mkg shared, kiosk (Mon to Fri), bicycle, gym, tennis (half court), non smoking property. D all meals ♦ $195 - $285, ♦♦ $360 - $440, AE BC DC EFT MC VI.

WARRACKNABEAL VIC 3393

Pop 2,500. (339km NW Melbourne), See map on pages 694/695, ref B4. Located on the banks of Yarriambiack Creek, it is one of the largest business centres of the Wimmera District. See also Wallup.

Hotels/Motels

★★★ **Warrack**, (M), 2 Lyle St (Dimboola Rd), ☎ 03 5398 1633, fax 03 5394 1488, 11 units [shwr, tlt, a/c, elec blkts, tel, TV, clock radio, t/c mkg, refrig, toaster], pool above ground, bbq, petrol, cots, non smoking rms. RO ♦ $50 - $55, ♦♦ $60 - $65, ♦♦♦ $75 - $85, ◊ $10, AE BC DC EFT MC VI.

★★★ **Warracknabeal Country Roads Motor Inn**, (M), Henty Hwy, 1.2km NE of PO, ☎ 03 5398 1811, fax 03 5398 1605, 14 units [shwr, tlt, hairdry, a/c-cool, heat, elec blkts, tel, TV, video-fee, clock radio, t/c mkg, refrig], pool, bbq, cots-fee, non smoking units (4). RO ♦ $58, ♦♦ $65 - $73, ◊ $11, AE BC DC EFT MC VI.

★★☆ **Werrigar Motel**, (M), Cnr Henty & Borung Hwys, 1km NE of PO, ☎ 03 5398 2144, fax 03 5398 2508, 9 units [shwr, tlt, a/c, heat, elec blkts, tel, TV, clock radio, t/c mkg, refrig], ☒, shop, petrol, cots. RO ♦ $41, ♦♦ $52, ◊ $11, ch con, pen con, AE BC DC EFT MC MP VI.

Pop 9,000. (103km SE Melbourne), See map on page 696, ref D6. Centre of a rich dairying & agricultural area, situated on the Princes Hwy. Bowls, Bush Walking, Croquet, Golf, Greyhound Racing, Horse Riding, Scenic Drives, Swimming (Pool), Tennis, Trotting.

Hotels/Motels

★★★★ **Edinburgh Motor Inn**, (M), 61 Princes Hwy, 800m W of PO, ☎ 03 5622 3339, fax 03 5622 3339, (2 stry gr fl), 16 units [shwr, tlt, hairdry, a/c, elec blkts, tel, cable tv, video-fee, clock radio, t/c mkg, refrig], iron, iron brd, conf fac, ✕, BYO, pool, bbq, dinner to unit, cots-fee, non smoking units (6). RO ♦ $70 - $100, ♦♦ $78 - $110, ◊ $15, ch con, AE BC DC EFT MC VI, ⴵᵴ.

★★★★ **Freeway Motor Inn Warragul**, (M), 50 Rulemount Rd, 2km S of PO, ☎ 03 5623 5222, fax 03 5622 3164, 18 units [shwr, spa bath (2), tlt, a/c, elec blkts, tel, TV, video-fee, clock radio, t/c mkg, refrig, mini bar], ldry, ☒ (Mon to Sat), bbq, dinner to unit (Mon to Sat), cots-fee, non smoking units (5). RO ♦ $69 - $80, ♦♦ $79 - $120, ◊ $12, AE BC DC EFT MC VI, ⴵᵴ.

★★★ **Warragul Motel**, (M), Princes Hwy, 1.7km W of PO, ☎ 03 5623 2189, fax 03 5622 2896, 14 units [shwr, tlt, hairdry, a/c-cool, heat, elec blkts, tel, cable tv, clock radio, t/c mkg, refrig], ldry, dinner to unit, cots, non smoking units (8). RO ♦ $57, ♦♦ $70, ◊ $14, AE BC DC EFT MC VI.

★☆ **Rowell's Club Hotel**, (LH), 51 Queen St, 300m S of PO, ☎ 03 5623 1636, fax 03 5622 2289, (2 stry), 15 rms [basin, fan], lounge (TV), ☒, t/c mkg shared, refrig, ☏, cots, non smoking rms (3). RO ♦♦ $35, ◊ $20, ch con, AE BC DC EFT MC VI.

Self Catering Accommodation

★★★★ **Bloomfield Cottages**, (Cotg), Number One Rd, Nilma 3821, 5km E of PO, off Bloomfield Rd, ☎ 03 5623 5188, 2 cotgs acc up to 2, (1 bedrm), [shwr, bath, tlt, c/fan, heat, elec blkts, TV, radio, CD, refrig, micro, toaster, doonas, linen, pillows], lounge firepl, bbq, breakfast ingredients, non smoking units. BLB ♦♦ $100 - $130, BC MC VI.

★★★★ **Mount Worth Cottage**, (Cotg), RMB 2788 McDonalds Trk, Seaview 3821, 23km SE of Warragul, ☎ 03 5626 4236, fax 03 5626 4236, 1 cotg acc up to 7, (3 bedrm), [shwr, tlt, hairdry, a/c, c/fan, heat, tel, TV, video, clock radio, CD, t/c mkg, refrig, cook fac, micro, elec frypan, d/wash, toaster, ldry], iron, iron brd, bbq, cots, non smoking property, Dogs allowed. BLB ♦♦ $132, Min book all holiday times, BC VI.

★★★★ **Springwood Park Nominees**, (Cotg), (Farm), 420 Lardner Rd, Warragul West 3820, 5km W of PO, ☎ 03 5623 1396, fax 03 5623 1396, 1 cotg acc up to 8, (4 bedrm), [shwr (2), tlt (2), hairdry, a/c-cool, c/fan, elec blkts, tel (local), TV, video, clock radio, t/c mkg, refrig, cook fac, micro, toaster, doonas, linen, pillows], iron, iron brd, rec rm, lounge firepl, bbq, c/park (garage), cots, non smoking property. D ♦♦ $90 - $100, ◊ $15 - $50, Farm activities included in tariff, BC MC VI.

B&B's/Guest Houses

★★★★☆ **Ann's Irish Shamrocks B & B**, (B&B), 41 Lilleys Rd, 2km W of PO, ☎ 03 5622 3063, fax 03 5622 3063, 1 rm [shwr, spa bath, tlt, hairdry, a/c-cool, fan, heat, elec blkts, tel, TV, video, clock radio, t/c mkg, refrig, toaster], rec rm, pool, spa (heated), plygr, non smoking property. BLB ♦ $95, ♦♦ $110 - $150, ◊ $10, ch con, BC MC VI.

★★★★☆ **Southside Bed and Breakfast**, (B&B), 20 Korumburra Rd, 1.5km S of PO, ☎ 03 5623 6885, fax 03 5623 6885, 2 rms [ensuite, hairdry, c/fan, heat, elec blkts, TV, clock radio, t/c mkg, refrig], spa (heated), non smoking property. BB ♦ $75, ♦♦ $100, ch con, BC MC VI.

★★★★ **Seven Oaks Country Gardens & Retreat**, (B&B), Grand Ridge Rd, Seaview 3821, 19km SE of Warragul PO, ☎ 03 5626 4260, fax 03 5626 2460, 3 rms (3 suites) [shwr, bath, tlt, hairdry, fan, cent heat, t/c mkg], ldry, bbq, cots. BB ♦ $75, BLB ♦♦ $150, 1 suite ★★★☆. Dinner by arrangement. Min book long w/ends and Easter, AE BC DC MC VI.

★★★☆ **Balmedie Bed & Breakfast**, (B&B), Nilma-Bona Vista Rd, Bona Vista 3820, 7km SE of PO, ☎ 03 5622 0016, fax 03 5622 0016, 2 rms [hairdry, heat, elec blkts, TV (1), clock radio, t/c mkg], lounge (TV), bbq, non smoking property. BB ♦ $50 - $55, ♦♦ $95 - $105, ch con.

Pop 26,050. (263km W Melbourne), See map on pages 694/695, ref B7. Coastal resort & largest city in Victoria's rich Western District. Woollen mills, and the Fletcher Jones gardens that are open to the public & illuminated at night. Flagstaff Hill Maritime Village a re-created 19th Century sea port, Aquarium & Performing Arts Centre. Tourist Information Centre, 600 Raglan Pde, 03 5564 7837. Art Gallery, Boating, Bowls, Croquet, Fishing, Golf, Greyhound Racing, Horse Racing, Horse Riding, Motor Racing, Rowing, Sailing, Scenic Drives, Shooting, Squash, Surfing, Swimming (Pool, Beach), Tennis, Water Skiing. See also Allansford & Koroit.

Hotels/Motels

★★★★☆ **Sundowner Chain Motor Inns**, (M), 525 Raglan Pde (Princes Hwy), 300m E of Visitors Centre, ☎ 03 5562 3866, fax 03 5562 0923, (2 stry gr fl), 69 units (8 suites) [shwr, spa bath (24), tlt, hairdry, a/c, elec blkts, tel, cable tv, movie, clock radio, t/c mkg, refrig, mini bar, toaster], ldry, iron, iron brd, conf fac, ☒, bar (cocktail), pool, spa, bbq, 24hr reception, rm serv, plygr, cots-fee. RO ♦ $99 - $200.50, ♦♦ $110.50 - $200.50, ◊ $11, ch con, Min book Christmas Jan long w/ends Easter May races, AE BC DC JCB MC VI, ⴵᵴ.

★★★★ **(Apartment Section)**, 6 apts acc up to 5, (2 bedrm), [shwr, tlt, hairdry, a/c, tel, cable tv, refrig, cook fac, micro, d/wash, blkts, linen, pillows]. D $153.58 - $173.02.

★★★★ **All Seasons Motor Inn & Apartments**, (M), 367 Raglan Pde (Princes Hwy), 1.6km E of Visitors Centre, ☎ 03 5561 2833, fax 03 5561 5999, 8 units [shwr, spa bath (3), tlt, hairdry, a/c, elec blkts, tel, TV, video-fee, movie, clock radio, CD, t/c mkg, refrig, mini bar, toaster], ldry-fee, bbq, rm serv, dinner to unit, plygr, cots-fee, non smoking units (3). RO ♦ $81 - $110, ♦♦ $86.50 - $130, ◊ $12, AE BC DC EFT MC MP VI.

★★★☆ **(Apartment Section)**, 16 apts acc up to 7, (2 bedrm), [shwr, spa bath (1), tlt, hairdry, a/c, tel, TV, clock radio, CD, refrig, mini bar, cook fac, micro, toaster, blkts, linen, pillows], ldry-fee, rm serv, cots-fee, non smoking units (8). D ♦ $110 - $150, ♦♦ $115 - $170, ◊ $12, ch con.

★★★★ **Anchor Belle Motel**, (M), 1 Darling St, 200m E of Visitors Centre, ☎ 03 5561 4977, fax 03 5561 1780, 16 units (5 suites) [shwr, bath (hip) (3), spa bath (6), tlt, hairdry, a/c, elec blkts, tel, cable tv, clock radio, t/c mkg, refrig, mini bar, cook fac (1), micro (6), toaster], ldry, iron, iron brd, conf fac, ✕, spa, bbq, dinner to unit, cots-fee, non smoking units (10). **RO** ♦ **$68 - $88**, ♦♦ **$77 - $110**, ch con, AE BC DC MC MP VI, ♿.

★★★★ **Central Court Motel**, (M), 581 Raglan Pde (Princes Hwy), opposite Visitors Centre, ☎ 03 5562 8555, fax 03 5561 1313, (2 stry), 40 units [shwr, bath (15), spa bath (5), tlt, a/c, elec blkts, tel, TV, movie, clock radio, t/c mkg, refrig], lift, ldry, ✕ (Mon to Sat), bar (cocktail), pool-heated, rm serv, cots. **RO $89 - $130**, ch con, AE BC DC EFT MC MP VI.

★★★★ **Hopkins House**, (M), Cnr Mortlake Rd & Whites Rd, 2.3km N of Visitors Centre, ☎ 03 5561 6630, fax 03 5561 6631, 14 units (2 suites) [shwr, bath (4), spa bath (5), tlt, hairdry, a/c, elec blkts, TV, video (8), clock radio, CD (2), t/c mkg, refrig, mini bar, cook fac (3), micro (3), toaster, ldry], iron, iron brd, res liquor license, bar (cocktail), pool-heated (salt water), spa (heated), bbq, dinner to unit (Mon to Fri), non smoking units (5). **BLB** ♦ **$85 - $135**, ♦♦ **$95 - $145**, ♀ **$12**, Suite **BLB** ♦♦♦♦ **$160 - $180**, ♀ **$12**, Min book long w/ends and Easter, AE BC DC EFT MC VI, ♿.

★★★★ **Olde Maritime Motor Inn**, (M), Cnr Banyan & Merri Sts, opp Flagstaff Hill Maritime Museum, ☎ 03 5561 1415, fax 03 5562 0767, (Multi-stry gr fl), 37 units [shwr, bath (1), spa bath (13), tlt, hairdry, a/c, elec blkts, tel, TV, movie, clock radio, t/c mkg, refrig, mini bar, micro (2), toaster (15)], ✕ (Mon to Sat), rm serv, cots-fee. **D $90 - $165**, ch con, 9 units ★★★☆, 11 units ★★★. AE BC DC MC MP VI.

★★★★ **(Holiday Unit Section)**, 4 units acc up to 6, (2 bedrm), [shwr, spa bath, tlt, hairdry, heat, tel, TV, video, clock radio, CD, refrig, cook fac, micro, d/wash, toaster, ldry (in unit), blkts, doonas, linen, pillows]. **D $150 - $160**, **W $980 - $1,100**.

★★★☆ **Centrepoint Motel**, (M), 75 Banyan St, 400m E of Visitors Centre, ☎ 03 5562 8044, fax 03 5560 5843, (2 stry gr fl), 22 units [shwr, spa bath (5), tlt, hairdry, a/c, elec blkts, tel, TV, video-fee, clock radio, t/c mkg, refrig, micro (2), toaster, ldry], iron, iron brd, dinner to unit (Mon to Sat), c/park (undercover) (2), cots-fee, non smoking units (13). **RO** ♦ **$68 - $110**, ♦♦ **$77 - $140**, ♀ **$10**, AE BC DC MC VI.

★★★☆ **City Heart Motel**, (M), 4 Spence St, 100m E of Visitors Centre, ☎ 03 5562 0500, fax 03 5561 3169, (2 stry gr fl), 17 units [shwr, spa bath (2), tlt, a/c, heat, elec blkts, tel, TV, video-fee, clock radio, t/c mkg, refrig], ldry, iron, iron brd, dinner to unit, cots-fee, non smoking units. **RO** ♦ **$61 - $88**, ♦♦ **$72 - $99**, ♀ **$10**, ch con, AE BC DC EFT MC MCH VI, ♿.

Medication and driving

Medication can effect your driving. Certain drugs can effect your mental alertness and/or co-ordination and therefore effect driving skills. Always check with your doctor the effect which any medication (over the counter or prescription) you are taking may have on your driving. There may be an alternative drug which will not affect your driving. It is best to avoid drinking alcohol while taking medication.

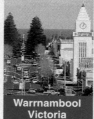

★★★☆ Tudor Motel Warrnambool, (M), Cnr Raglan Pde & Banyan St, 400m E of Visitors Centre, ☎ 03 5562 8877, fax 03 5561 1920, 22 units [shwr, spa bath (7), tlt, a/c, elec blkts, tel, TV, video-fee, clock radio, t/c mkg, refrig], iron, iron brd, ⊠, rm serv, cots-fee, non smoking units (5). **RO** ┃ **$88 - $150**, ┃┃ **$100 - $150**, AE BC DC EFT MC MP VI, ⅋⅌.

★★★☆ Warrnambool Gateway Motor Inn, (M), 69 Raglan Pde (Princes Hwy), 4.1km E of Visitors Centre, ☎ 03 5562 8622, fax 03 5561 2771, (2 stry gr fl), 24 units [shwr, spa bath, tlt, a/c, elec blkts, tel, cable tv, video-fee, clock radio, t/c mkg, refrig, mini bar], ldry, conf fac, ⊠, pool-heated (solar), bbq, rm serv, cots-fee. **RO** ┃ **$78 - $111**, ┃┃ **$88 - $121**, ┃ **$11**, AE BC BTC DC MC MP VI, ⅋⅌.

★★★☆ Western Coast Motel, (M), Cnr Raglan Pde & Bell St, 500m E of Fletcher Jones Gardens, ☎ 03 5562 2755, fax 03 5562 3353, (2 stry gr fl), 21 units [shwr, tlt, hairdry, a/c, elec blkts, tel, TV, video-fee, clock radio, t/c mkg, refrig, mini bar, toaster], ⊠ (Mon to Sat), cots. **RO** **$79 - $119**, ch con, AE BC DC JCB MC MP VI.

★★★ Chateau Lodge Motel, (M), 8 Spence St, 100m NE of Visitors Centre, ☎ 03 5562 7144, fax 03 5561 2966, (2 stry gr fl), 20 units [shwr, bath (hip) (3), spa bath (1), tlt, a/c-cool (13), a/c (7), heat (13), elec blkts, tel, TV, video-fee, clock radio, t/c mkg, refrig, toaster], ldry, rec rm, bbq, dinner to unit, cots-fee, non smoking units (7). **RO** ┃ **$55 - $88**, ┃┃ **$60.50 - $99**, ┃ **$11 - $14**, AE BC DC MC VI, ⅋⅌.

★★★ Flagstaff Hill Motel, (M), 762 Raglan Pde (Princes Hwy), 1.1km W of Visitors Centre, ☎ 03 5562 1166, fax 03 5562 1023, 14 units [shwr, tlt, a/c-cool (3), a/c (5), fan, heat, elec blkts, tel, TV, movie, clock radio, t/c mkg, refrig, toaster], bbq, cots, non smoking units (6). **RO** ┃ **$55 - $82.50**, ┃┃ **$66 - $88**, ┃ **$11**, ch con, BC EFT MC VI.

★★★ Mahogany Motel, (M), 463 Raglan Pde (Princes Hwy), 800m E of Visitors Centre, ☎ 03 5562 5722, fax 03 5562 9594, (2 stry gr fl), 14 units (2 bedrm), [shwr, tlt, hairdry, a/c-cool (7), heat, elec blkts, tel, TV, video (avail), clock radio, t/c mkg, refrig, cook fac (4), micro (12), toaster], iron, bbq, cots, non smoking rms (6). **BLB** ┃ **$55 - $82**, ┃┃ **$62 - $88**, ┃ **$11**, ch con, AE BC DC MC MP VI.

★★★ Motel Downtown Warrnambool, (M), 620 Raglan Pde (Princes Hwy), 100m W of Visitors Centre, ☎ 03 5562 1277, fax 03 5561 2171, (2 stry gr fl), 58 units [shwr, tlt, hairdry, a/c, elec blkts, tel, TV, clock radio, t/c mkg, refrig], ldry, rec rm, pool-heated, cook fac, bbq. **RO** ┃ **$70 - $200**, ┃┃ **$70 - $200**, ch con, AE BC DC MC MP VI, ⅋⅌.

★★★ Norfolk Lodge Motel, (M), 692 Raglan Pde (Princes Hwy), 600m W of Visitors Centre, ☎ 03 5562 6455, fax 03 5562 6757, (2 stry gr fl), 11 units [shwr, tlt, fan, heat, elec blkts, tel, TV, video-fee, movie, clock radio, t/c mkg, refrig, toaster], ldry, iron, iron brd, cots, non smoking units (2). **BLB** ┃ **$55 - $71**, ┃┃ **$65 - $87**, ┃ **$11**, ch con, AE BC DC EFT MC MCH VI.

★★★ Redwood Manor Motel Apartments, (M), 251 Koroit St, 500m NW of PO, ☎ 03 5562 3939, fax 03 5561 7203, (2 stry gr fl), 9 units (6 suites) [shwr, tlt, a/c-cool, heat, elec blkts, tel, TV, video-fee, clock radio, t/c mkg, refrig, cook fac ltd, micro, toaster], cots-fee, non smoking units (5). **RO** ┃ **$66 - $110**, ┃┃ **$77 - $120**, ┃ **$11**, AE BC DC EFT MC VI.

Operator Comment: The tranquility of home in the CBD, relax in our executive and family apartments with full lounge/dining fac and separate bedroom. Free pickup/delivery to rail/bus, 3 day packages and Seniors Card accepted.

★★★ Riverside Gardens Motor Inn, (M), Cnr Simpson & Verdon Sts, 2.5km E of Visitors Centre, ☎ 03 5562 1888, fax 03 5561 1459, (2 stry gr fl), 43 units [shwr, bath (3), tlt, hairdry, fan, heat, elec blkts, tel, TV, clock radio, t/c mkg, refrig], ldry, ✕, pool, spa, bbq. **RO** ┃ **$48 - $61**, ┃┃ **$55 - $87**, ┃ **$10**, ch con, 2 units ★★★☆. BC MC VI, ⅋⅌.

Operator Comment: Enjoy our facilities situated in 2 acres of pleasant garden surrounds near the Hopkins River and whale nursery. Featuring pool & heated spa, BBQ facilities and group dining rm. Quiet and comfortable units.

★★★ (Apartment Section), 2 apts acc up to 7, (2 bedrm), [shwr, bath (1), hairdry, c/fan, heat, elec blkts, tel, TV, clock radio, refrig, cook fac, micro, toaster, ldry, blkts, linen, pillows], pool, spa, bbq. **D $140**.

★★★ Southern Right Motor Inn, (M), 53 Raglan Pde, 4.7km E of Visitors Centre, ☎ 03 5561 1000, fax 03 5561 1022, 16 units [shwr, tlt, a/c, elec blkts, TV, video-fee, clock radio, t/c mkg, refrig, toaster], ldry, rec rm, bbq, plygr, cots, non smoking units (13). **BLB** ┃ **$50**, ┃┃ **$55 - $66**, ┃ **$11**, BC EFT MC VI.

★★★ Turn In Motel, (M), Cnr Simpson & Verdon Sts, 2.7km E of Visitors Centre, ☎ 03 5562 3677, fax 03 5562 3677, (2 stry gr fl), 17 units [shwr, bath (2), tlt, fan, heat, elec blkts, TV, video-fee, clock radio, t/c mkg, refrig, cook fac ltd (7), micro (7), toaster], ldry, bbq, cots, non smoking units (6). **RO** ┃ **$55**, ┃┃ **$60 - $65**, ┃ **$10**, AE BC DC EFT MC VI.

★★ Western Hotel, (M), Cnr Timor & Kepler Sts, 200m W of PO, ☎ 03 5562 2011, fax 03 5562 4324, (2 stry gr fl), 20 units [shwr, tlt, a/c (16), fan (4), heat (4), elec blkts, tel, TV, t/c mkg, refrig]. **BLB** ┃ **$49**, ┃┃ **$59**, ┃ **$6**, AE BC DC EFT MC MCH VI.

(Lodge Section), (2 stry), 15 rms lounge (TV), cook fac, t/c mkg shared. **BLB** ┃ **$16.50**.

★☆ Warrnambool Hotel, (LH), Cnr Koroit & Kepler Sts, 200m N of PO, ☎ 03 5562 2377, fax 03 5561 7248, (2 stry), 16 rms [basin (4), shwr (1), tlt (1), heat, elec blkts, TV (1), clock radio (1), refrig (1), cook fac (2)], ldry, lounge (TV), ⊠, t/c mkg shared, c/park (limited), cots. **BB** ┃ **$35**, ┃ **$35**, AE BC DC MC VI.

Self Catering Accommodation

★★★★★ Admirals Place, (Apt), 14 Pertobe Rd, 2km S of PO, ☎ 03 5562 8063, fax 03 5562 4990, 1 apt acc up to 4, (2 bedrm), [shwr, spa bath, tlt, hairdry, a/c, heat, elec blkts, tel (local), TV, video, clock radio, CD, t/c mkg, refrig, cook fac, micro, d/wash, toaster, ldry (in unit), blkts, doonas, linen, pillows], w/mach, dryer, iron, iron brd, bbq, non smoking property. **D** ┃┃ **$150 - $250**, ┃ **$20 - $35**, **W** ┃┃ **$1,050 - $1,500**, ┃ **$140 - $230**, Min book Christmas Jan long w/ends and Easter, BC MC VI.

★★★★★ Logans Beach Whale Nursery Apartments, (Apt), 7 Logans Beach Rd, 4km E of PO, ☎ 03 5561 3750, fax 03 5562 9901, (2 stry gr fl), 2 apts acc up to 4, (Studio & 2 bedrm), [shwr, spa bath, tlt, hairdry, a/c, c/fan, heat, elec blkts, tel (direct dial), TV, video, clock radio, CD, t/c mkg, refrig, cook fac, micro, elec frypan, d/wash, toaster, blkts, linen, pillows], ldry, w/mach, dryer, iron, iron brd, pool-heated (solar), spa (hydro)-fee, bbq, c/park (garage), bicycle, gym-fee, tennis, cots, non smoking property. **D** ┃┃ **$190 - $250**, ┃ **$27.50**, **W $1,338 - $1,650**, ch con, Min book applies, AE BC MC VI.

★★★★☆ Beachside Holiday Unit, (Apt), 14 Pertobe Rd, 2km S of PO, ☎ 03 5562 8063, fax 03 5562 4990, (Multi-stry), 1 apt acc up to 6, (3 bedrm), [shwr, tlt, hairdry, c/fan, heat, elec blkts, tel (local), cable tv, video, clock radio, t/c mkg, refrig, cook fac, micro, elec frypan, d/wash, toaster, ldry (in unit), blkts, linen, pillows], iron, iron brd, c/park (garage), non smoking property. **D $140 - $250**, **W $900 - $1,400**, Minimum booking long weekends, Easter & May races, AE BC MC VI.

★★★★☆ Guthrie Heights Apartment, (Apt), 8/148 Merri St, Warrnambool 3281, 500m SE of PO, ☎ 03 5562 1600, fax 03 5561 1974, 1 apt acc up to 8, [shwr, tlt, hairdry, fan, cent heat, tel (local), TV, radio, CD, refrig, cook fac, micro, d/wash, ldry, blkts, doonas, linen, pillows], iron, iron brd, bbq, c/park (garage). **D** ┃┃ **$160**, ┃ **$12**, **W $850 - $1,300**, AE DC MC VI.

★★★★ Cuttlefish Cottage, (Cotg), 15 Gibson St, 500m N of Flagstaff Hill, ☎ 03 5567 6457, fax 03 5565 1385, 1 cotg acc up to 4, (2 bedrm), [shwr, spa bath, tlt, hairdry, fan, heat (gas), elec blkts, tel (local), cable tv, video, clock radio, CD, refrig, cook fac, micro, toaster, ldry, blkts, doonas, linen], w/mach, dryer, bbq, c/park (undercover), non smoking property. **D $100 - $150**, **W $550 - $880**, Minium bookings Melbourne Cup & Warrnambool Races. BC MC VI.

Operator Comment: Very central to beach, shops, galleries & all tourist attractions.

★★★★ Kareja Apartments, (Apt), 282 Timor St, 450m W of PO, ☎ 03 5562 4244, fax 03 5562 4244, 2 apts acc up to 6, (2 bedrm), [shwr, bath (hip), tlt, hairdry, a/c, heat, elec blkts, tel, cable tv, clock radio, cook fac, micro, toaster, ldry (in unit), blkts, linen, pillows], c/park (carport), cots-fee. **D** ┃┃ **$82.50 - $121**, ┃ **$11**, **W** ┃┃ **$440 - $825**, ┃ **$66**, AE BC DC EFT JCB MC MP VI.

★★★★ **Kiki Holiday Apartments**, (HU), 6 Liebig St, 150m S of PO, mob 0417 990 660, 2 units acc up to 10, (2 bedrm), [shwr, tlt, hairdry, a/c, cent heat, TV, video, clock radio, t/c mkg, refrig, cook fac, micro, d/wash, toaster, ldry (in unit), blkts, doonas, linen, pillows], w/mach, dryer, iron, iron brd, c/park (garage). **D 👫 $120 - $170, 👤 $10 - $15, W $500 - $1,000**, Min book Christmas Jan long w/ends and Easter, AE BC DC EFT MC VI.

★★★★ **Seawaye Villas**, (HU), 73 Koroit St, 1km E of PO, ☎ 03 5562 4133, fax 03 5561 2121, 2 units acc up to 6, (2 bedrm), [shwr, bath, spa bath (1), tlt, hairdry, a/c-cool, heat, elec blkts, tel, TV, video, clock radio, cook fac, micro, blkts, linen, pillows]. **D 👫 $120 - $140, 👤 $10, W 👫 $756 - $840, 👤 $70**, AE BC DC MC VI.

★★★★ **The Gallery Apartments**, (Apt), 206 Lava St, 1km N of PO, ☎ 03 5560 5503, fax 03 5561 2909, (2 stry), 5 apts acc up to 5, (2 bedrm), [shwr, bath, tlt, hairdry, a/c, TV, video, clock radio, t/c mkg, refrig, cook fac, micro, toaster, ldry, blkts, doonas, linen, pillows], w/mach, dryer, iron, iron brd, pool-heated (solar - salt water), bbq, non smoking property. **D 👫 $100 - $150, 👤 $25 - $45, W $500 - $1,050**, Minimum booking long weekends, Easter & May races, AE BC DC EFT MC VI.

★★★★ **Warrnambool Heritage Cottage**, (Cotg), 26 MacDonald St, 2.2km S of PO, ☎ 03 5562 6531, fax 03 5562 6531, 1 cotg acc up to 4, (2 bedrm), [shwr, bath, tlt, hairdry, a/c-cool, heat, elec blkts, TV, video, clock radio, CD, refrig, cook fac, micro, toaster, ldry, blkts, linen, pillows], w/mach, dryer, iron, iron brd, bbq, breakfast ingredients, non smoking property. **D 👫 $120 - $160, 👤 $35, W $600 - $800, 👤 $100**, ch con, Min book Christmas Jan long w/ends and Easter, BC MC VI.

big Country APARTMENTS

★★★☆ **City Central Apartments**, (Apt), 14 King St, 1.5km NW of PO, ☎ 0500 522 140, fax 03 5561 7399, 6 apts acc up to 5, (1 & 2 bedrm), [shwr, bath (hip), tlt, hairdry, a/c (3), fan, heat, elec blkts, TV, video-fee, clock radio, refrig, cook fac, micro, toaster, ldry (in unit), blkts, doonas, linen, pillows], w/mach, iron, iron brd, bbq, c/park (carport) (4), cots. **D 👫 $66 - $110, 👤 $12 - $15, W $350 - $840**, ch con, AE BC DC EFT MC MP VI.

★★★☆ **(8 Jackman Ave Section)**, (2 stry gr fl), 6 apts acc up to 6, (2 & 3 bedrm), [shwr, spa bath, tlt, hairdry, fan, heat, elec blkts, TV, video-fee, clock radio, refrig, cook fac, micro, ldry (in unit), blkts, linen, pillows], w/mach, dryer, iron, iron brd, bbq, c/park (carport), cots-fee. **D 👫 $66 - $110, 👤 $12 - $15, W $350 - $840.**

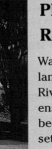

★★★★ **Fig Tree Holiday Village**, (Apt), 33 Lava St, 1km E of PO, ☎ 03 5561 1233, fax 03 5561 3068, 14 apts acc up to 6, (1 & 2 bedrm), [shwr, spa bath (3), tlt, c/fan, cent heat, tel, TV, video, clock radio, refrig, cook fac, micro, toaster, blkts, linen, pillows], ldry, rec rm, pool indoor heated-fee, spa-fee, bbq (covered), kiosk, ✆, plygr, tennis-fee. D ♦♦ $89 - $141, ◊ $11, W $578 - $850, ch con, Min book all holiday times, BC EFT MC VI.

★★☆ **(Holiday Flat Section)**, 4 flats acc up to 4, (Studio), [shwr, bath (hip), tlt, heat, TV, video-fee, refrig, cook fac, toaster, blkts reqd, linen reqd, pillows reqd]. D ♦♦ $60 - $100, ◊ $6, W $390 - $600, ch con.

★★★☆ **Ocean Beach Holiday Village**, (HF), Pertobe Rd, 1.8km S of PO, ☎ 03 5561 4222, fax 03 5562 0392, 23 flats acc up to 5, (Studio, 1 & 2 bedrm), [shwr, bath (hip), tlt, a/c, heat, elec blkts, TV, clock radio, refrig, cook fac, micro, toaster, blkts, linen, pillows], ldry, pool-heated, spa-fee, bbq (covered)-fee, kiosk, ✆, plygr. D ♦♦ $70 - $148, ◊ $15, Breakfast available. Min book Christmas Jan long w/ends and Easter, BC EFT MC VI.

★★★☆ **The Cottage Kerr Street**, (Cotg), 47 Kerr St, 1km W of PO, ☎ 03 5562 2282, fax 03 5562 0986, 1 cotg acc up to 4, (2 bedrm), [shwr, tlt, c/fan, elec blkts, TV, radio, refrig, cook fac, micro, toaster, ldry, blkts, linen, pillows], lounge firepl, bbq, c/park. D $88, W $440.

★★★ **Bayside Lodge**, (HF), 30 Pertobe Rd, 1.9km S of PO, ☎ 03 5562 7323, (2 stry gr fl), 11 flats acc up to 6, (2 bedrm), [shwr, tlt, heat, elec blkts, TV, clock radio, refrig, cook fac, micro, elec frypan, toaster, linen reqd-fee], ldry, bbq, plygr, cots. D ♦♦ $49.50 - $60.50, ◊ $5.50, W $297 - $660, ch con, BC MC VI.

★★★ **Cannon Hill Apartments**, (HF), 126 Merri St, 200m S of PO, ☎ 03 5561 1489, fax 03 5560 5943, 7 flats acc up to 5, (1 & 2 bedrm), [shwr, tlt, heat, tel, TV, clock radio, refrig, cook fac, micro, elec frypan, ldry (in unit), linen], c/park (carport). D $60 - $110, AE BC DC EFT MC VI.

★★★ **High View Horse Complex**, (Cotg), 229 Illowa Rd, Illowa 3282, 7km W of Warrnambool, ☎ 03 5565 9341, fax 03 5565 9341, 2 cotgs acc up to 5, (2 bedrm), [shwr, tlt, hairdry, fan, heat, TV, clock radio, t/c mkg, refrig, cook fac, micro, toaster, blkts, linen reqd-fee, pillows], ldry, iron, bbq. D ♦♦ $80 - $100, ◊ $10, W ♦♦ $350 - $625, Pets welcome. BC MC VI.

★★★ **Tea Tree Hill**, (Cotg), 374 Stafford St, Wangoom 3279, 10km E of PO, ☎ 03 5562 1763, 2 cotgs acc up to 6, (2 bedrm), [shwr, bath (1), tlt, hairdry, fan, heat, elec blkts, TV, video, clock radio, refrig, cook fac, micro, toaster, blkts, doonas, pillows], ldry, w/mach, bbq, cots-fee, non smoking property. D ♦♦ $75, ◊ $5, W ♦♦ $450, ◊ $25, Breakfast available.

★★★ **Warrnambool Holiday Park**, (HF), Cnr Raglan Pde & Simpson St, 2.7km E of Visitors Centre, ☎ 03 5562 5031, fax 03 5562 0552, 20 flats acc up to 6, (Studio, 1 & 2 bedrm), [shwr, tlt, heat, elec blkts, TV, clock radio, refrig, cook fac (14), cook fac ltd (6), micro (6), elec frypan (6), toaster, blkts, linen, pillows], ldry, rec rm, pool-heated (solar), bbq (covered), ✆, plygr, tennis (half court). D $62 - $106, ◊ $10, Min book Christmas Jan long w/ends and Easter, BC EFT MC VI.

B&B's/Guest Houses

★★★★☆ **Merton Manor Bed and Breakfast**, (B&B), 62 Ardlie St, ☎ 03 5562 0720, fax 03 5561 1220, 6 rms (6 suites) [ensuite, spa bath, hairdry, a/c, cent heat, elec blkts, TV, clock radio, t/c mkg, refrig], iron, iron brd, rec rm, lounge (TV, video, stereo), bbq, non smoking property. BB ♦ $130, ♦♦ $150 - $170, AE BC DC EFT JCB MC VI.

★★★★☆ **Seaviews Bed & Breakfast**, (B&B), 150 Merri St, 200m S of PO, ☎ 03 5562 1600, fax 03 5561 1974, (Multi-stry), 2 rms [ensuite, hairdry, cent heat, TV, clock radio, t/c mkg, refrig, toaster], iron, iron brd, lounge (TV, video, cd), spa (hydro spa). BLB ♦♦ $110 - $160, AE BC DC MC VI.

WARRNAMBOOL VIC continued...

★★★★ **Manor Gums**, (GH), Shadys La, Mailors Flat 3275, off Caramut Rd, 10km N of Visitors Centre, ☎ 03 5565 4410, fax 03 5565 4409, (2 stry), 3 rms [ensuite, bath (1), hairdry, a/c, heat, TV, video, clock radio, t/c mkg, refrig, cook fac (1), micro, toaster], lounge (cd player), lounge firepl, sauna, spa, bbq, gym, non smoking suites. **BLB** ♦♦ **$125 - $160**, Dinner by arrangement. AE BC DC MC VI.

★★★☆ **Casa D'Oro Bed & Breakfast**, (B&B), 42 Shady's La, Mailors Flat 3275, 10km N of PO, ☎ 03 5565 4243, 3 rms [ensuite (1), hairdry, elec blkts, clock radio], lounge (TV, cd, stereo, video), t/c mkg shared, bbq, Pets on application. **BB** ♦ **$50**, ♦♦ **$90**, ♦ **$40**, ch con, Dinner by arrangement.

★★★☆ **Nan Dodds Wollaston**, (B&B), c1854. No children's facilities, 84 Wollaston Rd, 4km N of PO, ☎ 03 5562 2430, fax 03 5562 2430, 2 rms [heat, elec blkts, TV, clock radio, refrig (communal), doonas], lounge, non smoking property. **BB** ♦♦ **$105 - $140**, BC MC VI.

★★★★ **(Cottage Section)**, 1 cotg acc up to 4, (1 bedrm), [shwr, tlt, heat, TV, clock radio, refrig, cook fac, micro, blkts, doonas, linen, pillows], iron, iron brd, lounge firepl, bbq, breakfast ingredients, non smoking property. **BB $110 - $150**.

★★★☆ **Whalesway**, (B&B), 6 Florence St, 3.5km SE of PO, ☎ 03 5561 2660, (2 stry), 2 rms [a/c, elec blkts, clock radio], lounge (TV, video), t/c mkg shared, refrig, non smoking property. **BB** ♦ **$40**, ♦♦ **$75 - $80**, ♦ **$10**.

WARTOOK VIC

See Grampians Region.

WATTLE POINT VIC 3875

Pop Nominal, (299km E Melbourne), See map on pages 694/695, ref J7. Agricultural district situated south of Bairnsdale. Boating, Bush Walking, Fishing, Scenic Drives, Swimming.

Self Catering Accommodation

★★★ **Wattle Point Holiday Retreat**, 200 Wattle Point Rd, 19km S of Bairnsdale PO, ☎ 03 5157 7517, fax 03 5157 7517, 9 cabins acc up to 10, (1, 2, 3 & 4 bedrm), [shwr, tlt, heat, elec blkts, TV, video (avail), clock radio, refrig, cook fac ltd, micro, toaster, ldry (in unit), blkts, linen, pillows], w/mach, pool indoor heated, spa (natural)-fee, bbq, ♦, jetty, tennis, cots. **D** ♦♦ **$69 - $180**, **RO** ♦ **$16**, ch con, Breakfast available. BC MC VI.

WEDDERBURN VIC 3518

Pop 700. (224km NW Melbourne), See map on pages 694/695, ref D4. Centre of old gold diggings. Many large nuggets found recently in this area. Annual Gold Dig (Mar). Bowls, Bush Walking, Fishing, Gold Prospecting, Golf, Scenic Drives, Shooting, Swimming (Pool), Tennis, Trotting.

Hotels/Motels

★★ **Wedderburn Motel**, (M), 43 High St (Calder Hwy), 100m E of PO, ☎ 03 5494 3002, fax 03 5494 3002, 19 units [shwr, tlt, a/c-cool, heat, tel, TV, clock radio, t/c mkg, refrig], cots-fee, non smoking units (5). **RO** ♦ **$38.50**, ♦♦ **$49.50**, ch con, BC MC VI.

B&B's/Guest Houses

★★★☆ **The Old Royal - Wedderburn**, (B&B), 118 High St (Calder Hwy), ☎ 03 5494 3493, fax 03 5494 3689, 3 rms [ensuite (1), elec blkts, clock radio], lounge (Cable TV, video), pool above ground, t/c mkg shared, tennis. **BB** ♦♦ **$82.50 - $104.50**, AE BC DC EFT MC VI.

WELSHPOOL VIC 3966

Pop 755. (208km SE Melbourne), See map on page 696, ref E8. Dairy farming area. Agnes Falls, Tarra Valley & Bulga National Parks, Bowls, Scenic Drives, Tennis.

Hotels/Motels

★★ **Welshpool Hotel Motel**, (LMH), 23 Main St, opposite PO, ☎ 03 5688 1209, fax 03 5688 1209, 10 units [shwr, tlt, heat, elec blkts, TV, t/c mkg, refrig], ⊠, bbq, ♦, cots. **RO** ♦ **$45**, ♦♦ **$60**, ♦ **$10**, ch con, BC MC VI.

Self Catering Accommodation

★★★ **Shady Creek Cottage**, (Cotg), 320 Woorarra Rd, ☎ 03 5688 1363, fax 03 5688 1363, 1 cotg acc up to 5, (2 bedrm), [shwr, bath, tlt, TV, video, clock radio, t/c mkg, refrig, cook fac, toaster, ldry, blkts, linen reqd-fee, pillows], w/mach, iron, iron brd, lounge firepl, bbq. **D $50 - $100**, **W $350 - $600**.

WILLAURA VIC

See Grampians Region.

WILSONS PROMONTORY NATIONAL PARK VIC

Pop Nominal. (230km SE Melbourne)

Waratah Park Country House

overlooking Wilsons Promontory National Park

Located on farmland with spectacular seascape views of Wilsons Prom and islands. Adjacent Cape Liptrap Park. 20 minutes to Prom. All rooms have king bed and double air spa. Licensed dinning room with huge open fire. see listing under Waratah Bay.

Thomson Rd. (off Walkerville-Fish Creek Rd.) **Waratah Bay 3959**
Ph: 03 5683 2575 Fax: 03 5683 2275
www.wpe.com.au

WINCHELSEA VIC 3241

Pop 1,050. (109km SW Melbourne), See map on pages 694/695, ref D7. Located on the Princes Hwy, adjacent to Barwon River.

★★☆ **Sea Mist Palomino Stud**, (M), 635 Wensleydale Station Rd, Wensleydale 3241, 20km SE of PO, ☎ 03 5288 7255, fax 03 5288 7357, 3 units [shwr, tlt, heat, elec blkts], ldry, rec rm, lounge, conf fac, ⊠, pool, spa (heated), t/c mkg shared, refrig, ♦. **D** all meals ♦ **$80 - $99**, ♦ **$80 - $99**, ch con, AE BC DC MC VI.

★★★ **(Park Cabin Section)**, 5 ▨ acc up to 5, [shwr, tlt, fan, heat, elec blkts, TV, clock radio, t/c mkg, refrig, cook fac ltd, micro, blkts, doonas, linen, pillows], cook fac. **D** ♦♦ **$77**, ♦ **$11**, ch con.

(Bunk Room Section), 14 rms acc up to 20, (Bunk Rooms), [blkts reqd, linen reqd, pillows reqd]. **D** all meals ♦ **$80 - $88**, ♦ **$80 - $88**.

★ **Winchelsea Motel - Roadhouse**, (M), Cnr Princes Hwy & Inverleigh Rd, 1.6km E of PO, ☎ 03 5267 2293, fax 03 5267 2293, 6 units [shwr, bath (hip), tlt, fan, heat, elec blkts, TV, clock radio, t/c mkg, refrig, toaster], ✕, ♦. **RO** ♦ **$38.50**, AE BC DC EFT MC MP VI.

WODONGA VIC 3690

Pop 25,850. (306km NE Melbourne), See map on pages 694/695, ref H4. Twin town to Albury, situated on the south bank of the Murray River, at the junction of the Hume & Murray Valley Hwys.

Hotels/Motels

★★★★ **Belvoir Village Motel**, (M), Cnr Melbourne & Moorefield Park Rds, 2.8km W of PO, ☎ 02 6024 5344, fax 02 6056 1918, 10 units [shwr, bath (hip) (4), tlt, a/c-cool, heat, elec blkts, tel, TV, video-fee, clock radio, t/c mkg, refrig, mini bar, toaster], iron, iron brd, pool, bbq, c/park (carport), cots-fee, non smoking rms (2). **RO** ♦ **$66 - $77**, ♦♦ **$77 - $88**, ♦ **$12**, AE BC DC EFT MC VI.

Operator Comment: 2 Bedroom Family Units Avail. 1 min. to Uni & TAFE.

★★★★ **Best Western Stagecoach Motel**, (M), 188 Melbourne Rd, 2.7km W of PO, ☎ 02 6024 3044, fax 02 6056 1013, 24 units [shwr, spa bath (2), tlt, hairdry (14), a/c-cool, heat, elec blkts, tel, cable tv, clock radio, t/c mkg, refrig, mini bar, ldry], iron (14), iron brd (14), pool, bbq, dinner to unit, plygr, cots, non smoking units (11). **RO** ♦ **$77 - $148**, ♦♦ **$87 - $148**, ♦ **$12**, ch con, 10 units ★★★. AE BC DC JCB MC MP VI.

Operator Comment: Collect Fly Buys points while relaxing in our quiet, modern, ground floor units. Enjoy our many facilities, including Free Austar TV Channels, In Ground Pool and BBQ Facilities in a large, pleasant setting.

★★★★ **The Blazing Stump Motel**, (M), Tallangatta Rd (Murray Valley Hwy), ☎ 02 6056 3433, fax 02 6056 3550, 31 units (2 suites) [shwr, spa bath (2), tlt, hairdry, a/c, elec blkts, tel, TV, video-fee, clock radio, t/c mkg, refrig, micro, toaster], ldry, iron, iron brd, pool, spa, bbq, rm serv, tennis, cots-fee, non smoking units (11). **RO** ♦ **$85**, ♦♦ **$95**, ♦ **$10**, **Suite D** ♦♦ **$120**, ♦ **$10**, ch con, AE BC DC MC MP VI, ♦&.

★★★★☆ **(Apartment Section)**, 6 apts acc up to 6, (2 bedrm), [shwr, bath (hip), tlt, hairdry, a/c, elec blkts, tel, TV, video-fee, clock radio, t/c mkg, refrig, cook fac, micro, d/wash, toaster, blkts, linen, pillows], c/park (undercover). **D** ♦♦♦♦ **$125**, ♦ **$10**.

True Country Style Atmosphere

Wodonga

BLAZING STUMP
MOTEL

- *Deluxe Units* • *Executive Units*
- *Self contained serviced apartments*

• SPA • POOL • 7 FULL DAY BISTRO SERVICE • TENNIS COURT • BBQ'S
• LAUNDRY • BUS SERVICE TO SNOWFIELDS

Murray Valley Highway Wodonga Victoria 3690
Telephone (02) 6056 3433 Facsimile (02) 6056 3550

★★★★ **Warrina Motor Inn**, (M), 31 High St, 1km N of PO, ☎ 02 6024 2211, fax 02 6024 4854, 14 units [shwr, tlt, hairdry, a/c, elec blkts, tel, TV, video-fee, clock radio, t/c mkg, refrig, cook fac (1), cook fac ltd (2), toaster], ldry, iron, iron brd, conf fac, ⊠ (Mon to Sat), pool, rm serv, plygr, cots, non smoking units (5). RO ♦ $66, ♦♦ $72 - $77, ⏰ $11, AE BC DC EFT MC VI.

★★★☆ **Border Gateway Motel Wodonga**, (M), 6 Moorefield Park Dve, 2.6km W of PO, ☎ 02 6056 1011, fax 02 6024 2084, 10 units [shwr, tlt, a/c, elec blkts, tel, TV, video-fee, clock radio, t/c mkg, refrig, mini bar, toaster, doonas], pool, bbq, rm serv, dinner to unit, cots, non smoking units (3). RO ♦ $68 - $79, ♦♦ $79 - $90, ⏰ $11, AE BC DC EFT MC MP VI.

★★★ **Motel Wellington Wodonga**, (M), 46 High St, 1km N of PO, ☎ 02 6024 2400, fax 02 6056 1505, 18 units (2 bedrm), [shwr, tlt, hairdry, a/c, elec blkts, tel, TV, video-fee, clock radio, t/c mkg, refrig, toaster], pool, bbq, dinner to unit (Mon to Sat), cots-fee, non smoking units (7). RO ♦ $61 - $72, ♦♦ $66 - $72, ⏰ $11, AE BC DC EFT MC MP VI.

★★★ **Murray Valley Motel**, (M), 196 Melbourne Rd, 2.8km W of PO, ☎ 02 6024 1422, fax 02 6024 1279, 19 units [shwr, tlt, a/c, elec blkts, tel, TV, video-fee, clock radio, t/c mkg, refrig, cook fac ltd (6), micro (2), toaster], ldry, iron (2), iron brd (2), pool, bbq, dinner to unit, c/park (carport) (16), plygr, cots-fee. RO ♦ $53 - $59, ♦♦ $62 - $70, ⏰ $9, ch con, AE BC DC EFT JCB MC VI.

★★★ **Provincial**, (M), 12 High St, 1.4km N of PO, ☎ 02 6024 1200, fax 02 6024 7412, 29 units [shwr, tlt, hairdry, a/c, c/fan, elec blkts, tel, TV, video-fee, clock radio, t/c mkg, refrig, toaster, doonas], ldry, iron, iron brd, ⊠ (Mon to Sat), pool, pool indoor heated, bbq, rm serv, c/park (carport), plygr, cots-fee. RO ♦ $60, ♦♦ $66, ⏰ $11, Units 31 to 33 not rated. AE BC DC EFT JCB MC MP VI.

★★★ **Twin City Motor Inn**, (M), 166 Melbourne Rd, 1.9km W of PO, ☎ 02 6024 2111, fax 02 6024 2855, (2 stry gr fl), 29 units [shwr, tlt, a/c-cool, c/fan, heat, elec blkts, tel, TV, video-fee, clock radio, t/c mkg, refrig, cook fac ltd (shared), doonas], ldry, pool, bbq, dinner to unit, cots-fee, non smoking units (11). RO ♦ $55, ♦♦ $66, ⏰ $11, ch con, AE BC DC EFT MC VI.

★★☆ **Sanctuary Park Motel**, (M), 11 High St, 1.2km N of PO, ☎ 02 6024 1122, fax 02 6024 1845, 21 units [shwr, tlt, a/c-cool (16), a/c (5), heat, elec blkts, tel, TV, video-fee, clock radio, t/c mkg, refrig, toaster], pool, bbq, dinner to unit, cots. RO ♦ $52 - $55, ♦♦ $60 - $66, ⏰ $11, 5 units ★★★. AE BC DC EFT MC MCH VI.

Self Catering Accommodation
★★★ **Albury-Wodonga Apartments**, (HU), 56 Huon Creek Rd, ☎ 02 6024 5844, fax 02 6056 2696, 12 units acc up to 6, (2 & 3 bedrm), [shwr, tlt, a/c-cool, heat, TV, clock radio, cook fac, micro, toaster], c/park (carport), cots-fee. D ♦♦ $80 - $90, ⏰ $20, W ♦♦ $490 - $560, ⏰ $140, AE BC DC MC VI.

Pop Part of Yarram, (234km SE Melbourne), See map on pages 694/695, ref G7. Dairy farming area. Bush Walking, Fishing, Scenic Drives.
★★★☆ **Chester Hill**, (Cotg), Bowdens Rd, 6km N of Won Wron school, off Hyland Hwy, ☎ 03 5189 1244, fax 03 5189 1288, 3 cotgs acc up to 8, (1 & 2 bedrm), [shwr, bath, tlt, a/c, elec blkts, TV, refrig, cook fac, ldry (in unit), blkts, linen, pillows], ✕, BYO, non smoking property. D ♦♦ $88, ⏰ $22, ch con, 1 cottage ★★☆. BC MC VI.

Pop 5,900. (132km SE Melbourne), See map on page 696, ref C7. Prosperous regional centre. Bowls, Bush Walking, Golf, Horse Riding.
★★★☆ **Wonthaggi Motel**, (M), 42 McKenzie St (Bass Hwy), 300m E of PO, ☎ 03 5672 2922, fax 03 5672 2221, 20 units [shwr, spa bath (7), tlt, hairdry, a/c, elec blkts, tel, TV, video-fee, clock radio, t/c mkg, refrig], cots, non smoking units (10). RO ♦ $60 - $88, ♦♦ $66 - $99, ⏰ $11 - $16.50, ch con, 9 units ★★★★. AE BC DC EFT MC MP VI, ♿.

★★☆ **Miners Rest Motel Hotel**, (LMH), 140 McKenzie St (Bass Hwy), 1.6km N of PO, ☎ 03 5672 1033, 26 units [shwr, tlt, a/c, elec blkts, tel, TV, radio, t/c mkg, refrig, cook fac (1)], conf fac, ⊠, bbq, plygr, cots-fee, non smoking units (10). RO ♦ $45, ♦♦ $55, ⏰ $6, ch con, AE BC DC MC VI.

Caledonian Hotel, (LH), 159 Graham St, 100m SE of PO, ☎ 03 5672 1002, (2 stry), 12 rms [basin (3)], lounge (TV), ⊠, ☎, cots. RO ♦ $30, ♦♦ $50, ch con, BC EFT MC VI. (Not yet classified)

B&B's/Guest Houses
★★★★ **Jongebloed's Bed & Breakfast**, (B&B), Berry's Rd, ☎ 03 5672 2028, (2 stry gr fl), 3 rms [ensuite (all rooms), bath (1), hairdry, fan, fire pl, heat, elec blkts], rec rm, lounge (TV), t/c mkg shared, tennis, non smoking property. BB ♦ $95, ♦♦ $115.

Pop 3,000. Part of Macedon Ranges, (69km NW Melbourne), See map on page 696, ref B4. Attractive town in forest country near Mt Macedon. Nearby - Hanging Rock Reserve.
★★★★★ **Pond Cottage**, (Cotg), Tariff includes seasonal farm activities, Glengrove Farm, 286 Chases La Pipers Creek via, 12km N of PO, ☎ 03 5422 1447, fax 03 5422 3530, (2 stry), 1 cotg acc up to 4, (2 bedrm), [shwr, tlt, hairdry, a/c, fan, elec blkts, tel, TV, video, clock radio, CD, refrig, cook fac, micro, elec frypan, toaster, ldry (in unit), blkts, doonas, linen, pillows], iron, iron brd, lounge firepl, pool (salt water), bbq, tennis, cots, breakfast ingredients, non smoking property. BB ♦♦ $185 - $215, ⏰ $55 - $65, ch con, Minimum booking weekends & public holidays, BC MC VI.

★★★★ **Swallow's Cottage**, (Cotg), c1850. 722 Romsey Rd, 8.5km E of PO, ☎ 03 5427 0327, 1 cotg acc up to 5, (2 bedrm - stone.), [shwr, bath, tlt, hairdry, evap cool, heat, wood heat, elec blkts, tel (Prepaid mobile), TV, video, clock radio, CD, refrig, cook fac, micro, elec frypan, toaster, blkts, linen, pillows], iron, iron brd, bbq, breakfast ingredients, non smoking property. BB ♦♦ $110 - $150, ⏰ $30, Min book Christmas Jan long w/ends and Easter.

★★★★ **The Woodend Shack**, (Cotg), 23A Old Lancefield Rd, ☎ 03 5427 1293, 1 cotg acc up to 2, (1 bedrm), [shwr, tlt, hairdry, fan, heat, elec blkts, TV, video, radio, CD, t/c mkg, refrig, cook fac, toaster, blkts, doonas, linen, pillows], lounge firepl, bbq, breakfast ingredients. D $150, W $700 - $1,000, AE VI.

★★★☆ **Country Carriage Retreat**, (Cotg), Restored 1891 Federation train carriage. Hesket - Boundary Rd, Heskett 3442, 10km E of PO, ☎ 03 5427 0420, 1 cotg acc up to 4, (2 bedrm - train carriage.), [shwr, tlt, hairdry, evap cool, fan, heat, elec blkts, tel, TV, video, clock radio, CD, refrig, cook fac, elec frypan, toaster, blkts, doonas, linen, pillows], iron, iron brd, bbq, breakfast ingredients, non smoking property. BB ♦♦ $120, ⏰ $35, ch con.

B&B's/Guest Houses
★★★★ **The Bentinck Country House**, (PH), 1 Carlisle St, 700m N of PO, ☎ 03 5427 2944, fax 03 5427 2232, (2 stry gr fl), 20 rms [ensuite (16), shwr (4), tlt (4), hairdry, heat, elec blkts, tel, TV, clock radio], rec rm, lounge, conf fac, lounge firepl, ⊠, pool, t/c mkg shared, tennis, non smoking rms. BB ♦ $135 - $165, ♦♦ $165 - $195, DBB ♦ $170 - $205, ♦♦ $250 - $285, AE BC DC EFT MC VI.

★★★★ **(Garden Cottage Section)**, 8 rms [ensuite, hairdry, cent heat, elec blkts, tel, clock radio], lounge (TV, video), lounge firepl, t/c mkg shared, refrig. BB ♦ $135, ♦♦ $165, DBB ♦ $175, ♦♦ $255.

★★★★ **Woodbury Cottage - Bed and Breakfast**, (B&B), 18 Jason Dve, 2km SW of PO, ☎ 03 5427 1876, 1 rm [shwr, bath, tlt, hairdry, fan, cent heat, elec blkts, clock radio, t/c mkg, refrig], iron, iron brd, lounge, lounge firepl (tv, cd player), non smoking property. BLB ♦ $80 - $90, ♦♦ $100 - $110, Children by arrangement. BC MC VI.
Operator Comment: www.geocities.com/woodbury_cottage

Pop Nominal, (245km SE Melbourne), See map on pages 694/695, ref H8. Small dairy and agricultural community.
★★ **Summer Breeze Motel**, (M), South Gippsland Hwy, opposite PO, ☎ 03 5187 1391, 5 units [shwr, tlt, fan, heat, elec blkts, TV, t/c mkg, refrig], cots. RO ♦ $49.50, ♦♦ $55, ⏰ $5 - $9, ch con.

WOOLSTHORPE VIC 3276

Pop Nominal, (282km W Melbourne), See map on pages 694/695, ref B7.
★★★★ **Quamby Homestead**, (GH), 3223 Caramut Rd, 10km N of PO, ☎ 03 5569 2395, fax 03 5569 2244, 7 rms [shwr, tlt, a/c, elec blkts, TV, clock radio, t/c mkg, refrig, doonas], ✉, cots (avail). **BB** ♦♦ **$115 - $145, DBB** ♦♦ **$192 - $222**, BC MC VI, ⚷.

WULGULMERANG VIC 3885

Pop Nominal, (418km E Melbourne), See map on pages 694/695, ref J6.
★★★☆ **Eagle Loft Gallery**, (B&B), Snowy River Rd, 1km N of Black Mountain Rd, ☎ 03 5155 0263, 2 rms [elec blkts], lounge firepl, t/c mkg shared, cots, non smoking property. **BB** ♦ **$55,** ♦♦ **$99,** ◊ **$49.50**, ch con, BC MC VI.

(Cottage Section), Limited facilities - no electricity. (2 stry gr fl), 1 cotg acc up to 8, (2 bedrm), [shwr (bush), bath (hip), heat, cook fac ltd, linen reqd-fee], lounge firepl, bbq, cots. **D** ♦ **$27.50,** ♦♦ **$55,** ◊ **$22, W $495**, ch con.

WYCHEPROOF VIC 3527

Pop 750. (285km NW Melbourne), See map on pages 694/695, ref C4. Unusual town in that the train line runs down the centre of the main street. Wheat producing area.
★★★ **Mount Wycheproof Motor Inn**, (M), 360 Broadway (Calder Hwy), 300m N of PO, ☎ 03 5493 7388, fax 03 5493 7402, 16 units [shwr, tlt, a/c-cool, heat, elec blkts, tel, TV, radio, t/c mkg, refrig, toaster], ldry, ✗ (Mon to Thurs), BYO, dinner to unit, cots. **RO** ♦ **$55,** ♦♦ **$60 - $66,** ◊ **$11**, BC EFT MC VI.
★ **Royal Mail Hotel**, (LH), 340 Broadway (Calder Hwy), 250m N of PO, ☎ 03 5493 7401, (2 stry), 12 rms [basin (2), a/c-cool (1), elec blkts, TV (1)], lounge (TV, video), ✉, refrig, c/park. **BLB** ♦ **$25,** ♦♦ **$35,** ◊ **$10**, BC EFT MC VI.

WYE RIVER VIC 3221

Pop Nominal, (158km SW Melbourne), See map on pages 694/695, ref D8. A tourist resort with surfing beach & good fishing.
★★ **Rookery Nook Hotel**, (LMH), Great Ocean Rd, ☎ 03 5289 0240, fax 03 5289 0393, 4 units [shwr, tlt, heat, elec blkts, TV, clock radio, t/c mkg, refrig], ✉, ☎. **RO** ♦ **$60 - $110,** ♦♦ **$65 - $130,** ◊ **$5**, Breakfast not available. Min book all holiday times, AE BC DC EFT MC VI.

Self Catering Accommodation
★★★★ **Wye in the Sky**, (Apt), Morley Ave, off Great Ocean Road, ☎ 03 5289 0234, fax 03 5289 0234, 1 apt acc up to 4, (2 bedrm), [shwr, tlt, hairdry, fan, heat, elec blkts, TV, video, clock radio, CD, t/c mkg, refrig, cook fac, micro, elec frypan, toaster, blkts, linen, pillows], iron, iron brd, lounge firepl, bbq, cots, non smoking property. **D** ♦♦ **$195,** ◊ **$22, W $1,000 - $1,600**, Min book applies.

YACKANDANDAH VIC 3749

Pop 600. (295km NE Melbourne), See map on pages 694/695, ref H4. Old gold mining area. The complete town is classified by the National Trust.
★★★★ **Yackandandah Motor Inn**, (M), 18 High St, 100m E of PO, ☎ 02 6027 1155, fax 02 6027 1644, 8 units [shwr, tlt, a/c, tel, TV, video (avail), clock radio, t/c mkg, refrig, toaster], bbq, cots, non smoking units (8). **BLB** ♦ **$60 - $79,** ♦♦ **$82 - $89,** ◊ **$20**, ch con, AE BC MC VI, ⚷.
★★★ **Yackandandah Townshiphill Motel**, (M), Dederang Rd, 1km S of PO, ☎ 02 6027 1467, fax 02 6027 0614, 10 units [shwr, tlt, a/c, tel, TV, clock radio, t/c mkg, refrig, toaster, doonas], ldry, non smoking property. **BLB** ♦ **$63 - $72,** ♦♦ **$72 - $82,** ◊ **$11**, ch con, AE BC DC EFT MC VI, ⚷.

Self Catering Accommodation
★★★★ **Creek Haven**, (Cotg), Osbornes Flat Rd, 6km SE of PO, ☎ 02 6027 1389, fax 02 6027 1026, 3 cotgs acc up to 4, (1 & 2 bedrm), [shwr, spa bath (1), tlt, hairdry, a/c-cool, c/fan, heat (wood fires), elec blkts, TV, clock radio, refrig, cook fac, micro, toaster, ldry, blkts, linen, pillows], w/mach, bbq, breakfast ingredients. **BB** ♦♦ **$95 - $110,** ◊ **$33**, ch con, 1 cottage ★★★. BC EFT MC VI.

B&B's/Guest Houses
★★★★☆ **Arcadia Cottage Yackandandah**, (B&B), Mongan La, Osbornes Flat 3691, 3.5km SE of PO, ☎ 02 6027 1713, 1 rm [ensuite, spa bath, hairdry, evap cool, c/fan, heat (wood), elec blkts, TV, clock radio, CD, t/c mkg, refrig, micro, toaster], iron, iron brd, bbq. **BB** ♦ **$80 - $90,** ♦♦ **$105 - $115,** ◊ **$20 - $30**, BC MC VI.

★★★★ **Serendipity Bed & Breakfast**, (B&B), 9 Windham St, 100m S of PO, ☎ 02 6027 1881, fax 02 6027 1881, 1 rm [shwr, bath, tlt, hairdry, fan, cent heat, elec blkts, clock radio, t/c mkg], lounge (TV, cd), non smoking property. **BB** ♦ **$60,** ♦♦ **$100**.
★★★ **(Cottage Section)**, 1 cotg acc up to 6, (1 bedrm), [shwr, tlt, hairdry, fan, c/fan, heat (wood & gas), TV, video, clock radio, CD, t/c mkg, refrig, micro, elec frypan, toaster, blkts, linen, pillows], ldry, w/mach, dryer, iron, bbq, cots, breakfast ingredients. **BB** ♦♦ **$90,** ◊ **$20**.

★★★☆ **Downham House**, (B&B), Racecourse Rd, 2.1km NE of PO, ☎ 02 6027 1690, fax 02 6027 1690, 3 rms [ensuite (1), shwr, tlt, evap cool, cent heat], lounge, t/c mkg shared, bbq, non smoking property. **BB** ♦ **$66 - $77,** ♦♦ **$99 - $121**, ch con.

Operator Comment: Comfort, tranquility and service. A beautiful B&B homestay on 8 acres.

YAMBUK VIC 3285

Pop 300. (308km W Melbourne), See map on pages 694/695, ref B7. Pastoral and agricultural district on the Shaw River, 17km W of Port Fairy. Fishing, Scenic Drives, Surfing, Swimming (Ocean).
★☆ **Yambuk Inn Hotel**, (LH), Princes Hwy, ☎ 03 5568 4310, (2 stry), 4 rms [hairdry, heat, heat, elec blkts], shwr, tlt, ldry, w/mach, dryer, ✗ (Fri to Sat), t/c mkg shared, bbq, ☎. **BLB** ♦ **$35,** ♦♦ **$65**.

Self Catering Accommodation
★★★★ **K-Elle Country Cottage**, (Cotg), 59 St Helens Rd, 1.5km N of PO, ☎ 03 5568 2116, 1 cotg acc up to 6, (3 bedrm), [shwr, bath, tlt, hairdry, c/fan, heat, elec blkts, tel (local calls only), TV, video, clock radio, refrig, cook fac, micro, elec frypan, toaster, ldry, blkts, doonas, linen, pillows], iron, iron brd, rec rm, lounge firepl, bbq, tennis (seasonal), cots, non smoking property. **D** ♦♦ **$80 - $155,** ◊ **$10, W $440 - $660**, ch con.

YANAKIE VIC 3960

Pop Part of Foster, (192km SE Melbourne), See map on page 696, ref E8. Gateway to Wilsons Promontory National Park.
Self Catering Accommodation
★★★★ **Shellcott Lodge**, (Cotg), 175 Shellcott Rd, ☎ 03 9816 4744, fax 03 9816 3579, 1 cotg acc up to 8, (4 bedrm), [ensuite (1), shwr, bath, tlt, hairdry, heat, elec blkts, TV, video, clock radio, CD, t/c mkg, refrig, cook fac, micro, elec frypan, toaster, ldry (in unit), blkts, doonas, linen reqd, pillows], w/mach, dryer, iron, iron brd, bbq, breakfast ingredients. **BLB $130 - $200**, BC EFT MC VI.
★★★☆ **Promhills Cabins**, Lot 2 Promontory Rd, 200m S of general store, ☎ 03 5687 1469, fax 03 5687 1469, 2 cabins acc up to 2, [shwr, tlt, hairdry, fire pl, elec blkts, cable tv, clock radio, t/c mkg, refrig, cook fac ltd, micro, toaster, blkts, linen, pillows], iron, iron brd, bbq, non smoking property. **D** ♦♦ **$90,** ◊ **$20, W** ♦♦ **$540,** ◊ **$120**, BC MC VI.
★★★ **Prom View Farm**, (Cotg), (Farm), 4295 Wilsons Promontory Rd, 7km S of PO, ☎ 03 5687 1460, 1 cotg acc up to 6, (2 bedrm), [shwr, tlt, cent heat, TV, clock radio, refrig, cook fac, micro, ldry, linen reqd-fee], bbq. **D $85 - $105, W $425 - $735**.
★★ **Prom Road Farmstay**, (Cotg), (Farm), 3895 Promontory Rd, 2km S of PO, ☎ 03 5687 1339, fax 03 5687 1288, 1 cotg acc up to 10, (4 bedrm), [shwr, bath, tlt, heat, TV, radio, refrig, cook fac, micro, toaster, ldry, linen reqd-fee], cots. **D $60 - $150, W $420 - $770**.

Yanakie House, (HU), 3630 Promontory Rd, adjacent to general store, ☎ 03 5687 1347, 4 units acc up to 6, (1 bedrm), [shwr, bath (1), tlt, fan, heat, TV, radio, refrig, cook fac (2), cook fac ltd (2), micro, toaster, doonas, linen, pillows], ldry, lounge firepl (1), bbq, breakfast ingredients. **BLB** ♦ **$70,** ♦♦ **$99,** ◊ **$16.50, W $800**, ch con, BC MC VI, (Rating under review).

B&B's/Guest Houses
★★★★ **Singapore Deep**, (B&B), No children's facilities, Foley Rd, ☎ 03 5687 1208, fax 03 5687 1208, 2 rms [ensuite, hairdry, c/fan, heat, elec blkts, clock radio, t/c mkg, micro, toaster], lounge (TV, video, cd), bbq, non smoking property. **BLB** ♦♦ **$195 - $230**, BC MC VI.
★★★★ **Tingara View Cottages & Teahouse**, (B&B), 10 Tingara Cl, ☎ 03 5687 1488, fax 03 5687 1488, 3 rms (Studio & 1 bedrm), [shwr, tlt, heat (wood) (1), elec blkts, TV, clock radio, t/c mkg, refrig], lounge (wood heater) (1), ✗ (available), BYO, non smoking property. **BB** ♦♦ **$132**, Dinner by arrangement, Minimum booking weekends, Easter & public holidays, BC MC VI.
★★★★ **Vereker House**, (B&B), 10 Iluka Close Foley Rd, ☎ 03 5687 1431, fax 03 5687 1480, 4 rms [ensuite], lounge (TV, radio, cd), lounge firepl, ✗, res liquor license, t/c mkg shared. **BB** ♦ **$80 - $100,** ♦♦ **$110 - $140**, Dinner by arrangement. BC EFT MC VI.

YANDOIT VIC 3461

Pop Part of Daylesford, (122km NW Melbourne), See map on page 696, ref A4. Mining township & agricultural district.

★★★ **Jajarawong Holiday Park**, (Cotg), Yandoit Creek Rd, 4km W of township, ☎ 03 5476 4362, fax 03 5476 4362, 5 cotgs acc up to 6, (2 bedrm), [shwr, tlt, heat (wood), refrig, cook fac, blkts, doonas, linen, pillows], sauna, spa (hot tub), bbq, plygr, cots, non smoking property. D ♯♯ $103 - $113, ◊ $30, W $540, ch con, Gas lighting & appliances - no electricity. Breakfast available. Min book applies.

(**Camping Area**), shwr (G/L) (3), tlt (G/L) (3). D ♯♯ $18, ◊ $6.

YARCK VIC 3719

Pop 148. (136km NE Melbourne), See map on page 696, ref D4.

★★★★ **Glenfield Cottage**, (Cotg), Middle Creek Rd, ☎ 03 5773 4304, fax 03 5773 4304, 1 cotg acc up to 4, (2 bedrm), [shwr, tlt, a/c, c/fan, heat, TV, refrig, cook fac, micro, blkts, linen, pillows], w/mach, bbq. D ♯♯ $85 - $100, ◊ $10.

YARRA GLEN VIC 3775

Pop 2,000. (51km NE Melbourne), See map on page 696, ref C5.

FLAG
FLAG CHOICE HOTELS

★★★★ **Grand Hotel**, (LH), 19 Bell St (Melba Hwy), ☎ 03 9730 1230, fax 03 9730 1124, (2 stry), 10 rms [shwr, bath (8), tlt, hairdry, a/c-cool, cent heat, tel, TV, clock radio, t/c mkg, refrig, mini bar], read rm, lounge (TV), conf fac, ☒ (Tue to Sat), cafe (Lic.), ⬦, cots, non smoking rms (4). RO ♦ $130 - $235, ♯♯ $130 - $235, ◊ $16, ch con, AE BC EFT MC VI.

Self Catering Accommodation

★★★★☆ **Kiltynane B & B**, (Cotg), Cnr School La & Yarra Glen - Healesville Rd, 6.8km E of PO, ☎ 03 5962 1897, fax 03 5962 1897, 2 cotgs acc up to 2, (1 bedrm), [shwr, spa bath, tlt, hairdry, a/c-cool, c/fan, heat, elec blkts, t/c mkg, refrig, cook fac, micro, toaster, blkts, doonas, linen, pillows], iron, iron brd, lounge (tv, video, cd player), lounge firepl, bbq, breakfast ingredients, non smoking property. BB ♯♯ $175 - $247.50, W ♯♯ $910, Min book long w/ends and Easter, BC EFT MC VI.

★★★ **Apple Porch Cottage**, (Cotg), 8 Irvine Cres, 1km NE of PO, ☎ 03 9440 6697, fax 03 9459 6753, 2 cotgs acc up to 2, (1 bedrm), [shwr, spa bath, tlt, hairdry, fan, heat, elec blkts, TV, clock radio, t/c mkg, refrig, cook fac ltd, micro, toaster, blkts, linen, pillows], lounge firepl, breakfast ingredients, non smoking property. BB ♯♯ $190 - $300.

B&B's/Guest Houses

★★★★☆ **Araluen Lodge**, (B&B), Children by arrangement, No children's facilities, 603 Steels Creek Rd, ☎ 03 5965 2013, fax 03 5965 2358, 5 rms [ensuite, spa bath, hairdry, evap cool, fan, heat, elec blkts, TV, clock radio, CD], lounge (TV, cd), lounge firepl, ✗, t/c mkg shared, refrig, bbq. BB ♯♯ $143 - $203, Dinner by arrangement. Min book long w/ends and Easter, AE BC MC VI.

★★★★☆ **Melba Lodge**, (B&B), 939 Melba Hwy, 700m N of PO, ☎ 03 9730 1511, fax 03 9730 1566, 6 rms [shwr, spa bath (2), tlt, hairdry, a/c, c/fan, cent heat, elec blkts, TV, video, CD], lounge firepl, ✗, spa. BB ♦ $121 - $154, ♯♯ $154 - $198, AE BC EFT MC VI.

★★★★☆ **Valley Guest House**, (GH), 319 Steels Creek Rd, 5km N of PO, ☎ 03 9730 1822, fax 03 9730 2019, 5 rms [ensuite, spa bath, hairdry, a/c-cool, c/fan (2), heat (wood), elec blkts, TV, CD, t/c mkg], refrig, non smoking property. BLB ♯♯ $145 - $195, ◊ $45, AE BC DC MC VI.

★★★☆ **Art at Linden Gate**, (B&B), 899 Healesville - Yarra Glen Rd, 3km E of PO, ☎ 03 9730 1861, fax 03 9730 1034, 1 rm (1 suite) [ensuite, hairdry, fan, heat, tel, TV, clock radio, t/c mkg, refrig, micro, elec frypan, toaster, doonas], bbq, non smoking property. BLB ♯♯ $104.50 - $126.50, ch con, BC MC VI.

YARRA JUNCTION VIC 3797

Pop 2,000. Part of Yarra Ranges, (68km E Melbourne), See map on page 696, ref D5.

★★★★★ **Langbrook Farm Cottage**, (Cotg), Stephensons La, 4.6km S of PO, off Lt Yarra Rd, ☎ 03 5967 1320, fax 03 5967 1182, 1 cotg acc up to 2, (1 bedrm), [shwr, tlt, a/c, c/fan, heat (wood), elec blkts, TV, video, CD, t/c mkg, refrig, cook fac, micro, d/wash, toaster, blkts, doonas, linen, pillows], w/mach, iron, iron brd, pool-heated (solar), spa (heated), bbq, c/park (carport), tennis, breakfast ingredients, non smoking property. BB ♦ $100, ♯♯ $160 - $220.

B&B's/Guest Houses

★★★☆ **Tarrango Farm**, (B&B), Tarrango Rd, 3km E of PO, ☎ 03 5967 2123, 2 rms [fan, heat, elec blkts, t/c mkg, doonas], lounge (TV). BB ♦ $60, ♯♯ $100, Cottage not listed or rated. Dinner by arrangement. BC MC VI.

YARRAGON VIC 3823

Pop 700. (115km E Melbourne), See map on page 696, ref D6.

Hotels/Motels

GOLDEN CHAIN

★★★☆ **Yarragon Motel**, (M), 119 Princes Hwy, opposite railway station, ☎ 03 5634 2655, fax 03 5634 2365, 14 units [shwr, tlt, hairdry, a/c, elec blkts, tel, TV (10), video-fee, clock radio, t/c mkg, refrig, mini bar, toaster], bar, dinner to unit, cots-fee, non smoking units (8). RO ♦ $57 - $88, ♯♯ $68 - $95, ◊ $11, pen con, AE BC DC EFT MC MCH MP VI.

Self Catering Accommodation

★★★★ **Yarragon Country Retreat**, (Cotg), Leongatha Rd, 9km S of PO, ☎ 03 5634 4282, fax 03 5634 4284, 1 cotg acc up to 2, (1 bedrm), [shwr, tlt, fan, heat, elec blkts, TV, radio, t/c mkg, refrig, cook fac ltd, toaster], breakfast ingredients, non smoking property. BB ♦ $100, ♯♯ $110, BC MC VI.

YARRAM VIC 3971

Pop 1,800. (225km SE Melbourne), See map on pages 694/695, ref G8. Dairy farming area. Tarra Valley & Bulga National Parks.

Hotels/Motels

GOLDEN CHAIN

★★★☆ **Ship Inn Motel**, (M), South Gippsland Hwy, 1.5km S of PO, ☎ 03 5182 5588, fax 03 5182 5072, 26 units [shwr, bath (2), spa bath (2), tlt, a/c, elec blkts, tel, TV, video-fee, clock radio, t/c mkg, refrig, mini bar, toaster], conf fac, ☒ (Mon to Sat), pool (solar heated), bbq, rm serv, cots, non smoking units (10). RO ♦ $59 - $115, ♯♯ $65 - $115, ◊ $11, ch con, AE BC DC EFT MC VI.

Country Haven

★★★☆ **Tarra Motel**, (M), 387 Commercial Rd (South Gippsland Hwy), 900m S of PO, ☎ 03 5182 5444, fax 03 5182 5444, 24 units [shwr, tlt, hairdry, a/c, elec blkts, tel, TV, video-fee, clock radio, t/c mkg, refrig, toaster], iron, iron brd, ☒ (Mon to Sat), pool-heated (solar), dinner to unit, plygr, cots-fee, non smoking units (12). RO ♦ $54 - $62, ♯♯ $65 - $75, ◊ $11, ch con, pen con, AE BC DC MC VI.

★★ **Commercial Hotel Motel**, (LMH), 238 Commercial Rd (South Gippsland Hwy), 50m S of PO, ☎ 03 5182 5419, fax 03 5182 6354, 10 units [shwr, tlt, heat, elec blkts, TV, t/c mkg, refrig], ☒, ⬦. RO ♯♯ $48, ◊ $6, BC EFT MC VI.

B&B's/Guest Houses

★★★★ **Rosewood Bed & Breakfast & SC Cottage**, (B&B), Hihos La, 1km SW of PO, ☎ 03 5182 5605, 1 rm [shwr, bath, tlt, hairdry, fan, heat, elec blkts, t/c mkg], lounge (TV), bbq. BB ♦ $115, ♯♯ $120, Min book long w/ends and Easter, BC MC VI.

★★★★ (**Cottage Section**), 1 cotg acc up to 4, (2 bedrm), [shwr, spa bath, tlt, heat (wood), elec blkts, TV, video, clock radio, CD, refrig, cook fac, micro, toaster, doonas, linen, pillows], bbq. D ♦ $95, ♯♯ $100, ◊ $22.

Other Accommodation

Forest Lodge Farm, (Lodge), Forest Lodge Rd, Alberton West 3971, 15km W of Yarram, ☎ 03 5184 1264, 15 rms acc up to 6, (Bunk Rooms), [heat], rec rm, lounge, lounge firepl, pool, cook fac, bbq, plygr, canoeing. D all meals ♦ $38.50, ♯♯ $38.50, ch con, Minimum booking for catered meals - 25 people. Self catering $15 per person.

(**Cottage**), 3 rms acc up to 12, [shwr, tlt, heat, refrig, cook fac, micro, ldry], lounge (TV, video). D $550.

YARRA VALLEY VIC

See: Healesville, Launching Place, Millgrove, Powelltown, Seville, Wandin, Warburton, Yarra Glen, Yarra Junction.

YARRAWONGA VIC 3730

Pop 3,450. (264km NE Melbourne), See map on page 696, ref E1. Located on the banks of the Murray River.

Hotels/Motels

★★★★ **Central Yarrawonga Motor Inn**, (M), 111 Belmore St, 150m S of PO, ☎ 03 5744 3817, fax 03 5744 2500, (2 stry gr fl), 34 units [shwr, tlt, hairdry, a/c, elec blkts, tel, TV, video-fee, t/c mkg, refrig], ldry, iron, iron brd, pool, spa, bbq, cots, non smoking units (12). RO ♦ $71.50 - $93.50, ♯♯ $71.50 - $93.50, ◊ $16.50, ch con, AE BC DC EFT MC MP VI, ♿.

★★★☆ **Belmore Motor Inn**, (M), 14 Belmore St, 50m N of PO, ☎ 03 5744 3685, fax 03 5743 3240, (2 stry gr fl), 12 units [shwr, tlt, hairdry, a/c, elec blkts, tel, TV, video (avail), clock radio, t/c mkg, refrig, micro (3), toaster], iron, iron brd, bbq, non smoking units (4). RO ♦ $55 - $85, ♯♯ $55 - $85, ◊ $12, AE BC DC EFT MC VI.

★★★☆ **Woodlands Lakeside Motor Inn**, (M), Murray Valley Hwy, 6.5km E of PO, on Lake Mulwala, ☎ 03 5744 2355, fax 03 5744 1039, 20 units [shwr, tlt, hairdry, a/c, elec blkts,tel, TV, video-fee, clock radio, t/c mkg, refrig, toaster], ldry, pool, spa-fee, bbq, tennis, cots-fee, non smoking units (4). RO ♦ $60 - $75, ♦ $60 - $85, ♦ $12, AE BC DC EFT MC VI, ⟨&.

★★★ **Quality Motel**, (M), 51 Telford St (Murray Valley Hwy), 700m S of PO, ☎ 03 5744 1956, fax 03 5744 1956, 10 units [shwr, tlt, a/c, elec blkts, tel, cable tv, clock radio, t/c mkg, refrig, micro (3)], cots-fee, non smoking units (3). RO ♦ $50 - $75, ♦ $60 - $85, ♦ $11, ch con, AE BC DC EFT MC MCH VI.

★★★ **Scalzo Lake-View Motel**, (M), 1 Hunt St, ☎ 03 5744 1555, fax 03 5743 1327, 38 units [shwr, tlt, a/c, elec blkts, tel, cable tv, video-fee, clock radio, t/c mkg, refrig, toaster], pool, bbq (covered), cots-fee. RO ♦ $60 - $80, ♦ $70 - $90, ♦ $10 - $20, ch con, AE BC DC EFT MC VI.

★★☆ **Burke's Hotel/Motel**, (LMH), 96 Belmore St, 100m S of PO, ☎ 03 5744 3033, fax 03 5743 1239, (2 stry gr fl), 20 units [shwr, tlt, a/c, c/fan (10), elec blkts, TV, clock radio, t/c mkg, refrig], ldry, conf fac, ☒, ☎, cots. BLB ♦ $49.50 - $69.50, ♦ $66 - $86, ♦ $15, fam con, AE BC DC EFT JCB MC MCH VI.

★★☆ **Ski-Land Motel**, (M), Murray Valley Hwy, 8km E of PO, ☎ 03 5744 3937, 12 units [shwr, tlt, a/c-cool, heat, elec blkts, TV, video-fee, clock radio, t/c mkg, refrig, cook fac ltd], iron, iron brd, pool, bbq, ☎, plygr, tennis, cots-fee. BB ♦ $35, ♦ $40, ♦ $20, ch con, *Operator Comment: The best sleep, the best breakfast, STAY HERE!*

Self Catering Accommodation
★★★★☆ **Murray Valley Resort (Yarrawonga)**, (HU), Murray Valley Hwy, 1.6km SW of PO, ☎ 03 5744 1844, fax 03 5744 2055, (2 stry gr fl), 10 units acc up to 6, (2 bedrm), [shwr, spa bath (10), tlt, a/c, elec blkts, tel, cable tv, movie, clock radio, refrig, cook fac, micro, d/wash, toaster, doonas, linen, pillows], ldry, rec rm, lounge, pool, pool indoor heated, sauna, spa (indoor & outdoor), bbq, ☎, plygr, bicycle-fee, gym, squash, tennis, cots-fee. D ♦ $120 - $153, ♦♦♦♦ $208 - $230, ♦ $24, Time share units not rated. Light breakfast available. AE BC DC MC MP VI.

★★★★ **Leigh Park**, (Cotg), (Farm), Cnr McPhails & Munros Rds, Bundalong 3730, 19.4km E of PO, ☎ 03 5726 8488, fax 03 5726 8480, 6 cotgs acc up to 6, (2 & 3 bedrm), [shwr, bath, tlt, a/c-cool, heat, elec blkts, tel, TV, clock radio, refrig, cook fac, micro, d/wash, toaster, ldry (in unit), doonas, linen, pillows], pool, spa, bbq, golf (pitch & putt), tennis, cots. D ♦♦ $114.40 - $140.80, ♦ $41.80, ch con, Min book Christmas Jan long w/ends and Easter, BC MC VI.

★★★ **Yarrawonga Waters**, (HU), 11 Hogans Rd, 6km E of PO, 200m S of Lake Mulwala, ☎ 03 5744 2000, fax 03 5743 2007, 8 units acc up to 5, (1 & 2 bedrm), [shwr, tlt, a/c-cool, heat, elec blkts, TV, clock radio, refrig, cook fac, micro, toaster, ldry (in unit) (4), linen], ldry, pool, spa, bbq (covered), shop (licensed), c/park (carport), plygr, cots. D ♦♦ $40 - $80, ♦ $14, W ♦♦ $280 - $690, ♦ $48, BC EFT MC VI.

★★☆ **Gillespies Cottages**, (Cotg), Cnr Murray Valley Hwy & Nevins Rd, 12.3km W of PO, ☎ 03 5748 4265, 2 cotgs acc up to 2, (1 bedrm - mudbrick.), [shwr, tlt, c/fan, heat, clock radio, refrig, cook fac, toaster, blkts, doonas, linen, pillows], bbq, non smoking property. D ♦♦ $90.

★★☆ **Yarrawonga Holiday Lodge**, (HF), 16 Piper St, 300m W of PO, ☎ 03 5743 3010, 3 flats acc up to 4, (Studio), [shwr, tlt, a/c-cool, c/fan, heat, elec blkts, TV, clock radio, refrig, cook fac, micro, toaster, ldry (in unit), linen, pillows]. D ♦♦ $43 - $60, ♦ $10, W ♦♦ $220 - $400, ♦ $50 - $80, Min book all holiday times, BC VI.

★★ **Yarrawonga Lakeside Lodges**, 31 Bank St, 1.5km NE of PO, ☎ 03 5744 2999, fax 03 5744 2900, 6 cabins acc up to 8, [shwr, tlt, a/c-cool, heat, elec blkts (double beds), TV, clock radio, refrig, cook fac, micro, toaster, blkts, linen reqd-fee, pillows]. D ♦♦ $45 - $70, ♦ $5, W ♦♦ $250 - $490, ♦ $35, Min book Christmas Jan long w/ends and Easter.

B&B's/Guest Houses
★★★☆ **Brae Side (Telford)**, (B&B), RMB 2100 Benalla Rd, ☎ 03 5744 3191, fax 03 5743 2988, 3 rms [ensuite, bath (1), a/c-cool, cent heat, elec blkts, doonas], lounge (TV), spa-fee, t/c mkg shared, refrig, bbq, non smoking property. BB ♦♦ $100, BC MC VI.

YEA VIC 3717
Pop 950. (105km NE Melbourne), See map on page 696, ref C4.
★★★ **Tartan Motel (Yea)**, (M), 17 High St (Goulburn Valley Hwy), 200m N of PO, ☎ 03 5797 2202, fax 03 5797 2406, 13 units [shwr, spa bath (1), tlt, a/c-cool, heat, elec blkts, tel, TV, clock radio, t/c mkg, refrig, mini bar, cook fac (1)], bbq, plygr. RO ♦ $55, ♦♦ $66, ♦ $10, ch con, AE BC EFT MC VI.

★★★ **Yea Motel**, (M), 8 Miller St, 500m N of PO, ☎ 03 5797 2660, fax 03 5797 2660, 8 units [shwr, tlt, a/c-cool, c/fan, heat, elec blkts, tel, TV, video (avail), clock radio, t/c mkg, refrig, toaster], pool, bbq, plygr, cots. RO ♦ $55, ♦♦ $65, ♦♦♦♦ $88, AE BC DC MC MCH VI.

Self Catering Accommodation

★★★★ **Cheviot Glen Cottages**, (Cotg), (Farm), No children's facilities, Limestone Rd, 4km SE of PO, ☎ 03 5797 2617, 2 cotgs acc up to 2, (1 bedrm), [shwr, spa bath, tlt, hairdry, c/fan, TV, video, clock radio, CD, t/c mkg, refrig, cook fac, toaster, doonas, linen, pillows], ldry, lounge firepl, bbq, non smoking property. BB ♦♦ $135, ♦ $30, BC MC VI.

B&B's/Guest Houses
★★★★☆ **Parra Homestead**, (B&B), RMB 4005 Frog Ponds Rd, 5km NE of Yea, off Limestone Rd, ☎ 03 5797 2216, fax 03 5797 3032, (2 stry), 1 rm [ensuite, bath, hairdry, c/fan, fire pl, heat, elec blkts, clock radio, t/c mkg], lounge (TV, Video, Cd Player), lounge firepl, non smoking property. BB ♦ $110, ♦ $115, ♦♦ $143, ♦♦ $150, Dinner by arrangement. Min book applies.

Other Accommodation
Billabong Angler, (Hbt), Permanently moored houseboat - solar power. 908 Killingworth Rd, 10km NE of PO, ☎ 03 5797 2045, fax 03 5797 2045, 1 houseboat acc up to 4, (2 bedrm), [shwr, tlt, heat, radio, t/c mkg, refrig, cook fac ltd, toaster, blkts, doonas, linen, pillows], bbq, cots. W $700, Min book applies, BC MC VI.

YELLINGBO VIC 3139
Pop Part of Yarra Ranges, (62km NE Melbourne), See map on page 696, ref C5. Small community situated in the Yarra Valley.
★★★ **Belltana Park Cottage Bed & Breakfast**, (Cotg), Previously Belltana Manor Bed & Breakfast (Farm), 185 Beenak Rd, 6km SW of general store, off Smiths Rd, ☎ 03 5964 8265, fax 03 5964 8181, 1 cotg acc up to 6, (2 bedrm), [shwr, bath, tlt, hairdry, fan, heat, elec blkts, clock radio, t/c mkg, refrig, cook fac, micro, toaster, blkts, doonas, linen, pillows], w/mach, iron, iron brd, lounge (TV, video, CD), pool, bbq. BB ♦♦ $140, ♦ $25, BC MC VI.

YERING VIC 3770
Pop Nominal, (55km E Melbourne), See map on page 696, ref C5.
★★★★★ **Chateau Yering Historic House Hotel**, (PH), 38 Melba Hwy, ☎ 03 9237 3333, fax 03 9237 3300, (2 stry gr fl), 20 rms (5 suites) [shwr, bath, spa bath (8), tlt, hairdry, a/c, fire pl (3), cent heat, elec blkts, tel, TV, video (DVD), clock radio, t/c mkg, refrig, mini bar], iron, iron brd, lounge, conf fac, ☒, cafe (licensed), pool (salt water), 24hr reception, rm serv, tennis, cots, non smoking rms (18). BB ♦ $407.50 - $867.50, ♦♦ $435 - $895, ♦ $55, ch con, AE BC DC EFT JCB MC VI.

VICTORIA

Western Australia is the biggest of Australia's states and territories. Its modern capital, Perth, lies on the Swan River, inland from the port of Fremantle and the restless Indian Ocean which first brought the inquisitive Dutch to Australia's West Coast in the 16th century. But it was not until 1829 that Captain James Stirling founded Perth.

Covering almost one third of Australia's total land mass WA's sheer size has been a curb on development, but the discovery of gold in Coolgardie brought boom times to the West in 1892, when Arthur Bayley struck it rich with a find of 554 ounces of golf at Fly Flat. Within six months, thousands were living in tents around Coolgardie and Western Australia's population had risen by 400 per cent.

Today mineral wealth still drives the economy. WA's mountain of iron, the Hamersley Range stretches for more than 300km's through the Pilbara.

West Australian's enjoy the outdoors and Rottnest Island is a holiday favourite, 20km off Fremantle. Kings Park bushland reserve, near the city centre, is also a popular attraction.

The southern corner of Western Australia is the "garden" of the state, with wildflowers colouring the landscape from September to November and forests of karri and jarrah reaching for the sky.

In the south-west, fine wineries, surf beaches and destinations like Albany, Margaret River, Busselton and Yallingup are part of the easy touring pleasure.

But the north and north-east of the state require planning before taking to the open road. Petrol water and food should be carried and attention paid to the distance to be travelled and the seasonal influences which bring monsoonal rains in October through March.

Tropical Broome leads the world in pearling and is the gateway to the West Kimberleys.

The region thrives on cattle and diamond mining. Golden history is to be found at Kalgoorlie-Boulder in the north east.

The limitless plain of the Nullarbor makes it a road "voyage" for drivers travelling from Adelaide in the east, bound for Perth.

To the north of Perth, Geraldton's reputation for fresh seafood attracts travellers.

Excellent fishing and coral reefs are found further north. The free-spirited dolphins of Monkey Mia give a contradiction to the disturbingly named Shark Bay.

The port of Carnarvon gives a new dimension to the enjoyment of fresh caught prawns. Exmouth, 220km off the North West Coastal Highway, is renowned for its beaches and fishing. Further north, Karratha has been developed as a centre for the Hamersley Iron Ore Project. Port Hedland is another iron ore boom town. From Broome, the Great Northern Highway passes through Fitzroy Crossing, and the old gold settlement of Halls Creek on its way to Wyndham, pastoral centre and port for the Ord River.

To the east, Kununurra, on the Victoria Highway, is the base for Lake Argyle diamond mining. Mirima and Purnululu National Parks are within striking distance. Purnululu includes the Bungle Bungles, thousands of beehive shaped rock formations, in black and orange.

And, like Western Australia itself, the Bungle Bungles are a natural wonder.

WESTERN AUSTRALIA

Experience the natural wonder of Western Australia

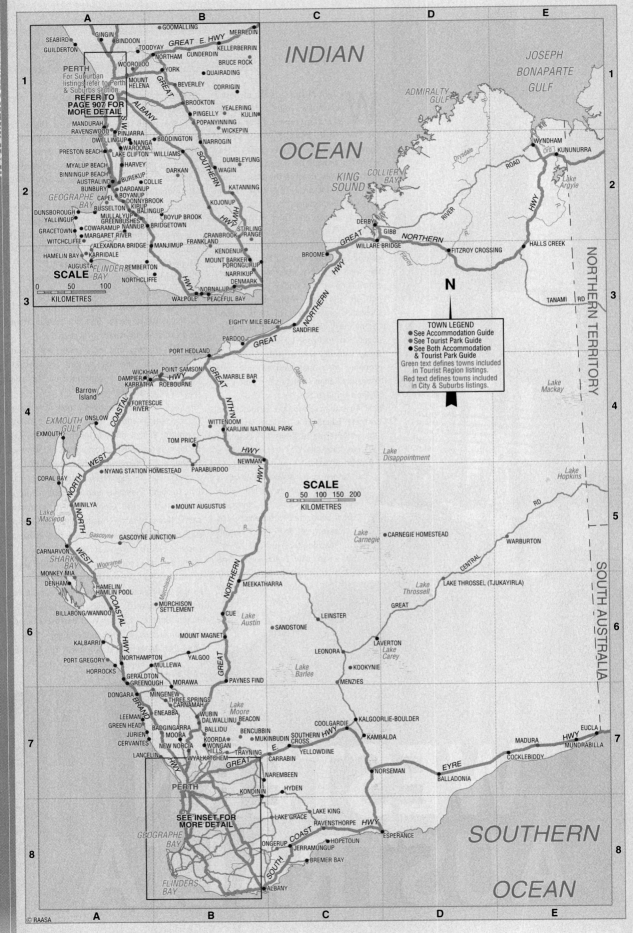

INDIAN

OCEAN

JOSEPH
BONAPARTE
GULF

ADMIRALTY
GULF

KING
SOUND

COLLIER
BAY

NORTHERN TERRITORY

SOUTH AUSTRALIA

SOUTHERN

OCEAN

PERTH
For Suburban
listings refer to Perth
& Suburbs section

**REFER TO
PAGE 907 FOR
MORE DETAIL**

SCALE

0   50   100

KILOMETRES

GEOGRAPHE
BAY

FLINDER
BAY

N

TOWN LEGEND
● See Accommodation Guide
● See Tourist Park Guide
● See Both Accommodation
   & Tourist Park Guide
Green text defines towns included
in Tourist Region listings.
Red text defines towns included
in City & Suburbs listings.

SCALE

0   50 100 150 200

KILOMETRES

**SEE INSET FOR
MORE DETAIL**

GEOGRAPHE
BAY

FLINDERS
BAY

© RAASA

Rates may change. Check before booking.

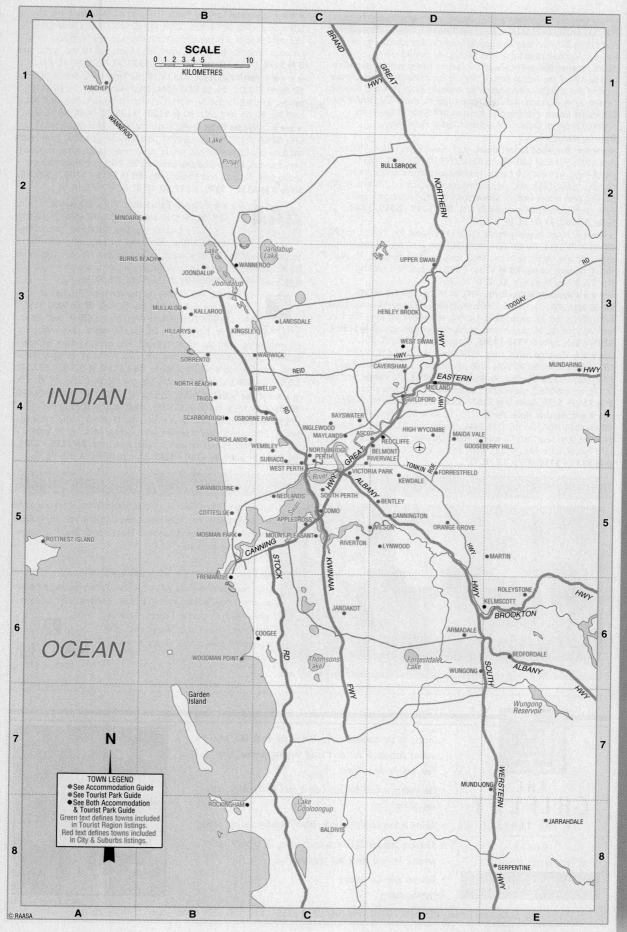

SCALE
0 1 2 3 4 5   10
KILOMETRES

A   B   C   D   E

1

2

3

4

5

6

7

8

INDIAN

OCEAN

N

TOWN LEGEND
● See Accommodation Guide
● See Tourist Park Guide
● See Both Accommodation
   & Tourist Park Guide
Green text defines towns included
in Tourist Region listings.
Red text defines towns included
in City & Suburbs listings.

YANCHEP

WANNEROO

Lake
Pinjar

BRAND   HWY

GREAT

NORTHERN

BULLSBROOK

MINDARIE

Lake
Jandabup
Lake

BURNS BEACH

JOONDALUP

Lake
Joondalup

WANNEROO

UPPER SWAN

TOODAY

RD

MULLALOO   KALLAROO

HILLARYS   KINGSLEY

LANDSDALE

HENLEY BROOK

WEST SWAN

SORRENTO

WARWICK

REID

CAVERSHAM

HWY

MUNDARING   HWY

NORTH BEACH

GWELUP

HWY

EASTERN

TRIGG

MIDLAND

GUILDFORD

SCARBOROUGH   OSBORNE PARK

INGLEWOOD

BAYSWATER

ASCOT

HIGH WYCOMBE

MAIDA VALE

CHURCHLANDS

MAYLANDS

REDCLIFFE

GOOSEBERRY HILL

WEMBLEY

NORTHBRIDGE
PERTH

BELMONT

RIVERVALE

SUBIACO

GREAT

TONKIN   RGE

FORRESTFIELD

WEST PERTH

River

HWY

VICTORIA PARK

KEWDALE

SWANBOURNE

NEDLANDS

Swan

SOUTH PERTH

ALBANY

BENTLEY

COTTESLOE

APPLECROSS

COMO

CANNINGTON

ORANGE GROVE

MOSMAN PARK

MOUNT PLEASANT

WILSON

CANNING

RIVERTON

LYNWOOD

HWY

MARTIN

ROTTNEST ISLAND

STOCK

KWINANA

FREMANTLE

HWY

ROLEYSTONE

HWY

KELMSCOTT

BROOKTON

JANDAKOT

COOGEE

ARMADALE

BEDFORDALE

WOODMAN POINT

RD

Thomsons
Lake

Forrestdale
Lake

WUNGONG

SOUTH

ALBANY

HWY

Garden
Island

FWY

Wungong
Reservoir

WESTERN

MUNDIJONG

ROCKINGHAM

Lake
Cooloongup

JARRAHDALE

BALDIVIS

SERPENTINE

HWY

© RAASA

A   B   C   D   E

PERTH WA 6000

Pop 1,000,000. See map on page 907, ref C4. The capital city of Western Australia situated on the Swan River, lies on rolling coastal plains between the green hills of the Darling Range and the sparkling blue waters of the Indian Ocean. The city has a Mediterranean climate making this a popular destination for tourists. Kings Park and Botanic Garden, Army Museum, Old Court House Law Museum, The Perth Mint, The Round House, Fire Brigades Museum, WA State Museum. Art Gallery, Canoeing, Catamaran, Gardens, Jetty, Parasailing.

Hotels/Motels

★★★★★ **Burswood Resort Hotel**, (LH), Great Eastern Hwy, Victoria Park 6100, 3km E of GPO, ☎ 08 9362 7777, fax 08 9470 2553, (Multi-stry), 413 rms (19 suites) [hairdry, a/c, tel, TV, movie, radio, t/c mkg, refrig, ldry], lift (/s), bathrm, conv fac, casino (24 hr), ✕ (9), bar (5), pool indoor heated, sauna, spa, rm serv, secure park, golf, gym, tennis, cots, non smoking flr (/s). D ♦♦ **$215 - $340**, ♦ **$49**, **Suite D $760**, AE BC DC MC VI, ⚹.

★★★★★ **Hyatt Regency Perth**, (LH), 99 Adelaide Tce, 2km SE of GPO, ☎ 08 9225 1234, fax 08 9325 8899, 367 rms [a/c, tel, TV, movie, radio, t/c mkg, refrig, mini bar, ldry], iron, iron brd, conf fac, ✕, pool, sauna, rm serv, tennis. RO ♦♦ **$230**, ♦ **$55**, ch con, Min booking Nov 1-5 & New Years Eve. AE BC DC MC VI.

★★★★★ **Parmelia Hilton Perth**, (LH), 14 Mill St, 700mSW of GPO, ☎ 08 9215 2000, fax 08 9215 2001, (Multi-stry), 273 rms (55 suites) [shwr, bath, tlt, a/c, tel, TV, movie, radio, t/c mkg, refrig, mini bar, ldry], lift, iron, iron brd, conv fac, ✕, pool-heated, sauna, rm serv, gym, cots. D ♦♦ **$295 - $395**, ♦ **$45**, **Suite D $335 - $545**, ch con, AE BC DC MC VI, ⚹.

★★★★★ **Sheraton Perth**, (LH), 207 Adelaide Tce, 1.4km SE of GPO, ☎ 08 9224 7777, fax 08 9224 7788, (Multi-stry), 388 rms (18 suites) [shwr, tlt, a/c, tel, TV, movie, radio, t/c mkg, refrig], lift, lounge, conf fac, ✕ (2), bar (cocktail), pool-heated, steam rm, rm serv, gym, cots. D ♦♦ **$145 - $259**, **Suite D ♦♦ $183 - $399**, AE BC DC JCB MC VI, ⚹.

★★★★☆ **Mercure Hotel Perth**, (LH), 10 Irwin St, 700mS of GPO, ☎ 08 9326 7000, fax 08 9221 3344, (Multi-stry), 232 rms (14 suites) [ensuite, a/c, heat, tel, TV, movie, radio, t/c mkg, mini bar, ldry], lift, conf fac, ✕, cafe, bar (/s) (2), pool, sauna, spa, rm serv, gym. D ♦♦ **$133 - $190**, AE BC DC MC VI.

★★★★☆ **Novotel Langley Perth**, (LH), Cnr Adelaide Tce & Hill St, 1.3km SE of GPO, ☎ 08 9221 1200, fax 08 9221 1669, (Multi-stry), 253 rms (28 suites) [shwr, bath, tlt, hairdry, a/c, tel, TV, movie, radio, t/c mkg, refrig, ldry], lift, iron, conv fac, sauna, spa, rm serv, gym, cots. D ♦♦ **$196**, ♦ **$32.50**, **Suite D $251 - $320**, AE BC DC MC VI, ⚹.

★★★★☆ **Perth Parkroyal**, (Ltd Lic H), 54 Terrace Rd, 2km SE of GPO, ☎ 08 9325 3811, fax 08 9221 1564, (Multi-stry), 191 rms [shwr, tlt, hairdry, a/c, tel, TV, movie, radio, t/c mkg, refrig], lift, iron, iron brd, conf fac, ✕, rm serv, cots. RO ♦♦ **$120 - $185**, AE BC DC MC VI, ⚹.

★★★★☆ **Rydges Hotel Perth**, (LH), Cnr Hay & King Sts, 0.5km E of GPO, ☎ 08 9263 1800, fax 08 9263 1801, 245 rms (6 suites) [shwr, bath, spa bath (6), tlt, hairdry, a/c, tel, TV, movie, clock radio, refrig, mini bar], iron, iron brd, business centre, conv fac, ✕, 24hr reception, rm serv, secure park, ☎, cots, non smoking rms. RO ♦♦ **$145 - $205**, ♦ **$27.50**, **Suite D ♦♦ $330 - $370**, ♦ **$27.50**, AE BC DC EFT JCB MC VI.

AAA TOURISM *Special Rates* ★★★★☆ **Saville Park Suites**, (LH), 201 Hay St, 1.5km E of GPO, ☎ 08 9267 4888, fax 08 9267 4838, (Multi-stry), 152 rms (1 & 2 bedrm), [ensuite, shwr, bath, tlt, hairdry, a/c, tel, TV, movie, clock radio, t/c mkg, refrig, cook fac, toaster, ldry, pillows], lift, w/mach, dryer, iron, iron brd, business centre, ✕, ✕, pool indoor heated, rm serv, secure park, cots, non smoking flr (/s). D ♦♦ **$167 - $194**, **$200 - $238**, AE BC DC JCB MC VI.

★★★★☆ **The Chifley on the Terrace**, (LH), 185 St Georges Tce, 500m SW of Hay St Mall, ☎ 08 9226 3355, fax 08 9226 1055, (Multi-stry), 85 rms [shwr, bath, spa bath, tlt, hairdry, a/c, tel, fax, TV, movie, clock radio, t/c mkg, refrig, mini bar, micro, pillows], lift, w/mach, dryer, lounge, business centre, conv fac, ✕, cafe, bar, 24hr reception, rm serv, meals avail, cots-fee, non smoking property. BB ♦ **$158**, ♦♦ **$169**, ♦ **$27.50**, RO **$152 - $300**, ch con, fam con, pen con, AE BC DC EFT MC VI, ⚹.

★★★★☆ **The Sebel of Perth**, (Ltd Lic H), 37 Pier St, 500mSE of GPO, ☎ 08 9325 7655, fax 08 9325 7383, (Multi-stry gr fl), 119 rms (19 suites) [shwr, tlt, hairdry, a/c-cool, tel, TV, movie, radio, t/c mkg, refrig], lift, w/mach-fee, dryer-fee, iron, lounge, conv fac, ✕, cafe, bar (mini), pool-heated, rm serv, bicycle, gym, cots. BB **$135 - $285**, RO ♦ **$110 - $260**, ♦♦ **$110 - $260**, ch con, AE BC DC JCB MC VI.

★★★★ **Holiday Inn City Centre Perth**, (LH), 778-788 Hay Street, 400m SW of GPO, ☎ 08 9261 7200, fax 08 9261 7277, (Multi-stry), 180 rms [shwr, bath (some), hairdry, a/c, tel, TV, movie, radio, t/c mkg, refrig, mini bar], lift, iron, iron brd, ✕, pool-indoor (heated), sauna, spa, rm serv, gym, cots. **BB** ⊪ **$137.50 - $229.90,** ⊪⊪ **$213.40 - $294.80, RO** ⊪ **$115.50 - $187,** ⊪⊪ **$170.50 - $209,** AE BC DC MC VI.

★★★★ **Hotel Grand Chancellor, Perth**, (LH), 707 Wellington St, 900m W of GPO, ☎ 08 9327 7000, fax 08 9327 7017, (Multi-stry), 273 rms (20 suites) [shwr, tlt, a/c-cool, tel, TV, video, t/c mkg, refrig, mini bar, ldry], lift, iron, iron brd, ✕, pool-heated, sauna, 24hr reception, rm serv, gym, cots. **D** $110, ⊪ $28, ch con, AE BC DC JCB MC VI, ♿.

★★★★ **The Melbourne Hotel**, (LH), Classified by National Trust, Cnr Hay & Milligan Streets, 1km W of GPO, ☎ 08 9320 3333, fax 08 9320 3344, (Multi-stry), 36 rms (3 suites) [shwr, tlt, hairdry, a/c, tel, cable tv, movie, clock radio, t/c mkg, refrig, mini bar, ldry (service)], iron, iron brd, conv fac, ✕, cafe, bar, 24hr reception, rm serv, secure park-fee, ☎, cots, non smoking rms. **BB** ⊪ $145, ⊪⊪ $145, **Suite D** $165, ch con, AE BC DC EFT MC VI.

★★★☆ **All Seasons Chateau Hotel**, (Ltd Lic H), Previously Chateau Commodore 417 Hay St, 1km SE of GPO, ☎ 08 9325 0461, fax 08 9221 2448, (Multi-stry), 119 rms [shwr, bath, tlt, a/c, tel, TV, clock radio, t/c mkg, refrig], lift, ✕, bar (cocktail), pool. **RO** ⊪⊪ $88 - $108, ⊪ $20, ch con, AE BC DC JCB MC VI.

★★★☆ **Criterion Hotel - Perth**, (LH), 560 Hay St, 500m SE of GPO, ☎ 08 9325 5155, fax 08 9325 4176, (Multi-stry), 69 rms [shwr, bath (9), tlt, hairdry, a/c, tel, TV, clock radio, t/c mkg, refrig, mini bar, ldry (services)], lift, ✕, bar, 24hr reception, rm serv (restricted hours), secure park, ☎. **BB** ⊪ $99, ⊪⊪ $132, ⊪⊪⊪ $198, ⊪ $66, ch con, Min book applies, AE BC DC EFT MC VI.

 Best Western

★★★☆ **Emerald Hotel**, (LMH), 24 Mount Street, 1km W of GPO, ☎ 08 9481 0866, fax 08 9321 4789, 102 units [shwr, bath (2), tlt, a/c, tel, TV, radio, t/c mkg, cook fac, ldry], ✕, sauna, spa, c/park (limited), gym. **D** $95 - $105, ⊪ $18, **Suite D** $160, AE BC DC MC VI.

★★★☆ **Hotel Ibis**, (LH), 334 Murray St, 300m W of GPO, ☎ 08 9322 2844, fax 08 9321 6314, (Multi-stry), 193 rms [shwr, tlt, hairdry, a/c, tel, cable tv, radio, t/c mkg, refrig], lift, conv fac, cots. **D** ⊪⊪ $85, ⊪ $25, AE BC DC MC VI.

★★★☆ **Kings Perth Hotel**, (LH), 517 Hay St, 600m SE of GPO, ☎ 08 9325 6555, fax 08 9221 1539, (Multi-stry), 119 rms (2 suites) [shwr, tlt, a/c-cool, tel, TV, radio, t/c mkg, refrig], lift, ✕, pool, rm serv, cots. **D** ⊪ $90, ⊪⊪ $95, ⊪ $22, **Suite D** $160, ch con, AE BC DC JCB MC VI.

FLAG FLAG CHOICE HOTELS METRO INNS

★★★☆ **Metro Hotel & Suites East Perth**, (LH), 22 Nile St, 2.5km E of GPO, ☎ 08 9325 1866, fax 08 9325 5374, (Multi-stry), 103 rms [shwr, tlt, a/c-cool, tel, TV, movie, radio, t/c mkg, refrig, cook fac, micro], conv fac, ✕, bar (Mini), pool, cots. **D** ⊪⊪ $95 - $130, ⊪⊪⊪ $130 - $195, ch con, AE BC DC MC VI.

★★★☆ **Park Inn International**, (LH), 70 Pier St, 250m S of GPO, ☎ 08 9325 2133, fax 08 9221 2936, (Multi-stry), 96 rms [shwr, bath (some), tlt, a/c, tel, TV, t/c mkg, refrig], lift, ✕, bar, shop (coffee), cots. **D** ⊪ $85, ⊪⊪ $85, ⊪ $10, AE BC DC JCB MC VI.

PERTH WA continued...

★★★☆ **Perth Ambassador**, (LH), 196 Adelaide Tce, 1.5km SE of GPO, ☎ 08 9325 1455, fax 08 9325 6317, (Multi-stry), 171 rms (52 suites) [shwr, bath, tlt, hairdry, a/c, tel, TV, movie, radio, t/c mkg, refrig], lift, ⊠, sauna, spa, rm serv (ltd), cots. **D** ♦♦ **$95 - $154,** ⚲ **$20, Suite D $110 - $120,** ch con, AE BC DC VI.

★★★☆ **Sullivans**, (Ltd Lic H) 166 Mounts Bay Rd, 1.2km SW of GPO, ☎ 08 9321 8022, fax 08 9481 6762, (Multi-stry), 70 rms [shwr, tlt, a/c, tel, TV, movie, radio, t/c mkg, refrig], lift, ldry, ⊠, pool, bbq, courtesy transfer, bicycle, cots. **D** ♦♦♦♦ **$110 - $130,** ch con, Some units of a higher rating. AE BC DC MC VI.

(Apartment Section), 2 apts acc up to 4, (2 bedrm), [shwr, bath, tlt, a/c-cool, tel, TV, video, clock radio, refrig, cook fac, micro, toaster], ldry, c/park. **D $150.**

★★★☆ **The Terrace Hotel**, (LMH), 195 Adelaide Tce, 1.4km SE of GPO, ☎ 08 9492 7777, fax 08 9492 7749, (Multi-stry), 179 units (3 suites) [shwr, bath (12), tlt, a/c, tel, TV, movie, clock radio, t/c mkg, refrig, cook fac, micro (160), toaster, ldry (services)], lift, ldry, w/mach-fee, dryer-fee, iron, business centre, conv fac, ⊠, coffee shop, bar, 24hr reception, cots, non smoking units (1 floor). **RO $95, Suite D $145 - $200,** AE BC DC MC VI, ♿.

★★★ **Miss Maud Swedish Hotel**, (LMH), 97 Murray St, 450m SE of GPO, ☎ 08 9325 3900, fax 08 9221 3225, (Multi-stry), 51 units [shwr, tlt, a/c, tel, TV, radio, t/c mkg, refrig, mini bar, ldry], lift, ⊠, coffee shop, rm serv, cots. **BB** ♦ **$96,** ♦♦ **$125,** ch con, AE BC DC MC VI.

★★★ **Pacific Motel**, (M), 111 Harold St, Mount Lawley 6050, 2.5km NE of GPO, ☎ 08 9328 5599, fax 08 9328 5268, (Multi-stry), 60 units [shwr, tlt, a/c, heat, tel, TV, t/c mkg, refrig, ldry], lift, conv fac, pool, bbq, cots. **D** ♦ **$60,** ♦♦ **$77,** ♦♦♦♦ **$121,** AE BC DC MC VI.

★★★ **Perth City Hotel**, (LMH), 200 Hay St, 150m E of East Perth PO, ☎ 08 9220 7000, fax 08 9220 7007, (Multi-stry), 94 units [shwr, tlt, hairdry, a/c, tel, fax, TV, movie, radio, t/c mkg, refrig], lift, w/mach-fee, dryer-fee, iron (10), iron brd, coffee shop, secure park, ✆, cots, non smoking flr, non smoking rms. **RO $82.50 - $115.50,** ⚲ **$11,** ch con, Minium booking New Years Eve, AE BC DC EFT JCB MC VI, ♿.

★★★ **The New Esplanade Hotel**, (M), 18 The Esplanade, 600m S of GPO, ☎ 08 9325 2000, fax 08 9221 2190, (Multi-stry), 65 units (12 suites) [shwr, bath (66), tlt, a/c-cool, tel, TV, radio, t/c mkg, refrig], lift, ⊠. **D** ♦ **$85,** ♦♦ **$95,** ⚲ **$15, Suite D $135,** ⚲ **$15,** AE DC MC VI.

★★★ **Wentworth Plaza Hotel**, (LH), 300 Murray St, 300m W of GPO, ☎ 08 9481 1000, fax 08 9321 2443, 96 rms (13 suites) [shwr, tlt, a/c, tel, TV, radio, t/c mkg, refrig (57), cook fac (10)], ⊠, cots-fee. **D** ♦ **$65 - $93,** ♦♦ **$115,** ⚲ **$13, Suite D $120 - $137,** ch con, Some units of a lower rating. AE BC DC MC VI.

★★☆ **CWA House Residential**, (M), 1174 Hay St, West Perth 6005, 2km W of GPO, ☎ 08 9321 6081, fax 08 9321 6024, (Multi-stry gr fl), 34 units [shwr, tlt, H & C, a/c, tel, TV, t/c mkg, refrig], lift, TV rm, ✗, cots. **BB** ♦ **$42 - $70,** ♦♦ **$75,** ch con, Some units of a lower rating. BC MC VI, ♿.

Adelphi Apartments, (M), 130A Mounts Bay Rd, 1.4km W of GPO, ☎ 08 9322 4666, fax 08 9322 4580, (Multi-stry), 62 units [shwr, tlt, a/c, tel, TV, radio, refrig, cook fac, ldry], lift, cots. **D** ♦♦ **$75,** ♦♦♦ **$85,** ♦♦♦♦ **$95, W** ♦ **$300,** ♦♦ **$360,** ♦♦♦ **$400,** ♦♦♦♦ **$430,** ch con, AE BC DC MC VI.

Duxton Hotel Perth, (LH), 1 St Georges Tce, 1km SE of GPO, ☎ 08 9261 8000, fax 08 9261 8020, (Multi-stry), 306 rms [ensuite, spa bath (12), hairdry, a/c, tel, TV, movie, clock radio, t/c mkg, refrig, mini bar], w/mach, dryer, iron, iron brd, business centre, conf fac, ⊠, coffee shop, pool, spa, 24hr reception, rm serv, secure park, ✆, gym, cots, non smoking rms. **RO** ♦♦ **$360 - $545,** AE BC DC MC VI.

Self Catering Accommodation

★★★★★ **Mounts Bay Waters Apartment Hotel**, (SA), 112 Mounts Bay Rd, 2km SW of GPO, ☎ 08 9486 7999, fax 08 9486 7998, (Multi-stry), 72 serv apts acc up to 5, (1 & 2 bedrm), [shwr, bath, tlt, a/c, tel, cable tv, video, movie, radio, refrig, cook fac, micro, d/wash, toaster, ldry, linen, pillows], lift, w/mach, dryer, iron, iron brd, conf fac, ✗, pool, spa, 24hr reception, rm serv, secure park, bicycle, gym, tennis, cots, non smoking units. **D** ♦♦ **$134 - $167, W** ♦♦ **$630 - $788,** AE BC DC EFT JCB MC VI.

★★★★★ **Perth Serviced Apartments**, (Apt), 112 Mounts Bay Rd, 1km SW of PO, ☎ 08 9486 7277, fax 08 9486 7404, (Multi-stry), 71 apts acc up to 6, (1, 2 & 3 bedrm), [shwr, bath, tlt, hairdry, a/c, tel, TV, movie, radio, t/c mkg, refrig, micro, d/wash, toaster, ldry, blkts, linen, pillows], lift, w/mach, dryer, iron, iron brd, conv fac, ✗, spa, freezer, bbq, 24hr reception, rm serv, secure park, bicycle, gym, tennis, cots. **W $630 - $893,** Min book applies, AE BC DC EFT JCB MC VI.

★★★★☆ **St James Quest Establishment**, (SA), 228 James St, Northbridge 6000, 1km W of GPO, ☎ 08 9227 2888, fax 08 9227 2800, (Multi-stry), 52 serv apts acc up to 6, (1, 2 & 3 bedrm), [shwr, bath, tlt, hairdry, a/c, tel, TV, movie, clock radio, refrig, cook fac, micro, d/wash, toaster, ldry], lift, w/mach, dryer, iron, ✗, pool, spa, bbq, 24hr reception, cots. **D $180 - $255,** AE BC DC MC VI, ♿.

★★★★☆ **West End Quest Establishment**, (SA), 50 Milligan St, 700m W of GPO, ☎ 08 9480 3888, fax 08 9480 3800, (Multi-stry), 41 serv apts acc up to 4, (1 & 2 bedrm), [shwr, bath, tlt, hairdry, a/c, tel, TV, movie, radio, t/c mkg, refrig, cook fac, micro, d/wash, ldry, blkts, linen, pillows], lift, w/mach, dryer, iron, ⊠, 24hr reception, rm serv, secure park, gym, cots (avail). **D $190 - $230,** AE BC DC MC VI.

Rates may change. Check before booking.

★★★★ **Lawson Apartments**, (SA), 2 Sherwood Crt, 600m S of GPO, ☎ 08 9321 4228, fax 08 9324 2030, 11 serv apts acc up to 4, [shwr, bath (some), tlt, a/c, tel, TV, video, cook fac, micro, d/wash, blkts, linen, pillows], w/mach, dryer. **D ⚤ $120 - $150, W ⚤ $500 - $600**, Min book.

★★★★ **Riverview On Mount Street**, (HU), 42 Mount St, 1.2km SW of GPO, ☎ 08 9321 8963, fax 08 9322 5956, (Multi-stry), 50 units acc up to 3, (1 bedrm), [shwr, tlt, a/c, tel, TV, refrig, cook fac, micro, ldry, blkts, linen, pillows], cafe, c/park. **D $82.50 - $90.**

★★★☆ **Brownelea Holiday Apartments**, (HU), 1/166 Palmerston St, 1.5km NW of GPO, ☎ 08 9227 1710, fax 08 9328 4840, 21 units acc up to 4, [shwr, tlt, a/c, fan, heat, tel, TV, radio, refrig, cook fac, ldry, blkts, linen, pillows], pool, sauna, spa, bbq, cots. **D ⚹ $72 - $83, ⚤ $72 - $83, ⛑ $11**, ch con, BC DC MC VI.

★★★☆ **City Stay Apartment Hotel**, (SA), 875 Wellington St, 1.5km W of GPO, ☎ 08 9322 6061, fax 08 9322 7348, (Multi-stry), 78 serv apts acc up to 5, (1 & 2 bedrm), [shwr, tlt, a/c, fan, tel, TV, movie, refrig, cook fac, micro, ldry], lift, w/mach, dryer, lounge, ✕ (bar), pool, spa, bbq, plygr, cots. **D $102 - $135, ⛑ $13,**, AE BC DC JCB MC VI.

★★★ **City Waters Lodge**, (HU), 118 Terrace Rd, 1.5km SE of GPO, ☎ 08 9325 1566, fax 08 9221 2794, 63 units (1 & 2 bedrm), [shwr, bath, tlt, a/c-cool, heat, tel, TV, refrig, cook fac], cots, non smoking units (some). **D ⚹ $73, ⚤ $78, ⛑ $10**, BC EFT JCB MC VI.

Mountway Holiday Flats, (HF), 36 Mount St, 1.2km W of GPO, ☎ 08 9321 8307, fax 08 9324 2147, (Multi-stry), 60 flats acc up to 3, (1 bedrm), [shwr, bath, tlt, fan, heat, TV, refrig, cook fac, blkts, linen, pillows], lift. **D ⚹ $54, ⚤ $63, W ⚹ $323, ⚤ $362**, ch con, AE BC DC EFT MC VI.

B&B's/Guest Houses

★★★★ **Parkside B&B**, (B&B), 21 Woolnough St, Daglish 6008, 4km W of GPO, ☎ 08 9388 6075, fax 08 9382 3878, (2 stry), 1 rm [ensuite, a/c, elec blkts, TV, video, t/c mkg, refrig, pillows], w/mach, dryer, iron, lounge, non smoking property. **BB ⚹ $65 - $75, ⚤ $90 - $120.**

★★★★ **Pension of Perth**, (B&B), 3 Throssell St, Opposite Hyde Park, ☎ 08 9228 9049, fax 08 9228 9290, 4 rms [shwr, bath, tlt, a/c, tel, fax, TV, clock radio, CD, refrig], lounge, pool, t/c mkg shared, secure park, courtesy transfer. **BB ⚤ $110, W⚤ $660**, BC MC VI.

★★ **YMCA Jewell House**, (PH), 180 Goderich St, 1km SE of GPO, ☎ 08 9325 8488, fax 08 9221 4694, 200 rms [heat, refrig (some rooms), ldry], shwr, tlt, TV rm (some rooms with TV), cafe. **RO ⚹ $39, ⚤ $46**, AE BC DC MC VI.

Other Accommodation

Aberdeen Lodge, No children's facilities, 79 Aberdeen St, Northbridge 6000, 800m N of GPO, ☎ 08 9227 6137, fax 08 9387 2892, 11 rms (Bunk Rooms), [c/fan, fire pl, cable tv, video, refrig, ldry, blkts, linen, pillows], shwr, tlt, w/mach-fee, dryer-fee, iron, rec rm, cook fac, bbq, ☎, non smoking rms. **D ⚹ $10 - $14, W $63 - $77, RO ⚹ $25 - $30, W ⚹ $150.**

Cheviot International Lodge, No children's facilities, 30 Bulwer St, 2km NE of GPO, ☎ 08 9227 6817, fax 08 9227 6826, (Multi-stry), 28 rms (Bunk Rooms), [shwr, bath, tlt, TV, video, radio, refrig, ldry, blkts, doonas, linen, pillows], w/mach-fee, dryer-fee, rec rm, read rm, cook fac (7.00am to 11.00pm), bbq, ☎, non smoking property. **RO ⚹ $15, ⚤ $36**, BC MC VI.

Rainbow Lodge International, 133 Summers St, 1km NE of GPO, ☎ 08 9227 1818, fax 08 9227 0719, 12 rms acc up to 8, (Studio, 1 & 2 bedrm), [a/c, fan, fire pl, tel, fax, TV, video, clock radio, refrig, blkts, linen reqd-fee, pillows], bathrm (private & communal), w/mach-fee, iron, iron brd, rec rm, read rm, lounge, cook fac, bbq, secure park, courtesy transfer, bicycle. **RO ⚹ $25 - $30, ⚤ $32 - $36, W ⚹ $150 - $180, ⚤ $190 - $216**, ch con, fam con, AE BC JCB MC VI.

PERTH - APPLECROSS WA 6153

Pop part of Perth, (8km SW Perth), See map on page 907, ref C5.

Hotels/Motels

Raffles Riverfront Hotel, (LH), Kintail Rd, ☎ 08 9364 7400, fax 08 9364 3633, 43 rms [shwr, tlt, a/c, tel, TV, movie, radio, t/c mkg, refrig], ✕, rm serv, cots. **D ⚹ $65, ⚤ $77**, AE BC DC MC VI.

Self Catering Accommodation

★★★☆ **Florina Lodge**, (SA), 6 Kintail Rd, 7km S of Perth GPO, ☎ 08 9364 5322, fax 08 9316 2596, 26 serv apts (1, 2 & 3 bedrm), [shwr, bath, tlt, a/c, tel, TV, radio, t/c mkg, refrig, cook fac, micro, blkts, linen, pillows], ldry, pool, cots-fee. **D ⚹ $71.50, ⚤ $93.50, ⚤⚤ $132**, AE BC DC MC VI.

★★★ **Canning Bridge Auto Lodge**, (SA), 891 Canning Hwy, Cnr Sleat Rd. 7km S of Perth GPO, ☎ 08 9364 2511, fax 08 9364 2477, 24 serv apts [shwr, tlt, a/c, tel, radio, refrig, cook fac, ldry, blkts, linen, pillows], pool, bbq, cots. **D ⚤ $87 - $156**, AE BC DC MC VI.

(Unit Section), 10 units [shwr, tlt, a/c-cool, tel, radio, t/c mkg, refrig, ldry, blkts, linen, pillows], pool, cots. **D ⚤ $65 - $106.**

PERTH - ARMADALE WA 6112

Pop Suburb of Perth, (27km SE Perth), See map on page 907, ref D6.

Hotels/Motels

★★★ **Heritage Country Motel Armadale**, (LMH), Cnr Albany & South West Hwys, 800m NE of PO, ☎ 08 9399 5122, fax 08 9497 1868, 30 units (2 suites) [shwr, bath, tlt, a/c, tel, TV, radio, refrig], ⊠, pool, cots-fee. **D ∮ $59, ∮∮ $77, Suite D $110.**

Self Catering Accommodation

Lake Side Country Resort, (HU), 70 Canns Rd, Bedfordale 6112, 2km NE of Armadale PO, ☎ 08 9399 7455, fax 08 9399 3424, 7 units acc up to 4, (1 bedrm), [shwr, tlt, a/c, TV, radio, refrig, cook fac, ldry, blkts, linen, pillows], bbq, plygr, tennis. **D ∮∮ $130 - $150, W ∮∮ $520 - $550.**

B&B's/Guest Houses

★★★★★ **Mimsbrook Farm Guest House**, (B&B), No children's facilities, 65 Keenan St Wungong, Darling Downs 6122, 1.5km W of South Western Hwy, ☎ 08 9497 1412, fax 08 9497 1582, 2 rms (2 suites) [ensuite, a/c, elec blkts, tel, TV, video, clock radio, t/c mkg, refrig, doonas], ldry, w/mach, lounge (TV), pool-heated, spa, bbq, breakfast ingredients, non smoking rms. **BB ∮∮ $120 - $130, ∮∮ W $600 - $650,** BC MC VI.

★★★★ **(Holiday Unit Section)**, 2 units acc up to 6, [shwr, spa bath, tlt, hairdry, a/c, wood heat, elec blkts, TV, video, clock radio, CD, refrig, cook fac, elec frypan, toaster, blkts, doonas, linen, pillows]. **BB ∮∮ $130 - $140, ∮ $40, ∮∮ W $650 - $700.**

★★★★☆ **Bungendore Hill Bed & Breakfast**, (B&B), 36 Corrigan Rise, Wungong 6112, 3km S of Albany, ☎ 08 9399 9373, 1 rm [ensuite, tlt, heat, c/fan, TV, radio, CD, t/c mkg, refrig], lounge, ✕, pool, bbq, bicycle-fee, non smoking property. **BB ∮ $55, ∮∮ $88.**

★★★★☆ **William Shakespeare Guest House**, (B&B), Classified by National Trust, 25 Canns Rd Strattford Park, Bedfordale 6112, Junction of SW Hwy & Albany Hwy, 2km NE of PO, ☎ 08 9497 4009, fax 08 9497 4544, (2 stry), 3 rms [shwr, tlt, hairdry, a/c, heat, elec blkts, tel, TV, clock radio, t/c mkg, refrig, doonas, pillows], ldry, lounge, ✕, bbq, non smoking rms. **BB ∮ $80 - $85, ∮∮ $105 - $115, ∮ $25, W ∮ $425 - $475, ∮∮ $550 - $625,** BC MC VI.

★★★★ **Armadale Cottage Bed & Breakfast**, (B&B), 3161 Albany Hwy, ☎ 08 9497 1663, fax 08 9399 5311, 6 rms [ensuite (4), tel, TV, t/c mkg, ldry, pillows], shwr, TV rm, ✕, pool. **BB ∮ $55, ∮∮ $82.50.**

PERTH - ASCOT WA 6104

Pop part of Perth, (7km E Perth), See map on page 907, ref D4.

Hotels/Motels

★★★☆ **Ascot Inn**, (LH), 1 Epsom Ave, ☎ 08 9277 8999, fax 08 9277 2037, 40 rms [shwr, a/c, TV, movie, radio, t/c mkg, mini bar], conf fac, ⊠, pool, rm serv, cots. **D ∮ $80 - $85, ∮∮ $90 - $95,** AE BC DC MC VI.

★★★★ **Aarn House B&B at Airport**, (B&B), 32 Tibradden Circle, 2km N of Airport, ☎ 08 9479 3556, fax 08 9479 3997, 2 rms [ensuite, shwr, tlt, a/c, tel, TV, clock radio, t/c mkg, refrig, doonas, pillows], ldry, ✕, non smoking property. **BLB ∮ $70, ∮∮ $85, ∮ $30,** fam con, Alcohol free establishment.

PERTH - BALDIVIS WA 6171

Pop Nominal, (48km S Perth), See map on page 907, ref C8. Vineyards, Wineries.

B&B's/Guest Houses

★★★★ **Peel Manor House**, (GH), 127 Fletcher Road, Between Rockingham & Mandurah, ☎ 08 9524 2838, fax 08 9524 2848, (2 stry), 15 rms [ensuite, spa bath, a/c, elec blkts, TV, video, t/c mkg, refrig], ldry, iron, iron brd, rec rm, lounge, non smoking property. **BB ∮∮ $120 - $195,** pen con, BC EFT MC VI.

PERTH - BAYSWATER WA 6053

Pop part of Perth, (4km N Perth), See map on page 907, ref C4.
Bayswater Motel Hotel, (LMH), 78 Railway Pde, 200m N of PO, ☎ 08 9271 7111, fax 08 9272 5204, 13 units [a/c, tel, TV, t/c mkg, refrig], bathrm. **D ∮ $60.50, ∮∮ $71.50.**

(Hotel Section), 14 rms [t/c mkg], shwr. **D ∮ $27.50, ∮∮ $38.50.**

PERTH - BEDFORDALE WA 6112

Pop part of Perth, (31km SE Perth), See map on page 907, ref E6.
★★★★☆ **Heritage View**, (B&B), Alcohol free establishment. 49 Canns Rd, 3km NE of Armadale PO, ☎ 08 9497 1635, fax 08 9497 1635, (2 stry), 4 rms [ensuite, TV, radio, refrig, doonas, pillows], lounge, ✕, t/c mkg shared, bbq, meals avail (by arrangement), non smoking property. **BB ∮∮ $75 - $85, W $525 - $595.**

PERTH - BELMONT WA 6104

Pop part of Perth, (8km E Perth), See map on page 907, ref D4.
Hotels/Motels

★★★★ **Inter City Motel**, (M), 249 Great Eastern Hwy, ☎ 08 9478 0888, fax 08 9478 0800, 44 units (2 suites) [shwr, tlt, a/c, tel, TV, t/c mkg, refrig, ldry (services)], ldry, w/mach-fee, dryer-fee, iron, business centre, conf fac, ⊠, pool, spa, bbq, plygr, gym, tennis, cots-fee, non smoking units. **RO ∮∮ $90.90, Suite D ∮∮ $151.50,** AE BC DC EFT MC VI, ⚿.

★★★☆ **Bel Eyre Motel**, (M), 285 Great Eastern Hwy, 8km E of GPO, ☎ 08 9277 2733, fax 08 9479 1113, 105 units [shwr, tlt, tel, TV, movie-fee, t/c mkg, refrig, ldry], ✕, pool, spa, bbq, cots. **D ∮∮ $89 - $155,** AE BC DC EFT MC MP VI, ⚿.

Self Catering Accommodation

★★★ **All Travellers Motel**, (SA), 169 Great Eastern Hwy, 7km E of GPO, ☎ 08 9479 4060, fax 08 9479 4509, 56 serv apts (1 & 2 bedrm), [shwr, tlt, tel, TV, refrig, cook fac, ldry, blkts, linen, pillows], pool, bbq, 24hr reception, security gates, tennis. **D ∮ $66, ∮∮ $77, ∮∮∮ $110, W ∮ $413, ∮∮ $500.50, ∮∮∮∮ $731.50.**

PERTH - BENTLEY WA 6102

Pop part of Perth, (10km SE Perth), See map on page 907, ref D5.
★★★ **Bentley Motor Inn**, (M), 1235 Albany Hwy, 9km SE of GPO, ☎ 08 9451 6344, fax 08 9458 6679, 46 units [shwr, tlt, a/c, tel, TV, radio, t/c mkg, refrig, cook fac (5), toaster, ldry], ⊠, pool, rm serv, plygr, cots-fee. **D ∮ $60.50 - $71.50, ∮∮ $66 - $77, ∮ $11 - $16.50,** AE BC DC MC VI, ⚿.

PERTH - CANNINGTON WA 6107

Pop part of Perth, (11km SE Perth), See map on page 907, ref D5.
★★★☆ **Astralodge Motel**, (M), 1514 Albany Hwy, 13km SE of GPO, ☎ 08 9351 9988, fax 08 9458 8427, 31 units [shwr, tlt, a/c, tel, TV, radio, t/c mkg, refrig], rec rm, ⊠, pool, bbq, cots. **D ∮∮ $55, ∮ $5,** AE BC DC MC VI.

PERTH - CHURCHLANDS WA 6018

Pop part of Perth, (5km NW perth) See map on page 907, ref B4.
★★★☆ **Kenwood Court**, (HU), 19 Flynn St, 5km NW of GPO, ☎ 08 9387 1711, fax 08 9387 8836, 14 units acc up to 6, (2 & 3 bedrm), [ensuite, shwr, tlt, a/c, heat (or gas), tel, TV, video, refrig, cook fac, micro, d/wash, toaster, ldry, blkts, doonas, linen, pillows], w/mach, dryer, iron, pool. **W $418 - $671.**

PERTH - COMO WA 6152

Pop part of Perth, (8km S Perth), See map on page 907, ref C5.

★★★★☆ **Broadwater Pagoda Hotel**, (LH), 112 Melville Parade, 4km S of GPO, ☎ 08 9367 0300, fax 08 9367 0388, (Multi-stry), 64 rms (Studio), [shwr, spa bath, tlt, hairdry, a/c, tel, TV, movie, clock radio, t/c mkg, refrig, mini bar, micro, ldry, pillows], iron, iron brd, conf fac, ⊠, pool-heated, sauna, 24hr reception, rm serv, secure park, bicycle, tennis, non smoking suites. **D $143 - $171,** AE BC DC MC VI.

★★★★★ **(Apartments Section)**, (Multi-stry), 37 serv apts acc up to 4, [ensuite, shwr, spa bath, tlt, hairdry, a/c, tel, TV, clock radio, refrig, cook fac, micro, elec frypan, d/wash, toaster, ldry, blkts, linen, pillows], lift, w/mach, dryer, iron, iron brd, secure park, non smoking units. **D $176 - $264.**

★★★☆ **Windsor Lodge Motel**, (M), 3 Preston St, 5km S of GPO, ☎ 08 9367 9177, fax 08 9474 1006, 44 units [shwr, tlt, tel, TV, radio, t/c mkg, refrig, cook fac, ldry], ⊠, pool, rm serv, secure park, cots. **RO ∮ $83 - $86, ∮∮ $88 - $91, ∮ $14,** AE BC DC MC VI.

★★★ **Swanview Motel**, (M), 1 Preston St, 5km S of GPO, ☎ 08 9367 5755, fax 08 9367 8025, 48 units [shwr, bath (some), tlt, tel, TV, t/c mkg, refrig, micro (some), ldry], pool, rm serv (b'fast), cots. **D ∮∮ $70, ∮∮∮∮ $90, ∮ $10,** AE BC DC.

Self Catering Accommodation

★★★★☆ **Broadwater Resort Apartments**, (SA), 137 Melville Pde, 5km S of GPO, ☎ 08 9474 4222, fax 08 9474 4216, (Multi-stry), 58 serv apts acc up to 6, [hairdry, a/c, tel, TV, video, refrig, cook fac, micro, d/wash, blkts, linen, pillows], w/mach, dryer, ⊠, pool-heated, spa, tennis, cots-fee. **D ∮∮ $160 - $269, ∮ $16,** AE BC DC MC VI.

PERTH - COOGEE WA 6166

Pop part of Perth, (27km SW Perth), See map on page 907, ref C6.

★★★ **Coogee Beach Short Term Accommodation**, (Apt), 16 Toulon Gve, 8km S of Fremantle, ☎ 08 9434 1691, fax 08 9434 4596, (2 stry), 1 apt acc up to 4, (2 bedrm), [shwr, tlt, hairdry, a/c, fan, c/fan, fax, TV, video, clock radio, refrig, cook fac, micro, blkts, doonas, linen, pillows], ldry, iron, iron brd, pool, bbq, c/park. **D** ♀♀ **$80**, ◊ **$20**, **W** ♀♀ **$400 - $500**, Min book.

PERTH - COTTESLOE WA 6011

Pop part of Perth, (11km SW Perth), See map on page 907, ref B5.

Hotels/Motels

Cottesloe Beach Hotel, (LH), 104 Marine Pde, 1km NW of PO, ☎ 08 9383 1100, fax 08 9385 2482, 13 rms [shwr, tlt, a/c, tel, t/c mkg, refrig], conv fac, cafe, bar. **RO** ♀ **$66**, ♀♀ **$88 - $99**, AE DC MC VI.

Self Catering Accommodation

★★★ **Cottesloe Beach Chalets**, (HU), 6 John St, 1 km NW of PO, ☎ 08 9383 5000, fax 08 9385 4196, 25 units acc up to 5, (2 bedrm), [shwr, tlt, a/c, fan, heat, tel, TV, refrig, cook fac, blkts, linen, pillows], pool. **D $162 - $180.**

★★★ **Cottesloe Waters Holiday Units**, (HU), 8 MacArthur St, 1km SW of PO, ☎ 08 9284 2555, fax 08 9284 2566, 9 units acc up to 6, (1 & 2 bedrm), [shwr, tlt, TV, clock radio, refrig, cook fac, ldry, blkts, linen, pillows]. **D $85 - $120.**

PERTH - FREMANTLE WA 6160

Pop 20,825. (18km SW Perth), See map on page 907, ref B6. Busy port and commercial centre, situated on the mouth of the Swan River.

Hotels/Motels

AAA TOURISM *Special Rates* ★★★★☆ **Esplanade Hotel Fremantle**, (LH), Cnr Marine Tce & Essex St, 300m S of PO, ☎ 08 9432 4000, fax 08 9430 4539, (2 stry), 259 rms (7 suites) [shwr, bath (145), spa bath (some), tlt, hairdry, tel, TV, movie-fee, radio, t/c mkg, refrig, mini bar, ldry (services)], business centre (fax), ✉ (2), bar, pool (2), sauna, spa (3), secure park, bicycle-fee, gym. **RO** ♀ **$157.50 - $174**, AE BC DC JCB MC VI, ♿.

★★★☆ **Tradewinds Hotel Fremantle**, (LH), 59 Canning Hwy, 2km NE of PO, ☎ 08 9339 8188, fax 08 9339 2266, 83 rms [shwr, tlt, a/c, tel, TV, radio, refrig, cook fac, micro], bathrm, iron, conv fac, ✉, bar, pool, spa, secure park, cots. **D** ♀♀ **$148**, AE BC DC MC VI, ♿.

Fremantle Hotel, (LH), Cnr High & Cliff Sts, 400m SW of PO, ☎ 08 9430 4300, fax 08 9335 2636, 35 rms [tel, TV, radio, refrig], bathrm, ✉, t/c mkg shared. **RO** ♀ **$55 - $80**, ♀♀ **$80 - $90**, BC MC VI.

Rosie O'Grady's, (LH), No children's facilities, 23 William St, 300m E of PO, ☎ 08 9335 1645, fax 08 9336 4650, (Multi-stry), 17 rms [ensuite (8), a/c (8), c/fan (9), TV (8), refrig], shwr, tlt, iron, iron brd, ✉, bar, t/c mkg shared, ☎. **BB** ♀ **$65 - $115**, ♀♀ **$60 - $125**, ◊ **$10**, AE BC EFT MC VI.

Self Catering Accommodation

★★★★☆ **Fremantle Colonial Accommodation**, (Cotg), Classified by National Trust, 215 High St, 200m E of Town Hall, ☎ 08 9430 6568, fax 08 9430 6405, 3 cotgs acc up to 5, (2 bedrm), [shwr, bath, tlt, TV, clock radio, refrig, cook fac, micro, toaster, ldry, blkts, doonas, linen, pillows], cots, non smoking property. **D** ♀♀ **$148.50 - $192.50**, ◊ **$22**, **W $770 - $891**, ch con, BC MC VI, ♿.

★★★★☆ **Harbour Village Quest Apartments**, (SA), Mews Rd, Challenger Habour, 1km S of PO, ☎ 08 9430 3888, fax 08 9430 3800, (2 stry gr fl), 56 serv apts acc up to 6, [shwr, bath, tlt, hairdry, a/c, tel, TV, movie, clock radio, t/c mkg, refrig, cook fac, micro, d/wash, ldry, blkts, linen, pillows], w/mach, dryer, iron, business centre, spa, bbq, bicycle-fee, cots. **D $160 - $260**, AE BC DC EFT MC VI.

Barbara's Cottage Fremantle, (Cotg), 26 Holdsworth St, 500m E of PO, ☎ 08 9430 9733, fax 08 9430 5535, 1 cotg acc up to 3, [shwr, tlt, a/c-cool, heat, tel, TV, radio, refrig, micro, elec frypan, toaster, blkts, linen, pillows], breakfast ingredients (hamper). **D $80 - $110**, **W $560 - $700**, AE BC MC VI.

Fremantle Executive Apartments, (SA), 1 High St, 300m W of PO, ☎ 08 9430 5530, fax 08 9430 5367, 15 serv apts acc up to 6, (2 & 3 bedrm), [shwr, bath, tlt, a/c-cool, fan, heat, tel, TV, video, clock radio, t/c mkg, refrig, cook fac, micro, d/wash, ldry, blkts, linen, pillows], w/mach, dryer, cots. **D $130 - $200**, Min book applies, AE BC MC VI.

B&B's/Guest Houses

★★★★☆ **Westerley**, (B&B), 74 Solomon St, 1.2km SE of PO, ☎ 08 9430 4458, fax 08 9430 4459, 2 rms (Studio), [ensuite, a/c (1), c/fan, elec blkts, tel, TV, clock radio, t/c mkg, refrig, cook fac (1), doonas], TV rm, bbq, bicycle, cots, non smoking property. **BB** ♀ **$95**, ♀♀ **$105 - $115**, ◊ **$15**, ch con, BC MC VI.

★★★★ **(88 Hampton Rd Section)**, (2 stry), 1 apt acc up to 6, (2 bedrm), [shwr, tlt, a/c, c/fan, tel, TV, clock radio, cook fac, micro, blkts, doonas, linen, pillows], w/mach, iron, iron brd, cots. **D** ♀♀♀♀ **$140**, Min book.

★★★★ **Danum House**, (B&B), No children's facilities, 6 Fothergill St, 700m E of PO, ☎ 08 9336 3735, fax 08 9335 3414, 2 rms [shwr (2), tlt (2), heat, c/fan, heat, tel, TV, pillows], t/c mkg shared, bbq, non smoking property. **BB** ♀ **$95 - $105**, ♀♀ **$100 - $110**, BC MC VI.

★★★★ **Fothergills Of Fremantle**, (B&B), 20-22 Ord St, 1km E of PO, ☎ 08 9335 6784, fax 08 9430 7789, (2 stry), 6 rms [ensuite (2), hairdry, a/c, TV, clock radio, t/c mkg, refrig, micro, ldry, pillows], TV rm. **BB** ♀♀ **$126 - $137**, ◊ **$20**, AE BC DC MC VI.

★★★☆ **Carnac Cottage**, (B&B), 127 Solomon Street, Beaconsfield, 3km SE of Fremantle Town Hall, ☎ 08 9336 3504, fax 08 9430 6390, (2 stry), 3 rms [a/c, c/fan, elec blkts, fax, clock radio, t/c mkg], shwr, tlt, ldry, iron, iron brd, rec rm, lounge (TV, video, cd, stereo), lounge firepl, ✕, refrig, bbq, cots. **BB** ♀ **$69 - $75**, ♀♀ **$98.50 - $105**, ◊ **$25**, BC MC VI.

★★☆ **The Flying Angel Club**, (PH), 76 Queen Victoria St, 1km N of PO, ☎ 08 9335 5000, fax 08 9335 5321, (2 stry), 20 rms [shwr, tlt, a/c, tel, TV, t/c mkg, refrig, ldry, pillows], rec rm, TV rm, conv fac, ✕, ☎. **D** ♀ **$60**, ♀♀ **$95**, AE BC DC EFT MC VI.

Fremantle Colonial Accommodation B&B, (B&B), Classified by National Trust, 215 High St, 300 metre E of PO, ☎ 08 9430 6568, fax 08 9430 6405, (Multi-stry), 6 rms [ensuite (2), a/c, fan, tel, TV, video (shared), clock radio, t/c mkg, refrig, doonas, pillows], shwr, tlt, bathrm, ldry, w/mach, iron, iron brd, TV rm, cook fac, bbq, cots (avail), non smoking property. **BLB** ♀♀ **$88 - $110**, ◊ **$22**, BC MC VI.

Holdsworth House, (B&B), Classified by National Trust, No children's facilities, 1 Bateman St, 800m E of PO, ☎ 08 9335 7729, fax 08 9335 7729, 2 rms [clock radio, t/c mkg, refrig, doonas, pillows], shwr, tlt, non smoking property. **BB** ♀♀ **$110**.

Kilkelly's, (B&B), No children's facilities, 82 Marine Tce, 1km S of Railway Station, ☎ 08 9336 1744, fax 08 9336 1571, 3 rms [fan, TV, refrig, pillows], shwr, tlt, ldry, TV rm, ✕, t/c mkg shared, bbq, non smoking property. **BB** ♀ **$93.50 - $105**, ♀♀ **$115.50 - $120**, weekly con, AE BC DC MC VI.

Other Accommodation

Cheviot Marina, 4 Beach St, Opposite Fremantle Passenger Terminal, ☎ 08 9433 2055, fax 08 9433 2066, (Multi-stry), 37 rms, (1, 2 & 4 bedrm), [fan, heat, clock radio, micro, toaster, blkts, doonas, linen, pillows], shwr (14), tlt (18), bathrm (2), w/mach-fee, dryer-fee, iron, iron brd, rec rm, lounge (TV, video, stereo), lounge firepl, ✕, cook fac, t/c mkg shared, refrig, bbq, c/park (25), courtesy transfer, ☎, non smoking property. **D** ♀ **$12 - $15**, **W** ♀ **$75 - $85**, BC EFT MC VI.

PERTH - GOOSEBERRY HILL WA 6076

Pop part of Perth, (26km E Perth), See map on page 907, ref D4.

B&B's/Guest Houses

★★★★☆ **Rosebridge House**, (B&B), 86 Williams St, 1km N of Kalamunda PO, ☎ 08 9293 1741, fax 08 9257 2778, 4 rms [ensuite, bath (1), spa bath (2), a/c, heat, tel, TV, clock radio, t/c mkg, refrig, doonas, pillows], ldry, ✕, pool, bbq, non smoking rms. **BB** ♀ **$100 - $150**, ♀♀ **$125 - $175**, ◊ **$30**.

Other Accommodation

★★★★☆ **Possum Creek Lodge**, (Lodge), 6 Lenori Rd, 2km N of Kalamunda PO, ☎ 08 9257 1927, fax 08 9257 1927, 4 rms (2 suites) acc up to 8, [ensuite, hairdry, a/c, TV, video, radio, refrig, cook fac, ldry (guest), blkts, linen, pillows], iron, iron brd, bbq, tennis, non smoking rms. **D** ♀♀ **$100 - $140**.

PERTH - GUILDFORD WA 6055

Pop part of Perth, (16km NE Perth), See map on page 907, ref D4. Swan Valley Vineyards - cellar tours.

★★★ **Rose & Crown Hotel**, (LMH), 105 Swan St, 400m N of PO, ☎ 08 9279 8444, fax 08 9377 1628, 28 units (3 suites) [shwr, tlt, a/c, tel, t/c mkg, refrig], conv fac, ✉, pool, cots. **D** ♀ **$55**, ♀♀ **$66**, AE BC DC VI.

PERTH – HENLEY BROOK WA 6055

Pop part of Perth, (26km NE Perth), See map on page 907, ref D3.

Self Catering Accommodation

★★★★ **Swan Valley Holiday Cottages**, (Cotg), 10070 West Swan Rd, 18km NE of PO, ☎ 08 9296 1007, fax 08 9296 3141, 4 cotgs acc up to 6, (2 bedrm), [shwr, bath, tlt, TV, clock radio, refrig, cook fac, micro, toaster, blkts, doonas, linen, pillows], ldry, w/mach-fee, dryer-fee, iron, ✕, pool, freezer, bbq, plygr, tennis, cots. D ♦♦ $88 - $121, ♦ $22, W ♦♦ $550, ♦ $104.50, ch con, Min book all holiday times, AE BTC DC JCB MC VI.

B&B's/Guest Houses

★★★★ **Hansons Swan Valley**, (GH), No children's facilities, 60 Forest Rd, 17km NE of GPO, ☎ 08 9296 3366, fax 08 9296 3332, (Multi-stry gr fl), 10 rms [ensuite, spa bath (6), a/c, TV, video, clock radio, t/c mkg, refrig, doonas, pillows], w/mach-fee, iron-fee, iron brd, ✕, pool, non smoking property. BB ♦♦ $175 - $250, BC EFT MC VI.

PERTH – GWELUP WA 6018

Pop part of Perth, (13km N Perth).

PERTH – HILLARYS WA 6025

Pop part of Perth, (21km NW Perth), See map on page 907, ref B3.

Self Catering Accommodation

★★★★☆ **Hillarys Harbour Resort**, (SA), 68 Southside Drive, 20km NW of GPO, ☎ 08 9262 7888, fax 08 9262 7800, (Multi-stry), 50 serv apts acc up to 6, [ensuite, shwr, bath, tlt, hairdry, a/c, tel, TV, movie, clock radio, refrig, cook fac, micro, d/wash, toaster, blkts, doonas, linen, pillows], w/mach, dryer, iron, iron brd, business centre, conv fac, pool, sauna, spa, bbq, secure park, cots. D ♦♦ $149 - $165, ♦♦♦♦ $173 - $192, ♦ $16, Min book all holiday times, Min book long w/ends, AE BC DC EFT MC VI, ♿.

B&B's/Guest Houses

★★★ **Hillary's Cottage**, (B&B), 14 Crossland Pl, 800m N of Hillarys Boat Harbour, ☎ 08 9401 8544, fax 08 9401 8544, 1 rm [shwr, tlt, heat, fax, TV, clock radio, t/c mkg, refrig], ldry, w/mach, dryer, iron, ✕, bbq, c/park. BLB ♦ $77 - $88, ♦♦ $93.50 - $104.50.

Beachside Bed and Breakfast, (B&B), 209 Flinders Ave, ☎ 08 9402 8638, 2 rms [fan, TV, CD], shwr, tlt, ldry, w/mach-fee, iron, iron brd, t/c mkg shared, refrig, bbq, non smoking property, Pets allowed. BB ♦ $65, ♦♦ $85, ♦ $350, ♦♦ $450, (not yet classified).

Whitfords By The Sea B & B and Cottages, (B&B), 25 Nautilus Way, Kallaroo 6025, 22km NNW of GPO, ☎ 08 9401 8149, fax 08 9307 2347, 3 rms [a/c, heat, tel, TV, clock radio, t/c mkg, pillows], bathrm, lounge. BB ♦ $50, ♦♦ $95.

(Amelia's Cottage Section), 2 Barque Place, Kallaroo 6025, 1 house acc up to 8, (3 bedrm), [shwr, bath, tlt, hairdry, heat, fan, c/fan, fire pl, tel, TV, clock radio, t/c mkg, refrig, cook fac, micro, elec frypan, toaster, ldry, blkts, doonas, linen, pillows], w/mach, iron, iron brd, bbq, trailer park, cots, non smoking property. D ♦ $100, W $700.

(Springfield Cottage Section), 29 Oleander Way, Kallaroo 6025, 1 house acc up to 5, (2 bedrm), [shwr, bath, tlt, hairdry, heat, fan, fire pl, tel, TV, clock radio, t/c mkg, refrig, cook fac, micro, elec frypan, ldry, blkts, doonas, linen, pillows], w/mach, iron, iron brd, bbq, trailer park, cots, non smoking property. D ♦ $95, W $630.

PERTH – INGLEWOOD WA 6052

Pop part of Perth, (5km NE Perth), See map on page 907, ref C4.

★★★★ **Crawford House Bed & Breakfast at Perth**, (B&B), No children's facilities, 303 Crawford Rd, 5km N of GPO, ☎ 08 9272 5305, fax 08 9272 5967, 1 rm (1 bedrm), [shwr, bath, tlt, a/c-cool, c/fan, elec blkts, TV, clock radio, t/c mkg, doonas, pillows], lounge, ✕, non smoking property. BB ♦ $60 - $65, ♦♦ $80 - $95, W ♦ $420, ♦♦ $560 - $630, BC MC VI.

PERTH – JANDAKOT WA 6164

Pop part of Perth, (21km S Perth), See map on page 907, ref C6.

Self Catering Accommodation

★★★ **Airport Chalet Centre**, (Chalet), 1 Wessex St, 17km S of GPO, ☎ 08 9414 1040, fax 08 9414 1171, 15 chalets acc up to 4, [shwr, tlt, a/c, heat, TV, refrig, cook fac, ldry, blkts, linen, pillows], bathrm, ✕, bbq, ☏, tennis, cots (avail). D ♦ $60, ♦♦ $70, ch con, BC VI.

B&B's/Guest Houses

★★★★ **N & J Webster Enterprises**, (B&B), 906 Gutteridge Road, 500m off Armadale Rd, ☎ 08 9417 8606, fax 08 9417 8606, 3 rms (2 suites) [ensuite, shwr, spa bath, tlt, hairdry, a/c-cool, heat, wood heat, tel, TV, video, clock radio, CD, t/c mkg], ldry, w/mach, dryer, iron, rec rm, lounge, lounge firepl, ✕, pool indoor heated, spa, bbq, secure park, plygr, picnic facilities, bicycle. BB ♦ $75, ♦♦ $95, ♦ $35.

PERTH - JOONDALUP WA 6027

Pop part of Perth, (26km NW Perth), See map on page 907, ref B3.

Hotels/Motels

★★★★★ **Joondalup Resort**, (LH), Country Club Boulevard, Connolly, ☎ 08 9400 8888, fax 08 9400 8889, (Multi-stry gr fl), 69 rms [shwr, bath (35), tlt, hairdry, a/c, tel, TV, video (4), clock radio, t/c mkg, refrig, mini bar, ldry (service)], lift, iron, conv fac, ⊠, ✕, coffee shop, pool, spa, 24hr reception, rm serv, secure park, courtesy transfer, ✆, golf, tennis, cots, non smoking rms. **RO** ♦ **$178 - $227, Suite D** ♦♦ **$378**, AE BC DC EFT JCB MC VI.

Self Catering Accommodation

★★★★ **Lakeside Cottages**, (Cotg), 17 Simcoe Crt, 1km N of PO and train station, ☎ 08 9300 4076, fax 08 9300 4076, 1 cotg acc up to 8, [shwr, bath, tlt, evap cool, heat, TV, video, clock radio, CD, refrig, cook fac, micro, blkts, linen, pillows], w/mach, iron, iron brd, non smoking property. **D** ♦♦♦♦ **$80 - $130, W** ♦♦♦♦ **$560 - $880**, Min book.
Joondalup Resort, (SA), Country Club Boulevard, Connolly 6027, Connolly, ☎ 08 9400 8888, 5 serv apts acc up to 6, (3 & 4 bedrm), [shwr, bath, tlt, a/c-cool, tel, TV, clock radio, t/c mkg, refrig, cook fac, micro, elec frypan, d/wash, toaster, ldry, blkts, linen, pillows], w/mach, dryer, iron, TV rm, conv fac, ✕, pool, spa, bbq, 24hr reception, secure park, courtesy transfer, ✆, golf, tennis, cots, non smoking units. **D $250 - $400, W $1,300 - $1,560**, Min book applies, AE BC DC EFT MC VI.

PERTH - KALLAROO WA 6025

Pop part of Perth, (24km NW Perth), See map on page 907, ref B3.

B&B's/Guest Houses

★★★☆ **Clareville House**, (B&B), 5 Clareville Cres, 3km N of Whitfords Shopping Centre, ☎ 08 9401 9437, fax 08 9401 9407, (2 stry), 3 rms [hairdry, evap cool, heat, c/fan, elec blkts, TV (shared), clock radio, t/c mkg], bathrm (guest), iron, iron brd, rec rm, lounge, ✕, pool, bbq, non smoking property. **BB** ♦ **$71.50**, ♦♦ **$93.50**, ch con, BC MC VI.

PERTH - KELMSCOTT WA 6111

Pop part of Perth, (24km SE Perth), See map on page 907, ref E6.

★★★★ **The Riverbend Bed & Breakfast**, (B&B), Lot 10 Cockram Rd, 3km W of PO, ☎ 08 9390 9609, fax 08 9390 1948, 1 rm (1 suite) [ensuite, a/c-cool, wood heat, TV, clock radio, t/c mkg, refrig, micro, doonas, pillows], ldry, iron, iron brd, pool, bbq, non smoking rms. **BLB** ♦ **$50**, ◊ **$20**.

PERTH - KEWDALE WA 6105

Pop part of Perth, (10km SE Perth), See map on page 907, ref D5.

Kewdale Motel Hotel, (LMH), 137 Kewdale Rd, 7km SE of PO, ☎ 08 9353 2224, fax 08 9353 1249, 13 units [shwr, tlt, a/c, fan, TV, movie, t/c mkg, refrig], ⊠, cots. **D** ♦ **$50**, ♦♦ **$55**, ch con, BC JCB MC VI.

PERTH - LYNWOOD WA 6155

Pop part of Perth, (13km SE Perth), See map on page 907, ref D5.

★★★ **Lynwood Arms Hotel**, (LH), 558 Metcalfe Rd, 14km S of GPO, ☎ 08 9451 8577, fax 08 9351 8433, 8 rms [shwr, tlt, a/c, tel, TV, radio, t/c mkg, refrig], conv fac, ⊠, cots-fee. **RO** ♦ **$60.50**, ♦♦ **$71.50**, ch con, AE BC DC MC VI.

PERTH - MAIDA VALE WA 6057

Pop part of Perth, (15km E Perth), See map on page 907, ref D4.

Self Catering Accommodation

★★★☆ **Vale House**, (House), 5 Casuarina Rd, 20km E of GPO, ☎ 08 9454 6462, fax 08 9454 6233, 1 house acc up to 6, (3 bedrm), [shwr, bath, tlt, a/c-cool, TV, video, radio, refrig, cook fac, micro, blkts, doonas, linen, pillows], w/mach, dryer, iron, iron brd, bbq, meals avail (by arrangement), non smoking rms. **D** ♦ **$100**, ◊ **$11, W** ♦♦ **$385**.

B&B's/Guest Houses

★★★☆ **Ridge View Guest House**, (GH), 317 Kalamunda Rd, 20km E of GPO, ☎ 08 9454 6129, fax 08 9454 6129, 1 rm [shwr, tlt, hairdry, fan, heat, elec blkts, tel, TV, video, clock radio, t/c mkg, refrig, pillows], pool, bbq, non smoking property. **BB** ♦ **$65**, ♦♦ **$85**, ◊ **$30**, ch con.

PERTH - MARTIN WA 6110

Pop part of Perth, (20km SE Perth), See map on page 907, ref E5.

★★★ **Sky Ship Lodge**, (B&B), 41 Milleara Rd, 20km SE of GPO, ☎ 08 9398 6174, fax 08 9398 6174, (2 stry), 2 rms (1 suite) [ensuite (1), shwr, tlt, evap cool, fan, c/fan, heat, elec blkts, TV, video, t/c mkg, refrig, cook fac], ldry, w/mach, iron, iron brd, rec rm, lounge, bbq, secure park, cots-fee, non smoking property. **BB** ♦ **$25**, ♦♦ **$35**, **Suite BB** ♦ **$60**, ♦♦ **$70**, ♦♦♦♦ **$90**, pen con.

PERTH - MAYLANDS WA 6051

Pop part of Perth, (5km NE Perth), See map on page 907, ref C4.

★★☆ **Maylands Motel**, (M), 14 Rowlands St, 5km NE of CBD, ☎ 08 9370 5505, fax 08 9370 5803, 15 units [shwr, tlt, a/c, TV, radio, t/c mkg, refrig], cots. **RO** ♦ **$49.50**, ♦♦ **$55**, ◊ **$11**, BC VI.

PERTH - MIDLAND WA 6056

Pop part of Perth, (19km E Perth), See map on page 907, ref D4.

Budget Motel Midland, (M), 51 Victoria St, 17km E of GPO, ☎ 08 9250 2688, fax 08 9250 2602, 32 units [shwr, bath, tlt, a/c, fan, heat, tel, TV, t/c mkg, refrig], pool, bbq, cots. **D** ♦♦ **$55**, BC DC MC VI.

PERTH - MINDARIE WA 6030

Pop Nominal, (38km N Perth), See map on page 907, ref A2.

Hotels/Motels

★★★☆ **Mindarie Marina Hotel**, (LH), Ocean Falls Blvd, ☎ 08 9305 1057, fax 08 9305 1678, (Multi-stry), 16 rms (5 suites) [shwr, tlt, a/c, heat, tel, TV, video, clock radio, t/c mkg, refrig, toaster], lift, bathrm, conv fac, ✕, spa, bbq, tennis, cots. **D $130 - $164, Suite D** ♦♦ **$98 - $130**, ◊ **$27.50**, AE BC DC MC VI.
   (Villa Section), 2 villas (2 bedrm), [shwr, tlt, hairdry, tel, TV, clock radio, refrig, cook fac, micro, d/wash, blkts, doonas, linen, pillows]. **D** ♦♦ **$164 - $197**.

B&B's/Guest Houses

★★★★ **Keys Kottage**, (B&B), 3 Caldera Cl, ☎ 08 9305 7576, 1 rm [ensuite, shwr, tlt, hairdry, fan, tel, TV, t/c mkg, refrig, doonas, pillows], TV rm, read rm, ✕, pool, bbq, rm serv, non smoking property. **RO** ♦ **$85**, ♦♦ **$85**.
Sunset Cottage, (B&B), 54 Savona Grove, 2km S of Mindarie Keys, ☎ 08 9407 8939, fax 08 9407 8939, 2 rms [evap cool, TV, clock radio, t/c mkg, refrig], shwr, tlt, ldry, w/mach, bbq, non smoking property. **BB** ♦ **$65 - $79**, ♦♦ **$85 - $95**, (not yet classified).

PERTH - MOSMAN PARK WA 6102

Pop part of Perth, (13km SW Perth), See map on page 907, ref B5.

★★★☆ **Rosemoore Bed & Breakfast**, (B&B), 2 Winifred St, 12km SW of GPO, ☎ 08 9384 8214, fax 08 9385 6373, 2 rms [ensuite, hairdry, a/c-cool, heat, c/fan, TV, clock radio, t/c mkg, doonas, pillows], w/mach, iron, iron brd, refrig, ✆, non smoking rms. **BB** ♦ **$80**, ♦♦ **$90**, ch con, BC MC VI.

PERTH - MOUNT PLEASANT WA 6153

Pop part of Perth, (8km S Perth), See map on page 907, ref C5.

Self Catering Accommodation

Annie's House, (HU), 25 Raymond St, 8km S of GPO, ☎ 08 9325 3520, fax 08 9364 2995, 7 units acc up to 10, (1, 2 & 3 bedrm), [shwr, bath, tlt, hairdry, a/c, fan, c/fan, tel, TV, video, refrig, cook fac, elec frypan, toaster, ldry, blkts, doonas, linen, pillows], w/mach, dryer, iron, bbq, meals avail (by arrangement), bicycle, cots, non smoking units. **D** ♦ **$85 - $105**, ♦♦ **$105 - $140**, ♦♦♦♦ **$150 - $170**.

B&B's/Guest Houses

★★★★★ **Mt Pleasant Bed & Breakfast**, (B&B), 11 Mt View Terrace, 1km S of Canning Bridge, ☎ 08 9316 9818, fax 08 9316 9718, 3 rms (1 suite) [ensuite, shwr, bath (1), tlt, hairdry, a/c, heat, fan, heat, elec blkts, TV, clock radio, t/c mkg, refrig, doonas, pillows], iron, iron brd, ✕, pool, ✆, non smoking rms. **BB** ♦♦ **$100 - $150**, ♦♦♦♦ **$180**, Min book all holiday times, BC DC MC VI.

PERTH - MULLALOO WA 6027

Pop part of Perth, (26km N Perth), See map on page 907, ref B3.

B&B's/Guest Houses

Ocean Sunset Bed & Breakfast, (B&B), 119 Mullaloo Drive, 500m W of Marmion Ave, ☎ 08 9307 7334, 2 rms [ensuite (1), spa bath (1), evap cool, heat, tel, TV, t/c mkg, micro, toaster], bathrm (1), w/mach-fee, iron, iron brd, lounge (cable TV), pool, refrig, bbq, non smoking property. **BB** ♦ **$35 - $55**, ♦♦ **$70 - $85**, ch con, fam con.

PERTH - MUNDARING WA 6073

Pop part of Perth, (34km E Perth), See map on page 907, ref E4.

Hotels/Motels

★★★☆ **The Mahogany Inn**, (M), Cnr Great Eastern Hwy & Homestead Rd, Mahogany Creek 6072, 3.5km W of PO, ☎ 08 9295 1118, fax 08 9295 2900, 12 units (12 suites) [ensuite, a/c, TV, t/c mkg, refrig], lounge, ✕, pool, ✆, cots, non smoking rms. **BLB** ♦ **$82**, ♦♦ **$120**, **Suite BLB** ♦♦♦♦ **$210**, BC DC MC VI.

PERTH - MUNDARING WA continued...

Mundaring Weir Hotel, (LH), Mundaring Weir Rd, 32km E of GPO, ☎ 08 9295 1106, fax 08 9295 3377, 13 rms [shwr, tlt, fire pl, TV, t/c mkg, refrig], ⊠, pool. **D ⋔ $35 - $70**.

Self Catering Accommodation
★★☆ **Travellers Rest Motel**, (HU), 8855 Great Eastern Hwy, 33km E of GPO, ☎ 08 9295 2950, fax 08 9295 2950, 17 units [shwr, tlt, a/c (2), TV, t/c mkg, refrig, cook fac, ldry], pool, cots. **DBB ⋔ $308, W ⓘ $44, RO ⋔ $55, ⋔ $71.50, ⓘ $220**, ch con, Min book applies, AE BC MC VI, ⓑ.

B&B's/Guest Houses
★★★★★ **Lion Mill Bed & Breakfast**, (GH), Cnr Johnston & Hummerston Street, Mount Helena 6082, 6KM E of PO, ☎ 08 9572 2252, fax 08 9386 5272, 2 rms [ensuite, hairdry, a/c-cool, heat, c/fan, elec blkts, tel, fax, TV, video, CD], w/mach, dryer, iron, iron brd, lounge, lounge firepl, pool, spa, t/c mkg shared, refrig, bbq, courtesy transfer, non smoking property. **BB ⋔ $120 - $150**, VI.
★★★★ **Faversham Cottages & Gardens**, (B&B), Classified by National Trust, 2075 Jacoby St, 32km E of GPO, ☎ 08 9295 1312, fax 08 9295 3127, 4 rms [shwr, tlt, a/c-cool, elec blkts, tel, clock radio, t/c mkg, refrig, toaster], ldry, pool, bbq. **BB ⋔ $160 - $200**, Accommodation provided in 4 seperate stone cottages. BC MC VI.

PERTH - NEDLANDS WA 6009
Pop part of Perth, (6km SW Perth), See map on page 907, ref C5.

Hotels/Motels
★★★ **Kingswood College**, (M), Cnr Hampden Rd & Stirling Hwy, 5km SW of GPO, ☎ 08 9423 9423, fax 08 9423 9422, 40 units [ensuite, a/c, tel, TV, t/c mkg, refrig, ldry]. **BB ⓘ $80, ⋔ $90**, BC MC VI.

Self Catering Accommodation
★★☆ **Kingswood College Holiday Flats**, (HF), Hampden Rd, 2km from Nedlands PO, ☎ 08 9423 9423, fax 08 9423 9422, 12 flats acc up to 4, (1 & 2 bedrm), [a/c, tel, TV, cook fac, linen], ldry, conf fac, meeting rm. **BB $90 - $120**, BC MC VI.

B&B's/Guest Houses
Caesia House Nedlands, (B&B), 32 Thomas St, 1km W of University of WA, ☎ 08 9389 8174, fax 08 9389 8173, 2 rms [ensuite, shwr, tlt, hairdry, a/c, heat, c/fan, TV, clock radio, t/c mkg, refrig], ✕, bbq, c/park. **BB ⋔ $85 - $95, ⋔ $95 - $105**, BC MC VI.

PERTH - NORTH BEACH WA 6020
Pop part of Perth, (8km NW Perth), See map on page 907, ref B4.

★★★☆ **Ocean View Motel**, (M), 10 Lawley St, 500m N of PO, ☎ 08 9246 4699, fax 08 9447 9555, (Multi-stry gr fl), 20 units [shwr, tlt, a/c, TV, clock radio, refrig, cook fac (2), toaster], ldry, spa (3), bbq. **RO ⓘ $75, ⋔ $85, ⋔⋔ $90 - $120**, AE BC DC MC MP VI.

PERTH - NORTHBRIDGE WA 6000
Pop part of Perth, (2km N Perth), See map on page 907, ref C4.

Hotels/Motels

Acacia Hotel, (LH), 15 Robinson Ave, 500m N of PO, ☎ 08 9328 0000, fax 08 9328 0100, (2 stry gr fl), 94 rms (10 suites) [shwr (82), bath, tlt (82), hairdry, a/c, tel, cable tv, clock radio, t/c mkg, refrig, doonas], lift, business centre, conf fac, ⊠, bar, 24hr reception, rm serv, secure park (undercover), gym, cots-fee, non smoking rms (36). **RO ⓘ $125 - $165, ⋔ $125 - $165, ⓘ $20, Suite RO ⓘ $195 - $225, ⋔ $195 - $225, ⓘ $20**, AE BC DC EFT JCB MC VI, (not yet classified).

B&B's/Guest Houses
Beaufort House, (B&B), 237 Beaufort St, 1km N of Perth GPO, ☎ 08 9227 8316, (Multi-stry), 2 rms bathrm. **BLB ⓘ $55, ⋔ $100, RO ⓘ $45, ⋔ $80**.

PERTH - OSBORNE PARK WA 6017
Pop part of Perth, (8km NW Perth), See map on page 907, ref C4.
★★☆ **Perth City Motel**, (HU), 29 - 33 Main St, 5km N of PO, ☎ 08 9444 6515, fax 08 9444 6183, 19 units acc up to 6, (1 & 2 bedrm), [shwr, tlt, a/c-cool, tel, TV, video (avail), clock radio, refrig, cook fac, micro, ldry, blkts, linen, pillows], w/mach, iron, rec rm, lounge, pool, bbq, plygr, cots. **D ⓘ $55, ⋔ $60, ⓘ $10, W ⓘ $350, ⋔ $385**, AE BC MC VI.

PERTH - REDCLIFFE WA 6104
Pop part of Perth, (7km E Perth), See map on page 907, ref D4.
Hotels/Motels
★★★ **Marracoonda Motel**, (M), 373 Great Eastern Hwy, Belmont 6104, 9km E of GPO, ☎ 08 9277 7777, fax 08 9479 1521, 130 units [shwr, tlt, a/c, tel, TV, video, radio, t/c mkg, refrig], ⊠, rm serv, courtesy transfer (airport), cots. **D ⓘ $77 - $99**, AE BC DC MC VI, ⓑ.

B&B's/Guest Houses
★★★☆ **Airport Accomodation Perth**, (B&B), Previously Airport B&B 103 Central Ave, 8km E of GPO, ☎ 08 9478 2923, fax 08 9478 2770, 4 rms [ensuite (2), hairdry, a/c-cool, heat, c/fan, elec blkts, TV (shared), clock radio, t/c mkg, doonas, pillows], bathrm (shared), ldry, w/mach-fee, dryer-fee, iron, iron brd, TV rm, ✕, ☏, non smoking property. **BLB ⓘ $55 - $65, ⋔ $75 - $85**, BC MC VI.

PERTH - RIVERTON WA 6155
Pop part of Perth, (14km S Perth), See map on page 907, ref C5.
Riverton Motel Hotel, (LMH), 361 High Rd, 13km SE of GPO, ☎ 08 9457 0477, fax 08 9354 2759, 7 units [shwr, tlt, a/c, TV, t/c mkg, refrig]. **RO ⓘ $50, ⋔ $60, ⓘ $10**.

PERTH - RIVERVALE WA 6103
Pop part of Perth, (6km E Perth), See map on page 907, ref C4.
★★★★ **Great Eastern Motor Lodge**, (M), 81 Great Eastern Hwy, 6.5km E of GPO, ☎ 08 9362 3611, fax 08 9470 2467, 200 units [shwr, tlt, a/c, tel, TV, radio, t/c mkg, refrig, cook fac, ldry], pool, cots-fee. **D ⓘ $72, ⋔ $80, ⋔⋔ $118, ⓘ $8**, ch con, Some units of a lower rating. AE BC DC MC VI, ⓑ.

★★★☆ **Flag Motor Lodge**, (M), Previously Flag Lodge Motel 129 Great Eastern Hwy, 7km E of GPO, ☎ 08 9277 2766, fax 08 9479 1304, 116 units [shwr, tlt, a/c-cool, heat, tel, TV, movie, radio, t/c mkg, refrig, cook fac (27), ldry], ✕, pool, rm serv, cots-fee. **D ⋔ $73 - $80, ⓘ $6 - $8**, AE BC DC MC VI, ⓑ.
★★★ **The Regency Motel**, (M), 61 Great Eastern Hwy, 6.5km E of GPO, ☎ 08 9362 3000, fax 08 9470 2087, 77 units [shwr, tlt, a/c, tel, TV, movie, radio, refrig, cook fac (59), ldry], ⊠, pool, spa, bbq, rm serv, shop (24 hr cafe), plygr, gym, tennis, cots. **D ⓘ $52.80 - $73.70, ⋔ $63.80 - $80.30, ⋔⋔ $85.80 - $107.80**, Some units of a lower rating. AE BC DC MC VI.
Toorak Lodge Motel, (M), 85 Great Eastern Hwy, 6.5km E of GPO, ☎ 08 9361 5522, fax 08 9472 3757, 51 units [shwr, tlt, a/c, tel, TV, radio, t/c mkg, refrig, ldry], ⊠, bar, pool, bbq, cots-fee. **D ⓘ $50 - $65, ⋔ $60 - $75, ⓘ $10**, ch con, AE BC DC EFT MC VI.

Self Catering Accommodation
Angelo Lodge, (HU), 66 Riversdale Rd, 6km E of GPO, ☎ 08 9361 7944, fax 08 9362 4415, 19 units acc up to 6, (1 & 2 bedrm), [shwr, tlt, a/c, tel, TV, refrig, cook fac, micro, blkts, linen, pillows], ldry, tennis, cots. **D ⓘ $65 - $75, ⋔ $87 - $98, ⋔⋔ $87 - $98**, ch con.
Eastway Lodge, (HU), 1 Minora Dve, 6km E of GPO, ☎ 08 9472 3411, fax 08 9361 2011, 27 units acc up to 6, (1 & 2 bedrm), [shwr, tlt, a/c, tel, TV, radio, refrig, cook fac, ldry, blkts, linen, pillows], pool, cots. **D $47 - $61, W $280 - $328**, ch con, AE BC DC JCB MC VI.
Glenvale Lodge, (SA), 6 Brighton Rd, 6km E of GPO, ☎ 08 9361 7800, fax 08 9361 7920, 30 serv apts acc up to 8, [shwr, tlt, a/c, tel, TV, refrig, cook fac, micro, ldry, blkts, linen, pillows]. **D ⋔ $73, ⋔⋔ $96.50 - $139**, ch con, BC MC VI.

PERTH - ROCKINGHAM WA 6168
Pop 49,917. (47km S Perth), See map on page 907, ref B8. Rockingham was one of the earliest settlements in WA.
Hotels/Motels
Leisure Inn, (LMH), Cnr Read St & Simpson Ave, 2km SE of PO, ☎ 08 9527 7777, fax 08 9527 7200, 10 units [shwr, tlt, a/c, tel, TV, radio, t/c mkg, refrig], rm serv. **D ⋔ $77, ⋔⋔ $88**, ch con, AE BC DC MC VI.
Self Catering Accommodation
★★★★☆ **Beachside Apartment Hotel**, (SA), 57 Rochingham Beach Rd, 2km NW of PO, ☎ 08 9529 3777, fax 08 9529 3444, (Multi-stry), 40 serv apts acc up to 5, (1, 2 & 3 bedrm), [shwr, tlt, hairdry, a/c, tel, TV, movie, clock radio, CD, t/c mkg, refrig, cook fac, micro, blkts, doonas, linen, pillows], lift, w/mach, dryer, iron, iron brd, ⊠, cafe, coffee shop, rm serv, meals to unit, secure park, non smoking units. **D $155 - $220, ⓘ $15 - $30, W $770 - $1,500 ⓘ $95 - $185**, ch con, fam con, pen con, AE BC DC EFT MC VI, ⓑ.

★★★ **Palm Holiday Apartments**, (HU), Cnr 153 Esplanade & Val St, 500m SW of PO, ☎ 08 9527 3374, fax 08 9527 3374, 1 unit acc up to 4, (2 bedrm), [shwr, bath, tlt, heat, fan, tel, TV, video, clock radio, refrig, micro, toaster, blkts, linen, pillows], ldry. **D** $70 - $100, **W** $350 - $550, Min book applies, BC MC VI.

Penguin Island Hideaway, (HU), 4/1 Penguin Rd, Shoalwater 6169, 5km W of PO, ☎ 08 9336 2208, 1 unit acc up to 2, (2 bedrm), [shwr, tlt, fan, heat, tel, TV, clock radio, refrig, cook fac, micro, ldry, blkts, doonas, linen, pillows], w/mach, iron, iron brd, non smoking units. **D** $80 - $150, **W** $400 - $600, Min book all holiday times, (not yet classified).

B&B's/Guest Houses

★★★★☆ **Palm Beach Bed & Breakfast**, (B&B), 42 Thorpe Street, 250m S of boardwalk, ☎ 08 9592 4444, fax 08 9591 1117, 2 rms [ensuite, a/c-cool, heat, elec blkts, fax, cable tv, clock radio, t/c mkg, refrig], ldry, w/mach, dryer-fee, iron, iron brd, rec rm, lounge (cd, stereo), ✕, spa, bbq, secure park, bicycle-fee, cots-fee, non smoking property. **BB** ⧫ $50 - $65, ⧫⧫ $75 - $85, ch con, fam con, pen con, BC MC VI.

★★★★☆ **The Anchorage**, (B&B), 2 Smythe St, 500m E of PO, ☎ 08 9527 4214, fax 08 9528 1750, (2 stry), 4 rms [ensuite, a/c-cool, heat, fire pl, tel, TV, video, clock radio, t/c mkg, refrig, doonas, pillows], w/mach-fee, dryer-fee, iron, TV rm, secure park, non smoking property. **BB** ⧫ $65 - $75, ⧫⧫ $85 - $95, BC MC VI.

★★★★ **Pelicans Landing**, (B&B), 352 Safety Bay Rd, Safety Bay 6169, 1.3km E of Safety Bay Yacht Club, ☎ 08 9592 3058, fax 08 9592 3058, (2 stry), 2 rms [ensuite (1), tlt, heat (gas), elec blkts, tel, TV, clock radio, micro, doonas, pillows], bathrm (Private) (1), ✕, t/c mkg shared, refrig, bbq, non smoking property. **BB** ⧫ $70, ⧫⧫ $90, **W** ⧫ $440 - $565, AE BC MC VI.

★★★★ **Rockingham Bed & Breakfast**, (B&B), 102 Penguin Rd, Safety Bay 6169, 1km S of PO, ☎ 08 9527 6842, fax 08 9527 6842, 3 rms [ensuite (1), shwr, tlt, a/c-cool, fire pl, elec blkts, tel, TV, video, clock radio, refrig, doonas, pillows], bathrm (1), TV rm, t/c mkg shared, bbq, bicycle, non smoking rms. **BB** ⧫ $65, ⧫⧫ $90, **W** ⧫ $350, ⧫⧫ $490, ch con, MC VI.

★★★☆ **Homestead Bed & Breakfast**, (B&B), 14 Palm Drive, Warnbro 6169, 3km S of PO, ☎ 08 9593 0928, fax 08 9593 0936, 3 rms [ensuite, hairdry, a/c, tel, TV (3), cable tv, clock radio, t/c mkg, refrig, doonas, pillows], ldry, w/mach, dryer, iron, TV rm, ✕, meals avail, non smoking rms. **BB** ⧫ $50 - $55, ⧫⧫ $80 - $85, **DBB** ⧫⧫ $110, fam con.

PERTH - ROLEYSTONE WA 6111

Pop part of Perth, (30km SE Perth), See map on page 907, ref E6.

★★★★☆ **Woodlands Bed & Breakfast**, (B&B), 9 Andreas Rd, 5km E of Kelmscott PO, ☎ 08 9397 5664, fax 08 9397 5329, 1 rm [ensuite, hairdry, a/c, tel, TV, video, t/c mkg, refrig, micro, doonas, pillows], iron, iron brd, pool, spa (outdoor), bbq, gym, cots, non smoking property. **BLB** ⧫ $65 - $75, ⧫⧫ $70 - $80, ⧫⧫⧫⧫ $90 - $100, **W** ⧫ $455, ⧫⧫ $490, ⧫⧫⧫⧫ $630, BC MC VI.

PERTH - ROTTNEST ISLAND WA 6161

Pop Nominal, (18km W Perth), See map on page 907, ref A5. Perth's most popular holiday resort, just 18km off the coast, can be reached in just fifteen minutes by air, or across the water on one of the ferries that regularly make the daily trip from either Perth, Fremantle or Hillarys.

Hotels/Motels

★★★☆ **Rottnest Lodge Resort**, (M), Rottnest Lodge, Rottnest Island, ☎ 08 9292 5161, fax 08 9292 5158, 80 units [shwr, tlt, tel, cable tv, t/c mkg, refrig], ✕, bar (Cocktail) (3), pool, cots. **D** ⧫⧫ $175 - $240, ⧫ $40, Some units of a lower rating. ⟨⟩.

Self Catering Accommodation

Allison & Caroline Thomson Camping Areas, Limited facilities, Rottnest Island, ☎ 08 9432 9111, fax 08 9432 9315, 30 cabins acc up to 6, [shwr, tlt, refrig, blkts reqd, linen reqd, pillows reqd]. **D** $75.20 - $81.90, Canvas Cabins. BC MC VI.

   (Allison Camping Area), 22 cabins acc up to 6, [blkts reqd, doonas reqd, linen reqd, pillows reqd], shwr, tlt. **D** $25.80 - $48.30.

   (Camping Area Section), [ldry], shwr, tlt, bbq. **D** ⧫ $5.50.

Other Accommodation

Rottnest Youth Hostel, Kingstown Barracks YHA, Rottnest Island, ☎ 08 9372 9780, fax 08 9292 5141, 9 rms acc up to 54, [refrig, cook fac, blkts, linen reqd-fee, pillows], shwr, tlt. **RO** ⧫ $20.90, BC MC MCH.

PERTH - SCARBOROUGH WA 6019

Pop part of Perth, (14km NW Perth), See map on page 907, ref B4.

Hotels/Motels

★★★★★ **Rendezvous Observation City Hotel**, (LH), The Esplanade, 200m W of PO, ☎ 08 9245 1000, fax 08 9245 1345, (Multi-stry), 327 rms (6 suites) [shwr, tlt, hairdry, a/c, tel, TV, movie, radio, t/c mkg, refrig, mini bar, toaster, ldry], lift, business centre, conv fac, night club, ✉, bar, pool, sauna, spa, rm serv (24 hr), courtesy transfer, tennis, cots. **RO** ⧫⧫ $160 - $190, ⧫ $45 - $67, **Suite RO** $350 - $1,200, AE BC DC EFT JCB MC VI, ⟨⟩.

★★★★ **Sunmoon Resort**, (LMH), 200 West Coast Highway, 250m NW of PO, ☎ 08 9245 8000, fax 08 9245 8055, 43 units [shwr, bath, spa bath, tlt, hairdry, a/c, tel, TV, movie, clock radio, t/c mkg, refrig, cook fac, micro, toaster, pillows], lift, ldry, w/mach, dryer, lounge, business centre, conv fac, ✉, bar, pool, rm serv, meals to unit, secure park, courtesy transfer, cots, non smoking property. **BB** $135 - $270, **W** $700 - $1,440, **RO** $115, **W** $660 - $1,155, ch con, AE BC DC EFT MC VI, ⟨⟩.

★★★☆ **Indian Ocean Hotel**, (Ltd Lic H), 27 Hastings St, 200m SE of PO, ☎ 08 9341 1122, fax 08 9341 1899, (Multi-stry gr fl), 60 rms [shwr, tlt, a/c, tel, cable tv, movie, radio, t/c mkg, refrig], lift, ✉, pool, spa, rm serv, cots-fee. **D** ⧫ $70 - $100, ⧫⧫ $88 - $115, ⧫ $15, ch con, AE BC DC MC VI.

Self Catering Accommodation

★★★★★ **Observation Rise**, (SA), 183 West Coast Hwy, 350m NW of PO, ☎ 08 9245 0800, fax 08 9341 1181, (Multi-stry), 55 serv apts acc up to 7, [shwr, bath (spa), tlt, a/c, tel, TV, clock radio, refrig, cook fac, micro, d/wash, blkts, linen, pillows], w/mach, dryer, pool, pool indoor heated, sauna, spa, bbq, gym, tennis, cots. **D** $185 - $286, AE BC DC MC VI.

★★★★☆ **Sandcastles On Scarborough**, (SA), 170 The Esplanade, 300m SW of PO, ☎ 08 9245 2030, fax 08 9341 7227, (Multi-stry gr fl), 13 serv apts acc up to 6, (2 & 3 bedrm), [shwr, spa bath, tlt, hairdry, a/c, tel, TV, video (some)-fee, clock radio, refrig, cook fac, micro, blkts, doonas, linen, pillows], lift, w/mach, dryer, iron, iron brd, pool, pool-heated, sauna-fee, bbq, secure park, courtesy transfer, cots. **D** ⧫⧫ $165 - $195, ⧫⧫⧫⧫ $210 - $265, Min book applies, AE BC DC MC VI.

★★★★☆ **Seashells Resort Apartments**, (HU), 178 The Esplanade, 300m SW of PO, ☎ 08 9341 6644, fax 08 9341 7227, 43 units (2 bedrm), [shwr, spa bath (30), tlt, a/c, tel, TV, movie, clock radio, refrig, cook fac, micro, blkts, linen, pillows], w/mach, dryer, pool (2), sauna, bbq, secure park, gym, cots. **D** $130 - $215, Min book applies, AE BC DC MC VI.

★★★★ **Observation Villas**, (Villa), 7 Manning St, 300m NW of PO, ☎ 08 9245 3111, fax 08 9245 3108, (2 stry gr fl), 6 villas acc up to 6, [shwr, bath, tlt, hairdry, a/c-cool, heat, tel, TV, video, refrig, cook fac, micro, ldry, blkts, doonas, linen, pillows], w/mach, dryer, iron, pool, spa, bbq, cots (avail)-fee. **D** $104.50 - $159.50, **W** $687.50 - $1,045, AE BC DC MC VI.

   (Paradiso Apartments Section), 46 Filburn Street, 3 apts acc up to 5, [shwr, bath, tlt, a/c-cool, c/fan, heat, tel, TV, video, refrig, cook fac, micro, blkts, doonas, linen, pillows], w/mach, dryer, iron, iron brd, bbq, secure park, cots (avail)-fee. **D** ⧫⧫ $77 - $121, ⧫ $20, **W** $522 - $825, Min book.

   (Surfside Apartments Section), 29-31 Hastings Street, 2 apts acc up to 3, (1 bedrm), [shwr, tlt, heat, fan, tel, TV, video (most), refrig, cook fac, micro, blkts, doonas, linen, pillows], ldry, iron, iron brd, pool, spa (shared), bbq, cots (avail)-fee. **D** ⧫⧫ $44 - $99, ⧫ $20, **W** $275 - $660, Min book.

S

PERTH & SUBURBS – WESTERN AUSTRALIA

★★★★ **Ocean Villas**, (HU), 17 Hastings St, 200m SW of PO, ☎ 08 9245 1066, fax 08 9245 1228, 12 units acc up to 5, [shwr, spa bath, tlt, hairdry, a/c-cool, heat (gas), tel, TV, clock radio, t/c mkg, refrig, micro, toaster, ldry, blkts, doonas, linen, pillows], w/mach, iron, iron brd, secure park, cots-fee. **D $100 - $125, W $650 - $850**, BC MC VI.

★★★★ **The Dunes**, (SA), 15 Filburn St, ☎ 08 9245 2797, fax 08 9245 5666, 3 serv apts acc up to 4, (2 bedrm) [shwr, bath, tlt, hairdry, a/c-cool, c/fan, heat, tel, fax, TV, video, clock radio, refrig, cook fac, micro, blkts, doonas, linen, pillows], w/mach, iron, iron brd, bbq, 24hr reception, cots, non smoking units. **D $132 - $165, W $715 - $1,149.50**, Min book applies, AE BC DC MC VI.

★★★☆ **Emerald Court & Mews Apartments**, (SA), 46 Scarborough Beach Rd, 12km N of GPO, ☎ 08 9245 2350, fax 08 9245 1347, (Multi-stry gr fl), 12 serv apts acc up to 4, (2 bedrm), [shwr, bath (6), tlt, a/c, heat, tel, TV, video, clock radio, refrig, cook fac, micro, toaster, blkts, linen, pillows], ldry, pool, bbq, cots. **D $88 - $135, W $550 - $880**, AE BC MC VI.

★★★☆ **West Beach Lagoon**, (SA), 251 West Coast Hwy, 400m SW of PO, ☎ 08 9341 6122, fax 08 9341 5944, (Multi-stry gr fl), 69 serv apts acc up to 4, (2 bedrm), [shwr, tlt, a/c, tel, TV, radio, refrig, cook fac, micro], pool, bbq, cots. **D $121 - $160**, ch con, AE BC DC VI.

★★★ **Nautilus Court Apartments**, (HU), 10 Nautilus Cres, 1km N of PO, ☎ 08 9245 2452, fax 08 9245 2451, 16 units acc up to 2, (1 bedrm), [ensuite, shwr, tlt, TV, clock radio, refrig, cook fac, toaster, blkts, linen, pillows], ldry, w/mach-fee, dryer-fee, iron, cots. **D ♦♦ $55, W ♦♦ $250 - $350**, Min book all holiday times, BC MC VI.

★★★ **West Coast Seas**, (HU), 177 West Coast Hwy, 700m N of PO, ☎ 08 9341 4101, fax 08 9341 5411, 6 units acc up to 4, (2 bedrm), [shwr, tlt, tel, TV, refrig, cook fac, ldry, blkts, linen, pillows]. **D $50 - $100, W $350 - $700**.

★★☆ **Scarborough Palms Apartments**, (HF), Previously Elsinore Holiday Flats 51 Pearl Pde, 1.2km N of PO, ☎ 08 9245 1272, or 08 9341 1122, fax 08 9341 5411, 19 flats [shwr, tlt, tel, TV, video-fee, refrig, cook fac, micro, blkts, linen, pillows], w/mach, dryer, pool, bbq, cots, Pets by arrangement. **D $50 - $100, W $290 - $700**.

★★☆ **Sunset Waters**, (HU), 38 Filburn St, 400m N of PO, ☎ 08 9364 8104, fax 08 9316 1088, 3 units acc up to 4, (2 bedrm), [shwr, tlt, a/c, tel, TV, clock radio, refrig, cook fac, micro, toaster, blkts, doonas, linen, pillows], ldry, iron, iron brd. **D $60 - $95, W $330 - $645**, Min book applies, BC MC VI.

Mandarin Gardens Holiday Units, (HU), Unit 1/20 Wheatcroft St, 500m NE of PO, ☎ 08 9341 5431, fax 08 9245 1553, 17 units acc up to 6, (1 & 2 bedrm), [shwr, tlt, a/c (10), tel, TV, movie, refrig, cook fac, blkts, linen, pillows], ldry, pool (25 metre), bbq, plygr. **D $61 - $99, ⓥ $10**, ch con, BC MC VI.

Mulloway Holiday Units, (HU), Cnr West Coast Hwy & Manning St, 300m NW of PO, ☎ 08 9341 2133, fax 08 9341 2133, 8 units acc up to 5, (1 & 2 bedrm), [shwr, tlt, a/c, tel, TV, radio, refrig, cook fac, micro, ldry, blkts, linen, pillows], pool, bbq, cots. **D $55 - $110, W $320 - $770**, Min book applies, BC MC VI.

B&B's/Guest Houses

Penny's By The Sea, (GH), 96A Stanley St, 800m S of PO, ☎ 08 9341 1411, 2 rms [fan, clock radio, t/c mkg, refrig, cook fac, pillows], shwr, tlt, rec rm, TV rm. **BLB ♦ $55, ♦♦ $80, ⓥ $30**, BC MC VI.

Other Accommodation

Mandarin Gardens Scarborough Beach Resort, 20-28 Wheatcroft St, 500m NE of PO, ☎ 08 9341 5431, fax 08 9245 1553, 19 rms [shwr, bath, tlt, a/c-cool, c/fan, TV, video, blkts reqd-fee, linen reqd-fee, pillows], ldry, w/mach-fee, dryer-fee, iron, rec rm, read rm, pool (25 metre), cook fac, refrig, bbq, ✆, plygr, non smoking rms. **D ♦ $16 - $31**, fam con, Min book all holiday times, BC MC VI.

Western Beach Lodge, 6 Westborough St, ☎ 08 9245 1624, 9 rms (1 bedrm), [ensuite (1), heat, c/fan, tel, TV, video, refrig, blkts, doonas, linen, pillows], shwr, tlt, ldry, w/mach-fee, iron, rec rm, read rm, cook fac, refrig, bbq, non smoking property. **D ♦ $12 - $14, ♦♦ $24 - $28, W ♦ $77 - $90, RO ♦♦ $28 - $38, ♦♦ $185 - $210**, BC MC VI.

PERTH - SORRENTO WA 6020

Pop part of Perth, (21km NW Perth), See map on page 907, ref B4.

Self Catering Accommodation

★★★☆ **All Seasons Sorrento Beach Resort**, (SA), 1 Padbury Circle, 17km N of GPO, ☎ 08 9246 8100, fax 08 9246 2481, 80 serv apts acc up to 6, (Studio, 1, 2 & 3 bedrm), [shwr, spa bath (26), tlt, a/c, tel, TV, movie, radio, refrig, cook fac, ldry, blkts, linen, pillows], ✗, pool, sauna, bbq. **D $99 - $174**, AE BC DC MC VI, ⓕ⅙.

B&B's/Guest Houses

★★★★ **Sorrento House Bed & Breakfast**, (B&B), 11 Sandpiper St, 1.5km E of Sorrento Quay/Hillarys, ☎ 08 9447 0995, fax 08 9447 0995, 2 rms [ensuite (2), a/c-cool, TV, clock radio, t/c mkg, refrig, cook fac, micro, doonas, pillows], lounge, pool-heated, non smoking property. **BB ♦ $65, ♦♦ $90, ⓥ $20**, ch con, fam con, VI.

PERTH - SOUTH PERTH WA 6151

Pop part of Perth, (5km S Perth), See map on page 907, ref C5.

Hotels/Motels

★★★☆ **Metro Inn Perth**, (LH), 61 Canning Hwy, 3km SE of GPO, ☎ 08 9367 6122, fax 08 9367 3411, (Multi-stry), 87 rms (1 suite) [shwr, bath, tlt, a/c, tel, TV, movie, radio, t/c mkg, refrig, mini bar], lift, conf fac, ✉, bar (cocktail), pool, bbq, rm serv, cots. **D ♦♦ $96 - $112**, AE BC DC MC VI, ⓕ⅙.

Self Catering Accommodation

★★★★☆ **Arlington Quest Apartments**, (SA), Cnr Arlington Ave & Mill Point Rd, 2km S of GPO, ☎ 08 9474 0200, fax 08 9368 1037, 45 serv apts (2 & 3 bedrm), [shwr, bath, tlt, hairdry, a/c, tel, TV, movie, clock radio, refrig, cook fac, micro, d/wash, blkts, doonas, linen, pillows], w/mach, dryer, iron, iron brd, pool, spa, bbq, cots. **D $170 - $220**, AE BC DC EFT MC VI.

★★★★☆ **Drakes Apartments with Cars**, (Apt), 7 Scenic Cres, ☎ 08 9367 5077, fax 08 9367 5970, 7 apts acc up to 6, [shwr, spa bath, tlt, hairdry, a/c, c/fan, tel, TV, video, clock radio, CD, refrig, cook fac, micro, d/wash, toaster, blkts, doonas, linen, pillows], w/mach, dryer, iron, iron brd, non smoking units. **D $280 - $300, W $1,820 - $1,960**, Exclusive use of car with each unit. AE BC EFT MC VI.
Operator Comment: See our ad in Perth Section.

★★★★ **(6 Scenic Cres Section)**, Reception: 7 Scenic Cres. 3 apts acc up to 6, [shwr, bath, tlt, hairdry, a/c, c/fan, tel, TV, video, clock radio, refrig, cook fac, micro, d/wash, toaster, blkts, doonas, linen, pillows], w/mach, dryer, iron, iron brd, non smoking units. **D $200 - $220, W $1,260 - $1,400**, Exclusive use of car with each unit.

★★★★ **(Swanview Tce Section)**, Reception: 7 Scenic Cres. 8 apts acc up to 4, [shwr, spa bath, tlt, hairdry, a/c, c/fan, tel, TV, video, clock radio, refrig, cook fac, refrig, micro, toaster, blkts, doonas, linen, pillows], w/mach, dryer, iron, iron brd, non smoking units. **D $160 - $180, W $980 - $1,120**, Exclusive use of car with each unit.

★★★☆ **(Mill Point Rd Section)**, Reception: 7 Scenic Cres. 10 apts acc up to 4, [shwr, tlt, hairdry, a/c, c/fan, tel, TV, video, clock radio, refrig, cook fac, micro, toaster, blkts, doonas, linen, pillows], ldry, iron, iron brd, non smoking units. **D $140 - $160, W $840 - $980**, Exclusive use of cars with each unit.

★★★ **(2 Scenic Cres Section)**, Reception: 7 Scenic Cres. 5 apts acc up to 5, [shwr, bath, tlt, hairdry, a/c, c/fan, tel, TV, video, clock radio, refrig, cook fac, micro, toaster, blkts, doonas, linen, pillows], ldry, iron, iron brd, 24hr reception, courtesy transfer, non smoking property. **D $120 - $200, W $735 - $1,260**, Exclusive use of car with each unit.

★★★★ **Waterside Apartments**, (Apt), 29 Melville Parade, 700m NW of PO, ☎ 08 9474 4474, fax 08 9474 4475, (2 stry), 42 apts acc up to 4, (1 & 2 bedrm), [shwr, tlt, a/c, tel, TV, clock radio, refrig, cook fac, micro, d/wash, toaster, ldry, blkts, linen, pillows], w/mach, dryer, iron, iron brd, bbq, secure park, cots, non smoking rms. **D $119 - $174**, AE BC DC MC VI.

★★★★ **Executive Apartments**, (SA), 19 Charles St, ☎ 08 9474 2255, fax 08 9474 2868, (Multi-stry), 160 serv apts acc up to 6, [shwr, bath (34), tlt, a/c (23), fan, heat, tel (90), TV, video-fee, clock radio, refrig, cook fac, d/wash (40), ldry (68), blkts, linen, pillows], lift, pool, bbq. **D $85 - $300**, Some units of a lower rating. Min book applies, BC MC VI.

★★★★ **The Peninsula**, (SA), 53 South Perth Esplanade, 100m of Ferry Port, ☎ 08 9368 6688, fax 08 9368 6689, 75 serv apts acc up to 4, (1 & 2 bedrm), [ensuite, shwr, a/c, tel, TV, clock radio, refrig, cook fac, micro, toaster, blkts, linen, pillows], ldry, w/mach-fee, dryer-fee, iron, iron brd, cots-fee, non smoking units. **D $110 - $165, W $654 - $847**, AE BC EFT MC VI.

★★★ **Lyall Holiday Apartments**, (HU), 2 Lyall St, 2km S of GPO, ☎ 08 9387 1711, fax 08 9387 8836, (Multi-stry), 7 units acc up to 2, (1 bedrm), [shwr, tlt, a/c (4), heat, fan, tel, refrig, cook fac, micro, blkts, linen, pillows], ldry, w/mach. **W $324.50 - $378**.

PERTH - SUBIACO WA 6008

Pop part of Perth, (3km W Perth), See map on page 907, ref C4.

Hotels/Motels

★★★☆ **Kings Park Motel**, (M), 255 Thomas St, 3.5km W of GPO, ☎ 08 9381 0000, fax 08 9381 4159, 33 units [shwr, tlt, hairdry, a/c, tel, TV, video, clock radio, t/c mkg, refrig, toaster, ldry], ✗ (b'fast), pool, spa (some), bbq, cots. **D ♦ $75, ♦♦ $80, ♦♦♦ $115 - $125**, AE BC DC MC VI.

Self Catering Accommodation

★★★★☆ **Victoria Quest Apartments**, (SA), 222 Hay St, 3km W of PO, ☎ 08 9380 0800, fax 08 9380 0888, 48 serv apts acc up to 6, (1, 2 & 3 bedrm), [shwr, bath, tlt, a/c, tel, TV, clock radio, refrig, cook fac, micro, d/wash, blkts, linen, pillows], w/mach, dryer, iron, ✉, pool, spa, bbq, rm serv, secure park, cots. **D ♦ $175, ♦♦ $208, ♦♦♦ $241**, AE BC DC EFT MC VI.

B&B's/Guest Houses

★★★★☆ **Amber Rose Bed & Breakfast**, (B&B), 102 Bagot Rd, 3km W of GPO, ☎ 08 9382 3669, 2 rms [shwr, tlt, a/c, cable tv, clock radio, CD, t/c mkg, refrig], w/mach, iron, iron brd, lounge, non smoking property. **BB ♦ $75, ♦♦ $105**, BC MC VI.

PERTH - SWAN VALLEY WA

See Guildford, Henely Brook, Midland, Upper Swan, West Swan.

PERTH - SWANBOURNE WA 6010

Pop part of Perth, (10km W Perth), See map on page 907, ref B5.
★★★☆ **Swanbourne Guest House**, (B&B), 5 Myera St, 9km W of GPO, ☎ 08 9383 1981, fax 08 9385 4595, 4 rms [ensuite, heat, fax, cable tv, video, clock radio, refrig, micro, ldry, pillows], lounge, cook fac, bbq. **BB** ♦ **$55**, ♦♦ **$95**, BC MC VI.

PERTH - TRIGG WA 6029

Pop part of Perth, (16km NW Perth), See map on page 907, ref B4.
★★★☆ **Gull Cottage**, (Cotg), 297 West Coast Dve, 1km N Karrinyup Rd & West Coast Dve, ☎ 08 9297 3481, fax 08 9297 3365, 1 cotg acc up to 6, [shwr, bath, tlt, fan, heat, tel, TV, video, clock radio, refrig, cook fac, micro, elec frypan, blkts, doonas, linen, pillows], w/mach, dryer, iron, iron brd, bbq, cots, non smoking property. **D** ♦♦ **$120**, ♦ **$20**, **W** ♦♦ **$720 - $840**, Minimum 3 day bookings. AE BC DC JCB MC VI.

PERTH - UPPER SWAN WA 6069

Pop part of Perth, (25km NE Perth), See map on page 907, ref D3.
Hotels/Motels
★★★★☆ **Novotel Vines Resort Hotel**, (LH), Verdelho Dve, The Vines, 30km NE of GPO, ☎ 08 9297 3000, fax 08 9297 3333, (2 stry), 103 rms (27 suites) [hairdry, a/c-cool, tel, fax, TV, movie, radio, t/c mkg, refrig, mini bar], lift, iron, iron brd, lounge, ⊠, ✗, pool, spa, bbq, ✎, plygr, golf, gym, squash, tennis, non smoking rms. **D RO** ♦♦ **$189**, ♦ **$27**, **Suite D** ♦♦ **$403**, ♦ **$27**, AE BC DC EFT MC VI, ⚷&.

Self Catering Accommodation
★★★ **Mill House Cottage**, (Cotg), Lot 107 Corona Way, Belhus 6069, 25km NE of GPO, ☎ 08 9297 3481, fax 08 9297 3365, 1 cotg acc up to 8, (3 bedrm), [shwr, bath, tlt, a/c-cool, heat, tel, TV, video, clock radio, refrig, cook fac, micro, toaster, blkts, doonas, linen, pillows], w/mach-fee, dryer-fee, bbq, non smoking property. **D** ♦♦ **$110**, ♦ **$20**, Min book long w/ends, AE BC DC JCB MC VI.
Novotel Vines Resort, (SA), Verdelho Drive, The Vines 6069, The Vines, 30km NE of GPO, ☎ 08 9297 3000, fax 08 9297 3333, 45 serv apts acc up to 6, (2 & 3 bedrm), [shwr, bath, tlt, hairdry, a/c, tel, TV, movie, clock radio, refrig, cook fac, d/wash, toaster, blkts, linen, pillows], w/mach, dryer, iron, iron brd, TV rm, conv fac, ⊠, ✗, bar, pool, spa, bbq, rm serv, ✎, plygr, golf (36 hole course), squash, tennis (4), cots. **D** ♦♦ **$250**, ♦♦♦♦ **$350**, AE BC DC EFT MC VI.

PERTH - VICTORIA PARK WA 6100

Pop part of Perth, (5km SE Perth), See map on page 907, ref C5.
★★★★★ **Durham Lodge**, (B&B), 165 Shepperton Rd, 5km E of GPO, ☎ 08 9361 8000, fax 08 9361 8000, 3 rms [shwr, bath, spa bath (2), tlt, hairdry, a/c, fire pl, tel, TV, video, clock radio, t/c mkg, refrig], ldry, ✗, t/c mkg shared, bbq, bicycle, cots (avail), non smoking property. **BB** ♦ **$75 - $95**, ♦♦ **$95 - $120**, **W** ♦ **$570 - $720**, AE BC DC MC VI.

PERTH - WANNEROO WA 6065

Pop 6,745. (26km N Perth), See map on page 907, ref B3.
B&B's/Guest Houses
Bebich House, (B&B), 84 Bebich Drive, ☎ 08 9306 3152, 3 rms [shwr, bath, evap cool, c/fan, elec blkts, TV, video], tlt, w/mach, dryer, iron, iron brd, lounge (cd), lounge firepl, pool, t/c mkg shared, refrig, bbq, non smoking property. **BB** ♦ **$50 - $60**, ♦♦ **$80 - $90**, BC MC VI, (not yet classified).

PERTH - WARWICK WA 6024

Pop part of Perth, (15km N Perth), See map on page 907, ref B4.
★★★☆ **Palms Bed & Breakfast**, (B&B), No children's facilities, 24 Dorchester Ave, 200m N of Warwick Grove Shopping Centre, ☎ 08 9246 9499, fax 08 9246 0686, 4 rms [ensuite (3), shwr, tlt, hairdry, heat, c/fan, elec blkts, tel, TV, clock radio, t/c mkg, ldry, doonas, pillows], ✗, pool-heated, non smoking property. **BB** ♦ **$69**, ♦♦ **$89**, ♦♦♦ **$99**, Min book applies, BC MC VI.

PERTH - WEMBLEY WA 6014

Pop part of Perth, (5km NW Perth), See map on page 907, ref C4.

★★★ **Cambridge Atrium**, (SA), 227 Cambridge St, 5km W of GPO, ☎ 08 9382 4299, fax 08 9381 4290, 24 serv apts acc up to 5, (1 bedrm), [shwr, tlt, a/c, tel, TV, refrig, cook fac, ldry, blkts, linen, pillows], dryer, pool. **D** **$99 - $110**.

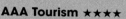

PERTH - WEST PERTH WA 6005

Pop part of Perth, (2km W Perth), See map on page 907, ref C4.
Hotels/Motels

★★★ **Murray Lodge Motel**, (M), 718 Murray St, 1.7km W of GPO, ☎ 08 9321 7441, fax 08 9321 7282, 27 units [shwr, tlt, a/c, heat, tel, TV, radio, t/c mkg, refrig], ⊠, cots-fee, non smoking rms. **D** ♦ **$64**, ♦♦ **$73**, ♦ **$9**, AE BC DC MC VI.

Other Accommodation
Beatty Lodge Budget Accommodation, (Lodge), No children's facilities, 235 Vincent St, West Perth 6872, ☎ 08 9227 1521, fax 08 9227 6509, (Multi-stry gr fl), 73 rms, [heat, fan, TV, video, refrig, blkts, doonas, linen, pillows], shwr, tlt, ldry, w/mach-fee, dryer-fee, iron, rec rm, ✗, cafe, pool, t/c mkg shared, ✎ (2), non smoking property. **RO** ♦ **$33**, ♦♦ **$46.20**, ♦♦♦ **$59.40**, **W** ♦ **$184.80**, ♦♦ **$258.50**, ♦♦♦ **$332.20**, Alcohol free establishment. BC EFT MC VI.

PERTH - WEST SWAN WA 6055

Pop part of Perth, (16km NE Perth), See map on page 907, ref D3.
★★★★ **Settlers Rest Farmstay**, (Cotg), 90 George Street, 1km off Swan Valley Tourist Drive 203, ☎ 08 9250 4540, fax 08 9250 4540, 1 cotg acc up to 6, [shwr, bath, tlt, hairdry, evap cool, wood heat, elec blkts, TV, clock radio, t/c mkg, refrig, cook fac, micro, elec frypan, blkts, doonas, linen, pillows], w/mach, iron, iron brd, bbq, trailer park, plygr, jetty, bicycle, canoeing, golf (driving range), cots, non smoking property. **D** ♦♦ **$130 - $140**, ♦♦♦ **$145 - $155**, ♦♦♦♦ **$160 - $170**, **W** ♦♦ **$780 - $840**, BC MC VI.

PERTH - WILSON WA 6107

Pop part of Perth, (11km S Perth), See map on page 907, ref D5.
★★★☆ **Langham Gardens Bed & Breakfast**, (B&B), 41 Langham Gardens, 7km SE of GPO, ☎ 08 9458 4382, fax 08 9458 4389, 4 rms [ensuite (1), shwr, tlt, c/fan, fire pl, heat, TV, t/c mkg, refrig, pillows], ldry, TV rm, pool, bbq, non smoking rms. **BB** ♦ **$33 - $38.50**, ♦♦ **$60.50 - $66**, **BLB** ♦ **$27.50 - $33**, ♦♦ **$49.50 - $60.50**, fam con.

PERTH - WUNGONG WA 6112

Pop part of Perth, (31km SE Perth), See map on page 907, ref D6. Outer

★★★★ **Waterway House Bed/Breakfast**, (B&B), 551 South Western Hwy, 5km S of Armadale PO, ☎ 08 9399 9283, fax 08 9399 9283, 3 rms (1 suite) [ensuite (1), a/c, fire pl, fax, TV, video, refrig, cook fac], shwr, tlt, lounge, bbq, c/park. **BB** ♦ **$70**, ♦♦ **$90**, ♦ **$20**, BC MC VI.

PERTH - YANCHEP WA 6035

Pop 486. (58km N Perth), See map on page 907, ref A1.

Hotels/Motels

★★★☆ **Lodge Capricorn**, (M), Two Rocks Rd, 56km N of GPO, ☎ 08 9561 1106, fax 08 9561 1163, 28 units (1 & 2 bedrm), [shwr, a/c, tel, cable tv, radio, t/c mkg, refrig, ldry], conv fac, ✕, bar, pool, sauna, spa, tennis. **D** ♦♦ **$130 - $160**.

Self Catering Accommodation

★★★☆ **Yanchep Holiday Village**, (HU), 56 Saint Andrews Dve, 53km N of GPO, ☎ 08 9561 2244, fax 08 9561 2338, 16 units acc up to 6, (1, 2 & 3 bedrm), [shwr, tlt, a/c-cool, fan, tel, TV, video, refrig, cook fac, micro, blkts, linen, pillows], rec rm, conv fac, pool, spa, bbq, plygr, bicycle-fee, gym, cots. **D $103 - $157, W $420 - $820**, AE BC DC MC VI, ♿.

Operator Comment: Please visit our website at: www.yanchepholidays.com

★★☆ **Club Capricorn Chalets**, (Chalet), Two Rocks Rd, 56km N GPO, ☎ 08 9561 1106, fax 08 9561 1163, 37 chalets acc up to 6, (2 & 3 bedrm), [shwr, tlt, refrig, cook fac, ldry, blkts, linen reqd, pillows], pool, bbq, golf (mini), tennis. **D $121 - $165**, Some units of a higher rating. Min book.

★★☆ **Two Rocks Harbour View Apartments**, (HU), Unit 1/Shop 18 Two Rocks, Two Rocks 6035, 63km N of GPO, ☎ 08 9561 1469, fax 08 9561 1218, 8 units acc up to 6, (1 & 2 bedrm), [shwr, tlt, TV, video-fee, clock radio, refrig, cook fac, micro, ldry, blkts, linen, pillows], w/mach, dryer. **D** ♦ **$70 - $90**, ♦♦♦♦ **$80 - $100, W** ♦♦ **$350 - $450**, ♦♦♦♦ **$450 - $550**.

B&B's/Guest Houses

★★★☆ **Glendale Park Lodge**, (B&B), Lot 53 Old Yanchep Rd, Carabooda 6033, 3km SE from junction of Old Yanchep & Wanneroo Rds, ☎ 08 9561 1247, fax 08 9561 2090, 3 rms [shwr, bath, tlt, c/fan, TV, video, refrig, doonas, pillows], w/mach reqd-fee, dryer reqd-fee, iron reqd-fee, rec rm, TV rm, pool, spa, t/c mkg shared, bbq, meals avail (by arrangement), secure park, non smoking property. **BB** ♦ **$65 - $75**, ♦♦ **$90 - $100, DBB** ♦ **$80 - $90**, ♦♦ **$120 - $130**, fam con, Farm Activities.

End of Perth & Suburbs

ALBANY WA 6330

Pop 20,493. (409km SE Perth), See map on page 906, ref B8. Albany is located on Princess Royal Harbour and is a delightful tourist retreat. It is the oldest settlement in Western Australia, preserving many of its historical buildings as a reminder of the settlement's early days. Bowls, Croquet, Fishing, Golf, Horse Riding, Squash, Swimming, Tennis, Vineyards, Wineries, Water Skiing.

Hotels/Motels

★★★★☆ **The Esplanade Hotel - Albany**, (LH), Flinders Pde Middleton Beach, 3km E of PO, ☎ 08 9842 1711, fax 08 9841 7527, 48 rms (8 suites) [shwr, bath, tlt, a/c, tel, TV, video (free videos), clock radio, t/c mkg, refrig, mini bar, ldry], iron, iron brd, lounge, conv fac, ✕, bar, pool, sauna (shared), spa, bbq, rm serv, plygr, bicycle, tennis, cots. **D** ♦♦ **$149 - $235**, ♦ **$20**, AE BC DC EFT MC VI, ♿.

★★★★ **Frederickstown Motel**, (M), Cnr Frederick St & Spencer St, 800m E of PO, ☎ 08 9841 1600, fax 08 9841 8630, 36 units [shwr, tlt, hairdry, a/c-cool, heat, tel, TV, movie, radio, t/c mkg, refrig, ldry], rm serv (b'fast), cots-fee, non smoking rms (avail). **RO** ♦ **$84 - $93**, ♦♦ **$92 - $102**, ♦ **$6 - $12**, AE BC DC MC VI.

★★★★ **(Apartment Section)**, 3 apts acc up to 6, (2 bedrm), [ensuite, shwr, tlt, hairdry, a/c, TV, clock radio, refrig, cook fac, micro, blkts, linen, pillows], iron, iron brd, non smoking property. **D** ♦♦♦♦ **$145**, ♦ **$6 - $12**, Min book long w/ends and Easter.

★★★★ **Travel Inn**, (M), 191 Albany Hwy, 1.3km NW of PO, ☎ 08 9841 4144, fax 08 9841 6215, 60 units [shwr, bath (3), tlt, hairdry, a/c, heat, tel, TV, video, t/c mkg, refrig, mini bar], iron (fac), ✕, rm serv, cots, non smoking rms (some). **D** ♦♦ **$93 - $130**, ♦♦♦ **$127**, ♦ **$11**, AE BC DC MC VI.

★★★☆ **Ace Motor Inn**, (M), 314 Albany Hwy, 3km NW of PO, ☎ 08 9841 2911, fax 08 9841 4443, 54 units (4 suites) [shwr, tlt, a/c-cool, heat, elec blkts, tel, TV, movie, t/c mkg, refrig, ldry], lounge, ✕, rm serv, cots-fee, non smoking units. **D** ♦ **$67 - $72**, ♦♦ **$78 - $83**, ♦ **$10**, Suite D **$93 - $137**, AE BC DC MC.

★★★☆ **Albany International Motel**, (M), 270 Albany Hwy, 2km NW of PO, ☎ 08 9841 7399, fax 08 9841 7579, 59 units [hairdry, a/c, heat, elec blkts, tel, TV, movie, clock radio, t/c mkg, refrig], ldry, ✕, bar, pool, bbq, rm serv, plygr, tennis, cots-fee. **D** ♦ **$68 - $78**, ♦♦ **$78 - $95**, ♦♦♦♦ **$98 - $125**, AE BC DC MC VI.

★★★☆ **Amity Motor Inn**, (M), 234 Albany Hwy, 2km NW of PO, ☎ 08 9841 2200, fax 08 9841 7941, (Multi-stry gr fl), 40 units [shwr, tlt, hairdry (4), a/c-cool, elec blkts, tel, TV, movie, clock radio, t/c mkg, refrig, toaster], ldry, w/mach-fee, dryer reqd-fee, iron, iron brd, ✕, bbq, rm serv, plygr, cots, non smoking units. **D** ♦ **$60.50 - $71.50**, ♦♦ **$71.50 - $88**, ♦♦♦♦ **$93.50 - $132**, ♦ **$11**, pen con, AE BC DC MC VI.

★★★☆ **Dog Rock Motel**, (M), 303 Middleton Rd, 600m N of PO, ☎ 08 9841 4422, fax 08 9842 1027, 81 units [shwr, tlt, heat, elec blkts, tel, TV, radio, t/c mkg, refrig], conf fac, ✕, rm serv, cots-fee. **RO** ♦ **$71 - $93**, ♦♦ **$82 - $103**, ♦ **$11**, Some units of a lower rating. AE BC DC MC VI.

★★★☆ **Quality Inn - Albany**, (M), 369 Albany Hwy, 2.5km N of PO, ☎ 08 9841 1177, fax 08 9841 8337, 49 units [shwr, tlt, a/c (16), heat, tel, TV, movie, radio, t/c mkg, refrig, mini bar, ldry], conv fac, ✕, bar, bbq, rm serv, plygr, cots. **RO** ♦ **$67.75 - $96.80**, ♦♦♦♦ **$88.55 - $126**, ♦ **$11 - $22**, pen con, AE BC DC EFT MC VI.

Emu Point Motel, (M), Cnr Medcalf & Mermaid Aves, Emu Point 6330, 6.5km SE of PO, ☎ 08 9844 1001, fax 08 9844 8026, 15 units [shwr, tlt, a/c-cool, heat, elec blkts, tel, TV, clock radio, t/c mkg, refrig, cook fac ltd, toaster, ldry], bbq, cots, non smoking property. **RO** ♦ **$59 - $69**, ♦♦ **$69 - $79**, ♦ **$10**, ch con, AE BC DC MC MCH VI, (not yet classified).

Motel Le Grande, (M), 479 Albany Hwy, ☎ 08 9841 3600, fax 08 9841 5755, 24 units (1, 2 & 3 bedrm), [shwr, spa bath, tlt, heat, tel, fax, movie, t/c mkg, refrig, cook fac (3), micro (3)], ✕, bar, rm serv, non smoking property. **D** ♦♦ **$77 - $120**, AE BC DC EFT MC VI, (not yet classified).

Royal George Motel Hotel, (LMH), 62 Stirling Tce, 600m S of PO, ☎ 08 9841 1013, fax 08 9842 2407, 10 units [shwr, tlt, elec blkts, TV, radio, t/c mkg, refrig], ✕, cots. **D** ♦ **$65**, ♦♦ **$77**, ♦ **$12**, DC MC VI.

(Hotel Section), 18 rms [TV, refrig], shwr, tlt. **RO** ♦ **$30**, ♦♦ **$45**, ♦ **$11**.

Torbay View Haven, (M), RMB 9377 Cosy Corner Rd, Torbay 6330, 26km W of Albany, ☎ 08 9845 1065, fax 08 9845 1254, 10 units (2 suites) [shwr, spa bath (2), tlt, a/c-cool, heat, elec blkts, TV, radio, t/c mkg, refrig], ✕, rm serv, cots. **D** ♦ **$55 - $65**, ♦♦ **$70 - $80**, Suite D **$69**, AE BC MC VI.

Self Catering Accommodation

★★★★☆ **Balneaire Seaside Resort**, (HU), 27 Adelaide Cres, 3km E of PO, ☎ 08 9842 2877, fax 08 9842 2899, 17 units acc up to 6, (2 & 3 bedrm), [shwr, tlt, hairdry, c/fan, wood heat, tel, TV, video, clock radio, CD, t/c mkg, refrig, cook fac, micro, toaster, blkts, linen, pillows], w/mach, dryer, cots, non smoking units. **D** ♦♦ **$130 - $180**, ♦ **$15**, Min book long w/ends, BC EFT MC VI.

★★★★☆ **Foreshore Apartments**, (SA), Unit 4, 81 Proudlove Pde, 100m E of Tourist Bureau, ☎ 08 9842 8800, fax 08 9842 3522, 9 serv apts acc up to 5, (1 bedrm), [ensuite, hairdry, heat, tel, TV, movie, clock radio, refrig, cook fac, blkts, linen, pillows], ldry, w/mach, dryer, non smoking units. **D** ♦♦ **$110 - $145**, Min book all holiday times, AE BC DC MC VI.

★★★★☆ **Pelicans Holiday Village**, (HU), 3 Golf Links Rd Middleton Beach, 3.5km E of PO, ☎ 08 9841 7500, fax 08 9841 7500, 8 units acc up to 6, [shwr, tlt, heat, elec blkts, TV, video, radio, t/c mkg, refrig, cook fac, micro, toaster, ldry, blkts, linen, pillows], w/mach, dryer, iron, bbq, ✆, cots-fee, non smoking units. **D** ♦♦ **$65 - $85**, ♦ **$10**, Min book long w/ends and Easter.

Pelicans Holiday Village ...continued
(Villa Section), 6 villas acc up to 6, (2 bedrm3 bedrm), [shwr, tlt, hairdry, a/c-cool, heat, elec blkts, TV, video, radio, refrig, cook fac, micro, ldry, blkts, linen, pillows], bbq, ☎, non smoking units. D ♠♠ $85 - $130, ⚲ $10.

★★★★☆ **The Castlereagh**, (HU), 9 Flinders Parade, 3km E of PO, ☎ 08 9842 0500, fax 08 9842 0555, (2 stry gr fl), 11 units acc up to 8, [shwr, tlt, hairdry, heat, elec blkts, tel, TV, video, clock radio, CD, t/c mkg, refrig, cook fac, micro, toaster, ldry, blkts, linen, pillows], bathrm, w/mach, dryer, iron, sauna, spa (pub/priv), bbq, gym, cots. D $170 - $290, ⚲ $30, Min book all holiday times, AE BC DC MC VI.

★★★★ **Banksia Gardens Resort**, (HU), 212 Albany Hwy, 1km N of PO, ☎ 08 9842 4111, fax 08 9842 5222, 38 units acc up to 8, (1, 2 & 3 bedrm), [shwr, spa bath, tlt, hairdry, heat, tel, TV, clock radio, refrig, cook fac, micro, toaster, blkts, linen, pillows], ldry, w/mach-fee, dryer-fee, iron, bbq. D ♠♠ $104.50 - $198, ⚲ $17, BC VI.

★★★★ **Dolphin Lodge**, (Apt), 1 Adelaide Cres Middleton Beach, 3.5km E of PO, ☎ 08 9841 6600, fax 08 9841 6600, 16 apts acc up to 7, (1, 2 & 3 bedrm), [shwr, spa bath, tlt, a/c, heat, elec blkts, TV, video, radio, refrig, cook fac, micro, ldry, blkts, linen, pillows], bbq, bicycle, cots. D ♠♠ $66 - $132, ⚲ $11, AE BC CC DC EFT JCB MC VI.

★★★★ **Middleton Mews**, (HU), 180 Middleton Rd, 1.5 km E of PO, ☎ 08 9841 4080, fax 08 9841 4080, 9 units acc up to 4, (1 & 2 bedrm), [shwr, tlt, heat, elec blkts, TV, clock radio, refrig, cook fac, micro, ldry, blkts, linen], bbq, non smoking units. D ♠♠ $75 - $85, ♠♠♠♠ $70 - $85, ⚲ $10, W ♠♠ $395, ♠♠♠♠ $465, ch con, Min book long w/ends, BC MC VI.

★★★★ **My Place**, (HU), 47-61 Grey St East, 200m SW of PO, ☎ 08 9842 3242, fax 08 9842 2326, 8 units acc up to 6, (1 & 2 bedrm), [shwr, tlt, cent heat, elec blkts, clock radio, refrig, cook fac, micro, toaster, ldry, blkts, doonas, linen, pillows], w/mach-fee, dryer-fee, iron, iron brd, read rm, bbq, cots (avail), non smoking units. D ♠♠ $75 - $120, ⚲ $6 - $12, W ♠♠ $472.50 - $756, ch con, Min book all holiday times, Min book long w/ends, BC EFT MC VI.

★★★★ **Ocean Pines Holiday Unit**, (HU), 10 Middleton Rd, 2.5km E of PO, ☎ 0417 182 242, 1 unit acc up to 6, (2 bedrm), [shwr, tlt, hairdry, heat, TV, video, clock radio, CD, refrig, cook fac, micro, toaster, ldry, blkts, doonas, linen, pillows], w/mach, iron, iron brd, bbq, c/park. D $95 - $105, ch con, Min book all holiday times & long w/ends.

★★★★ **Park Avenue Holiday Units**, (HU), 13 Golf Links Rd, Middleton Beach 3km SE of PO, ☎ 08 9842 5242, fax 08 9842 5242, 5 units acc up to 6, (1 & 2 bedrm), [shwr, tlt, hairdry, a/c, elec blkts, TV, video, clock radio, refrig, cook fac, micro, toaster, blkts, doonas, linen, pillows], ldry, bbq, cots, non smoking units. D ♠ $75 - $110, ♠♠ $75 - $121, ♠♠♠♠ $95 - $121, ⚲ $10, BC MC VI.

★★★★ **The Lilacs Holiday Homes**, (Cotg), 151 Frenchman Bay Rd, 3.5km WSW of PO, ☎ 08 9841 2390, fax 08 9842 2810, 9 cotgs acc up to 7, (2 & 3 bedrm), [shwr, tlt, heat (wood), elec blkts, TV, video, refrig, cook fac, micro, ldry, blkts, linen, pillows], bbq, ☎, plygr, cots. D ♠♠ $85 - $120, ♠♠♠♠ $450 - $1,090, ch con, Some units of a lower rating. Min book all holiday times, AE BC DC MC VI, ⚲⚲.

★★★★ **West Wind Drift**, (Chalet), Loc 2782 South Coast Highway, 18km W of PO, ☎ 08 9844 6070, fax 08 9844 6170, 2 chalets acc up to 6, [ensuite, shwr, tlt, hairdry, heat, fan, wood heat, TV, video, CD (shared)], w/mach, iron, iron brd, lounge, lounge firepl, cook fac, bbq. BB ♠ $60 - $80, ♠♠ $90 - $100, ♠♠♠♠ $110 - $120, BC EFT MC VI.

★★★☆ **Albany Holiday Units**, (HU), 17 Golf Links Rd Middleton Beach via, 3km E of PO, ☎ 08 9841 7817, fax 08 9841 7819, 10 units acc up to 6, [heat, elec blkts, TV, clock radio, refrig, cook fac, micro, ldry, blkts, linen, pillows], bbq, cots. D ♠♠ $80 - $90, ⚲ $10, BC MC VI.

★★★☆ **Coraki Holiday Cottages**, (Cotg), RMB 8552 Lower King River, 11km E of PO, ☎ 08 9844 7068, fax 08 9844 1468, 6 cotgs acc up to 8, [shwr, tlt, heat (wood), TV, refrig, cook fac, blkts, linen reqd-fee, pillows], w/mach, iron, bbq, canoeing-fee, cots, Dogs allowed on leash. D ♠♠ $75 - $105, W $450 - $770, ch con, Some units of a higher rating.

★★★☆ **Woody Grange Chalets**, (Chalet), Willyung Rd King River, 12km NW of PO, ☎ 08 9844 3458, fax 08 9844 3144, 4 chalets acc up to 6, [shwr, bath, tlt, heat (wood), TV, clock radio, refrig, cook fac, micro, ldry, doonas, linen reqd-fee, pillows], iron, bbq, plygr. D ♠♠ $75 - $110, ⚲ $12, W $475 - $690, ch con, BC MC VI.

★★★ **Albany Harbourside**, (Apt), Previously Harbourside Cottages. 8 Festing St, 800m W of PO, ☎ 08 9842 1769, fax 08 9842 1769, 3 apts acc up to 8, (2 bedrm), [shwr, bath, tlt, hairdry, a/c-cool, elec blkts, clock radio, refrig, cook fac, micro, toaster, ldry, blkts, doonas, linen, pillows], w/mach, dryer, iron, iron brd, bbq, c/park (undercover), plygr, non smoking units, Pets on application. D ♠ $80, ♠♠ $90 - $120, ⚲ $15, ch con, Min book long w/ends, BC MC VI.

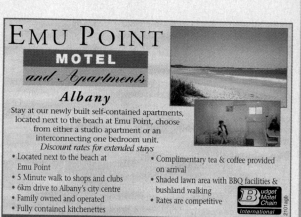
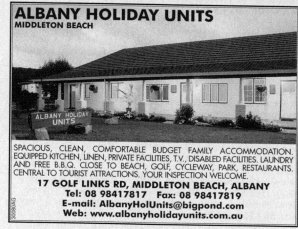
★★★ **Country Cottages**, (Cotg), RMB 8622 Nanarup Rd, 15km E of PO, ☎ 08 9846 4228, fax 08 9846 4400, 7 cotgs acc up to 15, [shwr, tlt, heat (wood), TV, refrig, cook fac, micro, blkts, linen reqd-fee, pillows], w/mach, iron, bbq, plygr, cots, Dogs welcome. D ♠♠ $66 - $88, ⚲ $11 - $16.50, W $374 - $550, BC MC VI, ⚲⚲.

★★★ **Nanarup Chalets**, (Chalet), Nanarup Rd, Nanarup, 25km E of PO, ☎ 08 9846 4444, fax 08 9846 4444, 3 chalets acc up to 7, (3 bedrm), [shwr, tlt, heat, TV, refrig, cook fac, micro, toaster, blkts, doonas, linen reqd-fee, pillows], w/mach, iron, iron brd, bbq, plygr, cots. D ♠♠ $65, ⚲ $5 - $10, BC MC VI.

★★★ **Settler's Chalet**, (Chalet), Riverside Dve, Kalgan 6330, 25km E of PO, ☎ 08 9846 4295, 1 chalet acc up to 10, [shwr, tlt, a/c-cool, wood heat, elec blkts, tel, TV, radio, refrig, cook fac, micro, toaster, blkts, doonas, linen reqd-fee, pillows], w/mach, iron, lounge, ✕, bbq, cots. D ♠ $27, ⚲ $11 - $25, ch con, Min book all holiday times.

★★☆ **Middleton Cottage**, (Cotg), 186 Middleton Beach Rd, 2km E of PO, ☎ 08 9841 1492, 1 cotg acc up to 6, [shwr, tlt, heat, TV, clock radio, refrig, cook fac, micro, toaster, blkts, doonas, linen, pillows], iron, cots (avail). D $70 - $100.

Acacia Grove Holiday House, (House), 3 Greeble St Emu Point via, 6km E of PO, ☎ 08 9761 7506, fax 08 9761 7606, 1 house acc up to 8, (3 bedrm), [shwr, bath, tlt, hairdry, fan, heat, elec blkts, TV, video, clock radio, refrig, cook fac, micro, blkts, doonas, linen, pillows], w/mach, iron, iron brd, rec rm, bbq. D ♠ $80, ♠♠ $95, ⚲ $15, Min book applies, (not yet classified).

Albany Apartments, (Apt), 280 Albany Hwy, ☎ 08 9841 5259, fax 1800 075 888, 8 apts acc up to 6, [ensuite, spa bath, a/c, TV, t/c mkg, cook fac, linen, pillows], ldry, w/mach-fee, iron, non smoking units. D ♠♠ $90 - $120, ♠♠♠♠ $100 - $130, W ♠♠ $300 - $400, AE BC MC VI, (not yet classified).

Channel Retreat, (HU), Unit 2, 3 Mermaid Ave, 7km NE of PO at Emu Point, ☎ 08 9837 1012, fax 08 9837 1012, 1 unit acc up to 8, [ensuite, a/c, heat, TV, video, clock radio, refrig, cook fac, micro, elec frypan, ldry, blkts, doonas, linen, pillows], w/mach, dryer, iron, iron brd, lounge. D ♠♠ $105 - $165, ♠♠♠♠ $120 - $165, ⚲ $15, BC MC VI.

Havana Villas, (Chalet), Cnr Birs & Firth Sts, Emu Point 6330, 8km NE of PO, ☎ 08 9844 1085, fax 08 9844 1685, 17 chalets acc up to 6, (2 bedrm), [shwr, tlt, TV, refrig, cook fac, ldry, blkts, linen reqd-fee, pillows], w/mach, dryer, bbq, cots. D $55 - $71.50, W $363 - $478.

Millbrook House, (Cotg), Lot 20 Millbrook Rd, 8km NE of PO, ☎ 08 9844 3359, fax 08 9844 3502, 1 cotg acc up to 4, [shwr, tlt, heat, TV, video, refrig, cook fac, blkts, linen, pillows], bbq, c/park (1), canoeing, non smoking property. D ♦♦ $126.50, ◊ $30.

  (**Chalet Section**), 1 chalet acc up to 4, [heat, TV, refrig, cook fac, blkts, linen, pillows]. D ♦♦ $99, ◊ $11.

Uhuru Chalets, (Chalet), Lot 213 Railway Rd, Torbay 6330, 25km SW of PO, ☎ 08 9845 1020, 2 chalets acc up to 4, [shwr, tlt, heat, TV, clock radio, t/c mkg, refrig, cook fac, micro, toaster, blkts, linen, pillows], non smoking property, Dogs allowed under control. D $75 - $85, W $525 - $595.

B&B's/Guest Houses

★★★★☆ **Flinders Park Lodge**, (GH), 3 Harbour Rd, Oyster Harbour, 6km NE of PO, ☎ 08 9844 7062, fax 08 9844 8044, 8 rms [shwr, tlt, heat, elec blkts, TV, t/c mkg, refrig, pillows], TV rm, ✕, non smoking property. BB ♦♦ $95 - $135, ◊ $25, Some units of a lower rating. BC MC VI.

★★★★ **Devine's English Style Bed & Breakfast**, (B&B), 20 Stirling Tce, 1km S of PO, ☎ 08 9841 8050, fax 08 9841 8050, 4 rms [ensuite, heat, elec blkts, TV, t/c mkg, refrig, micro, toaster, ldry, pillows], ✕ (shared). BB ♦ $49, ♦♦ $85 - $95, ♦♦♦ $110.

★★★★ **Munaleeun Farm**, (B&B), (Farm), Jackson Rd, Narrikup 6326, 13km E of Narrikup, ☎ 08 9853 2091, fax 08 9853 2090, 3 rms (1 & 2 bedrm) [fan, heat, tel, TV, radio, refrig, ldry, pillows], plygr. BB ♦♦ $110 - $130.

★★★★ **View Street Lodge B & B**, (B&B), 35 View St, 1km W of PO, ☎ 08 9842 8820, fax 08 9842 8820, 3 rms [ensuite (3), heat, tel, TV, t/c mkg, refrig, cook fac (1), pillows], non smoking property. BB ♦ $60, ♦♦ $90, ◊ $30.

★★★☆ **Doo-Kum-Inn Bed & Breakfast**, (B&B), No children's facilities, 87 Bayonet Head Rd, 7km NE of Albany PO, ☎ 08 9844 1261, 2 rms [heat, tel, TV (shared), video (shared), refrig (shared), pillows], shwr, tlt, w/mach reqd-fee, dryer reqd-fee, iron reqd-fee, iron brd reqd-fee, rec rm, TV rm, read rm, ✕, pool, t/c mkg shared, bbq, non smoking property. BB ♦♦ $55 - $60, ♦♦♦ $70 - $80, Alcohol free establishment. BC MC VI.

★★★☆ **King River Homestead**, (B&B), 64 Bushby Rd, Lower King 6330, 15km NNE of PO, ☎ 08 9844 7770, fax 08 9844 7770, 2 rms [ensuite, heat, elec blkts, tel, TV, radio, t/c mkg, refrig, pillows], lounge, bbq. BB ♦ $55, ♦♦ $75.

★★★☆ **Norman House**, (B&B), 28 Stirling Terrace, 500m S of PO, ☎ 08 9841 5995, fax 08 9841 5995, 8 rms [ensuite (3), H & C, fire pl, elec blkts, doonas, pillows], shwr, tlt, TV rm, t/c mkg shared, non smoking property. BB ♦ $50 - $60, ♦♦ $60 - $93, ♦♦♦ $99 - $121, ♿.

★★★☆ **Valencia Lodge**, (B&B), No children's facilities, 4 Valencia Cl, 4.5km NW of PO, ☎ 08 9842 3323, fax 08 9842 3323, 14 rms (2 suites) [ensuite (2), heat, elec blkts, TV, video, clock radio, refrig, doonas, pillows], shwr, tlt, ldry, w/mach, dryer, rec rm, lounge, ✕, t/c mkg shared, meals avail, ✆, non smoking property. BLB ♦ $25 - $30, ♦♦ $45 - $55, Min book long w/ends.

Albany's Cruize - Inn, (GH), 122 Middleton Rd, ☎ 08 9842 9599, fax 08 9842 9588, 3 rms [c/fan, wood heat, clock radio], shwr, tlt, ldry, w/mach-fee, dryer-fee, iron, iron brd, lounge (TV, video, cd), cook fac, t/c mkg shared, refrig, bbq, courtesy transfer, non smoking property. D ♦ $27.50, ♦♦ $55, ♦♦♦ $80, ◊ $25, W ♦♦ $330, ♦♦♦♦ $660, BC MC VI, (not yet classified).

Discovery Inn, (GH), No children's facilities, 9 Middleton Rd, 3.5km from PO, ☎ 08 9842 5535, fax 08 9842 2571, 12 rms [elec blkts, t/c mkg, pillows], TV rm, lounge (open fire), ✕. BB ♦ $41, ♦♦ $65.

Elizabeth House, (B&B), 9 Festing St, 1km S of PO, ☎ 08 9842 2734, fax 08 9842 2734, 3 rms [ensuite, tlt, heat, elec blkts, tel, TV, t/c mkg, cook fac, ldry, pillows], shwr, ✕, cots. BB ♦ $50, ♦♦ $83, ◊ $10 - $20.

Oakview Cottage Bed & Breakfast, (B&B), 34 Frederick St, 500m E of PO, ☎ 08 9841 4538, 2 rms [bath, tlt, fire pl, elec blkts, clock radio, refrig, pillows], lounge (TV, radio), shwr, iron, iron brd, ✕, t/c mkg shared. BB ♦ $55, ♦♦ $66.

AUGUSTA WA 6290

Pop 464. (320km S Perth), See map on page 906, ref A3. The State's third oldest settlement, in the south west corner of the State.

Hotels/Motels

★★★ **Augusta Motel Hotel**, (LMH), Blackwood Ave, 100m SE of PO, ☎ 08 9758 1944, fax 08 9758 1227, 52 units [shwr, tlt, heat, elec blkts, tel, TV, movie, radio, t/c mkg, refrig, cook fac (some), ldry], bathrm, ⊠, ✕, cots-fee. D ♦ $60 - $93, ♦♦ $71 - $104, ◊ $11, AE BC DC MC VI.

 ★★★ **Augusta's Georgiana Molloy Motel**, (M), 84 Blackwood Ave, 125 metres N of PO, ☎ 08 9758 1255, fax 08 9758 1033, 16 units [shwr, tlt, heat, elec blkts, tel, TV, clock radio, t/c mkg, refrig, cook fac, ldry], bbq, cots. D ♦ $70 - $85, ♦♦ $80 - $97, ♦♦♦♦ $104 - $121, ◊ $12, AE BC MC VI, ♿.

Self Catering Accommodation

 ★★★★ **Augusta Sheoak Chalets**, (Chalet), Lot 4555 Hillview Rd, 3.3km W of PO, ☎ 08 9758 1958, fax 08 9758 1901, (2 stry), 4 chalets acc up to 16, [shwr, tlt, fan, heat, TV, refrig, cook fac, ldry, doonas, linen, pillows], w/mach, bbq. D $88 - $150, ◊ $15, ch con, BC MC VI, ♿.

★★★★ **Leeuwin Ridge Chalets**, (Chalet), Lot 1 Hillview Rd, 2km W of PO, ☎ 08 9758 1443, 3 chalets acc up to 8, (3 bedrm) [shwr, tlt, H & C, heat, TV, video, radio, t/c mkg, refrig, micro, toaster, doonas, linen, pillows], w/mach, iron, iron brd, lounge, ✕, freezer, bbq, cots, non smoking property. D ♦♦ $85 - $110, ◊ $15, Min book all holiday times, BC MC VI.

★★★ **Augusta Holiday Cottages**, (Cotg), Ellis St, 100m E of PO, ☎ 08 9758 1944, fax 08 9758 1227, 5 cotgs acc up to 5, [shwr, tlt, tel, TV, movie, refrig, cook fac, ldry, blkts, linen, pillows]. D ♦♦ $110 - $132, ◊ $11, AE BC DC MC VI.

★★★ **Augusta Homes For Holidays**, (Chalet), 88 Blackwood Ave, 150m N of PO, ☎ 08 9758 1290, fax 08 9758 1291, 6 chalets acc up to 8, (2, 3 & 4 bedrm) [shwr, tlt, heat, TV, radio, cook fac, ldry, blkts, doonas, linen, pillows], w/mach, iron, lounge, ✕, bbq, boat park. D ♦♦ $80 - $160, ◊ $12 - $16, W ♦♦ $500 - $1,100, BC MC VI.

Clovelly Holiday Units, (HU), 78 Blackwood Ave, 100m N of PO, ☎ 08 9758 1577, 6 units acc up to 4, (1 & 2 bedrm) [shwr, tlt, a/c-cool, heat, refrig, cook fac, micro, blkts, linen, pillows], cots. D ♦♦ $55 - $71.50, ♦♦♦ $80, ♦♦♦♦ $90, ◊ $11, AE BC MC VI.

B&B's/Guest Houses

Maria's Budget Accommodation, (B&B), 20 Chamberlain Place, 300m N of PO, ☎ 08 9758 1049, 4 rms [hairdry, fan, tel, TV, radio, t/c mkg, doonas, pillows], shwr, tlt, w/mach-fee, iron, iron brd, lounge, ✕, cook fac, bbq, cots-fee, non smoking property. BB ♦♦ $80 - $85, ◊ $20 - $25.

Riversea Views Bed & Breakfast, (B&B), No children's facilities, 21 Ewing St, 300m NE of PO, ☎ 08 9758 1801, fax 08 9758 0104, 2 rms [hairdry, wood heat, TV, clock radio, t/c mkg, refrig, doonas, pillows], shwr, tlt, ldry, w/mach, iron, ✕, non smoking rms. BB ♦ $55, ♦♦ $75 - $82.50.

Other Accommodation

Baywatch Manor Resort, (Lodge), 88 Blackwood Ave, 150m N of PO, ☎ 08 9758 1290, fax 08 9758 1291, (Multi-stry), 12 rms [ensuite (2), c/fan, wood heat, TV, video, clock radio, refrig, blkts, doonas, linen, pillows], shwr, tlt, ldry, w/mach-fee, dryer-fee, iron, read rm, ✕, cook fac, bbq, ✆, bicycle-fee, non smoking property. RO ♦♦ $45 - $75, Min book long w/ends, BC MC VI.

AUSTRALIND WA 6233

Pop 3,666. (165km S Perth), See map on page 906, ref A2. Australind was the site for an ambitious but ill-fated plan to colonise the area and breed horses for the Indian Army. See also Bunbury.

★★★★ **Settlers Guest House**, (B&B), No children's facilities, 7 Watermass Place, 2km N of PO, ☎ 08 9725 9661, fax 08 9725 9661, 5 rms [ensuite, c/fan, wood heat, tel, TV, clock radio, refrig, doonas, pillows], ldry, rec rm, lounge, ✕, spa (indoor), t/c mkg shared, bbq, bicycle, non smoking property. BB ♦ $50 - $60, ♦♦ $85 - $90, ◊ $30 - $35, pen con, AE BC MC VI, ♿.

★★★☆ **Castlehead Bed & Breakfast**, (B&B), 44 Elinor Bell Rd, 10km NE of Bunbury, ☎ 08 9797 0272, fax 08 9797 0272, 4 rms [ensuite (1), a/c-cool, heat, elec blkts, TV, radio, t/c mkg, refrig, micro, pillows], shwr, tlt. BB ♦ $35 - $45, ♦♦ $60 - $75, BC MC VI.

The Lodge Bed & Breakfast, (B&B), 43 Elinor Bell Rd, 10km NE of Bunbury PO, ☎ 08 9797 0114, fax 08 9797 0114, 3 rms [tlt, a/c, fan, TV, video, refrig], bathrm, ldry, w/mach-fee, iron, lounge, t/c mkg shared, bbq, cots, non smoking property. BB ♦ $35 - $45, ♦♦ $60 - $70, ch con, pen con, (not yet classified).

Leschenault Bed & Breakfast, (B&B), 14 Old Coast Rd, 10km NE of Bunbury, ☎ 08 9797 1352, 4 rms [hairdry, fan, heat, TV, pillows], lounge (shared). BB ♦ $40, ♦♦ $70.

BALINGUP WA 6253

Pop part of Bridgetown, (241km S Perth), See map on page 906, ref A2. Is a small historic village situated on the famous Bibbulmun Walking Track in the heart of the Blackwood River Valley.

Self Catering Accommodation

★★★★ **Balingup Jalbrook Cottages & Alpacas**, (Cotg), Lot 1 Jayes Road, 1km E of General Store, ☎ 08 9764 1616, fax 08 9764 1615, 2 cotgs acc up to 6, [shwr, tlt, wood heat, elec blkts, radio, CD, t/c mkg, refrig, cook fac, micro, doonas, linen, pillows], bbq, cots, non smoking property. D ♦♦ $120 - $132, ◊ $10 - $15, W ♦♦ $550, BC MC VI.

★★★★ **Hillview Retreat - Balingup**, (Cotg), Lot 24 Eliott Rise, 1km E of South West Highway, ☎ 08 9764 1504, fax 08 9764 1508, 3 cotgs acc up to 15, [shwr, bath (2), spa bath (1), tlt, a/c-cool (2), c/fan, wood heat, TV, video, clock radio, CD, refrig, cook fac, micro, elec frypan (2), blkts, doonas, linen, pillows], iron, iron brd, bbq, breakfast ingredients. D ♦♦ $105 - $150, W ♦♦ $450 - $700.

★★★☆ **Woodlands Balingup**, (Cotg), (Farm), Woodlands Russell Rd, 2km N of PO, ☎ 08 9764 1272, fax 08 9764 1272, 1 cotg (3 bedrm), [shwr, tlt, a/c-cool, fire pl, tel, TV, t/c mkg, refrig, cook fac, blkts, linen, pillows], non smoking property. D ♦♦ $90, ◊ $20, ch con, BC MC VI.

★★★ **Balingup Heights**, (Chalet), Lot 6 Nannup Rd, 1 km W of PO, ☎ 08 9764 1283, fax 08 9764 1277, 4 chalets acc up to 4, [shwr, tlt, fan, wood heat, TV, refrig, cook fac, micro, doonas, linen, pillows], bbq. D ♦♦ $115 - $130, ◊ $15 - $20, ch con, BC MC VI.

Stoneridge Cottages, (Cotg), 18 Ewart Road, 9km SW of PO off Balingup-Nannup Rd, ☎ 08 9336 3250, fax 08 9463 6533, 1 cotg acc up to 4, (2 bedrm), [shwr, bath, tlt, hairdry, heat, c/fan, wood heat, radio, CD, t/c mkg, refrig, cook fac, micro, blkts, doonas, linen, pillows], lounge, bbq, non smoking property. D ♦♦ $80 - $110, ♦♦♦ $95 - $125, ♦♦♦♦ $110 - $140, W ♦♦ $350 - $450, ♦♦♦ $380 - $430, ♦♦♦♦ $410 - $460, (not yet classified).

Balinga Cottages, (Cotg), South West Hwy, 250m N of PO. On the Bibbulmun Track, ☎ 08 9764 1212, fax 08 9764 1259, 2 cotgs acc up to 6, [shwr, tlt, wood heat, tel, TV, refrig, cook fac, blkts, linen, pillows], tennis-fee, cots, Pets on application. D ♦♦ $115, ◊ $15, ch con.

Cottage Parks Lewana Valley, (Cotg), Lewana Park, Nannup Hwy via Balingup, 15km SW of PO, ☎ 08 9527 1844, fax 08 9592 5222, 6 cotgs acc up to 8, (1 & 3 bedrm), [shwr, tlt, heat, refrig, cook fac, linen reqd-fee, pillows], ldry, bbq, ✎, plygr, cots. D $60 - $80, Min book.

B&B's/Guest Houses

★★★★★ **Balingup Brook Bed & Breakfast**, (B&B), No children's facilities, Lot 109A Jayes Rd, 2km NE of PO, ☎ 08 9764 1191, fax 08 9764 1177, 3 rms [ensuite, a/c-cool, fan, heat (wood), clock radio, refrig, doonas, pillows], lounge, ✕, spa, t/c mkg shared, bbq, non smoking property. BB ♦ $120 - $150, ♦♦ $120 - $170, AE BC DC MC VI.

★★★★ **PJ's Bed & Breakfast**, (B&B), No children's facilities, Lot 1/109 Jayes Rd, 1.7km NE of PO, ☎ 08 9764 1205, fax 08 9764 1260, 3 rms [ensuite, fire pl (2), wood heat (1), tel, refrig, doonas, pillows], lounge, ✕, t/c mkg shared, bbq, non smoking rms. BB ♦ $83, ♦♦ $110, ◊ $38, BC MC VI.

Balingup Forest Lodge, (B&B), Lot 7120 Hay Rd, 4km S of PO, ☎ 08 9764 1273, 3 rms [ensuite, heat, c/fan, tel, t/c mkg, doonas, pillows], TV rm, ✕, bbq, meals avail (by arrangement), non smoking rms. BB ♦ $65, ♦♦ $100, ◊ $30, DBB ♦ $95, ♦♦ $160, ◊ $60, fam con, pen con, AE BC MC VI.

BALLADONIA WA 6443

Pop Nominal, (911km E Perth), See map on page 906, ref D7. A stopping place for tourists travelling between WA and SA.

★★★☆ **Balladonia Motel Hotel**, (LMH), Eyre Hwy, ☎ 08 9039 3453, fax 08 9039 3405, 26 units [shwr, tlt, a/c, heat, TV, video, t/c mkg, refrig (20)], ✉, cafe, bar, shop, cots-fee. D ♦ $69, ♦♦ $86 - $97, ♦♦♦♦ $105, BC.

BEVERLEY WA 6304

Pop 1,500. (129km E Perth), See map on page 906, ref B1. Standing on the banks of the Avon River, the town is situated at the southern end of the picturesque Avon Valley.

Hotels/Motels

★★☆ **Beverley Hotel**, (LH), 137 Vincent St, ☎ 08 9646 1190, fax 08 9646 1180, 14 rms bathrm, ✕, cots. RO ♦ $25, ♦♦ $50, ♦♦♦♦ $66.

Freemasons Hotel, (LH), 104 Vincent Street, 200m E of PO, ☎ 08 9646 1094, fax 08 9646 1094, 17 rms [TV, movie, t/c mkg], bathrm, lounge, ✉, bbq, cots. RO $27.50 - $66, EFT.

Self Catering Accommodation

Woonderlin Merino Stud Farmstay, (Cotg), (Farm), Lennards Rd, 6km SW of PO, ☎ 08 9646 1239, fax 08 9646 1239, 1 cotg acc up to 8, [shwr, tlt, wood heat, TV, radio, t/c mkg, refrig, micro, toaster, ldry, blkts, doonas, linen, pillows]. D $70 - $130.

BILLABONG/WANNOO WA 6530

Pop Nominal, See map on page 906, ref A6. A popular stopping place for motorists travelling to Carnarvon and north-west towns.

Billabong Homestead Hotel Motel, (LMH), Lot 3 North West Coastal Hwy, Geraldton 6530, 230 km N of Geraldton, ☎ 08 9942 5980, fax 08 9942 5983, 10 units [shwr, tlt, a/c], ldry, w/mach-fee, dryer-fee, iron-fee, TV rm, ✕, pool, bbq-fee, ✎. D ♦ $55, ♦♦ $65, ♦♦♦ $80, ◊ $15, BC EFT MC VI.

BINDOON WA 6502

Pop Nominal, (84km N Perth), See map on page 906, ref A1. Nestled in the fertile Chittering Valley.

Hotels/Motels

Bindoon Country Inn, (LMH), Lot 4 Great Northern Hwy, 3km N of Bindoon Townsite, ☎ 08 9576 1076, 4 units [shwr, tlt, heat, fan, c/fan, tel, TV, movie, t/c mkg, doonas, pillows], ldry, rec rm, lounge, lounge firepl, ✕, cafe, bar, bbq, meals to unit, c/park. D ♦ $40, ♦♦ $50, ch con, pen con, BC EFT MC VI.

B&B's/Guest Houses

★★★★ **The Chittering Bed & Breakfast**, (B&B), Lot 88 Parkside Gardens, 3km NW of PO, ☎ 08 9576 0161, fax 08 9576 0162, 3 rms [ensuite, hairdry, a/c-cool, heat, wood heat, elec blkts, tel, TV, radio, pillows], w/mach-fee, dryer-fee, iron, iron brd, ✕, t/c mkg shared, meals avail (by arrangement), non smoking property. BB ♦ $60, ♦♦ $80, ◊ $40, DBB ♦ $85, ♦♦ $130, ch con, BC EFT MC VI.

★★★☆ **The Laird's Lodge Accommodation Bindoon**, (GH), Lot 5 Great Northern Hwy, 3km N of Bindoon Townsite, ☎ 08 9576 1076, 4 rms [spa bath-fee, hairdry, heat, fan, c/fan, wood heat, tel] TV (shared), CD (shared), refrig (communal), shwr, tlt, ldry, w/mach-fee, iron, rec rm, lounge, cook fac, t/c mkg shared, bbq, plygr, picnic facilities, Pets on application. BB ♦ $60, ♦♦ $75, ♦♦♦ $80, fam con, pen con.

Windmill Farm, (B&B), Lot 101, Kay Rd, 2km N of PO, ☎ 08 9576 1136, fax 08 9576 1136, 7 rms [ensuite, shwr, tlt, a/c-cool, fan, tel, TV, video, pillows], cook fac. BB ♦ $55, ♦♦ $72, ♦♦♦♦ $80 - $110.

BODDINGTON WA 6390

Pop 367. (123km SE Perth), See map on page 906, ref B2. The Crossman and Bannister Rivers join here to form the Hotham.

Hotels/Motels

Boddington Motel, (M), 55 Bannister Rd, 10m N of PO, ☎ 08 9883 9383, fax 08 9883 8036, 9 units [shwr, tlt, a/c-cool, heat, TV, clock radio, t/c mkg, refrig, toaster], ldry, w/mach-fee, dryer-fee, iron. BB ♦ $50 - $60, ♦♦ $70 - $80, BC MC VI.

BOYANUP WA 6237

Pop 420. (195km S Perth), See map on page 906, ref A2. Small settlement located in a dairying, sheep farming and fruit growing district. See Also Bunbury.

Self Catering Accommodation

★★★★ **Meadowbrooke Farm**, (Chalet), 39 Turner St, 18km SW of Bunbury, ☎ 08 9731 5550, fax 08 9731 5771, 3 chalets acc up to 6, (2 bedrm), [shwr, bath, tlt, a/c-cool, refrig, cook fac, elec frypan, blkts, doonas, linen, pillows], ldry, rec rm, ✕, bbq, ✎, bicycle, mini golf, non smoking units. BLB ♦♦♦♦ $137.50, ◊ $10 - $20, ch con, MC, ♿.

B&B's/Guest Houses

★★★★ **Meadowbrooke Farm**, (B&B), 39 Turner St, 200metres N of PO, ☎ 08 9731 5550, fax 08 9731 5771, 3 rms [shwr, bath, tlt, a/c, t/c mkg], ldry, rec rm, ✕, plygr. BB ♦ $85 - $110, ♦♦ $93.50, ch con, MC.

BOYUP BROOK WA 6244

Pop 553. (269km SE Perth), See map on page 906, ref B2. Boyup Brook is situated on the Blackwood River in the heart of grass tree country.

Self Catering Accommodation

★★★★ **Tulip Cottage**, (Cotg), 2 Treloar St, 1km S of PO, ☎ 08 9765 1223, fax 08 9765 1223, 1 cotg acc up to 7, (4 bedrm), [shwr, bath, tlt, hairdry, a/c-cool, heat, elec blkts, tel, TV, video, clock radio, refrig, cook fac, micro, elec frypan, toaster, blkts, linen, pillows], w/mach, dryer, iron, iron brd, bbq, cots. D ♦♦ $80, ♦♦♦ $90, ♦♦♦♦ $100, ◊ $10, BC MC VI.

B&B's/Guest Houses

Boyup Brook Bed and Breakfast, (B&B), 30 Bridge Street, 0.5km S of PO, ☎ 08 9765 1223, fax 08 9765 1223, 3 rms [heat, fan, fire pl, wood heat, elec blkts, clock radio], shwr, tlt, ldry, iron, iron brd, lounge (TV, video), ✕, t/c mkg shared, refrig, bbq, non smoking property. BB ♦ $35, BC MC VI, (not yet classified).

Northlands Bed & Breakfast, (B&B), (Farm), RMB 153 Kojonup Rd, 5km SE of PO, ☎ 08 9765 1098, fax 08 9765 1520, 4 rms [fan, wood heat, elec blkts, TV, t/c mkg, pillows], bathrm, ldry, meals avail (by arrangement). BB ♦♦ $60, ch con, weekly con.

BREMER BAY WA 6338

Pop part of Gnowangerup, (515km SE Perth), See map on page 906, ref C8. Bremer Bay marks the south western corner of the magnificent Fitzgerald River National Park.

Hotels/Motels

★★★☆ **Bremer Bay Hotel**, (LH), 192 Frantom Way, 1km S of PO, ☎ 08 9837 4133, fax 08 9837 4133, 19 rms (1 suite) [shwr, tlt, a/c, heat, tel, TV, clock radio, t/c mkg, refrig, cook fac (1), toaster, ldry], ⊠, bbq, cots. D ♦ $62, ♦♦ $72, ♦♦♦ $98, ◊ $10, Suite D $110, BC MC VI, ⚹⚹.

B&B's/Guest Houses

★★★☆ **Adventurers Bed & Breakfast**, (B&B), 6 Roderick St, 200m N of PO, ☎ 08 9837 4067, fax 08 9837 4369, 3 rms [tlt, fire pl, TV, video, doonas, pillows], shwr, ldry, w/mach, iron, TV rm, ⊠, bbq, secure park, canoeing, non smoking property. BB ♦ $38.50, ♦♦ $60.50, BC MC VI.

BRIDGETOWN WA 6255

Pop 2,123. (267km S Perth), See map on page 906, ref B2. The town is in the midst of one of the prettiest areas in WA. The beautiful Blackwood river, rolling hills, rich farmland, jarrah forests, wildflowers and pine plantations.

Hotels/Motels

★★★★ **Nelson's of Bridgetown**, (M), 38 Hampton St, 700m S of PO, ☎ 08 9761 1641, fax 08 9761 2372, 40 units [shwr, tlt, a/c, heat, elec blkts, tel, clock radio, t/c mkg, refrig, mini bar, cook fac (some)], ldry, meeting rm, ⊠, spa, tennis, cots-fee. D ♦♦ $72 - $143, ◊ $15, RO ♦ $66 - $99. Some units of a lesser rating. AE BC DC MC VI, ⚹⚹.

Self Catering Accommodation

★★★☆ **Bridgetown Country Cottages**, (Cotg), Lot 419 Mattamattup St, 2km E of PO, ☎ 08 9761 1370, fax 08 9761 1370, 4 cotgs acc up to 8, (2 bedrm), [shwr, tlt, a/c-cool, wood heat, elec blkts, TV, refrig, cook fac, micro, blkts, linen, pillows], ldry, pool, bbq, ✆, tennis (half court), cots. D ♦♦ $66.50 - $88, ◊ $11, BC MC VI.

★★★☆ **Leyburn Farm Cottages**, (Cotg), (Farm), Winnejup Rd, 28km NE of PO, ☎ 08 9761 7506, fax 08 9761 7606, 2 cotgs acc up to 17, (2 & 4 bedrm), [shwr, tlt, a/c-cool, wood heat, TV, clock radio, cook fac, micro, ldry, blkts, linen reqd-fee, pillows], w/mach, bbq, cots. D ♦♦ $60 - $65, ◊ $5 - $10, W $380 - $420, ch con.

★★★☆ **Sunnyhurst Chalets**, (Chalet), (Farm), Lot 15 Doust St, 2.5km E of PO, ☎ 08 9761 1081, fax 08 9761 1081, 5 chalets acc up to 12, [shwr, tlt, a/c-cool, fire pl (log), elec blkts, tel, TV, clock radio, t/c mkg, refrig, cook fac, micro, blkts, linen reqd-fee, pillows], w/mach, pool, mini golf, cots (avail). D ♦♦ $75, ◊ $18, ch con, Min book long w/ends.

★★★ **Glenlynn Cottages**, (Cotg), Lot 12 Press Rd, 6km S of PO, ☎ 08 9761 1196, or 08 9761 2246, fax 08 9761 1196, 4 cotgs acc up to 6, (2 bedrm), [shwr, tlt, fan, wood heat, elec blkts, clock radio, refrig, micro, toaster, blkts, doonas, linen, pillows], w/mach, iron, iron brd, bbq, cots. D ♦♦ $75, W ♦♦ $330, Min book long w/ends, EFT.

Bridgetown Blues Bungalow, (House), 19 Hampton Street, 1km W of PO, ☎ 08 9757 7523, fax 08 9757 7523, 1 house acc up to 6, (2 bedrm), [ensuite, shwr, spa bath, tlt, hairdry, heat, c/fan, wood heat, TV, clock radio, CD, t/c mkg, refrig, cook fac, micro, elec frypan, blkts, doonas, linen, pillows], w/mach, iron, iron brd, lounge, bbq, c/park. D ♦♦ $95 - $135, pen con, Min book applies, (not yet classified).

Bridgetown Riverside Chalets, (Chalet), RMB 1338 Brockman Hwy, 5km W of Blackwood River Bridge, ☎ 08 9761 1040, fax 08 9761 1040, 4 chalets acc up to 8, (2 bedrm), [shwr, tlt, c/fan, wood heat, tel, TV, clock radio, refrig, cook fac, micro, elec frypan, toaster, ldry, blkts, doonas, linen reqd-fee, pillows], w/mach, tennis, cots. D ♦♦ $60, ◊ $10, Min book long w/ends.

Donnelly River Holiday Village, (Cotg), Limited facilities, Sears Rd, Manjimup 6258, 27km W of PO, ☎ 08 9772 1244, fax 08 9772 1309, 36 cotgs acc up to 12, (2, 3 & 4 bedrm), [shwr, tlt, fire pl, refrig, cook fac, blkts reqd-fee, linen reqd-fee], ldry, rec rm, TV rm, bbq, shop, plygr, tennis, D $65 - $135, W $295 - $750, AE BC DC MC VI.

Lucieville Farm Chalets, (Chalet), (Farm), RMB 390 South Western Hwy, 8km S of PO, ☎ 08 9761 1733, fax 08 9761 2213, 6 chalets acc up to 11, [shwr, tlt, fire pl, refrig, cook fac, micro, ldry, blkts, doonas, linen reqd-fee, pillows], bbq, plygr, canoeing. D ♦♦ $65 - $77, ♦♦♦♦ $71.50 - $85, ◊ $5.50, Farm activities, horse riding.

(Cottage Section), 1 cotg acc up to 14, [shwr, tlt, refrig, cook fac, blkts, doonas, linen reqd-fee, pillows], bbq. D ♦♦ $65 - $77.

B&B's/Guest Houses

★★★★☆ **Aislinn House of Ford House**, (B&B), Eedle Terrace, 500m S of PO, ☎ 08 9761 1816, fax 08 9761 1816, 2 rms [ensuite, shwr, bath, spa bath, tlt, fan, elec blkts, TV, video, clock radio], ldry, w/mach, iron, iron brd, lounge (cd, stereo), lounge firepl, ✗, cook fac, t/c mkg shared, refrig, bbq, canoeing, cots-fee, non smoking property. BB ♦♦ $135 - $145.

★★★★☆ **Woodlands of Bridgetown**, (B&B), No children's facilities, Lot 75 South West Highway, 1.5km N of PO, ☎ 08 9761 1106, fax 08 9761 4023, 3 rms [ensuite, shwr, spa bath, tlt, hairdry, a/c-cool, heat, fire pl, elec blkts, tel, TV, clock radio, t/c mkg, refrig, doonas, pillows], lounge, ✗, tennis, non smoking property. BB ♦♦ $132 - $165, AE BC DC MC VI.

★★★★ **Hi Life Guesthouse**, (GH), No children's facilities, 28 Carey St, 2km S of PO, ☎ 08 9761 2104, fax 08 9761 2104, 3 rms [ensuite, spa bath (1), hairdry, a/c-cool, cent heat, TV, clock radio, doonas, pillows], TV rm, ⊠, t/c mkg shared, bbq, meals avail, non smoking property. BB ♦♦ $100 - $120, AE BC DC MC VI.

★★★★ **Tortoiseshell Farm**, (B&B), Loc 5608 Polina Road, 14km E of PO via Kangaroo Gully, ☎ 08 9761 1089, fax 08 9761 1089, (2 stry), 3 rms [shwr (2), bath (2), tlt, heat, c/fan, wood heat, tel, TV, video, CD], iron, iron brd, lounge, lounge firepl, ✗, spa, t/c mkg shared, refrig, bbq, plygr, mini golf, non smoking property. BB ♦ $65 - $75, ♦♦ $85 - $95, ch con.

★★★☆ **Ford House**, (B&B), Eedle Tce, 1km S of PO, ☎ 08 9761 1816, fax 08 9761 1816, 3 rms [fan, heat, wood heat, elec blkts, TV, clock radio, CD, doonas, pillows], shwr, tlt, iron, lounge, ✗, refrig, bbq, cots, non smoking property. BB ♦ $55, DBB ♦ $88.

★★★☆ **Riverwood House**, (B&B), Lot 887 South Western Hwy, 2km S of PO, ☎ 08 9761 1862, fax 08 9761 1862, 2 rms [shwr, tlt, fan, heat, elec blkts, clock radio, t/c mkg, refrig, pillows], lounge, ✗. BB ♦ $55 - $60, ♦♦ $82 - $88.

★★★☆ **Windy Hollow**, (B&B), Henderson Rd, 6km E of PO, ☎ 08 9761 2523, fax 08 9761 2523, 3 rms [tlt, wood heat, elec blkts, t/c mkg, refrig, pillows], shwr, lounge, tennis. BB ♦♦ $99, ◊ $27.50.

(Tree House Section), 1 rm [shwr, tlt, wood heat, t/c mkg, refrig, toaster, pillows]. BB ♦♦ $99, ◊ $27.50.

★★★ **The Old Well**, (B&B), 16 Gifford Rd, 1km E of PO, ☎ 08 9761 2032, 2 rms [shwr, tlt, fan, heat, elec blkts, clock radio, t/c mkg, refrig, pillows], bbq, cots, Pets allowed. BB ♦ $40, ♦♦ $80.

Hampton House, (B&B), 26 Hampton St, 1km S of PO, ☎ 08 9761 2526, fax 08 9761 2536, 3 rms [shwr, tlt, heat, elec blkts, TV, clock radio, pillows], t/c mkg shared. BB ♦ $50, ♦♦ $80, BC MC VI.

Pamela's Retreat, (B&B), Lot 36 Bovell St, 2.5km SE of PO, ☎ 08 9761 1108, fax 08 9761 1108, 3 rms [shwr, bath, tlt, heat, elec blkts, tel, TV, radio, t/c mkg, cook fac ltd, pillows], w/mach, dryer, iron, spa (room), refrig, bbq. BB ♦ $38, ♦♦ $75, W ♦♦ $350.

Other Accommodation

Bridgetown Valley Lodge, (Lodge), Previously Blackwood Valley Lodge 43 Spencer St, 150m E of PO, ☎ 08 9761 4144, fax 08 9761 4400, 21 rms acc up to 8, [heat, fire pl (lounge), TV, clock radio, toaster, blkts, linen] refrig (communal), shwr, tlt, w/mach, dryer, iron, iron brd, lounge, ✗, cook fac, t/c mkg shared, non smoking property. RO ♦ $22, ◊ $11, BC EFT MC VI, (not yet classified).

BROOKTON WA 6306

Pop 595. (137km E Perth), See map on page 906, ref B1. A small country town located in the centre of a mixed farming district.

Bedford Arms Hotel, (LH), 12 Robinson Rd, Opposite Railway Station, ☎ 08 9642 1172, fax 08 9642 1362, 8 rms [heat, TV, t/c mkg, refrig, toaster], shwr, tlt, lounge, ✗, ⊠, bar, bbq, meals avail, c/park. BB ♦ $35, ♦♦ $50, ♦♦♦ $60, BC EFT VI, (not yet classified).

BROOME WA 6725

Pop 3,666. (2237km N Perth), See map on page 906, ref C3. Broome must surely be one of Western Australia's most interesting towns with its remarkable history and numerous local attractions. Broome's pearling sheds are an attraction unparalled elsewhere in Australia.

Hotels/Motels

★★★★★ **Cable Beach Inter-Continental Resort**, (Ltd Lic H), Cable Beach Rd, 4km NW of PO, ☎ 08 9192 0400, fax 08 9192 2249, 179 rms (3 suites) [shwr, bath, tlt, a/c, fan, tel, TV, clock radio, t/c mkg, refrig, ldry], conv fac, ✗ (4), bar, pool (2), plygr, tennis (8). D $286 - $371, Suite D $647 - $1,295, AE BC DC MC VI, ⚹⚹.

(Bungalow Section), 84 units acc up to 6, (1 & 2 bedrm), [shwr, bath, tlt, a/c-cool, fan, TV, clock radio, refrig, cook fac, blkts, linen, pillows]. D $369 - $419.

★★★★ **Broome Motel**, (M), 34 Frederick St, 600m SW of PO, ☎ 08 9192 7775, fax 08 9192 7772, 29 units [shwr, tlt, a/c-cool, c/fan, tel, fax, TV, clock radio, t/c mkg, refrig, micro, elec frypan, toaster], ldry, w/mach, dryer, iron, pool, bbq, cots-fee. D ♦♦ $72 - $115, ♦ $22 - $28, Min book all holiday times, BC MC VI.

★★★★ **Mercure Inn Continental Broome**, (LH), Weld St, 1km S of PO, ☎ 08 9192 1002, fax 08 9192 1715, 66 rms [shwr, bath (some), tlt, a/c, fan, tel, TV, movie, radio, t/c mkg, ldry], conv fac, ✕, pool, rm serv, tennis, cots. D ♦♦ $165 - $187, ♦♦♦♦ $220 - $242, AE BC DC MC VI, ♠⊟.

★★★★ **The Mangrove Hotel**, (LMH), 120 Carnarvon Street, 800m S of PO, ☎ 08 9192 1303, fax 08 9193 5169, 68 units [shwr, tlt, hairdry, a/c-cool, tel, TV, movie, radio, t/c mkg, refrig], iron, iron brd, conv fac (2), ✕, cafe, bar, pool (2), spa (2), cots. D ♦♦ $130 - $165, AE BC DC MC VI.

★★★☆ **Palms Resort - Broome**, (M), Cnr Hopkins & Herbert St, 2km SW of PO, ☎ 08 9192 1898, fax 08 9192 2424, 48 units (1 & 2 bedrm), [shwr, tlt, a/c, TV, movie, radio, refrig, cook fac, ldry], ⊠, ✕, bar, pool, spa. BLB $119 - $145, ♦ $25, Some units of a lower rating.

★★★ **Ocean Lodge**, (LMH), Cable Beach Rd, 1.8km W of PO, ☎ 08 9193 7700, fax 08 9193 7496, (2 stry gr fl), 58 units [shwr, tlt, a/c-cool, fan, tel, TV, clock radio, refrig, cook fac, ldry, pillows], pool, bbq, cots (avail). D ♦♦ $74 - $104, ♦♦♦♦ $86 - $120, ♦ $5 - $10, ch con, seasonal variation, AE BC DC JCB MC MCH VI.

★★★ **Tropicana Inn**, (LMH), Cnr Saville & Robinson Sts, 1km S of PO, ☎ 08 9192 1204, or 08 9321 9611, fax 08 9192 2583, 90 units [shwr, tlt, a/c, tel, TV, movie, t/c mkg, refrig], ⊠, pool, cots. D ♦♦ $80 - $135, ♦ $20, AE BC DC MC VI.

★★☆ **Roebuck Bay Hotel**, (LMH), Carnarvon St, 1km NE of PO, ☎ 08 9192 1221, fax 08 9192 2390, 37 units [a/c, tel, TV, movie, t/c mkg, refrig, ldry], ⊠, pool, cots. D ♦ $70 - $125, ♦♦ $88 - $125, Some units of a higher rating. AE BC DC MC VI.

Self Catering Accommodation

★★★★☆ **Bali Hai Resort**, (Villa), 6 Murray Road Cable Beach, 700m from Cable Beach, ☎ 08 9191 3100, fax 08 9191 3133, 15 villas acc up to 6, (1, 2 & 3 bedrm), [shwr, tlt, a/c-cool, c/fan, tel, TV, movie, refrig, cook fac, micro, d/wash, blkts, linen, pillows], w/mach, dryer, iron, iron brd, pool, spa (shared), bbq, bicycle-fee, non smoking property. D $140 - $275, AE BC DC EFT MC VI.

★★★★☆ **Blue Seas Resort**, (SA), 10 Sanctuary Road, 6.5km W of PO, ☎ 08 9192 0999, fax 08 9192 1900, 44 serv apts acc up to 4, (1 bedrm), [shwr, tlt, a/c-cool, c/fan, tel, TV, movie, clock radio, CD, refrig, cook fac, micro, d/wash, blkts, linen, pillows], w/mach, dryer, iron, iron brd, pool-heated, bbq, cots. D ♦♦♦♦ $128 - $186, ♦ $20, W ♦♦♦♦ $590 - $1,246, ch con, AE BC EFT MC VI.

★★★★☆ **Moonlight Bay**, (SA), Carnarvon St, 1.5km E of PO, ☎ 08 9193 7888, fax 08 9193 7999, (2 stry gr fl), 54 serv apts acc up to 6, (1 & 2 bedrm), [ensuite, bath, hairdry, a/c, c/fan, tel, TV, clock radio, t/c mkg, refrig, cook fac, toaster, ldry (services), blkts, linen, pillows], ldry, w/mach-fee, dryer-fee, pool, spa, cots. D ♦♦ $154 - $212, ♦ $22, ch con, BC DC MC VI.

★★★★☆ **Seashells Resort Broome**, (SA), 10 Challenor Drive, Sunset Park, Cable Beach 6726, 5km N of PO, ☎ 08 9192 6111, fax 08 9192 6166, 49 serv apts (1, 2 & 3 bedrm), [shwr, bath, spa bath (1 bedrm units), tlt, hairdry, a/c, tel, TV, movie, clock radio, refrig, cook fac, micro, d/wash, ldry, blkts, doonas, linen, pillows], w/mach, iron, iron brd, pool, wading pool, spa, bbq, plygr, cots. D $140 - $290, AE BC DC EFT MC VI.

★★★★ **Broome Beach Resort**, (HU), 4 Murray Rd, Cable Beach 6726, 5km NW of PO, ☎ 08 9158 3300, fax 08 9158 3339, 35 units acc up to 6, (1, 2 & 3 bedrm), [shwr, bath (27), tlt, a/c, tel, TV, movie, clock radio, refrig, cook fac, micro, d/wash, toaster, blkts, linen, pillows], w/mach, dryer, iron, pool, bbq, cots. D $140 - $176, AE BC DC MC VI.

★★★★ **Cable Beachside**, (HU), Murray Rd, Cable Beach 5km N of PO, ☎ 08 9193 5545, fax 08 9193 5549, 16 units acc up to 6, (1, 2 & 3 bedrm), [shwr, tlt, a/c-cool, c/fan, tel, TV, movie, clock radio, t/c mkg, refrig, cook fac, micro, toaster, ldry, blkts, doonas, linen, pillows], w/mach, iron, iron brd, pool, bbq, c/park (undercover), cots-fee, non smoking rms. D $120 - $230, AE BC DC MC VI.

★★★★ **Cocos Beach Bungalows**, (Chalet), 11 Sanctuary Rd, 300m from Cable Beach, ☎ 08 9192 3873, fax 08 9158 3339, 3 chalets acc up to 6, (3 bedrm), [shwr, bath, tlt, a/c-cool, c/fan, TV, video, clock radio, t/c mkg, refrig, micro, d/wash, blkts, linen, pillows], w/mach, dryer, iron, iron brd, bbq, c/park. D $180 - $220, W $900 - $1,400, Min book applies, AE BC DC MC VI.

★★★★ **Habitat Beach Resort**, (SA), Port Dr, 6km S of PO, ☎ 08 9158 3520, fax 08 9158 3599, 30 serv apts acc up to 6, (1, 2 & 3 bedrm), [shwr, tlt, a/c-cool, c/fan, TV, movie, clock radio, refrig, cook fac, micro, d/wash, toaster, ldry, blkts, linen, pillows], w/mach, dryer, iron, iron brd, pool, bbq, courtesy transfer, golf, cots, non smoking units. D $121 - $164, AE BC DC MC VI.

★★★☆ **Bayside Holiday Apartments**, (SA), Cnr Anne & Hammersley Sts, 1.5km E of PO, ☎ 08 9192 6426, fax 08 9193 7999, 12 serv apts acc up to 4, (1 & 2 bedrm), [ensuite, shwr, tlt, a/c, c/fan, TV, refrig, cook fac, toaster, blkts, linen, pillows], ldry, w/mach, dryer, bbq, cots. D ♦♦ $122, ♦♦♦♦ $190, BC MC VI.

★★★ **Broome Apartments Park Court**, (HU), 7 Haas St, 150m S of PO, ☎ 08 9193 5887, fax 08 9192 8299, 9 units acc up to 6, (1, 2 & 3 bedrm), [shwr, tlt, a/c, TV, t/c mkg, refrig, cook fac (7), blkts, linen, pillows], w/mach (7), bbq, cots (/s), non smoking units. D $60 - $185, W $414 - $1,165.

★★☆ **Lombadina Aboriginal Corporation**, Cape Leveque Rd Cape Leveque via, 200km N of Broome on Dampier Peninsula, ☎ 08 9192 4936, fax 08 9192 4116, 4 cabins acc up to 6, (2 bedrm), [shwr, tlt, a/c-cool, c/fan, tel, refrig, cook fac, blkts, doonas, linen, pillows], ldry, w/mach, iron, rec rm, bbq, meals avail, shop, ice, plygr. D $132, BC MC VI.

(Backpacker Section), 3 bunkhouses acc up to 4, (Bunk Rooms), [c/fan, refrig, blkts, doonas, linen, pillows], shwr (2), tlt (2), ldry, w/mach, iron, cook fac, bbq, ☎. RO ♦ $38.50.

B&B's/Guest Houses

★★★★ McAlpine House, (GH), No children's facilities, 84 Herbert St, 2km SE of GPO, ☎ 08 9192 3886, fax 08 9192 3887, 6 rms [ensuite (3), shwr, bath, tlt, H & C, hairdry, a/c-cool, fan, c/fan, tel, TV, video (shared), CD (shared), t/c mkg, refrig, ldry (service), doonas, pillows], shwr (2), tlt (2), ldry, w/mach, iron, iron brd, TV rm, business centre, ✕, pool, cook fac, bbq, secure park, non smoking rms. **BB** ♥♥ **$156 - $289, ♥♥♥♥ $980 - $1,540**, AE BC DC EFT MC VI.

★★★★ The Temple Tree B&B, (B&B), 31 Anne St, 1.5km SW of PO, ☎ 08 9193 5728, 2 rms [ensuite, a/c-cool, c/fan, tel, TV, clock radio, t/c mkg, refrig, pillows], ldry, w/mach, iron, iron brd, ✕, bbq, bicycle (/s). **BB ♥ $70 - $80, ♥♥ $85 - $95, ♥♥♥♥ $150 - $170**, BC MC VI.

Broometime Lodge, (GH), 59 Forrest St, 1km SW of PO, ☎ 08 9193 5067, fax 08 9193 5067, 26 rms [ensuite, a/c-cool, c/fan, refrig, ldry], TV rm, ✕, pool. **RO ♥ $55, ♥♥ $75**, BC EFT MC VI.

Harmony Broome, (B&B), Lot 5/1208 Broome Rd, 5km E of PO, ☎ 08 9193 7439, fax 08 9193 7429, 4 rms [a/c-cool, c/fan, tel, TV, video, t/c mkg, pillows], shwr, tlt, iron, iron brd, lounge, pool, meals avail (by arrangement). **BB ♥ $50, ♥♥ $80**.

BULLSBROOK WA 6084

Pop part of Perth, (44km N Perth), See map on page 906, ref D2. Small town in the vineyard district, adjoining Pearce R.A.A.F. Base. Walynuga National Park.

B&B's/Guest Houses

Peace Be Still Guest House, (GH), Lot 100 Chittering Rd, Lower Chittering 6084, 13km NE of PO, ☎ 08 9571 8108, fax 08 9571 8108, 18 rms [shwr, tlt (6), pillows], shwr, ✕, bbq. **RO ♥ $70 - $75, ♥♥ $140, ◊ $70**, Camping area.

BUNBURY WA 6230

Pop 24,944. (180km S Perth), See map on page 906, ref A2. Bunbury is the regional capital and gateway to Western Australia's beautiful South West. Fishing, Golf, Horse Riding, Sailing, Squash, Swimming, Tennis, Water Skiing. See Also Australind.

Hotels/Motels

★★★★☆ The Lord Forrest Hotel, (LH), 20 Symmons St, 400m N of PO, ☎ 08 9721 9966, fax 08 9721 1845, (Multi-stry), 115 rms (13 suites) [shwr, spa bath (some), tlt, a/c-cool, heat, tel, TV, movie, radio, t/c mkg], lift, conf fac, ✕, ✕, bar, pool-heated, sauna, spa, rm serv, c/park (undercover), gym. **D $132 - $209, Suite D $225 - $357**, AE BC DC MC VI, ♿.

★★★★ The Clifton, (M), 2 Molloy St, 800m NW of PO, ☎ 08 9721 4300, fax 08 9791 2726, 48 units (6 suites) [shwr, tlt, a/c, heat, tel, TV, movie, radio, t/c mkg, refrig], ✕, pool, sauna, spa, bbq, rm serv, cots. **D ♥♥ $93.50 - $122, ◊ $15, Suite D $154 - $187**, Some units of a lower rating. AE BC DC MC VI.

(Flat Section), 4 flats acc up to 6, (2 bedrm), [shwr, tlt, a/c-cool, heat, TV, clock radio, t/c mkg]. **D $132 ◊ $15,**.

★★★☆ Admiral Motor Inn, (M), 56 Spencer Street, 1km S of PO, ☎ 08 9721 7322, fax 08 9721 7185, 43 units (3 suites) [shwr, bath (3), tlt, a/c, tel, TV, movie, radio, t/c mkg, refrig], conv fac, ✕, bar (cocktail), pool, cots-fee. **RO ♥ $85, ♥♥ $105, ♥♥♥♥ $130, ◊ $10, Suite RO $115 - $140**, Min book long w/ends, AE BC DC MC VI.

★★★ Chateau La-Mer Motor Lodge, (M), 99 Ocean Dve, 1km SW of PO, ☎ 08 9721 3166, fax 08 9721 3963, 28 units [shwr, tlt, a/c, heat, tel, TV, video-fee, t/c mkg, refrig, cook fac (2)], ldry, pool, bbq, cots-fee. **D ♥ $50 - $72, ♥♥ $72 - $83, ♥♥♥♥ $99 - $121**, AE BC DC MC VI, ♿.

★★★ Bunbury Motel, (M), 45 Forrest Ave, 2km S of PO, ☎ 08 9721 7333, fax 08 9791 1065, 37 units [shwr, tlt, a/c, tel, TV, movie, radio, t/c mkg, refrig, toaster], ✕, pool, bbq, cots. **D ♥ $62 - $72, ♥♥ $70 - $83**, Min book long w/ends, AE BC DC MC MCH VI.

★★★ Fawlty Towers Lodge, (M), 205 Ocean Dve, 2.5km S of PO, ☎ 08 9721 2427, fax 08 9721 2427, 12 units [shwr, tlt, fan, heat, TV, movie, radio, t/c mkg, refrig], pool-heated. **BLB ♥ $65, ♥♥ $75, ♥♥♥♥ $105**, BC MC VI.

★★★ Ocean Drive Motel, (M), 121 Ocean Dve, 1.5km SW of PO, ☎ 08 9721 2033, fax 08 9721 2736, 26 units [ensuite, shwr, tlt, a/c, tel, TV, clock radio, t/c mkg, refrig, ldry], bbq, meals to unit (b'fast). **D ♥ $60 - $70, ♥♥ $70 - $80, ♥♥♥♥ $80 - $110, ◊ $10**, AE BC DC MC VI.

★★★ Welcome Inn Motel, (M), Ocean Dve, 1km SW of PO, ☎ 08 9721 3100, fax 08 9791 2858, 51 units [shwr, tlt, a/c, heat, tel, TV, video (22), radio, t/c mkg, refrig, cook fac (some), ldry], ✕, bar, pool, spa (10), bbq, cots-fee. **D ♥ $59 - $119, ♥♥ $65 - $129, ♥♥♥♥ $109, ◊ $5.50 - $11**, Some units of a higher rating. AE BC DC MC VI.

★★☆ Parade Hotel, (LH), Previously Parade Hotel Motel 100 Stirling St. 2km S of PO, ☎ 08 9721 2933, fax 08 9791 2245, 9 rms [shwr, tlt, a/c, TV, t/c mkg]. **RO ♥ $60.50, ♥♥ $88**.

(Hotel Section), 5 rms shwr, tlt. **RO ♥ $26.50, ♥♥ $42.75**.

Highway Motel Hotel, (LMH), Cnr Forrest Ave & Spencer St, 1.3km S of PO, ☎ 08 9721 4966, fax 08 9791 3746, 8 units [shwr, tlt, a/c, tel, TV, radio, t/c mkg, refrig], cots. **D $66**, AE BC MC VI.

(Hotel Section), 9 rms [tlt], shwr. **RO ♥ $33, ♥♥ $44**.

Rose Motel Hotel, (LMH), Victoria St, 250m N of PO, ☎ 08 9721 4533, fax 08 9721 8285, 25 units [shwr, tlt, TV, radio, t/c mkg, refrig], ✕. **BB ♥ $75.90, ♥♥ $86.90, ♥♥♥♥ $97.90**, AE BC MC VI.

Self Catering Accommodation

★★★★☆ Quest Bunbury, (SA), Cnr Koombana Dve & Lyons Dve, 500m E of PO, ☎ 08 9722 0777, fax 08 9791 7112, (2 stry), 52 serv apts acc up to 6, (Studio, 1, 2 & 3 bedrm), [shwr, bath, tlt, hairdry, a/c, c/fan, tel, fax, TV, clock radio, refrig, cook fac, micro, d/wash, blkts, linen, pillows], w/mach, dryer, iron, iron brd, pool, bbq, tennis (court), cots, non smoking units. **D $143**, AE BC DC EFT MC VI, ♿.

★★★★☆ The Sanctuary Resort, (SA), Resort, Old Coast Rd Pelican Point, 8km N of PO, ☎ 08 9725 2777, fax 08 9725 2998, (2 stry), 38 serv apts acc up to 5, (1 & 2 bedrm), [shwr, spa bath (10), tlt, a/c, c/fan, tel, TV, video, clock radio, refrig, cook fac, micro, toaster, blkts, doonas, linen, pillows], ldry, iron, iron brd, conv fac, ✕, ✕, cafe, bar, pool, golf (18 holes), tennis. **D ♥♥ $170 - $187, W ♥ $706 - $776, ♥♥ $953 - $1,048, Suite D $244 - $268**, AE BC DC MC VI.

★★★★ Ellens Cottage C.1878, (Cotg), Classified by National Trust, No children's facilities, 41 King Road, 3km SE of PO, ☎ 08 9721 4082, fax 08 9791 1620, 1 cotg acc up to 4, (2 bedrm), [shwr, bath, tlt, hairdry, heat, fire pl, elec blkts, radio, refrig, cook fac, micro, toaster, ldry, blkts, doonas, linen, pillows], w/mach, dryer, iron, non smoking property. **D ♥♥ $110, ◊ $33**.

Everview Chalets, (Chalet), RMB 237 Ratcliffe Rd, Ferguson 6236, 22km SE of PO, ☎ 08 9728 3098, fax 08 9728 3098, 3 chalets acc up to 5, [shwr, tlt, heat, fan, tel, TV, clock radio, refrig, cook fac, micro, toaster, blkts, doonas, linen, pillows], w/mach, iron, bbq, plygr, bicycle, cots, non smoking property. **D ♥ $40, ♥♥ $70, ♥♥♥♥ $80 - $95, ◊ $10, W $400**, pen con.

Ferguson Farmstay, (Chalet), Lot 2 Henty Rd, Ferguson 6236, 22km E of PO, ☎ 08 9728 1392, fax 08 9728 1392, 6 chalets acc up to 10, (2 bedrm), [wood heat, tel, TV, radio, refrig, cook fac, toaster, blkts, doonas, linen reqd-fee, pillows], ldry, w/mach, iron, bbq, cots. **D $90 - $100, W $540 - $600**.

Wellington Mill Farm, (Cotg), Weetman Rd, Wellington Mills 6236, 18km SE of PO, ☎ 08 9728 3077, fax 08 9728 3077, 1 cotg acc up to 8, (4 bedrm), [shwr (2), bath, tlt (2), hairdry, fan, wood heat, TV, clock radio, refrig, cook fac, micro, blkts, doonas, linen, pillows], w/mach, iron, iron brd, read rm, bbq, meals avail (by arrangement), canoeing, tennis, non smoking property. **D $150 - $200, ◊ $10, W $700 - $800**.

B&B's/Guest Houses

★★★★★ Grittleton Lodge, (B&B), No children's facilities, 2 Molloy St, 800m NW of PO, ☎ 08 9721 4300, fax 08 9791 2726, (2 stry), 4 rms (4 suites) [shwr, spa bath, tlt, hairdry, a/c, fire pl, elec blkts, tel, TV, video, movie, clock radio, t/c mkg, refrig, mini bar], ldry, w/mach, dryer, iron, lounge, ✕, pool-heated, sauna, spa, rm serv, secure park, cots-fee, non smoking property. **BB $80 - $240**, AE BC DC EFT JCB MC MP VI.

★★★★ Kingtree Lodge, (B&B), Kingtree Rd, Wellington Mills 6236, 33km E of PO, ☎ 08 9728 3050, fax 08 9728 3113, 4 rms [shwr, bath (1), tlt, fire pl, heat, tel, TV, t/c mkg, ldry (services), pillows], ✕, spa, tennis. **BB ♥♥ $198, DBB ♥♥ $275**.

★★★★ Joy & Peter's Bed & Breakfast, (B&B), Lot 103 Jaymon Rd, Stratham 6237, 15km S of PO, ☎ 08 9795 8336, fax 08 9795 8339, 2 rms [ensuite, a/c-cool, heat, TV, clock radio, refrig, doonas, pillows], ldry, lounge, ✕, t/c mkg shared, bbq, meals avail, plygr, non smoking property. **BB ♥ $38.50, ♥♥ $71.50**, Alcohol free establishment.

Marlston Hill Bed & Breakfast, (B&B), No children's facilities, 1 Sinclair Close, Marlston Hill, 1km N of PO, ☎ 08 9721 3914, 2 rms [ensuite, heat, fan, tel, TV, clock radio, refrig, doonas, pillows], ldry, lounge, ✕, t/c mkg shared, non smoking property. **BB ♥♥ $90**.

Other Accommodation

Wander Inn Budget Tourist Guest House, (Lodge), 16 Clifton St, 800m N of PO, ☎ 08 9721 3242, fax 08 9721 3242, 28 rms [fan, heat, fax, TV, video, refrig, ldry, blkts, linen, pillows], shwr, tlt, rec rm, read rm, lounge, ✕, cook fac, bbq, courtesy transfer, ✆, non smoking property. **RO ♥ $18 - $28, ♥♥ $45**.

BUREKUP WA 6227

(168km S Perth), See map on page 906, ref A2.
Evedon Park, (Chalet), Lennard Rd, 20km NE of Bunbury at Burekup, ☎ 08 9726 3012, fax 08 9726 3397, 6 chalets acc up to 5, [shwr, tlt, fire pl, TV, clock radio, refrig, cook fac, blkts, linen, pillows]. **D ♦♦ $88 - $99, ⚲ $11, W ♦♦ $432**, BC MC VI.

   (Holiday Unit Section), 10 units acc up to 4, (2 bedrm), [shwr, tlt, TV, clock radio, refrig, cook fac, blkts, linen, pillows]. **D ♦♦ $88 - $99, ⚲ $11, W ♦♦ $432**.

BUSSELTON WA 6280

*Pop 10,642. (229km S Perth), See map on page 906, ref A2.
Situated in a sheltered position on the shores of Geographe Bay.
The old jetty, 2km long, is the longest wooden jetty in the southern
hemisphere.*

Hotels/Motels

★★★★★ **Abbey Beach Resort**, (LH), 595 Bussell Hwy, 7km W of PO, ☎ 08 9755 4600, fax 08 9755 4610, 116 rms [shwr, bath, spa bath, tlt, hairdry, a/c, tel, TV, video, clock radio, CD, t/c mkg, refrig, cook fac (30), micro, toaster, doonas, pillows], lift, ldry, w/mach, dryer, lounge, business centre, conf fac, ✕, cafe, bar, pool indoor heated, wading pool, sauna, spa, bbq, 24hr reception, rm serv, bicycle-fee, gym, squash, tennis, cots-fee, non smoking property. **D ♦♦ $71 - $188, ♦♦♦♦ $135 - $209**, pen con, AE BC DC EFT MC VI, ♿.

★★★ **Amaroo Motor Lodge**, (M), 31 Bussell Hwy, 1km W of PO, ☎ 08 9752 1544, fax 08 9752 1979, 40 units [shwr, tlt, a/c (avail), heat, elec blkts, tel, TV, radio, t/c mkg, refrig], ✕, bbq, cots. **D ♦ $65 - $90, ♦♦ $75 - $95, ⚲ $8**, ch con, AE BC DC MC VI.

★★★ **Gale Street Motel and Villas**, (M), 40 Gale St, 300m W of PO, ☎ 08 9754 1200, fax 08 9754 2187, 13 units [shwr, tlt, a/c, tel, TV, video, movie, t/c mkg, refrig, mini bar], bbq, plygr, cots-fee. **D ♦ $50 - $77, ♦♦ $61 - $77, ⚲ $11**, AE BC DC EFT MC VI.

   ★★★★☆ **(Villa Section)**, 8 villas acc up to 6, (1, 2 & 3 bedrm), [ensuite, shwr, bath, tlt, a/c (1&2 bdrm), heat, fan, TV, clock radio, t/c mkg, refrig, mini bar, cook fac, micro, blkts, linen, pillows], w/mach, iron, iron brd, bbq, cots. **D ♦ $85 - $187, ♦♦ $90 - $197, ♦♦♦ $110 - $197, ♦♦♦♦ $120 - $197, ⚲ $11**.

★★★ **Paradise Motel**, (M), Pries Ave, 500m SW of PO, ☎ 08 9752 1200, fax 08 9754 1348, 32 units [shwr, tlt, tel, TV, video (7), radio, t/c mkg, refrig], ✕, pool, cots. **D ♦ $49.50 - $66, ♦♦ $55 - $77, ♦♦♦♦ $93.50 - $133.50, ⚲ $11**, BC MC VI.

★★★ **Restawile Motel**, (M), 340 Bussell Hwy, 4.5km W of PO, ☎ 08 9754 4600, fax 08 9754 4600, 12 units [shwr, tlt, heat, TV, radio, t/c mkg, refrig, cook fac (some), toaster, ldry], pool, bbq, plygr. **D ♦♦ $50 - $60, ⚲ $11**.

★★★ **Riviera Motor Inn**, (M), 44 Bussell Hwy, 1km W of PO, ☎ 08 9752 1555, fax 08 9752 4847, 30 units [shwr, tlt, a/c, elec blkts, tel, TV, video-fee, movie, radio, t/c mkg, refrig, ldry], ✕, pool, spa, bbq, rm serv, tennis, cots-fee. **D ♦ $50 - $65, ♦♦ $60 - $80, ♦♦♦♦ $85 - $120, ⚲ $10**, AE BC DC MC VI.

★★★ **The Geographe Bayview Resort**, (LMH), Bussell Hwy, 6km W of PO, ☎ 08 9755 4166, fax 08 9755 4075, 27 units [shwr, tlt, a/c, heat, tel, TV, video, radio, t/c mkg, refrig, mini bar, pillows], conv fac, ✕, cafe (breakfast), bar, pool (outdoor), pool indoor heated, sauna, spa, bbq, plygr, golf (putt/chipping green), gym (mini), squash, tennis, cots-fee. **D ♦ $112.20 - $132, ♦♦ $121.55 - $143, ⚲ $16.50**, AE BC DC EFT MC VI, ♿.

★★★ **Vasse River Resort Busselton**, (M), 70 Causeway Rd, 1km S of PO, ☎ 08 9752 3000, fax 08 9752 2554, 34 units (1 suite) [ensuite, shwr, tlt, a/c, elec blkts, tel, TV, movie, radio, t/c mkg, refrig, mini bar], ✕, pool, tennis, cots-fee. **D ♦ $81.40, ♦♦ $97.90, ⚲ $10**, AE BC DC JCB MC VI, ♿.

Commercial Hotel, (LH), 117 Queen St, 200m SW of PO, ☎ 08 9752 1166, fax 08 9752 1132, 23 rms [shwr (6), tlt (6), a/c-cool, t/c mkg, refrig], c/park. **RO ♦ $20 - $40, ♦♦ $40 - $60**.

Motel Busselton, (M), 90 Bussell Hwy, 1.5km W of PO, ☎ 08 9752 1908, 10 units [shwr, tlt, fan, heat, elec blkts, TV, t/c mkg, refrig], cots. **BB ♦ $33, ♦♦ $38.50**, ch con.

Self Catering Accommodation

★★★★★ **Abbey Beach Resort**, (SA), 595 Bussell Hwy, 7km W of PO, ☎ 08 9755 4600, fax 08 9755 4610, (2 stry gr fl), 69 serv apts acc up to 8, (1, 2 & 3 bedrm), [shwr, tlt, hairdry, a/c, tel, TV, video, clock radio, t/c mkg, refrig, cook fac, ldry, blkts, linen, pillows], w/mach, dryer, business centre, conf fac, ✕, cafe, bar (2), pool, pool-indoor (heated), sauna, spa, bbq, plygr, bicycle-fee, gym, ski hire (wave ski), squash, tennis, cots-fee. **D $135 - $209, W $835 - $1,332**, AE BC DC MC VI, ♿.

★★★★★ **Broadwater Beach Resort**, (HU), Cnr Bussell Hwy & Holgate Rd, 6km W of PO, ☎ 08 9754 1633, fax 08 9754 1151, 65 units acc up to 6, (1, 2 & 3 bedrm), [shwr, tlt, a/c, fan, heat, tel, TV, video, clock radio, t/c mkg, refrig, cook fac, ldry, blkts, linen, pillows], ✕, bar (cafe), pool indoor heated, spa, bbq, secure park, tennis, cots. **D $181 - $324**, Min book school holidays and Easter, AE BC DC MC VI.

★★★★☆ **Mandalay Holiday Resort**, (Villa), 652 Geographe Bay Road, 4km W of PO, ☎ 08 9752 1328, fax 08 9752 2835, 4 villas acc up to 6, (2 bedrm), [shwr, spa bath, tlt, a/c-cool, fan, heat, elec blkts, TV, video, refrig, cook fac, micro, d/wash, blkts, linen, pillows], w/mach, dryer, rec rm (games), pool, bbq, shop, plygr, cots. **D ♦♦ $136 - $218, ⚲ $12, W $815 - $1,300**, Min book applies, AE BC MC VI.

★★★★☆ **The Geographe Bayview Resort Villas**, (HU), Bussell Hwy, 6km W of PO, ☎ 08 9755 4166, fax 08 9755 4075, 58 units acc up to 8, (1, 2 & 3 bedrm), [shwr, tlt, fan, tel, TV, video, refrig, cook fac, micro, ldry, blkts, linen, pillows], w/mach, dryer, conv fac, ✕, cafe (b'fast), bar, pool (outdoor), pool indoor heated, sauna, spa (5 units), bbq, plygr, golf (putt/chipping green), gym (mini), squash, tennis, cots-fee. **D $113.15 - $242**, AE BC DC EFT MC VI, ♿.

★★★★ **Amalfi Resort**, (Villa), 13 Earnshaw Road, 3.5km W of Busselton turn off, off Bussell Highway, ☎ 08 9754 3311, fax 08 9754 3322, 48 villas acc up to 8, [shwr, tlt, a/c, fan, tel, fax, TV, video, clock radio, t/c mkg, refrig, cook fac, micro, d/wash (5), toaster, blkts, linen, pillows], w/mach, dryer, iron, iron brd, pool-heated, wading pool, spa (shared), bbq, tennis, cots-fee, non smoking property. **D ♦♦♦♦ $102 - $152, W ♦♦♦♦ $572 - $852**, pen con, Min book long w/ends, AE BC DC EFT MC VI.

★★★★ **Busselton Villas**, (HU), 163 Bussell Hwy, 1.5km W of PO, ☎ 08 9752 1175, fax 08 9752 1175, 20 units acc up to 6, (1 & 2 bedrm), [shwr, tlt, fan, heat, TV, video, refrig, cook fac, ldry, blkts, linen, pillows], plygr, cots (avail). **D ♦♦ $120, ⚲ $10, W $480 - $980**, BC MC VI.

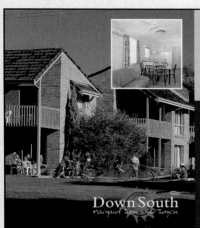

BUSSELTON WA continued...

★★★ **Busselton Jetty Chalets**, (Chalet), 94 Marine Tce, 800m NE of PO, ☎ 08 9752 3893, fax 08 9752 2149, 11 chalets acc up to 5, (2 bedrm), [shwr, tlt, fan, heat, elec blkts, TV, radio, refrig, cook fac, ldry, blkts, linen, pillows], bbq, plygr. **D** ♦♦ $85 - $160, ⊚ $12, **W** $480 - $1,120, pen con, BC MC VI.

★★★ **Kerriley Park Farmstyle Holidays**, (Cotg), Resort, Yelverton North Rd, Yelverton via Busselton, 14km S of Dunsborough PO, ☎ 08 9755 7524, fax 08 9755 7017, 4 cotgs acc up to 7, [shwr, tlt, heat, TV, refrig, cook fac, blkts, linen reqd-fee, pillows], bbq, canoeing, **D** ♦♦♦♦ $110, **W** ♦♦♦♦ $550, ⊚ $25, Farm activities. AE BC DC EFT MC VI.

Prospect Villa, (Cotg), No children's facilities, 1 Pries Ave, 150m S of South West Hwy, ☎ 08 9752 2273, fax 08 9752 2273, 1 cotg acc up to 3, [ensuite, bath, hairdry, a/c, c/fan, TV, video, t/c mkg, refrig, micro, blkts, linen, pillows], iron, iron brd, lounge, non smoking property. **D** ♦♦ $125, ♦♦♦ $145, **W** $750, ♦♦♦ $850, MC VI, (not yet classified).

Busselton Beach Resort, (HU), Cnr Geographe Bay Rd & Guerin St, 4km E of PO, ☎ 08 9752 3444, fax 08 9752 4701, 32 units acc up to 8, (2 & 3 bedrm), [ensuite (9), shwr, tlt, c/fan, heat (gas), tel, TV, clock radio, refrig, cook fac, micro, elec frypan, toaster, blkts, linen, pillows], ldry, w/mach-fee, dryer-fee, iron, pool, sauna, spa, bbq, rm serv-fee, plygr, bicycle, mini golf, squash, tennis. **D** $120 - $185, **W** $500 - $1,280, Min book all holiday times, BC MC VI.

Restawile Holiday Flats, (HF), 340 Bussell Hwy, 4.5km W of PO, ☎ 08 9754 4600, fax 08 9754 4600, 7 flats acc up to 5, (1 & 2 bedrm), [shwr, tlt, heat, fan, TV, radio, refrig, cook fac, ldry, blkts, linen, pillows], pool, bbq, plygr. **D** ♦♦ $55 - $77, Min book.

Seascape Holiday Apartments, (HU), 982 Geograph Bay Rd, 3km E of PO, ☎ 08 9752 1328, or 08 9752 1328, fax 08 9752 2835, 4 units acc up to 5, [shwr, tlt, fan, heat, TV, clock radio, refrig, cook fac, micro, ldry, blkts, linen, pillows], bbq, plygr. **D** ♦♦ $93 - $168, ⊚ $12, **W** ♦♦ $520 - $1,010, Min book all holiday times, AE BC MC VI.

Siesta Park Villas, (HU), Caves Rd, 12km W of PO, ☎ 08 9755 4016, or 08 9755 4722, (Multi-stry gr fl), 32 units acc up to 8, (1, 2 & 3 bedrm), [shwr, tlt, heat, elec blkts, TV, t/c mkg, refrig, cook fac, blkts, linen, pillows], bbq, shop, petrol, ☏, plygr, tennis, cots. **W** $330 - $960, pen con.

Tall Timbers Cottage, (Cotg), Carter Rd off Metricup Rd, Carbunup River 6280, Metricup, 8km N of Cowaramup, ☎ 08 9755 7539, fax 08 9755 7539, 2 cotgs acc up to 8, (1 & 2 bedrm), [shwr, tlt, heat, TV, refrig, cook fac, ldry, blkts, linen reqd-fee, pillows], bbq, Pets on application. **D** $81 - $102, **W** $486 - $648.

B&B's/Guest Houses

★★★★ **Geographe Guest House**, (GH), Not suitable for children under 8yrs. 28 West St, 1km NW of PO, ☎ 08 9752 1451, fax 08 9752 1451, 8 rms [ensuite (8), hairdry, c/fan, heat, elec blkts, t/c mkg, refrig, pillows], iron, TV rm (has wood stove), non smoking property, **BB** ♦ $60, ♦♦ $80, BC MC VI.

★★★★ **Kinvarra Park Lodge**, (GH), No children's facilities, Pries Rd, Vasse 6282, 1km S of junction of Caves Rd & Bussell Hwy, ☎ 08 9755 4203, 4 rms [ensuite (2), shwr, tlt, c/fan, wood heat, tel, TV, video, refrig, doonas, pillows], iron, iron brd, TV rm, read rm, ✕, t/c mkg shared, bbq, non smoking property. **BB** ♦ $60, ♦♦ $85 **Min book all holiday times.**

★★★★ **Martinfields**, (GH), Lot 25 Lockville Rd Wonnerup, 8km E of PO, ☎ 08 9754 2001, fax 08 9754 2034, (2 stry), 8 rms (7 suites) [ensuite, shwr, bath (1), tlt, heat, wood heat, elec blkts, tel, TV, t/c mkg, doonas, pillows], ldry, TV rm, ✕, bbq, meals avail (by arrangement), courtesy transfer, bicycle, non smoking suites. **BB** ♦ $65, ♦♦ $100.

★★★★ **Prospect Villa Historic House**, (B&B), 1 Pries Ave, 500m SW of PO, mob 0417 099 307, fax 08 9752 2273, 3 rms [ensuite (2), shwr, tlt, fan, heat, TV, t/c mkg, refrig, cook fac, pillows]. **BB** ♦ $75, ♦♦ $75 - $88, AE BC MC.

★★★ **Jacaranda Guest House**, (GH), 30 West St, 1km NW of PO, ☎ 08 9752 1246, fax 08 9754 2910, 7 rms [ensuite, fan, elec blkts, t/c mkg, refrig, doonas, pillows], TV rm, read rm, spa, meals avail. **BB** ♦ $55, ♦♦ $82 - $70, **DBB** ♦♦ $120, pen con.

★★★ **Villa Carlotta Country House Hotel**, (GH), 110 Adelaide St, 1km NW of PO, ☎ 08 9754 2026, fax 08 9754 2029, 22 rms [shwr, tlt, elec blkts, pillows], TV rm, ✕. **BB** ♦ $30, ♦♦ $45, ⊚ $15.

Ambergate Bed & Breakfast, (B&B), Edwards Rd, off Ambergate Rd, 11km S of PO, ☎ 08 9753 1132, fax 08 9753 1102, 3 rms [tlt, fan, c/fan, elec blkts, TV, video, t/c mkg, pillows], shwr, ldry, w/mach, dryer, iron, refrig, bbq, cots, non smoking property. **BB** ♦ $50, ♦♦ $70, ♦♦♦♦ $110.

Busselton Travellers' Rest, (GH), Limited facilities, 223 Bussell Hwy, 3km W of PO, ☎ 08 9752 2290, fax 08 9752 2290, 6 rms [tlt, fire pl, elec blkts, t/c mkg, refrig, pillows], shwr, TV rm. **BB** ♦♦ $50 - $65.

Just For You Bed & Breakfast, (B&B), 93 Bussell Hwy, 1.3km W of first set of traffic lights, ☎ 08 9754 7559, 4 rms [shwr, tlt, fan, wood heat, TV, clock radio, refrig], ldry, w/mach, iron, iron brd, ✕, t/c mkg shared, cots. **BB** ♦ $40, ♦♦ $60, ⊚ $15, pen con.

Wright's Place, (B&B), 9 Peaker Crt, 1km W of PO, ☎ 08 9752 1302, 1 rm [shwr, tlt, a/c-cool, fan, heat, elec blkts, tel, TV, t/c mkg, refrig, pillows], ldry. **BB** ♦♦ $60, **RO** ♦♦ $50, Min book.

Other Accommodation

Busselton Backpackers Hostel, 14 Peel Terrace, 500m from PO, ☎ 08 9754 2763, 7 rms [wood heat, tel, TV, blkts, doonas, linen, pillows], shwr, tlt, ldry, w/mach, iron, cook fac, refrig, bbq, non smoking property. **D** ♦ $15, ♦♦ $30, **RO** ♦ $20 - $25, ♦♦ $30 - $35.

CARNARVON WA 6701

Pop 6,357. (902km N Perth), See map on page 906, ref A5. The busy commercial centre for the rich Gascoyne District.

Hotels/Motels

★★★☆ **Fascine Lodge Motel Hotel**, (LMH), 1002 David Brand Dve, 1km NE of PO, ☎ 08 9941 2411, fax 08 9941 2491, 61 units [shwr, tlt, a/c, tel, TV, radio, refrig], conv fac, ✉, pool. **D** ♦ $99, ♦♦ $105, ♦♦♦♦ $121, Some units of a higher rating. AE BC DC MC VI.

★★★☆ **Gateway Motel**, (M), 379 Robinson St, 3km SE of PO, ☎ 08 9941 1532, fax 08 9941 2606, 66 units [shwr, tlt, a/c, TV, radio, t/c mkg, refrig], ✕, pool, cots. **D** ♦♦ $99, ♦♦♦♦ $126, ⊚ $20, AE BC DC MC VI.

★★★☆ **Hospitality Inn Carnarvon**, (M), West St, 1km W of PO, ☎ 08 9941 1600, fax 08 9941 2405, 45 units [shwr, tlt, a/c, tel, TV, movie, radio, t/c mkg, refrig], ✉, pool, bbq, rm serv, plygr, cots, non smoking units (avail). **D** ♦ $105, ♦♦ $105, ⊚ $22, ch con, pen con, Some units of a lower rating. AE BC DC MC VI.

★★ **Carnarvon Hotel**, (LMH), Olivia Tce, 300m W of PO, ☎ 08 9941 1181, fax 08 9941 2811, 27 units [shwr, tlt, a/c, TV, t/c mkg, refrig]. **D** ♦ $45, ♦♦ $65, ♦♦♦♦ $100.

(Hotel Section), 8 rms [fan, TV, t/c mkg, refrig], shwr, tlt. **RO** ♦ $30, ♦♦ $45.

Port Hotel, (LMH), Robinson St, 250m E of PO, ☎ 08 9941 1704, fax 08 9941 1835, 17 units [shwr, tlt, a/c-cool, TV, t/c mkg], bar, pool, bbq. **D** ♦ $30, ♦♦ $40, BC MC VI.

(Hotel Section), 34 rms shwr, tlt, shared fac. **D** ♦ $12.

Self Catering Accommodation

★★★ **Carnarvon Close Holiday Units**, (HU), 96-116 Robinson St, 1km NE of PO, ☎ 08 9941 1317, fax 08 9941 4184, 19 units acc up to 6, [shwr, evap cool, TV, refrig, cook fac, blkts, linen, pillows], w/mach. **D** ♦♦ $75, ch con, BC EFT MC VI.

Carnarvon Beach Holiday Resort, (HU), Pelican Point Rd Pelican Point, 6km NW of PO, ☎ 08 9941 2226, fax 08 9941 2216, 12 units acc up to 7, (2 bedrm), [shwr, tlt, fan, c/fan (1), TV, t/c mkg, refrig, cook fac, micro, elec frypan, toaster, blkts, doonas, linen], ldry, w/mach, iron, secure park (4), ☏, canoeing, cots (avail). **D** ♦ $65, ♦♦ $75, ⊚ $10, ch con, pen con, Min book all holiday times, BC MC VI.

Quobba Station, Quobba Station, 80km N of Carnarvon, ☎ 08 9941 2036, fax 08 9941 2036, 9 cabins acc up to 12, [shwr (4), tlt, refrig, cook fac, blkts reqd, linen reqd, pillows reqd], shwr. **D** ♦ $6.60 - $8.80, ♦♦ $39.60 - $48.40, ⊚ $20, Outback Station with camping area. Limited power.

Other Accommodation

Gnaraloo Station, (Lodge), (Farm), Limited facilities, Via Carnarvon, 145km N of Carnarvon, ☎ 08 9388 2881, fax 08 9388 2887, 1 rm acc up to 20, [refrig, cook fac, ldry, blkts reqd, linen reqd], shwr, tlt, bbq, mini mart, shop. **D** ♦ $30, ch con.

(Cabin Section), 1 cabin acc up to 15, [blkts, linen, pillows], shwr, tlt, cook fac. **D** ♦ $30, ch con.

Yalardy Station, (Bunk), Via Carnarvon, 25km N of Overlander Roadhouse & 94km E, ☎ 08 9942 5904, fax 08 9942 5904, 12 bunkhouses [blkts, linen], shwr, bbq. **DBB** ♦ $45, **D** ♦ $10, Camping area avail.

Carnarvon Backpackers, 97 Olivia Tce, 150m SW of PO, ☎ 08 9941 1095, fax 08 9941 1095, 12 rms acc up to 58, (Bunk Rooms), [a/c, fan, c/fan, TV, refrig, ldry, blkts, linen, pillows], shwr, w/mach-fee, dryer-fee, iron, rec rm, TV rm, read rm, cook fac, refrig, bbq, ☏, bicycle, canoeing. **D** ♦ $15 - $16.50, ch con, AE BC MC VI.

CARNEGIE HOMESTEAD WA 6646

Pop Nominal, (949km NE Perth), See map on page 906, ref D5.
Carnegie Homestead, Limited facilities, PMB 4 Western end of original Gunbarrel Hwy, Wiluna 6646, 353km E of Wiluna, ☎ 08 9981 2991, fax 08 9981 2994, 10 cabins [shwr, tlt, cook fac, linen]. **D ⋔ $8 - $30.**

CARRABIN WA 6423

Pop Nominal, (302km E Perth), See map on page 906, ref C7. A small town on the Great Eastern Highway between Merredin and Southern Cross.
Carrabin Motel Roadhouse, (LH), Great Eastern Hwy, ☎ 08 9046 7162, 4 rms [a/c], bathrm, ✕, mini mart (fuel). **D ⋔ $28, ⋔⋔ $35 - $40.**
(Camping Area Section), (Powered Site). **Powered Site D $9.**

CERVANTES WA 6511

Pop 242. (247km N Perth), See map on page 906, ref A7. A small but thriving fishing town.
Hotels/Motels

★★★☆ **Cervantes Pinnacles Motel**, (M), 227 Aragon St, 150m E of PO, ☎ 08 9652 7145, fax 08 9652 7214, 40 units (1 & 2 bedrm), [shwr, a/c, TV, radio, t/c mkg, refrig, cook fac (some)], w/mach, ✕, ☒, pool, cots.
RO ⋔⋔ $99 - $110, ⋔⋔⋔⋔ $132 - $148, AE BC DC MC VI, ₤&.
Self Catering Accommodation
Cervantes Beachfront Units, (HU), 34 Iberia St, 300m W of PO, ☎ 08 9652 7194, fax 08 9652 7579, 2 units acc up to 8, [shwr, tlt, heat, TV, refrig, cook fac, ldry, blkts reqd, linen reqd-fee], rec rm. **D $50 - $55, W $330 - $440.**
Cervantes Holiday Homes, (HU), 2 Valencia Rd, 500m SE of PO, ☎ 08 9652 7115, fax 08 9652 7115, 5 units acc up to 7, (2 & 3 bedrm), [shwr, tlt, refrig, cook fac, ldry, blkts, linen (supplied to some) reqd-fee], bbq. **D $58 - $66, ◊ $8, W $245 - $400.**
Other Accommodation
Pinnacles Beach Backpackers, 91 Seville St, 1km SW of PO, ☎ 08 9652 7377, fax 08 9652 7318, 9 rms [shwr, tlt, heat, fan, TV, video, radio, blkts, linen reqd, pillows], ldry, w/mach-fee, TV rm, cook fac, refrig, bbq, courtesy transfer reqd-fee, ✎, bicycle, non smoking property. **RO ⋔ $17, ⋔⋔ $45 - $55, ◊ $17, W ⋔ $110, ⋔⋔ $280**, BC MC VI, ₤&.

COCKLEBIDDY WA 6443

Pop Nominal, (1163km E Perth), See map on page 906, ref E7. A stopping point on the Eyre Highway 1163km east of Perth and 438km east of Norseman.
★☆ **Wedgetail Inn**, (LMH), Eyre Hwy, 438km E of Norseman, ☎ 08 9039 3462, fax 08 9039 3403, 24 units [shwr, tlt, a/c (20), t/c mkg, refrig (20)], ☒, bar, cots-fee. **D ⋔ $40 - $60, ⋔⋔ $48 - $70, ⋔⋔⋔⋔ $60 - $88**, Some units of a lower rating. BC.

COLLIE WA 6225

Pop 7,194. (202km S Perth), See map on page 906, ref A2. Collie, set in the heavily timbered jarrah country of the Darling Range, is the centre of the State's only coalfield.
★★★★ **Banksia Motel**, (M), 44 Wittenoom St, 1km NE of PO, ☎ 08 9734 5655, fax 08 9734 7080, 22 units [shwr, bath, tlt, hairdry (2), a/c-cool, tel, fax, TV, video (2), radio, t/c mkg, refrig], iron, iron brd, TV rm, business centre, conf fac, ✕, pool, bbq, c/park. **D ⋔ $99 - $143, ◊ $20**, AE BC DC EFT MC VI, ₤&.
Club Motel Hotel, (LMH), 63 Forrest St, 1km NW of PO, ☎ 08 9734 1722, fax 08 9734 3797, 21 units [shwr, tlt, a/c-cool, TV, t/c mkg], ☒. **RO ⋔ $55 - $66, ⋔⋔ $66 - $77**, AE BC DC MC VI.
Collie Forest Motor Lodge, (M), Atkinson St, 1.5km SW of PO, ☎ 08 9734 3388, fax 08 9734 4666, 18 units [shwr, tlt, a/c, elec blkts, tel, TV, clock radio, t/c mkg, refrig, cook fac, ldry], bbq. **D ⋔ $74, ⋔⋔ $87**, BC MC VI.
Collie Motel, (M), 127 Throssell St, 800m W of PO, ☎ 08 9734 1166, fax 08 9734 2713, 32 units [shwr, tlt, a/c, TV, radio, t/c mkg, refrig], ✕, ✎, cots-fee. **D ⋔ $40 - $60, ⋔⋔ $50 - $72, ⋔⋔⋔⋔ $84 - $96**, AE BC DC MC VI.

COOLGARDIE WA 6429

Pop 1,200. (557km E Perth), See map on page 906, ref C7. It is a pleasant inland town.
★★★ **Coolgardie Motel**, (M), 49 Bayley St, opposite PO, ☎ 08 9026 6080, fax 08 9026 6300, 27 units [shwr, tlt, a/c, tel, TV, clock radio, t/c mkg, refrig], ☒, pool, bbq, cots-fee. **D ⋔ $50, ⋔⋔ $65, ⋔⋔⋔⋔ $80, ◊ $10**, AE BC DC MC VI.

CORAL BAY WA 6701

Pop part of Exmouth, (1131km N Perth), See map on page 906, ref A5. WA's biggest and most accessible coral reef.
Ningaloo Reef Resort, (LMH), Robinson St, Coral Bay, ☎ 08 9942 5934, fax 08 9942 5953, 34 units [shwr, tlt, a/c, c/fan (9), TV, t/c mkg, refrig, cook fac (9)], ☒, pool, cots. **D ⋔ $104.50 - $120, ⋔⋔ $140 - $159.50.**
Self Catering Accommodation
Coral Bay Lodge, (HU), Robinson St, ☎ 08 9385 7411, fax 08 9385 7413, 24 units acc up to 6, [shwr, tlt, a/c, TV, refrig, cook fac, ldry, blkts, linen, pillows], bbq, tennis. **D ⋔⋔ $110 - $125**, BC MC VI.
Other Accommodation
Bayview Coral Bay Backpackers, French St, ☎ 08 9942 5932, fax 08 9385 7413, 25 rms acc up to 50, [a/c (15), fan, TV, refrig, blkts reqd-fee, linen, pillows], shwr, tlt, ldry, w/mach-fee, ✕, pool, cook fac, refrig, bbq, courtesy transfer, ✎, plygr, tennis. **D ⋔ $18 - $20, ◊ $18 - $20**, BC EFT MC VI.

CORRIGIN WA 6375

Pop 841. (230km SE Perth), See map on page 906, ref B1. It is the hub of a rich and progressive agricultural district.
Corrigin Windmill Motel, (M), Brookton Highway, 700m SE of PO, ☎ 08 9063 2390, fax 08 9063 2235, 10 units [ensuite, a/c (5), fan, heat, elec blkts, fax, TV, video-fee, movie, clock radio, t/c mkg, micro, toaster], ☒. **D ⋔⋔ $70 - $85**, AE BC DC MC VI.
(Lodge Section), 6 rms acc up to 2, [fan, heat, elec blkts, TV, refrig], lounge (TV). **RO ⋔ $38, ⋔⋔ $53.**

COWARAMUP WA 6284

Pop Nominal, (265km S Perth), See map on page 906, ref A2. The Northern Gateway to the Augusta/Margaret River shire. See Also Margaret River.
Self Catering Accommodation
★★★★ **Ellensbrook Cottages**, (Cotg), Ellensbrook Rd, 10km NW of PO, ☎ 08 9755 5880, fax 08 9755 5518, 2 cotgs acc up to 6, (2 bedrm), [shwr, spa bath, tlt, hairdry, a/c-cool, TV, video, clock radio, CD, t/c mkg, refrig, micro, toaster, ldry, blkts, doonas, linen, pillows], w/mach, iron, iron brd, TV rm, lounge, ✕, freezer, bbq, plygr, cots, non smoking rms. **D $150 - $175, W $968 - $1,078**, Min book all holiday times,Min book long w/ends, BC MC VI.
★★★★ **Forest Rise Chalets**, (Chalet), Yelverton Rd, Margaret River, ☎ 08 9384 1331, fax 08 9384 9626, 4 chalets acc up to 6, (1 & 2 bedrm), [shwr, spa bath, tlt, hairdry, fan (/s), wood heat, TV, video, clock radio, CD, cook fac, micro, linen, pillows], w/mach, dryer, iron, iron brd, bbq, bicycle (/s). **D ⋔⋔ $150 - $180, ⋔⋔⋔ $170 - $200, ⋔⋔⋔⋔ $190 - $220, ◊ $20**, Min book long w/ends and Easter, BC MC VI.
★★★★ **Sunset Ridge**, (HU), Peake St, 500m NW of PO, ☎ 08 9755 5239, fax 08 9755 5404, 1 unit acc up to 2, [shwr, tlt, fan, heat, elec blkts, TV, video, clock radio, t/c mkg, refrig, cook fac, micro, toaster, blkts, linen, pillows], ldry, w/mach, dryer, iron, bbq, ✎. **D $95 - $115, ◊ $15 - $25, W $450 - $600, ◊ $150 - $200**, Min book long w/ends.
Adinfern Farm, (Cotg), Bussell Hwy, 4km S of PO, ☎ 08 9755 5272, fax 08 9755 5206, 2 cotgs acc up to 6, (2 bedrm), [shwr, tlt, wood heat, elec blkts, tel, TV, clock radio, refrig, cook fac, micro, toaster, ldry, blkts, doonas, linen, pillows], w/mach, bbq, cots, non smoking units. **D ⋔⋔ $70 - $100, ◊ $10 - $15**, Min book all holiday times, BC MC VI.
Bettenay's Redgum Ridge, (Chalet), Harman's South Rd, 7km N of PO, ☎ 08 9755 5539, fax 08 9755 5539, 2 chalets acc up to 8, (2 & 3 bedrm), [ensuite (1), shwr, bath, tlt, fan, wood heat, tel, TV, video, clock radio, CD, refrig, cook fac, micro, toaster, ldry, doonas, linen], w/mach, iron, iron brd, bbq, tennis. **D ⋔⋔ $88 - $132, W ⋔ $510 - $792**, ch con, BC MC VI.
Gazebo Lake Chalets, (Chalet), RSM 431, Metricup Rd, Busselton 6280, 6km NW of PO, ☎ 08 9755 7575, fax 08 9755 7502, 10 chalets acc up to 6, [shwr, spa bath (3), tlt, hairdry, c/fan, fire pl, TV, clock radio, t/c mkg, refrig, cook fac, micro, toaster, blkts, linen, pillows]. **D ⋔⋔ $90 - $180, ◊ $20 - $50**, BC MC VI.
B&B's/Guest Houses
★★★★★ **Karriview Lodge**, (GH), Caves Rd, 600m S of Cowaramup Bay Rd, ☎ 08 9755 5553, fax 08 9755 5534, 12 rms [ensuite, a/c, fan, fire pl, TV, pillows], lounge (2), conv fac, ✕, spa (9), bbq, bicycle, golf, gym, tennis. **BB ⋔⋔ $170 - $300, ◊ $40**, AE BC DC MC VI.
(Cottage Section), 1 cotg acc up to 6, (2 bedrm), [shwr, tlt, TV, refrig, cook fac]. **D ⋔⋔⋔⋔ $240, ◊ $20.**

COWARAMUP WA continued...

★★★★ **Craythorne Country House**, (B&B), Worgan Rd, 7km N of PO, ☎ 08 9755 7477, fax 08 9755 7477, 4 rms [ensuite, hairdry, heat, c/fan, wood heat, elec blkts, fax, TV (shared), video (shared), clock radio, CD (shared), t/c mkg, refrig], lounge (guest), non smoking property. **BB** ♦ **$90**, ♦♦ **$120**, ♦♦♦ **$150**, BC EFT MC VI.

★★★★ **Sandyknowe Bed & Breakfast**, (B&B), Miamup Rd, 3km NW of PO, ☎ 08 9755 5336, fax 08 9755 5336, 3 rms [ensuite (2), c/fan, elec blkts, TV (2), video, clock radio, t/c mkg, refrig, pillows], shwr, lounge, ✕, cook fac, cots. **BB** ♦ **$66**, ♦♦ **$99**, ⚲.

★★★☆ **The Noble Grape**, (GH), Lot 18 Bussell Hwy, 500m N of PO, ☎ 08 9755 5538, fax 08 9755 5538, 6 rms [c/fan, heat, TV, t/c mkg, refrig, pillows], bathrm, cots, non smoking rms. **BLB** ♦ **$82**, ♦♦ **$99**, AE BC DC MC VI, ⚲.

Old Bakehouse, (B&B), Unsuitable for children under 10yrs. Bussell Hwy, 100m N of PO. ☎ 08 9755 5462, fax 08 9755 5671, 3 rms [ensuite, c/fan, heat (wood), elec blkts, TV, video, t/c mkg, refrig, pillows], lounge, ✕, bbq. **BB** ♦♦ **$82 - $90**, **D** ⚲ **$22**, Min book school holidays and Easter, Min book long w/ends and Easter, AE BC MC VI.

CUE WA 6640

Pop 374. (649km NE Perth), See map on page 906, ref B6. Cue, was once the most important mining centre in the Murchison Goldfields.

★★☆ **Murchison Club Motel Hotel**, (LMH), Austin St, 50m S of PO, ☎ 08 9963 1020, fax 08 9963 1277, 12 units [shwr, tlt, a/c, TV, t/c mkg, refrig, mini bar], pool. **RO** ♦ **$77**, ♦♦ **$99**, ♦♦♦ **$110**, BC DC MC VI.

(Hotel Section), 18 rms [tlt, a/c-cool, t/c mkg], shwr, TV rm. **RO** ♦ **$44**, ♦♦ **$55**.

DALWALLINU WA 6609

Pop 639. (251km NE Perth), See map on page 906, ref B7. Dalwallinu is the centre of a flourishing sheep and wheat farming area.

Hotels/Motels

★★☆ **Dalwallinu Hotel Motel**, (LMH), Johnston St, 200m S of PO, ☎ 08 9661 1102, fax 08 9661 1554, 11 units [shwr, tlt, a/c, elec blkts, TV, t/c mkg, refrig], cots. **D** ♦ **$50**, ♦♦ **$71.50**.

(Hotel Section), 15 rms shwr, tlt. **RO** ♦ **$35 - $40**, ♦♦ **$55**, ⚲ **$11**.

B&B's/Guest Houses

The Old Convent, (GH), Cnr Great Northern Hwy & Kalannie Rd, 1km S of PO, ☎ 08 9661 2072, fax 08 9661 2073, 6 rms [ensuite (1), heat, fan, elec blkts, tel, pillows] refrig (communal), shwr, tlt, iron, iron brd, rec rm, TV rm, t/c mkg shared, bbq, mini golf, cots (avail), non smoking property. **RO** ♦ **$44 - $55**, ♦♦ **$66 - $77**, ⚲ **$11 - $22**, BC MC VI.

(Cottage Section), 1 cotg acc up to 6, [shwr, tlt, fan, heat, wood heat, elec blkts, TV, t/c mkg, refrig, cook fac, linen], iron, iron brd, lounge, lounge firepl, bbq, cots, non smoking property. **D** **$66 - $88**, ⚲ **$11 - $22**.

DAMPIER WA 6713

Pop 1,424. (1555km NE Perth), See map on page 906, ref A4. Dampier has been developed as the iron ore port servicing the mines at Tom Price, Paraburdoo, Channar, Marandoo and Brockman.

★★★☆ **Mercure Inn Dampier**, (LH), The Esplanade, 200m S of PO, ☎ 08 9183 1222, fax 08 9183 1028, 63 rms [shwr, tlt, a/c, tel, TV, movie, t/c mkg, refrig, ldry], ✕, pool, bbq, cots. **D** ♦♦ **$80 - $130**, ♦♦♦♦ **$128 - $160**, ⚲ **$20**, Some units of a lower rating. AE BC DC MC VI.

★★★☆ **Peninsula Palms**, (LMH), The Esplanade, 1.5km N of PO, 10km NW of Airport, ☎ 08 9183 1888, fax 08 9183 1855, (2 stry) 110 units (2 suites) [shwr, tlt, hairdry, a/c-cool, tel, TV, clock radio, t/c mkg, refrig], ldry, conf fac, ✕, cafe, bar, pool, ☎, gym-fee, non smoking rms (50). **RO** ♦ **$93.50 - $145.20**, fam con, pen con, AE BC DC EFT MC VI.

(Budget Rooms Section), (2 stry) 200 units [a/c-cool, TV, video, pillows], shwr, tlt, ldry, rec rm, ✉, bar, ☎. **RO** ♦♦ **$38.50 - $145.20**.

DARDANUP WA 6236

Pop part of Bunbury, (200km S Perth), See map on page 906, ref A2. Small township just south of Bunbury.

Self Catering Accommodation

Cottage Parks Wellington Mills Cottages, (Cotg), Wellington Rd, off Ferguson Rd, 27km SE of PO, ☎ 08 9527 1844, fax 08 9592 5222, 8 cotgs acc up to 8, (3 bedrm), [shwr, tlt, heat, refrig, cook fac, ldry, linen reqd-fee, pillows], rec rm, ✕, bbq, ☎, plygr, cots. **D** **$60 - $110**, Min book.

B&B's/Guest Houses

Peppermint Lane Lodge, (B&B), Wellington Mill Rd, Wellington Mills 6236, 30km E PO via Dardanup, ☎ 08 9728 3138, 4 rms [shwr, tlt, hairdry, a/c, fax, TV, video, CD, refrig], iron, iron brd, lounge, ✕, pool, spa (shared), t/c mkg shared, c/park. **BB** ♦♦ **$132 - $160**, **DBB** ♦♦ **$209 - $235**, pen con, BC MC VI, (not yet classified).

DENHAM WA 6537

Pop Nominal, (831km N Perth), See map on page 906, ref A6. Denham is the western most town in Australia.

Hotels/Motels

★★★★ **Heritage Resort Shark Bay**, (LMH), Cnr Knights Tce & Durlacher St, 100m E of PO, ☎ 08 9948 1133, fax 08 9948 1134, (2 stry gr fl), 27 units [shwr, tlt, a/c, tel, TV, movie, clock radio, t/c mkg, refrig, mini bar, ldry], iron, iron brd, ✉, bar (cocktail & public), pool, bbq, cots. **RO** ♦ **$70 - $90**, ♦♦ **$100 - $130**, ♦♦♦ **$120 - $140**, ♦♦♦♦ **$120 - $140**, AE BC DC MC VI, ⚲.

★★☆ **Shark Bay Motel Hotel**, (LMH), 43 Knights Tce, 100m W of PO, ☎ 08 9948 1203, fax 08 9948 1304, 14 units [shwr, tlt, a/c-cool, TV, t/c mkg, refrig, toaster], ✉, bbq. **BLB** ♦ **$45**, ♦♦ **$70 - $85**.

Self Catering Accommodation

★★★★ **Denham Villas**, (HU), 4 Durlacher St, 100m E of PO, ☎ 08 9948 1264, fax 08 9948 1870, 10 units acc up to 6, (1 & 2 bedrm), [shwr, tlt, a/c, TV, clock radio, t/c mkg, refrig, cook fac, micro, blkts, linen, pillows], w/mach, iron, iron brd, bbq, cots. **D** **$88**, **W** **$495 - $595**, BC MC VI.

★★★ **Tradewinds Holiday Village**, (HU), Knights Tce, Shark Bay, 250m E of PO, ☎ 08 9948 1222, fax 08 9948 1161, 10 units acc up to 6, (1 & 2 bedrm), [shwr, tlt, hairdry, a/c, fan, refrig, cook fac, micro, ldry], bbq. **D** ♦♦ **$70 - $125**, **W** ♦♦ **$375 - $750**, AE BC MC VI.

Bay Lodge Holiday Units, (HU), 109 Knight Tce, 500m E of PO, ☎ 08 9948 1278, fax 08 9948 1031, 11 units acc up to 6, (2 bedrm), [shwr, tlt, a/c-cool, TV, radio, refrig, cook fac, micro, blkts, linen-fee, pillows], ldry, lounge. **D** ♦♦ **$77 - $120**, **W** ♦♦ **$400 - $700**.

(Motel Section), 6 units [shwr, tlt, a/c-cool, TV, cook fac ltd, ldry, pillows]. **D** ♦♦ **$77 - $100**, **W** ♦♦ **$360 - $550**.

Bay View Villas, (HU), Fry Crt, 500m N of PO, ☎ 08 9948 1323, fax 08 9948 1020, 1 unit acc up to 6, (3 bedrm), [shwr, tlt, fan, refrig, cook fac, ldry, blkts, linen reqd-fee, pillows]. **D** **$80**, **W** **$500**.

Denham Holiday Village, (HU), Sunter Pl & Capewell Dve, 500m N of PO, ☎ 08 9948 1323, fax 08 9948 1020, 6 units acc up to 8, [shwr, tlt, TV, refrig, cook fac, micro, ldry, blkts, linen reqd-fee, pillows], pool, bbq. **D** **$60 - $80**, **W** **$420 - $560**.

Mala Villas, (Chalet), Sunter Pl, 700m N of PO, ☎ 08 9948 1323, fax 08 9948 1020, 2 chalets acc up to 6, (2 bedrm), [shwr, tlt, TV, clock radio, t/c mkg, refrig, cook fac, micro, ldry, blkts, linen reqd-fee, pillows], bbq. **D** **$60 - $65**, **W** **$420 - $455**, AE BC MC VI.

Shark Bay Holiday Cottages, (Cotg), 13 Knight Tce, 500m N of PO, ☎ 08 9948 1206, fax 08 9948 1206, 14 cotgs acc up to 8, [shwr, tlt, a/c-cool, c/fan, TV, movie, refrig, cook fac, micro, blkts, doonas, linen reqd-fee, pillows], w/mach-fee, dryer-fee, pool, bbq, plygr, cots. **D** ♦♦ **$50 - $80**, **W** ♦♦ **$300 - $540**, BC MC VI.

Tropical Villas, (HU), Hartog Cres, 400m NE of PO, ☎ 08 9948 1323, fax 08 9948 1020, 3 units acc up to 6, (2 bedrm), [shwr, tlt, a/c, refrig, cook fac, micro, ldry, blkts reqd-fee, linen reqd-fee, pillows reqd-fee], bbq. **D** **$50 - $70**, **W** **$350 - $490**.

Whispering Waters, (Cotg), 17 Knight St, 200m W of PO, ☎ 08 9948 1323, fax 08 9948 1020, 1 cotg acc up to 9, [ensuite, shwr, bath, tlt, fan, TV, t/c mkg, refrig, micro, elec frypan, toaster, ldry, blkts, linen reqd-fee, pillows], w/mach. **D** **$90**, **W** **$630**, BC MC VI.

DENMARK WA 6333

Pop 4,120. (414km SE Perth), See map on page 906, ref B3.
Exciting seascapes and rugged coastline to tranquil forest walks and panoramic views.

Hotels/Motels

★★☆ **Denmark Unit Motel Hotel**, (LMH), Holling Rd, 250m N of PO, ☎ 08 9848 2206, fax 08 9848 1206, 22 units [shwr, tlt, heat, elec blkts, TV, radio, t/c mkg, refrig], lounge, ✕, res liquor license, bar. **D ♦ $55, ♦♦ $80, ♦♦♦ $100**, pen con, AE BC DC EFT MC VI.

(Hotel Section), 10 rms shwr, bathrm. **D ♦♦ $40, RO ♦ $25**.

The Koorabup Motel, (M), Previously Denmark Tavern Holiday Units South Coast Highway, 1km W of PO, ☎ 08 9848 1044, fax 08 9848 3408, 13 units [shwr, tlt, hairdry, heat, tel, fax, movie, clock radio, t/c mkg, refrig, toaster, pillows], ldry, w/mach-fee, dryer-fee, cots (avail). **BB ♦ $81, ♦♦ $85, ♦♦♦ $89, RO ♦ $77**, BC MC VI, (not yet classified).

★★★ **(Self Contained Section)**, 9 units acc up to 5, (1 & 2 bedrm), [shwr, tlt, heat, tel, TV, radio, t/c mkg, refrig, cook fac, ldry, blkts, linen, pillows], cots. **D $81 - $98, W $486 - $588**.

The Denmark Waterfront Motel, (M), 63 Inlet Dve, 3km S of PO, ☎ 08 9848 1147, fax 08 9848 1965, 8 units [shwr, tlt, heat (17), elec blkts, TV, radio, t/c mkg, refrig, doonas], ldry, ✕, cots. **D ♦♦ $70, ♦♦♦♦ $100**, pen con, BC DC MC VI, ⟨&.

(Apartment Section), 6 apts acc up to 4, [shwr, tlt, heat, elec blkts, TV, video, radio, t/c mkg, refrig, micro, toaster, ldry, doonas], cots. **D ♦♦ $85, ♦ $15, W ♦♦ $510**, pen con.

(Backpackers Section), 4 rms acc up to 4, [TV, cook fac, blkts, linen], rec rm. **RO ♦ $17, W ♦ $100**.

Self Catering Accommodation

★★★★☆ **Sahyma's A Frame Accommodation**, (Cotg), Illsley Dve, 10km NW of PO, ☎ 08 9840 9029, fax 08 9840 9029, (Multi-stry gr fl), 1 cotg acc up to 10, (6 bedrm), [shwr, bath, tlt, heat, tel, TV, video, refrig, cook fac, ldry, doonas, linen, pillows], w/mach, iron, bbq, non smoking property. **D $120 - $280, W $760 - $1,760**.

★★★★☆ **Tree-Elle Retreat**, (House), South Coast Hwy Bow Bridge, ☎ 08 9414 1314, fax 08 9414 1343, 4 houses acc up to 8, [shwr, bath, tlt, hairdry, heat, c/fan, wood heat, tel, fax, TV, video, clock radio, CD, t/c mkg, refrig, cook fac, micro, elec frypan, d/wash, toaster, blkts, doonas, linen, pillows], w/mach, dryer, iron, iron brd, bbq. **D ♦♦ $130 - $160, ♦ $20, W ♦♦ $780 - $960, ♦ $120**, One house of a lower rating. AE BC DC MC VI.

★★★★ **Bambrey Green Cottage**, (Cotg), No children's facilities, 3 Bambrey St, 300m NE of PO, ☎ 08 9848 1437, fax 08 9848 1437, 1 cotg acc up to 4, [hairdry, heat, c/fan, wood heat, elec blkts, tel, TV, video, clock radio, CD, refrig, cook fac, micro, toaster, ldry, blkts, doonas, linen, pillows], iron, non smoking property, **D $95 - $140, W $600 - $880**.

★★★★ **Hallowell Springs**, (Cotg), Lights Rd, 9.3km W of PO, ☎ 08 9848 1919, fax 08 9848 2626, 2 cotgs acc up to 6, [ensuite, wood heat, elec blkts, TV, video, radio, CD, refrig, cook fac, micro, elec frypan, toaster, blkts, doonas, linen, pillows], w/mach, iron, bbq, tennis. **D ♦♦ $99 - $165, W ♦♦ $660 - $990**, Min book.

★★★★ **Karma Chalets**, (Chalet), South Coast Hwy, 5km W of PO, ☎ 08 9848 1568, fax 08 9848 2124, (2 stry), 9 chalets acc up to 8, (2, 3 & 4 bedrm), [shwr, bath, spa bath (5), tlt, heat, TV (5), clock radio, CD, refrig, cook fac, micro, ldry, blkts, linen, pillows], w/mach (5), bbq, cots. **D $110 - $180, W $665**, Min book long w/ends and Easter, BC MC VI.

★★★★ **Kooringal**, (HU), No children's facilities, 6 Ridley Place, 5km SW of PO, ☎ 08 9848 2107, fax 08 9848 2107, 1 unit acc up to 6, (3 bedrm), [shwr, tlt, heat, elec blkts, TV, clock radio, refrig, cook fac, micro, blkts, doonas, linen, pillows], bbq, non smoking property. **D ♦ $40, ♦♦ $55 - $70, ♦ $10, W ♦ $250, ♦♦ $360 - $450**, Min book long w/ends, BC MC VI.

★★★★ **William Bay Country Cottages**, (Cotg), RMB 1070 South Coast Hwy, 16km W of PO, ☎ 08 9840 9221, fax 08 9840 9221, (2 stry), 6 cotgs acc up to 8, [shwr, tlt, heat, refrig, cook fac, ldry, blkts, linen, pillows], iron, rec rm, bbq, tennis, cots (avail). **D $121 - $143, ♦ $16.50 - $27.50, W $650 - $840**, Farm activities avail.

★★★☆ **Cape Howe Cottages**, (Cotg), RMB 9298 Tennessee Rd South Lowlands Beach, Albany 6330, 27km E of PO, ☎ 08 9845 1295, fax 08 9845 1396, 2 cotgs acc up to 4, (2 bedrm), [shwr, bath, tlt, heat (wood), tel, TV, video, clock radio, CD, refrig, micro, toaster, blkts, doonas, linen, pillows], iron, iron brd, lounge, bbq, cots, non smoking property, Pets on application. **D $110, W $770**, BC MC VI.

★★★☆ **Green Leaves**, (Cotg), 17 Adams Rd Wheedon Hill, 4km SW of PO, ☎ 08 9848 2055, fax 08 9848 2271, 1 cotg acc up to 6, (2 bedrm), [shwr, tlt, heat, heat (wood), CD, refrig, cook fac, micro, ldry, blkts, doonas, linen, pillows], w/mach, dryer, iron, iron brd, ✕, bbq (gas), c/park. **D $99 - $121, W $616 - $847**, Min book applies, Min book all holiday times, AE BC DC EFT MC VI, ⟨&.

★★★☆ **Rambling Rose Cottage**, (Cotg), 108 Scotsdale Rd, 1.6km NE of PO, ☎ 08 9848 1045, fax 08 9848 1045, 1 cotg acc up to 4, (2 bedrm), [shwr, spa bath, tlt, heat (wood), TV, video, radio, refrig, cook fac, micro, elec frypan, doonas, linen, pillows], bbq, non smoking property. **D ♦♦ $100 - $120, ♦ $15, W $600 - $790**, pen con.

★★★☆ **Riverview Cottage**, (Cotg), 96 Scotsdale Rd, 1.4km NE of PO, ☎ 08 9848 1873, 1 cotg acc up to 4, [wood heat, TV, video, radio, t/c mkg, refrig, cook fac, micro, ldry, blkts, doonas, linen reqd-fee, pillows], w/mach, iron, bbq. **D ♦♦ $75, W $500 - $550**.

★★★☆ **Winn Cottage**, (Cotg), 143 Minsterly Rd, 8km W of PO, ☎ 08 9848 1813, fax 08 9848 1813, 1 cotg acc up to 6, (3 bedrm), [shwr, bath, tlt, heat, TV, video, refrig, cook fac, micro, blkts, linen, pillows], w/mach. **D ♦♦♦♦ $80, ♦ $10, W ♦♦♦♦ $560**.

★★★ **Gum Grove Chalets**, (Chalet), Ocean Beach Rd, 3km S of PO, ☎ 08 9848 1378, fax 08 9848 1877, 10 chalets acc up to 9, (2 & 3 bedrm), [shwr, tlt, heat (gas & pot belly), TV, refrig, cook fac, micro, ldry, blkts, doonas, linen reqd-fee, pillows], w/mach, iron, iron brd, bbq, plygr, cots-fee. **D ♦♦ $55 - $95, W $330 - $665**, ⟨&.

★★★ **Kangaroo Valley Cottage**, (Cotg), Lot 7 Lantzke Rd, 5km N of PO, ☎ 08 9848 1710, 1 cotg acc up to 6, [shwr, tlt, heat, TV, video, refrig, cook fac, ldry, blkts, doonas, linen, pillows], w/mach, bbq, plygr, cots. **D $90 - $120, W $550 - $750**.

★★★ **Misty Valley Farmstay**, (Cotg), Lot 651 Scotsdale Rd, 13km W of PO, ☎ 08 9840 9239, fax 08 9840 9239, 3 cotgs acc up to 8, [shwr, bath, tlt, wood heat, TV, video, radio, t/c mkg, refrig, micro, toaster, doonas, linen, pillows], bbq, bicycle, cots. **D $88 - $198, W $539 - $1,287**, Farm activities. BC MC VI.

Chalet Arunga, (Chalet), No children's facilities, Hunwick Rd South, Torbay 6330, off Sth Coast Hwy, ☎ 08 9845 1025, fax 08 9845 1025, 1 chalet acc up to 4, (2 bedrm), [ensuite, shwr, tlt, evap cool, c/fan, wood heat, elec blkts, clock radio, CD, t/c mkg, refrig, cook fac, micro, blkts, doonas, linen, pillows], iron, iron brd, lounge, bbq, meals to unit (breakfast only), non smoking property. **D ♦♦ $140 - $180, ♦♦♦♦ $200 - $240**, BC MC VI, (not yet classified).

Osprey Cottage, (Cotg), 25 Adams Rd, 4km SW of PO, ☎ 08 9848 1344, fax 08 9848 1900, 1 cotg acc up to 6, [shwr, bath, tlt, heat, wood heat, TV, video, radio, CD, refrig, cook fac, blkts, doonas, linen], iron, iron brd, bbq, non smoking property. **D $120 - $140, W $550 - $1,000**, BC MC VI, (not yet classified).

Boat Harbour Chalets & Camping, (Chalet), RMB 1107A Boat Harbour Rd, 25km W of PO, ☎ 08 9840 8212, fax 08 9840 8212, 3 chalets acc up to 6, (2 bedrm), [tlt, wood heat, refrig, cook fac, blkts, linen reqd-fee, pillows reqd], shwr, bbq. **D $40 - $70, ♦ $5**.

Bombina Cottages, (Cotg), 349 Kearsley Rd, 1km W of PO, ☎ 08 9848 2144, fax 08 9848 2144, 2 cotgs acc up to 6, [shwr, tlt, wood heat, TV, video, clock radio, refrig, cook fac, toaster, ldry, doonas, linen, pillows], iron, iron brd, bbq, non smoking units, **D ♦♦ $100 - $120, ♦ $10, W ♦♦ $550 - $770**, ch con, AE BC DC MC VI.

Cinnamon Coloureds Farmstay, (Cotg), South Coast Hwy, 8km W of PO, ☎ 08 9848 1781, fax 08 9848 1231, 3 cotgs acc up to 6, (2 bedrm), [shwr, tlt, heat, tel, video, t/c mkg, refrig, micro, blkts, linen, pillows], bbq. **D $100 - $140, W $550 - $750**, ⟨&.

Denmark's Ocean Beach Chalets, (Chalet), Lot 51 Ocean Beach Rd, 8km S of PO, ☎ 08 9848 2248, fax 08 9848 2248, 5 chalets acc up to 8, (1, 2 & 3 bedrm), [shwr, tlt, a/c-cool (2), heat (wood) (2), TV, video, CD, refrig, cook fac, micro, ldry, blkts, linen, pillows], spa (2), bbq (4). **D $70 - $140**.

Karri Mia Resort, (Chalet), Mt Shadforth Rd, 4km W of PO, ☎ 08 9848 2233, fax 08 984841133, 10 chalets acc up to 6, (1 & 2 bedrm), [ensuite, shwr, spa bath (6), tlt, hairdry, heat, tel, TV, video, clock radio, CD, refrig, cook fac, micro, toaster, blkts, linen, pillows], ldry, w/mach, dryer, iron, ✕, bbq, meals avail, cots, Dogs allowed under control. **D $154 - $215, ♦ $20**, AE BC DC EFT MC VI.

Kate's Cottage, (Cotg), RMB 9411 Bolitho Rd Bornholm, Albany 6330, 25km E of PO, ☎ 08 9845 1027, fax 08 9845 1427, 1 cotg acc up to 6, [shwr, tlt, heat, clock radio, refrig, cook fac, blkts, doonas, linen reqd-fee, pillows], cots. **D $60 - $80, ♦ $10, W $420 - $490**.

Lakeside Holiday Villas, (HU), 31 Inlet Dve, 3km S of PO, ☎ 08 9848 1999, 2 units acc up to 4, [shwr, tlt, wood heat, TV, clock radio, refrig, cook fac, micro, toaster, ldry, blkts, doonas, linen, pillows], iron, iron brd, bbq. **D $60 - $75**, Min book.

DENMARK WA continued...

Rainbow House, (Chalet), 58 Minsterly Rd, 5km S of PO, ☎ 08 9291 8111, 2 chalets acc up to 6, [shwr, bath, tlt, heat, TV, refrig, cook fac, micro, toaster, doonas, linen, pillows], w/mach, iron, iron brd, non smoking property. **D** $60 - $75, ⓥ $10, **W** $350 - $500, AE BC DC EFT JCB MC MP VI.

Rudgyard Beach Holiday Park, (Chalet), Rudgyard Park, Rudgyard Rd, 9km E of PO, ☎ 08 9848 1169, 3 chalets acc up to 4, (2 bedrm) [ensuite, wood heat, refrig, cook fac, micro, doonas, pillows], tank water, bbq, bicycle, canoeing, cots. **D** $50 - $80, ⓥ $5, **W** $330.

Smith's A Frame Cottage, (Cotg), 4 Thorne Rd, 3km SW of PO, ☎ 08 9848 1265, 1 cotg acc up to 4, (2 bedrm), [shwr, tlt, wood heat, TV, video, t/c mkg, refrig, cook fac, micro, blkts, linen, pillows], w/mach, bbq. **D** $90, **W** $500.

Spring Bay Villas, (Chalet), Lot 6 Ocean Beach Rd, 7km S of PO, ☎ 08 9848 2456, fax 08 9848 3429, 10 chalets acc up to 6, (2 bedrm Studio), [shwr, spa bath (3), tlt, fire pl (log), TV, video, t/c mkg, refrig, cook fac, micro, toaster, ldry, blkts, doonas, linen, pillows], w/mach, iron, iron brd, cots, Pets on application. **D** $100 - $120, **W** $600 - $750, Studio **D** ♦♦ $140, Studio **W** ♦♦ $880, ch con, BTC EFT MC VI.

The Cove, (Chalet), Payne Rd, 3km SW of PO, ☎ 08 9848 1770, fax 08 9848 2990, (Multi-stry), 5 chalets acc up to 6, (1, 2 & 4 bedrm), [shwr, tlt, fire pl, refrig, cook fac, micro, blkts, linen, pillows], bbq, cots. **D** $95 - $210, ch con, Min book applies, BC MC VI, ⓘⓖ.

The Peppermints, (Cotg), Happy Valley Rd, 2.5km N of South Coast Hwy, ☎ 08 9840 9305, fax 08 9840 9305, 2 cotgs acc up to 7, [shwr, tlt, heat, video, refrig, cook fac, micro, ldry, blkts, doonas, linen, pillows], bbq, cots (avail). **D** ♦♦ $60 - $90, ⓥ $10, **W** $330 - $540, ch con.

  (Bed And Breakfast Section), 1 rm **BB** ♦ $50, ♦♦ $80.

Turicum Chalets, (Chalet), Wentworth Rd, 10km W of Denmark, ☎ 08 9840 9353, fax 08 9841 6727, 2 chalets acc up to 5, [shwr, tlt, wood heat, TV, video, clock radio, t/c mkg, refrig, cook fac, blkts, linen, pillows]. **D** $105 - $135, **W** $850, BC MC VI.

B&B's/Guest Houses

★★★★★ **Chimes at Karri Mia**, (GH), Previously Karri Mia Lodge No children's facilities, Mt Shadforth Rd, 3km W of PO, ☎ 08 9848 2255, fax 08 9848 2277, 10 rms (10 suites) [ensuite, spa bath, hairdry, a/c, tel, TV, video, clock radio, t/c mkg, refrig, mini bar, pillows], ldry, w/mach, dryer, iron, lounge, ✕, non smoking property. **Suite D** ♦♦ $170 - $297, AE BC DC MC VI.

★★★★☆ **Water's Edge**, (B&B), No children's facilities, 9 Inlet Dve, 2km S of PO, ☎ 08 9848 1043, 3 rms [ensuite, elec blkts, TV, t/c mkg, refrig, pillows], ✕, bbq, non smoking property. **BB** ♦ $55, ♦♦ $77, ♦♦♦ $105, ♦♦♦♦ $132, BC MC VI.

★★★★ **Edinburgh House**, (B&B), 31 South Coast Hwy, 300m NW of PO, ☎ 1800 671 477, fax 08 9848 1477, 9 rms [ensuite, fire pl, heat, TV, refrig, ldry, pillows], TV rm. **BB** ♦ $65, ♦♦ $86, AE BC DC MC VI.

★★★★ **Gumnuts Bed & Breakfast**, (B&B), No children's facilities, 62 Bracknell Cres, 4km SW of PO, ☎ 08 9848 1344, fax 08 9848 1900, 2 rms [shwr, tlt, tel, TV, video, t/c mkg, refrig, doonas], ldry, non smoking property. **BB** ♦ $65 - $75, ♦♦ $95 - $105, BC MC VI.

★★★☆ **Denmark Seaview Farm**, (B&B), Albany Rd, 6km E of PO, ☎ 08 9848 2354, fax 08 9848 2354, 2 rms [ensuite, tel, TV, radio, t/c mkg, refrig, doonas, pillows], ✕, bbq, plygr, cots, non smoking property, Pets allowed on leash. **BB** ♦ $45, ♦♦ $70, ch con.

★★★☆ **Rannoch West Farmstay**, (B&B), South Coast Hwy, 28km W of PO, ☎ 08 9840 8032, fax 08 9840 8032, 3 rms [ensuite (1), TV, video, refrig, doonas, pillows], shwr, tlt, TV rm, bbq. **BB** ♦♦ $85.

  (Cottage Section), (Farm), 2 cotgs acc up to 10, (3 & 5 bedrm), [TV, video, refrig, cook fac, doonas, linen reqd-fee, pillows]. **D** $55 - $66, **W** $450 - $805.

Stonehaus, (B&B), No children's facilities, 16 Gilbert Ave, 3km SW of PO, ☎ 08 9848 2247, fax 08 9848 2247, 1 rm [ensuite, heat, TV, clock radio, t/c mkg, refrig, toaster, doonas, pillows], non smoking rms. **BB** ♦ $70, ♦♦ $85 - $95.

DERBY WA 6728

Pop 3,236. (2391km N Perth), See map on page 906, ref C2. Situated on the shores of King Sound, Derby is a principal port, commercial and mining centre of the West Kimberleys.

Hotels/Motels

★★★☆ **King Sound Resort Hotel**, (LMH), Lock St, 1km SE of PO, ☎ 08 9193 1044, fax 08 9191 1649, 82 units [shwr, tlt, a/c-cool, tel, TV, movie, radio, t/c mkg, refrig, ldry], conv fac, ✕, pool, secure park, squash, cots (avail). **RO** ♦ $110, ♦♦ $126, ♦♦♦♦ $176, AE BC DC MC VI.

★★☆ **Derby Boab Inn**, (LH), Loch St, 1.5km SE of PO, ☎ 08 9191 1044, fax 08 9191 1568, 37 rms [shwr, a/c, tel, TV, t/c mkg, refrig], ✕, pool, bbq, cots. **D** ♦ $90, ♦♦♦ $90, ♦♦♦♦ $125, AE BC DC MC VI.

Spinifex Hotel, (LMH), Clarendon St, 600m W of PO, ☎ 08 9191 1233, fax 08 9191 1576, 20 units [shwr, tlt, a/c, tel, TV, t/c mkg, refrig], ✕. **D** $50 - $80, BC MC VI.

  (Hotel Section), 29 rms shwr, tlt. **RO** $30 - $50.

Self Catering Accommodation

Mt Elizabeth Station, (House), PMB Via Derby along Gibb River Rd, 338km E of PO, ☎ 08 9191 4644, fax 08 9191 4644, 9 houses acc up to 4, [shwr, tlt, t/c mkg, ldry, blkts, linen, pillows]. **DBB** $95 - $130, Camping areas avail.

B&B's/Guest Houses

Mt Hart Homestead, (GH), (Farm), 50km off Gibb River Rd, 250km NE of Derby, ☎ 08 9191 4645, fax 08 9191 4654, 12 rms [ensuite (1), tlt, fire pl, TV, doonas, pillows], shwr, ldry, w/mach, TV rm, t/c mkg shared, refrig, bbq, ☏, tennis, cots. **DBB** ♦ $105, ch con, Outback station accommodation. ⓘⓖ.

West Kimberley Lodge, (GH), Cnr Sutherland & Stanley Sts, 2.5km E of PO, ☎ 08 9191 1031, fax 08 9191 1028, 12 rms [ensuite (some), a/c, c/fan, TV, t/c mkg, refrig, ldry, pillows], pool, cook fac, bbq. **D** $60 - $80.

DONGARA WA 6525

Pop 1,874. (359km N Perth), See map on page 906, ref A7. Dongara Denison is a popular holiday resort. There is good fishing and the offshore reefs support a profitable rock lobster industry.

Hotels/Motels

★★☆ **Dongara Motor Hotel**, (LH), Moreton Tce, 100m N of PO, ☎ 08 9927 1023, fax 08 9927 1202, 28 rms [shwr, tlt, a/c, tel, TV, t/c mkg, refrig], ✕, pool, cots. **RO** ♦ $66, ♦♦ $77, ♦♦♦♦ $121, AE BC DC MC VI.

★★☆ **Old Mill Motel**, (M), Waldeck St, 500m NW of PO, ☎ 08 9927 1200, fax 08 9927 1879, 28 units [shwr, tlt, a/c, TV, t/c mkg, refrig], ✕, pool, rm serv, cots. **D** ♦ $55, ♦♦ $66, ♦♦♦♦ $82, ⓥ $10, AE BC DC MC VI.

Self Catering Accommodation

★★★★ **Seaspray Villas**, (HU), 81 Church St, 1km W of PO, ☎ 08 9927 2200, fax 08 9927 2426, 8 units acc up to 8, [shwr, tlt, a/c-cool, fan, heat, tel, TV, clock radio, refrig, cook fac, ldry, blkts, linen, pillows], pool, bbq, cots (avail). **D** ♦♦ $88, ⓥ $8, **W** $528, BC MC VI.

★★★ **Port Denison Holiday Units**, (HU), 14 Carnarvon St, 50m from marina, ☎ 08 9927 1104, 8 units acc up to 8, (1 & 2 bedrm), [shwr, tlt, a/c-cool, fan, heat, TV, refrig, cook fac, ldry, blkts, linen, pillows], bbq. **D** ♦♦ $75 - $95, ⓥ $8, **W** ♦♦ $385 - $525, BC MC VI.

Lazy Lobster, (HU), 45 Hampton Street, 3km S of PO, ☎ 08 9927 2177, fax 08 9927 2177, 6 units acc up to 6, (2 bedrm), [shwr, tlt, heat, c/fan, TV, refrig, cook fac, micro, elec frypan, blkts, doonas, linen, pillows], ldry, w/mach, iron, bbq, trailer park, plygr, cots, non smoking units (3). **D** ♦ $49.50 - $55, ♦♦ $55 - $66, ♦♦♦ $60.50 - $71.50, ♦♦♦♦ $66 - $77, **W** ♦ $346.50 - $385, ♦♦ $385 - $462, ♦♦♦ $423.50 - $500.50, ♦♦♦♦ $462 - $539.

B&B's/Guest Houses

Obawara, (B&B), Brand Hwy, 5km E of PO, ☎ 08 9927 1043, fax 08 9927 1043, 1 rm [ensuite (1), fan, elec blkts, t/c mkg, refrig, cook fac, micro, pillows], bbq. **BB** ♦♦ $77.

DONNYBROOK WA 6239

Pop 1,635. (210km S Perth), See map on page 906, ref A2. The Donnybrook district is the centre of the oldest and finest apple orchards in the State.

Hotels/Motels

Donnybrook Motel Motorlodge, (M), 28 South Western Hwy, 100m N of PO, ☎ 08 9731 1499, fax 08 9731 1499, 16 units [shwr, tlt, a/c, TV, radio, t/c mkg, refrig], pool, bbq, rm serv. **D** ♦ $55 - $65, ♦♦ $77 - $88, ⓥ $11 - $12.

Self Catering Accommodation

Boronia Farm, (Cotg), Farley Rd, 12km SE of PO, ☎ 08 9731 7154, 1 cotg acc up to 6, (3 bedrm), [shwr, tlt, wood heat, TV, clock radio, refrig, cook fac, micro, blkts, doonas, linen-fee, pillows], w/mach, iron, iron brd, bbq, cots. **D** ♦♦ $90 - $110, ⓥ $5 - $15, **W** ♦♦ $490 - $590, Min book all holiday times.

B&B's/Guest Houses

Marri Grove, (B&B), Lot 1 Hurst Rd, 10km NW of PO, ☎ 08 9731 1523, 3 rms [shwr, bath, tlt, heat, wood heat, elec blkts, TV, clock radio], iron, iron brd, lounge, t/c mkg shared, non smoking property. **BB** ♦ $35 - $70, ♦♦ $40 - $80, (not yet classified).

Rosedene Alpaca Farm, (B&B), No children's facilities, Rosedene Lane, Lowden, 14km E of PO, ☎ 08 9732 1332, fax 08 9732 1332, 2 rms [shwr, tlt, fan, fire pl, TV, video, clock radio, t/c mkg, refrig, ldry (service) reqd-fee, doonas, pillows], bbq, bicycle, non smoking property. **BB** ♦ $71.50, ♦♦ $93.50, Farm activities.

DUNSBOROUGH WA 6281

Pop 1,154. (255km S Perth), See map on page 906, ref A2. Situated on the coast of Geographe Bay, it provides a relaxing and enjoyable stopping place for a holiday.

Hotels/Motels

★★★★☆ **Radisson Beach Resort**, (LH), Lot 108 Caves Rd, 6km E of PO, ☎ 08 9756 9777, fax 08 9756 8788, 100 rms [shwr, bath, tlt, hairdry, a/c, tel, TV, video, clock radio, t/c mkg, refrig, mini bar, ldry (services)], w/mach, dryer, iron, iron brd, rec rm, business centre, conf fac, ☒, pool-heated, spa, bbq, ☏, plygr, golf, gym, tennis, cots, non smoking rms. **BB** ♠ **$199, RO** ♠ **$185 - $255**, pen con, Min book all holiday times,Min book long w/ends, AE BC DC EFT JCB MC VI, ⅄.

★★★★ **Mercure Inn Dunsborough**, (M), 2 Dunsborough Place, 500m S of PO, ☎ 08 9756 7711, fax 08 9756 7722, 47 units [ensuite, shwr, tlt, a/c, tel, cable tv, movie, radio, t/c mkg, refrig], lounge (guest), ☒, bar, pool, bbq (/s gas), cots. **D** ♠ **$76 - $153**, ♠♠ **$87 - $175**, ⍟ **$20**, Some rooms of a lower rating. AE BC DC MC VI, ⅄.

Self Catering Accommodation

★★★★☆ **Radisson Beach Resort**, (SA), Lot 108 Caves Rd, Marybrook 6280, 6km E of PO, ☎ 08 9756 9777, fax 08 9756 8788, 50 serv apts acc up to 4, (2 bedrm), [shwr, tlt, hairdry, a/c, tel, TV, video, clock radio, refrig, cook fac, micro, ldry (services), blkts, linen, pillows], w/mach, dryer, iron, rec rm, business centre, conv fac, ☒, pool-heated, spa, bbq, rm serv, plygr, bicycle, tennis, cots, non smoking units. **D $220 - $265**, pen con, Min book all holiday times,Min book long w/ends, AE BC DC EFT JCB MC VI, ⅄.

★★★★ **Bayshore Resort**, (SA), 330 Geographe Bay Rd, 3km from PO, ☎ 08 9756 8353, fax 08 9756 8354, (Multi-stry) 24 serv apts acc up to 8, (2 & 3 bedrm), [ensuite, shwr, bath, tlt, a/c-cool, c/fan, heat, TV, video, clock radio, CD, t/c mkg, refrig, micro, d/wash, toaster, blkts, doonas, linen, pillows], w/mach, dryer, iron, iron brd, rec rm, plygr, tennis (cots avail). **D $120 - $275**, ⍟ **$11**, BC DC MC VI.

★★★★ **Ocean View Villas**, (HU), 14 Geograhe Bay Rd, 500m E of PO, ☎ 08 9756 8934, fax 08 9756 8724, 4 units acc up to 8, (3 bedrm), [ensuite, shwr, fire pl, wood heat, TV, movie, clock radio, CD, t/c mkg, refrig, micro, elec frypan, d/wash, doonas, linen, pillows], w/mach, dryer, iron, iron brd, lounge, ☒, bbq, c/park. **D $180 - $350, W $950 - $1,900**.

★★★★ **Whalers Cove**, (Chalet), Lot 3 Lecaille Court, 1km NE of PO, ☎ 08 9755 3699, fax 08 9756 7287, 16 chalets acc up to 8, [ensuite, bath (3), spa bath (2), hairdry, c/fan, wood heat, tel, TV, clock radio, refrig, cook fac, micro, d/wash, ldry, doonas, linen, pillows], w/mach, dryer, iron, conv fac, non smoking units. **D $130 - $320, W $650 - $1,960**, Min book all holiday times, BC DC MC VI.

★★★☆ **Dunsborough Bay Village Resort**, (Chalet), 26 Dunn Bay Rd, 100m E of PO, ☎ 08 9755 3397, fax 08 9755 3790, 18 chalets acc up to 8, (2 & 3 bedrm), [shwr, tlt, fan, wood heat, tel, TV, video-fee, movie, refrig, cook fac, ldry, blkts, linen, pillows], rec rm, ☒, pool, spa, bbq, plygr, golf (mini), tennis. **D** ♠♠ **$163 - $314**, AE BC DC JCB MC VI.

Dunsborough Rail Carriages & Farm Cottages, RSM 100 Commonage Road, 3km S of Dunsborough, ☎ 08 9755 3865, fax 08 9756 7529, 5 cabins acc up to 3, [ensuite, heat, fan, TV, refrig, cook fac ltd, micro, elec frypan, doonas, linen, pillows], bbq, non smoking property, Pets on application. **D** ♠♠ **$86 - $107**, ⍟ **$7**, pen con, Refurbished rail carriages. Min book Christmas and Jan, BC MC VI.

(Cottage Section), 2 cotgs acc up to 8, [shwr, bath, tlt, fan, wood heat, TV, clock radio, cook fac, micro, elec frypan, toaster, ldry, doonas, linen, pillows], bathrm, w/mach, iron, bbq, non smoking property. **D** ♠♠♠♠ **$107 - $128**, ⍟ **$10**.

Dunsborough Windmill Cottages, (Cotg), Bronzewing Rd, 2km SW of PO, ☎ 08 9755 3258, fax 08 9756 8173, (Multi-stry gr fl), 4 cotgs acc up to 6, [shwr, tlt, wood heat, elec blkts, TV, clock radio, refrig, cook fac, micro, blkts, doonas, linen, pillows], iron, bbq (gas), cots. **D** ♠♠ **$85 - $95**, ⍟ **$15**, Min book all holiday times, BC MC VI.

White Sands Holiday Villas, (HU), 316 Geographe Bay Rd, 4km E of PO, ☎ 08 9755 3011, fax 08 9756 8886, 6 units acc up to 6, [shwr, tlt, heat, TV, refrig, cook fac, ldry, blkts, linen reqd-fee, pillows]. **D** ♠♠ **$60.50 - $104.50**, ⍟ **$11, W** ♠♠ **$363 - $1,039.50**.

Willowbank Farm Quindalup, (Cotg), Vasse Yallingup Rd, Busselton 6280, 9km SE of PO, ☎ 08 9755 1104, 1 cotg acc up to 6, (2 bedrm), [shwr, bath, tlt, tel, TV, t/c mkg, refrig, cook fac, micro, blkts, linen, pillows], iron, bbq, plygr. **D $100, W $350 - $600**.

B&B's/Guest Houses

★★★★☆ **Views Of The Bay**, (GH), No children's facilities, Lot 35 Rowan Place, 10km S of PO, ☎ 08 9755 2366, fax 08 9755 2366, 2 rms [ensuite, shwr, tlt, hairdry, fan, fire pl, elec blkts, TV, t/c mkg, refrig, doonas, pillows], w/mach-fee, dryer-fee, iron, iron brd, lounge, spa (hot tub), bbq, meals avail (by arrangement), bicycle, gym, non smoking property. **BB** ♠♠ **$148.50 - $165**, Min book long w/ends, BC MC VI.

★★★☆ **Carramar Rural Retreat**, (B&B), 3 Yungarra Dve, 5km S of PO, ☎ 08 9755 3063, 2 rms [fan, heat (wood), video, t/c mkg, ldry, pillows], shwr, tlt, lounge, ☒, pool. **BB** ♠ **$60 - $70**, ♠♠ **$85 - $99**.

★★★ **Grevillea Cove Bed & Breakfast**, (B&B), 5 Grevillea Cove, 300m W of Geographe Bay Rd, ☎ 08 9756 7861, fax 08 9756 7862, 2 rms [shwr, tlt, a/c-cool, heat, elec blkts, TV, clock radio, t/c mkg, refrig], bbq, c/park. **BLB** ♠ **$70 - $80**, ♠♠ **$80 - $90**.

Eagle Bay Retreat, (B&B), Lot 119 Water Lilly Cove Eagle Bay, 8km NW of PO, ☎ 08 9756 7000, 2 rms (2 suites) [shwr, spa bath, tlt, hairdry, heat, fan, TV, clock radio, t/c mkg, refrig, micro], w/mach-fee, dryer-fee, iron, bbq, picnic facilities, bicycle. **Suite BB** ♠ **$100 - $140**, ♠♠ **$154 - $187**, AE BC DC MC VI, (not yet classified).

Sea Shanty Bed & Breakfast, (B&B), 2 Dunsborough Lakes Dve, ☎ 08 9756 8272, 2 rms [shwr, bath, tlt, heat, c/fan, elec blkts, TV, refrig], iron, iron brd, lounge, t/c mkg shared, non smoking property. **BB** ♠ **$85 - $90**, ♠♠ **$90 - $95**, ♠♠♠ **$170**, Min book long w/ends and Easter, (not yet classified).

Other Accommodation

Dunsborough Inn, (Lodge), 50 Dunn Bay Rd, 100metres E of PO, ☎ 08 9756 7277, fax 08 9756 7377, 24 rms acc up to 4, [tlt, heat, c/fan, TV, video, micro], shwr (9), ldry, w/mach, dryer, iron, iron brd, ☒, cook fac, refrig, bbq, courtesy transfer, ☏, canoeing. **D** ♠ **$20 - $22**, ♠♠ **$40 - $85, RO** ♠ **$20 - $85**, ♠♠ **$45 - $85**, BC DC EFT MC VI, ⅄.

(Self Contained Section), 5 units acc up to 4, [shwr, tlt, cook fac, micro, blkts, doonas, linen, pillows]. **D** ♠♠ **$85 - $95**, ⍟ **$10**.

DWELLINGUP WA 6213

Pop 453. (97km S Perth), See map on page 906, ref A2. Dwellingup is in the timber and fruit growing district surrounded by majestic jarrah forests. Boating (White Water Rafting), Bush Walking, Canoeing, Fishing, Swimming.

Self Catering Accommodation

★★★★☆ **Dwellingup Forest Lodge**, (Chalet), Lot 2 Helio Rd, 4.5km W of PO, ☎ 08 9538 0333, fax 08 9538 0369, 8 chalets acc up to 6, (1 & 2 bedrm), [shwr, tlt, hairdry, evap cool, heat, wood heat, tel, TV, video, clock radio, CD, refrig, cook fac, micro, blkts, doonas, linen, pillows], ldry, w/mach-fee, dryer-fee, iron, iron brd, rec rm, bbq, trailer park, plygr, jetty, canoeing, gym, cots. **D** ♠♠ **$140**, ♠♠♠♠ **$180, W** ♠♠ **$840**, ♠♠♠♠ **$1,080**, pen con, BC EFT MC VI, ⅄.

B&B's/Guest Houses

★★★☆ **Berryvale Lodge**, (B&B), Lot 1082 Williams Rd, 1km W of PO, ☎ 08 9538 1239, fax 08 9538 1239, 3 rms [ensuite (1), a/c-cool, fire pl, elec blkts, tel, TV, doonas, pillows], shwr, tlt, ldry, read rm, lounge, t/c mkg shared, refrig, bbq, meals avail (by arrangement), non smoking property. **BB** ♠ **$55**, ♠♠ **$80 - $90, DBB** ♠ **$80**, ♠♠ **$130 - $140**, fam con, BC MC VI.

ESPERANCE WA 6450

Pop 6,375. (721km SE Perth), See map on page 906, ref D8. Serenely situated beside turquoise waters, the charms of the Esperance region have long been appreciated. Boating, Bush Walking, Fishing, Golf, Surfing, Swimming, Tennis.

Hotels/Motels

★★★★ **Bay Of Isles Motel**, (LMH), 32 The Esplanade, 500m NE of PO, ☎ 08 9071 3999, fax 08 9071 3800, 62 units [shwr, bath, tlt, a/c, tel, TV (satellite), movie, radio, refrig, ldry], lounge, conv fac, ☒ (A la Carte), bar, pool, spa. **D** ♠ **$85**, ♠♠ **$100, Suite D $130**, AE BC DC MC VI.

★★★☆ **Hospitality Inn Esperance**, (M), The Esplanade, 250m E of PO, ☎ 08 9071 1999, fax 08 9071 3915, 49 units [shwr, tlt, a/c, heat, tel, TV, radio, t/c mkg, refrig], ☒, pool, rm serv, plygr, non smoking units (avail). **D** ♠ **$102**, ♠♠ **$102**, ⍟ **$22**, ch con, pen con, AE BC DC MC VI, ⅄.

★★★ **Bayview Motel**, (M), 31 Dempster St, 900m NE of PO, ☎ 08 9071 1533, fax 08 9071 4544, 36 units [shwr, tlt, heat, elec blkts, tel, TV, movie, clock radio, t/c mkg, refrig, cook fac (6), toaster, ldry], ☒, bbq, rm serv, plygr, cots. **D** ♠ **$60.50**, ♠♠ **$75.90**, ♠♠♠♠ **$104.50**, ⍟ **$11**, pen con, BC DC EFT MC VI.

★★★ **Captain Huon Motel**, (M), 5 The Esplanade, 1.2km NE of PO, ☎ 08 9071 2383, fax 08 9071 2358, 15 units [shwr, tlt, a/c, elec blkts, tel, TV, radio, t/c mkg, refrig, cook fac (10)], ldry, ☒, bbq, rm serv, cots. **D** ♠ **$60.50 - $71.50**, ♠♠ **$71.50 - $82.50**, AE BC DC MC VI, ⅄.

(Holiday Unit Section), 6 units acc up to 6, (2 bedrm), [shwr, tlt, elec blkts, tel, TV, radio, cook fac, ldry, blkts, linen, pillows], bbq, cots. **D** ♠♠ **$93.50 - $115.50**.

★★★ **Jetty Motel**, (M), 1 The Esplanade, 1.3km NE of PO, ☎ 08 9071 5978, fax 08 9071 5540, 15 units (1 & 2 bedrm), [shwr, a/c, tel, TV, clock radio, t/c mkg, refrig, cook fac (11), toaster], ldry. **D** ⚊ **$72 - $82**, ⚊⚊ **$77 - $87**, ⚊⚊⚊⚊ **$99 - $109**, ⚊ **$6**, AE BC DC EFT MC VI, ♿.

★★★ **The Old Hospital Motel**, (M), No children's facilities, 1A William St, 400m S of PO, ☎ 08 9071 3587, fax 08 9071 5768, 8 units [shwr, tlt, fan, heat, TV, video, refrig, micro], bbq, non smoking property. **D** ⚊ **$66 - $77**, ⚊⚊ **$77 - $88**.

Esperance Motor Motel Hotel, (LMH), Andrew St, 100m S of PO, ☎ 08 9071 1555, fax 08 9071 1495, 27 units [shwr, tlt, a/c, tel, TV, radio, t/c mkg, refrig], ✉, spa (1), cots. **D** ⚊ **$60**, ⚊⚊ **$70**, AE BC VI.

(Hotel Section), 16 rms [tlt, H & C], shwr. **RO** ⚊ **$25**, ⚊⚊ **$40**.

Esperance Travellers Inn, (LH), Goldfields Rd, 3km NE of PO, ☎ 08 9071 1677, fax 08 9071 1190, 18 rms [shwr, tlt, heat, tel, TV, movie, radio, t/c mkg, refrig], ✕, cots (fee). **D** ⚊ **$49.50**, ⚊⚊ **$60.50**, ⚊⚊⚊⚊ **$77**, BC.

Self Catering Accommodation

★★★★☆ **Esperance Seaside Apartments**, (Apt), 15 The Esplanade, 700m NE of PO, ☎ 08 9072 0044, fax 08 9071 5313, 12 apts acc up to 6, (1, 2 & 3 bedrm), [ensuite (12), shwr, bath (4), spa bath (5), tlt, c/fan, heat, TV, video, clock radio, refrig, cook fac, micro, ldry, blkts, doonas, linen, pillows], w/mach, dryer, bbq, secure park (undercover). **D** ⚊⚊ **$99 - $130**, ⚊⚊⚊⚊ **$140 - $160**, ⚊ **$25**.

★★★★ **Anchorage Holiday Units**, (HU), 81 The Esplanade, 1.5km SE of PO, ☎ 08 9071 7338, fax 08 9071 7024, 5 units acc up to 6, (2 bedrm), [shwr, tlt, heat, fan, elec blkts, TV, video, clock radio, CD, refrig, cook fac, micro, blkts, doonas, linen, pillows], ldry, w/mach-fee, dryer-fee, bbq-fee, c/park (undercover). **D** **$80 - $110**, BC MC VI, ♿.

★★★★ **Archipelago Apartments**, (HU), 24 Goldfields Rd, 2km NE of PO, ☎ 08 9071 7100, fax 08 9071 7501, 6 units acc up to 8, (1, 2 & 3 bedrm), [shwr, tlt, a/c, elec blkts, TV, video, clock radio, t/c mkg, refrig, cook fac, micro, toaster, blkts, doonas, linen, pillows], bathrm, w/mach, dryer, bbq, plygr, cots (avail)-fee. **D** ⚊⚊ **$72 - $94**, ⚊ **$10 - $15**, AE BC DC EFT MC VI.

  ★★★★ **Crokers Park Holiday Resort**, (SA), 817 Harbour Rd, 3km N of PO, ☎ 08 9071 4100, fax 08 9071 5100, 2 serv apts acc up to 10, (2 & 4 bedrm), [shwr, bath, tlt, a/c, elec blkts, TV, video, clock radio, refrig, cook fac, micro, ldry, blkts, doonas, linen, pillows], w/mach, iron, iron brd, pool, bbq, ☎, plygr, cots-fee. **D** ⚊⚊ **$75 - $90**, ⚊ **$13 - $14**, ch con, Min book all holiday times, Min book long w/ends, AE BC DC EFT MC VI, ♿.

★★★★ **Ocean Beach Holiday Units**, (HU), 4 Dempster St, 200m W of Tanker Jetty, 1.2km NE of PO, ☎ 08 9071 5942, fax 08 9071 5942, 5 units acc up to 5, (1 bedrm), [shwr, tlt, heat, fan, c/fan (2), elec blkts, TV, clock radio, refrig, cook fac, micro, blkts, linen, pillows], baby bath, ldry, bbq, cots, non smoking rms. **D** ⚊ **$66 - $85**, ⚊⚊ **$72 - $95**, ⚊ **$15**, pen con, Min book all holiday times, AE BC MC VI.

 ★★★☆ **Esperance Beachfront Resort**, (HU), 19 The Esplanade, 1km NE of PO, ☎ 08 9071 2513, fax 08 9071 5442, 10 units acc up to 4, (1 bedrm), [heat, TV, refrig, cook fac, micro, ldry, blkts, linen, pillows], spa, bbq, shop (deli & cafe), plygr. **D** ⚊ **$71 - $93**, ⚊⚊ **$76 - $98**, ⚊⚊⚊ **$82 - $104**, ⚊⚊⚊⚊ **$87 - $109**, AE BC DC EFT MC VI.

★★★ **Great Ocean Drive Apartments**, (SA), 85 Pink Lake Rd, 1.7km W of PO, ☎ 08 9071 2075, fax 08 9071 4754, 4 serv apts acc up to 4, (1 bedrm), [ensuite, a/c, elec blkts, TV, clock radio, t/c mkg, refrig, micro, toaster, blkts, linen, pillows], ldry, w/mach-fee, dryer-fee, iron, iron brd, bbq, rm serv (ltd), ☎, plygr, cots (avail)-fee. **D** ⚊ **$60.50 - $71.50**, ⚊⚊ **$71.50 - $82.50**, ⚊ **$7.70**, BC MC VI.

Esperance Central Holiday Apartments, (Apt), 59 The Esplanade, 200m W of PO, ☎ 08 9071 7100, fax 08 9071 7501, 2 apts acc up to 3, [shwr, tlt, hairdry, a/c, heat, fan, elec blkts, TV, video, clock radio, t/c mkg, refrig, cook fac, micro, doonas, linen, pillows], w/mach, dryer, iron, iron brd, bbq, non smoking property. **D** ⚊ **$65**, ⚊⚊ **$80 - $100**, ⚊ **$10 - $15**, AE BC DC EFT MC VI, (not yet classified).

CWA Esperance Holiday Units, (HU), 23 The Esplanade, 600m NE of PO, ☎ 08 9071 2370, 2 units acc up to 6, (3 bedrm), [shwr, tlt, heat, TV, refrig, cook fac, ldry, blkts, linen reqd-fee, pillows], cots. **D** **$40 - $50**, ♿.

De La Grande Holiday Resort, (Cotg), Fisheries Rd, 9km NE of PO, ☎ 08 9071 3222, fax 08 9071 4191, 9 cotgs acc up to 6, [shwr, tlt, TV, refrig, cook fac, blkts, linen, pillows], pool, bbq. **D $50**.

Esperance All Seasons Esplanade Apartments, (HU), Previously Esperance All Seasons Holiday Units. No children's facilities, 73 The Esplanade, Loc 500m S of PO, ☎ 08 9071 2257, fax 08 9071 2331, 8 units acc up to 6, (1, 2 & 3 bedrm), [shwr, tlt, a/c-cool, heat, elec blkts, TV, video, clock radio, refrig, cook fac, micro, ldry, blkts, linen, pillows], w/mach, dryer, iron, iron brd, non smoking units, **D** ⚊⚊ **$75 - $100**, ⚊ **$15 - $20**, AE BC DC EFT MC VI.

Esperance Chalet Village, (Chalet), Frank Freeman Dve, 5km E of PO, ☎ 08 9071 1861, fax 08 9072 1021, 17 chalets acc up to 6, [shwr, tlt, TV, refrig, cook fac, ldry, linen, pillows], bbq, plygr, canoeing-fee, mini golf, tennis. **D** ⚊⚊ **$55 - $65**, ⚊ **$9**, AE BC DC EFT MC VI.

B&B's/Guest Houses

★★★★ **Dempster Charm Cottage**, (B&B), No children's facilities, 12 Dempster St, 1.1km NE of PO, ☎ 08 9071 1413, 2 rms [ensuite (1), shwr, bath, tlt, hairdry, heat, fan, wood heat, tel, TV, clock radio, refrig, doonas, pillows], ldry, w/mach, dryer, iron, TV rm, ✕, t/c mkg shared, bbq, bicycle, non smoking property. **BB** ⚊ **$95**, **BLB** ⚊⚊ **$88**, Alcohol free establishment. BC MC VI.

★★★★ **Rosehill Cottage**, (B&B), 30 Crossland St, 500m S of PO, ☎ 08 9071 5050, fax 08 9071 5050, 1 rm [shwr, bath, tlt, heat, TV, clock radio, t/c mkg, refrig, doonas, pillows], iron, iron brd, meals avail, non smoking property. **BB** ⚊ **$65 - $70**, ⚊⚊ **$80 - $90**.

★★★☆ **The Doo Drop Inn**, (B&B), No children's facilities, 3 Norseman Rd, 1.5km NE of PO, ☎ 08 9071 5043, fax 08 9071 5043, 3 rms [a/c-cool, heat (3), c/fan, heat (lounge), tel, TV, video, t/c mkg, refrig (3), doonas, pillows], shwr (1), tlt (2), bathrm (shared) (1), w/mach-fee, iron, iron brd, TV rm, bbq, meals avail, non smoking rms. **BB** ⚊ **$40**, ⚊⚊ **$75**, BC MC VI.

★★★☆ **The Old Hospital Motel B & B**, (B&B), Heritage, 1A William Street, 400m S of PO, ☎ 08 9071 3587, fax 08 9071 5768, 2 rms [spa bath, evap cool, heat, fan, wood heat, TV, video, clock radio, t/c mkg, refrig], shwr, tlt, iron, iron brd, lounge, ✕, bbq, non smoking property. **BLB** ⚊ **$66 - $77**, ⚊⚊ **$99 - $110**, ⚊⚊⚊ **$165 - $175**, ⚊⚊⚊⚊ **$190 - $200**, pen con, BC MC VI.

Pink Lake Lodge, (GH), 85 Pink Lake Rd, 1.7km W of PO, ☎ 08 9071 2075, fax 08 9071 4754, 23 rms [a/c (8), heat, TV, t/c mkg, refrig, pillows], ldry, w/mach-fee, dryer-fee, TV rm, ✕, bbq, ☎, plygr, cots. **D** ⚊⚊⚊⚊ **$60.50 - $86.90**, **RO** ⚊ **$27.50 - $60.50**, ⚊⚊ **$44 - $71.50**, BC MC VI.

Pink Lake Lodge ...continued

(Motel Section), 4 units [ensuite, a/c-cool, heat, t/c mkg, refrig].
D ♂♀ $60.50 - $71.50, ⓘ $7.70.

Western Heights Bed & Breakfast, (B&B), 4 Mills Place, 2km SE of PO,
☎ 08 9071 3164, 2 rms [shwr, bath, tlt, heat, tel, TV, video, clock radio,
t/c mkg, refrig, pillows], ldry, w/mach-fee, iron-fee, TV rm, ✕, non
smoking rms. BB ♂ $65 - $75, ♂♀ $80 - $90, Min book all holiday times.

Other Accommodation

Esperance Backpackers, No children's facilities, Emily St, 1km S of PO,
☎ 08 9071 4724, fax 08 9071 4724, 10 rms [heat, tel, TV, video,
t/c mkg, ldry, blkts, linen, pillows], shwr, tlt, w/mach-fee, dryer-fee,
iron-fee, rec rm, TV rm, read rm, cook fac, refrig, bbq, courtesy transfer,
plygr, non smoking rms. RO ♂ $16 - $18, ⓘ $39 - $42, BC MC VI.

EUCLA WA 6443

*Pop Nominal, (1436km E Perth), See map on page 906, ref E7.
On the Eyre Highway 11km from the WA/SA border.*

★★★☆ **Eucla Motor Hotel**, (LMH), Eyre Hwy, 726km E of Norseman,
☎ 08 9039 3468, fax 08 9039 3401, 23 units [shwr, tlt, a/c, heat,
TV, t/c mkg, refrig, ldry], ✕, bar, pool, cots. D ♂ $71, ♂♀ $82, BC
EFT MC VI, ⚐&.

EXMOUTH WA 6707

*Pop 3,058. (1260km N Perth), See map on page 906, ref A4.
Exmouth boasts some of the most unique natural-tourism attributes
within Australia.*

Hotels/Motels

★★★☆ **Potshot Hotel Resort**, (LMH), Murat Rd, 100m E of PO,
☎ 08 9949 1200, fax 08 9949 1486, 45 units [ensuite, a/c-cool, tel,
t/c mkg, refrig], conv fac, ✕ (2), bar (2), pool, bbq. RO ♂ $70 - $75,
♂♀ $85 - $89, AE BC DC MC VI.

★★★☆ **(Apartment Section)**, 32 apts acc up to 6, (2 & 3 bedrm),
[shwr, tlt, a/c-cool, TV, refrig, cook fac, ldry, blkts, linen, pillows],
✕ (2), bar (2), pool, bbq, cots-fee. D $98 - $185, ⓘ $12.

★★★ **Sea Breeze Resort**, (LH), 116 North C St H E Holt Navy Base,
inside Navy base, 5km N of PO, ☎ 08 9949 1800, fax 08 9949 1300,
24 rms [ensuite, a/c-cool, tel, TV, t/c mkg, refrig], ldry, rec rm, lounge,
✕, bar, pool, bbq, bicycle (free hire), gym, squash, tennis, non
smoking property. RO ♂ $90 - $115, ♂♀ $100 - $120, ⓘ $10, ch con,
fam con, BC EFT MC VI.

B&B's/Guest Houses

★★★★ **Ningaloo Lodge Exmouth**, (GH), Lot 1 Lefroy St, 800metres S
of PO, ☎ 08 9949 4949, fax 08 9949 4900, 36 rms [ensuite, shwr, tlt,
a/c-cool, fan, TV, clock radio, refrig, pillows], rec rm (/games), ✕ (/self
catering), pool, bbq, ⚐, non smoking rms. RO ♂♀ $66 - $90, EFT.

Giralia Station, (GH), Burkett Rd, Off Exmouth Rd, Carnarvon 6701,
126km SE of PO, ☎ 08 9942 5937, fax 08 9942 5937, 5 rms [a/c-cool,
TV, ldry, pillows], shwr, tlt, ✕. DBB ♂ $66 - $120.

(Cabin Section), 15 cabins acc up to 2, [a/c-cool, blkts, linen,
pillows], shwr, tlt. D ♂ $22.

(Camping Section), (Bunk Rooms).

Other Accommodation

Pete's Exmouth Backpackers, Truscott Cres, 1km S of PO,
☎ 08 9949 1101, fax 08 9949 1402, 44 rms acc up to 8, (1 bedrm),
[ensuite, shwr, tlt, a/c-cool, c/fan, tel, refrig, cook fac, micro, blkts, linen,
pillows], bathrm, ldry, w/mach, dryer, pool, bbq, kiosk, courtesy transfer,
bicycle, tennis, non smoking rms. RO ♂ $16.50, ♂♀ $39.60, W♂ $99,
♂♀ $237.60, pen con, BC EFT MC VI.

FITZROY CROSSING WA 6765

*Pop 1,147. (2566km N Perth), See map on page 906, ref D3.
Fitzroy Crossing is a small town serving the pastoral industry,
mining, tourism and Aboriginal communities.*

★★★☆ **Fitzroy River Lodge**, (LMH), Great Northern Hwy,
5km SE of PO, ☎ 08 9191 5141, fax 08 9191 5142,
38 units (2 suites) [shwr, bath, tlt, a/c-cool, tel, TV,
radio, t/c mkg, refrig, ldry], conv fac, ✕, bar, pool, bbq,
tennis, cots-fee. D ♂ $159, ♂♀ $159, ♂♂♂♂ $203, ⚐&.

Crossing Motor Inn, (LMH), Skuthorpe Rd Northern Hwy, 4km NE of PO,
☎ 08 9191 5080, fax 08 9191 5208, 27 units [shwr, tlt, a/c, t/c mkg,
refrig]. D ♂ $82, ♂♀ $85 - $100.

GASCOYNE JUNCTION WA 6705

*Pop Nominal, (951km N Perth), See map on page 906, ref A5.
Gascoyne Junction lies at the junction of the Gascoyne and Lyons
Rivers.*

Hotels/Motels

The Junction Hotel, (LH), Classified by National Trust, Meekatharra Rd,
1km from Police Station, ☎ 08 9943 0504, fax 08 9943 0564, 20 rms
[tlt, a/c, fax, t/c mkg, refrig, toaster], shwr, ldry, ✕, pool, bbq, petrol,
⚐, tennis. BB ♂ $45, ♂♀ $55, fam con, pen con, BC EFT MC VI.

Self Catering Accommodation

Erong Springs Station, (Cotg), 170km S of Mount Augustus,
☎ 08 9981 2910, fax 08 9981 2210, 1 cotg acc up to 8, (4 bedrm),
[cook fac, ldry, blkts, linen, pillows], shwr, tlt. D ♂ $38.50, **Powered
Site** D ♂♀ $15, ch con.

GERALDTON WA 6530

*Pop 24,243. (424km N Perth), See map on page 906, ref A6. The
largest town in the mid-west region. The off-shore islands and reef
support a rock lobster industry worth millions of dollars. See Also
Greenough.*

Hotels/Motels

★★★★ **African Reef Resort Hotel**, (LMH), 5 Broadhead Ave, Tarcoola
Beach 6530, 3km S of PO, ☎ 08 9964 5566, fax 08 9964 5544, 6 units
[shwr, tlt, a/c, tel, fax, TV, clock radio, t/c mkg, refrig, toaster], ldry,
w/mach-fee, dryer-fee, conv fac, ✕, pool, plygr, cots-fee, non smoking
rms. RO ♂ $88 - $100, ♂♀ $105 - $115, ⓘ $17, AE BC DC EFT MC VI.

★★★★ **Hospitality Inn Geraldton**, (M), Cathedral Ave,
1.5km S of PO, ☎ 08 9921 1422, fax 08 9921 1239,
48 units [shwr, tlt, a/c, heat, tel, TV, movie, radio, t/c mkg,
refrig, ldry], ✕, pool, bbq, rm serv, plygr, non smoking
units (avail). D ♂♀ $97 - $118, ⓘ $21.50, pen con, Some units of a
lower rating. AE BC DC MC VI, ⚐&.

(Serviced Apartment Section), 4 serv apts acc up to 6, (2 & 3
bedrm), [ensuite, hairdry, a/c, tel, TV, video, movie, clock radio,
refrig, cook fac, micro, toaster, ldry, pillows], spa. D $132 - $218.

★★★★ **Ocean Centre Hotel**, (LH), Cnr Foreshore Dve & Cathedral Ave,
☎ 08 9921 7777, fax 08 9964 1990, 92 rms [shwr, tlt, a/c, tel, TV, movie,
t/c mkg, refrig, mini bar], iron, iron brd, conv fac, ✕. D ♂♀ $85 - $160,
ⓘ $15, AE BC DC MC VI, ⚐&.

★★★☆ **Batavia Motor Inne**, (LMH), 54 Fitzgerald St, 500m SW of PO,
☎ 08 9921 3500, fax 08 9964 1061, 76 units [shwr, tlt, a/c, tel, TV,
radio, t/c mkg, refrig], ✕, pool, rm serv, cots. D ♂ $92, ♂♀ $92,
♂♂♂♂ $104, ⓘ $11, AE BC DC MC VI.

★★★☆ **Geraldton Motor Inn**, (M), 107
Brand Hwy, 3km S of PO, ☎ 08 9964 4777,
fax 08 9921 6969, (Multi-stry gr fl), 40 units
[shwr, tlt, a/c, tel, TV, movie, t/c mkg, refrig,
mini bar, toaster, ldry (services)], iron, iron brd, ✕. D ♂♀ $90 - $105,
ⓘ $15, AE BC DC EFT MC VI.

★★★☆ **Mercure Inn Wintersun Geraldton**, (LH), 441 Chapman Rd,
Bluff Point, 7km N of PO, ☎ 08 9923 1211, fax 08 9923 1411, 36 rms
[shwr, tlt, a/c, tel, TV, movie, radio, t/c mkg, refrig], ✕, pool, bbq,
cots. D ♂♀ $84, ♂♂♂♂ $94, ⓘ $10, AE BC DC MC VI.

★★★ **Hacienda Motel**, (M), Classified by National Trust, Durlacher St,
2km S of PO, ☎ 08 9921 2155, fax 08 9964 1018, 30 units [shwr, tlt,
a/c, tel, TV, clock radio, t/c mkg, refrig], ✕, pool, rm serv. D ♂ $60 - $70,
♂♀ $77 - $80, ♂♂♂♂ $130, ⓘ $15, BC MC VI.

★★★ **Sun City Motel-Geraldton**, (M), 137 Cathedral Ave, 1km S of PO,
☎ 08 9921 6111, fax 08 9921 6126, 20 units [shwr, tlt, a/c, tel, TV, movie,
radio, refrig], pool, pool-indoor, sauna, spa, bbq, gym. D ♂ $60 - $80,
♂♀ $68 - $90, Some units of a lower rating, AE BC DC MC VI.

★★☆ **Mercure Inn Geraldton**, (M), Brand Hwy, 3.5km S of PO,
☎ 08 9921 2455, fax 08 9921 5830, 60 units [shwr, tlt, a/c, tel, TV,
movie, t/c mkg, refrig, mini bar, cook fac (some), ldry], ✕, pool, bbq,
plygr, cots. D ♂♀ $84 - $105, ♂♂♂♂ $108 - $135, ⓘ $20, Some units of
a higher rating. AE BC DC MC VI.

★☆ **Mariner Motor Hotel**, (LMH), 298 Chapman Rd, 3km N of PO,
☎ 08 9921 2544, fax 08 9921 7466, 18 units [shwr, tlt, a/c, tel, TV,
radio, t/c mkg, refrig], ✕, pool, cots-fee. D ♂ $44 - $49, ♂♀ $55 - $60,
♂♂♂♂ $66 - $72, AE BC DC MC VI.

Queens Motor Hotel, (LH), Durlacher St, 500m S of PO,
☎ 08 9921 1064, fax 08 9921 8427, 24 rms [shwr, tlt, a/c, fan, tel,
TV, t/c mkg, refrig], ✕. D ♂ $55, ♂♀ $70, ⓘ $15.

GERALDTON WA continued...

Self Catering Accommodation

★★★☆ **Mahomets Village**, (HU), Willcock Dve, 3km S of PO,
☎ 08 9921 6652, fax 08 9921 6653, 14 units acc up to 6, [shwr, tlt, tel, TV, refrig, cook fac, blkts, linen, pillows], w/mach, bbq. **D $68.20 - $108.90, W $412.50 - $693**, Min book all holiday times.

★★★ **Abrolhos Reef Lodge**, (HU), 126 Brand Hwy, 3km S of PO,
☎ 08 9921 3811, fax 08 9921 3005, 30 units acc up to 6, (1 & 2 bedrm), [shwr, tlt, a/c, tel, TV, video-fee, refrig, cook fac, micro, ldry, blkts, linen, pillows], pool, bbq, plygr, cots (avail). **D ⚫ $80 - $95, ⚫⚫ $110 - $130**, ◊ $15, AE BC DC MC VI.

★★★ **Geraldton's Ocean West Units**, (HU), 1 Hadda Way, 2km S of PO,
☎ 08 9921 1047, fax 08 9923 9628, 24 units acc up to 6, (1 & 3 bedrm), [shwr, tlt, heat, tel, TV, refrig, micro, ldry, blkts, linen, pillows], bbq (communal area), plygr. **D $77 - $120, W $385 - $600**, BC MC VI, &⟨⟩.

★★★ **Goodwood Lodge**, (HU), Cnr Brand Hwy & Durlacher St, 2km S of PO, ☎ 08 9921 5666, fax 08 9964 5665, 19 units acc up to 5, (1 & 2 bedrm), [shwr, tlt, a/c, tel, TV, radio, refrig, cook fac, blkts, linen, pillows], pool, cots-fee. **D ⚫ $60, ⚫⚫ $68.**

★★★ **Tarcoola Beach Resort**, (HU), 5 Broadhead Ave Mount Tarcoola, 3km S of PO, ☎ 08 9964 5566, fax 08 9964 5544, 16 units acc up to 6, (1 & 2 bedrm), [shwr, tlt, a/c, tel, TV, clock radio, t/c mkg, refrig, cook fac, micro, toaster, blkts, linen, pillows], w/mach, dryer, pool, cots-fee. **D $77 - $105**, ◊ $8 - $17, AE BC DC EFT MC VI.

B&B's/Guest Houses

★★★☆ **Greengables Lodge**, (B&B), No children's facilities, 7 Hackett Rd, 15km NE of PO, ☎ 08 9938 2332, fax 08 9938 3134, 4 rms [ensuite (1), bath, spa bath, hairdry, a/c, c/fan, TV, video, clock radio, t/c mkg, refrig, pillows], shwr, tlt, ldry, lounge, ⊠, BYO, pool, bbq, meals avail (by arrangement), non smoking rms. **BB ⚫ $74 - $98, ⚫⚫ $87 - $113, DBB ⚫ $93 - $117, ⚫⚫ $138 - $151**, ch con, AE BC DC MC VI.

GINGIN WA 6503

Pop 549. (84km N Perth), See map on page 906, ref A1. A popular point of call for travellers on day trips from Perth, and those heading north.

Hotels/Motels

Gingin Motel Hotel, (LMH), 5 Jones St, 500m SW of PO,
☎ 08 9575 2214, fax 08 9575 2636, 6 units [shwr, tlt, TV, t/c mkg, refrig]. **D ⚫ $35 - $45, ⚫⚫ $55 - $65, ⚫⚫⚫⚫ $70.**

B&B's/Guest Houses

★★★★ **Cheriton Estate**, (GH), Lot 101 Cheriton Road, 1km N of Gingin Townsite, ☎ 08 9575 2463, fax 08 9575 1140, 7 rms [ensuite, shwr, bath, tlt, a/c-cool, heat, fire pl, wood heat, fax, TV, video, CD, t/c mkg], w/mach, dryer, iron, iron brd, lounge, lounge firepl, ⟨, pool above ground, secure park, picnic facilities, golf, non smoking property. **BLB ⚫⚫ $300**, fam con, pen con, AE BC DC EFT MC.

GRACETOWN WA 6284

Pop Nominal, (277km S Perth), See map on page 906, ref A2. A pleasant, seaside settlement on the shore of Cowaramup Bay.

BJ's at Gracetown, (Chalet), Unit 2 42 Osborne St, 4km W turn off Caves Rd, ☎ 08 9430 6383, fax 08 9336 2019, 2 chalets acc up to 6, [shwr, tlt, hairdry, wood heat, TV, video, clock radio, refrig, cook fac, micro, toaster, blkts, doonas, pillows], w/mach, iron, iron brd, bbq, non smoking property. **D $100 - $150, W $525 - $950**, Min book applies, (not yet classified).

GREENBUSHES WA 6254

Pop 321. (251km S Perth), See map on page 906, ref A2. The discovery of tin led to the town's founding.

Exchange Hotel, (LH), Blackwood Rd, 200m SE of PO, ☎ 08 9764 3509, fax 08 9764 3694, 9 rms [shwr, tlt, a/c-cool, heat, elec blkts, TV, t/c mkg, refrig], ⊠, cots. **D ⚫ $44, ⚫⚫ $55**, ◊ $10, AE BC DC MC VI.

GREENOUGH WA 6529

Pop 100. (400km N Perth), See map on page 906, ref A6. The historic hamlet of Greenough was the centre of several hundred small farms. Today, the hamlet has been extensively restored and visitors are encouraged.

Hotels/Motels

★★★☆ **Greenough River Motel Resort**, (M), Dover Crt, Geraldton 6530, 10km S of Geraldton PO, ☎ 08 9921 5888, fax 08 9921 8245, 16 units [shwr, bath, tlt, a/c, tel, TV, clock radio, refrig, cook fac, ldry], rec rm, ⊠, pool, bbq, plygr, tennis. **D ⚫⚫ $110**, ◊ $10, AE BC DC MC VI.

B&B's/Guest Houses

★★★☆ **Rock Of Ages Cottage B&B**, (B&B), Phillips Rd, off Brand Hwy, Geraldton 6530, 18km S of Geraldton PO, ☎ 08 9926 1154, fax 08 9926 1154, 3 rms [heat, fan, fire pl, TV, radio, t/c mkg, refrig, doonas, pillows], shwr, tlt, ldry, TV rm, spa, bbq, non smoking property. **BB ⚫ $60, ⚫⚫ $80, BLB ⚫ $55, ⚫⚫ $70**, BC MC VI.

GUILDERTON WA 6041

Pop part of Lancelin, (94km N Perth), See map on page 906, ref A1. A small peaceful and picturesque seaside town at the mouth of the Moore River. Fishing, Surfing, Swimming.

CWA Guilderton, (Cotg), 41 Gordon St, 500m SW of PO, ☎ 08 9651 9040, fax 08 9651 9040, 1 cotg acc up to 6, (3 bedrm), [heat, refrig, cook fac, ldry, blkts, linen reqd, pillows], bathrm, bbq. **D $55.**

Matilda Lake Farm Chalets, (Chalet), (Farm), 1484 Telephone Rd, Gingin 6503, 19km NE of PO, ☎ 08 9575 7657, fax 08 9575 7657, 6 chalets acc up to 14, [shwr, tlt, a/c-cool, heat, TV, refrig, cook fac, micro, toaster, ldry, blkts, linen, pillows], w/mach, iron, bbq, cots (avail). **D ⚫⚫⚫⚫ $88**, ◊ $11, Min book Christmas Jan long w/ends and Easter, BC MC VI.

HALLS CREEK WA 6770

Pop 966. (2855km N Perth), See map on page 906, ref E3. It was the site of the first goldrush in Western Australia.

FLAG
FLAG CHOICE HOTELS

★★★☆ **Kimberley Hotel Motel**, (LH), Roberta Ave, 500m S of PO, ☎ 08 9168 6101, fax 08 9168 6071, 50 rms [shwr, bath, tlt, hairdry, a/c, tel, TV, t/c mkg, refrig], iron, ⊠, pool, spa (shared), bbq. **RO ⚫ $155, ⚫⚫ $155**, AE BC DC MC VI.

★★ **Halls Creek Motel**, (M), Great Northern Hwy, 300m NW of PO, ☎ 08 9168 6001, fax 08 9168 6044, 30 units [shwr, tlt, a/c, heat, TV, t/c mkg, refrig], ⊠, pool. **RO ⚫ $70, ⚫⚫ $88, ⚫⚫⚫ $99, ⚫⚫⚫⚫ $110**, BC MC VI.

HARVEY WA 6220

Pop 2,570. (140km S Perth), See map on page 906, ref A2. Harvey is the central town and major part of the south-west irrigation area. Bowls, Bush Walking, Canoeing, Fishing, Golf, Scenic Drives.

Hotels/Motels

★★☆ **Harvey Hotel**, (LH), Cnr Harper & Harvey Sts, 2.5km E of PO, ☎ 08 9729 1034, fax 08 9729 3055, 27 rms [shwr (14), tlt (14), H & C (12), elec blkts, TV, t/c mkg, refrig], ⊠, cots. **RO ⚫ $25 - $50, ⚫⚫ $45 - $60**, ◊ $15, BC MC.

Self Catering Accommodation

Cottage Parks Myalup Pines, (Cotg), 365 Forestry Rd, 5km W of Harvey PO, ☎ 08 9720 1026, fax 08 9592 5222, 7 cotgs acc up to 8, (3 bedrm), [shwr, tlt, heat, refrig, cook fac, ldry, linen reqd, pillows], lounge (communal hall), ⟨, bbq, ⟨, plygr, cots. **D $60 - $80.**

Harvey Hills Farm Stay Holidays, (Cotg), Weir Rd, 6km E of PO, ☎ 08 9729 1434, fax 08 9729 1434, 3 cotgs acc up to 6, [shwr, a/c-cool, wood heat, elec blkts, TV, refrig, cook fac, ldry, blkts, linen reqd, pillows], bathrm, pool, bbq, plygr. **D $85 - $95.**

Mornington Farmstays, (Cotg), Lot 9 Cnr Martin & Sandalwood Road, Brunswick Junction 6224, 17km S of Harvey, ☎ 08 9726 9202, fax 08 9726 9202, 6 cotgs acc up to 10, [shwr, tlt, c/fan, wood heat, tel, refrig, micro, elec frypan, toaster, blkts, doonas, linen-fee], ⟨, freezer, bbq, plygr, canoeing, cots, non smoking units. **D $71.50 - $93.50**, ◊ $5.50 - $11, Min book long w/ends, BC MC VI.

HOPETOUN WA 6348

Pop 319. Nominal, (585km SE Perth), See map on page 906, ref C8. A picturesque and pleasant waterfront holiday destination.

Hopetoun Motel Village, (M), Lot 458 Veal St, 300m N of PO, ☎ 08 9838 3219, fax 08 9838 3220, 11 units [shwr, tlt, fan, TV, clock radio, t/c mkg, refrig], bbq, plygr. **D ⚫⚫ $65 - $75**, ◊ $9, BC MC VI.

HORROCKS WA 6535

Pop part of Northampton, (496km NW Perth), See map on page 906, ref A6. Horrocks Beach is a popular holiday and fishing community and a centre for the rock-lobster industry.

Killara Cottages, (Cotg), Glance St, Northampton 6535, next to PO, ☎ 08 9934 3031, fax 08 9934 3097, 12 cotgs acc up to 7, (2 & 3 bedrm), [shwr, tlt, TV, refrig, cook fac, micro, ldry, blkts, linen reqd-fee, pillows], bbq. **D ⚫⚫ $40, ⚫⚫⚫⚫ $60, W ⚫⚫ $200 - $330.**

HYDEN WA 6359

Pop 100. (339km SE Perth), See map on page 906, ref C7. Synonymous with the famous Wave Rock, Hippo's Yawn and The Breakers - unique formations created by wind action over the past three million years.

Hotels/Motels

★★★ **Hyden Wave Rock Hotel**, (LH), 2 Lynch St, 100m S of PO, ☎ 08 9880 5052, fax 08 9880 5041, 58 rms (3 suites) [shwr, tlt, a/c, tel, TV, t/c mkg, refrig, mini bar], bathrm, ⊠, pool, spa. **D ∮ $70, ♦♦ $98.**

Self Catering Accommodation

★★★ **Wave Rock Lakeside Cottages**, (Cotg), Wave Rock Rd, 4km E of PO, ☎ 08 9880 5400, fax 08 9889 5018, 14 cotgs acc up to 8, (2 bedrm), [shwr, tlt, a/c-cool, TV, clock radio, refrig, cook fac, micro, blkts, linen, pillows], ldry, canoeing. **D ∮ $99, ♦♦ $102, ∮ $16**, ch con, AE BC EFT MC VI, ⌂⌕.

Omeo Farm, (Cotg), (Farm), Cnr Kent & Hadden Rds, Pingaring 6357, 12.6km SE of Pingaring, ☎ 08 9866 8023, fax 08 9866 8089, 1 cotg acc up to 8, [shwr, bath, tlt, fan, heat, elec blkts, refrig, cook fac, blkts, linen, pillows], meals avail. **BB ∮ $38**, ch con.

B&B's/Guest Houses

★★★☆ **Wave-A-Way Getaway**, (B&B), Previously Joycraft Farmstay Bed & Breakfast Cnr Karlgarin Lake & Worland Rds, 22km NW of PO, ☎ 08 9880 5129, fax 08 9880 5103, 3 rms [a/c-cool, c/fan, wood heat, doonas, pillows], shwr, tlt, ldry, TV rm, ✗, t/c mkg shared, bbq, meals avail (by arrangement), non smoking rms. **BB ∮ $38.50, ♦♦ $77, DBB ∮ $55, ♦♦ $110**, ch con, Farm activities. MC VI.

Other Accommodation

Wave-A-Way Getaway-BP, Previously Wave-A-Way Backpackers Cnr Karlgarin Lake & Worland Rds, Karlgarin 6358, 22km NW of PO, ☎ 08 9880 5129, fax 08 9880 5103, 3 rms acc up to 24, [shwr, tlt, wood heat, TV (shared), t/c mkg, refrig, cook fac, blkts, linen reqd-fee, pillows], lounge, bbq, meals avail (by arrangement), non smoking rms. **D ∮ $16.50 - $18.70**, ch con, Farm Activities. MC VI.

JARRAHDALE WA 6203

Pop Nominal, (51km S Perth), See map on page 906, ref E8. Jarrahdale is the last of the timber towns near Perth and surprisingly, is still surrounded by Jarrah forrest.

Jarrahdale Holiday Carriages, 324 Jarrahdale Rd, 3.3km off South West Hwy, ☎ 08 9525 5780, fax 08 9525 5792, 4 cabins acc up to 4, [a/c-cool, refrig, cook fac ltd, ldry, blkts, linen, pillows], shwr, tlt, bbq. **D ♦♦ $60, W ♦♦ $240.**

JERRAMUNGUP WA 6337

Pop 332. (454km SE Perth), See map on page 906, ref C8. A small wheat and sheep farming community.

Fitzgerald River National Park B&B, (B&B), (Farm), Quiss Rd, 32km E of PO, ☎ 08 9835 5026, fax 08 9835 5026, 2 rms [shwr, tlt, a/c-cool, heat, fan, elec blkts, tel (hosts), TV, video, clock radio, t/c mkg, refrig], ldry, w/mach, dryer, iron, iron brd, lounge, picnic facilities, non smoking property. **BB ∮ $50, ♦♦ $75, DBB ∮ $72.**

Glentarkie Bed & Breakfast, (B&B), Gnowangerup-Jerramungup Rd, 1km W of PO, ☎ 08 9835 1006, fax 08 9835 1236, 3 rms [hairdry, fire pl, tel, TV, clock radio, t/c mkg, doonas, pillows], shwr, tlt, rec rm, meals avail (by arrangement). **BB ∮ $50, ♦♦ $70**, BC MC VI.

Jerramungup Farmstay, (B&B), (Farm), 1 South Coast Hwy, 2km S of PO, ☎ 08 9835 1002, fax 08 9835 1919, 1 rm [shwr, tlt, fan, heat, elec blkts, TV, clock radio, t/c mkg, refrig, ldry, pillows], bbq, plygr. **BB ∮ $55, ♦♦ $75, D ∮ $20.**

JURIEN WA 6516

Pop 449. (266km N Perth), See map on page 906, ref A7. Jurien Bay is the largest sheltered bay along the Central West Coast, which is protected by reefs and islands a few kilometres from the shoreline. Lions Lookout, Pinnacles. Boating, Bowls, Fishing, Golf, Squash, Swimming, Tennis.

Hotels/Motels

Jurien Bay Motel Hotel, (LMH), Padbury St, 250m E of PO, ☎ 08 9652 1022, fax 08 9652 1425, 32 units [shwr, tlt, a/c, heat, TV, clock radio, t/c mkg, refrig, cook fac (4)], ⊠, pool, bbq, tennis. **D ∮ $66, ♦♦ $77, ♦♦♦♦ $121**, BC DC MC VI.

Self Catering Accommodation

★★ **Top Spot Jurien Cottages**, (Cotg), Bashford St, 500m S of PO, ☎ 08 9652 1290, fax 08 9964 4745, 4 cotgs acc up to 6, (2 & 3 bedrm), [shwr, tlt, fan, heat, TV, refrig, cook fac, ldry, linen reqd-fee, pillows], lounge, cots. **D ♦♦ $70, ∮ $10 - $12, W ♦♦ $280 - $350.**

Jurien Beachfront Holiday Units, (HF), 12 Grigson St, adjacent to PO. ☎ 08 9652 1172, fax 08 9652 1366, 4 flats acc up to 6, [shwr, tlt, TV, refrig, cook fac, micro, ldry, blkts reqd-fee, linen reqd-fee, pillows reqd-fee]. **D $60 - $70, W $300 - $350.**

KALBARRI WA 6536

Pop 1,788. (589km N Perth), See map on page 906, ref A6. Situated at the mouth of the Murchinson River. The town is most famous for the spectacular scenery along the river, where nature has carved magnificent gorges, some over 130m deep.

Hotels/Motels

★★★☆ **Kalbarri Palm Resort**, (M), Porter St, 400m E of PO, ☎ 08 9937 2333, fax 08 9937 1324, 78 units [shwr, tlt, a/c, tel, TV, video, clock radio, t/c mkg, refrig, cook fac], ⊠, pool (2), spa, bbq, bowls, tennis, cots-fee. **D ♦♦ $65 - $90, ♦♦♦♦ $75 - $110**, AE BC DC MC VI.

Self Catering Accommodation

★★★★ **Kalbarri Beach Resort**, (HU), Cnr Grey & Clotworthy Sts, 1km NE of PO, ☎ 08 9937 1061, fax 08 9937 1323, 82 units acc up to 5, (2 bedrm), [shwr, tlt, a/c-cool, TV, movie, refrig, cook fac, blkts, linen, pillows], ⊠, pool, sauna, spa, bbq, tennis. **D $95, W $455**, AE BC DC MC VI.

★★★★ **Kalbarri Murchison View Apartments**, (HU), Cnr Grey & Rushton Sts, 150m W of PO, ☎ 08 9937 1096, fax 08 9937 1522, 19 units acc up to 6, (2 & 3 bedrm), [shwr, tlt, a/c-cool, fan, tel, TV, refrig, cook fac, micro, ldry, blkts, linen, pillows], pool, bbq, cots. **D $75.90 - $143, W $517 - $863.50**, BC MC VI.

★★★★ **Kalbarri Reef Villas**, (HU), Coles St, 700m NE of PO, ☎ 08 9937 1165, fax 08 9937 1465, 8 units acc up to 5, (2 bedrm), [shwr, tlt, a/c-cool (1), fan, heat, TV, movie, radio, refrig, cook fac, micro, ldry, blkts, linen, pillows], pool, bbq, courtesy transfer. **W $510 - $835**, pen con, BC MC VI.

★★★☆ **Kalbarri Seafront Villas**, (HF), 108 Grey St, 500m NE of PO, ☎ 08 9937 1025, fax 08 9937 1525, 13 flats acc up to 5, (1 & 2 bedrm), [shwr, tlt, a/c-cool, fan, heat, tel, TV, video, clock radio, refrig, cook fac, micro, toaster, ldry, blkts, linen, pillows], iron, pool, bbq, cots. **D $77 - $198, W $420 - $1,295**, BC EFT MC VI, ⌂⌕.

(Bed & Breakfast Section), 98 Grey St, 1 rm [shwr, spa bath, tlt, a/c-cool, heat, c/fan, TV, video, clock radio, t/c mkg, refrig], ldry, w/mach-fee, dryer-fee, iron, pool, c/park. **BLB ♦♦ $95 - $125**, (not yet classified).

★★★ **Kalbarri Gardens Apartments**, (HU), 33 Glass Street, ☎ 08 9937 2211, fax 08 9937 2200, (Multi-stry 2 stry gr fl), 18 units acc up to 6, [shwr, tlt, a/c, c/fan, TV, video, clock radio, t/c mkg, refrig, cook fac, ldry, blkts, linen, pillows], pool, bbq, ☎, plygr, cots. **D $60 - $120, W $380 - $750**, ⌂⌕.

★★★ **Pelican Shore Villas**, (HU), Cnr Grey and Kaiber Sts, 500m W of PO, ☎ 08 9937 1708, fax 08 9937 2057, (Multi-stry gr fl), 20 units acc up to 6, [shwr, bath, tlt, a/c, c/fan, TV, clock radio, refrig, cook fac, micro, toaster, ldry, blkts, linen, pillows], w/mach, iron, pool, bbq. **D $80 - $175, W $500 - $1,150**, BC MC VI.

★★★ **Sunsea Villas**, (HU), 38 Grey St, 200m W of PO, ☎ 08 9937 1187, fax 08 9937 1187, (2 stry gr fl), 9 units acc up to 6, [shwr, tlt, a/c-cool, fan, heat, TV, video, refrig, cook fac, micro, ldry, blkts, linen, pillows], w/mach, iron, bbq. **D $85 - $110, ∮ $11, W $490 - $690**, BC EFT MC VI.

★★☆ **Sun River Chalets**, (Cotg), Nanda Dve, 700m SW of PO, ☎ 08 9937 1119, fax 08 9937 1119, 7 cotgs acc up to 6, [shwr, tlt, a/c, fan, TV, refrig, cook fac, blkts, linen, pillows], bbq, plygr. **D $55 - $88, W $330 - $616**, BC MC VI.

Av-Er-Rest Duplex Holiday Homes, (HU), Previously Av-Er-Rest Holiday Units 17 Mortimer St, 800m NE of PO, ☎ 08 9937 1101, fax 08 9937 1455, 20 units acc up to 6, [shwr, tlt, a/c (some), fan, TV, refrig, cook fac, micro, ldry, blkts reqd-fee, linen reqd-fee], bbq. D ♦♦ $50 - $80, ◊ $11, W ♦♦ $300 - $480.

(Lodge Section), 1 rm acc up to 12, [shwr (2), fan, TV, refrig, cook fac, micro, blkts reqd-fee, linen reqd-fee], tlt. D ♦ $16 - $20, Min book applies, (not yet classified).

(Cottage Section), 2 cotgs acc up to 8, (3 bedrm), [shwr, tlt, a/c-cool, TV, refrig, cook fac, micro, ldry, blkts reqd-fee, linen reqd-fee]. D ♦♦ $60 - $100, ◊ $11.

(Villa Section), 3 villas acc up to 8, (3 bedrm), [shwr, tlt, a/c, TV, video, refrig, cook fac, micro, ldry, blkts, linen, pillows], bbq, c/park. D ♦♦ $100, ◊ $17, W ♦♦ $600 - $660.

Kalbarri Riverfront Units, (HU), 16 Grey St, 300m W of PO, ☎ 08 9937 1032, fax 08 9937 1509, 2 units acc up to 5, [shwr, bath, tlt, a/c, fan, TV, video, clock radio, refrig, cook fac, micro, ldry, blkts, linen, pillows], bbq, cots. D $90 - $105, W $480 - $700.

Riverfront Budget Units, (Cotg), 26 Grey St, 200m W of PO, ☎ 08 9937 1144, fax 08 9937 1509, 6 cotgs acc up to 6, [shwr, tlt, a/c-cool, TV, clock radio, refrig, cook fac, micro, ldry, blkts, linen reqd], bbq, cots. D ♦♦ $55 - $77, ◊ $5.50, W $385 - $539.

Wagoe Farm, (Chalet), Limited facilities, Grey Rd, 25km S of PO, ☎ 08 9936 6060, fax 08 9936 6067, 7 chalets acc up to 9, [shwr, tlt, refrig, cook fac, blkts reqd, linen reqd, pillows], cook fac, kitchen. D ♦♦ $44 - $55, W ♦♦ $198 - $308, Camping area available.

B&B's/Guest Houses

Lola - Rose Bed & Breakfast, (B&B), 21 Patrick Crescent, 1km NE of PO, ☎ 08 9937 2224, fax 08 9937 2324, (2 stry), 6 rms (3 suites) [ensuite (3), a/c-cool, TV (Shared), video (Shared), refrig (Shared)], shwr, tlt, ldry, lounge, ✕, cook fac, t/c mkg shared, bbq, cots (avail), non smoking property. BB ♦ $45 - $75, ◊ $11.

Other Accommodation

Kalbarri Backpackers & Bunks, 52 Mortimer St, 500m NE of PO, ☎ 08 9937 1430, fax 08 9937 1563, (Multi-stry), 15 rms acc up to 8, [c/fan, TV, refrig, blkts, linen, pillows], shwr, ldry, w/mach-fee, iron, pool, cook fac, bbq, ✆, bicycle, non smoking property. D ♦ $18, RO ♦♦ $44, W ♦ $108, BC MC VI.

KALGOORLIE-BOULDER WA 6430

Pop 28,087. (569km E Perth), See map on page 906, ref C7. One of the most important mining areas in Australia, Kalgoorlie and its twin city of Boulder played a major part in the development of Western Australia.

Hotels/Motels

★★★★ **Hannan's View Motel**, (M), 430 Hannan St, 1km SW of PO, ☎ 08 9091 3333, fax 08 9091 3331, (2 stry gr fl), 65 units [shwr, tlt, a/c, heat, elec blkts, tel, TV, video-fee, movie, t/c mkg, refrig, cook fac, micro (12), ldry], business centre, ✕, spa, rm serv, cots, non smoking units. D ♦ $95, ♦♦ $110 - $160, ◊ $20, ch con, AE BC DC EFT MC MP VI.

★★★★ **Mercure Hotel Plaza Kalgoorlie**, (LH), 45 Egan St, 400m E of PO, ☎ 08 9021 4544, fax 08 9091 2195, 100 rms [shwr, tlt, hairdry, a/c, tel, TV, movie, radio, t/c mkg, refrig, mini bar, ldry (guest)], lift, iron, iron brd, conf fac, ✕, bar, pool, 24hr reception, rm serv, golf, cots. D ♦♦ $131 - $257, ♦♦♦♦ $210 - $262, ◊ $20, AE BC DC MC VI, ♿.

★★★★ **Railway Motel & Function Centre**, (M), 51 Forrest St, 900m E of PO, ☎ 08 9088 0000, fax 08 9088 0290, 95 units [shwr, bath (53), spa bath (38), tlt, hairdry, a/c, tel, TV, radio, t/c mkg, refrig, micro (6)], ldry, w/mach-fee, dryer-fee, iron, iron brd, business centre, conv fac, ✕, pool-heated, spa, 24hr reception, courtesy transfer, non smoking units. D ♦♦ $153 - $185, ◊ $15.30 - $18.50, AE BC DC EFT MC MP VI.

★★★★ **Tower Hotel**, (LMH), Cnr Bourke & Maritana Sts, 1.2km NW of PO, ☎ 08 9021 3211, fax 08 9021 7115, 33 units [shwr, tlt, a/c, tel, TV, movie, radio, t/c mkg, refrig], ✕, pool, rm serv, cots. D $75 - $105, ◊ $10, AE BC DC MC VI.

★★★☆ **Albion Shamrock Motor Hotel**, (LMH), Cnr Lane & Piesse St, 300m S of Boulder PO, ☎ 08 9093 1399, fax 08 9093 1502, (Multi-stry gr fl), 51 units (14 suites) [shwr, tlt, a/c, heat, elec blkts, tel, TV, movie, radio, t/c mkg, refrig, cook fac (14), ldry], lounge, conv fac, ✕, pool, sauna, spa, bbq, rm serv, plygr, cots-fee. D ♦ $75, ♦♦ $85, ◊ $15, Suite D $115, AE BC MC VI.

★★★☆ **Hospitality Inn Kalgoorlie**, (M), 560 Hannan St, 2km SW of PO, ☎ 08 9021 2888, fax 08 9021 1237, 56 units (2 suites) [shwr, tlt, a/c, heat, tel, TV, movie, radio, t/c mkg, refrig, ldry], bathrm, ✕, pool, bbq, rm serv, plygr, cots, non smoking units (avail). D ♦ $109, ♦♦ $116 - $144, ◊ $22, Suite D $141 - $148, ch con, pen con, AE BC DC MC VI, ♿.

★★★☆ **Mercure Inn Overland Kalgoorlie**, (M), Hannan St, 2.5km SW of PO, ☎ 08 9021 1433, fax 08 9021 1121, 87 units [shwr, tlt, a/c, tel, TV, movie, radio, t/c mkg, refrig], conv fac, ✕, pool, cots. D ♦♦ $83 - $152, ♦♦♦♦ $125 - $152, ◊ $20, ch con, AE BC DC MC VI, ♿.

★★★☆ **Midas Motel**, (M), 409 Hannan St, 700m S of PO, ☎ 08 9021 3088, fax 08 9021 3125, 55 units [shwr, tlt, a/c, tel, cable tv, movie, radio, t/c mkg, refrig], ✕, pool, sauna, spa, rm serv, cots. D ♦ $95 - $115, ♦♦ $110 - $135, ch con, AE BC DC MC VI.

Piccadilly Hotel, (LH), 164 Piccadilly St, 1km E of PO, ☎ 08 9021 2109, fax 08 9091 4032, 19 rms [a/c, t/c mkg]. RO ♦ $25, ♦♦ $40.

Star & Garter, (LMH), 497 Hannan St, 1.3km SW of PO, ☎ 08 9026 3399, fax 08 9091 3555, 28 units [shwr, tlt, a/c, heat, TV, movie, radio, t/c mkg, refrig, ldry], ✕, pool, cots. D ♦ $71.50, ♦♦ $82.50, ♦♦♦♦ $110.

Self Catering Accommodation

★★★★☆ **The Yelverton Apartment Motel**, (SA), 210 Egan Street, 150m SE of Town Hall, ☎ 08 9022 8181, fax 08 9022 8191, (2 stry) 49 serv apts acc up to 6, (1 & 2 bedrm), [ensuite, shwr, spa bath, tlt, hairdry, a/c, tel, cable tv, clock radio, t/c mkg, refrig, cook fac, micro, linen, pillows], ldry, w/mach-fee, dryer-fee, iron, iron brd, pool, bbq, kiosk, secure park, courtesy transfer, cots, non smoking rms. D $152 - $175, ch con, fam con, pen con, AE BC DC EFT MC VI.

B&B's/Guest Houses

★★★★ **The Old Australia Private Hotel**, (PH), Previously Old Australia 138 Hannan St, 100m NE of PO, ☎ 08 9021 1320, fax 08 9091 2720, 24 rms [ensuite (13), a/c, fan, TV, radio, t/c mkg, refrig], shwr (11), tlt, TV rm, meals avail, cots. RO ♦ $86, ♦♦ $100 - $145, ♦♦♦♦ $170 - $220, ◊ $25, AE BC DC MC VI.

★★★☆ **Barb's Place**, (GH), No children's facilities, 41 Federal Rd, 2km SE of PO, ☎ 08 9021 6898, fax 08 9021 6893, 7 rms [ensuite (5), a/c-cool, heat, elec blkts, tel, TV, video, clock radio, refrig], shwr (1), tlt, ldry, w/mach, dryer, TV rm, cook fac, bbq, c/park. BLB ♦ $63, ♦♦ $84.

KAMBALDA WA 6442

Pop 4,463. (632km E Perth), See map on page 906, ref C7.

Hotels/Motels

Kambalda Motor Hotel, (LH), Bluebush Rd, 200m N of PO, ☎ 08 9027 1333, fax 08 9027 1803, 26 rms [shwr, tlt, a/c, tel, TV, radio, t/c mkg, refrig], ✕, rm serv. D ♦ $80, ♦♦ $90, ♦♦♦♦ $100, AE BC DC MC VI.

KARIJINI NATIONAL PARK WA 6751

Pop Nominal, (1468km NE Perth), See map on page 906, ref B4.

Hotels/Motels

Auski Tourist Village Motel, (M), Cnr Gt Northern Hwy & Wittenoom turn off, Port Hedland 6721, ☎ 08 9176 6988, fax 08 9176 6973, 20 units [shwr, tlt, a/c-cool, fan, tel, TV, t/c mkg, refrig], ldry, ✕, bbq. RO ♦ $110, ♦♦ $120, ◊ $20, BC EFT MC VI.

KARRATHA WA 6714

Pop 8,341. (1535km N Perth), See map on page 906, ref B4. Karratha, aptly named for the Aboriginal word meaning 'good country', lies beside Nickol Bay and is the youngest and fastest-growing town in the Pilbara.

Hotels/Motels

★★★★ **Karratha International Hotel**, (LH), Cnr Millstream & Hillview Rds, 500m W of PO, ☎ 08 9185 3111, fax 08 9185 4472, 80 rms [shwr, tlt, a/c-cool, tel, TV, movie, radio, t/c mkg, refrig], conv fac, ✕ (/Alfresco), ✕, pool, rm serv, shop, non smoking rms. RO ♦♦ $188 - $342, ◊ $45.

★★★☆ **Mercure Inn Karratha**, (LH), Searipple Rd, 200m N of PO, ☎ 08 9185 1155, fax 08 9185 4325, 60 rms [shwr, tlt, a/c-cool, tel, TV, movie, radio, t/c mkg, refrig], conf fac, ✕, pool, bbq, rm serv, cots. D ♦♦ $120 - $150, ♦♦♦♦ $128 - $160, ◊ $20, AE BC DC, ♿.

Self Catering Accommodation

★★★★☆ **Karratha Central Apartment Hotel**, (SA), Cnr Warambie & Searipple Rds, 200m E of PO, ☎ 08 9143 9888, fax 08 9143 9800, 84 serv apts acc up to 4, (1 & 2 bedrm), [ensuite, shwr, tlt, hairdry, a/c-cool, fan, tel, TV, movie, clock radio, refrig, cook fac, micro, d/wash, toaster, blkts, linen, pillows], w/mach, dryer, iron, iron brd, pool, bbq, cots-fee, non smoking units (avail). BLB $150 - $220, AE BC DC EFT MC VI, ♿.

KARRIDALE WA 6288

Pop Nominal, (306km S Perth), See map on page 906, ref A3.
See also Augusta and Hamelin Bay.

★★★ **Karridale Cottages**, (Cotg), Lot 4016 Brockman Hwy, 3km E of PO, ☎ 08 9758 5598, fax 08 9758 5598, 4 cotgs acc up to 6, [shwr, tlt, TV, video, clock radio, refrig, cook fac, ldry, blkts, linen, pillows], iron, rec rm, bbq, tennis, cots. **D** $80 - $140, **W** $375 - $650, Min book long w/ends, BC MC VI.

Brilea Cottages, (Cotg), RMB 102, off Bussell Hwy, ☎ 08 9758 5001, fax 08 9758 5001, 2 cotgs acc up to 5, (2 bedrm), [shwr, spa bath, tlt, fan, wood heat, TV, video, radio, refrig, cook fac, micro, blkts, doonas, linen, pillows], w/mach, iron, bbq, c/park. **D** ♦♦ $120, ◊ $10, **W** $720, ch con, fam con.

KATANNING WA 6317

Pop 4,413. (295km SE Perth), See map on page 906, ref B2. It is the largest country stock-selling centre in the State.

Hotels/Motels

★★★☆ **New Lodge Motel**, (M), 170 Clive St, 700m SW of PO, ☎ 08 9821 1788, fax 08 9821 1364, 16 units [shwr, tlt, a/c, elec blkts, tel, TV, radio, t/c mkg, refrig], conv fac, ⌧, cots. **D** ♦ $70 - $75, ♦♦ $85 - $90, AE BC DC MC VI.

★★★ **Katanning Motel**, (M), Albion St, 500m SW of PO, ☎ 08 9821 1657, fax 08 9821 1930, 34 units [shwr, tlt, a/c (26), fan, heat, elec blkts, TV, radio, t/c mkg, refrig], ⌧. **RO** ♦ $65, ♦♦ $76, ♦♦♦ $88, Some units of a lower rating. AE BC DC MC VI.

Federal Hotel, (LMH), Clive St, 20m SW of PO, ☎ 08 9821 1010, fax 08 9821 5045, 4 units [shwr, tlt, heat, TV, radio, t/c mkg, refrig], ⌧, c/park. **D** $60.

(**Hotel Section**), (Multi-stry), 21 rms [elec blkts, TV, clock radio, refrig], shwr, tlt. **RO** ♦ $22 - $25.

B&B's/Guest Houses

★★★★ **Woodchester Bed & Breakfast**, (B&B), 19 Clive St, 600m E of PO, ☎ 08 9821 7007, fax 08 9821 5226, 2 rms (2 suites) [ensuite, hairdry, heat, fan, fire pl, elec blkts, tel, TV, radio, t/c mkg, refrig, doonas, pillows], ldry, ⌧, non smoking property. **BB** ♦ $75, ♦♦ $110, ◊ $35, BC MC VI.

KELLERBERRIN WA 6410

Pop 1,091. (203km E Perth), See map on page 906, ref B1. A pleasantly situated sheep and wheat farming centre on the Great Eastern Highway.

Daystar Cottage & Cabins, (Cotg), 69 James St, 1km N of PO, ☎ 08 9045 4551, fax 08 9045 4551, 5 cotgs acc up to 4, (1 & 2 bedrm), [shwr, tlt, hairdry, a/c-cool, heat, fan, c/fan, TV, video-fee, clock radio, refrig, cook fac, micro, toaster, blkts, doonas, linen, pillows], ldry, w/mach, dryer, bbq, cots-fee. **D** ♦ $71.50, ♦♦ $82.50, ♦♦♦♦ $126.50.

KENDENUP WA 6323

Pop Nominal, (345km SE Perth), See map on page 906, ref B3.

Danebo, (B&B), No children's facilities, Second Ave, 500m NW of PO, ☎ 08 9851 4328, fax 08 9851 4328, 2 rms [hairdry, tel, clock radio, refrig, doonas, pillows], shwr, tlt, ldry, w/mach-fee, iron-fee, TV rm, ⌧, bbq, meals avail (by arrangement), non smoking rms. **BB** ♦♦ $90, **DBB** ♦ $55, ♦♦ $100, fam con.

Sharing the roads - Trucks and cars

Trucks are different from cars. They take up more road space than cars, especially when turning, and are slower to accelerate, turn and reverse. Here are some hints in sharing our roads safely with trucks:

- Don't cut in on trucks. Because trucks need a greater braking distance than cars, truck drivers leave more space in front of them when approaching a red light or stop sign than a car.
- Allow extra time and space to overtake trucks. You will need about 1.5 kilometres of clear road space to pass a truck.
- Don't pass a left-turning truck on the inside. Trucks sometimes need more than one lane to turn tight corners, so watch for a truck swinging out near intersections.
- Be patient - follow at a safe distance. Truck drivers may not see you because of blind spots, particularly if you travel right behind them.

KIRUP WA 6251

Pop Nominal, (228km SW Perth), See map on page 906, ref A2.

Kirup Kabins Farmstay, (Chalet), (Farm), Lot 3, Mailman Rd, 13km SW of Kirup, ☎ 08 9731 6272, fax 08 9731 6272, 4 chalets acc up to 8, (2 & 3 bedrm), [shwr, tlt, wood heat, TV-fee, refrig, cook fac, micro, toaster, blkts, doonas, linen reqd-fee, pillows], bbq, cots. **D** ♦♦ $99 - $115, ◊ $17, ch con.

KOJONUP WA 6395

Pop 1,102. (256km S Perth), See map on page 906, ref B2. Kojonup is situated in a thriving sheep farming and mixed agricultural region.

Hotels/Motels

★★★☆ **Hillview Motel**, (M), Albany Hwy, 600m N of PO, ☎ 08 9831 1160, fax 08 9831 1695, 14 units [shwr, tlt, a/c, heat, tel, TV, video, radio, t/c mkg, refrig], ✕ (byo). **D** ♦ $55, ♦♦ $60, ♦♦♦♦ $72, BC MC VI.

(**Holiday Unit Section**), 4 units acc up to 6, (2 bedrm), [shwr, tlt, hairdry, a/c, TV, clock radio, refrig, cook fac, micro, toaster, ldry, blkts, linen, pillows], iron. **D** $83.

Kojonup Commercial Motel Hotel, (LMH), 118 Albany Hwy, 200m S of PO, ☎ 08 9831 1044, fax 08 9831 1640, 18 units [shwr, tlt, a/c, TV, t/c mkg, refrig, ldry], ⌧, cots. **D** ♦ $40, ♦♦ $55, ♦♦♦♦ $70.

Self Catering Accommodation

★★★☆ **Kalpara Farmstay**, (Cotg), (Farm), Tenner Rd, 38km W on Blackwood Rd & 11km S on Tenner Rd, ☎ 08 9832 3016, fax 08 9832 3038, 1 cotg acc up to 5, (2 bedrm), [shwr, tlt, heat, elec blkts, TV, clock radio, t/c mkg, refrig, cook fac, micro, ldry, blkts, linen, pillows], bbq, tennis. **BB** ♦ $45, **D** ♦♦ $50 - $70.

Karana, (HU), (Farm), Hart Rd RMB 119A, 38km W of PO, ☎ 08 9832 3072, fax 08 9832 3058, 1 unit acc up to 6, [shwr, tlt, fan, heat, elec blkts, TV, clock radio, refrig, cook fac, ldry, blkts, linen, pillows], plygr, cots, Dog allowed on leash only. **BLB** ♦ $35, ♦♦ $50, ♦♦♦♦ $60 - $80, **RO** ♦ $30, ♦♦ $40, ♦♦♦♦ $50, ◊ $10, **W** $200.

Proandra Flowers Farmstay, (Cotg), (Farm), Albany Hwy, 20km N of PO, ☎ 08 9832 8065, fax 08 9832 8085, 1 cotg acc up to 7, (3 bedrm), [shwr, bath, tlt, heat, TV, clock radio, refrig, cook fac, blkts, linen, pillows], pool, cots. **D** $55, ◊ $11, **W** $277.50.

B&B's/Guest Houses

Kemminup Farm, (B&B), RMB 214 Kemminup Road, 14km NE of Kojonup, ☎ 08 9831 1286, fax 08 9831 1907, 2 rms [ensuite, fan, heat, elec blkts, tel, TV, video, clock radio, CD, t/c mkg], w/mach, dryer, iron, iron brd, lounge, lounge firepl, refrig, bbq, cots-fee. **BB** ♦♦ $99 - $110, ◊ $18, BC MC VI.

KONDININ WA 6367

Pop 400. (276km ESE Perth), See map on page 906, ref B7.

★★☆ **Kondinin Roadhouse**, (M), Cnr Graham & Gordon Sts, 200m W of PO, ☎ 08 9889 1190, fax 08 9889 1137, 6 units [shwr, tlt, a/c, elec blkts, tel, TV, t/c mkg, refrig], ✕. **BLB** ♦ $45, ♦♦ $60, BC EFT MC VI.

Kondinin Hotel, (LH), Cnr Rankin & Gordon Sts, 100m W of PO, ☎ 08 9889 1009, fax 08 9898 1112, 4 rms [shwr, tlt, a/c, elec blkts, TV, radio, t/c mkg, refrig], ⌧. **BLB** ♦ $49.50, ♦♦ $66, ♦♦♦ $88, BC EFT MC VI.

KOOKYNIE WA 6431

Pop part of Leonora, (796km NE Perth), See map on page 906, ref C6.

Hotels/Motels

Grand Hotel, (LH), Limited facilities, 200km N of Kalgoorlie PO, ☎ 08 9031 3010, fax 08 9031 3010, 6 rms [tlt], shwr, ⌧. **RO** ♦ $30, ♦♦ $50.

KULIN WA 6365

Pop 346. (285km SE Perth), See map on page 906, ref B1.

Kulin Motel Hotel, (LMH), Limited facilities, Johnson St, 100m SW of PO, ☎ 08 9880 1201, fax 08 9880 1010, 6 units [a/c, TV, t/c mkg, refrig]. **D** ♦ $50, ♦♦ $60, BC EFT MC VI.

(**Hotel Section**), 6 rms [shwr (male & female), t/c mkg], G, L, TV rm. **D** ♦ $55, ♦♦ $65.

KUNUNURRA WA 6743

Pop 6,000. (3214km NE Perth), See map on page 906, ref E2. This pleasantly shaded modern town sheltered by Kelly's Knob is the centre of the giant Ord River Project.

Hotels/Motels

★★★★☆ **Country Club Hotel**, (M), Limited facilities, Coolibah Dve, adjacent to PO, ☎ 08 9168 1024, fax 08 9168 1189, 90 units [shwr, tlt, a/c, tel, TV, movie, t/c mkg, refrig, ldry (2)], ⊠ (3), bar, pool, bbq. D $158.60 - $209.60, AE BC DC MC VI.

★★★☆ **Kununurra Lakeside Resort**, (M), Lot 2263 Casuarina Way, 1km SE of PO, ☎ 08 9169 1092, fax 08 9168 2741, 50 units [shwr, tlt, a/c, tel, TV, clock radio, t/c mkg, refrig], ldry, ⊠, ✕, pool, courtesy transfer, cots. D ♦ $152, ◊ $17, AE BC DC EFT MC VI.

★★★☆ **Mercure Inn Kununurra**, (Ltd Lic H), Victoria Hwy, 1km S of PO, ☎ 08 9168 1455, fax 08 9168 2622, 60 rms [shwr, tlt, a/c, tel, TV, movie, radio, t/c mkg, refrig, mini bar, ldry], conv fac, ⊠, pool, spa (1), bbq, rm serv, cots. D ♦♦ $112 - $160, ♦♦♦♦ $160 - $200, $20, ch con, AE BC DC MC.

★★★ **Hotel Kununurra**, (LMH), Messmate Way, 400m S of PO, ☎ 08 9168 1344, fax 08 9168 1946, 52 units [shwr, tlt, a/c-cool, tel (45), TV (45), movie, clock radio, t/c mkg, refrig], ldry, ⊠, bar, pool, bbq, courtesy transfer, plygr, cots, non smoking units (avail). D ♦ $38, ♦♦ $49.50 - $99, ♦♦♦♦ $121, ◊ $20, ch con, Some units of a lower rating. AE BC DC MC VI.

El Questro Station, (M), Gibb River Rd, 100km W of PO, ☎ 08 9169 1777, or 08 9161 4318, fax 08 9169 1383, 12 units [a/c-cool, ldry], w/mach-fee, ✕, bbq, kiosk, LPG, ice, ☎, D ♦♦ $170, ◊ $33, AE BC DC MC VI.

  (Camp Section), D ♦ $11 - $16.50.

Emma Gorge, (M), Limited facilities, Gibb River Rd, 70km W of PO, ☎ 08 9169 1777, fax 08 9169 1383, 45 units [ensuite (17), ldry, pillows], shwr, tlt, w/mach-fee, dryer-fee, iron, ✕, pool, ☎. D ♦♦ $133, ♦♦♦♦ $198, Safari Tent style accommodation. No camping or vans, AE BC DC MC VI.

Self Catering Accommodation

★★★★ **Lakeview Apartments Kununurra**, (SA), 224 Victoria Highway, Opposite Lily Creek Lagoon, ☎ 08 9168 0000, fax 08 9168 0088, 16 serv apts acc up to 6, (2 & 3 bedrm), [shwr, tlt, a/c-cool, c/fan, tel, fax, TV, clock radio, t/c mkg, refrig, cook fac, micro, elec frypan, toaster, blkts, linen, pillows], ldry, w/mach, dryer, iron, iron brd, pool, spa (shared), bbq, cots (avail), non smoking property. D $154 - $242, W $924 - $1,452, AE BC DC EFT MCH VI, ♿.

Home Valley Station, (House), Gibb River Rd, 125km W of PO, ☎ 08 9161 4322, fax 08 9161 4340, 10 houses [shwr, tlt, fan, tel, blkts, linen, pillows], w/mach, conf fac, ✕, pool above ground. DBB ♦ $80, ch con, Open March to December. Camping area also avail.

B&B's/Guest Houses

★★★★☆ **Duncan House**, (B&B), 167 Coolibah Dve, 500m W of PO, ☎ 08 9168 2436, fax 08 9168 2437, 9 rms [ensuite, hairdry, a/c-cool, fan, tel, TV, clock radio, t/c mkg, refrig, ldry, doonas, pillows], iron, bar (mini), spa (outdoor), bbq, secure park, non smoking rms. BB ♦ $105, ♦♦ $125, AE BC DC MC VI.

LANCELIN WA 6044

Pop 597. (127km N Perth), See map on page 906, ref B7. Lancelin is rated as one of the best surfing and windsurfing venues in the world.

Hotels/Motels

Lancelin Inn, (LMH), Gingin Rd, 700m N of PO, ☎ 08 9655 1005, fax 08 9655 1401, 25 units [shwr, tlt, a/c-cool, heat, TV, t/c mkg, refrig]. D ♦ $40 - $75, ♦♦ $65 - $75, ♦♦♦♦ $95, ◊ $10, BC.

Self Catering Accommodation

★★ **Lancelin Family Villas**, (HU), Gingin Rd, 200m SE of PO, ☎ 08 9655 1100, fax 08 9655 1100, (2 stry), 5 units acc up to 6, (1 & 2 bedrm), [shwr, tlt, TV, refrig, cook fac, micro, ldry, blkts, linen reqd-fee, pillows], bathrm, w/mach. D ♦ $64, ♦♦ $75.

Windsurfer Beach Chalets, (HU), 1 Hopkins St, 1.4km S of PO, ☎ 08 9655 1454, fax 08 9655 2454, 6 units acc up to 10, (2 & 3 bedrm), [shwr, tlt, heat, fan, TV, refrig, cook fac, blkts, linen, pillows], ldry, w/mach, bbq, ☎, Pets allowed under control. D ♦♦ $75 - $85, ◊ $10, BC MC VI.

Other Accommodation

Lancelin Lodge, 10 Hopkins St, 2km S of PO, ☎ 08 9655 2020, fax 08 9655 2021, 12 rms acc up to 6, [shwr, tlt, TV, doonas, linen, pillows], w/mach-fee, iron, cook fac, refrig, bbq, ☎. D ♦ $17, ♦♦ $45 - $55, $60 - $70, ch con, BC MC VI.

LAVERTON WA 6440

Pop 872. (957km E Perth), See map on page 906, ref C6. Laverton began as one of the richest gold finds in the State. Today tourists are using Laverton as the starting point for the trip across the Great Victorian Desert to Ayers Rock and Alice Springs.

Hotels/Motels

★★ **Desert Inn**, (LMH), 2 Laver St, 50m W of PO, ☎ 08 9031 1188, fax 08 9031 1165, 26 units [shwr, tlt, a/c, radio, t/c mkg, refrig], ⊠, cots. D ♦ $65, ♦♦ $85, AE BC DC MC VI.

Self Catering Accommodation

Laverton Chalet Accommodation, (Apt), 29 Augusta St, Opposite Police Station, ☎ 08 9031 1130, fax 08 9031 1130, 16 apts acc up to 6, [shwr, bath, tlt, evap cool, heat, heat, fax, TV, t/c mkg, refrig, cook fac, micro, blkts, linen, pillows], w/mach, iron brd, bbq, non smoking units (4). D ♦ $69, ♦♦ $98, ♦♦♦♦ $117, ◊ $39, ch con, fam con, BC MC VI, (not yet classified).

B&B's/Guest Houses

Laverton Downs Station, (GH), Laverton Downs Station, 25km N of Laverton PO, ☎ 08 9037 5998, fax 08 9037 5998, 19 rms [wood heat, t/c mkg, refrig, pillows], shwr, tlt, ✕, cook fac, bbq, meals avail (by arrangement), ☎, non smoking rms. BB ♦ $55, ♦♦ $99, DBB ♦ $72, ♦♦ $132, RO ♦ $39, ♦♦ $55.

LEEMAN WA 6514

Pop 531. (295km N Perth), See map on page 906, ref A7.

★★★ **Tamarisk Court Holiday Units**, (HU), Cnr Tamarisk & Nairn Sts, 100m NE of PO, ☎ 08 9953 1190, fax 08 9953 1185, 15 units acc up to 6, (1 & 2 bedrm), [shwr, tlt, evap cool, TV, video, refrig, cook fac, micro, ldry, blkts, linen, pillows], pool, bbq, plygr. D $75 - $110, W $280 - $500, BC MC VI.

LEINSTER WA 6347

Pop 997. (968km NE Perth), See map on page 906, ref C6.

Leinster Lodge, (M), Cnr Mansbridge St & Agnew Rd, 300m E of PO, ☎ 08 9037 9040, fax 08 9037 9459, 16 units [shwr, tlt, a/c, TV, t/c mkg, refrig], cots. D ♦ $80, ♦♦♦♦ $90.

LEONORA WA 6438

Pop 3,000. (833km NE Perth), See map on page 906, ref C6.

Whitehouse Hotel, (LH), Limited facilities, Tower St, 50m S of PO, ☎ 08 9037 6030, fax 08 9037 6168, 8 rms shwr, tlt, ⊠. RO ♦ $44, ♦♦ $77.

MADURA WA 6483

Pop Nominal, (1254km E Perth), See map on page 906, ref E7. A pleasantly situated stopping place below the cliffs on the Eyre Highway.

Madura Pass Oasis Motel, (LMH), Eyre Hwy, ☎ 08 9039 3464, fax 08 9039 3489, 38 units [ensuite, a/c-cool (20), TV, t/c mkg, refrig], ⊠, bar, pool. D ♦♦ $99.50, RO ♦♦ $60 - $69.50, ch con, pen con, AE BC DC MC VI.

MANDURAH WA 6210

Pop 35,945. (74km S Perth), See map on page 906, ref A1. Situated at the entrance to Peel Inlet, Mandurah deserves its reputation as the Year-Round holiday resort. Boating, Bowls, Fishing, Golf, Sailing, Swimming, Tennis, Water Skiing.

Hotels/Motels

★★★★ **Metro Suites Meadow Springs Resort**, (LH), 21 Oakmont Ave, 3km N of PO, off Fremantle Rd, ☎ 08 9582 5400, fax 08 9582 0489, 106 rms [shwr, spa bath, tlt, hairdry, a/c, c/fan, tel, TV, movie, clock radio, t/c mkg, refrig, mini bar, rec rm, coffee shop, bar, pool, wading pool, spa, bbq, kiosk, golf, tennis, non smoking rms (106). RO $88 - $160, AE BC DC EFT MCH VI, ♿.

★★★★ **Quest Mandurah**, (M), 20 Apollo Place, 2.5km W of Mandurah Forum, ☎ 08 9535 9599, fax 08 9535 9699, 22 units [shwr, a/c, tel, fax, TV, clock radio, t/c mkg, refrig, cook fac ltd, micro], ldry, w/mach, dryer, meeting rm, pool, spa, bbq, boat park. D $115 - $138, AE BC DC EFT MC VI, ♿.

★★★☆ **Mandurah Gates Resort**, (LMH), 110 - 116 Mandurah Tce, 700m N of PO, ☎ 08 9581 1222, fax 08 9581 1285, (Multi-stry), 34 units [shwr, spa bath (4), tlt, a/c, tel, TV, clock radio, t/c mkg, refrig, pillows], ldry, conv fac, ⊠, pool, sauna, spa, bbq, rm serv, plygr, golf (mini), tennis, cots. **D ♥♥ $109 - $129**, ◊ **$15**, AE BC DC VI, ⅃⅌.

(Self Contained Section), 18 units acc up to 6, [shwr, tlt, tel, TV, clock radio, refrig, cook fac, micro, blkts, linen, pillows], ldry, c/park. **D $169**.

★★★☆ **The Atrium Resort Hotel Mandurah**, (LH), 65 Ormsby Tce, 500m N of PO, ☎ 08 9535 6633, fax 08 9581 4151, (Multi-stry), 117 rms [shwr, tlt, a/c, tel, TV, movie, radio, t/c mkg, refrig, cook fac (88), toaster, ldry], lift, conv fac, ⊠, pool, pool indoor heated, sauna, spa, bbq, cots. **D ♥♥ $128 - $139, ♥♥♥♥ $159 - $203**, Some units of a lower rating. AE BC DC JCB MC VI.

★★★ **Mandurah Foreshore Motel**, (M), 2 Gibson St, town centre. 500m N of PO, ☎ 08 9535 5577, fax 08 9535 9863, 18 units [shwr, tlt, a/c, elec blkts, tel, TV, radio, t/c mkg, refrig], pool, cots-fee. **D ♥♥ $66 - $85, ♥♥♥♥ $85 - $100**, AE BC DC MC VI.

Blue Bay Motel, (M), 15 Oversby St, Halls Head. 2.5km W of PO, ☎ 08 9535 2743, fax 08 9535 3781, 14 units [shwr, tlt, evap cool, heat, TV, t/c mkg, refrig], lounge, pool, bbq, non smoking property. **D ♦ $55 - $65, ♥♥ $80 - $90, ♥♥♥ $95 - $115**, BC MC VI.

Self Catering Accommodation

★★★★☆ **Quest Mandurah**, (SA), 20 Apollo Place, 2.5km W of Mandurah Forum, ☎ 08 9535 9599, fax 08 9535 9699, (2 stry), 40 serv apts acc up to 8, (1, 2 & 3 bedrm), [ensuite, hairdry, a/c, tel, fax, TV, clock radio, t/c mkg, refrig, micro, d/wash, blkts, doonas, linen, pillows], w/mach, dryer, iron, iron brd, pool, spa (shared), cook fac, bbq, kiosk, secure park, trailer park, jetty, cots (avail). **D $138, W $966**, AE BC DC EFT MC VI, ⅃⅌.

★★★★☆ **Silver Sands Resort**, (HU), Mandurah Tce, 2km NE of PO, ☎ 08 9535 7722, fax 08 9535 7390, 52 units acc up to 6, (1 & 2 bedrm), [shwr, bath, a/c, tel, TV, movie, radio, refrig, cook fac, d/wash, ldry, blkts, linen, pillows], pool indoor heated, sauna, spa (4), bbq, mini golf, squash, tennis. **D $110 - $214, W $770 - $1,498**, BC MC VI.

★★★★ **Mandurah Quay Resort**, (SA), 1 Marina Quay Drive, 4km S of PO, ☎ 08 9582 8300, fax 08 9582 8100, 31 serv apts acc up to 6, (2 & 3 bedrm), [shwr, spa bath, tlt, a/c, TV, clock radio, refrig, cook fac, micro, ldry, blkts, doonas, linen, pillows], w/mach, dryer, iron, iron brd, bbq, ✆, bicycle, canoeing, gym, tennis, cots, non smoking units. **D $159 - $189**, Min book all holiday times, AE BC DC MC VI.

★★★★ **Metro Suites Meadow Springs Resort**, (SA), 21 Oakmont Ave, 3km N of PO off Fremantle Rd, ☎ 08 9582 5400, fax 08 9582 0489, 53 serv apts acc up to 6, [ensuite, spa bath, hairdry, a/c, tel, TV, video (12), movie, clock radio, t/c mkg, refrig, mini bar, cook fac, micro, d/wash, blkts, linen, pillows], w/mach, dryer, iron, iron brd, rec rm, coffee shop, pool, bbq, kiosk, plygr, golf, tennis, cots, non smoking units (avail). **D $111 - $235**, pen con, AE BC DC EFT MC VI, ⅃⅌.

★★★ **Mandurah Holiday Village**, (HU), 124 Mandurah Tce, 1km N of PO, ☎ 08 9535 4633, fax 08 9535 4429, (Multi-stry), 72 units acc up to 8, (2 bedrm), [shwr, tlt, a/c, heat, TV, movie, t/c mkg, refrig, cook fac, micro, toaster, blkts, doonas, linen, pillows], ldry, w/mach-fee, dryer-fee, pool, spa (suites avail), bbq, ✆, plygr, tennis, cots. **D ♥♥ $80 - $200**, ◊ **$10**, **W ♥♥ $400 - $1,400**, ch con, BC MC VI.

★★★ **Rosevale Self Contained Estuary Frontage Unit**, (HU), 41 John St, 8km E of PO, ☎ 0403 042 223, fax 08 9337 4776, 2 units acc up to 8, (4 bedrm), [shwr, bath, tlt, TV, refrig, cook fac, ldry, blkts, doonas, linen reqd-fee, pillows], w/mach, iron, iron brd, bbq, c/park. **D $90 - $130, W $450 - $600**.

Oaktune Holdings, (HU), Cnr Old Mill Lne & Leslie St, 800m S of PO, ☎ 08 9581 2244, fax 08 9581 2244, 3 units acc up to 6, (1, 3 & 4 bedrm), [ensuite (1), shwr, bath, tlt, TV, refrig, cook fac, micro, elec frypan, toaster, blkts, linen, pillows], w/mach (2), non smoking units, **D $75, W $340 - $650**, BC MC VI, (not yet classified).

B&B's/Guest Houses

★★★★☆ **Singleton Beach Guest House**, (B&B), 108 Foreshore Drive, Singleton 6175, 14 km N of PO, ☎ 08 9537 3427, fax 08 9537 3427, 3 rms [ensuite, hairdry, c/fan, fire pl, TV, clock radio, t/c mkg, refrig, doonas, pillows], ✕, spa, secure park, non smoking rms. **BB ♦ $75, ♥♥ $99 - $135**, BC.

Fawlty Wooducks B&B, (B&B), 7 Dawesville Rd, Dawesville 6210, 17km S of PO, ☎ 08 9582 2778, 2 rms [evap cool, c/fan, heat, TV, video, clock radio], bathrm (shared), iron, iron brd, t/c mkg shared, non smoking property. **BB ♥♥ $75, ♥♥♥♥ $140**, BC MC VI, (not yet classified).

Oaktune Holdings, (B&B), Cnr Old Mill Lne & Leslie St, 800m S of PO, ☎ 08 9581 2244, fax 08 9581 2244, 2 rms [ensuite, heat, fan, TV, t/c mkg, refrig], ldry, iron, iron brd, lounge, ✕, pool-heated, non smoking property. **BB ♥♥ $120, BLB ♥♥ $95**, BC MC VI, (not yet classified).

Other Accommodation

★★★★☆ **Yalgorup Country Lodge**, (Lodge), 1184 Estuary Rd South Mandurah, South Mandurah, 23km S of PO, ☎ 08 9739 1322, fax 08 9739 1322, 6 rms acc up to 2, [hairdry, a/c-cool, fire pl, tel, t/c mkg, blkts, linen, pillows], TV rm, ✕, pool, spa, non smoking rms. **BB ♦ $80, ♥♥ $110 - $130**, BC MC VI.

Dolphin Houseboat Holidays, (Hbt), Mandurah Ocean Marina, 1.5km NW of PO, ☎ 08 9535 9898, fax 08 9581 5888, 6 houseboats acc up to 10, [ensuite (1), TV, CD, refrig, cook fac, blkts, pillows], bathrm, c/park. **D $181.50 - $357.50, W $1,237 - $2,079**.

MANJIMUP WA 6258

Pop 5,000. (304km S Perth), See map on page 906, ref B3. Manjimup is regarded as the Gateway to the Tall Timber Country.

Hotels/Motels

★★★☆ **Kingsley Motel**, (M), 1 Chopping St, 1.2km S of PO, ☎ 08 9771 1177, fax 08 9777 1121, 30 units [ensuite, a/c, tel, TV, movie, clock radio, t/c mkg, refrig], ⊠, bbq (gas), cots-fee. **D ♦ $66 - $77, ♥♥ $66 - $88**, ◊ **$15**, ch con, Some units of a lower rating. AE BC DC MC VI.

Manjimup Motor Inn, (M), Cnr Mottram St & Hospital Ave, 400m NE of PO, ☎ 08 9771 1900, fax 08 9771 2818, 56 units [shwr, tlt, heat, elec blkts, TV, radio, t/c mkg, refrig, ldry], ⊠, cots. **D ♦ $40 - $52, ♥♥ $50 - $68, ♥♥♥♥ $70**, ◊ **$10**, AE BC DC MC VI.

Self Catering Accommodation

Greenfields Farm Stay, (Cotg), (Farm), Jones Rd, West Manjimup, 18km W of PO, ☎ 08 9772 1364, fax 08 9772 1440, 1 cotg acc up to 8, [shwr, tlt, hairdry, heat, TV, clock radio, refrig, cook fac, blkts, linen, pillows], w/mach, bbq. **D ♥♥ $70**, ◊ **$10**, ch con.

Kin Kin Holiday Resort, Cutting Rd Via Muir Hwy & Wheatly Coast Rd, 27km SE of PO, ☎ 08 9773 1268, fax 08 9773 1268, 15 cabins [shwr, tlt, heat, elec blkts, t/c mkg, blkts, linen, pillows]. **BB ♦ $32, ♥♥ $64, DBB ♦ $52, ♥♥ $104**, ◊ **$10 - $15**, ch con.

Tone River Wilderness Cottages, (Cotg), Muir Hwy via Manjimup, 42km SE of PO, ☎ 08 9387 9733, fax 08 9773 1358, 20 cotgs [shwr, tlt, wood heat, refrig, cook fac, blkts, linen reqd, pillows], ldry, rec rm (communal hall), bbq, plygr, bicycle-fee, canoeing-fee, tennis, cots. **D $55 - $85, W $385 - $420**, pen con, ⅃⅌.

B&B's/Guest Houses

★★★ **The Loco Shed Lodge**, (GH), Cnr Sears & Andrew Rds Donnelly River Mill, Donnelly River 6256, 25km NW of PO, ☎ 08 9772 1220, 10 rms [ensuite, shwr, tlt, fan, elec blkts, pillows], rec rm, ✕, t/c mkg shared, refrig. **BB ♥♥ $95, D ♦ $65**, Min book long w/ends and Easter, BC MC VI, ⅃⅌.

Glenoran Valley Guesthouse, (B&B), RMB 37, Hodgsons Rd, One Tree Bridge 18km W of PO, ☎ 08 9772 1382, fax 08 9772 1482, (2 stry), 2 rms [fan, heat, TV, t/c mkg, doonas, pillows], bathrm (2), lounge (private), meals avail, non smoking property. **BB ♥♥ $99**.

MARBLE BAR WA 6760

Pop 318. (1476km N Perth), See map on page 906, ref B4. An extraordinary colourful Jasper Bar crosses the Coongan River just south of the town.

★★☆ **Marble Bar Travellers' Stop**, (M), Lot 232 Halse Rd, 1km E of PO, ☎ 08 9176 1166, fax 08 9176 1138, 19 units [shwr, tlt, a/c, tel, TV, t/c mkg, refrig (7), ldry], shwr, tlt, ⊠, pool, cots. **D ♦ $77, ♥♥ $88**, ◊ **$20**, AE BC DC EFT MC VI.

(Bunkhouse Section), 7 bunkhouses [refrig], shwr, tlt. **RO ♦ $35**.

Children and road safety

For the safety of children on the roads, the three main ingredients are supervision, teaching by example and talking with the children about how to use the road safely.

If your family is holidaying away from home, take a walk around the area when you arrive, show children the safest places to play and identify any potential dangers.

Because children pick up clues from adults around them, parents must be sure always to set a good example whether crossing a road, riding a bike or driving the car.

MARGARET RIVER WA 6285

Pop 2,500. (277km S Perth), See map on page 906, ref A2. Margaret River lies in a rich dairy, cattle and wine region. See Also Cowaramup, Gracetown & Witchcliffe.

Hotels/Motels

★★★★☆ **Margaret River Resort**, (LH), 40 Wallcliffe Rd, 1km W of PO, ☎ 08 9757 0000, fax 08 9757 0099, 6 rms (1 suite) [shwr, bath, tlt, hairdry, a/c, tel, cable tv, video, t/c mkg, mini bar, ldry (services)], iron, iron brd, ✉, bar, pool, sauna, spa, rm serv, secure park, plygr, tennis, cots-fee, non smoking rms. RO ♦♦ $145 - $175, ⋔ $20, Suite D $275, AE BC DC EFT MC VI.

(Motel Section), 24 units [ensuite, spa bath, hairdry, a/c, tel, cable tv, video, clock radio, t/c mkg, refrig, mini bar, cook fac (12), micro, elec frypan, toaster], iron, iron brd, lounge, secure park, cots-fee, non smoking units. D ♦♦ $160 - $195, ⋔ $20.

 ★★★☆ **Emerald Colonial Lodge**, (M), Wallcliffe Rd, 1.5km W of PO, ☎ 08 9757 2633, fax 08 9757 9001, 53 units (10 suites) [shwr, tlt, fan, heat, elec blkts, tel, TV, movie, t/c mkg, refrig, ldry], conf fac, ✗, pool, spa, plygr, mini golf. D ♦♦ $109, Suite D $139 - $179, AE BC DC MC MP VI, ⱱㅎ.

 ★★★☆ **Grange on Farrelly**, (M), Previously Margaret River 1885 Motel & Restaurant Farrelly St, 500m W of PO, ☎ 08 9757 3177, fax 08 9757 3076, 29 units (8 suites) [shwr, tlt, heat, elec blkts, tel, TV, movie, clock radio, t/c mkg, refrig, mini bar, ldry (shared)], ✉, spa (8). D $105 - $120, Suite D $150 - $180, AE BC DC EFT JCB MC VI, ⱱㅎ.

★★★☆ **Margaret River Hotel**, (LMH), 139 Bussell Hwy, 100m W of PO, ☎ 08 9757 2655, fax 08 9757 2994, 11 units [shwr, tlt, heat, tel, TV, movie, t/c mkg, refrig, mini bar], conv fac, ✉, shop (bottle). BB ♦ $85 - $95, ♦♦ $95 - $105, ♦♦♦♦ $120, ⋔ $20 - $25, AE BC DC MC VI.

 ★★★☆ **The Freycinet Inn - Margaret River**, (M), Cnr Bussell Hwy & Tunbridge St, 400m NW of PO, ☎ 08 9757 2033, fax 08 9757 2959, 62 units [shwr, tlt, heat, tel, TV, movie, radio, t/c mkg, refrig, ldry], conv fac, ✉, pool, cots. D ♦ $79 - $106, ♦♦ $102 - $145, ♦♦♦♦ $146 - $189, ch con, AE BC DC MC VI.

Vintages Accommodation, (M), Cnr Willmott Ave & LeSouef St, 200m E of PO, ☎ 08 9758 8333, fax 08 9758 8344, 8 units [shwr, spa bath (2), tlt, heat, c/fan, elec blkts, TV, clock radio, t/c mkg, refrig, micro, toaster, pillows], cots (avail), non smoking units. BB ♦♦ $95 - $130, ♦♦♦ $125, ♦♦♦♦ $140, AE BC EFT MC VI, (not yet classified).

Adamsons Riverside Accommodation, (M), 71 Bussell Hwy, 300m N of PO, ☎ 08 9757 2013, fax 08 9757 2013, 9 units [shwr, tlt, c/fan, heat, elec blkts, TV, radio, t/c mkg, refrig, toaster], rm serv, cots-fee. BLB ♦ $80 - $90, ♦♦ $85 - $95, ⋔ $20, BC MC VI.

Edge Of The Forest, (M), 25 Bussell Hwy, 1.5km N of PO, ☎ 08 9757 2351, fax 08 9757 2351, 5 units [shwr, tlt, fan, fire pl, heat, elec blkts, TV, radio, t/c mkg, refrig], lounge, bbq. BLB ♦ $77 - $85, ♦♦ $85 - $90, ⋔ $20, BC DC MC VI.

Self Catering Accommodation

★★★★★ **Margaret River Resort**, (Villa), 40 Wallcliffe Rd, 1km W of PO, ☎ 08 9757 0000, fax 08 9757 0099, 8 villas acc up to 6, [shwr, bath, tlt, hairdry, a/c, tel, fax, cable tv, video, clock radio, refrig, mini bar, cook fac, micro, d/wash, toaster, ldry, blkts, linen, pillows], w/mach, dryer, iron, iron brd, ✉, bar, pool, sauna, spa, secure park, plygr, tennis, cots-fee, non smoking units. D ♦♦♦♦ $265 - $310, ⋔ $20, W ♦♦♦♦ $1,300 - $1,700, AE BC DC EFT MC VI.

★★★★☆ **Margarets Beach Resort**, (Apt), Wallcliffe Rd Gnarabup Beach, off Wallcliffe Rd, 9km W of PO, ☎ 08 9757 1227, fax 08 9757 1226, 68 apts acc up to 8, [ensuite, shwr, bath, tlt, c/fan, fire pl, tel, TV, movie, clock radio, refrig, cook fac, micro, d/wash, toaster, ldry, blkts, doonas, linen, pillows], w/mach, dryer, iron, iron brd, conv fac, pool, bbq, cots, non smoking units. D ♦♦ $149 - $198, ⋔ $15, $140 - $212, Min book long w/ends, AE BC DC MC VI.

★★★★ **Bushy Lake Chalets**, (Chalet), 22 Eucalyptus Crt, 5km W of PO, ☎ 08 9757 9677, fax 08 9757 9688, 6 chalets acc up to 6, (1 & 3 bedrm), [shwr, spa bath, tlt, c/fan, wood heat, tel, TV, radio, CD, t/c mkg, refrig, micro, toaster, ldry, blkts, linen, pillows], w/mach, iron, iron brd, freezer, cots. D ♦♦ $132 - $170.50, ⋔ $16.50, Min book all holiday times, Min book long w/ends, BC MC VI.

★★★★ **Half Moon Corner**, (Cotg), RMB 204 Rosa Brook Rd, 3.5km SE of PO, ☎ 08 9757 3384, fax 08 9757 3581, 3 cotgs acc up to 4, (2 bedrm), [shwr, tlt, hairdry, wood heat, tel, TV, video, clock radio, CD, refrig, cook fac, micro, toaster, doonas, linen, pillows], dryer, iron, iron brd, bbq, tennis, cots, non smoking units. D $132 - $187, AE BC MC VI.

★★★★ **Margaret River Farmstay**, (Chalet), RSM 268A Osmington Road, 4km N of PO, ☎ 08 9758 8005, fax 08 9757 3015, 3 chalets acc up to 4, (2 & 3 bedrm), [ensuite, shwr, spa bath (1), tlt, a/c, heat, c/fan, TV, video, clock radio, CD, t/c mkg, refrig, cook fac, micro, ldry, blkts, doonas, linen, pillows], bbq, courtesy transfer, plygr, canoeing, cots-fee. D ♦♦ $120 - $148, ⋔ $20, W ♦♦ $720 - $924, Min book applies, BC MC VI.

★★★★ **Margaret River Waterfall Cottages**, (Cotg), Kevill Rd, 4km W of PO, ☎ 08 9757 3228, fax 08 9757 2658, 9 cotgs acc up to 6, [shwr, tlt, hairdry, c/fan, heat, elec blkts, tel, TV, clock radio, t/c mkg, refrig, cook fac, micro, toaster, blkts, linen, pillows], w/mach, dryer, iron, bbq, cots (avail)-fee. D ♦♦ $90 - $190, Min book Christmas and Jan, Min book long w/ends, AE BC MC VI.

★★★★ **Riverglen Chalets**, (Chalet), 321 Carters Rd, 2km NW of PO, ☎ 08 9757 2101, fax 08 9757 3141, 14 chalets acc up to 8, [shwr, tlt, c/fan, fire pl, tel, TV, clock radio, refrig, cook fac, micro, toaster, doonas, linen, pillows], w/mach, dryer, iron, spa (2), bbq, cots-fee, non smoking units. D ♦♦ $110 - $165.

★★★ **Margaret River Chalets**, (Chalet), Lot 106 Bussell Hwy, 3km S of PO, ☎ 08 9757 2905, fax 08 9757 2905, 3 chalets acc up to 6, (2 bedrm), [shwr, tlt, wood heat, TV, clock radio, CD, refrig, cook fac, micro, blkts, linen, pillows], w/mach, bbq, plygr, cots (avail). D ♦♦ $100 - $130, ⋔ $15, W $630 - $820, AE BC MC VI.

★★★ **Margaret River Holiday Cottages**, (Cotg), Boodjidup Rd, 2.5km S of PO, ☎ 08 9757 2185, fax 08 9757 2185, 8 cotgs acc up to 6, (2 bedrm), [shwr, tlt, a/c, TV, t/c mkg, refrig, cook fac, blkts, linen, pillows], w/mach, rec rm, pool indoor heated, spa, bbq, plygr. D ♦♦ $110 - $150, ⋔ $20, ch con, BC MC VI.

★★★ **Sea & Soul Beachside Apartments**, (HU), 54 Mitchell Dve Prevelly Park, Prevelly Park 10km W of PO, ☎ 08 9757 2026, fax 08 9757 2026, 2 units acc up to 2, [ensuite, spa bath (1), heat, tel (portable), TV, video, t/c mkg, refrig, cook fac, micro, toaster, blkts, doonas, linen, pillows], iron, cots, non smoking property. D ♦♦ $70 - $150, Min book long w/ends.

Margarets Forest, (SA), 96 Bussell Hwy, 100m N of PO, ☎ 08 9758 7188, or 08 6210 0011, fax 08 9758 5807, (2 stry), 31 serv apts acc up to 4, (1 & 2 bedrm), [ensuite, spa bath (24), hairdry, a/c, tel, TV, video, clock radio, CD, refrig, cook fac, micro, d/wash, linen, pillows], w/mach, dryer, iron, iron brd, bbq, bicycle-fee, canoeing. D $145 - $280, ch con, pen con, AE BC DC EFT MC VI, (not yet classified).

Bramley Wood Cottages, (Cotg), RMB 205 Rosa Brook Rd, 5km SE of PO, ☎ 08 9757 2427, fax 08 9757 2427, 2 cotgs acc up to 6, [shwr, tlt, fan, heat, elec blkts, tel, TV, clock radio, refrig, cook fac, micro, toaster, blkts, doonas, linen reqd-fee, pillows], bbq. D ♦♦ $77 - $88, ⋔ $11 - $14, Min book applies, BC MC VI.

Burnside Bungalows, (Cotg), RMB 291A Burnside Rd, 7km N of PO, ☎ 08 9757 2139, fax 08 9757 3623, 4 cotgs acc up to 6, (1 & 2 bedrm), [shwr, bath (2), spa bath (2), tlt, hairdry, wood heat, tel, TV, video, clock radio, CD, refrig, cook fac, micro, elec frypan, blkts, doonas, linen, pillows], w/mach, dryer, iron, iron brd, bbq, breakfast ingredients, non smoking property. D $120 - $185, Min book.

Margaret House, (Cotg), Cnr Wallcliffe & Devon Dve, 2km W of PO, ☎ 08 9757 2692, 2 cotgs acc up to 6, [shwr, tlt, fan, heat, TV, radio, CD, t/c mkg, refrig, cook fac, micro, blkts, linen, pillows], cots, Pets on application. BB ♦ $70 - $85, ♦♦ $70 - $90, D ⋔ $15, Min book applies, BC MC VI.

Marri Lodge, (Cotg), Rosa Brook Rd, 3km SE of PO, ☎ 08 9757 3293, fax 08 9757 3293, 3 cotgs acc up to 7, (2 & 3 bedrm), [shwr, spa bath (1), tlt, wood heat, TV, CD (1), refrig, cook fac, micro, blkts, doonas, linen reqd-fee, pillows], w/mach, non smoking property. D ♦♦ $80 - $130, MC VI.

Olive Hill Farm, (Cotg), RMB 261A Bramley River Rd, 13 km NE of PO, ☎ 08 9757 4569, fax 08 9757 4569, 1 cotg acc up to 6, (3 bedrm), [shwr, bath, tlt, hairdry, fan, c/fan, wood heat, TV, clock radio, CD, refrig, cook fac, micro, ldry, blkts, doonas, linen, pillows], w/mach, iron, iron brd, bbq, trailer park, bowls, canoeing, non smoking property. D $120 - $265, W $840 - $1,800, Min book applies, BC MC VI.

Peppermint Brook Cottages, (Cotg), 1 Mann St, 1km W of PO, ☎ 08 9757 2485, 8 cotgs acc up to 6, (2 bedrm), [shwr, tlt, TV, refrig, cook fac, micro, blkts, linen, pillows], bbq. D $85 - $140, W $440 - $860, BC MC VI.

Prevelly Villas, (House), Lot 2 Papadakis Ave, 10km W of PO at Prevelly Park, ☎ 08 9757 2277, fax 08 9757 2277, 4 houses acc up to 6, (3 bedrm), [shwr, tlt, heat, wood heat, TV, video, refrig, cook fac, micro, elec frypan, ldry, blkts, linen reqd-fee, pillows], w/mach, iron, bbq, ✆, cots, Pets allowed. **D** $90 - $200, **W** $700 - $1,100, BC MC VI.
  (Beachside House Section), 1 chalet acc up to 7, (4 bedrm), [shwr, bath, tlt, wood heat, TV, video, radio, refrig, cook fac, micro, elec frypan, d/wash, toaster, ldry, blkts, doonas, linen reqd-fee, pillows], w/mach, iron, lounge, bbq, ✆, cots, non smoking property. **D** $132 - $165, **W** $770 - $1,100.

Station House, (HU), 208 Railway Tce, 1km W of PO, ☎ 08 9757 3175, fax 08 9757 2261, 6 units acc up to 8, (1 & 2 bedrm), [ensuite, shwr, tlt, heat, tel, TV, clock radio, refrig, cook fac, micro, elec frypan, toaster, blkts, doonas, linen, pillows], w/mach, iron, spa (2), bbq, bicycle, cots, non smoking units. **D** ♦♦ $75 - $83, ⋔ $10 - $20, AE BC MC VI.

B&B's/Guest Houses

★★★★★ **Basildene Manor**, (GH), Lot 100 Wallcliffe Rd, 2km W of PO, ☎ 08 9757 3140, fax 08 9757 3383, 17 rms [shwr, tlt, a/c-cool, heat (to all rooms), elec blkts, tel, TV, video, t/c mkg, refrig, pillows], lounge (s/guest), spa (8). **BB** ♦ $178 - $274, ♦♦ $193 - $289, Min book applies, AE BC DC MC VI.
★★★★★ **Heritage Trail Lodge**, (B&B), 31 Bussell Highway, 1km N of PO, ☎ 08 9757 9595, fax 08 9757 9596, 10 rms [ensuite, spa bath, hairdry, a/c, tel, cable tv, clock radio, t/c mkg, refrig, pillows], ldry, w/mach, dryer, iron, iron brd, ✕, bbq, non smoking property. **BB** ♦ $155 - $175, ♦♦ $198 - $230, ⋔ $30, BC DC MC VI, ⏏&.
★★★★☆ **Gilgara Homestead**, (GH), Cnr Caves Rd & Carters Rd, 9km W of PO, ☎ 08 9757 2705, fax 08 9757 3259, 6 rms [ensuite, fan, fire pl, elec blkts], lounge, ✕, t/c mkg shared. **BB** ♦ $165 - $181.50, ♦♦ $220 - $272.50, AE BC DC MC VI.
★★★★☆ **Rosewood Cottage**, (B&B), 54 Wallcliffe Rd, 1km W of PO, ☎ 08 9757 2845, fax 08 9757 3509, 4 rms [heat, elec blkts, TV, t/c mkg, refrig, doonas, pillows], lounge, non smoking rms. **BB** ♦ $77 - $88, ♦♦ $88 - $105.
★★★★☆ **Vat 107**, (B&B), 107 Bussell Highway, 500m N of PO, ☎ 08 9758 8877, fax 08 9758 8899, 4 rms [shwr, spa bath, tlt, hairdry, a/c, c/fan, tel, fax, TV, video, clock radio, CD, t/c mkg, refrig], ldry, w/mach, dryer, iron, cafe, c/park. **BB** ♦♦ $160 - $200, ⋔ $20, ⏏&.
★★★★☆ **Willowwood Cottages**, (B&B), No children's facilities, RMB 207 Rosa Brook Rd, 9km SE of Margaret River, ☎ 08 9757 5080, fax 08 9757 5008, 1 rm (1 bedrm), [ensuite, shwr, tlt, hairdry, fan, wood heat, tel, TV, video, radio, t/c mkg, refrig, doonas, pillows], ldry, meals avail (by arrangement), non smoking property, **D** ♦♦ $130 - $150, **W** ♦♦ $650 - $750, Min book.
★★★★ **Blue Gum Farm Stay**, (B&B), Mill Rd, Witchcliffe 6286, 9km SW of PO, ☎ 08 9757 6338, fax 08 9757 6444, 2 rms [ensuite, heat, fan, fire pl, pillows], ✕, t/c mkg shared, non smoking property. **BB** ♦ $50, ♦♦ $90, AE BC MC VI.
★★★★ **Kangaridge**, (GH), No children's facilities, Lot 2 275 Devon Drive, 2km W of Town, ☎ 08 9757 3939, fax 08 9757 3939, 4 rms [ensuite, tel, TV, video, clock radio, doonas, pillows], lounge, pool indoor heated, spa, bicycle, mini golf, non smoking rms. **BB** ♦♦ $109 - $129, ⋔ $45, AE BC DC MC VI.
★★★★ **Margaret House**, (B&B), Cnr Wallcliffe & Devon Dve, 2km W of PO, ☎ 08 9757 2692, 2 rms [shwr, tlt, a/c, TV, CD, t/c mkg, refrig], cots (avail). **BB** ♦♦ $85 - $100, **BLB** ♦ $80 - $95, BC MC VI.
★★★☆ **Margaret River Bed & Breakfast**, (B&B), 28 Fearn Ave, 300m W of PO, ☎ 08 9757 2118, 3 rms [TV, video, refrig, pillows], shwr, tlt, lounge, ✕. **BB** ♦ $50, ♦♦ $70 - $90.
★★★☆ **Margaret River Guest House**, (GH), 22 Valley Rd, 500m NW of PO, ☎ 08 9757 2349, fax 08 9757 2349, 8 rms [ensuite (5), shwr, tlt, fan, heat, wood heat, elec blkts, TV], ✕, t/c mkg shared, cots. **BB** ♦ $60 - $80, ♦♦ $75 - $95, ⋔ $20.
Bridgefield Guest House, (GH), 73 Bussell Hwy, 300m N of PO, ☎ 08 9757 3007, 4 rms [ensuite, fan, fire pl, heat, elec blkts, TV, video, t/c mkg, refrig, ldry, pillows], iron, read rm, lounge, ✕. **BB** ♦ $80, ♦♦ $95, ♦♦♦ $125.

AAA TOURISM *Special Rates*

Marri Lodge, (GH), No children's facilities, Rosa Brook Rd, 3km SE of PO, ☎ 08 9757 3293, 8 rms [ensuite, spa bath (3), a/c-cool (4), heat, elec blkts, TV, CD (3), t/c mkg, refrig, cook fac (3), pillows], lounge, meals avail (light breakfast)-fee, non smoking property. **RO** ♦♦ $77 - $130, MC VI,
Operator Comment: Tranquil retreat, central to wine region, beaches and forest. Views of roses, trees and cows. Web: www.obverse.com.au/marrilodge
Valley Views Bed & Breakfast, (B&B), (Farm), Lot 2 Jindon Treeton Rd, 16km NE of Margaret River, ☎ 08 9757 4573, fax 08 9757 8181, 3 rms [heat, wood heat, tel, doonas, pillows], shwr, tlt, ldry, TV rm, t/c mkg shared, refrig, bbq, meals avail (by arrangement), non smoking rms. **BB** ♦ $66, ♦♦ $88 - $90, Min book.

Other Accommodation
Glenbrook, (Lodge), Darch Rd, 5km S of PO, ☎ 08 9757 2791, fax 08 9757 2791, 8 rms acc up to 6, [tlt, wood heat, tel, radio, refrig, cook fac, blkts, linen, pillows], shwr, rec rm, bbq. **BLB** ♦ $38.50, ♦♦ $71.50, **RO** ♦♦♦♦ $66 - $77.
Margaret River Lodge, (Lodge), 220 Railway Tce, 2km SW of PO, ☎ 08 9757 9532, fax 08 9757 2532, 26 rms [shwr, tlt, TV, t/c mkg, refrig, cook fac, ldry, blkts reqd-fee, linen reqd-fee, pillows], w/mach-fee, dryer-fee, iron, rec rm, pool, bbq, courtesy transfer, ✆, bicycle. **RO** ♦ $17.60 - $19.80, ♦♦ $49.50 - $60.50, EFT.

Pop 989. (765km NE Perth), See map on page 906, ref B6.
★★★ **Auski Inland**, (LMH), Cnr Main & Robert Sts, 500m S of PO, ☎ 08 9981 1433, fax 08 9981 1478, 28 units [shwr, tlt, a/c, tel, TV, t/c mkg, refrig], ⊠, cots. **D** ♦♦ $104.50, ⋔ $5.50, AE BC DC MC VI.
  (Hotel Section), 18 rms [a/c, TV (some), radio, t/c mkg], shwr, tlt. **RO** $35 - $58.
Commercial Hotel, (LH), Main St, 100m S of PO, ☎ 08 9981 1020, fax 08 9981 1021, 12 rms bathrm. **RO** ♦ $35, ♦♦ $45, AE BC MC VI.

MERREDIN WA 6415

Pop 3,520. (260km E Perth), See map on page 906, ref B1. The largest town and commercial centre of the eastern wheat belt.

Hotels/Motels

★★★☆ **Merredin Motel**, (M), 10 Gamenya Ave, 1km W of PO, ☎ 08 9041 1886, fax 08 9041 1336, 12 units [shwr, tlt, a/c, heat, elec blkts, TV, video (avail), clock radio, t/c mkg, refrig], ✗, pool, spa, rm serv, cots. **D ∮ $55, ∮∮ $65**, ch con, AE BC DC MC VI.

★★★ **Merredin Olympic Motel**, (M), Great Eastern Hwy, 1km W of PO, ☎ 08 9041 1588, fax 08 9041 3124, 28 units [shwr, tlt, a/c, tel, TV, video, radio, t/c mkg, refrig], ✗, ✗, pool, rm serv, cots. **D ∮ $50, ∮∮ $60, ◊ $10**, AE BC MC VI.

★★★ **Potts Motor Inn**, (M), Great Eastern Hwy, 1km E of PO, ☎ 08 9041 1755, fax 08 9041 2366, 36 units [shwr, tlt, a/c, elec blkts, tel, TV, movie, radio, t/c mkg, mini bar], ✗, pool, rm serv, cots. **RO ∮ $72.60, ∮∮ $83.60**, ch con, AE BC DC MC VI.

Commercial Hotel, (LH), 62 Barrack St, 100m W of PO, ☎ 08 9041 1052, fax 08 9041 1050, 29 rms [a/c-cool (19), elec blkts], bathrm, ✗, c/park. **RO ∮ $27.50, ∮∮ $49.50**, AE BC MC VI.

Merredin Oasis Hotel, (LH), 8 Great Eastern Hwy, 1km W of PO, ☎ 08 9041 1133, fax 08 9041 1823, 18 rms [shwr, tlt, a/c, tel, TV, radio, t/c mkg, refrig], ✗, pool, rm serv, cots. **D ∮ $55, ∮∮ $66, ∮∮∮ $88**, AE BC DC MC.

MONKEY MIA WA

See Denham & Nanga.

MOORA WA 6510

Pop 1,677. (172km N Perth), See map on page 906, ref B7. Situated on the Midlands Road via New Norcia, Moora is the largest town between the Perth metropolitan area and Geraldton.

Hotels/Motels

Watheroo Station Tavern, (LH), Limited facilities, Railway Stn, George St, Watheroo 6510, 37km N of PO, ☎ 08 9651 7007, fax 08 9651 7170, 4 rms [t/c mkg, refrig, toaster], shwr, tlt, ✗ (cafe), bbq. **RO ∮ $35 - $50, ∮∮ $45 - $55**, EFT.

(Motel Section), 6 units [shwr, tlt, a/c-cool, TV, t/c mkg]. **D ∮ $60, ∮∮ $75**.

B&B's/Guest Houses

Hillend Farm, (GH), Watheroo West Rd, Watheroo 6510, 40km N of PO, ☎ 08 9651 7082, fax 08 9651 7175, 3 rms [pillows], pool. **BB ∮ $35, ∮∮ $65**.

MORAWA WA 6623

Pop 814. (370km N Perth), See map on page 906, ref B7. A small township positioned in a sheep and wheat farming area. During August and September there is an abundance of wildflowers throughout the region.

Hotels/Motels

Morawa Motel Hotel, (LMH), Cnr Solomon & Manning Sts, 100m E of PO, ☎ 08 9971 1060, fax 08 9971 1324, 10 units [shwr, tlt, a/c, heat, TV, clock radio, t/c mkg, refrig], ✗. **D ∮∮ $60, ∮∮∮∮ $85**, BC MC.

(Hotel Section), 13 rms **RO ∮ $20 - $45**.

MOUNT AUGUSTUS WA 6705

Pop Nominal, (1131km N Perth), See map on page 906, ref B5. According to the Guinness Book of Records, 1986 edition, Mount Augustus is the largest isolated monocline in the world - in other words the world's biggest rock.

Self Catering Accommodation

Mt Augustus Outback Tourist Resort, (HU), Cobra & Mt Augustus Rd, Meekatharra 6642, 4km from the foot of Mt. Augustus, ☎ 08 9943 0527, fax 08 9943 0527, 21 units acc up to 2, [a/c, refrig (16), ldry, blkts, linen, pillows], shwr, tlt, ✗, bar (tavern license), shop, petrol, Dogs allowed on leash. **D $30, RO ∮ $40 - $60**, ch con.

(Cabin Section), 2 cabins acc up to 4, (Powered Site), [shwr, tlt, refrig, blkts, linen, pillows]. **D $120, Powered Site D ∮∮ $10**.

B&B's/Guest Houses

Cobra Station Stay, (GH), PMB 28 Cobra Station, Carnarvon 6701, 37km W of Mount Augustus Nat/Park, ☎ 08 9943 0565, fax 08 9943 0992, 3 rms [shwr, tlt, t/c mkg, refrig, ldry], ✗, bbq, shop, LPG (bottle refills), ice, Dogs allowed on leash. **RO ∮ $49.50, ∮∮ $66, ∮∮∮ $82.50**.

(Unit Section), 6 units [ensuite, shwr, tlt]. **D ∮ $66, ∮∮ $88, ∮∮∮ $115.50**.

MOUNT BARKER WA 6324

Pop 1,648. (359km SE Perth), See map on page 906, ref B3. The town is located in the centre of a prosperous rural district.

Hotels/Motels

★★★ **Valley Views Motel**, (M), Albany Hwy, 700m N of PO, ☎ 08 9851 1899, fax 08 9851 1204, 20 units [shwr, tlt, heat, elec blkts, tel, TV (satelite), radio, t/c mkg, refrig], cots-fee. **D ∮ $63, ∮∮ $76, ∮∮∮ $87 - $98**, ch con, ⚿.

Plantagenet Motel Hotel, (LMH), 9 Lowood Rd, 150m N of PO, ☎ 08 9851 1008, fax 08 9851 2108, 6 units [shwr, tlt, TV, radio, t/c mkg, refrig], TV rm. **D ∮ $45, ∮∮ $65**.

(Hotel Section), 8 rms shwr, tlt, t/c mkg shared. **RO ∮ $25, ∮∮ $40 - $50**.

B&B's/Guest Houses

★★★★☆ **Abbeyholme**, (B&B), Classified by National Trust, No children's facilities, Lot 20 Mitchell Street, 1km from PO, ☎ 08 9851 1101, fax 08 9851 1771, 3 rms (1 suite) [shwr, bath, spa bath (1), tlt, wood heat, elec blkts, tel, TV, radio, t/c mkg, doonas, pillows], iron, iron brd, ✗, refrig, bbq, meals avail (by arrangement), non smoking rms. **BB ∮ $70, ∮∮ $90, ∮∮∮ $420, DBB ∮ $95, ∮∮ $140 - $155, Suite BB ∮∮ $125**, (Farm).

★★★★☆ **Hayrocks**, (B&B), 3925 St Werburghs Rd, 11km SW of PO, ☎ 0500 512 196, fax 08 9851 2496, 2 rms [ensuite, heat, fan, elec blkts, tel, TV, video, clock radio, refrig, micro, pillows], iron, iron brd, ✗, t/c mkg shared, meals avail (by arrangement), non smoking property. **BB ∮ $77 - $82.50, ∮∮ $93.50 - $104.50, ◊ $16.50 - $22, DBB ∮ $93.50 - $99, ∮∮ $137.50, ◊ $33 - $38.50, ◊ $198 - $236.50**, ch con, BC EFT MC VI.

MOUNT HELENA WA 6082

Pop part of Perth, (38km NE Perth), See map on page 906, ref A1.

B&B's/Guest Houses

Catton Hall Country Homestead, (B&B), 1641 Wilkins Rd, 3km E of PO, ☎ 08 9572 1375, fax 08 9572 1393, 3 rms [ensuite (1), fire pl, wood heat, tel, TV, video, radio, t/c mkg, refrig, doonas, pillows], shwr, tlt, ldry, w/mach, dryer, iron, iron brd, pool, spa, bbq, meals avail, bowls (carpet), golf, non smoking rms. **BB ∮ $99, ∮∮ $132 - $165, DBB ∮ $120 - $145, ∮∮ $162 - $195**, pen con.

MOUNT MAGNET WA 6638

Pop 618. (569km N Perth), See map on page 906, ref B6. Mount Magnet is the oldest-surviving gold settlement of the Murchison.

Grand Hotel, (LMH), Hepburn St, 250m SE of PO, ☎ 08 9963 4110, fax 08 9963 4268, 17 units [shwr, tlt, a/c-cool, t/c mkg, refrig], ✗, c/park. **BB ∮ $82, ∮∮ $99**, BC DC EFT MC VI.

MULLALYUP WA 6252

Pop Nominal, (237km SW Perth), See map on page 906, ref A2. Located on the South West Highway, in a mixed farming area which includes fruit, vegetables, beef cattle and sheep. Blackwood Inn built around 1860, Old Stables Pottery - both classified by the National Trust, Potters Shed.

B&B's/Guest Houses

★★★★★ **Blackwood Inn**, (B&B), No children's facilities, South Western Hwy, Balingup 6253, 5km NW of Balingup PO, ☎ 08 9764 1138, fax 08 9764 1135, 8 rms [shwr, tlt, hairdry, a/c-cool, fan, fire pl, elec blkts, TV, video (3), radio, t/c mkg, refrig, pillows], iron, iron brd, ✗, spa (bath) (4), ✆, non smoking rms. **BB ∮ $99 - $264, ∮∮ $132 - $264**, Some units of a lower rating. AE BC DC MC VI.

MULLEWA WA 6630

Pop 591. (450km N Perth), See map on page 906, ref A6. Mullewa is in the heart of wildflower country.

Hotels/Motels

★★☆ **Railway Motel Hotel**, (LMH), Grey St, 200m S of PO, ☎ 08 9961 1050, fax 08 9961 1068, 11 units [shwr, tlt, a/c, t/c mkg, refrig, ldry], c/park. **D ∮ $60, ∮∮ $80, ∮∮∮ $90**, Grading applies to motel section only.

(Hotel Section), 11 units shwr, tlt. **RO ∮ $45**.

Self Catering Accommodation

Tallering Station, (House), (Farm), Pindar-Beringara Rd, 40km NE of PO, ☎ 08 9962 3045, fax 08 9962 3045, 1 house acc up to 18, (6 bedrm), [tlt, t/c mkg, blkts, linen, pillows], shwr, ✗, meals avail, Dogs allowed on leash. **BB ∮ $38, DBB ∮ $77**, No firearms allowed.

(Bunkhouse), 1 bunkhouse acc up to 14, shared fac. **RO ∮ $16**.

MUNDIJONG WA 6123

Pop part of Perth, (47km S Perth), See map on page 906, ref E7.
Whitby Falls Railway Carriage Accommodation, (B&B), Lot 101
Keirnan St, 45km S of GPO, ☎ 08 9525 5256, 4 rms [a/c, elec blkts,
TV, clock radio, t/c mkg, refrig, cook fac ltd, micro, toaster, pillows],
bathrm, spa (shared), bbq. **BLB** ♦♦ **$80,** ♦ **$560,** MC VI.

MUNDRABILLA WA 6443

*Pop Nominal, (1368km E Perth), See map on page 906, ref E7. A
stopover point on the Eyre Highway. Fuel & home cooked meals at
the restaurant & service station.*
★☆ **Mundrabilla Motor Hotel**, (LMH), Eyre Hwy, 80km W of WA/SA
Border, ☎ 08 9039 3465, fax 08 9039 3200, 10 units [shwr, tlt, TV,
radio, t/c mkg, refrig], ✕, pool, cots. **RO** ♦♦ **$65.50,** ♦ **$10.**

MURCHISON SETTLEMENT WA 6630

*Pop 250. (644km N Perth), See map on page 906, ref B6.
Murchison Settlement is the focal point of Murchison Shire, 'the
only shire in Australia without a town.'*
Wooleen Station, (B&B), (Farm), 191km N of Mullewa and 25km
Murchison Settlement, ☎ 08 9963 7973, fax 08 9963 7684, 5 rms
[fan, heat, video, t/c mkg, ldry, pillows], shwr, w/mach, iron, rec rm,
lounge, ✕, pool, bbq, rm serv, plygr. **D all meals** ♦ **$120.**

NANGA WA 6537

*Pop Nominal, (785km N Perth), See map on page 906, ref A2. A
popular fishing resort on the beautiful beaches of the peninsula
which divides Shark Bay.*
Hotels/Motels
★★★ **Nanga Bay Resort**, (M), Nanga Station, Denham 6537, 55km S
of Denham, ☎ 08 9948 3992, fax 08 9948 3996, 24 units (1 bedrm),
[shwr, tlt, a/c, TV, clock radio, t/c mkg, refrig], ldry, w/mach-fee,
dryer-fee, iron, ✕ (byo), pool, spa, bbq, courtesy transfer, ☎, tennis,
cots (avail). **BB** ♦♦ **$57,** ♦♦♦ **$30, DBB** ♦♦ **$73 - $83,** ♦♦♦ **$59 - $69,**
RO ♦ **$71.50,** ♦♦ **$44 - $93.50,** ♦♦♦ **$30 - $104.50,** ch con, Min book
all holiday times, BC EFT MC VI.

Self Catering Accommodation
Nanga Bay Resort, (HU), Nanga Station, 55km S of Denham,
☎ 08 9948 3992, fax 08 9948 3996, 3 units acc up to 4, [shwr, tlt,
a/c-cool, TV, radio, refrig, cook fac, blkts, doonas, linen, pillows], ldry,
✕ (byo), pool, spa, bbq, tennis. **D** ♦♦♦♦ **$125 - $145,** Min book all
holiday times, BC EFT MC VI.

NANNUP WA 6275

*Pop 552. (282km S Perth), See map on page 906, ref A2. Nannup is
situated in a timber, dairy farming and fruit growing district.*
Self Catering Accommodation
★★★★ **Beyonderup Falls Adult Country Escape**, (Chalet), Previously
Beyonderup Falls Cottages. No children's facilities, Balingup Rd, 16km
NE of PO, ☎ 08 9756 2034, fax 08 9756 2034, 4 chalets acc up to 2,
[shwr, tlt, a/c-cool, wood heat (kent), refrig, cook fac, micro, doonas,
linen, pillows], spa (heated private), bbq. **D** ♦♦ **$145 - $170, W $805,**
Min book.
★★★★ **Nannup Nature Stays**, (Chalet), Brockman Highway, 4km E of
PO, ☎ 08 9756 0140, fax 08 9756 0000, (2 stry) 1 chalet acc up to
6, (2 bedrm), [shwr, tlt, hairdry, a/c-cool, heat, elec blkts, TV, video,
clock radio, t/c mkg, refrig, micro, toaster, ldry, blkts, doonas, linen,
pillows], w/mach, iron, bbq, meals to unit (breakfast), cots, non
smoking property, Pets on application. **D** ♦♦ **$65 - $95,** ♦ **$10,**
W ♦♦ **$522.50,** pen con, BTC MC VI.
Billabong Cottages, (Cotg), RMB 742 Brockman Hwy, 23km S of PO,
☎ 08 9756 3027, fax 08 9756 1425, 3 cotgs acc up to 6, (1 & 2
bedrm), [shwr, tlt, wood heat, CD, t/c mkg, refrig, cook fac, doonas,
linen, pillows], bbq, meals avail, bicycle, canoeing, breakfast ingredients,
non smoking units. **D** ♦ **$85,** ♦♦♦ **$100 - $130,** ♦♦♦♦ **$115 - $155,**
♦ **$15 - $25,** ch con.
Blackwood River Cottages, (Cotg), River Rd, 12km SW of PO,
☎ 08 9756 1252, fax 08 9756 1252, 3 cotgs acc up to 6, [shwr, tlt,
a/c-cool (2), heat, TV, CD, refrig, cook fac, micro, ldry (1), doonas,
linen, pillows], rec rm, spa (/s), bbq, canoeing, cots (avail).
D ♦♦ **$125 - $165,** ♦ **$17.**

Nannup Bush Cabins, Barrabup Rd, 6km W of PO, ☎ 08 9756 1170,
fax 08 9756 1170, 3 cabins acc up to 8, [shwr, bath, tlt, fan, heat (pot
belly), refrig, cook fac, doonas, linen, pillows], bbq. **D** ♦♦ **$80,** ♦ **$15,**
ch con, BC MC VI.
Nannup Tiger Cottages, (Cotg), East Nannup Rd, 4km S of PO,
☎ 08 9756 1188, fax 08 9756 1188, 3 cotgs acc up to 6, [shwr, tlt,
heat, elec blkts, TV, video, clock radio, refrig, cook fac, micro, ldry,
blkts, linen, pillows], pool-heated, bbq, c/park (undercover), plygr,
cots (avail). **D** ♦♦♦♦ **$90 - $100,** ♦ **$10, W $450 - $500.**
Redgum Hill Cottages, (Cotg), Balingup Rd, 15km NE of PO,
☎ 08 9756 2056, fax 08 9756 2067, (2 stry), 2 cotgs acc up to 4,
[shwr, tlt, a/c-cool, fan, wood heat, tel, TV, clock radio, t/c mkg, refrig,
cook fac, micro, elec frypan, toaster, blkts, doonas, linen, pillows],
w/mach, iron, iron brd, spa (hot tub) (2), bbq. **D** ♦♦ **$135,** ♦ **$25,**
W ♦♦ **$765,** Min book long w/ends, AE BC DC MC VI.

B&B's/Guest Houses
★★★★★ **Redgum Hill Guest House**, (GH), Balingup Rd, 15km NE of
PO, ☎ 08 9756 2056, fax 08 9756 2067, 3 rms [shwr, tlt, a/c, fan, TV,
radio, t/c mkg, refrig, mini bar]. **BB** ♦ **$120,** ♦♦ **$140, DBB** ♦ **$160,**
♦♦ **$220,** Min book long w/ends, AE BC DC MC VI.
★★★★☆ **Moss Brook**, (B&B), No children's facilities, Roberts Rd via
Vasse Hwy, 10km S of PO, ☎ 08 9756 1515, fax 08 9756 0081, 1 rm
[ensuite, evap cool, fan, heat (under floor), tel, TV, video, clock radio,
t/c mkg, refrig, doonas, pillows], ldry, ✕, bicycle, non smoking
property. **BB** ♦ **$95,** ♦♦ **$125, DBB** ♦ **$125,** ♦♦ **$195,** Min book long
w/ends, BC MC VI.
★★★★☆ **The Lodge Guest House**, (GH), No children's facilities, 14
Grange Rd, 200m NE of PO, ☎ 08 9756 1276, fax 08 9756 1394, 6 rms
[ensuite (4), evap cool, radio], ✕, pool, spa (1), meals avail (evening),
non smoking property. **BB** ♦♦ **$132 - $165,** BC MC VI.
★★★★ **Argyll Cottage**, (B&B), No children's facilities, 121 Warren Rd,
1.5km S of PO, ☎ 08 9756 3023, fax 08 9756 3023, 4 rms [ensuite,
c/fan, wood heat, elec blkts, TV, video, clock radio, refrig, ldry, doonas,
pillows], w/mach, dryer, iron, ✕, pool above ground, t/c mkg shared,
meals avail (by arrangement), bicycle, non smoking property. **BB** ♦ **$80,**
♦♦ **$90, DBB** ♦ **$95 - $105,** ♦♦ **$120 - $140,** pen con, Min book all
holiday times, Min book long w/ends, BC MC VI, ♿.
★★★★ **Tathra Hill Top Retreat**, (B&B), wildlife sanctuary, No
children's facilities, Blackwood River Tourist Drive (Route 251), 14km
NE of Nannup, ☎ 08 9756 2040, fax 08 9756 2040, 2 rms [ensuite,
shwr, spa bath, tlt, hairdry, c/fan, wood heat, elec blkts, TV, video,
clock radio, CD, t/c mkg, refrig, micro], ✕, bbq, picnic facilities, jetty,
non smoking property, **DBB** ♦♦ **$120,** ♦ **$30,** BC MC VI.

NAREMBEEN WA 6369

*Pop 459. (282km E Perth), See map on page 906, ref B7. Located
predominantly in a sheep and wheat farming district.*
Hotels/Motels
Narembeen Motel, (M), 18 Thomas St, ☎ 08 9064 7051,
fax 08 9064 7140, 6 units [shwr, tlt, a/c, c/fan, TV, clock radio, t/c mkg,
refrig, toaster], cots. **RO** ♦ **$45 - $55,** ♦♦ **$50 - $60,** ♦♦♦ **$65,** BC MC VI.

NARRIKUP WA 6326

*Pop Nominal, (376km SE Perth), See map on page 906, ref B3.
Small township just north of Albany.*
★★★★ **Coot Farm**, (Cotg), No children's facilities, Lake Barnes Rd,
7km W of PO/Store, ☎ 08 9853 2042, fax 08 9853 2042, 1 cotg acc
up to 4, [hairdry, heat, elec blkts, tel, TV, clock radio, refrig, cook fac,
micro, toaster, ldry, blkts, doonas, linen, pillows], w/mach, bbq, non
smoking property, **D $72 - $85,** ♦ **$10 - $20,** Min book long w/ends.

NARROGIN WA 6312

*Pop 4,491. (192km SE Perth), See map on page 906, ref B2.
Narrogin is the commercial hub of a flourishing agricultural area.*
Hotels/Motels
★★★☆ **Albert Facey Motor Inn**, (M), 78 Williams Rd, 1.5km W of PO,
☎ 08 9881 1899, fax 08 9881 3585, 29 units [shwr, tlt, a/c, tel, TV,
video (in house), t/c mkg, refrig], ✕, cots. **D** ♦ **$62 - $81,** ♦♦ **$74.50 -
$96,** ♦♦♦♦ **$145 - $135,** AE BC MC VI.
★★★ **Narrogin Motel**, (M), 56 Williams Rd, 1km W of PO,
☎ 08 9881 1660, fax 08 9881 3008, 43 units [shwr, tlt, a/c, tel, TV,
radio, t/c mkg, refrig, ldry], ✕, pool-heated, spa. **D** ♦ **$55,** ♦♦ **$66,**
♦ **$12,** ch con, AE BC DC EFT MC VI.

Self Catering Accommodation

Dryandra Lions Village, (Cotg), Limited facilities, Dryandra Rd, off Wandering-Narrogin Rd, 26km NW of PO, ☎ 08 9884 5231, fax 08 9884 5277, 8 cotgs acc up to 12, [refrig, cook fac, blkts reqd, linen, pillows reqd], bbq, plygr, tennis, **D ♦ $12.50 - $15**, ch con, No firearms allowed.

(Bunkhouse Section), 4 bunkhouses acc up to 56, [refrig, blkts, linen, pillows], shwr, tlt, cook fac. **D ♦ $12.50.**

B&B's/Guest Houses

★★★★ **Chuckem**, (B&B), Chomley Rd Highbury, 27km S of PO, ☎ 08 9885 9050, fax 08 9885 9060, 2 rms [shwr, bath, tlt, hairdry, heat, c/fan, fire pl, elec blkts, tel, TV, video, clock radio, t/c mkg, pillows], ldry, w/mach, dryer, iron, ✕, bbq, courtesy transfer. **BB ♦ $77 - $82.50, ♦♦ $121 - $132**, ch con, BC MC VI.

★★★☆ **Stoke Farm**, (GH), RMB 702, 10km S of PO, ☎ 08 9885 9018, fax 08 9885 9040, 3 rms [fan, heat, elec blkts, tel, TV, video, clock radio, ldry, pillows], shwr, tlt, tennis, cots. **BB ♦ $55, DBB ♦ $90 - $110.**

Hubbles Guest House, (GH), 46 Herald St, 1.5km SE of PO, ☎ 08 9881 1997, fax 08 9881 3409, 10 rms [ensuite (3), shwr (6), tlt (6), hairdry, fire pl, heat, elec blkts, tel, TV, radio, t/c mkg, refrig, pillows], TV rm, ✕, cook fac, meals avail (by arrangement), non smoking property. **BB ♦ $35 - $50, ♦♦ $65 - $80**, ch con.

NEW NORCIA WA 6509

Pop Nominal, (132km N Perth), See map on page 906, ref B7.

Hotels/Motels

New Norcia Hotel, (LH), Great Northern Hwy, 200m S of PO, ☎ 08 9654 8034, fax 08 9654 8011, 16 rms (1 suite) [t/c mkg], shwr, golf (winter only), tennis. **D ◊ $11, RO ♦ $45, ♦♦ $65, Suite D $90**, BC MC VI.

Self Catering Accommodation

★★★★ **Napier Downs Farm**, (Cotg), (Farm), Napier Downs Great Northern Hwy, 15km S of New Norcia, ☎ 08 9655 9015, fax 08 9655 9033, 1 cotg acc up to 6, (2 bedrm), [shwr, tlt, a/c-cool, wood heat, elec blkts, TV, video, clock radio, t/c mkg, refrig, cook fac, ldry, blkts, linen, pillows], bathrm, ✕, cots. **D ♦♦ $110 - $132, ◊ $16.50**, BC VI.

NEWMAN WA 6753

Pop 5,500. (1184km N Perth), See map on page 906, ref B4. Located in the heart of the Pilbara, built primarily to house the workforce at the site of Mt Whaleback, the largest single open cut Iron Ore Mine in the world.

★★★☆ **All Seasons Newman Hotel**, (LH), Newman Drive, 700m SE of PO, ☎ 08 9177 8666, fax 08 9177 8655, (Multi-stry), 83 rms [shwr, tlt, a/c, tel, TV, radio, t/c mkg, refrig, ldry (services)], ldry, w/mach-fee, dryer, iron, meeting rm, ✕, bar (cocktail), pool, bbq, ✎, non smoking rms. **BB ♦ $129 - $158, ♦♦ $140 - $169, ◊ $31, RO ♦♦ $118, ◊ $20**, AE BC DC MC VI.

(Bunkhouse Section), 27 bunkhouses acc up to 54, (Bunk Rooms), non smoking rms (shared facilities). **D ♦ $30, ♦♦ $49.**

★★★☆ **Mercure Inn Newman**, (LMH), Newman Dve, 300m SW of PO, ☎ 08 9175 1101, fax 08 9175 2779, 60 units [shwr, tlt, a/c, tel, TV, radio, t/c mkg, refrig, ldry], conf fac, ✉, bar, pool, bbq, cots. **RO ♦♦ $122 - $162, ♦♦♦♦ $137 - $177**, AE BC DC MC VI.

NORNALUP WA 6333

Pop Nominal, (436km S Perth), See map on page 906, ref B3. Situated on the Frankland River.

Nornalup Riverside Chalets Cafe & Shop, (Cotg), Limited facilities, Cnr Riverside Drive & South Coast Hwy, 10km E of Walpole PO, ☎ 08 9840 1107, fax 08 9840 1107, 1 cotg acc up to 6, [shwr, tlt, fan, heat, t/c mkg, refrig, cook fac, micro, toaster, blkts, doonas, linen, pillows], w/mach. **D ♦♦ $80 - $120**, Min book all holiday times, BC EFT MC VI.

(Chalet Section), 2 chalets acc up to 4, [ensuite, fan, heat, TV, video, t/c mkg, refrig, cook fac, micro, toaster, ldry, doonas, linen, pillows], w/mach, ✕, ice. **D $60 - $75.**

NORSEMAN WA 6443

Pop 1,516. (726km E Perth), See map on page 906, ref C7. A major stopping point for travellers to the Eastern States.

★★★☆ **Norseman Eyre Motel**, (LMH), Cnr Prinsep St & Eyre Hwy, 1.5km N of PO, ☎ 08 9039 1130, fax 08 9039 1547, 44 units [shwr, tlt, a/c, tel, TV, t/c mkg, refrig, ldry], ✉, cots. **RO ♦ $69, ♦♦ $76 - $87**, ch con, Some rooms of a lower rating. AE BC DC MC VI.

★★★ **Great Western Motel**, (M), Prinsep St, 1km N of PO, ☎ 08 9039 1633, fax 08 9039 1692, 25 units [shwr, tlt, a/c, heat, tel (some), TV, t/c mkg, refrig], ✉, pool, bbq, cots. **D ♦ $71 - $75, ♦♦ $85 - $89, ◊ $11**, AE BC DC MC VI.

NORTHAM WA 6401

Pop 6,300. (97km E Perth), See map on page 906, ref B1. Northam lies in the heart of the lush verdant Avon Valley.

Hotels/Motels

★★★☆ **Shamrock Hotel**, (LH), 112 Fitzgerald St, 500m N of PO, ☎ 08 9622 1092, fax 08 9622 5707, 14 rms (2 suites) [ensuite, a/c, TV], ✕ (2), bar (2), spa (5), rm serv. **D ♦♦ $99 - $155.**

Avon Bridge Hotel, (LH), Fitzgerald St, 300m SW of PO, ☎ 08 9622 1023, fax 08 9622 1122, 16 rms [tlt], shwr, TV rm, ✉. **RO ♦ $20, ♦♦ $45 - $50.**

Northam Motel, (M), 13 John St, 1km W of PO, ☎ 08 9622 1755, fax 08 9622 5166, 31 units [shwr, tlt, a/c, tel, TV, t/c mkg, refrig], ✕ (Mon to Thu), rm serv, cots. **D ♦ $55, ♦♦ $65, ◊ $10**, ch con, AE BC DC MC VI.

B&B's/Guest Houses

★★★★ **Brackson House Bed & Breakfast**, (B&B), 2 Old York Rd, 1.6km N of PO, ☎ 08 9622 5262, fax 08 9622 5262, 4 rms [ensuite, shwr, tlt, a/c-cool, fire pl, tel, TV, clock radio, refrig, doonas, pillows], spa, t/c mkg shared, bbq, plygr, cots, non smoking property. **BB ♦ $73, ♦♦ $91, ◊ $28, BLB ♦ $65, ♦♦ $75, ◊ $20**, BC MC VI.

Egoline Reflections, (B&B), Classified by National Trust, Toodyay Rd, 7km NW of PO, ☎ 08 9622 5811, fax 08 9622 1537, 4 rms [heat, elec blkts, tel, clock radio, t/c mkg, pillows], shwr, tlt, ldry, lounge, ✕, pool, bbq, non smoking property, **BB ♦♦ $132, ◊ $55.**

(Cottage Section), 2 cotgs acc up to 5, [shwr, tlt, heat, refrig, cook fac, blkts, linen, pillows]. **D ♦♦ $154, ◊ $55.**

Sir James Mitchell House, (B&B), Classified by National Trust, 112 Fitzgerald St, 1km E of PO, ☎ 08 9622 1092, fax 08 9622 5707, 4 rms [ensuite, fan, fire pl, clock radio, doonas, pillows], lounge, t/c mkg shared, non smoking rms. **BB ♦ $109 - $114, ♦♦ $119 - $129**, AE BC DC EFT MC VI.

Stackallan Homestead, (B&B), No children's facilities, Lot 1005 Henty Pl, 2km SW of PO, ☎ 08 9622 7206, fax 08 9622 1893, 4 rms [bath, tlt, a/c-cool, wood heat, TV, t/c mkg, doonas, pillows], shwr, ldry, iron, iron brd, read rm, lounge, ✕, bbq, meals avail (by arrangement), non smoking property. **BB ♦ $70, ♦♦ $110.**

Other Accommodation

Spring Hill Rural Retreat, (Lodge), Previously Northam Camp School. Spencers Brook Rd, 8km S of PO, ☎ 08 9622 5568, fax 08 9622 5123, 26 rms acc up to 2, [TV, video, ldry, blkts, linen, pillows], shwr, tlt, rec rm, pool, cook fac, bbq, ✎, plygr, golf, tennis. **D ♦ $28.60**, Group bookings only.

(Dormitory Section), 5 rms acc up to 64, [blkts, linen reqd-fee, pillows], shwr, tlt, cook fac. **D ♦ $12.10 - $15.40.**

Northam Guest House, Classified by National Trust, 51 Wellington St, 500m SE of PO, ☎ 08 9622 2301, (2 stry), 29 rms acc up to 2, [shwr, bath, tlt, tel, TV-fee, refrig, cook fac (some), ldry, blkts, linen, pillows], w/mach-fee, dryer-fee, secure park. **RO ♦ $20, W $71.50 - $82.50.**

NORTHAMPTON WA 6535

Pop 842. (474km N Perth), See map on page 906, ref A6. Northampton is a former lead mining centre, located in a sheep and wheat farming region.

Eurardy Station, (House), Caravan and camp sites available. North West Coastal Hwy, 100km N of Northhampton, ☎ 08 9936 1038, fax 08 9936 1054, 3 houses [tel, refrig, blkts, linen, pillows], shwr, tlt, ldry, pool, cook fac, t/c mkg shared, meals avail (by arrangement), non smoking rms. **BB ♦ $33, DBB ♦ $49.50, D $16.50.**

Glenorie Lookout Lodge, (HU), Swamps Rd, 34km NW Northampton, ☎ 08 9935 1017, fax 08 9935 1075, 1 unit acc up to 4, (2 bedrm), [shwr, tlt, fire pl, tel (portable), TV, clock radio, t/c mkg, refrig, cook fac, micro, toaster, blkts, linen reqd-fee, pillows], bbq, non smoking units. **D $82.50, ◊ $16.50, W $495.**

NORTHCLIFFE WA 6262

Pop 239. (366km S Perth), See map on page 906, ref B3. Situated amidst virgin karri forests, reputed to contain some of the oldest and tallest trees in the world, it is the gateway to an excellent south coastal recreation area.

★★★ **Riverway Chalets**, (Chalet), Riverway Rd, 7km SE of PO, ☎ 08 9776 7183, fax 08 9776 7337, 4 chalets acc up to 8, [shwr, tlt, fan, heat, radio, refrig, cook fac, micro, blkts, doonas, linen, pillows], ldry, w/mach, dryer, iron, bbq, ✎, plygr, cots. **D ♦♦ $85, ◊ $17, W $465 - $925**, ch con, Min book.

Meerup Springs Farm Cabins, Double Bridge Rd, 6km W of PO, ☎ 08 9776 7216, fax 08 9776 7216, 5 cabins [shwr, tlt, fire pl, refrig, cook fac, ldry, blkts, linen, pillows], bbq, plygr. **D $82.50 - $110**, BC MC VI.

NYANG STATION HOMESTEAD WA 6701

Pop Nominal, (1222km N Perth) See map on page 906, ref A5. Nyang Homestead is an ideal stopover for travellers.

Nyang Station Homestead, (House), Nyang Station Homestead, Carnarvon 6701, E of North West Coastal Hwy, 320km N of Carnarvon, ☎ 08 9943 0534, fax 08 9943 0534, 4 houses acc up to 2, [blkts, linen, pillows], tank water. **BB ♦ $38.50, ♦♦ $55.**

(Bunkhouse Section), 1 bunkhouse acc up to 15, (Bunk Rooms), [cook fac, blkts reqd, linen reqd, pillows reqd], shwr, tlt. **D ♦ $11.**

ONSLOW WA 6710

Pop 650. (1386km N Perth), See map on page 906, ref A4. Onslow is a pleasant tree-shaded town, situated on the coast at Beadon Creek.

Hotels/Motels

★★★ **Onslow Mackerel Motel**, (M), Cnr Second Ave & Third St, 500m E of PO, ☎ 08 9184 6444, fax 08 9184 6400, 17 units (4 suites) [shwr, tlt, a/c-cool, tel, TV, clock radio, t/c mkg, refrig, elec frypan (4), toaster], ldry, w/mach, dryer, c/park. **D ♦ $93.50 - $110, ♦♦ $110 - $121, ♦ $16.50, Suite D ♦♦ $143**, EFT, ♿.

Self Catering Accommodation

Onslow Sun Chalets, (Chalet), Second Ave, 100m E of PO, ☎ 08 9184 6058, fax 08 9184 6263, 9 chalets (2 bedrm), [shwr, tlt, a/c-cool, TV, refrig, cook fac, ldry, blkts, linen, pillows], pool. **RO ♦ $75, ♦ $10**, BC MC VI.

(Motel Section), 7 units acc up to 2, [ensuite, TV, t/c mkg, refrig, blkts, linen, pillows]. **RO ♦ $75.**

PARABURDOO WA 6754

Pop 2,357. (1536km NE Perth), See map on page 906, ref B4. Paraburdoo is the site of a major iron ore deposit.

Paraburdoo Inn, (LH), Cnr Tom Price & Rocklea Rd, 400m S of PO, ☎ 08 9189 5303, fax 08 9189 5624, 34 rms [a/c, tel, TV, radio, t/c mkg, refrig], ⊠, pool. **D ♦♦ $101 - $139, ♦ $22**, ch con, AE BC DC MC VI.

PARDOO WA 6721

Pop Nominal, (1778km NE Perth), See map on page 906, ref B3. A welcome stopping point on the long drive between Port Hedland and Broome.

Pardoo Station, (GH), Limited facilities, 133km N of Port Hedland, ☎ 08 9176 4930, fax 08 9176 4940, 11 rms [ensuite (1), tlt, a/c-cool, refrig, ldry, pillows], shwr, cook fac, shop (limited supplies). **RO ♦ $33 - $49.50, ♦♦ $49.50 - $60.50, ♦ $11 - $17.60**, BC MC VI.

(Camping Section), Weekly Rates Available. (Powered Site) pool, bbq, LPG, petrol. **D ♦♦ $15.40, Powered Site D ♦♦ $17.60.**

PAYNES FIND WA 6612

Pop Nominal, (425km NE Perth), See map on page 906, ref B6. A small community marking the centre of pastoral and mining activity on the Great Northern Highway.

Ninghan Station, (GH), Great Northern Hwy, 48km SE of Paynes Find, ☎ 08 9963 6517, fax 08 9963 6517, 3 rms [refrig (1), cook fac (1)], Pets on application. **DBB ♦ $71.50, RO ♦ $38.50**, ch con, Rooms in Homestead. No firearms allowed.

(Bunkhouse Section), 1 bunkhouse [blkts reqd, linen reqd, pillows reqd]. **D ♦ $11.**

(Cottage Section), 2 cotgs [refrig, cook fac, blkts reqd-fee, linen reqd-fee, pillows]. **D ♦ $22 - $24.20.**

PEACEFUL BAY WA 6333

Pop part of Denmark, (456km SE Perth), See map on page 906, ref B3.

Peaceful Bay Chalets, (HU), Bow Bridge, 42 km W of Denmark, 10km S of Hwy 1, ☎ 08 9840 8169, 15 units acc up to 7, [shwr, tlt, heat, TV, refrig, cook fac, ldry, blkts reqd, linen reqd, pillows reqd]. **D ♦♦ $48 - $75, W ♦♦ $300 - $400.**

Trouble-free travel tips - **Fluids**

Check all fluid levels and top up as necessary. Look at engine oil, automatic transmission fluid, radiator coolant (only check this when the engine is cold), power steering, battery and windscreen washers.

PEMBERTON WA 6260

Pop 871. (335km S Perth), See map on page 906, ref A3. Pemberton, is set in the heart of magnificent karri forests, crystal clear streams and, in the Spring, a profusion of wildflowers.

Hotels/Motels

★★★★ **Karri Forest Motel**, (M), Widdeson Street, 1.1km E of PO, ☎ 08 9776 1019, fax 08 9776 1710, 26 units [shwr, tlt, hairdry, a/c (some), c/fan, heat, elec blkts, tel, TV, movie, clock radio, t/c mkg, refrig, cook fac (4), toaster, ldry], iron, iron brd, ⊠, pool-heated, spa, bbq, rm serv, plygr, cots-fee, non smoking property. **D ♦♦ $98 - $120, ♦♦♦♦ $149 - $160, ♦ $20**, AE BC DC EFT MC VI.

★★★☆ **Forest Lodge Resort**, (M), Vasse Hwy, 2km NE of PO, ☎ 08 9776 1113, fax 08 9776 1315, 8 units [shwr, tlt, a/c (4), c/fan, heat, elec blkts, tel, TV, movie, clock radio, t/c mkg, refrig, cook fac (4), cook fac ltd (4), ldry], ⊠, spa (2), bbq, plygr, canoeing-fee, cots. **BB ♦♦ $132 - $170, D ♦♦ $99, ♦ $16.50**, Min book long w/ends and Easter, AE BC DC MC VI.

★★★☆ **Gloucester Motel**, (M), Ellis St, 700m SE of PO, ☎ 08 9776 1266, fax 08 9776 1552, 51 units [shwr, tlt, a/c (24), heat, elec blkts, TV, radio, t/c mkg, refrig, toaster], conv fac, ✕, bar (cocktail), rm serv. **D ♦♦ $65 - $77, ♦♦♦ $77 - $82.50, ♦♦♦♦ $82.50 - $99, ♦ $10 - $15**, AE BC DC MC VI.

★★☆ **Karri Valley Resort**, (Ltd Lic H), Vasse Hwy, 20km W of PO, ☎ 08 9776 2020, or 08 9387 4988, fax 08 9776 2012, 32 rms [shwr, tlt, fan, heat, tel, TV, t/c mkg, refrig, ldry], ⊠, bbq, plygr, mini golf, tennis, cots. **D ♦♦ $183, ♦ $22**, AE BC DC MC VI.

Pemberton Hotel, (LH), Brockman St, 100m NE of PO, ☎ 08 9776 1017, fax 08 9776 1600, 11 rms [TV, t/c mkg, refrig], shwr, tlt, ⊠. **D ♦ $25, ♦♦ $110 - $160**, ch con.

Self Catering Accommodation

★★★★☆ **Donnelly Lakes**, (Chalet), Storry Rd, 36km NW of PO, ☎ 08 9776 2005, fax 08 9776 2005, 5 chalets acc up to 7, [shwr, tlt, fan, fire pl, tel, CD, refrig, cook fac, micro, doonas, linen, pillows], iron, spa (hot outdoor) (5), bbq, canoeing, cots. **D ♦♦ $156 - $172, ♦♦♦♦ $200 - $225, ♦ $22**, ch con, Min book applies, AE BC DC MC VI.

★★★★☆ **Pemberton Old Picture Theatre Holiday Apts**, (SA), Heritage, Ellis St, Opposite PO, ☎ 08 9776 1513, fax 08 9776 0258, 5 serv apts acc up to 6, (1, 2 & 3 bedrm), [shwr, bath (2), tlt, hairdry, a/c, tel, TV, video, clock radio, refrig, cook fac, micro, elec frypan, toaster, blkts, linen, pillows], ldry, spa, bbq, non smoking property. **D ♦♦ $110 - $143, ♦ $16.50**, Children under 12 years not catered for. Min book all holiday times, AE BC DC EFT MC VI, ♿.

★★★★ **Diamond Forest Cottages**, (Cotg), Lot 1 South West Hwy, 17km N of PO, ☎ 08 9772 3170, fax 08 9772 3170, 4 cotgs acc up to 6, [shwr, tlt, c/fan, wood heat, tel, TV, video, clock radio, refrig, cook fac, micro, toaster, blkts, doonas, linen, pillows], bbq, canoeing, cots-fee, non smoking property. **D ♦♦ $85.50 - $93.50, ♦ $5.50 - $11**, MC VI.

★★★★ **Karri Valley Hideaway Cottages**, (Cotg), Lot 16 Hopgarden Rd, 21km W of PO, ☎ 08 9776 2049, fax 08 9776 2049, 6 cotgs acc up to 4, [shwr, tlt, fan, heat, refrig, cook fac, micro, ldry, blkts, linen, pillows], ✕, spa (/s), bbq, golf. **D ♦ $120, ♦♦ $120 - $145, ♦ $15**, BC MC VI.

★★★★ **Marima Cottages**, (Chalet), Old Vasse Rd, Warren National Park, ☎ 08 9776 1211, fax 08 9776 1211, 2 chalets acc up to 6, (2 bedrm), [shwr, tlt, c/fan, wood heat, tel, radio, CD, refrig, cook fac, micro, elec frypan, toaster, blkts, doonas, linen, pillows], cafe, non smoking property. **D ♦♦ $121, ♦♦♦♦ $165, ♦ $22**, BC MC VI.

★★★★ **Pump Hill Farm Cottages**, (Cotg), Pump Hill Rd, 1.5km W of PO, ☎ 08 9776 1379, fax 08 9776 1879, 12 cotgs acc up to 10, (1, 2 & 3 bedrm), [shwr, tlt, fire pl, TV, clock radio, t/c mkg, refrig, micro, toaster, blkts, doonas, linen, pillows], ldry, bbq, ✆, cots-fee. **D ♦ $90 - $145, ♦ $11 - $17**, ch con, Min book all holiday times, BC MC VI.

★★★★ **Treenbrook Cottages**, (Cotg), Lot 6785 Vasse Hwy, 4.5km W of PO, ☎ 08 9776 1638, fax 08 9776 0459, 4 cotgs acc up to 6, (2 bedrm), [shwr, tlt, hairdry, fire pl, TV, video, radio, refrig, cook fac, micro, blkts, doonas, linen, pillows], iron, bbq. **D ♦♦ $95 - $130, ♦ $10 - $15**, AE BC DC MC VI.

★★★★ **Warren National Park Chalets**, (Cotg), Lot 300 Hawke Rd, 18km SW of PO, ☎ 08 9776 1188, fax 08 9776 1061, 4 cotgs acc up to 6, (2 bedrm), [shwr, tlt, elec blkts, TV, clock radio, t/c mkg, refrig, cook fac, doonas, linen, pillows], ldry, w/mach, dryer, iron, lounge firepl, bbq, ✎, plygr, cots-fee, non smoking property. **D ♦♦ $90 - $120, ◊ $7.50 - $15, W ♦♦ $450 - $720, ◊ $37.50 - $90**, Min book all holiday times, BC MC VI.

★★★★ **Warren River Resort**, (Cotg), Pemberton Northcliffe Rd, 9km SW of PO, ☎ 08 9776 1400, fax 08 9776 1581, 11 cotgs acc up to 8, (1, 2 & 3 bedrm), [shwr, tlt, heat (wood), TV, movie, radio, refrig, micro, ldry, blkts, linen, pillows], w/mach, iron, rec rm, pool, spa (heated), bbq, plygr, cots. **D $115.50 - $148, ◊ $13 - $35**, BC MC VI.

★★★☆ **Pemberton Lavender & Berry Farm**, (Cotg), Browns Rd, 5km E of PO, ☎ 08 9776 1661, fax 08 9761 1661, 4 cotgs acc up to 5, (2 bedrm), [hairdry, c/fan, fire pl, TV, clock radio, t/c mkg, refrig, micro, toaster, blkts, doonas, linen, pillows], ldry, w/mach-fee, cots (avail), non smoking units. **D $98 - $132, ◊ $12**, ch con, Min book all holiday times, Min book long w/ends, BC MC VI.

★★★ **Peerabeelup Farm Cottages**, (Cotg), No children's facilities, Vasse Hwy, 36km NW of PO, ☎ 08 9776 2025, fax 08 9776 2024, 5 cotgs acc up to 4, (2 bedrm), [shwr, spa bath (5), tlt, c/fan, wood heat, refrig, cook fac, micro, toaster, doonas, linen], bbq. **D $135 - $175**, Min book applies, BC MC VI.

★★★ **Pemberton Break-Away Cottages**, (Cotg), Lot 1 Roberts Rd, 5km S of PO, ☎ 08 9776 1580, fax 08 9776 1580, 4 cotgs acc up to 6, (2 & 3 bedrm), [shwr, tlt, wood heat, TV, video, clock radio, cook fac, blkts, doonas, linen, pillows], iron, iron brd, bbq, courtesy transfer. **D ♦ $82.50 - $99, ♦♦ $93.50 - $110, ♦♦♦ $104.50 - $132, W ♦♦♦ $495 - $594, ♦♦♦♦ $627 - $737**, BC EFT MC VI.

★★★ **Pemberton Farm Chalets**, (Chalet), Vasse Hwy, 1.5km NE of PO, ☎ 08 9776 1290, fax 08 9776 1290, 8 chalets acc up to 6, (2 & 4 bedrm), [shwr, tlt, wood heat, TV, radio, refrig, cook fac, micro, ldry, blkts, linen reqd-fee, pillows], pool, spa (1), bbq, tennis. **D ♦♦ $85 - $95, ◊ $10**.

Beedelup House, (Cotg), Hop Garden Rd, 21km W of PO, ☎ 08 9776 2010, fax 08 9776 2010, 6 cotgs acc up to 4, [shwr, tlt, hairdry, a/c, fire pl (open), tel, TV, video, clock radio, CD, refrig, cook fac, micro, toaster, doonas, linen, pillows], w/mach, dryer, iron, pool, spa (4), bbq, cots (avail). **D ♦♦ $135 - $154**, AE BC DC MC VI.

Forest Lodge Resort, (Chalet), Vasse Hwy, 2km NE of PO, ☎ 08 9776 1113, fax 08 9776 1315, 5 chalets acc up to 8, [shwr, spa bath (1), tlt, fan, heat (log fire), elec blkts, tel, TV, movie, clock radio, t/c mkg, refrig, cook fac, micro, ldry, blkts, doonas, linen, pillows], ✕, ⌧, bbq, plygr, canoeing-fee, cots. **D ♦♦ $154, ◊ $16.50**, Min book long w/ends and Easter, AE BC DC MC VI.

Karri Valley Resort Chalets, (Chalet), Vasse Hwy, 20km W of PO, ☎ 08 9776 2020, fax 08 9776 2012, 36 chalets acc up to 7, (2 & 3 bedrm), [shwr, tlt, wood heat, cook fac, micro, ldry, blkts, linen, pillows], ⌧, bbq, plygr, mini golf, tennis, cots. **RO ♦ $183, ♦♦ $228, ♦♦♦ $257**, AE BC DC MC VI.

Pemberton Blue Loft Cottages, (Cotg), Channybearup Rd, 12km N of PO, ☎ 08 9776 1566, fax 08 9776 1566, (2 stry), 2 cotgs acc up to 6, (2 bedrm), [shwr, tlt, fan, wood heat, video, clock radio (cassette), t/c mkg, refrig, micro, elec frypan, toaster, blkts, doonas, linen, pillows], iron, iron brd, bbq, cots, non smoking property. **D ♦♦ $95, ◊ $11**, pen con.

B&B's/Guest Houses

Glenhaven Bed & Breakfast, (B&B), 25 Browns Rd, 3km E of PO, ☎ 08 9776 0028, fax 08 9776 0028, 3 rms [shwr, tlt, hairdry, fan, c/fan, fire pl, wood heat, elec blkts, TV (shared), video (shared), clock radio (shared), refrig], iron, iron brd, lounge, t/c mkg shared, bbq, c/park. **BB ♦ $65, ♦♦ $90**, BC MC VI, ⌂⌧, (not yet classified).

Treen Ridge Estate, (B&B), Packer Rd, 10km W of PO, ☎ 08 9776 1131, fax 08 9776 0442, 3 rms [shwr, bath, tlt, hairdry, wood heat, elec blkts, TV, video, clock radio, CD, refrig], iron, iron brd, lounge firepl, t/c mkg shared, bbq, cots, non smoking property. **BB ♦ $60, ♦♦ $95 - $121**, AE BC DC MC VI, (not yet classified).

PINGELLY WA 6308

Pop 937. (158km SE Perth), See map on page 906, ref B1. Located in a wheat and sheep district.

★★★☆ **Pingelly Farm Stay**, (GH), (Farm), Harper St, 158km SE of Perth, ☎ 08 9887 1375, fax 08 9887 1196, 3 rms [fan, heat, elec blkts, TV, video, pillows], shwr, tlt, bbq. **BB $45**.

PINJARRA WA 6208

Pop 1,892. (87km S Perth), See map on page 906, ref A1. Pinjarra, on the banks of the Murray River, first settled in 1833 and is one of the oldest towns in the State.

Pinjarra Motel, (M), South Western Hwy, opposite Hospital. 1km S of PO, ☎ 08 9531 1811, fax 08 9531 1355, 10 units [shwr, tlt, TV, t/c mkg, refrig], ✕ (licensed), pool, bbq. **D ♦ $55 - $65, ♦♦ $69 - $75, ♦♦♦♦ $110 - $130**.

POINT SAMSON WA 6720

Pop 255. Part of Roebourne, (1578km N Perth), See map on page 906, ref B4. Located on the tip of the Point Samson Peninsula.

★★★★ **Point Samson Lodge**, (M), 56 Samson Rd, 58km NE Karratha, ☎ 08 9187 1052, fax 08 9187 1603, 12 units [shwr, tlt, a/c-cool, fan, tel, TV, movie, clock radio, t/c mkg, refrig, cook fac, micro, toaster, ldry, pillows], ✕, pool, bbq, rm serv, c/park. **D ♦ $127 - $394, ♦♦ $140 - $394, ◊ $25**, ch con, AE BC DC EFT MC VI.

PORONGURUP WA 6324

Pop part of Mt Barker, (383km S Perth), See map on page 906, ref B3. This very popular range of hills offers some breathtaking scenery for the energetic climber, as well as for those who prefer to take it a bit easy.

Self Catering Accommodation

★★★★ **Thorn's Hillside Cottage**, (Cotg), RMB 1280 Porongurup Rd, 2km E of PO, ☎ 08 9853 1105, fax 08 9853 1105, 1 cotg acc up to 4, [shwr, tlt, wood heat, tel, video, radio, refrig, cook fac, micro, ldry, blkts, linen, pillows]. **D ♦♦ $85 - $95, ◊ $10, W $425 - $450**, Min book all holiday times, BC MC VI.

★★☆ **Bolganup Homestead**, (Cotg), (Farm), RMB 1336 Porongurup Rd, 300m behind shop, ☎ 08 9853 1049, fax 08 9853 1049, 2 cotgs acc up to 6, [shwr, bath (2), tlt, heat, elec blkts (3), refrig, cook fac, blkts, linen, pillows], ldry, rec rm, plygr, cots. **D $90 - $100**.

Karribank Country Retreat Chalets, (Chalet), RMB 1332 Porongurup Rd, ☎ 08 9853 1022, fax 08 9853 1122, 11 chalets acc up to 8, (2 & 3 bedrm), [shwr, tlt, heat, TV-fee, t/c mkg, refrig, cook fac, ldry, blkts, doonas, linen reqd-fee, pillows], w/mach-fee, dryer-fee, iron, non smoking units. **D ♦♦♦♦ $150 - $200, ◊ $6 - $12**, Min book all holiday times, Min book long w/ends, BC MC VI.

Moolabar Retreat, (Cotg), No children's facilities, Millinup Rd, 5km S of shop, ☎ 08 9853 2077, fax 08 9853 2077, 1 cotg acc up to 2, (1 bedrm), [ensuite, wood heat, elec blkts, tel, clock radio, CD, refrig, cook fac, micro, elec frypan, doonas, linen, pillows], iron, bbq, non smoking rms. **D ♦♦ $77, W ♦♦ $360**.

Porongurup Chalets, (Chalet), Cnr Bolganup & Porongurup Rds, 500m E of shop, ☎ 08 9853 1034, fax 08 9853 1034, 10 chalets acc up to 8, (1 & 2 bedrm), [shwr, tlt, refrig, cook fac, ldry, blkts, linen-fee, pillows], bbq, Pets allowed. **D $55 - $88, W $297 - $528**, ⌂⌧.

The Sleeping Lady Cottage, (Cotg), RMB 1044 Porongurup Road, 1km W of Chester Pass Rd, ☎ 08 9853 1113, fax 08 9853 1113, 1 cotg acc up to 4, (2 bedrm), [shwr, tlt, c/fan, wood heat, elec blkts, video, radio, CD, t/c mkg, refrig, cook fac, micro, blkts, doonas, linen, pillows], w/mach, bbq, c/park. **D ♦♦ $110, ♦♦♦ $120, ♦♦♦♦ $130, W ♦♦ $650 - $750, ♦♦♦♦ $750 - $840**, Min book applies, BC MC VI.

B&B's/Guest Houses

★★★★★ **The Sleeping Lady**, (B&B), No children's facilities, RMB 1044 Porongurup Rd, 1.5km W of Chester Pass Rd, ☎ 08 9853 1113, fax 08 9853 1113, 1 rm (1 suite) [shwr, bath, tlt, hairdry, a/c-cool, heat, fire pl, elec blkts, tel, TV, video, clock radio, t/c mkg, refrig, doonas, pillows], ldry, w/mach-fee, dryer-fee, iron-fee, iron brd, lounge, ✕, bbq, meals avail (by arrangement), non smoking rms. **BB ♦♦ $100**, BC MC VI.

★★★★☆ **Peacehaven Mountain Escape**, (B&B), No children's facilities, 4 Millinup Rd, 8km S of shop, ☎ 08 9853 2141, fax 08 9853 2141, 3 rms [ensuite, hairdry, fan, fire pl, elec blkts, tel, clock radio, t/c mkg, ldry (on request), doonas, pillows], read rm, lounge, meals avail (by arrangement), non smoking property. **BB ♦ $55 - $60, ♦♦ $90**.

★★★★ **Karribank Country Retreat**, (GH), RMB 1332 Porongurup Rd, ☎ 08 9853 1022, fax 08 9853 1122, 26 rms [shwr, tlt, heat, elec blkts], rec rm, ✕, cots. **D ◊ $13, RO ♦♦ $82 - $150**, Some rooms of a lower rating. BC MC VI.

PORT HEDLAND WA 6721

Pop 16,000. (1635km N Perth), See map on page 906, ref B4. Once an old pearling port, Port Hedland is one of the largest ports by tonnage in Australia. The town revolves around the mining and shipping of the Pilbara's most valuable commodity - iron ore.

★★★☆ **Hospitality Inn Port Hedland**, (M), Webster St, 4.5km E of PO, ☎ 08 9173 1044, fax 08 9173 1464, 40 units [shwr, tlt, a/c, tel, TV, movie, radio, t/c mkg, refrig, ldry], ⊠, pool, bbq, rm serv, plygr, cots, non smoking units (avail). **D** ♦♦ **$155,** ◊ **$22**, pen con, AE BC DC MC VI.

★★★☆ **Mercure Inn Port Hedland**, (LH), Cnr Lukis & McGregor Sts, 5km E of PO, ☎ 08 9173 1511, fax 08 9173 1545, 60 rms [shwr, bath (3), tlt, a/c-cool, tel, TV, movie, radio, t/c mkg, refrig], ✗ (licensed), pool, cots. **D** ♦♦ **$144 - $192**, AE BC DC MC VI, 👜.

★★★☆ **South Hedland Motel**, (M), Court Pl, South Hedland 6722, 200m NE of PO, ☎ 08 9172 2222, fax 08 9140 1067, 54 units [shwr, tlt, a/c, tel, TV, t/c mkg, refrig], ldry, conv fac, ⊠, pool, spa, rm serv, cots. **D** ♦ **$100,** ♦♦ **$110,** ♦♦♦♦ **$125,** ◊ **$15**, ch con, AE BC DC MC VI, 👜.

★★★☆ **The Lodge Motel & Offices**, (LMH), Brand St, South Hedland 6722, 100metres N of shopping centre, ☎ 08 9172 2188, fax 08 9172 1857, 132 units [shwr, tlt, hairdry, a/c-cool, tel, fax, TV, clock radio, t/c mkg, refrig, toaster], ldry, ⊠, bar, pool, bbq, courtesy transfer, gym. **DBB** ♦ **$120 - $147.50,** ♦♦ **$142 - $158.50,** ◊ **$27**, AE BC DC EFT MC VI.

★★★ **Port Hedland Walkabout Hotel**, (LH), Previously Mrecure Inn Port Hedland Airport North West Coastal Hwy, 10km SE of PO, ☎ 08 9172 1222, fax 08 9140 1245, 63 rms (2 suites) [shwr, tlt, tel, TV, radio, t/c mkg, refrig], ⊠, pool, rm serv, cots-fee. **D** ♦ **$110,** ♦♦ **$120,** ♦♦♦ **$140, Suite D** ♦♦♦♦ **$120 - $150**, ch con, AE BC DC VI.

PRESTON BEACH WA 6215

Pop Nominal, (133km S Perth), See map on page 906, ref A2. A holiday community located between Lake Preston and the Indian Ocean.

★★★☆ **Preston Beach Guest House**, (B&B), No children's facilities, 6 Styles Road, 57 km S of Mandurah PO, ☎ 08 9739 1550, fax 08 9739 1550, 3 rms [ensuite (1), bath, tlt, hairdry, heat, c/fan, TV, video, clock radio, refrig, doonas, pillows], shwr, ldry, TV rm, ✗, t/c mkg shared, meals avail (by arrangement), non smoking property. **BB** ♦ **$60 - $80,** ♦♦ **$70 - $90, DBB** ♦♦ **$100 - $120**, Min book long w/ends, BC MC VI.

QUAIRADING WA 6383

Pop 741. (166km E Perth), See map on page 906, ref B1. Located in a sheep and wheat farming district.

★★☆ **Quairading Motel**, (M), 55 Jennaberring Rd, 700m E of PO, ☎ 08 9645 1054, fax 08 9645 1054, 6 units [shwr, tlt, a/c-cool, heat, TV, t/c mkg, refrig], rm serv. **D** ♦ **$45,** ♦♦ **$50,** ◊ **$8**.

RAVENSTHORPE WA 6346

Pop 354. (532km SE Perth), See map on page 906, ref C8. Located in a mining, mixed farming district, via Wagin and Lake Grace. The town is circled by the Ravensthorpe Ranges amid stately Salmon Gums. Bowls, Golf, Tennis.

Hotels/Motels

★☆ **Ravensthorpe Motel**, (M), Cnr Hopetoun Rd & Jamieson St, 1km E of PO, ☎ 08 9838 1053, fax 08 9838 1366, 12 units [shwr, tlt, a/c-cool, elec blkts, TV, radio, t/c mkg, refrig], cots-fee. **D** ♦ **$49.50,** ♦♦ **$60.50,** ♦♦♦ **$71.50,** ♦♦♦♦ **$80**, ch con, AE BC DC EFT MC VI.

Ravensthorpe Palace Motor Hotel, (LMH), 28 Morgan St, next door to PO, ☎ 08 9838 1005, fax 08 9838 1200, 14 units [shwr, tlt, a/c, elec blkts, tel, TV, clock radio, t/c mkg, refrig], TV rm, ✗, cots. **RO** ♦ **$45,** ♦♦ **$60,** ◊ **$10**, BC DC EFT MC VI.

(Hotel Section), 12 rms [H & C], shwr. **BB** ♦ **$28,** ♦♦ **$51, RO** ♦ **$20,** ♦♦ **$35**.

Self Catering Accommodation

Chambejo Farm, (Cotg), South Coast Hwy, 34km W of PO, ☎ 08 9835 7015, fax 08 9835 7012, 1 cotg acc up to 8, [shwr, bath, tlt, fire pl, elec blkts, radio, refrig, cook fac, ldry, blkts, linen, pillows], cots. **D** ♦♦ **$50,** ◊ **$10**.

SANDFIRE WA 6721

Pop Nominal, (1915km N Perth), See map on page 906, ref C3. Sandfire originated in 1970 when a truck carrying petrol broke down 1,915km north of Perth, midway between Port Hedland and Broome. Such was the demand for fuel from passing motorists that the idea for a more-permanent installation developed.

★★ **Sandfire Roadhouse**, (LMH), Great Northern Hwy, Port Hedland 6721, 291km N of Port Hedland, ☎ 08 9176 5944, fax 08 9176 5942, 6 units [shwr, tlt, a/c, refrig], ⊠. **RO** ♦ **$70,** ♦♦ **$70,** ◊ **$10**.

(Hotel Section), 10 rms shwr, tlt. **RO** ♦ **$35,** ♦♦ **$35,** ◊ **$10**.

SOUTHERN CROSS WA 6426

Pop 936. (369km E Perth), See map on page 906, ref C7. Southern Cross has had a colourful history since the discovery of gold there in 1888.

Hotels/Motels

★★☆ **Palace Hotel**, (LMH), Cnr Antares St & Great Eastern Hwy, 250m S of PO, ☎ 08 9049 1555, fax 08 9049 1509, 34 units shwr, tlt. **RO** ♦ **$44,** ♦♦ **$55,** ◊ **$11**, ch con, BC MC VI.

(Motel Section), 6 units [shwr, tlt, a/c, fan, heat, tel, TV, video, t/c mkg, refrig], rec rm, TV rm, ✗, bbq, cots-fee. **RO** ♦ **$55,** ♦♦ **$66,** ◊ **$11**, 👜.

★★☆ **Southern Cross Motel**, (M), Canopus St, 300m NW of PO, ☎ 08 9049 1144, fax 08 9049 1140, 29 units [shwr, tlt, a/c, TV, t/c mkg, refrig], ⊠, pool, cots. **RO** ♦ **$60.50 - $71.50,** ♦♦ **$71.50 - $82.50**.

THREE SPRINGS WA 6519

Pop 638. (314km N Perth), See map on page 906, ref B7. As the geographical and rail centre for the North Midlands, Three Springs has had a steady growth, based mainly on sheep and wheat.

★★☆ **Commercial Motel Hotel**, (LMH), Railway Rd, 250m NW of PO. ☎ 08 9954 1041, fax 08 9954 1328, 19 units [shwr, tlt, a/c-cool, heat, TV, t/c mkg, refrig], cots. **RO** ♦ **$45,** ♦♦ **$70**, Grading applies to motel section only.

(Hotel Section), 10 rms shwr, tlt. **RO** ♦ **$30,** ♦♦ **$45**.

TOM PRICE WA 6751

Pop 3,540. (1553km NE Perth), See map on page 906, ref B4. The town of Tom Price is the administrative centre of the Shire of Ashburton. Bush Walking, Swimming.

★★★☆ **Karijini Lodge Motel**, (M), Stadium Rd, 400m NE of PO, ☎ 08 9189 1110, fax 08 9189 1625, 120 units [shwr, tlt, a/c, tel, TV, radio, t/c mkg, refrig], ldry, conv fac, ⊠, pool, bbq, cots. **D** ♦♦ **$129**, AE BC DC MC VI.

★★☆ **Mercure Inn Tom Price**, (LH), Central Rd, 100m S of PO, ☎ 08 9189 1101, fax 08 9189 1164, 45 rms [shwr, tlt, a/c, tel, TV, movie, t/c mkg, refrig], ⊠, bbq, cots. **RO** ♦ **$102 - $128,** ♦♦ **$102 - $128,** ♦♦♦ **$146 - $172**, ch con, AE BC DC MC VI.

TOODYAY WA 6566

Pop 678. (85km NE Perth), See map on page 906, ref A1. A wheat, sheep and cattle farming area located in the Avon Valley.

Self Catering Accommodation

Hoddywell Cottage, (Cotg), 440 Clackline Rd, 4.4km S of Toodyay & Clackline Rd Corner, ☎ 08 9227 1106, fax 08 9227 1249, 1 cotg acc up to 6, [shwr, bath, tlt, fire pl, CD, refrig, cook fac, micro, doonas, linen, pillows], w/mach, iron, bbq, cots. **D** ♦♦ **$100 - $120,** ♦♦♦ **$105 - $130,** ♦♦♦♦ **$110 - $140,** ◊ **$5 - $10, W** ♦♦ **$500,** ♦♦♦♦ **$600,** ◊ **$50**, AE BC DC MC VI, (not yet classified).

B&B's/Guest Houses

★★★★★ **The Bush Estate**, (B&B), Lot 3 Black Wattle Rd, 19km W of PO, ☎ 08 9574 4086, fax 08 9574 4088, 2 rms [shwr, tlt, hairdry, evap cool, heat, elec blkts, TV, video, t/c mkg, refrig], w/mach-fee, dryer-fee, iron, rec rm, bbq, c/park. **BB** ♦ **$100 - $150,** ♦♦ **$140 - $190,** ◊ **$70**, ch con.

★★★★ **Avalon Holiday Retreat**, (GH), No children's facilities, Lot 45 Julimar Rd, 4km W of PO, ☎ 08 9574 5050, fax 08 9574 5051, 16 rms [ensuite, tlt, a/c, fire pl, tel (public), TV, video, doonas, pillows], ldry, w/mach, dryer, iron, iron brd, lounge, ✗, t/c mkg shared, meals avail (by arrangement), c/park. **BB** ♦ **$60.50, DBB** ♦ **$82.50**, pen con, Min book long w/ends.

TOODYAY WA continued...

★★★★ **Ipswich View Homestead**, (B&B), Lot 45 Folewood Rd, 4km W of PO, ☎ 08 9574 4038, fax 08 9574 4292, 5 rms [shwr, bath (2), tlt, hairdry, a/c-cool, elec blkts, clock radio, t/c mkg, ldry, pillows], w/mach, dryer-fee, iron, ✗, pool, bbq, mini golf, tennis. **BB ∲ $115 - $105, DBB ♁ $150 - $135**, Min book long w/ends, BC JCB MC VI.

★★★★ **Pecan Hill Guesthouse**, (B&B), No children's facilities, Lot 59 Beaufort St, 4km W of PO, ☎ 08 9574 2636, fax 08 9574 2636, 4 rms [ensuite, shwr, tlt, hairdry, a/c, fire pl, elec blkts, tel, TV, video, t/c mkg, pillows], w/mach-fee, dryer-fee, read rm, lounge, ✗, pool (with spa), bbq, meals avail (by arrangement), non smoking rms. **BB ∲ $55 - $78, ♁ $75 - $106, DBB ♁ $110 - $142**, pen con, Min book long w/ends and Easter.

Katrine, (B&B), No children's facilities, Toodyay-Northam Rd, 10km from town across Avon River, ☎ 08 9622 3790, fax 08 9622 1205, 3 rms [ensuite, t/c mkg], pool, meals avail (by arrangement), tennis, non smoking rms. **BB ♁ $100 - $140.**

WAGIN WA 6315

Pop 1,488. (229km SE Perth), See map on page 906, ref B2. Wagin is the centre of a good, rich wheat and sheep farming district.

★★★ **Wagin Motel**, (M), Tudhoe St, 300m NE of PO, ☎ 08 9861 1888, fax 08 9861 1800, 12 units [shwr, tlt, a/c, elec blkts, tel, TV, movie, radio, t/c mkg, refrig], ✗. **D ∲ $65, ♁ $75.**

Moran's Wagin Hotel, (LH), 77 Tudor St, 300m S of PO, ☎ 08 9861 1017, fax 08 9861 1607, 15 rms [tlt], shwr, ✗, rm serv, cots. **BB ∲ $37, DBB ∲ $53, RO ∲ $27, ♁ $50.**

WALPOLE WA 6398

Pop 291. (423km S Perth), See map on page 906, ref B3. Lying on the banks of an inlet and surrounded by magnificent red tingle and karri forests, Walpole is a most inviting haven for the tourist.

Hotels/Motels

★★★★ **Tree Top Walk Motel & Restaurant**, (M), Nockolds St, 100m E of PO, ☎ 08 9840 1444, fax 08 9840 1555, 35 units [hairdry, heat, c/fan, elec blkts, tel, TV, movie, clock radio, t/c mkg, refrig, toaster], ldry, w/mach-fee, dryer-fee, iron, iron brd, ✗, pool, bbq, 24hr reception, rm serv, cots-fee, non smoking property. **D ♁ $114, ♁♁ $149 - $174, ◊ $20**, AE BC DC EFT MC VI, ⚹.

Walpole Motel Hotel, (LMH), South Coast Highway, 500m N of PO, ☎ 08 9840 1023, fax 08 9840 1589, 30 units [shwr, tlt, heat, TV, movie, t/c mkg, refrig, toaster], ✗, bbq, ✎, cots. **D ∲ $70, ♁ $80, ◊ $10**, AE BC DC EFT MC VI.

Self Catering Accommodation

★★★☆ **Che Sara Sara Chalets**, (Chalet), Hazelvale Rd, Denmark 6333, 15km NE of PO, ☎ 08 9840 8004, fax 08 9840 8004, 4 chalets acc up to 8, (2 & 3 bedrm), [shwr, tlt, wood heat, refrig, cook fac, micro, ldry, blkts, linen reqd-fee, pillows], w/mach, bbq, canoeing, tennis, cots. **D ♁ $80 - $105**, ch con, BC MC VI.

★★★ **Bow River Cottage**, (Cotg), Lot 3 Valley of The Giants Rd, rear of Bow Bridge Roadhouse, 24km E of PO, ☎ 08 9840 8062, fax 08 9840 8251, 1 cotg acc up to 5, (2 bedrm), [shwr, bath, tlt, heat (gas), elec blkts, TV, video, clock radio, t/c mkg, refrig, cook fac, micro, toaster, ldry, blkts, doonas, linen, pillows], w/mach, iron, ✗, ✎. **D ♁ $72 - $83, ◊ $5 - $10, W ♁ $430 - $495.**

★★★ **Riverside Retreat**, (Chalet), South Coast Highway, 8km E of Walpole PO, ☎ 08 9840 1255, fax 08 9840 1388, 6 chalets acc up to 5, (2 bedrm3 bedrm), [shwr, tlt, c/fan, wood heat, clock radio, refrig, cook fac, micro, elec frypan, ldry, blkts, doonas, linen, pillows], bbq, c/park (undercover), canoeing, tennis, cots, non smoking units. **D $88 - $99**, Min book all holiday times, BC MC VI.

★★ **Billa Billa Farm Cottages**, (Cotg), Hunter Rd, 19km N of PO, ☎ 08 9840 1131, fax 08 9840 1131, 4 cotgs acc up to 6, (2 bedrm), [shwr, tlt, wood heat, refrig, cook fac, ldry, doonas, linen reqd-fee, pillows], bbq, ✎, plygr, cots. **D $77 - $90, W $460 - $520**, BC VI.

Walpole Bayside Villas, (Villa), Lot 2 Boronia Avenue, 1km W of PO, ☎ 08 9840 1888, or 08 9840 1188, 6 villas acc up to 7, [shwr, spa bath, tlt, a/c, elec blkts, TV, video, clock radio, t/c mkg, refrig, cook fac, micro, elec frypan, toaster, blkts, doonas, linen, pillows], w/mach, iron, iron brd, bbq, cots (avail), non smoking property. **D ♁ $95 - $145, ♁♁ $105 - $155, ♁♁ $115 - $165, W $510 - $870**, AE BC DC EFT MC VI, (not yet classified).

Hideaway Cottage, (Cotg), (Farm), Armstrong Rd, 10km N of PO, ☎ 08 9840 1138, fax 08 9840 1138, 1 cotg acc up to 6, [shwr, bath, tlt, heat, TV, refrig, cook fac, micro, ldry, linen, pillows], plygr. **D $70, ◊ $5, W $350 - $450**, Min book Christmas and Jan.

Sheoak Cottage, (Cotg), 342 Sheoak Street, 1km W of Tourist Bureau off SW Highway, ☎ 08 9840 1309, 1 cotg acc up to 4, (2 bedrm), [shwr, tlt, hairdry, heat, fan, heat, elec blkts, TV, video, clock radio, CD, t/c mkg, refrig, cook fac, micro, blkts, doonas, linen, pillows], w/mach, iron, iron brd, bbq, 24hr reception, trailer park, bicycle, cots, non smoking property. **D ∲ $50, ♁ $70, ♁♁ $75, ♁♁ $80, W ♁ $420, ♁♁ $460 - $420.**

Tinglewood Cabins, (Cotg), Lot 10221 Bridge Rd, 8km N of PO, ☎ 08 9840 1367, 2 cotgs acc up to 8, (3 bedrm), [shwr, tlt, wood heat, tel, TV, t/c mkg, refrig, cook fac, micro, toaster, doonas, linen reqd-fee, pillows], w/mach, bbq, plygr. **D ♁ $65 - $70, ◊ $5 - $10.**

Walpole Wilderness Resort, (Cotg), Gardiner Road, 15km N of Walpole ☎ 08 9840 1481, fax 08 9840 1482, 4 cotgs acc up to 10, (3 bedrm), [shwr, tlt, wood heat, elec blkts, tel, TV, video, movie, radio, CD, t/c mkg, refrig, cook fac, micro, blkts, doonas, linen, pillows], w/mach, dryer, iron, iron brd, rec rm, spa, bbq, meals avail (to unit), secure park, trailer park, plygr, bicycle-fee, cots. **D ∲ $125 - $170, ♁♁ $136 - $181, ♁♁ $147 - $192, W ∲ $787 - $1,070, ♁♁ $857 - $1,040, ♁♁ $926 - $1,210**, BC DC EFT MC VI, ⚹.

B&B's/Guest Houses

★★★★☆ **Nornalup Views B&B**, (B&B), No children's facilities, Lot 100 MacPherson Dve, Nornalup 6333, 10km SE of Walpole PO, ☎ 08 9840 1373, fax 08 9840 1373, 1 rm [ensuite, heat, fan, wood heat, tel, TV, video, clock radio, t/c mkg, refrig, doonas, pillows], ldry, dryer, iron, bbq, meals avail (by arrangement), non smoking property. **BB ♁ $75 - $85**, BC MC VI.

★★★☆ **Inlet View**, (B&B), 58 Walpole St, 500m S of PO, ☎ 08 9840 1226, fax 08 9840 1226, 2 rms [shwr, tlt, fire pl, TV, pillows], lounge, ✗. **BB ∲ $40, ♁ $70**, ch con.

★★★☆ **Ridgeway Bed & Breakfast**, (B&B), Lot 162 Walpole St, 700m S of PO, ☎ 08 9840 1036, fax 08 9840 1536, 1 rm [ensuite, hairdry, heat, fan, elec blkts, t/c mkg, refrig, doonas, pillows], non smoking property. **BLB ∲ $38, ♁ $75.**

Tingledale Cottage, (B&B), Loc 1224 Settlers Boundary Rd, 27km E of PO, ☎ 08 9840 8181, fax 08 9840 8329, 1 rm [shwr, tlt, fan, wood heat, elec blkts, TV, video, clock radio, t/c mkg, refrig], spa, non smoking property. **BB ♁ $99**, Seperate cottage. (not yet classified).

Other Accommodation

Tingle All Over Budget Accommodation, (Lodge), Cnr Inlet & Nockolds St, South Coast Hwy, ☎ 08 9840 1041, fax 08 9840 1041, 10 rms acc up to 5, [shwr, tlt, fire pl, TV, cook fac (kitchen 7am to 10pm), blkts, linen, pillows], ldry, w/mach-fee, dryer-fee, iron, rec rm, refrig, bbq, non smoking rms. **RO ∲ $33, ♁ $44, ♁♁ $70 - $77**, BC MC VI.

WAROONA WA 6215

Pop 1,833. (112km S Perth), See map on page 906, ref A2. Waroona stretches from the Indian ocean to the darling range.

Drakesbrook Motel Hotel, (LMH), 342 South Western Hwy, 1km N of PO, ☎ 08 9733 1566, fax 08 9733 1620, 16 units [shwr, tlt, a/c, fan, heat, elec blkts, tel, TV, t/c mkg, refrig, ldry], conv fac, ✗, pool, cots-fee. **D ∲ $55, ♁ $75, ♁♁ $120, ◊ $11**, BC MC VI.

WICKHAM WA 6720

Pop 2,387. (1570km N Perth), See map on page 906, ref B4.

Wickham Lodge, (SA), 6 Wickham Dve, 1.2km from turnoff at Roebourne-Samson Rd, ☎ 08 9187 1439, fax 08 9187 1496, (Multi-stry), 21 serv apts acc up to 4, (1 bedrm), [ensuite, shwr, tlt, a/c-cool (18), a/c (3), TV, clock radio, t/c mkg, refrig, toaster, blkts, doonas, linen, pillows], ldry, w/mach, dryer, iron, iron brd, bbq, ✎, plygr, tennis. **D ♁ $70, ♁♁ $75**, AE BC DC MC VI.

WILLARE BRIDGE WA 6728

Pop Nominal, (2334km N Perth), See map on page 906, ref D2. A pleasant tree shaded spot where the Great Northern Highway crosses the Fitzroy River. Bird Watching, Bush Walking, Fishing.

Willare Bridge Roadhouse, (PH), Limited facilities, Great Northern Hwy, 14km W of Derby turnoff, ☎ 08 9191 4775, fax 08 9191 4775, 9 rms [a/c], ✗, ✉, pool. **RO ∲ $30, ♁ $45.**

WILLIAMS WA 6391

Pop 453. (160km SE Perth), See map on page 906, ref B2. An attractive small town on the Williams River, in a timber, sheep and cereal grain growing region. Bush Walking, Trotting.

Hotels/Motels

★★★☆ **Williams Motel**, (M), Cnr Albany Hwy & Narrogin Rd, 800m S of PO, ☎ 08 9885 1192, fax 08 9885 1298, 10 units [shwr, tlt, a/c, heat, elec blkts, tel, TV, movie, t/c mkg, refrig, ldry], w/mach, dryer, ✗, pool, rm serv, cots. D ⧍ $55, ⧍⧍ $66, ⧍ $14.30, ch con, AE BC DC MC VI.

Williams Hotel, (LH), Albany Hwy, 300m S of PO, ☎ 08 9885 1016, fax 08 9885 1343, 12 rms [a/c-cool, fan, TV, t/c mkg, refrig]. D ⧍ $35 - $55, ⧍⧍ $50 - $60.50, ⧍⧍⧍⧍ $75, VI.

B&B's/Guest Houses

★★★★ **The Gully Farmstay**, (GH), Crossman-Dwarda Rd, 40km N of PO, ☎ 08 9884 1076, fax 08 9884 1507, 3 rms [fan, heat, elec blkts, tel, TV, ldry, pillows], shwr, tlt (2). BB ⧍ $60, ⧍⧍ $95, ch con, Min book.

★★★☆ **Gelfro Holiday Farm**, (GH), (Farm), 14 Mile Brook Road, 33km from PO, ☎ 08 9884 5245, fax 08 9884 5245, 2 rms [pillows]. BB ⧍ $71.50, DBB ⧍⧍ $132.

Other Accommodation

Kievi Farm Lodge, (Lodge), RMB 853 Marradong Rd, 25km NW of PO, ☎ 08 9885 6026, fax 08 9885 6026, (2 stry) 10 rms acc up to 25, [tlt, a/c, ldry, blkts, linen, pillows], shwr, rec rm, ✗, pool, ☎, tennis, cots. BLB ⧍⧍ $143, BC MC VI.

WITCHCLIFFE WA 6286

Pop Nominal, (281km S Perth), See map on page 906, ref A2. A small township in a farming area. Wineries. See also Margaret River.

★★★★ **Harmony Forest Villas**, (Cotg), Sebbes Rd, Margaret River 6285, 15km S of Margaret River, ☎ 08 9757 7516, or 08 9757 7053, fax 08 97577055, 8 cotgs acc up to 6, [shwr, spa bath, tlt, hairdry, wood heat, elec blkts, video, clock radio, CD, t/c mkg, refrig, cook fac, micro, blkts, linen, pillows], w/mach, iron, bbq. D ⧍⧍ $239, ⧍ $49, W ⧍⧍ $1,490, AE BC DC MC VI.

★★★ **Margaret River Stone Cottages**, (Cotg), Warner Glen Rd, Forest Grove 6286, 15km SE of PO, ☎ 08 9757 7544, fax 08 9757 7544, (2 stry), 4 cotgs acc up to 6, (2 bedrm), [shwr, tlt, heat, TV, refrig, cook fac, ldry, blkts, linen, pillows], ldry, bbq, Pets allowed. D $80 - $132, Min book Christmas Jan long w/ends and Easter, BC MC VI.

WITTENOOM WA 6752

Pop Nominal, (1418km N Perth), See map on page 906, ref B4. The township of Wittenoom and surrounding areas are contaminated by asbestos fibres. Exposure to asbestos has been linked to lung diseases. There are special risks for children. Travellers intending visiting the township of Wittenoom and surrounding environs are strongly advised to seek expert medical advice before entering the area. See Also Karijini National Park.

Wittenoom Holiday Homes, (Cotg), Fifth Ave, ☎ 08 9189 7096, fax 08 9189 7096, 3 cotgs acc up to 7, (3 bedrm), [shwr, tlt, evap cool, TV, refrig, cook fac, ldry, blkts, linen, pillows], bbq. D ⧍⧍ $80, ⧍ $20, W ⧍⧍ $325, ⧍ $77, ch con, BC MC VI.

WONGAN HILLS WA 6603

Pop 947. (180km NE Perth), See map on page 906, ref B7. The town takes its name from the range of flat topped hills to the north-west.

Civic Motel Hotel, (LMH), Fenton St, 250m S of PO, ☎ 08 9671 1022, fax 08 9671 1186, 10 units [shwr, tlt, a/c, t/c mkg, refrig], TV rm, ✗, cots. D ⧍ $66, ⧍⧍ $77, AE BC MC VI.

(Hotel Section), 19 rms shwr, tlt. RO ⧍ $38.50, ⧍⧍ $55.

★ ★ ★ *Trouble-free travel tips* - **Fluids**

Check all fluid levels and top up as necessary. Look at engine oil, automatic transmission fluid, radiator coolant (only check this when the engine is cold), power steering, battery and windscreen washers.

WOOROLOO WA 6558

Pop Nominal, (59km E Perth), See map on page 906, ref A1. Situated in the rolling hills of the Darling Range. Here at Wooroloo is the Bodeguera Stud, the only breeding stock of Andalusian horse in Australia.

El Caballo Golf Resort, (LMH), Great Eastern Hwy, 60km E of GPO, ☎ 08 9573 1870, fax 08 9573 1055, (Multi-stry), 58 units [shwr, tlt, a/c, TV, clock radio, t/c mkg, refrig, toaster], rec rm, conv fac, ✗, bar, pool-indoor, spa, golf-fee, mini golf-fee, tennis-fee, cots, non smoking rms. D ⧍ $72.95 - $89.50, ⧍⧍ $83.50 - $116.95, ⧍⧍⧍⧍ $144.95 - $174.95, AE BC DC MC VI.

WUBIN WA 6612

Pop Nominal, (272km NE Perth), See map on page 906, ref B7. Wubin is on the edge of the vast station country to the north and east.

★★☆ **The Wubin Motel Hotel**, (LMH), Great Northern Hwy, 50m N of PO, ☎ 08 9664 1040, fax 08 9664 1079, 16 units [shwr, tlt, a/c (16), heat, TV, t/c mkg, refrig], ✗, ☎, cots-fee. D ⧍ $65, ⧍⧍ $85, ⧍⧍⧍ $95, RO ⧍⧍⧍⧍ $115, BC EFT MC VI.

WYNDHAM WA 6740

Pop 1,509. (3229km NE Perth), See map on page 906, ref E2. Situated on Cambridge Gulf, it is the northernmost port and major town in the State.

Wyndham Community Club, (Ltd Lic H), 6 Mile Peg Great Northern Hwy, 4km E of PO, ☎ 08 9161 1130, fax 08 9161 1022, 8 rms [shwr, tlt, a/c, TV, t/c mkg, refrig, toaster, ldry], bbq. RO ⧍ $55, ⧍⧍ $66, ⧍⧍⧍ $77, ch con, BC MC VI.

Wyndham Town Hotel, (LH), O'Donnell St, 4km N of PO, ☎ 08 9161 1003, fax 08 9161 1190, 27 rms [shwr, tlt, a/c, TV, movie, t/c mkg, refrig], ✗, pool, cots. RO ⧍ $65, ⧍⧍ $80, ⧍ $10, AE BC DC MC VI.

YALGOO WA 6635

Pop Nominal, (498km N Perth), See map on page 906, ref B6. Situated on the Mount Magnet-Geraldton Highway, in a mining and sheep farming area.

Thundelarra Station, (Cotg), Paynes Find Thundelara Rd, Between Paynes Find & Yalgoo, 80km SE of PO, ☎ 08 9963 6574, fax 08 9963 6575, 2 cotgs acc up to 10, [refrig, cook fac, blkts reqd-fee, linen reqd-fee, pillows], pool, tennis. D $77 - $99, Open April to October.

(Bunkhouse Section), 8 bunkhouses (Bunk Rooms), [blkts reqd-fee, linen reqd-fee, pillows], pool, tennis. D ⧍ $16.50.

YALLINGUP WA 6282

Pop Nominal, (263km S Perth), See map on page 906, ref A2. The area is noted for its magnificent caves and breathtaking coastal and forest scenery.

Hotels/Motels

★★★☆ **Caves House Hotel**, (LH), Yallingup Beach Rd, 100m W of PO, ☎ 08 9755 2131, fax 08 9755 2041, 14 rms (5 suites) [ensuite, shwr, spa bath (some), tlt, fan, heat, TV, t/c mkg, refrig], ldry, lounge, ✗ (a la carte), ✗, bar, tennis, cots (avail)-fee. D $135, Suite D $170, Some units of a lower rating. AE BC DC MC VI.

(Hotel Section), 14 rms [heat, elec blkts, TV, t/c mkg, refrig], shwr, tlt. RO $85 - $195.

Self Catering Accommodation

★★★★ **Canal Rocks Beach Resort Serviced Apartments**, (SA), Smiths Beach Rd, 5km S of PO, ☎ 08 9755 2116, fax 08 9754 1663, (2 stry), 16 serv apts acc up to 6, [shwr, spa bath, tlt, c/fan, wood heat, tel, TV, clock radio, CD, t/c mkg, refrig, cook fac, micro, toaster, doonas, linen, pillows], ldry (4), w/mach (12), dryer (12), rec rm, conv fac, ✗ (cafe), bbq, plygr, tennis, cots-fee. D ⧍⧍ $145 - $175, ⧍⧍⧍⧍ $180 - $270, W ⧍⧍ $770 - $1,225, ⧍⧍⧍⧍ $850 - $1,890, Min book all holiday times, BC MC VI.

★★★★ **Yallingup Forest Resort**, (Chalet), Lot 3 Hemsley Rd, 3km NE Yallingup PO, ☎ 08 9755 2550, fax 08 9756 6016, 16 chalets acc up to 5, (2 bedrm), [ensuite, shwr, bath, tlt, c/fan, heat, TV, video, clock radio, t/c mkg, refrig, micro, toaster, ldry, blkts, linen, pillows], w/mach, iron, iron brd, pool, freezer, 24hr reception, plygr, gym, tennis, cots (avail). D ⧍⧍⧍⧍ $130 - $160, ⧍ $20, W $820 - $1,008, Min book applies, AE BC DC MC VI.

★★★☆ **Canal Rocks Beach Resort**, (HU), Smith's Beach Rd, 5km S of PO, ☎ 08 9755 2116, fax 08 9754 1663, 13 units acc up to 6, (2 bedrm), [shwr, tlt, heat, wood heat, TV, video, refrig, cook fac, blkts, linen, pillows], rec rm, ⊠, bbq, plygr, tennis. **D $99 - $210, W $500 - $1,470.**

(**Cottage Section**), 8 cotgs acc up to 6, (2 bedrm), [shwr, tlt, wood heat, TV, refrig, cook fac, blkts, linen reqd, pillows]. **D $60 - $135, W $385 - $945.**

★★★ **Wyadup Brook Cottages**, (Cotg), Location 678 Caves Rd, 6km S of PO, ☎ 08 9755 2294, or 08 9755 2149, fax 08 9755 2294, 4 cotgs acc up to 6, (2 bedrm), [shwr, bath, tlt, fan (3), c/fan (1), fire pl, TV, clock radio, refrig, cook fac, micro, toaster, ldry, doonas, linen, pillows], baby bath, w/mach, iron, freezer, bbq, cots, non smoking units, **D ♦♦ $88 - $132, W ♦♦ $470 - $880**, ch con, ♿.

Chandlers Smiths Beach Villas, (HU), Smiths Beach Rd, 4km S of PO, ☎ 08 9755 2062, fax 08 9755 2062, 15 units acc up to 6, [shwr, tlt, heat, TV, t/c mkg, refrig, cook fac, micro, ldry, blkts, linen, pillows], bbq, cots. **D ♦♦ $88 - $148, ◊ $22, W $550 - $1,045**, ch con, BC MC VI.

Hideaway Holiday Homes, (HU), Limited facilities, 24 Elsegood Ave, 1.5km NW of PO, ☎ 08 9755 2145, fax 08 9755 2145, 6 units acc up to 6, (2 bedrm), [shwr, tlt, TV, refrig, cook fac, ldry, blkts reqd, linen reqd, pillows], rec rm, bbq. **D ♦♦ $55, W ♦♦ $253.**

B&B's/Guest Houses

★★★★★ **Cairnhill Homestead**, (GH), No children's facilities, Koorabin Drive, 4km SSE of PO, ☎ 08 9755 2828, fax 08 9755 2829, 3 rms [shwr, spa bath, tlt, hairdry, a/c, fire pl, tel, TV, video, clock radio, t/c mkg, refrig, pillows], ⊠, meals avail, non smoking property. **BB ♦♦ $170 - $235**, AE BC MC VI.

★★★★★ **Cape Lodge**, (GH), No children's facilities, Caves Rd, 10km S of PO, ☎ 08 9755 6311, fax 08 9755 6322, 18 rms [shwr, bath (2), tlt, a/c, tel, TV, video, t/c mkg, mini bar, pillows], ⊠, spa (11), tennis. **BB ♦♦ $235 - $350**, AE BC DC MC VI.

★★★★★ **Laughing Clown Lodge**, (GH), No children's facilities, Lot 1 Cnr Caves and Hemsley Rds, 3km E of PO, ☎ 08 9755 2341, fax 08 9755 2339, 13 rms [shwr, spa bath (6), tlt, a/c, elec blkts, tel, cable tv, radio, t/c mkg, pillows], ldry, w/mach, dryer, iron brd, ⊠, bar, bbq, gym, tennis, **BB ♦♦ $165 - $259, ♦♦ $990 - $1,554**, Min book all holiday times, AE BC DC MC VI.

★★★★☆ **Crayfish Lodge**, (GH), Cnr Caves Road & Canal Rocks Road, 2km S of PO, ☎ 08 9755 2028, fax 08 9755 2406, (Multi-stry), 7 rms [ensuite, bath (2), hairdry, fan, fire pl, elec blkts, tel, TV, video, clock radio, t/c mkg, refrig, cook fac ltd (3), ldry, doonas, pillows], w/mach, dryer, iron, lounge, ⊠, bbq, cots (avail). **BB ♦♦ $126.50 - $170**, Min book long w/ends, AE BC MC VI.

★★★★☆ **Wildwood Valley Guesthouse**, (GH), Wildwood Rd, 8km SE of PO, ☎ 08 9755 2120, fax 08 9754 2725, (Multi-stry), 5 rms [ensuite (3), shwr, bath (1), tlt, a/c-cool, evap cool, c/fan, fire pl, tel, TV, video, radio, refrig, doonas, pillows], w/mach, iron, iron brd, rec rm (billiards), TV rm, read rm, lounge, ⊠, t/c mkg shared, bbq, non smoking property. **BB ♦♦ $135 - $175, ◊ $35**, Min book long w/ends, BC MC VI.

(**Holiday Flat Section**), 1 flat acc up to 5, (2 bedrm), [a/c-cool, wood heat, tel, TV, refrig, cook fac, toaster, blkts, doonas, linen, pillows], ldry. **D $170 - $205.**

★★★★ **Yallingup Lodge**, (B&B), No children's facilities, 3 Hemsley Rd, Dunsborough 6281, 3km E of PO, ☎ 08 9755 2411, fax 08 9755 2511, 5 rms (5 suites) [ensuite, spa bath (3), hairdry, heat, c/fan, fire pl, TV, clock radio, t/c mkg, refrig, doonas, pillows], dryer, iron, iron brd, rec rm, TV rm, pool, spa, bbq, gym, tennis, non smoking property. **Suite BB ♦♦ $145 - $190**, Farm activities. AE BC DC MC VI.

YORK WA 6302

Pop 1,923. (97km E Perth), See map on page 906, ref B1. York is Western Australia's first inland town. First settled in 1831. It is now a popular tourist and festival town and a reminder of life in the pioneering days.

Hotels/Motels

★★★ **Avon Motel**, (M), 10 William St, 700m S of PO, ☎ 08 9641 2066, 6 units [shwr, tlt, a/c, elec blkts, TV, t/c mkg, refrig, ldry], cots. **D ♦ $60 - $70, ♦♦ $88 - $100, ♦♦♦ $105 - $115**, BC MC VI.

Self Catering Accommodation

★★★☆ **Glenrowan Farmstay**, (Cotg), Doodenanning Rd via Greenhills, 32km SE of PO, ☎ 08 9641 7051, fax 08 9641 7051, 1 cotg acc up to 7, (3 bedrm), [shwr, bath, tlt, a/c, fire pl, TV, clock radio, refrig, cook fac, micro, toaster, ldry, blkts, linen, pillows], w/mach, iron, bbq, cots. **D ♦♦ $88 - $99, ◊ $16.50.**

★★★☆ **Quellington School House Farmstay**, (Cotg), Sees Rd, Quellington, 20km NE of York PO, ☎ 08 9641 1343, fax 08 9641 1343, ⟨acc up to 7, (2 bedrm), [shwr, tlt, heat, c/fan, fire pl, clock radio, CD, t/c mkg, refrig, micro, blkts, doonas, baby bath, w/mach, iron, iron brd, cots (avail), non ⟩ **$50, ♦♦ $75, ◊ $15**, ch con.

★★★ **York Cottages**, (Cotg), 2 Morris Edwards Dve (cnr Ulster Road), 1km W of PO, ☎ 08 9641 2125, fax 08 9641 2125, 2 cotgs acc up to 6, [shwr, bath, tlt, a/c, fire pl, TV, refrig, cook fac, micro, toaster, doonas, linen, pillows], w/mach, iron, iron brd, rec rm, trailer park, tennis (court), cots. **D ♦♦♦♦ $120 - $180, ◊ $20.**

Khaelan, (HU), (Farm), Gilgering, Great Southern Hwy, 16km S of PO, ☎ 08 9641 4015, fax 08 9641 4015, 1 unit acc up to 4, [shwr, tlt, a/c, TV, clock radio, t/c mkg, refrig, cook fac, micro, toaster, blkts, linen, pillows], iron, bbq, cots (avail). **D ♦ $55, ♦♦ $70, ◊ $10 - $15**, ch con.

B&B's/Guest Houses

★★★★★ **The Grandhouse York**, (B&B), No children's facilities, 48 Panmure Rd, 500m E of PO, ☎ 08 9641 2880, fax 08 9641 2881, 6 rms [ensuite, hairdry, a/c, fire pl, tel, TV, video, clock radio, refrig, doonas, pillows], ldry, w/mach, dryer, iron, iron brd, lounge, ✕, spa (heated), t/c mkg shared, non smoking rms. **BB ♦ $85, ♦♦ $120 - $140, ◊ $40**, BC DC MC VI.

★★★★☆ **Lavender Hill**, (B&B), Lot 1 Great Southern Highway, 1.5km W of PO, ☎ 08 9641 2332, fax 08 9641 1335, 4 rms [ensuite (2), shwr, spa bath (1), tlt, a/c-cool, wood heat, tel, TV, video, refrig, ldry (services), doonas, pillows], lounge, ✕, t/c mkg shared, cots, non smoking property. **BB ♦ $80, ♦♦ $150**, fam con, AE BC MC VI.

★★★★ **Bucklands View**, (B&B), No children's facilities, Lot 341 Gt Southern Hwy, 2km SW of PO, ☎ 08 9641 2069, fax 08 9641 2069, 4 rms [shwr, spa bath (1), tlt, a/c, fire pl, TV, refrig, pillows], lounge, ✕, t/c mkg shared, bbq, meals avail (by arrangement), non smoking property. **BB ♦♦ $120 - $140.**

(**Cottage Section**), 1 cotg acc up to 4, (2 bedrm), [shwr, tlt, cook fac, blkts, doonas, linen, pillows]. **D $140 - $130.**

★★★★ **Hope Farm Guest House**, (GH), 15 Carter Rd, 3km N of PO, ☎ 08 9641 2183, fax 08 9641 1437, (2 stry gr fl), 3 rms [shwr, tlt, hairdry, a/c-cool, fan, c/fan, heat, elec blkts, tel, video, clock radio, t/c mkg, refrig, ldry, doonas, pillows], TV rm, lounge, lounge firepl, ✕, pool, bbq. **BB ♦ $80, ♦♦ $130**, BC MC VI.

★★★★ **Langsford House**, (B&B), Classified by National Trust,Heritage, 18 Avon Terrace, 500metres S of PO, ☎ 08 9641 1440, fax 08 9641 1846, (2 stry), 3 rms [ensuite (1), shwr, tlt, a/c, fire pl, elec blkts, TV, video, clock radio, refrig, doonas], ldry, w/mach, dryer, iron, iron brd, lounge (guest), t/c mkg shared, bbq, c/park. **BB ♦ $85 - $105, ♦♦ $125 - $170**, pen con, BC MC VI.

★★★★ **The Hillside Country Homestead**, (GH), Classified by National Trust, Forrest St, 1.3km S of PO, ☎ 08 9641 1065, fax 08 9641 2417, 5 rms [ensuite, wood heat, elec blkts, TV, video, t/c mkg, refrig, pillows], lounge, pool, bbq, tennis. **BB ♦ $60.**

★★★☆ **Imperial Inn**, (PH), 83 Avon Tce, opposite PO, ☎ 08 9641 1010, fax 08 9641 2201, 12 rms [fan, fire pl, heat, elec blkts, t/c mkg], lounge, ✕, ⊠, cafe. **BB ♦ $50 - $60, ♦♦ $90 - $100, RO ♦ $40 - $50, ♦♦ $80 - $90**, Some units of a higher rating.

(**Private Hotel Section**), 4 units [shwr, tlt, a/c, fan, heat, elec blkts, TV, t/c mkg, refrig], ⊠. **BB ♦♦ $80 - $90, RO ♦ $30 - $40, ♦♦ $70 - $80.**

★★★☆ **King's Head**, (B&B), 37 Avon Tce, 1km S of PO, ☎ 08 9641 1234, fax 08 9641 1234, 1 rm [ensuite, hairdry, a/c-cool, fan, heat, elec blkts, tel, TV, clock radio, t/c mkg, refrig, doonas, pillows], iron, iron brd, non smoking property. **BB ♦ $50, ♦♦ $75.**

Out Of Town Inn York, (B&B), No children's facilities, 58 Newcastle St, 1.4km N of PO, ☎ 08 9641 2214, fax 08 9641 2214, 3 rms [fan, c/fan, fire pl, tel, TV, video, radio, refrig, doonas, pillows], shwr, tlt, ldry, w/mach, lounge, t/c mkg shared, bbq, meals avail (by arrangement), non smoking rms. **BB ♦ $65, ♦♦ $100, DBB ♦ $85, ♦♦ $150.**

Children in cars

Here are some hints to make things safer and more comfortable when travelling with children in your car.

- Ensure that child restraints are correctly fitted and adjusted, and suitable for the size of the children. Nothing will irritate a child more on a long trip than being uncomfortable in their child restraint and an irritated child means extra stress and distraction for the driver.
- Make sure to take a supply of games that children can play in the car without distracting the driver. Card games and board games with magnetic pieces are useful. Avoid sharp toys as these can be dangerous missiles in a crash.
- Remember that children require more frequent breaks for toilet stops and drinks.
- Don't leave children in the car while you attend to other business, especially in hot weather. Children dehydrate much more easily than adults. Even in the shade, the temperature inside a parked car can build up to dangerously high levels.

...ange. Check before booking.